Chambers Family Dictionary

Chambers

CHAMBERS
An imprint of Chambers Harrap Publishers Ltd
7 Hopetoun Crescent, Edinburgh, EH7 4AY

First published by Chambers Harrap Publishers Ltd 2007

A CIP catalogue record for this book is available from the British Library.

ISBN 978 0550 10273 7

Typeset by Charlesworth

Printed and bound in Italy by Rotolito Lombarda SpA

Contents

Contributors

Managing Editor
Mary O'Neill

Editors
Vicky Aldus
Ian Brookes
Gary Dexter
Alison Pickering

Design
Heather Macpherson
Sharon McTeir

Data Management
Gerry Breslin
Patrick Gaherty

Prepress
Nicolas Echallier
Isla Maclean

Preface

Chambers Family Dictionary is a new dictionary that is specially designed to give everyone in the family the answers they need, whether it is the spelling of a word for an important e-mail or a little extra help with homework.

It covers not only everyday words and their meanings, but also hundreds of words and terms from school curriculum subjects such as mathematics, geography, history, and the sciences. Fun reminders of difficult spellings and useful tips on correct grammar are given in usage notes after some entries.

The pages have an exceptionally clean, modern design, and they are arranged so that you can easily find the word you are looking for. Entries are set out so as to be clear and self-explanatory, and the definitions are in straightforward English. In addition, the language content is appropriate for the whole family to look up, so the book can be used with ease and confidence.

And with its special colour supplement, this dictionary has even more to offer the family. Packed with facts about places, people and events, as well as illustrative maps, flags and photographs, it supplies the kind of information that is needed and appreciated by adults and children alike.

All these features make *Chambers Family Dictionary* a pleasure to look up or browse, and an essential addition to the family reference shelf.

Using the dictionary

anger *noun* a feeling of great displeasure or annoyance. ▸ *verb* to cause this kind of feeling in someone; to displease. [13c: from Norse *angr* trouble]

angina /anˈdʒaɪnə/ *noun, pathol* severe pain behind the chest-bone, usu induced by insufficient blood supply to the heart muscle during exertion. Also called **angina pectoris**. [16c: from Latin *angina* a throat disease]

angiogram *noun, med* a type of X-ray photograph that is achieved by **angiography**.

angiography *noun, med* the examination of the condition of blood vessels by X-ray.

Angle *noun* a member of a N German tribe who settled in N and E England in the 5c, forming the kingdoms of Northumbria, Mercia and East Anglia. See also **Saxon**, **Anglo-Saxon**. [Anglo-Saxon *engle* the people of *Angulus*, a district of Holstein so called because of its hook shape]

angle[1] *noun* **1** *maths* a measure of the rotation of a line about a point, usu measured in degrees, radians or revolutions. **2** the point where two lines or planes intersect. **3** the extent to which one line slopes away from another. **4** a corner. **5** a point of view. ▸ *verb* **1** *tr* & *intr* to move in or place at an angle. **2** to present a news story, information, etc from a particular point of view. [14c: from Latin *angulum* a corner]

angle[2] *verb* **1** to use a rod and line for catching fish. **2** (**angle for sth**) to try to get it in a devious or indirect way. ▪ **angler** *noun*. [Anglo-Saxon *angul* hook]

avenge *verb* to carry out some form of retribution for (some previous wrongdoing). ▪ **avenger** *noun*. [14c: from French *avengier*]

avenue *noun* **1 a** a broad road or street, often with trees along the sides; **b** (**Avenue**) a street title in an address. **2** a tree-lined approach to a house. **3** a means, way or approach. [17c: French]

aver *verb* (***averred, averring***) to state firmly and positively. [14c: from French *averer*]

average *noun* **1** the usual or typical amount, extent, quality, number, etc. **2** *stats* any number that is representative of a group of numbers or other data, esp the arithmetic mean, which is obtained by adding several amounts and dividing the total by the number of amounts. Same as **mean**[3] (sense 2a). Compare **median** (sense 3), **mode** (sense 5). ▸ *adj* **1** usual or ordinary. **2** estimated by taking an average. **3** mediocre: *gave a pretty average performance*. ▸ *verb* **1** to obtain the numerical average of (several numbers). **2** to amount to on average: *Her speed averaged 90mph on the motorway.* [15c: from Arabic *awariya* damaged goods]

IDIOMS **on average** usually; normally; typically.

PHRASAL VERBS **average out** to result in an average or balance.

averse *adj* (*always* **averse to sth**) reluctant about or opposed to it. [16c: from Latin *aversus*]

- Entry word (or headword)
- Pronunciation guidance (see page viii)
- Place, subject, or type of language in which the word is used
- Cross-reference to information in another entry
- Part of speech (or word class) – *noun*, *verb*, etc.
- Cross-reference to an entry in another part of the dictionary
- Superscript numbers distinguish between words spelt the same way
- Indication that a verb is, or can be, intransitive (ie it does not need an object)
- Word derived from the entry word
- Word history, including date of first use in English
- Numbers indicating different meanings, and letters indicating subsenses of the meaning
- Different forms of a verb or adjective, or plural of a noun
- Alternative form
- Example of the word in use
- Idioms that feature the entry word
- Phrasal verbs formed using the entry word

Abbreviations used in the dictionary

abbrev	abbreviation	*myth*	mythology
adj	adjective	*N*	North
adv	adverb	*naut*	nautical
archit	architecture	*N Am*	North American
astrol	astrology	*NZ*	New Zealand
astron	astronomy	*orig*	originally
Aust	Australia, Australian	*pathol*	pathology
bacteriol	bacteriology	*philos*	philosophy
biochem	biochemistry	*photog*	photography
biol	biology	*physiol*	physiology
Brit	Britain, British	*pl*	plural
c	century (eg 15c)	*poss*	possibly
c.	circa (ie approximately)	*prep*	preposition
Can	Canada, Canadian	*prob*	probably
chem	chemistry	*psychoanal*	psychoanalysis
cinematog	cinematography	*psychol*	psychology
comput	computing	*RC*	Roman Catholic
conj	conjunction	*relig*	religion
derog	derogatory	*S*	South
E	East	*S Afr*	South Africa, South African
ecol	ecology	*sb*	somebody
econ	economics	*Scot*	Scottish
elec	electricity, electrical	*sing*	singular
Eng	English	*sociol*	sociology
eng	engineering	*stats*	statistics
esp	especially	*sth*	something
EU	European Union	*telecomm*	telecommunications
euphem	euphemistic	*tr*	transitive
exclam	exclamation	*trig*	trigonometry
geog	geography	*TV*	television
geol	geology	*US*	United States
geom	geometry	*USA*	United States of America
hist	history, historical	*usu*	usually
intr	intransitive	*vet*	veterinary
maths	mathematics	*W*	West
mech	mechanics, mechanical	*zool*	zoology
med	medicine		
meteorol	meteorology		

Pronunciation guide

The pronunciations that appear after some entry words are written in the International Phonetic Alphabet. In this system, the consonants *b, d, f, g, h, k, l, m, n, p, r, s, t, v, w* and *z* are pronounced with their usual English sounds.

However, the following symbols may be not be familiar, and these are pronounced as you would say them in the words shown alongside:

Sounds in English

a	hat	eɪ	bay
ɑː	baa	ɔɪ	boy
ɛ	bet	aʊ	now
ə	ago	oʊ	go
ɜː	fur	ɪə	here
ɪ	fit	ɛə	hair
iː	me	ʊə	poor
ɒ	lot	θ	thin
ɔː	raw	ð	the
ʌ	cup	j	you
ʊ	put	ŋ	ring
uː	too	ʃ	she
aɪ	by	ʒ	vision

Common sounds in foreign words

ɑ̃	*French* grand	y	*French* sur
ɛ̃	*French* vin	ɥ	*French* huit
ɔ̃	*French* bon	ʀ	*French* rue
œ̃	*French* un	ç	*German* ich
ø	*French* peu	x	*Scottish* loch
œ	*French* coeur	ɬ	*Welsh* Llan-

Stress

Stress is extra weight that is put on a syllable of a word, so you pronounce it more strongly than the other syllables. In the pronunciations given for words with more than one syllable in them, a stress mark (') is shown before the syllable that has the main stress, for example /'neɪvɪ/ (*navy*).

Pronunciation of a final 'r'

If a letter 'r' appears in brackets at the end of a pronunciation, as in /'eɪkə(r)/ (*acre*), this tells you that the 'r' is sounded only when the following word begins with a vowel, as in *acre of land*. However, in Scottish, Irish and some American forms of pronunciation, the final 'r' is sounded whenever it occurs.

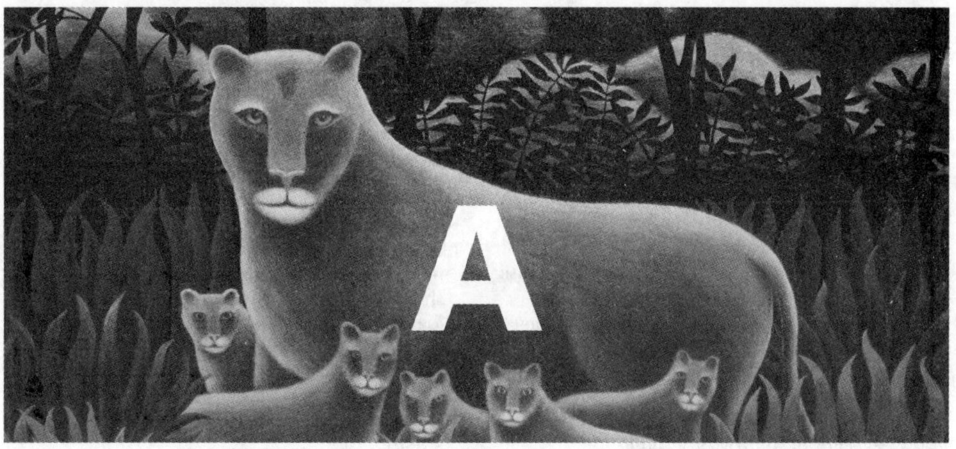

A[1] *or* **a** *noun* (***As, A's*** *or* ***a's***) **1** the first letter of the English alphabet. **2** (*usu* **A**) the highest grade or quality, or a mark indicating this. **3** (**A**) *music* the sixth note on the scale of C major. **4** (*usu* **A**) someone or something that is first in a sequence, or belonging to a class arbitrarily designated A. **5** the principal series of paper sizes, ranging from **A0** (841 × 1189mm) to **A10** (26 × 37mm).
IDIOMS **from A to B** from one place or point to another. **from A to Z** from beginning to end.

A[2] *abbrev* **1** ammeter. **2** ampere or amperes. **3** angstrom.

a[1] (used before a consonant or consonant sound, eg *a boy, a one*) or (used before a vowel or vowel sound, eg *an egg, an hour*) **an** *indefinite article* **1** used chiefly with a singular noun, usu where the thing referred to has not been mentioned before, or where it is not a specific example known to the speaker or listener: *Pass me a CD.* Compare **the**. **2** used before a word describing quantity: *a dozen eggs.* **3 a** any or every: *A fire is hot;* **b** (used after *not* or *never*): any at all: *not a chance.* **4** each or every; per: *once a day.* **5** one of a specified type: *He's a real Romeo.*

---

a, an
Some people use **an** rather than **a** before words beginning with an *h* sound, eg *an hotel, an historic occasion*. However, this is no more correct than using **a**, and it can sound old-fashioned.

---

a[2] *abbrev* **1** acceleration. **2** adjective. **3** *ante* (Latin), before.

a[3] see **A**[1]

a-[1] *prefix, signifying* **1** to or towards: *ashore.* **2** in the process or state of something: *abuzz* • *a-roving.* **3** on: *afire.* **4** in: *asleep.*

a-[2] *or* (*before a vowel, and in scientific compounds before* **h**) **an-** *prefix, signifying* not; without; opposite to: *amoral* • *anaemia.* [Greek]

Å *symbol* Ångström or angstrom.

AA *abbrev* **1** Alcoholics Anonymous. **2** anti-aircraft. **3** *Brit* Automobile Association.

AAA *abbrev* **1** *Brit* Amateur Athletic Association. **2** *US* American Automobile Association.

A & R *abbrev* artists and repertoire.

aardvark /'ɑːdvɑːk/ *noun* a nocturnal African mammal with a large snout and donkey-like ears. [19c: from Dutch *aarde* earth + *vark* pig]

AB *abbrev, Brit* able seaman.

ab- *prefix, signifying* opposite to; from; away from: *abnormal.* [Latin]

aback *adv* (*always* **taken aback**) surprised or shocked.

abacus *noun* an arithmetical calculating device consisting of several rows of beads strung on horizontal wires or rods mounted in a frame. [17c: Latin, from Greek *abax* drawing board]

abaft *naut, adv* in or towards the stern of a ship. ▸ *prep* behind. [Anglo-Saxon **a-**[1] + *beæftan* after]

abalone /abə'lounɪ/ *noun* marine gastropod mollusc with an oval shell lined with **mother-of-pearl**. [19c: from American Spanish *abulón*]

abandon *verb* **1** to give something up completely: *abandon hope.* **2** to leave or desert (a person, post of responsibility, etc). **3** (*usu* **abandon oneself to sth**) to let oneself be overcome by (strong emotion, passion, etc). ▸ *noun* uncontrolled or uninhibited behaviour. ▪ **abandonment** *noun.* [14c: from French *abandoner* to put under someone's control]
IDIOMS **abandon ship** of the crew and passengers: to leave a ship at sea when it is in danger of sinking.

abandoned *adj* **1** deserted. **2** having, or behaving as if one has, no sense of shame or morality.

abase *verb* to humiliate or degrade (someone or oneself). ▪ **abasement** *noun.* [15c: from French *abaissier*]

abashed *adj* embarrassed, esp because of shyness. [14c: from French *esbahir* to astound]

abate *verb, tr & intr* to become or make less strong or severe. ▪ **abatement** *noun.* [13c: from French *abatre* to demolish]

abattoir /'abətwɑː(r)/ *noun* a slaughterhouse. [19c: from French *abatre* to demolish]

abbacy *noun* (***-ies***) the office or authority of an abbot or abbess. [15c: from Latin *abbatia*]

abbess *noun* a woman in charge of a group of nuns living in an abbey. [13c: from French *abbesse*]

abbey /'abɪ/ *noun* **1** a group of nuns or monks living as a community under an abbot or abbess. **2** the buildings occupied by such a community. **3** a church associated with such a community. [13c: from French *abeie*]

abbot *noun* the man in charge of a group of monks living in an abbey. [Anglo-Saxon *abbod*]

abbr. *or* **abbrev.** *abbrev* **1** abbreviated. **2** abbreviation.

abbreviate *verb* to shorten, esp to represent (a long word) by a shortened form. [15c: from Latin *abbreviare* to shorten]

abbreviation *noun* **1** a shortening of a word used instead of a whole word, eg *approx.* for *approximately.* **2** the act or process of abbreviating something, or the result of this.

ABC[1] *noun* (***ABCs*** *or* ***ABC's***) **1** the alphabet. **2** the basic facts about a subject. **3** an alphabetical guide.

ABC[2] *abbrev* **1** American Broadcasting Company. **2** Australian Broadcasting Corporation.

abdicate *verb* **1** *tr & intr* to give up one's right to (the throne). **2** to refuse or fail to carry out (one's responsibilities). ▪ **abdication** *noun.* [16c: from Latin *ab-* away + *dicare, dicatum* to proclaim]

abdomen *noun, zool, anatomy* **1** in vertebrates: the lower part of the main body cavity, containing the stomach, bowels and reproductive organs. **2** in arthropods, eg insects: the rear part of the body, behind the head and the thorax. ▪ **abdominal** /ab'dɒmɪnəl/ *adj.* [17c: Latin]

abduct *verb* **1** to take someone away illegally by force or deception. **2** of a muscle: to draw a part of the body (such as an arm or finger) away from another or away from the centre line of the body. ▪ **abduction** *noun.* ▪ **abductor** *noun.* [19c: from Latin *abducere* to lead away]

abeam *adv* in a line at right angles to the length of a ship or aircraft.

Aberdeen Angus *noun* an early-maturing breed of hornless beef cattle with short black hair.

Aberdonian *noun* a citizen or inhabitant of, or person born in, Aberdeen, NE Scotland. ▸ *adj* relating or belonging to Aberdeen. [17c: from Latin *Aberdonia* Aberdeen]

aberrant *adj* differing or departing from what is normal or accepted as standard. ▪ **aberrance** *noun.* [19c: from Latin *aberrare* to wander away]

aberration *noun* **1** a temporary and usu brief change from what is normal or accepted as standard. **2** a usu temporary, brief and sudden drop in standards of behaviour, thought, etc. **3** *optics* the failure of a lens in an optical system to form a perfect image, usu due to the properties of the lens material.

abet *verb* (***abetted, abetting***) to help or encourage someone to do something wrong, esp to commit an offence. See also **aid and abet** at **aid.** ▪ **abetter** *or* (*esp law*) **abettor** *noun.* [14c: from French *abeter* to bait]

abeyance *noun* of laws, customs, etc: the condition of not being used or followed, usu only temporarily: *fall into abeyance.* [16c: from French *abeance,* from *abeer* to gape after]

ABH *abbrev* actual bodily harm.

abhor *verb* (***abhorred, abhorring***) to hate or dislike (usu something one considers morally wrong) very much. [15c: from Latin *ab-* from + *horrere* to shudder]

abhorrent *adj* (*esp* **abhorrent to sb**) hated or disliked by them. ▪ **abhorrence** *noun.*

abide *verb* (***abided*** *or* ***abode***) **1** (*esp with negatives and in questions*) to put up with or tolerate someone or something: *We cannot abide dishonesty.* **2** *intr* (**abide by something**) to follow, stay faithful to or obey (a decision, rule, etc). **3** *intr, old use* to remain. [Anglo-Saxon]

abiding *adj* permanent, lasting or continuing for a long time.

ability *noun* (***-ies***) **1** the power, skill or knowledge to do something. **2** great skill or intelligence. [14c: from Latin *habilitas* suitability]

-ability see under **-able**

abject *adj* **1** of living conditions, etc: extremely sad, miserable or poor. **2** of people or their actions: showing lack of courage or pride, etc: *an abject apology.* ▪ **abjectly** *adv.* [15c: from Latin *abjectus* thrown away]

abjure *verb, formal* to promise solemnly, esp under oath, to stop believing or doing something. ▪ **abjuration** *noun.* [16c: from Latin *ab* away + *jurare* to swear]

ablation *noun* **1** *med* the removal of an organ, tumour, etc, esp by surgical means. **2** any loss or removal of material caused by melting, erosion, weathering, etc. [16c: from Latin *ablatio* taking away]

ablative *grammar, noun* (abbrev **abl.**) **1** in eg Latin: the form or **case**[2] (sense 7) of a noun, pronoun or adjective that expresses the place, means, manner or instrument of an action. **2** a noun, etc in this case. ▸ *adj* belonging to or in this case. [15c: from Latin *ablitavus,* from *ablatus* carried off]

ablaze *adj* **1** burning, esp strongly. **2** brightly lit. **3** (*usu* **ablaze with sth**) feeling (an emotion) with great passion.

able *adj* **1** having the necessary knowledge, power, time, opportunity, etc to do something. **2** clever or skilful. ▪ **ably** *adv.* [14c: from Latin *habilis* handy]

-able *suffix, forming adjectives, denoting* **1** that may or must be: *eatable* • *payable.* **2** that may be the subject of something: *objectionable.* **3** that is suitable for something: *fashionable.* See also **-ible.** ▪ **-ability** *suffix, forming nouns.* ▪ **-ably** *suffix, forming adverbs.*

able-bodied *adj* fit and healthy.

abled *adj* characterized by having a specified type of ability or range of abilities: *holidays for the fully abled older person* • *Having dyslexia means being differently abled, not disabled.*

able seaman *noun* (abbrev **AB**) a sailor able to perform all duties, with more training and a higher rating than an **ordinary seaman.**

ablution *noun* (*usu* **ablutions**) **1** the washing of the body, the hands or ritual vessels as part of a religious ceremony. **2** *informal or facetious* the ordinary washing of oneself. [14c: from Latin *abluere* to wash away]

ably see under **able**

-ably see under **-able**

ABM *abbrev* anti-ballistic missile, a type of rocket which can destroy an enemy's ballistic missile in the air.

abnegation *noun, formal* **1** the act of giving up something one has or would like to have. **2** the act of renouncing a doctrine, etc. [16c: from Latin *abnegare* to deny]

abnormal *adj* not normal; different from what is expected or usual. ▪ **abnormality** *noun* (***-ies***). ▪ **abnormally** *adv.*

aboard *adv, prep* **1** on, on to, in or into (a ship, train, aircraft, etc). **2** *naut* alongside. [16c as *aborde*]

abode[1] *noun, formal* the house or place where one lives; a dwelling. [17c: from **abide**]

IDIOMS **of no fixed abode** *Brit law* having no regular home or address.

abode[2] *past tense, past participle of* **abide**

abolish *verb* to stop or put an end to (customs, laws, etc). [15c: from French *abolir*]

abolition *noun* the act of abolishing something; the state of being abolished.

abolitionist *noun* someone who seeks to abolish a custom or practice, esp capital punishment or (*formerly*) slavery. ▪ **abolitionism** *noun.*

A-bomb short for **atom bomb**

abominable *adj* **1** greatly disliked or found loathsome, usu because morally bad. **2** *informal* very bad. ▪ **abominably** *adv.*

abominable snowman *noun* a **yeti**. [1920s: a loose translation of Tibetan *metohkangmi*, literally 'snow-field man-bear']

abominate *verb* to dislike or hate something greatly; to find it loathsome. ▪ **abomination** *noun.* [17c: from Latin *abominari* to turn away from something believed to be ill-omened]

aboriginal /abəˈrɪdʒɪnəl/ *adj* **1** of inhabitants: earliest known; indigenous. **2** referring to the Aboriginals of Australia or one of their languages. ▸ *noun* (**Aboriginal**) a member of a people who were the original inhabitants of Australia.

Aboriginal, Aborigine

If you are speaking or writing about the original inhabitants of Australia, it is best to use **Aborigine** as the singular noun and **Aboriginals** as the plural. **Aboriginal** is preferred for the adjective.

---

aborigine /abəˈrɪdʒɪnɪ/ *noun* **1** (*also* **Aborigine**) an Aboriginal. **2** a member of any people who were the first to live in a country or region. [16c: from Latin *aborigines* a race of pre-Roman inhabitants of Italy, from *ab origine* from the beginning]

abort *verb* **1** *intr* to expel (an embryo or fetus) spontaneously from the uterus before it is capable of surviving independently. **2** *intr* of a baby: to be lost in this way. **3** to induce termination of pregnancy before the embryo or fetus is capable of surviving independently. **4** *tr & intr* to stop (a plan, etc), or to be stopped, earlier than expected and before reaching a successful conclusion. **5** *intr, biol* to fail to grow or develop to maturity. [16c: from Latin *abortus* miscarried]

abortion *noun* **1** the removal of an embryo or fetus from the uterus before it is sufficiently developed to survive independently. Also called **termination, induced abortion**. **2** the spontaneous expulsion of an embryo or fetus from the uterus before it is sufficiently developed to survive independently. Also called **miscarriage, spontaneous abortion**. **3** the failure of a plan, project, etc. **4** anything which has failed to grow properly or enough. ▪ **abortionist** *noun.*

abortive *adj* **1** unsuccessful. **2** checked in its development.

abound *verb, intr* **1** to exist in large numbers. **2** (**abound in** *or* **with sth**) to be rich in it or filled with it. [14c: from Latin *abundare* to overflow]

about *prep* **1** concerning or relating to someone or something; on the subject of them or it. **2** near to something. **3** around or centring on something. **4** here and there in or at points throughout something. **5** all around or surrounding someone or something. ▸ *adv* **1** nearly or just over; approximately. **2** nearby; close: *Is there anyone about?* **3** scattered here and there. **4** all around; in all directions. **5** in or to the opposite direction: *turn about.* **6** on the move; in action: *be up and about again after an illness.* [Anglo-Saxon *onbutan*]

IDIOMS **about to do sth** on the point of doing it.

about turn *or* **about face** *noun* **1** a turn made so that one is facing in the opposite direction. **2** a complete change of direction.

above *prep* **1** higher than or over something. **2** more or greater than something in quantity or degree. **3** higher or superior to someone in rank, importance, ability, etc. **4** too good or great for a specified thing: *above petty quarrels.* **5** too good, respected, etc to be affected by or subject to something: *above criticism.* **6** too difficult to be understood by, or beyond the abilities of, someone. ▸ *adv* **1** at, in or to a higher position, place, rank, etc. **2 a** in an earlier passage of written or printed text; **b** *in compounds*: *above-mentioned.* ▸ *adj* appearing or mentioned in an earlier or preceding passage of written or printed text. ▸ *noun* (**the above**) something already mentioned. [Anglo-Saxon *abufan*]

IDIOMS **above all** more than anything else.

above-board *adj* honest; open; not secret.

abracadabra *exclam* a word which supposedly has magic power, often used by people when doing magic tricks. [17c: first appearance is in a 2nd-century Latin poem]

abrasion *noun* **1** the action of rubbing off. **2** a graze on the body. **3** *geog* erosion caused by rocks and other material in a river or glacier scraping the surfaces they are in contact with. Also called **corrasion**.

abrasive *adj* **1** of a material: capable of wearing something away by rubbing and scraping. **2** of a material: used to smooth or polish another surface by rubbing. **3** of people or their actions: likely to offend others by being harsh and rude. ▸ *noun* any hard material that is used to wear away the surface of other materials, usu in order to smooth or shape them. [17c: from Latin *abradere* to scrape away]

abreast *adv* side by side and facing in the same direction.

IDIOMS **abreast of sth** up to date concerning it.

abridge *verb* to make (a book, etc) shorter. ▪ **abridged** *adj.* ▪ **abridgement** *or* **abridgment** *noun.* [14c: from French *abregier*]

abroad *adv* **1** in or to a foreign country or countries. **2** in circulation; at large. **3** over a wide area; in different directions.

abrogate *verb* to cancel (a law, agreement, etc) formally or officially. ▪ **abrogation** *noun.* [16c: from Latin *abrogare*]

abrupt *adj* **1** sudden and unexpected. **2** esp of speech, etc: rather sharp and rude. ▪ **abruptly** *adv.* ▪ **abruptness** *noun.* [16c: from Latin *abrumpere* to break off]

ABS *abbrev* anti-lock braking system.

abscess /ˈabsɛs/ *noun, pathol* a localized collection of pus in a cavity surrounded by inflamed tissue, usu caused by bacterial infection. [17c: from Latin *abscessus* going away]

abscissa /abˈsɪsə/ *noun* (***abscissas*** *or* ***abscissae*** /-ˈsɪsiː/) in coordinate geometry: the first of a pair of numbers x and y, known as the x-coordinate, which specifies the distance of a point from the vertical or y-axis. See also **ordinate**. [17c: from Latin *abscissus* cut off]

abscond *verb, intr* to depart or leave quickly and usu secretly. [16c: from Latin *abscondere* to hide]

abseil /ˈabseɪl/ *verb, intr* to go down a steep drop using a double rope wound round the body and fixed to a point higher up. ▸ *noun* an act of abseiling. ▪ **abseiling** *noun*. [20c: from German *abseilen*]

absence *noun* **1** the state of being away. **2** the time when a person is away. **3** the state of not existing or of being lacking. [14c: from Latin *abesse* to be away]

absent *adj* /ˈabsənt/ **1** not in its or one's expected place; not present. **2** not existing, esp where normally to be expected. **3** not paying attention or concentrating. ▸ *verb* /abˈsɛnt/ (*now always* **absent oneself**) to stay away from a meeting, gathering, etc. ▪ **absently** *adv*.

absentee *noun* someone who is not present at a particular or required time, or in a particular place. ▪ **absenteeism** *noun* continual absence from work, school, etc.

absent-minded *adj* not noticing what one is doing or what is going on around one, esp because one is thinking about something else; preoccupied or forgetful. ▪ **absent-mindedly** *adv*. ▪ **absent-mindedness** *noun*.

absinthe *or* **absinth** *noun* a strong green alcoholic drink flavoured with substances from certain plants, such as aniseed and wormwood. [17c: from Latin *absinthium* wormwood]

absolute *adj* **1** complete; total; perfect. **2** without limits; not controlled by anything or anyone else. **3** certain; undoubted. **4** not measured in comparison with other things; not relative: *an absolute standard*. **5** pure. **6** *grammar* **a** of a clause or phrase: standing alone, ie not dependent on the rest of the sentence. Compare **relative** (*adj* sense 5b); **b** of an adjective or a transitive verb: standing alone, ie without a noun or an object respectively. ▸ *noun* **1** a rule, standard, etc which is thought to be true or right in all situations. **2** (**the absolute** *or* **the Absolute**) that which can exist without being related to anything else. [14c: from Latin *absolutus* loosened or separate]

absolutely *adv* **1** completely. **2** independently of anything else. **3** *informal* in actual fact; really; very much. **4** *with negatives* at all: *absolutely nothing* • *absolutely no use*. ▸ *exclam* yes; certainly.

absolute majority *noun* in an election: a number of votes for a candidate which is greater than the number of votes received by all the other candidates put together.

absolute pitch see **perfect pitch**

absolute temperature *noun* temperature measured from **absolute zero** on the **Kelvin scale**.

absolute value *noun, maths* the value of a number irrespective of whether it is positive or negative, eg the absolute value of −5 is 5.

absolute zero *noun, physics* the lowest temperature theoretically possible, 0 K on the **Kelvin scale**, equivalent to −273.15°C or −459.67°F.

absolution *noun* the formal forgiving of a person's sins. [12c: from Latin *absolutio* acquittal]

absolutism *noun* the theory or practice of government by a person who has total power. See also **autocracy, despotism**. ▪ **absolutist** *noun, adj*.

absolve *verb* **1** (*usu* **absolve sb from** *or* **of sth**) to release them or pronounce them free from a promise, duty, blame, etc. **2** of a priest: to forgive someone formally for the sins they have committed. [16c: from Latin *absolvere* to loosen]

absorb *verb* **1** to take in or suck up (knowledge, etc). **2** *scientific* to take up or receive (matter or energy, eg water or radiation). **3** to receive or take something in as part of oneself or itself. **4** to engage all of (someone's attention or interest). **5** to reduce or lessen (the shock, force, impact, etc of something). **6** *physics* to take up (energy) without reflecting or emitting it. ▪ **absorbed** *adj* engrossed; intently interested. ▪ **absorbing** *adj*. [15c: from Latin *ab* away or from + *sorbere* to suck in]

absorbent *adj* able to absorb liquids, etc. ▸ *noun, med, etc* something that absorbs liquids, etc. ▪ **absorbency** *noun*.

absorption *noun* **1** the act of absorbing, or the process of being absorbed. **2** the state of having all one's interest or attention occupied by something. ▪ **absorptive** *adj*.

abstain *verb, intr* (*usu* **abstain from sth** *or* **from doing sth**) **1** to choose not to take, have or do it. **2** to formally record one's intention not to vote in an election. See also **abstention**, **abstinence**. [14c: from Latin *ab* away or from + *tenere* to hold]

abstemious *adj* of people, habits, etc: taking food, alcohol, etc in very limited amounts. ▪ **abstemiously** *adv*. ▪ **abstemiousness** *noun*. [17c: from Latin *abs* away + *temetum* strong drink]

abstention *noun* **1** the act of choosing not to do something. **2** an instance of abstaining from voting.

abstinence *noun* the practice or state of choosing not to do or take something, esp to drink alcohol. ▪ **abstinent** *adj*. ▪ **abstinently** *adv*.

abstract *adj* /ˈabstrakt/ **1** referring to something which exists only as an idea or quality. **2** concerned with ideas and theory rather than with things which really exist or could exist. **3** of an art form, esp painting: that represents the subject by shapes and patterns, etc rather than in the shape or form it actually has. Compare **concrete** (*adj* sense 2), **figurative** (sense 4). **4** *grammar* of a noun: denoting a quality, condition or action rather than a physical thing. Compare **concrete** (*adj* sense 4). ▸ *noun* /ˈabstrakt/ **1** a brief statement of the main points (of a book, speech, etc). **2** an abstract idea, theory, etc. **3** an example of abstract painting, etc. ▸ *verb* /abˈstrakt/ **1** to take out or remove something. **2** to summarize (a book, speech, etc). [14c: from Latin *abs* away or from + *trahere* to draw]

abstracted *adj* of a person: thinking about something so much that they do not notice what is happening around them. ▪ **abstractedly** *adv*.

abstraction *noun* **1** the act, or an example, of abstracting something. **2** something which exists as a general idea rather than as an actual example. **3** the state of thinking about something so much that one does not notice what is happening around one. **4** the process of taking something from a source: *abstraction of water from rivers*.

abstruse *adj* hard to understand. [16c: from Latin *abstrusus* pushed away]

absurd *adj* **1** not at all suitable or appropriate. **2** ridiculous; silly. ▪ **absurdity** *noun* (**-ies**). ▪ **absurdly** *adv.* [16c: from Latin *absurdus* out of tune]

abundance *noun* **1** a large amount, sometimes more than is needed. **2** wealth. [14c: from Latin *abundare* to overflow]

abundant *adj* existing in large amounts. ▪ **abundantly** *adv.*

IDIOMS **abundant in sth** having or providing a large amount or variety of something.

abuse *verb* /əˈbjuːz/ **1** to use (one's position, power, etc) wrongly. **2** to treat someone or something cruelly or wrongly. **3** to betray (a confidence). **4** to speak rudely or insultingly to or about someone. ▸ *noun* /əˈbjuːs/ **1** wrong use of one's position, power, etc. **2** bad or cruel treatment of someone or something. **3** (*also* **child abuse**) the physical, mental or emotional maltreatment of a child. **4** an evil or corrupt practice. **5** rude or insulting words said to or about someone. [15c: from Latin *abusus* misused]

abusive *adj* insulting or rude; using insulting or rude language. ▪ **abusively** *adv.*

abut *verb* (**abutted, abutting**) **1** *intr* (*usu* **abut against** *or* **on sth**) of countries, areas of land, buildings, etc: to join, touch or lean against another. **2** to lean on or touch something: *a wall abutting the house.* [15c: from French *abouter* to touch with an end]

abutment *noun, archit, eng* the support at the end of an arch, bridge, etc.

abuzz *adj* in a state of noisy activity or excitement.

abysmal *adj, informal* extremely bad. ▪ **abysmally** *adv.* [19c: from French *abisme* abyss]

abyss /əˈbɪs/ *noun* **1** a very large and deep chasm. **2** anything that seems to be bottomless or unfathomable. [14c: from Greek *abyssos* bottomless]

Abyssinian /abɪˈsɪnɪən/ *adj* of or relating to Abyssinia, the former name of Ethiopia. ▸ *noun* an inhabitant of, or a person born in, Abyssinia.

AC *abbrev* **1 alternating current**. Compare **DC**, **AC/DC**. **2** appellation contrôlée.

Ac *symbol, chem* actinium.

a/c *abbrev* **1** account. **2** account current.

acacia /əˈkeɪʃə/ *noun* a tree or shrub found mainly in Australia, Africa and S America, most of which bear clusters of small yellow flowers. Also called **wattle**. [16c: from Greek *akakia*]

academia *noun* the scholarly world or life.

academic *adj* **1** to do with learning, study, education or teaching. **2** to do with a university or college. **3** theoretical rather than practical. **4** of no practical importance, eg because impossible or unreal: *What we would do with a car is academic, since we can't afford one.* **5** of a person: fond of or having an aptitude for intellectual pursuits. ▸ *noun* a member of the teaching or research staff at a university or college. ▪ **academically** *adv.*

academy *noun* (**-ies**) **1** a school or college that gives training in a particular subject or skill. **2** a society that encourages the study of science, literature, art or music. **3** in Scotland: a secondary school. [16c: from Greek *Akademeia* the garden outside Athens where the philosopher Plato taught]

Academy Award *trademark* see **Oscar**

acanthus *noun* **1** a plant with spiny leaves and bracts, and white, pink or purple flowers. **2** *archit* a conventionalized carving of an acanthus leaf used as a decoration, eg on columns or plaster mouldings. [17c: from Greek *akanthos*]

ACAS /ˈeɪkas/ *abbrev, Brit* Advisory, Conciliation and Arbitration Service.

accede *verb, intr* (*often* **accede to sth**) **1** to take office, esp (as **accede to the throne**) to become king or queen. **2** to agree: *accede to the proposal.* **3** to join with others in a formal agreement. [15c: from Latin *accedere* to go near]

accelerando *adv, adj, music* increasingly faster. [19c: Italian]

accelerate *verb* **1** *tr & intr* to increase the speed of something. **2** to make something happen sooner. [16c: from Latin *accelerare*]

acceleration *noun* **1** *physics* the rate of change of velocity with time, equal to **force** (*noun* sense 9) divided by **mass**[1] (*noun* sense 1). **2** any increase in the speed or rate at which a vehicle moves or a process occurs. **3** the ability of a motor vehicle, etc, to accelerate.

accelerator *noun* **1** a pedal or lever designed to control the speed of an electric motor or engine. **2** *physics* a piece of apparatus designed to increase the velocity of charged atomic particles.

accent *noun* /ˈaksənt/ **1** the particular way words are pronounced by people who live in a particular place, belong to a particular social group, etc. **2** emphasis or stress put on a particular syllable in speaking. **3** a mark put over a vowel to show how it is pronounced, eg **acute**, **grave**[3] or **circumflex**. Compare **diacritic**. **4** a feature, mark or characteristic that makes something distinct or special. **5** *music* emphasis or stress placed on certain notes or chords. ▸ *verb* /əkˈsɛnt/ **1** to pronounce something with an accent. **2** to mark an accent on (a written letter or syllable). **3** to emphasize or stress. [14c: from Latin *accentus*]

accentuate *verb* **1** to emphasize or make something more evident or prominent. **2** to mark something with an accent. ▪ **accentuation** *noun.* [18c: from Latin *accentuare*]

accept *verb* **1** to agree or be willing to take or receive (something offered). **2** *tr & intr* to agree to (a suggestion, proposal, etc). **3** to agree to do (a job, etc) or take on (a responsibility, etc). **4** to believe something to be true or correct. **5** to be willing to listen to and follow (advice, etc). **6** to be willing to suffer or take (blame, etc). **7** to allow someone into a group, treat them as a colleague, etc. **8** to tolerate something calmly. [14c: from Latin *acceptare* to receive]

---

accept, except

Be careful not to use the spelling **accept** when you mean **except**:

> *I know nothing about first aid, except what I learned at school.*

---

acceptable *adj* **1** worth accepting. **2** welcome or pleasing; suitable. **3** good enough, but usu only just; tolerable. ▪ **acceptability** *noun.* ▪ **acceptably** *adv.*

acceptance *noun* **1** the act or state of accepting something. **2** favourable reception of something. **3** a written or formal answer to an invitation, etc accepting it.

access *noun* **1** a means of approaching or entering a place. **2** the right, opportunity or ability to use, approach, meet with or enter something. **3** *comput* the right and opportunity to **log on** (see under **log**) to a computer system, and to read and edit files that are held within it, often requiring the entry of a password. **4** *comput* the possibility of transferring data to and from a memory device. ▸ *verb* to locate or retrieve (information stored in the memory of a computer). [14c: from Latin *ad* to + *cedere* to go]

accessary see **accessory**

accessible *adj* **1** able to be reached or entered easily. **2** willing to talk to or have friendly discussions with other people. **3** easy to understand and enjoy or get some benefit from. ▪ **accessibility** *noun.*

accession *noun* the act or process of taking up a new office or responsibility, or of becoming a king or queen. [17c: from Latin *accedere* to accede]

accessory *noun* (**-*ies***) **1** something additional to, but less important than, something else. **2** an item of dress, such as a bag, hat, etc which goes with a dress, coat, etc. **3** (*sometimes* **accessary**) *law* someone who helps a criminal do something wrong. [17c: from Latin *accessorius*]

access road *noun* a minor road built specially to give access to a house, motorway, etc.

access time *noun, comput* the time interval between the issue of a command requesting the retrieval of data from memory, and the stage at which data is obtained.

accident *noun* **1** an unexpected event that causes damage or harm. **2** something that happens without planning or intention; chance: *managed it by accident.* [14c: from Latin *accidere* to happen]

accidental *adj* **1** happening or done by accident; not planned. **2** incidental; not essential. ▸ *noun* **1** in written music: a sign, such as a sharp or flat, put in front of a note to show that it is to be played higher or lower than the key signature indicates. **2** something that is not a necessary feature of something. ▪ **accidentally** *adv.*

accident-prone *adj* of a person: frequently causing or involved in accidents, usu minor ones.

acclaim *verb* **1** (*usu* **acclaim sb as sth**) to declare them to be a specified thing, with noisy enthusiasm. **2** to receive or welcome someone or something with noisy enthusiasm. ▸ *noun* enthusiastic approval. [17c: from Latin *acclamare*]

acclamation *noun* approval or agreement demonstrated by applause or shouting.

acclimatize *or* **-ise** /ə'klaɪmətaɪz/ *verb, tr & intr* to make or become accustomed to a new place, situation, climate, etc. *US equivalent* **acclimate** /'akləmeɪt, ə'klaɪmət/. ▪ **acclimatization** *noun.* [19c: from French *acclimater*]

accolade *noun* **1** a sign or expression of great praise or approval. **2** a touch on the shoulder with a sword when giving a person a knighthood. [17c: French]

accommodate *verb* **1** to provide someone with a place in which to stay. **2** to be large enough to hold something. **3** to oblige someone; to do them a favour. **4** to adapt or adjust something in order to make it more acceptable to or appropriate for something else. [16c: from Latin *accommodare* to adapt]

accommodating *adj* helpful; willing to do what another person wants.

accommodation *noun* **1** (also *N Am* **accommodations**) a room or rooms in a house or hotel in which to live. **2** willingness to accept other people's wishes, etc. **3** adaptation or adjustment. **4** (also *N Am* **accommodations**) a reserved place on a bus, train, ship or aircraft. **5** *biol* adjustment of the shape of the lens of the eye, in order to focus on distant or nearby objects.

accommodation

This word is often misspelt. It has two *m*'s as well as two *c*'s. It might help you to remember the following sentence:

*Good a**ccomm**odation has **c**omfortable **c**hairs and **m**odern **m**achines.*

accommodation address *noun* an address used on letters to a person who cannot give, or does not want to give, their permanent address.

accompaniment *noun* **1** something that happens or exists at the same time as something else, or which comes with something else. **2** music played to accompany a singer or another instrument.

accompanist *noun* someone who plays a musical instrument to accompany a singer or another player.

accompany *verb* (**-*ies*, -*ied***) **1** to come or go with someone. **2** to be done or found with something: *The series is accompanied by a workbook.* **3** to play a musical instrument to support someone who is playing another instrument or singing. [15c: from French *accompagnier*]

accomplice *noun* someone who helps another commit a crime. [15c as *complice*, from Latin *complex* joined]

accomplish *verb* **1** to manage to do something. **2** to complete. [14c: from French *acomplir*]

accomplished *adj* **1** expert or skilled. **2** completed or finished.

accomplishment *noun* **1** a social or other skill developed through practice. **2** something special or remarkable which has been done; an achievement. **3** the finishing or completing of something.

accord *verb* **1** *rather formal* to give someone (a welcome, etc) or grant them (permission, a request, etc). **2** *intr* (*usu* **accord with sb** *or* **sth**) to agree or be in harmony with them. ▸ *noun* agreement or harmony. [12c: from French *acorder*]

IDIOMS **of one's own accord** willingly; without being told to or forced to. **with one accord** with everyone in agreement and acting at the same time.

accordance *noun* agreement or harmony: *in accordance with the law.*

according *adv* **1** (*usu* **according to sb**) as said or told by them: *According to my doctor I am getting better.* **2** (*usu* **according to sth**) **a** in agreement with it: *live according to one's principles;* **b** in proportion to it: *Give to each according to his need.* **3** (*usu* **according as**) *formal* in proportion as; depending on whether: *pay according as one is able.*

accordingly *adv* **1** in an appropriate way: *act accordingly.* **2** therefore; for that reason.

accordion *noun* a musical instrument with metal reeds blown by bellows, the melody being produced by means of buttons or a keyboard. ▪ **accordionist** *noun.* [19c: from German *Akkordion*]

accost *verb* to approach someone and speak to them, esp boldly or in a threatening way. [16c: from French *acoster*]

account *noun* **1** a description or report. **2** an explanation, esp of one's behaviour. **3 a** an arrangement by which a bank or building society allows a person to have banking or credit facilities; **b** a deposit of money in a bank or building society. **4** a statement of the money owed to a person or company for goods or services. **5** (*usu* **accounts**) a record of money received and spent. **6** an arrangement by which a shop allows a person to buy goods on credit and pay for them later. ▶ *verb, formal* to consider someone or something to be as specified: *accounted them all fools.* [14c: from French *aconter* to count]

IDIOMS **bring sb to account** to punish them for something wrong that has been done. **by all accounts** according to general opinion. **call sb to account** to demand an explanation from them for their action or behaviour. **hold sb to account** to consider them responsible. **on account of sth** because of it. **on no account** not for any reason. **take sth into account** *or* **take account of sth** to make allowances for or consider (a problem, opinion or other factor) when making a decision or assessment.

PHRASAL VERBS **account for sth 1** to give a reason or explanation for it. **2** to make or give a reckoning of (money spent, etc). **account for sth** *or* **sb** to succeed in destroying or disposing of it or them.

accountable *adj* responsible; having to explain or defend one's actions or conduct. ▪ **accountability** *noun.*

accountant *noun* a person whose profession is to prepare, keep or audit the financial records of a business, company, etc. ▪ **accountancy** *noun.*

accounting *noun* the skill or practice of preparing or keeping the financial records of a company, etc.

accoutrements /ə'kuːtrəmənts/ *plural noun* **1** equipment. **2** a soldier's equipment apart from clothing and weapons. [16c: from French *accoustrer* to equip]

accredit *verb* **1** (*usu* **accredit sth to sb** *or* **accredit sb with sth**) to attribute (a saying, action, etc) to them. **2** (*usu* **accredit sb to** *or* **at a place**) to send (an ambassador or diplomat) to (a foreign country) with official authority. **3** to state officially that something is of a satisfactory standard. **4** *NZ* to accept (a student) for university on the basis of work done in school rather than a public examination. ▪ **accreditation** *noun.* [17c: from French *accréditer*]

accredited *adj* officially recognized.

accretion *noun, formal or technical* **1** an extra layer of material that has formed on something else. **2** the process of separate things growing into one. ▪ **accretive** *adj.* [17c: from Latin *accretio* growing together]

accrue *verb* **1** *intr* **a** to come in addition, as a product, result or development; **b** to be added as interest. **2** (*often* **accrue to sb** *or* **sth**) to fall to them or it naturally. **3** to collect: *accrued a collection of antique vases.* ▪ **accrual** *noun.* [15c: from French *acrue*]

accumulate *verb* **1** to collect or gather something in an increasing quantity. **2** *intr* to grow greater in number or quantity. [16c: from Latin *accumulare* to heap]

accumulation *noun* **1** the activity or process of accumulating. **2** a heap or mass.

accumulative *adj* **1** becoming greater over a period of time. **2** tending to gather or buy, etc many things.

accumulator *noun* **1** *elec eng* a storage battery that can be recharged by passing a current through it from an external direct current supply. **2** *horse-racing* (*also* **accumulator bet**) *Brit* a bet on four or more races, where the original money bet and any money won are bet on the next race.

accuracy *noun* the state of being absolutely correct and making no mistakes, esp through careful effort.

accurate *adj* **1** absolutely correct; making no mistakes. **2** agreeing exactly with the truth or a standard. ▪ **accurately** *adv.* [17c: from Latin *accuratus* performed with care]

accursed /ə'kɜːsɪd, ə'kɜːst/ *adj* **1** *informal* disliked or hated. **2** having been cursed.

accusation *noun* **1** the act of accusing someone of having done something wrong. **2** *law* a statement charging a person with having committed a crime. ▪ **accusatory** *adj.*

accusative (abbrev **acc.** *or* **accus.**) *grammar, noun* **1** in certain languages: the form or **case²** (sense 7b) of a noun, pronoun or adjective when it is the object of an action. **2** a noun, etc in this case. ▶ *adj* belonging to or in this case.

accuse *verb* (*usu* **accuse sb of sth**) to charge them with (an offence). ▪ **accuser** *noun.* ▪ **accusing** *adj.* ▪ **accusingly** *adv.* [13c: from Latin *accusare*]

IDIOMS **stand accused** *law* to appear in court charged with an offence. **the accused** the person or people accused of an offence.

accustom *verb* (*usu* **accustom sb** *or* **oneself to sth**) to make them or oneself familiar with it. [15c: from French *acostumer*]

accustomed *adj* usual; customary.

IDIOMS **accustomed to sb** used to them. **accustomed to sth** familiar with or experienced in it.

AC/DC *or* **ac/dc** *abbrev, elec* alternating current/direct current. Compare **AC**, **DC**.

ace *noun* **1** *cards* the card in each of the four suits with a single symbol on it. **2** *informal* someone who is extremely good at something. **3** a fighter pilot who has shot down many enemy aircraft. **4** *tennis* a serve that is so fast and cleverly placed that the opposing player cannot hit the ball back. ▶ *adj, informal* excellent. [13c: from Latin *as* a unit]

IDIOMS **an ace up one's sleeve** a hidden or secret advantage, argument, etc that will help one to beat an opponent. **within an ace of sth** *or* **of doing sth** very close to it: *came within an ace of winning.*

acerbic /ə'sɜːbɪk/ *adj* **1** bitter and sour in taste. **2** bitter and harsh in manner, speech, etc.

acerbity *noun* **1** applied to taste: sourness; bitterness. **2** applied to language or temper: harshness; sharpness. [17c: from Latin *acerbus* sour]

acetaldehyde /asɪ'taldɪhaɪd/ *noun, chem* a colourless volatile liquid used as a solvent and reducing agent. Also called **ethanal**.

acetate /'asəteɪt/ *noun* **1** a salt or ester of acetic acid. Also called **ethanoate**. **2** any of various synthetic fibres that are made from cellulose acetate, a tough thermoplastic resin.

acetic /ə'siːtɪk, ə'sɛtɪk/ *adj* consisting of or like vinegar. [19c: from Latin *acetum* vinegar]

acetic acid *noun* a clear colourless pungent liquid present in vinegar. Also called **ethanoic acid**.

acetone /ˈasətoun/ *noun, chem* a colourless flammable volatile liquid with a characteristic pungent odour, widely used as a solvent for paints and varnishes, and as a raw material in the manufacture of plastics. Also called **propanone**.

acetyl /ˈasətaɪl, -tɪl/ *noun, chem* the radical (*noun* sense 3) of acetic acid. Also called **ethanoyl**.

acetylene /əˈsɛtɪliːn/ *noun, chem* a colourless highly flammable gas, used mostly in lighting and in the manufacture of organic compounds. Also called **ethyne**.

ache *verb, intr* **1** to feel a dull continuous pain. **2** to be the source of a dull continuous pain. **3** to want very much: *aching to tell him my news.* ▸ *noun* a dull continuous pain. ▪ **aching** *or* **achy** *adj* (**-*ier*, -*iest***). [Anglo-Saxon *acan* to ache]

achieve *verb* to reach, realize or attain (a goal, ambition, etc), esp through hard work. ▪ **achievable** *adj.* ▪ **achiever** *noun.* [14c: from French *achever*]

achievement *noun* **1** the gaining of something, usu after working hard for it. **2** something that has been done or gained by effort.

Achilles' heel /əˈkɪliːz/ *noun* a person's weak or vulnerable point. [19c: named after Achilles, a hero in Homer's *Iliad*, who was invulnerable to weapons except in his heel]

Achilles' tendon *noun, anatomy* the tendon situated at the back of the ankle, that connects the muscles in the calf of the leg to the heelbone.

achromatic *adj* **1** without colour. **2** of a lens: capable of transmitting light without separating it into its constituent colours.

acid *noun* **1** *chem* any of a group of compounds that have a sour or sharp taste, turn blue litmus paper red, and react with bases to form salts. **2** any sour substance. **3** *slang* **LSD**. ▸ *adj* **1** sour to taste. **2** of remarks, etc: expressing bitterness or anger. **3** *chem* containing or having the properties of an acid. ▪ **acidic** *adj.* ▪ **acidly** *adv.* [17c: from Latin *acidus* sour]

acidify *verb* (**-*ies*, -*ied***) *tr & intr* to make or become acid. ▪ **acidification** *noun.*

acidity *noun* (**-*ies***) **1** the quality of being acid or sour. **2** *chem* the extent to which a given solution is acid, as indicated by its **pH**.

acid rain *noun, ecol* rain containing dissolved pollutants that have been released into the atmosphere as a result of the burning of fossil fuels.

the acid test *noun* a decisive test to determine whether something is genuine or valid. [20c: from a test using acid to determine whether a substance contained gold]

acidulous *adj* slightly sour. [18c: from Latin *acidulus*]

acknowledge *verb* **1** to admit or accept the truth of (a fact or situation). **2** to report that one has received (what has been sent). **3** to express thanks for something. **4** to show that one has noticed or recognized someone, by greeting them, nodding one's head, etc. [16c: from earlier *acknow* to acknowledge]

acknowledgement *or* **acknowledgment** *noun* **1** the act of acknowledging someone or something. **2** something done, given or said to acknowledge something.

acme /ˈakmɪ/ *noun* the highest point of achievement, success, etc. [16c: from Greek *akme* point]

acne /ˈaknɪ/ *noun, pathol* a skin disorder caused by overactivity of the sebaceous glands, esp on the face, chest and back. [19c: perhaps from Greek *akme* point]

acolyte *noun* **1** *Christianity* someone who assists a priest. **2** an assistant or attendant. [16c: from Latin *acolytus*]

aconite *noun* **1** a plant which has hooded bluish-purple flowers. **2** the narcotic analgesic drug obtained from the roots of this plant. [16c: from Latin *aconitum*]

acorn *noun* the nut-like fruit of the oak tree, which has a cup-shaped outer case. [Anglo-Saxon *æcern*]

acoustic *or* (*esp in senses 1 and 3*) **acoustical** *adj* **1** relating to, producing or operated by sound. **2** relating to the sense of hearing. **3** of a musical instrument, eg a guitar or piano: amplifying the sound by means of its body, not using an electrical amplifier. **4** of building materials, etc: designed so as to reduce the disturbance caused by excessive noise. ▪ **acoustically** *adv.* [17c: from Greek *akouein* to hear]

acoustics *plural noun* the characteristics of a room, theatre, etc that determine the nature and quality of sounds heard within it. ▸ *singular noun* the scientific study of the production and properties of sound waves.

acquaint *verb* (*usu* **acquaint sb with sth**) to make them aware of or familiar with it. [13c: from French *acointer*]

IDIOMS **be acquainted with sb** to know them personally but only slightly. **be acquainted with sth** to be familiar with it. **become acquainted with sb** to get to know them personally.

acquaintance *noun* **1** slight knowledge of something or someone. **2** someone whom one knows slightly.

IDIOMS **make sb's acquaintance** to get to know them.

acquiesce /akwɪˈɛs/ *verb, intr* (*usu* **acquiesce in** *or* **to sth**) to accept it or agree to it without objection. ▪ **acquiescence** *noun.* ▪ **acquiescent** *adj.* [17c: from Latin *acquiescere*]

acquire *verb* **1** to get or develop something, esp through skill or effort. **2** to achieve or reach (a reputation). ▪ **acquirement** *noun.* [15c: from Latin *acquirere*]

acquired immune deficiency syndrome *or* **acquired immunodeficiency syndrome** see **AIDS**

acquired taste *noun* **1** a liking for something that develops as one has more experience of it. **2** a thing liked in this way.

acquisition *noun* **1** something obtained or acquired, esp through hard work or effort. **2** a valuable addition to a group, a collection, etc. **3** the act of obtaining, developing or acquiring a skill, etc.

acquisitive *adj* very eager to obtain and possess things.

acquit *verb* (***acquitted*, *acquitting***) (*often* **acquit sb of sth**) of a court or jury, etc: to declare a person accused of a crime to be innocent. [13c: from French *aquiter*]

IDIOMS **acquit oneself** to behave or perform in a specified way: *acquitted themselves well.*

acquittal *noun* **1** a declaration in a court of law that someone is not guilty of the crime, etc of which they have been accused. **2** performance of a duty.

acre /ˈeɪkə(r)/ *noun* **1** a measure of land area equal to 4840 square yards (4047 sq m). **2** (*usu* **acres**) *infor-*

mal, loosely a large area. ▪ **acreage** *noun* the number of acres in a piece of land. [Anglo-Saxon *æcer* field]

acrid *adj* **1** having a very bitter and pungent smell or taste. **2** of speech, manner, etc: sharp or bitter. ▪ **acridity** /a'krɪdɪtɪ/ *noun*. ▪ **acridly** *adv*. [18c: from Latin *acer* sharp or keen]

acrimony *noun* bitterness in feeling, temper or speech. ▪ **acrimonious** *adj*. [16c: from Latin *acrimonia*]

acrobat *noun* an entertainer, eg in a circus, who performs skilful balancing acts and other athletic tricks. ▪ **acrobatic** *adj*. ▪ **acrobatically** *adv*. [19c: from French *acrobate*]

acrobatics *singular noun* the art or skill of an acrobat. ▸ *plural noun* acrobatic movements.

acronym /'akrənɪm/ *noun* a word made from the first letters or syllables of other words, and usu pronounced as a word in its own right, eg *NATO*. [1940s: from Greek *akron* point or tip + *onyma* name]

acrophobia *noun, psychol* fear of heights or high places. ▪ **acrophobic** *adj, noun*.

acropolis /ə'krɒpəlɪs/ *noun* the upper fortified part or citadel of an ancient Greek city, now esp Athens. [19c: from Greek *akron* summit + *polis* city]

across *prep* **1** to, at or on the other side of something. **2** from one side of something to the other. **3** so as to cross something: *arms folded across the chest*. ▸ *adv* **1** to, at or on the other side. **2** from one side to the other. **3** in a crossword: in the horizontal direction: *6 across*. Compare **down** (*adv* sense 10). [15c: **a-**[1] + **cross**]

IDIOMS **across the board** *adv or* **across-the-board** *adj* generally or general; applying in all cases.

across

This word is often misspelt. It has only one c. It might help you to remember the following sentence:

There is only one sea (one **c***) to get* **across***.*

acrostic *noun* a poem or puzzle in which the first, last or middle letters in each line, or a combination of these, form a word or proverb. [16c: from Greek *akron* end + *stichos* line]

acrylic *noun* any of various synthetic products derived from acrylic acid. ▸ *adj* relating to, containing or derived from acrylic acid. [20c: from Latin *acer* sharp + *olere* to smell]

acrylic acid *noun, chem* a highly reactive colourless liquid with a pungent odour and acidic properties.

acrylic fibre *noun* a synthetic fibre derived from acrylic acid, used for making knitwear and other clothing, etc. Often shortened to **acrylic**.

acrylic resin *noun* any of numerous synthetic resins used to make artificial fibres, paints and adhesives.

ACT *abbrev, Aust territory* Australian Capital Territory.

act *noun* **1** a thing done; a deed. **2** the process of doing something: *caught in the act*. **3** behaviour that is not a sincere expression of feeling: *Her shyness is just an act*. **4 a** a short piece of entertainment, usu one of a series in a variety show; **b** the person or people performing this. **5** a major division of a play, opera, etc. **6** (*often* **Act**) a law passed by a law-making body. ▸ *verb* **1** *intr* to behave or function in a specified way: *act tough*. **2** *intr* to do something: *need to act fast*. **3** *intr* to perform in a play or film. **4 a** to perform (a part) in a play or film; **b** to perform (a play). **5** to play the part of someone or something: *to act the fool*. **6** *intr* (**act as sb** *or* **sth**) to perform the actions or functions of (a specified person or thing): *He acted as caretaker until an appointment was made*. **7** *intr* (**act for sb**) to stand in as substitute for them. **8** *intr* to show feelings one does not really have. [14c: from Latin *actum* thing done]

IDIOMS **get in on the act** *informal* to start taking part in some profitable activity, plan, etc in order to share in the benefits. **get one's act together** *informal* to become organized and ready for action.

PHRASAL VERBS **act on** *or* **upon sth** to follow (advice, instructions, etc).

acting *noun* the profession or art of performing in a play or film. ▸ *adj* temporarily doing someone else's job or duties: *the acting headmaster*.

actinide *noun* any of a series of radioactive elements from actinium to lawrencium.

actinium *noun, chem* (symbol **Ac**) a radioactive metallic element found in uranium ores, used as a source of **alpha particle**s. [19c: from Greek *aktis* ray]

action *noun* **1** the process of doing something: *put ideas into action*. **2** something done. **3** activity, force or energy: *a woman of action*. **4** a movement or gesture. **5** the working part of a machine, instrument, etc; a mechanism. **6** a battle; fighting: *saw action in Korea*. **7** (**the action**) the events of a play, film, etc. **8** *informal* (**the action**) exciting activity or events going on around one: *get a piece of the action*. **9** a legal case. [14c: from Latin *actio*]

IDIOMS **out of action** not working.

actionable *adj* giving reasonable grounds for legal action.

action-packed *adj, informal* filled with exciting activity.

action painting *noun* an American version of **tachism** in which paint is dripped, spattered or smeared on to the canvas.

action replay *noun* on television: the repeating of a piece of recorded action, eg the scoring of a goal in football, usu in slow motion or from another angle. *N Am equivalent* **instant replay**.

action stations *plural noun* **1** positions taken by soldiers ready for battle. **2** *informal* posts assumed or manned in readiness for any special combined task or action.

activate *verb* **1** to make something start working or go into operation. **2** to make (a material) radioactive. **3** to increase the speed of or to cause (a chemical reaction). ▪ **activation** *noun*. ▪ **activator** *noun*.

active *adj* **1** of a person, etc: full of energy. **2** of a machine, etc: operating; working. **3** having an effect: *the active ingredients*. **4** of a volcano: liable to erupt; not extinct. **5** *physics* radioactive. **6** *grammar* (abbrev **act.**) **a** denoting or relating to a verbal construction in which the subject performs the action or has the state described by the verb, as in *the man fell, smoking kills you* and *God exists*. Compare **passive** (*adj* sense 3); **b** denoting or relating to the verb in such a construction. ▸ *noun, grammar* **1** (*also* **active voice**) the form or forms that an active verb takes. **2** an active verb or construction. ▪ **actively** *adv*. [14c: from Latin *activus*]

active service *noun* military service in the battle area.

activist *noun* someone who is very active, esp as a member of a political group. ▪ **activism** *noun*.

activity *noun* (**-*ies***) **1** the state of being active or busy. **2** (*often* **activities**) something that people do, esp for pleasure, interest, exercise, etc. **3** *physics* the rate at which the atoms of a radioactive substance disintegrate.

Act of Parliament *noun, Brit* a statute that has passed through both the House of Commons and the House of Lords, and received royal assent.

actor *noun* a man or woman who performs in plays or films, esp as their profession.

actress *noun* a female actor.

actual *adj* **1** existing as fact; real. **2** not imagined, estimated or guessed. **3** current; present. [14c: from Latin *actualis*]

actual bodily harm *noun* (abbrev **ABH**) *law* a criminal offence involving a less serious attack than **grievous bodily harm**.

actuality *noun* (**-*ies***) fact; reality.

actually *adv* **1** really; in fact. **2** usu said in surprise or disagreement: as a matter of fact.

actuary *noun* (**-*ies***) someone who calculates insurance risks, and gives advice to insurance companies, etc on what premiums to set. ▪ **actuarial** /-ˈɛərɪəl/ *adj*. [19c: from Latin *actuarius* clerk]

actuate *verb* to make (a mechanism, etc) go into action. ▪ **actuator** *noun*. [17c: from Latin *actuare*]

acuity /əˈkjuːɪtɪ/ *noun* **1** sharpness or acuteness, eg of the mind or senses. **2** (*esp* **visual acuity**) sharpness of vision. [16c: Latin, literally 'point', from *acus* needle]

acumen /ˈakjʊmən/ *noun* the ability to judge quickly and well; keen insight. [16c: Latin]

acupressure *noun* a treatment similar to acupuncture, pressure instead of needles applied at specified points (**acupoints**). See also **shiatsu**. [1950s: from **acupuncture** + **pressure** (sense 2)]

acupuncture *noun* a traditional Chinese method of healing in which symptoms are relieved by the insertion of thin needles at specified points (**acupoints**) beneath the skin. ▪ **acupuncturist** *noun*. [17c: from Latin *acus* needle + **puncture**]

acute *adj* **1** of the senses: keen, good or sharp; penetrating. **2** of mental powers, etc: quick and very good. **3** of a disease or symptoms: arising suddenly and often severe: *acute pain* • *acute bronchitis*. Compare **chronic**. **4** of any bad condition or situation: extremely severe: *acute drought*. **5** of hospital accommodation: intended for patients with acute illnesses. **6** *geom* of an angle: less than 90°. Compare **reflex** (*adj* sense 5), **obtuse** (sense 3). ▸ *noun* (*also* **acute accent**) a sign placed above a vowel in some languages, to indicate a particular pronunciation of the vowel, as with é in French, or, as in Spanish, to indicate that the vowel is to be stressed. ▪ **acutely** *adv*. ▪ **acuteness** *noun*. [16c: from Latin *acuere* to sharpen]

acyl group /ˈeɪsɪl, ˈasɪl/ *noun, chem* the radical RCO-, where R is **aliphatic**. [20c: from **acid** + **-yl**]

AD *abbrev* in dates: *Anno Domini* (Latin), in the year of our Lord, used together with a figure to indicate a specified number of years after that in which Christ was once thought to have been born. Compare **BC**, **BCE**. See also **Common Era**.

ad *noun, informal* an **advertisement**.

adage /ˈadɪdʒ/ *noun* a proverb or maxim. [16c: French]

adagio /əˈdɑːdʒɪoʊ/ *music, adv* slowly. ▸ *adj* slow. ▸ *noun* a piece of music to be played in this way; a slow movement. [18c: Italian]

adamant *adj* completely determined; not likely to change one's mind or opinion.

Adam's apple *noun, anatomy* the projection of the **thyroid** cartilage, lying just beneath the skin at the front of the throat.

adapt *verb* **1** *tr & intr* to change something, oneself, etc so as to fit new circumstances, etc; to make something suitable for a new purpose. **2** to alter or modify something. [17c: from Latin *ad* to + *aptare* to fit]

adaptable *adj* **1** of a person: good at fitting into new circumstances, situations, etc. **2** of a machine, device, etc: that can be adapted. ▪ **adaptability** *noun*.

adaptation *noun* **1** a thing that is adapted. **2** the process of adapting. **3** *biol* a change in the structure or behaviour of a living organism that improves its chances of survival in its environment.

adaptor *or* **adapter** *noun* **1** a device designed to connect two parts of different sizes. **2** a device that enables a plug and socket with incompatible terminals to be connected, or that allows more than one electrical appliance to be powered from a single socket.

ADC *abbrev* aide-de-camp.

ADD *or* **ADHD** *abbrev* attention deficit (hyperactivity) disorder.

add *verb* **1** (*also* **add sth together** *or* **add sth to sth else**) to put together or combine (two or more things). **2** (*also* **add sth up**) **a** to calculate the sum of two or more numbers or quantities in order to obtain their total value; **b** *intr* (*also* **add up**) to carry out the process of addition. **3** (**add sth on**) to attach it to something else. **4** (**add sth in**) to include it, esp as an extra. **5** to say or write something further: *They added a remark about the bad weather.* [14c: from Latin *addere*]

PHRASAL VERBS **add up** *informal* to make sense; to be coherent. See also *verb* (sense 2b) above.

addendum *noun* (***addenda***) **1** an addition. **2** (*usu* **addenda**) an extra piece of text added to the end of a book.

adder *noun* the common European **viper**, a poisonous snake with a dark zigzag line running down its back. [Anglo-Saxon *nædre*]

addict *noun* **1** someone who is dependent on the habitual intake of a drug. **2** *informal* someone who is extremely fond of a hobby, etc: *a chess addict*. ▪ **addictive** *adj*.

addicted *adj* **1** (*esp* **addicted to sth**) dependent on it (esp a drug). **2** unable to give it up, eg a habit. [16c: from Latin *addicere* to surrender]

addiction *noun* **1** the state of being addicted. **2** a habit that has become impossible to break, esp one involving physical and psychological dependence on the intake of harmful substances such as alcohol or drugs.

addition *noun* **1** the act or operation of adding. **2** someone or something that is added. **3** *maths* the combination of two or more numbers in such a way as to obtain their sum.

IDIOMS **in addition (to)** as well (as); besides.

additional *adj* extra; more than usual. ▪ **additionally** *adv*.

additive *noun* any chemical substance that is deliberately added to another substance, usu in small quantities, for a specific purpose, eg a food flavouring or colouring. ▸ *adj, maths* relating to addition.

addle *verb* **1** to confuse or muddle. **2** *intr* of an egg: to go bad. ▪ **addled** *adj.* [Anglo-Saxon *adela* mud]

addle-brained, addle-headed *or* **addle-pated** *adj* of a person: confused; crazy.

address *noun* /əˈdrɛs; also *N Am* ˈadrɛs/ **1** the number or name of the house or building, and the name of the street and town, where a person lives or works. **2** *rather formal* a speech or lecture. **3** *comput* a number giving the place in a computer memory where a particular piece of information is stored. ▸ *verb* /əˈdrɛs/ **1** to put the name and address on (an envelope, etc). **2** to make a speech, give a lecture, etc to (a group of people). **3** to speak to someone. **4** (**address oneself to sb**) to speak or write to them. **5** (*also* **address oneself to sth**) to give one's attention to (a problem, etc). [15c: from French *adresser*]

---

address

This word is often misspelt. It has two *d*'s as well as two *s*'s. It might help you to remember the following sentence:

*Your a**dd**re**ss** is where letters are **d**irectly **d**elivered, **s**afe and **s**ound.*

---

address book *noun* **1** a notebook in which names and addresses can be entered. **2** *comput* a facility on a computer for storing e-mail addresses.

addressee *noun* the person to whom a letter, etc is addressed.

adduce *verb* to mention (a fact) as a supporting reason, piece of evidence, etc. [17c: from Latin *ducere* to lead]

adduct *verb* of a muscle: to bring a part of the body (such as an arm or finger) towards another or towards the centre line of the body. Compare **abduct** (sense 2). ▪ **adduction** *noun.* ▪ **adductor** *noun.*

adenine /ˈadəniːn/ *noun, biochem* a base that is one of the four bases found in **nucleic acid**. See also **cytosine, guanine, thymine**.

adenoidal *adj* of the voice: having the blocked nasal tone normally associated with swollen adenoids.

adenoids *plural noun, anatomy* a pair of lymph glands located in the upper part of the throat at the back of the nasal cavity. [19c: from Greek *adenoiedes*]

adept *adj* (*often* **adept at sth**) skilful at doing it; proficient. ▸ *noun* an expert at something. [17c: from Latin *adeptus* having attained something]

adequate *adj* **1** enough; sufficient. **2** only just satisfactory. ▪ **adequacy** *noun.* ▪ **adequately** *adv.* [17c: from Latin *adaequatus* made equal]

à deux /a dø/ *adv* for or consisting of two people: *dinner à deux.* [19c: French]

ADHD see **ADD**

adhere *verb, intr* (*often* **adhere to sth**) **1** to stick or remain fixed to something. **2** to remain loyal to (a religion, etc). **3** to follow (a plan, rule, etc) exactly. [16c: from Latin *adhaerere*]

adherent *noun* a follower; a supporter. ▸ *adj* sticking or adhering. ▪ **adherence** *noun.*

adhesion *noun* **1** the process of sticking or adhering. **2** the sticking together of two surfaces, esp by means of an adhesive. **3** *pathol* (*often* ***adhesions***) a mass or band of fibrous connective tissue that develops, esp after surgery or injury, between membranes or other structures which are normally separate.

adhesive *adj* sticky; able to make things stick together. ▸ *noun* any substance that is used to bond two surfaces together.

ad hoc *adj, adv* for one particular purpose, situation, etc only: *employed on an ad hoc basis.* [17c: Latin, meaning 'for this purpose']

adieu /əˈdjuː/ *noun* (***adieus*** *or* ***adieux*** /-z/) a goodbye. ▸ *exclam* goodbye. [14c: French, from *à* to + *dieu* God]

Adi-Granth see **Guru Granth Sahib**

ad infinitum /ad ɪnfɪˈnaɪtəm/ *adv* for ever; without limit. [17c: Latin]

adipose *adj, technical* relating to, containing or consisting of fat; fatty. [18c: from Latin *adeps* soft fat]

adipose tissue *noun, anatomy* body tissue that stores fat, and provides insulation and an energy reserve.

adj. *abbrev* adjective.

adjacent *adj* (*often* **adjacent to sth**) lying beside or next to it. ▪ **adjacency** *noun.* [15c: from Latin *adjacere* to lie by the side of]

adjective *grammar, noun* (abbrev **adj.**) a word that describes or modifies a noun or pronoun, as *dark* describes *hair* in *She has dark hair.* ▪ **adjectival** /-ˈtaɪvəl/ *adj.* [16c: from Latin *adjicere* to attach or associate]

adjoin *verb* to be next to and joined to something. ▪ **adjoining** *adj.*

adjourn *verb* **1** to put off (a meeting, etc) to another time. **2** to finish (a meeting, etc), intending to continue it at another time or place. **3** *intr* to move to another place, usu for refreshment or rest. ▪ **adjournment** *noun.* [14c: from French *ajorner*]

adjudge *verb* to declare or judge officially.

adjudicate *verb* **1** *intr* to act as judge in a court, competition, etc. **2** to give a decision on (a disagreement between two parties, etc). ▪ **adjudication** *noun.* ▪ **adjudicator** *noun.* [17c: from Latin *adjudicare*]

adjunct /ˈadʒʌŋkt/ *noun* **1** something attached or added to something else but not an essential part of it. **2** a person who is below someone else in rank. [16c: from Latin *adjungere* to join to]

adjure *verb, formal* to request, beg or command someone formally or solemnly. ▪ **adjuration** *noun.* [14c: from Latin *adjurare* to swear with an oath]

adjust *verb* **1** to change something or oneself, etc slightly so as to be more suitable for a situation, etc. **2** to change or alter something, esp only slightly, to make it more correct or accurate. **3** to calculate or assess (the amount of money payable in an insurance claim, etc). **4** *intr* (*often* **adjust to sth**) to change so that one fits in with it or becomes suited to it. ▪ **adjustable** *adj.* ▪ **adjuster** *noun.* ▪ **adjustment** *noun.* [17c: from French *ajuster*]

adjutant /ˈadʒʊtənt/ *noun* an army officer who does administrative work. ▪ **adjutancy** *noun* (***-ies***). [17c: from Latin *adjutare* to assist]

ad-lib *verb* (***ad-libbed, ad-libbing***) *tr & intr* **1** to say something without preparation, esp as a departure from a prepared text or to fill time. **2** to improvise (music, etc). ▸ *adj* of speeches, etc: improvised. ▸ *adv* (**ad lib**) **1** without preparation. **2** *informal* without limit; freely. ▪ **ad-libber** *noun*. ▪ **ad-libbing** *noun*. [19c: short for Latin *ad libitum* at pleasure]

Adm. *abbrev* Admiral.

adman *noun, informal* a person whose job is to produce advertisements.

admin *noun, informal* **administration** (sense 1).

administer *verb* **1** to manage, govern or direct (one's affairs, an organization, etc). **2** to give out something formally: *administer justice*. **3** to supervise a person taking (an oath). **4** to apply or provide (medicine). [14c: from Latin *administrare*]

administrate *verb, tr & intr* to administer.

administration *noun* **1** the directing, managing or governing of a company's affairs, etc. **2** a period of government by a particular party, etc. **3** a period of government by a particular US president: *the Nixon administration*. **4** the group of people who manage a company's affairs or run the business of government.

administrative *adj* relating to or concerned with administration. ▪ **administratively** *adv*.

administrator *noun* someone who manages, governs, etc the affairs of an organization, estate, etc.

admirable *adj* **1** worthy of being admired. **2** very good; excellent. ▪ **admirably** *adv*.

admiral *noun* **1** a high-ranking officer in the navy. **2** a name applied to several species of butterfly: *red admiral*. [15c: from Arabic *amir-al-bahr* lord of the sea]

Admiralty *noun* (*usu* **the Admiralty**) *Brit, hist* the government department that managed the Royal Navy until the responsibility passed to the Ministry of Defence in 1964.

admire *verb* to regard with respect or approval. ▪ **admiration** /admɪ'reɪʃən/ *noun*. ▪ **admirer** *noun*. ▪ **admiring** *adj*. [16c: from Latin *admirari*]

admissible *adj* that can be allowed or accepted, esp as proof in a court of law. ▪ **admissibility** *noun*.

admission *noun* **1** the act of allowing someone or something in or of being allowed in. **2** the cost of entry. **3 a** an act of admitting the truth of something; **b** something admitted or conceded.

admit *verb* (***admitted, admitting***) **1** *tr & intr* to confess the truth of something. **2** (*also* **admit to sth**) to agree that one is responsible for (a deed or action, esp an offence or wrongdoing). **3** *intr* (**admit of sth**) *formal* to allow it as possible or valid. **4** to allow someone to enter. **5** (*also* **admit sb to sth**) to allow them to take part in it; to accept them as a member or patient of it. **6** *formal* to have the capacity for something: *a room admitting forty people*. [15c: from Latin *admittere*]

admittance *noun* **1** the right to enter; permission to enter. **2** the act of entering; entry.

admittedly *adv* as is known to be true; as one must admit.

admixture *noun, chiefly technical* **1** anything that is added to the main ingredient of a mixture. **2** the mixture itself.

admonish *verb* to scold or tell someone off firmly but mildly. ▪ **admonition** *noun*. ▪ **admonitory** *adj*. [14c: from French *amonester*]

ad nauseam /ad 'nɔːzɪam/ *adv* **1** to a disgusting or objectionable extent. **2** excessively. [17c: Latin, meaning 'to the point of sickness']

ado *noun* difficulty or trouble.

IDIOMS **without more** *or* **further ado** without any more delay.

adobe /ə'doʊbɪ/ *noun* **1** a building material made of clay and straw, and dried in the sun. **2** a sun-dried brick made from such material. **3** a building made from such bricks. [18c: Spanish]

adolescent *adj* **1** of a young person: between puberty and adulthood. **2** relating to or typical of this state. **3** *informal* of behaviour: silly and immature. ▸ *noun* a young person between puberty and adulthood. ▪ **adolescence** *noun* this stage of development. [15c: from Latin *adolescere* to grow up]

Adonis *noun* a handsome young man. [17c: in Greek mythology, the name of a handsome youth]

adopt *verb* **1** *tr & intr* to take (a child of other parents) into one's own family, becoming its legal parent. **2** to take up (a habit, position, policy, etc). **3** to take (an idea, etc) over from someone else. ▪ **adoption** *noun*. [16c: from Latin *adoptare*]

adoptive *adj* that adopts or is adopted.

adorable *adj, informal* very charming and attractive.

adore *verb* **1** to love someone deeply. **2** *informal* to like something very much. **3** to worship (a god). ▪ **adoration** *noun*. ▪ **adoring** *adj*. ▪ **adoringly** *adv*. [14c: from Latin *adorare*]

adorn *verb* **1** to decorate. **2** to add beauty to something. ▪ **adornment** *noun*. [14c: from Latin *adornare* to fit something out]

ADP *abbrev* **1** *comput* automatic data processing, the use of computer systems to process information with little or no human assistance. **2** *chem* adenosine diphosphate, an organic compound formed by the breakdown of **ATP**.

adrenal /ə'driːnəl/ *adj, anatomy* **1** referring or relating to the kidneys. **2** situated on or near the kidneys. **3** referring or relating to the adrenal glands. [19c: from Latin *ad* to + **renal**]

adrenal gland *noun, zool, anatomy* in mammals: either of a pair of glands, situated one above each kidney, that secrete adrenaline.

adrenaline *or* **adrenalin** *noun, biol* a hormone secreted by the adrenal glands in response to fear, excitement or anger, which causes an increase in heartbeat and blood pressure.

adrift *adj, adv* **1** of a boat: not tied up. **2** without help or guidance. **3** *informal* off course.

adroit *adj* quick and clever in action or thought. ▪ **adroitly** *adv*. ▪ **adroitness** *noun*. [17c: from French *à droit* rightly]

adsorb *verb, technical* of a solid: to accumulate a thin layer of atoms or molecules of (a solid, liquid, or gas) on its surface. ▪ **adsorbent** *adj*. ▪ **adsorption** *noun*. [19c: from Latin *sorbere* to suck in]

adulate *verb* to praise or flatter someone far too much. ▪ **adulation** *noun*. ▪ **adulatory** *adj*. [18c: from Latin *adulari* to fawn upon]

adult *adj* **1** fully grown; mature. **2** typical of, or suitable for, a fully grown person. ▸ *noun* a fully grown person, animal, bird or plant. ▪ **adulthood** *noun*. [16c: from Latin *adultus* grown-up]

adulterate *verb* to debase something by mixing it with something inferior or harmful. ▪ **adulteration** *noun*. [16c: from Latin *adulterare* to defile]

adultery *noun* sexual relations willingly undertaken between a married person and a person who is not their spouse. ▪ **adulterer** *noun*. ▪ **adulteress** *noun*. ▪ **adulterous** *adj*. [15c: from Latin *adulterare* to defile]

adumbrate *verb, formal* to indicate or describe in a general way. [16c: from Latin *adumbrare* to shade in or sketch]

adv. *abbrev, grammar* adverb.

advance *verb* **1** *tr & intr* to put, move or go forward. **2** *intr* to make progress. **3** to help the progress of something. **4** to propose or suggest (an idea, etc). **5** to put something at an earlier time or date than that previously planned. **6** *tr & intr* of a value, price or rate: to increase. ▸ *noun* **1** progress. **2** a payment made before it is due. **3** money lent to someone. **4** an increase, esp in price. **5** (*esp* **advances**) a friendly or sexual approach to a person. ▸ *adj* done, made or given beforehand. [16c: from Latin *abante* in front]
IDIOMS **in advance** ahead in time, place or development.

advanced *adj* **1** having progressed or developed well or far. **2** modern; new or revolutionary.

Advanced Higher *noun, Scot* **1** an examination at a more advanced level than a **Higher**. **2** a pass in such an examination.

Advanced level see **A level**

Advanced Subsidiary level see **AS level**

advancement *noun* promotion in rank or improvement in status.

advantage *noun* **1** a favourable circumstance; benefit. **2** a circumstance that may help one to succeed, win, etc. **3** superiority over another. **4** *tennis* the point scored after **deuce**. ▸ *verb* to benefit someone or improve their position. [14c: from French *avantage*]
IDIOMS **take advantage of sb** *or* **sth** **1** to make use of a situation, a person's good nature, etc in such a way as to benefit oneself. **2** *old use* to seduce someone. **to advantage** in such a way as to emphasize the good qualities: *shows off her figure to advantage*.

advantaged *adj* having a good social or financial situation.

advantageous *adj* giving help or benefit in some way. ▪ **advantageously** *adv*.

advent *noun* **1** coming or arrival; first appearance. **2** (**Advent**) *Christianity* the period that includes the four Sundays before Christmas. **3** (**Advent**) *Christianity* the first or second coming of Christ. [12c: from Latin *adventus* arrival]

Adventist *noun, Christianity* a member of a group that believes in the imminent second coming of Christ.

adventitious *adj* **1** happening by chance. **2** *biol* denoting tissues or organs that grow in an unusual position, eg a root growing upwards from a stem. [17c: from Latin *adventicius* coming from the outside]

adventure *noun* **1** an exciting and often dangerous experience. **2** the excitement of risk or danger: *a sense of adventure*. [13c: from Latin *adventura* something about to happen]

adventure playground *noun* a playground with things for children to climb on and equipment for them to build with.

adventurer *or* **adventuress** *noun* **1** a man or woman who is willing to use any means to make money, obtain power, etc. **2** a man or woman who is eager for adventure.

adventurous *adj* **1** enjoying adventure; daring. **2** full of excitement, danger, etc.

adverb *grammar, noun* (abbrev **adv.**) a word that describes or adds to the meaning of a verb, adjective or another adverb, such as *very* and *quietly* in *They were talking very quietly*. ▪ **adverbial** *adj*. [16c: from Latin *advium* a word added after]

adversary /ˈadvəsərɪ/ *noun* (**-ies**) **1** an opponent in a competition, etc. **2** an enemy. [14c: from Latin *adversarius*]

adverse *adj* **1** unfavourable to one's interests. **2** disapproving. **3** hurtful. ▪ **adversely** *adv*. [14c: from Latin *adversus* hostile]

---

adverse, averse

Be careful not to use the word **adverse** when you mean **averse**. **Averse** means reluctant about or opposed to:

> *We're not averse to giving the children extra pocket money, as long as they spend it on something worthwhile.*

---

adversity *noun* (**-ies**) **1** circumstances that cause trouble or sorrow. **2** a misfortune.

advert *noun, informal* an **advertisement**.

advertise *or* (*US sometimes*) **-ize** /ˈadvətaɪz, advəˈtaɪz/ *verb* **1** to draw attention to or describe (goods for sale, services offered, etc) to encourage people to buy or use them. **2** (*usu* **advertise for sth** *or* **sb**) to ask for or seek it or them by putting a notice in a newspaper, shop window, etc. **3** to make something known publicly or generally. ▪ **advertiser** *noun*. ▪ **advertising** *noun*. [16c: from French *avertir*]

advertisement *noun* **1** a public notice, announcement, etc, which advertises something. **2** a short television film advertising something. Often shortened to **ad**, **advert**.

advice *noun* **1** suggestions or opinions given to someone about what they should do in a particular situation. **2** *business* an official note about a transaction, etc. [13c: from French *avis*]

advisable *adj* of action to be taken, etc: to be recommended; sensible. ▪ **advisability** *noun*.

advise *verb* **1** to give advice to someone. **2** to recommend something. **3** (*usu* **advise sb of sth**) to inform them about it. ▪ **adviser** *or* **advisor** *noun*. [13c: from French *aviser*]

advised *adj, esp in compounds* considered; judged: *well-advised*.

advisedly *adv* after careful thought; on purpose.

advisory *adj* appointed in order to give advice.

advocaat /ˈadvoʊkɑː, -kɑːt/ *noun* a liqueur made from raw eggs, sugar and brandy. [20c: from Dutch *advocaatenborrel* lawyers' drink (so called because it supposedly cleared the throat)]

advocacy *noun* (**-ies**) recommendation or active support of an idea, etc.

advocate *noun* /ˈadvəkət/ **1** esp in Scotland: a lawyer who speaks for the defence or prosecution in a trial. See also **barrister**, **solicitor**. **2** someone who supports or recommends an idea, proposal, etc. ▸ *verb* /ˈadvəkeɪt/ to recommend or support (an idea, proposal, etc), esp in public. ▪ **advocation** *noun*. [14c: from French *avocat*]

adze *or* (*US*) **adz** *noun* a tool with an arched blade set at right angles to its handle, used for cutting and shaping wood. [Anglo-Saxon *adesa*]

aegis /ˈiːdʒɪs/ *noun* protection or patronage. [18c: from Greek *aigis* the shield of Zeus]
IDIOMS **under the aegis of sb** *or* **some organization** under their supervision, support or patronage.

-aemia, (*US*) **-emia** *or* **-haemia**, (*US*) **-hemia** *combining form, denoting* the presence of specified substances, esp to excess, in the blood: *leukaemia*.

aeolian deposits /ɪˈoʊlɪən/ *plural noun, geog* sediments carried and deposited by wind, eg desert sands, loess, etc. [From Greek *Aiolus*, god of the winds]

aeolian harp /ɪˈoʊlɪən/ *noun* a box-like musical instrument which has strings stretched across a hole, and which makes musical sounds when the wind passes through it. [18c: from Greek *Aiolus*, god of the winds]

aeon see **eon**

aerate *verb* to charge (a liquid) with carbon dioxide or some other gas, eg when making fizzy drinks. ▪ **aeration** *noun*.

aerial *noun* a wire, rod or other device, esp on a radio or television receiver, used to receive or transmit signals. Also called **antenna**. ▸ *adj* **1** relating to or found in the air. **2** like air. **3** relating to or using aircraft. [17c: from Latin *aer* air]

aerie see **eyrie**

aero- *combining form, signifying* **1** air: *aerodynamics*. **2** aircraft: *aerodrome*. [From Greek *aer* air]

aerobatics *plural noun* spectacular or dangerous manoeuvres in an aircraft or glider. ▸ *singular noun* the art of performing such manoeuvres in the air. ▪ **aerobatic** *adj*. [1917: from **aero-**, modelled on **acrobatics**]

aerobe *noun, biol* any organism that requires oxygen in order to survive. Compare **anaerobe**. [19c: from French *aérobie*]

aerobic *adj* **1** *biol* of an organism: requiring oxygen in order to obtain energy by respiration, and so to survive. Compare **anaerobic**. **2** relating to aerobics. **3** of some forms of physical exercise, eg walking, jogging, and swimming: producing an increase in the rate at which the body uses oxygen.

aerobic respiration *noun, biol* the process in which cells use oxygen to break down foodstuffs, releasing energy and creating carbon dioxide and water. Compare **anaerobic respiration**.

aerobics *singular noun* a system of physical exercise aimed at increasing the supply of oxygen in the blood and strengthening the heart and lungs. ▸ *plural noun* energetic exercises.

aerodrome *noun, Brit* a small area of land and its associated buildings, used by private and military aircraft.

aerodynamic *adj* **1** relating to **aerodynamics**. **2** making effective use of aerodynamics so as to minimize air resistance and drag.

aerodynamics *singular noun* the study of the movement of air relative to moving objects, eg aircraft, cars, etc. ▸ *plural noun* the qualities required for fast and efficient movement through the air.

aerofoil *noun* any body or part shaped so as to provide lift or thrust when it is moving through the air, eg the wings of an aeroplane.

aerogramme *or* **aerogram** *noun* a thin piece of paper on which to write letters for sending by air, and which can be folded and sealed without being put into an envelope. Also called **air letter**.

aeronautics *singular noun* the scientific study of travel through the Earth's atmosphere. ▪ **aeronautic** *or* **aeronautical** *adj*.

aeroplane *noun* a powered machine used for travelling in the air, that is heavier than air and supported in its flight by fixed wings. [19c: French]

aerosol *noun* **1** a suspension of fine particles of a solid or liquid in a gas. **2** a can containing a product, eg paint, polish or insecticide mixed with a **propellant**, that can be sprayed to produce such a suspension. [1920s: from **aero-** + *sol*ution]

aerospace *noun* the Earth's atmosphere and the space beyond it. ▸ *adj* referring to the design and development of aircraft and spacecraft: *the aerospace industry*.

aesthete /ˈiːsθiːt/ *or* (*US*) **esthete** /ˈɛsθiːt/ *noun* someone who has or claims to have a special appreciation of art and beauty. [19c: from Greek *aisthetes* one who perceives]

aesthetic *or* (*US*) **esthetic** /ɪsˈθɛtɪk, ɛs-/ *adj* **1** able to appreciate beauty. **2** artistic; tasteful. ▪ **aesthetically** *adv*. [19c: from Greek *aisthetikos*]

aesthetics *singular noun* **1** the branch of philosophy concerned with the study of the principles of beauty, esp in art. **2** the principles of good taste and the appreciation of beauty.

aestival *or* (*US*) **estival** /ˈiːstɪvəl, ˈɛstɪ-/ *adj* referring or relating to summer.

aestivate *or* (*US*) **estivate** /ˈiːstɪveɪt, ˈɛstɪ-/ *verb, biol* of certain animals: to survive the hot summer months in a dormant or torpid state. Compare **hibernate**. ▪ **aestivation** *or* (*US*) **estivation** *noun*. [17c, meaning 'to spend the summer', from Latin *aestivare*, from *aestas* summer]

aether see under **ether** (*noun* senses 3, 4)

aetiology *or* (*US*) **etiology** /iːtɪˈɒlədʒɪ/ *noun* (**-ies**) **1** the science or philosophy of causes. **2** the scientific study of the causes or origins of disease. **3** the cause of a specific disease. ▪ **aetiological** *adj*. [17c: from Greek *aitia* cause]

afar *adv* at a distance.
IDIOMS **from afar** from a great distance.

affable *adj* pleasant and friendly in manner. ▪ **affability** *noun*. ▪ **affably** *adv*. [16c: from Latin *affabilis*]

affair *noun* **1** a concern, matter or thing to be done. **2** an event or connected series of events. **3** a sexual relationship between two people, usu when at least one of them is married to someone else. **4** (**affairs**) matters of importance and public interest: *current affairs*. **5** (**affairs**) private or public business matters: *put my affairs in order*. [13c: from French *afaire*]

affect[1] *verb* **1** to have an effect on someone or something. **2** to cause someone to feel strong emotions, esp sadness or pity. **3** of diseases: to attack or infect. [17c: from Latin *afficere*]

affect, effect
Be careful not to use **affect** when you mean the noun **effect**:
the damaging effects of smoking
special effects used in the film

affect[2] *verb* **1** to pretend to feel or have (eg an illness or emotion). **2** to use, wear, etc something in a way that is intended to attract attention: *affect an accent*. [15c: from Latin *affectare* to aim at]

affectation *noun* unnatural behaviour or pretence which is intended to impress people.

affected *adj* **1** not genuine; pretended. **2** of a manner of speaking or behaving: put on to impress people.

affecting *adj* causing people to feel strong emotion.

affection *noun* **1** a feeling of love or strong liking. **2** (**affections**) feelings.

affectionate *adj* showing love or fondness.

affiance /ə'faɪəns/ *verb* (*usu* **be affianced to sb**) *old use* to be or become engaged to be married to them. [17c: from French *afiancer* to pledge in marriage]

affidavit /afɪ'deɪvɪt/ *noun, law* a written statement, sworn to be true by the person who makes it, for use as evidence in a court of law. [17c: Latin, meaning 'he or she has sworn on oath']

affiliate *verb* /ə'fɪlɪeɪt/ *tr & intr* (*usu* **be affiliated with** *or* **to sth**) to connect or associate a person or organization with a group or a larger organization. ▸ *noun* /ə'fɪlɪət/ a person or organization, etc that has an association with a group or larger body. ▪ **affiliation** *noun*. [18c: from Latin *affiliatus* adopted]

affiliation order *noun, law* a court order instructing a man to pay money towards the support of his illegitimate child.

affinity *noun* (**-ies**) **1** a strong natural liking for or feeling of attraction or closeness towards someone or something. **2** (*usu* **affinity with sb**) relationship to them, esp by marriage. **3** similarity in appearance, structure, etc, esp one that suggests relatedness. **4** (*usu* **affinity for sth**) chemical attraction between substances. [14c: from Latin *affinitas*]

affirm *verb* **1** to state something as a fact. **2** to uphold or confirm (an idea, belief, etc). ▪ **affirmation** *noun*. [14c: from French *afermer*]

affirmative *adj* expressing agreement; giving the answer 'yes'. Opposite of **negative**. ▸ *noun* an affirmative word or phrase.

affix *verb* /ə'fɪks/ to attach or fasten. ▸ *noun* /'afɪks/ *grammar* a word-forming element of one or more syllables which can be added to a word to form another, related, word, eg *un-* in *unhappy* or *-ness* in *sadness*; a **prefix** or **suffix**. [16c: from Latin *affigere* to fasten to]

afflict *verb* to cause someone physical or mental suffering. [14c: from Latin *affligere* to cast down]

affliction *noun* **1** distress or suffering. **2** a cause of this.

affluent *adj* having more than enough money; rich. ▪ **affluence** *noun*. [18c: from Latin *affluere* to flow freely]

afford *verb* **1** (*used with can, could, be able to*) **a** to have enough money, time, etc to spend on something; **b** to be able to do something, or allow it to happen, without risk. **2** to give; to provide: *a room affording a view of the sea*. ▪ **affordability** *noun*. ▪ **affordable** *adj*. [Anglo-Saxon *geforthian* to promote]

afforest *verb* to establish a forest on bare or cultivated land. ▪ **afforestation** *noun*.

affray *noun* a fight in a public place. [14c: from French *esfrei*]

affront *noun* an insult, esp one delivered in public. ▸ *verb* **1** to insult someone, esp in public. **2** to offend the pride of someone. [14c: from French *afronter* to slap in the face]

Afghan *adj* belonging or relating to Afghanistan, its inhabitants or their language. ▸ *noun* **1** (*also* **Afghani**) a citizen or inhabitant of, or person born in, Afghanistan. **2** the official language of Afghanistan. **3** (*also* **Afghan hound**) a type of tall thin dog with long silky hair. [18c: Pashto, the official language of Afghanistan]

aficionado /əfɪʃɪə'nɑːdoʊ/ *noun* someone who takes an enthusiastic interest in a particular sport or pastime. [19c: Spanish]

afield *adv* to or at a distance; away from home: *far afield*.

aflame *adj* **1** in flames; burning. **2** very excited.

aflatoxin *noun, biol* a toxic substance, produced by a fungus, which contaminates stored corn, soya beans, peanuts, etc in warm humid regions. [20c: from *A*spergillus *fla*vus (one of the fungi producing this) + **toxin**]

afloat *adj, adv* **1** floating. **2** at sea; aboard ship. **3** out of debt; financially secure.

afoot *adj, adv* being prepared or already in progress or operation: *There is trouble afoot*.

afore *adv, prep, old use or dialect* before.

afore- *combining form, signifying* before; previously.

aforementioned *adj* already mentioned.

aforesaid *adj* said or mentioned already.

aforethought *adj* premeditated.

IDIOMS **with malice aforethought** *law* of a criminal act: done deliberately; planned beforehand.

a fortiori /eɪ fɔːtɪ'ɔːraɪ/ *adv* for a stronger reason. *as adj*: *an a fortiori argument*. [17c: Latin]

afraid *adj* **1** (*often* **afraid of sb** *or* **sth**) frightened of them or it. **2** (*usu* **afraid to do sth**) reluctant to do it out of fear or concern for the consequences. **3** as a polite formula of regret: sorry: *I'm afraid we're going to be late*. [14c as *afrayed*]

afresh *adv* again, esp from the start.

African *adj* belonging or relating to the continent of Africa, its inhabitants, or their languages. ▸ *noun* a citizen or inhabitant of, or person born in, Africa.

African-American *or* (*dated*) **Afro-American** *noun* an American whose ancestors were orig brought from Africa as slaves. ▸ *adj* belonging or relating to African-Americans, their culture, etc. Also called **Black American**.

African elephant see under **elephant**

Afrikaans *noun* one of the official languages of S Africa, developed from Dutch. [20c: Dutch, meaning 'African']

Afrikaner *noun* a white inhabitant of S Africa, esp one of Dutch descent, whose native language is Afrikaans.

Afro *noun* a hairstyle consisting of thick bushy curls standing out from the head.

Afro- *combining form, signifying* African.

Afro-American see **African-American**

Afro-Caribbean *noun* a person living in the Caribbean whose ancestors orig came from Africa. ▸ *adj* relating to Afro-Caribbeans, their culture, etc.

aft /ɑːft/ *adv, adj, chiefly naut* at or towards the stern, rear or tail. [Anglo-Saxon *æftan* behind]

after *prep* **1** coming later in time than something. **2** following someone or something in position. **3** next to and following something in importance, order, etc. **4** because of something; considering: *You can't expect to be promoted after that mistake.* **5** in spite of something: *He's still no better after all that medicine.* **6** about someone or something: *ask after her.* **7** in pursuit of someone or something: *run after him.* **8** of a painting or other work of art: in the style or manner of (someone else). **9** with a name derived from that of (someone else): *called her Mary after her aunt.* **10** *N Am, esp US* past (an hour): *It's twenty after six.* ▸ *adv* **1** later in time. **2** behind in place. ▸ *conj* after the time when. ▸ *adj* **1** later: *in after years.* **2** *naut* further towards the stern of a ship: *the after deck.* See also **aft.** [Anglo-Saxon *æfter*]

IDIOMS **after all 1** in spite of all that has happened or has been said or done. **2** contrary to what is or was expected.

afterbirth *noun, zool, med* the placenta, blood and ruptured membranes expelled from the uterus after the birth of a mammal.

aftercare *noun* care and support given to someone after a period of treatment, a surgical operation, a prison sentence, etc.

afterdamp *noun* a poisonous gas arising in coal mines after an explosion of **firedamp**.

after-effect *noun* a circumstance or event that follows as the result of something.

afterglow *noun* **1** a glow remaining in the sky after the sun has set. **2** a pleasant impression or feeling that remains when the experience, etc that caused it is over.

afterlife *noun* the continued existence of one's spirit or soul after one's death.

aftermath *noun* circumstances that follow and are a result of something, esp a great and terrible event. [16c, meaning 'second mowing']

afternoon *noun* the period of the day between noon and the evening.

afters *singular noun, Brit informal* dessert; pudding.

aftershave *noun* a perfumed lotion for a man to put on his face after shaving. Also called **aftershave lotion**.

aftershock *noun* a small earthquake that follows the main shock of a large earthquake.

aftersun *noun* a lotion applied to damaged skin after sunbathing.

aftertaste *noun* the taste that remains in the mouth or comes into it after one has eaten or drunk something.

afterthought *noun* an idea thought of after the main plan, etc has been formed.

afterwards *or* (*esp US*) **afterward** *adv* later.

Ag *symbol, chem* silver. [From Latin *argentum* silver]

again *adv* **1** once more; another time. **2** back to (a previous condition or situation, etc): *get well again.* **3** in addition: *twice as much again.* **4** however; on the other hand: *He might come, but then again he might not.* **5** further; besides. [Anglo-Saxon *ongean* back]

against *prep* **1** close to or leaning on something. **2** into collision with something or someone. **3** in opposition to something. **4** in contrast to something: *against a dark background.* **5** with a bad or unfavourable effect on someone or something: *His age counts against him.* **6** as a protection from someone or something. **7** in return for something: *the exchange rate against the dollar.* [12c as *ageines*, meaning 'in front of']

agape [1] *adj* **1** of the mouth: gaping; open wide. **2** of a person: very surprised.

agape [2] /'agəpeɪ/ *noun, Christianity* selfless love, or the love of God for man. [17c: Greek, meaning 'love']

agar /'eɪgɑː(r)/ *or* **agar-agar** *noun, med, cookery* a gelatinous substance extracted from seaweed, used as a thickening agent in food. [19c: Malay]

agaric *noun, botany* any of various fungi that produce an umbrella-shaped spore-bearing structure with a central vertical stem supporting a circular cap, eg **death cap**. [16c: from Latin *agaricum*]

agate /'agət/ *noun* a variety of chalcedony consisting of concentrically arranged bands of two or more colours. [16c: from French *agathes*]

agave /ə'geɪvɪ/ *noun, botany* an evergreen plant, native to Central and S America, with fleshy leaves and tall flower stalks. [19c: Greek female name]

age *noun* **1** the period of time during which a person, animal or thing has lived or existed. **2** a particular stage in life: *old age.* **3** the fact or time of being old. **4** in the Earth's history: an interval of time during which specific life forms, physical conditions, geological events, etc were dominant: *the Ice Age.* **5** (*usu* **ages**) *informal* a very long time. ▸ *verb* (***ageing*** *or* ***aging***) **1** *intr* to show signs of growing old. **2** *intr* to grow old. **3** *intr* to mature. **4** to make someone seem older or look old. ▪ **ageing** *or* **aging** *noun, adj.* [13c: from French *aage*]

IDIOMS **come of age** to become legally old enough to have an adult's rights and duties. **under age** too young to be legally allowed to do something.

-age *suffix, forming nouns, signifying* **1** a collection, set or group: *baggage.* **2** an action or process: *breakage.* **3** the result of an action or event: *wreckage.* **4** a condition: *bondage.* **5** a home, house or place: *orphanage* . **6** cost or charge: *postage.* **7** rate: *dosage.* [French]

aged /eɪdʒd in sense 1, 'eɪdʒɪd in senses 2 and 3/ *adj* **1** having a specified age. **2** very old. **3** (**the aged**) old people as a group.

age group *or* **age bracket** *noun* the people between two particular ages, considered as a group.

ageism *or* **agism** *noun* the practice of treating people differently, and usu unfairly, on the grounds of age only. ▪ **ageist** *or* **agist** *noun, adj.*

ageless *adj* never growing old; never looking older.

age limit *noun* the age under or over which one may not do something.

agency *noun* (***-ies***) **1** an office or business that provides a particular service, eg matching workers with employers in specific areas. **2** an active part played by someone or something in bringing something about. **3** *N Am* a government department providing a particular service. [17c: from Latin *agere* to do]

agenda *singular noun* **1** a list of things to be done or discussed. **2** a written list of subjects to be dealt with at a meeting, etc. [20c: Latin, meaning 'things needing to be done']

agent *noun* **1 a** someone who represents an organization and acts on its behalf; **b** someone who deals with someone else's business matters, etc. **2** (*also* **secret agent**) a spy. **3** a substance that produces a particular effect. **4** someone who is the cause of something. [16c: from Latin *agere* to do]

agent provocateur /*French* aʒɑ̃pʀɔvɔkatœʀ/ *noun* (***agents provocateurs*** /*French* aʒɑ̃pʀɔvɔkatœʀ/) someone employed to lead others in illegal acts for which they will be punished. [19c: French]

age of consent *noun* the age at which consent to sexual intercourse is permitted by law.

age-old *adj* done, known, etc for a very long time.

agglomerate *verb, tr & intr* to make into or become a mass. ▸ *noun* **1** a mass or collection of things. **2** *geol* a type of volcanic rock consisting of a mass of coarse angular fragments of solidified lava. ▸ *adj* formed into a mass. ▪ **agglomeration** *noun.* [17c: from Latin *agglomerare* to wind on to a ball]

agglutinate *verb* **1** to stick or glue together. **2** *biol* of red blood cells, bacteria, etc: to clump together and form a visible precipitate. ▪ **agglutination** *noun.* [16c: from Latin *agglutinare* to glue together]

aggrandize *or* **-ise** *verb* to make someone or something seem greater than they really are. ▪ **aggrandizement** *noun.* [17c: from French *aggrandir*]

aggravate *verb* **1** to make (a bad situation, an illness, etc) worse. **2** *informal* to make someone angry; to annoy them. ▪ **aggravating** *adj.* ▪ **aggravation** *noun.* [16c: from Latin *aggravare* to make heavier or worse]

aggregate *noun* /ˈagrəgət/ **1** a collection of separate units brought together; a total. **2** *civil eng, building* any material, esp sand, gravel or crushed stone, that is mixed with cement to form concrete. **3** *geol* a mass of soil grains or rock particles, or a mixture of both. ▸ *adj* /ˈagrəgət/ formed of separate units combined together. ▸ *verb* /-geɪt/ **1** *tr & intr* to combine or be combined into a single unit or whole. **2** *informal* to amount in total to something. ▪ **aggregation** *noun.* [15c: from Latin *aggregare* to herd or bring together]

aggression *noun* **1** the act of attacking another person or country without being provoked. **2** an instance of hostile behaviour towards someone. **3** the tendency to make unprovoked attacks. **4** hostile feelings or behaviour. [17c: from Latin *aggredi* to attack]

aggressive *adj* **1** always ready to attack; hostile. **2** strong and determined. **3** of an action: hostile.

aggressor *noun* the person, group or country that attacks first in a fight, war, etc.

aggrieved *adj* angry, hurt or upset. [13c: from French *agrever* to press heavily upon]

aggro *noun, Brit slang* **1** violent or threatening behaviour. **2** problems or difficulties. [1960s: shortening of **aggravation**]

aghast *adj* filled with fear or horror. [Anglo-Saxon *gæstan* to frighten]

agile /ˈadʒaɪl *or* (*US*) ˈadʒəl/ *adj* able to move, change direction, etc quickly and easily; nimble. ▪ **agilely** *adv.* ▪ **agility** *noun.* [16c: from Latin *agilis*]

aging see under **age**

agism see **ageism**

agitate *verb* **1** to excite or trouble (a person, their feelings, etc). **2** *intr* to stir up public opinion for or against an issue. **3** to stir or shake (a liquid) vigorously. ▪ **agitated** *adj.* ▪ **agitatedly** *adv.* ▪ **agitator** *noun.* [16c: from Latin *agitare*]

agitation *noun* **1** public discussion for or against something. **2** a disturbed or nervous state of mind; anxiety.

aglow *adj* shining with colour or warmth; glowing.

AGM *abbrev* **annual general meeting**.

agnostic *noun* someone who believes that one can know only about material things and so believes that nothing can be known about the existence of God. ▸ *adj* relating to this view. ▪ **agnosticism** *noun.* [19c: from Greek *agnostos* not known]

ago *adv* in the past; earlier. [14c: orig (as *agon*) past participle of Anglo-Saxon *agan* to pass by]

agog *adj* very interested and excited; eager to know more. ▸ *adv* eagerly; expectantly. [16c: from French *en gogues* in fun]

agonist *noun, physiol* a muscle the relaxation of which opposes the contraction of another muscle (the **antagonist**).

agonize *or* **-ise** *verb, intr* (*esp* **agonize about** *or* **over sth**) to worry intensely or suffer great anxiety about it. ▪ **agonized** *adj.* ▪ **agonizing** *adj.* [16c: from Greek *agonizesthai* to struggle]

agony *noun* (***-ies***) severe bodily or mental pain. [14c: from Greek *agonia* struggle]

agony aunt *noun, informal* a person who answers letters sent in to an agony column, or who gives similar advice on radio or TV.

agony column *noun* part of a newspaper or magazine where advice is offered to readers who write in with their problems.

agoraphobia *noun, psychol* an irrational fear of open spaces or public places. ▪ **agoraphobe** *noun.* ▪ **agoraphobic** *adj, noun.* [19c: from Greek *agora* marketplace + *phobos* fear]

agrarian *adj* **1** relating to land or its management. **2** relating to the uses of land, esp agriculture. [18c: from Latin *agrarius*]

agree *verb* (***agreed, agreeing***) *usu intr* **1** (*often* **agree with sb** *or* **sth** *or* **about sth**) to be of the same opinion as them about it. **2** (*usu* **agree to sth**) to say yes to (a suggestion, request or instruction). **3** (*usu* **agree on** *or* **upon sth**) to reach a joint decision about it after discussion. **4** to reach agreement about something. **5** (*often* **agree with sth**) *grammar* to have the same number, person, gender or case. [14c: from French *agreer*]

IDIOMS **agree to differ** of two or more people, groups, etc: to agree to accept each other's different opinions.

agreeable *adj* **1** of things: pleasant. **2** of people: friendly. **3** (*usu* **agreeable to sth**) of people: willing to accept (a suggestion, etc). ▪ **agreeably** *adv.*

agreement *noun* **1** a contract or promise. **2** a joint decision made after discussion. **3** the state of holding the same opinion. **4** *grammar* the state of having the same number, person, gender or case. Also called **concord**.

agribusiness *noun* all the operations involved in supplying the market with farm produce, including growing, providing farm machinery, distribution, etc. [20c, orig US: from *agriculture* or *agro-* + **business**]

the Agricultural Revolution *noun, hist* the gradual movement in Britain, from the 18c, away from subsistence farming towards intensive farming.

agriculture *noun* the cultivation of the land in order to grow crops or raise animal livestock as a source of food or other useful products. ▪ **agricultural** *adj*. ▪ **agriculturalist** *or* **agriculturist** *noun*. [17c: from Latin *ager* field + *cultura* cultivation]

agrimony *noun* (*-ies*) an erect plant with small yellow flowers in long terminal spikes. [15c: from Greek *argemone* a type of poppy]

agroforestry *noun* the cultivation of trees and shrubs and the raising of agricultural crops or animals on the same land.

agronomy *noun* the scientific study of the cultivation of crops and soil management. ▪ **agronomist** *noun*.

aground *adj, adv* of ships: stuck on the bottom of the sea or rocks, usu in shallow water.

ague /ˈeɪgjuː/ *noun* **1** a fit of shivering. **2** malaria. [14c: from French *fièvre ague* acute fever]

AH *abbrev* used in the Islamic dating system: *anno Hegirae* (Latin), in the year of the Hegira, ie counting from AD 622.

ah *exclam* expressing surprise, sympathy, admiration, pleasure, etc.

aha *exclam* expressing pleasure, satisfaction, triumph, surprise, etc.

ahead *adv* **1** at or in the front; forwards. **2** earlier in time; before: *arrived ahead of me*. **3** in the lead; further advanced: *ahead on points*.

IDIOMS **get ahead** to make progress, esp socially.

ahem *exclam* a sound made in the back of the throat, used to gain people's attention or to express doubt or disapproval.

-aholic *or* **-oholic** *informal, combining form, forming adjectives and nouns, signifying* addicted to, or a person addicted to (a specified thing): *workaholic*. ▪ **-aholism** *or* **-oholism** *noun*. [Modelled on **alcoholic**]

ahoy *exclam, naut* a shout to greet or attract the attention of another ship.

AI *abbrev* **1** artificial insemination. **2** artificial intelligence.

aid *noun* **1** help. **2** help or support in the form of money, supplies or services given to people who need it, eg in developing countries. **3** *often in compounds* a person or thing that helps do something: *a hearing-aid*. ▸ *verb* to help or support someone. [15c: from French *aidier*]

IDIOMS **aid and abet** *law* to help and encourage someone to do something wrong, esp disobey the law. **in aid of sb** *or* **sth** in support of them or it.

aide *noun* a confidential assistant or adviser. [18c: short form of **aide-de-camp**]

aide-de-camp /eɪddəˈkɑ̃/ *or* (*chiefly US*) **aid-de-camp** *noun* (***aides-de-camp, aids-de-camp*** /eɪddəˈkɑ̃/) an officer in the armed forces who acts as assistant to a senior officer. [17c: French]

AIDS *or* **Aids** *abbrev* acquired immune deficiency (or immunodeficiency) syndrome, a disease which destroys the immune system.

AIDS-related complex *noun* (abbrev **ARC**), *pathol* a condition that manifests prior to the onset of full-blown AIDS.

ail *verb* **1** *intr* to be ill and weak. **2** *old use* to cause pain or trouble to someone. ▪ **ailing** *adj* ill; in poor health. [Anglo-Saxon *eglan* to trouble]

aileron *noun, aeronautics* one of a pair of hinged flaps at the rear edge of each wing of an aircraft, used to control roll. [20c: French diminutive of *aile* wing]

ailment *noun* an illness, esp a minor one.

aim *verb* **1** *tr & intr* (*usu* **aim at** *or* **for sb** *or* **sth**) to point or direct a weapon, remark, etc at them or it. **2** *intr* to plan, intend or try. ▸ *noun* **1** what a person, etc intends to do; the achievement aimed at. **2** the ability to hit what is aimed at: *good aim*. [14c: from French *esmer*]

IDIOMS **take aim** to point a weapon at a target so as to be ready to fire.

aimless *adj* without any purpose. ▪ **aimlessly** *adv*.

ain't *contraction, informal* **1** am not; is not; are not. **2** has not; have not.

air *noun* **1** the invisible odourless tasteless mixture of gases that forms the atmosphere surrounding the Earth, consisting mainly of nitrogen and oxygen. **2** the space above and around the Earth, where birds and aircraft fly. **3** moving air; a light breeze. **4** an appearance, look or manner: *a nonchalant air*. **5** (**airs**) behaviour intended to impress others, to show off, etc: *put on airs*. **6** a tune. **7** *in compounds* **a** relating to air or the air; **b** relating to aircraft. ▸ *verb* **1** *tr & intr* to hang (laundry) in a warm dry place to make it completely dry or to remove unpleasant smells. **2** *tr & intr* **a** to let fresh air into (a room, etc); **b** of a room, etc: to become cooler or fresher in this way. **3** to make (one's thoughts, opinions, etc) known publicly. **4** *tr & intr, N Am* to broadcast something, or be broadcast, on radio or television. [13c: French]

IDIOMS **by air** in an aircraft. **into thin air** completely; mysteriously and leaving no trace. **off the air** no longer or not yet being broadcast on radio or TV. **on the air** being broadcast on radio or TV.

air bag *noun* in a vehicle: a safety device consisting of a bag that inflates automatically in a collision to protect the occupants.

air base *noun* an operational centre for military aircraft.

air bed *noun* an inflated mattress.

air bladder *noun, biol* **1** a cavity or sac containing air. **2** a **swim bladder**.

airborne *adj* **1** of aircraft, etc: flying in the air. **2** transported by air.

air brake *noun* in heavy lorries, etc: a brake operated by compressed air.

air brick *noun* a brick with small holes, put into the side of a building to allow ventilation.

airbrush *noun* **1** a device for painting which uses compressed air to form a spray. **2** in computer graphics: a tool for achieving a similar effect. ▸ *verb* **1** to paint something using an airbrush. **2** to improve (the image of someone or something) by masking defects.

air chief marshal *noun* an officer in the Royal Air Force.

air commodore *noun* an officer in the Royal Air Force.

air-conditioning *noun* **1** any system that is used to control the temperature, relative humidity or purity of air, and to circulate it in an enclosed space such as a room, building or motor vehicle. **2** the control of room temperature, etc using such a system. ▪ **air-conditioned** *adj*. ▪ **air-conditioner** *noun*.

aircraft *singular or plural noun* any machine that is designed for travelling through air, eg an aeroplane or helicopter.

aircraft carrier *noun* a large naval warship with a flat deck which aircraft can take off from and land on.

aircraftman *or* **aircraftwoman** *noun, Brit* a person of the lowest rank in the air force.

aircrew *noun* the people in an aircraft who are responsible for flying it and looking after the passengers.

air cushion *noun* **1** a cushion that can be filled with air. **2** a pocket of down-driven air used for supporting a hovercraft, etc.

air-drop *noun* a delivery of supplies, etc by parachute. ► *verb* to deliver (supplies, etc) by parachute.

Airedale terrier *noun* a breed of large terrier.

airfield *noun* an open expanse that is used by aircraft for landing and take-off. Compare **airstrip**.

air force *noun* that part of a country's defence forces which uses aircraft for fighting.

airgun *noun* a gun that uses air under pressure to fire small pellets.

airhead *noun, slang* an idiot.

air hostess *noun, Brit* a female **flight attendant**.

airing *noun* **1** the act of airing (laundry, a room, the sheets, etc on a bed, etc) or fact of being aired. **2** the stating and discussing of opinions, etc publicly.

airing-cupboard *noun* a heated cupboard in which laundry is put to become completely dry and warm.

airless *adj* **1** of the weather: unpleasantly warm, with no wind. **2** of a room: lacking fresh air; stuffy.

air letter see **aerogramme**

airlift *noun* the transporting of large numbers of people or large amounts of goods in aircraft when other routes are blocked. ► *verb* to transport (people, goods, etc) in this way.

airline *noun* a company or organization that provides a regular transport service by aircraft.

airliner *noun* a large passenger aircraft.

airlock *noun* **1** a bubble of air or gas that obstructs or blocks the flow of liquid through a pipe. **2** an airtight chamber with two entrances, on either side of which are different air pressures, eg between a space vehicle and outer space, or a submarine and the sea.

airmail *noun* **1** the system of carrying mail by air. **2** mail carried by air. ► *verb* to send something by airmail.

airman *or* **airwoman** *noun* a pilot or member of the crew of an aeroplane, esp in an air force.

air marshal *noun, Brit* an officer in the Royal Air Force. *Also Aust, NZ.*

air mass *noun* a vast horizontal body of air.

air miles *or* **Air Miles** *plural noun* credits that are awarded with certain transactions, eg in shopping, the purchase of air tickets, etc, and which are saved up to be redeemed for reduced-price air travel.

airplane *noun, N Am* an aeroplane.

airplay *noun* the broadcasting of recorded music on the radio.

air pocket *noun* an area of reduced pressure in the air, or a downward current, which can cause an aircraft to suddenly lose height.

airport *noun* a place where civil aircraft arrive and depart, with facilities for passengers and cargo, etc.

air pump *noun* a device for pumping air out or in.

air quotes *plural noun* an up and down gesture made with curled fingers to indicate that what is being said is a quote or to suggest the speaker's scepticism, uneasiness, etc.

air raid *noun* an attack by enemy aircraft.

air-rifle *noun* a rifle that is fired by air under pressure.

airship *noun* a power-driven aircraft that consists of a streamlined envelope containing helium gas, with an engine and a **gondola** (sense 2) suspended from it. Also called **dirigible**.

airshow *noun* a flying display, especially one at an **air base**.

airside *noun* in aviation: the area of an airport with direct access to the aircraft, entry to which is controlled. Compare **landside**.

airspace *noun* the part of the atmosphere directly above a country, considered as part of that country.

airspeed *noun* the speed of an aircraft, missile, etc in relation to the air through which it is moving.

airstrip *noun* a strip of ground where aircraft can land and take off but which has no facilities. Compare **airfield**.

air terminal *noun* a building in a town from which passengers are transported to an airport nearby.

airtight *adj* **1** of a container, etc: which air cannot get into, out of, or through. **2** of an opinion, argument, etc: having no weak points.

airtime *noun* on TV or radio: the length of time given to a particular item, programme or topic.

air-traffic control *noun* a system or organization that manages the movement of aircraft and sends instructions to aircraft by radio communication. ▪ **air-traffic controller** *noun.*

air vice-marshal *noun, Brit* an officer in the Royal Air Force. *Also Aust, NZ.*

airwaves *plural noun* **1** *informal* the **radio waves** used for radio and television broadcasting. **2** the particular frequencies used for such broadcasting.

airway *noun* **1** in the body: the route by which oxygen reaches the lungs, from the nose or mouth via the windpipe. **2** a route regularly followed by aircraft.

airwoman see **airman**

airy *adj* (*-ier, -iest*) **1** with plenty of fresh cool air. **2** unconcerned. **3** light-hearted. ▪ **airily** *adv.* ▪ **airiness** *noun.*

airy-fairy *adj, informal* not based on facts or on awareness of real situations. [19c: alluding to a phrase in Tennyson, 'airy, fairy Lilian' (*Lilian*, 1830)]

aisle /aɪl/ *noun* **1** a passage between rows of seats, eg in an aircraft, theatre, etc. **2** the side part of the inside of a church. [14c in the form *ele*, from Latin *ala* wing]

aitch *noun* the letter H or h. [16c: from French *ache*]
IDIOMS **drop one's aitches** to fail to pronounce the sound of the letter *h* at the beginning of words.

aitchbone *noun* **1** the rump bone in cattle. **2** a cut of beef from this. [15c: from Latin *natis* buttocks]

ajar *adj, adv* partly open. [Anglo-Saxon *on* on + *cierr* turn]

AKA *or* **aka** *abbrev* also known as.

akimbo /ə'kɪmbou/ *adj, adv* with hands on hips and elbows bent outward. [15c as *in kenebowe* in a sharp bend]

akin *adj* **1** similar; being of the same kind. **2** related by blood.

Al *symbol, chem* aluminium.

-al *suffix* **1** *forming adjectives, signifying* related to someone specified: *parental*. **2** *forming nouns, signifying* the action of doing something specified: *arrival*. See also **-ial**. [From Latin *-alis*]

à la *prep* in the manner or style of someone or something specified: *mushrooms à la Grecque*. [16c: French]

alabaster *noun* a type of white stone used for ornaments, etc. ▸ *adj* made of or like alabaster. [14c: from Greek *alabastros*]

à la carte *adv, adj* of a meal in a restaurant: with each dish priced and ordered separately. Compare **table d'hôte**. [19c: French]

alacrity *noun* quick and cheerful enthusiasm. [16c: from Latin *alacritas*]

à la mode *adj, adv* in fashion; according to current fashion. [17c: French]

alarm *noun* **1** sudden fear produced by awareness of danger. **2** a noise warning of danger. **3** a bell, etc which sounds to warn of danger or, eg on a clock, to wake a person from sleep. **4** an alarm clock. ▸ *verb* **1** to frighten. **2** to warn someone of danger. **3** to fit or switch on an alarm on (a house, car, etc). [14c: from French *alarme*]

IDIOMS **give, raise** *or* **sound the alarm** to give warning of danger by shouting, ringing a bell, etc.

alarm clock *noun* a clock that can be set to make a noise at a particular time, usu to wake someone up.

alarming *adj* disturbing or frightening.

alarmist *noun* someone who spreads unnecessary alarm. ▸ *adj* causing unnecessary alarm.

alas *exclam, old or literary* expressing grief or misfortune. [13c: from French *ha* ah + *las* wretched]

alb *noun* a long white garment reaching to the feet, worn by some Christian priests. [Anglo-Saxon]

Albanian *adj* belonging or relating to Albania, its inhabitants, or their language. ▸ *noun* **1** a citizen or inhabitant of, or person born in, Albania. **2** the official language of Albania.

albatross *noun* **1** a large seabird with very long wings. **2** *golf* a score of three under par. Compare **birdie** (sense 2), **eagle** (sense 2), **bogey**[2]. [17c: from Portuguese *alcatraz* pelican]

albeit /ɔːl'biːɪt/ *conj* even if; although. [14c as *al be it* although it be]

albinism /'albɪnɪzəm/ *noun, biol* the inherited lack of pigmentation. [19c]

albino /al'biːnoʊ *or* (*US*) al'baɪnoʊ/ *noun, biol* **1** a person or other animal with an abnormal lack of pigmentation in the hair, skin and eyes. **2** a plant with a total or partial lack of **chlorophyll** or other pigments. [18c: Portuguese, from Latin *albus* white]

album *noun* **1** a book with blank pages for holding photographs, stamps, autographs, etc. **2** a record, CD, etc which contains multiple tracks. [17c: Latin, meaning 'blank tablet']

albumen *noun, zool* in the eggs of birds and some reptiles: the nutritive material surrounding the yolk; the white of an egg. [16c: Latin]

albumin *noun, biochem* any of various water-soluble globular proteins that coagulate when heated, found in egg white, milk, blood serum, etc.

alchemy *noun* the forerunner of modern chemistry, which centred around attempts to convert ordinary metals into gold, and to discover a universal remedy for illness, known as the elixir of life. ▪ **alchemist** *noun*. [14c: from Arabic *al* the + *kimiya* transmutation]

alcohol *noun* **1** *chem* any of numerous organic chemical compounds containing one or more hydroxyl groups, used as solvents for dyes, resins, varnishes, perfume oils, etc, and as fuels. **2** **ethanol**, esp when used as an intoxicant in alcoholic beverages. **3** any drink containing this liquid, such as wine or beer. [19c: from Arabic *al* the + *kohl* kohl]

alcoholic *adj* **1** relating to, containing or having the properties of alcohol. **2** relating to alcoholism. ▸ *noun* a person who suffers from alcoholism.

alcoholism *noun, pathol* a condition caused by physical dependence on alcohol, habitual and extensive consumption of which impairs physical and mental health.

alcopop *noun* an alcoholic drink bought ready-mixed with lemonade, etc. [20c: a blend of *alco*hol and **pop**[1]]

alcove *noun* a recess in the wall of a room or garden. [17c: from Spanish *alcoba*]

aldehyde *noun* any of numerous organic chemical compounds formed by the oxidation of alcohols. [19c: abbrev of Latin *alcohol dehydrogenatum*]

al dente /al 'dɛnte/ *adj, cookery* of pasta and vegetables: cooked so as to remain firm when bitten. [20c: Italian, literally 'to the tooth']

alder *noun* **1** any of various deciduous trees and shrubs with oval or rounded toothed leaves, and **catkins**. **2** the timber of this tree. [Anglo-Saxon *alor*]

alderman *noun* **1** in England and Wales until 1974: a member of a town, county or borough council elected by fellow councillors, below the rank of mayor. **2** in the US and Canada: a member of the governing body of a city. ▪ **aldermanship** *noun*. [Anglo-Saxon *ealdormann* a nobleman of the highest rank]

ale *noun* **1** a light-coloured beer, higher in alcohol content than **lager** and with a fuller body, flavoured with hops. **2** beer. [Anglo-Saxon *ealu*]

aleatory *or* **aleatoric** *adj, technical* **1** depending on chance. **2** of music: in which chance influences the choice of notes. [17c: from Latin *aleator* dice-player]

alehouse *noun, old use* an inn or public house.

alert *adj* **1** thinking and acting quickly. **2** (*esp* **alert to sth**) watchful and aware of (a danger, etc). ▸ *noun* **1** a warning of danger. **2** the period of time covered by such a warning. ▸ *verb* (*usu* **alert sb to sth**) to warn them of (a danger); to make them aware of (a fact or circumstance). ▪ **alertness** *noun*. [17c: from French *alerte*]

IDIOMS **on the alert** watchful.

A level (*in full* **Advanced level**) *noun* **1** in England, Wales and N Ireland: an advanced examination in a single subject, usually taken about the age of 18. **2** a pass in such an examination.

alexandrine *noun, poetry* a verse of six iambic feet (in English) or twelve syllables (in French). ▸ *adj* of verse: written in alexandrines. [16c: French, from the name *Alexandre*, Alexander the Great being the subject of an Old French romance written in this metre]

alexia *noun, pathol* loss of the ability to read, caused by brain disease. Compare **aphasia**, **dyslexia**. [19c: from **a-**[2] + Greek *lexis* speech]

alfalfa *noun* a plant of the pulse family with purple flowers and spirally twisted pods, widely cultivated as a forage crop. Also called **lucerne**. [19c: Spanish]

alfresco *adv* in the open air. ▸ *adj* open-air. [18c: Italian *al fresco* in the fresh air]

algae /ˈalgiː, ˈaldʒiː/ *plural noun* (*singular* ***alga*** /ˈalgə/) a large and very diverse group of mainly aquatic organisms. [16c as *alga*: Latin, meaning 'seaweed']

algebra *noun* the branch of mathematics that uses letters and symbols to represent variable quantities and numbers, and to express generalizations about them. ▪ **algebraic** /-ˈbreɪɪk/ *adj*. [16c: from Arabic *al-jebr*, from *al* the + *jebr* reunion of broken parts]

-algia *combining form, med, signifying* pain in the part of the body specified: *neuralgia*. [From Greek *algos* pain]

ALGOL *or* **Algol** *noun, comput* a high-level programming language, formerly widely used for scientific problem solving. [1950s: contraction of *algo*rithmic *l*anguage]

Algonquian /alˈgɒŋkwɪən/ *or* **Algonkian** *noun* **1** a family of Native American languages, including Natick, Shawnee, Ojibwa, Cheyenne, etc, spoken in the valley of the Ottawa and around the northern tributaries of the St Lawrence river. **2** a member of any Native American people (**Algonquin**) that speaks one of these languages. ▸ *adj* relating to this family of languages or its speakers. [19c: from *Algonquin*, 17c, from French Canadian]

algorithm *noun* any procedure involving a series of steps that is used to find the solution to a specific problem, eg to solve a mathematical equation. ▪ **algorithmic** *adj*. [1930s: from Latin *algorismus*, named after Al-Khwarizmi, a 9c Arab mathematician]

alias /ˈeɪlɪəs/ *noun* a false or assumed name. ▸ *adv* also known as: *John Smith, alias Mr X*. See also **AKA**. [16c: Latin, meaning 'otherwise']

alibi /ˈalɪbaɪ/ *noun* **1** a plea of being somewhere else when a crime was committed. **2** *informal* an excuse. ▸ *verb* (***alibied, alibiing***) to provide an alibi for someone. [18c: Latin, meaning 'elsewhere']

Alice band *noun* a wide hair-band of coloured ribbon or other material, worn flat round the head.

alien *noun* **1** a foreign-born resident of a country who has not adopted that country's nationality. **2** *esp sci fi* an inhabitant of another planet. ▸ *adj* **1** foreign. **2** (*usu* **alien to sb** *or* **sth**) not in keeping with them or it; unfamiliar. [14c: from Latin *alienus* foreign]

alienable *adj, law* of property: able to be transferred to another owner.

alienate *verb* **1** to make someone become unfriendly or estranged. **2** to make someone feel unwelcome or isolated. **3** *law* to transfer ownership of (property) to another person. ▪ **alienation** *noun*.

alight[1] *adj* **1** on fire. **2** lighted up; excited.

alight[2] *verb* (***alighted*** *or* ***alit***) *intr* **1** (*often* **alight from sth**) to get down from or out of (a vehicle). **2** of a bird, etc: to land. [Anglo-Saxon *alihtan*]

align *verb* **1** to put something in a straight line or bring it into line. **2** to bring (someone, a country, etc) into agreement with others, or with a political belief, cause, etc. **3** *intr* to come into alignment with someone or something. ▪ **alignment** *noun*. [17c: from French *à ligne* into line]

alike *adj* like one another; similar. ▸ *adv* in a similar manner. [Anglo-Saxon *gelic*]

alimentary *adj* **1** relating to digestion. **2** relating to food, diet or nutrition.

alimentary canal *noun, anatomy* a tubular organ extending from the mouth to the anus, along which food passes, and in which it is digested. Also called **digestive tract**.

alimony *noun, law* money for support paid by a man to his wife or by a woman to her husband, when they are legally separated or divorced. See also **maintenance**. [17c: from Latin *alimonia* nourishment]

aliphatic *adj, chem* of an organic compound: having carbon atoms arranged in chains rather than in rings. Compare **aromatic** (sense 2). [19c: from Greek *aleiphar* oil]

aliquot *noun* (*also* **aliquot part**) *maths* a number or quantity into which a given number or quantity can be exactly divided without any remainder: *3 is an aliquot part of 9*. [16c: Latin, meaning 'some' or 'several']

alit *past tense, past participle of* **alight**[2]

alive *adj* **1** living; having life; in existence. **2** lively. **3** (*usu* **alive to sth**) aware of it. **4** (*usu* **alive with sth**) full of it; abounding in it. [Anglo-Saxon *on life* in life]

alkali /ˈalkəlaɪ/ *noun* (***alkalis*** *or* ***alkalies***) *chem* a hydroxide of any of various metallic elements that dissolves in water to produce an alkaline solution, and neutralizes acids to form salts. [14c: from Arabic *al-qali* calcinated ashes]

alkaline *adj, chem* **1** relating to or having the properties of an alkali. **2** denoting a solution with a pH greater than 7. ▪ **alkalinity** /-ˈlɪnɪtɪ/ *noun*.

alkaloid *noun, biochem* any of numerous organic compounds that contain nitrogen, and which have toxic or medicinal properties.

alkane *noun, chem* the general name for a hydrocarbon of the series of general formula C_nH_{2n+2}, the carbon atoms of which form chains linked by single bonds.

alkene /ˈalkiːn/ *noun, chem* any of the unsaturated hydrocarbons of the series of general formula C_2H_{2n}, the carbon atoms of which form chains linked by one or more double bonds.

all *adj* **1** the whole amount, number or extent of something; every. **2** the greatest possible: *run with all speed*. **3** any whatever: *beyond all doubt*. ▸ *noun* **1** every one of the people or things concerned; the whole of something. **2** one's whole strength, resources, etc: *give one's all*. ▸ *adv* **1** entirely; quite. **2** *informal* very: *go all shy*. **3** used in giving the score in various games: on each side: *30 all*. [Anglo-Saxon *eall*]
IDIOMS **all along** the whole time. **all but** very nearly: *He all but drowned*. **all for sth** extremely enthusiastic about it. **all in all** considering everything. **all over** finished. **all over sb** *informal* excessively demonstrative towards them. **all over sth** everywhere in or on it: *all over the world*. **all over the place** *informal* in a disorganized muddle. **at all** *with negatives and in questions* **1** in the least. **2** in any way. **in all** all together. **that's her, etc all over** *informal* that's exactly what one would expect from her, etc.

Allah *noun, Islam* the name of God.

all-American *adj* typically American.

allay *verb* to make (pain, fear, suspicion, etc) less intense. [Anglo-Saxon *alecgan*]

all clear *noun* a signal or statement that the threat of danger is over.

allegation *noun* an unsupported claim, statement or assertion. [15c: from Latin *allegatio*]

allege *verb* to claim or declare something to be the case, usu without proof. ▪ **alleged** *adj* presumed and claimed, but not proved, to be as stated. ▪ **allegedly** /ə'lɛdʒɪdlɪ/ *adv.* [13c: from French *aleguer* to allege]

allegiance *noun* commitment and duty to obey and be loyal to a government, sovereign, etc. [14c: from French *liege* liege]

allegory /'aləgərɪ/ *noun* (**-ies**) **1** a story, play, poem, picture, etc in which the characters represent moral or spiritual ideas or messages. **2** symbolism of this sort. ▪ **allegorical** *adj.* ▪ **allegorize** *or* **-ise** *verb.* [14c: from French *allegorie*]

allegretto *music, adv* in a fairly quick and lively manner (less brisk than **allegro**). ▸ *adj* fairly quick and lively. ▸ *noun* a piece of music to be played in this way. [18c: Italian]

allegro *music, adv* in a quick lively manner. ▸ *adj* quick and lively. ▸ *noun* a piece of music to be played in this way. [18c: Italian]

allele /ə'liːl/ *noun, genetics* any of the possible alternative forms of the same gene, of which every individual inherits two (one from each parent), different combinations of which produce different characteristics. [20c: from Greek *allelos* one another]

alleluia see **hallelujah**

allergen /'alədʒən/ *noun, med* any foreign substance that induces an allergic reaction in someone.

allergic /ə'lɜːdʒɪk/ *adj* **1** (**allergic to sth**) having an allergy caused by abnormal sensitivity to it. **2** relating to or caused by an allergy: *an allergic reaction.*

allergy *noun* (**-ies**) **1** *pathol* a hypersensitive reaction of the body to certain foreign substances known as **allergens**, eg specific foods, dust or pollen. **2** *informal* a dislike. [20c: from Greek *allos* other + *ergia* activity]

alleviate *verb* to make (pain, a problem, suffering, etc) less severe. ▪ **alleviation** *noun.* [16c: from Latin *alleviare* to lighten]

alley *noun* **1** (*also* **alleyway**) a narrow passage behind or between buildings. **2** a long narrow channel used for bowling or skittles. **3** a path through a garden or park. [14c: from French *alee* passage]

All Fools' Day *noun* April Fool's Day.

All Hallows Eve see **Hallowe'en**

alliance *noun* **1** the state of being allied. **2** an agreement or treaty by which people, countries, etc ally themselves with one another. [14c: French]

allied *adj* **1 a** joined by political agreement or treaty; **b** (**Allied**) belonging or referring to Britain and her allies in World Wars I and II: *Allied troops.* **2** similar; related.

alligator *noun* a large reptile similar to a crocodile but with a broader head and blunter snout, and teeth that do not protrude over its jaws. [16c: from Spanish *el lagarto* the lizard]

all-important *adj* essential; crucial.

all-in wrestling *noun* a style of wrestling with few rules or restrictions.

alliteration *noun* the repetition of the same sound at the beginning of each word or each stressed word in a phrase, as in *sing a song of sixpence*. Compare **assonance.** ▪ **alliterate** *verb.* ▪ **alliterative** *adj.* [17c: from Latin *alliteratio*]

allo- *combining form, chiefly technical, signifying* other. [From Greek *allos* other or different]

allocate *verb* to give, set apart or assign something to someone or for some particular purpose. ▪ **allocation** *noun.* [17c: from Latin *ad* to + *locus* place]

allot *verb* (***allotted, allotting***) **1** to give (a share of or place in something) to each member of a group. **2** to assign something to a specific purpose. [16c: from French *aloter*]

allotment *noun* **1** *Brit* one of the subdivisions of a larger piece of public ground rented to individuals to grow vegetables, etc. **2** the act of allotting. **3** an amount allotted.

allotrope *noun, chem* any of the two or more structural forms in which some elements can exist, eg graphite and diamond (allotropes of carbon). ▪ **allotropic** *adj.*

allotropy /ə'lɒtrəpɪ/ *noun, chem* the existence of an element in **allotropes**. [19c: from Greek *allotropia* variation]

all-out *adj* **1** using all one's strength, powers, etc. *as adv* (**all out**): *going all out to win.* **2** eg of a strike: with everyone participating.

allow *verb* **1** to permit (someone to do something, something to happen, etc). **2** to assign or allocate: *allow £10 for food.* **3** to admit or agree to (a point, claim, etc). **4** *intr* (**allow for sth**) to take it into consideration when judging or deciding something. [16c: from French *alouer*]

allowable *adj* able to be admitted or accepted. ▪ **allowably** *adv.*

allowance *noun* **1** a fixed sum of money, amount of something, etc given regularly. **2** money given for expenses. **3** something allowed.

IDIOMS **make allowances for sb** to expect less of them because of particular circumstances applying to them. **make allowances for sth** to take it into consideration in one's plans.

alloy *noun* /'alɔɪ/ a material consisting of a mixture of two or more metals, or a metal and a non-metal. ▸ *verb* /ə'lɔɪ/ to mix (one metal with another). [16c: from French *alei*]

all-powerful *adj* supremely powerful; omnipotent.

all-purpose *adj* useful for many different purposes.

all right *or sometimes* **alright** *adj* **1** unhurt; safe; feeling fine. **2** just about adequate, satisfactory, etc. **3** (**all-right**) *informal* genuine; cool: *an all-right kind of a guy.* ▸ *exclam* **1** used simply as a greeting: *All right? How's it going?* **2** used to signal agreement or approval. ▸ *adv* **1** satisfactorily; properly. **2** *informal* used to reinforce what has just been said: *It's broken all right.*

alright, all right

Although it is becoming more common, many people still consider the spelling **alright** to be incorrect. Therefore it is best to use the spelling **all right**, especially if you are writing for readers who are precise about language.

all-round *adj* **1** having many different skills: *an all-round player.* **2** including everyone or everything:

an all-round education. ▸ *adv* (**all round**) everywhere; in every respect: *All round, the situation of the refugees looks desperate.*

all-rounder *noun* **1** someone who has a lot of different skills. **2** someone who shows ability in many aspects of a sport, esp a cricket player who can both bat and bowl.

All Saints' Day *noun* a Christian festival held on 1 November to commemorate all church saints collectively.

all-seater *adj* of a sports stadium, esp a football ground: having no space for standing spectators.

all-singing all-dancing *adj, informal or facetious* having many special features, esp ones that are gimmicky or not absolutely necessary: *an all-singing all-dancing video recorder.*

allspice *noun* **1** an aromatic spice prepared from the dried unripe berries of a small tropical evergreen tree, used to flavour foods, esp meat. **2** the **pimento** tree, cultivated mainly in Jamaica, that yields this spice.

all-time *adj, informal* **1** of a record, esp a sporting one: best to date; unsurpassed. **2** of great and permanent importance: *the all-time greats of jazz.*

allude *verb, intr* (*usu* **allude to sth**) to mention it indirectly or speak about it in passing. [16c: from Latin *alludere* to play with]

allure *noun* attractiveness, appeal or charm. ▸ *verb* to attract, charm or fascinate. [15c: from French *alurer*]

alluring *adj* enticing; seductive; attractive.

allusion *noun* any indirect reference to something else. [16c: from Latin *allusio*]

allusion, illusion

Be careful not to use the word **allusion** when you mean **illusion**. An **illusion** is a false appearance or idea:

Painting the walls white creates an illusion of extra space.

allusive *adj* referring indirectly to something.

alluvium *noun* (***alluvia***) fine particles of silt, clay, mud and sand that are carried and deposited by rivers. ▪ **alluvial** *adj.* [17c: from Latin *alluvius* washed against]

ally *noun* /ˈalaɪ/ (***-ies***) a country, state, etc that has formally agreed to help and support another. ▸ *verb* /əˈlaɪ/ (***-ies, -ied***) **1** of a country, state, etc: to join or become joined politically or militarily with another, esp with a formal agreement. **2** of an individual or group: to join or become joined with someone else or another group. [13c: from French *alier*]

alma mater *noun* the school, college or university that someone used to attend. See also **alumnus**. [19c: Latin, literally 'bountiful mother']

almanac *noun* a book, published yearly, with a calendar, information about the phases of the Moon and stars, dates of religious festivals, public holidays, etc. [14c: from Latin *almanach*]

almighty *adj* **1** having complete power: *an almighty god.* **2** *informal* very great: *an almighty crash.* ▸ *noun* (**the Almighty**) *Christianity* God. [Anglo-Saxon *ælmihtig*]

almond /ˈɑːmənd/ *noun* **1** a kind of small tree related to the peach. **2** the nut-like seed from the fruit of this tree. [14c: from French *almande*]

almoner *noun, hist, Brit* a medical social worker. [14c: from French *aumoner*]

almost *adv* nearly but not quite. [Anglo-Saxon *ælmæst*]

alms /ɑːmz/ *plural noun* charity donations of money, food, etc to the poor. [Anglo-Saxon *ælmesse*]

almshouse *noun, Brit, hist* a place where the aged, poor, etc were supported by charity.

aloe *noun* **1** a plant with long fleshy leaves with spiny edges. **2** (*usu* **aloes**) the dried juice of the leaves of this plant, formerly used as a purgative drug known as **bitter aloes**. [14c: from Latin *aloe*]

aloe vera /ˈaloʊ ˈveɪrə/ *noun* **1** a species of **aloe** plant, the leaves of which contain a juice that is said to have healing properties. **2** the juice of the leaves of this plant, used in skin lotions, shampoos, etc.

aloft *adv* **1** in the air; overhead: *held the trophy aloft.* **2** *naut* in a ship's rigging. [13c: from Norse *a lopti* in the sky]

alone *adj, adv* **1** by oneself. **2** without anyone else: *The idea was mine alone.* **3** lonely. [13c: from English *al one* wholly by oneself]

IDIOMS **go it alone** *informal* to act on one's own and without help.

along *adv* **1** in some direction: *Her old banger just chugs along.* **2** in the company of someone else or with others: *went along with him to the gig.* **3** into a more advanced state: *coming along nicely.* ▸ *prep* **1** by the side of something or near something. **2** down the length of or down part of the length of something: *The shops are just along that street.* [Anglo-Saxon *andlang*]

IDIOMS **along with sth** *or* **sb 1** in addition to it or them. **2** in conjunction with it or them.

alongside *prep* close to the side of something. ▸ *adv* to or at the side.

aloof *adj* unfriendly and distant. [16c: from **a-**[1] + nautical *loof* the after-part of a ship's bow]

alopecia /aləˈpiːʃə/ *noun, pathol* baldness, either of the hereditary type, such as the normal gradual loss of head hair in men, or of the type caused by disease or old age. [14c: from Greek *alopekia* fox-mange]

aloud *adv* loud enough to be able to be heard: *reading aloud.*

alp *noun* **1** a high mountain. **2** in Switzerland: pasture land on a mountainside. [16c: from Latin *Alpes* the name for the Alps, a mountain range in Switzerland, France and Italy]

alpaca *noun* **1** a S American mammal, closely related to the **llama**, reared mainly for its long straight fleece. **2 a** the fine silky wool obtained from this animal; **b** cloth made from it. [Early 19c: Spanish]

alpenstock *noun* a long stout stick, usu with a metal point at the bottom end, used by hikers and mountain climbers. [19c: German]

alpha *noun* **1** the first letter of the Greek alphabet. **2** *Brit* a mark given to an exam paper or other piece of work that denotes a first class grade. ▸ *adj, zool* referring to the most dominant member of a hierarchical group: *That gorilla is the alpha male.* [14c: Greek]

IDIOMS **alpha and omega** the beginning and the end.

alphabet *noun* a set of letters, characters, symbols, etc, usu arranged in a fixed order that, by convention, are used to represent the spoken form of a language in writing and printing. [16c: from Latin *alphabetum*]

alphabetical *or* **alphabetic** *adj* **1** in the order of the letters, characters, symbols, etc of an alphabet. **2** in the form of an alphabet. ▪ **alphabetically** *adv.*

alphabetize *or* **-ise** *verb* to arrange or list in the correct alphabetical order.

alpha decay *noun, physics* a form of radioactive decay in which a radioactive nucleus emits an alpha particle.

alphanumeric *or* **alphanumerical** *adj, comput* denoting characters, codes or data that consist of letters of the alphabet and numerals. [1950s: from *alpha*bet + *numeric*al]

alpha particle *noun, physics* a positively charged particle with a low energy content, produced by radioactive decay. See also **beta particle**.

alpha ray *noun, physics* a stream of **alpha particles**.

alpine *adj* **1** belonging or relating to alps or high mountains. **2** (**Alpine**) belonging or relating to the Alps. ▸ *noun* a plant that grows in high mountain areas. [17c: from Latin *alpinus*]

already *adv* **1** before the present time or the time in question: *We've already paid.* **2** so soon or so early: *It's already lunchtime.*

---

already, all ready
Be careful not to use **already** when you mean **all ready**, completely prepared:
He was all ready to go by 6 o'clock.

---

alright *adj* an alternative spelling of **all right**.

---

alright, all right
Although it is becoming more common, many people still consider the spelling **alright** to be incorrect. Therefore it is best to use the spelling **all right**, especially if you are writing for readers who are precise about language.

Alsatian *noun* a German shepherd dog. [1920s: from Latin *Alsatia* Alsace]

also *adv* in addition; as well as; besides. [Anglo-Saxon *alswa* all so or wholly]

also-ran *noun* **1** a horse, dog, person, etc not finishing in one of the top three places in a race. **2** someone who is considered to be unimportant, etc.

Altaic /al'teɪɪk/ *adj* denoting a family of languages spoken from the Balkan Peninsula to the NE of Asia, which includes Turkic and Mongolian. ▸ *noun* the languages that form this family. [19c: from French *altaïque* of the Altai mountains in Asia]

altar *noun* **1** a table, raised structure, etc where sacrifices are made to a god. **2** *Christianity* the table at the front of a church, consecrated for use during communion. [Anglo-Saxon]

altarpiece *noun* a religious picture or carving, often in either two or three parts, that is placed above and behind an altar. See also **diptych**, **triptych**.

alter *verb, tr & intr* to change; to become, or make something or someone become, different. ▪ **alterable** *noun.* ▪ **alteration** *noun.* [14c: from French *alterer*]

altercate *verb, intr* to argue or dispute, esp angrily, heatedly, etc. ▪ **altercation** *noun.* [16c: from Latin *altercari* to dispute with another]

alter ego *noun* **1** someone's second or alternative character: *Her aggressive alter ego surfaces when she drinks too much.* **2** a close and trusted friend. [16c: Latin, literally 'another I']

alternate *adj* /ɒl'tɜːnət/ **1** of two feelings, states, conditions, etc: arranged or coming one after the other in turn: *alternate layers of pasta and sauce.* **2** every other; one out of two. **3** *botany* of leaves, petals, etc: appearing singly and regularly at either side of a stem. ▸ *verb* /'ɔːltəneɪt/ **1** *tr & intr* of two things: to succeed or make them succeed each other by turns: *they alternate their days off.* **2** *intr* (**alternate between sth and sth else**) to change from one thing to another by turns. ▸ *noun* /'ɔːltəneɪt; *also* (*orig US*) 'ɔːltənət/ a substitute, esp a person who covers in someone's absence. ▪ **alternately** *adv.* ▪ **alternation** *noun.* [16c: from Latin *alternare* to do one thing after another]

alternate angles *plural noun, geom* a pair of angles that lie on opposite sides and at opposite ends of a line that cuts two other lines.

alternating current *noun* (abbrev **AC**) an electric current that reverses its direction of flow with a constant frequency, and is therefore continuously varying. Compare **direct current**.

alternative *adj* **1** of two or more possibilities: secondary or different, esp in terms of being less favourable as a choice: *had to make alternative travel plans.* **2** of a lifestyle, etc: outside the conventionally accepted ways of doing something and therefore thought of by adherents as preferable. ▸ *noun* **1** the possibility of having the option to choose, strictly speaking, between two things but often used of more than two or of an unknown number: *We had no alternative but to take the train.* **2** something that represents another possible option. ▪ **alternatively** *adv.* [16c: from Latin *alternare*]

alternative energy *noun, ecol* energy derived from sources other than nuclear power or the burning of fossil fuels, eg **solar energy**.

alternative medicine *or* **complementary medicine** *noun* the treatment of diseases and disorders using procedures other than those practised in orthodox medicine, eg **acupuncture**.

alternator *noun, elec eng* an electricity generator that produces **alternating current** by means of one or more coils rotating in a magnetic field.

although *conj* in spite of the fact that; apart from the fact that; though. [14c as *al thogh* all though]

altimeter *noun, aeronautics* a device used in aircraft for measuring height above sea or ground level. [Early 20c: from Latin *altus* high + **-meter** (sense 1)]

altitude *noun* **1** height, esp above sea level, of a mountain, aircraft, etc. **2** *geom* in a plane or solid figure: the distance from a vertex to the side opposite to it (the **base**). [14c: from Latin *altitudo* height]

alto *noun* **1** the lowest female singing voice. Also called **contralto**. **2** the singing voice of a **countertenor**. **3** someone with either of these types of singing voice. **4** a part or piece of music written for a voice or instrument at this pitch. ▸ *adj* of a musical instrument, etc: having a high pitch: *alto sax.* [16c: Italian]

altogether *adv* **1** completely. **2** **a** on the whole: *Altogether it was a wonderful holiday;* **b** taking everything into consideration: *Altogether the holiday cost*

£500. [Anglo-Saxon *al togædere*]
IDIOMS **in the altogether** *informal* naked.

altogether, all together
Be careful not to use **altogether** when you mean **all together**. **All together** means in a group:
We put the sheep all together in one field.
Ask yourself if you could separate the words without changing the meaning:
We put all the sheep together in one field.

altruism *noun* an unselfish concern for the welfare of others. ▪ **altruist** *noun*. ▪ **altruistic** *adj*. [19c: from French *altruisme*]

ALU *abbrev, comput* arithmetic logic unit.

alum *noun, chem* aluminium potassium sulphate, a white crystalline compound used in dyeing and tanning, and as a medical astringent to stop bleeding. [14c: from Latin *alumen*]

alumina *noun, chem* a white crystalline compound that is the main ingredient of bauxite. [14c: from Latin *alumen* alum]

aluminium *or* (*N Am*) **aluminum** /əˈluːmɪnəm/ *noun, chem* (symbol **Al**) a silvery-white light metallic element that forms strong alloys which are used in the construction of aircraft and other vehicles, door and window frames, household utensils, drink cans, etc. See also **bauxite**. [1812: from Latin *alumen* **alum**]

aluminize *or* **-ise** *verb* to coat (a mirror or other surface) with aluminium.

alumna /əˈlʌmnə/ *noun* (***alumnae*** /-niː/) a female **alumnus**. [19c: Latin]

alumnus /əˈlʌmnəs/ *noun* (***alumni*** /-naɪ/) a former pupil or student of a school, college or university. See also **alma mater**. [17c: Latin, meaning 'a foster-child']

alveolus /alvɪˈoʊləs/ *noun* (***alveoli*** /-laɪ/) **1** *anatomy* in the lungs: any of many tiny air sacs in which oxygen from inhaled air is exchanged for carbon dioxide from the bloodstream. **2** *anatomy* a tooth socket in the jaw bone. **3** *zool* any small depression in the surface of an organ. ▪ **alveolar** *adj*. [18c: Latin, meaning 'small cavity']

always *adv* **1** on every occasion. **2** continually; time and time again. **3** whatever happens; if necessary: *signed the letter 'Always yours'.* [Anglo-Saxon *ealne weg*]

alyssum /ˈalɪsəm, əˈlɪsəm/ *noun* a bushy plant with white, yellow or purple cross-shaped flowers. [16c: from Greek *alysson*]

Alzheimer's disease /ˈaltshaɪməz/ *noun, pathol* a disease in which degeneration of the brain cells results in gradual loss of memory, confusion, etc, eventually leading to total disintegration of the personality. [Early 20c: named after the German neurologist, Alois Alzheimer, who first identified it]

AM *abbrev* **amplitude modulation**.

Am *symbol, chem* americium.

am *verb* (used with *I*): the first person singular of the present tense of **be**.

a.m., **am**, **A.M.** *or* **AM** *abbrev* **ante meridiem**.

amalgam *noun* **1** a mixture or blend. **2** *chem* an alloy of mercury with one or more other metals, which forms a soft paste on mixing but later hardens, used in dentistry to fill holes in drilled teeth. [15c: from Latin *amalgama*]

amalgamate *verb* **1** *tr & intr* to join together or unite to form a single unit, etc. **2** *intr* of metals: to form an alloy with mercury. ▪ **amalgamation** *noun*.

amanita /amɪˈnaɪtə/ *noun, biol* any of various fungi some of which, eg fly agaric, are poisonous. [19c: from Greek *amanitai*, a type of fungus]

amanuensis /əmanjʊˈɛnsɪs/ *noun* (**-*ses*** /-siːz/) a literary assistant or secretary, esp one who writes from dictation or copies from manuscripts. [17c: Latin, from *servus a manu* a handwriting servant]

amaranth *noun* **1** any of various species of plant that produce spikes of small brightly coloured flowers. **2** *poetic* a fabled flower that never fades. [17c: from Greek *amarantos* everlasting]

amaryllis *noun* any of various plants, esp a S African species with strap-shaped leaves and large pink or white trumpet-shaped scented flowers. [18c: Latin]

amass *verb* to gather (money, possessions, etc), esp in great quantity. [15c: from French *amasser*]

amateur *noun* **1** someone who takes part in a sport, pastime, etc as a hobby and without being paid for it. **2** someone who is not very skilled in an activity, etc. ▸ *adj* **1** unskilled or non-professional: *playing the amateur detective*. **2** for, relating to or done by those who are not professional: *amateur dramatics*. ▪ **amateurism** *noun*. [18c: French]

amateurish *adj* not particularly skilful; inexperienced.

amatory *adj* belonging or relating to, or showing, sexual love or desire. [16c: from Latin *amatorius* loving]

amaze *verb* to surprise someone greatly; to astonish them. ▪ **amazement** *noun*. ▪ **amazing** *adj*. ▪ **amazingly** *adv*. [Anglo-Saxon *amasian*]

Amazon *noun* **1** a member of a legendary nation of women warriors, eg from S America. **2** (*usu* **amazon**) any tall, well-built, strong woman. [14c: Greek]

ambassador *noun* **1** a diplomat of the highest rank permanently appointed by a government, head of state, sovereign, etc to act on their behalf or to be their official representative in some foreign country, state, etc. **2** a representative, messenger or agent. ▪ **ambassadorial** /ambasəˈdɔːrɪəl/ *adj*. ▪ **ambassadorship** *noun*. [14c: from French *ambassateur*]

ambassadress *noun* **1** a woman ambassador. **2** the wife of an ambassador.

amber *noun, geol* **1** a transparent yellow or reddish fossilized resin, often carved and polished and used to make jewellery. *as adj*: *amber beads*. **2** the yellow or reddish-brown colour of this. **3** a traffic light that serves as a means of delaying the change-over in traffic flow, in the UK appearing on its own between green for 'go' and red for 'stop' but appearing simultaneously with red to mark the transition the other way between red and green. [14c: from Latin *ambar*]

ambergris *noun* a pale-grey waxy substance with a strong smell, produced in the intestines of sperm whales, and widely used until recently in the perfume industry. [15c: from French *ambre gris* grey amber]

ambi- *prefix, denoting* both; on both sides. [Latin, from *ambo* both]

ambidextrous *adj* able to use both hands equally well. [17c: from Latin *ambidexter*]

ambience *or* **ambiance** *noun* the surroundings or atmosphere of a place. ▪ **ambient** *adj*.

ambiguity *noun* (*-ies*) **1** uncertainty of meaning. **2** a word or statement that can be interpreted in more than one way. [15c: from Latin *ambiguus*]

ambiguous *adj* having more than one possible meaning. ▪ **ambiguously** *adv.* [16c: from Latin *ambiguus*]

ambit *noun* **1** range or extent. **2** circumference or boundary. [14c: from Latin *ambitus* a going round]

ambition *noun* **1** a strong desire for success, fame or power. **2** a thing someone wants to do or achieve. [14c: French]

ambitious *adj* **1** having a strong desire for success, etc. **2** enterprising or daring, but requiring hard work and skill: *an ambitious plan.*

ambivalence *or* **ambivalency** *noun* the concurrent adherence to two opposite or conflicting views, feelings, etc about someone or something. ▪ **ambivalent** *adj.*

amble *verb, intr* **1** to walk without hurrying; to stroll. **2** of a horse, etc: to walk by lifting the two feet on the same side together and then lifting the two feet on the other side together and so move in a smooth, flowing way. ▸ *noun* **1** a leisurely walk. **2** a horse's ambling walk (see *verb* sense 2). [14c: from French *ambler*]

ambrosia *noun* **1** *Greek myth* the food of the gods, believed to give them eternal youth and beauty. **2** something with a delicious taste or smell. ▪ **ambrosian** *adj.* [16c: Greek, from *ambrotos* immortal]

ambulance *noun* a specially equipped vehicle for carrying sick or injured people to hospital. [1920s: from Latin *ambulare* to walk about]

ambulatory *adj* **1** belonging or relating to or designed for walking. **2** moving from place to place. [17c: from Latin *ambulator* a walker]

ambush *noun* **1** the act of lying in wait to attack someone by surprise. **2** an attack made in this way. ▸ *verb* to lie in wait for someone or attack them in this way. [14c: from French *embuschier* to place men in the woods]

ameba an alternative *N Am* spelling of **amoeba**.

ameliorate /ə'miːlɪəreɪt/ *verb, tr & intr* to make or become better. ▪ **amelioration** *noun.* [18c: from French *ameillorer*]

amen *exclam* usu said at the end of a prayer, hymn, etc: so be it. [Anglo-Saxon: Hebrew, literally 'certainly']

amenable /ə'miːnəbəl/ *adj* (*esp* **amenable to sth**) ready to accept (someone else's idea, proposal, advice, guidance, etc). ▪ **amenably** *adv.* [16c: Anglo-French]

amend *verb* to correct, improve or make minor changes to (a book, document, etc). Compare **emend**. ▪ **amendable** *adj.* [14c: from French *amender*]
IDIOMS **make amends for sth** to make up for or compensate for (some injury, insult, etc).

amendment *noun* **1** an addition or alteration, esp to a motion, official document, etc. **2** an act of correcting or improving something.

amenity *noun* (*-ies*) **1** a valued public facility. **2** anything that makes life more comfortable and pleasant. [15c: from Latin *amoenus* pleasant]

American *adj* **1** belonging or relating to the United States of America or its inhabitants. **2** belonging or relating to the American continent, its inhabitants, or their languages. ▸ *noun* a citizen or inhabitant of, or person born in, the United States of America, or the American continent. [16c: named after the Italian navigator, Amerigo Vespucci]

American football *noun* **1** a team game with 11 players on both sides, similar to **rugby** but with forward passing and much emphasis on set-piece moves. **2** the oval ball used in this sport.

American Indian see **Native American**

Americanism *noun* a word, phrase, custom, etc that is characteristic of Americans.

Americanize *or* **-ise** *verb* to make or become more typical or characteristic of America, esp in terms of culture, customs, language, etc. ▪ **Americanized** *adj.*

American plan see **full board**

americium *noun, chem* (symbol **Am**) a silvery-white radioactive metallic element that is produced artificially, used as a source of **alpha particles**. [1945: named after America, where it was discovered]

Amerindian *adj* **1** relating or referring to any of the indigenous peoples of America. **2** denoting a family of over 1000 languages used by the indigenous peoples of N, Central and S America. ▸ *noun* **1** a member of any of the indigenous peoples of America. **2** the languages forming the Amerindian family.

amethyst *noun* **1** a pale- to deep-purple transparent or translucent variety of the mineral **quartz** used as a gemstone. **2** the purple or violet colour of this gemstone. [13c: from Greek *amethystos* not drunken]

Amharic *noun* the official language of Ethiopia, related to Hebrew and Arabic. [17c: named after Amhara, a province of Ethiopia]

amiable *adj* friendly, pleasant and good-tempered. ▪ **amiability** *noun.* ▪ **amiably** *adv.* [14c: from Latin *amicabilis* amicable]

amicable *adj* **1** friendly. **2** done in a reasonably friendly manner: *an amicable parting.* ▪ **amicability** *noun.* ▪ **amicably** *adv.* [16c: from Latin *amicabilis*]

amid *or* **amidst** *prep* in the middle of something; among. [Anglo-Saxon *onmiddan* in the centre]

amide *noun, chem* **1** any member of a class of organic compounds that contain the $CONH_2$ group, formed when one or more of the hydrogen atoms of ammonia is replaced by an acyl group. **2** any member of a class of inorganic compounds that contain the NH_2^- ion, formed when one of the hydrogen atoms of ammonia is replaced by a metal. [19c: from *ammonia* + **-ide**]

amidships *adv* in, into or near the middle of a ship.

amine /'amiːn/ *noun, chem* any member of a class of organic compounds, produced by decomposing organic matter, in which one or more of the hydrogen atoms of ammonia has been replaced by an organic group. [19c: from *ammonia*]

amino acid /ə'miːnoʊ/ *noun* any of a group of water-soluble organic compounds that contain an amino ($-NH_2$) group and a carboxyl ($-COOH$) group, and form the individual subunits of proteins.

amir see **emir**

amiss *adj* wrong; out of order. ▸ *adv* wrongly.
IDIOMS **take sth amiss** to be upset or offended by it.

amity *noun* friendship; friendliness. [15c: from French *amitie*]

ammeter *noun, elec eng* a device used for measuring electric current in a circuit, usu in amperes. [19c: from *ampere* + **-meter** (sense 1)]

ammo *noun, informal* short form of **ammunition**. [Early 20c]

ammonia *noun, chem* **1** a colourless pungent gas formed naturally by the bacterial decomposition of proteins, etc. **2** an alkaline solution of ammonia in water, used as a bleach and cleaning agent. Also called **ammonium hydroxide, liquid ammonia**. [18c: from Latin *sal ammoniacus* = **sal ammoniac**]

ammonite *noun* **1** *zool* an extinct marine cephalopod mollusc, widespread during the Mesozoic era. **2** *geol* the fossilized remains, esp the shell, of this animal. [18c: from Latin *Cornu Ammonis* horn of Ammon]

ammonium *noun, chem* a positively charged ion formed by the reaction of ammonia with acid, found in many salts, esp ammonium chloride (**sal ammoniac**) and ammonium carbonate (**sal volatile**).

ammunition *noun* **1** bullets, shells, bombs, etc made to be fired from a weapon. See also **ammo**. **2** anything that can be used against someone in an argument, etc. [17c: from French *amunition*]

amnesia *noun, pathol* the loss or impairment of memory. ▪ **amnesiac** *noun* someone suffering from amnesia. ▪ **amnesic** /-'niːzɪk/ *adj.* [17c: from Greek *amnestia* forgetfulness]

amnesty *noun* (**-ies**) **1** a general pardon, esp for people convicted or accused of political crimes. **2** a period of time when people can admit to crimes, hand in weapons, etc in the knowledge that they will not be prosecuted. [16c: from Greek *amnestia* oblivion]

amniocentesis *noun* (**-ses**) *obstetrics* a procedure that involves the insertion of a hollow needle through the abdominal wall into the uterus of a pregnant woman, enabling a small quantity of **amniotic fluid** to be drawn off in order to test for fetal abnormalities. [1950s: from **amnion** + Greek *kentesis* puncture]

amnion *noun* (***amnia***) *anatomy* the innermost membrane that surrounds the embryo. [17c: from Greek *amnos* a little lamb]

amniotic fluid *noun, zool* the clear fluid that surrounds and protects the embryo.

amoeba *or* (*N Am*) **ameba** /ə'miːbə/ *noun* (***amoebae*** /ə'miːbiː/ *or* ***amoebas***) *zool* a microscopic **protistic** animal that inhabits water or damp soil and has no fixed shape. ▪ **amoebic** *or* **amebic** *adj.* [19c: from Greek *amoibe* change]

amok *or* **amuck** *adv* (*usu* **run amok** *or* **amuck**) to rush about violently and out of control. [19c: from Malay *amoq* frenzied]

among *or* **amongst** *prep* used of more than two things, people, etc: **1** in the middle of them: *among friends*. **2** between them: *divide it among them*. **3** in the group or number of them: *among his best plays*. **4** with one another: *decide among yourselves*. [Anglo-Saxon *ongemang* mingling in]

---

among, between
See the Usage Note at **between**.

---

amoral /eɪ'mɒrəl/ *adj* having no moral standards or principles. Compare **immoral**. ▪ **amorality** *noun.*

amorous *adj* showing, feeling or relating to love, esp sexual love. [14c: from Latin *amorosus*]

amorphous *adj* **1** without definite shape or structure. **2** of rocks, chemicals, etc: without a crystalline structure. **3** without any clearly defined or thought-out purpose, identity, etc. [18c: from Greek *amorphos* shapeless]

amortize *or* **-ise** *verb* **1** to gradually pay off (a debt) by regular payments of money. **2** to gradually write off (the initial cost of an asset) over a period. ▪ **amortization** *noun.* [14c: from French *amortir* to bring to death]

amount *noun* a quantity; a total or extent: *a large amount of money*. ▸ *verb* (*always* **amount to sth**) to be equal to it or add up to it in size, number, significance, etc. [14c: from French *amonter* to climb up]

amour *noun, old use* a love affair, esp one that is secret. [13c: French, meaning 'love']

amour-propre /*French* amuʀpʀɔpʀ/ *noun* self-esteem.

amp *noun* **1** an **ampere**. **2** *informal* an **amplifier**.

amperage *noun* the magnitude or strength of an electric current expressed in **ampere**s.

ampere /'ampɛə(r)/ *noun* (symbol **A**) the SI unit of electric current. [19c: named after the French physicist André Marie Ampère]

ampersand *noun* the symbol &, which means 'and'. [1830s: from *and per se and* meaning '& when it appears by itself means *and*']

amphetamine /am'fɛtəmiːn, -mɪn/ *noun, med* a potentially addictive synthetic drug, often used illegally as a stimulant. Also (*slang* called) **speed**. [1930s: from the chemical name alpha*m*ethyl*phe*nethyl*amine*]

amphi- *combining form, denoting* both, or on both sides or ends. [Greek, meaning 'both' or 'on both sides']

amphibian *noun* **1** *zool* a cold-blooded animal, eg frog, toad and newt, that lives partly or entirely on land but returns to water to lay its eggs. **2** a vehicle that can operate both on land and in water. [17c: from Greek *amphibia* creatures that live in both environments]

amphibious *adj* **1** *zool* of a living organism: capable of living both on land and in water. **2** of vehicles, equipment, etc: designed to be operated or used both on land, and on or in water. **3** of a military operation: using troops that have been conveyed across the sea.

amphitheatre *noun* **1** an oval or round building without a roof, with tiers of seats built around a central open area. **2** *archit* a tiered gallery in a theatre, lecture hall, etc. [16c: from Greek *amphitheatron*]

amphora /'amfərə/ *noun* (***amphoras*** *or* ***amphorae*** /'amfəriː/) *archaeol, etc* a large narrow-necked Greek or Roman jar with a handle on either side, used for storing liquids. [15c: Greek]

ample *adj* **1** more than enough; plenty. **2** abundant. ▪ **amply** *adv.* [15c: from Latin *amplus* abundant]

amplification *noun* **1** the act, process or result of amplifying something. **2 a** material added to a report, story, etc to expand or explain it; **b** a story or account with details added. **3** *electronics* the magnification or the amount of magnification of a sound's loudness or the strength of an electrical current, signal, etc. **4** *genetics* the formation of multiple copies of a particular gene or DNA sequence. Also called **gene amplification**. [16c]

amplifier *noun* an electronic device that amplifies the strength of an electrical or radio signal, used in audio equipment, radio and television sets, etc.

amplify *verb* (***-ies, -ied***) **1** *electronics* to increase the strength of (an electrical or radio signal) by transferring power from an external energy source. **2** *tr & intr* to add details or further explanation to an account, story, etc. [15c: from Latin *amplificare*]

amplitude *noun* **1** spaciousness, wide range or extent. **2** abundance. **3** *physics* in any quantity that varies in periodic cycles, such as a wave or vibration: the maximum displacement from its mean position, eg the angle between the vertical and the peak position in the swing of a pendulum. [16c: from Latin *amplitudo*]

amplitude modulation *noun, telecomm* (abbrev **AM**) in radio transmission: the process whereby the amplitude of the carrier wave (the signal-carrying wave) is made to increase or decrease instantaneously in response to variations in the characteristics of the signal being transmitted. Compare **frequency modulation**.

ampoule *or* (*US*) **ampule** *noun, med* a small sealed container, usu of glass or plastic, containing one sterile dose of a drug for injection. [17c: French]

ampulla *noun* (***ampullae*** /am'pʊliː/) **1** *anatomy* the dilated end of a duct or canal. **2** a container for oil, water or wine used in religious ceremonies. [14c: Latin]

amputate *verb, surgery* to remove (all or part of a limb). ▪ **amputation** *noun*. [17c: from Latin *amputare* to cut off]

amputee *noun* someone who has had a limb surgically removed.

amrit *noun, Sikhism* **1** a ceremonial drink made of sugar and water. **2** the initiation ceremony in which amrit is drunk.

amuck see **amok**

amulet *noun* a small object, charm or jewel worn to protect the wearer from witchcraft, evil, disease, etc. [15c: from Latin *amuletum*]

amuse *verb* **1** to make someone laugh. **2** to keep someone entertained and interested. [15c: from French *amuser* to cause to muse]

amusement *noun* **1** the state of being amused. **2** something that amuses. **3** a machine for riding on or playing games of chance.

amusement arcade *noun, Brit* a place where people can play fruit machines, video games, etc.

amusement park *noun, N Am* a place of outdoor entertainment with side shows, stalls, shooting ranges and rides. *Brit equivalent* **funfair**.

amusing *adj* mildly funny, diverting or entertaining.

amylase *noun, biochem* any of various enzymes present in digestive juices, which play a part in the breakdown of starch and glycogen. [19c: from Greek *amylon* starch]

an see **a**[1]

---

an, a
See the Usage Note at **a**[1].

---

an- see **a-**[2]

-an, -ean *or* **-ian** *suffix* **1** *forming adjectives and nouns, signifying* belonging to, relating to or coming from a specified place: *Roman remains*. **2** *forming adjectives and nouns, signifying* dating from or typical of the reign of a specified ruler: *Georgian architecture*. **3** *forming adjectives and nouns, signifying* adhering to the beliefs or teachings of a specified leader: *the Lutheran church*. **4** *biol, forming adjectives and nouns, signifying* belonging to a specified class or order: *crustacean*. **5** *forming nouns, denoting* an expert in a specified subject: *politician*.

-ana *or* **-iana** *suffix, denoting* things belonging to or typical of a particular person or period: *Victoriana*. See also **-ia**[2]. [17c: from Latin *-anum* belonging or referring to someone specified]

Anabaptist *noun, Christianity* a member of various groups of believers who advocated the baptism of believing adults only. ▪ **Anabaptism** *noun*. [16c: from Latin *anabaptismus*]

anabolic steroid *noun, biochem* a synthetic hormone that increases muscle bulk and strength.

anabolism *noun, biochem* in the cells of living organisms: the process whereby complex molecules are manufactured from smaller molecules. Compare **catabolism**. ▪ **anabolic** /anə'bɒlɪk/ *adj*. [19c: from Greek *ana* up + *bole* throw + **-ism** (sense 3)]

anachronism *noun* **1** the attribution of something to a historical period in which it did not exist. **2** a person, thing or attitude that is or appears to be out of date and old-fashioned. ▪ **anachronistic** *adj*. [17c: from Greek *ana* backwards + *chronos* time]

anaconda *noun* a non-venomous S American snake of the **boa** family.

anaemia *or* **anemia** *noun, pathol* an abnormal reduction in the amount of **haemoglobin** in the red blood cells, characterized by pallid skin, fatigue and breathlessness. [19c: from Greek *an* without + *haima* blood]

anaemic *adj* **1** suffering from anaemia. **2** pale or weak. **3** spiritless; lacking in energy.

anaerobe *noun, biol* any organism that does not require oxygen for respiration, or that cannot survive in the presence of oxygen. Compare **aerobe**. [19c: from French *anaerobie*]

anaerobic *adj, biol* of an organism, especially a bacterium: not requiring oxygen in order to obtain energy by respiration, or unable to survive in the presence of oxygen. Compare **aerobic**.

anaerobic respiration *noun, biol* the process in which cells use oxygen to break down foodstuffs, releasing energy and creating carbon dioxide and water. Compare **aerobic respiration**.

anaesthesia *or* (*US*) **anesthesia** /anɪs'θiːzɪə/ *noun* a reversible loss of sensation in all or part of the body, usu induced by drugs. [18c: from **an-** + Greek *aisthesis* feeling]

anaesthetic *or* (*US*) **anesthetic** /anəs'θɛtɪk/ *noun* any agent, esp a drug, capable of producing anaesthesia. See also **general anaesthetic**, **local anaesthetic**. ▸ *adj* denoting an agent or procedure that is capable of producing anaesthesia.

anaesthetist /ən'iːsθətɪst/ *or* (*US*) **anesthetist** /ə'nɛs-/ *noun* someone who has been specifically trained in the administration of anaesthetics to patients.

anaesthetize, **-ise** /ə'niːsθətaɪz/ *or* (*US*) **anesthetize** /ə'nɛs-/ *verb* to give an anaesthetic to someone.

anagram *noun* a word, phrase or sentence that is formed by changing the order of the letters of another word, phrase or sentence. Compare **palin-**

drome. [16c: from Greek *ana* back + *gramma* a letter]

analgesia /anəl'dʒiːzɪə, -sɪə/ *noun, physiol* a reduction in or loss of the ability to feel pain. [18c: from **an-** + Greek *algeein* to feel pain]

analgesic *noun* a drug or other agent that relieves pain. ▸ *adj* having the effect of relieving pain.

analog an alternative *N Am* spelling of **analogue**.

analogize *or* **-ise** *verb* to use analogy, esp in order to clarify a point or for rhetorical effect.

analogous /ə'naləgəs/ *adj* **1** similar or alike in some way. **2** *biol* denoting plant or animal structures that are similar in function, but have evolved independently of each other in different groups, eg the wings of insects and birds. Compare **homologous**. [17c: from Latin *analogus*]

IDIOMS **be analogous to sth** to have similar characteristics to it or to function in the same way as it.

analogue *or* (*US*) **analog** *noun* **1** something regarded in terms of its similarity or parallelism to something else. **2** *biol* any part of an animal or plant that is similar in function, though not in origin, to a part in a different organism. ▸ *adj* of a device or physical quantity: changing continuously rather than in a series of discrete steps, and therefore capable of being represented by an electric voltage: *analogue computer.* Compare **digital**. [Early 19c: from Greek *analogos* proportionate]

analogy *noun* (***-ies***) **1** a similarity in some ways. **2** a way of reasoning which makes it possible to explain one thing or event by comparing it with something else. ▪ **analogical** *adj*. [16c: from Greek *analogia*]

analyse *or* (*US*) **analyze** /'anəlaɪz/ *verb* **1** to examine the structure or content of something in detail. **2** to resolve or separate something into its component parts. **3** to detect and identify the different chemical compounds present in (a mixture). **4** to psychoanalyse someone. [18c: from Greek *ana* up + *lyein* to loosen]

analysis /ə'nalɪsɪs/ *noun* (***-ses*** /-siːz/) **1** a detailed examination of the structure and content of something. **2** a statement of the results of such an examination. **3** short for **psychoanalysis**. [16c: from Greek *ana* up + *lyein* to loosen]

analyst /'anəlɪst/ *noun* **1** someone who is skilled in analysis, esp chemical, political or economic. **2** short form of **psychoanalyst** (see **psychoanalysis**).

analytic *or* **analytical** *adj* **1** concerning or involving analysis. **2** examining or able to examine things in detail to learn or make judgements about them. ▪ **analytically** *adv*.

analytical geometry see **co-ordinate geometry**

anaphylaxis /anafɪ'laksɪs/ *noun, med* a sudden severe hypersensitive reaction to the injection of a particular foreign substance or antigen. ▪ **anaphylactic** *adj*. [Early 20c: from Greek *ana* back + *phylaxis* protection]

anarchist *noun* **1** someone who believes that governments and laws are unnecessary and should be abolished. **2** someone who tries to overthrow the government by violence. **3** someone who tries to cause disorder of any kind. ▪ **anarchism** *noun*. ▪ **anarchistic** *adj*.

anarchy *noun* **1** confusion and lack of order, esp because of the failure or breakdown of law and government. **2** the absence of law and government. ▪ **anarchic** /an'ɑːkɪk/ *adj*. [16c: from Greek *anarchia* lack of a ruler]

anathema /ə'naθəmə/ *noun* **1** someone or something that is detested or abhorred. **2** a curse. [16c: Latin, meaning 'an excommunicated person']

anathematize *or* **-ise** *verb* to curse or denounce.

Anatolian *noun* a group of extinct languages, including Hittite, spoken c.2000 BC in Anatolia, an area now in present-day Turkey and Syria. ▸ *adj* relating to this group of languages.

anatomy *noun* (***-ies***) **1** the scientific study of the structure of plants and animals. **2** the physical structure of a plant or animal, esp the internal structure. **3** any close examination, analysis or study of something. **4** *non-technical* someone's body. ▪ **anatomical** /anə'tɒmɪkəl/ *adj*. ▪ **anatomist** *noun*. [14c: from Greek *ana* up + *temnein* to cut]

ANC *abbrev* African National Congress, a South African movement opposed to white minority rule that later become the governing party.

-ance *suffix, forming nouns, denoting* a state, quality, condition or action: *abundance* • *performance*.

ancestor *noun* **1** someone, usu more distant than a grandparent, from whom a person is descended. **2** a plant or animal that another type of plant or animal has evolved from. [13c: from Latin *antecessor*]

ancestral *adj* belonging to or inherited from one's ancestors: *the ancestral home*.

ancestry *noun* (***-ies***) lineage or family descent, esp when it can be traced back over many generations.

anchor *noun* **1** a heavy piece of metal attached by a cable to a ship and put overboard so that the barbs catch in the seabed or riverbed to restrict the ship's movement. **2** anything that acts as a weight to secure something else. **3** anything that gives security or stability. ▸ *verb* **1** to fasten (a ship) using an anchor. **2** to fasten anything securely. **3** *intr* to drop an anchor and become moored by it; to be moored by an anchor. [Anglo-Saxon *ancor*]

anchorage *noun* a place where a ship may anchor.

anchorite *noun* someone who lives alone or separate from other people, usu for religious reasons. [15c: from Greek *anachoretes*]

anchorman *noun* **1** *TV, radio* the person in the studio who provides the links with outside broadcast reporters, between commercial breaks, etc. **2** *athletics* the last person to run in a relay race.

anchovy /'antʃəvɪ/ *noun* (***-ies***) a small fish related to the herring, with a pungent flavour. [16c: from Spanish and Portuguese *anchova* a small fish]

ancien régime /*French* ɑ̃sjɛ̃ reʒim/ ▸ *noun* (***anciens régimes*** /ɑ̃sjɛ̃ reʒim/) **1** the French political, social and royal systems that were in place before the Revolution of 1789. **2** any outmoded system. [18c: French, meaning 'old rule']

ancient *adj* **1** dating from very long ago. **2** very old. **3** dating from before the end of the Western Roman Empire in AD 476. Compare **medieval**, **modern** (sense 1). [14c: from French *ancien* old]

ancient history *noun* **1** the history of the countries surrounding the Mediterranean Sea, esp Greece, Asia Minor, Italy and Egypt, esp that prior to the end of the Western Roman Empire in AD 476. **2** *informal* information, news, etc that has been well known for a long time.

ancillary /an'sɪlərɪ/ *adj* **1** helping or giving support to something else, eg medical services. **2** being used as an extra. ▸ *noun* someone or something used as support or backup. [17c: from Latin *ancillaris*]

-ancy *suffix* forming nouns corresponding to adjectives in **-ant**: *expectancy* • *vacancy.* [From Latin *-antia*]

and *conj* **1 a** used to show addition: *dogs and cats;* **b** used in sums of addition: *two and two make four.* **2 a** used to connect an action that follows as a result or reason of a previous one: *fall and bang one's head;* **b** used to connect an action that follows sequentially on from another: *boil the kettle and make the tea.* **3** used to show repetition or duration: *She cried and cried.* **4** used to show progression: *The crowd got bigger and bigger.* **5** used to show variety or contrast: *discussed the ins and outs of it.* **6** used after some verbs instead of *to*: *come and try* • *go and get it.* ▸ *noun* an unspecified problem or matter: *no ifs or ands about it.* [Anglo-Saxon]

---

and

Although some people think it is a bad use of English, it is not incorrect to begin a sentence with **and**.

---

andante /an'dantɪ, -teɪ/ *music, adv, adj* in a slow, steady manner. ▸ *noun* a piece of music to be played in this way. [18c: Italian]

andiron /'andaɪən/ *noun* a decorated iron bar, usu one of a pair, for supporting logs and coal in a big fireplace. [14c: from French *andier*]

and/or *conj* either or both of two possibilities stated: *cakes and/or biscuits.*

andro- *or (before a vowel)* **andr-** *combining form, denoting* male. [From Greek *andro-* male]

androecium /an'driːsɪəm/ *noun* (***androecia***) *botany* the male reproductive parts of a flower, consisting of the stamens. [19c: from **andro-** + Greek *oikion* house]

androgen *noun, physiol* any of a group of steroid hormones, produced mainly by the testes, that control the growth and functioning of the male sex organs and the appearance of male secondary sexual characteristics. Compare **oestrogen**.

androgynous *adj* **1** *biol* denoting an animal or plant that shows both male and female characteristics, esp one that possesses both male and female sex organs; hermaphrodite. **2** showing both male and female traits, eg someone who could be mistaken for either sex. [17c: from Greek *androgynos*]

android *noun* a robot that resembles a human being in form or features.

andrology *noun, med* the diagnosis and treatment of diseases and disorders that affect the reproductive organs of the male body. [1980s: modelled on **gynaecology**]

-ane *suffix, chem, forming nouns, denoting* a hydrocarbon derivative: *propane.*

anecdote *noun* a short entertaining account of an incident. ▪ **anecdotal** *adj.* [17c: from Greek *anekdota* unpublished things]

anemia an alternative *N Am* spelling of **anaemia**.

anemometer *noun* a device for measuring wind speed. Also called **wind gauge**. [18c: from Greek *anemos* wind + **-meter** (sense 1)]

anemone /ə'nɛmənɪ/ *noun* **1** *botany* any of several plants of the buttercup family, esp with red, purple, blue or white cup-shaped flowers. **2** *zool* short form of **sea anemone**. [16c: Greek, meaning 'daughter of the wind']

aneroid *noun, meteorol* a type of barometer used to measure atmospheric pressure and to estimate altitude. Also called **aneroid barometer**. [19c: from French *anéroïde*]

anesthesia an alternative *N Am* spelling of **anaesthesia**.

anesthesiologist see **anaesthetist**

anesthetic an alternative *N Am* spelling of **anaesthetic**.

aneurysm *or* **aneurism** /'anjərɪzəm/ *noun, pathol* a balloon-like swelling in the wall of an artery. [17c: from Greek *aneurysma*]

anew *adv* **1** once more, again. **2** in a different way. [Anglo-Saxon *of niowe*]

angel *noun* **1** a messenger or attendant of God or Allah. See also **order** (sense 20). **2** a representation of this in the form of a human being with a halo and wings. **3** *informal* a good, helpful, pure or beautiful person. **4** *informal* someone who puts money into an enterprise, particularly a theatrical production. [Anglo-Saxon]

angel cake *noun* a light sponge cake.

angelfish *noun* a S American freshwater fish with a very deep body, flattened from side to side and covered with dark vertical stripes, and elongated pectoral fins.

angelic *adj* of someone's face, expression, behaviour, etc: like that of an angel, esp in being innocent, beautiful, etc. ▪ **angelically** *adv.*

angelica *noun* a tall plant whose stem and leaf stalks are crystallized in sugar and used as a food flavouring and cake decoration. [16c: from Latin *herba angelica* angelic herb]

angelus /'andʒələs/ *noun, Christianity* **1** a Roman Catholic prayer said in the morning, at noon and at sunset. **2** a bell rung to announce these prayers. [18c: from Latin *Angelus domini* the angel of the Lord, the opening words of the prayer]

anger *noun* a feeling of great displeasure or annoyance. ▸ *verb* to cause this kind of feeling in someone; to displease. [13c: from Norse *angr* trouble]

angina /an'dʒaɪnə/ *noun, pathol* severe pain behind the chest-bone, usu induced by insufficient blood supply to the heart muscle during exertion. Also called **angina pectoris**. [16c: from Latin *angina* a throat disease]

angiogram *noun, med* a type of X-ray photograph that is achieved by **angiography**.

angiography *noun, med* the examination of the condition of blood vessels by X-ray.

Angle *noun* a member of a N German tribe who settled in N and E England in the 5c, forming the kingdoms of Northumbria, Mercia and East Anglia. See also **Saxon**, **Anglo-Saxon**. [Anglo-Saxon *engle* the people of *Angulus*, a district of Holstein so called because of its hook shape]

angle[1] *noun* **1** *maths* a measure of the rotation of a line about a point, usu measured in degrees, radians or revolutions. **2** the point where two lines or planes intersect. **3** the extent to which one line slopes away from another. **4** a corner. **5** a point of view. ▸ *verb* **1** *tr & intr* to move in or place at an angle. **2** to present a news story, information, etc from a particular point of view. [14c: from Latin *angulum* a corner]

angle² *verb* **1** to use a rod and line for catching fish. **2** (**angle for sth**) to try to get it in a devious or indirect way. ▪ **angler** *noun*. [Anglo-Saxon *angul* hook]

angle of incidence *noun, physics* the angle between the point where a ray strikes a reflecting surface, and a line drawn perpendicular to the surface at that point.

angle of reflection *noun, physics* the angle between the point where a ray leaves a reflecting surface, and a line drawn perpendicular to the surface at that point.

angle of refraction *noun, physics* the angle between the point where a ray is refracted at an interface between two different media, eg water and glass, and a line drawn perpendicular to the surface at that point.

Anglican *adj* relating to the Church of England or another Church in communion with it. ▶ *noun* a member of an Anglican Church. ▪ **Anglicanism** *noun*. [13c: from Latin *Anglicanus*]

Anglicism *noun* **1** a specifically English word, phrase or idiom. **2** a custom or characteristic that is peculiar to the English.

anglicize *or* **-ise** *verb* to make something English in form or character. [18c: from Latin *Anglus* English]

angling *noun* the action or sport of catching fish with rod, line and hook.

Anglo *noun* **1** someone who is neither black nor of Latin-American descent, esp in the US. **2** an English-speaking Canadian.

Anglo- *combining form, denoting* **1** English: *Anglophobic*. **2** British: *Anglo-American*. [16c: from Latin *Anglus* English]

Anglo-Catholic *noun* a member of an Anglican Church which emphasizes the Church's Catholic traditions. *as adj*: *Anglo-Catholic priests*. ▪ **Anglo-Catholicism** *noun*.

Anglocentric *adj* having a focus that is skewed in favour of things that are English or British, esp to the exclusion of other things.

Anglo-Indian *noun* **1** someone of British descent who has lived in India for a long time. **2** someone of mixed English and Indian descent. ▶ *as adj*: *Anglo-Indian traditions*.

Anglo-Irish *adj* **1 a** referring or relating to the community of people living in Ireland who are of English descent; **b** (**the Anglo-Irish**) such people as a group. **2** referring or relating to anything that is of joint concern to the English or British and the Irish. ▶ *noun* the variety of English spoken in Ireland.

Anglo-Norman *noun* **1** a blending of Norman French and English, used in England for around two centuries after the conquest. *Anglo-Norman literature*. **2** someone of Norman descent who settled in England, Scotland or Wales after 1066.

anglophile *or* **Anglophile** *noun* someone who admires England and the English. ▪ **anglophilia** /-ˈfɪlɪə/ *noun*.

anglophone *or* **Anglophone** *noun* someone who speaks English. ▶ *adj* belonging or relating to English-speaking people, countries, etc.

Anglo-Saxon *noun* **1** a member of any of the Germanic tribes who settled in England in the 5c. **2** the English language before about 1150. Also called **Old English**. **3** English as thought of in terms of its plain, usu monosyllabic, words including most of the taboo ones. **4** any English-speaking White person, usu one of Germanic descent. ▶ *adj* **1 a** belonging or relating to the Germanic peoples who settled in England; **b** belonging or relating to the early form of the English language. **2** of any English speech or writing: blunt and to the point. **3** belonging or relating to the shared cultural, legal, political, etc aspects of British and American life: *traditional Anglo-Saxon values*. [Anglo-Saxon, as plural noun *Angulseaxan*]

angora *or* **Angora** *noun* the wool or cloth made from the soft silky wool of the Angora goat or rabbit. ▶ *adj* denoting a breed of domestic goat, rabbit or domestic cat with long white silky hair. [Early 19c: an earlier form (used until 1930) of the placename Ankara]

Angostura bitters *plural noun, trademark* a blend of **gentian** and herbs, used as a flavouring in alcoholic drinks. [1870s: named after Angostura, a town in Venezuela where it was first made]

angry *adj* (*-ier, -iest*) **1** feeling or showing annoyance, resentment, wrath, disapproval, etc. **2** irritable, cross, etc: *an angry expression*. **3** of a wound, rash, etc: red and sore. **4** dark and stormy: *an angry sky, sea, etc*. ▪ **angrily** *adv*.

angst *noun* a feeling of apprehension or anxiety. [19c: German, meaning 'fear']

angstrom *or* **ångström** /ˈaŋstrəm/ *noun* (symbol **Å**) a unit of length equal to 10^{-10}m, but in the SI system now replaced by the **nanometre**. [19c: named after the Swedish physicist Anders J Ångström]

anguish *noun* severe mental distress or torture. ▶ *verb, tr & intr* to suffer or cause to suffer severe mental distress or torture. [13c: from Latin *angustia* tightness]

angular *adj* **1** of someone or part of someone's body, etc: thin and bony. **2** of actions, movement, etc: awkward or ungainly. **3** having sharp edges or corners. **4** measured by an angle: *angular distance*. ▪ **angularity** *noun*. [16c: from Latin *angularis*]

anhydride *noun, chem* any chemical compound formed by the removal of water from another compound, esp an acid.

anhydrous *adj* denoting a chemical compound that contains no water.

anil *noun* **1** a leguminous W Indian plant from which indigo is obtained. **2** the indigo dye itself. [18c: from Arabic *al* the + *nila* dark blue]

aniline *noun* a colourless oily highly toxic liquid organic compound, used in the manufacture of rubber, plastics, drugs and dyes.

animal *noun* **1 a** *zool* any member of the kingdom of organisms that are capable of voluntary movement, have specialized sense organs that allow rapid response to stimuli; **b** any of these excluding human beings. **2** someone who behaves in a rough uncivilized way. **3** *informal* (*usu* **an altogether different animal**) a person or thing: *This new multimedia PC is an altogether different animal*. ▶ *adj* **1** belonging or relating to, from or like, an animal: *animal fat*. **2** relating to physical desires; brutal; sensual: *animal passions*. [14c: Latin]

animal husbandry *noun* the branch of agriculture concerned with the breeding, care and feeding of domestic animals.

animalism *noun* **1** an obsession with anything that is physical as opposed to spiritual or intellectual. **2** the belief that humans are no better than other animals.

animality *noun* **1** someone's animal nature or behaviour. **2** the state of being an animal.

animalize *or* **-ise** *verb* to make someone brutal or sensual.

animal kingdom *noun* **1** *biol* in the classification of living organisms: the rank which includes all **animal**s (sense 1a). **2** all of the animals thought of collectively.

animate *verb* /ˈanɪmeɪt/ **1** to give life to someone or something. **2** to make something lively. **3** to record (drawings) on film in such a way as to make the images seem to move. *adj* /ˈanɪmət/ alive. [16c: from Latin *animare* to breathe]

animated *adj* **1** lively; spirited: *an animated discussion.* **2** living. **3** moving as if alive: *animated cartoons.* ▪ **animatedly** *adv.*

animation *noun* **1** liveliness; vivacity. **2** **a** the techniques used to record still drawings on film in such a way as to make the images seem to move; **b** any sequence of these images.

animator *noun* someone who makes animated films or cartoons.

animatronics *singular noun, cinematog* in film-making: the art of animating a life-like figure of a person, animal, etc, by means of computer technology.

animism *noun* the belief that plants and natural phenomena such as rivers, mountains, etc have souls. ▪ **animist** *noun.* ▪ **animistic** *adj.* [19c: from Latin *anima* soul]

animosity *noun* (**-ies**) a strong dislike or hatred.

animus *noun* a feeling of strong dislike or hatred. [Early 19c: Latin, meaning 'spirit', 'soul']

anion /ˈanaɪən/ *noun, chem* any negatively charged **ion**. Compare **cation.** ▪ **anionic** /anaɪˈɒnɪk/ *adj.* [19c: Greek, meaning 'going up']

anise /ˈanɪs/ *noun* an annual plant with small greyish-brown aromatic fruits containing liquorice-flavoured seeds. [14c: from Greek *anison*]

aniseed *noun* the liquorice-flavoured seeds of the anise plant, used as a food flavouring.

ankh *noun* the ancient Egyptian symbol of life in the form of a T-shaped cross with a loop above the horizontal bar. [19c: Egyptian, meaning 'life']

ankle *noun* **1** the joint that connects the leg and the foot. **2** the part of the leg just above the foot. [Anglo-Saxon *ancleow*]

anklet *noun* a chain or ring worn around the ankle.

ankylosis /aŋkɪˈloʊsɪs/ *noun* a disorder characterized by immobility or stiffening of a joint, the bones of which often become fixed in an abnormal position, as a result of injury, disease, surgery, etc. [18c: from Greek *ankylos* crooked]

annals *plural noun* **1** **a** yearly historical records of events; **b** recorded history in general. **2** regular reports of the work of an organization. ▪ **annalist** *noun.* [16c: from Latin *libri annales* yearly books]

anneal *verb, eng* to heat (a material such as metal or glass) and then slowly cool it in order to make it softer, less brittle and easier to work. ▪ **annealing** *noun.* [Anglo-Saxon *onælan* to burn]

annelid *noun, zool* a worm with a long soft cylindrical body composed of many ring-shaped segments, eg the earthworm. [19c: from Latin *annellus* little ring]

annex *verb* **1** to take possession of land or territory, esp by conquest or occupation. **2** to add or attach something to something larger. **3** *informal* to take without permission. ▸ *noun* the *N Am* spelling of **annexe.** ▪ **annexation** *noun.* [14c: from Latin *adnectere* to tie or bind]

annexe *or* (*N Am*) **annex** *noun* **1** an additional room, building, area, etc. **2** anything that has been added to something else, esp an extra clause, appendix, etc in a document. [17c: French, meaning 'something joined']

annihilate *verb* **1** to destroy something completely. **2** to defeat, crush or humiliate someone, esp in an argument, debate, sporting contest, etc. **3** *physics* of a particle: to be destroyed by a collision with its corresponding antiparticle. ▪ **annihilation** *noun.* [16c: from Latin *annihilare*]

anniversary *noun* (**-ies**) **1** a date on which some event took place in a previous year. **2** the celebration of this event on the same date each year. *as adj*: *an anniversary present.* [13c: from Latin *anniversarius*]

Anno Domini *or* **anno Domini** *adv* AD. ▸ *noun, informal* old age. [16c: Latin, meaning 'in the year of our Lord']

annotate *verb* to add notes and explanations to (a book, article, etc). ▪ **annotation** *noun.* [18c: from Latin *annotare* to put a note to something]

announce *verb* **1** to make something known publicly. **2** to make (an arrival, esp of a guest or some form of transport) known. **3** to declare in advance: *The sign announced next week's sale.* **4** to be a sign of something: *dark clouds announcing a storm.* **5** *intr, US* to declare oneself to be running as a candidate, esp for the presidency or a governorship: *She announced for governor.* ▪ **announcement** *noun.* [15c: from Latin *annuntiare* to report]

announcer *noun* someone who introduces programmes or reads the news on radio or TV.

annoy *verb* **1** to anger or distress. **2** to harass or pester. ▪ **annoyance** *noun.* ▪ **annoying** *adj.* ▪ **annoyingly** *adv.* [13c: from Latin *inodiare* to cause aversion]

annual *adj* **1** done or happening once a year or every year. **2** lasting for a year. ▸ *noun* **1** *botany* a plant that germinates, flowers, produces seed, and dies within a period of one year. See also **biennial**, **perennial.** **2** a book published every year. ▪ **annually** *adv.* [14c: from Latin *annualis*]

annual general meeting *noun* (abbrev **AGM**) a meeting of a public company, society, etc held once a year.

annualize *or* **-ise** *verb* to calculate (rates of interest, inflation, etc) for a year based on the figures for only part of it.

annuity /əˈnjuːɪtɪ/ *noun* (**-ies**) **1** a yearly grant or allowance. **2** money that has been invested to provide a fixed amount of interest every year. [15c: from Latin *annuitas*]

annul *verb* (***annulled, annulling***) to declare publicly that a marriage, legal contract, etc is no longer valid. [15c: from Latin *annullare*]

annular *adj* ring-shaped. [16c: from Latin *annularis*]

annular eclipse *noun, astron* an eclipse in which a thin ring of sunlight remains visible around the Moon's shadow. Compare **total eclipse**.

annulate *adj* formed from or marked with rings.

annulment *noun* **1** the act of annulling. **2** the formal ending of a marriage, legal contract, etc.

annulus /'anjʊləs/ *noun* (***annuli*** /-laɪ/), *geom* the figure formed by two concentric circles, ie a disc with a central hole. [16c: medieval Latin, meaning 'a ring or ring-shaped object']

annunciate *verb* to declare publicly or officially. [16c: from Latin *annuntiare* to report]

the Annunciation *noun, Christianity* **1** the announcement by the Angel Gabriel to Mary that she would be the mother of Christ. **2** the festival, held on 25 March, celebrating this. [15c: from Latin *annuntiare* to report]

anode *noun* **1** in an electrolytic cell: the positive electrode, towards which negatively charged ions, usu in solution, are attracted. **2** the negative terminal of a battery. Compare **cathode**. [19c: from Greek *anodos* way up]

anodize *or* **-ise** *verb* to coat (an object made of metal, esp aluminium) with a thin protective oxide film by making that object the **anode** in a cell to which an electric current is applied.

anodyne *noun* **1** a medicine or drug that relieves or alleviates pain. **2** anything that has a palliative effect, esp to hurt feelings, mental distress, etc. ► *adj* able to relieve physical pain or mental distress. [16c: from Greek *an-* without + *odyne* pain]

anoint *verb* to put oil or ointment on (someone's head, feet, etc), usu as part of a religious ceremony, eg baptism. ▪ **anointment** *noun*. [14c: from Latin *inungere* from *ungere* to smear with oil]

anomalous *adj* different from the usual; irregular; peculiar. [17c: from Greek *an-* not + *homalos* even]

anomaly /ə'nɒməlɪ/ *noun* (***-ies***) **1** something that is unusual or different from what is expected. **2** divergence from what is usual or expected.

anomie *or* **anomy** /'anəmɪ/ *noun* (***-ies***) *sociol* a lack of regard for the generally accepted social or moral standards. [First coined by the French sociologist Emile Durkheim in *Suicide* (1897): from Greek *anomia* lawlessness]

anon[1] *abbrev* anonymous.

anon[2] *adv, old use* some time soon. [Anglo-Saxon *on an* into one]

anonymous /ə'nɒnɪməs/ *adj* **1** having no name. **2** of a piece of writing, an action, etc: from or by someone whose name is not known or not given. **3** without character; nondescript. ▪ **anonymity** /anə'nɪmɪtɪ/ *noun*. ▪ **anonymously** *adv*. [17c: from Greek *an-* without + *onoma* name]

anorak *noun* **1** a hooded waterproof jacket. **2** *slang* someone who is obsessively involved in something that is generally regarded as boring or unfashionable. [1920s: from Inuit *anoraq*]

anorexia *noun* **1** loss of appetite. **2** the common name for **anorexia nervosa**. [16c: Latin]

anorexia nervosa *noun* a psychological disorder characterized by a significant decrease in body weight, deliberately induced by refusal to eat because of an obsessive desire to lose weight. See also **bulimia nervosa**. ▪ **anorexic** *noun, adj*.

another *adj,* ► *pronoun* **1** one more. **2** one of a different kind: *I've tried that wine, now let me try another.* [14c: orig *an other*]

ansaphone see **answering machine**

Anschluss /'anʃlʊs/ *noun, hist* the political union of Germany and Austria in 1938.

answer *noun* **1** something said or done in response to a question, request, letter, particular situation, etc. **2** (**the answer**) **a** the solution: *Winning the lottery would be the answer to all our problems;* **b** the solution to a mathematical problem. ► *verb* **1** *tr & intr* to make a spoken or written reply to something or someone. **2** to react or respond to something (esp a doorbell, the telephone, someone calling one's name, etc). **3** to solve (esp a maths problem), write in response to (an exam question), etc. **4** *intr* (**answer to sb**) to have to account to them. **5** to put up a defence to or offer an explanation for something. [Anglo-Saxon *andswaru*]

PHRASAL VERBS **answer back** to reply rudely.

answerable *adj* (*usu* **answerable to sb for sth**) accountable to them for it.

answering machine, **answerphone** *or* **ansaphone** *noun* a recording device attached to a telephone, which automatically answers incoming calls by playing a pre-recorded message to the caller and recording the caller's message for subsequent playback.

answering service *noun* a business that takes messages and answers telephone calls for its clients.

ant *noun* a small often wingless social insect that lives in colonies. [Anglo-Saxon *æmette*]

-ant *combining form* **1** *forming adjectives, signifying* **a** being in a specified state; **b** performing a specified action or function. **2** *forming nouns, signifying* someone or something that performs a specified action: *assistant*. [Latin present participle ending]

antacid *med, noun* an alkaline substance that neutralizes acidity in the stomach. ► *adj* of a substance, esp a medicine: able to neutralize excess acid in the stomach.

antagonism *noun* **1** openly expressed dislike or opposition. **2** *physiol* the opposing action between one muscle or group of muscles and another. **3** *biochem* interference with the growth or action of one organism or substance by another. [19c: from **antagonize**]

antagonist *noun* **1** an opponent. **2** an enemy. **3** *physiol* a muscle the contraction of which opposes the relaxation of another muscle (the **agonist**). **4** *med* a substance or organism that interferes with the growth or action of another. ▪ **antagonistic** *adj*. [19c]

antagonize *or* **-ise** *verb* **1** to make someone feel anger or hostility. **2** to irritate. [17c: from Greek *antagonizesthai* to oppose or rival]

Antarctic *noun* (**the Antarctic**) the area round the South Pole. ► *adj* relating to this area. [14c: from Greek *antarktikos* opposite the Arctic or North]

ante *noun* **1** a stake put up by a player, usu in poker, but also in other card games, before receiving any cards. **2** an advance payment. ► *verb* **1** (***anted, anteing***) to put up as a stake. **2** *tr & intr* (*usu* **ante up**) *informal, esp N Am* to pay. [19c: from Latin *ante* before]

IDIOMS **raise** *or* **up the ante 1** to increase the stakes in a card game, esp poker. **2** to elevate the importance of something.

ante- *prefix* before in place or time: *anteroom* • *antenatal*. [Latin, meaning 'before']

anteater *noun* a mammal that has a long cylindrical snout and an untidily bushy tail.

antecedent /antɪˈsiːdənt/ *noun* **1** an event or circumstance that precedes another. **2** *grammar* a word or phrase that some other word, usu a **relative** pronoun, relates to, eg *in the man who came to dinner, who* is a relative pronoun and its antecedent is *the man*. **3** (*usu* **antecedents**) **a** someone's past history; **b** someone's ancestry. ▸ *adj* going before in time. ▪ **antecedence** *noun*. [14c: from Latin *antecedens, -entis* going before]

antechamber *noun* an **anteroom**.

antedate *verb* **1** to belong to an earlier period than (some other date). **2** to put a date (on a document, letter, etc) that is earlier than the actual date.

antediluvian *adj* **1** belonging to the time before the flood as described in the Bible. **2** *facetious* very old or old-fashioned. [17c: from **ante-** + Latin *dilivium* flood]

antelope *noun* (***antelope*** *or* ***antelopes***) any of various species of hoofed mammal, usu with paired horns, found mainly in Africa. [15c: from Greek *antholops*]

ante meridiem *adj* (abbrev **a.m.**, **am**, **A.M.** *or* **AM**) indicating the time from midnight to midday. Compare **post meridiem**. [16c: Latin, meaning 'before noon']

antenatal *adj* **1** formed or occurring before birth. **2** relating to the health and care of women during pregnancy. [19c: from **ante-** + Latin *natalis* pertaining to birth]

antenna *noun* **1** (***antennae*** /anˈtɛniː/) in esp insects and crustaceans: one of a pair of long slender jointed structures on the head which act as feelers but are also concerned with the sense of smell. **2** (***antennas***) an **aerial**. [15c: Latin, meaning 'yard of a mast']

antepenultimate *adj* third from last. ▸ *noun* anything that is in third last position.

anterior *adj* **1** earlier in time. **2** **a** at or nearer the front; **b** *zool* at or near the head; **c** *botany* on the side next to the axis. Compare **posterior**. [17c: Latin, meaning 'fore']

anteroom *noun* a small room that opens into another, more important, room.

anthem *noun* **1** a song of praise or celebration, esp a **national anthem**. **2** a piece of music for a church choir, usu set to a Biblical text, sung at church services. [Anglo-Saxon *antefn*]

anther *noun* the structure at the tip of the stamen which contains the pollen sacs within which the pollen grains are produced. [16c: from Greek *anthos* flower]

ant hill *noun* a heap of earth, leaves, twigs, etc that ants pile up over their nest.

anthology *noun* (***-ies***) a collection of poems, usu by different authors but with some kind of thematic link. ▪ **anthologist** *noun*.

anthracite *noun* a hard shiny black coal that burns with a short blue flame, generating much heat but little or no smoke. [Early 19c: from Greek *anthrax* coal]

anthrax *noun, pathol* an acute infectious disease, mainly affecting sheep and cattle, which can be transmitted to humans and is often fatal if left untreated. [14c: from Greek *anthrax* coal or a carbuncle]

anthropocentric *adj* having or regarding mankind as the central element of existence. ▪ **anthropocentrism** *or* **anthropocentricism** *noun*.

anthropoid *adj* belonging or relating to, or like, a human being in form. ▸ *noun* (also **anthropoid ape**) any of the apes that shows a relatively close resemblance to a human, eg a chimpanzee or gorilla.

anthropology *noun* the study and analysis of the origins and characteristics of human beings and their societies, customs and beliefs. ▪ **anthropological** *adj*. ▪ **anthropologist** *noun*.

anthropomorphism *noun* the ascribing of a human form or human characteristics or attributes such as behaviour, feelings, etc to animals, objects, etc. ▪ **anthropomorphic** *adj*. ▪ **anthropomorphous** *adj*.

anti *adj, informal* opposed to (a particular policy, party, ideology, etc). ▸ *noun* someone who is opposed to something, esp a particular policy, party, ideology, etc. Compare **pro**[1]. [18c: from Greek *anti* against]

anti- *prefix, signifying* **1** opposed to: *antiwar*. **2** opposite to: *anticlockwise* • *anticlimax*. **3** mainly of drugs, remedies, etc: having the effect of counteracting, resisting or reversing: *antidepressant* • *antibiotic*. **4** of a device, product, etc: preventing; having a counteracting effect: *antifreeze* • *anti-lock braking system*. **5** set up as a rival or alternative: *Antichrist* • *antipope*. Compare **pro-**[1]. [Greek, meaning 'against']

anti-aircraft *adj* of a gun or missile: designed for use against enemy aircraft.

antibiotic *noun* a substance that can selectively destroy or inhibit other bacteria or fungi. ▸ *adj* having the property of or relating to antibiotics.

antibody *noun* (***-ies***) a protein that is produced in the blood, and forms an important part of the body's immune response.

antic *noun* (*often* **antics**) a playful caper or trick. [16c: from Italian *antico* ancient]

Antichrist *noun* **1** an enemy of Christ. **2** *Christianity* the great enemy of Christ, expected by the early Church to appear and reign over the world before Christ's **Second Coming**.

anticipate *verb* **1** to see what will be needed or wanted in the future and do what is necessary in advance. **2** to predict something and then act as though it is bound to happen. **3** to expect something. **4** to look forward to something. **5** to know beforehand: *could anticipate his every move*. **6** *tr & intr* to mention or think something before the proper time. **7** to foil or preclude: *anticipated the attack*. ▪ **anticipatory** *adj*. [16c: from Latin *anticipare*]

anticipation *noun* **1** a feeling of excited expectation. **2** knowledge gained in advance; a foretaste.

anticlerical *adj* opposed to public and political power being held by members of the clergy. ▪ **anticlericalism** *noun*.

anticlimax *noun* a dull or disappointing end to a series of events, a film, etc. ▪ **anticlimactic** *adj*.

anticline *noun, geol* a fold in the form of an arch, formed as a result of compressional forces acting in a horizontal plane on rock strata. Compare **syncline**. [1860s: from **anti-** (sense 2) + Greek *klinein* to lean]

anticlockwise *adv, adj* in the opposite direction to the direction that the hands of a clock move.

anticoagulant *noun, med* a drug or other substance that prevents or slows the clotting of blood.

anticonvulsant *noun, med* a drug that is used to prevent or reduce convulsions, esp in epilepsy.

antics see under **antic**

anticyclone *noun, meteorol* an area of relatively high atmospheric pressure from which light winds spiral outward in the opposite direction to that of the Earth's rotation. Also called **high**. Compare **cyclone** (sense 1).

antidepressant *noun, med* any drug that prevents or relieves the symptoms of depression. ▸ *adj* having or relating to this effect.

antidote *noun* **1** any agent, eg a drug, that counteracts or prevents the action of a poison. **2** anything that acts as a means of preventing or counteracting something bad. [15c: from Greek *antidoton* a remedy]

antifreeze *noun* any substance that is added to water or some other liquid in order to lower its freezing point, used eg in the radiators of motor vehicles.

antigen /'antɪdʒən/ *noun, biol* a foreign substance, eg a bacterium or virus, that stimulates the production of antibodies. [Early 20c: from *anti*body + Greek *-genes* born]

Antiguan *adj* belonging or relating to Antigua, an island in the Caribbean Sea, or its inhabitants. ▸ *noun* a citizen or inhabitant of, or person born in, Antigua.

antihero *noun* (***antiheroes***) a principal character in a novel, play, film, etc who lacks the conventional qualities of a hero. ▪ **antiheroine** *noun*.

antihistamine *noun, med* a drug that counteracts the effects of histamines produced in allergic reactions such as hay fever.

antiknock *noun* any substance that is added to petrol in order to reduce **knock** (noun 5), esp in the engines of motor vehicles.

anti-lock *or* **anti-locking** *adj* of a braking system: fitted with a special sensor that prevents the wheels of a vehicle locking when the brakes are applied vigorously. See also **ABS**.

antilogarithm *noun, maths* the number whose logarithm to a specified base is a given number. See also **logarithm**.

antimacassar /antɪmə'kasə(r)/ *noun* a covering for the back of a chair to stop it getting dirty. [19c: **anti-** (sense 4) + *macassar* the name for a hair oil]

antimatter *noun* a substance that is composed entirely of **antiparticle**s.

antimony /'antɪmənɪ/ *noun, chem* (symbol **Sb**) a brittle bluish-white metallic element used to increase the hardness of lead alloys. [15c: from Latin *antimonium*]

antinode *noun, physics* a point halfway between the nodes in a **standing wave**, indicating a position of maximum displacement or intensity. [19c]

antinomian *adj* denoting the view that Christians do not have to observe moral law. ▸ *noun* someone who holds this view. [17c: from *Antinomi*, the Latin name of a 16c German sect that believed this]

antinomy /an'tɪnəmɪ/ *noun* (***-ies***) **1** a contradiction between two laws or beliefs that are reasonable in themselves. **2** a conflict of authority. [16c: from Greek *nomos* law]

antinuclear *adj* **1** opposed to the use of nuclear weapons. **2** opposed to the building of nuclear power stations and to the use of nuclear power as a fuel.

antioxidant *chem, noun* a substance that slows down the process of oxidation. ▸ *adj* having this effect.

antiparticle *noun, physics* a subatomic particle that has the opposite electrical charge, magnetic moment and spin from other subatomic particles of the same mass.

antipasto *noun* (***antipasti*** /antɪ'pastiː/) a starter of a meal. [1930s: Italian, meaning 'before food']

antipathy /an'tɪpəθɪ/ *noun* (***-ies***) a feeling of strong dislike or hostility. [17c: from Greek *antipatheia*]

anti-personnel *adj* of weapons and bombs: designed to attack and kill people rather than destroy buildings, other weapons, etc.

antiperspirant *noun* a substance applied to the skin, esp under the armpits, in order to reduce perspiration.

antiphon *noun* a hymn or psalm sung alternately by two groups of singers. [16c: from Greek *antiphonos* sounding in response]

antipodes /an'tɪpədiːz/ *plural noun* (*usu* **the Antipodes**) two points on the Earth's surface that are diametrically opposite each other, esp Australia and New Zealand as being opposite Europe. ▪ **antipodean** /-'dɪən/ *adj, noun*. [14c: from Greek *antipous*]

antipope *noun* a pope elected in opposition to one already canonically chosen.

antipyretic /antɪpaɪə'rɛtɪk/ *adj* reducing or preventing fever. ▸ *noun* any drug that has this effect.

antiquarian /antɪ'kwɛərɪən/ *adj* referring or relating to, or dealing in, antiques and/or rare books. ▸ *noun* an antiquary.

antiquary /'antɪkwərɪ/ *noun* (***-ies***) someone who collects, studies or deals in antiques or antiquities. [16c: from Latin *antiquarius*]

antiquated *adj* old and out of date; old-fashioned. [17c: from Latin *antiquare* to make old]

antique *noun* a piece of furniture, china, etc that is old and often valuable. ▸ *adj* **1** old and often valuable. **2** *informal* old-fashioned. [16c: from Latin *antiquus* ancient]

antiquity *noun* (in sense 3 only ***-ies***) **1** ancient times, esp before the end of the Roman Empire in AD 476. **2** great age. **3** (**antiquities**) works of art or buildings surviving from ancient times. [14c: from Latin *antiquitas*]

antiracism *noun* opposition to prejudice or persecution on grounds of race. ▪ **antiracist** *adj, noun*.

antirrhinum /antɪ'raɪnəm/ *noun* a bushy plant with large brightly coloured two-lipped flowers. Also called **snapdragon.** [16c: from Greek *antirrhinon*]

antiscorbutic *adj* of a drug, remedy, etc: having the effect of preventing or curing scurvy. ▸ *noun* a drug or remedy that has this effect.

anti-Semite *noun* someone who is hostile to or prejudiced against Jews. ▪ **anti-Semitic** *adj*. ▪ **anti-Semitism** *noun*.

antiseptic *adj* denoting any substance that kills or inhibits the growth of bacteria and other micro-organisms. ▸ *noun* a drug or other substance that has this effect.

antiserum *noun* (***antisera***) a blood serum containing antibodies that are specific for, and neutralize the effects of, a particular antigen, used in vaccines. [19c: a contraction of *antitoxin serum*]

antisocial *adj* **1** reluctant to mix socially with other people. **2** of behaviour: harmful or annoying to the community in general. ▪ **antisocially** *adv.*

antistatic *adj* preventing the accumulation of static electric charges.

antitank *adj* of weapons: designed to destroy or immobilize military tanks.

antithesis /an'tɪθəsɪs/ *noun* (***-ses***) **1** a direct opposite of something. **2** the placing together of contrasting ideas, words or themes in any oral or written argument, esp to produce an effect. ▪ **antithetic** /antɪ'θɛtɪk/ *or* **antithetical** *adj.* [16c: Greek, meaning 'opposition']

antitoxin *noun, med* an antibody which neutralizes a toxin.

antitrades *plural noun* winds that blow above and in the opposite direction to **trade wind**s.

anti-trust *adj, N Am, esp US* said of a law, policy, etc: having the effect of protecting small companies and trade from domination by monopolies. [19c]

antler *noun* either of a pair of usu branched solid bony outgrowths on the head of an animal belonging to the deer family. ▪ **antlered** *adj.* [14c: from French *antoillier* the branch of a stag's horn]

antonym *noun* a word that in certain contexts is the opposite in meaning to another word, eg *straight* has the antonyms *curved* and *unconventional.* ▪ **antonymous** *adj.* [19c: from **anti-** (sense 2) + Greek *onoma* name; compare **synonym**]

antrum *noun* (***antra***) *anatomy* **1** a cavity or sinus, esp in a bone. **2** the part of the stomach next to the opening that leads into the duodenum. [14c: from Greek *antron* cave]

anus /'eɪnəs/ *noun* the opening at the end of the alimentary canal, through which the faeces are expelled from the body. ▪ **anal** *adj.* [17c: Latin, meaning 'ring']

anvil *noun* a heavy iron block on which metal objects can be hammered into shape. [Anglo-Saxon *anfilte*]

anxiety *noun* (***-ies***) **1** a strong feeling of fear or distress. **2** *informal* a worry. [16c: from Latin *anxietas;* see also **anxious**]

anxious *adj* **1** worried, nervous or fearful. **2** causing worry, fear or uncertainty: *an anxious moment.* **3** very eager: *anxious to do well.* ▪ **anxiously** *adv.* [17c: from Latin *anxius* troubled in the mind]

any *adj* **1** one, no matter which: *can't find any answer.* **2** some, no matter which: *have you any apples?* **3** *with negatives and in questions* even a very small amount of something: *won't tolerate any nonsense.* **4** indefinitely large: *have any number of dresses.* **5** every, no matter which: *Any child could tell you.* ▸ *pronoun* any one or any amount. ▸ *adv, with negatives and in questions* in any way whatever: *It isn't any better.* [Anglo-Saxon *ænig*]

anybody *pron* **1** any person, no matter which: *There wasn't anybody home.* **2** an important person: *Everybody who is anybody will be invited.* **3** some ordinary person: *She's not just anybody, you know.*

anyhow *adv* **1** anyway. **2** carelessly; in an untidy state.

anyone *pron* anybody.

anyplace *adv, N Am* **anywhere**.

anything *pron* a thing of any kind; a thing, no matter which. ▸ *adv* in any way; to any extent: *She isn't anything like her sister.*

IDIOMS **anything but** not at all: It *was anything but straightforward.*

anyway *conj* used as a sentence connector or when resuming an interrupted piece of dialogue: *Anyway, you'll never guess what he did next.* ▸ *adv* nevertheless; in spite of what has been said, done, etc.

---

anyway, any way

Be careful not to use **anyway** when you mean **any way**. **Any way** means in any manner:

Do it any way you can.

---

anywhere *adv* in, at or to any place. ▸ *pronoun* any place.

Anzac *noun* (*sometimes* **ANZAC**) a soldier serving in the Australia and New Zealand Army Corps during World War I. [1915: acronym]

AOB *or* **a.o.b.** *abbrev* any other business, the last item on the agenda for a meeting, when any matter not already dealt with may be raised.

A1 *adj* first-rate or excellent.

aorta /eɪ'ɔːtə/ *noun, anatomy* the main artery in the body, which carries oxygenated blood from the heart to the smaller arteries. ▪ **aortic** *adj.* [16c: from Greek *aorte* something that is hung]

apace *adv, literary* quickly.

Apache /ə'patʃɪ/ *noun* **1** a Native N American people who formerly lived nomadically in New Mexico and Arizona. **2** a member of this people. **3** the language of this people. [18c: from Zuni (the language of another N American native people) *apachu* enemy]

apart *adv* **1** in or into pieces: *come apart.* **2** separated by a certain distance or time: *The villages are about 6 miles apart.* **3** to or on one side: *set apart for special occasions.* **4** disregarded, not considered, taken account of, etc: *joking apart.* **5** distinguished by some unique quality: *a breed apart.* [14c: from French *à part* to one side]

IDIOMS **apart from sb** *or* **sth** not including them or it.

apartheid /a'pɑːtheɪt, -haɪt/ *noun* an official state policy, esp that operating in South Africa until 1992, of keeping different races segregated. [1940s: Afrikaans, from *apart* apart + *-heid* hood]

apartment *noun* **1** (abbrev **apt**) a single room in a house or flat. **2** (**apartments**) a set of rooms used for accommodation, usu in a large building. **3** *N Am* a self-contained set of rooms for living in, usu all on one floor, in a large building that is divided into a number of similar units. *Brit equivalent* **flat**. [17c: from French *appartement*]

apathy *noun* **1** lack of interest or enthusiasm. **2** lack of emotion. ▪ **apathetic** *adj.* [17c: from **a-**[2] + Greek *pathos* feeling]

apatosaurus *noun* a huge herbivorous dinosaur of the Jurassic period that had massive limbs, a small head, and a long neck and tail. Formerly called **brontosaurus**. [From Greek *apate* deceit + *sauros* lizard]

ape *noun* **1** any of several species of primate that differ from most monkeys, and resemble humans in that they have a highly developed brain, lack a tail and are capable of walking upright. **2** *non-technical* any monkey or primate. **3** a mimic. **4** an ugly, stupid or clumsy person. ▸ *verb* to imitate (someone's behaviour, speech, habits, etc). ▪ **apery** *noun*. [Anglo-Saxon as *apa*]
IDIOMS **go ape** *slang* to go completely crazy.

aperient /ə'pɪərɪənt/ *adj* having a mild laxative effect. ▸ *noun* a drug or other remedy that has this effect. [17c: from Latin *aperire* to open]

aperitif /əpɛrɪ'tiːf/ *noun* an alcoholic drink taken before a meal to stimulate the appetite. [19c: from French *apéritif*]

aperture *noun* **1** a small hole or opening. **2** the opening through which light enters an optical instrument such as a camera or telescope. [17c: from Latin *apertura*]

APEX *abbrev* Advance Purchase Excursion, a reduced fare that is available on some air and train tickets when they are booked a certain period in advance.

apex *noun* (***apexes*** *or* ***apices*** /'eɪpɪsiːz/) **1** the highest point or tip. **2** *geom* the highest point of a plane or solid figure relative to some line or plane. **3** a climax or pinnacle. See also **apical**. [17c: Latin, meaning 'peak']

aphasia *noun, psychol* loss or impairment of the ability to speak or write, or to understand the meaning of spoken or written language. [19c: from **a-**[2] + Greek *phanai* to speak]

aphelion /ap'hiːlɪən/ *noun* (***aphelia***) the point in a planet's orbit when it is farthest from the Sun. Compare **perihelion**. [17c: from Greek *apo* from + *helios* Sun]

aphid /'eɪfɪd/ *or* **aphis** *noun* (***aphids*** *or* ***aphides*** /-diːz/) a small insect which feeds by piercing plant tissues and sucking the sap.

aphorism *noun* a short and often clever or humorous saying expressing some well-known truth. ▪ **aphoristic** *adj*. [16c: from Greek *aphorizein* to define]

aphrodisiac /afrə'dɪzɪak/ *noun* a food, drink or drug that is said to stimulate sexual desire. ▸ *adj* sexually exciting or arousing.

apian /'eɪpɪən/ *adj* referring or relating to bees.

apiary /'eɪpɪərɪ/ *noun* (***-ies***) a place where honey bees are kept. ▪ **apiarist** *noun*. [17c: from Latin *apiarium*]

apical /'apɪkəl, 'eɪ-/ *adj* belonging to, at or forming an apex.

apiculture *noun* the rearing and breeding of honey bees. ▪ **apicultural** *adj*. ▪ **apiculturist** *noun*. [19c: from Latin *apis* bee + *cultura* tending]

apiece *adv* to, for, by or from each one: *They all chipped in £5 apiece.*

apish *adj* **1** like an ape. **2** affected; silly.

aplenty *adv* in great numbers or abundance.

aplomb /ə'plɒm/ *noun* calm self-assurance and poise. [19c: from French *à plomb* straight up and down]

apnoea *or* (*N Am*) **apnea** /ap'nɪə/ *noun, pathol* a temporary cessation of breathing. [18c: from Greek *apnoia* breathlessness]

apocalypse /ə'pɒkəlɪps/ *noun* **1** (**Apocalypse**) the last book of the New Testament, also called the **Revelation** of St John, which describes the end of the world. **2** any revelation of the future, esp future destruction or violence. ▪ **apocalyptic** *adj*. [12c: from Greek *apocalypsis* uncovering]

Apocrypha /ə'pɒkrɪfə/ *plural noun* those books of the Bible included in the ancient Greek and Latin versions of the Old Testament but not in the Hebrew version, and excluded from modern Protestant Bibles but included in Roman Catholic and Orthodox Bibles. [14c: from Greek *apocryphos* hidden]

apocryphal *adj* **1** being of doubtful authenticity. **2** of a story, etc: unlikely to be true; mythical. **3** (**Apocryphal**) relating or referring to the Apocrypha.

apogee /'apoʊdʒiː/ *noun, astron* the point in the orbit of the Moon or a satellite around the Earth when it is at its greatest distance from the Earth. Compare **perigee**. [16c: from Greek *apo* away + *gaia* Earth]

apolitical *adj* not interested or active in politics.

apologetic *adj* showing or expressing regret for a mistake or offence. ▪ **apologetically** *adv*.

apologia *noun* a formal statement in defence of a belief, cause, etc.

apologist *noun* someone who formally defends a belief or cause.

apologize *or* **-ise** *verb, intr* to acknowledge a mistake or offence and express regret for it.

apology *noun* (***-ies***) **1** an expression of regret for a mistake or offence. **2** a formal defence of a belief or cause. [16c: from Greek *apologia*]
IDIOMS **apology for sth** a poor example of it.

apophthegm *or* **apothegm** /'apəθɛm/ *noun* a short saying expressing some general truth. [16c: from Greek *apophthegma*]

apoplectic *adj* **1** suffering from, causing or relating to apoplexy. **2** *informal* red-faced and seething with anger.

apoplexy *noun* the former name for a **stroke** (sense 9) caused by a cerebral haemorrhage. [14c: from Greek *apoplexia* being struck down]

apostasy /ə'pɒstəsɪ/ *noun* (***-ies***) the rejection of one's religion or principles or of one's affiliation to a political party, etc. [14c: from Greek *apo* away + *stasis* standing]

apostate *noun* someone who rejects a religion, belief, political affiliation, etc that they previously held. ▸ *adj* relating to or involved in this kind of rejection.

a posteriori /eɪ pɒstɛrɪ'ɔːraɪ/ *adj, adv* of an argument or reasoning: working from effect to cause or from particular cases to general principles. Compare **a priori**. [17c: Latin, meaning 'from the latter']

apostle *noun* **1** *Christianity* (*often* **Apostle**) someone sent out to preach about Christ in the early church, esp one of the twelve **disciples**. **2** any enthusiastic supporter of a cause, belief, etc. [Anglo-Saxon *apostol*]

apostolic *adj* **1** relating to the apostles in the early Christian Church, or to their teaching. **2** relating to the teaching that the church was founded by Christ's apostles, and that the Pope is the successor to the Apostle Peter.

apostrophe[1] /ə'pɒstrəfɪ/ *noun* a punctuation mark (') that in English is used to show that there has been an omission of a letter or letters, eg in a contraction such as *I'm* for *I am*, or as a signal for the possessive such as *Ann's book*. [16c: from Greek *apostrephein* to turn away]

apostrophe² /ə'pɒstrəfɪ/ *noun, rhetoric* a passage in a speech, poem, etc which digresses to pointedly address a person (esp dead or absent) or thing. ▪ **apostrophize** *or* **-ise** /ə'pɒstrəfaɪz/ *verb*. [16c: from Greek, meaning 'a turning away']

apothecary *noun* (**-ies**) *old use* a chemist. [14c: from Greek *apotheke* storehouse]

apothegm see **apophthegm**

apotheosis /əpɒθɪ'oʊsɪs/ *noun* (***-ses*** /-siːz/) **1** the action of raising someone to the rank of a god. **2 a** glorification or idealization of someone or something; **b** an ideal embodiment. [16c: Greek]

appal *or* (*N Am*) **appall** *verb* (***appals*** *or* ***appalls, appalled, appalling***) to shock, dismay or horrify. [14c: from French *appallir* to grow pale]

appalling *adj* **1** causing feelings of shock or horror. **2** *informal* extremely bad. ▪ **appallingly** *adv*.

apparatchik /apə'ratʃɪk/ *noun* (***apparatchiks*** *or* ***apparatchiki***) an active member of an organization, esp a political party. [20c: Russian, from *apparat* apparatus or machine]

apparatus *noun* (***apparatuses*** *or* ***apparatus***) **1** the equipment needed for a specified purpose, esp in a science laboratory, gym, etc. **2** an organization or system made up of many different parts. **3** a machine with a specified purpose: *breathing apparatus*. [16c: Latin]

apparel /ə'parəl/ *noun, old use, formal* clothing. [14c: from French *apareiller* to make fit]

apparent *adj* **1** easy to see or understand; obvious. **2** seeming to be real but perhaps not actually so. ▪ **apparently** *adv*. See also **heir apparent**. [14c: from Latin *apparere* to come into sight]

apparition *noun* **1** a sudden unexpected appearance, esp of a ghost. **2** a ghost. [16c: from Latin *apparitio* an appearance]

appeal *noun* **1 a** an urgent or formal request for help, money, medical aid, etc; **b** a request made in a pleading or heartfelt way. **2** *law* **a** an application or petition to a higher authority or law court to carry out a review of a decision taken by a lower one; **b** a review and its outcome as carried out by such an authority or court. **3** the quality of being attractive, interesting, pleasing, etc. **4** *cricket* a request made to the umpire from the fielding side to declare that a batsman is out. ▸ *verb, intr* **1** to make an urgent or formal request: *appealed for calm*. **2** *law* to request a higher authority or law court to review a decision given by a lower one. **3** *cricket* to ask the umpire to call a batsman out. **4** to be attractive, interesting, pleasing, etc. ▪ **appealing** *adj* attractive. [14c: from Latin *appellare* to address]

appear *verb, intr* **1** to become visible or come into sight. **2** to develop: *Flaws in his design soon appeared*. **3** to seem. **4** to present oneself formally or in public, eg on stage. **5** to be present in a law court as either accused or counsel. **6** to be published. [14c: from Latin *apparere* to come forth]

appearance *noun* **1** an act or instance of appearing. **2** the outward or superficial look of someone or something. **3** illusion; pretence: *the appearance of being a reasonable person*. **4** (**appearances**) the outward show or signs by which someone or something is judged or assessed: *appearances can be deceptive*.

IDIOMS **keep up appearances** to put on an outward public show that things are normal, stable, etc when they are not. **put in** *or* **make an appearance** to attend a meeting, party, etc only briefly. **to all appearances** so far as it can be seen.

appease *verb* **1** to calm, quieten, pacify, etc, esp by making some kind of concession. **2** to satisfy or allay (a thirst, appetite, doubt, etc). ▪ **appeasement** *noun*. [14c: from French *apesier* to bring to peace]

appellant *noun* someone who makes an appeal to a higher court to review the decision of a lower one. ▸ *adj* belonging, relating or referring to an appeal or appellant. [14c: from Latin *appellare* to address]

appellate /ə'pɛlɪt/ *adj, law* **1** concerned with appeals. **2** of a court, tribunal, etc: having the authority to review and, if necessary, overturn the earlier decision of another court. [18c: from Latin *appellare* to address]

appellation *noun, formal* a name or title.

append *verb* to add or attach something to a document, esp as a supplement, footnote, etc. [17c: from Latin *appendere* to hang]

appendage *noun* **1** anything added or attached to a larger or more important part. **2** *zool* a part or organ, eg a leg, antenna, etc, that extends from the main body of insects, etc. **3** *botany* an offshoot, eg a branch, leaf, etc, that sprouts from the stem of a plant.

appendectomy *or* **appendicectomy** *noun* (**-ies**) *surgery* an operation to remove the appendix.

appendicitis *noun, pathol* inflammation of the appendix.

appendix *noun* (***appendixes*** *or* ***appendices*** /ə'pɛndɪsiːz/) **1** a section containing extra information, notes, etc at the end of a book or document. **2** *anatomy* a short tube-like sac attached to the lower end of the caecum at the junction of the small and large intestines. [16c: Latin]

appertain *verb, intr* (*usu* **appertain to sth**) to belong or relate to it. [14c: from Latin *pertinere* to belong]

appetite *noun* **1** a natural physical desire, esp for food. **2** the extent to which someone enjoys their food: *He has a very poor appetite*. [14c: from Latin *appetitus*]

appetizer *or* **-iser** *noun* a small amount of food or drink taken before a meal to stimulate the appetite.

appetizing *or* **-ising** *adj* stimulating the appetite, esp by looking or smelling delicious; tasty. [17c: from French *appetissant*]

applaud *verb* **1** *intr* to show approval by clapping. **2** to express approval of something: *He applauded her brave decision*. [16c: from Latin *applaudere*]

applause *noun* approval or appreciation shown by clapping.

apple *noun* **1** a small deciduous tree with pink or white flowers and edible fruit. **2** the firm round edible fruit of this tree, which has a green, red or yellow skin and white flesh. [Anglo-Saxon *æppel*]

IDIOMS **in apple-pie order** neat and tidy. **the apple of one's eye** someone's favourite person. **upset the apple cart** to disrupt carefully made plans.

apple jack *noun* the US name for **cider**.

apple-pie bed *noun* a bed that, as a joke, has been made up with the sheets doubled up so that the person cannot get into it.

applet *noun, comput* a small program that runs within another application. [From *appl*ication+ diminutive ending *-let*]

appliance *noun* any electrical device, usu a tool or machine, that is used to perform a specific task, esp in the home.

applicable *adj* **1** relevant; to the point. **2** suitable; appropriate. [17c: from Latin *applicare* to apply]

applicant *noun* someone who has applied for a job, a university place, a grant, etc. [15c: from Latin *applicare* to apply]

application *noun* **1** a formal written or verbal request, proposal or submission, eg for a job. **2 a** the act of putting something on (something else); **b** something put on (something else): *stopped the squeak with an application of oil.* **3** the act of using something for a particular purpose: *the application of statistics to interpret the data.* [15c: from Latin *applicare* to apply]

applications program *noun, comput* a computer program written to perform a specific task, eg word-processing.

applicator *noun* a device, eg on a tube of cream, etc, designed for putting something on to or into something else. [17c: from Latin *applicare* to apply]

applied *adj* of a skill, theory, etc: put to practical use: *applied linguistics.* Compare **pure** (sense 5).

appliqué /ə'pliːkeɪ/ *noun* a decorative technique whereby pieces of differently textured and coloured fabrics are cut into various shapes and stitched onto each other. ▸ *verb* (***appliquéd, appliquéing***) to use this technique to create (a decorative article). [19c: French, meaning 'applied']

apply *verb* (***-ies, -ied***) **1** *intr* to make a formal request, proposal or submission, eg for a job. **2** to put something on to something else. **3** to put or spread something on a surface: *applied three coats of paint.* **4** *intr* to be relevant or suitable: *thinks the rules don't apply to her.* **5** to put (a skill, rule, theory, etc) to practical use. **6** (*usu* **apply oneself to sth**) to give one's full attention or energy to (a task, etc). [14c: from Latin *applicare* to attach]

appoint *verb* **1** *tr & intr* to give someone a job or position. **2** to fix or agree on (a date, time or place). **3** to equip or furnish. ▪ **appointee** *noun.* [14c: from French *apointer*]

appointment *noun* **1** an arrangement to meet someone. **2 a** the act of giving someone a job or position; **b** the job or position someone is given; **c** the person who is given a job or position. **3** (**appointments**) *formal* equipment and furnishings.

apportion *verb* to share out fairly or equally. [16c: from French *portioner* to share]

apposite *adj* suitable; well chosen; appropriate. ▪ **appositely** *adv.* ▪ **appositeness** *noun.* [17c: from Latin *appositus*]

apposition *noun, grammar* a construction in which a series of nouns or noun phrases have the same grammatical status and refer to the same person or thing and give further information about them or it, eg *Poppy, the cat.* [15c: from Latin *appositio*]

appraisal *noun* **1** evaluation; estimation of quality. **2** any method of doing this.

appraise *verb* to decide the value or quality of (someone's skills, ability, etc). [16c: from French *aprisier*]

appreciable *adj* noticeable; significant; able to be measured or noticed: *an appreciable difference.*

appreciate *verb* **1** to be grateful or thankful for something. **2** to be aware of the value, quality, etc of something. **3** to understand or be aware of something. **4** *usu intr* to increase in value. ▪ **appreciative** *adj.* ▪ **appreciatively** *adv.* [17c: from Latin *appretiare*]

appreciation *noun* **1** gratitude or thanks. **2** sensitive understanding and enjoyment of the value or quality of something. **3** the state of knowing or being aware of something. **4** an increase in value.

apprehend *verb* **1** to arrest. **2** to understand. [14c: from Latin *apprehendere* to lay hold of]

apprehension *noun* **1** fear or anxiety. **2** the act of capturing and arresting someone or something: *called for the immediate apprehension of the fugitive.* **3** understanding.

apprehensive *adj* anxious or worried. ▪ **apprehensively** *adv.*

apprentice *noun* **1** someone, usu a young person, who works for an agreed period of time in order to learn a craft or trade. **2** anyone who is relatively unskilled at something or just beginning to learn something. ▸ *verb* to take someone on as an apprentice. ▪ **apprenticeship** *noun.* [14c: from French *apprentis*]

apprise *verb* (*usu* **apprise sb of sth**) to give them information about it. [17c: from French *appris*]

appro *noun*

IDIOMS **on appro** *informal* on approval. See under **approval**.

approach *verb* **1** *tr & intr* to come near or nearer in space, time, etc. **2** to begin to deal with, think about, etc (a problem, subject, etc): *They approached the project from a new angle.* **3** to contact someone, esp when wanting to suggest, propose, etc something. ▸ *noun* **1** the act of coming near. **2** a way to, or means of reaching, a place. **3** a suggestion or proposal. **4** a way of considering or dealing with a problem, etc. **5** the course that an aircraft follows as it comes in to land. ▪ **approachable** *adj.* [14c: from Latin *appropiare* to draw near]

approbation *noun* approval; consent. [14c: from Latin *approbatio*]

appropriate *adj* /ə'proʊprɪət/ suitable or proper. ▸ *verb* /-eɪt/ **1** to take something as one's own, esp without permission. **2** to put (money) aside for a particular purpose. ▪ **appropriately** *adv.* [16c: from Latin *appropriare*]

approval *noun* **1** a favourable opinion; esteem. **2** official permission.

IDIOMS **on approval** of goods for sale: able to be returned if not satisfactory.

approve *verb* **1** to agree to or permit. **2** *intr* (**approve of sb** *or* **sth**) to be pleased with or think well of them or it. ▪ **approving** *adj.* ▪ **approvingly** *adv.* [14c: from Latin *approbare* to approve of]

approx. *abbrev* approximate, approximately.

approximate *adj* /ə'prɒksɪmət/ almost exact or accurate. ▸ *verb* /-meɪt/ *tr & intr* to come close to something in value, quality, accuracy, etc. ▪ **approximately** *adv.* ▪ **approximation** *noun.* [17c: from Latin *approximare*]

appurtenance *noun* (*usu* **appurtenances**) an accessory to, or minor detail of, something larger, esp in reference to property-owning rights. [14c: from French *apertenance*]

APR *abbrev* annual percentage rate.

Apr. *abbrev* April.

après-ski /aprɛ'skiː/ *noun* the relaxation and entertainment that is enjoyed after a day's skiing. [1950s: French, meaning 'after-ski']

apricot *noun* **1** a small deciduous tree with oval toothed leaves and white or pale pink flowers. **2** the small edible fruit of this plant, which has yellow flesh and a soft furry yellowish-orange skin, eaten raw, or used to make jams, preserves, etc. **3** the colour of this fruit. [16c: from Portuguese *albricoque*]

April *noun* (abbrev **Apr.**) the fourth month of the year.

April Fool's Day *or* **All Fools' Day** *noun* 1 April, traditionally the day when people play practical jokes on one another.

a priori /eɪ praɪ'ɔːraɪ/ *adj, adv* of an argument or reasoning: working from cause to effect or from general principles to particular cases. Compare **a posteriori**. [18c: Latin, meaning 'from what is before']

apron *noun* **1** a piece of cloth, plastic, etc tied around the waist and worn over the front of clothes to protect them. **2** a hard-surface area at an airport where aircraft are loaded. **3** *theatre* the part of the stage that can still be seen when the curtain is closed. [15c: from 14c *napron*, from French *naperon*]

IDIOMS **tied to sb's apron strings** usu of a boy or man: completely dominated by and dependent on them, esp a mother or wife.

apropos /aprə'pou/ *adj* of remarks: suitable or to the point. ▸ *adv* by the way; appropriately. [17c: French, meaning 'to the purpose']

IDIOMS **apropos of sth** with reference to it.

apse *noun* a semicircular recess, esp when arched and domed and at the east end of a church. [19c: from Greek *apsis* arch]

apt *adj* **1** suitable. **2** clever or quick to learn. ▪ **aptly** *adv.* ▪ **aptness** *noun.* [14c: from Latin *aptus* fit]

IDIOMS **apt to do sth** inclined or likely to do it.

aptitude *noun* **1** (*usu* **aptitude for sth**) a natural skill or talent. **2** intelligence; speed in learning or understanding: *Her aptitude in maths is astounding*. [17c: from Latin *aptitudo*]

aqua fortis *noun, old use* the early scientific name for **nitric acid**. [17c: Latin, meaning 'strong water']

aqualung *noun* a device that enables a diver to breathe under water, consisting of a mouth tube connected to cylinders of compressed air.

aquamarine *noun* **1** *geol* a transparent bluish-green gemstone. **2** the colour of this gemstone. ▸ *adj* bluish-green in colour. [16c: Latin, meaning 'sea water']

aquaplane *noun* a board, similar to a water ski, on which the rider is towed along at high speed by a motor boat. ▸ *verb, intr* **1** to ride on an aquaplane. **2** of a vehicle: to slide along out of control on a thin film of water, the tyres having lost contact with the road surface.

aquarium *noun* (***aquariums*** *or* ***aquaria***) **1** a glass tank that fish, other water animals and water plants are kept in so that they can be observed or displayed. **2** a building in a zoo, etc with several of these tanks. [19c: from Latin *aquarius* of water]

Aquarius *noun, astrol* **a** the eleventh sign of the zodiac; **b** a person born between 21 January and 19 February, under this sign. ▪ **Aquarian** *noun, adj.* [14c: Latin, meaning 'water-carrier']

aquatic *adj* **1** living or growing in, on or near water. **2** of sports: taking place in water. ▸ *noun* **1** an aquatic animal or plant. **2** (**aquatics**) water sports. [15c: from Latin *aquaticus* watery]

aquatint *noun* **1** a method of **intaglio** etching that gives a transparent granular effect similar to that of watercolour. **2** a picture produced using this method of etching. ▸ *verb, tr & intr* to etch using this technique. [18c: from Italian *aqua tinta*]

aqua vitae /'akwə 'viːtaɪ/ *noun* a strong alcoholic drink, esp brandy. [15c: Latin, meaning 'water of life']

aqueduct *noun* a channel or canal that carries water, esp one that is in the form of a tall bridge across a valley, river, etc. [16c: from Latin *aqua* water + *ducere* to lead]

aqueous *adj* **1** relating to water. **2** denoting a solution that contains water, or in which water is the solvent. [17c: from Latin *aqua* water]

aqueous humour *noun, anatomy* the clear liquid between the lens and the cornea of the eye.

aqueous solution *noun, chem* a solution in which the solvent is water.

aquifer *noun, geol* any body of water-bearing rock that is highly porous and permeable to water, and can be tapped directly by sinking wells or pumping the water into a reservoir. [Early 20c: from Latin *aqua* + *ferre* to carry]

aquiline *adj* **1** referring or relating to, or like, an eagle. **2** of someone's nose: curved like an eagle's beak. Also called **Roman nose**. [17c: from Latin *aquila* eagle]

Ar *symbol, chem* argon.

Arab *noun* a member of a Semitic people living in the Middle East and N Africa. ▸ *adj* referring or relating to the Arabs. [17c: from Greek *Araps*]

arabesque *noun* **1** *ballet* a position in which the dancer stands with one leg stretched out backwards and the body bent forwards from the hips. **2** a complex flowing design of leaves, flowers, etc woven together. **3** a short ornate piece of music. [17c: from Italian *arabesco* in the Arabian style]

Arabian *adj* belonging, referring or relating to Arabia or the Arabs. ▸ *noun* an **Arab**.

Arabic *noun* the Semitic language of the Arabs. ▸ *adj* belonging, relating or referring to Arabs, their language or culture.

Arabic numeral *noun* any of the symbols 0, 1, 2, 3, 4, 5, 6, 7, 8 and 9, which are based on Arabic characters. Compare **Roman numeral**s.

arable *adj* **1** of land: suitable or used for ploughing and growing crops. **2** of a crop: able to be sown on arable land, eg cereals, potatoes, root crops. [16c: from Latin *arare* to plough]

arachnid *noun* any eight-legged invertebrate animal belonging to the class that includes spiders, scorpions and ticks. [19c: from Greek *arachne* spider]

arachnoid *adjective* **1** relating to or resembling an arachnid. **2** resembling a spider's web. **3** *botany* covered in, or made up of, thin delicate fibres.

arachnophobia *noun* a strong and usu irrational fear of spiders. ▪ **arachnophobe** *noun.* [20c: from Greek *arachne* spider + *phobos* fear]

arak see under **arrack**

Aramaic *noun* any of a group of ancient northern Semitic languages that are still spoken in parts of the Middle East today. ▸ *adj* referring or relating to, or written in, Aramaic. [1830s: from Greek *Aramaios* of Aram, an ancient name for Syria]

Aran *adj, knitting* denoting a type of knitwear originating from the Aran islands and characterized by its use of undyed wool and complex cabled patterns. ▸ *noun* a jumper or cardigan of this type.

arbiter *noun* **1** someone who has the authority or influence to settle arguments or disputes between other people. **2** someone who has great influence in matters of style, taste, etc.

arbitrary *adj* **1** capricious; whimsical. **2** based on subjective factors or random choice and not on objective principles. ▪ **arbitrarily** *adv.* [16c: from Latin *arbitrarius* uncertain]

arbitrate *verb, intr* to submit to or settle by arbitration. ▪ **arbitrator** *noun.* [16c: from Latin *arbitrari* to give a judgement]

arbitration *noun* the settling of a dispute between two or more groups by some neutral person who is acceptable to all concerned.

arbor[1] *noun* **1** the axle or spindle on which a revolving cutting tool is mounted. **2** the axle of a wheel in a clock or watch. [17c: Latin, meaning 'tree']

arbor[2] an *N Am* spelling of **arbour**

arboreal /ɑːˈbɔːrɪəl/ *adj* **1** relating to or resembling a tree. **2** denoting an animal that lives mainly in trees. [17c: from Latin *arbor* tree]

arboretum /ɑːbəˈriːtəm/ *noun* (***arboreta*** /-tə/) *botany* a botanical garden where trees and shrubs are grown. [19c: Latin, meaning 'a place where trees are grown']

arboriculture *noun* the cultivation of trees and shrubs. ▪ **arboricultural** *adj.* ▪ **arboriculturist** *noun.* [19c: from Latin *arbor* tree + *cultura* tending]

arborio /ɑːˈbɔːrɪoʊ/ *noun* a round-grained rice, used in making risotto. [20c: Italian]

arbour *or* (*N Am*) **arbor** *noun* a shady area in a garden formed by trees or climbing plants, usu with a seat. [14c: from Latin *herba* grass, influenced by Latin *arbor* tree]

ARC *abbrev* **AIDS-related complex**.

arc *noun* **1** a section of a curve or the circumference of a circle. **2** the graduated scale of an instrument or device that is used to measure angles. **3** a continuous electric discharge, giving out heat and light, that is maintained across the space between two electrodes, used in welding, etc. ▸ *verb* **1** to form an arc. **2** to move in an apparent arc. [16c: from Latin *arcus* bow]

arcade *noun* **1** a covered walk or passage, usu lined with shops. **2** a row of arches supporting a roof, wall, etc. **3** an **amusement arcade**. [17c: French]

arcade game *noun* any of a variety of electronic or mechanical games that are played in an amusement arcade.

Arcadian *adj* characterized by simple rural pleasures. ▸ *noun* someone who enjoys such pleasures. [16c: from Greek *Arcadia*, a hilly area in the Peloponnesus]

arcane *adj* mysterious, secret or obscure; understood only by a few. [16c: from Latin *arcanus*]

arch[1] *noun* **1** a curved structure forming an opening, used to sustain an overlying weight such as a roof or bridge, or for ornament. **2** anything shaped like an arch. **3** the bony structure of the foot between the heel and the toes, normally having an upward curve. ▸ *verb* **1** to form an arch. **2** to span something like an arch. [14c: from Latin *arcus* bow]

arch[2] *adj* **1** *usu in compounds* chief; principal: *arch enemy.* **2** cunning; knowing: *an arch look.* **3** self-consciously playful or coy. ▪ **archly** cleverly; slyly. [17c: from **arch-** as in such combinations as 'arch-villain']

arch- *or* **archi-** *combining form* **1** chief; most important: *archduke.* **2** most esteemed, feared, extreme, etc of its kind: *arch-criminal.* [Anglo-Saxon *arce*]

Archaean *or* (*N Am*) **Archean** *adj, geol* denoting the earlier of the two geological eons into which the **Precambrian** period is divided, extending from the time of formation of the Earth to about 2500 million years ago. [19c: from Greek *archaios* ancient]

archaebacterium /ɑːkɪbakˈtɪərɪəm/ *noun* (***archaebacteria***) *biol* any of various kinds of microorganisms that resemble ordinary bacteria in size and structure, but which evolved separately and have a unique organization of molecules. [20c]

archaeo- *or* (*N Am*) **archeo-** *combining form, indicating* ancient; primitive: *archaeology.* [From Greek *archaios*]

archaeology *or* (*N Am*) **archeology** *noun* the study of the physical remains of earlier civilizations, esp buildings and artefacts. ▪ **archaeological** *or* **archeological** *adj.* ▪ **archaeologist** *or* **archeologist** *noun.*

archaeopteryx /ɑːkɪˈɒptərɪks/ *noun* the oldest fossil bird which differed from modern birds in having a long bony tail supported by vertebrae, and sharp teeth on both jaws. [19c: **archaeo-** + Greek *pteryx* wing]

archaic /ɑːˈkeɪɪk/ *adj* **1** relating or referring to, or from, a much earlier period. **2** out of date; old-fashioned. **3** of a word, phrase, etc: no longer in general use. [19c: from Greek *archaikos*]

archaism *noun* an archaic word, expression or style. [17c: from Greek *archaizein* to copy the language of the ancient writers]

archangel *noun* an angel of the highest rank.

archbishop *noun* a chief **bishop** who is in charge of all the other bishops, clergy and churches in a particular area. [Anglo-Saxon *arcebiscop*]

archbishopric *noun* **1** the office of an archbishop. **2** the area that is governed by an archbishop. Also called **see, diocese**.

archdeacon *noun,* in the Church of England: a member of the clergy who ranks just below a bishop. See also **archidiaconal**. ▪ **archdeaconry** *noun.* [Anglo-Saxon *arcediacon*]

archdiocese *noun,* in the Church of England: the area under the control of an archbishop.

archduchess *noun* **1** *hist* a princess in the Austrian royal family. **2** the wife of an archduke.

archduchy *noun* the area ruled by an archduke.

archduke *noun* the title of some princes, esp formerly the son of the Emperor of Austria.

archeology an alternative *N Am* spelling of **archaeology**.

archer *noun* **1** someone who uses a bow and arrow. **2** (**the Archer**) the sign of the zodiac **Sagittarius**. [13c: from French *archier*]

archery *noun* the art or sport of shooting with a bow and arrow.

archetype /'ɑːkɪtaɪp/ *noun* **1** an original model; a prototype. **2** a perfect example. ▪ **archetypal** *adj.* [16c: from Greek *arche* beginning + *typos* model]

archi- see **arch-**

archidiaconal /ɑːkɪdaɪ'akənəl/ *adj* referring or relating to an archdeacon or archdeaconry.

archiepiscopal *adj* relating or referring to an archbishop. [17c: from Greek *archiepiskopos* archbishop]

archipelago /ɑːkɪ'pɛləgoʊ/ *noun, geog* a group or chain of islands separated from each other by narrow bodies of water. [16c: from Italian *arcipelago*]

architect *noun* **1** someone who is professionally qualified to design buildings and other large structures and supervise their construction. **2** someone who is responsible for creating or initiating something: *the architect of modern Europe*. [16c: from Greek *architekton* master-builder]

architecture *noun* **1** the art, science and profession of designing and constructing buildings, ships and other large structures. **2 a** a specified historical, regional, etc style of building design: *Victorian architecture*; **b** the buildings built in any particular style. **3** the way in which anything is physically constructed or designed. **4** *comput* the general specification and configuration of the internal design of a computer or local area network. ▪ **architectural** *adj.* [16c: from Latin *architectura*]

architrave /'ɑːkɪtreɪv/ *noun* **1** *archit* a beam that forms the bottom part of an **entablature** and which rests across the top of a row of columns. **2** a moulded frame around a door or window. [16c: French]

archive /'ɑːkaɪv/ *noun* **1** (*usu* **archives**) **a** a collection of old public documents, records, etc; **b** a place where such documents are kept. **2** *comput* a place for keeping data or files that are seldom used or needed. ▸ *verb* to store (documents, etc) in an archive. [17c: French]

archivist /'ɑːkɪvɪst/ *noun* someone who collects, keeps, catalogues, records, etc archives.

archway *noun* a passage or entrance under an arch or arches.

Arctic *noun* (**the Arctic**) the area round the North Pole. ▸ *adj* **1** belonging or relating to this area. **2** (**arctic**) *informal* extremely cold: *arctic conditions*. [14c: from Greek *arktikos*]

Arctic Circle *noun* the imaginary circular line parallel to the equator at a latitude of 66° 32′ N, which forms a boundary around the area of the north pole.

arc welding *noun, eng* a form of welding in which two pieces of metal are joined by means of a continuous electric arc.

ardent *adj* **1** enthusiastic; eager. **2** burning; passionate. ▪ **ardently** *adv.* [14c: from Latin *ardere* to burn]

ardour *or* (*N Am*) **ardor** *noun* a great enthusiasm or passion. [14c: from Latin *ardor*]

arduous *adj* **1** difficult; needing a lot of work, effort or energy. **2** steep. [16c: from Latin *arduus* steep]

are[1] *verb* used with *you, we* and *they*: the second person singular and first, second and third person plural of the present tense of **be**: *You are here* • *We are alive* • *Here they are.*

are[2] *noun* a unit of land measure equal to $100m^2$. [Early 19c: from French *are*]

area *noun* **1** a measure of the size of any surface, measured in square units. **2** a region or part. **3** any space set aside for a particular purpose. **4** the range of a subject, activity or topic. **5** an open space in front of a building's basement. [16c: Latin, meaning 'open space']

arena *noun* **1** an area surrounded by seats, for public shows, sports contests, etc. **2** a place of great activity, esp conflict: *the political arena*. **3** the open area in the middle of an amphitheatre. [17c: Latin, meaning 'sanded area for combats', 'sand']

aren't *contraction* **1** are not: *They aren't coming*. **2** *in questions* am not: *Aren't I lucky?*

areola *noun* (***areolae*** /ə'rɪəliː/ *or* ***areolas***) *anatomy* **1** the ring of pigmented tissue surrounding a nipple. **2** the part of the iris surrounding the pupil of the eye. [17c: from Latin, a diminutive of *area* open space]

arête *noun, geog, mountaineering* a sharp ridge or mountain ledge, between two corries. [19c: French, from Latin *arista* meaning 'ear of corn' or 'fish bone']

Argentinian *or* **Argentine** *adj* belonging, relating or referring to Argentina, a republic in SE South America, or its inhabitants. ▸ *noun* a citizen or inhabitant of, or person born in, Argentina.

argon *noun, chem* (symbol **Ar**) a colourless odourless inert gas, one of the noble gases. [19c: from **a-**[2] + Greek *ergon* work]

argot /'ɑːgoʊ/ *noun* slang that is only used and understood by a particular group of people. [19c: French, of obscure origin and once confined only to the slang spoken by thieves]

argue *verb* **1** *tr & intr* to put forward one's case, esp in a clear and well-ordered manner. **2** *intr* to quarrel or disagree. **3** to show or be evidence for something: *It argues a degree of enthusiasm on their part*. ▪ **arguable** *adj.* ▪ **arguably** *adv.* [14c: from Latin *arguere* to prove]

argument *noun* **1** a quarrel or unfriendly discussion. **2** a reason for or against an idea, etc. **3** *maths, comput* a quantity or element to which a function, operation, etc applies. [14c: from Latin *argumentum*]

argumentation *noun* sensible and methodical reasoning.

argumentative *adj* fond of arguing; always ready to quarrel.

argy-bargy *noun* a dispute. ▸ *verb* (***-ies, -ied***) *intr* to dispute or disagree.

aria /'ɑːrɪə/ *noun, music* a long accompanied song for one voice, esp in an opera or oratorio. [18c: Italian, meaning 'air']

arid *adj* **1** of a region or climate: characterized by very low rainfall. **2** lacking interest; dull. ▪ **aridity** /ə'rɪdɪtɪ/ *noun.* [17c: from Latin *aridus*]

Aries *noun, astrol* **a** the first sign of the zodiac; **b** a person born between 21 March and 20 April, under this sign. ▪ **Arian** *noun, adj.* [14c: from Latin *aries* ram]

aright *adv, old use* correctly. [Anglo-Saxon *ariht*]

arise *verb* (***arose*** /ə'roʊz/, ***arisen*** /ə'rɪzən/) *intr* **1** to come into being. **2** (*usu* **arise from** *or* **out of sth**) to result from or be caused by it. **3** to get up or stand up. **4** to come to notice. **5** to move or grow in an upward direction. [Anglo-Saxon *arisan*]

aristocracy *noun* (***-ies***) **1** the highest social class. **2 a** this class as a ruling body; **b** government by this class. **3** people considered to be the best representatives of something. [16c: from Greek *aristos* best + **-cracy**]

aristocrat *noun* a member of the aristocracy.

aristocratic *adj* **1** referring or relating to the aristocracy. **2** proud and noble-looking.

Aristotelian /arɪstə'tiːlɪən/ *adj* relating to Aristotle or his ideas. ▸ *noun* a student or follower of Aristotle. ▪ **Aristotelianism** *noun*. [17c: named after the Greek philosopher, Aristotle (384–322 BC)]

arithmetic *noun* /ə'rɪθmətɪk/ **1** the branch of mathematics that uses numbers to solve theoretical or practical problems, mainly by the processes of addition, subtraction, multiplication and division. **2** any calculation that involves the use of numbers. **3** skill, knowledge or understanding in this field. ▸ *adj* /arɪθ'mɛtɪk/ (*also* **arithmetical**) relating to arithmetic. ▪ **arithmetically** *adv*. ▪ **arithmetician** /ərɪθmə'tɪʃən/ *noun*. [13c: from Greek *arithmeein* to reckon]

arithmetic logic unit *noun, comput* (abbrev **ALU**) in the central processing unit of a computer: the circuit or set of circuits that performs arithmetic operations and logical operations.

arithmetic mean see under **mean**[3]

arithmetic progression *or* **arithmetic sequence** *noun* a sequence of numbers such that each number differs from the preceding and following ones by a constant amount, eg 4, 10, 16, 22.

ark *noun, Bible* the vessel built by Noah in which his family and animals survived the Flood. [Anglo-Saxon *arc*]

arm[1] *noun* **1 a** in humans: either of the two upper limbs of the body, from the shoulders to the hands; **b** a limb of an octopus, squid, etc. **2** anything shaped like or similar to this. **3** the sleeve of a garment. **4** the part of a chair, etc that supports a person's arm. **5** a section or division of a larger group, eg of the army, etc. **6** power and influence: *the long arm of the law.* [Anglo-Saxon *earm*]

IDIOMS **arm in arm** with arms linked together. **at arm's length** at a distance, esp to avoid becoming too friendly. **with open arms** wholeheartedly.

arm[2] *noun* (*usu* **arms**) **1** a weapon: *nuclear arms.* **2** fighting; soldiering. **3** a heraldic design that, along with others, makes up the symbol of a family, school, country, etc. ▸ *verb* **1** to equip (with weapons). **2** to prepare (a bomb) for use. [14c: from Latin *arma*]

IDIOMS **lay down one's arms** to stop fighting. **take up arms** to begin fighting. **up in arms** openly angry and protesting.

armada *noun* **1** a fleet of ships. **2** (**the Armada**) *hist* the fleet of Spanish ships sent to attack England in 1588. [16c: Spanish]

armadillo *noun* a small nocturnal burrowing mammal, the head and body of which are covered with horny plates. [16c: Spanish]

Armageddon *noun* **1** a large-scale and bloody battle, esp the final battle between good and evil, as described in the New Testament (Revelation 16.16). **2** any war, battle or conflict. [Early 19c: from Hebrew *har megiddon* a place in northern Palestine]

armament *noun* **1** (**armaments**) weapons or military equipment. **2** preparation for war. [17c: from Latin *armamenta*]

armature *noun* **1** *eng* the moving part of an electromagnetic device in which a voltage is induced by a magnetic field. **2** a wire or wooden framework that forms the support for a sculpture as it is being modelled. [16c: from Latin *armatura* armour]

armband *noun* **1** a strip of cloth worn round the arm, usually to indicate an official position, such as being captain of a team, or as a sign of mourning. **2** an inflatable plastic band worn round the arm by someone who is learning to swim.

armchair *noun* a comfortable chair with arms at each side. ▸ *adj* taking no active part; taking an interest in the theory of something rather than its practice: *an armchair detective.*

armed *adj* **1** supplied with arms. **2** of a weapon or bomb: ready for use.

IDIOMS **armed to the teeth** very heavily armed.

armed forces *noun* the military forces of a country, such as the army, air force and navy, thought of collectively.

Armenian *adj* belonging or relating to Armenia, its inhabitants, or their language. ▸ *noun* **1** a citizen or inhabitant of, or person born in, Armenia. **2** the official language of Armenia.

armful *noun* an amount that can be held in the arms.

armistice *noun* an agreement between warring factions to suspend all fighting so that they can discuss peace terms; a truce. [17c: from Latin *armistitium*]

armlet *noun* a band or bracelet worn round the arm.

armorial *adj* relating to heraldry or coats of arms. [16c: from Latin *arma* arms]

armour *or* (*N Am*) **armor** *noun* **1** *hist* a metal or chainmail, etc suit or covering worn by men or horses to protect them against injury in battle. **2** metal covering to protect ships, tanks, etc against damage from weapons. **3** armoured fighting vehicles as a group. **4** a protective covering on some animals and plants. ▪ **armoured** *or* (*N Am*) **armored** *adj*. [13c: from French *armure*]

armourer *or* (*N Am*) **armorer** *noun* **1** someone whose job is to make or repair suits of armour, weapons, etc. **2** someone in charge of a regiment's arms.

armour-plate *noun* strong metal or steel for protecting ships, tanks, etc. ▪ **armour-plated** *adj*. ▪ **armour-plating** *noun*.

armoury *or* (*N Am*) **armory** *noun* (**-ies**) **1** a place where arms are kept. **2** a collection of arms and weapons. **3** *US* a place where arms are manufactured.

armpit *noun* the hollow under the arm at the shoulder.

army *noun* (**-ies**) **1** a large number of people armed and organized for fighting on land. **2** the military profession. **3** a large number: *an army of Rangers supporters.* [14c: from French *armee*]

arnica *noun* **1** a composite plant with yellow flowers, found in N temperate and arctic zones and valued for its medicinal properties. **2** a tincture made from the dried heads of the flowers of this plant.

A-road *noun* in the UK: a main or principal road that can either be a dual or a single carriageway. Compare **B-road**.

aroma *noun* **1** a distinctive, usu pleasant, smell. **2** a subtle quality or charm. [13c: Greek, meaning 'spice']

aromatherapy *noun* a form of therapy involving the use of essential plant oils, generally in combination with massage. ▪ **aromatherapist** *noun*.

aromatic *adj* **1** having a strong, but sweet or pleasant smell. **2** *chem* of an organic compound: having carbon atoms arranged in one or more rings rather than in chains. Compare **aliphatic.** ▸ *noun* anything, such as a herb, drug, etc, that gives off a strong fragrant smell. ▪ **aromatically** *adv.*

arose *past tense of* **arise**

around *adv* **1** on every side; in every direction: *threw his money around.* **2** here and there; in different directions; in or to different places; with or to different people, etc: *could see for miles around* • *It's best to shop around.* **3** approximately: *This cinema seats around 100.* **4** somewhere in the vicinity: *waited around.* ▸ *prep* **1** on all sides of something. **2** in all directions from (a specified point): *The land around here is very fertile.* **3** over; in all directions: *Toys were scattered around the floor.* **4** so as to surround or encircle. **5** reached by making a turn or partial turn about: *The shop is around the corner.* **6** somewhere in or near. **7** approximately in or at; about.
IDIOMS **get around to sth** *or* **to doing sth** to do it, esp eventually or reluctantly. **have been around** *informal* to have had a great deal of experience of life.

arouse *verb* **1** to cause or produce (an emotion, reaction, response, etc). **2** to cause to become awake or active. ▪ **arousal** *noun.*

arpeggio /ɑː'pɛdʒɪoʊ/ *noun* a chord whose notes are played one at a time in rapid succession rather than simultaneously. Also called **broken chord.** [18c: from Italian *arpeggiare* to play the harp]

arquebus /'ɑːkwɪbəs/ *or* **harquebus** /hɑː-/ *noun, hist* an early type of portable gun. [15c: from Dutch *hakebusse*]

arrack *or* **arak** *noun* an alcoholic drink made in Eastern and Middle Eastern countries from grain or rice. [16c: from Arabic *araq* sweat]

arraign /ə'reɪn/ *verb* **1** to bring someone (usu someone who is already in custody) to a court of law to answer a criminal charge or charges. **2** to accuse someone. ▪ **arraignment** *noun.* [14c: from French *aresnier*]

arrange *verb* **1** to put into the proper or desired order. **2** to settle the plans for something: *arranged their holiday.* **3** to make a mutual agreement. **4** to make (a piece of music) suitable for particular voices or instruments. **5** to adapt (a play, novel, etc), esp for broadcast on TV or radio. [14c: from French *arangier*]

arrangement *noun* **1** a plan or preparation for some future event. **2** the act of putting things into a proper order. **3** an agreement. **4** a piece of music that has been made suitable for particular voices or instruments. **5** a play, novel, etc that has been specially adapted for broadcast on TV or radio.

arrant *adj* out-and-out; notorious: *an arrant liar.* [14c: a variant of **errant**, meaning 'wandering']

arras *noun* a colourful woven tapestry often used as a wall hanging. [14c: named after Arras in N France]

array *noun* **1** a large and impressive number, display or collection. **2** a well-ordered arrangement, esp a military one: *troops in battle array.* **3** *maths* an arrangement of numbers or other items of data in rows and columns, eg a matrix. **4** *comput* an arrangement of individual elements of data in such a way that any element can be located and retrieved. ▸ *verb* to put in order; to display. [13c: from French *areer* to arrange]

arrears *plural noun* an amount or quantity that still needs to be done or paid back. [17c: from French *arere*]
IDIOMS **in arrears** late in paying money that is owed.

arrest *verb* **1** to take someone into custody. **2** to stop or slow down the progress of (growth, development, etc). **3** to catch or attract (someone's attention). **4** *intr, pathol* to suffer a **cardiac arrest.** **5** to seize (assets, property, freight, etc) by legal warrant. ▸ *noun* **1** the act of taking, or state of being taken, into custody, esp by the police. **2** a stopping. **3** a halting or slowing down in the progress, development or growth of something; the act of doing this. [14c: from French *arester*]
IDIOMS **under arrest** taken into police custody.

arresting *adj* strikingly individual or attractive.

arrival *noun* **1** the act of coming to a destination. *as adj*: *the arrival lounge.* **2** someone or something that has arrived.

arrive *verb, intr* **1** to reach a place during a journey or come to a destination at the end of a journey. **2** (**arrive at sth**) to come to (a conclusion, decision, etc). **3** *informal* to be successful or to attain recognition. **4** of a baby: to be born. **5** of a thing: to be brought, delivered, etc. **6** to come about or occur at last: *The day arrived when a decision had to be made.* [13c: from French *ariver*]

arrogant *adj* having or showing too high an opinion of one's own abilities or importance. ▪ **arrogance** *noun.* [14c: from Latin *arrogare* to claim as one's own]

arrogate *verb* to claim a responsibility, power, etc without having any legal right to do so. ▪ **arrogation** *noun.* [16c: from Latin *arrogare* to claim as one's own]

arrow *noun* **1** a thin straight stick with a sharp point at one end and feathers at the other, which is fired from a bow. **2** any arrow-shaped symbol or sign, esp one showing the way to go or the position of something. [Anglo-Saxon *arwe*]

arrowhead *noun* the pointed tip of an arrow.

arrowroot *noun* **1** a tropical plant cultivated for its swollen underground tubers, which produce a highly digestible form of starch. **2** the fine-grained starch obtained from the tubers of this plant, used as a food thickener. [17c: named after its former use by S American Indians to treat wounds made by poisoned arrows]

arsenal *noun* **1** a store for weapons, explosives, etc. **2** a factory or workshop where weapons are made, repaired or serviced. **3** the weapons, etc available to a country or group. [16c: from Arabic *dar* house + *sina'ah* of handicrafts]

arsenic *noun, chem* **1** (symbol **As**) a metalloid chemical element. **2** a powerful poison, an oxide of arsenic, used in insecticides, rodent poisons, etc. ▪ **arsenical** /ɑː'sɛnɪkəl/ *adj, noun.* [14c: from Greek *arsenikon*]

arson *noun* the crime of deliberately setting fire to a building, etc. ▪ **arsonist** *noun.* [17c: from Latin *arsio*]

art *noun* **1 a** the creation of works of beauty, esp visual ones; **b** such creations thought of collectively. **2** human skill and work as opposed to nature. **3** a skill, esp one gained through practice: *the lost art of conversation.* **4** *informal* cunning schemes. See also **fine art.** [13c: from Latin *ars*]

art deco *or* **Art Deco** *noun* a style of interior design, orig of the 1920s and 1930s, characterized by highly angular geometric shapes and strong colours. [1960s: from French *art décoratif* decorative art]

artefact *or* **artifact** *noun* a handcrafted object, eg a tool, esp one that is historically or archaeologically interesting. [19c: from Latin *arte factum*]

arterial *adj* **1** affecting, relating to or like an artery or arteries. **2** of a road, etc: connecting large towns or cities; main, esp with lots of minor branches.

arteriole *noun, anatomy* a small artery.

arteriosclerosis /ɑːtɪərɪoʊsklə'roʊsɪs, -sklɪə-/ *noun* (**-ses** /-siːz/) *pathol* a disease of the arteries characterized by thickening of the artery walls, loss of elasticity, and eventual obstruction of blood flow. See also **atherosclerosis**.

artery *noun* (**-ies**) **1** *anatomy* a blood vessel that carries oxygenated blood from the heart to the body tissues. Compare **vein**. **2** a main road, railway or shipping lane. [14c: from Greek *arteria* windpipe]

artesian well *noun, geol* a deep well that is drilled so that the water trapped there under pressure is forced to flow upward in the well. [19c: named after *Arteis* (now called *Artois*), an old province in France where such wells were common]

artful *adj* **1** cunning, esp in being able to achieve what one wants. **2** skilful. ▪ **artfully** *adv.*

arthritic *noun* someone who is suffering from arthritis. ▸ *adj* relating to or typical of arthritis.

arthritis *noun, pathol* inflammation of one or more joints, characterized by swelling, pain and often restricted movement of the affected part. [16c: from Greek *arthron* joint + **-itis** (sense 1)]

arthropod *noun, zool* any invertebrate animal such as an insect, crustacean, **arachnid** and **myriapod**. [19c: from Greek *arthron* joint + *pous, podos* foot]

Arthurian *adj* relating to King Arthur, a 6c ruler of the Britons, whose court is the centre of many legends, but who himself probably had real existence.

artic *abbrev, informal* articulated lorry.

artichoke *noun* **1** a **globe artichoke**. **2** a **Jerusalem artichoke**. [16c: from Arabic *al-kharshuf*]

article *noun* **1** a thing or object. **2** a short written composition in a newspaper, magazine, etc. **3** a clause or paragraph in a document, legal agreement, etc. **4** *grammar* the definite article 'the' or the indefinite article 'a' or 'an'. [13c: from Latin *articulus* little joint]

articled *adj* of a trainee lawyer, accountant, etc: bound by a legal contract while working in an office to learn the job.

articular *adj* relating to or associated with a joint of the body. [15c: from Latin *articularis*]

articulate *verb* /ɑː'tɪkjʊleɪt/ **1** *tr & intr* to pronounce (words) or speak clearly and distinctly. **2** to express (thoughts, feelings, ideas, etc) clearly. **3** *intr, physiol* to be attached by way of a joint: *The carpals articulate with the metacarpals.* ▸ *adj* /ɑː'tɪkjʊlət/ **1 a** skilled at expressing one's thoughts clearly; **b** of a speech or a piece of writing: clearly presented, well-argued and to the point. **2** having joints. ▪ **articulately** *adv.* [16c: from Latin *articulare* to divide into distinct parts]

articulated lorry *noun* a large lorry consisting of two or more separate parts, joined by a pivot. Sometimes shortened to **artic**.

articulation *noun* **1** the act of speaking or expressing an idea in words. **2** *phonetics* **a** the process involved in uttering separate speech sounds; **b** the speech sound produced. **3** a joint.

artifact see **artefact**

artifice *noun* **1** a clever trick or plan. **2** clever trickery; cunning. [16c: from Latin *artificium*]

artificer /ɑː'tɪfɪsə(r)/ *noun* **1** a skilled craftsman. **2** a mechanic in the army or navy.

artificial *adj* **1** made by human effort; not occurring naturally. **2** imitating something natural, esp in order to become a cheaper substitute for the natural product. **3** of someone, their behaviour, etc: not genuine or sincere. ▪ **artificiality** *noun.* ▪ **artificially** *adv.* [14c: from Latin *artificialis*]

artificial intelligence *noun* (abbrev **AI**) the development and use of computer systems that can perform some of the functions normally associated with human intelligence, such as learning and problem-solving.

artificial respiration *noun* respiration that is stimulated and maintained manually or mechanically, by forcing air in and out of the lungs when normal spontaneous breathing has stopped. See **mouth-to-mouth**.

artillery *noun* (**-ies**) **1** large guns for use on land. **2** the part of an army equipped with such guns. [14c: from French *artillier* to arm]

artisan *noun* someone who does skilled work with their hands. [16c: French]

artist *noun* **1** someone who produces works of art, esp paintings. **2** someone who is skilled at some particular thing. **3** an artiste. ▪ **artistic** *adj.* ▪ **artistically** *adv.*

artiste *noun* a professional performer, esp a singer or dancer, in a theatre, circus, etc. [19c: French]

artistry *noun* artistic skill and imagination.

artless *adj* **1** simple and natural in manner. **2** honest, not deceitful. ▪ **artlessly** *adv.*

art nouveau /ɑː nuː'voʊ/ *noun* a style of art, architecture and interior design that flourished towards the end of the 19c, characterized by the use of flowing curved lines that resemble plant stems interlaced with highly stylized flowers and leaves. [1899: French, meaning 'new art']

artwork *noun* any illustrations, drawings, designs, etc in a book, magazine or other printed medium.

arty *adj* (**-ier, -iest**) *informal* affectedly or ostentatiously artistic.

arum lily *noun* a plant with large leaves shaped like arrow-heads and a yellow cylindrical **spadix** surrounded by a white, yellow or pink petal-like **spathe**.

arvo *noun, Aust informal* afternoon. [1930s abbrev]

-ary *suffix* **1** *forming adjectives, denoting* connected with or pertaining to something: *customary.* **2** *forming nouns, denoting* someone who is connected with or engaged in something: *adversary* • *secretary.* **3** *forming nouns, denoting* something connected with or employed in something; a place for something: *dictionary* • *apiary.* [From Latin *-arius*]

Aryan *noun* **1** *hist* in Nazi ideology: a European not of Jewish descent, esp someone of the northern European type with blonde hair and blue eyes. **2** a member of the peoples speaking any of the Indo-European languages, now esp the Indo-Iranian languages. ▸ *adj* belonging, relating or referring to Aryans or the Aryan languages. [19c: from Sanskrit *arya* noble]

As *symbol, chem* arsenic.

as *conj* **1** when; while; during: *met him as I was leaving the shop.* **2** because; since: *didn't go as it was raining.* **3** in the manner that: *fussing as only a mother can.* **4** that which; what: *Do as you're told.* **5** to the extent that: *Try as he might, he still couldn't reach.* **6** for instance: *large books, as this one for example.* **7** in the same way that: *married late in life, as his father had done.* **8** used to refer to something previously said, done, etc: like; just like: *As Frank says, the job won't be easy.* ▸ *prep* in the role of something: *speaking as her friend.* ▸ *adv* equally: *It was really hot yesterday, but I don't think today is as hot.* [Anglo-Saxon *eallswa* just as]

IDIOMS **as ... as ...** used in similes and for comparison: denoting that the things compared are the same or share the expected quality or characteristic: *as sly as a fox.* **as for** *or* **to sth** *or* **sb** with regard to it or them; concerning it or them. **as if** *or* **as though** as he, she, etc would if: *behaved as if nothing had happened.* **as well** also. **as yet** until now.

ASA *abbrev* **1** *Brit* Advertising Standards Authority. **2** *Brit* Amateur Swimming Association.

ASAP *or* **asap** *abbrev* as soon as possible.

asbestos *noun, geol* a fibrous silicate mineral that is highly resistant to heat. [14c: Greek, meaning 'inextinguishable']

asbestosis *noun* an inflammatory disease of the lungs, caused by inhalation of asbestos dust over a long period. Compare **silicosis**.

ASBO /'azbou/ *abbrev* Anti-Social Behaviour Order, a court order that places restrictions on a person who has been found guilty of antisocial acts. [21c]

ascend *verb* **1** *tr & intr* to climb, go or rise up. **2** *intr* to slope upwards. **3** *intr* to rise to a higher level, rank, etc. [14c: from Latin *ascendere* to climb up]

IDIOMS **ascend the throne** to become king or queen.

ascendancy *or* **ascendency** *noun* controlling or dominating power.

ascendant *or* **ascendent** *adj* **1** having more influence or power. **2** *astrol* rising over the eastern horizon. ▸ *noun, astrol* the sign of the zodiac rising over the eastern horizon at the time of an event, esp birth.

IDIOMS **in the ascendant** showing an increase in power, domination, authority, wealth, etc.

ascension *noun* **1** an act of climbing or moving upwards. **2** (**the Ascension**) Christ's believed passing into heaven. [14c: from Latin *ascensio*]

IDIOMS **Ascension Day** the fortieth day after Easter Sunday, when Christ's Ascension is celebrated.

ascent *noun* **1** the act of climbing, ascending or rising. **2** an upward slope.

ascertain *verb* to find out; to discover (the truth, etc). ▪ **ascertainment** *noun.* [15c: from French *acertener* to make certain]

ascetic /ə'sɛtɪk/ *noun* someone who abstains from all physical comfort and pleasure, esp someone who does so in solitude and for religious reasons. ▸ *adj* characterized by the abstinence from physical pleasure and comfort; self-denying. [17c: from Greek *asketikos*]

ASCII /'askiː/ *noun, comput* in digital computing systems: a code used for storage of text and for transmission of data between computers. [1960s: an acronym of *A*merican *S*tandard *C*ode for *I*nformation *I*nterchange]

ascorbic acid *noun* **vitamin C**. [1930s: from **a-**[2] + *scorbutic*]

ascribe *verb* to attribute; assign. ▪ **ascribable** *adj.* [15c: from Latin *ascribere* to enrol]

-ase *suffix, chem, forming nouns, indicating* an enzyme: *amylase.*

asepsis /eɪ'sɛpsɪs/ *noun* (**-ses** /-siːz/) the condition of being free from germs or other infection-causing micro-organisms. ▪ **aseptic** *adj, noun.*

asexual *adj* **1** denoting reproduction that does not involve sexual processes, with new individuals produced from a single parent rather than the union of male and female cells. **2** without functional sexual organs. ▪ **asexuality** *noun.* ▪ **asexually** *adv.*

ash[1] *noun* **1** the dusty residue that remains after something has been burnt. **2** the powdery dust that is put out by an erupting volcano. **3** (**ashes**) the remains of a body after cremation. ▪ **ashy** *adj.* [Anglo-Saxon *asce*]

ash[2] *noun* **1** a deciduous tree or shrub with strong grey bark, small clusters of greenish flowers and winged fruits. **2** the timber of this tree. [Anglo-Saxon *æsc*]

ashamed *adj* **1** troubled by feelings of guilt, embarrassment, etc. **2** (*usu* **ashamed of sb** *or* **sth**) embarrassed or humiliated by them or it. **3** hesitant or reluctant (to do something) because of embarrassment, guilt, fear of disapproval, etc. ▪ **ashamedly** /ə'ʃeɪmɪdlɪ/ *adv.* [Anglo-Saxon *ascamian* to feel shame]

ashcan *noun, N Am* a dustbin.

ashen *adj* of a face: very pale, usu from shock.

Ashkenazim *plural noun* the Polish and German Jews (as distinguished from the **Sephardim**, the Spanish and Portuguese Jews). ▸ *adj* of the Ashkenazim. [From Hebrew *Ashkenaz* a northern people (identified in Genesis 10), and identified by later Jews with Germany]

ashlar *or* **ashler** *noun* **1** a large square-cut stone that is used for building or facing walls. **2** masonry made of ashlars. [14c: from French *aiseler*]

ashore *adv* to, towards or onto the shore or land.

ashram *noun, Hinduism* **1** a hermitage for a holy man. **2** a place of retreat for a religious community. **3** a religious community in an ashram. [Early 20c: from Sanskrit *asrama* a hermitage]

ashtray *noun* a dish or other container for the ash, butts, etc from cigarettes, etc.

Ash Wednesday *noun, Christianity* the first day of **Lent**, so called because of the practice of sprinkling ashes on the heads of penitents.

Asian *adj* belonging or relating to the continent of Asia, its inhabitants or its languages. ▸ *noun* **1** an inhabitant of, or person born in, Asia. **2** someone of Asian descent. [16c: from Greek *Asianos*]

Asiatic *adj* belonging or relating to Asia or Asians. ▸ *noun, offensive* an Asian. [17c: from Greek *Asiatikos*]

aside *adv* **1** on, to, towards or over to one side. **2** away from everyone else: *took him aside to give him the news.* **3** in a direction away from oneself: *tossed the magazine aside in disgust.* **4** out of mind, consideration, etc, esp temporarily: *put his worries aside.* ▸ *noun* **1** words said by a character in a play that the audience can hear, but which the other characters cannot. **2** a remark that is not related to the main subject of a conversation.

IDIOMS **aside from sth** apart from or not including it.

asinine *adj* **1** relating to or resembling an ass. **2** stupid; idiotic; stubborn. [17c: from Latin *asininus*]

ask *verb* **1** *tr & intr* to question someone about something: *asked her name.* **2** to call for an answer to (a question): *asked what qualifications she had.* **3** to inquire about: *ask the way.* **4** to invite. **5** to expect: *I don't ask a lot of him.* [Anglo-Saxon *ascian*]

PHRASAL VERBS **ask after sb** to show concern about their health. **ask sb out** to invite them on a date.

askance *adv* sideways.

IDIOMS **look askance at sb** *or* **sth** to consider them or it with suspicion or disapproval.

askew *adv, adj* squint; not properly straight or level.

asking price *noun* the proposed selling price of something, set by the seller.

asleep *adj* **1** in a sleeping state. **2** *informal* not paying attention. **3** of limbs, hands, feet, etc: numb. ▸ *adv* into a sleeping state: *fall asleep.* [Anglo-Saxon *on slæpe*]

IDIOMS **sound asleep** in a very deep sleep.

AS level *or* (*in full*) **Advanced Subsidiary level** *noun* **1** an examination taken by sixth-form students after one year of study, either for its own sake or as a preliminary to the A-level examination. **2** a pass in such an examination.

asp *noun* **1** a small venomous S European snake. **2** the Egyptian cobra. [14c: from Greek *aspis*]

asparagus *noun* **1** a plant with cylindrical green shoots or 'spears' that function as leaves. **2** the harvested shoots of this plant, which can be cooked and eaten as a vegetable. [15c: from Greek *asparagos*]

aspartame *noun* an artificial sweetener, widely used in the food industry and by diabetics and dieters.

aspect /'aspɛkt/ *noun* **1** a particular or distinct part or element of a problem, subject, etc. **2** a particular way of considering a matter: *It's a very serious matter from all aspects.* **3 a** the appearance something has to the eye: *a lush green aspect*; **b** a look or appearance, esp of a face: *a worried aspect*. **4** the direction something faces: *a southern aspect*. [14c: from Latin *aspectus*]

aspen *noun* a deciduous tree of the poplar family, with smooth greyish-brown bark and leaves that tremble in the slightest breeze. [Anglo-Saxon *æspe*]

Asperger's syndrome /'aspɜːgəz/ *noun, med* a mild psychiatric disorder characterized by poor social interaction and obsessive behaviour. [Late 20c: named after Hans Asperger, an Austrian psychiatrist]

asperity *noun* (**-*ies***) roughness, bitterness or harshness, esp of temper. [17c: from Latin *asper* rough]

aspersion *noun* [16c: from Latin *aspergere* from *spergere* to sprinkle]

IDIOMS **cast aspersions on sb** *or* **sth** to make a damaging or spiteful remark.

asphalt *noun* a brown or black semi-solid bituminous material used in the construction industry for roofing, or mixed with rock chips or gravel to make paving and road-surfacing materials. ▸ *verb* to cover with asphalt. [14c: from Greek *asphaltos*]

asphodel *noun* a plant of the lily family with long narrow leaves and yellow or white star-shaped flowers. [16c: from Greek *asphodelos*]

asphyxia /as'fɪksɪə/ *noun* suffocation caused by any factor that interferes with respiration and prevents oxygen from reaching the body tissues, such as choking, drowning or inhaling poisonous gases. [18c: Greek, orig meaning 'absence of pulse' from *sphyxis* pulse]

asphyxiate *verb, tr & intr* **1** to stop or cause to stop breathing. **2** to suffocate. ▪ **asphyxiation** *noun.*

aspic *noun* a savoury jelly made from meat or fish stock, used as a mould for terrines, fish, eggs, etc.

aspidistra *noun* an evergreen house plant with broad leathery leaves, and dull-purple bell-shaped flowers. [19c: from Greek *aspis* shield]

aspirate *noun* /'aspɪrət/ *phonetics* the sound represented in English and several other languages by the letter *h*. ▸ *verb* /'aspɪreɪt/ **1** *phonetics* to pronounce the *h* sound in a word, or pronounce a word giving this sound its full phonetic value. **2** to withdraw (liquid, gas or solid debris) from a cavity by suction. [17c: from Latin *aspirare*]

aspiration *noun* **1** eager desire; ambition. **2** the removal of fluid from a cavity in the body by suction using an aspirator.

aspirator *noun* a device used to withdraw liquid, gas or solid debris from a cavity of the body.

aspire *verb* (*usu* **aspire to** *or* **after sth**) to have a strong desire to achieve or reach (an objective or ambition): *aspired to greatness.* [15c: from Latin *aspirare*]

aspirin *noun* **1** an analgesic drug that is widely used to relieve pain and to reduce inflammation and fever. **2** a tablet of this drug.

aspiring *adj* ambitious; hopeful of becoming something specified: *an aspiring novelist.*

ass *noun* **1** a hoofed mammal resembling, but smaller than, a horse, with longer ears. **2** *informal* a stupid person. [Anglo-Saxon *assa*]

assail *verb* **1** to make a strong physical attack. **2** to criticize fiercely. **3** to agitate, esp mentally. **4** to face up to something with the intention of mastering it. ▪ **assailant** *noun.* [13c: from Latin *ad* to + *salire* to leap]

assassin *noun* someone who kills someone else, esp for political or religious reasons. [16c: from Arabic *hashshashin* hashish-eaters]

assassinate *verb* to murder, esp for political or religious reasons. ▪ **assassination** *noun.*

assault *noun* **1** a violent physical or verbal attack. **2** *law* any act that causes someone to feel physically threatened. Compare **assault and battery**. **3** *euphem* rape or attempted rape. ▸ *verb* to make an assault on someone or something. [13c: from French *asaut*]

assault and battery *noun, law* the act of threatening to physically attack someone which is then followed by an actual physical attack.

assault course *noun* an obstacle course used esp for training soldiers.

assay *noun, metallurgy* the analysis of the composition and purity of a metal in an ore or mineral, or of a chemical compound in a mixture of compounds. ▸ *verb* to perform such an analysis on, or to determine the commercial value of (an ore or mineral) on the basis of such an analysis. [14c: from French *assaier* to attempt]

assegai *or* **assagai** *noun* a thin light iron-tipped wooden spear used in southern Africa. [17c: from Arabic *az-zagayah* the spear]

assemblage *noun* **1** a collection of people or things. **2** the act of gathering together.

assemble *verb* **1** *tr & intr* to gather or collect together. **2** to put together (the parts of something, such as a machine). [13c: from French *assembler*]

assembler *noun, comput* a computer program designed to convert a program written in assembly language into one written in machine code.

assembly *noun* (**-*ies***) **1** a group of people gathered together, esp for a meeting. **2 a** the act of assembling; **b** the state of being assembled. **3** the procedure of putting together the parts of something, such as a machine.

assembly language *noun, comput* a programming language used for programs controlling the processor's basic operations.

assembly line *noun* a continuous series of machines and workers that an article, product, etc passes along in the stages of its manufacture.

assent *noun* consent or approval, esp official. See also **royal assent**. ▸ *verb* (*often* **assent to sth**) to agree to it. [13c: from Latin *assentari*]

assert *verb* **1** to state firmly. **2** to insist on or defend (one's rights, opinions, etc). [17c: from Latin *asserere*]

IDIOMS **assert oneself** to state one's wishes, defend one's opinions, etc confidently and vigorously.

assertion *noun* **1** a positive or strong statement or claim. **2** the act of making such a claim or statement.

assertive *adj* of someone or their attitude: inclined to expressing wishes and opinions in a firm and confident manner. ▪ **assertively** *adv*. ▪ **assertiveness** *noun*.

assess *verb* **1** to judge the quality or importance of something. **2** to estimate the cost, value, etc of something. **3** to fix the amount of (a fine or tax). ▪ **assessment** *noun*. [15c: from Latin *assidere* to sit by]

assessor *noun* **1** someone who assesses the importance or quality of something. **2** someone who assesses the value of property, etc for taxation. **3** someone who advises a judge, etc on technical matters.

asset *noun* anything that is considered valuable or useful, such as a skill, quality, person, etc.

assets *plural noun, accounting* the total value of the property and possessions of a person or company, esp when thought of in terms of whether or not it is enough to cover any debts. [16c: from French *asetz* enough]

asset-stripping *noun* the practice of buying an unsuccessful company at a low price and selling off its assets separately for a profit.

asseverate *verb* to state solemnly. [18c: from Latin *asseverare* to assert solemnly]

assiduous *adj* **1** hard-working. **2** done carefully and exactly. ▪ **assiduity** /asɪ'djuːɪtɪ/ *noun*. [17c: from Latin *assiduus* sitting down to, and hence, persistent]

assign *verb* **1** to give (a task, etc) to someone. **2** to appoint someone to a position or task. **3** to fix (a time, place, etc) for a purpose. **4** to attribute or ascribe. **5** *law, formerly* to transfer (a title, property, interest, etc) to someone else. [13c: from Latin *assignare*]

assignation *noun* **1** a secret appointment to meet, esp between lovers. **2** *Scots law* an **assignment** (sense 3).

assignee *noun, law* someone to whom property, interest, etc is given by contract.

assignment *noun* **1 a** a task or duty that has been selected for someone to do; **b** an exercise that is set for students, etc. **2** the act of assigning. **3** *law* a transfer of property, interest, etc to someone else.

assimilate /'əsɪmɪleɪt/ *verb* **1** to become familiar with and understand (information, etc) completely. **2** *tr & intr* to become part of, or make (people) part of, a larger group, esp when they are of a different race, etc. **3** to cause something to become similar to something else. **4** *biol* of a plant, animal, or bacterium: to manufacture complex organic compounds from simple molecules obtained from the environment or from food. ▸ *noun* /-lət/ *biol* any of the organic compounds produced by green plants and certain bacteria that manufacture complex molecules from simple molecules obtained from the environment. ▪ **assimilation** *noun*. [17c: from Latin *ad* to + *similis* like]

assist *verb, tr & intr* to help. [16c: from Latin *assistere*]

assistance *noun* **1** help. **2** an act of helping.

assistant *noun* **1** a person whose job is to help someone of higher rank, position, etc. **2** a person whose job is to serve customers in a shop: *sales assistant*.

assistant referee *noun, football* one of the two officials who assist the referee by judging whether players are **offside** and awarding **throw-in**s. Formerly called **linesman**.

assisted suicide *noun* helping someone to commit suicide because he or she cannot do so unaided, eg because they are very ill.

assizes /ə'saɪzɪz/ *plural noun, formerly* in England and Wales: court sittings which used to be held at regular intervals in each county. [14c: from Latin *assidere* to sit beside]

assoc. *abbrev* **1** associated. **2** association.

associate *verb* /ə'soʊʃɪeɪt, -sɪ-/ **1** to connect in the mind: *associate lambs with spring*. **2** *intr* to mix socially: *don't associate with him*. **3** to involve (oneself) in a group because of shared views or aims. **4** *intr* to join with people for a common purpose. ▸ *noun* /-ət/ **1** a business partner or colleague. **2** a companion or friend. **3** someone who is admitted to a society, institution, etc without full membership. ▸ *adj* /-ət/ **1** joined with another, esp in a business: *an associate director*. **2** not having full membership of a society, institution, etc. [14c: from Latin *associare*]

association *noun* **1** an organization or club. **2** a friendship or partnership. **3** a connection in the mind. **4** the act of associating.

Association Football see under **football**

associative *adj, maths* of an arithmetical process: resulting in the same answer, no matter which way the elements are grouped together.

assonance *noun, prosody* a correspondence or resemblance in the sounds of words or syllables, either between their vowels, eg in *meet* and *bean*, or between all their consonants, eg in *keep* and *cape*. Compare **alliteration**, **rhyme**. [18c: from Latin *assonare* to sound]

assorted *adj* **1** mixed; consisting of various different kinds: *assorted chocolates*. **2** arranged in sorts; classified. [18c: from French *assorter*]

assortment *noun* a mixed collection.

assuage /ə'sweɪdʒ/ *verb* to make (a pain, sorrow, hunger, etc) less severe. [14c: from Latin *suavis* mild, sweet]

assume *verb* **1** to accept something without proof; to take for granted. **2** to take on (a responsibility, duty, etc). **3** to take on or adopt (an appearance, quality, etc): *an issue assuming immense importance*. **4** to pretend to have or feel. [15c: from Latin *assumere*]

assumed *adj* false; not genuine: *an assumed name*.

assuming *adj* of someone or their attitude: arrogant; presumptuous. ▸ *conj* if it is taken as a fact: *Assuming that the meal won't cost too much, we should have enough money left*.

assumption *noun* **1** something that is accepted as true without proof. **2** the act of accepting something as true without proof. **3** the act of assuming in other senses. [13c: from Latin *assumptio*]

assurance *noun* **1** a promise, guarantee or statement that something is true. **2** confidence and poise. **3** *Brit* insurance that allows for a certainty rather than a possibility, esp life insurance.

assure *verb* **1** to state positively and confidently; to guarantee. **2** to make (an event, etc) certain: *Her hard work assured her success*. **3** *Brit* to insure something (esp one's life). ▪ **assurer** *noun*. [14c: from French *aseurer*]

assured *adj* **1** of someone or their attitude, behaviour, etc: confident and poised. **2** certain to happen. ▪ **assuredly** /ə'ʃɔːrɪdlɪ/ *adv*.

Assyrian *noun* **1** an inhabitant of Assyria, an ancient empire that, from 1530–612 BC, extended from the E Mediterranean to Iran, and from the Persian Gulf to E Turkey. **2** the now extinct Semitic language of Assyria. ▸ *adj* belonging, relating or referring to Assyria. [16c: from Greek *Assyrios*]

AST *abbrev* Atlantic Standard Time.

astatine /'astətiːn/ *noun, chem* (symbol **At**) a radioactive chemical element that occurs naturally in trace amounts and is produced artificially by bombarding bismuth with alpha particles. [1940s: from Greek *astatos* unstable]

aster *noun* a plant with blue, purple, pink or white daisy-like flowers. [18c: from Greek *aster* star]

asterisk *noun* a star-shaped symbol (*) used in printing and writing: to mark a cross-reference to a footnote, an omission, etc. ▸ *verb* to mark with an asterisk. [17c: from Greek *asteriskos* small star]

astern *adv, adj* **1** in or towards the stern. **2** backwards. **3** behind.

asteroid *noun* any of thousands of small rocky objects that orbit around the Sun, mainly between the orbits of Mars and Jupiter. Also called **minor planet**. [Early 19c: from Greek *asteroeides* star-like]

asthma /'asmə *or* (*NAm*) 'azmə/ *noun* a respiratory disorder in which breathlessness and wheezing occur, caused by excessive contraction of muscles in the walls of the air passages. ▪ **asthmatic** *noun, adj*. [14c: Greek, meaning 'laboured breathing']

asthma
This word is often misspelt. It might help you to remember the following sentence:
*A**sth**m**a** may be caused by **s**ensitivity **t**o **h**ousehold **m**ites.*

astigmatic *adj* relating to, affected by or correcting astigmatism.

astigmatism /ə'stɪgmətɪzəm/ *noun* a defect in a lens, esp abnormal curvature of the lens or cornea of the eye, causing distortion of an image.

astir *adj, adv* **1** awake and out of bed. **2** in a state of motion or excitement.

astonish *verb* to surprise greatly. ▪ **astonishing** *adj*. ▪ **astonishment** *noun*. [16c: related to French *estoner*]

astound *verb* to amaze or shock. ▪ **astounding** *adj*.

astral *adj* belonging or relating to, consisting of, or like, the stars. [17c: from Latin *astralis*]

astray *adj, adv* out of the right or expected way.

astride *adv* **1** with a leg on each side. **2** with legs apart. ▸ *prep* **1** with a leg on each side of something. **2** stretching across.

astringent *adj* **1** severe and harsh. **2** of a substance: causing cells to shrink. ▸ *noun* an astringent substance. ▪ **astringency** *noun*. [16c: from Latin *astringere* to draw tight]

astro- *combining form, denoting* stars or space. [From Greek *astron* star]

astrolabe *noun, astron, formerly* a navigational instrument used to observe the positions of the Sun and bright stars, and to estimate the local time by determining the altitude of the Sun or specific stars above the horizon. [14c: from **astro-** + Greek *lambanein* to take]

astrology *noun* the study of the movements of the stars and planets, and of how they are thought to exert influences on people's lives, character traits, etc. ▪ **astrologer** *noun*. ▪ **astrological** *adj*. [14c: **astro-** + Greek *logos* word or reason]

astronaut *noun* someone who is trained to travel in space. See also **cosmonaut**. [1920s: from **astro-**]

astronautics *singular noun* the science of travel in space. ▪ **astronautical** *or* **astronautic** *adj*.

astronomical *or* **astronomic** *adj* **1** very large; vast. **2** relating to astronomy. ▪ **astronomically** *adv*.

astronomy *noun* the scientific study of celestial bodies, including the planets, stars and galaxies, and the universe as a whole. [13c: **astro-** + Greek *-nomia* administration or regulation]

astrophysics *singular noun* the application of physical laws and theories to astronomical objects and phenomena. ▪ **astrophysical** *adj*. ▪ **astrophysicist** *noun*.

astute *adj* mentally perceptive; shrewd. ▪ **astutely** *adv*. ▪ **astuteness** *noun*. [17c: from Latin *astutus* crafty]

asunder *adv* apart or into pieces. [Anglo-Saxon *onsundran*]

asylum *noun* **1** a place of safety or protection. **2** *hist* a mental hospital. [15c: from Greek *asylon* sanctuary]

asylum seeker *noun* a person who migrates to another country seeking political asylum.

asymmetry *noun* a lack of symmetry. ▪ **asymmetric** *and* **asymmetrical** *adj*.

asymptote /'asɪmtoʊt, 'asɪmp-/ *noun, geom* a straight line that is continually approached by a curve that never actually meets the line. ▪ **asymptotic** *adj*. [17c: from Greek *asymptotos* not falling together]

asynchronism *noun* the absence of a correspondence in time. ▪ **asynchronous** *adj*. ▪ **asynchrony** *noun*.

asystole /eɪ'sɪstəlɪ, a'sɪstəlɪ/ *noun, pathol* absence or stopping of the heartbeat. ▪ **asystolic** /asɪs'tɒlɪk/ *adj.* [19c]

At *symbol, chem* astatine.

at *prep* **1** used to indicate position or place: in, within, on, near, etc: *worked at a local factory.* **2** towards, in the direction of something: *working at getting fit.* **3** used to indicate a position in time: **a** around; on the stroke of: *The train arrives at six;* **b** having reached the age of: *At 17 you can start to drive.* **4** with, by, beside, next to, etc: *annoyed at her.* **5** engaged in; occupied with: *children at play.* **6** for; in exchange for: *sold it at a profit.* **7** in a state of: *at liberty.* [Anglo-Saxon æt]

atavism /'atəvɪzəm/ *noun* **1** a resemblance to ancestors rather than immediate parents. **2** reversion to an earlier type. ▪ **atavistic** *adj.* [19c: from Latin *atavus* great-great-great-grandfather]

ataxia /ə'taksɪə/ *or* **ataxy** /ə'taksɪ/ *noun, pathol* inability of the brain to co-ordinate voluntary movements of the limbs. [17c: Greek, meaning 'disorder']

ate *past tense of* **eat**

-ate[1] /-eɪt, -ət/ *suffix* **1** *forming verbs, denoting* cause to be or have: *hyphenate.* **2** *chem forming nouns, denoting* a salt: *carbonate.* **3** *forming adjectives, denoting* having, showing features of, like or related to: *passionate.* [From the Latin participial ending *-atus*]

-ate[2] *suffix, forming nouns, denoting* rank, profession, or group: *doctorate* • *magistrate* • *electorate.* [From the Latin collective noun ending *-atus*]

atelier /ə'tɛlɪeɪ; *French* atəlje/ *noun* a workshop or artist's studio. [19c: French]

Atharva-veda see **Veda**

atheism *noun* the belief that there is no god. ▪ **atheist** *noun.* [16c: from Greek *atheos* godless]

Athenian /ə'θiːnɪən/ *adj* belonging or relating to Athens, the capital city of Greece, or its inhabitants. ▸ *noun* a citizen or inhabitant of, or person born in, Athens.

atherosclerosis *noun* (***-ses***) *pathol* a form of **arteriosclerosis** in which fatty substances are deposited on the inner walls of arteries, eventually obstructing the flow of blood. ▪ **atherosclerotic** /-'rɒtɪk/ *adj.* [Early 20c: from Greek *athere* gruel + **sclerosis**]

athlete *noun* **1** someone who trains for and competes in field and track events. **2** someone who is good at sports. [16c: from Greek *athlos* contest]

athlete's foot *noun, informal* a fungal infection of the foot.

athletic *adj* **1** of someone or their build: physically fit and strong. **2** relating to athletics. **3** of a physical type: distinguished by having well-developed muscles and a body that is in proportion. ▪ **athletically** *adv.* ▪ **athleticism** *noun.*

athletics *singular noun* competitive track and field sports such as running, jumping and throwing events.

-atic *suffix, forming adjectives, denoting* belonging, relating or tending to do or be something specific: *Asiatic* • *systematic* • *lunatic.*

-ation *suffix, forming nouns, denoting* an action, process, condition, result, etc: *expectation* • *mechanization* • *representation.* See also **-ion**.

atishoo *exclam, indicating* the sound of a sneeze.

-ative *suffix, forming adjectives, denoting* having a specified attribute or tendency: *authoritative* • *talkative.*

Atlantic *noun* (**the Atlantic**) the Atlantic Ocean, an ocean bounded by Europe and Africa to the East, and by N and S America to the West. ▸ *adj* belonging, relating or referring to the area of the Atlantic Ocean: *Atlantic fishing.* [17c: from Greek *Atlantikos*, from *Atlas*, so named because the ocean lies beyond this range of mountains in N Africa]

Atlantic Standard Time *noun* (abbrev **AST**) the most easterly of the **time zones** of the US and Canada, 4 hours behind **Greenwich Mean Time**.

atlas *noun* a book of maps and geographical charts. [16c: in Greek mythology Atlas was a Titan who was condemned to support the sky on his shoulders]

ATM *abbrev* automated or automatic telling machine. See **cash machine**.

atman /'ɑːtmən/ *noun, Hinduism* the human soul or essential self, which is seen as being one with the Absolute, and is identified with Brahma. [18c: Sanskrit, meaning 'self' or 'soul']

atmosphere *noun* **1** the layer of gas surrounding a planet, esp the Earth, and held to it by gravity. **2** the air in a particular place. **3** the mood of a book, film, painting, piece of music, etc or the general impression that it gives. **4** the general or prevailing climate or mood: *an atmosphere of jubilation.* **5** a unit of pressure equal to normal air pressure at sea level. ▪ **atmospheric** *adj.* ▪ **atmospherically** *adv.* [17c: from Greek *atmos* vapour + *sphaira* ball]

atmospheric pressure *noun* the pressure exerted by the atmosphere at any point on the earth's surface, due to the weight of the air above it.

atmospherics *plural noun* radio-frequency electromagnetic radiation, produced by natural electrical disturbances in the Earth's atmosphere. Also called **atmospheric interference**.

atoll *noun* a circle of coral reef that surrounds a lagoon, and is itself surrounded by open sea. [17c: from *atollon*, a native name applied to the Maldive Islands]

atom *noun* **1** the smallest unit of a chemical element that can display the properties of that element, and which is capable of combining with other atoms to form molecules. **2** *non-technical* a very small amount. [15c: from Greek *atomos* something that cannot be divided]

atom bomb *or* **atomic bomb** *noun* a powerful explosive device that derives its force from the sudden release of enormous amounts of nuclear energy during nuclear fission. Also called **nuclear bomb**.

atomic *adj* **1** relating to atoms. **2** obtained by atomic phenomena, esp nuclear fission: *atomic weapons.* ▪ **atomically** *adv.*

atomic energy see **nuclear energy**

atomicity /atə'mɪsɪtɪ/ *noun, chem* **1** existence in the form of atoms. **2** the number of atoms in a molecule of an element.

atomic mass see **relative atomic mass**

atomic mass unit *noun, chem* an arbitrary unit, used to denote the masses of individual atoms or molecules, which is equal to one twelfth of the mass of an atom of the carbon-12 isotope of carbon.

atomic number *noun, chem* (symbol **Z**) the number of protons in the nucleus of an atom of an element.

atomic pile *noun, formerly* a **nuclear reactor**.

atomic theory *noun, chem* the hypothesis that all atoms of the same element are alike and that a compound can be formed by the union of atoms of different elements in some simple ratio.

atomic weight see **relative atomic mass**

atomize *or* **-ise** *verb* **1** to reduce to atoms or small particles. **2** to reduce (a liquid) to a spray or mist of fine droplets by passage through a nozzle or jet under pressure. **3** to destroy by means of atomic weapons. [17c]

atomizer *or* **-iser** *noun* a container that releases liquid, containing eg perfume, as a fine spray.

atonal *adj, music* lacking tonality; not written in a particular key. ▪ **atonality** *noun.*

atone *verb* (*also* **atone for sth**) to make amends for (a wrongdoing, crime, sin, etc). [17c: back-formation from **atonement**]

atonement *noun* **1** an act of making amends for, making up for, or paying for a wrongdoing, etc. **2** (**Atonement**) *Christianity* the reconciliation of God and man through the sufferings and death of Christ. [16c: from earlier *at onement*, meaning 'in harmony']

atop *adv* on top; at the top. ▸ *prep* on top of, or at the top of, something.

ATP *abbrev, biochem* adenosine triphosphate, a compound that is the main form in which energy is stored in living organisms.

atrium *noun* (*atria* /ˈeɪtrɪə, ˈɑːtrɪə/ *or* *atriums*) **1** a central court or entrance hall in an ancient Roman house. **2** a court in a public space, such as an office block, hotel, etc, that has galleries around it, and is often several storeys high. **3** *anatomy* either of the two upper chambers of the heart that receive blood from the veins. Also called **auricle**. **4** *anatomy* any of various other chambers or cavities in the body. ▪ **atrial** *adj.* [16c: Latin]

atrocious *adj* **1** *informal* very bad. **2** extremely cruel or wicked. ▪ **atrociously** *adv.* [17c: from Latin *atrox* cruel]

atrocity *noun* (**-ies**) **1** wicked or cruel behaviour. **2** an act of wickedness or cruelty. [16c: from Latin *atrox* cruel]

atrophy /ˈatrəfɪ/ *verb* (**-ies, -ied**) *tr & intr* to diminish or die away; to cause to diminish or die away. ▸ *noun* the process of atrophying. [17c: from Greek *atrophia* lack of nourishment]

atropine *or* **atropin** *noun, med* a poisonous alkaloid drug, obtained from **deadly nightshade**. Also called **belladonna**. [1830s: from *Atropos* the name of the Fate who, in Greek mythology, cut the thread of life]

attach *verb* **1** to fasten or join. **2** to associate (oneself) with or join. **3** to attribute or assign: *attach great importance to detail.* [14c: from French *atachier* to fasten]
IDIOMS **be attached to sb** *or* **sth** to be fond of them or it.

attaché /əˈtaʃeɪ/ *noun* someone who is connected to a diplomatic department, etc because they have some specialized knowledge. [19c: French, meaning 'attached']

attaché-case *noun* a small rigid leather case for holding documents, etc.

attached *adj* of someone: in a steady romantic relationship.

attachment *noun* **1** **a** an act or means of fastening; **b** the state of being fastened. **2** liking or affection. **3** an extra part that can be fitted to a machine, often used for changing its function slightly.

attack *verb* **1** to make a sudden violent attempt to hurt, damage or capture. **2** to criticize strongly in speech or writing. **3** *intr* to make an attack. **4** to begin to do something with enthusiasm or determination. **5** *intr* to take the initiative in a game, contest, etc to attempt to score a goal, points, etc. ▸ *noun* **1** an act or the action of attacking. **2** a sudden spell of illness: *an attack of flu.* **3** (**the attack**) the players, eg the strikers, forwards, etc in a team sport whose job is to score goals, points, etc. ▪ **attacker** *noun* someone who makes a physical, verbal, sporting, etc attack. [17c: from Italian *attaccare*]

attain *verb* **1** to complete successfully; to achieve. **2** to reach (in space or time): *attained the summit.* ▪ **attainable** *adj.* [14c: from Latin *tangere* to touch]

attainment *noun* **1** achievement, esp after some effort. **2** the act of achieving something. **3** something that is achieved.

attar *noun* a fragrant essential oil that is distilled from rose petals. [18c: from Persian *atir* perfumed]

attempt *verb* **1** to try. **2** to try to master, tackle, answer, etc (a problem, etc). ▸ *noun* an effort; an endeavour. [14c: from Latin *attemptare* to strive after]
IDIOMS **make an attempt on sb's life** to try to kill them.

attend *verb* **1** *tr & intr* to be present at something. **2** to go regularly to (eg school, church, etc). **3** *intr* (**attend to sb** *or* **sth**) to take care of them or it or to take action over them or it. ▪ **attender** *noun.* [13c: from Latin *attendere*]

attendance *noun* **1** the act of attending. **2** the number of people attending. **3** regularity of attending.

attendant *noun* **1** someone whose job is to help, guide or give some other service, esp to the public: *museum attendant.* **2** someone who serves or waits upon someone else. ▸ *adj* **1** being in or giving attendance. **2** accompanying: *attendant responsibilities.*

attention *noun* **1** the act of concentrating or directing the mind. **2** notice; awareness: *The problem has recently come to my attention.* **3** special care and consideration: *attention to detail.* **4** (**attentions**) *old use* an act of politeness or courtship. [14c: from Latin *attentio, attentionis*]
IDIOMS **pay attention to sth** **1** to listen to or concentrate on it closely. **2** to take care or heed of it.

attention deficit disorder *or* **attention deficit hyperactivity disorder** *noun, med* (abbrev **ADD** *or* **ADHD**) an abnormal inability in a child or young person to concentrate for more than very short periods of time.

attentive *adj* **1** showing close concentration; alert and watchful. **2** considerate; polite and courteous. ▪ **attentively** *adv.* ▪ **attentiveness** *noun.*

attenuate *verb* **1** to make or become thin or weak. **2** to reduce the value or something. **3** *physics* of sound, radiation, etc: to decrease in intensity after passing through a medium. ▪ **attenuation** *noun.* [16c: from Latin *attenuare* to make thin]

attenuated *adj* **1** thin. **2** thinned; diluted. **3** tapering.

attest *verb* **1** to affirm or be proof of the truth or validity of something. **2** *intr* (**attest to sth**) to certify that it is so; to witness or bear witness to it, esp by giving a sworn written or verbal statement. **3** to be evidence of something. ▪ **attestation** *noun*. [16c: from Latin *attestari*]

attic *noun* a space or room at the top of a house under the roof. [17c: from *Attic*, denoting ancient Athens or Attica, because, in classical Greek architecture, the decoration of the topmost part of a building was particularly important]

attire *noun* clothes, esp formal or elegant ones. [13c: from French *atirier* to put in order]

attitude *noun* **1** a way of thinking or behaving. **2** a hostile or resentful manner. **3** a position of the body. **4** a pose, esp adopted for dramatic effect. [17c: French]

attitudinize *or* **-ise** *verb* to adopt an opinion or position for effect.

attorney /ə'tɜːnɪ/ *noun* **1** someone able to act for another in legal or business matters. **2** *N Am* a lawyer. [14c: from French *atourner* to turn over to]

Attorney General *noun* (***Attorneys General*** *or* ***Attorney Generals***) in the UK, the US, Australia, New Zealand, etc: the chief law officer or chief government law officer.

attract *verb* **1** to cause (attention, notice, a crowd, interest, etc) to be directed towards oneself, itself, etc. **2** of a magnet: to draw or pull (towards itself), esp by exerting some force or power. **3** to arouse liking or admiration in someone; to be attractive to them. [15c: from Latin *trahere* to draw]

attraction *noun* **1** the act or power of attracting. **2** someone or something that attracts. **3** *physics* a force that tends to pull two objects closer together, such as that between opposite electric charges or opposite magnetic poles. Opposite of **repulsion**.

attractive *adj* **1** appealing; enticing: *an attractive salary.* **2** appealing in looks or character. ▪ **attractively** *adv*. ▪ **attractiveness** *noun*.

attribute *verb* /ə'trɪbjuːt/ (*always* **attribute sth to sb** *or* **sth**) to think of it as being written, said, or caused by them or it; to ascribe it to them or it: *attributed the accident to human error.* ▸ *noun* /'atrɪbjuːt/ **1** a quality, characteristic, feature, etc, usu one that has positive or favourable connotations. **2** *comput* an item of information about a file stored by the operating system, eg the date and time last saved. ▪ **attributable** *adj*. ▪ **attribution** *noun*. [15c: from Latin *attribuere*]

attributive /ə'trɪbjʊtɪv/ *adj, grammar* of an adjective or noun in a noun phrase: placed before the noun it modifies, eg the adjective 'young' in *young girl*.

attrition *noun* **1** a rubbing together; friction. **2** *geog* erosion involving rocks scraping against each other and being worn down. **3** *military* a relentless wearing down of an enemy's strength, morale, etc, esp by continual attacks: *war of attrition*. [14c: from Latin *attritio*]

attune *verb* (*often* **attune to** *or* **become attuned to sth**) to adjust to or prepare for (a situation, etc). ▪ **attunement** *noun*.

atypical *adj* not typical, representative, usual, etc. ▪ **atypically** *adv*.

Au *symbol, chem* gold. [From Latin *aurum*]

aubergine *noun* **1** a bushy plant with large leaves and funnel-shaped violet flowers, widely cultivated for its edible fruit. **2** the large egg-shaped fruit of this plant, with a smooth skin that is usu deep purple in colour, eaten as a vegetable. *N Am & Aust equivalent* **eggplant**. **3** a deep purple colour. ▸ *adj* deep purple in colour.

aubrietia /ɔː'briːʃə/ *noun* a dwarf plant with greyish leaves and purple, lilac, blue or pink cross-shaped flowers, widely cultivated as an ornamental plant in rock gardens. [19c: named after the French painter of flowers and animals, Claude Aubriet]

auburn *adj* of hair: reddish-brown. [15c: from Latin *alburnus* whitish]

auction *noun* a public sale in which each item is sold to the person who offers the most money. ▸ *verb* (*often* **auction sth off**) to sell something in an auction. [17c: from Latin *auctio* an increase]

auctioneer *noun* a person whose job is to conduct an auction by cataloguing and announcing the **lots** (sense 6) and presiding over the bids.

audacious *adj* **1** bold and daring. **2** disrespectful; impudent. ▪ **audaciously** *adv*. ▪ **audacity** *noun*. [16c: from Latin *audax* bold]

audible *adj* loud enough to be heard. ▪ **audibility** *noun*. ▪ **audibly** *adv*. [16c: from Latin *audire* to hear]

audience *noun* **1** a group of people watching a performance, eg of a play, concert, etc. **2** the people reached by a film, TV or radio broadcast, book, magazine, etc. **3** a formal interview with an important person. [14c: from Latin *audientia*]

audio *adj* **1** relating to hearing or sound. **2** relating to the recording and broadcasting of sound. [Early 20c: from Latin *audire* to hear]

audio- *combining form, denoting* **1** sound, esp broadcast sound. **2** hearing.

audiotypist *noun* a person whose job is to listen to a recording that has been made on a dictation machine and transfer the data into the form of typed letters, etc. ▪ **audiotyping** *noun*.

audiovisual *adj* of a device or teaching method: using both sound and vision.

audit *noun* an official inspection of an organization's accounts by an accountant. ▸ *verb* to examine (accounts) officially. [15c: from Latin *audire* to hear]

audition *noun* a test of the suitability of an actor, singer, musician, etc for a particular part or role, by way of a short performance. ▸ *verb* to test or be tested by means of an audition. [19c: from Latin *auditio*]

auditor *noun* a person who is professionally qualified to audit accounts.

auditorium *noun* (***auditoriums*** *or* ***auditoria***) the part of a theatre, hall, etc where the audience sits. [18c: Latin, meaning 'a lecture-room']

auditory *adj* belonging, relating or referring to hearing or the organs involved in hearing. [16c: from Latin *audire* to hear]

au fait /oʊ 'feɪ/ *adj* (*usu* **au fait with sth**) well informed about or familiar with it. [18c: French, meaning 'to the point']

Aug. *abbrev* August.

auger *noun* a hand-tool with a corkscrew-like point for boring holes. [Anglo-Saxon *nafogar*]

augment *verb, tr & intr* to make or become greater in size, number, strength, amount, etc. ▪ **augmentation** *noun*. [15c: from Latin *augere* to increase]

au gratin /oʊ 'gratɛ̃/ *adj, cookery* of a dish: covered with breadcrumbs, or grated cheese, or a combination of both. [Early 19c: French, meaning 'with the burnt scrapings']

augur /'ɔːgə(r), 'ɔːgjə(r)/ *verb, intr* (*usu* **augur well** *or* **ill**) to be a good or bad sign for the future. [15c: Latin, meaning 'a soothsayer']

augury *noun* (***-ies***) **1** a sign or omen. **2** the practice of predicting the future.

August *noun* (abbrev **Aug.**) the eighth month of the year. [Anglo-Saxon]

august /ɔː'gʌst/ *adj* noble; imposing. [17c: from Latin *augustus* grand]

Augustan *adj* **1** belonging, relating or referring to, or characteristic of, the reign of the Roman emperor Augustus Caesar. **2** of literature: having a classical style, such as that which flourished in 17c France and 18c England. [18c: from Latin *Augustanus* relating to Augustus Caesar]

auk *noun* a species of small diving seabird with a heavy body, black and white plumage, and short wings. [16c: from Norse *alka*]

auld *adj, Scot* old. [Anglo-Saxon *ald*]

auld lang syne *noun, Scot* days of long ago, esp those remembered nostalgically. [17c: Scots, literally 'old long since']

Aum see **Om**

au naturel *adv, adj* **1** of food: uncooked or cooked in a simple way, usu without seasoning. **2** naked. [Early 19c: French, meaning 'naturally']

aunt *noun* **1** the sister of one's father or mother. **2** the wife of one's uncle. **3** a close female friend of a child's parents. [13c: from Latin *amita* father's sister]

auntie *or* **aunty** *noun* (***-ies***) *informal* an aunt.

Aunt Sally *noun* (***Aunt Sallies***) **1** a game in which sticks or balls are thrown at a dummy. **2** any target of abuse.

au pair *noun* a young person from abroad, usu female, who, in order to learn the language, helps with housework, looking after children, etc in return for board and lodging. [19c: French, meaning 'on equality']

aura *noun* (***auras*** *or* ***aurae*** /'ɔːriː/) **1** a distinctive character or quality around a person or in a place. **2** a fine substance coming out of something, esp that supposedly coming from and surrounding the body, which many mystics claim is visible as a faint light. **3** *pathol* an unusual sensation that precedes the onset of an attack, eg of a migraine or an epileptic seizure. [14c: Greek, meaning 'breeze']

aural *adj* relating to the sense of hearing or to the ears. ▪ **aurally** *adv.* [1840s: from Latin *auris* ear]

aureate *adj* **1** **a** made of or covered in gold; gilded; **b** golden in colour. **2** of a speech, someone's writing style, etc: elaborate. [15c: from Latin *aureus* golden]

aureole *or* **aureola** *noun* **1** a bright disc of light that surrounds the head of a holy figure in Christian painting and iconography. **2** *astron* a hazy bluish-white halo surrounding the Sun or Moon. [13c: from Latin *aureolus* golden]

au revoir /oʊ rəv'wɑː(r)/ *exclam* goodbye. [17c: French, meaning 'until the next seeing']

auricle *noun, anatomy* **1** the outer part of the ear. **2** the ear-shaped tip of an **atrium** of the heart. **3** another word for an **atrium** of the heart. ▪ **auricular** *adj.* [17c: from Latin *auricula* little ear]

aurochs /'ɔːrɒks, 'ɑʊərɒks/ *noun* (***aurochs***) an extinct wild ox. Also called **urus**. [18c: from German *urohso*]

aurora *noun* (***auroras*** *or* ***aurorae*** /ə'rɔːriː/) **1** *astron* the appearance of bands of coloured lights in the night sky, most often observed from the Arctic and Antarctic regions. **2** *poetic* the dawn. [15c: Latin, meaning 'dawn']

aurora australis *noun* the name given to the aurora visible in the southern hemisphere. Also called **the southern lights**. [18c: Latin, meaning 'southern aurora']

aurora borealis *noun* the name given to the aurora visible in the northern hemisphere. Also called **the northern lights**. [17c: Latin, meaning 'northern aurora']

auscultation *noun, med* the practice of listening, esp with a stethoscope, to the sounds produced by the movement of blood or air within the heart, lungs, etc, in order to ascertain their physical state and diagnose any abnormalities. ▪ **auscultate** *verb.* [19c; 17c, meaning 'the act of listening']

auspice *noun* (*usu* **auspices**) protection; patronage. [17c: from Latin *auspicium* the action of foretelling the future by watching birds]

IDIOMS **under the auspices of sb** *or* **sth** with their or its help, support or guidance.

auspicious *adj* promising future success; favourable.

Aussie *noun, adj, informal* Australian.

austere *adj* **1** severely simple and plain. **2** serious; severe; stern. **3** severe in self-discipline. ▪ **austerely** *adv.* [14c: from Greek *austeros* making the tongue dry and rough]

austerity *noun* (***-ies***) **1** the state of being austere; strictness or harshness. **2** severe simplicity of dress, lifestyle, etc.

austral *adj* southern. [14c: from Latin *Auster* the south wind]

Australasian *adj* belonging or relating to Australia, New Zealand and the nearby Pacific islands, their inhabitants, or their language. ▸ *noun* a citizen or inhabitant of, or person born in, Australia, New Zealand or the nearby Pacific islands.

Australian *adj* belonging or relating to Australia, a continent and country in the southern hemisphere, or its inhabitants. ▸ *noun* a citizen or inhabitant of, or person born in, Australia. [18c: from **austral**]

Austrian *adj* belonging or relating to Austria, a republic in central Europe, or its inhabitants. ▸ *noun* a citizen or inhabitant of, or person born in, Austria. [18c: from German *Österreich* Eastern Kingdom]

autarchy *noun* (***-ies***) government of a country by a ruler who has absolute power. ▪ **autarchic** *or* **autarchical** *adj.* ▪ **autarchist** *noun.* [17c: from Greek *autarchos* an absolute ruler]

autarky *noun* (***-ies***) a system or policy of economic self-sufficiency in a country, state, etc. ▪ **autarkic** *or* **autarkical** *adj.* ▪ **autarkist** *noun.* [1930s; 17c, meaning 'self-sufficiency']

authentic *adj* **1** genuine. **2** reliable; trustworthy; true to the original. ▪ **authentically** *adv.* ▪ **authenticity** *noun.* [14c: from Greek *authentikos* original]

authenticate *verb* to prove something to be true or genuine. ▪ **authentication** *noun.*

author *noun* **1** the writer of a book, article, play, etc. **2** the creator or originator of an idea, event, etc: *the* *author of the peace plan.* ▸ *verb* to be the author of (a book, article, play, etc). [14c: from Latin *auctor*]

authoring *noun* an act or the process of composing, writing, compiling, etc using information technology, esp in the production of multimedia documents: *He did a course in web authoring.*

authoritarian *adj* in favour of, insisting on, characterized by, etc strict authority. ▸ *noun* an authoritarian person. ▪ **authoritarianism** *noun.*

authoritative *adj* **1** accepted as a reliable source of knowledge. **2** having authority; official. ▪ **authoritatively** *adv.*

authority *noun* (**-*ies***) **1** the power or right to control or judge others, or to have the final say in something. **2** a position that has such a power or right. **3** (*sometimes* **authorities**) the person or people who have power, esp political or administrative: *reported them to the authorities.* **4** the ability to influence others, usu as a result of knowledge or expertise. **5** well-informed confidence: *she delivered her lecture with authority.* **6** an expert. [14c: from French *autorite*]

IDIOMS **have it on authority** to know about something from a reliable source.

authorize *or* **-ise** *verb* **1** to give someone the power or right to do something. **2** to give permission for something. ▪ **authorization** *noun.* [14c: from French *autoriser*]

Authorized Version *noun* (abbrev **AV**) the English translation of the Bible that was first published in 1611 under the direction of King James VI and I. Also called **King James Bible**, **King James Version**.

authorship *noun* **1** the origin or originator of a particular piece of writing. **2** the profession of writing.

autism *noun, psychol* a mental disorder that develops in early childhood, characterized by learning difficulties and inability to relate to other people and the outside world. ▪ **autistic** *adj.* [Early 20c: from **auto-** + **-ism** (sense 5)]

auto *noun, N Am* a motor car. [19c: a shortened form of **automobile**]

auto- *or* (*before a vowel*) **aut-** *combining form* **1** self; same; by or of the same person or thing: *autobiography.* **2** self-acting: *automatic.* **3** self-induced. [From Greek *autos* self]

autobahn /ˈɔːtoʊbɑːn; *German* ˈɑʊtobaːn/ *noun* a motorway in Austria, Switzerland or Germany. [1930s: German *Auto* car + *Bahn* road]

autobiography *noun* (**-*ies***) someone's own account of their life. ▪ **autobiographer** *noun.* ▪ **autobiographical** *adj.* [18c: **auto-** (sense 1) + **biography**]

autoclave *noun* a strong steel container that can be made airtight and filled with pressurized steam in order to sterilize equipment, eg surgical instruments. [19c: from **auto-** (sense 1) + Latin *clavis* key or *clavus* nail]

autocracy *noun* (**-*ies***) **1** absolute government by one person; dictatorship. **2** the rule of such a person. **3** a country, state, society, etc that is governed by one person. [17c: from **auto-** (sense 1) + Greek *kratos* power]

autocrat *noun* **1** a ruler with absolute power. **2** an authoritarian person. ▪ **autocratic** *adj.* ▪ **autocratically** *adv.* [19c: from Greek *autokrates* absolute]

autocross *noun* a motor-racing sport for cars that takes place over a rough grass track. Compare **motocross**, **rallycross**.

Autocue *noun, trademark, TV* a screen hidden from the camera that slowly displays a script line by line, so that the newscaster or speaker can read the script.

auto-da-fé /ɔːtoʊdəˈfeɪ/ *noun* (***autos-da-fé***) **1** *hist* the ceremonial passing of sentence on heretics by the Spanish Inquisition. **2** the public burning of a heretic who had been sentenced by the Inquisition. [18c: Portuguese, meaning 'act of the faith']

autodidact /ɔːtoʊˈdaɪdakt/ *noun* someone who has taught himself or herself to do something. ▪ **autodidactic** /-ˈdaktɪk/ *adj.* [16c: from **auto-** (sense 1) + Greek *didaskein* to teach]

autogamy /ɔːˈtɒgəmɪ/ *noun, botany* in flowering plants: self-fertilization. ▪ **autogamic** /ɔːtoʊˈgamɪk/ *or* **autogamous** /ɔːˈtɒgəməs/ *adj.* [19c]

autogiro *or* **autogyro** /ɔːtoʊˈdʒaɪroʊ/ *noun* a type of aircraft with a propeller and rotor blades which are not mechanically powered but produce lift through being turned by the air when the aircraft is moving forwards. [1920s: from Greek *auto-* + Spanish *giro*, from Latin *gyrus* circle]

autograph *noun* someone's signature, esp that of a famous person. ▸ *verb* to sign (a photograph, book, poster, etc). [17c: from Greek *autographos* written with one's own hand]

autoimmunity *noun, physiol* the production by the body of antibodies that attack constituents of its own tissues, treating them as foreign material. ▪ **autoimmune** *adj.*

autolysis /ɔːˈtɒlɪsɪs/ *noun, biol* the breakdown of cells or tissues by enzymes produced within them. [20c]

automat *noun, N Am* an automatic vending machine.

automate *verb* to apply automation to (a technical process). [1950s: a back-formation from **automation**]

automatic *adj* **1** of a machine or device: capable of operating on its own and requiring little human control once it has been activated. **2** of an action: done without thinking; unconscious. **3** happening as a necessary result: *The gravity of the offence meant an automatic driving ban.* **4** of a firearm: able to reload itself and so fire continuously. Compare **semi-automatic**. **5** of a motor vehicle: having automatic transmission. ▸ *noun* **1** an automatic firearm. **2** a vehicle with automatic transmission. **3** a washing machine that operates automatically. ▪ **automatically** *adv.* [18c: from Greek *automatos* acting independently]

automatic pilot *or* **autopilot** *noun* an electronic control device that automatically steers a vehicle, esp an aircraft, space vehicle or ship.

IDIOMS **on automatic pilot** displaying automatic or involuntary actions or behaviour resulting from fatigue, boredom or abstraction.

automatic transmission *noun* in a motor vehicle: a system that allows the gears to be selected and engaged automatically in response to variations in speed, gradient, etc.

automation *noun* the use of automatic machinery in manufacturing and data-processing, so that entire procedures can be automatically controlled with minimal or no human intervention.

automaton *noun* (***automatons*** *or* ***automata***) **1** a machine or robot that has been programmed to perform specific actions in a manner imitative of a human or animal. **2** someone who acts like a machine, according to routine and without thinking. [17c: from Greek *automatos* acting independently]

automobile *noun, N Am* a motor car. [19c: French]

automotive *adj* **1** relating to motor vehicles. **2** self-propelling. [19c: from **auto-** (sense 1) + Latin *movere* to move]

autonomous *adj* **1** of a country, state, etc: self-governing. **2** independent of others. ▪ **autonomously** *adv.*

autonomy *noun* (***-ies***) **1** the power or right of self-government, administering one's own affairs, etc. **2** freedom from the intervention of others. **3** personal freedom or independence. [17c: from **auto-** (sense 1) + Greek *nomos* law]

autopilot see **automatic pilot**

autopsy *noun* (***-ies***) **1** a **postmortem**. **2** any dissection and analysis. [17c: from Greek *autopsia* seeing with one's own eyes]

autoroute *noun* in France and other French-speaking countries: a motorway. [1960s: French, meaning 'car road']

autosave *noun, comput* a computer program that causes newly recorded data to be automatically saved at regular intervals.

autostrada *noun* in Italy: a motorway. [1920s: Italian, meaning 'car road']

auto-suggestion *noun, psychol* a form of psychotherapy that involves repeating ideas to oneself in order to change attitudes or habits, eg to reduce anxiety. ▪ **auto-suggestive** *adj.*

autotrophic /ɔːtə'troʊfɪk/ *adj, biol* of an organism such as a plant: manufacturing complex organic compounds from simple inorganic substances such as carbon dioxide and nitrogen. ▪ **autotroph** *noun* an autotrophic organism. ▪ **autotrophism** *noun.* [20c: from Greek *trophe* food]

autumn *noun* **1** (*also* **Autumn**) the season of the year, between summer and winter, when leaves change colour and fall, and harvests ripen. *N Am equivalent* **fall**. **2** a period of maturity before decay. ▪ **autumnal** /ɔː'tʌmnəl/ *adj.* [14c: from Latin *autumnus*]

auxiliary *adj* **1** helping or supporting. **2** additional or extra. ▸ *noun* (***-ies***) **1** a helper. **2** (**auxiliaries**) foreign troops that help and support another nation that is engaged in a war. **3** *grammar* an **auxiliary verb**. [17c: from Latin *auxiliarius*]

auxiliary verb *noun, grammar* a verb, such as *be, do, have, can, shall, may* or *must,* used with other verbs (**lexical verbs**, such as *come, eat, sing* or *use*), to indicate **tense**[1], **mood**[2], **voice** (*noun* sense 9), etc, as in *I must go, you will go, they are going, they have been sent, I do not know.* See also **modal**.

AV *abbrev* **1** (*also* **av**) audiovisual. **2** Authorized Version (of the Bible).

av. *abbrev* **1** average. **2** avoirdupois.

avail *verb* **1** *tr & intr* to help or be of use. **2** (**avail oneself of sth**) to make use of it or take advantage of it. ▸ *noun* use; advantage. [14c: from French *valoir* to be worth]

available *adj* able or ready to be obtained or used. ▪ **availability** *noun.* ▪ **availably** *adv.*

avalanche *noun* **1** the rapid movement of a large mass of snow or ice down a mountain slope. **2** a sudden appearance or a large amount of something: *His book met with an avalanche of criticism.* [18c: French]

avant-garde /avɑ̃'gɑːd/ *noun* the writers, painters, musicians, etc whose ideas and techniques are considered the most modern or advanced of their time, regarded collectively. ▸ *adj* of a work of art, a piece of literature, a film, idea, movement, etc: characterized by daring modernity; innovative. [15c: French, meaning 'vanguard']

avarice /'avərɪs/ *noun* excessive desire for money, possessions, etc; greed. ▪ **avaricious** /avə'rɪʃəs/ *adj.* [14c: from Latin *avaritia*]

avatar *noun* **1** *Hinduism* the appearance of a god in human or animal form. **2** the visual manifestation of something abstract. [18c: from Sanskrit *ava* down + *tarati* he passes over]

Ave[1] *or* **Av.** *abbrev* used in addresses: Avenue.

Ave[2] /'ɑːvɪ/ *or* **Ave Maria** /mə'riːə/ *noun* (***Aves*** *or* ***Ave-Marias***) a prayer to the Virgin Mary. See also **hail Mary**. [13c: Latin, meaning 'Hail Mary', the opening words of the angel's greeting to Mary in Luke 1.28]

avenge *verb* to carry out some form of retribution for (some previous wrongdoing). ▪ **avenger** *noun.* [14c: from French *avengier*]

avenue *noun* **1 a** a broad road or street, often with trees along the sides; **b** (**Avenue**) a street title in an address. **2** a tree-lined approach to a house. **3** a means, way or approach. [17c: French]

aver *verb* (***averred, averring***) to state firmly and positively. [14c: from French *averer*]

average *noun* **1** the usual or typical amount, extent, quality, number, etc. **2** *stats* any number that is representative of a group of numbers or other data, esp the arithmetic mean, which is obtained by adding several amounts and dividing the total by the number of amounts. Same as **mean**[3] (sense 2a). Compare **median** (sense 3), **mode** (sense 5). ▸ *adj* **1** usual or ordinary. **2** estimated by taking an average. **3** mediocre: *gave a pretty average performance.* ▸ *verb* **1** to obtain the numerical average of (several numbers). **2** to amount to on average: *Her speed averaged 90mph on the motorway.* [15c: from Arabic *awariya* damaged goods]

IDIOMS **on average** usually; normally; typically.

PHRASAL VERBS **average out** to result in an average or balance.

averse *adj* (*always* **averse to sth**) reluctant about or opposed to it. [16c: from Latin *aversus*]

---

adverse, averse

Be careful not to use the word **averse** when you mean **adverse**. **Adverse** means unfavourable or hurtful:

All this worry will have an adverse effect on her health.

---

aversion *noun* **1** a strong dislike. **2** someone or something that is the object of strong dislike.

avert *verb* **1** to turn away: *avert one's eyes.* **2** to prevent (esp danger): *Quick reactions averted the accident.* [15c: from Latin *avertere*]

Avesta *noun* the holy scriptures of **Zoroastrianism**.

avian /ˈeɪvɪən/ *adj* belonging, relating or referring to birds. [19c: from Latin *avis* bird]

avian flu *or* **avian influenza** see **bird flu**

aviary *noun* (**-*ies***) a large enclosed area where birds are kept. ▪ **aviarist** *noun*. [16c: from Latin *aviarium*]

aviation *noun* **1** the science or practice of mechanical flight through the air, esp by powered aircraft. **2** the production, design and operation of aircraft. **3** the aircraft industry. [19c: from Latin *avis* bird]

aviator *noun, old use* an aircraft pilot.

avid *adj* very enthusiastic: *an avid filmgoer.* ▪ **avidity** *noun*. ▪ **avidly** *adv*. [18c: from Latin *avidus*]

avocado *noun* **1** a tropical evergreen tree of the laurel family, with a pear-shaped fruit. **2** the edible pear-shaped fruit of this tree, which has a rough thick greenish-brown skin and creamy flesh. Also called **avocado pear**. [17c: from Nahuatl *ahuacatl* testicle]

avocation *noun, old use* **1** a hobby. **2** *informal* someone's usual occupation. [17c: from Latin *avocatio*]

avocet /ˈavəsɛt/ *noun* any of various large wading birds with long legs and a long slender upward curving bill. [18c: from French *avocette*]

avoid *verb* **1** to keep away from (a place, person, action, etc). **2** to stop, prevent, manage not to do, or escape something. ▪ **avoidable** *adj*. ▪ **avoidably** *adv*. ▪ **avoidance** *noun*. [14c: from French *avoidier* to empty out]

avoirdupois /avwɑːdjʊˈpwɑː, avədəˈpɔɪz/ *noun* (abbrev **av.**) a system of units of mass based on a pound (0.45kg) consisting of 16 ounces, formerly widely used in English-speaking countries, but now increasingly replaced by SI units. ▶ *adj* referring or relating to this system of units. [14c: from French *aveir de peis* goods of weight]

avow *verb* to state openly; to declare or admit. ▪ **avowed** /əˈvaʊd/ *adj*. ▪ **avowedly** /əˈvaʊɪdlɪ/ *adv*. [13c: from Latin *advocare* to appeal to]

avuncular *adj* relating to or like an uncle, esp in having a kindly disposition. [19c: from Latin *avunculus* maternal uncle]

AWACS /ˈeɪwaks/ *abbrev* airborne warning and control system.

await *verb* **1** *formal* to wait for something. **2** to be in store for someone. [14c: from French *awaitier* to lie in wait for]

awake *verb* (***awoke, awoken***) *tr & intr* **1** to stop sleeping or cause to stop sleeping. **2** to become active or cause to become active. ▶ *adj* **1** not sleeping. **2** alert or aware. [Anglo-Saxon *awacian*]

awaken *verb, tr & intr* **1** to wake up. **2** to arouse (feelings, etc). **3** to stir or evoke: *The photo awakened happy memories.* [Anglo-Saxon *awacian*]

award *verb* (*always* **award sth to sb** *or* **award sb sth**) **1** to present or grant them it, esp in recognition of some achievement. **2** *law* to decide and declare (a right or claim to something): *The judge awarded custody to the father.* ▶ *noun* **1** a payment, prize, etc, esp one given in recognition of an achievement, etc. **2** a legal judgement granting something. [14c: from French *awarder*]

aware *adj* **1** (*often* **aware of sth** *or* **sb**) acquainted with or mindful of it or them. **2** (**aware that**) conscious that. **3** well informed: *These days everyone is more ecologically aware.*
▪ **awareness** *noun*. [Anglo-Saxon *gewær*]

awash *adj, adv, informal* covered or flooded with water.

away *adv* **1** from one place, position, person or time towards another; off. **2** in or to the usual or proper place: *put the books away.* **3** into the distance; into extinction: *fade away.* **4** apart; remote: *stay away from the bustle of the city.* **5** continuously; repeatedly; relentlessly: *talk away.* **6** aside; in another direction: *looked away.* **7** of a sporting event: on the opponent's ground. ▶ *adj* **1** not present; not at home. **2** distant: *not far away.* **3** of a sporting event: played on the opponent's ground: *away game.* ▶ *noun* a match played or won by a team playing on their opponent's ground. [Anglo-Saxon *aweg, onweg*]
IDIOMS **right** *or* **straight away** immediately.

awe *noun* admiration, fear and wonder. ▶ *verb* to fill with awe. [13c: from Norse *agi* fear]
IDIOMS **in awe of sb** *or* **sth** filled with admiration for them or it, but often slightly intimidated too.

aweigh *adv, naut* of an anchor: in the process of being raised from the bottom of the sea.

awe-inspiring *adj* **1** causing or deserving awe. **2** *informal* wonderful.

awesome *adj* **1** causing awe; dreaded. **2** *informal* completely and utterly wonderful.

awestruck *adj* filled with awe.

awful *adj* **1** *informal* very bad. **2** *informal* very great: *an awful shame.* **3** terrible or shocking. ▶ *adv, nonstandard* very: *I'm awful busy.* ▪ **awfully** *adv* **1** very badly. **2** very: *been awfully ill.* ▪ **awfulness** *noun*.

awhile *adv* for a short time. [Anglo-Saxon *æne hwil* a while]

awkward *adj* **1** clumsy and ungraceful. **2** embarrassed or embarrassing: *an awkward moment.* **3** difficult and dangerous: *Careful, it's an awkward turning.* **4** difficult or inconvenient to deal with. ▪ **awkwardly** *adv*. ▪ **awkwardness** *noun*. [14c, meaning 'turned the wrong way': from Norse *ofugr* turned the wrong way + **-ward**]

awl *noun* a pointed tool used for boring small holes, esp in leather. [Anglo-Saxon *æl*]

awn *noun, botany* in some grasses, eg barley: a small stiff bristle projecting from the lemma or glumes. ▪ **awned** *adj*. [14c: from Norse *ogn*]

awning *noun* a plastic or canvas covering over the entrance or window of a shop, etc, that can be extended to give shelter from the sun or rain. [17c: orig applied to this structure on the deck of a boat]

awoke, awoken see under **awake**

AWOL /ˈeɪwɒl/ *or* **A.W.O.L.** *abbrev* absent without leave, temporarily absent from one's place of duty, esp in the armed forces, without official permission.

awry *adj, adv* **1** twisted to one side. **2** wrong; amiss.

axe *or* (*N Am*) **ax** *noun* a hand-tool with a long handle and a heavy metal blade, used for cutting down trees, chopping wood, etc. ▶ *verb* **1** to get rid of, dismiss or put a stop to something: *30 jobs were axed.* **2** to reduce (costs, services, etc). [Anglo-Saxon *æcs*]
IDIOMS **have an axe to grind** to have a personal, often selfish, reason for being involved in something.

axes *pl of* **axe**, **axis**

axial *adj* relating to, forming or placed along an axis. ▪ **axially** *adv*.

axil *noun, botany* the angle between the upper surface of a leaf or stem and the stem or branch from which it grows. [18c: from Latin *axilla* armpit]

axiom *noun* **1** a proposition, fact, principle, etc which, because it is long-established, is generally accepted as true. **2** a self-evident statement. [15c: from Greek *axios* worthy]

axiomatic *or* **axiomatical** *adj* **1** obvious; self-evident. **2** containing or based on axioms.

axis *noun* (***axes*** /ˈaksiːz/) **1** an imaginary straight line around which an object, eg a planet, rotates. **2** (*also* **axis of symmetry**) an imaginary line through a figure on which the opposite sides are symmetrical. **3** *geom* one of the lines of reference used to specify the position of points on a graph, eg the horizontal *x*-axis and vertical *y*-axis in **co-ordinates**. **4** (**Axis**) *hist* the political alliance made in 1936 between Germany and Italy. ▪ **axial** *adj*. ▪ **axially** *adv*. [16c: from Latin *axis* axletree, the Earth's axis]

axle *noun* a fixed or rotating rod designed to carry a wheel or one or more pairs of wheels which may be attached to it, driven by it, or rotate freely on it. [16c: from Norse *oxul*]

ayah *noun, formerly* in India and other parts of the British Empire: a governess, lady's maid or children's nurse, esp one who is of Asian origin. [18c: from Hindi *aya*]

ayatollah *or* **Ayatollah** *noun* **1** in the hierarchy of Shiite religious leaders in Iran: someone who can demonstrate a highly advanced knowledge of the Islamic religion and laws. **2** any dictatorial or influential person. [1950s: from Arabic *ayatullah* miraculous sign of God]

aye *or* **ay** *adv, chiefly dialect* yes. ▸ *noun* **1** a vote in favour of something, esp in the House of Commons. **2** someone who votes in favour of something. Opposite of **nay**.

ayurveda /ˈɑːjʊveɪdə/ *noun, Hinduism* an ancient system of Hindu medicine, still widely practised in India, involving numerous forms of treatment, eg herbal remedies, fasting, bathing, enemas, massage, prayers and yoga. ▪ **ayurvedic** *adj*. [Early 20c: Sanskrit, from *ayur* life + *veda* knowledge]

azalea /əˈzeɪljə/ *noun* **1** a deciduous shrub with large clusters of funnel-shaped flowers. **2** the flower of this plant. [18c: from Greek *azaleos* dry, because it is supposed to prefer drier soil conditions]

Azerbaijani *adj* belonging or relating to Azerbaijan, its inhabitants, or their language. ▸ *noun* **1** a citizen or inhabitant of, or person born in, Azerbaijan. **2** the language spoken in Azerbaijan.

azimuth *noun* in astronomy and surveying: the bearing of an object, eg a planet or star, measured in degrees as the angle around the observer's horizon clockwise from north, which is the zero point. [14c: from Arabic *al* the + *sumut* directions]

Aztec *noun* **1** a group of Mexican Indian peoples whose great empire was overthrown by the Spanish in the 16c. **2** an individual belonging to this group of peoples. **3** their language. Also called **Nahuatl**. ▸ *adj* belonging or referring to this group or their language. ▪ **Aztecan** *adj*. [18c: from Nahuatl *Aztecatl*]

azure *adj* deep sky-blue in colour. ▸ *noun* **1** a deep sky-blue colour. **2** *poetic* the sky. [14c: from Persian *lajward* lapis lazuli]

B[1] *or* **b** *noun* (***Bs, B's*** *or* ***b's***) **1** the second letter of the English alphabet. **2** (*usu* **B**) the second highest grade or quality, or a mark indicating this. **3** (**B**) *music* the seventh note on the scale of C major.

B[2] *abbrev* on pencils: black.

B[3] *symbol* **1** *chess* bishop. **2** *chem* boron. **3** *physics* bel.

b. *abbrev* **1** born. **2** *cricket* bowled.

BA *abbrev* Bachelor of Arts.

Ba *symbol, chem* barium.

baa *noun* the cry of a sheep or lamb. ► *verb, intr* to make this cry; to bleat. [16c: imitating the sound]

baba *or* **rum baba** *noun* a type of small sponge cake soaked in a rum-flavoured syrup. [19c: French, from Polish, meaning 'old woman']

babble *verb* **1** *tr & intr* to talk or say something quickly, esp in a way that is hard to understand. **2** *intr, informal* to talk foolishly. **3** *intr, formal, literary* of a stream, etc: to make a low murmuring sound. **4** to give away (a secret) carelessly. ▪ **babbling** *adj.* [13c: prob imitating the sound]

babe *noun* **1** *informal* (often used as a term of affection) a girl or young woman. **2** *literary & old use* a baby. [14c]

babel /ˈbeɪbəl/ *noun* **1** a confused sound of voices. **2** a scene of noise and confusion. [17c: from Hebrew]

baboon *noun* any of various large ground-dwelling monkeys, which have a long dog-like muzzle, large teeth and a long tail. [14c: from French *babuin*]

baby *noun* (***-ies***) **1** a newborn or very young child or animal. **2** an unborn child. **3** the youngest member of a group. **4** *derog* a childish person. **5** *informal* a person's own particular project, etc. **6** *informal, esp N Am* a term of affection for a girl or woman. ► *verb* (***-ies, -ied***) to treat someone as a baby. ▪ **babyhood** *noun.* ▪ **babyish** *adj.* [14c: prob imitating the sound a baby makes]

IDIOMS **be left holding the baby** *informal* to be left with the responsibility for something.

Babylonian *noun* an inhabitant of Babylon, a city in ancient Mesopotamia. ► *adj* relating to Babylon or its citizens.

baby-sit *verb, tr & intr* to look after a child, usu in its own home, while the parents are out. ▪ **baby-sitter** *noun.* ▪ **baby-sitting** *noun.* [20c]

baccalaureate /bakəˈlɔːrɪət/ *noun* **1** *formal* a Bachelor's degree (see **bachelor** sense 2). **2** a diploma of a lower status than a degree. [17c: from Latin *baccalaureus* bachelor]

baccarat /ˈbakərɑː/ *noun* a card game in which players bet money against the banker. [19c: French]

bacchanalia /bakəˈneɪlɪə/ *plural noun* drunken celebrations; orgies. ▪ **bacchanalian** *adj.* [17c: Latin, meaning 'feasts in honour of Bacchus', the god of wine and pleasure in ancient Greece and Rome]

baccy *noun* (***-ies***) *informal* tobacco. [18c]

bachelor *noun* **1** an unmarried man. **2** (**Bachelor**) a person who has taken a first university degree: *Bachelor of Arts/Science*. See also **master** (*noun* sense 7). ▪ **bachelorhood** *noun.* [13c: from French *bacheler* a young man aspiring to knighthood]

---

bachelor

This word is often misspelt. It has no *t* in the middle. It might help you to remember that the word b**ache**lor contains the word **ache**.

---

bacillus /bəˈsɪləs/ *noun* (***bacilli*** /-laɪ/) *biol* any of a large group of rod-shaped bacteria including many species that cause food spoilage and serious diseases. [19c: Latin, meaning 'little stick']

back *noun* **1 a** the rear part of the human body from the neck to the base of the spine; **b** the spinal column itself. **2** the upper part of an animal's body. **3** the part of an object that is opposite to or furthest from the front: *The back of the house faces north.* **4** the side of an object that is not normally seen or used. **5** the upright part of a chair. **6** *sport* a player whose usual position is behind the forwards, and who in most sports is a defender, but who (eg in rugby) may also attack. Compare **forward** (*noun*). ► *adj* **1** located or situated behind or at the back: *through the back door.* **2** concerning, belonging to or from an earlier date: *back pay.* **3** away from or behind something, esp something more important: *back roads.* ► *adv* **1** to or towards the rear; away from the front. **2** in or into an original position or condition: *when I get back from holiday.* **3** in return or in response: *hit back.* **4** in or into the past: *look back to happier days.* ► *verb* **1** to help or support someone or something, usu with money. **2** *tr & intr* (*usu* **back away**, **out** *or* **out of sth**, *or* **back up**) to move or cause something to move backwards, away from or out of something. **3** to bet on the success of (a horse, etc). **4** (*sometimes* **back sb** *or* **sth up**) to provide a back or support for them. **5** to accompany (a singer) with music. **6** to lie at the back of something. **7** *intr, naut* of the wind: to change direction anticlockwise. Compare **veer. 8** to countersign or endorse (eg a cheque). [Anglo-Saxon *bæc*]

IDIOMS **back to front 1** with the back where the front should be. **2** in the wrong order. **have one's back to the wall** *informal* to be in a very difficult or desperate situation. **put sb's back up** *informal* to make them annoyed or resentful.

PHRASAL VERBS **back down** to concede an argument or claim, esp under pressure or opposition. **back off 1** to move backwards or retreat. **2** to back down. **back onto sth** of a building, etc: to have its back next to or facing it. **back out of sth** to withdraw from (a promise or agreement, etc). **back sb up** to support or assist them. **back sth up** to copy (computer data) onto a disk or tape. See also **backup**.

backbench *noun* a seat in the House of Commons for members who do not hold an official position either in the government or in the opposition. *as adj*: *backbench spokesperson.* ▪ **backbencher** *noun*. Compare **cross bench**, **front bench**.

backbite *verb, intr, informal* to speak unkindly about someone who is absent. ▪ **backbiting** *noun*. [12c]

backbone *noun* **1** the spine. **2** in both physical and abstract senses: the main support of something: *the backbone of a company.* **3** strength of character. [13c]

backbreaking *adj* of a task, etc: extremely hard or tiring.

back burner *noun* the rear burner on a stove.

IDIOMS **keep** *or* **put sth on the back burner** to set it aside or keep it in reserve for later consideration or action.

backchat *noun, Brit* impertinent or rude replies, esp to a superior. [20c: orig military slang]

backcloth *or* **backdrop** *noun* **1** the painted cloth at the back of a stage, forming part of the scenery. **2** the background to any situation, activity, etc.

backcomb *verb* to comb (the hair) towards the roots to make it look thicker.

back-cross *noun, genetics* a cross between a hybrid and a parent. [20c]

backdate *verb* **1** to put a date on (a document, etc) that is earlier than the actual date. **2** to make (something) effective from a date in the past.

backdoor *adj* applied to an activity done secretly and often dishonestly: *a backdoor deal.* ▸ *noun* (*usu* **the back door**) a clandestine or illicit means of achieving an objective: *got into power by the back door.* [16c]

backer *noun* a person who gives financial support to a project, etc.

backfire *verb, intr* **1** of an engine or vehicle: to make a loud bang as the result of an explosion of accumulated unburnt or partially burned gases in the exhaust or inlet system. **2** of a plan, etc: to go wrong and have a bad effect on the person who originated it. [20c]

backgammon *noun* a board game for two people, with pieces moved according to the throws of a dice. [17c: from **back** + *gamen* game]

background *noun* **1** the space behind the main figures of a picture. **2** the events or circumstances that precede and help to explain an event, etc. **3** a person's social origins or education, etc. **4** a less noticeable or less public position: *prefers to stay in the background.* [17c]

background radiation *noun, physics, astron* naturally occurring radiation detectable anywhere on the Earth.

backhand *noun, tennis, squash, etc* a stroke made with the back of the hand turned towards the ball. Compare **forehand**.

backhanded *adj* **1** *tennis* of a stroke: made with or as a backhand. **2** of a compliment: ambiguous or doubtful in effect.

backhander *noun* **1** *tennis* a backhand stroke of a ball. **2** *informal* a bribe. [17c]

backing *noun* **1** support, esp financial support. **2** material, etc that supports the back of something. **3** music accompanying a singer. *as adj*: *backing group.*

backing store *noun, comput* a large-capacity computer data store supplementary to a computer's main memory.

backlash *noun* **1** a sudden violent reaction to an action or situation, etc. **2** a jarring or recoil between parts of a machine that do not fit together properly.

backlog *noun* a pile or amount of uncompleted work, etc. [20c]

backpack *noun* a rucksack. ▸ *verb, intr* to travel about carrying one's belongings in a pack on one's back. ▪ **backpacker** *noun*. ▪ **backpacking** *noun*. [20c]

back-pedal *verb, intr* **1** to turn the pedals on a bicycle backwards. **2** to withdraw rapidly or suddenly from one's previous opinion or course of action.

back room *noun* a place where secret work or activity takes place. ▸ *adj* (*usu* **backroom**) applied to important work done secretly behind the scenes, or to someone who does such work: *backroom boys.*

back seat *noun* an inferior or unimportant position.

back-seat driver *noun, derog* a person, esp a passenger in a car, who gives unwanted advice.

backside *noun, informal* the buttocks. [16c]

backslide *verb, intr* to relapse into former bad behaviour, habits, etc. ▪ **backslider** *noun*. [16c]

backspace *verb, intr* to move the carriage of a typewriter, or a computer cursor, back one or more spaces.

backspin *noun, sport* the spinning of a ball in the opposite direction to the way it is travelling, which reduces its speed when it hits a surface. See also **topspin**.

backstabbing *noun* behaving treacherously towards someone with whom one pretends to be friendly. ▪ **backstabber** *noun*.

backstage *adv* behind a theatre stage. ▸ *adj* not seen by the public.

backstreet *noun* a street away from a town's main streets. ▸ *adj* secret or illicit; going on or carried out in, or as if in, a backstreet.

backstroke *noun* a swimming stroke performed on the back, with the arms raised alternately in a backward circular motion. [17c, meaning 'a return stroke or blow']

backtrack *verb, intr* **1** to return in the direction from which one came. **2** to reverse one's previous opinion or course of action. [20c: orig US]

backup *noun* **1** support; assistance. **2** *comput* **a** a procedure for copying data onto a disk or tape for security purposes; **b** a copy made by this procedure.

backward *adj* **1** directed behind or towards the back. **2** less advanced than normal in mental, physical or intellectual development. **3** reluctant or shy. ▸ *adv* backwards. [13c: orig a variant of *abackward*]

backwards *or sometimes* **backward** *adv* **1** towards the back or rear. **2** with one's back facing the direction of movement. **3** in reverse order: *counting backwards.* **4** in or into a worse state: *felt her career going backwards.* [16c: from **backward**]

IDIOMS **bend over backwards** *informal* to try extremely hard to please or accommodate someone.

backwash *noun* **1** a backward current, such as one caused by an outgoing wave. Compare **swash**. **2** a repercussion.

backwater *noun* **1** a pool of stagnant water connected to a river. **2** *derog* an isolated place, not affected by what is happening elsewhere.

backyard *noun* **1** *Brit* a yard at the back of a house. **2** *N Am* a garden at the rear of a house.

bacon *noun* meat from the back and sides of a pig, usu salted or smoked. [14c: French]

IDIOMS **bring home the bacon** *informal* **1** to earn enough money to support a household. **2** to accomplish a task successfully. **save sb's bacon** *informal* to rescue them from a difficult situation.

bacteria *plural noun* (*sing* ***bacterium***) *biol* an extremely diverse group of microscopic organisms that occur in water, soil, and air, including many that can cause decay, fermentation, and a number of diseases. ▪ **bacterial** *adj.* [19c: from Greek *bakterion* little stick]

bacteriology *noun* the scientific study of bacteria and their effects. ▪ **bacteriologist** *noun.* [19c]

bacteriophage /bak'tɪərɪoʊfeɪdʒ/ *noun* any of numerous viruses that infect bacteria. Often shortened to **phage**. [1920s: from Greek *phagein* to eat]

Bactrian camel *noun* a camel with two humps, native to central Asia. Compare **dromedary**. [17c: from Bactria, an ancient country forming part of modern Afghanistan]

bad *adj* (***worse, worst***) **1** not good. **2** wicked; immoral. **3** naughty. **4** (**bad at sth**) not skilled or clever (at some activity). **5** (**bad for sb**) harmful to them. **6** unpleasant; unwelcome. **7** rotten; decayed. **8** serious; severe: *a bad cold.* **9** unhealthy; injured; painful: *a bad leg.* **10** sorry, upset or ashamed. **11** not valid; worthless: *a bad cheque.* **12** (***badder, baddest***) *US slang* very good. ▸ *adv, N Am informal* badly; greatly; hard: *needs the money bad.* ▸ *noun* **1** evil; badness. **2** unpleasant events. ▪ **badness** *noun.* [13c]

IDIOMS **not bad** *informal* quite good. **not half bad** *informal* very good. **too bad** *informal* unfortunate (often used to dismiss a problem or unsatisfactory situation that cannot, or will not, be put right): *She's still not happy with it, but that's just too bad.*

bad blood *or* **bad feeling** *noun* angry or bitter feelings.

baddy *noun* (***-ies***) *informal* a criminal or villain, esp one in a film or book, etc.

bade *past tense of* **bid**[2]

badge *noun* **1** a small emblem or mark worn to show rank, membership of a society, etc. **2** any distinguishing feature or mark. [14c as *bage*: orig a knight's emblem]

badger *noun* a stocky burrowing mammal with black and white stripes on its head. ▸ *verb* to pester someone. [16c]

badinage /'badɪnɑːʒ/ *noun* playful bantering talk. [17c: French, from *badiner* to jest]

bad language *noun* coarse words and swearing.

badly *adv* (***worse, worst***) **1** poorly; inefficiently. **2** unfavourably: *came off badly in the review.* **3** extremely; severely: *badly in arrears with the rent.*

IDIOMS **badly off** poor; hard up.

badminton *noun* a game played with rackets and a **shuttlecock** which is hit across a high net. [19c: named after Badminton House in SW England, where it was first played]

badmouth *verb, informal, esp N Am* to criticize or malign someone or something. [20c]

bad news *noun, slang* a troublesome or irritating person or thing.

bad-tempered *adj* easily annoyed or made angry.

baffle *verb* to confuse or puzzle. ▸ *noun* a device for controlling the flow of gas, liquid or sound through an opening. ▪ **bafflement** *adj.* ▪ **baffling** *adj.* [16c: perhaps related to French *befe* mockery]

BAFTA /'baftə/ *noun* British Academy of Film and Television Arts.

bag *noun* **1** a container made of a soft material with an opening at the top, for carrying things. **2** a **bagful**. **3** a **handbag**. **4** an amount of fish or game caught. **5** (**bags**, *esp* **bags of sth**) *informal* a large amount of it. **6** *offensive informal* a woman, esp an unpleasant or ugly one. **7** (**bags**) loose wide-legged trousers. **8** *slang* a quantity of drugs, esp heroin, in a paper or other container. ▸ *verb* (***bagged, bagging***) **1** *tr & intr* (*also* **bag sth up**) to put (something) into a bag. **2** to kill (game): *bagged six pheasants.* **3** *informal* to obtain or reserve (a seat, etc). **4** *tr & intr* esp of clothes: to hang loosely or bulge. [13c]

IDIOMS **bag and baggage** completely: *clear out bag and baggage.* **bags I** *or* **bags** *or* **bagsy** *children's slang* I want to do or have, etc (the thing specified); I lay claim to it: *Bags I sit in the front.* **in the bag** *informal* as good as secured or done.

bagatelle *noun* **1** a game played on a board with holes into which balls are rolled. **2** an unimportant thing. **3** a short piece of light music. [17c: French]

bagel *or* **beigel** /'beɪgəl/ *noun* a hard, ring-shaped bread roll. [20c: from Yiddish *beygel*]

bagful *noun* the amount a bag can hold.

baggage *noun* (*pl*, in sense 2 only, ***baggages***) **1** a traveller's luggage. **2** *usu humorous, informal* an annoying or unpleasant woman. **3** the portable equipment of an army. [15c: from French *bagage* luggage]

baggy *adj* (***-ier, -iest***) hanging loose or bulging.

bag lady *noun* a homeless woman who carries her belongings around in carrier bags.

bagpipes *plural noun* a wind instrument consisting of a bag into which air is blown through a reed pipe (the **chanter**) by means of which the melody is also created.

baguette /ba'gɛt/ *noun* a long narrow French loaf. [French]

bah *exclam* expressing displeasure, scorn or disgust.

bail[1] *noun* **1** the temporary release of a person awaiting trial, secured by the payment of money and/or the imposition of special conditions. **2** money required as security for such a release. ▸ *verb* (*usu* **bail sb out**) **1** to provide bail for them. **2** *informal* to help them out of difficulties, esp by lending them money. [14c: French, meaning 'custody']

IDIOMS **forfeit bail** *or informal* **jump bail** to fail to return for trial after being released on bail. **on bail** of a person: released once bail money has been given to the court. **put up** *or* **stand** *or* **go bail** to provide bail for a prisoner.

bail[2] *or* **bale** *verb* (*usu* **bail out** *or* **bale out**) **1** *tr & intr* to remove (water) from a boat with a bucket or scoop. **2** *intr* to escape from an aeroplane by jumping out. [17c: from French *baille* bucket]

bail[3] *noun* (*usu* **bails**) *cricket* one of the cross-pieces laid on top of the stumps (see **stump** *noun* sense 3).

bail[4] *noun* on a typewriter or printer, etc: a hinged bar that holds the paper against the **platen**.

bailey *noun* the courtyard or outer wall of a castle. [13c: from French *baille* enclosure]

Bailey bridge *noun* a temporary bridge that can be assembled rapidly from prefabricated pieces of welded steel. [20c: designed by Sir Donald Bailey]

bailiff *noun* **1** an officer of a lawcourt, esp one with the power to seize the property of a person who has not paid money owed to the court. **2** a person who looks after property for its owner. [13c: from French *baillier*]

bailiwick *noun, now often slightly facetious* one's area of jurisdiction. [15c, orig meaning 'a bailiff's area of jurisdiction']

bain-marie /*French* bɛ̃mariː/ *noun* (***bain-maries***) *cookery* a pan filled with hot water in which a container of food can be cooked gently or kept warm. [19c: French, literally 'bath of Mary', from medieval Latin *balneum Mariae*, 'Maria' being the name of an alleged alchemist]

bairn *noun, dialect* a child. [Anglo-Saxon]

bait *noun* **1** food put on a hook or in a trap to attract fish or animals. **2** anything intended to attract or tempt. ▸ *verb* **1** to put food on or in (a hook or trap). **2** to harass or tease (a person or animal) wilfully. **3** to set dogs on (another animal, eg a badger). ▪ **baiting** *noun, esp in compounds*: *bear-baiting*. [13c: from Norse *beita* to make something bite]

bated, baited

Be careful not to use the spelling **baited** when you mean **bated**:

I waited with bated breath for the winner to be announced.

baize *noun* a woollen cloth, usu green and used as a covering on snooker and card tables, etc. [16c: from French *baies*, from Latin *badius* chestnut-coloured]

bake *verb* **1** *tr & intr* to cook (cakes, bread, vegetables, etc) using dry heat in an oven. **2** *tr & intr* to dry or harden by heat from the sun or a fire. **3** *intr, informal* to be extremely hot. [Anglo-Saxon *bacan*]

baked beans *plural noun* haricot beans baked in tomato sauce and usu tinned.

Bakelite /'beɪkəlaɪt/ *noun, trademark* a type of hard plastic formerly used to make dishes, buttons, etc. [20c: named after L H Baekeland, its inventor]

baker *noun* a person who bakes or sells bread and cakes, etc, esp as their profession.

baker's dozen *noun* thirteen. [16c: the term derives from the practice common among bakers in medieval times of supplying an extra loaf or roll with every batch of twelve]

bakery *noun* (***-ies***) a place where bread, cakes, etc are made or sold.

baking powder *or* **baking soda** see under **bicarbonate of soda**

baksheesh *noun* in some Eastern countries: money given as a tip or present. [18c: from Persian *bakshish*]

balaclava *or* **balaclava helmet** *noun* a knitted hat that covers the head and neck, with an opening for the face. [19c: from *Balaklava* in the Crimea]

balalaika /balə'laɪkə/ *noun* a Russian musical instrument with a triangular body and normally three strings. [18c: Russian]

balance *noun* **1** a state of physical stability in which the weight of a body is evenly distributed. **2** an instrument for weighing. **3** the amount by which the two sides of a financial account (money spent and money received) differ. **4** an amount left over. **5** a state of mental or emotional stability. **6** a state existing when two opposite forces are equal. **7** something that is needed to create such equality. **8** a device that regulates the speed of a clock or watch. ▸ *verb* **1** *tr & intr* to be in, or put (something) into, a state of physical balance. **2** (*often* **balance sth against sth else**) to compare two or more things in one's mind; to compare their respective advantages and disadvantages. **3** to find the difference between money put into an account and money taken out of it, and to make them equal: *balance the books*. **4** *intr* (*also* **balance out**) to be or become equal in amount. ▪ **balanced** *adj*. [14c as *noun* sense 2: from Latin *bilanx* having two scales]

IDIOMS **in the balance** not yet decided. **on balance** having taken all the advantages and disadvantages into consideration.

balance of payments *noun, econ* the difference in value between the amount of money coming into a country and the amount going out of it.

balance of trade *noun, econ* the difference in value of a country's imports and exports.

balance sheet *noun* a summary and balance of financial accounts.

balcony *noun* (***-ies***) **1** a platform surrounded by a wall or railing, projecting from the wall of a building. **2** an upper tier in a theatre or cinema. [17c: from Italian *balcone*]

bald *adj* **1** of a person: having little or no hair on their head. **2** of birds or animals: **a** not having any feather or fur; **b** having white markings on the face. **3** bare or plain: *the bald truth*. ▪ **balding** *adj* becoming bald. ▪ **baldly** *adv*. ▪ **baldness** *noun*. [14c: perhaps from *balled* rounded]

baldacchino /bɔːldə'kiːnoʊ/, **baldachin** *or* **baldaquin** /-kɪn/ *noun* **1** a canopy, especially one supported at each corner by a pole and carried over a sacred object in a religious procession, or placed over a throne, altar or pulpit. **2** *archit* esp over the high altar in a baroque church: a fixed structure with a canopy supported at each corner by a column. [16c: from Italian *baldacchino*, from *Baldacco* Baghdad, where the silk used for such canopies originally came from]

bald eagle *noun* a large white-headed N American eagle, the national emblem of the USA.

balderdash *noun, dated* nonsense. [16c]

bale[1] *noun* a large tied bundle of a commodity such as hay or cloth. ▸ *verb* to make (hay, etc) into bales. [14c: French]

bale[2] see **bail**[2]

baleen *noun* whalebone. [14c: from Latin *balaena* whale]

baleen whale *noun* any of various whales that have strips of whalebone in their mouths to enable them to strain **krill** from the water.

baleful *adj* **1** evil; harmful. **2** threatening; gloomy. ▪ **balefully** *adv.* [Anglo-Saxon *bealufull*, from *bealu* evil]

balk *or* **baulk** *verb* **1** *intr* (*usu* **balk at sth**) to hesitate, or refuse to go on, because of some obstacle. **2** to check or block. ▸ *noun, snooker, etc* the part of the table behind a line (called the **balk line**) near one end, from within which the start and restarts are made. [14c: from Anglo-Saxon *balca* ridge]

Balkan *adj* belonging or relating to the peninsula in SE Europe (called the **Balkans**) which is surrounded by the Adriatic, Aegean and Black seas, or to its peoples or its countries. [19c]

ball[1] *noun* **1** a round or roundish object used in some sports. **2** anything round or nearly round in shape: *a ball of wool.* **3** the act of throwing a ball, or the way a ball is thrown. **4** a rounded fleshy part of the body: *the ball of the foot.* ▸ *verb, tr & intr* to form or gather into a ball. [13c: from Norse *böllr*]

IDIOMS **have the ball at one's feet** to have the opportunity to do something. **on the ball** *informal* well-informed; alert. **play ball** *informal* to co-operate. **start** *or* **set** *or* **keep the ball rolling** to begin or continue an activity, conversation, etc.

ball[2] *noun* **1** a formal social meeting for dancing. **2** *informal* an enjoyable time: *We had a ball.* [17c: from French *bal*]

ballad *noun* **1** a slow, usu romantic song. **2** a poem or song with short verses, which tells a popular story. [15c: from Provençal *balada* dance]

ballade /baˈlɑːd/ *noun* **1** a poem consisting of verses grouped in threes, with a repeated refrain and a short concluding verse. **2** *music* a short lyrical piece for piano. [14c: an earlier form of **ballad**]

ballast *noun* **1** heavy material used to keep a ship steady or to weigh down and stabilize a hot-air balloon. **2** broken rocks or stones used as a base for roads and railway lines. **3** anything used to give a steadying influence, or lend weight or stability. [16c]

ball-bearing *noun* **1** an arrangement of small steel balls between the moving parts of some machines, to help reduce friction. **2** one of these balls.

ball-boy *or* **ball-girl** *noun, sport* a boy or girl who collects balls that go out of play, supplies balls to the players, etc.

ballcock *noun* a floating ball that rises and falls with the water level in a tank or cistern and, by means of a hinged rod to which it is attached, operates a valve controlling the inflow of water. [18c]

ballerina *noun* a female ballet-dancer. [18c: Italian, from *ballare* to dance]

ballet *noun* **1** a classical style of dancing and mime, using set steps and body movements. **2** a single performance or work in this style. ▪ **balletic** *adj.* [17c: French, diminutive of *bal* dance]

ball game *noun* **1 a** a game played with a ball; **b** *N Am* a baseball game. **2** *informal* a situation or state of affairs: *a whole new ball game.*

ballistic *adj* **1** referring or relating to projectiles: *ballistic weapons.* **2** operating under the force of gravity. [18c: from Latin *ballista* a military machine for throwing rocks at buildings, etc]

IDIOMS **go ballistic** *slang* of a person: to fly into a rage; to lose control.

ballistic missile *noun* a type of missile which is initially guided but drops on its target under the force of gravity.

ballistics *singular noun* the scientific study of the movement, behaviour and effects of projectiles. [18c]

balloon *noun* **1** a small rubber pouch with a neck, that can be inflated with air or gas and used as a toy or decoration, etc. **2** a large bag made of light material and filled with a light gas or hot air, designed to float in the air carrying people, weather-recording instruments, etc in a basket underneath. **3** a balloon-shaped outline containing the words or thoughts of a character in a cartoon. ▸ *verb* **1** *intr* to travel by balloon. **2** *intr* to increase dramatically: *Food prices ballooned this spring.* ▪ **balloonist** *noun.* [16c: from Italian *ballone*]

ballot *noun* **1 a** a method or system of voting, usu in secret, by putting a marked paper into a box or other container; **b** an act or occasion of voting by this system. **2** the total number of votes recorded in an election: *The ballot supported the management.* ▸ *verb* **1** to take the vote or ballot of (a group of people). **2** *intr* (*esp* **ballot for sth**) to vote by ballot (in favour of it). [16c: from Italian *ballotta* little ball]

ball park *noun, orig US* **1** a baseball field. **2** a sphere of activity. ▸ *adj* (*usu* **ballpark**) approximate: *ballpark figures.*

IDIOMS **in the right ballpark** approximately correct or relevant.

ballpoint *or* **ballpoint pen** *noun* a pen that has a tiny ball as the writing point.

ballroom *noun* a large room with a spacious dance floor, in which balls (see **ball[2]**) are held.

ballroom dancing *noun* a formal kind of social dancing, in which couples dance to music with a strict rhythm.

bally *adj, adv, dated Brit informal* a mild form of **bloody**, but almost meaningless. [19c]

ballyhoo *noun, informal* **1** a noisy confused situation. **2** noisy or sensational publicity or advertising. [20c]

balm *noun* **1** an oil obtained from certain types of trees, having a pleasant smell and used in healing or reducing pain. **2** a fragrant and healing ointment. **3 a** an aromatic plant, esp one of the mint family; **b** (*also* **lemon balm**) a plant with an aroma similar to that of lemon. **4** something comforting to either the body or the spirit. [14c: from French *basme*]

balmy *adj* (**-ier, -iest**) of the air: warm and soft.

baloney *or* **boloney** *noun, slang* nonsense. ▸ *exclam* nonsense! [20c: perhaps from the *Bologna* sausage]

balsa /ˈbɔːlsə/ *noun* **1** a tropical American tree. **2** (*also* **balsa-wood**) the very lightweight wood of this tree. [18c: from Spanish, meaning 'raft']

balsam *noun* **1** a pleasant-smelling thick sticky substance obtained from some trees and plants, used to make medicines and perfumes. **2** a tree or plant from which this substance is obtained. **3** an aromatic, sticky or oily ointment, or similar healing and soothing preparation made from this substance. ▪ **balsamic** *adj.* [Anglo-Saxon: from Greek *balsamon*]

balsamic vinegar *noun, cookery* a rich-flavoured, dark Italian vinegar matured in wooden barrels.

balti /ˈbɔːltɪ/ *noun* in Indian cookery: a style of curry in which the food is cooked in a two-handled wok-like dish. [20c: Hindi, meaning 'bucket' or 'scoop']

Baltic *adj* belonging or relating to the sea between Scandinavia and the rest of NE Europe, or the states bordering it. [16c: from Latin *Balticus*]

baluster *noun* any one of a series of posts or pillars supporting a rail. [17c: from French *balustre*]

balustrade *noun* a row of posts or pillars, joined by a rail, on the edge of a balcony, staircase, bridge, etc. [17c: French, from *balustre* **baluster**]

bamboo *noun* **1** a tall tropical grass with hollow stems. **2** the stems of this grass, used in furniture-making, etc and as a garden cane. [16c: prob from Malay *bambu*]

bamboozle *verb, informal* **1** to cheat (someone). **2** to confuse (someone). ▪ **bamboozlement** *noun*. [18c]

ban *noun* an official order stating that something is not allowed. ▸ *verb* (***banned, banning***) **1** to forbid (something). **2** to forbid (someone) from going somewhere or doing something, esp officially or formally: *ban you from driving*. [Anglo-Saxon *bannan*]

banal /bəˈnɑːl/ *adj* lacking in interest or originality. ▪ **banality** /bəˈnalɪtɪ/ *noun* (***-ies***). [18c: French]

banana *noun* **1** a large SE Asian tree-like plant, that is cultivated throughout the tropics as a staple food crop. **2** the long curved fruit of this plant. [16c: from the native name in Guinea]

band[1] *noun* **1** a flat narrow strip of cloth, metal, paper, etc used to hold things together or as a decoration. **2** a stripe of colour or strip of material differing from its background or surroundings. **3** a belt for driving machinery. **4** a group or range of radio frequencies between two limits. **5** a range of values between two limits. ▸ *verb* to fasten or mark (something) with a band. [12c: from French *bande*]

band[2] *noun* **1** a group of people with a common purpose or interest. **2** a group of musicians who play music other than classical music. ▸ *verb* (*usu* **band (sb) together**) to act as a group, or to organize (people) to act as a group or to work for a common purpose. [15c: from French *bande*]

bandage *noun* a strip of cloth for winding round a wound or an injured limb. ▸ *verb* to wrap (esp a wound or an injured limb) in a bandage. [16c: French]

Band-aid *noun, trademark, esp N Am* a type of sticking-plaster with attached dressing, for covering minor wounds. *Brit equivalent* **Elastoplast, plaster**.

bandana *or* **bandanna** *noun* a large brightly-coloured cotton or silk square, folded and worn around the neck or head. [18c: from Hindi *bandhnu*]

B and B *or* **B & B** *or* **b & b** *noun* (***B and B's, B & B's*** *or* ***b & b's***) a **bed and breakfast**.

bandbox *noun* a light round box for holding hats.

bandeau /ˈbandoʊ/ *noun* (***bandeaux*** /-doʊz/) a narrow band of material worn around the head. [18c: French]

bandicoot *noun* an Australian **marsupial**, with elongated hindlegs and a long flexible snout. [18c: from Telugu (a language of India) *pandikokku* pig-rat]

bandit *noun* an armed robber, esp a member of a gang. [16c: from Italian *bandito* outlaw]

bandmaster *noun* the conductor of a musical band.

bandoleer *or* **bandolier** /bandəˈlɪə(r)/ *noun* a leather shoulder belt, esp one for carrying bullets. [16c: from French *bandouillere*]

band-saw *noun* a saw consisting of a blade with teeth attached to a metal band which moves around two wheels.

bandsman *noun* a member of a musical band.

bandstand *noun* a platform with a roof, often in a park, where bands play music.

bandwagon *noun, hist* a wagon carrying a musical band in a procession or parade. [19c]

IDIOMS **jump** *or* **climb on the bandwagon** to join, or show interest in, an activity or movement only after it becomes fashionable or likely to succeed.

bandwidth *noun* **1** the width or spread of the range of frequencies used for transmitting TV or radio signals. **2** the capacity for transmitting information over a link between computers.

bandy[1] *verb* (***-ies, -ied***) (*usu* **bandy about** *or* **around**) **1** to pass (a story, etc) from one person to another. **2** to mention (someone's name) in rumour. [16c]

IDIOMS **bandy words with sb** to exchange angry words with them.

bandy[2] *adj* (***-ier, -iest***) of a person's or animal's legs: curved or bending wide apart at the knees. Compare **knock knee**. [17c]

bane *noun* the cause of trouble or evil: *the bane of my life*. ▪ **baneful** *adj*. [Anglo-Saxon *bana* murderer]

bang[1] *noun* **1** a sudden loud explosive noise. **2** a heavy blow. ▸ *verb, tr & intr* **1** to make, or cause (something) to make, a loud noise by hitting, dropping or closing (it) violently, etc. **2** to hit (something) sharply, esp by accident: *banged her elbow*. **3** to make, or cause (something) to make, the sound of an explosion. ▸ *adv, informal* **1** exactly: *bang on time*. **2** suddenly. [16c: from Norse *banga* to hammer]

IDIOMS **go (off) with a bang** to be a great success.

bang[2] *noun, N Am* (*usu* **bangs**) hair cut in a straight line across the forehead. *Brit equivalent* **fringe**. [19c: prob from *bangtail* a short tail]

banger *noun* **1** *informal* a sausage. **2** *informal* an old car, usu one that is in poor condition. **3** a loud firework.

Bangla see under **Bengali**

bangle *noun* a piece of jewellery in the form of a solid band, worn round the arm or leg. [18c: from Hindi *bangri* glass ring]

banian see **banyan**

banish *verb* **1** to send (someone) away from a place. **2** to put (thoughts, etc) out of one's mind. ▪ **banishment** *noun*. [14c: from French *bannir*]

banister *or* **bannister** *noun* (*usu* **banisters**) a row of posts and the hand-rail they support, running up the side of a staircase. [17c: from **baluster**]

banjo *noun* (***banjos*** *or* ***banjoes***) a stringed musical instrument with a long neck and a round body, played like a guitar. ▪ **banjoist** *noun*. [18c: prob of African origin]

bank[1] *noun* **1** a financial organization that keeps money in accounts for its clients, lends money, etc. **2** a box in which money can be saved, esp by children. See also **piggy bank**. **3** *also in compounds* a place where something is stored or collected for later use: *databank*. **4** in some games: a stock of money controlled by one of the players (the **banker**).

▸ *verb* **1** to put (money) into a bank. **2** *intr* to have a bank account: *We bank with Lloyds.* [15c, meaning 'a moneylender's shop': from French *banque*]

PHRASAL VERBS **bank on sth** to rely on it or expect it.

bank[2] *noun* **1** the side or slope of a hill. **2** *also in compounds* the ground at the edge of a river or lake, etc. **3** a long raised pile of earth or snow, etc. ▸ *verb* **1** to enclose something with a bank, or form a bank to it. **2** *tr & intr* of an aircraft: to change direction, with one wing higher than the other. **3** (*also* **bank up**) to cover (a fire) with a large amount of coal to keep it burning slowly for a long time. [13c]

bank[3] *noun* a collection of similar things arranged in rows: *a bank of switches.* [16c: from French *banc* bench]

bankable *adj* (*used esp in the film industry*) likely to ensure profitability. ▪ **bankability** *noun.*

bank account *noun* an arrangement by which a person or company keeps money in a bank and takes it out when needed.

bank card *or* **banker's card** *noun* a **cheque card** or **debit card**.

bank draft *noun* a written order sent from one bank to another bank for paying money to a customer.

banker[1] *noun* **1** a person who owns or manages a bank. **2** in some games: a person in charge of the bank (see **bank**[1] *noun* sense 4).

banker[2] *noun, Aust, NZ* a river that has risen up to, or is overflowing, its banks.

IDIOMS **run a banker** of a river: to be overflowing or reaching up to its banks.

banker's order see **standing order** (sense 1)

bank holiday *noun* in the UK: any one of several days in the year on which banks are closed, usu observed as a public holiday.

banking *noun* the business done by a bank or banker.

banknote *noun* a special piece of paper, issued by a bank, which serves as money, being payable to the bearer on demand. Also called **bill** (see **bill**[1] *noun* sense 3).

bankroll *noun* financial resources. ▸ *verb, informal* to provide financial resources for (someone or something).

bankrupt *noun* **1** someone who is legally recognized, by a court adjudication order, as not being able to pay their debts. **2** someone whose character is completely lacking in a specified respect: *a moral bankrupt.* ▸ *adj* **1** not having money to pay one's debts; insolvent. **2** exhausted of or lacking (some quality, etc): *bankrupt of ideas.* ▸ *verb* (***bankrupted, past participle bankrupt***) to make (someone) bankrupt. ▪ **bankruptcy** *noun* (***-ies***). [16c: from French *banqueroute*]

bank switching *noun, comput* a method of accessing extra random access memory by switching between one bank of memory and another.

banner *noun* **1** a large piece of cloth or cardboard, with a design or slogan, etc, carried or displayed at public meetings and parades. **2** *comput* an advertisement or graphic across the width of a Web page. [13c: from French *baniere*]

banner headline *noun* a newspaper headline written in large letters across the width of the page.

bannister see **banister**

bannock *noun, dialect* a small flat round cake, usu made from oatmeal. [Anglo-Saxon *bannuc*]

banns *plural noun* the public announcement of an intended marriage. [14c: from Anglo-Saxon *bannan* to summon]

banquet *noun* **1** a sumptuous formal dinner. **2** *loosely* an elaborate meal. ▸ *verb, intr* to eat or take part in a banquet. [15c: French, from *banc* a seat]

banshee *noun, esp Irish & Scot folklore* a female spirit whose wailing warns of a death in a house. [18c: from Irish Gaelic *bean sídhe* woman of the fairies]

bantam *noun* **1** a small breed of farm chicken. **2** a small but forceful person. [18c: prob from *Bantam* in Java, from where such chickens may have been first imported]

bantamweight *noun* **1** a class for boxers, wrestlers and weightlifters of not more than a specified weight, which is 53.5 kg (118 lb) in professional boxing, slightly more in the other sports. **2** a boxer, etc of this weight. [19c]

banter *noun* light-hearted friendly talk. ▸ *verb, intr* to engage in banter. [17c]

Bantu *noun* (*pl* ***Bantu***) **1** a group of languages spoken in southern and central Africa. **2** *pl* the group of peoples who speak these languages. **3** *offensive* a Black speaker of one of these languages. ▸ *adj* belonging or relating to the Bantu languages or Bantu-speaking people. [19c: a Bantu word, meaning 'people']

Bantustan *noun, hist, often offensive* (official term later **homeland**) any of the partially self-governing regions of South Africa populated and administered by Blacks before the end of apartheid in 1994. [20c: from **Bantu** + *-stan*, modelled on Hindustan]

banyan *or* **banian** *noun* an Indian fruit tree with branches from which shoots grow down into the ground and take root. [17c: from Portuguese *banian*]

baobab /'beɪoubab/ *noun* a large deciduous African tree with a massive soft trunk. [17c]

bap *noun, Scot & N Eng dialect* a large flat bread roll. [16c]

baptism *noun* the religious ceremony of baptizing a person by immersion in, or sprinkling with, water. ▪ **baptismal** *adj.*

baptism of fire *noun* (***baptisms of fire***) **1** a soldier's first experience of battle. **2** a difficult or frightening first experience of something.

Baptist *noun* a member of a Christian group which believes that only adults should be baptized into the Church, and that this should be by complete immersion in water.

baptistery *or* **baptistry** *noun* (***baptisteries*** *or* ***baptistries***) **1** the part of a church where baptisms are carried out, or a separate building for this. **2** a tank of water for baptisms in a Baptist church.

baptize *or* **-ise** *verb* **1** to immerse (someone) in, or sprinkle (them) with, water as a sign of them having become a member of the Christian Church (in the case of babies, this is usu accompanied by name-giving). **2** to give a name to (someone). Compare **christen** (sense 1). [13c: from Greek *baptizein* to immerse]

bar[1] *noun* **1** a block of some solid substance: *bar of soap.* **2** a rod or long piece of a strong rigid material used as a weapon, obstruction, etc. **3** anything that prevents, restricts or hinders, such as a non-physical barrier: *a bar on alcohol.* **4** a line or band of colour or light, etc, esp a stripe on a heraldic shield. **5** a room or counter in a restaurant or hotel, etc, or a separate establishment, where alcoholic drinks are sold and drunk. **6** *in compounds* a small café where drinks and snacks are served: *snack bar.* **7 a** (*also* **bar-line**) a vertical line marked on music, dividing it into sections of equal value; **b** one of these sections. **8** the rail in a law court where the accused person stands. **9** (**the Bar**) the profession of barristers. **10** *geog* a **berm** (sense 2). ▸ *verb* (***barred, barring***) **1** to fasten (something) with a bar. **2** (*often* **bar sb from sth**) to forbid, prohibit, prevent them from entering, eg a place or event, doing something, etc. **3** to hinder, obstruct or prevent (someone's progress). **4** to mark (something) with a stripe or bar. ▸ *prep* except; except for: *CID have interviewed every suspect, bar one.* See also **barring**. [12c: from French *barre*]

IDIOMS **be called to the Bar** in the UK: to be admitted as a barrister. **behind bars** in prison.

bar[2] *noun, physics, meteorol, etc* in the metric system: a unit of pressure equal to 10^5 newtons per square metre. See also **millibar**. [20c: from Greek *baros* weight]

barb *noun* **1** a point on a hook facing in the opposite direction to the main point. **2** a humorous but hurtful remark. ▸ *verb* to provide (something) with barbs or a barb. ▪ **barbed** *adj*. [14c: from Latin *barba* beard]

barbarian *noun* **1** someone who is cruel and wild in behaviour. **2** an uncivilized and uncultured person. ▸ *adj* cruel and wild; uncivilized. ▪ **barbaric** *adj*. [14c: from Greek *barbaros* foreign]

barbarism *noun* **1** the state of being uncivilized, coarse, etc. **2** a cruel, coarse or ignorant act. **3** a word or expression that is considered coarse or ungrammatical. [15c]

barbarity *noun* (***-ies***) **barbarism** (in senses 1 and 2). [16c]

barbarous *adj* **1** uncultured and uncivilized. **2** extremely cruel or brutal. [15c: from Greek *barbaros* foreign]

barbecue *noun* **1** a frame on which food is grilled over an open fire, esp a charcoal one. **2** food cooked in this way. **3** a party held out of doors at which food is cooked on a barbecue. ▸ *verb* to cook (food) on a barbecue. [18c: from S American Arawak *barbacòa* a framework of sticks]

barbed wire *noun* wire with short sharp points twisted on at intervals, used for making fences, etc.

barbel *noun* **1** a freshwater fish of the carp family, which has four long sensory feelers or **barbels** around its mouth. **2** a whisker-like outgrowth found around the mouth of some fishes, esp catfish and barbels. [15c: from Latin *barba* beard]

barbell *noun* a bar with heavy metal weights at each end, used for weightlifting exercises.

barber *noun* someone who cuts and styles men's hair and shaves their beards. [14c: from French *barbeor*, from Latin *barba* beard]

barbershop *noun* **1** a type of singing in which usu four men sing in close harmony without musical accompaniment. **2** the premises in which a barber works.

barbican *noun* a tower over the outer gate of a castle or town, for the purpose of defending the gate. [13c: from French *barbacane*]

barbie *noun, Aust informal* a barbecue. [20c]

barbiturate *noun, med* a salt or ester of **barbituric acid**, used as a source of sedative drugs. [20c]

barbituric acid *noun, chem* a crystalline solid used in the preparation of barbiturates.

Barbour jacket *noun, trademark* a waterproof jacket, esp one made of green waxed cotton.

barbule *noun, zool* **1** any of the hairlike filaments on the barb of a bird's feather. **2** a **barbel** (sense 2). [19c]

barcarole *or* **barcarolle** *noun* a gondolier's song, or a piece of music with a similar rhythm. [18c: from Italian *barcarola* boat-song]

bar chart *or* **bar graph** *noun* a graph that shows values or amounts by means of vertical bars. Compare **pie chart**.

bar code *noun* a series of numbers and parallel lines of varying thickness, commonly used on product labels, that represents information about the product for sales checkouts, etc. See also **EPOS**. [20c]

bard *noun* **1** *literary* a poet. **2** a poet who has won a prize at the Eisteddfod in Wales. [15c: Scottish and Irish Gaelic, meaning 'poet']

bare *adj* **1** not covered by clothes; naked. **2** without the usual or natural covering: *bare trees.* **3** empty. **4** simple; plain: *the bare facts.* **5** basic; essential: *the bare necessities.* ▸ *verb* to uncover. ▪ **bareness** *noun*. [Anglo-Saxon *bær*]

bareback *adv, adj* on a horse without a saddle.

bare bones *plural noun* the essential facts of a situation.

barefaced *adj* having no shame or regret; impudent: *a barefaced lie.*

barefoot *or* **barefooted** *adj, adv* not wearing shoes or socks.

bareheaded *adj, adv* not wearing a hat, scarf or other head-covering.

bareknuckle *adj* **1** without boxing gloves on: *bareknuckle fighter.* **2** fiercely aggressive.

barely *adv* **1** scarcely or only just: *barely enough food.* **2** plainly or simply: *barely furnished.*

bargain *noun* **1** an agreement made between people buying and selling things, offering and accepting services, etc: *strike a bargain.* **2** something offered for sale, or bought, at a low price. ▸ *verb, intr* (*often* **bargain with sb**) to discuss the terms for buying or selling, etc. [14c: from French *bargaine*]

IDIOMS **into the bargain** in addition; besides.

PHRASAL VERBS **bargain for** *or* **on sth** to expect it.

barge *noun* **1** a long flat-bottomed boat used on rivers and canals. **2** a large boat, often decorated, used in ceremonies, celebrations, etc. ▸ *verb, intr* (*esp* **barge about** *or* **around**) to move in a clumsy ungraceful way. [14c: French, from Latin *barga*]

PHRASAL VERBS **barge in** to interrupt, esp rudely or abruptly.

bargee *noun* a person in charge of a barge.

bargepole *noun* a long pole used to move a barge.

IDIOMS **not touch sth** *or* **sb with a bargepole** *informal* to refuse to have anything to do with it or them.

bar graph see **bar chart**

barite /'bɛəraɪt/ *noun, geol* **barytes**.

baritone *noun, music* **1** the second lowest male singing voice, between bass and tenor. **2** a singer with such a voice. ▸ *adj* referring to the pitch and compass of a baritone. [17c: from Italian *baritono*]

barium *noun, chem* (symbol **Ba**) a soft silvery-white metallic element. [19c: from Greek *barys* heavy]

barium meal *noun, med* a preparation of barium sulphate and water, drunk by a patient prior to X-ray of their digestive system. It cannot be penetrated by X-rays and so forms an opaque shadow showing the outline of the stomach and intestines.

bark[1] *noun* the short sharp cry of a dog, fox, etc. ▸ *verb* **1** *intr* to make this sound. **2** *tr & intr* to speak loudly and sharply. [Anglo-Saxon *beorcan*]
IDIOMS **bark up the wrong tree** *informal* to have the wrong idea, follow a mistaken course of action or investigation, etc.

bark[2] *noun, botany* the tough protective outer layer consisting mainly of dead cells, that covers the stems and roots of woody plants, eg trees. ▸ *verb* **1** to scrape or rub off the skin from (one's leg, etc): *barked her shin when she fell.* **2** to strip or remove the bark from (a tree, etc). [14c: from Norse *börkr*]

barker *noun* a person outside a circus or show, etc who shouts to attract customers.

barley *noun* **1** a cereal of the grass family which bears a dense head of grains. **2** (*also* **barleycorn**) the grain of this plant, used as feed for animal livestock and in the brewing of beer and the production of whisky. [Anglo-Saxon *bærlic* referring to barley]

barley sugar *noun* a kind of hard orange-coloured sweet, made by melting and cooling sugar.

barley water *noun* a drink made from water in which barley has been boiled, usu with orange or lemon juice added.

bar-line see **bar**[1] (*noun* sense 7)

barm *noun* the froth formed on fermenting liquor. [Anglo-Saxon *beorma*; see also **barmy**]

barmaid *or* **barman** *noun* a woman or man who serves drinks in a bar or public house. Also called **barperson**. *N Am equivalent* **bartender**.

bar mitzvah *noun* a Jewish ceremony in which a boy (usu aged 13) formally accepts full religious responsibilities. [19c: Hebrew, literally 'son of the law']

barmy *adj* (*-ier, -iest*) *informal* crazy; mentally unsound. [16c in original sense 'bubbling or fermenting' or 'full of **barm**']

barn *noun* a building in which grain or hay, etc is stored, or for housing cattle, etc. [Anglo-Saxon *beren*, from *bere* barley + *ærn* house]

barnacle *noun* a marine **crustacean** which clings firmly to rocks, hulls of boats, etc. [16c]

barn dance *noun* **1** a kind of party at which there is music and country dancing, orig held in a barn. **2** a particular kind of country dance, esp a **square dance**.

barney *noun, informal* a rough noisy quarrel. [19c]

barn owl *noun* an owl that has a pale heart-shaped face and feathered legs.

barnstorm *verb, intr* **1** to tour a district, stopping briefly in each town to give theatrical performances. **2** *N Am* to travel about the country making political speeches just before an election. ▪ **barnstorming** *adj* impressively dashing or flamboyant. [19c]

barnyard *noun* the area around or adjoining a barn.

barograph *noun, meteorol* a type of **barometer** that produces a continuous printed chart of fluctuations in atmospheric pressure. [19c: from Greek *baros* weight + **-graph**]

barometer *noun, meteorol* an instrument that measures atmospheric pressure, esp in order to predict changes in the weather or to estimate height above sea level. See also **aneroid**. ▪ **barometric** *adj.* [17c: from Greek *baros* weight + **-meter**]

baron *noun* **1** a man holding the lowest rank of the British nobility. **2** a powerful businessman: *oil baron*. ▪ **baronial** *adj.* [13c: from Latin *baro, baronis* man]

baroness *noun* **1** a baron's wife. **2** a woman holding the title of baron in her own right.

baronet *noun* (abbrev **Bart**) in the UK: **a** a hereditary title ranking below that of baron, not part of the **peerage**; **b** a man holding such a title. ▪ **baronetcy** *noun* (*-ies*). [17c: diminutive of **baron**]

baronial /bəˈroʊnɪəl/ *adj* **1** relating to or suitable for a baron or barons. **2** grand; stately: *a baronial hall.* **3** *archit* referring to a turreted building style especially favoured formerly in Scotland.

barony *noun* (*-ies*) **1** the rank of baron. **2** land belonging to a baron.

baroque *noun* (*also* **Baroque**) a bold complex decorative style of architecture, art and music, popular in Europe from the late 16c to the early 18c. ▸ *adj* **1** (*also* **Baroque**) built, designed or written, etc in such a style. **2** of ornamentation, etc: flamboyant or extravagant. [18c: French, from Portuguese *barroco* an irregularly shaped pearl]

barperson see under **barmaid**

barque *noun* **1** a small sailing ship with three masts. **2** *literary* any boat or small ship. [15c: French, from Latin *barca* small boat]

barrack[1] *noun* (*usu* **barracks**) a building or group of buildings for housing soldiers. ▸ *verb* to house (soldiers) in barracks. [17c: from French *baraque* hut]

barrack[2] *verb, tr & intr, chiefly Brit* to shout and laugh rudely or hostilely at (a speaker, sports team, etc). ▪ **barracking** *noun.* [19c]

barracuda *noun* (***barracuda*** *or* ***barracudas***) a large tropical sea fish which feeds on other fish and sometimes attacks people. [17c: Spanish]

barrage *noun* **1** *military* a long burst of gunfire which keeps an enemy back while soldiers move forward. **2** a large number of things, esp questions or criticisms, etc, coming in quickly one after the other. **3** an artificial barrier across a river. [19c: French, from *barrer* to block]

barrage balloon *noun* a large balloon attached to the ground by a cable and often with a net hanging from it, used to prevent attack by low-flying aircraft. [20c]

barre /bɑː(r)/ *noun, ballet* a rail fixed to a wall at waist level, which dancers use to balance themselves while exercising. [20c: French, literally 'bar']

barrel *noun* **1** a large round container with a flat top and bottom and curving out in the middle, usu made of planks of wood held together with metal bands. **2** a **barrelful**. **3** a measure of capacity, esp of industrial oil. **4** the long hollow tube-shaped part of a gun or pen, etc. ▸ *verb* (***barrelled, barrelling***; *N Am also* ***barreled, barreling***) to put (something) in barrels. [14c: from French *baril*]
IDIOMS **over a barrel** powerless or at a disadvantage.

barrelful *noun* the amount a barrel can hold.

barrel organ *noun* a large mechanical instrument that plays music when a handle is turned.

barren *adj* **1** of a woman or female animal: not able to bear offspring. **2** of land or soil, etc: not able to produce crops or fruit, etc. **3** not producing results. **4**

dull; unresponsive. ▪ **barrenness** *noun*. [13c: from French *brahaigne*]

barricade /'barɪkeɪd/ *noun* a barrier, esp an improvised one erected hastily. ▸ *verb* to block or defend (something) with a barricade. [17c: French, from *barrique* barrel, barricades often being made from barrels]

barrier *noun* **1** a fence, gate or bar, etc put up to defend, block, protect, separate, etc. **2** something that separates people, items, etc. [14c: from French *barriere*]

barrier cream *noun* cream used to protect the skin from damage or infection.

barrier reef *noun* a long narrow actively-growing coral reef, separated from the land by a deep lagoon.

barring *prep* except for; leaving a specified thing out of consideration.

barrister *noun* in England and Wales: a lawyer qualified to act for someone in the higher law courts. [15c: either from Latin *barra* bar, or from **bar**[1]]

barrow[1] *noun* **1** a small one-wheeled cart used to carry tools, earth, etc. **2** a larger cart, with two or four wheels, from which goods are often sold in the street. [14c: from Anglo-Saxon *bearwe* a bier]

barrow[2] *noun, archaeol* a pile of earth over an ancient grave. [Anglo-Saxon *beorg*, orig meaning 'hill']

barrow boy *noun* a boy or man who sells goods from a barrow.

Bart *abbrev* (*also* **Bart.**) Baronet.

bartender *noun, N Am* someone who serves drinks in a bar; a barperson.

barter *verb, tr & intr* to trade or exchange (goods or services) without using money. ▸ *noun* trade by exchanging goods rather than by selling them for money. [15c: from French *barater* to trick or cheat]

baryon /'barɪɒn/ *noun, physics* a heavy subatomic particle whose mass is greater than or equal to that of the proton. [20c: from Greek *barys* heavy]

barytes /bə'raɪtiːz/ *noun, geol* the mineral form of barium sulphate, the chief ore of barium. Also called **barite**. [18c: from Greek *barys* heavy]

basal /'beɪsəl/ *adj* **1** at, referring to or forming a base. **2** at the lowest level.

basalt /'basəlt/ *noun, geol* a fine-grained dark volcanic rock. ▪ **basaltic** *adj*. [17c: from Greek *basanites*]

base[1] *noun* **1** the lowest part or bottom; the part that supports something or on which something stands. **2** the origin, root or foundation of something. **3** the headquarters or centre of activity or operations. **4** a starting point. **5** the main part of a mixture: *Rice is the base of this dish.* **6** *chem* any of a group of chemical compounds that can neutralize an acid to form a salt and water. **7** *baseball* any one of four fixed points on the pitch which players must run around to score. **8** *maths* in a numerical system: the number of different symbols used, eg in the **binary** number system the base is two, because only the symbols 0 and 1 are used. **9** *maths* in logarithms: the number that, when raised to a certain power (see **power** *noun* sense 12), has a logarithm equal in value to that power. **10** *geom* the line or surface, usu horizontal, on which a geometric figure rests. ▸ *verb* to use as a base or basis. [14c: French, from Latin *basis* pedestal]

base[2] *adj* **1** lacking morals; wicked. **2** not pure. **3** low in value. [14c as *bas*: from Latin *bassus* low or short]

base 2 *noun* binary.

baseball *noun* **1** a team game using a truncheon-shaped bat and a ball, in which the person batting attempts to run as far as possible round a diamond-shaped pitch formed by four bases (see **base**[1] *noun* sense 7), aiming to get back to the home plate to score a run. **2** the ball used in this game. [19c]

baseball cap *noun* a tight-fitting cap with a long peak, as worn by baseball players.

baseless *adj* having no cause or foundation.

baseline *noun* **1** one of the two lines that mark the ends of a tennis court. **2** an amount or value taken as a basis for comparison.

basement *noun* the lowest floor of a building, usu below ground level.

base metal *noun* any metal that readily corrodes, tarnishes or oxidizes on exposure to air, moisture or heat, eg zinc, copper, lead. Opposite of **noble metal**.

base rate *noun, finance* the rate used by a bank as the base or starting point in fixing its **interest rate**s to customers.

bases *pl of* **base**[1], **base**[2], **basis**

bash *verb, informal* **1** to strike or smash (something) bluntly. **2** to attack (something or someone) harshly or maliciously with words. ▸ *noun* **1** a heavy blow or knock. **2** a mark made by a heavy blow. **3** *slang* a noisy party. [17c]

IDIOMS **have a bash (at sth)** *informal* to have a try; to make an attempt (at it).

bashful *adj* lacking confidence; shy; self-conscious. ▪ **bashfully** *adv*. ▪ **bashfulness** *noun*. [16c: from obsolete *bash* to disconcert, abash or lose confidence]

bashing *noun, informal* **1** *sometimes in compounds* an instance of severe physical or verbal assault. **2** *esp in compounds* the practice or activity of making strong and often unjustified physical or verbal attacks on members of a group: *gay-bashing*.

BASIC *or* **Basic** *noun* a high-level computer programming language that has been widely adopted as a standard language by microcomputer manufacturers. [20c: *B*eginner's *A*ll-purpose *S*ymbolic *I*nstruction *C*ode]

basic *adj* **1** referring to or forming the base or basis of something. **2** belonging to, or at, a very simple or low level: *Her grasp of French is basic.* **3** without additions: *basic salary.* **4** *chem* referring or relating to, or forming, a base or bases. ▸ *noun* (*usu* **the basics**) the essential parts or facts; the simplest principles. ▪ **basically** *adv*. [19c: from **base**[1]]

basil *noun* an aromatic plant widely cultivated as a culinary herb. [15c: from Greek *basilikon*, meaning 'royal']

basilica *noun* **1** an ancient Roman public hall, with a rounded wall at one end and a row of stone pillars along each side, used as a lawcourt, for public assemblies or commerce. **2** a church shaped like this. [16c: from Greek *basilike* hall, from *basilikos* royal]

basilisk *noun, myth* a snake that can kill people by breathing on them or looking at them. [14c: from Greek *basiliskos* little king]

basin *noun* **1** a wide open dish, esp one for holding water. **2** a bowl or sink in a bathroom, etc for washing oneself in. **3** a valley or area of land drained by a river, or by the streams running into a river. **4** the deep part of a harbour; a dock. **5** *geol* a large depression into which sediments deposit. [13c: from French *bacin*]

basis *noun* (**-ses** /-siːz/) **1** a principle on which an idea or theory, etc is based. **2** a foundation or starting point: *a basis for discussion.* [16c in its original meaning 'the lowest part']

bask *verb, intr* **1** to lie in comfort, esp in warmth or sunshine. **2** to enjoy and take great pleasure: *basking in her success.* [14c: from Norse *bathask* to bathe]

basket *noun* **1** a container made of plaited or interwoven twigs, rushes, canes, etc, often with a handle across the top. **2** a **basketful**. **3** *basketball* **a** either of the nets into which the ball is thrown to score a goal; **b** a goal scored. [13c]

basketball *noun* **1** a team game in which players score by throwing a ball into a net fixed high up at each end of the court. **2** the ball used in this game. [19c]

basketful *noun* the amount a basket can hold.

basketweave *noun* a form of weaving using two or more yarns in the warp and weft.

basketwork *singular noun* **1** articles made of strips of wood, cane, twigs, etc, woven together. **2** the art of making such articles.

basking shark *noun* a large but harmless marine shark that feeds entirely on plankton.

basmati *or* **basmati rice** *noun* a type of long-grain rice that is naturally aromatic, eaten esp with Indian food.

Basque *noun* **1** a member of a people living in the western Pyrenees, in Spain and France. **2** the language spoken by these people. ▸ *adj* belonging or relating to the Basque people or their language. [19c: French, from Latin *Vasco*]

basque *noun* a tight-fitting bodice for women. [19c: from part of the **Basque** national costume]

bas-relief /bɑːrɪ'liːf/ *noun, art* sculpture in which the relief figures are only slightly raised. See **relief** (sense 6). [17c: French, literally 'low relief']

bass[1] /beɪs/ *noun, music* **1** the lowest male singing voice. **2** a singer with such a voice. **3** a musical part written for such a voice or for an instrument of the lowest range. **4** *informal* a bass instrument, esp a bass guitar or a double-bass. **5** **a** low frequency sound as output from an amplifier, etc: *The bass is too heavy on this track;* **b** a dial that adjusts this sound. ▸ *adj* of a musical instrument, voice or sound: low in pitch and range. [15c: see **base**[2]]

bass[2] /bas/ *noun* (***bass*** or ***basses***) **1** an edible marine fish. **2** a similar freshwater fish. [16c as *bace*: from Anglo-Saxon *bærs* perch]

bass clef *noun, music* a sign (𝄢) placed at the beginning of a piece of written music, which fixes the note F below middle C on the fourth line of the stave that follows. Also called **F-clef**.

bass drum /beɪs/ *noun* a large drum that produces a very low sound.

basset *or* **basset hound** *noun* a breed of dog with a long body, smooth hair, short legs and long drooping ears. [17c: French, from *bas* low or short]

bass guitar *or* (*esp informal*) **bass** *noun* a guitar, usu an electric one, similar in pitch and range to the double-bass.

bassinet *noun* a baby's basket-like bed or pram, usu hooded. [19c: French diminutive of *bassin* basin]

bassist /'beɪsɪst/ *noun* a person who plays a bass guitar or double-bass.

bassoon *noun* a large woodwind instrument which produces a very low sound. ▪ **bassoonist** *noun.* [18c: from Italian *bassone*, from *basso* low]

bastard *noun dated, often offensive* a child born of parents not married to each other. ▸ *adj* **1** of a person: **illegitimate**. **2** not genuine, standard, original or pure. [13c: French]

bastardize *or* **-ise** *verb* to make (something) less genuine or pure. ▪ **bastardization** *noun.*

baste[1] *verb* to pour hot fat, butter or juices over (esp roasting meat) during cooking. [15c]

baste[2] *verb* to sew (eg a seam) with temporary loose stitches. [15c: from French *bastir*]

baste[3] *verb* to beat soundly. [16c]

bastion *noun* **1** a kind of tower which sticks out at an angle from a castle wall. **2** a person, place or thing regarded as a defender of a principle, etc: *a bastion of religious freedom.* [16c: French]

bat[1] *noun* **1** a shaped piece of wood, with a flat or curved surface, for hitting the ball in cricket, baseball, etc. **2** *chiefly cricket* a batsman or batswoman. **3** a quick and usu gentle or inoffensive blow with a flat hand or other flat-sided object, etc. ▸ *verb* (***batted, batting***) **1** *intr, cricket, baseball, etc* to take a turn at hitting a ball with a bat. **2** to hit (something) with, or as if with, a bat. [Anglo-Saxon *batt* club or stick]

IDIOMS **off one's own bat** without prompting or help.

bat[2] *noun* any of various small nocturnal flying mammals. [16c; 14c as *bakke*]

bat[3] *verb* (***batted, batting***) to open and close (one's eyelids) very quickly. [17c as a variant of *bate* to flutter]

IDIOMS **not bat an eye** *or* **eyelid** *informal* to show no surprise or emotion.

batch *noun* a number of things or people dealt with at the same time. ▸ *verb* **1** to arrange or treat (something) in batches. **2** *comput* to deal with (data) by batch processing. [15c: from Anglo-Saxon *bacan* to bake]

batch file *noun, comput* a text file containing a series of commands that are executed in order when the name of the file is called.

batch processing *noun, comput* the processing of several batches of similar data by a single computer at the same time.

bated *adj, archaic* diminished; restrained. [14c: from *bate* to lessen, moderate or beat down, from **abate**]

IDIOMS **with bated breath** hushed and tense with excitement, fear or anxiety.

bath *noun* **1** a large open container for water, in which to wash the whole body while sitting in it. **2** an act of washing the body in a bath. **3** the water filling a bath. **4** (**the baths**) a public swimming pool. **5** a liquid with or in which something is washed, heated or steeped, etc, as a medicinal or cleansing treatment, etc or as part of a technical process such as developing photographs. ▸ *verb* to wash (someone or something) in a bath. [Anglo-Saxon *bæth*]

Bath chair *or* **bath chair** *noun, esp formerly* a large wheeled and usu hooded chair in which an invalid can be pushed. [19c: named after Bath in SW England where they were used at the spa]

bathe *verb* **1** *intr* to swim in the sea, etc for pleasure. **2** *intr, chiefly N Am* to wash (oneself) in a bath; to take a bath. **3** to wash or treat (part of the body, etc) with water, or with a liquid, etc to clean it or to lessen pain. **4** of light, etc: to cover and surround (someone or something); to suffuse: *Sunlight bathed the room.* ▸ *noun* an act of swimming in the sea, etc; a swim or dip. ▪ **bather** *noun.* [Anglo-Saxon *bathian* to wash]

bathos /'beɪθɒs/ *noun* in speech or writing: a sudden descent from very important, serious or beautiful ideas to very ordinary or trivial ones. ▪ **bathetic** *adj.* [18c: Greek, meaning 'depth']

bathrobe *noun* a loose towelling coat used esp before and after taking a bath.

bathroom *noun* **1** a room containing a bath and now usu other washing facilities, a lavatory, etc. **2** *esp N Am* a room with a lavatory.

bathyscaphe *or* **bathyscape** /'baθɪskeɪf/ *noun* an electrically-powered crewed vessel with an observation cabin on its underside, used for exploring the ocean depths. [20c: from Greek *bathys* deep + *skaphos* ship]

bathysphere *noun* a deep-sea observation chamber, consisting of a watertight steel sphere that is lowered and raised from a surface vessel. [20c]

batik /bə'tiːk/ *noun* **1** a technique of printing cloth in which those parts not to be coloured are covered with wax. **2** cloth coloured by this method. [19c: Malay, literally 'painted']

batman *noun* an officer's personal servant in the armed forces. [18c: from French *bât* pack-saddle]

baton /'batən, -tɒn; *N Am* bə'tɑːn/ *noun* **1** a light thin stick used by the conductor of an orchestra or choir, etc to direct them. **2** a short heavy stick carried by a policeman as a weapon. Also called **truncheon. 3** a short stick passed from one runner to another in a relay race. **4** a stick carried, tossed and twirled, etc by a person at the head of a marching band. [16c, meaning 'a stick used as a weapon': from French *bâton* stick]

baton round *noun, formal* a plastic or rubber bullet.

bats *adj, informal* crazy; **batty.** [20c: from **bat**[2]]

batsman *noun, chiefly cricket* (*also* **batswoman**) a person who bats or is batting. Also called **bat.**

battalion *noun* an army unit made up of several smaller companies (see **company** *noun* sense 6), and forming part of a larger **brigade.** [16c: Italian *battaglione*]

batten *noun* **1** a long flat piece of wood used for keeping other pieces in place. **2** a strip of wood used to fasten the covers over the hatches in a ship's deck, etc. ▸ *verb* to fasten, strengthen or shut (eg a door) with battens. [17c: a variant of **baton**]

IDIOMS **batten down the hatches 1** *informal* to prepare for a danger or crisis. **2** *naut* to fasten covers over the hatches in a ship's deck using battens.

batter[1] *verb* **1** *tr & intr* to strike or hit (something or someone) hard and often, or continuously. **2** to damage or wear (something) out through continual use. ▪ **battering** *noun.* [14c: from French *battre* to beat]

batter[2] *noun* a mixture of eggs, flour and either milk or water, used in cooking. [15c: prob from **batter**[1]]

batter[3] *noun, esp baseball* a person who bats or is batting.

battering-ram *noun* a large wooden beam, formerly used in war for breaking down walls or gates.

battery *noun* (*-ies*) **1** a device that converts chemical energy into electrical energy in the form of direct current. **2** a number of similar things: *a battery of press photographers.* **3** a long line of small tiered cages in which hens are kept. **4** *law* intentional physical attack on a person, including touching the clothes or body in a threatening manner, not necessarily involving damage. See also **assault and battery. 5 a** a group of heavy guns with their equipment; **b** the place where they are mounted. [16c: from French *batterie*, from *battre* to strike or beat]

battle *noun* **1** a fight between opposing armies, naval or air forces, etc or people. **2** a competition between opposing groups or people: *a battle of wits.* **3** a long or difficult struggle: *a battle for equality.* ▸ *verb, intr* **1** to fight. **2** to struggle; to campaign vigorously or defiantly. [13c: ultimately from Latin *battuere* to beat]

battle-axe *noun* **1** *informal* a fierce and domineering older woman. **2** *hist* a large broad-bladed axe.

battle-cruiser *noun* a large warship, the same size as a battleship but faster and with fewer guns.

battle-cry *noun* **1** a shout given by soldiers charging into battle. **2** a slogan used to strengthen or arouse support for a cause or campaign, etc.

battledress *noun* a soldier's ordinary uniform.

battlefield *or* **battleground** *noun* **1** the place at which a battle is or was fought. **2** a site, subject or area of intense disagreement: *a political battlefield.*

battlement *noun* a low wall around the top of a castle, etc with gaps for shooting through. [14c: French]

battle royal *noun* (***battles royal***) **1** a general brawl or melee. **2** a long heated argument. [17c: orig referring to a fight continuing until only one contestant remained standing]

battleship *noun* the largest type of warship.

batty *adj* (*-ier, -iest*) *informal* crazy; eccentric.

bauble *noun* **1** a small cheap trinket. **2** a round coloured decoration hung on Christmas trees. [14c as *babel*: French, meaning 'a child's toy']

baud *or* **baud rate** *noun* **1** *comput* in a computer system: the number of bits or other signalling elements that can be transmitted between computers per second. **2** *telecomm* in telegraphy: the number of pulses and spaces that can be transmitted per second. [20c: named after the French inventor J M E Baudot]

Bauhaus /'baʊhaʊs/ *noun* a German school of art and architecture (1919–33) having as its aim the integration of art and technology in design. [20c: from German, literally, 'building-house']

baulk see **balk**

bauxite *noun, geol* a clay-like substance which is the main ore of aluminium. [19c: French, named after Les Baux in S France, where it was first found]

bawdy *adj* (*-ier, -iest*) of language or writing, etc: containing coarsely humorous references to sex; lewd. ▪ **bawdily** *adv.* ▪ **bawdiness** *noun.* [16c: from *bawd* the now archaic word for a woman who keeps a brothel]

bawl *verb, intr* **1** to cry loudly in distress, pain, etc. **2** (*also* **bawl out**) to shout loudly. ▸ *noun* a loud shout. [15c: imitative]

bay[1] *noun* a body of water that forms a wide-mouthed indentation in the coastline. [14c: from French *baie*]

bay² *noun* **1** an enclosed or partly enclosed area within a building, vessel, etc for storage or some other purpose. **2** *in compounds* a compartment for storing or carrying, eg in an aircraft: *bomb bay.* **3 a** a parking bay; **b** a loading bay. **4** a small area of a room set back into a wall. [14c: from French *baer* to gape]

bay³ *adj* of a horse: reddish-brown in colour, usu with black mane and tail. ▸ *noun* a bay-coloured horse. [14c: from Latin *badius* chestnut-coloured]

bay⁴ *noun* **1** any of various evergreen trees of the **laurel** family with shiny dark-green leaves. Also called **bay tree**, **sweet bay**. **2** (*usu* **bays**) a wreath of bay leaves, traditionally worn on the head by champions in some competitions, etc. [15c: from Latin *baca*]

bay⁵ *verb* **1** *intr* esp of large dogs: to make a deep howling bark or cry. **2** *intr* of a crowd, etc: to howl or shout loudly. ▸ *noun* the baying sound of a dog, etc. [14c: from French *abai* barking]

IDIOMS **at bay** of a hunted animal: not able to escape. **keep sth** *or* **sb at bay 1** to fight it or them off; to keep it or them from overwhelming (usu oneself). **2** to keep it or them at a distance.

bayonet *noun* **1** a steel knife that fixes to the muzzle of a soldier's rifle. **2** (*also* **bayonet fitting**) a type of fitting for a light bulb or camera lens, etc in which prongs on its side fit into slots to hold it in place. ▸ *verb* to stab (someone or something) with a bayonet. [17c: named after Bayonne in SW France, where they were first made]

bay window *noun* a three-sided or rounded window that juts out from the wall of a building.

bazaar *noun* **1** a sale of goods, etc usu in order to raise money for a particular organization or purpose. **2** a shop selling miscellaneous goods. **3** in Eastern countries: a market place or exchange. [16c in sense 3: from Persian *bazar* market]

bazooka *noun* a portable anti-tank gun that fires small rockets. [20c: from the name of a toy wind-instrument similar to the **kazoo**]

BBC *abbrev* British Broadcasting Corporation.

BBQ *abbrev* barbecue.

BC *abbrev* in dates: before Christ, used together with a figure to indicate a specified number of years before that in which Christ was once thought to have been born. Compare **AD**, **BCE**. See also **Common Era**.

BCC *or* **Bcc** *abbrev* blind carbon copy, used to mark a copy of a message sent without the knowledge of the main recipient.

BCE *abbrev* in dates: before the Common Era, sometimes used instead of **BC**, as a culturally neutral notation. Compare **CE**.

BCG *or* **bcg** *abbrev* bacillus Calmette-Guérin, a vaccine given to a person to prevent tuberculosis.

Be *symbol, chem* beryllium.

be *verb* (*past participle* ***been***; *present participle* ***being***; *present tense* ***am, are, is***; *past tense* ***was, were***) *intr* **1** to exist or live: *I think, therefore I am.* **2** to occur or take place: *Lunch is in an hour.* **3** to occupy a position in space: *She is at home.* **4** *in past tense* to go: *He's never been to Italy.* **5** to remain or continue without change: *Let it be.* **6** (as a **copula**) used to link a subject and what is said about it: *She is a doctor* • *He is ill.* **7** used with the **infinitive** form of a verb to express a possibility, command, intention, outcome, etc: *if it were to rain* • *We are to come tomorrow* • *It was not to be.* ▸ *auxiliary verb* **1** used with a past **participle** to form a **passive** construction: *The film was shown last night.* **2** used with a present **participle** to form the **progressive** tenses: *He was running.* [From Anglo-Saxon *beon* to live or exist, and Anglo-Saxon *weran* to be]

IDIOMS **be sb** to suit them: *That hat really isn't her.*

be- *prefix, signifying* **1** all over or all around; thoroughly or completely: *beset* • *bedeck.* **2** considering something or someone as, or causing it or them to be or feel, a specified thing *befriend* • *belittle.* **3** having or being affected by a specified thing *bejewel* • *bedevil.* **4** affecting someone or something by a particular action *bereave* • *bewail.* [16c, originally meaning 'about': from Anglo-Saxon *bi-* by]

beach *noun* the sandy or stony shore of a sea or lake. ▸ *verb* to push, pull or drive (esp a boat) onto a beach. [16c]

beach-ball *noun* a large colourful and usually inflatable ball for playing games with at the beach, in the swimming pool, etc.

beachcomber /ˈbiːtʃkoʊmə(r)/ *noun* someone who searches beaches for things of interest or value washed up by the tide. ▪ **beachcombing** *noun.* [19c: orig meaning 'a long rolling wave']

beachhead *noun, military* an area of shore captured from the enemy, on which an army can land men and equipment. [20c]

beacon *noun* **1** a warning or guiding device for aircraft or ships, eg a lighthouse or (*in full* **radio beacon**) a radio transmitter that broadcasts signals. **2** a fire on a hill, mountain or high ground, lit as a signal. **3** a **Belisha beacon**. [Anglo-Saxon *beacen*]

bead *noun* **1** a small and usu round ball made of glass or stone, etc strung with others, eg in a necklace. **2** (**beads**) a string of beads worn as jewellery, or one used when praying (a **rosary**). **3** a small drop of liquid. **4 beading**. **5** the front sight of a gun. ▸ *verb* to decorate (something) with beads or beading. ▪ **beaded** *adj.* [Anglo-Saxon *bed* in obsolete sense 'a prayer', from *biddan* to pray]

beading *noun* thin strips of patterned wood used to decorate the edges of furniture or walls, etc. Also called **bead**.

beadle *noun, Brit* **1** a person who leads formal processions in church or in some old universities and institutions. **2** in Scotland: a church officer who attends the minister. **3** *formerly* in England: a minor parish official who had the power to punish minor offences. [16c]

beady *adj* (***-ier, -iest***) *usu derog* of a person's eyes: small, round and bright.

beagle *noun* a breed of small hunting-dog with a short-haired coat. [15c: possibly from French *béguele*]

beak *noun* **1** the horny projecting jaws of a bird. **2** any pointed projection that resembles this, eg the projecting jaws of certain fishes and other animals. **3** *slang* a nose, esp a big pointed one. **4** *Brit, slang* a headmaster, judge or magistrate. [13c: from French *bec*]

beaker *noun* **1** a large drinking-glass, or a large cup without a handle. **2** a glass container, usu one with a lip for pouring, used in laboratory work. [14c: from Norse *bikarr*]

beam *noun* **1** a long straight thick piece of wood, used eg as a main structural component in a building. **2** a ray of light. **3** a broad radiant smile. **4** the widest part of a ship or boat. **5** a raised narrow horizontal wooden bar on which gymnasts perform balancing exercises. **6** *physics* a directed flow of electromagnetic radiation (eg radio or X-rays) or of particles (eg atoms or electrons). ▸ *verb* **1** *intr* to smile broadly with pleasure. **2** *intr* (*often* **beam down** *or* **out**) to shine. **3** to send out or transmit (eg rays of light, radio waves, etc). [Anglo-Saxon, meaning 'tree']

IDIOMS **off beam** *informal* wrong; misguided.

bean *noun* **1** a general name applied to the edible seed of plants belonging to the pea family. **2** any plant belonging to the pea family that bears such seeds, such as the **broad bean** or **runner bean**. **3** (*usu* **beans**) *cookery* a seed or young pod of such a plant, used as food. **4** any other seed that superficially resembles those of the pea family: *coffee bean*. **5** *informal, with negatives* a small coin; a tiny amount of money: *I haven't got a bean*. [Anglo-Saxon]

IDIOMS **full of beans** *informal* full of energy; very lively and cheerful.

bean bag *noun* **1** a small cloth bag filled with dried beans used like a ball in children's games. **2** a very large cushion filled with polystyrene chips or balls, etc, kept on the floor as seating.

beanfeast *noun, Brit informal* a party or celebration. [19c]

beano *noun, Brit informal* a beanfeast. [19c: printers' abbreviation of **beanfeast**]

beanpole *noun, informal* a tall thin person.

beansprout *or* **beanshoot** *noun* a young shoot of a bean plant eaten as a vegetable, esp in Chinese food.

beanstalk *noun* the stem of a bean plant.

bear[1] *verb* (*past tense* ***bore,*** *past participle* ***borne*** *or* (*in sense 7b*) ***born***) **1** to support or sustain (a weight or load). **2** to take or accept: *bear the blame*. **3** to put up with or tolerate (something or someone). **4 a** to allow; to be fit or suitable for (something): *It doesn't bear thinking about*; **b** to stand up to or be capable of withstanding (something): *will not bear close scrutiny*. **5** to bring or take (something) with one; to carry: *bearing gifts*. **6** to produce. **7 a** to give birth to (a child or offspring); **b** in the passive using past participle *born*: *He was born in 1990*; **c** in the past tense using past participle *borne*: *Has she borne children?* **8** to carry (something) in one's thought or memory: *bearing grudges*. **9** to have: *bears no resemblance to his father*. **10** to show or be marked by (something): *Her cheeks bore the traces of tears*. **11** *intr* to turn slightly in a given direction: *bear left*. ▪ **bearable** *adj*. [Anglo-Saxon *beran* to carry or support]

IDIOMS **bring sth to bear** to apply or exert esp pressure or influence, or bring something into operation.

PHRASAL VERBS **bear down on** *or* **upon sb** *or* **sth** to move threateningly towards them or it. **bear on sth** to affect, concern or relate to it. **bear sb** *or* **sth out** to support or confirm them or it. **bear up** to remain strong or brave, etc under strain or difficult circumstances. **bear with sb** to be patient with them.

bear[2] *noun* (***bears*** *or* ***bear***) **1** any of various large carnivorous animals with a heavily built body, covered with thick fur. **2** a rough ill-mannered person. **3** a teddy bear. **4** *stock exchange* someone who sells shares, hoping to buy them back later at a much lower price. Compare **bull**[1] (*noun* sense 4). ▸ *verb, stock exchange* **1** to act as a bear (sense 4 above). **2** to lower the price of (a stock) or to depress (a market) by selling speculatively. ▪ **bearish** *adj*. [Anglo-Saxon *bera*]

IDIOMS **like a bear with a sore head** *informal* of a person: exceptionally touchy and bad-tempered.

beard *noun* **1** the hair that grows on a man's chin and neck. **2** a beard-like growth on the lower jaw of some animals, esp goats. ▸ *verb* to face or oppose (somebody) boldly or impudently. ▪ **bearded** *adj*. [Anglo-Saxon]

bearer *noun* **1** a person or thing that bears, carries or brings something. **2** a person who holds a banknote, cheque or other money order that can be exchanged for money.

bear hug *noun, informal* a rough tight embrace.

bearing /ˈbɛərɪŋ/ *noun* **1** the way a person stands, walks, behaves, etc: *a proud bearing*. **2** relevance. **3 a** the horizontal direction of a fixed point, or the path of a moving object, measured from a reference point on the Earth's surface, and normally expressed as an angle measured in degrees clockwise from the north; **b** (*usu* **bearings**) position or a calculation of position: *compass bearing*. **4** (**bearings**) *informal* a sense or awareness of one's own position or surroundings. **5** any part of a machine or device that supports another part, and allows free movement between the two parts, eg a **ball-bearing**. [13c: from **bear**[1]]

bearskin *noun* **1** the skin of a bear. **2** a tall fur cap worn as part of some military uniforms. See also **busby**.

beast *noun* **1** any large animal, esp a wild one. **2** *informal* a cruel brutal person. **3** *informal* a difficult or unpleasant person or thing. [13c as *beste*: French]

beastly *adj* (***-ier, -iest***) *informal* unpleasant; disagreeable.

beat *verb* (*past tense* ***beat,*** *past participle* ***beaten*** *or* (*now rare*) ***beat***) **1** to hit (a person, animal, etc) violently and repeatedly, esp to harm or punish them. **2** to strike (something) repeatedly, eg to remove dust or make a sound. **3** *intr* (*usu* **beat against** *or* **at** *or* **on sth**) to knock or strike repeatedly: *rain beating against the window*. **4** to defeat; to do something better, sooner or quicker than (someone else): *always beats me at chess*. **5** to be too difficult to be solved or understood by (someone). **6** (*sometimes* **beat sth up**) to mix or stir thoroughly: *Beat two eggs in a bowl*. **7** (*also* **beat out**) **a** to make or shape (something) by repeatedly striking the raw material: *beating out horseshoes on the forge*; **b** to flatten or reduce the thickness of (something) by beating. **8** *intr* to move in a regular pattern of strokes, etc: *heard my heart beating*. **9** *tr & intr* to move rhythmically up and down: *tent-flaps beating in the wind*. **10** (*usu* **beat time** *or* **beat out time**) to mark or show (musical time or rhythm) with the hand or a baton, etc. **11** (**beat sb** *or* **sth back** *or* **down** *or* **off**) to push, drive or force them or it away. **12** (*also* **beat up**) *tr & intr* to strike (bushes or trees, etc) to force birds or animals into the open for shooting. ▸ *noun* **1** a regular recurrent stroke, or its sound: *the beat of my heart*. **2 a** in music and poetry, etc: the basic pulse, unit of rhythm or accent: *two beats to the bar;* **b** the conductor's stroke of the hand or baton indicating such a pulse: *Watch the beat;* **c** in popular music: rhythm; a strong rhythmic pulse. **3** a regular or usual course or journey: *a policeman's beat.* ▸ *adj, informal, esp N Am* worn out; exhausted. ▪ **beater** *noun* a person or thing that beats, eg a person who rouses game for shooting, an electric or hand-operated device for beating, etc. ▪ **beating** *noun.* [Anglo-Saxon *beatan*]

IDIOMS **beat about the bush** to talk tediously about a subject without coming to the main point. **beat it** *slang* to go away immediately and quickly. **off the beaten track** away from main roads and towns; isolated.

PHRASAL VERBS **beat down 1** of the sun: to give out great heat. **2** of rain: to fall heavily. **beat sb down** to force them to reduce the price of something by bargaining. **beat sb up** *or* (*US*) **beat up on sb** to punch, kick or hit them severely and repeatedly.

beat box *noun, informal* a drum machine.

beaten *adj* **1** defeated or outmanoeuvred. **2** *informal, esp Aust & NZ* exhausted or worn out. **3** made smooth or hard by beating or treading: *beaten path.* **4** shaped and made thin by beating: *beaten gold.*

beatific /bɪə'tɪfɪk/ *adj* expressing or revealing supreme peaceful happiness. [17c: from Latin *beatificus*, from *beatus* blessed + *facere* to make]

beatify /bɪ'atɪfaɪ/ *verb* (**-ies, -ied**) **1** *RC Church* to declare the blessed status of (someone who has died), usu as the first step towards full canonization. **2** to make (someone) eternally or supremely happy. ▪ **beatification** *noun.* [16c]

beatitude /bɪ'atɪtjuːd/ *noun* **1** (**the Beatitudes**) *Bible* the group of statements made by Christ during the Sermon on the Mount (in Matthew 5.3–11) about the kinds of people who receive God's blessing. **2** a state of blessedness or of extreme happiness and peace. [15c: from Latin *beatitudo*]

beatnik *noun, dated* **1** a young person with scruffy or unconventional clothes, long hair, unusual lifestyle, etc. **2** in the 1950s and 60s: a young person who rejected the accepted social and political ideas, etc of the time. [20c: **beat** (*adj*) + **-nik**]

beat-up *adj, informal* in a dilapidated condition.

beau /boʊ/ *noun* (***beaux*** *or* ***beaus*** /boʊz/) **1** *N Am or dated Brit* a boyfriend or male lover. **2** *old use* a **dandy**. [17c: French, meaning 'beautiful']

Beaufort scale /'boʊfət/ *noun, meteorol* a system for estimating wind speeds without using instruments. [19c: devised by Sir Francis Beaufort]

beauteous *adj, poetic* beautiful. [15c]

beautician *noun* a person who gives beauty treatment such as hair and skin treatments, make-up application, etc to women, esp in a beauty parlour. [20c]

beautiful *adj* **1** having an appearance or qualities that please the senses or give rise to admiration in the mind. **2** *informal* very enjoyable; excellent. ▪ **beautifully** *adv.*

---

beautiful

This word is often misspelt. It might help you to remember the following sentence:

Big elephants are usually beautiful.

---

beautify *verb* (**-ies, -ied**) to make (something or someone) beautiful; to adorn or grace. [16c]

beauty *noun* (**-ies**) **1** a quality pleasing to the senses, esp to the eye or ear, or giving aesthetic pleasure generally. **2** *informal* an excellent example of something: *a beauty of a black eye.* **3** a benefit or particular strength or quality: *The beauty of the plan is its flexibility.* **4** a beautiful person, usu a woman or girl. [13c: from French *biauté*]

beauty queen *noun* a woman judged the most beautiful in a contest.

beauty spot *noun* **1** a place of great natural beauty. **2** a small dark natural or artificial mark on the face, believed to enhance beauty.

beaver *noun* **1** a large semi-aquatic rodent with soft dark-brown fur, large incisor teeth, webbed hind feet and a broad flat scaly tail. **2** its valuable fur. **3** a hat made of beaver fur. ▸ *verb, intr* (*esp* **beaver away at sth**) *informal, chiefly Brit* to work very hard and persistently at something. [Anglo-Saxon *beofor*]

bebop *noun* (*often shortened to* **bop**) a variety of jazz music which added new harmonies, melodic patterns and highly syncopated rhythms to accepted jazz style. [20c: in imitation of its rhythm]

becalmed *adj* of a sailing ship: motionless and unable to move because of lack of wind. [16c]

became *past tense of* **become**

because *conj* for the reason that. [14c: shortened from the phrase *'by cause of'*]

IDIOMS **because of sth** *or* **sb** by reason of, or on account of, it or them.

béchamel /beɪʃəmɛl/ *or* **béchamel sauce** *noun, cookery* a white sauce flavoured with onion and herbs. [18c: named after the Marquis de Béchamel]

beck[1] *noun, archaic* a beckoning gesture. [14c from Anglo-Saxon *biecnan* to beckon]

IDIOMS **at sb's beck and call** having to be always ready or at hand to carry out their orders or wishes.

beck[2] *noun, N Eng dialect* a stream or brook. [12c: from Norse *bekkr*]

beckon *verb, tr & intr* to summon (someone) with a gesture. [Anglo-Saxon *biecnan*, from *beacen* a sign]

become *verb* (*past tense* ***became,*** *past participle* ***become***) **1** *intr* to come or grow to be (something); to develop into (something). **2** *formal* esp of clothing: to suit, look good on or befit (someone): *That hat becomes you.* [Anglo-Saxon *becuman*]

becoming *adj* **1** attractive. **2** of behaviour, etc: suitable or proper.

becquerel /'bɛkərɛl/ *noun, physics* (symbol **Bq**) in the SI system: the unit of activity of a radioactive source per second. Formerly called **curie**. [20c: named after the French physicist A H Becquerel]

BEd *abbrev* Bachelor of Education.

bed *noun* **1** a piece of furniture for sleeping on. **2** a place in which anything (eg an animal) sleeps or rests. **3** *informal* sleep or rest: *ready for bed.* **4** the bottom of a river, lake or sea. **5** an area of ground in a garden, for growing plants. **6** a flat surface or base, esp one made of slate, brick or tile, on which something can be supported or laid down. **7** a layer, eg of oysters, sedimentary rock, etc. **8** a place available for occupancy in a residential home, nursing home or hospital. ▸ *verb* (***bedded, bedding***) **1** *tr & intr* (*usu* **bed down**) to go to bed, or put (someone) in bed or in a place to sleep: *bedded down on the sofa.* **2** (*usu* **bed out**) to plant (something) in the soil, in a garden, etc. **3** to place or fix (something) firmly: *Its base was bedded in concrete.* **4** *tr & intr* to arrange (something) in or to form, layers. [Anglo-Saxon *bedd*]

IDIOMS **get out of bed on the wrong side** *informal* to start the day in a bad mood.

bed and breakfast *noun* (abbrev **B and B, B & B** *or* **b & b**) **1** at a guesthouse, hotel, etc: overnight accommodation with breakfast included in the price. *US equivalent* **room and board**. **2** a guesthouse, etc that provides accommodation and breakfast.

bedbug *noun* the common name for any of various species of household pest that infest bedding and feed on human blood.

bedclothes *plural noun* sheets, blankets, etc for a bed.

bedcover see **bedspread**

bedding *noun* **1** bedclothes, and sometimes also a mattress and pillows, etc. **2** straw or hay, etc for animals to sleep on. **3** *geol* stratification.

bedding plant *noun* a young plant that is sufficiently well-grown for planting out in a garden.

bedeck *verb* to cover (something or someone) with decorations; to adorn. [16c: from **deck**[2]]

bedevil *verb* (***bedevilled, bedevilling***; *N Am also* ***bedeviled, bedeviling***) **1** to cause continual difficulties or trouble to (someone or something). **2** to throw (something or someone) into confusion. ▪ **bedevilment** *noun*. [19c]

bedfellow *noun* **1** a partner or associate. **2** a person with whom one shares a bed. [15c in sense 2]

bedlam *noun, informal* a very noisy confused place or situation. [16c as *Bedlam*, the popular name for St Mary of Bethlehem, a former mental hospital in London; 17c in current sense]

bed linen *noun* sheets and pillowcases for a bed.

bed of roses *noun* an easy or comfortable place or situation: *Her life is no bed of roses.*

Bedouin /ˈbɛduɪn/ *noun* (***Bedouin*** *or* ***Bedouins***) a member of a nomadic tent-dwelling Arab tribe. Also **Beduin**. [15c: from French *beduin*]

bedpan *noun* a wide shallow pan used as a toilet by someone who is unable to get out of bed.

bedraggled *adj* of a person or animal: very wet and untidy. [18c]

bedridden *adj* not able to get out of bed, esp because of old age or sickness. [Anglo-Saxon]

bedrock *noun* **1** the solid rock forming the lowest layer under soil and rock fragments. **2** the basic principle or idea, etc on which something rests.

bedroom *noun* a room for sleeping in. ▸ *adj* **1** for a bedroom: *bedroom furniture*. **2** esp of a comedy or farce: including references to sexual activity.

Beds. *abbrev, English county* Bedfordshire.

bedside *noun* the place or position next to a bed.

bedside manner *noun* a doctor's way of talking to, and generally dealing with, a patient.

bedsitting-room *(formal)*, **bedsit** *or* **bedsitter** *noun, Brit* a single room used as a combined bedroom and sitting-room.

bedsore *noun* an ulcer on a person's skin, caused by lying in bed for long periods. Also called **pressure sore**.

bedspread *or* **bedcover** *noun* a top cover for a bed.

bedstead *noun* the frame of a bed.

Beduin see **Bedouin**

bed-wetting *noun* accidental urination in bed at night.

bee[1] *noun* any of numerous four-winged insects, some species of which live in colonies and are often kept for their honey. [Anglo-Saxon *beo*]

IDIOMS **a bee in one's bonnet** an idea that has become an obsession. **the bee's knees** *Brit informal* a person or thing considered to be extremely special or good, etc.

bee[2] *noun, N Am* a meeting of friends to work on a particular task together (eg a **quilting bee**) or in competition (eg a **spelling bee**). [18c]

the Beeb *noun, Brit informal* the British Broadcasting Corporation. [20c: colloquial shortening of the abbreviation **BBC**]

beech *noun* **1** (*also* **beech tree**) a deciduous tree or shrub with smooth grey bark. **2** (*also* **beechwood**) the hard wood of this tree, widely used for furniture making. [Anglo-Saxon *bece*]

beef *noun* (*pl* in sense 3 ***beefs***, in sense 4 ***beeves***) **1** the flesh of a bull, cow or ox, used as food. **2** *informal* muscle; vigorous muscular force or strength **3** *slang* a complaint or argument. **4 a** a steer or cow, esp one fattened for butchering; **b** its butchered carcass. ▸ *verb, intr, slang* to complain or grumble, esp vigorously or at length. [13c: from French *boef* ox]

PHRASAL VERBS **beef sth up** *informal* to make it stronger, more interesting or exciting.

beefburger *noun* a piece of minced beef made into a flat round shape and grilled or fried. See also **burger**.

beefeater *or* **Beefeater** *noun, Brit* a Yeoman Warder at the Tower of London. [17c]

beef tea *noun* a drink made from beef stock or the juice of chopped beef.

beef tomato *noun* a large fleshy variety of tomato.

beefy *adj* (***-ier, -iest***) **1** made of or like beef. **2** *informal* eg of a person: fleshy or muscular. ▪ **beefiness** *noun*.

beehive *noun* a box or hut in which bees are kept.

beekeeper *noun* a person who keeps bees for their honey, as a hobby, etc. ▪ **beekeeping** *noun*.

beeline *noun* a straight line between two places.

IDIOMS **make a beeline for sth** *or* **sb** to go directly or purposefully to it or them.

been *past participle of* **be**

beep *noun* a short high-pitched sound, like that made by a car horn. ▸ *verb, tr & intr* to produce a beep on or with (something). [20c: imitating the sound]

beer *noun* **1** an alcoholic drink brewed by the slow fermentation of malted cereal grains, usu barley, flavoured with hops, eg **ale**, **lager** and **stout**. **2** a glass, can or bottle of this drink. [Anglo-Saxon *beor*]

beer garden *noun* a garden, usu attached to a pub, where beer and other refreshments can be drunk.

beer-mat *noun* a small table mat, usually made of cardboard, for standing a glass of beer etc on.

beery *adj* (***-ier, -iest***) **1** made of or like beer. **2** *informal* affected by drinking beer.

beeswax *noun* **1** a solid yellowish substance produced by bees for making the cells in which they live. **2** this substance in a refined form, used esp as a wood-polish.

beet *noun* **1** any of several types of plant with large round or carrot-shaped roots which are cooked and used as food, or for making sugar (called **beet sugar**). **2** (*also* **red beet**) *N Am* beetroot. [Anglo-Saxon *bete*]

beetle[1] *noun* an insect with thickened forewings that are not used for flight but modified to form rigid horny cases which cover and protect the hindwings. ▸ *verb, intr* (*usu* **beetle about, around** *or* **away**) *Brit* to move quickly or as if in a hurry to get away; to scurry. [Anglo-Saxon *bitela*, from *biten* to bite]

beetle[2] *verb, intr* to project or jut out; to overhang. ▪ **beetling** *adj*. [17c: apparently first used as a verb by Shakespeare; derived from **beetle-browed**]

beetle-browed *adj* having bushy or overhanging eyebrows. [14c as *bitel-browed*: perhaps related to **beetle**[1]]

beetroot *noun* a type of plant with a round dark-red root which is cooked and used as a vegetable. *N Am equivalent* **beet**. [16c]

beeves *pl of* **beef** (*noun* sense 4)

BEF *abbrev* British Expeditionary Force.

befall *verb* (*past tense* ***befell***, *past participle* ***befallen***) *old or literary* **1** *intr* to happen. **2** to happen to (someone or something): *I alone knew what had befallen him.* [Anglo-Saxon *befeallan*]

befit *verb* (***befitted, befitting***) *formal* to be suitable or right for (something or someone). ▪ **befitting** *adj*. [15c: from Anglo-Saxon *bi-* by + **fit**[1]]

before *prep* **1** earlier than something: *before noon.* **2** ahead of or in front of someone or something. **3** in the presence of, or for the attention of, someone: *The question before us is a complex one.* **4** rather than or in preference to someone or something: *Never put money before friendship.* ▸ *conj* **1** earlier than the time when something occurs: *Tidy up before Mum gets back.* **2** rather than or in preference to doing something: *I'd die before I'd surrender.* ▸ *adv* previously; in the past. [Anglo-Saxon *beforan*]

beforehand *adv* **1** in advance; before a particular time or event. **2** in preparation or anticipation. [13c]

befriend *verb* **1** to become the friend of or start a friendship with (someone). **2** to be friendly and helpful towards (a stranger, etc). [16c]

befuddle *verb* (*used esp in the passive*) to confuse (someone), eg with the effects of alcohol. [19c]

beg *verb* (***begged, begging***) *tr & intr* **1** to ask for (money or food, etc). **2** to ask earnestly or humbly: *Give me one chance, I beg you.* **3** of a dog: to sit up on the hindquarters with paws raised (as if asking for a reward). [13c]

IDIOMS **beg the question** in an argument: to assume the truth of something which is in fact a part of what is still to be proved. **go begging** *informal* to be unused or unwanted.

beget *verb* (*past tense* ***begot*** or, esp in the Authorized Version of the Bible, ***begat***, *past participle* ***begotten***, *present participle* ***begetting***) **1** *rather formal* to cause; to give rise to (something): *Envy begets strife.* **2** esp in the Authorized Version of the Bible: to be the father of (someone): *Abraham begat Isaac*. [Anglo-Saxon]

beggar *noun* **1** a person who lives by begging. **2** *informal, chiefly Brit* an affectionate or gently reproachful term for a person: *cheeky beggar.* ▪ **beggarly** *adj*.

IDIOMS **beggar description** *or* **belief** to be impossible to describe or believe: *That story beggars belief.*

beggar-my-neighbour *noun, cards* a game that goes on until one player has gained all the others' cards.

begin *verb* (*past tense* ***began***, *past participle* ***begun***, *present participle* ***beginning***) **1** *tr & intr* to start. **2** *tr & intr* to bring or come into being: *Our story begins in the summer of 1970.* **3** *intr* to start speaking. **4** *intr* to be the first or to take the first step: *Vernon, will you begin?* **5** *intr, informal* to have the ability or possibility to do something: *I can't even begin to understand.* [Anglo-Saxon]

beginner *noun* someone who is just starting to learn, or is still learning, how to do something.

IDIOMS **beginner's luck** success achieved by someone inexperienced, eg in sport or a game of skill.

beginning *noun* **1** the point or occasion at which something begins. **2** an opening or first part of something.

begone *exclam, poetic or old use* go away! [14c]

begonia *noun* a tropical plant with brightly coloured waxy flowers. [18c: Latin, named after Michel Bégon, a French patron of botany]

begot *and* **begotten** see under **beget**

begrudge *verb* **1** to do, give or allow (something) unwillingly or with regret. **2** (**begrudge sb sth**) to envy or resent them for it. ▪ **begrudgingly** *adv*. [14c]

beguile /bɪˈgaɪl/ *verb* to charm or captivate. ▪ **beguiling** *adj*. [13c: from obsolete verb *guile* to deceive]

begum /ˈbeɪgəm/ *noun* **1** *Indian subcontinent* a Muslim woman of high rank. **2** (**Begum**) a title of respect given to a married Muslim woman. [18c: Urdu]

begun see under **begin**

behalf *noun* interest, part or benefit. [14c: from Anglo-Saxon *be* by + *healfe* side]

IDIOMS **on** *or* (*N Am*) **in behalf of somebody** *or* **something** *and* **on** *or* (*N Am*) **in somebody's** *or* **something's behalf 1** as a representative of them or it. **2** in the interest of them or it.

behave *verb* **1** *intr* to act in a specified way. **2** *tr & intr* (**behave oneself**) to act or conduct oneself in a suitable, polite or orderly way. [15c]

behaviour *or* (*N Am*) **behavior** *noun* **1** way of behaving; manners. **2** *psychol* a response to a stimulus. ▪ **behavioural** *adj*. [15c]

behaviourism *or* (*N Am*) **behaviorism** *noun, psychol* the psychological theory that aims to interpret behaviour as being governed by conditioning (see **condition** *verb* sense 2) as opposed to internal processes (eg thoughts). ▪ **behaviourist** *noun*.

behead *verb* to cut off the head of (someone), esp as a form of capital punishment. [Anglo-Saxon *beheafdian*]

beheld *past tense, past participle of* **behold**

behemoth /bɪˈhiːmɒθ/ *noun* something huge or monstrous. [14c: from Hebrew *b'hemoth* beasts]

behest /bɪˈhɛst/ *noun, formal or old use* a command or request. [12c: from Anglo-Saxon *behæs* a vow or promise]

IDIOMS **at the behest of someone** *or* **at someone's behest** at their request.

behind *prep* **1** at or towards the back or the far side of something or someone. **2** later or slower than something; after in time: *behind schedule.* **3** supporting: *We're all behind you.* **4** in the past with respect to someone or something: *Those problems are all behind me now.* **5** not as far advanced as someone or something: *Technologically, they are way behind the Japanese.* **6** being the cause or precursor of something: *reasons behind the decision.* ▸ *adv* **1** in or to the back or far side of something or someone. **2** remaining; in a place, etc that is or was being left or departed from: *Wait behind after class.* **3** following: *the dog was running behind.* **4** in or into arrears: *fell behind with the rent.* ▸ *adj* **1** not up to date; late: *behind with the payments.* **2** not having progressed enough: *I got behind with my work.* ▸ *noun, informal* the buttocks. [Anglo-Saxon *behindan*]

IDIOMS **behind sb's back** without their knowledge.

behindhand *adj* (following a verb) *dated* **1** not up to date with regard to it; in arrears; behind. **2** late; occurring later or progressing more slowly than expected.

behold *literary or old use, verb* (***beheld***) to see; to look at (something or someone). ▸ *exclam* see!; look! See also **lo**. ▪ **beholder** *noun*. [Anglo-Saxon *behealdan* to hold or observe]

beholden *adj* (**beholden to**) *formal* owing a debt or favour to (someone or something).

behove or (*chiefly N Am*) **behoove** *verb* (***behove, behoving; behooved, behooving***) *old use or formal* to be necessary or fitting: *It behoves me to tell you the truth.* [Anglo-Saxon *behofian* to stand in need of]

beige *noun* a very pale pinkish-brown or yellowish-brown colour. ▸ *adj* having, referring to, made in, etc this colour. [19c: French]

beigel see **bagel**

being *noun* **1** existence; life: *come into being.* **2** a living person or thing. **3** essence; essential self or nature, esp that of a person: *She was like part of my very being.* [14c]

bejewelled *adj* wearing or decorated with jewels.

bel *noun, physics* (symbol **B**) a unit used to represent the ratio of two different power levels, eg of sound, equal to 10 decibels. [20c: named after the Scots-born US inventor Alexander Graham Bell]

belabour or (*N Am*) **belabor** *verb* **1** to argue about or discuss (something) at excessive length. **2** to attack or batter (someone or something) thoroughly, either physically or with words. [16c]

Belarussian or **Belorussian** *adj* belonging or relating to the Republic of Belarus (formerly Belorussia, a region of the Soviet Union), its inhabitants or their language. ▸ *noun* a citizen or inhabitant of Belarus. [20c: from Russian *Belorussiya* White Russia]

belated *adj* happening or coming late, or too late: *belated birthday greetings.* ▪ **belatedly** *adv*. [17c: from obsolete *belate* to make something late]

belay *verb* **1** *mountaineering* to make (a climber) safe by tying their rope to a rock or a wooden or metal pin. **2** *naut* to make (a rope) secure by winding it round a hook or peg, etc. [Anglo-Saxon verb *belecgan*]

belch *verb* **1** *intr* to give out air noisily from the stomach through the mouth; to burp. **2** (*also* **belch out**) of a chimney or volcano, etc: to send out (eg smoke) forcefully or in quantity. ▸ *noun* an act of belching. [Anglo-Saxon *bealcan*]

beleaguer *verb* **1** to cause (someone) bother or worry; to beset: *beleaguered her parents with constant demands.* **2** to surround (eg a city) with an army and lay siege to it. ▪ **beleaguered** *adj*. [16c: from Dutch *belegeren* to besiege]

belfry *noun* (**-*ies***) **1** the upper part of a tower or steeple, where the bells are hung. **2** a tower for bells, usu attached to a church. [15c: from French *berfroi*]

Belgian *adj* belonging or relating to Belgium or its inhabitants. ▸ *noun* a citizen or inhabitant of, or person born in, Belgium. [17c]

belie /bɪˈlaɪ/ *verb* (***belying***) **1** to show (something) to be untrue or false: *The new figures belied previous impressive reports.* **2** to give a false idea or impression of (something): *Her cheerful face belied the seriousness of the situation.* **3** to fail to fulfil or justify (a hope, etc). [Anglo-Saxon *beleogan* to deceive by lying]

belief *noun* **1** a principle or idea, etc accepted as true, esp without proof. **2** trust or confidence: *has no belief in people.* **3** a person's religious faith. **4** a firm opinion. [12c]

believe *verb* **1** to accept (something) as true. **2** (**believe sth of sb**) to accept what is said or proposed, eg about someone, as true. **3** *intr* to have trust or confidence. **4** *intr* (**believe in sth**) to be convinced of the existence of: *Do you believe in ghosts?* **5** *intr* to have religious faith. ▪ **believable** *adj*. ▪ **believer** *noun*. [Anglo-Saxon *belyfan*]

---

believe

This word is often misspelt. The letter *i* comes before the letter e. It might help you to remember the following sentence:

*Don't be**lie**ve a **lie**.*

---

belittle *verb* to treat (something or someone) as unimportant, or of little or no significance; to speak or write disparagingly about (it or them). [18c]

bell *noun* **1** a deep hollow object, usu one made of metal, rounded at one end and wide and open at the other, which makes a ringing sound when struck by the small **clapper** fixed inside it. **2** any other device that makes a ringing or buzzing sound, eg an electric doorbell. **3** the sound made by such an object or device. **4** *Brit informal* a telephone call: *Give me a bell soon.* **5** anything shaped like a bell. [Anglo-Saxon *belle*]

belladonna *noun* **1 deadly nightshade**. **2** a compound, used medicinally, obtained from the deadly nightshade plant. [16c: from Italian *bella donna* beautiful lady; so called because ladies once used the drug as a cosmetic]

bell-bottoms *plural noun* trousers that are much wider at the bottom of the leg than at the knee. ▪ **bell-bottomed** *adj*. [19c]

bellboy or (*chiefly N Am*) **bellhop** *noun* a man or boy who works in a hotel, carrying guests' bags and delivering messages, etc.

belle *noun, dated* a beautiful woman. [17c: French, feminine of *beau* beautiful or fine]

IDIOMS **the belle of the ball** the most beautiful woman or girl at a dance or similar occasion.

belles-lettres /bɛlˈlɛtrə/ *plural noun* works of literature, esp poetry and essays, valued for their elegant style rather than their content. [18c: French, literally 'beautiful letters']

bellicose *adj* likely to, or seeking to, cause an argument or war; aggressive; warlike. [15c: from Latin *bellicosus*, from *bellum* war]

belligerent *adj* **1** aggressive and unfriendly; ready to argue. **2** fighting a war; engaged in conflict. ▸ *noun* a person, faction or country fighting a war. ▪ **belligerence** *noun*. [16c: from Latin *belligerare* to wage war]

bell jar *noun* a bell-shaped glass cover put over apparatus, experiments, etc in a laboratory, to stop gases escaping, etc, or used to protect a delicate decorative object from dust and damage. Also called **bell glass**.

bellow *verb* **1** *intr* to make a loud deep cry like that of a bull. **2** *tr & intr* (*often* **bellow out**) to shout (something) out loudly. ▸ *noun* **1** the loud roar of a bull. **2** a deep loud sound or cry. [14c: from Anglo-Saxon *bylgan*]

bellows *singular or plural noun* **1** (*also* **a pair of bellows**) a device consisting of a bag-like or box-like part with folds in it, which is squeezed to create a current of air, used eg to fan a fire. **2** on some cameras: a sleeve with bellows-like folds connecting the body of the camera to the lens. [13c: from Anglo-Saxon *belg* or *baelig* bag]

bells and whistles *plural noun, informal* additional features which are largely decorative rather than functional.

belly *noun* (**-*ies***) **1** the part of the human body below the chest, containing the organs used for digesting food. **2** the stomach. **3** the lower or under part of an animal's body, which contains the stomach and other organs. **4** the deep interior of something, esp an interior space. **5** a swelling exterior part of something, eg the underside of a plane, etc. ▸ *verb* (**-*ies*, -*ied***) *tr & intr* (*usu* **belly out**) to bulge out, or make (something) bulge or swell out. [Anglo-Saxon *belg* or *baelig* bag]

bellyache *noun, informal* a pain in the belly. ▸ *verb, intr, slang* to complain repeatedly. [Late 19c]

belly button *noun, informal* the navel. Also called **tummy button**.

belly dance *noun* a sensual dance performed by women, in which the belly and hips are moved around in a circling motion. ▸ *verb* (**belly-dance**) *intr* to perform a belly dance. ▪ **belly-dancer** *noun*. [Late 19c]

belly flop *noun* a dive into water in which the body hits the surface flat, instead of at an angle. ▸ *verb* (**belly-flop**) *intr* to perform a belly flop. [Late 19c]

bellyful *noun* **1** enough to eat. **2** *slang* (**a bellyful of sth** *or* **sb**) more than enough, or more than one can bear of it, them, or their behaviour, etc.

belly laugh *noun* a deep unrestrained laugh.

belong *verb, intr* **1** (**belong to sb** *or* **sth**) to be the right or property of. **2** (**belong to sth**) to be a member of (a group, club, etc) or a native of (a place). **3 a** to have a proper place, or have the right qualities to fit (esp with or in something or someone); to go along or together (with something or someone); **b** to be properly classified (in a class, section, under a heading, etc). **4** to be entirely acceptable on a social or personal level; to be at home, or to fit in: *It's a nice place, but somehow I just don't belong*. ▪ **belonging** *noun* (*esp in* **a sense of belonging**) fitting in or acceptability within a group. [14c intensive of *longen* to belong or to be suitable]

belongings *plural noun* personal possessions.

Belorussian see **Belarussian**

beloved /bɪˈlʌvd, bɪˈlʌvɪd/ *adj, often in compounds* much loved; very dear: *my beloved wife*. ▸ *noun, chiefly literary or old use* a person who is much loved. [14c: from an obsolete verb *belove* to love]

below *prep* **1** lower in position, rank, amount, degree, number or status, etc than a specified thing: *40 degrees below zero*. **2** not worthy of someone; beneath them. **3** under the surface of something: *below deck*. ▸ *adv* **1** at, to or in a lower place, point or level. **2** further on in a book, etc: *See paragraph below*. [14c as *bilooghe*, from *bi-* by + *looghe* low]

belt *noun* **1** a long narrow piece of leather or cloth worn around the waist. **2** a **seat belt**. **3** an area or zone, usu a relatively long and narrow one: *a belt of rain*. **4** *often in compounds* a band of rubber, etc moving the wheels, or round the wheels, of a machine: *fan belt* • *conveyor belt*. **5** *slang* a hard blow. ▸ *verb* **1** to put a belt around (someone or something). **2** to beat (someone or something) with a belt. **3** *tr & intr* (*often* **belt into**) *informal* to hit someone repeatedly. **4** *intr* (*esp* **belt along**) *informal* to move very fast, esp in a specified direction. **5** (*also* **belt sth on**) to fasten it with, or on with, a belt. [Anglo-Saxon: from Latin *balteus*]

IDIOMS **below the belt** *informal* unfair; not following the accepted rules of behaviour. **under one's belt** *informal* of an achievement, qualification, valuable experience, etc: firmly secured and in one's possession.

PHRASAL VERBS **belt sth out** *informal* to sing or say it very loudly. **belt up** *informal* **1** to stop talking; to be quiet. **2** to fasten one's seat-belt.

belter *noun, informal* something or someone that stands out from the others: *That goal was a belter.*

beluga /bəˈluːgə/ *noun* **1** a kind of large sturgeon. **2** caviar from this type of sturgeon. **3** a white whale. [16c: Russian, from *beliy* white]

belvedere *noun, archit* **1** a turret, lantern or room built on the top of a house, with open or glazed sides to provide a view or to let in light and air. **2** a **summerhouse** on high ground. [16c: Italian, from *bel* beautiful + *vedere* to see]

BEM *abbrev* British Empire Medal.

bemoan *verb* to express great sadness or regret about (something). [Anglo-Saxon]

bemused *adj* bewildered; confused. [18c]

ben *noun, Scot* esp in place names: a mountain or mountain peak: *Ben Nevis*. [18c: from Gaelic *beann*]

bench *noun* **1** a long seat for seating several people. **2** a work-table for a carpenter, scientist, etc. **3** (**the bench** *or* **the Bench**) **a** the place where the judge or magistrate sits in court; **b** judges and magistrates as a group or profession. See also **Queen's Bench**. [Anglo-Saxon *benc*]

IDIOMS **on the bench 1** of a person: holding the office of, or officiating as, a judge or bishop. **2** of a football, etc player: listed as a substitute.

benchmark *noun* **1** anything taken or used as a standard or point of reference. **2** *surveying* a permanent mark cut on a post, building, etc giving the height above sea level of the land at that exact spot. **3** *comput* a standard program used to compare the performance of different makes of computer.

bench test *noun* a test carried out on something, eg computer hardware or software, before it is installed or released.

bend *verb* (***bent***) **1** *tr & intr* to make or become angled or curved. **2** *intr* to move or stretch in a curve.

3 *intr* (*usu* **bend down** *or* **over**) to move the top part of the body forward and down towards the ground. **4** *tr & intr* to submit or force (someone or something) to submit: *bent them to his will.* **5** to aim or direct (one's attention, etc) towards something. See also **bent**. ▸ *noun* **1** a curve or bent part. **2** the act of curving or bending. See also **the bends**. ▪ **bendy** *adj* (**-*ier*, -*iest***). [Anglo-Saxon]

IDIOMS **bend the rules** to interpret the rules in one's favour, without actually breaking them. **round the bend** *informal* mad; crazy.

bender *noun, slang* a drunken spree; a spell of uncontrolled drinking.

the bends *singular or plural noun* a non-technical name for **decompression sickness**. [Late 19c]

beneath *prep* **1** under; below. **2** not worthy of (someone or something): *He thinks the job is beneath him.* ▸ *adv, rather formal or archaic* below; underneath. [Anglo-Saxon *beneothan*]

Benedictine *noun* **1** a member of the Christian religious order (the **Order of St Benedict**) that follows the teachings of St Benedict. *as adj*: *a Benedictine monk.* **2** a liqueur first made by Benedictine monks. [15c]

benediction *noun, Christianity* **1** a prayer giving blessing, esp at the end of a religious service. **2** *RC Church* a service in which the congregation is blessed. ▪ **benedictory** *adj.* [15c: from Latin *benedicere* to bless]

benefaction *noun* **1** a gift or donation from a benefactor. **2** an act of doing good; help or charity given. [17c]

benefactor *noun* a person who gives help, esp financial help, to an institution, cause or person. Also (if a female benefactor) **benefactress**. [15c: from Latin *bene* good + *facere* to do]

benefice *noun* a position as a priest or minister, or other church office, and the income that goes with it. [14c: from Latin *beneficium* a favour, service or benefit]

beneficent /bɪˈnɛfɪsənt/ *adj* kind and generous. ▪ **beneficence** *noun.* [16c: from Latin *beneficentia*]

beneficial *adj* having good results or benefits; advantageous. [15c: from Latin *beneficialis* generous]

beneficiary *noun* (**-*ies***) **1** a person who benefits from something. **2** *law* **a** a person who is entitled to estate or interest held for them by trustees; **b** a person who receives property or money, etc in a will, or benefits under an insurance policy, etc. [17c]

benefit *noun* **1** something good gained or received. **2** advantage or sake. **3** (*often* **benefits**) a payment made by a government or company insurance scheme, usu to someone who is ill or out of work. **4** a concert, football match, etc from which the profits are given to a particular cause, person or group in need. ▸ *verb* (***benefited, benefiting***; *N Am also* ***benefitted, benefitting***) **1** *intr* (*esp* **benefit from** *or* **by**) to gain an advantage from (something). **2** to do good to (someone). [14c: from French *benfet*, from Latin *benefactum* good deed]

IDIOMS **give sb the benefit of the doubt** in a case where some doubt remains: to assume that they are telling the truth, or are innocent, because there is not enough evidence to be certain that they are not.

benefit society *noun* a **friendly society**.

benevolence *noun* **1** the desire to do good; kindness; generosity. **2** an act of kindness or generosity. ▪ **benevolent** *adj.* [14c: from Latin *bene* good + *volens* wishing]

Bengali *adj* belonging or relating to Bangladesh and the state of W Bengal, their inhabitants, or their language. ▸ *noun* **1** a citizen or inhabitant of, or person born in, Bangladesh or W Bengal. **2** (*also* **Bangla**) the official language of Bangladesh and the chief language of W Bengal. [19c: from Hindi *Bangali*]

benign /bɪˈnaɪn/ *adj* **1** kind; gentle. **2** *med* **a** of a disorder: not having harmful effects; of a mild form; **b** specifically of a cancerous tumour: of a type that does not invade and destroy the surrounding tissue. Compare **malignant**. **3** favourable; promising. ▪ **benignly** *adv.* [14c: from Latin *benignus*]

benignant /bəˈnɪgnənt/ *adj* **1** *med* of a disease or growth, etc: not fatal; a later and less common word for **benign**. **2** kind. **3** favourable. ▪ **benignancy** *noun* (**-*ies***).

benignity /bəˈnɪgnɪtɪ/ *noun* (**-*ies***) kindness; benevolence. [14c]

bent *adj* **1** not straight; curved or having a bend. **2** *Brit slang* **a** dishonest; corrupt; **b** obtained dishonestly; stolen: *selling bent videos.* **3** (*usu* **bent on** *or* **upon sth**) having all one's attention or energy directed on it, or on doing it: *bent on revenge.* ▸ *noun* a natural inclination, liking or aptitude: *shows a real bent for music.* ▸ *verb, past tense, past participle of* **bend**. [14c]

benthos /ˈbɛnθɒs/ *noun, biol* the living organisms that are found at the bottom of a sea or lake. ▪ **benthic** *adj* living at the bottom of a sea or lake. Compare **pelagic**. [19c: Greek, literally 'depth']

benumb *verb* **1** to make (someone or something) numb. **2** to stupefy (esp the senses or the mind). [15c]

Benzedrine *noun, trademark* an **amphetamine** drug. [20c]

benzene *noun, chem* an inflammable colourless liquid **hydrocarbon**, mainly obtained from petroleum, that is widely used as a solvent. [19c]

benzine *or* **benzin** *noun* a volatile mixture of **hydrocarbon**s distilled from petroleum, used as a motor fuel and solvent, etc. [19c]

benzodiazepine /bɛnzoʊdaɪˈazəpiːn, -ˈeɪzəpiːn/ *noun, med* any of various potentially addictive minor tranquillizer and hypnotic drugs. [20c]

benzoin /ˈbɛnzoʊɪn, -zɔɪn/ *noun* the aromatic resinous sap of a tree native to Java and Sumatra, used in medicines, perfumes, incense, etc. [16c in the form *benjoin*: ultimately from Arabic *luban jawa* incense of Java]

bequeath *verb* **1** to leave (personal property) in a will (to someone). **2** to pass on or give to posterity. [Anglo-Saxon *becwethan*]

bequest *noun* **1** an act of leaving personal property in a will. **2** anything left or bequeathed in someone's will. [14c: from Anglo-Saxon *becwethan* (see **bequeath**)]

berate *verb* to scold (someone) severely. [16c: from Anglo-Saxon *bi-* by + old verb *rate* to scold]

Berber *noun* **1** any of several native Muslim tribes of N Africa. **2** an individual belonging to any of these tribes. **3** any of a group of Afro-Asiatic languages spoken by these people. ▸ *adj* belonging or relating to this group or their language. [18c: from Arabic *barbar*]

bereave *verb* to widow, orphan or deprive (someone) of a close relative or friend by death. ▪ **bereaved** *adj.* ▪ **bereavement** *noun.* [Anglo-Saxon *bereafian* to rob or plunder]

bereft *adj* (*usu* **bereft of sth**) deprived of it. [16c *past participle* of **bereave**]

beret /ˈbɛreɪ, *N Am* bəˈreɪ/ *noun* a round flat cap made of soft material. [19c: from French *béret* cap]

berg *noun* short form of **iceberg**. [19c]

bergamot *noun* **1** a small citrus tree that produces acidic pear-shaped fruits. **2** (*also* **bergamot oil**) the oil extracted from the rind of the fruit of this tree, used in perfumery. [17c: named after Bergamo in N Italy]

beriberi *noun, pathol, med* a deficiency disease caused by lack of **thiamine**. [18c: from Sinhalese *beri* weakness]

berkelium *noun, chem* (symbol **Bk**) a radioactive metallic element manufactured artificially. [20c: after Berkeley in California, where it was first made]

Berks. /bɑːks/ *abbrev, English county* Berkshire.

Berlin Wall *noun, hist* a wall separating East Berlin, Germany, from the part of the city occupied by Western powers, built in 1961 to stop emigration from East to West, but mostly taken down when Germany was reunified in 1990.

berm *noun* **1** a narrow ledge or path beside an embankment, road or canal, etc. **2** *geog* a ridge of sand or stones on a beach, formed by incoming tides. Also called **bar**.

Bermuda shorts *or* **Bermudas** *plural noun* knee-length shorts. [20c]

berry *noun* (**-ies**) **1** *botany* an **indehiscent** fleshy fruit that contains seeds that are not surrounded by a stony protective layer, eg grape, cucumber, tomato. **2** *loosely* any of the various small fleshy edible fruits that are not true berries, eg strawberry. [Anglo-Saxon *berie*]

berserk *adj* (*esp* **go berserk**) **1** violently angry; wild and destructive. **2** *informal & facetious* furious; crazy. [19c: from Norse *berserkr*]

berth *noun* **1** a sleeping-place in a ship or train, etc. **2** a place in a port where a ship or boat can be tied up. **3** enough room for a ship to be able to turn round in. ▸ *verb* **1** to tie up (a ship) in its berth. **2** *intr* of a ship: to arrive at its berth; to moor. **3** to provide a sleeping-place for (someone). [17c]

IDIOMS **give sb** *or* **sth a wide berth** to stay well away from them or it.

beryl *noun, geol* a hard mineral, used as a source of **beryllium** and as a gemstone, the most valuable varieties being **aquamarine** and **emerald**. [14c: ultimately from Greek *beryllos*]

beryllium *noun, chem* (symbol **Be**) a silvery-grey metallic element, obtained from the mineral **beryl**. [19c]

beseech *verb* (***besought*** *or* ***beseeched***) *formal or literary* to ask (someone) earnestly; to beg. [12c: from Anglo-Saxon *bi-* by + obsolete *sechen* to seek]

beset *verb* (***beset, besetting***) *now chiefly literary or formal* **1** to worry or harass (someone), or to hamper or complicate (something). **2** to surround, attack or besiege (a person or people) on every side. [Anglo-Saxon *besettan* to surround or set about]

beside *prep* **1** next to, by the side of or near something or someone. **2** not relevant to something: *beside the point.* **3** as compared with something or someone: *All beauty pales beside hers.* [13c: from Anglo-Saxon *be* by + *sidan* side]

IDIOMS **beside oneself** in a state of uncontrollable anger, excitement or other emotion.

besides *prep* in addition to, as well as or apart from something or someone. ▸ *adv* **1** also; as well. **2** (often as a sentence connector) moreover; in any case: *I don't want to go; besides, I'm not dressed.* [13c]

besiege *verb* **1** to surround (a town or stronghold) with an army in order to force it to surrender. **2** to gather round (something or someone) in a crowd; to surround: *besieged by excited fans.* **3** to annoy (someone) constantly or thoroughly; to plague or bother: *She besieged me with questions.* **4** to inundate or overwhelm (someone): *besieged with offers of help.* [13c]

besmirch *verb, formal* to spoil or stain (the reputation, character, name, etc of someone). [16c]

besom *noun* a large brush made from sticks tied to a long wooden handle. [Anglo-Saxon *besma*]

besotted *adj* **1** foolishly infatuated (with or by someone or something). **2** *archaic* confused, esp through having drunk too much alcohol. [16c: from old verb *besot* to make foolish or sottish]

besought *past tense, past participle of* **beseech**

bespatter *verb* to cover (something or someone) with splashes, esp of a dirty liquid. [17c]

bespeak *verb, formal* **1** to claim, engage or order (something) in advance. See also **bespoke**. **2** to show or be evidence of (something). **3** to indicate (something) in advance; to foretell: *This worrying news bespoke trouble ahead.* [16c]

bespectacled *adj* wearing spectacles.

bespoke *adj* **1** of clothes: made to fit a particular person. **2** of a tailor: making clothes to order, to fit individual customers and their requirements. **3** *comput* of software: specially created for a specific situation. [18c]

best *adj* (*superlative of* **good**) **1** most excellent, suitable or desirable. **2** most successful, clever, able or skilled, etc. **3** the greatest or most: *took the best part of an hour.* ▸ *adv* (*superlative of* **well**[1]) **1** most successfully or skilfully, etc: *Who did best in the test?* **2** more than, or better than, all others: *Which hat looks best?* ▸ *noun* **1** (**the best**) the most excellent or suitable person or thing; the most desirable quality or result, etc: *the best of the bunch.* **2** the greatest effort; one's utmost: *Do your best.* **3** a person's finest clothes: *Sunday best.* **4** (**the best**) victory or success: *get the best of an argument.* **5** (*usu* **the best of sth**) a winning majority from (a given number, etc): *the best of three.* ▸ *verb, informal* to beat or defeat (someone). [Anglo-Saxon *betst*]

IDIOMS **at best** considered in the most favourable way; in the best of circumstances. **for the best** likely or intended to have the best results possible, esp in the long term or over all. **make the best of** to do, etc as well as possible from (what is available or possible).

best boy *noun, cinema & TV, orig N Am* the chargehand electrician in a production crew, chief assistant to the **gaffer** (sense 2). [20c]

bestial *adj* **1** *derog* cruel; savage; brutish. **2** rude; unrefined; uncivilized. **3** like or referring to an animal in character, behaviour, etc. [14c: from Latin *bestia* animal]

bestiality *noun* (**-ies**) disgusting or cruel behaviour.

bestiary *noun* (**-ies**) a kind of book popular in Europe in the Middle Ages, containing pictures and descriptions of animals, often used for moral instruction. [19c: from Latin *bestiarium* a menagerie]

bestir *verb* (**bestir oneself**) to make an effort to become active; to get oneself moving or busy. [14c]

best man *noun* a bridegroom's chief attendant at a wedding. [18c]

bestow *verb* (**bestow on** *or* **upon**) *formal* to give or present (a title, award, etc) to (someone). ▪ **bestowal** *noun.* [14c: from Anglo-Saxon *stowen* to place]

bestrewn *adj, esp formal or literary* of a surface, eg the ground, a floor, or table-top: littered or covered loosely. [19c: from Anglo-Saxon *bestreowian* to strew]

bestride *verb* (*past tense* ***bestrode***, *past participle* ***bestridden***) *formal or literary* to sit or stand across (eg a horse) with one leg on each side. [Anglo-Saxon *bestridan*, from *stridan* to straddle]

bestseller *noun* a book or other item that sells in large numbers. ▪ **bestselling** *adj.* [Early 19c]

bet *verb* (***bet*** *or* ***betted, betting***) **1** *tr & intr* to risk (a sum of money or other asset) on predicting the outcome or result of a future event, esp a race or other sporting event. **2** (*usu* **bet sb sth**) to make a bet (with someone) of (a specified amount). **3** *informal* to feel sure or confident: *I bet they've forgotten.* ▶ *noun* **1** an act of betting. **2** a sum of money, or other asset, betted. **3** *informal* an opinion or guess: *My bet is that he's bluffing.* **4** *informal* a choice of action or way ahead: *Our best bet is to postpone the trip.* [16c]

IDIOMS **you bet** *slang, esp N Am* certainly; definitely; of course.

beta *noun* **1** the second letter of the Greek alphabet. **2** a mark indicating the second highest grade or quality. **3** the second in a series, or the second of two categories or types. [14c: Greek]

beta-blocker *noun, med* a drug that slows the heartbeat, used to treat high blood pressure, angina, and abnormal heart rhythms. [20c]

betacarotene *noun, biochem* a form of the pigment **carotene**, found in yellow and orange fruits and vegetables, that is converted to vitamin A in the body.

beta decay *noun, physics* a form of radioactive decay in which a neutron in an atomic nucleus spontaneously breaks up into a **proton** (which remains within the nucleus) and an **electron** (which is emitted).

beta particle *noun, physics* an **electron** or **positron** produced when a neutron inside an unstable radioactive nucleus turns into a proton, or a proton turns into a neutron. [20c]

betatron *noun, physics* a device that is used to accelerate charged subatomic particles, used in medicine and industry, which continuously increases the magnetic **flux** within the orbit of a charged particle. [20c]

betel /ˈbiːtəl/ *noun* an Asian palm, the fruit of which (the **betel nut**) is mixed with lime and chewed as a mild stimulant. [16c: Portuguese, from Malayalam *vettila*]

bête noire /bɛt nwɑː(r)/ *noun* (***bêtes noires***) a person or thing that esp bothers, annoys or frightens someone. [19c: French, literally 'black beast']

betide *verb* (now limited to this form, as infinitive and 3rd person subjunctive) *literary or archaic* **1** *intr* to happen; to come to pass: *whate'er may betide.* **2** to happen to (someone); to befall (them): *Woe betide you.* [13c: from Anglo-Saxon *tidan* to befall]

betoken *verb, formal* to be evidence of (something); to signify. [15c: from Anglo-Saxon *tacnian* to signify]

betray *verb* **1** to hand over or expose (a friend or one's country, etc) to an enemy. **2** to give away or disclose (a secret, etc). **3** to break (a promise, etc) or to be unfaithful to (someone). **4** to be evidence of (something, esp something intended to be hidden): *Her face betrayed her unhappiness.* ▪ **betrayal** *noun.* ▪ **betrayer** *noun.* [13c: ultimately from Latin *tradere* to hand over]

betrothal *noun, formal* engagement to be married. [19c]

betrothed *formal or facetious, adj* of a person: engaged to marry someone. ▶ *noun* a person to whom someone is betrothed. [16c: from the archaic verb *betroth* to plight one's **troth**]

better *adj* (*comparative of* **good**) **1** more excellent, suitable or desirable, etc. **2** (*usu* **better at sth**) more successful, skilful, etc in doing it. **3** (*comparative of* **well**[1]) (*esp* **be** *or* **feel** *or* **get better**) improved in health or recovered from illness. **4** greater: *the better part of a day.* ▶ *adv* (*comparative of* **well**[1]) **1** more excellently, successfully or fully, etc. **2** in or to a greater degree. ▶ *noun* **1** (*esp* **betters**) a person superior in quality or status, etc. **2** (**the better**) the person or thing that is the more excellent or suitable, etc of two comparable things or people. ▶ *verb* **1** to beat or improve on (something). **2** to make (something) more suitable, desirable or excellent, etc. [Anglo-Saxon *betera*]

IDIOMS **get the better of sb** to gain the advantage over them; to outwit them. **had better do sth** ought to do it, esp to avoid some undesirable outcome.

better half *noun, jocular or patronizing* one's own, or someone else's, partner or spouse.

betterment *noun* improvement or advancement.

betting *noun* gambling by predicting the outcome of some future event, esp a race or other sporting event.

betting-shop *noun, Brit* a licensed establishment where the public can place bets; a bookmaker's.

between *prep* **1** in, to, through or across the space dividing (two people, places, times, etc). **2** to and from: *travelling between Leeds and Bradford.* **3** in combination; acting together: *They bought the house between them.* **4** shared out among: *Divide the money between you.* **5** involving a choice between alternatives: *choose between right and wrong.* **6** including; involving: *a fight between rivals.* ▶ *adv* (*also* **in between**) in or into the middle of (two points in space or time, etc): *time for a quick lunch between appointments.* [Anglo-Saxon *betweonum*, from *be* by + *twegen* two]

between, among

It is acceptable to use the word **between** rather than **among** when you are referring to more than two people or things:

Viewers tend to switch between channels.

Between is also usual when individual people or things are named:

Duties are divided between John, Margaret and Catherine.

However, the word **among** is sometimes more appropriate when there are more than two people or things, and they are not individually named. It is also more appropriate for the notion of sharing or distributing:

Hand these out among all of you.

---

betwixt *prep,* ▸ *adv, old use* between. [Anglo-Saxon *betweox*]

IDIOMS **betwixt and between** undecided; in a middle position.

bevel *noun* a sloping edge to a surface, meeting another surface at an angle between the horizontal and the vertical. ▸ *verb* (***bevelled, bevelling***; *N Am also* ***beveled, beveling***) **1** to give a bevel to (eg a piece of wood). **2** *intr* to slope at an angle. [16c: from French *baer* to gape]

beverage *noun, formal* a prepared drink. [14c: from French *bevrage*, from *beivre* to drink]

bevvy *or* **bevy** *noun* (***-ies***) *informal* **1** alcoholic drink, or an individual alcoholic drink. **2** a drinking session. [19c: a colloquial shortening of **beverage**]

bevy *noun* (***-ies***) **1** a group, orig a group of women or girls. **2** a flock of larks, quails or swans. [15c]

bewail *verb, chiefly literary* to express great sorrow about (something), or to lament over (it). [14c]

beware *verb* (not inflected in modern use, but used as an imperative or infinitive) **1** *intr* (*usu* **beware of**) to be careful of (something); to be on one's guard. **2** *old use or literary* to be on one's guard against (something or someone): *Beware the cruel hand of fate.* [13c: from **be** (imperative) + *ware* cautious or wary]

bewilder *verb* to confuse, disorientate or puzzle (someone or something) thoroughly. ▪ **bewildering** *adj.* ▪ **bewilderment** *noun.* [17c: from obsolete verb *wilder* to lose one's way]

bewitch *verb* **1** to charm, fascinate or enchant. **2** to cast a spell on (someone or something). ▪ **bewitching** *adj.* [From Anglo-Saxon *wiccian* to use witchcraft]

beyond *prep* **1** on the far side of something: *beyond the hills.* **2** farther on than something in time or place. **3** out of the range, reach, power, understanding, possibility, etc of someone or something. **4** greater or better than something in amount, size, or level: *beyond all our expectations.* **5** other than, or apart from, something: *unable to help beyond giving money.* ▸ *adv* farther away; to or on the far side of something. ▸ *noun* (**the beyond**) the unknown, esp life after death. [Anglo-Saxon *begeondan*]

bezel *noun* **1** the sloped surface of a cutting tool. **2** a grooved rim that holds a watch-glass, precious gem, etc in its setting. **3** an oblique side or face of a cut gem. [17c: from French]

B-film see **B-movie**

Bh *noun, chem* bohrium.

bhaji /ˈbɑːdʒiː/ *noun, cookery* an Indian appetizer consisting of vegetables in a batter of flour and spices, formed into a ball and deep-fried. [20c: Hindi]

bhangra *noun* a style of pop music created from a mix of traditional Punjabi and Western pop. [20c: Punjabi, the name of a traditional harvest dance]

bhp *abbrev* brake horsepower.

bhuna *or* **bhoona** /ˈbuːnə/ *noun* in Indian cookery: a dish of meat or vegetables sautéed in oil and a mix of spices. [19c: Hindi and Urdu]

Bi *symbol, chem* bismuth.

bi- *or* (*before a vowel*) **bin-** *prefix, denoting* **1** having, involving, using or consisting of two things or elements, etc: *bifocal.* **2** happening twice in every one (of something), or once in every two (of something): *bi-monthly.* **3** on or from both sides: *bilateral.* **4** *chem* applied to a salt or compound: containing twice the amount of the acid, etc shown in the prefixed word (eg **bicarbonate** of soda indicates the presence of twice the quantity of carbonic acid present in **carbonate** of soda). *Technical equivalent* **di-**. [14c: from Latin *bis* twice]

biannual *adj* occurring or produced, etc twice a year. ▪ **biannually** *adv.*

bias *noun* **1** an inclination to favour or disfavour one side against another in a dispute, competition, etc; a prejudice. **2** a tendency or principal quality in a person's character. **3** *bowls, etc* a weight on or in an object (eg a bowl) which makes it move in a particular direction. **4** *dressmaking, etc* a line cut across the grain of a fabric. **5** *stats* an unevenness in a sample due to a systematic error. ▸ *verb* (***biased, biasing***; *also* ***biassed, biassing***) **1** to influence or prejudice, esp unfairly or without objective grounds. **2** to give a bias to (something). ▪ **biased** *or* **biassed** *adj.* [16c: from French *biais* slant]

biathlon *noun* an outdoor sporting event involving skiing and shooting. [20c]

biaxial *adj* esp of a crystal: having two axes (see **axis** sense 2). [19c]

bib *noun* **1** a piece of cloth or plastic fastened under a baby's or child's chin to protect its clothes while eating or drinking. **2** the top part of an apron or overalls. [16c]

bibl. *abbrev* **1** biblical. **2** bibliographical. **3** bibliography.

Bible *noun* **1 a** (**the Bible**) the sacred writings of the Christian Church, consisting of the Old and New Testaments; **b** (*sometimes* **bible**) a copy of these writings. **2 a** (**the Bible**) the Jewish Scriptures; the Old Testament or Hebrew Bible; **b** (*sometimes* **bible**) a copy of these. **3** (*usu* **bible**) an authoritative and comprehensive book on a particular subject, regarded as definitive. ▪ **biblical** *adj.* [14c: ultimately from Greek *biblos* a scroll or papyrus]

Bible-basher *or* **Bible-thumper** *noun, slang* a vigorous, aggressive or dogmatic Christian preacher. ▪ **Bible-bashing** *noun.*

Bible belt *noun* areas of the southern USA where the population is predominantly Christian fundamentalist. [20c]

biblio- *combining form, denoting* book or books. [From Greek *biblion* book]

bibliography *noun* (***-ies***) **1** a list of books by one author or on one subject. **2** a list of the books used as sources during the writing of a book or other written work, usu printed at the end of it. **3** the study, description or knowledge of books, in terms of their subjects, authors, editions, history, format, etc. ▪ **bib-**

liographer *noun.* ▪ **bibliographic** *or* **bibliographical** *adj.* [17c; 19c in the current senses]

bibliophile *noun* an admirer or collector of books. [19c]

bibulous *adj, humorous* liking alcohol too much. [17c: from Latin *bibulus* drinking freely]

bicameral *adj* of a legislative body: made up of two chambers. [19c: from Latin *camera* a chamber]

bicarbonate *noun, chem* an acid salt of carbonic acid. [19c]

bicarbonate of soda *noun, informal* (often shortened to **bicarb**) sodium bicarbonate, a white powder used in baking to make cakes, etc rise (as **baking soda** and **baking powder**), and as an indigestion remedy.

bicentenary *noun* (**-ies**) *esp Brit* **1** a two-hundredth anniversary of an event. **2** a celebration held in honour of such an anniversary. ▸ *adj* marking, belonging to, referring to or in honour of a bicentenary. [19c]

bicentennial *noun, adj, chiefly N Am, esp US* bicentenary. [19c]

biceps *noun* (*pl* ***biceps***) *anatomy* any muscle that has two points of origin, esp the muscle at the front of the upper arm. [17c: Latin, meaning 'two-headed']

bicker *verb, intr, informal* to argue or quarrel in a petty way (esp about or over something trivial). ▪ **bickering** *noun.* [14c as *biker*, meaning 'to fight or skirmish']

biconcave *adj, physics* of a lens: concave on both sides. [19c]

biconvex *adj, physics* of a lens: convex on both sides. [19c]

bicuspid /baɪˈkʌspɪd/ *adj* esp of a tooth: having two cusps or points. ▸ *noun, N Am* a **premolar** tooth. [19c]

bicycle *noun* a vehicle consisting of a metal frame with two wheels one behind the other, and a saddle between and above them, which is driven by turning pedals with the feet and steered by handlebars attached to the front wheel. Often shortened to **bike,** *sometimes* **cycle**. ▸ *verb, intr, rather formal* to ride a bicycle. Usually shortened to **cycle**, *sometimes* **bike**. [19c: French, from **bi-** (sense 1) + Greek *kyklos* a wheel or circle]

bicycle kick *noun, football* a kick made backwards over the player's head while both feet are off the ground.

bid[1] *verb* (***bid, bidding***) **1** *tr & intr* to offer (an amount of money) when trying to buy something, esp at an auction. **2** *tr & intr, cards* to state in advance (the number of tricks one will try to win). **3** *intr* (*esp* **bid for sth**) to state a price one will charge for work to be done. ▸ *noun* **1** an offer of an amount of money in payment for something, esp at an auction. **2** *cards* a statement of how many tricks one proposes to win. **3** *informal* an attempt to obtain or achieve something: *a bid for freedom.* ▪ **bidder** *noun.* [Anglo-Saxon *beodan* meaning 'to command' or 'summon']

bid[2] *verb* (*past tense* ***bade*** /bad, beɪd/, *past participle* ***bidden***, *present participle* ***bidding***) *formal, archaic or literary* **1** to express (a wish or greeting, etc) (to someone): *We bid you welcome.* **2** (with an imperative) to command (someone) (to do a specified thing): *The king bade him kneel.* **3** (*often* **bid sb to sth** *or* **to do sth**) to invite them to it, or to do it. [Anglo-Saxon *biddan*, meaning 'to beg' or 'to pray']

biddable *adj* compliant; obedient; docile.

bidding *noun* **1** a command, request or invitation. **2** the offers at an auction. **3** *cards* the act of making bids.

IDIOMS **do sb's bidding** to obey their orders.

biddy *noun* (**-ies**) *slang, chiefly derog* (*esp* **old biddy**) a woman, esp an old, doddery, fussy or cantankerous one. [18c, meaning 'an Irish maid-servant']

bide *verb* (*past tense* ***bided*** *or* ***bode,*** *past participle* ***bided***) *intr, Scot or old use* to wait or stay. [Anglo-Saxon *bidan*]

IDIOMS **bide one's time** to wait patiently for a good opportunity or for the right moment.

bidet /ˈbiːdeɪ/ *noun* a small low basin with taps, for washing the genital and anal areas. [17c: French, meaning 'a pony']

biennial *adj* **1** of an event: occurring once in every two years. **2** esp of a plant: lasting two years. ▸ *noun* **1** *botany* a plant that takes two years to complete its life cycle. See also **annual, perennial**. **2** an event that takes place, or is celebrated, every two years. [17c: from Latin *biennium* two years]

bier *noun* a movable stand on which a coffin rests or is transported. [Anglo-Saxon *bær*]

biff *slang, esp Brit, verb* to hit (someone or something) very hard, usu with the fist. ▸ *noun* a hard sharp blow. [Late 19c: imitating the sound]

bifid *adj, biol* divided into two parts by a deep split. [17c: from Latin *bifidus*, from *findere, findus* to split]

bifocal *adj* of a lens: **1** having two different focal lengths. **2** of spectacle or contact lenses: having two separate sections with different focal lengths, one for near vision, and one for viewing distant objects. [19c]

bifocals *plural noun* a pair of glasses with **bifocal** lenses.

bifurcate /ˈbaɪfəkeɪt/ *verb, intr, formal* of roads, etc: to divide into two parts or branches; to fork. ▸ *adj* forked or branched into two parts. ▪ **bifurcation** *noun.* [17c: from Latin *bifurcatus*, from *furca* fork]

big *adj* (***bigger, biggest***) **1** large or largest in size, amount, weight, number, power, etc. **2** significant or important to someone. **3** important, powerful or successful. **4** elder: *my big sister.* **5** adult; grown-up: *not big enough to go on your own.* **6** *often ironic* generous or magnanimous: *That was big of him.* **7** boastful; extravagant; ambitious: *big ideas.* **8** (*usu* **big on sth**) *informal, esp N Am* fond of or enthusiastic (about it). **9** *old use* in an advanced stage of pregnancy: *big with child.* ▸ *adv, informal* **1** in a boastful, extravagant or ambitious way: *act big.* **2** greatly or impressively: *Your idea went over big with the boss.* [14c]

IDIOMS **big deal!** *ironic slang* an expression indicating that one is indifferent to, or not at all impressed by, what has just been said or done. **in a big way** *informal* very much; strongly and enthusiastically.

bigamy *noun* (**-ies**) the crime of being married to two wives or husbands at the same time. ▪ **bigamist** *noun.* ▪ **bigamous** *adj.* [13c: ultimately from Latin *bi-* twice + Greek *gamos* marriage]

the Big Apple *noun, US informal* New York City. [20c]

Big Bang *noun* **1** a hypothetical model of the origin of the universe which postulates that all matter and energy were once concentrated into an unimaginably dense state, which underwent a gigantic explosion between 13 and 20 billion years ago. **2** *Brit informal* the introduction of major changes to the rules controlling the British Stock Exchange in 1986. [20c in sense 1]

Big Brother *noun* an all-powerful government or organization, etc, or its leader, keeping complete control over, and a continual watch on, its citizens. [20c: the name of the tyrannical leader in George Orwell's novel *Nineteen Eighty-Four*]

big business *noun* powerful commercial and industrial organizations, esp considered as a group.

big dipper *noun* (**the Big Dipper**) *esp N Am* **the Plough** (see under **plough**).

big game *noun* large animals, such as lions, tigers and elephants, etc hunted for sport.

bighead *noun, informal, derog* a conceited or arrogant person. ▪ **bigheaded** *adj*.

bight /baɪt/ *noun* **1** a stretch of gently curving coastline. **2** a loose curve or loop in a rope. [Anglo-Saxon *byht*]

big name *noun, informal* a celebrity.

big noise *or* (*chiefly Brit*) **big shot** *noun, informal* an important, powerful or influential person.

bigot *noun* someone who is persistently prejudiced, esp about religion, politics or race, and refuses to tolerate the opinions of others. ▪ **bigoted** *adj*. ▪ **bigotry** *noun* (***-ies***). [16c, first meaning 'a superstitious hypocrite': French]

the Big Smoke *noun, informal* a large city, esp London. [19c]

big time *noun, informal* success in an activity or profession, esp in show business.

big top *noun* the main tent of a circus.

bigwig *noun, informal* an important person. [18c]

bijou /ˈbiːʒuː/ *noun* (***bijoux*** *or* ***bijous***) a small delicate jewel or trinket. ▸ *adj* small and elegant. [17c: French, from Breton *bizou* a ring]

bike *noun, informal* **1** a bicycle. **2** a motorcycle. ▸ *verb, intr* to ride a bicycle or motorcycle. ▪ **biker** *noun* someone who rides a motorcycle, esp a member of a motorcycle gang or group. *Aust & NZ informal equivalent* **bikie**. [19c: colloquial short form of **bicycle**]

bikini *noun* a small two-piece swimming costume for women. [20c: named after Bikini, an atoll in the Pacific where atom-bomb experiments were first held]

bilateral *adj* **1** of a treaty, agreement, conference, talks, etc: involving the participation of, affecting, or signed or agreed by, two countries, parties or groups, etc. **2** having, belonging or referring to, or on, two sides. ▪ **bilaterally** *adv*. [18c in sense 2]

bilberry *noun* **1** a small deciduous shrub that has bright green oval leaves and pink globular flowers. **2** its edible round black berry. [16c]

bile *noun* **1** *biol* a thick yellowish-green alkaline liquid produced by the liver to aid the digestion of fats. **2** *literary* anger, irritability or bad temper. See also **bilious**. [17c: from Latin *bilis*]

bilge *noun* **1** **a** the broadest part of a ship's bottom; **b** (*usu* **bilges**) the lowest parts on the inside of a ship's hull. **2** (*also* **bilge-water**) the dirty water that collects in a ship's bilge. **3** *dated informal* nonsense. [16c: prob a variant of **bulge**]

bilharzia /bɪlˈhɑːtzɪə/ *noun, pathol* another name for the parasitic disease **schistosomiasis**. [19c: Latin, named after Theodor Bilharz, a German parasitologist]

biliary *adj* concerned with, relating or belonging to bile, the bile ducts or the gall bladder.

bilingual *adj* **1** written or spoken in two languages. **2** of a person: able to speak two languages. ▪ **bilingualism** *noun*. [19c: from **bi-** (sense 1) + Latin *lingua* tongue]

bilious *adj* **1** affected by a disorder relating to the secretion of **bile**. **2** of a colour: unpleasant and sickly. **3** peevish; bad-tempered. [16c: from Latin *biliosus*]

bilk *verb* **1** to avoid paying (someone) money owed. **2** (**bilk sb out of sth**) to make them lose something, usu money, by dishonest means. [17c]

bill[1] *noun* **1** **a** a printed or written statement of the amount of money owed for goods or services received; an invoice; **b** such a statement for food and drink received in a restaurant or hotel. *US equivalent* **check**; **c** the amount of money owed. **2** a written plan or draft for a proposed law. **3** *N Am* a **banknote**. **4** an advertising poster. **5** a list of items, events or performers, etc; a programme of entertainment. ▸ *verb* **1** to send or give a bill to (someone), requesting payment for goods, etc. **2** to advertise (a person or event) in a poster, etc: *was billed as Britain's best new comedy act*. [14c: from Latin *bulla* a seal or a document bearing a seal]

IDIOMS **fit** *or* **fill the bill** *informal* to be suitable, or what is required.

bill[2] *noun* **1** the beak of a bird. **2** any structure that resembles this. **3** a long thin piece of land that extends into the sea, eg Portland Bill. ▸ *verb, intr* (*esp* **bill and coo**) *informal* **1** of lovers: to kiss and whisper together affectionately. **2** of birds such as doves: to touch and rub bills together. [Anglo-Saxon *bile*]

billabong *noun, Aust* **1** a pool of water left when most of a river or stream has become dry. **2** a branch of a river that comes to an end without flowing into a sea, lake, or another river. [19c: from Australian Aboriginal *billa* river + *bung* dead]

billboard *noun, esp N Am* a **hoarding**.

billet[1] *noun* **1** a house, often a private home, where soldiers are given food and lodging temporarily. **2** *informal, chiefly Brit* a job or occupation. ▸ *verb* to give or assign lodging to, or to accommodate (soldiers, etc). [15c: from French *billette* a letter or note]

billet[2] *noun* **1** a thick chunk of wood, eg for firewood. **2** a small bar of metal. [15c: from French *billette*]

billet-doux /bɪlɪˈduː, bɪleɪˈduː/ *noun* (***billets-doux*** /-ˈduː, -ˈduːz/) *old use, literary or humorous* a love-letter. [17c: French, from *billet* letter + *doux* sweet]

billhook *noun* a cutting tool with a long curved blade, used for pruning, lopping, etc. Also called **bill**.

billiards *singular noun* an indoor game played with a **cue**[2] and coloured balls on a cloth-covered table, which has pockets at the sides and corners into which the balls can be struck to score points. [16c: from French *billard*, from *bille* a narrow stick]

billion *noun* (***billions*** or after a number ***billion***) **1** **a** the cardinal number 10^9; **b** the quantity that this represents, being a thousand million. **2** *formerly* in the UK and France, etc: a million million (ie unit and twelve zeros). **3** a set of a billion people or things:

one billion pounds. **4** (*usu* **a billion** *or* **billions of sth**) *informal* a great number; lots. [17c: French, modelled on **million**]

billionaire *or* **billionairess** *noun* a person who owns money and property worth over a billion pounds, dollars, etc. [19c: modelled on **millionaire**]

billionth *adj* **1** the last of one billion people or things. **2** the billionth position in a sequence of numbers. ▸ *noun* one of one billion equal parts.

bill of exchange *noun* (***bills of exchange***) *finance* esp in international trade: a document promising payment of a specified sum of money to a certain person on a certain date or when payment is asked for.

bill of fare *noun* (***bills of fare***) a menu.

bill of lading *noun* (***bills of lading***) an official receipt detailing a ship's cargo.

billow *verb, intr* **1** eg of smoke: to move in large waves or clouds. **2** (*usu* **billow out**) to swell or bulge, like a sail in the wind. ▸ *noun* **1** a rolling upward-moving mass of smoke or mist, etc. **2** *literary* a large wave. ▪ **billowing** *or* **billowy** *adj.* [16c as *noun* sense 2: from Norse *bylgja*]

billposter *or* **billsticker** *noun* a person who puts up advertising posters on walls or hoardings, etc. ▪ **billposting** *and* **billsticking** *noun.*

billy *or* **billycan** *noun* (***billies***; ***billycans***) *Brit & esp Aust* a metal cooking pot with a lid and wire handle used esp when camping. [19c: prob from Scottish and Northern English dialect *billypot*]

billy goat *noun* a male goat. Often shortened to **billy**. Compare **nanny goat**. [19c: from the name Billy]

bimbo *noun, derog slang* a young woman who is physically attractive, but empty-headed. [20c: Italian, meaning 'baby' or 'small child']

bimetallic *adj* made of or using two metals. [19c]

bimetallism *noun, econ* a monetary system in which two metals (usu gold and silver) are used in fixed relative values. [19c]

bimodal *adjective, stats* having two modes. ▪ **bimodality** *noun.*

bimonthly *adj* **1** occurring or produced, etc once every two months. **2** occurring or produced, etc twice a month. ▸ *adv* **1** every two months. **2** twice a month. [19c]

bin *noun* **1** a container for depositing or storing rubbish. **2** a container for storing some kinds of food: *bread bin.* **3** a large industrial container for storing goods in large quantities. **4** a stand or case for storing bottles of wine. ▸ *verb* (***binned, binning***) **1** to put (eg rubbish) into a bin. **2** to store (eg wine) in a bin. [Anglo-Saxon]

bin- see **bi-**

binary /'baɪnərɪ/ *adj* **1** consisting of or containing two parts or elements. **2** *comput, maths* denoting a system that consists of two components, esp a number system that uses the digits 0 and 1. See also **binary system**. ▸ *noun* (***-ies***) **1** a thing made up of two parts. **2** *astron* a **binary star**. [16c: from Latin *bini* two by two]

binary code *noun, comput* a code of numbers that involves only two digits, 0 and 1. See also **binary system**.

binary star *noun, astron* (*also* **binary**) a system of two stars that share and orbit around the same centre of mass. Also called **double star**.

binary system *noun, maths & esp comput* a number system to the base 2 that uses only the binary digits 0 and 1, and that forms the basis of the internal coding of information in electronics and computers. Also called **binary notation**.

bind *verb* (***bound***) **1** to tie or fasten tightly. **2** (*often* **bind up**) to tie or pass strips of cloth or bandage, etc around (something). **3** to control or prevent (someone or something) from moving; to restrain (them or it). See also **bound**[1]. **4** to make (someone) promise to do something. **5** to require or oblige (someone) to do something: *He is legally bound to reply.* **6** to fasten together and put a cover on (the separate pages of a book). **7** to put a strip of cloth on the edge of (something) to strengthen it. **8** to cause (dry ingredients) to stick together. **9** *intr* to stick together. ▸ *noun, informal* **1** a difficult, tedious or annoying situation. **2** a restriction; something that limits or hampers one: *What a bind! The train's late again.* [Anglo-Saxon *bindan*]

PHRASAL VERBS **bind sb over** *Brit law* to make them legally obliged to do a particular thing.

binder *noun* **1** a hard book-like cover in which loose pieces of paper can be kept in order. **2** a person or business that binds books. Also called **bookbinder**. **3** a reaping machine that ties cut grain into bundles. ▪ **bindery** *noun* (***-ies***) a place where books are bound.

bindi *or* **bindhi** /'bɪndiː/ *noun* a circular mark, usually red, traditionally worn as a facial decoration by Hindu women. [Hindi *bindi*, from Sanskrit *bindu* point or dot]

binding *noun* **1** the part of a book cover onto which the pages are stuck. **2** cloth or tape, etc used to bind something. ▸ *adj* formally or legally obliging someone to do something: *a binding contract.*

bindweed *noun* any of numerous plants with funnel-shaped flowers, including many climbing species which twine around the stems of other plants. See also **convolvulus**.

binge *noun, informal* a bout of over-indulgence, usu in eating and drinking. ▸ *verb* (***bingeing*** *or* ***binging***) *intr* to indulge in a binge. [19c: apparently from a dialect word meaning 'to soak']

bingo *noun* a game in which each player has a card with a set of numbers on it, and may cover a number if it is called out at random by the **bingo-caller**, the winner being the first player with a card on which all or a certain sequence of the numbers have been called. Formerly called **housey-housey** and **lotto**. [20c]

bin-liner *noun* a disposable plastic bag used as a lining inside a rubbish bin.

binnacle *noun, naut* a case for a ship's compass. [17c; its earlier form *bittacle* derived from Latin *habitaculum* a habitation or dwelling-place]

binocular *adj* relating to the use of both eyes simultaneously. [18c: from Latin *bini* two by two + *oculus* eye]

binoculars *plural noun* an optical instrument designed for viewing distant objects, consisting of two small telescopes arranged side by side.

binomial *noun* **1** *maths* an algebraic expression that contains two **variables**, eg 6x−3y. **2** *biol* in the taxonomic system (known as **binomial nomenclature**): a two-part name for an animal or plant, made up of two Latin words, first the genus name and then the species name, eg *Homo sapiens.* ▸ *adj* **1** *maths* containing two variables. **2** consisting of two names or terms. [16c: from **bi-** (sense 1) + Latin *nomen* name]

binomial theorem *noun, maths* a formula for finding any power of a **binomial** without lengthy multiplication, eg $(a + b)^2 = (a^2 + 2ab + b^2)$.

bio- *combining form, denoting* **1** relating to or involving, etc life or living things: *biology.* **2** relating to or like a life: *biography.* **3** biological: *biorhythms.* [From Greek *bios* life]

biochemistry *noun* the scientific study of the chemical compounds and chemical reactions that occur within the cells of living organisms. ▪ **biochemical** *adj.* ▪ **biochemist** *noun.* [19c]

biodegradable *adj* of a substance or waste product, etc: capable of being broken down by bacteria, fungi or other living organisms. [20c]

biodiversity *noun, biol* a measure of the number of different species of living organism that are present within a given area.

bioenergetics *singular noun, biol* the scientific study of the use of energy by living organisms, including its conversion from one form to another. [20c]

bioengineering *or* **biological engineering** *noun* **1** *med* the application of engineering methods and technology to biology and medicine, esp in the field of designing and manufacturing artificial limbs, hip joints, heart pacemakers, etc. Also called **biomedical engineering**. **2** *biol* the application of engineering methods and technology to the biosynthesis of plant and animal products. See also **biotechnology**. [20c]

bioflavonoid *noun, biochem* vitamin P, a vitamin that regulates the permeability of the capillary walls, and is found naturally in citrus fruit, blackcurrants and rose-hips. Also called **citrin**. [20c]

biofuel *noun* any fuel produced from organic matter. See also **biogas, biomass** (sense 2).

biogas *noun* domestic or commercial gas produced by bacterial fermentation of naturally occurring materials such as animal manure and other organic waste; a type of **biofuel**. [20c]

biogenesis *noun, biol* the theory that living matter always arises from other, pre-existing, living matter. ▪ **biogenetic** *adj.* [19c]

biogeography *noun, biol* the scientific study of the distributions of plants and animals. [19c]

biography *noun* (**-ies**) **1** an account of a person's life, written by someone else and published or intended for publication. **2** biographies as a genre. ▪ **biographer** *noun.* ▪ **biographical** *adj.* [17c]

biological *adj* **1** relating to biology. **2** physiological. **3** of a detergent: containing enzymes that remove dirt of organic origin, eg blood or grass. ▪ **biologically** *adv.*

biological clock *noun* a supposed natural mechanism of the body that controls the rhythm of its functions. Also called **body clock**. [20c]

biological engineering see **bioengineering**

biological warfare *noun* the use of toxins and micro-organisms as weapons of war, to kill or incapacitate the enemy. [20c]

biology *noun* the scientific study of living organisms. ▪ **biologist** *noun.* [19c]

biomass *noun, biol, ecol* **1** the total mass of living organisms in an ecosystem, population or designated area at a given time. **2** vegetation or other plant material that can be converted into useful fuel, considered as a potential source of energy. [20c]

biome /ˈbaɪoʊm/ *noun, biol* a major ecological community of living organisms, usually defined by the plant habitat with which they are associated, eg grassland, rainforest. [20c: **bio-** (sense 1) + **-ome**]

biomechanics *singular noun* the mechanics of movement in living things. [20c]

biomedical engineering see under **bioengineering**

bionic *adj* **1** using, or belonging or relating to, **bionics**. **2** *informal, sci fi* having extraordinary superhuman powers of speed or strength, etc. [20c]

bionics *singular noun* **1** the study of how living organisms function, and the application of the principles observed to develop computers and other machines that work in similar ways. **2** the replacement of damaged parts of the body, such as limbs and heart valves, by electronic devices. [20c: from **bio-** (sense 1), modelled on **electronics**]

biophysics *singular noun* the application of the ideas and methods of physics to the study of biological processes. ▪ **biophysical** *adj.* ▪ **biophysicist** *noun.* [19c]

biopic *noun* a film telling the life-story of a famous person. [20c: short for *bio*graphical *pic*ture]

biopsy *noun* (**-ies**) *pathol* the removal and examination of a small piece of living tissue from an organ or part of the body in order to determine the nature of any suspected disease. [19c: from **bio-** (sense 1) + Greek *opsis* sight or appearance]

biorhythm *noun, biol* **1** a periodic change in the behaviour or physiology of many animals and plants (eg hibernation and migration). **2** a **circadian** rhythm associated eg with sleep, and independent of daylength. **3** any of three cyclical patterns which have been suggested as influencing physical, intellectual and emotional aspects of human behaviour. [20c]

BIOS /ˈbaɪɒs/ *abbrev, comput* Basic Input-Output System, an essential part of a computer operating system on which more complex functions are based.

biosphere *noun* that part of the Earth's surface and its atmosphere in which living organisms are known to exist. Also called **ecosphere**. [19c]

biosynthesis *noun* the manufacture by living organisms of complex organic compounds such as proteins and fats, etc from simpler molecules. ▪ **biosynthetic** *adj.* [20c]

biotechnology *noun, biol* the use of living organisms (eg bacteria), or the enzymes produced by them, in the industrial manufacture of useful products, or the development of useful processes. [20c]

biotin *noun, biochem* a member of the vitamin B complex, found in yeast, liver, egg yolk, cereals and milk. Also called **vitamin H**. [20c: from Greek *biotos* means of living]

bipartisan *adj* belonging to, involving, supported by or consisting of two groups or political parties. [20c]

bipartite *adj* **1** consisting of or divided into two parts. **2** of an agreement, etc: involving, affecting or agreed by two parties. [16c: from Latin *bipartitus*, from **bi-** (sense 1) + *partire* to divide]

biped /ˈbaɪpɛd/ *noun* an animal with two feet, eg man. ▸ *adj* (*also* **bipedal**) /baɪˈpiːdəl/ of an animal: having two feet; walking on two feet. [17c: from **bi-** (sense 1) + Latin *pes, pedis* foot]

biplane *noun* an early type of aeroplane with two sets of wings, one above the other. [19c]

bipolar *adj* having two poles or extremes. ▪ **bipolarity** *noun*. [19c]

birch *noun* **1** a slender deciduous tree or shrub with silvery-white bark that often peels off in long papery strips. **2** (*also* **birchwood**) the strong fine-textured wood of this tree. **3** (**the birch**) **a** a birch rod, or a bundle of birch branches, formerly used to inflict physical punishment; **b** the punishment of being beaten with the birch. ▸ *adj* made of birch wood. ▸ *verb* to flog (someone) with a birch. [Anglo-Saxon *berc* or *beorc*]

bird *noun* **1** any member of a class of warm-blooded vertebrate animals that have feathers, front limbs modified to form wings, and projecting jaws modified to form a beak. **2** *Brit slang, often considered offensive* a girl or woman. **3** *Brit slang* prison or a prison sentence: *just out of bird*. **4** *informal, old use* a person, esp a strange or unusual one: *He's a funny old bird*. [Anglo-Saxon *bridd* young bird]

IDIOMS **birds of a feather** *Brit informal* people who are like each other, who share the same ideas, habits or lifestyle, etc.

bird-brained *adj, informal* of a person: silly or flighty; daft.

bird flu *noun* a highly contagious strain of influenza that affects poultry and can be transmitted to humans. Also called **avian flu** or **avian influenza**.

birdie *noun* **1** *informal* used by or to a child: a little bird. **2** *golf* a score of one stroke under **par** for a particular hole on a course. Compare **albatross** (sense 2), **bogey**[2], **eagle** (sense 2). ▸ *verb* (***birdying***) *tr & intr, golf* to complete (a hole) with a birdie score.

bird-lime *noun* a sticky substance put on the branches of trees to catch small birds. Also called **lime**.

bird of paradise *noun* (***birds of paradise***) any of various brilliantly coloured birds, native to New Guinea and Australia. [17c]

bird of prey *noun* (***birds of prey***) any of several types of bird that kill other birds and small mammals for food, eg the owl, hawk and eagle. Also called **raptor**. [14c]

birdseed *noun* seed used for feeding cagebirds etc, eg a mixture of small seeds such as hemp.

bird's-eye view *noun* **1** a wide general overall view from above. **2** a general impression. [18c]

birdwatcher *noun* a person who studies wild birds in their natural habitat, esp as a hobby.

biretta *noun* a stiff square cap worn by Roman Catholic clergy. [16c: Italian *berretta*]

biriani *or* **biryani** *noun, cookery* a type of spicy Indian dish consisting mainly of rice, with meat or fish and vegetables, etc. [20c: Urdu]

Biro *noun, Brit trademark* a type of **ballpoint** pen. [20c: named after a Hungarian journalist, Laszlo Biró, its inventor]

birth *noun* **1** the act or process of bearing offspring. **2** the act or process of being born. **3** ancestry; descent: *of humble birth*. **4** beginning; origins: *the birth of socialism*. [13c: from Norse *byrthr*]

IDIOMS **give birth** to bear or produce (offspring). **give birth to sth** to produce or be the cause or origin of it.

birth certificate *noun* an official document that records a person's birth, stating the date and place, the parents, etc.

birth control *noun* the prevention of pregnancy, esp by means of **contraception**. Also called **family planning**.

birthday *noun* **1** the anniversary of the day on which a person was born. **2** (*also* **birth day**) the day on which a person was born. [14c]

birthday suit *noun, informal* a state of complete nakedness: *He came to the door in his birthday suit*.

birthmark *noun* a blemish or mark that is present on the skin at birth. *Technical equivalent* **naevus**.

birthplace *noun* the place where a person was born or where something important or well known began.

birthright *noun* the rights a person may claim by being born into a particular family or social class, etc.

birth sign *noun, astrol* the **sign of the zodiac** under which a person was born.

birthstone *noun* a gemstone associated with the month in which a person was born, or with their **birth sign**.

biryani see **biriani**

biscuit *noun* **1** *esp Brit* **a** a small sweet cake, in any of numerous varieties or flavours, etc. *N Am equivalent* **cookie**; **b** a small thin crisp plain or savoury cake. *N Am equivalent* **cracker**. **2** objects made from baked clay that have not been glazed. Also called **biscuit-ware** and **bisque**. **3** a pale golden brown or pale tan colour. Also called **bisque**. ▸ *adj* pale golden brown or pale tan in colour. [14c: ultimately from Latin *bis* twice + *coquere* to cook]

bisect *maths, etc, verb* to divide (something) into two equal parts. ▪ **bisection** *noun*. [17c: from Latin *secare* to cut]

bisector *noun, maths* a line that divides an angle, etc into two equal parts.

bisexual *adj* **1** sexually attracted to both males and females. **2** having the sexual organs of both sexes. Also **hermaphrodite**. ▸ *noun* a bisexual person or organism, etc. ▪ **bisexuality** *noun*. [19c]

bishop *noun* **1** (*often* **Bishop**) *Christianity* a senior priest or minister in the Roman Catholic, Anglican and Orthodox Churches, in charge of a group of churches in an area or a **diocese**. See also **archbishop**, **suffragan**. **2** *chess* (symbol **B**) a piece shaped like a bishop's mitre at the top, which may only be moved diagonally across the board. [Anglo-Saxon *bisceop*]

bishopric *noun, Christianity* **1** the post or position of bishop. **2** the area under the charge of a bishop; a diocese. Also called **see**. [Anglo-Saxon *bisceoprice*]

bismuth *noun, chem* (symbol **Bi**) a hard silvery-white metallic element with a pinkish tinge, used to make lead alloys, and the insoluble compounds of which are used in medicine. [17c: German]

bison *noun* (*pl* ***bison***) either of two species of large hoofed mammal with a dark-brown coat, broad humped shoulders and long shaggy hair on its head, neck, shoulders and forelegs. [14c: Latin, prob of Germanic origin]

bisque¹ *noun, cookery* a thick rich shellfish soup. [17c: French]

bisque² *noun* a type of baked clay or china, which has not been glazed. ▸ *adj* pale golden-brown or pale tan in colour, like unglazed pottery. Also (in both *noun* and *adj* senses) **biscuit**. [17c as *noun*; 20c as *adj*: shortened and altered from **biscuit**]

bistable /ˈbaɪsteɪbəl/ *adj, telecomm, etc* of a valve or transistor circuit: having two stable states. [20c]

bistro *noun* a small bar or informal restaurant. [20c: French]

bit¹ *noun* a small piece, part or amount of something. [Anglo-Saxon *bita*]

IDIOMS **a bit** *informal* **1** a short time or distance: *Wait a bit*. **2** a little: *feel a bit of a fool*. **3** a lot: *takes a bit of doing*. **bit by bit** gradually. **do one's bit** *informal* to do one's fair share.

bit² *noun* **1** a small metal bar that a horse holds in its mouth as part of the bridle with which it is controlled. **2** (*also* **drill bit**) a tool with a cutting edge, which can be fitted into a drill and turned at high speed. See also **brace and bit**. [14c: from Anglo-Saxon *bite*]

bit³ *noun, comput* a binary digit with a value of either 0 or 1, representing the smallest piece of information that can be dealt with by a computer. [20c: a contraction of *binary digit*]

bit⁴ *past tense of* **bite**

bitch *noun* **1** a female of the dog family. **2** *offensive or derog slang* an unpleasant or spiteful woman. **3** *slang* a difficult or unpleasant thing: *Life's a bitch*. ▸ *verb, intr* (*also* **bitch about**) to complain or talk maliciously (about someone or something). [Anglo-Saxon *bicce*]

bitchy *adj* (***-ier, -iest***) *informal* spiteful; petulantly bad-tempered or malicious. ▪ **bitchiness** *noun*. [20c]

bite *verb* (*past tense* **bit,** *past participle* **bitten**) **1** *tr & intr* (*sometimes* **bite sth away** *or* **off** *or* **out**) to grasp, seize or tear with the teeth. **2** *tr & intr* of snakes and insects: to puncture (a victim's skin) with the fangs, mouthparts, etc. **3** *tr & intr* to smart or sting, or to make (something) do so. **4** *informal* to annoy or worry: *What's biting him?* **5** of acid, etc: to eat into (something) chemically; to have a corrosive effect. **6** *intr* to start to have an effect, usu an adverse one: *The spending cuts are beginning to bite*. **7** *intr, angling* of fish: to be caught on the hook on a fishing line, by taking the bait into the mouth. **8** *intr* of a wheel or screw, etc: to grip firmly. ▸ *noun* **1** an act or an instance of biting. **2** a wound or sting caused by biting. **3** a piece of something removed or taken, etc by biting; a mouthful. **4** *informal* a small amount of food. **5** strength, sharpness or bitterness of taste. **6** sharpness or incisiveness of words. **7** *angling* of a fish: an act or an instance of biting or nibbling at the bait. [Anglo-Saxon *bitan*]

IDIOMS **bite the dust** *informal* **1** of a plan or project, etc: to fail or come to nothing; to be unsuccessful. **2** of a person: to fall down dead; to be killed.

biting *adj* **1** bitterly and painfully cold. **2** of a remark: sharp and hurtful; sarcastic.

bit-mapping *noun, comput* a method of organizing the display on a computer screen so that each **pixel** is assigned to one or more bits (see **bit³**) of memory, depending on the shading or number of colours required. ▪ **bit map** *noun*. ▪ **bit-mapped** *adj*. [20c]

bit-part *noun* a small acting part in a play or film.

bits and pieces *or* **bits and bobs** *plural noun, Brit informal* small objects or possessions; odds and ends.

bitten *past participle of* **bite**

bitter *adj* **1** having a sharp, acid and often unpleasant taste. Compare **salt**, **sour**, **sweet**, **smooth**. **2** feeling or causing sadness or pain: *bitter memories*. **3** difficult to accept: *a bitter disappointment*. **4** showing an intense persistent feeling of dislike, hatred or opposition: *bitter resentment*. **5** of words, etc: sharp; acrimonious. **6** of the weather, etc: extremely and painfully cold. ▸ *noun, Brit* a type of beer with a slightly bitter taste. Compare **mild** (*noun*). ▪ **bitterly** *adv*. ▪ **bitterness** *noun*. [Anglo-Saxon *biter*, from *bitan* to bite]

bittern *noun* a long-legged European bird that lives on or near water, the male of which has a distinctive booming call. [14c: from French *butor*]

bitters *plural noun* a liquid made from bitter herbs or roots, used to flavour certain alcoholic drinks.

bittersweet *adj* pleasant and unpleasant, or bitter and sweet, at the same time: *a bittersweet love story*. [14c]

bitty *adj* (***-ier, -iest***) *informal* consisting of small unrelated bits or parts, esp when put together awkwardly or untidily; scrappy; disjointed. ▪ **bittiness** *noun*. [19c]

bitumen *noun* any of various black solid or tarry flammable substances composed of an impure mixture of hydrocarbons and which is used for surfacing roads and pavements, etc. ▪ **bituminous** *adj*. [15c: the Latin word for **pitch²** or **asphalt**]

bituminous coal *noun, geol* a dark brown or black coal that burns with a smoky yellowish flame.

bivalve *zool, adj* of a mollusc: having a shell composed of two valves hinged together. ▸ *noun* any of numerous mainly marine species of mollusc with a shell composed of two valves hinged together, eg clam, cockle, mussel and scallop. [17c]

bivariate *adj, maths* involving two variables. [20c]

bivouac *noun* a temporary camp or camping place without tents. ▸ *verb* (***bivouacked, bivouacking***) *intr* **1** to camp out temporarily at night without a tent. **2** to make such a camp. [18c, orig meaning a **night watch** by a whole army: French]

bizarre *adj* weirdly odd or strange. ▪ **bizarrely** *adv*. [17c: French, from Spanish *bizarro* gallant or brave]

Bk *symbol, chem* berkelium.

blab *verb* (***blabbed, blabbing***) **1** *tr & intr* (*usu* **blab sth out**) to tell or divulge (a secret, etc). **2** *intr* to chatter foolishly or indiscreetly. ▪ **blabbing** *noun, adj*. [16c]

blabber *verb, intr* to talk nonsense, esp without stopping or without being understood; to babble. ▸ *noun* a blabbermouth. [14c]

blabbermouth *noun, slang, orig US* a person who talks foolishly and indiscreetly. [20c]

black *adj* **1** having the darkest colour, the same colour as coal; reflecting no light. **2** without any light; totally dark. **3** (*now usu* **Black**) used of people: dark-skinned, esp of African, West Indian or Australian Aboriginal origin. **4** (*usu* **Black**) belonging or relating to Black people. **5** of coffee or tea: without added milk. **6** angry; threatening. **7** of hands, clothes etc:

dirty; soiled. **8** sad, gloomy or depressed; dismal. **9** promising trouble: *The future looks black.* **10** wicked or sinister; grim or macabre: *black comedy.* ▸ *noun* **1** the colour of coal, etc, the darkest colour, or absence of colour. **2** anything that is black in colour, eg a black chess piece. **3** (*usu* **Black**) a dark-skinned person, esp one of African, West Indian or Australian Aboriginal origin. **4** black clothes worn when in mourning. **5** a black pigment or dye. **6** the credit side of an account; the state of not being in debt, eg to a bank. Compare **red** (*noun* sense 5). ▸ *verb* **1** to **blacken**. **2** to clean (shoes, etc) with black polish. **3** of a trade union: to forbid work to be done on or with (certain goods). ▪ **blackish** *adj.* ▪ **blackness** *noun.* [Anglo-Saxon *blæc*]

PHRASAL VERBS **black out 1** of a person: to lose consciousness. **2** to deprive (something) of light; to extinguish or cover (lights), or all lights in (a place). **3** to prevent (information) from being broadcast or published. See also **blackout**.

black and blue *adj, informal* of a person or of a person's skin: covered in bruises.

black and white *adj* **1** used of photographs or TV images: having no colours except black, white, and shades of grey. **2** either good or bad, right or wrong, etc, with no compromise.

blackball *verb* **1** to vote against (a candidate for membership of something), orig by putting a black ball in the ballot box. **2** to refuse to see or speak to (someone). [18c]

black bear *noun* a bear belonging to either of two species, the American and the Asiatic black bear, usu black but sometimes brown in colour.

black belt *noun, judo, karate, etc* **1** a belt indicating that the wearer has reached the highest possible level of skill. **2** a person who is entitled to wear a black belt.

blackberry *noun* a thorny shrub or one of the dark purple-coloured berries it produces. Also called (*esp Scot*) **bramble**.

blackbird *noun* a small European bird, the male of which is black with a yellow beak.

blackboard *noun* a black or dark-coloured board for writing on with chalk.

black box *noun* a **flight recorder** in an aircraft.

the Black Country *noun* an industrialized region in the West Midlands of England. [19c: from the smoke and grime produced by the heavy industries]

blackcurrant *noun* a widely cultivated shrub or one of the small round black fruits it produces.

the Black Death *noun, hist* a virulent pneumonic and **bubonic plague** that spread across Europe from Asia in the 14c. [18c]

black economy *noun* unofficial business or trade not declared for tax purposes. Compare **black market**.

blacken *verb* **1** *tr & intr* (also **black**) to become or cause (something) to become black or very dark in colour. **2** to damage or ruin (someone's reputation or good name). [14c]

black eye *noun* an eye with darkened bruised swollen skin around it, usu caused by a blow.

blackguard /ˈblagɑːd/ *noun, dated or facetious* a rogue or villain; a contemptible scoundrel. [16c in obsolete sense 'the lowest form of servant']

blackhead *noun* a small black spot on the skin caused by sweat blocking one of the skin's tiny pores or hair follicles.

black hole *noun, astron* a region in space, believed to be formed when a large star has collapsed in on itself at the end of its life, with such a strong gravitational pull that not even light waves can escape from it. [20c]

black ice *noun* a thin transparent layer of ice that forms on road surfaces, making driving hazardous.

blacking *noun, dated* black polish, esp for shining shoes or fireplaces, etc.

blackjack *noun* **1** *cards* **pontoon**[2] or a similar game. **2** *N Am* a length of hard flexible leather, esp one used for hitting people; a cosh.

black lead *noun* **graphite**.

blackleg *noun, chiefly Brit derog* a person who refuses to take part in a strike, or who works in a striker's place during a strike. Also called (*derog slang*) **scab**. ▸ *verb* (***blacklegged, blacklegging***) *intr* to refuse to take part in a strike; to work as a blackleg. [19c; 18c meaning 'a swindler']

blacklist *noun* a list of people convicted or suspected of something, or not approved of, to be boycotted or excluded, etc. ▸ *verb* to put (someone or someone's name) on such a list. [17c as *noun*]

black magic *noun* magic that supposedly invokes the power of the devil to perform evil.

blackmail *verb* **1** to extort money, etc illegally from (someone) by threatening to reveal harmful information about them. **2** to try to influence (someone) by using unfair pressure or threats. ▸ *noun* an act of blackmailing someone. ▪ **blackmailer** *noun.* [16c: from **black** (*adj* sense 6) + obsolete *mail* payment of money]

Black Maria /məˈraɪə/ *noun, informal* a police van for transporting prisoners. [19c]

black mark *noun* a sign or demonstration, etc of disapproval or criticism towards someone, or of a failure on their part.

black market *noun* the illegal buying and selling, at high prices, of goods that are scarce, strictly regulated or in great demand. ▪ **black-marketeer** *noun.*

blackout *noun* **1** an enforced period during which all the lights in an area are turned out, eg during World War II as a precaution during an air raid at night. **2** an electrical power-failure or power-cut. **3** a sudden loss of memory or of consciousness. **4** a suppression or stoppage of news, information, communications, etc. See also **black out** at **black**.

black pepper *noun* pepper produced by grinding the dried fruits of the pepper plant without removing their dark outer covering.

Black Power *or* **black power** *noun* a movement seeking to increase the political, economic and social power and influence of Black people. [20c]

black pudding *noun* a dark sausage made from pig's blood and fat, cereal, etc. Also called **blood pudding**.

Black Rod *noun* in the UK: the chief usher to the House of Lords and to the Chapter of the Garter.

black sheep *noun* a member of a family or group who is disapproved of in some way. [18c]

Blackshirt *noun* **1** a member of the Italian Fascist Party before and during World War II. **2** *loosely* a Fascist. [20c: a translation of the Italian *camicia nera* black shirt (a distinctive part of the Fascist Party uniform)]

blacksmith *noun* a person who makes and repairs by hand things made of iron, such as horseshoes.

black spot *noun, chiefly Brit* **1** a dangerous stretch of road where accidents often occur. **2** an area where an adverse social condition is prevalent: *an unemployment black spot.*

blackthorn *noun* a thorny shrub or small tree, with conspicuous black twigs, white flowers and rounded bluish-black fruits known as **sloe**s.

black tie *noun* a black **bow tie**, esp one worn with a dinner jacket. ▸ *adj* (*usu* **black-tie**) of a celebration or function: formal; at which guests are expected to wear evening dress.

black widow *noun* any of various venomous spiders, esp a N American species, the female of which commonly eats the male after mating. [20c]

bladder *noun* **1** *anatomy* in all mammals, and some fish, amphibians and reptiles: a hollow sac-shaped organ in which urine is stored before it is discharged. **2** any of various similar hollow organs in which liquid or gas is stored, eg the gall bladder of animals, or the swim bladder of bony fish. **3** a hollow bag made eg of leather, which can be stretched by filling it with air or liquid. **4** in certain plants: a hollow sac-like structure, esp one of the air-filled sacs at the tips of the fronds of **bladder wrack**. [Anglo-Saxon *blædre* blister or pimple]

bladder wrack *noun* a tough brown seaweed, so called because its fronds bear air-filled bladders that provide buoyancy in the water.

blade *noun* **1** the cutting part of a knife or sword, etc. **2** the flat, usu long and narrow, part of a leaf, petal or sepal. **3** the wide flat part of an oar, bat or propeller, or of certain tools and devices. **4** a broad flat bone, eg the **shoulder blade**. **5** the runner of an ice-skate, that slides on the surface of the ice. [Anglo-Saxon *blæd*]

blag *verb* (***blagged, blagging***) *slang* **1** to rob or steal (something). **2** to scrounge (something); to get (something) for nothing: *blagged his way into the club.* ▪ **blagger** *noun.* [20c]

blain *noun* a boil or blister. [Anglo-Saxon *blegen*]

blame *verb* **1** to consider (someone) as responsible for (something bad, wrong or undesirable). **2** to find fault with (someone). ▸ *noun* (*esp* **the blame**) responsibility for something bad, wrong or undesirable: *I refuse to take the blame.* ▪ **blameless** *adj.* [13c: from Latin *blasphemare* to blaspheme]

blameworthy *adj* deserving blame.

blanch *verb* **1** to make (something) white by removing the colour. **2** *usu intr* to become pale or white, esp out of fear. **3** *cookery* to prepare (vegetables or meat) by boiling in water for a few seconds. **4** *cookery* to remove the skins from (almonds, etc) by soaking in boiling water. [15c: from French *blanc* white]

blancmange /blə'mɒndʒ/ *noun* a cold sweet jelly-like pudding made with milk. [14c: from French *blanc* white + *manger* food]

bland *adj, derog* **1** of food: having a very mild taste; tasteless. **2** insipid; lacking interest. **3** of a person or their actions: mild or gentle; showing no strong emotion. [17c: from Latin *blandus* soft or smooth]

blandish *verb* to persuade (someone) by gentle flattery; to coax or cajole. [14c: Latin *blandus* (see **bland**)]

blandishments *plural noun* flattery intended to persuade. [16c]

blank *adj* **1** of paper: not written or printed on. **2** of magnetic tape, etc: with no sound or pictures yet recorded on it. **3** with spaces left for details, information, a signature, etc: *a blank form.* **4** not filled in; empty: *Leave that space blank.* **5** showing no expression or interest. **6** having no thoughts or ideas: *My mind went blank.* **7** without a break or relieving feature: *a blank wall.* **8** sheer; absolute: *blank refusal.* ▸ *noun* **1** an empty space; a void. **2** an empty space left (on forms, etc) to be filled in with particular information. **3** a printed form with blank spaces left for filling in. **4** a state of having no thoughts or ideas: *My mind went a complete blank.* **5** a dash written in place of a word or letter. **6** a **blank cartridge**. ▸ *verb* **1** to ignore (someone). **2** to obscure or hide (something): *tried to blank the incident from my mind.* **3** (*usu* **blank out**) to blot or cross (something) out. ▪ **blankly** *adv.* [14c: from French *blanc* white]

IDIOMS **draw a blank** *informal* to get no results.

blank cartridge *noun* a cartridge containing an explosive but no bullet.

blank cheque *noun* **1** a cheque that has been signed but on which the amount to be paid has been left blank. **2** complete freedom or authority.

blanket *noun* **1** a thick covering of wool or other material, used to cover beds or for wrapping a person in for warmth. **2** a thick layer or mass that covers or obscures: *a blanket of fog.* ▸ *adj* (*used before the noun it describes*) general; applying to or covering all cases, people, etc: *blanket coverage.* ▸ *verb* **1** to cover (something) with, or as if with, a blanket. **2** to cover or apply (something) in a general, comprehensive or indiscriminate way. [14c: from French *blankete*, from *blanc* white]

blanket stitch *noun* a type of stitch used to strengthen and bind the edge of thick fabric, esp a blanket.

blank verse *noun, prosody* poetry that does not rhyme.

blare *verb* (*often* **blare out**) **1** *intr* to make a sound like a trumpet. **2** *tr & intr* to sound or say (something) loudly and harshly. ▸ *noun* a loud harsh sound. [15c, orig meaning 'to roar or howl (like a crying child), or bellow (like a calf)']

blarney *noun* flattering words used to persuade, deceive or cajole. [19c: named after the Blarney Stone in Ireland, said to endow whoever kisses it with the gift of charmingly persuasive talk]

blasé /'blɑːzeɪ/ *adj* lacking enthusiasm or interest, or unconcerned, esp as a result of over-familiarity. [19c: French]

blaspheme *verb* **1** *tr & intr* to show disrespect for (God or sacred things) in speech. **2** *intr* to swear or curse using the name of God or referring to sacred things. ▪ **blasphemer** *noun.* [14c]

blasphemy *noun* (*-ies*) **a** a speaking about God or sacred matters in a disrespectful or rude way; **b** an action, word or sign that intentionally insults God, or something held sacred, in such a way. ▪ **blasphemous** *adj.* [13c: from Latin *blasphemos* evil-speaking]

blast *noun* **1** an explosion, or the strong shock waves spreading out from it. **2** a strong sudden stream or gust (of air or wind, etc). **3** a sudden loud sound of a trumpet or car horn, etc. **4** a sudden and violent outburst of anger or criticism. **5** *informal* a highly enjoyable or exciting event, occasion or activity, esp a party. ▸ *verb* **1** to blow up (a tunnel or rock, etc) with explosives. **2** *tr & intr* (*esp* **blast out**) to make or cause (something) to make a loud or harsh sound. **3** to criticize (someone) severely. ▸ *exclam* (*also* **blast it!**) *informal* expressing annoyance or exasperation, etc. [Anglo-Saxon *blæst*]

IDIOMS **at full blast** at full power or speed, etc; with maximum effort or energy.

PHRASAL VERBS **blast off** of a spacecraft: to take off from its launching pad. See also **blast-off**.

blasted *adj, informal* (often used as an intensifier) annoying; damned; stupid; infuriating.

blast furnace *noun* a tall furnace that is used to extract iron from iron ores such as haematite and magnetite.

blast-off *noun* **1** the moment at which a spacecraft or rocket-propelled missile is launched. **2** the launching of a spacecraft or rocket-propelled missile. See **blast off** at **blast**.

blastula /'blastjʊlə/ *noun* (**-las** *or* **-lae** /-liː/) *biol* a hollow sphere of cells, one cell thick, formed during the division process early in the development of a multicellular embryo. Also called **blastosphere**. [19c: Latin, from Greek *blastos* bud]

blatant *adj* **1** very obvious and without shame. **2** very noticeable and obtrusive. ▪ **blatantly** *adv.* [16c: prob invented by Edmund Spenser]

blather see **blether**

blaze[1] *noun* **1** a bright strong fire or flame. **2** a brilliant display. **3** a sudden and sharp bursting out of feeling or emotion. **4** an intense burst or spate: *a blaze of publicity*. ▸ *verb, intr* **1** to burn or shine brightly. **2** *informal* to show great emotion, esp to be furious. **3** (*often* **blaze away**) *intr* **a** of a person: to fire a gun rapidly and without stopping; **b** of a gun: to fire rapidly and without stopping. [Anglo-Saxon *blæse* torch]

blaze[2] *noun* **1** a white mark or band on an animal's face. **2** a mark made on the bark of a tree, esp to show a route or path. ▸ *verb* to mark (a tree or path, etc) with blazes. [17c]

IDIOMS **blaze a trail** to be the first to do, study or discover something, etc.

blaze[3] *verb* (*esp* **blaze abroad**) to make (news or information) widely known. [14c: from Dutch *blasen*]

blazer *noun* a light jacket, often in the colours of a school or club. [19c]

blazon *verb* **1** (*often* **blazon abroad**) to make (something) public. **2** *heraldry* to describe (a coat of arms) in technical terms. **3** *heraldry* to paint (names, designs, etc) on (a coat of arms). ▸ *noun, heraldry* a shield or coat of arms. [14c: from French *blason* shield]

bleach *verb, tr & intr* to whiten or remove colour from (a substance) by exposure to sunlight or certain chemicals. ▸ *noun* a liquid chemical used to bleach clothes, etc. [Anglo-Saxon *blæcan*]

bleachers *plural noun, N Am* at a sports ground, etc: cheap open-air seats for spectators. [19c]

bleak *adj* **1** exposed and desolate. **2** cold and unwelcoming. **3** offering little or no hope. ▪ **bleakly** *adv.* ▪ **bleakness** *noun.* [16c: from Anglo-Saxon *blac* pale]

bleary *adj* (**-ier, -iest**) **1** of a person's eyes: red and dim, usu from tiredness or through crying. **2** blurred, indistinct and unclear. ▪ **blearily** *adv.* [14c]

bleat *verb* **1** *intr* to cry like a sheep, goat or calf. **2** *intr, informal* to complain whiningly (about something). [Anglo-Saxon *blætan*]

bleed *verb* (***bled***) **1** *intr* to lose or let out blood. **2** to remove or take blood from (someone, etc). **3** *intr* of plants, etc: to lose juice or sap. **4** to empty liquid or air from (a radiator, hydraulic brakes, etc). **5** *informal* to obtain money from (someone), usu illegally. **6** *intr* of dye or paint: to come out of the material when wet; to run. [Anglo-Saxon *bledan*]

IDIOMS **one's heart bleeds for sb** *usu ironic* one feels great pity for them, or is very sad on their account.

bleeding *adj, adv, Brit slang* (*used as an intensifier*) expressing anger or disgust; bloody: *a bleeding idiot*.

bleep *noun* **1** a short high-pitched burst of sound, usu made by an electronic machine. **2** a **bleeper**. ▸ *verb* **1** *intr* of an electronic machine, etc: to give out a short high-pitched sound. **2** to call (someone) using a bleeper. [20c: prob imitating the sound]

bleeper *noun* a portable radio receiver that emits a bleeping sound, used esp to call a doctor or police officer carrying such a device. Also called **pager**.

blemish *noun* a stain, mark or fault. ▸ *verb* to stain or spoil the beauty of (something). [14c: from French *blesmir* or *blamir* to wound or to make pale]

blench *verb, intr* to start back or move away, esp in fear. [Anglo-Saxon *blencan*]

blend *verb* **1** to mix (different sorts or varieties) into one. **2** *intr* (*often* **blend in**, *also* **blend with**) to form a mixture or harmonious combination; to go well together. **3** to mix together, esp intimately or harmoniously. **4** *intr* esp of colours: to shade gradually into another. ▸ *noun* a mixture or combination. [14c]

blende *noun* any naturally occurring metal sulphide, eg zinc blende. [17c: from German *blenden* to deceive, because of its deceptive resemblance to **galena**]

blender *noun* a machine for mixing food or esp for making it into a liquid or purée. See also **food processor**.

blenny *noun* (**-ies**) the common name for any of various small fishes that have a long tapering scaleless body and long fins. [18c: from Greek *blennos* slime]

bless *verb* (*past tense* ***blessed,*** *past participle* ***blessed*** *or* ***blest***) **1** to ask for divine favour or protection for (someone or something). **2 a** to make or pronounce (someone or something) holy; to consecrate; **b** to make the sign of the cross over (someone or something) or to cross (oneself). **3** to praise; to give honour or glory to (a deity). **4** to thank or be thankful for (something): *I bless the day I met him.* [Anglo-Saxon *bletsian* or *bledsian* to bless with sacrificial blood]

IDIOMS **be blessed with** to have the benefit or advantage of (some natural quality or attribute). **bless me** *or* **bless my soul** an expression of surprise, pleasure or dismay, etc. **bless you!** said to a person who has just sneezed.

blessed /ˈblɛsɪd, blɛst/ *adj* **1 a** (*also* **blest**) holy; **b** consecrated. **2** /ˈblɛsɪd/ *RC Church* of a dead person, and used as a title: pronounced holy by the Pope, usu as the first stage towards becoming a saint. **3** *euphem, informal* (pronounced /ˈblɛsɪd/ when preceding its noun) damned; confounded: *This blessed zip's stuck.* **4** very fortunate or happy.

blessing *noun* **1** a wish or prayer for happiness or success. **2** *relig* **a** an act that invites the goodness of God to rest upon someone; **b** a short prayer said before or after a meal or church service, etc. **3** a cause of happiness, or sometimes of relief or comfort; a benefit or advantage. **4** approval or good wishes.

blether *or* **blather** *chiefly Scot, verb, intr* **1** to talk foolishly and long-windedly. **2** to chat or gossip idly. ▸ *noun* **1** long-winded nonsense. **2** a chat or gossip. ▪ **blethering** *noun, adj.* [16c: from Norse *blathra*]

blew see under **blow**[1]

blight *noun* **1** a fungal disease of plants that usu attacks an entire crop, or (*in compounds*) one specific crop throughout a particular region: *potato blight.* **2** a fungus that causes blight. **3** (*esp* **cast a blight on sth**) someone or something that has a damaging, distressing, or destructive effect on something, or that spoils it. **4** *often in compounds* an ugly, decayed or neglected state or condition: *urban blight.* ▸ *verb* **1** to affect (something) with blight. **2** to harm or destroy (someone or something). **3** to disappoint or frustrate (someone or something): *All our hopes were blighted.* [17c]

blighter *noun, informal, old use* **1** (often used as a term of mild abuse) a scoundrel or contemptible person, usu a man. **2** a person, esp a man one feels some sympathy for or envy of: *lucky blighter.*

blimey *exclam, Brit slang* expressing surprise or amazement. [19c: a corruption of the phrase *God blind me*]

Blimp *or* **blimp** *noun* a conservative old-fashioned reactionary person. [20c: from the cartoon character Colonel Blimp]

blimp *noun* **1** a type of large balloon or airship, used for publicity, observation or defence. **2** a soundproof cover for a film camera. [20c]

blind *adj* **1** not able to see. **2** (*always* **blind to sth**) unable or unwilling to understand or appreciate something: *blind to his faults.* **3** unthinking; without reason or purpose: *blind hatred.* **4** hidden from sight: *blind entrance.* **5** not allowing sight of what is beyond: *blind summit.* **6** of flying, landing, navigating or bombing, etc: relying completely on instruments inside the craft. **7 a** having no openings or windows, etc: *blind wall;* **b** blocked or walled up: *blind arch.* **8** closed at one end: *blind alley.* ▸ *adv* **1** blindly; without being able to see. **2** without having gained proper knowledge of the item concerned: *I can't believe that you bought the car blind.* ▸ *noun* **1** (**the blind**) blind people as a group; people suffering from serious or total loss of vision in one or both eyes. **2** a screen to stop light coming through a window. **3** a person, action or thing that hides the truth or deceives. **4** anything that prevents sight or blocks out light. ▸ *verb* **1** to make (someone) blind. **2** to make (someone) unreasonable or foolish, etc. **3** (*usu* **blind sb with sth**) to confuse or dazzle them with it: *tried to blind me with science.* ▪ **blinding** *adj.* ▪ **blindly** *adv.* ▪ **blindness** *noun.* [11c]
IDIOMS **blind as a bat** completely blind. **blind drunk** *informal* completely and helplessly drunk. **turn a blind eye to sth** to pretend not to notice it.

blind alley *noun* **1** a narrow road with an opening at one end only. **2** a situation, course of action or job, etc that is leading or will lead nowhere.

blind date *noun* **1** a date with a person whom one has not met before. **2** the person met on such a date.

blinder *noun, informal* a spectacular performance in a sporting activity or event: *Campbell played a blinder in goal.*

blindfold *noun* a piece of cloth used to cover the eyes to prevent a person from seeing. ▸ *adj, adv* with one's eyes covered with a blindfold. ▸ *verb* to cover the eyes of (someone) to prevent them from seeing. [16c: from earlier *blindfellen* to strike someone blind]

blindman's-buff *noun* a children's game in which one child wears a blindfold and tries to catch the other children. [16c: traditionally the blindfolded child would give three slaps or *buffs* to anyone they caught]

blind spot *noun* **1** on the retina of the eye: a small area from which no visual images can be transmitted. **2** a place where sight or vision is obscured. **3** any subject that a person either cannot understand, or refuses even to try to understand.

blindworm see **slowworm**

bling *noun, chiefly US Black slang* showy or expensive jewellery that attracts attention. [20c]

blink *verb* **1** *intr* to shut and open the eyes again quickly, esp involuntarily. **2** to shut and open (an eyelid or an eye) very quickly. **3** *intr* of a light: to flash on and off; to shine unsteadily. ▸ *noun* **1** an act of blinking. **2** a gleam or quick glimmer of light, such as a brief moment of sunshine. [14c: a variant of **blench**]
IDIOMS **on the blink** *informal* not working properly.

blinker *noun* (*usu* **blinkers**) one of two small flat pieces of leather attached to a horse's bridle to prevent it from seeing sideways. ▸ *verb* **1** to put blinkers on (a horse). **2** to limit or obscure the vision or awareness of (a person, etc).

blinkered *adj* **1** of a horse: wearing blinkers. **2** *derog* of a person: narrow in outlook.

blinking *adj, adv, slang* used to express mild annoyance, frustration or disapproval, or as a general intensifier: *broke the blinking thing.* [20c: euphemism for **bloody**]

blip *noun* **1** a sudden sharp sound produced by a machine such as a monitor or radar screen. **2** a spot of bright light on a radar screen, showing the position of an object. **3 a** a short interruption, pause or irregularity in the expected pattern or course of something; **b** an unforeseen phenomenon, esp an economic one, that is claimed or expected to be temporary. [20c: imitating the sound]

bliss *noun* **1** very great happiness. **2** the special happiness of heaven. ▪ **blissful** *adj.* ▪ **blissfully** *adv.* [Anglo-Saxon, from **blithe**]

B-list *adjective, informal* said of celebrities, etc: not belonging to the most important or famous group. [20c]

blister *noun* **1** a small swelling on or just beneath the surface of the skin, containing watery fluid. **2** a bubble in a thin surface coating of paint or varnish, etc. ▸ *verb* **1** to make a blister or blisters occur on (something). **2** *intr* of hands or feet, etc: to come up in blisters. **3** to criticize or attack (someone) with sharp scathing language. ▪ **blistering** *adj.* [14c: most prob from French *blestre*]

blister pack see under **bubble pack**

blithe *adj* **1** happy; without worries or cares. **2** heedless or thoughtless; casual. ▪ **blithely** *adv.* [Anglo-Saxon]

blithering *adj, derog informal* stupid; jabbering; half-witted. [19c: from *blither*, a form of **blether**]

blitz *noun* **1** a sudden strong attack, or period of such attacks, esp from the air. **2** (*esp* **have a blitz on sth**) *informal* a period of hard work, etc to get something finished or done quickly. ▶ *verb* **1** to attack, damage or destroy (something) as if by an air raid. **2** *informal* to work hard at (something) for a short period. [20c: from **blitzkrieg**]

blitzkrieg /'blɪtskriːg/ *noun* a blitz; a sudden and intensive attack to win a quick victory in war. [20c: German, literally 'lightning war']

blizzard *noun* a severe snowstorm characterized by low temperatures and strong winds. [19c]

bloat *verb* **1** *tr & intr* to swell or make (something) swell or puff out with air, pride, food, etc, esp unpleasantly or uncomfortably. **2** to prepare (fish, esp herring) by salting and half-drying in smoke. ▪ **bloated** *adj.* [17c: perhaps from 13c adjective *bloat* soft]

bloater *noun* a herring that has been salted in brine and partially smoked. [19c]

blob *noun* **1** a small soft round mass of something. **2** a small drop of liquid. [15c: imit of the sound of dripping]

bloc *noun* a group of countries or people, etc that have a common interest, purpose or policy. [20c: French, meaning 'block' or 'group']

block *noun* **1** a mass of solid wood, stone, ice or other hard material, usu with flat sides. **2** a piece of wood or stone, etc used for chopping and cutting on. **3** a wooden or plastic cube, used as a child's toy. **4** *slang* a person's head. **5** a large building containing offices, flats, etc. **6 a** a group of buildings with roads on all four sides: *Let's go round the block*; **b** the distance from one end of such a group of buildings to the other: *lives about a block away.* **7** *comput* a group of data units treated as a complete unit for transfer or modification. **8** *Aust, NZ* an extensive area of land for settlement or farming, etc. **9** a compact mass, group or set. **10** a group of seats, tickets, votes, data, shares, etc thought of as a single unit. **11** something that causes or acts as a stopping of movement or progress, etc; an obstruction. **12** *athletics, often in pl* a starting-block: *fast off the block.* **13** a piece of wood or metal that has been cut to be used in printing. **14** *eng* a pulley or set of pulleys mounted in a case. See also **block and tackle**. ▶ *verb* **1** (*often* **block sb** *or* **sth in** *or* **out**) to obstruct or impede; to put an obstacle in the way of (someone or something). **2** to print (a design, title, etc) on (the cover of a book, etc). **3** (*usu* **block sth out** *or* **in**) to draw or sketch (something) roughly. **4** *cricket* to stop (a ball) with one's bat held vertically. [14c: from French *bloc*]

blockade *noun* the closing off of a port or region, etc by surrounding it with troops, ships and/or air-power, in order to prevent people or goods, etc from passing in and out. ▶ *verb* to impose a blockade on (a port or country, etc). [17c]

blockage *noun* **1** anything that causes a pipe or roadway, etc to be blocked. **2** the state of being blocked or the act of blocking.

block and tackle *noun, mech, eng* **1** a device used for lifting heavy objects, consisting of a case or housing (the **block**) containing a pulley or system of pulleys and a rope or chain passed over it (the **tackle**). **2** a series of such ropes and blocks.

blockboard *noun, building* plywood board made from thin strips of soft wood bonded together and enclosed by two outer layers of veneer.

blockbuster *noun, informal* **1** a highly popular and successful film, book or TV drama, etc. **2** an extremely powerful bomb that could destroy a whole block of buildings. [20c in sense 2]

block capital *or* **block letter** *noun* a plain capital letter written in imitation of printed type.

blockhead *noun, derog informal* a stupid person. [16c]

blog *or* (*in full*) **weblog** *noun* a personal journal that is published on the Internet. ▶ *verb* (***blogged, blogging***) to write a blog. ▪ **blogger** *noun.* ▪ **blogging** *noun.* [20c]

bloke *noun, Brit informal* a man or chap. ▪ **blokeish** *or* **blokey** *adj.* [19c: Shelta *loke* a man]

blond *or* (*the feminine form*) **blonde** *adj* **1** of a person or people: having light-coloured hair and usu fair or pale skin and blue or grey eyes. **2** of a person's hair: light-coloured; fair. ▶ *noun* a person with fair hair. [15c: from Latin *blondus* yellow]

blood *noun* **1** a fluid tissue that circulates in the arteries, veins, and capillaries of the body as a result of muscular contractions of the heart. **2** relationship through belonging to the same family or race, etc; descent: *of royal blood.* **3** near family: *my own flesh and blood.* **4** bloodshed or murder; violence. **5 a** life or vitality; lifeblood; **b** (*esp* **new blood** and **young blood**) a group of people seen as adding new strength, youth, young ideas, etc to an existing group. ▶ *verb* **1** *hunting* to give (a young hound) its first taste of a freshly killed animal. **2** to give someone the first experience of (war or battle, etc). [Anglo-Saxon *blod*]

IDIOMS **in cold blood** deliberately or cruelly; showing no concern. **in sb's blood** in their character. **make sb's blood boil** to make them extremely angry. **make sb's blood run cold** to frighten or horrify them.

blood-and-thunder *adj* of a film or story, etc: including much violent action and excitement.

blood bank *noun* a place where blood collected from donors is stored prior to transfusion. [20c]

bloodbath *noun* a massacre.

blood brother *noun* **1** a man or boy who has promised to treat another as his brother, usu in a ceremony in which some of their blood has been mixed. **2** a true brother, by birth.

blood cell *noun* any of the cells that are present in the blood, ie an **erythrocyte** or a **leucocyte**.

blood count *noun, med* a numerical calculation to determine the number of red or white blood cells in a known volume of blood.

bloodcurdling *adj* causing a chilling fear or horror.

blood donor *noun* a person who donates blood to be used for transfusion.

blood group *or* **blood type** *noun, med* any one of the various types into which human blood is classified.

bloodhound *noun* **1** a large breed of dog, known for its keen sense of smell. **2** *informal* a detective, or anyone who follows a trail intently. [14c]

bloodless *adj* **1** without violence or anybody being killed. **2** pale and lifeless; weak and sickly. **3** dull and tedious; without emotion or spirit.

bloodletting *noun* **1** killing; bloodshed. **2** the removal of blood by opening a vein, formerly used to treat numerous diseases and disorders.

blood money *noun* money gained at the cost of someone's life: **a** money paid for committing murder; **b** money earned by supplying information that will cause someone to be convicted on a charge punishable by death; **c** money paid in compensation to the relatives of a murdered person. [16c]

blood orange *noun* a type of orange with flesh that is red or flecked with red.

blood poisoning *noun* a serious condition caused by the presence of either bacterial toxins or large numbers of bacteria in the bloodstream. *Technical equivalent* **septicaemia** and *esp* **toxaemia**.

blood pressure *noun* the pressure of the blood within the blood vessels, esp the pressure within the arteries.

blood pudding see **black pudding**

blood relation *or* **blood relative** *noun* a person related to one by birth, rather than by marriage.

bloodshed *noun* the shedding of blood or killing of people; slaughter.

bloodshot *adj* of the eyes: red and irritated. [15c]

blood sports *plural noun* sports that involve the killing of animals, eg fox-hunting.

bloodstock *noun* pedigree horses.

bloodstream *noun* the flow of blood through the arteries, veins and capillaries of an animal's body.

bloodsucker *noun* **1** an animal that sucks blood, eg the leech. **2** *informal* a person who extorts money from another, or who persistently sponges off them.

bloodthirsty *adj* **1** eager for or fond of killing or violence. **2** of a film, etc: including much violence and killing. [16c]

blood transfusion *noun, med* the introduction of a volume of donated blood directly into a person's bloodstream. See also **transfusion**.

blood type see **blood group**

blood vessel *noun* in the body of an animal: any tubular structure through which blood flows.

bloody *adj* (*-ier, -iest*) **1** stained or covered with blood. **2** involving or including much killing. **3** *slang* used as an intensifier expressing annoyance, etc. **4** murderous or cruel. ▸ *adv, slang* used as an intensifier: **a** expressing annoyance, etc but sometimes almost meaningless: *I wish you'd bloody listen*; **b** extremely: *We're bloody angry about it*. ▸ *verb* (*-ies, -ied*) to stain or cover (something) with blood. ▪ **bloodiness** *noun*. [Anglo-Saxon as *blodig*]

bloody-minded *adj, derog* of a person: deliberately unco-operative.

bloom *noun* **1 a** a flower, esp one on a plant valued for its flowers; **b** such flowers or blossoms collectively. **2** the state of being in flower. **3** a state of perfection or great beauty: *in the full bloom of youth*. **4** a glow or flush on the skin. **5** a powdery or waxy coating on the surface of certain fruits (eg grapes) or leaves. **6** *biol* a rapid seasonal increase in the rate of growth of certain algae in lakes and ponds etc. ▸ *verb, intr* **1** of a plant: to be in or come into flower. **2** to be in or achieve a state of great beauty or perfection. **3** of a person, eg a child or an expectant mother: to be healthy; to flourish. [13c: from Norse *blom*]

bloomer[1] *noun, Brit informal* an embarrassing mistake. [19c: a slang contraction of *blooming error*]

bloomer[2] *noun, Brit* a crusty loaf of white bread. [20c]

bloomers *plural noun* **1** *informal, facetious or old use* women's knickers, esp large or baggy ones. **2** (*also* **bloomer trousers**) *hist* loose trousers for women, gathered at the knee or ankle. [19c in sense 2: named after Amelia Bloomer, an American social reformer]

blooming *adj* **1** of a plant: flowering. **2** of someone or something: healthy and flourishing. **3** *slang* used as an intensifier: **a** expressing annoyance, etc; a euphemism for **bloody** (*adj* sense 3); **b** complete and utter: *a blooming idiot*. ▸ *adv, slang* used as an intensifier: **a** expressing annoyance, etc; **b** very or completely.

blossom *noun* **1** a flower or mass of flowers, esp on a fruit tree. **2** the state of being in flower. ▸ *verb, intr* **1** of a plant, esp a fruit tree: to produce blossom or flowers. **2** (*sometimes* **blossom out**) to grow well or develop successfully. [Anglo-Saxon *blostm*]

blot *noun* **1** a spot or stain, esp of ink. **2** a spot or blemish that spoils the beauty of something. **3** a stain on a person's good reputation or character. ▸ *verb* (***blotted, blotting***) **1** to make a spot or stain on (something), esp with ink. **2 a** to dry (something) with blotting-paper; **b** (*sometimes* **blot up**) to soak up (excess liquid) by pressing eg a cloth, towel or tissue against it. [14c]

IDIOMS **blot one's copybook** to spoil one's good reputation, etc, esp by some foolish or unfortunate mistake.

PHRASAL VERBS **blot out 1** to hide (something) from sight. **2** to refuse to think about or remember (a painful memory). **3** to destroy or obliterate (something).

blotch *noun* a large irregular-shaped coloured patch or mark on the skin, etc. ▸ *verb* to mark (something) with blotches. ▪ **blotchy** *adj* (*-ier, -iest*). [17c: perhaps from **blot**]

blotter *noun* a large sheet or pad of blotting paper.

blotting paper *noun* soft thick unsized paper for absorbing excess ink.

blotto *adj, dated Brit slang* helplessly drunk. [20c]

blouse *noun* **1** a woman's garment very similar to a shirt. **2** *esp formerly* a loose jacket belted or gathered in at the waist, forming part of a soldier's or airman's uniform. ▸ *verb* to arrange (a garment or drapery, etc) in loose folds. [19c: French]

blouson /ˈbluːzɒn/ *noun* a loose jacket or top gathered in tightly at the waist. [20c: French]

blow[1] *verb* (*past tense* ***blew***, *past participle* ***blown*** *or* (*only in sense 13*) ***blowed***) **1** *intr* of a current of air or wind, etc: to be moving, esp rapidly. **2** *tr & intr* to move or cause (something) to move by a current of air or wind, etc. **3** to send (a current of air) from the mouth. **4** to form or shape (eg bubbles, glass) by blowing air from the mouth. **5** to shatter or destroy (something) by an explosion. **6** to produce a sound from (an instrument, etc) by blowing into it. **7** to clear (something) by blowing through it: *blow one's nose*. **8** *informal* **a** to make (an electric fuse) melt and so interrupt the circuit; **b** (*also* **blow out**) *intr* of an electric fuse: to melt, causing an interruption in the flow of current. **9** to break into (a safe, etc) using explosives. **10** *slang* to spoil or bungle (an opportunity, etc): *He had his chance, and he blew it*. **11** *slang* to spend (a large amount of money), esp quickly or recklessly. **12** *slang* to disclose or give away (something secret or confidential). **13** *intr* to breathe heavily: *puffing and blowing after the jog*. ▸ *noun* **1** an act or example of blowing. **2** a spell of exposure to fresh air: *Let's go for a blow on the cliffs*. ▸ *exclam* (*also* **blow it!**) expressing annoyance; damn! [Anglo-Saxon *blawan*]

IDIOMS **blow hot and cold on** *informal* to keep changing one's mind about (an idea, plan, person, etc). **blow one's** *or* **sb's mind** *slang* to make someone become intoxicated or ecstatic under the influence of a drug or of some exhilarating experience. **blow one's own trumpet** *informal* to praise oneself or one's own abilities and achievements. **blow one's stack** *or* **top** *informal* to explode in anger; to lose one's temper. **blow the whistle on** *informal* to inform against (someone or something). **I'll be blowed, blow me!** *or* **blow me down!** *Brit slang* expressions of surprise, etc (see *verb* sense 12 above).

PHRASAL VERBS **blow sb away** *N Am slang* **1** to murder them by shooting them. **2** to surprise and excite them. **blow out 1** to put out (a flame, etc) by blowing. **2** of a tyre: to burst; to puncture suddenly and forcibly when in use. **3** of an electric fuse: to melt or blow (see *verb* sense 8b above). See also **blow-out**. **blow over** of an incident, quarrel, threat, storm, etc: to pass by, esp without having any harmful or lasting effect. **blow up 1** *informal* of a person: to explode in anger. **2** to fill up or swell up with air or gas. **3** to explode. See also **blow-up**. **4** to inflate (eg a balloon). **5** to produce a larger version of (a photograph, etc). **6** *informal* to make (something) seem more serious or important than it really is. **7** to destroy (something) by way of an explosion.

blow[2] *noun* **1** a forceful stroke or knock with the hand or with a weapon. **2** a sudden shock or misfortune. [15c, first as Northern English and Scots *blaw*]

IDIOMS **come to blows** to start or end up fighting.

blow-by-blow *adj* of a description or account, etc: giving all the details precisely and in order.

blow-dry *verb* to dry (hair) in a particular style using a hand-held hairdrier. ▸ *noun* an act or process of blow-drying. ▪ **blow-drier** *noun*. [20c]

blower *noun* **1** a device or machine that blows out a current of air. **2** (**the blower**) *Brit informal* the telephone.

blowfly *noun* any of various flies whose eggs are laid in rotting flesh or excrement.

blowhole *noun* **1** a hole in an area of surface ice, where marine mammals, eg seals, can go to breathe. **2** a hole or modified nostril on top of a whale's head. **3** *geol* a natural vent from the roof of a sea cave up to the ground surface.

blowlamp *or* (*esp N Am*) **blowtorch** *noun* a small portable burner, that produces an intense hot flame, used for paint-stripping, melting soft metal, etc.

blow-out *noun* **1** *informal* a tyre-burst. **2** *oil industry* a violent escape of gas and oil from a well or on a rig, etc. **3** *informal* a large meal at which one over-indulges. **4** *elec eng* **a** an incident in which a circuit is broken by a fuse blowing; **b** a blown fuse.

blowpipe *noun* **1** in glass-blowing: an iron tube used to blow air into molten glass which can then be shaped as it cools. **2** a small tube that carries a stream of air into a flame in order to concentrate and direct it. **3** a long tube from which someone blows a dart, pellet, etc.

blow-up *noun, informal* **1** an enlargement of a photograph. **2** a sudden explosion of temper.

blowy *adj* (***-ier, -iest***) blustery; windy.

blowzy *or* **blowsy** /ˈblaʊzɪ/ *adj* (***-ier, -iest***) *derog, informal* of a woman: **1** fat and red-faced or flushed. **2** dirty and dishevelled; slovenly. [18c: from old dialect *blowze* a beggar woman or wench]

blubber *noun* **1** the fat of sea animals such as the whale. **2** *informal* excessive body fat; flab. ▸ *verb, derog informal* **1** *intr* to weep, esp noisily or unrestrainedly. **2** to say or try to say (words, etc) while weeping. [14c]

bludge *Aust & NZ slang, verb* **1** (*often* **bludge on**) *tr & intr* to scrounge; to impose on or sponge off (someone). **2** *intr* to loaf about; to avoid work or other responsibilities. ▸ *noun* an easy job that requires no effort. [20c: back-formation from **bludger**]

bludgeon *noun* a stick or club with a heavy end. ▸ *verb* **1** to hit (someone or something) with or as if with a bludgeon. **2** (*usu* **bludgeon sb into sth**) to force or bully them into doing it. [18c]

bludger *noun, Aust & NZ slang* a scrounger or loafer; a person who bludges. [19c in the obsolete sense 'someone living off a prostitute's earnings']

blue *adj* **1** with the colour of a clear cloudless sky; having any of the shades of this colour. **2** sad or depressed. See also **blues**. **3** of a film or joke etc: pornographic or indecent. **4** politically conservative. **5** with a skin that is pale blue or purple because of the cold or from bruising, etc. ▸ *noun* **1** the colour of a clear cloudless sky; any blue shade or hue. **2** blue paint or dye. **3** blue material or clothes. **4** a person who has been chosen to represent a college or university at sport, esp at Oxford or Cambridge. **5** *Brit informal* a supporter of the Conservative Party. **6** *Aust & NZ slang* an argument or fight. **7** *Aust & NZ informal* a mistake. **8** (**Blue**) *Aust & NZ informal* a nickname commonly given to a person with red hair, esp a man. ▸ *verb* (***bluing*** *or* ***blueing***) to make (something) blue. ▪ **blueish** *or* **bluish** *and* **bluey** *adj*. ▪ **blueness** *noun*. [13c as *blew*: from French *bleu*]

IDIOMS **out of the blue** unexpectedly.

blue baby *noun* a newborn baby suffering from congenital heart disease which leads to lack of oxygen in the blood, giving the skin and lips a bluish tinge. See **cyanosis**.

bluebell *noun* **1** a bulbous spring-flowering plant with clusters of bell-shaped flowers that are usu blue (also called **wild hyacinth**). **2** *Scot, N Eng* the **harebell**.

blueberry *noun* **1** any of various deciduous shrubs, native to N America, with white or pinkish flowers and edible berries. **2** the bluish-black edible berry produced by this plant. Also called **huckleberry**.

bluebird *noun* any of various birds of the thrush family, the male of which has bright blue plumage on its back.

blue blood *noun* royal or aristocratic ancestry.

bluebottle *noun* a large blowfly, so called because its abdomen has a metallic blue sheen.

blue cheese *noun* cheese with veins of blue mould running through it, eg **Stilton** or **Gorgonzola**.

blue-chip *orig US, adj* **1** *stock exchange* of industrial stocks and shares: considered reliable, secure and strong, though less secure than **gilt-edged** ones. **2** *loosely* prestigious and valuable. ▸ *noun* a blue-chip stock. [20c: from the (high-value) *blue chip* in poker]

blue-collar *adj* of workers: doing manual or unskilled work. Compare **white-collar**.

blue-eyed boy *noun, chiefly Brit, derog informal* a boy or man who is especially favoured.

blue funk *noun, slang* a state of great terror.

bluegrass *noun* **1** a simple style of country music originating in Kentucky, played on stringed instruments. **2** any of several bluish-green grasses of Europe and N America, especially Kentucky. [18c in sense 2; 20c in sense 1]

blue-pencil *verb* to correct, edit or cut parts out of (a piece of writing); to censor.

Blue Peter *or* **blue peter** *noun* a blue flag with a white square, flown on a ship that is about to set sail. [19c]

blueprint *noun* **1 a** a pattern, model or prototype; **b** a detailed original plan of work to be done to develop an idea, project or scheme, etc. **2** *technical* a photographic print of plans, engineering or architectural designs, etc consisting of white lines on a blue background. ▸ *verb* to make a blueprint of (a plan or project, etc). [19c in sense 2]

blue ribbon *or* **blue riband** *noun* **1** a first prize awarded in a competition, or some other very high distinction. **2** *Brit* the blue silk ribbon of the Order of the Garter.

blues *singular or plural noun* (*usu* **the blues**) **1** a feeling of sadness or depression. **2** slow melancholy jazz music of Black American origin. ▪ **bluesy** *adj*. [18c, short for 'the blue devils']

bluestocking *noun, often derog* a highly educated woman who is interested in serious academic subjects. [18c: from the 'Blue Stocking Society' literary meetings in London (c.1750)]

blue tit *noun* a small bird with a bright blue crown, wings and tail, and yellow underparts.

blue whale *noun* a rare **baleen whale**, the largest living animal, which has a bluish body with pale spots.

bluff[1] *verb, tr & intr* to deceive or try to deceive (someone) by pretending to be stronger, cleverer or more determined, etc than one really is. ▸ *noun* an act of bluffing. [19c: from Dutch *bluffen* to brag or boast]

IDIOMS **call sb's bluff** to challenge them by making them prove the genuineness of their claim, threat or promise, etc.

bluff[2] *adj* **1** of a person, character, manner, etc: rough, cheerful and honest; outspoken and hearty. **2** usu of a cliff or of the bow of a ship: broad, steep and upright. ▸ *noun* a steep cliff or high bank of ground. [17c in sense 2: perhaps from obsolete Dutch *blaf* broad or flat]

blunder *noun* a foolish or thoughtless mistake. ▸ *verb* **1** *intr* to make a blunder. **2** *intr* to act or move about awkwardly and clumsily. ▪ **blundering** *adj*. [14c: poss from Norse *blunda* to shut one's eyes]

blunderbuss *noun, hist* a type of musket with a wide barrel and a flared muzzle. [17c: from Dutch *donderbus*, from *donder* thunder + *bus* gun]

blunt *adj* **1** of a pencil, knife or blade, etc: having no point or sharp edge. **2** dull; imperceptive. **3** of a person, character or manner, etc: honest and direct in a rough way. ▸ *verb* to make (something) blunt or less sharp. ▪ **bluntly** *adv*. ▪ **bluntness** *noun*. [13c]

blur *noun* **1** a thing not clearly seen or heard, or happening too fast or too distantly, etc to be clearly seen, comprehended or recognized. **2** a smear or smudge. ▸ *verb* (***blurred, blurring***) **1** *tr & intr* to become or cause (something) to become less clear or distinct. **2** to rub over and smudge (something). **3** to make (one's memory or judgement, etc) less clear. ▪ **blurred** *or* **blurry** *adj* (***-ier, -iest***). [16c]

blurb *noun* a brief description of a book, usu printed on the jacket in order to promote it. [20c: invented by Gelett Burgess, an American author]

blurt *verb* (*usu* **blurt out**) to say (something) suddenly or without thinking of the effect or result. [16c: prob imitating this action]

blush *verb, intr* to become red or pink in the face because of shame, embarrassment, excitement, joy, etc. ▸ *noun* **1** a red or pink glow on the skin of the face, caused by shame, embarrassment, excitement, etc. **2** *esp literary* a pink rosy glow. [14c, from Anglo-Saxon *blyscan* to shine or redden]

blusher *noun* a cosmetic cream or powder used to give colour to the cheeks.

bluster *verb, intr* **1** to speak in a boasting, angry or threatening way. **2** of the wind or waves, etc: to blow or move roughly. ▸ *noun* speech that is ostentatiously boasting, angry or threatening. ▪ **blustery** *adj*. [16c: prob from German dialect *blustern* to blow violently]

Blu-Tack /ˈbluːtak/ *noun, trademark* a re-usable pliable adhesive used to fix paper temporarily to walls, noticeboards, etc. [20c]

BMA *abbrev* British Medical Association.

B-movie *noun, dated* a film, usu cheaply-produced and of mediocre or poor quality, made to support the main film in a cinema programme. Also (*chiefly Brit*) called **B-film**.

BMX *noun* **1** the sport of bicycle riding and racing over a rough track with obstacles. **2** (*also* **BMX bike**) a bicycle designed for BMX racing and also used for stunt-riding. [20c: abbrev of *bicycle motocross*]

b.o. *abbrev* (*also* **BO**) body odour.

boa *noun* **1** a **boa constrictor**, or any similar snake of the mainly S American type that kill by winding themselves round their prey and crushing it. **2** *popularly* any large constricting snake. **3** a woman's long thin scarf, usu made of feathers or fur. [14c: Latin, meaning 'a kind of snake']

boar *noun* (***boars*** *or* ***boar***) **1** a wild ancestor of the domestic pig. **2** a mature uncastrated male pig. [Anglo-Saxon *bar*]

board *noun* **1** a long flat strip of wood. **2** *often in compounds* a piece of material resembling this, made from fibres compressed together: *chipboard*. **3** *often in compounds* **a** a flat piece of wood or other hard solid material, used for a specified purpose or of a specified kind: *ironing board*; **b** a slab, table or other flat surface prepared for playing a game on: *chessboard*. **4** thick stiff card used eg for binding books. **5** a person's meals, provided in return for money: *bed and board*. **6** **a** an official group of people controlling or managing an organization, etc, or examining or interviewing candidates: *a board of examiners*; **b** (*also* **board of directors**) a group of individual directors appointed by a company, who are collectively responsible for its management. **7** (**the boards**) a theatre stage: *tread the boards*. **8** *naut* the side of a ship. ▸ *verb* **1** to enter or get onto (a ship, aeroplane, bus, etc). **2** (*usu* **board up**) to cover (a gap or entrance) with boards. **3** *intr* **a** to receive accommodation and meals in someone else's house, in return for payment; **b** to receive accommodation and meals at school; to attend school as a **boarder**. **4** to provide (someone) with accommodation and meals in return for payment. **5** (*also* **board sb out**) to arrange for them to receive accommodation and meals away from home. [Anglo-Saxon *bord*]

IDIOMS **go by the board** *informal* to be given up or ignored. **on board** on or into a ship or aeroplane, etc. **sweep the board** to win everything or all the prizes.

boarder *noun* a pupil who lives at school during term time.

board game *noun* a game (such as chess or draughts) played with pieces or counters that are moved on a specially designed board.

boarding *noun* **1** a structure or collection of wooden boards laid side by side. **2** the act of boarding a ship or aeroplane, etc.

boarding house *noun* a house in which people live and take meals as paying guests.

boarding school *noun* a school at which all or most of the pupils live during term time.

boardroom *noun* a room in which the directors of a company meet.

boardwalk *noun, N Am* a footpath made of boards, esp on the seafront.

boast *verb* **1** *intr* (*often* **boast about** *or* **of**) to talk with excessive pride about (one's own abilities or achievements, etc). **2** to own or have (something it is right to be proud of): *The hotel boasts magnificent views*. ▸ *noun* **1** an act of boasting; a brag. **2** a thing one is proud of. ▪ **boasting** *noun, adj*. [14c as *bost*]

boastful *adj, usu derog* given to boasting.

boat *noun* **1** a small vessel for travelling over water. **2** *informal, loosely* a larger vessel; a ship. **3** *in compounds* a boat-shaped dish for serving sauce, etc: *gravy boat*. ▸ *verb, intr* to sail or travel in a boat, esp for pleasure. [Anglo-Saxon *bat*]

IDIOMS **in the same boat** of people: finding themselves in the same difficult circumstances. **miss the boat** to lose an opportunity. **rock the boat** to disturb the balance or calmness of a situation.

boater *noun* a straw hat with a flat top and a brim.

boathook *noun* a metal hook fixed to the end of a pole, used by someone on a boat for pushing off, pulling or pushing on something, etc.

boathouse *noun* a building in which boats are stored, esp by a lake or river.

boating *noun* the sailing or rowing, etc of boats for pleasure.

boatman *noun* a man who is in charge of, or hires out, etc a small passenger-carrying boat or boats.

boat people *plural noun* refugees who have fled their country by boat.

boatswain *or* **bosun** /ˈbousən/ *noun* a warrant officer in the navy, or the foreman of a crew, who is in charge of a ship's equipment. [15c: from Anglo-Saxon *batswegen* boatman]

boat train *noun* a train that takes passengers to or from a ship.

bob[1] *verb* (***bobbed, bobbing***) *intr* **1** (*sometimes* **bob along** *or* **past,** *etc*) to move up and down quickly. **2** (*usu* **bob up**) to appear or reappear suddenly. **3** (*usu* **bob for**) to try to catch (esp an apple floating on water or suspended on a string) with one's teeth, as a game. ▸ *noun* a quick up-and-down bouncing movement. [14c]

bob[2] *noun* **1** a short hairstyle for women and children, with the hair cut evenly all round the head. **2** a hanging weight on a clock's pendulum or plumbline, etc. ▸ *verb* (***bobbed, bobbing***) **1** to cut (hair) in a bob. **2** to dock (a tail). [14c]

bob[3] *noun* (*pl* ***bob***) *Brit informal* **1** *old use* a shilling. **2** *loosely* (*usu* **a few bob** *or* **a bob or two**) a sum of money, esp a large amount. [18c]

bobbin *noun* a small cylindrical object on which thread or yarn, etc is wound. [16c: from French *bobine*]

bobble *noun* **1** a small ball, often fluffy or made of tufted wool, used to decorate clothes or furnishings, etc, esp on the top of a knitted **bobble-hat**. **2** a little ball formed on the surface of a fabric during use, through rubbing, etc. ▪ **bobbly** *adj*. [20c: diminutive of **bob[2]**]

bobby *noun* (***-ies***) *Brit informal* a policeman. [19c: after Sir Robert Peel who founded the Metropolitan Police]

bobcat *noun* a solitary nocturnal member of the cat family.

bobsleigh *or* (*esp N Am*) **bobsled** *noun, sport* a sledge for two or more people, for racing on an ice-covered track. Compare **luge**. ▸ *verb, intr* to ride or race on a bobsleigh. [19c]

bobtail *noun* **1** a short or cropped tail. **2** an animal having such a tail. [17c: see **bob[2]**]

bod *noun, informal* **1** a person. **2** a body.

bode[1] *verb* to be a sign of (something); to portend. [Anglo-Saxon]

IDIOMS **bode ill** *or* **well** to be a bad or good sign for the future.

bode[2] see under **bide**

bodge *informal, verb, tr & intr* to make a mess of (something). ▸ *noun* a piece of poor or clumsy workmanship. [16c: a variant of **botch**]

bodhi tree /ˈbɒdɪ/ *or* **bo tree** *noun, Buddhism* the holy tree of the Buddhists, under which Buddha found enlightenment. [From Pali *bodhi* enlightenment]

bodhran /bouˈrɑːn/ *noun* a shallow one-sided drum played in Scottish and Irish folk-music. [Irish Gaelic]

bodice *noun* **1** the close-fitting upper part of a dress, from shoulder to waist. **2** a woman's close-fitting waistcoat, worn over a blouse. **3** *formerly* a similar tight-fitting stiffened undergarment for women. [16c: from *bodies*, pl of **body**]

bodily *adj* belonging or relating to, or performed by, the body. ▸ *adv* **1** as a whole; taking the whole body: *carried me bodily to the car.* **2** in person.

bodkin *noun* a large blunt needle. [14c as *bodekin* a small dagger or stiletto]

body *noun* (**-ies**) **1** the whole physical structure of a person or animal. **2** the physical structure of a person or animal excluding the head and limbs. **3** a corpse. **4** the main or central part of anything, such as the main part of a vehicle that carries the load or passengers. **5** a person's physical needs and desires as opposed to spiritual concerns. **6** a substantial section or group: *a body of opinion.* **7** a group of people regarded as a single unit. **8** a quantity or mass: *a body of water.* **9** a distinct mass or object: *a foreign body.* **10** applied to wine, music, etc: a full or strong quality or tone; fullness. **11** thickness; substantial quality. **12** a legless tight-fitting one-piece garment for women. **13** *informal* a person. ▸ *verb* (**-ies, -ied**) (*often* **body forth**) to give (something) body or form. [Anglo-Saxon as *bodig*]

IDIOMS **keep body and soul together** *often facetious* to remain alive, esp not to die of hunger.

body bag *noun* a bag in which a dead body, esp that of a war casualty or accident victim, is transported.

body blow *noun* **1** *boxing* a blow to the torso. **2** a serious setback or misfortune.

body-building *noun* physical exercise designed to develop the muscles. ▪ **bodybuilder** *noun.*

body clock see under **biological clock**

bodyguard *noun* a person or group of people whose job is to accompany and give physical protection to an important person, etc.

body language *noun* the communication of information by means of conscious or unconscious gestures, attitudes, facial expressions, etc, rather than by words.

body politic *noun* (*usu* **the body politic**) all the people of a nation in their political capacity. [16c]

body shop *noun* a vehicle-body repair or construction shop.

body snatcher *noun, hist* a person who steals dead bodies from their graves, usu to sell them for dissection.

body stocking *noun* a tight-fitting one-piece garment worn next to the skin, covering all of the body and often the arms and legs.

body warmer *noun* a padded sleeveless jacket.

bodywork *noun* the outer shell of a motor vehicle.

Boer *noun* a descendant of the early Dutch settlers in S Africa. ▸ *adj* belonging or relating to the Boers. [19c: Dutch, literally 'farmer']

boffin *noun, Brit informal* **1** a scientist engaged in research, esp for the armed forces or the government. **2** an intelligent or studious person. [1940s]

bog *noun* **1** *ecol* an area of wet spongy poorly-drained ground, composed of acid peat and slowly decaying plant material. **2** *Brit slang* a toilet. ▸ *verb* (***bogged, bogging***) (*usu* **bog down**) **1** to become or cause (someone or something) to become stuck. **2** to hinder (someone or something) or hold up the progress of (them or it). ▪ **bogginess** *noun.* ▪ **boggy** *adj* (**-ier, -iest**). [14c: from Irish and Scottish Gaelic *bog* soft]

bogey[1] *or* **bogy** *noun* (***bogeys*** *or* ***bogies***) **1** an evil or mischievous spirit. **2** something esp feared or dreaded; a bugbear. **3** *slang* a piece of nasal mucus. [19c: prob from *bogle*, a dialect word meaning 'a spectre or goblin']

bogey[2] *golf, noun* **1** a score of one over **par** on a specific hole. Compare **albatross** (sense 2), **birdie** (sense 2), **eagle** (sense 2). **2** *formerly* the number of strokes that a competent golfer might expect to take for a given hole or course. ▸ *verb* to complete (a specified hole) in one over par. [19c]

bogeyman *or* **bogyman** *noun* a cruel or frightening person or creature, existing or imaginary, used to threaten or frighten children. [19c: from **bogey**[1]]

boggle *verb, intr, informal* **1** to be amazed or unable to understand or imagine: *the mind boggles.* **2** (*usu* **boggle at**) to hesitate or equivocate over (something), out of surprise or fright, etc. [16c: from *bogle*; see **bogey**[1]]

bogie *or* **bogey** *noun, mainly Brit* a frame with four or six wheels used as part of a pivoting undercarriage, supporting a railway carriage. [19c]

bog-standard *adj, informal* mediocre; ordinary.

bogus *adj* false; not genuine. [19c US slang]

bohemian *noun* **1** someone who lives in a way that ignores standard customs and rules of social behaviour. **2** (**Bohemian**) a person from Bohemia, formerly a kingdom, later a part of the Czech Republic. ▸ *adj* **1** ignoring standard customs and rules of social behaviour. **2** (**Bohemian**) from or belonging or relating to Bohemia. ▪ **bohemianism** *noun.* [19c; 16c in sense 2: from French *bohémien* a Bohemian or Gypsy]

bohrium /ˈbɔːrɪəm/ *noun, chem* (symbol **Bh**) an artificially manufactured radioactive chemical element. [20c: named after the Danish physicist Niels Bohr]

boil[1] *verb* **1** *intr* of a liquid: to change rapidly to a vapour on reaching a certain temperature. **2** *intr* of a container, eg a kettle: to have contents that are boiling. **3** **a** to make (a liquid) reach its boiling point rapidly; **b** to boil the contents of (a container). **4** *tr* to cook (food) by heating in boiling liquid. **5** (*sometimes* **boil up**) to bring (a container or its contents) to boiling point. **6** (*usu* **be boiling**) *informal* **a** to be very hot: *It's boiling in the car*; **b** to be extremely angry. **7** *intr* of the sea, etc: to move and bubble violently as if boiling. ▸ *noun* (*usu* **a boil** *or* **the boil**) the act or point of boiling. [13c: from French *boillir*, from Latin *bullire* to bubble]

PHRASAL VERBS **boil down to** *informal* to mean (something); to have (something) as the most important part or factor. **boil over 1** of a liquid: to boil and flow over the edge of its container. **2** *informal* to speak out angrily.

boil[2] *noun* a reddened pus-filled swelling in the skin, caused by bacterial infection of a hair follicle. [Anglo-Saxon *byl*]

boiler *noun* **1** any closed vessel that is used to convert water into steam, in order to drive machinery. **2** an apparatus for heating a building's hot water supply.

boilersuit *noun* a one-piece suit worn over normal clothes to protect them while doing manual or heavy work. Also called **overalls**.

boiling point *noun* **1** the temperature at which a particular substance changes from a liquid to a vapour. **2** a point of great anger or high excitement.

boisterous *adj* **1** of people, behaviour, etc: very lively, noisy and cheerful. **2** of the sea, etc: rough and stormy. [15c variant *boistous* meaning 'rough' or 'coarse']

bold *adj* **1** daring or brave; confident and courageous. **2** not showing respect; impudent. **3** striking and clearly marked; noticeable. ▪ **boldly** *adv.* ▪ **boldness** *noun.* [Anglo-Saxon *beald*]

bole *noun* the trunk of a tree. [14c: from Norse *bolr*]

bolero *noun* **1** /bəˈlɛəroʊ/ **a** a traditional Spanish dance; **b** the music for this dance, usu in triple time. **2** /ˈbɒləroʊ/ a short open jacket reaching not quite to the waist. [18c: Spanish]

Bolivian *adj* belonging or relating to Bolivia, a republic in South America, or its inhabitants. ▸ *noun* a citizen or inhabitant of, or person born in, Bolivia.

boll *noun* a rounded capsule containing seeds, esp of a cotton or flax plant. [14c: from *bolla* a bowl]

bollard *noun* **1** *Brit* a small post used to mark a traffic island or to keep traffic away from a certain area. **2** a short but strong post on a ship or quay, etc around which ropes are fastened.

boloney see **baloney**

Bolshevik *noun* **1** *hist* a member of the radical faction of the Russian socialist party, which became the Communist Party in 1918. **2** a Russian communist. **3** (*often* **bolshevik**) *derog informal* any radical socialist or revolutionary. ▸ *adj* **1** belonging or relating to the Bolsheviks. **2** communist. ▪ **Bolshevism** *noun.* ▪ **Bolshevist** *noun, adj.* [20c: Russian, from *bolshe* greater]

bolshie *or* **bolshy** *Brit derog informal, adj* (**-ier, -iest**) **1** bad-tempered and unco-operative; difficult or rebellious. **2** left-wing. ▸ *noun* a Bolshevik.

bolster *verb* (*often* **bolster sth up**) to support it, make it stronger or hold it up. ▸ *noun* **1** a long narrow pillow. **2** any pad or support. [Anglo-Saxon]

bolt[1] *noun* **1** a bar or rod that slides into a hole or socket to fasten a door, etc. **2** a small thick round bar of metal, with a screw thread, used with a **nut** to fasten things together. **3** a sudden movement or dash away, esp to escape from someone or something: *make a bolt for it*. **4** a flash of lightning. **5** a short arrow fired from a crossbow. ▸ *verb* **1** to fasten (a door, etc) with a bolt. **2** to fasten (two or more things) together with bolts. **3** to eat (a meal, etc) very quickly. **4** *intr* to run or dash away suddenly and quickly. **5** *intr* of a horse: to run away out of control. **6** *intr* of a plant: to flower and produce seeds too early. [Anglo-Saxon]

IDIOMS **a bolt from the blue** a sudden, completely unexpected and usu unpleasant, event. **bolt upright** absolutely straight and stiff.

bolt[2] *or* **boult** *verb* **1** to pass (flour, etc) through a sieve. **2** to examine, sift or investigate (information, etc). [13c: from French *bulter*]

bolthole *noun, Brit informal* a secluded private place to hide away in.

bomb *noun* **1** a hollow case or other device containing a substance capable of causing an explosion, fire or smoke, etc. **2** (**the bomb**) the atomic bomb, or nuclear weapons collectively. **3** (**a bomb**) *Brit informal* a lot of money. **4** *N Am informal* a failure, flop or fiasco. **5** *comput* a piece of programming, inserted into software, that can be activated to sabotage the system. ▸ *verb* **1** to attack or damage, etc (something) with a bomb or bombs. **2** (*esp* **bomb along** *or* **off,** *etc*) *intr, informal* to move or drive quickly. **3** *intr, N Am informal* to fail or flop badly. ▪ **bombing** *noun.* [17c: from Greek *bombos* a humming sound]

IDIOMS **go down (like) a bomb** *informal* to be a great success; to be received enthusiastically. **go like a bomb** *informal, chiefly Brit* **1** to move very quickly. **2** to go or sell, etc extremely well; to be very successful.

bombard *verb* **1** to attack (a place, target, etc) with large, heavy guns or bombs. **2** to direct questions or abuse at (someone) very quickly and without stopping. **3** to batter or pelt (something or someone) heavily and persistently. **4** *physics* to subject (a target, esp an atom) to a stream of high-energy particles. ▪ **bombardment** *noun.* [16c, meaning 'to fire or attack with a *bombard*' (an early type of cannon for throwing stones)]

bombardier /bɒmbəˈdɪə(r)/ *noun* **1** *Brit* a noncommissioned officer in the Royal Artillery. **2** the member of a bomber's crew who aims and releases the bombs.

bombast *noun* pretentious, boastful or insincere words having little real force or meaning. ▪ **bombastic** *adj.* [16c, orig meaning 'cotton padding or wadding']

Bombay duck *noun* a dried fish eaten as an accompaniment to curry.

bomber *noun* **1** an aeroplane designed for carrying and dropping bombs. **2** a person who bombs something or who plants bombs.

bombshell *noun* **1** a piece of surprising and usu devastating news. **2** *informal* a stunningly attractive woman.

bombsite *noun* **1** an area where buildings, etc have been destroyed by a bomb. **2** *informal* a chaotically untidy place.

bona fide /ˈboʊnə ˈfaɪdɪ/ *adj* genuine or sincere; done or carried out in good faith: *a bona fide offer*. ▸ *adv* genuinely or sincerely. [16c: Latin]

bonanza *noun* **1** an unexpected and sudden source of good luck or wealth. **2** a large amount, esp of gold from a mine. **3** *N Am* a rich mine or vein of precious ore such as gold or silver. [19c: Spanish, literally 'calm sea']

bonce *noun, Brit slang* the head. [19c, at first meaning 'a large marble']

bond *noun* **1** something used for tying, binding or holding. **2** (*usu* **bonds**) something that restrains or imprisons someone. **3** something that unites or joins people together: *a bond of friendship*. **4** a binding agreement or promise. **5** *finance* a **debenture. 6** *law* a written agreement to pay money or carry out the terms of a contract. **7** *chem* the strong force of attraction that holds together two atoms in a molecule or a crystalline salt. ▸ *verb* **1** to join, secure or tie (two or more things) together. **2** *intr* to hold or stick together securely. **3** *intr* esp of a mother and newborn baby: to form a strong emotional attachment. **4** to put (goods) into a **bonded warehouse**. [13c: from Norse *band*]

IDIOMS **in** *or* **out of bond** of goods: held in or out of a **bonded warehouse**.

bondage *noun* **1** slavery. **2** the state of being confined or imprisoned, etc; captivity. [14c]

bonded warehouse *noun* a building in which goods are kept until customs or other duty on them is paid.

bond energy *noun, chem* the energy released or absorbed during the formation of a chemical bond.

bond paper *noun* very good quality writing paper.

bone *noun* **1** the hard dense tissue that forms the skeleton of vertebrates. **2** any of the components of the skeleton, made of this material. **3** (**bones**) the skeleton. **4** (*chiefly* **one's bones**) the body as the place where feelings or instincts come from. **5** a substance similar to human bone, such as ivory and whalebone, etc. **6** (**bones**) the basic or essential part. ▸ *verb* **1** to take bone out of (meat, etc). **2** to make (a piece of clothing, eg a corset or bodice) stiff by adding strips of bone or some other hard substance. [Anglo-Saxon *ban*]

IDIOMS **have a bone to pick with sb** to have something to disagree about with them. **make no bones about sth 1** to admit or allow it without any fuss or hesitation. **2** to be quite willing to say or do it openly. **near** *or* **close to the bone** *informal* of speech, etc: **1** referring too closely to a subject that it would have been kind or tactful to avoid. **2** rather indecent or risqué.

PHRASAL VERBS **bone up on** *informal* to learn or collect information about (a subject).

bone china *noun* a type of fine china or **porcelain** made from clay mixed with ash from bones.

bone-dry *adj* completely dry.

bone-idle *adj, informal* utterly lazy.

bone marrow see **marrow** (sense 1)

bone meal *noun* dried and ground bones, used as a plant fertilizer and as a supplement to animal feed.

boneshaker *noun, informal* an old uncomfortable and unsteady vehicle, esp an early type of bicycle.

bonfire *noun* a large outdoor fire. [15c as *bonefire*, from **bone** + **fire**: bones were formerly used as fuel]

bongo *noun* (***bongos*** *or* ***bongoes***) each of a pair of small drums held between the knees and played with the hands. [20c: from American Spanish *bongó*]

bonhomie /ˈbɒnɒmiː/ *noun* easy good nature; cheerful friendliness. [19c: French]

bonk *verb* to hit (something or someone). ▸ *noun* a blow.

bonkers *adj, chiefly Brit slang* mad or crazy. [20c, at first meaning 'slightly drunk']

bon mot /bɔ̃ˈmoʊ/ *noun* (***bons mots*** /bɔ̃ˈmoʊ/) a short clever remark. [18c: French, literally 'good word']

bonnet *noun* **1** a type of hat fastened under the chin with ribbon, worn esp by babies. **2** *Brit* the hinged cover over a motor vehicle's engine. *N Am equivalent* **hood**. **3** *Scot* a brimless cap made of soft fabric, worn by men or boys. [14c as *bonet*: French]

bonny *adj* (***-ier, -iest***) **1** *chiefly Scot & N Eng* attractive; pretty. **2** looking very healthy. [15c]

bonsai *noun* (*pl* ***bonsai***) a miniature tree cultivated in a small container. [20c: Japanese, from *bon* tray or bowl + *sai* cultivation]

bonus *noun* **1** an extra sum of money given on top of what is due as wages, interest or dividend, etc. **2** an unexpected extra benefit gained or given with something else. **3** *insurance* an additional sum of money payable to the holder of a policy when it matures. [18c: Latin, meaning 'good']

bon voyage /*French* bɔ̃vwajaʒ/ *exclam* said to a person about to travel: expressing good wishes for a safe and pleasant journey. [15c: French, literally 'good journey']

bony *adj* (***-ier, -iest***) **1** consisting of, made of or like bone. **2** full of bones. **3** of a person or animal: thin, so that the bones are very noticeable.

boo *exclam, noun* a sound expressing disapproval, or made when trying to frighten or surprise someone. ▸ *verb* (***booed***) *tr & intr* to shout 'boo' to express disapproval (of someone or something). [19c]

boob *noun, informal* (*also* **booboo**) a stupid or foolish mistake. ▸ *verb, intr, informal* to make a stupid or foolish mistake. [20c: short for **booby**]

boob tube *noun, slang* **1** a woman's tight-fitting garment made of stretch fabric covering the torso from midriff to armpit. **2** *N Am* a TV set.

booby *noun* (***-ies***) **1** any of various seabirds of the gannet family. **2** *old use, informal* a stupid or foolish person.

booby prize *noun* a prize (usu a joke prize) for the lowest score in a competition.

booby trap *noun* **1** a bomb or mine that is disguised so that it is set off by the victim. **2** a trap, esp one intended as a practical joke. ▸ *verb* (**booby-trap**) to put a booby trap in or on (a place). [19c: from **booby**]

boogie *informal verb* (***boogieing*** *or* ***boogying***) *intr* to dance to pop, rock or jazz music. ▸ *noun* **1** a dance, or dancing, to pop, rock or jazz music. **2** **boogie-woogie**. [20c as *noun*]

boogie-woogie *noun, music, orig US* a style of jazz piano music with a constantly repeated, strongly rhythmic bass. [20c]

boo-hoo *exclam, noun* the sound of noisy weeping. ▸ *verb* (***boo-hooed***) *intr* to weep noisily. [16c: imit]

book *noun* **1** a number of printed pages bound together along one edge and protected by covers. **2** a piece of written work intended for publication, eg a novel, etc. **3** a number of sheets of blank paper bound together. **4** (*usu* **the books**) a record or formal accounts of the business done by a company, society, etc. **5** a record of bets made with different people. **6** (**the book**) *informal* the current telephone directory. **7** (*usu* **Book**) a major division of a long literary work. **8** a number of stamps, matches or cheques, etc bound together. **9** the words of an opera or musical. ▸ *verb* **1** *tr & intr* to reserve (a ticket, seat, etc), or engage (a person's services) in advance. **2** of a police officer, traffic warden, etc: to record the details of (a person who is being charged with an offence). **3** *football* of a referee: to enter (a player's name) in a notebook as a record of an offence. ▪ **bookable** *adj*. [Anglo-Saxon *boc*]

IDIOMS **be in sb's good** *or* **bad books** to be in or out of favour with them. **bring sb to book** to punish them or make them account for their behaviour. **by the book** strictly according to the rules. **in my book** in my opinion. **take a leaf out of sb's book** to benefit from their example.

PHRASAL VERBS **book in** *esp Brit* **1** to sign one's name on the list of guests at a hotel. **2** to report one's arrival at a hotel, etc. *N Am equivalent* **check in**. **book sb in** to reserve a place or room for them in a hotel, etc. *N Am equivalent* **check sb in**. **book up** to fix and reserve in advance the tickets and other arrangements for (a holiday, show, meal, etc).

bookbinder *noun* a person or business that binds books (see **bind** *verb* sense 6). ▪ **bookbinding** *noun*.

bookcase *noun* a piece of furniture with shelves for books.

book club *noun* a club that sells books to its members at reduced prices and generally by mail order.

book end *noun* each of a pair of supports used to keep a row of books standing upright.

book group *noun* a group of people who meet regularly to discuss a book, usually a novel.

bookie *noun, mainly Brit informal* a bookmaker.

booking *noun* **1** a reservation of a theatre seat, hotel room, etc. **2** esp in sport: the recording of an offence with details of the offender. **3** an engagement for the services of a person or company, esp for a theatrical or musical performance, etc.

bookish *adj, often derog* **1** extremely fond of reading and books. **2** having knowledge or opinions based on books rather than practical experience.

bookkeeper *noun* a person who keeps a record of the financial transactions of a business or organization, etc. ▪ **bookkeeping** *noun.* [16c]

booklet *noun* a small book with a paper cover.

bookmaker *noun, mainly Brit* (often shortened to **bookie**) **1** a person whose job is to take bets on horse races, etc and pay out winnings. Also called **turf accountant**. **2** *informal* a shop or premises used by a bookmaker for taking bets, etc. ▪ **bookmaking** *noun.*

bookmark *noun* **1** (*sometimes* **bookmarker**) a strip of leather, card, etc put in a book, esp to mark one's place. **2** *comput* a record of the location of a favourite Internet site, web page, etc. ▸ *verb comput* to make an electronic record of (a favourite Internet site etc).

bookstall *noun* a small shop in a station, etc where books, newspapers, magazines, etc are sold.

bookworm *noun* **1** *informal* a person who is extremely fond of reading. **2** a type of small insect that feeds on the paper and glue used in books.

Boolean algebra /'bu:lɪən/ *noun* a form of algebra, used to work out the logic for computer programs, that uses algebraic symbols and set theory to represent logical operations.

boom[1] *noun* a deep resounding sound. ▸ *verb, intr* to make a deep resounding sound. [15c: prob imit]

boom[2] *noun* **1** a sudden increase or growth in business, prosperity, activity, etc. **2** a period of such rapid growth or activity, etc. ▸ *verb, intr* **1** esp of a business: to become rapidly and suddenly prosperous. **2** of a commodity, etc: to increase sharply in value. [19c, orig US]

boom[3] *noun* **1** *naut* a pole to which the bottom of a ship's sail is attached, keeping the sail stretched tight. **2** a heavy pole or chain, or a barrier of floating logs, etc across the entrance to a harbour or across a river. **3** *cinema, TV, etc* a long pole with a microphone, camera or light attached to one end, held above the heads of people being filmed. [17c: Dutch, meaning 'beam']

boomerang *noun* **1** a piece of flat curved wood used by Australian Aborigines for hunting, often so balanced that, when thrown to a distance, it returns towards the person who threw it. **2** a malicious act or statement that harms the perpetrator rather than the intended victim. ▸ *verb, intr* of an act or statement, etc: to go wrong and harm the perpetrator rather than the intended victim. [19c: from Aboriginal *bumariny*]

boon[1] *noun* an advantage, benefit or blessing; something to be thankful for. [12c: from Norse *bon* a prayer]

boon[2] *adj* close, convivial, intimate or favourite: *a boon companion.* [14c: from French *bon* good]

boor *noun, derog* a coarse person with bad manners. ▪ **boorish** *adj.* [15c: from Dutch *boer* farmer]

boost *verb* **1** to improve or encourage (something or someone). **2** to make (something) greater or increase it; to raise: *boost profits.* **3** to promote (something) by advertising. ▸ *noun* **1** a piece of help or encouragement, etc. **2** a push upwards. **3** a rise or increase: *a boost in sales.* [19c, orig US]

booster *noun* **1** (*also* **booster shot**) a dose of vaccine that is given in order to renew or increase the immune response to a previous dose of the same vaccine. **2** *aerospace* an engine in a rocket that provides additional thrust at some stage of the vehicle's flight. **3** (*also* **booster rocket**) a rocket that is used to launch a space vehicle, before another engine takes over. **4** *electronics* a radio-frequency amplifier that is used to amplify a weak TV or radio signal.

boot[1] *noun* **1** an outer covering, made of leather or rubber, etc, for the foot and lower part of the leg. **2** *Brit* a compartment for luggage in a car, usu at the back. *N Am equivalent* **trunk**. **3** *informal* a hard kick. **4** (**the boot**) *informal* dismissal from a job. ▸ *verb* **1** to kick (something or someone). **2** (*usu* **boot sb** *or* **sth out**) to throw them or it out, or remove them or it by force. **3** (*often* **boot up**) *comput* to start or restart (a computer) by loading the programs which control its basic functions. [14c: from French *bote*]

IDIOMS **put the boot in** *informal* **1** to kick viciously. **2** to deliver further humiliation, hurt, torment, etc.

boot[2] *noun, archaic* an advantage. [Anglo-Saxon *bot* an advantage or help]

IDIOMS **to boot** as well; in addition.

bootee *noun* a soft knitted boot for a baby.

booth *noun* **1** a small temporary roofed structure or tent, esp a covered stall at a fair or market. **2** a small partly-enclosed compartment, eg one in a restaurant containing a table and seating, or one intended for a specific purpose. [13c, meaning 'a temporary dwelling': from Norse *buth*]

bootleg *verb* (***bootlegged, bootlegging***) **1** to make, sell or transport (alcoholic drink) illegally, esp in a time of prohibition. **2** to make or deal in (illicit goods such as unofficial recordings of copyright music, videos, etc). ▸ *noun* illegally produced, sold or transported goods. ▪ **bootlegger** *noun.* [17c: a *bootlegger* would conceal bottles of illegal liquor in the legs of high boots]

bootlicker *noun, informal* a person who tries to gain the favour of someone in authority by flattery, excessive obedience, etc. [19c]

boot sale see **car boot sale**

booty *noun* (***-ies***) valuable goods taken in wartime or by force; plunder. [15c *botye*: from Norse *byti*]

booze *slang, noun* alcoholic drink. ▸ *verb, intr* to drink a lot of alcohol, or too much of it. ▪ **boozy** *adj* (***-ier, -iest***). [14c: from Dutch *busen* to drink to excess]

boozer *noun, slang* **1** *Brit, Aust & NZ* a public house or bar. **2** a person who drinks a lot of alcohol.

booze-up *noun, Brit, Aust & NZ slang* a drinking-bout or an occasion when a lot of alcohol is drunk.

bop[1] *informal verb* (***bopped, bopping***) *intr* to dance to popular music. ▸ *noun* **1** a dance to popular music. **2** **bebop**. [1940s, shortened from **bebop**]

bop[2] *informal, often humorous, verb* (***bopped, bopping***) to hit (someone or something). ▸ *noun* a blow or knock. [20c: imitating the sound]

boracic *and* **boracic acid** see **boric** and **boric acid**

borage *noun* a plant with oval hairy leaves widely cultivated as a herb for use in salads and medicinally. [13c: from French *bourache*]

borate /ˈbɔːreɪt/ *noun* a salt or ester of **boric acid**.

borax *noun* a colourless crystalline salt, found in saline lake deposits, used in the manufacture of glass, and as a mild antiseptic and source of **boric acid**. Also called **sodium borate**. [14c as *boras*: from Latin *borax*]

border *noun* **1** a band or margin along the edge of something. **2** the boundary of a country or political region, etc. **3** the land on either side of a country's border. See also **the Borders**. **4** a narrow strip of ground planted with flowers, surrounding an area of grass. **5** any decorated or ornamental edge or trimming. ▸ *adj* belonging or referring to the border, or on the border. ▸ *verb* **1** to be a border to, adjacent to, or on the border of (something). **2** to provide (something) with a border. [14c as *bordure*: French, from the same root as **board**]

borderland *noun* **1** land at or near a country's border. **2** the undefined margin or condition between two states, eg between sleeping and waking.

borderline *noun* **1** the border between one thing, country, etc and another. **2** a line dividing two things: *the borderline between passing and failing*. ▸ *adj* on the border between one thing, state, etc and another; marginal: *a borderline result*.

the Borders *plural noun* the area of Scotland bordering on England.

bore[1] *verb* **1** to make a hole in (something) by drilling. **2** to produce (a borehole, tunnel or mine, etc) by drilling. ▸ *noun* **1** the hollow barrel of a gun, or the cavity inside any such tube. **2** **a** *in compounds* the diameter of the hollow barrel of a gun, esp to show which size bullets the gun requires: *12-bore shotgun*; **b** the diameter of the cavity inside any such tube or pipe. Also called **calibre**, **gauge**. **3** a **borehole**. [Anglo-Saxon *borian*]

bore[2] *verb* to make (someone) feel tired and uninterested, by being dull, tedious, uninteresting, etc. ▸ *noun* a dull, uninteresting or tedious person or thing. ▪ **boredom** *noun*. ▪ **boring** *adj*. [18c]

bore[3] *noun* a solitary high wave of water caused by constriction of the spring tide as it enters a narrow estuary. [17c: from Norse *bara* a wave or swell]

bore[4] see under **bear**[1]

boreal forest see **taiga**

borehole *noun* a deep narrow hole made by boring, esp one made in the ground to find oil or water, etc.

boric *or* **boracic** *adj* relating to or containing **boron**.

boric acid *or* **boracic acid** *noun, chem* a water-soluble white or colourless crystalline solid obtained from **borax**, used in pharmaceutical products, glazes, enamels, and glass.

born *adj* **1** brought into being by birth. **2** having a specified quality or ability as a natural attribute: *a born leader*. **3** (**born to sth**) destined to do it: *born to lead men*. ▸ *verb, past participle of* **bear**[1].

IDIOMS **not born yesterday** not naive or foolish.

born, borne

Be careful not to use the spelling **born** when you mean **borne. Born** is used for the past participle when referring to the birth of a child, idea, etc:

When were you born?

This form is also used in the passive, unless it is followed by the word **by**:

The child was born last week.

Otherwise the form is **borne**:

I couldn't have borne it any longer/the baby borne by Ms Smith.

born-again *adj* converted or re-converted, esp to a fundamentalist or evangelical Christian faith. [20c]

borne see under **bear**[1]

boron *noun, chem* (symbol **B**) a non-metallic element found only in compounds, eg **borax** and **boric acid**, and used in hardening steel. [19c: from *bor*ax + *carbon*]

borough *noun* **1** (*also* **parliamentary borough**) in England: a town or urban area represented by at least one member of Parliament. **2** *hist* in England: a town with its own municipal council and special rights and privileges granted by royal charter. See also **burgh**. **3** a division of a large town, esp of London or New York, for local-government purposes. [Anglo-Saxon *burg* a city or fortified town]

borrow *verb* **1** to take (something) temporarily, usu with permission and with the intention of returning it. **2** *intr* to get (money) in this way, from a bank, etc. **3** to take, adopt or copy (words or ideas, etc) from another language or person, etc. ▪ **borrower** *noun*. ▪ **borrowing** *noun*. [Anglo-Saxon *borgian*, from *borg* a pledge or security]

borscht, **bortsch** *or* **borsh** *noun* a Russian and Polish beetroot soup. [19c: Russian]

borstal *noun, Brit, formerly* an institution to which young criminals were sent. [20c: named after Borstal in Kent, where the first of these was established]

borzoi *noun* a large breed of dog with a tall slender body, a long thin muzzle, a long tail and a long soft coat. [19c: Russian, literally 'swift']

bosh *noun, exclam, informal* nonsense; foolish talk. [19c: from Turkish *boş* worthless or empty]

Bosman *noun, informal* the free transfer of a footballer whose contract has expired to another club within the EU in accordance with the Bosman ruling, a decision of the European Court of Justice in 1995. [Jean-Marc Bosman, Belgian footballer]

Bosnian *adj* belonging or relating to Bosnia or its inhabitants. ▸ *noun* a citizen or inhabitant of, or person born in, Bosnia. [18c]

bosom *noun* **1** a person's chest or breast, now esp that of a woman. **2** (*sometimes* **bosoms**) *informal* a woman's breasts. **3** a loving or protective centre: *return to the bosom of one's family*. **4** *chiefly literary* the seat of emotions and feelings; the heart. [Anglo-Saxon *bosm*]

bosom friend *or* **bosom buddy** *noun* a close or intimate friend.

boss[1] *informal, noun* a person who employs others, or who is in charge of others. ▸ *verb* **1** (*esp* **boss sb about** *or* **around**) to give them orders in a domineering way **2** to manage or control (someone). [17c, orig US: from Dutch *baas* master]

boss[2] *noun* **1** a round raised knob or stud on a shield, etc, usu for decoration. **2** *archit* a round raised decorative knob found where the ribs meet in a vaulted ceiling. [14c: from French *boce*]

bossa nova *noun* **1** a dance like the **samba**, orig from Brazil. **2** music for this dance. [20c: Portuguese, from *bossa* trend + *nova* new]

boss-eyed *adj, Brit informal* **1** having only one good eye. **2** cross-eyed. **3** crooked; squint. [19c: from the dialect word *boss* a mistake or bungle]

bossy *adj* (***-ier, -iest***) *informal* inclined to give orders like a **boss**[1]; disagreeably domineering. ▪ **bossiness** *noun.*

bosun see **boatswain**

bot *noun, comput* a computer program designed to perform routine tasks, such as searching the Internet, with some autonomy. [Late 20c: short form of **robot**]

bot. *abbrev* **1** botanical. **2** botany.

botany *noun* (***-ies***) the branch of biology concerned with the scientific study of plants. ▪ **botanic** *or* **botanical** *adj.* ▪ **botanist** *noun.* [17c: from Greek *botane* a plant or herb]

botch *informal, verb* (*esp* **botch up**) **1** to do (something) badly and unskilfully; to make a mess or bad job of (something). **2** to repair (something) carelessly or badly. ▶ *noun* (also **botch-up**) a badly or carelessly done piece of work, repair, etc. [14c as *bocchen*, meaning 'to patch']

both *adj, pron* (*sometimes* **both of sth**) the two; the one and the other: *I'd like you both to help.* ▶ *adv* as well. [12c: from Norse *bathir*]

IDIOMS **both ... and ...** not only ... but also ...

bother *verb* **1** to annoy, worry or trouble (someone or something). **2** *tr & intr* (*usu* **bother about sth**) to worry about it. **3** *intr* (*esp* **bother about** *or* **with sth**) to take the time or trouble to do it or consider it, etc: *We never bother with convention here.* ▶ *noun* **1** a minor trouble or worry. **2** a person or thing that causes bother. ▶ *exclam, mainly Brit* expressing slight annoyance or impatience.

IDIOMS **be bothered** to take the trouble (to do something).

bothersome *adj* causing bother or annoyance. [19c]

bothy *noun* (***-ies***) *chiefly Scot* **1** a simple cottage or hut used as temporary shelter. **2** a basically furnished dwelling for farm workers, etc. [18c: prob altered from Gaelic *bothan* a hut]

Botox /ˈboʊtɒks/ *noun, trademark* a substance injected into the skin as a temporary treatment to make lines on the face less apparent. [20c: shortened from *bo*tulinum *tox*in type A]

bottle *noun* **1** a hollow glass or plastic container with a narrow neck, for holding liquids. **2** a **bottleful**. **3** a baby's feeding bottle or the liquid in it. **4** *Brit, slang* courage, nerve or confidence **5** (*usu* **the bottle**) *slang* drinking of alcohol, esp to excess (*esp* **hit** *or* **take to the bottle**). ▶ *verb* to put (something) into a bottle. [14c: ultimately Latin *buttis* a cask]

PHRASAL VERBS **bottle out** *Brit slang* to lose one's courage and decide not to do something. **bottle up** to suppress (one's feelings about something).

bottle bank *noun* a large purpose-built container into which people can put empty glass bottles and jars, etc to be collected and **recycled**. [20c]

bottle-feed *verb* to feed (a baby) with milk from a bottle rather than the breast.

bottleful *noun* the amount a bottle can hold.

bottle green *noun* a dark-green colour. ▶ *adj* (**bottle-green**) dark green.

bottleneck *noun* **1** a place or thing that impedes or is liable to impede the movement of traffic, esp a narrow or partly-blocked part of a road. **2** something that causes congestion and is an obstacle to progress.

bottle party *noun* a party to which the guests each bring a bottle of wine or some other alcohol, etc.

bottom *noun* **1** the lowest position or part. **2** the point farthest away from the front, top, most important or most successful part: *the bottom of the garden* • *bottom of the class.* **3** the buttocks. **4** the base on which something stands or rests. **5** the ground underneath a sea, river or lake. ▶ *adj* lowest or last. [Anglo-Saxon *botm*]

IDIOMS **at bottom** in reality; fundamentally. **be at the bottom of sth** to be the basic cause of it. **get to the bottom of sth** to discover the real cause of (a mystery or difficulty, etc).

PHRASAL VERBS **bottom out** of prices, etc: to reach and settle at the lowest level, esp before beginning to rise again.

bottomless *adj* extremely deep or plentiful.

bottom line *noun* **1** *informal* the essential or most important factor or truth in a situation. **2** the last line of a financial statement, showing profit or loss.

botulism *noun, pathol* a severe form of food poisoning, caused by a bacterial toxin that is found in poorly preserved foods. [19c: from Latin *botulus* sausage (from the shape of the bacteria)]

bouclé /ˈbuːkleɪ/ *noun* **1** a type of wool with curled or looped threads. **2** a material made from this. [19c: French, literally 'buckled' or 'curly']

boudoir /ˈbuːdwɑː(r)/ *noun, dated* a woman's private sitting-room or bedroom. [18c: French, literally 'a place for sulking in']

bouffant /ˈbuːfɒnt; *French* bufɑ̃/ *adj* of a hairstyle, or a skirt, sleeve, dress, etc: very full and puffed out. [French, from *bouffer* to puff out]

bougainvillaea *or* **bougainvillea** /buːgənˈvɪlɪə/ *noun* a S American climbing shrub with flower heads surrounded by large brightly coloured bracts. [19c: named after L A de Bougainville, French navigator]

bough /baʊ/ *noun* a branch of a tree. [Anglo-Saxon]

bought *past tense, past participle of* **buy**

bouillon /ˈbuːjɔ̃/ *noun* a thin clear soup or stock. [17c: French, from *bouillir* to boil]

boulder *noun* a large piece of rock that has been rounded and worn smooth by weathering and abrasion. [17c, shortened from 14c *bulderston*]

boulder clay *noun, geog* a glacial deposit consisting of boulders of different sizes embedded in hard clay.

boules /buːl/ *singular noun* a form of **bowls** popular in France, played on rough ground, in which players throw metal bowls to land as close as possible to a target bowl (the **jack**). [20c: French]

boulevard *noun* a broad street in a town or city, esp one lined with trees. [18c: French, from German *Bollwerk* bulwark]

boult see **bolt**[2]

bounce *verb* **1** *intr* of a ball, etc: to spring or jump back from a solid surface. **2** to make (a ball, etc) spring or jump back from a solid surface. **3** *intr* (*often* **bounce about** *or* **up**) to move or spring suddenly: *the dog bounced about the room excitedly.* **4** (*often* **bounce in** *or* **out**) to rush noisily, angrily or with a lot of energy, etc, in the specified direction: *bounced out in a temper.* **5** *informal* **a** of a bank, etc: to return (a cheque) to the payee because of insufficient funds in the drawer's account; **b** *intr* of a cheque: to be returned to the payee in this way. ▸ *noun* **1** the ability to spring back or bounce well; springiness. **2** *informal* energy and liveliness. **3** a jump or leap. **4** the act of springing back from a solid surface. ▪ **bouncy** *adj* (***-ier, -iest***). [16c: from Dutch *bonzen*]

PHRASAL VERBS **bounce back** to recover one's health or good fortune after a difficult or adverse period.

bouncer *noun* **1** *informal, orig US* a person employed by a club or restaurant, etc to stop unwanted guests entering, and to throw out troublemakers. **2** *cricket* a ball bowled so as to bounce and rise sharply off the ground.

bouncing *adj* esp of a baby: strong, healthy, and lively.

bouncy castle *noun* a children's amusement in the form of a large structure that is inflated with air to form a cushion with sides in the shape of a castle. [20c]

bound[1] *adj* **1** tied with or as if with a rope or other binding. **2** *in compounds* restricted to or by the specified thing: *housebound* • *snowbound.* **3** obliged. **4** of a book: fastened with a permanent cover. ▸ *verb, past participle of* **bind**. [14c, meaning 'confined by bonds', 'in prison']

IDIOMS **bound to do sth** certain or obliged to do it. **bound up with sth** closely linked with it.

bound[2] *adj* **1** **a** (*usu* **bound for somewhere** *or* **sth**) on the way to or going towards it; **b** *following an adv*: *homeward bound.* **2** *in compounds* going in a specified direction: *southbound* • *Manchester-bound.* [13c: from Norse *buinn*]

bound[3] *noun* **1** (*usu* **bounds**) a limit or boundary, eg of that which is reasonable or permitted: *His arrogance knows no bounds.* **2** (*usu* **bounds**) a limitation or restriction. **3** (**bounds**) land generally within certain understood limits; the district. ▸ *verb* **1** to form a boundary to or of (something); to surround. **2** to set limits or bounds to (something); to restrict. ▪ **boundless** *adj*. [13c: from Latin *bodina*]

IDIOMS **out of bounds** usu of a place: not to be visited or entered, etc; outside the permitted area or limits.

bound[4] *noun* **1** a jump or leap upwards. **2** a bounce (eg of a ball). ▸ *verb, intr* **1** (*often* **bound across, in, out, over** *or* **up,** *etc*) to spring or leap in the specified direction; to move energetically. **2** to move or run with leaps. **3** of a ball: to bounce back. [16c: from French *bondir* to spring]

boundary *noun* (***-ies***) **1** a line or border marking the farthest limit of an area, etc. **2** a final or outer limit to anything: *the boundary of good taste.* **3** the marked limits of a cricket field. **4** *cricket* a stroke that hits the ball across the boundary line, scoring four or six runs. [17c: from **bound**[3]]

bounder *noun, dated informal* a person who behaves in a presumptuous and dishonourable way. [19c]

bounteous *adj, literary* **1** generous; beneficent. **2** of things: freely given; plentiful. [14c, from **bounty**]

bountiful *adj, now chiefly literary* **1** of a person, etc: bounteous; generous. **2** ample; plentiful. [16c, from **bounty**]

bounty *noun* (***-ies***) **1** a reward or premium given, esp by a government. **2** *chiefly literary* generosity. **3** a generous gift. [13c as *bounte*, meaning 'goodness']

bouquet *noun* **1** a bunch of flowers arranged in an artistic way. **2** the delicate smell of wine, etc. [18c: French, diminutive of *bois* a wood]

bouquet garni /'buːkeɪ 'gɑːniː/ *noun* (***bouquets garnis*** /'buːkeɪ 'gɑːniː/) *cookery* a small packet or bunch of mixed herbs used eg in stews to add flavour during cooking. [19c: French, literally 'garnished bouquet']

bourbon /'bɜːbən/ *noun* a type of whisky made from maize and rye, popular in the US. [19c: named after Bourbon county, Kentucky, where it was first made]

bourgeois /'bɔːʒwɑː/ *noun* (*pl* **bourgeois**) *usu derog* **1** a member of the middle class, esp someone regarded as politically conservative and socially self-interested. **2** a person with capitalist, materialistic or conventional values. ▸ *adj* **1** characteristic of the bourgeoisie. **2** belonging to the middle class or bourgeoisie. **3** in Marxist use: capitalist and exploitative of the working classes. [16c: French, meaning 'a citizen' or 'townsman']

the bourgeoisie /bɔːʒwɑː'ziː/ *noun, derog* **1** the middle classes, esp regarded as politically conservative and socially self-interested, etc. **2** in Marxist use: the capitalist classes. [18c: French, from **bourgeois**]

bourn *or* **bourne** *noun, chiefly Southern Eng* a small stream, esp one that only flows after heavy rains. [14c: a variant of **burn**[2]]

bourse /bɔːs/ *noun* (*usu* **Bourse**) a European stock exchange, esp that in Paris. [16c: French, literally 'purse']

bout *noun* **1** a period or turn of some activity; a spell or stint. **2** an attack or period of illness. **3** a boxing or wrestling match. [16c: from obsolete *bought* a bend or turn]

boutique *noun* a small shop, esp one selling fashionable clothes and accessories. [18c: French]

bouzouki *noun* a Greek musical instrument with a long neck and metal strings, related to the mandolin. [20c: modern Greek]

bovine *adj* **1** belonging or relating to, or characteristic of, cattle. **2** *derog* of people: dull or stupid. [19c: from Latin *bovinus*, from *bos, bovis* an ox]

bovine spongiform encephalopathy /'spʌndʒɪfɔːm ɛŋkefə'lɒpəθɪ/ *noun* (abbrev **BSE**) a fatal brain disease of cattle. Also (*informal*) *called* **mad cow disease**.

bow[1] /baʊ/ *verb* **1** (*also* **bow down**) to bend (the head or the upper part of the body) forwards and downwards. **2** (*also* **bow down before sb** *or* **sth**) *intr* to bend the head or the upper part of the body forwards and downwards, usu as a sign of greeting, respect, shame, etc or to acknowledge applause. **3** (*usu* **bow to**) to accept or submit to (something), esp unwillingly. ▸ *noun* an act of bowing. [Anglo-

Saxon *bugan* to bend]

IDIOMS **bow and scrape** *derog* to behave with excessive politeness or deference. **take a bow** to acknowledge applause or recognition.

PHRASAL VERBS **bow out** to stop taking part; to retire or withdraw.

bow² /boʊ/ *noun* **1 a** a knot made with a double loop, to fasten the two ends of a lace or string, etc; **b** a lace or string, etc tied in such a knot; **c** a looped knot of ribbons, etc used to decorate anything. **2** a weapon made of a piece of flexible wood or other material, bent by a string stretched between its two ends, for shooting arrows. **3** a long, thin piece of wood with horsehair stretched along its length, for playing the violin, etc. **4** anything that is curved or bent in shape, eg a rainbow. ▸ *verb, tr & intr* to bend or make (something) bend into a curved shape. [Anglo-Saxon]

bow³ /baʊ/ *naut noun* **1** (*often* **bows**) the front part of a ship or boat. **2** *rowing* the rower nearest the bow. [17c]

bowdlerize *or* **-ise** /baʊdləraɪz/ *verb* to remove passages or words from (a book or play, etc), esp on moral and social rather than aesthetic grounds. ▪ **bowdlerization** *noun*. [19c: named after Dr Thomas Bowdler, who published an expurgated edition of Shakespeare in 1818]

bowel *noun* **1** an intestine, esp the large intestine in humans. **2** (*usu* **bowels**) the depths or innermost part of something: *the bowels of the earth*. [14c: from French *buel*, from Latin *botellus* sausage]

bower *noun* a place in a garden, etc that is enclosed and shaded from the sun by plants and trees. [Anglo-Saxon *bur* a chamber]

bowerbird *noun* any of various species of bird native to Australia and New Guinea, so called because the males construct elaborate bowers to attract the females.

bowie knife *noun* a strong single-edged curved sheath-knife. [19c: named after the US adventurer Colonel James Bowie]

bowl¹ *noun* **1** a round deep dish for mixing or serving food, or for holding liquids or flowers, etc. **2** a **bowlful**. **3** the round hollow part of an object, eg of a spoon, pipe, lavatory, etc. [Anglo-Saxon *bolla*]

bowl² *noun* **a** a heavy wooden ball for rolling, esp one for use in the game of **bowls**; **b** a similar metal ball used in tenpin bowling. ▸ *verb* **1** to roll (a ball or hoop, etc) smoothly along the ground. **2** *intr* to play bowls, or tenpin bowling, etc. **3** *tr & intr, cricket* to throw (the ball) towards the person batting at the wicket. **4** (*often* **bowl sb out**) *cricket* to put (the batsman) out by hitting the wicket with the ball. **5** (*sometimes* **bowl along** *or* **on,** *etc*) *intr* to roll or trundle along the ground. **6** (*usu* **bowl along**) to move smoothly and quickly. [15c as *boule*: French, from Latin *bulla* a ball]

PHRASAL VERBS **bowl sb over 1** *informal* to surprise, delight or impress them thoroughly. **2** to knock them over.

bow legs /baʊ/ *plural noun* legs that curve out at the knees. ▪ **bow-legged** *adj* of a person: having bow legs.

bowler¹ *noun* **1** a person who bowls the ball in cricket, etc. **2** a person who plays bowls or goes bowling.

bowler² *noun* (*also* **bowler hat**) a hard, usu black, felt hat, with a rounded crown and a narrow curved brim. [19c: named after Bowler, a 19c English hatter]

bowlful *noun* the amount a bowl can hold.

bowline /ˈbaʊlɪn/ *noun, naut* **1** a rope used to keep a sail taut against the wind. **2** (*also* **bowline knot**) a knot that makes a loop that will not slip at the end of a piece of rope. [14c: from German dialect *boline*]

bowling *noun* **1** the game of **bowls**. **2** a game (eg esp **tenpin bowling**) played indoors, in which a ball is rolled along an alley at a group of skittles. **3** *cricket* the act, practice or a turn or spell of throwing the ball towards the person batting at the wicket.

bowls *singular noun* a game played on smooth grass with bowls (see **bowl²**), the object being to roll these as close as possible to a smaller ball called the **jack**.

bowsprit /ˈbaʊsprɪt/ *noun, naut* a strong spar projecting from the front of a ship, often with ropes from the sails fastened to it. [14c as *bouspret*: from German]

bowstring *noun, archery* the string on a bow.

bow tie /boʊ/ *noun* a necktie which is tied in a double loop to form a horizontal bow at the collar.

bow window /boʊ/ *noun* a window which projects towards the centre, forming a curved shape.

box¹ *noun* **1** a container made from wood, cardboard or plastic, etc, usu square or rectangular and with a lid. **2** a **boxful**. **3 a** *in compounds* a small enclosed area, shelter or kiosk, etc for a specified purpose: *telephone box* • *witness box*; **b** in a theatre, etc: a separate compartment for a group of people, containing several seats; **c** (*often* **horse box**) an enclosed area for a horse in a stable or vehicle. **4** an area in a field, pitch, road, printed page, etc marked out by straight lines. **5** (**the box**) *Brit informal* **a** the television; **b** *football* the penalty box. **6** an individually allocated pigeonhole or similar container at a newspaper office or other agency, in which mail is collected to be sent on to, or collected by, the person it is intended for: *Reply to box number 318*. ▸ *verb* **1** (*also* **box up**) to put (something) into a box or boxes. **2** (**box sb** *or* **sth in** *or* **up**) to confine or enclose them or it. ▪ **boxlike** *adj*. [Anglo-Saxon: from Latin *buxis*]

box² *verb* **1** *tr & intr* to fight (someone) with the hands formed into fists and protected by thick leather gloves, esp as a sport. **2** *informal* to hit (esp someone's ears) with the fist, or sometimes the hand. ▸ *noun, informal* (*usu* **a box on the ears**) a punch with the fist, or sometimes a cuff or slap, esp on the ears.

box³ *noun* **1** (*also* **boxtree**) an evergreen shrub or small tree with small leathery paired leaves, widely used as a hedging plant, and for topiary. **2** (*also* **boxwood**) the hard durable fine-grained yellow wood of this tree, used eg for fine carving and inlay work. [Anglo-Saxon: from Latin *buxus*]

boxer *noun* **1** a person who boxes, esp as a sport. **2** a breed of dog with a muscular body and a short broad muzzle with pronounced jowls.

boxer shorts *plural noun* (*also* **boxers**) underpants resembling shorts, with a front opening. [20c]

boxful *noun* the amount a box can hold.

box girder *noun, eng* a hollow girder made of steel, timber or concrete.

boxing *noun* the sport or practice of fighting with the fists.

Boxing Day *noun* in the UK and the Commonwealth: the first weekday after Christmas, observed as a public holiday. [19c: so called because of the tradition of giving boxes to the poor, apprentices, etc on that day]

box junction *noun, Brit* an area at the intersection of a road junction, marked with a grid of yellow lines, which vehicles may enter only if the exit is clear.

box office *noun* **1** an office at which theatre, cinema or concert tickets, etc are sold. **2 a** theatrical entertainment seen in terms of its commercial value, ie its takings: *The new show is wonderful box office*; **b** theatrical entertainment seen in terms of its popular appeal, ie its ability to attract an audience. *as adj*: *box-office appeal*.

box pleat *noun* on a skirt or dress: a large double pleat formed by folding the material in two pleats facing in opposite directions.

boxroom *noun, chiefly Brit* a small room, usu without a window, used esp for storage.

boy *noun* **1** a male child. **2** a son: *He's our youngest boy.* **3** a young man, esp one regarded as still immature. **4** (**the boys**) *informal* a group of male friends with whom a man regularly socializes. **5** *informal, usu in compounds* a man or youth with a specified function or skill, etc: *backroom boy.* **6** *S Afr, offensive* a black male servant. ▪ **boyhood** *noun.* ▪ **boyish** *adj.* [14c as *boi*]

boycott *verb* **1** to refuse to have any business or social dealings with (a company or a country, etc), usu as a form of disapproval or coercion. **2** to refuse to handle or buy (goods), as a way of showing disapproval or of exerting pressure, etc. ▸ *noun* an act or instance of boycotting. [19c: named after Captain C C Boycott, an English land agent in Ireland, who was treated in this way because of his harsh treatment of tenants]

boyfriend *noun* a regular male friend and companion, esp as a partner in a romantic relationship.

Boyle's law *noun, physics* a law which states that the volume of a given mass of gas at a constant temperature is inversely proportional to its pressure. [19c: named after Robert Boyle, Anglo-Irish chemist]

Boy Scout see under **scout** (*noun* sense 2)

bozo *noun, slang, esp US* a dim-witted person. [20c]

BP *abbrev* British Pharmacopoeia.

bp *abbrev* (*also* **BP**) blood pressure.

bpi *abbrev, comput* **1** bits per inch. **2** bytes per inch.

bps *abbrev, comput* bits per second.

Bq *symbol,* becquerel.

Br[1] *abbrev* **1** Britain. **2** British.

Br[2] *symbol, chem* bromine.

bra *noun* a woman's undergarment that supports and covers the breasts. [20c: shortened from **brassière**]

brace *noun* **1** a device, usu made from metal, that supports, strengthens or holds two things together. **2** (**braces**) *Brit* straps worn over the shoulders, for holding trousers up. *US equivalent* **suspenders**. **3** a wire device worn on the teeth to straighten them. **4** *building, etc* a tool used by carpenters and metalworkers to hold a **bit**[2] and enable it to be rotated (see also **brace and bit**). **5** *printing* either of two symbols, **{** and **}**, used to connect lines, figures, staves of music, parts of text, etc. **6** (*in pl also* ***brace***) a pair or couple, esp of game birds. **7** *naut* a rope attached to a ship's **yard**[1] (sense 2), used for adjusting the sails. See also **mainbrace**. ▸ *verb* **1** to make (something) tight or stronger, usu by supporting it in some way. **2** (**brace oneself**) to prepare and steady oneself for a blow or shock, etc. [14c, meaning 'a pair of arms': from Latin *brachium* arm]

brace and bit *noun* a hand tool for drilling holes, consisting of a **brace** with the drilling **bit**[2] in place.

bracelet *noun* **1** a band or chain worn as a piece of jewellery round the arm or wrist. **2** (**bracelets**) *slang* handcuffs. [15c: French from Latin *brachium* arm]

brachiate /ˈbreɪkɪeɪt/ *adj, botany* having opposite widely spreading branches. [19c]

brachiopod /ˈbreɪkɪəpɒd/ *noun* (***brachiopods*** *or* ***brachiopoda*** /-ˈɒpədə/) *zool* an invertebrate marine animal with a shell consisting of two unequal valves. [19c: from Greek *brachion* arm + *pous, podos* foot]

brachiosaurus /breɪkɪəˈsɔːrəs, bra-/ *noun* the heaviest of the dinosaurs, that lived in the late Jurassic period and had a massive body, a small head and longer forelegs than hindlegs. [20c: from Greek *brachion* arm + *sauros* lizard]

bracing *adj* of the wind, air, etc: stimulatingly cold and fresh.

bracken *noun* the commonest fern in the UK, which has tall fronds, and spreads rapidly. [14c]

bracket *noun* **1** *non-technical* either member of several pairs of symbols, **( )**, **[ ]**, **{ }**, **< >**, used to group together or enclose words, figures, etc. **2** *usu in compounds* a group or category falling within a certain range: *out of my price bracket*. **3** an L-shaped piece of metal or strong plastic, used for attaching shelves, etc to walls. ▸ *verb* **1** to enclose or group (words, etc) together in brackets. **2** (*usu* **bracket sb** *or* **sth together**) to put them or it into the same group or category. [From French *braguette*]

brackish *adj* of water: slightly salty. [16c: from Dutch *brak* salty]

bract *noun, botany* a modified leaf, usu smaller than a true leaf and green in colour, in whose **axil** an **inflorescence** develops. [18c: from Latin *bractea* gold leaf]

brae /breɪ/ *noun, Scot* a slope or a hill. [14c as *bra*: Norse, meaning 'eyelash']

brag *verb* (***bragged, bragging***) *intr, derog* to talk boastfully about oneself. ▸ *noun* **1** a boastful statement or boastful talk. **2** a card game similar to poker. [14c]

braggart *noun* someone who brags a lot. ▸ *adj* boastful. [16c: from French *bragard* vain or bragging]

Brahma *noun, Hinduism* **1** the creator God, the first god of the Hindu **Trimurti** of deities. **2** (*also* **Brahman**) in Hindu thought: the guiding principle beneath all reality. [18c: Sanskrit]

Brahman *or* (*esp formerly*) **Brahmin** *noun* **1** a Hindu who belongs to the highest of the four major **castes**, traditionally the priestly order. **2** **Brahma** (sense 2). ▪ **Brahmanic** *or* **Brahmanical** *adj.* ▪ **Brahmanism** *noun* **1** the religion and practices of the Brahmans. **2** the worship of **Brahma**, one of the early religions of India, from which Hinduism evolved. [15c: from Sanskrit *brahma* prayer or worship]

braid *noun* **1** a band or tape, often made from threads of gold and silver twisted together, used as a decoration on uniforms, etc. **2** *now chiefly N Am* a length of interwoven hair. *Brit equivalent* **plait**. ▸ *verb* **1** to interweave (several lengths of thread or hair, etc) together. **2** to decorate (something) with braid. ▪ **braiding** *noun*. [Anglo-Saxon *bregdan*]

Braille *or* **braille** *noun* a system of printing for the blind, consisting of dots that can be read by touch. [19c: named after Louis Braille, its inventor]

brain *noun* **1** the highly developed mass of nervous tissue that co-ordinates and controls the activities of the central nervous system of animals. **2** (*esp* **brains**) *informal* cleverness; intelligence. **3** (*esp* **brains** *or* **the brains**) *informal* a very clever person. **4** (*usu* **the brains**) *informal* a person who thinks up and controls a plan, etc. ▸ *verb, informal* to hit (someone) hard on the head. ▪ **brainless** *adj*. [Anglo-Saxon *brægen*]

IDIOMS **have sth on the brain** *informal* to be unable to stop thinking about it; to be obsessed by it.

brainchild *noun* a person's particular and original theory, idea or plan.

brain death *noun* the functional death of the centres in the brainstem that control breathing and other vital reflexes, so that the affected person is incapable of surviving without the aid of a ventilator. Also called **clinical death**. ▪ **brain-dead** *adj*.

brain drain *noun, informal* the steady loss of scientists, academics, professionals, etc to another country.

brainstem *noun, anatomy* the part of the brain that is connected to the tip of the spinal cord.

brainstorm *noun, informal* a sudden loss of the ability to think clearly and act properly or sensibly. [19c]

brainstorming *noun* the practice of trying to solve problems or develop new ideas and strategies, etc by intensive and spontaneous group discussion.

brainteaser *noun* a difficult exercise or puzzle.

brainwash *verb* to force (someone) to change their beliefs or ideas, etc by applying continual and prolonged mental pressure. ▪ **brainwashing** *noun*. [20c]

brainwave *noun* **1** *informal* a sudden, bright or clever idea; an inspiration. **2** a wave representing the pattern of electrical activity in the brain.

brainy *adj*, (***-ier, -iest***) *informal* clever; intelligent.

braise *verb* to cook (meat, vegetables, etc) slowly with a small amount of liquid in a closed dish. [18c: from French *braise* live coals]

brake[1] *noun* **1** a device used to slow down or stop a moving vehicle or machine, or to prevent the movement of a parked vehicle. **2** anything that makes something stop or prevents or slows down progress, etc: *a brake on public spending*. ▸ *verb* **1** *intr* to apply or use a brake. **2** to use a brake to make (a vehicle) slow down or stop. [18c: related to **break**]

brake[2] *noun* an area of wild rough ground covered with low bushes, brushwood, etc; a thicket. [15c]

brake horsepower *noun, eng* (abbrev **bhp**) the power developed by an engine as measured by the force that must be applied to a friction brake in order to stop it.

brake shoe *noun, eng* either of two semicircular metal structures that act as a brake on a wheel.

bramble *noun* **1** (*also* **bramble-bush**) a blackberry bush. **2** any other wild prickly shrub. **3** *esp Scot* a blackberry. ▪ **brambly** *adj*. [Anglo-Saxon *bremel*]

bran *noun* the outer covering of cereal grain, removed during the preparation of white flour. [14c: French]

branch *noun* **1** an offshoot arising from the trunk of a tree or the main stem of a shrub. **2** a main division of a railway line, river, road or mountain range. **3** a local office of a large company or organization. **4** a subdivision or section in a family, subject, group of languages, etc. ▸ *verb, intr* (*esp* **branch off**) **1** to divide from the main part: *a road branching off to the left*. **2** (*sometimes* **branch out** *or* **branch out from sth**) to send out branches, or spread out from it as a branch or branches. [14c: from French *branche*]

PHRASAL VERBS **branch out** to develop different interests or projects, etc.

brand *noun* **1** a distinctive maker's name or trademark, symbol or design, etc used to identify a product or group of products. **2** a variety or type. **3** an identifying mark on cattle, etc, usu burned on with a hot iron. **4** (*also* **branding-iron**) a metal instrument used for branding animals. **5** a sign or mark of disgrace or shame. ▸ *verb* **1** to mark (cattle, etc) with a hot iron. **2** to give (someone) a bad name or reputation. **3** to fix a brand or trademark, etc upon (a product or group of products). [Anglo-Saxon]

brandish *verb* to flourish or wave (a weapon, etc) as a threat or display. [14c: from French *brandir*]

brand-new *adj* completely new.

brandy *noun* (***-ies***) **1** a strong alcoholic drink distilled from grape wine. See also **cognac**. **2** a glass of this drink. [17c: from Dutch *brandewijn*]

brandy snap *noun* a thin crisp cylindrical biscuit flavoured with ginger.

brant goose see **brent goose**

brash *adj* **1** very loud, flashy or showy. **2** rude; impudent, overbearingly forward. ▪ **brashness** *noun*. [19c]

brass *noun* (*pl* ***brasses*** or when treated as pl in collective senses 3 and 5 ***brass***) **1** an alloy of copper and zinc. **2** an ornament, tool or other object made of brass, or such objects collectively. **3** (*singular or plural noun*) **a** wind instruments made of brass, such as the trumpet and horn; **b** the people who play brass instruments in an orchestra. **4** a piece of flat engraved brass, usu found in a church, in memory of someone who has died. **5** (*usu* **top brass** *or* **the brass**) *informal* people in authority or of high military rank collectively. **6** (*esp* **the brass** *or* **the brass neck**) *informal* over-confidence or effrontery. **7** *informal, esp N Eng* money; cash. ▸ *adj* made of brass. [Anglo-Saxon *bræs*]

IDIOMS **brassed off** *Brit slang* fed up; annoyed.

brass band *noun* a band consisting mainly of brass instruments.

brasserie *noun* a small and usu inexpensive restaurant, serving food, and orig beer. [19c: French, meaning 'brewery']

brass hat *noun, Brit informal* a high-ranking military officer or other top official. [19c: so called because of the gold trimming on the hats of senior officers]

brassica *noun* any member of a genus of plants that includes cabbage, cauliflower, broccoli, brussels sprout, turnip, swede. [19c: Latin, meaning 'cabbage']

brassière /ˈbrazɪə(r)/ *noun* the full name for **bra**. [20c: French]

brass rubbing *noun* **1** a copy of the design on a **brass** (sense 4) made by putting paper on top of it and rubbing with coloured wax or charcoal. **2** the process of making such a copy.

brass tacks *plural noun, informal* the essential details; the basic principles or practicalities.

brassy *adj* (**-ier, -iest**) **1** esp of colour: like brass in appearance. **2** of sound: similar to a brass musical instrument; hard, sharp or strident. **3** *informal* of a person: loudly confident and rude; insolent. **4** flashy or showy.

brat *noun, derog* a child, esp a badly-behaved one.

bravado *noun* (***bravados*** *or* ***bravadoes***) a display of confidence or daring, often a boastful and insincere one. [16c: from Spanish *bravada*]

brave *adj* **1** of a person, or their character, actions, etc: having or showing courage in facing danger or pain, etc; daring or fearless. **2** *chiefly literary or old use* fine or excellent, esp in appearance. ▸ *noun, formerly* a warrior, esp one from a Native American tribe. ▸ *verb* to meet or face up to (danger, pain, etc) boldly or resolutely; to defy. ▪ **bravery** *noun*. [15c: French]

bravo *exclam* shouted to express one's appreciation at the end of a performance, etc: well done! excellent! ▸ *noun* a cry of 'bravo'. [18c: Italian]

bravura *noun* **1** a display of great spirit, dash or daring. **2** *music* esp in vocal music: virtuosity, spirit or brilliance in performance. *as adj*: *a bravura performance*. [18c: Italian]

brawl *noun* a noisy quarrel or fight, esp in public; a punch-up. ▸ *verb, intr* to quarrel or fight noisily. [14c as *verb*: perhaps from Dutch *brallen* to brag]

brawn *noun* **1** muscle; muscular or physical strength. **2** jellied meat made from pig's head and ox-feet. ▪ **brawny** *adj* (**-ier, -iest**) [14c: from French *braon* meat]

bray *verb* **1** *intr* of a donkey: to make its characteristic loud harsh cry. **2** *intr* of a person: to make a loud harsh sound. **3** to say (something) in a loud harsh voice. ▸ *noun* **1** the loud harsh braying sound made by a donkey. **2** any loud harsh grating cry or sound. [14c: from French *braire*]

braze *verb, eng* to join (two pieces of metal) by melting an alloy with a lower melting point than either of the metals to be joined, and applying it to the joint. [16c: from French *braise* live coals]

brazen *adj* **1** (*also* **brazen-faced**) bold; impudent; shameless. **2** made of brass or like brass. ▪ **brazenly** *adv*. [Anglo-Saxon *bræsen* made of brass]
PHRASAL VERBS **brazen out** to face (an embarrassing or difficult situation) boldly and shamelessly.

brazier[1] /ˈbreɪzɪə(r)/ *noun* a portable metal frame or container for holding burning coal or charcoal. [17c: from French *braise* live coals]

brazier[2] /ˈbreɪzɪə(r)/ *noun* a person who works in brass. [15c: from **braze**]

Brazil *or* **brazil** *noun* **1** (*also* **Brazil nut**) an edible type of nut with a hard three-sided shell, obtained from a tropical American tree. **2** (*sometimes* **Brazil wood**) a type of red wood from any of several tropical trees. [14c: the country of Brazil in S America was so named from the similarity of the red wood found there to that found in the East and known as *brasil*]

Brazilian *adj* belonging or relating to the country of Brazil or its inhabitants. ▸ *noun* a citizen or inhabitant of, or person born in, Brazil. [17c]

breach *noun* **1** an act of breaking, esp breaking of a law or promise, etc. **2** a serious disagreement. **3** a gap, break or hole. ▸ *verb* **1** to break (a promise, etc). **2** to make an opening or hole in (something). [Anglo-Saxon *bryce*]

breach of the peace *noun, law* a riot or disturbance that violates the public peace.

bread *noun* **1** a staple food prepared from flour mixed with water or milk, kneaded into a dough with a leavening agent, eg yeast, and baked. **2** (*often* **daily bread**) food and the other things one needs to live. **3** *slang* money. ▸ *verb* to cover (a piece of food) with breadcrumbs before cooking. [Anglo-Saxon]

bread and butter *noun* a means of earning a living.

breadboard *noun* **1** a wooden board on which bread is cut. **2** a board for making a model of an electric circuit.

breadcrumb *noun* **1** (*usu* **breadcrumbs**) **a** bread crumbled into small pieces, used in cooking; **b** a commercially-produced version of this, usually coloured orange, used for dressing fish, etc. **2** a crumb of bread.

breadfruit *noun* (***breadfruit*** *or* ***breadfruits***) **1** a SE Asian tree. **2** the large oval edible starchy fruit of this tree, which can be baked whole and eaten. [17c: so called because it has a texture similar to that of bread]

breadline *noun, orig US* a queue of poor or down-and-out people waiting for handouts of food.
IDIOMS **on the breadline** of a person or people: having hardly enough food and money to live on.

breadstick *noun* a long thin stick of bread dough baked until crisp. Also called **grissino**.

breadth *noun* **1** the measurement from one side of something to the other. Compare **length**. **2** an area, section or extent (eg of cloth) taken as the full or standard width. **3** openness and willingness to understand and respect other people's opinions and beliefs, etc. **4** extent, size. [16c]

breadwinner *noun* the person who earns money to support a family.

break *verb* (*past tense* ***broke,*** *past participle* ***broken***) **1** *tr & intr* to divide or cause (something) to become divided into two or more parts as a result of stress or a blow. **2** **a** *intr* of a machine or tool, etc: to become damaged, so as to stop working and be in need of repair; **b** to damage (a machine or tool, etc) in such a way. **3** to fracture a bone in (a limb, etc). **4** to burst or cut (the skin, etc). **5** to do something not allowed by (a law, agreement, promise, etc); to violate (something). **6** to exceed or improve upon (a sporting record, etc). **7** *intr* to stop work, etc for a short period of time. **8** to interrupt (a journey, one's concentration, etc). **9** *intr* of a boy's voice: to become lower in tone on reaching puberty. **10** to defeat or destroy (something): *break a strike*. **11** to force (something) open with explosives: *break a safe*. **12** *intr* of a storm: to begin violently. **13** *tr & intr* of news, etc: to make or cause (something) to become known: *He was away when the story broke.* **14** *intr* (*also* **break up**) to disperse or scatter: *The crowd broke up.* **15** to reduce the force of (a fall or a blow, etc). **16** *intr* of waves, etc: to collapse into foam. **17**

to lose or disrupt the order or form of (something): *break ranks.* **18** *intr* of the weather: to change suddenly, esp after a fine spell. **19** *tr & intr* to cut or burst through: *sun breaking through the clouds.* **20** *intr* to come into being: *day breaking over the hills.* **21** *tr & intr* to make or become weaker. **22** to make (someone) bankrupt; to destroy (them) financially. **23** to decipher (a code, etc). **24** to disprove (an alibi, etc). **25** to interrupt the flow of electricity in (a circuit). **26** *intr, snooker* to take the first shot at the beginning of a game. **27** *tr & intr, tennis* to win a game when one's opponent is serving. **28** *intr, boxing* to come out of a clinch. **29** to make (someone) give up (a bad habit, etc). ▸ *noun* **1** an act or result of breaking. **2 a** a pause, interval or interruption in some ongoing activity or situation; **b** (*also* **breaktime**) a short interval in work or lessons, etc. *N Am equivalent* **recess**. **3** a change or shift from the usual or overall trend: a *break in the weather.* **4** a sudden rush, esp to escape: *make a break for it.* **5** *informal* a chance or opportunity to show one's ability, etc, often a sudden or unexpected one. **6** *informal* a piece of luck: *lucky break.* **7** *snooker, billiards, etc* a series of successful shots played one after the other. **8** *snooker, billiards, etc* the opening shot of a game. **9** *tennis* an instance of winning a game when one's opponent is serving. **10** an interruption in the electricity flowing through a circuit. **11** *music* in jazz, etc: a short improvised solo passage. ▪ **breakable** *adj.* [Anglo-Saxon *brecan*]

IDIOMS **break camp** to pack up the equipment after camping. **break even** to make neither a profit nor a loss in a transaction. **break into song, laughter**, *etc* to begin singing or laughing, etc, esp unexpectedly. **break new** *or* **fresh ground** to do something in an original way. **break the ice** *informal* to overcome the first awkwardness or shyness, etc, esp on a first meeting or in a new situation. **break wind** to expel gas from the body through the anus.

PHRASAL VERBS **break away 1** to escape from control, esp suddenly or forcibly. **2** to put an end to one's connection with a group or custom, etc, esp suddenly. See also **breakaway**. **break down 1** of a machine, etc: to stop working properly; to fail. **2** to collapse, disintegrate or decompose. **3** of a person: to give way to emotions; to burst into tears. **4** of human relationships: to be unsuccessful and so come to an end. **5** of a person: to suffer a nervous breakdown. See also **breakdown**. **break sth down 1** to use force to crush, demolish or knock it down. **2** to divide it into separate parts and analyse it. See also **breakdown**. **break in 1** to enter a building by force, esp to steal things inside. See also **break-in**. **2** (*also* **break in on sth**) to interrupt (a conversation, etc). **break sb in** to train or familiarize them in a new job or role. **break sth in 1** to use or wear (new shoes or boots, etc) so that they lose their stiffness, etc. **2** to train (a horse) to carry a saddle and a rider. See also **broken-in**. **break off 1** to become detached by breaking. **2** to come to an end abruptly. **3** to stop talking. **break sth off 1** to detach it by breaking. **2** to end a relationship, etc abruptly. **break out 1** to escape from a prison, etc using force. **2** to begin suddenly: *War broke out.* **3** (*esp* **break out in sth**) to become suddenly covered in (spots or a rash, etc). See also **breakout**. **break through 1** to force a way through. **2** to make a new discovery or be successful, esp after a difficult or unsuccessful period. See also **breakthrough**. **break up 1** to break into pieces. **2** to come to an end; to finish. **3** of people: to end a relationship or marriage. **4** of a school or a pupil: to end term and begin the holidays. See also **break-up**. **break sth up 1** to divide it into pieces. **2** to make it finish or come to an end. See also **break-up**.

breakage *noun* **1** the act of breaking. **2** a broken object; damage caused by breaking.

breakaway *noun* an act of breaking away or escaping. ▸ *adj, always before its noun* that has broken away; separate: *a breakaway republic.*

breakdown *noun* **1** a failure in a machine or device. *as adj: a breakdown van.* **2** a failure or collapse of a process: *a breakdown in communications.* **3** a process or act of dividing something into separate parts for analysis. **4** (*also* **nervous breakdown**) a failure or collapse in a person's mental health.

breaker *noun* **1** a large wave that breaks on rocks or on the beach. **2** *slang* a person who broadcasts on Citizens' Band radio.

breakfast *noun* the first meal of the day. ▸ *verb, intr* to have breakfast. [15c: from *break fast*, ie to begin eating again after a time of fasting]

break-in *noun* an illegal entry by force into a building, esp to steal property inside.

breaking point *noun* the point at which something, esp a person or relationship, can no longer stand up to a stress or strain, and breaks down.

breakneck *adj* of speed: extremely, and usu dangerously, fast.

breakout *noun* an act or instance of breaking out, esp an escape by force: *a mass breakout from the city jail.*

breakthrough *noun* **1** a decisive advance or discovery. **2** an act of breaking through something.

breaktime see **break** (*noun* sense 2b)

break-up *noun* **1** the ending of a relationship or situation. **2** the scattering or dividing up of something.

breakwater *noun* a strong wall or barrier built out from a beach to break the force of the waves. See also **groyne** and **mole**[5].

bream *noun* (*pl* ***bream***) **1** any of various freshwater fish of the carp family that have a deep body covered with silvery scales. **2** (*usu* **sea bream**) an unrelated deep-bodied marine fish. [14c: from French *bresme*]

breast *noun* **1** *anatomy* in women: each of the two mammary glands, which form soft protuberances on the chest. **2** the front part of the body between the neck and the belly: *clutched it to his breast.* **3** the part of a garment covering the breast. ▸ *verb* **1** to face, or fight against (something): *breasting his troubles bravely.* **2** to come to the top of (a hill, etc). [Anglo-Saxon *breost*]

breastbone *noun, non-technical* the **sternum**.

breastfeed *verb, tr & intr* to feed (a baby) with milk from the breast.

breastplate *noun* a piece of armour that protects the chest.

breaststroke *noun* a style of swimming breast-downwards in the water, in which the arms are pushed out in front and then pulled outward and backward together.

breath *noun* **1** *physiol* the air drawn into, and then expelled from, the lungs. **2** exhaled air as odour, vapour or heat. **3** a single inhalation of air: *a deep breath.* **4** a faint breeze. **5** a slight hint or rumour. **6** a slight trace of perfume, etc. **7** life: *not while I have* *breath in my body.* [Anglo-Saxon *bræth*]

IDIOMS **catch one's breath 1** to stop breathing for a moment, from fear, amazement or pain, etc. **2** to stop doing something until one's normal breathing rate returns. **out of** *or* **short of breath** breathless, esp after strenuous exercise. **take one's** *or* **sb's breath away** *informal* to astound or amaze one or them. **under one's breath** in a whisper.

breath, breathe
Be careful not to use **breath** when you mean the verb **breathe**:
He was finding it difficult to breathe.

breathable *adj* **1** of a fabric, etc: able to **breathe** (sense 4). **2** of air, etc: fit for breathing.

Breathalyser *or* (*chiefly US*) **Breathalyzer** *noun, trademark* a device used to test the amount of alcohol on a driver's breath. ▪ **breathalyse** *verb.* [20c: from *breath* + *analyser*]

breathe *verb* **1** *tr & intr* to respire by alternately drawing air into and expelling it from the lungs. **2** *tr & intr* to say, speak or sound quietly; to whisper. **3** *intr* to take breath; to rest or pause: *haven't had a moment to breathe.* **4** *intr* of fabric or leather, etc: to allow air and moisture, etc to pass through. **5** *intr* of wine: to develop flavour when exposed to the air. **6** to live; to continue to draw breath. **7** *intr* to blow softly. [13c as *brethen*, from **breath**]

IDIOMS **breathe again** *or* **easily** *or* **easy** *or* **freely** *informal* to relax or feel relieved after a period of anxiety, tension or fear. **breathe one's last** *euphem* to die.

breathe, breath
See the Usage Note at **breath**.

breather *noun, informal* a short rest or break from work or exercise.

breathing-space *noun* a short time allowed for rest; a brief respite. [17c]

breathless *adj* **1** having difficulty in breathing normally, because of illness or from hurrying, etc. **2** very eager or excited. **3** with no wind or fresh air. ▪ **breathlessly** *adv.* ▪ **breathlessness** *noun.*

breathtaking *adj* very surprising, exciting or impressive. [19c]

breath test *noun, chiefly Brit* a test given to drivers to check the amount of alcohol in their blood, esp one using a **Breathalyser**.

breathy *adj* (**-ier, -iest**) of a voice: accompanied by a sound of unvocalized breathing.

bred *past tense, past participle of* **breed**

breech *noun* **1** the back part of a gun barrel, where it is loaded. **2** *old use* the buttocks. [Anglo-Saxon]

breech birth *or* **breech delivery** *noun* the birth of a baby buttocks or feet first.

breeches *or* (*chiefly N Am*) **britches** *plural noun* **1** short trousers fastened usu just below the knee: *riding breeches.* **2** *humorous, informal* trousers.

breed *verb* (***bred***) **1** *intr* of animals and plants: to reproduce sexually. **2** to make (animals or plants) reproduce sexually. **3** to make or produce (something): *Dirt breeds disease.* **4** to train, bring up or educate (children, etc) in a specified way. ▸ *noun* **1** an artificially maintained subdivision within an animal species, produced by domestication and selective breeding, eg Friesian cattle. **2** a race or lineage. **3** a kind or type. ▪ **breeder** *noun.* [Anglo-Saxon *bredan*]

breeder reactor *noun* a type of nuclear reactor that produces more **fissile** material than it consumes as fuel. Compare **fast-breeder reactor**. [20c]

breeding *noun* **1** *biol* the process of controlling the manner in which plants or animals reproduce. **2** the result of a good education and training, social skills, manners, etc; upbringing. **3** the act of producing offspring.

breeze[1] *noun* **1** a gentle wind. **2** *informal, esp N Am* a pleasantly simple task. ▸ *verb, intr, informal* to move briskly, in a cheery and confident manner. [16c: prob from Spanish *briza*]

breeze[2] *noun* ashes from coal, coke or charcoal. [18c: from French *braise* live coals]

breezeblock *noun* a type of brick made from **breeze**[2] and cement, used for building houses, etc.

breezy *adj* (**-ier, -iest**) **1** rather windy. **2** of a person: lively, confident and casual: *You're bright and breezy today.*

bren gun *or* **Bren gun** *noun* a light quick-firing machine-gun used during World War II. [20c: from *Br*no in the Czech Republic, and *En*field in England, where it was made]

brent goose *or* (*esp N Am*) **brant goose** *noun* the smallest and darkest of the black geese, which has a white marking on each side of the neck. [16c]

brethren see under **brother**

Breton *adj* belonging or relating to Brittany, its inhabitants, or their language. ▸ *noun* **1** a citizen or inhabitant of, or person born in, Brittany. **2** the Celtic language spoken in Brittany. [14c]

breve *noun* **1** a mark (˘) sometimes put over a vowel to show that it is short or unstressed. **2** *music* a note twice as long as a **semibreve** (now only rarely used). [14c: from Latin *brevis* short]

breviary *noun* (**-ies**) *RC Church* a book containing the hymns, prayers and psalms which form the daily service. [17c: from Latin *breviarum* a summary]

brevity *noun* (***-ies***) **1** the use of few words. **2** shortness of time. [16c: prob from Anglo-French *brevete*]

brew *verb* **1** to make (eg beer) by mixing, boiling and fermenting. **2** (*also* **brew up**) *tr & intr* to make (tea, etc) by mixing the leaves, grains, etc with boiling water. **3** *intr* to be in the process of brewing. **4** (*also* **brew up**) *intr* to get stronger and threaten: *There's a storm brewing.* ▸ *noun* **1** a drink produced by brewing, esp tea or beer. **2** a concoction or mixture: *a heady brew of passion and intrigue.* ▪ **brewer** *noun.* [Anglo-Saxon *breowan*]

brewery *noun* (***-ies***) a place where beer and ale are brewed.

briar[1] *or* **brier** *noun* any of various prickly shrubs, esp a wild rose bush. [Anglo-Saxon *brer*]

briar[2] *or* **brier** *noun* **1** a shrub or small tree, native to S Europe, with a woody root. **2** a tobacco pipe made from this root. [19c: from French *bruyère* heath]

bribe *noun* **1** a gift, usu of money, offered to someone to persuade them to do something illegal or improper. **2** something offered to someone in order to persuade them to behave in a certain way. ▸ *verb* **1** *usu tr* to offer or promise a bribe, etc to (someone). **2** to gain influence over or co-operation from (someone), by offering a bribe. ▪ **bribery** *noun.* [14c: from French]

bric-à-brac *noun* small objects of little financial value kept as decorations or ornaments. [19c: French, from *à bric et à brac* at random]

brick *noun* **1** a rectangular block of baked clay used for building. **2** the material used for making bricks. **3** a child's plastic or wooden building block. **4** something in the shape of a brick: *a brick of ice cream.* **5** (**a brick**) *Brit dated informal* a trusted, helpful, supportive person. ▸ *adj* **1** made of brick or of bricks. **2** (*also* **brick-red**) having the dull brownish-red colour of ordinary bricks. ▸ *verb* (*usu* **brick in** *or* **over** *or* **up**) to close, cover, fill in or wall up (eg a window) with bricks. [15c: from French *brique*]

brickbat *noun* **1** an insult or criticism. **2** a piece of brick or anything hard thrown at someone. [16c in sense 2]

bricklayer *noun* in the building trade: a person who builds with bricks. Often *(informal) shortened to* **brickie**.

bridal *adj* belonging or relating to a bride or a wedding. [Anglo-Saxon *brydeala*, meaning 'wedding feast']

bride *noun* a woman who has just been married, or is about to be married. [Anglo-Saxon *bryd*]

bridegroom *noun* a man who has just been married, or is about to be married. [Anglo-Saxon *brydguma*]

bridesmaid *noun* a girl or unmarried woman who attends the bride at a wedding.

bridge[1] *noun* **1** a structure that spans a river, road, railway, etc, providing a continuous route across it for pedestrians, motor vehicles or trains. **2** anything that joins or connects two separate things or parts of something, or that connects across a gap. **3** on a ship: the narrow raised platform from which the captain and officers direct its course. **4** the hard bony upper part of the nose. **5** in a pair of spectacles: the part of the frame that rests on the bridge of the nose, connecting the two lenses. **6** on a violin or guitar, etc: a thin, movable, upright piece of wood, etc that supports the strings and keeps them stretched tight. **7** *dentistry* a fixed replacement for one or more missing teeth, consisting of a partial denture that is permanently secured to one or more adjacent natural teeth. Also called **bridgework**. **8** *comput* a piece of hardware that connects networks or parts of a network. ▸ *verb* **1** to form or build a bridge over (eg a river or railway). **2** to make a connection across (something), or close the two sides of (a gap, etc): *managed to bridge our differences.* [Anglo-Saxon *brycg*]

IDIOMS **cross a bridge when one comes to it** to deal with a problem when it arises and not before.

bridge[2] *noun, cards* a game that developed from **whist**, for four people playing in pairs. [19c]

bridgehead *noun, military* a fortified position held at the end of a bridge which is nearest to the enemy. [19c]

bridging loan *noun* a loan of money made, usu by a bank, to cover the period between having to pay for one thing, eg a new house, and receiving the funds to do so, eg the money from selling another house.

bridle *noun* **1** the leather straps put on a horse's head that help the rider to control the horse. **2** anything used to control or restrain someone or something. ▸ *verb* **1** to put a bridle on (a horse). **2** to bring (something) under control. **3** (*esp* **bridle at sth** or *sometimes* **bridle up**) *intr* to show anger or resentment, esp by moving the head upwards proudly or indignantly. [Anglo-Saxon *bridel*]

bridle path *or* **bridle way** *noun* a path for riding or leading horses along.

Brie *noun* a soft creamy French cheese. [19c: the name of the area in NE France where it is made]

brief *adj* **1** lasting only a short time. **2** short or small: *a brief pair of shorts.* **3** of writing or speech: using few words; concise. ▸ *noun* **1** *law* **a** a summary of the facts and legal points of a case, prepared for the barrister who will be dealing with the case in court; **b** a case taken by a barrister; **c** *informal* a barrister. **2** (*also* **briefing**) instructions given for a job or task. **3** (**briefs**) a woman's or man's close-fitting underpants without legs. **4** (*also* **papal brief**) *RC Church* a letter from the Pope written on a matter of discipline. ▸ *verb* **1** to prepare (someone) by giving them instructions in advance. **2** *law* **a** to inform (a barrister) about the facts of a case; **b** to retain (a barrister) as counsel. ▪ **briefly** *adv.* [14c as *bref*: French, from Latin *brevis* short]

IDIOMS **in brief** in few words; briefly.

briefcase *noun* a light, usu flat, case for carrying papers, etc.

brier see **briar**[1], **briar**[2]

Brig. *abbrev* Brigadier.

brig *noun* a type of sailing ship with two masts and square sails. [18c: shortened from **brigantine**]

brigade *noun* **1** one of the subdivisions in the army, consisting eg of a group of regiments, usu commanded by a **brigadier**. **2** *esp in compounds* a group of people organized for a specified purpose: *the fire brigade.* [17c: ultimately from Latin *briga* conflict or strife]

brigadier *noun* **a** an officer commanding a brigade; **b** a senior officer in the British Army and Royal Marines.

brigand *noun* a member of a band of robbers, esp one operating in a remote mountain area. [15c: French]

brigantine *noun* a type of sailing ship with two masts. [16c: from Italian *brigantino* a pirate ship]

bright *adj* **1** giving out or shining with much light. **2** of a colour: strong, light and clear. **3** lively; cheerful. **4** *informal* clever and quick to learn. **5** full of hope or promise: *a bright future.* ▸ *adv* brightly. ▪ **brightly** *adv.* ▪ **brightness** *noun.* [Anglo-Saxon *beorht* or *byrht*]

brighten *verb, tr & intr* (*often* **brighten up**) **1** to become, or make (something or someone), bright or brighter. **2** to become or make (someone) become happier or more cheerful.

brill[1] *noun* (*brills* or *brill*) a large flatfish that has a freckled sandy brown body. [15c]

brill[2] *adj, Brit slang* excellent. [20c: short for **brilliant** (sense 4)]

brilliance *or* **brilliancy** *noun* **1** intense or sparkling brightness. **2** outstanding intelligence or technical skill.

brilliant *adj* **1** very bright and sparkling. **2** of a colour: bright and vivid. **3** of a person: showing outstanding intelligence or talent. **4** *informal* excellent; exceptionally good. **5** (*usu* **brilliant-cut**) *technical* of a gem, esp a diamond: cut so as to have a lot of facets, so that it sparkles brightly. ▸ *noun* a diamond or other gem. [17c: from French *brillant*, from *briller* to shine]

brim *noun* **1** the top edge or lip of a cup, bowl, etc. **2** the projecting edge of a hat. ▸ *verb* (***brimmed, brimming***) *intr* to be, or become, full to the brim. ▪ **brimless** *adj*. [13c]

brimful *or* **brimfull** *adj, following its noun* (*sometimes* **brimful of** *or* **with sth**) full to the brim.

brimstone *noun, old use* sulphur. [Anglo-Saxon *brynstan*, literally 'burning stone']

brindled *adj* of animals: brown or grey, and marked with streaks or patches of a darker colour. [15c]

brine *noun* **1** very salty water, used for preserving food. **2** *literary* the sea. See also **briny**. [Anglo-Saxon *bryne*]

bring *verb* (***brought***) **1** to carry or take (something or someone) to a stated or implied place or person. **2** to make (someone or something) be in, or reach, a certain state: *It brought him to his senses.* **3** to make or result in (something): *War brings misery.* **4** (*esp* **bring oneself**) *usu with negatives* to persuade, make or force oneself (to do something unpleasant). **5** (*esp* **bring in**) to be sold for (a stated price); to produce (a stated amount) as income. **6** to make (a charge or action, etc) against someone. [Anglo-Saxon *bringan*]

IDIOMS **bring home sth** (*often* **bring sth home to sb**) to prove or show it clearly. **bring to mind** to make (something) be remembered or thought about.

PHRASAL VERBS **bring about** to make (something) happen; to cause (it). **bring back** to make (a thought or memory) return. **bring sb down 1** to make them sad or disappointed, etc. **2** to demean them. **bring sth down** to make it fall or collapse. **bring forward 1** to move (an arrangement, etc) to an earlier date or time. **2** *bookkeeping* to transfer (a partial sum) to the head of the next column. **bring in 1** to introduce (something) or make (it) effective, etc. **2** to produce (income or profit). **bring off** *informal* to succeed in doing (something difficult). **bring sb over** *or* **round** *or* **around** to convince them that one's own opinions, etc are right; to convert them to one's own side. **bring sb round** to cause them to recover consciousness. **bring to** *naut* to bring (a ship) to a standstill. **bring sb to** to make (someone who is asleep or unconscious) wake up. **bring sb up** to care for and educate them when young. **bring up 1** to introduce (a subject) for discussion. **2** to vomit or regurgitate (something eaten).

brink *noun* **1** the edge or border of a steep dangerous place or of a river. **2** the point immediately before something dangerous, unknown or exciting, etc starts or occurs: *the brink of disaster.* [13c: prob Danish, meaning 'steepness' or 'slope']

IDIOMS **on the brink of sth** at the very point or moment when it might start or occur, etc.

brinkmanship *or* **brinksmanship** *noun* esp in politics and international affairs: the art or practice of going to the very edge of a dangerous situation (eg war) before moving back or withdrawing. [20c]

briny *adj* (***-ier, -iest***) of water: very salty. ▸ *noun* (**the briny**) *informal* the sea. [17c: from **brine**]

briquette *or* **briquet** *noun* a brick-shaped block made of compressed coal-dust or charcoal, etc, used for fuel. [19c: French, meaning 'little brick']

bris *or* **brith** *noun, Judaism* a circumcision ceremony. [From Hebrew, meaning 'covenant']

brisk *adj* **1** lively, active or quick: *a brisk walk.* **2** of the weather: pleasantly cold and fresh. ▪ **briskly** *adv.* [16c: perhaps related to Welsh *brysg* brisk of foot]

brisket *noun* meat from the breast of a bull or cow. [14c as *brusket*]

brisling *noun* a small marine fish of the herring family. [19c: Norwegian]

bristle *noun* **1** a short stiff hair on an animal or plant. **2** something similar to this but artificial, used eg for brushes. ▸ *verb* **1** *tr & intr* of an animal's or a person's hair: to stand upright and stiff. **2** (*usu* **bristle with sth**) *intr* to show obvious anger or rage, etc: *bristling with resentment.* **3** (*usu* **bristle with sth**) *intr* to be covered or closely-packed with (upright objects). ▪ **bristly** *adj* (***-ier, -iest***). [14c as *brustel*, from Anglo-Saxon *byrst*]

Brit *noun, informal* a British person.

Brit. *abbrev* **1** Britain. **2** British.

Britannic *adj, formal* in some official titles: belonging or relating to Britain: *His Britannic Majesty.*

britches see **breeches**

British *adj* **1** belonging or relating to **Great Britain** or its inhabitants. **2** belonging or relating to the British Empire or to the Commonwealth. **3** belonging or relating to the variety of English used in Britain. **4** (**the British**) the people of Great Britain as a group. [Anglo-Saxon *Bryttisc*]

British Expeditionary Force *noun, hist* (abbrev **BEF**) an army established to support the left wing of the French armies under German attack during World War I and again in World War II.

British Summer Time *noun* (abbrev **BST**) the system of time (one hour ahead of **Greenwich Mean Time**) used in Britain during the summer to give extra daylight in the evenings.

Briton *noun* **1** a British person. **2** (*also* **ancient Briton**) *hist* one of the Celtic people living in Southern Britain before the Roman conquest. [13c]

brittle *adj* **1** of a substance: hard but easily broken or likely to break. **2** sharp or hard in quality: *a brittle laugh.* **3** of a condition or state, etc: difficult to keep stable or controlled. ▸ *noun* a type of hard crunchy toffee made from caramelized sugar and nuts. [14c: from Anglo-Saxon *breotan* to break in pieces]

brittle bone disease *noun, med* a hereditary disease characterized by extreme fragility of the bones.

broach *verb* **1** to raise (a subject) for discussion. **2** to open (a bottle, barrel, etc) to remove liquid. **3** to open (a bottle or other container) and start using its contents. ▸ *noun* **1** a long tapering pointed tool for making and rounding out holes. **2** a roasting-spit. [13c as *broche*: ultimately from Latin *brochus* projecting]

B-road *noun* in the UK: a secondary road. Compare **A-road**.

broad *adj* **1** large in extent from one side to the other: *The sink is two foot broad.* Compare **deep**. **2** wide and open; spacious. **3** general, not detailed: *a broad inquiry.* **4** clear; full: *in broad daylight.* **5** strong; obvious: *a broad hint.* **6** main; concentrating on the main elements rather than on detail: *the broad facts of the case.* **7** tolerant or liberal: *take a broad view.* **8** of an accent or speech: strongly marked by local dialect or features: *broad Scots.* **9** usu of a joke, etc: rather rude and vulgar. ▸ *noun* **1** *US offensive slang* a woman. **2** (**the Broads**) a series of low-lying shallow lakes connected by rivers in E Anglia. ▪ **broadly** *adv* widely; generally. [Anglo-Saxon *brad*]

broadband *adj* **1** *telecomm* across, involving or designed to operate across a wide range of frequencies. **2** *comput* capable of accommodating data from a variety of input sources, such as voice, telephone, TV, etc.

broad bean *noun* **1** an annual plant of the bean family. **2** one of the large flattened pale green edible seeds growing in pods on this plant. [18c]

broadcast *verb* **1** *tr & intr* to transmit (a radio or TV programme, speech, etc) for reception by the public. **2** *intr* to take part in a radio or TV broadcast. **3** to make (something) widely known. **4** to sow (seeds) by scattering them in all directions. ▸ *noun* a radio or TV programme. ▸ *adj* **1** communicated or sent out by radio or TV: *on broadcast news.* **2** widely known or scattered. ▪ **broadcaster** *noun.* ▪ **broadcasting** *noun.*

broaden *verb* (*also* **broaden out**) *tr & intr* to become or make (something) broad or broader.

broad gauge *noun* a railway track that is wider than that of **standard gauge** (see **gauge** *noun* sense 3a). *as adj*: *a broad-gauge line.*

broadloom *adj* esp of a carpet: woven on a wide loom to give broad widths.

broad-minded *adj* tolerant and accepting of other people's opinions, preferences, habits, etc; liberal.

broadsheet *noun* a newspaper printed on large sheets of paper. Compare **tabloid**.

broadside *noun* **1** a strongly critical verbal attack. **2** *navy* **a** all of the guns on one side of a warship; **b** the firing of all of these guns simultaneously. [16c, literally 'the broadside' (of a ship)]

broadsword *noun, old use* a heavy sword with a broad blade, chiefly used for cutting with a two-handed swinging action.

brocade *noun* a heavy silk fabric with a raised design on it, often one using gold or silver threads. [16c: from Italian *brocco* a twisted thread or spike]

broccoli *noun* a type of cultivated cabbage or its immature flower buds eaten as a vegetable. [17c: pl of Italian *broccolo* 'little shoot']

---

broccoli

This word is often misspelt. It has two *c*'s and one *l*. It might help you to remember the following sentence:

Broccoli may cause cramp or light indigestion.

---

brochure *noun* a booklet or pamphlet, esp one giving information or publicity about holidays, products, etc. [18c: French, from *brocher* to stitch]

broderie anglaise *noun* open embroidery used for decorating cotton and linen. [19c: French, literally 'English embroidery']

brogue[1] *noun,* (*usu* **brogues**) a type of strong heavy-soled leather outdoor shoe, with decorative punched holes. [16c: from Gaelic *bròg* shoe]

brogue[2] *noun* a strong but gentle accent, esp the type of English spoken by an Irish person. [18c]

broil *verb* **1** *chiefly N Am* to grill (food). **2** *intr* to be extremely hot. [14c: from French *bruiller* to burn]

broiler *noun* **1** a small chicken suitable for broiling. **2** *esp N Am* a grill.

broke *adj, informal* **1** having no money; bankrupt. **2** short of money; hard-up. ▸ *verb, past tense, old past participle of* **break**. [17c]

broken *adj* **1** smashed; fractured. **2** disturbed or interrupted. **3** not working properly. **4** of a promise, agreement or law, etc: not kept; violated or infringed. **5** of a marriage or family, etc: split apart by divorce. **6** of language, esp speech: not perfect or fluent; halting. **7** usu of a person: brought down, weakened and tired out. **8** **broken-in** (sense 1). **9** with an uneven rough surface: *broken ground.* ▸ *verb, past participle of* **break**. [14c]

broken chord *noun, music* an **arpeggio**.

broken-down *adj* **1** of a machine, etc: not in working order. **2** of an animal or person: not in good condition, spirits or health.

broken-hearted *adj* deeply hurt emotionally, or overwhelmed with sadness or grief.

broken home *noun* a home that has been disrupted by the separation or divorce of parents.

broken-in *adj* **1** (*also* **broken**) of an animal, esp a horse: made tame through training. **2** of shoes, etc: made comfortable by being worn.

broker *noun* **1** a person employed to buy and sell stocks and shares; a stockbroker. **2** *in compounds* a person who acts as an agent for other people in buying and selling goods or property: *insurance broker.* **3** a negotiator or middleman. [14c: from Anglo-French *brocour*]

brokerage *noun* **1** the profit taken by, or fee charged by, a broker for transacting business for other people; commission. **2** the business or office of a broker.

brolly *noun* (***-ies***) *chiefly Brit informal* an **umbrella** (sense 1). [19c]

bromide *noun* **1** *chem* a compound of bromine, esp one used medicinally as a sedative. **2** *dated* a platitude. [19c: *bromine* + *-ide*]

bromide paper *noun* a type of paper with a surface that has been coated with silver bromide to make it sensitive to light, used for printing photographs.

bromine *noun, chem* (symbol **Br**) a non-metallic element consisting of a dark-red highly-corrosive liquid with a pungent smell, used in photographic film. [19c: from Greek *bromos* stink]

bronchi *pl of* **bronchus**

bronchial *adj, anatomy* relating to either of the **bronchi**.

bronchiole *noun, anatomy* any of the minute branches of the **bronchi**. [19c]

bronchitis *noun, pathol* inflammation of the mucous membrane of the bronchi. ▪ **bronchitic** *noun, adj.* [19c: from **bronchus** + **-itis**]

bronchus /ˈbrɒŋkəs/ *noun* (***bronchi*** /-kaɪ/) either of the two main airways to the lungs that branch off the lower end of the **trachea**. [18c: from Greek *bronchos* windpipe]

bronco *noun* a wild or half-tamed horse from the western US. [19c: Spanish meaning 'rough']

brontosaurus /brɒntəˈsɔːrəs/ *or* **brontosaur** *noun* (***brontosauri*** /-raɪ/ *and* ***brontosaurs***) the former names for **apatosaurus**. [19c: from Greek *bronte* thunder + *sauros* lizard]

bronze *noun* **1** an alloy of copper and tin. **2** the dark orangey-brown colour of bronze. **3** a **bronze medal**. **4** a work of art made of bronze. ▸ *adj* **1** made of bronze. **2** having the colour of bronze. ▸ *verb* **1** to give a bronze colour, surface or appearance to (something). **2** *intr* to become the colour of bronze, or tanned. [18c: French, from Italian *bronzo*]

Bronze Age *noun* the period in the history of humankind, between about 3000 and 1000 BC, when tools, weapons, etc were made out of bronze.

bronze medal *noun* in athletics, etc: a medal given to the competitor who comes third.

brooch *noun* a decoration or piece of jewellery with a hinged pin at the back for fastening it to clothes. [13c as *broche*: French; see **broach** (*noun*)]

brood *noun* **1** a number of young animals, esp birds, that are produced or hatched at the same time. **2** *informal, usu humorous* all the children in a family. **3** a kind, breed or race of something. ▸ *verb, intr* **1** of a bird: to sit on (eggs) in order to hatch them. **2** (*often* **brood about, on** *or* **over**) to think anxiously or resentfully about (something) for a period of time. ▪ **brooding** *adj*. [Anglo-Saxon *brod*]

broody *adj* (**-ier, -iest**) **1** of a bird: ready and wanting to brood. **2** of a person: introspective; moody. **3** *informal* of a woman: eager to have a baby. [16c]

brook[1] *noun* a small stream. [Anglo-Saxon *broc*]

brook[2] *verb, formal, usu with negatives* to tolerate or accept (something): *I shall brook no criticism*. [16c]

broom *noun* **1 a** a long-handled sweeping brush, formerly made from the stems of the broom plant; **b** a **besom**. **2** any of various deciduous shrubby plants of the pea family. [Anglo-Saxon *brom*]

broomstick *noun* the handle of a **broom** (sense 1).

Bros *abbrev* (*used esp in the name of a company*) Brothers.

broth *noun* **1** a thin clear soup made by boiling meat, fish or vegetables, etc in water. **2** *scientific* broth (sense 1) used as a medium for the culture of bacteria. [Anglo-Saxon, from *breowan* to brew]

brothel *noun* a house where men can go to have sexual intercourse with prostitutes. [14c, meaning 'a worthless person' and later 'a prostitute', from Anglo-Saxon *brothen* ruined or worthless]

brother *noun* (***brothers*** *or* (*archaic or formal except in sense 3*) ***brethren***) **1** a boy or man with the same natural parents as another person or people. **2** a man belonging to the same group, trade union, etc as another or others. **3** (*pl* ***brethren***) a man who is a member of a religious group, esp a monk. [Anglo-Saxon *brothor*]

brotherhood *noun* **1** an association of men formed for a particular purpose, esp a religious purpose. **2** friendliness, or a sense of companionship or unity, etc felt towards people one has something in common with. **3** the state of being a brother. See also **fraternity**.

brother-in-law *noun* (***brothers-in-law***) **1** the brother of one's husband or wife. **2** the husband of one's sister. **3** the husband of the sister of one's own wife or husband.

brotherly *adj* like a brother; kind, affectionate. Compare **fraternal**.

brougham /ˈbruːəm/ *noun* a type of light, closed carriage pulled by four horses, with a raised open seat for the driver. [19c: named after Lord Brougham]

brought *past tense, past participle of* **bring**

brouhaha /ˈbruːhɑːhɑː/ *noun* noisy, excited and confused activity; a commotion or uproar. [19c: French]

brow *noun* **1** (*usu* **brows**) short form of **eyebrow**. **2** the forehead. **3** the top of a hill, road or pass, etc. **4** the edge of a cliff, etc. [Anglo-Saxon *bru*]

browbeat *verb* to frighten or intimidate (someone) by speaking angrily or sternly, or by looking fierce. [16c]

brown *adj* **1** having the colour of dark soil or wood, or any of various shades of this colour tending towards red or yellow. **2** of bread, etc: made from wholemeal flour. **3** having a dark skin or complexion. **4** having a skin tanned from being in the sun. ▸ *noun* **1** any of various dark earthy colours, like those of bark, tanned skin or coffee, etc. **2** brown paint, dye, pigment, material or clothes. ▸ *verb, tr & intr* to become or cause (something) to become brown by cooking, tanning in the sun, etc. ▪ **brownish** *and* **browny** *adj*. ▪ **brownness** *noun*. [Anglo-Saxon *brun*]

brown bear *noun* a bear, native to the N hemisphere, that has a thick brown coat and a pronounced hump on its shoulders.

browned off *adj, informal* bored, depressed or discouraged.

brownfield site *noun* an area that has been redeveloped for another use. Compare **greenfield site**.

brown goods *plural noun* electrical equipment of a type used for leisure, eg radio, TV, audio equipment. Compare **white goods**. [20c]

Brownian movement *or* **Brownian motion** *noun, physics* the ceaseless random movement of small particles suspended in a liquid or gas, caused by the continual bombardment of the particles by molecules of the liquid or gas.

brownie *noun* **1** *folklore* a friendly goblin or fairy, traditionally said to help with domestic chores. **2** a small square piece of chewy chocolate cake containing nuts. [16c, orig meaning a 'little brown man']

Brownie Guide *or* **Brownie** *noun* a young girl belonging to the junior section of the Guides Association in Britain (see **guide** *noun* sense 4), or of the Girl Scouts in the US. Compare **cub** (*noun* sense 2).

brownie point *or* **Brownie point** *noun, informal, usu ironic or facetious* an imaginary mark of approval awarded for doing something helpful, etc. [20c]

browning *noun, cookery, chiefly Brit* a substance used to turn gravy a rich brown colour.

Brownshirt *noun* **1** *hist* in Nazi Germany: a member of the Nazi political militia. Also called **stormtrooper**. **2** a member of any fascist organization. [1930s]

browse *verb, tr & intr* **1** to look through a book, etc, or look around a shop, etc in a casual, relaxed or haphazard way. **2** of certain animals, eg deer: to feed by continually nibbling on young buds, shoots, leaves, etc as opposed to grazing. **3** *comput* to examine information stored in (a database, etc). ▸ *noun* an act of browsing. [16c: from French *broust* a new shoot]

brucellosis *noun, vet med* an infectious disease, mainly affecting cattle. [20c: named after Sir David Bruce, an Australian-born bacteriologist]

bruise *noun* **1** an area of skin discoloration and swelling caused by the leakage of blood from damaged blood vessels following injury. *Technical equivalent* **contusion**. **2** a similar injury to a fruit or plant, shown as a soft discoloured area. ▸ *verb* **1** to mark and discolour (the surface of the skin or of a fruit, etc) in this way. **2** *intr* to develop bruises. **3** *tr & intr* to hurt (someone's feelings, pride, etc) or be hurt emotionally or mentally. [Anglo-Saxon *brysan* to crush]

bruiser *noun, informal* a big strong person, esp one who likes fighting or who looks aggressive.

Brummie *or* **Brummy** *Brit informal, adj* belonging or relating to Birmingham, a city in central England, or its inhabitants. ▸ *noun* (***-ies***) a citizen or inhabitant of, or person born in, Birmingham. [1940s: from *Brummagem* (often shortened to *Brum*), the informal local name for Birmingham]

brunch *noun, informal* a meal that combines breakfast and lunch, eaten around midday or late in the morning. [19c: from *b*reakfast + l*unch*]

brunette *noun* a woman or girl with brown or dark hair. ▸ *adj* (also *N Am* **brunet**) of hair colour: brown, usu dark brown. [18c: French, from *brun* brown]

brunt *noun* (*esp* **the brunt of**) the main force or shock of (a blow, attack, etc): *bore the brunt of the expense.* [14c, meaning 'a sharp blow']

brush[1] *noun* **1** a tool with lengths of stiff nylon, wire, hair, bristles or something similar set into it, used for tidying the hair, cleaning, painting, etc. **2** an act of brushing. **3** a light grazing contact. **4** a short encounter, esp a fight or disagreement: *a brush with the law.* **5** a fox's bushy tail. **6** *elec* a metal or carbon conductor that maintains sliding contact between the stationary and moving parts of an electric motor or generator. ▸ *verb* **1** to sweep, groom or clean (the hair, teeth, a floor, etc) with a brush. **2** (*also* **brush against**) *tr & intr* to touch (someone or something) lightly in passing. [14c: from French *brosse* brushwood]

PHRASAL VERBS **brush sth** *or* **sb aside** to dismiss or pay no attention to it or them. **brush sth** *or* **sb off** to ignore or refuse to listen to it or them. See also **brush-off**. **brush up** to make oneself clean or tidy one's appearance, etc. **brush up (on)** to improve or refresh one's knowledge of (a language or subject, etc).

brush[2] *noun* **brushwood**.

brushed *adj* of a fabric: treated by a brushing process so that it feels soft and warm.

brush-off *noun* (*usu* **the brush-off**) *informal* an act of ignoring, rebuffing or dismissing someone or something in an abrupt or offhand manner.

brushwood *noun* **1** dead, broken or lopped-off branches and twigs, etc from trees and bushes. **2** small trees and bushes on rough land. **3** rough land covered by such trees and bushes. Also called **brush**.

brushwork *noun* a particular technique or manner a painter uses to apply the paint to a canvas, etc.

brusque *adj* of a person or their manner, etc: blunt and often impolite; curt. ▪ **brusquely** *adv.* ▪ **brusqueness** *noun.* [17c: from Italian *brusco* sour or rough]

Brussels sprout *or* **brussels sprout** *noun* (*usu as pl* **Brussels sprouts** *or* (*informal*) **sprouts**) a type of cabbage or one of its swollen edible buds cooked and eaten as a vegetable. [18c: first grown near Brussels]

brut *adj* of wines, esp champagne: very dry. [19c: French, literally 'rough' or 'raw']

brutal *adj* **1** savagely cruel or violent. **2** ruthlessly harsh or unfeeling. **3** like, or belonging or relating to, a brute. ▪ **brutality** *noun* (***-ies***). ▪ **brutally** *adv.* [15c: from Latin *brutalis*]

brutalism *noun* applied to art, architecture and literature, etc: deliberate crudeness or harshness of style.

brutalize *or* **-ise** *verb* **1** to make (someone or something) brutal. **2** to treat (someone or something) brutally. ▪ **brutalization** *noun.*

brute *noun* **1** a cruel, brutal or violent person. **2** an animal other than a human; a beast. ▸ *adj* **1** instinctive, not involving rational thought: *brute force.* **2** coarse, crudely sensual or animal-like. **3** in its natural or raw state; unrefined or unworked: *brute nature.* ▪ **brutish** *adj.* [15c: from Latin *brutus* heavy or irrational]

bryony *noun* (***-ies***) a climbing plant that has tiny yellowish-green flowers followed by highly poisonous red berries. [14c: from Latin *bryonia*]

BS *abbrev* British Standard or Standards.

BSc *abbrev* Bachelor of Science.

BSE *abbrev* bovine spongiform encephalopathy.

BSI *abbrev* British Standards Institution.

BST *abbrev* British Summer Time.

Bt *abbrev* Baronet.

BTW *or* **btw** *abbrev* by the way.

bubble *noun* **1** a thin film of liquid forming a hollow sphere filled with air or gas. **2** a ball of air or gas that has formed in a solid or liquid. **3** a dome made of clear plastic or glass. **4** a sound of or like bubbling liquid. ▸ *verb, intr* **1** to form or give off bubbles, or to rise in bubbles. **2** (*often* **bubble away**) to make the sound of bubbling liquid. **3** (*often* **bubble over with sth**) to be full of or bursting with (happiness, excitement, enthusiasm, good ideas, etc). [14c as *bobel*]

bubble and squeak *noun, cookery, chiefly Brit* cooked cabbage and potatoes fried together.

bubble bath *noun* a scented soapy liquid that is added to running bath water to make it bubble.

bubble chamber *noun, physics* a device for detecting the movement of charged subatomic particles through a liquid.

bubble gum *noun* a type of chewing gum that can be blown into bubbles.

bubble-jet printer *noun* a type of **inkjet printer** that heats the ink in a fine tube to form a bubble, which then bursts and projects the ink onto the paper.

bubble pack *noun* a clear plastic bubble, usu stuck onto a cardboard backing, in which an article for sale is packed and displayed. Also called **blister pack**.

bubbly *adj* (***-ier, -iest***) **1** having bubbles, or being like bubbles. **2** of a person or their character: very lively and cheerful. ▸ *noun, informal* champagne.

bubo /ˈbjuːboʊ/ *noun* (***buboes***) *pathol* a swollen tender lymph node, esp in the armpit or groin. ▪ **bubonic** *adj.* [14c: Latin, from Greek *boubon* the groin]

bubonic plague *noun, pathol* the commonest form of plague, characterized by the development of buboes, and known in the Middle Ages as the Black Death. [19c]

buccaneer *noun, hist & literary* a pirate, esp in the Caribbean during the 17c. [17c: from French *boucanier*]

buck[1] *noun* (***bucks*** or in sense 1 only ***buck***) **1** a male animal, esp a male deer, goat, antelope, rabbit, hare or kangaroo. Compare **doe**. **2** an act of bucking.

▸ *verb* **1** *intr* of a horse, etc: to make a series of rapid jumps into the air, with the back arched and legs held stiff. **2** of a horse, etc: to throw (a rider) from its back in this way. **3** *informal* to oppose or resist (an idea or trend, etc). [Anglo-Saxon *buc* or *bucca*]

PHRASAL VERBS **buck up** *informal* **1** to become more cheerful. **2** to hurry up. **3** *informal* to make (someone) more cheerful. **4** *informal* to improve or liven up (one's ways or ideas, etc).

buck[2] *noun, informal* **1** *N Am, Aust, NZ, etc* a dollar. **2** *S Afr* a rand. [19c]

buck[3] *noun, cards* in the game of poker: a token object placed before the person who is to deal the next hand. [19c, from *buckhorn knife*, an item that used to be used as a *buck* in poker]

IDIOMS **pass the buck** *informal* to shift the responsibility for something onto someone else.

bucket *noun* **1** a round open-topped container for holding or carrying liquids and solids such as sand, etc. **2** (*also* **bucketful**) the amount a bucket holds. **3** *informal* a rubbish-bin or waste-paper basket. **4** *Aust informal* an ice-cream tub. **5** *comput* a subdivision of a data file, used to locate data. **6** the scoop of a dredging machine. ▸ *verb, informal* **1** (*also* **bucket down**) *intr* of rain: to pour down heavily. **2** (*esp* **bucket along** *or* **down**) to drive or ride very hard or bumpily. **3** to put, lift or carry (something) in a bucket. [13c: related to Anglo-French *buket* a pail, and Anglo-Saxon *buc* a pitcher]

bucketful *noun* the amount a bucket can hold.

bucket shop *noun, derog informal* **1** *chiefly Brit* a travel agent that sells cheap airline tickets. **2** *chiefly N Am* a firm of stockbrokers with questionable or dishonest methods of dealing. [19c: orig US, meaning 'a shop or bar selling alcoholic drink from open buckets']

buckle *noun* a flat piece of metal or plastic, etc usu attached to one end of a strap or belt, with a pin in the middle which goes through a hole in the other end of the strap or belt to fasten it. ▸ *verb, tr & intr* **1** to fasten (something) with a buckle. **2** to bend (metal, etc) out of shape, using or as a result of great heat or force. [14c: from Latin *buccula* 'the cheek-strap of a helmet']

PHRASAL VERBS **buckle down to sth** *informal* to begin working seriously on it. **buckle to** *or* **buckle down** *informal* to get down to some serious work.

buckler *noun, hist* a small round shield, usu with a raised centre. [13c: from French *bocler*, from *bocle* a **boss**[2]]

buckram *noun* cotton or linen stiffened with **size**[2], used to line clothes or cover books, etc. [13c as *bukeram*, meaning 'a fine cotton or linen fabric']

Bucks. *abbrev, English county* Buckinghamshire.

buckshee *adj, adv, slang* free of charge; gratis. [20c, orig military slang: from **baksheesh**]

buckshot *noun* a large type of lead shot used in hunting.

buckskin *noun* **1** a strong greyish-yellow leather made from deerskin. **2** a strong smooth twilled woollen fabric.

buckthorn *noun* any of various shrubs or small trees, esp a thorny deciduous shrub with black berries. [16c]

bucktooth *noun* a large front tooth that sticks out. ▪ **bucktoothed** *adj*. [18c: **buck**[1] (*noun* sense 1) + **tooth**]

buckwheat *noun* **1** a fast-growing plant with leathery leaves and clusters of tiny pink or white flowers. **2** the greyish-brown triangular seeds of this plant, which can be cooked whole, or ground into flour. [16c: from Dutch *boekweit* beech wheat, because the nuts are similar in shape to beechnuts]

bucolic /bjuˈkɒlɪk/ *adj* concerned with the countryside or people living there; pastoral; rustic. [16c: from Greek *boukolos* herdsman]

bud *noun* **1** in a plant: an immature knob-like shoot that will eventually develop into a leaf or flower. **2** a flower or leaf that is not yet fully open. **3** *biol* in yeasts and simple animals, eg hydra: a small outgrowth from the body of the parent that becomes detached and develops into a new individual capable of independent existence. ▸ *verb* (***budded, budding***) *intr* of a plant, etc: to put out or develop buds. [14c]

IDIOMS **nip sth in the bud** to put a stop to it, or destroy it, at a very early stage.

Buddhism *noun* a world religion that originated in ancient India, founded by the Buddha, Siddhartha Gautama, in the 6c BC, and based on his teachings regarding spiritual purity and freedom from human concerns and desires. ▪ **Buddhist** *noun, adj*. [19c: from Sanskrit *buddha* wise or enlightened]

budding *adj* of a person: developing; beginning to show talent in a specified area: *a budding pianist*.

buddleia /ˈbʌdlɪə/ *noun* any of various deciduous shrubs or small trees with long pointed fragrant flower heads which attract butterflies. [18c: named after the English botanist Adam Buddle]

buddy *noun* (**-ies**) *informal, esp N Am* (sometimes shortened to **bud**, esp when used as a term of address in these senses) **a** a friend or companion; **b** a term of address used to a man, often expressing a degree of annoyance or aggression, etc. [19c]

budge *verb, tr & intr* **1** to move, or to make (something or someone) move. **2** to change one's mind or opinions, or make (someone) change their mind or opinions. [16c: from French *bouger*]

budgerigar *noun* (*also informal* **budgie**) a type of small parrot native to Australia and popular as a cagebird. [19c: from Australian Aboriginal *gijirrigaa*]

budget *noun* **1** a plan, esp one covering a particular period of time, specifying how money coming in will be spent and allocated. **2** (**the Budget**) *Brit* a periodic assessment of and programme for national revenue and expenditure, proposed by the government. **3** the amount of money set aside for a particular purpose. ▸ *adj* low in cost; economical: *budget holidays*. ▸ *verb* **1** *intr* to calculate how much money one is earning and spending, so that one does not spend more than one has; to draw up a budget. **2** (*usu* **budget for**) *intr* to plan, arrange or allow for (a specific expense) in a budget. **3** to provide (an amount of money, or sometimes time, etc) in a budget. ▪ **budgetary** *adj*. [15c in obsolete sense 'wallet' or 'bag': from French *bougette*]

buff[1] *noun, informal, usu in compounds* a person who is enthusiastic about and knows a lot about a specified subject: *an opera buff*. [20c, orig US; keen attenders at fires came to be nicknamed buffs because of the buff overcoats (see **buff**[2] *adj* sense 2) formerly worn by New York volunteer firemen]

buff[2] *noun* **1** a dull-yellowish colour. **2** a soft undyed leather. **3** (*sometimes* **buffer**) a cloth or pad of buff (*noun* sense 2) or other material, used for polishing. ▸ *adj* **1** dull yellow in colour: *a buff envelope*. **2** made of buff (*noun* sense 2): *a military buff coat*. ▸ *verb* **1** (*also* **buff up**) to polish (something) with a buff or a piece of soft material. **2** to make (leather) soft like buff. [16c]

IDIOMS **in the buff** *Brit informal* naked.

buffalo *noun* (***buffalo*** *or* ***buffaloes***) **1** (*also* **African buffalo**) a member of the cattle family, native to S and E Africa, which has a heavy black or brown body and thick upward-curving horns. **2** (*also* **Indian buffalo**) a member of the cattle family, native to SE Asia, the wild form of which has a black coat. **3** sometimes used generally to refer to the American **bison**. [16c: Italian, or from Portuguese *bufalo*]

buffer[1] *noun* **1** an apparatus designed to take the shock when an object such as a railway carriage or a ship hits something. Also (*US*) called **bumper**. **2** a person or thing that protects from harm or shock, etc, or makes its impact less damaging or severe. **3** *comput* a temporary storage area for data that is being transmitted from the central processing unit to an output device such as a printer. **4** *chem* a chemical solution that maintains its pH at a constant level when an acid or alkali is added to it. [19c: from obsolete verb *buff* to strike or make a dull-sounding impact]

buffer[2] *noun, Brit informal* a rather foolish or dull person, esp a man.

buffer state *or* **buffer zone** *noun* a neutral country or zone situated between two others that are or may become hostile towards each other, making the outbreak of war less likely.

buffet[1] /ˈbʊfeɪ; *US* bəˈfeɪ/ *noun* **1** a meal set out on tables from which people help themselves. **2** a place, room or counter, etc where light meals and drinks may be bought and eaten. [18c: French]

buffet[2] /ˈbʌfɪt/ *noun* **1** a blow with the hand or fist. **2** a stroke or blow, esp a heavy or repeated one: *a sudden buffet of wind*. ▸ *verb* **1** to strike or knock (someone or something) with the hand or fist. **2** to knock (someone or something) about; to batter (them or it) repeatedly: *a ship buffeted by the waves*. [13c: from French *buffe* a blow]

buffoon *noun* **1** a person who sets out to amuse people with comic behaviour; a clown. **2** someone who does stupid or foolish things; a fool. ▪ **buffoonery** *noun*. [16c: from Italian *buffone*]

bug *noun* **1** the common name for any of thousands of insects with a flattened oval body and mouthparts modified to form a beak for piercing and sucking, eg aphids. **2** *N Am* a popular name for any kind of insect. **3** *informal* a popular name for a bacterium or virus that causes infection or illness. **4** *informal* a small hidden microphone. **5** *informal* a fault in a machine or computer program that stops it from working properly. **6** *informal* an obsession or craze: *She caught the skiing bug*. ▸ *verb* (***bugged, bugging***) **1** *informal* to hide a microphone in (a room, telephone, etc) so as to be able to listen in to any conversations carried on there. **2** *slang* to annoy or worry (someone). [17c: perhaps connected with Anglo-Saxon *budda* a beetle]

bugbear *noun* an object of fear, dislike or annoyance, esp when that fear, etc is irrational or needless.

buggy *noun* (***-ies***) **1** a light open carriage pulled by one horse. **2** a light folding pushchair for a small child. **3** (*also* **baby buggy**) *N Am* a pram. **4** *often in compounds* a small motorized vehicle, used for a specified purpose: *beach buggy*. [18c]

bugle *noun* a brass or copper instrument similar to a small trumpet, used mainly for sounding military calls. ▸ *verb, intr* to sound a bugle. ▪ **bugler** *noun*. [14c, short for *bugle horn*, a hunting horn made from the horn of a buffalo or wild ox]

build *verb* (***built***) **1** to make or construct (something) from parts. **2** (*also* **build up**) *intr* to increase gradually in size, strength, amount, intensity, etc; to develop: *Outside the excitement was building*. **3** to make (something) in a specified way or for a specified purpose: *built to last*. **4** to control the building of (something); to have (something) built: *The government built two new housing schemes*. ▸ *noun* physical form, esp that of the human body. [Anglo-Saxon *byldan*]

PHRASAL VERBS **build sb** *or* **sth up** to speak with great enthusiasm about them or it. **build sth up** to build or amass it in stages or gradually.

builder *noun* a person who builds, or organizes and supervises the building of, houses, etc.

builders' merchant *noun* a trader who supplies building materials.

building *noun* **1** the business, process, art or occupation of constructing houses, etc. **2** a structure with walls and a roof, such as a house.

building society *noun, Brit* a finance company that lends money to its members for buying or improving houses, and in which customers can invest money in accounts to earn interest. [19c]

build-up *noun* **1** a gradual increase. **2** a gradual approach to a conclusion or climax. **3** publicity or praise of something or someone given in advance of its or their appearance.

built *past tense, past participle of* **build**

built-in *adj* **1** built to form part of the main structure or design of something, and not as a separate or free-standing object: *built-in wardrobes*. **2** included as, forming or designed as a necessary or integral part of something: *built-in insurance cover*. **3** inherent; present naturally, by genetic inheritance, etc.

built-up *adj* **1** of land, etc: covered with buildings, esp houses. **2** increased in height by additions to the underside: *built-up shoes*. **3** made up of separate parts.

bulb *noun* **1** in certain plants, eg tulip and onion: a swollen underground organ that functions as a food store and consists of a modified shoot and roots growing from its lower surface. **2** a flower grown from a bulb. **3** a light-bulb. **4** anything that is shaped like a pear or a bulb (sense 1). [16c: from Greek *bolbos* onion]

bulbous *adj* **1** like a bulb in shape; fat, bulging or swollen. **2** having or growing from a bulb. [16c]

bulge *noun* **1** a swelling, esp where one would expect to see something flat. **2** a sudden and usu temporary increase, eg in population. ▸ *verb, intr* (*often* **bulge out** *or* **bulge with sth**) to swell outwards: *a sack bulging with presents*. [13c: from Latin *bulga* knapsack]

bulghur *or* **bulgur** *noun* wheat that has been boiled, dried, lightly milled and cracked. [20c: Turkish]

bulimia /bʊˈlɪmɪə, bjʊˈlɪmɪə/ *noun, med, psychol* **1** compulsive overeating. **2** **bulimia nervosa**. [14c: from Greek *boulimia*, from *bous* ox + *limos* hunger]

bulimia nervosa *noun, med* a psychological disorder in which episodes of excessive eating are followed by self-induced vomiting or laxative abuse. [19c: from **bulimia** + Latin *nervosus* nervous]

bulimic *adj* suffering from or relating to **bulimia nervosa**. ▸ *noun* a person suffering from bulimia nervosa.

bulk *noun* **1** size, esp when large and awkward. **2** the greater or main part of something. **3** a large body, shape, structure or person. **4** a large quantity: *buy in bulk*. **5** roughage; dietary fibre. [15c: from Norse *bulki* a heap or cargo]

bulk buying *noun* purchase of a commodity in a large quantity, usu at a reduced price.

bulkhead *noun* a wall in a ship or aircraft, etc that separates one section from another. [15c: from *bulk* a stall or framework + **head**]

bulky *adj* (***-ier, -iest***) large in size, filling a lot of space and awkward to carry or move. ▪ **bulkiness** *noun*.

bull[1] *noun* **1** the uncastrated male of animals in the cattle family. **2** the male of the elephant, whale and some other large animals. **3** (**a** *or* **the Bull**) *astrol* **Taurus**. **4** *stock exchange* someone who buys shares hoping to sell them at a higher price at a later date. Compare **bear**[2] (*noun* sense 4). **5** *informal* a **bull's-eye** (sense 1). **6** (*esp* **a bull of a man**) a well-built, powerful or aggressive man. ▸ *adj* **1** male: *a bull walrus*. **2** *stock exchange* of a market: favourable to the bulls (sense 4); rising. **3** massive; coarse; strong. [13c]

IDIOMS **take the bull by the horns** to deal boldly and positively with a challenge or difficulty.

bull[2] *noun* **1** *slang* nonsense; meaningless, pretentious talk. **2** an illogical nonsensical statement. **3** tedious and sometimes unnecessary routine tasks. [17c]

bull[3] *noun* an official letter or written instruction from the Pope. [14c: from Latin *bulla* a lead seal]

bull bar *noun, Brit informal* a strong metal bar or grid fitted to the front of a vehicle.

bulldog *noun* a breed of dog with a heavy body and a large square head with a flat upturned muzzle. [16c]

Bulldog clip *noun, trademark* a clip with a spring, used to hold papers together.

bulldoze *verb* **1** to use a bulldozer to move, flatten or demolish (something). **2** (**bulldoze sb into sth**) to force them to do something they do not want to do; to intimidate or bully them. **3** to force or push (something) through against all opposition: *bulldozed his scheme through the Council*. [19c, orig US]

bulldozer *noun* a large, powerful, heavy tractor with a vertical blade at the front, for pushing heavy objects, clearing the ground or making it level.

bullet *noun* a small metal cylinder with a pointed or rounded end, for firing from a small gun or rifle. See also **cartridge**. [16c: from French *boulette* little ball]

bulletin *noun* **1** a short official statement of news issued as soon as the news is known. **2** a short printed newspaper or leaflet, esp one produced regularly by a group or organization. [17c: from Italian *bullettino*, a diminutive ultimately from *bulla* **bull**[3]]

bulletin board *noun* **1** *N Am* a noticeboard. **2** *comput* an electronic data system containing messages and programs accessible to a number of users.

bullet point *noun, printing* a solid dot used to highlight items in a list.

bullet-proof *adj* of a material, etc: strong enough to prevent bullets passing through.

bullfight *noun* a public show, esp in Spain and Portugal, etc in which people bait, and usu ultimately kill, a bull. ▪ **bullfighter** *noun*. ▪ **bullfighting** *noun*.

bullfinch *noun* a small bird of the finch family, the male of which has a conspicuous red breast. [13c]

bullfrog *noun* any of various large frogs with a loud call.

bullion *noun* gold or silver that has not been coined, esp in large bars, or in mass. [14c as an Anglo-French word for **mint**[2]]

bullish *adj* aggressively confident.

bullock *noun* a castrated bull. Also called **steer**.

bullring *noun* an arena where bullfights take place.

bull's-eye *noun* **1** the small circular centre of a target used in shooting or darts, etc. **2** *darts, etc* a shot that hits this. **3** *informal* anything that hits its target or achieves its aim, etc. **4** a large hard round peppermint sweet.

bull terrier *noun* a breed of dog with a heavy body and a short smooth coat.

bully[1] *noun* (***-ies***) a person who hurts, frightens or torments weaker or smaller people. ▸ *verb* (***-ies, -ied***) **1** to act like a bully towards (someone); to threaten or persecute (them). **2** (**bully sb into sth**) to force them to do something they do not want to do. ▪ **bullying** *noun*. [16c, orig meaning 'sweetheart']

IDIOMS **bully for you!** *informal, ironic* good for you!

bully[2] *or* **bully beef** *noun* esp in the armed services: corned beef; tinned or pickled beef. [18c: from French *bouilli* boiled beef]

bully[3] *verb* (***-ies, -ied***) *intr* (*usu* **bully off**) *hockey, formerly* to begin or re-start a game by performing a **bully** *or* **bully-off**, a move involving hitting one's stick three times against an opponent's before going for the ball. [19c]

bulrush *noun* **1** a tall waterside plant with one or two spikes of tightly packed dark-brown flowers. **2** *Bible* a papyrus plant. [15c]

bulwark /ˈbʊlwək/ *noun* **1** a wall built as a defence, often one made of earth; a rampart. **2** a **breakwater** or sea-wall. **3** someone or something that defends a cause or way of life, etc. **4** (*esp* **bulwarks**) *naut* the side of a ship projecting above the deck. [15c: from Dutch *bolwerc*, from German *bol* plank + *werc* work]

bum[1] *noun, Brit informal* **1** the buttocks. **2** *coarse* the anus. [14c as *bom*]

bum[2] *informal, esp N Am & Aust, noun* **1** someone who lives by begging; a tramp. **2** someone who is lazy and shows no sense of responsibility; a loafer. ▸ *adj* worthless; dud or useless. ▸ *verb* (***bummed, bumming***) **1** to get (something) by begging, borrowing or cadging: *bum a lift*. **2** (*usu* **bum around** *or* **about**) *intr* to spend one's time doing nothing in particular. ▪ **bummer** *noun*. [19c]

bum bag *noun, Brit informal* a small bag on a belt, worn round the waist. [20c in skiing use]

bumble *verb, intr* **1** (*often* **bumble about**) to move or do something in an awkward or clumsy way. **2** to speak in a confused or confusing way. ▪ **bumbling** *adj.* [16c]

bumble-bee *noun* a large hairy black and yellow bee. [16c: from the old verb *bumble* to boom or buzz]

bumf *or* **bumph** *noun, Brit informal* miscellaneous useless leaflets, official papers and documents, etc. [19c: short for *bum-fodder,* ie lavatory paper]

bump *verb* **1** *tr & intr* to knock or hit (someone or something), esp heavily or with a jolt. **2** to hurt or damage (eg one's head) by hitting or knocking it. **3** (*usu* **bump together**) *intr* of two moving objects: to collide. **4** (*also* **bump along**) *intr* to move or travel with jerky or bumpy movements. ▸ *noun* **1** a knock, jolt or collision. **2** a dull sound caused by a knock or collision, etc. **3** a lump or swelling on the body, esp one caused by a blow. **4** a lump on a road surface. ▪ **bumpy** *adj* (*-ier, -iest*). [17c]

PHRASAL VERBS **bump into sb** *informal* to meet them by chance. **bump sb off** *slang* to kill them. **bump up** *informal* to increase or raise (eg production or prices).

bumper *noun* **1** *Brit* a bar on the front or back of a motor vehicle which lessens the shock or damage if it hits anything. **2** *US* a railway **buffer**. **3** an exceptionally good or large example or measure. ▸ *adj* exceptionally good or large: *a bumper edition.*

bumpkin *noun, informal, usu derog* an awkward, simple or stupid person, esp a simple fellow who lives in the country. Also called **country bumpkin**. [16c: perhaps from Dutch *bommekijn* little barrel]

bump-start *verb* to start (a car) by pushing it and engaging the gears while it is moving. ▸ *noun* (**bump start**) an act or instance of bump-starting a car. See also **jump-start**.

bumptious *adj* offensively or irritatingly conceited or self-important. [19c: prob a combination of **bump** + **fractious**]

bun *noun* **1** *esp Brit* **a** a small, round, usu sweetened, roll, often containing currants, etc; **b** a small round cake of various types, eg an individual sponge cake. **2** a mass of hair fastened in a round shape on the back of the head. **3** (**buns**) *US informal* the buttocks. [14c]

bunch *noun* **1** a number of things fastened or growing together: *a bunch of roses.* **2** (*usu* **bunches**) long hair divided into two sections and tied separately at each side or the back of the head. **3** *informal* a group or collection. **4** *informal* a group of people; gang: *The drama students are a strange bunch.* ▸ *verb, tr & intr* (*sometimes* **bunch up**) to group (people or things) together in, or to form a bunch or bunches. [14c]

buncombe see **bunkum**

bundle *noun* **1** a number of things loosely fastened or tied together. **2** a loose parcel, esp one contained in a cloth. **3** (*also* **vascular bundle**) *botany* one of many strands of conducting vessels or fibres in the stems and leaves of plants. **4** *slang* a large amount of money: *made a bundle on the deal.* ▸ *verb* **1** (*often* **bundle up**) to make (something) into a bundle or bundles. **2** to put quickly and unceremoniously, roughly or untidily; to hustle: *bundled him into a taxi.* **3** (**bundle with**) *marketing* to sell (a product) along with (another related product) as a single package. [14c]

IDIOMS **go a bundle on sb** *or* **sth** *slang* to be enthusiastic about, or like, them or it very much.

bun fight *noun, Brit informal* **1** a noisy tea party. **2** a noisy occasion or function.

bung *noun* a small round piece of wood, rubber or cork, etc used to close a hole eg in the top of a jar or other container. Also called **stopper**, **plug**. ▸ *verb* **1** (*esp* **bung up**) **a** to block (a hole) with a bung; **b** *informal, esp in passive* to block, plug or clog (something): *My nose is bunged up.* **2** *slang* to throw or put (something) somewhere in a careless way: *Just bung my coat in there.* [15c: from Dutch *bonge* stopper]

bungalow *noun* a single-storey house. [17c: from Gujarati *bangalo,* from Hindi *bangla* in the style of Bengal]

bungee jumping *noun* the sport or recreation in which a person jumps from a height with strong rubber ropes or cables attached to their ankles to ensure that they bounce up before they reach the ground. [20c: from slang *bungie* or *bungy* india-rubber]

bunghole *noun* a hole by which a barrel, etc is emptied or filled and into which a **bung** is fitted.

bungle *verb, tr & intr* to do (something) carelessly or badly; to spoil or mismanage (a job or procedure). ▸ *noun* carelessly or badly done work; a mistake or foul-up. ▪ **bungler** *noun.* ▪ **bungling** *noun, adj.* [16c]

bunion *noun* a painful swelling on the first joint of the big toe. [18c: perhaps from French *buigne* a bump on the head]

bunk[1] *noun* **1** a narrow bed attached to the wall in a cabin in a ship, caravan, etc. **2** a **bunk bed**. ▸ *verb, intr, informal* **1** (*esp* **bunk down**) to lie down and go to sleep, esp in some improvised place. **2** to occupy a bunk. [18c: prob from **bunker**]

bunk[2] *Brit slang, noun* (*usu* **do a bunk**) the act of running away; leaving the place where one ought to be, usu furtively: *He did a bunk from gym.* [19c]

PHRASAL VERBS **bunk off** to stay away from school or work, etc when one ought to be there.

bunk bed *noun* each of a pair of single beds fixed one on top of the other. Often shortened to **bunk**.

bunker *noun* **1** an obstacle on a golf course consisting of a hollow area containing sand. **2** a large container or compartment for storing fuel. **3** an underground shelter. [16c Scots as *bonker,* meaning 'box', 'chest', or 'seat']

bunkum *or* (*chiefly N Am*) **buncombe** *noun, informal* nonsense; foolish talk; claptrap. Often shortened to **bunk**. See also **debunk**. [19c: named after Buncombe, a county in N Carolina, whose congressman is said to have excused a rambling speech in Congress on the grounds that he was only speaking for Buncombe]

bunny *noun* (*-ies*) (*also* **bunny rabbit**) a pet name or child's word for a **rabbit**. [17c: from Scottish Gaelic *bun* bottom, or the tail of a rabbit, etc]

Bunsen burner /ˈbʌnsən/ *noun* a gas burner, used mainly in chemistry laboratories, with an adjustable inlet hole that allows the gas-air mixture to be controlled so as to produce a very hot flame with no smoke. [19c: named after its inventor R W Bunsen, a German chemist]

bunting[1] *noun* **1** a row of small cloth or paper flags on a string; streamers or other similar decorations hung on string. **2** thin loosely-woven cotton used to make flags, esp for ships. [18c]

bunting[2] *noun* any of various small finch-like birds with a short stout bill and a sturdy body. [13c]

buoy /bɔɪ; *N Am* 'buːɪ/ *noun* a brightly-coloured floating object fastened to the bottom of the sea by an anchor, to warn ships of rocks, etc or to mark channels, etc. See also **lifebuoy**. ▶ *verb* **1** to mark (eg an obstruction or a channel) with a buoy or buoys. **2** (*usu* **buoy up**) to keep (something) afloat. **3** (*usu* **buoy up**) to raise or lift the spirits of (someone); to encourage, cheer or excite (them). **4** (*often* **buoy up**) to sustain, support or boost (something): *Profits were buoyed by the new economic confidence.* **5** *intr* to rise or float to the surface. [15c as *boye* a float]

buoyant /'bɔɪənt; *N Am* buːjənt/ *adj* **1** of an object: able to float in or on the surface of a liquid. **2** of a liquid or gas: able to keep an object afloat. **3** of a person: cheerful; bouncy; resilient. ▪ **buoyancy** *noun* (**-*ies***). [16c]

bur *or* **burr** *noun* **1** any seed or fruit with numerous hooks or prickles. **2** any plant that produces such seeds or fruits. [14c]

burble *verb* **1** (*often* **burble on** *or* **away**) *intr* to speak at length but with little meaning or purpose. **2** *intr* of a stream, etc: to make a bubbling murmuring sound. **3** to say (something) in a way that is hard to understand, esp very quickly or incoherently. ▶ *noun* **1** a bubbling murmuring sound. **2** a long incoherent or rambling stream of speech. [14c]

burbot *noun* (***burbot*** *or* ***burbots***) a large fish, the only freshwater species in the cod family. [14c: from French *bourbotte*]

burden[1] *noun* **1** something to be carried; a load. **2** a duty or obligation, etc that is time-consuming, difficult, costly, exacting or hard to endure. **3** the carrying of a load or loads: *a beast of burden.* ▶ *verb* to weigh (someone) down (with a burden, difficulty, problem, etc); to trouble or impose upon (them). ▪ **burdensome** *adj.* [Anglo-Saxon from *beran* to bear]

burden[2] *noun* **1** the main theme, esp of a book or speech, etc. **2** a line repeated at the end of each verse of a song. [16c: from French *bourdon* a droning sound]

burdock *noun* any of various plants, with heart-shaped lower leaves and spiny fruits or burrs. [16c: **bur** + **dock**[3]]

bureau /'bjʊroʊ/ *noun* (***bureaux*** *or* ***bureaus*** /-roʊz/) **1** *Brit* a desk for writing at, with drawers and usu a front flap which opens downwards to provide the writing surface. **2** *N Am, esp US* a chest of drawers. **3** an office or department for business, esp for collecting and supplying information. **4** *esp US* a government or newspaper department. [17c: French]

bureaucracy *noun* (**-*ies***) **1** a system of government by officials who are responsible to their department heads and are not elected. **2** these officials as a group, esp when regarded as oppressive. **3** any system of administration in which matters are complicated by complex procedures and trivial rules. **4** a country governed by officials. [19c: **bureau** + **-cracy**]

bureaucrat *noun* **1** a government official. **2** an official who follows rules rigidly, so creating delays and difficulties; someone who practises or believes in bureaucracy. ▪ **bureaucratic** *adj.*

burette *noun, chem* a long vertical glass tube marked with a scale and having a tap at the bottom, used to deliver controlled volumes of liquid. [15c, meaning 'small cruet' or 'jug': French]

burgeon *verb, intr* (*sometimes* **burgeon forth**) **1** to grow or develop quickly; to flourish. **2** of a plant: to bud or sprout. [14c: from French *burjon* bud or shoot]

burger *noun* **1** a hamburger. **2** *esp in compounds* a hamburger covered or flavoured with something: *cheeseburger.* **3** *esp in compounds* an item of food shaped like a hamburger but made of something different: *nutburger.* [20c: shortening of **hamburger**]

burgh /'bʌrə/ *noun* in Scotland until 1975: an incorporated town or borough, with a certain amount of self-government under a town council. [14c: Scots form of **borough**]

burgher *noun, dated or facetious* a citizen of a town, esp a town on the Continent, or of a borough. [16c: from German *burger*, from *burg* borough]

burglar *noun, law* a person who commits the crime of **burglary**. [16c: from Anglo-French *burgler*]

burglary *noun* (**-*ies***) *law* the crime of entering a building illegally in order to steal, or to commit another crime. Compare **robbery**. [16c: see **burglar**]

burgle *verb* **1** to enter (a building, etc) illegally and steal from it. **2** *intr* to commit burglary. [19c]

burgundy *noun* (**-*ies***) **1** a French wine made in the Burgundy region, esp a red wine. **2** any similar red wine. **3** a deep or purplish-red colour. ▶ *adj* deep or purplish-red in colour. [17c]

burial *noun* the burying of a dead body in a grave. [Anglo-Saxon *byrgels* tomb]

burlesque *noun* **1** a piece of literature, acting or some other presentation that exaggerates, demeans or mocks a serious subject or art form. **2** a type of theatrical entertainment involving humorous sketches, songs and usu striptease. ▶ *adj* belonging to or like a burlesque. ▶ *verb* to make fun of (something) using burlesque. [17c: French]

burly *adj* (**-*ier*, -*iest***) of a person: strong and heavy in build; big and sturdy. [13c]

Burmese *adj* belonging or relating to Burma (since 1989 officially called Myanmar), its inhabitants or their language. ▶ *noun* **1** a citizen or inhabitant of, or person born in, Burma. **2** the official language of Burma. **3** a Burmese cat. [19c]

burn[1] *verb* (***burned*** *or* ***burnt***) **1** *tr & intr* to be on fire or set (something) on fire. **2** *tr & intr* to damage or injure (someone or something), or be damaged or injured, by fire or heat. **3** to use (something) as fuel. **4** *tr & intr* to char or scorch (someone or something), or become charred or scorched. **5** to make (a hole, etc) by or as if by fire or heat, etc: *Acid can burn holes in material.* **6** *intr* to be or feel hot. **7** *tr & intr* to feel or make (something) feel a hot or stinging pain: *Vodka burns my throat.* **8** (*usu* **be burning to do sth**) *intr, informal* to want to do it very much: *burning to get his revenge.* **9** (*esp* **be burning with sth**) *intr* to feel strong emotion: *burning with shame.* **10** to use (coal, oil, etc) as fuel. **11** *tr & intr* to kill (someone) or die by fire. ▶ *noun* **1** an injury or mark caused by fire, heat, acid, friction, etc. **2** an act of firing the engines of a space rocket so as to produce thrust. [Anglo-Saxon *biernan*, and *bærnan*]

IDIOMS **burn one's boats** *or* **bridges** *informal* to do something which makes it impossible for one to return to one's former situation or way of life, etc. **burn one's fingers** *or* **get one's fingers burnt** *informal* to suffer as a result of getting involved in or interfering with something foolish, dangerous, risky, etc. **burn the candle at both ends** to exhaust oneself by trying to do too much, usu by starting work very early in the morning and staying up late at night. **burn the midnight oil** to work late into the night.

PHRASAL VERBS **burn sb** *or* **oneself out** to exhaust them or oneself by too much work or exercise. **burn sth out** to make it stop working from overuse or overheating.

burn[2] *noun, chiefly Scot* a small stream. [Anglo-Saxon *burna* brook]

burner *noun* **1** the part of a gas lamp or stove, etc that produces the flame. **2** a piece of equipment, etc for burning something.

burning *adj* **1** on fire. **2** feeling extremely hot. **3** very strong or intense. **4** very important or urgent: *the burning question.*

burnish *verb* to make (metal) bright and shiny by polishing. ▸ *noun* polish; lustre. [14c: from French *brunir* to burnish, literally 'to make brown']

burnous *noun* (***burnouses*** *or* ***burnous***) a long cloak with a hood, worn by Arabs. [17c: from Arabic *burnus*]

burn-out *noun* **1** physical or emotional exhaustion caused by overwork or stress. **2** the point at which a rocket engine stops working when the fuel is used up.

burnt *a past tense & past participle of* **burn**[1]

burp *informal, verb* **1** *intr* to let air escape noisily from one's stomach through one's mouth. Also called **belch**. **2** to rub or pat (a baby) on the back to help get rid of air in its stomach. ▸ *noun* a belch. [20c: imitating the sound]

burr[1] *noun* **1** in some accents of English: a rough 'r' sound pronounced at the back of the throat. **2** a continual humming sound made eg by a machine. **3** a rough edge on metal or paper. **4** a small rotary drill used by a dentist or surgeon.

burr[2] see **bur**

burrito /bəˈriːtoʊ/ *noun* a Mexican dish consisting of a **tortilla** folded around a filling. [20c: American Spanish, literally 'little donkey']

burrow *noun* **1** a hole in the ground, esp one dug by a rabbit or other small animal for shelter or defence. **2** *informal* a cosy little refuge or bolt-hole. ▸ *verb* **1** (*esp* **burrow in** *or* **into** *or* **through** *or* **under sth**) *tr & intr* to make (a hole) or tunnel in or under it. **2** *intr* of an animal: to make burrows or live in a burrow. **3** (*esp* **burrow away, down, in** *or* **into sth**) *tr & intr* of a person: to keep (oneself, or something belonging to oneself, etc) cosy, protected or hidden away, as if in a burrow. **4** *intr* (*usu* **burrow into sth**) to search or investigate deeply into it. [13c as *borow*]

bursar *noun* **1** a treasurer in a school, college or university. **2** in Scotland and New Zealand: a student or pupil who has a bursary. [13c: from Latin *bursarius*, from *bursa* a bag or purse]

bursary *noun* (***-ies***) **1** esp in Scotland and New Zealand: an award or grant of money made to a student; a scholarship. **2** the bursar's room in a school, college, etc.

burst *verb* (***burst***) **1** *tr & intr* to break or fly open or into pieces, usu suddenly and violently, or cause (something) to do this. **2** (*esp* **burst in, into** *or* **out of somewhere** *or* **sth**) *intr* to make one's way suddenly or violently into or out of it, etc: *burst into the room.* **3** (*usu* **burst onto**) *intr* to appear suddenly in (a specified circle or area) and be immediately important or noteworthy: *burst onto the political scene.* **4** *intr* **a** to be completely full; **b** to break open; to overflow, etc: *My suitcase is bursting;* **c** to be overflowing with or unable to contain (one's excitement, vitality, anger or other emotion). ▸ *noun* **1** an instance of bursting or breaking open. **2** the place where something has burst or broken open, or the hole or break, etc made by it bursting. **3** a sudden, brief or violent period of some activity, eg speed, gunfire, applause. [Anglo-Saxon *berstan*]

IDIOMS **burst into flames** to begin burning suddenly and violently. **burst into song** to begin singing, esp suddenly or unexpectedly. **burst into tears** to begin weeping suddenly or unexpectedly. **burst open** to open suddenly and violently. **burst out laughing** to begin laughing suddenly or unexpectedly.

burton *noun, Brit slang* now only in the phrase **gone for a burton** meaning: **1** lost for good. **2** dead, killed or drowned. **3** broken or destroyed. [20c air force slang]

bury *verb* (***buries, buried***) **1** to place (a dead body) in a grave, the sea, etc. **2** to hide (something) in the ground. **3** to put something out of sight; to cover: *bury one's face in one's hands.* **4** to put (something) out of one's mind or memory; to blot out: *Let's bury our differences.* **5** to occupy (oneself) completely with something: *She buried herself in her work.* [Anglo-Saxon *byrgan*]

IDIOMS **bury the hatchet** to stop quarrelling and become friends again.

bus *noun* (***buses*** *or* (*N Am*) ***busses***) **1** a road vehicle, usu a large one, that carries passengers to and from established stopping points along a fixed route for payment. Originally called **omnibus**. **2** *informal* a car or aeroplane, esp one that is old and shaky. **3** *comput* a set of electrical conductors that form a channel or path along which data or power may be transmitted to and from all the main components of a computer. ▸ *verb* (***bused*** *or* ***bussed, busing*** *or* ***bussing***) **1** (*also* **bus it**) *intr* to go by bus. **2** *esp US* to transport (children) by bus to a school in a different area, as a way of promoting racial integration. [19c: short for **omnibus**]

busby *noun* (***-ies***) **1** a tall fur hat worn as part of some military uniforms. **2** *informal* a **bearskin** (sense 2). [18c in the obsolete sense 'a large bushy wig']

bush[1] *noun* **1** a low woody perennial plant, esp one having many separate branches originating at or near ground level. **2** (*usu* **the bush**) wild uncultivated land covered with shrubs or small trees, esp in Africa, Australia or New Zealand. **3** something like a bush, esp in thickness, shape or density. [13c: from Norse *buskr*]

bush[2] *noun* a sheet of thin metal lining a cylinder in which an axle revolves. ▸ *verb* to provide (eg a bearing) with a bush. [16c: from Dutch *bussche* box]

bushbaby *noun* an agile nocturnal African primate with thick fur, large eyes and a long tail. [20c]

bushed *adj, informal* extremely tired.

bushel *noun* **1** in the imperial system: a unit for measuring dry or liquid goods by volume, equal to 8 gallons or 36.4 l in the UK (35.2 l in the USA). **2** a container with this capacity. **3** *informal, esp US* a large amount or number. [14c: from French *boissiel*]
IDIOMS **hide one's light under a bushel** to keep one's talents or good qualities hidden from other people.

bushman *noun* **1** *Aust, NZ* someone who lives or travels in the bush. **2** (**Bushman**) a member of an almost extinct, small-statured, aboriginal race of nomadic hunters in S Africa. [18c in sense 2: from Afrikaans *boschjesman*]

bushranger *noun* **1** *Aust, hist* an outlaw or escaped convict living in the bush. **2** *N Am* someone who lives far from civilization.

bush telegraph *noun, chiefly Brit, humorous* the rapid spreading of information, rumours, etc, usu by word of mouth.

bushy *adj* (***-ier, -iest***) **1** covered with bush or bushes. **2** of hair, etc: thick and spreading. [14c: from **bush**[1]]

business *noun* **1** the buying and selling of goods and services. **2** a shop, firm or commercial company, etc. **3** a regular occupation, trade or profession. **4** the things that are one's proper or rightful concern: *mind your own business.* **5** serious work or activity: *get down to business.* **6** an affair or matter: *a nasty business.* **7** *informal* a difficult or complicated problem. **8** (**the business**) *slang* exactly what is required; the perfect thing or person, etc for the job. **9** commercial practice or policy: *Prompt invoicing is good business.* **10** economic or commercial dealings, activity, custom or contact: *I have some business with his company.* **11** (*also* **stage business**) *theatre* action on stage, as distinguished from dialogue. [Anglo-Saxon as *bisignes* meaning 'busyness']
IDIOMS **on business** of a person: in the process of doing business or something official. **out of business** no longer able to function as a business; bankrupt.

business card *noun* a card carried by a person in business showing their name and business details.

businesslike *adj* practical and efficient; methodical.

businessman *or* **businesswoman** *noun* a man or woman working in trade or commerce, esp at quite a senior level.

business park *noun* an area, usu on the edge of a town, esp designed to accommodate business offices and light industry.

busk *verb, intr, chiefly Brit* to sing, play music, etc in the street for money. ▪ **busker** *noun.* [19c]

busman's holiday *noun* leisure time spent doing what one normally does at work.

bus shelter *noun* an open-sided structure at a bus stop.

bus stop *noun* **1** a stopping place for a bus. **2** a post or sign marking such a place.

bust[1] *noun* **1** the upper, front part of a woman's body; breasts or bosom. **2** a sculpture of a person's head, shoulders and upper chest. [17c in sense 2: from French *buste*, from Italian *busto*]

bust[2] *informal, verb* (***bust*** *or* ***busted***) **1** *tr & intr* to break or burst (something). **2** of the police: to arrest (someone). **3** to raid or search (someone or somewhere), esp in a search for illegal drugs: *The club was busted last night.* **4** *N Am, usu military* to demote (someone). ▸ *noun, slang* **1** a police raid. **2** a drinking bout; a spree. ▸ *adj, informal* **1** broken or burst. **2** having no money left; bankrupt or ruined. [19c: colloquial form of **burst**]
IDIOMS **go bust** *informal* to become bankrupt.

bustard *noun* a large ground-dwelling bird with speckled grey or brown plumage and long powerful legs. [15c: from French *bistarde*]

bustier *noun, fashion* a short tight-fitting strapless bodice for women. [20c: French, meaning 'bodice']

bustle[1] *verb* **1** (*usu* **bustle about**) *intr* to busy oneself in a brisk, energetic and/or noisy manner. **2** to make (someone) hurry or work hard, etc: *bustled her out of the room.* ▸ *noun* hurried, noisy and excited activity. ▪ **bustling** *adj* lively and busy. [16c]

bustle[2] *noun, hist* a frame or pad for holding a skirt out from the back of the waist. [18c]

bust-up *noun, informal* **1** a quarrel; the ending of a relationship or partnership. **2** an explosion or collapse.

busty *adj* (***-ier, -iest***) *informal* of a woman: having large breasts.

busy *adj* (***-ier, -iest***) **1** fully occupied; having much work to do. **2** full of activity: *a busy street.* **3** *N Am* of a telephone line, etc: in use. *Brit equivalent* **engaged. 4** constantly working or occupied. **5** of a person: fussy and tending to interfere in the affairs of others. **6** of a picture or design, etc: unrestful to the eye because too full of detail. ▸ *verb* (***-ies, -ied***) to occupy (someone or oneself) with a task, etc. ▪ **busily** *adv.* [Anglo-Saxon *bisig*]

busybody *noun* someone who is always interfering in other people's affairs. [16c]

busy Lizzie *noun* any of various ornamental hybrid plants, usu with pink, red or white flowers. [20c: so called because it is fast-growing]

but *conj* **1** contrary to expectation: *She fell down but didn't hurt herself.* **2** in contrast: *You've been to Spain but I haven't.* **3** other than: *You can't do anything but wait.* **4** used to emphasize the word that follows it: *Nobody, but nobody, must go in there.* ▸ *prep* except: *They are all here but him.* ▸ *adv* only: *I can but try.* ▸ *noun* an objection or doubt: *no buts about it.* [Anglo-Saxon]
IDIOMS **but for** were it not for; without: *I couldn't have managed but for your help.* **but that** *formal or dated* were it not that; except that: *There seemed no explanation but that he had done it.*

but
Although some people think it is a bad use of English, it is not incorrect to begin a sentence with **but**.

butane *noun* a colourless highly flammable gas, belonging to the alkane series of hydrocarbons, that is used in the manufacture of synthetic rubber, and in liquid form as a fuel. [19c: from *butyric acid*]

butch /bʊtʃ/ *adj, slang* of a person: tough and strong-looking; aggressively masculine in manner or looks, etc. [20c]

butcher *noun* **1** a person or shop that sells meat. **2** someone whose job is slaughtering animals and preparing the carcasses for use as food. **3** a person who kills people needlessly and savagely. ▸ *verb* **1** to kill and prepare (an animal) for sale as food. **2** to kill (esp a large number of people or animals) cruelly or indiscriminately. **3** *informal* to ruin or make a botch of (something): *completely butchered his solo.* [13c: from French *bochier* or *bouchier*]

butchery *noun* (*-ies*) **1** the preparing of meat for sale as food; the trade of a butcher. **2** senseless, cruel or wholesale killing. **3** a slaughterhouse.

butler *noun* the chief male servant in a house. [13c: from French *bouteillier*, from *botele* bottle]

butt[1] *verb, tr & intr* **1** to push or hit (someone or something) hard or roughly with the head, in the way a ram or goat might. See also **head-butt**. **2** (*esp* **butt against** *or* **on sth**) to join or be joined end to end with it. ▸ *noun* **1** a blow with the head or horns. **2** the place where two edges join. [13c: from French *boter* to push or strike]

PHRASAL VERBS **butt in** *informal* to interrupt or interfere. **butt into** to interrupt (eg a conversation, or someone's private affairs).

butt[2] *noun* **1** the unused end of a finished cigar or cigarette, etc. **2** the thick, heavy or bottom end of a tool or weapon: *a rifle butt*. **3** *chiefly N Am informal* the buttocks. [15c as *bott* or *but* in senses 2 and 3; related to **buttock**]

butt[3] *noun* **1** a person who is often a target of jokes, ridicule or criticism, etc. **2** a mound of earth behind a target on a shooting range. [15c in sense 2: from French *but* a target or goal]

butt[4] *noun* a large barrel for beer or rainwater, etc. [14c: from French *botte*, from Latin *buttis* cask]

butte /bjuːt/ *noun, geol* an isolated flat-topped hill with steep sides. [19c: French]

butter *noun* **1** a solid yellowish edible food, made from the fats in milk by churning, and used for spreading on bread, and in cooking. **2** *in compounds* any of various substances that resemble this food in appearance or texture: *peanut butter*. ▸ *verb* to put butter on or in (something). ▪ **buttery** *adj*. [Anglo-Saxon *butere*]

PHRASAL VERBS **butter sb up** *informal* to flatter them, usu in order to gain a favour.

butter bean *noun* any of several varieties of bean plants or one of their large edible seeds.

buttercup *noun* any of various plants with bright yellow cup-shaped flowers. [18c]

butterfingers *singular noun, informal* a person who often drops things, or who fails to catch things. [19c]

butterfly *noun* **1** an insect that has four broad, often brightly coloured wings, and a long proboscis for sucking nectar from flowers. **2** a person who is not very serious, but is only interested in enjoying themselves: *a social butterfly*. **3** (**butterflies**) *informal* a nervous or fluttering feeling in the stomach. **4 butterfly stroke**. [Anglo-Saxon *buter-fleoge*, from **butter** + **fly**[1]]

butterfly nut *or* **butterfly screw** *noun* a screw or nut with two flat projections that allow it to be turned with the fingers. Also called **wing nut**.

butterfly stroke *noun* a swimming stroke in which both arms are brought out of the water and over the head at the same time. Often shortened to **butterfly**.

buttermilk *noun* the slightly sharp-tasting liquid left after all the butter has been removed from milk after churning.

butterscotch *noun* **1** a kind of hard toffee made from butter and sugar. **2** a flavouring made from butterscotch or similar to it.

buttery *noun* (*-ies*) *Brit* a room, esp in a college or university, where food is kept and supplied to students.

buttock *noun* (*usu* **buttocks**) each of the fleshy parts of the body between the base of the back and the top of the legs. [14c: prob from **butt**[2]]

button *noun* **1** a small round piece of metal or plastic, etc sewn onto a piece of clothing, which fastens it by being passed through a buttonhole. **2** (*sometimes* **push button**) a small round disc pressed to operate a door, bell, electrical appliance, etc. **3** a small round object worn as decoration or a badge. **4** any small round object more or less like a button. ▸ *verb* **1** (*also* **button up**) to fasten or close (something) using a button or buttons. **2** *intr* to be capable of being fastened with buttons or a button: *This dress buttons at the back*. [14c: from French *bouton*]

IDIOMS **on the button** *informal* exactly right or correct; spot on.

PHRASAL VERBS **button up** *slang* to stop talking; to shut up. **button sth up** *slang* to bring it to a successful conclusion.

buttonhole *noun* **1** a small slit or hole through which a button is passed to fasten a garment. **2** a flower or flowers worn in a buttonhole or pinned to a lapel. ▸ *verb* **1** to stop (someone), and force conversation on them. **2** to make buttonholes in (something).

buttress *noun* **1** *archit, civil eng* a projecting support made of brick or masonry, etc built onto the outside of a wall. See also **flying buttress**. **2** any support or prop. ▸ *verb* **1** to support (a wall, etc) with buttresses. **2** to support or encourage (an argument, etc). [14c: from French *bouter* to push]

butty *noun* (*-ies*) *Brit, esp N Eng, informal* a sandwich; a piece of bread and butter. [19c: from **butter**]

buxom *adj* of a woman: **1** attractively plump, lively and healthy-looking. **2** having large or plumply rounded breasts; busty. [12c as *buhsum*, in obsolete sense 'pliant' or 'obedient']

buy *verb* (***bought***) **1** to obtain (something) by paying a sum of money for it. **2** to be a means of obtaining (something): *There are some things money can't buy.* **3** to obtain (something) by giving up or sacrificing something else: *success bought at the expense of happiness.* **4** *informal* to believe (something): *I didn't buy his story.* **5** (*also* **buy off**) to bribe (somebody): *He can't be bought, he's thoroughly honest*. ▸ *noun* (*usu in* **a good buy** *or* **a bad buy**) a thing bought. [Anglo-Saxon *bycgan*]

IDIOMS **buy time** *informal* to gain more time before a decision or action, etc is taken. **have bought it** *slang* to have been killed.

PHRASAL VERBS **buy sth in 1** to buy a stock or supply of it. **2** at an auction: to buy it back for the owner when the **reserve price** is not reached. **buy into** to buy shares or an interest in (a company, etc). **buy off** to get rid of (a threatening person, etc) by paying them money. **buy oneself out** to pay to be released from the armed forces. **buy sb out** to pay to take over possession of something from them, esp to buy all the shares that they hold in a company. See also **buy-out**. **buy sth up** to buy the whole stock of it.

buyer *noun* **1** a person who buys; a customer. **2** a person employed by a large shop or firm to buy goods on its behalf.

buy-out *noun, commerce* the purchase of all the shares in a company in order to get control of it.

buzz *verb* **1** *intr* to make a continuous, humming or rapidly vibrating sound, like that made by the wings of an insect such as the bee. **2** *intr* to be filled with activity or excitement. **3** (*often* **buzz about** *or* **around**) *intr* to move quickly or excitedly. **4** *informal* to call (someone) using a **buzzer**. **5** *informal* to call someone on the telephone. **6** *informal* of an aircraft: to fly very low over or very close to (another aircraft or a building, etc). ▸ *noun* **1** a humming or rapidly vibrating sound, such as that made by a bee. **2** *informal* a telephone call. **3** *informal* a very pleasant, excited, or exhilarated feeling; a kick or thrill: *Joy-riding gives him a real buzz.* **4** a low murmuring sound such as that made by many people talking. **5** *informal* a rumour. [14c: imitating the sound]

PHRASAL VERBS **buzz off** *informal* to go away.

buzzard *noun* **1** any of several large hawks that resemble eagles in their effortless gliding flight. **2** *N Am* a vulture. [13c: from French *busard*]

buzzer *noun* an electrical device that makes a buzzing sound, used as a signal or for summoning someone.

buzz word *noun, informal* a fashionable new word or expression, usu in a particular subject, social group, or profession. [20c]

by *prep* **1** next to, beside or near: *standing by the door.* **2** past: *I'll drive by the house.* **3** through, along or across: *entered by the window.* **4** (esp after a passive verb) used to indicate the person or thing that does, causes or produces, etc something: *destroyed by fire.* **5** used to show method or means: *sent by registered post.* **6** not later than: *I'll be home by 10pm.* **7** during: *escape by night.* **8** used to show extent or amount: *worse by far.* **9** used in stating rates of payment, etc: *paid by the hour.* **10** according to: *It's 8.15 by my watch.* **11** used to show the part of someone or something held, taken or used, etc: *pulling me by the hand.* **12** used to show the number that must perform a mathematical operation on another: *multiply three by four.* **13** used in giving measurements and compass directions, etc: *a room measuring six feet by ten.* **14** used to show a specific quantity or unit, etc that follows another to bring about an increase or progression: *two by two.* **15** with regard to someone or something: *do his duty by them.* **16** in oaths, etc: in the name of, or strictly 'with the witness of' or 'in the presence of' (a specified deity, thing or person): *By God, you're right!* **17** fathered by: *two children by her first husband.* ▸ *adv* **1** near: *live close by.* **2** past: *drive by without stopping.* **3** aside; away; in reserve: *some money put by.* **4** *chiefly N Am* to or at one's or someone's home, etc: *Come by for a drink later.* ▸ *noun* (***byes***) same as **bye**[1]. [Anglo-Saxon *be* or *bi*]

IDIOMS **by and by** *rather literary or old use* after a short time; at some time in the not-too-distant future. **by and large** generally; all things considered. **by oneself** **1** alone: *Sit by yourself over there.* **2** without anyone else's help: *can't do it by myself.* **by the by** *or* **by the bye** *or* **by the way** *informal* while I think of it; incidentally.

by- *or* **bye-** *prefix, denoting* **1** minor, supplementary or less important: *by-election.* **2** indirect; running past, beside or apart from something: *bypass.* **3** incidental; occurring by way of something else: *by-product.*

bye[1] *noun* **1** *sport, etc* a pass into the next round of a competition, given to a competitor or team that has not been given an opponent in the current round. **2** *cricket* a run scored from a ball which the batsman has not hit or touched. [18c: an altered form of **by**]

IDIOMS **by the bye** see **by the by** at **by**.

bye[2] *or* **bye-bye** *exclam, informal* goodbye.

by-election *noun* an election held during the sitting of parliament, in order to fill a seat that has become empty because the member has died or resigned.

bygone *adj* former: *in bygone days.* ▸ *noun* (**bygones**) events, troubles or arguments that occurred in the past. [15c]

by-law *or* **bye-law** *noun, Brit* a law or rule made by a local authority or other body, rather than by the national government. [13c: probably from the obsolete word *byrlaw* local custom, from Norse *byjar-log* town law]

byline *noun* **1** *journalism* a line under the title of a newspaper or magazine article which gives the name of the author. **2** *football* the touchline.

bypass *noun* **1** a major road that carries traffic on a route that avoids a city centre, town or congested area. **2** *med* the redirection of blood flow so as to avoid a blocked or diseased blood vessel, esp a coronary artery. **3** a channel or pipe, etc that carries gas or electricity, etc when the main channel is blocked or congested. ▸ *verb* **1** to avoid (a congested or blocked place) by taking a route that goes round or beyond it. **2** to leave out or avoid (a step in a process), or ignore and not discuss something with (a person): *managed to bypass the usual selection procedure.* **3** to provide (something) with a bypass. **4** to direct (eg fluid, traffic or electricity) along a bypass.

by-play *noun* esp in a play: less important action that happens at the same time as the main action.

by-product *noun* **1** a secondary product that is formed at the same time as the main product during a chemical reaction or manufacturing process. **2** an unexpected or extra result; a side effect.

byre *noun, mainly Scot* a cowshed. [Anglo-Saxon]

byroad *or* **byway** *noun* **1** a minor, secondary or secluded road. Also called **sideroad**. **2** (*esp* **byway**) a line of thought or activity, etc not often taken by other people; an obscure area of interest. [17c]

bystander *noun* a person who happens to be standing by, who sees but does not take part in what is happening; an onlooker. [17c]

byte *noun, comput* **1** a group of adjacent binary digits (see **bit**[3]) that are handled as a single unit, esp a group of eight. **2** the amount of storage space occupied by such a group. [20c: possibly from *binary digit eight*, or from **bit**[3]]

byword *noun* **1** a person or thing that is well known as an example of something: *a byword for luxury.* **2** a common saying or proverb. [Anglo-Saxon in sense 2]

Byzantine *adj* **1** *hist* relating to Byzantium or the eastern part of the Roman Empire from AD 395 to 1453. **2** belonging or relating to the style of architecture and painting, etc developed in the Byzantine Empire, with domes, arches, stylized mosaics and icons, etc. **3** belonging or relating to the **Byzantine Church**, ie the Eastern or Orthodox Church. **4** secret, difficult to understand, and extremely intricate and complex; tortuous. **5** eg of attitudes or policies: rigidly hierarchic; inflexible. ▸ *noun, hist* an inhabitant of Byzantium. [18c: from Latin *byzantinus*]

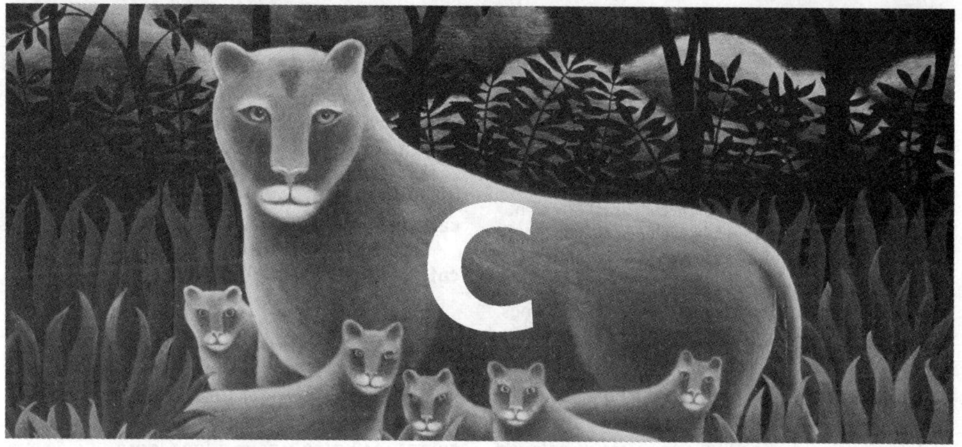

C[1] *or* **c** *noun* (***Cs, C's*** *or* ***c's***) **1** the third letter of the English alphabet. **2** (*usu* **C**) the third highest grade or quality, or a mark indicating this. **3** (**C**) *music* a musical key with the note C as its base. **4** (**C**) *comput* a high-level programming language.

C[2] *abbrev* **1** Celsius. **2** centigrade. **3** century: *C19.*

C[3] *symbol* **1** (*also* **c**) *centum* (Latin), the Roman numeral for 100. **2** *chem* carbon.

c *abbrev* **1** centi-. **2** cubic.

c. *abbrev* **1** *cricket* caught. **2** cent. **3** century. **4** chapter. **5** (*also* **ca**) *circa* (Latin), approximately.

Ca *symbol, chem* calcium.

cab *noun* **1** a taxi. **2** the driver's compartment in a lorry, railway engine, etc. [19c: shortened from **cabriolet**]

cabal /kə'bal/ *noun* **1** a small group formed within a larger body, for secret, esp political, discussion, etc. **2** a political plot or conspiracy. [17c: from French *cabale*]

cabala see **cabbala**

cabaret /'kabəreɪ/ *noun* **1** entertainment with songs, dancing, etc at a restaurant or nightclub. **2** a restaurant or nightclub providing this. [20c: French, meaning 'tavern']

cabbage *noun* **1** a leafy plant, grown for its compact head of green, white or red edible leaves. **2** the leaves of this plant eaten as a vegetable. **3** *derog* a dull inactive person. [14c: from French *caboche* head]

cabbala *or* **cabala** *noun* (also **kabala, kabbala** *or* **kabbalah**) a mystical Jewish lore, based on interpreting hidden meanings in the Old Testament. [17c: Latin, from Hebrew *qabbalah* tradition]

cabby *or* **cabbie** *noun* (***-ies***) *informal* a taxi-driver.

caber *noun, Scot athletics* a heavy wooden pole of 3–4m in length, that must be carried upright and then tipped end over end, during a contest called **tossing the caber**. [16c: from Scottish Gaelic *cabar* pole]

cabin *noun* **1** a small house, esp one made of wood. **2** a small room on a ship for living, sleeping or working in. **3** the section of a plane for passengers or crew. **4** the driving compartment of a large commercial vehicle. [14c: from French *cabane*]

cabin boy *noun, hist* a boy who serves officers and passengers on board ship.

cabin crew *noun* the members of an aircraft crew who attend to the passengers.

cabinet *noun* **1** a piece of furniture with shelves and doors, for storing or displaying items. **2** (*often* **the Cabinet**) *Brit* a body of senior ministers in charge of the various departments of government, who meet regularly for discussion with the prime minister. [16c: diminutive of **cabin**]

cabinet-maker *noun* a skilled craftsman who makes and repairs fine furniture. ▪ **cabinet-making** *noun.*

cable *noun* **1** a strong wire cord or rope. **2** two or more electrical wires bound together but separated from each other by insulating material, and covered by a protective outer sheath, used to carry electricity, television signals, etc. **3** (*also* **cablegram**) a telegram sent by cable. **4** (*also* **cable stitch**) a pattern in knitting that looks like twisted cable. **5** short for **cable television.** ▸ *verb* **1** to tie up or provide with a cable or cables. **2** *tr & intr* to send a cable, or send (a message) to someone by cable. [13c: from Latin *capulum* halter]

cable car *noun* a small carriage suspended from a continuous moving cable, for carrying passengers up or down a steep mountain, across a valley, etc.

cable TV, cable television *or* **cablevision** *noun* a television broadcasting system in which television signals are relayed directly to individual subscribers by means of cables. Often shortened to **cable**.

caboodle *noun, informal* (*esp* **the whole caboodle**) the whole lot; everything.

caboose *noun, N Am* a guard's van on a railway train. [18c: from Dutch *cabuse* ship's galley]

cabriolet /kabrɪoʊ'leɪ/ *noun* **1** *hist* a light two-wheeled carriage drawn by one horse. **2** a car with a folding roof. [18c: French, meaning 'little leap']

cacao /kə'kɑːoʊ/ *noun* the edible seed of a small evergreen tree, used in the manufacture of chocolate, cocoa and cocoa butter. [16c: Spanish]

cache /kaʃ/ *noun* **1** a hiding place, eg for weapons. **2** a collection of hidden things. ▸ *verb* to put or collect in a cache. [19c: from French *cacher* to hide]

cache memory *noun, comput* an extremely fast part of the main store of computer memory.

cachet /'kaʃeɪ/ *noun* **1** something which brings one respect or admiration; a distinction. **2** a distinguishing mark. [17c: from French *cacher* to hide]

cack-handed *adj, informal* **1** clumsy; awkward. **2** left-handed. [19c: from dialect *cack* excrement]

cackle *noun* **1** the sound made by a hen or a goose. **2** *derog* a raucous laugh like this. **3** shrill, silly chatter.

► *verb, intr* **1** to laugh raucously. **2** to chatter noisily. **3** to utter as a cackle. [13c: imitating the sound]

cacophony /kəˈkɒfənɪ/ *noun* (**-*ies***) a disagreeable combination of loud noises. ▪ **cacophonous** *adj.*

cactus *noun* (***cacti*** /ˈkaktaɪ/ *or* ***cactuses***) any of numerous mostly spiny plants which usu store water in swollen, often barrel-like stems. [18c: Latin]

CAD *abbrev* computer-aided design, the use of a computer system to create and edit design drawings.

cad *noun, Brit informal* a man who behaves discourteously or dishonourably.

cadaver /kəˈdɑːvə(r)/ *noun, med* a human corpse, esp one used for dissection. [16c: Latin]

cadaverous *adj* corpse-like in appearance; pale and gaunt.

caddie *or* **caddy** *noun* (**-*ies***) someone whose job is to carry the golf clubs around the course for a golfplayer. ► *verb* (***caddies, caddied, caddying***) *intr* to act as a caddie. [18c: from French *cadet* cadet]

caddy *noun* (**-*ies***) **1** a small container for loose tea. **2** *N Am* any storage container. [18c: from Malay *kati* a unit of weight equal to a small packet of tea]

cadence /ˈkeɪdəns/ *noun* **1** the rising and falling of the voice in speaking. **2** rhythm or beat. **3** *music* a succession of notes that closes a musical passage. [14c: French]

cadenza *noun, music* an elaborate virtuoso passage given by a solo performer towards the end of a movement. [19c: Italian]

cadet *noun* **1** a student undergoing preliminary training for the armed forces or police. **2** a school pupil undergoing military training in an organized group, not necessarily as preparation for the armed forces. [17c: French]

cadge *verb, tr & intr, informal* (*also* **cadge sth from** *or* **off sb**) to get (something, esp money or food) by scrounging or begging. ▪ **cadger** *noun.*

cadi, **kadi** *or* **qadi** *noun* in Muslim countries: a judge or magistrate. [16c: from Arabic *qadi*]

cadmium *noun, chem* (symbol **Cd**) a soft bluish-white metallic element. [19c: from Latin *cadmia*]

cadre /ˈkadə(r)/ *noun* **1** *military* a permanent core unit which can be expanded when required, eg by conscription. **2** an inner group of activists in a revolutionary party, esp a Communist one. [19c: French, meaning 'framework']

CAE *abbrev, comput* computer-aided engineering, the use of computers to replace the manual control of machine tools by automatic control.

caecum *or* (*esp US*) **cecum** /ˈsiːkəm/ *noun* (***caeca*** /-kə/) *anatomy* a blind-ended pouch at the junction of the small and large intestines. ▪ **caecal** *or* (*esp US*) **cecal** *adj.* [18c: Latin]

Caenozoic see **Cenozoic**

caesarean (section) *or* (*US*) **cesarean (section)** *noun* a surgical operation in which a baby is delivered through an incision in the lower abdomen. Also spelt **caesarian** *or* (*US*) **cesarian**. [17c: apparently named after Julius Caesar, said to have been the first child delivered by this method]

caesium *or* (*N Am*) **cesium** /ˈsiːzɪəm/ *noun, chem* (symbol **Cs**) a soft silvery-white metallic element. [19c: Latin]

caesura *or* **cesura** /sɪˈzjʊərə/ *noun* (***caesuras*** *or* ***caesurae*** /-riː/) a pause near the middle of a line of verse. [16c: Latin]

café *or* **cafe** *noun* a usu small restaurant that serves light meals or snacks. [19c: French]

cafeteria *noun* a self-service restaurant. [19c: American Spanish, meaning 'coffee shop']

cafetière /kafəˈtjɛə(r)/ *noun* a coffee-pot with a plunger for separating the grounds from the liquid. [19c: French]

caffeine *noun* a bitter-tasting alkaloid, found in coffee beans, tea leaves and cola nuts, a stimulant of the central nervous system. ▪ **caffeinated** *adj.* See also **decaffeinate**. [19c: from French *caféine*]

caftan *or* **kaftan** *noun* a long loose-fitting robe, often tied at the waist. [16c: from Turkish *qaftan*]

cage *noun* an enclosure, usu with bars, in which eg captive birds and animals are kept. ► *verb* (*also* **cage sb in**) to put them in a cage; to confine them. ▪ **caged** *adj.* [13c: French]

cagebird *noun* a bird, such as a canary, that is often kept in a cage.

cagey *or* **cagy** *adj* (***cagier, cagiest***) *informal* secretive and cautious; not forthcoming. ▪ **cagily** *adv.*

cagoule *or* **kagoule** *noun* a lightweight waterproof hooded anorak. [1950s: French, meaning 'cowl']

cahoots *plural noun.*

IDIOMS **in cahoots with sb** *usu derog, informal* working in close partnership with them, esp in the planning of something unlawful.

caiman see **cayman**

Cainozoic see **Cenozoic**

cairn[1] *noun* a heap of stones piled up to mark something, eg a grave or pathway. [16c: from Scottish Gaelic *carn*]

cairn[2] *or* **cairn terrier** *noun* a small breed of dog with short legs, a thick shaggy brown coat and erect ears. [20c: from Scottish Gaelic *carn*]

cairngorm *noun, geol* a yellow or smoky-brown variety of the mineral quartz, often used as a gemstone. [18c: named after the Cairngorm Mountains of Scotland where it is found]

caisson /ˈkeɪsən/ *noun* **1** a watertight rectangular or cylindrical chamber used to protect construction workers during the building of underwater foundations, etc. **2** the pontoon or floating gate used to close a dry dock. [18c: French, meaning 'large box']

cajole *verb* (*usu* **cajole sb into sth**) to persuade them using flattery, promises, etc; to coax. ▪ **cajolery** *noun.* [17c: from French *cajoler* to coax]

Cajun /ˈkeɪdʒən/ *noun* a member of a group of people of French descent living in Louisiana. ► *adj* of or relating to the Cajuns or their culture. [19c: from *Acadian*, from Acadia, a French colony in Canada]

cake *noun* **1** a solid food made by baking a mixture of flour, fat, eggs, sugar, etc. **2** an individually baked portion of this food. **3** a portion of some other food pressed into a particular shape: *fish cake.* **4** a solid block of a particular substance, eg soap. ► *verb* **1** *intr* to dry as a thick hard crust. **2** to cover in a thick crust: *skin caked with blood.* [13c: from Norse *kaka*]

IDIOMS **a piece of cake** *informal* a very easy task. **have one's cake and eat it** *informal* to enjoy the advantages of two alternative courses of action. **sell** *or* **go like hot cakes** to be bought enthusiastically in large numbers.

CAL *abbrev* computer-aided learning, a tutorial method using a computer to teach, question and assess a student.

cal. *abbrev* calorie.

calabash *noun* the dried hollowed-out shell of the flask-shaped woody fruit of the **calabash tree**, used as a bowl or water container. [17c: from French *calebasse*]

calabrese /kalə'breɪzeɪ/ *noun* a type of green sprouting broccoli, eaten as a vegetable. [20c: Italian]

calamari *plural noun* in Mediterranean cookery: squid. [Italian, pl of *calamaro* squid]

calamine *noun* a fine pink powder containing zinc oxide and small amounts of ferric oxide, used in the form of a lotion or ointment. [17c: French]

calamitous *adj* disastrous, tragic or dreadful.

calamity *noun* (***-ies***) **1** a catastrophe, disaster or serious misfortune causing great loss or damage. **2** a state of great misery or disaster. [15c: from French *calamité*]

calcareous /kal'kɛərɪəs/ *adj* containing or resembling calcium carbonate. [17c: from Latin *calcarius*]

calces *pl of* **calx**

calciferol *noun* **vitamin D_2** (see **vitamin D**).

calciferous *adj* **1** *chem* containing lime. **2** *biol* containing or producing calcium or calcium salts.

calcify *verb* (***-ies, -ied***) *tr & intr* **1** to harden as a result of the deposit of calcium salts. **2** to change or be changed into lime. ▪ **calcification** *noun*. [19c]

calcite *noun, geol* a white or colourless mineral, composed of crystalline calcium carbonate.

calcium *noun, chem* (symbol **Ca**) a soft, silvery-white metallic element which occurs mainly in the form of calcium carbonate minerals such as chalk, limestone and marble. [19c: from **calx**]

calcium carbonate *noun, chem* a white powder or colourless crystals, occurring naturally as limestone, marble, chalk, etc, which is used in the manufacture of glass, cement, etc.

calcium hydroxide *noun, chem* a white crystalline powder that dissolves sparingly in water to form an alkaline solution, and which is used in the manufacture of mortar, whitewash and water softeners, and as a neutralizer for acid soil. Also called **slaked lime**.

calcium oxide *noun, chem* a white chemical compound used in producing other calcium compounds, such as **slaked lime**, and in agriculture as an alkali to reduce acidity in soil. Also called **lime**, **quicklime**, **unslaked lime**, **calx**.

calculate *verb* **1** to work out, find out or estimate, esp by mathematical means. **2** (*often* **calculate on sth**) *intr* to make plans that depend on or take into consideration some probability or possibility. **3** to intend or aim: *The measures were calculated to avoid mass redundancy.* [16c: from Latin *calculare*]

calculated *adj* intentional; deliberate: *a calculated insult*.

calculating *adj, derog* deliberately shrewd and selfish.

calculation *noun* **1** the act or process of calculating. **2** something estimated or calculated. **3** *derog* the cold and deliberate use of people or situations.

calculator *noun* a small usu hand-held electronic device that is used to perform numerical calculations.

calculus *noun* (***calculuses*** *or* ***calculi*** /'kalkjʊlaɪ, -liː/) **1** the branch of mathematics concerned with the differentiation and integration of functions. See **differential calculus**, **integral calculus**. **2** *med* a hard stone-like mass that forms within hollow body structures such as the kidney, urinary bladder, gall bladder or bile ducts. Also called **concretion**. [17c: Latin, meaning 'pebble']

Caledonian *adj, esp formerly* belonging or relating to Scotland or its inhabitants. [17c: from Latin *Caledonia* Scotland]

calendar *noun* **1** any system by which the beginning, length and divisions of the year are fixed. **2** a booklet, chart, etc that shows such an arrangement. **3** a timetable or list of important dates, events, appointments, etc. [13c: from Latin *calendrium* account book]

---

calendar

This word is often misspelt. It has *en* in the middle and *ar* at the end. It might help you to remember the following sentence:

*A cal**endar** shows you the **end** of the ye**ar**.*

---

calendar month see **month**

calender *noun* a machine through which paper or cloth is passed in order to give it a smooth shiny finish. ▸ *verb* to give a smooth finish to (paper or cloth) by passing it through such a machine. [16c: from French *calandre*]

calends *or* **kalends** *plural noun* in the ancient Roman calendar: the first day of each month. [14c: from Latin *kalendae*]

calf[1] *noun* (***calves***) **1** the young of any bovine animal, esp domestic cattle. **2** the young of certain other mammals, eg the elephant and whale. [Anglo-Saxon *cælf*]

calf[2] *noun* (***calves***) the thick fleshy part of the back of the leg, below the knee. [14c: from Norse *kálfi*]

calf love see **puppy love**

calibrate *verb* to mark a scale on (a measuring instrument) so that it can be used to take readings in suitable units. ▪ **calibration** *noun*.

calibre /'kalɪbə(r)/ *noun* **1** the internal diameter of a gun barrel or tube. **2** the outer diameter of a bullet, shell or other projectile. **3** quality; standard; ability. [16c: French]

calico *noun* (***calicoes***) a kind of cotton cloth, usu plain white or in its natural unbleached state. [16c: named after Calicut in India from where it was first brought]

californium *noun, chem* (symbol **Cf**) a synthetic radioactive metallic element of the **actinide** series. [1950: named after California, where it was first made]

caliph, **calif**, **kalif** *or* **khalif** *noun* the chief Muslim civil and religious leader. ▪ **caliphate** *noun*. [14c: from Arabic *khalifah* successor (of Muhammad)]

call *verb* **1** *tr & intr* (*also* **call out**) to shout or speak loudly in order to attract attention or in announcing something. **2** to ask someone to come, esp with a shout. **3** to ask for a professional visit from someone: *call the doctor.* **4** to summon or invite someone. **5** *tr & intr* to telephone. **6** *intr* to make a visit: *call at the grocer's.* **7** to give a name to someone or something. **8** to regard or consider something as something specified: *I call that strange.* **9** to summon or assemble people for (a meeting). **10** (*often* **call for sth**) *tr &*

intr to make a demand or appeal for it: *call a strike*. **11** *intr* to predict which way a coin will land when tossed. **12** *intr* of a bird, etc: to make its typical or characteristic sound. **13** *comput* to transfer control (of a function) to a different part of a program. ▸ *noun* **1** a shout or cry. **2** the cry of a bird or animal. **3** an invitation; a summons. **4** a demand, request or appeal. **5** (*usu* **call on sth**) a claim or demand for it: *too many calls on my time*. **6** a brief visit. **7** an act of contacting someone by telephone; a telephone conversation. **8** a need or reason: *not much call for Latin teachers*. **9** a player's turn to bid or choose trumps in a card game. ▪ **caller** *noun*. [Anglo-Saxon *ceallian*]

IDIOMS **on call** eg of a doctor: available if needed, eg to deal with an emergency.

PHRASAL VERBS **call for sth** *or* **sb 1** to require it or them. **2** to collect or fetch it or them. **call sth off 1** to cancel a meeting, arrangement, etc. **2** to give orders for something to be stopped. **call sb up 1** to conscript them into the armed forces. **2** *informal* to telephone them. **call sth up 1** to cause (memories, etc) to come into the mind. **2** to retrieve (data) from a computer.

call box *noun* a public telephone box.

call centre *noun* a building where workers provide services to a company's customers by telephone.

calligraphy *noun* **1** handwriting as an art. **2** beautiful decorative handwriting. ▪ **calligrapher** *noun*. [17c: from Greek *kallos* beauty + *graphein* to write]

calling *noun* **1** a trade or profession. **2** an urge to follow a particular profession, esp the ministry or one involving the care of other people.

calling card *noun, N Am* a **visiting card**.

calliper *noun* **1** a measuring device, consisting of two hinged prongs attached to a scale, which is used to measure the linear distance between the prongs. **2** a splint for supporting a leg. [16c: variant of **calibre**]

callisthenics *plural noun* a system of physical exercises to increase the strength and grace of the body. ▪ **callisthenic** *adj*. [19c: from Greek *kallos* beauty + *sthenos* strength]

callous *adj* unconcerned for the feelings of others; deliberately cruel. ▪ **callously** *adv*. ▪ **callousness** *noun*. [15c: from Latin *callosus* thick-skinned]

callow *adj* young and inexperienced. [Anglo-Saxon *calu* bald]

call sign *or* **call signal** *noun, communications* a word, letter or number that identifies a ship, plane, etc when communicating by radio, etc.

callus *noun* **1** a thickened hardened pad of skin. **2** a mass of tissue that forms around a wound on the surface of a plant or around the exposed ends of a fractured bone as part of the healing process. [16c: Latin, meaning 'hardened skin or tissue']

calm *adj* **1** relaxed and in control; not anxious, upset, angry, etc. **2** of the weather, etc: still, quiet or peaceful. ▸ *noun* **1** peace, quiet and tranquillity. **2** stillness of weather. ▸ *verb, tr & intr* **1** (*usu* **calm down**) to become calmer. **2** (*usu* **calm sb** *or* **sth down**) to make them calmer. ▪ **calmly** *adv*. ▪ **calmness** *noun*. [14c: from French *calme*]

calorie *noun* **1** a metric unit denoting the amount of heat required to raise the temperature of one gram of water by 1°C (1K) at one atmospheric pressure, now replaced by the SI unit **joule**. Also called **small calorie**. **2** (**Calorie**) *old use* a **kilocalorie**. [19c: French]

calorific *adj* referring or relating to heat or calories.

calumet /'kaljʊmɛt/ *noun* a tobacco-pipe, smoked as a token of peace by Native Americans. Also called **peace pipe**. [18c: French dialect, meaning 'pipe stem']

calumniate *verb* to accuse someone falsely; to slander.

calumny *noun* (**-ies**) **1** an untrue and malicious spoken statement about a person. **2** the act of uttering such a statement. [16c: from Latin *calumnia* false accusation]

calve *verb, intr* **1** to give birth to (a calf). **2** of a glacier or iceberg: to release (masses of ice) on breaking up.

calves *pl of* **calf**[1], **calf**[2]

calx /kalks/ *noun* (***calces*** /'kalsiːz/ *or* ***calxes*** /'kalksɪz/) **1** the powdery metal oxide that remains after an ore has been roasted in air. **2** **calcium oxide**. [15c: Latin, meaning 'lime']

calypso *noun* a type of popular song originating in the West Indies. [20c]

calyx /'keɪlɪks/ *noun* (***calyces*** /-lɪsiːz/, ***calyxes*** /-lɪksiːz/) *botany* the outermost whorl of a flower, consisting of the **sepal**s, that protects the developing flower bud. [17c: Latin]

calzone /kalt'soʊnɪ/ *noun* (***calzones***) a folded round of pizza dough stuffed with a savoury filling. [20c: Italian, meaning 'trouser leg']

CAM *abbrev, comput* computer-aided manufacture (or manufacturing), the use of computers to control any part of a manufacturing process.

cam *noun, eng* an irregular projection on a wheel or rotating shaft, shaped so as to transmit regular movement to another part in contact with it. [18c: from Dutch *kam* comb]

camaraderie *noun* a feeling of friendship and cheerful support between friends. [19c: French]

camber *noun* a slight convexity on the upper surface of a road. [17c: from French *cambre*]

Cambodian *adj* belonging or relating to Cambodia, a republic in SE Asia, or its inhabitants. ▸ *noun* a citizen or inhabitant of, or person born in, Cambodia.

Cambrian *geol, adj* **1** relating to the earliest geological period of the **Palaeozoic** era. **2** relating to rocks formed during this period. ▸ *noun* the Cambrian period. [17c: from Latin *Cambria*]

cambric *noun* a fine white cotton or linen fabric. [16c: from Flemish *Kameryk* Cambrai, the town in N France where the cloth was first made]

Cambs. *abbrev, English county* Cambridgeshire.

camcorder *noun* a portable video camera that is used to record images and sound. [1980s: a shortening of **camera** + **recorder**]

came *past tense of* **come**

camel *noun* **1** a large mammal with a long neck and legs, and one or two humps on its back which contain fat and act as a food reserve. **2** the pale brown colour of this animal. [Anglo-Saxon]

camelhair *noun* a soft, usu pale-brown cloth made from camels' hair.

camellia /kə'miːlɪə/ *noun* **1** an evergreen shrub with attractive white, pink or crimson flowers and glossy leaves. **2** the flower of this plant. Also called **japon-**

ica. [18c: named after the plant collector Josef Kamel]

Camembert /'kaməmbɛə(r)/ *noun* a soft white French cheese with a rich flavour and strong smell. [19c: named after the village in N France where it was originally made]

cameo *noun* **1** a smooth rounded gemstone with a raised design of a head in profile carved on it, esp one where the design is a different colour from the gemstone. Compare **intaglio** (sense 1). **2** a piece of jewellery containing such a gemstone. **3** (*also* **cameo role**) a small part in a play or film performed by a well-known actor. [14c: from Italian *cammeo*]

camera *noun* **1** an optical device that records images as photographs. **2** a device in a television broadcasting system that converts visual images into electrical signals for transmission. [19c: Latin, meaning 'vaulted chamber']

cameraman *noun* in TV or film-making: someone who operates a camera.

camera obscura *noun* (***camera obscuras***) a darkened box or room with a small hole in one wall or the roof, through which light from outside can enter, pass through a lens, and form an inverted image of the scene outside, which is projected onto the opposite wall or the floor, etc of the chamber. [18c: Latin, meaning 'dark chamber']

camera phone *or* **camphone** *noun* a mobile phone incorporating a camera, enabling the transmission of digital images.

camerawork *noun* the process or technique of filming or taking photographs.

camisole *noun* a woman's loose vest-like undergarment, with narrow shoulder straps. [19c: French]

camomile *or* **chamomile** *noun* **1** a strongly scented plant which has finely divided leaves, and white and yellow daisy-like flower heads. **2** the dried crushed flowers or leaves of this plant, used for their soothing medicinal properties, esp in the form of a herbal tea. [14c: from Greek *chamaimelon* earth apple]

camouflage *noun* **1** any device or means of disguising or concealing a person or animal, or of deceiving an adversary, esp by adopting the colour, texture, etc, of natural surroundings or backgrounds. **2** the use of such methods to conceal or disguise the presence of military troops, equipment, vehicles or buildings, by imitating the colours of nature. **3** the colour pattern or other physical features that enable an animal to blend with its natural environment and so avoid detection by predators. ▸ *verb* to disguise or conceal with some kind of camouflage. [20c: French]

camp[1] *noun* **1** a piece of ground on which tents have been erected. **2** a collection of buildings, huts, tents, etc used as temporary accommodation or for short stays for a particular purpose. **3** a permanent site where troops are housed or trained. **4** a party or side in a dispute, etc; a group having a particular set of opinions, beliefs, etc. ▸ *verb, intr* to stay in a tent or tents. ▪ **camping** *noun*. [16c: French]

camp[2] *adj, informal, sometimes derog* of a man or his behaviour: effeminate, esp in an exaggerated way. [20c]

campaign *noun* **1** an organized series of actions intended to gain support for or build up opposition to a particular practice, group, etc. **2** the operations of an army while fighting in a particular area or to achieve a particular goal or objective. ▸ *verb, intr* (*usu* **campaign for** *or* **against sth**) to organize or take part in a campaign. ▪ **campaigner** *noun*. [17c: from French *campagne* open countryside]

campanile /kampə'niːlɪ/ *noun* esp in Italy: a bell tower that is free-standing. [17c: Italian]

campanology *noun* the art of bell-ringing. ▪ **campanologist** *noun*. [19c: from Latin *campana* bell + Greek *logos* word or reason]

camp bed *noun* a light portable folding bed.

camper *noun* **1** someone who camps. **2** a motor vehicle equipped for sleeping in.

camp-follower *noun, derog* someone who travels about with an army in order to earn money, eg by doing odd jobs.

camphor *noun* a white or colourless crystalline compound with a strong aromatic odour, used as a medicinal liniment and inhalant, and to make Celluloid. [14c: from Latin *camphora*]

campion *noun* a plant which has bright pink or white flowers.

campsite *noun* a piece of land on which people are allowed to camp.

campus *noun* the grounds of a college or university. [18c: Latin, meaning 'field']

campylobacter /'kampɪlɒbaktə(r)/ *noun, biol* a spiral-shaped bacterium that occurs in the reproductive and digestive tracts of humans and animals, causing diarrhoea and gastritis in humans, and genital diseases in cattle and sheep. [20c: from Greek *kampylos* bent + *bacterion* a little rod (from its shape)]

camshaft *noun, eng* a shaft to which one or more **cam**s are attached.

Can. *abbrev* **1** Canada. **2** Canadian.

can[1] *verb* (*past tense* ***could***) **1** to be able to: *Can you lift that?* **2** to know how to: *He can play the guitar.* **3** to feel able to; to feel it right to: *How can you believe that?* **4** to have permission to: *Can I take an apple?* **5** used when asking for help, etc: *Can you give me the time?* See also **cannot**, **can't**, **could**, **couldn't**. [Anglo-Saxon *cunnan* to know]

---

can, may

In traditional grammar, you use **may** when permission is being asked or given, and you use **can** if you are saying that someone is able or something is possible:

Can I have another doughnut?
You can, but you may not.

However, in modern English it is acceptable to use **can** for all meanings:

Hospital trusts can set their own pay rates.

---

can[2] *noun* **1** a sealed container, usu of tin plate or aluminium, used to contain food and esp fizzy drinks. **2** a large container made of metal or another material, for holding liquids, eg oil or paint. **3** a **canful**. **4** (**the can**) *slang* prison. **5** *N Am, slang* (*usu* **the can**) a lavatory. ▸ *verb* (***canned, canning***) to seal (food or drink) in metal containers in order to preserve it. [Anglo-Saxon *canne*]

Canadian *adj* belonging or relating to Canada, an independent country in N America, or its inhabitants. ▸ *noun* a citizen or inhabitant of, or person born in, Canada.

canal *noun* **1** an artificial channel or waterway, usu constructed for navigation or irrigation. **2** *anatomy* any tubular channel or passage that conveys food, air or fluids from one part of the body to another: *alimentary canal*. [17c: from Latin *canalis* water pipe]

canalize *or* **-ise** *verb* **1** to make or convert into a canal or system of canals. **2** to guide or direct into a useful, practical or profitable course. ▪ **canalization** *noun*.

canapé /ˈkanəpeɪ/ *noun* a small piece of bread or toast spread or topped with something savoury. [19c: French, meaning 'sofa']

canard *noun* a false report or piece of news. [19c: French, meaning 'duck']

canary *noun* (**-ies**) a small finch with bright yellow plumage, very popular as a caged bird. [16c: named after the Canary Islands]

canasta *noun* a card game similar to rummy played with two packs of cards. [20c: Spanish, meaning 'basket']

cancan *noun* a lively dance which is usu performed by dancing girls, who execute high kicks, raising their skirts to reveal their petticoats. [19c: French]

cancel *verb* (***cancelled, cancelling***) **1** to stop (something already arranged) from taking place. **2** to stop (something in progress) from continuing. **3** *intr* to tell a supplier that one no longer wants something. **4** to delete or cross out something. **5** to put an official stamp on (eg a cheque or postage stamp) so that it cannot be re-used. **6** *maths* to eliminate (common numbers or terms), esp to strike out (equal quantities) from opposite sides of an equation, or (common factors) from the **numerator** and **denominator** of a fraction. **7** (*usu* **cancel sth out**) to remove the effect of it, by having an exactly opposite effect; to counterbalance. ▪ **cancellation** *noun*. [14c: from French *canceller*]

Cancer *noun, astrol* **a** the fourth sign of the zodiac; **b** a person born between 22 June and 22 July, under this sign. See also **tropic**. ▪ **Cancerian** *noun, adj*. [14c: Latin, meaning 'crab']

cancer *noun* **1** *pathol* any form of malignant tumour that develops when the cells of a tissue or organ multiply in an uncontrolled manner. **2** *pathol* a diseased area produced when a malignant tumour invades and destroys the surrounding tissues. **3** an evil within an organization, community, etc that is gradually destroying it. ▪ **cancerous** *adj*. [17c: Latin, meaning 'crab' or 'cancerous growth']

candela /kanˈdiːlə/ *noun* (symbol **cd**) the SI unit of luminous intensity. [20c: Latin, meaning 'candle']

candelabrum *or* (*sometimes used wrongly as sing*) **candelabra** *noun* (***candelabrums, candelabra*** *or* ***candelabras***) a candle-holder with branches for several candles, or a light-fitting for overhead lights designed in the same way. [19c: Latin, meaning 'candlestick']

candid *adj* **1** honest and open about what one thinks; outspoken. **2** *informal* of a photograph: taken without the subject's knowledge so as to catch them unawares. [17c: from Latin *candidus* shining white]

candidate *noun* **1** someone who is competing with others for a job, prize, parliamentary seat, etc. **2** someone taking an examination. **3** a person or thing considered suitable for a particular purpose or likely to suffer a particular fate. ▪ **candidacy** (**-ies**) *or* **candidature** *noun*. [17c: from Latin *candidatus* clothed in white, because Roman candidates always wore white]

candle *noun* a piece of wax or (esp formerly) tallow, formed around a wick, which is burnt to provide light. [Anglo-Saxon *candel*]

candlelight *noun* the light given by a candle or candles. ▪ **candlelit** *adj*.

candlestick *noun* a holder, usu portable, for a candle.

candlewick *noun* a cotton fabric with a tufted surface formed by cut loops of thread, used for bedcovers, etc.

candour *or* (*N Am*) **candor** *noun* the quality of being candid; frankness and honesty. [17c: from Latin *candor* purity, sincerity]

candy *noun* (**-ies**) *N Am* **1** a sweet. **2** sweets or confectionery. ▸ *verb* (**-ies, -ied**) to preserve (fruit, peel, etc) by boiling in sugar or syrup. ▪ **candied** *adj*. [18c: from French *sucre candi* candied sugar]

candy floss *noun* a fluffy mass of coloured spun sugar served on a stick. *US equivalent* **cotton candy**.

candy stripe *noun* a textile fabric patterned with narrow stripes, usu pink or red, on a white background. ▪ **candy-striped** *adj*.

cane *noun* **1** the long jointed hollow or pithy stem of certain plants, esp various small palms (eg rattan) and larger grasses (eg bamboo and sugar cane). **2** **sugar cane**. **3** thin stems or strips cut from stems, eg of rattan, for weaving into baskets, etc. **4** a walking-stick. **5** a long slim stick for beating people as a punishment. ▸ *verb* to beat (someone) with a cane as a punishment. ▪ **caning** *noun*. [14c: French]

cane sugar *noun* **sucrose**, esp that obtained from sugar cane.

canful *noun* the amount a can can hold.

canine *adj* **1** relating to or resembling a dog. **2** relating to the dog family in general. ▸ *noun* **1** any animal belonging to the dog family, esp a domestic dog. **2** a **canine tooth**. [17c: from Latin *caninus*]

canine tooth *noun* in most mammals: any of the long sharp pointed teeth, two in each jaw, located between the incisors and premolars. Also called **eye tooth**.

canister *noun* a metal or plastic container for storing tea or other dry foods. [17c: from Latin *canistrum*]

canker *noun* **1** a fungal, bacterial or viral disease of trees and woody shrubs, eg fruit trees. **2** an ulcerous disease of animals that causes eg inflammation of the ears of cats and dogs. **3** an evil, destructive influence, etc. ▪ **cankerous** *adj*. [Anglo-Saxon *cancer*]

cannabis *noun* a narcotic drug, prepared from the leaves and flowers of the hemp plant. Also called **marijuana**, **hashish**, **pot**. [18c: Latin]

canned *adj* **1** contained or preserved in cans. **2** *slang* drunk. **3** *informal* previously recorded: *canned laughter*.

cannelloni *plural noun* a kind of pasta in the form of large tubes, served with a filling of meat, cheese, etc. [20c: Italian, from *cannello* tube]

cannery *noun* (**-ies**) a factory where goods are canned.

cannibal *noun* **1** someone who eats human flesh. **2** an animal that eats others of its own kind. ▪ **cannibalism** *noun*. [16c: from Spanish *Canibales*]

cannibalize *or* **-ise** *verb, informal* to take parts from (a machine, vehicle, etc) for use in repairing another.

cannon *noun* (*pl* ***cannons*** or in senses 1 and 2 ***cannon***) **1** *hist* a large gun mounted on wheels. **2** a rapid-firing gun fitted to an aircraft or ship. **3** in billiards, pool and snooker: a shot in which the cue ball strikes one object ball and then strikes another. ▸ *verb, intr* in billiards, pool and snooker: to play a cannon shot. [16c: from French *canon*]

cannonade *noun* a continuous bombardment by heavy guns. [17c: from French *canonnade*]

cannonball *noun, hist* a ball, usu of iron, for shooting from a cannon.

cannot *verb* can not. See also **can't**.

canny *adj* (***-ier, -iest***) **1** wise and alert; shrewd. **2** careful; cautious. ▪ **cannily** *adv.*

canoe *noun* a light narrow boat propelled manually by one or more single- or double-bladed paddles. ▸ *verb* (***canoeing***) *intr* to travel by canoe. ▪ **canoeing** *noun.* ▪ **canoeist** *noun.* [16c: from Spanish *canoa*]

canon *noun* **1** a basic law, rule or principle. **2** **a** a member of the clergy attached to a cathedral; **b** in the Church of England: a member of the clergy who has special rights with regard to the election of bishops. **3** an officially accepted collection of writing, or work considered to be by a particular writer. **4** the books of the Bible accepted as the standard by the Jewish or Christian faiths. **5** in the Christian Church: a list of saints. **6** a piece of music, similar to a round, in which a particular sequence is repeated with a regular overlapping pattern. [Anglo-Saxon]

canonical *adj* **1** according to, of the nature of or included in a canon. **2** orthodox or accepted.

canonical hours *plural noun, now esp RC Church* **a** the hours appointed for prayer and devotion; **b** the services prescribed for these times, which are **matins, lauds, terce, sext, none**[2], **vespers** and **compline**.

canonize *or* **-ise** *verb* **1** to officially declare someone to be a saint. **2** to treat someone as a saint. ▪ **canonization** *noun.*

canon law *noun* the law of the Christian Church.

canoodle *verb, intr, informal* to hug and kiss.

canopy *noun* (***-ies***) **1** an ornamental covering hung over a bed, throne, etc. **2** a covering hung or held up over something or someone, usu for shelter. **3** *archit* a roof-like structure over an altar, recess, etc. **4** a transparent cover over the cockpit of an aeroplane. **5** *botany* the topmost layer of a wood or forest, consisting of the uppermost leaves and branches of trees. [14c: from Greek *konopeion* a couch with a mosquito net]

cant[1] *noun* **1** *derog* insincere talk, esp with a false display of moral or religious principles. **2** the special slang or jargon of a particular group of people, eg lawyers, etc. ▸ *verb, intr* to talk using cant. [17c: from Latin *cantare* to chant]

cant[2] *noun* a slope. ▸ *verb, tr & intr* to tilt, slope or tip up. [14c]

can't *contraction* cannot.

cantabile /kan'tɑːbɪleɪ/ *music, adv* in a flowing and melodious manner. ▸ *adj* flowing and melodious. [18c: Italian, meaning 'suitable for singing']

cantaloup *or* **cantaloupe** *noun* a type of melon with a thick ridged skin and orange-coloured flesh. [18c: French]

cantankerous *adj* bad-tempered; irritable.

cantata /kan'tɑːtə/ *noun* a musical work, esp on a religious theme, which is sung, with parts for chorus and soloists. [18c: Italian, meaning 'a thing to be sung']

canteen *noun* **1** a restaurant attached to a factory, office, etc for the use of employees. **2** **a** a case containing cutlery; **b** the full set of cutlery contained in the case. [18c: from French *cantine*]

canter *noun* a horse-riding pace between trotting and galloping. ▸ *verb, tr & intr* to move or cause to move at this pace. [18c: shortened from *Canterbury gallop,* the pace used by the pilgrims riding to Canterbury in the Middle Ages]

canticle *noun* a non-metrical hymn or chant with a text taken from the Bible. [13c: from Latin *canticulum*]

cantilever *noun* a beam or other support that projects from a wall to support a balcony, staircase, etc.

cantilever bridge *noun* a fixed bridge consisting of two outer spans that project towards one another and support a suspended central span.

canto *noun* a section of a long poem. [16c: Italian, meaning 'song']

canton *noun* a division of a country, esp one of the separately governed regions of Switzerland. [16c: French]

cantor *noun* **1** *Judaism* in a synagogue service: a man who chants the liturgy and leads the congregation in prayer. **2** *Christianity* in a church service: someone who leads the choir. [16c: Latin, meaning 'singer']

canvas *noun* **1** a thick heavy coarse cloth, made from hemp or flax, used to make sails, tents, etc and for painting pictures on. **2** a painting done on a piece of canvas. [14c: from French *canevas*]

IDIOMS **under canvas** **1** in tents. **2** *naut* with sails spread.

canvas, canvass

Be careful not to use the spelling **canvas** when you mean **canvass**.

canvass *verb* **1** *tr & intr* to ask for votes or support from (someone). **2** to find out the opinions of (voters, etc). ▸ *noun* a solicitation of information, votes, opinions, etc. ▪ **canvasser** *noun.*

canyon *noun* a deep gorge or ravine with steep sides. [19c: from Spanish *cañón*]

cap *noun* **1** any of various types of hat, eg with a flat or rounded crown and a peak. **2** a small hat often worn as an indication of occupation, rank, etc. **3** a lid, cover or top, eg for a bottle or pen. **4** (*also* **percussion cap**) a little metal or paper case containing a small amount of gunpowder that explodes when struck, used eg to make a noise in toy guns. **5** a protective or cosmetic covering fitted over a damaged or decayed tooth. **6** the top or top part. **7** (**the cap** *or* **Dutch cap**) a contraceptive device used by a woman, consisting of a rubber cover that fits over the **cervix** (sense 1) and prevents the sperm entering. Also called **diaphragm**. ▸ *verb* (***capped, capping***) **1** to put a cap on, or cover the top or end of, (something) with a cap. **2** to be or form the top of. **3** to do better than, improve on or outdo (someone or something). **4** to set an upper limit to (a tax), or to the tax-gathering powers of (a local authority). See also **rate-cap**. [Anglo-Saxon *cæppe*]

cap. *abbrev* **1** capacity. **2** capital. **3** capital letter.

capability *noun* (**-*ies***) **1** ability or efficiency. **2** a power or ability, often one that has not yet been made full use of: *The USA has a strong nuclear capability.*

capable *adj* **1** clever; able; efficient. **2** (**capable of sth**) **a** having the ability to do it; **b** having the disposition or temperament to do it. ▪ **capably** *adv.* [16c: French]

capacious *adj, formal* having plenty of room for holding things; roomy. [17c: from Latin *capere* to take]

capacitance *noun, elec* (SI unit **farad**) the ability of the conductors in a capacitor to store electric charge.

capacitor *noun, elec* a device consisting of two conducting surfaces separated by a dielectric material, that can store energy in the form of electric charge.

capacity *noun* (**-*ies***) **1** the amount that something can hold. **2** the amount that a factory, etc can produce. **3** (**capacity for sth**) the ability or power to achieve it: *capacity for change.* **4** function; role. **5** mental ability or talent. [15c: from French *capacité*]

cape[1] *noun* **1** a short cloak. **2** an extra layer of cloth attached to the shoulders of a coat, etc. [16c: French]

cape[2] *noun* a part of the coast that projects into the sea. [14c: from French *cap*]

caper[1] *verb, intr* to jump or dance about playfully. ▸ *noun* a playful jump. [16c]

caper[2] *noun* a young flower bud of a small deciduous shrub, pickled in vinegar and used as a condiment.

capercaillie *or* **capercailzie** /kapə'keılı/ *noun* a large game bird. [16c: from Scottish Gaelic *capull coille* horse of the wood]

capillarity *noun* the phenomenon, caused by surface tension effects, whereby a liquid such as water rises up a narrow tube placed in the liquid. Also called **capillary action**. [19c: from French *capillarité*]

capillary /kə'pılərı; *US* 'kapılərı/ *noun* (**-*ies***) **1** a tube, usu made of glass, which has a very small diameter. **2** in vertebrates: the narrowest type of blood vessel. [17c: from Latin *capillaris*]

capita see **per capita**

capital[1] *noun* **1** the chief city of a country, usu where the government is based. **2** a capital letter (see *adj* sense 2 below). **3** the total amount of money or wealth possessed by a person or business, etc, esp when used to produce more wealth. ▸ *adj* **1** principal; chief. **2** of a letter of the alphabet: in its large form, as used eg at the beginnings of names and sentences. Also called **upper-case**. **3** of a crime: punishable by death. [13c: from Latin *caput* head]

IDIOMS **make capital out of sth** to use a situation or circumstance to one's advantage.

capital[2] *noun, archit* the slab of stone, etc that forms the top section of a column or pillar. [13c: from Latin *capitellum*]

capital gains tax *noun, commerce* (abbrev **CGT**) in the UK: a tax on the profit obtained by selling assets.

capital-intensive *adj, econ, geog* of an industry: requiring a large amount of capital for machinery etc compared to the amount of labour involved. Compare **labour-intensive**.

capitalism *noun* an economic system based on private, rather than state, ownership of businesses, services, etc, with free competition and profit-making.

capitalist *noun* **1** someone who believes in capitalism. **2** *derog* a wealthy person, esp one who is obviously making a great deal of personal profit from business, etc. ▸ *adj* **1** believing in capitalism. **2** relating to capitalism. ▪ **capitalistic** *adj.*

capitalize *or* **-ise** *verb* **1** *intr* (*esp* **capitalize on sth**) to exploit (an asset, achievement, etc) to one's advantage. **2** to write with a capital letter or in capital letters. **3** to sell (property, etc) in order to raise money. **4** to supply (a business, etc) with needed capital. ▪ **capitalization** *noun.*

capital punishment *noun* punishment of a crime by death.

capital sum *noun* a sum of money paid all at once, eg to someone insured.

capitation *noun* a tax of so much paid per person. [17c: from Latin *capitatio*]

capitulate *verb, intr* **1** to surrender formally, usu on agreed conditions. **2** to give in to argument or persuasion. ▪ **capitulation** *noun.* [16c: from Latin *capitulare* to set out under headings]

capon /'keıpən, -pɒn/ *noun* a castrated male chicken fattened for eating. [Anglo-Saxon *capun*]

cappuccino /kapʊ'tʃiːnoʊ/ *noun* coffee made with frothy hot milk and usu dusted with chocolate powder on top. [20c: Italian, meaning **Capuchin**, because the colour was thought to resemble the monks' habits]

caprice /kə'priːs/ *noun* **1** a sudden change of mind for no good or obvious reason. **2** the tendency to have caprices. [17c: French]

capricious *adj* subject to sudden changes in behaviour, mood or opinion, often for no good reason.

Capricorn *noun, astrol* **a** the tenth sign of the zodiac; **b** a person born between 22 December and 19 January, under this sign. See also **tropic**. [14c: from Latin *Capricornus*]

caprine *adj* belonging or relating to, or characteristic of, a goat. [17c: from Latin *caprinus*]

caps. *abbrev* capital letters.

capsicum *noun* **1** a tropical shrub belonging to the potato family. **2** the red, green or yellow fruit of this plant, which has a hollow seedy interior, and is eaten raw in salads or cooked as a vegetable. See also **pepper** *noun* (sense 2). [18c: from Latin *capsa* box or case]

capsize *verb* **1** *intr* usu of a boat: to tip over completely; to overturn. **2** to cause (a boat) to capsize.

capstan *noun* **1** a cylinder-shaped apparatus that is turned to wind a heavy rope or cable, eg that of a ship's anchor. **2** in a tape recorder: either of the shafts or spindles round which the tape winds. [14c: from Provençal *cabestan*]

capsule *noun* **1** a hard or soft soluble case, usu made of gelatine, containing a single dose of a powdered drug to be taken orally. **2** (*also* **space capsule**) a small spacecraft or a compartment within a spacecraft that contains the instruments and crew for the duration of a space flight. **3** *anatomy* a membranous sheath, sac or other structure that surrounds an organ or tissue. **4** *botany* in some flowering plants: a dry fruit, formed by the fusion of two or more carpels, that splits open to release its many seeds. **5** *biol* a jelly-like envelope of protein or polysaccharide that surrounds and protects certain bacteria. ▪ **capsular** *adj.* [17c: French]

Capt. *abbrev* Captain.

captain *noun* **1** a leader or chief. **2** the commander of a ship. **3** the commander of a company of troops. **4** a naval officer below a commodore and above a commander in rank. **5** an army officer of the rank below major. **6** the chief pilot of a civil aircraft. **7** the leader of a team or side, or chief member of a club. ▸ *verb* to be captain of something. ▪ **captaincy** *noun* (*-ies*). [14c: from French *capitain*]

caption *noun* **1** the words that accompany a photograph, cartoon, etc to explain it. **2** a heading given to a chapter, article, etc. **3** wording appearing on a television or cinema screen as part of a film or broadcast. **4** *comput* the wording on an object on the screen, eg on a command button. ▸ *verb* to provide a caption or captions for something. [18c: from Latin *captio* act of seizing]

captious *adj* inclined to criticize and find fault. [14c: from Latin *captiosus* arguing falsely]

captivate *verb* to delight, charm or fascinate. ▪ **captivating** *adj.* ▪ **captivation** *noun.* [16c: from Latin *captivare* to take captive]

captive *noun* a person or animal that has been caught or taken prisoner. ▸ *adj* **1** kept prisoner. **2** held so as to be unable to get away. ▪ **captivity** *noun* (*-ies*) the condition or period of being captive or imprisoned. [14c: from Latin *captivus* prisoner]

captor *noun* someone who takes a person or animal captive. [17c: Latin]

capture *verb* **1** to catch; to take prisoner; to gain control of someone or something. **2** in a game, eg chess: to gain possession or control of (a piece, etc). **3** to succeed in recording (a subtle quality, etc): *The novel accurately captured the mood.* **4** *comput* to transfer (data) into a computer. ▸ *noun* **1** the capturing of someone or something. **2** the person or thing captured. **3** *physics* the process whereby a neutron is absorbed by a nucleus, and the excess energy produced is released as gamma radiation. [16c: French]

Capuchin *noun* a friar belonging to an austere Franciscan order which stresses poverty. ▸ *adj* belonging or relating to this order. [16c: French, from Italian *cappuccio* hood]

capuchin *noun* an acrobatic intelligent New World monkey with a prehensile tail. [18c: French, from Italian *cappuccio* hood (because its hair resembles a monk's cowl)]

capybara /kapɪ'bɑːrə/ *noun* the largest living rodent, native to S America, which has partially webbed toes and no tail.

car *noun* **1** a four-wheeled road vehicle designed to carry passengers and powered by an internal combustion engine. Also called **motor car, automobile**. **2** *N Am* a railway carriage or van: *dining car.* **3** a passenger compartment in eg a balloon, airship, lift or cable railway. [14c: from French *carre*]

carafe /kə'raf/ *noun* a wide-necked bottle or flask for wine, etc, for use on the table. [18c: French]

carambola /karəm'boulə/ *noun* **1** a SE Asian tree. **2** the fruit of this tree, known as the **star fruit**. [16c: Portuguese, from Marathi (an Indian language) *karambal*]

caramel *noun* **1** a brown substance produced by heating sugar solution until it darkens, used as a food colouring and flavouring. **2** a toffee-like sweet made from sugar, animal fat and milk or cream. **3** the pale yellowish brown colour of this. ▸ *adj* **1** caramel-coloured. **2** made from caramel. [18c: French]

caramelize or **-ise** *verb* **1** to change (sugar) into caramel. **2** *intr* to turn into caramel.

carapace *noun, zool* the hard thick shell that covers the upper part of the body of some tortoises, turtles and crustaceans. [19c: French]

carat *noun* **1** a unit of mass, equal to 0.2g, used to measure the mass of gemstones, esp diamonds. **2** a unit used to express the purity of gold in an alloy with another metal (usu copper), equal to the number of parts of gold in 24 parts of the alloy. [16c: French]

caravan *noun* **1** a large vehicle fitted for living in, designed for towing by a motor vehicle. **2** a large covered van, formerly pulled by horses, used as a travelling home by Romanies, etc. **3** *hist* a group of travellers, merchants, etc, usu with camels, crossing the desert as a large company for safety. ▸ *verb* (***caravanned, caravanning***) *intr* to go travelling with or stay in a caravan. ▪ **caravanning** *noun.* [16c: from Persian *karwan*]

caravanserai or (*N Am*) **caravansery** *noun* (***caravanserais*** or ***caravanseries***) in some Eastern countries: an inn with a central courtyard for receiving caravans crossing the desert, etc. [16c: from Persian *karwansarai* caravan inn]

caraway seed *noun* the dried ripe fruit of the caraway plant which contains an aromatic oil and is widely used as a flavouring.

carbide *noun, chem* any chemical compound consisting of carbon and another element (except for hydrogen), usu a metallic one.

carbine *noun* a short light rifle. [17c: from French *carabine*]

carbohydrate *noun* any of a group of organic compounds, present in the cells of all living organisms, which consist of carbon, hydrogen and oxygen and are formed in green plants during photosynthesis.

carbolic acid see **phenol**

carbon *noun* **1** (symbol **C**) a non-metallic element that occurs in all organic compounds, and as two crystalline **allotrope**s, namely **diamond** and **graphite**. **2** a sheet of carbon paper. **3** a carbon copy. [18c: from French *carbone*]

carbonaceous *adj* containing large amounts of, or resembling, carbon.

carbonate *noun, chem* any salt of carbonic acid. ▸ *verb* to combine or treat (eg a liquid) with carbon dioxide, to make it fizzy. ▪ **carbonated** *adj* of a drink: made fizzy by adding carbon dioxide.

carbon black *noun, chem* a form of finely divided carbon, used in pigments and printer's ink.

carbon copy *noun* **1** an exact duplicate copy made using carbon paper. **2** *informal* a person or thing that looks exactly like someone or something else.

carbon dating *noun, archaeol* a scientific method of estimating the age of archaeological specimens, based on measurements of the radioactive **isotope** carbon-14, which is present in all living organisms, but on their death gradually decays and is not replaced.

carbon dioxide *noun, chem* a colourless odourless tasteless gas, present in the atmosphere and formed during respiration.

carbonic *adj* of a compound: containing carbon, esp carbon with a valency of four.

carboniferous *adj* **1** producing carbon or coal. **2** (**Carboniferous**) *geol* relating to the fifth geological period of the **Palaeozoic** era, characterized by extensive swampy forests which subsequently formed coal deposits. **3** *geol* relating to rocks formed during this period. ▸ *noun, geol* the Carboniferous period.

carbonize *or* **-ise** *verb* **1** *tr & intr* to convert or reduce (a substance containing carbon) into carbon, either by heating or by natural methods such as fossilization. **2** to coat (a substance) with a layer of carbon. ▪ **carbonization** *noun*.

carbon monoxide *noun, chem* a poisonous colourless odourless gas formed by the incomplete combustion of carbon, eg in car-exhaust gases.

carbon paper *noun* paper coated on one side with an ink-like substance containing carbon, which is placed between two or more sheets of paper so that a copy of what is on the top sheet is made on the lower sheets.

carbonyl group *noun, chem* in certain organic chemical compounds: the C=O group, consisting of a carbon atom joined to an oxygen atom by a double bond.

car boot sale *or* **boot sale** *noun* a sale, usu in the open air, where people sell second-hand goods from their car boots or from stalls.

Carborundum *noun, trademark, chem* an extremely hard black crystalline substance, consisting of silicon carbide, that is used as an abrasive and semiconductor.

carboxyl group *noun, chem* in certain organic chemical compounds: the -COOH group.

carboxylic acid /kɑːbɒk'sɪlɪk/ *noun, chem* an organic acid containing a carboxyl (–COOH) group bonded to hydrogen or a hydrocarbon, eg methanoic acid.

carboy *noun* a large glass or plastic bottle, usu protected by a basketwork casing. [18c: from Persian *qaraba* glass flagon]

carbuncle *noun* **1** a boil on the skin. **2** a rounded red gemstone, esp a garnet in uncut form. [13c: from Latin *carbunculus*]

carburettor *noun* part of an internal-combustion engine in which the liquid fuel and air are mixed in the correct proportions and vaporized before being sucked into the cylinders. [19c: from obsolete *carburet* carbide]

carcass *or* **carcase** *noun* **1** the dead body of an animal. **2** *informal* the body of a living person. [14c: from French *carcasse*]

carcinogen /kɑː'sɪnədʒən/ *noun, pathol* any substance capable of causing cancer in living tissue. ▪ **carcinogenic** /kɑːsɪnə'dʒənɪk/ *adj*. [19c: from Greek *karkinos* cancer + *-genes* born]

carcinoma *noun, pathol* any cancer that occurs in the skin or in the tissue that lines the internal organs of the body. [18c: Latin]

card¹ *noun* **1** a kind of thick, stiff paper or thin cardboard. **2** (*also* **playing card**) a rectangular piece of card bearing a design, usu one of a set, used eg for playing games, fortune-telling, etc. **3** a small rectangular piece of card or plastic, showing eg one's identity, job, membership of an organization, etc. **4** a small rectangular piece of stiff plastic issued by a bank, etc to a customer, used eg instead of cash or a cheque when making payments, as a guarantee for a cheque, for operating a cash machine, etc. See also **credit card**, **debit card**. **5** *comput* a piece of card on which information is stored in the form of punched holes or magnetic codes. **6** a piece of card, usu folded double and bearing a design and message, sent to someone on a special occasion. [15c: from French *carte*]

IDIOMS **on the cards** *informal* likely to happen.

card² *noun* a comb-like device with sharp teeth for removing knots and tangles from sheep's wool, etc before spinning, or for pulling across the surface of cloth to make it fluffy. ▸ *verb* to treat (wool, fabric) with a card. ▪ **carding** *noun*. [15c: from French *carde* teasel head]

cardamom, **cardamum** *or* **cardamon** *noun* the dried aromatic seeds of a tropical shrub, which are used as a spice. [15c: from Greek *kardamomum*]

cardboard *noun* a stiff material manufactured from pulped waste paper, used for making boxes, card, etc.

card-carrying *adj* officially registered as a member of a political party, etc and openly supporting it.

cardiac *adj* relating to or affecting the heart. [17c: from Greek *kardia* heart]

cardiac arrest *noun, pathol* the stopping of the heartbeat and therefore the pumping action of the heart.

cardigan *noun* a long-sleeved knitted jacket that fastens down the front. [19c: named after the 7th Earl of Cardigan]

cardinal *noun, RC Church* one of a group of leading clergy, who elect and advise the pope. ▸ *adj* highly important; principal. [12c: from Latin *cardinalis* relating to a hinge]

cardinal number *noun* one of a series of numbers expressing quantity (eg 1, 2, 3, ...). Compare **ordinal number**.

cardinal point *noun* any of the four main points of the compass: north, south, east and west.

cardinal virtue *noun* any of the most important virtues, usu listed as justice, prudence, temperance, fortitude, faith, hope and charity.

cardio- *or* (*before a vowel*) **cardi-** *combining form, denoting* heart. [From Greek *kardia* heart]

cardiographer *noun* someone who operates an **electrocardiograph**.

cardiography *noun* the branch of medicine concerned with the recording of the movements of the heart.

cardiology *noun* the branch of medicine concerned with the study of the structure, function and diseases of the heart. ▪ **cardiologist** *noun*.

cardiopulmonary *adj, anatomy* relating to the heart and lungs.

cardiopulmonary resuscitation *noun* (abbrev **CPR**) an emergency lifesaving technique, involving heart massage alternating with the kiss of life.

cardiovascular *adj, anatomy* relating to the heart and blood vessels.

care *noun* **1** attention and thoroughness. **2** caution; gentleness; regard for safety. **3** the activity of looking after someone or something, or the state of being looked after. **4** worry or anxiety. **5** a cause for worry; a responsibility. ▸ *verb, intr* **1** to mind or be upset by something, or the possibility of something. **2** (*usu* **care about** *or* **for sb** *or* **sth**) to concern oneself about them or it or be interested in them or it. **3** (*always* **care for sth**) to have a wish or desire for it: *Would you care for a drink?* **4** to wish or be willing: *Would you care to come?* **5** (*always* **care for sth**) to like or approve of it. **6** (*always* **care for sb** *or* **sth**) to look after them or it. [Anglo-Saxon *caru* anxiety or sorrow]

IDIOMS **care of** (abbrev **c/o**) written on letters, etc addressed to a person at someone else's address. **take care** to be cautious, watchful or thorough. **take care of sb** *or* **sth 1** to look after them or it. **2** to attend to or organize them or it.

careen *verb, intr* of a ship: to lean over to one side; to keel over. [17c: ultimately from Latin *carina* keel]

career *noun* **1** one's professional life; one's progress in one's job. **2** a job, occupation or profession. **3** one's progress through life generally. ► *verb, intr* to rush in an uncontrolled or headlong way. [16c: from French *carrière* racecourse]

careerist *noun, sometimes derog* someone who is chiefly interested in the advancement of their career. ▪ **careerism** *noun*.

carefree *adj* having few worries; cheerful.

careful *adj* **1** giving or showing care and attention; thorough. **2** gentle; watchful or mindful; cautious. **3** taking care to avoid harm or damage.

careless *adj* **1** not careful or thorough enough; inattentive. **2** lacking or showing a lack of a sense of responsibility.

carer *noun* the person who has the responsibility for looking after an ill, disabled or dependent person.

caress *verb* to touch or stroke gently and lovingly. ► *noun* a gentle loving touch or embrace. [17c: from French *caresse*]

caret *noun* a mark (ʌ) made on written or printed material to show where a missing word, letter, etc should be inserted. [18c: Latin, meaning 'there is missing']

caretaker *noun* a person whose job is to look after a house or a public building, eg a school, esp at times when the building would otherwise be unoccupied. ► *adj* temporary; stopgap: *caretaker president*.

careworn *adj* worn out with or marked by worry and anxiety.

carfuffle, **kefuffle** *or* **kerfuffle** *noun, informal* a commotion; agitation. [From Gaelic *car-* twist + Scots *fuffle* to disorder]

cargo *noun* (***cargoes***) the goods carried by a ship, aircraft or other vehicle. [17c: Spanish, meaning 'burden']

Carib *noun* (***Caribs*** *or* ***Carib***) **1** a group of Native American peoples of the Southern West Indies or Central and S America. **2** an individual belonging to this group of peoples. **3** their language. ► *adj* belonging or relating to this group or their language.

Caribbean *adj* belonging or relating to **the Caribbean**, the part of the Atlantic and its islands between the West Indies and Central and S America, or its inhabitants.

caribou *noun* (***caribous*** *or* ***caribou***) a large deer belonging to the same species as the reindeer, found in N America and Siberia. [17c: Canadian French]

caricature *noun* **1** a representation, esp a drawing, of someone with their most noticeable and distinctive features exaggerated for comic effect. **2** a ridiculously poor attempt at something. ► *verb* to make or give a caricature of someone. ▪ **caricaturist** *noun*. [18c: French]

caries /'kɛəriːz/ *noun* (*pl* ***caries***) the progressive decomposition and decay of a tooth or bone. [17c: Latin, meaning 'decay']

carillon /kə'rɪljən/ *noun* **1** a set of bells hung usu in a tower and played mechanically or with a keyboard. **2** a tune played on such bells. [18c: French]

caring *adj* **1** showing concern for others; sympathetic and helpful. **2** professionally concerned with social, medical, etc welfare.

Carmelite *noun* **1** a member of a Christian order of monks founded in Mount Carmel in the 12c. **2** a member of a contemplative order of nuns founded in the 15c. ► *adj* belonging or relating to these orders.

carmine *noun* a deep red colour; crimson. ► *adj* carmine-coloured. [18c: from French *carmin*]

carnage *noun* great slaughter. [16c: French]

carnal *adj* **1** belonging to the body or the flesh, as opposed to the spirit or intellect. **2** sexual. ▪ **carnality** *noun*. [15c: from Latin *caro* flesh]

carnassial tooth *noun* a molar or premolar tooth that is adapted for tearing flesh. [19c: from French *carnassier* flesh-eating]

carnation *noun* **1** a plant with strongly scented pink, white, red, yellow, orange or multicoloured flowers. **2** the flower of this plant. [16c: from Latin *carnatio* flesh colour]

carnelian see **cornelian**

carnival *noun* **1** a period of public festivity with eg street processions, colourful costumes, singing and dancing. **2** a circus or fair. [16c: from Italian *carnevale*]

carnivore *noun* an animal that feeds mainly on the flesh of other animals. ▪ **carnivorous** *adj*. [19c: French]

carob /'karəb, 'karɒb/ *noun* **1** an evergreen Mediterranean tree with large reddish-brown seedpods. Also called **locust tree**. **2** the edible seedpod of this tree, ground and used as a substitute for chocolate or as a feed for livestock. [16c: from French *carobe*, from Arabic *kharrub*]

carol *noun* a religious song, esp one sung at Christmas. ► *verb* (***carolled, carolling***) **1** *intr* to sing carols. **2** to sing joyfully. [16c: from French *carole*]

carotene *or* **carotin** *noun, biochem* any of a number of reddish-yellow pigments, widely distributed in plants, that are converted to vitamin A in the body. [19c: from Latin *carota* carrot]

carotid /kə'rɒtɪd/ *noun* (*also* **carotid artery**) either of the two major arteries that supply blood to the head and neck. ► *adj*. [17c: from Greek *karos* stupor, because pressure on these arteries causes unconsciousness]

carousal *noun* a drinking bout or party; a noisy revel.

carouse /kə'raʊz/ *verb, intr* to take part in a noisy drinking party. ► *noun* **carousal**. [16c: from German *gar aus* all out, ie completely emptying the glass]

carousel /karə'sɛl/ *noun* **1** a revolving belt in an airport, etc onto which luggage is unloaded for passengers to collect. **2** *N Am* a merry-go-round. [17c: from French *carrousel*]

carp[1] *noun* (***carps*** *or* ***carp***) a deep-bodied freshwater fish. [15c: from French *carpe*]

carp[2] *verb, intr* (*often* **carp at sb** *or* **sth**) to complain, find fault or criticize, esp unnecessarily. ▪ **carper** *noun*. [16c: from Norse *karpa* to boast or dispute]

carpal *anatomy, adj* relating to the **carpus**. ▸ *noun* in terrestrial vertebrates: any of the bones that form the carpus. [18c: from Latin *carpalis*]

car park *noun* a building or piece of land where motor vehicles can be parked.

carpel *noun, botany* the female reproductive part of a flowering plant, consisting of a **stigma** (sense 2), **style** (sense 6) and **ovary** (sense 2). ▪ **carpellary** *adj*. [19c: from Greek *karpos* fruit]

carpenter *noun* someone skilled in working with wood, eg in building houses, etc or in making and repairing fine furniture. ▪ **carpentry** *noun*. [14c: from French *carpentier*]

carpet *noun* **1** a covering for floors and stairs, made of heavy fabric. **2** something that covers a surface like a carpet does: *a carpet of rose petals*. ▸ *verb* **1** to cover something with or as if with a carpet. **2** *informal* to reprimand or scold. [14c: from French *carpite*]

IDIOMS **on the carpet** *informal* scolded or reprimanded verbally, by someone in authority.

carpetbagger *noun, derog* a politician seeking election in a place where he or she is a stranger, with no local connections.

carpus *noun* (***carpi*** /ˈkɑːpaɪ, -piː/) *anatomy* the eight small bones that form the wrist. [17c: Latin]

carrageen *or* **carragheen** /ˈkarəgiːn/ *noun* a type of purplish-red, edible seaweed found in the N Atlantic. Also called **Irish moss**.

carriage *noun* **1** a four-wheeled horse-drawn passenger vehicle. **2** a railway coach for carrying passengers. **3** a moving section of a machine, eg a typewriter, that carries some part into the required position. **4** the way one holds oneself when standing or walking. [14c: from French *cariage*]

carriage clock *noun* a small ornamental clock with a handle on top, orig used by travellers.

carriageway *noun* the part of a road used by vehicles, or a part used by vehicles travelling in one direction.

carrier *noun* **1** a person or thing that carries. **2** a person or firm that transports goods. **3** an individual who may transmit a disease or hereditary disorder to other individuals or to his or her offspring, but who may remain without symptoms. **4** a carrier bag.

carrier bag *noun* a plastic or paper bag with handles, supplied to shop customers for carrying purchased goods.

carrion *noun* dead and rotting animal flesh. [13c: from French *charogne*]

carrot *noun* **1** a plant with divided leaves, small white, pink, or yellow flowers, and an edible orange root. **2** the large fleshy orange root of this plant, eaten as a vegetable. **3** *informal* something offered as an incentive. ▪ **carroty** *adj* of hair: having a strong reddish colour. [16c: from French *carrotte*]

carry *verb* (**-*ies*, -*ied***) **1** to hold something in one's hands, have it in a pocket, bag etc, or support its weight on one's body, while moving from one place to another. **2** to bring, take or convey something. **3** to have on one's person: *He always carried a credit card*. **4** to be the means of spreading (a disease, etc): *Mosquitos carry malaria*. **5** to be pregnant with (a baby or babies). **6** to hold (oneself or a part of one's body) in a specified way: *She really carries herself well*. **7** to bear the burden or expense of something. **8** to do the work of (someone who is not doing enough) in addition to one's own. **9** to print or broadcast: *The story was first carried by the tabloids*. **10** *intr* of a sound or the source of a sound: to be able to be heard a distance away. **11** to take to a certain point: *carry politeness too far*. **12** *maths* to transfer (a figure) in a calculation from one column to the next. ▸ *noun* (**-*ies***) **1** an act of carrying. **2** *N Am* the land across which a vessel has to be transported between one navigable stretch and another. [14c: from French *carier*]

IDIOMS **be** *or* **get carried away** *informal* to become over-excited or over-enthusiastic.

PHRASAL VERBS **carry sth forward** to transfer (a number, amount, etc) to the next column, page or financial period. **carry sth off 1** to manage (an awkward situation, etc) well. **2** to win (a prize, etc). **3** to take something away by force. **carry on 1** to continue; to keep going. **2** *informal* to make a noisy or unnecessary fuss. See also **carry-on**. **carry sth out** to accomplish it successfully. **carry sth through** to complete or accomplish it.

carrycot *noun* a light box-like cot with handles, for carrying a baby.

carry-on *noun* an excitement or fuss.

carry-out *noun, Scot informal* **1** cooked food bought at a restaurant, etc for eating elsewhere. **2** a shop or restaurant supplying such food. **3** alcohol bought in a shop, pub, etc for drinking elsewhere.

cart *noun* **1** a two- or four-wheeled, horse-drawn vehicle for carrying goods or passengers. **2** a light vehicle pushed or pulled by hand. ▸ *verb* **1** to carry in a cart. **2** (*often* **cart sth around** *or* **off**, *etc*) *informal* to carry or convey it. [13c: from Norse *kartr*]

carte blanche *noun* complete freedom of action or discretion. [18c: French, meaning 'blank paper']

cartel *noun* a group of firms that agree, esp illegally, on similar fixed prices for their products, so as to reduce competition and keep profits high. [20c: French]

Cartesian co-ordinates *plural noun, maths* a set of coordinates specifying the position of a point in a plane or in space by its distances from two or three intersecting axes. [17c: named after French philosopher René Descartes, who developed the system]

Carthaginian /kɑːθəˈdʒɪnɪən/ *adj* of or relating to Carthage, an ancient city state in N Africa. ▸ *noun* an inhabitant of Carthage.

carthorse *noun* a large strong horse bred for pulling heavy loads on farms, etc.

Carthusian *noun* a member of a strict Christian order of monks founded in 1084. ▸ *adj* belonging or relating to this order.

cartilage *noun* in humans: a tough flexible material that forms the skeleton of the embryo, but is converted into bone before adulthood, persisting in adults in structures such as the larynx and trachea. ▪ **cartilaginous** /kɑːtɪˈladʒɪnəs/ *adj*. [16c: French]

cartography *noun* the art or technique of making or drawing maps. ▪ **cartographer** *noun*. ▪ **cartographic**

adj. [19c: from French *carte* chart + Greek *graphein* to write]

carton *noun* **1** a plastic or cardboard container in which certain foods or drinks are packaged for sale. **2** a cardboard box. [19c: French, meaning 'pasteboard']

cartoon *noun* **1** a humorous drawing in a newspaper, etc, often ridiculing someone or something. **2** a film made by photographing a series of drawings, each showing the subjects in a slightly altered position, giving the impression of movement when the film is run at normal speed. **3** a strip of drawings in a newspaper, etc showing a sequence of events. ▪ **cartoonist** *noun.* [17c: from Italian *cartone* strong paper, or a drawing on it]

cartouche *noun* **1** *archit* a scroll-like ornament or decorative border with rolled ends. **2** in Egyptian hieroglyphics: an oval figure enclosing a royal or divine name. [17c: French]

cartridge *noun* **1** a metal case containing the propellant charge for a gun. **2** the part of the pick-up arm of a record player that contains the stylus. **3** a small plastic tube containing ink for loading into a fountain pen. **4** a plastic container holding a continuous loop of magnetic tape which can be easily inserted into and removed from a tape deck, video recorder, etc. **5** a plastic container holding photographic film, which can be inserted into and removed from a camera. [16c: variant of **cartouche**]

cartridge belt *noun* a wide belt with a row of loops or pockets for gun cartridges.

cartridge paper *noun* a type of thick rough-surfaced paper for drawing or printing on, or for making cartridges.

cartwheel *noun* **1** the wheel of a cart. **2** an acrobatic movement in which one throws one's body sideways with the turning action of a wheel, supporting one's body weight on each hand and foot in turn. ▸ *verb, intr* to perform a cartwheel.

carve *verb* **1** to cut (wood, stone, etc) into a shape. **2** to make something from wood, stone, etc by cutting into it. **3** *tr & intr* to cut (meat) into slices; to cut (a slice) of meat. ▪ **carver** *noun.* [Anglo-Saxon *ceorfan*]

PHRASAL VERBS **carve sth up 1** to cut it up into pieces. **2** *informal* to divide (territory, spoils, etc), esp in a crude or wholesale manner. See also **carve-up**.

carvery *noun* (*-ies*) a restaurant where meat is carved from a joint for customers on request.

carve-up *noun, slang* a wholesale division, often dishonest, of territory or spoils.

carving *noun* a figure or pattern, etc produced by carving wood, stone, etc.

carving-knife *noun* a long sharp knife for carving meat.

car wash *noun* a drive-through facility at a petrol station, etc with automatic equipment for washing cars.

caryatid /karɪ'atɪd/ *noun* (***caryatids*** *or* ***caryatides*** /karɪ'atɪdiːz/) *archit* a carved female figure used as a support for a roof, etc, instead of a column or pillar. [16c: from Greek *Karyatides* priestesses of the goddess Artemis at Caryae in S Greece]

casbah see **kasbah**

cascade *noun* **1** a waterfall or series of waterfalls. **2** something resembling a waterfall in appearance or manner of falling: *a cascade of hair.* **3** a large number of things arriving or to be dealt with suddenly. ▸ *verb, intr* to fall like a waterfall. [17c: French]

case[1] *noun* **1** *often in compounds* a box, container or cover, used for storage, transportation, etc: *suitcase.* **2** an outer covering, esp a protective one. **3** *printing* a tray with compartments containing individual types, divided up in terms of their style and size. See **upper case**, **lower case.** ▸ *verb* to put something in a case. [13c: from French *casse*]

case[2] *noun* **1** a particular occasion, situation or set of circumstances. **2** an example, instance or occurrence. **3** someone receiving some sort of treatment or care. **4** a matter requiring investigation. **5** a matter to be decided in a law court. **6** (*sometimes* **case for** *or* **against sth**) the set of arguments, statements, etc, for or against something. **7** *grammar* **a** the relationship of a noun, pronoun or adjective to other words in a sentence; **b** one of the forms or categories indicating the relationship: *nominative case.* [13c: from French *cas*]

IDIOMS **in any case** no matter what happens. **in case** so as to be prepared or safe (if a certain thing should happen).

casebook *noun* a written record of cases dealt with by a doctor, lawyer, etc.

case history *noun* a record of relevant details from someone's past kept by a doctor, social worker, etc.

casein /'keɪsiːn/ *noun* a milk protein that is the main constituent of cheese. [19c: from Latin *caseus* cheese]

case law *noun* law based on decisions made about similar cases in the past, as distinct from **statute law**.

caseload *noun* the number of cases a doctor, lawyer, etc has to deal with at any particular time.

casement *or* **casement window** *noun* a window with vertical hinges that opens outwards like a door. [16c: from Latin *cassimentum*]

casework *noun* social work concerned with the close study of the background and environment of individuals and families.

cash *noun* **1** coins or paper money, as distinct from cheques, credit cards, etc. **2** *informal* money in any form. ▸ *verb* to obtain or give cash in return for (a cheque, traveller's cheque, postal order, etc). [16c: from French *casse* box]

PHRASAL VERBS **cash in on sth** *informal* to make money by exploiting a situation, etc.

cash-and-carry *noun* (*-ies*) a large, often wholesale, shop where customers pay for goods in cash and take them away immediately.

cashback *noun* **1** a facility offered by some retailers whereby a person paying for goods by debit card may also withdraw cash. **2** a sum of money offered as an incentive to someone entering into a financial agreement, eg a mortgage.

cash book *noun* a written record of all money paid out and received by a business, etc.

cash crop *noun* a crop that is grown for sale rather than for consumption by the farmer's household or by livestock.

cash desk *noun* a desk in a shop, etc at which one pays for goods.

cashew *noun* (*also* **cashew nut**) the curved edible seed of a small evergreen tree. [17c: from Portuguese *cajú*]

cash flow *noun* the amount of money coming into and going out of a business, etc.

cashier[1] *noun* in a business firm, bank, etc: any person who receives, pays out and generally deals with the cash. [16c: from French *caissier* treasurer]

cashier[2] *verb* to dismiss (an officer) from the armed forces in disgrace. [16c: from Dutch *kasseren*]

cash machine *or* **cash dispenser** *noun* an electronic machine, often in the outside wall of a bank, from which one can obtain cash using a cash card. Also called **ATM**, **hole-in-the-wall**.

cashmere *noun* **1** a type of very fine soft wool from a longhaired Asian goat. **2** a fabric made from this. [19c: named after Kashmir in N India]

cash point *noun* **1** the place in a shop, etc where money is taken for goods purchased. **2** a **cash machine**.

cash register *noun* a machine in a shop, etc that calculates and records the amount of each sale and from which change and a receipt are usu given.

casing *noun* a protective covering.

casino *noun* a public building or room for gambling. [18c: Italian diminutive of *casa* house]

cask *noun* a barrel for holding liquids, esp alcoholic liquids. [15c: from French *casque*]

casket *noun* **1** a small case for holding jewels, etc. **2** *N Am* a coffin. [15c: perhaps from French *cassette*, diminutive of *cassa* box]

cassava *noun* **1** a shrubby plant cultivated throughout the tropics for its fleshy tuberous edible roots. Also called **manioc**. **2** a starchy substance obtained from the root of this plant. [16c: from Spanish *cazabe*]

casserole *noun* **1** an ovenproof dish with a lid, in which meat, vegetables, etc can be cooked and served. **2** the food cooked and served in this kind of dish. ▸ *verb* to cook in a casserole. [18c: French]

cassette *noun* **1** a small plastic case containing a long narrow ribbon of magnetic tape wound around two reels, that can be inserted into an audio or video tape recorder. **2** a small lightproof plastic cartridge containing photographic film for loading into a camera. [18c: French, diminutive of *casse* box]

cassette recorder *or* **cassette player** *noun* a machine that records or plays material on audio cassette.

cassock *noun* a long black or red garment worn in church by clergymen and male members of a church choir. [17c: from French *casaque* type of coat]

cast *verb* (*past tense & past participle* ***cast***) **1** to throw. **2** to direct (one's eyes, a glance, etc) on or over something. **3** to throw off or shed something: *She cast her clothes in a heap.* **4** to project; to cause to appear: *cast a shadow.* **5** *tr & intr* to throw (a fishing line) out into the water. **6** to let down (an anchor). **7** (*usu* **cast sth off, aside** *or* **out**) to throw it off or away; to get rid of it. **8** to give (an actor) a part in a play or film; to distribute the parts in a film, play, etc. **9** to shape (molten metal, plastic, etc) by pouring it into a mould and allowing it to set. **10** to give or record (one's vote). ▸ *noun* **1** a throw; an act of throwing (eg dice, a fishing line). **2** an object shaped by pouring metal, plastic, etc, into a mould and allowing it to set. **3** (*also* **plaster cast**) a rigid casing, usu of plaster of Paris, moulded round a broken limb or other body part while the plaster is still wet, and then allowed to set in order to hold the broken bone in place while it heals. **4** the set of actors or performers in a play, opera, etc. **5** *formal* type, form, shape or appearance. **6** a slight tinge; a faint colour. [13c: from Norse *kasta* to throw]

PHRASAL VERBS **cast about** *or* **around for sth 1** to look about for it. **2** to try to think of it: *cast about for ideas.* **cast off 1** to untie a boat ready to sail away. **2** to finish off and remove knitting from the needles. See also **cast-off**. **cast on** to form (stitches or knitting) by looping and securing wool, etc over the needles.

castanets *plural noun* a musical instrument used by Spanish dancers, consisting of two hollow pieces of wood or plastic attached to each other by string, which are held in the palm and struck together rhythmically. [17c: from Spanish *castañeta*]

castaway *noun* someone who has been shipwrecked.

caste *noun* **1 a** any of the four hereditary social classes into which Hindu society is divided; **b** this system of social class division. **2** any system of social division based on inherited rank or wealth. [17c: from Latin *castus* pure]

castellated *adj* of a building: having turrets and battlements like those of a castle. [17c: from Latin *castellare*]

caster see **castor**

caster sugar *noun* finely crushed white sugar used in baking, etc.

castigate *verb* to criticize or punish severely. ▪ **castigation** *noun*. [17c: from Latin *castigare* to chastise]

casting *noun* an object formed by pouring molten material into a mould and allowing it to cool and solidify.

casting vote *noun* the deciding vote, used by a chairperson when the votes taken at a meeting, etc are equally divided.

cast iron *noun* any of a group of hard heavy alloys of iron, containing more carbon than steels, and cast into a specific shape when molten. ▸ *adj* (**cast-iron**) **1** made of cast iron. **2** of a rule or decision: firm; not to be altered.

castle *noun* **1** a large, fortified building with battlements and towers. **2** a large mansion. **3** *chess* a piece that can be moved any number of empty squares forwards or backwards, but not diagonally. Also called **rook**. [11c: from Latin *castellum* fort or fortress]

cast-off *noun* something, esp a garment, discarded or no longer wanted. See also **cast off** at **cast**. ▸ *adj* no longer needed; discarded.

castor *or* **caster** *noun* a small swivelling wheel fitted to the legs or underside of a piece of furniture so that it can be moved easily.

castor oil *noun* a yellow or brown non-drying oil obtained from the seeds of a tropical African plant, used as a lubricant and formerly as a laxative.

castrate *verb* **1** to remove the testicles of a male person or animal. **2** to deprive of vigour or strength. ▪ **castrated** *adj*. ▪ **castration** *noun*. [17c: from Latin *castrare*]

castrato *noun* (***castrati*** *or* ***castratos***) in 17c and 18c opera: a male singer castrated before puberty to preserve his soprano or contralto voice. [18c: Italian]

casual *adj* **1** happening by chance. **2** careless; showing no particular interest or concern. **3** without serious intention or commitment. **4** of clothes: informal. ▸ *noun* **1** an occasional worker. **2** (*usu* **casuals**) clothes suitable for informal wear. ▪ **casually** *adv.* ▪ **casualness** *noun.* [14c: from French *casuel*]

casualty *noun* (*-ies*) **1** someone killed or hurt in an accident or war. **2** the casualty department of a hospital. **3** something that is lost, destroyed, sacrificed, etc as a result of some event.

casuist *noun* someone who uses cleverly misleading arguments, esp to make things that are morally wrong seem acceptable. ▪ **casuistic** *adj.* ▪ **casuistry** *noun.* [17c: from French *casuiste*]

CAT *abbrev* **1** computer-aided training. **2** a **CT scanner.**

cat *noun* **1** any of a wide range of wild carnivorous mammals, including the lion, leopard and tiger, as well as the domestic cat. **2** the domestic cat. See also **feline. 3 cat-o'-nine-tails.** [Anglo-Saxon *catte*]
IDIOMS **let the cat out of the bag** *informal* to give away a secret unintentionally. **put** *or* **set the cat among the pigeons** to cause trouble or upset.

catabolism *noun, biochem* the metabolic process whereby complex organic compounds in living organisms are broken down into simple molecules. [19c: from Greek *katabole* throwing down]

cataclysm *noun* **1** an event, esp a political or social one, causing tremendous change or upheaval. **2** a terrible flood or other disaster. ▪ **cataclysmic** *adj.* [17c: from Greek *kataklysmos* flood]

catacomb /ˈkatəkuːm, ˈkatəkoʊm/ *noun* (*usu* **catacombs**) an underground burial place, esp one consisting of a system of tunnels with recesses dug out for the tombs. [Anglo-Saxon *catacumbe*]

catafalque /ˈkatəfalk/ *noun* a temporary platform on which the body of an important person lies in state, before or during the funeral. [17c: French]

Catalan *adj* belonging or relating to Catalonia, an autonomous region of NE Spain, its inhabitants, or their language. ▶ *noun* **1** a citizen or inhabitant of, or person born in, Catalonia. **2** the official language of Catalonia.

catalepsy *noun* (*-ies*) a trance-like state characterized by the abnormal maintenance of rigid body postures. ▪ **cataleptic** *adj, noun.* [14c: from Latin *catalepsia*]

catalogue *noun* **1** a list of items arranged in a systematic order, esp alphabetically. **2** a brochure, booklet, etc containing a list of goods for sale. **3** a list or index of all the books in a library. ▶ *verb* (***cataloguing***) **1** to make a catalogue of (a library, books, etc). **2** to enter (an item) in a catalogue. **3** to list or mention one by one: *He catalogued her virtues.* ▪ **cataloguer** *noun.* [15c: French]

catalyse *or* (*US*) **-lyze** *verb, chem* of a **catalyst**: to alter the rate of (a chemical reaction) without itself undergoing any permanent chemical change.

catalysis *noun* (***catalyses***) *chem* the process effected by a catalyst. ▪ **catalytic** /katəˈlɪtɪk/ *adj.* [19c: from Greek *katalysis* breaking up]

catalyst *noun* **1** *chem* any substance that accelerates a chemical reaction. **2** something or someone that speeds up the pace of something, or causes change.

catalytic converter *noun* a device fitted to the exhaust system of a motor vehicle that is designed to reduce toxic and polluting emissions from the engine.

catalytic cracking *noun* in the petrochemical industry: the process by which heavier oils produced during petroleum refining are broken down into lighter, more useful products, using a catalyst.

catamaran *noun* a sailing-boat with two hulls parallel to each other. [17c: from Tamil *kattumaram* tied wood]

catapult *noun* **1** a Y-shaped stick with an elastic or rubber band fitted between its prongs, used esp by children for firing stones, etc. **2** *hist* a weapon of war designed to fire boulders. ▶ *verb* **1** to fire or send flying with, or as if with, a catapult. **2** *intr* to be sent flying as if from a catapult. [16c: from Greek *katapeltes*]

cataract *noun* **1** *pathol* an opaque area within the lens of the eye that produces blurring of vision. **2** an immense rush of water, eg from a large waterfall that consists of a single vertical drop. [16c: from Greek *kataractes* waterfall]

catarrh /kəˈtɑː(r)/ *noun* inflammation of the mucous membranes lining the nose and throat, causing an excessive discharge of thick mucus. [16c: from French *catarrhe*]

catastrophe /kəˈtastrəfɪ/ *noun* a terrible blow, calamity or disaster. ▪ **catastrophic** /katəˈstrɒfɪk/ *adj.* ▪ **catastrophically** *adv.* [16c: Greek]

catatonia *noun, pathol* an abnormal mental state characterized either by stupor or by excessive excitement and violent activity. ▪ **catatonic** *adj, noun.* [19c: from Greek *kata* down + *tonos* tension]

cat burglar *noun* a burglar who breaks into buildings by climbing walls, water pipes, etc.

catcall *noun* a long shrill whistle expressing disagreement or disapproval.

catch *verb* (*past tense, past participle* ***caught***) **1** to stop (a moving object) and hold it. **2** to manage to get hold of or trap, esp after a hunt or chase. **3** to be in time to get, reach, see, etc something: *catch the last post.* **4** to overtake or draw level with someone or something. **5** to discover someone or something in time to prevent, or encourage, the development of something: *The disease can be cured if caught early.* **6** to surprise someone doing something wrong or embarrassing. **7** to trick or trap. **8** to become infected with (a disease, etc). **9** *tr & intr* to become or cause to become accidentally attached or held: *My dress caught on a nail.* **10** to manage to hear, see or understand something: *I didn't quite catch your third point.* **11** *cricket* to put (a batsman) out by gathering the ball he has struck before it touches the ground. ▶ *noun* **1** an act of catching. **2** a small device for keeping a lid, door, etc closed. **3** something caught. **4** the total amount of eg fish caught. **5** a hidden problem or disadvantage; a snag. **6** someone or something that it would be advantageous to get hold of, eg a certain person as a husband or wife. **7** a children's game of throwing and catching a ball. [13c: from French *cachier*]
IDIOMS **catch fire** to start burning. **catch sight of** *or* **catch a glimpse of sb** *or* **sth** to see them only for a brief moment.
PHRASAL VERBS **catch on** *informal* **1** to become popular. **2** (*sometimes* **catch on to sth**) to understand it. **catch sb out 1** to trick them into making a mistake. **2** to discover them or take them unawares in embarrassing circumstances. **catch up 1** (*often* **catch up with sb**) to draw level with someone ahead. **2** (*sometimes* **catch up on sth**) to bring oneself up to date with one's work, the latest news, etc. **3** to immerse or occupy: *caught up in her studies.*

catching *adj* **1** infectious. **2** captivating.

catchment *noun* **1** the area of land that is drained by a particular river system or lake. **2** the population within the catchment area of a school, hospital, etc.

catchment area *noun* **1** the area served by a particular school, hospital, etc, encompassing those people who are expected to make use of the facilities within it. **2** (*also* **drainage basin**) *geog* the area of land whose rainfall feeds a particular river, lake or reservoir.

catchpenny *adj* of a product: poor in quality but designed to appeal to the eye and sell quickly.

catch phrase *noun* a well-known phrase or slogan, esp one associated with a particular celebrity.

catch-22 *noun* a situation in which one is frustrated and from which one cannot escape, since all possible courses of action either have undesirable consequences or lead inevitably to further frustration of one's aims. [20c: named after the novel by Joseph Heller]

catchword *noun* a much-repeated well-known word or phrase.

catchy *adj* (*-ier, -iest*) of a song, etc: tuneful and easily remembered.

catechism *noun* a series of questions and answers about the Christian religion, or a book containing this, used for instruction. ▪ **catechist** *noun*. [16c: from Latin *catechismus*]

catechize *or* **-ise** *verb* **1** to instruct someone in the ways of the Christian faith, esp by means of a catechism. **2** to question someone thoroughly. [15c: from Greek *katechizein*]

categorical *or* **categoric** *adj* **1** of a statement, refusal, denial, etc: absolute or definite. **2** relating or belonging to a category. ▪ **categorically** *adv*.

categorize *or* **-ise** *verb* to put something into a category or categories. ▪ **categorization** *noun*.

category *noun* (*-ies*) a group of things, people or concepts classed together because of some quality or qualities they have in common. [16c: from Latin *categoria*]

catena *noun* **1** a chain or connected series. **2** (*in full* **soil catena**) *geog* the differences in the moisture, acidity, etc of soil along a slope. [17c in sense 1, 20c in sense 2; from Latin *catena* chain]

cater *verb*

PHRASAL VERBS **cater for sb** *or* **sth 1** to supply food, accommodation or entertainment for them or it. **2** to make provision for them or it; to take them or it into account. **cater to sth** to indulge or pander to (unworthy desires, etc). [17c: from French *acater* to buy]

caterer *noun* a person whose professional occupation is to provide food, etc for social occasions.

catering *noun* **1** the provision of food, etc. **2** the activity or job of a caterer.

caterpillar *noun* **1** the larva of a butterfly or moth. **2** (*usu* **Caterpillar**) *trademark* **a** a continuous band or track made up of metal plates driven by cogs, used instead of wheels on heavy vehicles for travelling over rough surfaces; **b** a vehicle fitted with such tracks. [15c: prob from French *chatepelose* hairy cat]

caterwaul *verb, intr* **1** of a cat: to make a loud high wailing noise. **2** to wail or shriek in this way. ▸ *noun* a loud high wail. [14c: imitating the sound]

catfish *noun* a freshwater fish with long whisker-like sensory barbels around the mouth.

catflap *noun* a small door or flap set into a door to allow a cat exit and entry.

catgut *noun* a strong cord made from the dried intestines of sheep and other animals, used in surgery for making stitches, and also used for stringing violins, etc.

catharsis /kə'θɑːsɪs/ *noun* (*-ses* /-siːz/) **1** the emotional relief that results either from allowing repressed thoughts and feelings to surface, as in psychoanalysis, or from an intensely dramatic experience. **2** *med* the process of clearing out or purging the bowels. [19c: Latin]

cathartic *adj* (*also* **cathartical**) **1** resulting in catharsis. **2** cleansing; purgative. ▸ *noun, med* a purgative drug or medicine.

cathedral *noun* the principal church of a **diocese**, in which the bishop has his throne. [13c: from Greek *kathedra* seat]

catheter *noun, med* a hollow slender flexible tube that can be introduced into a narrow opening or body cavity, usu in order to drain a liquid, esp urine. [17c: Latin]

cathode *noun* **1** in an electrolytic cell: the negative electrode, towards which positively charged ions, usu in solution, are attracted. **2** the positive terminal of a battery. Compare **anode**. [19c: from Greek *kathodos* descent]

cathode rays *plural noun* a stream of electrons emitted from the surface of a cathode in a vacuum tube.

cathode-ray tube *noun* (abbrev **CRT**) an evacuated glass tube in which streams of **cathode rays** are produced, used to display images in television sets, visual display units, etc.

catholic *adj* **1** (**Catholic**) relating or belonging to the Roman Catholic Church. **2** esp of a person's interests and tastes: broad; wide-ranging. ▸ *noun* (**Catholic**) a member of the Roman Catholic Church. [14c: from Greek *katholikos* universal]

Catholicism *noun* **1** the faith, dogma, etc of any Catholic Church. **2** short for **Roman Catholicism** (see under **Roman Catholic**).

cation /'katɪaɪən/ *noun, chem* any positively charged ion, which moves towards the **cathode** during **electrolysis**. Compare **anion**. [19c: from Greek *katienai* to go down]

catkin *noun, botany* in certain tree species, eg birch, hazel: a flowering shoot that bears many small unisexual flowers, adapted for wind pollination. [16c: from Dutch *kateken* kitten]

catmint *or* **catnip** *noun, botany* a plant with oval toothed leaves and spikes of white two-lipped flowers spotted with purple. [13c: so called because its strong scent is attractive to cats]

catnap *noun* a short sleep. ▸ *verb, intr* to doze; to sleep briefly, esp without lying down.

cat-o'-nine-tails *noun* (*pl* ***cat-o'-nine-tails***) *hist* a whip with nine knotted rope lashes. Often shortened to **cat**.

CAT scanner *abbrev, med* a **CT scanner**.

Cat's-eye *noun, trademark* a small glass reflecting device, one of a series set into the surface along the centre and sides of a road to guide drivers in the dark.

cat's paw *noun* a person used by someone else to perform an unpleasant job.

catsuit *noun* a close-fitting one-piece garment, combining trousers and top, usu worn by women.

catsup another spelling of **ketchup**

cattery *noun* (***-ies***) a place where cats are bred or looked after in their owner's absence.

cattle *plural noun* large heavily built grass-eating mammals, including wild species and the domestic varieties which are farmed for their milk, meat and hides. [13c: from French *chatel*]

cattle grid *noun* a grid of parallel metal bars that covers a trench in a road where it passes through a fence, designed to allow pedestrians and wheeled vehicles to pass while preventing the passage of animal livestock.

catty *adj* (***-ier, -iest***) *informal* malicious; spiteful. ▪ **cattily** *adv.* ▪ **cattiness** *noun.*

catwalk *noun* the narrow raised stage along which models walk at a fashion show.

Caucasian *adj* **1** relating to the Caucasus, a mountain range between the Black Sea and the Caspian Sea. **2** belonging to one of the light- or white-skinned races of mankind. ▸ *noun* **1** an inhabitant or native of the Caucasus. **2 a** a member of the Caucasian race; **b** *loosely* a white-skinned person.

caucus *noun* **1** a small dominant group of people taking independent decisions within a larger organization. **2** *US* a group of members of a political party, or a meeting of such a group for some purpose. [18c]

caudal *adj, anatomy* **1** relating to, resembling, or in the position of a tail. **2** relating to the tail end of the body. [17c: from Latin *caudalis*]

Caught *past tense, past participle of* **catch**

caul *noun, anatomy* a membrane that sometimes surrounds an infant's head at birth. [14c: from French *cale* little cap]

Caught *past tense, past participle of* ***catch***

cauldron *noun* a very large metal pot, often with handles, for boiling or heating liquids. [13c: from French *cauderon*]

cauliflower *noun* the firm head of a type of cabbage, made up of white florets and eaten as a vegetable. [16c: from Latin *cauliflora*]

cauliflower ear *noun* an ear permanently swollen and misshapen by injury, esp from repeated blows.

caulk *verb* to fill up (seams or cracks) with **oakum**. [15c: from French *cauquer* to press with force]

causal *adj* **1** relating to or being a cause. **2** relating to cause and effect. ▪ **causally** *adv.* [16c: from Latin *causa* cause]

causality *noun* (***-ies***) **1** the relationship between cause and effect. **2** (*also* **causation**) the principle that everything has a cause.

causative *adj* **1** making something happen; producing an effect. **2** *grammar* expressing the action of causing. [15c: from Latin *causativus*]

cause *noun* **1** something which produces an effect; the person or thing through which something happens. **2** a reason or justification: *no cause for concern.* **3** an ideal, principle, aim, etc, that people support and work for. ▸ *verb* to produce as an effect; to bring about something. [13c: from Latin *causa*]

cause célèbre /kouz sə'lɛb, kɔːz sɛ'lɛbrə/ *noun* (***causes célèbres*** /kouz sə'lɛb, kɔːz sɛ'lɛbrə/) a legal case, or some other matter, that attracts much attention and causes controversy. [18c: French, meaning 'famous case']

causeway *noun* **1** a raised roadway crossing low-lying marshy ground or shallow water. **2** a stone-paved pathway. [15c: from French *caucie*]

caustic *adj* **1** *chem* of a chemical substance, eg sodium hydroxide: strongly alkaline and corrosive to living tissue. **2** of remarks, etc: sarcastic; cutting; bitter. ▸ *noun* a caustic substance. ▪ **caustically** *adv.* [14c: from Latin *causticus*]

caustic lime see **slaked lime**

caustic soda see **sodium hydroxide**

cauterize *or* **-ise** *verb* to destroy (living tissue) by the direct application of a heated instrument or a caustic chemical. ▪ **cauterization** *noun.* [14c: from Latin *cauterizare*]

caution *noun* **1** care in avoiding danger; prudent wariness. **2** a warning. **3** a formal reprimand for an offence, accompanied by a warning not to repeat it. ▸ *verb* **1** *tr & intr* to warn or admonish someone. **2** to give someone a legal caution. ▪ **cautionary** *adj.* [17c: French]

cautious *adj* having or showing caution; careful; wary. ▪ **cautiously** *adv.* ▪ **cautiousness** *noun.*

Cava /'kava/ *noun* a white sparkling wine, similar to champagne, produced mainly in NE Spain. [20c: Spanish *cava* cellar]

cavalcade *noun* **1** a ceremonial procession of cars, horseback riders, etc. **2** any procession or parade. [17c: from Latin *caballicare* to ride on horseback]

cavalier *noun* **1** a courtly gentleman. **2** (**Cavalier**) *hist* a supporter of Charles I during the 17c English Civil War. ▸ *adj, derog* of a person's behaviour, attitude, etc: thoughtless, offhand, casual or disrespectful. [16c: from Italian *cavaliere*]

cavalry *noun* (***-ies***) **1** *usu hist* the part of an army consisting of soldiers on horseback. **2** the part of an army consisting of soldiers in armoured vehicles. Compare **infantry**. ▪ **cavalryman** *noun.* [16c: from French *cavallerie*]

cave *noun* a large natural hollow chamber either underground or in the side of a mountain, hillside or cliff. [13c: from Latin *cavus* hollow]

PHRASAL VERBS **cave in 1** of walls, a roof, etc: to collapse inwards. **2** *informal* of a person: to give way to persuasion.

caveat *noun* **1** a warning. **2** *law* an official request that a court should not take some particular action without warning the person who is making the request. [16c: Latin, meaning 'let him or her beware']

cave-in *noun* **1** a collapse. **2** a submission or surrender.

caveman *noun* **1** (*also* **cave-dweller**) a person of prehistoric times, who lived in caves, etc. **2** *derog* a man who behaves in a crude, brutish way.

cavern *noun* a large cave or an underground chamber. [14c: from French *caverne*]

cavernous *adj* of a hole or space: deep and vast.

caviar *or* **caviare** *noun* the salted hard roe of the sturgeon, used as food and considered a delicacy. [16c: perhaps from Turkish *havyar*]

cavil *verb* (***cavilled, cavilling***) *intr* (*usu* **cavil at** *or* **about sth**) to make trivial objections to something. ▸ *noun* a trivial objection. [16c: from Latin *cavillari* to scoff]

caving *noun* the sport of exploring caves.

cavitation *noun* **1** the formation of cavities in a structure. **2** *physics* the formation of gas bubbles in a liquid.

cavity *noun* (**-*ies***) **1** a hollow or hole. **2** a hole in a tooth, caused by decay. [16c: from French *cavité*]

cavort *verb, intr* to jump or caper about.

caw *noun* the loud harsh cry of a crow or rook. ▸ *verb, intr* to make such a cry. [16c: imitating the sound]

cay see **key**^{2}

cayenne /keɪ'ɛn/ *or* **cayenne pepper** *noun* a hot spice made from the seeds of various types of **capsicum**. [18c as *cayan*, from Tupí (a S American native language), but popularly associated with Cayenne in French Guiana]

cayman *or* **caiman** *noun* a S American reptile closely related to the alligator. [16c: from Spanish *caimán*]

CBE *abbrev* Commander of the Order of the British Empire.

cc *abbrev* **1** carbon copy, used to mark a copy of a message sent to people other than the main recipient. **2** cubic centimetre.

CCTV *abbrev* closed-circuit television.

CD *abbrev* compact disc.

Cd *symbol, chem* cadmium.

cd *abbrev* candela.

CD-i *or* **CDI** *abbrev* compact disc interactive, a type of CD-ROM that responds intelligently to instructions given by the user. Also written **ICD**.

CD-R *abbrev* compact disc recordable.

CD-ROM *abbrev, comput* compact disc read-only memory, a compact disc allowing examination, but not alteration, of text.

CD-RW *abbrev* compact disc rewritable.

CE *or* **C.E.** *abbrev* **1** Church of England. **2** Common Era.

Ce *symbol, chem* cerium.

cease *verb, tr & intr* to bring or come to an end. [14c: from French *cesser*]

ceasefire *noun* **1** a break in the fighting during a war, agreed to by all sides. **2** the order to stop firing.

ceaseless *adj* continuous; going on without a pause or break. ▪ **ceaselessly** *adv.*

cecal *and* **cecum** see **caecum**

cedar *noun* **1** a tall coniferous tree with widely spreading branches, cones, needle-like leaves and reddish-brown bark. **2** (*also* **cedarwood**) the hard yellow sweet-smelling wood of this tree. ▸ *adj* made of cedar. [11c: from French *cedre*]

cede *verb* to hand over or give up something formally. [17c: from Latin *cedere* to yield]

cedilla /sə'dɪlə/ *noun* **1** in French and Portuguese: a **diacritic** put under *c* in some words, eg *façade*, to show that it is to be pronounced like *s*, not like *k*. **2** the same mark used under other letters in other languages to indicate various sounds. [16c: Spanish, meaning 'little z']

ceilidh /'keɪlɪ/ *noun* in Scotland and Ireland: an informal social gathering, with traditional music and dancing. [19c: Scottish Gaelic, meaning 'a visit']

ceiling *noun* **1** the inner roof of a room, etc. **2** an upper limit.

---

ceiling

This word is often misspelt. The letter *e* comes before the letter *i*. It might help you to remember the following sentence:

*The **ceiling** covers **e**verything **i**nside.*

---

celandine *noun* a plant with heart-shaped dark-green leaves, and flowers with glossy golden-yellow petals. [13c: from Greek *chelidon* swallow, as the flowering of the plant was supposed to coincide with the arrival of the swallows in spring]

celebrant *noun* someone who performs a religious ceremony.

celebrate *verb* **1** to mark (an occasion, esp a birthday or anniversary) with festivities. **2** *intr* to do something enjoyable to mark a happy occasion, anniversary, etc. **3** to give public praise or recognition to someone or something, eg in the form of a poem. **4** to conduct (a religious ceremony, eg a marriage or mass). ▪ **celebration** *noun.* ▪ **celebratory** *adj.* [15c: from Latin *celebrare* to honour]

celebrated *adj* famous; renowned.

celebrity *noun* (**-*ies***) **1** a famous person. **2** fame or renown. [17c: from Latin *celebritas* fame]

celeriac /sə'lɛrɪak/ *noun* **1** a variety of celery, widely cultivated for the swollen edible base of its stem. **2** the swollen base of the stem of this plant, which is eaten raw in salads or cooked as a vegetable.

celerity /sə'lɛrɪtɪ/ *noun, formal* quickness; rapidity of motion or thought. [15c: from Latin *celeritas*]

celery *noun* (**-*ies***) a plant with segmented leaves, and deeply grooved swollen leaf stalks that can be eaten raw or cooked as a vegetable. [17c: from French *céleri*]

celestial *adj* **1** belonging or relating to the sky: *celestial bodies.* **2** heavenly; divine: *celestial voices.* ▪ **celestially** *adv.* [14c: from Latin *celestialis*]

celiac see **coeliac**

celibate *adj* **1** unmarried, esp in obedience to a religious vow. **2** having no sexual relations with anyone. ▸ *noun* someone who is unmarried, esp because of a religious vow. ▪ **celibacy** *noun.* [17c: from Latin *caelebs* unmarried]

cell *noun* **1** a small room occupied by an inmate in a prison or monastery. **2** *biol* the basic structural unit of all living organisms, consisting of a mass of protein material which is composed of the **cytoplasm** and usu a **nucleus** (sense 2). **3** *elec* a device consisting of two **electrode**s immersed in an **electrolyte**, for converting electrical energy into chemical energy. **4** one of the compartments in a honeycomb or in a similarly divided structure. **5** *comput* a unit or area of storage, eg the smallest unit capable of storing a single bit. **6** *comput* a location on a computerized spreadsheet. [12c: from Latin *cella* room or small apartment]

cellar *noun* **1** a room, usu underground, for storage, eg of wine. **2** a stock of wines. ▸ *verb* to store in a cellar. [13c: from French *celer*]

cell membrane see **membrane** (sense 2)

cello *noun* a large stringed musical instrument of the violin family, which is played held between the knees of a seated player. ▪ **cellist** *noun.* [19c: short for **violoncello**]

Cellophane *noun, trademark* a thin transparent sheeting manufactured from regenerated **cellulose**, used mainly as a wrapping material. [20c: from **cellulose** + Greek *phainein* to shine or appear]

cellphone *noun, radio* a portable telephone for use in a cellular radio system.

cellular *adj* **1** composed of cells or divided into cell-like compartments. **2** containing many cavities or holes; porous. **3** knitted with an open pattern. **4** relating to cellular radio. [18c: from Latin *cellularis*]

cellular radio *noun* a system of radio communication used esp for mobile phones, based on a network of small geographical areas called cells, each of which is served by a transmitter.

cellulite *noun* deposits of fat cells said to be resistant to changes in diet or exercise regime, and which give the skin a dimpled, pitted appearance. [1960s: French]

Celluloid *noun, trademark* **1** a transparent highly flammable plastic material made from cellulose nitrate and **camphor**. **2** cinema film.

cellulose *noun* a complex carbohydrate that is the main constituent of plant cell walls, and is used in the manufacture of paper, rope, textiles and plastics.

cell wall *noun* the outermost layer of cells in plants, bacteria, etc.

Celsius *adj* (abbrev **C**) relating to the Celsius scale.

Celsius scale *noun* a scale of temperature in which the freezing point of water is 0°C and its boiling point is 100°C. [18c: named after Anders Celsius, the Swedish inventor of the centigrade thermometer]

Celt *or* **Kelt** *noun* **1** a member of one of the ancient peoples that inhabited most parts of Europe in pre-Roman and Roman times, or of the peoples descended from them, eg in Scotland, Wales and Ireland. **2** someone who speaks a Celtic language. [17c: from Latin *Celtae*]

Celtic *or* **Keltic** *adj* relating to the Celts or their languages. ▸ *noun* a branch of the Indo-European family of languages, including Gaelic, Welsh, and Breton.

cement *noun* **1** a fine powder, composed of a mixture of clay and limestone, that hardens when mixed with water, and is used to make mortar and concrete. **2** any of various substances used as adhesives for bonding to a hard material. **3** *dentistry* any of various substances used to fill cavities in teeth. ▸ *verb* **1** to stick together with cement. **2** to apply cement to. **3** to bind or make firm (eg a friendship). [13c: from French *ciment*]

cemetery *noun* (**-*ies***) a burial ground. [14c: from Latin *cemeterium*]

cemetery

This word is often misspelt. It has an e in the middle and ends in *ery*. It might help you to remember that the word ce**metery** contains the word **meter**.

cenotaph *noun* a tomb-like monument in honour of a person or persons buried elsewhere, esp soldiers killed in war. [17c: from French *cenotaphe*]

Cenozoic *or* **Caenozoic** /siːnoʊˈzoʊɪk/ *or* **Cainozoic** /kaɪnoʊˈzoʊɪk/ *geol, adj* denoting the most recent era of the Phanerozoic eon. ▸ *noun* (**the Cenozoic**) the Cenozoic era. [19c: from Greek *kainos* new + *zoe* life]

censer *noun* a container in which incense is burnt, used eg in some churches. Also called **thurible**. [13c: from French *censier*]

censor *noun* an official who examines books, films, newspaper articles, etc, with the power to cut out any parts thought politically sensitive or offensive, and to forbid publication or showing altogether. ▸ *verb* **1** to alter or cut out parts of something, or forbid its publication, showing or delivery. **2** to act as a censor. [16c: Latin, from *censere* to estimate or assess]

censorious *adj* inclined to find fault; severely critical. [16c: from Latin *censorius* relating to a censor]

censorship *noun* **1** the practice of censoring. **2** the job of a censor.

censure *noun* severe criticism or disapproval. ▸ *verb* to criticize severely or express strong disapproval of someone or something. [17c: from Latin *censura*]

census *noun* an official count of a population, carried out at periodic intervals, which covers information such as sex, age, job, etc. [17c: from Latin *censere* to estimate or assess]

cent *noun* **1** a currency unit of several countries, worth one hundredth of the standard unit, eg of the US dollar. **2** a unit of currency of most countries of the European Union, worth one hundredth of a **euro**. [16c: from Latin *centum* a hundred]

centaur *noun, Greek myth* a creature with a man's head, arms and trunk, joined to the body and legs of a horse. [14c: from Latin *centaurus*]

centenarian *noun* someone who is 100 years old or more. ▸ *adj* **1** 100 years old or more. **2** relating to a centenarian.

centenary *noun* (**-*ies***) the one-hundredth anniversary of some event, or the celebration of it. ▸ *adj* **1** occurring every 100 years. **2** relating to a period of 100 years. [17c: from Latin *centenarius* composed of one hundred]

centennial *noun, N Am* a centenary. ▸ *adj* **1** relating to a period of 100 years. **2** occurring every 100 years. **3** lasting 100 years. [18c: from Latin *centum* 100 + *annus* year, modelled on **biennial**]

center the *US* spelling of **centre**.

centi- *or* (*before a vowel*) **cent-** *combining form* (abbrev **c**) **1** one hundredth: *centigram* • *centilitre*. **2** one hundred: *centipede*. [From Latin *centum* hundred]

centigrade *adj, noun* (abbrev **C**) the former name for the **Celsius** scale of temperature.

centigram *or* **centigramme** /ˈsɛntɪgram/ *noun* (abbrev **cg**) a unit of measurement of mass, equal to one hundredth of a gram.

centilitre *or* (*US*) **centiliter** *noun* (abbrev **cl**) a unit of measurement of volume, equal to one hundredth of a litre.

centime /ˈsɒntiːm/ *noun* a currency unit of several countries, worth one hundredth of the standard unit, eg of the Swiss franc. [19c: French, from *centiesme*]

centimetre *or* (*US*) **centimeter** *noun* (abbrev **cm**) a unit of measurement of length, equal to one hundredth of a metre.

centipede *noun* any of numerous species of terrestrial arthropod which have a long rather flat segmented body and usu a pair of legs for each body segment. [17c: from Latin *centipeda*]

central *adj* **1** at or forming the centre of something. **2** near the centre of a city, etc; easy to reach. **3** principal or most important. ▪ **centrality** *noun*. ▪ **centrally** *adv*. [17c: from Latin *centralis*]

central bank *noun* a national bank acting as banker to the government, issuing currency, controlling the amount of credit in the country and having control over interest rates.

central government *noun* the government that has power over a whole country, as distinct from local government.

central heating *noun* a system for heating a whole building, by means of pipes, radiators, etc connected to a central source of heat.

centralism *noun* the policy of bringing the administration of a country under central control, with a decrease in local administrative power. ▪ **centralist** *noun, adj.*

centralize *or* **-ise** *verb, tr & intr* to bring under central control. ▪ **centralization** *noun.*

central locking *noun* in a motor vehicle: a system whereby all the doors are locked or unlocked automatically when the driver's door is locked or unlocked.

central nervous system *noun* in vertebrates: the part of the nervous system that is responsible for the co-ordination and control of the various body functions; it consists of the brain and spinal cord.

central processing unit *noun, comput* (abbrev **CPU**) the part of a computer that controls and co-ordinates the operation of all the other parts, and that performs arithmetical and logical operations on data. Also called **central processor**. See also **microprocessor**.

central reservation *noun, Brit* a narrow strip of grass, concrete, etc dividing the two sides of a dual carriageway or motorway.

centre *or* (*US*) **center** *noun* **1** a part at the middle of something. **2** a point inside a circle or sphere that is an equal distance from all points on the circumference or surface, or a point on a line at an equal distance from either end. **3** a point or axis round which a body revolves or rotates. **4** a central area. **5** *chiefly in compounds* a place where a specified activity is concentrated or specified facilities, information, etc are available: *a sports centre.* **6** something that acts as a focus: *the centre of attraction.* **7** a point or place from which activities are controlled: *the centre of operations.* **8** a position that is at neither extreme, esp in politics. **9** in some field sports, eg football: **a** a position in the middle of the field; **b** a player in this position. ▸ *adj* at the centre; central. ▸ *verb* **1** to place in or at the centre. **2** *tr & intr* (*often* **centre on** *or* **upon sth**) to concentrate on it. [14c: French]

centrefold *noun* the sheet that forms the two central facing pages of a magazine, etc.

centre of gravity *noun, physics* a theoretical point in an object about which its weight is evenly distributed.

centrepiece *noun* **1** a central or most important item. **2** an ornament or decoration for the centre of a table.

centrifugal /sɛntrɪ'fjuːgəl, sɛn'trɪfjʊgəl/ *adj, physics* acting or moving away from the centre of a circle along which an object is moving, or away from the axis of rotation. Compare **centripetal**. [18c: from Latin *centrum* + *fugere* to flee]

centrifugal force *noun* an apparent force that seems to exert an outward pull on an object that is moving in a circular path. Compare **centripetal force**.

centrifuge *noun* a device containing a rotating device that is used to separate solid or liquid particles of different densities. ▸ *verb* to subject something to centrifugal action. [19c: from Latin *centrum* + *fugere* to flee]

centripetal /sɛn'trɪpɪtəl, sɛntrɪ'piːtəl/ *adj, physics* acting or moving towards the centre of a circle along which an object is moving, or towards the axis of rotation. Compare **centrifugal**. [18c: from Latin *centrum* + *petere* to seek]

centripetal force *noun* the force that is required to keep an object moving in a circular path. Compare **centrifugal force**.

centrist *adj* having moderate, non-extreme political opinions. ▸ *noun* someone holding such opinions. ▪ **centrism** *noun.*

centurion *noun, hist* in the army of ancient Rome: an officer in charge of a **century** (*noun* sense 5). [14c: from Latin *centurio*]

century *noun* (**-ies**) **1** a period of 100 years. **2** any 100-year period counted forwards or backwards from an important event, esp the birth of Christ. **3** *cricket* a score of 100 runs made by a batsman in a single innings. **4** a score of 100. **5** *hist* in the army of ancient Rome: a company of (orig) 100 foot soldiers. [16c: from Latin *centuria* a division of 100 things]

cephalic /sɪ'falɪk/ *adj* relating to the head or the head region. [16c: from French *céphalique*]

cephalopod /'sɛfələpɒd/ *noun* any invertebrate animal with a head and many tentacles surrounding its mouth, eg squid, octopus, and cuttlefish.

ceramic *noun* **1** any of a number of hard brittle materials produced by moulding or shaping and then baking or firing clays at high temperatures. **2** an object made from such a material. ▸ *adj* relating to or made of such a material. [19c: from Greek *keramikos*]

ceramics *singular noun* the art and technique of making pottery.

cereal *noun* **1** a grass that is cultivated as a food crop for its nutritious edible seeds, ie grains, eg barley, wheat, rice, etc. **2** the grain produced. **3** a breakfast food prepared from this grain. ▸ *adj* relating to edible grains. [19c: from Latin *Cerealis* relating to Ceres, goddess of agriculture]

cerebellum /sɛrə'bɛləm/ *noun* (***cerebella*** /-lə/) *anatomy* in vertebrates: the main part of the hindbrain, concerned primarily with the co-ordination of movement. ▪ **cerebellar** *adj.* [16c: Latin diminutive of *cerebrum* brain]

cerebral /'sɛrəbrəl, sə'riːbrəl/ *adj* **1** relating to or in the region of the brain. **2** intellectual; using the brain rather than appealing to the emotions: *a cerebral argument.*

cerebral palsy *noun, pathol* a failure of the brain to develop normally in young children due to brain damage before or around the time of birth, resulting in weakness and lack of co-ordination of the limbs.

cerebrate *verb, intr, facetious* to think; to use one's brain. ▪ **cerebration** *noun.*

cerebrospinal *adj* relating to the brain and spinal cord together: *cerebrospinal fluid.*

cerebrum /'sɛrəbrəm, sə'riːbrəm/ *noun* (***cerebrums*** *or* ***cerebra*** /-brə/) *anatomy* in higher vertebrates: the larger part of the brain, situated at the front, which controls thinking, emotions and personality. [17c: Latin]

ceremonial *adj* relating to, used for or involving a ceremony. ▸ *noun* a system of rituals. ▪ **ceremonially** *adv.* [14c: from Latin *caerimonia* rite]

ceremonious *adj* excessively formal. ▪ **ceremoniously** *adv.* [16c: from Latin *caerimoniosus* full of ceremony]

ceremony *noun* (**-*ies***) **1** a ritual performed to mark a particular, esp public or religious, occasion. **2** formal politeness. [14c: from Latin *caerimonia* sacredness or rite]

IDIOMS **stand on ceremony** to insist on behaving formally.

cerise /sə'riːz, sə'riːs/ *noun* a bright cherry-red colour. ▸ *adj* cerise-coloured. [19c: French, meaning 'cherry']

cerium *noun, chem* (symbol **Ce**) a soft silvery-grey metallic element used in catalytic converters, alloys for cigarette-lighter flints, etc. [19c: named after the asteroid Ceres]

cert *noun, informal* (*usu* **dead cert**) a certainty, esp a horse that is bound to win a race.

cert. *abbrev* **1** certificate. **2** certified.

certain *adj* **1** proved or known beyond doubt. **2** (*sometimes* **certain about** *or* **of sth**) having no doubt about it; absolutely sure. **3** used with reference to the future: definitely going to happen, etc; able to rely on or be relied on. **4** particular and, though known, not named or specified: *a certain friend of yours.* **5** of a quality: undeniably present without being clearly definable: *The beard gave his face a certain authority.* **6** some, though not much: *That's true to a certain extent.* [13c: French]

IDIOMS **for certain** definitely; without doubt.

certainly *adv* **1** without any doubt. **2** definitely. **3** in giving permission: of course.

certainty *noun* (**-*ies***) **1** something that cannot be doubted or is bound to happen. **2** freedom from doubt; the state of being sure.

certifiable *adj* **1** capable of or suitable for being certified. **2** *informal* of a person: mad; crazy.

certificate /sə'tɪfɪkət/ *noun* an official document that formally acknowledges or witnesses a fact, an achievement or qualification, or one's condition: *marriage certificate.* ▸ *verb* /sə'tɪfɪkeɪt/ to provide with a certificate. See also **certify.** [15c: from Latin *certificare* to certify]

certificated *adj* qualified by a particular course of training.

certified *adj* **1** possessing a certificate. **2** endorsed or guaranteed. **3** of a person: insane.

certify *verb* (**-*ies*, -*ied***) **1** *tr & intr* to declare or confirm officially. **2** to declare someone legally insane. **3** to declare to have reached a required standard, passed certain tests, etc. See also **certificate**. [14c: from Latin *certificare*]

certitude *noun* a feeling of certainty. [15c: from Latin *certitudo*]

cervical *adj* relating to or in the region of the cervix.

cervine *adj* relating to or resembling a deer. [19c: from Latin *cervinus*]

cervix *noun, anatomy* (***cervixes*** *or* ***cervices*** /sɜː'vaɪsiːz/) **1** the neck of the uterus, consisting of a narrow passage leading to the inner end of the vagina. **2** the neck. [18c: Latin, meaning 'neck']

cesarean *or* **cesarian** the *US* spelling of **caesarean**

cesium the *N Am* spelling of **caesium**

cessation *noun* a stopping or ceasing; a pause. [14c: from Latin *cessatio*]

cession *noun* the giving up or yielding of territories, rights, etc to someone else. [15c: from Latin *cessio*]

cesspit *noun* **1** a pit for the collection and storage of sewage. **2** a foul and squalid place.

cesspool *noun* a tank, well, etc for the collection and storage of sewage and waste water.

cesura see **caesura**

cetacean /sɪ'teɪʃən/ *noun* any animal belonging to the order which includes dolphins, porpoises and whales. ▸ *adj* relating or belonging to this group. [19c: from Greek *ketos* whale]

cetane /'siːteɪn/ *noun* a colourless liquid hydrocarbon found in petroleum, used as a solvent. Also called **hexadecane.** [19c: from Latin *cetus* whale]

cetane number *noun* a measure of the ignition quality of diesel fuel when it is burnt in a standard diesel engine.

Cf *symbol, chem* californium.

cf *abbrev*: *confer* (Latin), compare.

CFC *abbrev* chlorofluorocarbon.

cg *abbrev* centigram.

CGI *abbrev* computer-generated imagery.

cgs unit *abbrev, physics* centimetre-gram-second unit, a system of measurement based on the use of the centimetre, gram and second as the fundamental units of length, mass and time, respectively, for most purposes now superseded by SI units.

ch *abbrev* **1** chapter. **2** church.

cha-cha *or* **cha-cha-cha** *noun* **1** a Latin American dance. **2** a piece of music for this dance. ▸ *verb, intr* to perform this dance. [1950s: American Spanish]

Chadic *adj* belonging or relating to a group of more than 100 languages spoken in parts of Ghana and the Central African Republic. ▸ *noun* this group of languages.

chador, **chadar** *or* **chuddar** /'tʃʌdə(r)/ *noun* a thick veil worn by some Muslim women that covers the head and body. [17c: Persian]

chafe *verb* **1** *tr & intr* to make or become sore or worn by rubbing. **2** *intr* (*also* **chafe at** *or* **under sth**) to become angry or impatient: *chafe at the rules.* [14c: from French *chaufer* to heat]

chafer *noun* any of various species of large slow-moving nocturnal beetle, found mainly in the tropics. [Anglo-Saxon *ceafor*]

chaff¹ *noun* **1** the husks that form the outer covering of cereal grain, and are separated from the seeds during threshing. **2** chopped hay or straw used as animal feed or bedding. **3** worthless material. [Anglo-Saxon *ceaf*]

chaff² *noun* light-hearted joking or teasing. ▸ *verb* to tease or make fun of someone in a good-natured way. [19c: prob from **chaff¹**]

chaffinch *noun* a finch with a blue crown, reddish body, stout bill and conspicuous white wing bars. [Anglo-Saxon *ceaffinc*]

chagrin *noun* acute annoyance or disappointment. ▸ *verb* to annoy or embarrass someone. [18c: French]

chain *noun* **1** a series of interconnecting links or rings, esp of metal, used for fastening, binding or holding, or, eg in jewellery, for ornament. **2** a series or progression: *a chain of events.* **3** a number of shops, hotels, etc under common ownership or management. **4** (**chains**) something that restricts or frustrates. **5** *chem* a number of atoms of the same type that are joined in a line to form a molecule. ▶ *verb* (*often* **chain sb** *or* **sth up** *or* **down**) to fasten, bind or restrict with, or as if with, chains. [13c: from French *chaeine*]

chain gang *noun* a group of prisoners chained together for working outside the prison.

chain letter *noun* a letter copied to a large number of people, esp with a request for and promise of something, eg money, with each recipient being asked to send out further copies.

chainmail see **mail[2]**

chain reaction *noun* **1** *physics* a nuclear reaction that is self-sustaining, eg nuclear fission. **2** *chem* a chemical reaction that is self-sustaining because a change in one molecule causes many other molecules to undergo change, eg during combustion. **3** a series of events, each causing the next.

chainsaw *noun* a portable power-driven saw with cutting teeth linked together in a continuous chain.

chain-smoke *verb, tr & intr* to smoke (cigarettes, etc) continuously, esp lighting each one from its predecessor. ▪ **chain-smoker** *noun.*

chain store *noun* one of a series of shops, esp department stores, owned by the same company and selling the same range of goods.

chair *noun* **1** a seat for one person, with a back-support and usu four legs. **2** the office of chairman or chairwoman at a meeting, etc, or the person holding this office. **3** a professorship. **4** (**the chair**) *informal, N Am, esp US* the electric chair as a means of capital punishment. ▶ *verb* to control or conduct (a meeting) as chairman or chairwoman. [13c: from French *chaiere*]

IDIOMS **in the chair** acting as chairman. **take the chair** to be chairman or chairwoman.

chairlift *noun* a series of seats suspended from a moving cable, for carrying skiers, etc up a mountain.

chairman, **chairwoman** *or* **chairperson** *noun* **1** someone who conducts or controls a meeting or debate. **2** someone who presides over a committee, board of directors, etc.

chaise /ʃeɪz/ *noun, hist* a light open two-wheeled horse-drawn carriage, for one or more persons. [18c: French, meaning 'chair']

chaise longue /ʃeɪz 'lɒŋ/ *noun* (***chaises longues*** /ʃeɪz 'lɒŋ, lɒŋz/) a long seat with a back and one armrest, on which one can recline at full length. [19c: French, meaning 'long chair']

chalcedony /kal'sɛdənɪ/ *noun* (***-ies***) *geol* a fine-grained variety of the mineral quartz, which occurs in various forms, eg agate, jasper, and onyx. [14c: from Latin *chalcedonius*]

chalet /'ʃaleɪ/ *noun* **1** a style of house typical of Alpine regions, built of wood, with window-shutters and a heavy sloping roof. **2** a small cabin for holiday accommodation. [19c: Swiss French]

chalice *noun* **1** *poetic* a wine cup; a goblet. **2** in the Christian Church: the cup used for serving the wine at Communion or Mass. [Anglo-Saxon]

chalk *noun* **1** a soft fine-grained porous rock, composed of calcium carbonate. **2** a material similar to this, usu calcium sulphate, in stick form, used for writing and drawing, esp on a blackboard. ▶ *verb* to write or mark in chalk. ▪ **chalky** *adj* (***-ier, -iest***). [Anglo-Saxon *cealc*]

IDIOMS **as different** *or* **as like as chalk and cheese** *informal* completely different. **not by a long chalk** *informal* not at all.

PHRASAL VERBS **chalk sth up to someone** to add it to the account of money owed by or to them.

chalkboard *noun, N Am* a blackboard.

challenge *verb* **1** to call on someone to settle a matter by any sort of contest. **2** to cast doubt on something or call it in question. **3** to test, esp in a stimulating way: *a task that challenges you.* **4** of a guard or sentry: to order someone to stop and show official proof of identity, etc. **5** *law* to object to the inclusion of someone on a jury. ▶ *noun* **1** an invitation to a contest. **2** the questioning or doubting of something. **3** a problem or task that stimulates effort and interest. **4** an order from a guard or sentry to stop and prove identity. **5** *law* an objection to the inclusion of someone on a jury. ▪ **challenger** *noun.* ▪ **challenging** *adj.* [13c: from French *chalenge*]

challenged *adj, usu in compounds* a supposedly neutral term, denoting some kind of handicap, impairment or disability: *physically challenged.*

chamber *noun* **1** *old use* a room, esp a bedroom. **2** a hall for the meeting of an assembly, esp a legislative or judicial body. **3** one of the houses of which a parliament consists. **4** (**chambers**) a suite of rooms used by eg a judge or lawyer. **5** an enclosed space or hollow; a cavity. **6** the compartment in a gun into which the bullet or cartridge is loaded. **7** a room or compartment with a particular function: *a decompression chamber.* [13c: from French *chambre*]

chamberlain *noun* someone who manages a royal or noble household. Sometimes given the title **Lord Chamberlain**. [13c: from French *chambrelenc*]

chambermaid *noun* a woman who cleans bedrooms in a hotel, etc.

chamber of commerce *noun* an association of business people formed to promote local trade.

chamberpot *noun* a receptacle for urine, etc for use in a bedroom.

chameleon /kə'miːlɪən/ *noun* **1** lizard whose granular skin changes colour rapidly in response to changes in its environment. **2** *derog* a changeable unreliable person. [14c: from Greek *chamaileon*]

chamfer *verb* to give a smooth rounded shape to (an edge or corner). ▶ *noun* a rounded or bevelled edge. [16c: from French *chanfrein*]

chamois *noun* (*pl* ***chamois***) **1** *sing and pl* /'ʃamwɑː/ an agile antelope, native to S Europe and Asia. **2** /'ʃamɪ/ soft suede leather, formerly made from the skin of this animal, but now usu made from the hides of sheep, lambs or goats. **3** /'ʃamɪ/ (*pl* /-mɪz/) a piece of this used as a polishing cloth for glass, etc. Also written **shammy** (*pl* ***shammies*** /-mɪz/) and **shammy leather** *or* **chamois leather**. [16c: French]

chamomile see **camomile**

champ[1] *verb, tr & intr* to munch noisily. ▶ *noun* the sound of munching. [16c: imitative]

IDIOMS **champ at the bit** to be impatient to act.

champ[2] *noun, informal* a champion.

champagne *noun* **1** *strictly* a sparkling white wine made in the Champagne district of France. **2** *loosely* any sparkling white wine. **3** a pale pinkish-yellow colour. ▸ *adj* **1** champagne-coloured. **2** relating to champagne: *champagne bottle*. **3** denoting an extravagant way of life: *champagne lifestyle*. [17c: named after Champagne, the French district where the wine was orig made]

champion *noun* **1** in games, competitions, etc: a competitor that has defeated all others. **2** the supporter or defender of a person or cause. ▸ *verb* to strongly support or defend (a person or cause). ▸ *adj, N Eng dialect* excellent. [13c: from Latin *campus* battlefield or place for exercise]

championship *noun* **1** a contest held to find the champion. **2** the title or position of champion. **3** the strong defence or support of a cause or person.

chance *noun* **1** the way that things happen unplanned and unforeseen. **2** fate or luck; fortune. **3** an unforeseen and unexpected occurrence. **4** a possibility or probability. **5** a possible or probable success. **6** an opportunity: *your big chance*. **7** risk; a gamble: *take a chance*. ▸ *verb* **1** to risk something. **2** *intr* to do or happen by chance: *I chanced to meet her*. [13c: from French *cheance*]

IDIOMS **be in with a chance** to have some hope of success. **on the off chance** in hope rather than expectation. **stand a good chance** to have a reasonable expectation of success. **take a chance on sth** to act in the hope of its being the case. **take one's chance** *or* **chances** to risk an undertaking; to accept whatever happens.

PHRASAL VERBS **chance on** *or* **upon sb** *or* **sth** to meet or find them or it by accident.

chancel *noun* the eastern part of a church containing the altar, usu separated from the nave by a screen or steps. [14c: from Latin *cancellus*]

chancellery *or* **chancellory** *noun* (**-ies**) **1** the rank of chancellor. **2** a chancellor's department or staff. **3** (*also* **chancery**) **a** the offices or residence of a chancellor; **b** the office of an embassy or consulate.

chancellor *noun* **1** the head of the government in certain European countries. **2** a state or legal official of various kinds. **3** in the UK: the honorary head of a university. **4** in the US: the president of a university or college. ▪ **chancellorship** *noun*. [11c: from French *chanceler*]

chancer *noun, informal, derog* someone inclined to take any opportunity to profit, whether honestly or dishonestly.

chancery *noun* (**-ies**) **1** (*also* **Chancery**) a division of the High Court of Justice. **2** a record office containing public archives. **3** a **chancellery**. [14c]

chancre /ˈʃaŋkə(r)/ *noun, pathol* a small hard growth that develops in the primary stages of syphilis and certain other diseases. [17c: French]

chancy *adj* (**-ier, -iest**) risky; uncertain.

chandelier /ʃandəˈlɪə(r)/ *noun* an ornamental light-fitting hanging from the ceiling, with branching holders for candles or light-bulbs. [17c: French]

chandler *noun* a dealer in candles, oil, groceries, etc. ▪ **chandlery** *noun* (**-ies**) goods sold by a chandler. [14c: from French *chandelier* dealer in candles]

change *verb* **1** *tr & intr* to make or become different. **2** to give, leave or substitute one thing for another. **3** to exchange (usu one's position) with another person, etc. **4** *tr & intr* to remove (clothes, sheets, a baby's nappy, etc) and replace them with clean or different ones. **5** *tr & intr* (*sometimes* **change into sth**) to make into or become something different. **6** to obtain or supply another kind of money: *change pounds into francs*. **7** *tr & intr* to go from one vehicle, usu a train or bus, to another to continue a journey. **8** *tr & intr* to put a vehicle engine into (another gear). ▸ *noun* **1** the process of changing or an instance of it. **2** the replacement of one thing with another. **3** a variation, esp a welcome one, from one's regular habit, etc: *Let's eat out for a change*. **4** the leaving of (one vehicle) for another during a journey. **5** a fresh set (of clothes) for changing into. **6** (*also* **small** *or* **loose change**) coins as distinct from notes. **7** coins or notes given in exchange for ones of higher value. **8** money left over or returned from the amount given in payment. **9** (**the change**) *informal* see **change of life**. [13c: French]

IDIOMS **change hands** to pass into different ownership. **change one's mind** *or* **tune** to adopt a different intention or opinion.

PHRASAL VERBS **change over 1** to change from one preference or situation to another. **2** to exchange (jobs, roles, etc).

changeable *adj* **1** inclined or liable to change often; fickle. **2** able to be changed. ▪ **changeability** *or* **changeableness** *noun*.

changeless *adj* never-changing. ▪ **changelessly** *adv*. ▪ **changelessness** *noun*.

changeling *noun, folklore* a child substituted by the fairies for an unbaptized human baby.

change of heart *noun* a change of attitude often resulting in the reversal of a decision.

change of life *noun* the menopause. Also called **the change**.

changing room *noun* a room in a sports centre, etc where one can change one's clothes.

channel *noun* **1** any natural or artificially constructed water course. **2** the part of a river, waterway, etc, that is deep enough for navigation by ships. **3** a wide stretch of water, esp between an island and a continent, eg the English Channel. **4** the bed of a stream, canal or river. **5** *electronics* **a** the frequency band that is assigned for sending or receiving a clear radio or television signal; **b** a path along which electrical signals flow. **6** a groove, furrow or any long narrow cut, esp one along which something moves. **7** *comput* the path along which electrical signals representing data flow. **8** (*often* **channels**) a means by which information, etc is communicated, obtained or received. **9** a course, project, etc into which some resource may be directed: *a channel for one's energies*. **10** (**the Channel**) the English Channel, the stretch of sea between England and France. ▸ *verb* (***channelled, channelling***) **1** to make a channel or channels in something. **2** to convey (a liquid, information, etc) through a channel. **3** to direct (a resource, eg talent, energy, money) into a course, project, etc. [13c: from French *chanel*]

chant *verb, tr & intr* **1** to recite in a singing voice. **2** to keep repeating, esp loudly and rhythmically. ▸ *noun* **1** a type of singing used in religious services for passages in prose, with a simple melody and several words sung on one note. **2** a phrase or slogan constantly repeated, esp loudly and rhythmically. ▪ **chanting** *noun, adj*. [14c: from French *chanter*]

chanter *noun* on a set of bagpipes: the pipe on which the melody is played.

chantry *noun* (*-ies*) a chapel or part of a church provided for the chanting of masses. [14c: from French *chanterie*, from *chanter* sing]

chanty another spelling of **shanty**[2]

Chanukkah *or* **Hanukkah** /ˈhɑːnəkə; *Hebrew* ˈxanuka/ *noun* an eight-day Jewish festival held annually in December commemorating the rededication of the temple at Jerusalem in 165 BC. Also called **Festival of Dedication, Festival of Lights**. [19c: Hebrew *hanukkah* consecration]

chaos *noun* **1** complete confusion or disorder. **2** *physics* a state of irregularity between highly ordered motion and entirely random motion. ▪ **chaotic** *adj*. ▪ **chaotically** *adv*. [16c: Greek]

chaos
This word is often misspelt. It might help you to remember the following sentence:
*Cyclones, **h**urricanes **a**nd **o**ther **s**torms cause chaos.*

chap[1] *noun, informal* (*also* **chappie**) a man or boy; a fellow. [18c: shortened from **chapman**]

chap[2] *verb* (***chapped, chapping***) *tr & intr* of the skin: to make or become cracked, roughened and red as a result of rubbing or exposure to cold. ▸ *noun* a cracked roughened red patch on the skin, formed in this way.

chap. *abbrev* chapter.

chaparajos *or* **chaparejos** see under **chaps**

chaparral /ʃapəˈral/ *noun* in the south-western USA: a dense growth of low evergreen thorny shrubs and trees. [19c: Spanish]

chapati *or* **chapatti** /tʃəˈpɑːtɪ/ *noun* (***chapati, chapatis*** *or* ***chapaties***) in Indian cooking: a thin flat portion of unleavened bread. [19c: Hindi]

chapel *noun* **1** a recess within a church or cathedral, with its own altar. **2** a place of worship attached to a house, school, etc. **3** in England and Wales: a place of Nonconformist worship. **4** in Scotland and N Ireland: the place of worship for Roman Catholics or Episcopalians. **5** an association of workers in a newspaper office, or a printing- or publishing-house. [13c: from French *chapele*]

chaperone *or* **chaperon** /ˈʃapəroʊn/ *noun* **1** *formerly* an older woman accompanying a younger unmarried one on social occasions. **2** an older person accompanying and supervising a young person or group of young people. ▸ *verb* to act as chaperone to someone. [18c: French, from *chape* hood]

chaplain *noun* a member of the clergy attached to a school, hospital or other institution, sometimes having a chapel, or to the armed forces. ▪ **chaplaincy** *noun* (***-ies***) the position or office of chaplain. [12c: from French *chapelain*]

chaplet *noun* a wreath of flowers or a band of gold, etc worn on the head. [14c: from French *chapel* hat]

chapman *noun, hist* a travelling dealer; a pedlar. [Anglo-Saxon *ceapman*]

chapped *adj* of the skin and lips: dry and cracked.

chappie see **chap**[1]

chaps, **chaparajos** *or* **chaparejos** /ʃapəˈreɪoʊs/ *plural noun* a cowboy's protective leather riding leggings, worn over the trousers. [19c: from Spanish *chaparejos*]

chapter *noun* **1** one of the numbered or titled sections into which a book is divided. **2** a period associated with certain happenings: *University was an exciting chapter in my life*. **3** a sequence or series: *a chapter of accidents*. **4** *N Am* a branch of a society. **5** the body of canons of a cathedral, or of the members of a religious order. [13c: from French *chapitre*]
IDIOMS **chapter and verse** an exact reference, description of circumstances, etc.

char[1] *verb* (***charred, charring***) *tr & intr* to blacken or be blackened by burning; to scorch. [17c: shortened from **charcoal**]

char[2] *verb* (***charred, charring***) *intr* to do paid cleaning work in someone's house, an office, etc. ▸ *noun, informal* a charwoman. [Anglo-Saxon *cierran*]

char[3] *noun, slang* tea. [20c: from Chinese *cha*]

char[4] *or* **charr** *noun* (***char, charr, chars*** *or* ***charrs***) a fish related to and resembling the salmon, native to cool northern lakes and rivers.

charabanc /ˈʃarəbaŋ/ *noun, dated* a single-decker coach for tours, sightseeing, etc. [19c: from French *char à bancs* carriage with seats]

character *noun* **1** the combination of qualities that makes up a person's nature or personality. **2** the combination of qualities that typifies anything. **3** type or kind. **4** strong admirable qualities such as determination, courage, honesty, etc. **5** interesting qualities that make for individuality: *a house with character*. **6** someone in a story or play. **7** an odd or amusing person. **8** reputation: *blacken someone's character*. **9** a letter, number or other written or printed symbol. **10** *comput* a symbol represented by a unique finite length bit pattern (see **bit**[3]). ▪ **characterless** *adj*. [14c: Latin]
IDIOMS **in** *or* **out of character** typical or untypical of a person's nature.

character code *noun, comput* the particular binary code used to represent a character in a computer, eg ASCII.

characteristic *noun* **1** a distinctive quality or feature. **2** *maths* the integral part of a logarithm. ▸ *adj* indicative of a distinctive quality or feature; typical: *a characteristic feature*. ▪ **characteristically** *adv*.

characterize *or* **-ise** *verb* **1** to describe or give the chief qualities of someone or something. **2** to be a typical and distinctive feature of someone or something. ▪ **characterization** *noun*.

charade /ʃəˈrɑːd, ʃəˈreɪd/ *noun* **1** *derog* a ridiculous pretence; a farce. **2** (**charades**) a party game in which players mime each syllable of a word, or each word of a book title, etc, while the watching players try to guess the complete word or title. [18c: French]

charbroil see **chargrill**

charcoal *noun* **1** a black form of carbon produced by heating organic material, esp wood, in the absence of air. **2** a stick of this used for drawing. **3** a drawing done in charcoal. **4** (*also* **charcoal grey**) a dark grey colour. ▸ *adj* charcoal-coloured. [14c]

Chardonnay /ˈʃɑːdəneɪ/ *noun* **1** a white grape variety, originally from the Burgundy region of France. **2** a dry white wine made from this grape. [20c: French]

charge *verb* **1** to ask for an amount as the price of something. **2** to ask someone to pay an amount for something. **3** to accuse someone officially of a crime. **4** *intr* to rush at someone or something in attack. **5** to rush. **6** *formal* to officially order someone to do something: *She was charged to appear in court*. **7** to load (a gun, furnace, etc) with explosive, fuel, etc. **8** *formal & old use* to fill up: *charge your glasses.* **9** *intr* of a battery, capacitor, etc: to take up or store electricity. **10** to cause (a battery, capacitor, etc) to take up or store electricity. **11** to fill: *The moment was charged with emotion.* ▸ *noun* **1** an amount of money charged. **2** control, care or responsibility: *in charge of repairs.* **3** supervision or guardianship: *The police arrived and took charge.* **4** something or someone, eg a child, that is in one's care. **5** something of which one is accused: *a charge of murder.* **6** a rushing attack. **7** (*also* **electrical charge**) a deficiency or excess of electrons on a particular object, giving rise to a positive or negative charge, respectively. **8** the total amount of electricity stored by an insulated object such as an accumulator or capacitor. **9** a quantity of material appropriate for filling something. **10** an amount of explosive, fuel, etc, for loading into a gun, furnace, etc. **11** an order. **12** a task, duty or burden. **13** a debt or financial liability. ▪ **chargeable** *adj.* [13c: French]

IDIOMS **press** *or* **prefer charges** to charge someone officially with a crime, etc.

charge card *noun* a small card issued by a store, which entitles the holder to buy goods on credit.

chargé d'affaires /ˈʃɑːʒeɪ daˈfɛə/ *noun* (***chargés d'affaires*** /ˈʃɑːʒeɪ daˈfɛə/) a deputy to, or substitute for, an ambassador. [18c: French, meaning 'person in charge of affairs']

charge hand *noun* the deputy to a foreman in a factory, etc.

charge nurse *noun* a nurse in charge of a hospital ward, esp if a male; the equivalent of a **sister**.

charger *noun, hist* a strong horse used by a knight in battle, etc.

chargrill *or* (*N Am*) **charbroil** *verb, cookery* to grill over charcoal.

chariot *noun, hist* a two-wheeled vehicle pulled by horses, used in ancient times for warfare or racing. ▪ **charioteer** *noun* a chariot-driver. [14c: diminutive of French *char* carriage]

charisma /kəˈrɪzmə/ *noun* a strong ability to attract people, and inspire loyalty and admiration. [17c: from Greek *charis* grace]

charismatic /karɪzˈmatɪk/ *adj* **1** full of charisma or charm. **2** denoting a Christian movement based on belief in God-given gifts of speaking in tongues, healing, etc.

charitable *adj* **1** having a kind and understanding attitude to others. **2** generous in assisting people in need. **3** relating to, belonging to, or in the nature of a charity: *charitable institutions.* ▪ **charitably** *adv.*

charity *noun* (***-ies***) **1** assistance given to those in need. **2** an organization established to provide such assistance. **3** a kind and understanding attitude towards, or judgement of, other people. [13c: from French *charite*]

charlady see **charwoman**

charlatan /ˈʃɑːlətən/ *noun, derog* someone posing as an expert in some profession, esp medicine. [17c: from French]

Charles's law *noun, physics* the law which states that at a constant pressure the volume of a mass of gas is directly proportional to its absolute temperature. [Named after Jacques *Charles*, French physicist]

Charleston /ˈtʃɑːlstən/ *noun* a vigorous dance popular in the 1920s, its characteristic step being a pivot on one leg with a side-kick of the other from the knee. [20c: named after the town in South Carolina, USA, where the dance originated]

charlie *noun* (***-ies***) *Brit informal* a fool: *a right charlie.*

charm *noun* **1** the power of delighting, attracting or fascinating. **2** (**charms**) delightful qualities possessed by a person, place, thing, etc. **3** an object believed to have magical powers. **4** a magical saying or spell. **5** a small ornament, esp of silver, worn on a bracelet. ▸ *verb* **1** to delight, attract or fascinate someone. **2** (*usu* **charm sb into** *or* **out of sth**) to influence or persuade them by charm. ▪ **charmer** *noun.* ▪ **charmless** *adj.* [13c: French *charme*]

charming *adj* delightful; pleasing; attractive; enchanting. ▪ **charmingly** *adv.*

charnel house *noun, hist* a building where dead bodies or bones are stored. [14c: French *charnel* burial place]

chart *noun* **1** a map, esp one designed as an aid to navigation by sea or air. **2** a sheet of information presented as a table, graph or diagram. **3** (**the charts**) *informal* a weekly list of top-selling recordings, usu of pop music. ▸ *verb* **1** to make a chart of something, eg part of the sea. **2** to plot (the course or progress of something). **3** *intr, informal* to appear in the recording charts. [16c: from French *charte*]

charter *noun* **1** a formal deed guaranteeing the rights and privileges of subjects, issued by a sovereign or government. **2** a document in which the constitution and principles of an organization are presented. **3** a document creating a borough or burgh. **4** the hire of aircraft or ships for private use, or a contract for this. ▸ *verb* **1** to hire (an aircraft, etc) for private use. **2** to grant a charter to someone. [13c: from French *chartre*]

chartered *adj* **1** qualified according to the rules of a professional body that has a royal charter: *chartered accountant.* **2** having been granted a **charter** (*noun* sense 4): *a chartered plane.*

charter flight *noun* a flight in a chartered aircraft.

Chartism *noun, hist* a movement in England supporting political reform, most active between 1838 and 1849, which presented 'the People's Charter' twice to parliament. ▪ **Chartist** *noun, adj.*

chartreuse /ʃɑːˈtrɜːz/ *noun* a green or yellow liqueur made from aromatic herbs and brandy. [19c: named after the monastery of Chartreuse in France where it is produced]

charwoman *or* **charlady** *noun* a woman employed to clean a house, office, etc. [19c: from **char**[2]]

chary /ˈtʃɛərɪ/ *adj* (***-ier, -iest***) (*usu* **chary of sth**) **1** cautious or wary. **2** sparing; rather mean: *chary of praise.* [Anglo-Saxon *cearig* sorrowful or anxious]

chase[1] *verb* **1** (*often* **chase after sb**) to follow or go after them in an attempt to catch them. **2** (*often* **chase sb away** *or* **off**, *etc*) to drive or force them away, off, etc. **3** *intr* to rush; to hurry. **4** *informal* to try to obtain or achieve something, esp with difficulty: *too many applicants chasing too few jobs.* **5** *informal* to pursue a particular matter urgently with someone: *chase the post office about the missing parcel.* ▸ *noun* a pursuit. [13c: from French *chasser*]

chase[2] *verb* to decorate (metal) with engraved or embossed work. ▪ **chasing** *noun.* [14c]

chasm *noun* **1** a deep crack or opening in the ground or in the floor of a cave. **2** a very wide difference in opinion, feeling, etc. [17c: from Greek *chasma*]

chassis /ˈʃasɪ/ *noun* (*pl* ***chassis*** /ˈʃasɪz/) the structural framework of a motor vehicle, to which the body and movable working parts eg wheels are attached. [20c: French, meaning 'frame']

chaste *adj* **1** sexually virtuous or pure. **2** of behaviour, etc: modest; decent. **3** of clothes, jewellery, style, etc: simple; unadorned. ▪ **chastely** *adv.* ▪ **chasteness** *noun.* See **chastity**. [13c: from Latin *castus* pure]

chasten *verb* **1** to free someone from faults by punishing them. **2** to moderate or restrain something. [16c: from French *chastier* to punish]

chastise *verb* **1** to scold someone. **2** to punish someone severely, esp by beating. ▪ **chastisement** *noun.* [14c, from obsolete *chastien* to chasten]

chastity *noun* **1** the state of being **chaste**. **2** simplicity or plainness of style.

chasuble /ˈtʃazjʊbəl/ *noun, Christianity* a long sleeveless garment, worn by a priest when celebrating Mass or Communion. [13c: French]

chat *verb* (***chatted, chatting***) *intr* to talk or converse in a friendly informal way. ▸ *noun* informal familiar talk; a friendly conversation. [16c: shortened from **chatter**]

PHRASAL VERBS **chat sb up** *informal* to speak to them flirtatiously, or with an ulterior motive.

château /ˈʃatoʊ/ *noun* (***châteaux*** /-toʊz) a French castle or country seat. [18c: French]

chat room *noun, comput* a place on the Internet where people can exchange messages, often about a specific topic.

chat show *noun* a TV or radio programme in which well-known people are interviewed informally.

chattel *noun* any kind of **movable** (sense 2) property. [13c: French *chatel*]

chatter *verb, intr* **1** to talk rapidly and unceasingly, usu about trivial matters. **2** of the teeth: to keep clicking together as a result of cold or fear. **3** eg of monkeys or birds: to make rapid continuous high-pitched noises. ▸ *noun* **1** a sound similar to this. **2** idle talk or gossip. ▪ **chatterer** *noun.* [13c: imitating the sound]

chatterbox *noun, derog* someone who is inclined to chatter.

chatty *adj* (***-ier, -iest***) *informal* **1** given to amiable chatting. **2** of writing: friendly and informal in style. ▪ **chattily** *adv.* ▪ **chattiness** *noun.*

chauffeur *noun* someone employed to drive a car for someone else. ▸ *verb, tr & intr* to act as a driver for someone. [20c: French, meaning 'stoker']

chauvinism /ˈʃoʊvənɪzəm/ *noun, derog* an unreasonable belief, esp if aggressively expressed, in the superiority of one's own nation, sex, etc. ▪ **chauvinist** *noun, adj.* ▪ **chauvinistic** *adj.* [19c: named after Nicolas Chauvin, a fanatically patriotic soldier under Napoleon]

chav /tʃav/ *noun, derog slang* a boorish uneducated person, especially one regarded as having little taste. [Prob from Romany *chavi* child]

cheap *adj* **1** low in price; inexpensive. **2** being or charging less then the usual. **3** low in price but of poor quality. **4** having little worth. **5** vulgar or nasty. ▸ *adv, informal* cheaply: *Good houses don't come cheap.* ▪ **cheaply** *adv.* ▪ **cheapness** *noun.* [Anglo-Saxon *ceap* trade, price or bargain]

cheapen *verb* **1** to cause to appear cheap or not very respectable. **2** *tr & intr* to make or become cheaper.

cheapjack *noun, derog* a seller of cheap poor-quality goods. ▸ *adj* of poor quality.

cheapskate *noun, derog informal* a mean, miserly person.

cheat *verb* **1** to trick, deceive or swindle. **2** (*usu* **cheat sb of** *or* **out of sth**) to deprive them of it by deceit or trickery. **3** *intr* to act dishonestly so as to gain an advantage: *cheat at cards.* **4** *intr* (*often* **cheat on sb**) *informal* to be unfaithful to (one's spouse, lover etc). ▸ *noun* **1** someone who cheats. **2** a dishonest trick. ▪ **cheater** *noun.* [14c: shortened from **escheat**]

check *verb* **1** *tr & intr* to establish that something is correct or satisfactory, esp by investigation or enquiry; to verify. **2** to hold back, prevent or restrain: *He was about to complain, but checked himself.* **3** *informal* to reproach or rebuke someone. **4** *N Am* to mark something correct, etc with a tick. ▸ *noun* **1** an inspection or investigation made to find out about something or to ensure that something is as it should be. **2** a standard or test by means of which to check something. **3** a stoppage in, or control on, progress or development. **4** a pattern of squares: *cotton with a purple check.* **5** *N Am, esp US* a tick marked against something. **6** *N Am, esp US* a cheque. **7** *N Am* a restaurant bill. **8** *chess* the position of the king when directly threatened by an opposing piece. ▪ **checker** *noun.* [14c: from French *eschec*, meaning 'check' in chess]

PHRASAL VERBS **check in** to report one's arrival at an air terminal or a hotel. **check sb** *or* **sth in 1** to register or report the arrival of someone, especially guests at a hotel or passengers at an air terminal. **2** to hand in (luggage for weighing and loading) at an air terminal. See also **check-in**. **check sth off** to mark (an item on a list) as dealt with. **check out 1** to register one's departure, esp from a hotel on paying the bill. **2** *chiefly N Am* of information etc: to be satisfactory or consistent. **check sb** *or* **sth out** to investigate them or it thoroughly. **check up on sb** *or* **sth** to enquire into or examine them or it (eg evidence). See also **check-up**.

check box *noun, comput* a square on a screen on which the user can click the mouse to activate a feature.

checked *adj* having a squared pattern: *purple-checked cotton.*

checker[1] *noun* **1** someone who checks. **2** *N Am* someone who operates a checkout at a supermarket.

checker[2] see **chequer**

check-in *noun* at an air terminal: the desk at which passengers' tickets are checked and luggage weighed and accepted for loading. See also **check in**, **check sb** or **sth in** at **check**.

checklist *noun* a list of things to be done or systematically checked.

checkmate *chess, noun* a winning position, putting one's opponent's king under inescapable attack. ▸ *verb* to put the (opposing king) into checkmate. [14c: from Persian *shah mata* the king is dead]

checkout *noun* the pay desk in a supermarket.

checkpoint *noun* a place, eg at a frontier, where vehicles are stopped and travel documents checked.

check-up *noun* a thorough examination, esp a medical one. See also **check up on sb** *or* **sth** at **check**.

Cheddar /ˈtʃɛdə(r)/ *noun* a hard English cheese made from cow's milk. [17c: named after Cheddar in Somerset, where it was originally made]

cheek *noun* **1** either side of the face below the eye; the fleshy wall of the mouth. **2** impudent speech or behaviour. **3** *informal* either of the buttocks. [Anglo-Saxon *ceace* or *cece*]

IDIOMS **cheek by jowl** very close together. **turn the other cheek** to refuse to retaliate.

cheekbone *noun* either of a pair of bones that lie beneath the prominent part of the cheeks.

cheeky *adj* (**-ier, -iest**) impudent or disrespectful. ▪ **cheekily** *adv.* ▪ **cheekiness** *noun.*

cheep *verb, intr* esp of young birds: to make high-pitched noises; to chirp. ▸ *noun* a sound of this sort. [16c: imitating the sound]

cheer *noun* **1** a shout of approval or encouragement. **2** *old use* disposition; frame of mind: *be of good cheer.* ▸ *verb* **1** *intr* to shout in approval or encouragement. **2** (*sometimes* **cheer sb** *or* **sth on**) to show approval or encouragement of them or it by shouting. [13c: from French *chere* face]

PHRASAL VERBS **cheer up** to become more cheerful. **cheer sb up** to make them more cheerful.

cheerful *adj* **1** happy; optimistic. **2** bright and cheering. **3** willing; glad; ungrudging.

cheering *adj* bringing comfort; making one feel glad or happier.

cheerio *exclam, Brit informal* goodbye. [20c: from **cheer**]

cheerleader *noun* esp in the US: someone who leads organized cheering, applause, etc, esp at sports events.

cheerless *adj* dismal, depressing, dreary or dull.

cheers *exclam, Brit informal* **1** used as a toast before drinking. **2** thank you. **3** goodbye. [20c: from **cheer**]

cheery *adj* (**-ier, -iest**) cheerful; lively; jovial. ▪ **cheerily** *adv.* ▪ **cheeriness** *noun.*

cheese *noun* **1** a solid or soft creamy food that is prepared from the curds of milk. **2** a wheel-shaped solid mass of this substance. [Anglo-Saxon *cyse*]

IDIOMS **cheesed off** *Brit slang, dated* fed up or annoyed. **hard cheese!** *Brit slang* bad luck!

cheeseburger *noun* a hamburger served with a slice of cheese.

cheesecake *noun* a sweet cake with a pastry base, topped with cream cheese, sugar, eggs etc.

cheesecloth *noun* **1** a type of thin cloth used for pressing cheese. **2** a loosely woven cloth used for shirts, etc.

cheeseparing *adj, derog* mean with money; miserly. ▸ *noun* miserliness.

cheesy *adj* (**-ier, -iest**) **1** like cheese eg in smell, flavour, etc. **2** *informal* cheap, inferior; hackneyed, trite. **3** of a smile: wide, but prob insincere: *a cheesy grin.*

cheetah *noun* a large member of the cat family and the fastest land mammal, found in Africa and Asia, which has a tawny or grey coat with black spots. [18c: from Hindi *cita*]

chef *noun* a cook in a restaurant etc, esp the principal one. [19c: French, meaning 'chief']

chef d'oeuvre /ʃeɪ ˈdɜːvrə/ *noun* (***chefs d'oeuvre*** /ʃeɪ ˈdɜːvrə/) an artist's or writer's masterpiece. [17c: French, meaning 'chief (piece of) work']

Cheka *noun, hist* a secret police force formed in Russia in 1917 to investigate and punish anti-Bolshevik activities. [From Russian *che ka*, names of the initial letters of the words meaning 'extraordinary commission']

chemical *adj* **1** relating to or used in the science of chemistry. **2** relating to a substance or substances that take part in or are formed by reactions in which atoms or molecules undergo changes. **3** relating to the properties of chemicals. ▸ *noun* a substance that has a specific molecular composition, and takes part in or is formed by reactions in which atoms or molecules undergo changes. ▪ **chemically** *adv.*

chemical element *noun* a substance which cannot be broken down into simpler substances by chemical means, and which is composed of similar atoms that all have the same **atomic number**.

chemical engineering *noun* the branch of engineering concerned with the design, manufacture, operation and maintenance of machinery in industrial chemical processing plants.

chemical warfare *noun* warfare involving the use of toxic chemical substances as weapons.

chemise *noun* a woman's shirt or loose-fitting dress. [13c: French]

chemist *noun* **1** a scientist who specializes in chemistry. **2** someone qualified to dispense medicines; a pharmacist. **3** a shop dealing in medicines, toiletries, cosmetics, etc. [16c: earlier *chymist* from Latin *alchimista* alchemist]

chemistry *noun* (**-ies**) the scientific study of the composition, properties, and reactions of chemical elements and their compounds. [17c]

chemoreceptor *noun, biol* any sense organ that responds to stimulation by chemical substances.

chemotherapy *noun, med* the treatment of a disease or disorder by means of drugs or other chemical compounds. Compare **radiotherapy**.

chenille /ʃəˈniːl/ *noun* a soft shiny velvety fabric. [18c: French, meaning 'caterpillar']

cheque *noun* a printed form on which to fill in instructions to one's bank to pay a specified sum of money from one's account to another account. [18c: from **check**]

chequebook *noun* a book of cheques ready for use, printed with the account-holder's name and that of the bank issuing it.

cheque card *noun* a card issued to customers by a bank, guaranteeing payment of their cheques up to a stated amount.

chequer *or* (*US*) **checker** *noun* **1** a pattern of squares alternating in colour as on a chessboard. **2** one of the pieces used in the game of Chinese chequers. **3** *N Am* one of the round pieces used in the game of draughts. See **chequers**. ▸ *verb* to mark in squares of different colours. [13c: from French *escheker* chessboard]

chequered *adj* **1** patterned with squares or patches of alternating colour. **2** of a person's life, career, etc: eventful, with alternations of good and bad fortune.

chequered flag *noun* a black-and-white checked flag waved in front of the winner and subsequent finishers in a motor race.

chequers *or* (*US*) **checkers** *singular noun* the game of draughts.

cherish *verb* **1** to care for lovingly. **2** to cling fondly to (a hope, belief or memory). [14c: from French *cherir*]

cheroot *noun* a cigar that is cut square at both ends. [17c: from French *cheroute*]

cherry *noun* (**-ies**) **1** a small round red or purplish fruit containing a small stone surrounded by pulpy flesh. **2** any of various small deciduous trees which bear this fruit. **3** a bright red colour. [Anglo-Saxon *ciris*]

cherry-picking *noun, informal* the practice of choosing only the best among assets, staff members, etc, and discarding the rest.

cherub *noun* **1** (*pl also* ***cherubim*** /ˈtʃɛrəbɪm/) **a** an angel, represented in painting and sculpture as a winged child; **b** in the traditional medieval hierarchy of angels: an angel of the second-highest rank. **2** a sweet, innocent and beautiful child. ▪ **cherubic** /tʃəˈruːbɪk/ *adj.* [Anglo-Saxon]

chervil *noun* a plant that is widely cultivated for its aromatic leaves, which are used as a garnish and for flavouring salads, etc. [Anglo-Saxon *cherfelle*]

Ches. *abbrev, English county* Cheshire.

chess *noun* a game of skill played on a chequered board by two people, each with 16 playing-pieces, **chessmen**, the object of which is to trap the opponent's king. [13c: from French *esches*, pl of *eschec* meaning 'check' in chess]

chessboard *noun* the board on which chess or draughts is played, divided into 64 squares alternately white and another colour (usually black).

chest *noun* **1** the front part of the body between the neck and the waist; the non-technical name for the thorax. **2** a large strong box used for storage or transport. [Anglo-Saxon *cist, cest* box]

IDIOMS **get sth off one's chest** *informal* to relieve one's anxiety about a problem, wrongdoing, etc by talking about it openly.

chesterfield *noun* a heavily padded leather-covered sofa with arms and back of the same height. [19c: named after a 19c Earl of Chesterfield]

chestnut *noun* **1** (*also* **sweet chestnut**) a deciduous tree which has simple toothed glossy leaves, and prickly globular fruits containing large edible nuts. **2** the large reddish-brown edible nut produced by this tree. **3** (*also* **horse chestnut**) a large deciduous tree which has brown shiny inedible seeds, popularly known as **conkers**. **4** the hard timber of either of these trees. **5** a reddish-brown colour, esp of hair. **6** a reddish-brown horse. [16c: from the earlier *chesten nut*]

chest of drawers *noun* a piece of furniture fitted with drawers.

chesty *adj* (**-ier, -iest**) *informal, Brit* liable to, suffering from or caused by illness affecting the lungs: *a chesty cough*. ▪ **chestiness** *noun.*

chevron *noun* **1** a V-shaped mark or symbol, esp one worn on the sleeve of a uniform to indicate non-commissioned rank. **2** on a road sign: a horizontal row of black and white V-shapes indicating a sharp bend ahead. [14c: French, literally 'rafter']

chew *verb* **1** *tr & intr* to use the teeth to break up (food) inside the mouth before swallowing. **2** *tr & intr* (*sometimes* **chew at** *or* **on sth**) to keep biting or nibbling it. ▸ *noun* **1** an act of chewing. **2** something for chewing, eg a sweet. [Anglo-Saxon *ceowan*]

PHRASAL VERBS **chew on sth** *or* **chew sth over** *informal* to consider it or discuss it at length.

chewing-gum *noun* a sticky sweet-flavoured substance for chewing without swallowing.

chewy *adj* (**-ier, -iest**) *informal* requiring a lot of chewing. ▪ **chewiness** *noun.*

chez /ʃeɪ/ *prep* at the home of someone. [18c: French]

chi *or* **ch'i** see **qi**

chiaroscuro /kɪɑːroʊˈskʊəroʊ/ *noun, art* the management of light and shade in a picture. [17c: Italian, meaning 'light-dark']

chic /ʃiːk/ *adj* of clothes, people, etc: appealingly elegant or fashionable. ▸ *noun* stylishness; elegance. [19c: French]

chicane /ʃɪˈkeɪn/ *noun, motor sport* on a motor-racing circuit: a series of sharp bends. [17c: French, meaning 'quibble']

chicanery *noun* (**-ies**) **1** clever talk intended to mislead. **2** trickery; deception.

chick *noun* **1** the young of a bird, esp a domestic fowl. **2** *dated slang* a young woman. [14c: shortened from **chicken**]

chicken *noun* **1** the domestic fowl, bred for its meat and eggs. **2** the flesh of this animal used as food. **3** *derog slang* a cowardly person. ▸ *adj, derog informal* cowardly. [Anglo Saxon *cicen*]

PHRASAL VERBS **chicken out of sth** to avoid or withdraw from (an activity or commitment) from lack of nerve or confidence.

chickenfeed *noun* **1** food for poultry. **2** something small and insignificant, esp a paltry sum of money.

chicken-hearted *or* **chicken-livered** *adj, derog, informal* cowardly.

chickenpox *noun* an infectious viral disease which mainly affects children, characterized by a fever and an itchy rash of dark red spots.

chicken wire *noun* wire netting.

chickpea *noun* a leafy plant grown for its wrinkled yellow pea-like edible seeds. [16c: from earlier *chich pea*]

chickweed *noun* a sprawling plant with oval pointed leaves and tiny white flowers.

chicory *noun* (**-ies**) **1** a plant with stalked lower leaves, stalkless upper leaves and a long stout tap root. **2** the dried root of this plant, which is often ground, roasted and blended with coffee. **3** the leaves of this plant, eaten raw as a salad vegetable. [14c: from Greek *kichoreion*]

chide *verb* (*past tense* ***chided*** *or* ***chid,*** *past participle* ***chidden*** *or* ***chided***) *chiefly literary* to scold or rebuke. ▪ **chiding** *noun* a scolding or a rebuke. [Anglo-Saxon *cidan*]

chief *noun* **1** the head of a tribe, clan, etc. **2** a leader. **3** the person in charge of any group, organization, department, etc. ▸ *adj* **1** used in titles, etc: first in rank; leading: *chief inspector.* **2** main; most important; principal. [13c: from French *chef*]

chief executive officer *noun* a **managing director**.

chiefly *adv* **1** mainly. **2** especially; above all.

chieftain *noun* the head of a tribe or clan. [14c: from French *chevetaine*]

chiffchaff *noun* an insect-eating warbler. [18c: imitating its call]

chiffon /'ʃɪfɒn/ *noun* a very fine transparent silk or nylon fabric. [18c: French]

chiffonier *or* **chiffonnier** /ʃɪfə'nɪə(r)/ *noun* **1** a tall elegant chest of drawers. **2** a low wide cabinet with an open or grille front. [19c: French, meaning 'a container for scraps of fabric']

chigger, **chigoe** /'tʃɪgoʊ/ *or* **jigger** *noun* a tropical flea, the pregnant female of which burrows under the skin of the host. [17c: from Carib (a S American native language) *chigo*]

chignon /'ʃiːnjɒn/ *noun* a soft bun or coil of hair worn at the back of the neck. [18c: French, meaning 'nape of the neck']

chihuahua /tʃɪ'wɑːwɑː/ *noun* a tiny dog which has a disproportionately large head with large widely spaced eyes and large ears. [19c: named after the place in Mexico that it orig came from]

chi kung see **qi gong**

chilblain *noun* a painful itchy swelling of the skin, esp on the fingers, toes or ears, caused by exposure to cold. [16c: from **chill** + **blain**]

child *noun* (***children***) **1** a boy or girl between birth and physical maturity. **2** one's son or daughter. **3** *derog* an innocent or naive person. **4** someone seen as a typical product of a particular historical period, etc: *He was a child of his time.* ▪ **childless** *adj.* ▪ **childlessness** *noun.* ▪ **childlike** *adj.* [Anglo-Saxon *cild*]

IDIOMS **with child** *old use* pregnant.

childbearing *noun* the act of giving birth to a child. ▸ *adj* suitable for or relating to the bearing of children: *childbearing hips.*

childbirth *noun* the process at the end of pregnancy whereby a mother gives birth to a child.

childhood *noun* the state or time of being a child.

childish *adj* **1** *derog* silly; immature. **2** relating to children or childhood; like a child.

child-lock *noun* **1** a device designed to prevent a child opening something such as a car door or a drawer. **2** a feature on equipment, eg a video recorder, which prevents settings being altered by a child playing with it.

childminder *noun* an officially registered person who looks after children in return for payment.

child's play *noun, informal* a basic or simple task.

chill *noun* **1** a feeling of coldness. **2** a cold that causes shivering, chattering teeth, etc, commonly caused by exposure to a cold damp environment. **3** a feeling, esp sudden, of depression or fear. ▸ *verb* **1** *tr & intr* to make or become cold. **2** to cause to feel cold. **3** to scare, depress or discourage. [Anglo-Saxon *ciele* cold]

PHRASAL VERBS **chill out** *slang* to relax or calm oneself, esp after a period of hard work or exercise.

chilled *adj* **1** made cold. **2** hardened by chilling. **3** preserved by chilling.

chilli *or* **chili** *noun* (***chillis*** *or* ***chillies***) **1** the fruit or pod of one of the varieties of capsicum, which has a hot spicy flavour and is used in cooking, often in a powdered form. **2 chilli con carne.** [17c: Aztec]

chilli con carne *noun* a spicy Mexican dish of minced meat and beans, flavoured with chilli. Also called **chilli.**

chilling *adj* frightening. ▪ **chillingly** *adv.*

chilly *adj* (***-ier, -iest***) **1** rather cold. **2** *informal* unfriendly; hostile. ▪ **chilliness** *noun.*

chime *noun* **1** the sound made by a clock, set of tuned bells, etc. **2** (*usu* **chimes**) a percussion instrument consisting of hanging metal tubes that are struck with a hammer. ▸ *verb* **1** *intr* of bells: to ring. **2** *tr & intr* of a clock: to indicate (the time) by chiming. [13c: from Anglo-Saxon *cimbal* cymbal]

PHRASAL VERBS **chime in 1** to interrupt or join in a conversation, esp to repeat or agree with something. **2** to agree with someone or to fit in with them.

chimera *or* **chimaera** /kaɪ'mɪərə/ *noun* **1** a wild or impossible idea. **2** (**Chimera**) *Greek myth* a fire-breathing monster, with the head of a lion, the body of a goat and the tail of a serpent. **3** a beast made up from various different animals, esp in art. **4** *biol* an organism made up of two or more genetically distinct tissues. ▪ **chimeric** *or* **chimerical** *adj.* [14c: from Greek *chimaira* she-goat]

chimney *noun* (***-ies***) **1** a vertical structure made of brick, stone or steel, that carries smoke, steam, fumes or heated air away from a fireplace, stove, furnace or engine. **2** the top part of this structure, rising from a roof. [14c: from French *cheminee*]

chimney breast *noun* a projecting part of a wall built round the base of a chimney.

chimneypot *noun* a short hollow rounded fitting, usu made of pottery, that sits in the opening at the top of a chimney.

chimney stack *noun* **1** a stone or brick structure rising from a roof, usu carrying several chimneys. **2** a very tall factory chimney.

chimney-sweep *noun* someone whose job is to clean soot out of chimneys.

chimp *noun, informal* a **chimpanzee.**

chimpanzee *noun* the most intelligent of the great apes, found in tropical rainforests of Africa. [18c: from W African]

chin *noun* the front protruding part of the lower jaw. [Anglo-Saxon *cinn*]

IDIOMS **keep one's chin up** *informal* to stay cheerful in spite of misfortune or difficulty.

china *singular noun* **1** articles made from a fine translucent earthenware, orig from China. **2** articles made from similar materials. ▸ *adj* made of china. [17c: from Persian *chini* Chinese]

china clay see **kaolin**

chinchilla *noun* **1** a small S American mammal with a thick soft grey coat, a bushy tail and large round ears. **2** the thick soft grey fur of this animal. **3** a breed of cat or a breed of rabbit with grey fur. [17c: Spanish diminutive of *chinche* bug]

chine *noun* **1** the backbone. **2** a cut, esp of pork, which consists of part of the backbone and adjoining parts. [14c: from French *eschine* backbone]

Chinese *adj* belonging or relating to China, a state in central and E Asia, its inhabitants, or their language. ▸ *noun* **1** a citizen or inhabitant of, or person born in, China. **2** any of the closely related languages of the main ethnic group of China.

Chinese gooseberry see **kiwi fruit**

chink[1] *noun* **1** a small slit or crack. **2** a narrow beam of light shining through such a crack. [16c: related to **chine**]

chink[2] *noun* a faint short ringing noise; a clink: *a chink of glasses.* ▸ *verb, tr & intr* to make or cause to make this noise. [16c: imitating the sound]

chinless *adj, derog* having a weak indecisive character.

chinoiserie /ʃɪn'wɑːzəriː/ *noun* a European style of design and decoration which imitates or uses Chinese motifs and methods. [19c: French]

chinos /'tʃiːnoʊz/ *plural noun* trousers made from the material **chino**, a strong khaki-like twilled cotton.

chintz *noun* a cotton fabric printed generally in bright colours on a light background, esp used for soft furnishings. [17c: Gujarati *chints*, pl of *chint*]

chintzy *adj* (**-ier, -iest**) *derog* sentimentally or quaintly showy.

chinwag *noun, informal* a chat.

chip *verb* (***chipped, chipping***) **1** (*sometimes* **chip at sth**) to knock or strike small pieces off (a hard object or material). **2** *intr* to be broken off in small pieces; to have small pieces broken off. **3** to shape by chipping. **4** *tr & intr, golf, football* to strike the ball so that it goes high up in the air over a short distance. ▸ *noun* **1** a small piece chipped off. **2** a place from which a piece has been chipped off: *a chip in the vase.* **3** *Brit* (*usu* **chips**) strips of deep-fried potato. See also **French fries**. **4** *N Am* (*also* **potato chip**) a potato crisp. **5** in gambling: a plastic counter used as a money token. **6** *comput* a **silicon chip**. **7** a small piece of stone. **8** *golf, football* a short high shot or kick. ▪ **chipped** *adj* **1** shaped or damaged by chips. **2** shaped into chips: *chipped potatoes.* [Anglo-Saxon *cipp* log, ploughshare or beam]

IDIOMS **a chip off the old block** *informal* someone who strongly resembles one of their parents in personality, behaviour or appearance. **have a chip on one's shoulder** *informal* to feel resentful about something, esp unreasonably. **have had one's chips** *informal* **1** to have failed or been beaten. **2** to have been killed. **when the chips are down** *informal* at the moment of crisis; when it comes to the point.

PHRASAL VERBS **chip in** *informal* **1** to interrupt. **2** *tr & intr* to contribute (eg money): *We all chipped in for the car.*

chip and PIN *noun* a system of payment by credit or debit card in which the card holder keys in a personal identification number to authorize the payment.

chipboard *noun* thin solid board made from compressed wood chips.

chipmunk *noun* a small ground squirrel, found in N America and N Asia, which has reddish-brown fur. [19c: from earlier *chitmunk*, from Ojibwa (a N American native language)]

chipolata *noun* a small sausage. [19c: French]

chipper *adj, N Am informal* of a person: cheerful and lively.

chippy *noun* (**-ies**) *Brit informal* **1** a chip shop, where take-away meals of chips and other fried foods are sold. **2** a carpenter or joiner.

chirography *or* **cheirography** *noun* handwriting or penmanship.

chiromancy *noun* **palmistry**.

chiropodist /kɪ'rɒpədɪst, ʃɪ-/ *noun* someone who treats minor disorders of the feet, eg corns. ▪ **chiropody** *noun.* [19c: from Greek *cheir* hand + *pous*, *podos* foot; the original practitioners treated hands as well as feet]

chiropractic /kʌɪroʊ'praktɪk/ *noun* a method of treating pain by manual adjustment of the spinal column, etc, so as to release pressure on the nerves. ▪ **chiropractor** *noun.* [19c: from Greek *cheir* hand + *praktikas* practical]

chirp *verb* **1** *intr* of birds, grasshoppers, etc: to produce a short high-pitched sound. **2** *tr & intr* to chatter or say something merrily. ▸ *noun* a chirping sound. [15c: imitating the sound]

chirpy *adj* (**-ier, -iest**) *informal* lively and merry. ▪ **chirpiness** *noun.*

chirrup *verb, intr* of some birds and insects: to chirp, esp in little bursts. ▸ *noun* a burst of chirping. [16c: lengthened form of **chirp**]

chisel *noun* a hand tool which has a strong metal blade with a cutting edge at the tip, used for cutting and shaping wood or stone. ▸ *verb* (***chiselled, chiselling***) to cut or shape (wood or stone) with a chisel. [14c: from French *cisel*]

chit[1] *noun* **1** a short note or voucher recording money owed or paid. **2** a note. Also called **chitty** (**-ies**). [18c: from Hindi *citthi*]

chit[2] *noun, derog* **a** a cheeky young girl; **b** a mere child. [17c: related to **kitten**]

chitchat *noun, informal* **1** chatter. **2** gossip. ▸ *verb, intr* to gossip idly. [18c: reduplicated form of **chat**]

chitterlings *or* **chitlings** *singular or plural noun* the intestines of a pig or another edible animal prepared as food.

chivalrous *adj* **1** **a** brave or gallant; **b** courteous or noble. **2** relating to medieval chivalry.

chivalry *noun* **1** courtesy and protectiveness, esp as shown by men towards women. **2** *hist* a code of moral and religious behaviour followed by medieval knights. [13c: from French *chevalerie*]

chive *noun* a plant of the onion family with purple flowers and long thin hollow leaves used as a flavouring or garnish. [14c: from French *cive*]

chivvy *or* **chivy** *verb* (**-ies, -ied**) to harass or pester someone. [19c: a form of *chevy*, perhaps from the ballad *Chevy Chase*]

chlorate *noun, chem* any salt of chloric acid.

chloric /'klɔːrɪk/ *adj, chem* relating to, containing or obtained from chlorine. [19c]

chloride *noun* **1** *chem* **a** a compound of chlorine with another element or **radical** (*noun* sense 3); **b** a salt of hydrochloric acid. **2** chloride of lime, a bleaching agent.

chlorinate *verb* to treat (eg water) with, or cause (a substance) to combine with, chlorine. ▪ **chlorination** *noun.*

chlorine *noun, chem* (symbol **Cl**) a greenish-yellow poisonous gas with a pungent smell, widely used as a disinfectant and bleach, and in the chemical industry.

chloro- *or (before vowels)* **chlor-** *combining form, denoting* **1** green. **2** chlorine. [Greek *chloros* green]

chlorofluorocarbon *noun, chem* (abbrev **CFC**) a compound composed of chlorine, fluorine and carbon, formerly used as an aerosol propellant and refrigerant, but now widely banned because of the damage such compounds cause to the ozone layer. [1940s]

chloroform *noun, chem* a sweet-smelling liquid, formerly used as an anaesthetic, and still used as a solvent. Also called **trichloromethane**. [19c: from **chloro-** + Latin *formica* ant]

chlorophyll *noun, botany* the green pigment, found in the chloroplasts of all green plants, that absorbs light energy from the Sun during **photosynthesis**. [19c: from **chloro-** + Greek *phyllon* leaf]

chloroplast *noun, botany* in the cytoplasm of photosynthetic cells of all green plants: any of many specialized structures containing the green pigment chlorophyll. [19c: from **chloro-** + Greek *plastos* moulded]

chocaholic *or* **chocoholic** *noun, facetious* someone who has an uncontrollable craving for chocolate. [20c: from **chocolate**, modelled on **alcoholic**]

chock *noun* a heavy block or wedge used to prevent movement of a wheel, etc.

chock-a-block *or* **chock-full** *adj* tightly jammed; crammed full.

chocolate *noun* **1** a food product, made from **cacao** beans, that may be eaten on its own or used as a coating or flavouring. **2** an individual sweet made from or coated with this substance. **3** a drink made by dissolving a powder prepared from this substance in hot water or milk. Also called **hot chocolate**. **4** a dark-brown colour. ▸ *adj* **1** made from or coated with chocolate. **2** dark brown. ▪ **chocolaty** *or* **chocolatey** *adj*. [17c: from Aztec *chocolatl*]

choice *noun* **1** the act or process of choosing. **2** the right, power, or opportunity to choose. **3** something or someone chosen. **4** a variety of things available for choosing between: *a wide choice*. ▸ *adj* select; worthy of being chosen: *choice cuts of meat*. [13c: from French *chois*]

choir *noun* **1** an organized group of trained singers, esp one that performs in church. **2** the area, esp in a church, occupied by a choir. [13c: from French *cuer*]

choirboy *or* **choirgirl** *noun* a young boy or girl who sings in a church choir.

choirmaster *or* **choirmistress** *noun* the trainer of a choir.

choke *verb* **1** *tr & intr* to prevent or be prevented from breathing by an obstruction in the throat. **2** to stop or interfere with breathing in this way. **3** to fill up, block or restrict something. **4** (*often* **choke something up**) to fill up, block or restrict it. **5** to restrict the growth or development of: *plants choked by weeds*. ▸ *noun* **1** the sound or act of choking. **2** *eng* a valve in the carburettor of a petrol engine that reduces the air supply and so gives a richer fuel/air mixture while the engine is still cold. [Anglo-Saxon *aceocian* to suffocate]

PHRASAL VERBS **choke sth back** to suppress something indicative of feelings, esp tears, laughter or anger.

choker *noun* a close-fitting necklace or broad band of velvet, etc worn round the neck.

cholecalciferol /kɒlɪkal'sɪfərɒl/ *noun* **vitamin D_3** (see **vitamin D**).

choler /'kɒlə(r)/ *noun, dated* anger or irritability. ▪ **choleric** *adj* irritable or bad-tempered. [16c: from Greek *chole* bile]

cholera /'kɒlərə/ *noun, pathol* an acute and potentially fatal bacterial infection of the small intestine. [16c: from Greek *chole* bile]

cholesterol /kə'lɛstərɒl/ *noun, biochem* in animal cells: a **sterol** present in all cell membranes, and associated with **atherosclerosis** when present at high levels in the blood. [19c: from Greek *chole* bile + **sterol**]

chomp *verb, tr & intr* to munch noisily. ▸ *noun* an act or sound of chomping.

choose *verb* (*past tense* ***chose***, *past participle* ***chosen***) **1** *tr & intr* to take or select (one or more things or persons) from a larger number. **2** to decide; to think fit. **3** *intr* to be inclined; to like: *I will leave when I choose*. [Anglo-Saxon *ceosan*]

choosy *adj* (***-ier, -iest***) *informal* difficult to please; fussy.

chop¹ *verb* (***chopped, chopping***) **1** to cut with a vigorous downward or sideways slicing action, with an axe, knife, etc. **2** to hit (a ball) with a sharp downwards stroke. ▸ *noun* **1** a slice of pork, lamb or mutton containing a bone, esp a rib. **2** a chopping action or stroke. **3** a sharp downward stroke given to a ball. **4** in boxing, karate etc: a short sharp blow. [14c: variant of **chap²**]

chop² *verb* (***chopped, chopping***) to change direction or have a change of mind. [Anglo-Saxon *ceapian* to bargain or trade]

IDIOMS **chop and change** to keep changing one's mind, plans, etc.

chop-logic *noun* **1** over-subtle or complicated and confusing arguments. **2** someone who argues in this way.

chopper *noun* **1** *informal* a helicopter. **2** *informal* a motorcycle with high handlebars. **3** a short-handled axe. **4** (**choppers**) *informal* the teeth.

choppy *adj* (***-ier, -iest***) of the sea, weather etc: rather rough. ▪ **choppiness** *noun*.

chops *plural noun* the jaws or mouth, esp of an animal. [16c: from *chap* the lower half of the cheek]

chopsticks *plural noun* a pair of slender sticks made from wood, plastic or ivory, which are held in one hand and used for eating with, chiefly in Oriental countries. [17c: from Pidgin English *chop* quick + **stick¹**]

chop suey *noun* a Chinese-style dish of chopped meat and vegetables fried in a sauce, usu served with rice. [19c: from Cantonese Chinese *jaahp seui* mixed bits]

choral *adj* relating to, or to be sung by, a choir or chorus. Compare **vocal**, **instrumental**.

chorale *or* **choral** /kɒ'rɑːl/ *noun* **1** a hymn tune with a slow dignified rhythm. **2** *N Am, esp US* a choir or choral society. [19c: German *Choral*]

chord¹ *noun, music* a combination of musical notes played together. ▪ **chordal** *adj*. [16c: shortened from **accord**]

chord² *noun* **1** *anatomy* another spelling of **cord**. **2** *maths* a straight line joining two points on a curve or curved surface. [16c: from Greek *chorde* string or gut]

chordate *noun, zool* any animal that possesses a **notochord** at some stage in its development. [19c: from Greek *chorde* a string or intestine]

chore *noun* **1** a domestic task. **2** a boring or unenjoyable task. [18c: see **char²**]

chorea /kɔː'rɪə/ *noun, pathol* either of two disorders of the nervous system that cause rapid involuntary movements of the limbs and sometimes of the face. [19c: Greek *choreia* dance]

choreograph *verb* to plan the choreography for (a dance, ballet, etc).

choreography *noun* **1** the arrangement of the sequence and pattern of movements in dancing. **2** the steps of a dance or ballet. ▪ **choreographer** *noun*. ▪ **choreographic** *adj*. [18c: from Greek *choreia* dance + *graphein* to write]

chorister *noun* a singer in a choir, esp a church or cathedral choir.

choroid /ˈkɔːrɔɪd/ *noun, anatomy* a layer of coloured cells in the eye, between the retina and the sclerotic. [18c: from Greek *chorion* membrane]

chortle *verb, intr* to laugh joyfully. ▸ *noun* a joyful laugh. [19c: invented by Lewis Carroll in *Through the Looking-glass*, combining **chuckle** + **snort**]

chorus *noun* **1** a set of lines in a song, sung as a refrain after each verse. **2** a large choir. **3** a piece of music for such a choir. **4** the group of singers and dancers supporting the soloists in an opera or musical show. **5** something uttered by a number of people at the same time: *a chorus of 'No's'.* **6** *theatre* an actor who delivers an introductory or concluding passage to a play. **7** *Greek theatre* a group of actors, always on stage, who comment on developments in the plot. ▸ *verb* to say, sing or utter simultaneously. [16c: Latin, meaning 'band of dancers, singers, etc']

chose *past tense of* **choose**

chosen *past participle of* **choose**

choux pastry /ʃuː/ *noun* a very light pastry made with eggs. [19c: from French *pâte choux* cabbage paste]

chow *noun* a breed of dog with thick fur, a curled tail and a blue tongue. [19c: prob from Pidgin English]

chowder *noun, chiefly N Am* a thick soup or stew made from clams or fish with vegetables. [18c: from French *chaudière* pot]

chow mein *noun* a Chinese-style dish of chopped meat and vegetables, served with fried noodles. [Early 20c: Chinese, meaning 'fried noodles']

chrism *or* **chrisom** *noun, relig* holy oil used for anointing in the Roman Catholic and Greek Orthodox Churches. [13c: from Greek *chrisma* anointing]

Christ *noun* **1** the Messiah whose coming is prophesied in the Old Testament. **2** Jesus of Nazareth, or Jesus Christ, believed by Christians to be the Messiah. **3** a figure or picture of Jesus. [Anglo-Saxon *Crist*]

christen *verb* **1** to give a person, esp a baby, a name as part of the religious ceremony of receiving them into the Christian Church. Compare **baptize**. **2** to give a name or nickname to someone. **3** *humorous, informal* to use something for the first time: *Shall we christen the new wine glasses?* ▪ **christening** *noun*. [Anglo-Saxon *cristnian*]

Christendom *noun* all Christian people and parts of the world.

Christian *noun* **1** someone who believes in, and follows the teachings and example of, Jesus Christ. **2** *informal* someone having Christian qualities. ▸ *adj* **1** relating to Jesus Christ, the Christian religion or Christians. **2** *informal* showing virtues associated with Christians, such as kindness, patience, tolerance and generosity. ▪ **Christianity** *noun*. [16c: from Latin *Christianus*]

christian name *noun* **1** *loosely* anyone's first or given name; a forename. Compare **first name**, **forename**. **2** the personal name given to a Christian at baptism.

Christmas *noun* **1** the annual Christian festival held on 25 December, which commemorates the birth of Christ. Also called **Christmas Day**. **2** the period of, mostly non-religious, celebration surrounding this date. ▪ **Christmassy** *adj*. [Anglo-Saxon *Cristesmæsse* Christ's Mass]

chromatic *adj* **1** relating to colours; coloured. **2** *music* relating to, or using notes from, the **chromatic scale**. See also **diatonic**. [17c: from Greek *chroma* colour]

chromatic scale *noun, music* a scale which proceeds by **semitones**.

chromatin *noun, biol* in a cell nucleus: the material, composed of **DNA**, **RNA** and proteins, which becomes organized into visible chromosomes at the time of cell division. [19c: from Greek *chroma* colour]

chromato- see **chromo-**

chromatography *noun, chem* a technique for separating the components of a mixture of liquids or gases by allowing them to pass through a material through which different substances are adsorbed at different rates. [1930s: from Greek *chroma* colour + *graphein* to write]

chrome *noun, non-technical* chromium, esp when used as a silvery plating for other metals. ▸ *verb* **1** in dyeing: to treat with a chromium solution. **2** to plate with chrome. [19c: French]

chromite *noun, geol* a mineral that is the main source of chromium.

chromium *noun, chem* (symbol **Cr**) a hard silvery metallic element that is resistant to corrosion, used in electroplating and in alloys with iron and nickel to make stainless steel. [19c: a Latinized form of **chrome**]

chromo- *or* **chromato-** *combining form, signifying* **1** colour. **2** chromium. [From Greek *chroma* colour]

chromosome *noun* in the nucleus of a cell: any of a number of microscopic thread-like structures that become visible as small rod-shaped bodies at the time of cell division, and which contain, in the form of DNA, all the genetic information needed for the development of the cell and the whole organism. [19c: from German *chromosom*]

chromosphere *or* **chromatosphere** *noun, astron* a layer of gas, mainly hydrogen, that lies above the Sun's **photosphere**. [19c: from Greek *chroma* colour + **sphere**]

chronic *adj* **1** of a disease or symptoms: long-lasting, usu of gradual onset and often difficult to treat: *chronic pain*. Compare **acute**. **2** *Brit informal* very bad; severe: *The film was chronic*. **3** habitual: *a chronic dieter*. [16c: from Greek *chronikos* relating to time]

chronic fatigue syndrome see **myalgic encephalomyelitis**

chronicle *noun* (*often* **chronicles**) a record of historical events year by year in the order in which they occurred. ▸ *verb* to record (an event) in a chronicle. ▪ **chronicler** *noun*. [14c: diminutive of French *chronique*]

chronological *adj* **1** according to the order of occurrence. **2** relating to chronology. ▪ **chronologically** *adv*.

chronology *noun* (*-ies*) **1** the study or science of determining the correct order of historical events. **2** the arrangement of events in order of occurrence. **3** a table or list showing events in order of occurrence. ▪ **chronologist** *noun.*

chronometer *noun* a type of watch or clock, used esp at sea, which is designed to keep accurate time in all conditions.

chrysalis /'krɪsəlɪs/ *or* **chrysalid** *noun* (***chrysalises*** *or* ***chrysalides*** /-'salɪdiːz/) **1** the pupa of insects that undergo **metamorphosis**, eg butterflies, moths. **2** the protective case that surrounds the pupa. [17c: from Greek *chrysallis*]

chrysanthemum *noun* a garden plant of the daisy family, with large bushy flowers. [16c: from Greek *chrysos* gold + *anthemon* flower]

chub *noun* a small fat river-fish of the carp family.

chubby *adj* (*-ier, -iest*) plump. ▪ **chubbiness** *noun.* [18c]

chuck[1] *verb* **1** *informal* to throw or fling. **2** to give (someone) an affectionate tap under the chin. ▸ *noun* **1** *informal* a toss, fling or throw. **2** an affectionate tap under the chin.

PHRASAL VERBS **chuck sth in** *informal* to give it up or abandon it. **chuck sb** *or* **sth out** *informal* to get rid of them or it.

chuck[2] *noun* a device for holding a piece of work in a lathe, or for holding the blade or bit in a drill. [17c: variant of **chock**]

chuckle *verb, intr* to laugh quietly, esp in a half-suppressed private way. ▸ *noun* an amused little laugh. [17c: prob from *chuck* to cluck like a hen]

chuddar see **chador**

chuff *verb, intr* of a steam train: to progress with regular puffing noises. [Early 20c: imitating the sound]

chuffed *adj, Brit informal* very pleased. [19c: from dialect *chuff* plump or swollen with pride]

chug *verb* (***chugged, chugging***) *intr* of a motor boat, motor car, etc: to progress while making a quiet thudding noise. [19c: imitating the sound]

chukker *or* **chukka** *noun* any of the six periods of play in polo each of which normally lasts for seven and a half minutes. [19c: from Hindi *cakkar* round]

chum *noun, informal* a close friend. ▸ *verb* (***chummed, chumming***) **1** *intr* (*usu* **chum up with sb**) to make friends with them. **2** to accompany someone: *She chummed me to the clinic.* ▪ **chummy** *adj* (*-ier, -iest*). [19c: perhaps from *chamber fellow* a fellow student]

chump *noun* **1** *informal* an idiot; a fool. **2** the thick end of anything, esp of a loin cut of lamb or mutton: *a chump chop.* **3** a short thick heavy block of wood. [18c: perhaps a combination of **chunk** + **lump**]

IDIOMS **off one's chump** *Brit informal* crazy.

chunk *noun* **1** a thick, esp irregularly shaped, piece. **2** *informal* a large or considerable amount. [17c]

chunky *adj* (*-ier, -iest*) **1** thick-set; stockily or strongly built. **2** of clothes, fabrics, etc: thick; bulky. **3** solid and strong.

church *noun* **1** a building for public Christian worship. **2** the religious services held in a church. **3** (**the Church**) the clergy as a profession: *enter the Church.* **4** (*often* **the Church**) the clergy considered as a political group: *quarrels between Church and State.* **5** (*usu* **Church**) any of many branches of Christians with their own doctrines, style of worship, etc: *the Methodist Church.* **6** the whole Christian establishment. [Anglo-Saxon *cirice*]

churchgoer *noun* someone who regularly attends church services.

churchman *or* **churchwoman** *noun* a member of the clergy or of a church.

churchwarden *noun* in the Church of England: either of two lay members of a congregation elected to look after the church's property, money, etc.

churchyard *noun* the burial ground round a church.

churl *noun* an ill-bred surly person. ▪ **churlish** *adj* ill-mannered or rude. ▪ **churlishly** *adv.* [Anglo-Saxon *ceorl* peasant]

churn *noun* **1** a machine in which milk is vigorously shaken to make butter. **2** a large milk can. ▸ *verb* **1 a** to make (butter) in a churn; **b** to turn (milk) into butter in a churn. **2** (*often* **churn sth up**) to shake or agitate it violently. [Anglo-Saxon *ciern*]

PHRASAL VERBS **churn sth out** to keep producing things of tedious similarity in large quantities.

chute[1] *noun* **1** a sloping channel down which to send water, rubbish, etc. **2** a slide in a children's playground or swimming-pool. **3** a waterfall or rapid. [19c: French]

chute[2] *noun, informal* short for **parachute**.

chutney *noun* a type of pickle, made with fruit, vinegar, spices, sugar, etc. [19c: from Hindi *chatni*]

chutzpah /'xʊtspə/ *noun, chiefly N Am informal* self-assurance bordering on impudence. [19c: Yiddish]

Ci *symbol, physics* curie.

CIA *abbrev* Central Intelligence Agency.

ciabatta /tʃə'batə/ *noun* (***ciabattas*** *or* ***ciabatte*** /-teɪ/) **1** Italian bread with an open texture, made with olive oil. **2** a loaf of this bread. [20c: Italian, meaning 'slipper']

ciao /tʃaʊ/ *exclam* an informal greeting used on meeting and parting. [20c: Italian, a dialect alteration of *schiavo* I am your slave]

cicada /sɪ'kɑːdə/ *or* **cicala** /sɪ'kɑːlə/ *noun* (***cicadas*** *or* ***cicadae*** /-diː/; ***cicalas*** *or* ***cicale*** /-leɪ/) a large insect of mainly tropical regions, the male of which is noted for its high-pitched warbling sound. [19c: Latin]

cicatrice /'sikətrɪs/ *or* **cicatrix** /'sɪkətrɪks/ *noun* (***cicatrices*** /-trɪsiːz, -traɪsiːz/ *or* ***cicatrixes***) *med* the scar tissue that lies over a healed wound. [15c: Latin *cicatrix*]

CID *abbrev* Criminal Investigation Department.

-cide *or* **-icide** *combining form, forming nouns, denoting* a person, substance or thing that kills: *pesticide.* [From Latin *caedere* to cut down]

cider *or* **cyder** *noun* an alcoholic drink made from apples. [14c: from Hebrew *shekhar* intoxicating liquor]

cigar *noun* a long slender roll of tobacco leaves for smoking. [18c: from Spanish *cigarro*]

cigarette *noun* a tube of finely cut tobacco rolled in thin paper, for smoking. [19c: French diminutive of *cigare* cigar]

cigarillo *noun* a small cigar. [19c: Spanish diminutive of *cigarro* cigar]

ciggy *or* **cig** *noun* (***ciggies***) *informal* short for **cigarette.**

cilium *noun* (***cilia*** /'sɪlɪə/) *biol* any of the short hair-like appendages that project from the surface of certain cells, and whose rhythmic movement aids cell movement. [18c: Latin, meaning 'eyelash']

cinch /sɪntʃ/ *noun, informal* **1** an easily accomplished task. **2** a certainty. [19c: from Spanish *cincha* saddle girth]

cinchona /sɪŋ'koʊnə/ *noun* any tree of the type yielding bark from which quinine and related by-products are obtained. [18c: named after Countess of Chinchon]

cincture *noun, chiefly literary* a belt or girdle. [16c: from Latin *cinctura*]

cinder *noun* **1** a piece of burnt coal or wood. **2** (**cinders**) ashes. [Anglo-Saxon *sinder* slag]

Cinderella *noun* **1** someone who achieves recognition or fame after being unknown. **2** someone or something whose charms or merits go unnoticed. [19c: named after the heroine of the fairy tale *Cinderella*]

cinema *noun* **1** a theatre in which motion pictures are shown. **2** (*usu* **the cinema**) **a** motion pictures or films generally; **b** the art or business of making films. ▪ **cinematic** *adj*. [19c: shortened from **cinematograph**]

cinematograph *noun* an apparatus for taking and projecting a series of still photographs in rapid succession so as to present a single moving scene. [19c: from Greek *kinema* motion + **-graph** (sense 1)]

cinematography *noun* the art of making motion pictures. ▪ **cinematographer** *noun*.

cinerarium /sɪnə'rɛərɪəm/ *noun* (***cineraria*** /-rɪə/) a place for keeping the ashes of the dead.

cinnabar *noun* **1** *geol* a bright red mineral form of mercury sulphide. **2** a bright orange-red colour. [15c: from Greek *kinnabari*]

cinnamon *noun* a spice obtained from the cured dried bark of a SE Asian tree.

cinquefoil *noun* **1** a plant of the rose family with five-petalled flowers, and leaves divided into five sections. **2** *archit* a design composed of five petal-like arcs. [14c: from French *cincfoille*]

cipher *or* **cypher** *noun* **1** a secret code. **2** something written in code. **3** the key to a code. **4** an interlaced set of initials; a monogram. **5** *maths, old use* the symbol 0, used to fill blanks in writing numbers, but of no value itself. **6** a person or thing of no importance. ▶ *verb* to write (a message, etc) in code. [14c: from Latin *ciphra*]

circa *prep* (abbrev **c.** and **ca.**) used esp with dates: about; approximately: *circa 1250*. [19c: Latin, meaning 'about' or 'around']

circadian *adj, biol* relating to a biological rhythm that is more or less synchronized to a 24-hour cycle. [20c: from Latin *circa* around + *dies* day]

circle *noun* **1** a perfectly round two-dimensional figure that is bordered by the **circumference**, every point of which is an equal distance from a fixed point within the figure called the **centre**. **2** anything in the form of a circle. **3** a circular route. **4** in a theatre, auditorium etc: a gallery of seats above the main stalls: *the dress circle*. **5** a series or chain of events, steps or developments, ending at the point where it began. See also **vicious circle**. **6** a group of people associated in some way: *his circle of acquaintances*. ▶ *verb* **1** *tr & intr* **a** to move in a circle; **b** to move in a circle round something. **2** to draw a circle round something. [Anglo-Saxon *circul*]

IDIOMS **go round in circles** to be trapped in a frustrating cycle of repetitive discussion or activity.

circlet *noun* **1** a simple band or hoop of gold, silver, etc worn on the head. **2** a small circle. [15c: from French *cerclet*, diminutive of *cercle* circle]

circuit *noun* **1** a complete course, journey or route round something. **2** a race track, running-track, etc. **3** (*sometimes* **electric circuit**) a path consisting of various electrical devices joined together by wires, to allow an electric current to flow continuously through it. **4** a round of places made by a travelling judge. **5** *sport* the round of tournaments in which competitors take part. ▶ *verb* to go round. [14c: French]

circuit-breaker *noun* in an electric circuit: a device that automatically interrupts the circuit if the current exceeds a certain value.

circuitous /sə'kjuːɪtəs/ *adj* indirect; roundabout.

circuitry *noun* (***-ies***) *elec* **1** a plan or system of circuits used in a particular electronic or electrical device. **2** the equipment or components making up such a system.

circular *adj* **1** having the form of a circle. **2** moving or going round in a circle, leading back to the starting point. **3** of reasoning, etc: illogical, since the truth of the premise cannot be proved without reference to the conclusion. **4** of a letter, etc: addressed and copied to a number of people. ▶ *noun* a circular letter or notice. ▪ **circularity** *noun*. [14c: from Latin *circularis*]

circular function *noun, maths* a **trigonometric function**.

circularize *or* **-ise** *verb* to send circulars to (people).

circular saw *noun* a power-driven saw which has a rotating disc-shaped blade with a serrated edge.

circulate *verb* **1** *tr & intr* to move or cause to move round freely, esp in a fixed route: *traffic circulating through the town*. **2** *tr & intr* to spread; to pass round: *circulate the report*. **3** *intr* to move around talking to different people, eg at a party. ▪ **circulatory** *adj*. [17c: from Latin *circulare* to encircle]

circulation *noun* **1** the act or process of circulating. **2** *anatomy* in most animals: the system of blood vessels that supplies oxygenated blood pumped by the heart to all parts of the body, and that transports deoxygenated blood to the lungs. **3** **a** the distribution of a newspaper or magazine; **b** the number of copies of it that are sold.

IDIOMS **in** *or* **out of circulation 1** of money: being, or not being, used by the public. **2** taking part, or not taking part, in one's usual social activities.

circum- *combining form, signifying* round about. [Latin, meaning 'about']

circumcircle *noun, geom* a circle drawn round another figure, especially round a triangle and touching all its points.

circumcise *verb* **1** to cut away all or part of the foreskin of the penis of (a male), as a religious rite or medical necessity. **2** to cut away the clitoris and sometimes the labia of (a woman). ▪ **circumcision** *noun*. [13c: from Latin *circumcidere*]

circumference *noun* **1** *geom* the length of the boundary of a circle. **2** the boundary of an area of any shape. **3** the distance represented by any of these. [14c: from **circum-** + Latin *ferre* to carry]

circumflex *noun* (*also* **circumflex accent**) in some languages, eg French: a mark placed over a vowel, eg *ô, û*, as an indication of pronunciation, length or the omission of a letter formerly pronounced. [16c: from Latin *circumflexus* bent]

circumlocution *noun* an unnecessarily long or indirect way of saying something. ▪ **circumlocutory** *adj.*

circumnavigate *verb* to sail or fly round, esp the world. ▪ **circumnavigation** *noun.* ▪ **circumnavigator** *noun.*

circumscribe *verb* **1** to put a boundary, or draw a line, round something. **2** to limit or restrict something. **3** *geom* to draw (a figure) around another figure so that they touch at as many points as possible but do not intersect. Compare **inscribe.** ▪ **circumscription** *noun.* [15c: from Latin *circumscribere*]

circumspect *adj* cautious; prudent; wary. ▪ **circumspection** *noun.* [15c: from Latin *circumspicere*]

circumstance *noun* **1** (*usu* **circumstances**) a fact, occurrence or condition, esp when relating to an act or event: *died in mysterious circumstances.* **2** (**circumstances**) one's financial situation. **3** events that one cannot control; fate. **4** ceremony: *pomp and circumstance.* [13c: from Latin *circumstantia*]

IDIOMS **in** *or* **under no circumstances** never, not for any reason at all. **in** *or* **under the circumstances** the situation being what it is or was.

circumstantial *adj* **1** relating to or dependent on circumstance. **2** of an account of an event: full of detailed description, etc.

circumstantiate *verb* to support or prove by citing circumstances. ▪ **circumstantiation** *noun.*

circumvent *verb* **1** to find a way of getting round or evading (a rule, law, etc). **2** to outwit or frustrate someone. ▪ **circumvention** *noun.* [16c: from Latin *circumvenire* to surround, beset, deceive]

circus *noun* **1 a** a travelling company of performers including acrobats, clowns and often trained animals, etc; **b** a performance by such a company. **2** *informal* a scene of noisy confusion. **3** in ancient Rome: an oval or circular open-air stadium for chariot-racing and other competitive sports. [16c: Latin, meaning 'circle', 'ring' or 'stadium']

cirque /sɜːk/ *noun, geog* a deep semicircular hollow with steep side and back walls, located high on a mountain slope. [19c: French]

cirrhosis /səˈroʊsɪs/ *noun, pathol* a progressive disease of the liver, esp alcohol related, which results in a wasting away of normal tissue. [19c: from Greek *kirrhos* tawny, the colour of diseased liver]

cirrocumulus /sɪroʊˈkjuːmjʊləs/ *noun* (***cirrocumuli*** /-laɪ/) *meteorol* a type of high cloud which consists of small masses of white clouds that form a rippled pattern.

cirrostratus /sɪroʊˈstrɑːtəs/ *noun* (***cirrostrati*** /-taɪ/) *meteorol* a type of high cloud which forms a thin whitish layer with a fibrous appearance.

cirrus /ˈsɪrəs/ *noun* (***cirri*** /-raɪ/) **1** *meteorol* a common type of high cloud composed of ice crystals, with a wispy fibrous or feathery appearance. **2** *zool* a curved filament, found in barnacles. **3** *botany* a **tendril.** [19c: Latin, meaning 'curl']

cissy see **sissy**

Cistercian *noun* a member of a strict Christian order formed in 1098. ▸ *adj* belonging or relating to this order. [17c: from the Latin place name *Cistercium*, now Cîteaux, France]

cistern *noun* **1** a tank storing water, usu in the roof-space of a house, or connected to a flushing toilet. **2** *archaeol* a natural underground reservoir. [13c: from Latin *cisterna* reservoir]

citadel *noun* a fortress built close to or within a city, for its protection and as a place of refuge. [16c: from Italian *cittadella*, diminutive of *città* city]

citation *noun* **1** the quoting or citing of something as example or proof. **2** a passage quoted from a book, etc. **3 a** a special official commendation or award for merit, bravery, etc; **b** a list of the reasons for such an award.

cite *verb* **1** to quote (a book, its author or a passage from it) as an example or proof. **2** to mention as an example or illustration. **3** *law* to summon someone to appear in court. **4** to mention someone in an official report by way of commendation: *cited for bravery.* ▪ **citable** *adj.* [15c: from French *citer* to summon]

citizen *noun* **1** an inhabitant of a city or town. **2** a native of a country, or a naturalized member of it.

citizenry *noun* (***-ies***) the citizens of a town, country, etc.

citizen's arrest *noun* an arrest made without a warrant by a member of the public.

citizenship *noun* **1** the status or position of a citizen. **2** the rights and duties of a citizen. **3** a person's conduct in relation to such duties.

citrate *noun, chem* a salt or ester of citric acid.

citric *adj* **1** derived from citric acid. **2** relating to or derived from citrus fruits. [19c: see **citrus**]

citric acid *noun, chem* an organic acid present in the juice of citrus fruit, which is used as a food flavouring and **antioxidant**.

citrin *noun* **bioflavonoid**. [20c]

citron *noun* **1** a fruit like a large lemon, with a thick sweet-smelling yellow rind. **2** the candied rind of this fruit, used for flavouring or decorating cakes, etc. **3** the small thorny evergreen Asian tree bearing the fruit. [16c: from Latin *citrus* the citron tree]

citrus *noun* any of a group of edible fruits with a tough outer peel enclosing juicy flesh rich in vitamin C, citric acid and water. Also called **citrus fruit**. [19c: Latin, meaning 'the citron tree']

city *noun* (***-ies***) **1** any large town. **2** in the UK: a town with a royal charter and usu a cathedral. **3** the body of inhabitants of a city. **4** (**the City**) the business centre of a city, esp London. [13c: from French *cité*]

city fathers *plural noun* **a** the magistrates of a city; **b** the members of a city's council.

city hall *noun* (*often* **City Hall**) **a** the local government of a city; **b** the building in which it is housed.

city-state *noun, hist* a sovereign state consisting of a city and its dependencies.

civet *noun* **1** (*also* **civet cat**) a small spotted and striped carnivorous mammal found in Asia and Africa. **2** a strong-smelling fluid secreted by this animal, used in perfumes to make their scent last. See also **musk**. **3** the fur of the animal. [16c: from French *civette*]

civic *adj* relating to a city, citizen or citizenship. ▪ **civically** *adv.*

civic centre *noun* a place, sometimes a specially designed complex, where the administrative offices and chief public buildings of a city are grouped.

civics *singular noun* the study of local government and of the rights and duties of citizenship.

civil *adj* **1** relating to the community: *civil affairs.* **2** relating to or occurring between citizens: *civil disturbances.* **3 a** relating to ordinary citizens; **b** not military, legal or religious. **4** *law* relating to cases about individual rights, etc, not criminal cases. **5** polite. ▪ **civilly** *adv.* [14c: from Latin *civilis* relating to citizens]

civil defence *noun* the organization and training of ordinary citizens to assist the armed forces in wartime.

civil disobedience *noun* the refusal to obey regulations, pay taxes, etc as a form of non-violent protest, usu against the government.

civil engineering *noun* the branch of engineering concerned with the design, construction, and maintenance of roads, bridges, railways, tunnels, docks, etc as carried out by a **civil engineer**.

civilian *noun* anyone who is not a member of the armed forces or the police force. [14c: from French *civilien* relating to civil law]

civility *noun* (**-ies**) **1** politeness. **2 a** an act of politeness; **b** a polite remark or gesture. [16c: from French *civilité*]

civilization *or* **-isation** *noun* **1** a stage of development in human society that is socially, politically, culturally and technologically advanced. **2** the parts of the world that have reached such a stage. **3** the state of having achieved or the process of achieving such a stage. **4** *usu hist* a people and their society and culture: *the Minoan civilization.* **5** built-up areas as opposed to wild, uncultivated or sparsely populated parts. **6** intellectual or spiritual enlightenment, as opposed to brutishness or coarseness.

civilize *or* **-ise** *verb* **1** to lead out of a state of barbarity to a more advanced stage of social development. **2** to educate and enlighten morally, intellectually and spiritually. ▪ **civilized** *adj.* [16c: French *civiliser*]

civil law *noun* the part of a country's law that deals with the rights etc of its citizens, rather than crimes. Compare **criminal law**.

civil liberty *noun* (*often* **civil liberties**) personal freedom of thought, word, action, etc and the right to exercise it.

civil list *noun* in the UK: the annual Parliamentary allowance to the sovereign and certain members of the Royal family for household expenses.

civil partnership *or* **civil union** *noun* an agreement between two people, usu of the same sex, giving them a legal status similar to that of a married couple.

civil rights *plural noun* the personal rights of any citizen of a country to freedom and equality, regardless of race, religion, sex or sexuality.

civil service *noun* the body of officials employed by a government to administer the affairs of a country, excluding the military, naval, legislative and judicial areas. ▪ **civil servant** *noun.*

civil war *noun* a war between citizens of the same state.

civvy *noun* (**-ies**) *informal* **1** a civilian. **2** (**civvies**) ordinary civilian clothes as opposed to a military uniform.

CJD *abbrev* Creutzfeldt-Jakob disease.

Cl *symbol, chem* chlorine.

cl *abbrev* centilitre.

clack *noun* a sharp noise made by one hard object striking another. ▸ *verb* **1** *tr & intr* to make or cause something to make this kind of noise. **2** *intr* to talk noisily. [13c: imitating the sound]

clad *adj, literary* **1** clothed. **2** *also in compounds* covered: *velvet-clad* • *stone-clad.* ▸ *verb* (**clad, cladding**) to cover one material with another, eg brick or stonework with a different material, esp to form a protective layer. [14c: past tense & past participle of **clothe**]

cladistics *singular noun, biol* a system of classification in which organisms are grouped together on the basis of similarities. [20c: from Greek *klados* branch]

claim *verb* **1** to state something firmly, insisting on its truth. **2** to declare oneself (to be, to have done, etc). **3** to assert that one has something: *He claimed no knowledge of the crime.* **4** *tr & intr* to demand or assert as a right: *He claimed his prize.* **5** to take or use up something: *The hurricane claimed 300 lives.* **6 a** to need; **b** to have a right to something: *The baby claimed its mother's attention.* **7** to declare that one is the owner of something. ▸ *noun* **1** a statement of something as a truth. **2** a demand, esp for something to which one has, or believes one has, a right: *lay claim to the throne.* **3** a right to or reason for something: *a claim to fame.* **4** something one has claimed, eg a piece of land or a sum of money. **5** a demand for compensation, in accordance with an insurance policy, etc. ▪ **claimable** *adj.* ▪ **claimant** *noun.* [13c: from Latin *clamare* to cry out]

clairvoyance *or* **clairvoyancy** *noun* the alleged ability to see into the future, or know things that cannot be discovered through the normal range of senses. [19c: French, literally 'clear-seeing']

clairvoyant *adj* involving or claiming the power of clairvoyance. ▸ *noun* someone who claims to have the power of clairvoyance.

clam *noun* **1 a** any of various **bivalve** shellfish; **b** its edible flesh. **2** *informal* an uncommunicative person. ▸ *verb* (**clammed, clamming**) *intr, chiefly US* to gather clams. [16c: a shortening of *clamshell* a shell which clamps]

PHRASAL VERBS **clam up** *informal* **1** to stop talking suddenly. **2** to refuse to speak.

clamber *verb, intr* to climb using one's hands as well as one's feet. ▸ *noun* an act of clambering. [15c: related to **climb**]

clammy *adj* (**-ier, -iest**) **1** moist or damp, esp unpleasantly so. **2** of the weather: humid. [Anglo-Saxon *clæman* to smear]

clamour *or* (*N Am*) **clamor** *noun* **1** a noise of shouting or loud talking. **2** loud protesting or loud demands. ▸ *verb, intr* to make a loud continuous outcry. ▪ **clamorous** *adj.* [14c: French]

clamp *noun* **1** a tool with adjustable jaws for gripping things firmly or pressing parts together. **2** (*usu* **wheel clamp**) a heavy metal device fitted to the wheels of an illegally parked car, to prevent its being moved. ▸ *verb* **1** to fasten together or hold with a clamp. **2**

to fit a clamp to a wheel of (a parked car) to prevent its being moved. **3** to hold, grip or shut tightly. [14c: from Dutch *klampe*]

PHRASAL VERBS **clamp down on sth** *or* **sb** to put a stop to or to control it or them strictly.

clampdown *noun* **a** a suppressive measure; **b** repression of activity: *a clampdown on drugs.*

clamshell phone *noun* a mobile phone consisting of two working parts joined by a hinge so that it can be folded and unfolded.

clan *noun* **1** in Scotland or among people of Scots origin: a group of families, generally with the same surname, and (esp formerly) led by a chief. **2** *humorous* one's family or relations. **3** a group of people who have similar interests, concerns, etc. [14c: from Scottish Gaelic *clann* family]

clandestine *adj* kept secret; furtive; surreptitious. ▪ **clandestinely** *adv.* [16c: from Latin *clandestinus*]

clang *verb, tr & intr* to ring or make something ring loudly and deeply. ▸ *noun* this ringing sound. [16c: from Latin *clangere* to resound]

clanger *noun, informal* a tactless, embarrassing and obvious blunder.

clangour *or* (*US*) **clangor** *noun, poetic* a loud resounding noise. [16c: from Latin *clangor*]

clank *noun* a sharp metallic sound like pieces of metal striking together. ▸ *verb, tr & intr* to make or cause something to make such a sound. [17c: imitating the sound]

clannish *adj, derog* of a group of people: closely united, with little interest in people not belonging to the group.

clansman *or* **clanswoman** *noun* a member of a clan.

clap *verb* (***clapped, clapping***) **1** *tr & intr* to strike the palms of (one's hands) together with a loud noise, in order to mark (a rhythm), gain attention, etc. **2** *tr & intr* to applaud someone or something by clapping. **3** to strike someone softly with the palm of the hand, usu as a friendly gesture. **4** to place forcefully: *clapped the book on the table.* ▸ *noun* **1** an act of clapping. **2** the sudden loud explosion of noise made by thunder. [Anglo-Saxon *clæppan*]

clapped out *adj, informal* **1** of a machine, etc: old, worn out and no longer working properly. **2** *Aust, NZ* of a person: exhausted.

clapper *noun* the dangling piece of metal inside a bell that strikes against the sides to make it ring.

IDIOMS **like the clappers** *informal* very quickly; at top speed.

clapperboard *noun* a pair of hinged boards clapped together in front of the camera before and after shooting a piece of film, to help synchronize sound and vision.

claptrap *noun* meaningless or pompous talk.

claque *noun* **1** a group of people paid to applaud a speaker at a meeting or performer in a theatre, etc. **2** a circle of flatterers or admirers. [19c: from French *claquer* to clap]

claret *noun* **1** a French red wine, esp from the Bordeaux area in SW France. **2** the deep reddish-purple colour of this wine. [14c: from French *clairet* clear wine]

clarify *verb* (***-ies, -ied***) *tr & intr* **1** to make or become clearer or easier to understand. **2** of butter, fat, etc: to make or become clear by heating. ▪ **clarification** *noun.* [19c: from Latin *clarus* clear]

clarinet *noun, music* a woodwind instrument with a cylindrical tube and a single **reed** (sense 2). ▪ **clarinettist** *noun.* [18c: French *clarinette*]

clarion *noun, chiefly poetic, hist* an old kind of trumpet with a shrill sound: *a clarion call.* [14c: French]

clarity *noun* **1** the quality of being clear and pure. **2** the quality of being easy to see, hear or understand. [17c: from Latin *claritas* clearness]

clash *noun* **1** a loud noise, like that of metal objects striking each other. **2** a serious disagreement; a quarrel or argument. **3** a fight, battle or match. ▸ *verb* **1** *tr & intr* of metal objects, etc: to strike against each other noisily. **2** *intr* to come into physical or verbal conflict. **3** *intr* of commitments, etc: to coincide, usu not fortuitously. **4** *intr* of colours, styles, etc: to be unpleasing or unharmonious together. [16c: imitating the sound]

clasp *noun* **1** a fastening on jewellery, a bag, etc made of two parts that link together. **2** a firm grip, or act of gripping. ▸ *verb* **1** to hold or take hold of someone or something firmly. **2** to fasten or secure something with a clasp.

class *noun* **1** a lesson or lecture. **2** a number of pupils taught together. **3** *esp US* the body of students that begin or finish university or school in the same year: *class of '94.* **4** a category, kind or type, members of which share common characteristics. **5** a grade or standard. **6** any of the social groupings into which people fall according to their job, wealth, etc. **7** the system by which society is divided into such groups. **8** *informal* **a** stylishness in dress, behaviour, etc; **b** good quality. **9** *biol* in taxonomy: any of the groups into which a **phylum** in the animal kingdom or a **division** (sense 7) in the plant kingdom is divided, and which is in turn subdivided into one or more **order**s (sense 11). ▸ *verb* **a** to regard someone or something as belonging to a certain class; **b** to put into a category. [17c: from Latin *classis* rank, class, division]

IDIOMS **in a class of its own** with no equal.

class-conscious *adj, derog* aware of one's own and other people's social class.

classic *adj* **1** made of or belonging to the highest quality; established as the best. **2** entirely typical. **3** simple, neat and elegant, esp in a traditional style. ▸ *noun* **1** an established work of literature. **2** an outstanding example of its type. **3** something, eg an item of clothing, which will always last, irrespective of fashions and fads. ▪ **classically** *adv.* [17c: from Latin *classicus* relating to classes, esp the best]

classical *adj* **1** of literature, art, etc: **a** from ancient Greece and Rome; **b** in the style of ancient Greece and Rome. **2** of architecture or the other arts: showing the influence of ancient Greece and Rome: *a classical façade.* **3** of music and arts related to it: having an established, traditional and somewhat formal style and form. **4** of a shape, design, etc: simple; pure; without complicated decoration. **5** of a language: being the older literary form. **6** of an education: concentrating on Latin, Greek and the humanities.

classicism *noun* **1** in art and literature: a simple elegant style based on the Roman and Greek principles of beauty, good taste, restraint and clarity. **2** a Latin or Greek idiom or form.

classicist *noun* someone who has studied classics, esp as a university subject.

classics *singular noun* (*often* **the Classics**) **a** the study of Latin and Greek; **b** the study of the literature and history of ancient Greece and Rome.

classification *noun* **1** the arrangement and division of things and people into classes. **2** a group or class into which a person or thing is put.

classified *adj* **1** arranged in groups or classes. **2** of information: kept secret or restricted by the government.

classify *verb* (**-ies, -ied**) **1** to put into a particular group or category. **2** of information: to declare it secret and not for publication. ▪ **classifiable** *adj.*

classless *adj* **1** of a community, society etc: not divided into social classes. **2** not belonging to any particular social class.

classmate *noun* a fellow pupil or student in one's class at school or college.

classroom *noun* a room in a school or college where classes are taught.

class war *noun* hostility between the various classes of society.

classy *adj* (**-ier, -iest**) *informal* **a** stylish or fashionable; **b** superior.

clatter *noun* a loud noise made by hard objects striking each other, or falling onto a hard surface. ▸ *verb, tr & intr* to make or cause to make this noise. [Anglo-Saxon *clatrunge* clattering]

clause *noun* **1** *grammar* **a** a group of words that includes a subject and its related finite verb, and which may or may not constitute a sentence (eg *if time permits* and *we will come tomorrow*). See **main clause**, **subordinate clause**; **b** a group of words with a similar grammatical function, but which has no expressed subject (eg *while running for the bus*), no finite verb (eg *time permitting*), or neither a subject nor a verb (eg *if possible*). **2** *law* a paragraph or section in a contract, will or act of parliament. ▪ **clausal** *adj.* [13c: from Latin *claudere* to close]

claustrophobia *noun* an irrational fear of being in confined spaces. ▪ **claustrophobic** *adj.* [19c: from Latin *claustrum* bolt or barrier + Greek *phobos* fear]

clavichord *noun* an early keyboard instrument with a soft tone. [15c: from Latin *clavis* key + *chorda* string]

clavicle *noun, anatomy* in vertebrates: either of two short slender bones linking the shoulder-blades with the top of the breastbone. [17c: from Latin *clavicula*, diminutive of *clavis* key]

claw *noun* **1** a hard curved pointed nail on the end of each digit of the foot in birds, most reptiles and many mammals. **2** the foot of an animal or bird with a number of such nails. **3** something with the shape or action of a claw, eg part of a mechanical device. ▸ *verb, tr & intr* (*often* **claw at sth**) to tear or scratch it with claws, nails or fingers. [Anglo-Saxon *clawu*]

PHRASAL VERBS **claw sth back 1** of a government: to recover money given away in benefits and allowances by imposing a new tax. **2** to regain something with difficulty (eg commercial advantage etc): *She clawed her way back to solvency.*

clay *noun* **1** *geol* a poorly draining soil consisting mainly of aluminium **silicate**s, which is pliable when wet and is used to make pottery, bricks, ceramics, etc. **2** earth or soil generally. **3** *poetic* the substance of which the human body is formed. [Anglo-Saxon *clæg*]

claymore *noun, hist* a two-edged broadsword used by Scottish highlanders. [18c: from Scottish Gaelic *claidheamh mór* large sword]

clay pigeon *noun* a clay disc that is thrown up mechanically as a target in the sport of **clay pigeon shooting**.

clean *adj* **1** free from dirt or contamination. **2** not containing anything harmful to health; pure. **3** pleasantly fresh: *a clean taste.* **4** recently washed. **5** hygienic in habits: *a clean animal.* **6** unused; unmarked. **7** neat and even: *a clean cut.* **8** simple and elegant: *a ship with good clean lines.* **9** clear of legal offences: *a clean driving licence.* **10** morally pure; innocent. **11** of humour, etc: not offensive or obscene. **12** fair: *a clean fight.* **13** *slang* not carrying drugs or offensive weapons. **14** absolute; complete: *make a clean break.* ▸ *adv* **1** *informal* completely: *I clean forgot.* **2** straight or directly; encountering no obstruction: *sailed clean through the window.* ▸ *verb, tr & intr* to make or become free from dirt. ▸ *noun* an act of cleaning. [Anglo-Saxon *clæne*]

IDIOMS **come clean** *informal* to admit or tell the truth about something that one has previously concealed or lied about. **make a clean breast of sth** to confess or admit to having done it, esp through feelings of guilt.

PHRASAL VERBS **clean sth out** to clean (a room or cupboard, etc) thoroughly. **clean up 1** to clean a place thoroughly. **2** *slang* to make a large profit.

clean-cut *adj* **1** pleasingly regular in outline or shape: *clean-cut features.* **2** neat; respectable.

cleaner *noun* **1** someone employed to clean inside buildings, offices, etc. **2** a machine or substance used for cleaning. **3** (*usu* **cleaners**) a shop where clothes, etc can be taken for cleaning.

IDIOMS **take sb to the cleaners** *informal* to take away, esp dishonestly, all of their money.

clean-living *adj* leading a decent healthy existence.

cleanly *adv* **1** in a clean way. **2** tidily; efficiently; easily. ▪ **cleanliness** /ˈklɛnlɪnəs/ *noun.*

cleanse *verb* **1** to clean or get rid of dirt from someone or something. **2 a** to purify someone or something; **b** to remove sin or guilt from someone. ▪ **cleanser** *noun.* [Anglo-Saxon *clænsian*]

clean-shaven *adj* of men: with facial hair shaved.

clean sheet *noun* a record with no blemishes.

clean sweep *noun* **1** a complete or overwhelming success. **2** a complete change or clear-out.

clear *adj* **1** transparent; easy to see through. **2** of weather, etc: not misty or cloudy. **3** of the skin: healthy; unblemished by spots, etc. **4 a** easy to see, hear or understand; **b** lucid. **5** bright; sharp; well-defined: *a clear photograph.* **6** of vision: not obstructed. **7** certain; having no doubts or confusion. **8** definite; free of doubt, ambiguity or confusion. **9** evident; obvious. **10** free from obstruction: *a clear path.* **11** well away from something; out of range of or contact with it: *well clear of the rocks.* **12** free of something; no longer affected by it. **13** of the conscience, etc: free from guilt, etc. **14** free of appointments, etc. ▸ *adv* **1** in a clear manner. **2** completely: *get clear away.* **3** *N Am* all the way: *see clear to the hills.* **4** well away from something; out of the way of it: *steer clear of trouble.* ▸ *verb* **1** *tr & intr* to make or become clear, free of obstruction, etc. **2** to remove or move out of the way. **3** to prove or declare to be innocent or free from suspicion. **4** to get over or past something without touching it: *clear the fence*. **5** to make as profit over expenses. **6** to pass inspection by (customs). **7** to give or get official permission for (a plan, etc). **8** to approve someone for a special assignment, access to secret information, etc. **9** *tr & intr* of a cheque: to pass from one bank to another through a clearing-house. **10** to pay a debt. **11** *tr & intr* to give or receive clearance: *The aeroplane was cleared for take-off.* [13c: from French *cler*]

IDIOMS **clear the air** *informal* to get rid of bad feeling, suspicion or tension, esp by frank discussion. **in the clear** no longer under suspicion, in difficulties, etc.

PHRASAL VERBS **clear sth away** to remove it. **clear off** *informal* to go away. **clear out** *informal* to go away. **clear sth out** to rid it of rubbish, etc. **clear up 1** of the weather: to brighten after rain, a storm, etc. **2** to get better. **clear sth up 1** to tidy up a mess, room, etc. **2** to solve a mystery, etc.

clearance *noun* **1** the act of clearing. **2** the distance between one object and another passing beside or under it. **3** permission, or a certificate granting this: *The plane was given clearance to land.*

clear-cut *adj* clear; sharp.

clear-headed *adj* capable of, or showing, clear logical thought. ▪ **clear-headedly** *adv.*

clearing *noun* an area in a forest, etc that has been cleared of trees, etc.

clearing bank *noun* a bank using the services of a central clearing-house.

clearing-house *noun* **1** an establishment that deals with transactions between its member banks. **2** a central agency that collects, organizes and distributes information.

clearly *adv* **1** in a clear manner: *speak clearly.* **2** obviously: *Clearly, he's wrong.*

clear-out *noun* a clearing out of something, eg rubbish, possessions, etc.

clear-sighted *adj* capable of, or showing, accurate observation and good judgement.

clearstory see **clerestory**

clearway *noun* a stretch of road on which cars may not stop except in an emergency.

cleat *noun* **1** a wedge. **2** a piece of wood attached to a structure to give it extra support. [14c: prob from **clot**]

cleavage *noun* **1** *informal* the hollow between a woman's breasts, esp as revealed by a top with a low neck. **2** *geol* **a** the splitting of rocks into thin parallel sheets; **b** the splitting of a crystal in one or more specific directions to give smooth surfaces. [19c: from **cleave**[1]]

cleave[1] *verb* (*past tense* ***clove, cleft*** *or* ***cleaved,*** *past participle* ***cloven, cleft*** *or* ***cleaved***) *tr & intr, formal or literary* **1** to split or divide. **2** to cut or slice. [Anglo-Saxon *cleofan*]

cleave[2] *verb, intr* to cling or stick. [Anglo-Saxon *cleofian*]

cleaver *noun* a knife with a large square blade, used esp by butchers for chopping meat.

clef *noun, music* a symbol placed on a **stave** to indicate the pitch of the notes written on it. [16c: French, meaning 'key']

cleft[1] *noun* a split, fissure, wide crack or deep indentation. [13c: from **cleave**[1]]

cleft[2] *adj* split; divided. ▸ *verb* see **cleave**[1]. [14c]

IDIOMS **in a cleft stick** in a difficult or awkward situation.

cleft palate *noun, pathol* a split in the palate caused by the failure of the two sides of the mouth to meet and fuse together in the developing fetus. See also **harelip**.

clematis /ˈklɛmətɪs, kləˈmeɪtɪs/ *noun* a garden climbing plant with purple, yellow or white flowers. [16c: from Greek *klematis*]

clemency *noun* **1** the quality of being clement. **2** mercy.

clement *adj* of the weather: mild; not harsh or severe. [15c: from Latin *clemens* calm or merciful]

clementine *noun* a citrus fruit which is a type of small tangerine or a hybrid of a tangerine and an orange. [20c: French]

clench *verb* **1** to close one's teeth or one's fists tightly, esp in anger. **2** to hold or grip firmly. [Anglo-Saxon *beclencan* to hold fast]

clerestory *or* **clearstory** /ˈklɪəstɔːrɪ/ *noun* (***-ies***) *archit* in a church: a row of windows in the nave wall, above the roof of the aisle. [15c: from **clear** + **storey**]

clergy *singular or plural noun* (***-ies***) the ordained ministers of the Christian Church, or the priests of any religion. [13c: French]

clergyman *or* **clergywoman** *noun* a member of the clergy.

cleric *noun* a clergyman. [17c: from Latin *clericus* priest, clergyman]

clerical *adj* **1** relating to clerks, office workers or office work. **2** relating to the clergy.

clerihew /ˈklɛrɪhjuː/ *noun* a humorous poem about a famous person, consisting of two short couplets. [20c: named after E Clerihew Bentley, the English journalist and novelist who invented it]

clerk /klɑːk; *US* klɜːrk/ *noun* **1** in an office or bank: someone who deals with accounts, records, files, etc. **2** in a law court: someone who keeps records or accounts. **3** a public official in charge of the records and business affairs of the town council. **4** an unordained or lay minister of the Church. **5** *N Am* a shop assistant or hotel receptionist. ▪ **clerkship** *noun.* [Anglo-Saxon *clerc*]

clerk of works *noun* the person in charge of the construction and care of a building.

clever *adj* **1** good or quick at learning and understanding. **2** skilful, dexterous, nimble or adroit. **3** well thought out; ingenious. ▪ **cleverly** *adv.* ▪ **cleverness** *noun.* [16c as *cliver*]

cliché /ˈkliːʃeɪ/ *noun, derog* a once striking and effective phrase or combination of words which has become stale and hackneyed through overuse. ▪ **clichéd** *or* **cliché'd** *adj.* [19c: French, meaning 'a stereotype plate or stencil']

click *noun* a short sharp sound like that made by two parts of a mechanism locking into place. ▸ *verb* **1** *tr & intr* to make or cause to make a click. **2** *intr, informal* to meet with approval. **3** *intr, informal* to become clear or understood: *The meaning clicked after a while.* **4** *comput* to press and release one of the buttons on a **mouse**. **5** *intr* of two or more people: to instantly get along very well. [17c: imitating the sound]

client *noun* **1** someone using the services of a professional institution, eg a bank. **2** a customer. **3** *comput* a program used to contact and download data from a server. [17c: from Latin *cliens* dependant]

clientele /kliːɒn'tɛl/ *noun* **1** the clients of a professional person, customers of a shopkeeper, etc. **2** people habitually attending a theatre, pub, etc. [16c: from Latin *clientela*]

cliff *noun* a high steep rock face, esp on the coast or the side of a mountain. [Anglo-Saxon *clif*]

cliffhanger *noun* **1** a story that keeps one in suspense. **2** the ending of an episode of a serial story which leaves the audience in suspense.

climacteric *noun* **1** *biol* in living organisms: a period of changes, eg those associated with the menopause in women. **2** a critical period. [16c: from Greek *klimakter* critical period]

climactic see under **climax**

climate *noun* **1** the average weather conditions of a particular region of the world over a long period of time. **2** a part of the world considered from the point of view of its weather conditions: *move to a warmer climate.* **3** a current trend in general feeling, opinion, policies, etc. ▪ **climatic** *adj.* ▪ **climatically** *adv.* [14c: from Greek *klima* slope or inclination]

climax *noun* **1** the high point or culmination of a series of events or of an experience. **2 a** *rhetoric* the arrangement of a series of sentences, etc, in order of increasing strength; **b** *loosely* the final term of the arrangement. **3** the final stage in the development of a series of plant and animal communities in an area, when it remains relatively stable. *as adj*: *climax vegetation.* ▸ *verb, tr & intr* to come or bring to a climax. ▪ **climactic** *or* **climactical** *adj.* [16c: Latin]

climb *verb* **1** (*often* **climb up**) to mount or ascend (a hill, ladder, etc), often using hands and feet. **2** *tr & intr* to rise or go up. **3** *intr* to increase. **4** *intr* to slope upwards: *The path started to climb suddenly.* **5** of plants: to grow upwards using tendrils, etc. ▸ *noun* **1** an act of climbing. **2** a slope to be climbed. ▪ **climbable** *adj.* ▪ **climbing** *noun.* [Anglo-Saxon *climban*]

PHRASAL VERBS **climb down 1** to descend. **2** to concede one's position on some issue, etc.

climb-down *noun* a dramatic change of mind or concession, often humiliating.

climber *noun* **1** a climbing plant. **2** a mountaineer. **3** *derog* a **social climber**.

clime *noun, chiefly poetic or humorous* a region of the world: *foreign climes.* [16c: from Greek *klima* region or latitude]

clinch *verb* **1** to settle something finally and decisively, eg an argument, deal, etc. **2** *intr, boxing, wrestling* of contestants: to hold each other in a firm grip. **3** *intr, informal* to embrace. **4** to bend over and hammer down the projecting point of a nail, etc, so as to secure it. ▸ *noun* **1** an act of clinching. **2** *boxing, wrestling* an act of clinging to each other to prevent further blows, create a breathing space, etc. **3** *informal* an embrace between lovers. [16c: variant of **clench**]

clincher *noun* a point, argument or circumstance that finally settles or decides a matter.

cline *noun, biol* a gradual change in the form of an animal or plant species across different parts of its geographical or environmental range. [20c: from Greek *klinein* to lean]

cling *verb* (***clung***) *intr* **1** to hold firmly or tightly; to stick. **2** to be emotionally over-dependent. **3** to refuse to drop or let go. [Anglo-Saxon *clingan*]

clingfilm *noun* a thin clear plastic material that adheres to itself, used for wrapping food, etc.

clingy *adj* (***-ier, -iest***) liable or tending to cling. ▪ **clinginess** *noun.*

clinic *noun* **1** a private hospital or nursing home that specializes in the treatment of particular diseases or disorders. **2** a department of a hospital or a health centre which specializes in one particular area, eg a family planning clinic. **3** the instruction in examination and treatment of patients that is given to medical students, usu at the patient's bedside in a hospital ward. **4** a session in which an expert is available for consultation. [19c: from Greek *klinikos* relating to a sickbed]

clinical *adj* **1** relating to, or like, a clinic or hospital. **2** of medical studies: based on, or relating to, direct observation and treatment of the patient. **3** of manner, behaviour, etc: cold; impersonal; unemotional or detached. **4** of surroundings, etc: severely plain and simple, with no personal touches. ▪ **clinically** *adv.*

clinical death see **brain death**

clink[1] *noun* a short sharp ringing sound. ▸ *verb, tr & intr* to make or cause to make such a sound. [14c: perhaps from Dutch *klinken* to ring]

clink[2] *noun, slang* prison. [16c: orig the name of a prison in Southwark]

clinker *noun* **1** a mass of fused ash or slag left unburnt in a furnace. **2** the cindery crust on a lava flow. [17c: from Dutch *klinker* hard brick]

clinker-built *adj* of the hull of a boat: built with planks, each of which overlaps the one below it on the outside.

clip[1] *verb* (***clipped, clipping***) **1** to cut (hair, wool, etc). **2** to trim or cut off the hair, wool or fur of (an animal). **3** to punch out a piece from (a ticket) to show that it has been used. **4** to cut (an article, etc) from a newspaper, etc. **5** *informal* to hit or strike someone or something sharply. **6** to excerpt a section from (a film, etc). ▸ *noun* **1** an act of clipping. **2** a short sequence extracted from a film, recording, etc. **3** *informal* a sharp blow: *a clip round the ear.* **4** *informal* speed; rapid speed: *going at a fair clip.* [12c: from Norse *klippa* to cut]

clip[2] *noun* **1** *often in compounds* any of various devices, usu small ones, for holding things together or in position: *paper clip.* **2** (*also* **cartridge clip**) a container for bullets attached to a gun, that feeds bullets directly into it. **3** a piece of jewellery in the form of a clip which can be attached to clothing. ▸ *verb* (***clipped, clipping***) to fasten something with a clip. [Anglo-Saxon *clyppan* to embrace or clasp]

clipboard *noun* **1** a firm board with a clip at the top for holding paper, forms, etc which can be used as a portable writing surface. **2** *comput* a temporary store for text or graphics being transferred between documents or programs.

clipped *adj* **1** of the form of a word: shortened, eg *deli* from *delicatessen.* **2** of speaking style: **a** tending to shorten vowels, omit syllables, etc; **b** curt and distinct.

clipper *noun* **1** *hist* a fast sailing ship with large sails. **2** someone or something which clips.

clippers *plural noun, often in compounds* a clipping device: *nail clippers.*

clipping *noun* **1** a piece clipped off: *hair clippings.* **2** a cutting from a newspaper, etc.

clique /kliːk/ *noun, derog* a group of friends, professional colleagues, etc who stick together and are hostile towards outsiders. ▪ **cliquey** (***cliquier, cliquiest***) *adj.* [18c: French from *cliquer* to click]

clitoris /ˈklɪtərɪs/ *noun, anatomy* a small highly sensitive organ in front of the vaginal opening. ▪ **clitoral** *adj.* [17c: from Greek *kleitoris*]

cloaca /kloʊˈeɪkə/ *noun* (***cloacae*** /-ˈeɪsiː, -ˈɑːkaɪ/) **1** *zool* in most vertebrates apart from mammals: the terminal region of the gut, into which the alimentary canal and the urinary and reproductive systems all open and discharge their contents. **2** a sewer. ▪ **cloacal** *adj.* [18c: Latin meaning 'sewer']

cloak *noun* **1** a loose outdoor garment, usu sleeveless, fastened at the neck so as to hang from the shoulders. **2** a covering: *a cloak of mist.* ▸ *verb* to cover up or conceal something. [13c: French *cloke*]

cloak-and-dagger *adj* of stories, situations, etc: full of adventure, mystery, plots, spying, etc.

cloakroom *noun* **a** a room where coats, hats, etc may be left; **b** a room containing a WC; **c** a room offering both these facilities.

clobber[1] *verb, informal* **1** to beat or hit someone very hard. **2** to defeat someone completely. **3** to criticize someone severely.

clobber[2] *noun, slang* clothing; personal belongings, equipment, etc.

cloche /klɒʃ/ *noun* **1** a transparent glass or plastic covering for protecting young plants from frost, etc. **2** a woman's close-fitting dome-shaped hat. [19c: French, meaning 'bell' and 'bell jar']

clock *noun* **1** a device for measuring and indicating time. **2** *comput* an electronic device that synchronizes processes within a computer system, by issuing signals at a constant rate. **3** a device that synchronizes the timing in switching circuits, transmission systems, etc. **4** (**the clock**) *informal* **a** a **mileometer**; **b** a **speedometer**. **5** (in full **time clock**) a device for recording the arrival and departure times of employees. **6** the downy seedhead of a dandelion. ▸ *verb* **1** to measure or record (time) using such a device. **2** to record with a stopwatch the time taken by (a racer, etc) to complete a distance, etc. **3** *informal* to travel at (a speed as shown on a speedometer). **4** *slang* to hit someone. [14c: from Dutch *clocke* bell or clock]

IDIOMS **round the clock** throughout the day and night.

PHRASAL VERBS **clock in** *or* **on** to record one's time of arrival at a place of work. **clock out** *or* **off** to record one's time of departure from a place of work.

clock tower *noun* a four-walled tower with a clock face on each wall.

clockwise *adj, adv* moving, etc in the same direction as that in which the hands of a clock move.

clockwork *noun* a mechanism like that of some clocks, working by means of gears and a spring that must be wound periodically. ▸ *adj* operated by clockwork: *a clockwork mouse.*

IDIOMS **like clockwork** smoothly and with regularity; without difficulties.

clod *noun* **1** a lump of earth, clay, etc. **2** *informal* a stupid person. [15c as *clodde*, from Anglo-Saxon *clod-*, found in compounds]

clodhopper *noun, informal* **1** a clumsy person. **2** a large heavy boot or shoe. ▪ **clodhopping** *adj.* [19c]

clog *noun* **1** a shoe carved entirely from wood, or having a thick wooden sole. **2** *Scot* a heavy block of wood. ▸ *verb* (***clogged, clogging***) *tr & intr* to obstruct or become obstructed so that movement is difficult or impossible.

IDIOMS **pop one's clogs** *slang* to die.

PHRASAL VERBS **clog up** to block or choke up.

cloister *noun* **1** a covered walkway built around a garden or quadrangle. **2** **a** a place of religious retreat, eg a monastery or convent; **b** the quiet secluded life of such a place. ▸ *verb* to keep someone away from the problems of normal life in the world. ▪ **cloistered** *adj* secluded. [13c: from French *cloistre*]

clone *noun* **1** *biol* any of a group of genetically identical cells or organisms derived from a single parent cell or organism by asexual reproduction. **2** *biol* any of a large number of identical copies of a gene produced by genetic engineering. **3** *comput* an imitation of an existing computer or software product, usu cheaper, and produced by a different manufacturer. **4** *informal* a person or thing that looks like someone or something else. ▸ *verb* **1** to produce a set of identical cells or organisms from (a single parent cell or organism). **2** to produce many identical copies of (a gene) by genetic engineering. **3** to produce replicas of, or to copy something: *cloned ideas.* [20c: from Greek *klon* twig]

close[1] *adj* **1** near in space or time; at a short distance. **2** **a** near in relationship: *a close relation*; **b** intimate. **3** touching or almost touching. **4** tight; dense or compact; with little space between: *a close fit.* **5** near to the surface. **6** thorough; searching: *a close reading.* **7** of a contest, etc: with little difference between entrants, etc. **8** (*often* **close to sth**) about to happen, on the point of doing it, etc: *close to tears.* **9** similar to the original, or to something else: *a close resemblance.* **10** uncomfortably warm; stuffy. **11** secretive. **12** mean. **13** heavily guarded: *under close arrest.* **14** of an organization, etc: restricted in membership. ▸ *adv* **1** *often in compounds* in a close manner; closely: *follow close behind.* **2** at close range. ▪ **closely** *adv.* ▪ **closeness** *noun.* [14c: from French *clos* closed]

IDIOMS **close at** *or* **to hand** near by; easily available.

close[2] *verb* **1** *tr & intr* to shut. **2** (*sometimes* **close sth off**) to block (a road, etc) so as to prevent use. **3** *tr & intr* of shops, etc: to stop or cause to stop being open to the public for a period of time. **4** *tr & intr* of a factory, business, etc: to stop or cause to stop operating permanently. **5** *tr & intr* to conclude; to come or bring to an end: *He closed with a joke.* **6** *tr & intr* to join up or come together; to cause edges, etc, of something to come together. **7** to settle or agree on something: *close a deal.* **8** *intr, econ* of currency, shares, etc: to be worth (a certain amount) at the end of a period of trading. ▸ *noun* an end or conclusion. [13c: from French *clos*]

PHRASAL VERBS **close down** of a business: to close permanently. **close in on sb** to approach and surround them.

closed *adj* **1** shut; blocked. **2** of a community or society: exclusive, with membership restricted to a chosen few.

closed-circuit television *noun* a TV system serving a limited number of receivers, eg within a building, the signal being transmitted by cables or telephone links.

closed shop *noun* an establishment, eg a factory, which requires its employees to be members of a trade union.

close harmony *noun, music* harmony in which the notes of chords lie close together.

close-knit *adj* of a group, community, etc: closely bound together.

close-range *adj* **1** in, at or within a short distance. **2** eg of a gun: fired from very close by.

close-run *adj* of a competition, election, etc: fiercely contested; having close results.

close season *noun* the time of year when it is illegal to kill certain birds, animals or fish for sport.

close shave *or* **close call** *noun* a narrow or lucky escape.

closet *noun* **1** *chiefly N Am* a cupboard. **2** *old use* a small private room. **3** *old use* a **water closet**. ▸ *adj* not openly declared: *a closet gambler.* ▸ *verb* to shut away in private, eg for confidential discussion. [14c: French diminutive of *clos*]

close-up *noun* **1** a photograph, television shot, etc taken at close range. **2** a detailed look at, or examination of, something.

clostridium *noun* (***-dia***) *biol* a rod-shaped bacterium that occurs in soil and in the digestive tract of humans and animals, and which can cause botulism and tetanus. [19c: from Greek *clostrum* spindle]

closure *noun* **1** the act of closing something, eg a business or a transport route. **2** a device for closing or sealing something. **3** a parliamentary procedure for cutting short a debate and taking an immediate vote. [16c: French]

clot *noun* **1** a soft semi-solid mass, esp one formed during the coagulation of blood. **2** *Brit informal* a fool. ▸ *verb* (***clotted, clotting***) *tr & intr* to form into clots. [Anglo-Saxon *clott* lump or mass]

cloth *noun* **1** woven, knitted or felted material. **2** *often in compounds* a piece of fabric for a special use: *tablecloth.* **3** (**the cloth**) the clergy. [Anglo-Saxon *clath*]

clothe *verb* (***clothed*** *or* ***clad***) **1** to cover or provide someone with clothes. **2** to dress someone. **3** to cover, conceal or disguise someone or something: *hills clothed in mist*. See also **clad**. [Anglo-Saxon *clathian*]

clothes *plural noun* **1** articles of dress for covering the body, for warmth, decoration, etc. **2** **bedclothes**. [Anglo-Saxon *clathas*]

clothes horse *noun* a hinged frame on which to dry or air clothes indoors.

clothesline *noun* a rope, usu suspended outdoors, on which washed clothes, etc are hung to dry.

clothes peg *noun* a small clip made from wood or plastic used for securing clothes to a clothesline.

clothing *noun* clothes collectively.

clotted cream *noun* thick cream made by slowly heating milk and taking the cream from the top.

cloud *noun* **1** *meteorol* a visible floating mass of small water droplets or ice crystals suspended in the atmosphere above the Earth's surface. **2** a visible mass of particles of dust or smoke in the atmosphere. **3** a circumstance that causes anxiety. **4** a state of gloom, depression or suspicion. ▸ *verb* **1** *tr & intr* (*usu* **cloud over** *or* **cloud sth over**) to make or become misty or cloudy. **2** *intr* (*often* **cloud over**) of the face: to develop a troubled expression. **3** to make dull or confused. **4** to spoil or mar. ▪ **cloudless** *adj.* [Anglo-Saxon *clud* hill or mass of rock]

IDIOMS **on cloud nine** *informal* extremely happy. **with one's head in the clouds** *informal* preoccupied with one's own thoughts.

cloudburst *noun* a sudden heavy downpour of rain over a small area.

cloud-cuckoo-land *noun* the imaginary dwelling-place of over-optimistic unrealistic people.

cloudy *adj* (***-ier, -iest***) **1** full of clouds; overcast. **2** eg of a liquid: not clear; muddy. **3** confused; muddled.

clout *noun* **1** *informal* a blow or cuff. **2** *informal* influence or power. ▸ *verb, informal* to hit or cuff. [Anglo-Saxon *clut* piece of cloth]

clove[1] *noun* the strong-smelling dried flower-bud of a tropical evergreen tree, used as a spice. [14c: from French *clou* nail, from the shape of the bud]

clove[2] *noun* one of the sections into which a compound bulb, esp of garlic, naturally splits. [Anglo-Saxon *clufu* bulb]

clove[3] *past tense of* **cleave**[1]

cloven *adj, old use, poetic* split; divided. ▸ *verb* see under **cleave**[1].

cloven hoof *or* **cloven foot** *noun* the partially divided hoof of various mammals, including cattle, deer, sheep, goats and pigs.

clover *noun* a small plant that grows wild in temperate regions and which has leaves divided into usu three leaflets and small dense red or white flowers. [Anglo-Saxon *clæfre*]

IDIOMS **in clover** *informal* in great comfort and luxury.

clown *noun* **1** in a circus or pantomime, etc: a comic performer, usu wearing ridiculous clothes and make-up. **2** someone who behaves comically. **3** *derog* a fool. ▸ *verb, intr* (*often* **clown about** *or* **around**) to play the clown.

cloy *verb* **1** *intr* to become distasteful through excess, esp of sweetness. **2** to satiate to the point of disgust. ▪ **cloying** *adj.* [16c: from Latin *clavus* nail]

club *noun* **1** a stick, usu thicker at one end, used as a weapon. **2** in various sports, esp golf: a stick with a specially shaped head, used to hit the ball. **3** an **Indian club**. **4** a society or association. **5** the place where such a group meets. **6** a building with dining, reading and sleeping facilities for its members. **7** a **nightclub**. **8** (**clubs**) one of the four suits of playing-cards, with a black cloverleaf-shaped symbol (♣), the others being the **diamond**, **heart** and **spade**[2]. **9** one of the playing-cards of this suit. ▸ *verb* (***clubbed, clubbing***) to beat (a person, animal, etc) with a club. ▪ **clubber** *noun.* ▪ **clubbing** *noun.* [13c: from Norse *klubba* cudgel]

club foot *noun, non-technical* a congenital deformity in which the foot is twisted down and turned inwards.

clubhouse *noun* a building where a club meets, esp the premises of a sports club.

club soda *noun, chiefly US* soda water.

cluck *noun* **1** the sound made by a hen. **2** any similar sound. ▸ *verb, intr* **1** of a hen: to make such a sound. **2** to express disapproval by making a similar sound with the tongue. [17c: imitating the sound]

clue *noun* **1** a fact or circumstance which helps towards the solution of a crime or a mystery. **2** in a crossword puzzle: a word or words representing, in a more or less disguised form, a problem to be solved. [17c: from Anglo-Saxon *cliewen* ball of thread]
IDIOMS **not have a clue** *informal* to be completely ignorant about something.

clued-up *adj, informal* shrewd; knowledgeable.

clueless *adj, derog* stupid, incompetent or ignorant.

clump *noun* **1** a group or cluster of something, eg trees or people standing close together. **2** a dull heavy sound, eg of treading feet. **3** a shapeless mass: *a clump of weeds.* ▶ *verb* **1** *intr* to walk with a heavy tread. **2** *tr & intr* to form into clumps. [16c: related to Dutch *klompe* lump or mass]

clumpy *adj* (**-ier, -iest**) large and heavy: *clumpy shoes.*

clumsy *adj* (**-ier, -iest**) **1** unskilful with the hands or awkward and ungainly in movement. **2** badly or awkwardly made. ▪ **clumsily** *adv.* ▪ **clumsiness** *noun.* [16c as *clumse*, meaning 'numb with cold']

clung *past tense, past participle of* **cling**

clunk *noun* the sound of a heavy object, esp a metal one, striking something. ▶ *verb, tr & intr* to make or cause to make such a sound. [19c: imitating the sound]

clunky *adj* (**-ier, -iest**) *informal* clumsy and awkward. [20c]

cluster *noun* **1** a small group or gathering. **2** a number of flowers growing together on one stem. ▶ *verb, tr & intr* to form into a cluster or clusters. [Anglo-Saxon *clyster* bunch]

clutch[1] *verb* **1** to grasp something tightly. **2** *intr* (*usu* **clutch at sth**) to try to grasp it. **3** *US* in a motor vehicle: to press the clutch pedal. ▶ *noun* **1** (*usu* **clutches**) control or power. **2** any device for connecting and disconnecting two rotating shafts, esp the device in a motor vehicle that transmits or prevents the transmission of the driving force from engine to gearbox. **3** in a motor vehicle: the pedal operating this device. **4** a grasp. [Anglo-Saxon *clyccan*]
IDIOMS **clutch** *or* **grasp at straws** to try anything, however unlikely, in one's desperation.

clutch[2] *noun* **1** a number of eggs laid at the same time. **2** a brood of newly hatched birds, esp chickens. [18c: from Norse *klekja* to hatch]

clutter *noun* an untidy accumulation of objects, or the confused overcrowded state caused by it. ▶ *verb* (*often* **clutter sth up**) to overcrowd it or make it untidy with accumulated objects. ▪ **cluttered** *adj.* [16c variant of earlier *clotter* from **clot**]

Cm *symbol, chem* curium.

cm *abbrev* centimetre.

Co *symbol, chem* cobalt.

co- *prefix, indicating* with; together; jointly: *co-starring* • *co-operate.* [Shortened from **con-**]

c/o *abbrev* care of: see under **care**.

coach *noun* **1** a railway carriage. **2** a bus designed for long-distance travel. **3** *hist* a closed horse-drawn carriage. **4** a trainer or instructor, esp in sport. **5** a private tutor, esp one who prepares pupils for examinations. ▶ *verb, tr & intr* **a** to train in a sport, etc; **b** to teach privately. ▪ **coaching** *noun.* [16c: from French *coche*]

coachman *noun, hist* the driver of a horse-drawn coach.

coachwork *noun* the painted outer bodywork of a motor or rail vehicle.

coagulant *noun* a substance which causes or facilitates coagulation.

coagulate /koʊˈagjʊleɪt/ *verb, tr & intr* of a liquid: to become clotted or curdled, or to form a soft semi-solid mass. ▶ *noun* the soft semi-solid mass produced by this process. ▪ **coagulation** *noun.* [17c: from Latin *coagulare*]

coal *noun* **1** a hard brittle **carbonaceous** rock, usu black or brown in colour, formed from partially decomposed plant material and used as a fuel. **2** a piece of this. [Anglo-Saxon *col*]
IDIOMS **coals to Newcastle** something brought to a place where it is already plentiful. **haul sb over the coals** *informal* to scold them severely.

coalesce /koʊəˈlɛs/ *verb, intr* to come together to form a single mass. ▪ **coalescence** *noun.* ▪ **coalescent** *adj.* [17c: from Latin *co-* together + *alescere* to grow]

coalface *noun* in a coal mine: the exposed surface from which coal is being cut.

coalfield *noun* an area where there is coal underground.

coalfish see **coley**

coal gas *noun* a flammable gas, consisting mainly of hydrogen and methane, which is obtained by the distillation of coal and was formerly used as a fuel.

coalition /koʊəˈlɪʃən/ *noun, politics* a combination or temporary alliance, esp between political parties. [18c: Latin *coalitio*]

coal mine *noun* an underground deposit of coal prepared for excavation.

coal scuttle *noun* a fireside container for coal, usu in a domestic household.

coal tar *noun* a thick black liquid obtained as a by-product during the manufacture of coke, and used in the manufacture of drugs, dyes, etc.

coarse *adj* **1** rough or open in texture. **2** rough or crude; not refined. **3** of behaviour, speech, etc: rude or offensive. ▪ **coarsely** *adv.* ▪ **coarseness** *noun.* [15c]

coarse fish *noun* a freshwater fish, other than trout and salmon. ▪ **coarse fishing** *noun.*

coarsen *verb, tr & intr* to make or become coarse.

coast *noun* the zone of land that borders the sea. ▶ *verb, intr* **1** to travel downhill, eg on a bicycle or in a motor vehicle, relying on gravity or momentum rather than power. **2** to progress smoothly and satisfactorily without much effort. ▪ **coastal** *adj.* [14c: from French *coste*]
IDIOMS **the coast is clear** *informal* there is no danger of being seen or caught.

coaster *noun* **1** a vessel that sails along the coast taking goods to coastal ports. **2** a small mat or tray placed under a cup, glass, etc to protect the table surface.

coastguard *noun* **1** an official organization stationed on the coast which rescues people at sea, prevents smuggling, etc. **2** a member of this organization.

coastline *noun* the shape of the coast, esp as seen on a map, or from the sea or air.

coat *noun* **1** an outer garment with long sleeves, typically reaching below the waist. **2** any similar garment, eg a jacket. **3** the hair, fur or wool of an animal. **4** a covering or application of something eg paint, dust, sugar, etc. ▶ *verb* to cover with a layer of something. ▪ **coating** *noun* a covering or outer layer. [13c: from French *cote*]

coat-hanger *noun* a shaped piece of wood, plastic or metal with a hook, on which to hang clothes.

coat of arms *noun* (***coats of arms***) a heraldic design consisting of a shield bearing the special insignia of a particular person, family, organization or town.

coat-tails *plural noun* the two long pieces of material which hang down at the back of a man's tailcoat.

coax *verb* **1** (*often* **coax sb into** *or* **out of sth**) to persuade them, using flattery, promises, kind words, etc. **2** to get something by coaxing. **3** to manipulate something patiently: *I coaxed the key into the lock.* [16c: from earlier *cokes* fool]

coaxial *adj* **1** having or mounted on a common axis. **2** *elec* of a cable: consisting of a conductor in the form of a metal tube surrounding and insulated from a second conductor. [20c: from **co-** + **axis**]

cob *noun* **1** a short-legged sturdy horse used for riding. **2** a male swan. See also **cygnet**, **pen**[4]. **3** a hazelnut or hazel tree. **4** a **corncob**. **5** *Brit* a loaf with a rounded top.

cobalt *noun, chem* (symbol **Co**) a hard silvery-white metallic element commonly used in **alloy**s to produce cutting tools and magnets. [17c: from German *Kobold* goblin of the mines, the name given to the material by frustrated miners looking for silver]

cobber *noun, Aust & NZ informal* used as a form of address: a pal or mate.

cobble[1] *noun* a rounded stone used esp formerly to surface streets. Also called **cobblestone**. ▸ *verb* to pave with cobblestones. ▪ **cobbled** *adj.*

cobble[2] *verb* **1** to mend (shoes). **2** (*often* **cobble sth together** *or* **up**) to assemble or put it together roughly or hastily.

cobbler *noun* someone who makes or mends shoes. [13c]

cobblers *plural noun, Brit slang* nonsense. [20c]

COBOL /ˈkoʊbɒl/ *abbrev* Common Business-Oriented Language, an English-based computer programming language used in commerce.

cobra *noun* any of various species of venomous snake found in Africa and Asia which, when threatened, rear up and spread the skin behind the head to form a flattened hood. [19c: shortened from Portuguese *cobra de capello* snake with hood]

cobweb *noun* **1** a web of fine sticky threads spun by a spider. **2** a single thread from this. [Anglo-Saxon *atorcoppe* spider + **web**]

coca *noun* **1** either of two S American shrubs whose leaves contain cocaine. **2** the leaves of the shrub chewed as a stimulant. [17c: Spanish]

cocaine *noun, med* an addictive narcotic drug, obtained from the leaves of the coca plant, used medicinally as a local anaesthetic and illegally as a stimulant. Also called (*informal*) **coke**.

coccus /ˈkɒkəs/ *noun* (***cocci*** /ˈkɒk(s)aɪ/) *biol* a spherical bacterium. [19c: Latin]

coccyx /ˈkɒksɪks/ *noun* (***coccyges*** /kɒkˈsaɪdʒiːz/) *anatomy* in humans and certain apes: a small triangular tail-like bone at the base of the spine. [17c: Latin]

cochineal *noun* a bright red pigment widely used as a food colouring. [16c: from Spanish *cochinilla*]

cochlea /ˈkɒklɪə/ *noun* (***cochleae*** /-iː/) *anatomy* in the inner ear of vertebrates: a hollow spirally coiled structure which converts the vibrations of sound waves into nerve impulses. ▪ **cochlear** *adj.* [17c: Latin, meaning 'snail or snail shell']

cock[1] *noun* **1** a male bird, esp an adult male chicken. **2** a **stopcock**. **3** the hammer of a gun which, when raised and let go by the trigger, produces the discharge. ▸ *verb* **1** to turn in a particular direction: *cock an ear towards the door.* **2** to draw back the hammer of a gun. **3** to set (one's hat) at an angle. [Anglo-Saxon *cocc*]

cock[2] *noun* a small heap of hay, etc. ▸ *verb* to pile into such heaps. [15c: perhaps related to Norse *kökkr* lump]

cockade *noun, hist* a feather or a rosette of ribbon worn on the hat as a badge. [18c: from French *coquarde*, from *coq*; see **cock**[1]]

cock-a-doodle-doo *noun* an imitation of the sound of a cock crowing.

cock-a-hoop *adj, informal* **1** jubilant; exultant. **2** boastful.

cockamamie *adj, US slang* ridiculous or incredible.

cock-and-bull story *noun, informal* an unlikely story, esp one used as an excuse or explanation.

cockatiel *noun* a small, crested parrot of the cockatoo family. [19c: Dutch, from a diminutive of **cockatoo**]

cockatoo *noun* a light-coloured parrot with a brightly coloured erectile crest on its head, usu found in woodland areas in Australasia. [17c: from Malay *kakatua*]

cock-crow *noun* dawn; early morning.

cocked hat *noun, hist* a three-cornered hat with upturned brim.

cockerel *noun* a young cock. [15c: diminutive of **cock**[1]]

cock-eyed *adj, informal* **1** crooked; lopsided. **2** senseless; crazy; impractical. [19c: from **cock**[1]]

cockfight *noun* a fight between cocks wearing sharp metal spurs. ▪ **cockfighting** *noun.*

cockle *noun* an edible **bivalve** shellfish with a rounded and ribbed shell. [14c: French *coquille* shell]

IDIOMS **warm the cockles of the heart** *informal* to delight and gladden someone.

cockney *noun* **1** (*often* **Cockney**) **a** *loosely* a native of London, esp of the East End; **b** *strictly* someone born within the sound of Bow Bells. **2** the dialect used by Cockneys. ▸ *adj* relating to Cockneys or their dialect. [17c: from earlier *cokeney* a cock's egg, ie a misshapen egg, later used as a contemptuous name for a town-dweller]

cockpit *noun* **1** in an aircraft: the compartment for the pilot and crew. **2** in a racing-car: the driver's seat. **3** *naut* the part of a small yacht, etc which contains the wheel and tiller. **4** *hist* a pit into which cocks were put to fight.

cockroach *noun* a large insect which infests houses, etc. [17c: from Spanish *cucaracha*]

cockscomb *or* **coxcomb** *noun* **1** the fleshy red crest on a cock's head. **2** (**coxcomb**) *old use, derog* a foolishly vain or conceited man. [15c]

cocksure *adj* foolishly over-confident.

cocktail *noun* **1** a mixed drink of spirits and other liquors. **2** a mixed dish esp of seafood and mayonnaise. **3** a mixture of different things: *a cocktail of drink and drugs.*

cocktail stick *noun* a short thin pointed stick on which small items of food are served at parties, etc.

cocky *adj* (**-*ier*, -*iest***) *derog* cheekily self-confident. ▪ **cockily** *adv.* ▪ **cockiness** *noun.* [18c: from **cock**[1]]

coco see **coconut**

cocoa *noun* **1** the seed of the **cacao** tree. **2** a powder prepared from the seeds of this tree after they have been fermented, dried and roasted. **3** a drink prepared by mixing this powder with hot milk or water. [18c: variant of **cacao**]

cocoa bean *noun* one of the seeds from the **cacao** tree.

cocoa butter *noun* a pale yellow fat obtained from cocoa beans, which is used in the manufacture of chocolate, cosmetics, etc.

coconut *noun* **1** (*also* **coconut palm**, **coco**) a tropical palm tree cultivated for its edible fruit. **2** the large single-seeded fruit of this tree, with a thick fibrous outer husk and a hard woody inner shell enclosing a layer of white edible flesh and a central cavity. [18c: from Portuguese *coco* grimace or ugly face, from the face-like markings on a coconut]

cocoon *noun* **1** the protective silky covering that many animals, eg spiders, spin around their eggs. **2** a similar covering that a larva spins around itself before it develops into a pupa. ▸ *verb* **1** to wrap someone or something up as if in a cocoon. **2** to protect someone from the problems of everyday life. [17c: French *cocon*]

cocotte *noun* a small lidded pot for oven and table use, usu intended for an individual portion. [20c: French, from *cocasse* a kind of pot]

cod[1] *noun* (*pl* ***cod***) a large food fish, found mainly in the N Atlantic Ocean.

cod[2] *noun, slang* **1** a hoax. **2** a parody. [20c]

c.o.d. *abbrev* cash on delivery.

coda /ˈkoʊdə/ *noun, music* a passage added at the end of a movement or piece, to bring it to a satisfying conclusion. [18c: Italian, meaning 'tail']

coddle *verb* **1** to cook something (esp eggs) gently in hot, rather than boiling, water. **2** to pamper, mollycoddle or over-protect someone or something. [16c]

code *noun* **1** a system of words, letters or symbols, used in place of those really intended, for secrecy's or brevity's sake. **2** a set of signals for sending messages, etc. **3** *comput* the set of written instructions or statements that make up a computer program. **4** a set of principles of behaviour. **5** a systematically organized set of laws. **6** *telecomm* the number dialled before a personal telephone number when making a non-local call, in order to connect with the required area. ▸ *verb* **1** to put something into a code. **2** *comput* to generate a set of written instructions or statements that make up a computer program. [14c: French]

codeine /ˈkoʊdiːn/ *noun, med* a morphine derivative that relieves pain and has a sedative effect. [19c: from Greek *kodeia* poppy head]

codex *noun* (***codices*** /koʊdɪsiːz/) an ancient manuscript volume, bound in book form. [19c: Latin, meaning 'set of tablets' or 'book']

codger *noun, informal* a man, esp an old one. [18c: perhaps a variant of **cadge**]

codicil /ˈkoʊdɪsɪl, ˈkɒdɪsɪl/ *noun, law* a supplement to a will. [15c: from Latin *codicillus*, from *codex* book]

codify *verb* (**-*ies*, -*ied***) to arrange something into a systematic code, eg laws, etc. ▪ **codification** *noun.*

codling *noun* a young cod.

cod-liver oil *noun* a medicinal oil obtained from the livers of cod, rich in vitamins A and D.

codpiece *noun, hist* a pouch attached to the front of a man's breeches, covering his genitals. [15c: from an earlier sense of *cod* scrotum]

codswallop *noun, Brit slang* nonsense.

co-ed *abbrev, informal* coeducation or coeducational.

coeducation *noun* the teaching of pupils of both sexes in the same school or college. ▪ **coeducational** *adj.*

coefficient *noun* **1** *algebra* a number or other constant factor placed before a variable to signify that the variable is to be multiplied by that factor. **2** *physics* a number or other constant that measures a specified property of a particular substance under certain conditions.

coelacanth /ˈsiːləkanθ/ *noun* a primitive bony fish believed extinct until a live specimen was found in 1938. [19c: from Greek *koilos* hollow + *akantha* spine]

coelenterate /siːˈlɛntəreɪt/ *noun, zool* any member of the **phylum** of invertebrate animals which have a single body cavity, eg jellyfish, sea anemones, etc. [19c: from Greek *koilos* hollow + *enteron* intestine]

coeliac or (*esp US*) **celiac** /ˈsiːlɪak/ *adj* **1** relating to the abdomen. **2** relating to coeliac disease. ▸ *noun* someone suffering from coeliac disease. [17c: from Greek *koilia* belly]

coeliac disease *noun, pathol* a condition in which the lining of the small intestine is abnormally sensitive to **gluten**, leading to improper digestion and absorption of food.

coenobite /ˈsiːnəbaɪt/ *noun* a member of a monastic community. [17c: from Greek *koinos* common + *bios* life]

coerce /koʊˈɜːs/ *verb* (*often* **coerce sb into sth**) to force or compel them to do it. ▪ **coercion** /koʊˈɜːʃən/ *noun.* ▪ **coercive** *adj.* [17c: from Latin *coercere* to restrain]

coeval /koʊˈiːvəl/ *adj, formal* belonging to the same age or period of time. [17c: from **co-** + Latin *aevum* age]

co-exist *verb, intr* **1** to exist together, or simultaneously. **2** to live peacefully side by side in spite of differences, etc. ▪ **co-existence** *noun.* ▪ **co-existent** *adj.*

coffee *noun* **1** an evergreen tree or shrub which has red fleshy fruits. **2** the seeds, or beans, of this plant, roasted whole or ground to a powder. **3** a drink, usu containing **caffeine**, which is prepared from the roasted and ground beans of the coffee plant. [17c: from Turkish *kahveh*]

coffee bean *noun* the seed of the coffee plant, esp roasted for grinding to make coffee.

coffee mill *noun* a machine for grinding coffee beans.

coffee table *noun* a small low table.

coffer *noun* **1** a large chest for holding valuables. **2** (**coffers**) a treasury or supply of funds. **3** *archit* a hollow or sunken section in the elaborate panelling or plasterwork of a ceiling. [13c: from French *cofre*]

cofferdam *noun* a watertight chamber allowing construction workers to carry out building work underwater. Compare **caisson**.

coffin *noun* a box in which a corpse is cremated or buried. *N Am equivalent* **casket**. [16c: French *cofin*]

cog *noun* **1** one of a series of teeth on the edge of a wheel or bar which engage with another series of teeth to bring about motion. **2** a small gear wheel. **3** someone unimportant in, though necessary to, a process or organization. [13c: perhaps from Scandinavian origin]

cogent /ˈkoudʒənt/ *adj* of arguments, reasons, etc: strong; persuasive; convincing. ▪ **cogency** *noun*. [17c: French]

cogitate /ˈkɒdʒɪteɪt/ *verb, intr* to think deeply; to ponder. ▪ **cogitation** *noun*. ▪ **cogitative** *adj*. [17c: from Latin *cogitare* to think]

cognac /ˈkɒnjak/ *noun* a high-quality French brandy. [18c: named after the area in SW France]

cognate *adj* **1** descended from or related to a common ancestor. **2** of words or languages: derived from the same original form. **3** related; akin. ▸ *noun* something that is related to something else. ▪ **cognation** *noun*. [17c: Latin *cognatus*]

cognition *noun, psychol* the mental processes, such as perception, reasoning, problem-solving, etc, which enable humans to experience and process knowledge and information. ▪ **cognitive** *adj*. [15c: Latin *cognitio* study or knowledge]

cognizance *or* **cognisance** *noun* **1** knowledge; understanding. **2** the range or scope of awareness or knowledge. ▪ **cognizant** *adj*. [14c: from French *conoisance*]

IDIOMS **take cognizance of sth** to take it into consideration.

cognomen /kɒgˈnoumən/ *noun* (***cognomens*** *or* ***cognomina*** /-ˈnoumɪnə/) **1** *Roman history* a Roman's third name, often in origin an epithet or nickname, which became their family name. **2** a nickname or surname. [19c: from Latin *co-* with + (g)nomen name]

cognoscenti /kɒnjouˈʃɛntiː/ *plural noun* knowledgeable people; connoisseurs. [18c: Italian]

cogwheel *noun* a toothed wheel.

cohabit *verb, intr* to live together as husband and wife, usu without being married. ▪ **cohabitation** *noun*. ▪ **cohabiter** *or* **cohabitee** *noun*. [16c: from Latin *cohabitare* to live together]

cohere *verb, intr* **1** to stick together. **2** to be consistent; to have a clear logical connection. [16c: from Latin *cohaerere* to be connected]

coherent *adj* **1** of a description or argument: logical and consistent. **2** speaking intelligibly. **3** sticking together; cohering. **4** *physics* of two or more radiating waves: having the same frequency, and either the same **phase** (*noun* sense 4) or a constant phase difference. ▪ **coherence** *noun*. [16c: French]

cohesion *noun* **1** sticking together. **2** *physics* the attraction between atoms or molecules of the same substance, which produces **surface tension**. See also **adhesion**. ▪ **cohesive** *adj*. [17c: French]

cohort *noun* **1** *hist* in the ancient Roman army: one of the ten divisions of a legion. **2** a group of people sharing a common quality or belief. [15c: from Latin *cohors* enclosure or company of soldiers]

coif[1] /kɔɪf/ *noun* a close-fitting cap worn esp by women in medieval times. [14c: French *coiffe*]

coif[2] /kwɑːf/ *noun* a hairstyle. ▸ *verb* (***coiffed, coiffing***) to dress (hair); to dress someone's hair. [19c in this sense; prob from **coiffure**]

coiffeur /kwɑːˈfɜː(r)/ *or* **coiffeuse** /kwɑːˈfɜːz/ *noun* a male and female hairdresser respectively. [19c: French]

coiffure /kwɑːˈfuə(r) *noun* a hairstyle. [17c: French]

coil[1] *verb, tr & intr* (*sometimes* **coil up**) to wind round and round in loops to form rings or a spiral. ▸ *noun* **1** something looped into rings or a spiral: *a coil of rope*. **2** a single loop in such an arrangement. **3** *elec* a conducting wire wound into a spiral, used to provide a magnetic field, or to introduce inductance into an electrical circuit. **4** *non-technical* an IUD. [17c: from French *cueillir* to gather together]

coil[2] *noun, old use* trouble and tumult.

IDIOMS **this mortal coil** the troubles of the world.

coin *noun* **1** a small metal disc stamped for use as currency. **2** coins generally. ▸ *verb* **1 a** to manufacture (coins) from metal; **b** to make (metal) into coins. **2** to invent (a new word or phrase). [14c: French meaning 'wedge' or 'die']

IDIOMS **be coining it in** *informal* to be making a lot of money. **to coin a phrase** *ironic* used to introduce an over-used expression.

coinage *noun* **1** the process of coining. **2** coins.

coincide *verb, intr* **1** to happen at the same time. **2** to be the same; to agree. **3** to occupy the same position. [18c: from Latin *co-* together + *incidere* to happen]

coincidence *noun* **1** the striking occurrence of events together or in sequence, without any causal connection. **2** the fact of being the same.

coincident *adj* **1** coinciding in space or time. **2** in agreement.

coincidental *adj* happening by coincidence. ▪ **coincidentally** *adv*.

coir /kɔɪə(r)/ *noun* fibre from coconut shells, used for making ropes, matting, etc. [16c: from Malayalam (a language of S India) *kayaru* cord]

coition /kouˈɪʃən/ *or* **coitus** /ˈkouɪtəs, kɔɪ-/ *noun* sexual intercourse. ▪ **coital** /ˈkouɪtəl, kɔɪ-/ *adj*. [17c: from Latin *coire* to unite]

coke[1] *noun* a brittle greyish-black solid left after gases have been extracted from coal. ▸ *verb, tr & intr* to convert (coal) into this material. [17c: perhaps from N Eng dialect *colk* core]

coke[2] *noun, informal* cocaine.

Col. *abbrev* Colonel.

col *noun, geol* in a mountain range: a pass between two adjacent peaks, or the lowest point in a ridge. [19c: French, meaning 'neck']

col- see **con-**

cola *or* **kola** *noun* **1** a tree, native to Africa but cultivated in other tropical regions for its seeds called **cola nuts**. **2** a soft drink flavoured with the extract obtained from the seeds of this tree. [18c: from W African *kolo* nut]

colander *noun* a perforated bowl used to drain the water from cooked vegetables, etc. [15c: from Latin *colare* to strain]

cold *adj* **1** low in temperature. **2** lower in temperature than is normal, comfortable or pleasant. **3** of food: cooked, but not eaten hot: *cold meat*. **4** unfriendly. **5** comfortless; depressing. **6** *informal* unenthusiastic: *The suggestion left me cold*. **7** without warmth or emotion: *a cold calculating person*. **8** of colours: producing a feeling of coldness. **9** *informal* unconscious: *out cold*. **10** dead. **11** of a trail or scent: not

fresh. ▸ *adv* without preparation or rehearsal. ▸ *noun* **1** lack of heat or warmth; cold weather. **2** a highly contagious viral infection whose symptoms include a sore throat, coughing and sneezing, and a congested nose. Also called **the common cold**. ▪ **coldly** *adv*. ▪ **coldness** *noun*. [Anglo-Saxon *ceald*]
IDIOMS **get cold feet** *informal* **1** to lose courage. **2** to become reluctant to carry something out. **give someone the cold shoulder** *informal* to respond aloofly to them; to rebuff or snub them. **in cold blood** deliberately and unemotionally. **pour** *or* **throw cold water on sth** *informal* to be discouraging or unenthusiastic about a plan, idea, etc.

cold-blooded *adj* **1** of all animals except mammals and birds: having a body temperature that varies with the temperature of the surrounding environment. **2 a** lacking emotion; **b** callous or cruel.

cold comfort *noun* no comfort at all.

cold front *noun, meteorol* the leading edge of an advancing mass of cold air moving under a retreating mass of warm air.

cold-hearted *adj* unkind. ▪ **cold-heartedness** *noun*.

cold-shoulder *verb* to give someone the cold shoulder.

cold sore *noun* a patch of small blister-like spots on or near the lips, caused by the herpes simplex virus.

cold storage *noun* **1** the storage of food, etc under refrigeration, in order to preserve it. **2** the state of being put aside or saved till another time.

cold sweat *noun* a chill caused by a feeling of fear or nervousness.

cold turkey *noun* a way of curing drug addiction by suddenly and completely stopping the use of drugs.

cold war *noun* a state of hostility and antagonism between nations, without actual warfare.

cole *noun* any of various vegetables belonging to the cabbage family. [Anglo-Saxon *cawl*]

coleslaw *noun* a salad made with finely-cut raw cabbage, onion and carrots, etc, bound together, usu with mayonnaise. [19c: from Dutch *koolsla* cabbage salad]

coley *noun* a large edible fish of the cod family, with white or grey flesh. Also called **coalfish**, **saithe**.

colic *noun, pathol* severe spasmodic abdominal pain. ▪ **colicky** *adj*. [15c: from French *colique*]

colitis *noun* inflammation of the **colon²**.

collaborate *verb, intr* **1** to work together with another or others on something. **2** *derog* to co-operate or collude with an enemy. ▪ **collaboration** *noun*. ▪ **collaborative** *adj*. ▪ **collaborator** *noun*. [19c: from Latin *com-* together + *laborare* to work]

collage /kɒˈlɑːʒ, ˈkɒlɑːʒ/ *noun* **1** a design or picture made up of pieces of paper, cloth, photographs, etc glued onto a background surface. **2** the art of producing such works. ▪ **collagist** *noun*. [20c: French, meaning 'pasting' or 'gluing']

collagen *noun, biol* a tough fibrous protein of **connective tissue** found in skin, bones, teeth, cartilage, ligaments, etc, and used in skin cream or plastic surgery to make the skin look younger. [19c: from Greek *kolla* glue]

collapse *verb* **1** *intr* of buildings, etc: to fall or cave in. **2** *intr* of people: **a** to fall or drop in a state of unconsciousness; **b** to drop in a state of exhaustion or helplessness. **3** *intr* to break down emotionally. **4** *intr* to fail suddenly and completely: *Several firms collapsed.* **5** *tr & intr* to fold up compactly esp for storage. ▸ *noun* **1** a process or act of collapsing. **2** a breakdown. ▪ **collapsible** *adj*. [18c: from Latin *collabi, collapsus* to fall]

collar *noun* **1 a** a band or flap of any of various shapes, folded over or standing up round the neck of a garment; **b** the neck of a garment generally. **2** something worn round the neck. **3** a band of leather, etc worn round the neck by an animal. **4** a distinctively coloured ring of fur or feathers round the neck of certain mammals and birds. **5** a cut of meat, esp bacon, from the neck of an animal. **6** a ring-shaped fitting for joining two pipes, etc together. ▸ *verb, informal* **1** to catch or capture someone or something. **2** to grab something for oneself. [13c: from French *colier*]

collarbone *noun, non-technical* the **clavicle**.

collate *verb* **1** to study and compare. **2** to check and arrange (sheets of paper) in order. ▪ **collator** *noun*. [17c: from Latin *collatus*]

collateral *adj* **1** descended from a common ancestor, but through a different branch of the family. **2** additional; secondary in importance. ▸ *noun* **1** a collateral relative. **2** assets offered to a creditor as security for a loan. [14c: from Latin *collateralis*]

collateral damage *noun, military* incidental unintended civilian casualties or damage to property.

collation *noun* **1** the act of collating. **2** a light meal.

colleague *noun* a fellow-worker, esp in a profession. [16c: from French *collègue*]

collect¹ *verb* **1** *tr & intr* to bring or be brought together. **2** to build up a collection of things of a particular type as a hobby: *collect stamps.* **3** to call for someone or something: *I'll collect you in the evening.* **4** *tr & intr* to get something from people, eg money owed or voluntary contributions, etc. **5** to calm (oneself); to get one's thoughts, etc under control. ▪ **collected** *adj*. [16c: from Latin *collectus*]

collect² *noun, Christianity* a short prayer. [13c: from Latin *collecta*]

collectable *adj* desirable to a collector.

collection *noun* **1** the act of collecting. **2** an accumulated assortment of things of a particular type: *a stamp collection.* **3** an amount of money collected. **4** the removal of mail from a postbox at scheduled times.

collective *adj* of, belonging to or involving all the members of a group: *a collective effort.* ▸ *noun* an organized group or unit who run some kind of business, etc.

collective bargaining *noun* negotiations between a trade union and a company's management to settle questions of pay and working conditions.

collective farming *noun* **1** the running of a farm by a group of individuals, with profits shared by the whole group. **2** *hist* in the former Soviet bloc: state-controlled farming, usually on large farms formed by the merging of several privately-owned farms.

collective noun *noun* a singular noun which refers to a group of people, animals, things, etc, such as *cast, flock, gang.*

collectivism *noun* the economic theory that industry should be carried on with collective capital.

collectivize *or* **-ise** *verb* to group (farms, factories, etc) into larger units and bring them under state control and ownership. ▪ **collectivization** *noun*.

collector *noun, often in compounds, denoting* someone who collects, as a job or hobby: *debt-collector* • *stamp-collector.*

collector's item *or* **collector's piece** *noun* an object which would interest a collector.

colleen *noun, Irish* a girl. [19c: from Irish Gaelic *cailín*]

college *noun* **1** an institution, either self-contained or part of a university, which provides higher education, further education or professional training. **2** one of a number of self-governing establishments that make up certain universities. **3** the staff and students of a college. **4** the buildings which make up a college. **5** (*often* **College**) a name used by some larger secondary schools. **6** a body of people with particular duties and rights. **7** an official body of members of a profession, concerned with maintaining standards, etc. [14c: from Latin *collegium* group of associates or fellowship]

collegiate *adj* **1** of, relating to or belonging to a college. **2** having the form of a college. **3** of a university: consisting of individual colleges. [16c: from Latin *collegiatus*]

collide *verb, intr* **1** to crash together or crash into someone or something. **2** of people: to disagree or clash. [17c: Latin *collidere*]

collie *noun* a longhaired dog, orig used for herding sheep. [17c: perhaps from Scots *colle* coal, the breed having once been black]

collier *noun* **1** a coal-miner. **2** a ship that transports coal.

colliery *noun* (***-ies***) a coal mine with its surrounding buildings.

collision *noun* **1** a violent meeting of objects; a crash. **2** a disagreement or conflict. [15c: Latin, from *collidere* to strike together]

collocate *verb* **1** to arrange or group together in some kind of order. **2** *grammar* of a word: to occur frequently alongside another word. ▪ **collocation** *noun.* [16c: from Latin *collocare* to place together]

colloid *noun, chem* an intermediate state between a **suspension** (sense 5) and a true **solution** (sense 3), in which fine particles of one substance are spread evenly throughout another. ▪ **colloidal** *adj.* [19c: from Greek *kolla* glue]

colloquial *adj* of language or vocabulary: **a** informal; **b** used in familiar conversation rather than in formal speech or writing. ▪ **colloquially** *adv.* [18c: from Latin *colloquium* conversation]

colloquialism *noun* a word or expression used in informal conversation.

colloquium /kəˈloʊkwɪəm/ *noun* (***colloquia*** /-ə/ *or* ***colloquiums***) an academic conference; a seminar. [19c: Latin, meaning 'conversation']

colloquy *noun* (***-quies***) a conversation; talk. [16c: from Latin *colloquium* conversation]

collude *verb, intr* to plot secretly with someone, esp with a view to committing fraud. [16c: from Latin *colludere*]

collusion *noun* secret and illegal co-operation for the purpose of fraud or other criminal activity, etc. ▪ **collusive** *adj.* [14c: French]

collywobbles *plural noun* (*usu* **the collywobbles**) *informal* **1** pain or discomfort in the abdomen. **2** nervousness; apprehensiveness. [19c: prob from **colic** + **wobble**]

cologne see **eau de Cologne**

Colombian *adj* belonging or relating to Colombia or its inhabitants. ▶ *noun* a citizen or inhabitant of, or person born in, Colombia.

colon[1] *noun* a punctuation mark (:), properly used to introduce a list, an example or an explanation. [16c: Greek, meaning 'clause' or 'limb']

colon[2] *noun, anatomy* in vertebrates: the large intestine lying between the **caecum** and **rectum.** ▪ **colonic** *adj.* [16c: Latin]

colonel /ˈkɜːnəl/ *noun* a senior army officer, in charge of a regiment. ▪ **colonelcy** *noun* (***-ies***). [16c: from Italian *colonello* leader of a regiment]

colonial *adj* **1** relating to, belonging to or living in a colony or colonies. **2** possessing colonies. ▶ *noun* an inhabitant of a colony.

colonialism *noun, often derog* the policy of acquiring colonies, esp as a source of profit. Compare **imperialism.** ▪ **colonialist** *noun, adj.*

colonize *or* **-ise** *verb* **1** *tr & intr* to establish a colony in (an area or country). **2** to settle (people) in a colony. ▪ **colonist** *noun.* ▪ **colonization** *noun.*

colonnade *noun, archit* a row of columns placed at regular intervals. ▪ **colonnaded** *adj.* [18c: French]

colony *noun* (***-ies***) **1 a** a settlement abroad established and controlled by the founding country; **b** the settlers living there; **c** the territory they occupy. **2** a group of the same nationality or occupation forming a distinctive community within a city, etc: *writers' colony.* **3** *zool* a group of animals or plants of the same species living together in close proximity. **4** *bacteriol* an isolated group of bacteria or fungi growing on a solid medium, usu from the same single cell. [16c: from Latin *colonia*]

colophon *noun* a publisher's ornamental mark or device. [17c: Latin]

color an *N Am* spelling of **color**

Colorado beetle *noun* a small black and yellow striped beetle which is a pest of potato crops.

colorant *or* **colourant** *noun* a substance used for colouring. [19c: French]

coloration *or* **colouration** *noun* arrangement or combination of colours. [17c: from Latin *colorare* to colour]

coloratura /kɒlərəˈtʊərə/ *noun, music* **1** an elaborate and intricate passage or singing style. **2** (*also* **coloratura soprano**) a soprano specializing in such singing. [18c: Italian, meaning 'colouring']

colossal *adj* **1** huge; vast. **2** *informal* splendid; marvellous: *a colossal view.*

colossus *noun* (***colossi*** /kəˈlɒsaɪ/ *or* ***colossuses***) **1** a gigantic statue. **2** an overwhelmingly powerful person or organization. [14c: Latin]

colostomy *noun* (***-ies***) *surgery* an operation in which part of the colon is brought to the surface of the body through an incision in the abdomen, through which the colon can be emptied. [19c: from **colon**[2] + Greek *stoma* a mouth]

colour *or* (*N Am*) **color** *noun* **1 a** the visual sensation produced when light of different wavelengths is absorbed by the cones of the retina and relayed, in the form of nerve impulses, to the brain; **b** the particular visual sensation produced in this way, depending upon the wavelength. **2** any of these variations or colours, often with the addition of black and white. **3** *photog, art* the use of some or all colours, as distinct from black and white only: *in full colour.* **4** a colouring substance, esp paint. **5** the shade of a person's skin, as related to race. **6** pinkness of the face or cheeks, usu indicating healthiness. **7** lively or convincing detail: *add local colour to the story.* See also **colours**. ▸ *verb* **1** **a** to put colour on to something; **b** to paint or dye. **2** (*often* **colour sth in**) to fill in (an outlined area or a black and white picture) with colour. **3** to influence: *Personal feelings can colour one's judgement.* **4** *intr* to blush. [13c: French]

IDIOMS **off colour** *informal* unwell.

colour bar *noun* social discrimination against people of different races.

colour-blind *adj* unable to distinguish between certain colours, most commonly red and green. ▪ **colour-blindness** *noun.*

coloured *or* (*N Am*) **colored** *adj* **1** *also in compounds* having colour, or a specified colour: *coloured paper.* **2** **a** belonging to a dark-skinned race; **b** non-white. **3** (**Coloured**) *S Afr* being of mixed white and non-white descent. **4** distorted: *Her judgement was coloured because of past experiences.* ▸ *noun* **1** *often offensive* someone of a dark-skinned race. **2** (**Coloured**) *S Afr* a person of mixed white and non-white descent.

colour-fast *adj* of fabrics: dyed with colours that will not run or fade when washed.

colourful *or* (*N Am*) **colorful** *adj* **1** full of esp bright colour. **2** lively; vivid; full of interest or character. ▪ **colourfully** *adv.*

colouring *or* (*N Am*) **coloring** *noun* **1** a substance used to give colour, eg to food. **2** the applying of colour. **3** arrangement or combination of colour. **4** facial complexion, or this in combination with eye and hair colour.

colourist *noun* someone skilled in the use of colour, esp an artist.

colourless *or* (*N Am*) **colorless** *adj* **1** without or lacking colour. **2** uninteresting; dull; lifeless: *a colourless existence.* **3** pale.

colours *or* (*N Am*) **colors** *plural noun* **1** the flag of a nation, regiment or ship. **2** the coloured uniform or other distinguishing badge awarded to team-members in certain games. **3** a badge of ribbons in colours representing a particular party, etc, worn to show support for it.

IDIOMS **in one's true colours** as one really is. **with flying colours** with great success.

colour sergeant *noun* a sergeant who carries the company's colours.

colour therapy *noun* a form of therapy which involves the selection and use of appropriate colours that are said to promote healing and wellbeing.

colt *noun* **1** a male horse or pony less than four years old. **2** *sport* an inexperienced young player. [Anglo-Saxon, meaning 'young ass']

coltsfoot *noun* (***coltsfoot*** *or* ***coltsfoots***) a wild plant with yellow flowers and heart-shaped leaves. [16c: so called because of the shape of its leaves]

columbine *noun* a wild flower related to the buttercup. [13c: from French *colombine*]

column *noun* **1** *archit* a vertical pillar, usu cylindrical, with a base and a **capital**[2]. **2** something similarly shaped; a long and more or less cylindrical mass. **3** a vertical row of numbers. **4** a vertical strip of print on a newspaper page, etc. **5** a regular section in a newspaper concerned with a particular topic, or by a regular writer. **6** a troop of soldiers or vehicles standing or moving a few abreast. ▪ **columnar** *adj.* [15c: from Latin *columna* pillar]

columnist *noun* someone who writes a regular section of a newspaper.

com- see **con-**

coma *noun* a prolonged state of deep unconsciousness from which a person cannot be awakened, caused by head injury, etc. [17c: from Greek *koma* deep sleep]

comatose *adj* **1** in a coma. **2** *facetious* sound asleep.

comb *noun* **1** **a** a rigid toothed device for tidying and arranging the hair; **b** a similar device worn in the hair to keep it in place. **2** a toothed implement or part of a machine for disentangling and cleaning wool or cotton. **3** an act of combing. **4** a honeycomb. **5** the fleshy serrated crest on the head of a fowl. ▸ *verb* **1** to arrange, smooth or clean something with a comb. **2** to search (a place) thoroughly. [Anglo-Saxon *camb*]

combat *noun* fighting; a struggle or contest. ▸ *verb* to fight against someone or something; to oppose something. [16c: French]

combatant *adj* involved in or ready for a fight. ▸ *noun* someone involved in or ready for a fight.

combative *adj* inclined to fight or argue.

combination *noun* **1** the process of combining or the state of being combined. **2** **a** two or more things, people, etc combined; **b** the resulting mixture or union. **3** a sequence of numbers or letters for opening a combination lock. **4** *Brit* a motorcycle with sidecar. **5** *maths* a **subset** selected from a given set of numbers or objects, regardless of the order of selection. **6** *chem* **a** a union of chemical substances which forms a new compound; **b** the new compound formed.

combination lock *noun* a lock which will only open when the numbered dial on it is turned to show a specific sequence of numbers.

combine /kəm'baɪn/ *verb, tr & intr* **1** to join together. **2** *chem* to coalesce or make things coalesce so as to form a new compound. ▸ *noun* /'kɒmbaɪn/ **1** a group of people or businesses associated for a common purpose. **2** *informal* a combine harvester. [15c: from Latin *combinare*]

combine harvester *noun* a machine used to both reap and thresh crops.

combining form *noun, grammar* a word-forming element that occurs in combinations or compounds, eg *-lysis* in *electrolysis.*

combo *noun, informal* a small jazz band. [20c: from **combination**]

combustible *adj* **a** liable to catch fire and burn readily; **b** capable of being burnt as fuel. ▸ *noun* a combustible object or material. [16c: from Latin *combustibilis*]

combustion *noun* **1** the process of catching fire and burning. **2** *chem* a chemical reaction in which a gas, liquid or solid is rapidly **oxidize**d, producing heat and light. [15c: French]

come *verb* (*past tense* ***came,*** *past participle* ***come***) *intr in most senses* **1** to move in the direction of a speaker or hearer. **2** to reach a place; to arrive. **3** (*usu* **come to** *or* **into sth**) to reach (a certain stage or state). **4** to travel or traverse (a distance, etc). **5** to enter one's consciousness or perception: *come into view.* **6** to occupy a specific place in order, etc: *In* *'ceiling', 'e' comes before 'i'.* **7** to be available; to exist or be found: *Those purple jeans come in several sizes.* **8** to become: *come undone.* **9** on the arrival of (a particular point in time): *Come next Tuesday, I'll be free.* ▸ *exclam* used to reassure or admonish: *Oh, come now, don't exaggerate.* [Anglo-Saxon *cuman*]

IDIOMS **come again?** *informal* could you repeat that?

PHRASAL VERBS **come about** to happen. **come across** to make a certain impression: *Her speech came across well.* **come across sth** *or* **sb** to meet or discover it or them accidentally. **come at sth** *or* **sb** to attack it or them. **come back 1** to be recalled to mind. **2** to become fashionable again. **come between sb** *or* **sth and sb** *or* **sth else** to create a barrier or division between them. **come by sth** to obtain it, esp accidentally. **come down 1** to lose one's social position. **2** of an heirloom, etc: to be inherited. **3** to decide. **4** to descend. **come down on** *or* **upon sb** *or* **sth** to deal with them or it severely. **come down to sth** to be equivalent to it, in simple terms: *It comes down to this: we stay or we leave.* **come down with sth** to develop (an illness). **come in 1** to arrive; to be received. **2** to have a particular role, function or use: *This is where you come in.* **3** to become fashionable. **come in for sth** to deserve or incur it. **come off 1** to become detached. **2** to succeed. **3** *informal* to take place. **come on 1** to start. **2** to prosper or make progress. **3** to appear or make an entrance on stage. **4** *informal* to begin: *He could feel the flu coming on.* **come out 1** to become known; to become public. **2** to be removed. **3** to be released or made available. **4** to go on strike. **5** to emerge in a specified position or state: *come out well from the affair.* **6** *informal* to declare openly that one is a homosexual. Compare **out** (*verb* sense 2). **7** *old use* of a girl: to be launched in society. **come out in sth** to develop (a rash, etc). **come out with sth** to make a remark, etc. **come over 1** to change one's opinion or side. **2** to make a specified impression: *comes over well on television.* **3** *informal* to feel or become: *come over a bit faint.* **come round 1** to regain consciousness. **2** to change one's opinion. **come through 1** to survive. **2** to emerge successfully. **come to** to regain consciousness. **come to sth** to reach or total (a sum of money). **come up 1** to occur; to happen. **2** to be considered or discussed: *The question didn't come up.* **come up against sb** *or* **sth** to be faced with them or it as an opponent, challenge, etc. **come upon sth** *or* **sb** to discover it or them by chance. **come up to sth** to extend to or reach (a level, standard, etc). **come up with sth** to offer it; to put it forward.

comeback *noun* **1** a return to former success, or to the stage, etc after a period of retirement, etc. **2** a retort.

comedian *or* **comedienne** *noun* **1** a male or female entertainer who tells jokes, performs comic sketches, etc. **2** an actor in comedy. [17c: from **comedy**]

comedown *noun* **1** a decline in social status. **2** an anticlimax.

comedy *noun* (*-ies*) **1** a light amusing play or film. **2** in earlier literature: a play with a fortunate outcome. **3** such plays as a group or genre. Compare **tragedy**. **4** funny incidents. [14c: from Greek *komoidia*]

comedy of manners *noun* a satirical comedy dealing with the manners or fashions of a social class.

come-hither *adj, informal* flirtatious; seductive: *a come-hither look.*

comely *adj* (*-ier, -iest*) *dated* of a person: attractive in a wholesome way. ▪ **comeliness** *noun.* [Anglo-Saxon *cymlic* beautiful]

comestible *noun* (*usu* **comestibles**) *affected* something to eat. [19c: from Latin *comedere* to eat up]

comet *noun, astron* in the solar system: a small body which follows an elliptical orbit around the Sun, leaving a trail. [13c: from Greek *kometes* longhaired]

come-uppance *noun, informal* justified punishment or retribution.

comfit *noun* a type of sweet, containing a sugar-coated nut, liquorice, etc. [15c: from French *confit*]

comfort *noun* **1** a state of contentedness or wellbeing. **2** relief from suffering, or consolation in grief. **3** a person or thing that provides such relief or consolation. **4** (*usu* **comforts**) something that makes for ease and physical wellbeing. ▸ *verb* to relieve from suffering; to console or soothe. [13c: from French *conforter*]

comfortable *adj* **1** in a state of wellbeing, esp physical. **2** at ease. **3** providing comfort. **4** *informal* financially secure. **5** of a hospital patient, etc: in a stable condition. ▪ **comfortably** *adv.* [18c: from French *confortable*]

comforter *noun* **1** someone who comforts. **2** *old use* a warm scarf. **3** *old use* a baby's dummy.

comfrey *noun* a bristly, robust plant with tubular white, pink or purple flowers, traditionally used medicinally. [13c: from Latin *conferva* healing water plant]

comfy *adj* (*-ier, -iest*) *informal* comfortable.

comic *adj* **1** characterized by or relating to comedy. **2** funny. ▸ *noun* **1** a comedian. **2** a paper or magazine which includes strip cartoons, illustrated stories, etc. Also called **comic book**. [16c: from Greek *komikos*]

comical *adj* funny; amusing; humorous; ludicrous. ▪ **comically** *adv.*

comic strip *noun* in a newspaper, magazine, etc: a brief story or episode told through a short series of cartoon drawings.

coming *noun* an arrival or approach. ▸ *adj* **1** *informal* likely to succeed: *the coming man.* **2** approaching: *in the coming months.*

IDIOMS **have it coming to one** to deserve what is about to happen to one. **up and coming** promising; progressing well.

comity *noun* (*-ies*) civility; politeness; courtesy. [16c: from Latin *comitas*]

comma *noun* a punctuation mark (,) indicating a slight pause or break made for the sake of clarity, to separate items in a list, etc. [16c: Latin]

command *verb* **1** to order formally. **2** to have authority over or be in control of someone or something. **3** to deserve or be entitled to something. **4** to look down over something: *The window commands a view of the bay.* ▸ *noun* **1** an order. **2** control; charge. **3** knowledge of and ability to use something: *a good command of the English language.* **4** a military unit or a district under one's command. **5** *comput* an instruction to initiate a specific operation. [13c: from French *commander*]

commandant /ˈkɒməndant/ *noun* a commanding officer, esp of a prisoner-of-war camp or a military training establishment. [17c: French, present participle of *commander* to command]

commandeer *verb* **1** to seize (property) for military use. **2** to seize without justification. [19c: from Afrikaans *kommandeer*]

commander *noun* **1** a naval officer just below captain in rank. **2** a high-ranking police officer. **3** a senior member in some orders of knighthood.

commander in chief *noun* (***commanders in chief***) the officer in supreme command of a nation's forces.

commanding *adj* **1** powerful; leading; controlling. **2** in charge. **3** inspiring respect or awe. **4** giving good views all round: *a house with a commanding position.*

commandment *noun* **a** a divine command; **b** (**Commandment**) a religious rule for living by, especially one of the Ten Commandments.

commando *noun* **1** a unit of soldiers specially trained to carry out dangerous and difficult attacks or raids. **2** a member of such a unit. [18c: Portuguese]

commemorate *verb* **1** to honour the memory of (a person or event) with a ceremony, etc. **2** to be a memorial to someone or something. ▪ **commemoration** *noun.* ▪ **commemorative** *adj.* [16c: from Latin *commemorare* to keep in mind]

commence *verb, tr & intr* to begin. [14c: from French *commencier*]

commencement *noun* **1** a beginning. **2** *N Am* a graduation ceremony.

commend *verb* **1** to praise. **2** to recommend. **3** (*usu* **commend sth to sb**) to entrust it to them. ▪ **commendable** *adj.* ▪ **commendation** *noun.* ▪ **commendatory** *adj.* [14c: from Latin *commendare*]

commensalism *noun, biol,* a close association of two living organisms of different species, with one gaining from the relationship, and the other remaining unaffected by it. Compare **mutualism**, **parasitism**. ▪ **commensal** *adj, noun.* [19c in this sense; French, from Latin *com-* together + *mensa* table]

commensurable *adj* **1** *maths* having a common factor. **2** denoting quantities whose ratio is a **rational number**. **3** denoting two or more quantities that can be measured in the same units. [16c: from Latin *commensurabilis*]

commensurate *adj* **1** in equal proportion to something; appropriate to it. **2** equal in extent, quantity, etc to something. [17c: from Latin *commensuratus*]

comment *noun* **1** a remark or observation, esp a critical one. **2** talk, discussion or gossip. **3** an explanatory or analytical note on a passage of text. ▸ *verb, tr & intr* (*often* **comment on sth**) to make observations, remarks, etc. [15c: French]

IDIOMS **no comment** I have nothing to say.

commentary *noun* (***-ies***) **1** an ongoing description of an event, eg a football match, as it happens. **2** a set of notes explaining or interpreting points in a text, etc. [16c: from Latin *commentarium* notebook]

commentate *verb, intr* to act as a commentator.

commentator *noun* **1** a broadcaster who gives a commentary on an event, etc. **2** the writer of a textual commentary. [17c: Latin, meaning 'inventor' or 'author']

commerce *noun* the buying and selling of commodities and services. [16c: French]

commercial *adj* **1** relating to, engaged in or used for commerce. **2** profitable; having profit as the main goal. **3** paid for by advertising. ▸ *noun* a radio or TV advertisement. [17c: from Latin *commercium* trade]

commercial break *noun* on some TV and radio stations: a periodic interruption of programmes to allow the advertising of various products.

commercialism *noun* **1** commercial attitudes and aims. **2** undue emphasis on profit-making.

commercialize *or* **-ise** *verb* **1** *derisive* to exploit for profit, esp by sacrificing quality. **2** to make commercial. ▪ **commercialization** *noun.*

commis *or* **commis chef** *noun* (*pl* ***commis*** *or* ***commis chefs***) a trainee waiter or chef. [20c: French, meaning 'deputy']

commiserate *verb, tr & intr* (*often* **commiserate with sb**) to express one's sympathy for them. ▪ **commiseration** *noun.* [17c: from Latin *commiserari*]

commissar *noun* in the former Soviet Union: a Communist Party official responsible for the political education of military units. [20c: from Russian *komissar*]

commissariat *noun* in the army: a department responsible for food supplies. [18c: from Latin *commissarius* officer in charge]

commissary *noun* (***-ies***) **1** *US* a store supplying provisions and equipment to a military force. **2** a deputy, esp one representing a bishop. [14c: from Latin *commissarius* officer in charge]

commission *noun* **1 a** a formal or official request to someone to perform a task or duty; **b** the authority to perform such a task or duty; **c** the task or duty performed. **2** a military rank above the level of officer. **3** an order for a piece of work, esp a work of art. **4** a board or committee entrusted with a particular task: *the equal rights commission.* **5** a fee or percentage given to an agent for arranging a sale, etc. ▸ *verb* **1** to give a commission or authority to someone. **2** to grant a military rank above a certain level to someone. **3** to request someone to do something. **4** to place an order for something, eg a work of art, etc. **5** to prepare (a ship) for active service. [14c: French]

IDIOMS **in** *or* **out of commission** in or not in use or working condition.

commissionaire *noun, chiefly Brit* a uniformed attendant at the door of a cinema, theatre, office or hotel. [19c: French]

commissioned officer *noun* a military officer who holds a commission.

commissioner *noun* **1** a representative of the government in a district, department, etc. **2** a member of a commission.

commit *verb* (***committed, committing***) **1** to carry out or perpetrate (a crime, offence, error, etc). **2** to have someone put in prison or a mental institution. **3** to promise or engage, esp oneself, for some undertaking, etc. **4** to dedicate oneself to a cause, etc from a sense of conviction: *She committed herself to Christ.* [14c: from Latin *committere* to put together or to join]

IDIOMS **commit oneself** to make an irrevocable undertaking. **commit sth to memory** to memorize it.

commitment *noun* **1** the act of committing someone or oneself. **2** dedication or devotion; strong conviction. **3** a usu irrevocable undertaking or responsibility.

committal *noun* the action of committing someone to a prison or mental institution.

committee *noun* a group of people selected by and from a larger body, eg a club, to undertake certain duties on its behalf.

committee

This word is often misspelt. It has two *m*'s as well as two *t*'s, and two *e*'s. It might help you to remember the following sentence:

***M**any **m**eetings **t**ake **t**ime – **e**veryone's **e**xhausted!*

commode *noun* **1** a chair with a hinged seat, designed to conceal a chamber pot. **2** an ornate chest of drawers. [18c: French]

commodious *adj* comfortably spacious. [15c: from Latin *commodus* convenient]

commodity *noun* (**-*ies***) **1** something that is bought and sold, esp a manufactured product or raw material. **2** something, eg a quality, from the point of view of its value or importance in society: *Courtesy is a scarce commodity.* [15c: from French *commodité*]

commodore *noun* **1** a naval officer just below a rear admiral in rank. **2** the president of a yacht club. [17c: perhaps from Dutch]

common *adj* **1** frequent; familiar: *a common mistake.* **2** shared by two or more people, things, etc: *characteristics common to both animals.* **3** publicly owned. **4** widespread: *common knowledge.* **5** *derog* lacking taste or refinement; vulgar. **6 a** of the ordinary type: *the common cold;* **b** esp of plants and animals: general or ordinary: *common toad.* **7** *maths* shared by two or more numbers: *highest common factor.* ► *noun* a piece of land that is publicly owned or available for public use. ▪ **commonly** *adv.* [13c: from French *comun*]

IDIOMS **in common 1** of two people with regard to their interests, etc: shared. **2** in joint use or ownership.

common denominator *noun* **1** *maths* a whole number that is a multiple of each of the **denominator**s of two or more **vulgar fraction**s, eg 15 is a common denominator of 13 and 35. See also **lowest common denominator**. **2** something that enables comparison, agreement, etc between people or things.

commoner *noun* someone who is not a member of the nobility.

Common Era *noun* (abbrev **CE**) a culturally neutral term for the era reckoned from the birth of Christ, sometimes used instead of **Anno Domini**. See also **BCE**.

common fraction see **vulgar fraction**

common law *noun, law* law based on custom and decisions by judges, in contrast to **statute** law.

common-law *adj* denoting the relationship of two people who have lived together as husband and wife for a certain number of years but who have not been through a civil or religious ceremony.

common multiple *noun, maths* a multiple shared by two or more numbers, *eg* 18 is a common multiple of 2, 3, 6 and 9.

common-or-garden *adj* ordinary; everyday.

commonplace *adj* **1** ordinary; everyday. **2** *derog* unoriginal; lacking individuality; trite. ► *noun* **1** *derog* a trite comment; a cliché. **2** an everyday occurrence.

common ratio *noun, maths* a constant that is the quotient of successive numbers in a geometric sequence.

common room *noun* in a college, school, etc: a sitting-room for general use by students or one used by staff.

commons *plural noun* **1** *hist* (**the commons**) the ordinary people. **2** *old use, facetious* shared food rations. ► *singular noun* (**the Commons**) the House of Commons.

common sense *noun* practical wisdom and understanding. ▪ **common-sense** *adj.*

common time *noun, music* a rhythm with four beats to the bar.

commonwealth *noun* **1** a country or state. **2** an association of states that have joined together for their common good. **3** a state in which the people hold power; a republic. **4** (**the Commonwealth**) an association of countries or states which were formerly ruled by Britain. **5** a title used by certain US states.

commotion *noun* **1** a disturbance; an upheaval. **2** noisy confusion. [15c: from Latin *commovere* to move]

communal /ˈkɒmjʊnəl, kəˈmjuːnəl/ *adj* **1** relating or belonging to a community. **2** relating to a commune or communes. ▪ **communally** *adv.* [19c: French]

commune[1] /ˈkɒmjuːn/ *noun* **1** a number of unrelated families and individuals living together as a mutually supportive community, with shared accommodation, responsibilities, etc. **2** in some European countries: the smallest administrative unit locally governed. [18c: French]

commune[2] /kəˈmjuːn/ *verb, intr* **1** to communicate intimately. **2** to get close to or relate spiritually to (eg nature). [16c: from French *comuner* to share]

communicable *adj* **1** of a disease: easily transmitted from one organism to another. **2** capable of being communicated. [16c: French]

communicant *noun, Christianity* someone who receives communion.

communicate *verb* **1** *tr & intr* **a** to impart (information, ideas, etc); to make something known or understood; **b** to get in touch. **2** to pass on or transmit (a feeling, etc). **3** *intr* to understand someone; to have a comfortable social relationship. **4** *intr, Christianity* to receive communion. ▪ **communicative** *adj.* [16c: from Latin *communicare* to share]

communication *noun* **1 a** the process or act of communicating; **b** the exchanging or imparting of ideas and information, etc. **2** a piece of information, a letter or a message. **3** social contact. **4** (**communications**) the various means by which information is conveyed from one person or place to another.

communications satellite *noun, astron* an artificial satellite which orbits the Earth relaying radio, TV and telephone signals.

communion *noun* **1** the sharing of thoughts, beliefs or feelings. **2** a group of people sharing the same religious beliefs. **3** (*also* **Holy Communion**) *Christianity* **a** a church service at which bread and wine are taken as symbols of Christ's body and blood; **b** the consecrated bread and wine. See also **Eucharist**. [14c: from Latin *communio* mutual participation]

communiqué /kəˈmjuːnɪkeɪ/ *noun* an official announcement. [19c: French, meaning 'something communicated']

communism *noun* **1** a political ideology advocating a classless society where all sources of wealth and production are collectively owned and controlled by the people. **2** (**Communism**) a political movement founded on the principles of communism set out by Karl Marx. **3** the political and social system established on these principles in the former Soviet Union and other countries. ▪ **communist** *and* **Communist** *noun*. [19c: from French *communisme*]

community *noun* (**-ies**) **1** the group of people living in a particular place. **2** a group of people bonded together by a common religion, nationality or occupation: *the Asian community*. **3** a group of states with common interests. **4** the public; society in general. **5** *biol* a naturally occurring group of different plant or animal species that occupy the same habitat and interact with each other. [14c: from Latin *communitas* fellowship]

community centre *noun* a place where members of a community may meet for social, sporting or educational activities.

community charge *noun, formerly* in Britain: a tax levied on individuals to pay for local services, known informally as the **poll tax**. See also **rates**, **council tax**.

community service *noun* unpaid work of benefit to the local community, sometimes prescribed for offenders as an alternative to a prison sentence.

commutative *adj, maths* of an arithmetical process: performed on two quantities, the order of which does not affect the result, eg addition and multiplication.

commutator *noun* a device used for reversing electrical currents.

commute *verb* **1** *intr* to travel regularly between two places which are a significant distance apart, esp between home and work in a city, etc. **2** to alter (a criminal sentence) to one less severe. **3** to substitute; to convert. **4** to exchange (one type of payment) for another, eg a single payment for one made in instalments. ▪ **commutable** *adj*. ▪ **commutation** *noun*. [17c: from Latin *commutare* to alter or exchange]

commuter *noun* someone who regularly travels a significant distance to work.

compact[1] *adj* /ˈkɒmpakt/ **1** firm and dense in form or texture. **2** small, but with all essentials neatly contained. **3** concise. **4** denoting a quality newspaper printed in a smaller format than a broadsheet. ▸ *verb* /kəmˈpakt/ to compress. ▸ *noun* /ˈkɒmpakt/ a small case for women's face powder, usu including a mirror. ▪ **compactly** *adv*. ▪ **compactness** *noun*. [14c: from Latin *compactus*]

compact[2] /ˈkɒmpakt/ *noun* a contract or agreement. [16c: from Latin *compactum*]

compact disc *noun* (abbrev **CD**) a small disc used to record audio and/or visual information in the form of digital data, which can be read by laser. See also **CD-ROM**.

companion *noun* **1** a friend or frequent associate. **2** *hist* a woman employed by another woman to live or travel with her and to keep her company. **3** esp as a title: a handbook or guide. **4** one of a pair. ▪ **companionship** *noun*. [13c: from French *compagnon*]

companionable *adj* friendly; sociable; comfortable as a companion. ▪ **companionably** *adv*.

companionway *noun* on a ship: a staircase from a deck to a cabin, or between decks.

company *noun* (**-ies**) **1** the presence of another person or other people; companionship. **2** the presence of guests or visitors, or the people involved: *expecting company*. **3** one's friends or associates: *get into bad company*. **4** a business organization. **5** a troop of actors or entertainers. **6** a military unit of about 120 men. **7** a gathering of people, at a social function, etc. [13c: from French *compaignie*]

IDIOMS **keep sb company** to act as their companion. **part company with sb 1** to separate from them. **2** to disagree with them.

comparable *adj* **1** being of the same or equivalent kind. **2** able to be compared. ▪ **comparability** *noun*.

comparative *adj* **1** as compared with others. **2** relating to, or using the method of, comparison. **3** relative: *their comparative strengths*. **4** *grammar* of adjectives and adverbs: in the form denoting a greater degree of the quality in question but not the greatest, formed either by using the suffix *-er* or the word *more*, eg *larger* or *more usual*. Compare **positive**, **superlative**. ▸ *noun, grammar* **1** a comparative adjective or adverb. **2** the comparative form of a word. ▪ **comparatively** *adv*. [15c: from Latin *comparativus*]

compare *verb* **1** to examine (items, etc) to see what differences or similarities they have. **2** *intr* (*often* **compare with sth** *or* **sb**) to be comparable with it or them: *He can't compare with his predecessor in ability*. **3** (*often* **compare sb** *or* **sth to sb** *or* **sth else**) to liken them to each other: *compare her to an angel*. **4** *intr* to relate (well, badly, etc) when examined: *The two books compare well*. [15c: from Latin *comparare* to match]

IDIOMS **beyond** *or* **without compare** *formal* without equal; incomparable. **compare notes** to exchange ideas and opinions.

comparison *noun* **1** the process of, an act of or a reasonable basis for, comparing: *There can be no comparison between them*. **2** *grammar* the **positive** (sense 13), **comparative** (*adj* sense 4) and **superlative** (*adj* sense 1) forms of adjectives and adverbs. Also called **degrees of comparison**. [14c: from French *comparaison*]

compartment *noun* a separated-off or enclosed section. [16c: from French *compartiment*]

compartmentalize *or* **-ise** *verb* to divide, distribute or force into categories.

compass *noun* **1** any device for finding direction, esp one consisting of a magnetized needle that swings freely on a pivot and points to magnetic north, from which true north can be calculated. **2** (*usu* **compasses**) a device consisting of two hinged legs, for drawing circles, measuring distances on maps, etc. Also called **pair of compasses**. **3** range or scope: *within the compass of philosophy*. ▸ *verb* **1** to pass or go round. **2** to surround or enclose. **3** to accomplish or obtain. **4** to comprehend. [13c: from French *compas*]

compassion *noun* a feeling of sorrow and pity for someone in trouble. ▪ **compassionate** *adj*. ▪ **compassionately** *adv*. [14c: French]

compassionate leave *noun* special absence from work granted in cases of bereavement.

compatible *adj* (*often* **compatible with sth** *or* **sb**) **1** able to associate or co-exist agreeably. **2** consistent or congruous: *His actions were not compatible with his beliefs*. **3** *comput* of a program or device: capable of being used with a particular computer system. **4** *eng* of a device or piece of machinery: capable of being used in conjunction with another. ▪ **compatibility** *noun*. [16c: French]

compatriot *noun* someone from one's own country; a fellow-citizen. [17c: from Latin *compatriota*]

compel *verb* (***compelled, compelling***) **1** to force; to drive. **2** to arouse; to elicit or evoke: *Their plight compels sympathy.* [14c: from Latin *compellere*]

compelling *adj* **1** powerful; forcing one to agree, etc. **2** irresistibly fascinating.

compendious *adj* concise but comprehensive. [14c: from Latin *compendiosus*]

compendium *noun* (***compendiums*** *or* ***compendia*** /kəmˈpɛndɪə/) **1** a concise summary; an abridgement. **2** a collection of boardgames, puzzles, etc in a single container. [16c: Latin]

compensate *verb* **1** to make amends to someone for loss, injury or wrong, esp by a suitable payment. **2** *intr* (*often* **compensate for sth**) to make up for (a disadvantage, loss, imbalance, etc). ▪ **compensatory** *adj.* [17c: from Latin *compensare* to counterbalance]

compensation *noun* **1** the process of compensating. **2** something that compensates. **3** a sum of money awarded to make up for loss, injury, etc.

compere *or* **compère** *noun* someone who hosts a radio or television show, introduces performers, etc. ▸ *verb, tr & intr* to act as compere for (a show). [1930s: French, meaning 'godfather']

compete *verb, intr* **1** to take part in a contest. **2** to strive or struggle: *compete with other firms.* [17c: from Latin *competere* to coincide, ask for or seek]

competence *or* **competency** *noun* **1** capability; efficiency. **2** legal authority or capability.

competent *adj* **1** efficient. **2** having sufficient skill or training to do something. **3** legally capable. [14c: from Latin *competere* to meet, be sufficient]

competition *noun* **1** an event in which people compete. **2** the process or fact of competing. **3** rivals, eg in business or their products. **4** *biol* the demand for the same limited resource, eg light or water, among organisms or species in a community. [16c: from Latin *competitio* meeting together]

competitive *adj* **1** involving rivalry. **2** characterized by competition; aggressive; ambitious. **3** of a price or product: reasonably cheap; comparing well with those of market rivals. ▪ **competitiveness** *noun.* [19c: from Latin *competere* to meet together]

competitor *noun* **a** a person, team, firm or product that competes; **b** a rival. [16c: Latin, from *competere* to meet together]

compile *verb* **1 a** to collect and organize (information, etc) from different sources; **b** to produce (a list, reference book, etc) from information collected. **2** *comput* to create (a set of instructions written in machine code) from a source program written in a high-level programming language, using a compiler. ▪ **compilation** *noun.* [14c: from Latin *compilare* to plunder]

compiler *noun* **1** someone who compiles information, etc. **2** *comput* a program that converts a program in a high-level programming language into machine code.

complacent *adj* **1** self-satisfied; smug. **2** too easily satisfied; disinclined to worry. ▪ **complacence** *or* **complacency** *noun.* ▪ **complacently** *adv.* [15c: from Latin *complacere* to be pleasing]

complain *verb, intr* **1** to express dissatisfaction or displeasure. **2** (*always* **complain of sth**) to say that one is suffering from (a pain, disease, etc). [14c: from French *complaindre*]

complainant *noun, law* a plaintiff.

complaint *noun* **1** the act of complaining. **2** an expression of dissatisfaction. **3** a grievance. **4** a disorder, illness, etc.

complaisant /kəmˈpleɪzənt/ *adj* eager to please; obliging; amenable. ▪ **complaisance** *noun.* [17c: French]

complement *noun* **1** something that completes or perfects; something that provides a needed balance or contrast. **2** (*often* **full complement**) the number or quantity required to make something complete, eg the crew of a ship. **3** *grammar* a word or phrase added to a verb to complete the **predicate** of a sentence, eg *dark* in *It grew dark*. **4** *geom* the amount by which an angle or arc falls short of a right angle or **quadrant**. ▸ *verb* to be a complement to something. [14c: from Latin *complementum*]

---

complement, compliment

Be careful not to use the spelling **complement** when you mean **compliment**:

Her pretty dress received many compliments.

---

complementary *adj* **1** serving as a complement to something. **2** of two or more things: complementing each other.

---

complementary, complimentary

Be careful not to use the spelling **complementary** when you mean **complimentary**:

lots of complimentary comments

You will be sent a complimentary copy of the book.

---

complementary angles *plural noun, geom* a pair of angles whose sum is 90°. Compare **conjugate angles, supplementary angles**.

complementary medicine see **alternative medicine**

complete *adj* **1** whole; finished; with nothing missing. **2** thorough; absolute; total: *a complete triumph.* **3** perfect. ▸ *verb* **1 a** to finish; **b** to make complete or perfect. **2** to fill in (a form). ▪ **completely** *adv.* ▪ **completion** *noun.* [14c: from Latin *complere* to fill up]

IDIOMS **complete with …** having the additional feature of …

complex *adj* **1** composed of many interrelated parts. **2** complicated; involved; tangled. ▸ *noun* **1** something made of interrelating parts, eg a multi-purpose building: *a leisure complex.* **2** *psychoanal* a set of repressed thoughts and emotions that strongly influence an individual's behaviour and attitudes. **3** *informal* an obsession or phobia. [17c: from Latin *complexus*]

complexion *noun* **1** the colour or appearance of the skin, esp of the face. **2** character or appearance: *That puts a different complexion on the matter.* [16c: French]

complexity *noun* (**-ies**) **1** the quality of being complex. **2** a complication; an intricacy.

complex number *noun, maths* the sum of a real and an imaginary number.

compliance *noun* **1** yielding. **2** agreement; assent. **3** submission. ▪ **compliant** *adj.* [17c: see **comply**]

complicate *verb* to add difficulties to something; to make complex or involved. [17c: from Latin *complicare* to fold together]

complicated *adj* **1** difficult to understand or deal with. **2** intricate; complex.

complication *noun* **1** a circumstance that causes difficulties. **2** *pathol* a second and possibly worse disease or disorder that arises during the course of, and often as a result of, an existing one.

complicity *noun* the state of being an accomplice in a crime or wrongdoing. [17c: from Latin *complex* closely connected]

compliment *noun* **1** an expression of praise, admiration or approval. **2** a gesture implying approval: *paid her the compliment of dancing with her.* **3** (**compliments**) formal regards accompanying a gift, etc. ▸ *verb* (*often* **compliment sb on sth**) **1** to congratulate them for it. **2** to praise them; to pay them a compliment.

compliment, complement
Be careful not to use the spelling **compliment** when you mean **complement**:
This sauce is an ideal complement to fish.

complimentary *adj* **1** paying a compliment; admiring or approving. **2** given free.

complimentary, complementary
Be careful not to use the spelling **complimentary** when you mean **complementary**:
She decorated the living room with complementary colours.

compline *or* **complin** /ˈkɒmplɪn/ *noun, now esp RC Church* the seventh of the **canonical hours**, completing the set hours for prayer. [13c: from French *complie*]

comply *verb* (**-*ies*, -*ied***) *intr* (*usu* **comply with sth**) to act in obedience to an order, command, request, etc; to agree. [17c: from Italian *complire*]

component *noun* any of the parts or elements that make up a machine, engine, instrument, etc. ▸ *adj* functioning as one of the parts of something. [17c: from Latin *componere* to assemble into a whole]

comport *verb* **1** (*always* **comport oneself**) to behave in a specified way. **2** *intr* (*always* **comport with sth**) to suit or be appropriate to it. ▪ **comportment** *noun* behaviour. [16c: from Latin *comportare* to carry together]

compose *verb* **1** *tr & intr* to create (music). **2** to write (a poem, letter, article, etc). **3** to make up or constitute something. **4** to arrange as a balanced, artistic whole. **5** to calm (oneself); to bring (thoughts, etc) under control. **6** to settle (differences between people in dispute). **7** *printing* to arrange (type) or set (a page, etc) in type ready for printing. [16c: from French *composer*]

composed *adj* of a person: calm; controlled.

composer *noun* someone who composes, esp music.

composite *adj* **1** made up of different parts, materials or styles. **2** *botany* belonging or relating to the *Compositae* (see *noun* 2 below) family. ▸ *noun* **1** something made up of different parts, materials or styles. **2** *botany* a member of the largest family of flowering plants (*Compositae*) with a flower head consisting of a crowd of tiny florets often surrounded by a circle of bracts, eg daisy. [16c: from Latin *compositus*]

composite volcano *noun* a volcano with steep sides formed from alternating layers of ash and lava. Also called **stratovolcano**.

composition *noun* **1** something composed, esp a musical or literary work. **2** the process of composing. **3** *art* arrangement, esp with regard to balance and visual effect: *photographic composition.* **4** *old use* a school essay. **5** the constitution of something. **6** a synthetic material of any of various kinds.

compositor *noun, printing* someone who sets or arranges pages of type ready for printing.

compos mentis *adj, law* sound in mind; perfectly rational. [17c: Latin]

compost *noun* a mixture of decomposed organic substances such as rotting vegetable matter, etc, which is used to enrich soil and nourish plants. ▸ *verb* **1** to treat with compost. **2** to convert (decaying organic matter) into compost. [14c: from Latin *composita*]

composure *noun* mental and emotional calmness; self-control. [17c: from **compose**]

compound[1] /ˈkɒmpaʊnd/ *noun* **1** (*in full* **chemical compound**) *chem* a substance composed of two or more elements combined in fixed proportions and held together by chemical bonds. **2** something composed of two or more ingredients or parts. **3** a word made up of two or more words, eg *tablecloth*. Compare **derivative** (*noun* sense 2). ▸ *adj* composed of a number of parts or ingredients. ▸ *verb* /kəmˈpaʊnd/ **1 a** to make (esp something bad) much worse; **b** to complicate or add to (a difficulty, error, etc). **2** *law* to agree to overlook (an offence, etc) in return for payment. [14c: from French *compondre*]

compound[2] /ˈkɒmpaʊnd/ *noun* **1** an area enclosed by a wall or fence, containing a house or factory. **2 a** an enclosed area in a prison, used for a particular purpose; **b** a similar area in a concentration camp, prisoner-of-war camp, etc. [17c: prob from Malay *kampong* village]

compound fracture *noun, med* a type of bone fracture in which the overlying skin is pierced by the broken bone. Compare **simple fracture**.

compound interest *noun* interest calculated on the original sum of money borrowed and on any interest already accumulated. Compare **simple interest**.

compound time *noun, music* a **time** (*noun* sense 14) that has three, or a multiple of three, beats to a bar.

comprehend *verb* **1** to understand; to grasp with the mind. **2** to include. ▪ **comprehensible** *adj.* [14c: from Latin *comprehendere* to grasp or seize]

comprehension *noun* **1 a** the process or power of understanding; **b** the scope or range of someone's knowledge or understanding. **2** a school exercise for testing students' understanding of a passage of text. [16c: from Latin *comprehensio*]

comprehensive *adj* **1** covering or including a large area or scope. **2** of a school or education: providing teaching for pupils of all abilities aged between 11 and 18. ▸ *noun* a comprehensive school. [17c: from Latin *comprehensivus*]

compress *verb* /kəmˈprɛs/ **1** to press, squeeze or squash together. **2** to reduce in bulk; to condense. **3** *comput* to pack (data) into the minimum possible space in computer memory. ▸ *noun* /ˈkɒmprɛs/ a cloth or pad soaked in water and pressed against a part of the body to reduce swelling, stop bleeding, etc. [14c: from Latin *comprimere* to squeeze together]

compression *noun* **1** the process of compressing or the state of being compressed. **2** the reduction in the volume of a substance, esp a gas, as a result of an increase in pressure. ▪ **compressional** *adj.*

compressor *noun, eng* a device that compresses a gas.

comprise *verb* **1** to contain, include or consist of something specified. **2** to go together to make up something. [15c: from French *compris*]

comprise

When you say that A comprises Bs, you mean that Bs are the parts or elements of A:

✓ *The village school comprises one old building and two modern buildings.*

Because it means the same as **consist of**, it is sometimes confused with this and followed by 'of', but this use is not correct:

✗ *The instructions comprised of two sheets of A5 paper.*

compromise *noun* **1** a settlement of differences agreed upon after concessions have been made on each side. **2** anything of an intermediate type which comes halfway between two opposing stages. ▶ *verb* **1** *intr* to make concessions; to reach a compromise. **2** to endanger or expose to scandal, by acting indiscreetly. **3 a** to settle (a dispute) by making concessions; **b** to relax (one's principles, etc). [15c: from French *compromis*]

comptroller see **controller**

compulsion *noun* **1** the act of compelling or condition of being compelled. **2** an irresistible urge to perform a certain action, esp an irrational one. [15c: French]

compulsive *adj* **1** having the power to compel. **2** of an action: resulting from a compulsion. **3** of a person: acting on a compulsion. **4** of a book, film, etc: holding the attention; fascinating. ▪ **compulsively** *adv.* [17c: from Latin *compulsivus*]

compulsory *adj* required by the rules, law, etc; obligatory. [16c: from Latin *compulsorius*]

compulsory purchase *noun* the purchase of property or land required for some public project, etc by a local authority, irrespective of the wishes of the owner.

compunction *noun* a feeling of guilt or regret. [14c: from Latin *compungere* to prick sharply or sting]

computation *noun* **1** the process or act of calculating or computing. **2** a result calculated or computed. ▪ **computational** *adj.*

compute *verb, tr & intr* **1** to calculate or estimate, esp with the aid of a computer. **2** to carry out (a computer operation). [17c: from Latin *computare* to reckon]

computer *noun* an electronic device which processes data at great speed according to a **program** (see under **programme**) stored within the device. See also **analogue** (*adj*), **digital** (sense 2).

computer-aided design *noun* (abbrev **CAD**) the use of a computer system to create and edit design drawings, by employing many of the techniques of **computer graphics**.

computerize *or* **-ise** *verb* **a** to transfer (a procedure, system, etc) to control by computer; **b** to organize (information, data, etc) by computer; **c** to install (computers) for this purpose. ▪ **computerization** *noun.*

computer-literate *adj* able to use computers, programs, etc.

computer virus see **virus** (sense 4)

computing *noun* the act or process of using a computer.

comrade *noun* **1 a** a friend or companion; **b** an associate, fellow worker, etc. **2** a fellow communist or socialist. ▪ **comradely** *adj.* ▪ **comradeship** *noun.* [16c: from French *camarade*]

Con. *abbrev* Conservative.

con[1] *informal, noun* a **confidence trick**. ▶ *verb* (***conned, conning***) to swindle or trick someone, esp after winning their trust.

con[2] *noun* an argument against something. See also **pros and cons**. [16c: shortened from Latin *contra* against]

con[3] *noun, prison slang* a prisoner or inmate. [19c: shortened from **convict**]

con-, col-, com- *or* **cor-** *prefix* found usu in words derived from Latin: with or together, sometimes used with emphatic or intensifying effect. [From Latin *com-*, form of *cum* together with]

concatenation *noun, formal* a series of items linked together in a chain-like way. ▪ **concatenate** *verb.* [16c: from Latin *concatenare* to chain]

concave *adj* of a surface or shape: inward-curving, like the inside of a bowl. Compare **convex.** ▪ **concavity** *noun.* [14c: French]

conceal *verb* **1** to hide; to place out of sight. **2** to keep secret. ▪ **concealer** *noun.* ▪ **concealment** *noun.* [14c: from Latin *concelare*]

concede *verb* **1** to admit to be true or correct. **2** to give or grant. **3** to yield or give up. **4** *intr* to admit defeat in (a contest, etc) before, or without continuing to, the end. [17c: from Latin *concedere* to yield]

conceit *noun* **1 a** an inflated opinion of oneself; **b** vanity. **2** *old use* a witty, fanciful or ingenious thought or idea. [16c: from **conceive**, by analogy with *deceive, deceit*]

conceited *adj* **a** having too good an opinion of oneself; **b** vain. ▪ **conceitedness** *noun.*

conceivable *adj* imaginable; possible: *try every conceivable method.* ▪ **conceivably** *adv.*

conceive *verb* **1** *tr & intr* to become pregnant. **2** *tr & intr* (*often* **conceive of sth**) to think of or imagine (an idea, etc). [13c: from French *concever*]

concentrate *verb* **1** *intr* (*often* **concentrate on sth** *or* **sb**) to give full attention and energy to it or them. **2** to focus: *concentrate our efforts.* **3** *chem* to increase the strength of (a dissolved substance in a solution), either by adding more of it or by evaporating the solvent in which it is dissolved. ▶ *noun* a concentrated liquid or substance. ▪ **concentrated** *adj.* [17c: from Latin *con-* together + *centrum* centre]

concentration *noun* **1** intensive mental effort. **2** the act of concentrating or the state of being concentrated. **3** the number of molecules or ions of a substance present in unit volume or weight of a solution or mixture. **4** a concentrate.

concentration camp *noun* a prison camp used to detain civilians, esp as in Nazi Germany.

concentric *adj, geom* of circles, spheres, etc: having a common centre. [14c: from Latin *concentricus*]

concept *noun* a notion; an abstract or general idea. [17c: from Latin *conceptum*]

conception *noun* **1** an idea or notion. **2** the origin or start of something, esp something intricate. **3** the act or an instance of conceiving. **4** *biol* the fertilization of an ovum by a sperm, representing the start of pregnancy. [13c: French]

conceptual *adj* relating to or existing as concepts or conceptions.

conceptual art *noun* a revolutionary type of art of the 1960s and 1970s, concentrating not so much on a completed image as on the means of producing an image or concept.

conceptualize *or* **-ise** *verb* to form a concept or idea of something. ▪ **conceptualization** *noun.*

concern *verb* **1** to have to do with someone or something; to be about someone or something: *It concerns your son.* **2** (*often* **be concerned about sth** *or* **sb**) to worry, bother or interest. **3** to affect; to involve. ▸ *noun* **1 a** worry or a cause of worry; **b** interest or a subject of interest. **2** someone's business or responsibility: *That's my concern.* **3** an organization; a company or business. [16c: from Latin *concernere* to distinguish or relate to]

concerned *adj* worried.

IDIOMS **concerned with sth** *or* **sb** having to do with it or them; involving it or them.

concerning *prep* regarding; relating to; about.

concert *noun* /ˈkɒnsət/ **1** a musical performance given before an audience by singers or players. **2** agreement; harmony. ▸ *verb* /kənˈsɜːt/ to endeavour or plan by arrangement. [16c: French]

IDIOMS **in concert 1** jointly; in co-operation. **2** of singers, musicians, etc: in a live performance.

concerted /kənˈsɜːtɪd/ *adj* planned and carried out jointly.

concertina *noun* a musical instrument like a small accordion. ▸ *verb, tr & intr* to fold or collapse like a concertina. [19c: from **concert** + *-ina*]

concerto /kənˈtʃɛətoʊ/ *noun* (***concertos*** *or* ***concerti*** /-tiː/) *music* a composition for an orchestra and one or more solo performers. [18c: Italian, meaning 'concert']

concerto grosso *noun* (***concerti grossi*** /-tiː -siː/) *music* **1** an orchestral work performed by solo musicians as well as the main body of the orchestra. **2** the main body of instruments in an orchestral work of this kind. [18c: Italian, meaning 'large concert']

concession *noun* **1** the act of conceding. **2** something conceded or allowed. **3** the right, granted under government licence, to extract minerals, etc in an area. **4** the right to conduct a business from within a larger concern. **5** a reduction in ticket prices, fares, etc for categories such as students, the elderly, etc. ▪ **concessionary** *adj.* [17c: from Latin *concessio* yielding]

concessionaire *or* (*US*) **concessioner** *noun* the holder of a concession.

conch *noun* (***conchs*** *or* ***conches***) **1** any of a family of large marine snails, native to warm shallow tropical waters, with large colourful shells. **2** the shell of this animal often used as a trumpet. [16c: from Latin *concha*]

concierge /kɒnsiːˈɛəʒ/ *noun* a warden or caretaker of a block of flats, esp one who lives on the premises.

conciliate *verb* **1** to overcome the hostility of someone. **2** to reconcile (people in dispute, etc). ▪ **conciliation** *noun.* ▪ **conciliator** *noun.* ▪ **conciliatory** *adj.* [16c: from Latin *conciliare* to unite in friendship]

concise *adj* brief but comprehensive. ▪ **concisely** *adv.* ▪ **conciseness** *or* **concision** *noun.* [16c: from Latin *concisus* cut short]

conclave *noun* **1** a private or secret meeting. **2** *RC Church* the body of cardinals gathered to elect a new pope. [14c: Latin, meaning 'a room that can be locked']

conclude *verb* **1** *tr & intr* to come or bring to an end. **2** to reach an opinion based on reasoning. **3** to settle or arrange: *conclude a treaty with a neighbouring state.* [15c: from Latin *concludere*]

conclusion *noun* **1** an end. **2** a reasoned judgement; an opinion based on reasoning: *draw a conclusion.* **3** *logic* a statement validly deduced from a previous **premise**. **4** a result or outcome (of a discussion, event, etc). [14c: French]

IDIOMS **in conclusion** finally. **jump to conclusions** to presume something without adequate evidence.

conclusive *adj* of evidence, proof, etc: decisive, convincing; leaving no room for doubt. ▪ **conclusively** *adv.* [17c: from Latin *conclusivus*]

concoct *verb* **1** to make something, esp ingeniously from a variety of ingredients. **2** to invent (a story, excuse, etc). ▪ **concoction** *noun.* [17c: from Latin *concoctus* cooked together]

concomitant *adj* accompanying because of or as a result of something else. ▸ *noun* a concomitant thing, person, etc. [17c: from Latin *concomitari* to accompany]

concord *noun* **1** agreement; peace or harmony. **2** *grammar* **agreement** (sense 4). **3** *music* a combination of sounds which are harmonious to the ear. Opposite of **discord**. ▪ **concordant** *adj.* [13c: from French *concorde*]

concordance *noun* **1** a state of harmony. **2** a book containing an alphabetical index of principal words used in a major work, usu supplying citations and their meaning. [14c: from Latin *concordantia*]

concordat *noun* an agreement between church and state, esp the Roman Catholic Church and a secular government. [17c: French]

concourse *noun* **1** in a railway station, airport, etc: a large open area where people can gather. **2** a throng; a gathering. [14c: from French *concours*]

concrete *noun* a building material consisting of a mixture of cement, sand, gravel and water, which forms a hard rock-like mass when dry. ▸ *adj* **1** relating to such a material. **2** relating to items which can be felt, touched, seen, etc: *concrete objects*. Compare **abstract** (*adj* sense 3), **figurative** (sense 4). **3** definite or positive, as opposed to vague or general: *concrete evidence.* **4** *grammar* of a noun: denoting a physical thing, eg *house*, rather than a quality, condition or action. Compare **abstract** (*adj* sense 4). ▸ *verb* **1** to cover with or embed in concrete. **2** *tr & intr* to solidify. [16c: from Latin *concretus*]

concretion *noun, pathol* a hard stony mass which forms in body tissues or natural cavities. See also **calculus** (sense 2). [17c: from Latin *concretio*]

concubine *noun* **1** *hist* a woman who lives with a man and has sexual intercourse with him, without being married to him. **2** in polygamous societies: a secondary wife. [13c: from Latin *concubina*]

concupiscence /kəŋˈkjuːpɪsəns/ *noun* strong desire, esp sexual. ▪ **concupiscent** *adj.* [14c: from Latin *concupiscere* to long for]

concur *verb* (***concurred, concurring***) *intr* **1** to agree. **2** to happen at the same time; to coincide. [16c: from Latin *con-* together + *currere* to run]

concurrent *adj* **1** happening or taking place simultaneously. **2** of lines: meeting or intersecting; having a common point. **3** in agreement. ▪ **concurrence** *noun*. ▪ **concurrently** *adv*.

concuss *verb* to cause concussion in someone. [16c: from Latin *concutere* to shake together]

concussion *noun* a violent shaking or jarring of the brain, caused by injury to the head eg as a result of a severe blow or fall, and usu resulting in temporary loss of consciousness.

condemn *verb* **1** to declare something to be wrong or evil. **2** to pronounce someone guilty; to convict someone. **3** (*usu* **condemn sb to sth**) **a** to sentence them to (a punishment, esp death); **b** to force them into (a disagreeable fate). **4** to show the guilt of someone; to give away or betray someone: *His obvious nervousness condemned him.* **5** to declare (a building) unfit to be used or lived in. ▪ **condemnation** *noun*. ▪ **condemnatory** *adv*. [13c: from French *condemner*]

condensation *noun* **1** *chem* the process whereby a gas or vapour turns into a liquid as a result of cooling. **2** *meteorol* the production of water droplets in the atmosphere.

condense *verb* **1** to decrease the volume, size or density of (a substance). **2** to concentrate something. **3** *tr & intr* to undergo or cause to undergo condensation. **4** to express something more briefly; to summarize. [15c: from Latin *condensare* to compress]

condensed milk *noun* milk that has been concentrated and thickened by evaporation and to which sugar has been added as a preservative.

condenser *noun* **1** *elec* a **capacitor**. **2** *chem* an apparatus for changing a vapour into a liquid by cooling it and allowing it to condense. **3** *optics* a lens or series of lenses that is used to concentrate a light source.

condescend *verb, intr* **1** to act in a gracious manner towards those one regards as inferior. **2** to be gracious enough to do something, esp as though it were a favour. ▪ **condescending** *adj*. ▪ **condescension** *noun*. [15c: from Latin *condescendere*]

condiment *noun* any seasoning or sauce, eg salt, pepper, mustard, etc, added to food at the table. [15c: from Latin *condimentum*]

condition *noun* **1** a particular state of existence. **2** a state of health, fitness or suitability for use: *out of condition.* **3** an ailment or disorder: *a heart condition.* **4** (**conditions**) circumstances: *poor working conditions.* **5** a requirement or qualification. **6** a term of contract. ▸ *verb* **1** to accustom or train someone or something to behave or react in a particular way; to influence them or it. **2** to prepare or train (a person or animal) for a certain activity or for certain conditions of living. **3** to affect or control; to determine. **4** to improve (the physical state of hair, skin, fabrics, etc) by applying a particular substance. ▪ **conditioning** *noun*. [14c: from Latin *conditio*]

IDIOMS **on condition that** only if: *I will go on condition that you come too.*

conditional *adj* **1** dependent on a particular condition, etc. **2** *grammar* expressing a condition on which something else is dependent, as in the first clause in 'If it rains, I'll stay at home'. Compare **indicative**, **imperative**, **subjunctive**.

conditioner *noun, often in compounds* a substance which improves the condition of something, esp hair: *hair conditioner* • *fabric conditioner.*

condolence *noun* (*usu* **condolences**) an expression of sympathy: *offer my condolences.* ▪ **condole** *verb*. [17c: from Latin *con-* with + *dolere* to grieve]

condom *noun* a thin rubber sheath worn on the penis during sexual intercourse, to prevent conception and the spread of sexually transmitted diseases. [18c]

condominium *noun* **1** *N Am* **a** a building, eg office block, apartment block, etc in which each apartment is individually owned and any common areas, eg passageways, etc are commonly owned; **b** an apartment in such a block. Often shortened to **condo**. **2** a country which is controlled by two or more other countries. [18c: from Latin *con-* with + *dominium* lordship]

condone *verb* **1** to pardon or overlook (an offence or wrong). **2** *loosely* to tolerate. [19c: from Latin *condonare* to present or overlook]

condor *noun* either of two species of large American vulture. [17c: Spanish]

conducive *adj* (*often* **conducive to sth**) likely to achieve a desirable result; encouraging.

conduct *verb* /kən'dʌkt/ **1** to lead or guide. **2** to manage; to control: *conduct the firm's business.* **3** *tr & intr* to direct the performance of an orchestra or choir by movements of the hands or by using a baton. **4** to transmit (heat or electricity) by **conduction**. **5** to behave (oneself) in a specified way: *One should always conduct oneself with dignity.* ▸ *noun* /'kɒndʌkt/ **1** behaviour. **2** the managing or organizing of something. [15c: from Latin *conductus* guide]

conductance *noun* **a** the ability of a material to conduct heat or electricity; **b** in a direct current circuit: the reciprocal of **resistance**. See also **conductivity**.

conduction *noun* **1** the transmission of heat through a material from a region of higher temperature to one of lower temperature, without any movement of the material itself. **2** the flow of electricity through a material under the influence of an electric field, without any movement of the material itself.

conductivity *noun* **1** a measure of the ability of a material to conduct electricity. Also called **electrical conductivity**. **2** the ability of a material to conduct heat.

conductor *noun* **1** the person who conducts a choir or orchestra. **2** a material that conducts heat or electricity. **3** someone who collects fares from passengers on a bus, etc. **4** *N Am* the official in charge of a train.

conduit /'kɒndjuɪt/ *noun* a channel, pipe, tube or duct through which a fluid, a liquid or a gas may pass. [14c: French]

cone *noun* **1** *geom* a solid, three-dimensional figure with a flat base in the shape of a circle or ellipse, and a curved upper surface that tapers to a fixed point. **2** something similar to this in shape, eg a hollow pointed wafer for holding ice cream. **3** *anatomy* in the retina: a type of light-sensitive receptor cell specialized for the detection of colour, and which functions best in bright light. Compare **rod** (*noun* sense 6). **4** *botany* the oval fruit of a coniferous tree, consisting of overlapping woody scales. **5** a plastic cone-shaped bollard which is placed on the road temporarily, to divert traffic, cordon off an area, etc. Also called **traffic cone**. [16c: from Greek *konos* pine cone or geometrical cone]

confab *noun, informal* a conversation.

confabulate *verb, intr, formal* to talk, discuss or confer. ▪ **confabulation** *noun*. [17c: from Latin *confabulari* to talk together]

confection *noun* **1** any sweet food, eg a cake, sweet, biscuit or pudding. **2** *dated, facetious* a fancy or elaborate garment. [14c: French]

confectioner *noun* someone who makes or sells sweets or cakes.

confectionery *noun* (**-ies**) **1** sweets, biscuits and cakes. **2** the work or art of a confectioner.

confederacy *noun* (**-ies**) **1** a league or alliance of states. **2** (**the Confederacy**) *US* the union of eleven southern states that seceded from the USA in 1860–1, so causing the American Civil War. [14c: from Latin *confoederatio* league]

confederate *noun* /kən'fɛdərət/ **1** a member of a confederacy. **2** a friend or an ally; an accomplice or a fellow conspirator. **3** (**Confederate**) *US hist* a supporter of the Confederacy. ▸ *adj* /-rət/ **1** allied; united. **2** (**Confederate**) *US hist* belonging to the Confederacy. ▸ *verb* /-reɪt/ *tr & intr* to unite into or become part of a confederacy. [14c: from Latin *confoederatus*]

confederation *noun* **1** the uniting of states into a league. **2** the league so formed.

confer *verb* (***conferred, conferring***) **1** *intr* to consult or discuss together. **2** (*usu* **confer sth on sb**) to grant them (an honour or distinction). ▪ **conferment** *noun*. [16c: from Latin *conferre* to bring together]

conference *noun* **1** a formally organized gathering for the discussion of matters of common interest or concern. **2** consultation: *in conference with the Prime Minister*. [16c: from Latin *conferentia*]

confess *verb* **1** *tr & intr* **a** to own up to (a fault, wrongdoing, etc); **b** to admit (a disagreeable fact, etc) reluctantly. **2** *tr & intr, Christianity* to declare (one's sins) to a priest or directly to God, in order to gain absolution. [14c: from French *confesser*]

confession *noun* **1** the admission of a sin, fault, crime, distasteful or shocking fact, etc. **2** *Christianity* the formal act of confessing one's sins to a priest. **3** a declaration of one's religious faith or principles.

confessional *noun* in a church: the small enclosed stall in a church where a priest sits when hearing confessions. ▸ *adj* relating to a confession.

confessor *noun* **1** *Christianity* a priest who hears confessions and gives spiritual advice. **2** *hist* someone whose holy life serves as a demonstration of his or her religious faith, but who does not suffer martyrdom. [13c: Latin, meaning 'martyr' or 'witness']

confetti *noun* tiny pieces of coloured paper traditionally thrown over the bride and groom by wedding guests. [19c: Italian, pl of *confetto* sweetmeat]

confidant *or* **confidante** *noun* a close friend (male or female, respectively) with whom one discusses personal matters. [18c: from Latin *confidere* to trust]

confide *verb* **1** to tell (a secret, etc) to someone. **2** to entrust someone (to someone's care). **3** (*usu* **confide in sb**) to speak freely and confidentially with them about personal matters. [15c: from Latin *confidere* to trust]

confidence *noun* **1** trust or belief in a person or thing. **2** faith in one's own ability; self-assurance. **3** a secret, etc confided to someone. **4** a relationship of mutual trust. [15c: from Latin *confidentia*]

IDIOMS **in confidence** in secret; confidentially.

confidence trick *noun* a form of swindle in which the swindler first wins the trust of the victim. Often shortened to **con**[1].

confident *adj* **1** (*sometimes* **confident of sth**) certain; sure: *confident of success*. **2** self-assured.

confidential *adj* **1** secret; not to be divulged. **2** trusted with private matters. **3** indicating privacy or secrecy: *a confidential whisper*. ▪ **confidentiality** *noun*. ▪ **confidentially** *adv*. [18c: from Latin *confidentia* confidence]

confiding *adj* trusting. ▪ **confidingly** *adv*.

configuration *noun* **1** the positioning or distribution of the parts of something, relative to each other. **2** an outline or external shape. [17c: from Latin *configuratio*]

confine *verb* **1** to restrict or limit. **2** to keep prisoner. **3** eg of ill health: to restrict someone's movement.

confinement *noun* **1** the state of being shut up or kept in an enclosed space. **2** *old use* the period surrounding childbirth.

confirm *verb* **1** to provide support for the truth or validity of something. **2** to finalize or make definite (a booking, arrangement etc). **3** of an opinion, etc: to strengthen it or become more convinced in it. **4** to give formal approval to something. **5** *Christianity* to accept someone formally into full membership of the Church. [13c: from Latin *confirmare*]

confirmation *noun* **1** the act of confirming. **2** proof or support. **3** finalization. **4** *Christianity* the religious ceremony in which someone is admitted to full membership of the Church.

confirmed *adj* so firmly settled into a state, habit, etc as to be unlikely to change: *confirmed bachelor*.

confiscate *verb* to take away something from someone, usu as a penalty. ▪ **confiscation** *noun*. [16c: from Latin *confiscare* to transfer to the state treasury]

conflagration *noun* a large destructive blaze. [17c: from Latin *conflagrare* to burn up]

conflate *verb* to blend or combine (two things, esp two different versions of a text, story, etc) into a single whole. ▪ **conflation** *noun*. [17c: from Latin *conflare* to fuse]

conflict *noun* /'kɒnflɪkt/ **1** disagreement; fierce argument; a quarrel. **2** a clash between different interests, ideas, etc. **3** a struggle or battle. ▸ *verb* /kən'flɪkt/ *intr* to be incompatible or in opposition. ▪ **conflicting** *adj*. [15c: from Latin *confligere* to dash together or clash]

confluence *or* **conflux** *noun* **1** the point where two rivers flow into one another. **2** an act of meeting together. ▪ **confluent** *adj* flowing together. [15c: from Latin *confluentia* flowing together]

conform *verb, intr* **1** (*often* **conform to sth**) to meet or comply with (rules, laws, standards, etc). **2** to behave, dress, etc in obedience to some standard considered normal by the majority. **3** (*often* **conform with sth**) to be in agreement with it; to match or correspond to it. ▪ **conformist** *noun*. ▪ **conformity** *noun*. [14c: from Latin *conformare* to shape]

conformation *noun* a shape, structure or arrangement of something.

confound *verb* **1** to puzzle; to baffle. **2** to mix up or confuse (one thing with another). [14c: from Latin *confundere* to pour together, throw into disorder or overthrow]

IDIOMS **confound it!** damn it!

confounded *adj* **1** confused. **2** *informal* damned: *That boy's a confounded nuisance!*

confrère /ˈkɒnfrɛə(r)/ *noun* a fellow member of one's profession, etc; a colleague. [18c: French]

confront *verb* **1** to face someone, esp defiantly or accusingly. **2** (*usu* **confront sb with sth**) to bring them face to face with it, esp when it is damning or revealing. **3** to prepare to deal firmly with something. **4** of an unpleasant prospect: to present itself to someone. ▪ **confrontation** *noun*. [16c: from Latin *confrontari*]

Confucianism *noun* a school of Chinese thought, with emphasis on morality, consideration for others, obedience and good education. ▪ **Confucian** *adj, noun*. ▪ **Confucianist** *noun*. [19c: named after the Chinese philosopher Confucius]

confuse *verb* **1** to put into a muddle or mess. **2** to mix up or fail to distinguish (things, ideas, people, etc): *confuse 'ascetic' with 'aesthetic'*. **3** to puzzle, bewilder or muddle. **4** to complicate. ▪ **confusing** *adj*. ▪ **confusingly** *adv*. [18c: from Latin *confundere* to mix]

confusion *noun* **1** the act of confusing or state of being confused. **2** disorder; muddle. **3** mental bewilderment.

confute *verb* to prove (a person, theory, etc) wrong or false. ▪ **confutation** *noun*. [16c: from Latin *confutare* to refute]

conga *noun* **1** an orig Cuban dance of three steps followed by a kick, performed by people moving in single file. **2** music for this dance. **3** a tall narrow drum beaten with the fingers. ▸ *verb* (***congaed, congaing***) *intr* to dance the conga. [20c: Spanish]

congeal *verb, tr & intr* of a liquid, eg blood: to thicken or coagulate, esp through cooling. [15c: from Latin *congelare* to freeze completely]

congenial *adj* **1** of people: compatible; having similar interests. **2** pleasant or agreeable. ▪ **congeniality** *noun*. [17c: from Latin *con-* same + *genius* spirit]

congenital *adj* **1** of a disease or deformity: present at or before birth, but not inherited. **2** complete, as if from birth: *a congenital liar*. ▪ **congenitally** *adv*. [18c: from Latin *congenitus*]

conger *noun* a large marine eel. [14c: Latin]

congest *verb, tr & intr* **1** to excessively crowd or become excessively crowded. **2** of an organ: to accumulate or make something accumulate with blood, often causing inflammation. **3** of the nose or other air passages: to block up with mucus. ▪ **congested** *adj*. ▪ **congestion** *noun*. [19c: from Latin *congerere* to heap up]

conglomerate *noun* /kəŋˈglɒmərət/ **1** a miscellaneous collection or mass. **2** *geol* a sedimentary rock consisting of small rounded pebbles embedded in a fine matrix of sand or silt. **3** a business group composed of a large number of firms with diverse and often unrelated interests. ▸ *adj* /-rət/ composed of miscellaneous things. ▸ *verb* /-reɪt/ *intr* to accumulate into a mass. ▪ **conglomeration** *noun*. [17c: from Latin *conglomerare* to roll together]

congrats *plural noun, informal* a short form of **congratulations**.

congratulate *verb* (*usu* **congratulate sb on sth**) **1** to express pleasure to someone at their success, good fortune, happiness, etc. **2** to consider (oneself) lucky or clever to have managed something. ▪ **congratulatory** *adj*. [16c: from Latin *congratulari*]

congratulations *plural noun* often as an exclamation: an expression used to congratulate someone.

congregate *verb, tr & intr* to gather together into a crowd. [15c: from Latin *congregare*]

congregation *noun* a gathering or assembly of people, esp for worship in church. ▪ **congregational** *adj*.

Congregationalism *noun, Christianity* a form of church government in which each individual congregation is responsible for the management of its own affairs. ▪ **Congregationalist** *noun*.

congress *noun* **1** a large, esp international, assembly of delegates, gathered for discussion. **2** in some countries: a name used for the law-making body. **3** (**Congress**) in the US: the federal legislature, consisting of two elected chambers called the Senate and the House of Representatives. ▪ **congressional** *adj*. [16c: from Latin *congredi* to go together]

congressman *or* **congresswoman** *noun* someone who is a member of a congress.

congruent *adj* **1** *geom* of two or more figures: identical in size and shape. **2** (*often* **congruent with sth**) suitable or appropriate to it. ▪ **congruence** *or* **congruency** *noun*. [15c: from Latin *congruere* to meet together]

congruous *adj* (*often* **congruous with sth**) **1** corresponding. **2** fitting; suitable. ▪ **congruity** *noun*. [16c: from Latin *congruus*]

conic *or* **conical** *adj, geom* **a** relating to a cone; **b** resembling a cone.

conic section *noun, geom* the curved figure produced when a plane (see **plane**[2], *noun* sense 1) intersects a cone.

conifer *noun* an evergreen tree or shrub with narrow needle-like leaves, which produce their pollen and seeds in cones, eg pine, spruce, etc. ▪ **coniferous** *adj*. [19c: Latin, from *conus* cone + *ferre* to carry]

conjecture *noun* **1** an opinion based on incomplete evidence. **2** the process of forming such an opinion. ▸ *verb, intr* to make a conjecture. ▪ **conjectural** *adj*. [16c: from Latin *conjectura* conclusion]

conjoin *verb, tr & intr* to join together, combine or unite. [14c: from French *conjoindre*]

conjoined twins *plural noun* the formal or technical name for **Siamese twins**.

conjugal *adj* relating to marriage, or to the relationship between husband and wife. [16c: from Latin *conjugalis*]

conjugate *verb* /ˈkɒndʒʊgeɪt/ **1** *grammar* **a** to give the inflected parts of (a verb), indicating number, person, tense, **mood**[2] and **voice** (*noun* sense 9); **b** *intr* of a verb: to undergo inflection. **2** *intr, biol* to reproduce by conjugation. ▸ *adj* /-gət/ **1** joined or connected. **2** *grammar* of a word: having the same root as another word. ▸ *noun* /-gət/ **1** *grammar* a word with the same root as another word. **2** something joined or connected with something else. [15c: from Latin *conjugare* to yoke together]

conjugate angles *plural noun, geom* a pair of angles whose sum is 360°. Compare **complementary angles, supplementary angles**.

conjugation *noun* **1** *grammar* **a** the inflection of a verb to indicate number, person, tense, **voice** (*noun* sense 9) and **mood**[2]; **b** a particular class of verbs having the same set of inflections. See also **declension**. **2** a uniting, joining or fusing. **3** *biol* a method of sexual reproduction which involves the fusion of **gametes**.

conjunction *noun* **1** *grammar* a word used to link sentences, clauses or other words, eg *and, but, if, or, because*, etc. **2** a joining together; combination. **3** the coinciding of two or more events. **4** *astron, astrol* the alignment of two or more heavenly bodies, as seen from Earth. [14c: from Latin *conjunctio*]
IDIOMS **in conjunction with sth** together with it.

conjunctiva /kɒndʒʌŋk'taɪvə/ *noun* (***conjunctivas*** *or* ***conjunctivae*** /-viː/) *anatomy* in the eye of vertebrates: the thin mucous membrane that lines the eyelids and covers the exposed surface of the cornea at the front of the eyeball. ▪ **conjunctival** *adj.* [16c: from Latin *membrana conjunctiva* conjunctive membrane]

conjunctive *adj* **1** connecting; linking. **2** *grammar* relating to conjunctions. ▸ *noun, grammar* a word or phrase used as a conjunction. [15c: from Latin *conjunctivus*]

conjunctivitis *noun* inflammation of the conjunctiva. Also called **pink eye**.

conjuncture *noun* a combination of circumstances, esp one leading to a crisis. [17c: from Latin *conjungere* to join together]

conjure /'kʌndʒə(r)/ *verb* **1** *intr* to perform magic tricks. **2** to summon (a spirit, demon, etc) to appear. **3** /kɒn'dʒʊə(r)/ *old use* to beg someone earnestly to do something. ▪ **conjurer** *or* **conjuror** *noun* someone who performs magic tricks, etc. ▪ **conjuring** *noun.* [13c: from Latin *conjurare* to swear together]
PHRASAL VERBS **conjure sth up 1** to produce it as though from nothing. **2** to call up, evoke or stir (images, memories, etc).

conk[1] *noun, slang* **1** the nose. **2** the head. **3** a blow, esp on the head or nose. ▸ *verb* to hit someone on the nose or head. [19c: prob a variant of **conch**]

conk[2] *verb, intr, slang* (*usu* **conk out**) **1** of a machine, etc: to break down. **2** of a person: to collapse with fatigue, etc.

conker *noun, informal* the brown shiny seed of the **horse chestnut** tree. [19c: prob dialectal, meaning 'snail shell']

conkers *singular noun, Brit* a game played with conkers threaded onto strings, the aim being to shatter one's opponent's conker by hitting it with one's own.

con man *noun, informal* a swindler who uses a **confidence trick**.

connect *verb* (*usu* **connect to** *or* **with sb** *or* **sth**) **1** *tr & intr* (*sometimes* **connect sth up** *or* **connect up**) to join; to link. **2** to associate or involve: *is connected with advertising.* **3** *tr & intr* to associate or relate mentally: *We connected immediately.* **4** to join by telephone. **5** to relate by marriage or birth. **6** *intr* of aeroplanes, trains, buses, etc: to be timed to allow transfer from one to another. ▪ **connective** *adj.* ▪ **connector** *or* **connecter** *noun.* [17c: from Latin *con-* together + *nectere* to fasten]

connection *or* **connexion** *noun* **1** the act of connecting or state of being connected. **2** something that connects; a link. **3** a relationship through marriage or birth. **4** an esp influential person whom one meets through one's job, etc; a contact. **5 a** a train, bus, etc timed so as to allow transfer to it from another passenger service; **b** the transfer from one vehicle to another.
IDIOMS **in connection with sth** to do with it; concerning it.

connective tissue *noun, anatomy* any of several widely differing tissues that provide the animal body and its internal organs with structural support, eg bone, cartilage, tendons, ligaments.

conning tower *noun* the raised part of a submarine containing the periscope, which is additionally used as an entrance or exit. [19c]

connive *verb, intr* (*often* **connive with sb**) to conspire or plot. ▪ **connivance** *noun.* [17c: from Latin *connivere* to blink or shut the eyes]

connoisseur *noun* someone who is knowledgeable about and a good judge of a particular subject, eg the arts, wine, food, etc. [18c: French]

connotation *noun* an idea, association or implication additional to the main idea or object expressed. ▪ **connote** *verb.* [17c: from Latin *connotare* to mark in addition]

connubial *adj* pertaining to marriage, or to relations between a husband and wife. [17c: from Latin *connubialis*]

conquer *verb* **1** to gain possession or dominion over (territory) by force. **2** to defeat or overcome. **3** to overcome or put an end to (a failing, difficulty, evil, etc). ▪ **conquering** *adj.* ▪ **conqueror** *noun.* [13c: from French *conquerre*]

conquest *noun* **1** the act of conquering. **2** a conquered territory. **3** something won by effort or force. **4** someone whose affection or admiration has been won. [13c: from French *conqueste*]

conquistador /kəŋ'kwɪstədɔː(r)/ *noun* (***conquistadores*** /kəŋkwɪstə'dɔːreɪz/ *or* ***conquistadors***) an adventurer or conqueror, esp one of the 16th-century Spanish conquerors of Peru and Mexico. [19c: Spanish, meaning 'conqueror']

consanguinity *noun* relationship by blood. ▪ **consanguine** *or* **consanguineous** *adj.* [14c: from Latin *consanguinitas* blood relationship]

conscience *noun* the moral sense of right and wrong that determines someone's thoughts and behaviour. [13c: French]
IDIOMS **in all conscience** by any normal standard of fairness. **on one's conscience** making one feel guilty.

conscience-stricken *adj* feeling guilty over something one has done.

conscientious *adj* **1** careful; thorough; painstaking. **2** guided by conscience. ▪ **conscientiously** *adv.* ▪ **conscientiousness** *noun.* [17c: from Latin *conscientiosus*]

conscientious objector *noun* someone who refuses to serve in the armed forces on moral grounds.

conscious *adj* **1** awake, alert and aware of one's thoughts and one's surroundings. **2** aware; knowing: *She was conscious that someone was watching her.* **3**

deliberate: *I made a conscious effort to be polite.* ▸ *noun* the part of the human mind which is responsible for such awareness, and is concerned with perceiving and reacting to external objects and events. ▪ **consciously** *adv.* ▪ **consciousness** *noun.* [17c: from Latin *conscius* knowing something with others]

conscript *verb* /kən'skrɪpt/ to enlist for compulsory military service. ▸ *noun* /'kɒnskrɪpt/ someone who has been conscripted. ▪ **conscription** *noun.* [18c: from Latin *conscribere* to enlist]

consecrate *verb* **1** to set something apart for a holy use; to make sacred. **2** *Christianity* to sanctify (bread and wine) for the **Eucharist**. **3** to devote something to a special use. ▪ **consecration** *noun.* [15c: from Latin *consecrare* to make sacred]

consecutive *adj* following one after the other; in sequence. ▪ **consecutively** *adv.* [17c: from French *consécutif*]

consensus *noun* general feeling or agreement; the majority view. [19c: Latin, meaning 'agreement']

consent *verb* **1** *intr* (*often* **consent to sth**) to give one's permission for it. **2** to agree to do something. ▸ *noun* agreement; assent; permission. [13c: from Latin *consentire* to agree]

consequence *noun* **1** something that follows from, or is caused by, an action or set of circumstances. **2** a conclusion reached from reasoning. **3** importance or significance: *of no consequence.* [14c: French]
IDIOMS **take the consequences** to accept the (often unpleasant) results of one's decision or action.

consequent *adj* **1** following as a result. **2** following as an inference.

consequential *adj* **1** significant or important. **2** following as a result. [17c: from Latin *consequentia*]

consequently *adv* as a result; therefore.

conservancy *noun* (**-ies**) an area under special environmental protection. [18c: from Latin *conservare* to **conserve**]

conservation *noun* **1** the act of conserving; the state of being conserved. **2** the protection and preservation of the environment, its wildlife and its natural resources. **3** the preservation of historical artefacts, eg books, paintings, monuments, for future generations. ▪ **conservationist** *noun.* [14c: from Latin *conservatio*]

conservative *adj* **1** favouring that which is established or traditional, with an opposition to change. **2** of an estimate or calculation: deliberately low, for the sake of caution. **3** of tastes, clothing, etc: restrained or modest. **4** (**Conservative**) belonging or relating to a Conservative Party. ▸ *noun* **1** a traditionalist. **2** (**Conservative**) a member or supporter of any political party with *Conservative* in its title, eg the Conservative Party of the UK. ▪ **conservatism** *noun.* [14c: from Latin *conservare* to preserve]

Conservative Party *noun* **1** in the UK: a political party on the right of the political spectrum, whose policies include a commitment to privatization and the advocation of free enterprise. Also called **Conservative and Unionist Party**. See also **Tory**. **2** in other countries: any of various right-leaning political parties.

conservatoire /kən'sɜːvətwɑː(r)/ *noun* a school specializing in the teaching of music. Also called **conservatory**. [18c: French]

conservatory *noun* (**-ies**) **1** **a** a greenhouse for plants; **b** a similar room used as a lounge, which is attached to and entered from, the house. **2** a conservatoire. [17c: from Latin *conservare* to conserve]

conserve *verb* /kən'sɜːv/ **1** to keep safe from damage, deterioration, loss or undesirable change. **2** to preserve (fruit, etc) with sugar. ▸ *noun* /'kɒnsɜːv/ a type of jam, esp one containing chunks of fresh fruit. [14c: from Latin *conservare* to save]

consider *verb* **1** to go over something in one's mind. **2** to look at someone or something thoughtfully. **3** to call to mind for comparison, etc. **4** to assess with regard to employing, using, etc: *consider someone for a job.* **5** to contemplate doing something. **6** to regard as something specified: *He considered Neil to be his best friend.* **7** to think; to have as one's opinion. [14c: from Latin *considerare* to examine]

considerable *adj* **1** large; great. **2** having many admirable qualities; worthy: *a considerable person.* ▪ **considerably** *adv* largely; greatly. [17c: from Latin *considerabilis* worthy to be considered]

considerate *adj* thoughtful regarding the feelings of others; kind. [17c: from Latin *consideratus*]

consideration *noun* **1** thoughtfulness on behalf of others. **2** careful thought. **3** a fact, circumstance, etc to be taken into account. **4** a payment, reward or recompense. [14c: from Latin *consideratio*]
IDIOMS **take sth into consideration** to allow for it; to bear it in mind. **under consideration** being considered.

considered *adj* **1** carefully thought about: *my considered opinion.* **2** *with an adverb* thought of or valued in a specified way: *highly considered.*

considering *prep* in view of; when one considers. ▸ *conj* taking into account. ▸ *adv* taking the circumstances into account: *Her results were pretty good, considering.*

consign *verb* **1** to hand over; to entrust. **2** to send, commit or deliver formally. **3** to send (goods). ▪ **consignee** *noun.* ▪ **consigner** *or* **consignor** *noun.* [16c: from Latin *consignare* to put one's seal to]

consignment *noun* **1** a load of goods, etc sent or delivered. **2** the act of consigning.

consist *verb, intr* **1** (*always* **consist of sth**) to be composed or made up of several elements or ingredients. **2** (*always* **consist in** *or* **of sth**) to have it as an essential feature. [16c: from Latin *consistere* to stand firm]

consistency *or* **consistence** *noun* (**-ies**) **1** the texture or composition of something, with regard to thickness, firmness, etc. **2** agreement; harmony. [16c: from Latin *consistere* to stand firm]

consistent *adj* **1** (*usu* **consistent with sth**) in agreement or in keeping with it. **2** reliable; regular; steady. **3** of people or their actions: not contradictory. ▪ **consistently** *adv.* [17c: from Latin *consistere* to stand firm]

consolation *noun* **1** a circumstance or person that brings one comfort. **2** the act of consoling.

consolation prize *noun* a prize given to someone who has otherwise failed to win anything.

console[1] /kən'soul/ *verb* to comfort in distress, grief or disappointment. ▪ **consolable** *adj.* [17c: from French *consoler*]

console[2] /'kɒnsoul/ *noun* **1** *music* the part of an organ with the keys, pedals and panels of stops. **2** a panel of dials, switches, etc for operating electronic equipment. **3** a freestanding cabinet for audio or video equipment. **4** an ornamental bracket for a shelf, etc. [18c: French]

consolidate *verb, tr & intr* **1** to make or become solid or strong. **2** of businesses, etc: to combine or merge into one. ▪ **consolidation** *noun.* ▪ **consolidator** *noun.* [16c: from Latin *consolidare* to make firm]

consommé /kɒn'sɒmeɪ/ *noun* a type of thin clear soup made usu from meat stock. [19c: French, from *consummare* to finish]

consonance *noun* the state of agreement.

consonant *noun* **a** any speech-sound produced by obstructing the passage of the breath in any of several ways; **b** a letter of the alphabet representing such a sound. Compare **vowel**. ▸ *adj* (**consonant with sth**) in harmony or suitable with it. [14c: from Latin *consonans*]

consort[1] *noun* /'kɒnsɔːt/ a wife or husband, esp of a reigning sovereign. ▸ *verb* /kən'sɔːt/ (*usu* **consort with sb**) (usu with unfavourable implications) to associate with them. [16c: from Latin *consors* sharer]

consort[2] /'kɒnsɔːt/ *noun* a group of singing or playing musicians, particularly specializing in early music.

consortium /kən'sɔːtɪəm/ *noun* (***consortia*** /-ɪə/ *or* ***consortiums***) an association or combination of several banks, businesses, etc, usu for a specific purpose. [19c: Latin, meaning 'partnership']

conspectus *noun* **1** a comprehensive survey or report. **2** a summary or synopsis. [19c: Latin, meaning 'a view']

conspicuous *adj* **1** visibly noticeable or obvious. **2** notable; striking; glaring. ▪ **conspicuously** *adv.* [16c: from Latin *conspicuus* visible]

conspiracy *noun* (***-ies***) **1** the act of plotting in secret. **2** a plot. [14c: from Latin *conspiratio* plot]

conspire *verb, intr* **1** to plot secretly together, esp for an unlawful purpose. **2** of events: to seem to be working together to achieve a certain end: *Everything conspired to make me miss my train.* ▪ **conspirator** *noun.* ▪ **conspiratorial** *adj.* [13c: from Latin *conspirare* literally 'to breathe together']

constable *noun* a police officer of the most junior rank. [13c: from French *conestable*]

constabulary *noun* (***-ies***) the police force of a district or county. [19c: from Latin *constabularius*]

constant *adj* **1** never stopping. **2** frequently recurring. **3** unchanging. **4** faithful; loyal. ▸ *noun, maths* a symbol representing an unspecified number, which remains unchanged, unlike a **variable** (noun 3). ▪ **constancy** *noun.* ▪ **constantly** *adv.* [14c: French]

constellation *noun* **1** *astron* a named group of stars seen as forming a recognizable pattern in the night sky. **2** a group of associated people or things. [14c: from Latin *constellatio*]

consternate *verb* to fill with anxiety, dismay or confusion. ▪ **consternation** *noun.* [17c: from Latin *consternare* to dismay]

constipated *adj* suffering from constipation. [16c: from Latin *constipare* to press closely together]

constipation *noun* a condition in which the faeces become hard, and bowel movements occur infrequently or with pain or difficulty.

constituency *noun* (***-ies***) **1** the district represented by a member of parliament or other representative in a legislative body. **2** the voters in that district. [19c: from **constituent**]

constituent *adj* **1** forming part of a whole. **2** having the power to create or alter a constitution: *a constituent assembly.* **3** having the power to elect. ▸ *noun* **1** a necessary part; a component. **2** a resident in a constituency. [17c: from Latin *constituens*]

constitute *verb* **1** to be; to make up. **2** to establish formally. [15c: from Latin *constituere* to establish]

constitution *noun* **1** a set of rules governing an organization. **2** the supreme laws and rights upon which a country or state is founded. **3** (*often* **Constitution**) in the US, Australia, etc: the legislation which states such laws and rights. **4** one's physical make-up, health, etc. [16c: from Latin *constitutio* arrangement or physical make-up]

constitutional *adj* **1** legal according to a given constitution. **2** relating to, or controlled by, a constitution. **3** relating to one's physical make-up, health, etc. **4** inherent in the natural make-up or structure of a person or thing. ▸ *noun, dated* a regular walk taken for the sake of one's health.

constrain *verb* **1** to force; to compel. **2** to limit the freedom, scope or range of someone. [14c: from French *constraindre*]

constrained *adj* awkward; embarrassed; forced.

constraint *noun* **1** a limit or restriction. **2** force; compulsion. **3** awkwardness, embarrassment or inhibition.

constrict *verb* **1 a** to squeeze or compress; **b** to enclose tightly, esp too tightly; **c** to cause to tighten. **2** to inhibit. ▪ **constriction** *noun.* ▪ **constrictive** *adj.* [18c: from Latin *constrictus*]

constrictor *noun* **1** a snake that kills by coiling around its prey and squeezing it until it suffocates. See also **boa**. **2** *anatomy* any muscle that compresses an organ or narrows an opening.

construct *verb* /kən'strʌkt/ **1** to build. **2** to form, compose or put together. **3** *geom* to draw (a figure). ▸ *noun* /'kɒnstrʌkt/ **1** something constructed, esp in the mind. **2** *psychol* a complex idea or thought constructed from a number of simpler ideas or thoughts. ▪ **constructor** *noun.* [17c: from Latin *construere* to heap together]

construction *noun* **1** the process of building or constructing. **2** something built or constructed; a building. **3** *grammar* the arrangement of words in a particular grammatical relationship. **4** interpretation: *put a wrong construction on someone's words.* ▪ **constructional** *adj.*

constructive *adj* **1** helping towards progress or development; useful. **2** *law* of facts: inferred rather than directly expressed.

construe *verb* **1** to interpret or explain. **2** *grammar* to analyse the grammatical structure of (a sentence, etc). **3** *grammar* (*often* **construe with**) to combine words grammatically. [14c: from Latin *construere* to heap together]

consul *noun* **1** an official representative of a state, stationed in a foreign country. **2** *hist* in ancient Rome: either of the two joint chief magistrates. ▪ **consular** *adj.* ▪ **consulship** *noun.* [14c: Latin, prob related to *consulere* to take counsel]

consulate *noun* the post or official residence of a consul.

consult *verb* **1** to ask the advice of. **2** to refer to (a map, book, etc). **3** *intr* (*often* **consult with sb**) to have discussions with them. [16c: from Latin *consultare*]

consultant *noun* **1** someone who gives professional advice. **2** in a hospital or clinic: a doctor or surgeon holding the most senior post in a particular field of medicine. ▪ **consultancy** *noun* (*-ies*).

consultation *noun* **1** the act or process of consulting. **2** a meeting for the obtaining of advice or for discussion. ▪ **consultative** *adj.*

consulting *adj* acting as an adviser: *a consulting architect.*

consulting room *noun* the room in which a doctor sees patients.

consume *verb* **1** to eat or drink. **2** to use up. **3** to destroy. **4** to devour or overcome completely. ▪ **consumable** *adj.* ▪ **consuming** *adj* overwhelming. [14c: from Latin *consumere* to take up completely]

consumer *noun* someone who buys goods and services for personal use or need.

consumer durables *plural noun* goods that are designed to last for a relatively long time, eg furniture, television sets, etc.

consumerism *noun* **1** the protection of the interests of consumers. **2** *econ* the theory that steady growth in the consumption of goods is necessary for a sound economy.

consummate *verb* /'kɒnsəmeɪt, 'kɒnsjʊmeɪt/ **1** to finish, perfect or complete something. **2** to complete (a marriage) in its full legal sense through the act of sexual intercourse. ▸ *adj* /kən'sʌmət/ **1** supreme; very skilled. **2** complete; utter: *a consummate idiot.* ▪ **consummately** *adv.* ▪ **consummation** *noun.* [16c: from Latin *consummare* to complete or perfect]

consumption *noun* **1** the act or process of consuming. **2** the amount consumed. **3** the buying and using of goods. **4** *dated* another name for **tuberculosis** of the lungs. [14c: from Latin *consumptio*]

consumptive *adj* **1** relating to consumption; wasteful or destructive. **2** suffering from **tuberculosis** of the lungs. ▸ *noun* someone suffering from tuberculosis of the lungs.

cont. *or* **contd.** *abbrev* continued.

contact *noun* **1** the condition of touching physically. **2** communication or a means of communication. **3** an acquaintance whose influence or knowledge may prove useful, esp in business. **4** in an electrical device: a connection made of a conducting material that allows the passage of a current by forming a junction with another conducting part. Also called **electric contact**. **5** someone who has been exposed to an infectious disease. **6** a contact lens. ▸ *verb* to get in touch with someone; to communicate with someone. ▪ **contactable** *adj.* [17c: from Latin *contactus*]

contact lens *noun* a small lens which is placed in direct contact with the eyeball to correct vision.

contagion *noun* **1** the transmission of a disease by direct physical contact with an infected person. **2** *dated* a disease that is transmitted in this way. **3** a harmful influence. [14c: from Latin *contagio* touching, contact]

contagious *adj* **1** of a disease: only able to be transmitted by direct contact with or close proximity to an infected individual, eg the common cold. Also called **communicable**. **2** of a mood, laughter, etc: spreading easily from person to person; affecting everyone in the vicinity.

---

contagious, infectious

Be careful not to use the word **contagious** when you mean **infectious**. A **contagious** disease is spread by touch, while an **infectious** disease can be spread through the air. However, if you use these words figuratively, describing laughter for example, they mean the same thing.

---

contain *verb* **1** to hold or be able to hold. **2** to consist of something specified. **3** to control, limit, check or prevent the spread of something: *They were eventually able to contain the riot.* **4** to control (oneself or one's feelings). **5** to enclose or surround. ▪ **containable** *adj.* [13c: from Latin *continere* to hold together]

container *noun* **1** an object designed for holding or storing, such as a box, tin, carton, etc. **2** a huge sealed metal box of standard size and design for carrying goods by lorry or ship.

containerize *or* **-ise** *verb* **1** to put (cargo) into containers. **2** to convert so as to be able to handle containers. ▪ **containerization** *noun.*

containment *noun* the action of preventing the expansion of a hostile power, etc.

contaminate *verb* **1** to pollute or infect (a substance). **2** to make something radioactive. ▪ **contaminant** *noun.* ▪ **contamination** *noun.* [16c: from Latin *contaminare* to corrupt]

contemn *verb, literary* to despise, disdain or scorn. [15c: from Latin *contemnere*]

contemplate *verb* **1** *tr & intr* to think about; to meditate. **2** to look thoughtfully at something. **3** to consider something as a possibility. ▪ **contemplation** *noun.* [16c: from Latin *contemplari* to survey or look at carefully]

contemplative *adj* thoughtful; meditative. ▸ *noun* someone whose life is spent in religious contemplation.

contemporaneous *adj* (*often* **contemporaneous with sth**) existing or happening at the same time.

contemporary *adj* **1** (*often* **contemporary with sth**) belonging to the same period or time as something. **2** (*often* **contemporary with sb**) around the same age as them. **3** modern. ▸ *noun* (*-ies*) **1** someone who lives or lived at the same time as another. **2** someone of about the same age as another. [17c: from Latin *contemporarius*]

contempt *noun* **1** scorn. **2** *law* disregard of or disobedience to the rules of a court of law. [14c: from Latin *con-* intensive + *temnere, temptum* to scorn]

IDIOMS **hold sb in contempt** to despise them.

contemptible *adj* despicable; disgusting; vile.

contemptuous *adj* (*often* **contemptuous of sb** *or* **sth**) showing contempt or scorn.

contend *verb* **1** *intr* (*often* **contend with sb** *or* **sth**) to fight or compete. **2** *intr* to argue earnestly. **3** to say, maintain or assert something. ▪ **contender** *noun.* [15c: from Latin *con-* with + *tendere* to strive]

content[1] /kɒn'tɛnt/ *adj* (*often* **content with sth**) satisfied; happy; uncomplaining. ▸ *verb* to satisfy or make (oneself or another) satisfied. ▸ *noun* peaceful satisfaction; peace of mind. ▪ **contentment** *noun.* [14c: from Latin *contentus* contained]

content² /'kɒntɛnt/ *noun* **1** the subject-matter of a book, speech, etc. **2** the proportion in which a particular ingredient is present in something: *a diet with a high starch content*. **3** (**contents**) **a** the text of a book, divided into chapters; **b** a list of these chapters, given at the beginning of the book. [15c: from Latin *contenta* things contained]

contented *adj* peacefully happy or satisfied. ▪ **contentedly** *adv.* ▪ **contentedness** *noun.*

contention *noun* **1** a point that one asserts or maintains in an argument. **2** argument or debate. [14c: from Latin *contentio* strife, controversy]

contentious *adj* **1** likely to cause argument or quarrelling. **2** quarrelsome or argumentative. [15c: from Latin *contentiosus*]

contest *noun* /'kɒntɛst/ **1** a competition. **2** a struggle. ▸ *verb* /kən'tɛst/ **1** to enter the competition or struggle for something. **2** *tr & intr* to dispute (a claim, a will, etc). ▪ **contestable** *adj.* [16c: from Latin *contestari* to call to witness]

contestant *noun* someone who takes part in a contest; a competitor.

context *noun* **1** the pieces of writing in a passage which surround a particular word, phrase, etc and which contribute to the full meaning of the word, phrase, etc in question. **2** circumstances, background or setting. ▪ **contextual** *adj.* [16c: from Latin *contextus* connection]

contiguous *adj* (*often* **contiguous with** *or* **to sth**) touching. [17c: from Latin *contiguus*]

continent¹ *noun* **1 a** any of the seven main land masses of the world (Europe, Asia, N America, S America, Africa, Australia and Antarctica); **b** the mainland portion of one of these land masses. **2** (**the Continent**) the mainland of Europe, as regarded from the British Isles. [16c: from Latin, representing the phrase *terra continens* continuous land]

continent² *adj* **1** able to control one's bowels and bladder. **2** self-controlled, esp with regard to one's passions. ▪ **continence** *noun.* [14c: from Latin *continere* to hold together]

continental *adj* **1** of a continent. **2** *Brit* European.

continental breakfast *noun* a light breakfast of rolls and coffee.

continental climate *noun, geog* the climate characteristic of the inland area of a continent, with hot summers, cold winters, and little rainfall.

continental crust *noun, geol* the part of the earth's crust lying underneath the large landmasses.

continental drift *noun, geol* the theory that the continents were formed by the break-up of a single land mass, the constituent parts of which drifted apart horizontally across the Earth's surface.

continental quilt *noun* a **duvet**.

continental shelf *noun, geol* the part of a continent that is submerged in an area of relatively shallow sea.

contingency *noun* (**-ies**) **1** something liable, but not certain, to occur; a chance happening. **2** something dependent on a chance future happening.

contingent *noun* **1** a body of troops. **2** any identifiable body of people: *There were boos from the Welsh contingent*. ▸ *adj* **1** (*usu* **contingent on** *or* **upon sth**) dependent on some uncertain circumstance. **2** liable but not certain to occur. **3** accidental. [14c: from Latin *contingere* to touch together]

continual *adj* **1** constantly happening or done; frequent. **2** constant; never ceasing. ▪ **continually** *adv.* [14c: from Latin *continuus* uninterrupted]

---

continual, continuous
See the Usage Note at **continuous.**

---

continuance *noun* **1** the act or state of continuing. **2** duration. [14c: from Latin *continuare* to make continuous]

continuation *noun* **1** the act or process of continuing. **2** that which adds to something or carries it on, eg a further episode of or sequel to a story.

continue *verb* **1** *tr & intr* to go on without stopping. **2** *tr & intr* to last or cause to last. **3** *tr & intr* to start again after a break. **4** *intr* to keep moving in the same direction. [14c: from Latin *continuare* to make continuous]

continuity *noun* **1** the state of being continuous, unbroken or consistent. **2** *TV, cinema* the arrangement of scenes so that one progresses smoothly from another, without any inconsistencies. [16c: from Latin *continuitas*]

continuo *noun, music* **a** a bass part for a keyboard or stringed instrument; **b** the instrument or instruments playing this. Also called **thorough bass.** [18c: Italian, meaning 'continuous']

continuous *adj* **1** incessant. **2** unbroken; uninterrupted. ▪ **continuously** *adv.* [17c: from Latin *continuus* unbroken]

---

continuous, continual
Be careful not to use the word **continual** when you mean **continuous**. Something that is **continuous** exists or happens for a period without a break, and something that is **continual** exists or happens repeatedly over a period. *A continuous disturbance* goes on for a time without a break, whereas *continual disturbances* are a number of disturbances with gaps between them.

---

continuum /kɒn'tɪnjʊʌm/ *noun* (***continua*** /-jʊə/ *or* ***continuums***) a continuous sequence; an unbroken progression. [17c: Latin, from *continuus* unbroken]

contort *verb, tr & intr* to twist violently out of shape. ▪ **contorted** *adj.* ▪ **contortion** *noun.* [16c: from Latin *contorquere* to twist]

contortionist *noun* an entertainer who is able to twist their body into spectacularly unnatural positions.

contour *noun* **1** (*often* **contours**) the distinctive outline of something. **2** a line on a map joining points of the same height or depth. Also called **contour line.** ▸ *verb* **1** to shape the contour of, or shape so as to fit a contour. **2** to mark the contour lines on (a map). [17c: French]

contra- *prefix* **1** against: *contraception.* **2** opposite: *contraflow.* **3** *music* lower in pitch: *contrabass.* [Latin]

contraband *noun* smuggled goods. ▸ *adj* **1** prohibited from being imported or exported. **2** smuggled. [16c: from Spanish *contrabanda*]

contrabass *noun* the **double bass.**

contrabassoon *noun, music* a **bassoon** which sounds an octave lower than the standard instrument. Also called **double bassoon.** [19c: from Latin *contra-* against + **bassoon**]

contraception *noun* the deliberate prevention of pregnancy by artificial or natural means. [19c: from **contra-** + **conception**]

contraceptive *noun* a drug or device that prevents pregnancy resulting from sexual intercourse. ▸ *adj* having the effect of preventing pregnancy.

contract *noun* /ˈkɒntrakt/ **1** an agreement, esp a legally binding one. **2** a document setting out the terms of such an agreement. ▸ *verb* /kənˈtrakt/ **1** *tr & intr* to make or become smaller. **2** *tr & intr* of muscles: to make or become shorter, esp in order to bend a joint, etc. **3** to catch (a disease). **4** to enter into (an alliance or marriage). **5** *tr & intr* of a word, phrase, etc: to reduce to a short form: *'Are not' is contracted to 'aren't'.* **6** *tr & intr* (*often* **contract with sb**) to enter a legal contract concerning them. ▪ **contractable** *adj* of a disease, habit, etc: likely to be contracted. ▪ **contractible** *adj* of a muscle, word, etc: capable of being contracted. [14c: from Latin *contractus* agreement]

PHRASAL VERBS **contract in** *or* **out** to arrange to participate, or not to participate, eg in a pension scheme. **contract sth out** of a company, etc: to arrange for part of a job to be done by another company.

contraction *noun* **1** the process of contracting or state of being contracted. **2** a decrease in length, size or volume. **3** a tightening of the muscles caused by a shortening in length of the muscle fibres. **4** (**contractions**) the regular painful spasms of the muscles of the uterus that occur during labour. **5** a shortened form of a word or phrase which includes at least the last letter of the word or phrase: *'Aren't' is a contraction of 'are not'.*

contractor *noun* a person or firm that undertakes work on contract.

contractual *adj* relating to a contract or binding agreement.

contradict *verb* **1** to assert the opposite of or deny (a statement, etc) made by (a person). **2** of a statement, action, etc: to disagree or be inconsistent with another. ▪ **contradiction** *noun.* [16c: from Latin *contradicere* to speak against]

contradictory *adj* **1** inconsistent. **2** denying. **3** contrary.

contradistinction *noun* a distinction made in terms of a contrast between qualities, properties, etc. ▪ **contradistinctive** *adj.*

contraflow *noun* a form of traffic diversion whereby streams of traffic moving in opposite directions share the same carriageway of a motorway, dual carriageway, etc.

contralto /kənˈtraltəʊ/ *noun* (***contraltos*** *or* ***contralti*** /-tiː/) **a** the female singing voice that is lowest in pitch; **b** a singer with this voice; **c** a part to be sung by this voice. [18c: Italian, meaning, 'lower in pitch than alto']

contraption *noun, informal* a machine or apparatus which is usu ingenious rather than effective. [19c]

contrapuntal *adj, music* relating to or arranged as **counterpoint**. [19c: from Italian *contrappunto* counterpoint]

contrariwise *adv* **1** on the other hand. **2** the opposite way round. **3** in the opposite direction.

contrary *adj* **1** /ˈkɒntrərɪ/ (*often* **contrary to sth**) opposite; quite different; opposed. **2** /ˈkɒntrərɪ/ of a wind: blowing against one; unfavourable. **3** /kɒnˈtrɛərɪ/ obstinate, perverse, self-willed or wayward. ▸ *noun* /ˈkɒntrərɪ/ (***-ies***) **1** an extreme opposite. **2** either of a pair of opposites. ▪ **contrariness** *noun.* [14c: from Latin *contrarius*]

IDIOMS **on the contrary** in opposition or contrast to what has just been said. **to the contrary** to the opposite effect; giving the contrasting position.

contrast *noun* /ˈkɒntrɑːst/ **1** difference or dissimilarity between things or people that are being compared. **2** a person or thing that is strikingly different from another. **3** the degree of difference in tone between the colours, or the light and dark parts, of a photograph or television picture. ▸ *verb* /kənˈtrɑːst/ **1** to compare so as to reveal differences. **2** (*often* **contrast with sth**) to show the difference. [17c: from Latin *contra-* against + *stare* to stand]

IDIOMS **in contrast to** *or* **with sth** *or* **sb** as an opposite to it or them or something distinct from it or them.

contravene *verb* to break or disobey (a law or rule, etc). ▪ **contravention** *noun* (*often* **in contravention of sth**) infringement of a law, etc. [16c: from Latin *contravenire* to come against, oppose]

contretemps /ˈkɒntrətɑ̃/ *noun* (*pl* ***contretemps*** /-tɑ̃z/) **1** an awkward or embarrassing moment, situation, etc. **2** a slight disagreement. [19c: French, meaning 'bad or false time']

contribute *verb* (*usu* **contribute to sth**) **1** *tr & intr* to give (money, time, etc) for some joint purpose. **2** *intr* to be one of the causes of something. **3** to supply (an article, etc) for publication in a magazine, etc. ▪ **contribution** *noun.* ▪ **contributor** *noun.* ▪ **contributory** *adj.* [16c: from Latin *contribuere* to bring together]

con trick *noun, informal* short for a **confidence trick**.

contrite *adj* **1** sorry for something one has done. **2** resulting from a feeling of guilt: *a contrite apology.* ▪ **contrition** *noun.* [14c: from Latin *contritus* crushed]

contrivance *noun* **1** the act or power of contriving. **2** a device or apparatus, esp an ingenious one. **3** a scheme; a piece of cunning.

contrive *verb* **1** to manage or succeed. **2** to bring about something: *contrive one's escape.* **3** to make or construct something, esp with difficulty. [14c: from French *controver* to find]

contrived *adj* forced or artificial.

control *noun* **1** authority or charge; power to influence or guide: *take control.* **2** a means of limitation. **3** (**controls**) a device for operating, regulating, or testing (a machine, system, etc). **4** the people in control of some operation: *mission control.* **5** the place where something is checked: *passport control.* **6** (*in full* **control experiment**) a scientific experiment in which the variable being tested in a second experiment is held at a constant value, in order to establish the validity of the results of the second experiment. ▸ *verb* (***controlled, controlling***) **1** to have or exercise power over someone or something. **2** to regulate. **3** to limit. **4** to operate, regulate or test (a machine, system, etc). ▪ **controllable** *adj.* [15c: from French *contrerolle* duplicate account or register]

control freak *noun, informal* someone who is obsessively reluctant to share power or responsibility with others.

controller *noun* **1** a person or thing that controls. **2** someone in charge of the finances of an enterprise, etc. Also called **comptroller**. **3** an official in charge of public finance.

control tower *noun* a tall building at an airport from which take-off and landing instructions are given to aircraft pilots by air-traffic controllers.

controversy *noun* (*-ies*) a usu long-standing dispute or argument, esp one where there is a strong difference of opinion. ▪ **controversial** *adj*. [14c: from Latin *contra* against + *vertere* to turn]

controvert *verb* **1** to oppose or contradict. **2** to argue against something. [17c: from Latin *controversus*]

contumacy /ˈkɒntjʊməsɪ/ *noun, formal* obstinate refusal to obey. ▪ **contumacious** /-ˈmeɪʃəs/ *adj*. [14c: from Latin *contumacia* stubbornness]

contumely /ˈkɒntjuːmlɪ/ *noun* (*-ies*) *formal* **1** scornful or insulting treatment or words. **2** a contemptuous insult. [14c: from Latin *contumelia* outrage or insult]

contusion *noun, technical* a bruise.

conundrum *noun* **1** a confusing problem. **2** a riddle, esp one involving a pun.

conurbation *noun* an extensive cluster of towns, the outskirts of which have merged resulting in the formation of one huge urban development. [20c: from Latin *con-* together + *urbs* city]

convalesce *verb, intr* to recover one's strength after an illness, operation or injury, esp by resting. ▪ **convalescence** *noun* **1** the gradual recovery of health and strength. **2** the period during which this takes place. ▪ **convalescent** *noun, adj*. [15c: from Latin *convalescere* to grow strong]

convection *noun* **1** the process by which heat is transferred through a liquid or gas as a result of movement of molecules of the fluid itself. **2** *geog* the movement of hot currents of molten rock in the earth's mantle, causing the plates on its crust to move. [17c: from Latin *convectio*]

convector *noun* an electrical device used to heat the surrounding air in rooms, etc, by convection. [20c: from Latin *con-* together + *vehere, vectum* to carry]

convene *verb, tr & intr* to assemble or summon to assemble. [15c: from Latin *convenire* to come together]

convener *or* **convenor** *noun* someone who convenes or chairs a meeting.

convenience *noun* **1** the quality of being convenient. **2** something useful or advantageous. **3** *Brit euphem* a lavatory, esp a public one.

IDIOMS **at one's convenience** when and where it suits one.

convenient *adj* **1** fitting in with one's plans, etc; not causing trouble or difficulty. **2** useful; handy; saving time and trouble. **3** available; at hand. ▪ **conveniently** *adv*. [14c: from Latin *conveniens*]

convent *noun* **1** **a** a community of nuns; **b** the building they occupy. **2** a school where the teaching is done by nuns. Also called **convent school**. [13c: from Latin *conventus* assembly]

conventicle *noun, hist* a secret, esp unlawful, religious meeting. [14c: from Latin *conventiculum* assembly]

convention *noun* **1** a large and formal conference or assembly. **2** a formal treaty or agreement. **3** a custom or generally accepted practice, esp in social behaviour. **4** *US politics* a meeting of delegates from one party to nominate a candidate for office. [15c: from Latin *conventio* meeting or agreement]

conventional *adj* **1** traditional; normal; customary. **2** conservative or unoriginal. **3** of weapons or warfare: non-nuclear. ▪ **conventionally** *adj*.

conventionality *noun* (*-ies*) **1** the state of being conventional. **2** something which is established by use or custom.

conventionalize *or* **-ise** *verb* to make conventional.

converge *verb, intr* **1** (*often* **converge on** *or* **upon sb** *or* **sth**) to move towards or meet at one point. **2** eg of opinions: to tend towards one another; to coincide. [17c: from Latin *convergere* to incline together]

convergent *adjective* **1** meeting, coming together. **2** *maths* of an infinite sequence, series, etc: having a limit. ▪ **convergence** *noun*.

conversant *adj* (*usu* **conversant with sth**) having a thorough knowledge of it. [16c: from Latin *conversari* to associate with]

conversation *noun* informal talk between people; communication. [16c: from Latin *conversatio*]

conversational *adj* **1** relating to conversation. **2** used in conversation rather than formal language. **3** communicative; talkative. ▪ **conversationalist** *noun*.

conversation piece *noun* a striking object that stimulates conversation.

converse[1] /kənˈvɜːs/ *verb, intr* (*often* **converse with sb**) *formal* **1** to hold a conversation; to talk. **2** to commune spiritually. [17c: from Latin *conversari* to associate with]

converse[2] /ˈkɒnvɜːs/ *adj* reverse; opposite. ▸ *noun* opposite. ▪ **conversely** *adv*. [16c: from Latin *conversus* turned about]

conversion *noun* **1** the act of converting. **2** something converted to another use. **3** *rugby, Amer football* the scoring of further points after a **try** or **touchdown** by kicking the ball over the goal.

convert *verb* /kənˈvɜːt/ **1** *tr & intr* to change the form or function of one thing into another. **2** *tr & intr* to win over, or be won over, to another religion, opinion, etc. **3** to change into another measuring system or currency. **4** *rugby, American football* to achieve a conversion after (a try or touchdown). ▸ *noun* /ˈkɒnvɜːt/ someone who has been converted to a new religion, practice, etc. [13c: from Latin *convertere* to transform]

converter *or* **convertor** *noun* **1** a person or thing that converts. **2** an electrical device for converting alternating current into direct current, or more rarely, direct current into alternating current. **3** a device for converting a signal from one frequency to another. **4** *comput* a device that converts coded information from one form to another.

convertible *adj* **1** capable of being converted. **2** of a currency: capable of being freely converted into other currencies. ▸ *noun* a car with a fold-down top.

convex *adj* of a surface or shape: outward-curving, like the surface of the eye. Compare **concave**. ▪ **convexity** *noun*. [16c: from Latin *convexus* arched]

convey *verb* **1** to carry; to transport. **2** to communicate. **3** *law* to transfer the ownership of (property). **4** of a channel, etc: to lead or transmit. ▪ **conveyable** *adj*. ▪ **conveyor** *noun*. [14c: from French *conveier*]

conveyance *noun* **1** the process of conveying. **2** a vehicle of any kind. **3** *law* **a** the transfer of the ownership of property; **b** the document setting out such a transfer. ▪ **conveyancer** *noun*.

conveyor belt *noun* an endless moving rubber or metal belt for the continuous transporting of articles, eg in a factory.

convict *verb* /kən'vɪkt/ to prove or declare someone guilty (of a crime). ▸ *noun* /'kɒnvɪkt/ **1** someone serving a prison sentence. **2** someone found guilty of a crime. [14c: from Latin *convincere* to conquer]

conviction *noun* **1** the act of convicting; an instance of being convicted. **2** the state of being convinced; a strong belief.

convince *verb* to persuade someone of something; to make them believe it. ▪ **convinced** *adj*. ▪ **convincing** *adj*. ▪ **convincingly** *adv*. [17c: from Latin *convincere* to overcome wholly]

convivial *adj* **1** lively, jovial, sociable and cheerful. **2** festive. ▪ **conviviality** *noun*. [17c: from Latin *convivialis*]

convocation *noun* **1** the act of summoning together. **2** an assembly. **3** a formal assembly of graduates of a college or university. [14c: from Latin *convocatio* summoning together]

convoke *verb* to call together; to assemble. [16c: from Latin *convocare* to call together]

convoluted *adj* **1** coiled and twisted. **2** complicated; difficult to understand. [19c: from Latin *convolvere* to roll together]

convolution *noun* **1** a twist or coil. **2** *anatomy* any of the sinuous folds of the brain. **3** a complication.

convolvulus /kɒn'vɒlvjʊləs/ *noun* (***convolvuluses*** or ***convolvuli*** /-laɪ/) a trailing or twining plant native to temperate regions, with funnel-shaped flowers. [16c: Latin, from *convolvere* to roll up]

convoy *noun* a group of vehicles or merchant ships travelling together, or under escort. [14c: from French *convoier*]

convulse *verb, tr & intr* to jerk or distort violently by or as if by a powerful spasm. ▪ **convulsive** *adj*. [17c: from Latin *convellere* to pull violently]

convulsion *noun* **1** (*often* **convulsions**) a violent involuntary contraction of the muscles of the body, or a series of such contractions, resulting in contortion of the limbs and face. **2** (**convulsions**) *informal* spasms of uncontrollable laughter. [17c: from Latin *convulsio*]

cony *or* **coney** *noun* (***conies*** *or* ***coneys***) **1** *dialect* a rabbit. **2** rabbit fur. [13c: from French *conil*]

coo[1] *noun* the soft murmuring call of a dove. ▸ *verb* (***cooed***) **1** *intr* to make this sound. **2** *tr & intr* to murmur affectionately. See also **bill and coo** at **bill**[2]. [17c: imitating the sound]

coo[2] *exclam, Brit informal* used to express amazement.

cooee *exclam* a usu high-pitched call used to attract attention. [19c: from a signal orig used by Australian Aborigines and later adopted by colonists]

cook *verb* **1** *tr & intr* to prepare (food) or be prepared by heating. **2** *informal* to alter (accounts, etc) dishonestly. ▸ *noun* someone who cooks or prepares food. [Anglo-Saxon *coc*]

IDIOMS **cook the books** to falsify accounts, records, etc.

PHRASAL VERBS **cook sth up** *informal* to concoct or invent it.

cook-chill *adj* denoting foods, esp individual meals, that are cooked, rapidly chilled, then packaged and stored in a refrigerated state, requiring reheating before being served.

cooker *noun* **1** an apparatus for cooking food; a stove. **2** *Brit informal* a **cooking apple**.

cookery *noun* (*pl* in sense 2 only ***-ies***) **1** the art or practice of cooking food. **2** *US* a place equipped for cooking.

cookie *noun* **1** *chiefly N Am* a biscuit. **2** *informal* a person: *a smart cookie*. **3** *comput* a small piece of basic information on a user, sent to a web browser when a certain web page is accessed by them. [18c: from Dutch *koekje*]

IDIOMS **that's the way the cookie crumbles** *N Am informal* that's the way it goes.

cooking apple *or* **cooker** *noun* an apple sour in taste, which is used for cooking rather than eating raw.

cool *adj* **1** between cold and warm; fairly cold. **2** pleasantly fresh; free of heat: *a cool breeze*. **3** calm; laid-back: *He was very cool under pressure*. **4** lacking enthusiasm; unfriendly: *a cool response*. **5** of a large sum: exact; at least: *made a cool million*. **6** *informal* admirable; excellent. **7** of colours: suggestive of coolness, typically pale and containing blue. **8** sophisticated. ▸ *noun* **1** a cool part or period; coolness: *the cool of the evening*. **2** *informal* self-control; composure: *keep your cool*. ▸ *verb, tr & intr* (*often* **cool down** *or* **off**) **1** to become cool. **2** to become less interested or enthusiastic. ▪ **coolly** *adv*. ▪ **coolness** *noun*. [Anglo-Saxon *col*]

coolant *noun* a liquid or gas used as a cooling agent, esp to absorb and remove heat from its source in a system such as a car radiator, nuclear reactor, etc.

cool box *or* **cool bag** *noun* an insulated container, used to keep food cool.

cooler *noun* **1** a container or device for cooling things. **2** *slang* prison.

cooling tower *noun* a tall, hollow structure in which water heated during industrial processes is cooled for re-use.

coomb, **coombe**, **comb** *or* **combe** /kuːm/ *noun* **1** in S England: a short deep valley. **2** a deep hollow in a hillside. [Anglo-Saxon *cumb* valley]

coop *noun* **1** a cage for hens. **2** any confined or restricted space. ▸ *verb* (*usu* **coop sb** *or* **sth up**) to confine in a small space. [15c: prob related to Anglo-Saxon *cypa* basket]

co-op *noun, informal* a co-operative society or a shop run by one.

cooper *noun* someone who makes or repairs barrels. [14c: from Latin *cuparius*]

co-operate *verb, intr* **1** (*often* **co-operate with sb**) to work together with them. **2** to be helpful, or willing to fit in with the plans of others. ▪ **co-operation** *noun*. [17c: from Latin *cooperari* to work together]

co-operative *adj* **1** relating to or giving co-operation. **2** helpful; willing to fit in with others' plans, etc. **3** of a business or farm: jointly owned by workers, with profits shared equally. ▸ *noun* a co-operative business or farm.

co-operative society *noun* a profit-sharing association for the cheaper purchase of goods.

co-opt *verb* of the members of a body, etc: to elect an additional member, by the votes of the existing ones. [17c: from Latin *cooptare* to choose together]

co-ordinate *verb* **1** to integrate and adjust (a number of different parts or processes) so as to relate smoothly one to another. **2** to bring (one's limbs or bodily movements) into a smoothly functioning relationship. ▸ *adj* relating to or involving co-ordination or co-ordinates. ▸ *noun* (*also* **coordinate**) **1** *maths, geog* either of a pair of numbers taken from a vertical and horizontal axis which together establish the position of a fixed point on a map. **2** *geom* any of a set of numbers, esp either of a pair, that are used to define the position of a point, line or surface by reference to a system of axes that are usu drawn through a fixed point at right angles to each other. ▪ **co-ordination** *noun*. ▪ **co-ordinator** *noun*.

co-ordinate geometry *noun maths* a system of geometry in which points, lines and surfaces are located by co-ordinates. Also called **analytical geometry**.

coot *noun* **1** an aquatic bird with dark plumage, a characteristic white shield above the bill and large feet with lobed toes. **2** *dated, informal* a fool.

cop *noun, slang* **1** a policeman. **2** an arrest: *a fair cop.* ▸ *verb* (***copped, copping***) **1** to catch. **2** to grab; to seize. **3** to suffer (a punishment, etc). [18c: from French *caper* to seize]

IDIOMS **cop it** *slang* to be punished.

PHRASAL VERBS **cop out** *informal* to avoid a responsibility; to escape. See also **cop-out**.

cope[1] *verb, intr* to manage; to deal with (a problem, etc) successfully: *She coped well with the difficulties.* [14c: from French *couper* to hit]

cope[2] *noun* a long sleeveless cape worn by clergy on ceremonial occasions. [13c: from Latin *capa*]

cope[3] *verb, building* to cut (a piece of moulding) so that it fits over another piece. [17c: from French *couper* to cut]

Copernican system *noun, astron* a model of the Solar System in which the Sun is at the centre, with the Earth and other planets moving around it, in perfectly circular orbits.

copier see under **copy**

co-pilot *noun* the assistant pilot of an aircraft.

coping *noun* a capping along the top row of stones in a wall, designed to protect it from the weather.

coping saw *noun* a small saw used for cutting curves in relatively thick wood or metal. Compare **fretsaw**.

coping-stone *noun* one of the stones forming the top row in a wall, etc.

copious *adj* plentiful. ▪ **copiously** *adv*. [14c: from Latin *copiosus*]

cop-out *noun, informal* an avoidance of a responsibility; an escape or withdrawal. See also **cop out** at **cop**.

copper[1] *noun* **1** *chem* (symbol **Cu**) a soft reddish-brown metallic element, which is an excellent conductor of heat and electricity. **2** (*usu* **coppers**) any coin of low value made of copper or bronze. **3** a large metal vessel for boiling water in. **4** a reddish-brown colour. ▸ *adj* **1** made from copper. **2** copper-coloured. [Anglo-Saxon *coper*]

copper[2] *noun, slang, chiefly Brit* a policeman. Often shortened to **cop**. [19c: from **cop**]

copper-bottomed *adj* **1** eg of ships or pans: having the bottom protected by a layer of copper. **2** *informal* reliable, esp financially.

copperplate *noun* **1** *printing* **a** a copper plate used for engraving or etching; **b** a print made from it. **2** fine regular handwriting of the style formerly used on copperplates.

copper sulphate *noun, chem* a white compound which is used in electroplating and as an antiseptic, pesticide and wood preservative.

coppice *noun, botany* an area of woodland in which trees are regularly cut back to ground level to encourage the growth of side shoots. [14c: from French *copeiz*]

copra *noun* the dried kernel of the coconut, rich in coconut oil. [16c: Portuguese]

copse *noun* a **coppice**.

Copt *noun* **1** a member of the Coptic Church. **2** an Egyptian descended from the ancient Egyptians.

Coptic *noun* the language of the Copts, now used only in the Coptic Church. ▸ *adj* relating to the Copts or their language. [17c: from Greek *Aigyptios* Egyptian]

copula /ˈkɒpjʊlə/ *noun* (***copulas*** *or* ***copulae*** /-liː/) *grammar* a verb that links the subject and **complement** of a sentence, eg *is* in *She is a doctor* or *grew* in *It grew dark*. [17c: Latin, meaning 'bond']

copulate *verb, intr* to have sexual intercourse. ▪ **copulation** *noun*. [17c: from Latin *copulare* to couple]

copy *noun* (***-ies***) **1** an imitation or reproduction. **2** one of the many specimens of a book or of a particular issue of a magazine, newspaper, etc. **3** written material for printing, esp as distinct from illustrations, etc. **4** the wording of an advertisement. **5** *informal* material suitable for a newspaper article. ▸ *verb* (***-ies, -ied***) **1** to imitate. **2** to make a copy of something; to transcribe. ▪ **copier** *noun* a person or machine which makes copies. [14c: from Latin *copia* abundance]

copybook *noun* a book of handwriting examples for copying. ▸ *adj* **1** *derog* unoriginal. **2** faultless; perfect.

IDIOMS **blot one's copybook** to spoil one's good record by misbehaviour or error.

copycat *noun, informal derisive* an imitator or person who copies the work of another.

copyist *noun* **1** someone who copies (documents, etc) in writing, esp as an occupation. **2** an imitator.

copyright *noun* the sole right, granted by law, to print, publish, translate, perform, film or record an original literary, dramatic, musical or artistic work. ▸ *adj* protected by copyright. ▸ *verb* to secure the copyright of something.

copywriter *noun* someone who writes advertising copy.

coquette *noun* a flirtatious woman. ▪ **coquettish** *adj*. [17c: French, diminutive of *coq* cock]

cor *exclam, informal* expressing surprise or pleasure.

cor- see **con-**

coracle *noun* a small oval rowing-boat made of wickerwork covered with hides or other waterproof material. [16c: from Welsh *corwgl*]

coral *noun* **1** a tiny invertebrate marine animal, consisting of a hollow tube with a mouth surrounded by tentacles at the top, which is found mainly in tropical seas. **2** a hard chalky substance of various colours, formed from the skeletons of this animal. **3** a pinkish-orange colour. ▸ *adj* pinkish-orange in colour. [14c: from Latin *coralium*]

coralline /ˈkɒrəlaɪn/ *adj* consisting of, containing, or like coral.

coral reef *noun* a rock-like mass of coral built up gradually from the seabed.

cor anglais /kɔːr ˈɑŋgleɪ, ˈɒŋgleɪ/ *noun* (***cors anglais*** /kɔːz/) *music* a woodwind instrument similar to, but lower in pitch than, the oboe. [19c: French, meaning 'English horn']

corbel *noun, archit* a projecting piece of stone or timber, coming out from a wall and taking the weight of eg a parapet, arch or bracket. [15c: French]

corbie *noun, Scot* a crow or raven. [15c: from French *corbin*]

cord *noun* **1** a thin rope or string consisting of several separate strands twisted together. **2** *anatomy* any long flexible structure resembling this: *umbilical cord*. **3** *N Am* the cable of an electrical appliance. **4** a ribbed fabric, esp corduroy. **5** (**cords**) corduroy trousers. **6** a unit for measuring the volume of cut wood, equal to 128 cubic ft (3.63 m^3). ▸ *verb* to bind with a cord. [13c: from Latin *chorda*]

cordate *adj* heart-shaped. [17c: from Latin *cordatus*]

corded *adj* **1** fastened with cords. **2** of fabric: ribbed.

cordial *adj* **1** warm and affectionate. **2** heartfelt; profound. ▸ *noun* a concentrated fruit-flavoured drink, which is usu diluted before being drunk. ▪ **cordially** *adv*. [14c: from Latin *cordialis*]

cordite *noun* any of various smokeless explosive materials used as a propellant for guns, etc.

cordless *adj* of an electrical appliance: operating without a flex connecting it to the mains, powered instead by an internal battery: *cordless phone*.

cordon *noun* **1** a line of police or soldiers, or a system of road blocks, encircling an area so as to prevent or control passage into or out of it. **2** a ribbon bestowed as a mark of honour. **3** *horticulture* a fruit tree trained to grow as a single stem. ▸ *verb* (*often* **cordon sth off**) to close off (an area) with a cordon. [15c: from French *cordon*]

cordon bleu *adj* of a cook or cookery: being of the highest standard. [19c: French, meaning 'blue ribbon']

corduroy *noun* **1** a thick ribbed cotton fabric. **2** (**corduroys**) trousers made of corduroy. See also **cord** (sense 5). **3** *N Am* a road made of logs lying side by side. Also called **corduroy road**. ▸ *adj* made from corduroy.

core *noun* **1** the fibrous case at the centre of some fruits, eg apples and pears, containing the seeds. **2** the innermost, central, essential or unchanging part. **3** the central region of a star or planet, esp the Earth. **4** the central part of a nuclear reactor, containing the fuel, where the nuclear reaction takes place. **5** *elec* a piece of magnetic material that, when placed in the centre of a wire coil through which an electric current is being passed, increases the intensity of the magnetic field and the inductance of the coil. **6** the main memory of a computer, where instructions and data are stored in such a way that they are available for immediate use. Also called **core memory**. **7** a cylindrical sample of rock, soil, etc, removed with a hollow tubular drill. ▸ *verb* to remove the core of (an apple, etc).

co-respondent *noun, law* in divorce cases: someone alleged to have committed adultery with the **respondent** (*noun* sense 2).

corgi *noun* a sturdy short-legged breed of dog with a thick coat and fox-like head. [20c: from Welsh *cor* dwarf + *ci* dog]

coriander *noun* **1** a plant with narrowly lobed leaves and globular aromatic fruits. **2** the leaves and dried ripe fruit of this plant, widely used as a flavouring in cooking. [14c: from Latin *coriandrum*]

Corinthian *adj* **1** relating to ancient Corinth in Greece. **2** *archit* denoting an **order** (*noun* sense 19) of classical architecture characterized by a style of column with a fluted shaft and a heavily carved capital having a distinctive acanthus-leaf design. Compare **Doric**, **Ionic**, **Tuscan**.

corium see **dermis**

cork *noun* **1** *botany* a layer of tissue that forms below the epidermis in the stems and roots of woody plants, eg trees, which is often cultivated for commercial use. **2** a piece of this used as a stopper for a bottle, etc. ▸ *verb* (*often* **cork up** *or* **cork sth up**) to stop up (a bottle, etc) with a cork. [14c: from Arabic *qurq*]

corkage *noun* the fee charged by a restaurant for serving customers wine, etc that they have bought off the premises.

corked *adj* of wine: spoiled as a result of having a faulty cork.

corkscrew *noun* a tool with a spiral spike for screwing into bottle corks to remove them. ▸ *verb, tr & intr* to move spirally. [18c]

corm *noun, botany* in certain plants, eg crocus: a swollen underground stem. [19c: from Greek *kormos* lopped tree trunk]

cormorant *noun* a seabird with dark brown or black plumage, webbed feet, a long neck and a slender bill. [14c: from French]

corn[1] *noun* **1** in the UK: the most important cereal crop of a particular region, esp wheat in England, and oats in Scotland and Ireland. **2** in N America, Australia and New Zealand: **maize**. **3** the harvested seed of cereal plants; grain. **4** *slang* a song, film, etc, that is trite and sentimental. [Anglo-Saxon]

corn[2] *noun* a small painful area of hard thickened skin, usu on or between the toes, which is caused by pressure or friction. [15c: French]

Corn. *abbrev, English county* Cornwall.

corn circle see **crop circle**

corncob *noun* the woody core of an ear of maize, to which the rows of kernels are attached.

corncrake *noun* a bird of the rail family with a rasping cry.

corn dolly *noun* a decorative figure made of plaited straw.

cornea /ˈkɔːnɪə/ *noun* (***corneas*** *or* ***corneae*** /-iː/) in vertebrates: the convex transparent membrane that covers the front of the eyeball. ▪ **corneal** *adj*. [14c: Latin, short for *cornea tela* horny tissue]

corned beef *noun* beef that has been cooked, salted and then canned.

cornelian /kɔːˈniːlɪən/ *or* **carnelian** /kɑː-/ *noun, geol* a red and white form of agate, used as a semi-precious stone. [15c: from French *corneline*]

corner *noun* **1** **a** a point or place where lines or surface-edges meet; **b** the inside or outside of the angle so formed. **2** an intersection between roads. **3** a quiet or remote place. **4** an awkward situation: *in a tight corner.* **5** *boxing* either of the angles of the ring used as a base between bouts by contestants. **6** in some sports, esp football: a free kick from a corner of the field. ▸ *verb* **1** to force into a place or position from which escape is difficult. **2** to gain control of (a market) by obtaining a monopoly of a certain commodity or service. **3** *intr* of a driver or vehicle: to turn a corner. [13c: from French]

IDIOMS **cut corners** to spend less money, effort, etc on something than one should, esp to save time.

cornerstone *noun* **1** a stone built into the corner of the foundation of a building. **2** a crucial or indispensable part; a basis.

cornet *noun* **1** a brass musical instrument similar to the trumpet. **2** an edible cone-shaped holder for ice cream. ▪ **cornetist** *or* **cornettist** *noun* someone who plays the cornet. [14c: French]

cornflakes *plural noun* toasted maize flakes, usu eaten as a breakfast cereal.

cornflour *noun, cookery* a finely ground flour, usu made from maize, which is used for thickening sauces, etc. *N Am equivalent* **cornstarch**.

cornflower *noun* a plant with narrow hairy leaves and deep blue flowers.

cornice *noun* **1** a decorative border of moulded plaster round a ceiling. **2** *archit* the projecting section of an **entablature**. [16c: Italian, meaning 'crow']

Cornish *adj* belonging to Cornwall, a county in SW England, its people or language. ▸ *noun* the Celtic language once spoken in Cornwall, related to Welsh.

Cornish pasty *noun* a semicircular folded pastry case containing meat, vegetables, etc.

corn on the cob *noun* a **corncob** cooked and served as a vegetable.

cornstarch see under **cornflour**

cornucopia *noun* **1** *art* in painting, sculpture, etc: a horn full to overflowing with fruit and other produce, used as a symbol of abundance. Also called **horn of plenty**. **2** an abundant supply. [16c: from Latin *cornu* horn + *copiae* abundance]

corny *adj* (**-ier, -iest**) *informal* **1** of a joke: old and stale. **2** embarrassingly old-fashioned or sentimental. [20c: from **corn**[1]]

corolla *noun, botany* the collective name for the petals of a flower. Also called **whorl**. [18c: Latin, diminutive of *corona* garland or crown]

corollary /kəˈrɒlərɪ/ *noun* (**-ies**) **1** something that directly follows from another thing that has been proved. **2** a natural or obvious consequence. [14c: from Latin *corollarium* gift of money, orig for a garland]

corona /kəˈroʊnə/ *noun* (**coronae** /-iː/ *or* **coronas**) **1** *astron* the outer atmosphere of the Sun, consisting of a halo of hot luminous gases that boil from its surface, visible during a total solar eclipse. **2** *astron* a circle of light which appears around the Sun or the Moon. **3** *botany* in certain plants, eg the daffodil: a trumpet-like outgrowth from the petals. **4** *physics* the glowing region produced by ionization of the air surrounding a high-voltage conductor. [16c: Latin, meaning 'crown']

coronary /ˈkɒrənərɪ/ *adj, physiol* denoting vessels, nerves, etc which encircle a part or organ, esp the arteries which supply blood to the heart muscle. ▸ *noun* (**-ies**) *pathol* a **coronary thrombosis**. [17c: from Latin *coronarius* pertaining to a crown]

coronary artery *noun, med* either of the two arteries which supply the muscle of the heart wall with blood.

coronary thrombosis *noun, pathol* the formation of a blood clot in one of the two coronary arteries, which blocks the flow of blood to the heart and usu gives rise to a heart attack.

coronation *noun* the ceremony of crowning a monarch or **consort**[1] (*noun*). [14c: from French]

coroner *noun* a public official whose chief responsibility is the investigation of sudden, suspicious or accidental deaths. [14c: from French *corouner*]

coronet *noun* **1** a small crown. **2** a circlet of jewels for the head. [15c: from Old French *coronete*]

corp. *or* **Corp.** *abbrev* **1** corporal. **2** corporation.

corporal[1] *noun* a non-commissioned officer in the army or air force. [16c: French]

corporal[2] *adj* relating or belonging to the body. [14c: French]

corporal punishment *noun* physical punishment such as beating or caning.

corporate *adj* **1** shared by members of a group; joint: *corporate membership.* **2** belonging or relating to a corporation: *corporate finance.* **3** formed into a corporation: *a corporate body.* [16c: from Latin *corporare* to form into one body]

corporation *noun* **1** a body of people acting jointly, eg for administration or business purposes. **2** the council of a town or city. [16c: from Latin *corporatio*]

corporatism *or* **corporativism** *noun, politics* the control of a country's economy by groups of producers who have the authority to implement social and economic policies.

corporeal *adj* **1** relating to the body as distinct from the soul; physical. **2** relating to things of a material nature. [17c: from Latin *corporeus*]

corps /kɔː(r)/ *noun* (*pl* **corps**) **1** a military body or division forming a tactical unit: *the intelligence corps.* **2** a body of people engaged in particular work: *the diplomatic corps.* [18c: French]

corps de ballet /*French* kɔʀ də balɛ/ *noun* a company of ballet dancers, eg at a theatre. [19c: French]

corpse /kɔːps/ *noun* the dead body of a human being. [14c: from Latin *corpus* body]

corpulent *adj* fat; fleshy; obese. ▪ **corpulence** *or* **corpulency** *noun*. [15c: French]

corpus *noun* (**corpora** /ˈkɔːpərə/) **1** a body of writings, eg by a particular author, on a particular topic, etc. **2** a body of written and/or spoken material for language research. [18c: Latin, meaning 'body']

corpuscle /ˈkɔːpʌsəl/ *noun, anatomy* any small particle or cell within a tissue or organ, esp a red or white blood cell. ▪ **corpuscular** *adj*. [17c: from Latin *corpusculum*]

corral /kəˈrɑːl/ *chiefly N Am, noun* **1** an enclosure for driving horses or cattle into. **2** a defensive ring of wagons. ▸ *verb* (**corralled, corralling**) to herd or pen into a corral. [16c: Spanish, meaning 'courtyard']

corrasion see under **abrasion**

correct *verb* **1** to set or put right; to remove errors from something. **2** to mark the errors in. **3** to adjust or make better. **4** *old use* to rebuke or punish. ▸ *adj* **1** free from error; accurate. **2** appropriate; conforming to accepted standards: *very correct in his behaviour.* ▪ **correctly** *adv.* ▪ **correctness** *noun.* [14c: from Latin *corrigere* to make straight]

IDIOMS **stand corrected** to acknowledge one's mistake.

correction *noun* **1** the act of correcting. **2** an alteration that improves something. **3** *old use* punishment. ▪ **correctional** *adj.*

corrective *adj* having the effect of correcting or adjusting. ▸ *noun* something that has this effect.

correlate *verb* **1** *tr & intr* of two or more things: to have a connection or correspondence. **2** to combine, compare or show relationships between (information, reports, etc). ▸ *noun* either of two things which are related to each other. [17c: from Latin *cor-* with + *relatum* referred]

correlation *noun* **1** a connection or correspondence. **2** an act of correlating. **3** *stats* the strength of the relationship between two random variables, eg **positive correlation**, where if one variable has a high or low value so does the other, and **negative correlation**, where if one variable has a high value, the other has a low value.

correlative *adj* **1** mutually linked. **2** *grammar* of words: used as an interrelated pair, although not necessarily together, eg like *either* and *or.* ▸ *noun* a correlative word or thing.

correspond *verb, intr* **1** (*usu* **correspond to sth**) to be similar or equivalent. **2** (*usu* **correspond with** *or* **to sth** *or* **sb**) to be compatible or in agreement; to match. **3** (*usu* **correspond with sb**) to communicate, esp by letter. ▪ **corresponding** *adj.* ▪ **correspondingly** *adv.* [16c: from Latin *correspondere*]

correspondence *noun* **1** similarity; equivalence. **2** agreement. **3 a** a communication by letters; **b** the letters received or sent.

correspondence course *noun* a course of study conducted by post.

correspondent *noun* **1** someone with whom one exchanges letters. **2** someone employed by a newspaper, radio station, etc to send reports from a particular part of the world or on a particular topic: *political correspondent.*

corresponding angles *plural noun, geom* angles that are in similar positions and on the same side of a transversal.

corridor *noun* a passageway in a building or on a train. [17c: French]

corrie *noun* in the Scottish Highlands: **1** a semicircular hollow on a hillside. **2** a **cirque**. [18c: from Gaelic *coire* cauldron]

corrigendum /kɒrɪˈdʒɛndəm/ *noun* (***corrigenda*** /-də/) **1** an error for correction, eg in a book. **2** (**corrigenda**) errata (see **erratum**). [19c: Latin, meaning 'that which is to be corrected']

corroborate *verb* to confirm (eg someone's statement), esp by providing evidence. ▪ **corroboration** *noun.* ▪ **corroborative** *adj.* [16c: from Latin *corroborare* to strengthen]

corrode *verb* **1** *tr & intr* of a material or object: to eat or be eaten away, esp by rust or chemicals. **2** to destroy gradually. [14c: from Latin *corrodere* to gnaw away]

corrosion *noun* **1** the process of corroding, eg of a metal or alloy. **2** a corroded part or patch. **3** *geog* another word for **solution** (sense 5).

corrosive *adj* **1** capable of eating away. **2** of a substance: tending to cause corrosion. **3** of language: hurtful, sarcastic. ▸ *noun* a corrosive thing or substance.

corrugate *verb* to fold into parallel ridges, so as to make stronger. ▪ **corrugated** *adj.* ▪ **corrugation** *noun.* [17c: from Latin *corrugare* to wrinkle]

corrugated iron *noun* a sheet of iron which has been bent into a wavy shape in order to strengthen it.

corrupt *verb* **1** *tr & intr* to change for the worse, esp morally. **2** to spoil, deform or make impure. **3** to bribe. **4** of a text: to change it from the original, usu for the worse. **5** *comput* to introduce errors into (a program or data) so that it is no longer reliable. ▸ *adj* **1** morally evil. **2** involving bribery. **3** of a text: so full of errors and alterations as to be unreliable. **4** *comput* of a program or data: containing errors and therefore no longer reliable. ▪ **corruptive** *adj.* ▪ **corruptly** *adv.* [13c: from Latin *corrumpere* to spoil]

corruptible *adj* capable of being or liable to be corrupted.

corruption *noun* **1** the process of corrupting or condition of being corrupt. **2** a deformed or altered form of a word or phrase: *'Santa Claus' is a corruption of 'Saint Nicholas'.* **3** dishonesty. **4** impurity.

corsage /kɔːˈsɑːʒ/ *noun* a small spray of flowers for pinning to the bodice of a dress. [19c: French, from *cors* body]

corsair /ˈkɔːsɛə(r)/ *noun, old use* **1** a pirate or pirate ship. **2** a privately owned warship. [16c: from French *corsaire*]

corselet *noun* **1** *hist* a protective garment or piece of armour for the upper part of the body. **2** (*usu* **corselette**) a woman's undergarment combining girdle and bra. [15c: French, from *cors* body or bodice]

corset *noun* **1** a tightly fitting women's undergarment used for shaping or controlling the figure. **2** a similar garment worn to support an injured back. ▪ **corsetry** *noun.* [13c: French, diminutive of *cors* body or bodice]

cortège /kɔːˈtɛʒ/ *noun* a procession, esp at a funeral. [17c: French]

cortex /ˈkɔːtɛks/ *noun* (***cortices*** /-tɪsiːz/) *anatomy* the outer layer of an organ or tissue, when this differs in structure or function from the inner region. ▪ **cortical** *adj.* [17c: Latin, meaning 'tree bark']

cortisone /ˈkɔːtɪzoʊn/ *noun, biochem* a naturally occurring steroid hormone which, in synthetic form, is used to treat rheumatoid arthritis, certain eye and skin disorders, etc. [20c: from *corticosteron* a hormone]

corundum *noun, geol* a hard aluminium oxide mineral, used as an abrasive. Its coloured crystalline forms include the gemstones ruby and sapphire. [18c: from Tamil *kuruntam*]

coruscate *verb, intr* to sparkle; to give off flashes of light. ▪ **coruscating** *adj.* ▪ **coruscation** *noun.* [18c: from Latin *coruscare*]

corvette *noun* a small warship for escorting larger vessels. [17c: French]

corvine *adj* relating to or resembling a crow. [17c: from Latin *corvinus*]

cos[1] *or* **cos lettuce** *noun* a type of lettuce with crisp slim leaves. [17c: named after Cos, the Greek island where it originated]

cos[2] *abbrev* cosine.

'cos, cos, 'coz *or* **coz** *contraction, informal* because.

cosecant /koʊ'siːkənt/ *noun, trig* (abbrev **cosec**) for a given angle in a right-angled triangle: a **function** (*noun* sense 4) that is the ratio of the length of the **hypotenuse** to the length of the side opposite the angle under consideration; the reciprocal of the sine of an angle.

cosh *noun* a club, esp a rubber one filled with metal, used as a weapon. ▸ *verb, informal* to hit with a cosh or something heavy. [19c]

cosine /'koʊsaɪn/ *noun, trig* (abbrev **cos**) in a right-angled triangle: a **function** (*noun* sense 4), that is the ratio of the length of the side adjacent to the angle to the length of the **hypotenuse**.

cosmetic *noun* (*often* **cosmetics**) any application intended to improve the appearance of the body, esp the face. See also **make-up**. ▸ *adj* **1** used to beautify the face, body or hair. **2** improving superficially, for the sake of appearance only. ▪ **cosmetically** *adv.* [17c: from Greek *kosmetikos* relating to adornment]

cosmetic surgery *noun* surgery, eg a facelift, which is performed purely to improve the patient's appearance, rather than for any medical reason. Compare **plastic surgery**.

cosmic *adj* **1** relating to the Universe; universal. **2** coming from outer space: *cosmic rays*.

cosmogony *noun* (**-*ies***) the study of the origin and development of the Universe. [18c: from Greek *kosmogonia*]

cosmology *noun* (**-*ies***) **1** the scientific study of the origin, nature, structure and evolution of the Universe. **2** a particular theory or model of the origin and structure of the Universe. ▪ **cosmological** *adj.* ▪ **cosmologist** *noun.* [17c: from Greek *kosmos* world + *logos* word or reason]

cosmonaut *noun* **a** *formerly* a Russian astronaut; **b** an astronaut from any of the countries of the former Soviet Union. [20c: from Greek *kosmos* world + *nautes* sailor]

cosmopolitan *adj* **1** belonging to or representative of all parts of the world. **2** free of national prejudices; international in experience and outlook. **3** composed of people from all different parts of the world. ▸ *noun* someone of this type; a citizen of the world. [17c: from Greek *kosmos* world + *polites* citizen]

cosmos *noun* the Universe seen as an ordered system. [17c: from Greek *kosmos* world or order]

cosset *verb* (***cosseted, cosseting***) to pamper. [16c]

cost *verb* (in senses 1 and 2 *past tense, past participle* ***cost***) **1** to be obtainable at a certain price. **2** *tr & intr* to involve the loss or sacrifice of someone or something. **3** (*past tense, past participle* ***costed***) to estimate or decide the cost of something. ▸ *noun* **1** what something costs. **2** loss or sacrifice: *The war was won but the cost of human life was great.* **3** (**costs**) *law* the expenses of a case, generally paid by the unsuccessful party. [13c: from Latin *constare* to stand firm or cost]

IDIOMS **at all costs** no matter what the risk or effort may be. **count the cost 1** to consider all the risks before taking action. **2** to realize the bad effects of something done.

cost accountant *noun, business* an accountant who analyses the costs for a product or operation, often with the aim of establishing a current standard or norm against which actual cost may be compared. ▪ **cost accounting** *noun.*

co-star *noun* a fellow star in a film, play, etc. ▸ *verb* **1** *intr* of an actor: to appear alongside another star. **2** of a production: to feature as fellow stars: *The play co-starred Gielgud and Olivier.*

cost-effective *adj* giving acceptable financial return in relation to initial outlay.

costermonger *noun, Brit* someone who sells fruit and vegetables from a barrow. Also called **coster**. [16c: from *costard* a type of apple + **-monger** (sense 1)]

costive *adj, old use* **1** constipated. **2** mean; stingy. [14c: from French *costivé*]

costly *adj* (**-*ier, -iest***) **1** involving much cost; expensive. **2** involving major losses or sacrifices. ▪ **costliness** *noun.*

cost of living *noun* the expense to the individual of the ordinary necessities such as food, clothing, etc.

cost price *noun* the price paid for something by the retailer, before resale to the public at a profit.

costume *noun* **1** a set of clothing of a special kind, esp of a particular historical period or country. **2** a garment or outfit for a special activity: *a swimming costume*. ▸ *verb* **1** to arrange or design the clothes for (a play, film, etc). **2** to dress in a costume. [18c: Italian, meaning 'custom' or 'habit']

costume jewellery *noun* inexpensive jewellery made from artificial materials.

costumier *noun* someone who makes or supplies costumes. [19c: French]

cosy *adj* (**-*ier, -iest***) **1** warm and comfortable. **2** friendly, intimate and confidential: *a cosy chat.* ▸ *noun* (**-*ies***) a cover to keep something warm, esp a teapot or boiled egg. ▪ **cosily** *adv.* ▪ **cosiness** *noun.*

cot[1] *noun* **1** a small bed with high, barred sides for a child. **2** a portable bed. [17c: from Hindi *khat* bedstead]

cot[2] *noun* **1** *poetic* a cottage. **2** *usu in compounds* a shortened form of **cote**: *dovecot*. [Anglo-Saxon]

cotangent *noun, trig* (abbrev **cot**) for a given angle in a right-angled triangle: a **function** (*noun* sense 4) that is the ratio of the length of the side adjacent to the angle under consideration, to the length of the side opposite it; the reciprocal of the tangent of an angle.

cot death see **sudden infant death syndrome**

cote *noun, usu in compounds* a small shelter for birds or animals: *dovecote*. [Anglo-Saxon]

coterie /'koʊtərɪ/ *noun* a small exclusive group of people who have the same interests. [18c: French]

cotoneaster /kətoʊnɪ'astə(r)/ *noun* a shrub or small tree with clusters of white or pink flowers, followed by red or orange berries. [18c: from Latin *cotonea* quince]

cottage *noun* a small house, esp one in a village or the countryside. ▪ **cottager** *noun.* [13c: from **cot**[2]]

cottage cheese *noun* a type of soft white cheese made from the curds of skimmed milk.

cottage industry *noun* a craft industry, such as knitting, employing workers in their own homes.

cottar *or* **cotter** *noun, Scot hist* a farm labourer occupying a cottage rent-free, in return for working on the farm. [16c: from **cot**[2]]

cotton *noun* **1** a shrubby plant cultivated for the creamy-white downy fibres which surround its seeds. **2** the soft white fibre obtained from this plant, used in the production of textiles. **3** the cloth or yarn that is woven from these fibres. ▸ *adj* made from cotton. ▸ *verb* (*often* **cotton on to sth**) *informal* to begin to understand it. ▪ **cottony** *adj*. [14c: from French *coton*]

cotton candy *noun, US* **candy floss**.

cotton wool *noun* soft fluffy wadding made from cotton fibre, which is used in the treatment of injuries, application of cosmetics, etc.

cotyledon /kɒtɪ'liːdən/ *noun, botany* in flowering plants: one of the leaves produced by the embryo. [17c: Latin]

couch[1] /kaʊtʃ/ *noun* **1** a sofa or settee. **2** a bed-like seat with a headrest, eg for patients to lie on when being examined or treated by a doctor or psychiatrist. ▸ *verb* to express in words of a certain kind. [14c: from French *coucher* to lay down]

couch[2] /kaʊtʃ, kuːtʃ/ *or* **couch grass** *noun* a grass with rough dull green or bluish-green leaves. Also called **quitch**. [Anglo-Saxon *cwice*]

couchette /kuː'ʃɛt/ *noun* **a** on a ship or train: a sleeping-berth, converted from ordinary seating; **b** a railway carriage with such berths. [20c: French, diminutive of *couche* bed]

couch potato *noun, informal* someone who spends their leisure time watching television.

cougar /'kuːgə(r)/ *noun, N Am* a **puma**. [18c: from French *couguar*]

cough *verb* **1** *intr* to expel air, mucus, etc from the throat or lungs with a rough sharp noise. **2** *intr* of an engine, etc: to make a similar noise. **3** to express with a cough. ▸ *noun* **1** an act or sound of coughing. **2** a condition of lungs or throat causing coughing.

PHRASAL VERBS **cough up** *slang* to provide (money, information, etc), esp reluctantly. **cough sth up** to bring up mucus, phlegm, blood, etc by coughing.

could *verb* **1** *past tense of* **can**: *I found I could lift it*. **2** used to express a possibility: *You could be right*. **3** used to express a possible course of action: *You could try telephoning her*. **4** used in making requests: *Could you help me?* **5** to feel like doing something or able to do something: *I could have strangled him*.

couldn't *contraction* could not.

coulis /kuːliː/ *noun* (*pl* ***coulis*** /-liːz/) a pureé of fruit, vegetables, etc often served as a sauce.

coulomb /'kuːlɒm/ *noun* (symbol **C**) the SI unit of electric charge.

council *noun* **1 a** a body of people whose function is to advise, administer, organize, discuss or legislate; **b** the people making up such a body. **2** the elected body of people that directs the affairs of a town, borough, district, region, etc. [12c: from French *concile*]

council house *noun* a house built, owned and rented out by a local council.

councillor *noun* an elected member of a council, esp of a town, etc.

council tax *noun* in the UK: a local-government tax based on property values.

counsel *noun* **1** advice. **2** consultation, discussion or deliberation. **3** a lawyer or group of lawyers that gives legal advice and fights cases in court. ▸ *verb* (***counselled, counselling***) to advise. [13c: from French *conseil*]

counsellor *or* (*N Am*) **counselor** *noun* **1** an adviser. **2** *N Am* a lawyer.

count[1] *verb* **1** *intr* to recite numbers in ascending order. **2** to find the total amount of (items), by adding up item by item. **3** to include: *Did you remember to count Iain?* **4** *intr* to be important: *Good contacts count in the music business*. **5** to consider: *He counted himself lucky that he still had a job*. ▸ *noun* **1** an act of counting. **2** the number counted. **3** a charge brought against an accused person. ▪ **countable** *adj*. [14c: from French *cunter*]

IDIOMS **keep** *or* **lose count** to keep, or fail to keep, a note of the running total. **out for the count 1** *boxing* of a floored boxer: unable to rise to his feet within a count of ten. **2** unconscious. **3** *facetious* fast asleep.

PHRASAL VERBS **count against sb** to be a disadvantage to them. **count on sb** *or* **sth** to rely on them or it. **count sb out 1** *boxing* to declare (a floored boxer) to have lost the match if they are unable to get up within ten seconds. **2** to exclude them from consideration.

count[2] *noun* a European nobleman, equal in rank to a British earl. [16c: from French *conte*]

countdown *noun* a count backwards from a certain number, with zero as the moment for action, used eg in launching a rocket.

countenance *noun* face; expression or appearance. ▸ *verb* **1** to favour or support. **2** to allow; to tolerate. [13c: from French *contenance*]

counter[1] *noun* **1** a long flat-topped fitting in a shop, cafeteria, bank, etc over which goods are sold, food is served or business is transacted. **2** in various board games: a small flat disc used as a playing-piece. **3** a disc-shaped token used as a substitute coin. [14c: from Latin *computare* to reckon]

IDIOMS **under the counter** by secret illegal sale, or by unlawful means.

counter[2] *verb, tr & intr* to oppose, act against or hit back. ▸ *adv* (*often* **counter to sth**) in the opposite direction to it; in contradiction of it. ▸ *adj* contrary; opposing. ▸ *noun* **1** a return blow; an opposing move. **2** an opposite or contrary. **3** something that can be used to one's advantage in negotiating or bargaining. **4** *naut* the curved, overhanging part of a ship's stern. [14c: from French *contre*]

IDIOMS **run counter to sth** to act in a way contrary to it.

counter- *prefix, denoting* **1** opposite; against: *counter-attack*. **2** matching or corresponding: *counterpart*. [From French *contre*]

counteract *verb* to reduce or prevent the effect of something. ▪ **counteraction** *noun*. ▪ **counteractive** *adj*.

counter-attack *noun* an attack in reply to an attack. ▸ *verb, tr & intr* to attack in return.

counterbalance *noun* a weight, force or circumstance that balances another or cancels it out. ▸ *verb* to act as a counterbalance to; to neutralize or cancel out.

counterblast *noun* a vigorous and indignant verbal or written response.

counter-clockwise *adj, adv, esp N Am* anticlockwise.

counter-espionage *noun* activities undertaken to frustrate spying by an enemy or rival. Also called **counter-intelligence**.

counterfeit /'kaʊntəfɪt/ *adj* **1** made in imitation of a genuine article, esp with the purpose of deceiving; forged. **2** not genuine; insincere. ▸ *noun* an imitation, esp one designed to deceive; a forgery. ▸ *verb*

1 to copy for a dishonest purpose; to forge. **2** to pretend. [13c: from French *contrefait*]

counterfoil *noun* the section of a cheque, ticket, etc retained as a record by the person who issues it.

counter-intelligence *noun* another name for **counter-espionage**.

countermand *verb* to cancel or revoke (an order or command). ▸ *noun* a command which cancels a previous one. [15c: from French *contremander*]

counter-measure *noun* an action taken to counteract a threat, dangerous development or move.

counterpane *noun, dated* a bedspread. [17c: from French *coitepoint* quilt]

counterpart *noun* **1** one of two parts which form a corresponding pair. **2** a person or thing which is not exactly the same as another, but which is equivalent to it in a different place or context.

counterpoint *noun, music* **1** the combining of two or more melodies sung or played simultaneously into a harmonious whole. **2** a part or melody combined with another. ▸ *verb* to set in contrast to. See also **contrapuntal**. [16c: from French *contrepoint*]

counterpoise *noun* **1** a weight which balances another weight. **2** a state of equilibrium. ▸ *verb* to balance with something of equal weight. [14c: from French *contrepois*]

counter-productive *adj* tending to undermine productiveness and efficiency; having the opposite effect to that intended.

Counter-Reformation *noun, hist* a reform movement within the Roman Catholic Church, following and counteracting the **Reformation**.

counter-revolution *noun* a revolution to overthrow a system of government established by a previous revolution. ▪ **counter-revolutionary** *adj, noun.*

countersign *verb* to sign (a document, etc already signed by someone else) by way of confirmation. ▸ *noun* a password or signal used in response to a sentry's challenge; a sign or signal given in response to another sign or signal. [16c: from French *contresigne*]

countersink *verb* **1** to widen the upper part of (a screw hole) so that the top of the screw, when inserted, will be level with the surrounding surface. **2** to insert (a screw) into such a hole.

counter-tenor *noun, music* an adult male voice, higher than the **tenor**.

counterweight *noun* a counterbalancing weight.

countess *noun* **1** the wife or widow of an earl or count. **2** a woman with the rank of earl or count. [12c: from French *contesse*]

countless *adj* numerous; so many as to be impossible to count.

count noun *noun, grammar* a noun which can be qualified in the singular by the indefinite article and can also be used in the plural, eg *car* (as in *a car* or *cars*) but not *furniture*. Compare **mass noun**.

countrified *adj* rural; rustic in appearance or style.

country *noun* (***-ies***) **1** an area of land distinguished from other areas by its culture, inhabitants, political boundary, etc. **2** the population of such an area of land. **3** a nation or state. **4** one's native land. **5** (*often* **the country**) open land, away from the towns and cities, usu characterized by moors, woods, hills, fields, etc. [13c: from French *contrée*]

IDIOMS **across country** not keeping to roads. **go to the country** *Brit* of a government in power: to dissolve parliament and hold a general election.

country and western *noun* a style of popular music, based on the white folk music of the Southern USA, characterized by its use of instruments like banjos, fiddles and pedal steel guitar.

country bumpkin see **bumpkin**

country club *noun* a club in a rural area with facilities for sport and recreation.

country dance *noun* any one of many traditional British dances in which partners face each other in lines or sometimes form circles. ▪ **country dancing** *noun.*

country house *or* **country seat** *noun* a large house in the country, esp one belonging to a wealthy landowner.

countryman *or* **countrywoman** *noun* **1** someone who lives in a rural area. **2** someone belonging to a particular country, esp the same country as oneself.

country music *noun* a category of popular music, including **country and western**.

countryside *noun* rural land situated outside or away from towns.

county *noun* (***-ies***) **1** any of the geographical divisions within England, Wales and Ireland that form the larger units of local government. **2** in the USA: the main administrative subdivision within a state. [15c: from French *conté*]

county court *noun* a local court dealing with non-criminal cases.

coup /kuː/ *noun* **1** a successful move; a masterstroke. **2** a **coup d'état**. [18c: French]

coup de grâce /kuː də ˈgrɑːs/ *noun* (***coups de grâce*** /kuː də ˈgrɑːs/) a final decisive blow, esp one which puts an end to suffering. [17c: French, meaning 'blow of mercy']

coup d'état /kuː deɪˈtɑː/ *noun* (***coups d'état*** /kuː deɪˈtɑː/) the sudden, usu violent, overthrow of a government. Often shortened to **coup**. [17c: French, meaning 'stroke of the state']

coupé /ˈkuːpeɪ/ *noun* a car with four seats, two doors and a sloping rear. [19c: from French *couper* to cut]

couple *noun* **1** a pair of people attached in some way, often romantically. **2** a pair of partners, eg for dancing. **3** (*usu* **a couple of**) two, or a few: *I'll call you in a couple of weeks.* **4** *physics* a pair of equal but opposite forces applied to different points on the same object, producing a turning effect. ▸ *verb* **1** to associate; to link. **2** to connect (two things). **3** *intr* to have sexual intercourse. [13c: from French *cople*]

couplet *noun* a pair of consecutive lines of verse, esp ones which rhyme and have the same metre. [16c: diminutive of **couple**]

coupling *noun* a link for joining things together.

coupon *noun* **1** a slip of paper entitling one to something, eg a discount. **2** a detachable order form, competition entry form, etc printed on packaging, etc. **3** a printed betting form for football pools. [19c: French]

courage *noun* **1** bravery. **2** cheerfulness or resolution in coping with setbacks. [14c: from French *corage*]

IDIOMS **have the courage of one's convictions** to be brave enough to act in accordance with one's beliefs, no matter what the outcome.

courageous *adj* having or showing courage. ▪ **courageously** *adv.*

courgette /kɔːˈʒɛt/ *noun* a variety of small marrow. Also called **zucchini**. [20c: French, diminutive of *courge* gourd]

courier *noun* **1** a guide who travels with, and looks after, parties of tourists. **2** a messenger, esp one paid to deliver special or urgent messages or items. [15c: French]

course *noun* **1** the path in which anyone or anything moves. **2** a direction taken or planned: *go off course*. **3** the channel of a river, etc. **4** the normal progress of something. **5** the passage of a period of time: *in the course of the next year.* **6** a line of action: *Your best course is to wait.* **7** **a** a series of lessons, etc; a curriculum; **b** the work covered in such a series. **8** a prescribed treatment, eg medicine to be taken, over a period. **9** any of the successive parts of a meal. **10** *often in compounds* the ground over which a game is played or a race run: *golf course*. **11** *building* a single row of bricks or stones in a wall, etc. ▸ *verb* **1** *intr* to move or flow. **2** to hunt (hares, etc) using dogs. [13c: from French *cours*]

IDIOMS **a matter of course** a natural or expected action or result. **in due course** at the appropriate or expected time. **in the course of sth** while doing it; during it. **of course 1** as expected. **2** naturally; certainly; without doubt. **stay the course** to endure to the end.

coursebook *noun* a book to accompany a course of instruction.

courser *noun* **1** **a** someone who courses hares, etc; **b** a hound used for this. **2** *poetic* a swift horse.

court *noun* **1** the judge, law officials and members of the jury gathered to hear and decide on a legal case. **2** the room or building used for such a hearing. **3** an area marked out for a particular game or sport, or a division of this: *basketball court*. **4** an open space or square surrounded by houses or by sections of a building. **5** (*often* **Court**) used in names: **a** a group of houses arranged around an open space; **b** a block of flats; **c** a country mansion. **6** the palace, household, attendants, and advisers of a sovereign. ▸ *verb* **1** *tr & intr, old use* to try to win the love of someone. **2** to try to win the favour of someone. **3** to risk or invite: *court danger.* [12c: from French *cort*]

IDIOMS **go to court** to take legal action. **hold court** to be surrounded by a circle of admirers. **out of court** without legal action being taken. **pay court to sb** to pay them flattering attention. **take sb to court** to bring a legal case against them.

court card *noun* in a pack of playing cards: the king, queen or jack. Also called **face card, picture card**.

courteous *adj* polite; considerate; respectful. ▪ **courteously** *adv.* [13c: from French *corteis*]

courtesan /ˈkɔːtɪzan/ *noun, hist* a prostitute with wealthy or noble clients. [16c: from French *courtisane*]

courtesy *noun* (**-ies**) **1** courteous behaviour; politeness. **2** a courteous act. [13c: from French *corteisie*]

IDIOMS **by courtesy of sb 1** with their permission. **2** *informal* from them.

courthouse *noun* a building in which the lawcourts are held.

courtier *noun* **1** someone in attendance at a royal court. **2** an elegant flatterer. [13c: ultimately from French *cortoyer* to be at or frequent the court]

courtly *adj* (**-ier, -iest**) **1** having fine manners. **2** flattering.

court-martial *noun* (***courts-martial*** *or* ***court-martials***) a military court which tries members of the armed forces for breaches of military law. ▸ *verb* (***court-martialled, court-martialling***) to try by court-martial.

Court of Appeal *noun* in England and Wales: a court with civil and criminal divisions which hears appeals from other courts.

court of law see **lawcourt**

court order *noun* a direction or command of a judiciary court which, if not complied with, may lead to criminal proceedings against the offender or offenders.

courtroom *noun* a room in which a lawcourt is held.

courtship *noun, dated* **1** the courting or wooing of an intended spouse. **2** the period for which this lasts.

courtyard *noun* an open space surrounded by buildings or walls.

couscous /ˈkʊskʊs/ *noun* a N African dish of crushed semolina, which is steamed and served with eg vegetables, chicken, fish, etc. [17c: French]

cousin *noun* a son or daughter of one's uncle or aunt. Also called **first cousin**. Compare **second cousin**. [13c: from French *cosin*]

couture /kuːˈtʊə(r)/ *noun* the designing, making and selling of fashionable clothes. [Early 20c: French, meaning 'sewing' or 'dressmaking']

couturier /kuːˈtʊərɪeɪ/ *or* **couturière** /-rɪɛə(r)/ *noun* a male, or female, fashion designer.

covalency *adj, chem* the union of two or more atoms by the sharing of one or more pairs of electrons. ▪ **covalent** *adj.* ▪ **covalently** *adv.*

covalent bond *noun, chem* a chemical bond in which two atoms are held together by sharing a pair of electrons between them.

cove[1] *noun* a small and usu sheltered bay or inlet on a rocky coast. [Anglo-Saxon *cofa* room]

cove[2] *noun, Brit & Aust, dated, informal* a fellow. [16c]

coven /ˈkʌvən/ *noun* a gathering of witches. [17c: from Latin *convenire* to meet]

covenant /ˈkʌvənənt/ *noun* **1** *law* a formal sealed agreement to do something, eg pay a sum of money regularly to a charity. **2** a formal binding agreement. **3** *Bible* an agreement made between God and a person or a people. ▸ *verb, tr & intr* to agree by covenant to do something. [13c: French, from *convenir* to agree]

covenanter *noun* **1** a person who makes a covenant. **2** (**Covenanter**) *Scot hist* an adherent of either of two 17c religious covenants defending Presbyterianism in Scotland. [17c: from French *convenir* to agree]

cover *verb* **1** to form a layer over someone or something. **2** to protect or conceal someone or something by putting something over them or it. **3** to clothe. **4** to extend over something. **5** to strew, sprinkle, spatter, mark all over, etc. **6** to deal with (a subject). **7** of a reporter, etc: to investigate or report on (a story). **8** to have as one's area of responsibility. **9** to travel (a distance). **10** to be adequate to pay: *He had enough money to cover the meal.* **11** to insure; to insure against something. **12** to shield with a firearm at the ready or with actual fire. **13** *sport* to protect (a fellow team-member) or obstruct (an opponent). **14** to record a cover version of (a song, etc). **15** *intr* (*usu* **cover for sb**) to take over the duties of an ab-

sent colleague, etc. ▸ *noun* **1** something that covers. **2** a lid, top, protective casing, etc. **3** the covering of something. **4** (**covers**) the sheets and blankets on a bed. **5** the paper or board binding of a book, magazine, etc; one side of this. **6** an envelope: *a first-day cover.* **7** shelter or protection. **8** insurance. **9** service: *emergency cover.* **10** a pretence; a screen; a false identity: *His cover as a salesman was blown.* **11** armed protection; protective fire. **12** *cricket* see **cover point**. **13** a **cover version**. [13c: from French *covrir*]
IDIOMS **under cover 1** in secret. **2** within shelter.
PHRASAL VERBS **cover sth up 1** to cover it entirely. **2** to conceal (a dishonest act, a mistake, etc). See also **cover-up**.

coverage *noun* **1** an amount covered. **2** the extent to which a news item is reported in any of the media, etc.

cover charge *noun* in a restaurant, café, etc: a service charge made per person.

covering *noun* something that covers, eg a blanket, protective casing, etc.

covering letter *noun* a letter explaining the documents or goods it accompanies.

coverlet *noun* a thin top cover for a bed; a bedspread. [13c: prob from French *cuver-lit*]

cover note *noun* a temporary certificate of insurance, giving cover until the issue of the actual policy.

cover point *noun, cricket* the fielding position forward and to the right of the batsman.

covert *adj* /'kʌvət, 'koʊvɜːt/ secret; concealed. ▸ *noun* /'kʌvət/ **1** a thicket or woodland providing cover for game. **2** a shelter for animals. **3** any of the small feathers that surround the bases of the large quill feathers of the wings and tails of a bird. ▪ **covertly** *adv.* [14c: French, from *covrir* to cover]

cover-up *noun* an act of concealing or withholding information about something suspect or illicit. See also **cover sth up** at **cover**.

cover version *noun* a recording of a song which has already been recorded by another artist.

covet *verb* to long to possess something (esp something belonging to someone else). [13c: from French *coveitier*]

covetous *adj* envious; greedy. ▪ **covetously** *adv.*

covey /'kʌvɪ/ *noun* **1** a small flock of game birds of one type, esp partridge or grouse. **2** a small group of people. [15c: from Old French *covée*]

cow[1] *noun* **1** the mature female of any bovine animal, esp domesticated cattle. See also **bull**[1] (*noun* sense 1), **calf**[1]. **2** the mature female of certain other mammals, eg the elephant, whale and seal. **3** loosely used to refer to any domestic breed of cattle. **4** *derog slang* a woman. [Anglo-Saxon *cu*]
IDIOMS **till the cows come home** *informal* for an unforeseeably long time.

cow[2] *verb* to frighten something into submission. [17c: from Norse *kuga* to subdue]

coward *noun* someone easily frightened, or lacking courage to face danger or difficulty. ▪ **cowardice** *noun.* ▪ **cowardly** *adv.* [13c: from Latin *cauda* tail]

cowboy *noun* **1** in the western USA: a man who tends cattle, usu on horseback. **2** this kind of man as a character in films of the Wild West. **3** *slang, derog* someone who undertakes building or other work without proper training or qualifications; a dishonest businessman.

cowcatcher *noun, US* a concave metal fender fixed onto the front of a railway engine for clearing cattle and other obstacles from the line.

cower *verb, intr* to shrink away in fear. [13c]

cowhide *noun* leather made from the hide of a cow.

cowl *noun* **1** a monk's large loose hood or hooded habit. **2** any large loose hood. **3** a revolving cover for a chimney-pot for improving ventilation. [Anglo-Saxon *cugele* hood]

cowlick *noun* a tuft of hair that grows in a different direction from the rest, usu hanging over the forehead.

cowling *noun* the streamlined metal casing, usu having hinged or removable panels, that houses the engine of an aircraft or other vehicle.

co-worker *noun* a fellow worker; a colleague.

cow parsley *noun* a plant with small white flowers borne in **umbel**s. Also called **Queen Anne's lace**.

cowpat *noun* a flat deposit of cow dung.

cowpox *noun, med* a viral infection of cows that can be transmitted to humans by direct contact, and used to formulate a vaccine against smallpox.

cowrie *or* **cowry** *noun* (***-ries***) **1** a marine snail, found mainly in tropical waters. **2** the brightly coloured glossy egg-shaped shell of this animal. [17c: from Hindi *kauri*]

cowslip *noun* a plant with a cluster of yellow sweet-smelling flowers. [Anglo-Saxon *cuslyppe* cow dung]

cox *noun* short for **coxswain**. ▸ *verb, tr & intr* to act as cox of (a boat). ▪ **coxless** *adj.*

coxcomb see **cockscomb**

coxswain *or* **cockswain** /'kɒksən/ *noun* someone who steers a small boat. Often shortened to **cox**. [15c: from *cock* ship's boat + **swain**]

coy *adj* **1** shy; modest; affectedly bashful. **2** irritatingly uncommunicative about something. ▪ **coyly** *adv.* ▪ **coyness** *noun.* [14c: from French *coi* calm]

coyote /'kɔɪoʊtiː/ *noun* (***coyotes*** *or* ***coyote***) a small N American wolf, found mainly in deserts, prairies and open woodland. Also called **prairie wolf**. [19c: Mexican Spanish]

coypu *noun* (***coypus*** *or* ***coypu***) **1** a large rat-like aquatic rodent which has a broad blunt muzzle and webbed hind feet. **2** the soft fur of this animal. Also called **nutria**. [18c: from a native S American language]

'coz *or* **coz** see **'cos**

CPR *abbrev* cardiopulmonary resuscitation.

CPU *abbrev, comput* central processing unit.

Cr *abbrev* Councillor.

Cr *symbol, chem* chromium.

crab[1] *noun* **1** a marine crustacean with a hard flattened shell and five pairs of jointed legs, the front pair being developed into pincers. **2 a** another name for the **crab louse**; **b** (**crabs**) infestation by this. **3** (**Crab**) *astron, astrol* **Cancer**. [Anglo-Saxon *crabba*]
IDIOMS **catch a crab** in rowing: to sink the oar too deeply or to miss the water completely.

crab[2] *noun* **1** short for **crab apple**. **2** a grumpy or irritable person.

crab apple *noun* **1** a large deciduous shrub or small tree with thorny branches, oval toothed leaves and white flowers. **2** the small hard round sour fruit of this tree.

crabbed /'krabɪd, krabd/ *adj* **1** bad-tempered; grouchy. **2** of handwriting: cramped and hard to decipher. [13c: from **crab**[1]; the crooked gait of the crab is said to express a contradictory nature]

crabby *adj* (**-ier, -iest**) *informal* bad-tempered.

crab louse *noun* a crab-shaped parasitic louse which infests the hair of the human pubic area. Often shortened to **crab** (see **crab**[1] *noun* sense 2).

crack *verb* **1** *tr & intr* to fracture or cause to fracture without breaking into pieces. **2** *tr & intr* to split or make something split. **3** *tr & intr* to make or cause to make a sudden sharp noise. **4** to strike sharply. **5** *tr & intr* to give way or make someone or something give way: *He finally cracked under the pressure.* **6** to force open (a safe). **7** to solve (a code or problem). **8** to gain unauthorized access to (computer files). **9** to tell (a joke). **10** *intr* of the voice: to change pitch or tone suddenly and unintentionally. **11** *chem, tr & intr* to break down long-chain hydrocarbons produced during petroleum refining into lighter more useful short-chain products. ▸ *noun* **1** a sudden sharp sound. **2** a partial fracture in a material produced by an external force or internal stress. **3** a narrow opening. **4** a resounding blow. **5** *slang* (*in full* **crack cocaine**) a highly addictive derivative of cocaine, consisting of hard crystalline lumps that are heated and smoked. **6** (*usu* **the crack** *or* **the craic**) the latest news or gossip. **7** *Irish* (*also* **craic**) fun, enjoyable activity and conversation, often in a pub: *We had some good crack at the races.* ▸ *adj, informal* expert: *a crack shot*. [Anglo-Saxon *cracian* to resound]

IDIOMS **a fair crack of the whip** a fair opportunity. **at the crack of dawn** *informal* at daybreak; very early. **get cracking** *informal* to make a prompt start with something. **have a crack at sth** *informal* to attempt it.

PHRASAL VERBS **crack down on sb** *or* **sth** *informal* to take firm action against them or it. **crack up** *informal* **1** to suffer an emotional breakdown. **2** to collapse with laughter.

crackdown *noun* a firm action taken against someone or something.

cracked *adj* **1** *informal* crazy; mad. **2** of a voice: harsh; uneven in tone. **3** damaged by splitting.

cracker *noun* **1** a thin crisp unsweetened biscuit. **2** a party toy in the form of a paper tube usu containing a paper hat, gift and motto, that pulls apart with an explosive bang. **3** a small, noisy firework. **4** *informal* an exceptional person or thing.

crackers *adj, informal* mad.

cracking *adj, informal* **1** very good: *a cracking story.* **2** very fast: *a cracking pace.* ▸ *noun, chem* short for **catalytic cracking**.

crackle *verb, intr* to make a faint continuous cracking or popping sound. ▸ *noun* this kind of sound. ▪ **crackly** *adj* (**-ier, -iest**). [16c: diminutive of **crack**]

crackling *noun* the crisp skin of roast pork.

cracknel *noun* **1** a light brittle biscuit. **2** a hard nutty filling for chocolates.

crackpot *informal, adj* crazy. ▸ *noun* a crazy person.

-cracy *combining form, denoting* rule, government or domination by a particular group, etc: *democracy* • *autocracy* • *bureaucracy.* [From Greek *kratos* power]

cradle *noun* **1** a cot for a small baby, esp one that can be rocked. **2** a place of origin; the home or source of something: *the cradle of civilization.* **3** a suspended platform or cage for workmen engaged in the construction, repair or painting of a ship or building. ▸ *verb* **1** to rock or hold gently. **2** to nurture. [Anglo-Saxon *kradol*]

IDIOMS **from the cradle to the grave** throughout the whole of one's life.

cradle-snatcher *noun, derog* someone who chooses a much younger person as a lover or spouse.

craft *noun* **1** a skill, trade or occupation, esp one requiring the use of the hands. **2** skilled ability. **3** cunning. ▸ *plural noun, often in compounds* boats, ships, air or space vehicles collectively. ▸ *verb* to make something skilfully. [Anglo-Saxon *cræft* strength]

craftsman *or* **craftswoman** *noun* someone skilled at a craft.

craftsmanship *noun* the skill of a craftsman or craftswoman.

crafty *adj* (**-ier, -iest**) clever, shrewd, cunning or sly. ▪ **craftily** *adv.* ▪ **craftiness** *noun.*

crag *noun* a rocky peak or jagged outcrop of rock. ▪ **craggy** *adj* (**-ier, -est**). [13c: Celtic]

craic see **crack** (*noun* senses 6, 7)

cram *verb* (***crammed, cramming***) **1** to stuff full. **2** (*sometimes* **cram sth in** *or* **together**) to push or pack it tightly. **3** *tr & intr* to study intensively, or prepare someone rapidly, for an examination. [Anglo-Saxon *crammian*]

cram-full *adj* full to bursting.

crammer *noun* a person or school that prepares pupils for examinations by rapid or intensive study.

cramp[1] *noun* **1** a painful involuntary prolonged contraction of a muscle or group of muscles. **2** (**cramps**) severe abdominal pain. ▸ *verb* to restrict with or as with a cramp. [14c: from French *crampe*]

IDIOMS **cramp sb's style** to restrict or prevent them from acting freely or creatively.

cramp[2] *noun* a piece of metal bent at both ends, used for holding stone or timbers together. Also called **cramp-iron**. ▸ *verb* to fasten with a cramp. [16c: from Dutch *crampe* hook]

cramped *adj* **1** overcrowded; closed in. **2** of handwriting: small and closely written.

crampon *noun* a spiked iron attachment for climbing boots, to improve grip on ice or rock. [15c: French]

cranberry *noun* **1** a shrub with oval pointed leaves, pink flowers and red berries. **2** the sour-tasting fruit of this plant. [17c: from German dialect *kraanbeere* crane berry]

crane *noun* **1** a machine with a long pivoted arm from which lifting gear is suspended, allowing heavy weights to be moved both horizontally and vertically. **2** a large wading bird with a long neck and long legs. ▸ *verb, tr & intr* to stretch (one's neck), or lean forward, in order to see better. [Anglo-Saxon *cran*]

cranefly *noun* a long-legged, two-winged insect. Also (*informal*) *called* **daddy-long-legs**. See also **leatherjacket**.

cranesbill *noun* a plant with white, purple or blue flowers and slender beaked fruits.

cranial *adj* relating to or in the region of the skull.

cranium /ˈkreɪnɪəm/ *noun* (***crania*** /-nɪə/ *or* ***craniums***) **1** the dome-shaped part of the skull, consisting of several fused bones, that encloses and protects the brain. **2** the skull. [16c: Latin]

crank *noun* **1** a device consisting of an arm connected to and projecting at right angles from the shaft of an engine or motor. **2** a handle bent at right angles and incorporating such a device, used to start an engine

or motor by hand. Also called **crank handle, starting handle**. **3** *derog* an eccentric person. **4** *N Am derog* a bad-tempered person. ▸ *verb* **1** to rotate (a shaft) using a crank. **2** (*sometimes* **crank sth up**) to start (an engine, a machine, etc) using a crank. [Anglo-Saxon *cranc-stæf* weaving implement]
PHRASAL VERBS **crank sth up** to increase its volume, intensity, etc.

crankshaft *noun* the main shaft of an engine or other machine, bearing one or more cranks, used to transmit power from the cranks to the connecting rods.

cranky *adj* (**-ier, -iest**) **1** *informal* eccentric or faddy. **2** *N Am* bad-tempered.

cranny *noun* (**-ies**) a narrow opening; a cleft or crevice. [15c: related to French *cran*]

crap *noun* **1** (*usu* **craps**) a gambling game in which the player rolls two dice. **2** a losing throw in this game.

crape see **crêpe** (*noun* sense 1)

crapulent *or* **crapulous** *adj* **1** suffering from sickness caused by overdrinking. **2** relating to or resulting from intemperance. ▪ **crapulence** *noun*. [17c: from Latin *crapulentus*]

crash *verb* **1** *tr & intr* to fall or strike with a banging or smashing noise. **2** *tr & intr* (*often* **crash into sth**) of a vehicle: to collide or cause it to collide with something. **3** *intr* to make a deafening noise. **4** *intr* to move noisily. **5** *intr* of a business or stock exchange: to collapse. **6** *intr* of a computer or program: to fail completely, because of a malfunction, fluctuation in the power supply, etc. **7** to cause a computer system or program to break down completely. **8** *slang* to gatecrash (a party, etc). **9** (*often* **crash out**) *slang* to fall asleep. ▸ *noun* **1** a violent impact or breakage, or the sound of it. **2** a deafening noise. **3** a traffic or aircraft accident. **4** the collapse of a business or the stock exchange. **5** the failure of a computer or program. [14c: imitating the sound]

crash barrier *noun* a protective metal barrier along the edge of a road, carriageway, the front of a stage, etc.

crash dive *noun* **1** a rapid emergency dive by a submarine. **2** a sudden dive by an aircraft, ending in a crash.

crash helmet *noun* a protective helmet worn eg by motorcyclists, motor-racing drivers, etc.

crashing *adj, informal* utter; extreme: *a crashing bore*.

crash-land *verb, tr & intr* of an aircraft or pilot: to land or cause (an aircraft) to land, usu without lowering the undercarriage and with the risk of crashing. ▪ **crash-landing** *noun*.

crass *adj* **1** gross; vulgar. **2** colossally stupid. **3** utterly tactless or insensitive. ▪ **crassly** *adv*. ▪ **crassness** *noun*. [16c: from Latin *crassus* thick or solid]

-crat *combining form, denoting* a person who takes part in or supports government, rule or domination by a particular group: *democrat* • *autocrat* • *bureaucrat*.

crate *noun* **1** a strong wooden, plastic or metal case with partitions, for storing or carrying breakable or perishable goods. **2** *derog slang* a decrepit vehicle or aircraft. ▸ *verb* to pack in a crate. [17c: from Latin *cratis* wickerwork barrier]

crater *noun* **1** the bowl-shaped mouth of a volcano or geyser. **2** a hole left in the ground where a meteorite has landed, or a bomb or mine has exploded. **3** *astron* a circular, rimmed depression in the surface of the Moon. ▸ *verb, tr & intr* to form craters in (a road, a surface, etc). ▪ **cratered** *adj*. [17c: Latin]

-cratic *or* **-cratical** *combining form, indicating* a person who takes part in or supports government, rule or domination by a particular group: *democratic* • *autocratic* • *bureaucratic*.

craton *noun, geog* a relatively rigid and stable area of rock in the Earth's crust.

cravat /krə'vat/ *noun* a formal style of neckerchief worn instead of a tie. [17c: from French *cravate*]

crave *verb* **1** (*often* **crave for** *or* **after sth**) to long for it; to desire it overwhelmingly. **2** *old use, formal* to ask for politely; to beg. ▪ **craving** *noun*. [Anglo-Saxon *crafian*]

craven *adj* cowardly; cringing. [14c]

craw *noun* **1** the **crop** (*noun* sense 6). **2** the stomach of a lower animal. [14c]
IDIOMS **stick in one's craw** *informal* to be difficult for one to swallow or accept.

crawl *verb, intr* **1** of insects, worms, etc: to move along the ground slowly. **2** of a human: to move along on hands and knees. **3** eg of traffic: to progress very slowly. **4** to be, or feel as if, covered or overrun with something: *the place was crawling with police*. **5** (*often* **crawl to sb**) *derog informal* to behave in a fawning way, often to someone in a senior position. ▸ *noun* **1** a crawling motion. **2** a very slow pace. **3** *swimming* a stroke with an alternate overarm action together with a kicking leg action. [13c]

crawler *noun* **1** someone or something which crawls. **2** *derog informal* someone who behaves in a fawning and ingratiating way, esp to those in senior positions. **3** a computer program that extracts information from sites on the World Wide Web in order to create entries for a search engine index.

crayfish *or* **crawfish** *noun* an edible, freshwater crustacean, similar to a small lobster. [14c: from French *crevice*]

crayon *noun* **1** a pencil or stick made from coloured wax, chalk or charcoal and used for drawing. **2** a drawing made using crayons. ▸ *verb, tr & intr* to draw or colour with a crayon. [17c: French, from *craie*]

craze *noun* an intense but passing enthusiasm or fashion. ▸ *verb* **1** to make crazy. **2** *tr & intr* eg of a glazed or varnished surface: to develop or cause to develop a network of fine cracks. [15c]

crazy *adj* (**-ier, -iest**) **1** mad; insane. **2** foolish; absurd; foolhardy. ▪ **crazily** *adv*. ▪ **craziness** *noun*.
IDIOMS **be crazy about sb** *or* **sth** to be madly enthusiastic about them or it. **like crazy** *informal* keenly; fast and furious.

crazy paving *noun* a type of paving made up of irregularly shaped slabs of stone or concrete.

creak *noun* a shrill squeaking noise made typically by an unoiled hinge or loose floorboard. ▸ *verb, intr* to make or seem to make this noise. ▪ **creakily** *adv*. ▪ **creakiness** *noun*. ▪ **creaky** *adj* (**-ier, -iest**). [16c]

cream *noun* **1** the yellowish fatty substance that rises to the surface of milk, and yields butter when churned. **2** any food that resembles this substance in consistency or appearance. **3** any cosmetic substance that resembles cream in texture or consistency. **4** the best part of something; the pick. **5** a yellowish-white colour. ▸ *verb* **1** to beat (eg butter and sugar) till creamy. **2** to remove the cream from (milk). **3** (*often* **cream sth off**) to select or take away (the best part). ▪ **creamy** *adj* (**-*ier*, -*iest***). [14c: from French *cresme*]

cream cheese *noun* a soft cheese made from soured milk or cream.

creamer *noun* **1** a powdered milk substitute, used in coffee. **2** *N Am, esp US* a jug for serving cream. **3** a device for separating cream from milk.

creamery *noun* (**-*ies***) a place where dairy products are made or sold.

cream of tartar *noun* a white crystalline powder, soluble in water, which is used in baking powder, soft drinks, laxatives, etc.

crease *noun* **1** a line made by folding, pressing or crushing. **2** a wrinkle, esp on the face. **3** *cricket* a line marking the position of batsman or bowler. ▸ *verb, tr & intr* **1** to make a crease or creases in (paper, fabric, etc); to develop creases. **2** to graze with a bullet. PHRASAL VERBS **crease up** *or* **crease sb up** *informal* to be or make helpless or incapable with laughter.

create *verb* **1** to form or produce from nothing: *create the universe*. **2** to bring into existence: *create a system*. **3** to cause. **4** to produce or contrive. **5** *tr & intr* said of an artist, etc: to use one's imagination to make something. **6** *intr, Brit informal* to make a fuss. [14c: from Latin *creare*]

creation *noun* **1** the act of creating. **2** something created, particularly something special or striking. **3** the universe. **4** (*often* **the Creation**) *Christianity* God's act of creating the universe.

creationism *noun* the theory or belief that everything that exists was created by God, as described in the Book of Genesis in the Bible, as opposed to being formed by evolution. [19c]

creative *adj* **1** having or showing the ability to create. **2** inventive or imaginative. ▪ **creativity** *noun*.

creator *noun* **1** someone who creates. **2** (**the Creator**) *Christianity* God.

creature *noun* **1** a bird, beast or fish. **2** a person: *a wretched creature*. **3** the slavish underling or puppet of someone. [13c: from Latin *creatura* a thing created]

creature comforts *plural noun* material comforts or luxuries such as food, clothes, warmth, etc which add to one's physical comfort.

creature of habit *noun* a person of unchanging routines.

crèche /krɛʃ/ *noun* **1** a nursery where babies can be left and cared for while their parents are at work, shopping, exercising, etc. **2** a model representing the scene of Christ's nativity. [19c: French, meaning 'manger']

cred *noun, slang* credibility: *street cred*.

credence *noun* faith or belief placed in something: *give their claims no credence*. [14c: from Latin *credentia*]

credentials *plural noun* **1** personal qualifications and achievements that can be quoted as evidence of one's trustworthiness, competence, etc. **2** documents or other evidence of these. [17c: from Latin *credentia* belief]

credibility gap *noun* the discrepancy between what is claimed and what is actually or likely to be the case.

credible *adj* **1** capable of being believed. **2** reliable; trustworthy. ▪ **credibility** *noun*. [14c: from Latin *credibilis*]

credit *noun* **1** faith placed in something. **2** honour or a cause of honour: *To her credit, she didn't say anything*. **3** acknowledgement, recognition or praise. **4** (**credits**) a list of acknowledgements to those who have helped in the preparation of a book, film, etc. **5** trust given to someone promising to pay later for goods already supplied: *buy goods on credit*. **6** one's financial reliability, esp as a basis for such trust. **7** the amount of money available to one at one's bank. **8** **a** an entry in a bank account acknowledging a payment; **b** the side of an account on which such entries are made. Compare **debit**. **9** **a** a certificate of completion of a course of instruction; **b** a distinction awarded for performance on such a course. ▸ *verb* **1** to believe; to place faith in someone or something. **2** (*often* **credit sth to sb** *or* **sb with sth**) to enter a sum as a credit on someone's account, or allow someone a sum as credit. **3** (*often* **credit sb with sth**) to attribute a quality or achievement to someone. [16c: from French *crédit*]

creditable *adj* praiseworthy; laudable. ▪ **creditably** *adv*.

credit card *noun* a card issued by a bank, finance company, etc authorizing the holder to purchase goods or services on credit. Compare **debit card**.

credit note *noun* a form issued by a company or shop, stating that a particular customer is entitled to a certain sum as credit, instead of a cash refund, replacement goods, etc.

creditor *noun* a person or company to whom one owes money. Compare **debtor**.

credit rating *noun* an assessment of a person's or company's creditworthiness.

creditworthy *adj* judged as deserving financial credit on the basis of earning ability, previous promptness in repaying debts, etc. ▪ **creditworthiness** *noun*.

credo /ˈkriːdoʊ/ *noun* a belief or set of beliefs. [12c: Latin, meaning 'I believe']

credulity *noun* a tendency to believe something without proper proof.

credulous *adj* apt to be too ready to believe something, without sufficient evidence. ▪ **credulously** *adv*. [16c: from Latin *credulus*]

creed *noun* **1** (*often* **Creed**) a statement of the main points of Christian belief. **2** (**the Creed**) the statement of the main principles and ideology of the Christian faith. **3** any set of beliefs or principles, either personal or religious. [Anglo-Saxon *creda*]

creek *noun* **1** a small narrow inlet or bay in the shore of a lake, river, or sea. **2** *N Am, Aust, NZ* a small natural stream or tributary, larger than a brook and smaller than a river. [13c: from Norse *kriki* nook] IDIOMS **up the creek** *informal* in desperate difficulties.

creel *noun* a large basket for carrying fish. [15c]

creep *verb* (***crept***) *intr* **1** to move slowly, with stealth or caution. **2** to move with the body close to the ground. **3** of a plant: to grow along the ground, up a wall, etc. **4** to enter slowly and almost imperceptibly: *Anxiety crept into her voice*. **5** esp of the flesh: to have a strong tingling sensation as a response to fear or disgust. **6** to act in a fawning way. ▸ *noun* **1** an act of creeping. **2** *derog* an unpleasant person. ▪ **creep-**

ing *adj.* [Anglo-Saxon *creopan*]

IDIOMS **give sb the creeps** *informal* to disgust or frighten them.

creeper *noun* a creeping plant.

creepy *adj* (**-ier, -iest**) *informal* slightly scary; spooky.

creepy-crawly *noun* (**-ies**) *informal* a small creeping insect.

cremate *verb* to burn (a corpse) to ashes. ▪ **cremation** *noun* the act or process of cremating a corpse, as an alternative to burial. [19c: from Latin *cremare* to burn]

crematorium /krɛmə'tɔːrɪəm/ *noun* (***crematoria*** /-rɪə/ *or* ***crematoriums***) a place where corpses are cremated.

crème de la crème /krɛm də la 'krɛm/ *noun* the very best; the elite. [19c: French, literally meaning 'cream of the cream']

crème de menthe /krɛm də 'mɒnθ/ *noun* (***crème de menthes***) a green peppermint-flavoured liqueur.

crème fraîche /krɛm 'frɛʃ/ *noun* cream thickened with a culture of bacteria, used in cooking. [1990s: French, meaning 'fresh cream']

crenellate *verb, archit* to furnish with battlements. ▪ **crenellated** *adj.* ▪ **crenellation** *noun.*

creole *noun* **1** a **pidgin** language that has become the accepted language of a community or region. **2** (**Creole**) the French-based creole spoken in the US states of the Caribbean Gulf. **3** (**Creole**) a native-born West Indian or Latin American of mixed European and Negro blood. **4** (**Creole**) a French or Spanish native of the US Gulf states. [17c: French]

creosote *noun* **1** a thick dark oily liquid, obtained by distilling coal tar, used as a wood preservative. **2** a colourless or pale yellow oily liquid with a penetrating odour, obtained by distilling wood tar, used as an antiseptic. ▸ *verb* to treat (wood) with creosote. [19c: from Greek *kreas* flesh + *soter* saviour]

crêpe *or* **crepe** /kreɪp, krɛp/ *noun* **1** (*also* **crape** /kreɪp/) a thin finely-wrinkled silk fabric. **2** rubber with a wrinkled surface, used for shoe soles. Also called **crêpe rubber.** **3** a thin pancake, often containing a filling. [19c: French]

crêpe paper *noun* a type of thin paper with a wrinkled elastic texture, used for making decorations, etc.

crept *past tense, past participle of* **creep**

crepuscular *adj* **1** relating to or like twilight; dim. **2** denoting animals that are active before sunrise or at dusk. [17c: from Latin *crepusculum* twilight]

Cres. *abbrev* Crescent.

crescendo /krɛ'ʃɛndoʊ/ *noun* **1** a gradual increase in loudness. **2** a musical passage of increasing loudness. **3** a high point or climax. ▸ *adv, music* played with increasing loudness. Compare **diminuendo.** [18c: Italian, meaning 'increasing']

crescent *noun* **1** the curved shape of the Moon during its first or last quarter, when it appears less than half illuminated. **2** something similar in shape to this, eg a semicircular row of houses. **3** (*often* **Crescent**) *chiefly Brit* used in names: a street of houses arranged in a crescent shape. [14c: from Latin *crescere* to grow]

cress *noun* a plant cultivated for its edible seed leaves which are eaten raw in salads, sandwiches, etc, and used as a garnish. [Anglo-Saxon *cressa*]

crest *noun* **1** a comb or a tuft of feathers or fur on top of the head of certain birds and mammals. **2** a ridge of skin along the top of the head of certain reptiles and amphibians. **3** a plume on a helmet. **4** the topmost part of something, esp a hill, mountain or wave. ▸ *verb* **1** to reach the top of (a hill, mountain, etc). **2** to crown; to cap. **3** *intr* of a wave: to rise or foam up into a crest. ▪ **crested** *adj.* [14c: from Latin *crista* plume]

crestfallen *adj* dejected as a result of a blow to one's pride or ambitions.

cretaceous *geol, adj* **1** (**Cretaceous**) relating to the last period of the **Mesozoic** era, during which the first flowering plants appeared, and dinosaurs and many other reptiles became extinct. **2** (**Cretaceous**) relating to rocks formed during this period. **3** composed of or resembling chalk. ▸ *noun* (*usu* **the Cretaceous**) the Cretaceous age or rock system. [17c: from Latin *creta* chalk]

cretin *noun* **1** someone suffering from cretinism. **2** *offensive, loosely* an idiot. ▪ **cretinous** *adj.* [18c: from Swiss dialect *crestin*]

cretinism *noun* a chronic condition caused by a congenital deficiency of thyroid hormone resulting in dwarfism and mental retardation.

cretonne *noun* a strong cotton material, usu with a printed design, used for curtains, chair-covers, etc. [19c: French]

Creutzfeldt-Jakob disease /krɔɪtsfɛlt 'jakɒb/ *noun, pathol* a rare degenerative brain disease, characterized by dementia, wasting of muscle tissue and various neurological abnormalities. [1960s: named after the German physicians H G Creutzfeldt and A Jakob]

crevasse /krə'vas/ *noun* **1** *geol* a deep vertical crack in a glacier. **2** *US* a breach in the bank of the river. ▸ *verb* to make a fissure in (a wall, a dyke, etc). [19c: from French *crevace* crevice]

crevice /'krɛvɪs/ *noun* **1** a narrow crack or fissure, esp in a rock. **2** a narrow opening. [14c: from French *crevace*]

crew[1] *noun* **1** the team of people manning a ship, aircraft, train, bus, etc. **2** a ship's company excluding the officers. **3** a team engaged in some operation: *camera crew.* **4** *informal, usu derog* a bunch of people: *a strange crew.* ▸ *verb, intr* to serve as a crew member on a yacht, etc. [16c: from Latin *crescere* to increase or grow]

crew[2] *past tense of* **crow**

crewcut *noun* a closely cropped hairstyle. [1930s: apparently first adopted by the boat crews at the universities of Harvard and Yale]

crewel *noun* thin loosely twisted yarn for tapestry or embroidery. ▪ **crewelwork** *noun.* [15c]

crew neck *noun* a firm round neckline on a sweater. ▸ *adj* (**crew-neck**).

crib *noun* **1** a baby's cot or cradle. **2** a manger. **3** a model of the nativity, with the infant Christ in a manger. **4** a literal translation of a text, used as an aid by students. **5** something copied or plagiarized from another's work. **6** short for **cribbage.** ▸ *verb* (***cribbed, cribbing***) **1** *tr & intr* to copy or plagiarize. **2** to put in or as if in a crib. [Anglo-Saxon *cribb* stall or manger]

cribbage *noun* a card game for two to four players, who each try to be first to score a certain number of points. Sometimes shortened to **crib.**

crick *informal, noun* a painful spasm or stiffness of the muscles, esp in the neck. ▸ *verb* to wrench (eg one's neck or back). [15c: prob imitating the sound]

cricket[1] *noun* an outdoor game played using a ball, bats and wickets, between two sides of eleven players, the object of which is for one team to score more runs (see **run** *noun* sense 17) than the other by the end of the period of play. ▪ **cricketer** *noun.* [16c]
IDIOMS **not cricket** *informal* unfair; unsporting.

cricket[2] *noun* a species of mainly nocturnal insect related to the grasshopper, which has long slender antennae and whose males can produce a distinctive chirping sound by rubbing their forewings together. [14c: imitating the sound]

cried *and* **cries** see under **cry**

crier *noun, hist* an official who announces news by shouting it out in public.

crikey *exclam, dated slang* an expression of astonishment. [19c: perhaps euphemistic for **Christ**]

crime *noun* **1** an illegal act; an act punishable by law. **2** such acts collectively. **3** an act which is gravely wrong in a moral sense. **4** *informal* a deplorable act; a shame. [14c: French]

criminal *noun* someone guilty of a crime or crimes. ▸ *adj* **1** against the law. **2** relating to crime or criminals, or their punishment. **3** *informal* very wrong; wicked. ▪ **criminality** *noun.* ▪ **criminalize** *or* **-ise** *verb.* ▪ **criminally** *adv.* [15c: from Latin *criminalis*]

criminal law *noun* the branch of law dealing with unlawful acts. Compare **civil law**.

criminology *noun* the scientific study of crime and criminals. ▪ **criminologist** *noun.* [19c: from Latin *crimen* crime + Greek *logos* word or reason]

crimp *verb* **1** to press into small regular ridges; to corrugate. **2** to wave or curl (hair) with crimping-irons. **3** *US* to thwart or hinder. ▸ *noun* a curl or wave in the hair. ▪ **crimped** *adj.* [Anglo-Saxon *crympan* to curl]

crimping irons *or* **crimpers** *plural noun* a tong-like device with two metal plates each with a series of ridges, which are used to form waves in hair that is pressed between the heated plates.

Crimplene *noun, trademark* a crease-resistant clothing fabric made from a thick polyester yarn.

crimson *noun* a deep purplish red colour. [15c: from Spanish *cremesin*]

cringe *verb, intr* **1** to cower away in fear. **2** *derog* to behave in a submissive, over-humble way. **3** *loosely* to wince in embarrassment, etc. ▸ *noun* an act of cringing. [Anglo-Saxon *cringan* to fall in battle]

crinkle *verb, tr & intr* to wrinkle or crease. ▸ *noun* a wrinkle or crease; a wave. [related to Anglo-Saxon *crincan* to yield]

crinkly *adj* (**-ier, -iest**) wrinkly. ▸ *noun* (**-ies**) *informal* an elderly person.

crinoline *noun, hist* a petticoat fitted with hoops to make the skirts stick out. [19c: French]

cripple *verb* **1** to make lame; to disable. **2** to damage, weaken or undermine: *policies which crippled the economy.* ▸ *noun* **1** *offensive* someone who is lame or badly disabled. **2** someone damaged psychologically: *an emotional cripple.* [Anglo-Saxon *crypel*]

crisis /ˈkraɪsɪz/ *noun* (**-ses** /-siːz/) **1** a crucial or decisive moment. **2** a turning-point, eg in a disease. **3** a time of difficulty or distress. **4** an emergency. [16c: Latin]

crisp *adj* **1** dry and brittle. **2** of vegetables or fruit: firm and fresh. **3** of weather: fresh; bracing. **4** of a person's manner or speech: firm; decisive; brisk. **5** of fabric, etc: clean; starched. ▸ *noun, Brit* (*usu* **crisps**) thin deep-fried slices of potato, usu flavoured and sold in packets as a snack. Also called **potato crisps**. ▸ *verb, tr & intr* to make or become crisp. ▪ **crisply** *adv.* ▪ **crispness** *noun.* ▪ **crispy** *adj* (**-ier, -iest**). [Anglo-Saxon]

crispbread *noun* a brittle unsweetened biscuit made from wheat or rye.

criss-cross *adj* **1** of lines: crossing one another in different directions. **2** of a pattern, etc: consisting of criss-cross lines. ▸ *adv* in a criss-cross way or pattern. ▸ *noun* a pattern of criss-cross lines. ▸ *verb, tr & intr* to form, mark with or move in a criss-cross pattern.

criterion /kraɪˈtɪərɪən/ *noun* (**criteria** /-rɪə/) a standard or principle on which to base a judgement. [17c: from Greek *kriterion*]

---

criterion, criteria

The word **criteria** is plural. 'A criteria' is often used, but is not correct:

✗ *A good price was the main criteria for our choice.*

✓ *A good price will be the main criterion for our choice.*

---

critic *noun* **1** a professional reviewer of literature, art, drama, music, etc. **2** someone who finds fault with or disapproves of something. [16c: from Latin *criticus*]

critical *adj* **1** fault-finding; disapproving. **2** relating to a critic or criticism. **3** involving analysis and assessment. **4** relating to a crisis; decisive; crucial. **5** urgent; vital. **6** of a patient: so ill or seriously injured as to be at risk of dying. **7** *physics* denoting a state, level or value at which there is a significant change in the properties of a system: *critical mass.* **8** *nuclear physics* of a fissionable material, a nuclear reactor, etc: having reached the point at which a nuclear chain reaction is self-sustaining. ▪ **critically** *adv.*

critical mass *noun, physics* the smallest amount of a given fissile material that is needed to sustain a nuclear chain reaction.

criticism *noun* **1** fault-finding. **2** reasoned analysis and assessment, esp of art, literature, music, drama, etc. **3** the art of such assessment. **4** a critical comment or piece of writing.

criticize *or* **-ise** *verb, tr & intr* **1** to find fault; to express disapproval of someone or something. **2** to analyse and assess.

critique *noun* **1** a critical analysis. **2** the art of criticism. [17c: French]

croak *noun* the harsh throaty noise typically made by a frog or crow. ▸ *verb* **1** *intr* to make this sound. **2** to utter with a croak. **3** *intr* to grumble or moan. **4** *intr, slang* to die. [15c: prob imitating the sound]

Croatian /kroʊˈeɪʃən/ *or* **Croat** /ˈkroʊat/ *adj* belonging or relating to Croatia, its inhabitants, or their language. ▸ *noun* a citizen or inhabitant of, or person born in, Croatia.

crochet /ˈkroʊʃeɪ/ *noun* decorative work consisting of intertwined loops, made with wool or thread and a hooked needle. ▸ *verb tr & intr* to make this kind of work. [19c: French, diminutive of *croche* hook]

crock[1] *noun, informal* a decrepit person or an old vehicle, etc. [19c]

crock[2] *noun* an earthenware pot. [Anglo-Saxon *crocc* pot]

crockery *noun* earthenware or china dishes collectively.

crocodile *noun* **1** a large amphibious reptile. **2** *informal* a line of schoolchildren walking in twos. [13c: from Latin *crocodilus*]

crocodile tears *noun* a show of pretended grief. [16c: from the belief that crocodiles wept either to allure potential victims or while eating them]

crocus *noun* a small plant with yellow, purple or white flowers and an underground **corm**. [17c: Latin]

croft *noun* esp in the Scottish Highlands: a small piece of enclosed farmland attached to a house. [Anglo-Saxon]

croissant /'krwasɑ̃/ *noun* a flaky crescent-shaped bread roll, made from puff pastry or leavened dough. [19c: French, meaning 'crescent']

Cro-Magnon *adj* relating to an early type of **Homo sapiens**, long-skulled but short-faced, of late Palaeolithic times. [From Cro-Magnon, in France, where the first skulls of this type were found]

cromlech /'krɒmlɛk/ *noun, archaeol* **1** a prehistoric stone circle. **2** *loosely* a **dolmen**. [17c: Welsh, from *crwm* curved + *llech* stone]

crone *noun, derog* an old woman. [14c: from French *carogne*]

crony *noun* (**-ies**) a close friend. [17c: orig university slang, from Greek *kronios* long-lasting]

crook *noun* **1** a bend or curve. **2** a shepherd's or bishop's hooked staff. **3** *informal* a thief or swindler; a professional criminal. ▸ *adj, Aust & NZ informal* **1** ill. **2** not working properly. **3** nasty; unpleasant. ▸ *verb* to bend or curve. [13c: from Norse *krokr* hook]

crooked /'krʊkɪd/ *adj* **1** bent, curved, angled or twisted. **2** not straight; tipped at an angle. **3** *informal* dishonest. ▪ **crookedly** *adv.* ▪ **crookedness** *noun.*

croon *verb, tr & intr* to sing in a subdued tone and sentimental style. ▸ *noun* this style of singing. ▪ **crooner** *noun.* [15c: prob from Dutch *cronen* to lament]

crop *noun* **1** a plant that is cultivated to produce food for people, fodder for animals, or raw materials, eg cereals, barley, etc. **2** the total yield produced by or harvested from such a plant, or from a certain area of cultivated land, such as a field. **3** a batch; a bunch: *this year's crop of graduates.* **4** a very short style of haircut. **5** **a** a whip handle; **b** a horserider's short whip. **6** *zool* in the gullet of birds: the thin-walled pouch where food is stored before it is digested. Also called **craw**. ▸ *verb* (**cropped, cropping**) **1** to trim; to cut short. **2** of animals: to feed on grass, etc. **3** to reap or harvest a cultivated crop. **4** *intr* of land: to produce a crop. [Anglo-Saxon *cropp*]

PHRASAL VERBS **crop up** *informal* to occur or appear unexpectedly.

crop circle *noun* a flattened circle, of uncertain origin, in a field of arable crop. Also called **corn circle**.

cropper *noun* a person or thing that crops.

IDIOMS **come a cropper** *informal* **1** to fall heavily. **2** to fail disastrously.

crop top *noun* a garment for the upper body, cut short to reveal the wearer's stomach.

croquet /'kroʊkeɪ/ *noun* a game played on a lawn, in which the players use mallets to drive wooden balls through a sequence of hoops. [19c: apparently French, diminutive of *croc* hook]

croquette /kroʊ'kɛt/ *noun* a ball or round cake made from eg minced meat, fish, potato, etc which is coated in breadcrumbs and fried. [18c: French, from *croquer* to crunch]

crosier *or* **crozier** *noun* a bishop's hooked staff, carried as a symbol of office. [15c: from French *crossier* one who bears a cross]

cross *noun* **1** **a** a mark, structure or symbol composed of two lines, one crossing the other in the form + or ×; **b** the mark × indicating a mistake or cancellation. Compare **tick**[1] (*noun* sense 3); **c** the mark × used to symbolize a kiss in a letter, etc. **2** a vertical post with a shorter horizontal bar fixed to it, on which criminals were crucified in antiquity. **3** (**the Cross**) *Christianity* **a** the cross on which Christ was crucified, or a representation of it; **b** this as a symbol of Christianity. **4** a variation of this symbol, eg the **Maltese cross**. **5** a burden or affliction: *have one's own cross to bear.* **6** **a** a monument in the form of a cross; **b** as a place name: the site of such a monument. **7** a medal in the form of a cross. **8** a plant or animal produced by crossing two different strains, breeds or varieties of a species in order to produce an improved hybrid offspring. **9** a mixture or compromise: *a cross between a bedroom and a living room.* **10** *sport, esp football* a pass of (a ball, etc) from the wing to the centre. ▸ *verb* **1** *tr & intr* (*often* **cross over**) to move, pass or get across (a road, a path, etc). **2** to place one across the other: *cross one's legs.* **3** *intr* to meet; to intersect. **4** *intr* of letters between two correspondents: to be in transit simultaneously. **5** to make the sign of the Cross upon (someone or oneself), usu as a blessing. **6** to make (a cheque) payable only through a bank by drawing two parallel lines across it. **7** (*usu* **cross out, off** *or* **through**) to delete or cancel something by drawing a line through it. **8** to cross-breed (two different strains, breeds or varieties of a species of animal or plant): *cross a labrador with a collie.* **9** to frustrate or thwart. **10** to cause unwanted connections between (telephone lines). **11** *sport, esp football* to pass (the ball, etc) from the wing to the centre. ▸ *adj* **1** angry; in a bad temper. **2** *in compounds* **a** across: *cross-country;* **b** intersecting or at right angles: *crossbar;* **c** contrary: *cross purposes;* **d** intermingling: *cross-breeding.* [Anglo-Saxon *cros*]

IDIOMS **cross one's heart** to make a crossing gesture over one's heart as an indication of good faith. **cross sb's mind** to occur to them.

crossbar *noun* **1** a horizontal bar between two upright posts. **2** the horizontal bar on a man's bicycle.

crossbeam *noun* a beam which stretches across from one support to another.

cross bench *noun* a seat in the House of Commons for members not belonging to the government or opposition. ▪ **cross bencher** *noun.* Compare **backbench, front bench**.

crossbill *noun* a finch with a beak in which the points cross instead of meeting.

crossbones *plural noun* a pair of crossed femurs appearing beneath the skull in the **skull and crossbones**.

crossbow *noun* a bow placed crosswise on a **stock** (*noun* sense 5), with a crank to pull back the bow and a trigger to release arrows.

cross-breed *biol, verb* to mate (two animals or plants of different pure breeds) in order to produce offspring in which the best characteristics of both parents are combined. ▸ *noun* an animal or plant that has been bred from two different pure breeds.

crosscheck *verb* to verify (information) from an independent source. ▶ *noun* a check of this kind.

cross-country *adj, adv* across fields, etc rather than on roads.

cross cut *noun* a transverse or diagonal cut. ▶ *adj* cut transversely. ▶ *verb* (**cross-cut**) to cut across.

cross-dress *verb, intr* esp of men: to dress in the clothes of the opposite sex. ▪ **cross-dressing** *noun*. Compare **transvestite**.

cross-examine *verb* **1** *law* to question (esp a witness for the opposing side) so as to develop or throw doubt on his or her statement. **2** to question very closely. ▪ **cross-examination** *noun*. ▪ **cross-examiner** *noun*.

cross-eyed *adj* **1** squinting. **2** having an abnormal condition in which one or both eyes turn inwards towards the nose.

cross-fertilization *or* **-isation** *noun* **1** in animals: the fusion of male and female **gamete**s from different individuals to produce an offspring. **2** in plants: another name for **cross-pollination**. **3** the fruitful interaction of ideas from different cultures, etc. ▪ **cross-fertilize** *or* **-ise** *verb*.

crossfire *noun* **1** gunfire coming from different directions. **2** a bitter or excited exchange of opinions, arguments, etc.

cross-grained *adj* of timber: having the grain or fibres crossing or intertwined.

crosshatch *verb, tr & intr, art* to shade with intersecting sets of parallel lines.

crossing *noun* **1** the place where two or more things cross each other. **2** a place for crossing a river, road, etc. **3** a journey across something, esp the sea: *a rough crossing*. **4** an act of cross-breeding.

cross-legged *adj, adv* sitting, usu on the floor, with the ankles crossed and knees wide apart.

cross-over *adj* **1** referring or relating to something moving from one side to another. **2** referring or relating to something which spans two different genres (see **genre** sense 1).

crosspatch *noun, informal* a bad-tempered or grumpy person.

cross-ply *adj* of a tyre: having fabric cords in the outer casing that run diagonally to stiffen and strengthen the side walls. See also **radial-ply tyre** under **radial**.

cross-pollination *noun, botany* the transfer of pollen from the **anther** of one flower to the **stigma** (sense 2) of another flower of the same species, by wind dispersal, formation of pollen tubes, etc.

cross-purposes *plural noun* confusion in a conversation or action by misunderstanding.
IDIOMS **be at cross purposes** to misunderstand or clash with one another.

cross-question *verb* to cross-examine. ▶ *noun* a question asked during a cross-examination.

cross-refer *verb, tr & intr* to direct (the reader) from one part of a text to another. ▪ **cross-reference** *noun*.

crossroads *singular noun* **1** the point where two or more roads cross or meet. **2** a point at which an important choice has to be made.

cross section *noun* **1 a** the surface revealed when a solid object is sliced through, esp at right angles to its length; **b** a diagram representing this. **2** a representative sample. ▪ **cross-sectional** *adj*.

cross-stitch *needlecraft, noun* an embroidery stitch made by two stitches crossing each other. ▶ *verb* to embroider with this stitch.

crosstalk *noun* **1** unwanted interference between communication channels. **2** fast and clever conversation; repartee.

crosswind *noun* a wind blowing across the path of a vehicle or aircraft.

crosswise *or* **crossways** *adj, adv* **1** lying or moving across, or so as to cross. **2** in the shape of a cross.

crossword *or* **crossword puzzle** *noun* a puzzle in which numbered clues are solved and their answers in words inserted into their correct places in a grid of squares that cross vertically and horizontally.

crotch *noun* **1** (*also* **crutch**) **a** the place where the body or a pair of trousers forks into the two legs; **b** the human genital area. **2** the fork of a tree. [16c: variant of **crutch**]

crotchet *noun, music* a note equal to two **quaver**s or half a **minim** (sense 1) in length. [15c: French, meaning 'hooked staff']

crotchety *adj, informal* irritable; peevish.

crouch *verb, intr* (*sometimes* **crouch down**) **1** to bend low or squat with one's knees and thighs against one's chest. **2** of animals: to lie close to the ground ready to spring up. ▶ *noun* a crouching position or action. [14c]

croup[1] /kruːp/ *noun* a condition, esp in young children, characterized by inflammation and consequent narrowing of the larynx, resulting in a hoarse cough, difficulty in breathing and fever. [18c: imitating the sound]

croup[2] /kruːp/ *noun* the rump or hindquarters of a horse. [13c: from French *croupe*]

croupier /ˈkruːpɪeɪ/ *noun* in a casino: someone who presides over a gaming-table, collecting the stakes, dealing the cards, paying the winners, etc. [18c: French, literally meaning 'one who rides pillion on a horse']

croûton *noun* a small cube of fried or toasted bread, served in soup, etc. [19c: French, diminutive of *croûte* crust]

crow *noun* **1** a large black bird, usu with a powerful black beak and shiny feathers. **2** the shrill drawn-out cry of a cock. ▶ *verb* (*past tense* ***crowed*** *or* ***crew***) *intr* **1** of a cock: to cry shrilly. **2** of a baby: to make happy inarticulate sounds. **3** (*usu* **crow over sb** *or* **sth**) to triumph gleefully over them or it; to gloat. [Anglo-Saxon *crawa*]
IDIOMS **as the crow flies** in a straight line.

crowbar *noun* a heavy iron bar with a bent flattened end, used as a lever.

crowd *noun* **1** a large number of people gathered together. **2** the spectators or audience at an event. **3** (*usu* **crowds**) *informal* a large number of people. **4** (**the crowd**) the general mass of people. ▶ *verb* **1** *intr* to gather or move in a large, usu tightly-packed, group. **2** to fill. **3** to pack; to cram. **4** to press round, or supervise someone too closely. ▪ **crowded** *adj*. [Anglo-Saxon *crudan* to press]
PHRASAL VERBS **crowd sb** *or* **sth out** to overwhelm and force them out.

crown *noun* **1** the circular, usu jewelled, gold headdress of a sovereign. **2** (**the Crown**) **a** the sovereign as head of state; **b** the authority or jurisdiction of a sovereign or of the government representing a sovereign. **3** a wreath for the head or other honour, awarded for victory or success. **4** a highest point of achievement: *the crown of one's career.* **5** the top, esp of something rounded. **6 a** the part of a tooth projecting from the gum; **b** an artificial replacement for this. **7** a representation of a royal crown used as an emblem, symbol, etc. **8** an old British coin worth 25 pence (formerly 5 shillings). ▸ *verb* **1** to place a crown ceremonially on the head of someone, thus making them a monarch. **2** to be on or round the top of someone or something. **3** to reward; to make complete or perfect: *efforts crowned with success.* **4** to put an artificial crown on (a tooth). **5** *informal* to hit on the head. **6** *draughts* to give (a piece) the status of king, by placing another piece on top of it. [11c: from French *coroune*]

IDIOMS **to crown it all** *informal* as the finishing touch to a series of esp unfortunate events.

crown colony *noun* a colony under the direct control of the British government.

crown jewels *plural noun* the crown, sceptre and other ceremonial regalia of a sovereign.

crown prince *noun* the male heir to a throne.

crown princess *noun* **1** the wife of a crown prince. **2** the female heir to a throne.

crow's feet *plural noun* the wrinkles at the outer corner of the eye.

crow's nest *noun* at the top of a ship's mast: a lookout platform.

crozier see **crosier**

cruces see **crux**

crucial *adj* **1** decisive; critical. **2** very important; essential. **3** *slang* very good; great. ▪ **crucially** *adv.* [19c: from Latin *crux* cross]

crucible *noun* **1** an earthenware pot in which to heat metals or other substances. **2** a severe test or trial. [15c: from Latin *crucibulum* a night lamp]

crucifix *noun* a representation, esp a model, of Christ on the cross. [13c: from Latin *crucifixus* one fixed to a cross]

crucifixion *noun* **1** execution by crucifying. **2** (**Crucifixion**) *Christianity* the crucifying of Christ, or a representation of this. [17c: from Latin *crucifixio*]

cruciform *adj* cross-shaped. [17c: from Latin *crux* cross + **-form**]

crucify *verb* (**-ies, -ied**) **1** to put to death by fastening or nailing to a cross by the hands and feet. **2** to torture or persecute someone. **3** *slang* to defeat or humiliate someone utterly. [13c: from French *crucifier*]

crud *noun, slang* dirt or filth, esp if sticky. ▪ **cruddy** *adj* (**-ier, -iest**). [20c: variant of the earlier **curd**]

crude *adj* **1** in its natural unrefined state. **2** rough or undeveloped: *a crude sketch.* **3** vulgar; tasteless. ▸ *noun* (also **crude oil**) petroleum in its unrefined state. ▪ **crudely** *adv.* [14c: from Latin *crudus* raw]

cruel *adj* (**crueller, cruellest**) **1** deliberately and pitilessly causing pain or suffering. **2** painful; distressing: *a cruel blow.* ▪ **cruelly** *adv.* ▪ **cruelty** *noun* (**-ies**) [13c: French]

cruet *noun* **1** a small container which holds salt, pepper, mustard, vinegar, etc, for use at table. **2** a stand for a set of such jars. [14c: French, diminutive of *crue* jar]

cruise *verb* **1** *tr & intr* to sail about for pleasure, calling at a succession of places. **2** *intr* eg of a vehicle or aircraft: to go at a steady comfortable speed. ▸ *noun* an instance of cruising, esp an ocean voyage undertaken for pleasure. [17c: from Dutch *kruisen* to cross]

cruise missile *noun* a low-flying, long-distance, computer-controlled winged missile.

cruiser *noun* **1** a large fast warship. **2** (*also* **cabin-cruiser**) a large, esp luxurious motor boat with living quarters.

cruiserweight *noun* **1** a class for boxers, wrestlers and weightlifters of not more than a specified weight, which is 86kg (190 lb) in professional boxing, and similar weights in the other sports. **2** a boxer, etc of this weight.

crumb *noun* **1** a particle of dry food, esp bread. **2** a small amount: *a crumb of comfort.* [Anglo-Saxon *cruma*]

crumble *verb* **1** *tr & intr* to break into crumbs or powdery fragments. **2** *intr* to collapse, decay or disintegrate. ▸ *noun* a baked dessert of stewed fruit covered with a crumbled mixture of sugar, butter and flour. ▪ **crumbly** *adj* (**-ier, -iest**). [15c as *kremelen*]

crumby *adj* (**-ier, -iest**) **1** full of or in crumbs. **2** soft like the inside of a loaf. **3** see **crummy**. [18c: from **crumb**]

crummy *adj* (**-ier, -iest**) *informal, derog* shoddy, dingy, dirty or generally inferior. [19c: variant of **crumby**]

crumpet *noun* **1** a thick round cake made of soft light dough, eaten toasted and buttered. **2** *offensive slang* **a** a woman; **b** female company generally.

crumple *verb* **1** *tr & intr* to make or become creased or crushed. **2** *intr* of a face or features: to pucker in distress. **3** *intr* to collapse; to give away. [From Anglo-Saxon *crump* crooked]

crumple zone *noun* part of a car, usu at the front or rear, designed to absorb the impact in a collision.

crunch *verb* **1** *tr & intr* to crush or grind noisily between the teeth or under the foot. **2** *intr* to produce a crunching sound. **3** *tr & intr, comput, informal* to process (large quantities of data, numbers, etc) at speed. ▸ *noun* **1** a crunching action or sound. **2** (**the crunch**) *informal* the moment of decision or crisis. ▸ *adj* crucial or decisive: *crunch talks.* [19c: imitating the sound]

crunchy *adj* (**-ier, -iest**) able to be crunched; crisp. ▪ **crunchiness** *noun.*

crusade *noun* **1** a strenuous campaign in aid of a cause. **2** (**Crusades**) *hist* any of the eight Holy Wars from 1096 onwards, which were fought to recover the Holy Land from the Muslims. ▸ *verb, intr* to engage in a crusade; to campaign. ▪ **crusader** *noun.* [16c: from French *croisade*]

crush *verb* **1** to break, damage, bruise, injure or distort by compressing violently. **2** to grind or pound into powder, crumbs, etc. **3** *tr & intr* to crumple or crease. **4** to defeat, subdue or humiliate. ▸ *noun* **1** violent compression. **2** a dense crowd. **3** a drink made from the juice of crushed fruit: *orange crush.* **4** *informal* **a** an amorous passion, usu an unsuitable one; an infatuation; **b** the object of such an infatuation. ▪ **crushing** *adj.* [14c: from French *croissir*]

crush barrier *noun* a barrier for separating a crowd, eg of spectators, into sections.

crust *noun* **1 a** the hard-baked outer surface of a loaf of bread; **b** a piece of this; a dried-up piece of bread. **2** the pastry covering a pie, etc. **3** a crisp or brittle covering. ▸ *verb, tr & intr* to cover with or form a crust.

crustacean *noun, zool* any invertebrate animal which typically possesses two pairs of antennae and a segmented body covered in a chalky **carapace**, eg crabs, lobsters, woodlice, etc. ▸ *adj* relating to these creatures. [19c: from Latin *crusta* shell]

crusty *adj* (**-ier, -iest**) **1** having a crisp crust. **2** irritable, snappy or cantankerous. ▪ **crustiness** *noun.*

crutch *noun* **1** a stick, usu one of a pair, used as a support by a lame person, with a bar fitting under the armpit or a grip for the elbow. **2** a support, help or aid. **3** *Brit* another word for **crotch** (sense 1). ▸ *verb, Aust, NZ* to cut off wool from the hindquarters of a sheep. [Anglo-Saxon *crycc*]

crux *noun* (**cruces** /ˈkruːsiːz/ *or* **cruxes**) a decisive, essential or crucial point. [18c: Latin, meaning 'cross']

cry *verb* (**cries, cried**) **1** *intr* to shed tears; to weep. **2** *intr* (*often* **cry out**) to shout or shriek, eg in pain or fear, or to get attention or help. **3** (*often* **cry out**) to exclaimation (words, news, etc). **4** *intr* of an animal or bird: to utter its characteristic noise. ▸ *noun* (**cries**) **1** a shout or shriek. **2** an excited utterance or exclamation. **3** an appeal or demand. **4** a bout of weeping. **5** the characteristic utterance of an animal or bird. [13c: from French *crier*]

IDIOMS **a far cry 1** a great distance. **2** very different. **cry one's eyes** *or* **heart out** to weep long and bitterly. **cry over spilt milk** to cry over something which cannot be changed.

PHRASAL VERBS **cry off** *informal* to cancel an engagement or agreement. **cry out for sth** to be in obvious need of it.

crybaby *noun, derog, informal* a person, esp a child, who weeps at the slightest upset.

crying *adj* demanding urgent attention: *a crying need.*

cryogenics *singular noun* the branch of physics concerned with very low temperatures, and of the phenomena that occur at such temperatures. [1950s]

cryopreservation *or* **cryonics** /kraɪˈɒnɪks/ *noun, biol* the preservation by freezing of living cells, esp the practice of freezing human corpses with the idea that advances in science will enable them to be revived at a later date.

crypt *noun* an underground chamber or vault, esp one beneath a church, often used for burials. [18c: from Latin *crypta*]

cryptic *adj* **1** puzzling, mysterious, obscure or enigmatic. **2** secret or hidden. **3** of a crossword puzzle: with clues in the form of riddles, puns, anagrams, etc. ▪ **cryptically** *adv.* [17c: from Greek *kryptikos*]

cryptogam *noun, botany* a general term for a plant that reproduces by means of spores, eg a seaweed, moss or fern. [19c: from Greek *kryptein* to hide + *gamos* marriage]

cryptogram *noun* something written in a code.

cryptography *noun* the study of writing in and deciphering codes. ▪ **cryptographer** *noun.* ▪ **cryptographic** *adj.*

crystal *noun* **1** (*also* **rock crystal**) colourless transparent quartz. **2 a** a brilliant, highly transparent glass used for cut glass; **b** cut-glass articles. **3** *chem* any solid substance consisting of a regularly repeating arrangement of atoms, ions or molecules. **4** *elec* a crystalline element, made of piezoelectric or semiconductor material, that functions as a transducer, oscillator, etc in an electronic device. ▸ *adj* belonging or relating to, or made of, crystal. [11c: from Latin *crystallum*]

IDIOMS **crystal clear** as clear or obvious as can be.

crystal ball *noun* a globe of rock crystal or glass into which a fortune-teller or clairvoyant gazes, apparently seeing visions of the future.

crystal-gazing *noun* **1** a fortune-teller's practice of gazing into a crystal ball long and hard enough to apparently conjure up a vision of the future. **2** *derog* guesswork about the future. ▪ **crystal-gazer** *noun.*

crystalline *adj* **1** composed of or having the clarity and transparency of crystal. **2** *chem* displaying the properties or structure of crystals, eg with regard to the regular internal arrangement of atoms, ions or molecules.

crystallize *or* **-ise** *verb* **1** *tr & intr* to form crystals. **2** to coat or preserve (fruit) in sugar. **3** *tr & intr* of plans, ideas, etc: to make or become clear and definite. ▪ **crystallization** *noun.*

crystallography *noun* the scientific study of the structure, forms and properties of crystals. ▪ **crystallographer** *noun.*

Cs *symbol, chem* caesium.

c/s *abbrev* cycles per second.

CSA *abbrev* Child Support Agency.

CS gas *noun* an irritant vapour which causes a burning sensation in the eyes, choking, nausea and vomiting, used in riot control. [1928: named from the initials of its US inventors, B Carson & R Staughton]

Ct *abbrev* in addresses, etc: Court.

ct *abbrev* **1** carat. **2** cent. **3** court.

CT scanner *noun* a computer-assisted tomography or computed axial tomography scanner, a machine that produces X-ray images of cross-sectional 'slices' through the brain or other soft body tissues. Formerly called a **CAT scanner**.

Cu *symbol, chem* copper.

cu *abbrev* cubic.

cub *noun* **1** the young of certain carnivorous mammals, such as the fox, wolf, lion and bear. **2** (**Cub**) a member of the junior branch of the Scout Association. Also called **Cub Scout**. Compare **Brownie Guide**. ▸ *verb* (**cubbed, cubbing**) *tr & intr* to give birth to cubs. [16c]

Cuban *adj* belonging or relating to Cuba, an island republic in the Caribbean Sea, or its inhabitants. ▸ *noun* a citizen or inhabitant of, or person born in, Cuba.

cubbyhole *noun, informal* **1** a tiny room. **2** a cupboard, nook or recess in which to accumulate miscellaneous objects. [19c: from dialect *cub* stall or pen]

cube *noun* **1** *maths* a solid figure having six square faces of equal area. **2** a block of this shape. **3** *maths* the product of any number or quantity multiplied by its square, ie the third power of a number or quantity. ▸ *verb* **1** to raise (a number or quantity) to the third power. **2** to form or cut into cubes. [16c: French]

cube root *noun, maths* the number or quantity of which a given number or quantity is the cube, eg 3 is the cube root of 27 since $3 \times 3 \times 3 = 27$.

cubic *adj* **1** relating to or resembling a cube. **2** having three dimensions. **3** *maths* of or involving a number or quantity that is raised to the third power, eg a cubic equation (in which the highest power of the unknown variable is three). **4** *maths* of a unit of volume: equal to that contained in a cube of specified dimensions.

cubicle *noun* a small compartment for sleeping or undressing in, screened for privacy. [15c: from Latin *cubiculum* bedchamber]

Cubism *noun, art* an early-20c movement in painting which represented natural objects as geometrical shapes. ▪ **Cubist** *noun, adj.*

cubit *noun* an old unit of measurement equal to the length of the forearm. [14c: from Latin *cubitum* elbow]

cuboid *adj* (*also* **cuboidal**) resembling a cube in shape. ▸ *noun, maths* a solid body having six rectangular faces, the opposite faces of which are equal.

Cub Scout see **cub** (*noun* sense 2)

cuckold *old use, derisive, noun* a man whose wife is unfaithful. ▸ *verb* to make a cuckold of (a man). [13c: from French *cocu* cuckoo]

cuckoo *noun* an insectivorous bird which lays its eggs in the nests of other birds. ▸ *adj, informal* insane; crazy. [13c: from French *cucu*, imitating the sound of the bird's two-tone call]

cuckoo clock *noun* a clock from which a model cuckoo springs on the hour, uttering the appropriate number of cries.

cuckoo-pint *noun* a European plant with large leaves shaped like arrow-heads, and a pale-green **spathe** partially surrounding a club-shaped **spadix**.

cuckoo spit *noun* a white frothy mass found on the leaves and stems of plants, surrounding and secreted by the larvae of some insects. Also called **frog-spit**.

cucumber *noun* **1** a creeping plant cultivated for its edible fruit. **2** a long green fruit of this plant, containing juicy white flesh, which is often used raw in salads, etc. [14c: from Latin *cucumis*]

cud *noun* in ruminant animals: partially digested food that is regurgitated from the first stomach into the mouth to be chewed again. [Anglo-Saxon *cwidu*]
IDIOMS **chew the cud** *informal* to meditate, ponder or reflect.

cuddle *verb* **1** *tr & intr* to hug or embrace affectionately. **2** (*usu* **cuddle in** *or* **up**) to lie close and snug; to nestle. ▸ *noun* an affectionate hug. ▪ **cuddly** *adj* (***-ier, -iest***) pleasant to cuddle.

cudgel *noun* a heavy stick or club used as a weapon. ▸ *verb* (***cudgelled, cudgelling***) to beat with a cudgel. [Anglo-Saxon *cycgel*]

cue[1] *noun* **1** the end of an actor's speech, or something else said or done by a performer, that serves as a prompt for another to say or do something. **2** anything that serves as a signal or hint to do something. ▸ *verb* (***cueing***) to give a cue to someone. [16c: thought to be from 'q', a contraction of Latin *quando* meaning 'when' which was formerly written in actors' scripts to show them when to begin]
IDIOMS **on cue** at precisely the right moment.

cue[2] *noun* in billiards, snooker and pool: a stick tapering almost to a point, used to strike the ball. ▸ *verb* (***cueing***) *tr & intr* to strike (a ball) with the cue. [18c: variant of **queue**]

cue ball *noun* in billiards, snooker and pool: the ball which is struck by the cue.

cuff[1] *noun* **1** a band or folded-back part at the lower end of a sleeve, usu at the wrist. **2** *N Am* the turned-up part of a trouser leg. **3** (**cuffs**) *slang* handcuffs. [15c]
IDIOMS **off the cuff** *informal* without preparation or previous thought.

cuff[2] *noun* a blow with the open hand. ▸ *verb* to hit with an open hand. [16c]

cufflink *noun* one of a pair of decorative fasteners for shirt cuffs, used in place of buttons.

cuisine /kwɪ'ziːn/ *noun* **1** a style of cooking. **2** the range of food prepared and served at a restaurant, etc. [18c: French, meaning 'kitchen']

cul-de-sac /'kʌldəsak/ *noun* (***culs-de-sac*** /'kʌldəsak/ *or* ***cul-de-sacs***) a street closed at one end; a blind alley. [18c: French, meaning 'sack-bottom']

culinary *adj* relating to cookery or the kitchen. [17c: from Latin *culinarius*]

cull *verb* **1** to gather or pick up (information or ideas). **2** to select and kill (weak or surplus animals) from a group, eg seals or deer, in order to keep the population under control. ▸ *noun* **1** an act of culling. **2** an inferior animal eliminated from the herd, flock, etc. [14c: from French *cuillir* to gather]

culminate *verb, tr & intr* (*often* **culminate in** *or* **with sth**) to reach the highest point or climax. ▪ **culmination** *noun.* [17c: from Latin *culminare*]

culottes *plural noun* wide-legged trousers for women, intended to look like a skirt. [20c: French, meaning 'knee-breeches']

culpable *adj* deserving blame. ▪ **culpability** *noun.* [14c: from Latin *culpare* to blame]

culprit *noun* someone guilty of a misdeed or offence. [17c: from the fusion of French *culpable* guilty + *prest* ready]

cult *noun* **1 a** a system of religious belief; **b** the sect of people following such a system. **2** an esp extravagant admiration for a person, idea, etc. ▪ **cultic** *adj.* [17c: from Latin *cultus* worship]

cultivate *verb* **1** to prepare and use (land or soil) for growing crops. **2** to grow (a crop, plant, etc). **3** to develop or improve: *cultivate a taste for literature.* **4** to try to develop a friendship, a relationship, etc with (someone), esp for personal advantage. [17c: from Latin *cultivare*]

cultivated *adj* well bred and knowledgeable.

cultivation *noun* **1** the act of cultivating. **2** education, breeding and culture.

cultivator *noun* **1** a tool for breaking up the surface of the ground. **2** someone or something which cultivates.

cultural *adj* **1** relating to a culture. **2** relating to the arts. ▪ **culturally** *adv.*

culture *noun* **1** the customs, ideas, values, etc of a particular civilization, society or social group, esp at a particular time. **2** appreciation of art, music, literature, etc. **3** improvement and development through care and training: *beauty culture.* **4** *biol* a population of micro-organisms (esp bacteria), cells or tissues grown in a **culture medium** usu for scientific study or medical diagnosis. ▸ *verb* to grow (micro-organisms, cells, etc) in a **culture medium** for study. [15c: from Latin *cultura*]

cultured *adj* **1** well-educated; having refined tastes and manners. **2** of micro-organisms, cells or tissues: grown in a **culture medium**.

culture medium *noun, biol* a solid or liquid nutrient medium in which micro-organisms, cells or tissues can be grown under controlled conditions in a laboratory. Sometimes shortened to **medium**.

culture shock *noun, sociol* disorientation caused by a change from a familiar environment, culture, ideology, etc, to another that is radically different or alien.

culture vulture *noun, informal* someone who is extremely interested in the arts.

culvert *noun* a covered drain or channel carrying water or electric cables underground.

-cum- *combining form* combined with; also used as: *kitchen-cum-dining room.* [Latin *cum* with]

cumbersome *adj* unwieldy or unmanageable.

cumin *or* **cummin** /ˈkʌmɪn/ *noun* **1** an umbelliferous plant of the Mediterranean region. **2** the seeds of this plant used as an aromatic herb or flavouring. [Anglo-Saxon *cymen*]

cummerbund *noun* a wide sash worn around the waist, esp one worn with a dinner jacket. [17c: from Hindi *kamarband* loin band]

cumulative /ˈkjuːmjʊlətiv/ *adj* increasing in amount, effect or strength with each successive addition.

cumulonimbus /kjuːmjʊloʊˈnɪmbəs/ *noun, meteorol* a type of cumulus cloud, with a dark and threatening appearance, and associated with thunderstorms.

cumulus /ˈkjuːmjʊləs/ *noun* (***cumuli*** /-laɪ/) *meteorol* a fluffy heaped cloud with a rounded white upper surface and a flat horizontal base, which usu develops over a heat source, eg a volcano or hot land.

cuneiform /ˈkjuːnɪfɔːm/ *adj* **1** relating to any of several ancient Middle-Eastern scripts with wedge-shaped characters. **2** wedge-shaped. ▸ *noun* cuneiform writing. [17c: from Latin *cuneus* wedge + **-form**]

cunning *adj* **1** clever, sly or crafty. **2** ingenious, skilful or subtle. ▸ *noun* **1** slyness; craftiness. **2** skill; expertise. [From Anglo-Saxon *cunnan* to know]

cup *noun* **1** a small, round, open container, usu with a handle, used to drink from. **2** the amount a cup will hold, used as a measure in cookery. **3** a container or something else shaped like a cup: *egg cup.* **4** an ornamental trophy awarded as a prize in sports competitions, etc. **5** a competition in which the prize is a cup. **6** a wine-based drink, with added fruit juice, etc: *claret cup.* **7** *literary* something that one undergoes or experiences: *one's own cup of woe.* ▸ *verb* (***cupped, cupping***) **1** to form (one's hands) into a cup shape. **2** to hold something in one's cupped hands. [Anglo-Saxon *cuppe*]

IDIOMS **one's cup of tea** *informal* one's personal preference.

cupboard *noun* a piece of furniture or a recess, fitted with doors, shelves, etc, for storing provisions, etc. [Anglo-Saxon *cuppebord* table for crockery]

cupboard love *noun* an insincere show of affection towards someone or something in return for some kind of material gain.

cupful *noun* the amount a cup will hold.

cupid *noun* a figure of Cupid, the Roman god of love, represented in art or sculpture. [14c: from Latin *cupido* desire or love]

cupidity *noun* greed for wealth and possessions. [15c: from Latin *cupiditas*]

cupola /ˈkjuːpələ/ *noun* **1** a small dome or turret on a roof. **2** a domed roof or ceiling. **3** an armoured revolving gun turret. [16c: Italian]

cuppa *noun, Brit informal* a cup of tea. [20c: altered form of *cup of*]

cupric /ˈkjuːprɪk/ *adj, chem* denoting any compound of copper in which the element has a **valency** of two, eg cupric chloride. Compare **cuprous**. [18c: from Latin *cuprum* copper]

cupro-nickel /kjuːproʊˈnɪkəl/ *noun* an alloy of copper and nickel that is resistant to corrosion, used to make silver-coloured coins in the UK.

cuprous /ˈkjuːprəs/ *adj, chem* denoting any compound of copper in which the element has a **valency** of one, eg cuprous chloride. Compare **cupric**. [17c: from Latin *cuprum* copper]

cup tie *noun, sport* a knockout match in a round of a competition for a cup.

cup-tied *adj, sport, esp football* said of a player who is ineligible to play in a cup competition having already represented another team at some previous stage in the competition.

cur *noun, derog, old use* **1** a surly mongrel dog. **2** a scoundrel. [13c as *curdogge*]

curable *adj* capable of being cured.

curacy /ˈkjʊərəsɪ/ *noun* (***-ies***) the office or benefice of a curate.

curare /kjʊˈrɑːrɪ/ *noun* **1** a poisonous black resin obtained from certain tropical plants in South America, which has medicinal uses as a muscle relaxant. **2** any of the plants from which this resin is obtained. [18c: Portuguese and Spanish]

curate *noun* **1** in the Church of England: a clergyman who acts as assistant to a vicar or rector. **2** in Ireland: an assistant barman. [14c: from Latin *curatus*]

curate's egg *noun* anything of which some parts are excellent and some parts are bad. [1895: named after a cartoon in the magazine *Punch* depicting a modest curate who is served a bad egg, and states that 'parts of it are excellent']

curative *adj* able or tending to cure. ▸ *noun* a substance that cures. [16c: from Latin *curativus*]

curator *noun* the custodian of a museum or other collection. [17c: from Latin *curator* overseer]

curb *noun* **1** something that restrains or controls. **2 a** a chain or strap passing under a horse's jaw, attached at the sides to the bit; **b** a bit with such a fitting. **3** a raised edge or border. **4** *N Am* a kerb. ▸ *verb* **1** to restrain or control. **2** to put a curb on (a horse). [15c: from French *courb*]

curd *noun* **1** (*often* **curds**) the clotted protein substance, as opposed to the liquid component, formed when fresh milk is curdled, and used to make cheese, etc. Compare **whey**. **2** any of several substances of similar consistency. ▸ *verb, tr & intr* to make or turn into curd. [14c as *crud*]

curdle *verb, tr & intr* to turn into curd; to coagulate. [16c]

cure *verb* **1** to restore someone to health or normality; to heal them. **2** to get rid of (an illness, harmful habit, or other evil). **3** to preserve (food, eg meat, fish, etc) by salting, smoking, etc. **4** to preserve (leather, tobacco, etc) by drying. **5** to vulcanize (rubber). ▸ *noun* **1** something that cures or remedies. **2** restoration to health. **3** a course of healing or remedial treatment. [14c: from French *curer*]

cure-all *noun* a universal remedy.

curettage *noun* the process of using a curette. See also **dilatation and curettage**.

curette *or* **curet** *noun, surgery* a spoon-shaped device used to scrape tissue from the inner surface of an organ or body cavity. ▶ *verb* to scrape with a curette. [18c: French]

curfew *noun* **1 a** an official order restricting people's movements, esp after a certain hour at night; **b** the time at which such an order applies. **2** *hist* **a** the ringing of a bell as a signal to put out fires and lights; **b** the time at which such a ringing took place. [13c: from French *cuevrefeu*, literally 'cover the fire']

curie *noun, physics* (abbrev **Ci**) the former unit of radioactivity, which has now been replaced by the **becquerel** in SI units. [20c: named after the French physicists Marie and Pierre Curie]

curio /ˈkjʊərɪoʊ/ *noun* an article valued for its rarity or unusualness. [19c: shortened from **curiosity**]

curiosity *noun* (**-ies**) **1** eagerness to know; inquisitiveness. **2** something strange, rare, exotic or unusual. [14c: from Latin *curiositas*]

curious *adj* **1** strange; odd. **2** eager or interested. **3** inquisitive (often in an uncomplimentary sense). ▪ **curiously** *adv.* [14c: from Latin *curiosus* full of care]

curium /ˈkjʊərɪəm/ *noun, chem* (symbol **Cm**) a radioactive element formed by bombarding plutonium-239 with alpha particles. [20c: named after Marie and Pierre Curie]

curl *verb* **1** to twist, roll or wind (hair) into coils or ringlets. **2** *intr* to grow in coils or ringlets. **3** *tr & intr* to move in or form into a spiral, coil or curve. **4** *intr* to take part in the game of curling. ▶ *noun* **1** a small coil or ringlet of hair. **2** a twist, spiral, coil or curve.

IDIOMS **curl one's lip** to sneer.

PHRASAL VERBS **curl up 1** to sit or lie with the legs tucked up. **2** *informal* to writhe in embarrassment, etc.

curler *noun* **1** a type of roller for curling the hair. **2** someone who takes part in the sport of curling.

curlew *noun* a large wading bird, with a slender down-curved bill and long legs. [14c: from French *corlieu*, perhaps imitating the bird's call]

curlicue *noun* **a** a fancy twist or curl; **b** a flourish made with a pen. [19c: from **curly** + **cue**^{2}]

curling *noun* a team game played on ice with smooth heavy stones with handles, that are slid towards a circular target marked on the ice.

curling tongs *plural noun* a device which is heated up before a lock of hair is twisted around it for a short time to make a curl.

curly *adj* (**-ier, -iest**) **1** having curls; full of curls. **2** tending to curl.

curmudgeon /kəˈmʌdʒən/ *noun* a bad-tempered or mean person. ▪ **curmudgeonly** *adj.* [16c]

currant *noun* **1** a small dried seedless grape. **2** a shrub which produces a certain kind of fruit eg blackcurrant, redcurrant, etc. [16c: shortened from French *raisins de Corinthe* grapes of Corinth]

---

currant, current

Be careful not to use the spelling **currant** when you mean **current**:

current trends in music

The river has strong currents.

---

currency *noun* (**-ies**) **1** the system of money, or the coins and notes, in use in a country. **2** general acceptance or popularity, esp of an idea, theory, etc. [17c: from Latin *currere* to run]

current *adj* **1** generally accepted. **2** belonging to the present: *current affairs*. **3** in circulation; valid. ▶ *noun* **1** the continuous steady flow of a body of water, air, heat, etc, in a particular direction. **2** the rate of flow of electric charge through a conductor per unit time. **3** an **electric current**. **4** a popular trend or tendency. ▪ **currently** *adv* at the present time. [15c: from French *corant*]

---

current, currant

Be careful not to use the spelling **current** when you mean **currant**:

The cake contains currants and raisins.

---

current account *noun* a bank account from which money or cheques can be drawn without notice, and on which little or no interest is paid.

curriculum /kəˈrɪkjʊləm/ *noun* (**curricula** /-lə/ *or* **curriculums**) **1** a course of study, esp at school or university. **2** a list of all the courses available at a school, university, etc. ▪ **curricular** *adj.* [17c: Latin, from *currere* to run]

curriculum vitae /kəˈrɪkjələm ˈviːtaɪ, ˈvaɪtiː/ *noun* (**curricula vitae**) (abbrev **CV**) a written summary of one's personal details, education and career, produced to accompany job applications, etc. [20c: from **curriculum** + Latin *vita* life]

curry^{1} *noun* (**-ies**) a dish, orig Indian, of meat, fish, or vegetables usu cooked with hot spices. ▶ *verb* (**-ies, -ied**) to prepare (food) using curry powder or a curry sauce. [16c: from Tamil *kari* sauce]

curry^{2} *verb* **1** to groom (a horse). **2** to treat (tanned leather) so as to improve its flexibility, strength and waterproof quality. [13c: from French *correier* to make ready]

IDIOMS **curry favour with sb** to use flattery to gain their approval; to ingratiate oneself with them.

curry powder *noun* a preparation of various spices used to give curry its hot flavour.

curse *noun* **1** a blasphemous or obscene expression, usu of anger; an oath. **2** an appeal to God or some other divine power to harm someone. **3** the resulting harm suffered by someone: *under a curse*. **4** an evil; a cause of harm or trouble. **5** *informal* (**the curse**) menstruation; a woman's menstrual period. ▶ *verb* **1** to utter a curse against; to revile with curses. **2** *intr* to use violent language; to swear. [Anglo-Saxon *curs*]

IDIOMS **be cursed with sth** to be burdened or afflicted with it.

cursed /ˈkɜːsɪd, kɜːst/ *adj* **1** under a curse. **2** *old use* damnable; hateful.

cursive *adj* of handwriting: flowing; having letters which are joined up rather than printed separately. ▶ *noun* cursive writing. [18c: from Latin *cursivus*]

cursor *noun* **1** on the screen of a visual display unit: an underline character or a rectangular box that flashes on and off to indicate where the next character to be entered on the keyboard will appear. **2** the transparent movable part of a measuring device, esp a slide rule, which can be set at any point along the graduated scale. [16c: from Latin *cursor* runner]

cursory *adj* hasty; superficial; not thorough. ▪ **cursorily** *adv.* [17c: from Latin *cursorius* pertaining to a runner]

curt *adj* rudely brief; dismissive; abrupt. ▪ **curtly** *adv.* ▪ **curtness** *noun.* [17c: from Latin *curtus* cut]

curtail *verb* to reduce; to cut short. ▪ **curtailment** *noun*. [16c: as *curtal* something shortened]

curtain *noun* **1** a hanging cloth over a window, round a bed, etc for privacy or to exclude light. **2** *theatre* a hanging cloth in front of the stage to screen it from the auditorium. **3** *theatre* (*often* **the curtain**) the rise of the curtain at the beginning, or fall of the curtain at the end, of a stage performance, act, scene, etc. **4** something resembling a curtain: *a curtain of thick dark hair*. **5** (**curtains**) *informal* the end; death. ▸ *verb* **1** (*often* **curtain sth off**) to surround or enclose it with a curtain. **2** to supply (windows, etc) with curtains. [13c: from French *courtine*]

curtain call *noun* an audience's demand for performers to appear in front of the curtain after it has fallen, to receive further applause.

curtain-raiser *noun* **1** *theatre* a short play, etc before the main performance. **2** any introductory event.

curtsy *or* **curtsey** *noun* (***curtsies*** *or* ***curtseys***) a slight bend of the knees with one leg behind the other, performed as a formal gesture of respect by women. ▸ *verb* (***-ies, -ied***) *intr* to perform a curtsy. [16c: variant of **courtesy**]

curvaceous *adj, informal* of a woman: having a shapely figure.

curvature *noun* **a** the condition of being curved; **b** the degree of curvedness. [17c: from Latin *curvatura*]

curve *noun* **1** a line no part of which is straight, or a surface no part of which is flat. **2** any smoothly arched line or shape, like part of a circle or sphere. **3** (**curves**) *informal* the rounded contours and shapes of a woman's body. **4** any line representing measurable data, eg birth-rate on a graph. **5** *maths* any line (including a straight line) representing a series of points whose co-ordinates satisfy a particular equation. ▸ *verb, tr & intr* to form or form into a curve; to move in a curve. ▪ **curvy** *adj* (***-ier, -iest***). [16c: from Latin *curvare*]

curvilinear *adj* consisting of or bounded by a curved line.

cushion *noun* **1** a fabric case stuffed with soft material, used for making a seat comfortable, for kneeling on, etc. **2** a thick pad or something having a similar function. **3** something that gives protection from shock, reduces unpleasant effects, etc. **4** the resilient inner rim of a billiard table. ▸ *verb* **1** to reduce the unpleasant or violent effect of something. **2** to protect from shock, injury or the extremes of distress. **3** to provide or furnish with cushions. [14c: from French *cuissin*]

Cushitic *adj* belonging or relating to a group of about 30 languages spoken by people in Somalia, Kenya, Sudan and Ethiopia.

cushty /ˈkʊʃtiː/ *adj, slang* highly satisfactory, excellent. [20c: possibly related to **cushy**]

cushy *adj* (***-ier, -iest***) *informal* comfortable; easy; undemanding. [20c: from Hindi *khush* pleasant]

cusp *noun* **1** *geom* a point formed by the meeting of two curves, corresponding to the point where the two tangents coincide. **2** *astron* either point of a crescent Moon. **3** *anatomy* a sharp raised point on the grinding surface of a molar tooth. **4** *astrol* the point of transition between one sign of the zodiac and the next. [16c: from Latin *cuspis* point]

cuss *old use, informal, noun* **1** a curse. **2** a person or animal, esp if stubborn. ▸ *verb, tr & intr* to curse or swear. [19c: orig a vulgar pronunciation of **curse**]

cussed /ˈkʌsɪd/ *adj* **1** obstinate, stubborn, awkward or perverse. **2** cursed. ▪ **cussedness** *noun*.

custard *noun* **1** a sauce made with sugar, milk and cornflour. **2** (*also* **egg custard**) a baked dish or sauce of eggs and sweetened milk. [15c: altered from *crustade* pie with a crust]

custard apple *noun* a **papaw**.

custodian *noun* someone who has care of something, eg a public building or ancient monument; a guardian or curator. ▪ **custodianship** *noun*. [18c: from Latin *custodia* watch or watchman]

custody *noun* (***-ies***) **1** protective care, esp the guardianship of a child, awarded to someone by a court of law. **2** the condition of being held by the police; arrest or imprisonment. ▪ **custodial** *adj*. [15c: from Latin *custodia* watch]

custom *noun* **1** a traditional activity or practice. **2** a personal habit. **3** the body of established practices of a community; convention. **4** an established practice having the force of a law. **5** the trade or business that one gives to a shop, etc by regular purchases. ▸ *adj* made to order. [12c: from French *costume*]

customary *adj* usual; traditional; according to custom. ▪ **customarily** *adv*.

custom-built *or* **custom-made** *adj* built or made to an individual customer's requirements.

customer *noun* **1** someone who purchases goods from a shop, uses the services of a business, etc. **2** *informal* a person, usu with a specified quality: *an awkward customer*.

custom house *noun* the office at a port, etc where customs duties are paid or collected.

customs *plural noun* taxes or duties paid on imports. ▸ *singular noun* **1** the government department that collects these taxes. **2** the place at a port, airport or frontier where baggage is inspected for goods on which duty must be paid and illegal goods.

cut *verb* (***cut, cutting***) **1** *tr & intr* (*also* **cut sth off** *or* **out**) to slit, pierce, slice or sever (a person or thing) using a sharp instrument. **2** (*often* **cut sth up**) to divide something by cutting. **3** to trim (hair, nails, etc). **4** to reap or mow (corn, grass, etc). **5** to prune (flowers or plants). **6** (*sometimes* **cut sth out**) to make or form it by cutting. **7** to shape the surface of (a gem) into facets, or decorate (glass) by cutting. **8** to shape the pieces of (a garment): *He cuts clothes so that they hang perfectly.* **9** to make (a sound recording). **10** to hurt: *cut someone to the heart*. **11** to reduce (eg prices, wages, interest rates, working hours, etc). **12** to shorten or abridge (eg a book or play). **13** to delete or omit. **14** to edit (a film). **15** *intr* to stop filming. **16** *intr, cinema* of a film or camera: to change directly to another shot, etc. **17** *maths* to cross or intersect. **18** to reject or renounce: *cut one's links with one's family.* **19** *informal* to ignore or pretend not to recognize someone. **20** to stop: *The alcoholic was told to cut his drinking.* **21** *informal* to absent oneself from something: *cut classes*. **22** to switch off (an engine, etc). **23** of a baby: to grow (teeth). **24** *intr* (*usu* **cut across** *or* **through**) to go off in a certain direction; to take a short route. **25** to dilute (eg an alcoholic drink) or adulterate (a drug). **26** to divide; to partition: *a room cut in half by a book-*

case. ▸ *noun* **1** an act of cutting; a cutting movement or stroke. **2** a slit, incision or injury made by cutting. **3** a reduction. **4** a deleted passage in a play, etc. **5** the stoppage of an electricity supply, etc. **6** *slang* one's share of the profits. **7** a piece of meat cut from an animal. **8** the style in which clothes or hair are cut. **9** a sarcastic remark. **10** a refusal to recognize someone; a snub. **11** a short cut. **12** a channel, passage or canal. [13c as *cutten*]

IDIOMS **a cut above sth** *informal* superior to it. **cut a long story short** to come straight to the point. **cut and dried** decided; definite; settled beforehand. **cut and run** *informal* to escape smartly. **cut both ways** to have advantages and disadvantages; to bear out both sides of an argument. **cut sb dead** to ignore them completely. **cut it fine** *informal* to have or leave barely enough time, space, etc for something. **cut it out** *slang* to stop doing something bad or undesirable. **cut out for** *or* **to be sth** having the qualities needed for it. **cut sb short** to silence them by interrupting. **cut up** *informal* distressed; upset.

PHRASAL VERBS **cut across sth 1** to go against (normal procedure, etc). **2** to take a short cut through it, eg a field, etc. **cut back on sth** to reduce spending, etc. See also **cutback**. **cut down on sth** to reduce one's use of it; to do less of it. **cut in 1** to interrupt. **2** of a vehicle: to overtake and squeeze in front of another vehicle. **cut sb off** to disconnect them during a telephone call. **cut sth off 1** to separate or isolate it. **2** to stop (the supply of gas, electricity, etc). **3** to stop it or cut it short. See also **cut-off**. **cut out 1** of an engine, etc: to stop working. **2** of an electrical device: to switch off or stop automatically, usu as a safety precaution. See also **cut-out**. **cut sth out 1** to remove or delete it. **2** to clip pictures, etc out of a magazine, etc. **3** *informal* to stop doing it. **4** to exclude it from consideration. **5** to block out the light or view. See also **cut-out**.

cutaway *adj* of a diagram, etc: having outer parts omitted so as to show the interior.

cutback *noun* a reduction in spending, use of resources, etc. See also **cut back on sth** at **cut**.

cute *adj, informal* **1** attractive; pretty. **2** clever; cunning; shrewd. ▪ **cuteness** *noun*. [18c: shortened from **acute**]

cuticle /ˈkjuːtɪkəl/ *noun, anatomy* the outer layer of cells in hair, and the dead hardened skin at the base of fingernails and toenails. [17c: from Latin *cuticula*]

cutis /ˈkjuːtɪs/ *noun* the anatomical name for the skin. [17c: Latin]

cutlass *noun, hist* a short, broad, slightly curved sword. [16c: from French *coutelas*]

cutler *noun* someone who manufactures and sells cutlery. [14c: from French *coutelier*]

cutlery *noun* knives, forks and spoons used to eat food.

cutlet *noun* **1 a** a small piece of meat with a bone attached, usu cut from a rib or the neck; **b** a piece of food in this shape, not necessarily containing meat: *nut cutlet*. **2** a slice of veal. **3** a rissole of minced meat or flaked fish. [18c: from French *costelette*]

cut-off *noun* **1** the point at which something is cut off or separated. **2** a stopping of a flow or supply. **3** (**cut-offs**) *informal* shorts which have been made by cutting jeans to above the knee. See also **cut sth off** at **cut**.

cut-out *noun* **1** something which has been cut out of something else, eg a newspaper clipping. **2** a safety device for breaking an electrical circuit. See also **cut out** and **cut sth out** at **cut**.

cutter *noun* **1** a person or thing that cuts. **2** a small single-masted sailing ship.

cut-throat *adj* **1** of competition, etc: very keen and aggressive. **2** of a card game: played by three people. ▸ *noun* **1** a murderer. **2** (*also* **cut-throat razor**) a long-bladed razor that folds into its handle.

cutting *noun* **1** an extract, article or picture cut from a newspaper, etc. **2** *horticulture* a piece cut from a plant for rooting or grafting. **3** a narrow excavation made through high ground for a road or railway. ▸ *adj* **1** hurtful; sarcastic: *a cutting comment*. **2** of wind: penetrating.

cutting edge *noun* a part or area (of an organization, branch of study, etc) that breaks new ground, effects change and development, etc.

cuttlefish *noun* a mollusc related to the squid and octopus, which has a shield-shaped body containing an inner chalky plate, and a small head bearing eight arms and two long tentacles. [Anglo-Saxon *cudele* + **fish**]

CV *or* **cv** *abbrev* (***CVs***, ***cvs***) curriculum vitae.

cwm /kuːm/ *noun* in Wales: a valley. [19c: Welsh]

cwt. *abbrev* hundredweight.

cyan *noun* **1** a greenish blue colour. **2** *printing* a blue ink used as a primary colour. ▸ *adj* cyan-coloured. [19c: from Greek *kyanos* blue]

cyanide *noun* any of the poisonous salts of hydrocyanic acid, which contain the CN^- ion and smell of bitter almonds, esp potassium cyanide, which is extremely toxic.

cyanocobalamin *noun* **vitamin B_{12}**. [20c: from **cyanide** + **cobalt** + **vitamin**]

cyanogen *noun, chem* a colourless inflammable poisonous gas. [19c: from French *cyanogène*]

cyanosis *noun, pathol* a bluish discoloration of the skin usu caused by lack of oxygen in the blood. [19c]

cyber- *combining form, denoting* computers or computer networks, esp **the Internet**: *cyberspace* • *cyberterrorist*. [From cybernetic]

cybernetics *singular noun* the comparative study of communication and automatic control processes in mechanical or electronic systems, eg machines or computers, and biological systems, eg the nervous system of animals, esp humans. ▪ **cybernetic** *adj*. [1940s: from Greek *kybernetes* steersman]

cyberspace *noun* the three-dimensional artificial environment of **virtual reality**. [20c: from **cyber-** + **space**]

cyclamen /ˈsɪkləmən/ *noun* a plant with heart-shaped leaves and white, pink or red flowers with turned-back petals. ▸ *adj* coloured like a pink cyclamen. [16c: Latin]

cycle *noun* **1** a constantly repeating series of events or processes. **2** a recurring period of years; an age. **3** *physics* one of a regularly repeated set of similar changes, eg in the movement of a wave, with the duration of one cycle being equal to the **period** (*noun* sense 10) of the motion, and the rate at which a cycle is repeated per unit time being equal to its **frequency** (*noun* sense 3). **4** a series of poems, songs, plays, etc centred on a particular person or happening. **5** short for **a bicycle**; **b motorcycle**; **c**

tricycle. ▸ *verb, tr & intr* to ride a bicycle. [14c: from Greek *kyklos* circle]

cycle path *or* **cycleway** *noun, chiefly Brit* a lane or road, etc specially designed or set aside for the use of pedal cycles.

cyclic *or* **cyclical** *adj* **1** relating to, containing, or moving in a cycle. **2** recurring in cycles. **3** *chem* an organic chemical compound whose molecules contain one or more closed rings of atoms.

cyclist *noun* the rider of a bicycle, motorcycle, etc.

cyclo- *or* (*before a vowel*) **cycl-** *combining form, denoting* **1** circle; ring; cycle: *cyclometer*. **2** *chem* cyclic compound: *cyclopropane*. **3** bicycle. [From Greek *kyklos* circle]

cycloid *noun, geom* the curve traced by a point on the circumference of a circle as the circle rolls along a straight line. Compare **trochoid.** ▸ *adj* resembling a circle. ▪ **cycloidal** *adj.*

cyclone *noun* **1** *meteorol* an area of low atmospheric pressure, often associated with stormy weather, in which winds spiral inward towards the centre. Also called **depression, low.** Compare **anticyclone. 2** a violent tropical storm with torrential rain and extremely strong winds. ▪ **cyclonic** /saɪˈklɒnɪk/ *adj.* [19c: from Greek *kyklon* a whirling round]

cyclopedia *or* **cyclopaedia** *noun* an **encyclopedia.**

cyclotron *noun, physics* a circular type of **particle accelerator.** [20c]

cyder see **cider**

cygnet *noun* a young swan. See also **cob** (sense 2), **pen**[4]. [15c: from Latin *cygnus* swan]

cylinder *noun* **1** *geom* a solid figure of uniform circular cross-section, in which the curved surface is at right angles to the base. **2** a container, machine part or other object of this shape, eg a storage container for compressed gas. **3** *eng* in an internal-combustion engine: the tubular cylinder within which the chemical energy of the burning fuel is converted to the mechanical energy of a moving piston. ▪ **cylindrical** *adj.* [16c: from Latin *cylindrus*]

cymbal *noun* a thin plate-like brass percussion instrument, either beaten with a drumstick, or used as one of a pair that are struck together to produce a ringing clash. ▪ **cymbalist** *noun.* [9c: from Latin *cymbalum*]

Cymric /ˈkʌmrɪk, ˈkɪmrɪk/ *adj* belonging or relating to Wales, its inhabitants or their language. [19c: from Welsh *Cymru* Wales]

cynic *noun* **1** someone who takes a pessimistic view of human goodness or sincerity. **2** (**Cynic**) *philos* a member of a sect of ancient Greek philosophers who scorned wealth and enjoyment of life. ▸ *adj* another word for **cynical.** [16c: from Latin *cynicus*]

cynical *adj* disinclined to believe in the goodness or sincerity of others. ▪ **cynically** *adv.*

---

cynical, sceptical
Be careful not to use the word **cynical** when you mean **sceptical**. A **cynical** person is suspicious of apparently good things and people, whereas a person who is **sceptical** about something is cautious about believing or accepting it.

---

cynicism *noun* **1** the attitude, beliefs or behaviour of a cynic. **2** a cynical act, remark, etc.

cynosure /ˈsaɪnəʃʊə(r)/ *noun* the focus of attention; the centre of attraction. [16c: from Greek *Kynosoura* dog's tail, ie the Ursa Minor constellation, used as a guide by sailors]

cypher see **cipher**

cypress *noun* **a** a dark-green coniferous tree, sometimes associated with death and mourning; **b** the wood of this tree. [13c: from French *cypres*]

Cypriot *adj* belonging or relating to Cyprus, an island republic in the NE Mediterranean, its inhabitants, or their dialect. ▸ *noun* **1** a citizen or inhabitant of, or person born in, Cyprus. **2** the dialect of Greek spoken in Cyprus.

Cyrillic *adj* belonging or relating to the alphabet used for Russian, Bulgarian and other Slavonic languages. [19c: named after St Cyril who was said to have devised it]

cyst /sɪst/ *noun* **1** *pathol* an abnormal sac that contains fluid, semi-solid material or gas. **2** *anatomy* any normal sac or closed cavity. **3** *biol* a tough outer membrane which surrounds and protects certain organisms, eg bacteria, protozoa, etc, during the resting stage in their life cycle. [18c: from Greek *kystis* bladder or pouch]

cystic fibrosis *noun, pathol* a hereditary disease in which the **exocrine** glands produce abnormally thick mucus that blocks the bronchi, pancreas and intestinal glands, causing recurring bronchitis and other respiratory problems.

cystitis *noun, pathol* inflammation of the urinary bladder, which is usu caused by bacterial infection and is characterized by a desire to pass urine frequently, accompanied by a burning sensation.

-cyte *combining form, denoting* a cell: *erythrocyte* • *lymphocyte*. [From Greek *kytos* vessel]

cyto- *combining form, denoting* a cell: *cytoplasm*. [From Greek *kytos* vessel]

cytology *noun* the scientific study of the structure and function of individual cells in plants and animals. ▪ **cytological** *adj.* ▪ **cytologist** *noun.* [19c]

cytoplasm *noun, biol* the part of a living cell, excluding the **nucleus** (sense 2), that is enclosed by the cell membrane. ▪ **cytoplasmic** *adj.* [19c: from **cyto-** + Greek *plasma* body]

cytosine *noun, biochem* one of the four bases found in **nucleic acid.** See also **adenine, guanine, thymine.** [19c]

czar see **tsar**

czarina see **tsarina**

Czech /tʃɛk/ *adj* **a** belonging or relating to the Czech Republic or to its inhabitants or their language; **b** *formerly* (also **Czechoslovak, Czechoslovakian**) belonging or relating to Czechoslovakia (1918–93), its inhabitants, or their language; **c** *hist* belonging or relating to Bohemia or Moravia, their inhabitants, or their language. ▸ *noun* **1 a** a citizen or inhabitant of, or person born in, the Czech Republic; **b** *formerly* (also **Czechoslovak**) a citizen or inhabitant of, or person born in, Czechoslovakia; **c** an inhabitant of, or person born in, Bohemia or Moravia. **2** the official language of the Czech Republic. [19c: Polish]

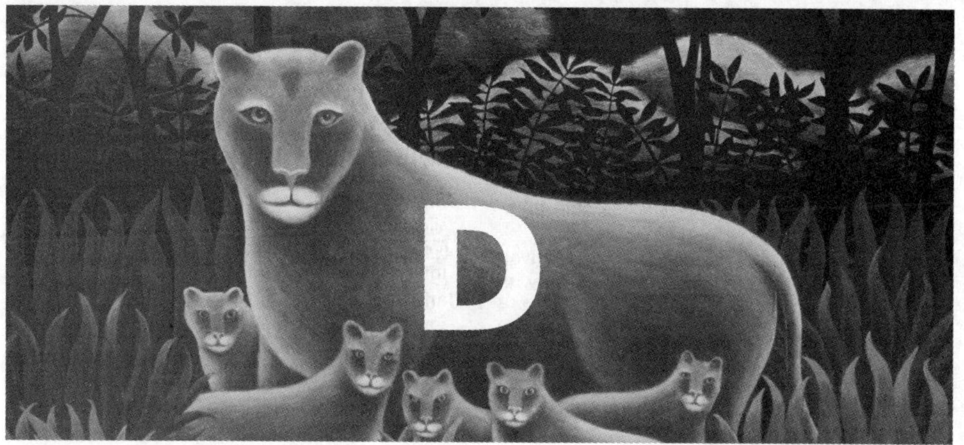

D[1] *or* **d** *noun* (***Ds, D's*** *or* ***d's***) **1** the fourth letter of the English alphabet. **2** (**D**) *music* the second note on the scale of C major. **3** (*usu* **D**) the fourth highest grade.

D[2] *symbol* **1** the Roman numeral for 500. **2** *chem* deuterium.

d *abbrev* **1** daughter. **2** day. **3** deci-. **4** *denarius* (Latin), (in the UK before 1971) a penny, or pence. **5** died.

'd *contraction* **1** would: *I'd go.* **2** had: *He'd gone.* **3** *informal* did: *Where'd they go?*

da *abbrev* deca-.

dab[1] *verb* (***dabbed, dabbing***) *tr & intr* (*often* **dab at sth**) to touch something lightly with a cloth, etc. ▸ *noun* **1** a small amount of something creamy or liquid. **2** a light touch. **3** (**dabs**) *slang* fingerprints. [14c: prob imitating the sound]

dab[2] *noun* a small brown flatfish with rough scales. [15c: from French *dabbe*]

dab[3] *noun* (*usu* **a dab hand at** *or* **with sth**) an expert. [17c]

dabble *verb* **1** *tr & intr* to move or shake (a hand, foot, etc) about in water. **2** *intr* (*often* **dabble at, in** *or* **with sth**) to do or study something without serious effort. ▪ **dabbler** *noun*. [16c: from **dab**[1] or Dutch *dabbelen*]

dace *noun* (***dace*** *or* ***daces***) a small European river fish. [15c: from French *dars* dart]

dachshund /ˈdaksənd/ *noun* a small dog with a long body and short legs. [19c: German, meaning 'badger-dog']

dactyl *noun, poetry* a foot consisting of a long or stressed syllable followed by two short or unstressed ones. ▪ **dactylic** *adj*. [14c: from Greek *daktylos* finger, a finger having one long and two short bones]

dad *or* **daddy** *noun* (***-ies***) *informal* father. [16c: from the sound *da da* made by a baby]

Dada *or* **Dadaism** *noun* a short-lived movement in art and literature, from 1916 to c.1920, which aimed to abandon all form and throw off all tradition. ▪ **Dadaist** *noun*. ▪ **Dadaistic** *adj*. [20c: from French *dada* hobby-horse]

daddy-long-legs *noun* (*pl* ***daddy-long-legs***) *Brit, Austral, NZ informal* a **cranefly**.

dado /ˈdeɪdoʊ/ *noun* (***dadoes*** *or* ***dados***) **1** the lower part of an indoor wall when different from the upper part. **2** *archit* the plain square part of the base of a column or pedestal. [17c: Italian, meaning 'dice']

daemon /ˈdiːmən/ *noun* a spirit, often a guardian spirit. Also called **demon**. ▪ **daemonic** /diːˈmɒnɪk/ *adj*. [16c: from Greek]

daffodil *noun* a plant with yellow trumpet-shaped flowers. [15c as *affodille*, from Latin *asphodelus*]

daft *adj, informal* **1** silly; foolish. **2** mad. **3** (**daft about** *or* **on sth**) enthusiastic about it; keen on it. [Anglo-Saxon *gedæfte* meek]

dag *noun, Austral informal* a scruffy, untidy person. ▪ **daggy** *adj* (***-ier, -iest***). [17c]

dagger *noun* **1** a pointed knife for stabbing. **2** *printing* the symbol †. [14c]

IDIOMS **at daggers drawn** openly showing hostility. **look daggers at sb** to give them a hostile look.

dahl see **dal**[1]

dahlia /ˈdeɪlɪə/ *noun, botany* a garden plant with large, brightly coloured flowers. [19c: named after the Swedish botanist Anders Dahl]

Dáil /dɔɪl/ *or* **Dáil Éireann** /ˈɛərən/ *noun* the lower house of the parliament of the Republic of Ireland. [20c: Irish, from *Dáil* assembly + *Éireann* of Ireland]

daily *adj* **1** happening, appearing, etc every day, or every day except Sunday, or except Saturday and Sunday. **2** relating to a single day. ▸ *adv* every day, or every weekday. ▸ *noun* (***-ies***) **1** a newspaper published every day except Sunday. **2** *informal* a person who comes in to clean and tidy a house. [Anglo-Saxon *dæglic*]

dainty *adj* (***-ier, -iest***) **1** small, pretty or delicate. **2** particularly nice to eat. **3** *often derog* very careful and sensitive about what one does or says. ▸ *noun* (***-ies***) something small and nice to eat. ▪ **daintily** *adv*. ▪ **daintiness** *noun*. [13c: from French]

daiquiri /ˈdakərɪ/ *noun* a drink made with rum, lime juice and sugar. [20c: named after Daiquiri in Cuba]

dairy *noun* (***-ies***) **1** a farm building where milk is stored or where butter and cheese are made. **2** a business or factory that bottles and distributes milk and manufactures dairy products. **3** a shop which sells milk, butter, etc. ▸ *adj* relating to milk production or milk products: *a dairy farm* • *dairy products*. [13c]

dais /ˈdeɪɪs/ *noun* a raised platform in a hall, eg for speakers. [13c: from French]

daisy *noun* (***-ies***) a small flower with heads consisting of a yellow centre surrounded by white petals. [Anglo-Saxon *dæges eage* day's eye]

daisy-wheel *noun* a rotating metal disc in a typewriter, etc consisting of spokes with letters at the end which print when the keys are struck.

dal[1], **dahl** *or* **dhal** /dɑːl/ *noun* **1** any of various edible dried split pea-like seeds. **2** a cooked dish made of these. [17c: from Hindi]

dal[2] *abbrev* decalitre or decalitres.

Dalai Lama /'dalaɪ/ *noun* the head of Tibetan Buddhism. [17c: Mongolian *dalai* ocean + **lama**]

dale *noun* a valley. [Anglo-Saxon *dæl*]

dalliance *noun, old use* **1** flirtation. **2** idle time-wasting.

dally *verb* (*-ies, -ied*) *intr* **1** to waste time idly or frivolously. **2** (*often* **dally with sb**) *old use* to flirt with them. [14c: from French]

Dalmatian /dal'meɪʃən/ *noun* a large short-haired breed of dog, white with dark spots. [19c: from *Dalmatia* in Croatia]

dam[1] *noun* **1** a barrier built to hold back water. **2** the water confined behind such a structure. ▸ *verb* (***dammed, damming***) to hold back (water, etc) with a dam. [14c: prob Dutch]

dam[2] *noun* of horses, cattle and sheep: a female parent. [14c]

dam[3] *abbrev* decametre or decametres.

damage *noun* **1** harm or injury, or loss caused by injury. **2** (**damages**) *law* payment due for loss or injury. **3** *informal* amount owed: *What's the damage?* ▸ *verb* to cause harm, injury or loss to someone or something. ▪ **damaging** *adj*. [14c: French, from Latin *damnum* loss]

damask *noun* a patterned silk or linen cloth, used for tablecloths, curtains, etc.

dame *noun* **1** a woman who has been honoured by the Queen or the Government for service or merit. See also **knight**. **2** *N Am slang* a woman. **3** a comic female character in a pantomime, usu played by a man. [13c: French]

damn *verb* **1** *relig* to sentence someone to punishment in hell. **2** to declare someone or something to be useless or worthless. **3** to prove someone's guilt. ▸ *exclam* (*often* **damn it**) expressing annoyance. ▸ *adj, informal* annoying; hateful: *the damn cold*. ▸ *adv, informal* extremely; very: *It's damn cold*. ▪ **damning** *adj*. [13c: from Latin *damnare* to condemn]

IDIOMS **damn sb** *or* **sth with faint praise** to praise them or it so unenthusiastically as to seem disapproving. **not give a damn** *informal* not to care at all.

damnable *adj* **1** hateful; awful. **2** annoying.

damnation *noun, relig* punishment in hell. ▸ *exclam* expressing annoyance.

damned *adj* **1** *relig* sentenced to damnation. **2** *informal* annoying, hateful, etc. **3** (**the damned**) those sentenced to punishment in hell. ▸ *adv, informal* extremely; very: *damned cold*.

IDIOMS **do one's damnedest** *informal* to try as hard as possible.

damp *adj* slightly wet. ▸ *noun* slight wetness, esp if cold and unpleasant. ▸ *verb* **1** to wet something slightly. **2** (*often* **damp down**) to make (emotions, interest, etc) less strong. **3** (*often* **damp down**) to make (a fire) burn more slowly. **4** *music* to press (the string or strings of an instrument) to stop or lessen vibration. ▪ **damply** *adv*. ▪ **dampness** *noun*. [16c: from German *Dampf* steam]

damp-course *or* **damp-proof course** *noun* a layer of material in a wall of a building which stops damp rising up through the wall.

dampen *verb* **1** to make something slightly wet. **2** *tr & intr* (*usu* **dampen down** *or* **dampen sth down**) of emotions, interest, etc: to make or become less strong. **3** to make (a fire) burn more slowly. ▪ **dampener** *noun*.

damper *noun* **1** something which lessens enthusiasm, interest, etc. **2** a movable plate controlling air flow to a fire, etc. **3** *music* in a piano, etc: a pad which silences a note after it has been played.

IDIOMS **put a damper on sth** to lessen enthusiasm for it or interest in it.

damp-proof *adj* not allowing wetness through. ▸ *verb, building* to make something damp-proof.

damsel *noun, old use or literary* a girl or young woman. [16c: from French]

damson *noun* **1** a small purple plum. **2** the tree it grows on. [15c: from Latin *Damascenus* of Damascus]

dan *noun* **1** any of the ten grades of **black belt** in judo, karate, etc. **2** someone who has such a grade. [20c: Japanese]

dance *verb* **1** *intr & tr* to make rhythmic steps or movements (usu in time to music). **2** *intr* (*usu* **dance about** *or* **around**) to move or jump about quickly. ▸ *noun* **1** a pattern of rhythmic steps, usu in time to music. **2** a social gathering for dancing. **3** music played for dancing. *as adj*: *dance-band*. ▪ **dancer** *noun*. ▪ **dancing** *noun*. [13c: from French]

IDIOMS **dance attendance on sb** *derog* to follow them closely and do whatever they want.

D and C *abbrev, med* **dilatation and curettage**.

dandelion *noun* a plant with notched leaves and yellow flowerheads on hollow stems. [15c: from French *dent de lion* lion's tooth, referring to the leaves]

dander *noun* (*only* **get one's** *or* **sb's dander up**) *informal* to become angry, or make someone angry. [19c]

dandle *verb* to bounce or dance (usu a small child) on one's knee.

dandruff *noun* whitish flakes of dead skin shed from the scalp. [16c]

dandy *noun* (*-ies*) a man who is concerned to dress very fashionably or elegantly. Also called **beau**. ▸ *adj, informal* (*-ier, -iest*) good; fine.

Dane *noun* **1** a citizen or inhabitant of, or person born in, Denmark. **2** *hist* a Viking. See also **Danish**. [Anglo-Saxon *Dene*]

danger *noun* **1** a situation or state of possible harm, injury, loss or unpleasantness. **2** a possible cause of harm, injury or loss. [13c: from French 'power to harm']

danger money *noun* extra money paid to a person doing a dangerous job.

dangerous *adj* likely or able to cause harm or injury. ▪ **dangerously** *adv*. ▪ **dangerousness** *noun*.

dangle *verb* **1** *tr & intr* to hang loosely, sometimes swinging or swaying. **2** to offer (an idea, a possible reward, etc) to someone. [16c]

Danish *adj* **1** belonging or relating to Denmark, its inhabitants or their language. **2** (**the Danish**) the people of Denmark. ▸ *noun* the official language of Denmark. See also **Dane**. [Anglo-Saxon]

Danish pastry *noun* a flat cake of rich light pastry, with a sweet filling or topping.

dank *adj* unpleasantly wet and cold. ▪ **dankness** *noun*. [15c]

dapper *adj* smart in appearance and lively in movement. [15c: Dutch, meaning 'brave']

dappled *adj* with spots or patches of a different, usu darker, colour. [15c]

dare *verb* **1** *intr* to be brave enough to do something. **2** to challenge someone to do something difficult, dangerous, etc. ▶ *auxiliary verb* used in questions and negative statements, as in *Daren't he tell her?* and *I dared not look at him.* ▶ *noun* a challenge to do something dangerous, etc. [Anglo-Saxon]

IDIOMS **I dare say** *or* **daresay** probably; I suppose.

dare to

If you use the word **dare** to mean 'to be brave enough to do something', you can use it either as an ordinary verb or as an auxiliary (helping) verb, that is, a verb that is used with other verbs to form tenses etc.

As an ordinary verb, **dare** may be followed by 'to' or by a verb without 'to':

She did not dare to push her bike through the gate.
I did not dare make a noise.

When **dare** is used as an auxiliary verb in questions and negative statements, there is no 'to' before the following verb:

Dare she push her bike through the gate?
I dared not make a noise.

daredevil *noun* a daring person not worried about taking risks. ▶ *adj* of actions, etc: daring and dangerous.

daring *adj* **1** courageous or adventurous. **2** intended to shock or surprise. ▶ *noun* boldness, courage.

dark *adj* **1** without light. **2** closer to black than to white. **3** of a person or skin or hair colour: not light or fair. **4** sad or gloomy. **5** evil or sinister: *dark powers.* **6** mysterious and unknown: *a dark secret.* ▶ *noun* **1** (*usu* **the dark**) the absence of light. **2** the beginning of night-time. **3** a dark colour. ▪ **darkly** *adv.* ▪ **darkness** *noun.* [Anglo-Saxon]

IDIOMS **in the dark** not knowing or not aware of something. **keep it dark** to keep something secret.

the Dark Ages *noun* the period of European history from about the 5c to the 11c.

darken *verb, tr & intr* to make or become dark or darker.

IDIOMS **darken sb's door** to appear as an unwelcome visitor.

dark horse *noun* someone who keeps their past, life, abilities, etc secret.

darkroom *noun* a room into which no ordinary light is allowed, used for developing photographs.

darling *noun* **1** used esp. as a form of address: a dearly loved person. **2** a lovable person or thing. ▶ *adj* **1** well loved. **2** *informal* delightful. [Anglo-Saxon]

darmstadtium *noun, chem* (symbol **Ds**) an artificially produced metallic element. [19c: from Darmstadt in Germany, where it was first discovered]

darn[1] *verb* to mend (a hole, a garment, etc) by sewing with rows of stitches which cross each other. ▶ *noun* a darned place. [17c]

darn[2] *exclam* a substitute for **damn.** ▪ **darned** *adj.*

dart *noun* **1** a narrow pointed weapon that can be thrown or fired. **2** a small sharp-pointed object thrown in the game of **darts. 3** a sudden quick movement. **4** a fold sewn into a piece of clothing. ▶ *verb* **1** *intr* to move suddenly and quickly. **2** to send or give (a look or glance) quickly. [14c: French]

dartboard *noun* a circular target at which darts are thrown in the game of **darts.**

darts *singular noun* a game in which darts are thrown at a dartboard.

Darwinism *noun, biol* the theory of evolution proposed by Charles Darwin (1809–82). ▪ **Darwinian** *and* **Darwinist** *adj, noun.*

dash *verb* **1** *intr* to run quickly *I had to dash off to catch my train.* **2** *intr* to crash or smash. **3** (*often* **dash against sth**) to hit it or smash into it violently. **4** to put an end to (hopes, etc). ▶ *noun* **1** a quick run or sudden rush. **2** a small amount of something, esp a liquid. **3** a patch of colour. **4** a short line (–) used in writing to show a break in a sentence, etc. **5** in **Morse** code: the longer of the two lengths of signal element. Compare **dot** (sense 2). **6** confidence, enthusiasm and stylishness. **7** *sport* a short race for fast runners. **8** a **dashboard.** [14c: from *daschen* to rush or strike violently]

PHRASAL VERBS **dash sth off** to produce or write it hastily.

dashboard *noun* a panel with dials, switches, etc in front of the driver's seat in a car, boat, etc. [19c]

dashing *adj* **1** smart; stylish. **2** lively and enthusiastic. **3** rushing. ▪ **dashingly** *adv.*

dastardly *adj, old use* cowardly, mean and cruel. [16c: prob connected with **dazed**]

DAT *abbrev* digital audio tape.

dat. *abbrev* dative.

data *noun* (orig *pl* of **datum** but now generally treated as *sing*) **1** information or facts, esp if obtained by scientific observation or experiment. **2** information in the form of numbers, characters, electrical signals, etc, that can be supplied to, stored in or processed by a computer. [17c: Latin, meaning 'things given']

data, datum

In strict contexts, for example in science, **data** is a plural, and the singular is **datum.** However, **data** is becoming more common as singular noun, followed by a singular verb:

The data is entered by a keyboarder.

database *noun, comput* a collection of computer **data.**

data capture *noun, comput* changing information into a form which can be fed into a computer.

data mining *noun, comput* the gathering of electronically stored information, eg about shopping patterns from loyalty cards.

date[1] *noun* **1** the day of the month and/or the year, given as a number or numbers. **2** the day on which a letter, etc was written, sent, etc, an event took place or is planned to take place, etc. **3** a particular period of time in history: *tools of an earlier date.* **4** *informal* a planned meeting or social outing, usu with a person one is romantically attached to. **5** *informal, esp N Am* a person whom one is meeting or going out with, esp romantically. **6** *informal* an agreed time and place of performance. ▶ *verb* **1** to put a date on (a letter, etc). **2** to find, decide on or guess the date of something. **3** to show the age of someone or something; to make (esp a person) seem old. **4** *intr* to become old-fashioned. **5** *intr* (*always* **date from** *or* **back to**) to have begun or originated (at a specified time). **6** *tr & intr, informal* to go out socially with someone, esp regularly for romantic reasons. ▪ **datable** *or* **dateable** *adj*. ▪ **dated** *adj* old-fashioned. [15c: French, from Latin *datum* given]

IDIOMS **to date** up to the present time.

date² *noun* the fruit of the **date palm**. [13c: from French *datte*]

dateline *noun* a line, usu at the top of a newspaper article, which gives the date and place of writing.

date line see **International Date Line**

date palm *noun* a tall tree with a crown of leaves, cultivated for its edible fruit.

dative *grammar, noun* **1** in certain languages: the **case²** (*noun* sense 7) of a noun, pronoun or adjective which is used chiefly to show that the word is the indirect object of a verb. **2** a noun, etc in this case. ▸ *adj* belonging to or in this case. [15c: from Latin *dativus*, from *dare* to give]

datum *noun* (***data***) a piece of information. See also **data**. [18c: Latin, meaning 'something given']

daub *verb* **1** to spread something roughly or unevenly onto a surface. **2** to cover (a surface) with a soft sticky substance or liquid. **3** *tr & intr, derog* to paint carelessly or without skill. ▸ *noun* **1** soft, sticky material such as clay, often used as a covering for walls (see also **wattle and daub**). **2** *derog, informal* an unskilful or carelessly done painting. [14c: from French *dauber*]

daughter *noun* **1** a female child. **2** a woman closely associated with, involved with or influenced by a person, thing or place: *a faithful daughter of the Church*. ▸ *adj* **1** derived from something: *French is a daughter language of Latin*. **2** *biol* of a cell: formed by division. **3** *physics* of an element: formed by nuclear fission. ▪ **daughterly** *adj*. [Anglo-Saxon *dohtor*]

daughter-in-law *noun* (***daughters-in-law***) the wife of one's son.

daunt *verb* to frighten, worry or discourage someone. ▪ **daunting** *adj* intimidating; discouraging. ▪ **dauntless** *adj* fearless; not easily discouraged. [14c: from French]

dauphin /ˈdɔfɪn/ *noun* (in France, from 1349–1830) the eldest son of the king. [From Old French *daulphin*, from *Delphinus*, a family name]

davenport *noun* **1** *Brit* a type of desk. **2** *N Am* a large sofa. [19c: possibly named after a Captain Davenport]

davit /ˈdavɪt/ *noun* either of a pair of crane-like devices on a ship on which a lifeboat is hung. [15c: from the name *David*]

Davy (***-ies***) *or* **Davy lamp** *noun* a miner's safety lamp. [19c: named after the inventor, Sir Humphry Davy]

Davy Jones's locker *noun* the bottom of the sea. [19c: named after Davy Jones, a sailors' name for the evil spirit of the sea]

dawdle *verb, intr* **1** to walk unnecessarily slowly. **2** to waste time, esp by taking longer than necessary to do something. [17c]

dawn *noun* **1** the time of day when light first appears. **2** the beginning of (a new period of time, etc). ▸ *verb, intr* **1** of the day: to begin. **2** (*usu* **dawn on sb**) to begin to be realized by them. [15c: prob from Norse]

dawn chorus *noun* the singing of birds at dawn.

day *noun* **1** a period of 24 hours, esp from midnight to midnight. **2** the period from sunrise to sunset. **3** the period in any 24 hours normally spent doing something: *the working day*. **4** (**day** *or* **days**) a particular period of time, usu in the past: *childhood days*. **5** time of recognition, success, influence, power, etc: *Their day will come*. [Anglo-Saxon]

IDIOMS **all in a** *or* **the day's work** a normal or acceptable part of one's work or routine. **at the end of the day** when all is said and done. **call it a day** to leave off doing something. **day in, day out** continuously and tediously without change. **from day to day** concerned only with the present and not with any long-term plans. **make sb's day** to satisfy or delight them. **that will be the day** *informal* that is unlikely to happen. **those were the days** that was a good or happy time.

day-boy *or* **day-girl** *noun* a pupil who studies at a boarding school but lives at home.

daybreak *noun* dawn.

day care *noun* supervision and care given to young children, the elderly or handicapped people during the day.

daydream *noun* pleasant thoughts which take one's attention away from what one is, or should be, doing. ▸ *verb, intr* to be engrossed in daydreams. ▪ **daydreamer** *noun*.

dayglo *adj* luminously brilliant green, yellow, pink or orange. [1950s: from the name of a brand of paint]

daylight *noun* **1** the light given by the sun. **2** the time when light first appears in the sky.

IDIOMS **beat** *or* **knock the living daylights out of sb** *informal* to beat them severely. **in broad daylight 1** during the day. **2** openly. **scare** *or* **frighten the living daylights out of sb** *informal* to frighten them greatly. **see daylight 1** to begin to understand. **2** to be close to completing a difficult or long task.

daylight robbery *noun, informal* greatly overcharging for something.

daylight-saving time *noun* time, usu one hour ahead of standard time, adopted, usu in summertime, to increase the hours of daylight at the end of the day.

Day of Atonement see **Yom Kippur**

Day of Judgement *or* **Last Judgement** *noun* the end of the world, when God will judge humankind.

day of reckoning *noun* a time when mistakes, failures, bad deeds, etc are punished.

day release *noun* a system by which employees are given time off work (usu one day a week) to study at college, etc.

day shift *noun* **1** a period of working during the day. **2** the people who work during this period. See also **night shift**.

days of grace *plural noun* days allowed for payment of bills, etc, beyond the day named.

daytime *noun* the time between sunrise and sunset.

day-to-day *adj* daily; routine.

day trader *noun, finance* a person who buys and sells securities on the same day with a view to making quick profits from price movements.

daze *verb* to make someone confused or unable to think clearly (eg by a blow or shock). ▸ *noun* a confused, forgetful or inattentive state of mind. ▪ **dazed** *adj*. [14c: from Norse *dasask* to be weary]

dazzle *verb* **1** to make someone unable to see properly, with or because of a strong light. **2** to impress someone greatly by one's beauty, charm, skill, etc. ▪ **dazzling** *adj*. ▪ **dazzlingly** *adv*. [15c: from **daze**]

Db *symbol, chem* dubnium.

dB *abbrev* decibel, or decibels.

DBE *abbrev* Dame Commander of the Order of the British Empire.

dbl. *abbrev* double.

DC[1] *noun* (***DCs*** *or* ***DC's***) District Commissioner.

DC[2] *abbrev* direct current. Compare **AC**, **AC/DC**.

DCC *abbrev* digital compact cassette.

DCI *abbrev* Deputy Chief Inspector.

DCM *abbrev* Distinguished Conduct Medal.

DD *abbrev*: *Divinitatis Doctor* (Latin), Doctor of Divinity.

D-Day *noun* **1** the date of the Allied invasion of Europe in World War II, 6 June 1944. **2** any critical day of action. ['D' for 'unnamed day']

DDR *abbrev*: *Deutsche Demokratische Republik* (German), the former German Democratic Republic or East Germany.

DDS *abbrev* Doctor of Dental Surgery.

DDT *abbrev* dichlorodiphenyltrichloroethane, a highly toxic insecticide, now restricted or banned in most countries.

de- *prefix, signifying* **1** down or away: *debase*. **2** reversal or removal: *decriminalize*. [Sense 1 from Latin *de* off, from; sense 2 from French *des-*]

deacon *noun* **1** a member of the lowest rank of clergy in the Roman Catholic and Anglican churches. **2** in some other churches: a person with certain duties, such as looking after the church's financial affairs. See also **diaconate**. [Anglo-Saxon, from Greek *diakonos* servant]

deaconess *noun* **1** in some churches: a woman who has similar duties to those of a deacon (sense 2). **2** in some churches: a woman who acts as an assistant minister. [16c]

deactivate *verb* to remove or lessen the capacity of (something such as a bomb) to function or work. ▪ **deactivation** *noun*. [Early 20c]

dead *adj* **1** no longer living. **2** not alive. **3** no longer in existence. **4** with nothing living or growing in or on it. **5** not, or no longer, functioning; not connected to a source of power. **6** no longer burning. **7** no longer in everyday use: *a dead language*. **8** no longer of interest or importance: *a dead issue*. **9** having little or no excitement or activity. **10** without feeling; numb. **11** complete; absolute. **12** of a sound: dull. **13** *sport* of a ball: out of play. ▸ *noun* (**the dead**) dead people. ▸ *adv, slang* absolutely; very: *dead drunk*. [Anglo-Saxon]

IDIOMS **dead on** exact; exactly. See also **dead-on**. **over my dead body** not if I can prevent it. **the dead of night** the middle of the night, when it is darkest. **the dead of winter** the middle of winter, when it is coldest.

deadbeat *noun, informal* a useless person; a down-and-out.

dead beat *adj, informal* exhausted.

dead duck *noun, informal* someone or something with no chance of success or survival.

deaden *verb* **1** to lessen or weaken something or make it less sharp, strong, etc. **2** to make something soundproof.

dead end *noun* **1** a passage, road, etc, closed at one end. **2** a situation or activity with no possibility of further progress or movement. ▸ *adj* (**dead-end**) allowing no progress or improvement.

deadhead *noun, chiefly N Am* **1** someone who enjoys free privileges. **2** an ineffective unproductive person. **3** a train, etc, travelling empty. **4** a sunken or semi-submerged log in a waterway. ▸ *verb* to remove withered or dead flowers from (plants).

dead heat *noun* the result when two or more competitors produce equally good performances or finish a race in exactly the same time.

dead letter *noun* **1** a rule or law no longer obeyed or in force. **2** a letter that can neither be delivered nor returned to the sender because it lacks the necessary address details.

deadline *noun* a time by which something must be done. [19c, meaning 'a line around a prison beyond which an escaping prisoner could be shot']

deadlock *noun* a situation in which no further progress towards an agreement is possible. ▸ *verb, tr & intr* to make or come to a deadlock. [18c]

dead loss *noun, informal* someone or something that is totally useless.

deadly *adj* (***-ier, -iest***) **1** causing or likely to cause death. **2** *informal* very dull or uninteresting. **3** very great: *in deadly earnest*. ▸ *adv* very; absolutely.

deadly nightshade *noun* a plant with bell-shaped purple flowers and poisonous black berries from which the drug **belladonna** is obtained.

deadly sins see **the seven deadly sins**

dead man's handle *or* **dead man's pedal** *noun* a device on a machine, eg a railway engine, which stops the machine if pressure on it is released.

dead march *noun, music* a piece of solemn music played at funeral processions, esp those of soldiers.

dead men *or* (*Austral & NZ*) **dead marines** *plural noun, informal* bottles of alcoholic drink that have been emptied.

dead-nettle *noun* any of various plants superficially like a nettle but without a sting.

dead-on *adj, informal* accurate; spot-on.

deadpan *adj* showing no emotion or feeling, esp when joking but pretending to be serious. [1920s]

dead reckoning *noun* estimating the position of a ship, etc from the distance and direction travelled, without looking at the position of the stars, Sun or Moon.

dead set *adj* determined.

dead weight *noun* **1** a heavy load. **2** *technical* (*also* **deadweight**) the difference in the displacement of a ship when unloaded and loaded.

dead wood *noun, informal* someone or something that is no longer useful or needed.

deaf *adj* **1** unable to hear at all or to hear well. **2** (*usu* **deaf to sth**) not willing to listen to (advice, appeals, criticism, etc). **3** (**the deaf**) deaf people in general. ▪ **deafness** *noun*. [Anglo-Saxon]

deaf aid *noun* a **hearing aid**.

deafen *verb* to make someone deaf or temporarily unable to hear. ▪ **deafening** *adj* **1** extremely loud. **2** causing deafness. ▪ **deafeningly** *adv*.

deaf-mute *noun, often considered offensive* someone who is both deaf and unable to speak. ▸ *adj* unable to hear or speak.

deal[1] *noun* **1** a bargain, agreement or arrangement. **2** particular treatment of or behaviour towards someone: *a rough deal*. **3** the act or way of, or a player's turn of, sharing out cards among the players in a card game. ▸ *verb* (***dealt*** /dɛlt/) *tr & intr* **1** (*always* **deal in sth**) to buy and sell it. **2** (*also* **deal out**) to divide the cards among the players in a card game. **3** (*also* **deal out**) to give something out to a number of people, etc. [Anglo-Saxon *dæl* a part]

IDIOMS **a good** *or* **great deal 1** a large quantity. **2** very much or often. **deal sb a blow** to hit or distress them.

PHRASAL VERBS **deal with sth** *or* **sb 1** to take action regarding it or them. **2** to be concerned with it or them.

deal² *noun* a plank or planks of fir or pine wood. [15c: from German dialect]

dealer *noun* **1** a person or firm dealing in retail goods. **2** the player who deals in a card game. **3** someone who sells illegal drugs. ▪ **dealership** *noun* **1** a business which buys and sells things. **2** a business licensed to sell a particular product by its manufacturer.

dealings *plural noun* **1** one's manner of acting towards others. **2** business, etc, contacts and transactions.

dealt *past tense, past participle of* **deal¹**

dean *noun* **1** a senior clergyman in an Anglican cathedral. **2** a senior official in a university or college. **3** the head of a university or college faculty. See also **rural dean**. [14c: from French *deien*]

deanery *noun* (***-ies***) **1** the house of a dean. **2** a group of parishes for which a rural dean has responsibility. [15c]

dear *adj* **1** high in price; charging high prices. **2** lovable; attractive. **3** used in addressing someone at the start of a letter. **4** (*usu* **dear to sb**) greatly loved by, or very important or precious to, them. ▸ *noun* (*also* **deary**, **dearie**) (***-ies***) **1** a charming or lovable person. **2** used esp as a form of address: a person one loves or likes. ▸ *exclam* (*also* **deary**, **dearie**) used as an expression of dismay, etc: *Dear me!* ▪ **dearly** *adv*. [Anglo-Saxon]

IDIOMS **cost sb dear** to result in a lot of trouble or suffering. **dear knows** *informal* no one knows. **pay dearly** to be made to suffer.

dearth /dɜːθ/ *noun* a scarceness or lack. [13c: from **dear**]

death *noun* **1** the time, act or manner of dying; the state of being dead. **2** *often humorous* something which causes a person to die: *His antics will be the death of me*. **3** the end or destruction of something. **4** (**Death**) the figure of a skeleton, as a symbol of death. ▪ **deathless** *adj, often ironic* immortal; unforgettable: *deathless prose*. ▪ **deathly** *adj*. [Anglo-Saxon]

IDIOMS **at death's door** near death; gravely ill. **catch one's death (of cold)** *informal* to catch a very bad cold. **do sth to death** to overuse it. **like death warmed up** *informal* very unwell. **put sb to death** to kill them or have them killed. **to death** extremely: *bored to death*. **to the death 1** until one or one's opponent is dead. **2** to the very end.

deathbed *noun* the bed in which a person died or is about to die.

deathblow *noun* **1** a blow which causes death. **2** an action, etc which puts an end to (hopes, plans, etc).

death cap *noun* an extremely poisonous toadstool. Also called **death cup**, **death angel**.

death certificate *noun* a certificate stating the time and cause of someone's death.

death duty *noun* (*often* **death duties**) *Brit* a former tax paid on the value of property left by a person who has died, replaced by **inheritance tax**.

death knell *noun* **1** the ringing of a bell when someone has died. **2** an action, announcement, etc that heralds the end or destruction of (hopes, plans, etc).

death mask *noun* a mask made from the cast of a person's face after they have died.

death penalty *noun* punishment of a crime by death.

death rattle *noun* a rattling noise noise in the throat that sometimes precedes death.

death row *noun, esp US* the part of a prison where people who have been sentenced to death are kept.

death's-head *noun* a human skull, or a picture, mask, etc representing one.

deathtrap *noun* a building, vehicle, place, etc which is very unsafe.

death warrant *noun* an official order for a death sentence to be carried out.

IDIOMS **sign one's own death warrant** to do something that makes one's downfall inevitable.

deathwatch beetle *noun* a beetle which makes a ticking sound once believed to herald a death in the building where it was heard.

death wish *noun* a desire to die, or that someone else should die.

deb *noun, informal* a **debutante**.

debacle *or* **débâcle** /deɪˈbɑːkəl/ *noun* total disorder, defeat, collapse of an organization, etc. [19c: French]

debar *verb* (***-barred, -barring***) to stop someone from joining, taking part in, doing, etc something. [15c: from French]

debase *verb* **1** to lower the value, quality, or status of something. **2** to lower the value of (a coin) by adding metal of a lower value. ▪ **debasement** *noun*. [16c: **de-** (sense 1) + **abase**]

debate *noun* **1** a formal discussion. **2** a general discussion. ▸ *verb, tr & intr* **1** to hold or take part in a debate. **2** to consider the arguments for or against something. ▪ **debatable** *or* **debateable** *adj* doubtful; not agreed; uncertain. [13c: from French]

IDIOMS **open to debate** not certain or agreed.

debauch /dɪˈbɔːtʃ/ *verb* to cause or persuade someone to take part in immoral, esp sexual, activities or excessive drinking. ▸ *noun* a period of debauched behaviour. ▪ **debauched** *adj* corrupted; immoral. ▪ **debauchery** *noun*. [16c: from French *desbaucher* to corrupt]

debenture *noun, finance* **1** a type of loan to a company or government agency which is usu made for a set period of time and carries a fixed rate of interest. **2** the document or bond acknowledging this loan. [15c: from Latin *debentur* there are due or owed]

debilitate *verb* to make someone weak or weaker. ▪ **debilitating** *adj*. ▪ **debilitation** *noun*. ▪ **debility** *noun* (***-ies***). [16c: from Latin *debilis* weak]

debit *noun* **1** an entry in an account recording what is owed or has been spent. **2** a sum taken from a bank, etc account. **3** a deduction made from a bill or account. Compare **credit** (sense 8). ▸ *verb* **1** to take from (an account, etc). **2** to record something in a debit entry. [15c: from Latin *debitum* what is due]

debit card *noun* a plastic card used by a purchaser to transfer money directly from their account to the retailer's. Compare **credit card**. [1970s]

debonair *adj* esp of a man: cheerful, charming, elegant and well-mannered. [18c: from French *de bon aire* of good manners]

debouch *verb, intr, technical* of troops or a river, etc: to come out of a narrow place or opening into a wider or more open place. ▪ **debouchment** *noun*. [18c: from French *de* from + *bouche* mouth]

debrief *verb* to gather information from (a diplomat, astronaut, soldier, etc) after a battle, event, mission, etc. ▪ **debriefing** *noun*. [1940s]

debris *or* **débris** /ˈdɛbriː/ *noun* **1** what remains of something crushed, smashed, destroyed, etc. **2** rubbish. **3** small pieces of rock. [18c: French]

debt *noun* **1** something owed. **2** the state of owing something. [13c: from French *dette*]

IDIOMS **in sb's debt** under an obligation to them.

debt of honour *noun* a debt one is morally but not legally obliged to pay.

debtor *noun* someone owing money. Compare **creditor**.

debug *verb* **1** to remove secret microphones from (a room, etc). **2** to remove faults in (a computer program). [20c]

debunk *verb* to show (a person's claims, good reputation, etc) to be false or unjustified. [1920s]

debut *or* **début** /ˈdeɪbjuː/ *noun* **1** the first public appearance of a performer. **2** the formal presentation of a debutante. [18c: French *début*]

debutante *or* **débutante** /ˈdeɪbjʊtɒnt/ *noun* a young woman making her first formal appearance as an adult in upper-class society, usu at a ball. [19c: French, from *débuter* to start off]

Dec. *abbrev* December.

deca- *or* (*before a vowel*) **dec-** *combining form* (abbrev **da**) ten: *decagon* • *decalitre*. [From Greek *deka* ten]

decade *noun* **1** a period of 10 years. **2** a group or series of 10 things, etc. [15c: from Greek *deka* ten]

decadence *noun* **1** a falling to low standards in morals, art, etc. **2** the state of having low or immoral standards of behaviour, etc. ▪ **decadent** *adj*. ▪ **decadently** *adv*. [16c: from French *décadence*]

decaff *or* **decaf** *informal, adj* decaffeinated. ▸ *noun* decaffeinated coffee.

decaffeinate *verb* to remove all or part of the caffeine from (eg coffee). ▪ **decaffeinated** *adj*. [1920s]

decagon *noun, geom* a polygon with 10 sides. ▪ **decagonal** *adj*. [17c: from **deca-** + Greek *gonia* angle]

decahedron *noun* a solid figure with ten faces. ▪ **decahedral** *adj*. [19c: from **deca-** + Greek *hedra* seat]

decalitre *or* (*US*) **decaliter** /ˈdɛkəliːtə(r)/ *noun* (abbrev **dal**) a unit of measurement of volume, equal to ten litres.

the Decalogue *noun, Bible* the Ten Commandments. [14c: from **deca-** + Greek *logos* word]

decametre *or* (*US*) **decameter** *noun* (abbrev **dam**) a unit of measurement of length, equal to ten metres.

decamp *verb, intr* **1** to go away suddenly, esp secretly. **2** to break camp. [17c: from French *décamper*]

decant *verb* **1** to pour (wine, etc) from one container to another, leaving sediment behind. **2** to remove (people) from where they usu live to some other place. [17c: from French *décanter*]

decanter *noun* an ornamental bottle with a stopper, used for decanted wine, sherry, etc.

decapitate *verb* to cut off the head of someone. ▪ **decapitation** *noun*. [17c: from **de-** (sense 1) + Latin *caput* head]

decapod *noun, zool* **1** a crustacean with 10 limbs. **2** a sea creature with ten arms, eg a squid. [19c: from **deca-** + Greek *pous, podos* foot]

decarbonize *or* **-ise** *or* **decarburize** *or* **-ise** *verb* to remove carbon from (an internal-combustion engine).

decathlon *noun* an athletic competition involving 10 events over two days. ▪ **decathlete** *noun*. [1912: from **deca-** + Greek *athlon* contest]

decay *verb* **1** *tr & intr* to make or become rotten, ruined, weaker in health or power, etc. **2** *intr, physics* of a radioactive substance: to break down into radioactive or non-radioactive **isotopes**. ▸ *noun* **1** the natural breakdown of dead organic matter. **2** *physics* the breakdown of a radioactive substance into one or more **isotopes**. **3** a gradual decrease in health, power, quality, etc. **4** rotten matter in a tooth, etc. [15c: from French *decair*]

decease *noun, formal, law* death. [14c: from Latin *decessus* departure or death]

deceased *adj, formal, law* **1** dead, esp recently dead. **2** (**the deceased**) the dead person or dead people in question.

deceit *noun* **1** an act of deceiving or misleading. **2** dishonesty; willingness to deceive. ▪ **deceitful** *adj*. ▪ **deceitfully** *adv*. ▪ **deceitfulness** *noun*. [14c: French]

deceive *verb* **1** to mislead or lie to someone. **2** to convince (oneself) that something untrue is true. See also **deception**. [13c: from French *décevoir*]

decelerate *verb, tr & intr* to slow down, or make something slow down. ▪ **deceleration** *noun*. [19c: from **de-** (sense 1) + **accelerate**]

December *noun* (abbrev **Dec.**) the twelfth month of the year. [13c: from Latin *decem* ten, because it was at one time the tenth month of the Roman year]

decennial *adj* **1** happening every 10 years. **2** consisting of 10 years. [17c: from Latin *decem* ten + *annus* year]

decent *adj* **1** respectable; not vulgar or immoral. **2** kind, tolerant or likeable. **3** fairly good; adequate. ▪ **decency** *noun* (*-ies*) **1** decent behaviour or character. **2** (**decencies**) the generally accepted rules of respectable or moral behaviour. ▪ **decently** *adv*. [16c: from Latin *decere* to be fitting]

decentralize *or* **-ise** *verb, tr & intr* to change (eg a government department, an industry, etc) from having one central place of control into several smaller centres. ▪ **decentralist** *or* **decentralizer** *noun*. ▪ **decentralization** *noun*. [19c]

deception *noun* **1** deceiving or being deceived. **2** something which deceives. ▪ **deceptive** *adj*. ▪ **deceptiveness** *noun*. [15c: from Latin *decipere* to deceive]

deci- *combining form* (abbrev **d**) *signifying* one tenth: *decilitre*. [From Latin *decimus* tenth]

decibel *noun* (symbol **dB**) a unit equal to ¹⁄₁₀ of a **bel**, used for comparing levels of power, esp sound.

decide *verb* **1** *intr* (*sometimes* **decide on** *or* **about sth**) to establish an intention or course of action regarding it. **2** (**decide to do sth**) to make up one's mind to do it. **3** to settle something, or make its final result certain. **4** to make someone decide in a certain way. **5** to make a formal judgement. [14c: from Latin *decidere* to cut down, settle]

decided *adj* **1** clear and definite. **2** determined; showing no doubt. ▪ **decidedly** *adv.*

decider *noun* **1** someone or something that decides. **2** something that decides a result, eg a winning goal.

deciduous *adj* **1** *botany* of a plant: shedding leaves once a year. Compare **evergreen**. **2** of a forest: comprising deciduous trees. **3** *biol* shed after a period of growth, eg milk teeth. [17c: from Latin *decidere* to fall down]

decigram *or* **decigramme** *noun* (abbrev **dg**) a unit of measurement of mass, equal to one tenth of a gram.

decilitre *or* (*US*) **deciliter** *noun* (abbrev **dl**) a unit of measurement of volume, equal to one tenth of a litre.

decimal *adj* **1** based on the number 10 or powers of 10. **2** denoting a system of units related to each other by multiples of 10. ▸ *noun* a decimal fraction. [17c: from Latin *decimalis*, from *decem* ten]

decimal fraction *noun* a fraction in which tenths, hundredths, etc are written in figures after a decimal point, eg 0.5 = 5/10 or 1/2. Compare **vulgar fraction**.

decimalize *or* **-ise** *verb* to convert (numbers, a currency, etc) to a decimal form. ▪ **decimalization** *noun.* [19c]

decimal point *noun* the point which precedes the **decimal fraction**.

decimal system *noun* a system of units related by multiples of 10. [17c: from Latin *decem* ten]

decimate *verb* to destroy a large part or number of something. ▪ **decimation** *noun.* [17c: orig 'to execute one in every ten': from Latin *decem* ten]

decimetre *or* (*US*) **decimeter** *noun* (abbrev **dm**) a unit of measurement of length, equal to one tenth of a metre.

decipher *verb* **1** to translate (eg a message in code) into ordinary language. **2** to work out the meaning of something obscure or difficult to read. ▪ **decipherable** *adj.* ▪ **decipherment** *noun.* [16c]

decision *noun* **1** the act of deciding. **2** something decided. **3** the ability to make decisions and act on them firmly: *act with decision in a crisis.* [15c: from Latin *decisio* cutting off]

decisive *adj* **1** putting an end to doubt or dispute. **2** having or showing decision. ▪ **decisively** *adv.* ▪ **decisiveness** *noun.*

deck[1] *noun* **1** a platform forming a floor or covering across a ship. **2** a floor or platform in a bus, bridge, etc. **3** *N Am, esp US* a pack of playing-cards. **4** the part of a tape recorder, record player or computer which contains the mechanism for operation. [15c: from Dutch *dec* roof or covering]

IDIOMS **clear the decks** to clear away obstacles or deal with preliminary jobs in preparation for further activity.

deck[2] *verb* (*usu* **deck sth out**) to decorate or embellish it. [15c: from Dutch *dekken* to cover]

deckchair *noun* a light folding chair made of wood and a length of heavy fabric. [19c]

-decker *adj, in compounds, signifying* having a specified number of decks or layers: *a double-decker bus.* ▸ *as noun*: *a double-decker.*

decking *noun* a wooden floor in a garden or the material used to make it.

deckle edge *noun* the rough edge of handmade paper, or an imitation of this.

decko see **dekko**

declaim *verb* **1** *tr & intr* to make (a speech) in an impressive and dramatic manner. **2** *intr* (*usu* **declaim against sth**) to protest about it loudly and passionately. ▪ **declamation** *noun.* ▪ **declamatory** *adj.* [14c: from Latin *declamare*]

declare *verb* **1** to announce something publicly or formally. **2** to say something firmly or emphatically. **3** *intr* (*often* **declare for** *or* **against sth**) to state one's support or opposition regarding it. **4** to make known (goods on which duty must be paid, income on which tax should be paid, etc). **5** *intr, cricket* to end an innings voluntarily before 10 wickets have fallen. **6** *tr & intr, cards* to state or show that one is holding (certain cards). ▪ **declaration** *noun.* ▪ **declaratory** *adj.* [14c: from Latin *declarare*]

declassify *verb* (**-ies, -ied**) to state that (an official document, etc) is no longer secret. ▪ **declassification** *noun.* [19c]

declension *noun, grammar* **1** in certain languages: any of various sets of forms taken by nouns, adjectives or pronouns to indicate case, number and gender. **2** the act of stating these forms. See also **conjugation**, **decline** (sense 3). **3** any group of nouns or adjectives showing the same pattern of forms. [16c: from French, from Latin *declinatio* bending aside]

declination *noun* **1** *technical* the angle between **true north** and **magnetic north**. **2** *astron* the angular distance of a star or planet north or south of the celestial equator. [16c: from Latin *declinatio* bending aside]

decline *verb* **1** to refuse (an invitation, etc), esp politely. **2** *intr* to become less, less strong, less healthy or less good. **3** *grammar* to state the **declension** of (a word). See also **conjugate**. ▸ *noun* a lessening of strength, health, quality, quantity, etc. [14c: from Latin *declinare* to bend aside]

declivity *noun* (**-ies**) *formal* a downward slope. ▪ **declivitous** *adj.* [17c: from Latin *declivitas*]

declutch *verb, intr* to release the clutch of (a motor vehicle). [Early 20c]

decoct *verb* to extract the essence, etc of (a substance) by boiling. ▪ **decoction** *noun.* [14c: from Latin *coquere* to cook]

decode *verb* to translate (a coded message) into ordinary language. ▪ **decoder** *noun.* [19c]

decoke *verb, informal* to **decarbonize**.

décolletage /deɪkɒl'tɑːʒ/ *noun* **1** a low-cut neckline on a woman's dress, etc. **2** the resulting exposure of the neck and shoulders. [19c: French]

décolleté *or* **décolletée** /deɪ'kɒləteɪ/ *adj* **1** of a dress, etc: low-cut. **2** of a woman: wearing such a dress, etc. [19c: from French *décolleter* to bare the neck and shoulders]

decolonize *or* **decolonise** *verb* to grant independence to (a colony). ▪ **decolonization** *noun.*

decommission *verb* to take (eg a warship or atomic reactor) out of use or operation. [1920s]

decompose *verb* **1** *intr* of a dead organism: to rot. **2** *tr & intr, technical* to separate or break down into smaller or simpler elements. ▪ **decomposition** *noun.* [18c: from French]

decompress *verb, technical* to decrease or stop the pressure on something. ▪ **decompression** *noun.* ▪ **decompressor** *noun.* [Early 20c]

decompression sickness *noun* a disorder suffered by a person who has been breathing air under high pressure returning too quickly to normal atmospheric pressure. Also called **the bends, caisson disease.**

decongestant *med, noun* a drug which reduces nasal congestion. ▸ *adj* relieving congestion. [1950s]

decontaminate *verb* to remove poisons, radioactivity, etc from something. ▪ **decontamination** *noun.* [1930s]

décor /'deɪkɔː(r)/ *noun* **1** scenery, etc; a theatre set. **2** the style of decoration, furnishings, etc in a room or house. [19c: French, meaning 'decoration']

decorate *verb* **1** to beautify something with ornaments, etc. **2** to put paint or wallpaper on (a wall, etc). **3** to give a medal or badge to someone as a mark of honour. ▪ **decorative** *adj.* ▪ **decorator** *noun.* [16c: from Latin *decorare* to beautify]

decoration *noun* **1** something used to decorate. **2** the act of decorating. **3** the state of being decorated. **4** a medal or badge given as a mark of honour.

decorous *adj* socially correct or acceptable; showing proper respect. ▪ **decorously** *adv.* [17c: from Latin *decorus* becoming or fitting]

decorum /dɪ'kɔːrəm/ *noun* correct or socially acceptable behaviour. [16c: from Latin *decorus* becoming or fitting]

decoy *verb* to lead or lure into a trap. ▸ *noun* someone or something used to lure (a person or animal) into a trap. [16c: prob from Dutch *de kooi* the cage]

decrease *verb* /dɪ'kriːs/ *tr & intr* to make or become less. ▸ *noun* /'diːkriːs/ a lessening or loss. ▪ **decreasingly** *adv.* [14c: from Latin *decrescere*]

decree *noun* **1** a formal order or ruling. **2** *law* a ruling made in a law court. ▸ *verb* (***decreed, decreeing***) to order or decide something formally or officially. [14c: from Latin *decretum*]

decree absolute *noun, law* a decree in divorce proceedings which officially ends a marriage.

decree nisi /'naɪsaɪ/ *noun, law* a decree of divorce which will become a **decree absolute** after a period of time unless some reason is shown why it should not.

decrepit *adj* **1** weak or worn out because of old age. **2** in a very poor state because of age or long use. ▪ **decrepitude** *noun.* [15c: from Latin *decrepitus* very old]

decretal *noun* a papal decree. [15c: from Latin *decretalis* of a decree]

decriminalize *or* **-ise** *verb, law* to make (something) no longer a criminal offence. ▪ **decriminalization** *noun.* [1940s as *noun*]

decry *verb* (***-cries, -cried***) to express disapproval of someone or something; to criticize someone or something as worthless or unsuitable. [17c: from French *décrier*]

decrypt /diː'krɪpt/ *verb* to convert information (eg computer data or TV signals) from a coded into a readable form. ▪ **decryption** *noun.* [20c: from **de-** (sense 2) + Greek *kryptos* hidden]

dedicate *verb* (*usu* **dedicate oneself** *or* **sth to sb** *or* **sth**) **1** to give or devote (oneself or one's time, money, etc) to some purpose, cause, etc. **2** to devote or address (a book, piece of music, etc) to someone as a token of affection or respect. **3** to set something apart for some sacred purpose. [15c: from Latin *dedicare*]

dedicated *adj* **1** committing a great deal of time and effort to something. **2** committed to a cause, etc. **3** assigned to a particular purpose: *a dedicated phone line.* **4** *technical* of a computer: designed to carry out one function.

dedication *noun* **1** the quality of being dedicated. **2** the act of dedicating. **3** the words dedicating a book, etc to someone.

deduce *verb* to think out or judge on the basis of what one knows or assumes to be fact. ▪ **deducible** *adj.* [15c: from **de-** (sense 1) + Latin *ducere* to lead]

deduct *verb* to take away (a number, amount, etc). ▪ **deductible** *adj.* [15c: from Latin *deducere*]

deduction *noun* **1** the act or process of deducting or deducing. **2** something, esp money, which has been or will be deducted. **3** something that has been deduced. Compare **induction** (sense 5). ▪ **deductive** *adj.*

deed *noun* **1** something done. **2** a brave action or notable achievement. **3** *law* a signed statement recording an agreement, esp about a change in ownership of property. [Anglo-Saxon]

deed poll *noun, law* a deed made and signed by one person only, esp when changing their name.

deejay *noun, informal* a **disc jockey**. [1950s]

deem *verb, formal, old use* to judge, think or consider. [Anglo-Saxon *deman* to form a judgement]

deep *adj* **1** far down from the top or surface; with a relatively great distance from the top or surface to the bottom. **2** far in from the outside surface or edge. **3** *usu in compounds* far down by a specified amount: *knee-deep in mud.* **4** in a specified number of rows or layers: *lined up four deep.* **5** coming from or going far down; long and full: *a deep sigh.* **6** very great: *deep trouble.* **7** of a colour: strong and relatively dark. **8** low in pitch: *deep-toned.* **9** of emotions, etc: strongly felt. **10** obscure; hard to understand: *deep thoughts.* **11** of a person: mysterious; keeping secret thoughts. **12** *cricket* not close to the wickets. **13** *football* well behind one's team's front line of players. ▸ *adv* **1** deeply. **2** far down or into. **3** late on in or well into (a period of time). ▸ *noun* **1** (**the deep**) the ocean. **2** (*also* **deeps**) *old use* a place far below the surface of the ground or the sea. See also **depth.** ▪ **deeply** *adv* very greatly. ▪ **deepness** *noun.* [Anglo-Saxon *deop*]

IDIOMS **deep in sth** fully occupied or involved with it: *deep in thought.* **go off (at) the deep end** *informal* to lose one's temper suddenly and violently. **in deep water** *informal* in trouble or difficulties.

deepen *verb, tr & intr* to make or become deeper, greater, more intense, etc. [16c]

deep-freeze *noun* a refrigeration unit, or a compartment in a refrigerator, designed for storing perishables below −18°C (0°F). ▸ *verb* to preserve perishable material, esp food, by storing it in a frozen state. [1940s]

deep-fry *verb* to fry something by completely submerging it in hot fat or oil.

deep-laid *adj* secretly plotted or devised.

deep-rooted *or* **deep-seated** *adj* of ideas, habits, etc: deeply and firmly established.

deep-vein thrombosis *noun* (abbreviation **DVT**) the formation of a blood clot in a deep vein, sometimes affecting people who travel in cramped conditions on long-distance flights.

deer *noun* (*pl* ***deer***) a **ruminant** mammal, the male of which has antlers. [Anglo-Saxon *deor* animal]

deerstalker *noun* a hat with peaks at the front and back and flaps at the side that can cover the ears.

def. *abbrev* **1** defendant. **2** definition.

deface *verb* to deliberately spoil the appearance of something (eg by marking or cutting). ▪ **defacement** *noun*. [14c: from French *desfacier*]

de facto *adj, adv* actual or actually, though not necessarily legally so. Compare **de jure**. [17c: Latin, meaning 'in fact']

defame *verb* to attack the good reputation of someone. ▪ **defamation** *noun*. ▪ **defamatory** *adj*. [14c: from Latin *diffamare* to spread bad reports about]

default *verb, intr* **1** (*usu* **default on sth**) to fail to do what one should do, esp to fail to pay what is due. **2** *law* to fail to appear in court when called upon. ▸ *noun* **1** a failure to do or pay what one should. **2** *comput* a preset option which will always be followed unless the operator enters a command to the contrary. ▪ **defaulter** *noun*. [13c: from French *defaillir* to fail]

IDIOMS **by default** because of someone's failure to do something. **in default of sth** in the absence of it; for lack of it.

defeat *verb* **1** to beat someone, eg in a war, competition, game or argument. **2** to make (plans, etc) fail. ▸ *noun* defeating or being defeated. [16c: from French *desfait*]

defeatism *noun* a state of mind in which one too readily expects or accepts defeat or failure. ▪ **defeatist** *adj, noun*. [Early 20c]

defecate *verb* to empty the bowels of waste matter. ▪ **defecation** *noun*. [19c: from Latin *defaecare* to cleanse]

defect *noun* /ˈdiːfɛkt/ a flaw or fault. ▸ *verb* /dɪˈfɛkt/ *intr* to leave one's country, political party, etc, esp to go to or join an opposing one. ▪ **defection** *noun*. ▪ **defector** *noun*. [15c: from Latin *deficere* to fail]

defective *adj* having a defect or defects. ▪ **defectively** *adv*. ▪ **defectiveness** *noun*.

defence *or* (*US*) **defense** *noun* **1** the act of defending against attack. **2** the method or equipment used to protect against attack or when attacked. **3** the armed forces of a country. **4** (**defences**) fortifications. **5** a person's answer to an accusation, justifying or denying what they have been accused of. **6** (**the defence**) *law* in a court: the person or people on trial and the lawyer or lawyers acting for them. **7** (**the defence**) *sport* the players in a team whose main task is to prevent their opponents from scoring. ▪ **defenceless** *adj*. [13c: from Latin *defendere* to defend]

defend *verb* **1** to guard or protect someone or something against attack or when attacked. **2** to explain, justify or argue in support of the actions of someone accused of doing wrong. **3** to be the lawyer acting on behalf of (the accused) in a trial. **4** *tr & intr, sport* to try to prevent one's opponents from scoring. **5** *sport* to take part in a contest against a challenger for (a title, etc one holds). ▪ **defender** *noun*. [13c: from Latin *defendere*]

defendant *noun* someone against whom a charge is brought in a law-court. See also **plaintiff**. [16c]

defensible *adj* able to be defended or justified. ▪ **defensibility** *noun*.

defensive *adj* **1** defending or ready to defend. **2** attempting to justify one's actions when criticized or when expecting criticism. ▪ **defensively** *adv*. ▪ **defensiveness** *noun*.

IDIOMS **on the defensive** defending oneself or prepared to defend oneself against attack or criticism.

defer[1] *verb* (***deferred, deferring***) to put off something until a later time. ▪ **deferment** *or* **deferral** *noun*. [14c: from Latin *differre* to delay or postpone]

defer[2] *verb* (***deferred, deferring***) *intr* (*usu* **defer to sb**, *etc*) to yield to their wishes, opinions or orders. [15c: from Latin *deferre* to carry away]

deference *noun* **1** willingness to consider or respect the wishes, etc of others. **2** the act of deferring. ▪ **deferential** *adj*. ▪ **deferentially** *adv*. [17c]

IDIOMS **in deference to sb** *or* **sth** deferring to them; showing recognition of or respect for them.

defiance *noun* open disobedience or opposition. ▪ **defiant** *adj*. ▪ **defiantly** *adv*.

deficiency *noun* (***-ies***) **1** a shortage or lack in quality or amount. **2** the thing or amount lacking.

deficient *adj* not good enough; not having all that is needed. [16c: from Latin *deficere* to fail or be lacking]

deficit *noun* the difference between what is required and what is available. [18c: from Latin *deficere* to fail or be lacking]

defile[1] *verb* **1** to make something dirty or polluted. **2** to take away or spoil the goodness, purity, holiness, etc of something. ▪ **defilement** *noun*. [14c: from French *defouler* to trample or violate]

defile[2] *noun* a narrow valley or passage between mountains. ▸ *verb, intr* to march in file. [17c: from French *défilé*, from *défiler* to march in file]

define *verb* **1** to fix or state the exact meaning of (a word, etc). **2** to fix, describe or explain (opinions, duties, the qualities or limits of something, etc). **3** to make clear the outline or shape of something. ▪ **definable** *adj*. [14c: from Latin *definire* to set boundaries to]

definite *adj* **1** fixed or firm; not liable to change. **2** sure; certain. **3** clear and precise. **4** having clear outlines. ▪ **definitely** *adv* **1** as a definite fact; certainly. **2** in a definite way. [16c: from Latin *definire* to set boundaries to]

definite article *noun, grammar* the word **the**, or any equivalent word in other languages. Compare **indefinite article**.

definition *noun* **1** a statement of the meaning of a word or phrase. **2** the act of defining a word or phrase. **3** the quality of having clear precise limits or form. **4** clearness and preciseness of limits or form. [14c: from Latin *definitio*]

definitive *adj* **1** settling a matter once and for all. **2** complete and authoritative. ▪ **definitively** *adv*. [14c: from Latin *definitivus* definite]

deflate *verb* **1** *tr & intr* to collapse or grow smaller by letting out gas. **2** to reduce or take away the hopes, excitement, feelings of importance or self-confidence, etc of someone. **3** *tr & intr, econ* to undergo or make something undergo **deflation**. Compare **inflate**, **reflate**. [19c: from **de-** (sense 2) + *-flate*, from **inflate**]

deflation *noun* **1** deflating or being deflated. **2** the state of feeling deflated. **3** *econ* a reduction in the amount of available money in a country, lowering economic activity, industrial output, employment, and wage rises. See also **inflation**, **reflation**, **stagflation**. ▪ **deflationary** *adj.*

deflect *verb, tr & intr* to turn aside from the correct or intended course. ▪ **deflection** *noun.* ▪ **deflector** *noun.* [16c: from Latin *deflectere* to bend aside]

deflower *verb, literary* to take away someone's virginity. [14c: from Latin *deflorare*]

defoliant *noun, technical* a herbicide that makes the leaves of plants fall off. ▪ **defoliate** *verb.* ▪ **defoliation** *noun.* [1940s: from Latin *de* off + *folium* leaf]

deforest *verb* to clear forested land, eg for agriculture. ▪ **deforestation** *noun.* [16c]

deform *verb* to change the shape of something, making it look ugly, unpleasant, unnatural or spoiled. ▪ **deformed** *adj.* [15c: from Latin *deformis* ugly]

deformity *noun* (**-ies**) **1** being deformed or misshapen. **2** ugliness; disfigurement; an ugly feature.

defragment *or* **defrag** *verb* (***defragged, defragging***) *comput* to move files or parts of files together on a hard disk.

defraud *verb* (*usu* **defraud sb of sth**) to dishonestly prevent someone getting or keeping something which belongs to them or to which they have a right. [14c: from Latin *defraudare*]

defray *verb, formal* to provide the money to pay (someone's costs or expenses). ▪ **defrayal** *or* **defrayment** *noun.* [16c: from French *deffroier* to pay costs]

defrock *verb* to remove (a priest) from office. [17c: from French *défroquer*]

defrost *verb, tr & intr* **1** to remove ice from something. **2** to thaw or unfreeze. [19c]

deft *adj* skilful, quick and neat. ▪ **deftly** *adv.* ▪ **deftness** *noun.* [Anglo-Saxon *gedæfte* meek]

defunct *adj* no longer living, existing, active, usable or in use. [16c: from Latin *defungi* to finish]

defuse *verb* **1** to remove the fuse from (a bomb, etc). **2** to make (a situation, etc) harmless or less dangerous. [1940s]

defuse, diffuse

Be careful not to use the word **defuse** when you mean **diffuse**. To **diffuse** something is to send it out in all directions:

The news was diffused rapidly around the town.

defy *verb* (**-*ies*, -*ied***) **1** to resist or disobey someone boldly and openly. **2** to dare or challenge someone. **3** *formal* to make something impossible or unsuccessful: *defying explanation.* See also **defiance**. [14c: from French *defier*]

degenerate *adj* /dɪ'dʒɛnərət/ **1** physically, morally or intellectually worse than before. **2** *biol* having lost former structure; having become simpler. ▸ *noun* /dɪ'dʒɛnərət/ a degenerate person or animal. ▸ *verb* /dɪ'dʒɛnəreɪt/ *intr* to become degenerate. ▪ **degeneracy** *noun.* ▪ **degeneration** *noun.* ▪ **degenerative** *adj.* [15c: from Latin *degenerare* to become unlike one's kind]

degrade *verb* **1** to disgrace or humiliate someone. **2** to reduce someone or something in rank, status, etc. **3** *tr & intr, chem* to change or be converted into a substance with a simpler structure. ▪ **degradable** *adj.* ▪ **degradation** *noun.* ▪ **degrading** *adj* humiliating; debasing. [14c: from French *degrader*]

degree *noun* **1** an amount or extent. **2** *physics* (symbol °) a unit of temperature. **3** *geom* (symbol °) a unit by which angles are measured, equal to 1⁄360 of a circle. **4** an award given by a university or college. **5** a comparative amount of severity or seriousness. [13c: from French]

IDIOMS **by degrees** gradually.

dehiscent /dɪ'hɪsənt/ *adj, botany* bursting open to release seeds or pollen. Compare **indehiscent**. ▪ **dehiscence** *noun.* [17c: from Latin *dehiscere* to split open]

dehumanize *or* **-ise** *verb* to remove the human qualities from someone ▪ **dehumanization** *noun.* [19c]

dehydrate *verb* **1** to remove water from (a substance or organism). **2** *tr & intr* to lose or make someone or something lose too much water from the body. ▪ **dehydrated** *adj.* ▪ **dehydration** *noun.* [19c: **de-** (sense 2) + Greek *hydor* water]

de-ice *verb* to make or keep something free of ice. ▪ **de-icer** *noun.* [1930s]

deify /'deɪɪfaɪ/ *verb* (**-*ies*, -*ied***) to regard or worship someone or something as a god. ▪ **deification** *noun.* [14c: from French *deifier*]

deign /deɪn/ *verb, intr* to do something in a way that shows that one considers the matter unimportant or beneath one's dignity. [13c: from French *daigner*]

deindustrialize *or* **-ise** *verb* to reduce the industrial organization and potential of a nation, area, etc. ▪ **deindustrialization** *noun.* [19c]

deionization *noun, chemistry* a process involving exchange of ions that is used to purify a solution, especially water obtained from the mains supply.

deism /'deɪɪzəm, 'diː-/ *noun* belief in the existence of God without acceptance of any religion or message revealed by God to man. ▪ **deist** *noun.* ▪ **deistic** *or* **deistical** *adj.* [17c: from Latin *deus* god + **-ism** (sense 1)]

deity /'deɪɪtɪ, 'diː-/ *noun* (**-*ies***) *formal* **1** a god or goddess. **2** the state of being divine. **3** (**the Deity**) God. [14c: from Latin *deitas*, from *deus* god]

déjà vu /deɪʒɑː 'vuː/ *noun* the feeling or illusion that one has experienced something before, although one is actually experiencing it for the first time. [Early 20c: French, meaning 'already seen']

dejected *adj* sad; miserable. ▪ **dejectedly** *adv.* ▪ **dejection** *noun.* [16c: from Latin *deicere* to disappoint]

de jure /diː 'dʒʊərɪ/ *adv, adj, law* according to law; by right. Compare **de facto**. [16c: Latin, meaning 'by law']

dekko *or* **decko** *noun* (*usu* **have** *or* **take a dekko**) *slang* a look. [19c: from Hindi *dekhna* to see]

delay *verb* **1** to slow someone or something down or make them late. **2** to put off to a later time. **3** *intr* to be slow in doing something. ▸ *noun* **1** delaying or being delayed. **2** the amount of time by which someone or something is delayed. [13c: from French *delaier*]

delectable *adj* delightful; delicious. ▪ **delectably** *adv.* [14c: from Latin *delectare* to delight]

delectation *noun, formal* delight, enjoyment or amusement. [14c: from Latin *delectare* to delight]

delegate *verb* /ˈdɛlɪgeɪt/ **1** to give (part of one's work, power, etc) to someone else. **2** to send or name someone as a representative, as the one to do a job, etc. ▸ *noun* /ˈdɛlɪgət/ someone chosen to represent others, eg at a meeting. [14c: from Latin *delegare*]

delegation *noun* **1** a group of delegates. **2** delegating or being delegated.

delete *verb* to rub out, score out or remove something, esp from something written or printed. ▪ **deletion** *noun.* [16c: from Latin *delere* to blot out]

deleterious /dɛlɪˈtɪərɪəs/ *adj, formal* harmful or destructive. [17c: from Greek *deleterios*]

delf, delph, **delft** /dɛlft/ *or* **Delftware** *noun* a type of earthenware orig made at Delft in the Netherlands, typically with a blue design on white. [17c]

deli *noun* a **delicatessen**.

deliberate *adj* /dɪˈlɪbərət/ **1** done on purpose. **2** slow and careful. ▸ *verb* /dɪˈlɪbəreɪt/ *tr & intr* to think about something carefully. ▪ **deliberately** *adv.* [16c: from Latin *deliberare* to consider carefully]

deliberation *noun* **1** careful thought. **2** (**deliberations**) formal and thorough thought and discussion. **3** slowness and carefulness.

delicacy *noun* (**-*ies***) **1** the state or quality of being delicate. **2** something considered particularly delicious to eat.

delicate *adj* **1** easily damaged or broken. **2** not strong or healthy. **3** having fine texture or workmanship. **4** small and attractive. **5** small, neat and careful: *delicate movements.* **6** requiring tact and careful handling: *a delicate situation.* **7** careful not to offend others. **8** of colours, flavours, etc: light; not strong. ▪ **delicately** *adv.* ▪ **delicateness** *noun.* [14c: from Latin *delicatus*]

delicatessen *noun* a shop or counter selling eg cheeses, cooked meats, and unusual or imported foods. Often shortened to **deli**. [19c: German, from French *délicatesse* delicacy]

delicious *adj* **1** with a very pleasing taste or smell. **2** giving great pleasure. ▪ **deliciously** *adv.* [14c: from French *delicious*]

delight *verb* **1** to please greatly. **2** *intr* (**delight in sth**) to take great pleasure from it. ▸ *noun* **1** great pleasure. **2** something or someone that gives great pleasure. ▪ **delighted** *adj.* ▪ **delightedly** *adv.* [13c: from French *deliter*; modern spelling influenced by **light**]

delightful *adj* giving great pleasure. ▪ **delightfully** *adv.*

delimit *verb* to mark or fix the limits of (powers, etc). ▪ **delimitation** *noun.* [19c: from Latin *delimitare*]

delineate *verb* **1** to show something by drawing. **2** to describe something in words. ▪ **delineation** *noun.* [16c: from Latin *delineare* to sketch out]

delinquent *noun* someone, esp a young person, guilty of a minor crime. ▸ *adj* guilty of a minor crime or misdeed. ▪ **delinquency** *noun* (**-*ies***) **1** minor crime, esp committed by young people. **2** delinquent nature or behaviour. [15c: from Latin *delinquere* to fail in one's duty]

deliquesce *verb, intr, chem* esp of salts: to dissolve slowly in water absorbed from the air. ▪ **deliquescence** *noun.* ▪ **deliquescent** *adj.* [18c: from Latin *deliquescere* to dissolve]

delirious *adj* **1** affected by **delirium**. **2** very excited or happy. ▪ **deliriously** *adv.* [16c: from Latin *delirare* to rave]

delirium *noun* **1** a state of madness or mental confusion and excitement, often caused by fever, drugs, etc. **2** extreme excitement or joy. [16c: see **delirious**]

delirium tremens /ˈtrɛmɛnz/ *noun* (abbrev **DTs**) delirium caused by chronic alcoholism.

deliver *verb* **1** to carry (goods, letters, etc) to a person or place. **2** to give or make (a speech, etc). **3** to help (a woman) at the birth of (a child). **4** *tr & intr, informal* to keep or fulfil (a promise or undertaking). **5** *formal* to aim or direct (a blow, criticism, etc). [13c: from French *délivrer*]

IDIOMS **deliver the goods** *informal* to fulfil a promise or undertaking.

deliverance *noun, formal* the act of rescuing, freeing or saving from danger or harm. [13c]

delivery *noun* (**-*ies***) **1** the carrying of (goods, letters, etc) to a person or place. **2** the thing or things being delivered. **3** the process or manner of giving birth to a child. **4** the act of making, or the manner of making, a speech, etc. **5** the act or manner of throwing a ball.

dell *noun* a small valley or hollow, usu wooded. [Anglo-Saxon]

delph see **delf**

delphinium *noun* (***delphiniums*** *or* ***delphinia*** /dɛlˈfɪnɪəm/) a garden plant with tall spikes of usu blue flowers. [17c: from Greek *delphinion* larkspur]

delta *noun* **1** the fourth letter of the Greek alphabet. **2** *geog* an area of silt, sand, gravel or clay, often roughly triangular, at a river mouth. **3** in classification systems: the fourth grade. [15c: Greek]

delude *verb* to deceive or mislead someone. [15c: from Latin *deludere* to cheat]

deluge /ˈdɛljuːdʒ/ *noun* **1** a flood. **2** a downpour of rain. **3** a great quantity of anything pouring in. ▸ *verb, formal* to flood; to cover in water. [14c: French]

IDIOMS **be deluged with sth** to be overwhelmed by it.

delusion *noun* **1** the act of deluding or the state of being deluded. **2** *psychol* a false or mistaken belief. Compare **illusion**, **hallucination**. ▪ **delusive** *and* **delusory** *adj.* [15c: from Latin *delusio*]

de luxe *or* **deluxe** *adj* **1** very luxurious or elegant. **2** with special features or qualities. [19c: French, literally 'of luxury']

delve *verb, intr* **1** (*usu* **delve into sth**) to search it for information. **2** (*usu* **delve through sth**) to search through it. [Anglo-Saxon *delfan* to dig]

demagnetize *or* **-ise** *verb* to remove the magnetic properties of something. ▪ **demagnetization** *noun.* [19c]

demagogue *noun, derog* someone who tries to win power or support by appealing to people's emotions and prejudices. ▪ **demagogic** *adj.* ▪ **demagoguery** *or* **demagogy** *noun.* [17c: from Greek *demos* people + *agogos* leading]

demand *verb* **1** to ask or ask for firmly, forcefully or urgently. **2** to require or need something. **3** to claim something as a right. ▸ *noun* **1** a forceful request or order. **2** an urgent claim for action or attention: *demands on one's time.* **3** people's desire or ability to buy or obtain goods, etc. **4** *econ* the amount of any article, commodity, etc, which consumers will buy. Compare **supply** (*noun* sense 6). [15c: from French *demander* to ask]

IDIOMS **in demand** very popular; frequently asked for. **on demand** when asked for.

demanding *adj* **1** requiring a lot of effort, ability, etc. **2** needing or expecting a lot of attention.

demarcation *noun* **1** the marking out of limits or boundaries. **2** the strict separation of the areas or types of work to be done by the members of the various trade unions in a factory, etc. *as adj*: *a demarcation dispute*. ▪ **demarcate** *verb*. [18c: from Spanish *demarcar* to mark the boundaries of]

demean *verb* to lower the dignity of or lessen respect for (esp oneself). [17c]

demeanour *or* (*N Am*) **demeanor** *noun* way of behaving. [15c: from French *demener* to treat]

demented *adj* mad; out of one's mind. ▪ **dementedly** *adv*. [17c: from Latin *de* from + *mens* mind]

dementia /dɪ'mɛnʃə/ *noun, psychol* a loss or severe lessening of normal mental ability and functioning, esp in the elderly. See also **senile dementia**. [18c: from Latin *de* from + *mens* mind]

demerara *or* **demerara sugar** *noun* a form of crystallized brown sugar. [19c: named after Demerara in Guyana, where it orig came from]

demerit *noun, formal* a fault or failing. [16c: from Latin *demereri* to deserve]

demi- *combining form, signifying* half or partly: *demigod*. Compare **semi-**. [From French *demi* half]

demigod *or* **demigoddess** *noun* **1** *myth* someone part human and part god; a lesser god. **2** a person idolized as if they were a god. [16c]

demijohn *noun* a large bottle with a short narrow neck and one or two small handles, used for storing eg wine. [18c: from French *dame-jeanne* Dame Jane]

demilitarize *or* **-ise** *verb* to remove armed forces from (an area) and/or not allow any military activity in it. ▪ **demilitarization** *noun*. [19c]

demi-monde *noun* **1** women in an unrespectable social position. **2** any group considered not completely respectable. [19c: French, meaning 'half-world']

demise *noun* **1** *formal or euphem* death. **2** a failure or end. [16c: from French]

demisemiquaver *noun, music* a note equal in time to half a **semiquaver**.

demist /diː'mɪst/ *verb* to free (a vehicle's windscreen, etc) from condensation by blowing warm air over it. ▪ **demister** *noun*. [1930s]

demo *noun, informal* **1** a public demonstration of opinion on a political or moral issue. **2** (*also* **demo tape**) a recording made usu by unsigned musicians to demonstrate their music to record companies. [1930s]

demob *verb, Brit informal* (***demobbed, demobbing***) to **demobilize**. [1920s]

demobilize *or* **-ise** *verb* to release someone from service in the armed forces, eg after a war. ▪ **demobilization** *noun*. [19c]

democracy *noun* (***-ies***) **1** a form of government in which the people govern themselves or elect representatives to govern them. **2** a country, state or other body with such a form of government. [16c: from French *démocratie*]

democrat *noun* **1** someone who believes in **democracy**. **2** (**Democrat**) a member or supporter of any political party with *Democratic* in its title, eg the Democratic Party of the USA. Compare **Republican** (*noun* sense 2).

democratic *adj* **1** concerned with or following the principles of democracy. **2** believing in or providing equal rights and privileges for all. **3** (**Democratic**) belonging or relating to the Democratic Party, one of the two chief political parties of the USA. Compare **Republican** (*adj* sense 3). ▪ **democratically** *adv*. [17c]

demodulation *noun, electronics* the inverse of **modulation**, a process by which an output wave is obtained that has the characteristics of the original modulating wave. [1920s]

demography *noun, technical* the scientific study of population statistics. ▪ **demographer** *noun*. ▪ **demographic** *adj*. [19c: from Greek *demos* people + *graphein to write*]

demolish *verb* **1** to pull down (a building, etc). **2** to destroy (an argument, etc). **3** *facetious* to eat up. ▪ **demolition** *noun*. [16c: from Latin *demoliri* to throw down]

demon *noun* **1** an evil spirit. **2** a cruel or evil person. **3** someone who has great energy, enthusiasm or skill: *a demon at football*. **4** a **daemon**. ▪ **demonic** *adj*. [15c: from Greek *daimon* spirit]

demoniac /dɪ'moʊnɪak/ *or* **demoniacal** /diːmə'naɪəkəl/ *adj* **1** of or like a demon or demons. **2** influenced by demons; frenzied or very energetic.

demonize *or* **demonise** /'diːmənaɪz/ *verb* (***demonized, demonizing***) to portray (a person) as evil or corrupt. ▪ **demonization** *noun*. [19c]

demonstrate *verb* **1** to show or prove something by reasoning or evidence. **2** *tr & intr* to show how something is done, operates, etc. **3** *tr & intr* to show (support, opposition, etc) by protesting, marching, etc in public. ▪ **demonstrable** *adj*. ▪ **demonstrably** *adv*. ▪ **demonstration** *noun*. [16c: from Latin *demonstrare* to show]

demonstrative *adj* **1** showing one's feelings openly. **2** (*usu* **demonstrative of sth**) showing evidence of it; proving it to be so. ▪ **demonstratively** *adv*. [16c]

demonstrative pronoun *or* **demonstrative adjective** *noun, grammar* a word indicating which person or thing is referred to, ie **this**, **that**, **these**, **those**.

demonstrator *noun* **1** someone who demonstrates equipment, etc. **2** someone who takes part in a public demonstration. [17c]

demoralize *or* **-ise** *verb* to take away the confidence, courage or enthusiasm of someone. ▪ **demoralization** *noun*. [19c: from French *démoraliser*]

demote *verb* to reduce someone to a lower rank or grade. ▪ **demotion** *noun*. [19c: from **de-** (sense 2) + *promote*]

demotic *adj* of a language: popular, everyday. ▸ *noun* colloquial language. [19c: from Greek *demotikos*, from *demos* people]

demur *verb* (***demurred, demurring***) *intr* to object or show reluctance. ▪ **demurral** *noun*. [17c: from French *demorer* to wait]

IDIOMS **without demur** without objecting.

demure *adj* quiet, modest and well-behaved. ▪ **demurely** *adv*. ▪ **demureness** *noun*. [17c: from French *demorer* to wait]

demutualize *or* **demutualise** /diːˈmjuːtʃuːəlaɪz/ *verb intr* of a financial institution that is owned by its members, eg a building society: to become a public company. ▪ **demutualization** *noun*. [20c]

demystify *verb* (**-ies, -ied**) to remove the mystery from something. ▪ **demystification** *noun*. [1960s]

den *noun* **1** a wild animal's home. **2** a centre (often secret) of illegal or immoral activity. **3** *informal* a room or hut used as a place to work or play. [Anglo-Saxon *denn* cave or lair]

denar see **dinar**

denarius /dɪˈnɛərɪəs/ *noun* (***denarii*** /-rɪaɪ, -rɪiː/) an ancient Roman silver coin. [16c: Latin]

denary /ˈdiːnərɪ/ *adj* decimal. [19c: from Latin *denarius* containing ten]

denationalize *or* **-ise** *verb* to transfer (an industry) to private ownership from state ownership. ▪ **denationalization** *noun*. [19c]

denature *or* **denaturize** *or* **-ise** *verb* **1** to change the structure or composition of (something). **2** to add an unpalatable substance to (alcohol), so that it is unfit for human consumption. [17c, orig meaning 'to make something unnatural']

dendrology *noun* the scientific study of trees. ▪ **dendrological** *adj*. ▪ **dendrologist** *noun*. [18c: from Greek *dendron* tree]

dengue /ˈdɛŋgeɪ/ *noun* an acute tropical viral fever transmitted by mosquitos. [19c: prob from Swahili *dinga*]

denial *noun* **1** denying something; declaring something not to be true. **2** an act of refusing something to someone. **3** a refusal to acknowledge connections with somebody or something.

denier /ˈdɛnɪə(r)/ *noun* the unit of weight of silk, rayon or nylon thread, usu used as a measure of the fineness of stockings or tights. [19c: French]

denigrate *verb* to attack or belittle someone's reputation, character or worth. ▪ **denigration** *noun*. ▪ **denigrator** *noun*. [16c: from Latin *denigrare* to blacken]

denim *noun* **1** a hard-wearing twilled cotton cloth. **2** (**denims**) clothing, esp jeans, made of denim. ▸ *adj* made of denim. [17c: from French *de* of + Nîmes, a town in southern France]

denizen *noun* **1** *formal* an inhabitant. **2** *biol* a species of animal or plant which has become well established in a place to which it is not native. [15c: from French *deinzein*]

denominate *verb, formal* to give a specific name or title to something. [16c: from Latin *denominare* to name]

denomination *noun* **1** a religious group with its own beliefs, organization and practices. **2** a particular unit of value of a postage stamp, coin or banknote, etc. ▪ **denominational** *adj*. [15c]

denominator *noun, maths* in a **vulgar fraction**, the number below the line. Compare **numerator**. [16c]

denote *verb* **1** to mean; to be the name of or sign for something. **2** to be a sign, mark or indication of something. ▪ **denotation** *noun*. [16c: from Latin *denotare* to mark out]

denouement *or* **dénouement** /deɪˈnuːmɑ̃/ *noun* **1** the final part of a story or plot, in which uncertainties, problems and mysteries are resolved. **2** *loosely* any resolution. [18c: French, from *dénouer* to untie a knot]

denounce *verb* **1** to inform against or accuse someone publicly. **2** to condemn (an action, proposal, etc) strongly and openly. See also **denunciation**. [15c: from French *dénoncier*]

dense *adj* **1** closely packed or crowded together. **2** thick: *dense fog*. **3** *informal* stupid; slow to understand. ▪ **densely** *adv*. [15c: from Latin *densus* thick]

density *noun* (**-ies**) **1** the state of being dense; the degree of denseness. **2** the ratio of the mass of a substance to its volume. **3** the number of items within a specific area or volume. **4** *comput* the number of bits that can be stored on one track of a disk or within a specific area of magnetic tape, etc.

dent *noun* **1** a hollow made by pressure or a blow. **2** a noticeable, usu bad, effect; a lessening (eg of resources, money, etc). ▸ *verb* **1** to make a dent in something. **2** *intr* to become dented. **3** to injure (someone's pride, etc). [Anglo-Saxon *dynt* blow]

dental *adj* **1** concerned with the teeth or dentistry. **2** *phonetics* of a sound: produced by putting the tongue to the teeth. ▸ *noun, phonetics* a dental sound. [16c: from Latin *dentalis*, from *dens* tooth]

dental floss *noun* a soft thread used for cleaning between the teeth.

dental surgeon *noun* a dentist.

dentate *adj, technical* with tooth-like notches round the edge. [19c: from Latin *dentatus*]

dentifrice /ˈdɛntɪfrɪs/ *noun* paste or powder for cleaning the teeth. [16c: French]

dentine *or* **dentin** *noun, anatomy* the hard material that forms the bulk of a tooth. [19c: from Latin *dens* tooth]

dentist *noun* someone who diagnoses, treats and prevents diseases of the oral cavity and teeth. ▪ **dentistry** *noun*. [18c: from French *dentiste*]

dentition *noun, technical* the number, arrangement and type of teeth in a human or animal. [16c: from Latin *dentitio* teething]

denture *noun* a false tooth or (usu **dentures**) set of false teeth. [19c: French]

denude *verb* **1** to make someone or something completely bare. **2** to strip (land) through weathering and erosion. ▪ **denudation** *noun*. [15c: from Latin *denudare* to lay bare or uncover]

denunciation *noun* a public condemnation or accusation. See also **denounce**. [16c: from Latin *denuntiare* to announce]

deny *verb* (**-ies, -ied**) **1** to declare something not to be true. **2** to refuse to give or allow something to someone. **3** to refuse to acknowledge. See also **denial**. ▪ **deniable** *adj*. [14c: from French *denier*]

IDIOMS **deny oneself sth** to do without (something that one wants or needs).

---

deny, refute

Be careful not to use the word **deny** when you mean **refute**. If you **refute** something, you prove it is wrong or use a reasoned argument against it:

The evidence will refute any allegation of wrongdoing.

---

deodorant *noun* a substance that prevents or conceals unpleasant smells, esp on the human body. [19c]

deodorize *or* **-ise** *verb* to remove, conceal or absorb the unpleasant smell of something. [19c]

deoxygenate *verb, chem* to remove oxygen from something.

deoxyribonucleic acid /diːˈɒksɪraɪboʊnjuːˈkleɪɪk/ *noun, biochem* (abbrev **DNA**) the nucleic acid that forms the material that chromosomes and genes are composed of. [1930s]

depart *verb, intr* **1** to leave. **2** (*usu* **depart from sth**) to stop following or decline to follow a planned or usual course of action. ▪ **departed** *adj, formal* **1** dead. **2** (**the departed**) a person or people recently dead. [13c: from French *departir*]

department *noun* **1** a section of an organization. **2** a subject or activity which is someone's special skill or responsibility. ▪ **departmental** *adj.* [18c: from French *département*]

department store *noun* a large shop with many departments selling a wide variety of goods.

departure *noun* **1** an act of going away or leaving. **2** (*often* **departure from sth**) a change from a planned or usual course of action. **3** (*often* **new departure**) a new and different activity. [16c]

depend *verb, intr* (*usu* **depend on** *or* **upon sb** *or* **sth**) **1** to trust or rely on them or it. **2** to rely on financial or other support from someone. **3** to be decided by or vary according to something else. [15c: from Latin *dependere* to hang down]

dependable *adj* trustworthy; reliable. ▪ **dependability** *noun.* ▪ **dependably** *adv.*

dependant *noun* a person who is kept or supported financially by another. [16c]

---

dependant, dependent

Be careful not to use the spelling **dependant** when you mean the adjective **dependent**:

We are increasingly dependent on television for entertainment.

---

dependence *noun* (*usu* **dependence on sth** *or* **sb**) **1** the state of being dependent on it or them. **2** trust and reliance. [17c]

dependency *noun* (**-ies**) **1** a country governed or controlled by another. **2** excessive dependence on someone or something, eg addiction to a drug. [16c]

dependent *adj* (*often* **dependent on sth** *or* **sb**) **1** relying on it or them for financial or other support. **2** to be decided or influenced by them or it: *Success is dependent on all our efforts.*

---

dependent, dependant

Be careful not to use the spelling **dependent** when you mean the noun **dependant**:

If you have an accident, your dependants will be looked after.

---

dependent clause *noun, grammar* a **subordinate clause**.

depict *verb* **1** to paint or draw something. **2** to describe something, esp in detail. ▪ **depiction** *noun.* [17c: from Latin *depingere* to paint]

depilate *verb* to remove hair from (a part of the body). ▪ **depilation** *noun.* ▪ **depilatory** /dɪˈpɪlətərɪ/ *noun, adj.* [16c: from Latin *depilare* to remove hair]

deplete *verb* to reduce greatly in number, quantity, etc; to use up (money, resources, etc). ▪ **depletion** *noun.* [19c: from Latin *deplere* to empty]

deplorable *adj* very bad, shocking or regrettable. ▪ **deplorably** *adv.*

deplore *verb* to feel or express great disapproval of or regret for something. [16c: from French *déplorer*]

deploy *verb* **1** *tr & intr* to position (troops) ready for battle. **2** to organize and bring (resources, arguments, etc) into use. ▪ **deployment** *noun.* [18c: from French *déployer*]

deponent *noun, law* someone who makes a deposition (see **deposition** sense 3), esp under oath. [16c: from Latin *deponere* to lay aside or put down]

depopulate *verb* to greatly reduce the number of people living in (an area, country, etc). ▪ **depopulation** *noun.* [16c: from Latin *depopulari* to deprive of people]

deport[1] *verb* to legally remove or expel (a person) from a country. ▪ **deportation** *noun.* ▪ **deportee** *noun.* [17c: from Latin *deportare* to carry away]

deport[2] *verb, formal* to behave (oneself) in a particular way. ▪ **deportment** *noun* **1** one's bearing. **2** behaviour. [16c: from Latin *deportare* to carry away]

depose *verb* to remove (someone) from a high office or powerful position. [15c: from French *deposer* to put down or away]

deposit *verb* **1** to put down or leave something. **2** to put (money, etc) in a bank, etc. **3** to give (money) as the first part of the payment for something. **4** to pay (money) as a guarantee against loss or damage. ▸ *noun* **1** money, etc, deposited in a bank, etc. **2** money given as part payment for something or as a guarantee against loss or damage. **3** solid matter that has settled at the bottom of a liquid, or is left behind by a liquid. **4** *geol* a layer (of coal, oil, minerals, etc) occurring naturally in rock. ▪ **depositor** *noun.* [16c: from Latin *depositum*]

deposit account *noun* a bank account in which money gains interest but which cannot be used for money transfers by eg cheque or standing order.

depositary *noun* (**-ies**) **1** *formal* a person, etc to whom something is given for safekeeping. **2** a **depository** (sense 1). [17c: from Latin *depositarius*]

deposition *noun* **1** deposing or being deposed. **2** the act of depositing or process of being deposited. **3** *law* a written statement made under oath and used as evidence in a court of law. **4** *geog* the laying down of eroded material, eg rocks, that has been transported by wind, rivers, glaciers, avalanches, etc. [14c: from Latin *depositio* putting down]

depository *noun* (**-ies**) **1** a place where anything may be left for safe-keeping, eg a furniture store. **2** a **depositary** (sense 1). [17c: from Latin *depositorium*]

depot /ˈdɛpoʊ; *N Am* ˈdiːpoʊ/ *noun* **1** a storehouse or warehouse. **2** a place where buses, trains and other vehicles are kept and repaired. **3** *N Am* a bus or railway station. [18c: from French *dépôt*]

depraved *adj* morally corrupted. ▪ **depravity** *noun* (**-ies**). [15c: from Latin *depravare* to pervert]

deprecate *verb* to express or feel disapproval of something. ▪ **deprecatingly** *adv.* ▪ **deprecation** *noun.* ▪ **deprecatory** *adj* **1** showing or expressing disapproval. **2** apologetic; trying to avoid disapproval. [17c: from Latin *deprecari* to try to avert]

depreciate *verb* **1** *tr & intr* to fall, or make something fall, in value. **2** to belittle someone or something. ▪ **depreciatory** *adj.* [15c: from Latin *depretiare* to lower the price of]

depreciation *noun* **1** *econ* a fall in value of a currency against the value of other currencies. **2** the reduction in the value of assets through use or age. **3** the process of depreciating.

depredation *noun* (*often* **depredations**) damage, destruction or violent robbery. [15c: from Latin *praedari* to plunder]

depress *verb* **1** to make someone sad and gloomy. **2** *formal* to make (prices, etc) lower. **3** *formal* to press down. **4** to weaken something. ▪ **depressing** *adj.* ▪ **depressingly** *adv.* [16c: from French *depresser*]

depressant *adj, med* of a drug: able to reduce mental or physical activity. ▸ *noun* a depressant drug. [19c]

depressed *adj* **1** sad and gloomy. **2** *psychol* suffering from depression. **3** of a region, etc: suffering from high unemployment and low standards of living. **4** of trade, etc: not flourishing.

depression *noun* **1** *psychol* a mental state characterized by prolonged and disproportionate feelings of sadness, pessimism, helplessness, apathy, low self-esteem and despair. **2** a period of low business and industrial activity accompanied by a rise in unemployment. **3** (**the Depression**) the period of worldwide economic depression from 1929 to 1934. **4** a **cyclone**. **5** a hollow, esp in the ground. **6** *maths* an angle measuring a point below a horizontal line. Compare **elevation** (sense 3).

depressive *adj* **1** depressing. **2** suffering from frequent bouts of depression. ▸ *noun* someone who suffers from depression.

depressor *noun* **1** something or someone that depresses. **2** *anatomy* a muscle that draws down the part it is connected to.

depressurize *or* **-ise** *verb* to reduce the air pressure in (eg an aircraft). ▪ **depressurization** *noun.* [1940s]

deprive *verb* (*usu* **deprive sb of sth**) to prevent them from having or using it. ▪ **deprivation** *noun.* [14c: from Latin *deprivare* to degrade]

deprived *adj* **1** lacking money, reasonable living conditions, etc. **2** of a district, etc: lacking good housing, schools, medical facilities, etc.

dept *abbrev* department.

depth *noun* **1** the distance from the top downwards, from the front to the back or from the surface inwards. **2** intensity or strength. **3** extensiveness: *the depth of one's knowledge.* **4** (*usu* **the depths**) somewhere far from the surface or edge of somewhere: *the depths of the ocean.* **5** (*usu* **the depths**) an extreme feeling (of despair, sadness, etc) or great degree (of deprivation, etc). **6** (*often* **the depths**) the middle and severest or most intense part (of winter, etc). **7** (**depths**) serious aspects of a person's character that are not immediately obvious. **8** of sound: lowness of pitch. [14c: from Anglo-Saxon *deop* **deep**]

IDIOMS **in depth** deeply and thoroughly. **out of one's depth 1** in water deeper than one's height. **2** not able to understand information or an explanation; in a situation too difficult to deal with.

depth charge *noun* a bomb which explodes underwater, used to attack submarines.

deputation *noun* a group of people appointed to represent and speak on behalf of others. [16c: from Latin *deputare* to select]

depute *verb* /dɪ'pjuːt/ *formal* **1** to formally appoint someone to do something. **2** (*usu* **depute sth to sb**) to give (eg part of one's work) to someone else to do. [15c: from French *deputer*]

deputize *or* **-ise** *verb* **1** *intr* (*often* **deputize for sb**) to act as their deputy. **2** to appoint someone as a deputy.

deputy *noun* (**-ies**) **1** a person appointed to act on behalf of, or as an assistant to, someone else. **2** in certain countries: a person elected to the lower house of parliament. ▸ *adj* in some organizations: next in rank to the head. [16c: from French *deputer* to appoint]

derail *verb, tr & intr* to leave or make (a train, etc) leave the rails. ▪ **derailment** *noun.* [19c: from French *dérailler*]

derange *verb* **1** to make someone insane. **2** to disrupt or throw into disorder or confusion. ▪ **deranged** *adj.* ▪ **derangement** *noun.* [18c: from French *déranger* to disturb]

Derby *abbrev, English county* Derbyshire.

derby[1] /'dɑːbɪ/ *noun* (**-ies**) **1** (**the Derby**) a horse race held annually at Epsom Downs. **2** a race or a sports event, esp a contest between teams from the same area. [19c: named after the Earl of Derby]

derby[2] /'dɜːbɪ/ *noun* (**-ies**) *N Am* a bowler hat. [19c: from **derby**[1]]

deregulate *verb* to remove controls and regulations from (a business or business activity). ▪ **deregulation** *noun.*

derelict *adj* **1** abandoned. **2** of a building: in ruins. ▸ *noun* **1** a tramp with no home or money. **2** anything, esp a ship, forsaken or abandoned. [17c: from Latin *derelinquere* to abandon]

dereliction *noun* **1** (*usu* **dereliction of duty**) neglect or failure. **2** the state of being abandoned.

derestrict *verb* to remove a restriction from (something), esp a speed limit from (a road). ▪ **derestriction** *noun.* [20c]

deride *verb* to laugh at or make fun of someone. ▪ **derision** *noun.* [16c: from Latin *deridere*]

de rigueur /də rɪ'gɜː(r)/ *adj* required by fashion, custom or the rules of politeness. [19c: French, meaning 'of strictness']

derisive *adj* scornful; mocking. ▪ **derisively** *adv.*

derisory *adj* ridiculous and insulting, esp ridiculously small. [20c: from Latin *derisorius* derisive]

derivation *noun* **1** deriving or being derived. **2** the source or origin (esp of a word).

derivative *adj* not original; derived from or copying something else. ▸ *noun* **1** something which is derived from something else. **2** *grammar* a word formed by adding one or more **affix**es to another word. Compare **compound**[1] (*noun* sense 3). **3** *chem* a compound, usu organic, that is made from another compound. **4** *maths* the rate of change of one variable quantity in relation to small changes in another. Also called **differential coefficient**. **5** *stock exchange* (**derivatives**) **future**s and **option**s.

derive *verb* **1** *intr* (*usu* **derive from sth**) to have it as a source or origin. **2** (*usu* **derive sth from sth else**) to obtain or produce one thing from another. [14c: from French *dériver*]

dermatitis *noun, med* inflammation of the skin in the absence of infection, eg eczema and psoriasis. [19c]

dermato- *or* (*before a vowel*) **dermat-** *combining form, denoting* the skin: *dermatitis.* [From Greek *derma* skin]

dermatology *noun* the study of the skin and treatment of its diseases. ▪ **dermatologist** *noun.* [19c]

dermis *noun, anatomy* the thick lower layer of skin beneath the epidermis, containing blood capillaries, nerve endings, hair follicles, sweat glands, and lymph vessels. Also called **corium**. [19c: from Greek *derma* skin]

derogate *verb, intr* (**derogate from sth**) *formal* to make it appear inferior; to show one's low opinion of it. ▪ **derogation** *noun.* [15c: from Latin *derogare* to detract from]

derogatory /dɪˈrɒɡətərɪ/ *adj* showing dislike, scorn or lack of respect. ▪ **derogatorily** *adv.* ▪ **derogatoriness** *noun.* [16c: from Latin *derogatorius*]

derrick *noun* **1** a type of crane with a movable arm. **2** a framework built over an oil-well, for raising and lowering the drill. [18c: named after a 17c hangman]

derring-do *noun, old use, literary* daring deeds. [16c: from *derrynge do,* meaning 'daring to do']

derv *noun, Brit* diesel oil used as a fuel for road vehicles. [1940s: from *d*iesel-*e*ngine *r*oad *v*ehicle]

dervish *noun* a Muslim ascetic, noted for performing spinning dances as a religious ritual. [16c: from Persian *darvish* poor man]

desalinate *verb, technical* to remove salt from (esp seawater). ▪ **desalination** *and* **desalinization** *or* **-isation** *noun.* [1940s]

descale *verb* to remove encrusted deposits from (a pipe, kettle, etc). [1950s]

descant /ˈdɛskant/ *music, noun* a melody played or harmony sung above the main tune. ▸ *adj* of a musical instrument: having a higher pitch and register than others of the same type. [14c: French, from Latin *dis-* apart + *cantus* song]

descend *verb* **1** *tr & intr* to move from a higher to a lower place or position. **2** *intr* to lead or slope downwards. **3** *intr* (*often* **descend on sb** *or* **sth**) to invade or attack them or it. [13c: from French *descendre*]
IDIOMS **be descended from sb** to have them as an ancestor.

descendant *adj* (*also* **descendent**) descending. ▸ *noun* a person or animal, etc that is the child, grandchild, etc of another.

descent *noun* **1** the act or process of coming or going down. **2** a slope downwards. **3** family origins or ancestry; being descended from someone. **4** a sudden invasion or attack. [14c: from French *descente*]

describe *verb* **1** to say what someone or something is like. **2** *technical, geom* to draw or form (eg a circle). [16c: from Latin *describere*]

description *noun* **1** the act of describing. **2** a statement of what someone or something is like. **3** *informal* a sort, type or kind: *toys of every description.* [15c: from Latin *descriptio*]

descriptive *adj* describing, esp describing vividly. ▪ **descriptively** *adv.*

descry /dɪˈskraɪ/ *verb* (**-ies, -ied**) *formal* **1** to see or catch sight of something. **2** to see or discover by looking carefully. [14c: from French *descrier* to announce and *descrire* to describe]

desecrate *verb* to treat or use (a sacred object) or behave in (a holy place) in a way that shows a lack of respect. ▪ **desecration** *noun.* [17c: from **de-** (sense 2) + **consecrate**]

desegregate *verb* to end segregation, esp racial segregation in (public places, schools, etc). ▪ **desegregation** *noun.* [1950s]

deselect *verb* not to reselect (eg a sitting MP or councillor, an athlete). ▪ **deselection** *noun.*

desensitize *or* **-ise** *verb* to make someone or something less sensitive to light, pain, suffering, etc. ▪ **desensitization** *noun.* [Early 20c]

desert[1] *verb* **1** to leave or abandon (a place or person). **2** *intr* to leave (esp a branch of the armed forces) without permission. **3** to take away support from (a person, cause, etc). ▪ **deserter** *noun.* ▪ **desertion** *noun.* [15c: from French *déserter*]

desert, dessert
Be careful not to use the spelling **desert** when you mean **dessert**:
We are having trifle for dessert.

desert[2] *noun* an area of land with little rainfall and scarce vegetation. *as adj*: *a desert island.* [13c: French, from Latin *deserere* to abandon]

desertification *noun* the process by which new desert is formed. [1970s]

deserts *plural noun* (*usu* **just deserts**) what one deserves, usu something bad. [13c: from French *deservir* to deserve]

deserve *verb* to have earned or be worthy of (a reward or punishment, etc). ▪ **deservedly** /dɪˈzɜːvɪdlɪ/ *adv.* [13c: from French *deservir*]

deserving *adj* (*usu* **deserving of sth**) worthy of being given support, a reward, etc. ▪ **deservingly** *adv.*

déshabille /deɪzəˈbiː/ *or* **dishabille** /disəˈbiːl/ *noun* the state of being only partly dressed. [17c: French, meaning 'undress']

desiccate *verb* **1** to dry or remove the moisture from something, esp from food in order to preserve it. **2** *intr* to dry up. ▪ **desiccated** *adj.* ▪ **desiccation** *noun.* [16c: from Latin *desiccare* to dry up]

design *verb* **1** to make a preparatory plan, drawing or model of something. **2** *formal* to plan, intend or develop something for a particular purpose. ▸ *noun* **1** a plan, drawing or model showing how something is to be made. **2** the art or job of making such drawings, plans, etc. **3** the way in which something has been made. **4** a decorative picture, pattern, etc. **5** a plan, purpose or intention. ▪ **designedly** /dɪˈzaɪnɪdlɪ/ *adv* intentionally; on purpose. ▪ **designing** *adj, derog* using cunning and deceit to achieve a purpose. ▪ **designingly** *adv.* [16c: from French *désigner*]
IDIOMS **by design** intentionally. **have designs on sb** *or* **sth** to have plans to appropriate them or it.

designate *verb* /ˈdɛzɪɡneɪt/ **1** to choose or specify someone or something for a purpose or duty. **2** to mark or indicate something. **3** to be a name or label for someone or something. ▸ *adj* /-nət/ *usu following its noun* appointed to some official position but not yet holding it: *editor designate.* ▪ **designation** *noun.* [18c: from Latin *designare* to plan or mark out]

designer *noun* someone who makes plans, patterns, drawings, etc. ▸ *adj* **1** designed by and bearing the name of a famous fashion designer: *designer dresses.* **2** *informal, sometimes derog* following current fashion.

desirable *adj* **1** pleasing; worth having. **2** of a person: attractive. ▪ **desirability** *noun.* ▪ **desirably** *adv.*

desire *noun* **1** a longing or wish. **2** strong sexual interest and attraction. ▸ *verb* **1** *formal* to want. **2** to feel sexual desire for someone. [13c: from French *desirer*]

desirous *adj, formal* (*usu* **desirous of sth**) wanting it keenly.

desist *verb, intr, formal* (*often* **desist from sth**) to stop. [15c: from French *desister*]

desk *noun* **1** a table, often with drawers, for sitting at while writing, reading, etc. **2** a service counter in a public building. **3** a section of a newspaper etc office with responsibility for a particular subject: *news desk*. [14c: from Latin *discus* disc or table]

deskilling *noun* the process of removing the element of human skill from a job, process, etc, through automation, computerization, etc.

desktop *adj* small enough to fit on the top of a desk. ▸ *noun* **1** a desktop computer. **2** *comput* a screen showing the files and programs available for working with.

desktop publishing *noun* (abbrev **DTP**) the preparation and production of typeset material using a desktop computer and printer.

desolate *adj* /ˈdɛsələt/ **1** barren and lonely. **2** very sad. **3** lacking pleasure or comfort: *a desolate life*. **4** lonely; alone. ▸ *verb* /-leɪt/ **1** to overwhelm someone with sadness or grief. **2** to lay waste (an area). ▪ **desolately** *adv.* ▪ **desolation** *noun*. [14c: from Latin *desolare*, desolatum to forsake]

despair *verb, intr* (*often* **despair of sth** *or* **despair of doing sth**) to lose or lack hope. ▸ *noun* the state of having lost hope. [14c: from French *desperer*]

despatch see **dispatch**

desperado *noun* (***desperados*** *or* ***desperadoes***) a bandit or outlaw. [17c: prob formed from **desperate**]

desperate *adj* **1** extremely anxious, fearful or despairing. **2** willing to take risks because of hopelessness and despair. **3** very serious, difficult, dangerous and almost hopeless: *a desperate situation*. **4** dangerous and likely to be violent: *a desperate criminal*. **5** extreme and carried out as a last resort: *desperate measures*. **6** very great: *desperate need*. **7** extremely anxious or eager: *desperate to go to the concert*. ▪ **desperately** *adv.* ▪ **desperation** *noun*. [15c: from Latin *desperare* to despair]

IDIOMS **desperate for sth** in great need of it.

---

desperate

This word is often misspelt. It has an e in the middle. It might help you to remember the following sentence:

*I'm in desp**er**ate **per**il!*

---

despicable *adj* contemptible; mean. ▪ **despicably** *adv.* [16c: from Latin *despicabilis*]

despise *verb* to scorn or have contempt for someone or something. [13c: from Latin *despicere*]

despite *prep* in spite of. [13c: French]

despoil *verb, formal, literary* to steal everything valuable from (a place). ▪ **despoliation** *noun*. [13c: from French *despoiller*]

despondent *adj* sad; dejected. ▪ **despondency** *noun*. ▪ **despondently** *adv.* [17c: from Latin *despondere* to lose heart]

despot *noun* someone who has great or total power, esp if cruel or oppressive. ▪ **despotic** *adj*. ▪ **despotically** *adv.* [18c: from Greek *despotes* master]

despotism *noun* **1** complete or absolute power. **2** a state governed by a despot.

dessert *noun* a sweet food served after the main course of a meal. [16c: French, from *desservir* to clear the table]

---

dessert, desert

Be careful not to use the spelling **dessert** when you mean **desert**:

The travellers were lost in the desert.

She has been deserted by her friends.

---

dessertspoon *noun* (abbrev **dsp**) **1** a spoon about twice the size of a **teaspoon**. **2** the amount a dessertspoon will hold. Also called **dessertspoonful**.

destabilize *or* **-ise** *verb* to make (a country, an economy, etc) less stable. ▪ **destabilization** *noun*. [20c]

destination *noun* the place to which someone or something is going. [16c: from Latin *destinatio* purpose]

destine *verb, formal* (*usu* **be destined for sth** *or* **to do sth**) to have it as one's fate. [14c: from French *destiner*]

destiny *noun* (***-ies***) **1** the purpose or future as arranged by fate or God. **2** (*also* **Destiny**) fate. [14c: from French *destinee*]

destitute *adj* extremely poor. ▪ **destitution** *noun*. [15c: from Latin *destitutus*]

de-stress /diːˈstrɛs/ *verb, tr & intr* to relax after a period of psychological stress or hard work.

destroy *verb* **1** to break something into pieces, completely ruin it, etc. **2** to put an end to something. **3** to defeat someone totally. **4** to ruin the reputation, health, financial position, etc of someone. **5** to kill (a dangerous, injured or unwanted animal). [13c: from French *destruire*]

destroyer *noun* **1** someone or something that destroys. **2** a type of small fast warship.

destruction *noun* **1** the act or process of destroying or being destroyed. **2** something that destroys. ▪ **destructible** *adj*. [14c: from Latin *destruere* to destroy]

destructive *adj* **1** causing destruction or serious damage. **2** of criticism, etc: pointing out faults, etc without suggesting improvements. ▪ **destructively** *adv.*

desuetude /dɪˈsjuːɪtʃuːd/ *noun* disuse; discontinuance. [17c: from Latin *desuescere* to become unaccustomed]

desultory /ˈdɛzəltərɪ/ *adj* jumping from one thing to another with no plan, purpose or logical connection. ▪ **desultorily** *adv.* [16c: from Latin *desultorius*]

detach *verb* **1** *tr & intr* to unfasten or separate. **2** *military* to select and separate (soldiers, etc) from a larger group, esp for a special task. ▪ **detachable** *adj*. [17c: from French *destachier*]

detached *adj* **1** of a building: not joined to another on either side. **2** feeling no personal or emotional involvement; showing no prejudice or bias. ▪ **detachedly** *adv.*

detachment *noun* **1** the state of being emotionally detached or free from prejudice. **2** a group (eg of soldiers) detached for a purpose. **3** detaching or being detached.

detail *noun* **1** a small feature, fact or item. **2** something considered unimportant. **3** all the small features and parts of something: *an eye for detail*. **4** a part of a painting, map, etc considered separately, often enlarged to show small features. **5** *military* a group of eg soldiers given a special task. ▸ *verb* **1** to describe or list fully. **2** to appoint someone to do a particular task. ▪ **detailed** *adj* **1** of a list, etc: itemized. **2** of a story, picture, etc: intricate. [17c: from French *detailler* to cut up]

IDIOMS **in detail** giving or looking at all the details.

detain *verb* **1** to delay someone or something. **2** of the police, etc: to keep someone in a cell, prison, etc. See also **detention**. ▪ **detainee** *noun*. ▪ **detainment** *noun*. [15c: from French *detenir* to hold]

detect *verb* **1** to see or notice. **2** to discover, and usu indicate, the presence or existence of (something). ▪ **detectable** *or* **detectible** *adj*. ▪ **detector** *noun*. [16c: from Latin *detegere* to uncover]

detection *noun* **1** detecting or being detected. **2** the work of a detective, investigating and solving crime.

detective *noun* a police officer whose job is to solve crime by observation and gathering evidence.

détente /deɪ'tɑ̃t/ *noun* a lessening of tension, esp between countries. [Early 20c: French]

detention *noun* **1** the act of detaining or the state of being detained, esp in prison or police custody. **2** a punishment in which a pupil is kept at school after the other pupils have gone home. [15c: from Latin *detinere* to detain]

deter *verb* (***deterred, deterring***) to discourage or prevent something or someone from doing something, because of possible unpleasant consequences. [16c: from Latin *deterrere* to frighten off]

detergent *noun* a soap-like cleansing agent. ▸ *adj* having the power to clean.

deteriorate *verb, intr* to grow worse. ▪ **deterioration** *noun*. [17c: from Latin *deterior* worse]

determinant *noun* **1** a determining factor or circumstance. **2** *maths* in a square matrix of elements, the difference between the multiplied diagonal terms. ▸ *adj* determining.

determinate *adj* having definite fixed limits, etc.

determination *noun* **1** firmness or strength of will, purpose or character. **2** the act of determining or process of being determined.

determine *verb* **1** to fix or settle the exact limits or nature of something. **2** to find out or reach a conclusion about something by gathering facts, making measurements, etc. **3** *tr & intr* to decide or make someone decide. **4** to be the main or controlling influence on someone or something. [14c: from French *determiner*]

determined *adj* **1** (**determined to do sth**) firmly intending to do it. **2** having or showing a strong will. ▪ **determinedly** *adv*.

determiner *noun, grammar* a word that precedes a noun and limits its meaning in some way, eg **a**[1], **the**, **this**, **every**, **some**.

determinism *noun, philos* the theory that whatever happens has to happen and could not be otherwise. ▪ **determinist** *noun*.

deterrent *noun* something which deters, eg a weapon that deters attack. ▸ *adj* capable of deterring. ▪ **deterrence** *noun*.

detest *verb* to dislike someone or something intensely. ▪ **detestable** *adj* hateful. [15c: from French *detester*]

dethrone *verb* **1** to remove (a monarch) from the throne. **2** to remove someone from a position of power or authority. ▪ **dethronement** *noun*. [17c]

detonate *verb, tr & intr* to explode or make something explode. ▪ **detonation** *noun*. [18c: from Latin *detonare* to thunder down]

detonator *noun* an explosive substance or a device used to make a bomb, etc explode.

detour *noun* a route away from and longer than a planned or more direct route. ▸ *verb, intr* to make a detour. [18c: from French *détour*]

detoxify *verb* (***-ies, -ied***) **1** to remove poison, drugs or harmful substances from (a person, etc). **2** to treat (a patient) for alcoholism or drug addiction. Often shortened to **detox**. ▪ **detoxification** *noun*. [1940s: from Latin *toxicum* poison]

detract *verb, intr* (*chiefly* **detract from sth**) to take away from it or lessen it. ▪ **detraction** *noun*. ▪ **detractor** *noun*. [15c: from Latin *detrahere* to pull away]

detriment *noun* harm or loss. ▪ **detrimental** *adj* harmful; damaging. ▪ **detrimentally** *adv*. [15c: from Latin *detrimentum*]

detritus /dɪ'traɪtəs/ *noun* bits and pieces of rubbish left over from something. [19c: from Latin *deterere* to rub away]

de trop /də troʊ/ ▸ *adj* not wanted; in the way. [18c: French, meaning 'too much']

deuce /dʒuːs/ *noun* **1** *tennis* a score of forty points each in a game or five games each in a match. **2** a card, dice throw, etc, of the value two. [15c: from French *deus* two]

deus ex machina /'diːəs ɛks mə'ʃiːnə, 'deɪʊs ɛks 'makɪnə/ *noun* in literature: someone or something providing a contrived solution to a difficulty. [17c: Latin, meaning 'god out of a machine']

deuterium *noun, chem* (symbol **D**) one of the three isotopes of hydrogen. Also called **heavy hydrogen**. See also **tritium**. [1930s: from Greek *deuteros* second]

deuterium oxide *noun, chem* a compound of deuterium and hydrogen, used to slow down neutrons in nuclear reactors. Also called **heavy water**.

deutero-, **deuto-** *or* (*before a vowel*) **deuter-** *or* **deut-** *combining form, signifying* **1** second or secondary. **2** *chem* that one or more hydrogens in a compound is the **deuterium** isotope. [17c: Greek, from *deuteros* second]

deuteron *noun, physics* the nucleus of an atom of deuterium, composed of a proton and a neutron.

Deutschmark /'dɔɪtʃmɑːk/ *or* **Deutsche Mark** /'dɔɪtʃə/ *noun* the former standard unit of currency of Germany, replaced in 2002 by the euro. [20c: German, meaning 'German mark']

devalue *or* **devaluate** *verb* **1** *tr & intr* to reduce the value of (a currency) in relation to the values of other currencies. **2** to make (a person, action, etc) seem less valuable or important. ▪ **devaluation** *noun*. [20c]

devastate *verb* **1** to cause great destruction in or to something. **2** to overwhelm someone with grief or shock. ▪ **devastated** *adj*. ▪ **devastating** *adj*. ▪ **devastation** *noun*. [17c: from Latin *devastare* to lay waste]

develop *verb* **1** *tr & intr* to make or become more mature, advanced, complete, organized, detailed, etc. **2** to change to a more complex structure. **3** to begin to have, or to have more, of something: *develop an* *interest in politics.* **4** *tr & intr* to appear and grow; to have or suffer from something which has appeared and grown: *developing a cold.* **5** to convert an invisible image on (exposed photographic film or paper) into a visible image. **6** to bring into fuller use (the natural resources, etc of a country or region). **7** to build on (land) or prepare (land) for being built on. [17c: from French *développer*]

developer *noun* **1** a chemical used to develop film. **2** someone who builds on land or improves and increases the value of buildings.

developing country *noun, econ* a country with a low level of economic development which is trying to industrialize.

development *noun* **1** the act of developing or the process of being developed. **2** a new stage, event or situation. **3** a result or consequence. **4** land which has been or is being developed, or the buildings built or being built on it. ▪ **developmental** *adj.*

deviant *adj* not following the normal patterns, accepted standards, etc. ► *noun* someone who behaves in a way not considered normal or acceptable. ▪ **deviance** *and* **deviancy** *noun.* [15c]

deviate *verb* /ˈdiːvɪeɪt/ *intr* to move away from what is considered a correct or normal course, standard of behaviour, way of thinking, etc. ▪ **deviation** *noun.* [17c: from Latin *deviare* to turn from the road]

device *noun* **1** a tool or instrument. **2** a plan or scheme, sometimes involving trickery or deceit. **3** *heraldry* a sign, pattern or symbol eg on a crest or shield. [13c: from French *devis* and *devise*]

IDIOMS **be left to one's own devices** to be left alone and without help.

devil *noun* **1** (**the Devil**) *relig* the most powerful evil spirit; Satan. **2** any evil spirit. **3** *informal* a mischievous or bad person. **4** *informal* a person: *lucky devil.* **5** someone or something difficult to deal with. **6** someone who excels at something. **7** (**the devil**) used for emphasis in mild oaths and exclamations: *What the devil is he doing?* ► *verb* (***devilled, devilling***; *US* ***deviled, deviling***) **1** to prepare or cook (meat, etc) with a spicy seasoning. **2** to be a drudge. [Anglo-Saxon *deofol*]

IDIOMS **between the devil and the deep blue sea** in a situation where the alternatives are equally undesirable. **give the devil his due** to admit the good points of a person one dislikes. **speak** *or* **talk of the devil** said on the arrival of someone one has just been talking about.

devilish *adj* **1** characteristic of, like, or as if produced by a devil. **2** very wicked. ► *adv, old use* very.

devil-may-care *adj* cheerfully heedless of danger, etc.

devilment *noun* mischievous fun.

devilry *noun* (***-ies***) **1** mischievous fun. **2** wickedness or cruelty. **3** witchcraft; black magic.

devil's advocate *noun* someone who argues for or against something simply to encourage discussion or argument.

devious *adj* **1** not totally open or honest. **2** cunning, often deceitfully. **3** not direct: *came by a devious route.* ▪ **deviously** *adv.* [17c: from Latin *devius*]

devise *verb* to think up (a plan, etc). [14c: from French *deviser*]

devoid *adj* (*always* **devoid of sth**) free from it or lacking it. [15c: from French *devoidier* to take away]

devolution *noun* the act of devolving, esp of giving certain powers to a regional government by a central government. ▪ **devolutionary** *adj.* ▪ **devolutionist** *noun, adj.* [18c: from Latin *devolvere* to roll down]

devolve *verb* (*usu* **devolve to** *or* **on** *or* **upon sb**) **1** *tr & intr* of duties, power, etc: to be transferred or to transfer them to someone else. **2** *intr, law* to pass by succession. [15c: from Latin *devolvere* to roll down]

Devonian *adj,* **1** *geol* relating to the fourth period of the **Palaeozoic** era. **2** relating to the rocks formed during this period. [17c: from Devon in SW England]

devote *verb* to use or give up (eg time or money) to a purpose. [17c: from Latin *devovere* to consecrate]

devoted *adj* **1** (*usu* **devoted to sb**) loving and loyal to them. **2** (*usu* **devoted to sth**) given up to it; totally occupied by it. ▪ **devotedly** *adv.*

devotee /dɛvoʊˈtiː/ *noun* **1** a keen follower or enthusiastic supporter. **2** a keen believer in a religion. [17c]

devotion *noun* **1** great love or loyalty. **2** devoting or being devoted. **3** religious enthusiasm and piety. **4** (**devotions**) *relig* worship and prayers. ▪ **devotional** *adj.*

devour *verb* **1** to eat up something greedily. **2** to completely destroy something. **3** to read (a book, etc) eagerly. **4** (*usu* **be devoured**) to be taken over totally: *devoured by guilt.* [14c: from French *devorer*]

devout *adj* **1** sincerely religious. **2** deeply felt; earnest. ▪ **devoutly** *adv.* [13c: from Latin *devovere* to consecrate]

dew *noun* tiny droplets of water deposited on eg leaves close to the ground on cool clear nights. ▪ **dewy** *adj* (***-ier, -iest***). [Anglo-Saxon *deaw*]

dewberry *noun* **1** a trailing type of **bramble**. **2** the fruit of this plant.

dewclaw *noun* a small functionless toe or claw on the legs of dogs and some other animals. [16c]

dewlap *noun* a flap of loose skin hanging down from the throat of certain animals. [14c: prob from **dew** + Anglo-Saxon *læppa* loose hanging piece]

dewy-eyed *adj, often ironic* naive and too trusting.

dexter *adj, heraldry* on the side of the shield on the bearer's right-hand side. Compare **sinister** (sense 2). [16c: Latin, meaning 'right']

dexterity *noun* **1** skill in using one's hands. **2** quickness of mind. [16c: from French *dextérité*]

dexterous *or* **dextrous** *adj* having, showing or done with dexterity. ▪ **dexterously** *or* **dextrously** *adv.*

dextrin *or* **dextrine** *noun, biochem* a substance produced during the breakdown of starch or glycogen, used as a thickener in foods and adhesives. [19c: from French *dextrine*]

dextro- *or* (*before a vowel*) **dextr-** *combining form, signifying* to or towards the right.

dextrose *noun* a type of **glucose**. [19c]

DFC *abbrev* Distinguished Flying Cross.

DFM *abbrev* Distinguished Flying Medal.

dg *abbrev* decigram or decigrams.

dhal see **dal**[1]

dharma /ˈdɑːmə/ *noun* **1** *Buddhism* truth. **2** *Hinduism* the universal laws, esp the moral laws. [18c: Sanskrit, meaning 'decree' or 'custom']

dhoti /'doʊtɪ/ *or* **dhooti** /'duːtɪ/ *noun* a long strip of cloth wrapped around the waist and between the legs, worn by some Hindu men. [17c: Hindi]

DI *abbrev* **1** Detective Inspector. **2** donor insemination.

di- *prefix* **1** two or double: *dicotyledon*. **2** *chem* containing two atoms of the same type: *dioxide*. [From Greek *dis* twice]

dia- *prefix, denoting* **1** through. **2** across. **3** during. **4** composed of. [Greek]

diabetes /daɪə'biːtiːz/ *noun* a disorder characterized by thirst and excessive production of urine. [16c: Greek, meaning 'siphon']

diabetes mellitus /mɛ'laɪtəs/ *noun, med* a metabolic disorder in which insulin is not produced sufficiently to control sugar metabolism.

diabetic *noun* someone suffering from diabetes. ▸ *adj* **1** relating to or suffering from diabetes. **2** for people who have diabetes. [18c]

diabolic *adj* **1** satanic; devilish. **2** very wicked or cruel. [14c: from Greek *diabolos* slanderer or devil]

diabolical *adj, Brit informal* very shocking, annoying, bad, difficult, etc. ▪ **diabolically** *adv*.

diabolism *noun* Satanism; witchcraft. ▪ **diabolist** *noun*.

diaconal /daɪ'akənəl/ *adj* relating to a deacon. [17c: from Latin *diaconus* deacon]

diaconate /daɪ'akəneɪt/ *noun* **1** the position of deacon. **2** one's period of time as a deacon. **3** deacons as a group. [18c: from Latin *diaconus* deacon]

diacritic *noun* a mark over, under or through a letter to show that it has a particular sound, as in *é, è, ç, ñ*. Compare **accent** (*noun* sense 3). [17c: from Greek *diakritikos* able to distinguish]

diadem /'daɪədɛm/ *noun* a crown or jewelled headband. [13c: from French *diademe*]

diaeresis *or* (*N Am*) **dieresis** /daɪ'ɛrəsɪs/ *noun* (***-ses*** /-siːz/) a mark (¨) placed over a vowel to show that it is to be pronounced separately, as in **naïve**. [17c: from Greek *diairesis* separation]

diagnosis /daɪəg'noʊsɪs/ *noun* (***-ses*** /-siːz/) *med* the identification of a medical disorder on the basis of its symptoms. ▪ **diagnose** *verb*. ▪ **diagnostic** *adj*. [17c: Greek, from *diagignoskein* to distinguish]

diagonal *adj* **1** *maths* of a straight line: joining non-adjacent corners of a **polygon** or vertices not on the same face in a **polyhedron**. **2** sloping or slanting. ▸ *noun* a diagonal line. ▪ **diagonally** *adv*. [16c: from Greek *dia* through + *gonia* angle]

diagram *noun* a drawing that shows something's structure or the way in which it functions. ▪ **diagrammatic** *adj*. [17c: from Greek *diagramma*]

dial *noun* **1** a plate on a clock, radio, meter, etc with numbers or symbols on it and a movable indicator, used to indicate eg measurements or selected settings. **2** the round numbered plate on some telephones and the movable disc fitted over it. ▸ *verb* (***dialled, dialling***; *US* ***dialed, dialing***) *tr & intr* to use a telephone dial or keypad to call (a number). [14c: from Latin *dialis* daily, perhaps from the dial of a sundial]

dialect *noun* a form of a language spoken in a particular region or by a certain social group. ▪ **dialectal** *adj*. [16c: from Greek *dialektos* manner of speech]

dialectic *noun, philos* **1** (*also* **dialectics**) the establishing of truth by discussion. **2** (*also* **dialectics**) a debate which aims to resolve the conflict between two opposing theories rather than to disprove either of them. **3** the art of arguing logically. ▪ **dialectical** *adj*. [17c: from Greek *dialektike* (*techne*) (the art) of debating]

dialling code *noun* the part of a telephone number that represents a town or area.

dialling tone *or* (*N Am*) **dial tone** *noun* the sound heard on picking up a telephone receiver which indicates that the equipment is ready to accept an input telephone number.

dialogue *or sometimes* (*US*) **dialog** *noun* **1** a conversation, esp a formal one. **2** the words spoken by the characters in a play, book, etc. **3** a discussion with a view to resolving conflict or achieving agreement. [13c: French, from Greek *dialogos* conversation]

dialogue box *or* **dialog box** *noun, comput* a small on-screen box that prompts the user to give information or enter an option.

dial-up *adj, comput* of a connection: using a modem to connect to another computer or to the Internet.

dialysis /daɪ'alɪsɪs/ *noun* (***-ses*** /-siːz/) **1** *chem* the separation of particles in a solution by diffusion through a semipermeable membrane. **2** *med* the removal of toxic substances from the blood by such a process in an artificial kidney machine. Also called **haemodialysis**. ▪ **dialyse** *or* (*chiefly N Am*) **dialyze** *verb*. ▪ **dialyser** *noun*. [16c: Greek, meaning 'separation']

diamanté /daɪə'mɒnteɪ, -'mantɪ/ *adj* decorated with small sparkling ornaments. [Early 20c: French, meaning 'decorated with diamonds']

diameter *noun, geom* **1** a straight line drawn across a circle through its centre. **2** the length of this line. [14c: from Greek *dia* across + *metron* measure]

diametric *or* **diametrical** *adj* **1** relating to or along a diameter. **2** of opinions, etc: directly opposed; very far apart. ▪ **diametrically** *adv*.

diamond *noun* **1** a colourless crystalline form of carbon, the hardest mineral and a gemstone. **2** a **rhombus**. **3** *cards* **a** (**diamonds**) one of the four suits of playing-cards, with red rhombus-shaped symbols (◆); **b** a playing-card of this suit. **4** a baseball pitch, or the part of it between the bases. ▸ *adj* **1** resembling, made of or marked with diamonds. **2** rhombus-shaped. [14c: from French *diamant*]

diamond anniversary *noun* a sixtieth, or occasionally seventy-fifth, anniversary.

diamond wedding *noun* the **diamond anniversary** of a marriage.

dianthus *noun* any plant of the family of flowers to which carnations and pinks belong. [18c: Latin]

diapason /daɪə'peɪzən/ *noun, music* **1** the whole range or compass of tones. **2** a standard of pitch. **3** a full volume of various sounds in concord. **4** an organ stop extending through its whole compass. [16c: from Greek *dia pason chordon symphonia* concord through all the notes]

diaper *noun, N Am* a baby's nappy. [15c: from French *diaspre*]

diaphanous /daɪ'afənəs/ *adj* of cloth: light and fine, and almost transparent. [17c: from Greek *dia* through + *phanein* to show]

diaphoretic *adj* promoting sweating. ▸ *noun* a diaphoretic substance.

diaphragm /'daɪəfram/ *noun* **1** *anatomy* the sheet of muscle that separates the **thorax** from the **abdo-**

men. **2** *optics* an opaque disc with an adjustable aperture that is used to control the amount of light entering eg a camera or microscope. **3** a thin vibrating disc or cone that converts sound waves to electrical signals in a microphone, or electrical signals to sound waves in a loudspeaker. **4** a **cap** (*noun* sense 7). [14c: from Greek *diaphragma* partition]

diapositive *noun* a transparent photographic slide. [19c]

diarist *noun* a person who writes a diary, esp one which is published.

diarrhoea *or* (*N Am*) **diarrhea** /daɪə'rɪə/ *noun* **1** *med* a condition in which the bowels are emptied frequently and the faeces are very soft or liquid. **2** an excessive flow of anything: *verbal diarrhoea*. [16c: from Greek *dia* through + *rhoia* flow]

diary *noun* (**-*ies***) **1 a** a written record of daily events in a person's life; **b** a book containing this. **2** *Brit* a book with separate spaces or pages for each day of the year in which appointments, daily notes and reminders may be written. [16c: from Latin *diarium*, from *dies* day]

the Diaspora /daɪ'aspərə/ *noun* **1** the scattering of the Jewish people to various countries following their exile in Babylon in the 6c BC. **2** the resulting new communities of Jews in various countries. **3** the Jews who do not live in the modern state of Israel. **4** (*also* **diaspora**) a dispersion of people of the same nation or culture. [19c: from Greek *dia* through + *speirein* to scatter]

diastole /daɪ'astəlɪ/ *noun, med* the rhythmic expansion of the chambers of the heart during which they fill with blood. See also **systole**. ▪ **diastolic** /daɪə'stɒlɪk/ *adj*. [16c: from Greek *dia* apart + *stellein* to place]

diatom *noun* a microscopic one-celled alga. [19c: from Greek *diatomos* cut through]

diatomic *adj, chem* denoting a molecule that consists of two identical atoms.

diatonic *adj, music* relating to, or using notes from, the **diatonic scale**, a scale consisting of only the basic notes proper to a particular key with no additional sharps, flats or naturals. See also **chromatic**. [17c: from **dia-** + Greek *tonos* tone]

diatribe *noun* a bitter or abusive critical attack. [19c: Greek, meaning 'discourse']

diazepam /daɪ'azəpam, daɪ'eɪ-/ *noun, med* a tranquillizing drug which relieves anxiety and acts as a muscle relaxant. [1960s: from benzo*diazepine*]

dibasic *adj, chem* denoting an acid that contains two replaceable atoms, allowing the formation of two types of salt, the normal and the acid salt. [19c]

dibble *noun* a short pointed hand-tool used for making holes in the ground, etc for seeds, young plants, etc. Also called **dibber**.

dice *noun* (*pl* ***dice***) **1** a small cube with 1 to 6 spots on each of its faces, used in games of chance. **2** a game of chance played with dice. See also **die**[2]. ▸ *verb* **1** to cut (vegetables, etc) into small cubes. **2** *intr* to play or gamble with dice. [14c: orig the pl of **die**[2]]
IDIOMS **dice with death** to take a great risk.

dicey *adj* (***dicier, diciest***) *informal* risky.

dichlorodiphenyltrichloroethane see **DDT**

dichotomy /daɪ'kɒtəmɪ/ *noun* (**-*ies***) a division or separation into two groups or parts, esp when these are sharply opposed or contrasted. ▪ **dichotomous** *adj*. [16c: from Greek *dicha* in two + *tome* cut]

dichromatic *adj* **1** of eg animals: having two variant colours or colourings. **2** able to see only two colours and combinations of these. [19c]

dick *noun, slang* a detective. [18c: from the name *Dick*]

dickens *noun, informal* (*usu* **the dickens**) the devil, used esp for emphasis: *What the dickens are you doing?* [16c: from the name *Dickon* or *Dicken*, from *Richard*]

Dickensian *adj* **1** resembling the 19c English social life depicted in the novels of Charles Dickens, eg the poor living and working conditions. **2** characteristic of or relating to Charles Dickens or to his writings.

dicky[1], **dickey** *or* **dickie** *noun* (**-*ies*** *or* **-*eys***) **1** a false shirt front worn with evening dress. **2** a bow tie. Also called **dicky bow**.

dicky[2] *adj* (**-*ier, -iest***) *informal* **1** shaky; unsteady. **2** not in good condition. [19c]

dicotyledon /daɪkɒtɪ'liːdən/ *noun, botany* a flowering plant with an embryo that has two **cotyledons**. Compare **monocotyledon**. [18c]

dicta see **dictum**

Dictaphone *noun, trademark* a small tape recorder for use esp when dictating letters.

dictate *verb* /dɪk'teɪt/ **1** to say or read out something for someone else to write down. **2** to state or lay down (rules, terms, etc) forcefully or with authority. **3** *tr & intr, derog* to give orders to or try to impose one's wishes on someone. ▸ *noun* /'dɪkteɪt/ (*usu* **dictates**) **1** an order or instruction. **2** a guiding principle. ▪ **dictation** *noun*. [16c: from Latin *dictare*]

dictator *noun* **1** a ruler with total power. **2** someone who behaves in a dictatorial manner. ▪ **dictatorial** *adj* fond of imposing one's wishes on or giving orders to other people. ▪ **dictatorially** *adv*. ▪ **dictatorship** *noun*.

diction *noun* **1** the way in which one speaks. **2** one's choice or use of words. [17c: from Latin *dicere* to say]

dictionary *noun* (**-*ies***) **1** a book containing the words of a language arranged alphabetically with their meanings etc, or with the equivalent words in another language. **2** an alphabetically arranged book of information. **3** *comput* a dictionary contained on the disk that a program can check against for spelling errors in text. [16c: from Latin *dictionarium*]

dictum *noun* (***dictums*** *or* ***dicta*** /'dɪktə/) **1** a formal or authoritative statement of opinion. **2** a popular saying or maxim. [16c: Latin]

did *past tense of* **do**[1]

didactic /daɪ'daktɪk/ *adj* intended to teach or instruct. ▪ **didactically** *adv*. ▪ **didacticism** *noun*. [17c: from Greek *didaskein* to teach]

diddle *verb, informal* to cheat or swindle. [19c: prob from Jeremy Diddler, a character in a play]

didgeridoo *noun, music* a native Australian wind instrument, consisting of a long tube which, when blown into, produces a low droning sound. [Early 20c: from an Australian Aboriginal language]

didn't *contraction of* did not.

die[1] *verb* (***died, dying***) *intr* **1** to stop living. **2** to come to an end or fade away. **3** of an engine, etc: to stop working suddenly and unexpectedly. **4** (*usu* **die of**

sth) to suffer or be overcome by the effects of it: *die of laughter.* [14c: from Norse *deyja*]

IDIOMS **be dying for sth** *or* **to do sth** *informal* to have a strong desire or need for it or to do it. **die hard** to be difficult to change or remove. See also **diehard**. **to die for** *informal* highly desirable: *a dress to die for.*

PHRASAL VERBS **die away 1** to fade away from sight or hearing until gone. **2** to become steadily weaker and finally stop. **die back** *botany* of a plant's soft shoots: to die or wither from the tip back to the hard wood. **die down** to lose strength or force. **die off** to die one after another; to die in large numbers. **die out** to cease to exist anywhere.

die[2] *noun* **1** (*pl* ***dies***) **a** a metal tool or stamp for cutting or shaping metal or making designs on coins, etc. **b** a metal device for shaping or moulding a semi-soft solid material. **2** (*pl* ***dice***) a **dice**. [14c: from French *de*]

IDIOMS **straight as a die 1** completely straight. **2** completely honest. **the die is cast** an irreversible decision has been made or action taken.

diehard *noun* a person who stubbornly refuses to accept new ideas or changes. *as adj*: *a diehard traditionalist.*

dielectric *physics, noun* a non-conducting material whose molecules align or polarize under the influence of applied electric fields, used in capacitors. ▸ *adj* denoting such a material. [19c]

dieresis an alternative *N Am, esp US* spelling of **diaeresis**.

diesel *noun* **1 diesel fuel**. **2** a **diesel engine**. **3** a train, etc driven by a diesel engine. [19c: named after the German engineer Rudolf Diesel]

diesel engine *noun* a type of internal-combustion engine in which air in the cylinder is compressed until it reaches a sufficiently high temperature to ignite the fuel.

diesel fuel *or* **diesel oil** *noun, eng* liquid fuel for use in a diesel engine.

diet[1] *noun* **1** the food and drink habitually consumed by a person or animal. **2** a planned or prescribed selection of food and drink, eg for weight loss. ▸ *adj* containing less sugar than the standard version: *diet lemonade.* ▸ *verb, intr* to restrict the quantity or type of food that one eats, esp in order to lose weight. ▪ **dietary** *adj.* ▪ **dieter** *noun.* [13c: from French *diete*]

diet[2] *noun* a legislative assembly. [14c: from Latin *dieta* public assembly]

dietary fibre *noun* indigestible plant material, found in eg wholemeal bread, cereals, fruit and vegetables. Also called **roughage**.

dietetic *adj* **1** concerning or belonging to **diet**[1]. **2** for use in a special medical diet.

dietetics *singular noun* the scientific study of **diet**[1] and its relation to health. ▪ **dietician** *or* **dietitian** *noun.*

differ *verb, intr* **1** to be different or unlike in some way. **2** (*often* **differ with sb**) to disagree. [14c: from French *differer*]

difference *noun* **1** something that makes one thing or person unlike another. **2** the state of being unlike. **3** a change from an earlier state, etc. **4** the amount by which one quantity or number is greater or less than another. **5** a quarrel or disagreement. [14c: from Latin *differentia*]

IDIOMS **make a** *or* **no,** *etc* **difference** to have some or no, etc effect on a situation.

different *adj* **1** (*usu* **different from** *or* **to sth** *or* **sb**) not the same; unlike. **2** separate; distinct; various. **3** *informal* unusual. ▪ **differently** *adv.* [15c]

different from, to, than

In current British English, **different** can be followed by 'from' or 'to':

That car is different from the one he had yesterday.
Is that car different to the one you had yesterday?

In American English, **different** is often followed by 'than', but it is best not to use this in British English:

It was all very different than they had imagined.

differential *adj* **1** constituting, showing, relating to or based on a difference. **2** *maths* an infinitesimal change in the value of one or more variables as a result of a similarly small change in another variable or variables. ▸ *noun* **1** a difference in the rate of pay between one category of worker and another in the same industry or company. Also called **wage differential**. **2** a **differential gear**. [17c: from Latin *differentialis*]

differential calculus *noun, maths* the branch of calculus concerned with finding derivatives, used to find velocities, gradients of curves, etc.

differential coefficient see **derivative** (*noun* sense 4)

differential equation *noun, maths* an equation involving derivatives.

differential erosion *noun, geog* different rates of erosion in the same piece of rock, where some parts are softer than other parts.

differential gear *noun* an arrangement of gears that allows the wheels on either side of a vehicle to rotate at different speeds, eg when cornering.

differentiate *verb* **1** *tr & intr* (*usu* **differentiate between things**, or **one thing from another**) to establish a difference between them; to be able to distinguish one from another. **2** (*usu* **differentiate one thing from another**) to constitute a difference between things, or a difference in (one thing as against another). **3** to become different. **4** *maths* to calculate the changes in one variable quantity produced by small changes in another, ie to find the **derivative** (*noun* sense 4) of a **function** (sense 4) or variable. **5** *biol* of an unspecialized cell or tissue: to become increasingly specialized in structure and function. ▪ **differentiation** *noun.* [19c: from Latin *differentiare*]

difficult *adj* **1** requiring great skill, intelligence or effort. **2** not easy to please; unco-operative. **3** of a problem, situation, etc: potentially embarrassing; hard to resolve or get out of. [14c: from Latin *difficultas* difficulty]

difficulty *noun* (**-*ies***) **1** the state or quality of being difficult. **2** a difficult thing to do or understand. **3** a problem, obstacle or objection. **4** (*usu* **difficulties**) trouble or embarrassment, esp financial trouble.

diffident *adj* lacking in confidence; too modest or shy. ▪ **diffidence** *noun.* ▪ **diffidently** *adv.* [15c: from Latin *diffidere* to distrust]

diffraction *noun, physics* the spreading out of waves (eg light or sound waves) as they emerge from a small opening or slit. ▪ **diffract** *verb.* ▪ **diffractive** *adj.* [19c: from Latin *diffringere* to shatter]

diffuse *verb* /dɪ'fjuːz/ *tr & intr* to spread or send out in all directions. ▸ *adj* /dɪ'fjuːs/ **1** widely spread; not concentrated. **2** using too many words. ▪ **diffusely** *adv.* ▪ **diffuseness** *noun.* ▪ **diffuser** *noun.* ▪ **diffusible** *adj.* ▪ **diffusive** *adj.* [15c: from Latin *diffundere* to pour out in various directions]

diffuse, defuse
Be careful not to use the word **diffuse** when you mean **defuse**. To **defuse** something is to make it less dangerous:
Police were brought in to defuse the situation.

diffusion *noun* **1** diffusing or being diffused. **2** *physics, chem* the gradual and spontaneous dispersal of a liquid or gas from a region of high concentration to one of low concentration. **3** *anthropol* the spread of cultural elements from one community, region, etc, to another.

dig *verb* (***dug, digging***) **1** *tr & intr* to turn up or move (earth, etc) esp with a spade. **2** to make (a hole, etc) by digging. **3** *tr & intr* to poke. **4** *old slang* to appreciate. **5** *tr & intr, old slang* to understand. ▸ *noun* **1** a remark intended to irritate, criticize or make fun of someone. **2** a place where archaeologists are digging. **3** a poke. **4** an act of digging. [13c]
IDIOMS **dig in one's heels** to refuse to change one's mind. **dig one's own grave** to be the cause of one's own failure or downfall.
PHRASAL VERBS **dig in 1** *informal* to start to eat. **2** to work hard. **dig oneself in** to establish a firm or protected place for oneself. **dig into sth 1** *informal* to start eating (a meal, etc). **2** to examine or search through it for information. **dig sth out** to find it by extensive searching. **dig sth up 1** to find or reveal something buried or hidden by digging. **2** *informal* to search for and find (information, etc).

digest[1] /daɪ'dʒɛst/ *verb* **1** *tr & intr* to break down (food), or be broken down, in the stomach, intestine, etc into a form which the body can use. **2** to hear and consider the meaning and implications of (information). **3** *tr & intr, chem* to soften or disintegrate in heat and moisture. ▪ **digestible** *adj.* [14c: from Latin *digerere* to dissolve]

digest[2] /'daɪdʒɛst/ *noun* **1** a collection of summaries or shortened versions of news stories or current literature, etc. **2** a summary or shortened version. **3** a systematically arranged collection of laws. [14c: from Latin *digerere* to arrange]

digestion *noun* **1** the process whereby food is broken down by enzymes in the **alimentary canal**. **2** the process of absorbing information, etc. [14c]

digestive *adj* concerned with or for digestion.

digestive tract *noun* the **alimentary canal**.

digger *noun* **1** a machine for digging and excavating. **2** someone who digs, esp a gold-miner. **3** *informal* an Australian or New Zealander.

Digibox /'dɪdʒɪbɒks/ *noun, trademark* a brand of set-top box for receiving digital satellite television. [*digi*tal + **box**]

digicam /'dɪdʒɪkam/ *noun* a **digital camera**. [20c]

digit *noun* **1** any of the figures 0 to 9. **2** *technical* a finger or toe. [15c: from Latin *digitus* finger or toe]

digital *adj* **1** showing numerical information in the form of **digit**s, rather than by a pointer on a dial. **2** operating by processing information supplied and stored in the form of a series of binary digits: *digital recording*. **3** *electronics* denoting an electronic circuit that responds to and produces signals which at any given time are in one of two possible states. Compare **analogue**. [20c]

digital audio tape *noun, electronics* (abbrev **DAT, Dat** *or* **dat**) a magnetic audio tape on which sound has been recorded after it has been converted into a binary code.

digital camera *noun* a camera which stores images in digital form so that they can be viewed, manipulated and printed using a computer.

digital compact cassette *noun* (abbrev **DCC**) a **digital audio tape** in standard cassette format.

digital compact disc *noun* a **compact disc**.

digitalis /dɪdʒɪ'teɪlɪs/ *noun* **1** *botany* any plant of the genus that includes the foxglove. **2** *med* a collective term for drugs that stimulate the heart muscle, orig obtained from foxglove leaves. [17c]

digital radio *noun* a form of radio broadcasting in which the sounds are compressed into and transmitted in digital form.

digital television *noun* a form of television broadcasting in which the signal is transmitted in digital form and decoded by a special receiver.

digital versatile disc *noun* (abbreviation **DVD**) a small disc which can store many times more information than a standard **compact disc**. [20c]

digitate *or* **digitated** *adj, botany* of leaves: consisting of several finger-like sections.

digitize *or* **-ise** *verb* to convert (data) into **binary** form. ▪ **digitization** *noun.* ▪ **digitizer** *noun.* [1950s]

diglossia /daɪ'glosɪə/ *noun* the existence of both a colloquial and a formal or literary form of a language in a community. [Greek *diglossos* bilingual]

dignify *verb* (***-ies, -ied***) **1** to make something impressive or dignified. **2** to make something seem more important or impressive than it is. ▪ **dignified** *adj* **1** showing or consistent with dignity. **2** stately; noble; serious. [15c: from Latin *dignus* worthy + *facere* to make]

dignitary *noun* (***-ies***) someone of high rank or position. [17c]

dignity *noun* **1** stateliness, seriousness and formality of manner and appearance. **2** goodness and nobility of character. **3** calmness and self-control. **4** high rank or position. [13c: from Latin *dignitas*]
IDIOMS **beneath one's dignity 1** not worthy of one's attention or time, etc. **2** degrading.

digraph *noun* a pair of letters that represent a single sound, eg the *ph* of *digraph*. [18c: from Greek *di-* twice + *graphe* mark or character]

digress *verb, intr* to wander from the point, or from the main subject in speaking or writing. ▪ **digression** *noun.* [16c: from Latin *digredi* to move away]

digs *plural noun, Brit informal* lodgings.

dihedral *adj, geom* formed or bounded by two planes. [18c: from Greek *di-* twice + *hedra* seat]

dike see **dyke**

dilapidated *adj* falling to pieces; in great need of repair. ▪ **dilapidation** *noun.* [16c: from Latin *dilapidare* to demolish]

dilatation and curettage *noun* (abbrev **D and C**) *med* a gynaecological operation in which the **cervix** is dilated and a **curette** is passed into the uterus to scrape the lining.

dilate *verb, tr & intr* to make or become larger, wider or further open. ▪ **dilatation** *or* **dilation** *noun.* [14c: from Latin *dilatare* to spread out]

dilatory /ˈdɪlətərɪ/ *adj* slow in doing things; inclined to or causing delay. ▪ **dilatorily** *adv.* ▪ **dilatoriness** *noun.* [15c: from Latin *dilatorius*]

dilemma *noun* **1** a situation in which one must choose between two or more courses of action, both/all equally undesirable. **2** *informal* a problem or difficult situation. [16c: from Greek *di-* twice + *lemma* assumption]

dilettante /dɪləˈtantɪ/ *noun* (***dilettantes*** *or* ***dilettanti*** /-tiː/) *often derog* someone who is interested in a subject but who does not study it in depth. ▪ **dilettantism** *noun.* [18c: Italian, from *dilettare* to delight]

diligent *adj* **1** hard-working and careful. **2** showing or done with care and serious effort. ▪ **diligence** *noun.* ▪ **diligently** *adv.* [14c: French, from Latin *diligens* careful]

dill *noun* a herb used in flavouring and to relieve wind. [Anglo-Saxon *dile*]

dilly-dally *verb* (***-ies, -ied***) *intr, informal* **1** to be slow or waste time. **2** to be unable to make up one's mind. [18c: from **dally**]

diluent /ˈdɪljʊənt/ *noun, chem* any solvent used to dilute a solution. [18c]

dilute *verb* **1** to decrease the concentration of a **solute** in a solution by adding more **solvent**, eg water. **2** to reduce the strength, influence or effect of something. ▸ *adj, chem* of a solution: containing a relatively small amount of **solute** compared to the amount of **solvent** present. ▪ **dilution** *noun.* [16c: from Latin *diluere* to wash away]

diluvial *or* **diluvian** *adj* **1** concerning or pertaining to a flood, esp the Flood mentioned in the Book of Genesis. **2** caused by a flood. [17c: from Latin *diluvium* flood]

dim *adj* **1** not bright or distinct. **2** lacking enough light to see clearly. **3** faint; not clearly remembered: *a dim memory.* **4** *informal* not very intelligent. **5** of eyes: not able to see well. **6** *informal* not good; not hopeful: *dim prospects.* ▸ *verb* (***dimmed, dimming***) *tr & intr* to make or become dim. ▪ **dimly** *adv.* ▪ **dimness** *noun.* [Anglo-Saxon *dimm*]

IDIOMS **take a dim view of sth** *informal* to disapprove of it.

dime *noun* **1** a coin of the US and Canada worth ten cents. **2** ten cents. [18c: from Latin *decima* tenth]

dimension *noun* **1** a measurement of length, width or height. **2** a measurable quantity. **3** *geom* any of the parameters needed to specify the size of a geometrical figure and the location of points on it, eg a triangle has two dimensions and a pyramid has three. **4** (*often* **dimensions**) size or extent. **5** a particular aspect of a problem, situation, etc: *the religious dimension of the problem.* ▪ **dimensional** *adj.* [14c: from Latin *dimensio* measuring]

dimer *noun, chem* a chemical compound composed of two **monomers**. ▪ **dimeric** *adj.* [20c]

dime store *noun, N Am* a shop selling cheap goods.

diminish *verb* **1** *tr & intr* to become or make something less or smaller. **2** to make someone or something seem less important, valuable or satisfactory. [15c: ultimately from Latin *deminuere* to make less]

diminished responsibility *noun, law* limitation of criminal responsibility on the grounds of mental weakness or abnormality.

diminuendo *music, adj, adv* with gradually lessening sound. ▸ *noun* **1** a gradual lessening of sound. **2** a musical passage with gradually lessening sound. Compare **crescendo**. [18c: Italian, from Latin *deminuere* to make less]

diminution *noun* a lessening or decrease. [14c: from Latin *diminutio*]

diminutive *adj* very small. ▸ *noun, grammar* **1** an ending added to a word to indicate smallness, eg *-let* in *booklet*. Also called **diminutive suffix**. **2** a word formed in this way. [14c: from Latin *deminuere* to make less]

dimmer *or* **dimmer switch** *noun* a control used to modify the brightness of a light.

dimple *noun* a small hollow, esp in the skin of the cheeks, chin or, esp in babies, at the knees and elbows. ▸ *verb, tr & intr* to show or form into dimples. [15c]

dim sum *noun* a selection of Chinese foods, usu including steamed dumplings with various fillings, often served as an appetizer. [20c: Chinese]

dimwit *noun, informal* a stupid person. ▪ **dim-witted** *adj.* [1920s]

din *noun* a loud, continuous and unpleasant noise. ▸ *verb* (***dinned, dinning***) (*usu* **din sth into sb**) to repeat something forcefully to someone over and over again so that it will be remembered. [Anglo-Saxon *dyne*]

dinar /ˈdiːnɑː(r)/ *noun* the standard unit of currency in Macedonia (usu in the form **denar**), Serbia, and several Arab countries. [19c]

dine *verb, formal* **1** *intr* to eat dinner. **2** *intr* (*usu* **dine off, on** *or* **upon sth**) to eat it for one's dinner. **3** to give dinner to someone: *wining and dining his girlfriend.* [13c: from French *disner*]

PHRASAL VERBS **dine out** to have dinner somewhere other than one's own house, eg in a restaurant. **dine out on sth** to be invited out to dinner so that others may hear one tell (an amusing story).

diner *noun* **1** someone who dines. **2** a restaurant car on a train. **3** *N Am* a small cheap restaurant. [19c]

dinette /daɪˈnɛt/ *noun* an alcove or other small area of a room, etc, set apart for meals. [1920s]

dingbat *noun, N Am slang except sense* 3 **1** something whose name one has forgotten or wishes to avoid using. **2** a foolish or eccentric person. **3** *Austral & NZ informal* (**the dingbats**) **delirium tremens**. ▪ **dingbats** *adj, Austral & NZ informal* daft; crazy. [19c]

ding-dong *noun* **1** the sound of bells ringing. **2** *informal* a heated argument or fight. [16c]

dinghy /ˈdɪŋgɪ, ˈdɪŋɪ/ *noun* (***-ies***) **1** a small open boat. **2** a small collapsible rubber boat. [19c: from Hindi *dingi* small boat]

dingle *noun* a deep wooded hollow. [17c]

dingo *noun* (***dingoes***) an Australian wild dog. [18c: from an Australian Aboriginal language]

dingy /ˈdɪndʒɪ/ *adj* (***-ier, -iest***) **1** faded and dirty-looking: *dingy clothes.* **2** dark and rather dirty: *a dingy room.* ▪ **dinginess** *noun.* [18c]

dining car see **restaurant car**

dinkum *adj, Austral & NZ informal* real; genuine; honest. ▸ *adv* genuinely; honestly. [19c: from English dialect *dinkum* fair share of work]

dinky *adj* (**-ier,-iest**) **1** *informal* neat; dainty. **2** *N Am informal* trivial; insignificant. [18c: from Scots *dink* neat]

dinner *noun* **1** the main meal of the day, eaten in the middle of the day or in the evening. **2** a formal meal, esp in the evening. [13c: see **dine**]

dinner jacket *noun* a jacket, usu black, worn by men at formal social gatherings, esp in the evening. Compare **tuxedo**.

dinner service *or* **dinner set** *noun* a complete set of plates and dishes for serving dinner to several people.

dinosaur *noun* **1** a prehistoric reptile. **2** *often jocular* a chance survivor of a type characteristic of past times. [19c: from Greek *deinos* terrible + *sauros* lizard]

dint *noun* a dent. [Anglo-Saxon *dynt* blow]
IDIOMS **by dint of sth** by means of it.

diocese /'daɪəsɪs/ *noun* the district over which a bishop has authority. ▪ **diocesan** /daɪ'ɒsɪzən/ *adj.* [14c: from Greek *dioikesis* housekeeping]

diode *noun, electronics* an electronic device containing an **anode** and a **cathode**, allowing current to flow in one direction only. [19c: from Greek *di-* twice + *hodos* way]

dioptre *or* (*esp N Am*) **diopter** /daɪ'ɒptə(r)/ *noun, optics* (abbrev **dpt**) a unit used to express the power of a lens, defined as one divided by the focal length of the lens in metres. [19c: from Greek *dioptron* spyglass]

dioxide *noun, chem* a compound formed by combining two atoms of oxygen with one atom of another element. [19c: from Greek *di-* twice + **oxide**]

dioxin *noun* a highly toxic hydrocarbon which has been associated with allergic skin reactions, cancer, birth defects and miscarriages. [1919]

dip *verb* (***dipped, dipping***) **1** to put something briefly into a liquid. **2** *intr* to go briefly under the surface of a liquid. **3** *intr* to drop below a surface or level. **4** *tr & intr* to go, or push something, down briefly and then up again. **5** *intr* to slope downwards. **6** *tr & intr* to put (one's hand, etc) into a dish, etc and take out some of the contents. **7** to immerse (an animal) in disinfectant that kills parasites. **8** *Brit* to lower the beam of (a vehicle's headlights). ▸ *noun* **1** an act of dipping. **2** a downward slope or hollow (eg in a road). **3** a short swim or bathe. **4** a chemical liquid for dipping animals. **5** a type of thick sauce into which biscuits, raw vegetables, etc are dipped. [Anglo-Saxon *dyppan*]
PHRASAL VERBS **dip into sth 1** to take or use part of it. **2** to look briefly at a book or study a subject in a casual manner.

Dip Ed *abbrev* Diploma in Education.

dipeptide *noun, chem* a peptide formed by combining two amino acids.

diphtheria /dɪp'θɪərɪə, dɪf-/ *noun, med* a disease which affects the throat, causing difficulty in breathing and swallowing. [19c: from Greek *diphthera* leather (from the leathery covering formed in the throat)]

diphthong /'dɪpθɒŋ, 'dɪf-/ *noun* **1** two vowel sounds pronounced as one syllable, such as the sound represented by the *ou* in *sounds*. Compare **monophthong**. **2** a **digraph**. [15c: from Greek *di-* twice + *phthongos* sound]

diplodocus /dɪ'plɒdəkəs/ *noun* a gigantic herbivorous dinosaur with a particularly long neck and tail. [19c: from Greek *diplo-* twice + *dokos* bar or beam]

diploid *adj, genetics* having two sets of chromosomes, one from each parent. [19c: from Greek *diploos* double + *eidos* form]

diploma *noun* a document certifying that one has passed a certain examination or completed a course of study. [17c: Latin, from Greek, meaning 'letter folded over']

diplomacy *noun* **1** the art or profession of making agreements, treaties, etc between countries, or of representing and looking after the affairs and interests of one's own country in a foreign country. **2** skill and tact in dealing with people. ▪ **diplomatic** *adj.* ▪ **diplomatically** *adv.* [18c: from French *diplomatie*]

diplomat *noun* **1** a government official or representative engaged in diplomacy. **2** a very tactful person. [19c: from French *diplomate*]

diplomatic corps *noun* the diplomats and staff of all the embassies in the capital of a country.

diplomatic immunity *noun* the privilege granted to members of the diplomatic corps by which they may not be taxed, arrested, etc by the country in which they are working.

dipole *noun, physics* a separation of electric charge, in which two equal and opposite charges are separated from each other by a small distance. ▪ **dipolar** *adj.* [Early 20c]

dipper *noun* **1** a type of ladle. **2** a small songbird which can swim under water and feeds on riverbeds.

dippy *adj* (**-ier, -iest**) *informal* crazy; mad. [20c]

dipsomania *noun, med* an insatiable craving for alcoholic drink. ▪ **dipsomaniac** *noun.* Also called (*informal*) **dipso**. [19c: from Greek *dipsa* thirst + *mania* madness]

dipstick *noun* **1** a stick used to measure the level of a liquid in a container, esp the oil in a car engine. **2** *slang* a stupid person.

dipswitch *noun* a switch used to dip the headlights of a motor vehicle.

diptych /'dɪptɪk/ *noun* a work of art, esp on a church altar, consisting of a pair of pictures painted on hinged wooden panels which can be folded together like a book. See also **triptych**. [19c: from Greek *diptychos* folded together]

dire *adj* **1** dreadful; terrible. **2** extreme; very serious; very difficult. ▪ **direly** *adv.* [16c: from Latin *dirus*]

direct *adj* **1** following the shortest path. **2** open, straightforward and honest; going straight to the point. **3** actual: *the direct cause of the accident*. **4** not working or communicating through other people, organizations, etc: *a direct link with the chairman*. **5** exact; complete: *a direct opposite*. **6** in an unbroken line of descent from parent to child to grandchild, etc: *a direct descendant of Sir Walter Raleigh*. ▸ *verb* **1** to point, aim or turn something in some direction. **2** to show the way to someone. **3** *tr & intr* (*usu* **direct sb to do sth** *or* **that sth be done**) to give orders or instructions. **4** to control, manage or be in charge of something. **5** *tr & intr* to supervise the production of (a play or film). **6** *formal* to put a name and address on (a letter, etc). ▸ *adv* by the quickest or shortest path. ▪ **directness** *noun*. [14c: from Latin *dirigere* to direct or guide]

direct current *noun* (abbrev **DC**) electric current which flows in one direction. Compare **alternating current**.

direct debit *noun, finance* an order to one's bank which allows someone else to withdraw sums of money from one's account, esp in payment of bills. Compare **standing order**.

direction *noun* **1** the place or point towards which one is moving or facing. **2** the way in which some-one or something is developing. **3** (*usu* **directions**) information, instructions or advice, eg on how to construct or operate a piece of equipment. **4** (**directions**) instructions about the way to go to reach a place. **5** management or supervision. **6** the act, style, etc of directing a play or film. [16c: from Latin *directio*]

directional *adj* relating to direction in space.

directive *noun* an official instruction issued by a higher authority. [16c: from Latin *directivus*]

directly *adv* **1** in a direct manner. **2** by a direct path. **3** at once; immediately. **4** very soon. **5** exactly: *directly opposite*.

direct object *noun, grammar* the noun, phrase or pronoun which is directly affected by the action of a transitive verb, eg *the dog* in *the boy kicked the dog*. Compare **indirect object**.

director *noun* **1** a senior manager of a business firm. **2** the person in charge of an organization, institution or special activity. **3** the person directing a play, film, etc. **4** *music, esp N Am* a **conductor** (sense 1). ▪ **directorial** *adj*. ▪ **directorship** *noun*.

directorate *noun* **1** the directors of a business firm. **2** the position or office of director.

director-general *noun* (***directors-general*** *or* ***director-generals***) the chief administrator of an organization.

directory *noun* (***-ies***) **1** a book with a (usu alphabetical) list of names and addresses. **2** *comput* a named grouping of files on a disk. [15c: from Latin *directorium*]

directrix *noun* (***directrices***) *maths* a straight line from which the distance to any point on a conic section is in a constant ratio to the distance between that point and the **focus**.

direct speech *noun, grammar* speech reported in the actual words of the speaker, eg *'Hello'* in the sentence *'Hello', said Henry*. Compare **indirect speech**.

direct tax *noun* a tax paid directly to the government by a person or organization, eg **income tax**. Compare **indirect tax**.

dirge *noun* **1** a funeral song or hymn. **2** *sometimes derog* a slow sad song or piece of music. [16c: from Latin *dirige*, the first word of the Office of the Dead]

dirigible /ˈdɪrɪdʒɪbəl/ *noun, technical* an airship. [19c: from Latin *dirigere* to direct]

dirk *noun* a small knife or dagger. [16c: Scots]

dirndl /ˈdɜːndəl/ *noun* **1** a traditional alpine peasant-woman's dress, with a tight-fitting bodice and a very full skirt. **2** a skirt that is tight at the waist and wide at the lower edge. Also called **dirndl skirt**. [20c: German dialect, from *dirne* girl]

dirt *noun* **1** mud, dust, etc. **2** soil; earth. **3** a mixture of earth and cinders used to make road surfaces. **4** *euphem* excrement. **5** *informal* obscene speech or writing. **6** *informal* scandal. [13c: from Norse *drit* excrement]

IDIOMS **eat dirt** to submit to humiliation. **treat sb like dirt** to treat them with no consideration or respect.

dirt-cheap *adj, adv, informal* very cheap.

dirt track *noun* **1** a rough unsurfaced track. **2** a motorcycle racing course made of cinders, etc.

dirty *adj* (***-ier, -iest***) **1** marked with dirt; soiled. **2** making one become soiled with dirt: *a dirty job*. **3** unfair; dishonest: *dirty tricks*. **4** obscene, lewd or pornographic: *dirty films*. **5** of weather: rainy or stormy. **6** of a colour: dull. **7** showing dislike or disapproval: *a dirty look*. **8** unsportingly rough or violent: *a dirty tackle*. ▸ *verb* (***-ies, -ied***) to make dirty. ▸ *adv* **1** dirtily: *fight dirty*. **2** very: *dirty great stains*. ▪ **dirtiness** *noun*.

IDIOMS **do the dirty on sb** *informal* to cheat or trick them.

dirty money *noun* **1** money earned by immoral, corrupt or illegal means. **2** extra pay for handling dirty materials or working in dirty conditions.

dirty trick *noun* a dishonest or despicable act.

dirty tricks campaign *noun* underhanded intrigue intended to discredit someone.

dirty word *noun* **1** a vulgar word. **2** *informal* an unpopular concept: *Ambition is a dirty word*.

dirty work *noun* **1** work that makes a person dirty. **2** *informal* unpleasant or dishonourable tasks.

dis- *prefix, forming words denoting* **1** the opposite of the base word: *disagree* • *dislike*. **2** reversal of the action of the base word: *disassemble*. **3** removal or undoing: *dismember* • *disrobe*. [Latin]

disability *noun* (***-ies***) **1** the state of being disabled. **2** a physical or mental handicap.

disable *verb* **1** to deprive someone of a physical or mental ability. **2** to make (eg a machine) unable to work; to make something useless. ▪ **disablement** *noun*. [15c]

disabled *adj* **1** having a physical or mental handicap. **2** made unable to work. **3** designed or intended for people with physical disabilities.

disabuse *verb* (*always* **disabuse sb of sth**) to rid them of a mistaken idea or impression. [17c]

disaccharide /daɪˈsakəraɪd/ *noun, biochem* a carbohydrate that consists of two **monosaccharides**, eg **sucrose**, **lactose**. [19c]

disadvantage *noun* **1** a difficulty, drawback or weakness. **2** an unfavourable situation. ▸ *verb* to put someone at a disadvantage. ▪ **disadvantaged** *adj* in an unfavourable position; deprived of normal social or economic benefits. ▪ **disadvantageous** *adj*. [14c]

disaffected *adj* dissatisfied and no longer loyal or committed. ▪ **disaffection** *noun*. [17c]

disafforest *or* **disforest** *verb* to clear (land) of forest. ▪ **disafforestation** *or* **disafforestment** *noun*. [16c]

disagree *verb, intr* **1** to have conflicting opinions. **2** (*often* **disagree with sth**) to be opposed to it. **3** to conflict with each other. **4** (*always* **disagree with sb**) of food: to give them digestive problems. **5** *euphem* to quarrel. [15c: from French *desagréer*]

disagreeable *adj* **1** unpleasant. **2** bad-tempered; unfriendly. ▪ **disagreeably** *adv*.

disagreement *noun* **1** the state of disagreeing. **2** *euphem* a quarrel.

disallow *verb* **1** to formally refuse to allow or accept something. **2** to judge something to be invalid. ▪ **disallowance** *noun*. [14c: from French *desalouer*]

disappear *verb* **1** *intr* to vanish. **2** *intr* to cease to exist. **3** *intr* to go missing. **4** to make someone vanish, esp by imprisoning them or killing them secretly, usu for political reasons. ▪ **disappearance** *noun*. [16c]

> **disappear**
> This word is often misspelt. It has one *s* and two *p*'s. It might help you to remember the following phrase:
> *a single* **s** *and a* **p***air of* **p***'s*

disappoint *verb* **1** to fail to fulfil the hopes or expectations of someone. **2** *formal* to prevent (eg a plan) from being carried out. ▪ **disappointed** *adj*. ▪ **disappointing** *adj*. ▪ **disappointment** *noun*. [15c: from French *desapointer*

> **disappoint**
> This word is often misspelt. It has one *s* and two *p*'s. It might help you to remember the following phrase:
> *a single* **s** *and a* **p***air of* **p***'s*

disapprobation *noun, formal* disapproval, esp on moral grounds. [17c]

disapprove *verb, intr* (*usu* **disapprove of sth** *or* **sb**) to have a low opinion of it or them; to think it or them bad or wrong. ▪ **disapproval** *noun*. ▪ **disapproving** *adj*. ▪ **disapprovingly** *adv*. [17c]

disarm *verb* **1** to take weapons away from someone. **2** *intr* to reduce or destroy one's own military capability. **3** to take the fuse out of (a bomb). **4** to take away the anger or suspicions of someone. [15c: from French *desarmer*]

disarmament *noun* the reduction or destruction by a nation of its own military forces. [18c]

disarming *adj* taking away anger or suspicion; quickly winning confidence or affection. ▪ **disarmingly** *adv*.

disarrange *verb* to make something untidy or disordered. ▪ **disarrangement** *noun*. [18c]

disarray *noun* a state of disorder or confusion. ▸ *verb* to throw something into disorder. [15c]

disassociate *verb, tr & intr* to **dissociate**. ▪ **disassociation** *noun*. [17c]

disaster *noun* **1** an event causing great damage, injury or loss of life. **2** a total failure. **3** extremely bad luck: *Disaster struck*. ▪ **disastrous** *adj*. ▪ **disastrously** *adv*. [16c: orig meaning 'bad influence of the stars', from French *desastre, from astre* star]

disavow *verb, formal* to deny knowledge of, a connection with, or responsibility for something or someone. ▪ **disavowal** *noun*. [14c: from French *desavouer*]

disband *verb, tr & intr* to stop operating as a group; to break up. ▪ **disbandment** *noun*. [16c: from French *desbander* to unbind]

disbar *verb* (**-barred, -barring**) to expel (a barrister) from the Bar (see **bar**[1]*noun* sense 9). [17c]

disbelieve *verb* **1** to believe something to be false or someone to be lying. **2** *intr* to have no religious faith. ▪ **disbelief** *noun*. [17c]

disburse *verb* to pay out (a sum of money), esp from a fund. ▪ **disbursement** *noun*. [16c: from French *desbourser*]

disc *noun* **1** a flat thin circular object. **2** any disc-shaped recording medium, such as a **record** (*noun* sense 4) or **compact disc**. **3** *anatomy* a plate of fibrous tissue between two adjacent vertebrae in the spine. **4** *comput* see **disk**. [17c: from Greek *diskos*]

discard *verb* **1** to get rid of something useless or unwanted. **2** *cards* to put down (a card of little value) eg when unable to follow suit. [16c]

disc brake *noun* a brake in which pads are pressed against a metal disc attached to the wheel.

discern *verb* to perceive, notice or make out something; to judge. ▪ **discernible** *adj*. ▪ **discernibly** *adv*. ▪ **discerning** *adj* having or showing good judgement. ▪ **discernment** *noun* good judgement. [14c: from Latin *discernere*]

discharge *verb* /dɪs'tʃɑːdʒ/ **1** to allow someone to leave; to dismiss or send away (a person). **2** to perform or carry out (eg duties). **3** *tr & intr* to flow out or make something flow out or be released. **4** *law* to release someone from custody. **5** *tr & intr* to fire (a gun). **6** *law* to pay off (a debt). **7** *tr & intr* to unload (a cargo). ▸ *noun* /'dɪstʃɑːdʒ/ **1** the act of discharging. **2** something discharged. **3** *formal, law* release or dismissal. **4** *physics* the flow of electric current through a gas, often resulting in luminescence of the gas. **5** *elec* the release of stored electric charge from a capacitor, battery or accumulator. **6** *elec* a high-voltage spark of electricity. **7 a** an emission of a substance, liquid, etc; **b** the substance, etc emitted. **8** *geog* the volume of water passing a specific point in a river over a specific amount of time. [14c: from French *descharger*]

disciple /dɪ'saɪpəl/ *noun* **1** someone who believes in, and follows, the teachings of another. **2** one of the twelve close followers of Christ. ▪ **discipleship** *noun*. [Anglo-Saxon: from Latin *discipulus*]

discipline *noun* **1 a** a strict training, or the enforcing of rules, intended to produce controlled behaviour; **b** the ordered behaviour resulting from this. **2** punishment designed to create obedience. **3** an area of learning or study, or a branch of sport. ▸ *verb* **1** to train or force (oneself or others) to behave in an ordered and controlled way. **2** to punish someone. ▪ **disciplinarian** *noun* someone who enforces strict discipline on others. ▪ **disciplinary** *adj* characteristic of, relating to or enforcing discipline; intended as punishment. [13c: from Latin *disciplina*]

disc jockey *noun* someone who presents recorded popular music on the radio, at a club, etc. Also called **DJ**. [1940s]

disclaim *verb* **1** to deny (eg involvement with or knowledge of something). **2** to give up a legal claim to something. ▪ **disclaimer** *noun* **1** a written statement denying legal responsibility. **2** a denial. [14c: from French *desclaimer*]

disclose *verb* to make something known or visible. ▪ **disclosure** *noun*. [14c: from French *desclore*]

disco *noun* **1** a night-club where people dance to recorded pop music. **2** a party with dancing to recorded music. **3** mobile hi-fi and lighting equipment. ▸ *adj* suitable for, or designed for, discotheques. [1960s: shortened from **discotheque**]

discography *noun* (**-ies**) a catalogue of sound recordings, esp those of one composer or performer. [1930s]

discolour *or* (*N Am*) **discolor** *verb, tr & intr* to stain or dirty something; to change in colour. ▪ **discoloration** *or* **discolouration** *noun.* [14c: from French *descolorer*]

discomfit *verb* **1** to make someone feel embarrassed, uneasy or perplexed. **2** to frustrate the plans of someone. ▪ **discomfiture** *noun.* [13c: from French *desconfire*]

discomfort *noun* a slight physical pain or mental uneasiness. [19c: from French *desconfort*]

discompose *verb* to upset, worry or agitate someone. ▪ **discomposure** *noun.* [15c]

disconcert *verb* to make someone feel anxious, uneasy or flustered. ▪ **disconcerting** *adj.* [17c: from French *disconcerter*]

disconnect *verb* **1** to break the connection between (esp an electrical device and a power supply). **2** to stop the supply of (eg a public service such as the gas supply or the telephone) to (a building, etc). ▪ **disconnection** *noun.* [18c]

disconnected *adj* esp of speech: not correctly constructed, and often not making sense.

disconsolate *adj* deeply sad or disappointed; not able to be consoled. ▪ **disconsolately** *adv.* [14c: from Latin *disconsolatus*]

discontent *noun* dissatisfaction; lack of contentment. ▪ **discontented** *adj.* ▪ **discontentedly** *adv.* [16c]

discontinue *verb* **1** *tr & intr* to stop or cease. **2** to stop producing something. ▪ **discontinuance** *or* **discontinuation** *noun.* [15c: from French *discontinuer*]

discontinuous *adj* having breaks or interruptions. ▪ **discontinuity** *noun* (**-*ies***).

discord *noun* **1** disagreement; conflict. **2** *music* an unpleasant combination of notes; lack of harmony. **3** uproarious noise. ▪ **discordant** *adj.* ▪ **discordantly** *adv.* [13c: from Latin *discordia*]

discotheque *noun, dated, formal* a **disco**. [1950s: French *discothèque*, orig meaning 'a record library']

discount *noun* /ˈdɪskaʊnt/ **1** an amount deducted from the normal price. **2** the rate or percentage of the deduction granted. ▸ *verb* /dɪsˈkaʊnt/ **1** to disregard as unlikely, untrue or irrelevant. **2** to make a deduction from (a price). [17c: from French *descompter*]

IDIOMS **at a discount 1** for less than the usual price. **2** of shares: below par.

discountenance *verb* **1** to refuse support to someone or something. **2** to show disapproval of someone or something. **3** to embarrass someone. [16c]

discourage *verb* **1** to deprive someone of confidence, hope or the will to continue. **2** to seek to prevent (a person or an action) with advice or persuasion. ▪ **discouragement** *noun.* ▪ **discouraging** *adj.* [15c: from French *descourager*]

discourse *noun* /ˈdɪskɔːs/ **1** a formal speech or essay on a particular subject. **2** serious conversation. ▸ *verb* /dɪsˈkɔːs/ *intr* to speak or write at length, formally or with authority. [16c: from Latin *discursus*]

discourse markers *plural noun, linguistics* words and terms which are guidelines to the structure of a text or argument, eg *later, however, on the other hand*.

discourteous *adj* impolite. ▪ **discourteously** *adv.* ▪ **discourtesy** *noun* (**-*ies***). [16c]

discover *verb* **1** to be the first person to find something or someone. **2** to find by chance. **3** to learn of or become aware of for the first time. ▪ **discoverer** *noun.* [16c: from French *descouvrir*]

discovery *noun* (**-*ies***) **1** the act of discovering. **2** a person or thing discovered.

discredit *noun* loss of good reputation, or the cause of it. ▸ *verb* **1** to make someone or something be disbelieved or regarded with doubt or suspicion. **2** to damage the reputation of someone. ▪ **discreditable** *adj.* [16c]

discreet *adj* **1** careful to prevent suspicion or embarrassment, eg by keeping a secret. **2** avoiding notice; inconspicuous. ▪ **discreetly** *adv.* [14c: from Latin *discretus*]

---

discreet, discrete

Be careful not to use the spelling **discreet** when you mean **discrete**:

The pattern is formed from thousands of discrete dots of colour.

---

discrepancy *noun* (**-*ies***) a failure (eg of sets of information) to correspond or be the same. ▪ **discrepant** *adj.* [17c: from Latin *discrepare* to differ in sound]

discrete *adj* separate; distinct. ▪ **discretely** *adv.* ▪ **discreteness** *noun.* [14c: from Latin *discretus*]

---

discrete, discreet

Be careful not to use the spelling **discrete** when you mean **discreet**:

Can I rely on you to be discreet about this matter?

---

discretion *noun* **1** behaving discreetly. **2** the ability to make wise judgements. **3** the freedom or right to make decisions and do as one thinks best. ▪ **discretional** *or* **discretionary** *adj.* [14c: from Latin *discretio*]

discriminate *verb, intr* **1** to see a difference between two people or things. **2** (*usu* **discriminate in favour of** *or* **against sb**) to give different treatment to different people or groups, esp without justification and on political, racial or religious grounds. ▪ **discriminating** *adj* showing good judgement; seeing even slight differences. ▪ **discrimination** *noun.* ▪ **discriminatory** *adj* displaying or representing unfairly different treatment. [17c: from Latin *discriminare* to separate]

discursive *adj* of spoken or written style: wandering from the main point; moving from point to point. ▪ **discursively** *adv.* ▪ **discursiveness** *noun.* [17c: from Latin *discursus* conversation]

discus *noun* (***discuses*** *or* ***disci*** /ˈdɪskaɪ/) **1** a heavy disc thrown in athletic competitions. **2** the competition itself. [17c: from Greek *diskos*]

discuss *verb* **1** to examine or consider something in speech or writing. **2** to talk or argue about something in conversation. ▪ **discussion** *noun.* [14c: from Latin *discutere* to shake to pieces]

disdain *noun* dislike due to a feeling that something is not worthy of attention; contempt; scorn. ▸ *verb* **1** to refuse or reject someone or something out of disdain. **2** to regard someone or something with disdain. ▪ **disdainful** *adj.* ▪ **disdainfully** *adv.* [13c: from French *desdaigner*]

disease *noun* **1** a disorder or illness caused by infection rather than by an accident. **2** any undesirable phenomenon: *the social disease of drug addiction.* ▪ **diseased** *adj.* [14c: from French *desaise* unease]

diseconomy *noun* (***-ies***) an economic drawback. [1930s]

disembark *verb, tr & intr* to take or go from a ship on to land. ▪ **disembarkation** *noun.* [16c: from French *desembarquer*]

disembodied *adj* **1** separated from the body; having no physical existence. **2** seeming not to come from, or be connected to, a body. [18c]

disembowel *verb* (***disembowelled, disembowelling***) to remove the internal organs of someone or something. ▪ **disembowelment** *noun.* [17c]

disenchant *verb* **1** to free someone from illusion. **2** to make someone dissatisfied or discontented. ▪ **disenchanted** *adj.* ▪ **disenchantment** *noun.* [16c: from French *desenchanter*]

disenfranchise see **disfranchise**

disengage *verb* **1** to release or detach someone or something from a connection. **2** *tr & intr* to withdraw (troops) from combat. ▪ **disengaged** *adj.* ▪ **disengagement** *noun.* [17c: from French *desengager*]

disentangle *verb* **1** to free something from complication, difficulty or confusion. **2** to take the knots or tangles out of (eg hair). ▪ **disentanglement** *noun.* [16c]

disestablish *verb* to take away the official status or authority of (an organization, etc), esp the national status of (a church). ▪ **disestablishment** *noun.* [16c]

disfavour *or* (*N Am*) **disfavor** *noun* **1** a state of being disliked, unpopular or disapproved of. **2** dislike or disapproval. [16c]

disfigure *verb* to spoil the beauty or general appearance of something. ▪ **disfigurement** *noun.* [14c: from French *desfigurer*]

disforest see **disafforest**

disfranchise *or* **disenfranchise** *verb* to deprive someone of the right to vote or other rights and privileges of a citizen. ▪ **disfranchisement** *noun.* [15c]

disgorge *verb* **1** *tr & intr* to vomit. **2** to discharge or pour out something. [15c: from French *desgorger*]

disgrace *noun* **a** shame or loss of favour or respect; **b** the cause of it; **c** an example of it. ▸ *verb* to bring shame upon someone. ▪ **disgraceful** *adj.* ▪ **disgracefully** *adv.* [16c: from French *disgrâce*]

IDIOMS **in disgrace** out of favour.

disgruntled *adj* annoyed and dissatisfied; in a bad mood. [17c: from obsolete *gruntle* to complain]

disguise *verb* **1** to hide the identity of someone or something by a change of appearance. **2** to conceal the true nature of (eg intentions). ▸ *noun* **1** a disguised state. **2** something, esp a combination of clothes and make-up, intended to disguise. [14c: from French *desguiser*]

disgust *verb* to sicken; to provoke intense dislike or disapproval in someone. ▸ *noun* intense dislike; loathing. ▪ **disgusted** *adj.* ▪ **disgusting** *adj.* [16c: from French *desgouster*]

dish *noun* **1** a shallow container in which food is served or cooked. **2** its contents, or the amount it can hold. **3** anything shaped like this. **4** a particular kind of food, esp food prepared for eating. **5** (**dishes**) the used plates and other utensils after the end of a meal. **6** a **dish aerial**. **7** *informal* a physically attractive person. ▸ *verb* to put (food) into a dish for serving at table. [Anglo-Saxon *disc* plate, bowl, table]

PHRASAL VERBS **dish sth out** *informal* **1** to distribute it. **2** (*esp* **dish it out**) to give out punishment. **dish sth up** *informal* **1** to serve (food). **2** to offer or present (eg information), esp if not for the first time.

dishabille see **déshabille**

dish aerial *noun* a large dish-shaped aerial. Also called **dish**, **dish antenna**, **satellite dish**.

disharmony *noun* disagreement; lack of harmony. ▪ **disharmonious** *adj.* [17c]

dishcloth *noun* a cloth for washing or drying dishes.

dishearten *verb* to dampen the courage, hope or confidence of someone. ▪ **disheartening** *adj.* [16c]

dishevelled *adj* of clothes or hair: untidy; in a mess. [15c: from French *descheveler*]

dishonest *adj* not honest; likely to deceive or cheat; insincere. ▪ **dishonestly** *adv.* ▪ **dishonesty** *noun.* [14c: from French *deshoneste*]

dishonour *or* (*US*) **dishonor** *noun* **a** shame or loss of honour; **b** the cause of it. ▸ *verb* **1** to bring dishonour on someone or something. **2** to treat someone or something with no respect. **3** *commerce* to refuse to honour (a cheque). ▪ **dishonourable** *adj.* [14c: from French *deshonneur*]

dishwasher *noun* **1** a machine that washes and dries dishes. **2** someone employed to wash dishes.

dishwater *noun* **1** water in which dirty dishes have been washed. **2** any liquid like it.

dishy *adj* (***-ier, -iest***) *informal* of a man: attractive. [1960s]

disillusion *verb* to correct the mistaken beliefs or illusions of someone. ▸ *noun* (also **disillusionment**) a state of being disillusioned. ▪ **disillusioned** *adj.* [19c]

disincentive *noun* something that discourages or deters. [1940s]

disinclined *adj* unwilling. ▪ **disinclination** *noun.* [17c]

disinfect *verb* to clean something with a substance that kills germs. ▪ **disinfectant** *noun, adj.* [17c]

disinformation *noun* false information intended to deceive or mislead. [1950s]

disingenuous *adj* not entirely sincere or open; creating a false impression of frankness. ▪ **disingenuously** *adv.* [17c]

disinherit *verb* to legally deprive someone of an inheritance. ▪ **disinheritance** *noun.* [15c]

disintegrate *verb, tr & intr* **1** to break into tiny pieces; to shatter or crumble. **2** to break up. **3** *physics* to undergo or make a substance undergo nuclear fission. ▪ **disintegration** *noun.* [18c]

disinter *verb* **1** to dig up (esp a body from a grave). **2** to discover and make known (a fact, etc). ▪ **disinterment** *noun.* [17c: from French *désenterrer*]

disinterested *adj* **1** not having an interest in a particular matter; impartial, objective. **2** *informal* showing no interest; uninterested. ▪ **disinterest** *noun.* [17c]

disjointed *adj* esp of speech: not properly connected; incoherent. [16c: from French *desjoindre*]

disjunctive *adj* marked by breaks; discontinuous. [16c: from Latin *disjunctivus*]

disk *noun* **1** *comput* a **magnetic disk**. See also **floppy disk**, **hard disk**. **2** *esp US* a **disc**. [18c: variant of **disc**]

disk drive *noun, comput* a part of a computer that can read and write data on a disk.

diskette *noun, comput* a **floppy disk**.

disk operating system *noun* (abbrev **DOS**) *comput* software that manages the storage and retrieval of information on disk.

dislike *verb* to consider someone or something unpleasant or unlikeable. ► *noun* **1** mild hostility; aversion. **2** something disliked. [16c]

dislocate *verb* **1** to dislodge (a bone) from its normal position. **2** to disturb or disrupt something. ▪ **dislocation** *noun*. [16c: from Latin *dislocare*]

dislodge *verb* to force something or someone out of a fixed position. [15c: from French *desloger*]

disloyal *adj* not loyal. ▪ **disloyalty** *noun*. [15c: from French *desloyal*]

dismal *adj* **1** not cheerful; causing or suggesting sadness. **2** *informal* third-rate; of poor quality. ▪ **dismally** *adv*. [16c: French, from Latin *dies mali* unlucky days]

dismantle *verb* **1** to take something to pieces. **2** to abolish or close down something, esp bit by bit. [16c: from French *desmanteller*]

dismay *noun* **1** a feeling of sadness arising from deep disappointment or discouragement. **2** alarm; consternation. ► *verb* to make someone discouraged, sad or alarmed. [13c: from French *desmaiier*]

dismember *verb* **1** to tear or cut the limbs from (the body). **2** to divide up (esp land). ▪ **dismemberment** *noun*. [13c: from French *desmembrer*]

dismiss *verb* **1** to refuse to consider or accept (an idea, claim, etc). **2** to put someone out of one's employment. **3** to send someone away; to allow them to leave. **4** to close (a court case). **5** *cricket* to bowl (a batsman) out. ▪ **dismissal** *noun*. ▪ **dismissive** *adj*. [15c: from **dis-** (sense 3) + Latin *mittere* to send]

dismount *verb* **1** *intr* to get off a horse, bicycle, etc. **2** to force someone off a horse, bicycle, etc. [16c: from French *desmonter*]

disobedient *adj* refusing or failing to obey. ▪ **disobedience** *noun*. [15c: French]

disobey *verb* to act contrary to the orders of someone; to refuse to obey (a person, a law, etc). [14c: from French *desobeir*]

disobliging *adj* unwilling to help. [17c]

disorder *noun* **1** lack of order; confusion or disturbance. **2** unruly or riotous behaviour. **3** a disease or illness. ▪ **disordered** *adj*. [16c: from French *desordre*]

disorderly *adj* **1** not neatly arranged; disorganized. **2** causing trouble in public.

disorganize *or* **-ise** *verb* to disturb the order or arrangement of something; to throw someone into confusion. ▪ **disorganization** *noun*. ▪ **disorganized** *adj*. [18c]

disorientate *or* **disorient** *verb* to make someone lose all sense of position, direction or time. ▪ **disorientation** *noun*. [17c]

disown *verb* to deny having any relationship to, or connection with, someone or something. [17c]

disparage *verb* to speak of someone or something with contempt. ▪ **disparagement** *noun*. ▪ **disparaging** *adj*. [14c: from French *desparager*]

disparate /ˈdɪspərət/ *adj* completely different; too different to be compared. [17c: from Latin *disparare* to separate]

disparity *noun* (**-ies**) great or fundamental difference; inequality. [16c: from French *disparité*]

dispassionate *adj* not influenced by personal feelings; impartial. ▪ **dispassionately** *adv*. [16c]

dispatch *or* **despatch** *verb* **1** to send (mail, a person, etc) to a place. **2** to finish off or deal with something quickly: *dispatch a meal*. **3** *euphem* to kill. ► *noun* **1** (*often* **dispatches**) an official (esp military or diplomatic) report. **2** a journalist's report sent to a newspaper. **3** the act of dispatching; the fact of being dispatched. **4** *old use* speed or haste. [16c: from French *despeechier* to set free]

dispatch box *or* **dispatch case** *noun* a box or case designed to carry dispatches or other valuable papers.

dispatch rider *noun* someone who delivers messages by motorcycle.

dispel *verb* (***dispelled, dispelling***) to drive away or banish (thoughts or feelings). [17c: from Latin *dispellere*]

dispensable *adj* **1** able to be done without. **2** able to be dispensed. [16c]

dispensary *noun* (**-ies**) a place where medicines are given out or dispensed. [17c]

dispensation *noun* **1** special exemption from a rule or obligation. **2** the act of dispensing. **3** *relig* God's management of human affairs.

dispense *verb* **1** to give out (eg advice). **2** to prepare and distribute (medicine). **3** to administer (eg the law). **4** (*always* **dispense with sth**) to do without it. ▪ **dispenser** *noun*. [14c: from Latin *dispendere* to weigh out]

dispensing optician see **optician**

disperse *verb, tr & intr* **1** to spread out over a wide area. **2** to break up, or make (a crowd) break up, and leave. **3** to vanish or make something vanish. **4** *physics* of white light: to break up into the colours of the spectrum. **5** *physics* of particles: to become evenly distributed throughout a liquid or gas. ▪ **dispersal** *noun*. ▪ **dispersion** *noun*. [15c: from Latin *dispergere* to scatter widely]

dispirit *verb* to dishearten or discourage someone. ▪ **dispirited** *adj*. [17c: **dis-** (sense 2) + **spirit**]

displace *verb* **1** to put or take something or someone out of the usual place. **2** to take the place of someone or something. **3** to remove someone from a post. [16c]

displaced person *noun* someone forced to leave their home through war or persecution.

displacement *noun* **1** the act of displacing. **2** *technical* the quantity of liquid, gas, etc displaced by an immersed object, eg of water by a floating ship.

display *verb* **1** to put someone or something on view. **2** to show or betray (eg feelings). ► *noun* **1** the act of displaying. **2** an exhibition or show, eg of talent or work. **3** the showing of information on a screen, calculator, etc, or the information shown. **4** a pattern of animal behaviour involving stereotyped sounds, movements, etc, that produces a specific response in another individual. [14c: from French *despleier*]

displease *verb* to annoy or offend someone. ▪ **displeasure** *noun*. [14c: from French *desplaisir*]

disport *verb, tr & intr, literary* to indulge (oneself) in lively amusement. [14c: from French *se desporter* to carry oneself away]

disposable *adj* **1** intended to be thrown away or destroyed after one use. **2** of income or assets: remaining after tax and other commitments are paid, so available for use. ▸ *noun* a product intended for disposal after one use.

disposal *noun* getting rid of something.
IDIOMS **at the disposal of sb** available for their use.

dispose *verb* **1** *intr* (*always* **dispose of sth**) to get rid of it. **2** *intr* (*always* **dispose of sth**) to deal with or settle it. **3** *intr* to place something in an arrangement or order. [14c: from French *disposer* to decide]
IDIOMS **be disposed to do sth** to be inclined or willing to do it: *am not disposed to try.* **be disposed to** *or* **towards sb** *or* **sth** to have specified feelings about or towards them or it: *ill-disposed towards us.*

disposition *noun* **1** temperament; personality; a tendency. **2** arrangement; position; distribution.

dispossess *verb* (*always* **dispossess sb of sth**) to take (esp property) away from them. ▪ **dispossessed** *adj.* ▪ **dispossession** *noun.* [15c: from French *despossesser*]

disproportion *noun* lack of balance or equality. [16c]

disproportionate *adj* unreasonably large or small in comparison with something else. ▪ **disproportionately** *adv.*

disprove *verb* to prove something to be false or wrong. [14c: from French *desprover*]

dispute *verb* /dɪs'pjuːt/ **1** to question or deny the accuracy or validity of (a statement, etc). **2** to quarrel over rights to or possession of something. **3** *tr & intr* to argue about something. ▸ *noun* /dɪs'pjuːt, 'dɪspjuːt/ an argument. ▪ **disputable** *adj.* ▪ **disputably** *adv.* ▪ **disputation** *noun.* ▪ **disputatious** *adj.* [13c: from Latin *disputare* to discuss]
IDIOMS **in dispute** being debated or contested.

disqualify *verb* (**-ies, ied**) **1** to ban someone from doing something. **2** to make someone or something unsuitable or ineligible. ▪ **disqualification** *noun.* [18c]

disquiet *noun* anxiety or uneasiness. ▸ *verb* to make someone anxious, uneasy, etc. ▪ **disquieting** *adj.* ▪ **disquietude** *noun.* [16c]

disquisition *noun, formal* a long and detailed discussion. [15c: from Latin *disquisitio*]

disregard *verb* **1** to pay no attention to someone or something. **2** to dismiss something as unworthy of consideration. ▸ *noun* dismissive lack of attention or concern. [17c]

disrepair *noun* bad condition or working order, showing a need for repair and maintenance. [18c]

disreputable *adj* not respectable; having a bad reputation. ▪ **disreputably** *adv.* ▪ **disrepute** *noun.* [18c]

disrespect *noun* lack of respect; impoliteness; rudeness. ▪ **disrespectful** *adj.* [17c]

disrobe *verb, tr & intr, literary* to undress. [16c]

disrupt *verb* to disturb the order or peaceful progress of (an activity, process, etc). ▪ **disruption** *noun.* ▪ **disruptive** *adj.* [17c: from Latin *disrumpere* to break into pieces]

diss *verb, slang, esp US* to mention someone with contempt. [20c urban slang, prob from **disrespect**]

dissatisfy *verb* (**-ies, ied**) **1** to fail to satisfy someone. **2** to make someone discontented. ▪ **dissatisfaction** *noun.* ▪ **dissatisfied** *adj.* [17c]

dissect /dɪ'sɛkt, daɪ-/ *verb* **1** to cut open (a plant or dead body) for scientific or medical examination. **2** to examine something in minute detail, esp critically. ▪ **dissection** *noun.* [16c: from Latin *dissecare* to cut into pieces]

dissemble *verb, tr & intr* to conceal or disguise (true feelings or motives). ▪ **dissemblance** *noun.* [16c: from Latin *dissimulare*]

disseminate *verb* to make (eg news or theories) widely known. ▪ **dissemination** *noun.* [17c: from Latin *disseminare* to sow widely]

dissension *noun* disagreement, esp if leading to strife. [13c: French, from Latin *dissentire* to disagree]

dissent *noun* **1** disagreement, esp open or hostile. **2** voluntary separation, esp from an established church. ▸ *verb, intr* (*often* **dissent from sb** *or* **sth**) **1** to disagree with them. **2** to break away, esp from an established church. ▪ **dissenter** *noun.* ▪ **dissenting** *adj.* [15c: from Latin *dissentire* to disagree]

dissentient /dɪ'sɛnʃənt/ *adj, formal* disagreeing with a majority or established view.

dissertation *noun* **1** a long essay. **2** a formal lecture. [17c: from Latin *disserere* to discuss]

disservice *noun* a wrong; a bad turn. [16c: from French *desservir*]

dissident *noun* someone who disagrees publicly, esp with a government. ▸ *adj* disagreeing; dissenting. ▪ **dissidence** *noun.* [16c: from Latin *dissidere* to sit apart]

dissimilar *adj* (*often* **dissimilar to sth**) unlike; different. ▪ **dissimilarity** *noun* (**-ies**). [16c]

dissimulate *verb, tr & intr* to disguise (esp feelings). ▪ **dissimulation** *noun.* [17c: from Latin *dissimulare*]

dissipate *verb* **1** *tr & intr* to separate and scatter. **2** to squander something. ▪ **dissipated** *adj* over-indulging in pleasure and enjoyment. ▪ **dissipation** *noun.* [16c: from Latin *dissipare*]

dissociate *verb* **1** to regard something or someone as separate. **2** to declare someone or oneself to be unconnected with someone or something else. **3** *chem* of a chemical substance: to break down into its constituent molecules, atoms or ions. ▪ **dissociation** *noun.* [16c: from Latin *dissociare*]

dissoluble *adj* **1** able to be disconnected. **2** soluble. [16c: from Latin *dissolubilis*]

dissolute *adj* indulging in pleasures considered immoral; debauched. ▪ **dissoluteness** *noun.* [16c: from Latin *dissolutus* lax]

dissolution *noun* **1** the breaking up of a meeting or assembly. **2** the ending of a formal or legal partnership. **3** abolition, eg of the monarchy. **4** breaking up into parts. [14c: from Latin *dissolvere* to loosen]

dissolve *verb* **1** *tr & intr* to merge with a liquid. **2** to bring (an assembly) to a close. **3** to end (a legal partnership). **4** *tr & intr* to disappear or make something disappear. **5** *intr* (*often* **dissolve into laughter, tears**, *etc*) to be overcome emotionally. **6** *intr, technical* of a film or television image: to fade out as a second image fades in. [14c: from Latin *dissolvere* to loosen]

dissonance *noun* **1** *music* an unpleasant combination of sounds. **2** disagreement; incompatibility. ▪ **dissonant** *adj.* [16c: from Latin *dissonare* to be discordant]

dissuade *verb* (*usu* **dissuade sb from doing sth**) to deter them by advice or persuasion. ▪ **dissuasion** *noun.* [15c: from Latin *dissuadere*]

dissyllable *or* **dissyllabic** see **disyllable**

distaff *noun* the rod on which wool, etc is held ready for spinning. [Anglo-Saxon *distæf*]

IDIOMS **the distaff side** *old use* the wife's or mother's side of the family.

distal *adj, biol* farthest from the point of attachment. Compare **proximal**. ▪ **distally** *adv.* [19c: formed from **distance** on the analogy of *central*]

distance *noun* **1** the length between two points in space. **2** the fact of being apart. **3** any faraway point or place; the furthest visible area. **4** coldness of manner. ▸ *verb* **1** to put someone or something at a distance. **2** (*usu* **distance oneself from sb** *or* **sth**) to declare oneself to be unconnected or unsympathetic to them or it. [13c: from Latin *distancia*]

IDIOMS **go the distance** *informal* to last out until the end. **keep one's distance** to stay away or refuse involvement; to avoid friendship or familiarity.

distance learning *noun* learning via correspondence courses, TV, etc.

distant *adj* **1** far away or far apart in space or time. **2** not closely related. **3** cold and unfriendly. **4** appearing to be lost in thought. ▪ **distantly** *adv.* [14c]

distaste *noun* dislike; aversion. ▪ **distasteful** *adj.* [16c]

distemper[1] *noun* any of several infectious diseases of animals, esp **canine distemper**, an often fatal viral infection of dogs. [16c: from French *destemprer* to derange]

distemper[2] *noun* a water-based paint, esp one mixed with glue or size. ▸ *verb* to paint (eg a wall) with distemper. [17c: from Latin *distemperare* to soak]

distend *verb, tr & intr* to make or become swollen, inflated or stretched. ▪ **distensible** *adj.* ▪ **distension** *noun.* [14c: from Latin *distendere*]

distil *or* (*N Am*) **distill** *verb* (***distilled, distilling***) **1** to purify a liquid by heating it to boiling point and condensing the vapour formed. **2** to produce alcoholic spirits in this way. **3** to create a shortened or condensed version of something. ▪ **distillate** *noun.* ▪ **distillation** *noun.* [14c: from Latin *destillare* to drip down]

distillery *noun* (***-ies***) a place where alcoholic spirits are distilled. ▪ **distiller** *noun.*

distinct *adj* **1** clear or obvious. **2** noticeably different or separate. ▪ **distinctly** *adv.* [14c: from Latin *distinguere* to distinguish]

distinction *noun* **1** exceptional ability or achievement, or an honour awarded in recognition of it. **2** the act of differentiating. **3** the state of being noticeably different. **4** a distinguishing feature. [14c: from Latin *distinctio*]

distinctive *adj* easily recognized because very individual. ▪ **distinctiveness** *noun.*

distinguish *verb* **1** (*often* **distinguish one thing from another**) to mark or recognize them as different. **2** *intr* (*often* **distinguish between things** *or* **people**) to see the difference between them. **3** to make out or identify something. **4** (*always* **distinguish oneself**) *often ironic* to be outstanding because of some achievement. ▪ **distinguishable** *adj.* ▪ **distinguishing** *adj.* [16c: from Latin *distinguere*]

distinguished *adj* **1** famous (and usu well respected). **2** with a noble or dignified appearance.

distort *verb* **1** to twist something out of shape. **2** to change the meaning or tone of (a statement, etc) by inaccurate retelling. **3** *radio, telecomm* to alter the quality of (a signal), eg making sound less clear. ▪ **distortion** *noun.* [15c: from Latin *distorquere*]

distract *verb* **1** (*usu* **distract sb** *or* **sb's attention from sth**) to divert their attention from it. **2** to entertain or amuse someone. ▪ **distracted** *adj.* [14c: from Latin *distrahere* to draw apart]

distraction *noun* **1** something that diverts the attention. **2** an amusement; recreation. **3** anxiety; anger. **4** madness.

distrain *verb, law* to seize (eg property) as, or in order to force, payment of a debt. ▪ **distraint** *noun.* [13c: from French *destraindre*]

distrait /dɪˈstreɪ/ *adj, literary* thinking of other things. [18c: French]

distraught *adj* in an extremely troubled state of mind. [14c: a form of **distract**]

distress *noun* **1** mental or emotional pain. **2** financial difficulty; hardship. **3** great danger; peril: *a ship in distress*. ▸ *verb* **1** to upset someone. **2** to give (fabric, furniture, etc) the appearance of being older than it is. ▪ **distressing** *adj.* [13c: from French *destresse*]

distributary *noun, geog* a branch that flows off from a river, eg in a delta.

distribute *verb* **1** to give out something. **2** to supply or deliver (goods). **3** to spread (something) widely. [15c: from Latin *distribuere*]

distribution *noun* **1** the process of distributing or being distributed. **2** the placing of things spread out. **3** *stats* a set of measurements or values, together with the observed or predicted frequencies with which they occur.

distributive *adj*, **1** relating to distribution. **2** *grammar* said of a word: referring individually to all members of a group, eg *each, every*. **3** *maths* following the law that the same result is gained by multiplying a set of numbers as multiplying each individual member of the set, so that $a \times (x + y + z) = (a \times x) + (a \times y) + (a \times z)$.

distributor *noun* **1** a person or company that distributes goods, esp between manufacturer and retailer. **2** a device in a vehicle ignition system that directs pulses of electricity to the spark plugs.

district *noun* a region; an administrative or geographical unit. [17c: from Latin *districtus* jurisdiction]

district attorney *noun, esp US* a lawyer employed by a district to conduct prosecutions. Often shortened to **DA**.

district nurse *noun* a nurse who treats patients in their homes.

distrust *verb* to have no trust in someone or something; to doubt them or it. ▸ *noun* suspicion; lack of trust. See also **mistrust**. ▪ **distrustful** *adj.* [15c]

disturb *verb* **1** to interrupt someone. **2** to inconvenience someone. **3** to upset the arrangement or order of something. **4** to upset the peace of mind of someone. ▪ **disturbed** *adj, psychol* emotionally upset or confused; maladjusted. ▪ **disturbing** *adj.* [13c: from Latin *disturbare*]

disturbance *noun* **1** an outburst of noisy or violent behaviour. **2** an interruption.

disunite *verb* to drive (people, etc) apart; to cause disagreement or conflict between (people) or within (a group). ▪ **disunity** *noun.* [16c]

disuse *noun* the state of no longer being used, practised or observed; neglect. ▪ **disused** *adj.* [16c]

disyllable *or* **dissyllable** /ˈdaɪsɪləbəl/ *noun* a word of two syllables. ▪ **disyllabic** *or* **dissyllabic** *adj.* [16c: from Greek *di-* twice + **syllable**]

ditch *noun* a narrow channel dug in the ground. ▸ *verb* **1** *slang* to get rid of or abandon someone or something. **2** *tr & intr, informal* of an aircraft or a pilot: to bring or come down in the sea. [Anglo-Saxon *dic*]

dither *verb, intr* to act in a nervously uncertain manner; to waver. ▸ *noun* a state of nervous indecision. ▪ **ditherer** *noun.* ▪ **dithery** *adj.* [20c: from *didderen* to tremble or shake]

ditto *noun* the same thing; that which has just been said. ▸ *adv* (abbrev **do.**) likewise; the same. [17c: Italian, meaning 'aforesaid']

ditto marks *noun* a symbol (") written immediately below a word, etc in a list to mean 'same as above'.

ditty *noun* (*-ies*) a short simple song or poem. [14c: from French *dité*]

diuretic /daɪjʊˈrɛtɪk/ *med, noun* a drug or other substance that increases the volume of urine produced and excreted. ▸ *adj* increasing the production and excretion of urine. [14c: from Greek *dia* through + *ouron* urine]

diurnal /daɪˈɜːnəl/ *formal, technical, adj* **1** daily. **2** during the day. **3** active during the day. [15c: from Latin *diurnus*]

div see **divvy**[1]

diva /ˈdiːvə/ *noun* (*divas or dive* /ˈdiːveɪ/) a great female singer. [19c: Latin, meaning 'goddess']

divalent *adj, chem* of an atom: able to combine with two atoms of hydrogen or the equivalent. [19c]

Divali see **Diwali**

divan *noun* **1** a sofa with no back or sides. **2** a bed without a headboard or footboard. [18c: from Persian *diwan* long seat]

dive[1] *verb* (***dived*** *or* (*N Am*) ***dove***) *intr* **1** to throw oneself into water, or plunge down through water. **2** of a submarine, etc: to become submerged. **3** to descend or fall steeply through the air. **4** to throw oneself to the side or to the ground. **5** to move quickly and suddenly out of sight: *diving behind a tree.* ▸ *noun* **1** an act of diving. **2** *slang* any dirty or disreputable place, esp a bar or club. **3** *boxing slang* a faked knockout: *take a dive.* [Anglo-Saxon *dyfan*]
PHRASAL VERBS **dive in** to help oneself to (food). **dive into sth 1** to plunge one's hands (eg into a bag). **2** to involve oneself enthusiastically in an undertaking.

dive[2] see **diva**

dive-bomber *noun* an aeroplane that releases a bomb while diving. ▪ **dive-bomb** *verb.*

diver *noun* **1** someone who dives. **2** someone who works underwater. **3** a duck-like diving bird. [16c]

diverge *verb, intr* **1** to separate and go in different directions. **2** to differ. **3** to depart or deviate (eg from a usual course). ▪ **divergence** *noun.* ▪ **divergent** *adj.* [17c: from Latin *divergere*]

diverse *adj* **1** various; assorted. **2** different; dissimilar. [13c: from Latin *diversus* turned different ways]

diversify *verb* (*-ies, -ied*) **1** *tr & intr* to become or make something diverse. **2** *intr* to engage in new and different activities. ▪ **diversification** *noun.* [15c]

diversion *noun* **1** the act of diverting; the state of being diverted. **2** a detour from a usual route. **3** something intended to draw attention away. **4** amusement. ▪ **diversionary** *adj.* [17c: from Latin *diversio*]

diversity *noun* (*-ies*) variety; being varied or different. [14c: from French *diversité*]

divert *verb* **1** to make someone or something change direction. **2** to draw away (esp attention). **3** to amuse someone. [15c: from Latin *divertere* to turn aside]

diverticulitis /daɪvətɪkjʊˈlaɪtɪs/ *noun* inflammation of a diverticulum. [Early 20c]

diverticulum /daɪvəˈtɪkjʊləm/ *noun* (***diverticula*** /-lə/) a pouch formed at a weak point in the muscular wall of the alimentary canal, esp the colon. [17c: Latin]

divertimento /dɪvɜːtɪˈmɛntoʊ/ *noun* (***divertimenti*** /-tiː/ *or* ***divertimentos***) a light musical composition. [19c: Italian, meaning 'entertainment']

divest *verb* (*usu* **divest sb of sth**) **1** to take away or get rid of it. **2** *rather formal* to take something off: *divested herself of her jacket.* [16c: from Latin *de-* away + *vestire* to clothe]

divi see **divvy**[1]

divide *verb* **1** *tr & intr* to split up or separate into parts. **2** (*also* **divide sth up**) to share. **3** *maths* **a** to determine how many times one number is contained in (another); **b** *intr* of a number: to be a number of times greater or smaller than another: *3 divides into 9.* **4** to bring about a disagreement among (people). **5** to serve as a boundary between something. **6** *intr* of an assembly, Parliament, etc: to form into groups voting for and against a motion. ▸ *noun* **1** a disagreement. **2** a gap or split. **3** *esp US* a ridge of high land between two rivers. [14c: from Latin *dividere* to force apart]

dividend *noun* **1** a portion of a company's profits paid to a shareholder. **2** a benefit: *Meeting her would pay dividends.* **3** *maths* a number divided by another number. [15c: from Latin *dividendum* what is to be divided]

dividers *plural noun* a V-shaped device with movable arms ending in points, used in geometry, etc for measuring.

divination *noun* the practice of foretelling the future by, or as if by, supernatural means. [14c: from **divine**]

divine *adj* **1** belonging or relating to, or coming from God or a god. **2** *informal* extremely good, pleasant or beautiful. ▸ *verb* **1** to foretell something. **2** to realize something by intuition; to guess it. **3** *tr & intr* to search for (underground water) with a divining rod. ▸ *noun* a member of the clergy who is expert in theology. ▪ **divinely** *adv.* ▪ **diviner** *noun.* [14c: from Latin *divinus*]

diving bell *noun* a large hollow bottomless container which traps air, and in which divers can descend into, and work under, water.

diving board *noun* a narrow platform from which swimmers can dive into a pool, etc.

diving suit *noun* a diver's waterproof suit, esp one with a helmet and heavy boots.

divining rod *noun* a stick held when divining for water, which moves when a discovery is made. Also called **dowsing rod**.

divinity *noun* (*-ies*) **1** theology. **2** a god. **3** the state of being God or a god. [14c: from Latin *divinitas*]

divisible *adj* able to be divided.

division *noun* **1** dividing or being divided. **2** something that divides or separates. **3** one of the parts into which something is divided. **4** a major unit of an organization such as an army or police force. **5** *maths* the process of determining how many times one number is contained in another. **6** a formal vote in Parliament. **7** *botany* any of the major groups into which the plant kingdom is divided. ▪ **divisional** *adj*. [14c]

division sign *noun* the symbol ÷, representing division in calculations.

divisive *adj* tending to cause disagreement or conflict. [16c: from late Latin *divisivus*]

divisor *noun, maths* a number by which another number is divided. [15c: Latin *divisor* divider]

divorce *noun* **1** the legal ending of a marriage. **2** a complete separation. ▸ *verb* **1** *tr & intr* to legally end marriage to someone. **2** to separate. [14c: from Latin *divortere* to leave one's husband]

divorcee *noun* someone who has been divorced.

divot *noun* a piece of grass and earth. [19c]

divulge *verb* to make something known; to reveal (a secret, etc). ▪ **divulgence** *noun*. [15c: from Latin *divulgare* to publish widely]

divvy[1] *slang, noun* (*-ies*) a dividend or share. Also called **div**, **divi**. ▸ *verb* (*-ies, -ied*) (*also* **divvy up sth**) to divide or share it. [19c]

divvy[2] *informal noun* (*-ies*) a fool. [20c]

Diwali /diː'wɑːliː/ *or* **Divali** /-'vɑːliː/ *noun* a Hindu festival held in honour of Lakshmi, goddess of wealth and good fortune. [17c: Hindi]

DIY *abbrev* do-it-yourself.

dizzy *adj* (*-ier, -iest*) **1** experiencing or causing a spinning sensation in the head. **2** *informal* silly; not reliable or responsible. **3** *informal* bewildered. ▸ *verb* (*-ies, -ied*) **1** to make someone dizzy. **2** to bewilder someone. ▪ **dizziness** *noun*. [Anglo-Saxon *dysig* foolish]

DJ *abbrev* **1** *slang* dinner jacket. **2** disc jockey.

djinn *or* **djinni** see **jinni**

dl *abbrev* decilitre or decilitres.

DLitt *abbrev*: *Doctor Litterarum* (Latin), Doctor of Letters.

dm *abbrev* decimetre or decimetres.

DNA *abbrev* deoxyribonucleic acid.

DNA fingerprinting *noun* **genetic fingerprinting**.

D-notice *noun* a notice sent by the government to newspapers asking them not to publish certain security information. [1940s: from *d*efence notice]

DNS *abbrev, comput* domain name system.

do[1] *verb* (**does**, *past tense* **did**, *past participle* **done**) **1** to carry out, perform or commit something. **2** to finish or complete something. **3** *tr & intr* (*also* **do for sb**) to be enough or suitable. **4** to work at or study: *Are you doing maths?* **5** *intr* to be in a particular state: *Business is doing well.* **6** to put in order or arrange. **7** *intr* to act or behave. **8** to provide something as a service: *do lunches.* **9** to bestow (honour, etc). **10** to cause or produce. **11** to travel (a distance). **12** to travel at (a speed). **13** *informal* to improve or enhance something or someone: *This dress doesn't do much for me.* **14** *informal* to cheat someone. **15** *informal* to mimic someone. **16** to visit (a place, etc) as a tourist. **17** *informal* to ruin something: *Now he's done it!* **18** *informal* to assault or injure someone: *I'll do you.* **19** *informal* to spend (time) in prison. **20** *informal* to convict someone. **21** *intr, informal* to happen: *There was nothing doing.* **22** *slang* to take (drugs). ▸ *auxiliary verb* **1** used in questions and negative statements or commands, as in *Do you smoke?*, *I don't like wine* and *Don't go!* **2** used to avoid repetition of a verb, as in *She eats as much as I do.* **3** used for emphasis, as in *She does know you've arrived.* ▸ *noun* (**dos** *or* **do's**) *informal* **1** a party or other gathering. **2** something done as a rule or custom: *dos and don'ts.* [Anglo-Saxon *don*]

IDIOMS **could do with sth** *or* **sb** would benefit from having it or them. **have** *or* **be to do with sb** *or* **sth** **1** to be related to or connected with them or it: *What has that to do with me?* **2** to be partly or wholly responsible for something: *I had nothing to do with it.*

PHRASAL VERBS **do away with sb** *or* **sth** **1** to murder them or it. **2** to abolish it. **do sb** *or* **sth down** to speak of them or it disparagingly. **do for sb** *informal* **1** to do household cleaning for them. **2** to defeat, ruin or kill them. **do sb in** *informal* **1** to kill them. **2** to exhaust them. **do sb out of sth** to deprive them of it, esp by trickery. **do sb over** *slang* to rob, attack or injure them. **do oneself up** to dress up. **do sth up** *informal* **1** to repair, clean or improve the decoration of (a building, etc). **2** to fasten it; to tie or wrap it up. **do without sth** to manage without it.

do[2] see **doh**

doable *adj* able to be done.

dob *abbrev* date of birth.

Dobermann pinscher /'doʊbəmən 'pɪnʃə(r)/ *or* **Dobermann** *noun* a large breed of dog with a smooth black-and-tan coat. [20c: from Ludwig Dobermann, the breeder + German *Pinscher* terrier]

doc *noun, informal* a doctor.

docile *adj* easy to manage or control. ▪ **docilely** *adv*. ▪ **docility** *noun*. [15c: from Latin *docilis* easily taught]

dock[1] *noun* **1** a harbour where ships are loaded, unloaded, and repaired. **2** (**docks**) the area surrounding this. ▸ *verb, tr & intr* **1** to bring or come into a dock. **2** of space vehicles: to link up in space. [16c: from Dutch *docke*]

dock[2] *verb* **1** to cut off all or part of (an animal's tail). **2** to make deductions from (eg someone's pay). **3** to deduct (an amount). [14c]

dock[3] *noun* a weed with large broad leaves. [Anglo-Saxon *docce*]

dock[4] *noun* the enclosure in a court of law where the accused sits or stands. [16c: from Flemish *dok* cage or sty]

docker *noun* a labourer who loads and unloads ships. [19c]

docket *noun* a label or note accompanying a parcel or package, eg detailing contents or recording receipt. ▸ *verb* to fix a label to something. [15c: possibly from **dock**[2]]

dockyard *noun* a shipyard, esp a naval one.

doctor *noun* **1** someone qualified to practise medicine. **2** *N Am* **a** a dentist; **b** a veterinary surgeon. **3** someone holding a **doctorate**. ▸ *verb* **1** to falsify (eg information). **2** to tamper with something; to drug (food or drink). **3** *informal* to sterilize or castrate (an animal). [14c: Latin, meaning 'teacher']

doctorate *noun* a high academic degree, awarded esp for research.

doctrinaire *adj, derog* adhering rigidly to theories or principles, regardless of practicalities or appropriateness. [19c: French]

doctrine /ˈdɒktrɪn/ *noun* something taught; a religious or political belief, or a set of such beliefs. ▪ **doctrinal** /dɒkˈtraɪnəl/ *adj.* [14c: from Latin *doctrina* teaching]

docudrama *noun* a play or film based on real events and characters. [1960s: from *documentary drama*]

document *noun* **1** any piece of writing of an official nature. **2** *comput* a text file. ▸ *verb* **1** to record something, esp in written form. **2** to provide written evidence to support or prove something. [15c: from Latin *documentum* lesson or proof]

documentary *noun* (**-ies**) a film or television or radio programme presenting real people in real situations. ▸ *adj* **1** connected with, or consisting of, documents: *documentary evidence.* **2** of the nature of a documentary; undramatized. [19c]

documentation *noun* **1** documents or documentary evidence. **2** the provision or collection of these.

dodder *verb, intr* to move in an unsteady trembling fashion, usu as a result of old age. ▪ **dodderer** *noun.* ▪ **doddery** *adj.* [19c]

doddle *noun, informal* something easily done. [20c]

dodeca- *combining form, signifying* twelve. [Greek *dodeka* twelve]

dodecagon /doʊˈdɛkəgɒn/ *noun* a flat geometric figure with 12 sides and angles. [17c: from Greek, from *dodeka* twelve + *gonia* angle]

dodecahedron /doʊdɛkəˈhiːdrən/ *noun* a solid geometric figure with twelve faces. [16c: from Greek, from *dodeka* twelve + *hedra* seat]

dodge *verb* **1** to avoid (a blow, a person, etc) by moving quickly away, esp sideways. **2** to escape or avoid something by cleverness or deceit. ▸ *noun* **1** a sudden movement aside. **2** a trick to escape or avoid something. [16c]

Dodgems *plural noun, trademark* a fairground amusement in which drivers of small electric cars try to bump each other.

dodger *noun* a shirker; a trickster.

dodgy *adj* (**-ier, -iest**) *informal* **1** difficult or risky. **2** untrustworthy; dishonest, or dishonestly obtained. **3** unstable; slightly broken. [19c]

dodo *noun* (***dodos*** *or* ***dodoes***) a large extinct flightless bird. [17c: from Portuguese *doudo* silly]

doe *noun* (***does*** *or* ***doe***) an adult female rabbit, hare or small deer. [Anglo-Saxon *da*]

doer *noun* a busy active person.

does see under **do**[1]

doesn't *contraction of* does not.

doff *verb, old use, literary* **1** to lift (one's hat) in greeting. **2** to take off (a piece of clothing). [14c: from **do**[1] + **off**]

dog *noun* **1** a carnivorous mammal such as a wolf, jackal or fox. **2** a domestic species of this family. **3** the male of any such animal. **4** *informal* a person. ▸ *verb* (***dogged, dogging***) **1** to follow someone very closely; to track someone. **2** to trouble or plague someone. [Anglo-Saxon *docga*]

IDIOMS **a dog's life** a life of misery. **go to the dogs** *informal* to deteriorate greatly. **like a dog's dinner** *informal, often disparaging* dressed smartly or showily.

dogcart *noun* a two-wheeled horse-drawn passenger carriage with seats back-to-back.

dog collar *noun* **1** a collar for a dog. **2** *informal* a stiff collar worn by certain clergy.

dog days *plural noun* the hottest period of the year, when **Sirius**, the **Dog Star**, rises and sets with the sun.

doge /doʊdʒ/ *noun* the chief magistrate of Venice or Genoa. [16c: Italian, meaning 'duke']

dog-eared *adj* of a book: with its pages turned down at the corners; shabby; scruffy.

dog eat dog *noun* ruthless pursuit of one's own interests. *as adj* (**dog-eat-dog**): *a dog-eat-dog struggle.*

dog-end *noun, slang* a cigarette end. [1930s]

dogfight *noun* **1** a battle at close quarters between two fighter aircraft. **2** any violent fight.

dogfish *noun* any of various kinds of small shark

dogged /ˈdɒgɪd/ *adj* determined; resolute. ▪ **doggedly** *adv.* ▪ **doggedness** *noun.* [16c]

doggerel *noun* **1** badly written poetry. **2** poetry with an irregular rhyming pattern for comic effect. ▸ *adj* of poor quality. [14c, meaning 'worthless']

doggo *adv* [19c: prob from **dog**]

IDIOMS **lie doggo** *informal* to hide; to lie low.

doggy *adj* (**-ier, -iest**) *informal* **1** belonging to, like or relating to dogs. **2** fond of dogs. ▸ *noun* (**-ies**) a child's word for a dog. Also **doggie**.

doggy-bag *noun* a bag in which a customer at a restaurant can take home uneaten food. [1960s]

doggy-paddle, doggie-paddle *or* **dog-paddle** *noun* a basic swimming stroke with short paddling movements. ▸ *verb, intr* to swim using this stroke.

doghouse *noun, now chiefly N Am* a **kennel**. [17c]

IDIOMS **in the doghouse** *informal* out of favour.

dog in the manger *noun* someone who has no need of something but refuses to let others use it.

dogleg *noun* a sharp bend, esp on a golf course. [19c]

dogma *noun* (***dogmas*** *or* ***dogmata*** /ˈdɒgmətə/) **1** a belief or principle laid down by an authority as unquestionably true. **2** such beliefs or principles in general. [16c: Greek, meaning 'opinion']

dogmatic *or* **dogmatical** *adj* **1** relating to dogma or a dogma. **2** of an opinion: forcefully and arrogantly stated as if unquestionable. **3** of a person: tending to make such statements of opinion. ▪ **dogmatically** *adv.* ▪ **dogmatism** *noun.* ▪ **dogmatist** *noun.*

do-gooder *noun, informal* an enthusiastic helper of other people, esp one whose help is not appreciated.

dog-paddle see **doggy-paddle**

dogsbody *noun* (**-ies**) *informal* someone who does menial tasks. [20c: naval slang for a junior officer]

dog's breakfast *or* **dinner** *noun* anything very messy or untidy.

Dog Star see **Sirius**

dog-tired *adj, informal* extremely tired.

doh *or* **do** /doʊ/ *noun, music* in sol-fa notation: the first note of the major scale. [18c: see **sol-fa**]

doily *or* **doyley** *noun* (**-ies** *or* **-eys**) a small decorative napkin of lace or lace-like paper laid on plates under sandwiches, cakes, etc. [17c: named after Doily, a London draper]

doings *plural noun* activities; behaviour. ▸ *singular noun, informal* something whose name cannot be remembered or is left unsaid.

do-it-yourself *noun* (abbrev **DIY**) the practice of doing one's own household repairs, etc without professional help. ▸ *adj* designed to be built, constructed, etc by an amateur rather than a fully trained professional. [1950s]

Dolby *or* **Dolby system** *noun, trademark* a system of noise reduction in audio tape-recording, used to reduce the background hissing heard during replay, and to improve the quality of stereophonic sound in cinemas. [1960s: named after the US engineer Raymond Dolby]

the doldrums *plural noun* **1** a depressed mood; low spirits. **2** a state of inactivity. **3** (*also* **the Doldrums**) *meteorol* a hot humid region on either side of the Equator where there is little wind. [19c: from obsolete *dold* stupid]

dole *noun, informal* (**the dole**) unemployment benefit. ▸ *verb, intr* (*always* **dole sth out**) to hand it out or give it out. [Anglo-Saxon *dal* share]

IDIOMS **on the dole** *informal* unemployed.

doleful *adj* sad; mournful. ▪ **dolefully** *adv.* ▪ **dolefulness** *noun.* [13c: from French *doel* grief + **-ful**]

doll *noun* **1** a toy in the form of a small model of a human being. **2** *derog, informal* a showy overdressed woman. **3** *slang, often offensive* any girl or woman, esp when considered pretty. **4** *informal* a term of endearment, esp for a girl. ▸ *verb* (*always* **doll oneself up**) to dress smartly or showily. [17c: from the name Dolly]

dollar *noun* (symbol $) the standard unit of currency in the US, Canada, Australia and other countries, divided into 100 **cents**. [18c: from German *Thaler*, a silver coin from Joachimsthal in Bohemia]

dollop *noun, informal* a small shapeless mass. [19c]

dolly *noun* (***-ies***) **1** *informal* a doll. **2** *cinema, TV* a frame with wheels on which a film or television camera is mounted for moving shots.

dolman sleeve *noun* a kind of sleeve that tapers from a very wide armhole to a tight wrist. [20c: from Turkish *dolaman* a robe with tight sleeves]

dolmen *noun* a simple prehistoric monument consisting of a large flat stone supported by several vertical stones. [19c: perhaps from Breton *dol* table + *men* stone]

dolphin *noun* a small toothed variety of whale. [16c: from Greek *delphinos*]

dolphinarium *noun* (***dolphinaria*** *or* ***dolphinariums***) a large open-air aquarium in which dolphins are kept. [20c]

dolt *noun, derog* a stupid person. ▪ **doltish** *adj.* [Anglo-Saxon *dol* stupid]

-dom *suffix, forming nouns, denoting* **1** a state or rank: *serfdom* • *dukedom.* **2** an area ruled or governed: *kingdom.* **3** a group of people with a specified characteristic: *officialdom.* [Anglo-Saxon *dom* judgement]

domain *noun* **1** the scope of any subject or area of interest. **2** a territory owned or ruled by one person or government. **3** *maths* the set of values specified for a given mathematical function. [17c: from French *domaine*]

domain name *noun, comput* the distinctive name of a specific computer network or service used as part of an Internet address, allowing its easy identification.

dome *noun* **1** a hemispherical roof. **2** anything of similar shape. ▪ **domed** *adj.* [17c: from Latin *domus* house]

domestic *adj* **1** belonging or relating to the home, the family or private life. **2** kept as a pet or farm animal. **3** within or relating to one's country: *domestic sales.* **4** enjoying home life. ▸ *noun* **1** *informal* a fight, usu in the home, between members of a household. **2** a household servant. ▪ **domestically** *adv.* [16c: from Latin *domesticus*, from *domus* house]

domesticate *verb* **1** to train (an animal) to live with people. **2** *often facetious* to make someone used to home life; to train someone in cooking, housework, etc. ▪ **domestication** *noun.* [17c]

domesticity *noun* home life, or a liking for it.

domestic science *noun* training in household skills, esp cooking; home economics.

domicile /ˈdɒmɪsaɪl/ *noun* **1** *formal* a house. **2** a legally recognized place of permanent residence. ▸ *verb, law* to establish or be settled in a fixed residence. [19c: from Latin *domicilium* dwelling]

domiciliary *adj* **1** relating to people and their homes. **2** dealing with or available to people in their own homes. [19c: from **domicile**]

dominant *adj* **1** most important, evident or active. **2** tending or seeking to command or influence others. **3** of a building, etc: overlooking others from an elevated position. **4** *biol* **a** denoting a gene whose characteristics are always fully expressed in an individual. See also **recessive**. **b** denoting a characteristic determined by such a gene. ▸ *noun* **1** *music* the fifth note on a musical scale. **2** *biol* a dominant gene. ▪ **dominance** *noun.*

dominate *verb, tr & intr* **1** to have command or influence over someone. **2** to be the most important, evident or active of (a group). **3** to stand above (a place). ▪ **dominating** *adj.* ▪ **domination** *noun.* [17c: from Latin *dominari* to be master]

domineering *adj* overbearing; arrogant. [16c: from Latin *dominari* to be master]

Dominican *noun* a member of a Christian order of friars and nuns orig founded by St Dominic in 1215. ▸ *adj* belonging or relating to this order.

dominion *noun* **1** rule; power; influence. **2** a territory or country governed by a single ruler or government. **3** *formerly* a self-governing colony within the British Empire. [15c: from Latin *dominium* ownership]

domino *noun* (***dominoes***) **1** any of the small rectangular tiles marked, in two halves, with varying numbers of spots, used in the game of **dominoes**. **2** (**dominoes**) a game in which these tiles are laid down, with matching halves end to end. **3** a black cloak with a hood and mask. [17c: perhaps from Italian *domino!*, master!, the winner's cry in the game of dominoes]

don¹ *noun* a university lecturer. [17c: from Latin *dominus* lord]

don² *verb* (***donned, donning***) to put on (clothing). [17c: **do¹** (*verb* sense 1) + **on**]

donate *verb* to give, esp to charity. ▪ **donation** *noun.* [18c: from Latin *donare* to give]

done *verb, past participle of* **do¹**. ▸ *adj* **1** finished; completed. **2** fully cooked. **3** socially acceptable. **4** used up. **5** *informal* exhausted. ▸ *exclam* expressing agreement or completion of a deal.

IDIOMS **done for** *informal* facing ruin or death.

doner kebab /ˈdɒnə(r)/ *noun* thin slices cut from a block of minced and seasoned lamb grilled on a spit and eaten on unleavened bread. [1950s: from Turkish *döner* rotating + **kebab**]

donkey *noun* **1** a hoofed herbivorous mammal related to but smaller than the horse. **2** *informal* a stupid person. [18c]

donkey jacket *noun* a heavy jacket made of a thick woollen fabric, usu black or dark blue.

donkey's years *plural noun, informal* a very long time.

donkey-work *noun* **1** heavy manual work. **2** preparation; groundwork.

donor *noun* **1** someone who donates something, esp money. **2** a person or animal that provides blood, semen, living tissue or organs for medical use. [15c]

donor card *noun* a card indicating that its carrier is willing, in the event of sudden death, to have their organs removed for transplantation.

don't *contraction of* do not. ▸ *noun, informal* something that must not be done: *dos and don'ts.*

donut see **doughnut**

doodah *or* (*N Am*) **doodad** *noun, informal* a thing whose name one does not know or cannot remember. [20c]

doodle *verb, intr* to scrawl or scribble aimlessly and meaninglessly. ▸ *noun* a meaningless scribble. [20c]

doodlebug *noun* **1** *US* the larva of certain insects. **2** any device used by prospectors to indicate the presence of minerals. **3** *war slang* a V-1 flying bomb, used by the Germans in World War II. [19c]

doolally *adj, slang* mentally unbalanced; crazy. [20c: from Deolali in India, where there was a sanitarium]

doom *noun* inescapable death, ruin or other unpleasant fate. ▸ *verb* to condemn someone to death or some other dire fate. [Anglo-Saxon *dom* judgement]

doomsday *noun* the last day of the world. [Anglo-Saxon *domes dæg*]

door *noun* **1** a movable barrier opening and closing an entrance. **2** an entrance. **3** a house considered in relation to others: *three doors away.* **4** a means of entry; an opportunity to gain access: *opened the door to stardom.* [Anglo-Saxon *duru*]
IDIOMS **close the door to sth** to make it impossible. **lay sth at sb's door** to blame them for it.

doorbell *noun* a bell on or next to a door, rung by visitors as a sign of arrival. [19c]

doorjamb *or* **doorpost** *noun* one of the two vertical side pieces of a door frame.

doorknocker see **knocker**

doorman *noun* a man employed to guard the entrance to a hotel, club, etc and assist guests or customers.

doormat *noun* **1** a mat for wiping shoes on before entering. **2** *informal* a person easily submitting to unfair treatment by others.

doorstep *noun* **1** a step in front of a building's door. **2** *slang* a thick sandwich or slice of bread. ▸ *verb* (***-stepped, -stepping***) **1** to go from door to door canvassing. **2** of journalists, etc: to pester someone by waiting at their door.

doorstop *noun* **1** a device, eg a wedge, for holding a door open. **2** a device, eg a fixed knob, for preventing a door opening too far.

doorway *noun* the space where there is or might be a door; an entrance.

dopamine *noun, biochem* an important compound that functions as a neurotransmitter. [20c]

dope *noun* **1** *informal* a drug taken for pleasure, esp cannabis. **2** *informal* a drug given to athletes, dogs or horses to affect performance. **3** *informal* a stupid person. **4** (**the dope**) *slang* information, esp when confidential. ▸ *verb* to give or apply drugs to (a person or animal), especially illegally. ▪ **doping** *noun.* [19c: from Dutch *doop* sauce]

dopey *or* **dopy** *adj, informal* (***dopier, dopiest***) **1** sleepy or inactive, as if drugged. **2** stupid.

doppelgänger /ˈdɒpəlgɛŋə(r)/ *noun* an apparition or double of a person. [19c: German, meaning 'double-goer']

Doppler effect *or* **Doppler shift** *noun, physics* the change in wavelength observed when the distance between a source of waves and the observer is changing, eg the sound change perceived as an aircraft or vehicle passes by. [19c: named after the Austrian physicist Christian Doppler]

Doric *adj, archit* denoting an order of classical architecture, characterized by thick fluted columns. Compare **Corinthian**, **Ionic**, **Tuscan**. [16c: from Greek *Dorikos*, from Doris, in ancient Greece]

dorm *noun, informal* a **dormitory**.

dormant *adj* **1** temporarily quiet, inactive or out of use. **2** *biol* in a resting state. ▪ **dormancy** *noun.* [16c: from Latin *dormire* to sleep]

dormer *or* **dormer window** *noun* a window fitted vertically into an extension built out from a sloping roof. [16c: from **dormitory**]

dormitory *noun* (***-ies***) **1** a large bedroom for several people. **2** *esp US* a hall of residence in a college or university. Often shortened to **dorm**. [15c: from Latin *dormitorium*]

dormitory town *noun* a town from which most residents travel to work elsewhere.

Dormobile *noun, trademark* a van equipped for living and sleeping in. [1950s: from **dormitory** + **automobile**]

dormouse *noun* a small nocturnal rodent with rounded ears, large eyes, velvety fur, and a bushy tail. [15c]

dorp *noun, S Afr* a small town or village. [15c: Dutch]

dorsal *adj, biol, physiol* belonging or relating to the back. Compare **ventral**. [15c: from Latin *dorsum* back]

dory *noun* (***-ies***) a golden-yellow fish of the mackerel family. Also called **John Dory**. [15c: from French *dorée* golden]

DOS /dɒs/ *abbrev, comput* disk-operating system, a program for handling information on a disk.

dos *or* **do's** see under **do**[1]

dosage *noun* the prescribed amount of a dose of a medicine or drug.

dose *noun* **1** *med* the measured quantity of medicine, etc that is prescribed by a doctor to be administered to a patient. **2** the amount of radiation a person is exposed to over a specified period of time. **3** *informal* a bout, esp of an illness or something unpleasant. ▸ *verb* (*also* **dose sb up with sth**) to give them medicine, esp in large quantities. [17c: from Greek *dosis* giving]

IDIOMS **like a dose of salts** *informal* extremely quickly and effectively.

dosh *noun, slang* money. [20c]

doss *verb, intr, slang* (*often* **doss down**) to settle down to sleep, esp on an improvised bed. [18c]

dosser *noun, slang* **1** a homeless person sleeping on the street or in a **dosshouse**. **2** a lazy person.

dosshouse *noun, slang* a cheap lodging-house for homeless people.

dossier /ˈdɒsɪeɪ, ˈdɒsɪə(r)/ *noun* a file of papers containing information on a person or subject. [19c: French]

dot *noun* **1** a spot; a point. **2** in **Morse** code: the shorter of the two lengths of signal element. Compare **dash** (sense 5). ▸ *verb* (***dotted, dotting***) **1** to put a dot on something. **2** to scatter; to cover with a scattering: *dotted with daisies*. [Anglo-Saxon *dott* head of a boil]

IDIOMS **dot the i's and cross the t's 1** to pay close attention to detail. **2** to finish the last few details of something. **on the dot** exactly on time.

dotage *noun* feeble-mindedness owing to old age; senility. [14c: see **dote**]

dotard *noun* someone in their dotage.

dotcom *adj* of a company: trading through the Internet. ▸ *noun* a company that trades through the Internet. [20c: pronunciation of *.com*, suffix in commercial Internet addresses]

dote *verb, intr* **1** (*always* **dote on** *or* **upon sb** *or* **sth**) to show a foolishly excessive fondness for them or it. **2** to be foolish or weak-minded, esp because of old age. ▪ **doting** *adj* foolishly or excessively fond of someone. [15c: from Dutch *doten* to be silly]

dot matrix printer *noun, comput* a computer printer using arrangements of pins from a matrix or set to form the printed characters. Compare **inkjet printer**, **laser printer**.

dotty *adj* (***-ier, -iest***) *informal* silly; crazy. ▪ **dottiness** *noun*.

double *adj* **1** made up of two similar parts; paired; in pairs. **2** twice the weight, size, or twice the usual weight, size, etc. **3** for two people: *a double bed*. **4** ambiguous: *double meaning*. **5** of a musical instrument: sounding an octave lower: *double bass*. ▸ *adv* **1** twice. **2** with one half over the other: *folded double*. ▸ *noun* **1** a double quantity. **2** a duplicate or lookalike. **3** an actor's stand-in. **4** a double measure of alcoholic spirit. **5** a racing bet in which winnings from the first stake become a stake in a subsequent race. **6** a win in two events on the same racing programme. See also **doubles**. ▸ *verb* **1** *tr & intr* to make or become twice as large in size, number, etc. **2** (*often* **double sth over**) to fold one half of it over the other. **3** *intr* to have a second use or function: *The spare bed doubles as a couch*. **4** *intr* to turn round sharply. **5** *intr* (*often* **double for sb**) to act as their substitute. [13c: from French *doble*]

IDIOMS **at** *or* **on the double** very quickly.

PHRASAL VERBS **double back** to turn and go back, often by a different route. **double up 1** to bend sharply at the waist, esp through pain. **2** (*also* **double up with sb**) to share a bedroom with another person.

double act *noun, theatre* two entertainers working together.

double agent *noun* a spy working for two opposing governments at the same time.

double-barrelled *or* (*N Am*) **double-barreled** *adj* **1** having two barrels. **2** of a surname: made up of two names. **3** eg of a compliment: ambiguous.

double bass *noun* the largest and lowest in pitch of the orchestral stringed instruments. Also called **string bass**.

double bassoon see **contrabassoon**

double bill *noun* two films, plays, bands, etc presented as a single entertainment, one after the other.

double bluff *noun* an action or statement which is meant to be seen as a bluff, but which is in fact genuine.

double bond *noun, chem* a covalent bond formed by the sharing of two pairs of electrons between two atoms.

double-breasted *adj* of a coat or jacket: having overlapping front flaps.

double-check *verb* to check twice or again.

double chin *noun* a chin with an area of loose flesh underneath.

double cream *noun* thick cream with a high fat content.

double-cross *verb* to cheat or deceive (esp a colleague or ally, or someone one is supposed to be helping). ▸ *noun* such a deceit.

double-dealing *noun* cheating; treachery.

double-decker *noun* **1** a bus with two decks. **2** *informal* anything with two levels or layers.

double Dutch *noun, informal* nonsense; incomprehensible jargon.

double-edged *adj* **1** having two cutting edges. **2** having two possible meanings or purposes.

double entendre /ˈduːbəl ɑ̃ˈtɑ̃drə/ *noun* a remark having two possible meanings, one of them usu sexually suggestive. [17c: French, meaning 'double meaning']

double-entry *noun, bookkeeping* a method by which two entries are made of each transaction.

double fault *noun, tennis, etc* two faults served in succession, resulting in loss of a point.

double figures *plural noun* the numbers between 10 and 99 inclusive.

double-glazing *noun* windows constructed with two panes separated by a vacuum, providing added heat insulation.

double-jointed *adj* having extraordinarily flexible body joints.

double negative *noun* an expression containing two negative words, esp where only one is logically needed: *He hasn't never asked me*.

double-park *verb* to park at the side of another vehicle parked alongside the kerb.

double-quick *adj, adv* very quick or quickly.

doubles *singular noun* a competition in tennis, etc between two teams of two players each.

double standard *noun* (*often* **double standards**) a principle or rule applied firmly to one person or group and loosely or not at all to another, esp oneself.

double star *noun, astron* **1** a **binary star**. **2** a pair of stars that appear close together but are in fact at very different distances from Earth.

doublet *noun* **1** *hist* a close-fitting man's jacket. **2** a pair of objects of any kind, or each of these. [14c: French]

double take *noun* an initial inattentive reaction followed swiftly by a sudden full realization.

double-talk *noun* ambiguous talk, or talk that seems relevant but is really meaningless, esp as offered up by politicians.

doublethink *noun* simultaneous belief in, or acceptance of, two opposing ideas or principles. [20c: coined by George Orwell in his novel *Nineteen Eighty-Four*]

double time *noun* **1** a rate of pay equal to double the basic rate. **2** *music* a time twice as fast as the previous time. **3** *music* **duple** time.

doubloon *noun* a gold coin formerly used in Spain and S America. [17c: from Spanish *doblón*]

doubly *adv* **1** to twice the extent; very much more. **2** in two ways.

doubt *verb* **1** to feel uncertain about something; to be suspicious or show mistrust of it. **2** to be inclined to disbelieve something. ▸ *noun* **1** a feeling of uncertainty, suspicion or mistrust. **2** an inclination to disbelieve; a reservation. ▪ **doubter** *noun*. [13c: from Latin *dubitare*]

IDIOMS **beyond doubt** *or* **beyond a shadow of a doubt** certain; certainly. **in doubt** not certain. **no doubt** surely; probably. **without a doubt** *or* **without doubt** certainly.

doubtful *adj* **1** feeling doubt. **2** uncertain; able to be doubted. **3** likely not to be the case. ▪ **doubtfully** *adv*.

doubtless *adv* probably; certainly. ▪ **doubtlessly** *adv*.

douche /duːʃ/ *noun* **1** a powerful jet of water that is used to clean a body orifice, esp the vagina. **2** an apparatus for producing such a jet. ▸ *verb, tr & intr* to apply or make use of a douche. [18c: French]

dough *noun* **1** a mixture of flour, liquid (water or milk) and yeast, used in the preparation of bread, pastry, etc. **2** *slang* money. [Anglo-Saxon *dah*]

doughnut *or* (*esp US*) **donut** *noun* **1** a portion of sweetened dough fried in deep fat, usu with a hole in the middle or with a filling. **2** anything shaped like a doughnut with a hole.

doughty /'daʊtɪ/ *literary adj* (**-ier, -iest**) brave; stout-hearted. [Anglo-Saxon *dyhtig*]

dour /dʊə(r)/ *adj* stern; sullen. ▪ **dourness** *noun*. [14c; orig Scots: from Latin *durus* hard]

douse *or* **dowse** /daʊs/ *verb* **1** to throw water over something; to plunge something into water. **2** to extinguish (a light or fire). [17c]

dove[1] *N Am past tense of* **dive**[1]

dove[2] /dʌv/ *noun* **1** any of various pigeons. **2** this bird as an emblem of peace. **3** *politics* a person favouring peace rather than hostility. Compare **hawk**[1] (sense 2). [Anglo-Saxon *dufe*]

dovecote *or* **dovecot** *noun* a building or shed in which domestic pigeons are kept.

dovetail *noun* a joint, esp in wood, made by fitting V-shaped parts into corresponding slots. Also called **dovetail joint**. ▸ *verb, tr & intr* **1** to fit using one or more dovetails. **2** to fit or combine neatly.

dowager *noun* a title given to a nobleman's widow, to distinguish her from the wife of her late husband's heir. [16c: from French *douagiere*]

dowdy *adj* (**-ier, -iest**) dull, plain and unfashionable. ▪ **dowdily** *adv*. ▪ **dowdiness** *noun*. [16c: from *dowd* a slut]

dowel *noun* a wooden peg, esp used to join two pieces by fitting into corresponding holes in each. [14c: from German *dovel*]

dower *noun* a widow's share, for life, in her deceased husband's property. [15c: from French *douaire*]

dower house *noun* a house smaller than, and within the grounds of, a large country house, orig one forming part of a **dower**.

Dow-Jones average *or* **Dow-Jones index** *noun, finance* an indicator of the relative prices of stocks and shares on the New York stock exchange. [Early 20c: named after Charles Dow and Edward Jones, American economists]

down[1] *adv* **1** towards or in a low or lower position, level or state; on or to the ground. **2** from a greater to a lesser size, amount or level: *scaled down*. **3** towards or in a more southerly place. **4** in writing; on paper: *take down notes*. **5** as a deposit: *put down five pounds*. **6** to an end stage or finished state: *hunt someone down*. **7** from earlier to later times: *handed down through generations*. **8** to a state of exhaustion, defeat, etc: *worn down by illness*. **9** not vomited up: *keep food down*. **10** in a crossword: in the vertical direction: *5 down*. Compare **across** (*adv* sense 3). ▸ *prep* **1** in a lower position on something. **2** along; at a further position on, by or through: *down the road*. **3** along in the direction of the current of a river. **4** from the top to or towards the bottom. **5** *dialect* to or in (a particular place): *going down the town*. ▸ *adj* **1** sad; in low spirits. **2** going towards or reaching a lower position: *a down pipe*. **3** made as a deposit: *a down payment*. **4** reduced in price. **5** of a computer, etc: out of action, esp temporarily. ▸ *verb* **1** to drink something quickly, esp in one gulp. **2** to force someone to the ground. ▸ *exclam* used as a command to animals, esp dogs: get or stay down. ▸ *noun* **1** an unsuccessful or otherwise unpleasant period: *Life has its ups and downs*. **2** (**downs**) an area of rolling (esp treeless) hills. [Anglo-Saxon *of dune* from the hill]

IDIOMS **down in the mouth** sad. **down on one's luck** in unfortunate circumstances. **down tools** *informal* to stop working, as a protest. **down to the ground** *informal* completely; perfectly. **down under** *informal* in or to Australia and/or New Zealand. **down with ...!** let us get rid of ...! **have a down on sb** *informal* to be ill-disposed towards them.

down[2] *noun* soft fine feathers or hair. ▪ **downy** *adj* (**-ier, -iest**). [14c: from Norse *dunn*]

down-and-out *adj* homeless and penniless. ▸ *noun* a down-and-out person.

down-at-heel *adj* shabby.

downbeat *adj* **1** pessimistic; cheerless. **2** calm; relaxed. ▸ *noun, music* the first beat of a bar or the movement of the conductor's baton indicating this.

downcast *adj* **1** glum; dispirited. **2** of eyes: looking downwards.

downer *noun* **1** *informal* a state of depression. **2** *slang* a tranquillizing or depressant drug.

downfall *noun* **1** failure or ruin, or its cause. **2** a **downpour**.

downgrade *verb* to reduce to a lower grade.

downhearted *adj* dispirited; discouraged; dismayed.

downhill *adv* **1** downwards. **2** to or towards a worse condition. ▸ *adj* downwardly sloping. ▸ *noun* a ski race down a hillside.

IDIOMS **go downhill** to deteriorate (in health, morality or prosperity).

down-in-the-mouth *adj* unhappy; depressed.

download *verb, comput* to transfer (data) from one computer to another or to a disk.

down-market *adj* cheap, of poor quality or lacking prestige.

down payment *noun* a deposit.

downpour *noun* a very heavy fall of rain.

downright *adj* utter: *downright idiocy.* ▸ *adv* utterly.

downshift *verb, intr* **1** to select a lower gear in a vehicle. **2** to choose a less affluent lifestyle in order to enhance one's life in non-material ways, eg by having more leisure time. ▪ **downshifter** *noun.* ▪ **downshifting** *noun.* [1950s in sense 1; 1990s sense 2]

downside *noun, informal* a negative aspect; a disadvantage.

downsizing *noun* reducing the size of a workforce, esp by redundancies. [1970s]

Down's syndrome *noun, pathol* a congenital disorder which results in mental retardation, flattened facial features, and slight slanting of the eyes. [19c: named after the UK physician John L H Down]

downstairs *adv* to or towards a lower floor; down the stairs. ▸ *adj* on a lower or ground floor. ▸ *noun* a lower or ground floor.

downstream *adj, adv* further along a river towards the sea; with the current.

downswing *noun* a decline in economic activity, etc.

downtime *noun* time during which work ceases because a machine, esp a computer, is not working.

down-to-earth *adj* sensible and practical.

downtown *adj, adv* in or towards either the lower part of the city or the city centre. ▸ *noun* this area of a city.

downtrodden *adj* oppressed; ruled or controlled tyrannically.

downturn *noun* a decline in economic activity.

downward *adj* leading or moving down; descending; declining. ▸ *adv* downwards. ▪ **downwardly** *adv.*

downward, downwards

Downward can be an adverb or an adjective. **Downwards** can be only an adverb. In British English the more usual adverb is **downwards**:

They slid downwards.

In American English the more usual adverb is **downward**:

They slid downward.

downwards *adv* to or towards a lower position or level. [15c]

downwind *adv* **1** in or towards the direction in which the wind is blowing. **2** with the wind carrying one's scent away from (eg an animal one is stalking). ▸ *adj* moving with, or sheltered from, the wind.

dowry *noun* (**-*ies***) an amount of wealth handed over by a woman's family to her husband on marriage. [15c]

dowse[1] *verb, intr* to search for underground water with a **divining rod**. ▪ **dowser** *noun.* [17c]

dowse[2] see **douse**

dowsing rod see **divining rod**

doxology *noun* (**-*ies***) a Christian hymn, verse or expression praising God. [17c: from Greek *doxa* glory + *logos* discourse]

doyen /ˈdɔɪən/ *noun, literary* the most senior and most respected member of a group or profession. [17c: French]

doyenne /dɔɪˈɛn/ *noun* a female **doyen**.

doyley see **doily**

doze *verb, intr* to sleep lightly. ▸ *noun* a brief period of light sleep. [17c: from Norse *dus* lull]

PHRASAL VERBS **doze off** to fall into a light sleep.

dozen *noun* (***dozens*** or, following a number, ***dozen***) **1** a set of twelve. **2** (*often* **dozens**) *informal* very many. ▪ **dozenth** *adj.* [13c: from French *dozeine*]

dozy *adj* (***-ier, -iest***) **1** sleepy. **2** *informal* stupid; slow to understand; not alert. [17c]

DPh *or* **DPhil** *abbrev* Doctor of Philosophy. See also **PhD**.

DPP *abbrev* Director of Public Prosecutions.

Dr *abbrev* Doctor.

Dr. *abbrev* in addresses: Drive.

drab *adj* (***drabber, drabbest***) **1** dull; dreary. **2** of a dull greenish-brown colour. ▪ **drabness** *noun.* [16c: perhaps from French *drap* cloth]

drachm /dram/ *noun* a measure equal to ⅛ of an ounce or fluid ounce. [14c: see **drachma**]

drachma *noun* (***drachmas*** *or* ***drachmae*** /ˈdrakmiː/) the former standard unit of currency of Greece, replaced in 2002 by the euro. [19c: from Greek *drakhme* handful]

draconian *or* **draconic** *adj* of a law, etc: harsh; severe. [19c: named after Draco, 7c BC Athenian lawgiver]

draft *noun* **1** a written plan; a preliminary sketch. **2** a written order requesting a bank to pay out money, esp to another bank. **3** a group of people drafted. **4** *esp US* conscription. ▸ *verb* **1** to set something out in preliminary sketchy form. **2** to select and send off (personnel) to perform a specific task. **3** *esp US* to conscript. [17c: a form of **draught**]

draft, draught

Be careful not to use the spelling **draft** when you mean **draught**:

There's a draught coming through the window.

He took a draught from his tea.

drag *verb* (***dragged, dragging***) **1** to pull someone or something along roughly, violently, slowly and with force. **2** *tr & intr* to move or make something move along scraping the ground. **3** *informal* (*usu* **drag sb away**) to force or persuade them to come away. **4** *comput* to move (an icon or file) across a screen by using a mouse with its key pressed down. **5** to search (eg a lake) with a hook or dragnet. ▸ *noun* **1** an act of dragging; a dragging effect. **2** a person or thing that makes progress slow. **3** *informal* a draw on a cigarette. **4** *informal* a dull or tedious person or thing. **5** *informal* women's clothes worn by a man. **6** the resistance to motion encountered by an object travelling through a liquid or gas. [Anglo-Saxon *dragan*]

IDIOMS **drag one's feet** *or* **heels** *informal* to delay; to be deliberately slow to take action.

PHRASAL VERBS **drag sth out** *informal* to make it last as long as possible. **drag sth up** *informal* to mention an unpleasant subject long forgotten or not usu introduced.

draggle *verb, tr & intr* to make or become wet and dirty eg through trailing on the ground. [16c: from **drag**]

dragnet *noun* **1** a heavy net pulled along the bottom of a river, lake, etc in a search for something. **2** a systematic police search for a wanted person.

dragon *noun* **1** a mythical, fire-breathing, reptile-like creature with wings and a long tail. **2** *informal* a frighteningly domineering woman. [13c: from Greek *drakon* serpent]

dragonfly *noun* an insect with a long slender brightly coloured body and gauzy translucent wings.

dragoon *noun, hist* but still used in regimental titles: a heavily armed mounted soldier. ▸ *verb* to force someone into doing something. [17c: from French *dragon*]

drag race *noun* a contest in acceleration between specially designed cars or motorcycles over a short distance. ▪ **drag-racing** *noun.*

drain *verb* **1** to empty (a container) by causing or allowing liquid to escape. **2** (**drain sth of liquid**) to remove liquid from it. **3** (*often* **drain sth off** *or* **away**) to cause or allow (a liquid) to escape. **4** *intr* (*often* **drain off**) of liquid, etc: to flow away. **5** *intr* (*often* **drain away**) to disappear. **6** to drink the total contents of (a glass, etc). **7** to use up the strength, emotion or resources of (someone). **8** of a river: to carry away surface water from (land). ▸ *noun* a device, esp a pipe, for carrying away liquid. [Anglo-Saxon *dreahnian*]
IDIOMS **a drain on sth** anything that exhausts or seriously depletes a supply. **down the drain** *informal* wasted; lost.

drainage *noun* the process or a system of draining.

drainage basin *noun* a **catchment area** (sense 2).

draining board *noun* a sloping, and often channelled, surface at the side of a sink allowing water from washed dishes, etc to drain away.

drainpipe *noun* a pipe carrying waste water or rainwater, esp water from a roof into a drain below ground.

drake *noun* a male duck. [13c]

dram *noun* **1** *informal* a small amount of alcoholic spirit, esp whisky. **2** a measure of weight equal to 1⁄16 of an ounce. [15c: see **drachm**]

drama *noun* **1** a play. **2** plays in general. **3** the art of producing, directing and acting in plays. **4** excitement and emotion; an exciting situation. [16c: Greek]

drama documentary see **faction**[2]

dramatic *adj* **1** relating to plays, the theatre or acting in general. **2** exciting. **3** sudden and striking; drastic. **4** of a person or behaviour: flamboyantly emotional. ▪ **dramatically** *adv.*

dramatics *singular or plural noun* activities associated with the staging and performing of plays. ▸ *plural noun* exaggeratedly emotional behaviour.

dramatis personae /ˈdramətɪs pɜːˈsoʊnaɪ/ *plural noun* (often functioning as *singular noun*) **1** a list of the characters in a play. **2** these characters. [18c: Latin, meaning 'persons of the drama']

dramatist *noun* a writer of plays.

dramatize *or* **-ise** *verb* **1** to make something into a work for public performance. **2** to treat something as, or make it seem, more exciting or important. ▪ **dramatization** *noun.*

drank *past tense of* **drink**

---

drank, drunk
See the Usage Note at **drink**.

---

drape *verb* **1** to hang cloth loosely over something. **2** to arrange or lay (cloth, etc) loosely. ▸ *noun, theatre or* (*esp* **drapes**) *N Am* a curtain or hanging. [19c: from French *draper*]

draper *noun* someone who sells fabric. [14c: orig meaning 'a maker of cloth']

drapery *noun* (**-ies**) **1** fabric; textiles. **2** curtains and other hanging fabrics. **3** a draper's business or shop.

drastic *adj* extreme; severe. ▪ **drastically** *adv.* [17c: from Greek *drastikos*]

drat *exclam, informal* expressing anger or annoyance. [19c: prob an alteration of *God rot*]

draught *noun* **1** a current of air, esp indoors. **2** a quantity of liquid swallowed in one go. **3** any of the discs used in the game of **draughts**. Also called **draughtsman**. **4** *informal* draught beer. **5** a dose of liquid medicine. ▸ *adj* **1** of beer: pumped direct from the cask to the glass. **2** *esp in compounds* of an animal: used for pulling loads. [Anglo-Saxon *draht*]

---

draught, draft
Be careful not to use the spelling **draught** when you mean **draft**:
This is just the first draft of my essay.
a bank draft
They were drafted into the navy.

---

draughts *singular noun* a game for two people played with 24 discs on a chequered board (a **draughtboard**).

draughtsman *noun* **1** someone skilled in drawing. **2** someone employed to produce accurate and detailed technical drawings. **3** see **draught** (*noun* sense 3). ▪ **draughtsmanship** *noun.*

draughty *adj* (**-ier, -iest**) prone to or suffering draughts of air.

draw *verb* (*past tense* **drew,** *past participle* **drawn**) **1** *tr & intr* to make a picture of something or someone, esp with a pencil. **2** to pull out or take out something: *draw water from a well.* **3** *intr* to move or proceed steadily in a specified direction: *draw nearer.* **4** to pull someone along or into a particular position: *drawing her closer to him.* **5** to open or close (curtains). **6** to attract (eg attention or criticism). **7** *tr & intr* (*also* **draw with sb**) to end a game equal with an opponent. **8** to choose or be given as the result of random selection. **9** to arrive at or infer (a conclusion). **10 a** *intr* (*also* **draw on**) to suck air (through a cigarette); **b** of a chimney: to make air flow through a fire, allowing burning. **11** *technical* of a ship: to require (a certain depth of water) to float. **12** *intr* of tea: to brew or infuse. **13** to disembowel: *hang, draw and quarter.* **14** to write (a cheque). ▸ *noun* **1** a result in which neither side is the winner. **2 a** the making of a random selection, eg of the winners of a competition; **b** a competition with winners chosen at random. **3** the potential to attract many people, or a person or thing having this. **4** the act of drawing a gun. [Anglo-Saxon *dragan*]
IDIOMS **be drawn on sth** to be persuaded to talk or give information: *He refused to be drawn on his plans.* **draw a blank** to get no result. **draw the line** to fix a limit, eg on one's actions or tolerance.

PHRASAL VERBS **draw in** of nights: to start earlier, making days shorter. **draw on sth** to make use of assets: *draw on reserves of energy.* **draw sb out** to encourage them to be less shy or reserved. **draw up** to come to a halt. **draw sth up** to plan and write (a contract or other document).

drawback *noun* a disadvantage.

drawbridge *noun* a bridge that can be lifted to prevent access across or allow passage beneath.

drawer *noun* **1** a sliding lidless storage box fitted as part of a desk or other piece of furniture. **2** someone who draws. **3** (**drawers**) *old use* knickers, esp large ones.

drawing *noun* **1** a picture made up of lines. **2** the act or art of making such pictures.

drawing pin *noun* a short pin with a broad flat head.

drawing room *noun* a sitting room or living room. [17c: orig *withdrawing room*]

drawl *verb, tr & intr* to speak or say in a slow lazy manner, esp with prolonged vowel sounds. [16c: possibly connected with **draw**]

drawn[1] *adj* showing signs of mental strain or tiredness.

drawn[2] *verb, past participle of* **draw**. ▸ *adj, in compounds* pulled by: *horse-drawn.*

drawn-out *adj* tedious; prolonged.

drawstring *noun* a cord sewn inside a hem eg on a bag or piece of clothing, closing up the hem when pulled.

dray[1] *noun* a low horse-drawn cart. [Anglo-Saxon *dræge*]

dray[2] see **drey**

dread *noun* great fear or apprehension. ▸ *verb* to look ahead to something with dread. [Anglo-Saxon *ondrædan*]

dreadful *adj* **1** inspiring great fear; terrible. **2** *loosely* very bad, unpleasant or extreme. ▪ **dreadfully** *adv* **1** terribly. **2** *informal* extremely; very.

dreadlocks *plural noun* thin braids of hair tied tightly all over the head, esp worn by a Rastafarian. Often shortened to **dreads**. [1960s]

dream *noun* **1** thoughts and mental images experienced during sleep. **2** a state of being completely engrossed in one's own thoughts. **3** a distant ambition, esp if unattainable. **4** *informal* an extremely pleasing person or thing: *He's a dream to work with.* ▸ *adj informal,* luxurious, ideal. ▸ *verb* (*past tense & past participle* ***dreamed*** /driːmd/ *or* ***dreamt*** /drɛmt/) **1** *tr & intr* to have thoughts and visions during sleep. **2** (*usu* **dream of sth**) **a** to have a distant ambition or hope; **b** to imagine or conceive of something. **3** *intr* to have extravagant and unrealistic thoughts or plans. **4** *intr* to be lost in thought. ▪ **dreamer** *noun.* [13c]

PHRASAL VERBS **dream sth up** to devise or invent something unusual or absurd.

dream ticket *noun, chiefly N Am* an ideal pair or list, esp of electoral candidates.

dreamy *adj* (***-ier, -iest***) **1** unreal, as if in a dream. **2** having or showing a wandering mind. **3** *informal* lovely. ▪ **dreamily** *adv.* ▪ **dreaminess** *noun.*

dreary *adj* (***-ier, -iest***) **1** dull and depressing. **2** uninteresting. ▪ **drearily** *adv.* ▪ **dreariness** *noun.* [Anglo-Saxon *dreorig* bloody or mournful]

dredge[1] *verb, tr & intr* to clear the bottom of or deepen (the sea or a river) by bringing up mud and waste. ▸ *noun* a machine for dredging. ▪ **dredger** *noun.* [15c]

PHRASAL VERBS **dredge sth up** *informal* to mention or bring up something long forgotten.

dredge[2] *verb* to sprinkle (food), eg with sugar or flour. ▪ **dredger** *noun.* [16c: from French *dragie* sugar-plum]

dregs *plural noun* **1** solid particles in a liquid that settle at the bottom. **2** worthless or contemptible elements. [14c: from Norse *dregg*]

drench *verb* **1** to make something or someone soaking wet. **2** to administer liquid medicine to (an animal). ▸ *noun* a dose of liquid medicine for an animal. [Anglo-Saxon *drencan* to cause to drink]

dress *verb* **1** *tr & intr* to put clothes on; to wear, or make someone wear, clothes (of a certain kind). **2** to treat and bandage (wounds). **3** to prepare, or add seasoning or a sauce to (food). **4** to arrange a display in (a shop window). **5** to shape and smooth (esp stone). **6** *intr* to put on or have on formal evening wear. ▸ *noun* **1** a woman's garment with top and skirt in one piece. **2** clothing; wear: *in evening dress.* ▸ *adj* formal; for wear in the evenings: *dress jacket.* [14c: from French *dresser* to prepare]

PHRASAL VERBS **dress sb down** to scold them. **dress up 1** to put on fancy dress. **2** to dress in smart or formal clothes. **dress sth up** to make it appear more pleasant or acceptable by making additions or alterations.

dressage /ˈdrɛsɑːʒ/ *noun* the training of a horse in, or performance of, set manoeuvres signalled by the rider. [1930s: from French]

dress circle *noun, theatre* a balcony in a theatre, esp the first above the ground floor.

dresser *noun* **1** a free-standing kitchen cupboard with shelves above. **2** *US* a chest of drawers or dressing-table. **3** a theatre assistant employed to help actors with their costumes. **4** a person who dresses in a particular way. **5** a tool used for dressing stone, etc.

dressing *noun* **1** *cookery* any sauce added to food, esp salad. **2** *N Amer, cookery* **stuffing**. **3** a covering for a wound. **4** an application of fertilizer to the soil surface.

dressing-down *noun* a reprimand.

dressing gown *noun* a loose robe worn informally indoors, esp over nightclothes.

dressing room *noun* **1** *theatre* a room backstage where a performer can change clothing, apply make-up, etc. **2** any room used when changing clothing.

dressing table *noun* a piece of bedroom furniture typically with drawers and a large mirror.

dressmaking *noun* the craft or business of making esp women's clothes. ▪ **dressmaker** *noun.*

dress rehearsal *noun* **1** *theatre* the last rehearsal of a performance, with full costumes, lighting and other effects. **2** a practice under real conditions.

dress shirt *noun* a man's formal shirt worn with a dinner jacket.

dressy *adj* (***-ier, -iest***) **1** dressed or dressing stylishly. **2** of clothes: for formal wear; elegant. **3** *informal* fancy; over-decorated. ▪ **dressily** *adv.*

drew *past tense of* **draw**

drey *or* **dray** *noun* a squirrel's nest. [17c]

dribble *verb* **1** *intr* to fall or flow in drops. **2** *intr* to allow saliva to run slowly down from the mouth. **3** *tr & intr, football, hockey, etc* to move along keeping (a ball) in close control with frequent short strokes. ▸ *noun* **1** a small quantity of liquid, esp saliva. **2** *football, hockey, etc* an act of dribbling a ball. [16c: from obsolete *drib* to fall or let fall in drops]

dribs and drabs *plural noun* very small quantities at a time.

drier *or* **dryer** *noun* **1** a device or substance that dries clothing, hair, paint, etc. **2** a person or thing that dries.

drift *noun* **1** a general movement or tendency to move. **2** degree of movement off course caused by wind or a current. **3** the general or essential meaning of something. **4 continental drift**. ▸ *verb, intr* **1** to float or be blown along or into heaps. **2** to move aimlessly or passively from one place or occupation to another. **3** to move off course. [13c: Norse, meaning 'snowdrift']

drifter *noun* **1** a fishing boat that uses a **drift net**. **2** someone who moves aimlessly from place to place.

drift net *noun* a large fishing net allowed to drift with the tide.

driftwood *noun* wood floating near, or washed up on, a shore.

drill[1] *noun* **1** a tool for boring holes. **2** a training exercise or session. **3** *informal* correct procedure; routine. ▸ *verb* **1** to make (a hole) in something with a drill. **2** to exercise or teach through repeated practice. [17c: prob from Dutch *drillen* to bore]

drill[2] *noun* thick strong cotton cloth. [18c: from German *Drillich* ticking]

drill[3] *noun* **1** a shallow furrow in which seeds are sown. **2** the seeds sown or plants growing in such a row. **3** a machine for sowing seeds in rows. ▸ *verb* to sow (seeds) in rows. [18c: possibly from **drill[1]**]

drilling platform *noun* a floating or fixed offshore structure supporting a **drilling rig**, the apparatus required for drilling an oil well.

drink *verb* (*past tense* ***drank,*** *past participle* ***drunk***) **1** *tr & intr* to take in or consume (a liquid) by swallowing. **2** *intr* to drink alcohol; to drink alcohol to excess. **3** to get oneself into a certain state by drinking alcohol: *drank himself into a stupor.* ▸ *noun* **1** an act of drinking. **2** liquid for drinking. **3** alcohol of any kind; the habit of drinking alcohol to excess. **4** a glass or amount of drink. **5** (**the drink**) *informal* the sea. ▪ **drinkable** *adj.* ▪ **drinker** *noun* someone who drinks, esp alcohol, and esp too much. [Anglo-Saxon *drincan*]

IDIOMS **drink** *or* **drink to (the health) of sb** to drink a toast to them.

PHRASAL VERBS **drink sth in 1** to listen to it eagerly. **2** to absorb it.

---

drank, drunk

Be careful not to confuse these two forms of the verb **drink**:

Drank is the past tense:

✓ *I drank one of the beers and she drank the other.*

✗ *You shouldn't have drank so much wine.*

Drunk is the past participle:

✓ *I'd have been okay if I hadn't drunk the water.*

✗ *Who drunk my juice?*

---

drink-driving *noun* the act or practice of driving while under the influence of alcohol. ▪ **drink-driver** *noun.*

drip *verb* (***dripped, dripping***) **1** *tr & intr* to release or fall in drops. **2** *intr* to release a liquid in drops. **3** *tr & intr, informal* to have a large amount of something: *a film dripping with sentimentality.* ▸ *noun* **1** the action or noise of dripping. **2** a device for passing a liquid solution slowly and continuously into a vein. Also called **drip-feed**. **3** *derog, informal* someone who lacks spirit or character. [Anglo-Saxon *dryppan*]

drip-dry *adj* requiring little or no ironing if hung up to dry by dripping. ▸ *verb, tr & intr* to dry in this way. [1950s]

drip-feed *noun* a **drip** (*noun* sense 2). ▸ *verb* to feed something or someone with a liquid using a drip.

dripping *noun* fat from roasted meat.

drive *verb* (*past tense* ***drove,*** *past participle* ***driven***) **1 a** to control the movement of (a vehicle); **b** to be legally qualified to do so. **2** *intr* to travel in a vehicle. **3** to take or transport someone or something in a vehicle. **4** to urge or force someone or something to move: *boats driven on to the beach by the storm.* **5** to make someone or something get into a particular state or condition: *It drove me crazy.* **6** to force by striking: *drove the nail into the wood.* **7** to produce motion in something; to make it operate: *machinery driven by steam.* **8** *sport* **a** in golf: to hit (a ball) from the tee; **b** in cricket: to hit (a ball) forward with an upright bat; **c** to hit or kick (a ball, etc) with great force. **9** to conduct or dictate: *drive a hard bargain.* ▸ *noun* **1** a trip in a vehicle by road. **2** a path for vehicles, leading from a private residence to the road outside. Also called **driveway**. **3** (**Drive**) a street title in an address. **4** energy and enthusiasm. **5** an organized campaign; a group effort: *an economy drive.* **6** operating power, or a device supplying this. **7** a forceful strike of a ball in various sports. **8** a united movement forward, esp by a military force. **9** a meeting to play a game, esp cards. ▪ **driver** *noun.* [Anglo-Saxon *drifan*]

IDIOMS **be driven by sth** to be motivated by it. **be driving at sth** to intend or imply it as a meaning or conclusion. **drive sth home 1** to make it clearly understood. **2** to force (a bolt, nail, etc) completely in.

drive-in *adj* providing a service or facility for customers remaining seated in vehicles. ▸ *as noun: get a burger at the drive-in.*

drivel *noun* nonsense. ▸ *verb* (***drivelled, drivelling***) *intr* **1** to talk nonsense. **2** to dribble or slaver. [Anglo-Saxon *dreflian* to dribble]

driver *noun,* **1** a person or thing that drives. **2** a golf club with a metal or wooden head used to hit the ball from the tee. **3** *comput* a piece of software that connects a peripheral device to a computer.

driveway see under **drive**

driving licence *noun* an official licence to drive a motor vehicle.

drizzle *noun* fine light rain. ▸ *verb, intr* to rain lightly. ▪ **drizzly** *adj.* [Anglo-Saxon *dreosan* to fall]

droll *adj* oddly amusing or comical. ▪ **drollery** *noun.* ▪ **drolly** *adv.* [17c: from French *drôle*]

dromedary /ˈdrɒmədərɪ/ *noun* (***-ies***) a single-humped camel. Compare **Bactrian camel**. [14c: from Greek *dromados* running]

drone *verb, intr* **1** to make a low humming noise. **2** (*usu* **drone on**) to talk at length in a tedious monotonous voice. ▶ *noun* **1** a deep humming sound. **2** a male honey bee whose sole function is to mate with the queen. Compare **queen** (sense 3), **worker** (sense 4). **3** a lazy person, esp one living off others. **4 a** the bass-pipe of a set of bagpipes; **b** the low sustained note it produces. [Anglo-Saxon *dran* drone (bee)]

drool *verb, intr* **1** to dribble or slaver. **2** (*usu* **drool over sth**) to show uncontrolled admiration for it or pleasure at the sight of it. [19c: alteration of **drivel**]

droop *verb, intr* **1** to hang loosely; to sag. **2** to be or grow weak with tiredness. ▶ *noun* a drooping state. ▪ **droopy** *adj* (**-ier, -iest**). [14c: from Norse *drupa*]

drop *verb* (***dropped, dropping***) **1** *tr & intr* to fall or allow to fall. **2** *tr & intr* to decline or make something decline; to lower or weaken. **3** to give up or abandon (eg a friend or a habit). **4** to stop discussing (a topic). **5** (*also* **drop sb** *or* **sth off**) to set them down from a vehicle; to deliver or hand them in. **6** to leave or take out someone or something. **7** to mention something casually: *drop a hint*. **8** to fail to pronounce (esp a consonant): *drop one's h's*. **9** *informal* to write informally: *Drop me a line*. **10** *rugby* to score (a goal) by a **drop kick**. **11** of an animal: to give birth to (a baby). **12** *slang* to beat to the ground. ▶ *noun* **1** a small round or pear-shaped mass of liquid; a small amount (of liquid). **2** a descent; a fall. **3** a vertical distance. **4** a decline or decrease. **5** any small round or pear-shaped object, eg an earring or boiled sweet. **6** (**drops**) liquid medication administered in small amounts. **7** a delivery. [Anglo-Saxon *droppian*]

IDIOMS **at the drop of a hat** *informal* promptly; for the slightest reason. **let sth drop** to make it known inadvertently or as if inadvertently.

PHRASAL VERBS **drop back** *or* **behind** to fall behind others in a group. **drop in** *or* **by** to pay a brief unexpected visit. **drop off 1** *informal* to fall asleep. **2** to become less; to diminish; to disappear. **drop out 1** (*often* **drop out of sth**) to withdraw from an activity. **2** *informal* to adopt an alternative lifestyle as a reaction against traditional social values.

drop-dead *adv, slang* stunningly or breathtakingly: *drop-dead gorgeous*.

drop-down menu *noun, comput* a menu on a computer screen viewed by making a single click on a button on the toolbar. Compare **pull-down menu**.

drop goal *noun, rugby* a goal scored by a **drop kick**.

drop-in *adj* of a café, day centre, clinic, etc: where clients are free to attend informally and casually.

drop kick *rugby, noun* a kick in which the ball is released from the hands and struck as it hits the ground. ▶ *verb* (**drop-kick**) to kick (a ball) in this way.

droplet *noun* a tiny drop.

dropout *noun* **1** a student who quits before completing a course of study. **2** a person whose alternative lifestyle is a reaction against traditional social values.

dropper *noun* a short narrow glass tube with a rubber bulb on one end, for applying liquid in drops.

droppings *plural noun* animal or bird faeces.

drop scone *noun* a small thick pancake.

drop-shot *noun* in tennis, badminton, etc: a shot hit so that it drops low and close to the net.

dropsy *noun* the former name for **oedema**. ▪ **dropsical** *adj*. [13c: from Greek *hydrops*, from *hydor* water]

dross *noun* **1** waste coal. **2** scum that forms on molten metal. **3** *derog informal* rubbish; any worthless substance. [Anglo-Saxon *dros*]

drought *noun* a prolonged lack of rainfall. [Anglo-Saxon *drugath* dryness]

drove[1] *past tense of* **drive**

drove[2] *noun* **1** a moving herd of animals, esp cattle. **2** a large moving crowd. [Anglo-Saxon *draf* herd]

drover *noun, hist* someone employed to drive farm animals to and from market.

drown *verb* **1** *intr* to die by suffocation as a result of inhaling liquid, esp water, into the lungs. **2** to kill by suffocation in this way. [Middle English *drounen*]

PHRASAL VERBS **drown sth out** to suppress the effect of one sound with a louder one.

drowse *verb, intr* to sleep lightly for a short while. [Anglo-Saxon *drusian* to be sluggish]

drowsy *adj* (**-ier, -iest**) **1** sleepy; causing sleepiness. **2** quiet and peaceful. ▪ **drowsily** *adv*. ▪ **drowsiness** *noun*.

drub *verb* (***drubbed, drubbing***) **1** to defeat severely. **2** to beat; to thump. ▪ **drubbing** *noun*. [17c: from Arabic *daraba* to beat]

drudge *verb, intr* to do hard, tedious or menial work. ▶ *noun* a servant; a labourer. ▪ **drudgery** *noun*. [16c]

drug *noun* **1** a medicine. **2** an illegal addictive substance; a narcotic. **3** anything craved for. ▶ *verb* (***drugged, drugging***) **1** to administer a drug to (a person or animal). **2** to poison or stupefy with drugs. **3** to mix or season (food) with drugs. [14c: from French *drogue*]

druggist *noun, now N Am, esp US* a pharmacist.

drugstore *noun, N Am, esp US* a chemist's shop, esp one also selling refreshments.

druid *or* **Druid** *noun* **1** a Celtic priest in pre-Christian times. **2** an eisteddfod official. ▪ **druidic** *or* **druidical** *adj*. [16c: from Gaulish *druides*]

drum *noun* **1** a percussion instrument consisting of a hollow frame with a membrane stretched tightly across it, sounding when struck. **2** any object resembling this in shape; a cylindrical container. **3** an eardrum. ▶ *verb* (***drummed, drumming***) **1** *intr* to beat a drum. **2** *tr & intr* to make or cause to make continuous tapping or thumping sounds. **3** (*usu* **drum sth into sb**) to force it into their mind through constant repetition. ▪ **drummer** *noun*. [16c: related to German *Trommel*; imitating the sound made]

PHRASAL VERBS **drum sb out** to expel them. **drum sth up** *informal* to achieve or attract it by energetic persuasion.

drumbeat *noun* the sound made when a drum is hit.

drum machine *noun* a **synthesizer** for simulating the sound of percussion instruments.

drum major *noun* the leader of a marching (esp military) band.

drum majorette see **majorette**

drumstick *noun* **1** a stick used for beating a drum. **2** the lower leg of a cooked fowl, esp a chicken.

drunk *verb, past participle of* **drink**. ▶ *adj* lacking control in movement, speech, etc through having consumed too much alcohol. ▶ *noun* a drunk person, esp one regularly so.

---

drunk, drank
See the Usage Note at **drink**.

---

drunkard *noun* someone who is often drunk.

drunken *adj* **1** drunk. **2** relating to, or brought on by, alcoholic intoxication. ▪ **drunkenly** *adv.* ▪ **drunkenness** *noun.*

drupe *noun, botany* a fleshy fruit with one or more seeds, eg cherry, peach. [18c: from Greek *dryppa* olive]

dry *adj* (***drier, driest***) **1** free from or lacking moisture or wetness. **2** with little or no rainfall. **3** from which all the water has evaporated or been taken: *a dry well.* **4** thirsty. **5** of an animal: no longer producing milk. **6** of wine, etc: not sweet. **7** not buttered: *dry toast.* **8** of humour: expressed in a quietly sarcastic or matter-of-fact way. **9** forbidding the sale and consumption of alcohol. **10** of eyes: without tears. **11** dull; uninteresting. **12** lacking warmth of character. **13** of a cough: not producing catarrh. ▸ *verb* (***dries, dried***) **1** *tr & intr* to make or become dry. **2** *tr* to preserve (food) by removing all moisture. ▸ *noun* (***dries*** *or* ***drys***) *informal* a staunch right-wing British Conservative politician. Compare **wet** (*noun* sense 4). ▪ **drily** *or* **dryly** *adv.* ▪ **dryness** *noun.* [Anglo-Saxon *dryge*]

PHRASAL VERBS **dry out 1** to become completely dry. **2** *informal* to be cured of addiction to alcohol. **dry up 1** to dry thoroughly or completely. **2** to cease to produce or be produced. **3** *informal* of a speaker or actor: to run out of words; to forget lines while on stage. **4** *slang* to shut up or be quiet.

dryad *noun, Greek myth* a woodland nymph. [16c: from Greek *dryados*]

dry cell *noun* a battery or electrolytic cell in which current is passed through an electrolyte consisting of a moist paste.

dry-clean *verb* to clean (esp clothes) with liquid chemicals, not water. ▪ **dry-cleaner** *noun.* ▪ **dry-cleaning** *noun.*

dry dock *noun* a dock from which the water can be pumped out to allow work on a ship's lower parts.

dryer see **drier**

dry ice *noun* solid carbon dioxide used as a refrigerating agent and also (*theatre*) for creating special effects.

dry riser *noun* (abbrev **DR**) a vertical pipe through which water can be pumped to the individual floors of a building in the event of fire.

dry rot *noun, botany* a serious type of timber decay caused by a fungus common in damp, poorly ventilated buildings, which ultimately reduces the wood to a dry brittle mass. Compare **wet rot**.

dry run *noun* **1** a rehearsal, practice or test. **2** *military* a practice exercise.

dry-stone *adj* of a wall: made of stones wedged together without mortar.

Ds *symbol, chem* darmstadtium.

DSC *abbrev* Distinguished Service Cross.

DSc *abbrev* Doctor of Science.

DSM *abbrev* Distinguished Service Medal.

DSO *abbrev* Distinguished Service Order.

DT *or* **DTs** *abbrev* delirium tremens.

DTP *abbrev* desktop publishing.

dual *adj* **1** consisting of or representing two separate parts. **2** double; twofold. See also **number** (*noun* sense 12). ▪ **duality** *noun.* [17c: from Latin *duo* two]

dual carriageway *noun* a road on which traffic moving in opposite directions is separated by a central barrier or strip of land. [1930s]

dual-purpose *adj* serving two purposes.

dub[1] *verb* (***dubbed, dubbing***) **1** to give a name, esp a nickname, to someone. **2** to smear (leather) with grease. [Anglo-Saxon *dubbian*]

dub[2] *verb* (***dubbed, dubbing***) **1** to add a new soundtrack to (eg a film), esp in a different language. **2** to add sound effects or music to (eg a film). ▸ *noun* a type of **reggae** music in which bass, drums and the artistic arrangement are given prominence over voice and other instruments. [20c: contraction of **double**]

dubbin *noun* a wax-like mixture for softening and waterproofing leather. [19c: from **dub**[1]]

dubiety /dʒʊ'baɪɪtɪ/ *noun, formal* dubiousness; doubt. [18c: from Latin *dubietas*]

dubious /'dʒuːbɪəs/ *adj* **1** feeling doubt; unsure; uncertain. **2** arousing suspicion; potentially dishonest or dishonestly obtained. ▪ **dubiously** *adv.* ▪ **dubiousness** *noun.* [16: from Latin *dubium* doubt]

dubnium /'dʌbnɪəm/ *noun, chem* **1** (symbol **Db**) a radioactive metallic element formed by bombarding **californium** with carbon nuclei. **2** a former name for **rutherfordium**. [20c: named after Dubna in Russia]

ducal /'dʒuːkəl/ *adj* belonging or relating to a duke. [15c: from Latin *ducalis*]

ducat /'dʌkət/ *noun* a former European gold or silver coin. [13c: from Latin *ducatus* duchy]

duchess *noun* **1** the wife or widow of a duke. **2** a woman of the same rank as a duke in her own right. [14c: from French *duchesse*]

duchy *noun* (***-ies***) the territory owned or ruled by a duke or duchess. [14c: from French *duché*]

duck[1] *noun* **1** a water bird with short legs, webbed feet, and a large flattened beak. **2** the flesh of this bird used as food. **3** the female of such a bird, as opposed to the male **drake**. **4** *informal* **a** a likeable person; **b** (*also* **ducks**) a term of endearment or address. **5** *cricket* a batsman's score of zero. [Anglo-Saxon *duce*]

IDIOMS **like water off a duck's back** *informal* having no effect at all.

duck[2] *verb* **1** *intr* to lower the head or body suddenly, esp to avoid notice or a blow. **2** to push someone or something briefly under water. [13c]

PHRASAL VERBS **duck out of sth** *informal* to avoid something unpleasant or unwelcome.

duck-billed platypus see **platypus**

duckling *noun* a young duck.

duckweed *noun* a plant with broad flat leaves that grows on the surface of water.

ducky *informal, noun* (***-ies***) a term of endearment. ▸ *adj* (***-ier, -iest***) excellent; attractive or pleasing. [19c: from duck[1]]

duct *noun* **1** *anatomy* a tube in the body, esp one for carrying glandular secretions. **2** a casing or shaft for pipes or electrical cables, or a tube used for ventilation and air-conditioning. [17c: from Latin *ducere* to lead]

ductile *adj* **1** denoting metals that can be drawn out into a thin wire without breaking. **2** easily influenced by others. ▪ **ductility** *noun.* [17c: from Latin *ducere* to lead]

dud *informal, noun* **1** a counterfeit article. **2** a bomb, firework, etc that fails to go off. **3** any useless or ineffectual person or thing. **4** (**duds**) clothes. ▸ *adj* **1** useless. **2** counterfeit. [15c]

dude *noun, informal, N Am, esp US, orig slang* **1** a man; a guy. **2** a city man, esp an Easterner holidaying in the West. **3** a man preoccupied with dressing smartly. [19c]

dudgeon *noun* (*usu* **in high dudgeon**) the condition of being very angry, resentful or indignant. [16c]

due *adj* **1** owed; payable. **2** expected according to timetable or pre-arrangement. **3** proper. ▸ *noun* **1** what is owed; something that can be rightfully claimed or expected. **2** (**dues**) subscription fees. ▸ *adv* directly: *due north.* [14c: from French *deu*, from *devoir* to owe]

IDIOMS **due to sth** *or* **sb 1** caused by it or them. **2** because of it or them. **give sb their due** to acknowledge their qualities or achievements, esp when disapproving in other ways. **in due course** in the ordinary way when the time comes.

duel *noun* **1** a pre-arranged fight between two people to settle a matter of honour. **2** any serious conflict between two people or groups. ▸ *verb* (***duelled, duelling***) *intr* to fight a duel. ▪ **duellist** *or* **dueller** *noun.* [15c: from Latin *duellum*, variant of *bellum* war]

duet *noun* **1** a piece of music for two singers or players. **2** a pair of musical performers. ▪ **duettist** *noun.* [18c: from Italian *duetto*, from Latin *duo* two]

duff[1] *adj, informal* useless; broken. [19c: perhaps from **duffer**]

duff[2] *verb, informal* **1** to bungle something. **2** *esp golf* to mishit (a shot). ▸ *adj* bungled. [19c: from **duffer**]

PHRASAL VERBS **duff sb up** *slang* to treat them violently.

duffel *or* **duffle** *noun* a thick coarse woollen fabric. [17c: Dutch, named after Duffel, a Belgian town]

duffel bag *noun* a cylindrical canvas shoulder bag with a drawstring fastening.

duffel coat *noun* a heavy, esp hooded, coat made of **duffel**.

duffer *noun, informal* a clumsy or incompetent person. [18c]

dug[1] *past tense, past participle of* **dig**

dug[2] *noun* an animal's udder or nipple. [16c]

dugong /ˈduːɡɒŋ/ *noun* a seal-like tropical sea mammal. [19c: from Malay *duyong*]

dugout *noun* **1** a canoe made from a hollowed-out log. **2** a soldier's rough shelter dug into a slope or bank or in a trench. **3** a covered shelter at the side of a sports field, for the trainer, substitutes, etc. [19c]

duke *noun* **1** a nobleman of the highest rank. **2** the ruler of a small state or principality. **3** *old slang use* (*often* **dukes**) a fist. See also **ducal, duchess**. ▪ **dukedom** *noun* the title or property of a duke. [12c: French *duc*]

dulcet /ˈdʌlsɪt/ *adj, literary* of sounds: sweet and pleasing to the ear. [15c: from Latin *dulcis* sweet]

dulcimer *noun, music* a percussion instrument consisting of a flattish box with tuned strings stretched across, struck with small hammers. [15c: from Latin *dulce melos* sweet song]

dull *adj* **1** of colour or light: lacking brightness or clearness. **2** of sounds: deep and low; muffled. **3** of weather: cloudy; overcast. **4** of pain: not sharp. **5** of a person: slow to learn or understand. **6** uninteresting; lacking liveliness. **7** of a blade: blunt. ▸ *verb, tr & intr* to make or become dull. ▪ **dullness** *noun.* ▪ **dully** *adv.* [Anglo-Saxon *dol* stupid]

dulse *noun* an edible red seaweed. [17c: from Irish Gaelic *duileasg*]

duly *adv* **1** in the proper way. **2** at the proper time. [14c: from **due**]

duma *noun* an elected council, *esp* the Russian parliament before and since the Communist era. [from Russian]

dumb *adj* **1** temporarily or permanently unable to speak. **2** of animals: not having human speech. **3** silent; not expressed in words. **4** *informal, esp US* foolish; unintelligent. **5** performed without words: *dumb show.* ▸ *verb, tr & intr* (*always* **dumb down**) to present (information) in a less sophisticated form in order to appeal to a large number of people. ▪ **dumbly** *adv.* [Anglo-Saxon]

dumbbell *noun* a short metal bar with a weight on each end, used in muscle-developing exercises.

dumbfound *or* **dumfound** *verb* to astonish or confound someone; to leave someone speechless. [17c: **dumb** + *-found* from **confound**]

dumbing-down *noun* the presentation of information in a less sophisticated form. See also **dumb** *verb.* [20c]

dumb show *noun* miming.

dumbstruck *adj* silent with astonishment or shock.

dumb waiter *noun* **1** a small lift for transporting laundry, dirty dishes, etc between floors in a restaurant or hotel. **2** a movable shelved stand for food. **3** a revolving food tray.

dumdum *noun* a bullet that expands on impact, causing severe injury. [19c: named after Dum-Dum, an arsenal in India]

dummy /ˈdʌmɪ/ *noun* (***-ies***) **1** a life-size model of the human body, eg used for displaying clothes. **2** a realistic copy, esp one substituted for something. **3** a rubber teat sucked by a baby for comfort. **4** *informal, chiefly N Am* a stupid person. **5** *sport* an act of dummying with the ball. **6** a person or company seemingly independent, but really the agent of another. **7** *bridge* an exposed hand of cards. ▸ *adj* false; sham; counterfeit. ▸ *verb* (***-ies, -ied***) *tr & intr, sport* **a** to make as if to move one way before sharply moving the other, in order to deceive (an opponent); **b** to do so with (a ball). [16c: from **dumb**]

dummy run *noun* a practice; a try-out.

dump *verb* **1** to put something down heavily or carelessly. **2** *tr & intr* to dispose of (rubbish), esp in an unauthorized place. **3** *slang* to break off a romantic relationship with someone. **4** *econ* to sell (goods not selling well on the domestic market) abroad at a much reduced price. **5** *comput* to transfer (computer data) from one program to another or onto disk or tape. ▸ *noun* **1** a place where rubbish may be dumped. **2** a military store, eg of weapons or food. **3** *comput* a printed copy of the contents of a computer's memory. **4** *informal* a dirty or dilapidated place. [14c: possibly from Norse]

dumpbin *noun* a display stand or a container.

dumper truck *or* **dumptruck** *noun* a lorry which can be emptied by raising one end of the carrier to allow the contents to slide out.

dumpling *noun* **1** a baked or boiled ball of dough served with meat. **2** a rich fruit pudding. **3** *informal* a plump person. [17c: from obsolete *dump* lump]

dumps *plural noun*
IDIOMS **down in the dumps** *informal* in low spirits; depressed.

dumpy *adj* (**-ier, -iest**) short and plump. [18c: perhaps from **dumpling**]

dun[1] *adj* (***dunner, dunnest***) greyish-brown. ▸ *noun* **1** a dun colour. **2** a horse of this colour. [Anglo-Saxon]

dun[2] *verb* (***dunned, dunning***) to press someone for payment. ▸ *noun* a demand for payment. [17c]

dunce *noun* a stupid person; a slow learner. [16c: from the *Dunses*, followers of the philosopher and theologian John Duns Scotus, who were opposed to the new classical studies]

dune *noun* a ridge or hill of windblown sand. [18c: from Dutch *duna*]

dung *noun* animal excrement. [Anglo-Saxon]

dungarees *plural noun* loose trousers with a bib and shoulder straps attached. [Late 19c: from Hindi *dungri* a coarse calico fabric]

dungeon *noun* a prison cell, esp underground. [14c: from French *donjon*]

dungheap *or* **dunghill** *noun* **1** a pile of dung. **2** any squalid situation or place.

dunk *verb* **1** to dip (eg a biscuit) into tea or a similar beverage. **2** to submerge or be submerged. [Early 20c: from German dialect *tunke*]

dunlin *noun* a small brown wading bird with a slender probing bill. [16c: a diminutive of **dun**[1]]

dunno *informal, contraction of* I do not know.

dunnock *noun* the hedge sparrow. [17c: from **dun**[1]]

duo *noun* **1** a pair of musicians or other performers. **2** any two people considered a pair. **3** *music* a duet. [16c: Latin, meaning 'two']

duodecimal *adj* relating to or based on the number twelve, or multiples of it. [17c: from Latin *duodecim* twelve]

duodenum /dʒuːoʊ'diːnəm/ *noun* (***duodena*** /-'diːnə/ *or* ***duodenums***) *anatomy* the first part of the small intestine, into which food passes after leaving the stomach. ▪ **duodenal** *adj*. [14c: from Latin *duodecim* twelve, the duodenum being twelve fingers' breadth in length]

duologue *or* (*sometimes US*) **duolog** *noun* **1** a dialogue between two actors. **2** a play for two actors. [18c: from Latin *duo* two + Greek *logos* discourse]

DUP *abbrev* in Northern Ireland: Democratic Unionist Party, a political party advocating the continued political union of Great Britain and Northern Ireland.

dupe *verb* to trick or deceive. ▸ *noun* a person who is deceived. [17c: French]

duple *adj* **1** double; twofold. **2** *music* having two beats in the bar. [16c: from Latin *duplus* double]

duplex *noun, N Am* **1** (*also* **duplex apartment**) a flat on two floors. **2** (*also* **duplex house**) a semi-detached house. ▸ *adj* **1** double; twofold. **2** of a computer circuit: allowing transmission of signals in both directions simultaneously. [19c: Latin, meaning 'double']

duplicate *adj* /'dʒuːplɪkət/ identical to another. ▸ *noun* /'dʒuːplɪkət/ **1** an exact copy. **2** another of the same kind. ▸ *verb* /'dʒuːplɪkeɪt/ **1** to make or be an exact copy or copies of something. **2** to repeat something. ▪ **duplication** *noun*. ▪ **duplicator** *noun*. [15c: from Latin *duplicare* to fold in two]
IDIOMS **in duplicate** in two exact copies.

duplicity *noun* (**-ies**) *formal* deception; trickery; double-dealing. ▪ **duplicitous** *adj*. [15c: from Latin *duplicis* double]

Dur *abbrev, English county* Durham.

durable *adj* **1** lasting a long time without breaking; sturdy. **2** long-lasting; enduring. ▸ *noun* a durable item. ▪ **durability** *noun* (**-ies**). [14c: from Latin *durare* to last]

dura mater /'dʒʊərə 'meɪtə(r); *Latin* 'duːra 'mɑːtɛr/ ▸ *noun, anatomy* the outermost and thickest of the three membranes that surround the brain and spinal cord. [15c: Latin *dura* hard + *mater* mother, a translation of the Arabic name]

duration *noun* the length of time that something lasts or continues. [14c: from Latin *durare* to last]

duress *noun* the influence of force or threats; coercion. [15c: from French *duresse*]

during *prep* **1** throughout the time of something. **2** in the course of something. [14c: from obsolete *dure* to last]

durum *or* **durum wheat** *noun* a kind of wheat whose flour is used for making pasta. [Early 20c: from Latin *durum* hard]

dusk *noun* twilight; the period of semi-darkness before night. [Anglo-Saxon *dox* dark]

dusky *adj* (**-ier, -iest**) **1** dark; shadowy. **2** dark-coloured; dark-skinned. ▪ **duskily** *adv*. ▪ **duskiness** *noun*.

dust *noun* **1** earth, sand or household dirt in the form of fine powder. **2** a cloud of this. **3** any substance in powder form. **4** *informal* an angry complaint; a commotion: *kick up a dust*. **5** *poetic* human remains; a dead body. ▸ *verb* **1** to remove dust from (furniture, etc). **2** to sprinkle something with powder. [Anglo-Saxon]
IDIOMS **let the dust settle** *informal* to wait until calm is restored before acting. **not see sb for dust** not to see them again because they have gone away rapidly and suddenly. **throw dust in sb's eyes** *informal* to deceive them.

dustbin *noun* a large lidded container for household rubbish.

dust bowl *noun* an area of land from which the topsoil has been removed by winds and drought.

dustcart *noun* a vehicle in which household rubbish is collected.

dust cover *noun* **1** a **dust jacket**. **2** a **dust sheet**.

duster *noun* a cloth for removing household dust.

dust jacket *or* **dust cover** *noun* a loose protective paper cover on a book, carrying the title and other information.

dustman *noun* someone employed to collect household rubbish.

dustpan *noun* a handled container into which dust is swept, like a flattish open-ended box.

dust sheet *or* **dust cover** *noun* a cloth or plastic sheet used to protect furniture from dust or paint.

dust-up *noun, informal* an argument or fight.

dusty *adj* (**-ier, -iest**) **1** covered with or containing dust. **2** of a colour: dull. **3** old-fashioned; dated. ▪ **dustily** *adj*. ▪ **dustiness** *noun*.

Dutch *adj* belonging or referring to the Netherlands, its inhabitants or their language. ▸ *noun* **1** the official language of the Netherlands. **2** (**the Dutch**) the people of the Netherlands. [16c; orig meaning 'German': from Dutch *dutsch*]

IDIOMS **go Dutch** *informal* each person to pay their own share of a meal, etc.

Dutch auction *noun* an auction at which the price is gradually lowered until someone agrees to buy.

Dutch cap see **cap** (*noun* sense 7)

Dutch courage *noun* artificial courage gained by drinking alcohol.

Dutch elm disease *noun, botany* a serious disease of elm trees, caused by a fungus and spread by a beetle.

Dutchman *or* **Dutchwoman** *noun* a native or citizen of, or a person born in, the Netherlands.

Dutch oven *noun* **1** an open-fronted metal box for cooking food in front of a fire. **2** a lidded earthenware or iron stewpot or casserole.

Dutch uncle *noun* someone who openly criticizes or reprimands where appropriate.

duteous *adj, literary* dutiful. [16c: from **duty**]

dutiable *adj* of goods: on which duty is payable.

duty *noun* (*-ies*) **1** an obligation or responsibility, or the awareness of it. **2** a task, esp part of a job. **3** tax on goods, esp imports. **4** respect for elders, seniors or superiors. ▪ **dutiful** *adj.* ▪ **dutifully** *adv.* [13c: from French *dueté*]

IDIOMS **off duty** not on duty. **on duty** working; liable to be called upon to go into action.

duty-bound *adj* obliged by one's sense of duty.

duty-free *adj* of goods, esp imports: non-taxable. ▸ *noun, informal* **1** a shop where duty-free goods are sold. **2** an article or goods for sale at such a shop.

duvet /'duːveɪ/ *noun* a thick quilt filled with feathers or man-made fibres, for use on a bed instead of a sheet and blankets. Also called **continental quilt**. [18c: French]

dux *noun, esp Scot* the top academic prize-winner in a school or class. [18c: Latin, meaning 'leader']

DV *abbrev*: *Deo volente* (Latin), God willing.

DVD *abbrev* digital versatile disc.

DVT *abbrev* deep-vein thrombosis.

dwarf *noun* (***dwarfs*** or *less often* ***dwarves***) **1** an abnormally small person. **2** an animal or plant that is much smaller or shorter than others of its species, usu as a result of selective breeding. *as adj*: *dwarf rabbits.* **3** a mythical man-like creature with magic powers. ▸ *verb* to make something seem small or unimportant. ▪ **dwarfism** *noun.* [Anglo-Saxon *dweorg*]

dwell *verb* (***dwelt*** *or* ***dwelled***) *intr, formal, literary* to reside. ▪ **dweller** *noun.* [Anglo-Saxon *dwellan* to delay or tarry]

PHRASAL VERBS **dwell on sth** to think or speak about it obsessively.

dwelling *noun, formal, literary* a place of residence.

dwindle *verb, intr* to shrink in size, number or intensity. [Anglo-Saxon *dwinan* to fade]

Dy *symbol, chem* dysprosium.

dye *verb* (***dyeing***) *tr & intr* to colour or stain something, or undergo colouring or staining. ▸ *noun* **1** a coloured substance that is used in solution to give colour to a material. **2** the solution used for dyeing. **3** the colour produced by dyeing. ▪ **dyer** *noun.* [Anglo-Saxon *deagian*]

dyed-in-the-wool *adj* of firmly fixed opinions.

dying *verb, present participle of* **die**[1]. ▸ *adj* **1** expressed or occurring immediately before death: *her dying breath.* **2** final: *the dying seconds of the match.*

dyke *or* **dike** *noun* **1** a wall or embankment built to prevent flooding. **2** *esp Scot* a wall, eg surrounding a field. **3** *Austral & NZ slang* a lavatory. [Anglo-Saxon *dic* ditch]

dynamic *adj* **1** full of energy, enthusiasm and new ideas. **2** relating to **dynamics**. ▪ **dynamically** *adv.* [19c: from Greek *dynamis* power]

dynamics *singular noun* the branch of mechanics that deals with motion and the forces that produce motion. ▸ *plural noun* **a** movement or change in any sphere; **b** the forces causing this: *political dynamics.* **c** *music* the signs indicating varying levels of loudness. [18c: from Greek *dynamis* power]

dynamism *noun* limitless energy and enthusiasm.

dynamite *noun* **1** a powerful explosive. **2** *informal* a thrilling or dangerous person or thing. ▸ *verb* to explode something with dynamite. [19c: from Greek *dynamis* power]

dynamo *noun* **1** an electric generator that converts mechanical energy into electrical energy. **2** *informal* a tirelessly active person. [19c: from Greek *dynamis* power]

dynasty *noun* (*-ies*) **1** a succession of rulers from the same family. **2** their period of rule. **3** a succession of members of a powerful family or other connected group. ▪ **dynastic** *adj.* [15c: from Greek *dynasteia* power or dominion]

dys- *combining form, signifying* ill, bad or abnormal: *dysfunction.* [Greek]

dysentery *noun, med* severe infection and inflammation of the intestines. [14c: from Greek *dysenteria* bad bowels]

dysfunction *noun* impairment or abnormality of functioning. ▪ **dysfunctional** *adj.* [Early 20c]

dyslexia *noun, psychol, med* a disorder characterized by difficulty in reading, writing and spelling correctly. ▪ **dyslexic** *adj, noun.* [19c: from **dys-** + Greek *lexis* word]

dysmenorrhoea *or* **dysmenorrhea** /dɪsmɛnə'rɪə/ *noun, med* pain in the lower abdomen, associated with menstruation. [19c: from **dys-** + Greek *men* month + *rhoia* flow]

dyspepsia *noun, pathol* indigestion. ▪ **dyspeptic** *adj* **1** suffering from dyspepsia. **2** *informal* bad-tempered. [18c: from **dys-** + Greek *pepsis* digestion]

dysphasia *noun, psychol, med* difficulty in expressing or understanding spoken or written words, caused by brain damage. ▪ **dysphasic** *adj, noun.* [19c: from **dys-** + Greek *phasis* speech]

dysprosium *noun* (symbol **Dy**) a soft, silvery-white magnetic metallic element. [19c: from Greek *dysprositos* difficult to reach]

dystrophy *noun* (*-ies*) *med* a disorder of organs or tissues, esp muscle, arising from an inadequate supply of nutrients. See also **muscular dystrophy**. [19c: from **dys-** + Greek *trophe* nourishment]

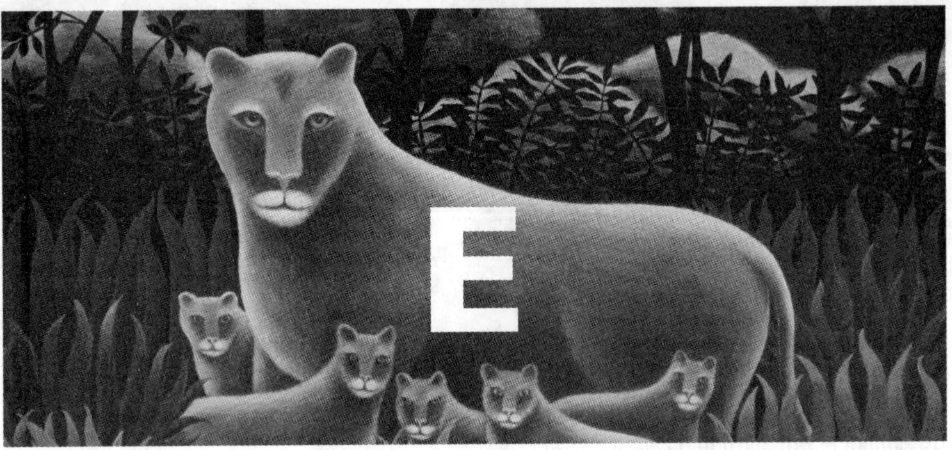

E[1] *or* **e** *noun* (***Es, E's*** *or* ***e's***) **1** the fifth letter and second vowel of the English alphabet. **2** *music* (**E**) the third note in the scale of C major.

E[2] *abbrev* **1** East. **2** Ecstasy. **3** *physics* electromotive force. **4** (*also* **e**) electronic: *E-mail.* **5** *physics* (*also* **E**) energy. **6** English. **7** *also in compounds* European: *E-number.*

e *symbol* **1** *in compounds* (with numbers) *denoting* any of a series of standard sizes of pack as set out in EU law. **2** *maths* the base of the natural system of logarithms, with an approximate value of 2.718281828. See **logarithm**.

each *adj* applied to every one of two or more people or items considered separately. ▸ *pronoun* every single one of two or more people, animals or things. ▸ *adv* to, for or from each one: *Give them one each.* [Anglo-Saxon *ælc*]

IDIOMS **each other** used as the object of a verb or preposition when an action takes place between two (or more than two) people, etc: *They talked to each other.*

---

each

There is sometimes uncertainty over whether to use a singular or a plural verb with **each**.

Use a plural verb when **each** comes after a plural noun or pronoun:

The children each have a PC of their own.

Use a singular verb when **each** is the subject of the sentence or clause:

There are twenty houses in the terrace. Each (house) has its own back and front garden.

---

eager *adj* **1** (*often* **eager for sth** *or* **to do sth**) feeling or showing great desire or enthusiasm; keen to do or get something. **2** excited by desire or expectancy: *an eager glance.* ▪ **eagerly** *adv.* ▪ **eagerness** *noun.* [13c: from French *aigre*]

eagle *noun* **1** any of various kinds of large birds of prey. **2** *golf* a score of two under par. Compare **albatross** (sense 2), **birdie** (sense 2), **bogey**[2]. [14c: from French *aigle*]

eagle eye *noun* **1** exceptionally good eyesight. **2** careful supervision, with an ability to notice small details. ▪ **eagle-eyed** *adj.*

eaglet *noun* a young eagle.

-ean see **-an**

ear[1] *noun* **1** the sense organ that is concerned with hearing. **2** the external part of the ear. **3** the ability to hear and appreciate the difference between sounds: *an ear for music.* **4** *formal or literary* attention; the act of listening: *give ear to me.* [Anglo-Saxon *eare*]

IDIOMS **be all ears** *informal* to listen attentively or with great interest. **fall on deaf ears** of a remark, etc: to be ignored. **in one ear and out the other** *informal* listened to but immediately disregarded. **lend an ear to sb** *or* **sth** to listen. **out on one's ear** *informal* dismissed swiftly and without politeness. **play it by ear** *informal* to act without a fixed plan, according to the situation that arises. **up to one's ears in sth** *informal* deeply involved in it or occupied with it.

ear[2] *noun* the part of a cereal plant, such as wheat, that contains the seeds. [Anglo-Saxon]

earache *noun* pain in the inner part of the ear.

eardrum *noun* the small thin membrane inside the ear, which transmits vibrations made by sound waves to the inner ear. *Technical equivalent* **tympanic membrane**.

earful *noun, informal* **1** a long complaint or telling-off. **2** as much talk or gossip as one can stand. [Early 20c]

earl *noun* a male member of the British nobility ranking below a marquess and above a viscount. See also **countess**. ▪ **earldom** *noun.* [Anglo-Saxon *eorl* a warrior or hero]

earlobe *noun* the soft, loosely hanging piece of flesh which forms the lower part of the ear.

early *adv, adj* (***-ier, -iest***) **1** characteristic of or near the beginning of (a period of time, period of development, etc). **2** sooner than others, sooner than usual, or sooner than expected or intended. **3** in the near future. **4** in the distant past. ▪ **earliness** *noun.* [Anglo-Saxon *ærlice*]

earmark *verb* to set aside something or someone for a particular purpose. ▸ *noun* a distinctive mark. [16c]

earmuffs *plural noun* coverings worn over the ears to protect them from cold or noise.

earn *verb* **1** *tr & intr* to gain (money, wages, one's living, etc) by working. **2** to gain. **3** to deserve. ▪ **earner** *noun.* [Anglo-Saxon *earnian*]

earnest[1] *adj* **1** serious or over-serious. **2** showing determination, sincerity or strong feeling. ▪ **earnestly** *adv.* ▪ **earnestness** *noun.* [Anglo-Saxon *eornust* seriousness]

IDIOMS **in earnest 1** serious or seriously. **2** sincere. **3** not as a joke; in reality.

earnest[2] *noun, literary or old use* a part payment made in advance, esp (*law*) one made to confirm an agreement. [13c: from French *erres* pledges]

earnings money earned.

earphones see under **headphones**

earpiece *noun* the part of a telephone or hearing-aid which is placed at or in the ear.

ear-piercing *adj* of a noise: loud and sharp; shrill.

earplug *noun* a piece of wax or rubber, etc placed in the ear as a protection against noise, cold or water.

earring *noun* a piece of jewellery worn attached to the ear, esp to the earlobe.

earshot *noun* the distance at which sound can be heard: *out of earshot*.

ear-splitting *adj* of a noise: extremely loud; deafening.

earth *noun* **1** (*often* **the Earth**) the planet on which we live, the third planet from the Sun. **2** the land and sea, as opposed to the sky. **3** dry land; the land surface; the ground. **4** soil. **5** a hole in which an animal lives, esp a badger or fox. **6 a** an electrical connection with the ground; **b** a wire that provides this. ▸ *verb, electronics* to connect to the ground. [Anglo-Saxon *eorthe*]

IDIOMS **come back** *or* **down to earth** to become aware of the realities of life. **on earth** used for emphasis: *What on earth is that?*

earthbound *adj* **1** attached or restricted to the earth. **2** of a spacecraft, etc: moving towards the Earth. **3** *sometimes derog* lacking imagination.

earthen *adj* **1** of a floor, etc: made of earth. **2** of a pot, etc: made of baked clay.

earthenware *noun* pottery made of a kind of baked clay.

earthling *noun* in science fiction: a native of the Earth.

earthly *adj* (**-ier, -iest**) **1** *literary* referring, relating or belonging to this world; not spiritual. **2** *informal, with negatives* used for emphasis: *have no earthly chance*. See also **unearthly**.

earthquake *noun* a succession of vibrations that shake the Earth's surface, caused by shifting movements in the Earth's crust, volcanic activity, etc.

earth science *noun* any of the sciences broadly concerned with the Earth, eg geology and meteorology.

earth-shattering *adj, informal* being of great importance.

earthwork *noun* **1** (*often* **earthworks**) *technical* excavation and embanking, eg as a process in road-building. **2** a fortification built of earth.

earthworm *noun* any of several types of worm which live in and burrow through the soil.

earthy *adj* (**-ier, -iest**) **1** consisting of, relating to, or like earth or soil. **2** coarse or crude; lacking politeness.

earwig *noun* an insect with pincers at the end of its body. [Anglo-Saxon *eare* ear + *wicga* insect]

ease *noun* **1** freedom from pain, anxiety or embarrassment. **2** absence of difficulty. **3** absence of restriction. **4** leisure; relaxation. **5** wealth; freedom from the constraints of poverty. ▸ *verb* **1** to free someone from pain, trouble or anxiety. **2** to make someone comfortable. **3** to relieve or calm something. **4** to loosen something. **5** to make something less difficult; to assist: *ease his progress*. **6** *intr* (*often* **ease off** *or* **up**) to become less intense. **7** *intr* to move gently or very gradually. [13c: from French *aise*]

IDIOMS **at ease 1** relaxed; free from anxiety or embarrassment. **2** *military* standing with legs apart and hands clasped behind the back.

easel *noun* a stand for supporting a blackboard or an artist's canvas, etc. [17c: from Dutch *ezel* ass]

east *noun* (abbrev **E**) (*also* **the east** *or* **the East**) **1** the direction from which the Sun rises at the equinox. **2** one of the four **cardinal point**s of the compass. **3** any part of the earth, a country or a town, etc lying in that direction. **4** (**the East**) **a** the countries of Asia, east of Europe; **b** *politics* the former communist countries of eastern Europe. ▸ *adj* **1** situated in the east; on the side which is on or nearest the east. **2** facing or towards the east. **3** esp of wind: coming from the east. ▸ *adv* in, to or towards the east. [Anglo-Saxon]

eastbound *adj* going or leading towards the east.

Easter *noun, Christianity* a religious festival celebrating the resurrection of Christ, held on the Sunday after the first full moon in spring, called **Easter Day** *or* **Easter Sunday**. [Anglo-Saxon *eastre*, perhaps from *Eostre*, the name of a goddess associated with spring]

Easter egg *noun* a chocolate egg given at Easter.

easterly *adj* **1** of a wind, etc: coming from the east. **2** looking or lying, etc towards the east; situated in the east. ▸ *adv* to or towards the east. ▸ *noun* (**-ies**) an easterly wind.

eastern *or* **Eastern** *adj* situated in, directed towards or belonging to the east or the East. ▪ **easterner** *or* **Easterner** *noun*. ▪ **easternmost** *adj*.

easting *noun, naut* the total distance travelled towards the east by a ship, etc.

eastward *adv* (*also* **eastwards**) towards the east. ▸ *adj* towards the east.

easy *adj* (**-ier, -iest**) **1** not difficult. **2** free from pain, trouble, anxiety, etc. **3** not stiff or formal; friendly. **4** tolerant. **5** not tense or strained; leisurely. **6** *informal* having no strong preference; ready to accept suggestions offered by others. **7** of financial circumstances: comfortable. ▸ *adv, informal* in a slow, calm or relaxed way: *take it easy*. ▪ **easily** *adv* **1** without difficulty. **2** clearly; beyond doubt; by far. **3** very probably. ▪ **easiness** *noun*. [12c: from French *aisie*]

IDIOMS **go easy on** *or* **with sb** to deal with them gently or calmly. **go easy on** *or* **with sth** to use, take, etc not too much of it.

easy-going *adj* not strict; relaxed, tolerant or placid.

eat *verb* (**ate** /ɛt, eɪt/, **eaten**) **1** to bite, chew and swallow (food). **2** *intr* to take in food; to take a meal. **3** to eat into something. **4** *informal* to trouble or worry someone: *What's eating you?* ▪ **eater** *noun*. [Anglo-Saxon *etan*]

IDIOMS **be eaten up by** *or* **with sth** to be greatly affected by it (usu a bad feeling): *be eaten up with jealousy*. **eat one's heart out** to suffer, esp in silence, from some longing or anxiety, or from envy. **what's eating you, him,** *etc*? what's wrong with you, him, etc?

PHRASAL VERBS **eat into** *or* **through sth 1** to use it up gradually. **2** to waste it. **3** to destroy its material, substance or form, etc, esp by chemical action; to corrode it. **eat out** to eat at a restaurant, cafe, etc rather than at home. **eat up** to finish one's food. **eat sth up 1** to finish (one's food). **2** to destroy it. **3** to absorb; to listen with real interest.

eatable *adj* fit to be eaten. ▸ *noun* (*usu* **eatables**) an item of food. Compare **edible**.

eau de Cologne /oʊ də 'kəloʊn/ *or* **cologne** *noun* a mild type of perfume, orig made in Cologne in Germany in 1709. [Early 19c: French, literally 'water of Cologne']

eaves *plural noun* the part of a roof that sticks out beyond the wall, or the underside of it. [Anglo-Saxon *efes* the clipped edge of thatch]

eavesdrop *verb, intr* (*also* **eavesdrop on sb**) to listen secretly to a private conversation. ▪ **eavesdropper** *noun*. [Anglo-Saxon *yfæsdrypæ* a person who stands under the eaves to listen to conversations]

ebb *verb, intr* **1** of the tide: to move back from the land. Compare **flow** *verb* (sense 7). **2** (*also* **ebb away**) to grow smaller or weaker. ▸ *noun* **1** the movement of the tide away from the land. **2** a decline. [Anglo-Saxon *ebba*]

IDIOMS **at a low ebb** in a poor or weak state, mentally or physically. **on the ebb** in decline; failing.

ebony *noun* (*-ies*) **1** a type of extremely hard, heavy and almost black wood. **2** any of various tropical trees from which it is obtained. ▸ *adj* **1** made from this wood. **2** black: *ebony skin*. [14c: from Latin *hebenus*]

ebullient *adj* very high-spirited; full of cheerfulness or enthusiasm. ▪ **ebullience** *noun*. [16c: from Latin *ebullire* to boil out]

EC *abbrev* European Commission.

eccentric *adj* **1** of a person or behaviour, etc: odd; unusual or unconventional. **2** *technical* of a wheel, etc: not having the axis at the centre. **3** *geom* of circles: not having a common centre; not concentric. **4** of an orbit: not circular. ▸ *noun* an eccentric person. ▪ **eccentricity** *noun* (*-ies*) [16c: from Latin *eccentricus*]

ecclesiastic *noun, formal* a clergyman or a member of a holy order. ▸ *adj* (*also* **ecclesiastical**) relating to the church or the clergy. ▪ **ecclesiastically** *adv*. [15c: from 15c Greek *ekklesiastikos*, meaning 'relating to the *ekklesia*' ie an assembly or gathering]

ECG *abbrev* **1** electrocardiogram. **2** electrocardiograph.

echelon /'ɛʃəlɒn/ *noun* **1** *formal* **a** a level or rank in an organization, etc; **b** the people at that level. **2** *technical* a roughly V-shaped formation, used by ships, planes, birds in flight, etc. [19c: French from *échelle* ladder]

echinacea /ɛkɪ'neɪsɪə/ *noun* **1** a N American composite plant of the genus **Echinacea**. **2** a herbal remedy prepared from this plant, thought to boost the immune system. [20c: from Latin, from Greek *echinos* hedgehog]

echinoderm /ɪ'kaɪnoʊdɜːm/ *noun* a sea animal noted for having tube feet and a body wall strengthened by calcareous plates, eg starfish and sea urchins. [19c: from Greek *echinos* sea urchin + *derma* skin]

echo *noun* (***echoes***) **1** the repeating of a sound caused by the sound waves striking a surface and coming back. **2** a sound repeated in this way. **3** an imitation or repetition, sometimes an accidental one. **4** (*often* **echoes**) a trace; something which brings to mind memories or thoughts of something else. **5** a reflected radio or radar beam, or the visual signal it produces on a screen. ▸ *verb* (***echoes, echoed***) **1** to send back an echo of something. **2** to repeat (a sound or a statement). **3** to imitate or in some way be similar to something. **4** *intr* to resound; to reverberate. [14c: Greek, meaning 'sound']

echocardiogram *noun, med* the record produced by **echocardiography**, the examination of the heart and its function by means of ultrasound. [20c]

echo chamber *noun* a room where the walls reflect sound. [20c]

echolocation *noun* the determining of the position of objects by measuring the time taken for an echo to return from them, and the direction of the echo. [20c]

echo-sounding *noun* a method used at sea, etc for determining the depth of water, locating shoals of fish, etc, by measuring the time taken for a signal sent out from the ship, etc to return as an echo.

éclair *noun* a long cake of choux pastry with a cream filling and chocolate icing. [19c: French, literally 'flash of lightning', perhaps because it is quickly eaten]

eclampsia *noun, pathol* a toxic condition which may develop during the last three months of pregnancy. See also **pre-eclampsia**. [19c: from Greek *eklampein* to shine out]

eclectic *adj* selecting material or ideas from a wide range of sources or authorities. ▸ *noun* a person who adopts eclectic methods. ▪ **eclectically** *adv*. ▪ **eclecticism** *noun*. [17c: from Greek *eklektikos*]

eclipse *noun* **1** the total or partial obscuring of one planet or heavenly body by another, eg of the Sun when the Moon comes between it and the Earth (a **solar eclipse**) or of the Moon when the Earth's shadow falls across it (a **lunar eclipse**). **2** a loss of fame or importance. ▸ *verb* **1** to cause an eclipse of (a heavenly body). **2** to surpass or outshine. **3** to obscure. [14c: French, from Greek *ekleipsis* failure to appear]

ecliptic *noun* (**the ecliptic**) the course which the Sun seems to follow in relation to the stars.

eco- *combining form, denoting* ecology or concern for the environment. [From **ecology**]

ecocide *noun* destruction of the aspects of the environment which enable it to support life. [20c]

eco-friendly *adj* not harmful to or threatening the environment.

E. coli *abbrev* Escherichia coli.

ecology *noun* **1** the relationship between living things and their surroundings. **2** the study of plants, animals, peoples and institutions, in relation to environment. ▪ **ecologic** *or* **ecological** *adj*. ▪ **ecologist** *noun*. [19c]

economic *adj* **1** relating to or concerned with economy or economics. **2** relating to industry or business. **3** of a business practice or industry, etc: operated at, or likely to bring, a profit. **4** economical. **5** *informal* cheap; not expensive.

economical *adj* not wasting money or resources. ▪ **economically** *adv*.

IDIOMS **economical with the truth** deceiving someone by not telling them some essential fact.

economics *singular noun* **1** the study of the production, distribution and consumption of money, goods and services. **2** the financial aspects of something. See also **home economics**. ▪ **economist** *noun* an expert in economics.

economize *or* **-ise** *verb, intr* to cut down on spending or waste. [17c]

economy *noun* (*-ies*) **1** the organization of money and resources within a nation or community, etc, esp in terms of the production, distribution and consumption of goods and services. **2** a system in which these are organized in a specified way: *a socialist economy*. **3** careful management of money or other resources. **4** (*usu* **economies**) an instance of economizing; a saving. **5** efficient or sparing use of something: *economy of movement*. ▸ *adj* **a** of a class of travel, esp air travel: of the cheapest kind; **b** (*also* **economy-size** *or* **economy-sized**) of a packet of food, etc: larger than the standard or basic size, and proportionally cheaper. [16c: from Greek *oikos* house + *nemein* to control]

ecosphere *noun, technical* **1** the parts of the universe, especially of the Earth, in which living things can exist. **2** the **biosphere**. [1950s]

ecosystem *noun* a community of living things and their relationships to their surroundings. [1930s]

ecoterrorism *noun* violence carried out to draw attention to environmental issues. ▪ **ecoterrorist** *noun*. [20c]

ecotourism *noun* the careful development and management of tourism in areas of unspoiled natural beauty, so that the environment is preserved and the income from tourists contributes to its conservation.

ecru *adj* off-white or greyish-yellow in colour; fawn. ▸ *noun* this colour. [19c: French *écru* the colour of unbleached linen]

Ecstasy *noun, slang* (abbrev **E**) a powerful hallucinatory drug.

ecstasy *noun* (***-ies***) a feeling of immense joy; rapture. ▪ **ecstatic** *adj*. [14c: from French *extasie*]

ECT *abbrev* electroconvulsive therapy.

ecto- /ɛktoʊ-, ɛktɒ-/ *combining form* outside. See also **endo-**, **ento-**, **exo-**. [From Greek *ektos* outside]

ectomorph *noun* a person of thin light body build. Compare **endomorph**, **mesomorph**. ▪ **ectomorphic** *adj*. [1940s]

-ectomy *combining form* (***-ectomies***) *med, signifying* removal by surgery: *hysterectomy*. [From Greek *ektome*, from *ektemnein* to cut out]

ectopic pregnancy *noun, pathol* the development of a fetus outside the uterus, esp in a Fallopian tube. [19c: from Greek *ek* out of + *topos* place]

ectoplasm *noun* **1** *biol* the outer layer of a cell's protoplasm, the material which makes up the living part. **2** the substance thought by some people to be given off by the body of a spiritualistic medium during a trance. [19c]

ecu *or* **Ecu** /'eɪkjuː/ *noun* the **European currency unit**, used as a trading currency in the European Union before the introduction of the euro.

ecumenical *or* **oecumenical** /iːkjʊ'mɛnɪkəl, ɛk-/ *or* **ecumenic** *or* **oecumenic** *adj* **1** bringing together different branches of the Christian Church. **2** working towards the unity of the Christian Church. **3** referring to or consisting of the whole Christian Church: *an ecumenical council*. ▪ **ecumenicalism** *or* **ecumenicism** *or* **ecumenism** *noun* the principles or practice of Christian unity. [16c: from Greek *oikoumenikos* relating to the inhabited world]

eczema /'ɛksɪmə/ *noun, pathol* a skin disorder in which red blisters form on the skin, usu causing an itching or burning sensation. [18c: from Greek *ekzema*, from *ek* out of + *zeein* to boil]

ed. *abbrev* **1** (***eds***) edition. **2** (*also* **Ed.**) (***eds*** *or* ***Eds***) editor.

-ed *suffix* **1** used to form past tenses and past participles: *walked*. **2** used to form adjectives from nouns: *bearded* • *bald-headed*.

Edam /'iːdam/ *noun* a type of mild yellow cheese, usually shaped into balls and covered with red wax. [19c: from Edam, near Amsterdam, where it was originally made]

eddy *noun* (***-ies***) **1** a current of water running back against the main stream or current, forming a small whirlpool. **2** a movement of air, smoke or fog, etc similar to this. ▸ *verb* (***-ies, -ied***) *tr & intr* to move or make something move in this way. [15c]

edelweiss /'eɪdəlvaɪs/ *noun* (*pl* ***edelweiss***) a small white mountain plant. [19c: German, from *edel* noble + *weiss* white]

edema see **oedema**

Eden *noun* **1** (*also* **Garden of Eden**) the garden where, according to the Bible, the first man and woman lived after being created. **2** a beautiful region; a place of delight. [14c: from Hebrew *eden* delight or pleasure]

edentate /iː'dɛnteɪt/ *biol, adj* having few or no teeth. ▸ *noun* an animal belonging to a group of mammals which have few or no teeth, such as the anteater, armadillo and sloth. [19c: from Latin *edentatus* toothless]

edge *noun* **1** the part farthest from the middle of something; a border or boundary; the rim. **2** the area beside a cliff or steep drop. **3** the cutting side of something sharp such as a knife. **4** *geom* the meeting point of two surfaces. **5** sharpness or severity: *bread to take the edge off his hunger*. **6** bitterness: *There was an edge to his criticism*. ▸ *verb* (***edged, edging***) **1** to form or make a border to something. **2** to shape the edge or border of something. **3** *tr & intr* to move gradually and carefully, esp sideways. ▪ **edging** *noun*. [Anglo-Saxon *ecg*]

IDIOMS **have the edge on** *or* **over sb** *or* **sth 1** to have an advantage over them. **2** to be better than them. **on edge** uneasy; nervous and irritable.

PHRASAL VERBS **edge out sth** *or* **sb 1** to remove or get rid of it or them gradually. **2** to defeat them by a small margin.

edgeways *or* **edgewise** *adv* **1** sideways. **2** with the edge uppermost or forwards.

IDIOMS **not get a word in edgeways** to be unable to contribute to a conversation because the others are talking continuously.

edgy *adj* (***-ier, -iest***) *informal* easily annoyed; anxious, nervous or tense. ▪ **edgily** *adv*. ▪ **edginess** *noun*.

edible *adj* fit to be eaten; suitable to eat. ▸ *plural noun* (**edibles**) food; things that are fit to be eaten. Compare **eatable**. ▪ **edibility** *noun*. [17c: from Latin *edibilis*]

edict /'iːdɪkt/ *noun* an order issued by any authority. [15c: from Latin *edictum*, from *edicere* to proclaim]

edifice *noun, formal* a building, esp an impressive one. [14c: French *édifice*, from Latin *aedificare* to build]

edify *verb* (***-ies, -ied***) *formal* to improve the mind or morals of someone. ▪ **edification** *noun*. ▪ **edifying** *adj*. [14c: from French *édifier*]

edit *verb* (***edited, editing***) **1** to prepare (a book, newspaper, film, etc) for publication or broadcasting, esp by making corrections or alterations. **2** to be in overall charge of the process of producing (a newspaper, etc). **3** to compile (a reference work). **4**

(*usu* **edit out sth**) to remove (parts of a work) before printing or broadcasting, etc. **5** to prepare (a cinema film, or a TV or radio programme) by putting together material previously photographed or recorded. **6** to prepare (data) for processing by a computer. ▶ *noun* a period or instance of editing. ▪ **edited** *adj*. [18c: from **editor**]

edition *noun* **1** the total number of copies of a book, etc printed at one time. **2** one of a series of printings of a book or periodical, etc, produced with alterations and corrections made by the author or an editor. **3** the form in which a book, etc is published: *paperback edition*. **4** the form given to a work by its editor or publisher: *the Cambridge edition*. [16c]

editor *noun* **1** a person who edits. **2** a person who is in charge of a newspaper or magazine, etc, or one section of it. **3** a person who is in charge of a radio or TV programme which is made up of different items, eg a news programme. **4** a person who puts together the various sections of a film, etc. ▪ **editorship** *noun*. [17c]

editorial *adj* referring or relating to editors or editing. ▶ *noun* an article written by or on behalf of the editor of a newspaper or magazine, usu one offering an opinion on a current topic. ▪ **editorially** *adv*.

educate *verb* **1** to train and teach. **2** to provide school instruction for someone. **3** to train and improve (one's taste, etc). ▪ **educative** *adj* **1** educating. **2** characteristic of or relating to education. [15c: from Latin *educare* to bring up]

educated *adj* **1** having received an education, esp to a level higher than average. **2** produced by or suggesting an education, usu a good one. **3** based on experience or knowledge: *an educated guess*.

education *noun* **1** the process of teaching. **2** the instruction received. **3** the process of training and improving (one's taste, etc). ▪ **educational** *adj*. ▪ **educationalist** *or* **educationist** *noun* an expert in methods of education. ▪ **educationally** *adv*.

Edwardian *adj* belonging to or characteristic of Britain in the years 1901–10, the reign of King Edward VII. ▶ *noun* a person living during this time.

-ee *suffix, forming nouns, signifying* **1** a person who is the object of an action of a specified verb: *payee* • *employee*. **2** a person in a specified condition: *absentee* • *escapee*. **3** a person with a specified association or connection: *bargee*. [From French *-é* or *-ée*]

EEG *abbrev* **1** electroencephalogram. **2** electroencephalograph.

eel *noun* any of several kinds of fish with a long smooth snake-like body and very small fins. [Anglo-Saxon *ǣl*]

EEPROM *abbrev, comput* electrically erasable programmable read-only memory. Compare **EPROM**.

-eer *suffix* **1** *forming nouns, denoting* a person concerned with or engaged in a specified thing or activity: *auctioneer* • *mountaineer*. **2** *forming verbs, denoting* actions or behaviour associated with a specified thing or activity: *electioneer*. [From French *-ier*]

eerie *adj* strange and disturbing or frightening. ▪ **eerily** *adv*. ▪ **eeriness** *noun*. [13c: from Northern English *eri*]

efface *verb* **1** to rub or wipe out something. **2** to block out (a memory, etc). **3** to avoid drawing attention to (oneself). See also **self-effacing**. ▪ **effacement** *noun*. [15c: from French *effacer*]

effect *noun* **1** a result. **2** an impression given or produced. **3** operation; a working state: *The ban comes into effect today*. **4** (*usu* **effects**) *formal* property. **5** (*usu* **effects**) devices, esp lighting and sound, used to create a particular impression in a film or on a stage, etc. ▶ *verb, formal* to do something; to make something happen, or to bring it about. [14c as *noun*: French]

IDIOMS **in effect** in reality; practically speaking. **take effect** to come into force.

---

effect, affect

Be careful not to use **effect** when you mean the verb **affect**:

All these interruptions have affected our schedule.

---

effective *adj* **1** having the power to produce, or producing, a desired result. **2** producing a pleasing effect. **3** impressive; striking. **4** in, or coming into, operation; working or active. **5** actual, rather than theoretical. ▶ *noun* a serviceman or body of servicemen equipped and prepared for action. ▪ **effectively** *adv*. ▪ **effectiveness** *noun*. [14c]

effector *biol, adj* causing a response to stimulus. ▶ *noun* an organ or substance which has this property. [20c]

effectual *adj* **1** producing the intended result. **2** of a document, etc: valid. ▪ **effectually** *adv*. [14c: from Latin *effectualis*]

effeminate *adj, derog* of a man: having features of behaviour or appearance more typical of a woman; not manly. ▪ **effeminacy** *noun*. ▪ **effeminately** *adv*. [15c: from Latin *effeminare* to make in the form of a woman]

efferent *adj, physiol* of a nerve: carrying impulses out from the brain. [19c: from Latin *efferre* to carry out]

effervesce /ɛfəˈvɛs/ *verb, intr* **1** of a liquid: to give off bubbles of gas. **2** to behave in a lively or energetic way. ▪ **effervescence** *noun*. ▪ **effervescent** *adj*. [18c: from Latin *effervescere* to boil up]

effete /ɪˈfiːt/ *adj, derog* **1** of an institution, organization, etc: lacking its original power or authority. **2** of a person: **a** lacking strength or energy; **b** decadent; **c** made weak by too much protection or refinement. [17c: from Latin *effetus* weakened by having given birth]

efficacious *adj, formal* producing, or certain to produce, the intended result. ▪ **efficacy** *noun*. [16c: from Latin *efficax, efficacis* powerful]

efficient *adj* **1** producing satisfactory results with an economy of effort and a minimum of waste. **2** of a person: capable of competent work within a relatively short time. **3** *in compounds* economical in the use or consumption of a specified resource: *energy-efficient*. ▪ **efficiency** *noun* (*-ies*). ▪ **efficiently** *adv*. [14c: from Latin *efficere* to accomplish]

effigy *noun* (*-ies*) **1** a crude doll or model representing a person, on which hatred of, or contempt for, the person can be expressed, eg by burning it. **2** *formal* a portrait or sculpture of a person used as an architectural ornament. [16c: from Latin *effigies*]

effloresce *verb, intr* **1** *botany* of a plant: to produce flowers. **2** *chem* of a chemical compound: to form an **efflorescence** (sense 2). [18c]

efflorescence *noun* **1** the act of efflorescing. **2** *chem* a powdery substance formed as a result of crystallization or loss of water to the atmosphere. **3** *botany* the period during which a plant is producing flowers. ▪ **efflorescent** *adj.* [17c: from Latin *efflorescere* to blossom]

effluent *noun* **1** liquid industrial waste or sewage released into a river or the sea, etc. **2** *geog, etc* a stream or river flowing from a larger body of water. [18c: from Latin *effluere* to flow out]

effluvium *noun* (***effluvia***) *formal* an unpleasant smell or vapour given off by something, eg decaying matter. [17c: Latin, meaning 'a flowing out']

efflux *noun* **1** the process of flowing out. **2** something that flows out. [17c: Latin, from *effluere* to flow out]

effort *noun* **1** hard mental or physical work, or something that requires it. **2** an act of trying hard. **3** the result of an attempt; an achievement. ▪ **effortless** *adj.* ▪ **effortlessly** *adv.* [15c: from French *esfort*, from Latin *fortis* strong]

effrontery *noun* (**-ies**) shameless rudeness; impudence. [18c: from Latin *effrons* shameless]

effusion *noun* **1** the act or process of pouring or flowing out. **2** something that is poured out. **3** an uncontrolled flow of speech or writing.

effusive *adj, derog* expressing feelings, esp happiness or enthusiasm, in an excessive or very showy way. ▪ **effusively** *adv.* ▪ **effusiveness** *noun.* [17c]

EFL *abbrev* English as a Foreign Language.

eg *abbrev*: *exempli gratia* (Latin), for example.

egalitarian *adj* relating to, promoting or believing in the principle that all human beings are equal and should enjoy the same rights. ▸ *noun* a person who upholds this principle. ▪ **egalitarianism** *noun.* [19c: from French *égalitaire*, from *égal* equal]

egg[1] *or* **egg cell** *noun* **1** the reproductive cell produced by a female animal, bird, etc, from which the young develops. Also called **ovum**. **2** a reproductive cell or developing embryo produced and deposited in a hard shell by female birds, reptiles, and certain animals. **3** a hen's egg, used as food. [14c: Norse] IDIOMS **have egg on one's face** *informal* to be made to look foolish. **put all one's eggs in one basket** to depend entirely on one plan, etc.

egg[2] *verb* (*usu* **egg sb on**) *informal* to urge or encourage them. [Anglo-Saxon *eggian*]

eggcup *noun* a small cup-shaped container for holding a boiled egg in its shell while it is being eaten.

egghead *noun, informal, sometimes derog* a very clever person; an intellectual. [20c]

eggnog *or* **egg-flip** *noun* a drink made from raw eggs, milk, sugar and an alcoholic spirit, esp rum or brandy.

eggplant *noun, N Am, esp US* an **aubergine**.

eggshell *noun* the hard thin porous covering of an egg. ▸ *adj* **1** of paint or varnish: having a slightly glossy finish. **2** of articles of china: very thin and fragile.

ego *noun* **1** personal pride. **2** *psychoanal* in Freudian theory: the part of a person that is conscious and thinks. Compare **id**, **superego**. **3** one's image of oneself. **4** egotism. [19c: Latin, meaning 'I']

egocentric *adj, derog* interested in oneself only.

egoism *noun* **1** *philos* the principle that self-interest is the basis of morality. **2** selfishness. **3** egotism.

egoist *noun* a person who believes in self-interest as a moral principle. ▪ **egoistic** *or* **egoistical** *adj.*

egomania *noun, psychol* extreme self-interest or egotism. ▪ **egomaniac** *noun.*

egotism *noun, derog* the fact of having a very high opinion of oneself. ▪ **egotist** *noun.* ▪ **egotistic** *or* **egotistical** *adj.* [18c]

ego trip *noun, informal* something carried out mainly to increase one's high opinion of oneself. [1960s]

egregious /ɪˈgriːdʒəs/ *adj, formal* outrageous; shockingly bad. ▪ **egregiously** *adv.* [16c: from Latin *egregius* standing out from the herd]

egress /ˈiːgrɛs/ *noun, formal or law* **1** the act of leaving a building or other enclosed place. **2** an exit. **3** the power or right to depart. Opposite of **ingress**. [16c: from Latin *egredi, egressus* to go out]

egret /ˈiːgrət/ *noun* any of various white wading birds similar to herons. [15c: from French *aigrette*]

Egyptian *adj* belonging or relating to Egypt, its inhabitants, or their language. ▸ *noun* a citizen or inhabitant of, or person born in, Egypt. [14c]

eh *exclam* **1** used to request that a question or remark, etc be repeated. **2** added to a question, often with the implication that agreement is expected. **3** used to express surprise.

Eid see **Id-ul-Fitr**

eider /ˈaɪdə(r)/ *or* **eider duck** *noun* a large sea duck from northern countries. [18c: from Icelandic *æthr*]

eiderdown *noun* **1** the down or soft feathers of the eider. **2** a quilt filled with this or some similar material.

Eid-ul-Adha see **Id-ul-Adha**

Eid-ul-Fitr see **Id-ul-Fitr**

eight *noun* **1 a** the cardinal number 8; **b** the quantity that this represents, being one more than seven. **2** any symbol for this, eg *8* or *VIII*. **3** the age of eight. **4** something, esp a garment, or a person, whose size is denoted by the number 8. **5** the eighth hour after midnight or midday: *Come at eight* • *8 o'clock*. **6** a set or group of eight people or things. **7** *rowing* a racing-boat manned by eight oarsmen or oarswomen; the crew of such a boat. ▸ *adj* **1** totalling eight. **2** aged eight. [Anglo-Saxon *æhta*]

eighteen *noun* **1 a** the cardinal number 18; **b** the quantity that this represents, being one more than seventeen. **2** any symbol for this, eg *18* or *XVIII*. **3** the age of eighteen. **4** something, esp a garment, or a person, whose size is denoted by the number 18. **5** a set or group of eighteen people or things. **6** (written **18**) a film classified as suitable for people aged 18 and over. ▸ *adj* **1** totalling eighteen. **2** aged eighteen. ▪ **eighteenth** *adj, noun, adv.* [Anglo-Saxon *æhtatene*]

eightfold *adj* **1** equal to eight times as much. **2** divided into or consisting of eight parts. ▸ *adv* by eight times as much.

eighth (often written **8th**) *adj* **1** in counting: **a** next after seventh; **b** last of eight. **2** in eighth position. **3** being one of eight equal parts: *an eighth share*. ▸ *noun* **1** one of eight equal parts: *an eighth share*. **2** a **fraction** equal to one divided by eight (usu written ⅛). **3** a person coming eighth, eg in a race or exam. **4** (**the eighth**) **a** the eighth day of the month; **b** *golf* the eighth hole. ▸ *adv* eighthly. ▪ **eighthly** *adv* used to introduce the eighth point in a list. [Anglo-Saxon]

eighties (often written **80s** *or* **80's**) *plural noun* **1** (**one's eighties**) the period of time between one's eightieth and ninetieth birthdays. **2** (**the eighties**) the range of temperatures between eighty and ninety degrees. **3** (**the eighties**) the period of time between the eightieth and ninetieth years of a century. *as adj*: *an eighties disco.*

eightsome reel *noun* **1** a lively Scottish dance for eight people. **2** the music for this dance.

eighty *noun* (**-*ies***) **1** **a** the cardinal number 80; **b** the quantity that this represents, being one more than seventy-nine, or the product of ten and eight. **2** any symbol for this, eg *80* or *LXXX*. **3** the age of eighty. **4** a set or group of eighty people or things: *a score of eighty points.* ▸ *adj* **1** totalling eighty. **2** aged eighty. See also **eighties**. ▪ **eightieth** *adj, noun, adv.* [Anglo-Saxon]

eighty- *combining form* **a** *forming adjectives and nouns* with cardinal numbers between *one* and *nine*: *eighty-two*; **b** *forming adjectives and nouns* with ordinal numbers between *first* and *ninth*: *eighty-second.*

einsteinium *noun* (symbol **Es**) an element produced artificially from plutonium. [20c: named after Albert Einstein, German-born physicist]

eisteddfod /aɪ'stɛdfəd, -'stɛðvɒd/ *noun* (***eisteddfods*** *or* ***eisteddfodau*** /aɪ'stɛðvɒdaɪ/) a Welsh festival during which competitions are held to find the best poetry, drama, songs, etc. [19c: Welsh, literally 'a session']

either *adj* **1** any one of two. **2** each of two: *a garden with a fence on either side.* ▸ *pronoun* any one of two things or people, etc. ▸ *adv, with negatives* **1** also; as well: *I thought him rather unpleasant, and I didn't like his wife either.* **2** what is more; besides: *He plays golf, and he's not bad, either.* [Anglo-Saxon *ægther*]

IDIOMS **either ... or ...** introducing two choices or possibilities: *I need either a pen or a pencil.*

---

either ... or ...

When **either** is followed by **or** and the two subjects it links are singular, use a singular verb:

Either Rosie or Bill is right.

If the second of the linked subjects is plural, use a plural verb:

If either Rosie or her sisters are not telling the truth, we'll soon know.

When both of the linked subjects are plural, use a plural verb:

I have either teenage children or elderly parents making demands on my time.

---

ejaculate *verb* **1** *tr & intr* of a man or male animal: to discharge (semen). **2** to exclaim. ▪ **ejaculation** *noun.* [16c: from Latin *ejaculari* to throw out]

eject *verb* **1** to throw out someone or something with force. **2** to force someone to leave. **3** *intr* to leave a moving aircraft using an ejector seat. ▪ **ejection** *noun.* ▪ **ejector** *noun.* [16c: from Latin *ejicere* to throw out]

ejector seat *or* (*US*) **ejection seat** *noun* a type of seat fitted in an aircraft, etc, designed to propel the occupant out of the aircraft at speed in case of emergency.

eke /iːk/ *verb* (*always* **eke sth out**) **1** to make (a supply) last longer, eg by adding something else to it or by careful use. **2** to manage with difficulty to make (a living, etc). [Anglo-Saxon *eacan* to increase]

elaborate *adj* /ɪ'labərət/ **1** complicated in design; complex. **2** carefully planned or worked out. ▸ *verb* /-reɪt/ **1** *intr* (*usu* **elaborate on** *or* **upon sth**) to add detail to it. **2** to work out something in great detail. ▪ **elaborately** *adv.* ▪ **elaboration** *noun.* [16c: from Latin]

élan /eɪ'lan; *French* elɑ̃/ *noun, literary* impressive and energetic style. [19c: French]

eland /'iːlənd/ *noun* (***elands*** *or* ***eland***) a large African antelope with spiral horns. [18c: Afrikaans]

elapse *verb, intr, formal* of time: to pass. [17c: from Latin *elabi* to slide away]

elastic *adj* **1** of a material or substance: able to return to its original shape or size after being pulled or pressed out of shape. **2** of a force: caused by, or causing, such an ability. **3** flexible. **4** made of elastic. ▸ *noun* stretchable cord or fabric woven with strips of rubber. ▪ **elastically** *adv.* ▪ **elasticated** *adj.* ▪ **elasticity** *noun.* [17c: from Greek *elastikos*]

elastic band *noun* a thin loop of rubber for keeping papers, etc together. Also called **rubber band**.

Elastoplast *noun, trademark* a dressing for a wound, of gauze on a backing of adhesive tape. [20c]

elate *verb* **1** to make someone intensely happy. **2** to fill someone with optimism. ▪ **elated** *adj.* [17c: from Latin *elatus* elevated or exalted]

elation *noun* **1** an elated state; euphoria. **2** pride resulting from success.

elbow *noun* **1** the joint where the human arm bends. **2** the part of a garment which covers this joint. **3** the corresponding joint in animals. ▸ *verb* **1** to push or strike something with the elbow. **2** to make (one's way through) by pushing with the elbows. [Anglo-Saxon *elnboga*]

elbow grease *noun, informal* hard work, esp hard polishing. [17c]

elbow room *noun* enough space for moving or doing something. [16c]

elder[1] *adj* **1** older. **2** (**the elder**) used before or after a person's name to distinguish them from a younger person of the same name. ▸ *noun* **1** a person who is older. **2** (*often* **elders**) an older person, esp someone regarded as having authority. **3** in some tribal societies: a senior member of a tribe, who is invested with authority. **4** in some Protestant Churches: a lay person who has some responsibility for pastoral care and decision-making. [Anglo-Saxon *eldra*]

---

elder, older

You would use the word **elder** about people in the family:

an elder brother/sister

You would not use **elder** if you are making a comparison using the word **than**. You would use **older** instead:

She is older than me.

---

elder[2] *noun* a bush or small tree with white flowers and purple-black or red berries. [Anglo-Saxon *ellærn*]

elderberry *noun* the fruit of the **elder**[2].

elderly *adj* **1** rather old. **2** bordering on old age. **3** (**the elderly**) old people as a group. [17c]

elder statesman *noun* an old and very experienced member of a group, esp a politician, whose opinions are respected.

eldest *adj* oldest. ▸ *noun* someone who is the oldest of three or more.

eldest, oldest
You would use the word **eldest** about people in the family:
my eldest brother/sister
In other examples, you would use **oldest** instead:
She is the oldest teacher in the school.

El Dorado /ɛldəˈrɑːdoʊ/ *noun* (*pl* in sense 2 ***eldorados***) **1** the golden land or city, imagined by the Spanish explorers of America. **2** (*also* **eldorado**) any place where wealth is easy to accumulate. [16c: Spanish, literally 'the gilded place']

eldritch *adj, orig Scot* weird; uncanny.

elect *verb* **1** to choose someone to be an official or representative by voting. **2** to choose something by vote, in preference to other options. ▸ *adj, following its noun* elected to a position, but not yet formally occupying it: *president elect*. ▪ **electable** *adj*. [15c: from Latin *eligere* to choose]
IDIOMS **elect to do sth** to do it by choice.

election *noun* **1** the process or act of choosing people for office, esp political office, by taking a vote. See also **general election**. **2** the act of electing or choosing.

electioneer *verb, intr* to work for the election of a candidate, esp in a political campaign. ▪ **electioneering** *noun, adj*. [18c]

elective *adj* **1** of a position or office, etc: to which someone is appointed by election. **2** optional.

elector *noun* someone who has the right to vote at an election. ▪ **electoral** *adj* concerning or relating to elections or electors. ▪ **electorally** *adv*.

electoral roll *or* **electoral register** *noun* the list of people in a particular area who are allowed to vote in local and general elections.

electorate *noun* all the electors of a city or country, etc.

electric *adj* **1** (*also* **electrical**) relating to, produced by, worked by or generating electricity. **2** of a musical instrument: amplified electronically. **3** having or causing great excitement, tension or expectation. ▸ *plural noun* (**electrics**) **1** electrical appliances. **2** *informal* wiring. ▪ **electrically** *adv*. [17c: from Greek *elektron* amber, which produces electricity when rubbed]

electrical engineering *noun* the branch of engineering concerned with the practical applications of electricity and magnetism. ▪ **electrical engineer** *noun*.

electric blanket *noun* a blanket incorporating an electric element, used for warming a bed.

electric chair *noun, US* a chair used for executing criminals by sending a powerful electric current through them. [Late 19c]

electric current *noun* the flow of electric charge, in the form of **electron**s, in the same direction through a conductor.

electric eel *noun* an eel-like fish, which is able to deliver electric shocks by means of an organ in its tail.

electrician *noun* a person whose job is to install, maintain and repair electrical equipment.

electricity *noun* **1** the energy which exists in a negative form in electrons and in a positive form in protons, and also as a flowing current usu of electrons. **2** an electric charge or current. **3** a supply of this energy to a household, etc, eg for heating and lighting. **4** the science or study of this energy. **5** excitement, tension or expectation. [17c]

electric shock see under **shock**[1]

electric shock therapy see under **electroconvulsive therapy**

electrify *verb* (***-ies, -ied***) **1** to give an electric charge to something. **2** to equip (eg a railway system) for the use of electricity as a power supply. **3** to cause great excitement in (eg a crowd). ▪ **electrification** *noun*. ▪ **electrifying** *adj* extremely exciting. [18c]

electro- *combining form, denoting* electricity. [From Greek *elektron* amber]

electrocardiogram *noun, med* (abbrev **ECG**) the diagram or tracing produced by an electrocardiograph. [Early 20c]

electrocardiograph *noun, med* (abbrev **ECG**) an apparatus which registers the electrical variations of the beating heart, as a diagram or tracing. [Early 20c]

electrochemistry *noun* the study of the relation between electricity and chemical change. ▪ **electrochemical** *adj*. ▪ **electrochemist** *noun*. [19c]

electroconvulsive therapy *noun, med* (abbrev **ECT**) the treatment of mental illness by passing small electric currents through the brain. Also called **electric shock therapy**. [20c]

electrocute *verb* **1** to kill someone or something by electric shock. **2** to carry out a death sentence on someone by means of electricity. ▪ **electrocution** *noun*. [19c]

electrode *noun, technical* either of the two conducting points by which electric current enters or leaves a battery or other electrical apparatus. [19c]

electrodynamics *singular noun* the study of electricity in motion, or of the interaction of currents and currents, or currents and magnets.

electroencephalogram *noun, med* (abbrev **EEG**) a diagram or tracing produced by an electroencephalograph. Also called **encephalogram**. [20c]

electroencephalograph *noun, med* (abbrev **EEG**) an apparatus which registers the electrical activity of the brain. Also called **encephalograph**. [20c]

electrolysis /ɛləkˈtrɒlɪsɪs/ *noun* **1** *chem* the decomposition of a chemical in the form of a liquid or solution by passing an electric current through it. **2** the removal of tumours or hair roots by means of an electric current. ▪ **electrolytic** *adj*. ▪ **electrolytically** *adv*. [19c]

electrolyte *noun, chem* a solution of chemical salts which can conduct electricity. ▪ **electrolytic** *adj*. [19c: from **electro-** + Greek *lytos* released]

electromagnet *noun, physics* a piece of soft metal, usu iron, made magnetic by the passage of an electric current through a coil of wire wrapped around the metal. ▪ **electromagnetic** *adj* having electrical and magnetic properties. ▪ **electromagnetism** *noun* magnetic forces produced by electricity. [19c]

electromotive *adj, physics* producing or tending to produce an electric current.

electromotive force *noun, physics* the energy which forces a current to flow in an electrical circuit.

electron *noun, physics* a particle, present in all atoms, which has a negative electric charge and is responsible for carrying electricity in solids. [19c]

electronegative *adj* carrying a negative charge, tending to form negative ions. [Early 19c]

electronic *adj* **1** operated by means of electrical circuits, usu several very small ones, which handle very low levels of electric current. **2** produced or operated, etc, using electronic apparatus. **3** concerned with electronics. ▪ **electronically** *adv.* [Early 20c]

electronic mail see under **e-mail**

electronic publishing *noun* the publishing of computer-readable texts on disk, CD-ROM, CD-I, etc. [20c]

electronics *singular noun* the science that deals with the study of the behaviour of electronic circuits and their applications in machines, etc. ▸ *plural noun* the electronic parts of a machine or system. [Early 20c]

electron microscope *noun* a microscope which operates using a beam of electrons rather than a beam of light, and is capable of very high magnification.

electronvolt *noun, nuclear physics* a unit of energy equal to that acquired by an electron when accelerated by a potential of one volt.

electroplate *verb* to coat (an object) with metal, esp silver, by electrolysis. ▸ *noun* articles coated in this way. ▪ **electroplated** *adj.* ▪ **electroplating** *noun.* [19c]

electrostatics *singular noun* the branch of science concerned with electricity at rest. ▪ **electrostatic** *adj.*

elegant *adj* **1** having or showing good taste in dress or style, combined with dignity and gracefulness. **2** of a movement: graceful. **3** of apparatus, work in science, a plan, etc: simple and ingenious. ▪ **elegance** *noun.* ▪ **elegantly** *adv.* [16c: from Latin *elegans*]

elegiac /ɛlə'dʒaɪək/ *adj, formal, literary* mournful or thoughtful.

elegy /'ɛlədʒɪ/ *noun* (***-ies***) a mournful or thoughtful song or poem, esp one whose subject is death or loss. [16c: from Latin *elegia*]

element *noun* **1** a part of anything; a component or feature. **2** *chem, physics* any substance that cannot be split by chemical means into simpler substances. **3** a person or small group within a larger group. **4** a slight amount. **5** the wire coil through which an electric current is passed to produce heat in various electrical appliances. **6** any one of the four basic substances (earth, air, fire and water) from which, according to ancient philosophy, everything is formed. **7** (**the elements**) weather conditions, esp when severe. **8** (**the elements**) basic facts or skills. **9** (**the elements**) *Christianity* bread and wine as the representation of the body and blood of Christ in the Eucharist. ▪ **elemental** *adj* **1** basic or primitive. **2** referring or relating to the forces of nature, esp the four elements (earth, air, fire and water). **3** immense; referring to the power of a force of nature. [13c: from Latin *elementum*]

IDIOMS **in one's element** in the surroundings that one finds most natural and enjoyable.

elementary *adj* **1** dealing with simple or basic facts; rudimentary. **2** belonging or relating to the elements or an element.

elementary particle *noun, chem, physics* any of the twenty or more particles (eg **electrons**, **protons** and **neutrons**) which make up an atom.

elementary school *noun, N Am, esp US* primary school.

elephant *noun* (***elephants*** *or* ***elephant***) the largest living land animal, with thick greyish skin, a nose in the form of a long hanging trunk, and two curved tusks, surviving in two species, the larger **African elephant** and the **Indian elephant**. See also **white elephant**. [14c: from Latin *elephantus*]

elephantiasis /ɛləfən'taɪəsɪs/ *noun, pathol* a disease in which the skin becomes thicker and the limbs become greatly enlarged. [16c]

elephantine *adj* **1** belonging to, or like, an elephant. **2** huge. **3** *derog* large and awkward; not graceful. [17c]

elevate *verb* **1** to raise or lift. **2** to give a higher rank or status to someone or something. **3** to improve (a person's mind, etc) morally or intellectually. **4** to make someone more cheerful. [15c: from Latin *elevare*]

elevated *adj* **1** of a rank or position, etc: very high; important. **2** of thoughts or ideas, etc: intellectually advanced or very moral. **3** of land or buildings: raised above the level of their surroundings.

elevation *noun* **1** the act of elevating or state of being elevated. **2** *technical* vertical height, eg of a place above sea-level. **3** *maths* an angle measuring a point above a horizontal line. Compare **depression** (sense 6). **4** *technical* a drawing or diagram of one side of a building, machine, etc. **5** *formal* a high place.

elevator *noun* **1** *N Am, esp US* a **lift** (*noun* sense 4). **2** *chiefly N Am, esp US* a tall building in which grain is stored. **3** a lift or machine for transporting goods to a higher level. **4** *anatomy* a muscle which lifts part of the body.

eleven *noun* **1 a** the cardinal number 11; **b** the quantity that this represents, being one more than ten. **2** any symbol for this, eg *11* or *XI*. **3** the age of eleven. **4** something, eg a garment or a person, whose size is denoted by the number 11. **5** the eleventh hour after midnight or midday: *Come at eleven • 11pm.* **6 a** a set or group of eleven people or things; **b** *football, cricket, hockey, etc* a team of players. ▸ *adj* **1** totalling eleven. **2** aged eleven. [Anglo-Saxon *endleofan*]

eleven-plus *noun, educ, esp formerly* in the UK: an examination taken at the age of 11 or 12 to determine which sort of secondary school a pupil should attend. [20c]

elevenses *plural noun* (*often used with singular verb*) *informal* a mid-morning snack. [19c]

eleventh (often written **11th**) *adj* **1** in counting: **a** next after tenth; **b** last of eleven. **2** in eleventh position. **3** (**the eleventh**) **a** the eleventh day of the month; **b** *golf* the eleventh hole. ▸ *noun* **1** one of eleven equal parts: *an eleventh share.* **2** a **fraction** equal to one divided by eleven (usu written $\frac{1}{11}$). **3** the position in a series corresponding to eleven in a sequence of numbers. **4** a person coming eleventh, eg in a race or exam.

elf *noun* (***elves***) *folklore* a tiny supernatural being with a human form, with a tendency to play tricks. [Anglo-Saxon *ælf*]

elfin *adj* **1** of physical features, etc: small and delicate. **2** like an elf; small and mischievous, but charming.

elicit *verb* **1** to cause something to happen; to bring something out into the open. **2** (*usu* **elicit sth from sb**) to succeed in getting information from them, usu with some effort or difficulty. [17c: from Latin *elicere*]

elide *verb, grammar* to omit (a vowel or syllable) at the beginning or end of a word. See also **elision**. [16c: from Latin *elidere* to strike out]

eligible *adj* **1** suitable, or deserving to be chosen (for a job, as a husband, etc). **2** having a right to something: *eligible for compensation*. ▪ **eligibility** *noun*. [15c: from Latin *eligere* to select]

eliminate *verb* **1** to get rid of or exclude. **2** to expel (waste matter) from the body. **3** to exclude someone or something from a competition by defeat. **4** *slang* to kill or murder someone. ▪ **elimination** *noun*. ▪ **eliminator** *noun*. [16c: from Latin *eliminare* to put out of the house]

elision *noun, grammar* the omission of a vowel or syllable, as in *I'm* and *we're*. See also **elide**. [16c: from Latin *elidere* to strike out]

elite *or* **élite** /ɛ'liːt/ *noun* **1** the best, most important or most powerful people within society. **2** the best of a group or profession. [18c: French]

elitism *noun* **1** the belief in the need for a powerful social elite. **2** the belief in the natural social superiority of some people. **3** *often derog* awareness of, or pride in, belonging to an elite group in society. ▪ **elitist** *adj, noun*. [20c]

elixir /ɪ'lɪksə(r)/ *noun* **1** in medieval times: a liquid chemical preparation believed to have the power to give people everlasting life or to turn base metals into gold. **2** any medical preparation which is claimed to cure all illnesses. **3** a liquid medicine mixed with honey or alcohol, to hide the unpleasant taste. [14c: from Arabic *al-iksir* the philosopher's stone]

Elizabethan *adj* relating to or typical of the reign of Queen Elizabeth, esp Queen Elizabeth I of England (1558–1603). ▸ *noun* a person living during this time.

elk *noun* (***elks*** *or* ***elk***) **1** a large deer with flat rounded antlers, found in Europe and Asia, and in N America where it is called the **moose**. **2** *N Am* the **wapiti**. [Probably Anglo-Saxon *elh*]

ellipse *noun, geom* a regular oval, as formed by a diagonal cut through a cone above the base. [18c: from Latin *ellipsis*]

ellipsis *noun* (***-ses*** /-siːz/) **1** *grammar* a figure of speech in which a word or words needed for the sense or grammar are omitted but understood. **2** in text: a set of three dots (...) that indicate the omission of a word or words, eg in a lengthy quotation. [16c: Latin, from Greek *elleipein* to fall short]

ellipsoid *noun, geom* a surface or solid object of which every plane section is an ellipse or a circle.

elliptical *or* **elliptic** *adj* **1** *maths* relating to, or having the shape of, an **ellipse**. **2** of speech or writing: **a** containing an **ellipsis**; **b** so concise as to be unclear or ambiguous. [17c]

elm *noun* **1** (*also* **elm tree**) a tall deciduous tree with broad leaves. **2** (*also* **elmwood**) the hard heavy wood of this tree. ▸ *adj* made of elm. [Anglo-Saxon]

elocution *noun* the art of speaking clearly and effectively. ▪ **elocutionist** *noun*. [15c: from Latin *eloqui* to speak out]

elongate *verb* to lengthen or stretch something out. ▪ **elongation** *noun*. [16c: from Latin *elongare*]

elope *verb, intr* to run away secretly in order to get married. ▪ **elopement** *noun*. [16c: from French *aloper*]

eloquence *noun* **1** the art or power of using speech to impress, move or persuade. **2** persuasive, fine and effectual language. ▪ **eloquent** *adj*. ▪ **eloquently** *adv*. [14c: French, from Latin *eloqui* to speak out]

else *adv, adj* different from or in addition to something or someone known or already mentioned: *Where else can you buy it?* [Anglo-Saxon *elles*]

IDIOMS **or else 1** or if not ... ; otherwise ... : *Hurry up, or else we'll be late*. **2** *informal* or there will be trouble: *Give me the money, or else!*

elsewhere *adv* somewhere else.

ELT *abbrev* English Language Teaching.

elucidate *verb* to make (a person or animal) extremely thin, esp through illness or starvation, etc. ▪ **elucidation** *noun*. [16c: from Latin *elucidare*]

elude *verb* **1** to escape or avoid something by quickness or cleverness. **2** to fail to be understood, discovered or remembered by someone. [16c: from Latin *eludere*]

elusive *adj* **1** difficult to find or catch. **2** difficult to understand or remember. ▪ **elusively** *adv*. ▪ **elusiveness** *noun*. [18c: from **elude**]

elver *noun* a young eel. [17c: variant of *eelfare*, literally 'eel journey']

elves *pl of* **elf**

Elysium /ɪ'lɪzɪəm/ *noun* **1** *Greek myth* the place where the blessed were supposed to rest after death. **2** *poetic* a state or place of perfect happiness. ▪ **Elysian** *adj*. [16c: Latin, from Greek *elysion*]

em- *prefix* a form of **en-** used before *b, m* and *p*.

emaciate /ɪ'meɪsɪeɪt/ *verb* to make (a person or animal) extremely thin, esp through illness or starvation, etc. ▪ **emaciated** *adj*. ▪ **emaciation** *noun*. [17c: from Latin *maciare* to make lean]

e-mail, **email** *or* **E-mail** *noun* (*in full* **electronic mail**) **1** a system for transmitting messages and computer files electronically from one computer to another, eg within an office computer network, over **the Internet**, etc. **2** correspondence sent in this way. ▸ *verb* to send someone an electronic message.

emanate *verb, intr* **1** of an idea, etc: to emerge or originate. **2** of light or gas, etc: to flow; to issue. ▪ **emanation** *noun*. [18c: from Latin *emanare* to flow out]

emancipate *verb* to set someone free from slavery, or from some other social or political restraint. ▪ **emancipation** *noun*. [17c: from Latin *emancipare* to give independence to (one's child or wife)]

emasculate *verb* **1** to reduce the force, strength or effectiveness of someone or something. **2** to castrate (a man or male animal). ▪ **emasculation** *noun*. [17c: from Latin e- away + *masculus*, diminutive of *mas* male]

embalm *verb* **1** to preserve (a dead body) from decay. **2** to preserve something unchanged. **3** to impregnate with balm; to perfume. [14c: from French *embaumer*]

embankment *noun* **1** a bank or wall of earth made to enclose a waterway. **2** a mound built to carry a road or railway over a low-lying place. **3** a slope of grass, earth, etc which rises from either side of a road or railway.

embargo *noun* (***embargoes***) **1** an official order forbidding something, esp trade with another country.

2 the resulting stoppage, esp of trade. **3** any restriction or prohibition. ▸ *verb* (***embargoes, embargoed***) **1** to place something under an embargo. **2** to take something for use by the state. [16c: from Spanish *embargar* to impede or restrain]

embark *verb* **1** *tr & intr* to go or put on board a ship or aircraft. **2** *intr* (*usu* **embark on** *or* **upon sth**) to begin (a task, esp a lengthy one). ▪ **embarkation** *noun*. [16c: from French *embarquer*]

embarrass *verb* **1** *tr & intr* to make someone feel, or become anxious, self-conscious or ashamed. **2** to confuse or perplex. ▪ **embarrassed** *adj*. ▪ **embarrassing** *adj*. ▪ **embarrassingly** *adv*. ▪ **embarrassment** *noun*. [17c: from French *embarrasser*]

---

embarrass
This word is often misspelt. It has two *m*'s as well as two *s*'s. It might help you to remember the following sentence:
*I went **r**eally **r**ed and **s**miled **s**hyly.*

---

embassy *noun* (***-ies***) **1** the official residence of an ambassador. **2** an ambassador and his or her staff. [16c: from French *ambassee*]

embattled *adj* **1** troubled by problems or difficulties; engaged in a struggle. **2** prepared for battle.

embed /ɪm'bɛd/ *verb* (***embedded, embedding***) (*also* **imbed**) to set or fix something firmly and deeply. ▸ *noun* /'ɛmbɛd/ a journalist who is given an official placement within a military unit (also **embedded reporter**). [18c]

embellish *verb* **1** to make (a story, etc) more interesting by adding details which may not be true. **2** to beautify something with decoration. ▪ **embellishment** *noun*. [14c: from French *embellir* to make beautiful]

ember *noun* **1** a piece of glowing or smouldering coal or wood. **2** (**embers**) red-hot ash; the smouldering remains of a fire. [Anglo-Saxon *æmerge*]

embezzle *verb* to take or use dishonestly (money or property with which one has been entrusted). ▪ **embezzlement** *noun*. ▪ **embezzler** *noun*. [15c: from French *embesiler* to make away with]

embitter *verb* **1** to make someone feel bitter. **2** to make someone more bitter or a difficult situation worse. ▪ **embittered** *adj*. [17c]

emblazon *verb* **1** to decorate with a coat of arms or some other bright design. **2** to display in a very obvious or striking way. [16c: from French *blason* shield]

emblem *noun* an object chosen to represent an idea, a quality, a country, etc. ▪ **emblematic** *adj*. [15c: from Greek *emblema* something inserted]

embody *verb* (***-ies, -ied***) **1** to be an expression or a representation of something in words, actions or form; to typify or personify. **2** to include or incorporate. ▪ **embodiment** *noun*. [16c, meaning 'to put into a body']

embolden *verb* **1** to make someone bold; to encourage. **2** *printing* to set in bold type. [15c]

embolism *noun, pathol* the blocking of a blood vessel by an air bubble, a blood clot, etc. [14c: from Greek]

embolus /'ɛmbələs/ *noun* (***emboli*** /-laɪ/) *pathol* any obstruction in a blood vessel, esp a blood clot. [19c: from Greek *embolos* a stopper]

emboss *verb* to carve or mould a raised design on (a surface). [14c: from French]

embrace *verb* **1** to hold someone closely in the arms, affectionately or as a greeting. **2** *intr* of two people: to hold each other closely in the arms. **3** to take (eg an opportunity) eagerly, or accept (eg a religion) wholeheartedly. **4** to include. ▸ *noun* **1** an act of embracing. **2** a loving hug. [14c: from French *embracer*]

embrasure *noun* **1** an opening in the wall of a castle, etc for shooting through. **2** an opening in a thick wall for a door or window, with angled sides which make it narrower on the outside. [18c: from French *embraser* to splay]

embrocation *noun* a lotion for rubbing into the skin, eg as a treatment for sore or pulled muscles. [16c: from Greek *embroche* lotion]

embroider *verb* **1** to decorate (cloth) with sewn designs. **2** to make (a story, etc) more interesting by adding details, usu untrue ones. [15c: from French *embroder*]

embroidery *noun* (***-ies***) **1** the art or practice of sewing designs on to cloth. **2** decorative needlework. **3** articles decorated with this work. **4** the addition of details, usu false ones, to a story, etc.

embroil *verb* to involve in a dispute or argument. ▪ **embroilment** *noun*. [17c: from French *embrouiller* to throw into confusion]

embryo /'ɛmbrɪoʊ/ *noun, biol* **1** in animals: the developing young organism until hatching or birth. **2** in humans: the developing young organism during the first seven weeks after conception (compare **fetus**). **3** anything in its earliest stages. [16c: from Greek *embryon*]

embryology *noun* the scientific study of embryos. [19c]

embryonic *adj* in an early stage of development.

emend *verb* to edit (a text), removing errors and making improvements. ▪ **emendation** *noun*. [18c: from Latin *emendare*]

emerald *noun* **1** a deep green variety of **beryl**, highly valued as a gemstone. **2** (*also* **emerald green**) its colour. [13c: from French *esmeralde*]

emerge *verb, intr* **1** to come out from hiding or into view. **2** to become known or apparent. **3** to survive a difficult or dangerous situation. ▪ **emergence** *noun*. ▪ **emergent** *adj*. [17c: from Latin *emergere* to rise up from]

emergency *noun* (***-ies***) **1** an unexpected and serious happening which calls for immediate and determined action. **2** **a** a serious injury needing immediate medical treatment; **b** a patient suffering such an injury.

emergency room *noun, N Am* (abbrev **ER**) the department in a hospital which deals with accidents and emergencies.

emeritus /ɪ'mɛrɪtəs/ *adj, often following its noun* retired or honourably discharged from office, but retaining a former title as an honour: *professor emeritus*. [19c: Latin, meaning 'having served one's term']

emery *noun* (***-ies***) a hard mineral, usu used in powder form, for polishing or abrading. [15c: from French *esmeril*]

emery board *noun* a strip of card coated with emery powder or some other abrasive, for filing one's nails.

emetic *adj, med* making one vomit. ▸ *noun* an emetic medicine. [17c: from Greek *emeein* to vomit]

EMF *abbrev* (*also* **emf**) electromotive force.

emigrate *verb, intr* to leave one's native country and settle in another. Compare **immigrate**. ▪ **emigrant** *noun, adj*. ▪ **emigration** *noun*. [18c: from Latin *emigrare* to move from a place]

émigré /ˈɛmɪgreɪ/ *noun* (*émigrés* /-greɪz/) a person who has emigrated, usu for political reasons. [18c: French]

eminence *noun* **1** honour, distinction or prestige. **2** an area of high ground. [17c: from Latin *eminere* to stand out]

IDIOMS **Your** *or* **His Eminence** (*Your or Their Eminences*) a title of honour used in speaking to or about a cardinal.

éminence grise /eminɑ̃s griz/ *noun* (*éminences grises* /eminɑ̃s griz/) a person who has great influence over a ruler or government, etc, without occupying an official position of power. [17c: French, literally 'grey eminence', first applied to Père Joseph, private secretary to Cardinal Richelieu]

eminent *adj* **1** famous and admired. **2** distinguished; outstanding. ▪ **eminently** *adv* **1** very. **2** obviously. [15c: from Latin *eminere* to stand out]

emir /ɛˈmɪə(r)/ *noun* a title given to various Muslim rulers. ▪ **emirate** *noun*. [17c: French, from Arabic *amir* ruler]

emissary /ˈɛmɪsərɪ/ *noun* (*-ies*) a person sent on a mission, esp on behalf of a government. [17c: from Latin *emissarius*]

emission *noun* **1** the act of emitting. **2** something emitted. [17c: from Latin *emissio* a sending out]

emit *verb* (*emitted, emitting*) to give out (light, heat, a smell, etc). [17c: from Latin *emittere* to send out]

emollient *adj* **1** *med* softening or soothing the skin. **2** *formal* advocating a calmer, more peaceful attitude. ▸ *noun, med* a substance which softens or soothes the skin. [17c: from Latin *emolliens*]

emolument *noun, formal* (*often* **emoluments**) money earned or otherwise gained through a job or position, eg salary or fees. [15c: from Latin *emolumentum*]

emote *verb, intr, derog informal* to display exaggerated or insincere emotion. [Early 20c]

emoticon *noun, comput* a combination of characters used in e-mails to express an emotional reaction, eg :-) for happiness or laughter. [From *emotion* + *icon*]

emotion *noun* a strong feeling. ▪ **emotionless** *adj*. [16c: from Latin *emovere* to stir up or disturb]

emotional *adj* **1** referring or relating to the emotions. **2** causing or expressing emotion. **3** of a person: tending to express emotions easily or excessively. **4** *often derog* based on emotions, rather than rational thought: *an emotional response*. ▪ **emotionally** *adv*.

emotive *adj* tending or designed to excite emotion.

empathize *or* **-ise** *verb, intr* (*usu* **empathize with sb**) to share their feelings; to feel empathy. [20c]

empathy *noun* the ability to share, understand and feel another person's feelings. ▪ **empathetic** *or* **empathic** *adj* able to share others' feelings. [Early 20c: from Greek *empatheia* passion or affection]

emperor *noun* the male ruler of an empire. See also **empress**. [13c: from French *emperere*]

emphasis *noun* (*-ses* /-siːz/) **1** (*usu* **emphasis on sth**) special importance or attention given to it. **2** greater force or loudness on certain words or parts of words to show that they are important or have a special meaning. **3** force or firmness of expression. [16c: Greek]

emphasize *or* **-ise** *verb* to put emphasis on something. [19c]

emphatic *adj* **1** expressed with or expressing emphasis. **2** of a person: speaking firmly and forcefully. ▪ **emphatically** *adv*. [18c: from Greek *emphatikos*]

emphysema /ɛmfɪˈsiːmə/ *noun, pathol* the presence of air in the body tissues. [17c: Latin, from Greek *emphysaein* to swell]

empire *noun* **1** a group of nations or states under the control of a single ruler or ruling power. **2** the period of time during which such control is exercised. **3** a large commercial or industrial organization which controls many separate firms, esp one headed by one person. See also **emperor**, **empress**. [13c: French, from Latin *imperium* command or power]

empire-builder *noun, informal, often derog* someone who seeks to acquire extra personal authority or responsibility, etc, within an organization. ▪ **empire-building** *noun, adj*.

empirical *or* **empiric** *adj* based on experiment, observation or experience, rather than on theory. ▪ **empirically** *adv*. [16c: from Latin *empiricus*, from Greek *empeiria* experience]

empirical formula *noun, chem* a formula showing the simplest possible ratio of atoms in a molecule.

empiricism *noun, philos* the theory or philosophy stating that knowledge can only be gained through experiment and observation. ▪ **empiricist** *noun*. [17c]

emplacement *noun, military* a strongly defended position from which a large gun may be fired. [19c: French]

employ *verb* **1** to give work, usu paid work, to someone. **2** to use. [15c: from French *employer*]

IDIOMS **be in sb's employ** *formal* to be employed by them.

employee *noun* a person who works for another in return for payment.

employer *noun* a person or company that employs workers.

employment *noun* **1** the act of employing or the state of being employed. **2** an occupation, esp regular paid work. Compare **unemployment**.

emporium *noun* (*emporiums or emporia*) *formal* a shop, esp a large one that sells a wide variety of goods. [16c: from Greek *emporion* trading station]

empower *verb* (*usu* **empower sb to do sth**) to give them authority or official permission to do it. [17c]

empress *noun* **1** the female ruler of an empire. **2** the wife or widow of an emperor. [12c: from French *emperesse*]

empty *adj* (*-ier, -iest*) **1** having nothing inside. **2** not occupied, inhabited or furnished. **3** not likely to be satisfied or carried out: *empty promises*. **4** (*usu* **empty of sth**) completely without it: *a life empty of meaning*. ▸ *verb* (*-ies, -ied*) *tr & intr* **1** to make or become empty. **2** to tip, pour or fall out of a container. ▸ *noun* (*-ies*) *informal* an empty container, esp a bottle. ▪ **emptiness** *noun*. [Anglo-Saxon *æmetig* unoccupied]

empty-handed *adj* **1** carrying nothing. **2** having gained or achieved nothing.

empty-headed *adj* foolish or frivolous; having no capacity for serious thought.

EMS *abbrev* European Monetary System.

EMU *abbrev* Economic and Monetary Union (between EU countries).

emu *noun* a large flightless but swift-running Australian bird. [17c: from Portuguese *ema* ostrich]

emulate *verb* **1** to try hard to equal or be better than someone or something. **2** to imitate. **3** *tr & intr* of a computer or a program: to imitate the internal design of another microprocessor-based device. ▪ **emulation** *noun*. [16c: from Latin *aemulari* to rival]

emulator *noun* **1** someone or something that emulates. **2** *comput* a computer or program that imitates the internal design of another device.

emulsifier *noun* a chemical substance that coats the surface of droplets of one liquid so that they can remain dispersed throughout a second liquid (eg margarine or ice cream) forming a stable emulsion.

emulsify *verb* (**-ies, -ied**) *tr & intr* to make or become an emulsion. ▪ **emulsification** *noun*. [19c]

emulsion *noun* **1** *chem* a **colloid** consisting of a stable mixture of two **immiscible** liquids (such as oil and water), in which small droplets of one liquid are dispersed uniformly throughout the other, eg salad cream and low-fat spreads. **2** *photog* the light-sensitive material used to coat photographic film and paper, etc. **3** emulsion paint. **4** a liquid mixture containing globules of fat or resinous or bituminous material. ▸ *verb, informal* to apply emulsion paint to something. [17c: from Latin *emulgere* from *mulgere* to milk]

emulsion paint *noun* water-based paint.

en- *prefix, forming verbs, signifying* **1** to put into, on or onto a specified thing: *entrust* • *enthrone*. **2** to cause someone or something to be a specified thing: *enrich* • *enfeeble*. **3** intensifying the meaning of the base verb: *entangle* • *enliven*. See also **em-**.

-en *suffix* **1** *forming verbs, signifying* **a** to make or become a specified thing, or make or become more so: *deepen* • *sadden*; **b** to give or endow with a specified thing: *strengthen*. **2** *forming adjectives, signifying* made or consisting of a specified thing: *wooden*. Compare **-ent**.

enable *verb* **1** to make someone able; to give them the necessary means, power or authority (to do something). **2** to make something possible. [15c]

enact *verb* **1** to act or perform something on stage or in real life. **2** to establish by law. ▪ **enactment** *noun*. [15c]

enamel *noun* **1** a hardened coloured glass-like substance applied as a decorative or protective covering to metal or glass. **2** any paint or varnish which gives a finish similar to this. **3** the hard white covering of the teeth. ▸ *verb* (***enamelled, enamelling***; *US* ***enameled, enameling***) to cover or decorate something with enamel. [15c: from French *enameler*]

enamoured *or* (*N Am*) **enamored** *adj* **1** (*usu* **enamoured with sb**) *formal or literary* in love with them. **2** (*usu* **enamoured of sth**) very fond of it, pleased with it, or enthusiastic about it. [14c: from French *amour* love]

en bloc /ɑ̃blɔk/ *adv* all together; as one unit. [19c: French, meaning 'in a block']

enc. *abbrev* **1** enclosed. **2** enclosure.

encamp *verb, tr & intr* to settle in a camp. ▪ **encampment** *noun*. [16c]

encapsulate *or* **incapsulate** *verb* **1** to express concisely the main points or ideas of something, or capture the essence of it. **2** to enclose something in, or as if in, a capsule. ▪ **encapsulation** *noun*. [Early 20c]

encase *verb* **1** to enclose something in, or as if in, a case. **2** to surround or cover. ▪ **encasement** *noun*. [17c]

-ence *suffix, forming nouns corresponding to adjectives in* **-ent**, *signifying* **1** a state or quality, or an action, etc which shows a state or quality: *confidence* • *diligence*. **2** an action: *reference*. [French, from Latin *-entia*]

encephalitis /ɛnsɛfəˈlaɪtɪs, ɛŋkɛ-/ *noun, pathol* inflammation of the brain. [19c]

encephalogram see **electroencephalogram**

encephalograph see **electroencephalograph**

enchant *verb* **1** to charm or delight. **2** to put a magic spell on someone or something. ▪ **enchanted** *adj*. ▪ **enchanting** *adj*. ▪ **enchantment** *noun*. [14c: from French *enchanter*]

enchilada /ɛntʃɪˈlɑːdə/ *noun, cookery* a Mexican dish consisting of a flour tortilla with a meat filling, served with a chilli-flavoured sauce. [19c: from Spanish *enchilar* to season with chilli]

encircle *verb* to surround, or form a circle round, something. ▪ **encirclement** *noun*. [16c]

enclave *noun* **1** a small country or state entirely surrounded by foreign territory. **2** a distinct racial or cultural group isolated within a country. [19c: French, from Latin *inclavare* to lock up]

enclose *or* **inclose** *verb* **1** to put something inside a letter or in its envelope. **2** to shut in or surround.

enclosure *or* **inclosure** *noun* **1** the process of enclosing or being enclosed, esp with reference to common land. **2** land surrounded by a fence or wall. **3** an enclosed space at a sporting event. **4** an additional paper or other item included with a letter. **5** *hist* the division of shared land into privately-owned plots. [16c]

encode *verb* to express something in, or convert it into, code. ▪ **encoder** *noun*. [Early 20c]

encomium *noun* (***encomiums*** *or* ***encomia*** /ɪŋˈkoumɪə/) a formal speech or piece of writing praising someone. [16c: Latin, from Greek *enkomion* song of praise]

encompass *verb* **1** to include or contain something, esp to contain a wide range or coverage of something. **2** to surround something. [16c]

encore *noun* a repetition of a performance, or an additional performed item, after the end of a concert, etc. ▸ *exclam* an enthusiastic call from the audience for such a performance. [18c: French, meaning 'again']

encounter *verb* **1** to meet someone or something, esp unexpectedly. **2** to meet with (difficulties, etc). **3** to meet someone in battle or conflict. ▸ *noun* **1** a chance meeting. **2** a fight or battle. [13c: from French *encontrer*]

encourage *verb* **1** to give support, confidence or hope to someone. **2** to urge someone to do something. ▪ **encouragement** *noun*. [15c: from French *encourager*]

encroach *verb, intr* (*usu* **encroach on sb** *or* **sth**) **1** to intrude or extend gradually (on someone else's land, etc). **2** to overstep proper or agreed limits. ▪ **en-**

croachment *noun.* [14c: from French *encrochier* to seize]

encrust *or* **incrust** *verb* to cover something with a thick hard coating, eg of jewels or ice. ▪ **encrustation** *noun.* [17c: from Latin *incrustare*]

encrypt *verb* to put information (eg computer data or TV signals) into a coded form. [20c]

encumber *verb* **1** to prevent the free and easy movement of someone or something; to hamper or impede. **2** to burden someone or something with a load or debt. [14c: from French *encombrer* to block]

encumbrance *or* **incumbrance** *noun* an impediment, hindrance or burden.

-ency *suffix, forming nouns, indicating* a state or quality, or something which shows a state or quality: *efficiency* • *inconsistency.* [From Latin *-entia*]

encyclical /ɛn'sɪklɪkəl/ *noun, RC Church* a letter sent by the Pope to all Roman Catholic bishops. [17c: from Greek *enkyklios*]

encyclopedia *or* **encyclopaedia** *noun* a reference work containing information on every branch of knowledge, or on one particular branch, usu arranged in alphabetical order. ▪ **encyclopedic** *adj* of knowledge: full and detailed. [16c: from Greek *enkyklios paideia* general education]

encyst *verb, tr & intr, biol* to enclose or become enclosed in a cyst. ▪ **encysted** *adj.* [19c]

end *noun* **1** the point or part farthest from the beginning, or either of the points or parts farthest from the middle, where something stops. **2** a finish or conclusion. **3** (**the end**) *informal* the last straw; the limit. **4** a piece left over: *a cigarette end.* **5** death or destruction: *meet one's end.* **6** an object or purpose: *The end justifies the means.* **7** *sport* one of the two halves of a pitch or court defended by a team or player, etc. **8** the part of a project, etc for which one is responsible: *had a few problems at their end.* ▸ *verb, tr & intr* **1** to finish or cause something to finish. **2** *intr* to reach a conclusion or cease to exist. ▪ **ended** *adj* **1** brought to an end. **2** *in compounds* having ends of a specified kind. [Anglo-Saxon *ende*]

IDIOMS **at the end of one's tether** exasperated; at the limit of one's endurance. **in the end** finally; after much discussion or work, etc. **make ends meet** to live within one's income and avoid debts. **no end** *informal* very much. **no end of people** *or* **things** very many; a lot. **on end 1** vertical; standing straight up. **2** continuously; without a pause.

PHRASAL VERBS **end up** *informal* **1** to arrive or find oneself eventually or finally. **2** to finish.

endanger *verb* to put someone or something in danger; to expose them to possible loss or injury. [16c]

endangered species *noun* any plant or animal species that is in danger of extinction.

endear *verb* (*usu* **endear sb to sb else**) to make them beloved or liked. ▪ **endearing** *adj.*

endearment *noun* **1** a word or phrase expressing affection. **2** a caress.

endeavour *or* (*N Am*) **endeavor** *verb* (*usu* **endeavour to do sth**) to try to do it, esp seriously and with effort. ▸ *noun* a determined attempt or effort. [14c as *endeveren* to exert oneself]

endemic *adj* **1** of a disease, etc: regularly occurring in a particular area or among a particular group of people. **2** *biol* of a plant or animal: native to, or restricted to, a particular area. [18c: from Greek *endemios* native]

ending *noun* **1** the end, esp of a story or poem, etc. **2** *grammar* the end part of a word, esp an **inflection**.

endive /'ɛndɪv/ *noun* a plant, related to chicory, whose crisp leaves are used in salads. [15c: French]

endless *adj* having no end, or seeming to have no end. ▪ **endlessly** *adv.*

endmost *adj* farthest; nearest the end.

endo- /ɛndoʊ-, ɛndɒ-/ *or* (before a vowel) **end-** *combining form* internal; inside. See also **ecto-**, **ento-**, **exo-**. [From Greek *endon* within]

endocarp *noun, botany* the inner layer of the pericarp of a fruit, usu hard, eg a plum stone. [19c]

endocrine *adj* of a gland: ductless, and producing and secreting one or more hormones directly into the bloodstream. See also **exocrine**. [Early 20c: from Greek *krinein* to separate]

endometrium /ɛndoʊ'miːtrɪəm/ *noun, anatomy* the mucous membrane which lines the **uterus**. [19c: from Greek *metra* womb]

endomorph *noun* a person of rounded or plump body build. Compare **ectomorph**, **mesomorph**. ▪ **endomorphic** *adj.* [1940s]

endoplasm *noun, biol* the central portion of the cytoplasm of a cell.

endorphin *noun, biochem* any of a group of chemical compounds that occur naturally in the brain and have similar pain-relieving properties to morphine. [20c]

endorse *or* **indorse** *verb* **1** to sign the back of (a document, esp the back of a cheque) to specify oneself or another person as payee. **2** to make a note of an offence on (a driving licence). **3** to state one's approval of or support for something. ▪ **endorsement** *noun.* [15c: from Latin *in* on + *dorsum* back]

endoscope *noun, med* a long thin flexible instrument containing bundles of optical fibres and having a light at one end, used for viewing internal body cavities and organs. ▪ **endoscopic** *adj.* ▪ **endoscopy** *noun* (*-ies*). [19c]

endoskeleton *noun, zool* in vertebrates: an internal skeleton made of bone or cartilage. [19c]

endosperm *noun, biol* nutritive tissue in the seed of some plants. ▪ **endospermic** *adj.* [19c]

endothermic reaction *noun, chem* any process, especially a chemical reaction, that involves the absorption of heat. Compare **exothermic reaction**. [19c]

endow *verb* **1** to provide a source of income for (a hospital or place of learning, etc), often by a bequest. **2** (*often* **be endowed with sth**) to have a quality or ability, etc. [14c: from French *endouer*]

endowment *noun* **1** a sum endowed. **2** a quality or skill, etc with which a person is endowed.

endowment assurance *or* **endowment insurance** *noun* a form of insurance to provide for payment of a set sum at a certain date, or earlier in the event of death.

endowment mortgage *noun* a form of mortgage in which the capital sum is repaid by the eventual proceeds from **endowment assurance**.

endpaper *noun, publishing, etc* one of the two leaves at the front or back of a hardback book, fixed with paste to the inside of the cover.

endurance *noun* **1** the capacity for, or the state of, patient toleration. **2** the ability to withstand physical hardship or strain.

endure *verb* **1** to bear something patiently; to put up with it. **2** *intr, formal* to continue to exist; to last. ▪ **enduring** *adj.* [14c: from French *endurer*]

endways *or* (*esp N Am*) **endwise** *adv* **1** with the end forward or upward. **2** end to end.

enema /ˈɛnəmə/ *noun* (***enemas*** *or* ***enemata*** /ɛˈnɛmətə/) *med* **1** the injection of a liquid into the rectum, eg to clean it out or to introduce medication. **2** the liquid injected. [15c: Latin, from Greek *enienai* to send in]

enemy *noun* (***-ies***) **1** a person who is actively opposed to someone else. **2** a hostile nation or force, or a member of it. **3** an opponent or adversary. **4** a person or thing that opposes or acts against someone or something: *Cleanliness is the enemy of disease.* ▸ *adj* hostile; belonging to a hostile nation or force. [13c: from French *enemi*]

energetic *adj* having or displaying energy; forceful or vigorous. ▪ **energetically** *adv.* [18c: from Greek *energetikos*]

energize *or* **-ise** *verb* **1** to stimulate, invigorate or enliven. **2** to provide energy for the operation of (a machine, etc). ▪ **energizer** *noun.* [18c]

energy *noun* (***-ies***) **1** the capacity for vigorous activity; liveliness or vitality. **2** force or forcefulness. **3** *physics* the capacity to do work. [16c: from Greek *energeia*]

enervate *verb* **1** to take energy or strength from something. **2** to deprive someone of moral or mental vigour. ▪ **enervating** *adj.* ▪ **enervation** *noun.* [17c: from Latin *enervare* to weaken]

enfant terrible /*French* ɑ̃fɑ̃tɛʀibl/ *noun* (***enfants terribles*** /ɑ̃fɑ̃tɛʀibl/) a person with a reputation for provocative or embarrassing behaviour in public. [19c: French, meaning 'dreadful child']

enfeeble *verb, formal* to make someone weak. [14c]

enfilade *noun, military* a continuous burst of gunfire sweeping from end to end across a line of enemy soldiers. [18c: French, from *enfiler* to thread on a string]

enfold *or* **infold** *verb* **1** to wrap up or enclose. **2** to embrace. [16c]

enforce *verb* **1** to cause (a law or decision) to be carried out. **2** (*usu* **enforce sth on sb**) to impose (one's will, etc) on them. **3** to press (an argument). **4** to persist in (a demand). ▪ **enforceable** *adj.* ▪ **enforcement** *noun.*

enfranchise *verb, formal* **1** to give someone the right to vote in elections. **2** to set someone free, esp from slavery. ▪ **enfranchisement** *noun.* [16c: from French *enfranchir* to set free]

Eng. *abbrev* **1** England. **2** English.

engage *verb* **1** to take someone on as a worker. **2** to book or reserve (eg a table or room). **3** to involve or occupy (a person or their attention): *She engaged me in small talk.* **4** *tr & intr, military* to come or bring something into battle: *engage with the enemy.* **5** *tr & intr* to cause part of a machine (eg the gears) to fit into and lock with another part. [15c: from French *engager*]

engaged *adj* **1** (*usu* **engaged to sb**) bound by a promise to marry them. **2** of a room or a telephone line, etc: not free or vacant; occupied; in use. **3** geared together; interlocked.

engagement *noun* **1** the act of engaging or state of being engaged. **2** a firm agreement between two people to marry. **3** an arrangement made in advance; an appointment. **4** *military* a battle.

engaging *adj* charming; attractive. ▪ **engagingly** *adv.*

engender *verb* to produce or cause (esp feelings or emotions). [14c: from French *engendrer*]

engine *noun* **1** a machine that is used to convert some form of energy into mechanical energy that can be used to perform useful work. **2** a railway locomotive. **3** *formal* a device or instrument: *an engine of destruction.* [13c: from French *engin*]

engineer *noun* **1** someone who designs, makes, or works with machinery, including electrical equipment. **2** an officer in charge of a ship's engines. **3** *N Am* the driver of a locomotive. **4** someone who contrives to bring something about: *the engineer of the scheme.* **5** a person, esp a member of the armed forces, who designs and builds military apparatus and is trained in construction work. ▸ *verb* **1** *often derog* to arrange or bring something about by skill or deviousness. **2** to design or construct something as an engineer. [14c: from French *engignier* to contrive]

engineering *noun* the application of scientific knowledge, esp that concerned with matter and energy, to the practical problems of design, construction, operation and maintenance of devices encountered in everyday life.

English *adj* **1** belonging or relating to England or its inhabitants. **2** relating to the English language. ▸ *noun* **1** (**the English**) the citizens or inhabitants of, or people born in, England, considered as a group. See also **Briton**. **2** the native language of Britain, N America, much of the Commonwealth and some other countries. ▪ **Englishman** *and* **Englishwoman** *noun.* [Anglo-Saxon *Englisc*, from *Engle* the Angles]

engorged *adj, pathol* congested with blood. ▪ **engorgement** *noun.* [16c: from 15c *engorge* to gorge]

engrain, engrained variant of **ingrain, ingrained**

engrave *verb* **1** to carve (letters or designs) on stone, metal, etc. **2** to decorate (stone, etc) in this way. **3** to fix or impress something deeply on the mind, etc. ▪ **engraver** *noun.* [16c, from obsolete *grave* to carve]

engraving *noun* **1** the art or process of carving or incising designs on wood or metal, etc, esp for the purpose of printing impressions from them. **2** a print taken from an engraved metal plate, etc. **3** a piece of stone, etc decorated with carving.

engross *verb* to take up someone's attention completely. [17c: from French *engrosser*, from *en gros* completely]

engulf *verb* **1** to swallow something up completely. **2** to overwhelm. [16c]

enhance *verb* to improve or increase the value, quality or intensity of something (esp something already good). ▪ **enhancement** *noun.* [14c: from French *enhauncer*]

enigma *noun* **1** a puzzle or riddle. **2** a mysterious person, thing or situation. ▪ **enigmatic** *adj.* [16c: Latin]

enjoin *verb, formal* **1** to order or command someone to do something. **2** *law* (*usu* **enjoin sb from sth**) to forbid them to do it, by means of an injunction. **3**

(*usu* **enjoin sth on sb**) to demand behaviour of a certain kind from them: *enjoin politeness on one's children*. [17c: from French *enjoindre*]

enjoy *verb* **1** to find pleasure in something. **2** to have, experience or have the benefit of something good: *The room enjoys sunlight all day.* ▪ **enjoyable** *adj.* ▪ **enjoyment** *noun.* [14c: from French *enjoir*; see **joy**]

enlarge *verb* **1** *tr & intr* to make or become larger. **2** to reproduce (a photograph, etc) in a larger form. **3** *intr* (*usu* **enlarge on** *or* **upon sth**) to speak or write about it at greater length or in greater detail. ▪ **enlarger** *noun.* [14c]

enlargement *noun* **1** something enlarged, especially a photographic print larger than the standard or original print. **2** the act of enlarging or the state of being enlarged. **3** *maths* a transformation that produces a larger figure with its dimensions in the same ratio. Compare **reflection**, **rotation**, **translation**.

enlighten *verb* **1** to give more information to someone. **2** to free someone from ignorance or superstition. **3** to make someone aware or uplift them by knowledge or religion. ▪ **enlightened** *adj.* [Anglo-Saxon *inlihtan*]

enlightenment *noun* **1** the act of enlightening or the state of being enlightened. **2** freedom from ignorance or superstition. **3** (**the Enlightenment**) the philosophical movement originating in 18c France, with a belief in reason and human progress, and a questioning of tradition and authority.

enlist *verb* **1** *intr & tr* to join or be enrolled in one of the armed forces. **2** to obtain the support and help of someone; to obtain (support and help). ▪ **enlistment** *noun.* [16c]

enlisted man *or* **enlisted woman** *noun, N Am, esp US* a member of the armed forces below the rank of officer.

enliven *verb* to make active or more active, lively or cheerful. [17c]

en masse /*French* ɑ̃mas/ *adv* all together; as a mass or group. [18c: French, literally 'in a body']

enmesh *verb* to catch or trap something in a net, or as if in a net; to entangle. [17c]

enmity *noun* (**-*ies***) **1** the state or quality of being an enemy. **2** ill-will; hostility. [13c: from French *enemistie*]

ennoble *verb* **1** to make something noble or dignified. **2** to make someone a member of the nobility. [15c]

ennui /ɒ'nwiː/ *noun, literary* boredom or discontent caused by a lack of activity or excitement. [18c: French]

enormity *noun* (**-*ies***) **1** outrageousness or wickedness. **2** an outrageous or wicked act. **3** immenseness or vastness. [15c: from Latin *enormitas*]

enormous *adj* extremely large; huge. ▪ **enormously** *adv.* [16c: from Latin *enormis* unusual]

enough *adj* in the number or quantity needed; sufficient: *enough food to eat.* ▸ *adv* **1** to the necessary degree or extent. **2** fairly: *She's pretty enough, I suppose.* **3** quite: *Oddly enough, I can't remember.* ▸ *pronoun* the amount needed. [Anglo-Saxon *genoh*]

en passant /ɑ̃pasɑ̃/ *adv* in passing; by the way. [17c: French]

enquire, enquiring, enquiry see **inquire**, etc

enrage *verb* to make someone extremely angry. [15c]

enrapture *verb* to give intense pleasure or joy to someone. ▪ **enraptured** *or* **enrapt** *adj.* [18c]

enrich *verb* **1** to make something rich or richer, esp better or stronger in quality, value or flavour, etc. **2** to make wealthy or wealthier. **3** to fertilize (soil, etc). **4** *physics* to increase the proportion of one or more particular isotopes in a mixture of the isotopes of an element. ▪ **enriched** *adj.* ▪ **enrichment** *noun.* [14c]

enrol *or* (*US*) **enroll** *verb* (***enrolled, enrolling***) **1** to add the name of (a person) to a list or roll, eg of members or pupils. **2** to secure the membership or participation of someone. **3** *intr* to add one's own name to such a list; to become a member. ▪ **enrolment** *noun.* [14c: from French *enroller*]

en route *adv* on the way: *stop en route for a meal.* [18c: French]

ensconce *verb, literary or humorous* (*often* **be ensconced**) **1** to settle comfortably or safely. **2** to hide safely. [16c: from *sconce* a small fort]

ensemble /ɒn'sɒmbəl; *French* ɑ̃sɑ̃bl/ *noun* **1** a small group of (usu classical) musicians who regularly perform together. **2** a passage in opera or ballet, etc performed by all the singers, musicians or dancers together. **3** a set of items of clothing worn together; an outfit. **4** all the parts of a thing considered as a whole. [15c: French, literally 'together']

enshrine *verb* **1** to enter and protect (a right or idea, etc) in the laws or constitution of a state, constitution of an organization, etc. **2** to place something in a shrine.

enshroud *verb* **1** to cover something completely; to hide something by covering it up. **2** to cover something or someone in a shroud. [16c]

ensign /'ɛnsaɪn, *in senses 1 and 2 also* 'ɛnsən/ *noun* **1** the flag of a nation or regiment. **2** a coloured flag with a smaller union flag in one corner. **3** *hist* the lowest rank of officer in the infantry, or an officer of this rank. **4** *N Am, esp US* **a** the lowest rank in the navy; **b** an officer of this rank. [14c: from Latin *insignia*, from *signum* sign]

enslave *verb* to make someone into a slave. ▪ **enslavement** *noun.* [17c]

ensnare *verb* to catch something or someone in, or as if in, a trap; to trick or lead them dishonestly (into doing something). [16c]

ensue *verb* (*usu* **ensue from sth**) *intr* **1** to follow it; to happen after it. **2** to result from it. ▪ **ensuing** *adj.* [14c: from French *ensuer*]

en suite *adv, adj* forming, or attached as part of, a single unit or set. ▸ *noun, informal* an en suite bathroom. [19c: French, literally 'in sequence']

ensure *verb* **1** to make something certain; to assure or guarantee it. **2** to make (a thing or person) safe and secure. See also **insure**. [14c: from French *enseurer*]

ENT *abbrev, med* ear, nose and throat.

ent- see **ento-**

-ent *suffix* **1** *forming adjectives corresponding to nouns in* **-ence**, *signifying* acting, causing an action, or existing in a certain state: *resident* • *different*. **2** *forming nouns, signifying* an agent. Compare **-en**. [From Latin *-ens*]

entablature *noun, archit* the part of a classical building directly supported by the columns. [17c: French]

entail *verb* **1** to have something as a necessary result or requirement. **2** (*usu* **entail sth on sb**) *law* to bequeath (property) to one's descendants, not allowing them the option to sell it. ▪ **entailment** *noun*. [14c: from **tail**[2]]

entangle *verb* **1** to cause something to get caught in some obstacle, eg a net. **2** to involve someone or something in difficulties. **3** to make something complicated or confused. ▪ **entanglement** *noun*. [17c]

entente /ɑ̃'tɑ̃t/ *noun* **1** an **entente cordiale**. **2** those who are collectively party to an **entente cordiale**. [19c: French, literally 'intent' or 'understanding']

entente cordiale /ɑ̃'tɑ̃t kɔːdɪ'ɑːl/ *noun* (***ententes cordiales***) a friendly agreement or relationship between nations or states. [19c: French]

enter *verb* **1** *tr & intr* to go or come in or into (eg a room). **2** *tr & intr* to register (another person, oneself, one's work, etc) in a competition. **3** to record something in a book, diary, etc. **4** to join (a profession or society, etc). **5** to submit or present something: *enter a complaint*. **6** *intr, theatre* to come on to the stage. [13c: from French *entrer*]

PHRASAL VERBS **enter into sth 1** to begin to take part in it. **2** to become involved in it; to participate actively or enthusiastically in it. **3** to agree to be associated in or bound by (eg an agreement).

enteric /ɛn'tɛrɪk/ *adj, anatomy* intestinal. [19c: from Greek *enteron* intestine]

enteritis /ɛntə'raɪtɪs/ *noun, pathol* inflammation of the intestines, esp the small intestine. [Early 19c]

enterprise *noun* **1** a project or undertaking, esp one that requires boldness and initiative. **2** boldness and initiative. **3** a business firm. [15c: from French *entreprendre* to undertake]

enterprise zone *noun* an economically depressed area in which the government encourages companies to invest by giving them financial incentives.

enterprising *adj* showing boldness and initiative.

entertain *verb* **1** to provide amusement or recreation for someone. **2** *tr & intr* to give hospitality to (a guest), esp in the form of a meal. **3** to consider or be willing to adopt (an idea or suggestion, etc). ▪ **entertainer** *noun* a person who provides amusement, esp one who does so as their profession. [15c: from French *entretenir* to maintain or hold together]

entertaining *adj* interesting and amusing; giving entertainment. ▸ *noun* provision of entertainment.

entertainment *noun* **1** something that entertains, eg a theatrical show. **2** the act of entertaining. **3** amusement or recreation.

enthalpy /ɛn'θalpɪ, 'ɛnθəlpɪ/ *noun, chem* the amount of heat energy possessed by a substance, expressed per unit mass. [20c: from Greek *enthalpein* to warm]

enthral or (*esp US*) **enthrall** *verb* (***enthralled, enthralling***) to fascinate; to hold the attention or grip the imagination of someone. ▪ **enthralment** *noun*. [16c]

enthrone *verb* to place someone on a throne. ▪ **enthronement** *noun*. [17c]

enthuse *verb, tr & intr* to be enthusiastic, or make someone enthusiastic. [19c]

enthusiasm *noun* lively or passionate interest or eagerness. [17c: from Greek *enthousiasmos* zeal inspired by a god]

enthusiast *noun* someone filled with enthusiasm, esp for a particular subject; a fan or devotee. ▪ **enthusiastic** *adj*. ▪ **enthusiastically** *adv*.

entice *verb* to tempt or persuade, by arousing hopes or desires or by promising a reward. ▪ **enticement** *noun*. ▪ **enticing** *adj*. [13c: from French *enticier* to provoke]

entire *adj* **1** whole or complete. **2** absolute or total. ▪ **entirely** *adv*. [14c: from French *entier*]

entirety *noun* (***-ies***) completeness; wholeness; the whole. [16c]

IDIOMS **in its entirety** totally; taken as a whole.

entitle *verb* **1** to give (someone) a right to have or to do (something). **2** to give a title or name to (a book, etc). ▪ **entitlement** *noun* having a right to something. [14c]

entity *noun* (***-ies***) **1** something that has a real existence. **2** the essential nature of something. [16c: from Latin *entitas*, from *ens* thing that exists]

ento- or (before a vowel) **ent-** *combining form, signifying* inside. See also **ecto-**, **endo-**, **exo-**. [From Greek *entos* within]

entomb *verb* **1** to put (a body) in a tomb. **2** to cover, bury or hide someone or something as if in a tomb. [16c]

entomology *noun* the scientific study of insects. ▪ **entomological** *adj*. ▪ **entomologist** *noun*. [18c: from Greek *entomon* insect]

entourage *noun* a group of followers or assistants, esp one accompanying a famous or important person. [19c: French, from *entourer* to surround]

entrails *plural noun* **1** the internal organs of a person or animal. **2** *literary* the inner parts of anything. [13c: from French *entrailles*]

entrance[1] /'ɛntrəns/ *noun* **1** a way in, eg a door. **2** *formal* the act of entering. **3** the right to enter. [16c: French, from *entrer* to enter]

entrance[2] /ɪn'trɑːns/ *verb* **1** to grip or captivate someone's attention and imagination. **2** to put someone into a trance. ▪ **entrancement** *noun*. ▪ **entrancing** *adj* gripping the imagination; fascinating; delightful. [16c]

entrant *noun* someone who enters something, esp an examination, a competition or a profession. [17c]

entrap *verb* **1** to catch something in a trap. **2** to trick someone into doing something. ▪ **entrapment** *noun*. [16c]

entreat *verb, tr & intr* to ask passionately or desperately; to beg. [15c: from French *entraiter*]

entreaty *noun* (***-ies***) a passionate or desperate request.

entrecôte /'ɒntrəkoʊt/ *noun, cookery* a boneless steak cut from between two ribs. [19c: French]

entrée /'ɒntreɪ/ *noun* **1** a small dish served after the fish course and before the main course at a formal dinner. **2** *chiefly US* a main course. **3** *formal* the right of admission or entry. [18c: French, literally 'entrance']

entrench or **intrench** *verb* **1** to fix or establish something firmly, often too firmly: *deeply entrenched ideas*. **2** to fortify something with trenches dug around. ▪ **entrenchment** *noun*. [16c]

entrepreneur *noun* someone who engages in business enterprises, often with some personal financial risk. ▪ **entrepreneurial** *adj*. [19c: French, literally 'someone who undertakes']

entropy /'ɛntrəpɪ/ *noun* (***-ies***) *physics* a measure of the amount of disorder in a system, or of the unavailability of energy for doing work. [19c: from German *Entropie*, from Greek *en* in + *tropos* turn or change]

entrust *or* **intrust** *verb* (*usu* **entrust sth to sb,** *or* **sb with sth**) to give it to them to take care of or deal with. [17c]

entry *noun* (**-*ies***) **1** the act of coming or going in. **2** the right to enter. **3** a place of entering such as a door or doorway. **4** a person, or the total number of people, entered for a competition, etc. **5** an item written on a list or in a book, etc, or the act of recording an item or items in this way. [14c]

entwine *verb* **1** to wind or twist (two or more things) together. **2** to make something by winding or twisting materials together. [16c]

E-number *noun* any of various identification codes, consisting of the letter E (for European) followed by a number, that are used to denote all food additives, except flavourings, that have been approved by the European Union. [20c]

enumerate *verb* **1** to list one by one. **2** to count. ▪ **enumeration** *noun*. [17c: from Latin *enumerare* to count up]

enumerator *noun* someone who issues and then collects census forms. [19c]

enunciate *verb* **1** *tr & intr* to pronounce words clearly. **2** to state something formally. ▪ **enunciation** *noun*. [17c: from Latin *enuntiare* to announce]

enure see **inure**

enuresis /ɛnjʊəˈriːsɪs/ *noun, pathol* involuntary urination, esp during sleep. [19c: from Greek *en* in + *ouresis* urination]

envelop *verb* (***enveloped, enveloping***) **1** to cover or wrap something or someone completely. **2** to obscure or conceal: *an event enveloped in mystery.* ▪ **envelopment** *noun*. [14c: from French *envoloper*]

envelop, envelope

Be careful not to use the noun spelling **envelope** when you mean the verb **envelop**, or vice versa:

the wrappings that envelop our food
send a self-addressed envelope

envelope *noun* **1** a thin flat sealable paper packet or cover, esp for a letter. **2** a cover or wrapper of any kind. **3** *biol* a plant or animal structure that contains or encloses something. **4** *technical* the glass casing that surrounds an incandescent lamp. [18c: from French *enveloppe*]

enviable *adj* likely to cause envy; highly desirable. ▪ **enviably** *adv*. [17c]

envious *adj* feeling or showing envy. Compare **jealous.** ▪ **enviously** *adv*. [14c]

environment *noun* **1** the surroundings or conditions within which something or someone exists. **2** the natural features which make up the earth, eg land, plants, animals, water, etc. **3** *comput* a program, set of programs or an operating system that allows a particular application to be employed. ▪ **environmental** *adj*. [17c: from French *environnement*]

environment

This word is often misspelt. It has an *n* in the middle. It might help you to remember the following sentence:

*There is **iron** in the env**iron**ment.*

environmentalist *noun* someone who is concerned about the harmful effects of human activity on the environment. ▪ **environmentalism** *noun*. [Early 20c]

environmentally friendly *adj* of a product, eg a detergent: designed to cause as little damage to the environment as possible.

environs *plural noun* surrounding areas, esp the outskirts of a town or city. [17c: from French *environ* around]

envisage *verb* **1** to picture something in the mind. **2** to consider as likely in the future. [19c: from French *envisager*, from *visage* face]

envoy *noun* **1** a diplomat ranking next below an ambassador. **2** a messenger or agent, esp on a diplomatic mission. [17c: from French *envoyer* to send]

envy *noun* (**-*ies***) **1** a feeling of resentment or regretful desire for another person's qualities, better fortune or success. **2** anything that arouses envy: *She is the envy of his friends.* ▸ *verb* (***-ies, -ied***) **1** to feel envy towards someone. **2** to covet; to wish to have something. **3** (**envy sb sth**) to feel envy towards them on account of (their success, etc). [14c: from French *envie*]

enzyme *noun, biochem* a specialized protein molecule that acts as a catalyst for the biochemical reactions that occur in living cells. ▪ **enzymatic** *or* **enzymic** *adj*. [19c: from Greek *zyme* leaven]

Eocene /ˈiːoʊsiːn/ *noun, geol* the second epoch of the **Tertiary** period, lasting from about 54 million to 38 million years ago. ▸ *adj* **1** relating to this epoch. **2** relating to rocks formed during this epoch. [19c: from Greek *eos* dawn + *kainos* new]

eolian harp see **aeolian harp**

eolithic *or* **Eolithic** *adj, archaeol* belonging to the early part of the Stone Age, when crude stone tools were first used. [19c: from Greek *eos* dawn + *lithos* stone]

eon *or* **aeon** *noun* **1** a long period of time; an endless or immeasurable period of time. **2** (*usu* **eon**) *geol* the largest unit of geological time, consisting of a number of **eras**. **3** *astron* a period of a thousand million years. [17c: from Greek *aion*]

-eous *suffix, forming adjectives, signifying* relating to, or of the nature of a specified thing. [From Latin *-eus*]

EP *noun* an extended-play record or compact disc.

epaulette *or* (*chiefly US*) **epaulet** /ɛpəˈlɛt/ *noun* a decoration on the shoulder of a coat or jacket, esp of a military uniform. [18c: from French *épaulette*, from *épaule* shoulder]

épée /ˈeɪpeɪ/ *noun* a sword with a narrow flexible blade, formerly used in duelling, now, with a blunted end, used in fencing. [19c: French]

ephedrine *noun* a drug with similar effects to adrenaline, now mainly used as a nasal decongestant. [19c: from Greek *ephedra* horsetail (the plant)]

ephemera¹ /ɪˈfɛmərə/ *noun* (***ephemeras*** *or* ***ephemerae*** /-riː/) **1** a mayfly. **2** something that lasts or is useful for only a short time; an **ephemeron** (sense 1). [17c: from Latin *ephemerus* lasting only a day]

ephemera² *pl of* **ephemeron**

ephemeral *adj* **1** lasting a short time. **2** *biol* denoting a plant or animal that completes its life cycle within weeks, days or even hours, eg the mayfly. ▸ *noun*, *biol* such a plant or animal. [16c]

ephemeron /ɪˈfɛmərən/ *noun* (***ephemera*** /-mərə/) **1** (*usu* **ephemera**) a thing that is valid or useful only for a short time, esp printed items such as tickets and posters. **2** an insect which lives for one day only. [16c: from Greek *ephemeros* living for a day]

epic *noun* **1** a long narrative poem telling of heroic acts, the birth and death of nations, etc. **2** a long adventure story or film, etc. ▸ *adj* referring to or like an epic. [16c: from Greek *epikos*, from *epos* word or song]

epicene *adj* **1** having characteristics of both sexes, or of neither sex. **2** relating to, or for use by, both sexes. [15c: from Latin *epicoenus* of both genders]

epicentre *or* (*US*) **epicenter** *noun* the point on the Earth's surface which is directly above the **focus** (sense 4) of an earthquake, or directly above or below a nuclear explosion. ▪ **epicentral** *adj.* [19c]

epicure *noun* someone who has refined taste, esp one who enjoys good food and drink. ▪ **epicurean** *noun, adj.* ▪ **epicurism** *noun.* [16c: from Epicurus, the ancient Greek philosopher who believed that the greatest good is pleasure]

epidemic *noun* **1** a sudden outbreak of infectious disease which spreads rapidly and widely in a particular area for a limited period of time. **2** a sudden and extensive spread of anything undesirable. ▸ *adj* referring to or like an epidemic: also used to describe a non-infectious condition such as malnutrition. See also **endemic**. [17c: from Greek *epi* among + *demos* the people]

epidemiology /ɛpɪdiːmɪˈɒlədʒɪ/ *noun, biol* the study of the distribution, effects and causes of diseases in populations. ▪ **epidemiologist** *noun.* [19c]

epidermis *noun, biol* the outermost layer of a plant or animal, which serves to protect the underlying tissues from infection, injury and water loss. ▪ **epidermal** *adj.* [17c: Latin, from Greek *derma* the skin]

epididymis /ɛpɪˈdɪdɪmɪs/ *noun* (***epididymides*** /-dɪˈdɪmɪdiːz/) *anatomy, zool* a long narrow coiled tube in the testis of mammals, birds and reptiles, that stores and conveys sperm to the **vas deferens**. [17c: Greek, from *didymos* a twin or testicle]

epidural *med, adj* situated on, or administered into, the **dura mater**. ▸ *noun* (*in full* **epidural anaesthetic**) the epidural injection of an anaesthetic to remove all sensation below the waist, used esp during childbirth. [19c as *adj*]

epiglottis *noun, anatomy* in mammals: a movable flap of cartilage hanging at the back of the tongue, which closes the opening of the larynx when food or drink is being swallowed. [17c: Greek; see **glottis**]

epigram *noun* **1** a witty or sarcastic saying. **2** a short poem with such an ending. ▪ **epigrammatic** *adj.* [16c: from Greek *epigramma*, from *gramma* writing]

epigraph *noun* **1** a quotation or motto at the beginning of a book or chapter. **2** an inscription on a building. [16c: from Greek *epigraphe*]

epilate *verb* to remove (hair) by any method. ▪ **epilation** *noun.* ▪ **epilator** *noun.* [19c: from French *épiler*, modelled on **depilate**]

epilepsy *noun, pathol* any of a group of disorders of the nervous system characterized by recurring attacks that involve impairment, or sudden loss, of consciousness. See also **grand mal**, **petit mal**. [16c: from Greek *epilepsia*]

epileptic *adj* **1** referring or relating to, or like epilepsy. **2** suffering from epilepsy. ▸ *noun* someone who suffers from epilepsy.

epilogue *or* (*US*) **epilog** *noun* **1** the closing section of a book or programme, etc. **2** **a** a speech addressed to the audience at the end of a play; **b** the actor making this speech. [15c: from Greek *epilogos*]

Epiphany /ɪˈpɪfənɪ/ *noun* (***-ies***) *Christianity* a festival on 6 January which, in the western Churches, commemorates the showing of Christ to the three wise men, and, in the Orthodox and other eastern Churches, the baptism of Christ. [14c: from Greek *epiphaneia* manifestation]

episcopacy /ɪˈpɪskəpəsɪ/ *noun* (***-ies***) **1** the government of the church by bishops. **2** bishops as a group. **3** the position or period of office of a bishop. [17c: from Greek *episkopos* overseer]

episcopal *adj* **1** belonging or relating to bishops. **2** of a church: governed by bishops.

episcopalian *adj* **1** belonging or relating to an episcopal church. **2** advocating church government by bishops. ▸ *noun* a member of an episcopal church, esp the Anglican Church. ▪ **episcopalianism** *noun.*

episcopate /ɪˈpɪskəpət/ *noun* **1** the position or period of office of a bishop. **2** bishops as a group. **3** an area under the care of a bishop; a diocese or bishopric.

episiotomy /ɪpɪzɪˈɒtəmɪ/ *noun* (***-ies***) *med* a surgical cut made at the opening of the vagina during childbirth, to assist the delivery of the baby. [19c]

episode *noun* **1** one of several events or distinct periods making up a longer sequence. **2** one of the separate parts in which a radio or TV serial is broadcast, or a serialized novel is published. **3** any scene or incident forming part of a novel or narrative poem. ▪ **episodic** *adj* **1** consisting of several distinct periods. **2** occurring at intervals; sporadic. [17c: from Greek *epeisodion*]

epistemology /ɪpɪstəˈmɒlədʒɪ/ *noun* the philosophical theory of knowledge. ▪ **epistemological** *adj.* ▪ **epistemologist** *noun.* [19c: from Greek *episteme* knowledge]

epistle *noun* **1** *literary* a letter, esp a long one, dealing with important matters. **2** a novel or poem written in the form of letters. **3** (*usu* **Epistle**) *Christianity* each of the letters written by Christ's Apostles, which form part of the New Testament. ▪ **epistolary** *adj, formal* relating to or consisting of letters. [Anglo-Saxon *epistol*]

epitaph *noun* **1** an inscription on a gravestone. **2** a short commemorative speech or piece of writing in a similar style. [14c: from Greek *epitaphion*, from *taphos* tomb]

epithelium /ɛpɪˈθiːlɪəm/ *noun* (***epithelia***) *anatomy* the layer of tissue that covers all external surfaces of a multicellular animal, and lines internal hollow structures. ▪ **epithelial** *adj.* [18c: from Greek *thele* nipple]

epithet *noun* an adjective or short descriptive phrase which captures the particular quality of the person or thing it describes. [16c: from Greek *epitheton*]

epitome /ɪˈpɪtəmɪ/ *noun* **1** a miniature representation of a larger or wider idea, issue, etc. **2** a person or thing that is the embodiment or a perfect example (of a quality, etc). **3** a summary of a written work. [16c: from Greek *tome* a cut]

epitomize *or* **-ise** *verb* **1** to typify or personify. **2** to make an epitome of something; to shorten. [16c]

EPNS *abbrev* electroplated nickel silver.

epoch /ˈiːpɒk/ *noun* **1** a major division or period of history, or of a person's life, etc, usu marked by some important event. **2** *geol* an interval of geological time representing a subdivision of a period, and during which a particular series of rocks was formed. ▪ **epochal** *adj.* [17c: from Greek *epoche* fixed point]

epoch-making *adj* highly significant or decisive.

eponymous /ɪˈpɒnɪməs/ *adj* of a character in a story, etc: having the name which is used as the title. [19c: from Greek *onyma* a name]

epoxy *chem, adj* consisting of an oxygen atom bonded to two carbon atoms. ▸ *noun* (**-ies**) (*also* **epoxy resin**) any of a group of synthetic thermosetting resins, that form strong adhesive bonds. [Early 20c: from Greek *epi* on or over + **oxygen**]

EPROM /ˈiːprɒm/ *abbrev, comput* erasable programmable read-only memory, a read-only memory in which stored data can be erased and reprogrammed.

epsilon /ɛpˈsaɪlən, ˈɛpsɪlɒn/ *noun* the fifth letter of the Greek alphabet. [14c: Greek *e psilon* bare, or mere, e]

Epsom salts *singular or plural noun* a preparation of magnesium sulphate, used as a medicine, eg for clearing the bowels. [18c: from Epsom in Surrey]

equable /ˈɛkwəbəl/ *adj* **1** of a climate: never showing very great variations or extremes. **2** of a person: even-tempered. ▪ **equably** *adv.* [17c: from Latin *aequabilis*, from *aequus* equal]

equal *adj* **1** the same in size, amount or value, etc. **2** evenly balanced; displaying no advantage or bias. **3** having the same status; having or entitled to the same rights. ▸ *noun* a person or thing of the same age, rank, ability, etc. ▸ *verb* (***equalled, equalling***) **1** to be the same in amount, value, size, etc as someone or something. **2** to be as good as someone or something; to match. **3** to achieve something which matches (a previous achievement or achiever). ▪ **equality** *noun* (**-ies**). ▪ **equally** *adv.* [14c: from Latin *aequus* level or equal]

IDIOMS **equal to sth** having the necessary ability for it.

equalize *or* **-ise** *verb* **1** *tr & intr* to make or become equal. **2** *intr* to reach the same score as an opponent, after being behind. ▪ **equalization** *noun.* ▪ **equalizer** *noun.* [17c]

equanimity *noun* calmness of temper; composure. [17c: from Latin *aequus* equal + *animus* mind]

equate *verb* **1** (*usu* **equate one thing to** *or* **with another**) to consider them as equivalent. **2** (*usu* **equate with sth**) to be equivalent to it. [19c]

equation *noun* **1** *maths* a mathematical statement of the equality between two expressions involving constants and/or variables. **2** *chem* a formula expressing a chemical reaction and the proportions of the substances involved. **3** the act of equating.

equator *noun* **1** (*often* **the Equator**) *geog* the imaginary great circle that passes around the Earth at latitude 0 at an equal distance from the North and South Poles. **2** *astron* the celestial equator. **3** a circle dividing a spherical body into two equal parts. ▪ **equatorial** *adj.* [14c: from Latin *aequator* equalizer (of day and night)]

equerry /ˈɛkwərɪ/ *noun* (**-ies**) an official who serves as a personal attendant to a member of a royal family. [16c: from French *esquierie* company of squires]

equestrian *adj* **1** belonging or relating to horse-riding or horses. **2** on horseback. ▪ **equestrianism** *noun.* [17c: from Latin *equestris* relating to horsemen]

equiangular *adj* having equal angles. [17c]

equidistant *adj* equally distant. ▪ **equidistantly** *adv.* [16c]

equilateral *adj* having all sides of equal length. [16c: from Latin *latus* side]

equilibrium *noun* (***equilibria*** *or* ***equilibriums***) **1** *physics* a state in which the various forces acting on an object or objects in a system balance each other. **2** a calm and composed state of mind. **3** a state of balance. [17c: from Latin *aequi librium*]

equine *adj, formal* belonging or relating to, or like, a horse or horses. [18c: from Latin *equinus*]

equinoctial *adj* happening on or near an equinox. ▸ *noun* a storm occurring at an equinox.

equinox *noun* either of the two occasions on which the Sun crosses the equator, making night and day equal in length, occurring about 21 March and 23 September. [14c: from Latin *aequi noctium*]

equip *verb* (***equipped, equipping***) to fit out or provide someone or something with the necessary tools, supplies, abilities, etc. ▪ **equipment** *noun* **1** the clothes, machines, tools or instruments, etc necessary for a particular kind of work or activity. **2** *formal* the act of equipping. [16c: from French *équiper*]

equipoise *noun, formal* **1** a state of balance. **2** a counterbalancing weight. [17c]

equitable /ˈɛkwɪtəbəl/ *adj* fair and just. ▪ **equitably** *adv.* [16c: from French *équitable*]

equitation *noun, formal* the art of riding a horse. [16c: from Latin *equitare* to ride]

equity *noun* (**-ies**) **1** fair or just conditions or treatment. **2** *law* the concept of natural justice, as opposed to common law or statute law. **3** the excess in value of a property over the mortgage and other charges held on it. Compare **negative equity. 4** (*usu* **equities**) an ordinary share in a company. **5** (**Equity**) the trade union for actors. [14c: from Latin *aequitas* equality]

equivalent *adj* equal in value, power, meaning, etc. ▸ *noun* an equivalent thing or amount, etc. ▪ **equivalence** *noun.* [15c: from Latin *aequus* equal + *valere* to be worth]

equivocal /ɪˈkwɪvəkəl/ *adj* **1** ambiguous; of doubtful meaning. **2** of an uncertain nature. **3** questionable, suspicious or mysterious. ▪ **equivocally** *adv.* ▪ **equivocate** *verb, intr* to use ambiguous words in order to deceive or to avoid answering a question. ▪ **equivocation** *noun* evasive ambiguity. [16c: from Latin *aequus* equal + *vox* voice or word]

ER *abbrev*: *Elizabeth Regina* (Latin), Queen Elizabeth.

Er *symbol, chem* erbium.

-er[1] *suffix* used to form the comparative of adjectives and adverbs: *happier* • *sooner.* [Anglo-Saxon *-ra* for adjectives and *-or* for adverbs]

-er[2] *suffix, forming nouns, signifying* **1** the person or thing performing the action of the verb: *driver* • *heater.* **2** a person from a specified town or city: *Londoner* • *New Yorker.* [Anglo-Saxon -ere]

era *noun* **1** a distinct period in history marked by or beginning at an important event. **2** *geol* the second largest unit of geological time, representing a subdivision of an **eon**. [17c: from Latin *aera* number]

eradicate *verb* to get rid of something completely. ▪ **eradicable** *adj*. ▪ **eradication** *noun*. ▪ **eradicator** *noun*. [16c: from Latin *eradicare* to root out]

erase *verb* **1** to rub out (pencil marks, etc). **2** to remove all trace of something. **3** to destroy (a recording) on audio or video tape. ▪ **erasable** *adj*. ▪ **eraser** *noun* something that erases, esp a rubber for removing pencil or ink marks. ▪ **erasure** *noun* **1** the act of rubbing out. **2** a place where something written has been erased. [17c: from Latin *eradere* to scratch out]

erbium *noun, chem* (symbol **Er**) a soft silvery metallic element. [19c: from Ytterby in Sweden, where it was first discovered]

ere /ɛə(r)/ *prep, conj, now only poetic* before. [Anglo-Saxon *ær*]

erect *adj* **1** upright; not bent or leaning. **2** *physiol* of the penis, clitoris or nipples: enlarged and rigid through being filled with blood, usu as a result of sexual excitement. ▸ *verb* **1** to put up or build something. **2** to set or put (a pole or flag, etc) in a vertical position. **3** to set up or establish something. ▪ **erection** *noun*. ▪ **erectly** *adv*. [14c: from Latin *erigere* to set upright]

erectile *adj, physiol* **1** of an organ, etc: capable of becoming erect. **2** capable of being erected. [19c]

ergo *adv, formal or logic* therefore. [14c: Latin]

ergonomics *sing noun* the study of the relationship between people and their working environment. ▪ **ergonomic** *adj*. ▪ **ergonomist** *noun*. [20c: from Greek *ergon* work, modelled on **economics**]

ergot *noun* **1** a disease of rye and other cereals caused by a fungus. **2** this fungus, now an important source of alkaloid drugs. [17c: French]

Erinys *noun* (***Erinyes***) *Greek myth* any of **the Furies**.

ermine *noun* (***ermine*** *or* ***ermines***) **1** the stoat in its winter phase, when its fur has turned white. **2** the fur of this animal. [12c: from French *hermine*]

erode *verb, tr & intr* to wear away, destroy or be destroyed gradually. [17c; see **erosion**]

erogenous /ɪˈrɒdʒənəs/ *adj* of areas of the body, usu called **erogenous zones**, sensitive to sexual stimulation. [Late 19c: from Greek *eros* love]

erosion *noun* the loosening, fragmentation and transport from one place to another of rock material by water, wind, ice, gravity, or living organisms. ▪ **erosive** *adj* causing erosion. [16c: from Latin *erodere* to gnaw away]

erotic *adj* arousing; referring or relating to sexual desire, or giving sexual pleasure. ▪ **erotically** *adv*. [17c: from Greek *erotikos*, from *eros* love]

erotica *plural noun* erotic literature or pictures, etc. [19c]

eroticism *noun* **1** the erotic quality of a piece of writing or a picture, etc. **2** interest in, or pursuit of, sexual sensations. **3** the use of erotic images and symbols in art and literature, etc.

err *verb, intr* **1** to make a mistake, be wrong, or do wrong. **2** to sin. [14c: from Latin *errare* to stray]

errand *noun* **1** a short journey made in order to get or do something, esp for someone else. **2** the purpose of such a journey. [Anglo-Saxon *ærende* verbal message]

IDIOMS **run an errand** *or* **errands** to perform small pieces of business, deliver messages, etc.

errant *adj, literary* **1** doing wrong; erring. **2** (*placed after the noun*) wandering in search of adventure: *a knight errant*. ▪ **errantry** *noun*. [14c: from French *errer*]

erratic *adj* **1** irregular; having no fixed pattern or course. **2** unpredictable in behaviour. ▸ *noun, geog* a mass of rock transported by ice and deposited elsewhere. ▪ **erratically** *adv*. [14c: from Latin *errare* to stray]

erratum *noun* (***errata***) *formal* an error in writing or printing. [16c: past participle of Latin *errare* to stray]

erroneous *adj* wrong or mistaken. ▪ **erroneously** *adv*. [14c, meaning 'straying from what is right']

error *noun* **1** a mistake, inaccuracy or misapprehension. **2** the state of being mistaken. **3** the possible discrepancy between an estimate and an actual value or amount: *a margin of error*. [14c: Latin, also meaning 'a wandering or straying']

ersatz /ˈɜːzats, ˈɛə-/ *adj, derog* substitute; imitation. [Late 19c: German]

Erse *noun* the name formerly used by lowland Scots for Scottish **Gaelic**; now also applied to Irish Gaelic. ▸ *adj* relating to, or spoken or written in, these languages. [15c: Lowland Scots *Erisch* Irish]

erstwhile *adj, formal or archaic* former; previous. [Anglo-Saxon]

eructation *noun, formal* a belch or the act of belching. [16c: from Latin *eructare* to belch out]

erudite /ˈɛrʊdaɪt/ *adj* showing or having a great deal of knowledge; learned. ▪ **erudition** *noun*. [15c: from Latin *erudire* to instruct]

erupt *verb, intr* **1** of a volcano: to throw out lava, ash and gases. **2** to break out suddenly and violently. **3** of a skin blemish or rash: to appear suddenly and in a severe form. ▪ **eruption** *noun*. ▪ **eruptive** *adj*. [17c: from Latin *erumpere* to break out]

-ery *or* **-ry** *suffix, forming nouns, indicating* **1** a place where work or an activity of the specified kind is carried out: *brewery*. **2** a class, group or type of the specified kind: *greenery* • *weaponry*. **3** an art, skill or practice of the specified kind: *dentistry*. **4** behaviour of the specified kind: *bravery*. **5** anything connected with the specified person or thing: *popery*. [From French *-erie*, from Latin *-arius*]

erysipelas /ɛrɪˈsɪpɪləs/ *noun, pathol* an infectious disease of the skin, esp of the face, which produces deep red sore patches, accompanied by fever. [16c: Latin]

erythrocyte *noun* a red blood corpuscle. [Late 19c]

Es *symbol, chem* einsteinium.

-es see **-s**[1], **-s**[2]

escalate *verb, tr & intr* to increase or be increased rapidly in scale or degree, etc. ▪ **escalation** *noun*. ▪ **escalatory** *adj*. [20c: from **escalator**]

escalator *noun* a type of conveyor belt which forms a continuous moving staircase. [1900: orig a trademark, modelled on **elevator**]

escallop see **scallop**

escalope /ˈɛskəlɒp/ *noun, cookery* a thin slice of boneless meat, esp veal. [19c: French, orig meaning 'shell']

escapade *noun* a daring, adventurous or unlawful act. [17c, meaning 'escape': French]

escape *verb* **1** *intr* to gain freedom. **2** to manage to avoid (punishment or disease, etc). **3** not to be noticed or remembered by someone: *Nothing escapes his notice.* **4** *intr* of a gas or liquid, etc: to leak out or get out. **5** of words, etc: to be uttered unintentionally by someone. ▸ *noun* **1** an act of escaping. **2** a means of escape. **3** the avoidance of danger or harm: *a narrow escape.* **4** a leak or release. **5** something providing a break or distraction. [14c: from French *escaper*]

escapee *noun* someone who has escaped, esp from prison. [19c]

escape key *noun, comput* a key that allows exit from a program or cancels a previous action, etc.

escapement *noun* the mechanism in a clock or watch which connects the moving parts to the balance. [18c: from French *échappement*]

escape velocity *noun, physics* the minimum velocity required for an object to escape from the pull of the gravitational field of the Earth, or of another celestial body.

escapism *noun* the means of escaping, or the tendency to escape, from unpleasant reality into daydreams or fantasy. ▪ **escapist** *adj, noun.* [20c]

escapology *noun* the art or practice of freeing oneself from chains and other constraints, esp as theatrical entertainment. ▪ **escapologist** *noun.* [20c]

escarpment *noun, geol* a more or less continuous line of very steep slopes, formed by faulting or erosion, esp around the sides of a plateau. Also called **scarp**. [19c: from French *escarper* to cut steeply]

eschatology /ɛskə'tɒlədʒɪ/ *noun* the branch of theology dealing with final things, eg death, divine judgement and life after death. ▪ **eschatological** *adj.* ▪ **eschatologist** *noun.* [19c: from Greek *eschatos* last]

escheat /ɪs'tʃiːt/ *law, noun* **1** *formerly* the handing over of property to the state or a feudal lord in the absence of a legal heir. **2** property handed over in this way. ▸ *verb* **1** *intr* of property: to be handed over in this way. **2** to confiscate (property). [14c: from French *eschete*, from *escheoir* to fall to someone]

Escherichia coli /ɛʃə'rɪkɪə 'koʊlaɪ/ *noun, biol* (abbrev **E. coli**) a species of bacterium that occurs naturally in the intestines of vertebrates including humans, and which sometimes causes disease. [19c: named after the German physicianT Escherich]

eschew /ɪs'tʃuː/ *verb, formal* to avoid, keep away from, or abstain from something. ▪ **eschewal** *noun.* [14c: from French *eschever*]

escort *noun* /'ɛskɔːt/ **1** one or more people or vehicles, etc accompanying another or others for protection, guidance, or as a mark of honour. **2** someone of the opposite sex asked or hired to accompany another at a social event. ▸ *verb* /ɪ'skɔːt/ to accompany someone or something as an escort. [16c: from French *escorte*]

escritoire /ɛskrɪ'twɑː(r)/ *noun* a writing desk, usually ornamented and with drawers and compartments, etc. [16c: French, from Latin *scriptorium* writing-room]

escudo /ɛ'skuːdoʊ/ *noun* the former standard unit of currency of Portugal, replaced in 2002 by the euro. [19c: from Latin *scutum* shield]

esculent /'ɛskjʊlənt/ *formal, adj* edible. ▸ *noun* any edible substance. [17c: from Latin *esculentus* eatable]

escutcheon *noun* a shield decorated with a coat of arms. [15c: from French *escuchon*]
IDIOMS **a blot on the escutcheon** *facetious* a stain on one's good reputation.

-ese *suffix, forming nouns and adjectives* **1** relating to a specified country or place: *Japanese* • *Vietnamese.* **2** indicating the people or language of a specified country: *Chinese.* **3** *often derog* the typical style or language of a particular group or profession: *journalese.* [From French *-eis*]

Eskimo *now often offensive, noun* (***Eskimos*** *or* ***Eskimo***) **Inuit.** ▸ *adj* **Inuit.** [16c: Native N American *esquimantsic* eaters of raw flesh]

esophagus the *N Am* spelling of **oesophagus**.

esoteric /iːsoʊ'tɛrɪk/ *adj* understood only by those few people who have the necessary special knowledge; secret or mysterious. ▪ **esoterically** *adv.* [17c: from Greek *esoterikos*, from *eso* within]

ESP *abbrev* extra-sensory perception.

espadrille /'ɛspədrɪl/ *noun* a light canvas shoe with a sole made of rope or other plaited fibre. [19c: French, from Provençal *espardillo*]

espalier /ɪ'spalɪə(r)/ *noun* **1** a trellis or arrangement of wires against which a shrub or fruit tree is trained to grow flat, eg against a wall. **2** such a shrub or tree. [17c: French]

especial *adj* special. ▪ **especially** *adv* principally; more than in other cases. [14c: French]

---

especially, specially
Be careful not to use the word **especially** when you mean **specially**.
Especially means 'above all':
I like making cakes, especially for birthdays.
Specially means 'for a special purpose':
I made this cake specially for your birthday.
You will sometimes find **especially** used wrongly to mean **specially**:
✗ *He had driven up especially to collect her.*

Esperanto *noun* a language invented for international use, based on European languages, and published in 1887. ▪ **Esperantist** *noun.* [19c: orig the pseudonym of its inventor, Dr Zamenhof, meaning 'the one who hopes']

espionage /'ɛspɪənɑːʒ/ *noun* the activity of spying, or the use of spies to gather information. [18c: from French *espionnage*]

esplanade *noun* **1** a long wide pavement next to a beach. **2** a level open area between a fortified place and the nearest houses. [17c: French]

espouse *verb* **1** *formal* to adopt or give one's support to (a cause, etc). **2** *old use* to marry, or to give (eg a daughter) in marriage. ▪ **espousal** *noun* **1** *formal* the act of espousing (a cause, etc). **2** *old use* a marriage or engagement. [15c: from French *espouser* to marry]

espresso *or* **expresso** *noun* **1** coffee made by forcing steam or boiling water through ground coffee beans. **2** the machine for making this. [20c: Italian, literally 'pressed out']

esprit /ɛspʀi/ *noun, formal or literary* liveliness or wit. [16c: French, literally 'spirit']

esprit de corps /ɛs'priː də kɔː(r)/ *noun* loyalty to, or concern for the honour of, a group or body to which one belongs. [18c: French, literally 'spirit of the group']

espy *verb, literary* to catch sight of someone or something; to observe. [14c: from French *espier* to spy]

Esq. *or* **esq.** *abbrev* esquire.

-esque *suffix, signifying* **1** in the style or fashion of the specified person or thing: *Byronesque.* **2** like or similar to the specified thing: *picturesque.* [French, from Italian *-esco*]

esquire *noun* (*pl* in sense 2 only ***esquires***) **1** (abbrev **Esq.** *or* **esq.**) a title used after a man's name when no other form of address is used, esp when addressing letters. **2** *now chiefly hist* a squire. [15c: from French *esquier* squire]

-ess *suffix, forming noun, signifying* a female of the specified type or class: *lioness* • *duchess.* [From French *-esse*, from Latin *-issa*]

essay *noun* /'ɛseɪ/ **1** a short formal piece of writing, usu dealing with a single subject. **2** *formal* an attempt. ▸ *verb* /ɛ'seɪ/ *formal* to attempt. ▪ **essayist** *noun* a writer of literary essays. [16c: from French *essayer* to try]

essence *noun* **1** the basic distinctive part or quality of something, which determines its nature or character. **2** a liquid obtained from a plant or drug, etc, which has its properties in concentrated form. [14c: French]

IDIOMS **in essence** basically or fundamentally. **of the essence** absolutely necessary or extremely important.

essential *adj* **1** absolutely necessary. **2** relating to the basic or inner nature of something or its essence. ▸ *noun* **1** something necessary. **2** (*often* **the essentials**) a basic or fundamental element, principle or piece of information. ▪ **essentially** *adv.* [14c]

essential oil *noun, botany* a mixture of volatile oils which have distinctive and characteristic odours, obtained from certain aromatic plants. [17c]

EST *abbrev* electric shock therapy.

est. *abbrev* **1** established. **2** estimated.

-est *suffix* forming the superlative of adjectives and some adverbs *quickest* • *soonest.* [Anglo-Saxon *-est* and *-ost*]

establish *verb* **1** to settle someone firmly in a position, place or job, etc. **2** to set up (eg a university or a business). **3** to find, show or prove something. **4** to cause people to accept (eg a custom or a claim). [14c: from French *establir*]

establishment *noun* **1** the act of establishing. **2** a business, its premises or its staff. **3** a public or government institution: *a research establishment.* **4** (**the Establishment**) the group of people in a country, society or community who hold power and exercise authority, and are regarded as being opposed to change.

estate *noun* **1** a large piece of land owned by a person or group of people. **2** an area of land on which development of a particular kind has taken place, eg houses on a **housing estate** or factories on an **industrial estate**. **3** *law* a person's total possessions (property or money, etc), esp at death. **4** an **estate car**. **5** *hist* any of various groups or classes within the social structure of society. [13c: from French *estat*]

estate agent *noun* a person whose job is the buying, selling, leasing and valuation of houses and other property.

estate car *noun* a car with a large area behind the rear seats for luggage, etc, and a rear door. Often shortened to **estate**.

estate duty *noun* **death duty**.

esteem *verb* **1** to value, respect or think highly of someone or something. **2** *formal* to consider someone to be a specified thing. ▸ *noun* high regard or respect. ▪ **esteemed** *adj* respected. [15c: from French *estimer*]

ester *noun, chem* an organic chemical compound formed by the reaction of an alcohol with an organic acid, with the loss of a water molecule. [19c: from German]

esthete the *US* spelling of **aesthete**.

esthetic the *US* spelling of **aesthetic**.

estimable *adj* highly respected; worthy of respect.

estimate *verb* /'ɛstɪmeɪt/ **1** to judge or calculate (size, amount or value, etc) roughly or without measuring. **2** to have or form an opinion; to think. **3** to submit to a possible client a statement of (the likely cost) of carrying out a job. ▸ *noun* /'ɛstɪmət/ **1** a rough assessment (of size, etc). **2** a calculation of the probable cost of a job. ▪ **estimation** *noun* **1** judgement; opinion. **2** the act of estimating. ▪ **estimator** *noun.* [16c: from Latin *aestimare*]

estival the *US* spelling of **aestival**.

Estonian *adj* belonging or relating to Estonia, a republic in E Europe, its inhabitants, or their language. ▸ *noun* **1** a citizen or inhabitant of, or person born in, Estonia. **2** the official language of Estonia. [18c]

estrange *verb* to cause someone to break away from a previously friendly state or relationship. ▪ **estranged** *adj* no longer friendly or supportive; alienated: *his estranged wife.* ▪ **estrangement** *noun.* [15c: from French *estranger*]

estrogen the *N Am* spelling of **oestrogen**.

estrus the *N Am* spelling of **oestrus**.

estuary *noun* (***-ies***) the broad mouth of a river that flows into the sea, where fresh water mixes with tidal sea water. ▪ **estuarine** *adj.* [16c: from Latin *aestus* commotion or tide]

ETA *abbrev* estimated time of arrival.

eta /'iːtə/ *noun* the seventh letter of the Greek alphabet.

et al. /ɛt al/ *abbrev* **1** *et alia* (Latin), and other things. **2** *et alii* (Latin), and other people. **3** *et alibi* (Latin), and in other places.

et cetera *or* **etcetera** *adv* (abbrev **etc**) **1** and the rest; and so on. **2** and/or something similar. [15c: Latin]

etch *verb* **1** *tr & intr* to make designs on (metal or glass, etc) using an acid to eat out the lines. **2** to make a deep or irremovable impression. ▪ **etcher** *noun.* ▪ **etching** *noun* **1** the act or art of making etched designs. **2** a print made from an etched plate. [17c: from German *ätzen* to eat away with acid]

eternal *adj* **1** without beginning or end; everlasting. **2** unchanging; valid for all time. **3** *informal* frequent or endless. **4** (**the Eternal**) a name for God. ▪ **eternally** *adv* for ever; without end or constantly. [14c: from French *éternel*]

eternity *noun* (**-*ies***) **1** time regarded as having no end. **2** the state of being eternal. **3** *relig* a timeless existence after death. **4** *informal* an extremely long time. [14c: from French *éternité*]

eternity ring *noun* a ring given as a symbol of lasting love, esp one set with stones all round the band.

ethanal see **acetaldehyde**

ethane *noun, chem* a colourless odourless flammable gas belonging to the alkane series of hydrocarbons, and found in natural gas. [19c]

ethanedioic acid /iːθeɪndaɪ'oʊɪk/ *noun* **oxalic acid**.

ethanoate see **acetate** (sense 2)

ethanoic acid see **acetic acid**

ethanol *noun, chem* a colourless volatile flammable alcohol that is produced by fermentation of the sugar in fruit or cereals, constitutes the intoxicant in alcoholic beverages, and is used as a fuel. Also called **ethyl alcohol**.

ethanoyl see **acetyl**

ethene see **ethylene**

ether *noun* **1** any of a group of organic chemical compounds formed by the dehydration of alcohols, that are volatile and highly flammable, and contain two hydrocarbon groups linked by an oxygen atom. **2** (*also* **diethyl ether**) the commonest ether, widely used as a solvent, and formerly employed as an anaesthetic. **3** (*also* **aether**) *physics* a hypothetical medium formerly believed to be necessary for the transmission of electromagnetic radiation. **4** (*also* **aether**) *poetic* the clear upper air or a clear sky. [17c: from Greek *aither* the heavens]

ethereal *adj* **1** having an unreal lightness or delicateness; fairy-like. **2** heavenly or spiritual. ▪ **ethereally** *adv.* [16c: from **ether**]

Ethernet *noun, trademark, comput* a type of local area network (see under **LAN**). [20c: **ether** (sense 3) + *network*]

ethic *noun* the moral system or set of principles particular to a certain person, community or group, etc. ▪ **ethical** *adj* **1** relating to or concerning morals, justice or duty. **2** morally right. **3** of a medicine or drug: not advertised to the general public, and available only on prescription. ▪ **ethically** *adv.* [15c: from Greek *ethikos* moral]

ethics *singular noun* the study or the science of morals. ▸ *plural noun* rules or principles of behaviour: *medical ethics*.

Ethiopian *adj* belonging or relating to Ethiopia, its inhabitants, or their group of Semitic languages. ▸ *noun* a citizen or inhabitant of, or person born in, Ethiopia. [16c: ultimately from Greek *Aithiops*, literally 'burnt-face']

ethnic *adj* **1** relating to or having a common race or cultural tradition: *an ethnic group*. **2** associated with or resembling an exotic, esp non-European, racial or tribal group: *ethnic clothes*. **3** seen from the point of view of race, rather than nationality: *ethnic Asians*. **4** between or involving different racial groups: *ethnic violence*. ▸ *noun, esp US* a member of a particular racial group or cult, esp a minority one. ▪ **ethnically** *adv.* [14c: from Greek *ethnos* nation]

ethnic cleansing *noun* **genocide** or forced removal inflicted by one ethnic group on all others in a particular area.

ethnocentric *adj* relating to or holding the belief that one's own cultural tradition or racial group is superior to all others. ▪ **ethnocentricity** *noun.* [20c]

ethnology *noun* the scientific study of different races and cultural traditions, and their relations with each other. ▪ **ethnological** *adj.* ▪ **ethnologist** *noun.* [19c]

ethology *noun, zool* the study of animal behaviour. [19c]

ethos *noun* the typical spirit, character or attitudes (of a group or community, etc). [19c: Greek, meaning 'custom' or 'culture']

ethyl /'ɛθɪl/ *noun, chem* in organic chemical compounds: the (C_2H_5-) group, as for example in ethylamine ($C_2H_5NH_2$). [19c]

ethyl alcohol see **ethanol**

ethylene *noun, chem* a colourless flammable gas with a sweet smell, belonging to the **alkene** series of hydrocarbons. Also called **ethene**. [19c]

ethylene glycol *noun, chem* a thick liquid alcohol used as an antifreeze.

ethyne see **acetylene**

etiolated /'iːtɪoʊleɪtɪd/ *adj* **1** *botany* of a plant: having foliage that has become yellow through lack of sunlight. **2** *formal or literary* of a person: pale and weak in appearance. ▪ **etiolation** *noun.* [18c: from French *étioler* to become pale]

etiology the *US* spelling of **aetiology**.

etiquette *noun* **1** conventions of correct or polite social behaviour. **2** rules, usu unwritten ones, regarding the behaviour of members of a particular profession, etc towards each other. [18c: from French *étiquette* a label]

Etruscan *noun* **1** a person inhabiting or from Etruria, an ancient state in Italy. **2** the language of the Etruscans. ▸ *adj* relating to Etruria, or to the language, culture, etc of the Etruscans.

-ette *suffix, forming nouns, indicating* **1** a female of the specified type: *usherette*. **2** a small thing of the specified type: *cigarette* • *kitchenette*. **3** an imitation of something specified: *leatherette*. [French]

étude /eɪ'tjuːd/ *noun, music* a short piece written for a single instrument, intended as an exercise or a means of showing talent. [19c: French, literally 'study']

etymology *noun* (**-*ies***) **1** the study of the origin and development of words and their meanings. **2** an explanation of the history of a particular word. ▪ **etymological** *adj.* ▪ **etymologist** *noun.* [15c: from Latin *etymologia*]

EU *abbrev* European Union.

Eu *symbol, chem* europium.

eucalyptus /juːkə'lɪptəs/ *noun* (***eucalyptuses*** *or* ***eucalypti*** /-taɪ/) **1** an evergreen tree, native to Australia, grown for timber, oil or ornamental appearance. **2** the hard durable wood of this tree. **3** eucalyptus oil. [19c: from Greek *eu* well + *kalyptos* covered]

Eucharist /'juːkərɪst/ *noun, Christianity* **1** the sacrament of **the Last Supper**. **2** **the Lord's Supper**. **3** the elements of the sacrament, the bread and wine. ▪ **Eucharistic** *adj.* [14c: from Greek *eucharistia* giving of thanks]

euchre /'juːkə(r)/ *noun* **1** a N American card-game. **2** an instance of euchring or being euchred. ▸ *verb* **1** to prevent (a player) from winning three tricks. **2** (*usu*

euchre sb out of sth) *N Am, Aust, NZ* to cheat or outwit them. [19c]

Euclidean *or* **Euclidian** /juːˈklɪdɪən/ *adj* referring or relating to or based on the geometrical system devised by Euclid, a Greek mathematician who lived in c.300 BC.

eugenics /juːˈdʒɛnɪks/ *singular noun* the now largely discredited science of improving the human race by selective breeding. ▪ **eugenic** *adj.* ▪ **eugenically** *adv.* [19c: from Greek *eugenes* well-born]

eukaryote /juːˈkarɪoʊt/ *noun, biol* an organism in which the cells have a distinct nucleus containing the genetic material and separated from the cytoplasm by a nuclear membrane. ▪ **eukaryotic** *adj.* [20c: from Greek *karyon* kernel]

eulogize *or* **-ise** *verb* to praise highly. ▪ **eulogistic** *adj.* [19c]

eulogy *noun* (***-ies***) **1** a speech or piece of writing in praise of someone or something. **2** high praise. [16c: from Latin *eulogium*]

eunuch /ˈjuːnək/ *noun* **1** a man who has been castrated. **2** *esp formerly* such a man employed as a guard of a harem in Eastern countries. [15c: from Greek *eunouchos*]

euphemism *noun* **1** a mild or inoffensive term used in place of one considered offensive or unpleasantly direct. **2** the use of such terms. ▪ **euphemistic** *adj.* ▪ **euphemistically** *adv.* [17c: from Greek *euphemismos*]

euphonium *noun* a four-valved brass instrument of the tuba family. [19c: from Greek *euphonos* sweet-sounding]

euphony *noun* (***-ies***) **1** a pleasing sound, esp in speech. **2** pleasantness of sound, esp of pronunciation. ▪ **euphonious** *or* **euphonic** *adj* pleasing to the ear. [17c: from Greek *euphonia*]

euphoria *noun* a feeling of wild happiness and well-being. ▪ **euphoric** *adj.* [19c: Greek, meaning 'ability to endure well']

Eur- see **Euro-**

Eurasian *adj* **1** of mixed European and Asian descent. **2** belonging, referring or relating to Europe and Asia. ▸ *noun* a Eurasian person. [19c]

eureka /jʊəˈriːkə/ *exclam* expressing triumph at finding something or solving a problem, etc. [17c: from Greek *heureka* I have found it]

Euro- *or* (*before a vowel*) **Eur-** *combining form, denoting* Europe; European; relating to the EU: *Europhile* • *Euromyth.*

euro /ˈjʊəroʊ/ *noun* (symbol €) (***euros*** *or* ***euro***) the basic monetary unit for most countries in the European Union, widely replacing former standard currencies in 2002, equal to 100 **cent**s. [1990s: from *Europe*]

Eurocentric *adj* centred, or concentrating, on Europe. [20c]

Euro-MP *noun* a member of the European Parliament.

European *adj* **1** belonging or relating to Europe. **2** showing or favouring a spirit of co-operation between the countries of Europe, esp those of the EU. ▸ *noun* **1** a citizen or inhabitant of Europe. **2** a person who favours close political and economic contact between the countries of Europe, esp those of the EU. Also called **Euro.** [17c]

European Commission *noun* (abbrev **EC**) an executive body composed of members of the European Union countries which is responsible for the formulation of EU policy, and initiates and drafts most EU legislation.

European currency unit see **ecu**

European Union *noun* (abbrev **EU**) an economic and political association of European states.

europium *noun, chem* (symbol **Eu**) a soft silvery metallic element belonging to the **lanthanide** series. [19c: Latin, named after Europe]

Eurosceptic *noun* someone who is not in favour of devolving powers from national government to the European Union.

Eustachian tube /juːˈsteɪʃən/ *noun, anatomy* either of the two tubes which connect the **middle ear** to the **pharynx**. [18c: named after the Italian anatomist B Eustachio]

eustasy /ˈjuːstəsɪ/ *noun, geog* worldwide change in sea-level caused by advancing or receding polar ice caps, and not by changes in land levels. ▪ **eustatic** *adj.* [20c: from Greek *eu* well + *stasis* standing]

euthanasia *noun* the act or practice of ending the life of a person who is suffering from an incurable illness. [19c: Greek, from *eu-* good + *thanatos* death]

evacuate *verb* **1** to leave (a place), esp because of danger. **2** to make (people) evacuate a place. **3** *technical* to empty (the bowels). **4** *physics* to create a vacuum in (a vessel). ▪ **evacuation** *noun.* ▪ **evacuee** *noun* an evacuated person. [16c: from Latin *evacuare* to empty out]

evade *verb* **1** to escape or avoid something or someone by trickery or skill. **2** to avoid answering (a question). See also **evasion**. [16c: from Latin *evadere* to go out]

evaluate *verb* **1** to form an idea or judgement about the worth of something. **2** *maths* to calculate the value of something. ▪ **evaluation** *noun.* [19c]

evanesce *verb, intr, literary* to disappear gradually; to fade from sight. ▪ **evanescent** *adj* **1** quickly fading. **2** short-lived; transitory. [19c: from Latin *evanescere* to vanish]

evangelical *adj* **1** based on the Gospels. **2** referring or relating to, or denoting any of various groups within the Protestant Church stressing the authority of the Bible and claiming that personal acceptance of Christ as saviour is the only way to salvation. **3** enthusiastically advocating a particular cause, etc. ▸ *noun* a member of an evangelical movement. ▪ **evangelicalism** *noun.* ▪ **evangelically** *adv.* [16c]

evangelism *noun* **1** the act or practice of evangelizing. **2** evangelicalism. [17c in sense 1]

evangelist *noun* **1** a person who preaches Christianity. **2** (*usu* **Evangelist**) any of the writers of the four Biblical Gospels. ▪ **evangelistic** *adj.*

evangelize *or* **-ise** *verb* **1** *tr & intr* to attempt to persuade someone to adopt Christianity. **2** *intr* to preach Christianity. ▪ **evangelization** *noun.* [14c]

evaporate *verb, tr & intr* **1** to change or cause something to change from a liquid into a vapour. **2** to disappear or make disappear. ▪ **evaporation** *noun* the process of evaporating; disappearance. [16c: from Latin *evaporare*]

evaporated milk *noun* unsweetened milk that has been concentrated by evaporation.

evapotranspiration *noun, geog* the loss of water from the earth's surface to the atmosphere as a result of evaporation and transpiration from plants. [20c]

evasion *noun* **1** the act of evading, esp evading a commitment or responsibility. **2** a trick or excuse used to evade (a question, etc). [15c: from Latin *evasio*]

evasive *adj* **1** intending or intended to evade something, esp trouble or danger. **2** not honest or open: *an evasive answer.* ▪ **evasively** *adv.* ▪ **evasiveness** *noun.*

eve *noun* **1** *esp in compounds* the evening or day before some notable event: *New Year's Eve.* **2** the period immediately before: *the eve of war.* [13c: from **even²**]

even¹ *adj* **1** smooth and flat. **2** constant or regular: *travelling at an even 50mph.* **3** *maths* of a number: divisible by two, with nothing left over. **4** designated or marked by an even number: *the even houses in the street.* **5** (*usu* **even with sth**) level, on the same plane or at the same height as it. **6** (*often* **even with sb**) having no advantage over or owing no debt to them. **7** of temper or character, etc: calm. **8** equal. ▶ *adv* **1** used with a comparative to emphasize a comparison with something else: *He's good, but she's even better.* **2** used with an expression stronger than a previous one: *He looked sad, even depressed.* **3** used to introduce a surprising piece of information: *Even John was there!* **4** used to indicate a lower extreme in an implied comparison: *Even a child would have known that!* ▶ *verb* (*often* **even sth up**) to make it equal. ▶ *noun* **1** (*usu* **evens**) an even number, or something designated by one. **2** (**evens**) same as **even money**. ▪ **evenly** *adv.* ▪ **evenness** *noun.* [Anglo-Saxon *efen*]

IDIOMS **even if, even so** *or* **even though** used to emphasize that whether or not something is or might be true, the following or preceding statement is or would remain true: *He got the job but, even so, he's still unhappy.* **get even with sb** to be revenged on them.

PHRASAL VERBS **even out** to become level or regular. **even sth out** *or* **up** to make it smooth or level.

even² *noun, old use or poetic* evening. [Anglo-Saxon *æfen*]

even-handed *adj* fair; impartial. [17c]

evening *noun* **1** the last part of the day, usu from late afternoon until bedtime. **2** *often in compounds* a party or other social gathering held at this time: *a poetry evening.* **3** *poetic* the latter part of something: *the evening of her life.* ▶ *adj* referring to or during the evening. ▪ **evenings** *adv, esp N Am* in the evening; in the evening on a number of days. [Anglo-Saxon *æfnung*]

evening dress *noun* clothes worn on formal occasions in the evening.

evening primrose *noun, botany* a plant with large scented yellow flowers that open at dusk.

evening star *noun* a planet, esp Venus, clearly visible in the west just after sunset. See also **morning star**.

even money *noun* gambling odds with the potential to win the same as the amount gambled.

evensong *noun* in the Church of England: the service of evening prayer. Compare **matins**. [Anglo-Saxon *æfensang* evening song]

event *noun* **1** something that occurs or happens; an incident, esp a significant one. **2** an item in a programme of sports, etc. [16c: from Latin *eventus* result or event]

IDIOMS **at all events** *or* **in any event** in any case; whatever happens. **in the event** in the end; as it happened, happens or may happen. **in the event of** *or* **that sth** if it occurs: *in the event of a power cut.*

even-tempered *adj* placid; calm.

eventful *adj* full of important or characterized by important or significant events. ▪ **eventfully** *adv.*

eventide *noun, poetic or old use* evening. [Anglo-Saxon *æfentid*]

eventing *noun* the practice of taking part in horse-riding events.

eventual *adj* happening after or at the end of a period of time or a process, etc. ▪ **eventuality** *noun* (**-ies**) a possible happening or result: *plan for every eventuality.* ▪ **eventually** *adv* after an indefinite period of time; in the end. [17c: from French *éventuel*]

ever *adv* **1** at any time. **2 a** *formal* always; continually; **b** *in compounds: ever-hopeful.* **3** *informal* used for emphasis: *She's ever so beautiful!* [Anglo-Saxon *æfre*]

IDIOMS **ever such a ...** *informal* a very ...: *ever such a good boy.* **for ever 1** always. **2** *informal* for a long time.

evergreen *adj, botany* of a plant: bearing leaves all the year round, eg pines or firs. Compare **deciduous**. ▶ *noun* an evergreen tree or shrub. [17c]

everlasting *adj* **1** without end; continual. **2** lasting a long time, esp so long as to become tiresome. ▶ *noun* **1** any of several kinds of flower that keep their shape and colour when dried. **2** eternity. ▪ **everlastingly** *adv.* [13c]

evermore *adv* (*often* **for evermore**) for all time to come; eternally. [13c]

every *adj* **1** each one or single of a number or collection; omitting none. **2** the greatest or best possible: *making every effort.* ▶ *adv* at, in, or at the end of, each stated period of time or distance, etc: *every six inches.* [Anglo-Saxon *æfre ælc* ever each]

IDIOMS **every bit** the whole; all of it; quite or entirely. **every last** (*used for emphasis*) every. **every now and then** *or* **every now and again** *or* **every so often** occasionally; from time to time. **every other** *or* **every second** one out of every two (things) repeatedly (the first, third, fifth, etc or second, fourth, sixth, etc): *comes every other day.* **every which way** *US* **1** in every direction. **2** in disorder.

everybody *pron* every person.

everyday *adj* **1** happening, done or used, etc daily, or on ordinary days, rather than on special occasions. **2** common or usual. [17c]

Everyman *noun* (*also* **everyman**) the ordinary or common person; mankind. [Early 20c: from the name of the hero of a medieval morality play]

everyone *pron* every person.

everyplace *adv, US* everywhere.

everything *pron* **1** all things; all. **2** the most important thing: *Fitness is everything in sport.*

IDIOMS **have everything** *informal* to be well endowed with possessions, good looks, etc.

everywhere *adv* in or to every place.

evict *verb* to put someone out of a house, etc or off land by force of law. ▪ **eviction** *noun*. [15c: from Latin *evincere* to overcome]

evidence *noun* **1** information, etc that gives grounds for belief; that which points to, reveals or suggests something. **2** written or spoken testimony used in a court of law. ▸ *verb, formal* to be evidence of something; to prove. [14c: from Latin *evidentia* clearness of speech]

IDIOMS **in evidence** easily seen; clearly displayed.

evident *adj* clear to see or understand; obvious or apparent. ▪ **evidently** *adv* **1** obviously; apparently. **2** as it appears; so it seems: *Evidently they don't believe us.*

evidential *adj, formal* relating to, based on or providing evidence. ▪ **evidentially** *adv*.

evil *adj* **1** morally bad or offensive. **2** harmful. **3** *informal* very unpleasant: *an evil stench*. ▸ *noun* **1** wickedness or moral offensiveness, or the source of it. **2** harm, or a cause of harm; a harmful influence. **3** anything bad or unpleasant, eg crime or disease. ▪ **evilly** *adv*. ▪ **evilness** *noun*. [Anglo-Saxon *yfel*]

the evil eye *noun* a glare, superstitiously thought to cause harm.

evince *verb, formal* to show or display something (usu a personal quality) clearly. [17c: from Latin *evincere* to overcome]

eviscerate /ɪ'vɪsəreɪt/ *verb, formal* to tear out the bowels of a person or animal; to gut. ▪ **evisceration** *noun, formal* disembowelling. [17c: from Latin *eviscerare* to disembowel]

evoke *verb* **1** to cause or produce (a response or reaction, etc). **2** to bring (a memory or emotion, etc) into the mind. ▪ **evocation** *noun*. ▪ **evocative** *adj*. [17c: from Latin *evocare* to call out]

evolution *noun* **1** the process of evolving. **2** a gradual development. **3** *biol* the cumulative changes in the characteristics of living organisms or populations of organisms from generation to generation. **4** *chem* the giving off of a gas. ▪ **evolutionary** *adj* relating to, or part of, evolution. ▪ **evolutionism** *noun, anthropol, biol* the theory of evolution. ▪ **evolutionist** *noun* a person who believes in the theory of evolution. [17c: from Latin *evolutio* unrolling]

evolve *verb* **1** *tr & intr* to develop or produce gradually. **2** *intr* to develop from a primitive into a more complex or advanced form. **3** *chem* to give off (heat, etc). [17c: from Latin *evolvere* to roll out or unroll]

ewe *noun* a female sheep. [Anglo-Saxon *eowu*]

ewer *noun* a large water jug with a wide mouth. [14c: from French *eviere*]

ex[1] *noun, informal* a person who is no longer what he or she was, esp a former husband, wife or lover. [19c: from words formed with **ex-**[1]]

ex[2] *prep, commerce* **1** direct from somewhere: *ex warehouse*. **2** excluding something: *ex VAT*. [19c: Latin, meaning 'out of']

ex-[1] *prefix, signifying* **1** former: *ex-wife* • *ex-president*. **2** outside: *ex-directory*. [From Latin *ex*, meaning 'out of']

ex-[2] see under **exo-**

exacerbate /ɪg'zasəbeɪt/ *verb* to make (a bad situation, anger or pain, etc) worse or more severe. ▪ **exacerbation** *noun*. [17c: from Latin *exacerbare* to irritate]

exact *adj* **1** absolutely accurate or correct. **2** insisting on accuracy or precision in even the smallest details. **3** dealing with measurable quantities or values: *Psychology is not an exact science*. ▸ *verb* **1** (*usu* **exact sth from** *or* **of sb**) to demand (payment, etc) from them. **2** to insist on (a right, etc). ▪ **exacting** *adj* making difficult or excessive demands. ▪ **exaction** *noun, formal* **1** the act of demanding payment, or the payment demanded. **2** illegal demands for money; extortion. ▪ **exactitude** *noun, formal* accuracy or correctness. ▪ **exactness** *noun*. [15c: from Latin *exigere* to demand]

exactly *adv* **1** just; quite, precisely or absolutely. **2** with accuracy; with attention to detail. **3** said in reply: you are quite right.

exaggerate *verb* **1** *tr & intr* to regard or describe something as being greater or better than it really is. **2** to emphasize something or make it more noticeable. **3** to do something in an excessive or affected way. ▪ **exaggeration** *noun*. [16c: from Latin *exaggerare* to heap up]

---

exaggerate

This word is often misspelt. It has two *g*'s in the middle. It might help you to remember the following sentence:

*A br**agger** will often ex**agger**ate.*

---

exalt *verb* **1** to praise (eg God) highly. **2** to fill someone with great joy. **3** to give a higher rank or position to someone or something. ▪ **exaltation** *noun*. ▪ **exalted** *adj* **1** noble; very moral. **2** elevated; high. ▪ **exaltedly** *adv*. [15c: from Latin *exaltare* to raise]

exam *noun, informal* an **examination** (sense 1).

examination *noun* **1** a set of tasks, esp in written form, designed to test knowledge or ability. **2** an inspection of a person's state of health, carried out by a doctor. **3** the act of examining, or process of being examined. **4** *law* formal questioning in a court of law.

examine *verb* **1** to inspect, consider or look into something closely. **2** to check the health of someone. **3** to test the knowledge or ability of (a person), esp in a formal examination. **4** *law* to question formally in a court of law. ▪ **examinable** *adj*. ▪ **examinee** *noun* a candidate in an examination. ▪ **examiner** *noun* someone who sets an examination. [14c: from French *examiner*]

example *noun* **1** someone or something that is a typical specimen. **2** something that illustrates a fact or rule. **3** a person or pattern of behaviour, etc as a model to be, or not to be, copied: *set a good example*. **4** a punishment given, or the person punished, as a warning to others: *make an example of someone*. [14c: French]

IDIOMS **for example** as an example or illustration.

exasperate *verb* to make someone annoyed and frustrated; to anger them. ▪ **exasperating** *adj*. ▪ **exasperation** *noun* a feeling of angry frustration. [16c: from Latin *exasperare* to make rough]

ex cathedra /ɛks kə'θiːdrə, ɛks 'kaθɛdrɑː/ *adv* with authority, esp the full authority of the Pope. ▸ *adj* (*usu* **ex-cathedra**) **1** of a papal pronouncement: stating an infallible doctrine. **2** made with, or as if with, authority. [17c: Latin, literally 'from the chair']

excavate *verb* **1** to dig up or uncover something (esp historical remains). **2** to dig up (a piece of ground, etc); to make (a hole) by doing this. ▪ **excavation** *noun* **1** *esp archaeol* the process of excavating or digging up ground. **2** an excavated area or site. ▪ **excavator** *noun*. [16c: from Latin *excavare* to make hollow]

exceed *verb* **1** to be greater than someone or something. **2** to go beyond; to do more than is required by something. ▪ **exceedingly** *adv* very; extremely. [14c: from French *exceder*]

exceed
This word is often misspelt. It ends in *eed*. It might help you to remember the following sentence:
*There's no **need** to exc**eed** the sp**eed** limit.*

excel *verb* (***excelled, excelling***) **1** *intr* (*usu* **excel in** *or* **at sth**) to be exceptionally good at it. **2** to be better than someone or something. [15c: from Latin *excellere* to rise up]
IDIOMS **excel oneself** *often ironic* to do better than usual or previously.

excellence *noun* great worth; very high or exceptional quality. ▪ **excellent** *adj* of very high quality; extremely good. ▪ **excellently** *adv*. [14c: French, from Latin *excellentia*]

Excellency *noun* (***-ies***) (*usu* **His, Her** *or* **Your Excellency** *or* **Your** *or* **Their Excellencies**) a title of honour given to certain people of high rank, eg ambassadors. [16c]

except *prep* leaving out; not including. ► *verb* to leave out or exclude: *present company excepted.* ▪ **excepting** *prep* leaving out; not including or counting. [14c: from Latin *excipere* to take out]
IDIOMS **except for sth** apart from it; not including or counting.

except, accept
Be careful not to use the spelling **except** when you mean **accept**:
I decided to accept the invitation.

exception *noun* **1** someone or something not included. **2** someone or something that does not, or is allowed not to, follow a general rule: *make an exception.* **3** an act of excluding. ▪ **exceptionable** *adj* **1** likely to cause disapproval, offence or dislike. **2** open to objection. [14c]
IDIOMS **take exception to sth** to object to it; to be offended by it.

exceptional *adj* **1** remarkable or outstanding. **2** being or making an exception. ▪ **exceptionally** *adv*.

excerpt *noun* /'ɛksɜːpt/ a short passage or part taken from a book, film or musical work, etc. ► *verb* /ɪk'sɜːpt/ to select extracts from (a book, etc). [17c: from Latin *excerptum*]

excess /ɪk'sɛs/ *noun* **1** the act of going, or the state of being, beyond normal or suitable limits. **2** an amount or extent greater than is usual, necessary or wise. **3** the amount by which one quantity, etc exceeds another; an amount left over. **4** (*usu* **excesses**) an outrageous or offensive act. ► *adj* /'ɛksɛs/ **1** greater than is usual, necessary or permitted. **2** additional; required to make up for an amount lacking: *excess postage* • *excess fare.* ▪ **excessive** *adj* too great; beyond what is usual, right or appropriate. ▪ **excessively** *adv* to an excessive degree. [14c: from French exces]
IDIOMS **in excess of sth** going beyond (a specified amount); more than it.

exchange *verb* **1** (*usu* **exchange one thing for another**) to give, or give up, something, in return for something else. **2** to give and receive in return: *exchange gifts.* ► *noun* **1** the giving and taking of one thing for another. **2** a thing exchanged. **3** a giving and receiving in return. **4** a conversation or argument, esp a brief one. **5** the act of exchanging the currency of one country for that of another. **6** a place where shares are traded, or international financial deals carried out. **7** (*also* **telephone exchange**) a central telephone system where lines are connected, or the building housing this. ▪ **exchangeable** *adj*. [14c: from French *eschangier*]
IDIOMS **in exchange for sth** in return for it.

exchange rate *or* **rate of exchange** *noun* the value of the currency of one country in relation to that of another country or countries.

exchequer *noun* **1** (*often* **Exchequer**) the government department in charge of the financial affairs of a nation. **2** *informal* one's personal finances or funds. [14c: from French *eschequier*]

excise[1] *noun* /'ɛksaɪz/ the tax or duty payable on goods, etc produced and sold within a country, and on certain trading licences: *excise duty.* ► *verb* /ɪk'saɪz/ **1** to charge excise on (goods, etc). **2** to force someone to pay excise. ▪ **excisable** *adj* liable to excise duty. [15c: from Dutch *excijs*]

excise[2] /ɪk'saɪz/ *verb* **1** to remove (eg a passage from a text). **2** to cut out something, or cut off something by surgery. ▪ **excision** *noun*. [16c: from Latin *excidere* to cut out]

excitable *adj* easily made excited, flustered, frantic, etc. ▪ **excitability** *noun*.

excite *verb* **1** to make someone feel lively expectation or a pleasant tension and thrill. **2** to arouse (feelings, emotions or sensations, etc). **3** to provoke (eg action). **4** *physics* to raise (a nucleus, atom or molecule) from the **ground state** to a higher level. **5** *physics* to produce electric or magnetic activity in something. ▪ **excitation** *noun*. ▪ **excited** *adj*. ▪ **excitedly** *adv*. [14c: from French *exciter*]

excitement *noun* **1** the state of being excited. **2** objects and events that produce such a state, or the quality they have which produces it. **3** behaviour or a happening, etc which displays excitement.

exciting *adj* arousing a lively expectation or a pleasant tension and thrill. ▪ **excitingly** *adv*.

exclaim *verb, tr & intr* to call or cry out suddenly and loudly, eg in surprise or anger. [16c: from Latin *exclamare*]

exclamation *noun* **1** a word or expression uttered suddenly and loudly. **2** the act of exclaiming. ▪ **exclamatory** *adj*. [14c: from Latin *exclamatio*]

exclamation mark *or* (*US*) **exclamation point** *noun* the punctuation mark (!), used to indicate an exclamation.

exclude *verb* **1** to prevent someone from sharing or taking part. **2** to shut someone or something out, or to keep them out. **3** to omit someone or something or leave them out of consideration. **4** to make something impossible. Opposite of **include**. ▪ **excluding** *prep* not counting; without including. [14c: from Latin *excludere* to shut out]

exclusion *noun* the act of excluding, or the state of being excluded. [17c: from Latin *exclusio*]
IDIOMS **to the exclusion of sb** *or* **sth** so as to leave out them or it.

exclusive *adj* **1** involving the rejection or denial of something else or everything else. **2** (**exclusive to sb** *or* **sth**) limited to, given to, found in, etc only that place, group or person. **3** (**exclusive of sb** *or* **sth**) not including a specified thing. **4** not readily accepting others into the group, esp because of a feeling of superiority: *an exclusive club.* **5** fashionable and expensive: *an exclusive restaurant.* ▸ *noun* a report or story published or broadcast by only one newspaper, programme, etc. ▪ **exclusively** *adv.* ▪ **exclusiveness** *or* **exclusivity** *noun.* [16c: from Latin *exclusivus*]

excommunicate *verb, Christianity* to exclude someone from membership of a church. ▪ **excommunication** *noun.* [15c: from Latin *excommunicare* to exclude from the community]

excoriate /ɛks'kɔːrɪeɪt/ *verb* **1** *technical* to strip the skin from (a person or animal). **2** to criticize someone severely. ▪ **excoriation** *noun.* [15c: from Latin *excoriare*]

excrement *noun* waste matter passed out of the body, esp faeces. ▪ **excremental** *adj.* [16c: from Latin *excrementum*]

excrescence *noun* **1** an abnormal, esp an ugly, growth on a part of the body or a plant. **2** an unsightly addition. ▪ **excrescent** *adj.* [16c: from Latin *excrescere* to grow up]

excreta *plural noun, formal* excreted matter; faeces or urine.

excrete *verb* of a plant or animal: to eliminate (waste products). ▪ **excretion** *noun, biol* in plants and animals: the removal of excess waste, or harmful material produced by the organism. ▪ **excretive** *or* **excretory** *adj.* [17c: from Latin *excernere* to sift out]

excruciating *adj* **1** causing great physical or mental pain. **2** *informal* extremely bad or irritating. ▪ **excruciatingly** *adv.* [16c: from Latin *excruciare* to torture]

exculpate /ɪks'kʌlpeɪt/ *verb, formal* to free someone from guilt or blame; to absolve or vindicate. Compare **inculpate.** ▪ **exculpation** *noun.* [17c: from Latin ex from + *culpa* fault or blame]

excursion /ɪks'kɜːʒən/ *noun* **1** a short trip, usu one made for pleasure. **2** a brief change from the usual course or pattern. [17c: from Latin *excurrere* to run out]

excuse *verb* /ɪk'skjuːz/ **1** to pardon or forgive someone. **2** to offer justification for (a wrongdoing). **3** to free someone from (an obligation or duty, etc). **4** to allow someone to leave a room, etc, eg in order to go to the lavatory. ▸ *noun* /ɪk'skjuːs/ **1** an explanation for a wrongdoing, offered as an apology or justification. **2** *derog* a very poor example: *You'll never sell this excuse for a painting!* ▪ **excusable** *adj.* ▪ **excusably** *adv.* [14c: from Latin *excusare*]
IDIOMS **excuse me** an expression of apology, or one used to attract attention. **make one's excuses** to apologize for leaving or for not attending.

ex-directory *adj* of a telephone number: not included in the directory at the request of the subscriber.

execrable /'ɛksəkrəbəl/ *adj* **1** detestable. **2** dreadful; of very poor quality. ▪ **execrably** *adv.* [14c: from Latin *execrabilis* detestable]

execrate *verb, formal* **1** to feel or express hatred or loathing of something. **2** to curse. ▪ **execration** *noun* an expression of loathing; cursing. [16c: from Latin *exsecrari* to curse]

executable *adj* **1** able be executed. **2** *comput* able to be run by computer: *executable file.* ▸ *noun, comput* an executable file or program.

execute *verb* **1** to put someone to death by order of the law. **2** to perform or carry out something. **3** to produce something, esp according to a design. **4** *law* to make something valid by signing. **5** *law* to carry out instructions contained in (a will or contract). ▪ **executable** *adj.* ▪ **executer** *noun* someone who carries out (a plan, etc) or puts (a law, etc) into effect. Compare **executor**. [14c: from Latin *exsequi* to follow up or carry out]

execution *noun* **1** the act, or an instance, of putting someone to death by law. **2** the act or skill of carrying something out; an instance or the process of carrying something out. ▪ **executioner** *noun* a person who carries out a sentence of death. [14c]

executive *adj* **1** in a business organization, etc: concerned with management or administration. **2** for the use of managers and senior staff. **3** *informal* expensive and sophisticated: *executive cars.* **4** *law, politics* relating to the carrying out of laws: *executive powers.* ▸ *noun* **1** someone in an organization, etc who has power to direct or manage. **2** (**the executive**) *law, politics* the branch of government that puts laws into effect. [17c]

executor *noun, law* a male or female person appointed to carry out instructions stated in a will. ▪ **executorship** *noun.* ▪ **executory** *adj.* [13c]

executrix /ɪg'zɛkjʊtrɪks/ *noun* (***executrices*** /-trɪsɪz/ *or* ***executrixes***) *law* a female **executor**. [15c]

exegesis /ɛksə'dʒiːsɪs/ *noun* (***-ses*** /-siːz/) a critical explanation of a text, esp of the Bible. [17c: Greek, meaning 'explanation']

exemplar *noun* **1** a person or thing worth copying; a model. **2** a typical example. [14c: from Latin *exemplum* example]

exemplary *adj* **1** worth following as an example. **2** serving as an illustration or warning. [16c]

exemplify *verb* (***-ies, -ied***) **1** to be an example of something. **2** to show an example of something, or show it by means of an example. ▪ **exemplification** *noun.* [15c]

exempt *verb* to free someone from a duty or obligation that applies to others. ▸ *adj* free from some obligation; not liable. ▪ **exemption** *noun.* [14c: from Latin *eximere* to take out]

exercise *noun* **1** physical training or exertion for health or pleasure. **2** an activity intended to develop a skill. **3** a task designed to test ability. **4** a piece of written work intended as practice for learners. **5** *formal* the act of putting something into practice or carrying it out: *the exercise of one's duty.* **6** (*usu* **exercises**) *military* training and practice for soldiers. ▸ *verb* **1** *tr & intr* to give exercise to (oneself, or someone or something else). **2** to use something or bring it into use: *exercised his right to appeal.* **3** to trouble, concern, or occupy someone's thoughts. ▪ **exercisable** *adj.* ▪ **exerciser** *noun.* [14c: from French *exercice*]

exert *verb* **1** to bring something into use or action forcefully: *exert one's authority.* **2** (**exert oneself**) to force oneself to make a strenuous, esp physical, effort. ▪ **exertion** *noun.* [17c: from Latin *exserere* to thrust out]

exeunt *verb, theatre* as a stage direction: leave the stage; they leave the stage. See also **exit**. [15c: Latin, meaning 'they go out']

IDIOMS **exeunt omnes** all leave the stage.

exfoliant /ɛks'foʊlɪənt/ *noun* a cosmetic preparation for removing dead layers of skin. [20c: see **exfoliate**]

exfoliate *verb, tr & intr* of bark, rocks or skin, etc: to shed or peel off in flakes or layers. ▪ **exfoliation** *noun.* ▪ **exfoliative** *adj.* [17c: from Latin *exfoliare* to strip of leaves]

ex gratia /ɛks 'greɪʃɪə/ *adv, adj* given as a favour, not in recognition of any obligation, esp a legal one. [18c: Latin, meaning 'as a favour']

exhale *verb, tr & intr* **1** to breathe out. **2** to give off or be given off. Compare **inhale**. ▪ **exhalation** *noun.* [14c: from French *exhaler*]

exhaust *verb* **1** to make (a person or animal) very tired. **2** to use something up completely. **3** to say all that can be said about (a subject, etc). **4** *eng* to empty (a container) or draw off (gas). ▸ *noun* **1** the escape of waste gases from an engine, etc. **2** the gases themselves. **3** the part or parts of an engine, etc through which the waste gases escape. ▪ **exhausted** *adj.* ▪ **exhaustible** *adj.* ▪ **exhausting** *adj.* ▪ **exhaustion** *noun.* [16c: from Latin *exhaurire* to draw off or drain away]

exhaustive *adj* complete; comprehensive or very thorough. ▪ **exhaustively** *adv.* [18c]

exhibit *verb* **1** to present or display something for public appreciation. **2** to show or manifest (a quality, etc). ▸ *noun* **1** an object displayed publicly, eg in a museum. **2** *law* an object or article produced in court as part of the evidence. ▪ **exhibitor** *noun* a person who provides an exhibit for a public display. [15c: from Latin *exhibere* to produce or show]

exhibition *noun* **1** a display, eg of works of art, to the public. **2** the act or an instance of showing something, eg a quality. [15c]

IDIOMS **make an exhibition of oneself** to behave foolishly in public.

exhibitionism *noun, derog* the tendency to behave so as to attract attention to oneself. ▪ **exhibitionist** *noun.*

exhilarate *verb* to fill someone with a lively cheerfulness. ▪ **exhilarating** *adj.* ▪ **exhilaration** *noun* a feeling of extreme cheerfulness. [16c: from Latin *exhilarare*, from *hilaris* cheerful]

exhort *verb* to urge or advise someone strongly and sincerely. ▪ **exhortation** *noun* a strong appeal or urging. [14c: from Latin *exhortari* to encourage]

exhume *verb, formal* **1** to dig up (a body) from a grave. **2** to reveal; to bring something up or mention it again. ▪ **exhumation** *noun* the digging up of a body from a grave. [18c: from Latin ex out of + *humus* the ground]

exigency /'ɛksɪdʒənsɪ/ *noun* (**-ies**) *formal* **1** (*usu* **exigencies**) urgent need. **2** an emergency. ▪ **exigent** *adj.* [16c: from Latin *exigere* to drive out]

exiguous /ɪg'zɪgjʊəs/ *adj, formal* scarce or meagre; insufficient. ▪ **exiguity** /ɛksɪ'gjuːɪtɪ/ *noun.* [17c: from Latin *exiguus* small or meagre]

exile *noun* **1** enforced or regretted absence from one's country or town, esp for a long time and often as a punishment. **2** someone who suffers such absence. ▸ *verb* to send someone into exile. [13c: from Latin *exsilium* banishment]

exist *verb, intr* **1** to be, esp to be present in the real world or universe rather than in story or imagination. **2** to occur or be found. **3** to manage to stay alive; to live with only the most basic necessities of life. [17c: from Latin *exsistere* to stand out]

existence *noun* **1** the state of existing. **2** a life, or a way of living. **3** everything that exists. ▪ **existent** *adj* having an actual being; existing. [14c, meaning 'actuality' or 'reality']

existential *adj* **1** relating to human existence. **2** *philos* relating to existentialism. [17c]

existentialism *noun* a philosophy that emphasizes freedom of choice and personal responsibility for one's own actions, which create one's own moral values and determine one's future. ▪ **existentialist** *adj, noun.* [20c: from German *Existentialismus*]

exit *noun* **1** a way out of a building, etc. **2** going out or departing. **3** an actor's departure from the stage. **4** a place where vehicles can leave a motorway or main road. ▸ *verb* (***exited, exiting***) *intr* **1** *formal* to go out, leave or depart. **2** *theatre* **a** to leave the stage; **b** as a stage direction: he or she leaves the stage. See also **exeunt**. **3** *comput* to leave (a program or system, etc). [16c: from Latin *exire* to go out]

exit poll *noun* a poll of a sample of voters in an election, taken as they leave a polling station.

exo- *or* (before a vowel) **ex-** *combining form* out or outside. See also **ecto-**, **endo-**, **ento-**. [From Greek *exo* outside]

exocrine *adj, physiol* of a gland, such as the sweat gland or salivary gland: discharging its secretions through a duct which opens onto an epithelial surface. See also **endocrine**. [Early 20c]

exodus *noun* **1** a mass departure of people. **2** (**Exodus**) the departure of the Israelites from Egypt, prob in the 13c BC. [17c: Latin]

ex officio *adv, adj* by virtue of one's official position. [16c: Latin]

exonerate *verb* to free someone from blame, or acquit them of a criminal charge. ▪ **exoneration** *noun.* ▪ **exonerative** *adj.* [16c: from Latin *exonerare*, to free from a burden]

exorbitant *adj* of prices or demands: very high, excessive or unfair. ▪ **exorbitantly** *adv.* [15c: from Latin *exorbitare* to go out of the track]

exorcize *or* **-ise** *verb* in some beliefs: **1** to drive away (an evil spirit or influence) with prayer or holy words. **2** to free (a person or place) from the influence of an evil spirit in this way. ▪ **exorcism** *noun.* ▪ **exorcist** *noun.* [16c: from Greek *exorkizein*]

exoskeleton *noun, zool* in some invertebrates: an external skeleton forming a rigid covering that is external to the body. ▪ **exoskeletal** *adj.* [19c]

exosphere *noun, astron* the outermost layer of the Earth's atmosphere, which starts at an altitude of about 500km. [20c]

exothermic reaction *noun, chem* any process, esp a chemical reaction, that involves the release of heat. Compare **endothermic reaction**. [19c]

exotic *adj* **1** introduced from a foreign country, esp a distant and tropical country: *exotic plants.* **2** interestingly different or strange, esp colourful and rich, and suggestive of a distant land. ▸ *noun* an exotic person or thing. ▪ **exotically** *adv.* ▪ **exoticism** *noun.* [16c: from Greek *exotikos*, from *exo* outside]

exotica *plural noun* strange or rare objects. [19c]

expand *verb* **1** *tr & intr* to make or become greater in size, extent or importance. **2** *intr, formal* to become more at ease or more open and talkative. **3** *tr & intr* (*often* **expand on** *or* **upon sth**) to give additional information; to enlarge on (a description, etc). **4** *tr & intr, formal* to fold out flat or spread out. **5** to write something out in full. **6** *maths* to multiply out (terms in brackets). ▪ **expandable** *adj.* [15c: from Latin *expandere* to spread out]

expanse *noun* a wide area or space. [17c: from Latin *expansum*]

expansible *adj* able to expand or be expanded. [17c]

expansion *noun* **1** the act or state of expanding. **2** the amount by which something expands. **3** *maths* the result of expanding terms in brackets. [15c]

expansion board *or* **expansion card** *noun, comput* a printed circuit board which can be inserted into an **expansion slot**, a connector on the motherboard of a computer which allows extra facilities to be added.

expansionism *noun,* the act or practice of increasing territory or political influence or authority, usu at the expense of other nations or bodies. ▪ **expansionist** *noun, adj.*

expansive *adj* **1** ready or eager to talk; open or effusive. **2** wide-ranging. **3** able or tending to expand. ▪ **expansiveness** *noun.*

expat *noun, informal* an **expatriate**. [20c]

expatiate *verb, intr, formal* to talk or write at length or in detail. ▪ **expatiation** *noun.* [17c: from Latin *exspatiari* to digress]

expatriate *adj* /ɛk'spatrɪət/ **1** living abroad, esp for a long but limited period. **2** exiled. ▸ *noun* a person living or working abroad. ▸ *verb* /ɛk'spatrɪeɪt/ **1** to banish or exile. **2** to deprive someone of citizenship. ▪ **expatriation** *noun.* [18c: from Latin ex out of + *patria* native land]

expect *verb* **1** to think of something as likely to happen or come. **2** *informal* to suppose: *I expect you're tired.* **3** (*usu* **expect sth from** *or* **of sb**) to require it of them; to regard it as normal or reasonable. ▪ **expectable** *adj.* [16c: from Latin *exspectare* to look out for]

IDIOMS **be expecting** *informal* to be pregnant.

expectancy *noun* (*-ies*) **1** the act or state of expecting. **2** a future chance or probability. *Also in compounds*: *life expectancy.*

expectant *adj* **1** eagerly waiting; hopeful. **2** not yet, but expecting to be something (esp a mother or father). ▪ **expectantly** *adv.*

expectation *noun* **1** the state, or an attitude, of expecting. **2** (*often* **expectations**) something expected, whether good or bad. **3** (*usu* **expectations**) money or property, etc that one expects to gain, esp by inheritance.

expectorant *med, adj* causing the coughing up of phlegm. ▸ *noun* an expectorant medicine.

expectorate *verb, tr & intr, med* to cough up and spit out (phlegm). ▪ **expectoration** *noun.* [17c: from Latin *expectorare*, from ex from + *pectus* the chest]

expedient *adj* **1** suitable or appropriate. **2** practical or advantageous, rather than morally correct. ▸ *noun* a suitable method or solution, esp one quickly thought of to meet an urgent need. ▪ **expediency** (*-ies*) *or* **expedience** *noun* **1** suitability or convenience. **2** practical advantage or self-interest, esp as opposed to moral correctness. ▪ **expediently** *adv.* [14c: from Latin *expediens* setting free]

expedite *verb* **1** to speed up, or assist the progress of something. **2** to carry something out quickly. [15c: from Latin *expedire* literally 'free the feet']

expedition *noun* **1** an organized journey with a specific purpose. **2** a group making such a journey. ▪ **expeditionary** *adj* relating to, forming, or for use on, an expedition. [15c: from Latin *expeditio*]

expeditious *adj, formal* carried out with speed and efficiency. [15c]

expel *verb* (***expelled, expelling***) **1** to dismiss from or deprive someone of membership of (a club or school, etc), usu permanently as punishment for misconduct. **2** to get rid of something; to force it out. ▪ **expellee** *noun* a person who is expelled. [14c: from Latin *expellere* to drive out]

expend *verb* to use or spend (time, supplies or effort, etc). [15c: from Latin *expendere* to weigh out]

expendable *adj* **1** able to be given up or sacrificed for some purpose or cause. **2** not valuable enough to be worth preserving.

expenditure *noun* **1** the act of expending. **2** an amount expended, esp of money.

expense *noun* **1** the act of spending money, or the amount of money spent. **2** something on which money is spent. **3** (**expenses**) a sum of one's own money spent doing one's job, or this sum of money or an allowance paid by one's employer to make up for this. [14c: from Latin *expensa*]

IDIOMS **at the expense of sth** *or* **sb 1** with the loss or sacrifice of them. **2** causing damage to their pride or reputation: *a joke at my expense.* **3** with the cost paid by them.

expense account *noun* **1** an arrangement by which expenses incurred during the performance of an employee's duties are reimbursed by the employer. **2** a statement of such incurred expenses.

expensive *adj* involving much expense; costing a great deal. ▪ **expensiveness** *noun.* [17c]

experience *noun* **1** practice in an activity. **2** knowledge or skill gained through practice. **3** wisdom gained through long and varied observation of life. **4** an event which affects or involves one. ▸ *verb* **1** to have practical acquaintance with someone or something. **2** to feel or undergo. ▪ **experienced** *adj.* [14c: from Latin *experientia*]

experiential *adj, philos* of knowledge or learning: based on direct experience. ▪ **experientially** *adv* in terms of direct experience. [19c]

experiment *noun* **1** a trial carried out in order to test a theory, a machine's performance, etc or to discover something unknown. **2** the carrying out of such trials. **3** an attempt at something original. ▸ *verb, intr* (*usu* **experiment on** *or* **with sth**) to carry out an experiment. ▪ **experimentation** *noun.* ▪ **experimenter** *noun.* [14c]

experimental *adj* **1** consisting of or like an experiment. **2** relating to, or used in, experiments. **3** trying out new styles and techniques. ▪ **experimentalism** *noun* use of, or reliance on, experiment. ▪ **experimentalist** *noun.* ▪ **experimentally** *adv.* [15c]

expert *noun* someone with great skill in, or extensive knowledge of, a particular subject. ▸ *adj* **1** highly skilled or extremely knowledgeable. **2** relating to or done by an expert or experts. ▪ **expertly** *adv.* [14c: from Latin *expertus*]

expertise *noun* special skill or knowledge. [19c]

expert system *noun, comput* a program that is designed to solve problems by utilizing both knowledge and reasoning derived from human expertise in a particular field. [20c]

expiate *verb* to make amends for (a wrong). ▪ **expiation** *noun.* ▪ **expiatory** *adj.* [16c: from Latin *expiare* to atone for]

expire *verb, intr* **1** to come to an end or cease to be valid. **2** to breathe out. **3** to die. ▪ **expiration** *noun, formal* **1** expiry. **2** the act or process of breathing out. [15c: from Latin *exspirare* to breathe out]

expiry *noun* (***-ies***) the ending of the duration or validity of something. [18c]

explain *verb, tr & intr* **1** to make something clear or easy to understand. **2** to give, or be, a reason for or account for. **3** (**explain oneself**) **a** to justify (oneself or one's actions); **b** to clarify one's meaning or intention. ▪ **explainable** *adj.* [15c: from Latin *explanare* to make flat]

PHRASAL VERBS **explain sth away** to dismiss it or lessen its importance by explanation.

explanation *noun* **1** the act or process of explaining. **2** a statement or fact that explains.

explanatory *adj* serving to explain.

expletive *noun* **1** a swearword or curse. **2** a meaningless exclamation. [17c: from Latin *explere* to fill up]

explicable *adj* able to be explained. [16c]

explicate *verb* **1** to explain (esp a literary work) in depth, with close analysis of particular points. **2** to unfold or develop (an idea or theory, etc). ▪ **explication** *noun.* [17c: from Latin *explicare* to fold out]

explicit *adj* **1** stated or shown fully and clearly. **2** speaking plainly and openly. ▪ **explicitly** *adv.* [17c: from Latin *explicitus* straightforward]

explode *verb* **1** *intr* of a substance: to undergo an explosion. **2** to cause something to undergo an explosion. **3** *intr* to undergo a violent explosion as a result of a chemical or nuclear reaction. **4** *intr* to suddenly show a strong or violent emotion, esp anger. **5** to disprove (a theory, etc) with vigour. **6** *intr* esp of population: to increase rapidly. [17c: from Latin *explodere* to force off stage by clapping]

exploded *adj* **1** blown up. **2** of a theory, etc: no longer accepted; proved false. **3** of a diagram: showing the different parts of something relative to, but slightly separated from, each other.

exploit *noun* /'ɛksplɔɪt/ (*usu* **exploits**) an act or feat, esp a bold or daring one. ▸ *verb* /ɪk'splɔɪt/ **1** to take unfair advantage of something or someone so as to achieve one's own aims. **2** to make good use of something. ▪ **exploitable** *adj.* ▪ **exploitation** *noun.* ▪ **exploitative** *or* **exploitive** *adj.* ▪ **exploiter** *noun.* [14c: from Latin *explicitum* unfolded]

exploratory *adj* **1** of talks, etc: serving to establish procedures or ground rules. **2** of surgery: aiming to establish the nature of a complaint rather than treat it.

explore *verb* **1** to search or travel through (a place) for the purpose of discovery. **2** to examine something carefully: *explore every possibility.* ▪ **exploration** *noun.* ▪ **explorative** *adj.* ▪ **explorer** *noun.* [16c: from Latin *explorare* to search out]

explosion *noun* **1** a sudden and violent increase in pressure, which generates large amounts of heat and destructive shock waves. **2** the sudden loud noise that accompanies such a reaction. **3** a sudden display of strong feelings, etc. **4** a sudden great increase. [17c: from Latin *explodere*]

explosive *adj* **1** likely, tending or able to explode. **2** likely to become marked by physical violence or emotional outbursts. **3** likely to result in violence or an outburst of feeling: *an explosive situation.* ▸ *noun* any substance that is capable of producing an explosion. ▪ **explosively** *adv.* ▪ **explosiveness** *noun.*

expo *noun, informal* a large public exhibition. [Early 20c: from **exposition**]

exponent *noun* **1** someone able to perform some art or activity, esp skilfully. **2** someone who explains and promotes (a theory or belief, etc). **3** *maths* a number that indicates how many times a given quantity, called the **base**, is to be multiplied by itself, usu denoted by a superscript number or symbol immediately after the quantity concerned, eg $6^4 = 6 \times 6 \times 6 \times 6$. Also called **power**, **index**. [16c: from Latin *exponere* to set out]

exponential *noun, maths* a function, equation, curve, etc that involves numbers raised to exponents. ▸ *adj* **1** *maths* to do with or involving numbers that are exponents. **2** having an increasingly steep rate of increase. ▪ **exponentially** *adv* on an exponential basis; very rapidly. [18c]

export *verb* /ɪk'spɔːt/ to send or take (goods, etc) to another country, esp for sale. ▸ *noun* /'ɛkspɔːt/ **1** the act or business of exporting. **2** something exported. ▪ **exportation** *noun* the exporting of goods. ▪ **exporter** *noun* a person or business that exports goods commercially. [17c: from Latin *exportare* to carry away]

expose *verb* **1** to remove cover, protection or shelter from something, or to allow this to be the case: *exposed to the wind* • *exposed to criticism.* **2** to discover something (eg a criminal or crime) or make it known. **3** (*always* **expose sb to sth**) to cause or allow them to have experience of it. **4** to allow light to fall on (a photographic film or paper) when taking or printing a photograph. [15c: from French *exposer* to set out]

exposé /ɛk'spoʊzeɪ/ *noun* **1** a formal statement of facts, esp one that introduces an argument. **2** an article or programme which exposes a public scandal or crime, etc. [19c: French, literally 'set out' or 'exposed']

exposition *noun* **1** an in-depth explanation or account (of a subject). **2** the act of presenting such an explanation, or a viewpoint. **3** a large public exhibition. **4** *music* the part of a sonata, fugue, etc, in which themes are presented. ▪ **expositional** *adj.* [14c: from Latin *expositio* a setting out]

expository *adj* explanatory; serving as, or like, an explanation.

ex post facto *adj* retrospective. ▸ *adv* retrospectively. [17c: Latin, meaning 'from what is done or enacted after']

expostulate *verb, intr* (*usu* **expostulate with sb about sth**) to argue or reason with them, esp in protest or so as to dissuade them. ▪ **expostulation** *noun.*

▪ **expostulative** *or* **expostulatory** *adj.* [16c: from Latin *expostulare* to demand]

exposure *noun* **1** the act of exposing or the state of being exposed. **2** the harmful effects on the body of extreme cold. **3** the number or regularity of someone's appearances in public, eg on TV. **4** the act of exposing photographic film or paper to light. **5** the amount of light to which a film or paper is exposed, or the length of time for which it is exposed. **6** the amount of film exposed or to be exposed in order to produce one photograph.

expound *verb* **1** to explain something in depth. **2** (*often* **expound on sth**) *intr* to talk at length about it. [14c: from Latin *exponere* to set out]

express *verb* **1** to put something into words. **2** to indicate or represent something with looks, actions, symbols, etc. **3** to show or reveal. **4** to press or squeeze out something. **5** to send something by fast delivery service. ▸ *adj* **1** of a train, etc: travelling esp fast, with few stops. **2** belonging or referring to, or sent by, a fast delivery service. **3** clearly stated: *his express wish.* **4** particular; clear: *with the express purpose of insulting him.* ▸ *noun* **1** an express train. **2** an express delivery service. ▸ *adv* by express delivery service. ▪ **expressible** *adj.* ▪ **expressly** *adv* **1** clearly and definitely. **2** particularly or specifically. [14c: from Latin *exprimere* to press out]

IDIOMS **express oneself** to put one's thoughts into words.

expression *noun* **1** the act of expressing. **2** a look on the face that displays feelings. **3** a word or phrase. **4** the indication of feeling, eg in a manner of speaking or a way of playing music. **5** *maths* a symbol or combination of symbols. ▪ **expressionless** *adj* of a face or voice: showing no feeling. [15c]

Expressionism *or* **expressionism** *noun* a movement in art, architecture and literature which aims to communicate the internal emotional realities of a situation, rather than its external 'realistic' aspect. ▪ **Expressionist** *noun* a person, esp a painter, who practises Expressionism. *as adj*: *an Expressionist painter.* ▪ **expressionistic** *adj.* [Early 20c]

expressive *adj* **1** showing meaning or feeling in a clear or lively way. **2** (*always* **expressive of sth**) expressing a feeling or emotion. ▪ **expressiveness** *noun.*

expresso see **espresso**

expressway *noun, N Am* a motorway.

expropriate *verb, formal or law* esp of the state: to take (property, etc) from its owner for some special use. ▪ **expropriation** *noun.* ▪ **expropriator** *noun.* [17c: from Latin *expropriare*]

expulsion *noun* **1** the act of expelling from school or a club, etc. **2** the act of forcing or driving out. ▪ **expulsive** *adj.* [14c: from Latin *expulsio* a forcing out]

expunge *verb* **1** to cross out or delete something (eg a passage from a book). **2** to cancel out or destroy something. [17c: from Latin *expungere* to mark for deletion by a row of dots]

expurgate *verb* **1** to revise (a book) by removing objectionable or offensive words or passages. **2** to remove (such words or passages). ▪ **expurgation** *noun.* ▪ **expurgator** *noun.* [17c: from Latin *expurgare* to purify]

exquisite *adj* **1** extremely beautiful or skilfully produced. **2** able to exercise sensitive judgement; discriminating: *exquisite taste.* **3** of pain or pleasure, etc: extreme. ▪ **exquisitely** *adv.* [15c: from Latin *exquisitus*]

extant *adj* still existing; surviving. [16c: from Latin *extans*, standing out]

extempore /ɪk'stɛmpərɪ/ *adv, adj* without planning or preparation. ▪ **extemporaneous** *or* **extemporary** *adj* **1** spoken or done, etc without preparation; impromptu. **2** makeshift or improvised. [16c: Latin *ex tempore* on the spur of the moment]

extemporize *or* **-ise** *verb, tr & intr* to speak or perform without preparation. ▪ **extemporization** *noun.* [17c]

extend *verb* **1** to make something longer or larger. **2** *tr & intr* to reach or stretch in space or time. **3** to hold out or stretch out (a hand, etc). **4** to offer (kindness or greetings, etc) to someone. **5** to increase something in scope. **6** (*always* **extend to sth**) *intr* to include or go as far as it: *Their kindness did not extend to lending money.* **7** to exert someone to their physical or mental limit: *extend oneself.* ▪ **extendable, extendible, extensible** *or* **extensile** *adj.* [14c: from Latin *extendere* to stretch out]

extended family *noun* the family as a unit including all relatives. Compare **nuclear family**.

extension *noun* **1** the process of extending something, or the state of being extended. **2** an added part, that makes the original larger or longer. **3** a subsidiary or extra telephone, connected to the main line. **4** an extra period beyond an original time limit. **5** range or extent. **6** *comput* a **file extension**. [14c]

extensive *adj* large in area, amount, range or effect. ▪ **extensively** *adv* to an extensive degree; widely. [17c]

extensor *noun, physiol* any of various muscles that straighten out parts of the body. Compare **flexor**. [18c: from Latin *extendere* to stretch out]

extent *noun* **1** the area over which something extends. **2** amount, scope or degree. [15c]

extenuate *verb* to reduce the seriousness of (an offence) by giving an explanation that partly excuses it. ▪ **extenuating** *adj* esp of a circumstance: reducing the seriousness of an offence by partially excusing it. ▪ **extenuation** *noun.* [16c: from Latin *extenuare* to make thin]

exterior *adj* **1** on, from, or for use on the outside. **2** foreign, or dealing with foreign nations. **3** *cinematog* outdoor. ▸ *noun* **1** an outside part or surface. **2** an outward appearance, esp when intended to conceal or deceive. **3** an outdoor scene in a film, etc. [16c: Latin, from *exterus* on the outside]

exterior angle *noun, maths* the angle between any extended side and the adjacent side of a polygon.

exterminate *verb* to get rid of or completely destroy (something living). ▪ **extermination** *noun.* ▪ **exterminator** *noun.* [16c: from Latin *exterminare* to drive away]

external *adj* **1** belonging to, for, from or on the outside. **2** being of the world, as opposed to the mind: *external realities.* **3** foreign; involving foreign nations: *external affairs.* **4** of a medicine: to be applied on the outside of the body. **5** taking place, or coming from, outside one's school or university, etc: *an external examination.* ▪ **externally** *adv.* [15c: from Latin *externus*]

externalize *or* **-ise** *verb* **1** to express (thoughts, feelings or ideas, etc) in words. **2** *psychol* to assign (one's feelings) to things outside oneself. [19c]

extinct *adj* **1** of a species of animal, etc: no longer in existence. **2** of a volcano: no longer active. ▪ **extinction** *noun* **1** the process of making or becoming extinct; elimination or disappearance. **2** *biol* the total elimination or dying out of any plant or animal species. [15c: from Latin *exstinguere* to extinguish]

extinguish *verb* **1** to put out (a fire, etc). **2** *formal* to kill off or destroy (eg passion). **3** *law* to pay off (a debt). ▪ **extinguishable** *adj.* ▪ **extinguisher** *noun* **1** a person or thing that extinguishes. **2** a **fire extinguisher**. [16c: from Latin *exstinguere*]

extirpate /ˈɛkstəpeɪt/ *verb, formal* **1** to destroy completely. **2** to uproot. ▪ **extirpation** *noun*. [16c: from Latin *exstirpare* to tear up by the roots]

extol *verb* (***extolled, extolling***) *rather formal* to praise enthusiastically. [15c: from Latin *extollere* to lift or raise up]

extort *verb* to obtain (money or information, etc) by threats or violence. ▪ **extortion** *noun*. [16c: from Latin *extorquere* to twist or wrench out]

extortionate *adj* of a price or demand, etc: unreasonably high or great. ▪ **extortionately** *adv.*

extra *adj* **1** additional; more than is usual, necessary or expected. **2** for which an additional charge is made. ▸ *noun* **1** an additional or unexpected thing. **2** **a** an extra charge; **b** an item for which this is made. **3** an actor employed for a small, usu non-speaking, part in a film. **4** a special edition of a newspaper containing later news. **5** *cricket* a run scored other than by hitting the ball with the bat. ▸ *adv* unusually or exceptionally. [17c: prob a shortening of **extraordinary**]

extra- *prefix, signifying* outside or beyond: *extramural* • *extra-curricular.* [From Latin *extra* outside]

extract *verb* /ɪkˈstrakt/ **1** to pull or draw something out, esp by force or with effort. **2** to separate (a substance) from a liquid or solid mixture. **3** to derive (pleasure, etc). **4** to obtain (money, etc) by threats or violence. **5** to select (passages from a book, etc). ▸ *noun* /ˈɛkstrakt/ **1** a passage selected from a book, etc. **2** *chem* a substance that is separated from a liquid or solid mixture by using heat, solvents or distillation, etc. ▪ **extractable** *adj.* ▪ **extractor** *noun* **1** a person or thing that extracts. **2** an extractor fan. [15c: from Latin *extrahere* to draw out]

extraction *noun* **1** the act of extracting. **2** the process whereby a metal is obtained from its ore. **3** the removal of a tooth from its socket. **4** family origin; descent: *of Dutch extraction.*

extractive industry *noun* an industry such as mining, forestry, agriculture, etc which draws out natural resources and processes them.

extractor fan *or* **extraction fan** *noun* an electric device for ventilating a room or building, etc.

extra-curricular *adj* not belonging to, or offered in addition to, the subjects studied in the main teaching curriculum of a school or college, etc.

extradite *verb* to return (a person accused of a crime) for trial in the country where the crime was committed. ▪ **extraditable** *adj.* ▪ **extradition** *noun.* [19c: from Latin *ex* from + *traditio* a handing over]

extramarital *adj* esp of sexual relations: taking place outside marriage. [20c]

extramural *adj* **1** of courses, etc: for people who are not full-time students at a college, etc. **2** outside the scope of normal studies. [19c: from Latin *murus* wall]

extraneous /ɪkˈstreɪnɪəs/ *adj* **1** not belonging; not relevant or related. **2** coming from outside. [17c: from Latin *extraneus* external]

extranet *noun, comput* a restricted network, eg in a company, which allows some access from users outside.

extraordinaire /ɪkˈstrɔːdɪnɛə(r)/ *adj* (*placed after the noun*) outstanding in a particular skill or area: *linguist extraordinaire.* [20c: French]

extraordinary *adj* **1** unusual; surprising or remarkable. **2** additional; not part of the regular pattern or routine: *extraordinary meeting.* **3** (*often following its noun*) *formal* employed to do additional work, or for a particular occasion: *ambassador extraordinary.* ▪ **extraordinarily** *adv.* [15c: from Latin *extra ordinem* outside the usual order]

extrapolate /ɪkˈstrapəleɪt/ *verb, tr & intr* **1** *maths* to estimate (a value that lies outside a known range of values), on the basis of those values and usu by means of a graph. **2** to make (estimates) or draw (conclusions) from known facts. ▪ **extrapolation** *noun.* [19c]

extrasensory *adj* achieved using means other than the ordinary senses of sight, hearing, touch, taste and smell: *extrasensory perception.* [20c]

extraterrestrial *adj* of a being or creature, etc: coming from outside the Earth or its atmosphere. ▸ *noun* an extraterrestrial being. [19c]

extravagant *adj* **1** using, spending or costing too much. **2** unreasonably or unbelievably great: *extravagant praise.* ▪ **extravagance** *noun.* ▪ **extravagantly** *adv.* [14c: from Latin *vagari* to wander]

extravaganza *noun* a spectacular display, performance or production. [18c: from Italian *estravaganza* extravagance]

extravert see **extrovert**

extreme *adj* **1** very high, or highest, in degree or intensity. **2** very far, or furthest, in any direction, esp out from the centre. **3** very violent or strong. **4** not moderate; severe: *extreme measures.* ▸ *noun* **1** either of two people or things as far, or as different, as possible from each other. **2** the highest limit; the greatest degree of any state or condition. ▪ **extremely** *adv* to an extreme degree. [15c: from Latin *extremus*]

IDIOMS **go to extremes** to take action beyond what is thought to be reasonable. **in the extreme** to the highest degree.

extreme sport *noun* an unconventional sport that exposes the participants to personal danger, eg bungee jumping. [20c]

extremist *noun* someone who has extreme opinions, esp in politics. ▸ *adj* relating to, or favouring, extreme measures. ▪ **extremism** *noun.* [19c]

extremity *noun* (***-ies***) **1** the furthest point. **2** an extreme degree; the quality of being extreme. **3** a situation of great danger. **4** (**extremities**) the hands and feet. [14c: from Latin *extremitas* end or farthest point]

extricate *verb* to free someone or something from difficulties; to disentangle. ▪ **extricable** *adj.* ▪ **extrication** *noun.* [17c: from Latin *extricare*]

extrinsic *adj* **1** external. **2** operating from outside. ▪ **extrinsically** *adv.* [16c: from Latin *extrinsecus* outwardly]

extrovert *or* **extravert** *noun* **1** *psychol* someone who is more concerned with the outside world and social relationships than with their inner thoughts and feelings. **2** someone who is sociable, outgoing and talkative. ▸ *adj* having the temperament of an extrovert; sociable or outgoing. Compare **introvert**. ▪ **extroversion** *noun.* ▪ **extroverted** *adj.* [Early 20c]

extrude *verb* **1** to squeeze something or force it out. **2** to force or press (a semi-soft solid material) through a **die**[2] (sense 1b) in order to mould it into a continuous length of product. ▪ **extrusion** *noun.* ▪ **extrusive** *adj.* [16c: from Latin *extrudere* to push out]

exuberant *adj* **1** in very high spirits. **2** enthusiastic and energetic. **3** of health, etc: excellent. **4** of plants, etc: growing abundantly. ▪ **exuberance** *noun* high spirits; enthusiasm. ▪ **exuberantly** *adv.* [15c: from Latin *exuberans*, from *uber* rich]

exudate *noun* **1** *biol* any substance released from a plant or animal through a gland, pore, or membrane, eg resin and sweat. **2** *pathol* a fluid that is discharged through small pores in membranes, usu as a result of inflammation. [19c; see **exude**]

exude *verb* **1** to give off or give out (an odour or sweat). **2** to show or convey (a quality or characteristic, etc) by one's behaviour. **3** *intr* to ooze out. ▪ **exudate** *noun.* ▪ **exudation** *noun.* [16c: from Latin *exsudare* to sweat out]

exult *verb, intr* **1** (*often* **exult in** *or* **at sth**) to be intensely joyful about it. **2** (*often* **exult over sth**) to show or enjoy a feeling of triumph. ▪ **exultant** *adj* joyfully or triumphantly elated. ▪ **exultation** *noun* a feeling or state of joyful elation. [16c: from Latin *exsultare* to jump up and down]

eye *noun* **1** the organ of vision, usu one of a pair. **2** the area of the face around the eye. **3** (*often* **eyes**) sight; vision: *Surgeons need good eyes.* **4** attention, gaze or observation: *catch someone's eye* • *in the public eye.* **5** the ability to appreciate and judge: *an eye for beauty.* **6** a look or expression: *a hostile eye.* **7** *botany* the bud of a tuber such as a potato. **8** an area of calm and low pressure at the centre of a tornado, etc. **9** any rounded thing, esp when hollow, eg the hole in a needle or the small wire loop that a hook fits into. ▸ *verb* (***eyeing*** *or* ***eying***) to look at something carefully. ▪ **eyed** *adj, esp in compounds* **1** having eyes of the specified kind. **2** spotted. ▪ **eyeless** *adj.* [Anglo-Saxon *eage*]

IDIOMS **an eye for an eye** retaliation; justice enacted in the same way or to the same degree as the crime. **be all eyes** *informal* to be vigilant. **be up to the** *or* **one's eyes in sth** to be busy or deeply involved in (work, a commitment, etc). **clap, lay** *or* **set eyes on sb** *or* **sth** *informal, usu with negatives* to see them or it: *I never want to set eyes on you again.* **have eyes for sb** to be interested in them. **have one's eye on sth** to be eager to acquire it. **in one's mind's eye** in one's imagination. **in the eyes of sb** in their estimation or opinion. **keep an eye on sb** *or* **sth** *informal* to keep them or it under observation. **keep one's eyes skinned** *or* **peeled** *informal* to watch or look out. **make eyes at sb** *informal* to look at them with sexual interest or admiration. **more than meets the eye** more complicated or difficult, etc than appearances suggest. **one in the eye for sb** *informal* a harsh disappointment or rebuff for them. **see eye to eye with sb** to be in agreement with them. **with an eye to sth** having it as a purpose or intention. **with one's eyes open** with full awareness of what one is doing.

PHRASAL VERBS **eye sb** *or* **sth up** *informal* to assess their worth or attractiveness.

eyeball *noun* the nearly spherical body of the eye. ▸ *verb, informal* **1** to face someone; to confront them. **2** to examine something closely.

eyebath *or* (*esp US*) **eyecup** *noun* a small vessel for holding and applying medication or cleansing solution, etc to the eye.

eyebright *noun* a small plant with white flowers marked with purple, used in herbal medicine to treat sore eyes. [16c]

eyebrow *noun* the arch of hair on the bony ridge above each eye. [15c]

IDIOMS **raise an eyebrow** *or* **one's eyebrows** to show surprise, interest or disbelief.

eye-catching *adj* drawing attention, esp by being strikingly attractive. ▪ **eye-catcher** *noun.*

eye contact *noun* a direct look between two people.

eyeful *noun, informal* **1** an interesting or beautiful sight. **2** an attractive woman. **3** a look or view. [19c]

eyeglass *noun* **1** a single lens in a frame, to assist weak sight. **2** (**eyeglasses**) *chiefly US* spectacles. [17c]

eyelash *noun* any of the short protective hairs that grow from the edge of the upper and lower eyelids. Often shortened to **lash**. [18c]

eyelet *noun* **1** a small hole in fabric, etc through which a lace, etc is passed. **2** the metal, etc ring reinforcing such a hole. [14c: from French *oillet*, diminutive of *oil* eye]

eyelid *noun* a protective fold of skin and muscle, lined with a membrane, that can be moved to cover or uncover the front of the eyeball. [13c]

eyeliner *noun* a cosmetic used to outline the eye. See also **kohl**.

eye-opener *noun* **1** *informal* a surprising or revealing sight or experience, etc. **2** *N Am* a drink of alcohol taken early in the morning.

eyepiece *noun, optics* the lens or group of lenses in an optical instrument that is nearest to the eye of the observer.

eye-rhyme *noun* a similarity of spelling but not pronunciation between words, as with *come* and *home*.

eyeshade *noun* a **visor**.

eyeshadow *noun* a coloured cosmetic for the eyelids.

eyesight *noun* the ability to see; power of vision.

eyesore *noun, derog* an ugly thing, esp a building. [16c]

eye tooth *noun* a **canine tooth**.

IDIOMS **give one's eye teeth for sth** to go to any lengths to obtain it.

eyewash *noun* **1** liquid for soothing sore eyes. **2** *informal, derog* nonsense; insincere or deceptive talk.

eyewitness *noun* someone who sees something happen, esp a crime.

eyrie *or* **aerie** /ˈɪərɪ/ *noun* **1** the nest of an eagle or other bird of prey, built in a high inaccessible place. **2** any house or fortified place, etc perched high up. [15c: from French *aire*]

F[1] *or* **f** *noun* (***Fs, F's*** *or* ***f's***) **1** the sixth letter of the English alphabet. **2** (**F**) *music* the fourth note in the scale of C major.

F[2] *abbrev* **1** Fahrenheit. **2** farad. **3** Fellow (of a society, etc). **4** *physics* force. **5** franc.

F[3] *symbol* **1** *chem* fluorine. **2** *genetics* filial generation, where F_1 is the first filial generation, etc.

f *abbrev* **1** fathom. **2** female. **3** feminine. **4** focal length. **5** (*pl* ***ff.***) folio. **6** (*pl* ***ff.***) following (page).

fa see **fah**

fab *adj, informal* fabulous. [20c]

Fabian /ˈfeɪbɪən/ *adj* **1** cautious; inclined to use delaying tactics. **2** relating to the **Fabian Society**, a body founded in 1884 for the gradual establishment of socialism. ▶ *noun* a member of this society. ▪ **Fabianism** *noun*. ▪ **Fabianist** *noun*. [18c: named after the Roman general, Q Fabius Maximus, who dealt with Hannibal by avoiding battle]

fable *noun* **1** a story with a moral, usu with animals as characters. **2** a lie; a false story. **3** myths and legends generally. ▪ **fabled** *adj*. [13c: from Latin *fabula* story]

fabric *noun* **1** woven, knitted or felted cloth. **2** quality; texture. **3** the walls, floor and roof of a building. **4** orderly structure: *the fabric of society*. **5** a type or method of construction. [15c: from Latin *fabrica* craft]

fabricate *verb* **1** to invent or make up (a story, evidence, etc). **2** to make something, esp from whatever materials are available. **3** to forge (a document, etc). ▪ **fabrication** *noun*. [16c: from Latin *fabricari* to construct]

fabulous *adj* **1 a** *informal* marvellous; wonderful; excellent; **b** immense; amazing. Often shortened to **fab**. **2** legendary; mythical. [16c: from Latin *fabulosus*]

façade *or* **facade** /fəˈsɑːd/ *noun* **1** the front of a building. **2** a false appearance that hides the reality. [17c: French, from Italian *faccia* face]

face *noun* **1** the front part of the head, from forehead to chin. **2** the features or facial expression. **3** a surface or side, eg of a mountain, gem, geometrical figure, etc. **4** the important or working side, eg of a golf-club head. **5 a** in a mine or quarry: the exposed surface from which coal, etc is mined; **b** on a cliff: the exposed surface, usu vertical; **c** *in compounds*: *coalface* • *cliff-face*. **6** the dial of a clock, watch, etc. **7** the side of a playing card that is marked with numbers, symbols, etc. **8** general look or appearance. **9** an aspect. **10** impudence; cheek. **11** *literary* someone's presence: *stand before his face*. **12** *printing* a typeface. ▶ *verb* **1** *tr & intr* to be opposite to something or someone; to turn to look at or look in some direction. **2** to have something unpleasant before one: *face ruin*. **3** to confront, brave or cope with (problems, difficulties, etc). **4** to accept (the unpleasant truth, etc). **5** to present itself to someone: *the scene that faced us*. **6** to cover with a surface: *bricks were faced with plaster*. See also **facial**. [13c: from Latin *facies* face]

IDIOMS **face the music** *informal* to accept unpleasant consequences at their worst; to brave a trying situation, hostile reception, etc. **face to face 1** in the presence of each other. **2** facing or confronting each other: *a face-to-face meeting*. **in the face of sth** in spite of a known circumstance, etc. **in your face 1** right in front of someone. **2** dealing with an issue in a direct and often provocative way. **on the face of it** superficially; at first glance. **put a good** *or* **brave face on sth** to try to hide disappointment, fear, etc concerning it. **save one's face** to preserve one's reputation, while avoiding humiliation or the appearance of giving in or climbing down. **set one's face against sth** to oppose an idea, course of action, etc, firmly. **show one's face** *often with negatives* to make an appearance: *didn't dare show his face*. **to sb's face** directly; openly, in someone's presence.

PHRASAL VERBS **face up to sth** *or* **sb** to accept an unpleasant fact, etc; to deal with it or them bravely.

face card see **court card**

facecloth *noun* a small square of towelling for washing with. Also called **flannel**.

faceless *adj* **1** of a person: with identity concealed; anonymous. **2** of bureaucrats, etc: impersonal.

facelift *noun* **1** a surgical operation to remove facial wrinkles by tightening the skin. **2** any procedure for improving the external appearance of something.

facer *noun* **1** a tool for smoothing or facing a surface. **2** *slang* a severe blow on the face. **3** *informal* a problem.

face-saving *adj* preserving a person's reputation, credibility, etc and avoiding humiliation or the appearance of climbing down. ▪ **face-saver** *noun*.

facet *noun* **1** a face of a cut jewel. **2** an aspect, eg of a problem, topic or someone's personality. ▶ *verb* (***faceted, faceting***) to cut a facet on (a jewel). [17c: from French *facette* small face]

facetious *adj* of a person or remark, etc: amusing or witty, esp unsuitably so. [16c: from Latin *facetus* witty]

face value *noun* **1** the stated value on a coin, stamp, etc. **2** the apparent meaning or implication, eg of a statement, which may not be the same as its real meaning.

facial *adj* belonging or relating to the face: *facial hair.* ▸ *noun* a beauty treatment for the face. ▪ **facially** *adv.* [17c: from Latin *facies* face]

facile *adj* **1** of success, etc: too easily achieved. **2** of remarks, opinions, etc: over-simple; showing a lack of careful thought. [15c: from Latin *facilis* easy]

facilitate *verb* to make something easy or easier to do. ▪ **facilitation** *noun.* [17c: from Latin *facilis* easy]

facility *noun* (**-ies**) **1** skill, talent or ability. **2** fluency; ease. **3** an arrangement, feature, attachment, etc that enables someone to do something. **4** (*chiefly* **facilities**) a building, service or piece of equipment for a particular activity. [16c: from Latin *facilitas* ease]

facing *noun* **1** an outer layer, eg of stone covering a brick wall. **2** a piece of material used to back and strengthen part of a garment.

facsimile /fak'sɪmɪlɪ/ *noun* **1** an exact copy made, eg of a manuscript, picture, etc. **2** electronic copying of a document and its transmission by telephone line. Usu called **fax**. **3** a copy made by facsimile. [17c: from Latin *fac simile* make the same]

fact *noun* **1** a thing known to be true, to exist or to have happened. **2** truth or reality, as distinct from mere statement or belief. **3** a piece of information. [16c: from Latin *facere* to do]

IDIOMS **after** *or* **before the fact** after or before a crime is committed. **as a matter of fact** *or* **in actual fact** *or* **in fact** *or* **in point of fact** in reality; actually.

faction[1] *noun* **1** an active or trouble-making group within a larger organization. **2** argument or dissent within a group. ▪ **factional** *adj.* [16c: from Latin *factio* party]

faction[2] *noun* **1** a play, programme, piece of writing, etc that is a mixture of fact and fiction. **2** this genre of writing, etc. Also called **drama documentary**. Compare **docudrama**. [1960s: from **fact** + *fiction*]

factitious *adj* **1** deliberately contrived rather than developing naturally. **2** insincere; false. [17c: from Latin *facticius*]

fact of life *noun* **1** an unavoidable truth, esp if unpleasant. **2** (**the facts of life**) basic information on sexual matters and reproduction.

factor *noun* **1** a circumstance that contributes to a result. **2** *maths* one of two or more numbers that, when multiplied together, produce a given number: *4 is a factor of 12.* **3** in Scotland: **a** the manager of an estate; **b** an agent responsible for renting property for an owner. [15c: Latin, meaning 'a person who acts']

factorial *noun, maths* (symbol **!**) the number resulting when a whole number and all whole numbers below it are multiplied together eg, 5! is $5 \times 4 \times 3 \times 2 \times 1 = 120$.

factorize *or* **-ise** *verb, maths* to find the factors of (a number). ▪ **factorization** *noun.*

factory *noun* (**-ies**) a building or buildings with equipment for the large-scale manufacture of goods. [16c: from Latin *factoria*, from **factor**]

factory farming *noun* farming in which animals are reared usu with a minimum of space and which uses highly industrialized machinery etc, in order to achieve maximum production.

factotum *noun* a person employed to do a large number of different jobs. [16c: from Latin *fac totum* do all]

factual *adj* **1** concerned with, or based on, facts. **2** actual. ▪ **factually** *adv.*

facultative *adj* **1** optional. **2** incidental. **3** relating to a faculty. **4** conferring privilege, permission or authority. ▪ **facultatively** *adv.*

faculty *noun* (**-ies**) **1** a mental or physical power. **2** a particular talent or aptitude for something. **3 a** a section of a university, comprising a number of departments: *the Faculty of Science*; **b** the professors and lecturers belonging to such a section. **4** *N Am* the staff of a college, school or university. [14c: from Latin *facultas* power or ability]

fad *noun, informal* **1** a short-lived fashion; a craze. **2** an odd idea, belief or practice. ▪ **faddy** *adj* (**-ier, -iest**). [19c]

fade *verb* **1** *tr & intr* to lose, or cause something to lose, strength, freshness, colour, etc. **2** *intr* of a sound, image, memory, feeling, etc: to disappear gradually. [13c: French, meaning 'dull' or 'pale']

PHRASAL VERBS **fade sth in** *or* **out** *cinematog, broadcasting* to make (a sound or picture) become gradually louder and more distinct, or gradually fainter and disappear.

faeces *or* (*N Am*) **feces** /'fiːsiːz/ *plural noun* waste matter discharged from the body through the anus. ▪ **faecal** *or* **fecal** /'fiːkəl/ *adj.* [17c: pl of Latin *faex* dregs]

faff *verb, intr, informal* (*also* **faff about**) to act in a fussy or dithering way. [19c]

fag *noun* **1** *informal* a cigarette. **2** *informal* a piece of drudgery; a bore. **3** *dated* a schoolboy who runs errands, etc for an older one. ▸ *verb* (**fagged, fagging**) **1** *tr* to tire out or exhaust. **2** *intr, dated* of a schoolboy: to act as fag. **3** *intr* to work hard; to toil. [15c: meaning 'something that hangs loose']

IDIOMS **fagged out** very tired; exhausted.

faggot *or* (*N Am*) **fagot** *noun* **1** a ball or roll of chopped pork and liver mixed with breadcrumbs and herbs, and fried or baked. **2** a bundle of sticks, twigs, etc, used for fuel, fascines, etc. [13c: from French *fagot* bundle of sticks]

fah *or* **fa** *noun, music* in sol-fa notation: the fourth note of the major scale. [14c; see **sol-fa**]

Fahrenheit /'farənhaɪt, 'fɑː-/ *noun* a scale of temperature on which water boils at 212° and freezes at 32° under standard atmospheric pressure. ▸ *adj* (abbrev **F**) on or relating to this scale. Compare **Celsius**. [18c: named after G D Fahrenheit, German physicist]

faience *or* **faïence** /faɪ'ɑ̃s/ *noun* glazed decorated pottery. [18c: from Faenza in Italy]

fail *verb* **1** *tr & intr* (*often* **fail in sth**) not to succeed; to be unsuccessful in (an undertaking). **2** to judge (a candidate) not good enough to pass a test, etc. **3** *intr* of machinery, a bodily organ, etc: to stop working or functioning. **4** *intr* not to manage (to do something): *failed to pay the bill in time.* **5** not to bother (doing something). **6** to let (someone) down; to disappoint. **7** of courage, strength, etc: to desert (one) at the time of need. **8** *intr* to become gradually weaker. **9** *intr* of a business, etc: to collapse; to become insolvent or bankrupt. ▸ *noun* a failure, esp in an exam. [13c: from Latin *fallere* to deceive or disappoint]

IDIOMS **without fail** for certain; with complete regularity and reliability.

failing *noun* a fault; a weakness. ▸ *prep* in default of; in the absence of: *Failing an agreement today, the issue will be referred for arbitration.*

fail-safe *adj* of a machine, system, etc: designed to return to a safe condition if something goes wrong.

failure *noun* **1** an act of failing; lack of success. **2** someone or something that is unsuccessful. **3** a stoppage in functioning, eg of a computer, machine, system, etc. **4** a poor result. **5** an instance or act of something not being done or not happening: *failure to turn up.*

fain *old use, adj* glad or joyful. ▸ *adv* gladly; willingly. [Anglo-Saxon *fægen*]

faint *adj* **1** pale; dim; indistinct; slight. **2** physically weak; on the verge of losing consciousness. **3** feeble; timid; unenthusiastic. ▸ *verb, intr* to lose consciousness; to collapse. ▸ *noun* a sudden loss of consciousness. [13c: from French *faindre* to feign]

faint-hearted *adj* timid; cowardly; spiritless.

fair[1] *adj* **1** just; not using dishonest methods or discrimination. **2** in accordance with the rules. **3 a** of hair and skin: light-coloured; **b** having light-coloured hair and skin. **4** *old use* beautiful. **5** quite good; reasonable. **6** sizeable; considerable. **7** of weather: fine. **8** of the wind: favourable. **9** of words: insincerely encouraging. ▸ *adv* **1** in a fair way. **2** *dialect* completely. ▪ **fairness** *noun.* [Anglo-Saxon *fæger* beautiful]

IDIOMS **be fair game** to deserve to be attacked or criticized. **by fair means or foul** using any possible means, even if dishonest. **fair-and-square 1** absolutely; exactly. **2** honest and open. **fair enough** all right. **in all fairness** *or* **to be fair** if one is fair; being scrupulously fair.

fair[2] *or* (*nostalgic*) **fayre** *noun* **1** a collection of sideshows and amusements, often travelling from place to place. **2** *hist* a market for the sale of produce, livestock, etc, with or without sideshows. **3** (*only* **fair**) an indoor exhibition of goods from different countries, firms, etc, held to promote trade. [14c: from Latin *feria* holiday]

fairground *noun* the piece of land on which sideshows and amusements are set up for a fair.

fairing *noun* an external structure fitted to an aircraft, vessel or other vehicle to improve streamlining and reduce drag. [1860s: from *fair* to make smooth]

fairly *adv* **1** justly; honestly. **2** quite; rather. **3** *informal* absolutely.

fair-minded *adj* impartial.

fair play *noun* honourable behaviour; just treatment.

fair trade *noun* a system of trade in which fair prices are paid for goods, especially those produced in developing countries.

fairway *noun* **1** *golf* a broad strip of short grass extending from the tee to the green. **2** a navigable deep-water channel.

fair-weather friend *noun* someone who cannot be relied on in times of trouble.

fairy *noun* (**-*ies***) **1** *myth* a supernatural being, usu with magical powers and of diminutive and graceful human form. **2** *slang, derog* a gay man. [14c: from French *faerie*]

fairy godmother *noun* someone who comes unexpectedly or magically to a person's aid.

fairyland *noun* **1** *myth* the home of fairies. **2** an entrancing place.

fairy ring *noun* a ring of darker grass marking the outer edge of an underground growth of fungi.

fairy tale *or* **fairy story** *noun* **1** a story about fairies, magic and other supernatural things. **2** a fantastical tale. **3** *euphem, informal* a lie. ▸ *adj* (**fairy-tale**) beautiful, magical or marvellous.

fait accompli /feɪt ə'kɒmpliː/ *noun* (***faits accomplis*** /-pliː/) something done and unalterable; an established fact. [19c: French, meaning 'accomplished fact']

faith *noun* **1** trust or confidence. **2** strong belief, eg in God. **3** a specified religion: *the Jewish faith.* **4** any set or system of beliefs. **5** loyalty to a promise, etc; trust: *break faith with someone.* [13c: from French *feid*]

faithful *adj* **1** having or showing faith. **2** loyal and true. **3** accurate. **4** loyal to a partner. **5** reliable; constant. ▸ *plural noun* **1** (**the Faithful**) the believers in a particular religion, esp Islam. **2** (**the faithful**) loyal supporters. ▪ **faithfully** *adv.* ▪ **faithfulness** *noun.*

faith healing *noun* the curing of illness through religious faith rather than medical treatment. ▪ **faith healer** *noun.*

faithless *adj* **1** disloyal; treacherous. **2** having no religious faith.

faith school *noun* a school that instructs its pupils in the teachings of a particular religion as part of its curriculum.

fajitas /fa'hiːtəz/ *plural noun* in Mexican cookery: a dish of strips of spiced chicken, beef, etc, served hot, wrapped in flour tortillas. [20c: from Mexican Spanish *fajo* a bundle]

fake *noun* someone or something that is not genuine. ▸ *adj* not genuine; false; counterfeit. ▸ *verb* **1** *tr* to alter something dishonestly; to falsify something or make something up. **2** *tr & intr* to pretend to feel (an emotion) or have (an illness). [18c]

fakir /'feɪkɪə(r)/ *noun* **1** a wandering Hindu or Muslim holy man, depending on begging for survival. **2** a member of any Muslim religious order. [17c: from Arabic *faqir* poor man]

falcon *noun* a type of long-winged bird of prey that can be trained to hunt small birds and animals. [13c: from Latin *falco* hawk]

falconry *noun* **1** the breeding and training of falcons for hunting. **2** the sport of using falcons to hunt prey. ▪ **falconer** *noun.*

the Fall *noun, Bible* the sinning of Adam and Eve when they disobeyed God by eating from the tree of knowledge, resulting in a state of sinfulness marking the human condition.

fall *verb* (***fell, fallen***) *intr* **1** to descend or drop freely and involuntarily, esp accidentally, by force of gravity. **2** (*also* **fall over** *or* **down**) of someone, or something upright: to drop to the ground after losing balance. **3** of a building, bridge, etc: to collapse. **4** of rain, snow, etc: to come down from the sky; to precipitate. **5** of hair, etc: to hang down. **6** (*usu* **fall on sth**) of a blow, glance, shadow, light, etc: to land. **7** to go naturally or easily into position. **8** of a government, leader, etc: to lose power; to be no longer able to govern. **9** of a stronghold: to be captured. **10** of defences or barriers: to be lowered or broken down. **11** to die or be badly wounded in battle, etc. **12** to give in to temptation; to sin. **13** of value, temperature, etc: to become less. **14** of sound: to diminish. **15** of silence: to intervene. **16** of darkness or night: to arrive. **17** to pass into a certain state; to begin to be in that state: *fall asleep* • *fall in love*. **18** to be grouped or classified in a certain way: *falls into two categories*. **19** to occur at a certain time or place: *The accent falls on the first syllable*. **20** of someone's face: to show disappointment. ▸ *noun* **1** an act or way of falling. **2** something, or an amount, that falls. **3** (*often* **falls**) a waterfall. **4** a drop in quality, quantity, value, temperature, etc. **5** a defeat or collapse. **6** (*also* **Fall**) *N Am* autumn. **7** *wrestling* a manoeuvre by which one pins one's opponent's shoulders to the ground. [Anglo-Saxon *feallan*]

IDIOMS **fall foul of sb** *or* **sth** to get into trouble or conflict with them or it. **fall head over heels** to fall hopelessly (in love). **fall over oneself** *or* **fall over backwards** *informal* to be strenuously or noticeably eager to please or help. **fall short** *or* **fall short of sth** **1** to turn out not to be enough; to be insufficient. **2** to fail to attain or reach what is aimed at. See also **shortfall**. **fall to pieces** *or* **bits** **1** of something: to break up; to disintegrate. **2** of someone: to be unable to function normally.

PHRASAL VERBS **fall about** *informal* to be helpless with laughter. **fall apart** **1** to break in pieces. **2** to fail; to collapse. **fall away** **1** of land: to slope downwards. **2** to become fewer or less. **3** to disappear. **fall back on sth** to make use of it in an emergency. **fall behind** *or* **fall behind with sth** to fail to keep up with someone, with one's work, with paying rent, etc. **fall down** of an argument, etc: to be shown to be invalid. **fall for sb** to fall in love with them. **fall for sth** to be deceived or taken in by it; to be conned by it. **fall in** **1** of a roof, etc: to collapse. **2** of a soldier, etc: to take his or her place in a parade. **fall into sth** to become involved in it, esp by chance or without having put much effort into getting there. **fall in with sb** to chance to meet or coincide with them. **fall in with sth** to agree to it; to support it. **fall off** to decline in quality or quantity; to become less. **fall out** **1** of a soldier: to come out of military formation. **2** to happen in the end; to turn out. **fall out with sb** to quarrel with them, and then not have contact with them for a period of time. **fall through** of a plan, etc: to fail; to come to nothing. **fall to sb** to become their job or duty.

fallacy *noun* (***-ies***) **1** a mistaken notion. **2** a mistake in reasoning that spoils a whole argument. See also **logic**, **syllogism**. ▪ **fallacious** *adj*. [15c: from Latin *fallax* deceptive]

fallen *adj* **1** *old use* having lost one's virtue, honour or reputation: *fallen woman*. **2** killed in battle.

fall guy *noun, informal* **1** someone who is easily cheated; a dupe. **2** someone who is left to take the blame for something; a scapegoat.

fallible *adj* capable of making mistakes. ▪ **fallibility** *noun* (***-ies***). [15c: from Latin *fallere* to deceive]

Fallopian tube *noun, anatomy, zool* in female mammals: either of the two long slender tubes through which the egg cells pass from the ovaries to the uterus. [18c: named after G Fallopius, Italian anatomist]

fallout *noun* **1** a cloud of radioactive dust caused by a nuclear explosion. **2** (**fall-out** *and* **falling-out**) a quarrel. **3** (**fall-out**) the act of leaving a military formation.

fallow *adj* of land: left unplanted after ploughing, to recover its natural fertility. [Anglo-Saxon *fealga*]

fallow deer *noun* a small deer with a reddish-brown coat that becomes spotted with white in summer. [Anglo-Saxon *fealu* tawny]

false *adj* **1** of a statement, etc: untrue. **2** of an idea, etc: mistaken. **3** artificial; not genuine. **4** of words, promises, etc: insincere. **5** treacherous; disloyal. **6** *botany* of a plant: resembling, but wrongly so called: *false acacia*. ▸ *adv* in a false manner; incorrectly; dishonestly. ▪ **falsely** *adv*. ▪ **falseness** *noun*. ▪ **falsity** *noun* (***-ies***). [12c: from Latin *fallere* to deceive]

IDIOMS **under false pretences** by giving a deliberately misleading impression.

false alarm *noun* an alarm given unnecessarily.

falsehood *noun* **1** dishonesty. **2** a lie.

false move *noun* a careless or unwise action.

false start *noun* **1** a failed attempt to begin something. **2** an invalid start to a race, in which one or more competitors begin before the signal is given.

falsetto *noun* **1** an artificially high voice, esp produced by a tenor above his normal range. **2** someone who uses such a voice. [18c: Italian]

falsify *verb* (***-ies, -ied***) to alter (records, accounts, evidence, etc) dishonestly, or make something up, in order to deceive or mislead. ▪ **falsification** *noun*. [15c: from French *falsifier*]

falter *verb* **1** *intr* to move unsteadily; to stumble. **2** *intr* to start functioning unreliably. **3** *intr* to lose strength or conviction. **4** *tr & intr* to speak, or say something, hesitantly. ▪ **faltering** *adj*. [14c]

fame *noun* **1** the condition of being famous; celebrity. **2** *old use* repute. ▪ **famed** *adj* renowned; famous. [13c: from Latin *fama* report or rumour]

familiar *adj* **1** well known or recognizable. **2** frequently met with. **3** (**familiar with**) well acquainted with or having a thorough knowledge of something. **4** friendly; close. **5** over-friendly. ▸ *noun* **1** a close friend. **2** a demon or spirit, esp one in the shape of an animal, that serves a witch. ▪ **familiarity** *noun*. ▪ **familiarly** *adv*. [14c: from Latin *familiaris* domestic or intimate]

familiarize *or* **-ise** *verb* **1** (*usu* **familiarize with sth**) to make (someone or oneself) familiar with it. **2** to make something well known or familiar.

family *noun* (***-ies***) **1** a group consisting of a set of parents and children. Compare **nuclear family**. **2** a group of people related to one another by blood or marriage. Compare **extended family**. **3** a person's children. **4** a household of people. **5** all those descended from a common ancestor. **6** a related group, eg of languages, etc. **7** *biol* in taxonomy: a division of an **order** (sense 11) which is subdivided into one or more genera (see **genus** sense 1). ▸ *adj* **a** belonging to or specially for a family: *family car*; **b** concerning the family: *family matters*; **c** suitable for the whole family: *family pub*. ▪ **familial** *adj*. [14c: from Latin *familia* household]

family

You can use either a singular or plural verb with a collective noun such as **family**. If you want to emphasize the family as a single unit, use a singular verb:

The family was faced with tragedy.

If you want to emphasize the family as a number of individuals, use a plural verb:

The family are very pleasant.

family name *noun* a surname.

family planning *noun* **birth control**.

family tree *noun* the relationships within a family throughout the generations, or a diagram showing these. Compare **genealogy**.

famine *noun* a great shortage of food, usually caused by an increase in population or failure of food crops. [14c: French, from Latin *fames* hunger]

famished *adj* **1** starving. **2** (*also* **famishing**) *informal* feeling very hungry. [14c: from Latin *fames* hunger]

famous *adj* **1** well known; celebrated; renowned. **2** great; glorious: *a famous victory*. ▪ **famously** *adv*. [14c: from Latin *fama* report or fame]

IDIOMS **famous last words** a remark or prediction likely to be proved wrong by events. **get on famously** to be on excellent terms (with someone).

fan[1] *noun* **1** a hand-held device, usu semicircular, and made of silk or paper, for creating a cool current of air. **2** any mechanical or electrical device that creates air currents, esp for ventilation. **3** any structure that can be spread into the shape of a fan, eg a bird's tail. ▸ *verb* (***fanned, fanning***) **1** to cool or ventilate with a fan or similar device. **2** to kindle (flames, resentment, etc). **3** (*often* **fan out** *or* **fan sth out**) to spread out, or cause to spread out, in the shape of a fan. [Anglo-Saxon *fann*]

fan[2] *noun* an enthusiastic supporter or devoted admirer, esp of a pop group, a football team, a sport, etc. [17c: from **fanatic**]

fanatic *noun* someone with an extreme or excessive enthusiasm for something, esp a religion, or religious issues. ▸ *adj* (*also* **fanatical**) extremely or excessively enthusiastic about something. ▪ **fanaticism** *noun*. [16c: from Latin *fanaticus* frenzied]

fan belt *noun* in a vehicle engine: the rubber belt that drives the cooling fan.

fancier *noun, esp in compounds* someone with a special interest in, or knowledge of, a specified bird, animal or plant: *pigeon fancier*.

fanciful *adj* **1** indulging in fancies; imaginative or over-imaginative. **2** existing in fancy only; imaginary. **3** designed in a curious or fantastic way. ▪ **fancifully** *adv*.

fan club *noun* a club of admirers of a pop star, etc.

fancy *noun* (***-ies***) **1** the imagination. **2** an image, idea or whim. **3** a sudden liking or desire for something. ▸ *adj* (***-ier, -iest***) **1** elaborate. **2** *informal* special, unusual or superior, esp in quality. **3** *informal, facetious* of prices: too high. ▸ *verb* (***-ies, -ied***) **1** to think or believe something. **2** to have a desire for something. **3** *informal* to be physically attracted to someone. **4** to consider likely to win or do well. **5** *tr & intr* to take in mentally; to imagine: *Fancy him getting married at last!* ▸ *exclam* (*also* **fancy that!**) expressing surprise. ▪ **fanciable** *adj*. ▪ **fancily** *adv*. [15c: shortened from **fantasy**]

fancy dress *noun* clothes for dressing up in, usu representing a historical, fictional, popular, etc character, esp for a **fancy-dress ball** *or* **fancy-dress party**.

fancy-free *adj* **1** not in love. **2** free to do as one pleases.

fandango *noun* **1** an energetic Spanish dance. **2** the music for this dance, in 3/4 time. [18c: Spanish]

fanfare *noun* a short piece of music played on trumpets to announce an important event or arrival. [18c: French, prob imitating the sound]

fang *noun* **1** a sharp pointed tooth, esp a large canine tooth of a carnivorous animal. **2** a tooth of a poisonous snake. [Anglo-Saxon, meaning 'something caught']

fanlight *noun* a semicircular window over a door or window.

fantasia *noun* **1** a musical composition that is free and unconventional in form. **2** a piece of music based on a selection of popular tunes. [18c: Italian, meaning 'imagination']

fantasize *or* **-ise** *verb, intr* (*often* **fantasize about sth**) to indulge in pleasurable fantasies or daydreams.

fantastic *or* **fantastical** *adj* **1** *informal* splendid; excellent. **2** *informal* enormous; amazing. **3** of a story, etc: absurd; unlikely; incredible. **4** fanciful; strange; unrealistic: *fantastic idea*. ▪ **fantastically** *adv*. [15c: from Greek *phantastikos* presenting to the mind]

fantasy *noun* (***-ies***) **1** a pleasant daydream. **2** something longed-for but unlikely to happen. **3** a mistaken notion. **4** the activity of imagining. **5** a fanciful piece of writing, music, film-making, etc. [14c: from Greek *phantasia* image in the mind, imagination]

fanzine *noun* a magazine written, published and distributed by and for a particular group of enthusiasts or fans. [1940s: **fan**[2] + maga*zine*]

FAQ *abbrev, comput* frequently asked questions.

far (***farther, farthest*** *or* ***further, furthest***) *adv* **1** at, to or from a great distance. **2** to or by a great extent: *My guess wasn't far out*. **3** at or to a distant time. ▸ *adj* **1** distant; remote. **2** the more distant of two things. **3** extreme: *the far Right of the party*. See also **farther**, **further**. [Anglo-Saxon *feorr*]

IDIOMS **as far as** up to a certain place or point. **by far** *or* **far and away** by a considerable amount; very much. **far and wide** extensively; everywhere. **far from** the opposite of; not at all. **far gone** in an advanced state, eg of illness or drunkenness. **go far** to achieve great things. **go so far** *or* **as far as to do sth** to be prepared to do it; to go to the extent of doing it. **go too far** to behave, speak, etc unreasonably. **in so far as** to the extent that.

farad *noun, electronics* (abbrev **F**) the SI unit of electrical **capacitance**, defined as the capacitance of a capacitor in which a charge of one **coulomb** produces a potential difference of one **volt** between its terminals. [19c: named after Michael Faraday, British physicist]

faraday *noun, physics* (abbrev **F**) a unit of electrical charge, defined as the charge on a **mole**[4], which is equal to 9.65×10^4 **coulomb**s. [20c: named after Michael Faraday, British physicist]

faraway *adj* **1** distant. **2** of a look or expression: dreamy; abstracted; absent-minded.

farce *noun* **1 a** a comedy involving a series of ridiculously unlikely turns of events; **b** comedies of this type. **2** an absurd situation; something ludicrously badly organized. ▪ **farcical** *adj*. ▪ **farcically** *adv*. [14c: French, meaning 'stuffing']

fare *noun* **1** the price paid by a passenger to travel on a bus, train, etc. **2** a taxi passenger. **3** food or the provision of food. ▸ *verb, intr, formal* **1** to get on (in a specified way): *She fared well.* **2** *archaic, poetic* to travel. [Anglo-Saxon *faran* to go]

the Far East *noun* a loosely-used term for the countries of E and SE Asia. ▪ **Far Eastern** *adj.*

farewell *exclam, old use* goodbye! ▸ *noun* an act of saying goodbye; an act of departure. ▸ *adj* parting; valedictory; final: *a farewell party.* [14c: **fare** + **well**[1]]

far-fetched *adj* of an idea, story, excuse, etc: unlikely; unconvincing.

far-flung *adj* **1** extensive. **2** distant: *the far-flung corners of the world.*

farina *noun* flour; meal. ▪ **farinaceous** *adj.* [14c: Latin, from *far* corn]

farm *noun* **1** a piece of land with its buildings, used for growing crops, breeding livestock, etc. **2** a farmer's house and the buildings round it. **3** a place specializing in the rearing or growing of a specified type of livestock, crop, etc: *dairy farm* • *fish farm.* ▸ *verb* **1 a** *tr* to prepare and use (land) for crop-growing, animal-rearing, etc. **b** *intr* to be a farmer. **2** *tr* to collect and keep the proceeds from (taxes, etc) in return for a fixed sum. **3** *tr* (*also* **farm out**) **a** to hand over (a child, old person, etc) temporarily to a carer; **b** to hand over (work, etc) to another to do. [14c: from Latin *firma* fixed payment]

farmer *noun* someone who earns a living by managing or operating a farm, either as owner or tenant.

farmers' market *noun* a market where food producers sell their products directly to local consumers.

farm hand, farm labourer *or* **farm worker** *noun* a person whose job is to work on a farm.

farming *noun* the business of running a farm.

farmyard *noun* the central yard at a farm, surrounded by farm buildings.

far-off *adj, adv* distant; remote.

far-out *adj, informal* **1** strange; weird. **2** excellent.

farrago /fəˈrɑːɡoʊ/ *noun* (***farragos*** *or* ***farragoes***) a confused mixture; a hotchpotch. [17c: Latin, meaning 'mixed fodder']

far-reaching *adj* extensive in scope, influence, etc: *far-reaching consequences.*

farrier *noun* **1** a person who shoes horses. **2** a person who treats horses for diseases or injuries. [16c: Latin *ferrarius* smith]

farrow *noun* a sow's litter of piglets. ▸ *verb, tr & intr* of a sow: to give birth to (piglets). [Anglo-Saxon *fearh*]

Farsi *noun* modern **Persian**, the official language of Iran. [19c: from Arabic *Fars,* the name of a province in SW Iran]

far-sighted *adj* **1** (*also* **far-seeing**) wise; prudent; forward-looking. **2** long-sighted.

fart *slang, verb, intr* to emit wind from the anus. ▸ *noun* **1** an emission of this kind. **2** a term of abuse for a person: *a boring old fart.* [Anglo-Saxon]

farther *adj, adv* further (with reference to physical distance). See also **far**.

---

farther, further

You can use either **farther** or **further** when you are talking about an actual physical distance:

I can't walk any farther/further.

However, you should always use **further** when you mean 'additional' or 'beyond this point':

I would like to make one further remark.

I want to take this complaint further.

---

farthest *adj, adv* furthest (with reference to physical distance). See also **far**.

farthing *noun, formerly* **1** one quarter of an old British penny. **2** a coin of this value. [Anglo-Saxon *feortha* quarter]

fasces /ˈfasiːz/ *plural noun, Roman hist* a bundle of rods with an axe in the middle, carried before magistrates as a symbol of authority. [16c: from Latin *fascis* bundle]

fascia /ˈfeɪʃɪə/ *noun* (***fasciae*** /-ʃiiː/ *or* ***fascias***) **1** the board above a shop entrance, bearing the shop name and logo, etc. **2** *Brit* the dashboard of a motor vehicle. **3** *archit* a long flat band or surface. **4** /ˈfaʃɪə/ *anatomy* connective tissue sheathing a muscle or organ. **5** any bandlike structure. [16c: from Latin *fascia* band]

fasciitis /faʃɪˈaɪtɪs/ *noun, med* inflammation of the **fascia** (sense 4).

fascinate *verb* **1** to interest strongly; to intrigue. **2** to hold spellbound; to enchant irresistibly. ▪ **fascinating** *adj.* ▪ **fascinatingly** *adv.* ▪ **fascination** *noun.* [17c: from Latin *fascinare* to bewitch]

---

fascinate

This word is often misspelt. It might help you to remember the following sentence:

***Sc**ience fa**sc**inates me.*

---

fascism /ˈfaʃɪzəm/ *noun* **1** a political movement or system characterized mainly by a belief in the supremacy of the chosen national group. **2** (**Fascism**) this system in force in Italy from 1922 to 1943. **3** any system or doctrine characterized by a belief in the supremacy of a particular way of viewing things. [1920s: from Latin *fascis* bundle or group]

fascist *noun* **1** an exponent or supporter of Fascism or (loosely) anyone with extreme right-wing nationalistic, etc views. **2** (**Fascist**) a member of the ruling party in Italy from 1922–43, or a similar party elsewhere, in particular the **Nazi** party in Germany. ▸ *adj* belonging or relating to Fascism. ▪ **fascistic** *adj.*

fashion *noun* **1** style, esp the latest style, in clothes, music, lifestyle, etc. **2** a currently popular style or practice; a trend. **3** a manner of doing something: *in a dramatic fashion.* **4** sort, type or kind. ▸ *verb* **1** to form or make something into a particular shape, esp with the hands. **2** to mould or influence something. [14c: from Latin *facere* to make]

IDIOMS **after a fashion** in a rather clumsy or inexpert way.

fashionable *adj* **1** of clothes, people, etc: following the latest fashion. **2** used by or popular with fashionable people. ▪ **fashionably** *adv.*

fast[1] *adj* **1** moving, or able to move, quickly. **2** taking a relatively short time. **3** of a clock, etc: showing a time in advance of the correct time. **4** allowing or intended for rapid movement: *the fast lane.* **5** of a photographic film: requiring only brief exposure. **6** *informal* seeking excitement; dissolute. **7** firmly fixed or caught; steadfast. **8** of friends: firm; close. **9** of fabric colours: not liable to run or fade. ▸ *adv* **1** quickly; rapidly. **2** in quick succession: *coming thick and fast.* **3** firmly; tight: *The glue held fast.* **4** deeply; thoroughly: *fast asleep.* [Anglo-Saxon *fæst* fixed or firm]

IDIOMS **play fast and loose** to behave irresponsibly

or unreliably. **pull a fast one** *informal* to cheat or deceive.

fast[2] *verb, intr* to go without food, or restrict one's diet, esp as a religious discipline. ▸ *noun* a period of fasting. ▪ **fast day** *noun.* ▪ **fasting** *noun.* [Anglo-Saxon *fæstan*]

fast-breeder reactor *noun* a type of nuclear reactor in which the neutrons produced during nuclear fission are not slowed down by a moderator, but are used to produce more of the same nuclear fuel, with as much fuel being produced as is consumed by the reactor. Compare **breeder reactor**.

fasten *verb* **1** (*also* **fasten up**) to make something firmly closed or fixed. **2** to attach something to something else. **3** *intr* to become fastened. **4** to be capable of being fastened. **5** *intr* (*usu* **fasten on** *or* **upon sth**) to concentrate on it eagerly; to dwell on it. ▪ **fastener** *or* **fastening** *noun.* [Anglo-Saxon *fæstnian*]

fast food *noun* ready-prepared food, such as hamburgers, fried fish, chips, etc, either to be eaten in the restaurant or taken away. *as adj*: *fast-food outlet*.

fast-forward *noun* a facility on a video player, cassette player, CD or DVD player, etc for advancing the tape or disc quickly. ▸ *verb* to advance a tape or disc quickly by this means.

fastidious *adj* **1** particular in matters of taste and detail, esp excessively so. **2** easily disgusted. [15c: from Latin *fastidium* disgust]

fastness *noun* **1** the quality of being firmly fixed or, with reference to fabric colours, fast. **2** *old use* a stronghold.

fast-talk *verb* to persuade with rapid talk and plausible arguments.

fast-track *informal, noun* **1** a routine for accelerating a proposal, etc through its formalities. **2** a quick route to advancement. ▸ *verb* to process something or promote someone speedily.

fat *noun* **1** any of a group of organic compounds that occur naturally in animals and plants, are solid at room temperature, and are insoluble in water. **2 a** in mammals: a layer of white or yellowish tissue that lies beneath the skin and between various organs, and which serves both as a thermal insulator and as a means of storing energy; **b** an excess of this. ▸ *adj* (***fatter, fattest***) **1** having too much fat on the body; plump; overweight. **2** containing a lot of fat. **3** thick or wide. **4** *informal* of a fee, profit, etc: large. **5** fertile; profitable: *a fat land*. **6** *facetious, slang* none at all: *a fat chance*. [Anglo-Saxon *fætt* fatted]

fatal *adj* **1** causing death; deadly. **2** bringing ruin; disastrous: *a fatal mistake*. **3** destined; unavoidable. ▪ **fatally** *adv.* [14c: from Latin *fatalis*, from *fatum* **fate**]

fatalism *noun* **1** a belief or the philosophical doctrine that all events are predestined and humans cannot alter them. **2** a defeatist attitude or outlook. ▪ **fatalist** *noun.* ▪ **fatalistic** *adj.* [17c: **fatal** + **-ism** (sense 1)]

fatality *noun* (***-ies***) **1** an accidental or violent death. **2** a person who has been killed in an accident, etc. **3** the quality of being fatal.

fate *noun* **1** (*also* **Fate**) the apparent power that determines the course of events, over which humans have no control. **2** the individual destiny or fortune of a person or thing. **3** ultimate outcome. **4** death, downfall, destruction or doom. [14c: from Latin *fatum* that which has been spoken, ie by an oracle]

fated *adj* **1** destined or intended by fate. **2** doomed.

fateful *adj* **1** of a remark, etc: prophetic. **2** decisive; critical; having significant results. **3** bringing calamity or disaster. ▪ **fatefully** *adv.*

the Fates *plural noun, myth* the three goddesses who determine the birth, life and death of humans.

father *noun* **1** a male parent. **2** (**fathers**) one's ancestors. **3** a founder, inventor, originator, pioneer or early leader. **4** (**Father**) a title or form of address for a priest. **5** (**Father**) *Christianity* **a** God; **b** the first person of the Trinity (see **trinity** sense 3); God. **6** (**fathers**) the leading or senior men of a city, etc. **7** the oldest member or member of longest standing of a profession or body. **8** (**Father**) used as a title in personifying something ancient or venerable: *Father Time*. ▸ *verb* **1** to be the father of (a child); to beget (offspring); to procreate. **2** to invent or originate (an idea, etc). ▪ **fatherhood** *noun.* [Anglo-Saxon *fæder*]

Father Christmas *noun* Santa Claus.

father figure *noun* an older man who is respected and admired.

father-in-law *noun* (***fathers-in-law***) the father of one's wife or husband.

fatherland *noun* one's native country.

fatherly *adj* benevolent, protective and encouraging, like a father should be to a child. ▪ **fatherliness** *noun.*

fathom *noun* in the imperial system: a unit of measurement of the depth of water, equal to 6ft (1.8m). ▸ *verb* (*also* **fathom sth out**) **1** to work out a problem; to get to the bottom of a mystery. **2** to measure the depth of water. ▪ **fathomable** *adj.* [Anglo-Saxon *fæthm*]

fatigue *noun* (*pl* in sense 4 only ***fatigues***) **1** tiredness after work or effort, either mental or physical; exhaustion. **2** *physiol* a decreased power of response to stimulus, resulting from work or effort. **3** weakness, esp in metals, caused by variations in stress. **4** (**fatigues**) military clothing. ▸ *verb, tr & intr* to exhaust or become exhausted. [17c: from Latin *fatigare* to weary]

fatten *verb, tr & intr* (*also* **fatten up**) to make or become fat. ▪ **fattening** *adj, noun.*

fatty *adj* (***-ier, -iest***) **1** containing fat. **2** greasy; oily. **3** of an acid: occurring in, derived from or chemically related to animal or vegetable fats. ▸ *noun* (***-ies***) *derog, informal* a fat person.

fatty acid *noun* any of a group of acids, obtained from animal and vegetable fats.

fatuous *adj* foolish, esp in a self-satisfied way; empty-headed; inane. ▪ **fatuity** *noun* (***-ies***). ▪ **fatuously** *adv.* [17c: from Latin *fatuus*]

fatwa *or* **fatwah** /ˈfatwə/ *noun* a formal legal opinion or decree issued by a Muslim authority. [17c as *fetfa*: Arabic, meaning 'a legal decision']

faucet /ˈfɔːsɪt/ *noun* **1** a **tap**[2] fitted to a barrel. **2** *N Am* a **tap**[2] on a bath, etc. [15c: from French *fausset* peg]

fault *noun* **1** a weakness or failing in character. **2** a flaw or defect in an object or structure. **3** a misdeed or slight offence. **4** responsibility for something wrong: *all my fault*. **5** *geol* a break or crack in the Earth's crust. **6** *tennis, etc* an incorrectly placed or delivered serve. **7** *showjumping* a penalty for refusing or failing to clear a fence. ▸ *verb* **1** *intr* to commit a fault. **2** to blame someone. ▪ **faultless** *adj.* [14c: from French *faute*]

IDIOMS **at fault** culpable; to blame. **find fault with sth** *or* **sb** to criticize it or them, esp excessively or unfairly. **to a fault** to too great an extent.

faulty *adj* (**-ier, -iest**) **1** having a fault or faults. **2** particularly of a machine or instrument: not working correctly.

faun *noun, Roman myth* a mythical creature with a man's head and body and a goat's horns, hind legs and tail. [14c: from Latin *Faunus* a rural deity]

fauna *noun* (***faunas*** *or* ***faunae*** /ˈfɔːniː/) the wild animals of a particular region, country, or time period. Compare **flora**. ▪ **faunal** *adj.* [18c: Latin *Fauna* goddess of living creatures, sister of Faunus (see **faun**)]

faux pas /foʊ pɑː/ *noun* (*pl* ***faux pas*** /foʊ pɑː/) an embarrassing blunder, esp a social one. [17c: French, meaning 'false step']

favour *or* (*N Am*) **favor** *noun* **1** a kind or helpful action. **2** liking, approval or goodwill. **3** unfair preference. **4** a knot of ribbons worn as a badge of support for a particular team, political party, etc. **5** *hist* something given or worn as a token of affection. ▸ *verb* **1** to regard someone or something with goodwill. **2** to treat someone or something with preference, or over-indulgently. **3** to prefer; to support. **4** of circumstances: to give an advantage to someone or something. **5** to look like (a relative, esp a mother or father). ▪ **favoured** *or* (*N Am*) **favored** *adj.* [14c: from Latin *favere* to favour]

IDIOMS **in favour of sth** *or* **sb** **1** having a preference for it or them. **2** to their benefit. **3** in support or approval of them. **in** *or* **out of favour with sb** having gained, or lost, their approval.

favourable *or* (*N Am*) **favorable** *adj* **1** showing or giving agreement or consent. **2** pleasing; likely to win approval. **3** (**favourable to sb**) advantageous or helpful to them. **4** of a wind: following. **favourably** *adv.*

favourite *or* (*N Am*) **favorite** *adj* best-liked; preferred. ▸ *noun* **1** a favourite person or thing. **2** someone unfairly preferred or particularly indulged. **3** *sport* a horse or competitor expected to win. [16c: from French *favorit*]

favouritism *or* (*N Am*) **favoritism** *noun* the practice of giving unfair preference, help or support to someone or something.

fawn[1] *noun* **1** a young deer. **2** a yellowish-beige colour. ▸ *adj* of this colour. ▸ *verb, intr* of deer: to give birth to young. [14c: from French *faon*]

fawn[2] *verb, intr* (*often* **fawn on** *or* **upon sb**) to flatter or behave over-humbly towards someone, in order to win approval. [Anglo-Saxon *fagnian*]

fax *noun* **1** a machine that scans documents electronically and transmits a photographic image of them to a receiving machine by telephone line. **2** a document sent or received by such a machine. ▸ *verb* **1** to transmit (a document) by this means. **2** to send a communication (to someone) by fax. [1940s: contraction and respelling of **facsimile**]

fayre *noun* a nostalgic spelling of **fair**[2].

faze *verb, informal* to disturb, worry or fluster. [19c: variant of the dialect word *feeze* to beat off]

FBI *abbrev* Federal Bureau of Investigation.

FD *abbrev* used on British coins: *Fidei Defensor* (Latin), Defender of the Faith, a title borne by the sovereign of England since 1521.

Fe *symbol, chem* iron. [19c: from Latin *ferrum* iron]

fealty /ˈfɪəltɪ/ *noun* (**-ies**) *hist* the loyalty sworn by a vassal or tenant to a feudal lord. [14c: from French *fealte*, from Latin *fidelitas* loyalty]

fear *noun* **1** anxiety and distress caused by the awareness of danger or expectation of pain. **2** a cause of this feeling. **3** *relig* reverence, awe or dread. ▸ *verb* **1** to be afraid of (someone or something). **2** to think or expect (something) with dread. **3** to regret; to be sorry to say something: *I fear you have misunderstood.* **4** *intr* (**fear for sth**) to be frightened or anxious about it: *feared for their lives.* [Anglo-Saxon *fær* calamity]

IDIOMS **no fear** *informal* no chance; definitely not.

fearful *adj* **1** afraid. **2** frightening. **3** *informal* very bad: *a fearful mess.* ▪ **fearfully** *adv.*

fearless *adj* without fear; brave. ▪ **fearlessly** *adv.*

fearsome *adj* **1** causing fear. **2** frightening.

feasible *adj* **1** capable of being done or achieved; possible. **2** *loosely* probable; likely. ▪ **feasibility** *noun* (**-ies**). ▪ **feasibly** *adv.* [15c: from Latin *facere* to do]

feast *noun* **1** a large rich meal, esp one prepared to celebrate something. **2** a pleasurable abundance of something. **3** *relig* a regularly occurring celebration commemorating a person or event. ▸ *verb* **1** *intr* to take part in a feast. **2** *old use* to provide a feast for someone; to entertain someone sumptuously. ▪ **feasting** *noun.* [13c: from Latin *festum* a holiday]

Feast of Tabernacles see under **Sukkoth**

feat *noun* a deed or achievement, esp one requiring extraordinary strength, skill or courage. [15c: from French *fait*, related to **fact**]

feather *noun* **1** any of the light growths that form the soft covering of a bird. **2** something with a feather-like appearance. **3** plumage. **4** condition; spirits: *in fine feather.* ▸ *verb* **1** to provide, cover or line with feathers. **2** to turn (an oar, blade, etc) in order to lessen the resistance of the air or water. ▪ **feathery** *adj.* [Anglo-Saxon]

IDIOMS **a feather in one's cap** something to be proud of. **feather one's own nest** to accumulate money for oneself, esp dishonestly.

feather bed *noun* a mattress stuffed with feathers. ▸ *verb* (**featherbed**) **1** to spoil or pamper someone. **2** to protect (an industry, workers, etc) by practices such as overmanning in order to create or save jobs.

featherbrain *noun* a silly, frivolous, feckless or empty-headed person. ▪ **feather-brained** *adj.*

featherweight *noun* **1** a class for boxers, wrestlers and weightlifters of not more than a specified weight, which is 57kg (126 lb) in professional boxing, and similar weights in the other sports. **2** a boxer, etc of this weight. **3** someone who weighs very little.

feature *noun* **1** any of the parts of the face, eg eyes, nose, mouth, etc. **2** (**features**) the face. **3** a characteristic. **4** a noticeable part or quality of something. **5** an extended article in a newspaper, discussing a particular issue. **6** an article or item appearing regularly in a newspaper. **7** (*also* **feature film**) a main film in a cinema programme. ▸ *verb* **1** to have as a feature or make a feature of something. **2** to give prominence to (an actor, a well-known event, etc) in a film.

3 *intr* (*usu* **feature in sth**) to play an important part or role in (a film, documentary, etc). ▪ **featureless** *adj*. [14c in the sense 'bodily form': from French *faiture*]

featured *adj* **1** of an actor, etc: prominent in a particular film, etc. **2** *in compounds* having features of a specified type: *sharp-featured*.

featurette *noun* a short additional item, such as a documentary about the making of the film, included on the DVD of a feature film.

Feb. *abbrev* February.

febrile /ˈfiːbraɪl/ *adj* relating to fever; feverish. [17c: from Latin *febris* fever]

February *noun* (abbrev **Feb.**) the second month of the year, which has 28 days, except in **leap years** when it has 29. [13c: from Latin *februa* the Roman festival of purification]

feces the *N Am* spelling of **faeces**.

feckless *adj* **1** helpless; clueless. **2** irresponsible; aimless. [16c: from Scots *feck* effect]

fecund *adj* fruitful; fertile; richly productive. ▪ **fecundity** *noun*. [15c: from Latin *fecundus*]

fed *past tense, past participle of* **feed**[1]. See also **fed up**.

federal *adj* **1** belonging or relating to a country consisting of a group of states independent in local matters but united under a central government for other purposes, eg defence, foreign policy: *the Federal Republic of Germany*. **2** relating to the central government of a group of federated states. ▪ **federalism** *noun*. ▪ **federalist** *noun*. [17c: from Latin *foedus* treaty]

federalize *or* **-ise** *verb* **1** *tr & intr* to bring together as a federal union or federation. **2** to subject to federal control. ▪ **federalization** *noun*.

federate /ˈfɛdəreɪt/ *verb, tr & intr* to unite to form a federation. [19c: from Latin *foedus* treaty]

federation *noun* **1** a **federal** union of states, ie a group of states united politically by a treaty. **2** a union of business organizations, institutions, etc. **3** the act of uniting in a league.

fedora /fɪˈdɔːrə/ *noun* a wide-brimmed felt hat. [19c: from *Fédora*, a play by Victorien Sardou]

fed up *adj* (*also* **fed up with** *or* (*informal*) **of sth**) bored; irritated.

fee *noun* **1** a charge made for professional services, eg by a doctor or lawyer. **2** a charge for eg membership of a society, sitting an examination, entrance to a museum, etc. **3** (*usu* **fees**) a payment for school or college education, or for a course of instruction. **4** a payment made to a football club for the transfer of one of its players. **5** *law* an estate in the form of land that is inheritable with either restricted rights (**fee tail**) or unrestricted rights (**fee simple**). ▸ *verb* to pay a fee to someone. [13c: from Latin *feodum*]

feeble *adj* **1** lacking strength; weak. **2** of a joke, an excuse, etc: lacking power, influence or effectiveness; unconvincing. **3** easily influenced. ▪ **feebly** *adv*. [12c: from French *foible*]

feed[1] *verb* (***fed***) **1** to give or supply food to (animals, etc). **2** to give something as food (to animals, etc). **3** to administer food (to an infant, young animal). **4** *in compounds* to administer food to someone in a specified way: *breast-feed*. **5** *intr* of animals: to eat food. **6** to supply a machine, etc with fuel or other material required for continued operation or processing. **7** *theatre* to provide (an actor, esp a comedian) with material or a cue. **8** *sport* to pass the ball to (a teammate). ▸ *noun* **1** an act or session of feeding. **2** an allowance of food for animals, eg cattle or babies. **3** food for livestock, etc. **4** *informal* a meal, esp a hearty one: *a good feed*. **5** the channel or mechanism by which a machine is supplied with fuel, etc. **6** *theatre* an actor who feeds or cues another one; a stooge. [Anglo-Saxon *fedan*]

PHRASAL VERBS **feed sb up** to fatten them up with nourishing food.

feed[2] *past tense, past participle* of **fee**

feedback *noun* **1** responses and reactions to an inquiry or report, etc that provide guidelines for adjustment and development. **2** the process by which part of the output of a system or device, or of a component of a living organism, is returned to the input, in order to regulate or modify subsequent output. **3** in a public-address system, etc: the partial return of the sound output to the microphone, producing a high-pitched whistle or howl. **4** the whistling noise so produced.

feeder *noun* **1** a person or animal with particular eating habits: *a poor feeder*. **2** any device used for feeding, esp a baby's bottle. **3** a stream that runs into a river; a tributary. **4** a minor road, railway line, etc leading to a main one; any channel of supply to a main system. **5** a power line with large current-carrying capacity, used to transmit electric power between a generating station and a distribution network.

feel *verb* (***felt***) **1** to become aware of something through the sense of touch. **2** *tr & intr* to have a physical or emotional sensation of something; to sense. **3** *tr & intr* to find out or investigate with the hands, etc. **4** *tr & intr* to have (an emotion). **5** *tr & intr* to react emotionally to something or be emotionally affected by something: *feels the loss very deeply*. **6** *intr* (**feel for sb**) to have sympathy or compassion for them. **7** *intr* to give the impression of being (soft, hard, rough, etc) when touched. **8** *intr* to be or seem (well, ill, happy, etc). **9** to instinctively believe in something: *She feels that this is a good idea*. **10** *tr & intr* (*also* **feel like sth**) to seem to oneself to be: *feel a fool* • *feel like an idiot*. ▸ *noun* **1** a sensation or impression produced by touching. **2** an impression or atmosphere created by something. **3** an act of feeling with the fingers, etc. **4** an instinct, touch or knack. [Anglo-Saxon *felan*]

IDIOMS **feel like sth** to have an inclination or desire for it. **feel oneself** to feel as well as normal: *felt herself again after a good sleep*. **feel one's feet** to get used to a new situation, job etc. **feel one's way** to make one's way cautiously. **feel up to sth** *usu with negatives or in questions* to feel fit enough for it. **get the feel of sth** to become used to it. **have a feel for sth** have a natural ability for or understanding of (an activity, etc).

feeler *noun* **1** a tentacle. **2** either of a pair of long slender jointed structures, sensitive to touch, on the head of certain invertebrate animals. Also called **antenna**.

IDIOMS **put out feelers** to sound out the opinion of others.

feeling *noun* **1** the sense of touch, a sensation or emotion. **2** emotion as distinct from reason. **3** strong emotion. **4** a belief or opinion. **5** (*usu* **a feeling for**

sth) a natural ability for, or understanding of, an activity, etc. **6** affection. **7** mutual interactive emotion between two people, such as **bad feeling** (resentment), **good feeling** (friendliness), etc. **8** (*often* **feeling for sth**) an instinctive grasp or appreciation of it. **9** (**feelings**) one's attitude to something: *have mixed feelings.* **10** (**feelings**) sensibilities: *hurt his feelings.* [Anglo-Saxon *felan* to feel]

feet *noun, pl of* **foot**

feign /feɪn/ *verb* to pretend to have (eg an illness) or feel (an emotion, etc); to invent. ▪ **feigning** *noun.* [13c: from Latin *fingere* to contrive]

feint[1] *noun* **1** in boxing, fencing, etc: a mock attack; a movement intended to deceive or distract one's opponent. **2** a misleading action or appearance. ▸ *verb, intr* to make a feint. [17c: from French *feinte* to feign]

feint[2] *adj* of paper: ruled with pale horizontal lines to guide writing. [19c: variant of **faint**]

feisty /ˈfaɪstɪ/ *adj* (**-ier, -iest**) *informal* **1** spirited; lively. **2** irritable; quarrelsome. [19c: US dialect *fist* an aggressive small dog]

feldspar *or* **felspar** *noun, geol* a rock-forming mineral found in most igneous and many metamorphic rocks. ▪ **feldspathic** *or* **felspathic** *adj.* [18c: from German *Feld* field + *Spat* spar]

felicitate *verb* to congratulate. ▪ **felicitation** *noun* **1** the act of congratulating. **2** (**felicitations**) congratulations. [17c: from Latin *felicitas* happiness]

felicitous *adj* **1** of wording: elegantly apt; well-chosen; appropriate. **2** pleasant; happy.

felicity *noun* (**-ies**) **1** happiness. **2** a cause of happiness. **3** elegance or aptness of wording; an appropriate expression. [14c: from Latin *felicitas* happiness]

feline *adj* **1** relating to the cat or cat family. **2** like a cat, esp in terms of stealth or elegance. ▸ *noun* a member of the cat family. [17c: from Latin *felis* cat]

fell[1] *verb* **1** to cut down (a tree). **2** to knock down someone or something. **3** *needlecraft* to turn under and stitch down the edges of, eg a seam. [Anglo-Saxon *fyllan* to make something fall]

fell[2] *noun* (*often* **fells**) a hill, moor or an upland tract of pasture or moorland. [14c: from Norse *fjall*]

fell[3] *adj, old use* destructive; deadly. [13c: from French *fel* cruel]

IDIOMS **at** *or* **in one fell swoop** with a single deadly blow; in one quick operation.

fell[4] *past tense of* **fall**

fellow *noun* **1** a companion or equal. **2** (*also informal* **fella, fellah** *or* **feller**) **a** a man or boy, sometimes used dismissively; **b** *informal* a boyfriend. **3** a senior member of a college or university; a member of the governing body of a college or university. **4** a postgraduate research student financed by a fellowship. **5** (**Fellow**) a member of a learned society. **6** one of a pair. ▸ *adj* relating to a person in the same situation or condition as oneself, or having the same status, etc: *a fellow worker.* [Anglo-Saxon *feolaga* partner]

fellowship *noun* **1** friendly companionship. **2** commonness or similarity of interests between people, often common religious interests. **3** a society or association. **4** the status of a fellow of a college, society, etc. **5** a salary paid to a research fellow.

felon *noun, law* a person guilty of **felony**.

felony *noun* (**-ies**) *law* a serious crime. ▪ **felonious** *adj.* [13c: from Latin *fello* traitor]

felspar see **feldspar**

felt[1] *noun* a fabric formed by matting or pressing fibres, esp wool, together. ▸ *verb* **1** *tr & intr* to make into felt; to mat. **2** to cover with felt. **3** *intr* to become felted or matted. [Anglo-Saxon]

felt[2] *past tense, past participle of* **feel**

felt pen, felt-tip pen *or* **felt tip** *noun* a pen with a nib made of felt. [20c]

fem. *abbrev* feminine.

female *adj* **1** belonging or relating to the sex that gives birth to young, produces eggs, etc. **2** denoting the reproductive structure of a plant that contains an egg cell, such as the pistil of flowering plants. **3** belonging or relating to, or characteristic of, a woman. **4** *eng* of a piece of machinery, etc: having a hole or holes into which another part (the **male** *adj* sense 5) fits. ▸ *noun* **1** *sometimes derog* a woman or girl. **2** a female animal or plant. ▪ **femaleness** *noun.* [14c: from Latin *femella* young woman]

feminine *adj* **1** typically belonging or relating to, or characteristic of, a woman. **2** having or reflecting qualities considered typical of a woman; effeminate. **3** *grammar* (abbrev **f.** *or* **fem.**) in some languages: belonging or relating to the **gender** into which most words for human and animal females fall, along with many other nouns. Compare **masculine**, **neuter**. ▸ *noun, grammar* **1** the feminine gender. **2** a word belonging to this gender. ▪ **femininity** *noun.* [14c: from Latin *feminina*, diminutive of *femina* woman]

feminism *noun* a belief or movement advocating women's rights and opportunities, particularly equal rights with men. ▪ **feminist** *noun.* [19c: from Latin *femina* woman]

feminize *or* **-ise** *verb, tr & intr* **1** to make or become feminine. **2** to make (a male animal) develop female characteristics.

femme fatale /fam fəˈtɑːl/ *noun* (***femmes fatales*** /fam fəˈtɑːl/) a woman with irresistible charm and fascination, who often brings despair or disaster to her lovers. [19c: French, meaning 'fatal woman']

femto- *combining form* a thousand million millionth (10^{-15}). [From Danish or Norwegian *femten* fifteen]

femur /ˈfiːmə(r)/ *noun* (***femurs*** *or* ***femora*** /ˈfɛmərə/) **1** the longest bone of the human skeleton, from hip to knee. Also called **thigh bone**. **2** the corresponding bone in the hind limb of four-limbed vertebrates. ▪ **femoral** /ˈfɛmərəl/ *adj.* [18c: Latin, meaning 'thigh']

fen *noun* a wet area of lowland, dominated by grasses, sedges and rushes, with an alkaline soil. Also called **fenland**. [Anglo-Saxon *fenn*]

fence *noun* **1** a barrier, eg of wood or wire, for enclosing or protecting land. **2** a barrier for a horse to jump. **3** *slang* someone who receives and disposes of stolen goods. **4** a guard or guide on a piece of machinery. ▸ *verb* **1** (*also* **fence sth in** *or* **off**) to enclose or separate with a fence, or as if with a fence. **2** *intr* to practise the art or sport of fencing. **3** to build fences. **4** *intr, slang* to be a receiver or purchaser of stolen goods. [14c: as *fens*, shortened from **defence**]

IDIOMS **sit on the fence** to be unable or unwilling to support either side in a dispute, etc.

fencing *noun* **1** the art, act or sport of attack and defence with a foil, épée or sabre. **2** material used for constructing fences. **3** fences collectively.

fend *verb* **1** (*usu* **fend sth** *or* **sb off**) to defend oneself from (blows, questions, etc). **2** *intr* (*esp* **fend for sb**) to provide for, esp oneself. [14c: shortened from **defend**]

fender *noun* **1** a low guard fitted round a fireplace to keep ash, coals, etc within the hearth. **2** *N Am* the wing or mudguard of a car. **3** a bundle of rope, tyres, etc hanging from a ship's side to protect it when in contact with piers, etc.

fenestra /fəˈnɛstrə/ *noun* (***fenestrae*** /-striː/) **1** *archit* a window or other wall opening. **2** *biol* a small opening, especially between the middle and inner ear. ▪ **fenestral** *adj.* [19c: Latin]

fenestration *noun, archit* the arrangement of windows in a building.

feng shui /fʌŋ ˈʃweɪ/ *noun* the process of making the correct decisions about the siting of a building, placing of furniture, etc in a building, room, etc, to ensure the optimum happiness for the occupants, based on the notion of balancing the natural energies of a locality. [18c: Chinese, meaning 'wind and water']

fenland see under **fen**

fennel *noun* a strong-smelling plant, whose seeds and leaves are used in cooking. [Anglo-Saxon *finul*]

fenugreek *noun* a white-flowered leguminous plant with strong-smelling seeds, used as animal fodder and in cooking. [Latin *fenum graecum* Greek hay]

feral *adj* of domesticated animals or cultivated plants: living or growing wild. [17c: from Latin *fera* wild beast]

ferment *noun* /ˈfɜːmɛnt/ **1** a substance, such as a yeast or mould, that causes fermentation. **2** fermentation. **3** a state of agitation or excitement. ▸ *verb* /fəˈmɛnt/ **1** *intr* to undergo fermentation. **2** to be, or make something be, in a state of excitement or instability. [15c: from Latin *fermentum* yeast]

fermentation *noun, chem* a biochemical process in which micro-organisms break down an organic compound, usu a carbohydrate, in the absence of oxygen, eg the conversion of sugar into alcohol.

fermium *noun, chem* (symbol **Fm**) an artificially produced metallic radioactive element. [20c: named after E Fermi, Italian physicist]

fern *noun* a flowerless feathery-leaved plant that reproduces by spores. ▪ **ferny** *adj* (***-ier, -iest***). [Anglo-Saxon *fearn*]

ferocious *adj* savagely fierce; cruel; savage ▪ **ferociously** *adv.* ▪ **ferocity** *noun.* [17c: from Latin *ferox* wild]

-ferous *combining form, denoting* bearing or containing: *carboniferous* • *umbelliferous.* [From Latin *ferre* to carry]

ferrate *noun* a salt of ferric acid. [19c: from Latin *ferrum* iron]

ferret *noun* **1** a small, half-tame, albino type of polecat, used for driving rabbits and rats from their holes. **2** an inquisitive and persistent investigator. ▸ *verb* (***ferreted, ferreting***) *tr & intr* to hunt (rabbits, etc) with a ferret. [14c: from Latin *fur* thief]

PHRASAL VERBS **ferret sth out 1** to drive (an animal, etc) out of a hiding place. **2** to find it out through persistent investigation.

ferric *adj* **1** referring or relating to iron. **2** *chem* denoting a compound that contains iron in its trivalent state. [18c: from Latin *ferrum* iron]

ferric oxide *noun* a reddish-brown or black solid, occurring naturally as **haematite**, used in magnetic tapes and as a catalyst and pigment. Also called **iron oxide**.

ferrite *noun, chem* any of a class of ceramic materials made of oxides of iron and some other metal, eg cobalt, nickel, etc, that have magnetic properties and a high electrical resistivity, and are used in loudspeaker magnets, tape-recorder heads, etc.

ferroconcrete *noun* reinforced concrete.

ferrous *adj, chem* **1** belonging or relating to iron. **2** denoting a chemical compound that contains iron in its divalent state. [19c: from Latin *ferrum* iron]

ferrule *noun* **1** a metal ring or cap at the tip of a walking-stick or umbrella. **2** a cylindrical fitting, threaded internally like a screw, for joining pipes, etc together. [15c: from Latin *viriola* little bracelet]

ferry *noun* (***-ies***) **1** (*also* **ferryboat**) a boat that carries passengers and often cars across a river or strip of water, esp as a regular service. **2** the service thus provided. **3** the place or route where a ferryboat runs. ▸ *verb* (***-ies, -ied***) **1** *tr & intr* (*sometimes* **ferry across**) to transport or go by ferry. **2** to convey (passengers, goods, etc) in a vehicle: *He ferried them to school each day.* [Anglo-Saxon *ferian* to convey]

fertile /ˈfɜːtaɪl, *N Am* ˈfɜːtəl/ *adj* **1** of land, soil, etc: containing the nutrients required to support an abundant growth of crops, plants, etc. **2** producing or capable of producing babies, young or fruit. **3** of an egg or seed: capable of developing into a new individual. **4** of the mind: rich in ideas; very productive. **5** providing a wealth of possibilities. **6** producing many offspring; prolific. ▪ **fertility** *noun.* [15c: from Latin *ferre* to bear]

fertilize *or* **-ise** *verb* **1** of a male gamete, esp a sperm cell: to fuse with (a female gamete, esp an egg cell) to form a **zygote**. **2** of a male animal: to inseminate or impregnate (a female animal). **3** of flowering/cone-bearing plants: to transfer (pollen) by the process of **pollination**. **4** to supply (soil) with extra nutrients in order to increase its fertility. ▪ **fertilization** *noun.*

fertilizer *or* **fertiliser** *noun* a natural or chemical substance, esp nitrogen, potassium salts or phosphates, added to soil to improve fertility.

fervent *adj* enthusiastic; earnest or ardent. ▪ **fervently** *adv.* [14c: from Latin *fervere* to boil or to glow]

fervid *adj* fervent; full of fiery passion or zeal. ▪ **fervidly** *adv.* [16c: from Latin *fervere* to boil or to glow]

fervour *or* (*N Am*) **fervor** *noun* passionate enthusiasm; intense eagerness or sincerity. [15c: from Latin *fervor* violent heat]

fescue *or* **fescue grass** *noun* a tufted grass with bristle-like leaves, which forms much of the turf on chalk downs. [14c: from Latin *festuca* a straw]

fest *noun, in compounds* a gathering or festival for a specified activity: *filmfest* • *thrill fest.* [19c: German, meaning 'festival']

fester *verb* **1** *intr* of a wound: to form or discharge pus. **2** of an evil: to continue unchecked or get worse. **3** *intr* to rot or decay. **4** *intr* of resentment or anger: to smoulder; to become more bitter, usu over time. [14c: from Latin *fistula* a kind of ulcer]

festival *noun* **1** a day or period of celebration, esp one kept traditionally. **2** *relig* a feast or saint's day. **3** a season or series of performances (of musical, theatrical or other cultural events). [15c: from Latin *festum* feast]

Festival of Dedication *or* **Festival of Lights** see **Chanukkah**

festive *adj* **1** relating to a festival. **2** celebratory; joyous; lively; cheerful. [17c: from Latin *festus* feast]

festivity *noun* (**-*ies***) **1** a lighthearted event; celebration, merrymaking. **2** (**festivities**) festive activities; celebrations.

festoon *noun* **1** a decorative chain of flowers, ribbons, etc looped between two points. **2** *archit* a carved or moulded ornament representing this. ▸ *verb* to hang or decorate with festoons. [17c: from Italian *festone* decoration for a feast]

feta *noun* a crumbly, white, ewe's- or goat's-milk cheese, orig made in Greece. [1950s: Modern Greek *pheta* a slice]

fetch *verb* **1** to go and get something, and bring it back. **2** to be sold for (a certain price). **3** *informal* to deal someone (a blow, slap, etc). **4** to bring forth (tears, blood, a sigh, etc). [Anglo-Saxon *feccan*]
IDIOMS **fetch and carry** to act as servant; to perform menial tasks.
PHRASAL VERBS **fetch up** *informal* to arrive; to end up.

fetching *adj, informal* of appearance: attractive, charming.

fête *or* **fete** /feɪt, fɛt/ *noun* **1** an outdoor event with entertainment, competitions, stalls, etc, usu to raise money for a charity. **2** a festival or holiday, esp to mark the feast day of a saint. ▸ *verb* to entertain or honour someone lavishly. [18c: French]

fetid *or* **foetid** *adj* having a strong disgusting smell. [16c: from Latin *fetere* to stink]

fetish *noun* **1** in some societies: an object worshipped for its perceived magical powers. **2** a procedure or ritual followed obsessively, or an object of obsessive devotion. ▪ **fetishism** *noun*. ▪ **fetishist** *noun*. [17c: from Latin *facere* to make]

fetlock *noun* the thick projection at the back of a horse's leg just above the hoof. [14c as *fetlak*]

fetter *noun* **1** (*usu* **fetters**) a chain or shackle fastened to a prisoner's ankle. Compare **manacle**. **2** (**fetters**) tiresome restrictions. ▸ *verb* **1** to put someone in fetters. **2** to restrict someone. [Anglo-Saxon *fetor*]

fettle *noun* spirits; condition; state of health. [Anglo-Saxon *fetel* belt]

fettuccine, **fettucine** *or* **fettucini** /fɛtʊ'tʃiːnɪ/ *noun* pasta made in long ribbons. [1920: Italian, from *fettucia* slice or ribbon]

fetus *or* (*non-technical*) **foetus** /'fiːtəs/ *noun* **1** the embryo of a **viviparous** mammal during the later stages of development in the uterus. **2** a human embryo from the end of the eighth week after conception until birth. ▪ **fetal** *adj*. [14c: from Latin *fetus* offspring]

feu /fjuː/ *noun* **1** *often as adj* **a** *legal hist, feudalism* a tenure of land where the **vassal** makes a return in grain or in money, in place of military service; **b** in modern use: a perpetual lease for a fixed rent: *feu-farm*; **c** a piece of land so held. **2** *Scots law* a right to the use of land, houses, etc in return for payment of **feu duty**, a fixed annual payment. ▸ *verb* to grant (land, etc) on such terms. [15c: French, variant of **fee**]

feud *noun* **1** a long-drawn-out bitter quarrel between families, individuals or clans. **2** a persistent state of private enmity. ▸ *verb, intr* (*often* **feud with sb**) to carry on a feud with them. ▪ **feuding** *noun, adj*. [13c: from French *feide* feud; see also **foe**]

feudal *adj* **1** relating to feudalism. **2** relating to a **feu**. [17c]

feudalism *or* **feudal system** *noun* a system of social and political organization prevalent in W Europe in the Middle Ages, in which powerful land-owning lords granted degrees of privilege and protection to lesser subjects holding a range of positions within a rigid social hierarchy. See also **fief**, **liege**, **vassal**.

fever *noun* **1** an abnormally high body temperature, often accompanied by shivering, thirst and headache. **2** a disease in which this is a marked symptom, eg scarlet fever, yellow fever. **3** an extreme state of agitation or excitement. ▸ *verb* (***fevered, fevering***) to affect with a fever or agitation. [Latin *febris*]

feverfew /'fiːvəfjuː/ *noun* a perennial plant of the daisy family, used in herbal medicine. [Anglo-Saxon *feferfuge*, from Latin *febris* fever and *fugare* to put to flight]

feverish *or* **feverous** *adj* **1** suffering from fever. **2** agitated or restless. ▪ **feverishly** *adv*.

fever pitch *noun* a state of high excitement.

few *adj* not many; a small number; hardly any. ▸ *pronoun* (*used as a pl*) hardly any things, people, etc. [Anglo-Saxon *feawe*]
IDIOMS **a few** a small number; some. **a good few** *or* **quite a few** *informal* a fairly large number; several. **as few as** no more than (a stated number). **few and far between** *informal* rare; scarce. **the few** the minority of discerning people, as distinct from *the many*.

---

fewer, less
See the Usage Note at **less**.

---

fey /feɪ/ *adj* **1** strangely fanciful; whimsical. **2** able to foresee future events. **3** *chiefly Scot* in a state of extravagantly high spirits believed to presage imminent death. [Anglo-Saxon *fæge* doomed to die]

fez *noun* (***fezzes*** *or* ***fezes***) a hat shaped like a flat-topped cone, with a tassel, worn by some Muslim men. Also called **tarboosh**. [19c: from Turkish *fes*, named after Fez, a city in Morocco]

ff *abbrev* **1** *music* fortissimo. **2** and the following (pages, etc). **3** folios.

fiancé *or* **fiancée** /fɪ'ɑ̃seɪ, fɪ'ɒnseɪ/ *noun* respectively, a man or woman to whom one is engaged to be married. [19c: from French *fiancer* to betroth]

Fianna Fáil /'fiːanɑ fɔɪl/ *noun* a political party in the Republic of Ireland. [Irish Gaelic, literally 'soldiers of destiny']

fiasco *noun* (***fiascos*** *or* ***fiascoes***) **1** a ludicrous or humiliating failure. **2** a bizarre or ludicrous happening: *What a fiasco!* [19c: Italian, meaning 'flask']

fiat /'faɪat/ *noun* **1** an official command; a decree. **2** a formal authorization for some procedure. [17c: Latin, meaning 'let it be done']

fib *informal, noun* a trivial lie. ▸ *verb* (***fibbed, fibbing***) *intr* to tell fibs. ▪ **fibber** *noun*. [17c: possibly shortened from *fible-fable* nonsense, from **fable**]

Fibonacci numbers, sequence *or* **series** /fiːboʊ'nɑːtʃi/ *noun, maths* the infinite series of numbers (0, 1, 1, 2, 3, 5, 8, etc) in which each term is the sum of the preceding two terms. [19c: named after Italian mathematician Leonardo Fibonacci, who discovered the series]

fibre *or* (*N Am*) **fiber** *noun* **1** a fine thread or thread-like cell of a natural or artificial substance, eg cellulose, nylon. **2** a material composed of fibres. **3** any fibrous material which can be made into textile fabrics. **4** *botany* in the stems of woody plants: a long, narrow, thick-walled cell that provides mechanical support for the plant. **5** the indigestible parts of edible plants or seeds, that help to move food quickly through the body: *dietary fibre*. **6** strength of character; stamina: *moral fibre*. [14c: from Latin *fibra* thread or fibre]

fibreboard or (*N Am*) **fiberboard** *noun* strong board made from compressed wood chips or other organic fibres.

fibreglass or (*N Am*) **fiberglass** *noun* **1** a strong light plastic strengthened with glass fibres, which is resistant to heat, fire and corrosion, and is used for boat-building, car bodies, etc. **2** material consisting of fine, tangled fibres of glass, used for insulation.

fibre optics or (*N Am*) **fiber optics** *singular noun* the technique of using flexible strands of glass or plastic (**optical fibres**) to carry information in the form of light signals. ▪ **fibre-optic** *adj*.

fibril /ˈfaɪbrɪl/ *noun* **1** a small fibre or part of a fibre. **2** a hair on a plant's root.

fibrillate /ˈfaɪbrɪleɪt/ *verb, intr, med* of the muscle fibres of the heart: to contract spontaneously, rapidly, and irregularly. ▪ **fibrillation** *noun*. [19c]

fibroid *adj* fibrous. ▸ *noun, pathol* a benign tumour, esp on the wall of the uterus. [19c]

fibrosis *noun, pathol* the formation of an abnormal amount of fibrous connective tissue over or in place of normal tissue of an organ or body part. See also **cystic fibrosis**. [19c]

fibrous *adj* consisting of, containing or like fibre.

fibula *noun* (***fibulae*** /ˈfɪbjʊliː/ or ***fibulas***) **1** the outer and narrower of the two bones in the lower leg, between the knee and the ankle. Compare **tibia**. **2** the corresponding bone in the hind limb of four-limbed vertebrates. [16c: Latin, meaning 'brooch']

fiche /fiːʃ/ *noun* short form of **microfiche**.

fickle *adj* inconstant or changeable in affections, loyalties or intentions. ▪ **fickleness** *noun*. [Anglo-Saxon *ficol* deceitful]

fiction *noun* **1** literature concerning imaginary characters or events, eg a novel or story. **2** a pretence; a lie. **3** *law* a misrepresentation of the truth, accepted for convenience. ▪ **fictional** *adj*. ▪ **fictionalize** or **-ise** *verb*. [14c: from Latin *fingere* to mould]

fictitious *adj* imagined; invented; not real. [17c]

fictive *adj* **1** concerned with fiction. **2** fictitious; imaginary. [15c in the obsolete sense 'disposed to feigning': from Latin *fingere, fictum* to fashion or fabricate]

fiddle *noun* **1** a violin, esp when used to play folk music or jazz. **2** *informal* a dishonest arrangement; a fraud. **3** a manually delicate or tricky operation. ▸ *verb* **1** *intr* (*often* **fiddle with sth**) to play about aimlessly with it; to tinker, toy or meddle with it. **2** *intr* (**fiddle around** or **about**) to waste time: *kept fiddling about and got nothing done*. **3** *tr & intr* to falsify (accounts, etc); to manage or manipulate dishonestly. **4** *tr & intr* to play a violin or fiddle; to play (a tune) on one. [Anglo-Saxon *fithele*; compare **viol**]

IDIOMS **as fit as a fiddle** in excellent health. **on the fiddle** *informal* making money dishonestly. **play second fiddle to sb** to be subordinate to them.

fiddler *noun* **1** a person who plays the fiddle. **2** a swindler. **3** (*also* **fiddler crab**) any of various small burrowing crabs, so called because the movements of a pincer-like claw in the male resemble those of a fiddler.

fiddling *adj* unimportant; trifling.

fiddly *adj* (***-ier, -iest***) awkward to handle or do, esp if the task requires delicate finger movements.

fidelity *noun* (***-ies***) **1** faithfulness; loyalty or devotion. **2** accuracy in reporting, describing or copying something. **3** precision in sound reproduction. [16c: from Latin *fidelitas*]

fidget *verb* (***fidgeted, fidgeting***) **1** *intr* to move about restlessly. **2** (*often* **fidget with sth**) to touch and handle it aimlessly. ▸ *noun* **1** a person who fidgets. **2** (**the fidgets**) nervous restlessness. ▪ **fidgety** *adj*. [17c: from earlier *fidge* to twitch]

fiduciary *law, noun* (***-ies***) someone who holds something in trust; a trustee. ▸ *adj* **1** held or given in trust. **2** relating to a trust or trustee. [17c: from Latin *fiducia* trust]

fie *exclam, facetious or old use* expressing disapproval or disgust, real or feigned. [13c: imitating the sound made on perceiving a disagreeable smell]

fief /fiːf/ *noun* **1** *feudalism* land granted to a **vassal** by his lord in return for military service, or on other conditions. **2** a person's own area of operation or control. [17c: from French *fie* or *fief* fee; see **fee**]

fiefdom *noun* **1** *feudalism* a piece of land held as a fief. **2** any area of influence autocratically controlled by an individual or organization.

field *noun* **1** a piece of land enclosed for growing crops or pasturing animals. **2** a piece of open grassland. **3** an area marked off as a ground for a sport, etc. **4** *in compounds* an area rich in a specified mineral, etc: *coalfield* • *oilfield*. **5** *in compounds* an expanse of something specified, usu from the natural world: *snowfields* • *poppy fields*. **6** an area of knowledge or study; speciality. **7** *physics* a region of space in which one object exerts force on another: *force field*. **8** the area included in something; the range over which a force, etc extends; the area visible to an observer at any one time: *field of vision*. **9** **a** the contestants in a race, competition, etc; **b** all contestants except for the favourite; the rivals of a particular contestant. **10** a battlefield: *fell on the field*. **11** any place away from the classroom, office, etc where practical experience is gained. See also **fieldwork**. **12** the background to the design on a flag, coin, heraldic shield, etc. **13** *comput* a set of characters comprising a unit of information in a database record. **14** *comput* an area in a database or screen display in which information may be entered. **15** *maths* a system or collection of elements upon which binary operations of addition, subtraction, multiplication and division can be performed (excluding division by 0). ▸ *verb* **1** *tr & intr, sport, esp cricket* **a** of a team: to be the team whose turn it is to retrieve balls hit by the batting team; **b** *tr & intr* of a player: to retrieve the ball from the field; **c** *intr* of a player: to play in the field. **2** to put forward as (a team or player) for a match. **3** to enter someone in a competition: *Each group fielded a candidate*. **4** to deal with a succession of (inquiries, etc): *to field questions*. [Anglo-Saxon *feld*]

IDIOMS **lead the field** to be in the foremost or winning position. **play the field** *informal* to try out the range of possibilities before making a choice.

field day *noun* **1** a day spent on some specific outdoor activity, such as a nature study. **2** *informal* any period of exciting activity.

fielder *noun, sport, particularly cricket* a player in the field; a member of the fielding side, as distinct from the batting side.

field event *noun, athletics* a contest involving jumping, throwing, etc, as distinct from a track event.

field glasses *plural noun* binoculars.

field hockey *noun, N Am* hockey played on grass, as distinct from ice hockey.

field marshal *noun* in Britain: an army officer of the highest rank.

fieldmouse *noun* any of various species of small mouse that live among dense vegetation.

field sports *plural noun* sports carried out in the countryside, such as hunting, shooting, fishing, etc.

field trip *noun* an expedition, esp by students, to observe and study something at its location.

fieldwork *noun* practical work or research done at a site away from the laboratory or place of study.

fiend *noun* **1** a devil; an evil spirit. **2** *informal* a spiteful person. **3** *informal* an enthusiast for something specified: *sun fiend.* [Anglo-Saxon *feond* enemy]

fiendish *adj* **1** like a fiend. **2** devilishly cruel. **3** extremely difficult or unpleasant. ▪ **fiendishly** *adv.*

fierce *adj* **1** violent and aggressive. **2** intense; strong: *fierce competition.* **3** severe; extreme: *a fierce storm.* ▪ **fiercely** *adv.* [13c: from Latin *ferus* savage]

fiery *adj* (*-ier, -iest*) **1** consisting of fire; like fire. **2** easily enraged: *a fiery temper.* **3** passionate; spirited; vigorous: *fiery oratory.* **4** of food: hot-tasting; causing a burning sensation. ▪ **fieriness** *noun.* [13c: from **fire**]

fiesta *noun* **1** esp in Spanish-speaking communities: a religious festival with dancing, singing, etc. **2** any carnival, festivity or holiday. [19c: Spanish, meaning 'feast']

fife *noun* a small type of flute played in military bands. [15c: from German *Pfifa* pipe]

fifteen *noun* **1 a** the cardinal number 15; **b** the quantity that this represents, being one more than fourteen or the sum of ten and five. **2** any symbol for this, eg *15* or *XV.* **3** the age of fifteen. **4** something, esp a garment, or a person, whose size is denoted by the number 15. **5 a** a set or group of fifteen people or things; **b** *rugby union* a team of players. **6** (written **15**) *Brit* a film classified as suitable for people aged 15 and over. ▸ *adj* **1** totalling fifteen. **2** aged fifteen. ▪ **fifteenth** *adj, noun, adv.* [Anglo-Saxon *fiftene*]

fifth (often written **5th**) *adj* **1** in counting: **a** next after fourth; **b** last of five. **2** in fifth position. **3** being one of five equal parts: *a fifth share.* ▸ *noun* **1** one of five equal parts: *a fifth share.* **2** a **fraction** equal to one divided by five (usu written ⅕). **3** a person coming fifth, eg in a race or exam. **4** (**the fifth**) **a** the fifth day of the month; **b** *golf* the fifth hole. **5** *music* **a** an interval consisting of three whole tones and a semitone; an interval of four diatonic degrees; **b** a note at that interval from another. ▸ *adv* fifthly. ▪ **fifthly** *adv* used to introduce the fifth point in a list. [Anglo-Saxon]

fifth column *noun* a body of citizens prepared to co-operate with an invading enemy. ▪ **fifth columnist** *noun.* [20c]

fifties (often written **50s** *or* **50's**) *plural noun* **1** (**one's fifties**) the period of time between one's fiftieth and sixtieth birthdays. **2** (**the fifties**) the range of temperatures between fifty and sixty degrees. **3** (**the fifties**) the period of time between the fiftieth and sixtieth years of a century. *as adj*: *a fifties hairstyle.*

fifty *noun* (*-ies*) **1 a** the cardinal number 50; **b** the quantity that this represents, being one more than forty-nine, or the product of ten and five. **2** any symbol for this, eg *50* or *L.* **3** the age of fifty. **4** something, esp a garment, or a person, whose size is denoted by the number 50. **5** a set or group of fifty people or things. **6** a score of fifty points. ▸ *adj* **1** totalling fifty. **2** aged fifty. See also **fifties.** ▪ **fiftieth** *adj, noun, adv.* [Anglo-Saxon *fiftig*]

fifty- *combining form* **a** *forming adjectives and nouns* with cardinal numbers between *one* and *nine*: *fifty-two*; **b** *forming adjectives and nouns* with ordinal numbers between *first* and *ninth*: *fifty-second.*

fifty-fifty *adj* **1** of a chance: equal either way. **2** half-and-half. ▸ *adv* divided equally between two; half-and-half.

fig *noun* **1** a tropical and sub-tropical tree or shrub with a soft pear-shaped fruit full of tiny seeds. **2** its green, brown or purple fleshy fruit. [13c: from Latin *ficus* fig or fig tree]

IDIOMS **not give** *or* **care a fig** *informal* not to care at all.

fig. *abbrev* **1** figurative or figuratively. **2** figure, ie a diagram, illustration.

fight *verb* (*fought*) **1** *tr & intr* to attack or engage (an enemy, army, etc) in combat. **2** to take part in or conduct (a battle, campaign, etc). **3** *tr & intr* (*sometimes* **fight against**) to oppose (eg an enemy, a person, an illness, a cause, etc) vigorously. **4** *intr* to quarrel; to disagree, sometimes coming to blows. **5** *intr* (*often* **fight for sth** *or* **sb**) to struggle or campaign on its or their behalf. **6** *intr* to make (one's way) with a struggle. ▸ *noun* **1** a battle; a physically violent struggle. **2** a quarrel; a dispute; a contest. **3** resistance. **4** the will or strength to resist. **5** a boxing match. **6** a campaign or crusade. [Anglo-Saxon *feohtan*]

IDIOMS **fight a losing battle** to continue trying for something even when there is little chance of succeeding. **fighting fit** *informal* in vigorous health.

PHRASAL VERBS **fight back** to resist an attacker; to counter an attack. **fight sth back** to try not to show (one's emotions, etc). **fight sb off** to repulse them (esp an attacker). **fight sth off** to get rid of or resist (an illness).

fighter *noun* **1** a person who fights, esp a professional boxer. **2** a person with determination. **3** (*also* **fighter plane**) an aircraft equipped to attack other aircraft.

fig leaf *noun* **1** the leaf of a fig tree. **2** *art* the traditional representation of a fig leaf covering the genitals of a statue, picture, etc of a nude figure. **3** any device used to cover up something considered embarrassing.

figment *noun* something imagined or invented. [15c: from Latin *figmentum* a fiction]

figuration *noun* **1** the act of giving figure or form. **2** representation by, or in, figures or shapes. **3** ornamentation with a design. **4** *music* **a** consistent use of particular melodic or harmonic series of notes; **b** florid treatment.

figurative *adj* **1** metaphorical; not literal. **2** of writing, etc: full of figures of speech, esp metaphor. **3** representing a figure; representing using an emblem or symbol, etc. **4** of art: showing things as they actually look. Compare **abstract** (*adj* sense 3), **concrete** (*adj* sense 2).

figure *noun* **1** the form of anything in outline. **2** a symbol representing a number; a numeral. **3** a number representing an amount; a cost or price. **4** an indistinctly seen or unidentified person. **5** a representation of the human form, esp in painting or sculpture. **6** (**figures**) arithmetical calculations; statistics. **7** a well-known person. **8** a specified impression that a person has or makes. **9** a diagram or illustration, esp in a text. **10** the shape of a person's body. **11** an image, design or pattern. **12** a geometrical shape, formed from a combination of points, lines, curves or surfaces. **13** *music* a short distinctive series of notes in music. **14** *dancing, sport, etc* a set pattern of steps or movements. See also **figure skating**. **15** a **figure of speech**. ▸ *verb* **1** *intr* (*usu* **figure in sth**) to play a part in it (eg a story, incident, etc). **2** *N Am* to think; to reckon. **3** to imagine; to envisage. **4** *intr, informal* to be probable or predictable; to make sense: *That figures!* [13c: from Latin *fingere* to mould]
PHRASAL VERBS **figure on sth** to count on, plan or expect it. **figure sb** *or* **sth out** to come to understand them or it.

figurehead *noun* **1** a leader in name only, without real power. **2** a carved wooden figure fixed to a ship's prow.

figure of speech *noun* a device such as a **metaphor**, **simile**, etc that enlivens language.

figure skating *noun* skating where prescribed patterns are performed on the ice. ▪ **figure skater** *noun*.

figurine *noun* a small carved or moulded figure, usu representing a human form. [19c: French, from Italian *figurina* small figure]

filament *noun* **1** a fine thread or fibre. **2** *elec* in electrical equipment: a fine wire with a high resistance that emits heat and light when an electric current is passed through it. **3** *botany* the stalk of a stamen, which bears the anther. [16c: from Latin *filum* thread]

filbert *noun* **1** the nut of the cultivated hazel. **2** (*also* **filbert tree**) the tree bearing the nut. [14c: prob named after St Philibert, whose feast day (August 22) fell in the nutting season]

filch *verb* to steal something small or trivial. [16c, meaning 'to take as booty']

file[1] *noun* **1** a folder or box in which to keep loose papers. **2** a collection of papers so kept, esp dealing with a particular subject. **3** *comput* an organized collection of data that is stored in the memory of a computer as a single named unit. **4** a line of people or things, esp soldiers, positioned or moving one behind the other: *single file*. **5** *chess* any of the eight lines of squares extending across the chessboard from player to player. Compare **rank**[1] (*noun* sense 8). ▸ *verb* **1** (*often* **file sth away**) to put (papers, etc) into a file. **2** (*often* **file for sth**) to make a formal application to a law court on (a specified matter): *file a complaint* • *file for divorce*. **3** to place (a document) on official or public record. **4** *intr* to march or move along one behind the other. **5** of a reporter: to submit (a story) to a newspaper. [16c: from Latin *filum* a thread]
IDIOMS **on file** retained in a file (*noun* sense 1 or 3 above) for reference; on record.

file[2] *noun* **1** a steel hand tool with a rough surface consisting of fine parallel grooves with sharp cutting edges, used to smooth or rub away wood, metal, etc. **2** a small object of metal or emery board used for smoothing or shaping fingernails. Also called **nailfile**. ▸ *verb* to smooth or shape (a surface) using a file. [Anglo-Saxon *fyl*]

file extension *noun, comput* a series of characters that follows the dot in a filename and identifies the file type.

filename *noun, comput* any name or reference used to specify a file stored in a computer.

filial *adj* **1** belonging or relating to, or resembling, a son or daughter: *filial duties*. **2** *biol, genetics* (abbrev F_1, F_2, etc) denoting any successive generation following a parental generation. [14c: from Latin *filia* daughter, and *filius* son]

filibuster *noun* esp in the US Senate: **a** the practice of making long speeches to delay the passing of laws; **b** a member of a law-making assembly who does this. Compare **obstructionism**. ▸ *verb, intr* esp in the US Senate: to obstruct legislation by making long speeches. [19c: prob from Spanish *filibustero*]

filigree *noun* **1** delicate work in gold or silver wire, twisted into convoluted forms and soldered together, used in jewellery, etc. **2** any delicate ornamentation. [17c: from Latin *filum* thread + *granum* grain]

filing cabinet *noun* a set of drawers, usu metal, for holding collections of papers and documents.

filings *plural noun* particles rubbed off with a file.

fill *verb* **1** (*also* **fill sth up**) to make it full. **2** *intr* (*also* **fill up**) to become full. **3** to take up all the space in something. **4** to satisfy (a need); to perform (a role) satisfactorily. **5** (*sometimes* **fill up**) to occupy (time). **6** (*also* **fill sth in** *or* **up**) to put material into (a hole, cavity, etc) to level the surface. **7** to appoint someone to (a position or post of employment). **8 a** to take up (a position or post of employment); **b** to work in (a job), sometimes temporarily. **9** *intr* of a sail: to billow out in the wind. ▸ *noun* **1** anything used to fill something. **2** *sometimes in compounds* material used to fill a space to a required level: *rock-fill*. [Anglo-Saxon *fyllan*]
IDIOMS **eat one's fill** to consume enough to satisfy. **to have had one's fill of sth** *or* **sb** to have reached the point of being able to tolerate no more of it or them.
PHRASAL VERBS **fill sb in** to inform them fully; to brief them. **fill sth in 1** to write information as required on to (a form, etc). **2** to complete a drawing, etc, esp by shading. **fill in for sb** to take over their work temporarily. **fill out** to put on weight and become fatter or plumper. **fill sth out 1** to enlarge it satisfactorily; to amplify it. **2** *chiefly N Am* to fill in (a form, etc). **fill sth up** to fill in (a form, etc).

filler *noun* **1** a person or thing that fills. **2** a paste-like substance used for filling cracks or holes, usu in walls of buildings. **3** a material or substance used to add bulk or weight to something, or to fill a gap or space, etc.

fillet *noun* **1 a** a piece of meat without bone, taken as an undercut of the **sirloin**, or the fleshy part of the thigh: *pork fillet*; **b** (*in full* **fillet steak**) the most highly valued cut of beef, cut from the lowest part of the **loin**. **2** a thin narrow strip of wood, metal or other material. **3** *archit* a narrow flat band, often between mouldings. ▸ *verb* (***filleted, filleting***) **1** **a** to cut fillets from (meat or fish); **b** to remove the bones from (a fish). **2** to decorate with or as if with a fillet. [14c: from Latin *filum* thread]

filling *noun* **1** *dentistry* a specially prepared substance, that is inserted into a cavity that has been drilled in a decaying tooth. **2** food put inside a pie, sandwich, etc. ▸ *adj* of food, a meal, etc: substantial and satisfying.

filling station *noun, orig US* a place where motorists can buy petrol and other supplies.

fillip *noun* **1** something that has a stimulating or brightening effect; a boost. **2** a movement of a finger when it is engaged under the thumb and then suddenly released away from the hand. [16c as *philippe*]

filly *noun* (***-ies***) **1** a young female horse or pony. **2** *informal* a young girl or woman. [15c: prob from Norse *fylja*]

film *noun* **1** a strip of thin flexible plastic, etc, coated so as to be light-sensitive and exposed inside a camera to produce still or moving pictures. **2** a series of images, often of moving objects, recorded and edited to tell a story, present a subject, etc, and shown in the cinema or on TV. **3** a fine skin, membrane or coating over something. **4** *sometimes in compounds* a thin sheet of plastic used for wrapping: *clingfilm*. ▸ *verb tr & intr* to record any series of images, usu moving objects, using a TV camera, video camera, camcorder, etc. [19c in modern senses: Anglo-Saxon *filmen* membrane]

filmic *adj* referring or relating to the cinema, film or cinematography. ▪ **filmically** *adv.*

film-maker *noun* a producer or director of cinema films. ▪ **film-making** *noun.*

film star *noun* a celebrated film actor or actress.

filmy *adj* (***-ier, -iest***) of a fabric, etc: thin, light and transparent.

filo *or* **phyllo** /ˈfiːloʊ/ *noun* (*in full* **filo pastry**) a type of Greek flaky pastry made in thin sheets. [1940s: from Modern Greek *phyllon* leaf]

Filofax *noun, trademark* (*often* **filofax**) a small loose-leaf personal filing system. Compare **personal organizer**. [1920s: colloquial pronunciation of *file of facts*]

filter *noun* **1** a porous substance that allows liquid, gas, smoke, etc through, but traps solid matter, impurities, etc. **2** a device containing this. **3** a fibrous pad at the unlit end of a cigarette that traps some of the smoke's impurities, such as tar. Also called **filter tip**. **4** a transparent tinted disc used to reduce the strength of certain colour frequencies in the light entering a camera or emitted by a lamp. **5** *elec, radio* a device for suppressing the waves of unwanted frequencies. **6** *comput* a device for blocking access to certain websites or e-mail addresses. **7** *Brit* a traffic signal at traffic lights that allows vehicles going in some directions to proceed while others are stopped. ▸ *verb* **1** *tr & intr* to pass something through a filter, often to remove impurities, particles, etc. **2** (*usu* **filter sth out**)to remove it (eg impurities from liquids, gases, etc) by filtering. **3** *intr* to go past little by little. **4** *intr* (*usu* **filter through** *or* **out**) of news: to leak out, often gradually. [16c as *filtre*: from Latin *filtrum* felt used as a filter]

filter tip *noun* **1** a **filter** (*noun* sense 3). **2** a cigarette with a filter. ▪ **filter-tipped** *adj.*

filth *noun* **1** repulsive dirt; any foul matter. **2** anything perceived as physically or morally obscene. **3** (**the filth**) *slang* the police. [Anglo-Saxon *fylth*, from *ful* foul]

filthy *adj* (***-ier, -iest***) **1** extremely dirty. **2** obscenely vulgar: *filthy language*. **3** offensive or vicious: *a filthy lie*. **4** *informal or dialect* extremely unpleasant: *filthy weather*. ▸ *verb* to make filthy. ▸ *adv, informal* used for emphasis, esp showing disapproval: *filthy rich*. ▪ **filthiness** *noun.*

filtrate *chem, noun* the clear liquid obtained after filtration. ▸ *verb, tr & intr* to filter. ▪ **filtration** *noun.* [17c: from Latin *filtrare* to filter]

fin *noun* **1** a thin wing-like projection on a fish's body for propelling it through the water, balancing, steering, etc. **2** anything that resembles a fin in appearance or function, eg the vertical projection in the tail of an aircraft, a blade projecting from the hull of a ship, a swimmer's flipper, an attachment on some cars, etc. ▪ **finned** *adj.* [Anglo-Saxon *finn*; Latin *pinna* feather or fin, is prob the same word]

finagle /fɪˈneɪgəl/ *verb* **1** *tr & intr* to obtain by guile or swindling, to wangle. **2** (*often* **finagle sb out of sth**) to cheat (them out of it). [20c: from an English dialect form *fainaigue* cheat]

final *adj* **1** occurring at the end; last in a series, after all the others. **2** completed; finished. **3** of a decision, etc: definite; not to be altered; conclusive. ▸ *noun* **1** **a** the last part of a competition at which the winner is decided; **b** (**finals**) the last round or group of contests resulting in a winner. **2** (**finals**) the examinations held at the end of a degree course, etc. ▪ **finality** *noun.* ▪ **finally** *adv.* [14c: from Latin *finalis finis* end]

finale /fɪˈnɑːlɪ/ *noun* **1** the grand conclusion to a show, etc. **2** the last or closing movement of a symphony or other piece of music. [18c: from Latin *finis* end]

finalist *noun* someone who reaches the final round in a competition.

finalize *or* **-ise** *verb* **1** to complete (an agreement or transaction). **2** to arrive at the final form of something. ▪ **finalization** *noun.*

finance *noun* **1** money affairs and the management of them. **2** the money or funds needed or used to pay for something. **3** (**finances**) a person's financial state. ▸ *verb* to provide funds for something. [14c: from Latin *finis* an end]

financial *adj* **1** relating to finance or finances. **2** *Aust & NZ slang* having money; financially solvent.

financial year *noun* **1** any annual period for which accounts are made up. **2** *chiefly Brit* the twelve-month period, in Britain starting 6 April, used in accounting, annual taxation, etc. Compare **fiscal year**.

financier *noun* someone engaged in large financial transactions. [17c: French]

finch *noun* a small songbird, eg a canary, chaffinch, goldfinch, etc, with a short conical beak. [Anglo-Saxon *finc*]

find *verb* (***found***) **1** to discover through search, enquiry, mental effort or chance. **2** to seek out and provide something. **3** to realize or discover something. **4** to experience something as being (easy, difficult, etc): *find it hard to express oneself.* **5** to consider; to think. **6** to get or experience: *find pleasure in reading*. **7** to become aware of something or someone:

found her beside him. **8** to succeed in getting (time, courage, money, etc for something). **9** to see or come across. **10** to reach: *find one's best form.* **11** *tr & intr, law* of a jury or court, etc: to decide on and deliver a specified verdict (about an accused person): *found the accused innocent.* ▸ *noun* something or someone that is found; an important discovery. [Anglo-Saxon *findan*]

IDIOMS **find one's feet** to establish oneself confidently in a new situation. **find out about sth** to discover or get information about it. **find sb out** to detect them in wrongdoing; to discover the truth about them.

finder *noun* **1** someone who finds something. **2** *astrol* a small telescope attached to a larger one for finding the required object and setting it in the centre of the field. **3** short for **viewfinder**.

finding *noun* **1** *law* a decision or verdict reached as the result of a judicial inquiry. **2** (*usu* **findings**) conclusions reached as the result of some research or investigation.

fine[1] *adj* **1** of high quality; excellent; splendid. **2** beautiful; handsome. **3** *facetious* grand; superior: *her fine relations.* **4** of weather: bright; not rainy. **5** well; healthy. **6** quite satisfactory: *That's fine by me.* **7** pure; refined. **8** thin; delicate. **9** close-set in texture or arrangement. **10** consisting of tiny particles. **11** intricately detailed: *fine embroidery.* **12** slight; subtle: *fine adjustments.* ▸ *adv* **1** *informal* satisfactorily. **2** finely; into fine pieces. ▪ **finely** *adv.* ▪ **fineness** *noun.* [13c: from French *fin* end, in the sense of 'boundary or limit']

IDIOMS **cut** *or* **run it fine** *informal* to leave barely enough time for something.

fine[2] *noun* an amount of money to be paid as a penalty for breaking a regulation or law. ▸ *verb* to impose a fine on someone. [12c: from French *fin* end, settlement or ending a dispute]

fine art *noun* **1** art produced for its aesthetic value. **2** (*usu* **fine arts**) painting, drawing, sculpture and architecture; arts that appeal to the sense of beauty.

Fine Gael /fiːnə 'geɪl/ *noun* a political party in the Republic of Ireland. [Irish Gaelic, literally 'family of Gaels']

finery *noun* splendour; very ornate and showy clothes, jewellery, etc. [17c]

finespun *adj* delicate; over-subtle.

finesse /fɪ'nɛs/ *noun* (*pl* ***finesses*** in sense 3 only) **1** skilful elegance or expertise. **2** tact and poise in handling situations. **3** *cards* an attempt by a player holding a high card to win a trick with a lower one. ▸ *verb* to attempt to win a trick by finesse. [15c: French, meaning 'fineness']

fine-tooth comb *or* **fine-toothed comb** *noun* a comb with narrow close-set teeth.

IDIOMS **go over** *or* **through sth with a fine-tooth comb** to search or examine it very thoroughly.

fine-tune *verb* to make slight adjustments to something to obtain optimum performance.

finger *noun* **1 a** one of the five jointed extremities of the hand; **b** any of the four of these other than the thumb; **c** *in compounds*: *fingerprint.* **2** the part of a glove that fits over a finger. **3** anything resembling or similar to a finger in shape. **4** a measure or quantity of alcoholic spirits in a glass, filling it to a depth which is equal to the width of a finger. ▸ *adj* relating to or suitable for fingers *finger buffet.* ▸ *verb* **1** to touch or feel something with the fingers, often affectionately or lovingly; to caress: *He fingered the velvet.* **2** *music* to indicate (on a part or composition) the choice and configuration of fingers to be used for a piece of music. **3** *slang* to identify (a criminal) to the police, etc. **4** *informal* to use the Internet or another network to obtain information about (another user). ▪ **fingerless** *adj*: *fingerless gloves.* [Anglo-Saxon]

IDIOMS **be all fingers and thumbs** *informal* to be clumsy in handling or holding things. **get one's fingers burnt** *informal* to suffer for one's over-boldness or mistakes. **have a finger in every pie** *informal* to have an interest, or be involved, in many different things. **not lay a finger on sb** not to touch or harm them. **point the finger at sb** *informal* to blame or accuse them. **pull** *or* **get one's finger out** *slang* to start working more efficiently. **put the finger on sb** *slang* to finger (*verb* sense 3) (a criminal, etc). **slip through sb's fingers** to manage to escape from them. **wrap** *or* **twist sb round one's little finger** *informal* to be able to get what one wants from them.

fingerboard *noun* the part of a violin, guitar, etc against which the strings are pressed by the fingers.

fingering *noun* **1** the correct positioning of the fingers for playing a particular musical instrument or piece of music. **2** the written or printed notation indicating this.

fingernail *noun* the nail at the tip of one's finger.

fingerprint *noun* **1** the print or inked impression made by the pattern of minute swirling ridges on the surface of the end joints of the fingers and thumbs, which is unique to each person, and can be used as a means of identification, esp of criminals. **2** any accurate and unique identifying feature or characteristic, esp that produced by analysis of a sample of a person's DNA, using a technique known as **DNA fingerprinting** or **genetic fingerprinting**. **3** a distinctive feature or identifiable characteristic, etc. ▸ *verb* to make an impression of the fingerprints of (someone).

fingerstall *noun* a covering for protecting the finger, esp after an injury.

fingertip *noun* the end or tip of one's finger.

IDIOMS **have sth at one's fingertips** to know a subject thoroughly and have information readily available.

finicky *or* **finickety** *adj* **1** too concerned with detail. **2** of a task: intricate; tricky. **3** fussy; faddy. [19c: prob derived from **fine**[1]]

finish *verb* (*often* **finish off** *or* **up**) **1** *tr & intr* to bring something to an end, or come to an end; to reach a natural conclusion. **2** to complete or perfect something. **3** to use, eat, drink, etc the last of something. **4** *intr* to reach or end up in a certain position or situation. **5** *intr* (*often* **finish with sb**) to end a relationship with them. **6** *intr* (**finish with sb** *or* **sth**) to stop dealing with or needing them or it. **7** to give a particular treatment to the surface of (cloth, wood, etc). ▸ *noun* **1** the last stage; the end. **2** the last part of a race, etc. **3** perfecting touches put to a product. **4** the surface texture given to cloth, wood, etc. [14c as *fenys*: from Latin *finire* to end]

IDIOMS **fight to the finish** to fight till one party is dead or so severely disabled that they are unable to continue.

PHRASAL VERBS **finish sb** *or* **sth off** *informal* **1** to exhaust them emotionally or physically. **2** to complete their defeat or killing.

finished *adj* **1** *informal* no longer useful, productive, creative, wanted or popular. **2** of a performer, performance, etc: very accomplished.

finishing-school *noun* a private school where girls are taught social skills and graces. [19c]

finishing touch *noun* (*also* **finishing touches**) a last minor improvement or detail that makes something perfect.

finite *adj* **1** having an end or limit. **2** *maths* having a fixed, countable number of elements. **3** *grammar* of a verb: being in a form that reflects person, number, tense, etc, as distinct from being an infinitive or participle. Compare **infinitive**. [15c: from Latin *finire* to end or limit]

Finnish *adj* belonging or relating to Finland, a republic in Scandinavia, its inhabitants or their language. ▶ *noun* the official language of Finland.

fiord see **fjord**

fir *noun* **1** a coniferous evergreen tree, with silvery or bluish foliage and leathery needle-like leaves. **2** any of various related trees, eg the Douglas fir. **3** the wood of any of these trees. [Anglo-Saxon *fyrh*]

fire *noun* (*pl* ***fires*** in senses 2, 3 and 4 only) **1** flames coming from something that is burning. **2** an occurrence of destructive burning of something: *a forest fire*. **3** mainly in homes: a mass of burning wood, coal or other fuel, usu in a grate, etc, used for warmth or cooking. Also called **open fire**. **4** a gas or electric room-heater. **5** the discharge of firearms. **6** the launching of a missile. **7** heat and light produced by something burning or some other source. **8** enthusiasm; passion. **9** fever; a burning sensation from inflammation, etc. **10** sparkle; brilliance (eg of a gem). ▶ *verb* **1** *tr & intr* to discharge (a gun); to send off (a bullet or other missile) from a gun, catapult, bow, etc: *fired the gun • The enemy fired on us*. **2** to launch (a rocket, missile, etc). **3** to detonate (an explosive). **4** of a gun, missile, etc: to be discharged, launched, etc: *The gun fired*. **5** to direct (eg questions) in quick succession at someone. **6** *informal* to dismiss someone from employment. **7** *intr* of a vehicle engine, boiler, etc: to start working when a spark causes the fuel to burn: *The motor fired*. **8** to put fuel into (a furnace, etc). **9** (*also* **fire sb up**) to inspire or stimulate (someone). **10** *pottery* to bake (pottery, bricks, etc) in a kiln, usu at a very high temperature. ▶ *exclam* **1** a cry, warning others of a fire. **2** the order to start firing weapons, etc. [Anglo-Saxon *fyr*]

IDIOMS **fire away** *informal* an expression inviting someone to start saying what they have to say, esp to begin asking questions. **play with fire** *informal* to take risks; to act recklessly. **pull sth out of the fire** to rescue the situation at the last minute. **set fire to sth** *or* **set sth on fire** to make it burn; to set light to it. **under fire 1** being shot at. **2** being criticized or blamed.

fire alarm *noun* a bell or other device activated to warn people of fire.

firearm *noun* (*often* **firearms**) a gun carried and used by an individual.

fireball *noun* **1** ball lightning. **2** a mass of hot gases at the centre of a nuclear explosion. **3** *informal* a lively energetic person. **4** *astron* a large bright meteor.

firebomb *noun* an incendiary bomb. ▶ *verb* to attack or destroy something with firebombs. [19c]

firebrand *noun* **1** a piece of burning wood. **2** someone who stirs up unrest; a troublemaker.

firebreak *noun* a strip of land in a forest which is cleared to stop the spread of fire.

fire brigade *noun, chiefly Brit* an organized team of people trained and employed to prevent and extinguish fires. *N Am equivalent* **fire department**. See also **firefighter**.

fire clay *noun* a type of clay that can withstand high temperatures, used for making fire-resistant pottery.

firecracker *noun* a small firework that bangs repeatedly.

firedamp *noun* an explosive mixture of methane gas and air, formed in coal mines by the decomposition of coal. See also **afterdamp**.

firedog *noun* an **andiron**.

fire door *noun* **1** a fire-resistant door between two parts of a building to prevent the spread of fire. **2** a door leading out of a building which can be easily opened from the inside, used as an emergency exit.

fire drill *noun* the routine of evacuating and checking a building, etc, to be followed in case of fire, or a practice of this routine.

fire-eater *noun* **1** a performer who pretends to swallow fire from flaming torches. **2** an aggressive or quarrelsome person.

fire engine *noun* a vehicle which carries firefighters and firefighting equipment to the scene of a fire.

fire escape *noun* an external metal staircase by which people can escape from a burning building.

fire extinguisher *noun* a portable device containing water, liquid carbon dioxide under pressure, foam, etc, for spraying on to a fire to put it out.

firefighter *noun* a person who is trained to put out large fires and rescue those endangered by them, usu as part of a **fire brigade**. ▪ **firefighting** *noun, adj*.

firefly *noun* (***-ies***) a small, winged, nocturnal beetle that emits light in a series of brief flashes.

fireguard *noun* a metal or wire-mesh screen for putting round an open fire to protect against sparks or falling coal, logs, etc.

fire hydrant *noun* a **hydrant**.

fire irons *plural noun* a set of tools for looking after a coal or log fire, usu including a poker, tongs, brush and shovel.

firelighter *noun* a block of flammable material placed underneath the fuel to help light a coal or log fire.

fireman *noun* **1** a male member of a **fire brigade**, officially called a **firefighter**. **2** on steam trains or steamboats: a person who stokes the fire or furnace.

fireplace *noun* mainly in homes: a recess for a coal or log fire or a tiled, marble, etc structure around it.

firepower *noun, military* the amount and effectiveness of the firearms possessed by a military unit, country etc.

fireproof *adj* resistant to fire and fierce heat. ▶ *verb* to make something resistant to fire.

fire-raiser *noun* someone who deliberately sets fire to buildings, etc. Compare **arsonist** at **arson**.

fire-raising *noun, Scots law* **arson**.

fireside *noun* the area round a fireplace, esp as a symbol of home. ▶ *adj* domestic; familiar.

fire sign *noun, astrol* any of the three signs of the zodiac, ie Aries, Leo and Sagittarius, associated with fire.

fire station *noun* a building where fire engines and equipment are housed and firefighters are stationed.

firewall *noun* **1** a fireproof wall installed in a building to prevent fires from spreading. **2** *comput* an item of software that protects a network against unauthorized users.

firewater *noun, informal* any strong alcoholic spirit.

firewood *noun* wood for burning as fuel.

firework *noun* **1** a device that, when lit, produces coloured sparks, flares, etc, often with accompanying loud bangs. **2** (**fireworks** *or* **firework display**) a show at which such devices are let off for entertainment, usu to mark a special event. **3** (**fireworks**) *informal* a show of anger or bad temper.

firing line *noun* **1** the position from which gunfire, etc is delivered, esp the front line of battle. **2** the position at which criticisms, complaints, etc are directed.

firing squad *noun* a detachment of soldiers with the job of shooting a condemned person.

firkin *noun* **1** *brewing* a measure equal to 9 gallons (c. 40 litres). **2** a small container with a capacity equal to quarter of a barrel, varying in amount depending on the commodity. [15c: from Dutch *vierde* fourth + Anglo-Saxon *cynn*]

firm[1] *adj* **1** strong; compact; steady. **2** solid; not soft or yielding. **3** definite: *a firm offer.* **4** of prices, markets, etc: steady or stable, with a slight upward trend. **5** determined; resolute. **6** of a mouth or chin: suggesting determination. ▸ *adv* in a determined and unyielding manner; with resolution: *hold firm to a promise.* ▸ *verb* to make something firm or secure. ▪ **firmly** *adv.* ▪ **firmness** *noun.* [14c: from Latin *firmus* firm or solid]

PHRASAL VERBS **firm up** of prices, markets, etc: to become more stable, usu with a slight upward trend: *Prices were firming up.*

firm[2] *noun* an organization or individual engaged in economic activity with the aim of producing goods or services for sale to others; a business or company. [16c: from Latin *firmare* to confirm by signature]

firmament *noun, literary, old use* the sky; heaven. [13c: from Latin *firmamentum,* from *firmus* firm or solid; relating to the earlier belief that the position of the stars was fixed]

firmware *noun, comput* a software program which cannot be altered and is held in a computer's read-only memory, eg the operating system. [1960s: from **firm**[1], modelled on **software**]

first (often written **1st**) *adj* **1** in counting: before all others; before the second and following ones. **2** earliest in time or order. **3** the most important; foremost in importance: *first prize.* **4** basic; fundamental: *first principles.* **5** *music* **a** having the higher part: *the first violins;* **b** being the principal player: *the first clarinet.* ▸ *adv* **1** before anything or anyone else. **2** foremost: *got in feet first.* **3** before doing anything else: *first make sure of the facts.* **4** for the first time: *since he first saw him.* **5** preferably; rather: *I'd die first.* **6** firstly. ▸ *noun* **1** the starting object of a series of objects. **2** a person or thing coming first, eg in a race or exam. **3** *informal* a first occurrence of something; something never done before: *That's a first for me!* **4** the beginning; the start: *from first to last.* **5** (**the first**) **a** the first day of the month; **b** *golf* the first hole. **6** (also **first gear**) the first or lowest forward gear in a gearbox, eg in a motor vehicle. **7** *education, chiefly Brit* first-class honours in a university degree. ▪ **firstly** *adv* **1** used to introduce the first point in a list of things. **2** in the first place; to begin with. [Anglo-Saxon *fyrest*]

IDIOMS **at first** at the start of something; early on in the course of something. **at first hand** directly from the original source. **in the first place** from the start; to begin with. **not have the first idea** *or* **not know the first thing about sth** *informal* to be completely ignorant about it; to know nothing about it.

first aid *noun* immediate emergency treatment given to an injured or ill person.

first-born *literary or old use, noun* the eldest child in a family. ▸ *adj* eldest.

first-class *adj* **1** referring to the best or highest grade in terms of value, performance or quality. **2** excellent. **3** referring to the most comfortable grade of accommodation in a train, plane, etc: *a first-class ticket from Edinburgh to Aberdeen.* **4** *chiefly Brit* the category of mail most speedily delivered. ▸ *noun* (**first class**) first-class mail, transport, etc. ▸ *adv* (**first class**) by first-class mail, transport, etc. [18c]

first cousin see **cousin**

first-day cover *noun, philately* an envelope bearing a newly-issued stamp postmarked with the stamp's date of issue.

first-degree *adj* **1** *med* denoting the least severe type of burn in which only the outer layer of the skin is damaged. **2** *N Amer law* denoting the most serious of the two levels of murder, ie unlawful killing with intent and premeditation.

first foot *Scot, noun* (*also* **first-footer**) the first person to enter a house in the New Year. ▸ *verb* (**first-foot**) to enter a house as a first foot. ▪ **first-footing** *noun.*

first-hand *adj, adv* direct; from the original source; without an intermediary.

first lady *noun, N Am, chiefly US* (*often* **First Lady**) **1** the wife or partner of the governor of a city, state or country, esp of the US President. **2** a woman who is highly regarded in a particular field or activity.

first lieutenant *noun* in the US army, air force and marine corps: an officer of the rank directly below captain.

First Minister *noun* the title given to the leader of the devolved administrations in Scotland, Northern Ireland and Wales.

first name *noun* a personal name as distinct from a family name or surname.

first-past-the-post *adj, politics* referring to an electoral system in which voters have one vote only, and the candidate with the most votes is declared the winner.

first person see under **person**

first-rate *adj* **1** being of the highest quality, as opposed to **second-rate**, etc. **2** excellent; fine.

first strike *noun, military, politics* a pre-emptive attack on an enemy, intended to destroy their nuclear weapons before they can be brought into use.

First World War see **World War I**

firth *noun* esp in Scotland: a river estuary or an inlet. [15c: from Norse *fjörthr* fjord]

fiscal *adj* **1** of or relating to government finances or revenue. **2** of or relating to financial matters generally. ▸ *noun, Scot* a **procurator fiscal**. ▪ **fiscally** *adv.* [16c: from Latin *fiscus* rush-basket or purse]

fiscal year *noun, chiefly N Am* the **financial year**, starting on 1 July.

fish *noun* (***fish*** *or* ***fishes***) **1** a cold-blooded aquatic vertebrate that breathes by means of gills, and has a bony or cartilaginous skeleton, a body covered with scales, and that swims using fins. **2** *in compounds* any of various water-inhabiting creatures: *shellfish* • *jellyfish*. **3** the flesh of fish used as food. **4** *derog, informal* a person: *an odd fish*. **5** (**the Fish**) *astron, astrol* **Pisces**. ▸ *verb* **1** *intr* to catch or try to catch fish. **2** to catch or try to catch fish in (a river, lake, etc). **3** *intr* to search or grope: *fished in his bag for a pen*. **4** *intr* to seek information, compliments, etc by indirect means. [Anglo-Saxon *fisc*]

IDIOMS **a fish out of water** someone in an unaccustomed, unsuitable situation which makes them ill at ease. **have other fish to fry** *informal* to have other, more important, things to do.

fishcake *noun* a round flat portion of cooked fish and mashed potato, coated in breadcrumbs.

fisherman *noun* a person who fishes as a job or hobby.

fishery *noun* (**-ies**) **1** an area of water where fishing takes place, particularly sea waters; a fishing ground. **2** the business or industry of catching, processing and selling fish.

fish-eye lens *noun, photog* a convex camera lens with an extremely wide angle and a small focal length, giving a scope of nearly 180°.

fish finger *noun* an oblong piece of filleted or minced fish coated in breadcrumbs.

fishing *noun* the sport or business of catching fish.

fishing rod *noun* a long flexible rod to which a fishing line, and usu a reel, is attached.

fishmonger *noun* a retailer of fish. [15c]

fishnet *noun* a net for catching fish. ▸ *adj* of clothes: having an open mesh, like netting: *fishnet tights*.

fish slice *noun* a kitchen utensil with a flat slotted head, for lifting and turning food in a frying pan, etc.

fishtail *adj* shaped like the tail of a fish. ▸ *verb, intr* **1** of an aircraft: to swing the aircraft's tail from side to side, to reduce speed while gliding downwards. **2** of a car, vehicle, etc: to skid when the back of the vehicle swings from side to side.

fishwife *noun, derog* a loud-voiced, coarse woman.

fishy *adj* (**-ier, -iest**) **1** relating to fish, like or consisting of fish. **2** *informal* dubious; questionable.

fissile *adj* **1** *geol* of certain rocks, eg shale: tending to split or capable of being split. **2** *nuclear physics* capable of undergoing nuclear fission. [17c: from Latin *fissilis* that can be split]

fission *noun* **1** a splitting or division into pieces. **2** *biol* the division of a cell or a single-celled organism into two or more new cells or organisms as a means of asexual reproduction. **3** *nuclear physics* see **nuclear fission**. ▪ **fissionable** *adj.* [19c: from Latin *fissio* splitting; compare **fissure**]

fissure *noun, geol* **1** a long narrow crack or fracture esp in a body of rock, the Earth's surface or a volcano. **2** *anatomy* a natural narrow cleft or groove that divides an organ such as the brain into lobes. [14c: from Latin *findere* to split]

fist *noun* a tightly closed or clenched hand with the fingers and thumb doubled back into the palm. [17c]

fistful *noun* an amount that can be held in a closed hand; a handful.

fisticuffs *plural noun, humorous* fighting with fists. [17c: from **fist** + **cuff²**]

fistula *noun* (***fistulas*** *or* ***fistulae*** /ˈfɪstjʊliː/) *pathol* an abnormal connection between two internal organs or body cavities. [14c: Latin, meaning 'tube' or 'pipe']

fit¹ *verb* (***fitted*** *or* (*N Am*) ***fit, fitting***) **1** *tr & intr* to be the right shape or size for something or someone. **2** *intr* (*usu* **fit in** *or* **into sth**) to be small or few enough to be contained in it. **3** to be suitable or appropriate for something. **4** *tr & intr* to be consistent or compatible with something. **5** to install or put something new in place. **6** to equip. **7** *tr & intr* (*also* **fit together** *or* **fit sth together**) to join together to form a whole. **8** to make or be suitable. **9** to try clothes on someone to see where adjustment is needed. ▸ *noun* the way something fits according to its shape or size: *a tight fit*. ▸ *adj* (***fitter, fittest***) **1 a** healthy; feeling good. **b** healthy, esp because of exercise. **2** about to do something, or apparently so: *looked fit to drop*. ▸ *adv* enough to do something: *laughed fit to burst*. ▪ **fitly** *adv.* ▪ **fitness** *noun.* [15c]

IDIOMS **fit for sth** suited to it; good enough for it. **fit like a glove** to fit perfectly. **fit the bill** to be perfectly suited to something; to be just right. **see** *or* **think fit** to choose to do something.

PHRASAL VERBS **fit in 1** of someone in a social situation: to behave in a suitable or accepted way. **2** to be appropriate or to conform to certain arrangements. **fit sb** *or* **sth in** to find time to deal with them or it. **fit sth out** to furnish or equip it with all necessary things for its particular purpose: *fit out the ship*. **fit sb up** *informal* to incriminate them; to frame them.

fit² *noun* **1** a sudden involuntary attack, of convulsions, coughing, hysterics, etc. **2** a burst, spell or bout: *a fit of giggles*. [Anglo-Saxon *fitt* struggle]

IDIOMS **by** *or* **in fits and starts** in irregular spells; spasmodically. **have** *or* **throw a fit** to become very angry. **in fits** *informal* laughing uncontrollably.

fitful *adj* irregular, spasmodic or intermittent; not continuous. ▪ **fitfully** *adv.* [17c]

fitment *noun* a piece of equipment or furniture which is fixed to a wall, floor, etc.

fitted *adj* **1** made to fit closely: *fitted sheets*. **2** of a carpet: covering the floor entirely. **3** fixed; built-in: *fitted cupboards*. **4** of a kitchen, etc: with built-in shelves, cupboards, appliances, etc.

fitter *noun* a person who installs, adjusts or repairs machinery, equipment, etc.

fitting *adj* suitable; appropriate. ▸ *noun* **1** an accessory or part: *a light fitting*. **2** (**fittings**) fitted furniture or equipment. **3** an act or an occasion of trying on a specially made piece of clothing, to see where adjustment is necessary. ▪ **fittingly** *adv.*

five *noun* **1 a** the cardinal number 5; **b** the quantity that this represents, being one more than four. **2** any symbol for this number, eg *5* or *V*. **3** the age of five. **4** something, esp a garment, or a person, whose size is denoted by the number 5. **5** the fifth hour after midnight or midday: *The meeting starts at five* • *5 o'clock* • *5am*. **6** a set or group of five people or things. ▸ *adj* **1** totalling five. **2** aged five. [Anglo-

Saxon *fif*]

IDIOMS **bunch of fives** *slang* the fist.

fivefold *adj* **1** equal to five times as much or many. **2** divided into, or consisting of, five parts. ▸ *adv* by five times as much.

fiver *noun, informal* **a** *Brit* a five-pound note; **b** *NAm* a five-dollar bill. [19c]

fix *verb* **1** to attach or place something firmly. **2** to mend or repair something. **3** to direct; to concentrate: *fixed his eyes on her.* **4** to transfix someone. **5** to arrange or agree (a time, etc). **6** to establish (the time of an occurrence). **7** *informal* to arrange (the result of a race, trial, etc) dishonestly. **8** *informal* to bribe or threaten someone into agreement. **9** *informal* to thwart, punish or kill someone. **10** *photog* to make (the image in a photograph) permanent by the use of chemicals which dissolve unexposed silver halides. **11** *informal* to prepare (a meal, etc): *I'll fix breakfast.* See also **fixed.** ▸ *noun* **1** *informal* a situation which is difficult to escape from; a predicament. **2** *slang* **a** an act of injecting a narcotic drug, etc; **b** the quantity injected or to be injected in this way. **3** a calculation of the position of a ship, etc, by radar, etc. [15c: from Latin *fixare*]

PHRASAL VERBS **fix sth up 1** to arrange a meeting, etc. **2** to get a place ready for some purpose. **3** to set it up, esp temporarily. **fix sb up (with sth)** to provide them with what is needed.

fixate *verb, tr & intr* to become or make something (eg the eyes) become fixed on something. [19c: from Latin *fixus* fixed]

fixated *adj* **1** *psychoanal* affected by or engaged in **fixation**: *He is fixated on his mother.* **2** obsessed; obsessively attached.

fixation *noun* **1** an (often abnormal) attachment, preoccupation or obsession. **2** *psychol* a strong attachment of a person to another person, an object or a particular means of gratification during childhood. **3** *biol* the procedure whereby cells or tissues have their shape and structure preserved with suitable chemical agents before being examined. **4** *chem* the conversion of a chemical substance into a form that does not evaporate, ie a non-volatile or solid form. **5** *psychol* inability to change a particular way of thinking or acting, which has become habitual as a result of repeated reinforcement or frustration.

fixative *noun* **1** a liquid sprayed on a drawing, painting or photograph to preserve and protect it. **2** a liquid used to hold eg dentures in place. **3** a substance added to perfume to stop it evaporating.

fixed *adj* **1** fastened; immovable. **2** unvarying; unchanging; set or established: *fixed ideas.* **3** of a gaze or expression: steady; concentrated; rigid. **4** of a point: stationary. **5** permanent: *a fixed address.* ▪ **fixedly** /ˈfɪksɪdlɪ/ *adv.*

fixed assets *plural noun, econ* assets that remain valuable for a long period, such as plant and buildings, brands, processes, patents and financial investments.

fixer *noun* **1** *photog* a chemical solution that **fix**es photographic images. **2** *slang* a person who arranges things, esp illegally.

fixity *noun* the quality of being fixed, steady, unchanging, unmoving or immovable.

fixture *noun* **1** a permanently fixed piece of furniture or equipment: *Fixtures and fittings are included in the house price.* **2** **a** a match, horse race or other event in a sports calendar; **b** the date for such an event. **3** someone or something permanently established in a place or position. [16c: from Latin *fixura* a fastening, modelled on **mixture**]

fizz *verb, intr* **1** of a liquid: to give off bubbles of carbon dioxide with a hissing sound. **2** to hiss. ▸ *noun* **1** a hiss or spluttering sound; fizziness. **2** vivacity; high spirits. **3** the bubbly quality of a drink; effervescence. **4** any effervescent drink. ▪ **fizziness** *noun.* ▪ **fizzy** *adj* (**-ier, -iest**). [17c: imitating the sound]

fizzle *verb, intr* **1** to make a faint hiss. **2** (*usu* **fizzle out**) to come to a feeble end; to come to nothing, esp after an enthusiastic start. ▸ *noun* a faint hissing sound. [16c: from *fysel* to fart]

fjord *or* **fiord** /ˈfiːɔːd/ *noun* a long narrow steep-sided inlet of the sea in a mountainous coast, eg in Norway, Greenland or New Zealand, formed by the flooding of a previously glaciated valley. [17c: from Norse *fjörthr*]

fl. *abbrev* **1** florin. **2** floruit. **3** fluid.

flab *noun, informal* excess flesh or fat on the body. [1920s: back-formation from **flabby**]

flabbergast *verb, informal* to amaze; to astonish: *I was flabbergasted at their impudence.* [18c]

flabby *adj* (**-ier, -iest**) *derog* **1** **a** of flesh: sagging, not firm; **b** of a person: having excess or sagging flesh. **2** lacking vigour; feeble; ineffective. ▪ **flabbiness** *noun.* [17c: altered form of **flappy**]

flaccid /ˈflasɪd, ˈflaksɪd/ *adj* limp and soft; not firm. ▪ **flaccidity** *noun.* [17c: from Latin *flaccus* feeble]

flag[1] *noun* **1** a piece of cloth with a distinctive design, flown from a pole to represent a country, political party, etc, or used for signalling. **2** national identity represented by a flag. **3** any kind of marker used to indicate and draw special attention to something, eg a code placed at a particular position in a computer program, a paper marker pinned onto a map, etc. ▸ *verb* (***flagged, flagging***) to mark something with a flag, tag or symbol.

IDIOMS **fly the flag** *or* **keep the flag flying** to maintain a show of support for or fight for something. **with flags flying** triumphantly.

PHRASAL VERBS **flag sb** *or* **sth down** to signal, usu with a hand, to a vehicle or driver to stop.

flag[2] *verb* (***flagged, flagging***) *intr* to grow weak or tired after a period of intense work or activity. [16c: prob derived from **flap**, in the sense of 'hang down']

flag[3] *noun* **1** (*also* **flagstone**) a large flat stone for paving. **2** a flat slab of any fine-grained rock which can be split into flagstones. [15c: from Norse *flaga* slab]

flagellate *verb* /fladʒəˈleɪt/ to whip someone or oneself, eg for the purpose of religious penance. ▸ *adj* /ˈfladʒələt/ **1** *biol* having or relating to a flagellum or flagella. **2** whip-like. ▸ *noun* a single-celled protozoan animal with one or more flagella. [17c: from Latin *flagellare* to whip]

flagellation *noun* an act of whipping.

flagellum /fləˈdʒɛləm/ *noun* (***flagella*** /-lə/) **1** *biol* a long whip-like structure that projects from the cell surface of sperm, certain bacteria, unicellular algae and protozoans, used for propulsion. **2** *botany* a long thin runner or creeping shoot. [19c: Latin, meaning 'a small whip']

flageolet[1] /fladʒoʊ'lɛt, -'leɪ/ *noun* a small pale green kidney bean. [19c: French, from Latin *faseolus* bean]

flageolet[2] /fladʒoʊ'lɛt, -'leɪ/ *noun* a high-pitched woodwind instrument similar to the recorder. [17c: French, from *flajol* pipe]

flag of convenience *noun* a flag of a foreign country where a ship is registered to avoid taxation, etc in its real country of origin.

flagon *noun* a large bottle or jug with a narrow neck, usu with a spout and handle. [15c: French, from Latin *flasconum* flask]

flagpole *or* **flagstaff** *noun* a pole from which a flag is flown.

flagrant *adj* of something or someone bad: undisguised; blatant; outrageous; brazen or barefaced: *a flagrant lie.* ▪ **flagrancy** *noun.* ▪ **flagrantly** *adv.* [16c: from Latin *flagrare* to blaze]

flagship *noun* **1** the ship that carries and flies the flag of the fleet commander. **2** the leading ship in a shipping line. **3** a commercial company's leading product, model, etc; the product considered most important. *as adj: their flagship branch.*

flagstone see **flag**[3]

flag-waving *noun* an excessive demonstration of patriotic feeling.

flail *noun* a threshing tool consisting of a long handle with a free-swinging wooden or metal bar attached to the end. ▸ *verb* to beat with or as if with a flail. [Anglo-Saxon *fligel*]

flair *noun* **1** (*often* **flair for sth**) a natural ability or talent for something: *a flair for maths.* **2** stylishness; elegance: *dresses with flair.* [19c: from Latin *fragrare* to smell sweet]

---

flair, flare

Be careful not to use the spelling **flair** when you mean **flare**:

Violence could flare at any time.

---

flak *noun* **1** anti-aircraft fire. **2** *informal* adverse criticism. [1930s: from German *Fliegerabwehrkanone* anti-aircraft gun, literally 'pilot defence gun']

flake *noun, often in compounds* **1** a small flat particle which has broken away or is breaking away from a larger object: *flakes of plaster.* **2** a small piece or particle: *snowflake • cornflake.* ▸ *verb* **1** *intr* to come off in flakes. **2** to break (eg cooked fish) into flakes. [14c: possibly related to Norse *floke* flock of wool]

PHRASAL VERBS **flake out** *informal* to collapse or fall asleep from exhaustion.

flaky *adj* (**-ier, -iest**) **1** made of flakes or tending to form flakes. **2** *chiefly US informal* crazy; eccentric.

flambé /'flɒmbeɪ/ *adj* of food: soaked in a spirit, usu brandy, and set alight before serving. ▸ *verb* (***flambéed, flambéing***) to serve (food) in this way. [19c: from French *flamber* to expose to flame]

flamboyant *adj* **1** of a person or behaviour: colourful, exuberant, and showy. **2** of clothing or colouring: bright, bold and striking. ▪ **flamboyance** *noun.* [19c: French, meaning 'blazing']

flame *noun* **1 a** a hot luminous flickering tongue shape of burning gases coming from something that is on fire; **b** (*often* **flames**) a mass of these: *burst into flames • go up in flames.* **2 a** a strong passion or affection: *the flame of love;* **b** *informal* a boyfriend or girlfriend. ▸ *verb* **1** *intr* to burn with flames; to blaze. **2** *intr* to shine brightly. **3** *intr* to explode with anger. **4** *intr* to get red and hot: *Her cheeks flamed with anger.* **5** to apply a flame to (an object or substance). [14c: from Latin *flamma*]

flamenco *noun* **1** a rhythmical, emotionally stirring type of Spanish Gypsy music, usu played on the guitar. **2** the dance performed to it. [19c: Spanish, meaning 'flamingo']

flameproof *verb* to make something resistant to burning or damage by high temperatures. ▸ *adj* not easily damaged by fire or high temperatures.

flame-thrower *noun* a device that discharges a stream of burning liquid, used as a weapon in war.

flaming *adj* **1** blazing. **2** bright; glowing, particularly a brilliant red. **3** *informal* very angry; furious; violent. **4** *informal* damned: *That flaming dog!*

flamingo *noun* (***flamingos*** *or* ***flamingoes***) a large wading bird with white or pinkish plumage, a long neck and long legs, webbed feet, and a broad curving bill. [16c: from Provençal *flamenc* flaming]

flammable *adj* liable to catch fire; inflammable. Opposite of **non-flammable**. ▪ **flammability** *noun.* [19c: from Latin *flammare* to blaze]

flan *noun* an open pastry or sponge case with a savoury or fruit filling. Compare **quiche**. [19c: from Latin *flado* a flat cake]

flange *noun* a broad flat projecting rim, eg round a wheel, added for strength or for connecting with another object or part. [17c: from French *flanc* flank]

flank *noun* **1 a** the side of an animal, between the ribs and hip; **b** the corresponding part of the human body. **2** a cut of beef from the flank, consisting of the abdominal muscles. **3** the side of anything, eg a mountain, building, etc. **4** of a body of things, esp of troops or a fleet drawn up in formation: the left or right extremities of that formation. ▸ *verb* **1 a** to be on the edge of (an object, a body of things, etc); **b** to move around the sides of a body of things. **2** *military* **a** to guard on or beside the flank of a formation; **b** to move into a position in the flanks or beside the flanks of a formation. [12c: from French *flanc*]

flannel *noun* **1** soft woollen cloth with a slight nap used to make clothes. **2** (*also* **face flannel**) a small square of towelling for washing with. Also called **face cloth**. **3** *informal* flattery or meaningless talk intended to hide one's ignorance or true intentions. **4** (**flannels**) **a** *dated* trousers made of flannel; **b** white trousers, orig made of flannel, worn by cricketers. ▸ *verb* (***flannelled, flannelling***; *N Am* ***flanneled, flanneling***) *tr & intr* to flatter or persuade by flattery, or to talk flannel. [16c: possibly from Welsh *gwlanen*, from *gwlan* wool]

flannelette *noun* a cotton imitation of flannel, with a soft brushed surface.

flap *verb* (***flapped, flapping***) **1** *tr & intr* to wave something up and down, or backwards and forwards. **2** *tr & intr* of a bird: to move (the wings) up and down; to fly with pronounced wing movements. **3** *intr, informal* (*often* **flap about** *or* **around**) to get into or be in a panic or flustered state. ▸ *noun* **1** a broad piece or part of something attached along one edge and hanging loosely, usu as a cover to an opening: *pocket flaps.* **2** an act, sound or impact of flapping. **3** *informal* a panic; a flustered state. **4** a hinged section on an aircraft wing adjusted to control speed. ▪ **flappy** *adj* (***-ier, -iest***). [14c: prob imitative]

flapjack *noun* **1** a thick biscuit made with oats and syrup. **2** *N Am* a pancake. [16c]

flapper *noun* **1** a fashionable and frivolous young woman of the 1920s. **2** something or someone that flaps.

flare *verb* **1** *intr* (*also* **flare up**) to burn with sudden brightness. **2** *intr* (*also* **flare up**) to explode into anger. **3** *tr & intr* to widen towards the edge. ▸ *noun* **1** a sudden blaze of bright light. **2** a device composed of combustible material that produces a sudden blaze of intense light, and is activated to give warning, emergency illumination (eg on an airfield), or a distress signal (eg at sea). **3** in chemical plants and oil refineries: a device for burning off superfluous combustible gas or oil, in order to ensure its safe disposal. **4** short for **solar flare**. **5** a widening out towards the edges: *sleeves with a wide flare*. [16c]

flare, flair

Be careful not to use the spelling **flare** when you mean **flair**:

a flair for music

flares *plural noun, informal* trousers with legs which widen greatly below the knee.

flare-up *noun* **1** *informal* a sudden explosion of emotion or violence. **2** a sudden burst into flames.

flash *noun* **1** a sudden brief blaze of light. **2** an instant; a very short length of time. **3** a brief but intense occurrence: *a flash of inspiration*. **4** a fleeting look on a face or in the eyes: *a flash of joy*. **5** *photog* **a** a bulb or electronic device attached to a camera which produces a momentary bright light as a picture is taken: *a camera with built-in flash*; **b** the bright light produced by it: *The flash made her blink*. **6** an emblem on a military uniform. **7** a sudden rush of water down a river. ▸ *verb* **1** *tr & intr* to shine briefly or intermittently. **2** *tr & intr* to appear or cause to appear briefly; to move or pass quickly. **3** *intr* of the eyes: to brighten with anger, etc. **4** to give (a smile or look) briefly. **5** to display briefly; to flourish, brandish, or flaunt. **6** *tr & intr* to send (a message) by radio, satellite, etc. **7** *tr & intr* to operate (a light) as a signal. ▸ *adj* **1** sudden and severe: *flash floods*. **2** quick: *flash freezing*. **3** *informal* smart and expensive.

IDIOMS **a flash in the pan** *informal* an impressive but untypical success, unlikely to be repeated.

flashback *noun* esp in a film, novel, etc: a scene depicting events which happened before the current ones.

flashbulb *noun* a small light bulb used to produce a brief bright light in photography.

flasher *noun* **1** **a** a light that flashes; **b** a device causing a light to do this. **2** *informal* a man who flashes (see **flash** *verb* sense 8).

flash flood *noun* a sudden, severe and brief flood caused by heavy rain. ▪ **flash flooding** *noun*.

flashlight *noun* **1** *N Am* a torch. **2** *photog* the momentary bright light emitted from an electronic flash or a flashbulb as a photograph is taken. Usu shortened to **flash**.

flash point *noun* **1** a stage in a tense situation, etc where tempers flare and people may become angry or violent. **2** *chem* the temperature at which the vapour above a volatile liquid will ignite.

flashy *adj* (***-ier, -iest***) *informal* ostentatiously smart and gaudy. ▪ **flashily** *adv*. ▪ **flashiness** *noun*.

flask *noun* **1** (*also* **hip flask**) a small flat pocket bottle for alcoholic spirits. **2** a **vacuum flask**. **3** a narrow-necked bottle used in chemical experiments, etc. [16c: from Latin *flasco*]

flat[1] *adj* (***flatter, flattest***) **1** level; horizontal; even. **2** without hollows or prominences. **3** lacking the usual prominence: *a flat nose*. **4** not bent or crumpled. **5** of feet: having little or no arch to the instep. **6** of shoes: not having a raised heel. **7** bored; depressed. **8** dull; not lively. **9** toneless and expressionless. **10** *informal* definite; downright; emphatic: *a flat refusal*. **11** *music* **a** of an instrument, voice, etc: lower than the correct **pitch**[1] (*noun* sense 5); **b** *following its noun* lowering the specified note by a **semitone**: *C flat*. Compare **sharp** (*adj* sense 11). **12** of a tyre: having too little air in it. **13** of a drink: having lost its fizziness. **14** of a battery: having little or no electrical charge remaining. **15** of a price, rate, economic indicator, etc: fixed; unvarying. **16** of a business, company, etc: commercially inactive. **17** of paint: matt, not glossy. ▸ *adv* **1** stretched out rather than curled up, crumpled, etc. **2** into a flat compact shape: *folds flat for storage*. **3** exactly: *in two minutes flat*. **4** bluntly and emphatically: *I can tell you flat*. **5** *music* at lower than the correct pitch: *He sang flat*. ▸ *noun* **1** something flat; a flat surface or part. **2** (**flats**) **a** an area of flat land; **b** a mud bank exposed at low tide. **3** *informal* a punctured tyre on a vehicle. **4** *music* **a** a sign (♭) that lowers a note by a **semitone** from the note that it refers to; **b** a note lowered in this way. **5** a flat upright section of stage scenery slid or lowered onto the stage. **6** (**the flat**) *horse-racing* **a** **flat racing**; **b** the season of flat racing, from March to November. ▪ **flatly** *adv* emphatically: *She flatly refused to go*. ▪ **flatness** *noun*. [14c: from Norse *flatr* flat]

IDIOMS **fall flat** *informal* to fail to achieve the hoped-for effect: *The joke fell flat*. **fall flat on one's face** *informal* to fail at something in a humiliating way. **flat broke** *informal* completely without money. **flat out** *informal* with maximum speed and energy. **that's flat** *informal* that's certain or final.

flat[2] *noun* a set of rooms for living in as a self-contained unit, in a building or tenement with a number of such units. *N Am equivalent* **apartment**. [19c; orig Anglo-Saxon *flett* floor, house]

flatbread *noun* any of various types of bread baked in flat, usually unleavened, loaves.

flatfish *noun* a horizontally flat-bodied fish, with both eyes on the upper surface, eg a sole, plaice, flounder, etc.

flat-footed *adj* **1** having flat feet. **2** *derog* clumsy or tactless.

flatlet *noun* a small **flat**[2].

flatmate *noun* a person one shares a **flat**[2] with.

flat racing *noun, horse-racing* the sport of racing horses on courses with no obstacles for the horses to jump. ▪ **flat race** *noun*.

flat spin *noun* **1** uncontrolled rotation of an aircraft or projectile in a horizontal plane around a vertical axis. **2** *informal* a state of agitated confusion; dither.

flatten *verb* **1** *tr & intr* to make or become flat or flatter. **2** *informal* **a** to knock someone to the ground in a fight; **b** to overcome, crush or subdue someone utterly. **3** *music* to lower the pitch of (a note) by one semitone.

flatter *verb* **1** to compliment someone excessively or insincerely, esp in order to win a favour from them. **2** of a picture or description: to represent someone or something over-favourably. **3** to show something off well: *a dress that flatters the figure*. **4** to make someone feel honoured; to gratify. ▪ **flatterer** *noun*. [13c]

flattery *noun* (**-ies**) **1** the act of flattering. **2** excessive or insincere praise.

flatulence *noun* **1** an accumulation of gas formed during digestion in the stomach or intestines, causing discomfort. **2** pretentiousness. ▪ **flatulent** *adj*. [18c: from Latin *flatus* blowing]

flatworm *noun* a type of worm (distinct from eg **roundworm**s) with a flattened body, a definite head but no true body cavity, eg the **tapeworm**.

flaunt *verb* to display or parade oneself or something, in the hope of being admired. [16c]

flaunt, flout
Be careful not to use the word **flaunt** when you mean **flout**. If you **flout** something, you defy it:
a rebel who flouted all the rules

flautist or (*chiefly N Am*) **flutist** *noun* someone skilled in playing the flute. [19c: from Italian *flauto* flute]

flavonoid /ˈfleɪvənɔɪd/ *noun, biochem* any of a group of organic compounds including numerous water-soluble plant pigments. [20c: from Latin *flavus* yellow]

flavour or (*N Am*) **flavor** *noun* **1** a sensation perceived when eating or drinking which is a combination of taste and smell. **2** any substance added to food, etc to give it a particular taste. **3** a characteristic quality or atmosphere. **4** *physics* an index which denotes different types of **quark**[1]. ▸ *verb* to add something (usu to food) to give it a particular flavour or quality. ▪ **flavourless** or (*N Am*) **flavorless** *adj*. ▪ **flavoursome** or (*N Am*) **flavorsome** *adj*. [14c: from French *flaour*]

flavouring or (*N Am*) **flavoring** *noun* any substance added to food, etc to give it a particular taste.

flaw *noun* **1** a fault, defect, imperfection or blemish. **2** a mistake, eg in an argument. ▪ **flawed** *adj*. ▪ **flawless** *adj*. [14c: prob from Norse *flaga* stone flag]

flax *noun* **1** a slender herbaceous plant cultivated in many parts of the world for the fibre of its stem and for its seeds. **2** the fibre of this plant, used to make thread and woven into **linen** fabrics. [Anglo-Saxon *fleax*]

flaxen *adj* **1** of hair: very fair. **2** made of or resembling flax. [16c]

flaxseed see **linseed**

flay *verb* **1** to strip the skin from (an animal or a person). **2** to whip or beat violently. **3** to criticize harshly. [Anglo-Saxon *flean*]

flea *noun* **1** a wingless blood-sucking jumping insect that lives as a parasite on mammals (including humans) and some birds. **2** *in compounds* referring to small **crustacean**s that leap like fleas: *sand flea* • *water flea*. [Anglo-Saxon *fleah*]

IDIOMS **a flea in one's ear** *informal* a reply that is unwelcome or surprisingly sharp; a severe scolding.

flea-bite *noun* **1** the bite of a flea, or an itchy swelling caused by it. **2** a trivial inconvenience. [15c]

flea-bitten *adj* **1** bitten by or infested with fleas. **2** dingy; squalid.

flea market *noun, informal* a street market that sells second-hand goods or clothes. [1920s]

flea-pit *noun, informal* a shabby cinema or other public building. [1930s]

fleck *noun* **1** a spot or marking: *a white coat with flecks of grey*. **2** a speck or small bit: *a fleck of dirt*. ▸ *verb* (*also* **flecker**) to spot or speckle. [16c: from Norse *flekkr* speck or spot]

fled *past tense, past participle of* **flee**

fledged *adj* **1** of a young bird: able to fly because the feathers are fully developed. **2** qualified; trained: *a fully-fledged doctor*. [Anglo-Saxon *flycge*]

fledgling or **fledgeling** *noun* **1** a young bird that has just grown its feathers and is still unable to fly. **2** an inexperienced person new to a situation; a recently formed organization. *as adj*: *a fledgling company*. [19c: from *fledge* ready to fly]

flee *verb* (**fled**) **1** *intr* to run away quickly. **2** to hurriedly run away from or escape from (danger or a dangerous place). [Anglo-Saxon *fleon*]

fleece *noun* **1** a sheep's woolly coat. **2** a sheep's wool cut from it at one shearing. **3** sheepskin or a fluffy fabric for lining garments, etc. **4** a garment made of fluffy acrylic thermal fabric and used like a jacket or pullover. ▸ *verb* **1** to cut wool from (sheep); to shear (sheep). **2** *slang* to rob, swindle or overcharge. ▪ **fleecy** *adj* (**-ier, -iest**). [Anglo-Saxon *flies*]

fleet[1] *noun* **1** a number of ships under one command and organized as a tactical unit. **2** a navy; all the ships of a nation. **3** a number of buses, aircraft, etc operating under the same ownership or management. [Anglo-Saxon *fleot* ship, from *fleotan* to float]

fleet[2] *verb, intr* to flit or pass swiftly. ▸ *adj, poetic* swift; rapid: *fleet of foot*. [Anglo-Saxon *fleotan* to float]

fleeting *adj* passing swiftly; brief; short-lived: *a fleeting smile*. ▪ **fleetingly** *adv*.

Fleet Street *noun* British newspapers or journalism collectively. [Late 19c: named after the street in London where many newspapers were produced]

Fleming *noun* a native of Flanders (a region in northern Europe comprising NW Belgium, part of northern France and a western part of the Netherlands) or of the Flemish-speaking part of Belgium. [15c in the form *flemmyng*]

Flemish *adj* belonging or relating to Flanders, an area of N Belgium, or to the Flemings or their language. ▸ *noun* the language of the Flemings, one of the two official languages of Belgium, which is virtually identical to Dutch. [15c in the form *Flemis*]

flesh *noun* **1** in animals: the soft tissues covering the bones, consisting chiefly of muscle. **2** the meat of animals, as distinct from that of fish, used as food; sometimes the meat of birds, used as food. **3** the pulp of a fruit or vegetable. **4** the body as distinct from the soul or spirit; bodily needs. **5** *poetic* humankind. **6** excess fat; plumpness. **7** a yellowish-pink colour. [Anglo-Saxon *flæsc*]

IDIOMS **flesh and blood** bodily or human nature. **in the flesh** in person; actually present. **one's (own) flesh and blood** one's family or relations.

PHRASAL VERBS **flesh sth out** to add descriptive detail to it.

fleshly *adj* relating to the body as distinct from the soul; worldly.

flesh wound *noun* a superficial wound, not deep enough to damage bone or a bodily organ.

fleshy *adj* (*-ier, -iest*) **1** plump. **2** relating to or like flesh. **3** of leaves, etc: thick and pulpy. ▪ **fleshiness** *noun*.

fletcher *noun* a person whose job is to make arrows. [14c: from French *flèche* arrow]

fleur-de-lis *or* **fleur-de-lys** /flɜːdəˈli, flɜːdəˈliːs/ *noun* (*fleurs-de-lis, fleurs-de-lys* /flɜːdəˈliz, flɜːdəˈliːz/) a stylized three-petal representation of a lily or iris, used as a heraldic design. [14c: from French *flour de lis* lily flower]

flew *past tense of* **fly²**

flex¹ *verb* **1** to bend (a limb or joint). **2** to contract or tighten (a muscle) so as to bend a joint. [16c: from Latin *flectere* to bend]

flex² *noun* flexible insulated electrical cable. [Early 20c: from **flexible**]

flexible *adj* **1** bending easily; pliable. **2** readily adaptable to suit circumstances. ▪ **flexibility** *noun*. ▪ **flexibly** *adv*. [16c: from Latin *flexibilis*]

flexion *noun* **1** the bending of a limb or joint, esp a flexor muscle. **2** a fold or bend.

flexitime *noun* a system of flexible working hours, allowing workers to choose when they put in their hours, usu including certain hours (**core time**) each day when everyone must be at work. [1970s: from *flex*ible + **time**]

flexor *noun, anatomy* any muscle that causes bending of a limb or other body part. Compare **extensor**. [17c: from **flex¹**]

flibbertigibbet *noun* a frivolous or over-talkative person. [16c: imitating fast talking]

flick *verb* **1** to move or touch something with a quick light movement. **2** to move the hand or finger quickly and jerkily against something small, eg a speck of dust, crumbs, etc, in order to remove it. **3** *intr* (*usu* **flick through sth**) to glance quickly through it (eg a book, a video, etc), in order to get a rough impression of it. ▸ *noun* **1** a flicking action. **2** *informal* (*often pl*) a cinema film. [15c: imitating the sound]

flicker *verb* **1** *intr* to burn or shine unsteadily by alternately flashing bright and dying away again. **2** *intr* to move lightly to and fro; to flutter. **3** to cause something to flicker. ▸ *noun* **1** a brief or unsteady light. **2** a fleeting appearance or occurrence: *a flicker of hope*. [Anglo-Saxon *flicorian* to flutter]

flick knife *noun* a knife whose blade is concealed in its handle and springs out at the touch of a button. [1950s]

flier *or* **flyer** *noun* **1** a leaflet used to advertise a product, promote an organization, etc, usu distributed on street corners or as an insert in a newspaper, etc. **2** an aviator or pilot. **3** *informal* a **flying start**. **4** someone or something that flies or moves fast. **5** *informal* a risky or speculative business transaction. [15c as *flyer*]

flies see under **fly¹**, **fly²**

flight¹ *noun* **1** the practice or an act of flying with wings or in an aeroplane or other vehicle. **2** the movement of eg a vehicle, bird or projectile through the air, supported by aerodynamic forces. **3** a flock of birds flying together. **4** a regular air journey made by an aircraft. **5** a journey of a spacecraft. **6** a group of aircraft involved in a joint mission. **7** a set of steps or stairs. **8** a feather or something similar attached to the end of a dart or arrow. [Anglo-Saxon *flyht*]
IDIOMS **a flight of fancy** *sometimes derog* a free use of the imagination. **in flight** flying.

flight² *noun* the act of fleeing; escape. [12c]

flight attendant *noun* a member of the **cabin crew** on a passenger aircraft.

flight deck *noun* **1** the forward part of an aeroplane where the pilot and flight crew sit. **2** the upper deck of an **aircraft carrier** where planes take off and land.

flightless *adj* of certain birds or insects: unable to fly.

flight lieutenant *noun* an officer in the Royal Air Force.

flight recorder *noun* an electronic device fitted to an aircraft, recording information about its performance in flight, prevailing weather conditions, etc, often used in determining the cause of an air crash. Also called **black box**. [1940s]

flighty *adj* (*-ier, -iest*) irresponsible; frivolous; flirtatious. ▪ **flightiness** *noun*.

flimflam *noun* **1** a trick or deception. **2** idle, meaningless talk; nonsense. [16c: reduplication of *flam*, possibly from Norse *flimska* mockery]

flimsy *adj* (*-ier, -iest*) **1** of clothing, etc: light and thin. **2** of a structure: insubstantially made; frail. **3** of an excuse, etc: inadequate or unconvincing. ▪ **flimsily** *adv*. ▪ **flimsiness** *noun*. [18c: perhaps from **film**]

flinch *verb, intr* **1** to start or jump in pain, fright, surprise, etc. **2** (*often* **flinch from sth**) to avoid something difficult such as a task, duty, etc. [16c: prob connected with French *flechir* to bend]

fling *verb* (*flung*) **1** to throw something, esp violently or vigorously. **2** *sometimes intr* to throw oneself or one's body about. ▸ *noun* **1** an act of flinging. **2** *informal* a sexual relationship with someone for a short period of time. **3** *informal* a spell of enjoyable self-indulgence. **4** a lively reel. [13c: prob related to Norse *flengja* and Swedish *flänga* to flog]
PHRASAL VERBS **fling sb out** to get rid of them. **fling sth out** to throw it away or reject it.

flint *noun* **1** *geol* a crystalline form of quartz consisting of hard dark-grey or black nodules encrusted with white. **2** *archaeol* a trimmed piece of this used as a tool. **3** a piece of a hard metal alloy from which a spark can be struck, eg in a cigarette lighter. ▪ **flinty** *adj* (*-ier, -iest*). [Anglo-Saxon]

flip *verb* (*flipped, flipping*) **1** to toss (eg a coin) so that it turns over in mid-air. **2** *intr, informal* (*also* **flip one's lid**) to become suddenly wild with anger; to lose one's temper. **3** *intr* (*usu* **flip through sth**) to look quickly through it. ▸ *noun* **1** a flipping action. **2** a somersault, esp performed in mid-air. **3** an alcoholic drink made with beaten egg. **4** *informal* a short air trip. ▸ *adj, informal* flippant; over-smart. [17c: prob imitating the sound]

flip-flop *noun* **1** *informal* a rubber or plastic sandal consisting of a sole held on to the foot by a thong that separates the big toe from the other toes. **2** *elec, comput* an electronic circuit that remains in one of two stable states until it receives a suitable electric pulse, which causes it to switch to the other state. [16c: reduplication of **flip** indicating the repetition of the movement]

flippant *adj* not serious enough about grave matters; disrespectful; irreverent; frivolous. ▪ **flippancy** *noun*. ▪ **flippantly** *adv*. [17c: prob from **flip**]

flipper *noun* **1** a limb adapted for swimming, eg in a whale, seal, etc. **2** a rubber foot-covering imitating an animal flipper, worn for underwater swimming. [19c]

flip phone *noun* a mobile phone with a hinged cover that protects it when it is not in use.

flip side *noun, informal* **1** of a coin: the reverse; tails. **2** a less familiar aspect of something. **3** a different, and sometimes opposite, aspect or effect of something.

flirt *verb, intr* **1** (*usu* **flirt with sb**) to behave in a playful manner (towards someone one finds attractive). **2** (*usu* **flirt with sth**) to take a fleeting interest in it; consider it briefly. **3** (*usu* **flirt with sth**) to treat it (eg death, danger, etc) lightly. ▸ *noun* someone who flirts. ▪ **flirtation** *noun*. ▪ **flirtatious** *adj*. ▪ **flirty** *adj*. [16c: compare **flick**, **flip**]

flit *verb* (***flitted, flitting***) *intr* **1 a** to move about lightly and quickly from place to place; **b** to fly silently or quickly from place to place. **2** *Scot & N Eng* to move house. **3** *Brit informal* to move house stealthily to avoid paying debts, etc. ▸ *noun* an act of flitting. [12c: from Norse *flytja* to carry]

flitch *noun* a salted and cured side of pork.

float *verb* **1** *tr & intr* to rest or move, or make something rest or move, on the surface of a liquid. **2** *intr* to drift about or hover in the air. **3** *intr* to move about in an aimless or disorganized way. **4** to start up or launch (a company, scheme, etc). **5** to offer (stocks) for sale. **6** *finance* to allow (a currency) to vary in value in relation to other currencies. ▸ *noun* **1** something that floats or is designed to keep something afloat. **2** *angling* a floating device fixed to a fishing-line, that moves to indicate a bite. **3** a low-powered delivery vehicle: *milk float*. **4** a vehicle decorated as an exhibit in a street parade. **5** an amount of money set aside each day for giving change, etc in a shop at the start of business. **6** a plasterer's trowel. [Anglo-Saxon *flotian*; compare **fleet**[2]]

floatation see **flotation**

floating *adj* **1** not fixed; moving about: *a floating population*. **2** of a voter: not committed to supporting any one party. **3** of a currency: free to vary in value in relation to other currencies. **4** of a bodily organ, eg a kidney: moving about abnormally.

floating capital *noun* goods, money, etc not permanently invested in **fixed assets**; working capital.

floating rib *noun* any of the lower two pairs of ribs in humans which do not reach the breastbone at all.

floats *plural noun, theatre* floodlights.

floccose *adj, botany* covered with downlike hairs.

flocculent *adj* **1** woolly; fleecy. **2** *chem* of a precipitate: aggregated in woolly cloudlike masses. **3** *botany* covered with tufts or flakes. ▪ **flocculence** *noun*. [18c: from Latin *floccus* tuft of wool]

flock[1] *noun* **1** a group of creatures, esp birds or sheep. **2** a crowd of people. **3** a body of people under the spiritual charge of a priest or minister. ▸ *verb, intr* to gather or move in a group or a crowd. [Anglo-Saxon *flocc*]

flock[2] *noun* **1** a tuft of wool, etc. **2** (*also* **flocks**) waste wool or cotton used for stuffing mattresses, etc. **3** fine particles of wool or nylon fibre applied to paper, esp wallpaper, or cloth to give a raised velvety surface. [14c: from Latin *floccus*]

floe *noun* a sheet of ice other than the edge of an ice shelf or glacier, floating in the sea. [19c: from Norwegian *flo* layer]

flog *verb* (***flogged, flogging***) **1** to beat; to whip repeatedly, particularly as a form of punishment. **2** *informal* to sell something. [17c: prob from Latin *flagellare*]

IDIOMS **flog a dead horse** *informal* to waste time and energy trying to do something that is impossible.

flood *noun* **1** an overflow of water from rivers, lakes or the sea on to dry land. **2** any overwhelming flow or quantity of something. **3** the rising of the tide. **4** *informal* a floodlight. ▸ *verb* **1** to overflow or submerge (land) with water. **2** to fill something too full or to overflowing. **3** (*usu* **flood sb out**) to force them to leave a building, etc because of floods. **4** *intr* to become flooded, esp frequently. **5** *intr* to move in a great mass: *Crowds flooded through the gates*. **6** *intr* to flow or surge. **7** *intr* to bleed profusely from the uterus, eg after childbirth. **8** to supply (a market) with too much of a certain kind of commodity. **9** to supply (an engine) with too much petrol so that it cannot start. [Anglo-Saxon *flod*]

floodgate *noun* a gate for controlling the flow of a large amount of water.

IDIOMS **open the floodgates** to remove all restraints.

floodlight *noun* (*also* **floodlamp**) a powerful light used to illuminate extensive areas, esp sports grounds or the outside of buildings. ▸ *verb* (***floodlit***) to illuminate with floodlights.

flood plain *noun, geog* an extensive level area beside a river, corresponding to the part of the river valley which becomes covered with water when the river floods.

floor *noun* **1** the lower interior surface of a room or vehicle. **2** all the rooms, etc on the same level in a building; the storey of a building. **3** *usu in compounds* the lowest surface of some open areas, eg the ground in a forest or cave, the bed of the sea, etc. **4** the debating area in a parliamentary assembly or the open area of a stock exchange as opposed to the viewing gallery. **5** the right to speak in a parliamentary assembly: *have the floor*. ▸ *verb* **1** to construct the floor of (a room, etc). **2** *informal* to knock someone down. **3** *informal* to baffle someone completely. [Anglo-Saxon *flor*]

IDIOMS **take the floor 1** to rise to speak in a debate, etc. **2** to start dancing.

floorboard *noun* one of the narrow boards that form a wooden floor.

flooring *noun* **1** material for constructing floors. **2** a platform.

floor show *noun* a series of performances such as singing and dancing at a nightclub or restaurant.

floosie, **floozie** *or* **floozy** *noun* (***-sies*** *or* ***-zies***) *informal, often facetious* a disreputable or immodest woman or girl. [Early 20c]

flop *verb* (***flopped, flopping***) *intr* **1** to fall, drop, move or sit limply and heavily. **2** of eg hair: to hang or sway about loosely. **3** *informal* of a play, project, business, etc: to fail dismally. **4** *slang* (*usu* **flop out**) to fall asleep, esp because of exhaustion. ▸ *noun* **1** a flopping movement or sound. **2** *informal* a complete failure. **3** *N Am informal* a place to sleep; temporary lodgings. ▸ *adv* with a flop: *He fell flop into the swimming pool*. [17c: variant of **flap**]

floppy *adj* (*-ier, -iest*) tending to flop; loose and insecure. ▸ *noun* (*-ies*) *comput* a floppy disk.

floppy disk *noun, comput* a small flexible magnetic disc, enclosed in a stiff plastic casing, used to store data. Compare **hard disk**. [1970s]

flor. *abbrev* floruit.

flora *noun* (**floras** *or* **florae** /ˈflɔːriː/) *botany* the wild plants of a particular region, country or time period. Compare **fauna**. [16c: after Flora, Roman goddess of flowers]

floral *adj* **1** consisting of or relating to flowers: *a floral tribute*. **2** patterned with flowers: *floral curtains*. [17c: from Latin *floralis*]

Florentine *adj* **1** belonging or relating to Florence, a city in Tuscany, Italy, or its inhabitants. **2** (*sometimes* **florentine**) *usu following its noun* of a cooked dish: containing or served with spinach: *eggs florentine*. ▸ *noun* **1** a citizen or inhabitant of, or person born in, Florence. **2** (*sometimes* **florentine**) a biscuit consisting of preserved fruit and nuts on a chocolate base. [16c]

florescence *noun, botany* the process, state or period of flowering. [18c: from Latin *florescere* to begin to blossom]

floret *noun, botany* **1** a small flower; one of the single flowers in the head of a composite flower, such as a daisy or sunflower. **2** each of the branches in the head of a cauliflower or of broccoli. [17c: from Latin *flos, floris* flower]

florid *adj* **1** over-elaborate: *a florid speech*. **2** of a complexion: pink or ruddy. [17c: from Latin *floridus* blooming]

florin *noun* **1** a former British coin worth two shillings. **2** (abbrev **fl.**) another name for the Dutch **guilder**. [14c: from Italian *fiorino*, from *fiore* a flower, because of the flower on one side of the first coins]

florist *noun* someone who grows, sells or arranges flowers. [17c: from Latin *flos, floris* flower]

floruit /ˈflɒruːɪt/ *noun* (abbrev **fl.** *or* **flor.**) a period during which someone was most active, used especially to provide chronological information when birth and death dates are unknown. [19c: Latin, meaning 'he or she flourished']

floss *noun* **1** loose strands of fine silk which are not twisted together, used in embroidery, for tooth-cleaning (**dental floss**), etc. **2** the rough silk on the outside of a silkworm's cocoon. **3** any fine silky plant substance. ▸ *verb, tr & intr* to clean the teeth with dental floss. ▪ **flossy** *adj* (*-ier, -iest*). [18c: prob from French *flosche* down]

flotation *or* **floatation** *noun* **1** the launching of a commercial company with a sale of shares to raise money. **2** the act of floating. **3** the science of floating objects. [19c]

flotilla *noun* a small fleet, or a fleet of small ships. [18c: Spanish, meaning 'little fleet']

flotsam *noun* goods lost by shipwreck and found floating on the sea. Compare **jetsam**. [16c: from French *floteson* something floating]

IDIOMS **flotsam and jetsam** odds and ends.

flounce[1] *verb, intr* to move in a way expressive of impatience or indignation. ▸ *noun* a flouncing movement. [16c: possibly related to Norse *flunsa* to hurry]

flounce[2] *noun* a deep frill on a dress, etc. [18c: altered from *frounce* plait or curl]

flounder[1] *verb, intr* **1** to thrash about helplessly, as if caught in a bog. **2** to stumble helplessly in thinking or speaking, struggling to find the appropriate words, etc. ▸ *noun* an act of floundering. [16c: partly imitating the action, partly a blend of **founder** + **blunder**]

---

flounder, founder

Be careful not to use the word **flounder** when you mean **founder**. If something **founders**, it sinks or fails:

The ship foundered on the rocks.

The business foundered.

---

flounder[2] *noun* a type of European **flatfish** with greyish-brown mottled skin with orange spots, used as food. [15c: from French *flondre*]

flour *noun* **1** the finely ground meal of wheat or other cereal grain. **2** a dried powdered form of any other vegetable material: *potato flour*. ▸ *verb* to coat, cover or sprinkle with flour. ▪ **floury** *adj*. [13c: a specific use of **flower**, best part of the **meal**[2]]

flourish *verb* **1** *intr* to be strong and healthy; to grow well. **2** *intr* to do well; to develop and prosper. **3** *intr* to be at one's most productive, or at one's peak. **4** to adorn with flourishes or ornaments. **5** to wave or brandish something. ▸ *noun* **1** a decorative twirl in handwriting. **2** an elegant sweep of the hand. **3** a showy piece of music; a fanfare. **4** a piece of fancy language. [13c: from French *florir* to flower]

flout *verb* **1** to defy (an order, convention, etc) openly; to disrespect (authority, etc). **2** (*usu* **flout at**) *intr* to jeer; to mock. [16c, meaning 'to play the flute']

---

flout, flaunt

Be careful not to use the word **flout** when you mean **flaunt**. If you **flaunt** something, you display it:

a rich woman who flaunted her wealth

---

flow *verb, intr* **1** to move along like water. **2** of blood or electricity: to circulate. **3** to keep moving steadily. **4** of hair: to hang or ripple in a loose shining mass. **5** of words or ideas: to come readily to mind or in speech or writing. **6** to be present in abundance. **7** of the tide: to advance or rise. Compare **ebb** *verb* (sense 1). ▸ *noun* **1** the action of flowing. **2** the rate of flowing. **3** a continuous stream or outpouring. **4** the rising of the tide. [Anglo-Saxon]

IDIOMS **in full flow** speaking energetically.

flow chart *noun* a diagram representing the nature and sequence of operations, esp in a computer program or an industrial process.

flower *noun* **1** in a flowering plant: the structure that bears the reproductive organs. **2** a plant that bears flowers, esp if cultivated for them. **3** the best part; the cream. **4** the most distinguished person or thing. ▸ *verb* **1** *intr* to produce flowers; to bloom. **2** *intr* to reach a peak; to develop to maturity. [13c: from French *flour*, from Latin *flos, floris* flower]

IDIOMS **in flower** blooming or blossoming.

flower bed *noun* a garden bed planted with flowering plants.

flowerpot *noun* a clay or plastic container for growing plants in.

flowery *adj* **1** decorated or patterned with flowers. **2** of language or gestures: excessively elegant or elaborate. ▪ **floweriness** *noun*.

flowing *adj* **1** moving as a fluid. **2** smooth and continuous; fluent. **3** falling or hanging in folds or waves: *a flowing dress.*

flown *past participle of* **fly**[2]

fl. oz. *abbrev* fluid ounce or fluid ounces.

flu *noun, informal* (*often* **the flu**) influenza. [19c]

fluctuate *verb, intr* of prices etc: to vary in amount, value, etc; to rise and fall. ▪ **fluctuation** *noun.* [17c: from Latin *fluere* to flow]

flue *noun* **1** an outlet for smoke or gas, eg through a chimney. **2** a pipe or duct for conveying heat. [16c]

fluent *adj* **1** having full command of a foreign language: *fluent in French.* **2** spoken or written with ease: *speaks fluent Russian.* **3** speaking or writing in an easy flowing style. **4** of a movement: smooth, easy or graceful. ▪ **fluency** *noun.* [17c: from Latin *fluere* to flow]

fluff *noun* **1** small bits of soft woolly or downy material. **2** *informal* a mistake, eg in speaking or reading aloud. **3** *informal* a stroke at golf, etc where the player misses or mishits the ball. ▸ *verb* **1** (*usu* **fluff sth out** *or* **up**) to shake or arrange it into a soft mass. **2** *tr & intr* of an actor, speaker, etc: to make a mistake in (lines, etc); to bungle. ▪ **fluffiness** *noun.* ▪ **fluffy** *adj* (**-ier, -iest**). [18c: from earlier *flue* a downy substance]

fluid *noun* a substance, such as a liquid or gas, which can move about with freedom and has no fixed shape. ▸ *adj* **1** able to flow like a liquid; unsolidified. **2** of movements, etc: smooth and graceful. **3** altering easily; adaptable. ▪ **fluidity** /flʊˈɪdɪtɪ/ *or* **fluidness** *noun.* [17c: from Latin *fluidus* flowing]

fluid ounce *noun* (abbrev **fl. oz.**) **1** in the UK: a unit of liquid measurement, equal to one twentieth of a British or imperial pint. **2** in the US: a unit of liquid measurement, equal to one sixteenth of a US pint.

fluke[1] *noun* a success achieved by accident or chance. ▸ *verb* to make, score or achieve something by a fluke. ▪ **flukey** *or* **fluky** *adj.* [19c: orig referring to a successful stroke made by chance in billiards]

fluke[2] *noun* **1** a parasitic flatworm, having a complex life cycle which may involve several different hosts including sheep, cattle and humans. **2** a **flounder**[2]. [Anglo-Saxon *floc* plaice]

fluke[3] *noun* **1** one of the triangular plates of iron on each arm of an anchor. **2** a barb, eg of an arrow, harpoon, etc. **3** a lobe of a whale's tail. [16c: prob a special use of **fluke**[2]]

flume *noun* **1 a** a descending chute with flowing water at a swimming pool, that people slide down, landing in the pool; **b** a ride at an amusement park with small boats which move through water-filled channels. **2** an artificial channel for water, used in industry, eg for transporting logs. [18c: from Latin *flumen* river]

flummery *noun* (**-ies**) **1** a jelly made with oatmeal, milk, egg and honey. **2** pompous nonsense; empty flattery. [17c: from Welsh *llymru*]

flummox *verb, informal* to confuse someone; to bewilder someone. [19c]

flung *past tense, past participle of* **fling**

flunk *verb, esp N Am informal* **1** *tr & intr* to fail (a test, examination, etc). **2** of an examiner: to fail (a candidate). [19c]

PHRASAL VERBS **flunk out** *intr* to be dismissed from a school or university for failing examinations.

flunkey *or* **flunky** *noun* (**-eys** *or* **-ies**) **1** a uniformed manservant, eg a footman. **2** *derog* a slavish follower. **3** *N Am* a person doing a humble or menial job. [18c: possibly from *flanker* someone who runs alongside]

fluor see **fluorspar**

fluoresce *verb, intr* to demonstrate fluorescence. [19c: from **fluorescence**]

fluorescence *noun, physics* **1** the emission of light and other radiation by an object after it has absorbed electrons or radiation of a different wavelength, esp ultraviolet light. **2** the radiation emitted as a result of fluorescence. Compare **luminescence**, **phosphorescence**. ▪ **fluorescent** *adj.* [19c: from **fluorspar**]

fluorescent light *or* **fluorescent lamp** *noun, elec* a type of electric light that emits visible light by the process of fluorescence. Also called **strip light**.

fluoridate *or* **fluoridize** *or* **-ise** *verb* to add small amounts of fluoride salts to drinking water supplies to help prevent tooth decay. [1940s]

fluoride *noun, chem* any chemical compound consisting of fluorine and another element, especially sodium fluoride, which is added to water or toothpaste to prevent tooth decay. [19c: from **fluorine**]

fluorine *noun* (symbol **F**) *chem* a highly corrosive poisonous yellow gas of the **halogen** group. [19c: from Latin *fluor* flow]

fluorocarbon *noun, chem* a compound of carbon and fluorine, formerly widely used as an aerosol propellant and refrigerant. See also **chlorofluorocarbon**. [1930s: from **fluorine** + **carbon**]

fluorspar, **fluorite** *or* **fluor** *noun, geol* calcium fluoride, a mineral that is transparent when pure, but commonly occurs as blue or purple crystals. [18c: from Latin *fluor* flow (from the use of fluorspar as a flux) + **spar**[2]]

flurry *noun* (**-ies**) **1** a sudden commotion; a sudden bustle or rush: *a flurry of activity.* **2** a sudden gust; a brief shower of rain, snow, etc: *a flurry of snowflakes.* ▸ *verb* (**-ies, -ied**) to agitate, confuse or bewilder someone. [17c: imitating the sound]

flush[1] *verb* **1** *usu intr* to blush or make someone blush or go red. **2** to clean out (esp a lavatory pan) with a rush of water. ▸ *noun* **1** a redness or rosiness, esp of the cheeks or face; a blush. **2** a rush of water that cleans a lavatory pan, or the mechanism that controls it. **3** high spirits: *in the first flush of enthusiasm.* **4** freshness; bloom; vigour: *the flush of youth.* [16c: possibly influenced by **flash**, **blush** and **flush**[4]]

flush[2] *adj* **1** (*often* **flush with sth**) level or even with an adjacent surface. **2** *informal* having plenty of money. **3** abundant or plentiful. **4** full to the brim. ▸ *adv* so as to be level with an adjacent surface: *fixed it flush with the wall.* [17c: perhaps from **flush**[1]]

flush[3] *noun, cards* a hand made up of cards from a single suit. [16c: from Latin *fluxus* flow, influenced by **flush**[1]]

flush[4] *verb, hunting* to startle (game birds) so that they rise from the ground. [13c: prob imitating the sound]

PHRASAL VERBS **flush sb** *or* **sth out** to drive them or it out of a hiding place.

fluster *verb* to agitate, confuse or upset. ▸ *noun* a state of confused agitation. [15c: related to Norse *flaustr* hurry]

flute *noun* **1** a wind instrument consisting of a wooden or metal tube with holes stopped by the fingertips or by keys, which is held horizontally and played by directing the breath across the hole in the mouthpiece. See also **flautist**. **2** *archit* a rounded concave groove or furrow in wood or stone, eg running vertically down a pillar. **3** a tall narrow wineglass, used esp for sparkling wine and champagne. ▸ *verb* to produce or utter (sounds) like the high shrill tones of a flute. ▪ **fluty** *adj* (***-ier, -iest***) like a flute in tone. [14c: from French *flahute*]

fluted *adj* ornamented with flutes (see **flute** sense 2).

fluting *noun* a series of parallel grooves cut into wood or stone.

flutist *noun, N Am* a **flautist**.

flutter *verb* **1** *tr & intr* of a bird, etc: to flap (its wings) lightly and rapidly; to fly with a rapid wing movement. **2** *intr* of a flag, etc: to flap repeatedly in the air. **3** *intr* to drift with a twirling motion. **4** *intr* of the heart: to race, from excitement or some medical disorder. ▸ *noun* **1** a quick flapping or vibrating motion. **2** agitation; excitement: *flutter of excitement*. **3** *informal* a small bet; a speculation. [Anglo-Saxon *floterian*]

fluvial *adj* relating to or found in rivers. [14c: from Latin *fluvialis*]

flux *noun* **1** a flow of matter; a process or act of flowing. **2** constant change; instability. **3** any substance added to another in order to aid the process of melting. **4** in the smelting of metal ores: any substance that is added so that it will combine with impurities which can then be removed as a flowing mass of slag. **5** any substance, such as a resin, that is used to remove oxides from the surfaces of metals that are to be soldered, welded or brazed. **6** *physics* the rate of flow of particles, energy, mass or some other quantity per unit cross-sectional area per unit time. See also **magnetic flux**. ▸ *verb* **1** to apply flux to (a metal, etc) when soldering. **2** *tr & intr* to make or become fluid. [14c: from Latin *fluxus* flow]

fly[1] *noun* (***flies***) **1** a two-winged insect, esp the common housefly. **2** *in compounds* any of various other flying insects: *dragonfly*. **3** *angling* a fish hook tied with colourful feathers to look like a fly, used in fly-fishing. [Anglo-Saxon *fleoge*]

IDIOMS **a fly in the ointment** a drawback or disadvantage to an otherwise satisfactory state of affairs. **a fly on the wall** the invisible observer, usu at a meeting or in a social situation, that one would like to be to find out what is happening without taking part. **no flies on sb** *informal* the person specified is cunning and not easily fooled.

fly[2] *verb* (*third person present tense* ***flies,*** *past tense* ***flew,*** *past participle* ***flown***) **1** *intr* **a** of birds, bats, insects and certain other animals: to move through the air using wings or structures resembling wings; **b** of an aircraft or spacecraft: to travel through the air or through space. **2** *tr & intr* to travel or convey in an aircraft: *They flew to Moscow* • *The company flew them to Moscow.* **3** to operate and control (an aircraft, kite, etc); to cause it to fly. **4** to cross (an area of land or water) in an aircraft: *They flew the Atlantic to New York*. **5 a** to raise (a flag). **b** *intr* of a flag: to blow or flutter in the wind. **6** *intr* to move or pass rapidly: *fly into a temper* • *rumours flying around.* **7** *intr, informal* to depart quickly; to dash off: *I must fly.* **8** *tr & intr* to escape; to flee (a country, a war zone, etc). ▸ *noun* (***flies***) **1** (*chiefly* **flies**) a zip or set of buttons fastening a trouser front, or the flap covering these. **2** a flap covering the entrance to a tent. **3** (**flies**) the space above a stage, concealed from the audience's view, from which scenery is lowered. [Anglo-Saxon *fleogan*]

IDIOMS **fly a kite** to release information about an idea, proposal, etc to find out what people's opinion might be about it. **fly in the face of sth** to oppose it; to be at variance with it. **fly off the handle** to lose one's temper. **let fly at** to lose one's temper with (someone).

fly[3] *adj, informal* cunning; smart. [19c]

flyblown *adj* **1** of food: covered with blowfly eggs; contaminated. **2** shabby, dirty or dingy. [16c]

fly-by *noun* (***fly-bys***) a flight, at low altitude or close range, past a place, target, etc, for observation, esp the close approach of a spacecraft to a planet, etc.

fly-by-night *adj, derog* of a person, business, etc: not reliable or trustworthy. ▸ *noun* an unreliable person, esp one who avoids debts by disappearing overnight.

flyer see **flier**

fly-fish *verb, intr* to fish using artificial flies as bait. ▪ **fly-fishing** *noun*.

flying *adj* **1** hasty; brief: *a flying visit*. **2** designed or organized for fast movement. **3** able to fly or glide. **4** of hair, a flag, etc: streaming; fluttering. ▸ *noun* **1** flight. **2** the activity of piloting, or travelling in, an aircraft.

flying boat *noun* a seaplane with a fuselage shaped like a boat hull.

flying buttress *noun, archit* a support structure forming an arch or half-arch built against the outside wall of a large building in order to resist the outward thrust of the wall. [17c]

flying colours *plural noun* triumphant success: *She passed the exam with flying colours.* [18c]

flying doctor *noun* esp in the remote parts of Australia: a doctor who can be called by radio and who travels by light aircraft to visit patients.

flying fish *noun* a fish with stiff, greatly enlarged pectoral fins that enable it to leap out of the water and glide for considerable distances.

flying officer *noun* an officer in the Royal Air Force.

flying picket *noun* a picket travelling from place to place to support local pickets during any strike.

flying saucer *noun* an unidentified circular flying object reported in the sky, believed by some to be a craft from outer space.

flying squad *noun* a body of police specially trained for quick response and fast action, and available for duty wherever the need arises.

flying start *noun*

IDIOMS **get off to a flying start** of a task, project, etc or of a person: to begin promisingly or with a special advantage.

flyleaf *noun* a blank page at the beginning or end of a book.

flyover *noun* a bridge that takes a road or railway over another. *N Am equivalent* **overpass**.

flypaper *noun* a strip of paper with a sticky poisonous coating that attracts, traps and kills flies.

flypast *noun* a ceremonial flight of military aircraft.

flypitch *noun, informal* a market stall for which the operator does not have a licence. ▪ **flypitcher** *noun.*

flyposting *noun* the putting up of advertising or political posters, etc illegally.

flysheet *noun* **1** a protective outer sheet for a tent which is fitted over the main body. **2** a single-sheet leaflet.

fly-tipping *noun* unauthorized disposal of waste materials.

flytrap *noun* **1** a device for catching flies. **2** *botany* a plant that traps flies and digests them.

flyweight *noun* **1** a class of boxers, wrestlers and weight-lifters of not more than a specified weight, which is 51kg (112 lb) in professional boxing, and similar weights in the other sports. **2** a boxer, etc of this weight.

flywheel *noun* a heavy wheel on a revolving shaft that stores kinetic energy and regulates the action of a machine by maintaining a constant speed of rotation over the whole cycle.

FM *abbrev* **1** Field Marshal. **2** frequency modulation.

Fm *symbol, chem* fermium.

fo *or* **fol.** *abbrev* folio.

foal *noun* the young of a horse or of a related animal. ▸ *verb, intr* to give birth to a foal. [Anglo-Saxon *fola*]
IDIOMS **in foal** *or* **with foal** of a mare: pregnant.

foam *noun* **1** a mass of tiny bubbles on the surface of liquids. **2** a substance composed of tiny bubbles formed by passing gas through it. **3** frothy saliva or perspiration. **4** a light cellular material used for packaging, insulation, etc. ▸ *verb, tr & intr* (*sometimes* **foam up**) to produce or make something produce foam. ▪ **foaming** *noun, adj.* ▪ **foamy** *adj* (**-ier, -iest**). [Anglo-Saxon *fam*]

fob[1] *verb* (***fobbed, fobbing***) now only in phrases below. [16c: related to German *foppen* to delude or jeer]
PHRASAL VERBS **fob sb off** to dismiss or ignore them: *tried to fob off his critics.* **fob sb off with sth** to provide them with something inferior (eg a poor substitute, or an inadequate explanation), usu in the hope that they will be satisfied. **fob sth off on sb** to manage to sell or pass off something inferior to someone.

fob[2] *noun* **1** a chain attached to a watch. **2** a decorative attachment to a key ring or watch chain. **3** *hist* a small watch pocket in a waistcoat or trouser waistband, for holding a **fob watch**. [17c: perhaps related to German dialect *fuppe* pocket]

focaccia /fə'katʃə/ *noun* a flat round of Italian bread made with olive oil and herbs or spices. [20c: Italian]

focal distance *or* **focal length** *noun* the distance between the surface of a mirror or centre of a lens and its focal point.

focal point *noun* **1** *optics* the point at which rays of light which are initially parallel to the axis of a lens or mirror converge, or appear to diverge, having been reflected or refracted. Also called **focus**. **2** a centre of attraction of some event or activity.

fo'c'sle /'foʊksəl/ *noun, naut* a spelling of **forecastle** suggested by its pronunciation.

focus *noun* (***focuses*** *or* ***foci*** /'foʊsaɪ/) **1** the point at which rays of light or sound waves converge or appear to diverge. **2** *optics* **focal point** (sense 1). **3 a** the condition in which an image is sharp; **b** the state of an instrument producing this image. **4** the location of the centre of an earthquake. See also **epicentre**. **5** a centre of interest or attention. **6** special attention paid to something. **7** *geom* a fixed point on a **conic section** from where the distance between it and any point on the curve is in a constant ratio to the distance between that point and the **directrix**. **8** the location of the centre of an earthquake, where the fracture takes place under the ground. ▸ *verb* (***focused, focusing***; ***focussed, focussing***) **1** *tr & intr* to bring or be brought into focus; to meet or make something meet or converge at a focus. **2** to adjust the thickness of the lens of (the eye) or to move the lens of (an optical instrument) so as to obtain the sharpest possible image of a particular object. **3** to cause (electron beams) to converge or diverge by varying the voltage or current that controls the magnetic or electric fields through which they pass. **4** (*often* **focus sth on sth**) *tr & intr* to concentrate attention, etc on it: *focused her energies on the problem.* ▪ **focal** *adj.* [17c: Latin, meaning 'hearth or fireplace']

focus group *noun* a small group of people brought together to examine some topic. [20c]

fodder *noun* **1** any bulk feed, esp hay and straw, for cattle and other animal livestock. **2** *informal* something that is constantly made use of: *fodder for the popular press.* See also **cannon fodder**. ▸ *verb* to supply (livestock) with fodder. [Anglo-Saxon *fodor*]

foe *noun, literary, old use* an enemy. [Anglo-Saxon *fah* hostile]

foetid see **fetid**

foetus see **fetus**

fog *noun* **1** a suspension of tiny water droplets or ice crystals forming a cloud close to the ground surface. **2** *photog* an unwanted blurred patch on a negative, print or transparency, etc. **3** a blur; cloudiness. **4** a state of confusion or bewilderment. ▸ *verb* (***fogged, fogging***) *tr & intr* (*often* **fog over** *or* **up**) to obscure or become obscured with, or as if with, fog or condensation. [16c]

fogey *or* **fogy** *noun* (**-eys** *or* **-ies**) someone with boring, old-fashioned and usu conservative ideas and attitudes. ▪ **fogeyish** *or* **fogyish** *adj.* [18c: prob from *foggy* moss-grown]

foggy *adj* (**-ier, -iest**) **1** covered with or thick with fog; misty, damp. **2** not clear; confused.
IDIOMS **not have the foggiest** *or* **not have the foggiest idea** *informal* not to know at all.

foghorn *noun* a horn that sounds at regular intervals to ships in fog as a warning of some danger or obstruction, eg land, other vessels, etc. [19c]

foible *noun* a slight personal weakness or eccentricity. [17c: French, variant of *faible* feeble or weak]

foie gras /fwɑː grɑː/ *noun* a pâté made from specially fattened goose liver. Also called **pâté de foie gras**. [19c: French, meaning '(pâté of) fat liver']

foil[1] *verb* to prevent, thwart or frustrate someone or something. [16c: from French *fuler* to trample]

foil[2] *noun* **1 a** metal beaten or rolled out into thin sheets; **b** *also in compounds*: *tinfoil* • *gold foil.* **2** a thin metallic coating (usu a mercury-alloy) on a piece of glass which produces a reflection, forming the backing of a mirror. [14c: from French *foil* leaf, from Latin *folium*]

foil[3] *noun, fencing* a long slender fencing sword with a blunt edge and a point protected by a button. [16c]

foist *verb* **1** (*usu* **foist sth on sb**) to inflict or impose something unwanted on them. **2** (*usu* **foist sth on sb**) to sell or pass on something inferior to them, while suggesting that it has value or is genuine. [16c: perhaps from Dutch *vuisten* to take in hand]

fol. *abbrev* folio.

fold[1] *verb* **1** (*also* **fold over, back, up,** *etc*) to double (something) over so that one part lies on top of another. **2** *intr* (*also* **fold away**) to be able to be folded, or closed up so that it takes up less space, usu making it flat. **3** of an insect, etc: to bring in (wings) close to its body. **4** (*often* **fold up**) to arrange (clothes, etc) for storage by laying them flat and doubling each piece of clothing over on itself. **5** *intr* of flower petals: to close. **6** to clasp (someone) in one's arms, etc. **7** (*also* **fold up**) *informal* of a business, etc: to collapse; to fail. ▸ *noun* **1** a doubling of one layer over another. **2** a rounded or sharp bend made by this, particularly the inside part of it; a crease. **3** a hollow in the landscape. **4** *geol* a buckling or contortion of stratified rocks as a result of movements of the Earth's crust. ▪ **foldable** *adj.* [Anglo-Saxon *faldan* to fold]

fold[2] *noun* **1** a walled or fenced enclosure or pen for sheep or cattle. **2** the body of believers within the protection of a church. [Anglo-Saxon *falod*]

-fold *suffix, forming advs and adjs* **1** multiplied by a specified number: *threefold.* **2** ▸ *adj* having a specified number of parts: *a twofold benefit.* [Anglo-Saxon *-feald*]

folder *noun* **1** a cardboard or plastic cover in which to keep loose papers. **2** *comput* another name for a **directory**. [Early 20c in sense 1, late 20c in sense 2]

foliage *noun* the green leaves on a tree or plant. [15c: from French *feuille* leaf]

foliate *adj* leaflike or having leaves. ▸ *verb* **1** to cover with leaf-metal or foils. **2** to hammer (metal) into thin sheets. **3** to mark the leaves or folios (not pages) of a book, etc with consecutive numbers. Compare **paginate**. [17c: from Latin *foliatus* leafy]

folic acid /ˈfoʊlɪk, ˈfɒlɪk/ *noun, biochem* a member of the **vitamin B complex** found in many foods, esp liver and green leafy vegetables, which is required for the manufacture of DNA and RNA and the formation of red blood cells, deficiency of which causes anaemia and retarded growth. [1940s: from Latin *folium* leaf (because of its presence in green leaves)]

folio *noun* **1** a leaf of a manuscript, etc, numbered on one side. **2 a** a sheet of paper folded once to make two leaves for a book; **b** a book composed of such sheets. ▸ *adj* of a book: composed of folios: *a folio edition.* [16c: from Latin *folium* leaf]

folk *plural noun* **1** people in general. **2** (*also informal* **folks**) a person's family: *going to visit the folks.* **3** people belonging to a particular group, nation, etc: *country folk.* ▸ *singular noun, informal* folk music. ▸ *adj* traditional among, or originating from, a particular group of people or nation: *folk music* • *folk art.* [Anglo-Saxon *folc*]

folklore *noun* the customs, beliefs, stories, traditions, etc of a particular group of people, usu passed down through the oral tradition. [19c]

folk music *noun* **1** traditional music handed down orally from generation to generation within a particular area or group of people. **2** contemporary music of a similar style.

folksy *adj* (**-*ier,* -*iest***) **1** simple and homely, esp in an over-sweet or twee way. **2** everyday; friendly; sociable; unpretentious. [19c: orig US]

folk tale *or* **folk story** *noun* a popular story handed down by oral tradition from generation to generation, and whose origin is often unknown.

follicle *noun* a small cavity or sac within a tissue or organ: *hair follicle.* ▪ **follicular** *adj.* [17c: from Latin *folliculus* a small bellows]

follow *verb* **1** *tr & intr* (*also* **follow after**) to go or come after (someone or something), either immediately or shortly afterwards. **2** to secretly go after (someone or something); to pursue stealthily. **3** to accept someone as leader or authority. **4** *intr* (*sometimes* **follow from**) to result from or be a consequence of (something). **5** to go along (a road, etc), alongside (a river, etc) or on the path marked by (signs). **6** to watch (someone or something moving): *His eyes followed her up the street.* **7** to do (something) in a particular way; to practise (something): *follow a life of self-denial* • *follow a trade.* **8** to conform to (something): *follows a familiar pattern.* **9** to obey (advice, etc). **10** *tr & intr* to copy: *follow her example.* **11** *tr & intr* to understand: *Do you follow me?* **12** to take a keen interest in (a sport, etc). [Anglo-Saxon *folgian*]

IDIOMS **follow suit** to do what someone else has done without thinking much about it.

PHRASAL VERBS **follow on** *cricket* of a side: to play a **follow-on**. **follow through** *or* **follow sth through** *tennis, golf* to continue the action of (a stroke) after hitting the ball. **follow sth through** *or* **up** to pursue (an idea, a project, etc) beyond its early stages, and often to fruition; to investigate or test it. **follow sth up** to take the next step after a particular procedure. See also **follow-up**.

follower *noun* **1** someone or something that follows or comes after others. **2** someone who copies. **3** an avid supporter or devotee, eg of a particular sport, celebrity, etc. **4** a disciple. **5** an attendant; someone who is part of someone's entourage.

following *noun* **1** a body of supporters, devotees, etc. **2** (**the following**) the thing or things, or the person or people, about to be mentioned or referred to: *I'll be discussing the following ...* ▸ *adj* **1** coming after; next. **2** about to be mentioned: *deal with the following points.* **3** of a wind, currents, etc: blowing in the direction in which a ship, etc is travelling. ▸ *prep* after.

follow-on *noun, cricket* a second innings batted immediately after the first, as a result of a team having scored a particular number of runs fewer than the competing team.

follow-up *noun* continuing something that is not completed; further action or investigation.

folly *noun* (**-*ies***) **1** foolishness; a foolish act. **2** a mock temple, castle, ruin, etc built eg as a romantic addition to a view. [13c: from French *folie* madness]

foment /foʊˈmɛnt/ *verb* to encourage or foster (ill-feeling, etc). ▪ **fomentation** *noun.* [17c: from Latin *fomentum*, from *fovere* to cherish or warm]

fond *adj* **1** loving; tender: *fond glances.* **2** happy: *fond memories.* **3** of desire, hopes, etc: foolishly impractical: *a fond hope.* ▪ **fondly** *adv.* ▪ **fondness** *noun.* [14c as *fonned*; from *fonnen* to act foolishly]

IDIOMS **fond of sb** *or* **sth** liking them or it.

fondant *noun* a soft sweet paste made with sugar and water, often flavoured and used in cake- and chocolate-making. [19c: French, from *fondre* to melt]

fondle *verb* to touch, stroke or caress someone or something lovingly, affectionately or lustfully. [17c: from **fond** (sense 1)]

fondue *noun, cookery* a dish, orig Swiss, consisting of hot cheese sauce into which bits of bread are dipped. [19c: from French *fondu* melted]

font[1] *noun* a basin in a church that holds water for baptisms. [Anglo-Saxon *fant*, from Latin *fons, fontis* fountain]

font[2] see **fount**[1]

fontanelle *or* (*chiefly US*) **fontanel** *noun, anatomy* a soft membrane-covered gap between the bones of the skull of a young infant. [16c: from French]

food *noun* **1** a substance taken in by a living organism that provides it with energy and materials for growth and repair of tissues. **2** something that provides stimulation: *food for thought*. [Anglo-Saxon *foda*]

food chain *noun, ecol* a sequence of organisms each of which feeds on the organism below it in the chain and is a source of food for the organism above it.

foodie *noun, informal* a person who is greatly or excessively interested in cookery and food. [1980s]

food poisoning *noun* an illness caused by eating food or drinking water containing toxins or micro-organisms, esp species of the **salmonella** bacterium.

food processor *noun* an electrical kitchen appliance for chopping, liquidizing, etc, food. [20c]

foodstuff *noun* a substance used as food. [19c]

food web *noun* a group of interrelated **food chains**.

fool[1] *noun* **1** someone who lacks common sense or intelligence. **2** someone made to appear ridiculous. **3** *hist* a person employed by kings, nobles, etc to amuse them; a jester. ▸ *verb* **1** to deceive someone so that they appear foolish or ridiculous. **2** (**fool sb into** *or* **out of sth**) to persuade them by deception to do something or not to do it. **3** *intr* (*often* **fool about** *or* **around**) to behave stupidly or playfully. [13c: from French *fol*]

IDIOMS **make a fool of oneself** to act in a way that makes one appear foolish. **make a fool of sb** to trick them or make them appear ridiculous; to humiliate them.

fool[2] *noun* a dessert of puréed fruit mixed with cream or custard. [16c]

foolery *noun* (**-ies**) ridiculous behaviour. [16c]

foolhardy *adj* taking foolish risks; rash; reckless. ▪ **foolhardiness** *noun*. [13c: from French *fol hardi*, literally 'foolish-bold']

foolish *adj* **1** unwise; senseless. **2** ridiculous; silly; comical. ▪ **foolishly** *adv*. ▪ **foolishness** *noun*.

foolproof *adj* **1** of a plan, etc: designed so that it is easy to follow and very unlikely to go wrong; unable to go wrong. **2** of a machine, etc: simple to use.

foolscap *noun* a large size of printing- or writing-paper, measuring 17 × 13½in (432 × 343mm). [17c: from *fool's cap*, the jester's cap used as a watermark in the 18c]

fool's errand *noun* a pointless or unprofitable task or venture; a futile journey.

fool's gold see under **pyrite**

fool's paradise *noun* a state of happiness or confidence based on false expectations. [15c]

foot *noun* (*pl usu* ***feet*** but see sense 7) **1** the part of the leg on which a human being or animal stands or walks. **2** in molluscs: a muscular organ used for locomotion, which can be retracted into the animal's shell. **3** the part of a sock, stocking, etc that fits over the foot. **4** the bottom or lower part of something: *the foot of a mountain*. **5** the part on which something stands; anything functioning as or resembling a foot. **6** the end of a bed where the feet go, as opposed to the head. **7** (*pl* ***feet*** or *often* ***foot***) (abbrev **ft** *or* ′, eg 6ft or 6′) in the imperial system: a unit of length equal to 12in (30.48cm): *The room is sixteen foot by ten*. **8** *prosody* a unit of rhythm in verse containing any of various combinations of stressed and unstressed syllables. **9** a part of a sewing machine that holds the fabric in position. [Anglo-Saxon *fot*]

IDIOMS **foot the bill** to pay the bill. **get a foot in the door** to gain entry into, or get accepted for the first time in, an organization, profession, etc. **get off on the wrong foot** to make a bad start. **have one foot in the grave** *informal* to be very old or near death. **not put a foot wrong** to make no mistakes. **on foot** walking. **put one's best foot forward** to set off with determination. **put one's foot down** to be firm about something. **put one's foot in it** *informal* to cause offence or embarrassment.

footage *noun* **1** measurement or payment by the foot. **2** **a** the length of film measured in feet; **b** a clip from a film, etc: *archive footage*.

football *noun* **1** any of several team games played with a large ball that players try to kick or head into the opposing team's goal. Also called **Association Football, soccer**. **2** the ball used in the game. **3** (**the football**) a football match: *Fiona is going to the football on Saturday*. ▪ **footballer** *noun*.

footbridge *noun* a bridge for pedestrians.

footed *adj* **1** having a foot or feet. **2** *in compounds* **a** having a specified number or type of feet: *four-footed*; **b** having a specified manner of walking: *light-footed*.

footer *noun* **1** *in compounds* a person or thing of a height or length specified in feet: *a six-footer*. **2** a line of information at the foot of a page.

footfall *noun* the sound of a footstep.

foothill *noun* (*usu* **foothills**) a lower hill on the approach to a high mountain or mountain range.

foothold *noun* **1** a place to put one's foot when climbing. **2** a firm starting position.

footie *or* **footy** *noun, informal* football.

footing *noun* **1** the stability of one's feet on the ground: *lost my footing*. **2** basis or status; position or rank. **3** relationship: *on a friendly footing*.

footlights *plural noun, theatre* **1** a row of lights set along the front edge of a stage to illuminate it. **2** the theatre in general, as a profession.

footloose *adj* free to go where, or do as, one likes; not hampered by any ties: *footloose and fancy-free*. [19c]

footman *noun* a uniformed male attendant. [18c]

footnote *noun* a comment at the bottom of a page, often preceded by a numbered mark or asterisk, etc which relates the comment to a part of the main text. [19c]

footpath *noun* **1** a path or track for walkers, usu in the countryside, eg alongside fields, through a wood, etc: *public footpath*. **2** a pavement.

footplate *noun* in a steam train: a platform for the driver and fireman, who are known as the **footplatemen**.

footprint *noun* **1** the mark or impression of a foot or shoe left eg in sand, in soft ground, etc. **2** *comput* the amount of space taken up by a computer and its hardware on a desk, etc.

foot soldier *noun* a soldier serving on foot; an infantry soldier or infantryman.

footsore *adj* having sore and tired feet from prolonged walking.

footstep *noun*
IDIOMS **follow in the footsteps of sb** to do the same as they did earlier; to copy or succeed them.

footstool *noun* a low stool for supporting the feet while sitting.

footwear *singular noun* shoes, boots, socks, etc.

footwork *noun* the agile use of the feet in dancing or sport.

fop *noun* a man who is very consciously elegant in his dress and manners; a dandy. ▪ **foppery** *noun*. ▪ **foppish** *adj*. [17c]

for *prep* **1** intended to be given or sent to someone: *This is for you.* **2** towards: *heading for home.* **3** throughout (a time or distance): *was writing for half an hour.* **4** in order to have, get, etc: *meet for a chat • fight for freedom.* **5** at a cost of something: *said he'd do it for £10.* **6** as reward, payment or penalty appropriate to something: *got six months for stealing • charge for one's work.* **7** with a view to something: *train for the race.* **8** representing; on behalf of someone: *the MP for Greenfield • speaking for myself.* **9** to the benefit of someone or something: *What can I do for you?* **10** in favour of someone: *for or against the proposal.* **11** proposing to oneself: *I'm for bed.* **12** because of something: *couldn't see for tears.* **13** on account of something: *famous for its confectionery.* **14** suitable to the needs of something: *books for children.* **15** having as function or purpose: *scissors for cutting hair.* **16** on the occasion of something: *got it for my birthday.* **17** meaning: *The German word for 'help' is 'helfen'.* **18** in place of; in exchange for something: *replacements for the breakages • translated word for word.* **19** in proportion to something: *one woman for every five men.* **20** up to someone: *It's for him to decide.* **21** as being: *took you for someone else • know for a fact.* **22** with regard to something: *can't beat that for quality.* **23** considering what one would expect: *serious for his age • warm for winter.* **24** about; aimed at: *proposals for peace • a desire for revenge.* **25** in spite of something: *quite nice for all his faults.* **26** available to be disposed of or dealt with by: *not for sale.* **27** with reference to time: **a** at or on: *an appointment for 12 noon on Friday*; **b** so as to be starting by: *7.30 for 8.00*; **c** throughout (a time): *in jail for 15 years.* ▸ *conj, archaic* because; as: *He left, for it was late.* [Anglo-Saxon]
IDIOMS **as for** as far as concerns. **be for it** *or* **be in for it** *informal* to be about to receive a punishment, etc.

fora see **forum**

forage /'fɒrɪdʒ/ *noun* **1** (*also* **forage crop**) a crop, eg grass, kale, swede, etc, grown as feed for livestock. **2** the activity or an instance of searching around for food, provisions, etc. ▸ *verb* **1** *intr* to search around, esp for food. **2** to rummage about (for something). [14c: from French *fourrage*; compare **fodder**]

foramen /fə'reɪmən/ *noun* (***foramina*** /fə'ramɪnə/ *or* ***foramens***) *zool, anatomy* a naturally occurring small opening, particularly in a bone. [17c: from Latin, from *forare* to pierce]

forasmuch as *conj, old use* since; seeing that.

foray /'fɒreɪ/ *noun* **1** a raid or attack. **2** a venture; an attempt. ▸ *verb, tr & intr* to raid; to pillage; to forage. [14c as *forrayen*: to pillage, from **forage**]

forbear[1] *verb* (*past tense* ***forbore***, *past participle* ***forborne***) **1** *archaic* to tolerate something. **2** *intr* (*usu* **forbear from** *or* **forbear to do**) to stop oneself going as far as; to refrain from: *forbear from answering • forbear to mention it.* ▪ **forbearance** *noun*. [Anglo-Saxon *forberan*]

forbear[2] see **forebear**

forbid *verb* (*past tense* ***forbade*** /fə'bad, -'beɪd/ *or* ***forbad*** /-'bad/, *past participle* ***forbidden*** *or* ***forbid***, *present participle* ***forbidding***) **1** to order not; to refuse to allow: *I forbid you to go.* **2** to prohibit: *It is forbidden to smoke here.* **3** to refuse access or entry. [Anglo-Saxon *forbeodan*]

forbidden *adj* prohibited; not allowed; not permitted: *forbidden territory • forbidden fruit.*

forbidding *adj* **1** threatening; grim. **2** uninviting; sinister; unprepossessing.

forbore *or* **forborne** see under **forbear**[1]

force *noun* **1** strength; power; impact or impetus. **2** compulsion, esp with threats or violence. **3** military power. **4** passion or earnestness. **5** strength or validity. **6** meaning. **7** influence. **8** a person or thing seen as an influence. **9** *physics* (SI unit **newton**) (abbrev **F**) **a** any external agent that produces a change in the speed or direction of a moving object, or that makes a stationary object move: *the force of gravity*; **b** any external agent that produces a strain on a static object. **10** any irresistible power or agency: *the forces of nature.* **11** the term used in specifying an index between 0 and 12 on the **Beaufort scale**, each of which corresponds to a different wind speed: *a gale of force 8 • a force-10 gale.* **12 a** a military body; **b** (**the forces**) a nation's armed services. **13** any organized body of workers, etc. **14** (**the force**) the police force. ▸ *verb* **1** to make or compel (someone to do something). **2** to obtain (something) by effort, strength, threats, violence, etc. **3** to produce (something) with an effort. **4** to inflict (eg views, opinions etc) (on someone). **5** to make (a plant) grow or (fruit) ripen unnaturally quickly or early so that it can appear on the market out of its normal season. **6** to strain. [13c: from Latin *fortia* strength]
IDIOMS **force sb's hand** to compel them to act in a certain way. **in force 1** of a law, etc: valid; effective. **2** in large numbers: *Protesters arrived in force.* **join forces** to come together or unite for a purpose.

forced *adj* **1** of a smile, laugh, etc: unnatural; unspontaneous. **2** done or provided under compulsion: *forced labour.* **3** carried out as an emergency: *a forced landing.*

force-feed *verb* to feed (a person or animal) forcibly, esp by passing liquid food through a soft rubber tube into the stomach via the mouth or nostril.

forceful *adj* powerful; effective; influential. ▪ **forcefully** *adv*. ▪ **forcefulness** *noun*.

forcemeat *noun* a mixture of chopped or minced ingredients, eg sausage meat, herbs, etc, used as stuffing. [17c: from *farce* 'stuffing' + **meat**]

forceps *singular noun* (*pl* ***forceps***) *biol, med, etc* an instrument like pincers, for gripping firmly, used esp in surgery, dentistry, etc. [16c: said to be from Latin *formus* warm + *capere* to take]

forcible *adj* **1** done by or involving force: *forcible entry.* **2** powerful: *a forcible reminder.* ▪ **forcibly** *adv.* [15c: French, from 16–18c sometimes spelt *forceable*]

ford *noun* a place where a river or stream may be crossed by passing through shallow water. ▸ *verb* to ride, drive or wade across (a stream, river, etc) by passing through shallow water. ▪ **fordable** *adj.* [Anglo-Saxon]

fore[1] *adj, usu in compounds* towards the front. ▸ *noun* **1** the front part. **2** *naut* the foremast. [Anglo-Saxon *fore*]

IDIOMS **to the fore** at or to the front; prominent; conspicuous.

fore[2] *exclam, golf* ball coming!; a warning shout to anybody who may be in the ball's path. [19c: prob a short form of **before**]

fore- *prefix* **1** before or beforehand: *forewarn.* **2** in front: *foreleg.* [Anglo-Saxon *fore*]

fore-and-aft *adj, naut* **1** at the front and rear of a vessel. **2** set lengthways, pointing to the bow and stern.

forearm *noun* the lower part of the arm between wrist and elbow. ▸ *verb* to prepare someone or arm someone beforehand. [18c]

forebear *or* **forbear** *noun* an ancestor, usu more remote than grandfather or grandmother. [15c]

forebode *verb tr & intr, old use* **1** to foretell; to prophesy. **2** to have a premonition of something, especially something bad. ▪ **foreboding** *noun* a feeling of approaching trouble. [17c: **fore-** + **bode**[1]]

forebrain *noun, anatomy* the largest part of the brain in vertebrates, consisting of the left and right cerebral hemispheres, the thalamus and the hypothalamus.

forecast *verb* (***forecast*** *or sometimes* ***forecasted***) *tr & intr* **1** to give warning of something; to predict something. **2** to gauge or estimate (weather, statistics, etc) in advance. ▸ *noun* **1** a warning, prediction or advance estimate. **2** a weather forecast. ▪ **forecaster** *noun.* [14c]

forecastle /'fouksəl/ *noun* **1** a short raised deck at the front of a vessel. **2** the bow section of a ship under the main deck, formerly the crew's quarters. Often shortened to **fo'c'sle**. [14c]

foreclose *verb* **1** of a mortgager, bank, etc: to repossess a property because of failure on the part of the mortgagee to repay agreed amounts of the loan. **2** to prevent or hinder. ▪ **foreclosure** *noun.* [15c]

forecourt *noun* a courtyard or paved area in front of a building, eg a petrol station. [16c]

forefather *noun* an ancestor.

forefinger *noun* the **index finger**. [15c]

forefoot *noun* either of the two front feet of a four-legged animal.

forefront *noun* **1** the very front. **2** the most prominent or active position.

foregather see **forgather**

forego[1] *verb, tr & intr* to precede. [Anglo-Saxon *foregan*]

forego[2] see **forgo**

foregoing *adj* just mentioned. ▸ *noun* the thing or person just mentioned. [15c]

foregone conclusion *noun* an inevitable or predictable result or conclusion. [17c]

foreground *noun* **1** the part of a picture or view nearest to the observer, as opposed to the **background**. **2** a position where one is noticeable. ▸ *verb* to spotlight or emphasize something. [19c]

forehand *adj* **1** *tennis, squash, etc* of a stroke: with the palm in front, as opposed to **backhand**. **2** done beforehand. ▸ *noun, tennis, squash, etc* **a** a stroke made with the palm facing forward; **b** the part of the court to the right of a right-handed player or to the left of a left-handed player.

forehead *noun* the part of the face between the eyebrows and hairline. [Anglo-Saxon *forheafod*]

foreign *adj* **1** concerned with or relating to, or coming from another country. **2** not belonging where found: *a foreign body in my eye.*

IDIOMS **foreign to sb 1** unfamiliar: *the technique was foreign to them.* **2** uncharacteristic: *Envy was foreign to his nature.*

foreigner *noun* **1** a person from another country. **2** an unfamiliar person.

foreign exchange *noun* foreign currency or dealing in foreign currencies.

foreign minister *or* **foreign secretary** *noun* the government minister responsible for a country's relationships with other countries. *US equivalent* **secretary of state**.

foreknow *verb* to know something before it happens; to foresee something. ▪ **foreknowledge** *noun.* [15c]

foreleg *noun* either of the two front legs of a four-legged animal.

forelock *noun* a lock of hair falling over the brow. [17c]

IDIOMS **pull, touch** *or* **tug the forelock** to raise one's hand to the forehead as a sign of respect or subservience to someone.

foreman, **forewoman** *or* **foreperson** *noun* **1** a worker who supervises other workers. **2** *law* the principal juror who presides over the deliberations of the jury and communicates their verdict to the court; the chairperson or spokesperson of a jury. [15c as *foreman*; *forewoman* and *foreperson* have been used since the 1970s]

foremast *noun, naut* the mast that is nearest to the bow of a ship. Compare **mainmast**.

foremost *adj* leading; best. ▸ *adv* leading; coming first. [Anglo-Saxon *formest*, from *forma* first]

forename *noun* used on official forms, etc: one's personal name as distinct from one's family name or surname.

forenoon *noun* the morning. [16c]

forensic *adj* **1** belonging or relating to courts of law, or to the work of a lawyer in court. **2** *informal* concerned with the scientific side of legal investigations: *forensic laboratory.* ▪ **forensically** *adv.* [17c: from Latin *forensis*, belonging to the *forum*, where law courts were held in Rome]

forensic medicine *noun* the branch of medicine concerned with the production of evidence in order to determine the cause of a death, the identity of a criminal, etc, used in law cases. Also called **medical jurisprudence**.

foreordain *verb* to determine (events, etc) in advance; to destine. [15c]

foreplay *noun* sexual stimulation, often leading up to sexual intercourse. [1920s]

forerunner *noun* **1** a person or thing that goes before; an earlier type or version; a predecessor. **2** a sign of what is to come. **3** an advance messenger or herald.

foresee *verb* to see that something will happen in advance, or know in advance, often by circumstantial evidence. ▪ **foreseeable** *adj.*

foreshadow *verb* to give or have some indication of something in advance.

foreshore *noun* the area on the shore between the high and low water marks. [18c]

foreshorten *verb* to draw or paint something as if it is shortened, in order to give it a realistic-looking perspective. [17c]

foresight *noun* **1** the ability to foresee. **2** wise forethought; prudence. **3** consideration taken or provision made for the future. ▪ **foresighted** *adj.*

foreskin *noun, anatomy* the retractable fold of skin that covers the tip of the penis. *Technical equivalent* **prepuce**.

forest *noun* **1** a large area of land dominated by trees. **2** the trees growing on such an area. **3** a large number or dense arrangement of objects. ▸ *verb* to cover (an area) with trees; to cover (an area) thickly with tall, upright objects. ▪ **forested** *adj.* [13c: from Latin *forestis silva* unfenced woodland]

forestall *verb* **1** to prevent something by acting in advance. **2** to anticipate (an event) or anticipate the action of (someone). [15c, meaning 'to waylay']

forester *noun* a person whose job is to manage a forest; someone trained in forestry.

forestry *noun* the science or management of forests and woodlands.

foretaste *noun* a brief experience of what is to come.

foretell *verb* to predict. [13c]

forethought *noun* **1** consideration taken or provision made for the future. **2** deliberate intent.

forever *adv* (*also* **for ever**) **1** always; eternally; for all time. **2** continually: *forever whining*. **3** *informal* for a very long time. ▸ *noun* **1** an endless or indefinite length of time. **2** a very long time.

forewarn *verb* to warn beforehand; to give previous notice.

foreword *noun* an introduction to a book, often by a writer other than the author; a preface. [19c]

forfeit *noun* **1** something that is surrendered, usu as a penalty. **2** a penalty or fine imposed for a breach of regulations. ▸ *verb* to lose (the right to something), or to hand (something) over, as a penalty. ▪ **forfeiture** *noun.* [14c: from Latin *forisfactum* penalty]

forgather *or* **foregather** *verb, intr* to meet together; to assemble. [16c]

forgave *past tense of* **forgive**

forge[1] *noun* **1** a furnace for heating metal, esp iron, prior to shaping it. **2** the workshop of a blacksmith. ▸ *verb* **1** to shape metal by heating and hammering, or by heating and applying pressure more gradually. **2** to make an imitation of (a signature, banknote, etc) for a dishonest or fraudulent purpose. ▪ **forger** *noun.* [13c: from Latin *fabrica* workshop]

forge[2] *verb, intr* **1** to progress swiftly and steadily. **2** (**forge ahead**) to progress or take the lead. [18c]

forgery *noun* (**-ies**) **1** the act or an instance of making a copy of a picture, document, signature, banknote, etc for a fraudulent purpose. **2** a copy of this kind. [17c]

forget *verb* (***forgot, forgotten, forgetting***) *tr & intr* **1** to fail to remember or be unable to remember (something). **2** to stop being aware of (something): *forgot his headache in the excitement*. **3** to neglect or overlook (something). **4** to leave (something) behind accidentally. **5** *informal* to dismiss something from one's mind. **6** to lose control over (oneself). [Anglo-Saxon *forgietan*]

forgetful *adj* inclined to forget.

forget-me-not *noun* a plant with small flowers, often pink in bud and turning blue as they open. [16c]

forgive *verb* (*past tense* **forgave,** *past participle* **forgiven**) **1** to stop being angry with (someone who has done something wrong) or about (an offence). **2** to pardon someone. **3** to spare (someone) the paying of (a debt). ▪ **forgivable** *adj.* ▪ **forgiving** *adj.* [Anglo-Saxon *forgiefan*]

fought *past tense, past participle of* **fight**

forgiveness *noun* **1** the act of forgiving or state of being forgiven. **2** readiness to forgive.

forgo *or* **forego** *verb* to do or go without (something); to sacrifice (something) or give (something) up. [Anglo-Saxon *forgan*]

forgot *or* **forgotten** see under **forget**

fork *noun* **1** an eating or cooking implement with prongs for spearing and lifting food. **2** a pronged digging or lifting tool. **3 a** a division in a road, etc with two branches; **b** one such branch: *take the left fork*. **4** something that divides similarly into two parts, eg the wheel support of a bicycle. ▸ *verb* **1** *intr* of a road, etc: to divide into two branches. **2** *intr* of a person or vehicle: to follow one such branch: *fork left at the church*. **3** to dig, lift or move with a fork. [Anglo-Saxon *forca*, from Latin *furca* a fork for hay]

PHRASAL VERBS **fork out for sth** *informal* to pay (a specified amount) for it, usu unwillingly.

forked *adj* **1** dividing into two branches or parts; like a fork. **2** of lightning: forming zigzagged lines.

forkful *noun* the amount that can be held on a fork.

fork-lift truck *noun* a small vehicle equipped with two horizontal prongs that can be raised and lowered to move or stack goods.

forlorn *adj* **1** exceedingly unhappy; miserable. **2** deserted; forsaken. **3** desperate. ▪ **forlornly** *adv.* [Anglo-Saxon *forloren*]

form *noun* **1** shape. **2** figure or outward appearance. **3** kind, type, variety or manifestation. **4** a document with printed text and spaces for the insertion of information. **5** a way, esp the correct way, of doing or saying something. **6** structure and organization in a piece of writing or work of art. **7** one's potential level of performance, eg in sport: *soon find your form again*. **8** a way that a word can be spelt or grammatically inflected: *the past tense form*. **9** a school class. **10** a bench. **11** *slang* a criminal record. **12** a hare's burrow. ▸ *verb* **1** to organize or set something up. **2** *intr* to come into existence; to take shape. **3** to shape; to make (a shape). **4** to take on the shape or function of. **5** to make up; to constitute. **6** to develop: *form a relationship*. **7** to influence or mould: *the environment that formed him*. **8** to construct, inflect grammatically or pronounce (a word). [13c: from Latin *forma* shape or model]

IDIOMS **good** *or* **bad form** polite or impolite social behaviour. **in** *or* **on good form** in good spirits; acting or speaking in a particularly animated or entertaining way. **on** *or* **off form** performing well or badly. **true to form** in the usual, typical or characteristic way.

-form *combining form* **1** having the specified appearance or structure: *cuneiform* • *cruciform*. **2** in the specified number of forms or varieties: *multiform* • *uniform*. [From Latin *-formis*, from *forma* shape]

formal *adj* **1** relating to or involving etiquette, ceremony or conventional procedure generally: *formal dress*. **2** stiffly polite rather than relaxed and friendly. **3** valid; official; explicit: *a formal agreement*. **4** of language: strictly correct with regard to grammar, style and choice of words, as distinct from conversational. **5** organized and methodical. **6** precise and symmetrical in design: *a formal garden*. **7** relating to outward form as distinct from content. ▪ **formally** *adv*.

formaldehyde /fɔːˈmaldɪhaɪd/ *noun, chem* a colourless pungent gas widely used as a disinfectant and preservative for biological specimens. Also called **methanal**. [19c: from Latin *formica* ant + **aldehyde**]

formalin *noun, chem* a clear solution of formaldehyde in water used as a disinfectant and as a preservative for biological specimens. [19c: from **formaldehyde**]

formalism *noun* **1** concern, esp excessive concern, with outward form, to the exclusion of content. **2** *maths* the mathematical or logical structure of a scientific argument, consisting of formal rules and symbols which are intrinsically meaningless. ▪ **formalist** *noun*. [19c]

formality *noun* (**-ies**) **1** a procedure gone through as a requirement of etiquette, ceremony, the law, etc. **2** a procedure gone through merely for the sake of correctness. **3** strict attention to the rules of social behaviour.

formalize *or* **-ise** *verb* **1** to make precise or give definite form to. **2** to make official, eg by putting in writing, etc. ▪ **formalization** *noun*.

format *noun* **1** the size and shape of something, esp a book or magazine. **2** the style in which a television programme, radio programme, etc is organized and presented. **3** *comput* a specific arrangement of data in tracks and sectors on a disk. ▸ *verb* (***formatted, formatting***) **1** to design, shape or organize in a particular way. **2** to organize (data) for input into a particular computer. **3** to prepare (a new disk) for use by marking out the surface into tracks and sectors. ▪ **formatter** *noun, comput* a program for formatting a disk, tape, etc. [19c: from Latin *liber formatus* a book formed in a certain way]

formation *noun* **1** the process of forming, making, developing or establishing something. **2** **a** a particular arrangement or order, particularly of troops, aircraft, players of a game, etc: *flew in formation*; **b** a shape or structure. **3** *geol* a mass or area of rocks which have common characteristics. [15c: from Latin *formatio* shape]

formative *adj* **1** relating to development or growth: *the formative years*. **2** having an effect on development. [15c: from French *formatif*]

former *adj* **1** belonging to or occurring at an earlier time. **2** of two people or things: mentioned, considered, etc first. **3** having once or previously been: *her former partner*. [Anglo-Saxon *formere*, the comparative of *forma* first or earliest]

IDIOMS **the former** of two people or things: the first one mentioned, considered, etc. Compare **latter**.

formerly *adv* previously; in the past. [16c]

Formica /fɔːˈmaɪkə/ *noun, trademark* a hard heat-resistant plastic, used for making easy-to-clean work surfaces in kitchens, laboratories, etc. [1920s]

formic acid *noun, chem* a colourless, pungent, toxic liquid, present in ant bites and stinging nettles. Also called **methanoic acid**. [18c: from Latin *formica* ant]

formidable *adj* **1** awesomely impressive. **2** of problems, etc: enormous; difficult to overcome. ▪ **formidably** *adv*. [16c: from Latin *formido* fear]

formless *adj* lacking a clear shape or structure.

formula *noun* (***formulae*** /ˈfɔːmjʊliː, -laɪ/ *or* ***formulas***) **1** the combination of ingredients used in manufacturing something. **2** a method or rule of procedure, esp a successful one. **3** *chem* a combination of chemical symbols that represents the chemical composition of a particular substance. **4** *maths, physics* a mathematical equation or expression, or a physical law, that represents the relationship between various quantities, etc. **5** an established piece of wording used by convention eg in religious ceremonies or legal proceedings. **6** a classification for racing cars according to engine size. **7** *N Am* powdered milk for babies. ▪ **formulaic** *adj*. [16c: Latin diminutive of *forma* form]

formularize *or* **-ise** *verb* to **formulate** (senses 1, 2).

formulate *verb* **1** to express something in terms of a formula. **2** to express something in systematic terms. **3** to express something precisely and clearly. ▪ **formulation** *noun*. [19c]

fornicate *verb, intr* to have sexual intercourse outside marriage. ▪ **fornication** *noun*. ▪ **fornicator** *noun*. [16c: from Latin *fornicari, fornicatus*]

forsake *verb* (***forsook, forsaken***) **1** to desert; to abandon. **2** to renounce, or no longer follow or indulge in. ▪ **forsaken** *adj*. [Anglo-Saxon *forsacan*, from *sacan* to strive]

forsooth *adv, archaic* indeed.

forswear *verb* (***forswore, forsworn***) *old use* **1** to give up or renounce (one's foolish ways, etc). **2** to perjure (oneself). [Anglo-Saxon *forswerian* to swear falsely]

fort *noun* a fortified military building, enclosure or position. [16c: from Latin *fortis* strong]

IDIOMS **hold the fort** to keep things running in the absence of the person normally in charge.

forte[1] /ˈfɔːteɪ/ *noun* something one is good at; a strong point. [17c: from French *fort* strong]

forte[2] /ˈfɔːteɪ/ (abbrev **f**) *music, adv* in a loud manner. ▸ *adj* loud. See also **fortissimo**. [18c: Italian]

forth *adv, old use* except in certain set phrases **1** into existence or view: *bring forth children*. **2** forwards: *swing back and forth*. **3** out: *set forth on a journey*. **4** onwards: *from this day forth*. [Anglo-Saxon]

IDIOMS **and so forth** and so on; et cetera. **hold forth** to speak, esp at length.

forthcoming *adj* **1** happening or appearing soon. **2** of a person: willing to talk; communicative. **3** available.

forthright *adj* firm, frank, straightforward and decisive. [Anglo-Saxon *forthriht*]

forthwith *adv* immediately; at once.

forties (often written **40s** *or* **40's**) *plural noun* **1** (**one's forties**) the period of time between one's fortieth and fiftieth birthdays. **2** (**the forties**) the range of temperatures between forty and fifty degrees. **3** (**the forties**) the period of time between the fortieth and fiftieth years of a century. *as adj*: *a forties look*.

fortification *noun* **1** the process of fortifying. **2** (**fortifications**) walls and other defensive structures built in preparation for an attack.

fortify *verb* (**-ies, -ied**) **1** to strengthen (a building, city, etc) in preparation for an attack. **2 a** to add extra alcohol to (wine) in the course of production, in order to produce sherry, port, etc; **b** to add extra vitamins, nutrients, etc to (food). **3** to strengthen or revive, either physically or mentally. [15c: ultimately from Latin *fortis* strong]

fortissimo (abbrev **ff**) *music, adv* in a very loud manner. ▸ *adj* very loud. See also **forte**[2]. [18c: Italian superlative of *forte* (see **forte**[2])]

fortitude *noun* uncomplaining courage in pain or misfortune. [16c: from Latin *fortitudo* strength]

fortnight *noun* a period of 14 days; two weeks. [Anglo-Saxon *feowertiene niht* fourteen nights]

fortnightly *adj* occurring, appearing, etc once every fortnight; bi-monthly. ▸ *adv* once a fortnight. ▸ *noun* (**-ies**) a publication which comes out every two weeks.

fortress *noun* a fortified town, or large fort or castle. [13c: from French *forteresse* strength]

fortuitous *adj* happening by chance; accidental. ▪ **fortuitously** *adv*. [17c: from Latin *fortuitus*, from *forte* by chance, from *fors* chance]

fortunate *adj* **1** lucky; favoured by fate. **2** timely; opportune. ▪ **fortunately** *adv*. [14c: from Latin *fortunatus*]

fortune *noun* **1** chance as a force in human affairs; fate. **2** luck. **3** (**fortunes**) unpredictable happenings that swing affairs this way or that: *the fortunes of war*. **4** (**fortunes**) the state of one's luck. **5** one's destiny. **6** a large sum of money. [13c: from Latin *fortuna*]

fortune-teller *noun* a person who claims to be able to tell people their destinies. ▪ **fortune-telling** *noun, adj*.

forty *noun* (**-ies**) **1 a** the cardinal number 40; **b** the quantity that this represents, being one more than thirty-nine, or the product of ten and four. **2** any symbol for this, eg *40* or *XL*. **3** the age of forty. **4** something, esp a garment or a person, whose size is denoted by the number 40. **5** a set or group of forty people or things. ▸ *adj* **1** totalling forty. **2** aged forty. See also **forties**. ▪ **fortieth** *adj, noun, adv*. [Anglo-Saxon *feowertig*]

forty- *combining form* **a** *forming adjectives and nouns* with cardinal numbers between *one* and *nine*: *forty-two*; **b** *forming adjectives and nouns* with ordinal numbers between *first* and *ninth*: *forty-second*.

forty-five *noun, dated* a **record** (*noun* sense 4), usu 7 inches in diameter, played at a speed of 45 revolutions per minute. Compare **LP**.

forty winks *plural noun, informal* a short sleep.

forum *noun* (**fora**) **1** *hist* a public square or market place, esp that in ancient Rome where public business was conducted and law courts held. **2** a meeting to discuss topics of public concern. **3** a place, programme or publication where opinions can be expressed and openly discussed. [15c: Latin]

forward *adv* **1** (*also* **forwards**) in the direction in front or ahead of one. **2** (*also* **forwards**) progressing from first to last. **3** on or onward; to a later time. **4** to an earlier time. **5** into view or public attention. ▸ *adj* **1** in the direction in front or ahead. **2** at the front. **3** advanced in development. **4** concerning the future. **5** *derog* inclined to push oneself forward; over-bold in offering one's opinions. ▸ *noun, sport* a player whose task is to attack rather than defend. Compare **back** *noun* (sense 6). ▸ *verb* **1** to send (mail) on to another address from the one to which it arrived. **2** to help the progress of something. [Anglo-Saxon *foreweard*]

fossil *noun* **1** an impression or cast of an animal or plant preserved within a rock. **2** a relic of the past. **3** *informal* a curiously antiquated person. ▸ *adj* **1** like or in the form of a fossil. **2** formed naturally through the decomposition of organic matter: *fossil fuels*. [17c: from Latin *fossilis* dug up]

fossil fuel *noun* a fuel, such as coal, petroleum and natural gas, derived from fossilized remains.

fossilize *or* **-ise** *verb, tr & intr* **1** to change or be changed into a fossil. **2** to become or make old-fashioned, inflexible, etc. ▪ **fossilization** *noun*.

foster *verb* **1** *tr & intr* to bring up (a child that is not one's own). **2** to put (a child) into the care of someone who is not its parent, usu for a temporary period of time. **3** to encourage the development of (ideas, feelings, etc). ▸ *adj* **1** concerned with or offering fostering: *foster home*. **2** related through fostering rather than by birth: *foster mother*. Compare **adopt**. [Anglo-Saxon *fostrian* to feed]

fought *past tense, past participle of* **fight**

foul *adj* **1** disgusting: *a foul smell*. **2** soiled; filthy. **3** contaminated: *foul air*. **4** *informal* very unkind or unpleasant. **5** of language: offensive or obscene. **6** unfair or treacherous: *by fair means or foul*. **7** of weather: stormy. **8** clogged. **9** entangled. ▸ *noun, sport* a breach of the rules. ▸ *verb* **1** *tr & intr, sport* to commit a foul against (an opponent). **2** to make something dirty or polluted. **3** *tr & intr* (*sometimes* **foul up** *or* **foul sth up**) to become or cause it to become entangled. **4** *tr & intr* (*sometimes* **foul up** *or* **foul sth up**) to become or cause it to become clogged. ▸ *adv* in a foul manner; unfairly. ▪ **foully** *adv*. ▪ **foulness** *noun*. [Anglo-Saxon *ful*]

foul-mouthed *or* **foul-spoken** *adj* of a person: using offensive or obscene language.

foul play *noun* **1** treachery or criminal violence, esp murder. **2** *sport* a breach of the rules.

found[1] *verb* **1** to start or establish (an organization, institution, city, etc), often with a provision for future funding. **2** to lay the foundation of (a building). ▪ **founder** *noun*. [13c: from Latin *fundare*, from *fundus* bottom or foundation]

found[2] *verb* **1** to cast (metal or glass) by melting and pouring it into a mould. **2** to produce (articles) by this method. [14c: from Latin *fundere* to pour]

found[3] *past tense, past participle of* **find**

foundation *noun* **1 a** an act or the process of founding or establishing an institution, etc; **b** an institution, etc founded or the fund providing for it. **2** (*usu* **foundations**) the underground structure on which a building is supported and built. **3** the basis on which a theory, etc rests or depends. [14c]

foundation course *noun* (*also* **foundation**) an introductory course, usu taken as a preparation for more advanced studies.

foundation school *noun* a **state school** whose governors are responsible for the property, the appointing of staff and for managing the admissions.

foundation stone *noun* a stone laid ceremonially as part of the foundations of a new building.

founder *verb, intr* **1** of a ship: to sink. **2** of a vehicle, etc: to get stuck in mud, etc. **3** of a horse: to go lame. **4** of a business, scheme, etc: to fail. [14c: from French *fondrer* to plunge to the bottom]

founder, flounder
Be careful not to use the word **founder** when you mean **flounder**. If someone **flounders**, they thrash about, or struggle to think or speak clearly:
She floundered in the water, gasping for breath.
He floundered as he tried to propose to her.

foundling *noun* an abandoned child of unknown parents. [13c: from **found**[3]]

foundry *noun* (**-ies**) a place where metal or glass is melted and cast. [17c: from French *fonderie*; see **found**[2]]

fount[1] *or* **font** *noun, printing* a set of printing type of the same design and size. [17c: from French *fonte* casting]

fount[2] *noun* **1** a spring or fountain. **2** a source of inspiration, etc. [16c: from **fountain**]

fountain *noun* **1** **a** a jet or jets of water for ornamental effect; **b** a structure supporting this, consisting of a basin and statues, etc. **2** a structure housing a jet of drinking water, eg, in an office, shopping mall or other public place. **3** a spring of water. **4** a source of wisdom, etc. [15c: from Latin *fons* fountain]

fountainhead *noun* **1** a spring from which a stream flows. **2** the principal source of something.

fountain pen *noun* a metal-nibbed pen equipped with a cartridge or reservoir of ink.

four *noun* **1** **a** the cardinal number 4; **b** the quantity that this represents, being one more than three. **2** any symbol for this, eg *4* or *IV*. **3** the age of four. **4** something, esp a garment, or a person, whose size is denoted by the number 4. **5** the fourth hour after midnight or midday: *Tea's at four • 4 o'clock • 4pm*. **6** a set or group of four people or things. **7** **a** the crew of a rowing boat with four sweep oars; **b** such a boat. **8** *cricket* a score of four runs awarded if the ball reaches the boundary having hit the ground. ▸ *adj* **1** totalling four. **2** aged four. [Anglo-Saxon *feower*]
IDIOMS **on all fours** on hands and knees.

four-by-four *noun* a vehicle in which the driving power is transmitted to all four wheels. Also called **four-wheel drive**. Compare **front-wheel drive**, **rear-wheel drive**.

fourfold *adj* **1** equal to four times as much or many. **2** divided into, or consisting of, four parts. ▸ *adv* by four times as much.

four-letter word *noun* **1** a short obscene English word. **2** a word that should be avoided for a specified reason or in a particular context: *He's on a diet, so chocolate is a four-letter word.*

four-poster *noun* a large bed with a post at each corner to support curtains and a canopy. Also called **four-poster bed**. [19c]

fourscore *adj, noun, archaic* eighty. [13c]

foursome *noun* **1** a set or group of four people. **2** *golf* a game between two pairs of players. [16c]

four-square *adj* **1** strong; steady; solidly based. **2** of a building: square and solid-looking. ▸ *adv* steadily; squarely.

four-stroke *adj* of an internal-combustion engine: with the piston making a recurring cycle of four strokes, intake, compression, combustion and exhaust.

fourteen *noun* **1** **a** the cardinal number 14; **b** the quantity that this represents, being one more than thirteen, or the sum of ten and four. **2** any symbol for this, eg *14* or *XIV*. **3** the age of fourteen. **4** something, esp a garment, or a person, whose size is denoted by the number 14. **5** a set or group of fourteen people or things. ▸ *adj* **1** totalling fourteen. **2** aged fourteen. ▪ **fourteenth** *adj, noun, adv*. [Anglo-Saxon *feowertiene*]

fourth (often written **4th**) *adj* **1** in counting: **a** next after third; **b** last of four. **2** in fourth position. **3** being one of four equal parts. Usually called **quarter**: *a fourth share*. ▸ *noun* **1** one of four equal parts. Usually called **quarter**. **2** a **fraction** equal to one divided by four (usu written ¼). Usually called **quarter**. **3** a person coming fourth, eg in a race or exam: *a good fourth*. **4** (**the fourth**) **a** the fourth day of the month; **b** *golf* the fourth hole. **5** *music* **a** an interval of three diatonic degrees; **b** a tone at that interval from another, or a combination of two tones separated by that interval. ▸ *adv* fourthly. ▪ **fourthly** *adv* used to introduce the fourth point in a list. [Anglo-Saxon]

fourth dimension *noun* **1** time regarded as a dimension complementing the three dimensions of space (length, width and depth). **2** **a** a dimension, such as a parallel universe, which may exist in addition to the three dimensions of space; **b** anything which is beyond ordinary experience.

fourth official *noun, football* an official who has responsibility for off-the-field activities such as substitutions, indicating additional time to be played, etc.

fowl *noun* (***fowls*** *or* ***fowl***) **1** a farmyard bird, eg a chicken or turkey. **2** the flesh or meat of one of these birds used as food. ▸ *verb, intr* to hunt or trap wild birds. [Anglo-Saxon *fugel* bird]

fox *noun* **1** a carnivorous mammal of the dog family, with a pointed muzzle, large pointed ears and a long bushy tail. **2** the fur of this animal. **3** *informal* a cunning person. See also **vixen**. **4** *N Am* an attractive woman. ▸ *verb* **1** to puzzle, confuse or baffle. **2** to deceive, trick or outwit. See also **outfox**. [Anglo-Saxon]

foxglove *noun* a biennial or perennial plant that produces tall spikes with many thimble-shaped purple or white flowers, and whose leaves are a source of **digitalis**. [Anglo-Saxon]

foxhole *noun, military* a hole dug in the ground by a soldier for protection from enemy fire. [Anglo-Saxon *foxhol*]

foxhound *noun* a breed of dog bred and trained to chase foxes.

fox hunt *noun* **1** a hunt for a fox by people on horseback using hounds. **2** a group of people who meet to hunt foxes. ▪ **foxhunting** *noun.*

fox terrier *noun* a breed of small dog orig trained to drive foxes out of their holes.

foxtrot *noun* **1** a ballroom dance with gliding steps, alternating between quick and slow. **2** the music for this dance. ▸ *verb, intr* to perform this dance.

foxy *adj* (*-ier, -iest*) **1** referring to foxes; fox-like. **2** cunning; sly. **3** reddish brown in colour. ▪ **foxily** *adv.* ▪ **foxiness** *noun.*

foyer *noun* an entrance hall of a theatre, hotel, etc. [19c: from Latin *focus* hearth]

fp *abbrev* freezing point.

Fr[1] *abbrev* Father, the title of a priest.

Fr[2] *symbol, chem* francium.

fr *abbrev* franc.

fracas /ˈfrakɑː/ *noun* (***fracas***) a noisy quarrel or brawl. [18c: from Italian *fracassare* to make an uproar]

fractal /ˈfraktəl/ *noun, maths* an intricate shape produced by repeated subdivision, according to a mathematical formula, of a basic geometric shape. *as adj*: *fractal geometry.* [1970s: from Latin *frangere, fractum* to break]

fraction *noun* **1** *maths* an expression that indicates one or more equal parts of a whole, usu represented by a pair of numbers separated by a horizontal or diagonal line, where the upper number (the **numerator**) represents the number of parts selected and the lower number (the **denominator**) the total number of parts. Compare **integer. 2** a portion; a small part of something. **3** *chem* a group of chemical compounds whose boiling points fall within a very narrow range, the components of which can be separated by **fractional distillation.** ▪ **fractional** *adj.* ▪ **fractionally** *adv.* [14c: from Latin *fractio* breaking]

fractional distillation *noun, chem* the separation of the constituents of a mixture of liquids by heating and condensing at their various boiling points.

fractious *adj* cross and quarrelsome; inclined to quarrel and complain. ▪ **fractiously** *adv.* [18c: modelled on **fraction**, in an earlier sense of 'dispute' or 'quarrel']

fracture *noun* **1** the breaking or cracking of anything hard, esp bone, rock or mineral. **2** the medical condition resulting from this. ▸ *verb* **1** to break or crack something, esp a bone. **2** *intr* of a bone, etc: to break or crack. [16c: from Latin *fractura* a break]

fragile *adj* **1** easily broken. **2** easily damaged or destroyed. **3** delicate. **4** in a weakened state of health. ▪ **fragility** *noun.* [17c: from Latin *fragilis* breakable]

fragment *noun* /ˈfragmənt/ **1** a piece broken off; a small piece of something that has broken. **2** something incomplete; a small part remaining. ▸ *verb* /fragˈmɛnt/ *tr & intr* to break into pieces. ▪ **fragmentation** *noun.* [16c: from Latin *frangere* to break]

fragmentary *or* **fragmented** *adj* **1** consisting of small pieces, not usu amounting to a complete whole; in fragments. **2** existing or operating in separate parts, not forming a harmonious unity.

fragrance *noun* **1** sweetness of smell. **2** a sweet smell or odour. ▪ **fragrant** *adj.* [15c: from Latin *fragrare* to give out a smell]

frail *adj* **1** easily broken or destroyed; delicate; fragile. **2** in poor health; weak. **3** morally weak; easily tempted. ▪ **frailness** *noun.* ▪ **frailty** *noun* (***-ies***). [14c: from Latin *fragilis* fragile]

frame *noun* **1** a hard main structure or basis to something, round which something is built or to which other parts are added. **2** a structure that surrounds and supports something. **3** something that surrounds. **4** a body, esp a human one, as a structure of a certain size and shape. **5** one of the pictures that make up a strip of film or comic strip. **6** a single television picture, eg a still picture seen when the pause button on a video player is pressed. **7** one of the pictures in a comic strip. **8** *comput* an independent section on a web page. **9** a low glass or semi-glazed structure for protecting young plants growing out of doors, which is smaller than a greenhouse. Also called **cold frame. 10** a framework of bars, eg in a playground for children to play on. **11** *snooker, etc* **a** a triangular structure for confining the balls for the **break** (*noun* sense 8) at the start of a round; **b** each of the rounds of play, a pre-determined number of which constitute the entire match. **12** the rigid part of a bicycle, usu made of metal tubes. ▸ *verb* **1** to put a frame round something. **2** to be a frame for something. **3** to compose or design something. **4** to shape or direct (one's thoughts, actions, etc) for a particular purpose. **5** *informal* to dishonestly direct suspicion for a crime, etc at (an innocent person). [Anglo-Saxon *framian* to benefit]

frame of mind *noun* (***frames of mind***) a mood; state of mind; attitude towards something.

frame of reference *noun* (***frames of reference***) **1** a set of facts, beliefs or principles that serves as the context within which specific actions, events or behaviour patterns can be analysed or described. **2** *maths* a set of points, lines or planes, esp three geometrical axes, used to locate the position of a point in space.

frame-up *noun, informal* a plot or arrangement to make an innocent person appear guilty. [Early 20c: orig US]

framework *noun* **1** a basic supporting structure. **2** a basic plan or system. **3** a structure composed of horizontal and vertical bars or shafts.

franc *noun* **1** the standard unit of currency of various countries including Switzerland and Liechtenstein. **2** the former standard unit of currency of France, Belgium and Luxembourg, replaced in 2002 by the euro. [14c: from French *Francorum rex* king of the Franks, the inscription on the first such coins]

franchise *noun* **1** the right to vote, esp in a parliamentary election. **2** a right, privilege, exemption from a duty, etc, granted to a person or organization. **3** an agreement by which a business company gives someone the right to market its products in an area. **4** a concession granted by a public authority to a TV, radio, etc company to broadcast in a certain area. ▸ *verb* to grant a franchise to (a person, a company, etc). ▪ **franchisee** *noun.* ▪ **franchiser** *or* **franchisor** *noun.* [13c: from French *franchir* to set free]

Franciscan *noun* a member of a Christian order of friars orig founded by St Francis of Assisi in the 13c. ▸ *adj* belonging or relating to this order.

francium *noun, chem* (symbol **Fr**) a radioactive metallic element, the heaviest of the alkali metals, present in uranium ore. [20c: from *France*, the country where it was discovered]

Franco- *combining form, signifying* France or the French, together with some other specified group: *Franco-Russian* • *Franco-Canadians*. [18c: from Latin *Francus* the Franks or the French]

francophone *noun* (*sometimes* **Francophone**) a French-speaking person, esp in a country where other languages are spoken. ▶ *adj* **1** speaking French as a native language. **2** using French as a second mother-tongue or lingua franca. [19c]

Frank *noun* a member of a W Germanic people that invaded Gaul (an ancient region of W Europe) in the late 5c AD, and founded France. ▪ **Frankish** *adj*. [Anglo-Saxon *Franca*, prob from *franca* javelin]

frank *adj* **1** open and honest in speech or manner; candid. **2** bluntly outspoken. **3** undisguised; openly visible. ▶ *verb* to mark (a letter), either cancelling the stamp or, in place of a stamp, to show that postage has been paid. ▶ *noun* a franking mark on a letter. ▪ **frankly** *adv*. ▪ **frankness** *noun*. [13c: from Latin *francus* free]

frankfurter *noun* a type of spicy smoked sausage, orig made in Frankfurt am Main. [19c: short for German *Frankfurter Wurst* Frankfurt sausage]

frankincense *noun* an aromatic gum resin obtained from certain E African or Arabian trees, burnt to produce a sweet smell, esp during religious ceremonies. [14c: from French *franc encens* pure incense]

frantic *adj* **1** desperate, eg with fear or anxiety. **2** hurried; rushed. ▪ **frantically** *adv*. [14c: from French *frenetique*; compare **frenetic**]

frappé /ˈfrapeɪ/ *adj* iced. ▶ *noun* an iced drink. [19c: French, from *frapper* to strike]

fraternal *adj* **1** concerning a brother; brotherly. **2** of twins: developed from two **zygote**s or fertilized eggs. Compare **identical** (sense 3). ▪ **fraternally** *adv*. [15c: from Latin *frater* brother]

fraternity *noun* (**-ies**) **1** a religious brotherhood. **2** a group of people with common interests. **3** the fact of being brothers; brotherly feeling. **4** *N Am* a social club for male students. Compare **sorority**. [14c: from Latin *frater* brother]

fraternize *or* **-ise** *verb, intr* (*often* **fraternize with sb**) to meet or associate together as friends. ▪ **fraternization** *noun*. [17c: from Latin *fraternus* brotherly]

fratricide *noun* **1** the act of killing one's own brother. **2** someone who commits this act. [15c: from Latin *frater* brother + **-cide**]

fraud *noun* **1** an act or instance of deliberate deception, with the intention of gaining some benefit. **2** *informal* someone who dishonestly pretends to be something they are not. [14c: from Latin *fraus, fraudis* trick]

fraudster *noun* a cheat; a swindler.

fraudulent *adj* involving deliberate deception; intended to deceive. ▪ **fraudulence** *or* **fraudulency** *noun*. ▪ **fraudulently** *adv*. [15c]

fraught *adj, informal* causing or feeling anxiety or worry. [14c: from Dutch *vracht* freight]

IDIOMS **fraught with danger**, *etc* full of or laden down with danger, difficulties, etc.

fray[1] *verb, tr & intr* **1** of cloth or rope: to wear away along an edge or at a point of friction, so that individual threads come loose. **2** of tempers, nerves, etc: to make or become edgy and strained. [15c: from Latin *fricare* to rub]

fray[2] *noun* **1** a fight, quarrel or argument. **2** any scene of lively action. [14c: short for **affray**]

frazzle *noun* **1** a state of nervous and physical exhaustion. **2** a scorched and brittle state: *burnt to a frazzle*. ▶ *verb* to tire out physically and emotionally. [19c: prob related to **fray**[1]]

freak *noun* **1** a person, animal or plant of abnormal shape or form. **2** someone or something odd or unusual. **3** *esp in compounds* someone highly enthusiastic about the specified thing: *health freak* • *film freak*. **4** a drug addict: *an acid freak*. **5** a whim or caprice: *a freak of fancy*. ▶ *adj* abnormal: *a freak storm*. ▶ *verb, tr & intr* (*also* **freak out** *or* **freak sb out**) *informal* **1 a** to become or make someone mentally or emotionally over-excited: *It really freaked him*; **b** to become frightened or paranoid, or make someone become so, esp through the use of hallucinatory drugs. **2** (*also* **freak out**) to become angry or make someone angry. ▪ **freaky** *adj* (**-ier, -iest**). [16c: possibly related to Anglo-Saxon *frician* to dance]

freckle *noun* a small yellowish-brown benign mark on the skin, usu becoming darker and more prominent with exposure to the sun. ▶ *verb, tr & intr* to mark, or become marked, with freckles. ▪ **freckled** *or* **freckly** *adj*. [14c as *frecken*: from Norse *freknur* freckles]

free *adj* **1** allowed to move as one pleases; not shut in. **2** not tied or fastened. **3** allowed to do as one pleases; not restricted, controlled or enslaved. **4** of a country: independent. **5** costing nothing. **6** open or available to all. **7** not working, busy, engaged or having another appointment. **8** not occupied; not being used. **9** of a translation: not precisely literal. **10** smooth and easy. **11** without obstruction. **12** *derog* of a person's manner: disrespectful, over-familiar or presumptuous. **13** *chem* not combined with another chemical element. **14** *in compounds* **a** not containing the specified ingredient, substance, factor, etc (which is usu considered to be undesirable): *sugar-free* • *nuclear-free*; **b** free from, or not affected or troubled by, the specified thing: *stress-free weekend* • *carefree*; **c** not paying or exempt from the specified thing: *rent-free* • *tax-free*. ▶ *adv* **1** without payment: *free of charge*. **2** freely; without restriction: *wander free*. ▶ *verb* **1** to allow someone to move without restriction after a period in captivity, prison, etc; to set or make someone free; to liberate someone. **2** (*usu* **free sb of** *or* **from sth**) to rid or relieve them of it. ▪ **freely** *adv*. ▪ **freeness** *noun*. [Anglo-Saxon *freo*]

IDIOMS **a free hand** scope to choose how best to act. **feel free** *informal* you have permission (to do something): *Feel free to borrow my bike*. **free and easy** cheerfully casual or tolerant. **free of** *or* **from sth** without; not or no longer having or suffering (esp something harmful, unpleasant or not wanted): *free from pain*. **free with sth** open, generous, lavish or liberal: *free with her money*. **make free with sth** to make too much, or unacceptable, use of something not one's own.

freebie *noun, informal* something given or provided without charge, particularly as a sales promotion.

freebooter *noun, hist* a pirate. [17c: from Dutch *vrijbuiter*]

freeborn *adj* born as a free citizen, not a slave.

Free Church *noun* **1** the branch of Presbyterians in Scotland which left the established church in 1843. **2** in England: a Nonconformist church.

freed *past tense, past participle of* **free**

freedman *or* **freedwoman** *noun* a man or woman who has been a slave and has been emancipated.

freedom *noun* **1** the condition of being free to act, move, etc without restriction. **2** personal liberty or independence, eg from slavery, serfdom, etc. **3** a right or liberty. **4** (*often* **freedom from sth**) the state of being without or exempt (from something). **5** autonomy, self-government or independence, eg of a state or republic. **6** unrestricted access to or use of something. **7** honorary citizenship of a place, entitling one to certain privileges: *was granted the freedom of Aberdeen*. **8** frankness; candour. **9** over-familiarity; presumptuous behaviour. [Anglo-Saxon *freodom*]

free enterprise *noun* business carried out between companies, firms, etc without interference or control by the government.

free fall *noun* **1** the fall of something acted on by gravity alone. **2** the part of a descent by parachute before the parachute opens.

free-for-all *noun* a fight, argument, or discussion in which everybody present feels free to join.

free-form *adj* freely flowing; spontaneous.

freehand *adj, adv* of a drawing, etc: done without the help of a ruler, compass, etc.

free hand *noun* complete freedom of action.

freehold *adj* of land, property, etc: belonging to the owner by **fee simple**, **fee tail**, (see under **fee**), or for life and without limitations. ▸ *noun* ownership of such land, property, etc. Compare **leasehold**. ▪ **freeholder** *noun*.

free house *noun* a hotel or bar not owned by a particular beer-producer and therefore free to sell a variety of beers.

free kick *noun, football* a kick awarded to one side with no tackling from the other, following an infringement of the rules.

freelance *noun* a self-employed person offering their services where needed, not under contract to any single employer. Also called **freelancer**. *as adj*: *freelance journalist*. ▸ *adv* as a freelance: *She works freelance now*. ▸ *verb, intr* to work as a freelance. [19c, meaning 'a medieval mercenary soldier', coined by Sir Walter Scott]

free-living *adj, biol* not parasitic or symbiotic.

freeload *verb, intr, informal* to eat, live, enjoy oneself, etc at someone else's expense. ▪ **freeloader** *noun*. [1960s: orig US]

freeman *or* **freewoman** *noun* **1** a man or woman who is free or enjoys liberty. **2** a respected man or woman who has been granted the freedom of a city.

Freemason *or* **Mason** *noun* a member of an international secret male society, organized into **lodge**s, having among its purposes mutual help and brotherly fellowship. ▪ **Freemasonry** *noun*. [17c]

freephone *or* **freefone** *noun, trademark* (*sometimes* **Freephone** *or* **Freefone**) a telephone service whereby calls made to a business or organization are charged to that business or organization rather than to the caller. [1950s]

free port *noun* **1** a port open on equal terms to all traders. **2** a port, or a zone adjacent to a port or airport, where goods may be imported free of tax or import duties, provided they are re-exported or used to make goods to be re-exported.

free radical *noun, chem* an uncharged atom or group of atoms containing at least one unpaired electron.

free-range *adj* **1** of animal livestock, esp poultry and pigs: allowed some freedom to move about and graze or feed naturally; not kept in a **battery**. **2** of eggs: laid by free-range poultry.

freesia *noun* a plant of the iris family, widely cultivated for its fragrant trumpet-shaped flowers. [19c: named after F H T Freese, German physician]

free speech *noun* the right to express any opinion freely, particularly in public.

free-standing *adj* not attached to or supported by a wall or other structure.

freestyle *sport, adj* **1** **a** denoting a competition or race in which competitors are allowed to choose their own style or programme; **b** *swimming* denoting the front crawl stroke, most commonly chosen by swimmers in a freestyle event. **2** denoting **all-in wrestling**. **3** of a competitor: taking part in freestyle competitions, etc. ▸ *noun* a freestyle competition or race.

freethinker *noun* someone who forms their own ideas, esp religious ones, rather than accepting the view of an authority. ▪ **freethinking** *noun, adj*. [18c]

free-to-air *or* **free-to-view** *adj* of a television channel: requiring no extra subscription before programmes can be viewed.

free trade *noun* trade between or amongst countries without protective tariffs, such as customs, taxes, etc.

free verse *noun* poetry with no regular pattern of rhyme, rhythm or line length.

freeware *noun, comput* software which is made available free of charge.

freeway *noun, N Am* a toll-free highway.

freewheel *verb, intr* **1** to travel, usu downhill, on a bicycle, in a car, etc without using mechanical power. **2** to act or drift about unhampered by responsibilities.

free will *noun* **1** **a** the power of making choices without the constraint of fate or some other uncontrollable force, regarded as a human characteristic; **b** the philosophical doctrine that this human characteristic is not illusory. Compare **determinism**. **2** a person's independent choice.

freewoman see under **freeman**

freeze *verb* (*past tense* ***froze***, *past participle* ***frozen***) **1** *tr & intr* to change (a liquid) into a solid by cooling it to below its freezing point, eg to change water into ice. **2** of a liquid: to change into a solid when it is cooled to below its freezing point. **3** *tr & intr* (*often* **freeze together**) to stick or cause to stick together by frost. **4** *intr* of the weather, temperature, etc: to be at or below the freezing-point of water. **5** *tr & intr, informal* to be or make very cold. **6** *intr* to die of cold. **7** *tr & intr* of food: to preserve, or be suitable for preserving, by refrigeration at below freezing-point. **8** *tr & intr* to make or become motionless or unable to move, because of fear, etc. **9** to fix (prices, wages, etc) at a certain level. **10** to prevent (money, shares, assets, etc) from being used. **11** to stop (a video, a moving film, etc) at a certain frame. **12** to anaesthetize (a part of the body). ▸ *noun* **1** a period of very cold weather with temperatures below freezing-point. **2** a period during which wages, prices, etc are controlled. ▸ *exclam, chiefly US* a command to stop instantly or risk being shot. ▪ **freezable** *adj.* [Anglo-Saxon *freosan*]

PHRASAL VERBS **freeze sb out** to exclude them from an activity, conversation, etc by persistent unfriendliness or unresponsiveness.

freeze-dry *verb* to preserve (perishable material, esp food and medicines) by rapidly freezing it and then drying it under high-vacuum conditions.

freezer *noun* a refrigerated cabinet or compartment in which to store or preserve food at a temperature below freezing point. Compare **deep-freeze**.

freezing point *noun* (abbrev **fp**) **1** the temperature at which the liquid form of a particular substance turns into a solid. **2** (*also* **freezing**) the freezing point of water (0°C at sea level).

freight *noun* **1** transport of goods by rail, road, sea or air. **2** the goods transported in this way. **3** the cost of such transport. ▸ *verb* **1** to transport (goods) by rail, road, sea or air. **2** to load (a vehicle, etc) with goods for transport. [16c: from Dutch *vrecht*]

freighter *noun* a ship or aircraft that carries cargo rather than passengers.

French *adj* **1** belonging or relating to France or its inhabitants. **2** relating to the French language. ▸ *noun* **1** (**the French**) the people of France. **2** the official language of France and various other countries. [Anglo-Saxon *frencisc*, from **Frank**]

French bean *noun* a widely cultivated species of bean plant whose pods and unripe seeds are eaten together as a vegetable. The mature seeds, known as haricot beans, are dried or processed, eg as baked beans.

French bread, **French loaf** *or* **French stick** *noun* white bread in the form of a long narrow loaf with tapered ends and a thick crisp crust.

French chalk *noun* a form of the mineral talc used to mark cloth or remove grease marks. See also **soapstone**.

French doors see **French windows**

French dressing *noun* a salad dressing made from oil, spices, herbs, and lemon juice or vinegar; vinaigrette.

French fries *or* **fries** *plural noun, chiefly N Am informal* long thin strips of potato deep-fried in oil, usu longer and thinner than chips (see **chip** *noun* sense 3). Also (*Brit formal*) called **French fried potatoes**.

French horn *noun* an orchestral **horn**.

French leave *noun* leave taken without permission from work or duty.

French polish *noun* a varnish for furniture, consisting of shellac dissolved in alcohol. ▸ *verb* (**French-polish**) to varnish (furniture, etc) with French polish.

French toast *noun* slices of bread dipped in beaten egg (sometimes mixed with milk), and fried.

French windows *or* (*N Am*) **French doors** *plural noun* a pair of glass doors that open on to a garden, etc.

frenetic *or* (*rare*) **phrenetic** *adj* frantic, distracted, hectic or wildly energetic. ▪ **frenetically** *or* (*rare*) **phrenetically** *adv.* [14c: from Greek *phren* heart or mind; compare **frantic, frenzy**]

frenzy *noun* (**-ies**) **1** wild agitation or excitement. **2** a frantic burst of activity. **3** a state of violent mental disturbance. ▪ **frenzied** *adj.* [14c: from Greek *phrenesis* madness; compare **frenetic**]

frequency *noun* (**-ies**) **1** the condition of happening often. **2** the rate at which a happening, phenomenon, etc, recurs. **3** *physics* (SI unit **hertz**; abbrev **f**) a measure of the rate at which a complete cycle of wave motion is repeated per unit time. **4** *radio* the rate of sound waves per second at which a particular radio signal is sent out. **5** *stats* the number of values, items, etc that occur within a specified category. [17c: from Latin *frequens* happening often]

frequency distribution *noun, stats* a set of data that includes values for the frequencies of different scores or results, ie the number of times that each particular score or result occurs.

frequency modulation *noun, radio* (abbrev **FM**) a method of radio transmission in which the frequency of the carrier wave (the signal-carrying wave) increases or decreases instantaneously in response to changes in the amplitude of the signal being transmitted, giving a better signal-to-noise ratio than **amplitude modulation**.

frequent *adj* /ˈfriːkwənt/ **1** recurring at short intervals. **2** habitual. ▸ *verb* /frɪˈkwɛnt/ to visit or attend (a place, an event, etc) often. ▪ **frequently** *adv.*

fresco *noun* (***frescoes*** *or* ***frescos***) a picture painted on a wall, usu while the plaster is still damp. ▪ **frescoed** *adj.* [17c: Italian, meaning 'cool' or 'fresh']

fresh *adj* **1** newly made, gathered, etc. **2** having just arrived from somewhere, just finished doing something or just had some experience, etc: *fresh from university.* **3** other or another; clean: *a fresh sheet of paper.* **4** new; additional: *fresh supplies.* **5** original: *a fresh approach.* **6** of fruit or vegetables: not tinned, frozen, dried, salted or otherwise preserved. **7** not tired; bright and alert. **8** cool; refreshing: *a fresh breeze.* **9** of water: not salty. **10** of air: cool and uncontaminated; invigorating. **11** of the face or complexion: youthfully healthy; ruddy. **12** not worn or faded. **13** *informal* of behaviour: offensively informal; cheeky. ▸ *adv* in a fresh way: *Milk keeps fresh in the fridge.* ▪ **freshly** *adv.* ▪ **freshness** *noun.* [Anglo-Saxon *fersc* not salt]

freshen *verb* **1** to make something fresh or fresher. **2** *tr & intr* (*also* **freshen up** *or* **freshen oneself** *or* **sb up**) to get washed and tidy; to wash and tidy (oneself or someone). **3** *intr* of a wind: to become stronger.

fresher *or* (*N Am*) **freshman** *noun* a student in their first year at university or college.

freshet *noun* **1** a stream of fresh water flowing into the sea. **2** the sudden overflow of a river. [16c: a diminutive of **fresh**]

freshwater *adj* referring to, consisting of or living in fresh as opposed to salt water: *freshwater lake* • *freshwater fish.*

fret[1] *verb* (***fretted, fretting***) **1** *intr* (*also* **fret about** *or* **over sth**) to worry, esp unnecessarily; to show or express anxiety. **2** to wear something away or consume something by rubbing or erosion. [Anglo-Saxon *fretan* to gnaw, from *etan* to eat]

fret[2] *noun* any of the narrow metal ridges across the neck of a guitar or similar musical instrument, onto which the strings are pressed in producing the various notes. [16c: prob from **fret**[3]]

fret[3] *noun* a type of decoration for a cornice, border, etc, consisting of lines which (usu) meet at right angles, the pattern being repeated to form a continuous band. ▸ *verb* (***fretted, fretting***) to decorate something with a fret, or carve with fretwork. [14c: from French *frete* interlaced design]

fretful *adj* anxious and unhappy; tending to fret; peevish. ▪ **fretfully** *adv.*

fretsaw *noun* a narrow-bladed saw for cutting designs in wood or metal. Compare **coping saw**. [19c]

fretwork *noun* fine decorative work in wood or metal including open spaces. [16c]

Freudian /ˈfrɔɪdɪən/ *adj* relating to the Austrian psychologist, Sigmund Freud (1856–1939), or to his theories or methods of psychoanalysis. ▪ **Freudianism** *noun.* [Early 20c]

Freudian slip *noun* an error or unintentional action, esp a slip of the tongue, taken as revealing an unexpressed or unconscious thought.

friable *adj* easily broken; easily reduced to powder. ▪ **friability** *noun.* [16c: from Latin *friare* to crumble]

friar *noun* a male member of any of various religious orders of the Roman Catholic Church, such as the Franciscans, Carmelites, etc. [13c: from Latin *frater* brother]

friary *noun* (***-ies***) **1** a building inhabited by a community of friars. **2** the community itself.

fricassee *noun* a cooked dish, usu of pieces of meat or chicken served in a sauce. ▸ *verb* to prepare meat as a fricassee. [16c: from French *fricasser* to cook chopped food in its own juice]

fricative *phonetics, adj* of a sound: produced partly by friction, the breath being forced through a narrowed opening. ▸ *noun* a fricative consonant, eg *sh, f* and *th.* [19c: from Latin *fricare* to rub]

friction *noun* **1** the rubbing of one thing against another. **2** *physics* the force that opposes the relative motion of two bodies or surfaces that are in contact with each other. **3** quarrelling; disagreement; conflict. ▪ **frictional** *adj.* [16c: from Latin *fricare* to rub]

Friday *noun* (abbrev **Fri.**) the sixth day of the week. [Anglo-Saxon *Frigedæg*, named after the Norse goddess Frigg]

fridge *noun, informal* a refrigerator. [1920s]

fried *past tense, past participle of* **fry**[1]

friend *noun* **1** someone whom one knows and likes, and to whom one shows loyalty and affection; a close or intimate acquaintance. **2** someone who gives support or help. **3** an ally as distinct from an enemy or foe. **4** someone or something already encountered or mentioned: *our old friend the woodworm.* **5** (**Friend**) a Quaker; a member of the Religious Society of Friends. **6** a member of an organization which gives voluntary financial or other support to an institution, etc: *Friends of the National Gallery.* ▪ **friendless** *adj.* [Anglo-Saxon *freond*]

friend

This word is often misspelt. The letter *i* comes before the letter *e*. It might help you to remember the following sentence:

Share your ***fri****es with your* ***fri****end.*

friendly *adj* (***-ier, -iest***) **1** kind; behaving as a friend. **2** (**friendly with sb**) on close or affectionate terms with them. **3** relating to, or typical of, a friend. **4** being a colleague, helper, partner, etc rather than an enemy: *friendly nations.* **5** *sport* of a match, etc: played for enjoyment or practice and not as part of a formal competition. **6** *in compounds, forming adjs* **a** denoting things that are made easy or convenient for those for whom they are intended: *user-friendly;* **b** indicating that something causes little harm to something, particularly something related to the environment: *eco-friendly.* ▸ *noun* (***-ies***) *sport* a friendly match. ▪ **friendliness** *noun.*

friendly society *noun, Brit* an organization which gives support to members in sickness, old age, widowhood, etc, in return for regular financial contributions. Also called **benefit society**.

friendship *noun* **1** the having and keeping of friends. **2** a particular relationship that two friends have.

frier see **fryer**

fries[1] see under **fry**[1]

fries[2] see **French fries**

Friesian /ˈfriːʒən/ *noun* a breed of black-and-white dairy cattle, originating in Friesland, in the Netherlands. [20c]

frieze *noun* **1** a decorative strip running along a wall. **2** *archit* **a** a horizontal band between the cornice and capitals of a classical temple; **b** the sculpture which fills this space. [16c: from Latin *Phrygium* a piece of Phrygian work, Phrygia being famous for embroidered garments]

frigate *noun* **1** a naval escort vessel, smaller than a destroyer. **2** *hist* a small fast-moving sailing warship. [16c: from French *fregate*]

fright *noun* **1** sudden fear; a shock. **2** *informal* a person or thing of ludicrous appearance. [Anglo-Saxon *fyrhto*]

IDIOMS **take fright** to become scared.

frighten *verb* **1** to make someone afraid; to alarm them. **2** (*usu* **frighten sb away** *or* **off**) to drive them away by making them afraid. ▪ **frightened** *adj.* ▪ **frightening** *adj.* [17c]

frightful *adj* **1** ghastly; frightening. **2** *informal* bad; awful. **3** *informal* great; extreme. ▪ **frightfully** *adv.*

frigid *adj* **1** cold and unfriendly; without feeling. **2** *geog* intensely cold. ▪ **frigidity** *noun.* [17c: from Latin *frigidus* cold]

frill *noun* **1** a gathered or pleated strip of cloth attached along one edge to a garment, etc as a trimming. **2** (*usu* **frills**) something extra serving no very useful purpose. ▪ **frilled** *adj.* ▪ **frilly** *adj* (***-ier, -iest***).

IDIOMS **without frills** straightforward; clear; with no superfluous additions.

fringe *noun* **1** a border of loose threads on a carpet, tablecloth, garment, etc. **2** hair cut to hang down over the forehead. **3** the outer area; the edge; the part farthest from the main area or centre. ▸ *adj* **a** bordering, or just outside, the recognized or orthodox form, group, etc: *fringe medicine;* **b** unofficial, not part of the main event: *fringe meeting* • *fringe festival;* **c** less important or less popular: *fringe sports.* ▸ *verb* **1** to decorate something with a fringe. **2** to form a fringe round something. [14c: from Latin *fimbriae* threads or fringe]

fringe benefits *plural noun* things that one gets from one's employer in addition to wages or salary, eg a cheap mortgage, a car, etc.

frippery *noun* (***-ies***) **1** showy but unnecessary adornment. **2** trifles; trivia. [16c: from French *frepe* a rag]

Frisbee /'frɪzbɪ/ *noun, trademark* a light, plastic, saucer-shaped object that spins when thrown and is used in catching games. [20c: based on the Frisbie bakery in Bridgeport, Connecticut, whose pie tins presumably inspired its invention]

frisk *verb* **1** *intr* (*also* **frisk about**) to jump or run about happily and playfully. **2** *slang* to search someone for concealed weapons, drugs, etc. ▸ *noun* **1** a frolic; spell of prancing about. **2** an act of searching a person for weapons, etc. [16c: orig from French *frisque* lively]

frisky *adj* (**-ier, -iest**) lively; playful; high-spirited; frolicsome. ▪ **friskily** *adv*.

frisson /'friːsɒn/ *noun* a shiver of fear or excitement. [18c: French *frisson*]

fritter[1] *noun* a piece of meat, fruit, etc coated in batter and fried: *spam fritter* • *banana fritter*. [15c: from French *friture*]

fritter[2] *verb* (*chiefly* **fritter sth away**) to waste (time, money, energy, etc) on unimportant things; to squander something. [18c: from *fitter* fragment]

frivolous *adj* **1** silly; not sufficiently serious. **2** trifling or unimportant; not useful and sensible. ▪ **frivolity** *noun* (**-ies**) [16c: from Latin *frivolus* worthless or empty]

frizz *noun* of hair: a mass of tight curls. ▸ *verb, tr & intr* (*also* **frizz sth up**) to form or make something form a frizz. [17c: French *friser* to curl]

frizzle *verb, tr & intr* of food: to fry till scorched and brittle. [19c: possibly imitating the sound]

frizzy *adj* (**-ier, -iest**) tightly curled.

fro see **to and fro** at **to**

frock *noun* **1** a woman's or girl's dress. **2** a priest's or monk's long garment, with large open sleeves. **3** a loose smock. [14c: from French *froc* monk's garment]

frog[1] *noun* a tailless amphibian with a moist smooth skin, protruding eyes, powerful hind legs for swimming and leaping, and webbed feet. [Anglo-Saxon *frogga*]

IDIOMS **a frog in one's throat** a throat irritation that temporarily interferes with one's speech.

frog[2] *noun* **1** an attachment to a belt for carrying a weapon. **2** a decorative looped fastener on a garment. ▪ **frogging** *noun* a set of such fasteners, esp on a military uniform. [18c]

frogman *noun* an underwater swimmer wearing a protective rubber suit and using breathing equipment.

frogmarch *verb* **1** to force someone forward, holding them firmly by the arms. **2** to carry someone horizontally in a face-downward position between four people, each holding one limb. [19c]

frogspawn *noun* a mass of frogs' eggs in nutrient jelly. [17c: from *frogs'* **spawn** (*noun* sense 1a)]

frog-spit see **cuckoo spit**

frolic *verb* (**frolicked, frolicking**) *intr* to frisk or run about playfully; to gambol about. ▸ *noun* **1** a spell of happy playing or frisking; a gambol. **2** something silly done as a joke; a prank. ▪ **frolicsome** *adj*. [16c: from Dutch *vrolijk* merry]

from *prep, indicating* **1** a starting-point in place or time: *from London to Glasgow* • *crippled from birth*. **2** a lower limit: *tickets from £12 upwards*. **3** repeated progression: *trail from shop to shop*. **4** movement out of: *took a letter from the drawer*. **5** distance away: *16 miles from Dover*. **6** a viewpoint: *can see the house from here*. **7** separation; removal: *took it away from her*. **8** point of attachment: *hanging from a nail*. **9** exclusion: *omitted from the sample*. **10** source or origin: *made from an old curtain*. **11** change of condition: *translate from French into English*. **12** cause: *ill from overwork*. **13** deduction as a result of observation: *see from her face she's angry*. **14** distinction: *can't tell one twin from the other*. **15** prevention, protection, exemption, immunity, release, escape, etc: *safe from harm* • *excused from attending* • *released from prison*. [Anglo-Saxon *fram*]

fromage frais /'frɒmɑːʒ 'freɪ/ *noun* a creamy low-fat cheese with the consistency of whipped cream. [1980s: French, meaning 'fresh cheese']

frond *noun, botany* a large compound leaf, esp of a fern or palm. [18c: from Latin *frons*]

front *noun* **1** the side or part of anything that is furthest forward or nearest to the viewer; the most important side or part, eg the side of a building where the main door is. **2** any side of a large or historic building. **3** the part of a vehicle, etc that faces or is closest to, the direction in which it moves. **4** *theatre* the auditorium of a theatre, etc. See also **front of house**. **5** the cover or first pages of a book. **6** a road or promenade in a town that runs beside the sea, or large lake, etc; sea front. **7** in war, particularly when fought on the ground: the area where the soldiers are nearest to the enemy: *eastern front*. See also **front line**. **8** a matter of concern or interest: *no progress on the job front*. **9** *meteorol* the boundary between two air masses that have different temperatures. See also **cold front**, **occluded front**, **warm front**. **10** an outward appearance. **11** (*usu* **Front**) a name given to some political movements, particularly when a number of organizations come together as a unified force against opponents. **12** *slang* an organization or job used to hide illegal or secret activity: *The corner shop was just a front for drug dealing*. **13** *archaic* the forehead; the face. ▸ *verb* **1** *tr & intr* of a building: to have its front facing or beside something specified: *The house fronts on to the main road*. **2** to be the leader or representative of (a group, etc). **3** to be the presenter of (a radio or television programme). **4** to cover the front of (a building, etc): *The house was fronted with grey stone*. **5** *intr* (*usu* **front for sth**) to provide a cover or excuse for it (eg an illegal activity, etc). ▸ *adj* **1** relating to, or situated at or in the front. **2** *phonetics* of a vowel: articulated with the front of the tongue in a forward position. [13c: French, from Latin *frons, frontis* forehead]

IDIOMS **in front 1** on the forward-facing side. **2** ahead. **in front of sb** *or* **sth 1** at or to a position in advance of them. **2** to a place towards which a vehicle, etc is moving: *ran in front of a car*. **3** ahead of them: *pushed in front of her*. **4** facing or confronting them: *stood up in front of an audience*. **5** in their presence. **up front** *informal* of money: paid before work is done or goods received, etc.

frontage *noun* the front of a building, esp in relation to the street, etc along which it extends.

frontal *adj* **1** relating to the front. **2** aimed at the front; direct: *a frontal assault*. **3** *anatomy* relating to the forehead. **4** *meteorol* relating to a **front** (*noun* sense 9): *frontal system*. ▸ *noun* **1** the façade of a building.

2 something worn on the forehead or face. **3** an embroidered hanging of silk, satin, etc, for the front of an altar, now usu covering only the top. [17c]

front bench *noun* the seats in the House of Commons closest to the centre of the House, occupied on one side by Government ministers and on the other by leading members of the Opposition. ▪ **frontbencher** *noun*. Compare **backbench**, **cross bench**. [19c]

fronted *adj* **1** formed with a front. **2** *phonetics* changed into or towards a **front** (*adj* sense 2) sound.

frontier *noun* **1 a** the part of a country bordering onto another country; **b** a line, barrier, etc marking the boundary between two countries. **2** (**frontiers**) limits: *the frontiers of knowledge*. **3** *N Amer hist* the furthest edge of civilization, habitation or cultivation. [15c: French, from *front* **front**]

frontiersman *or* **frontierswoman** *noun* someone who lives on the frontier of a country, particularly on the outlying edges of a settled society. [18c]

frontispiece *noun* **1** a picture at the beginning of a book, facing the title page. **2** *archit* the decorated pediment over a door, gate, etc. **3** *archit* the main front or façade of a building. [16c: from Latin *frons, frontis* front + *specere* to see, influenced by **piece**]

front line *noun* **1** in a war: the area of a **front** (*noun* sense 7) where soldiers are physically closest to the enemy. **2** that area in any concern where the important pioneering work is going on. ▸ *adj* (**front-line**) **1** belonging or relating to the front line: *front-line soldiers*. **2** relating to a state bordering on another state in which there is an armed conflict.

front of house *noun* in a theatre: the collective activities carried out in direct contact with the public, such as box-office activity, programme selling, ushering, etc. [19c]

front-runner *noun* **1** the person most likely or most favoured to win a competition, election, etc. **2** in a race: someone who runs best when they are in the lead.

front-wheel drive *noun* a system in which the driving power is transmitted to the front wheels of a vehicle.

frost *noun* **1** a white feathery or powdery deposit of ice crystals formed when water vapour comes into contact with a surface whose temperature is below the freezing point of water. **2** an air temperature below freezing point: *12 degrees of frost*. ▸ *verb* **1** *tr & intr* (*also* **frost up** *or* **over**) to cover or become covered with frost. **2** to damage (plants) with frost. [Anglo-Saxon]

frostbite *noun* damage to the body tissues, esp the nose, fingers or toes, caused by exposure to very low temperatures. ▪ **frostbitten** *adj*.

frosted *adj* **1** covered by frost. **2** damaged by frost. **3** of glass: patterned or roughened as though with frost, so as to be difficult to see through.

frosting *noun* **1** *N Am* cake icing. **2** a rough or matt finish on glass, silver, etc.

frosty *adj* (**-ier, -iest**) **1** covered with frost. **2** cold enough for frost to form. **3** of a person's behaviour or attitude: cold; unfriendly; unwelcoming. ▪ **frostily** *adv*.

froth *noun* **1** a mass of tiny bubbles forming eg on the surface of a liquid, or round the mouth in certain diseases. **2** writing, talk, etc that has no serious content or purpose. **3** glamour; something frivolous or trivial. ▸ *verb, tr & intr* to produce or make something produce froth. ▪ **frothy** *adj* (**-ier, -iest**). [14c: from Norse *frotha*]

frown *verb, intr* **1** to wrinkle one's forehead and draw one's eyebrows together in worry, disapproval, deep thought, etc. **2** (*usu* **frown at, on** *or* **upon sth**) to disapprove of it. ▸ *noun* **1** the act of frowning. **2** a disapproving expression or glance. [14c: from French *froignier*]

frowsty *adj* (**-ier, -iest**) stuffy; musty; fusty. [19c]

frowsy *or* **frowzy** *adj* (**-ier, -iest**) **1** of someone's appearance: untidy, dishevelled or slovenly. **2** of an atmosphere: stuffy; stale-smelling. [17c]

froze *past tense of* **freeze**

frozen *adj* **1** preserved by keeping at a temperature below freezing point. **2** very cold. **3** stiff and unfriendly. ▸ *verb past participle of* **freeze**.

fructify *verb* (**-ies, -ied**) to produce fruit. ▪ **fructification** *noun*. [17c: from Latin *fructus* fruit]

fructose *noun, biochem* a sugar found in fruit and honey. Also called **fruit sugar**. [19c]

frugal *adj* **1** thrifty; economical; not generous; careful, particularly in financial matters. **2** not large; costing little: *a frugal meal*. ▪ **frugality** *noun*. ▪ **frugally** *adv*. [16c: from Latin *frugalis* economical]

fruit *noun* **1** the fully ripened ovary of a flowering plant, containing one or more seeds that have developed from fertilized **ovules**, and sometimes including associated structures such as the **receptacle**. **2** an edible part of a plant that is generally sweet and juicy, esp the ovary containing one or more seeds, but sometimes extended to include other parts, eg the leaf stalk in rhubarb. See also **berry**, **soft fruit**. **3** plant products generally: *the fruits of the land*. **4** (*also* **fruits**) whatever is gained as a result of hard work, etc: *the fruit of his labour*. **5** *derog slang, chiefly US* a gay man. **6** *old use, informal* a person: *old fruit*. **7** *rare* offspring; young: *the fruit of her womb*. ▸ *verb, intr* to produce fruit. [12c: from Latin *fructus* fruit]

IDIOMS **bear fruit 1** to produce fruit. **2** to produce good results. **in fruit** of a tree: bearing fruit.

fruitcake *noun* **1** a cake containing dried fruit, nuts, etc. **2** *informal* a slightly mad person.

fruiterer *noun* a person who sells or deals in fruit. [15c]

fruitful *adj* producing useful results; productive; worthwhile. ▪ **fruitfully** *adv*. ▪ **fruitfulness** *noun*.

fruition *noun* **1** the achievement of something that has been aimed at and worked for: *The project finally came to fruition*. **2** the bearing of fruit. [15c: from Latin *frui* to enjoy]

fruitless *adj* **1** useless; unsuccessful; done in vain. **2** not producing fruit.

fruit machine *noun* a coin-operated gambling-machine with symbols in the form of fruits, that may be made to appear in winning combinations, found in amusement arcades, pubs, etc. [Early 20c]

fruit salad *noun* a dish of mixed chopped fruits, usu eaten as a dessert.

fruit sugar *noun* **fructose**.

fruity *adj* (**-ier, -iest**) **1** full of fruit; having the taste or appearance of fruit. **2** of a voice: deep and rich.

frump *noun* a woman who dresses in a dowdy way. ▪ **frumpish** *adj*. ▪ **frumpy** *adj* (**-ier, -iest**). [19c]

frustrate *verb* **1** to prevent (someone from doing something or from getting something); to thwart or foil (a plan, attempt, etc). **2** to make (someone) feel disappointed, useless, lacking a purpose in life, etc. ▪ **frustrating** *adj.* ▪ **frustratingly** *adv.* ▪ **frustration** *noun.* [15c: from Latin *frustrari, frustratus* to deceive or disappoint]

frustrated *adj* **1** a feeling of agitation and helplessness at not being able to do something. **2** disappointed; unhappy; dissatisfied. **3** unfulfilled in one's ambitions for oneself.

frustum /ˈfrʊstəm/ *noun* (***frustums*** *or* ***frusta*** /-tə/) **1** a slice of a solid body. **2** the part of a cone or pyramid between the base and a parallel plane, or between two planes. [17c: Latin, meaning 'a bit']

fry[1] *verb* (***fries, fried***) *tr & intr* to cook (food) in hot oil or fat, either in a frying pan, or by deep-frying. ▸ *noun* (***fries***) **1** a dish of anything fried. **2** a **fry-up**. **3** (**fries**) **French fries**. [14c: from Latin *frigere* to roast or fry]

fry[2] *plural noun* **1** young or newly spawned fish. **2** salmon in their second year. [14c: from French *frai* seed, offspring]

fryer *or* **frier** *noun* **1** a frying pan. **2** a chicken or fish suitable for frying. **3** someone who fries something (esp fish).

frying pan *noun* a shallow long-handled pan for frying food in.

IDIOMS **out of the frying pan into the fire** from a bad situation into an even worse one.

fry-up *noun* (***fry-ups***) **1** a mixture of fried foods. **2** the cooking of these.

FSA *abbrev* **1** Financial Services Authority. **2** Food Standards Agency.

ft *abbrev* foot or feet.

FTP *abbrev* file-transfer protocol, a means of transferring data across a computer network.

fuchsia /ˈfjuːʃə/ *noun* a shrub with purple, red or white hanging flowers. [18c: named after Leonard Fuchs, German botanist]

fuddle *verb* to muddle the wits of; to confuse or stupefy. ▸ *noun* a state of confusion or intoxication. [16c]

fuddy-duddy *informal, adj* quaintly old-fashioned or prim. ▸ *noun* (***-ies***) a fuddy-duddy person. [20c]

fudge[1] *noun* a soft toffee made from butter, sugar and milk. [19c]

fudge[2] *verb, informal* **1** to invent or concoct (an excuse, etc). **2** to distort or deliberately obscure (figures, an argument, etc), to cover up problems, mistakes, etc. **3** to dodge or evade something. **4** *intr* to avoid stating a clear opinion. ▸ *noun* the action of obscuring, distorting an issue, etc. [17c: perhaps from earlier *fadge* to succeed or turn out]

fuel *noun* **1** any material that releases energy when it is burned, which can be used as a source of heat or power. **2** fissile material that is used to release energy by nuclear fission in a nuclear reactor. **3** food, as a source of energy and a means of maintaining bodily processes. **4** something that feeds or inflames passions, etc. ▸ *verb* (***fuelled, fuelling***) **1** to fill or feed with fuel. **2** *intr* to take on or get fuel. **3** to inflame (anger or other passions). [14c: from Latin *focus* hearth]

fuel injection *noun* in an internal-combustion engine: a system that injects pure fuel under pressure directly into the cylinder, eliminating the need for a carburettor and producing improved performance.

fug *noun* a stale-smelling stuffy atmosphere, often very hot, close and airless. ▪ **fuggy** *adj* (***-ier, -iest***).

fugitive *noun* a person who is fleeing someone or something, usu some kind of authority, such as the law, an army, a political system, etc. ▸ *adj* **1** fleeing away. **2** lasting only briefly; fleeting. [17c: French, from Latin *fugitivus*]

fugue *noun, music* a style of composition in which a theme is introduced in one part and developed as successive parts take it up. ▪ **fugal** *adj.* [16c: from Italian *fuga* flight]

-ful *suffix* **1** *forming nouns* denoting an amount held by a container, or something thought of as one: *an armful of books* • *two mugfuls of coffee.* **2** *forming adjs* denoting **a** full of something specified: *meaningful* • *eventful*; **b** characterized by something specified: *merciful* • *graceful*; **c** having the qualities of something specified: *youthful*; **d** in accordance with something specified: *lawful*; **e** showing an inclination to do something: *forgetful.* [Anglo-Saxon, as in *handful*]

fulcrum *noun* (***fulcrums*** *or* ***fulcra*** /ˈfʊlkrə/) **1** *technical* the point on which a **lever** turns, balances or is supported. **2** a support; a means to an end. [17c: Latin, meaning 'prop']

fulfil *or* (*N Am*) **fulfill** *verb* (***fulfilled, fulfilling***) **1** to carry out or perform (a task, promise, etc). **2** to satisfy (requirements). **3** to achieve (an aim, ambition, etc). ▪ **fulfilment** *noun.* [Anglo-Saxon *fullfyllan*]

full *adj* **1** (*also* **full of sth**) holding, containing or having as much as possible, or a large quantity. **2** complete: *do a full day's work.* **3** detailed; thorough; including everything necessary: *a full report.* **4** occupied: *My hands are full.* **5** having eaten till one wants no more. **6** plump; fleshy: *the fuller figure* • *full lips.* **7** of clothes: made with a large amount of material: *a full skirt.* **8** rich and strong: *This wine is very full.* **9** rich and varied: *a full life.* **10** having all possible rights, privileges, etc: *a full member.* **11** of the Moon: at the stage when it is seen as a fully-illuminated disc. **12 a** of a brother or sister: having the same parents as oneself (compare **half-brother, half-sister**); **b** of a cousin: see **first cousin** under **cousin.** ▸ *adv* **1** completely; at maximum capacity: *Is the radiator full on?* **2** exactly; directly: *hit him full on the nose.* ▪ **fullness** *or* (*N Am or dated*) **fulness** *noun.* [Anglo-Saxon]

IDIOMS **be full up 1** to be full to the limit. **2** to have had enough to eat. **full of oneself** having too good an opinion of oneself and one's importance. **in full 1** completely. **2** at length; in detail. **in full swing** at the height of activity. **to the full** to the greatest possible extent.

fullback *noun, hockey, football, rugby* a defence player positioned towards the back of the field to protect the goal.

full-blast *adv* with maximum energy and fluency.

full-blooded *adj* **1** of pure breed; thoroughbred; not mixed blood. **2** enthusiastic; whole-hearted.

full-blown *adj* having all the features of the specified thing: *a full-blown war.*

full board *noun* accommodation at a hotel, guesthouse, etc including the provision of all meals, etc.

Also (*US*) called **American plan**. Compare **half board**.

full-bodied *adj* having a rich flavour or quality.

full-circle *adv* **1** round in a complete revolution. **2** back to the original starting position.

full house *noun* **1** a performance at a theatre, cinema, etc, at which every seat is taken. **2** *cards, esp poker* a set of five cards consisting of three cards of one kind and two of another. Also called **full hand**. **3** in bingo: having all the numbers needed to win.

full-length *adj* **1** complete; of the usual or standard length. **2** showing the whole body: *a full-length mirror.* **3** of maximum length; long: *a full-length skirt*.

full moon *noun* **1** one of the four phases of the Moon, when the whole of it is illuminated and it is seen as a complete disc. Compare **new moon**. **2** the time when the Moon is full.

full-scale *adj* **1** of a drawing, etc: the same size as the subject. **2** using all possible resources, means, etc; complete or exhaustive: *a full-scale search*.

full stop *noun* a punctuation mark (.) used to indicate the end of a sentence or to mark an abbreviation. Also (*esp Scot and N Am*) called **period**.

full time *noun* the end of the time normally allowed for a sports match, etc.

full-time *adj* occupied for or extending over the whole of the working week. ▸ *adv* (**full time**): *working full time*. Compare **part-time**. ▪ **full-timer** *noun*.

fully *adv* **1** to the greatest possible extent. **2** completely: *fully qualified*. **3** in detail: *deal with it more fully next week*. **4** at least: *stayed for fully one hour.*

fully-fledged *adj* **1** of a person: completely trained or qualified. **2** of a bird: old enough to have grown feathers.

fulminate *verb, intr* to utter angry criticism or condemnation. ▪ **fulminant** *adj, pathol* developing suddenly or rapidly. ▪ **fulmination** *noun*. [15c: from Latin *fulminare* to hurl lightning]

fulness see **fullness** under **full**

fulsome *adj* of praise, compliments, etc: so overdone as to be distasteful. [13c]

fumble *verb* **1** *intr* (*also* **fumble for sth**) to grope, clumsily. **2** to say or do awkwardly. **3** to fail to manage, because of clumsy handling: *The fielder fumbled the catch.* ▸ *noun* **1** an act of fumbling. **2** in ball sports: a dropped or fumbled ball.

fume *noun* **1** (*often* **fumes**) smoke, gases or vapour, esp if strong-smelling or toxic, emanating from heated materials, operating engines or machinery, etc. **2** the pungent toxic vapours given off by solvents or concentrated acids. **3** a rage; fretful excitement. ▸ *verb* **1** *intr* to be furious; to fret angrily. **2** *intr* to give off smoke, gases or vapours. **3** *intr* of gases or vapours: to come off in fumes, esp during a chemical reaction. **4** to treat (eg wood) with fumes. [16c: from Latin *fumus* smoke]

fumigant *noun* a gaseous form of a chemical compound that is used to fumigate a place.

fumigate *verb* to disinfect (a room, a building, etc) with fumes, in order to destroy pests, esp insects and their larvae. ▪ **fumigation** *noun*. ▪ **fumigator** *noun* an apparatus used to fumigate a place. [18c: from Latin *fumus* smoke]

fun *noun* **1** enjoyment; merriment. **2** a source of amusement or entertainment. ▸ *adj, informal* for amusement, enjoyment, etc: *fun run*. [17c, from earlier *fon* to make a fool of]

IDIOMS **make fun of** *or* **poke fun at sb** *or* **sth** to laugh at them or it, esp unkindly; to tease or ridicule them or it.

function *noun* **1** the special purpose or task of a machine, person, bodily part, etc. **2** *linguistics* the part played by a word, phrase, etc in a construction. **3** an organized event such as a party, reception, meeting, etc. **4** a duty particular to someone in a particular job. **5** *maths, logic* the relation of every element in a set (the **domain**) to a single element of a second set (the **codomain**), shown by $y = f(x)$, where x is an element of the first set and y is an element of the second. **6** *comput* any of the basic operations of a computer, usu corresponding to a single operation. ▸ *verb, intr* **1** to work; to operate. **2** to fulfil a function; to perform one's duty. **3** to serve or act as something. [16c: from Latin *functio*]

functional *adj* **1** of buildings, machines, etc: designed for efficiency rather than decorativeness; plain rather than elaborate. **2** in working order; operational. **3** referring to or performed by functions. ▪ **functionally** *adv*.

functionalism *noun* **1** the policy or practice of the practical application of ideas. **2** *art, archit* the theory that beauty is to be identified with functional efficiency. ▪ **functionalist** *noun*.

functionality *noun* **1** the capacity that a thing, idea, etc has to be functional or practical. **2** *comput* the specific application of a computer program.

functionary *noun* (*-ies*) *derog* someone who works as a minor official in the government, etc.

function key *noun, comput* any of the keys marked with an 'F' and a following numeral on a keyboard, pressed alone or in combination with other keys to perform a specific task within a program.

fund *noun* **1** a sum of money on which some enterprise is founded or on which the expenses of a project are supported. **2** a large store or supply: *a fund of jokes*. **3** (**funds**) *informal* money available for spending. **4** (**funds**) British government securities paying fixed interest, which finance the **national debt**. ▸ *verb* **1** to provide money for a particular purpose: *fund the project*. **2** to make (a debt) permanent, with fixed interest. [17c: from Latin *fundus* bottom]

IDIOMS **in funds** *informal* having plenty of cash.

fundament *noun, euphem* the buttocks. [13c]

fundamental *adj* **1** basic; underlying: *fundamental rules of physics*. **2** large; important: *fundamental differences*. **3** essential; necessary. ▸ *noun* **1** (*usu* **fundamentals**) a basic principle or rule. **2** *music* the lowest note of a chord. [15c: from Latin *fundare* to **found**[1]]

fundamentalism *noun* in religion, politics, etc: strict adherence to the traditional teachings of a particular doctrine. ▪ **fundamentalist** *noun*. [1920s]

fundamental particle *noun, physics* an elementary particle.

fundamental unit *noun* a unit in a system of measurement from which all other units are derived, eg in the SI system, the metre as a unit of length and the second as a unit of time.

fundraiser *noun* **1** someone engaged in fundraising for a charity, organization, etc. **2** an event held to raise money for a cause. ▪ **fundraising** *noun, adj*.

funeral *noun* **1** the ceremonial burial or cremation of a dead person. **2** *informal* one's own problem, affair, etc: *That's his funeral.* ▶ *adj* relating to funerals. [14c: from Latin *funeralia* funeral rites]

funeral director *noun* an undertaker.

funeral parlour *noun* **1** an undertaker's place of business. **2** a room that can be hired for funeral ceremonies.

funerary *adj* relating to or used for funerals. [17c: from Latin *funerarius*]

funereal *adj* **1** associated with or suitable for funerals. **2** mournful; dismal. **3** extremely slow. ▪ **funereally** *adv.* [18c: from Latin *funereus*]

funfair *noun* a fair with sideshows, amusements, rides, etc. [1920s]

fungal *and* **fungi** see **fungus**

fungicide *noun* a chemical that kills or limits the growth of fungi. ▪ **fungicidal** *adj.* [19c: **fungus** + **-cide**]

fungoid *adj, botany* resembling a fungus in nature or consistency. [19c: **fungus** + Greek *eidos* shape]

fungus *noun* (***fungi*** /ˈfʌŋgiː, -gaɪ, -dʒaɪ/ *or* ***funguses***) an organism that superficially resembles a plant, but does not have leaves and roots, and lacks **chlorophyll**, so that it must obtain its nutrients from other organisms, by living either as a parasite on living organisms, or as a **saprophyte** on dead organic matter. ▪ **fungal** *adj.* ▪ **fungous** *adj.* [16c: Latin, meaning 'mushroom' or 'fungus']

funicular /fjʊˈnɪkjʊlə(r)/ *adj* of a mountain railway: operating by a machine-driven cable, with two cars, one of which descends while the other ascends. ▶ *noun* a funicular railway. [Early 20c]

funk[1] *noun* **1** *informal* jazz or rock music with a strong rhythm and repeating bass pattern, with a down-to-earth bluesy feel. **2** *in compounds* a mix of the specified types of music, containing elements from both traditions: *jazz-funk • techno-funk.* [1950s: a back-formation from **funky**]

funk[2] *noun, informal* **1 a** (*also* **blue funk**) a state of fear or panic; **b** shrinking back or shirking because of a loss of courage. **2** a coward. ▶ *verb* to avoid doing something from panic; to balk at something or shirk from fear. [18c: possibly from Flemish *fonck*]

funky *adj* (***-ier, -iest***) *informal* **1** of jazz or rock music: strongly rhythmical and emotionally stirring. **2** trendy; good. **3** earthy; smelly.

funnel *noun* **1** a tube with a cone-shaped opening through which liquid can be poured into a narrow-necked container. **2** a vertical exhaust pipe on a steamship or steam engine through which smoke escapes. ▶ *verb* (***funnelled, funnelling***; (*US*) ***funneled, funneling***) **1** *intr* to rush through a narrow space: *wind funnelling through the streets.* **2** to transfer (liquid, etc) from one container to another using a funnel. [15c: from Latin *infundere* to pour in]

funny *adj* (***-ier, -iest***) **1** amusing; causing laughter. **2** strange; odd; mysterious. **3** *informal* dishonest; shady; involving trickery. **4** *informal* ill: *feeling a bit funny.* **5** *informal* slightly crazy. ▶ *noun* (***-ies***) *informal* a joke. ▪ **funnily** *adv.* ▪ **funniness** *noun.* [18c]

funny bone *noun* a place in the elbow joint where the ulnar nerve passes close to the skin and, if accidentally struck, causes a tingling sensation.

fur *noun* **1** the thick fine soft coat of a hairy animal. **2 a** the skin of such an animal with the hair attached, used to make, line or trim garments; **b** a synthetic imitation of this. **3** a coat, cape or jacket made of fur or an imitation of it. **4** a whitish coating on the tongue, generally a sign of illness. **5** a whitish coating that forms on the inside of water pipes and kettles in hard-water regions. ▶ *verb* (***furred, furring***) **1** *tr & intr* (*often* **fur up** *or* **fur sth up**) to coat or become coated with a fur-like deposit. **2** to cover, trim or line with fur. ▪ **furry** *adj* (***-ier, -iest***). [14c: from French *fuerre* sheath or case]

furbelow *noun* **1** a dress trimming in the form of a strip, ruffle or flounce. **2** (**furbelows**) fussy ornamentation. [18c: from French and Italian *falbala*]

furbish *verb* to restore, decorate or clean; to rub up; to renovate or revive (something). ▪ **furbishment** *noun.* [14c: from French *fourbir* to polish]

furcate *verb, intr* to fork or divide; to branch like a fork. ▶ *adj* forked. ▪ **furcation** *noun.* [Early 19c: from Latin *furca* fork]

the Furies *plural noun* the three spirits of vengeance, known in Greek mythology as the Erinyes (see **Erinys**).

furious *adj* **1** violently or intensely angry. **2** raging; stormy: *furious winds.* **3** frenzied; frantic: *furious activity.* ▪ **furiously** *adv.* [14c: from Latin *furiosus*]

furl *verb, tr & intr* of flags, sails or umbrellas: to roll up. [16c: from French *fer* **firm**[1] + *lier* to bind]

furlong *noun* a measure of distance now used mainly in horse-racing, equal to one eighth of a mile, or 220 yards (201.2m). [Anglo-Saxon *furlang*, from *furh* furrow + *lang* long]

furlough /ˈfɜːloʊ/ *noun* leave of absence, esp from military duty abroad. [17c: from Dutch *verlof*]

furnace *noun* **1 a** an enclosed chamber in which heat is produced, eg for smelting metal, heating water or burning rubbish; **b** a **blast furnace**. **2** *informal* a very hot place. [13c: from Latin *fornacis* kiln or oven]

furnish *verb* **1** to provide (a house, etc) with furniture. **2 a** to supply (what is necessary). **b** (**furnish sb with sth**) to supply or equip them with what they require (eg information, documents). ▪ **furnished** *adj.* [15c: from French *furnir* to provide]

furnishings *plural noun* articles of furniture, fittings, carpets, curtains, etc.

furniture *noun* movable household equipment such as tables, chairs, beds, etc. [16c: from French *fourniture*, from *fournir* to provide]

furore /fjʊˈrɔːrɪ/ *or* (*esp N Am*) **furor** /fʊəˈrɔː(r)/ *noun* a general outburst of excitement or indignation. [18c: Italian, from Latin *furor* frenzy]

furrier *noun* someone who makes or sells furs. [16c]

furrow *noun* **1** a groove or trench cut into the earth by a plough; a rut. **2** a wrinkle, eg in the forehead. ▶ *verb* **1** to plough (land) into furrows. **2** *intr* to become wrinkled. [Anglo-Saxon *furh*]

further *adj* **1** more distant or remote (than something else). **2** more extended than was orig expected: *further delay.* **3** additional: *no further clues.* ▶ *adv* **1** at or to a greater distance or more distant point. **2** to or at a more advanced point: *further developed.* **3** to a greater extent or degree: *modified even further.* **4** moreover; furthermore. ▶ *verb* to help the progress of something. See also **far.** ▪ **furtherance** *noun.* [Anglo-Saxon *furthra*]

IDIOMS **further to** following on from (our telephone conversation, your letter, etc).

further, farther
You can use either **further** or **farther** when you are talking about an actual physical distance:
I can't walk any farther/further.
However, you should always use **further** when you mean 'additional' or 'beyond this point':
I would like to make one further remark.
I want to take this complaint further.

further education *noun, Brit* post-school education other than at a university. Compare **higher education**.

furthermore *adv* in addition to what has already been said; moreover.

furthermost *adj* most distant or remote; farthest.

furthest *adj* most distant or remote. ▶ *adv* **1** at or to the greatest distance or most distant point. **2** at or to the most advanced point; to the greatest extent or degree. Compare **farthest**.

furtive *adj* secretive; stealthy; sly. ▪ **furtively** *adv.* [15c: from Latin *furtivus* stolen]

fury *noun* (*-ies*) **1** (an outburst of) violent anger. **2** violence: *the fury of the wind.* **3** a frenzy: *a fury of activity.* [14c: from French *furie*, from Latin *furere* to rage]

furze *noun* **gorse**. [Anglo-Saxon *fyrs*]

fuse[1] *noun, elec* a safety device consisting of a length of wire which melts when the current exceeds a certain value, thereby breaking the circuit. See also **blow**[1] (*verb* sense 8). ▶ *verb, tr & intr* **1** to melt as a result of the application of heat. **2** (*also* **fuse together**) to join by, or as if by, melting together. **3** of an electric circuit or appliance: to cease to function as a result of the melting of a fuse. [16c: from Latin *fundere, fusum* to melt]

IDIOMS **blow a fuse** *informal* to lose one's temper.

fuse[2] *or* (*US*) **fuze** *noun* a cord or cable containing combustible material, used for detonating a bomb or explosive charge. ▶ *verb* to fit with such a device. [17c: from Latin *fusus* spindle]

IDIOMS **have a short fuse** to be quick-tempered.

fuse box *noun* a box with the electrical switches and fuses for a whole building or part of it.

fuselage /'fjuːzəlɑːʒ/ *noun* the main body of an aircraft, which carries crew and passengers, and to which the wings and tail unit are attached. [Early 20c: from French *fuselé* spindle-shaped]

fusible *adj* able to be fused; easily fused.

fusilier /fjuːzɪ'lɪə(r)/ *noun, hist* an infantryman armed with a **fusil**, a light musket. [17c: from French *fuisil*]

fusillade /fjuːsɪ'leɪd/ *noun* **1** a simultaneous or continuous discharge of firearms. **2** an onslaught, eg of criticism. [19c: from French *fusiller* to shoot; see **fusilier**]

fusilli /fjuː'ziːliː/ *singular or plural noun* pasta shaped into short thick spirals. [20c: Italian]

fusion *noun* **1** *chem* the process of melting, whereby a substance changes from a solid to a liquid. **2** the act of joining together. **3** see **nuclear fusion**. [16c: from Latin *fusio* melting]

fuss *noun* **1** agitation and excitement, esp over something trivial. **2** a commotion, disturbance or bustle. **3** a show of fond affection. ▶ *verb, intr* (*also* **fuss over** *or* **about sth**) **1** to worry needlessly. **2** to concern oneself too much with trivial matters. **3** to agitate. [18c]

IDIOMS **make a fuss** *or* **make a fuss about sth** to complain about it. **make a fuss of sb** *informal* to give them a lot of affectionate or amicable attention.

fusspot *noun, informal* someone who makes too much of trivial things.

fussy *adj* (*-ier, -iest*) **1** choosy; discriminating. **2** over-concerned with details or trifles; finicky. **3** bustling and officious. **4** of clothes, etc: over-elaborate.

fustian *noun* **1** a kind of coarse twilled cotton fabric with a nap. **2** a pompous and unnatural style of writing or speaking; bombast. ▶ *adj* **1** made of fustian. **2** bombastic. [12c: from French *fustaigne*, prob named after El-Fustat (Old Cairo) where the cloth was made]

fusty *adj* (*-ier, -iest*) **1** stale-smelling; old and musty. **2** old-fashioned. ▪ **fustiness** *noun*. [14c: from French *fust* wine cask]

futile *adj* unproductive, unavailing, foolish, vain or pointless. ▪ **futility** *noun*. [16c: from Latin *futilis* 'easily pouring out' or 'leaky']

futon /'fuːtɒn/ *noun* a cloth-filled mattress used on the floor or on a wooden frame. [19c: Japanese]

future *noun* **1** the time to come; events that are still to occur. **2** *grammar* **a** the future tense; **b** a verb in the future tense. **3** prospects: *must think about one's future.* **4** likelihood of success: *no future in that.* **5** (**futures**) *stock exchange* commodities bought or sold at an agreed price, to be delivered and paid for at a later date. ▶ *adj* **1** yet to come or happen. **2** about to become: *my future wife.* **3** *grammar* of the tense of a verb: indicating actions or events yet to happen, in English formed with the auxiliary verb *will* and infinitive without *to*, as in *She will see him tomorrow.* [14c: from Latin *futurus* about to be]

IDIOMS **in future** from now on.

future perfect see under **perfect**

futurism *noun* an artistic movement concerned with expressing the movement of machines in all art forms, taking, as its reference point, the dynamism of modern technology. ▪ **futurist** *noun*. [Early 20c]

futuristic *adj* **1** of design, etc: so modern or original as to seem appropriate to the future, or considered likely to be fashionable in the future. **2** relating to futurism.

futurity *noun* (*-ies*) **1** the future. **2** a future event.

fuze an alternative *US* spelling of **fuse**[2]

fuzz *noun* **1** a mass of fine fibres or hair, usu curly. **2** a blur. ▶ *verb* (*also* **fuzz sth up**) to make or become fuzzy. [17c]

the fuzz *noun, slang* the police. [1920s]

fuzzy *adj* (*-ier, -iest*) **1** covered with fuzz. **2** forming a mass of tight curls. **3** indistinct; blurred.

fuzzy logic *noun, comput* a form of logic or reasoning that is a central part of artificial intelligence, used to process information that cannot be defined precisely as true or false but must be qualified by degrees, etc.

fwd *or* **FWD** *abbrev* forward.

fx *abbrev* effects.

fyi *or* **FYI** *abbrev* for your information.

G *or* **g** *noun* (***Gs, G's*** *or* ***g's***) **1** the seventh letter of the English alphabet. **2** (**G**) *music* the fifth note on the scale of C major.

g *abbrev* **1** gallon. **2** gram or grams. **3** gravity.

Ga *symbol, chem* gallium.

gab *informal, noun* idle talk; chat. ▸ *verb* (***gabbed, gabbing***) *intr* (*also* **gab on** *or* **away**) to talk idly, esp at length. [18c: prob from Irish Gaelic *gob* mouth]
IDIOMS **the gift of the gab** *informal* the ability to speak with ease, esp persuasively.

gabble *verb, tr & intr* to talk or say something quickly and unclearly. [16c: from Dutch *gabbelen*]

gaberdine *or* **gabardine** *noun* (*pl* ***gaberdines*** *or* ***gabardines*** in sense 2) **1** a closely woven twill fabric, esp one made of wool or cotton. **2** a coat or loose cloak made from this. [16c: from French *gauvardine* a pilgrim's garment]

gable *noun* **1** the triangular upper part of a side wall between the sloping parts of a roof. **2** a triangular canopy above a door or window. ▪ **gabled** *adj* having a gable or gables. [14c: from Norse *gafl*]

gad *verb* (***gadded, gadding***) *intr, informal* (*usu* **gad about** *or* **around**) to go from place to place busily, esp in the hope of finding amusement or pleasure. [15c: back-formation from Anglo-Saxon *gædeling* companion]

gadget *noun* any small device, esp one more ingenious than necessary. ▪ **gadgetry** *noun.* [19c]

gadolinium *noun, chem* (symbol **Gd**) a soft silvery-white metallic element, belonging to the **lanthanide** series. [19c: named after Johan Gadolin, Finnish mineralogist]

Gaelic *noun* any of the closely related Celtic languages spoken in the Scottish Highlands and Islands /ˈɡɑːlɪk/, or Ireland or the Isle of Man /ˈɡeɪlɪk/. ▸ *adj* relating to these languages or the people who speak them, or to their customs.

gaff[1] *noun* **1** a long pole with a hook, for landing large fish. **2** *naut* a vertical spar to which the tops of certain types of sail are attached. ▸ *verb* to catch (a fish) with a gaff. [13c: from Provençal *gaf* a boathook]

gaff[2] *noun, slang* nonsense.
IDIOMS **blow the gaff** *Brit* to give away a secret.

gaffe *noun* a socially embarrassing action or remark. [19c: French]

gaffer *noun* **1** *informal* a boss or foreman. **2** *cinema & TV* the senior electrician in a production crew. **3** *dialect* an old man. [Perhaps from **godfather** or **grandfather**]

gaffer tape *noun* a type of strong adhesive tape.

gag[1] *verb* (***gagged, gagging***) **1** to silence someone by putting something in or over their mouth. **2** to deprive someone of free speech. **3** *intr* to retch. **4** *intr* to choke. ▸ *noun* **1** something put into or over a person's mouth to prevent them from speaking. **2** any suppression of free speech. **3** a **closure** (sense 3) applied to a parliamentary debate. [15c in obsolete sense 'to suffocate']

gag[2] *informal, noun* a joke or trick. ▸ *verb* (***gagged, gagging***) *intr* to tell jokes. [19c]

gaga *adj, informal* **1** weak-minded through old age; senile. **2** silly; foolish. [20c: French]

gage[1] *noun* **1** an object given as security or a pledge. **2** *hist* something thrown down to signal a challenge, eg a glove. [14c: from French *guage*]

gage[2] see **gauge**

gaggle *noun* **1** a flock of geese. **2** *informal* a group of noisy people. [14c as verb: imitating the sound]

gaiety *noun* **1** the state of being merry or bright. **2** attractively bright appearance. **3** fun; merrymaking. [17c: from French *gaieté*]

gaily *adv* **1** in a light-hearted, merry way. **2** brightly; colourfully. [14c: from **gay**]

gain *verb* **1** to get, obtain or earn (something desirable). **2** to win (esp a victory or prize). **3** to have or experience an increase in something: *gain speed.* **4** *intr* (*usu* **gain on sb** *or* **sth**) to come closer to them or it; catch them up. **5** *tr & intr* of a clock, etc: to go too fast by (a specified amount of time). **6** to reach (a place), esp after difficulties. ▸ *noun* **1** (*often* **gains**) something gained, eg profit. **2** an increase, eg in weight. **3** an instance of gaining. [15c: from French *gaaignier* to earn, gain or till (land)]

gainful *adj* **1** profitable. **2** of employment: paid. ▪ **gainfully** *adv.*

gainsay *verb* (***gainsaid***) *formal* to deny or contradict. ▪ **gainsayer** *noun.* [13c: from Anglo-Saxon *gean* against + *sayen* to say]

gait *noun* **1** a way of walking. **2** the leg movements of an animal travelling at a specified speed, eg trotting. [16c: variant of obsolete *gate* manner of doing]

gaiter *noun* a leather or cloth covering for the lower leg and ankle. [18c: from French *guêtre*]

gal *noun, informal* a girl.

gala /ˈɡɑːlə/ *noun* **1** an occasion of special entertainment or a public festivity of some kind, eg a carnival *as adj*: *gala night at the theatre.* **2** a meeting for sports competitions, esp swimming. [17c: French, from *galer* to make merry]

galactic *adj* relating to a galaxy or the Galaxy. [19c]

galactose *noun, biochem* a soluble sugar obtained from lactose.

galaxy *noun* (*-ies*) **1** a huge collection of stars, dust and gas held together by mutual gravitational attraction. **2** (**the Galaxy**) the vast spiral arrangement of stars to which our solar system belongs, known as the Milky Way. **3** a fabulous gathering, eg of famous people. [14c as *the Galaxy*: from Greek *galaxias* the Milky Way]

gale *noun* **1 a** *loosely* any very strong wind; **b** *technical* a wind that blows with a speed of 51.5 to 101.4km per hour, corresponding to force 7 to 10 on the **Beaufort scale**. *as adj*: *gale warning*. **2** (*usu* **gales**) a sudden loud burst, eg of laughter. [16c]

galena *noun* the most important ore of **lead**[2] (*noun* sense 1) which occurs as compact masses of very dense dark grey crystals consisting mainly of lead sulphide. Also called **galenite**. [16c: Latin, meaning 'lead ore']

gall[1] *noun* **1** *informal* impudence; cheek. **2** bitterness or spitefulness. **3** something unpleasant. **4** *med, old use* bile. [Anglo-Saxon *gealla* bile]

gall[2] *noun* a small round abnormal growth on the stem or leaf of a plant, usu caused by invading parasitic fungi, or by insects, eg gall wasps. [14c: from Latin *galla* the oak apple]

gall[3] *noun* **1** a sore or painful swelling on the skin caused by chafing. **2** something annoying or irritating. **3** a state of being annoyed. ▶ *verb* **1** to annoy. **2** to chafe (skin). [14c as *gealla* a sore on a horse]

gallant /'galənt, *also* gə'lant/ *adj* **1** brave. **2** *literary or old use* splendid, grand or fine. **3** /gə'lant/ of a man: courteous and attentive to women. ▶ *noun, old use* a handsome young man who pursues women. [15c: from French *galant*, from *galer* to make merry]

gallantry *noun* **1** bravery. **2** *old use* politeness and attentiveness to women.

gall bladder *noun, anatomy* a small muscular pear-shaped sac lying beneath the liver that stores bile and releases it into the intestine.

galleon *noun, hist* a large Spanish ship, usu with three masts, used for war or trade from the 15c to 18c. [16c: from Spanish *galeón*]

gallery *noun* (*-ies*) **1** a room or building used to display works of art. **2** a balcony along an inside upper wall, eg of a church or hall, providing extra seating or reserved for musicians, etc: *minstrels' gallery*. **3 a** the upper floor in a theatre, usu containing the cheapest seats; **b** the part of the audience seated there. **4** a long narrow room or corridor. **5** an underground passage in a mine or cave. **6** a covered walkway open on one or both sides. **7** the spectators in the stand at a golf, tennis or other tournament. [15c: from French *galerie*]

galley *noun* **1** *hist* a long single-deck ship propelled by sails and oars. **2** *hist* a Greek or Roman warship. **3** *naut* the kitchen on a ship. [13c: from French *galie*, from Greek *galaia* a low flat boat]

galley slave *noun* **1** *hist* a slave forced to row a galley. **2** *informal* someone who is given menial tasks; a drudge.

Gallic *adj* **1** typically or characteristically French. **2** *hist* relating to ancient Gaul or the Gauls. [17c: from Latin *gallicus* Gaulish]

gallinaceous *adj, biol* relating or referring to the order of birds that includes domestic fowl, turkeys, pheasants, grouse, etc. [18c: from Latin *gallina* hen]

galling *adj* irritating. [17c: from **gall**[3]]

gallium *noun, chem* (symbol **Ga**) a soft silvery metallic element found in zinc blende, bauxite and kaolin. [19c: from Latin *gallus* cock, from the name of its French discoverer, Lecoq de Boisbaudran]

gallivant *verb, intr, humorous or derog, informal* to go out looking for entertainment or amusement. [19c]

gallon *noun* (abbrev **gal.**) an imperial unit of liquid measurement equal to four quarts or eight pints, equivalent to 4.546 l (an **imperial gallon**) in the UK, and 3.785 l in the USA. [13c: from French *galon*]

gallop *verb* **1** *intr* of a horse or similar animal: to move at a gallop. **2** *intr* to ride a horse, etc at a gallop. **3 a** to read, talk or do something quickly; **b** to make (a horse, etc) move at a gallop. **4** *intr, informal* to move, progress or increase very quickly: *inflation is galloping out of control*. ▶ *noun* **1** the fastest pace at which a horse or similar animal moves, during which all four legs are off the ground together. **2** a period of riding at this pace. **3** an unusually fast speed. ▪ **galloper** *noun*. ▪ **galloping** *noun, adj*. [16c: from French *galoper*]

gallows *singular noun* **1** a wooden frame on which criminals are put to death by hanging. **2** a similar frame for suspending things. **3** (**the gallows**) death by hanging. [Anglo-Saxon *gealga*]

gallstone *noun, pathol* a small hard mass that is formed in the gall bladder or one of its ducts.

galore *adv* (placed after the noun) in large amounts or numbers: *I read books galore*. [17c: from Irish Gaelic *go leór* to sufficiency]

galosh *or* **golosh** *noun, usu in pl* a waterproof overshoe. [14c: from Latin *gallicula* a small Gaulish shoe]

galvanic *adj* **1** *physics* relating to or producing an electric current, esp a direct current, by chemical means. **2** of behaviour, etc: sudden, or startlingly energetic, as if the result of an electric shock. ▪ **galvanically** *adv*. [18c: named after Luigi Galvani, Italian scientist]

galvanize *or* **-ise** *verb* **1** to stimulate or rouse to action. **2** *technical* to coat (a metallic surface, usu iron or steel) with a thin layer of zinc, in order to protect it from corrosion. **3** to stimulate by applying an electric current. ▪ **galvanization** *noun*.

gambit *noun* **1** *chess* a chess move made early in a game, in which a pawn or other piece is sacrificed in order to gain an overall advantage. **2** an initial action or remark, esp one intended to gain an advantage. **3** a piece of trickery; a stratagem. [17c: from Italian *gambetto* a tripping up]

gamble *verb* **1** *tr & intr* to bet (usu money) on the result of a card game, horse race, etc. **2** (*also* **gamble sth away**) to lose (money or other assets) through gambling. **3** *intr* (*often* **gamble on sth**) to take a chance or risk on it. ▶ *noun* **1** an act of gambling; a bet. **2** a risk or a situation involving risk. ▪ **gambler** *noun*. ▪ **gambling** *noun*. [18c: from Anglo-Saxon *gamen* to play]

gamboge /gam'boudʒ/ *noun* a gum resin obtained from various Asian trees, used as a source of a yellow pigment or as a laxative. [18c: from Latin *gambogium*, derived from Cambodia]

gambol *verb* (***gambolled, gambolling***; *N Am also* ***gamboled, gamboling***) *intr* to jump around playfully. ▸ *noun* jumping around playfully; a frolic. [16c: from Italian *gamba* leg]

game[1] *noun* **1** an amusement or pastime. **2** the equipment used for this, eg a board, cards, dice, etc. **3** a competitive activity with rules, involving some form of skill. **4** an occasion on which individuals or teams compete at such an activity; a match. **5** in some sports, eg tennis: a division of a match. **6** (**games**) an event consisting of competitions in various activities, esp sporting ones: *the Commonwealth games.* **7** *informal, often derog* a type of activity, profession, or business: *the game of politics.* **8** a person's playing ability or style: *her backhand game.* **9** *derog* an activity undertaken light-heartedly: *War is just a game to him.* **10 a** certain birds and animals that are killed for sport; **b** the flesh of such creatures. **11** *derog, informal* a scheme, trick or intention: *give the game away* • *What's your game?* ▸ *adj, informal* **1** (*also* **game for sth**) ready and willing to undertake it: *game for a try.* **2** *old use* having plenty of fighting spirit; plucky. ▸ *verb, intr* to gamble. ▪ **gamely** *adv* bravely, sportingly. ▪ **gameness** *noun.* [Anglo-Saxon *gamen* amusement]

IDIOMS **give the game away** to reveal the truth. **play the game** to behave fairly. **the game is up** the plan or trick has failed or has been found out.

game[2] *adj, old use* lame. See also **gammy**. [18c: perhaps from Irish Gaelic *cam* crooked]

gamekeeper *noun* a person employed to look after and manage the **game**[1] (*noun* sense 10a) on a country estate.

gamer /ɡeɪmə(r)/ *noun* **1** a person who plays games, especially computer games. **2** *US* an enthusiastic and persistent competitor. [Late 20c]

gamesmanship *noun, derog* the art, practice or process of winning games by trying to unsettle one's opponent or using unsporting tactics.

gamester *noun* a gambler. [16c: from **game**[1]]

gamete *noun, biol* in sexually reproducing organisms: a specialized sex cell, esp an **ovum** or **sperm**, that fuses with another gamete of the opposite type during fertilization. [19c: from Greek *gameein* to marry]

gamine /ˈɡamiːn/ *noun* a girl or young woman with a mischievous, boyish appearance. [19c: French, literally 'a female urchin']

gaming *noun* gambling. *as adj and in compounds*: *gaming-house.* [16c: from **game**[1] *verb*]

gamma *noun* **1** the third letter of the Greek alphabet. **2** a mark indicating the third highest grade or quality. **3** the third element, etc in a series. Compare **alpha**, **beta**.

gamma rays *plural noun, physics* electromagnetic radiation of very high frequency, consisting of high-energy **photon**s, often produced during radioactive decay. Also called **gamma radiation**.

gammon *noun* **1** cured meat from the upper leg and hindquarters of a pig. **2** the back part of a side of bacon including the whole back leg and hindquarters. [15c: from French *gambon*, from *gambe* leg]

gammy *adj* (***-ier, -iest***) *informal, old use* lame with a permanent injury. [19c: related to **game**[2]]

gamut /ˈɡamət/ *noun* **1** the whole range of anything, eg a person's emotions. **2** *music, hist* **a** a scale of notes; **b** the range of notes produced by a voice or instrument. [14c: from *gamma* the lowest note on a medieval six-note scale + *ut* the first note (now called **doh**) of an early sol-fa notation system]

gamy *or* **gamey** *adj* (***-ier, -iest***) of meat: having the strong taste or smell of game that has been kept for a long time.

gander *noun* **1** a male goose. **2** *informal* a look: *have a gander.* [Anglo-Saxon *gandra*]

gang *noun* **1** a group, esp of criminals or troublemakers. **2** a group of friends, esp children. **3** an organized group of workers. [From Anglo-Saxon *gong* a journeying]

PHRASAL VERBS **gang up on** *or* **against sb** to act as a group against them.

gangland *noun* the world of organized crime.

gangling *or* **gangly** *adj* (***-ier, -iest***) tall and thin, and usu awkward in movement. [19c: from Anglo-Saxon *gangan* to go]

ganglion *noun* (***ganglia*** *or* ***ganglions***) **1** *anatomy* in the central nervous system: a group of nerve cell bodies, usu enclosed by a sheath or capsule. **2** *pathol* a cyst or swelling that forms on the tissue surrounding a tendon, eg on the back of the hand. [17c: Greek, meaning 'cystic tumour']

gangplank *noun* a movable plank serving as a gangway for a ship.

gangrene *noun, pathol* the death and subsequent decay of part of the body due to some failure of the blood supply to that region as a result of disease, injury, frostbite, etc. ▪ **gangrenous** *adj.* [16c: from Greek *gangraina*]

gangster *noun* a member of a gang of violent criminals. ▪ **gangsterism** *noun.* [19c]

gangway *noun* **1 a** a small movable bridge used for getting on and off a ship; **b** the opening on the side of a ship into which this fits. **2** a passage between rows of seats, eg on an aircraft or in a theatre. ▸ *exclam* make way!

gannet *noun* **1** a large seabird that has a heavy body, white plumage with dark wing tips and webbed feet. **2** *informal* a greedy person. [Anglo-Saxon *ganot*]

ganoid *adj, zool* **1** of the scales of certain primitive fish: rhomboid-shaped with a hard shiny enamel-like outer layer. **2** of fish: having such scales. [19c: from Greek *ganos* brightness]

gantry *noun* (***-ies***) a large metal supporting framework, eg for railway signals, serving as a bridge for a travelling crane, or used at the side of a rocket's launch pad. [16c: from Latin *cantherius* a trellis]

gaol *and* **gaoler** see **jail**

gaolbird *and* **gaolbreak** see **jailbird** and **jailbreak**

gap *noun* **1** a break or open space, eg in a fence, etc. **2** a break in time; an interval. **3** a difference or disparity: *the generation gap.* **4** a ravine or gorge. ▪ **gappy** *adj* (***-ier, -iest***). [14c: Norse, meaning 'a chasm']

gape *verb, intr* **1** to stare with the mouth open, esp in surprise or wonder. **2** to be or become wide open. **3** to open the mouth wide. ▸ *noun* **1** a wide opening. **2** an open-mouthed stare. **3** the extent to which the mouth can be opened. ▪ **gaping** *adj.* ▪ **gapingly** *adv.* [13c: from Norse *gapa* to open the mouth]

gap year *noun, chiefly Brit* a year spent by a student between school and university doing non-academic activities such as voluntary work abroad.

garage *noun* **1** a building in which motor vehicles are kept. **2** an establishment where motor vehicles are bought, sold and repaired, often also selling petrol, etc. **3** a filling station. ▸ *verb* to put or keep (a car, etc) in a garage. [20c: from French *garer* to shelter]

garb *literary, noun* **1** clothing, esp as worn by people in a particular job or position: *priestly garb.* **2** outward appearance. ▸ *verb* to dress or clothe. [16c: from Italian *garbo* grace]

garbage *noun* **1** *N Am* domestic waste; refuse. **2** worthless or poor quality articles or matter. **3** nonsense. **4** *comput* erroneous, irrelevant or meaningless data. [15c]

garbage can *noun, N Am* a rubbish bin. Also called **trashcan.**

garble *verb* **1** to mix up the details of something unintentionally. **2** to deliberately distort the meaning of something, eg by making important omissions. ▪ **garbled** *adj* of a report or account: muddled. [15c: from Arabic *ghirbal* a sieve]

garden *noun* **1** an area of land, usu one adjoining a house, where grass, trees, ornamental plants, fruit, vegetables, etc, are grown. **2** (*usu* **gardens**) such an area of land, usu of considerable size, with flower beds, lawns, trees, walks, etc, laid out for enjoyment by the public: *botanical gardens.* **3** a fertile region: *Kent is the garden of England.* ▸ *adj* **1** of a plant: cultivated, not wild. **2** belonging to or for use in a garden, or in gardening: *garden fork.* ▸ *verb, intr* to cultivate, work in or take care of a garden, esp as a hobby. ▪ **gardener** *noun.* ▪ **gardening** *noun.* [14c: from French *gardin,* variant of *jardin*]

IDIOMS **lead sb up the garden path** *informal* to mislead or deceive them deliberately.

garden centre *noun* a place where plants, seeds, garden tools, etc are sold.

garden city *noun* a spacious modern town designed with trees, private gardens and public parks.

gardenia *noun* **1** an evergreen shrub with glossy leaves and large, usu white, fragrant flowers. **2** the flower produced by this plant. [18c: named after Dr Alexander Garden, US botanist]

Garden of Eden see **Eden** (sense 1)

gargantuan *or* **Gargantuan** *adj* enormous; colossal. [16c: named after *Gargantua,* the greedy giant in Rabelais's novel *Gargantua and Pantagruel* (1534)]

gargle *verb, tr & intr* to cleanse, treat or freshen the mouth and throat by breathing out through (a medicinal liquid) that is held there for a while before spitting it out. ▸ *noun* **1** gargling or the sound produced while gargling. **2** the liquid used. [16c: from French *gargouille* throat]

gargoyle *noun* a grotesque carved open-mouthed head or figure acting as a rainwater spout from a roof-gutter, esp on a church. [15c: from French *gargouille* throat]

garish *adj, derog* unpleasantly bright or colourful; very gaudy. ▪ **garishly** *adv.* ▪ **garishness** *noun.* [16c: from obsolete *gaurish,* from *gaure* to stare]

garland *noun* a circular arrangement of flowers or leaves worn round the head or neck, or hung up as a decoration. ▸ *verb* to decorate something or someone with a garland. [14c: from French *garlande*]

garlic *noun* **1** a plant of the onion family, widely cultivated for its underground bulb, which is divided into segments known as cloves. **2** the bulb of this plant, which is widely used as a flavouring in cooking. [Anglo-Saxon *garleac*]

garment *noun, now rather formal* an article of clothing. [14c: from French *garniment*]

garner *verb, formal or literary* to collect and usu store (information, knowledge, etc). [12c: from Latin *granarium* granary]

garnet *noun* any of various silicate minerals, esp a deep red variety used as a semi-precious stone. [13c: from Latin *granatum* pomegranate]

garnish *verb* to decorate (esp food to be served). ▸ *noun* a decoration, esp one added to food. [14c: from French *garnir* to supply]

garret *noun* an attic room, often a dingy one. [14c: from French *garite* refuge]

garrison *noun* **1** a body of soldiers stationed in a town or fortress. **2** the building or fortress they occupy. [13c: from French *garison,* from *garir* to protect]

garrotte *or* **garotte** *or* (*N Am*) **garrote** /gə'rɒt/ *noun* **1** a wire loop or metal collar that can be tightened around the neck to cause strangulation. **2** this method of execution. ▸ *verb* to execute or kill someone with a garrotte. [17c: from Spanish *garrote*]

garrulous *adj* **1** of a person: tending to talk a lot, esp about trivial things. **2** *derog* of a speech, etc: long and wordy. ▪ **garrulousness** *noun.* [17c: from Latin *garrulus,* from *garrire* to chatter]

garter *noun* **1** a band of tight material, usu elastic, worn on the leg to hold up a stocking or sock. **2** (**the Garter**) **a** the highest order of British knighthood; **b** membership of the order; **c** the emblem of the order, a blue garter. [14c: from French *gartier*]

gas *noun* **1** a state of matter other than **solid** and **liquid**, that has no fixed shape, is easily compressed, and which will expand to occupy all the space available. **2** a substance or mixture of substances that is in this state at ordinary temperatures, eg hydrogen, air. **3 natural gas** used as a source of fuel for heating, lighting or cooking. *as adj*: *gas cooker.* **4** a gas, esp nitrous oxide, used as an anaesthetic. **5 firedamp,** explosive in contact with air. **6** a poisonous gas used as a weapon in war. **7** *dated informal* gasoline; petrol. **8** *informal* an amusing or entertaining event, situation or person: *The film was a real gas!* **9** *derog, informal* foolish talk; boasting. ▸ *verb* (***gassed, gassing***) **1** to poison or kill (people or animals) with gas. **2** *intr, derog, informal* to chat, esp at length, boastfully or about trivial things. [17c: coined by J B van Helmont, Belgian chemist, after Greek *chaos* atmosphere]

gas chamber *noun* a sealed room that is filled with poisonous gas and used for killing people or animals.

gaseous /'gasɪəs, 'geɪʃəs/ *adj* in the form of, or like, gas. ▪ **gaseousness** *noun.*

gasfield *noun* a region that is rich in economically valuable **natural gas.**

gash *noun* a deep open cut or wound. ▸ *verb* to make a gash in something. [16c: from French *garser* to scratch or wound]

gasify *verb* (***-ies, -ied***) to convert something into gas. ▪ **gasification** *noun.*

gasket *noun* a compressible ring or sheet made of rubber, paper or asbestos that fits tightly in the join between two metal surfaces to form an airtight seal. [20c]

IDIOMS **blow a gasket** *informal* to become extremely angry.

gaslight *noun* **1** a lamp powered by gas. **2** the light from such a lamp.

gas mask *noun* a type of mask that is used in warfare and certain industries to filter out any poisonous gases.

gasoline *noun, N Am* petrol. Often shortened to **gas**.

gasometer *noun* a large metal tank used for storing gas for use as fuel.

gasp *verb* **1** *intr* to take a sharp breath in, through surprise, sudden pain, etc. **2** *intr* to breathe in with difficulty, eg because of illness, exhaustion, etc. **3** (*also* **gasp sth out**) to say it breathlessly. ▸ *noun* a sharp intake of breath. [14c: from Norse *geispa* to yawn]

gas ring *noun* a hollow ring with perforations that serve as gas **jet**s (see under **jet**[2]).

gassy *adj* (**-ier, -iest**) **1** like gas; full of gas. **2** *derog, informal* talking a lot, esp about unimportant things.

gasteropod see **gastropod**

gastric *adj, med, etc* relating to or affecting the stomach. [17c: from Greek *gaster* belly]

gastric juice *noun, biochem* a strongly acidic fluid produced by the gastric glands of the stomach wall during the digestion of food.

gastritis *noun, med* inflammation of the lining of the stomach.

gastroenteritis *noun, med* inflammation of the lining of the stomach and intestine.

gastronome *or* **gastronomist** *noun* a person who enjoys, and has developed a taste for, good food and wine. [19c: from Greek *gaster* belly + *nomos* law]

gastronomy *noun* the appreciation and enjoyment of good food and wine. ▪ **gastronomic** *adj.*

gastropod *or* **gasteropod** *noun, biol* a mollusc, eg snail, slug, whelk, winkle, that typically possesses a large flattened muscular foot and often has a single spirally coiled shell. [19c: from Greek *gaster* belly + *pous, podos* foot]

gasworks *singular noun* a place where gas is manufactured.

gate *noun* **1** a door or barrier, usu a hinged one, that is moved in order to open or close an entrance in a wall, fence, etc. **2** at an airport: any of the numbered exits from which passengers can board or leave a plane. **3** the total number of people attending a sports event or other entertainment. **4** (*also* **gate money**) the total money paid in admission fees to an entertainment. **5** *technical* an electronic circuit whose output is controlled by the combination of signals at the input terminals. ▸ *verb* to confine (pupils) to school after hours. [Anglo-Saxon *geat* a way]

-gate *suffix, attached to the name of a person or place, signifying* a scandal connected with them or it: *Irangate.* [20c: modelled on *Watergate*]

gateau *or* **gâteau** /ˈgatoʊ/ *noun* (***gateaux, gâteaux*** *or* ***gateaus*** /-toʊz/) a large rich cake, esp one filled with cream. [20c in this sense: French *gâteau* a cake]

gatecrash *verb, tr & intr, informal* to join or attend (a party, meeting, etc) uninvited. ▪ **gatecrasher** *noun.*

gatehouse *noun* a building at or above the gateway to a city, castle, etc, often occupied by the person who guards it.

gateleg table *noun* a table that has a hinged and framed leg or legs that can be swung out to support a leaf or leaves in order to make the table bigger.

gatepost *noun* either of the posts on each side of a gate.

gateway *noun* **1** an entrance with a gate across it. **2** a way in or to something: *the gateway to success.* **3** *comput, etc* a connection between computer networks, or between a computer network and a telephone line.

gather *verb* **1** *tr & intr* (*also* **gather together**) to bring or come together in one place. **2** (*also* **gather sth in**) to collect, pick or harvest it. **3** to pick something up. **4** to increase in (speed or force). **5** to accumulate or become covered with (eg dust). **6** to learn or understand something from information received. **7** to pull (material) into small folds. **8** to pull someone or something close to oneself: *She gathered the child into her arms.* **9** to wrinkle (the brow). **10** to draw together or muster (strength, courage, etc) in preparation for something. **11** *intr* of a boil, etc: to form a head. ▸ *noun* a small fold in material, often stitched. [Anglo-Saxon *gaderian*]

gathering *noun* **1** a meeting or assembly. **2** a series of gathers in material.

gauche /goʊʃ/ *adj* ill-at-ease, awkward in social situations. ▪ **gauchely** *adv.* ▪ **gaucheness** *noun.* [18c: French, meaning 'left, left-handed, awkward']

gaucho /ˈgaʊtʃoʊ/ *noun* a cowboy of the S American plains. [19c: American Spanish]

gaudy *adj* (**-ier, -iest**) *derog* coarsely and brightly coloured or decorated. ▪ **gaudiness** *noun.* [16c]

gauge *or* (*N Am*) **gage** /geɪdʒ/ *verb* **1** to measure something accurately. **2** to estimate or guess (a measurement, size, etc). **3** to judge or appraise. ▸ *noun* **1** any of various instruments that are used to measure a quantity: *pressure gauge.* **2** each of the standard sizes used in measuring articles (esp by diameter) such as wire, bullets or knitting needles. **3** on a railway: **a** the distance between the inner faces of the rails on a line, in Britain **broad gauge** and **narrow gauge** being broader and narrower respectively than the **standard gauge** of 56.5in (1.435m); **b** the distance between wheels on an axle. **4** a standard against which other things are measured or judged. [15c: French]

gauge
This word is often misspelt. It might help you to remember the following sentence:
*A **g**auge **i**s **a** **u**seful **g**eneral **e**stimate.*

Gaul *noun, hist* an inhabitant of, or a person born in, ancient Gaul. See also **Gallic**. [17c: from Latin *Gallus*]

gaunt *adj* **1** thin or thin-faced; lean, haggard. **2** of a place: barren and desolate. ▪ **gauntly** *adv.* ▪ **gauntness** *noun.* [15c]

gauntlet[1] *noun* **1** *hist* a metal or metal-plated glove worn by medieval soldiers. **2** a heavy protective leather glove covering the wrist. [15c: from French *gantelet*]

IDIOMS **take up the gauntlet** to accept a challenge. **throw down the gauntlet** to make a challenge.

gauntlet[2] *noun* [17c: from Swedish *gatlopp* passageway]

IDIOMS **run the gauntlet** to expose oneself to hostile treatment or criticism.

gauss /gaʊs/ *noun* (*pl* ***gauss***) *physics* the cgs unit of magnetic flux density, which in the SI system has been replaced by the **tesla**. [19c: named after J K F Gauss, German mathematician and physicist]

gauze *noun* **1** thin transparent fabric, esp cotton muslin as used to dress wounds. **2** thin wire mesh. ▪ **gauzy** *adj* (***-ier, -iest***). [16c: from French *gaze*]

gave *past tense of* **give**

gavel *noun* a small hammer used by a judge, auctioneer, etc to call attention. [19c]

gavotte /gə'vɒt/ *noun* **1** a lively French country dance that was popular during the 18c. **2** a piece of music for this or in this rhythm. [17c: French, meaning 'the dance of the Gavots or Alpine people']

gawk *informal, verb, intr* to stare blankly or stupidly; to gawp. ▸ *noun, derog* an awkward, clumsy or stupid person. [18c: perhaps from obsolete *gaw* to stare]

gawky *adj* (***-ier, -iest***) *informal, derog* awkward-looking, ungainly, and usu tall and thin. ▪ **gawkiness** *noun.*

gawp *verb, intr, informal* to stare stupidly, esp open-mouthed; to gape. [14c as *galpen* to yawn]

gay *adj* **1** homosexual; relating to, frequented by, or intended for, homosexuals: *a gay bar.* **2** happily carefree. **3** bright and attractive. **4** pleasure-seeking or fun-loving. ▸ *noun* a homosexual. [From French *gai*]

gaze *verb, intr* (*esp* **gaze at sth** *or* **sb**) to stare fixedly. ▸ *noun* a fixed stare. [14c as *gasen*]

gazebo /gə'ziːboʊ/ *noun* (***gazebos*** *or* ***gazeboes***) a small summerhouse usu situated in a place that offers pleasant views. [18c: perhaps coined from **gaze**]

gazelle *noun* (***gazelles*** *or* ***gazelle***) a fawn-coloured antelope with a white rump and belly found in Africa and Asia. [17c: French, from Arabic *ghazal* wild goat]

gazette *noun* **1** an official newspaper giving lists of government, military and legal notices. **2** *often facetious* a newspaper. [17c: from Venetian dialect *gazeta*, from *gazet* a small coin or the cost of an early news-sheet]

gazetteer *noun* a book or part of a book that lists place names and describes the places. [18c in this sense: from **gazette**]

gazump *verb, informal* to charge a prospective house buyer a higher price than has already been verbally agreed, usually because someone else has offered a higher price. [1970s]

gazunder *verb, informal* of a buyer: to lower the sum offered (to a seller of property) just before contracts are due to be signed. [1980s: humorously based on **gazump** and **under**]

GB *abbrev* Great Britain.

GBH *or* **gbh** *abbrev* grievous bodily harm.

Gbit *abbrev, comput* gigabit(s) (see **giga-**).

Gbyte *abbrev, comput* gigabyte(s) (see **giga-**).

GCE *abbrev* **General Certificate of Education**. ▸ *noun* **1** a subject in which an examination is taken at this level. **2** an examination pass or a certificate gained at this level.

GCSE *abbrev* **General Certificate of Secondary Education**. ▸ *noun* **1** a subject in which an examination is taken at this level. **2** an examination pass or a certificate gained at this level.

Gd *symbol, chem* gadolinium.

GDP *abbrev, econ* gross domestic product.

Ge *symbol, chem* germanium.

gear *noun* **1** (*also* **gearwheel**) a toothed wheel or disc that engages with another wheel or disc having a different number of teeth, and turns it, so transmitting motion from one rotating shaft to another. **2** the specific combination of such wheels or discs that is being used: *second gear* • *low gear* • *to change gear.* **3** *informal* the equipment or tools needed for a particular job, sport, etc. **4** *aeronautics* landing gear. **5** *informal* personal belongings. **6** *informal* clothes, esp young people's current fashion. **7** *slang* drugs. ▸ *verb* (*usu* **gear sth to** *or* **towards sth else**) to adapt or design it to suit (a particular need). [13c as *gere* in obsolete sense 'arms' or 'equipment': from Norse *gervi*]

PHRASAL VERBS **gear oneself up** to become or make oneself ready or prepared.

gearbox *noun* **1** esp in a motor vehicle: the set or system of gears that transmits power from the engine to the road wheels. **2** the metal casing that encloses such a set or system of gears.

gearing *noun* **1** a set of gearwheels as a means of transmission of motion. **2** *finance* the ratio of a company's equity to its debts.

gear lever *or* **gear stick** *or* (*N Am*) **gearshift** *noun* a lever for engaging and disengaging gears, esp in a motor vehicle.

gearwheel see under **gear**

gecko *noun* (***geckos*** *or* ***geckoes***) a nocturnal lizard found in warm countries. [18c: from Malay *gekoq*, imitating the sound it makes]

gee[1] *exclam* (*usu* **gee up**) used to encourage a horse to move, or to go faster. ▸ *verb* (***geed, geeing***) to encourage (a horse, etc) to move or move faster.

gee[2] *exclam, informal* expressing surprise, admiration or enthusiasm. Also **gee whiz**. [20c: from *Jesus*]

geek *noun, slang* **1** a strange or eccentric person. **2** a creep or misfit. [16c as *geke*: from Dutch *geck* a fool]

geese *pl of* **goose**

gee-string see **G-string**

geezer *noun, informal* a man. [19c: from *guiser* a masked actor in mime]

Geiger counter /'gaɪgə(r)/ *noun, physics* an instrument that is used to detect and measure the intensity of radiation. [1920s: named after Hans Geiger, German physicist]

geisha /'geɪʃə/ *noun* (***geisha*** *or* ***geishas***) a Japanese girl or woman who is trained to entertain men with music, dancing, conversation, etc. Also called **geisha girl**. [19c: from Japanese *gei* art + *sha* person]

gel *noun* **1** a **colloid** consisting of a solid and a liquid that are dispersed evenly throughout a material and have set to form a jelly-like mass, eg gelatine. **2** (*also* **hair gel**) such a substance used in styling the hair or fixing it in place. ▸ *verb* (***gelled, gelling***) **1** *tr & intr* to become or cause something to become a gel. **2** to style (hair) using gel. **3** to **jell**. [19c: from **gelatine**]

gelatine /'dʒɛlətiːn/ *or* **gelatin** /-tɪn/ *noun* a clear tasteless protein extracted from animal bones and hides and used in food thickenings, photographic materials, etc. [19c: from French *gélatine* jelly]

gelatinous /dʒə'latɪnəs/ *adj* like gelatine or jelly.

geld *verb* to castrate (a male animal, esp a horse) by removing its testicles. ▪ **gelding** *noun* a castrated male animal, esp a horse. [13c: from Norse *geldr* barren]

gelignite *noun* a powerful explosive. [19c: from **gelatine** + Latin *ignis* fire]

gem *noun* **1** (*also* **gemstone**) a semi-precious or precious stone or crystal, esp one that has been cut and polished for use in jewellery. **2** *informal* someone or something that is valued, admired, etc. [Anglo-Saxon as *gim*: from Latin *gemma* a bud or precious stone]

Gemini *singular noun* (*pl* in sense b ***Geminis***) *astrol* **a** the third sign of the zodiac; **b** a person born between 21 May and 20 June, under this sign. ▪ **Geminian** *adj, noun*. [14c: Latin, meaning 'twins']

gemsbok /'gɛmzbɒk; *S Afr* 'xɛmz-/ *noun* a large S African antelope with long straight horns and distinctive markings on its face and underparts. [18c: Dutch, meaning 'male chamois']

gemstone see under **gem**

gen *noun, informal* (*esp* **the gen**) the required or relevant information. [1940s: from *gen*eral information]

PHRASAL VERBS **gen up on sth** (***genned up, genning up***) to obtain the relevant information about it.

Gen. *abbrev* General.

gendarme /'ʒɒndɑːm/ *noun* a member of an armed police force in France and other French-speaking countries. [18c: French, from *gens d'armes* armed people]

gender *noun* **1** the condition of being male or female; one's sex. **2** *grammar* **a** in many languages: a system of dividing nouns and pronouns into different classes, often related to the sex of the persons and things denoted; **b** any of these classes, usu two or three in European languages (see **feminine**, **masculine** and **neuter**). [14c: from Latin *genus* kind or sort]

gene *noun* the basic unit of inheritance, consisting of a sequence of DNA that occupies a specific position on a **chromosome**. It is the means by which specific characteristics are passed on from parents to offspring. [20c: from German *Gen*]

genealogy *noun* (***-ies***) **1 a** a person's direct line of descent from an ancestor; **b** a diagram or scheme showing this. **2** the study of the history and lineage of families. **3** the study of the development of plants and animals into present-day forms. ▪ **genealogical** *adj*. ▪ **genealogically** *adv*. ▪ **genealogist** *noun*. [13c: from Greek *genealogia*]

genera *pl of* **genus**

general *adj* **1** relating to, involving or applying to all or most parts, people or things; widespread, not specific, limited, or localized: *as a general rule*. **2** not detailed or definite; rough; vague: *general description • in general terms*. **3** not specialized: *general knowledge*. **4** (**the general**) generalized non-specific ideas: *turn from the general to the particular*. **5** (esp before or after a job title) chief: *general manager • director-general*. ▸ *noun* **1** in Britain: an army officer of the rank below field marshal. **2** in the USA: an army officer of the rank below the General of the Army. **3** an officer in the US Air Force of the rank below the General of the Air Force. **4** the commander of a whole army. **5** any leader, esp when regarded as a competent one. **6** the head of a religious order, eg the Jesuits. [13c: from Latin *generalis* meaning 'applying to the whole group']

IDIOMS **in general** usually; mostly.

general anaesthetic *noun, med* a drug that causes a complete loss of consciousness. Compare **local anaesthetic**.

General Certificate of Education *noun* (abbrev **GCE**) in England and Wales: a qualification obtainable for various school subjects by passing an examination at Advanced (or A) level and Special (or S) level and, also formerly, at Ordinary level.

General Certificate of Secondary Education *noun* (abbreviation **GCSE**) in England and Wales: a school-leaving qualification in one or more subjects.

general election *noun* a national election in which the voters of every constituency in the country elect a member of parliament. Compare **by-election**.

generalissimo *noun* a supreme commander of the combined armed forces in some countries, who often also has political power. [17c: Italian, superlative of *generale* general]

generality *noun* (*pl* in sense 2 ***-ies***) **1** the quality or fact of being general. **2** a general rule or principle. **3** (**the generality**) the majority.

generalize *or* **-ise** *verb* **1** *intr* to speak in general terms or form general opinions, esp ones that are too general to be applied to all individual cases. **2** to make something more general, esp to make it applicable to a wider variety of cases. ▪ **generalization** *noun*.

generally *adv* **1** usually. **2** without considering details; broadly. **3** as a whole; collectively.

general practitioner *noun* (abbrev **GP**) a community doctor who treats most illnesses and complaints, and refers appropriate cases to specialists.

general staff *noun* military officers who advise senior officers on policy, administration, etc.

general strike *noun* a strike by workers in all or most of the industries in a country at the same time.

generate *verb* to produce or create something. [16c: from Latin *generare*]

generation *noun* **1** the act or process of producing something, eg electricity or ideas. **2** *biol* of living organisms: the act or process of producing offspring. **3** all the individuals produced at a particular stage in the natural descent of humans or animals: *the younger generation • generation differences*. **4** the average period between the birth of a person or animal and the birth of their offspring, which, in humans, is usu considered to be about 30 years: *three generations ago*. **5** a single stage in a person's descent. *as adj and in compounds*: *second-generation American*. ▪ **generational** *adj*.

generation gap *noun* the extent to which two, usu successive, generations differ, eg in lifestyles, ideas, values, etc and the lack of mutual understanding that results from these differences.

generative *adj, formal* **1** able to produce or generate. **2** relating to production or creation.

generator *noun, elec* a machine that converts mechanical energy into electrical energy, eg a **dynamo**.

generic *adj* **1** belonging, referring or relating to any member of a general class or group. **2 a** esp of a drug: not protected by a trademark and sold as a specific brand; non-proprietary: *generic aspirin*; **b** applied to supermarket products: sold without a brand name. **3** applied to a product name that was originally a trademark: now used as the general name for the product. **4** *biol* belonging, referring or relating to a **genus**. [17c: from **genus**]

generous *adj* **1** giving or willing to give or help unselfishly. **2** eg of a donation: large and given unselfishly. **3** large; ample; plentiful: *generous portions*. **4** kind; willing to forgive: *of generous spirit*. ▪ **generosity** *noun* (**-*ies***) ▪ **generously** *adv*. [16c: from Latin *generosus* of noble birth]

genesis *noun* (**-*ses*** /-siːz/) **1** a beginning or origin. **2** (**Genesis**) the title of the first book in the Old Testament which describes the creation of the world. [From Greek, meaning 'origin' or 'creation']

genetic *adj* **1** referring or relating to **genes** or **genetics**; inherited: *a genetic defect*. **2** belonging or relating to origin. ▪ **genetically** *adv*. [19c: from **gene**]

genetically modified *adj* (abbrev **GM**) altered as a result of **genetic manipulation**.

genetic fingerprinting *noun, genetics* the process of analyzing samples of DNA from body tissues or fluids in order to establish a person's identity in criminal investigations, paternity disputes, etc. Also called **DNA fingerprinting**.

genetic manipulation *or* (*informal*) **genetic engineering** *noun* a form of **biotechnology** in which the genes of an organism are deliberately altered by a method other than conventional breeding in order to change characteristics of the organism.

genetics *singular noun* the scientific study of heredity and of the mechanisms by which characteristics are transmitted from one generation to the next. ▪ **geneticist** *noun*.

genial *adj* **1** cheerful; friendly; sociable. **2** of climate: pleasantly warm or mild. ▪ **geniality** *noun*. ▪ **genially** *adv*. [16c: from Latin *genialis*]

genic *adj* relating to a **gene**.

genie *noun* (***genies*** *or* ***genii*** /-nɪaɪ/) in folk or fairy stories: a spirit with the power to grant wishes. [18c: from French *génie*]

genii *pl of* **genie**

genital *adj* **1** relating to or affecting the **genitals**. **2** connected with or relating to reproduction. [14c]

genitals *or* **genitalia** /-ˈteɪlɪə/ *plural noun* the external sexual organs. [14c: from Latin *genitalis*, from *gignere* to beget]

genitive *grammar, noun* (abbrev **gen.**) **1** in certain languages, eg Latin, Greek and German: the form or **case**[2] of a noun, pronoun or adj that shows possession or association. **2** a noun, etc in this case. ▸ *adj* belonging to or in this case. [14c: from Latin *genitivus*]

genito-urinary *adj* relating to both the **genital** and the **urinary** organs and functions.

genius *noun* **1** someone who has outstanding creative or intellectual ability. **2** such ability. **3** a person who exerts a powerful influence on another (whether good or bad). [16c: Latin, meaning 'guardian spirit' or 'deity']

genocide *noun* the deliberate killing of a whole nation or people. ▪ **genocidal** *adj*. [20c: from Greek *genos* race + **-cide**]

genome /ˈdʒiːnoum/ *noun, genetics* the complete set of genetic material in the cell of a living organism. [20c: from German *genom*]

genomics /dʒɪˈnɑmɪks/ *singular noun* the study of **genomes**.

genotype *noun, genetics* the particular set of genes possessed by an organism. [20c: from German *Genotypus*]

genre /ˈʒɑ̃rə/ *noun* **1** a particular type or kind of literature, music or other artistic work. **2** (*in full* **genre painting**) *art* a type of painting featuring scenes from everyday life. [19c: French, literally 'kind' or 'type']

gent *noun, informal* a gentleman. See also **gents**.

genteel *adj* **1** *derog* polite or refined in an artificial, affected way approaching snobbishness. **2** well-mannered. **3** *old use, facetious* referring to or suitable for the upper classes. [16c: from French *gentil* well-bred]

gentian /ˈdʒɛnʃən/ *noun* a low-growing plant with funnel-shaped or bell-shaped flowers, often deep blue in colour. [14c: from Latin *gentiana*]

gentile *noun* (*often* **Gentile**) **a** used esp by Jews: a person who is not Jewish; **b** used esp by Mormons: a person who is not Mormon. ▸ *adj* **1** (*often* **Gentile**) **a** used esp by Jews: not Jewish; **b** used esp by Mormons: not Mormon. **2** *now rare* relating to a nation or tribe. [15c: from Latin *gentilis*]

gentility *noun* **1** good manners and respectability. **2** *old use* **a** noble birth; **b** people of the upper classes. [14c: from French *gentilité*]

gentle *adj* **1** mild-mannered, not stern, coarse or violent. **2** light and soft; not harsh, loud, strong, etc: *a gentle breeze*. **3** moderate; mild: *a gentle reprimand*. **4** of hills, etc: rising gradually. ▪ **gentleness** *noun*. ▪ **gently** *adv*. [16c: from French *gentil* well-bred]

gentleman *noun* **1** a polite name for a man: *Ask that gentleman*. **2** a polite, well-mannered, respectable man. **3** a man from the upper classes. ▪ **gentlemanly** *adj*.

gentlemen's agreement *or* **gentleman's agreement** *noun* an agreement based on honour and thus not legally binding.

gentlewoman *noun, dated* an upper-class woman.

gentrify *verb* (**-*ies*, -*ied***) **1** to convert or renovate (housing) to conform to middle-class taste. **2** to make (an area) middle-class. ▪ **gentrification** *noun*. [1970s: from **gentry**]

gentry *plural noun* (*esp* **the gentry**) people belonging to the class directly below the nobility: *the landed gentry*. [14c: from French *genterise* nobility]

gents *singular noun* (*often* **the gents**) a men's public toilet.

genuflect *verb, intr* to bend one's knee in worship or as a sign of respect. ▪ **genuflection** *or* **genuflexion** *noun*. [17c: from Latin *genu* knee + *flectere* to bend]

genuine *adj* **1** authentic, not artificial or fake. **2** honest; sincere. [17c: from Latin *genuinus* natural]

genus /ˈdʒiːnəs, ˈdʒɛnəs/ *noun* (***genera*** /ˈdʒɛnərə/ *or* ***genuses***) **1** *biol* in taxonomy: any of the groups into which a **family** (sense 7) is divided and which in turn is subdivided into one or more **species** (sense 1). **2** a class divided into several subordinate classes. [16c: Latin, meaning 'race' or 'kind']

geo- *combining form, signifying* **1** the Earth. **2** geography or geographical. [From Greek ge earth]

geocentric *adj* **1** of a system, esp the universe or the solar system: having the Earth as its centre. **2** measured from the centre of the Earth. [17c]

geodesic *or* **geodetic** *adj* **1** relating to or determined by **geodesy**. **2** denoting an artificial structure composed of a large number of identical components, esp a dome. ▸ *noun* a geodesic line. [19c]

geodesic line *noun, maths, surveying, etc* a line on a plane or curved surface that represents the shortest distance between two points.

geodesy /dʒiːˈɒdəsɪ/ *noun* the scientific study of the Earth's shape and size. [16c: from Greek *geodaisia*]

geography *noun* (**-ies**) **1** the scientific study of the Earth's surface, esp its physical features, climate, resources, population, etc. **2** *informal* the layout of a place. ▪ **geographer** *noun*. ▪ **geographical** *adj*. [16c]

geological time *noun* a time scale in which the Earth's history is subdivided into units known as **eon**s, which are further subdivided into **era**s, **period**s, and **epoch**s.

geology *noun* **1** the scientific study of the origins and structure, composition, etc of the Earth, esp its rocks. **2** the distinctive geological features of an area, country, etc. ▪ **geological** *adj*. ▪ **geologist** *noun*. [18c]

geomagnetism *noun* **1** the Earth's magnetic field. **2** the scientific study of this. ▪ **geomagnetic** *adj*. [20c]

geometric *or* **geometrical** *adj* **1** relating to or using the principles of **geometry**. **2** of a pattern, design, style of architecture, etc: using or consisting of lines, points, or simple geometrical figures such as circles or triangles.

geometric mean see under **mean**[3]

geometric progression *noun, maths* a sequence of numbers in which the ratio between one term and the next remains constant, eg 1, 2, 4, 8 …

geometry *noun* the branch of mathematics dealing with lines, angles, shapes, etc and their relationships. [14c: from **geo-** + Greek *metron* a measure]

geomorphology *noun* the study of the nature and history of the landforms on the surface of the Earth. ▪ **geomorphological** *adj*. ▪ **geomorphologist** *noun*. [1890s]

geophysics *singular noun* the scientific study of the physical properties of the Earth. ▪ **geophysical** *adj*. ▪ **geophysicist** *noun*. [1880s]

Geordie *informal,noun* **1** someone who was born on or who lives on Tyneside. **2** the Tyneside dialect. ▸ *adj* belonging or relating to Tyneside, its people, or their dialect. [19c: diminutive of the name *George*]

georgette *noun* a kind of thin silk material. [20c: named after Georgette de la Plante, French dressmaker]

Georgian *adj* **1** belonging to or typical of the reigns of King George I, II, III and IV, ie the period 1714–1830. **2** of literature: typical of the kind that was written during the reign of King George V, especially the period 1910–20. **3** relating to the Caucasian republic of Georgia, its people or their language. **4** relating to the US state of Georgia or its people.

geosphere *noun* **1** the non-living part of the Earth, including the lithosphere, hydrosphere and atmosphere. **2** the solid part of the Earth, as opposed to the atmosphere and hydrosphere. [19c]

geostationary *adj, technical* of an artificial satellite above the Earth's equator: taking exactly 24 hours to complete one orbit and so appearing to remain stationary above a fixed point on the Earth's surface. [20c]

geothermal *adj, technical* **1** relating to the internal heat of the Earth. **2** relating to or using the energy that can be extracted from this heat. [19c]

geranium *noun, botany* a plant or shrub with divided leaves and large flowers with five pink or purplish petals. [16c]

gerbil *noun* a small burrowing rodent with long hind legs and a long furry tail. [19c: from Latin *gerbillus* little jerboa]

geriatric *adj* **1** for or dealing with old people; relating to **geriatrics**: *geriatric medicine*. **2** *derog, informal* very old. ▸ *noun* an old person.

geriatrics *singular noun* the branch of medicine concerned with the health and care of the elderly. [20c: from Greek *geras* old age + *iatros* physician]

germ *noun* **1** a micro-organism, esp a bacterium or virus that causes disease. *as adj*: *germ warfare*. **2** the embryo of a plant, esp of wheat. **3** an origin or beginning: *the germ of a plan*. [17c: from Latin *germen* bud or sprout]

German *adj* belonging or relating to Germany, its language, or its inhabitants. ▸ *noun* **1** a native of Germany. **2** the official language of Germany. [16c: from Latin *Germanus*]

Germanic *noun* a branch of the Indo-European family of languages that includes both the modern and historical varieties and which is divided into **East Germanic** (Gothic and other extinct languages), **North Germanic** (Norwegian, Danish, Swedish, Icelandic) and **West Germanic** (English, Frisian, Dutch, Low German, High German). ▸ *adj* **1** relating to these languages or to the people speaking them. **2** typical of Germany or the Germans. [17c, meaning 'German']

germanium *noun, chem* (symbol **Ge**) a hard greyish-white metalloid element, widely used as a semiconductor. [19c: named after Germany, the native country of its discoverer, C A Winkler]

German measles *singular noun* **rubella**.

German shepherd dog *noun* a large dog with a thick coat, a long pointed muzzle, and pointed ears. Also called **Alsatian**.

germicide *noun* any agent that destroys disease-causing micro-organisms such as bacteria and viruses. ▪ **germicidal** *adj*. [19c: **germ** + **-cide**]

germinate *verb* **1** *intr, biol* of a seed or spore: to show the first signs of development into a new individual. **2 a** to make (a seed, an idea, etc) begin to grow; **b** *intr* to come into being or existence. ▪ **germination** *noun*. [17c: from Latin *germinare*]

germ warfare *noun* the use of bacteria to inflict disease on an enemy in war.

gerontology *noun* the scientific study of old age, the ageing process and the problems of elderly people. ▪ **gerontological** *adj*. ▪ **gerontologist** *noun*. [Early 20c: from Greek *geron* old man + *logos* word or reason]

gerrymander *verb, derog* **1** to arrange or change the boundaries of (one or more electoral constituencies) so as to favour one political party. **2** to manipulate (eg data, a situation, etc) unfairly. ▪ **gerrymandering** *noun*. [19c: named after Massachusetts Governor Elbridge Gerry and **salamander**, from the shape on the map of one of his electoral districts after manipulation]

gerund *noun, grammar* a noun formed from a verb and which refers to an action. In English gerunds end in *-ing*, eg 'the *baking* of bread' and '*Smoking* damages your health'. [16c: from Latin *gerundium*, from *gerere* to carry]

gesso /'dʒɛsoʊ/ *noun* (***gessoes***) plaster for sculpting with or painting on. [16c: Italian, from Latin *gypsum*]

Gestapo /gə'stɑːpoʊ/ *noun*, **1** *hist* the secret police in Nazi Germany. **2** (**gestapo**) *derog* any similar secret police organization. [1930s: from German *Geheime Staatspolizei*, secret state police]

gestate *verb, tr & intr* **1** *zool* of a mammal: to carry (young) or be carried in the uterus, and to undergo physical development, in the period from fertilization to birth. **2** to develop (an idea, etc) slowly in the mind. ▪ **gestation** *noun*. [19c: from Latin *gestare* to carry]

gesticulate *verb* **1** *intr* to make gestures, esp when speaking. **2** to express (eg feelings) by gestures. ▪ **gesticulation** *noun*. [17c: from Latin *gesticulare*]

gesture *noun* **1** a movement of a part of the body as an expression of meaning, esp when speaking. **2** something done to communicate feelings or intentions, esp when these are friendly. **3** *derog* something done simply as a formality. ▸*verb* **1** *intr* to make gestures. **2** to express (eg feelings) with gestures. ▪ **gestural** *adj*. [15c: from Latin *gestus*]

get *verb* (***got***, *past participle* ***got*** *or* (*N Am*) ***gotten***, ***getting***) **1** to receive or obtain. **2** to have or possess. **3** *tr & intr* (*also* **get across** *or* **get sb across** *or* **away, to, through**, *etc*) to go or make them go, move, travel or arrive as specified: *tried to get past him* • *Will you get him to bed at 8?* • *got to Paris on Friday.* **4** (*often* **get sth down, in, out**, *etc*) to fetch, take, or bring it as specified: *Get it down from the shelf.* **5** to put into a particular state or condition: *Don't get it wet* • *got him into trouble.* **6** *intr* to become: *I got angry.* **7** to catch (a disease, etc): *She got measles and couldn't come.* **8** to order or persuade: *Get him to help us.* **9** *informal* to receive (a broadcast, etc): *can't get the World Service.* **10** *informal* to make contact with someone, esp by telephone: *never get him at home.* **11** *informal* to arrive at (a number, etc) by calculation. **12** *intr, informal* to receive permission (to do something): *Can you get to stay out late?* **13** *informal* to prepare (a meal): *I'll get the breakfast.* **14** *informal* to buy or pay for something: *got her some flowers for her birthday.* **15** *informal* to suffer: *got a broken arm.* **16** *informal* to receive something as punishment: *got ten years for armed robbery.* **17** (**get sb**) *informal* to attack, punish, or otherwise cause harm to them: *I'll get you for that!* **18** *informal* to annoy someone: *It really gets me.* **19** *informal* to understand something. **20** *informal* to hear something: *I didn't quite get his name.* **21** *informal* to affect someone emotionally. **22** *informal* to baffle someone: *You've got me there.* ▸*noun, derog slang* a stupid or contemptible person; a git. ▸*exclam* clear off! get lost! [13c: from Norse *geta* to obtain or beget]

IDIOMS **be getting on 1** of a person: to grow old. **2** of time, etc: to grow late. **be getting on for** *informal* to be approaching (a certain time or age). **get along with you!** *informal* **1** go away! **2** an expression of disbelief. **get by** *informal* **1** to manage to live. **2** to be just about acceptable. **get one's own back** *informal* to have one's revenge. **get somewhere** *informal* to make progress. **get there** *informal* to make progress towards or achieve one's final aim. **have got to** to have to, to be required to do something.

PHRASAL VERBS **get about** *or* **around** *informal* **1** to travel; to go from place to place. **2** of a rumour, etc: to circulate. **get sth across** to make it understood. **get along with sb** *informal* to be on friendly terms with them. **get at sb** *informal* **1** to criticize or victimize them persistently. **2** *informal* to influence them by dishonest means, eg bribery. **get at sth 1** to reach or take hold of it. **2** *informal* to suggest or imply it. **get away 1** to leave or be free to leave. **2** to escape. **3** *informal* as an exclamation: used to express disbelief, shock, etc. **get away with sth** to commit (an offence or wrongdoing, etc) without being caught or punished. **get back at sb** *or* **get sb back** *informal* to take revenge on them. **get sb down** *informal* to make them sad or depressed. **get sth down 1** to manage to swallow it. **2** to write it down. **get down to sth** to apply oneself to (a task or piece of work). **get in** of a political party: to be elected to power. **get into sth** *informal* to develop a liking or enthusiasm for it. **get off** *or* **get sb off** *informal* **1** to escape, or cause them to escape, with no punishment or with only the stated punishment: *was charged but got off* • *managed to get him off with a warning.* **2** to fall asleep or send (eg a child) to sleep. **get on** *informal* to make progress; to be successful. **get on with sb** to have a friendly relationship with them. **get on with sth** to continue working on it or dealing or progressing with it. **get over sb** *or* **sth** to be no longer emotionally affected by them or it. **get over sth** to recover from (an illness, disappointment, etc). **get sth over** to explain it successfully; to make it understood. **get sth over with** to deal with (something unpleasant) as quickly as possible. **get round** *informal* of information, a rumour, etc: to become generally known. **get round sb** *informal* to persuade them or win their approval or permission. **get round sth** to successfully pass by or negotiate (a problem, etc). **get round to sth** *or* **sb** to deal with it or them eventually. **get through sth 1** to complete (a task, piece of work, etc). **2** to use it steadily until it is finished: *got through a bottle of whisky every day.* **3** *informal* to pass (a test, etc). **get through to sb 1** to make contact with them by telephone. **2** to make them understand. **get to sb** *informal* to annoy them. **get up 1** to get out of bed. **2** to stand up. **3** of the wind, etc: to become strong. **get up to sth** *informal* to do or be involved in it, esp when it is bad, unwelcome or not approved of.

getaway *noun* an escape, esp after committing a crime. *as adj*: *getaway car.*

get-out *noun* a means or instance of escape. *as adj*: *a get-out clause.*

get-together *noun, informal* an informal meeting.

get-up *noun, informal* an outfit or clothes, esp when considered strange or remarkable.

get-up-and-go *noun, informal* energy.

geyser /'giːzə(r), 'gaɪzə(r)/ *noun* **1** *geol* in an area of volcanic activity: a type of hot spring that intermittently spouts hot water and steam into the air. **2** a domestic appliance for heating water rapidly. [18c: from Icelandic *Geysir*, the name of a famous hot spring]

ghastly *adj* (***-ier***, ***-iest***) **1** extremely frightening, hideous or horrific. **2** *informal* very bad. **3** *informal* very ill. ▸ *adv, informal* extremely; unhealthily: *ghastly pale.* ▪ **ghastliness** *noun.* [14c: from obsolete *gast* to terrify]

ghat /gɔːt/ *noun, Indian subcontinent* **1** a mountain pass. **2** a set of steps leading down to a river. **3** (in full **burning ghat**) the site of a Hindu funeral pyre at the top of a river ghat. [17c: Hindi, meaning 'descent']

ghee *or* **ghi** /giː/ *noun* in Indian cookery: clarified butter. [17c: from Hindi *ghi*]

gherkin *noun* **1** a variety of cucumber that bears very small fruits. **2** a small or immature fruit of a cucumber, used for pickling. [17c: from Dutch *augurkje*]

ghetto *noun* (***ghettos*** *or* ***ghettoes***) **1** *derog* a poor area densely populated by people from a deprived social group, esp a racial minority. **2** *hist* a part of a city to which Jews were formerly restricted. [17c: Italian]

ghetto blaster *noun, informal* a large portable radio and cassette or CD player. [1980s, orig US]

ghettoize *or* **-ise** *verb* to think of (a group of people or things) as being confined to a specific restricted function or area of activity. ▪ **ghettoization** *noun.*

ghi see **ghee**

ghillie see **gillie**

ghost *noun* **1** the spirit of a dead person when it is visible in some form to a living person. **2** a suggestion, hint or trace. **3** a faint shadow attached to the image on a television screen. ▸ *verb, tr & intr* to be a **ghost writer** for a person or of (some written work). [Anglo-Saxon *gast*]

ghostly *adj* **1** belonging to or like a ghost or ghosts. **2** relating to or suggesting the presence of ghosts. ▪ **ghostliness** *noun.*

ghost town *noun* a deserted town, esp one that was formerly thriving.

ghost writer *noun* someone who writes books, speeches, etc on behalf of another person who is credited as their author.

ghoul *noun* **1** someone who is interested in morbid or disgusting things. **2 a** in Arab mythology: a demon that robs graves and eats dead bodies; **b** an evil spirit or presence. ▪ **ghoulish** *adj.* [18c: from Arabic *ghul*]

GHz *abbrev* gigahertz (see **giga-**).

GI *noun, informal* a soldier in the US army, esp during World War II. [20c: from Government Issue]

giant *noun* **1** in stories: a huge, extremely strong creature of human form. **2** *informal* an unusually large person or animal. **3** a person, group, etc of exceptional ability, importance or size: *corporate giants.* ▸ *adj* **1** *informal* huge: *giant portions.* **2** belonging to a particularly large species: *giant tortoise.* ▪ **giantess** *noun* a female giant. [13c: from Greek *gigas*]

gib /dʒɪb/ *noun* a small metal or wooden wedge used for keeping a machine part in place. ▸ *verb* (***gibbed, gibbing***) to secure with a gib. [18c]

gibber *verb, intr* **1** to talk so fast that one cannot be understood. **2** *derog* to talk foolishly. ▪ **gibbering** *adj.* [17c: imitating the sound]

gibberish *noun* **1** speech that is meaningless or difficult to understand. **2** utter nonsense. [16c]

gibbet *noun, hist* **1** a gallows-like frame on which the bodies of executed criminals were hung as a public warning. **2** a gallows. [13c: from French *gibet* gallows]

gibbon /ˈgɪbən/ *noun* the smallest of the anthropoid apes, with very long arms. [18c: French]

gibbous /ˈgɪbəs/ *adj, technical* of the moon or a planet: not fully illuminated but more than half illuminated. [17c: from Latin *gibbus* hump]

gibe[1] *or* **jibe** /dʒaɪb/ *verb, intr* to mock, scoff or jeer. ▸ *noun* a jeer. [16c: from French *giber* to treat roughly]

gibe[2] see **gybe**

giblets *plural noun* the heart, liver and other internal organs of a chicken or other fowl. [15c: from French *gibelet* game stew]

giddy *adj* (***-ier, -iest***) **1** suffering an unbalancing spinning sensation. **2** causing such a sensation. **3** *literary* overwhelmed by feelings of excitement or pleasure. **4** light-hearted and carefree; frivolous. ▪ **giddily** *adv.* ▪ **giddiness** *noun.* [Anglo-Saxon *gidig* insane]

GIF /gɪf/ *abbrev, comput* graphic interchange format, a standard image file format.

gift *noun* **1** something given; a present. **2** a natural ability. **3** the act or process of giving: *the gift of a book.* **4** *informal* something easily obtained, made easily available or simply easy. ▸ *verb, formal* to give something as a present to someone. [13c: from Norse *gipt*]

IDIOMS **look a gift horse in the mouth** *usu with negatives* to find fault with a gift or unexpected opportunity.

gifted *adj* having a great natural ability.

gig[1] *noun* **1** *hist* a small open two-wheeled horse-drawn carriage. **2** a small rowing boat carried on a ship. [18c]

gig[2] *informal, noun* **1** a pop, jazz or folk concert. **2** a musician's booking to perform, esp for one night only. ▸ *verb* (***gigged, gigging***) *intr* to play a gig or gigs.

giga- *prefix, denoting* **1** in the metric system: ten to the power of nine (10^9), ie one thousand million: *gigahertz.* **2** *comput* two to the power of thirty (2^{30}): *gigabyte.* [1940s: from Greek *gigas* giant]

gigantic *adj* huge; enormous. ▪ **gigantically** *adv.* [17c: from Greek *gigantikos,* from *gigas* giant]

gigantism *noun, biol* **1** excessive overgrowth of the whole human body. **2** excessive size in plants. [19c]

giggle *verb, intr* to laugh quietly in short bursts or in a nervous or silly way. ▸ *noun* **1** such a laugh. **2** (**the giggles**) a fit of giggling. **3** *informal* a funny person, situation, thing, activity, etc: *the film was a right giggle.* ▪ **giggly** *adj* (***-ier, -iest***). [16c: imitating the sound]

gigolo /ˈdʒɪgəloʊ/ *noun, derog* a young, and usu attractive, man who is paid by an older woman to be her companion, escort and/or lover. [20c: French]

gigot /ˈdʒɪgət/ *noun* a leg of lamb or mutton. [16c: French]

gild[1] *verb* (***gilded*** *or* ***gilt***) **1** to cover something with a thin coating of gold or something similar. **2** to give something a falsely attractive or valuable appearance. [Anglo-Saxon, from *gyldan* gold]

IDIOMS **gild the lily** to try to improve something that is already beautiful enough.

gild[2] see **guild**

gilder see **guilder**

gill[1] /gɪl/ *noun* **1** in all fishes and many other aquatic animals: a respiratory organ that extracts dissolved oxygen from the surrounding water. **2** (**gills**) *informal* the flesh around the jaw. [14c]

gill[2] /dʒɪl/ *noun* in the UK: a unit of liquid measure equal to 142.1ml or a quarter of a pint. [13c: from French *gelle*]

gillie *or* **ghillie** *noun* a guide to a stalker or fisherman, esp in Scotland. [19c: from Gaelic *gille* boy]

gilt[1] *adj* covered with a thin coating of gold or apparently so covered; gilded. ▸ *noun* **1** gold or a gold-like substance used in gilding. **2** (**gilts**) gilt-edged securities. **3** glitter; superficial attractiveness; glamour. ▸ *verb, past tense, past participle of* **gild**[1]. [14c]

gilt[2] *noun* a young female pig. [15c: from Norse *gyltr*]

gilt-edged *adj* **1** of a book: having pages with gilded edges. **2** of the highest quality. **3** of government securities with a fixed rate of interest: able to be sold at face value. See also **gilts** at **gilt**[1].

gimcrack /ˈdʒɪmkrak/ *derog, adj* cheap, showy and badly made. ▸ *noun* a cheap and showy article. [18c: from 14c *gibecrake* fancy woodwork]

gimlet *noun* a T-shaped hand-tool for boring holes in wood. [15c: from French *guimbelet*]

gimmick *noun, derog* a scheme or object used to attract attention or publicity, esp to bring in customers. ▪ **gimmickry** *noun*. ▪ **gimmicky** *adj*. [20c]

gin[1] *noun* an alcoholic spirit made from barley, rye or maize and flavoured with juniper berries. [18c: from Dutch *genever* juniper]

gin[2] *noun* (*also* **gin trap**) a wire noose laid as a snare or trap for catching game. ▸ *verb* (***ginned, ginning***) to snare or trap (game) in a gin. [13c: from French *engin* engine or ingenuity]

gin[3] see **gin rummy**

ginger *noun* **1** an aromatic spicy swollen root, often dried and ground to a powder and widely used as a flavouring, or preserved in syrup. **2** the tropical plant from which this root is obtained. **3** a reddish-brown colour. ▸ *adj* **1** flavoured with ginger. **2 a** of hair: reddish-orange in colour; **b** reddish-brown in colour. ▸ *verb* (*usu* **ginger up**) *informal* to urge, persuade or force someone or something to become more lively, active, interesting or efficient. ▪ **gingery** *adj*. [Anglo-Saxon *ingifer*]

ginger ale *or* **ginger beer** *noun* a non-alcoholic fizzy drink flavoured with ginger.

gingerbread *noun* a type of cake flavoured with treacle and ginger.

ginger group *noun* a small group within a larger one (such as a political party) which urges stronger or more radical action.

gingerly *adv* with delicate caution. ▸ *adj* very cautious or wary. [17c: perhaps from French *gensor* delicate]

gingham /ˈgɪŋəm/ *noun* striped or checked cotton cloth. *as adj*: *a gingham frock*. [17c: from Malay *ginggang* striped]

gingivitis /dʒɪndʒɪˈvaɪtɪs/ *noun, med* inflammation of the gums. [19c: from Latin *gingiva* gum]

ginormous *adj, informal* exceptionally huge. [20c: from **gigantic** + **enormous**]

gin rummy *or* **gin** *noun, cards* a type of **rummy** in which players have the option of ending the round at any time when their unmatched cards count ten or less.

ginseng /ˈdʒɪnsɛŋ/ *noun* **1 a** a plant cultivated in E Asia for its roots; **b** a similar American species of this plant. **2** the aromatic root of either of these plants. **3** a preparation derived from the root of either or these plants, widely used as a tonic, stimulant and aphrodisiac. [17c: Chinese *ren-shen*]

gin trap see under **gin**[2]

gip same as **gyp**

Gipsy see **Gypsy**

giraffe *noun* (***giraffes*** *or* ***giraffe***) a very tall African mammal with an extremely long neck and legs, a small head, and large eyes. [17c: from Arabic *zarafah*]

gird *verb* (***girded*** *or* ***girt***) *literary* to encircle or fasten something (esp part of the body) with a belt or something similar. [Anglo-Saxon *gyrdan*]

IDIOMS **gird** *or* **gird up one's loins** to prepare oneself for action.

girder *noun* a large beam of wood, iron or steel used to support a floor, wall, road or bridge. [17c: from **gird**]

girdle[1] *noun* **1** a woman's close-fitting elasticated undergarment that covers the area from waist to thigh. **2** *old use* a belt or cord worn round the waist. **3** a surrounding part, esp such a part of the body: *pelvic girdle*. ▸ *verb* **1** to put a girdle on someone or something. **2** *literary* to surround something. [Anglo-Saxon *gyrdel*, from **gird**]

girdle[2] see **griddle**

girl *noun* **1** a female child. **2** a daughter. **3** *often offensive* a young woman, esp an unmarried one. **4** *often offensive* a woman of any age. **5** *informal* a sweetheart: *Dave is bringing his girl home for tea*. ▪ **girlhood** *noun*. [13c *gerle, girle* and *gurle* a child]

girlfriend *noun* **1** a female romantic partner. **2** a female friend.

girlie *or* **girly** *informal, adj* **1** of a magazine, picture, etc: featuring naked or nearly naked young women in erotic poses. **2** *derog* girlish, esp in being overly feminine.

girlish *adj* like a girl. ▪ **girlishly** *adv*. ▪ **girlishness** *noun*.

giro /ˈdʒaɪəroʊ/ *noun* **1** a banking system by which money can be transferred from one account directly to another. **2** *Brit informal* a social security benefit received in the form of a cheque. [19c: Italian, meaning 'turn' or 'transfer']

girt *past tense, past participle of* **gird**

girth *noun* **1** the distance round something such as a tree or a person's waist. **2** the strap round a horse's belly that holds a saddle in place. ▸ *verb* to put a girth on (a horse). [From Norse *gjörth* belt]

gismo *or* **gizmo** *noun, informal* a gadget. [1940s: US]

gist /dʒɪst/ *noun* the general meaning or main point of something said or written. [18c: French, third person of *gesir(en)* to consist (in)]

git *noun, derog slang* a stupid or contemptible person. [20c: variant of **get**, and now the commoner form]

gite *or* **gïte** /ʒiːt/ *noun* in France: a self-catering holiday cottage. [20c: French, from *giste* a resting place]

give *verb* (*past tense* ***gave,*** *past participle* ***given***) **1** to transfer ownership of something; to transfer possession of something temporarily: *gave him my watch* • *Give me your bags*. **2** to provide or administer: *give advice* • *give medicine*. **3** to produce: *Cows give milk*. **4** to perform (an action, service, etc): *give a smile* • *She gave a lecture on beetles*. **5** to pay: *gave £20 for it*. **6** *intr* to make a donation: *Please give gen-*

erously. **7** (*also* **give sth up**) to sacrifice it: *give one's life.* **8** to be the cause or source of something: *gives me pain.* **9** *intr* to yield or break: *give under pressure.* **10** to organize something at one's own expense: *give a party.* **11** to have something as a result: *four into twenty gives five.* **12** to reward or punish with something: *was given 20 years.* **13** *informal* to agree to or admit something; to concede: *I'll give you that.* **14** *sport* to declare someone to be a specified thing: *be given offside.* ► *noun* capacity to yield; flexibility: *a board with plenty of give.* [Anglo-Saxon *gefan*]

IDIOMS **give and take** to make mutual concessions. **give as good as one gets** *informal* to respond to an attack with equal energy, force and effect. **give or take sth** *informal* allowing for a (specified) margin of error: *We have all the money, give or take a pound.* **give up the ghost** *informal* to die. **give way 1** to allow priority. **2** to collapse under pressure.

PHRASAL VERBS **give sb away 1** to betray them. **2** to present (the bride) to the bridegroom at a wedding ceremony. **give sth away 1** to hand it over as a gift. **2** to sell it at an incredibly low price. **3** to allow (a piece of information) to become known, usu by accident. **give in to sb** *or* **sth** to yield to them; to admit defeat. **give sth off** to produce or emit (eg a smell). **give out** *informal* to break down or come to an end. **give sth out 1** to announce or distribute it. **2** to emit (a sound, smell, etc). **give over!** *informal* usually as a command: to stop (doing it): *Give over shouting!* **give sth over 1** to transfer it. **2** to set it aside or devote it to some purpose. **give up** to admit defeat. **give oneself up** to surrender. **give oneself up to sth** to devote oneself to (a cause, etc). **give sth up** to renounce or quit (a habit, etc): *give up smoking.*

give-and-take *noun* **1** mutual willingness to accept the other's point of view. **2** a useful exchange of views.

giveaway *informal, noun* **1** an act of accidentally revealing secrets, etc. **2** something obtained extremely easily or cheaply: *That goal was a giveaway.* **3** a free gift. ► *adj* **1** extremely cheap. **2** free.

given *adj* **1** stated or specified. **2** admitted, assumed or accepted as true. ► *prep, conj* accepting (a specified thing) as a basis for discussion; assuming: *given that he is guilty.* ► *noun* something that is admitted, assumed or accepted as true: *His guilt is a given.* ► *verb, past participle of* **give**.

IDIOMS **given to sth** prone to it; having it as a habit.

gizmo see **gismo**

gizzard *noun* in birds, earthworms and certain other animals: a muscular chamber specialized for grinding up indigestible food. [14c: from French *guisier* fowl's liver]

glacé /ˈglɑseɪ/ *adj* **1** coated with a sugary glaze; candied: *glacé cherries.* **2** applied esp to thin silk and kid leather: glossy, shiny. [19c: French]

glacial *adj* **1** *geol, geog* **a** relating to or resembling a glacier; **b** caused by the action of a glacier. **2** referring or relating to ice or its effects. **3** hostile: *a glacial stare.* [17c in sense 2: from Latin *glacialis* icy]

glacial trough *noun, geog* a U-shaped river valley, caused by erosion of its sides by a moving glacier. Also called **U-shaped valley**.

glaciate *verb, geol, geog* **1** of land, etc: to become covered with glaciers or ice sheets. **2** to subject (land, etc) to the eroding action of moving glaciers or ice sheets. **3** to polish (rock, etc) by the action of ice. ▪ **glaciation** *noun.* [19c in this sense: from Latin *glaciare* to freeze]

glacier *noun* a large slow-moving body of ice. [18c: French, from *glace* ice]

glad *adj* (***gladder, gladdest***) **1** (*sometimes* **glad about sth**) happy or pleased. **2** (**glad of sth**) grateful for it: *I was glad of your support.* **3** very willing: *We are glad to help.* **4** *old use* bringing happiness: *glad tidings.* ▪ **gladly** *adv.* ▪ **gladness** *noun.* [Anglo-Saxon *glæd*]

gladden *verb* to make someone (or their heart, etc) happy or pleased.

glade *noun, literary* an open space in a wood or forest. [16c]

gladiator *noun* in ancient Rome: a man trained to fight against other men or animals in an arena. ▪ **gladiatorial** *adj.* [16c: Latin, meaning 'swordsman']

glad rags *plural noun, informal* one's best clothes.

glam *slang, adj* glamorous. ► *noun* glamour. [20c shortening]

glamorize *or* **-ise** *verb* **1** to make someone or something glamorous. **2** to romanticize. ▪ **glamorization** *noun.*

glamorous *adj* full of glamour. ▪ **glamorously** *adv.*

glamour *or* (*N Am*) **glamor** *noun* **1** the quality of being fascinatingly, if falsely, attractive. **2** great beauty or charm, esp when created by make-up, clothes, etc. [18c: Scots variant of *gramarye*, grammar, in the sense of 'a spell', from the old association of magic with learning]

glance *verb, usu intr* **1** (*often* **glance at sth** *or* **sb**) to look quickly or indirectly at it or them. **2** (*often* **glance over** *or* **through sth**) to read or look at it cursorily. **3** *tr & intr* (*often* **glance off**) **a** of a blow or weapon: to be deflected; to hit (a target) obliquely; **b** of light: to shine or reflect in flashes; to glint: *The sunlight glanced off the table.* ► *noun* **1** a brief (and often indirect) look. **2** a deflection. **3** *literary* a brief flash of light. [15c]

IDIOMS **at a glance** at once; from one brief look.

gland *noun* **1** *zool* in humans and animals: an organ that produces a specific chemical substance (eg a hormone) for use inside the body. **2** *botany* in plants: a specialized cell or group of cells involved in the secretion of plant products such as nectar, oils and resins. [17c: from Latin *glans* acorn]

glandes *pl of* **glans**

glandular *adj, zool, botany, etc* relating to, containing or affecting a gland or glands. [18c: from French *glandulaire*]

glandular fever *noun* infectious mononucleosis, a disease caused by the Epstein-Barr virus and with symptoms including swollen glands, sore throat, headache and fatigue.

glans *noun* (***glandes*** /ˈglandiːz/) *anatomy* an acorn-shaped part of the body.

glare *verb* **1** *intr* to stare angrily. **2** *intr* to be unpleasantly bright or shiny. **3** to express something with a glare. ► *noun* **1** an angry stare. **2** dazzling light. **3** *comput* excessive luminance emitted from a VDU screen or from light reflecting off a terminal. **4** brash colour or decoration. [13c: from Dutch *glaren* to gleam]

glaring *adj* **1** unpleasantly bright. **2** very obvious. ▪ **glaringly** *adv.*

glasnost /ˈglaznɒst/ *noun* a policy of openness and willingness to provide information on the part of governments, esp the Soviet government under Mikhail Gorbachev (President 1988–91). [20c: Russian, meaning 'speaking aloud, openness']

glass *noun* **1** a hard brittle non-crystalline material that is usu transparent or translucent. **2** an article made from this, eg a mirror, a lens or, esp, a drinking cup. **3** (*also* **glassful**) the amount held by a drinking glass. **4** (*also* **glassware**) articles made of glass: *a collection of glass*. **5** (**glasses**) spectacles. ▸ *verb* to supply or cover something with glass. [Anglo-Saxon *glæs*]

glass-blowing *noun* the process of shaping molten glass by blowing air into it through a tube. ▪ **glass-blower** *noun*.

glass ceiling *noun* an invisible but unmistakable barrier on the career ladder that certain categories of employees (esp women) find they cannot progress beyond. [1990s]

glass fibre *noun* glass that has been melted and then drawn out into extremely fine fibres, often set in plastic resin and used to make strong lightweight materials.

glasshouse *noun* **1** a building constructed mainly or entirely of glass, esp a greenhouse. **2** *slang* a military prison.

glassware see under **glass**

glass wool *noun* glass that has been spun into fine thread-like fibres, forming a wool-like mass, used in air filters, insulation, fibreglass, etc.

glassy *adj* (***-ier, -iest***) **1** like glass. **2** expressionless: *glassy eyes*.

Glaswegian /glaːzˈwiːdʒən, glaz-, -s-/ *noun* a citizen or inhabitant of, or person born in, Glasgow, Scotland. *adj* belonging or relating to Glasgow, its inhabitants or its distinctive dialect. [19c: modelled on *Galwegian* a native of Galloway]

glaucoma *noun, med, ophthalmol, etc* an eye disease in which increased pressure within the eyeball causes impaired vision and which, if left untreated, can lead to blindness. [17c: from Greek *glaukoma* cataract]

glaucous *adj* **1** having a dull green or blue colour. **2** *botany* having a blue-green waxy coating that can be rubbed off, eg the bloom of grapes. [17c: from Greek *glaukos* bluish-green or bluish-grey]

glaze *verb* **1** to fit glass panes into (a window, door, etc). **2** to achieve a glaze on or apply a glaze to (pottery). **3** in painting: to apply a glaze to something. **4** *intr* (*usu* **glaze over**) of the eyes: to become fixed and expressionless. **5** to achieve a glaze on or apply a glaze to (eg pastry). ▸ *noun* **1** a hard glassy coating on pottery or the material for this coating before it is applied or fired. **2** in painting: a thin coat of semi-transparent colour. **3 a** a shiny coating of milk, eggs or sugar on food; **b** the material for this coating before it is applied or baked. ▪ **glazed** *adj*. ▪ **glazing** *noun*. [14c as *glase*: orig a variant of **glass**]

glazier *noun* someone whose job is to fit glass in windows, doors, etc.

gleam *noun* **1** a gentle glow. **2** a brief flash of light, esp reflected light. **3** a brief appearance or sign: *a gleam of excitement in his eyes*. ▸ *verb, intr* **1** to glow gently. **2** to shine with brief flashes of light. **3** of an emotion, etc: to be shown briefly. [Anglo-Saxon *glæm*]

glean *verb* **1** to collect (information, etc) bit by bit, often with difficulty. **2** *tr & intr* to collect (loose grain and other useful remnants of a crop left in a field) after harvesting. ▪ **gleaner** *noun*. ▪ **gleanings** *plural noun* things that have been or may be gleaned, esp bits of information. [14c: from French *glener* in sense 2]

glebe *noun* **1** a piece of church-owned land providing income in rent, etc for the resident minister. **2** *poetic* land; a field. [14c: from Latin *gleba* clod]

glee *noun* (*pl* in sense 2 ***glees***) **1** great delight; joy. **2** a song with different parts for three or four unaccompanied voices, esp male voices. [Anglo-Saxon *glio* mirth or jesting]

glee club *noun* esp in the US: a choral society or choir.

gleeful *adj* joyful; merry. ▪ **gleefully** *adv*.

glen *noun* esp in Scotland: a long narrow valley. [15c: from Gaelic *gleann*]

glib *adj* (***glibber, glibbest***) *derog* speaking or spoken readily and persuasively, but neither sincere nor reliable: *glib explanations*. ▪ **glibly** *adv*. ▪ **glibness** *noun*. [16c: compare Dutch *glibberig* slippery]

glide *verb, intr* **1** to move smoothly and often without any visible effort: *glide along the ice*. **2** of an aircraft: to travel through the air or to land without engine power. **3** to travel through the air by glider. **4** to pass gradually: *glide into sleep*. ▸ *noun* **1** a gliding movement. **2** the controlled descent of an aircraft without engine power. ▪ **gliding** *adj*. [Anglo-Saxon *glidan* to slip]

glider *noun* a fixed-wing aircraft designed to glide and soar in air currents without using any form of engine power. ▪ **gliding** *noun* the sport of flying gliders.

glimmer *verb, intr* to glow faintly. ▸ *noun* **1** a faint glow; a twinkle. **2** a hint or trace: *a glimmer of hope*. ▪ **glimmering** *noun, adj*. [14c as *glemern*]

glimpse *noun* a very brief look. ▸ *verb* to see something or someone momentarily. [14c as *glymsen*]

glint *verb, intr* to give off tiny flashes of bright light. ▸ *noun* a brief flash of light. [15c as *glent*, prob from Scandinavian]

glissade *noun* **1** a sliding ballet step. **2** *mountaineering* an act of sliding down a snowy or icy slope in a standing or squatting position, often with the aid of an ice axe. ▸ *verb, intr* to perform a glissade. [19c: French, from *glisser* to slide]

glissando *noun* (***glissandos*** *or* ***glissandi*** /-diː/) *music* **1** the effect produced by sliding the finger along a keyboard or a string. **2** a similar effect produced on the trombone. [19c: Italian]

glisten *verb, intr* often of something wet or icy: to shine or sparkle. ▪ **glistening** *adj*. [Anglo-Saxon *glisnian*]

glitch *noun, informal* a sudden brief irregularity or failure to function, esp in electronic equipment. [1960s]

glitter *verb, intr* **1** to shine with bright flashes of light; to sparkle. **2** *informal* to be sparklingly attractive or resplendent: *a party glittering with famous film stars*. ▸ *noun* **1** sparkle. **2** *informal* bright attractiveness, often superficial. **3** tiny pieces of shiny material used for decoration. ▪ **glittering** *adj*. ▪ **glittery** *adj*. [14c as *gliteren*]

glitterati /glɪtəˈrɑːtiː/ *plural noun, informal* famous, fashionable and beautiful people. [1950s: from **glitter**, modelled on **literati**]

glitz *noun, informal* showiness; garishness. [1970s: a back-formation from **glitzy**]

glitzy *adj* (**-ier, -iest**) *informal* extravagantly showy; flashy. [1960s: perhaps from German *glitzern* to glitter]

gloaming *noun, poetic or Scot* dusk; twilight. [Anglo-Saxon *glomung*]

gloat *verb, intr* (*often* **gloat over sth**) to feel or show smug or vindictive satisfaction, esp in one's own success or in another's misfortune. ▸ *noun* an act of gloating. [16c: perhaps from Norse *glotta* to grin]

global *adj* **1** affecting the whole world. **2** total; including everything. **3** *comput* affecting or applying to a whole program or file: *made a global exchange.* ▪ **globally** *adv.* [17c: meaning 'globe-shaped']

globalize *or* **globalise** /ˈgloʊbəlaɪz/ *verb, intr* to extend commercial activities or the same cultural and social values all over the world. ▪ **globalization** *noun.* [1940s]

global village *noun* the world perceived as a single community, largely because of mass communication. [1960s]

global warming *noun, ecol* a gradual increase in the average temperature of the Earth's surface and its atmosphere which has been attributed to the **greenhouse effect**. [1970s]

globe *noun* **1** (**the globe**) the Earth. **2** a sphere with a map of the world on it. **3** any approximately ball-shaped object. [16c: from Latin *globus*]

globe artichoke *noun* **1** a tall plant with deeply divided leaves and large purplish-blue flowers. **2** the fleshy base of the immature flower-head of this plant, eaten as a vegetable.

globetrotter *noun, informal* someone who travels all over the world, esp as a tourist. ▪ **globetrotting** *noun.*

globin *noun, biochem* in animals: any of a group of soluble proteins present in haemoglobin. [19c]

globular *adj* **1** shaped like a globe or globule. **2** consisting of globules.

globule *noun* a small drop, esp of liquid. [17c: from Latin *globulus*]

globulin *noun, biochem* a type of protein that is soluble in salt solutions but not in pure water.

glockenspiel /ˈglɒkənspiːl, -ʃpiːl/ *noun* a musical instrument consisting of tuned metal plates held in a frame, played with two small hammers. [19c: German, from *Glocke* bell + *Spiel* play]

gloom *noun* **1** near-darkness. **2** sadness or despair. ▸ *verb, intr* **1** of the sky: to be dark and threatening. **2** to behave in a sad or depressed way. [14c as *gloumbe*]

gloomy *adj* (**-ier, -iest**) **1** dark; dimly lit. **2** causing gloom. **3** sad or depressed. ▪ **gloomily** *adv.* ▪ **gloominess** *noun.*

glorified *adj, derog* given a fancy name or appearance: *a glorified skivvy.*

glorify *verb* (**-ies, -ied**) **1** to exaggerate the beauty, importance, etc of something or someone. **2** to praise or worship (God). **3** to make someone or something glorious. ▪ **glorification** *noun.* [14c: from Latin *glorificare*]

glorious *adj* **1** having or bringing glory. **2** splendidly beautiful. **3** *informal* excellent. **4** *humorous, informal* very bad: *glorious mess.* [14c: Anglo-French]

glory *noun* (**-ies**) **1** great honour and prestige. **2** great beauty or splendour. **3** praise and thanks given to God. **4** a greatly-admired asset: *Patience is her crowning glory.* **5** a halo eg round a saint's head in a painting. **6** the splendour and blessedness of heaven. ▸ *verb* (**-ies, -ied**) *intr* (*usu* **glory in sth**) to feel or show great delight or pride in it. [14c: from Latin *gloria*]

glory hole *noun, informal* a room, cupboard, drawer, etc where odds and ends are kept, esp in a disorganized way. [19c: perhaps related to 15c *glory* to defile]

Glos. *abbrev, English county* Gloucestershire.

gloss[1] *noun* **1** shiny brightness on a surface. **2** a superficial pleasantness or attractiveness. **3** (*in full* **gloss paint**) paint that produces a shiny finish. **4** a substance that adds shine: *lip gloss.* ▸ *verb* **1** to give a shiny finish to something. **2** to paint (a surface, etc) with gloss. [16c]

PHRASAL VERBS **gloss over sth** to disguise or mask (a deficiency, mistake, etc), esp by treating a subject briefly and dismissively.

gloss[2] *noun* **1** a short explanation of a difficult word, phrase, etc in a text, eg in the margin of a manuscript. **2** an intentionally misleading explanation. ▸ *verb* **1** to provide a gloss of (a word, etc) or add glosses to (a text). **2** (*also* **gloss sth over** *or* **away**) to explain it away; to give a different or false interpretation of it. [16c: from Latin *glossa* a word requiring explanation]

glossary *noun* (**-ies**) a list of explanations of words, often at the end of a book. [14c: from Latin *glossarium*]

glossy *adj* (**-ier, -iest**) **1** smooth and shiny. **2** superficially attractive. **3** of a magazine: printed on glossy paper. ▸ *noun* (**-ies**) *informal* such a magazine. ▪ **glossily** *adv.* ▪ **glossiness** *noun.*

glottal *adj, technical* relating to or produced by the **glottis**.

glottal stop *noun, phonetics* a sound produced when the glottis is closed and then opened sharply.

glottis *noun* (***glottises*** *or* (*anat*) ***glottides*** /ˈglɒtɪdiːz/) the opening through which air passes from the pharynx to the trachea, including the space between the vocal cords. [16c: Latin, from Greek *glotta* tongue]

glove *noun* **1** a covering for the hand which usu has individual casings for each finger. **2** a similar padded hand covering used in sports such as boxing, baseball, etc. ▸ *verb* to cover something with a glove or gloves. See also **kid glove**. [Anglo-Saxon *glof*]

glove compartment *noun* a small compartment in the dashboard of a car where small articles can be kept.

glow *verb, intr* **1** to give out a steady heat or light without flames. **2** to shine brightly, as if very hot. **3** to feel or communicate a sensation of intense contentment or well-being: *glow with pride.* **4** of the complexion: to be well-coloured (ie rosy or tanned) and healthy-looking: *cheeks glowing with health.* ▸ *noun* **1** a steady flameless heat or light. **2** bright, shiny appearance. **3** intensity of feeling, esp pleasant feeling. **4** a healthy colour of complexion. [Anglo-Saxon *glowan*]

glower *verb, intr* to stare angrily. ▸ *noun* an angry stare; a scowl. [16c as *glowr* or *glowir*]

glowing *adj* commendatory; full of praise: *glowing report*. ▸ *verb, present participle of* **glow**. ▪ **glowingly** *adv*.

glow-worm *noun* **1** a small nocturnal beetle, the wingless female of which attracts the male by giving out a bright greenish light from the underside of her abdomen. **2** *N Am* a luminous insect larva. [14c]

glucose *noun, biochem* the most common form of naturally occurring sugar, in animals the main form in which energy derived from carbohydrates is transported around the bloodstream.

glue *noun* **1** any adhesive obtained by extracting natural substances, esp from bone, in boiling water. **2** any adhesive made by dissolving synthetic substances such as rubber or plastic in a suitable solvent. ▸ *verb* (***glueing*** *or* ***gluing***) to use such an adhesive to stick (two materials or parts) together. ▪ **gluey** *adj* (***-ier, -iest***). [14c: from Latin *glus*]

IDIOMS **be glued to sth** *informal* to have one's eyes fixed on it: *eyes glued to the TV.*

glum *adj* (***glummer, glummest***) in low spirits; sullen. ▪ **glumness** *noun*. [16c: related to **gloom**]

gluon *noun, physics* a hypothetical particle with no mass, the carrier of the force that is believed to hold quarks together. [20c: from **glue** + **-on**]

glut *noun* **1** an excessive supply of goods, etc. **2** an act or instance of glutting. ▸ *verb* (***glutted, glutting***) **1** to feed or supply something to excess. **2** to block or choke up. [14c: from Latin *glutire* to swallow]

gluten *noun, biochem* a mixture of two plant storage proteins occurring in wheat flour that gives bread dough elastic properties. [16c: Latin, meaning 'glue']

gluteus *noun, anatomy* one of the three large muscles in the human buttock. ▪ **gluteal** *adj*. [17c: Latin, from Greek *gloutos* the rump]

glutinous *adj* like glue; sticky. ▪ **glutinously** *adv*. ▪ **glutinousness** *noun*. [16c: from Latin *gluten* glue]

glutton[1] *noun* **1** *derog* someone who eats too much. **2** someone whose behaviour suggests an eagerness (for something unpleasant): *a glutton for hard work*. ▪ **gluttonous** *adj*. ▪ **gluttony** *noun, derog* the habit or practice of eating too much. [13c: from Latin *gluttire* to swallow]

glutton[2] *noun* a **wolverine**.

glycerine /ˈglɪsəriːn/ *or* **glycerin** /-rɪn/ *noun, non-technical* **glycerol**. [19c: from Greek *glykeros* sweet]

glycerol /ˈglɪsərɒl/ *noun, chem* a colourless viscous sweet-tasting liquid that is a by-product in the manufacture of soap from naturally-occurring fats and is widely used in various foodstuffs and medicines. [19c: from Greek *glykeros* sweet]

glyco- *combining form, denoting* **1** sugar. **2** glycogen. [From Greek *glykys* sweet]

glycogen *noun, biochem* a highly branched chain of glucose molecules, the main form in which carbohydrate is stored (esp in the liver and muscles) in vertebrates. ▪ **glycogenic** *adj*. [19c: **glyco-** + Greek *-genes* born]

glycol /ˈglaɪkɒl/ *noun, chem* any of a class of compounds with two hydroxyl groups on adjacent carbon atoms, and so intermediate between *glycerine* and alcoh*ol*. [19c]

glycolysis /glaɪˈkɒlɪsɪs/ *noun, biochem* during respiration in cells: the breaking down of glucose, accompanied by the release of energy in the form of ATP. [19c: **glyco-** + **-lysis**]

GM *abbrev* genetically modified.

gm *abbrev* gram or grams.

GMO *abbrev* genetically modified organism.

GMT *abbrev* Greenwich Mean Time.

gnarled *or* **gnarly** *adj* (***-ier, -iest***) of tree trunks, branches, human hands, etc: twisted, with knotty swellings, usu as a result of age. [17c]

gnash *verb, tr & intr* to grind (the teeth) together, esp in anger or pain. [15c: from 13c *gnasten*]

gnashers *plural noun, humorous informal* teeth.

gnat *noun* a small biting fly. [Anglo-Saxon *gnætt*]

gnaw *verb* (*past participle* ***gnawed*** *or* ***gnawn***) **1** (*also* **gnaw at** *or* **gnaw away at sth**) to bite it with a scraping action, causing a gradual wearing away. **2** to make (eg a hole) in this way. **3** *tr & intr* (*also* **gnaw at sb**) of pain, anxiety, etc: to trouble them persistently: *He is gnawed by guilt*. ▪ **gnawing** *adj*. [Anglo-Saxon *gnagan*]

gneiss /naɪs/ *noun, geol* a coarse-grained metamorphic rock that contains bands of quartz and feldspar alternating with bands of mica. [18c: from German *Gneis*]

gnome *noun* **1** a fairy-tale creature, usu in the form of a small misshapen old man, who lives underground, often guarding treasure. **2** a statue of such a creature used as a garden ornament. [18c: from Latin *gnomus* dwarf]

gnomic *adj, formal* of speech or writing: **1** expressed in or containing short pithy aphorisms. **2** so terse or opaque as to be difficult to understand. [19c: from Greek *gnomikos*]

gnostic /ˈnɒstɪk/ *adj* **1** relating to knowledge, esp mystical or religious knowledge. **2** (**Gnostic**) relating to Gnosticism. ▸ *noun* (**Gnostic**) an early Christian heretic believing in redemption of the soul through special religious knowledge. [16c: from Greek *gnostikos* relating to knowledge]

Gnosticism /ˈnɒstɪsɪzəm/ *noun* the doctrines of the **Gnostics** (see under **gnostic**).

GNP *abbrev, econ* gross national product.

gnu /nuː/ *noun* (***gnus*** *or* ***gnu***) either of two species of large African antelope with horns, a long mane and tufts of hair growing from the muzzle, throat and chest. Also called **wildebeest**. [18c: from Hottentot]

go *verb* (***goes,*** *past tense* ***went,*** *past participle* ***gone***) *usu intr* **1** (*often* **go about** *or* **by** *or* **down,** *etc*) to walk, move or travel in the direction specified. **2** to lead or extend: *The road goes all the way to the farm.* **3** (*usu* **go to somewhere**) to visit or attend it, once or regularly: *go to the cinema* • *go to school*. **4 a** to leave or move away; **b** (*only as exclam*) said by someone signalling the start of a race: begin the race! **5** to be destroyed or taken away; to disappear: *The old door had to go* • *The peaceful atmosphere has gone*. **6** to proceed or fare: *The scheme is going well.* **7** to be used up: *All his money went on drink*. **8** to be given or sold for a stated amount: *went for £20.* **9** to leave or set out for a stated purpose: *go on holiday* • *gone fishing*. **10** *tr & intr* to perform (an action) or produce (a sound): *go like this* • *go bang*. **11** *informal* to break, break down, or fail: *The old TV finally went* • *His eyes have gone*. **12** to work or be in working order: *get it going*. **13** to become; to pass into a certain condition: *go mad*. **14** to belong; to be placed correctly: *Where does this go?* **15** to fit, or be contained: *Four into three won't go.* **16** to be or continue in a certain state: *go hungry.* **17** of time: to pass. **18** of a story or tune: to run: *How does it go?* **19** (*often* **go for sb** *or* **sth**) to apply to them; to be valid or accepted for them: *The same goes for you • In this office, anything goes.* **20** *informal* to carry authority: *What she says goes.* **21** (*often* **go with sth**) of colours, etc: to match or blend. **22** to subject oneself: *go to much trouble.* **23** to adopt a specified system: *go metric.* **24** *tr* to bet (a specified amount), esp at cards: *went five pounds.* **25** *informal* to be in general, for the purpose of comparison: *As girls go, she's quite naughty.* **26** to exist or be on offer: *the best offer going at the moment.* **27** *very informal* to say: *She goes, 'No, you didn't!' and I goes, 'Oh, yes I did!'* ▸ *noun* **1** a turn or spell: *It's my go.* **2** energy; liveliness: *She lacks go.* **3** *informal* busy activity: *It's all go.* **4** *informal* a success: *make a go of it.* [Anglo-Saxon *gan*]

IDIOMS **be going on for sth** *informal* to be approaching (a specified age): *She's going on for 60.* **from the word go** from the very beginning. **give it a go** *informal* to make an attempt at something. **go all out for sth** to make a great effort to obtain or achieve it. **go slow** to work slowly so as to encourage an employer to negotiate or meet a demand. See also **go-slow**. **have a go** *informal* to try; to make an attempt. **have a go at sb** to attack them verbally. **have sth going for one** *informal* to have it as an attribute or advantage. **no go** *informal* not possible. **on the go** *informal* busily active. **to be going on with** *informal* for the moment: *enough to be going on with.*

PHRASAL VERBS **go about 1** to circulate: *a rumour going about.* **2** *naut* to change course. **go about sth 1** to busy oneself with it. **2** to attempt or tackle it: *how to go about doing this.* **go against sb** to be decided unfavourably for them. **go against sth** to be contrary to it. **go ahead** to proceed. **go along with sb** *or* **sth** to agree with and support them or it. **go back on sth** to break (an agreement, etc). **go down 1** to decrease. **2** *informal* to be accepted or received: *The joke went down well.* **go down with sth** to contract an illness. **go for sb** *or* **sth** *informal* **1** to attack them. **2** to be attracted by them. **3** to choose them. **4** (*usu* **go for it**) *informal* to try very hard to achieve something. **go in for sth** *informal* **1** to take up (a profession). **2** to enter (a contest). **3** to be interested or attracted by something, as a rule: *don't usually go in for films with subtitles.* **go into sth 1** to take up or join (a profession). **2** to discuss or investigate something. **go off 1** to explode. **2** *informal* of perishables, eg food: to become rotten. **3** to proceed or pass off: *The party went off well.* **go off sb** *or* **sth** *informal* to stop liking them or it. **go on 1** to continue or proceed. **2** *informal* to talk too much. **3** (*only as exclam*) *informal* expressing disbelief. **go out 1** of a fire or light: to become extinguished. **2** to be broadcast. **go out with sb** to spend time with someone socially or (esp) romantically. **go over** to pass off or be received: *The play went over well.* **go over sth 1** to examine it. **2** to revise or rehearse it. **go over to** to transfer support or allegiance: *go over to the enemy.* **go round** to be enough for all. **go through** to be approved. **go through sth 1** to use it up. **2** to revise or rehearse it. **3** to examine it. **4** to suffer it: *went through hell.* **5** to search it: *went through all our bags.* **go through with sth** to carry it out to the end. **go under** *informal* to fail or be ruined. **go up 1** to increase. **2** of a building, etc: to be erected. **go with sb** *informal* to have a close romantic friendship with them. **go without sth** to suffer a lack of it.

goad *verb* (*usu* **goad sb into sth** *or* **to do sth**) to urge or provoke them to action. ▸ *noun* **1** a sharp-pointed stick used for driving cattle, etc. **2** anything that provokes or incites. [Anglo-Saxon *gad*]

go-ahead *informal, adj* energetically ambitious and far-sighted. ▸ *noun* (**the go-ahead**) permission to start.

goal *noun* **1 a** in various sports, esp football: a set of posts with a crossbar, through which the ball is struck to score points; **b** the area in which the goal stands. **2 a** an act of scoring in this way; **b** the point or points scored. **3** an aim or purpose: *You really should have a goal in life.* **4** a destination, etc: *Paris was our goal.* ▪ **goalless** *adj.* [16c]

IDIOMS **in goal** playing in the position of goalkeeper.

goalie *noun, informal* a goalkeeper.

goalkeeper *noun* in various sports: the player who guards the goal and tries to prevent the opposition from scoring.

goal kick *noun* **1** *football* a free kick awarded to the defending team when their opponents have put the ball over the **goal line** but a goal has not been scored. **2** *rugby* an attempt to kick a goal. ▪ **goal kicker** *noun.*

goal line *noun* in various sports: the line marking each end of the field of play.

goalpost *noun* in various sports: each of two upright posts forming the goal.

IDIOMS **move the goalposts** to change the accepted rules or aims of an activity during its course.

goat *noun* **1** a herbivorous mammal, noted for its physical agility and sure-footedness, the males of which have tufty beards on their lower jaws. **2** *derog informal* a lecherous man, esp an old one. **3** *derog, informal* a foolish person. **4** (**the Goat**) the constellation and sign of the zodiac **Capricorn**. [Anglo-Saxon *gat*]

IDIOMS **get sb's goat** *informal* to annoy or irritate them.

goatee *noun* a pointed beard growing only on the front of the chin. [19c]

goatherd *noun* someone who looks after goats out in the pastures.

gob *noun* **1** *coarse slang* the mouth. **2** a soft wet lump. **3** *coarse slang* spit. ▸ *verb* (***gobbed, gobbing***) *intr, coarse slang* to spit. [14c: from French *gobe* a lump or mouthful]

gobbet *noun* **1** a lump or chunk. **2** *informal* an extract from a text. [14c: from French *gobet*]

gobble[1] *verb, tr & intr* (*usu* **gobble sth up** *or* **down**) to eat hurriedly and noisily. [17c: from French *gober* to gulp down]

gobble[2] *verb, intr* of a male turkey: to make a loud gurgling sound in the throat. ▸ *noun* the loud gurgling sound made by a male turkey. [17c: imitating the sound]

gobbledygook *or* **gobbledegook** *noun, informal* **1** official jargon, meaningless to ordinary people. **2** nonsense; rubbish. [1940s: imitating the sound and based on **gobble[2]**]

gobbler *noun, N Am* a male turkey.

go-between *noun* a messenger between two people or sides; an intermediary.

goblet *noun* a drinking-cup with a base and stem but no handles. [14c: from French *gobelet*, diminutive of *gobel* cup]

goblin *noun* in folk-tales: an evil or mischievous spirit in the form of a small man. [14c: from French *gobelin*]

gobsmacked *adj, informal* astonished; dumbfounded. [From the action of clapping a hand to one's mouth in surprise]

gobstopper *noun, informal* a very large round sweet for lengthy sucking.

go-cart see **go-kart**

god *noun* **1** (**God**) in the Christian and other monotheistic religions: the unique supreme being, creator and ruler of the universe. **2** in other religions: a superhuman male being with power over nature and humanity; a male object of worship. Compare **goddess**. **3** a man greatly admired, esp for his fine physique or wide influence. **4** *often derog* an object of excessive worship or influence: *He made money his god.* **5** (**the gods**) superhuman beings collectively, both male and female. **6** (**the gods**) **a** the balcony or upper circle in a theatre; **b** the theatregoers in this area. ▸ *exclam* (**God!** *or* **my God!**) expressing amazement, anger, etc. ▪ **godlike** *adj*. [Anglo-Saxon]
IDIOMS **for God's sake 1** expressing pleading. **2** expressing irritation, disgust, etc.

godchild *noun* a child that a godparent is responsible for.

goddaughter *noun* a female godchild.

goddess *noun* **1** a superhuman female being who has power over nature and humanity; a female object of worship. Compare **god**. **2** a woman greatly admired for her beauty.

godfather *noun* **1** a male godparent. **2** the head of a criminal group, esp in the Mafia.

God-fearing *adj* respectful of God's laws; pious.

godforsaken (also **Godforsaken**) *adj, derog* of a place: remote and desolate.

godless *adj* **1** not religious; not believing in God. **2** having no god. **3** wicked; immoral. ▪ **godlessness** *noun*.

godly *adj* (**-ier, -iest**) religious; pious. ▪ **godliness** *noun*.

godmother *noun* a female godparent.

godparent *noun* someone who, at baptism, guarantees a child's religious education and generally takes a personal interest in them.

godsend *noun* someone or something whose arrival is unexpected but very welcome.

godson *noun* a male godchild.

goer *noun* **1** *in compounds* someone who makes visits, esp regular ones, to a specified place: *cinemagoer.* **2** *informal* something that travels fast or makes fast progress.

goes see under **go** *verb* and *noun*

gofer *noun, informal* a junior employee who runs errands. [1960s: from *go for*]

go-getter *noun, informal* an ambitious enterprising person. ▪ **go-getting** *adj*.

goggle *verb* **1** *intr* to look with wide staring eyes. **2** to roll (the eyes). **3** *intr* of the eyes: to stick out. ▸ *noun* a wide-eyed stare. [14c: meaning 'to turn the eyes to one side']

goggle-box *noun* (*usu* **the goggle-box**) *informal* the TV.

goggle-eyed *adj* having bulging or rolling eyes.

goggles *plural noun* **1** protective spectacles with edges that fit closely against the face. **2** *informal* spectacles.

going *noun* **1** leaving; a departure: *comings and goings of the lodgers.* **2** *horse-racing* the condition of the track. **3** progress: *made good going.* **4** *informal* general situation or conditions: *when the going gets tough.* **5** *in compounds* the act or practice of making visits, esp regular ones, to specified places: *theatre-going.* ▸ *verb, present participle of* **go 1** about or intending (to do something). **2** *in compounds* in the habit of visiting specified places: *the cinema-going public.* ▸ *adj* **1** flourishing, successful: *a going concern.* **2** usual or accepted: *the going rate.* **3** in existence; currently available: *These are the cheapest ones going.*
IDIOMS **be tough** *or* **hard going** to be difficult to do. **going on** *or* **going on for sth** approaching (a certain age or period of time): *going on for sixteen.*

going-over *noun* (***goings-over***) *informal* **1** a beating. **2** a close inspection.

goings-on *plural noun, informal* events or happenings, esp if they are strange or disapproved of.

goitre *or* (*N Am*) **goiter** /ˈgɔɪtə(r)/ *noun, pathol* an abnormal enlargement of the **thyroid** gland which results in a large visible swelling in the neck. [17c: French *goître*]

go-kart *or* **go-cart** *noun* a low racing vehicle consisting of a frame with wheels, engine and steering gear.

gold *noun* **1** (symbol **Au**) a soft yellow precious metallic element used for making jewellery, coins, etc. **2** articles made from it. **3** its value, used as a standard for the value of currency. **4** its deep yellow colour. **5** *informal* a gold medal. **6** precious or noble quality: *heart of gold.* **7** monetary wealth. ▸ *adj* **1** made of gold. **2** gold-coloured. ▪ **goldish** *and* **goldy** *adj*. [Anglo-Saxon]

gold-digger *noun* **1** *derog informal* someone who starts love affairs with rich people in order to get at their money. **2** someone who digs for gold.

golden *adj* **1** gold-coloured. **2** made of or containing gold. **3** happy; prosperous or thriving: *golden age.* **4** excellent; extremely valuable: *golden opportunity.* **5** greatly admired or favoured: *golden girl.* **6** denoting a 50th anniversary: *golden wedding* • *golden jubilee.*

golden age *noun* **1** an imaginary past time of innocence and happiness. **2** the period of highest achievement in any sphere.

golden eagle *noun* a large eagle with dark brown plumage and a golden nape.

golden handshake *noun, informal* a large sum received from an employer on retirement or in compensation for compulsory redundancy.

golden mean *noun* the midpoint between two extremes.

golden oldie *noun, informal* a song, recording, film, etc first issued years ago and still popular or well-known.

golden rule *noun* any essential principle or rule.

goldfinch *noun* a European finch that has a broad yellow bar across each wing.

goldfish *noun* a yellow, orange or golden-red freshwater fish of the carp family.

goldfish bowl *noun* **1** a spherical glass aquarium for fish. **2** a situation entirely lacking in privacy.

gold leaf *noun* gold that is rolled or beaten into very thin sheets and used to decorate books, etc.

gold medal *noun* a medal awarded to the winner of a sporting contest, or in recognition of excellence, eg of a wine. Often shortened to **gold**.

gold mine *or* **goldmine** *noun* **1** a place where gold is mined. **2** *informal* a source of great wealth.

gold plate *noun* **1** a thin coating of gold, esp on silver. **2** articles such as spoons and dishes made of gold. ▸ *verb* (**gold-plate**) to coat (another metal) with gold. ▪ **gold-plated** *adj*.

gold rush *noun* a frantic scramble by large numbers of people to reach and exploit an area where gold has been discovered.

goldsmith *noun* someone who makes articles out of gold.

gold standard *noun* a monetary system in which the unit of currency is assigned a value relative to gold.

golf *noun* a game played on a golf course, the object being to hit a small ball into each of a series of nine or eighteen holes using a set of clubs, taking as few strokes as possible. ▸ *verb, intr* to play this game. [15c Scots: perhaps from Dutch *colf* club]

golf ball *noun* **1** a small ball used in golf. **2** in some electric typewriters and printers: a small detachable metal sphere with the type characters moulded on to its surface.

golf club *noun* **1** any of the set of long-handled clubs used to play golf. **2 a** an association of players of golf; **b** its premises with a golf course attached.

golf course *noun* an area of specially prepared ground on which golf is played.

golfer *noun* someone who plays golf.

golosh see **galosh**

gonad *noun, biol* an organ in which eggs or sperm are produced, esp the **ovary** or **testis**. [19c: from Greek *gone* generation]

gondola *noun* **1** a long narrow flat-bottomed boat with pointed upturned ends, used to transport passengers on the canals of Venice. **2** the passenger cabin suspended from an airship, balloon or cable-railway. **3** a free-standing shelved unit for displaying goods in a supermarket. ▪ **gondolier** *noun* someone who propels a gondola in Venice. [16c: a Venetian dialect word, meaning 'to rock']

gone *verb, past participle of* **go**. ▸ *adj* **1** departed. **2** *informal* of time: past: *gone six*. **3** used up. **4** lost. **5** dead. **6** *informal* pregnant: *four months gone*. **7** *informal* in an exalted state, eg from drugs.

goner *noun, informal* someone or something that is considered beyond hope of recovery. [19c]

gong *noun* **1** a hanging metal plate that makes a resonant sound when struck: *a dinner gong*. **2** *slang* a medal. **3** an orchestral percussion instrument consisting of a flattened metal disc played by striking it with a softly padded mallet. [17c: from Malay]

gonna *contraction, informal, esp N Am* going to.

gonorrhoea *or* (*N Am*) **gonorrhea** /gɒnə'rɪə/ *noun, pathol* a sexually transmitted infection of the genital tract by a bacterium. ▪ **gonorrhoeal** *adj*. [16c]

gonzo /'gɒnzoʊ/ *adj, slang, esp N Am* applied especially to eccentric subjective journalism: bizarre; weird. [Coined by the US writer Hunter S Thompson in 1971]

goo *noun* (*pl* in sense 1 ***goos***) *informal* **1** any sticky substance. **2** *derog* excessive sentimentality. [20c]

good *adj* (***better, best***) **1 a** having desirable or necessary (positive) qualities; admirable; **b** *patronizing* used when addressing or referring to someone: *my good man* • *your good lady*. **2 a** morally correct; virtuous; **b** (**the good**) virtuous people in general. **3** kind and generous. **4** bringing happiness or pleasure: *good news*. **5** well-behaved. **6** wise; advisable: *a good buy*. **7** thorough. **8** finest compared with others: *my good china*. **9** adequate; satisfactory: *a good supply*. **10** enjoyable: *having a good time*. **11** valid. **12** well-respected. **13** sound; giving use; serviceable: *The roof is good for another winter*. **14** financially sound: *a good investment*. **15** considerable; at least: *waited a good while* • *lasted a good month*. **16** certain to provide the desired result: *good for a laugh*. **17** used to introduce exclamations expressing surprise, dismay, or exasperation: *good heavens* • *good grief*. ▸ *noun* **1** moral correctness; virtue. **2** benefit; advantage: *do you good* • *It turned out all to the good*. ▸ *exclam* expressing approval or satisfaction. ▸ *adv, informal* very well: *The boy done good*. [Anglo-Saxon *god*]

IDIOMS **as good as ...** almost ...; virtually ... **as good as gold** esp of children: extremely well-behaved. **good and ...** *informal* very ...; completely or absolutely ...: *good and ready*. **good for sb** *or* **sth** beneficial to them or it. **good for you,** *etc*! *or* (*Aust, NZ informal*) **good on you,** *etc*! **1** an expression of approval or congratulation. **2** an expression of snide resentment. **good morning** *or* **good afternoon** *or* **good evening** traditional expressions used when either meeting or parting from someone at the specified time of day. **good night** a traditional expression used when parting from someone in the evening or at night. **in sb's good books** in favour with someone. **make good** to be successful. **make sth good 1** to repair it. **2** to carry it out or fulfil it. **to the good** on the credit side.

the Good Book *noun* the Bible.

goodbye *exclam* used when parting from someone. ▸ *noun* an act or instance of saying goodbye: *said our goodbyes*. [16c as *God be wy you* God be with you]

good-for-nothing *adj* lazy and irresponsible. ▸ *noun* a lazy and irresponsible person.

Good Friday *noun* a Christian festival on the Friday before Easter, in memory of Christ's crucifixion. [13c: from **good** in the sense 'holy']

goodies *plural noun, informal* things considered pleasant or desirable: *a table laden with goodies*. See also **goody**.

goodly *adj* (**-ier, -iest**) *old use or jocular* **1** quite large: *a goodly measure of the amber nectar*. **2** physically attractive; fine. [13c in obsolete sense 'beautifully']

good nature *noun* natural goodness and mildness of disposition. ▪ **good-natured** *adj*.

goodness *noun* **1** the state or quality of being good; generosity; kindness; moral correctness. **2** *euphem* used in exclamations: God: *goodness knows*. **3** nourishing quality: *all the goodness of the grain*. ▸ *exclam* expressing surprise or relief: *Goodness! What a mess!*

goods *plural noun* **1** articles for sale; merchandise. **2** freight. *as adj*: *goods train.* **3** *informal* the required result: *deliver the goods.* **4** *old use* personal possessions.

IDIOMS **have the goods on sb** *informal* to have proof of wrongdoings or crimes committed by them.

goodwill *noun* **1** a feeling of kindness towards others. **2** the good reputation of an established business, seen as having an actual value.

goody *noun* (**-ies**) *informal* a hero in a film, book, etc.

goody-goody *informal, adj* virtuous in an ostentatious or self-satisfied way. ▸ *noun* (**-ies**) an ostentatiously virtuous person.

gooey (***gooier, gooiest***) *informal adj* sticky. ▪ **gooily** *adv.* ▪ **gooiness** *noun.* [20c: from **goo**]

goof *chiefly N Am informal, noun* **1** a silly or foolish person. **2** a stupid mistake. ▸ *verb, intr* **1** (*sometimes* **goof up**) to make a stupid mistake. **2** (*often* **goof about** *or* **around**) to mess about or behave in a silly way. **3** (**goof off**) to spend time idly when one should be working or doing something. [20c]

goofy *adj* (***-ier, -iest***) *informal* **1** silly; crazy. **2** of teeth: protruding.

googly *noun* (**-ies**) *cricket* a ball bowled so that it changes direction unexpectedly after bouncing.

goon *noun* **1** *informal* a silly person. **2** *slang* a hired thug. [1920s: from US cartoon character Alice the Goon, created by E C Segar]

goose *noun* (***geese*** in senses 1 to 4, ***gooses*** in sense 5) **1** any of numerous large wild or domesticated waterfowl, with a stout body, long neck, webbed feet and a broad flat bill. **2** the female of this, as opposed to the male (the **gander**). **3** the flesh of a goose cooked as food. **4** *informal, old use* a silly person. **5** *informal* a poke or pinch on the buttocks. ▸ *verb, informal* to poke or pinch someone on the buttocks. [Anglo-Saxon *gos*]

IDIOMS **cook sb's goose** *informal* to ruin their plans or chances.

gooseberry *noun* (**-ies**) **1** a low-growing deciduous shrub with spiny stems and greenish flowers. **2** one of the small sour-tasting yellowish-green or reddish berries produced by this plant.

IDIOMS **play gooseberry** *informal* to be an unwanted third person, esp in the company of an amorous couple.

goose pimples *or* **goose bumps** *plural noun or* **goose flesh** *singular noun* a condition of the skin caused by cold or fear, in which the body hairs become erect, pimples appear and there is a bristling feeling.

goose-step *noun* a military marching step in which the legs are kept rigid and swung very high. ▸ *verb, intr* to march with this step.

gopher *noun* a small burrowing rodent with a stocky body, short legs and large chisel-like incisor teeth. [19c]

Gordian knot *noun* a difficult problem or dilemma. [16c: named after Gordius, king of ancient Phrygia, who tied a complicated knot that no-one could untie]

IDIOMS **cut the Gordian knot** to resolve a difficulty by decisive and often evasive action.

gore[1] *noun* blood from a wound, esp when clotted. [Anglo-Saxon *gor* filth]

gore[2] *verb* to pierce something or someone with a horn or tusk. [Anglo-Saxon *gar* spear]

gore[3] *noun* a triangular piece of material, eg a section of an umbrella or a tapering piece in a garment, glove, etc. ▸ *verb* to construct something from, or shape it with, gores. ▪ **gored** *adj* made with gores. [Anglo-Saxon *gara* a triangular piece of land]

gorge *noun* **1** a deep narrow valley, usu containing a river. **2** the contents of the stomach. **3** a spell of greedy eating. ▸ *verb* **1** *tr & intr* to eat or swallow greedily. **2** (*usu* **gorge oneself**) to stuff oneself with food. [14c: French, meaning 'throat']

IDIOMS **make sb's gorge rise** to disgust or sicken them.

gorgeous *adj* **1** extremely beautiful or attractive; magnificent. **2** *informal* excellent; extremely pleasant. ▪ **gorgeously** *adv.* ▪ **gorgeousness** *noun.* [15c: from French *gorgias* fine or elegant]

gorgon *noun* **1** (**Gorgon**) *myth* any of the three female monsters that had live snakes for hair and were capable of turning people to stone. **2** *derog, informal* a fierce, frightening or very ugly woman. [14c: from Greek *gorgos* terrible]

Gorgonzola *noun* a blue-veined Italian cheese with a sharp flavour. [19c: named after the town near Milan where it was first made]

gorilla *noun* **1** the largest of the apes, native to African rainforests, which has a heavily built body and jet black skin covered with dense fur. **2** *informal* a brutal-looking man, esp a hired thug. [19c: from Greek *Gorillai* the hairy females supposedly seen on a voyage to Africa in the 6c BC]

gormless *adj, derog informal* stupid; dim. [19c: from *gaum* understanding]

gorse *noun* an evergreen shrub with leaves reduced to very sharp deeply furrowed spines and bright yellow flowers. Also called **furze** and **whin.** ▪ **gorsy** *adj.* [Anglo-Saxon *gors*]

gory *adj* (***-ier, -iest***) **1** causing or involving bloodshed. **2** *informal* unpleasant: *gory details.* **3** covered in **gore**[1]. ▪ **goriness** *noun.* [15c]

goshawk /'gɒshɔːk/ *noun* a large hawk with bluish-grey plumage, short rounded wings and a long tail. [Anglo-Saxon *gos* goose + *hafoc* hawk]

gosling *noun* a young goose. [15c]

go-slow *noun* an instance or the process of deliberately working slowly so as to encourage an employer to negotiate. See also **go slow** at **go.**

gospel *noun* **1** the life and teachings of Christ: *preach the gospel.* **2** (**Gospel**) each of the New Testament books ascribed to Matthew, Mark, Luke and John. **3** a passage from one of these read at a religious service. **4** (*also* **gospel truth**) *informal* the absolute truth. **5** a set of closely followed principles or rules. **6** (*also* **gospel music**) lively religious music of Black American origin. [Anglo-Saxon *god* good + *spel* story]

gossamer *noun* **1** fine filmy spider-woven threads seen on hedges or floating in the air. **2** any soft fine material. ▪ **gossamery** *adj.* [14c]

gossip *noun* **1** *derog* talk or writing about the private affairs of others, often spiteful and untrue. **2** *derog* someone who engages in or spreads such talk. **3** casual and friendly talk. ▸ *verb, intr* **1** to engage in, or pass on, malicious gossip. **2** to chat. ▪ **gossiping**

noun, adj. ▪ **gossipy** *adj.* [Anglo-Saxon *godsibb* godparent, hence a familiar friend one chats to]

got *past tense & past participle of* **get**

Goth *noun* **1** *hist* a member of an East Germanic people (see under **Germanic**) who invaded various parts of the Roman Empire between the 3c and 5c. **2** (**goth**) someone who dresses mainly in black, often having dyed hair and stark black and white make-up, and who favours gothic music. [Anglo-Saxon plural *Gotan*]

Gothic *adj* **1** belonging or relating to the Goths or their language. **2** belonging or relating to a style of architecture featuring high pointed arches, popular in Europe between the 12c and 16c. **3** belonging or relating to a type of literature dealing with mysterious or supernatural events in an eerie setting, popular in the 18c. **4** (*also* **gothick**) belonging or relating to a modern style of literature, films, etc which imitates this. **5** *printing* relating to various styles of heavy type with elaborate angular features. **6** (**gothic**) denoting a style of guitar-based rock music derived from punk and heavy metal, characterized by dark lyrics and occult iconography. ▸ *noun* **1** Gothic architecture or literature. **2** Gothic lettering. **3** the extinct Germanic language of the Goths. [17c]

gotta *contraction, very informal* **1** got to; must: *gotta get there before it shuts.* **2** got a: *gotta really sore head.*

gotten *N Am a past participle of* **get**

gouache /gʊ'ɑːʃ/ *noun* **1** a painting technique using a blend of watercolour and a glue-like substance, giving an opaque matt surface. **2** a painting done in this way. [19c: French]

Gouda /'gɑʊdə/ *noun* a flat round mild Dutch cheese. [19c: named after the town in Holland where it originated]

gouge /gɑʊdʒ/ *noun* **1** a chisel with a rounded hollow blade, used for cutting grooves or holes in wood. **2** a groove or hole made using, or as if using, this. ▸ *verb* **1** to cut something out with or as if with a gouge. **2** (*usu* **gouge sth out**) to force or press it out of position, eg the eye with the thumb. [15c: French, from Latin *gubia* chisel]

goujons /'guːdʒɒnz; *French* guʒɔ̃/ *plural noun, cookery* strips of meat or fish coated in flour, batter or breadcrumbs and deep-fried. [1940s: French]

goulash *noun, cookery* a thick meat stew heavily seasoned with paprika, orig from Hungary. [19c: from Hungarian *gulyas hus* herdsman's meat]

gourd *noun* **1 a** a climbing plant that produces a large fruit with a hard woody outer shell; **b** the large fruit of this plant. **2** the hard durable shell of this fruit, often hollowed out, dried, and used as an ornament, cup, bowl, etc. [14c: from French *gourde*]

gourmand /'gɔːmənd/ *noun* **1** a greedy eater; a glutton. **2** a gourmet. [15c: French]

gourmet /'gɔːmeɪ/ *noun* someone who has expert knowledge of, and a passion for, good food and wine. [19c: French, orig meaning 'a wine-merchant's assistant']

gout /gɑʊt/ *noun, med, pathol* a disease in which excess **uric acid** accumulates in the bloodstream and is deposited as crystals in the joints, causing acute **arthritis**, esp of the big toe. ▪ **gouty** *adj.* [13c: from French *goute* a drop]

govern *verb* **1** *tr & intr* to control and direct the affairs of (a country, state, or organization). **2** to guide or influence; to control or restrain: *govern his temper.* **3** *grammar* of a word or part of speech: to dictate the **case**[2] (sense 7), **mood**[2] (sense 1) or inflectional ending of another, closely associated word. ▪ **governable** *adj.* ▪ **governing** *adj.* [13c: from Latin *gubernare,* to steer]

governance *noun, formal* **1** the act or state of governing. **2** the system of government. **3** authority or control. [14c]

governess *noun, chiefly formerly* a woman employed to teach, and perhaps look after, children, usu while living in their home. [18c; 15c as 'a woman who governs']

government *noun* **1** (*often* **the Government**) a body of people, usu elected, with the power to control the affairs of a country or state. **2 a** the way in which this is done; **b** the particular system used. **3** the act or practice of ruling; control. **4** *grammar* the power of one word to determine the form, **case**[2] (sense 7) or **mood**[2] (sense 1) of another. ▪ **governmental** *adj.* [16c in senses 2 and 3]

government
This word is often misspelt. There is a *n* in the middle that isn't sounded in speech. It might help you to remember that gover**n**ments **govern**.

governor *noun* **1** (*also* **Governor**) the elected head of a US state. **2** the head of an institution, eg a prison. **3** a member of a governing body of a school, hospital, college, etc. **4** (*also* **Governor**) the head of a colony or province, esp the monarch's representative. **5** *mech* a regulator or other device for maintaining uniform speed in an engine. **6** (*also* **guvnor** *or* **guv'nor**) *informal* **a** (*often* **the governor**) a boss or father; **b** (*often* **guv**) a respectful, though now often ironical, form of address to a man. ▪ **governorship** *noun.* [13c]

Governor-General *noun* (***Governors-General*** *or* ***Governor-Generals***) the official representative of the British monarch in a Commonwealth country or British colony.

gown *noun* **1** a woman's long formal dress. **2** an official robe worn by clergymen, lawyers and academics. **3** a protective overall worn eg by surgeons, patients, hairdressers' clients, etc. [14c: from Latin *gunna* a garment made of fur or leather]

GP *abbrev* general practitioner.

GPO *abbrev* General Post Office.

gr. *abbrev* gram or grams.

Graafian follicle *noun, anatomy* in the ovary of female mammals: one of the many small sacs in which an egg cell develops before ovulation. [19c: named after Regnier de Graaf, Dutch anatomist who discovered these]

grab *verb* (***grabbed, grabbing***) **1** *tr & intr* (*also* **grab at sth**) to seize suddenly and often with violence. **2** to take something greedily. **3** to take something hurriedly or without hesitation: *grab a snack* • *grab an opportunity.* **4** *informal* to impress or interest someone: *How does that grab you?* ▸ *noun* **1** an act or an instance of grabbing something. **2** a mechanical device with scooping jaws, used eg for excavation. [16c: from German dialect or Dutch *grabben*]

IDIOMS **up for grabs** *informal* available, esp easily or cheaply.

grace *noun* **1** elegance and beauty of form or movement. **2** decency; politeness: *had the grace to offer.*

3 a short prayer of thanks to God said before or after a meal. **4** a delay allowed, esp to a debtor, as a favour: *gave us two days' grace.* **5** a pleasing or attractive characteristic: *completely lacking in social graces • a saving grace.* **6 a** *relig* the mercy and favour shown by God to mankind; **b** *relig* the condition of a person's soul when they have been made free from sin and evil by God. **7** (**His** *or* **Her Grace** *or* **Your Grace** (*pl* ***Their*** *or* ***Your Graces***)) a title used of or to a duke, duchess or archbishop. ▸ *verb* **1** *often facetious* to honour (an occasion, person, etc), eg with one's presence. **2** to add beauty or charm to something. [12c: from Latin *gratia* favour]

IDIOMS **with good** *or* **bad grace** willingly or unwillingly.

graceful *adj* having or showing elegance and beauty of form or movement. ▪ **gracefully** *adv.* ▪ **gracefulness** *noun.*

graceless *adj* **1** awkward in form or movement. **2** bad-mannered. ▪ **gracelessly** *adv.*

grace note *noun, music* a note introduced as an embellishment and not essential to the melody or harmony.

the Graces *plural noun, Greek myth* the three sister goddesses who have the power to grant beauty, charm and happiness. [16c: from Latin *Gratiae*; see **grace**]

gracing *present participle of* **grace**

gracious *adj* **1** kind and polite. **2** of God: merciful. **3** having qualities of luxury, elegance, comfort and leisure: *gracious living.* **4** *formal* used out of polite custom to describe a royal person or their actions: *Her Gracious Majesty.* ▸ *exclam* (*also* **gracious me!**) expressing surprise. ▪ **graciously** *adv.* ▪ **graciousness** *noun.* [14c: from Latin *gratiosus*]

gradation *noun* **1 a** a series of gradual and successive stages or degrees; **b** one step in this. **2** the act or process of forming grades or stages. **3** the gradual change or movement from one state, musical note, colour, etc to another. ▪ **gradational** *adj.* [16c: from **grade**]

grade *noun* **1** a stage or level on a scale of quality, rank, size, etc. **2** a mark indicating this. **3** *N Am, esp US* **a** a particular class or year in school; **b** the level of work taught in it. **4** a slope or gradient. **5** in stockbreeding: an improved variety of animal produced by crossing usu a native animal with one of purer breed. *as adj*: *grade lambs.* ▸ *verb* **1** to arrange (things or people) in different grades. **2** to award a mark indicating grade, eg on a piece of written work, essay, etc. **3** to produce a gradual blending or merging of (esp colours). **4** to adjust the gradients of (a road or railway). **5** *intr* to pass gradually from one grade, level, value, etc to another. [16c: from Latin *gradus* step]

IDIOMS **make the grade** *informal* to succeed; to reach the required or expected standard.

grader *noun* **1** a machine that makes a smooth surface for road-building. **2** *in compounds, N Am, esp US* a school pupil in a specified grade: *sixth-grader.* **3** someone or something that grades.

grade school *noun, N Am* elementary or primary school.

gradient *noun* **1** the steepness of a slope. **2** *formal* a slope. **3** *maths* the slope of a line or the slope of a tangent to a curve at a particular point. **4** *physics* the rate of change of a variable quantity over a specified distance. [19c: from Latin *gradiens* stepping]

gradual *adj* **1** developing or happening slowly, by degrees. **2** of a slope: not steep; gentle. ▪ **gradually** *adv.* [16c: from Latin *gradus* step]

graduand *noun* someone who is about to be awarded a higher-education degree. [19c: from Latin *graduare* to take a degree]

graduate *verb* /'gradʒueɪt/ **1** *intr or* (*N Am*) *sometimes* **be graduated** to receive an academic degree from a higher-education institution. **2** *intr, N Am* to receive a diploma at the end of a course of study at high school. **3** *intr* to move up from a lower to a higher level, often in stages. **4** to mark (eg a thermometer) with units of measurement or other divisions. **5** to arrange something into regular groups, according to size, type, etc. ▸ *noun* /-ɪt/ someone who has a higher-education degree or (*N Am*) a high-school diploma. [15c: from Latin *graduare* to take a degree]

graduation *noun* **1** the act of receiving a higher-education degree or (*N Am*) a high-school diploma. **2** the ceremony marking this. **3 a** a unit of measurement or other division marked on a ruler, thermometer, etc; **b** the process of making or marking such divisions.

graffiti *plural noun*, sometimes used as *singular* (*also* ***graffito***) words or drawings, usu humorous, political or rude, scratched, sprayed or painted on walls, etc in public places. [19c: Italian, literally 'little scratches or scribbles']

graft[1] *noun* **1** *horticulture* a piece of plant tissue that is inserted into a cut in the outer stem of another plant, resulting in fusion of the tissues and growth of a single plant. **2** *surgery* the transfer or transplantation of an organ or tissue from one individual to another, or to a different site within the same individual, usu to replace diseased or damaged tissue: *skin graft.* **3** a transplanted organ. Compare **implant.** ▸ *verb* **1** (*also* **graft in** *or* **into** *or* **on** *or* **together**) **a** to attach a graft in something or someone; **b** to attach something as a graft. **2** *intr* to attach grafts. [15c: from French *graffe*]

graft[2] *noun* **1** *informal* hard work. **2** *slang* **a** the use of illegal or unfair means to gain profit or advantage, esp by politicians or officials; **b** the profit or advantage gained. ▸ *verb, intr* **1** *informal* to work hard. **2** *slang* to practise graft. ▪ **grafter** *noun.* [19c, orig US]

grail *or* **Grail** ▸ *noun* **1** (*in full* **Holy Grail**) the plate or cup used by Christ at the Last Supper, the object of quests by medieval knights. **2** a cherished ambition or goal. [14c: from Latin *gradalis* a flat dish]

grain *noun* **1** a single small hard fruit, resembling a seed, produced by a cereal plant or other grass. **2** such fruits referred to collectively. **3** any of the cereal plants that produce such fruits, eg wheat, corn. **4** a small hard particle of anything. **5** a very small amount: *a grain of truth.* **6 a** the arrangement, size and direction of the fibres or layers in wood, leather, etc; **b** the pattern formed as a result of this arrangement. **7** the main direction of the fibres in paper or the threads in a woven fabric. **8** any of the small particles of metallic silver that form the dark areas of the image on a developed photograph. **9** in the avoirdupois system: the smallest unit of weight, equal to 0.065 grams, formerly said to be the average weight of a grain of wheat (7000 grains being equivalent to one pound avoirdupois). **10** in the troy system: a similar unit of weight (5760 grains being equivalent to one pound troy). ▸ *verb* **1** *tr & intr* to form into grains. **2** to give a rough appearance or texture to something. **3** to paint or stain something with a pattern like the grain of wood or leather. ▪ **grained** *adj.* ▪ **grainy** *adj* (**-ier, -iest**). [13c: from Latin *granum* seed]

IDIOMS **go against the grain** to be against someone's principles or natural character.

gram *or* **gramme** *noun* (abbrev **g, gm** *or* **gr.**) a unit of measurement of mass, equal to one thousandth of a kilogram or 0.035 ounces. [18c: from Greek *gramma* a small weight]

graminivorous *adj* of animals: feeding on grass or cereals. [18c: from Latin *gramen* grass]

grammar *noun* **1** the accepted rules by which words are formed and combined into sentences. **2** the branch of language study dealing with these. **3** **a** a description of these rules as applied to a particular language; **b** a book containing this. **4** a person's understanding of or ability to use these rules: *bad grammar.* ▪ **grammatical** *adj* **1** relating to grammar. **2** correct according to the rules of grammar. [14c: from Greek *gramma* something written]

grammarian *noun* an expert on grammar.

grammar school *noun, Brit, esp formerly* a secondary school that emphasizes the study of academic rather than technical subjects.

gramme see **gram**

gramophone *noun, dated* a record player, esp an old-fashioned one. [19c: from Greek *gramma* something written + *phone* 'sound' or 'voice']

Gram's stain *noun, biol* an important staining procedure used to distinguish between two major groups of bacteria. [20c: named after H J C Gram, Danish physician who devised the technique]

gran *noun, informal* short form of **granny**.

granary *noun* (**-ies**) **1** a building where grain is stored. **2** a region that produces large quantities of grain. **3** (**Granary**) *trademark* a make of bread containing malted wheat flour. ▸ *adj, loosely* of bread: containing whole grains of wheat. [16c: from Latin *granarium*]

grand *adj* **1** large or impressive in size, appearance or style. **2** *sometimes derog* dignified; self-important. **3** intended to impress or gain attention: *a grand gesture.* **4** complete; in full: *grand total.* **5** *informal* very pleasant; excellent. **6** greatest; highest ranking: *Grand Master.* **7** highly respected: *grand old man.* **8** main; principal: *the grand entrance.* **9** *in compounds* indicating a family relationship that is one generation more remote than that of the base word: *grandson.* See also **great** *adj* sense 5. ▸ *noun* (*pl* in sense 1 ***grand***) **1** *slang* a thousand dollars or pounds. **2** *informal* a grand piano. ▪ **grandly** *adv.* ▪ **grandness** *noun.* [16c: French]

grandad *or* **granddad** *noun, informal* **1** a grandfather. **2** *offensive* an old man.

grandchild *noun* a child of one's son or daughter.

granddad see **grandad**

granddaughter *noun* a daughter of one's son or daughter.

grand duchy *noun* a small European country or territory ruled by a grand duke or grand duchess.

grand duke *noun* a high-ranking nobleman who rules a grand duchy. ▪ **grand duchess** *noun.*

grandee *noun* **1** a Spanish or Portuguese nobleman of the highest rank. **2** any well-respected or high-ranking person. [16c: from Spanish *grande*]

grandeur /'grandjə(r)/ *noun* **1** greatness of character, esp dignity or nobility. **2** impressive beauty; magnificence. **3** *derog* self-importance; pretentiousness. [15c: French]

grandfather *noun* the father of one's father or mother.

grandfather clock *noun* a clock driven by a system of weights and a pendulum contained in a tall free-standing wooden case.

grandiloquent *adj, derog* speaking, or spoken or written in a pompous style. ▪ **grandiloquence** *noun.* [16c: from Latin *grandis* great + *loqui* to speak]

grandiose *adj* **1** *derog* exaggeratedly impressive or imposing, esp on a ridiculously large scale. **2** splendid; magnificent; impressive. ▪ **grandiosely** *adv.* [19c: from Italian *grandioso*]

grand jury *noun* in the US: a jury that decides whether there is enough evidence for a person to be brought to trial. ▪ **grand juror** *noun.*

grandma *informal or* (*old use*) **grandmamma** *noun* a grandmother.

grand mal /*French* gʀɑ̃mal/ *noun, med* a serious form of **epilepsy** in which there is sudden loss of consciousness followed by convulsions. Compare **petit mal**. [19c: French, meaning 'great illness']

grandmaster *noun, chess* the title given to an extremely skilled player.

grandmother *noun* the mother of one's father or mother.

grandmother clock *noun* a clock that is similar to a **grandfather clock**, but in a smaller case.

grandpa *informal or* (*old use*) **grandpapa** *noun* a grandfather.

grandparent *noun* either parent of one's father or mother.

grand piano *noun* a large, harp-shaped piano that has its strings arranged horizontally.

grand prix /grɑ̃ priː/ *noun* (*pl* ***grands prix*** /grɑ̃ priː/) **1** any of a series of races held annually in various countries to decide the motor racing championship of the world. **2** in other sports: any competition of similar importance. [19c: French, literally 'great prize']

grand slam *noun* **1** *sport, eg tennis, rugby* the winning in one season of every part of a competition or of all major competitions. **2** *cards, esp bridge* the winning of all thirteen tricks by one player or side.

grandson *noun* a son of one's son or daughter.

grandstand *noun* a large covered sports-ground stand that has tiered seating and which provides a good view for spectators. *as adj*: *a grandstand view.*

grange *noun* a country house with attached farm buildings. [13c: French, meaning 'barn']

granite *noun* a hard coarse-grained igneous rock, consisting mainly of quartz, feldspar and mica. ▪ **granitic** *adj.* [17c: from Italian *granito*, literally 'grained']

granny *or* **grannie** *noun* (**-ies**) *informal* a grandmother.

granny flat *noun, informal* a flat built on to or contained in a house, to accommodate an elderly relative.

granny knot *noun* a reef knot with the ends crossed the wrong way, allowing it to slip or undo easily.

grant *verb* **1** to give, allow or fulfil. **2** to admit something to be true. ▸ *noun* **1** something granted, esp an amount of money from a public fund for a specific purpose. **2** *law* the transfer of property by deed. [13c: from French *granter* or *greanter* to promise]

granted *verb, past participle of* **grant** (*used as a sentence substitute*) an admission that something is true or valid: *She's a good writer. – Granted. But rather limited.* ▸ *conj* though it is admitted that: *granted you gave it back later.* ▸ *prep* though (a specified thing) is admitted: *Granted his arrogance, still he gets results.*
IDIOMS **take sb for granted** to treat them casually and without appreciation. **take sth for granted** to assume it to be true or valid.

grantee *noun, law* the person to whom a **grant** is made.

grant-maintained *adj* (abbrev **GM**) of a school: funded by central rather than local government, and self-governing.

grantor *noun, law* the person who makes a **grant**.

granular *adj, technical* **1** made of or containing tiny particles or granules. **2** of appearance or texture: rough. [18c]

granulate *verb* **1** *tr & intr* to break down into small particles or granules. **2** to give a rough appearance or texture to something. ▪ **granulation** *noun.* [17c]

granulated sugar *noun* white sugar in coarse grains.

granule *noun* a small particle or grain. [17c: from Latin *granulum*]

grape *noun* **1** a pale green or purplish-black juicy edible berry which may be eaten fresh, pressed to make wine or dried to form currants, raisins, etc. **2** any species of climbing vine that bears this fruit. **3** (**the grape**) *affected or literary* wine. ▪ **grapey** *or* **grapy** *adj.* [13c: French, meaning 'bunch of grapes']

grapefruit *noun* (***grapefruit*** *or* ***grapefruits***) **1** an evergreen tree cultivated for its large edible fruits. **2** the round fruit produced by this tree which has acidic pale yellow or pink flesh. [19c: **grape** (because the fruit grow in clusters) + **fruit**]

grapeshot *noun* ammunition in the form of small iron balls which scatter when fired in clusters from a cannon.

grapevine *noun* **1** a vine on which grapes grow. **2** (**the grapevine**) *informal* an informal means of spreading information through casual conversation: *I heard on the grapevine that you're leaving.*

graph *noun* **1** a diagram that illustrates the way in which one quantity varies in relation to another, usu consisting of horizontal and vertical axes (see **axis** sense 3) that cross each other at a point called the **origin**. **2** a symbolic diagram. ▸ *verb* to represent something with or as a graph. [19c: short for the earlier *graphic formula*]

-graph *combining form, forming nouns, denoting* **1** an instrument for writing or recording information: *telegraph.* **2** information written, drawn or recorded by such an instrument: *cardiograph.* [From Greek *graphein* to write]

graphic *or* **graphical** *adj* **1** described or shown vividly and in detail. **2** referring to or composed in a written medium. **3** referring to the **graphic arts**, ie those concerned with drawing, printing and lettering: *graphic design.* **4** relating to graphs; shown by means of a graph. ▪ **graphically** *adv.*

graphical user interface *noun, comput* (abbrev **GUI**) mouse-controlled icons and other images on a desktop display.

graphics *singular noun* the art or science of drawing according to mathematical principles. ▸ *plural noun* **1** the photographs and illustrations used in a magazine. **2** the non-acted visual parts of a film or television programme, eg the credits. **3** *comput* **a** the use of computers to display and manipulate information in graphical or pictorial form, either on a visual-display unit or via a printer or plotter; **b** the images that are produced by this.

graphics card *noun, comput* a printed circuit board that stores visual data and conveys it to the screen.

graphite *noun* a soft black **allotrope** of carbon that is used as a lubricant and electrical contact, and is mixed with clay to form the 'lead' in pencils. [18c: from Greek *graphein* to write + **-ite**]

graphology *noun* **1** the study of handwriting, esp as a way of analysing the writer's character. **2** the study of the systems and conventions of writing. ▪ **graphologist** *noun.* [19c: from Greek *graphein* to write + *logos* word or reason]

graph paper *noun* paper covered in small squares, used for drawing graphs.

grapnel *noun* **1** a large multi-pointed hook on one end of a rope, used for securing a heavy object on the other end. **2** a light anchor for small boats. [14c: from French *grapin*]

grapple *verb* **1** struggle and fight, esp at close quarters, eg in hand-to-hand combat. **2** *intr* (**grapple with sth**) to struggle mentally with (a difficult problem). **3** to secure something with a hook, etc. ▸ *noun* **1** a hook or other device for securing. **2** an act of gripping; a way of gripping. [16c: from French *grappelle*]

grappling-iron *or* **grappling-hook** *noun* a **grapnel**.

grasp *verb* **1** to take a firm hold of something or someone; to clutch. **2** (*often* **grasp at** *or* **after sth**) to make a movement as if to seize it. **3** to understand. ▸ *noun* **1** a grip or hold. **2** power or control; ability to reach, achieve or obtain: *felt the promotion was within her grasp.* **3** ability to understand: *beyond their grasp.* [14c as *graspen*]

grasping *adj, derog* greedy, esp for wealth.

grass *noun* **1** any of a family of flowering plants (eg cereals, bamboos, etc) that typically have long narrow leaves with parallel veins, a jointed upright hollow stem and flowers (with no petals) borne alternately on both sides of an axis. **2** an area planted with or growing such plants, eg a lawn or meadow. **3** lawn or pasture. **4** *slang* marijuana. **5** *slang* someone who betrays someone else, esp to the police. ▸ *verb* **1** to plant something with grass or turf. **2** to feed (animals) with grass; to provide pasture for them. **3** *intr, slang* (*often* **grass on sb** *or* **grass sb up**) to inform on them, esp to the police. [Anglo-Saxon *gærs, græs*]
IDIOMS **let the grass grow under one's feet** to delay or waste time. **put out to grass 1** to give a life of grazing to (eg an old racehorse). **2** *informal* to put (eg a worker) into retirement.

grasshopper *noun* a large brown or green jumping insect, the male of which produces a characteristic chirping sound.

grassland *noun* permanent pasture.

grass roots *plural noun* **1** *esp politics* ordinary people, as opposed to those in a position of power. **2** bare essentials; fundamental principles.

grass snake *noun* a small non-venomous greenish-grey to olive-brown snake.

grass widow *or* **grass widower** *noun* someone whose partner is absent from home for long periods.

grassy *adj* (***-ier, -iest***) covered with, or like, grass.

grat see under **greet**[2]

grate[1] *verb* **1** to cut (eg vegetables or cheese) into shreds by rubbing them against a rough or perforated surface. **2** *tr & intr* to make, or cause something to make, a harsh grinding sound by rubbing. **3** *intr* (*usu* **grate on** *or* **upon sb**) to irritate or annoy them. [15c: from French *grater* to scrape]

grate[2] *noun* **1** a framework of iron bars for holding coal, etc in a fireplace or furnace. **2** the fireplace or furnace itself. [15c: from Latin *grata*]

grateful *adj* **1 a** feeling thankful; **b** showing or giving thanks. **2** *formal* pleasant and welcome: *grateful sleep.* ▪ **gratefully** *adv.* ▪ **gratefulness** *noun.* [16c: from Latin *gratus* pleasing or thankful]

grater *noun* a device with sharpened perforations for grating food.

gratify *verb* (***-ies, -ied***) **1** to please someone. **2** to satisfy or indulge (eg a desire). ▪ **gratification** *noun.* ▪ **gratifying** *adj.* ▪ **gratifyingly** *adv.* [16c: from Latin *gratus* pleasing or thankful + *facere* to make]

gratin see **au gratin**

grating[1] *noun* a framework of metal bars fixed into a wall (eg over a window) or into a pavement (eg over a drain). [17c]

grating[2] *adj* **1** of sounds, etc: harsh. **2** irritating. ▸ *noun* a grating sound.

gratis *adv, adj* free; without charge. [15c: Latin, from *gratia* favour]

gratitude *noun* the state or feeling of being grateful; thankfulness. [16c: from Latin *gratus* thankful]

gratuitous *adj* **1** done without good reason; unnecessary or unjustified: *gratuitous violence.* **2** given or received without charge; voluntary. ▪ **gratuitously** *adv.* [17c: from Latin *gratuitas*, from *gratia* favour]

gratuity *noun* (***-ies***) a sum of money given as a reward for good service; a tip. [16c: from Latin *gratus* thankful]

grave[1] /greɪv/ *noun* **1** a deep trench dug in the ground for burying a dead body. **2** the site of an individual burial. **3** (**the grave**) *literary* death. [Anglo-Saxon *græf* grave or trench]

grave[2] /greɪv/ *adj* **1** giving cause for great concern; very dangerous. **2** very important; serious. **3** solemn and serious in manner. ▪ **gravely** *adv.* ▪ **graveness** *noun* (more commonly **gravity** sense 3, 4). [16c: from Latin *gravis*]

grave[3] /grɑːv/ *or* **grave accent** *noun* a sign placed above a vowel in some languages, eg à and è in French, to indicate a particular pronunciation or extended length of the vowel. [17c: French]

gravel *noun* **1** a mixture of small loose rock fragments and pebbles, coarser than sand, found on beaches and in the beds of rivers, streams and lakes. **2** *pathol* small stones formed in the kidney or bladder. ▸ *verb* (***gravelled, gravelling***; *N Am also* ***graveled, graveling***) **1** to cover (eg a path) with gravel. **2** to puzzle or perplex someone. [13c: from French *gravele*]

gravelly *adj* **1** full of, or containing, small stones. **2** of a voice: rough and deep.

graven image *noun* a carved idol used in worship.

gravestone *noun* a stone marking a grave, usu having the dead person's name and dates of birth and death engraved on it. Also called **tombstone, headstone.**

graveyard *noun* a burial place; a cemetery.

gravid *adj, med* pregnant. [16c: from Latin *gravis* heavy]

gravimeter *noun* an instrument for measuring variations in the magnitude of the gravitational field at different points on the Earth's surface. [1790s: from Latin *gravis* heavy]

gravitas /ˈgravɪtɑːs/ *noun* seriousness of manner; solemnity, authoritativeness; weight. [20c: Latin]

gravitate *verb, intr* **1** to fall or be drawn under the force of gravity. **2** to move or be drawn gradually, as if attracted by some force: *gravitated towards a life of crime.* [17c: from **gravity**]

gravitation *noun* **1** *physics* the force of attraction that exists between any two bodies on account of their mass. **2** the process of moving or being drawn, either by this force or some other attracting influence. ▪ **gravitational** *adj.* ▪ **gravitationally** *adv.*

gravitational field *noun, physics* that region of space in which one object, by virtue of its mass, exerts a force of attraction on another object.

gravity *noun* **1** the observed effect of the force of attraction that exists between two massive bodies. **2** the force of attraction between any object situated within the Earth's gravitational field, and the Earth itself, on account of which objects feel heavy and are pulled down towards the ground. **3** seriousness; dangerous nature. **4** serious attitude; solemnity. [From Latin *gravitas* heaviness or seriousness]

gravy *noun* (***-ies***) **1** the juices released by meat as it is cooking. **2 a** a sauce made by thickening and seasoning these juices; **b** a similar sauce made with an artificial substitute. [14c]

gravy boat *noun* a small boat-shaped container with a handle, for serving gravy and other sauces.

gravy train *noun, slang* a job or scheme from which a lot of money is gained for little effort.

gray[1] *noun* (symbol **Gy**) the SI unit of absorbed dose of ionizing radiation, equivalent to one joule per kilogram. [1970s: named after L H Gray, British radiobiologist]

gray[2] see **grey**

grayling *noun* (***grayling*** *or* ***graylings***) a freshwater fish that has silvery scales and a large purplish spiny dorsal fin. [15c: **grey** + **-ling** sense 1]

graze[1] *verb* **1** *tr & intr* of animals: to eat grass. **2 a** to feed (animals) on grass; **b** to feed animals on (an area of pasture). **3** *intr, informal* to pilfer and eat food while shopping in a supermarket. **4** *tr & intr, informal* to browse through TV channels, etc. ▪ **grazer** *noun.* ▪ **grazing** *noun* **1** the act or practice of grazing. **2** pasture. [Anglo-Saxon *grasian*, from *græs* grass]

graze[2] *verb* **1** to suffer a break in (the skin of eg a limb), through scraping against a hard rough surface. **2** to brush against something lightly in passing. ▸ *noun* **1** an area of grazed skin. **2** the action of grazing skin. [17c]

grease *noun* **1** animal fat softened by melting or cooking. **2** any thick oily substance, esp a lubricant for the moving parts of machinery. ▸ *verb* to lubricate or dirty something with grease. [13c: from French *graisse*]

IDIOMS **grease sb's palm** *or* **hand** *informal* to bribe them.

greasepaint *noun* waxy make-up used by actors.

greasy *adj* (**-ier, -iest**) **1** containing, or covered in, grease. **2** having an oily appearance or texture. **3** slippery, as if covered in grease. **4** *informal* insincerely friendly or flattering. ▪ **greasily** *adv.* ▪ **greasiness** *noun.*

great *adj* **1** outstandingly talented and much admired and respected. **2** very large in size, quantity, intensity or extent. **3** (**greater**) (added to the name of a large city) indicating the wider area surrounding the city, sometimes including other boroughs, etc, as well as the city itself: *Greater Manchester.* **4** (*also* **greater**) *biol* larger in size than others of the same kind, species, etc: *great tit.* **5** *in compounds* indicating a family relationship that is one generation more remote than that of the base word: *great-grandmother.* See also **grand** (*adj* sense 9). **6** *informal* very enjoyable; excellent or splendid. **7** (*also* **great at sth**) *informal* clever; talented. **8** (*also* **great for sth**) *informal* very suitable or useful. **9** most important: *the great advantage of it.* **10** enthusiastic; keen: *a great reader.* **11** *informal* used to emphasize other adjectives describing size, esp *big*: *a great big dog.* **12** (**the Great**) in names and titles: indicating an importance or reputation of the highest degree: *Alexander the Great.* **13** (**the greatest**) *informal* **a** the best in their field; **b** a marvellous person or thing. **14** *old use* used in various expressions of surprise: *Great Scott!* ▸ *noun* a person who has achieved lasting fame, deservedly or not: *one of the all-time greats.* ▸ *adv, informal* very well. ▪ **greatly** *adv.* ▪ **greatness** *noun.* [Anglo-Saxon]

the Great Bear *noun* Ursa Major, a constellation of stars in the Northern hemisphere, whose seven brightest stars form the **Plough** (see under **plough**).

Great Britain *noun* the largest island in Europe, containing England, Wales and Scotland.

great circle *noun* a circle on the surface of a sphere, whose centre is the centre of the sphere.

greatcoat *noun* a heavy overcoat.

the Great War *noun* **World War I.**

greave *noun* (*usu* **greaves**) armour for the legs below the knee. [14c: from French *greve* shin]

grebe *noun* any of various waterfowl with short wings, a pointed bill and almost no tail. [18c: from French *grèbe*]

Grecian /ˈgriːʃən/ *adj* of a design, etc: in the style of ancient Greece. [16c: from Latin *Graecus* Greek]

greed *noun* **1** an excessive desire for, or consumption of, food. **2** selfish desire in general, eg for money. [17c: back-formation from **greedy**]

greedy *adj* (**-ier, -iest**) filled with greed. ▪ **greedily** *adv.* ▪ **greediness** *noun.* [Anglo-Saxon *grædig*]

Greek *adj* **1** belonging or relating to Greece, its inhabitants or their language. **2** belonging or relating to ancient Greece, its inhabitants or their language. ▸ *noun* **1** a citizen or inhabitant of, or person born in, Greece. **2 a** the official language of Greece (**Modern Greek**); **b** the language of the ancient Greeks (**Ancient Greek**), chiefly written in the Greek alphabet. **3** *informal* any language, jargon or subject one cannot understand. [Anglo-Saxon pl *Grecas*: from Latin *Graecus*]

Greek cross *noun* an upright cross with arms of equal length.

green *adj* **1** like the colour of the leaves of most plants. **2** covered with grass, bushes, etc: *green areas of the city.* **3** consisting mainly of leaves: *green salad.* **4** of fruit: not yet ripe. **5** *informal* of a person: young, inexperienced or easily fooled. **6** concerned with care of the environment: *the green movement.* **7** of someone's face: pale; showing signs of nausea. **8** not dried or dry: *green bacon* • *green timber.* **9** extremely jealous or envious. **10** healthy, vigorous, or flourishing: *green old age.* ▸ *noun* **1** the colour of the leaves of most plants. **2** something of this colour. **3** an area of grass, esp one in a public place: *the village green.* **4** an area of specially prepared turf: *bowling green* • *putting green.* **5** (**greens**) vegetables with edible green leaves and stems. **6** (*sometimes* **Green**) someone who supports actions or policies designed to protect or benefit the environment. ▸ *verb, tr & intr* to make or become green. ▪ **greenish** *and* **greeny** *adj.* ▪ **greenness** *noun.* [Anglo-Saxon *grene*]

greenback *noun, informal* a US dollar bill.

green bean *noun* any variety of bean, such as the French bean, string bean, etc, of which the narrow green unripe pod and contents can be eaten whole.

green belt *noun* open land surrounding a town or city, where building or development is strictly controlled.

green card *noun* **1** an international motorists' insurance document. **2** an official US work and residence permit issued to foreign nationals.

greenery *noun* green plants or their leaves.

the green-eyed monster *noun* jealousy. [16c: coined by Shakespeare in *Othello* (1604)]

greenfield site *noun* a site, separate from existing developments, that is to be developed for the first time. Compare **brownfield site**.

green fingers *plural noun, informal* natural skill at growing plants successfully.

greenfly *noun* (***greenfly*** *or* ***greenflies***) any of various species of **aphid**. [18c: so called because the female has a greenish body]

greengage *noun* **1** a cultivated variety of tree, sometimes regarded as a subspecies of the plum. **2** the small green plum-like edible fruit produced by this tree.

greengrocer *noun* a person or shop that sells fruit and vegetables.

greenhorn *noun, informal* an inexperienced person; a novice.

greenhouse *noun* a **glasshouse**, esp one with little or no artificial heating.

greenhouse effect *noun, meteorol, ecol, etc* the warming of the Earth's surface as a result of the trapping of radiation by carbon dioxide, ozone, and certain other gases (**greenhouse gases**) in the atmosphere.

greenhouse gas *noun* any of various gases, eg carbon dioxide, that are present in the atmosphere and contribute to the greenhouse effect.

greenkeeper *noun* someone who is responsible for the maintenance of a golf course or bowling green.

green light *noun* **1** a signal to drivers of cars, trains, etc that they can move forward. **2** (**the green light**) *informal* permission to proceed.

green paper *noun* (*often* **Green Paper**) *politics* in the UK: a written statement of the Government's proposed policy on a particular issue.

green party *or* **Green Party** *noun* a political party concerned with promoting policies for the protection and benefit of the environment.

Greenpeace *noun* an international environmental pressure group that campaigns against the dumping of toxic waste at sea, the testing of nuclear weapons, etc.

green pepper *noun* a green unripe sweet pepper, eaten as a vegetable.

green pound *noun* the pound's value compared with that of the other European currencies used in trading EU farm produce.

greenroom *noun* a backstage room in a theatre, etc where actors, musicians, etc can relax and receive visitors. [Early 18c]

greens see **green** (*noun* sense 5)

greenstick fracture *noun* a fracture where the bone is partly broken and partly bent.

green tea *noun* a sharp-tasting light-coloured tea made from leaves that have been dried quickly without fermenting.

Greenwich Mean Time /ˈgrɛnɪtʃ/ *noun* (abbrev **GMT**) the local time at the line of 0° longitude, which passes through Greenwich in England, used to calculate times in most other parts of the world.

greet[1] *verb* **1** to address or welcome someone, esp in a friendly way. **2** to receive or respond to something in a specified way: *His remarks were greeted with dismay.* **3** to be immediately noticeable to someone: *smells of cooking greeted me.* [Anglo-Saxon *gretan*]

greet[2] *Scot, N Eng dialect, verb* (*past tense* ***grat,*** *past participle* ***grat*** *or* ***grutten***) *intr* to weep or cry. [Anglo-Saxon *greotan* to weep]

greeting *noun* **1** a friendly expression or gesture used on meeting or welcoming someone. **2** (**greetings**) a good or fond wish; a friendly message. [Anglo-Saxon]

gregarious *adj* **1** liking the company of other people; sociable. **2** of animals: living in groups. ▪ **gregariously** *adv.* [17c: from Latin *gregarius,* from *grex* flock]

Gregorian calendar *noun* the system introduced by Pope Gregory XIII in 1582, and still widely in use, in which an ordinary year is divided into twelve months or 365 days, with a leap year of 366 days every four years. See also **Julian calendar**.

Gregorian chant *noun* a type of **plainsong** used in Roman Catholic religious ceremonies, introduced by Pope Gregory I.

gremlin *noun* an imaginary mischievous creature blamed for faults in machinery or electronic equipment. [1940s: orig RAF slang]

grenade *noun* a small bomb thrown by hand or fired from a rifle. [16c as *granade*: from Spanish *granada* pomegranate]

grenadier /grɛnəˈdɪə(r)/ *noun* a member of a regiment of soldiers formerly trained in the use of grenades.

grenadine *noun* a syrup made from pomegranate juice, used to flavour drinks. [19c: related to **grenade**]

grew *past tense of* **grow**

grey *or* (*esp N Am*) **gray** *adj* **1** of a colour between black and white, the colour of ash and slate. **2** of the weather: dull and cloudy. **3** **a** of a someone's hair: turning white; **b** of a person: having grey hair. **4** *derog* anonymous or uninteresting; having no distinguishing features: *a grey character.* **5** *informal* referring or relating to elderly or retired people: *the grey population.* ▸ *noun* **1** a colour between black and white. **2** grey material or clothes: *dressed in grey.* **3** dull light. **4** an animal, esp a horse, that is grey or whitish in colour. ▸ *verb, tr & intr* to make or become grey. ▪ **greyish** *adj.* ▪ **greyness** *noun.* [Anglo-Saxon *grei*]

grey area *noun* an unclear situation or subject, often with no distinct limits, guiding principles or identifiable characteristics.

greyhound *noun* a tall dog with a slender body, renowned for its speed and raced for sport. [Anglo-Saxon *grighund*]

greying *adj* **1** becoming grey: *greying hair.* **2** aging: *greying population.* ▸ *noun* **1** the process of becoming grey. **2** the process or phenomenon of having an increasing elderly or retired sector in the population.

grey matter *noun* **1** *anatomy* the tissue of the brain and spinal cord that appears grey in colour. Compare **white matter**. **2** *informal* intelligence or common sense.

grey whale *noun* a grey **baleen whale** with a mottled skin.

grid *noun* **1** a network of evenly spaced horizontal and vertical lines that can be superimposed on a map, chart, etc, esp in order to locate specific points. **2** such a network used for constructing a chart. **3** (**the grid** *or* **the national grid**) the network of power transmission lines, by means of which electricity is distributed from power stations across a region or country. **4** a network of underground pipes by which gas, water, etc is distributed across a region or country. **5** a framework of metal bars, esp one covering the opening to a drain. **6** an arrangement of lines marking the starting-points on a motor-racing track. **7** *electronics* an electrode that controls the flow of electrons from the cathode to the anode of a thermionic valve or vacuum tube. [19c: back-formation from **gridiron**]

griddle *or* (*Scot*) **girdle** *noun* a flat iron plate that is heated for baking or frying. [13c: from French *gridil*]

gridiron *noun* **1** a frame of iron bars used for grilling food over a fire. **2** *Amer football* the field of play. [13c as *gredire*]

gridlock *noun* **1** a severe traffic jam in which no vehicles are able to move. **2** a jammed-up situation, in which no progress is possible. ▪ **gridlocked** *adj.* [1980s]

grid reference *noun* a series of numbers and letters used to indicate the precise location of a place on a map.

grief *noun* **1** **a** great sorrow and unhappiness, esp at someone's death; **b** an event that is the source of this. **2** *informal* trouble or bother: *was getting grief from her parents for staying out late.* [13c: from French *grever* to grieve]

IDIOMS **come to grief** *informal* **1** to end in failure. **2** to have an accident.

grief-stricken *adj* crushed with sorrow.

grievance *noun* **1** a real or perceived cause for complaint, esp unfair treatment at work. **2** a formal complaint, esp one made in the workplace. [15c: from French *grevance*]

grieve *verb* **1** *intr* **a** to feel grief, esp at a death; **b** to mourn. **2** to upset or distress someone: *It grieves me to learn that he's still on drugs.* [13c: from French *grever* to grieve]

grievous *adj* **1** very severe or painful. **2** causing or likely to cause grief. **3** showing grief. **4** of a fault, etc: extremely serious. ▪ **grievously** *adv.* [13c: from French *grevos*]

grievous bodily harm *noun* (abbrev **GBH**) *law* **1** severe injury caused by a physical attack. **2** the criminal charge of causing such injury. Compare **actual bodily harm**.

griffin *or* **gryphon** *noun, myth* a winged monster with an eagle's head and a lion's body. [14c: from French *grifon*]

griffon *noun* **1** a small dog with a coarse wiry blackish or black and tan coat. **2** a large vulture with a bald head. [17c: French, meaning 'griffin']

grifter /ɡrɪftə(r)/ *noun, N Am slang* a con man; a swindler. [Early 20c: perhaps from **graft**[2]]

grill *verb* **1** to cook over or, more usu, under radiated heat. See also **broil**. **2** *informal* to interrogate someone, esp at length. **3** *intr* to suffer extreme heat. ▸ *noun* **1** a device on a cooker that radiates heat downwards. **2** a metal frame for cooking food over a fire; a gridiron. **3** a dish of grilled food: *mixed grill.* **4** (*also* **grillroom**) a restaurant or part of a restaurant that specializes in grilled food. [17c: from French *griller* to grill]

grille *or* **grill** *noun* a protective framework of metal bars or wires, eg over a window. [17c: French]

grilse *noun* (***grilse*** *or* ***grilses***) a young salmon returning from the sea to fresh water for the first time.

grim *adj* (***grimmer, grimmest***) **1** stern and unsmiling. **2** terrible; horrifying. **3** resolute; dogged: *grim determination.* **4** depressing; gloomy. **5** *informal* unpleasant. ▪ **grimly** *adv.* ▪ **grimness** *noun.* [Anglo-Saxon]

grimace *noun* an ugly twisting of the face that expresses pain or disgust, or that is pulled for amusement. ▸ *verb, intr* to make a grimace. [17c: French]

grime *noun* thick ingrained dirt or soot. ▸ *verb* to soil something heavily; to make something filthy. ▪ **grimy** *adj* (***-ier, -iest***). [15c: from Flemish *grijm*]

grin *verb* (***grinned, grinning***) **1** *intr* to smile broadly, showing the teeth. **2** to express (eg pleasure) in this way. ▸ *noun* a broad smile, showing the teeth. ▪ **grinning** *adj, noun.* [Anglo-Saxon *grennian*]

IDIOMS **grin and bear it** *informal* to endure something unpleasant without complaining.

grind *verb* (***ground***) **1** to crush something into small particles or powder between two hard surfaces. **2** to sharpen, smooth or polish something by rubbing against a hard surface. **3** *tr & intr* to rub something together with a jarring noise. **4** to press something hard with a twisting action: *ground his heel into the dirt.* **5** to operate something by turning a handle: *grinding his barrel-organ.* ▸ *noun* **1** *informal* steady, dull and laborious routine. **2** the act or sound of grinding. **3** a specified size or texture of crushed particles: *fine grind.* [Anglo-Saxon *grindan*]

IDIOMS **grind to a halt** to stop completely.

PHRASAL VERBS **grind sb down** to crush their spirit; to oppress them.

grinder *noun* **1** a person or machine that grinds. **2** a molar tooth.

grinding *adj* crushing; oppressive: *grinding poverty.*

grindstone *noun* a revolving stone wheel used for sharpening and polishing. [13c]

IDIOMS **have** *or* **keep one's nose to the grindstone** *informal* to work hard and with perseverance.

gringo *noun, derog* in Latin America, esp Mexico: an English-speaking foreigner. [19c: Spanish, from *griego* a Greek or a foreigner]

grip *verb* (***gripped, gripping***) **1** to take or keep a firm hold of something. **2** to capture the imagination or attention of a person. ▸ *noun* **1** a firm hold; the action of taking a firm hold. **2** a way of gripping. **3** a handle or part that can be gripped. **4** a U-shaped wire pin for keeping the hair in place. **5** a holdall. **6** *informal* understanding. **7** *informal* control; mastery: *lose one's grip of the situation.* **8** *theatre* a stagehand who moves scenery. **9** *cinema, TV* someone who manoeuvres a film camera. ▪ **gripper** *noun.* [Anglo-Saxon *gripe* a grasp]

IDIOMS **get to grips with sth** to begin to deal with it.

gripe *verb* **1** *intr, informal* to complain persistently. **2** *tr & intr* to feel, or cause someone to feel, intense stomach pain. ▸ *noun* **1** *informal* a complaint. **2** (*usu* **gripes**) *old use, informal* a severe stomach pain. [Anglo-Saxon *gripan*]

gripping *adj* holding the attention; exciting.

grisly *adj* (***-ier, -iest***) horrible; ghastly; gruesome. ▪ **grisliness** *noun.* [12c *grislic*]

grist *noun* grain that is to be, or that has been, ground into flour. [Anglo-Saxon]

IDIOMS **grist to the mill** anything useful or profitable.

gristle *noun* cartilage, esp in meat. ▪ **gristly** *adj.* [Anglo-Saxon]

grit *noun* **1** small particles of a hard material, esp of stone or sand. **2** *informal* courage and determination. ▸ *verb* (***gritted, gritting***) **1** to spread grit on (icy roads, etc). **2** to clench (the teeth), eg to overcome pain. [Anglo-Saxon *greot*]

grits *plural noun* coarsely ground grain with the husks removed. ▸ *singular noun* a dish of this, boiled and eaten for breakfast in the southern US. [Anglo-Saxon as *grytt* meaning 'bran']

gritty *adj* (***-ier, -iest***) **1** full of or covered with grit. **2** like grit. **3** determined; dogged.

grizzle *verb, intr, informal* **1** esp of a young child: to cry fretfully. **2** to sulk or complain. [19c]

grizzled *adj* **1** of the hair or a beard: grey or greying. **2** of a person: having such hair. [15c as *griseld*: from French *gris* grey]

grizzly *adj* (***-ier, -iest***) grey or greying; grizzled. ▸ *noun* (***-ies***) *informal* a grizzly bear. [16c as *gristelly*: see **grizzled**]

grizzly bear *noun* the largest of the bears, so called because its dark brown fur is frosted with white.

groan *verb* **1** *intr* to make a long deep sound in the back of the throat, expressing pain, distress, disapproval, etc. **2** to utter or express something with or by means of a groan. **3** *intr* to creak loudly. **4** *intr* to be weighed down or almost breaking: *tables groaning with masses of food.* ▸ *noun* an act, or the sound, of groaning. ▪ **groaning** *noun, adj.* [Anglo-Saxon *granian*]

groat *noun* an obsolete British silver coin worth four old pennies. [14c as *grote*: from Dutch *groot* thick]

groats *plural noun* crushed grain, esp oats, with the husks removed. [Anglo-Saxon *grotan*]

grocer *noun* **1** someone whose job is selling food and general household goods. **2** a grocer's shop. [15c: from French *grossier*; see **gross**]

grocery *noun* (*-ies*) **1** the trade or premises of a grocer. **2** (**groceries**) merchandise, esp food, sold in a grocer's shop. [15c]

grog *noun* **1** a mixture of alcoholic spirit (esp rum) and water. **2** *Aust & NZ informal* any alcoholic drink. [18c: from Old Grog, the nickname of British admiral Edward Vernon, who in 1740 ordered the naval ration of rum to be diluted with water]

groggy *adj* (*-ier, -iest*) *informal* weak, dizzy and unsteady on the feet, eg from the effects of illness or alcohol. ▪ **groggily** *adv.* [18c: in old sense 'intoxicated']

groin *noun* **1** the part of the body where the lower abdomen joins the upper thigh. **2** *archit* the edge formed by the joining of two vaults in a roof; the rib covering the intersection. ▸ *verb, archit* to build (a vault, etc) with groins. ▪ **groined** *adj.* ▪ **groining** *noun.* [15c as *grynde*]

grommet *or* **grummet** *noun* **1** a rubber or plastic ring around a hole in metal, to protect a tube or insulate a wire passing through. **2 a** a metal ring lining an eyelet; **b** the eyelet itself. **3** *med* a small tube passed through the eardrum to drain the middle ear. [17c: perhaps from French *grommette* the curb on a bridle]

groom *noun* **1** someone who looks after horses and cleans stables. **2** a bridegroom. **3** a title given to various officers in a royal household. ▸ *verb* **1** to clean, brush and generally smarten (animals, esp horses). **2** to keep (a person) clean and neat, esp regarding clothes and hair. **3** to train or prepare someone for a specified office, stardom or success in any sphere. [13c as *grom* boy, man, or manservant]

groove *noun* **1** a long narrow channel, esp one cut with a tool. **2** the continuous track cut into the surface of a **record** (*noun* sense 4), along which the **stylus** moves. **3** *informal* a set routine, esp a monotonous one. **4** repetitive, rhythmic, musical patterns used in creating dance music for clubs. ▸ *verb* **1** to cut a groove in something. **2** *intr, dated slang* to enjoy oneself. [14c as *grofe*: from Dutch *groeve* a furrow]

groovy *adj* (*-ier, -iest*) *dated slang* excellent, attractive or fashionable. [20c]

grope *verb* **1** *intr* to search by feeling about with the hands, eg in the dark. **2** *intr* to search uncertainly or with difficulty: *groping for answers.* **3** to find (one's way) by feeling. ▪ **groping** *adj, noun.* ▪ **gropingly** *adv.* [Anglo-Saxon *grapian*]

groper see **grouper**

gross *adj* (*grosser, grossest*, except in sense 1) **1** total, with no deductions: *gross weight.* Opposite of **net**[2]. **2** very great; flagrant; glaring: *gross negligence.* **3** *derog* vulgar; coarse. **4** *derog* unattractively fat. **5** *informal, derog* very unpleasant. **6** dense; lush: *gross vegetation.* **7** *derog* dull; lacking sensitivity or judgement. **8** solid; tangible; concrete; not spiritual or abstract. ▸ *noun* **1** (*pl* ***gross***) twelve dozen, 144. **2** (*pl* ***grosses***) the total amount or weight, without deductions. ▸ *verb* to earn (a specified sum) as a gross income or profit, before tax is deducted. ▪ **grossly** *adv.* ▪ **grossness** *noun.* [14c: from French *gros* large or fat]

PHRASAL VERBS **gross sb out** *slang* to disgust or offend them. **gross sth up** to convert (a net figure) into a gross one, eg for the purpose of calculating tax.

gross domestic product *noun* (abbrev **GDP**) *econ* the total value of all goods produced and all services provided by a nation in one year.

gross national product *noun* (abbrev **GNP**) *econ* gross domestic product plus the value of income from investments abroad.

grotesque *adj* **1** very unnatural or strange-looking, so as to cause fear or laughter. **2** exaggerated; ridiculous; absurd. ▸ *noun* **1** (**the grotesque**) a 16c style in art that features animals, plants and people mixed together in a strange or fantastic manner. **2** a work of art in this style. ▪ **grotesquely** *adv.* ▪ **grotesqueness** *noun.* [16c: from Italian *pittura grottesca* cave painting]

grotto *noun* (***grottos*** *or* ***grottoes***) **1** a cave, esp a small and picturesque one. **2** a man-made cave-like structure, esp in a garden or park. [17c: from Italian *grotta* cave]

grotty *adj* (*-ier, -iest*) *informal* **1** *derog* unpleasantly dirty or shabby. **2** slightly ill. ▪ **grottiness** *noun.* [1960s: short form of **grotesque**]

grouch *informal verb, intr* to grumble or complain. ▸ *noun* **1** a complaining person. **2 a** a bad-tempered complaint; **b** the cause of it. [19c: US variant of obsolete *grutch* grudge]

grouchy *adj* (*-ier, -iest*) bad-tempered; tending to grumble. ▪ **grouchily** *adv.* ▪ **grouchiness** *noun.*

ground[1] *noun* **1** the solid surface of the Earth, or any part of it; soil; land. **2** (*often* **grounds**) an area of land, usu extensive, attached to or surrounding a building. **3** an area of land used for a specified purpose: *football ground.* **4** distance covered or to be covered. **5** the substance of discussion: *cover a lot of ground.* **6** a position or standpoint, eg in an argument: *stand or shift one's ground.* **7** progress relative to that made by an opponent; advantage: *lose or gain ground.* **8** (*usu* **grounds**) a reason or justification. **9** *art* **a** the background in a painting; **b** a surface prepared specially before paint is applied. **10** *N Amer, elec* **earth** (*noun* sense 6). **11** (**grounds**) sediment or dregs, esp of coffee. **12** the bottom of the sea or a river. ▸ *verb* **1** *tr & intr* to hit or cause (a ship) to hit the seabed or shore and remain stuck. **2** to refuse to allow (a pilot or aeroplane) to fly. **3** to forbid (eg teenagers) to go out socially as a punishment. **4** to lay (eg weapons) on the ground. **5** (*usu* **ground sb in sth**) to give them basic instructions in (a subject). **6** (*usu* **ground sth on sth else**) to base (an argument, a complaint, etc) on it: *an argument grounded on logic.* **7** *N Amer, elec* to **earth**. ▸ *adj* on or relating to the ground: *ground forces.* [14c: from French *gros* large or fat]

IDIOMS **give ground** to give way; to retreat. **go to ground 1** of an animal: to go into a burrow to escape from hunters. **2** to go into hiding, eg from the police. **off the ground** started; under way: *get the project off the ground.* **on the ground** amongst ordinary people: *opinion on the ground.*

ground² *past tense, past participle of* **grind**

groundbreaking *adj* innovative.

ground control *noun* the control and monitoring from the ground of the flight of aircraft or spacecraft.

ground cover *noun* low-growing plants that cover the surface of the ground.

ground crew *noun* a team of mechanics whose job is to maintain aircraft.

groundhog *noun* the **woodchuck**.

Groundhog Day *noun* **1** (in the US and Canada) 2 February, supposed to mark the end of winter if a groundhog emerging from hibernation on that day does not see its shadow. **2** *informal* a day when things seem to happen in exactly the same way as on the previous day.

grounding *noun* a foundation of basic knowledge or instruction.

groundless *adj* having no reason or justification.

groundnut *noun* **1 a** a N American climbing plant of the pulse family that produces small edible underground tubers, seed pods, etc, eg the **peanut** plant; **b** one of the tubers produced by such a plant. **2** *US* a peanut.

ground rule *noun* a basic principle.

groundsheet *noun* a waterproof sheet spread on the ground, eg in a tent, to protect against damp.

groundsman *noun* someone whose job is to maintain a sports field.

ground state *noun, physics* the lowest energy state of an atom.

groundswell *noun* **1** a broad high swell of the sea, often caused by a distant storm or earthquake. **2** a rapidly growing indication of public or political feeling.

ground water *noun, geol* water that occurs in the rocks beneath the surface of the Earth and which can surface in springs.

group *noun* **1** a number of people or things gathered, placed or classed together. **2** (*sometimes* **Group**) a number of business companies under single ownership and central control. **3** a band of musicians and singers, esp one that plays pop music. **4** a division of an air force. **5** *chem* in the periodic table: a vertical column representing a series of chemical elements with similar chemical properties. **6** *chem* a combination of two or more atoms that are bonded together and tend to act as a single unit in chemical reactions. ▸ *verb, tr & intr* to form (things or people) into a group. [17c: from French *groupe*]

group captain *noun* an officer in the Royal Air Force below the rank of air commodore.

grouper or (*Aust, NZ*) **groper** *noun* a name given to various fishes, esp ones resembling **bass²**. [17c: from Portuguese *garupa*]

groupie *noun, informal* **1** *often derog* an ardent follower of a touring pop star or group. **2** *loosely* someone who follows a specified activity, sport, pastime, etc: *a religious groupie.*

group therapy *noun* a form of psychotherapy that involves the joint participation of several people who discuss their problems and ways of overcoming them.

groupware *noun, comput* software that is designed for use on several computers at the same time.

grouse¹ *noun* (*pl* ***grouse***) a gamebird with a plump body, feathered legs and a short curved bill.

grouse² *informal, verb, intr* to complain. ▸ *noun* **1** a complaint or spell of complaining. **2** a querulous person; a moaner. ▪ **grouser** *noun.* [19c as *verb* (orig army slang)]

grout *noun* thin mortar applied to the joints between bricks or esp ceramic tiles, as a decorative finish. ▸ *verb* to apply grout to the joints of something. ▪ **grouting** *noun.* [17c as *growt*]

grove *noun* **1** a small group of trees, often planted for shade or ornament. **2** an area planted with fruit trees, esp citrus and olive. [Anglo-Saxon as *graf*]

grovel *verb* (***grovelled, grovelling***; *N Am also* ***groveled, groveling***) *intr* **1** to act with exaggerated (and usu insincere) respect or humility, esp to gain the favour of a superior. **2** to lie or crawl face down, in fear or respect. ▪ **groveller** *noun.* ▪ **grovelling** *adj.* [16c]

grow *verb* (*past tense* ***grew,*** *past participle* ***grown***) **1** *intr* of a living thing: to develop into a larger more mature form. **2** *tr & intr* to increase, or allow (hair, nails, etc) to increase, in length. **3** *intr* **a** to increase in size, intensity or extent; **b** to increase in size in a specified direction: *grow upwards towards the light.* **4** to cultivate (plants). **5 a** to become … gradually: *Over the years they grew very lazy;* **b** (*usu* **grow to …**) to come gradually to (have a specified feeling): *grew to hate him.* [Anglo-Saxon *growan*]

PHRASAL VERBS **grow into sth** to become big enough to wear (clothes that were orig too large). **grow on sb** to gradually come to be liked by them. **grow out of sth 1** to become too big to wear (clothes that were orig the right size). **2** to lose a liking for it, or the habit of doing it, with age. **grow up 1** to become, or be in the process of becoming, an adult. **2** to behave in an adult way. **3** to come into existence; to develop.

growing pains *plural noun* **1** muscular pains sometimes experienced by growing children. **2** temporary problems or difficulties encountered in the early stages of a project, business or enterprise.

growl *verb* **1** *intr* of animals: to make a deep rough sound in the throat, showing hostility. **2** *tr & intr* of people: to make a similar sound showing anger or displeasure; to speak or say something angrily. ▸ *noun* an act or the sound of growling. ▪ **growling** *adj, noun.* [14c: meaning 'to rumble']

grown *adj* **1** mature: *a grown woman.* **2** *in compounds* developed to a specified degree: *fully grown.*

grown-up *informal, adj* adult. ▸ *noun* an adult.

growth *noun* **1 a** the process or rate of growing; **b** the increase in size, weight and complexity of a living organism that takes place as it develops to maturity. **2** an increase. **3** *econ* an increase in economic activity or profitability. **4** *med* a tumour formed as a result of the uncontrolled multiplication of cells.

groyne *noun* a **breakwater** built to stop erosion and drifting of sand. [16c: from French *groign* snout or promontory]

grub *noun* **1** the worm-like larva of an insect, esp a beetle. **2** food. ▸ *verb* (***grubbed, grubbing***) **1** *intr* (*usu* **grub about**) to dig or search in the soil. **2** *intr* (*usu* **grub around**) to search or rummage. **3** (*esp* **grub up**) to dig up (roots and stumps). **4** to clear (ground). [13c as *grube* (verb)]

grubby *adj* (***-ier, -iest***) *informal* dirty. ▪ **grubbily** *adv.* ▪ **grubbiness** *noun.* [19c: from **grub**]

grudge *noun* a long-standing feeling of resentment: *bear a grudge.* ▸ *verb* **1** (*esp* **grudge doing sth**) to be unwilling to do it; to do it unwillingly. **2** (**to grudge sb sth**) **a** to be unwilling to give them it; to give them it unwillingly; **b** to feel resentment at their good fortune. [15c: from French *grouchier* to grumble]

grudging *adj* **1** resentful. **2** unwilling. ▪ **grudgingly** *adv.*

gruel *noun* thin porridge. [14c: French, meaning 'groats']

gruelling *or* (*N Am*) **grueling** *adj* exhausting; punishing. [19c: from **gruel** in old sense 'to punish']

gruesome *adj* inspiring horror or disgust; sickening; macabre. ▪ **gruesomely** *adv.* [16c as *growsome*: from dialect *grue* to shiver]

gruff *adj* **1** of a voice: deep and rough. **2** rough, unfriendly or surly in manner. ▪ **gruffly** *adv.* ▪ **gruffness** *noun.* [16c Scots as *groiff*, meaning 'coarse']

grumble *verb, intr* **1** to complain in a bad-tempered way. **2** to make a low rumbling sound. ▸ *noun* **1** a complaint. **2** a rumbling sound. ▪ **grumbler** *noun.* ▪ **grumbling** *noun, adj.* ▪ **grumblingly** *adv.* ▪ **grumbly** *adj.* [16c: from Dutch *grommelen*]

grummet see **grommet**

grump *noun, informal* **1** a grumpy person. **2** (**the grumps**) a fit of bad temper or sulking. [18c: an imitation of a snort of displeasure]

grumpy *adj* (***-ier, -iest***) bad-tempered; surly. ▪ **grumpily** *adv.* ▪ **grumpiness** *noun.* [18c]

grunge *noun, slang, orig US* **1** dirt; rubbish; trash. **2** (*in full* **grunge rock**) a style of music with a strident discordant guitar-based sound. ▪ **grungy** *adj* (***-ier, -iest***). [1960s in sense 1; 1990s otherwise]

grunt *verb* **1** *intr* of animals, esp pigs: to make a low rough sound in the back of the throat. **2** *intr* of people: to make a similar sound, eg indicating disgust or unwillingness to speak fully. **3** to express or utter something with this sound. ▸ *noun* an act or the sound of grunting. [Anglo-Saxon *grunnettan*]

Gruyère /gruː'jɛə(r)/ *noun* a pale yellow holey cheese, originally made in Switzerland. [19c]

gryphon see **griffin**

GSOH *abbrev* good (or great) sense of humour.

G-string *noun* (*also* **gee-string**) a garment that barely covers the pubic area, consisting of a strip of cloth attached to a narrow waistband.

g-suit *or* **G-suit** *noun* a close-fitting inflatable garment worn by astronauts and the pilots of high-speed aircraft. [1940s: abbrev of *gravity suit*]

guacamole /gwakə'moʊlɪ/ *noun* a traditional Mexican dish of mashed avocado mixed with spicy seasoning. [1920s: American Spanish]

guanine /'gwɑːniːn/ *noun, biochem* a **base**[1] (*noun* sense 6) that is one of the four bases found in **nucleic acid**. See also **adenine**, **cytosine**, **thymine**.[19c: from **guano**]

guano /'gwɑːnoʊ/ *noun* the droppings of large colonies of bats, fish-eating seabirds or seals, used as a fertilizer. [17c: Spanish, from Quechua *huanu* dung]

guarantee *noun* **1 a** a formal agreement, usu in writing, that a product, service, etc will conform to specified standards for a particular period of time; **b** a document that records this kind of agreement. **2** an assurance that something will have a specified outcome, condition, etc: *no guarantee that there wouldn't be more pay cuts.* **3** *law* an agreement, usu backed up by some kind of collateral, under which one person, the **guarantor**, becomes liable for the debt or default of another. **4** someone who agrees to give a guarantee. ▸ *verb* **1** to provide (eg a product, service, etc) with a guarantee. **2** to ensure something: *Their reputation guarantees their success.* **3** to assure or promise: *I guarantee the script will be finished tomorrow.* **4** to act as a **guarantor** for something. See also **warranty**. ▪ **guaranteed** *adj.* [17c]

guarantor *noun* someone who gives a guarantee.

guaranty *noun* (***-ies***) a **guarantee** (sense 3). [16c: from French *guarantie* and related to **warranty**]

guard *verb* **1** to protect someone or something from danger or attack. **2** to watch over someone in order to prevent their escape. **3** to control or check: *guard your tongue.* **4** to control passage through (eg a doorway). **5** *intr* (**guard against sth**) to take precautions to prevent it. ▸ *noun* **1** a person or group whose job is to provide protection, eg from danger or attack, or to prevent escape. **2** *Brit* a person in charge of a railway train. **3** a state of readiness to give protection or prevent escape: *keep guard.* **4** *boxing, cricket, etc* a defensive posture. **5** *Amer football, etc* a defensive player or their position. **6** *esp in compounds* anything that gives protection from or to something: *fireguard* • *shinguard.* **7** the act or duty of protecting. **8** (*often* **Guard**) a soldier in any of certain army regiments orig formed to protect the sovereign. [15c: from French *garder* to protect]
IDIOMS **off guard** *or* **off one's guard** not on the alert; unwary about what one says or does: *caught you off guard.* **on guard 1** on sentry duty. **2** (*also* **on one's guard**) on the alert; wary about what one says or does: *be on your guard against thieves.*

guarded *adj* cautious. ▪ **guardedly** *adv.*

guardian *noun* **1** someone who is legally responsible for the care of another, esp an orphaned child. **2** a guard, defender or protector: *the Church's role as guardian of public morals.* ▪ **guardianship** *noun.* [15c: from Anglo-French *gardein*]

guardian angel *noun* an angel believed to watch over a particular person.

guardsman *noun* **1** *Brit* a member of a regiment of Guards. **2** *US* a member of the National Guard.

guava /'gwɑːvə/ *noun* **1** a small tropical tree cultivated for its edible fruits. **2** the pear-shaped fruit of this tree. [16c as *guiava*: from Spanish *guayaba*]

gubernatorial /gʌbənə'tɔːrɪəl/ *adj, formal, esp US* referring or relating to a **governor** (in senses 1–4, esp sense 1). [18c: from Latin *gubernator* steersman]

gudgeon[1] *noun* **1** a small freshwater fish. **2** *informal* a gullible person. [15c: from French *goujon*]

gudgeon[2] *noun* **1** a pivot or pin of any kind. **2** the socket part of a hinge or rudder that the pin part fits into. [15c: from French *goujon* pin of a pulley]

guernsey *noun* **1** a hand-knitted woollen pullover, orig one worn by sailors. **2** *Aust* a sleeveless football jersey worn by Australian rules players. [19c: *Guernsey* in the Channel Islands]

guerrilla *or* **guerilla** *noun* a member of a small, independent armed force making surprise attacks, eg against government troops. *as adj*: *guerrilla warfare*. [19c: Spanish diminutive of *guerra* war]

guess *verb* **1** *tr & intr* to make an estimate or form an opinion about something, based on little or no information. **2** to estimate something correctly. **3** to think or suppose: *I guess we could go*. ▸ *noun* an estimate based on guessing. [14c as *gess*: from Dutch *gissen*]

guesstimate *informal, noun* a very rough estimate, based on guesswork. ▸ *verb* to estimate something using a rough guess. [1930s: **guess** + **estimate**]

guesswork *noun* the process or result of guessing.

guest *noun* **1** someone who receives hospitality in the home of, or at the expense of, another. **2** someone who stays at a hotel, boarding-house, etc. **3** a person specially invited to take part: *guest star* • *guest speaker*. ▸ *verb, intr* to appear as a guest, eg on a television show. [Anglo-Saxon *gest*]

guesthouse *noun* a private home that offers accommodation to paying guests; a boarding-house.

guff *noun, informal, derog* nonsense. [19c: orig as **puff**, meaning 'a blow of air']

guffaw *noun* a loud coarse laugh. ▸ *verb, intr* to laugh in this way. [19c: imitating the sound]

GUI *abbrev, comput* graphical user interface.

guidance *noun* **1** help, advice or counselling; the act or process of guiding. **2** direction or leadership.

guide *verb* **1** to lead, direct or show the way to someone. **2** to control or direct the movement or course of something. **3** to advise or influence: *be guided by your parents*. ▸ *noun* **1** someone who leads the way for eg tourists or mountaineers. **2** any device used to direct movement. **3** a **guidebook**. **4** (**Guide**) a member of a worldwide youth organization for girls. Also called **Girl Guide**. *US equivalent* **Girl Scout**. **5** someone or something, esp a quality, that influences another person's decisions or behaviour: *Let truth be your guide*. [14c: from French *guider*]

guidebook *noun* a book containing information about a particular place or instructions for a practical activity.

guide dog *noun* a dog specially trained to guide a blind person safely.

guideline *noun* (*often* **guidelines**) an indication of what future action is required or recommended.

guild *or* **gild** *noun* **1** a medieval association of merchants or craftsmen for maintaining standards and providing mutual support. **2** a name used by various modern societies, clubs and associations. [Anglo-Saxon *gield*]

guilder *or* **gilder** *noun* (*pl* ***guilder*** *or* ***guilders***) the former standard unit of currency of the Netherlands, replaced in 2002 by the euro. [15c as *guldren*: from Dutch *gulden*]

guildhall *noun* **1** a hall where members of a guild or other association meet. **2** a town hall.

guile /gaɪl/ *noun* **1** the ability to deceive or trick. **2** craftiness or cunning. ▪ **guileful** *adj*. ▪ **guileless** *adj*. ▪ **guilelessly** *adv*. [13c as *gile*: French, meaning 'deceit']

guillemot /ˈgɪlɪmɒt/ *noun* a seabird with black and white plumage and a long narrow bill. [17c]

guillotine *noun* **1** an instrument for beheading, consisting of a large heavy blade that slides rapidly down between two upright posts. **2** a device with a large blade moved by a lever, for cutting paper or metal. **3** *politics* a time limit set to speed up discussion of, and voting on, a parliamentary bill. ▸ *verb* to use a guillotine in any of the senses above. [18c: named after French physician Joseph Guillotin, who proposed beheading by guillotine in the French Revolution]

guilt *noun* **1** a feeling of shame or remorse resulting from a sense of having done wrong. **2** the state of having done wrong or having broken a law. **3** blame. **4** *law* liability to a penalty. [Anglo-Saxon *gylt*]

guiltless *adj* innocent. ▪ **guiltlessly** *adv*.

guilt trip *noun, informal* a prolonged feeling of guilt.

guilty *adj* (***-ier, -iest***) (*often* **guilty of sth**) **1** responsible for a crime or wrongdoing, or judged to be so. **2** feeling, showing or involving guilt: *a guilty look*. **3** able to be justly accused of something: *guilty of working too hard*. ▪ **guiltily** *adv*. ▪ **guiltiness** *noun*.

guinea *noun* **1** an obsolete British gold coin worth 21 shillings (£1.05). **2** its value, still used as a monetary unit in some professions, esp horse-racing. [17c: named after Guinea, W Africa, where the gold for the coin was orig mined]

guinea fowl *noun* (*pl* ***guinea fowl***) a ground-living bird with a naked head and greyish plumage speckled with white. [18c: it was imported from Guinea, W Africa, in the 16c]

guinea pig *noun* **1** a tailless rodent, widely kept as a domestic pet and also used as a laboratory animal. **2** a person used as the subject of an experiment. [17c]

guise *noun* **1** assumed appearance; pretence: *under the guise of friendship*. **2** external appearance in general. [13c]

guitar *noun* a musical instrument with a body generally shaped like a figure eight, a long fretted neck and usu six strings that are plucked or strummed. ▪ **guitarist** *noun*. [17c as *guitarra*: from Spanish *guitarra*]

gulch *noun, N Am* a narrow rocky ravine with a fast-flowing stream running through it. [19c]

gulf *noun* **1** a very large and deeply indented inlet of the sea extending far into the land. **2** a vast difference or separation, eg between points of view, etc. **3** a deep hollow in the ground; a chasm. **4** (**the Gulf**) **a** the region around the Persian Gulf in the Middle East; **b** the area around the Gulf of Mexico in Central America. [14c: from French *golfe*]

gull *noun* an omnivorous seabird with a stout body and predominantly white or greyish plumage. Also called **seagull**. [15c]

gullet *noun* the **oesophagus** or throat. [14c: French diminutive of *goule* throat]

gullible *adj* easily tricked. ▪ **gullibility** *noun*. [18c]

gully *or* **gulley** *noun* (***gullies*** *or* ***gulleys***) **1** a small channel or cutting with steep sides formed by running water esp during heavy rain in tropical and semi-arid regions. **2** *cricket* a fielding position between cover point and the slips.

gulp *verb* **1** *tr & intr* (*also* **gulp down**) to swallow (food, drink, etc) eagerly or in large mouthfuls. **2** (*usu* **gulp sth back**) to stifle (tears, etc). **3** *intr* to make a swallowing motion, eg because of fear.

▸ *noun* **1** a swallowing motion. **2** an amount swallowed at once; a mouthful. [15c: from Dutch *gulpen*]

gum[1] *noun* the firm fibrous flesh surrounding the roots of the teeth. [Anglo-Saxon *goma* palate]

gum[2] *noun* **1** a substance found in certain plants, esp trees, that produces a sticky solution or gel when added to water, used in confectionery, gummed envelopes, etc. **2** this or any similar substance used as glue. **3** a gumdrop. **4** *informal* chewing gum. ▸ *verb* (***gummed, gumming***) to smear, glue or unite something with gum. [13c: from French *gomme*]

gum arabic *noun* a thick sticky water-soluble gum exuded by certain acacia trees. [16c]

gumbo *noun* a thick soup or stew thickened with okra. [19c: from Louisiana French *gombo*]

gumboil *noun* a small abscess on the gum.

gumboot *noun* a **wellington** boot.

gummy[1] *adj* (***-ier, -iest***) toothless. [Early 20c: from **gum[1]**]

gummy[2] *adj* (***-ier, -iest***) **1** sticky. **2** producing gum. [14c: from **gum[2]**]

gumption *noun, informal* **1** common sense; initiative. **2** courage. [18c]

gumshield *noun, sport* a flexible pad worn in the mouth to protect the teeth.

gum tree *noun*

IDIOMS **up a gum tree** *informal* in a difficult position.

gun *noun* **1** any weapon that fires bullets or shells from a metal tube. **2** any instrument that forces something out under pressure: *spray gun*. **3** *informal* a gunman: *a hired gun*. **4** a member of a party of hunters. **5** the signal to start a race, etc. ▸ *verb* (***gunned, gunning***) *informal* to rev up (a car engine) noisily. [14c]

IDIOMS **be gunning for sb** to be searching determinedly for them, usu with hostile intent. **go great guns** *informal* to function or be performed with great speed or success.

PHRASAL VERBS **gun sb** *or* **sth down** to shoot them or it with a gun.

gunboat *noun* a small warship with mounted guns.

gun cotton *noun* a highly explosive material formed by treating cotton with nitric acid and sulphuric acid.

gun dog *noun* a dog specially trained to **flush[4]** birds or small mammals and to retrieve them when they have been shot.

gunfight *noun* a fight involving two or more people with guns, esp formerly in the old American West. ▪ **gunfighter** *noun.*

gunfire *noun* **1** the act of firing guns. **2** the bullets fired. **3** the sound of firing. See also **gunshot**.

gunge *informal, noun* any messy, slimy or sticky substance. ▸ *verb* (*usu* **be gunged up**) to be covered or blocked with gunge. [1960s]

gung-ho *adj, derog, informal* excessively or foolishly eager, esp to attack an enemy. [1940s, orig US]

gunk *noun, informal* any slimy or oily semi-solid substance. [1930s: orig a US trademark of a grease-solvent]

gunlock *noun* the mechanism in some guns that causes the charge to explode.

gunman *noun* **1** an armed criminal. **2** an assassin. **3** a terrorist.

gunmetal *noun* **1** a dark-grey alloy, composed mainly of copper with small amounts of tin and zinc, formerly used to make cannons. **2** any of various other alloys that are used to make guns. **3** a dark-grey colour, esp if metallic. ▸ *adj* dark-grey.

gunnel see **gunwale**

gunner *noun* **1** any member of an armed force who operates a heavy gun. **2** a soldier in an artillery regiment.

gunnery *noun* **1** the use of guns. **2** the science of designing guns.

gunpoint *noun* (*only* **at gunpoint**) threatening, or being threatened, with a gun.

gunpowder *noun* the oldest known explosive, a mixture of potassium nitrate, sulphur and charcoal.

gunrunning *noun* the act of smuggling arms into a country. ▪ **gunrunner** *noun.*

gunshot *noun* **1** bullets fired from a gun. **2** the distance over which a gun can fire a bullet: *within gunshot*. **3** a sound of firing. See also **gunfire**.

gunslinger *noun, informal* an armed fighter in the lawless days of the American West.

gunsmith *noun* someone whose job is to make and/or repair firearms.

gunwale *or* **gunnel** /ˈgʌnəl/ *noun* the upper edge of a ship's side. [15c: from **gun** + *wale*, a course of planking running along the top edge of a ship's side]

guppy *noun* (***-ies***) a small brightly coloured freshwater fish that is a popular aquarium fish. [1940s: named after R J L Guppy, who sent the first specimens to the British Museum in the 19c]

gurdwara /gɜːˈdwɑːrə/ *noun* a Sikh place of worship. [Early 20c: from Punjabi *gurduara*]

gurgle *verb* **1** *intr* of water: to make a bubbling noise when flowing. **2** *intr* to make a bubbling noise in the throat. **3** to utter something with a gurgle. ▸ *noun* the sound of gurgling. [16c as *gurgull*: from Latin *gurgulare*]

guru *noun* **1** a Hindu or Sikh spiritual leader or teacher. See also **maharishi**, **swami**. **2** any greatly respected and influential leader or adviser. [17c: Hindi; from Sanskrit, meaning 'venerable']

Guru Granth Sahib /grʌnt sɑːɪb/ *noun* the sacred scripture of the Sikh religion. Also called **Adi-Granth** /ʌˈðɪ/, **Granth**, **Granth Sahib**. [18c: from Hindi *granth* book]

gush *verb* **1** *tr & intr* of a liquid: to flood out or make it flood out suddenly and violently. **2** *intr, derog, informal* to speak or act with affected and exaggerated emotion or enthusiasm. ▸ *noun* **1** a sudden violent flooding-out. **2** *derog, informal* exaggerated emotion or enthusiasm. ▪ **gushing** *adj, noun.* ▪ **gushingly** *adv.* [14c as *gosshe* or *gusche*: imitating the sound]

gusher *noun* **1** an oil well that oil flows from without the use of pumps. **2** someone who talks or behaves in a gushing way.

gusset *noun, dressmaking* a piece of material sewn into a garment for added strength or to allow for freedom of movement, eg at the crotch. [15c: from French *gousset*]

gust *noun* **1** a sudden blast or rush, eg of wind or smoke. **2** an emotional outburst. ▸ *verb, intr* of the wind: to blow in gusts. [16c: from Norse *gustr* blast]

gusto *noun* enthusiastic enjoyment; zest. [17c: Italian, meaning 'taste']

gusty *adj* (*-ier, -iest*) **1** blowing in gusts; stormy. **2** fitfully irritable or upset. ▪ **gustily** *adv.*

gut *noun* **1** *anatomy* the alimentary canal or part of it. **2** (**guts**) *informal* the insides of a person or animal. **3** *informal* the stomach or abdomen. **4** *informal* a fat stomach; a paunch. **5** (**guts**) *informal* courage or determination. **6** (**guts**) *informal* the inner or essential parts: *the guts of the scheme.* **7 a catgut**; **b** a fibre obtained from silkworms, used for fishing tackle. ▸ *verb* (***gutted, gutting***) **1** to take the guts out of (an animal, esp fish). **2** to destroy the insides of something; to reduce to a shell: *Fire gutted the building.* ▸ *adj, informal* based on instinct and emotion, not reason: *a gut reaction.* [Anglo-Saxon *gutt*]
IDIOMS **work** *or* **sweat** *or* **slave one's guts out** *informal* to work extremely hard.

gutless *adj, derog* cowardly; lacking determination.

gutsy *adj* (*-ier, -iest*) *informal* **1** courageous and determined. **2** gluttonous.

gutta-percha *noun* a whitish rubbery substance, obtained from the latex of certain Malaysian trees, used in dentistry and in electrical insulation. [19c: from Malay *getah* gum + *percha* the tree that produces it]

gutted[1] *adj, informal* extremely shocked or disappointed.

gutted[2] *past tense, past participle of* **gut**

gutter *noun* **1** a channel for carrying away rainwater, fixed to the edge of a roof or built between a pavement and a road. **2** *ten-pin bowling* either of the channels at the sides of a lane. **3** (**the gutter**) a state of poverty and social deprivation or of coarse and degraded living. **4** *printing* the inner margins between two facing pages. ▸ *verb* **1** *intr* of a candle: to have its melted wax, etc suddenly pour down a channel which forms on its side. **2** of a flame: to flicker and threaten to go out. ▪ **guttering** *noun.* [13c: from French *goutiere*]

gutter press *noun, derog* newspapers that specialize in sensationalistic journalism that deals largely with scandal and gossip.

guttersnipe *noun, derog, old use* a raggedly dressed or ill-mannered person, esp a child.

guttural *adj* **1** *non-technical* of sounds: produced in the throat or the back of the mouth. **2** of a language or style of speech: having or using such sounds; harsh-sounding. ▸ *noun, non-technical* a sound produced in the throat or the back of the mouth. [16c: from Latin *guttur* throat]

guv, guvnor *or* **guv'nor** see under **governor**

guy[1] *noun* **1** *informal* a man or boy. **2** *informal, orig US* **a** a person; **b** (**guys**) used to address or refer to a group of people: *What do you guys think?* **3** a crude model of Guy Fawkes that is burnt on a bonfire on Guy Fawkes Night. ▸ *verb* to make fun of someone. [19c: named after Guy Fawkes, leader of the plot to blow up Parliament in 1605]

guy[2] *noun* (*in full* **guy rope**) a rope or wire used to hold something, esp a tent, firm or steady. ▸ *verb* to secure something with guys. [17c: from French *guie* guide]

guzzle *verb, tr & intr* to eat or drink greedily. ▪ **guzzler** *noun.* [16c as *gossel*]

gybe, gibe *or* **jibe** /dʒaɪb/ *verb, tr & intr, naut* **1** of a sail: to swing, or make it swing, over from one side of a boat to the other. **2** of a boat: to change or make it change course in this way. [17c]

gym *noun, informal* **1 gymnastics**. **2 gymnasium**. [19c colloquial abbreviation]

gymkhana /dʒɪm'kɑːnə/ *noun* a local event consisting of competitions in sports, esp horse-riding. [19c: from Hindi *gend-khana* racket-court]

gymnasium *noun* (***gymnasiums*** *or* ***gymnasia*** /dʒɪm'neɪzɪə/) a building or room with equipment for physical exercise. [16c: from Greek *gymnasion* school for physical training]

gymnast *noun* someone who is skilled in gymnastics. [16c: from Greek *gymnastes* trainer of athletes]

gymnastic *adj* **1** relating to gymnastics. **2** athletic; agile. ▪ **gymnastically** *adv.* [16c: from Greek *gymnastikos*]

gymnastics *singular noun* physical training designed to strengthen the body and improve agility, usu using special equipment. ▸ *plural noun* **1** feats of agility. **2** difficult exercises that test or demonstrate ability of any kind: *mental gymnastics.*

gymnosperm *noun, botany* a plant that produces seeds borne on cones, eg the conifer. [19c: from Latin *gymnospermus*, from Greek *gymnos* naked + *sperma* seed]

gym shoe *noun* a **plimsoll**.

gym slip *noun* a belted **pinafore** dress worn (*esp formerly*) by schoolgirls as part of their uniform.

gynaecology *or* (*N Am*) **gynecology** /gaɪnə'kɒlədʒɪ/ *noun* the branch of medicine concerned with the diagnosis and treatment of diseases and disorders that affect the reproductive organs of the female body. ▪ **gynaecological** *adj.* ▪ **gynaecologist** *noun.* [19c: from Greek *gynaikos* woman]

gynoecium, gynaecium *or US* **gynecium** /gaɪ'niːsɪəm, dzaɪ-/ *noun* (***gynaecia*** *or* ***gynoecia***) *botany* the female reproductive parts of a flower. [17c: from Greek *gynaikeion* women's apartments]

gyp *or* **gip** *noun*
IDIOMS **give sb gyp** *informal* to cause them pain or discomfort: *This tooth's been giving me gyp.* [19c: possibly a contraction of **gee up**]

gypsum *noun* a soft mineral composed of calcium sulphate, used to make plaster of Paris, cement, rubber and paper. [17c: Latin]

Gypsy *or* **Gipsy** *noun* (*-ies*) **1** a member of a travelling people, orig from NW India, now scattered throughout Europe and N America. Also called **Romany. 2** (**gypsy**) someone who resembles or lives like a Gypsy. ▸ *adj* concerned with or relating to Gypsies. [17c: from *Egyptian*, because they were orig thought to have come from Egypt]

gyrate *verb, intr* to move with a circular motion. ▪ **gyration** *noun.* [19c: from Greek *gyros* circle]

gyroscope *noun* a device consisting of a small flywheel with a heavy rim, mounted so that once in motion it resists any changes in the direction of axis, used in ship stabilizers and in automatic steering systems. ▪ **gyroscopic** *adj.* ▪ **gyroscopically** *adv.* [19c]

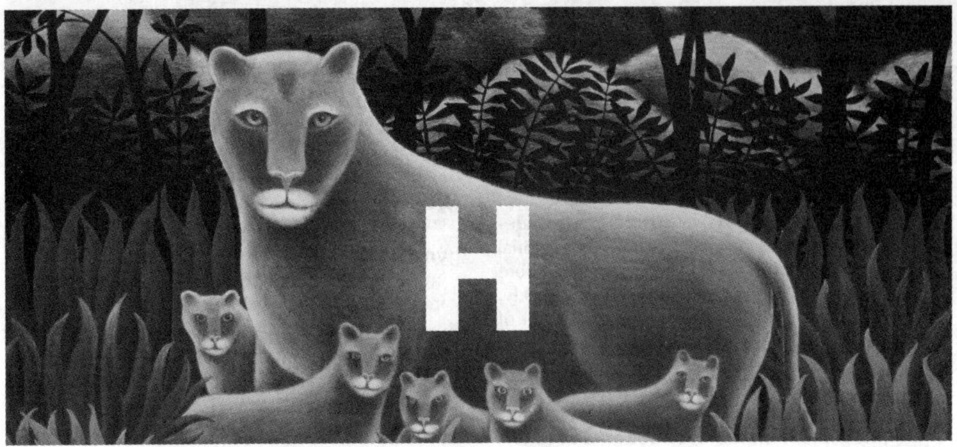

H[1] *or* **h** *noun* (***Hs, H's*** *or* ***h's***) **1** the eighth letter of the English alphabet. **2** the speech sound represented by this letter, an aspirate. **3** something shaped like an H. *Also in compounds*: *H-beam*.

H[2] *abbrev* **1** of pencils: hard. **2** height. **3** *slang* heroin. **4** hospital. **5** hydrant.

H[3] *symbol* **1** *chem* hydrogen. **2** *physics* magnetic field strength. **3** *electronics* henry.

h *symbol, physics* Planck's constant.

ha *abbrev* hectare or hectares.

haar /hɑː(r)/ *noun, Scot & NE Eng dialect* a cold mist or fog coming off the North Sea.

habeas corpus /ˈheɪbɪəs ˈkɔːpəs/ *noun, law* a writ requiring a person to be brought into court for a judge to decide if their imprisonment is legal. [15c: Latin, meaning 'have the body (brought before the judge)']

haberdasher *noun* **1** *Brit* a person or shop that deals in sewing items, eg ribbons, needles, buttons, etc. **2** *N Am* a men's outfitter. ▪ **haberdashery** *noun* (***-ies***). [14c: from French *hapertas*]

habit *noun* **1** a tendency to behave, think, etc in a specific way. **2** a usual practice or custom. **3** an addiction. **4** a mental attitude. **5** a long loose garment worn by monks and nuns. **6** a characteristic form, type of development, growth or existence; general appearance. **7** (*in full* **riding habit**) a woman's riding dress. [14c: from Latin *habitus* practice]

habitable *or* **inhabitable** *adj* suitable for living in; fit to live in. [14c: from Latin *habitabilis*]

habitat *noun* **1** *biol* the natural home of an animal or plant. **2** the place where a person, group, class, etc can usu be found. [18c: Latin from *habitare* to dwell]

habitation *noun* **1** the act of living in a particular dwelling place. **2** a house or home. [14c: from Latin *habitatio*]

habitual *adj* **1** done regularly and repeatedly. **2** done, or doing something, by habit. **3** customary; usual. ▪ **habitually** *adv.* [16c: from Latin *habitualis*]

habituate *verb* to accustom. ▪ **habituation** *noun.* [16c: from Latin *habituare*]

habitué /həˈbɪtʃʊeɪ/ *noun* a regular or frequent visitor to a specified place; a person who lives in a specified place. [19c: from French *habituer* to frequent]

háček /ˈhatʃɛk/ *noun* a diacritic (ˇ) placed over a letter in some Slavonic languages to modify the sound.

hachure /haˈʃʊə(r)/ *noun* **1** (**hachures**) parallel lines on a map where the closeness of the lines indicates the relative steepness of gradients. **2** one of these lines. [19c: from French *hacher* to chop up]

hacienda /hasɪˈɛndə/ *noun* in Spanish-speaking countries: **1** a ranch or large estate with a main dwelling-house on it. **2** this house. [18c: Spanish]

hack[1] *verb* **1** to cut or chop roughly: *hacked down the tree* • *hacked chunks out of the story.* **2** to cut (a path, one's way, etc) through undergrowth, etc. **3** *intr, informal* (*often* **hack into**) to use a computer with skill, esp to obtain unauthorized access to (computer files, etc). **4** *slang* to be able to bear, suffer, tolerate, etc. **5** *football, rugby* to kick the shin of (an opponent). ▸ *noun* **1** a kick on the shins. **2** a wound or rough cut. **3** a **mattock** or miner's **pick**[2]. **4** a short dry cough. **5** a chop or blow. [Anglo-Saxon *tohaccian*]

hack[2] *noun* **1** a horse kept for general riding, esp one for hire. **2** a ride on horseback. **3** an old or worn-out horse. **4** a writer who produces dull, mediocre or routine work. **5** a **dogsbody**. ▸ *verb* **1** *tr & intr* to ride a horse at a leisurely pace, usu for pleasure. **2** *intr* to work as a hack. [17c: short form of **hackney**]

hacker *noun* **1** someone or something that hacks. **2** *informal* someone skilled in using computers, particularly for unauthorized access.

hackles *plural noun* the hairs or feathers on the back of the neck of some animals and birds, which are raised when they are angry. [15c]

hackney *noun* **1** a **hack**[2]. **2** a horse with a high-stepping trot, bred to draw light carriages. **3** a vehicle that is for hire. [14c: named after Hackney, a borough in East London, where horses were formerly pastured]

hackney cab *or* **hackney carriage** *noun* **1** *hist* a horse-drawn carriage for public hire. **2** *formal* a taxi.

hackneyed *adj* of a word, phrase, etc: meaningless and trite through too much use. [18c]

hacksaw *noun* a saw for cutting metals.

had *past tense, past participle of* **have**

haddock *noun* (***haddock*** *or* ***haddocks***) a commercially important N Atlantic sea fish. [14c]

Hadith /ˈhadɪθ, hɑːˈdiːθ/ *noun* the collection of traditions about Muhammad which form a supplement to the Koran. [19c: Arabic]

hadj see **hajj**

hadji see **hajji**

hadn't *contraction* had not.

hadron *noun, physics* a subatomic particle that interacts strongly with other subatomic particles. ▪ **hadronic** *adj.* [1960s: from Greek *hadros* heavy]

haem /hiːm/ *or* (*US*) **heme** *noun, biochem* the iron compound that combines with the protein globin to form haemoglobin, and gives red blood cells their colour. [20c: from Greek *haima* blood]

haem- *or* **haema-** see **haemo-**

haemal *or* (*US*) **hemal** /ˈhiːməl/ *adj, med* **1** relating to the blood or blood-vessels. **2** *old use* denoting the region of the body that contains the heart. [19c]

haemat- see **haemato-**

haematite *or* (*US*) **hematite** /ˈhiːmətaɪt/ *noun* a mineral containing ferric oxide, the most important ore of iron. [17c; 16c as *ematites*]

haemato- *or* (*US*) **hemato-** /hiːmətoʊ/ *or* (*before a vowel*) **haemat-**, (*US*) **hemat-** *combining form, med, denoting* blood: *haematology.* [19c: from Greek *haima* blood]

haematology *or* (*US*) **hematology** /hiːməˈtɒlədʒɪ/ *noun* the branch of medicine concerned with the study of the blood and diseases of the blood. ▪ **haematologic** *or* **haematological** *adj.* ▪ **haematologist** *noun.* [19c]

-haemia see **-aemia**

haemo-, (*US*) **hemo-** /hiːmoʊ/ *or* **haema-**, (*US*) **hema-** *or* (*before a vowel*) **haem-**, (*US*) **hem-** *combining form, med, denoting* blood. [From Greek *haima* blood]

haemoglobin *or* (*US*) **hemoglobin** *noun, biochem* a protein in red blood cells that carries oxygen. [19c]

haemophilia *or* (*US*) **hemophilia** *noun* a hereditary disease, usu only affecting males, in which the blood does not clot as it should. ▪ **haemophiliac** *or* **haemophilic** *noun, adj.* [19c]

haemorrhage *or* **hemorrhage** /ˈhɛmərɪdʒ/ *noun* **1** *med* the escape of profuse amounts of blood, esp from a ruptured blood vessel. **2** persistent or severe loss or depletion of resources, staff, etc. ▸ *verb, intr* to lose copious amounts of blood. [17c: from **haemo-** + Greek *rhegnynai* to burst]

haemorrhoids *or* (*US*) **hemorrhoids** /ˈhɛmərɔɪdz/ *plural noun, med* swollen veins in the anus. Also called **piles**. ▪ **haemorrhoidal** *adj.* [14c: from **haemo-** + Greek *rheein* to flow]

haemostasis *or* (*US*) **hemostasis** *noun, med* stoppage of the flow of blood. ▪ **haemostatic** *adj.* [18c]

hafnium *noun, chem* (symbol **Hf**) a metallic element found mainly in zirconium minerals and used in electrodes. [1920s: from Latin *Hafnia* Copenhagen, where it was discovered]

haft *noun* a handle of a knife, sword, axe, etc. ▸ *verb* to fit with a haft. [Anglo-Saxon *hæft*]

hag *noun* **1** *offensive* an ugly old woman. **2** a witch. ▪ **haggish** *adj.* [Anglo-Saxon *hægtes*]

Haggadah *or* **Haggadoh** /həˈgɑːdə/ *noun* (***Haggadahs, Haggadas*** *or* ***Haggadoth*** /hagəˈdoʊt/) *Judaism* **1** the book that contains the text recited at the **Seder** on the first two nights of the Passover. **2** the narrative of the Exodus from Egypt which constitutes the main part of the Passover service. ▪ **Haggadic** *adj.* [18c: from Hebrew *hagged* to tell]

haggard *adj* looking very tired and upset, esp because of pain, worry, etc. ▪ **haggardly** *adv.* ▪ **haggardness** *noun.* [16c: from French *hagard* wild]

haggis *noun* a Scottish dish made from sheep's or calf's offal mixed with suet, oatmeal and seasonings and then boiled in a bag traditionally made from the animal's stomach. [16c: Scots]

haggle *verb, intr* (*often* **haggle over** *or* **about**) to bargain over or argue about (a price, etc). ▪ **haggler** *noun.* [16c: from Norse *heggra* to hew]

hagio- *or* (*before a vowel*) **hagi-** *combining form, signifying* a saint; saints; holiness. [18c: from Greek *hagios* holy]

hagiographer *or* **hagiographist** *noun* someone who writes about the lives of saints.

hagiography *noun* (***-ies***) **1** the writing of the lives of saints. **2** a biography that idealizes or overpraises its subject. ▪ **hagiographic** *or* **hagiographical** *adj.* [19c; 16c as *hagiographical*]

hagiolatry *noun* worship or reverence of saints. [19c]

hagiology *noun* (***-ies***) literature about the lives and legends of saints. ▪ **hagiological** *or* **hagiologic** *adj.* ▪ **hagiologist** *noun.* [19c]

hag-ridden *adj* tormented; mentally oppressed. [17c: ie as if possessed by a witch]

ha-ha[1] *or* **haw-haw** *exclam* **1** a conventional way of representing the sound of laughter. **2** expressing triumph, mockery, scorn, etc.

ha-ha[2] *or* **haw-haw** *noun* a wall or a fence separating areas of land in a large garden or park, but placed in a ditch to avoid interrupting the view. [18c: French]

haiku /ˈhaɪkuː/ *or* **hokku** /ˈhɒkuː/ *noun* (*pl* ***haiku*** *or* ***hokku***) a Japanese poem of 17 syllables. [19c: Japanese, from *hai* amusement + *ku* verse]

hail[1] *noun* **1** grains of ice that fall from the clouds when there are strong rising air currents. **2** a large quantity (of words, questions, missiles, etc) directed at someone or something with force: *a hail of criticism.* ▸ *verb* **1** *intr* of hail: to fall from the clouds: *It's hailing.* **2 a** to shower with words, questions, missiles, etc; **b** *intr* to come forcefully or in great numbers. [Anglo-Saxon *hagol*]

hail[2] *verb* **1** to attract attention by shouting or making gestures, eg to signal (esp a taxi) to stop. **2** to greet someone, esp enthusiastically. **3** to recognize or describe someone as being or representing something: *He was hailed a hero.* **4** *intr* (**hail from somewhere**) to come from or belong to (a place). ▸ *exclam, old use* an expression of greeting. ▸ *noun* the act or an instance of hailing. [13c: from Norse *heill* healthy]

hail-fellow-well-met *adj* friendly and familiar, esp overly so.

hail Mary *noun* (***hail Marys***) a prayer to the Virgin Mary, the English version of the Ave Maria (see **Ave**[2]).

hailstone *noun* a single grain of hail.

hair *noun* **1** a thread-like structure growing from the skin of animals. **2** a mass or growth of such strands, esp on a person's head. **3** an artificial strand similar to an animal's or person's hair. **4** *botany* a thread-like structure growing from the surface of a plant. **5** a hair's-breadth: *won by a hair.* [Anglo-Saxon *hær*]

IDIOMS **get in sb's hair** *informal* to annoy them incessantly. **keep your hair on!** *informal* keep calm and don't get angry. **let one's hair down** *informal* to enjoy oneself or behave without restraint. **make sb's hair curl** *informal* to shock them. **make sb's hair**

stand on end *informal* to frighten them. **not turn a hair** to remain calm and show no surprise, anger, etc. **split hairs** to make unnecessary petty distinctions.

haircut *noun* **1** the cutting of someone's hair. **2** the shape or style in which it is cut.

hairdo *noun, informal* a woman's haircut.

hairdresser *noun* **1** a person whose job is washing, cutting, styling, etc hair. **2** an establishment where this takes place. ▪ **hairdressing** *noun.*

hairdryer *or* **hairdrier** *noun* an electrical device that dries hair by blowing hot air over it.

hairgrip *noun, chiefly Brit* a small wire clasp for holding the hair in place.

hairline *noun* **1** the line along the forehead where the hair begins to grow. **2** a very fine line.

hairnet *noun* a fine-meshed net for keeping the hair in place.

hairpiece *noun* **1** a wig or piece of false hair worn over a bald area on the head. **2** an attachment of hair added to a person's own hair to give extra length or volume.

hairpin *noun* a thin flat U-shaped piece of wire for keeping the hair in place.

hairpin bend *noun* a sharp and often U-shaped bend, esp on a mountain road.

hair-raising *adj* extremely frightening or disturbing.

hair's-breadth *noun* a very small distance or margin.

hair shirt *noun* a shirt of coarse cloth made from horse hair, usu worn next to the skin as a religious penance.

hairspray *noun* lacquer for holding the hair in place.

hairspring *noun* a very small spiral spring that regulates a watch in conjunction with the balance wheel.

hairstyle *noun* the way in which someone's hair is cut or shaped. ▪ **hairstylist** *noun.*

hair trigger *noun* in a firearm: a trigger that responds to very light pressure.

hairy *adj* (***-ier, -iest***) **1** covered in hair. **2** *informal* **a** dangerous, frightening or exciting; **b** difficult or tricky. ▪ **hairiness** *noun.*

Haitian /ˈheɪʃən, hɑːˈiːʃən/ *noun* **1** a native or inhabitant of Haiti, a republic in the W part of the island of Hispaniola in the Caribbean Sea. **2** the form of French spoken in Haiti. *adj* belonging or relating to Haiti, its inhabitants, or the form of French they speak.

hajj *or* **hadj** /hɑːdʒ, hadʒ/ *noun* the Muslim pilgrimage to Mecca. [17c: from Arabic *hajj* pilgrimage]

hajji, haji *or* **hadji** /ˈhɑːdʒɪ, ˈhadʒɪ/ *noun* a Muslim who has been on pilgrimage to Mecca.

haka /ˈhɑːkɑː/ *noun, NZ* **1** a Maori war-dance accompanied by chanting. **2** a similar ceremonial dance performed at the start of a match by members of the New Zealand national rugby union team. [19c: Maori]

hake *noun* (***hake*** *or* ***hakes***) an edible sea fish. [15c: from Norse *haki* hook]

Halakah *or* **Halacha** /hɑːˈlɑːkɑː/ *noun, Judaism* the legal element in the Talmud, forming the complete body of Jewish religious law. ▪ **Halakic** /həˈlakɪk/ *adj.* [19c: Hebrew, from *halak* to walk]

halal /ˈhalal/ *noun* meat from an animal that has been killed according to Muslim holy law. [19c: from Arabic *halal* lawful]

halberd *or* **halbert** *noun, hist* a weapon of the Middle Ages that combines a spear with an axe blade. ▪ **halberdier** /halbəˈdɪə(r)/ *noun.* [15c: from German *helm* handle + *barde* hatchet]

halcyon /ˈhalsɪən/ *adj* peaceful, calm and happy: *halcyon days.* [14c: from Greek *halkyon* kingfisher]

hale *adj* strong and fit: *hale and hearty.* ▪ **haleness** *noun.* [Anglo-Saxon *hál* whole]

half *noun* (***halves***) **1 a** one of two equal parts which together form a whole; **b** a quantity that equals such a part. **2** a **fraction** equal to one divided by two (usu written ½). **3** *informal* a half pint, esp of beer. **4** *Scot* a measure of spirits, esp whisky. **5** one of two equal periods of play in a match. **6** *football, hockey, etc* the half of the pitch considered to belong to one team. **7** *golf* an equal score with an opponent. **8** a **half-hour**. **9** *sport* a **halfback**. **10** a half-price ticket, esp for a child. ▸ *adj* **1** forming or equal to half of something: *a half chicken.* **2** not perfect or complete: *We don't want any half measures.* ▸ *adv* **1** to the extent or amount of one half: *half finished.* **2** almost; partly; to some extent: *half dead with exhaustion.* **3** thirty minutes past the hour stated: *half three.* [Anglo-Saxon *healf*]

IDIOMS **by half** *informal* excessively: *He's too clever by half.* **by halves** without being thorough: *never do things by halves.* **go halves on sth** to share the cost or expenses of something: *go halves on a pizza.* **not half** *informal* **1** very: *It isn't half cold.* **2** not nearly: *I'm not half fit enough.* **3** yes, indeed. **one's other** *or* **better half** *informal* one's husband, wife or partner.

half- *prefix* **1** one of two equal parts: *half-day.* **2** having only one parent in common: *half-sister.* **3** partly; not completely or thoroughly: *a half-baked idea.*

half-and-half *adv, adj* in equal parts; in part one thing, in part another.

halfback *noun* **1** *football, hockey, etc* a player or position immediately behind the forwards and in front of the fullbacks. **2** *rugby* either the stand-off half or the scrum half.

half-baked *adj* **1** *informal* of an idea, scheme, etc: **a** not properly or completely thought out; **b** unrealistic or impractical. **2** foolish.

half-blood *noun* the relationship between individuals who have only one parent in common. ▪ **half-blooded** *adj.*

half board *noun, Brit* the provision of bed, breakfast and one other meal in a hotel or boarding house. Compare **full board**.

half-brother *noun* a brother with whom one has only one parent in common.

half-cock *noun* the position of a firearm's **hammer** when it cocks the trigger and therefore cannot reach the **primer**² (sense 2) to fire the weapon.

IDIOMS **to go off half-cocked** *or* **at half-cock** to fail due to insufficient preparation or premature starting.

half-crown *or* **half-a-crown** *noun* a former British coin worth two shillings and sixpence (12½p).

half-cut *adj, slang* drunk.

half-day *noun* a day on which someone only works, etc in the morning or in the afternoon.

half-dozen *or* **half a dozen** *noun* six, or roughly six.

half-hardy *adj* of a cultivated plant: able to grow outdoors except during severe winter weather.

half-hearted *adj* not eager; without enthusiasm. ▪ **half-heartedly** *adv.* ▪ **half-heartedness** *noun.*

half-hour *noun* **1** a period of thirty minutes. **2** the moment that is thirty minutes after the start of an hour: *Buses run on the hour and on the half-hour.* ▪ **half-hourly** *adj, adv.*

half-life *noun, physics* the period of time required for half the original number of atoms of a radioactive substance to undergo spontaneous radioactive decay.

half-light *noun* dull light, esp at dawn or dusk.

half mast *noun* the lower-than-normal position at which a flag flies as a sign of mourning.

half measures *plural noun* actions or means that are not sufficient or thorough enough to deal with a problem.

half-moon *noun* **1** the Moon when only half of it can be seen from the Earth. **2** the time when this occurs.

half nelson *noun, wrestling* a hold in which a wrestler puts an arm under one of their opponent's arms from behind, and pushes on the back of their neck. Compare **nelson**.

half note *noun, N Am* a **minim** (sense 1).

halfpenny *or* **ha'penny** /ˈheɪpnɪ/ (**-*ies*** *or* ***halfpence***) *noun* **1** *formerly* a small British coin worth half a new penny. **2** *hist* an old British coin worth half an old penny. ▸ *adj* **1** valued at a halfpenny: *a halfpenny loaf.* **2** of negligible value: *a halfpenny matter.*

half-rhyme *noun* a rhyme in which the consonants, but not the vowel, of the last stressed syllable have the same sound, eg *wild* and *field*. Also called: **pararhyme**.

half-sister *noun* a sister with whom one only has one parent in common.

half-term *noun, Brit education* a short holiday halfway through an academic term.

half-timbered *or* **half-timber** *adj* of a building, esp one in Tudor style: having a visible timber framework filled with brick, stone or plaster. ▪ **half-timbering** *noun.*

half-time *noun, sport* an interval between the two halves of a match.

half-title *noun* a short title on the right-hand page of a book which precedes the title page.

half-tone *noun* **1** a photographic process in which tones are broken up by a fine screen into dots of different sizes to produce varying shades. **2** the illustration obtained. **3** *N Am* a **semitone**.

half-track *noun* a vehicle, usu a military one, with wheels in front and caterpillar tracks behind.

half-truth *noun* a statement that is only partly true and is intended to mislead.

half volley *noun, sport* a stroke in which the ball is hit immediately after it bounces or as it bounces.

halfway *adj,* ▸ *adv* **1** at a point equally far from two others. **2** in an incomplete manner.

IDIOMS **meet sb halfway** to come to a compromise with them.

halfway house *noun* **1** *informal* something that is between two extremes, and which has some features of each. **2** a home where former prisoners, psychiatric patients, etc stay temporarily to readjust to life outside prison, hospital, etc.

halfwit *noun* a foolish or stupid person. ▪ **halfwitted** *adj.* ▪ **halfwittedly** *adv.*

half-yearly *adj, adv* done, occurring, etc every six months.

halibut *noun* (***halibut*** *or* ***halibuts***) a large edible flatfish found in the N Atlantic and N Pacific. [15c: Anglo-Saxon *halybutte*, from *haly* holy + *butt* flatfish, so called because it was eaten on holy days]

halide /ˈheɪlaɪd/ *noun, chem* a binary compound (eg sodium chloride) formed by a **halogen** and a metal or **radical** (*noun* sense 3). [19c: from Greek *hals* salt]

halite /ˈhalaɪt/ *noun* a mineral consisting of sodium chloride in cubic crystalline form, a source of table salt. Also called **rock salt**. [19c: from Greek *hals* salt]

halitosis *noun* unpleasant-smelling breath. [19c: from Latin *halitus* breath]

hall *noun* **1** a room or passage just inside the entrance to a house, which usu allows access to other rooms and the stairs. **2** a building or large room, used for concerts, public meetings, assemblies, etc. **3** (*usu* **Hall**) a large country house or manor. **4** *Brit* (*in full* **hall of residence**) a building where university or college students live. **5** *Brit* **a** the dining room in a college or university; **b** the dinner in such a room. **6** the main room of a great house, castle, etc. **7** *esp N Am* a corridor onto which rooms open. [Anglo-Saxon *heall*]

hallelujah *or* **halleluia** /halɪˈluːjə/ *or* **alleluia** /alɪ-/ *exclam* expressing praise to God. ▸ *noun* **1** the exclamation of 'hallelujah'. **2** a musical composition based on the word 'Hallelujah'. [16c: from Hebrew *hallelu* praise ye + *jah* Jehova]

halliard see **halyard**

hallmark *noun* **1** an official series of marks stamped on gold, silver and platinum articles to guarantee their authenticity. **2** any mark of genuineness or excellence. **3** a typical or distinctive feature, esp of quality. ▸ *verb* to stamp with a hallmark. [18c: named after Goldsmiths' Hall in London where articles were orig classed and stamped]

hallo see **hello**

halloo, hallo *or* **halloa** *noun,* ▸ *exclam* **1** a cry to encourage hunting dogs or call for attention. **2** a shout of 'halloo'. ▸ *verb* (***hallooed***) *intr* **1** to cry 'halloo', esp to dogs at a hunt. **2** to urge on hunting dogs with shouts. [16c]

hallow *verb* **1** to make or regard as holy. **2** to consecrate or set apart as being sacred. ▪ **hallowed** *adj.* [Anglo-Saxon *halgian*, from *halig* holy]

Hallowe'en *or* **Halloween** *noun* the evening of 31 October, the eve of All Saints Day. Also called **All Hallows Eve**. [18c: from *All-Hallow-Even* All Saints Eve]

hallucinate *verb, intr* to see something that is not actually present or that may not even exist. ▪ **hallucination** *noun.* ▪ **hallucinatory** *adj.* [17c: from Latin *(h)allucinari* to wander in the mind]

hallucinogen *noun* a drug that causes hallucination. ▪ **hallucinogenic** *adj.*

hallway *noun* an entrance hall or corridor.

halm see **haulm**

halo *noun* (***halos*** *or* ***haloes***) **1** in paintings etc: a ring of light around the head of a saint, angel, etc. **2** the glory or glamour that is attached to a famous or admired person or thing. **3** a ring of light that can be seen around the sun or moon, caused by the refraction of light by ice crystals. ▸ *verb* (***haloes, haloed***) to put a halo round someone or something. [16c: from Greek *halos* circular threshing floor]

halogen /ˈhalədʒɛn/ *noun, chem* any of the non-metallic elements, fluorine, chlorine, bromine, iodine and astatine, which form salts when in union with metals. [19c: from Greek *hals, halos* salt]

halon /ˈhalɒn, ˈheɪ-/ *noun* an organic chemical compound, containing bromine combined with other **halogens**, used in fire extinguishers.

halt *noun* **1** an interruption or stop to movement, progression or growth. **2** *Brit* a small railway station without a building. ▸ *verb, tr & intr* to come or bring to a halt. [17c: from German *Halt* stoppage]

IDIOMS **call a halt to sth** to put an end to it or stop it.

halter *noun* **1** a rope or strap for holding and leading a horse by its head. **2** a rope with a noose for hanging a person. **3** a **halterneck**. ▸ *verb* **1** to put a halter on (a horse, etc). **2** to hang someone with a halter. [Anglo-Saxon *hælfter*]

halterneck *noun* a woman's top or dress held in place by a strap which goes round her neck, leaving the shoulders and back bare.

halting *adj* unsure; hesitant. ▪ **haltingly** *adv*. [From Anglo-Saxon *healt* lame]

halve *verb* **1** to divide into two equal parts or halves. **2** to share equally. **3** *tr & intr* of costs, problems, etc: to reduce by half. **4** *golf* to take the same number of strokes as an opponent over (a hole or match). [Anglo-Saxon *halfen*]

halves *pl of* **half**

halyard *or* **halliard** *noun* a rope for raising or lowering a sail or flag on a ship. [14c: *halier* from French *haler* to haul in + **yard**[1]]

ham[1] *noun* **1** the top part of the back leg of a pig. **2** the meat from this part, salted and smoked. **3** *informal* the back of the thigh. [Anglo-Saxon *hamm*]

ham[2] *noun, informal* **1** *theatre* **a** a bad actor, esp one who overacts or exaggerates; **b** inexpert or clumsy acting. **2** an amateur radio operator. ▸ *verb* (***hammed, hamming***) *tr & intr* (*also* **ham up**) to overact or exaggerate. [19c: perhaps from *hamfatter* a third-rate minstrel]

hamburger *noun* a flat round cake of finely chopped beef, usu fried and served in a soft bread roll. [1930s: orig called *Hamburger steak*, from Hamburg, a city in N Germany]

ham-fisted *or* **ham-handed** *adj, informal* clumsy.

Hamitic *noun* a group of N African languages related to **Semitic**. ▸ *adj* **1** referring or relating to this group of languages. **2** belonging to or characteristic of the **Hamites**, a race of N Africa. [19c: named after Ham, one of Noah's sons and the supposed founder of this race]

hamlet *noun* a small village. [14c: from French *hamelet*]

hammer *noun* **1** a tool with a heavy metal head on the end of a handle, used for driving nails into wood, breaking hard substances, etc. **2** the part of a bell, piano, clock, etc that hits against some other part, making a noise. **3** the part of a gun that strikes the **primer**[2] or **percussion cap** when the trigger is pulled and causes the bullet to be fired. **4** *sport* **a** a metal ball on a long flexible steel chain, thrown in competitions; **b** the sport of throwing this. **5** the mallet with which an auctioneer announces that an article is sold. ▸ *verb* **1** *tr & intr* to strike or hit with or as if with a hammer. **2** *intr* to make a noise as of a hammer. **3** *Brit informal* to criticize or beat severely. **4** *informal* to defeat. [Anglo-Saxon *hamor*]

IDIOMS **come** *or* **go under the hammer** to be sold at auction. **hammer and tongs** *informal* with a lot of enthusiasm, effort or commotion.

PHRASAL VERBS **hammer sth out** to reconcile or settle problems, differences, etc after a great deal of effort and discussion.

hammer and sickle *noun* the sign of a hammer and a sickle laid across each other, symbolic of labour. [20c]

hammerhead *noun* a shark with a hammer-shaped head.

hammock *noun* a piece of canvas or net hung by the corners, used as a bed. [16c: from Spanish *hamaca*]

hammy *adj* (***-ier, -iest***) *informal* **1** of an actor: inclined to overact. **2** of a play, performance, etc: overacted or exaggerated.

hamper[1] *verb* to hinder the progress or movement of (someone or something). [14c]

hamper[2] *noun* **1** a large basket with a lid, used esp for carrying food. **2** *Brit* the food and drink packed in such a basket. [14c: from *hanypere* wicker basket]

hamster *noun* a small nocturnal Eurasian rodent with a short tail and pouches in its mouth for storing food, often kept as a pet. [17c: from German *hamustro*]

hamstring *noun* **1** in humans: a tendon at the back of the knee attached to muscles in the thigh. **2** in horses: the large tendon at the back of the hind leg. ▸ *verb* (***hamstringed*** *or* ***hamstrung***) **1** to make powerless or hinder. **2** to lame by cutting the hamstring. [17c: from **ham**[1] + **string**]

hand *noun* **1** in humans: the extremity of the arm below the wrist. **2** a corresponding part in higher vertebrates. **3** something that resembles this in form or function. **4** *in compounds* made by hand rather than by a machine: *hand-knitted*. **5** control, agency or influence: *the hand of fate*. **6** (**a hand**) help; assistance: *He gave us a hand.* **7** a part or influence in an activity: *They had a hand in the victory.* **8** a needle or pointer on a clock, watch or gauge. **9** *informal* a round of applause: *He got a big hand.* **10** a manual worker or assistant, esp in a factory, on a farm or on board ship: *All hands on deck!* **11** someone who is skilful at some specified activity: *a dab hand at baking*. **12** a specified way of doing something: *She has a light hand at pastry.* **13** *cards* **a** the cards dealt to a player in one round of a game; **b** a player holding such cards; **c** one round of a card game. **14** a specified position in relation to an object or onlooker: *on the right hand*. **15** a source of information considered in terms of closeness to the original source: *hear the news at first hand*. **16** an opposing aspect, point of view, etc: *on the other hand*. **17** someone's handwriting or style of handwriting. **18** a promise or acceptance of partnership, esp to marry: *He asked for her hand.* **19** in measuring the height of horses: a unit of measurement equal to 4in (about 10cm). ▸ *adj* **a** relating to or involving the hand: *hand grenade*; **b** worn on, for or carried in the hand: *hand lotion*; **c** operated by hand: *handsaw*. ▸ *verb* **1** (*often* **hand sth back** *or* **in** *or* **out** *or* **round**, etc) to deliver or give it using the hand or hands. **2** to lead, help or escort in a specified direction with the hand or hands: *He handed her into the carriage.* [Anglo-Saxon]

IDIOMS **a free hand** freedom to do as desired. **a hand's turn** *usu with negatives* the least amount of work: *He didn't do a hand's turn all day.* **at first hand** directly from the source. **at hand** near by; about to happen. **by hand 1** using the hands or tools held in the hand rather than by mechanical means. **2** delivered by messenger, not by post. **change hands** to pass to other ownership or custody. **come to hand** to arrive; to be received. **force sb's hand** to force them to act. **get one's hands on sb** *or* **sth** *informal* to catch or find them or it. **hand and foot** completely; in every possible way: *Servants wait on him hand and foot.* **hand in glove** very closely associated. **hand in hand 1** with hands mutually clasped. **2** in close association. **hand it to sb** *informal* to give them credit. **hand over fist** *informal* in large amounts and very quickly: *making money hand over fist.* **hands down** without effort; easily: *won hands down.* **hands off!** keep off!; do not touch! **hands up!** hold your hands up above your head. **have one's hands full** *informal* **1** to be very busy. **2** to be plagued with problems. **have one's hands tied** to be unable to act, usu because of instructions from a higher authority. **in good hands** in good keeping; in the care of someone who may be trusted. **in hand 1** under control. **2** being done or prepared. **3** available in reserve: *with half an hour in hand.* **keep one's hand in** *informal* to continue to have some involvement in an activity so as to remain proficient at it. **lend a hand** to give assistance. **lift a hand** *usu with negatives* to make the least effort: *He didn't lift a hand to help.* **live from hand to mouth 1** to live with only enough money and food for immediate needs. **2** to live without preparation or planning. **off one's hands** *informal* no longer one's responsibility. **on hand** near; available if required. **on one's hands** *informal* left over; not sold or used; to spare: *too much time on my hands.* **out of hand 1** beyond control. **2** immediately and without thinking: *to dismiss it out of hand.* **take sth off sb's hands** to relieve them of it. **to hand** within reach. **try one's hand at sth** to attempt to do it. **the upper hand** power or advantage.

PHRASAL VERBS **hand sth down 1** to pass on (an heirloom, tradition, etc) to the next generation. **2** to pass on (an outgrown item of clothing) to a younger member of a family, etc. **3** *N Amer, law* to pronounce (a verdict). **hand sth in** to return or submit (an examination paper, something found, etc). **hand sth out** to pass it by hand or distribute it to individuals. See also **handout**. **hand sth over** to transfer it or give possession of it to someone else. See also **handover**.

handbag *noun* a small bag, often with a strap, for carrying personal articles. *N Am equivalent* **purse**.

handball *noun* **1** a game in which two or four players hit a small ball against a wall with their hands. **2** the small hard rubber ball used in this game. **3** a game between goals in which the ball is struck with the palm of the hand. **4** *football* the offence a player other than a goalkeeper in their own penalty area commits if they touch the ball with their hand.

handbill *noun* a small printed notice or advertisement distributed by hand.

handbook *noun* **1** a manual that gives guidelines on maintenance or repair, eg of a car. **2** a guidebook that lists brief facts on a subject or place.

handbrake *noun* **1** a brake on a motor vehicle, operated by a lever. **2** the lever that operates the handbrake.

h and c *or* **h & c** *abbrev* hot and cold (water).

handcrafted *adj* made by hand.

handcuff *noun* a pair of steel rings, joined by a short chain, for locking round the wrists of prisoners, etc. ▸ *verb* to put handcuffs on someone. [18c]

handed *adj, in compounds* **1** using one hand in preference to the other: *left-handed.* **2** having or using a hand or hands as specified: *one-handed.* ▪ **handedly** *adv.* ▪ **handedness** *noun.*

handful *noun* **1** the amount or number that can be held in one hand. **2** a small amount or number. **3** *informal* **a** someone who is difficult to control; **b** a difficult task.

hand grenade *noun* a grenade to be thrown by hand.

handgun *noun* a firearm that can be held and fired in one hand, eg a revolver.

handicap *noun* **1** a physical or mental impairment. **2** something that impedes or hinders. **3 a** a disadvantage imposed on a superior competitor in a contest, race, etc, or an advantage given to an inferior one, so that everyone has an equal chance of winning; **b** a race or competition in which competitors are given a handicap. **4** the number of strokes by which a golfer's averaged score exceeds par for a course. ▸ *verb* (***handicapped, handicapping***) **1** to impede or hamper someone. **2** to impose special disadvantages or advantages on (a player, horse, etc) in order to make a better contest. ▪ **handicapper** *noun.* [17c: prob from *hand i'cap* an old lottery game]

handicapped *adj* **1** physically or mentally impaired. **2** (**the handicapped**) handicapped people in general. **3** of a competitor: given a handicap.

handicraft *noun* **1** an activity that requires skilful use of the hands, eg pottery. **2** (*usu* **handicrafts**) the work produced by this activity. [15c: changed from *handcraft* through the influence of **handiwork**]

handiwork *noun* **1** work, esp skilful work, produced by hand. **2** *often derog* the outcome of the action or efforts of someone or something. [Anglo-Saxon *handgeweorc*, from **hand** + ge-, collective prefix, + *woerc* work]

handkerchief *noun* (***handkerchiefs*** *or* ***handkerchieves***) a piece of cloth or soft paper used for wiping the nose, face, etc.

hand-knit *verb* to knit by hand.

handle *noun* **1** the part of a utensil, door, etc by which it is held so that it may be used, moved, picked up, etc. **2** an opportunity, excuse, etc for doing something: *Her shyness served as a handle for their bullying.* **3** *slang* a person's name or title. **4** of textiles, etc: the quality which is appreciated by touching or handling. ▸ *verb* **1** to touch, hold, move or operate with the hands. **2** to deal with, control, manage, discuss, etc: *She handles all the accounts.* **3** to buy, sell or deal in (specific merchandise). **4** *intr* to respond in a specified way to being operated: *This car handles very smoothly.* [Anglo-Saxon]

IDIOMS **fly off the handle** *informal* to become suddenly very angry.

handlebars *plural noun, sometimes singular* a bar for steering a bicycle, motorcycle, etc.

handler *noun* **1** someone who trains and controls an animal. **2** *in compounds* someone who handles something specified: *a baggage handler.*

handless *adj, dialect* awkward; clumsy.

handmade *adj* made by a person's hands or with hand-held tools.

handmaiden *or* **handmaid** *noun, old use* a female servant.

hand-me-down *noun, informal* something, esp a garment, passed down from one person to another.

handout *noun* **1** money, food, etc given to people who need it. **2** a leaflet, free sample, etc, given out as publicity for something. **3** a statement given to the press, students, etc as a supplement to or substitute for an oral address.

handover *noun* the transfer of power from one person or group of people to another.

hand-pick *verb* to choose carefully, esp for a particular purpose: *I hand-picked the grapes • He hand-picked the team.* ▪ **hand-picked** *adj.*

handsaw *noun* a saw worked with one hand.

handset *noun* a telephone mouthpiece and earpiece together in a single unit.

handshake *noun* an act of holding or shaking a person's hand, esp as a greeting or when concluding a deal.

hands-off *adj* **1** of a machine, etc: not touched or operated by the hands. **2** of a strategy, policy, etc: deliberately avoiding involvement.

handsome *adj* **1** of a man: good-looking. **2** of a woman: attractive in a strong, dignified, imposing way. **3** of a building, room, etc: well-proportioned; impressive. **4** substantial or generous: *a handsome donation.* **5** liberal or noble: *a handsome gesture.* ▪ **handsomely** *adv.* [15c: meaning 'easy to handle']

hands-on *adj* involving practical experience rather than just information or theory: *hands-on training.*

handspring *noun* a somersault or cartwheel in which one lands first on one's hands and then on one's feet.

handstand *noun* the act of balancing one's body on one's hands with one's legs in the air.

hand-to-hand *adj* of fighting: involving direct physical contact with the enemy.

hand-to-mouth *adj, adv* with just enough money or food for immediate needs only: *lives hand-to-mouth.*

handwriting *noun* **1** writing with a pen or pencil rather than by typing or printing. **2** the characteristic way a person writes. ▪ **handwritten** *adj.*

handy *adj* (***-ier, -iest***) **1** ready to use and conveniently placed. **2** easy to use or handle. **3** clever with one's hands. ▪ **handily** *adv.* ▪ **handiness** *noun.*

handyman *noun* a man skilled at, or employed to do, odd jobs around the house.

hang *verb* (***hung*** *or* (*in sense 3*) ***hanged***) **1** *tr & intr* to fasten or be fastened from above, esp with the lower part free. **2** *tr & intr* of a door, etc: to fasten or be fastened with hinges so that it can move freely. **3** *tr & intr* to suspend or be suspended by a rope around the neck until dead. **4** (*sometimes* **hang over**) to be suspended or hover, esp in the air or in a threatening way: *The smell of paint hung in the air • The fear of redundancy hung over me.* **5** *tr & intr* to droop or make something droop: *hang one's head in shame.* **6** to fix (wallpaper) to a wall. **7** *tr & intr* of a painting, etc: to place or be placed in an exhibition. **8** to decorate (a room, wall, etc) with pictures or other hangings. **9** *tr & intr, informal* to damn or be damned: *Hang the expense.* **10** *intr* of a piece of clothing: to sit in a specified way when worn: *a coat which hangs well.* **11** to suspend game from a hook to allow it to decompose slightly and become more flavoursome. **12** *comput* of a computer or a program: to stop functioning. ▸ *noun* **1** the way something hangs, falls or droops. **2** *usu with negatives, informal* a damn: *I couldn't give a hang.* See also **hanging**. [Anglo-Saxon *hangian*]

IDIOMS **get the hang of sth** *informal* to learn or begin to understand how to do it. **hang fire 1** to delay taking action. **2** to cease to develop or progress. **hang in the balance** to be uncertain or in doubt.

PHRASAL VERBS **hang about** *or* **around** *informal* **1** to waste time; to stand around doing nothing. **2** to stay or remain. **hang back** to be unwilling or reluctant to do something. **hang on** *informal* **1** to wait: *I'll hang on for a bit.* **2** to carry on bravely, in spite of problems or difficulties. **hang on sth 1** to depend on it: *It all hangs on the weather.* **2** to listen closely to it: *hanging on her every word.* **hang on to sth** to keep a hold or control of it. **hang out 1** to lean or bend out (eg of a window, etc). **2** *informal* to frequent a place: *He hangs out in local bars.* See also **hang-out**. **hang together 1** of two people: to be united and support each other. **2** of ideas, etc: to be consistent. **hang up** to finish a telephone conversation by replacing the receiver.

---

hanged, hung

Be careful not to confuse these two forms of the verb **hang**. The normal past tense and past participle of the verb **hang** is **hung**:

She hung the apron over the back of a chair.

Curtains could be hung from a pole across the wall.

However, if you are writing or speaking about killing by hanging, the correct form of the past tense and past participle is **hanged**:

He was hanged for his part in a bomb plot.

A man has hanged himself in his cell.

---

hangar *noun* a large shed or building in which aircraft are kept. [19c: French]

hangdog *adj* of someone's appearance or manner: ashamed, guilty or downcast.

hanger *noun* **1** (*in full* **coat-hanger**) a frame on which clothes are hung to keep their shape. **2 a** someone who hangs something; **b** *in compounds* a person or contraption that hangs a specified thing: *paper-hanger.*

hanger-on *noun* (***hangers-on***) a dependant or follower, esp one who is not wanted.

hang-glider *noun* **1** a large light metal frame with cloth stretched across it and a harness hanging below it for the pilot, which flies using air currents. **2** the pilot of this. ▪ **hang-gliding** *noun.*

hanging *noun* **1** the execution of someone by suspending their body by the neck. **2** (*usu* **hangings**) curtains, tapestries, etc hung on walls for decoration. ▸ *adj* **1** suspended; not fixed below; overhanging. **2** undecided: *a hanging question.*

hangman *noun* an official who carries out executions by hanging.

hangnail *noun* a piece of loose skin that has been partly torn away from the base or side of a fingernail. [17c: from Anglo-Saxon *ange* painful + *nægl* nail]

hang-out *noun, informal* a place where one lives or spends much time.

hangover *noun* **1** a collection of unpleasant physical symptoms that may follow a period of heavy drinking. See also **be hung over** at **hung**. **2** someone or something left over from or influenced by an earlier time.

hang-up *noun, informal* **1** an emotional or psychological problem or preoccupation. **2** a continual source of annoyance. See also **be hung up** at **hung**.

hank *noun* a coil, loop or skein of wool, string, rope, etc. [13c: from Norse *hanki* a hasp]

hanker *verb, intr* (*usu* **hanker after** *or* **for sth**) to have a longing or craving for it. ▪ **hankering** *noun*. [17c: perhaps from Dutch dialect *hankeren*]

hankie *or* **hanky** *noun* (**-ies**) *informal* a handkerchief.

hanky-panky *noun, informal* **1** slightly improper behaviour. **2** dubious or foolish conduct. [19c: prob a variant of **hocus-pocus**]

hansom *or* **hansom cab** *noun, hist* a small two-wheeled horse-drawn carriage with a fixed roof and the driver's seat high up at the back, used as a taxi. [19c: named after its inventor J A Hansom]

Hants *abbrev, English county* Hampshire. [From *Hantsharing*, the county's original name]

Hanukkah see **Chanukkah**

ha'penny see **halfpenny**

haphazard *adj* **1** careless. **2** random. ▶ *adv* at random. ▪ **haphazardly** *adv*. ▪ **haphazardness** *noun*. [16c]

hapless *adj* unlucky; unfortunate. [16c]

haploid *biol, adj* of a cell nucleus: having a single set of unpaired chromosomes. ▶ *noun* a haploid cell or organism. [20c]

happen *verb, intr* **1** to take place or occur. **2** (**happen to sb**) of an unforeseen, esp unwelcome, event: to be done to them or experienced by them. **3** to have the good or bad luck (to do something): *I happened to meet him on the way*. ▶ *adv, N Eng dialect* perhaps. [14c: from Norse *happ* good luck]

PHRASAL VERBS **happen on** *or* **upon sth** to discover or encounter it, esp by chance.

happening *noun* **1** an event. **2** a performance, esp one that takes place in the street, which has not been fully planned, and in which the audience is invited to take part. ▶ *adj* fashionable and up to the minute. [16c]

happy *adj* (**-ier, -iest**) **1** feeling or showing pleasure or contentment: *a happy smile*. **2** causing pleasure: *a happy day for the company*. **3** suitable; fortunate: *a happy coincidence*. **4** suitably expressed; appropriate: *a happy reply*. **5** *informal* slightly drunk. **6** *in compounds* overcome with the thing specified: *power-happy*. ▪ **happily** *adv*. ▪ **happiness** *noun*. [14c: from Norse *happ*]

happy-go-lucky *adj* carefree or easy-going.

happy hour *noun* in licensed premises: a period of time when drinks are sold at reduced prices.

happy medium *noun* a reasonable middle course between two extreme positions.

hara-kiri /harəˈkɪrɪ/ *or* **hari-kari** /harɪˈkɑːrɪ/ *noun* ritual suicide by cutting one's belly open with a sword, formerly practised in Japan to avoid dishonour. [19c: from Japanese *hara* belly + *kiri* cut]

harangue /həˈraŋ/ *noun* a loud forceful speech either to attack people or to try to persuade them to do something. ▶ *verb* to address such a speech to (someone or a crowd). [15c: from Italian *aringa* public speech]

harass *verb* **1** to pester, torment or trouble (someone) by continually questioning or attacking them. **2** to make frequent sudden attacks on (an enemy). ▪ **harassed** *adj*. ▪ **harassment** *noun*. [17c: from French *harasser* to **harry**, perhaps a derivative form of *harer* to set a dog on]

harbinger /ˈhɑːbɪndʒə(r)/ *noun* a person or thing that announces or predicts something to come; a forerunner. [12c: from French *herbergere* host]

harbour *or* (*N Am*) **harbor** *noun* **1** a place of shelter for ships. **2** a refuge or safe place. ▶ *verb* **1** to give shelter or protection to (someone, esp to a criminal). **2** to have (a feeling, etc) in one's head: *harbour a grudge*. [Anglo-Saxon from *here* army + *beorg* protection]

hard *adj* **1** of a substance: resistant to scratching or indentation; firm; solid. **2** toughened; not soft or smooth: *hard skin*. **3** difficult to do, understand, solve or explain. **4** using, needing or done with a great deal of effort. **5** demanding: *a hard master*. **6** harsh; cruel. **7** tough or violent: *a hard man*. **8** of weather: severe. **9** forceful: *a hard knock*. **10** cool or uncompromising: *took a long hard look at sales figures*. **11** causing hardship, pain or sorrow: *hard times*. **12** harsh and unpleasant to the senses: *a hard light*. **13** of information, etc: proven and reliable: *hard facts*. **14** shrewd or calculating: *a hard businesswoman*. **15** of water: containing calcium or magnesium salts, and tending to produce an insoluble scum instead of a lather with soap. **16** of a drug: highly addictive. **17** of an alcoholic drink: very strong, esp one which is a spirit rather than a beer, wine, etc. **18** politically extreme: *hard right* • *hard left*. **19** *phonetics, non-technical* of the sounds of certain consonants: produced as a stop rather than a fricative, as eg the *c* in *cat* and the *g* in *got*. Compare **soft**. **20** of currency: in strong demand due to having a stable value and exchange rate. **21** of credit: difficult to obtain. **22** as a classification of pencil leads: indicating durable quality and faintness in use. **23** of photographic paper: giving a high degree of image contrast. **24** of radiation: having high energy and the ability to penetrate solids. **1** with great effort or energy: *She works hard*. **2** *in compounds* achieved in the specified way with difficulty or as a result of great effort: *a hard-won victory* • *hard-earned results*. **3** earnestly or intently: *He thought hard to find a solution*. **4** with great intensity: *The news hit us hard*. ▪ **hardness** *noun*. [Anglo-Saxon *heard*]

IDIOMS **be hard going** to be difficult to do. **be hard put to do sth** to have difficulty doing it. **hard at it** working hard; very busy. **hard by** close by. **hard done by** *informal* unfairly treated. **hard of hearing** partially deaf. **hard up** *informal* in need of money.

hard-and-fast *adj* of a rule or principle: permanent or absolute.

hardback *noun* a book with a hard cover.

hardball *noun* no-nonsense tough tactics, used esp for political gain.

hard-bitten *adj, informal* of a person: tough and ruthless.

hardboard *noun* light strong board made by compressing wood pulp.

hard-boiled *adj* **1** of eggs: boiled until the yolk is solid. **2** *informal* of a person: tough; cynical.

hard cash *noun* coins and banknotes, as opposed to cheques and credit cards.

hard copy *noun* a printed version of information held in computer files. [1960s]

hardcore *noun* **1** pieces of broken brick, stone, etc used as a base for a road. **2** (*also* **hard core**) the central, most important group within an organization, resistant to change. ▸ *adj* (*often* **hard-core**) having long-lasting, strong and unchanging beliefs: *hard-core revolutionaries.*

hard disk *or* **hard disc** *noun, comput* a rigid aluminium disk, normally permanently sealed within a disk drive, with a large capacity for storing data. Compare **floppy disk**.

hard drive *noun, comput* a **disk drive** that controls the recording and reading of data on a hard disk.

hard-earned *adj* having taken a great deal of hard work to achieve or acquire.

harden *verb* **1** *tr & intr* to make or become hard or harder. **2** *tr & intr* to become or make less sympathetic or understanding. **3** to make or become stronger or firmer. **4** *intr, commerce* **a** of prices, a market, etc: to stop fluctuating; **b** of prices: to rise. ▪ **hardened** *adj* **1** rigidly set, eg in a behavioural pattern. **2** toughened through experience and not likely to change: *a hardened criminal.* ▪ **hardener** *noun.*
PHRASAL VERBS **harden sth off** to accustom (a plant) to cold, frost, etc by gradually exposing it to outdoor conditions.

hard-fought *adj* strongly contested.

hard hat *noun* **1** a protective helmet worn esp by building workers. **2** *chiefly US informal* a construction worker. **3** *chiefly US informal* a person with conservative or reactionary views.

hard-headed *adj* **1** tough, realistic or shrewd. **2** not influenced by emotion.

hard-hearted *adj* feeling no pity or kindness.

hardihood *noun* courage or daring.

hard labour *noun, law, formerly* a punishment involving heavy physical work in addition to a sentence of imprisonment.

hard line *noun* an uncompromising course, opinion, decision or policy. ▪ **hardliner** *noun.*

hardly *adv* **1** barely; scarcely: *I hardly knew the man.* **2** only just: *She could hardly keep her eyes open.* **3** *often ironic* certainly not: *They'll hardly come now.* **4** with difficulty: *I can hardly believe it.* **5** *rare* harshly.

hard-nosed *adj, informal* **1** tough and shrewd. **2** influenced by reason, not emotion.

hard palate *noun* the bony front part of the palate, which separates the mouth from the nasal cavities.

hard-pressed *or* **hard-pushed** *adj* **1** having problems; in difficulties. **2** threatened by severe competition or attack. **3** closely pursued.

hard science *noun* any of the physical or natural sciences.

the hard sell *noun* an aggressive and insistent way of promoting, selling or advertising.

hardship *noun* **1** living conditions that are difficult to endure. **2** severe suffering or pain, or a cause of this.

hard shoulder *noun, Brit* a hard verge along the side of a motorway, on which vehicles can stop if in trouble.

hardtack *noun* a kind of hard biscuit, formerly given to sailors as food on long journeys.

hardware *noun* **1** metal goods such as pots, cutlery, tools, etc. **2** *comput* the electronic, electrical, magnetic and mechanical components of a computer system, as opposed to the programs that form the **software**. **3** heavy military equipment, eg tanks and missiles. **4** mechanical equipment, components, etc.

hard-wearing *adj* durable; designed to last a long time and stay in good condition despite regular use.

hard-wired *adj* of computers: having functions that are controlled by hardware and cannot be altered by software programmes.

hardwood *noun* **1** the wood of a slow-growing deciduous tree, such as the oak, mahogany or teak. **2** any tree that produces such wood.

hardy *adj* (**-ier, -iest**) **1** tough; strong; able to bear difficult conditions. **2** of a plant: able to survive outdoors in winter. ▪ **hardily** *adv.* ▪ **hardiness** *noun.* [13c: from French *hardi*, from *hardir* to become bold]

hardy annual *noun* a plant that lives for up to a year and which can withstand severe climatic conditions.

hare *noun* a herbivorous mammal like a rabbit but slightly larger and with longer legs and ears. ▸ *verb, intr, informal* to run very fast or wildly. ▪ **harelike** *adj.* [Anglo-Saxon *hara*]

harebell *noun* a wild plant with violet-blue bell-shaped flowers. In Scotland called **bluebell**.

hare-brained *adj* of people, actions, etc: foolish; rash; heedless.

harelip *noun* a deformity of the upper lip, present from birth, in which there is a cleft on one or both sides of the centre.

harem /ˈhɑːriːm, hɑːˈriːm/ *noun* **1** a separate part of a traditional Muslim house in which wives, concubines, etc live. **2** the women living in this. [17c: from Arabic *harim* forbidden]

haricot /ˈharɪkoʊ/ *or* **haricot bean** *noun* a small white dried bean, used as food. [French]

hari-kari see **hara-kiri**

hark *verb, intr, literary & dialect* to listen attentively. [Anglo-Saxon, from *heorcnian* to hearken]
PHRASAL VERBS **hark back to sth** to refer to or remind one of (past experience): *hark back to one's childhood.*

harken see **hearken**

harlequin *noun* **1** (*also* **Harlequin**) *theatre* a humorous character from traditional Italian plays who is dressed in a black mask and a brightly coloured, diamond-patterned costume. **2** a clown or buffoon. ▸ *adj* in varied bright colours. [16c: from French *Hellequin* leader of a troop of demon horsemen]

harlequinade /hɑːləkwɪˈneɪd/ *noun* **1** (*also* **Harlequinade**) *theatre* a play in which a harlequin has a leading role. **2** buffoonery. [18c: from French *arlequinade*]

harlot *noun, old use* a prostitute. ▪ **harlotry** *noun.* [13c: from French *herlot* rascal]

harm *noun* physical, emotional, etc injury or damage. ▸ *verb* to injure or damage. [Anglo-Saxon *hearm*] IDIOMS **out of harm's way** in a safe place, not able to be harmed or cause harm.

harmful *adj* causing or tending to cause harm.

harmless *adj* not able or likely to cause harm.

harmonic *adj* **1** relating or referring to, or producing, harmony; harmonious. **2** *music* relating or belonging to harmony. **3** *maths* **a** able to be expressed in the form of **sine**[1] and **cosine** functions; **b** relating or referring to numbers whose reciprocals form an arithmetic progression; **c** *physics* relating to, or concerned with, a harmonic or harmonics. ▸ *noun* **1** *music* an overtone of a fundamental note, produced on a stringed instrument by touching one of the strings lightly at one of the points that divide the string into exact fractions. **2** *physics* a component of a sound whose frequency is an integral multiple of the base frequency. ▪ **harmonically** *adv.* [16c: from Latin *harmonicus* relating to **harmony**]

harmonica *noun* a small wind instrument with metal reeds along one side, played by being held against the mouth, blown or sucked, and moved from side to side to change the notes. Also called **mouth organ**. [18c: from Latin *harmonicus* relating to **harmony**]

harmonious *adj* **1** pleasant-sounding and tuneful. **2** forming a pleasing whole: *a harmonious arrangement of colours.* **3** without disagreement or bad feeling. ▪ **harmoniously** *adv.* [16c]

harmonium *noun* a musical instrument with a keyboard, in which air from bellows pumped by the feet makes the reeds vibrate to produce sound. [19c: French, from *harmonie* harmony]

harmonize *or* **-ise** *verb* **1** *tr & intr* to be in or bring into musical harmony. **2** *tr & intr* to form or be made to form a pleasing whole. **3** to add notes to (a simple tune) to form harmonies. **4** *intr* to sing in harmony, eg with other singers. ▪ **harmonization** *noun.*

harmony *noun* (**-ies**) **1** *music* **a** a pleasing combination of notes or sounds produced simultaneously; **b** the whole chordal structure of a piece as distinguished from its **melody** or its **rhythm**; **c** the art or science concerned with combinations of chords. **2** a pleasing arrangement of parts or things: *a harmony of colour.* **3** agreement in opinions, actions, feelings, etc. [14c: from Latin *harmonia* concord of sounds, from Greek *harmos* a joint]

harness *noun* **1** a set of leather straps used to attach a cart to a horse, and to control the horse's movements. **2** a similar set of straps for attaching to a person's body, eg to hold a child who is just learning to walk. ▸ *verb* **1** to put a harness on (a horse, person, etc). **2** to attach (a draught animal to a cart, etc). **3** to control (resources, esp natural ones) so as to make use of the potential energy or power they contain. ▪ **harnesser** *noun.* [13c: from French *herneis* equipment]

harp *noun* a large upright musical instrument with a series of strings stretched vertically across it, played by plucking the strings with the fingers. ▸ *verb, intr* **1** to play the harp. **2** *informal* (**harp on about sth**) to talk or write repeatedly and tediously about it. ▪ **harpist** *noun.* [Anglo-Saxon *hearpe*]

harpoon *noun* a barbed spear fastened to a rope, used for catching whales, etc. ▸ *verb* to strike (a whale, etc) with a harpoon. ▪ **harpooner** *or* **harpooneer** *noun.* [17c: from French *harpon* clamp]

harpsichord *noun* a triangular-shaped keyboard instrument in which the strings are plucked mechanically when the player presses the keys. ▪ **harpsichordist** *noun.* [17c: from Latin *harpa* harp + *chorda* string]

harpy *noun* (**-ies**) **1** *Greek myth* an evil creature with the head and body of a woman and the wings and feet of a bird. **2** a cruel, grasping woman. [16c: from Greek *harpyia* snatcher, from *harpazein* to seize]

harquebus see **arquebus**

harridan *noun* a bad-tempered, scolding old woman; a nag. [17c: prob from French *haridelle*, literally 'broken-down horse']

harrier[1] *noun* **1** a cross-country runner. **2** a hound used orig for hunting hares. [15c: from **hare** + *-er*, influenced by **harrier**[2]]

harrier[2] *noun* **1** a diurnal bird of prey with broad wings and long legs. **2** any person or thing that harries. [16c: from **harry**]

harrow *noun* a heavy metal framed farm implement with spikes or teeth, used to break up clods of soil and cover seed. ▸ *verb* **1** to pull a harrow over (land). **2** to distress greatly; to vex. [Anglo-Saxon *haerwe*]

harrowing *adj* extremely distressing.

harry *verb* (**-ies, -ied**) **1** to ravage or destroy (a town, etc), esp in war. **2** to annoy or worry someone. [Anglo-Saxon *hergian*, related to *here* army]

harsh *adj* **1** rough; grating; unpleasant to the senses. **2** strict, cruel or severe. ▪ **harshly** *adv.* ▪ **harshness** *noun.* [13c]

hart *noun* a male deer. [Anglo-Saxon *heorot*]

hartebeest /ˈhɑːtəbiːst/ *noun* a large African antelope with curved horns. [18c: Afrikaans, from Dutch *hert* **hart**+ *beest* **beast**]

harum-scarum /hɛərəmˈskɛərəm/ *adj* wild and thoughtless; reckless. ▸ *adv* recklessly. ▸ *noun* someone who is wild, impetuous or rash. [17c: from *hare* in obsolete sense 'harass' + **scare**]

harvest *noun* **1** the gathering in of ripened crops, usu in late summer or early autumn. **2** the season when this takes place. **3** the crop or crops gathered. **4** the product or result of some action, effort, etc. ▸ *verb* **1** *tr & intr* to gather (a ripened crop). **2** to receive or reap (benefits, consequences, etc). ▪ **harvester** *noun.* ▪ **harvesting** *noun.* [Anglo-Saxon *hærfest*]

harvest festival *noun* a religious service offering thanks for the crops gathered in the harvest.

harvest moon *noun* the full moon nearest to the autumnal equinox.

has see **have**

has-been *noun, informal* someone or something that once was, but is no longer, successful, important or influential. [17c]

hash[1] *noun* **1** a dish of cooked meat and vegetables chopped up together and recooked. **2** a re-using of old material. **3** *informal* a mess: *made a hash of it.* ▸ *verb* **1** to chop up into small pieces. **2** to mess up. [17c: from French *hacher* to chop, from *hache* hatchet]

hash[2] *noun, slang* hashish.

hashish *or* **hasheesh** /ˈhaʃiːʃ/ *noun* **cannabis**. [16c: from Arabic *hashish* dry leaves of hemp]

Hasid *or* **Hassid** *noun* (***Hasidim***) a member of one of a number of devout Jewish sects existing at various times throughout history. Also called **Chassid**. ▪ **Hasidic** *adj*. ▪ **Hasidism** *noun*.

hasn't *contraction* has not.

hasp *noun* a hinged metal fastening for a door, box, etc, often secured by a padlock. [Anglo-Saxon *hæpse*]

hassium /ˈhasɪəm/ *noun, chem* (symbol **Hs**) an artificially manufactured transuranic element. [20c: from *Hassia* the Latin name of Hesse in Germany]

hassle *informal, noun* **1** trouble, annoyance or inconvenience, or a cause of this. **2** a fight or argument. ▸ *verb* **1** to annoy or bother someone, esp repeatedly; to harass. **2** *intr* to argue or fight. [1940s]

hassock *noun* **1** a firm cushion for kneeling on, esp in church. **2** a tuft of grass. [Anglo-Saxon *hassuc*]

haste *noun* **1** speed, esp in an action. **2** urgency of movement. ▸ *verb* to hasten. [14c: French]

IDIOMS **in haste** in a hurry. **make haste** to hurry.

hasten *verb* **1** *tr & intr* to hurry or cause to hurry. **2** (*always* **hasten to do sth**) to do it eagerly and promptly: *He hastened to admit we were right*. [16c: from **haste**]

hasty *adj* (***-ier, -iest***) **1** hurried; swift; quick. **2** without enough thought or preparation; rash. **3** short-tempered. **4** conveying irritation or anger: *hasty words*. ▪ **hastily** *adv*. ▪ **hastiness** *noun*.

hat *noun* **1** a covering for the head, usu worn out of doors. **2** *informal* a role or capacity: *wearing her critic's hat*. ▪ **hatless** *adj*. [Anglo-Saxon *hæt*]

IDIOMS **keep sth under one's hat** *informal* to keep it secret. **take one's hat off to sb** *informal* to admire or praise them.

hatch[1] *noun* **1** a door covering an opening in a ship's deck. **2** a hatchway. **3** a door in an aircraft or spacecraft. **4** (*also* **serving hatch**) an opening in a wall between a kitchen and dining room, used esp for serving food. **5** the lower half of a divided door. [Anglo-Saxon *hæc*]

hatch[2] *verb* **1** *intr* (*also* **hatch out**) of an animal or bird: to break out of an egg. **2** *intr* of an egg: to break open, allowing young animals or birds to be born. **3** to produce (young animals or birds) from eggs. **4** (*often* **hatch up**) to plan or devise (a plot, scheme, etc), esp in secret. [13c]

hatch[3] *verb* to shade (the surface of a map, drawing, engraving, etc) with close parallel or crossed lines. ▪ **hatching** *noun*. [15c: from French *hacher* to chop]

hatchback *noun* **1** a sloping rear end of a car with a single door which opens upwards. **2** a car with such a rear end.

hatchery *noun* (***-ies***) a place where eggs, esp fish eggs, are hatched under artificial conditions.

hatchet *noun* a small axe held in one hand. [14c: from French *hachette*, from *hache* axe]

hatchet man *noun, informal* a person employed to carry out unpleasant or destructive assignments.

hatchling *noun* a newly hatched bird or reptile.

hatchway *noun* **1** an opening in a ship's deck for loading cargo through. **2** a similar opening in a wall, ceiling, floor, etc.

hate *verb* **1** to dislike intensely. **2** *informal* to regret: *I hate to bother you*. ▸ *noun* **1** an intense dislike. **2** (*esp* **pet hate**) *informal* an intensely disliked person or thing. ▪ **hatable** *or* **hateable** *adj*. [Anglo-Saxon *hatian*]

hate crime *noun* a crime motivated by hatred of the victim on the grounds of race, religion, etc.

hateful *adj* causing or deserving great dislike; loathsome; detestable.

hate mail *noun* correspondence containing an abusive or threatening message.

hatpin *noun* a long metal pin, often decorated, pushed through a woman's hat and hair to keep the hat in place.

hatred *noun* intense dislike; enmity; ill-will.

hatstand *or* (*esp US*) **hat tree** *noun* a piece of furniture with pegs for hanging hats, coats, etc on.

hatter *noun* someone who makes or sells hats.

IDIOMS **mad as a hatter** extremely mad or eccentric.

hat trick *noun* the scoring of three points, goals, victories, etc in a single period of time or match. [19c: prob because a cricketer taking three wickets with successive balls might win a hat for achieving this]

haughty *adj* (***-ier, -iest***) very proud; arrogant or contemptuous. ▪ **haughtily** *adv*. ▪ **haughtiness** *noun*. [16c: from Latin *altus* high]

haul *verb* **1** *tr & intr* to pull with great effort or difficulty. **2** to transport by road, eg in a lorry. **3** *naut* to alter the course of a vessel, esp so as to sail closer to the wind. **4** (*usu* **haul up**) to bring (someone before some authority) for punishment, reprimand etc: *was hauled up before the boss*. ▸ *noun* **1** a distance to be travelled: *Just a short haul now over the mountains* • *It's a long haul to Sydney*. **2** an act of dragging something with effort or difficulty. **3** an amount gained at any one time, eg of items stolen. **4** an amount of contraband seized at any one time: *drugs haul*. ▪ **hauler** *noun*. [16c: from French *haler* to drag]

haulage *noun* **1** the act or labour of hauling. **2** **a** the business of transporting goods by road, esp in lorries; **b** the money charged for this.

haulier *noun* a person or company that transports goods by road, esp in lorries.

haulm *or* **halm** /hɔːm/ *noun, botany* **1** the stalks or stems of potatoes, peas, beans or grasses, collectively. **2** one such stalk or stem. [Anglo-Saxon *healm*]

haunch *noun* **1** the fleshy part of the buttock or thigh. **2** the leg and loin, esp of a deer, as a cut of meat: *a haunch of venison*. [13c: from French *hanche*]

haunt *verb* **1** of a ghost or spirit: to be present in (a place) or visit (a person or place) regularly. **2** of unpleasant thoughts, etc: to keep coming back to someone's mind: *haunted by the memory of his death*. **3** to visit (a place) frequently. **4** to associate with someone frequently. ▸ *noun* **1** (*often* **haunts**) a place visited frequently. **2** the habitation or usual feeding-ground of deer, game, fowls, etc. ▪ **haunted** *adj* **1** frequented or visited by ghosts or spirits. **2** constantly worried or obsessed. [13c: from French *hanter*]

haunting *adj* of a place, memory, piece of music, etc: making a very strong and moving impression.

Hausa /ˈhaʊsə, -zə/ *noun* (***Hausas*** *or* ***Hausa***) **1** a Black people of W Africa, living mainly in N Nigeria. **2** a member of this people. **3** the language of this people, widely used in commerce throughout W Africa.

haute couture /oʊt kʊ'tjʊə(r)/ *noun* **1** the most expensive and fashionable clothes available. **2** the leading fashion designers or their products, collectively. [Early 20c: French, literally 'high dressmaking']

haute cuisine /oʊt kwɪ'ziːn/ *noun* cookery, esp French cookery, of a very high standard. [1920s: French, literally 'high cooking']

hauteur /oʊ'tɜː(r)/ *noun* haughtiness; arrogance. [17c: French, from *haut* high]

have *verb* (***has, had, having***) **1** to possess or own: *They have a big house.* **2** to possess as a characteristic or quality: *He has brown eyes.* **3** to receive, obtain or take: *I'll have a drink* • *He had a look.* **4** to think of or hold in the mind: *I have an idea.* **5** to experience, enjoy or suffer: *You'll have a good time* • *I have a headache* • *I had my car stolen.* **6** to be in a specified state: *The book has a page missing.* **7** to arrange or hold: *I'm having a party.* **8** to take part in something: *We had a conversation.* **9** to cause, order or invite someone to do something or something to be done: *You should have your hair cut* • *They had him fired.* **10** to state or assert: *Rumour has it that they've only just met.* **11** to place: *I'll have the fridge in this corner.* **12** to eat or drink: *I had beans and chips.* **13** to gain an advantage over or control of someone: *You have me on that point.* **14** *informal* to cheat or deceive: *You've been had.* **15** to show or feel: *I have no pity for them* • *She had the goodness to leave.* **16** *with negatives* to accept or tolerate: *I won't have any of that!* **17** to receive as a guest: *We're having people to dinner.* **18** to be pregnant with or give birth to (a baby, etc): *She had a boy.* **19** to possess a knowledge of something: *I have some French.* ▸ *auxiliary verb* used with a past **participle** to show that the action or actions described have been completed, as in *I have made the cake* and *She has been there many times.* ▸ *noun* (**haves**) *informal* people who have wealth and the security it brings: *the haves and the have-nots.* [Anglo-Saxon *habban*]

IDIOMS **have had it** *informal* **1** to be dead, ruined or exhausted. **2** to have missed one's opportunity. **3** to become unfashionable. **have it out** to settle a disagreement by arguing or discussing it frankly. **have to be** to surely be: *That has to be the reason.* **have to be** *or* **do sth** to be required to be or do it: *He had to run fast* • *We had to be gentle.* **I have it!** *or* **I've got it!** I have found the answer, solution, etc. **let sb have it** *informal* to launch an attack on them, either physical or verbal.

PHRASAL VERBS **have sb on** *informal* to trick or tease them. **have sth on** to have an engagement or appointment. **have sth on sb** to have information about them, esp adverse or incriminating information. **have sb up for sth** *Brit, informal* to bring them to court to answer (a charge): *He was had up for robbery.*

haven *noun* **1** a place of safety or rest. **2** a harbour or other sheltered spot for ships. [Anglo-Saxon *hæfen*]

have-nots *plural noun* people with relatively little material wealth. See also **have** ▸ *noun.*

haven't *contraction* have not.

haver /'heɪvə(r)/ *esp Scot & N Eng, verb, intr* **1** to babble; to talk nonsense. **2** to be slow or hesitant in making a decision. ▸ *noun* (*usu* **havers**) foolish talk; nonsense. [18c]

haversack *noun* a canvas bag carried over one shoulder or on the back. [18c: from German *Habersack*, literally 'oat-bag']

having *present participle of* **have**

havoc *noun* **1** great destruction or damage. **2** *informal* chaos; confusion. [15c: from French *havot* plunder]

IDIOMS **play havoc with sth** to cause a great deal of damage or confusion to it.

haw[1] see **hum and haw** at **hum**

haw[2] *noun* **1** a hawthorn berry. **2** the hawthorn. [Anglo-Saxon *haga*]

haw-haw see **ha-ha**[1], **ha-ha**[2]

hawk[1] *noun* **1** a relatively small diurnal bird of prey with short rounded wings. **2** *politics* a person favouring force and aggression rather than peaceful means of settling disputes. Compare **dove**[2] (sense 2). **3** a ruthless or grasping person. ▸ *verb* **1** *intr* to hunt with a hawk. **2** *intr* of falcons or hawks: to fly in search of prey. **3** to pursue or attack on the wing, as a hawk does. ▪ **hawking** *noun.* ▪ **hawkish** *adj.* ▪ **hawk-like** *adj.* [Anglo-Saxon *hafoc*]

hawk[2] *verb* to carry (goods) round, usu from door to door, trying to sell them. ▪ **hawker** *noun.* [16c]

hawk[3] *verb* **1** *intr* to clear the throat noisily. **2** to bring phlegm up from the throat. ▸ *noun* an act or an instance of doing this. [16c]

hawk-eyed *adj* **1** having very keen eyesight. **2** watchful; observant.

hawser *noun, naut* a thick rope or steel cable for tying ships to the quayside. [14c: from French *haucier* to hoist]

hawthorn *noun* a thorny tree or shrub with pink or white flowers and red berries (see **haw**[2] sense 1). *Also called* **may**, **may tree**, **mayflower**, **quickthorn**, **whitethorn**. [Anglo-Saxon *haguthorn*, from *haga* hedge + **thorn**]

hay *noun* grass, clover, etc that has been cut and dried in the field before being baled and stored for use as winter fodder for livestock. [Anglo-Saxon *hieg*]

IDIOMS **make hay while the sun shines** to take advantage of an opportunity while one has the chance.

hay fever *noun, non-technical* allergic **rhinitis**, an allergic response to pollen characterized by itching and watering of the eyes, dilation of nasal blood vessels and increased nasal mucus.

haystack *or* **hayrick** *noun* a large firm stack of hay built in an open field.

haywire *adj, informal* (*often* **go haywire**) **1** of things: out of order; not working properly. **2** of people: crazy or erratic. [1920s]

hazard *noun* **1** a risk of harm or danger. **2** something that is likely to cause harm or danger. **3** *golf* an obstacle on a golf course, such as water, a bunker, etc. **4** chance; accident. ▸ *verb* **1** to put forward (a guess, suggestion, etc). **2** to risk. **3** to expose to danger. ▪ **hazardous** *adj.* [13c: from French *hasard*]

haze *noun* **1** a thin mist, vapour or shimmer in the atmosphere which obscures visibility. **2** a feeling of confusion or of not understanding. ▸ *verb, tr & intr* to make or become hazy. [17c: a back-formation from **hazy**]

hazel *noun* **1** a small deciduous shrub or tree with edible nuts. **2** its wood. **3** a hazelnut. **4** a greenish-brown colour. [Anglo-Saxon *hæsel*]

hazelnut *noun* the edible nut of the hazel tree, with a smooth hard shiny shell.

hazy *adj* (**-ier, -iest**) **1** misty. **2** vague; not clear: *was a bit hazy about what happened.* ▪ **hazily** *adv.* ▪ **haziness** *noun.* [17c]

H-bomb see **hydrogen bomb**

He *symbol, chem* helium.

he *pron* **1** a male person or animal already referred to. **2** a person or animal of unknown or unstated sex, esp after pronouns such as 'someone' or 'whoever'. ► *noun, also in compounds* a male person or animal: *Is the kitten a he or a she?* • *he-goat.* [Anglo-Saxon *he*]

---

he or she, they

If you want to use a pronoun that does not specify a gender, you can use **he or she**:

There is a limit on what a teacher can achieve if he or she has no support.

However, this can sound awkward sometimes:

There is a limit on what a teacher can achieve if he or she has no support from his or her colleagues.

Because of this awkwardness, it is acceptable to use **they** and **their** as singular pronouns in less formal contexts:

If anyone has lost an umbrella, will they let me know?

---

head *noun* **1** the uppermost or foremost part of an animal's body, containing the brain and the organs of sight, smell, hearing and taste. **2** the head thought of as the seat of intelligence, imagination, ability, etc: *Use your head* • *a head for heights.* **3** something like a head in form or function, eg the top of a tool. **4** the person with the most authority in an organization, country, etc. **5** the position of being in charge. **6** *informal* a head teacher or principal teacher. **7** the top or upper part of something, eg a table or bed. **8** the highest point of something: *the head of the pass.* **9** the front or forward part of something, eg a queue. **10** the foam on top of a glass of beer, lager, etc. **11** the top part of a plant which produces leaves or flowers. **12** a culmination or crisis: *Things came to a head.* **13** the pus-filled top of a boil or spot. **14** (*pl* ***head***) a person, animal or individual considered as a unit: *600 head of cattle* • *The meal cost £10 a head.* **15** *informal* a headache. **16** the source of a river, lake, etc. **17** the height or length of a head, used as a measurement: *He won by a head* • *She's a head taller than her brother.* **18** a headland: *Beachy Head.* **19** **a** the height of the surface of a liquid above a specific point, esp as a measure of the pressure at that point: *a head of six metres;* **b** water pressure, due to height or velocity, measured in terms of a vertical column of water; **c** any pressure: *a full head of steam.* **20** an electromagnetic device in a tape recorder, video recorder, computer, etc for converting electrical signals into the recorded form on tapes or disks, or vice versa, or for erasing recorded material. **21** (**heads**) the side of a coin bearing the head of a monarch, etc. Compare **tails** at **tail**[1] (*noun* sense 7). **22** a headline or heading. **23** a main point of an argument, discourse, etc. **24** (*often* **heads**) *naut* a ship's toilet. **25** *informal* a user of a specified drug: *acid head* • *smack head.* **26** *also in compounds* the final point of a route: *railhead.* ► *adj* **1** for or belonging to the head: *headband* • *head cold.* **2** chief; principal: *head gardener.* **3** at, or coming from, the front: *head wind.* ► *verb* **1** to be at the front of or top of something: *to head the queue.* **2** to be in charge of, or in the most important position. **3** *tr & intr* to move or cause to move in a certain direction: *heading for work* • *heading home.* **4** *tr & intr* to turn or steer (a vessel) in a particular direction: *They headed into the wind.* **5** to provide with or be (a headline or heading) at the beginning of a chapter, top of a letter, etc. **6** *football* to hit (the ball) with the head. ▪ **headless** *adj.* [Anglo-Saxon *heafod*]

IDIOMS **above** *or* **over one's head** too difficult for one to understand. **bring** *or* **come to a head** to reach or cause to reach a climax or crisis. **give sb his** *or* **her head** to allow them to act freely and without restraint. **go to one's head 1** of alcoholic drink: to make one slightly intoxicated. **2** of praise, success, etc: to make one conceited. **head and shoulders** by a considerable amount; to a considerable degree: *head and shoulders above the rest.* **head over heels 1** rolling over completely with the head first. **2** completely: *head over heels in love.* **hold up one's head** to be confident or unashamed. **keep one's head** to remain calm and sensible in a crisis. **lose one's head** to become angry or excited or act foolishly, particularly in a crisis. **not make head or tail of sth** to be unable to understand it. **off one's head** *informal* mad; crazy. **off the top of one's head** *informal* without much thought or calculation. **on your,** *etc* **own head be it** you, etc will bear the full responsibility for your, etc actions. **out of one's head 1** *informal* mad, crazy. **2** of one's own invention. **over sb's head 1** without considering the obvious candidate: *He was promoted over the head of his supervisor.* **2** referring to a higher authority without consulting the person in the obvious position. **3** too difficult for them to understand: *Her jokes are always over my head.* **put our** *or* **your** *or* **their heads together** to consult. **take** *or* **get it into one's head 1** to decide to do something, usu foolishly. **2** to come to believe something, usu wrongly. **turn sb's head 1** to make them vain and conceited. **2** to attract their attention.

PHRASAL VERBS **head off** to leave: *headed off before it got too dark.* **head sb off** to get ahead of them so as to intercept them and force them to turn back. **head sth off** to prevent or hinder it.

headache *noun* **1** a continuous pain felt in the head. **2** *informal* someone or something that causes worry or annoyance. ▪ **headachy** *adj.*

headband *noun* a band worn round the head, especially for decoration.

headbanger *noun, informal* **1** a fan of heavy metal or rock music. **2** a stupid or fanatical person.

headboard *noun* a panel at the top end of a bed.

head-butt *verb* to strike someone deliberately and violently with the head. ► *noun* a blow of this kind.

headcase *noun, informal* **1** someone who behaves in a wild or irrational way. **2** a mentally ill person.

head count *noun* a count of people present.

headdress *noun* a covering for the head, esp a highly decorative one used in ceremonies.

headed *adj* **1** having a heading: *headed notepaper.* **2** *in compounds*: *clear-headed.*

header *noun* **1** *informal* a fall or dive forward. **2** *football* the hitting of the ball with the head. **3** *building* a brick or stone laid across a wall so that the shorter side shows on the wall surface. **4** a heading for a chapter, article, etc. **5** *comput* an optional piece of coded information preceding a collection of data, giving details about the data.

headfirst *adv* **1** moving esp quickly with one's head in front or bent forward. **2** without thinking; rashly.

headgear *noun* anything worn on the head: *protective headgear.*

headhunting *noun* **1** *anthropol* the practice in certain societies of taking the heads of one's dead enemies as trophies. **2** the practice of trying to attract a person away from their present job to work for one's own or a client's company. ▪ **headhunt** *verb.* ▪ **headhunter** *noun.*

heading *noun* **1** a title at the top of a page, letter, section of a report, etc. **2** a main division, eg in a speech. **3** *mining* a horizontal tunnel in a mine.

headland *noun* a strip of land that sticks out into a sea or other expanse of water.

headlight *or* **headlamp** *noun* a powerful light on the front of a vehicle.

headline *noun* **1 a** a title or heading of a newspaper article, written above the article in large letters; **b** a line at the top of a page, indicating the page number, title, etc. **2** (**headlines**) the most important points in a television or radio news broadcast, read out before the full broadcast. ▸ *verb, tr & intr* to have top billing in (a show, etc).

headlong *adj, adv* **1** moving esp quickly with one's head in front or bent forward. **2** quickly, and usu without thinking.

headman *noun* **1** *anthropol* a tribal chief or leader. **2** a foreman or supervisor.

headmaster *or* **headmistress** *noun* a **head teacher.**

head on *adv* **1** head to head; with the front of one vehicle hitting the front of another. **2** in direct confrontation. *as adj* (**head-on**): *a head-on crash.*

headphones *plural noun* a device consisting of two small sound receivers, held over the ears by a metal strap passed over the head, or inserted into the ear (**earphones**), for listening to a radio, CD player, MP3 player, etc.

headquarters *singular or plural noun* (abbrev **HQ, hq**) **1** the centre of an organization or group, from which activities are controlled. **2** *military* the residence of the commander-in-chief, from where orders are issued.

headrest *noun* a cushion that supports the head, fitted to the top of a car seat, etc.

headroom *noun* **1** the space between the top of a vehicle and the underside of a bridge. **2** any space overhead, below an obstacle, etc. Also called **headway.**

headscarf *noun* a scarf worn over the head and tied under the chin.

headset *noun* a pair of headphones, often with a microphone attached.

head start *noun* an initial advantage in a race or competition.

headstone *noun* **1** a **gravestone. 2** *archit* a keystone.

headstrong *adj* **1** of a person: difficult to persuade; determined; obstinate. **2** of an action: heedless; rash.

head teacher *noun* the principal teacher in charge of a school.

head to head *adv, informal* in direct competition. *as adj* (**head-to-head**): *a head-to-head clash.* ▸ *noun* a competition involving two people, teams, etc.

headwaters *plural noun* the tributary streams of a river, which flow from the area in which it rises.

headway *noun* **1** progress: *making headway with the backlog.* **2** a ship's movement forward. **3** headroom. **4** the interval between consecutive trains, buses, etc, on the same route in the same direction.

headwind *noun* a wind that is blowing towards a person, ship or aircraft, in the opposite direction to the chosen course of travel.

headword *noun* a word forming a heading, esp for a dictionary or encyclopedia entry.

heady *adj* (**-ier, -iest**) **1** of alcoholic drinks: tending to make one drunk quickly. **2** very exciting. **3** rash; impetuous. ▪ **headily** *adv.* ▪ **headiness** *noun.*

heal *verb* **1** to cause (a person, wound, etc) to become healthy again. **2** *intr* (*also* **heal up** *or* **over**) of a wound: to become healthy again by natural processes, eg by scar formation. **3** to make (sorrow, etc) less painful. **4** *tr & intr* to settle (disputes, etc) and restore friendly relations, harmony, etc. ▪ **healer** *noun.* ▪ **healing** *noun, adj.* [Anglo-Saxon *hælan*]

health *noun* **1** a state of physical, mental and social wellbeing accompanied by freedom from illness or pain. **2** a person's general mental or physical condition: *in poor health.* **3** the soundness, esp financial soundness, of an organization, country, etc. ▪ **healthful** *adj.* [Anglo-Saxon *hælth*]

health centre *noun, Brit* a centre where a group of doctors and nurses provide health care.

health farm *noun* a place where people go to improve their health through diet and exercise.

health food *noun* any food that is considered to be natural, free of additives and beneficial to health.

health service *noun* a public service providing medical care, usu without charge.

health visitor *noun* a trained nurse who visits people, eg new mothers and their babies, the elderly, etc, in their homes to check on their health and give advice on matters of health.

healthy *adj* (**-ier, -iest**) **1** having or showing good health. **2** causing good health. **3** in a good state: *a healthy economy.* **4** wise: *a healthy respect for authority.* **5** relating to soundness of body or mind: *a healthy appetite.* **6** *informal* considerable; satisfactory: *a healthy sum.* ▪ **healthily** *adv.* ▪ **healthiness** *noun.*

heap *noun* **1** a collection of things in an untidy pile or mass. **2** (*usu* **heaps**) *informal* a large amount or number: *heaps of time.* **3** *informal* something, esp a motor vehicle, that is very old and not working properly. ▸ *verb* **1** *tr & intr* (*also* **heap sth up** *or* **heap up**) to collect or be collected together in a heap. **2** (*often* **heap sth on sb** *or* **heap sb with sth**) to give them it in large amounts. ▸ *adv* (**heaps**) *informal* very much: *I'm heaps better.* ▪ **heaped** *adj* denoting a spoonful that forms a rounded heap on the spoon. [Anglo-Saxon *héap*]

hear *verb* (**heard**) **1** *tr & intr* to perceive (sounds) with the ear. **2** to listen to something: *Did you hear what he said?* **3** *intr* (*usu* **hear about, of** *or* **that**) to be told or informed (of it). **4** *intr* (*usu* **hear from**) to be contacted (by them), esp by letter or telephone. **5** *law* to listen to and judge (a case). ▪ **hearer** *noun.* [Anglo-Saxon *hieran*]

IDIOMS **hear! hear!** an expression of agreement or approval. **hear tell** *or* **hear tell of sth** *dialect* to be told about it. **not hear of sth** not to allow it to happen.

PHRASAL VERBS **hear sb out** to listen to them until they have said all they wish to say.

hearing *noun* **1** the sense that involves the perception of sound. **2** the distance within which something can be heard: *within hearing*. **3** an opportunity to state one's case: *We gave him a fair hearing*. **4** a judicial investigation and listening to evidence and arguments, esp without a jury.

hearing aid *noun* (*also* **deaf aid**) a small electronic device consisting of a miniature sound receiver, an amplifier and a power source, worn in or behind the ear by a partially deaf person to help them hear more clearly.

hearken *or* (*sometimes US*) **harken** *verb, intr* (*often* **hearken to**) *old use* to listen or pay attention (to someone or something). [Anglo-Saxon *heorcnian*]

hearsay *noun* rumour; gossip.

hearse *noun* a vehicle used for carrying a coffin at a funeral. [14c: from Latin *hirpex* harrow]

heart *noun* **1** in vertebrates: a muscular organ that contracts and pumps blood round the body. **2** the corresponding organ or organs that pump circulatory fluid in invertebrates. **3** this organ considered as the centre of a person's thoughts, emotions, conscience, etc. **4** emotional mood: *a change of heart*. **5** ability to feel tenderness or pity: *You have no heart*. **6** courage and enthusiasm: *take heart*. **7** the most central part: *the heart of the old town*. **8** the most important part: *the heart of the problem*. **9** the compact inner part of some vegetables, eg cabbages and lettuces. **10** a symbol (♥), usu red in colour, representing the heart, with two rounded lobes at the top curving down to meet in a point at the bottom. **11** *cards* **a** (**hearts**) one of the four suits of playing-cards, with the heart-shaped (♥) symbols on them; **b** one of the playing-cards of this suit. [Anglo-Saxon *heorte*]

IDIOMS **at heart** really; basically. **break sb's heart** to cause them great sorrow. **by heart** by or from memory. **lose heart** to become discouraged or disillusioned over something. **take sth to heart** to pay great attention to it or be very affected by it. **to one's heart's content** as much as one wants. **with all one's heart** very willingly or sincerely.

heartache *noun* great sadness or mental suffering.

heart attack *noun, non-technical* a sudden severe chest pain caused by failure of part of the heart muscle to function. See also **coronary thrombosis**.

heartbeat *noun* **1** the pulsation of the heart, produced by the alternate contraction and relaxation of the heart muscle. **2** a single pumping action of the heart.

heartbreak *noun* very great sorrow or grief. ▪ **heartbreaking** *adj*. ▪ **heartbroken** *adj*.

heartburn *noun* a feeling of burning in the chest caused by indigestion.

hearten *verb, tr & intr* to make or become happier, more cheerful or encouraged. ▪ **heartening** *adj*.

heart failure *noun* a condition in which the heart fails to pump sufficient blood.

heartfelt *adj* sincerely and deeply felt.

hearth *noun* **1** the floor of a fireplace, or the area surrounding it. **2** the home. **3** the lowest part of a blast-furnace, in which the molten metal is produced or contained. [Anglo-Saxon *heorth*]

heartland *noun* a central or vitally important area.

heartless *adj* cruel; very unkind. ▪ **heartlessly** *adv*. ▪ **heartlessness** *noun*.

heart murmur see **murmur** (*noun* sense 4)

heart rate *noun* the number of single heartbeats per minute.

heart-rending *adj* causing great sorrow or pity.

heart-searching *noun* the close examination of one's deepest feelings and conscience.

heartstrings *plural noun* a person's deepest feelings. [15c: from old notions of anatomy, in which the tendons were thought to support the heart]

heart-throb *noun, informal* someone, esp a male actor or singer, many people find very attractive.

heart-to-heart *adj* of a conversation: intimate, sincere and candid. ▸ *noun* an intimate and candid conversation.

heart-warming *adj* gratifying; pleasing; emotionally moving.

heartwood *noun, botany* the dark, hard wood at the centre of a tree.

hearty *adj* (**-ier, -iest**) **1** very friendly and warm in manner. **2** strong, vigorous or enthusiastic: *hale and hearty*. **3** heartfelt: *a hearty dislike*. **4** of a meal or an appetite: large. ▪ **heartily** *adv*. ▪ **heartiness** *noun*.

heat *noun* **1** a form of energy that is stored as the energy of vibration or motion (kinetic energy) of the atoms or molecules of a material. **2** a high temperature; warmth; the state of being hot. **3** hot weather. **4** intensity of feeling, esp anger or excitement: *the heat of the argument*. **5** the most intense part: *in the heat of the battle*. **6** *sport* **a** a preliminary race or contest which eliminates some competitors; **b** a single section in a contest. ▸ *verb, tr & intr* **1** to make or become hot or warm. **2** to make or become intense or excited. [Anglo-Saxon *hætu*]

IDIOMS **in** *or* **on heat** of some female mammals: ready to mate. See also **oestrus**. **in the heat of the moment** without pausing to think.

heated *adj* **1** having been made hot or warm. **2** angry or excited. ▪ **heatedly** *adv*. ▪ **heatedness** *noun*.

heater *noun* **1** an apparatus for heating a room, building, water in a tank, etc. **2** *US slang* a pistol.

heath *noun* **1** an area of open land, usu with acidic soil, dominated by low-growing evergreen shrubs, esp heathers. **2** a low evergreen shrub found esp on open moors and heaths. [Anglo-Saxon *hæth*]

heathen *noun* (***heathens*** *or* ***heathen***) **1** someone who does not adhere to a particular religion, esp when regarded by a person or community that does follow that religion. **2** *informal* an ignorant or uncivilized person. ▸ *adj* **1** having no religion; pagan. **2** *informal* ignorant; uncivilized. [Anglo-Saxon *hæthen*]

heather *noun* **1** a low evergreen moor or heath shrub with small pink or purple bell-shaped flowers. Also called **ling**. **2 heath** (sense 2). [14c: *hathir*]

Heath-Robinson *adj* of a machine or device: ludicrously complicated and impractical in design, esp when its function is a simple one. [19c: named after William Heath Robinson, the cartoonist who drew such machines]

heating *noun* **1** any of various systems for maintaining the temperature inside a room or building at a level higher than that of the surroundings. **2** the heat generated by such a system.

heat-seeking *adj* of a missile, etc: able to detect heat from its target and use this as a guide to hitting it. ▪ **heat-seeker** *noun*.

heatstroke *noun* a condition caused by overexposure to unaccustomed heat, characterized by progressively severe symptoms of lassitude, fainting and high fever. Also called **sunstroke**.

heatwave *noun* a prolonged period of unusually hot dry weather.

heave *verb* (***heaved*** or (*in naut senses*) ***hove***) **1** to lift or pull with great effort. **2** *informal* to throw something heavy. **3** *intr* to rise and fall heavily or rhythmically. **4** to make something rise and fall heavily or rhythmically. **5** *intr, informal* to retch or vomit. ▸ *noun* an act or instance of heaving. [Anglo-Saxon *hebban*]

IDIOMS **heave a sigh** to sigh heavily or with effort. **heave into sight** *esp naut* to move in a particular direction. **the heave** *or* **the heave-ho** *informal* dismissal or rejection.

PHRASAL VERBS **heave to** *esp naut* to bring or be brought to a stop or standstill.

heaven *noun* **1** the place believed to be the abode of God, angels and the righteous after death. **2** (*usu* **the heavens**) the sky. **3** a place or the state of great happiness or bliss. **4** often used in exclamations: God or Providence: *heaven forbid*. [Anglo-Saxon *heofon*]

heavenly *adj* **1** *informal* very pleasant; beautiful. **2** situated in or coming from heaven or the sky: *heavenly body*. **3** holy. ▪ **heavenliness** *noun*.

heaven-sent *adj* very lucky or convenient; timely.

heavy *adj* (***-ier, -iest***) **1** having great weight. **2** of breathing: loud, because of excitement, exhaustion, etc. **3** great in amount, size, power, etc: *heavy traffic* • *a heavy crop*. **4** great in amount, frequency, etc: *a heavy drinker*. **5** considerable: *heavy emphasis*. **6** hard to bear, endure or fulfil: *a heavy fate*. **7** ungraceful and coarse: *heavy features*. **8** severe, intense or excessive: *heavy fighting*. **9** sad or dejected: *with a heavy heart*. **10** of food: difficult to digest: *a heavy meal*. **11** having a great or relatively high density: *a heavy metal*. **12** striking or falling with force; powerful: *heavy rain*. **13** forceful or powerful: *a heavy sea*. **14** intense or deep: *a heavy sleep*. **15** of the sky: dark and cloudy. **16** needing a lot of physical or mental effort. **17** of literature, music, etc: **a** serious in tone and content; **b** not immediately accessible or appealing. **18** physically and mentally slow. **19** fat; solid. **20** of soil: wet and soft due to its high clay content. **21** *informal* strict; severe: *Don't be heavy on him*. **22** *military* **a** equipped with powerful weapons, armour, etc; **b** of guns: large and powerful. **23** of cakes and bread: dense through not having risen enough. ▸ *noun* (***-ies***) **1** *slang* a large, violent man: *They sent in the heavies*. **2** a villain in a play, film, etc. **3** *Scot* a beer like bitter but darker in colour and gassier. **4** (*usu* **the heavies**) serious newspapers. ▸ *adv* heavily: *Time hangs heavy on my hands*. ▪ **heavily** *adv* **1** in a heavy way; with or as if with weight. **2** intensely, severely or violently. ▪ **heaviness** *noun*. [Anglo-Saxon *hefig*]

heavy-duty *adj* designed to resist or withstand very hard wear or use.

heavy going *noun* difficult or slow progress. ▸ *adj* (**heavy-going**) difficult to deal with or to get further with.

heavy-handed *adj* **1** clumsy and awkward. **2** too severe or strict; oppressive. ▪ **heavy-handedly** *adv*. ▪ **heavy-handedness** *noun*.

heavy hydrogen see **deuterium**

heavy industry *noun* a factory or factories involving the use of large or heavy equipment, eg coal-mining, ship-building, etc.

heavy metal *noun* loud repetitive rock music with a strong beat.

heavy water *noun* deuterium oxide.

heavyweight *noun* **1** a class for boxers and wrestlers of more than a specified weight, which is 86kg (190 lb) in professional boxing, and similar but different weights in amateur boxing and wrestling. *as adj*: *heavyweight bout*. **2** a boxer, etc of this weight. **3** *informal* an important, powerful or influential person. **4** a person who is heavier than average.

hebdomadal /hɛb'dɒmədəl/ *adj* weekly. ▪ **hebdomadally** *adv*. [18c: from Greek *hebdomas* week]

Hebraic /hɪ'breɪɪk/ *adj* referring or relating to the Hebrews or the Hebrew language. [Anglo-Saxon: from Greek *hebraikos*]

Hebrew *noun* **1** the ancient Semitic language of the Hebrews, revived and spoken in a modern form as the formal language by Jews in Israel. **2** a member of an ancient Semitic people, orig based in Palestine, and claiming descent from Abraham, an Israelite. ▸ *adj* relating or referring to the Hebrew language or people. [13c: from Greek *Hebraios*, from Aramaic *Ibhraij* someone from the other side of the river]

heck *exclam, informal* mildly expressing anger, annoyance, surprise, etc. [19c: euphemistic alteration of **hell**]

heckle *verb, tr & intr* to interrupt (a speaker) with critical or abusive shouts and jeers, esp at a public meeting. ▪ **heckler** *noun*. [15c as *hekelen*]

hectare *noun* (abbrev **ha**) a metric unit of land measurement, equivalent to 100 ares (see **are**[2]), or 10,000 square metres (2.471 acres). [19c: from **hecto-** + **are**[2]]

hectic *adj* agitated; very excited, flustered or rushed. ▪ **hectically** *adv*. [14c: from Greek *hektikos* habitual]

hecto- *or* (*before a vowel*) **hect-** *combining form, denoting* one hundred times: *hectometre* • *hectogram* • *hectolitre*. [French, contraction of Greek *hekaton* a hundred]

hector *verb, tr & intr* to bully, intimidate or threaten. [17c: named after Hector, the Trojan hero in Homer's *Iliad*]

he'd *contraction* **1** he had. **2** he would.

hedge *noun* **1** a boundary formed by bushes and shrubs planted close together, esp between fields. **2** a barrier or protection against loss, criticism, etc. ▸ *verb* **1** to enclose or surround (an area of land) with a hedge. **2** to avoid making a decision or giving a clear answer. **3** to protect oneself from possible loss or criticism by backing both sides: *hedge one's bets*. **4** *intr* to make hedges. **5** *intr* to be evasive or shifty, eg in an argument. ▪ **hedged** *adj*. ▪ **hedger** *noun*. [Anglo-Saxon *hecg*]

hedgehog *noun* a small, prickly-backed, insectivorous, nocturnal mammal with a hoglike snout.

hedge-hop *verb, intr* to fly at a very low altitude as if hopping over hedges. [1920s]

hedgerow *noun* a row of bushes, hedges or trees forming a boundary.

hedonism *noun* **1** the belief that pleasure is the most important achievement or the highest good in life. **2** the pursuit of and devotion to pleasure. ▪ **hedonist** *noun*. ▪ **hedonistic** *adj*. [19c: from Greek *hedone* pleasure]

-hedron (***-hedra*** *or* ***-hedrons***) *combining form, geom, denoting* face, referring to a geometric solid with the specified number of faces or surfaces: *polyhedron*. [From Greek *hedra* base]

the heebie-jeebies *plural noun, slang* feelings or fits of nervousness or anxiety. [20c: coinage by W De Beck, American cartoonist]

heed *verb* **1** to pay attention to or take notice of (something, esp advice or a warning, etc). **2** *intr* to mind or care. ▸ *noun* careful attention; notice: *Take heed of what she says*. ▪ **heedful** *adj*. ▪ **heedfully** *adv*. ▪ **heedfulness** *noun*. [Anglo-Saxon *hedan*]

heedless *adj* taking no care; careless. ▪ **heedlessly** *adv*. ▪ **heedlessness** *noun*.

hee-haw *noun* the bray of a donkey, or an imitation of this sound. ▸ *verb, intr* to bray. [19c: imitating the sound]

heel[1] *noun* **1** the rounded back part of the foot below the ankle. **2** the part of a sock, stocking, etc that covers the heel. **3** the part of a shoe, boot, etc that supports the heel. **4** anything shaped or functioning like the heel, eg that part of the palm near the wrist. **5** a heel-like bend, as on a golf club. **6** the end of a loaf. **7** *slang* a despicable person; someone who is untrustworthy or who lets others down. ▸ *verb* **1** to execute or perform with the heel. **2** to strike using the heel. **3** to repair or fit a new heel on (a shoe, etc). **4** *intr* to move one's heels in time to a dance rhythm. **5** *intr, rugby* to kick the ball backwards out of the scrum with the heel. [Anglo-Saxon *hela*]

IDIOMS **at, on** *or* **upon sb's heels** following closely behind them. **cool** *or* **kick one's heels** to be kept waiting indefinitely. **dig one's heels in** to behave stubbornly. **down at heel** untidy; in poor condition or circumstances. **take to one's heels** to run away; to abscond. **to heel 1** esp of a dog: walking obediently at the heels of the person in charge of it. **2** under control; subject to discipline; submissive. **turn on one's heel** to turn round suddenly.

heel[2] *verb* **1** *intr* (*often* **heel over**) of a vessel: to lean over to one side; to list. **2** to cause (a vessel) to tilt. [Anglo-Saxon *hieldan* to slope]

heel[3] *verb* (*usu* **heel in**) to temporarily cover (the roots of a plant) with soil to keep them moist. [Anglo-Saxon *helian*, a combination of *hellan* and *helan*, both meaning 'to hide']

heelball *noun* a black waxy substance used for blacking and polishing the heels and soles of shoes and boots, and for doing brass rubbings. [19c]

hefty *adj* (***-ier, -iest***) *informal* **1** of a person: strong, robust or muscular. **2** of an object, blow, etc: large, heavy or powerful; vigorous. **3** large or considerable in amount: *a hefty sum of money*. ▪ **heftily** *adv*. ▪ **heftiness** *noun*. [19c: from **heave**]

hegemony /hɪ'gɛmənɪ/ *noun* (***-ies***) authority or control, esp of one state over another within a confederation. [16c: from Greek *hegemonia* leadership]

Hegira *or* **Hejira** /'hɛdʒɪrə, hɪ'dʒaɪərə/ *noun, relig* the flight of the prophet Muhammad from Mecca to Medina in AD 622, marking the beginning of the Muslim era. [16c: Arabic *hejira* flight]

heifer /'hɛfə(r)/ *noun* a cow over one year old that has either not calved, or has calved only once. [Anglo-Saxon *heahfore*]

heigh *exclam* expressing enquiry, encouragement or exultation. ▪ **heigh-ho** *exclam* expressing weariness. [16c]

height *noun* **1** the condition of being high, or the distance from the base of something to the top. **2** the distance above the ground from a recognized point, esp above sea level. **3** relatively high altitude. **4** a high place or location. **5** the highest point of elevation; the summit. **6** the most intense part or climax: *the height of battle*. **7** an extremely good, bad or serious example: *the height of stupidity*. ▪ **heighten** *verb* to make higher, greater, stronger, etc. [Anglo-Saxon *hiehthu*]

height
This word is often misspelt. The letter e comes before the letter *i*. It might help you to remember the following sentence:
*H**e**ight – **e**veryone **i**s **g**uessing **h**ow **t**all.*

Heimlich manoeuvre *or* **Heimlich procedure** /'haɪmlɪk/ *noun* an emergency method of dislodging an obstruction from a choking person's windpipe by applying a sharp thrust below the breastbone. [Mid 20c: after H J Heimlich, US physician]

heinous /'heɪnəs, 'hiː-/ *adj* extremely wicked or evil; odious. ▪ **heinously** *adv*. ▪ **heinousness** *noun*. [14c: from French *haineus*, from *hair* to hate]

heir /ɛə(r)/ *noun* **1** someone who by law receives or is entitled to receive property, wealth, a title, etc when the previous owner or holder dies. **2** someone who is successor to a position, eg leadership, or who continues a convention or tradition. ▪ **heirless** *adj*. [13c: from Latin *heres*]

IDIOMS **fall heir to sth** to inherit it.

heir apparent *noun* (***heirs apparent***) *law* an heir whose claim to an inheritance cannot be challenged by the birth of another heir.

heiress /'ɛərɛs/ *noun* a female heir, esp a woman who has inherited or will inherit considerable wealth.

heirloom *noun* **1** a personal article or piece of property that descends to the legal heir by means of a will or special custom. **2** an object that has been handed down through a family over many generations. [15c: **heir** + *lome* tool]

heir presumptive *noun* (***heirs presumptive***) *law* an heir whose claim to an inheritance may be challenged by the birth of another heir more closely related to the holder.

heist /haɪst/ *noun, N Am, slang* a robbery. ▸ *verb* to steal or rob in a heist. [1920s: variant of **hoist**]

hejab *or* **hijab** /hɪ'dʒab, hɛ'dʒɑːb/ *noun* a covering for a Muslim woman's face and head, sometimes reaching to the ground. [Arabic and Persian]

Hejira see **Hegira**

held *past tense, past participle of* **hold**[1]

heli-[1] *combining form, denoting* helicopter: *heliport* • *helipad*. [From Greek *helix*, *helikos* screw or spiral]

heli-² see **helio-**

helical *adj* relating to or like a helix; coiled.

helicopter *noun* an aircraft that is lifted and propelled by rotating blades above its body. [19c: from Greek *helikos* screw + *pteron* wing]

helio- *or (before a vowel)* **heli-** *combining form, denoting* the Sun: *heliograph.* [From Greek *helios* the Sun]

heliograph *noun* an instrument that uses mirrors to reflect light from the Sun in flashes as a way of sending messages. [19c]

heliotrope *noun* **1** a garden plant of the borage family, with small fragrant lilac-blue flowers that grow towards the sun. **2** the colour of these flowers. [17c: **helio-** + Greek *trepein* to turn]

helium *noun, chem* (symbol **He**) a colourless odourless inert gas found in natural gas deposits, also formed in stars by nuclear fusion. [19c: from Greek *helios* sun, so called because it was first identified in the Sun's atmosphere]

helix /ˈhiːlɪks/ *noun* (***helices*** /-siːz/ *or* ***helixes***) **1** a spiral or coiled structure, eg the thread of a screw. **2** *geom* a spiral-shaped curve that lies on the lateral surface of a cylinder or cone, and becomes a straight line if unrolled into a plane. [16c: Greek]

hell *noun* **1** the place or state of infinite punishment for the wicked after death. **2** the abode of the dead and evil spirits. **3** any place or state that causes extensive pain, misery and discomfort. ▶ *exclam, informal* **1** expressing annoyance or exasperation. **2** (**the hell**) an expression of strong disagreement or refusal: *The hell I will!* [Anglo-Saxon *hel*]

IDIOMS **a hell of a** *or* **one hell of a** *informal* a very great or significant: *one hell of a row.* **all hell breaks** *or* **is let loose** there is chaos and uproar. **as hell** absolutely; extremely: *He's as mad as hell.* **for the hell of it** *informal* for the fun or sake of it. **from hell** considered to be the most awful example of its kind imaginable: *boyfriend from hell.* **give sb hell** *informal* **1** to punish or rebuke them severely. **2** to make things extremely difficult for them. **hell for leather** *informal* at an extremely fast pace: *drove hell for leather to the airport.* **hell to pay** serious trouble or consequences. **like hell 1** very much, hard, fast, etc: *ran like hell.* **2** not at all or in any circumstances: *Like hell I will.* **to hell with sb** *or* **sth 1** an expression of angry disagreement with them or it. **2** an intention to ignore or reject them or it. **what the hell 1** what does it matter?; who cares? **2** an expression of surprise and amazement: *What the hell are you doing?*

he'll *contraction* **1** he will. **2** he shall.

hellbent *adj* (*usu* **hellbent on sth**) *informal* recklessly determined or intent about it.

Hellenic *adj* relating to the Greeks and their language. [17c: from Greek *Hellen*]

Hellenism *noun* **1** a Greek idiom, esp one used in another language. **2** the nationality or spirit of Greece. **3** conformity to the Greek character, language and culture, esp that of ancient Greece.

Hellenist *noun* a student of or expert in Greek language and culture.

Hellenistic *or* **Hellenistical** *adj* relating to Greek culture after Alexander the Great, that was greatly affected by foreign influences.

Hellenize *or* **-ise** *verb* **1** to make Greek. **2** *intr* to conform, or have a tendency to conform, to Greek usages. ▪ **Hellenization** *noun.*

hellfire *noun* **1** the fire of hell. **2** the punishment suffered in hell.

hellhole *noun* a disgusting, evil, frightening, etc place.

hellish *adj* **1** relating to or resembling hell. **2** *informal* very unpleasant, horrifying or difficult.

hello, hallo *or* **hullo** *exclam* **1** used as a greeting, to attract attention or to start a telephone conversation. **2** used to express surprise or discovery: *Hello! What's going on here?*

hellraiser *noun, informal* a boisterously debauched person.

helm *noun, naut* the steering apparatus of a boat or ship, such as a wheel or tiller. [Anglo-Saxon *helma*]

IDIOMS **at the helm** in a controlling position; in charge.

helmet *noun* a protective head covering, worn eg by police officers, firefighters, soldiers, motorcyclists, cyclists, etc. ▪ **helmeted** *adj.* [Anglo-Saxon *helm*]

helmsman *noun* someone who steers a boat or ship.

helot *noun* a member of the serf class, esp in ancient Sparta. [16c: from Greek *Heilotes* inhabitants of Helos, a town in the area around Sparta]

help *verb* **1** to contribute towards the success of something; to assist or aid. **2** to give the means to do something. **3** to relieve a difficult situation or burden; to improve or lighten (a predicament). **4** to provide or supply with a portion; to deal out. **5** (**help oneself to sth**) to take it without authority or permission. **6** to remedy; to mitigate or alleviate. **7** to refrain from something: *I couldn't help laughing.* **8** to prevent or control: *I can't help the bad weather.* **9** *intr* to give assistance. **10** *intr* to contribute. ▶ *noun* **1** an act of helping. **2** means or strength given to another for a particular purpose. **3** someone who is employed to help, esp a domestic help. **4** a remedy or relief. ▪ **helper** *noun.* [Anglo-Saxon *helpan*]

PHRASAL VERBS **help out** *or* **help sb out** to offer help, usu for a short time, and esp by sharing a burden or the cost of something.

helpful *adj* giving help or aid; useful.

helping *noun* a single portion of food served at a meal.

helping hand *noun* help or assistance.

helping verb *noun* an **auxiliary verb**.

helpless *adj* **1** unable or unfit to do anything for oneself. **2** weak and defenceless; needing assistance.

helpline *noun* a telephone service that people with a particular problem can call in order to contact advisers: *victim support helpline.*

helpmate *noun* a friend or partner, esp a husband or wife.

helter-skelter *adj* hurried and disorderly. ▶ *adv* in a hurried and disorientated manner. ▶ *noun, Brit* a spiral slide on the outside of a tower in a fairground or playground. [16c: a rhyming compound based on 14c *skelten* to hurry]

hem¹ *noun* a bottom edge or border of a garment, piece of cloth, etc, folded over and sewn down. ▶ *verb* (***hemmed, hemming***) *tr & intr* to form a border or edge on a garment, piece of cloth, etc. [Anglo-Saxon *hemm*]

PHRASAL VERBS **hem sth** *or* **sb in** to surround it or them closely, preventing movement.

hem² *exclam* a slight clearing of the throat or cough to show hesitation or to draw attention. ▸ *noun* such a sound. ▸ *verb* (***hemmed, hemming***) *intr* to utter this kind of cough or sound. [16c: imitating the sound]

hem- *or* **hema-** see **haemo-**

he-man *noun, informal* a man of exaggerated or extreme strength, stamina and virility.

hemat- see **haemato-**

hematite see **haematite**

hemato- see **haemato-**

hemi- *combining form, denoting* half: *hemisphere.* [Greek *hemi*]

-hemia see **-aemia**

hemiplegia *noun, pathol* paralysis of one side of the body only. Compare **paraplegia**, **quadriplegia**. ▪ **hemiplegic** *adj, noun.*

hemisphere *noun* **1** one half of a sphere. **2** either half of the Earth's sphere, when divided by the equator into the northern and southern hemispheres, or by a meridian into the eastern and western hemispheres. ▪ **hemispheric** *or* **hemispherical** *adj.* [14c]

hemline *noun* the height, level or line of a hem on a dress or skirt, etc.

hemlock *noun* **1** a poisonous plant with small white flowers and a spotted stem. **2** the poison extracted from this plant. [Anglo-Saxon *hymlic*]

hemo- see **haemo-**

hemp *noun* **1** (*in full* **Indian hemp**) an Asian plant grown commercially for its stem fibres, a drug and an oil. **2** any drug obtained from this plant, eg cannabis or marijuana. **3** the coarse fibre obtained from the stem of this plant, used to make rope, cord, tough cloth, etc. ▪ **hempen** *adj.* [Anglo-Saxon *hænep*]

hemstitch *noun* a decorative finishing stitch used on the inner side of a hem. ▸ *verb, tr & intr* to use this stitch to secure a hem.

hen *noun* a female bird of any kind, esp a domestic fowl. [Anglo-Saxon *henn*]

hence *adv* **1** for this reason or cause. **2** from this time onwards. **3** *old use* from this place or origin. [13c as *hennes*, from Anglo-Saxon *heonan*]

henceforth *or* **henceforward** *adv* from now on.

henchman *noun* a faithful supporter or right-hand man, esp one who obeys and assists without question. [Anglo-Saxon *hengest* a horse + *man*]

henge *noun* a prehistoric monument consisting of large upright stones or wooden posts, usu forming a circle. [18c: a back-formation from *Stonehenge*, a famous stone circle in S England]

hen harrier *noun* the common harrier.

hen house *noun* a house or coop for fowl.

henna *noun* **1** a small Asian and N African shrub with fragrant white flowers. **2** reddish-brown dye obtained from the leaves of this shrub, used for colouring the hair and decorating the skin. ▸ *verb* (***hennaed***) to dye or stain using henna. [16c: from Arabic *hinna*]

hen party *or* **hen night** *noun* a party attended by women only, esp one to celebrate the imminent marriage of one of the group.

henpecked *adj, informal* usu of a man: constantly harassed, criticized and dominated by a woman, esp a wife, girlfriend, etc. ▪ **henpecker** *noun.*

henry *noun* (***henry, henrys*** *or* ***henries***) (symbol **H**) the SI unit of electrical inductance. [19c: named after Joseph Henry, the US physicist]

heparin *noun, biochem* **1** a chemical substance formed in most tissues of the body (eg liver, lung, etc) that prevents the clotting of the blood. **2** an extracted and purified form of this used as an anticoagulant drug in the treatment of thrombosis. [20c: from Greek *hepar* liver]

hepatic *adj* **1** relating or referring to the liver. **2** liver-coloured. [15c: from Greek *hepar* liver]

hepatitis *noun* inflammation of the liver, the symptoms of that include jaundice, fever and nausea. [18c: from Greek *hepar, hepatos* liver + **-itis**]

hepta- *or* (*before a vowel*) **hept-** *combining form, denoting* seven. [Greek]

heptagon *noun* a plane figure with seven angles and sides. ▪ **heptagonal** *adj* heptagon-shaped. [16c: **hepta-** + Greek *gonia* angle]

heptane *noun, chem* a hydrocarbon with many isomers, belonging to the alkane series.

heptathlon *noun* an athletic contest comprising seven events. Compare **decathlon**, **pentathlon**. [1980s]

her *pron* **1** the objective form of **she**: *We all like her • send it to her.* **2** the possessive form of **she**: *Her car is outside.* ▸ *adj* referring to a female person or animal, or something personified or thought of as female, eg a ship: *went to her house • gave the cat her milk • tried to keep her head into the wind.* [Anglo-Saxon *hire*]

herald *noun* **1** a person who announces important news, or an officer whose task it is to make public proclamations and arrange ceremonies. **2** someone or something that is a sign of what is to come. **3** an officer responsible for keeping a record of the genealogies and coats of arms of noble families. ▸ *verb* to be a sign of the approach of something; to proclaim or usher in: *dark clouds heralding a storm.* ▪ **heraldic** *adj.* ▪ **heraldically** *adv.* [14c: from French *herault*]

heraldry *noun* the art of recording genealogies, and blazoning coats of arms. [14c]

herb *noun* **1** a flowering plant that, unlike a shrub or tree, has no woody stem above the ground. **2** an aromatic plant such as rosemary, mint and parsley, used in cookery or in herbal medicine. [13c: from Latin *herba* grass or green plant]

herbaceous *adj* of a plant: relating to or having the characteristics of a **herb** (sense 1). [17c: from Latin *herbaceus* relating to grass or green plants]

herbaceous border *noun* a garden border containing mainly perennial plants and flowers.

herbage *noun* herbs collectively; herbaceous vegetation covering a large area. [13c]

herbal *adj* composed of or relating to herbs. ▸ *noun* a book describing the use of plants, or substances extracted from them, for medicinal purposes. [16c: from Latin *herbalis* belonging to grass or herbs]

herbalist *or* **herbist** *noun* **1** a person who researches, collects and sells herbs and plants. **2** a person who practises herbal medicine. **3** an early botanist. ▪ **herbalism** *noun.*

herbarium /hɜːˈbɛərɪəm/ *noun* (***herbaria*** /-rɪə/ *or* ***herbariums***) **1** a classified collection of preserved plants (in a room or building, etc). **2** the room or building used to house such a collection.

herbicide *noun* a substance used to kill weeds, etc. ▪ **herbicidal** *adj*. [19c]

herbivore *noun* an animal that feeds on plants. ▪ **herbivorous** *adj*. [19c: from Latin *herba* grass or green plant + *vorare* to swallow]

Herculean /hɜːkjʊˈlɪən, hɜːˈkjuːlɪən/ *adj* (*also* **herculean**) requiring great strength or stamina or an enormous effort: *a herculean task*. [17c: from *Hercules*, Latin form of *Heracles*, the hero's Greek name]

herd *noun* **1** a company of animals, esp large ones, that habitually remain together. **2** a collection of livestock or domestic animals, esp cows or pigs. **3** (*also in combination*) a person who looks after a herd: *The herd grazed his flock on the hillside* • *a lonely goatherd*. **4** a large crowd of people. **5** (**the herd**) people in general, esp when considered as behaving in an unimaginative and conventional way. ▸ *verb* **1** *intr* to gather in a crowd like an animal in a herd. **2** to look after or tend a herd of (animals). **3** to group (animals) together. [Anglo-Saxon *heord*]

herdsman *noun* an owner, keeper or tender of a herd of animals.

here *adv* **1** at, in or to this place. **2** in the present life or state; at this point, stage or time. **3** used with *this, these*, etc for emphasis: **a** after a noun: *this chair here*; **b** *informal, dialect* between a noun and *this, that*, etc: *this here chair*. ▸ *noun* this place or location. ▸ *exclam* **1** calling for attention. **2** calling attention to one's own presence, or to something one is about to say. [Anglo-Saxon *her*]

IDIOMS **here and now** the present moment; straight away. **here and there** in various places; irregularly or thinly. **here goes!** an exclamation indicating that the speaker is about to proceed with something, often with apprehension. **here's to sb** *or* **sth** used when proposing a toast to them or it: *Here's to the happy couple*. **here today, gone tomorrow** a comment on the ephemeral or transient nature of something. **neither here nor there** of no particular importance or relevance.

---

here's

If you are using formal English, don't use **here's** if you are going to refer to more than one person or thing:

✗ *Here's Suzanne and Heather.*

✓ *Here are Suzanne and Heather.*

However, if you are talking about a quantity as a single amount, the singular verb **is** (rather than the plural **are**) is correct:

✓ *Here's seventy pence for your bus fare.*

---

hereabouts *or* **hereabout** *adv* around or near this place; within this area.

hereafter *adv, formal* **1** after this time; in a future time, life or state. **2** in a legal document or case: from this point on.

IDIOMS **the hereafter** a future stage or phase; the afterlife.

hereby *adv, formal* **1** not far off. **2** as a result of this or by this.

hereditable *adj* relating to something that may be inherited. [15c: from Latin *hereditas* inheritance]

hereditary *adj* **1** descending or acquiring by inheritance. **2** passed down or transmitted genetically to offspring: *a hereditary disease*. **3** succeeding to a title or position, etc by inheritance. **4** passed down according to inheritance. [16c: from Latin *hereditas* inheritance]

heredity *noun* (***-ies***) **1** the transmission of recognizable and genetically based characteristics from one generation to the next. **2** the total quantity of such characteristics inherited. Also called **inheritance**. [16c]

Herefs *abbrev, English county* Herefordshire.

herein *adv* **1** *formal* in this case or respect. **2** *law & formal* contained within this letter or document, etc.

hereinafter *adv, law & formal* later in this document or form, etc.

hereof *adv, law & formal* relating to or concerning this.

hereon *adv, formal* on, upon or to this point.

heresy /ˈhɛrəsɪ/ *noun* (***-ies***) **1** an opinion or belief contrary to the authorized teaching of a particular religion. **2 a** an opinion that contradicts a conventional or traditional belief; **b** an example of this. [13c: from Greek *hairesis* choice]

heretic /ˈhɛrətɪk/ *noun* **1** someone who believes in, endorses or practises heresy. **2** someone who has views and opinions that conflict with those commonly held. ▪ **heretical** *adj*. ▪ **heretically** *adv*. [14c: from Greek *hairein* to choose]

hereto *adv, law & formal* **1** to this place or document. **2** for this purpose.

heretofore *adv, law & formal* before or up to this time; formerly.

hereupon *adv, law & formal* **1** on this. **2** immediately after or as a result of this.

herewith *adv, law & formal* with this; enclosed or together with this letter, etc.

heritable *adj* **1** of property: able to be inherited or passed down. **2** of people: able or in a position to inherit property. ▪ **heritability** *noun*. ▪ **heritably** *adv*. [14c: from French *heriter* to inherit]

heritage *noun* **1** something that is inherited. **2** the characteristics, qualities, property, etc inherited at birth. **3** the buildings, countryside, cultural traditions, etc seen as a people's or country's defining qualities. [13c: French]

hermaphrodite *noun* **1** a person, plant or animal that has both male and female reproductive organs. **2** a compound of opposite qualities. ▸ *adj* combining the characteristics of both sexes or opposite qualities. ▪ **hermaphroditic** *adj*. ▪ **hermaphroditism** *noun*. [15c: named after Hermaphroditos, in Greek mythology, a youth who grew into one person with the nymph *Salmacis*]

hermetic *or* **hermetical** *adj* perfectly closed or sealed so as to be airtight. ▪ **hermetically** *adv*. [17c: named after the Greek Hermes Trismegistos, supposedly the inventor of a magic seal]

hermit *noun* **1** an ascetic who lives an isolated life for religious reasons. **2** someone who lives a solitary life. ▪ **hermitic** *adj*. [13c: from Greek *eremos* solitary]

hermitage *noun* **1** the dwelling-place of a hermit. **2** a secluded place or abode; a retreat.

hernia *noun* the protrusion of an organ (esp part of the viscera) through an opening or weak spot in the wall of its surroundings. ▪ **herniated** *adj*. [14c: Latin]

hero *noun* (***heroes***) **1** a man distinguished by his bravery and strength; any illustrious person. **2** in novels, plays, films, etc: a principal male character or one whose life is the theme of the story. See also **heroine**. [14c: from Greek *heros*]

heroic *adj* **1** supremely courageous and brave. **2** befitting or suited to a hero. **3** relating to or concerning heroes or heroines. ▪ **heroically** *adv.*

heroics *plural noun* **1** over-dramatic or extravagant speech. **2** excessively bold behaviour. [16c: from Greek *heroikos* relating to a hero]

heroin *noun* a powerful analgesic drug produced from **morphine**, used illegally as a highly addictive narcotic. *Technical equivalent* **diamorphine**. [19c: from German *Heroin,* from Greek *heros* hero, perhaps from the initial feeling of euphoria produced]

heroine *noun* **1** a woman distinguished by her bravery or her achievements; any illustrious woman. **2** in novels, plays, films, etc: a principal female character or one whose life is the theme of the story. See also **hero**. [17c: from Greek *heros*]

heroism *noun* the qualities of a hero or heroic behaviour.

heron *noun* a large wading bird with a long neck and legs, and usu with grey and white plumage. [14c: from French *hairon*]

hero-worship *noun* **1** an excessive fondness and admiration for someone. **2** the worship of heroes in antiquity. ▸ *verb* to idealize or to have a great admiration for someone.

herpes /ˈhɜːpiːz/ *noun* any of various contagious skin diseases caused by a virus that gives rise to watery blisters, esp **herpes simplex**, a sexually transmitted disease, and **herpes zoster** or **shingles**. ▪ **herpetic**. [17c: from Greek *herpein* to creep]

herpetology *noun* the study of reptiles and amphibians. ▪ **herpetologist** *noun.* [19c: from Greek *herpeton* a creeping animal]

herring *noun* (***herring*** *or* ***herrings***) a small edible silvery sea fish, found in large shoals in northern waters. [Anglo-Saxon *hæring*]

herringbone *noun* a zigzag pattern, like the spine of a herring, woven into cloth. [17c]

hers *pron* the one or ones belonging to **her**.
IDIOMS **of hers** relating to or belonging to **her**.

hers
Remember that **hers** does not have an apostrophe:
The coat on the chair is hers.

herself *pron* **1** the reflexive form of **her** and **she**: *She made herself a dress.* **2** used for emphasis: *She did it herself.* **3** her normal self or true character: *She isn't feeling herself.* **4** (*also* **by herself**) alone; without help. [Anglo-Saxon *hire self*]

Herts. /hɑːts/ *abbrev, English county* Hertfordshire.

hertz *noun* (*pl* ***hertz***) (abbrev **Hz**) the SI unit of frequency, equal to one cycle per second. [1920s: named after the German physicist, Heinrich Hertz]

he's *contraction* **1** he is. **2** he has.

hesitant *adj* uncertain; holding back; doubtful. ▪ **hesitance** *and* **hesitancy** *noun.* ▪ **hesitantly** *adv.*

hesitate *verb, intr* **1** to falter or delay in speaking, acting or making a decision; to be in doubt. **2** to be unwilling to do or say something, often because one is uncertain if it is right. ▪ **hesitatingly** *adv.* ▪ **hesitation** *noun.* [17c: from Latin *haesitare* to remain stuck]

hessian *noun* a coarse cloth, similar to sacking, made from hemp or jute. [18c: from *Hesse,* a state in central Germany]

hetero- *or* (*before a vowel*) **heter-** *combining form, denoting* **1** the other: *heterodox.* **2** different: *heterogeneous.* Compare **homo-**, **auto-**. [From Greek *heteros* other]

heterocyclic *adj, chem* of a compound: having a closed chain of atoms where at least one is not the same as the others. Compare **homocyclic**. [19c]

heterodoxy *noun* a belief, esp a religious one, that is different from the one most commonly accepted. ▪ **heterodox** *adj.* [17c]

heterodyne *adj, electronics* in radio communication: superimposing one wave on another continuous wave of slightly different wavelength, creating beats. [Early 20c: from Greek *dynamis* power]

heterogamy *noun* **1** *genetics* reproduction from unlike reproductive cells. **2** *botany* the presence of different kinds of flowers (eg male, female, neuter) in the same inflorescence. **3** *botany* **cross-pollination**. ▪ **heterogamous** *adj.* [19c]

heterogeneous *adj* composed of parts, people, things, etc that are not related to each other, or are of different kinds. ▪ **heterogeneity** *noun.* ▪ **heterogeneously** *adv.* ▪ **heterogeneousness** *noun.* [17c: from Greek *genos* a kind]

heterologous *adj* not homologous; different in form and origin. ▪ **heterology** *noun.* [19c]

heteromorphic *or* **heteromorphous** *adj, biol* **1** changing or differing in form from a given type. **2** of insects: undergoing changes in form at varying stages of life. ▪ **heteromorphism** *or* **heteromorphy** *noun.* [19c]

heterosexual *adj* **1** having a sexual attraction to people of the opposite sex. **2** of a relationship: between a man and a woman. ▸ *noun* a heterosexual person. Sometimes shortened to **hetero**. ▪ **heterosexuality** *noun.* ▪ **heterosexually** *adv.* [Early 20c]

heterotrophy *noun, biol* the dependence of most animals, fungi, etc on green plants, and organic compounds generally, for carbon. ▪ **heterotroph** *noun.* ▪ **heterotrophic** *adj.* [19c: from Greek *trophe* livelihood]

het up *adj, informal* angry; agitated. [19c: orig British and N American dialect past participle of **heat**, meaning 'heated']

heuristic /hjʊəˈrɪstɪk/ *adj* **1** serving or leading to discover or find out. **2** of a teaching method: encouraging a desire in learners to find their own solutions. **3** *comput* using a method of trial and error to solve a problem. [19c: from Greek *heuriskein* to find]

hew *verb* (*past participle* ***hewn***) **1** to cut, fell or sever something using an axe, sword, etc. **2** to carve or shape something from wood or stone. [Anglo-Saxon *heawan*]

hex *noun* **1** a witch, wizard or wicked spell. **2** anything that brings bad luck. **3** **hexadecimal**. ▸ *verb* to bring misfortune; to bewitch. [19c: from German *Hexe* witch]

hexa- *or* (*before a vowel*) **hex-** *combining form, denoting* six: *hexahedron.* [From Greek *hex*]

hexad *noun* any group or series of six.

hexadecane see under **cetane**

hexadecimal (*sometimes* **hex**) *comput, adj* relating to or being a number system with a base of 16 (see **base**[1] *noun* sense 8). ▸ *noun* **1** such a system. **2** the notation used in the system. **3** a number expressed using the system. [1950s]

hexagon *noun* a plane figure with six sides and angles. ▪ **hexagonal** /hɛk'sagənəl/ *adj.* [16c: **hexa-** + Greek *gonia* angle]

hexagram *noun* a star-shaped figure created by extending the lines of a uniform hexagon until they meet at six points. [19c]

hexameter /hek'samɪtə(r)/ *noun* a line or verse with six feet. [16c]

hexane *noun, chem* a toxic flammable liquid belonging to the alkane series of hydrocarbons.

hexose *noun, chem* a simple sugar with six carbon atoms in each molecule.

hey *exclam, informal* **1** a shout expressing joy, interrogation or dismay. **2** a call to attract attention. [13c: as *hei*]

IDIOMS **hey presto!** a conjuror's expression, usu used at the successful finale of a trick.

heyday *noun* a period of great success, power, popularity, etc. [16c: from German *heida* hey there]

Hf *symbol, chem* hafnium.

Hg *symbol, chem* mercury.

HGV *abbrev, Brit* heavy goods vehicle.

hi *exclam, informal* **1** a casual form of greeting. **2** a word used to attract attention. [19c: from **hey**]

hiatus /haɪ'eɪtəs/ *noun* (***hiatus*** *or* ***hiatuses***) **1** an opening or gap; a break in something that should be continuous. **2** *grammar* the use of two consecutive vowels in adjacent syllables without any intervening consonant. [16c: Latin, from *hiare* to gape]

hiatus hernia *noun* a hernia in which part of the stomach protrudes through an opening in the diaphragm intended for the oesophagus.

hibernal *adj* referring or belonging to the winter; wintry.

hibernate *verb, intr* of certain animals: to pass the winter in a dormant state; to be completely inactive. ▪ **hibernation** *noun.* [19c: from Latin *hibernus* wintry]

Hibernian *literary, adj* relating to Ireland. ▸ *noun* a native of Ireland. [17c: from Latin *Hibernia* Ireland]

hibiscus *noun* a tropical tree or shrub with large brightly coloured flowers. [18c: from Greek *ibiskos* marshmallow]

hiccup *or* **hiccough** /'hɪkʌp/ *noun* **1 a** an involuntary spasm of the diaphragm; **b** a burping sound caused by this. **2** *informal* a temporary and usu minor setback, difficulty or interruption. ▸ *verb* **1** *intr* to produce a hiccup or hiccups. **2** *intr* to falter, hesitate or malfunction. [16c: an alteration of French *hocquet* an abrupt interruption; the spelling *hiccough* is a result of confusion with *cough*]

hick *noun, informal* **1** someone from the country. **2** an unsophisticated person. [16c: a familiar form of *Richard*]

hickory *noun* (***-ies***) **1** a N American tree of the walnut family, with edible nutlike fruits. **2** its heavy strong wood. [17c: from Algonquian (a family of Native American languages)]

hide[1] *verb* (*past tense* ***hid,*** *past participle* ***hidden***) **1** to put, keep or conceal (something) from sight: *hid the key under the doormat.* **2** to keep secret: *hid her prison record from her employer.* **3** *intr* to conceal (oneself); to go into or stay in concealment: *hid in the cellar.* **4** to make (something) difficult to see; to obscure: *trees hid the cottage from the road.* ▸ *noun* a concealed shelter used for observing wildlife. ▪ **hidden** *adj.* See also **hiding**[1]. [Anglo-Saxon *hydan*]

hide[2] *noun* the skin of an animal, esp a large one, either raw or treated. [Anglo-Saxon *hyd*]

IDIOMS **not** *or* **neither hide nor hair of sb** *or* **sth** not the slightest trace of them or it.

hide-and-seek *or* (*N Am*) **hide-and-go-seek** *noun* a game in which one person seeks the others who have hidden themselves. [18c]

hideaway *or* **hideout** *noun* a refuge or retreat; concealment.

hidebound *adj, derog* reluctant to accept new ideas or opinions, esp because of a petty, stubborn or conservative outlook. [17c]

hideous *adj* **1** dreadful; revolting; extremely ugly. **2** frightening; horrific. [13c: from French *hisdos*]

hiding[1] *noun* **1** the state of being hidden or concealed. **2** concealment; a secret location. ▸ *verb, present participle of* **hide**[1].

hiding[2] *noun, informal* a severe beating. [19c: from **hide**[2]]

IDIOMS **be on a hiding to nothing** *informal* to be in a situation in which a favourable outcome is impossible.

hie *verb* (***hied, hieing*** *or* ***hying***) *archaic* **1** *intr* to hasten or hurry. **2** to urge. [Anglo-Saxon *higian*]

hierarchy *noun* (***-ies***) **1** a system that classifies people or things according to rank, importance, etc. **2** the operation of such a system or the people who control it. **3** *relig* the graded organization of priests or ministers. ▪ **hierarchical** *or* **hierarchic** *adj.* [16c]

hieroglyph *or* **hieroglyphic** *noun* a character or symbol representing a word, syllable, sound or idea, esp in ancient Egyptian. [16c: from Greek *hieros* sacred + *glyphein* to carve]

hi-fi *adj* of high fidelity. ▸ *noun* a set of equipment, usu consisting of an amplifier, tape deck, CD player, turntable, etc, for sound reproduction that has such a high quality that it is virtually indistinguishable from the original sound. [1940s: a shortening of **high fidelity**]

higgledy-piggledy *adv, adj, informal* haphazard; in confusion; disorderly. [16c]

high *adj* **1** elevated; tall; towering: *high buildings.* **2** being a specific height: *a hundred feet high.* **3** far up from a base point, such as the ground or sea level: *a high branch • a high mountain.* **4** intense or advanced; more forceful than normal: *a high wind.* **5** at the peak or climax: *high summer.* **6** (*also* **High**) of a period or era; at the height of its development: *High Renaissance.* **7** significant; exalted or revered: *high art.* **8** of sound: acute in pitch. **9** fully developed in terms of emotions and content: *high drama.* **10** of meat: partially decomposed or tainted. **11** elated or euphoric; over-excited. **12** *informal* under the influence of drugs or alcohol: *was high on E.* **13** taller or bigger than average: *a high-necked sweater.* ▸ *adv* at or to a height; in or into an elevated position: *The plane flew high.* ▸ *noun* **1** a high point or level. **2** the maximum or highest level. **3** *informal* a state of ecstasy and euphoria, often produced by drugs or alcohol: *on a high*. **4** *meteorol* an **anticyclone**. [Anglo-Saxon *heah*]

IDIOMS **high and dry 1** stranded or helpless; defenceless. **2** of boats: out of the water. **high and low 1** up and down; everywhere. **2** rich and poor alike. **high and mighty** arrogant; pompous. **high as a kite** *informal* **1** over-excited or ecstatic. **2** under the influence of drugs or alcohol. **on high** above or aloft; in heaven. **on one's high horse** *informal* having an attitude of arrogance and imagined superiority.

highball *noun, chiefly N Am* an alcoholic drink of spirits and soda served with ice in a long glass. [19c]

highbrow *often derog, noun* an intellectual or learned person. ▸ *adj* of art, literature, etc: intellectual; cultured. [19c]

highchair *noun* a tall chair with a small attached table for young children, used esp at mealtimes. [19c]

High Church *noun* a section within the Church of England that places great importance on holy ceremony and priestly authority. [17c]

high-class *adj* **1** of very high quality. **2** superior and distinguished. [19c]

High Commission *noun* an embassy representing one member country of the British Commonwealth in another country. ▪ **High Commissioner** *noun*. [19c]

high court *noun* **1** a supreme court. **2** (**the High Court**) the supreme court for civil cases in England and Wales. [13c]

high-density *adj, comput* of a disk: having a large data-storage capacity. [1950s]

Higher *noun, Scot* an examination, generally taken at the end of the fifth year of secondary education, more advanced than **Standard grade**.

higher education *noun, Brit* education beyond secondary school level, ie at university or college, usu studying for a degree. Compare **further education**. [19c]

high explosive *noun* a detonating explosive of immense power and extremely rapid action, eg dynamite, TNT, etc. [19c]

highfalutin *or* **highfaluting** *adj, informal* ridiculously pompous or affected. [19c: **high** + *falutin*, variation of *fluting*, present participle of **flute**]

high fidelity *noun* an accurate and high quality reproduction of sound. See also **hi-fi**. [1930s]

high-five *noun, esp N Am* a sign of greeting or celebration, involving the slapping together of raised palms.

high-flier *or* **high-flyer** *noun* **1** an ambitious person, likely to achieve their goals. **2** someone naturally skilled and competent in their career. ▪ **high-flying** *adj*. [17c]

high-flown *adj* often of language: sounding grand but lacking real substance; rhetorical; extravagant.

high frequency *noun* a radio frequency between 3 and 30 megahertz. [19c]

high-handed *adj* overbearing and arrogant; arbitrary. ▪ **high-handedly** *adv*. ▪ **high-handedness** *noun*. [17c]

high jump *noun* **1** an athletic event where competitors jump over a high bar which is raised after each successful jump. **2** *informal* a severe punishment or reproof: *He's for the high jump*. ▪ **high-jumper** *noun*. [19c]

highland *noun* **1** (*often* **highlands**) a mountainous area of land. **2** (**the Highlands**) the mountainous area of northern Scotland. ▸ *adj* referring to or characteristic of highland regions or the Scottish Highlands. ▪ **highlander** *or* **Highlander** *noun*. [Anglo-Saxon]

high-level language *noun, comput* a programming language which allows users to employ instructions that more closely resemble their own language, rather than machine code. See also **low-level language**. [1960s]

high life *noun* (*usu* **the high life**) luxurious living associated with the very wealthy. [18c]

highlight *noun* **1** the most memorable or outstanding feature, event, experience, etc. **2** (**highlights**) lighter patches or streaks in the hair, often bleached or dyed. ▸ *verb* **1** to draw attention to or emphasize something. **2** to overlay sections of (a text) with a bright colour for special attention. **3** to put highlights in (someone's hair). [19c; 1940s as *noun* sense 2]

highlighter *noun* (*in full* **highlighter pen**) a broad-tipped felt pen used to highlight parts of a text, etc. [20c]

highly *adv* **1** very; extremely: *highly gratified*. **2** with approval: *speak highly of her*. **3** at or to a high degree; in a high position: *He is rated highly in his office*.

highly strung *or* **highly-strung** *adj* excitable; extremely nervous; easily upset or sensitive. [18c]

High Mass *noun, RC Church* an esp elaborate form of the mass involving music, ceremonies and incense. [12c]

high-minded *adj* having or showing noble and moral ideas and principles, etc. [15c]

highness *noun* **1** (**Highness**) an address used for royalty, usu as **Her Highness**, **His Highness** and **Your Highness**. **2** the state of being high.

high-octane *adj* of petrol: having a high **octane number**.

high-pitched *adj* **1** of sounds, voices, etc: high or acute in tone. **2** of a roof: steeply angled. [16c]

high point *noun* the most memorable, pleasurable, successful, etc moment or occasion.

high-powered *adj* **1** very powerful or energetic. **2** very important or responsible. [Early 20c]

high-pressure *adj* **1** having, using or allowing the use of air, water, etc at a pressure higher than that of the atmosphere: *high-pressure water reactor*. **2** *informal* forceful and persuasive: *high-pressure negotiations*. **3** involving considerable stress or intense activity: *a high-pressure job*. [Early 19c]

high priest *or* **high priestess** *noun* the chief priest or priestess of a cult. [14c]

high-rise *adj* of a building: having many storeys: *high-rise flats*. ▸ *noun, informal* a building with many storeys; a tower block. [1950s]

high road *noun* a public or main road; a road for general traffic. [18c]

high school *noun* a secondary school in the UK, formerly often called **grammar school**. [Early 19c]

high seas *plural noun* the open ocean not under the control of any country. [Anglo Saxon *heah sae*]

high season *noun* the busiest time of year at a holiday resort, tourist town, etc; the peak tourist period.

high society *noun* fashionable wealthy society; the upper classes.

high-spirited *adj* daring or bold; naturally cheerful and vivacious. [17c]

high spirits *plural noun* a positive, happy and exhilarated frame of mind.

high spot *noun* an outstanding feature, moment, location, etc.

high street *noun* **1** (*also* **High Street**) the main shopping street of a town. **2** (**the high street**) **a** shops generally; the retail trade; **b** the public, when regarded as consumers.

hightail *verb, N Am informal* (*usu* **hightail it**) to hurry away: *Let's hightail it out of here.*

high tea *noun, Brit* a meal served in the late afternoon, usu consisting of a cooked dish, with bread, cakes and tea. [19c]

high-tech, **hi-tech** *or* **hi-tec** *adj* employing, designed by, etc advanced and sophisticated technology. [1960s: a shortening of *high technology*]

high-tension *adj* carrying high-voltage electrical currents. [Early 20c]

high tide *or* **high water** *noun* **1** the highest level of a tide. **2** the time when this occurs.

high time *adv, informal* the right or latest time by which something ought to have been done: *It's high time you went home.*

high treason *noun* treason against one's sovereign or country. [14c]

high-voltage *adj* having or concerning a voltage large enough to cause damage or injury. [1960s]

high-water mark *noun* **1** **a** the highest level reached by a tide, river, etc; **b** a mark indicating this. **2** the highest point reached by anything. [16c]

highway *noun, chiefly N Am* **1** a public road that everyone has the right to use. **2** the main or normal way or route. [Anglo-Saxon *heiweg*]

highwayman *noun, hist* a robber, usu on horseback, who robbed people travelling on public roads. [17c]

high wire *noun* a tightrope stretched high above the ground for performing. [19c]

hijab see **hejab**

hijack *verb* **1** to take control of a vehicle, esp an aircraft, and force it to go to an unscheduled destination, often taking any passengers present as hostages. **2** to stop and rob (a vehicle). **3** to steal (goods) in transit. ▪ **hijacker** *noun.* ▪ **hijacking** *noun.* [1920s]

hike *noun* a long walk or tour, often for recreation, and usu in the country. ▸ *verb* **1** *intr* to go on or for a hike. **2** (*often* **hike sth up**) to pull up, raise or lift it with a jerk. **3** to increase (prices) suddenly. ▪ **hiker** *noun.* [18c: formerly a dialect word for **hitch**]

hilarious *adj* extravagantly funny or humorous; merry. ▪ **hilariously** *adv.* ▪ **hilariousness** *noun.* ▪ **hilarity** *noun.* [19c: from Greek *hilaros* cheerful]

hill *noun* **1** a raised area of land, smaller than a mountain. **2** an incline on a road. ▪ **hilliness** *noun.* ▪ **hilly** *adj* (**-ier, -iest**). [Anglo-Saxon *hyll*]

IDIOMS **over the hill** *informal* past one's peak or best.

hillbilly *noun* (**-ies**) *esp US derog* any unsophisticated person, particularly from a remote, mountainous or rustic area. [Early 20c: **hill** + dialect *billy* a fellow]

hillock *noun* **1** a small hill. **2** a small heap or pile. ▪ **hillocky** *adj.* [14c: English *hilloc*]

hillside *noun* the sloping side of a hill. [15c]

hilltop *noun* the summit of a hill.

hillwalking *noun* the activity of walking in hilly or mountainous country. ▪ **hillwalker** *noun.*

hilt *noun* the handle, esp of a sword, dagger, knife, etc. [Anglo-Saxon *hilte*]

IDIOMS **up to the hilt** completely; thoroughly.

him *pron* the object form of **he**: *We saw him* • *We gave it to him.* [Anglo-Saxon *him*]

himself *pron* **1** the reflexive form of **him** and **he**: *He made himself a drink.* **2** used for emphasis: *He did it himself.* **3** his normal self: *He's still not feeling himself after the operation.* **4** (*also* **by himself**) alone; without help. [Anglo-Saxon *him selfum*]

hind[1] *adj* at the back; referring to the area behind: *hind legs.* [Anglo-Saxon *hindan*]

hind[2] *noun* (***hind*** *or* ***hinds***) a female red deer, usu older than three years of age. [Anglo-Saxon *hind*]

hindbrain *noun, anatomy* the lowest part of the brain, containing the **cerebellum** and the **medulla oblongata**.

hinder[1] /ˈhɪndə(r)/ *verb* **1** to delay or hold back; to prevent the progress of something. **2** *intr* to be an obstacle; to obstruct. [Anglo-Saxon *hindrian*]

hinder[2] /ˈhaɪndə(r)/ *adj* **1** placed at the back. **2** further back: *the hinder region.*

Hindi *noun* **1** one of the official languages of India, a literary form of Hindustani, and including terms from **Sanskrit**. **2** a group of Indo-European languages spoken in N India. ▸ *adj* relating or referring to any of these languages. [18c: from Persian *Hind* India]

hindquarters *plural noun* the rear parts of an animal, esp a four-legged one. [19c]

hindrance *noun* **1** someone or something that hinders; an obstacle or prevention. **2** the act or an instance of hindering. [15c: meaning 'damage or loss': from **hinder**[1]]

hindsight *noun* wisdom or knowledge after an event. [19c]

Hindu *noun* **1** someone who practises **Hinduism**. **2** a native or citizen of Hindustan or India. ▸ *adj* relating or referring to Hindus or Hinduism. [17c: from Persian *Hind* India]

Hinduism *noun* the main religion of India, that includes the worship of several gods, a belief in reincarnation, and the arrangement of society into a caste system.

hinge *noun* **1** the movable hook or joint by which a door is fastened to a door-frame or a lid is fastened to a box, etc and also on which they turn when opened or closed. **2** *biol* the pivoting point from which a **bivalve** opens and closes. **3** a principle or fact on which something depends or turns. ▸ *verb* **1** to provide a hinge or hinges for something. **2** *intr* (*usu* **hinge on sth**) to depend on it: *Everything hinges on their decision.* [14c as *henge*]

hinny *noun* (***-ies***) the offspring of a stallion and a female donkey or ass. [17c: from Greek *hinnos* mule]

hint *noun* **1** a distant or indirect indication or allusion; an insinuation or implication. **2** a helpful suggestion or tip. **3** a small amount; a slight impression or suggestion of something: *a hint of perfume.* ▸ *verb* **1** to indicate indirectly. **2** *intr* (*often* **hint at sth**) to suggest or imply it, esp indirectly. [Anglo-Saxon *hentan* to seize]

IDIOMS **take** *or* **get the hint** *informal* to understand and act on what a person is hinting at.

hinterland *noun* **1** the region lying inland from the coast or the banks of a river. **2** an area dependent on a nearby port, commercial site, or any centre of influence. [19c: German, from *hinter* behind + *Land* land]

hip[1] *noun* **1** the haunch or upper fleshy part of the thigh just below the waist. **2** the joint between the thigh bone and the pelvis. **3** *archit* the external angle created when the sloping end of a roof meets the sloping sides. [Anglo-Saxon *hype*]

hip[2] *noun* the red fruit of a rose, esp a wild variety. [Anglo-Saxon *heope*]

hip[3] *exclam* used to encourage a united cheer: *Hip, hip, hooray!* [18c]

hip[4] *adj* (***hipper, hippest***) *informal* informed about, knowledgeable of, or following current fashions in music, fashion, political ideas, etc. [Early 20c]

hip bath *noun* a bath for sitting in.

hip bone *noun* the **innominate bone**. [14c]

hip flask *noun* a flask, esp for alcoholic drink, small enough to be carried in the hip pocket.

hip-hop *noun* a popular culture movement originating in the US in the early 1980s, incorporating rap music, acrobatic dancing and graffiti art, etc. [1980s: from **hip**[4]]

hip joint *noun* the articulation of the head of the thigh bone with the **innominate bone**. [18c]

hipped *adj* **1** of a roof: with sloping sides and edges. **2** *usu in compounds* having hips of a specified kind: *wide-hipped.*

hippie *or* **hippy** *noun* (***-ies***) *informal* a member of a 1960s youth subculture, typically with long hair and wearing brightly-coloured clothes, stressing the importance of self-expression and love, and rebelling against the more conservative standards and values of society.

hippo *noun, informal* short for **hippopotamus**.

Hippocratic oath *noun* the oath taken by doctors obligating them to observe the code of medical ethics contained within it. [18c: named after Hippocrates, the Greek physician who devised it]

hippodrome *noun* **1** a variety theatre or circus. **2** in ancient Greece and Rome: a racecourse for horses and chariots. [16c: from Greek *hippos* horse + *dromos* course]

hippopotamus *noun* (***hippopotamuses*** *or* ***hippopotami*** /hɪpə'pɒtəmaɪ/) a hoofed mammal with a thick skin, large head and muzzle, and short stout legs, found in rivers and lakes in parts of Africa. [16c: from Greek *hippos* horse + *potamos* river]

hippy[1] see **hippie**

hippy[2] *adj* esp of a woman: having proportionally large hips.

hipsters *plural noun* trousers that hang from the hips rather than the waist. [1960s]

hire *verb* **1** to procure the temporary use of (something belonging to someone else) in exchange for payment. **2** to employ or engage (someone) for wages. **3** (**hire sth out**) to grant the temporary use of it for payment. ▸ *noun* **1** payment for the use or hire of something. **2** wages paid for services. **3** an act or instance of hiring. ▪ **hirable** *or* **hireable** *adj.* ▪ **hirer** *noun.* [Anglo-Saxon *hyr*]

IDIOMS **for hire** ready for hiring. **on hire** hired out.

hireling *noun, derog* **1** a hired servant. **2** someone whose work is motivated solely by money. [Anglo-Saxon *hyrling*]

hire-purchase *noun, Brit* (abbrev **HP** *or* **hp**) a system where a hired article becomes owned by the hirer after a specified number of payments.

hirsute /'hɜːsjuːt, hɜː'sjuːt/ *adj* hairy; shaggy. ▪ **hirsuteness** *noun.* [17c: from Latin *hirsutus* shaggy]

his *adj* referring or belonging to a male person or animal. ▸ *pronoun* the one or ones belonging to **him**. [Anglo-Saxon]

IDIOMS **of his** relating or belonging to **him**.

Hispanic *adj* relating to or deriving from Spain, the Spanish or Spanish-speaking communities. ▸ *noun, N Am, esp US* a Spanish-speaking American of Latin-American descent. [16c: from Latin *Hispania* Spain]

hiss *noun* **1** a sharp sibilant sound like a sustained *s*. **2** an unwanted noise in audio reproduction: *tape hiss.* ▸ *verb* **1** *intr* of an animal, such as a snake or goose, or a person: to make such a sound, esp as a sign of disapproval or anger. **2** to show (one's disapproval of someone or something) by hissing. [14c: imitating the sound]

hissy fit /'hɪsɪ/ *noun, chiefly US informal* a display of petulance; a tantrum. [1930s: perhaps from *hysterical fit*]

histamine *noun, biochem* a chemical compound released by body tissues during allergic reactions, injury, etc. [20c]

histo- *or* (*before a vowel*) **hist-** *combining form, denoting* animal or plant tissue. [From Greek *histos* web]

histogenesis *or* **histogeny** /hɪ'stɒdʒɪnɪ/ *noun, biol* the development and differentiation of tissues. ▪ **histogenetic** *or* **histogenic** *adj.* ▪ **histogenetically** *or* **histogenically** *adv.* [19c]

histogram *noun* a statistical graph in which vertical rectangles of differing heights are used to represent a frequency distribution. [19c]

histology *noun* the study of the microscopic structure of cells and tissues of living organisms. ▪ **histologic** *or* **histological** *adj.* ▪ **histologically** *adv.* ▪ **histologist** *noun.* [19c]

historian *noun* a person who studies or writes about history. [15c]

historic *adj* famous, important or significant in history. [17c: from Greek *historikos*]

historical *adj* **1** relevant to or about history. **2** relevant to or about people or events in history. **3** of the study of a subject: based on its development over a period of time. **4** referring to something that actually existed or took place; authentic. ▪ **historically** *adv.* [14c: from Latin *historicus*]

historicism *noun* **1** the idea that historical events are determined by natural laws. **2** the theory that sociological circumstances are historically determined. ▪ **historicist** *noun, adj.* [19c: **historic** + **-ism**]

historicity *noun* historical truth or actuality.

historiography *noun* the art or employment of writing history. ▪ **historiographer** *noun.* [16c: from Greek *historiographia*]

history *noun* (***-ies***) **1** an account of past events and developments. **2** a methodical account of the origin and progress of a nation, institution, the world, etc. **3**

the knowledge of past events associated with a particular nation, the world, a person, etc. **4** the academic discipline of understanding and interpreting past events. **5** a past full of events of more than common interest: *a building with a fascinating history.* **6** a play or drama representing historical events. [15c: from Greek *histor* knowing]

IDIOMS **be history** *informal* to be finished, over, dead, etc: *He's history.* **make history** to do something significant or memorable, esp to be the first person to do so.

histrionic *adj* **1** of behaviour, etc: theatrical; melodramatic; expressing too much emotion. **2** *formerly* referring or relating to actors or acting. ▸ *noun* (**histrionics**) theatrical or dramatic behaviour expressing excessive emotion and done to get attention. ▪ **histrionically** *adv.* [17c: from Latin *histrio* actor]

hit *verb* (*past tense, past participle* ***hit,*** *present participle* ***hitting***) **1** to strike (someone or something). **2** to come into forceful contact with (something). **3** of a blow, missile, etc: to reach (a target). **4** to knock (eg oneself or part of oneself) against something, esp hard or violently: *hit her head on the door.* **5** to affect suddenly and severely: *The sad news hit her hard.* **6** *intr* to strike or direct a blow. **7** *informal* to find or attain (an answer, etc) by chance: *You've hit it!* **8** to reach or arrive at: *hit an all-time low.* **9** *sport* to drive (a ball) with a stroke of the bat. **10** *informal* to reach (a place): *We'll hit the city tomorrow.* ▸ *noun* **1** a stroke or blow. **2** *sport* a successful stroke or shot. **3** *informal* something of extreme popularity or success: *The new cinema is a real hit.* **4** an effective remark, eg a sarcasm or witticism. **5** *slang* a murder, esp one by organized gangs. **6** *slang* a dose of a hard drug. [Anglo-Saxon *hittan*]

IDIOMS **hit it off (with sb)** to get on well (with them).

PHRASAL VERBS **hit back** to retaliate. **hit out at** *or* **against sb** *or* **sth** to attack them or it physically or verbally.

hit-and-miss *or* **hit-or-miss** *adj, informal* without any order or planning; random. [19c]

hitch *verb* **1** to move (something) jerkily. **2** (*also* **hitch up**) to move or lift (something, esp an article of clothing) with a jerk. **3** (*also* **hitch up**) to hook, fasten or tether: *hitched the caravan to the car.* **4** *informal* **a** *intr* to hitchhike; **b** to obtain (a lift) as a hitchhiker. ▸ *noun* **1** a small temporary setback or difficulty. **2** a jerk; a sudden movement. **3** a knot for attaching two pieces of rope together. ▪ **hitcher** *noun.* [15c]

IDIOMS **get hitched** *informal* to get married.

hitchhike *verb, intr* to travel, esp long distances, by obtaining free lifts from passing vehicles. ▪ **hitchhiker** *noun.* [1920s]

hi-tec *or* **hi-tech** see **high-tech**

hither *adv, old use* to this place. [Anglo-Saxon *hider*]

IDIOMS **hither and thither** in different directions; this way and that.

hitherto *adv* up to this or that time. [13c]

hit list *noun, informal* a list of targeted victims. [1970s]

hit man *noun, informal* someone hired to assassinate or attack others. [1960s]

Hittite *noun* **1** a member of an ancient people of Syria and Asia Minor. **2** an extinct language belonging to the Anatolian group of languages and discovered from documents in cuneiform writing. ▸ *adj* relating to the Hittites or their language.

HIV *abbrev* human immunodeficiency virus, a virus that breaks down the human body's natural immune system, often leading to **AIDS**.

hive *noun* **1** a box or basket for housing bees. **2** a colony of bees living in such a place. **3** a scene of extreme animation, eg where people are working busily: *a hive of activity.* [Anglo-Saxon *hyf*]

PHRASAL VERBS **hive sth off 1** to separate (a company, etc) from a larger organization. **2** to divert (assets or sectors of an industrial organization) to other organizations, esp private ones. **3** to assign (work) to a subsidiary company.

hives *plural noun, non-technical* **urticaria**. [16c]

HIV-positive *adj, med* denoting a person who has tested positively for the presence of HIV.

hiya *exclam, slang* a familiar greeting. [1940s: a contraction of *how are you?*]

HM *abbrev* Her or His Majesty or Majesty's.

Ho *symbol, chem* holmium.

ho *or* **hoh** *exclam* **1** a call or shout to attract attention or indicate direction or destination. **2** (*esp* **ho-ho**) representation of laughter. [13c]

hoar *adj, esp poetic* white or greyish-white, esp with age or frost. [Anglo-Saxon *har*]

hoard *noun* a store of money, food or treasure, usu one hidden away for use in the future. ▸ *verb, tr & intr* to store or gather (food, money or treasure), often secretly, and esp for use in the future. ▪ **hoarder** *noun.* [Anglo-Saxon *hord*]

hoard, horde

Be careful not to use the spelling **hoard** when you mean **horde**:

hordes of tourists

hoarding *noun* **1** a screen of light boards, esp round a building site. **2** a similar wooden surface for displaying advertisements, posters, etc. [19c: from French *hourd* palisade]

hoarfrost *noun* the white frost on grass, leaves, etc in the morning formed by freezing dew after a cold night. Also called **white frost.** [13c]

hoarse *adj* **1** of the voice: rough and husky, esp because of a sore throat or excessive shouting. **2** of a person: having a hoarse voice. ▪ **hoarsely** *adv.* ▪ **hoarsen** *verb.* ▪ **hoarseness** *noun.* [Anglo-Saxon *has*]

hoary *adj* (***-ier, -iest***) **1** white or grey with age. **2** ancient. **3** overused and trite. ▪ **hoariness** *noun.* [16c]

hoax *noun* a deceptive trick played either humorously or maliciously. ▸ *verb* to trick or deceive with a hoax. ▪ **hoaxer** *noun.* [18c: perhaps from *hocus* to trick; see **hocus-pocus**]

hob *noun* the flat surface on which pots are heated, either on top of a cooker or as a separate piece of equipment.

hobbit *noun* one of an imaginary race of people, half the size of humans and hairy-footed, living below the ground. [Created by J R R Tolkien in his novel *The Hobbit* (1937)]

hobble *verb* **1** *intr* to walk awkwardly and unsteadily by taking short unsteady steps. **2** to loosely tie the legs of (a horse) together, to inhibit its movement. **3** to hamper or impede. ▸ *noun* **1** an awkward and irregular gait. **2** something used to hamper an animal's feet. [14c]

hobbledehoy *noun* an awkward youth. [16c]

hobby[1] *noun* (**-ies**) an activity or occupation carried out in one's spare time for amusement or relaxation. [14c as *hobyn*, meaning 'a small horse', and also a variant of *Robin*]

hobby[2] *noun* (**-ies**) a small species of falcon. [15c: from French *hobe* falcon]

hobby-horse *noun* **1** a child's toy consisting of a long stick with a horse's head at one end that they prance about with, as if riding a horse. **2** a subject that a person talks about frequently.

hobgoblin *noun* a mischievous or evil spirit. [16c: from *hob*, a variant of *Rob*, short for *Robert* + **goblin**]

hobnail *noun* a short nail with a large strong head for protecting the soles of boots, shoes and horseshoes. ▪ **hobnailed** *adj*. [16c: from an old meaning of **hob**, meaning 'peg or pin']

hobnob *verb* (**hobnobbed, hobnobbing**) *intr* (*also* **hobnob with**) to associate or spend time socially or talk informally (with someone). [18c: from the phrase *hab or nab* have or have not]

hobo *noun* (**hobos** *or* **hoboes**) *N Am* **1** a tramp. **2** an itinerant worker, esp an unskilled one. [19c]

Hobson's choice *noun* the choice of taking the thing offered, or nothing at all. [17c: named after Thomas Hobson, a Cambridge carrier who hired out the horse nearest the door or none at all]

hock[1] *noun* **1** the joint on the hind leg of horses and other hoofed mammals, corresponding to the ankle joint on a human leg. Also called **hamstring**. **2** the joint of meat extending upwards from the hock joint. [16c: a contraction of *hockshin*, from Anglo-Saxon *hohsinu* heel sinew]

hock[2] *noun* a German white wine from the Rhine valley. [17c: from German *Hochheimer* of Hochheim]

hock[3] *verb, informal* to pawn. ▸ *noun* (*always* **in hock**) *informal* **1** in debt. **2** in prison. **3** in pawn; having been pawned. [19c: from Dutch *hok* prison, hovel or debt]

hockey *noun* **1** a ball game played by two teams of eleven players with long clubs curved at one end, each team attempting to score goals. **2** *N Am* **ice hockey**. **3** (also **hockey line**) see **oche**. [16c: from French *hoquet* a crook or staff]

hocus-pocus *noun, informal* **1** the skill of trickery or deception. **2** a conjurer's chant while performing a magic trick. [17c: sham Latin]

hod *noun* an open V-shaped box on a pole, used for carrying bricks, etc. [16c: from French *hotte* pannier]

hodgepodge see **hotchpotch**

Hodgkin's disease *or* **Hodgkin's lymphoma** *noun* a malignant disease in which the lymph nodes, spleen and liver become enlarged, the main symptoms being anaemia, fever and fatigue. [19c: named after Thomas Hodgkin, British physician]

hoe *noun* a long-handled tool with a narrow blade, used for loosening soil, weeding, etc. ▸ *verb* (**hoed, hoeing**) **1** to dig, loosen or weed (the ground, etc) using a hoe. **2** *intr* to use a hoe. [14c: from French *houe*]

hoedown *noun, esp US* **1** a country dance, esp a square dance. **2** a gathering for performing such dances. [19c: **hoe** + **down**[1]]

hog *noun* **1** *N Am, esp US* a general name for a **pig**. **2** a castrated boar. **3** a pig reared specifically for slaughter. **4** *informal* a greedy, inconsiderate and often coarse person. ▸ *verb* (**hogged, hogging**) *informal* to take, use, occupy, etc selfishly. [Anglo-Saxon *hogg*]

IDIOMS **go the whole hog** to carry out or do something completely.

hogback *or* **hog's-back** *noun* a steep-sided hill-ridge. [17c]

Hogmanay *noun, Scot* New Year's Eve or a celebration of this time. [17c: from French *aguillaneuf* a gift at New Year]

hogshead *noun* **1** a large cask for liquids. **2** a liquid or dry measure of capacity (usu about 63 gallons or 238 l). [14c]

hogtie *verb* **1** to tie (someone) up by fastening all four limbs together. **2** to frustrate, obstruct or impede. [Late 19c]

hogwash *noun, informal* nonsense. [Early 20c]

hoh see **ho**

hoi see **hoy**

hoick *or* **hoik** *verb, informal* to lift up abruptly. [19c]

hoi polloi *plural noun* (*usu* **the hoi polloi**) the masses; the common people. [Early 19c: Greek, meaning 'the many']

hoist *verb* **1** to lift or heave up. **2** to raise or heave up using lifting equipment. ▸ *noun* **1** *informal* the act of hoisting. **2** equipment for hoisting heavy articles. [16c: past tense of obsolete verb *hoise*]

hoity-toity *adj* arrogant; superciliously haughty. [17c: rhyming compound from obsolete *hoit* to romp]

hokku see **haiku**

hokum *noun, N Am slang* **1** nonsense. **2** pretentious or over-sentimental material in a play, film, etc. [20c: prob from **hocus-pocus**, modelled on **bunkum**]

hold[1] *verb* (*past tense & past participle* **held**) **1** to have or keep in one's hand or hands. **2** to have in one's possession. **3** to think or believe. **4** to retain or reserve. **5** *tr & intr* to keep or stay in a specified state or position: *hold firm*. **6** *intr* to remain in position, esp when under pressure. **7** to detain or restrain. **8** to contain or be able to contain: *This bottle holds three pints*. **9** to conduct or carry on: *hold a conversation* • *hold a meeting*. **10** to have (a position of responsibility, a job, etc): *held office for two years*. **11** to have or possess: *holds the world record*. **12** to keep or sustain (a person's attention). **13** to affirm or allege. **14** to maintain one's composure and awareness, and not suffer any bad effects, even after large amounts of (alcohol): *She can hold her drink*. **15** *intr* of weather: to continue. **16** to consider to be; to think or believe. **17** *intr* to continue to be valid or apply: *The law still holds*. **18** to defend from the enemy. **19** to cease or stop: *hold fire*. **20** *music* to continue (a note or pause). **21** *intr* of a telephone caller: to wait without hanging up while the person being called comes on the line. **22** of the future, regarded as a force: to have in store or readiness: *Who knows what the future holds?* ▸ *noun* **1** an act of holding. **2** a power or influence: *They have a hold over him*. **3** a way of holding someone, esp in certain sports, eg judo. **4** a place of confinement; a prison cell. **5** an object to hold on to. [Anglo-Saxon *healdan*]

IDIOMS **get hold of sb** *informal* to manage to find and speak to them. **get hold of sth** to find, obtain or buy it. **hold good** *or* **hold true** to remain true or valid; to apply. **hold one's own** to maintain one's position, eg in an argument, etc. **hold one's peace** *or* **tongue** to remain silent. **on hold** in a state of suspension; temporarily postponed: *She put the trip on hold.* **with no holds barred** without any restrictions.

PHRASAL VERBS **hold back** to hesitate; to restrain oneself. **hold sb back** to restrain them from doing something. **hold sth back** to keep it in reserve. **hold sth down** to manage to keep it: *hold down a job.* **hold sth in** to restrain or check it. **hold off** *or* **hold off doing sth** to delay or not begin to do it; to refrain from doing it. **hold on** *informal* to wait, esp during a telephone conversation. **hold on!** an exclamation requesting the other person to wait. **hold on to sth** to keep or maintain it in one's possession. **hold out 1** to stand firm, esp resisting difficulties: *held out against the enemy.* **2** to endure or last. **hold out for sth** to wait persistently for something one wants or has demanded. **hold out on sb** *informal* to keep back money, information, etc from them. **hold sth over** to postpone or delay it. **hold sb up 1** to delay or hinder them. **2** to stop and rob them. **hold sth up** to delay or hinder it. **hold sb** *or* **sth up as sth** to exhibit them or it as an example: *held them up as models of integrity.* **hold with sth** (*with negatives and in questions*) to endorse or approve of it: *I don't hold with violence.*

hold² *noun* a storage cavity in ships and aeroplanes. [16c: variant of **hole**]

holdall *noun* a large strong bag for carrying miscellaneous articles, esp clothes when travelling. [19c]

holder *noun* **1** someone or something that holds or grips. **2** *law* someone who has ownership or control of something, eg a shareholder. [14c]

holdfast *noun* **1** something that holds fast or firmly. **2** a device for fixing or holding something together, eg a long nail or a hook. [16c]

holding *noun* **1** land held by lease. **2** an amount of land, shares, etc owned by a person or company. [12c]

hold-up *noun* **1** a delay or setback. **2** a robbery, usu with violence or threats of violence. [Early 19c]

hole *noun* **1** a hollow area or cavity in something solid. **2** an aperture or gap in or through something: *a hole in the sock.* **3** an animal's nest or refuge. **4** *informal* an unpleasant or contemptible place. **5** *informal* an awkward or difficult situation. **6** *informal* a fault or error: *a hole in the argument.* **7** *golf* **a** a hollow in the middle of each green, into which the ball is hit; **b** each section of a golf course extending from the tee to the green. ▸ *verb* **1** to make a hole in something. **2** to hit or play (a ball, etc) into a hole. [Anglo-Saxon *hol*]

IDIOMS **in holes** full of holes. **make a hole in sth** *informal* to use up a large amount of it, eg money. **pick holes in sth** to find fault with it.

PHRASAL VERBS **hole out** *golf* to play the ball into the hole. **hole up** *informal* to go to earth; to hide.

hole-and-corner *adj* secret; underhand.

hole in one *noun, golf* a single hit of the ball which results in it going straight into the hole.

hole in the wall *noun, informal* an automated cash dispensing machine sited in a wall.

holey *adj* (***-ier, -iest***) full of holes.

Holi /ˈhoʊliː/ *noun, Hinduism* the spring festival in honour of Krishna, held in February or March over several days. [Early 20c: from Sanskrit]

holiday *noun* **1** (*often* **holidays**) a period of recreational time spent away from work, study or general routine. **2** a day when no work is done, orig a religious festival. ▸ *verb, intr* to spend or go away for a holiday in a specified place or at a specified time: *They holiday every year in Cornwall.* [Anglo-Saxon *haligdæg* holy day]

holiday camp *noun* a place, often near the sea, where activities and entertainment are organized for the people staying there on holiday in hotels, chalets, etc.

holidaymaker *noun* a person on holiday. [19c]

holier-than-thou *adj* of a person, attitude, etc: self-righteous, often sanctimoniously or patronizingly so.

holiness *noun* **1** the state of being holy; sanctity. **2** (**Holiness**) a title of the Pope, used to address or refer to him, in the form of **Your Holiness** and **His Holiness**.

holism *noun, philos* **1** the theory that a complex entity or system is more than merely the sum of its parts or elements. **2** the treatment of a disease, etc by taking social, economic, psychological, etc factors into consideration, rather than just the person's ailment or condition. ▪ **holist** *noun.* ▪ **holistic** *adj.* ▪ **holistically** *adv.* [20c: from Greek *holos* whole]

hollandaise sauce /ˈhɒləndeɪz/ *noun* a sauce made from egg yolks, butter and lemon juice or vinegar. [Early 20c: French]

holler *verb, tr & intr, informal* to shout or yell. ▸ *noun* a shout or yell. [16c: from French *holà* stop!]

hollow *adj* **1** containing an empty space within or below; not solid. **2** sunken or depressed: *hollow cheeks.* **3** of a sound: echoing as if made in a hollow place. **4** without any great significance: *a hollow victory.* **5** insincere: *hollow promises.* ▸ *noun* **1** a hole or cavity in something. **2** a valley or depression in the land. ▸ *adv, informal* completely: *beat someone hollow.* ▸ *verb* (*usu* **hollow out**) to make hollow. ▪ **hollowly** *adv.* ▪ **hollowness** *noun.* [Anglo-Saxon *holh*]

holly *noun* (***-ies***) an evergreen tree or shrub with dark shiny prickly leaves and red berries. [Anglo-Saxon *holen*]

hollyhock *noun* a tall garden plant of the mallow family, with thick hairy stalks and colourful flowers. [13c: from *holi* holy + *hoc* mallow]

holmium *noun, chem* (symbol **Ho**) a soft silver-white metallic element. [19c: from Latin *Holmia* Stockholm, since many minerals with this element were found there]

holo- *or* (*before a vowel*) **hol-** *combining form, denoting* whole or wholly. [From Greek *holos*]

holocaust *noun* **1** a large-scale slaughter or destruction of life, often by fire. **2** (**the Holocaust**) the mass murder of Jews by the Nazis during World War II. [13c: **holo-** + Greek *kaustos* burnt]

Holocene *noun* the most recent geological period, during which modern human civilization began. [19c]

hologram *noun, photog* a photograph produced without a lens, by the interference between two split laser beams which, when suitably illuminated, shows a three-dimensional image. [1940s]

holograph *adj* of a document: completely in the handwriting of the author. ▸ *noun* a holograph document. [17c]

holography *noun* the process or study of producing or using holograms. ▪ **holographic** *adj*.

hols *plural noun, informal* holidays.

holster *noun* a leather case for a handgun, often a belt round a person's hips or shoulders. [17c: Dutch]

holt *noun* an animal's den, esp that of an otter. [Anglo-Saxon: from **hold**[1]]

holy *adj* (**-ier, -iest**) **1** associated with God or gods; religious or sacred. **2** morally pure and perfect; saintly. **3** of ground, a place, etc: sanctified or sacred. ▪ **holily** *adv*. [Anglo-Saxon *halig*]

Holy Communion see **communion** (sense 2)

holy day *noun* a religious festival.

the Holy Father *noun* the Pope. [14c]

the Holy Ghost, **the Holy Spirit** *or* **the Spirit** *noun, Christianity* the third person in the Trinity.

Holy Grail see under **grail**

the Holy Land *noun, Christianity* Palestine, esp Judea, the scene of Christ's ministry in the New Testament.

holy of holies *noun* any place or thing regarded as especially sacred.

holy orders *plural noun* the office of an ordained member of the clergy. [14c]

Holy Roman Empire *noun* the empire held by the **Holy Roman Emperors** in Italy and central Europe, strictly from the 12c, but more generally so called from the reign of Charlemagne, King of the Franks, in the 9c.

the Holy See *noun, RC Church* the see or office of the Pope in Rome. [18c]

holy war *noun* a war waged in the name of or in support of a religion. [17c]

holy water *noun* water blessed for use in religious ceremonies. [Anglo-Saxon *haligwæter*]

Holy Week *noun, Christianity* the week before Easter Sunday, which includes Maundy Thursday and Good Friday. [18c]

homage *noun* a display of great respect towards someone or something; an acknowledgement of their superiority. [13c: French]

home *noun* **1** the place where one lives, often with one's family. **2** the country or area one orig comes from, either a birthplace or where one grew up. **3** a place where something first occurred, or was first invented. **4** an institution for people who need care or rest, eg the elderly, orphans, etc. **5** the den, base or finishing point in some games and races. ▸ *adj* **1** being at or belonging to one's home, country, family, sports ground, etc. **2** made or done at home or in one's own country: *home baking*. **3** of a sporting event: played on one's own ground, etc: *a home match*. ▸ *adv* **1** to or at one's home. **2** to the target place, position, etc: *hit the point home*. **3** to the furthest or final point; as far as possible: *hammer the nail home*. ▸ *verb, intr* **1** of an animal, esp a bird: to return home safely. **2** (*often* **home in on sth**) to identify (a target or destination) and focus on attempting to reach it. [Anglo-Saxon *ham*]

IDIOMS **bring sth home to sb** to make it clear or obvious to them. **home and dry** having achieved one's goal. **home from home** a place where one feels completely comfortable, relaxed, and happy, as if at home. **nothing to write home about** *informal* unremarkable.

homeboy *noun, US informal* **1** a male acquaintance from one's own neighbourhood or town. **2** a member of a youth gang.

home brew *noun* beer, etc brewed at home. [19c]

homecoming *noun* an arrival home, usu of someone who has been away for a long time. [14c: *homcomyng*]

home economics *singular noun* the study of domestic science, household skills and management. ▪ **home economist** *noun*. [19c]

home farm *noun, Brit* a farm, usu one of several on a large estate, set aside to produce food, etc for the owner of the estate.

the Home Guard *noun, hist* a volunteer army formed to defend Britain from invasion during World War II.

home help *noun, Brit* a person who is hired, often by the local authority, to help sick, aged, etc people with domestic chores.

homeland *noun* **1** one's native country; the country of one's ancestors. **2** *hist* in South Africa: an area of land reserved by the government for the Black population. [17c]

homeless *adj* **1** of a person: without a home and living, sleeping, etc in public places or squats. **2** of an animal: without an owner. ▪ **homelessness** *noun*.

homely *adj* (**-ier, -iest**) **1** relating to home; familiar. **2** making someone feel at home. **3** of a person: honest and unpretentious; pleasant. **4** *N Am* of a person: plain and unattractive. [14c]

home-made *adj* **1** of food, clothes, etc: made at home. **2** made in one's native country. [17c]

home movie *noun* a motion picture made by an amateur, usu using a portable cine camera or camcorder.

homeo-, **homoeo-** *or* **homoio-** *combining form, denoting* like or similar. [From Greek *homoios*]

homeopathy *or* **homoeopathy** *noun* a system of alternative medicine where a disease is treated by prescribing small doses of drugs that produce symptoms similar to those of the disease itself. ▪ **homeopath** *noun*. ▪ **homeopathic** *adj*. ▪ **homeopathically** *adv*. ▪ **homeopathist** *noun*. [19c]

homeostasis *or* **homoeostasis** /hoʊmɪˈɒstəsɪs, hɒmɪ-/ *noun, biol* the tendency of an animal or organism to maintain a stable internal condition regardless of changes in its environment. [20c]

homeothermic *or* **homoeothermic** *adj, zool* **warm-blooded**.

homer *noun* **1** a breed of pigeon that can be trained to return home from a distance. **2** *baseball* a home run. **3** *informal* an out-of-hours job illicitly done by a tradesman for cash-in-hand payment.

home rule *noun* **1** the government of a country and its internal affairs by its own citizens. **2** (**Home Rule**) the form of self-government claimed by Irish, Scottish and Welsh Nationalists, including a separate government to manage internal affairs. [19c]

homesick *adj* pining for one's home and family when away from them. ▪ **homesickness** *noun*.

homespun *adj* **1** of character, advice, thinking, etc: artless, simple and straightforward. **2** *old use* of cloth: woven at home. ▸ *noun* a cloth produced at home.

homestead *noun* **1** a dwelling-house and its surrounding land and buildings. **2** *N Am, esp US* an area of land (usu about 65ha) granted to a settler for development as a farm. [Anglo-Saxon *hamstede*]

home truth *noun* (*usu* **home truths**) a true but unwelcome fact, usu about oneself.

homeward *adj* going home. ▸ *adv* (*also* **homewards**) towards home. [Anglo-Saxon *hamweard*]

homework *noun* **1** work or study done at home, esp for school. **2** paid work, esp work paid for according to quantity rather than time, done at home. [17c]

homey[1] *or* **homy** *adj* (*-ier, -iest*) homelike; homely.

homey[2] *or* **homie** /ˈhoʊmɪ/ *noun* (***homeys*** *or* ***homies***) *US slang* a **homeboy**. [1980s]

homicide *noun* **1** the murder or manslaughter of one person by another. **2** a person who commits this act. ▪ **homicidal** *adj*. ▪ **homicidally** *adv*. [14c: from Latin *homo* man + **-cide**]

homily *noun* (*-ies*) **1** a sermon. **2** a long, tedious talk. [14c: from Greek *homilia* assembly or sermon]

homing *verb, present participle of* **home**. ▸ *adj* **1** of animals, esp pigeons: trained to return home, usu from a distance. **2** of navigational devices on missiles, crafts, etc: guiding towards a target.

homing instinct *noun, biol* the ability of several animal species to navigate their way home.

hominid *noun* a primate belonging to the family that includes modern humans and their fossil ancestors. [19c: from Latin *homo, hominis* man]

hominoid *adj* resembling a human. ▸ *noun* any animal resembling a human. [1920s: from Latin *homo, hominis* man + Greek *eidos* shape]

hominy *noun, N Am, esp US* coarsely ground maize boiled with milk or water to make a porridge. [17c: a Native American word]

homo- *combining form, denoting* same: *homogeneous*. Compare **hetero-**. [From Greek *homos*]

homocyclic *adj, chem* of a compound: having a closed chain of similar atoms. Compare **heterocyclic**. [Early 20c: from Greek *kyklos* a ring]

homoeopathy see **homeopathy**

homogeneous /hɒməˈdʒiːnɪəs, hoʊ-/ *adj* **1** made up of parts or elements that are all of the same kind or nature. **2** made up of similar parts or elements. **3** *maths* having the same degree or dimensions throughout in every term. ▪ **homogeneously** *adv*. ▪ **homogeneousness** *or* **homogeneity** *noun*. [17c: from Greek *genos* kind]

homogenize *or* **-ise** /həˈmɒdʒənaɪz/ *verb* **1** to make or become homogeneous. **2** to break up the fat droplets of (a liquid, esp milk) into smaller particles so that they are evenly distributed throughout the liquid. [19c: from Greek *genos* kind]

homogeny /həˈmɒdʒənɪ/ *noun, biol* a similarity owing to common descent or origin. ▪ **homogenous** *adj*. [17c: from Greek *homogeneia* similarity of origin]

homograph *noun* a word with the same spelling as another, but with a different meaning, origin, and sometimes a different pronunciation, eg *tear* (rip) and *tear* (teardrop). [19c]

homologous /həˈmɒləgəs/ *adj* **1** having a related or similar function or position. **2** of plant or animal structures: having a common origin, but having evolved in such a way that they no longer perform the same functions or resemble each other, eg a human arm and a bird's wing. Compare **analogous**. **3** *chem* denoting a series of compounds in which each member has one more of a chemical group in its molecule than the preceding member. **4** *genetics* of two chromosomes in a cell: pairing during meiosis, and containing genes for the same set of characteristics, but derived from different parents. ▪ **homology** *noun* (*-ies*). [17c]

homologue *or* (*US*) **homolog** *noun* anything that is homologous to something else. [19c]

homomorphic *or* **homomorphous** *adj* similar in form, esp if different otherwise. ▪ **homomorphism** *noun*.

homonym *noun* a word with the same sound and spelling as another, but with a different meaning, eg *kind* (helpful) and *kind* (sort). [17c: from Greek *onoma* name]

homophobe *noun* a person with a strong aversion to or hatred of homosexuals. ▪ **homophobia** *noun*. ▪ **homophobic** *adj*. [1950s: shortened from **homosexual** + Greek *phobos* fear]

homophone *noun* **1** a word that sounds the same as another word but is different in spelling and/or meaning, eg *bear* and *bare*. **2** a character or characters that represent the same sound as another, eg *f* and *ph*. [17c]

homophony *noun, music* a style of composition in which one part or voice carries the melody, and other parts or voices add texture with simple accompaniment. Compare **polyphony**. [19c]

homopterous *adj* relating or referring to insects that have wings of a uniform texture. ▪ **homopteran** *noun*. [19c: from Greek *pteron* wing]

Homo sapiens /ˈhoʊmoʊ ˈsapɪɛnz/ *noun* the species to which modern man belongs, and the only member of the Homo genus still in existence. [18c: Latin, meaning 'wise man']

homosexual *noun* a person who is sexually attracted to people of the same sex. ▸ *adj* **1** having a sexual attraction to people of the same sex. **2** relating to or concerning a homosexual or homosexuals. ▪ **homosexuality** *noun*. ▪ **homosexually** *adv*.

homunculus *or* **homuncule** *noun* (***homunculi*** /həˈmʌnkjuːlaɪ/) a small man; a dwarf. ▪ **homuncular** *adj*. [17c: Latin diminutive of *homo* man]

homy see **homey**[1]

Hon. *abbrev* **1** Honourable. **2** Honorary.

honcho *noun, N Am informal* an important person, esp someone in charge; a big shot. [1940s: from Japanese *han* squad + *cho* head or chief]

hone *noun* a smooth stone used for sharpening tools. ▸ *verb* to sharpen with or as if with a hone. [Anglo-Saxon *han*]

honest *adj* **1** not inclined to steal, cheat or lie; truthful and trustworthy. **2** fair or justified: *an honest wage*. **3** sincere and respectable: *an honest attempt*. **4** ordinary and undistinguished; unremarkable: *an honest wine*. ▸ *adv, informal* honestly: *I do like it, honest*. [13c: from Latin *honestus*]

honest broker *noun* an impartial and objective mediator in a dispute. [19c]

honestly *adv* **1** in an honest way. **2** in truth. **3** used for emphasis: *I honestly don't know*. ▸ *exclam* **1** expressing annoyance. **2** expressing disbelief.

honesty *noun* **1** the state of being honest and truthful. **2** integrity and candour. **3** a common garden plant with silvery leaf-like pods. [14c: from Latin *honestus*]

honey *noun* (**-eys**) **1** a sweet viscous fluid made by bees from the nectar of flowers, and stored in honeycombs. **2** a dark dull-yellow or golden-brown colour resembling that of honey. **3** *N Am informal* a term of endearment used to address a loved one. [Anglo-Saxon *hunig*]

honeycomb *noun* **1** the structure made up of rows of hexagonal wax cells in which bees store their eggs and honey. **2** anything like a honeycomb. **3** a bewildering maze of cavities, rooms, passages, etc. ▸ *verb* to form like a honeycomb. [Anglo-Saxon *hunigcamb*]

honeydew *noun* a sugar secretion from aphids and plants. [16c]

honeyed *or* **honied** *adj* of a voice, words, etc: sweet, flattering or soothing. [14c]

honeymoon *noun* **1** the first weeks after marriage, often spent on holiday, before settling down to the normal routine of life. **2** a period of unusual or temporary goodwill, enthusiasm and harmony at the start eg of a new business relationship. ▸ *verb, intr* to spend time on a honeymoon, usu on holiday. ▪ **honeymooner** *noun*. [16c: so called because the feelings of the couple were thought to wax and wane like the moon phases]

honeypot *or* **honeypot site** *noun* something or somewhere that attracts people in great numbers.

honeysuckle *noun* a climbing garden shrub with sweet-scented white, pale-yellow or pink flowers. [Anglo-Saxon *hunigsuce*, so called because honey is easily sucked from the flower by long-tongued insects]

honing *present participle of* **hone**

honk *noun* **1** the cry of a wild goose. **2** the sound made by a car horn. ▸ *verb, tr & intr* to make or cause something to make a honking noise. [19c: imitating the sound]

honky-tonk *noun, informal* **1** a style of jangly popular piano music based on **ragtime**. **2** *N Am slang* a cheap seedy nightclub. [1890s: a rhyming compound derived from **honk**]

honor an *N Am* spelling of **honour**

honorarium *noun* (***honorariums*** *or* ***honoraria*** /ɒnə'rɛərɪə/) a fee paid to a professional person in return for services carried out on a voluntary basis. [17c: Latin]

honorary *adj* **1** conferring or bestowing honour. **2** of a title, etc: given as a mark of respect, and without the usual functions, dues, etc. **3** of an official position: receiving no payment. [17c: from Latin *honorarius*]

honorific *adj* showing or giving honour or respect. ▸ *noun* a form of title, address or mention. ▪ **honorifically** *adv*. [17c: from Latin *honorificus*]

Honour *noun* a title of respect given to judges, mayors, etc, in the form of **Your Honour, His Honour** and **Her Honour**.

honour *or* (*N Am*) **honor** *noun* **1** the esteem or respect earned by or paid to a worthy person. **2** great respect or public regard. **3** a source of credit, such as fame, glory or distinction, or an award, etc in recognition of this. **4** a scrupulous sense of what is right; a high standard of moral behaviour or integrity. **5** a pleasure or privilege. **6** *old use* a woman's chastity or virginity, or her reputation for this. ▸ *verb* **1** to respect or venerate; to hold in high esteem. **2** to confer an award, title, etc on someone as a mark of respect for an ability, achievement, etc. **3** to pay (a bill, debt, etc) when it falls due. **4** to keep or meet (a promise or agreement). [12c: from Latin *honor*]

IDIOMS **do the honours** *informal* to perform or carry out a task, esp that of a host. **in honour of sb** *or* **sth** out of respect for or in celebration of them or it. **on one's honour** under a moral obligation.

honourable *or* (*N Am*) **honorable** *adj* **1** deserving or worthy of honour. **2** having high moral principles. **3** (**Honourable**) a prefix to the names of certain people as a courtesy title. See also **Right Honourable**. ▪ **honourableness** *or* (*N Am*) **honorableness** *noun*. ▪ **honourably** *or* (*N Am*) **honorably** *adv*. [14c]

honour-bound *adj* obliged to do something by duty or by moral considerations.

honours *plural noun* **1** a higher grade of university degree with distinction for specialized or advanced work. **2** a mark of civility or respect, esp at a funeral. **3** in some card games: any of the top four or five cards.

honours list *noun* a list of people who have received or are about to receive a knighthood, order, etc from the monarch.

hooch *or* **hootch** *noun, N Am informal* any strong alcoholic drink, esp when distilled or obtained illegally. [19c: a shortening of *Hoochinoo*, a Native American people who made alcoholic drink]

hood[1] *noun* **1** a flexible covering for the whole head and back of the neck, often attached to a coat at the collar. **2** a folding and often removable roof or cover on a car, pushchair, etc. **3** *N Am* a car bonnet. **4** an ornamental loop of material worn as part of academic dress, specifically coloured according to the university and degree obtained. **5** a covering of a hawk's head. **6** any projecting or protective covering. **7** an expanding section of a cobra's neck. ▸ *verb* to cover with a hood; to blind. [Anglo-Saxon *hod*]

hood[2] *noun, slang* a hoodlum.

hood[3] *or* **'hood** /hʊd/ *noun, US informal* a shortened form of **neighbourhood**. [1960s]

-hood *suffix, forming nouns, denoting* **1** a state or condition of being the specified thing: *manhood* • *motherhood*. **2** a collection or group of people: *priesthood*. [Anglo-Saxon *-had*]

hooded *adj* having, covered with, or shaped like a hood.

hoodie *noun, informal* a hooded jacket or top.

hoodlum *noun* **1** *N Am* a small-time criminal. **2** a violent, destructive or badly behaved youth. [19c: from German *Hudellump* a sloppy or careless person]

hoodoo *noun* **1** voodoo. **2** a jinx or bad luck. **3** a person or thing that brings such. ▸ *verb* (***hoodooed***) to bring bad luck to someone. [19c: variant of **voodoo**]

hoodwink *verb* to trick or deceive. [16c: meaning 'to blindfold', from **hood**[1] + **wink**]

hooey *noun, slang* nonsense.

hoof *noun* (***hoofs*** *or* ***hooves***) the horny structure that grows beneath and covers the ends of the digits in the feet of certain mammals, eg horses. [Anglo-Saxon *hof*]

IDIOMS **hoof it** *slang* **1** to go on foot. **2** to dance. **on the hoof** of cattle, horses, etc: alive.

hoofer *noun, slang* a professional dancer.

hoo-ha *or* **hoo-hah** *noun, informal* excited and noisy talk; a commotion. [1930s: prob from Yiddish *hu-ha* uproar]

hook *noun* **1** a curved piece of metal or similar material, used for catching or holding things. **2** a snare, trap, attraction, etc. **3** a curved tool used for cutting grain, branches, etc. **4** a sharp bend or curve, eg in land or a river. **5** *boxing* a swinging punch with the elbow bent. **6** *sport* a method of striking the ball causing it to curve in the air. **7** *cricket, golf* a shot that causes the ball to curve in the direction of the swing. **8** *pop music* a catchy or easily memorized phrase. ► *verb* **1** to catch, fasten or hold with or as if with a hook. **2** to form into or with a hook. **3** to ensnare, trap, attract, etc. **4 a** *golf, cricket* to hit (the ball) out round the other side of one's body, to the left if the player is right-handed, and vice versa; **b** of the ball: to curve in this direction. **5** in a rugby scrum: to catch (the ball) with the foot and kick it backwards. **6** *tr & intr* to bend or curve. **7** *tr & intr* to pull abruptly. [Anglo-Saxon *hoc*]

IDIOMS **by hook or by crook** by some means or other. **hook and eye** a device used to fasten clothes by means of a hook that catches in a loop or eye. **hook, line and sinker** *informal* completely. **off the hook 1** *informal* out of trouble or difficulty; excused of the blame for something. **2** of a telephone receiver: not on its rest, and so not able to receive incoming calls.

hookah *or* **hooka** *noun* an oriental tobacco pipe consisting of a tube which passes through water, used to cool the smoke before it is inhaled. [18c: from Arabic *huqqah* bowl]

hooked *adj* **1** curved like a hook. **2** *informal* physically, emotionally, etc dependent.

hooker *noun* **1** someone or something that hooks. **2** *informal* a prostitute. **3** *rugby* the forward whose job is to hook the ball out of a scrum.

Hooke's law *noun, physics* the law that states that, up to a certain limit, the extension produced by stretching an elastic material is proportional to the force that is producing the extension. [Named after Robert Hooke, English physicist]

hookey *or* **hooky** *noun, N Am informal* absence from school without permission: *played hookey.* [19c]

hook-up *noun* a temporary link-up of different broadcasting stations, esp the radio and a television channel, for a special transmission. [Early 20c]

hookworm *noun* a parasitic worm with hook-like parts in its mouth, which lives in the intestines of animals and humans, causing mild anaemia. [Early 20c]

hooligan *noun* a violent, destructive or badly-behaved youth. ▪ **hooliganism** *noun.* [19c: from *Houlihan*, an Irish surname]

hoop *noun* **1** a thin ring of metal, wood, etc, esp those used round casks. **2** anything similar to this in shape. **3** a large ring made of light wood or plastic, used for amusement, eg rolled along the ground, whirled round the body, or used by circus performers, etc to jump through. **4** an iron arch through which the ball is hit in croquet. **5** a ring for holding a skirt wide. **6** a horizontal band of colour running round a sportsperson's shirt. ► *verb* to bind or surround with a hoop or hoops. [Anglo-Saxon *hop*]

IDIOMS **go** *or* **be put through the hoops** *informal* to undergo or suffer a thorough and difficult test or ordeal.

hoop-la *noun* **1** *Brit* a fairground game in which small rings are thrown at objects, with the thrower winning any objects encircled by the rings. **2** *US slang* pointless activity or nonsense; a nuisance. [Early 20c: from French *houp la!* an order for someone to move]

hoorah *or* **hooray** see under **hurrah**

hoot *noun* **1** the call of an owl, or a similar sound. **2** the sound of a car horn, siren, steam whistle, etc, or a similar sound. **3** a loud shout of laughter, scorn or disapproval. **4** *informal* a hilarious person, event or thing. ► *verb* **1** *intr* of an owl: to make a hoot. **2** to sound (a car horn, etc). **3** *intr* of a person: to shout or laugh loudly, often expressing disapproval, scorn, etc. [13c: prob imitating the sound]

IDIOMS **not care** *or* **give a hoot** *or* **two hoots** *informal* not to care at all.

hootch see **hooch**

hooter *noun* **1** a person or thing that makes a hooting sound. **2** *Brit informal* a nose.

Hoover *noun, trademark* (*also* **hoover**) a **vacuum cleaner.** ► *verb* (**hoover**) *tr & intr* to clean (a carpet, etc) with or as if with a vacuum cleaner. [Early 20c: named after William Henry Hoover, US industrialist]

hooves see **hoof**

hop¹ *verb* (***hopped, hopping***) **1** *intr* of a person: to jump up and down on one leg, esp forward as a form of movement. **2** *intr* of certain small birds, animals and insects: to move by jumping on both or all legs simultaneously. **3** to jump over something. **4** *intr* (*usu* **hop in**, **out**, *etc*) *informal* to move in a lively or agile way in the specified direction. ► *noun* **1** an act of hopping; a jump on one leg. **2** *informal* a distance travelled in an aeroplane without stopping; a short journey by air. **3** *old use, informal* an informal dance. [Anglo-Saxon *hoppian* to dance]

IDIOMS **catch sb on the hop** *informal* to catch them unawares or by surprise. **hop it** *Brit slang* to take oneself off; to leave. **hopping mad** *informal* very angry or furious. **on the hop** in a state of restless activity.

hop² *noun* **1** a climbing plant of the mulberry family, grown for its green cone-shaped female flowers, which are used to give a bitter flavour to beer. **2** (*usu* **hops**) **a** the female flower of this plant, used in brewing and in medicine; **b** *US slang* any narcotic drug, esp opium. ► *verb* (***hopped, hopping***) **1** *intr* to pick or gather hops. **2** to flavour (beer) with hops. [15c as *hoppe*, from Dutch]

hope *noun* **1** a desire for something, with some confidence or expectation of success. **2** a person, thing or event that gives one good reason for hope. **3** a reason for justifying the belief that the thing desired will still occur. **4** something desired or hoped for. ► *verb* **1** (*also* **hope for sth**) to wish or desire that something may happen, esp with some reason to believe that it will. **2** *intr* to have confidence. [Anglo-Saxon *hopa*]

hopeful *adj* **1** feeling, or full of, hope. **2** having qualities that excite hope. **3** likely to succeed; promising. ► *noun* a person, esp a young one, who is ambitious or expected to succeed. ▪ **hopefulness** *noun.*

hopefully *adv* **1** in a hopeful way: *He waited hopefully for the weather to improve.* **2** *informal* it is to be hoped, if all goes according to plan: *Hopefully, I'll see him tomorrow.*

hopeless *adj* **1** without hope. **2** having no reason or cause to expect a good outcome or success. **3** *informal* having no ability; incompetent: *He is hopeless at maths.* **4** of a disease, etc: incurable. **5** of a problem: unresolvable. ▪ **hopelessly** *adv.* ▪ **hopelessness** *noun.*

hopper[1] *noun* **1** a person, animal or insect that hops. **2** *esp US* a grasshopper. **3** a funnel-like device used to feed material into a container below it, or on to the ground.

hopper[2] *noun* a person or machine that picks hops.

hopscotch *noun* a children's game in which players take turns at throwing a stone into one of a series of squares marked on the ground, and hopping in the others around it in order to fetch it. [Early 19c: **hop**[1] + **scotch**]

horde *noun* **1** *often derog* a huge crowd or multitude, esp a noisy one. **2** a group of nomads. [16c: from Turkish *ordu* camp]

---

horde, hoard

Be careful not to use the spelling **horde** when you mean **hoard**:

a hoard of old comics

---

horizon *noun* **1** the line at which the Earth and the sky seem to meet. **2** the limit of a person's knowledge, interests or experience. [14c: from Greek *horizon kyklos* limiting circle, from *horizein* to limit]

IDIOMS **on the horizon** about to happen, etc.

horizontal *adj* **1** at right angles to vertical. **2** relating to or parallel to the horizon; level or flat. **3** measured in the plane of the horizon. ▸ *noun* a horizontal line, position or object. ▪ **horizontally** *adv.* [16c: French]

hormone *noun* **1** a substance secreted by an endocrine gland, and carried in the bloodstream to organs and tissues in the body, where it performs a specific physiological action. **2** an artificially manufactured chemical compound that has the same function as such a substance. **3** a substance in plants that influences their growth and development. ▪ **hormonal** *adj.* [Early 20c: from Greek *horman* to stimulate]

hormone replacement therapy *noun, med* (abbrev **HRT**) a treatment rectifying an imbalance in hormone levels, used esp for post-menopausal women lacking oestrogen. [20c]

horn *noun* **1** one of a pair of hard hollow outgrowths, usu pointed, on the heads of many ruminant animals, such as cattle, sheep, etc. **2** any similar structure growing on the head of another animal, such as the growth on the snout of a rhinoceros, a male deer's antlers, or a snail's tentacle. **3** the bony substance (**keratin**) of which horns are made. **4** something resembling a horn in shape. **5** a horn-shaped area of land or sea. **6** an object made of horn, or an equivalent of horn, eg a drinking vessel. **7** *music* a wind instrument orig made from horn, now usu made of brass, specifically: **a** *Brit* a **French horn**; **b** *jazz* any wind instrument. **8** an apparatus for making a warning sound, esp on motor vehicles. **9** *US slang* a telephone. ▸ *verb* **1** to fit with a horn or horns. **2** to injure or gore with a horn or horns. ▸ *adj* made of horn. ▪ **horned** *adj* having a horn or horns, or something shaped like a horn. ▪ **horny** *adj* (***-ier, -iest***) relating to or resembling horn, esp in hardness. [Anglo-Saxon]

IDIOMS **on the horns of a dilemma** having to make a choice between two equally undesirable alternatives. **pull** *or* **draw in one's horns 1** to control one's strong emotions. **2** to restrict or confine one's activities, esp spending, etc.

hornbeam *noun* a tree similar to a beech, with hard tough wood. [16c: so called because of its hard wood]

hornblende *noun* a dark green or black mineral that is a major component of many metamorphic and igneous rocks. [18c: German, from *Horn* horn + **blende**]

hornet *noun* a large social wasp, with a brown and yellow striped body. [Anglo-Saxon *hyrnet*]

IDIOMS **stir up a hornets' nest** to do something that causes trouble or hostile reactions.

horn of plenty see **cornucopia** (sense 2)

hornpipe *noun* **1** a lively solo jig, conventionally regarded as popular amongst sailors. **2** a tune for this dance. [14c]

horology *noun* the art of measuring time or of making clocks, watches, etc. ▪ **horological** *adj.* ▪ **horologist** *noun.* [19c: from Greek *hora* hour]

horoscope *noun* **1** an astrologer's prediction of someone's future based on the position of the stars and planets at the time of their birth. **2** a map or diagram showing the positions of the stars and planets at a particular moment in time. ▪ **horoscopic** *adj.* ▪ **horoscopy** *noun.* [16c: from Greek *hora* hour + *skopos* observer]

horrendous *adj* causing great shock, fear or terror; dreadful or horrifying. [17c: from Latin *horrere* to shudder]

horrible *adj* **1** causing horror, dread or fear. **2** *informal* unpleasant, detestable or foul. ▪ **horribleness** *noun.* ▪ **horribly** *adv.* [14c: from Latin *horribilis*]

horrid *adj* **1** revolting; detestable or nasty. **2** *informal* unpleasant; distasteful. **3** spiteful or inconsiderate. [16c: from Latin *horridus*]

horrific *adj* **1** causing horror; terrible or frightful. **2** *informal* very bad; awful. ▪ **horrifically** *adv.* [17c: from Latin *horror* horror+ *facere* to make]

horrify *verb* (***-ies, -ied***) to shock greatly; to cause a reaction of horror. ▪ **horrified** *adj.* ▪ **horrifying** *adj.* [18c: from Latin *horror* **horror**+ *facere* to make]

horror *noun* **1** intense fear, loathing or disgust. **2** intense dislike or hostility. **3** someone or something causing horror. **4** *informal* a bad, distasteful or ridiculous person or thing. ▸ *adj* of literature, films, etc: depicting horrifying, frightening or bloodcurdling events: *a horror film.* [14c: Latin, meaning 'a shudder with fear']

horror-stricken *or* **horror-struck** *adj* shocked, horrified or dismayed.

hors de combat /*French* ɔʀdəkɔ̃ba/ ▸ *adv* **1** unfit to fight. **2** no longer in the running. [18c: French, literally 'out of the fight']

hors d'oeuvre /ɔː ˈdɜːvr/ *noun* (*pl* ***hors d'oeuvre*** *or* ***hors d'oeuvres***) a savoury appetizer, usu served at the beginning of a meal, to whet the appetite. [18c: French, literally 'out of the work']

horse *noun* **1** a large hoofed mammal, with a long neck, a mane and long legs. **2** an adult male of this species. **3** cavalry. **4** *gymnastics* a piece of apparatus used for vaulting over, etc. **5** *in compounds* any of various types of supporting apparatus: *clothes-horse* • *saw-horse*. **6** *slang* heroin. [Anglo-Saxon as *hors*]

IDIOMS **hold your horses** wait a moment; not so fast or hasty. **straight from the horse's mouth** directly from a well-informed and reliable source.

PHRASAL VERBS **horse about** *or* **around** *informal* to fool about.

horseback *noun* the back of a horse.

IDIOMS **on horseback** mounted on or riding a horse.

horsebox *noun* a closed trailer pulled by a car or train, designed to carry horses.

horse chestnut see under **chestnut**

horsefly *noun* a large biting fly, especially troublesome to horses.

horsehair *noun* hair from the mane or tail of a horse, formerly used as padding or stuffing.

horseman *or* **horsewoman** *noun* **1** a horse rider. **2** a person skilled in riding and managing horses. ▪ **horsemanship** *noun*.

horseplay *noun* rough boisterous play.

horsepower *noun* (abbrev **HP** *or* **hp**) **1** an imperial unit of power, replaced in the SI system by the watt, with one horsepower equal to 745.7 watts. **2** the power of a vehicle's engine so expressed.

horseradish *noun* a plant with a pungent root, which is crushed and used to make a savoury sauce.

horse sense *noun, informal* plain common sense.

horseshoe *noun* **1** a piece of curved iron nailed to the bottom of a horse's hoof to protect the foot. **2** anything shaped like a horseshoe, esp as a symbol of good luck.

horse-trading *noun* hard bargaining.

horsewhip *noun* a long whip, used for driving or managing horses. ▸ *verb* to beat, esp severely, with a horsewhip.

horsey *or* **horsy** *adj* (**-ier, -iest**) **1** referring or relating to horses. **2** *often derog* of people: like a horse, esp in appearance. **3** *Brit informal* very interested in or devoted to horses, or to racing or breeding them. ▪ **horsiness** *noun*.

hortative *or* **hortatory** *adj* giving advice or encouragement. [16c: from Latin *hortari* to incite to action]

horticulture *noun* **1** the intensive cultivation of fruit, vegetables, flowers and ornamental shrubs. **2** the art of gardening or cultivation. ▪ **horticultural** *adj*. ▪ **horticulturist** *noun*. [17c: from Latin *hortus* garden + *cultura* cultivation]

hosanna *noun, exclam* a shout of adoration and praise to God. [Anglo-Saxon *osanna*: from Hebrew *hoshiah nna* save now, I pray]

hose¹ *noun* (*also* **hosepipe**) a flexible tube for conveying water, eg for watering plants. ▸ *verb* (*often* **hose down**) to water, clean or soak with a hose. [Anglo-Saxon *hosa*]

hose² *noun* (***hose*** *or* (*archaic*) ***hosen***) a covering for the legs and feet, such as stockings, socks and tights. [Anglo-Saxon *hosa*]

hosier *noun* a person who makes or deals in hosiery. [15c]

hosiery *noun* **1** stockings, socks and tights collectively. **2** knitted underwear. [18c]

hospice *noun* **1** a home that specializes in the care of the sick, esp the terminally ill. **2** *hist* a **hospital** (sense 3). [19c: from Latin *hospes* guest]

hospitable *adj* **1** generous and welcoming towards guests. **2** showing kindness to strangers. ▪ **hospitableness** *noun*. ▪ **hospitably** *adv*. [16c: from Latin *hospes* guest]

hospital *noun* **1** an institution, staffed by doctors and nurses, for the treatment and care of people who are sick or injured. **2** *archaic* a charitable institution providing shelter for the old and destitute, and education for the young. **3** *hist* a hostel offering lodging and entertainment for travellers, esp one kept by monks or a religious order. [13c: from Latin *hospes* guest]

hospitality *noun* (**-ies**) the friendly welcome and entertainment of guests or strangers, which usu includes offering them food and drink. [14c: from Latin *hospes* guest]

hospitalize *or* **-ise** *verb* **1** to take or admit (someone) to hospital for treatment. **2** to injure (someone) so badly that hospital treatment is necessary. ▪ **hospitalization** *noun*. [Early 20c]

hospitaller *or* (*US*) **hospitaler** *noun* **1** a member of a religious order that does charity work, esp for the sick in hospitals. **2** (**Hospitaller**) a member of the Knights of St John, an order founded when it built a hospital for pilgrims in Jerusalem in the 11c. [14c: from Latin *hospes* guest]

host¹ *noun* **1** someone who entertains someone. **2** *old use* an innkeeper or publican. **3** someone who introduces performers and participants, chairs discussions and debates, etc on a TV or radio show. **4** *biol* a plant or animal on which a parasite lives. **5** *med* the recipient of a tissue graft or organ transplant. **6** *comput* a computer in control of a multi-terminal computer system. **7** *comput* a computer attached to a multi-computer network and able to provide access to a number of databases. ▸ *verb* to be the host of (an event, programme, show, etc). [13c: from French *hoste*, from Latin *hospes* guest]

host² *noun* **1** a very large number; a multitude. **2** *old use* an army. [13c: from French *hoste*, from Latin *hostis* enemy]

host³ *noun, RC Church* the consecrated bread of the Eucharist, used in a Holy Communion service. [14c: from French *oiste*, from Latin *hostia* victim]

hostage *noun* **1** someone who is held prisoner as a guarantee or security that the captor's demands and conditions are carried out and fulfilled. **2** the condition of being a hostage. **3** any guarantee or security. [13c: from French *otâge*, from Latin *obses*]

hostel *noun* **1** a residence providing shelter for the homeless, esp one run for charitable rather than for profitable purposes. **2** a residence for students, nurses, etc. **3** a **youth hostel**. [13c: French, from Latin *hospes* guest]

hosteller *or* (*US*) **hosteler** *noun* **1** someone who lives in or regularly uses a hostel, esp a youth hostel. **2** *archaic* the keeper of a hostel or inn. [13c: from French *hostelier*]

hostelling *noun* the use of youth hostels when on holiday.

hostelry *noun* (**-ies**) *old use, now facetious* an inn or public house. [14c: a variant of French *hostellerie*]

hostess *noun* **1** a female host. **2** a woman employed as a man's companion for the evening at a nightclub, dance hall, etc. **3** *old use* an air hostess. [13c: from French *ostesse*]

hostile *adj* **1** expressing enmity, aggression or angry opposition. **2** relating or belonging to an enemy. **3** resistant or strongly opposed to something. **4** of a place, conditions, atmosphere, etc: harsh, forbidding or inhospitable. [16c: from Latin *hostis* enemy]

hostility *noun* (**-ies**) **1** enmity, aggression or angry opposition. **2** (**hostilities**) acts of warfare; battles. [14c: from Latin *hostilitas*]

hot *adj* (***hotter, hottest***) **1** having or producing a great deal of heat; having a high temperature. **2** having a higher temperature than is normal or desirable. **3** of food: spicy or fiery. **4** easily made angry; excitable or passionate: *a hot temper.* **5** *slang* of a person: very attractive. **6** of a contest or fight: intense and animated. **7** of news: recent, fresh and of particular interest. **8** strongly favoured: *a hot favourite.* **9** of jazz music: having strong and exciting rhythms, with complex improvisations. **10** of a colour: bright and fiery. **11** *slang* of goods: recently stolen or illegally acquired. **12** of a scent in hunting: fresh and strong, suggesting the quarry is not far ahead. **13** *slang* of information: up-to-date and reliable: *a hot tip.* **14** *informal* of a situation: difficult, unpleasant, or dangerous: *make life hot for him.* **15** *slang* highly radioactive. **16** in certain games, etc: very close to guessing the answer or finding the person or thing sought. ▸ *adv* in a hot way; hotly: *a dish served hot.* ▸ *verb* (***hotted, hotting***) *informal* to heat. ▪ **hotly** *adv.* ▪ **hotness** *noun.* [Anglo-Saxon *hat*]

IDIOMS **go** *or* **sell like hot cakes** to sell or disappear rapidly; to be extremely popular. **hot and bothered** *informal* anxious and confused; agitated. **hot on sth** interested in, skilled at or well-informed about it. **hot on the heels of sb** *informal* following or pursuing them closely. **hot under the collar** *informal* indignant or annoyed; uncomfortable. **in hot pursuit** chasing as fast or as closely as one can.

PHRASAL VERBS **hot up** *or* **hot sth up** to increase in excitement, energy, danger, etc.

hot air *noun, informal* empty, unsubstantial or boastful talk.

hotbed *noun* **1** a glass-covered bed of earth heated by a layer of fermenting manure, to encourage rapid plant growth. **2** a place where something, esp something undesirable, flourishes: *a hotbed of discontent.*

hot-blooded *adj* having strong and passionate feelings; high-spirited.

hot chocolate see **chocolate** (sense 2)

hotchpotch *or* **hodgepodge** *noun* **1** a confused mass or jumble. **2** a mutton stew, containing many different vegetables. [15c: from French *hochepot*]

hot cross bun *noun* a fruit bun marked with a pastry cross on top, customarily eaten on Good Friday.

hot dog *noun* a sausage in a long soft bread roll.

hotel *noun* a commercial building providing accommodation, meals and other services to visitors for payment. [17c: from French *hostel*, from Latin *hospes* guest]

hotelier /hoʊ'tɛlɪeɪ/ *noun* a person who owns or manages a hotel.

hotfoot *informal, adv* in haste; as fast as possible. ▸ *verb* (*usu* **hotfoot it**) to rush or hasten.

hothead *noun* **1** an easily angered or agitated person. **2** an impetuous or headstrong person. ▪ **hotheaded** *adj.* ▪ **hotheadedness** *noun.*

hothouse *noun* **1** a greenhouse that is kept warm for growing tender or tropical plants. **2** any establishment or environment promoting rapid growth or development, eg of skills, ideas, etc.

hot key *noun, comput* a key that activates a program when pressed, either alone or in combination with other keys.

hotline *noun* **1** a direct and exclusive telephone link, eg, between leaders of governments, allowing prompt communication in an emergency. **2** an emergency telephone number for inquiries about a particular incident, accident, etc.

hotplate *noun* **1** the flat top surface of a cooker on which food is cooked. **2** a portable heated surface for keeping food, dishes, etc hot.

hotpot *noun* chopped meat and vegetables, seasoned and covered with sliced potatoes, and cooked slowly in a sealed pot.

hot potato *noun, informal* a difficult or controversial problem or situation.

hot rod *noun* a motor car modified for extra speed by increasing the engine power.

the hot seat *noun* **1** *informal* an uncomfortable or difficult situation. **2** *N Am slang* the electric chair.

hotshot *noun, chiefly US* a person who is, often boastfully or pretentiously, successful or skilful.

hot spot *noun* **1** an area with higher than normal temperature, eg, in an engine, etc. **2** *informal* a popular or trendy nightclub. **3** an area of potential trouble or conflict. **4** *geog* an area of the earth where there is isolated volcanic activity due to hot material rising up through the mantle.

hot spring *noun* a spring of water heated naturally underground.

hot-tempered *adj* easily angered or provoked.

hot water *noun, informal* trouble; bother: *get into hot water.*

hot-water bottle *noun* a container, usu made of rubber, filled with hot water and used to warm a bed. [19c]

hot-wire *verb, informal* to start (a vehicle engine) by touching electrical wires together, rather than using the ignition switch.

houdah see **howdah**

hoummos *or* **houmus** see **hummus**

hound *noun* **1** *informal* a dog. **2** a type of dog used in hunting. **3** an assiduous hunter, tracker or seeker of anything. **4** *informal* a despicable or contemptible man. **5** *often in compounds* **a** a hunting dog: *foxhound*; **b** an addict or devotee: *newshound.* **6** (**the hounds**) a pack of foxhounds. ▸ *verb* **1** to chase or bother relentlessly. **2** to set or urge on in chase. [Anglo-Saxon *hund*]

houndstooth *noun* a textile pattern of small broken checks. Also called **dog's-tooth**.

hour *noun* **1** sixty minutes, or a twenty-fourth part of a day. **2** the time indicated by a clock or watch. **3** an occasion or a point in time: *an early hour.* **4** a special occasion or point in time: *his finest hour.* **5** (**hours**) the time allowed or fixed for a specified activity: *of-*

fice hours. **6** the distance travelled in an hour: *two hours away from the airport.* **7** a time for action: *The hour has come.* **8** (**hours**) **canonical hours**. [13c: from Greek *hora*]

IDIOMS **after hours** after the usual opening or working hours. **at all hours** at irregular times, esp late at night. **at the eleventh hour** at the last or latest moment. **on the hour** at exactly one, two, etc, o'clock: *The train departs on the hour.* **out of hours** before or after usual working hours.

hourglass *noun* an instrument that measures time, consisting of two reversible glass containers connected by a narrow glass tube, and filled with sand that takes a specified time, not necessarily an hour, to pass from one container to the other.

houri /'hʊərɪ/ *noun* **1** a nymph in the Muslim Paradise. **2** any voluptuous and beautiful young woman. [18c: from Arabic *hur*, pl of *haura* gazelle-eyed]

hourly *adj* **1** happening or done every hour. **2** measured by the hour: *an hourly wage.* **3** frequent or constant: *live in hourly fear of discovery.* ▸ *adv* **1** every hour. **2** frequently.

house *noun* /haʊs/ **1** a building in which people, esp a single family, live. **2** the people living in such a building. **3** an inn or public house. **4** *in compounds* a building used for a specified purpose: *an opera-house.* **5** a business firm: *a publishing house.* **6** the audience in a theatre, a theatre itself or a performance given there. **7** (*often* **the House**) the legislative body that governs a country, esp either chamber in a bicameral system. **8** (**the House**) **a** in Oxford: Christ Church College; **b** in London: the Stock Exchange; **c** in London: the Houses of Parliament. **9** (**House**) a family, esp a noble or royal one: *the House of Hanover.* **10** *astrol* one of the twelve divisions of the heavens. **11** *Brit* one of several divisions of pupils at a large school. **12** **a** a college or university building in which students live; **b** a building at a boarding-school in which pupils live. **13** a building in which members of a religious community live; a convent. **14** **house music**. ▸ *verb* /haʊz/ **1** to provide with a house or similar shelter. **2** to store. **3** to protect by covering. [Anglo-Saxon *hus*]

IDIOMS **bring the house down** *informal* to evoke loud applause in a theatre; to be a great success. **keep house** to manage a household. **keep open house** to be hospitable or provide entertainment for all visitors. **like a house on fire** *informal* **1** very well: *They get on like a house on fire.* **2** very quickly. **on the house** of food, drink, etc: at the expense of the manager or owner; free of charge. **put** *or* **set one's house in order** to organize or settle one's affairs.

house arrest *noun* confinement in one's own home instead of imprisonment.

houseboat *noun* a barge or boat, usu stationary, with a deck-cabin designed and built for living in.

housebound *adj* confined to one's house because of illness, carer's duties, etc.

housebreaking *noun* the act or process of unlawfully breaking into and entering a house or building with the intention to steal. ▪ **housebreaker** *noun.*

housecoat *noun* a woman's long loose garment similar to a dressing-gown, worn in the home.

house guest *noun* a guest staying in a private house, usu for several nights.

household *noun* **1** the people who live together in a house, making up a family. **2** (**the Household**) the royal domestic establishment or household. ▸ *adj* relating to the house or family living there; domestic.

householder *noun* **1** the owner or tenant of a house. **2** the head of a family or household.

household name *or* **household word** *noun* a familiar name, word or saying.

house husband *noun* a man who looks after the house and family instead of having a paid job. [1950s: orig US]

housekeeper *noun* a person who is paid to manage a household's domestic arrangements.

housekeeping *noun* **1** the management of a household's domestic arrangements. **2** money set aside to pay for this. **3** *comput* operations carried out on or within a computer program or system ensuring its efficient functioning.

house lights *plural noun* the lights that illuminate the auditorium of a cinema, theatre, etc.

housemaid *noun* a maid employed to keep a house clean and tidy.

houseman *noun* a recently qualified doctor holding a junior resident post in a hospital to complete their training.

housemaster *or* **housemistress** *noun* in Britain: a male or female teacher in charge of a house in a school, esp a boarding-school.

house music *noun* a style of dance music that features a strong beat in 4/4 time and often incorporates edited fragments of other recordings. Often shortened to **house**. [1980s]

the House of Commons *noun* in the UK and Canada: the lower, elected assembly in parliament.

house of God, **house of prayer** *or* **house of worship** *noun* a place of worship and prayer.

the House of Lords *noun* in the UK: the unelected upper assembly in parliament, made up of peers and bishops.

houseparent *noun* a man or woman in charge of children in an institution.

houseplant *noun* a plant grown indoors.

house-proud *adj* taking an often excessive amount of pride in the appearance of one's house.

houseroom *noun*

IDIOMS **not give sth houseroom** to refuse to have anything to do with it.

house-sit *verb, intr* to look after someone's house by living in it while they are away. ▪ **housesitter** *noun.*

housetrain *verb* to train (a puppy, kitten, etc) to urinate and defecate outside or in a special tray, etc. ▪ **housetrained** *adj.*

house-warming *noun* a party given to celebrate moving into a new house.

housewife *noun* **1** a woman who looks after the house and family and who often does not have a paid job outside the home. **2** /'hʌzɪf/ a pocket sewing-kit. ▪ **housewifery** *noun.* [13c]

housework *noun* the work involved in keeping a house clean and tidy.

housing *verb, present participle of* **house**. ▸ *noun* **1** houses and accommodation collectively. **2** the act, or process of providing living accommodation. **3**

anything designed to cover, contain or protect machinery, etc.

housing estate *noun* a planned residential estate, esp one built by a local authority.

housing scheme *noun, Scot* a local-authority housing estate.

hove see **heave**

hovel *noun* a small, dirty, run-down dwelling. [15c]

hover *verb, intr* **1** of a bird, helicopter, etc: to remain in the air without moving in any direction. **2** (*also* **hover about, around** *or* **round**) to linger, esp anxiously or nervously (near someone or something). **3** to be or remain undecided (usu between two options). ▸ *noun* **1** an act or state of hovering. **2** a condition of uncertainty or indecision. [14c: from English *hoveren*]

hovercraft *noun* a vehicle that is able to move over land or water, supported by a cushion of air.

hoverfly *noun* a wasp-like fly that hovers and feeds on pollen and nectar.

how *adv* **1** in what way; by what means: *How did it happen?* **2** to what extent: *How old is he?* • *How far is it?* **3** in what condition, esp of health: *How is she feeling now?* **4** to what extent or degree is something good, successful, etc: *How was your holiday?* **5** for what cause or reason; why: *How can you behave like that?* **6** using whatever means are necessary: *Do it how best you can.* ▸ *conj* **1** *informal* that: *He told me how he'd done it on his own.* **2** in which manner or condition: *How did you get there?* ▸ *noun* a manner or means of doing something: *The hows and whys of it.* [Anglo-Saxon *hu*]

IDIOMS **how about** would you like; what do you think of: *How about another piece of cake?* • *How about going to see a film?* **how are you?** a conventional greeting to someone, sometimes referring specifically to their state of health. **how come?** *informal* for what reason?; how does that come about?: *How come you're not going tomorrow?* **how do you do?** a formal greeting to a person one is meeting for the first time. **how's that? 1** what is your opinion of that? **2** *cricket* an appeal to the umpire to give the batsman out. Also written **howzat**.

howdah *or* **houdah** *noun* a seat, usu with a sunshade, used for riding on an elephant's back. [18c: from Arabic *haudaj*]

howdy *exclam, N Am, informal* hello. [16c: a colloquial form of *how do you do?*]

however *adv, conj* **1** in spite of that; nevertheless. **2** *informal* esp implying surprise: in what way; by what means: *However did you do that?* **3** by whatever means: *Do it however you like.* **4** to no matter what extent: *You must finish this however long it takes.* [14c]

howitzer *noun* a short heavy gun that fires shells high in the air and at a steep angle, esp used in trench warfare. [17c: from Czech *houfnice* sling, catapult]

howl *noun* **1** a long mournful cry of a wolf or dog. **2** a long loud cry made by the wind, etc. **3** a prolonged cry of pain or distress. **4** a loud peal of laughter. **5** *electronics* a vibrant sound made by loudspeakers caused by feedback. ▸ *verb, intr* **1** to make a howl. **2** to laugh or cry loudly. [14c]

PHRASAL VERBS **howl sb down** to prevent a speaker from being heard by shouting loudly and angrily.

howler *noun* **1** the largest of the S American monkeys, with black, brown or reddish fur. **2** *informal* an outrageous and amusing blunder.

howling *adj, informal* very great; tremendous: *a howling success.*

howzat see **how's that?** at **how**

hoy *or* **hoi** *exclam* used to attract someone's attention. [14c variant of **hey**]

hoyden *noun* a wild lively girl; a tomboy. ▪ **hoydenish** *adj.* [16c: from Dutch *heyden* boor]

HP *or* **hp** *abbrev* **1** high pressure. **2** *Brit* hire purchase. **3** horsepower.

HQ *or* **hq** *abbrev* headquarters.

HR *abbrev* Human Resources.

hr *abbrev* hour.

HRH *abbrev* His or Her Royal Highness.

HRT *abbrev* hormone replacement therapy.

Hs *symbol, chem* hassium.

http *abbrev* in Internet addresses: hypertext transfer protocol.

hub *noun* **1** the centre of a wheel. **2** the focal point of activity, interest, discussion, etc. **3** *comput* a device on a server that connects the parts of a network. [17c: perhaps a variant of **hob**]

hubbub *noun* **1** a confused noise of many sounds, esp voices. **2** uproar; commotion. [16c: perhaps Irish; compare Scottish Gaelic *ub! ub!* an exclamation expressing contempt]

hubby *noun* (**-ies**) *informal* an affectionate contraction of **husband**. [17c]

hubcap *noun* the metal covering over the hub of a wheel.

hubris /ˈhjuːbrɪs/ *noun* arrogance or excessive confidence, esp when likely to result in disaster or ruin. ▪ **hubristic** *adj.* ▪ **hubristically** *adv.* [19c: from Greek *hybris*]

huckleberry *noun* **1** a low-growing American woodland plant. **2** its dark blue or blackish fruit. [17c: prob a variant of American *hurtleberry* whortleberry]

huckster *noun* **1** *old use* a street trader; a hawker or pedlar. **2** an aggressive seller. **3** a mercenary person. ▸ *verb* **1** *intr* to hawk or peddle (goods, etc). **2** to sell aggressively. **3** *intr* to haggle meanly. [12c as *huccstere*, from Dutch *hoekster*]

huddle *verb* **1** *tr & intr* (*usu* **huddle together** *or* **up**) to nestle or crowd closely, eg because of cold. **2** *intr* to sit curled up or curl oneself up. ▸ *noun* **1** a confused mass or crowd. **2** *informal* a secret or private conference: *go into a huddle.* **3** a gathering together of esp football players during a game, in order to receive instructions, etc. [16c: from *hoder* to wrap up, prob related to **hide**[1]]

hue *noun* **1** a colour, tint or shade. **2** the feature of a colour that distinguishes it from other colours. **3** a view or aspect. [Anglo-Saxon *hiw*]

hue and cry *noun* a loud public protest or uproar. [16c]

huff *noun* a fit of anger, annoyance or offended dignity: *in a huff.* ▸ *verb* **1** *intr* to blow or puff loudly. **2** *tr & intr* to give or take offence. **3** *draughts* to remove (an opponent's piece) for failing to capture one's own piece. [16c: imitating the sound of blowing or puffing loudly]

IDIOMS **huffing and puffing** loud empty threats or objections.

huffy *or* **huffish** *adj* (**-ier, -iest**) **1** offended. **2** easily offended; touchy. ▪ **huffily** *or* **huffishly** *adv*. ▪ **huffiness** *noun*.

hug *verb* (***hugged, hugging***) **1** *tr & intr* to hold tightly in one's arms, esp to show love. **2** to keep close to something: *The ship was hugging the shore.* **3** to hold or cherish (a belief, etc) very firmly. ▸ *noun* **1** a tight grasp with the arms; a close embrace. **2** *wrestling* a squeezing type of grip. [16c: perhaps from Norse *hugga* to soothe]

huge *adj* very large or enormous. ▪ **hugely** *adv*. ▪ **hugeness** *noun*. [13c: from French *ahuge*]

hugger-mugger *noun* **1** confusion or disorder. **2** secrecy. ▸ *adj, adv* **1** secret; in secret. **2** confused; in confusion or disorder. [16c: from *mokeren* to hoard]

Huguenot /ˈhjuːɡənoʊ, -nɒt/ *noun* a French Protestant, especially of the 16c or 17c. *adj* relating or belonging to the Huguenots. [16c: perhaps from *Hugues* a Genevan political leader + French *eidgenot*, from Swiss German *Eidgenoss* confederate]

huh *exclam, informal* expressing disgust, disbelief or inquiry. [17c]

hula *or* **hula-hula** *noun* a Hawaiian dance in which the dancer, usu a woman, sways their hips and moves their arms gracefully. [19c: Hawaiian]

hula hoop *noun* a light hoop, usu made of plastic, which is kept spinning round the waist by a swinging movement of the hips.

hulk *noun* **1** the dismantled body of an old ship. **2** a ship that is or looks unwieldy or difficult to steer. **3** *derog, informal* a large, awkward and ungainly person or thing. **4** *hist* the body of an old ship used as a prison. [Anglo-Saxon *hulc*]

hulking *adj, informal* big and clumsy.

hull[1] *noun* **1** the frame or body of a ship or airship. **2** the armoured body of a tank, missile, rocket, etc. [14c: prob from **hull[2]**]

hull[2] *noun* **1** the outer covering or husk of certain fruit and seeds, esp the pods of beans and peas. **2** the calyx of a strawberry, etc. ▸ *verb* to remove the hulls from (strawberries, etc). [Anglo-Saxon *hulu* husk]

hullabaloo *noun, informal* an uproar or clamour. [18c: a rhyming compound derived from Scottish *baloo* lullaby]

hullo see **hello**

hum *verb* (***hummed, humming***) **1** *intr* to make a low, steady murmuring sound similar to that made by a bee. **2** *tr & intr* to sing (a tune) with closed lips. **3** *intr* to speak indistinctly or stammer, esp through embarrassment or hesitation. **4** *intr, informal* to be full of activity: *The whole building was humming.* **5** *intr, slang* to have an unpleasant smell or odour. ▸ *noun* **1** a humming sound. **2** an inarticulate sound or murmur. **3** *slang* a bad smell. [14c: imitating the sound]

IDIOMS **hum and haw** *or* **hum and ha** to make inarticulate sounds expressing doubt, uncertainty or hesitation; to hesitate.

human *adj* **1** relating or belonging to people. **2** having or showing the qualities and limitations typical of a person. **3** having or showing the better qualities of people, eg in being kind, thoughtful, etc. ▸ *noun* a human being. ▪ **humanness** *noun*. See also **humanity**. [14c: from Latin *humanus*, from *homo* man; by 18c the forms *human* and *humane* began to be differentiated]

human being *noun* a member of the human race.

humane *adj* **1** kind and sympathetic. **2** of a killing: done with as little pain and suffering as possible. **3** of a branch of learning: aiming to civilize and make more elegant and polite. ▪ **humanely** *adv*.

human immunodeficiency virus see **HIV**

human interest *adj* of newspaper articles, broadcasts, etc: featuring events in people's lives and the emotions related to them.

humanism *noun* a system of thought that rejects the divine, the supernatural, etc, in favour of the notion that human beings are paramount, esp in their capability to decide what is or is not moral. ▪ **humanist** *noun*.

humanitarian *adj* concerned with improving people's lives and welfare: *humanitarian aid.* ▸ *noun* a person who tries to improve the quality of people's lives by means of reform, charity, etc; a philanthropist. ▪ **humanitarianism** *noun*. [19c]

humanity *noun* (**-ies**) **1** humans as a species or a collective group. **2** typical human nature. **3** the typical qualities of human beings, eg kindness, mercy, etc. **4** (**humanities**) the subjects involving the study of human culture, esp language, literature, philosophy, and Latin and Greek. [14c: from French *humanité*, from Latin *humanitas*]

humanize *or* **-ise** *verb* **1** to render, make or become human. **2** to make humane. ▪ **humanization** *noun*. [17c]

humankind *noun* **1** the human species. **2** people generally or collectively.

humanly *adv* **1** in a human or humane way. **2** by human agency or means. **3** with regard to human limitations: *if it is humanly possible.*

humanoid *noun* **1** any of the ancestors from which modern human beings are descended and to which they are more closely related than to **anthropoid**s. **2** an animal or machine with human characteristics. [Early 20c: from **human** + Greek *eidos* shape]

human resources *plural noun* **1** people collectively in terms of their skills, training, knowledge, etc in the work place. **2** the workforce of an organization. Compare **personnel**.

human rights *plural noun* the rights every person has to justice, freedom, etc.

humble *adj* **1** having a low opinion of oneself and one's abilities, etc. **2** having a low position in society. **3** lowly, modest or unpretentious. ▸ *verb* **1** to make humble or modest. **2** to abase or degrade. ▪ **humbleness** *noun*. ▪ **humbling** *adj*. ▪ **humbly** *adv*. [13c: from Latin *humilis* low, from *humus* the ground]

humble pie *or* **umble pie** *noun* a pie made from deer offal. [17c: ultimately from 14c *numbles* the offal of a deer]

IDIOMS **eat humble pie** to be forced to humble or abase oneself, or to make a humble apology.

humbug *noun* **1** a trick or deception. **2** nonsense or rubbish. **3** an impostor or fraud. **4** *Brit* a hard, peppermint-flavoured sweet. [18c]

humdinger /hʌmˈdɪŋə(r)/ *noun, slang* an exceptionally good person or thing. [19c]

humdrum *adj* dull or monotonous; ordinary. [16c: a rhyming compound derived from **hum**]

humerus *noun* (***humeri*** /ˈhjuːməraɪ/) **1** the bone in the human upper arm. **2** the corresponding bone in vertebrates. ▪ **humeral** *adj*. [17c: from Latin *umerus* shoulder]

humid *adj* damp; moist. ▪ **humidly** *adv.* ▪ **humidness** *noun.* [16c: from Latin *umidus*]

humidifier *noun* a device for increasing or maintaining the humidity of a room, etc. [19c]

humidify *verb* (**-ies, -ied**) to make (eg the air or atmosphere) damp or humid. ▪ **humidification** *noun.* [19c]

humidity *noun* **1** the amount of water vapour in the atmosphere, usu expressed as a percentage. **2** moisture; dampness. [15c: from Latin *umiditas*]

humiliate *verb* to injure (someone's pride), or make (someone) feel ashamed or look foolish, esp in the presence of others. ▪ **humiliating** *adj.* ▪ **humiliatingly** *adv.* ▪ **humiliation** *noun.* [16c: from Latin *humiliatus*, from *humilis* humble]

humility *noun* (**-ies**) **1** the quality or state of being humble. **2** a lowly self-opinion; modesty or meekness. [13c: from French *humilité*, from Latin *humilis* humble]

hummingbird *noun* a small S American bird with brilliant plumage. [17c: so called because its wings beat so rapidly that they produce a low humming sound]

hummock *noun* a low hill; a hillock. ▪ **hummocky** *adj.* [16c]

hummus, hoummos *or* **houmus** /ˈhʊməs, ˈhʌ-/ *noun* a Middle-Eastern hors d'oeuvre or dip made from puréed cooked chickpeas, oil and tahini, flavoured with lemon juice and garlic. [1950s: Arabic, meaning 'chickpeas']

humongous *or* **humungous** *adj, informal* huge or enormous. [1960s: perhaps from *huge* + *monstrous*]

humoresque *noun* a humorous piece of music; a musical caprice. [19c: from German *humoreske*, from Latin *humor*]

humorist *noun* someone with a talent for talking or writing humorously. [16c: from French *humoriste*]

humorous *adj* **1** funny or amusing. **2** of a person, joke, etc: having the ability or quality to cause humour. ▪ **humorously** *adv.* ▪ **humorousness** *noun.* [16c]

humour *or* (*N Am*) **humor** *noun* **1** the quality of being amusing. **2** the ability to appreciate and enjoy something amusing. **3** a specified temperament or state of mind: *He is in good humour today.* **4** a specified type of fluid in the body: *aqueous humour.* **5** *old* any of the four bodily fluids formerly believed to determine a person's physical health and character. ▸ *verb* **1** to please or gratify someone by doing what they wish. **2** to adapt to eg the mood or ideas of someone else. ▪ **humourless** *adj.* [14c: from Latin *humor* liquid]

hump *noun* **1** a large rounded lump of fat on the back of a camel that serves as an energy store when food is scarce. **2** an abnormal curvature of the spine that gives the back a hunched appearance, due to spinal deformity. **3** a rounded raised area of a road, etc. **4** *Brit informal* a feeling of despondency or annoyance. ▸ *verb* **1** to hunch or bend in a hump. **2** (*usu* **hump about** *or* **around**) to shoulder or carry (esp something awkward or heavy) with difficulty. ▪ **humpy** *adj.* [18c]

IDIOMS **have** *or* **give sb the hump** to be in, or put someone in, a bad mood or sulk. **over the hump** *informal* past the crisis; over the worst.

humpback *noun* **1** a back with a hump or hunch. **2** someone whose back has a hump; a hunchback. **3** a whale with a fin on its back which forms a hump. ▪ **humpbacked** *adj.* [17c]

humph *exclam* expressing doubt, displeasure or hesitation. [17c: imitating a snorting sound]

humus /ˈhjuːməs/ *noun* dark-brown organic material produced in the topmost layer of soil due to the decomposition of plant and animal matter. [18c: Latin]

Humvee /ˈhʌmviː/ *noun* (***Humvees***) *US trademark* a military vehicle similar to but larger than a **Jeep**. [20c: altered from *HMMWV*, abbreviated form of *H*igh-*M*obility *M*ultipurpose *W*heeled *V*ehicle]

Hun *noun* (***Huns*** *or* ***Hun***) **1** *hist* a member of a powerful, warlike and nomadic people from Asia who, led by Attila, invaded and controlled Europe in the 4c and 5c. **2** a barbarian or vandal. [Anglo-Saxon *Hune*]

hunch *noun* **1** an idea, guess or belief based on feelings, suspicions or intuition rather than on actual evidence. **2** a hump. ▸ *verb* **1** to bend or arch; to hump. **2** *intr* (*also* **hunch up** *or* **over**) to sit with the body hunched or curled up. [16c]

hunchback *noun* someone with a large rounded lump on their back, due to spinal deformity. ▪ **hunchbacked** *adj.* [18c as *hunchback*; 16c as *hunchbacked*]

hundred *noun* (***hundreds*** *or after a number* ***hundred***) **1 a** the cardinal number 100; **b** the quantity that this represents, being ten times ten. **2** a numeral, figure or symbol representing this, eg *100* or *C*. **3** a set of a hundred people or things. **4** (**hundreds**) *informal* a large but indefinite number: *hundreds of people.* **5** (**hundreds**) *in compounds* the hundred years of a specified century: *the thirteen-hundreds.* **6** *hist* a division of an English county orig containing a hundred families. ▸ *adj* **1** totalling one hundred. **2** aged one hundred. **3** *informal* very many: *I've told you a hundred times to stop.* [Anglo-Saxon, from *hund* a hundred + suffix *-red* a reckoning]

IDIOMS **a** *or* **one hundred per cent** completely. **one, two,** *etc* **hundred hours** one, two, etc o'clock.

hundredfold *adj* **1** equal to one hundred times as much or many. **2** divided into, or consisting of, one hundred parts. ▸ *adv* by one hundred times as much.

hundredth *adj* **1** the last of one hundred people or things. **2** the hundredth position in a sequence of numbers. ▸ *noun* one of one hundred equal parts.

hundredweight *noun* (***hundredweight*** *or* ***hundredweights***) **1** *Brit* (abbrev **cwt**) a measure of weight equal to 112 pounds (50.8kg). Also called **long hundredweight**. **2** *N Am* (abbrev **cwt**) a measure of weight equal to 100 pounds (45.4kg). Also called **short hundredweight**. **3** a metric measure of weight equal to 50kg. Also called **metric hundredweight**.

hung *verb, past tense, past participle of* **hang**. ▸ *adj* of a parliament or jury: with neither side having a majority.

IDIOMS **be hung over** *informal* to be suffering from a hangover. See also **hangover**. **be hung up on** *or* **about sb** *or* **sth** *informal* **1** to be extremely anxious or upset about it **2** to be obsessed with them or it: *She is completely hung up on him.* See also **hang-up**.

hung, hanged

See the Usage Note at **hang**.

Hungarian *adj* **1** belonging or relating to Hungary, a republic in central Europe, or its inhabitants. **2** belonging or relating to the official language of Hungary, also spoken in parts of Romania, belonging to the Finno-Ugric language family. ▸ *noun* **1** a citizen or inhabitant of, or person born in, Hungary. **2** the Magyar or Hungarian language. See also **Magyar**.

hunger *noun* **1** the desire or need for food. **2** a strong desire for anything. ▸ *verb, intr* (*usu* **hunger for** *or* **after**) to crave. [Anglo-Saxon *hungor*]

hunger strike *noun* a prolonged refusal to eat, esp by a prisoner, as a form of protest. ▪ **hunger-striker** *noun*.

hungry *adj* (**-ier, -iest**) **1** having a need or craving for food. **2** (*usu* **hungry for**) having a great desire (for something): *He is hungry for success.* **3** eager; greedy: *hungry eyes.* ▪ **hungrily** *adv*. ▪ **hungriness** *noun*. [Anglo-Saxon *hungrig*]

IDIOMS **go hungry** to remain without food.

hunk *noun* **1** a lump or piece, sometimes broken or cut off from a larger piece. **2** *informal* a strong, muscular, attractive man. ▪ **hunky** *adj* (**-ier, -iest**). [19c: from Flemish *hunke*]

hunky-dory *adj, informal* of a situation, condition, etc: fine; excellent. [19c]

hunt *verb* **1** *tr & intr* to chase and kill (wild birds or animals) for food or sport. **2** *Brit* to hunt and kill (an animal, esp a fox) on horseback, using hounds. **3** to seek out and pursue game over (a certain area). **4** of an animal or bird: to search for and chase (its prey). **5** *mech* to oscillate around a middle point, or to vary in speed. ▸ *noun* **1** an act of hunting. **2** a group of people meeting together, often on horses, to hunt animals for sport, eg foxes. **3** a search. ▪ **hunting** *noun*. [Anglo-Saxon *huntian*]

PHRASAL VERBS **hunt sb** *or* **sth down 1** to pursue and capture them or it. **2** to persecute them or it out of existence. **hunt sb** *or* **sth out** *or* **up** to search or seek for them or it.

hunter *noun* **1 a** someone who hunts; **b** *esp in compounds* someone who seeks someone or something out: *bounty hunter.* **2** an animal that hunts (usu other animals) for food. **3** a horse used in hunting, esp fox-hunting. **4** a watch with a hinged metal cover to protect the glass over its face.

hunter-gatherer *noun, anthropol* a member of a society that lives by hunting animals from the land and sea, and by gathering wild plants.

huntress *noun* a female hunter.

huntsman *noun* **1** someone who hunts. **2** an official who manages the hounds during a fox-hunt.

hurdle *noun* **1** *athletics, horse-racing* one of a series of portable frames, hedges or barriers to be jumped in a race. **2** an obstacle, problem or difficulty to be overcome. **3** (**hurdles**) a race with hurdles. **4** a light frame with bars or wire across it, used as a temporary fence. ▸ *verb* **1** *tr & intr* to jump over (a hurdle in a race, an obstacle, etc). **2** to enclose with hurdles. ▪ **hurdler** *noun*. ▪ **hurdling** *noun*. [Anglo-Saxon *hyrdel*]

hurdy-gurdy *noun* (**-ies**) a musical instrument that makes a droning sound when a wheel is turned by a handle. Also called **barrel organ**. [18c: a variant of Scots *hirdy-girdy* uproar]

hurl *verb* **1** to fling violently. **2** to utter with force and spite: *hurl abuse.* ▸ *noun* an act of hurling. [13c]

hurling *or* **hurley** *noun* a traditional Irish game resembling hockey. [16c: from **hurl**]

hurly-burly *noun* noisy activity; confusion or uproar. [16c: from *hurling* and *burling*, a rhyming compound based on *hurling* in its obsolete meaning 'uproar']

hurrah *or* **hoorah** *exclam* a shout of joy, enthusiasm or victory. ▸ *noun* such a shout. Also **hooray** *and* **hurray**. [17c: from German *hurra*]

hurricane *noun* a cyclonic tropical storm of the N Atlantic or NE Pacific Ocean east of the International Date Line. Compare **typhoon**. [16c: from West Indian *huracán*]

hurricane lamp *noun* an oil lamp whose flame is enclosed in glass to protect it from the wind.

hurry *verb* (**-ies, -ied**) **1** to urge forward or hasten; to make (someone or something) move or act quickly. **2** *intr* to move or act with haste, esp with excessive speed. ▸ *noun* **1** great haste or speed. **2** the necessity for haste or speed. ▪ **hurried** *adj*. [16c: from English *horyen*]

IDIOMS **in a hurry 1** rushed; in haste. **2** readily; willingly: *I won't do that again in a hurry.*

hurt *verb* (*past tense & past participle* **hurt**) **1** to injure or cause physical pain to. **2** to cause emotional, etc pain to: *hurt her feelings.* **3** *intr* to be injured or painful: *The wound hurts.* ▸ *noun* **1** an injury or wound. **2** mental or emotional pain or suffering. ▸ *adj* **1** injured: *a hurt leg.* **2** aggrieved; upset: *a hurt expression.* [12c: from French *hurter* to knock against something]

hurtful *adj* causing mental pain.

hurtle *verb, tr & intr* to move or throw very quickly or noisily. [13c: *hurtlen*, from French *hurtler* to knock against]

husband *noun* a man to whom a woman is married. ▸ *verb* to manage (money, resources, etc) wisely and economically. [Anglo-Saxon *husbonda*, from Old Norse *hus* a house and *buandi* inhabiting]

husbandry *noun* **1** the farming business. **2** the economical and wise management of money, resources, etc. [14c: from English *housebondrie*]

hush *exclam* silence!; be still! ▸ *noun* silence or calm, esp after noise. ▸ *verb, tr & intr* to make or become silent, calm or still. ▪ **hushed** *adj* silent; very quiet or calm. [16c: from the obsolete adj *husht*, whose final -*t* was thought to indicate a past participle]

hush-hush *adj, informal* top-secret or private.

hush money *noun, informal* money paid to someone to guarantee that something remains secret.

husk *noun* **1** the thin dry covering of certain fruits and seeds. **2** a case, shell or covering, esp one that is worthless. [14c]

husky[1] *adj* (**-ier, -iest**) **1** of a voice: rough and dry in sound. **2** *informal* usu of a man: big, tough and strong. **3** resembling or full of husks. ▪ **huskily** *adv*. ▪ **huskiness** *noun*. [19c: from **husk**]

husky[2] *noun* (**-ies**) a dog with a thick coat and curled tail, used as a sledge-dog in the Arctic. [19c: perhaps an alteration and contraction of **Eskimo**]

hussar /hʊ'zɑː(r)/ *noun* a soldier in a cavalry regiment who carries only light weapons. [15c: from Hungarian *huszar*]

hussy *noun* (**-ies**) *derog* a forward or promiscuous girl or woman. [16c: contraction of *hussif* housewife]

hustings *singular or plural noun* speeches, campaigning, etc prior to a political election, or a platform, etc from which such speeches are given. [Anglo-Saxon *husting* tribunal, from *hus* house + *thing* assembly]

hustle *verb* **1 a** to push or shove quickly and roughly; to jostle; **b** to push or shove in a specified direction or into a specified position: *He hustled her out of the room.* **2** to act hurriedly or hastily. **3** *informal* to coerce or pressure someone to act or deal with something quickly: *They hustled us into agreeing.* **4** to earn money or one's living illicitly. **5** *intr, slang* to work as a prostitute. ▸ *noun* **1** lively or frenzied activity. **2** *slang* a swindle or fraud. [17c: from Dutch *husselen* to shake]

hustler *noun, slang* **1** a lively person. **2** a swindler.

hut *noun* **1** a small and crudely built house, usu made of wood. **2** a small temporary dwelling. [17c: from German *hutta*]

hutch *noun* a box, usu made of wood and with a wire-netting front, in which small animals, eg rabbits, are kept. [14c: from French *huche*]

hyacinth *noun* a bulbous plant with sweet-smelling clusters of blue, pink or white flowers. [16c: named after *Hyakinthos*, a youth in Greek myth killed by Apollo, and from whose blood a blue flower sprang]

hyaena see **hyena**

hyalite *noun* a transparent colourless opal.

hybrid *noun* **1** an animal or plant produced by crossing two different species, varieties, etc. **2** something composed of disparate elements, eg, a word with elements taken from different languages. ▸ *adj* bred or produced by combining elements from different sources. ▪ **hybridism** *or* **hybridity** *noun*. ▪ **hybridization** *noun*. ▪ **hybridize** *or* **-ise** *verb*. [17c: from Latin *hibrida* the offspring of a tame sow and wild boar]

hydr- see **hydro-**

hydra *noun* (***hydras*** *or* ***hydrae*** /ˈhaɪdriː/) **1** a freshwater polyp with a tube-like body and tentacles round the mouth, remarkable for its ability to multiply when cut or divided. **2** any manifold or persistent evil. [14c: from Greek *hydor* water]

hydrant *noun* a pipe connected to the main water supply, esp in a street, with a nozzle for attaching, eg, a firefighter's hose. [19c]

hydrate *chem, noun* a compound containing water that is chemically combined, and which may be expelled without affecting the composition of the other substance. ▸ *verb* **1** to form (such a compound) by combining with water. **2** to cause something to absorb water. [19c]

hydration *noun, chem* the process whereby water molecules become attached to the ions of a **solute** as it is being dissolved in water.

hydraulic *adj* **1** relating to hydraulics. **2** worked by the pressure of water or other fluid carried in pipes: *hydraulic brakes.* **3** relating to the movement of water or other liquid: *hydraulic action.* **4** relating to something that sets in water: *hydraulic cement*. ▪ **hydraulically** *adv.* [17c: from Greek *hydor* water + *aulos* pipe]

hydraulics *singular noun, eng* the science of the mechanical properties of fluids, esp water, at rest or in motion, and their practical applications, eg to water pipes.

hydride *noun* a chemical compound of hydrogen with another element or **radical** (*noun* sense 3). [19c]

hydro[1] *noun* hydroelectric power. [20c]

hydro[2] *noun, Brit* a hotel or clinic, often situated near a spa, providing hydropathic treatment. [1880s]

hydro- *or* (*before a vowel*) **hydr-** *combining form, denoting* **1** water: *hydroelectricity.* **2** hydrogen. [From Greek *hydor* water]

hydrocarbon *noun, chem* an organic chemical compound containing carbon and hydrogen. [19c]

hydrocephalus *noun, med* an accumulation of fluid in the brain, usu occurring in young children. ▪ **hydrocephalic** *or* **hydrocephalous** *adj.* [17c: from Greek *kephale* head]

hydrochloric acid *noun, chem* a strong corrosive acid, formed by dissolving hydrogen and chlorine in water. [19c]

hydrodynamics *singular noun* the science of the movement, equilibrium and power of liquids. See also **hydrostatics**. [18c]

hydroelectricity *or* **hydroelectric power** *noun* electricity generated by turbines that are driven by the force of falling water. ▪ **hydroelectric** *adj.* [19c]

hydrofoil *noun* **1** a device on a boat that raises it out of the water as it accelerates. **2** a boat fitted with such a device. [Early 20c: modelled on **aerofoil**]

hydrogen *noun* (symbol **H**) a flammable colourless odourless gas which is the lightest of all known substances and by far the most abundant element in the universe. ▪ **hydrogenous** *adj.* [18c: from French *hydrogène*, from **hydro-** + Greek *gennaein* to produce]

hydrogenation *noun, chem* any chemical reaction where hydrogen is combined with another substance. ▪ **hydrogenate** *verb*. [19c]

hydrogen bomb *or* **H-bomb** *noun* a bomb that releases vast amounts of energy as a result of hydrogen nuclei being converted into helium nuclei by fusion. Also called **thermonuclear bomb**.

hydrogen bond *noun, chem* a weak chemical bond between an electronegative atom with a lone pair of electrons (eg oxygen, nitrogen) and covalently bonded hydrogen atoms.

hydrogen peroxide *noun, chem* an unstable colourless viscous liquid, a strong oxidizing agent, soluble in water and used as an oxidant in rocket fuel and a bleach for hair and textiles. Also called **peroxide**.

hydrogen sulphide *noun, chem* a colourless, toxic gas composed of hydrogen and sulphur with a characteristic smell of bad eggs, produced by decaying organic matter, and also found in natural gas.

hydrography *noun* the science of charting and mapping seas, rivers and lakes, and of studying tides, currents, winds, etc. ▪ **hydrographer** *noun*.

hydroid *zool, adj* belonging, referring or similar to a hydra. ▸ *noun* a type of **coelenterate** that reproduces asexually; a polyp.

hydrology *noun* the scientific study of the occurrence, movement and properties of water on the Earth's surface, and in the atmosphere. [18c]

hydrolysis /haɪˈdrɒlɪsɪs/ *noun* the chemical decomposition of organic compounds caused by the action of water. ▪ **hydrolytic** *adj.* [19c]

hydrometer *noun, physics* a device used for measuring the density of a liquid. [17c]

hydropathy /haɪˈdrɒpəθɪ/ *noun* the treatment of disease or illness using large amounts of water both internally and externally. ▪ **hydropathic** /haɪdroʊ-

'paθɪk/ *adj*. ▪ **hydropathically** *adv*. ▪ **hydropathist** *noun*. [19c]

hydrophilic *adj, chem* relating to a substance that absorbs, attracts or has an affinity for water. [20c]

hydrophobia *noun* **1** a fear or horror of water. **2** the inability to swallow water, esp as a symptom of rabies. **3** rabies. ▪ **hydrophobic** *adj*. [16c]

hydrophyte *noun, botany* a plant that grows in water or very moist conditions. ▪ **hydrophytic** /-'fɪtɪk/ *adj*. [19c]

hydroplane *noun* **1** a motor boat with a flat bottom or hydrofoils which, at high speeds, skims along the surface of the water. **2** a fin-like device on a submarine allowing it to rise and fall in the water. [Early 20c]

hydroponics *singular noun, botany* the practice of growing plants without using soil, by immersing the roots in a chemical solution of essential nutrients. ▪ **hydroponic** *adj*. [1930s: from Greek *ponos* work or toil]

hydrosphere *noun* the water, such as seas and rivers, on the surface of the Earth. [19c]

hydrostatics *singular noun* the branch of hydrodynamics that deals with the behaviour and power of fluids that are not in motion. [17c]

hydrotherapy *noun, med* the treatment of diseases and disorders by the external use of water, esp through exercising in water. [19c]

hydrous *adj* of a substance: containing water. [19c]

hydroxide *noun, chem* a chemical compound containing one or more hydroxyl groups.

hydroxyl *noun, chem* a compound **radical** (*noun* sense 3) containing one oxygen atom and one hydrogen atom. [19c: from *hyd*rogen + *ox*ygen + Greek *hyle* matter]

hyena *or* **hyaena** *noun* a carrion-feeding doglike mammal. [14c: from Greek *hyaina*, from *hys* pig]

hygiene *noun* **1** the practice or study of preserving health and preventing the spread of disease. **2** sanitary principles and practices. ▪ **hygienic** *adj*. ▪ **hygienically** *adv*. [16c: from Greek *hygieia* health]

---

hygiene
This word is often misspelt. It might help you to remember the following sentence:
*You get ill if you don't follow the rules of **hygi**ene.*

---

hygienist *noun* a person skilled in the practice of hygiene.

hygrometer *noun, meteorol* a device for measuring the humidity of gases or of the air. [17c]

hygroscope *noun* a device that indicates changes in air humidity without measuring it. [17c]

hygroscopic *or* **hygroscopical** *adj* **1** relating to the hygroscope. **2** of a substance: able to absorb moisture from the air. **3** of some movements of plants: indicating or caused by absorption or loss of moisture. ▪ **hygroscopically** *adv*. ▪ **hygroscopicity** *noun*. [18c]

hying see under **hie**

hymen *noun, anatomy* a thin membrane partially covering the opening of the vagina, that is usu broken during the first instance of sexual intercourse. ▪ **hymenal** *adj*. [17c: Greek]

hymn *noun* a song of praise, esp to God, but also to a nation, etc. ▸ *verb* **1** to celebrate in song or worship. **2** *intr* to sing in adoration. [Anglo-Saxon: from Greek *hymnos*]

hymnal *noun* a book containing hymns. [17c]

hymnbook *noun* a book or collection of hymns.

hype[1] *informal, noun* **1** intensive, exaggerated or artificially induced excitement about, or enthusiasm for, something or someone. **2** exaggerated and usu misleading publicity or advertising; a sales gimmick. ▸ *verb* to promote or advertise intensively. [20c]

hype[2] *verb, slang* (*usu* **hype up**) to stimulate or excite (someone or something) artificially. [1920s]

hyper *adj, informal* of a person: over-excited; overstimulated. [1940s: short form of **hyperactive**]

hyper- *combining form, denoting* over, excessive, more than normal: *hyperactive*. [Greek, meaning 'over']

hyperactive *adj* of, esp, a child: abnormally or pathologically active. ▪ **hyperactivity** *noun*. [19c]

hyperbola /haɪ'pɜːbələ/ *noun* (***hyperbolas, hyperbolae*** /-liː/) *geom* the curve produced when a **plane**[2] cuts through a cone so that the angle between the base of the cone and the plane is greater than the angle between the base and the sloping side of the cone. ▪ **hyperbolic** *adj*. [17c: Latin, from Greek *hyperbole*, from *hyper* over + *ballein* to throw]

hyperbole /haɪ'pɜːbəlɪ/ *noun, rhetoric* an overstatement or exaggeration used for effect and not meant to be taken literally. ▪ **hyperbolic** *adj*. ▪ **hyperbolically** *adv*. [16c: Greek, literally 'exaggeration']

hyperbolic function *noun, maths* any of a set of **function**s (*noun* sense 5) analogous to the trigonometrical functions.

hypercritical *adj* too critical, esp of small faults. [17c]

hyperglycaemia *or* (*NAm*) **hyperglycemia** /haɪpəglaɪ'siːmɪə/ *noun, pathol* a condition in which the sugar concentration in the blood is abnormally high. Compare **hypoglycaemia**. [20c]

hyperinflation *noun, econ* rapid inflation that cannot be controlled by normal economic measures.

hyperlink *noun, comput* a link between documents or items within a document created using hypertext.

hypermarket *noun, Brit* a very large supermarket with a wide range of goods, usu on the edge of a town. [1960s: a translation of French *hypermarché*]

hypermedia *noun, comput* a computer file and related software that identifies and links information in various media, such as text, graphics, sound, video clips, etc. [1990s: from *hyper*text + multi*media*]

hypersensitive *adj* excessively sensitive; more sensitive than normal. ▪ **hypersensitiveness** *or* **hypersensitivity** *noun*. [19c]

hypersonic *adj* **1** of speeds: greater than Mach number 5. **2** *aeronautics* of an aircraft or rocket: capable of flying at such speeds. **3** of sound waves: having a frequency greater than 1000 million hertz. ▪ **hypersonics** *plural noun*. [1930s]

hypertension *noun* **1** *pathol* a condition in which the blood pressure is abnormally high. Compare **hypotension**. **2** a state of great emotional tension. ▪ **hypertensive** *adj, noun*. [19c]

hypertext *noun, comput* computer-readable text in which cross-reference links (**hyperlink**s) have been inserted, enabling the user to call up relevant data from other files, or parts of the same file, by clicking on a coded word or symbol, etc.

hypertonic *adj* **1** of muscles: having excessive tone. **2** *chem* of a solution: having a higher **osmotic pres-**

sure than another solution with which it is being compared. Compare **hypotonic**. [19c]

hypertrophy *biol* (*-ies*) *noun* an abnormal increase in an organ's size resulting from overnourishment. ▸ *verb* (*-ies, -ied*) to subject or be subjected to hypertrophy. ▪ **hypertrophic** *or* **hypertrophied** *adj*. [19c]

hyperventilation *noun* a condition in which the speed and depth of breathing becomes abnormally rapid. ▪ **hyperventilate** *verb*. [1920s]

hyphen *noun* a punctuation mark (-) used to join two words to form a compound (eg, *booby-trap, double-barrelled*) or, in texts, to split a word between the end of one line and the beginning of the next. ▸ *verb* to hyphenate. [19c: from Greek *hypo* under + *hen* one]

hyphenate *verb* to join or separate (two words or parts of words) with a hyphen. ▪ **hyphenated** *adj*. ▪ **hyphenation** *noun*. [19c]

hypno- *or* (*before a vowel*) **hypn-** *combining form, denoting* **1** sleep. **2** hypnosis. [From Greek *hypnos* sleep]

hypnosis *noun* (*-ses* /-siːz/) an induced sleep-like state in which a person is deeply relaxed, and in which the mind responds to external suggestion and can recover subconscious memories. [19c: from Greek *hypnos* sleep]

hypnotherapy *noun* the treatment of illness or altering of habits, eg smoking, by hypnosis. ▪ **hypnotherapist** *noun*. [19c]

hypnotic *adj* **1** relating to, causing or caused by, hypnosis. **2** causing sleepiness; soporific. ▸ *noun* **1** a drug that produces sleep. **2** someone who is subject to hypnosis. **3** someone in a state of hypnosis. ▪ **hypnotically** *adv*. [17c]

hypnotism *noun* **1** the science or practice of hypnosis. **2** the art or practice of inducing hypnosis. ▪ **hypnotist** *noun*. [19c: a shortening of *neuro-hypnotism*, a term introduced by James Braid, a British surgeon]

hypnotize *or* **-ise** *verb* **1** to put someone in a state of hypnosis. **2** to fascinate, captivate or bewitch.

hypo- *or* (*before a vowel*) **hyp-** *combining form, denoting* **1** under. **2** inadequate. **3** defective. [Greek, meaning 'under']

hypochondria *or* **hypochondriasis** *noun* a condition characterized by excessive or morbid concern over one's health and sometimes belief that one is seriously ill. ▪ **hypochondriac** *noun, adj*. [17c: from Greek *hypochondrion* abdomen, formerly believed to be the source of melancholy]

hypocrisy *noun* (*-ies*) **1** the practice of pretending to have feelings, beliefs or principles which one does not actually have. **2** an act or instance of this. [13c: from Greek *hypokrisis* play-acting]

hypocrite *noun* a person who practises hypocrisy. ▪ **hypocritical** *adj*. ▪ **hypocritically** *adv*. [13c: from Greek *hypokrites* an actor]

hypodermic *adj* **a** of a drug: injected under the skin; **b** of a syringe: designed for use under the skin. ▸ *noun* a hypodermic injection or syringe. [19c: from Greek *hypo* under + *derma* skin]

hypoglycaemia *or* **hypoglycemia** /haɪpouglaɪ'siːmɪə/ *noun, pathol* a condition in which the sugar content of the blood is abnormally low, usu occurring in diabetics after an insulin overdose. ▪ **hypoglycaemic** *adj*. [19c: **hypo-** + **glyco-** + **-aemia**]

hypotension *noun, pathol* a condition in which the blood pressure is abnormally low. Compare **hypertension**. ▪ **hypotensive** *adj, noun*. [19c]

hypotenuse /haɪ'pɒtənjuːz/ *noun, maths* the longest side of a right-angled triangle, opposite the right angle. [16c: from Greek *hypoteinousa* subtending or stretching under]

hypothalamus *noun* (***hypothalami*** /-maɪ/) *anatomy* the region of the brain that is involved in the regulation of involuntary functions, such as body temperature. ▪ **hypothalamic** *adj*. [19c]

hypothermia *noun* a condition where the body temperature becomes abnormally and sometimes dangerously low. [19c: from Greek *therme* heat]

hypothesis *noun* (*-ses* /-siːz/) **1** a statement or proposition assumed to be true for the sake of argument. **2** a statement or theory to be proved or disproved by reference to evidence or facts. **3** a provisional explanation of anything. [16c: Greek]

hypothesize *or* **-ise** *verb* **1** *intr* to form a hypothesis. **2** to assume as a hypothesis.

hypothetical *or* **hypothetic** *adj* **1** based on or involving hypothesis. **2** assumed but not necessarily true. ▪ **hypothetically** *adv*.

hypotonic *adj* **1** of muscles: lacking normal tone. **2** *chem* of a solution: having a lower osmotic pressure than another solution with which it is being compared. Compare **hypertonic**. [19c]

hyssop *noun* a small shrubby aromatic plant with narrow leaves and clusters of long blue flowers, formerly cultivated as a medicinal herb. [Anglo-Saxon: from Greek *hyssopos*]

hyster- see **hystero-**

hysterectomy *noun* (*-ies*) the surgical removal of the womb. [19c]

hysteria *noun* **1** *psychol* a psychoneurosis characterized by hallucinations, convulsions, amnesia or paralysis. **2** any state of emotional instability caused by acute stress or a traumatic experience. **3** any extreme emotional state, such as laughter or weeping. [19c: from Greek *hystera* womb, from the former belief that disturbances in the womb caused emotional imbalance]

hysteric *noun* **1** (**hysterics**) *psychol* a bout of hysteria. **2** (**hysterics**) *informal* a bout of uncontrollable laughter: *The film had us in hysterics.* **3** someone suffering from hysteria. [17c]

hysterical *adj* **1** relating to or suffering from hysteria. **2** characterized by hysteria: *a hysterical laugh.* **3** *informal* extremely funny or amusing: *a hysterical joke.* ▪ **hysterically** *adv*. [17c]

hystero- *or* (*before a vowel*) **hyster-** *combining form, denoting* womb. [From Greek *hystera*]

Hz *abbrev* hertz.

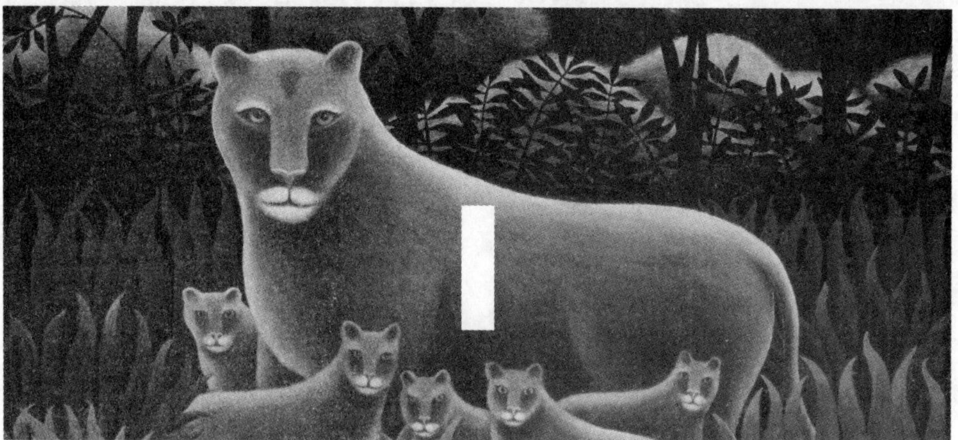

I[1] *or* **i** *noun* (***Is, I's*** *or* ***i's***) the ninth letter of the English alphabet.

I[2] *pron* used to refer to oneself. [Anglo-Saxon *ic*]

I, me

After a preposition, you should always use the word **me** (rather than **I**) as the object:

✓ *between you and me*
✗ *between you and I*
✓ *for John and me*
✗ *for John and I*

If you are not sure, try the phrase without the *you*, and you will see that *for I* and *with I* are wrong.

I[3] *abbrev* **1** Institute, or Institution. **2** International. **3** Island, or Isle.

I[4] *symbol* **1** *chem* iodine. **2** as a Roman numeral: one.

-ia[1] *suffix, forming nouns, signifying* **1** *med* a diseased or pathological condition: *anaemia • pneumonia*. See also **-iasis**. **2** *biol* a genus or class of plants or animals: *Magnolia*. **3** a state or type of society or world: *Utopia • suburbia*. **4** the name of a country or place: *Australia*. [Latin and Greek noun suffix]

-ia[2] *suffix, forming pl and collective nouns, signifying* **1** *biol* a taxonomic **division** (sense 7): *Mammalia*. **2** items belonging or relating to, or derived from, a specified thing: *militaria • regalia*. See also **-ana**. **3** used in the plural form of certain nouns of Latin and Greek origin: *effluvia • media*. [Latin and Greek]

-ial *suffix* **1** *forming adjectives, signifying* belonging or relating to a specified thing: *managerial*. **2** *forming nouns, signifying* the action of a specified thing: *tutorial*. See also **-al**. [From Latin *-ialis*]

iambus /aɪ'ambəs/ *or* **iamb** /'aɪamb/ *noun* (***iambuses, iambi*** /-baɪ/ *and* ***iambs***) a metrical foot containing a short or unstressed syllable followed by a long or stressed one. ▪ **iambic** *adj* of or using iambuses. ▸ *noun* **1** an iambus. **2** (*usu* **iambics**) iambic verse. [16c: from Greek *iambos*]

-ian, -ean *or* **-an** *suffix* **1** *forming adjectives, signifying* relating to or similar to a specified thing, person, etc: *Dickensian*. **2** *forming nouns, signifying* someone interested or skilled in a specified thing: *grammarian*. [From Latin *-ianus*]

-iana see **-ana**

-iasis *or* (*sometimes*) **-asis** *med, combining form, forming nouns, denoting* a diseased condition: *psoriasis*. [From Greek suffix denoting 'state or condition']

ib. *or* **ibid.** /'ɪbɪd/ *abbrev* **ibidem**.

Iberian *adj* relating to Portugal and Spain, their inhabitants, languages or culture. ▸ *noun* a Spanish or Portuguese person. [17c: from Latin *Iberia*]

ibex *noun* (***ibex, ibexes*** *or* ***ibices*** /'aɪbɪsiːz/) a wild mountain goat with backward-curving horns. [17c: Latin]

ibidem /'ɪbɪdəm/ *adv* (abbrev ***ib.*** *or* ***ibid.***) in the same book, article, passage, etc as previously mentioned or cited. [17c: Latin, meaning 'in the same place']

ibis /'aɪbɪs/ *noun* (***ibis*** *or* ***ibises***) a large wading bird with a long slender downward-curving beak. [14c: Greek, from Egyptian]

-ible *suffix, forming adjectives, signifying* that may be or is capable of being dealt with as specified: *expressible • possible*. See also **-able**. ▪ **-ibility** *suffix* (***-ibilities***) *forming nouns*: *possibility*. ▪ **-ibly** *suffix, forming adverbs*: *inexpressibly*. [From Latin *-ibilis*]

-ic *suffix, forming adjectives, signifying* **1** (*also* **-ical**, often with some difference in meaning) belonging or relating to, or in terms of, a specified thing: *historic • historical • photographic • political*. **2** *chem* formed with an element in its higher **valency**: *sulphuric*. Compare **-ous**. See also **-ics**. ▸ *suffix, forming nouns,* especially corresponding to adjectives in **-ic**: *cosmetic • lunatic*. See also **-aholic**. ▪ **-ically** ▸ *suffix, forming adverbs*: *historically • graphically*. [From French *-ique*]

-ical *suffix, forming adjectives* often, but not always, the same as **-ic**. Compare **economic** and **economical**. ▪ **-ically** see under **-ic**.

ice *noun* **1** solid frozen water. **2** **ice cream** or **water ice**, or a portion of this. **3** coldness of manner; reserve. ▸ *verb* **1** to cover (a cake) with icing. **2** *intr* (*usu* **ice over** *or* **up**) to become covered with ice. **3** to cool or mix something with ice. [Anglo-Saxon *is*]

IDIOMS **on ice 1** to be used later. **2** awaiting further attention.

ice age *noun, geol* **1** any period when ice sheets and glaciers covered large areas of the Earth. **2** (**the Ice Age**) the period during which this happened in the **Pleistocene** epoch.

iceberg *noun* **1** a huge mass of ice floating in the sea. **2** an iceberg lettuce. [19c: from Scandinavian or Dutch]

icebreaker *noun* **1** a ship that cuts channels through ice. **2** someone or something that breaks down shyness or formality. ▪ **ice-breaking** *adj, noun*.

icecap *noun* a thick permanent covering of ice.

ice cream *noun* a sweet creamy flavoured frozen dessert.

iced *adj* **1** covered or cooled with, or affected by, ice. **2** covered with icing.

ice dance *or* **ice dancing** *noun* a form of ice-skating based on the movements of ballroom dancing.

iced tea *or* **ice tea** *noun* chilled sweetened tea flavoured with lemon.

ice field *noun* **1** an **ice sheet**. **2** a large **ice floe**.

ice floe *noun* a sheet of ice floating on the sea.

ice hockey *noun* a form of hockey played on ice, with a **puck**[2] instead of a ball.

Icelandic *adj* relating to the Republic of Iceland, its inhabitants or their language. ▸ *noun* the official language of Iceland.

ice lolly *noun, Brit informal* a portion of flavoured water or ice cream frozen on a small stick.

ice pack *noun* **1** *med* a bag of crushed ice, used to reduce swelling, lower a patient's temperature, etc. **2** *geog* an area of **pack ice**. **3** a gel-filled pack that stays frozen for long periods, used in a **cool box**, etc.

ice rink see **rink** (sense 2)

ice sheet *noun* a layer of ice covering a whole region.

ice skate *noun* a boot with a metal blade, used for skating on ice. ▸ *verb* (**ice-skate**) *intr* to skate on ice. ▪ **ice-skater** *noun*. ▪ **ice-skating** *noun*.

ice tea see **iced tea**

ichthyology /ɪkθɪ'ɒlədʒɪ/ *noun* the study of fishes. ▪ **ichthyological** *adj*. ▪ **ichthyologist** *noun*. [17c: from Greek *ichthys* fish + *logos* word or reason]

-ician *suffix, forming nouns, especially based on nouns ending in -ic or -ics, denoting* someone who is skilled or trained in a specified area or activity: *beautician* • *technician*. See also **-ic**, **-ian**. [From French *-icien*]

icicle *noun* a long hanging spike of ice. [Anglo-Saxon, from *is* ice + *gicel* icicle]

icing *noun* a sugar-based coating for cakes, etc. IDIOMS **the icing on the cake** *informal* an agreeable addition to something which is already satisfactory.

icing sugar *noun* very fine powdered sugar.

icky *adj* (*-ier, -iest*) *informal* **1** sickly; cloying or sticky. **2** repulsive, nasty or unpleasant. [20c]

icon *or* (*sometimes*) **ikon** *noun* **1** *relig art* esp in the Orthodox Church: an image of Christ, the Virgin Mary or a saint. **2 a** a person or thing uncritically revered or admired; **b** someone or something regarded as a symbol of a particular culture, sphere, etc. **3** *comput* a symbol on a computer screen. **4** a picture, image or representation. ▪ **iconic** *adj*. [16c: from Greek *eikon* image]

iconoclast *noun* **1** *esp church hist* someone who rejects the use of religious images, often destroying them. **2** someone who is opposed to, and attacks, traditional and cherished beliefs and superstitions. ▪ **iconoclasm** *noun*. ▪ **iconoclastic** *adj*. [17c: from Greek *eikon* image + *klastes* breaker]

iconography *noun, art hist* **1** the branch of study concerned with the form and representation of the subject. **2** a generally recognized set of objects that are considered to symbolize a particular movement, genre, etc. **3** a collection of portraits. ▪ **iconographer** *noun*. ▪ **iconographic** /aɪkɒnə'grafɪk/ *or* **iconographical** *adj*. [17c]

icosahedron *noun* (***icosahedrons*** *or* ***icosahedra*** /aɪkɒsə'hiːdrə/) *geom* a solid figure with twenty faces. [16c: Greek, from *eikosi* twenty + *hedra* seat]

-ics *suffix, usu forming singular nouns, denoting* a subject or subjects of study, a specific activity, art or science: *athletics* • *mathematics* • *politics*. [From French *-iques*]

icy *adj* (*-ier, -iest*) **1** very cold. **2** covered with ice. **3** unfriendly; hostile. ▪ **icily** *adv*. ▪ **iciness** *noun*.

ID *abbrev* identification or identity.

I'd *contraction* **1** I had. **2** I would.

id *noun, psychoanal* the unconscious source of primitive biological instincts and urges. Compare **ego**, **superego**. [20c: Latin, meaning 'it']

id. *abbrev* **idem**.

-id[1] *suffix, forming nouns, denoting* **1** *biol* a member of a particular zoological or racial group: *arachnid* • *hominid*. **2** a member of a particular dynastic line: *Fatimid*. **3** *astron* a meteor that has come from a particular constellation: *Perseid*. [From Greek *-ides* son of …]

-id[2] *suffix, forming nouns* **1** *technical* used in the names of bodies, formations, particles, etc: *hydatid*. **2** *botany* used in the names of plants belonging to a particular family: *orchid*. [From French *-ide*]

-id[3] see **-ide**

-ide *chem suffix, forming nouns, denoting* a compound of an element with some other element: *chloride*. Compare **-ite**.

idea *noun* **1** a thought, image or concept formed by the mind. **2** a plan or notion. **3** an aim or purpose: *The idea of the game is to win cards*. **4** an opinion, belief, or vague fancy. **5** someone's conception of something: *not my idea of fun*.

ideal *adj* **1** perfect; best possible or conceivable. **2** existing only in the mind. **3** theoretical; conforming to theory. ▸ *noun* **1** the highest standard of behaviour, perfection, beauty, etc. **2** someone or something considered perfect. **3** something existing only in the imagination. ▪ **ideally** *adv*. [17c: from French *idéal*]

idealism *noun* **1** a tendency to see or present things in an ideal or idealized form rather than as they really are. **2** the practice of forming, and living according to, ideals. **3** impracticality. **4** *philos* the theory that objects and the external world are products of the mind. Compare **realism**. ▪ **idealist** *noun*. ▪ **idealistic** *adj*.

idealize *or* **-ise** *verb* to regard or treat someone or something as perfect or ideal. ▪ **idealization** *noun*.

idée fixe /iːdeɪ'fiːks/ *noun* (***idées fixes*** /iːdeɪ'fiːks/) a dominant idea or obsession. [19c: French, literally 'fixed idea']

idem /'aɪdɛm, 'ɪ-/ (abbrev **id.**) *pron* the same author, place, etc as previously mentioned. ▸ *adv* in the same place as previously mentioned. [14c: Latin, meaning 'the same']

identical *adj* **1** exactly similar in every respect. **2** being the very same one. **3** of twins: developed from a single fertilized egg, therefore of the same sex and closely resembling each other. Compare **fraternal** (sense 2). ▪ **identically** *adv*. [17c: from Latin *identicus*]

identification parade *noun, Brit* a line of people containing one person who is suspected of a crime and others who are innocent of it, from which a witness is asked to try and identify the criminal. Also called **identity parade**.

identify *verb* (*-ies, -ied*) **1** to recognize or establish someone or something as being a particular person or thing. **2** to associate (one person, thing or group) closely with another. **3** to see clearly or pinpoint (a problem, method, solution, etc). **4** *intr* (**identify with sb**) to feel sympathy and understanding for someone because of shared personal characteristics or experiences. ▪ **identifiable** *adj*. ▪ **identification** *noun*. [17c: from Latin *identificare*]

Identikit *noun, trademark* (*often* **identikit**) a series of transparent strips showing different facial features, from which one can put together a rough picture of a criminal or suspect from witnesses' descriptions. ▸ *adj* composed from Identikit. [20c]

identity *noun* (*-ies*) **1** who or what a person or thing is: *The winner's identity is not yet known.* **2** the characteristics by which a person or thing can be identified. **3** the state of being exactly the same: *identity of interests.* **4** *maths* **a** (*in full* **identity element**) an element that, when combined with another element *x*, leaves *x* unchanged; **b** an equation that is valid for all possible values of the variables involved. ▸ *adj* serving to identify someone (eg the wearer or holder) or to give information about them: *identity bracelet*. [16c: from French *identité*]

identity card *noun* a card bearing information about the holder, used as proof of their identity.

identity crisis *noun, psychol* a mental conflict involving the loss of a person's sense of self.

identity parade see under **identification parade**

ideogram *noun* a symbol for a concept or object, but not a direct representation of it. Also called **ideograph**. [19c: from Greek *idea* idea + *gramma* letter]

ideologue *noun, usu derog* someone who supports a particular ideology very rigidly. [19c: from French *idéologue*]

ideology *noun* (*-ies*) **1** the ideas and beliefs that form the basis for a social, economic or political system. **2** the opinions, beliefs and way of thinking characteristic of a particular person, group or nation. ▪ **ideological** *adj*. ▪ **ideologically** *adv*. ▪ **ideologist** *noun*. [18c: from French *idéologie*]

Ides /aɪdz/ *plural or singular noun* (*also* **ides**) in the ancient Roman calendar: the fifteenth day of March, May, July and October, and the thirteenth day of the other months. [14c: French, from Latin *idus*]

idiocy *noun* (*-ies*) **1** a foolish action or foolish behaviour. **2** *non-technical* the state of being extremely retarded mentally.

idiom *noun* **1** an expression with a meaning that cannot be derived from the meanings of the words which form it. **2** the forms of expression peculiar to a language, dialect, group, etc. **3** the characteristic style or forms of expression of a particular artist, musician, artistic or musical school, etc. ▪ **idiomatic** *adj* **1** characteristic of a particular language. **2** tending to use idioms; using idioms correctly. ▪ **idiomatically** *adv*. [16c: from French *idiome*]

idiosyncrasy *noun* (*-ies*) a personal peculiarity or eccentricity. ▪ **idiosyncratic** *adj*. ▪ **idiosyncratically** *adv*. [17c: from Greek *idiosynkrasis*]

idiot *noun* **1** *informal* a foolish or stupid person. **2** *non-technical* a severely mentally retarded person. ▪ **idiotic** *adj*. ▪ **idiotically** *adv*. [14c: from Greek *idiotes* a person lacking skill or expertise]

idiot savant /ˈɪdɪət ˈsavənt; *French* idjosavɑ̃/ ▸ *noun* (***idiot savants*** /ˈɪdɪət ˈsavənts/ *or* ***idiots savants*** /idjosavɑ̃/) someone with a mental disability who shows a remarkable talent in some specific respect, such as rapid calculation. [20c: French, literally 'clever idiot']

idle *adj* **1** not in use; unoccupied. **2** not wanting to work; lazy. **3** worthless: *idle chatter.* **4** without cause, basis or good reason: *an idle rumour.* **5** having no effect or result; not taken seriously: *an idle threat.* ▸ *verb* **1** (*usu* **idle away time**, *etc*) to spend (time) idly. **2** *intr* to do nothing or be idle. **3** *intr* of an engine, machinery, etc: to run gently while out of gear or without doing any work. **4** to make (an engine, etc) idle. ▪ **idleness** *noun*. ▪ **idler** *noun*. ▪ **idly** *adv*. [Anglo-Saxon *idel*, meaning 'empty' or 'worthless']

idol *noun* **1** an image or symbol used as an object of worship. **2** an object of excessive love, honour or devotion. [14c: from Latin *idolum*]

idolatry /aɪˈdɒlətrɪ/ *noun* (*-ies*) **1** the worship of idols. **2** excessive love, honour, admiration or devotion. ▪ **idolater** *and* (*now rare*) **idolatress** *noun*. ▪ **idolatrous** *adj*. ▪ **idolatrously** *adv*. [13c: from Latin *idololatria*]

idolize *or* **-ise** *verb* **1** to love, honour, admire, etc someone or something too much. **2** to make an idol of someone or something. ▪ **idolization** *noun*.

Id-ul-Adha *or* **Eid-ul-Adha** /iːd al aːdˈhaː/ *noun* a Muslim festival celebrating Abraham's willingness to sacrifice his son. [Arabic, literally 'Feast of Sacrifice']

Id-ul-Fitr *or* **Eid-ul-Fitr** /iːd al ˈfɪtə(r)/ *noun* a Muslim festival celebrating the end of Ramadan. Also called **Eid**. [18c: Arabic, literally 'Feast of Breaking Fast']

idyll /ˈɪdɪl/ *noun* **1** a short poem or prose work describing a simple, pleasant, usu rural or pastoral scene. **2** a story, episode or scene of happy innocence or love. **3** a work of this character in another art form, esp music. ▪ **idyllic** /ɪˈdɪlɪk/ *adj* **1** relating to or typical of an idyll. **2** charming; picturesque. [17c: from Latin *idyllium*]

ie *or* **i.e.** *abbrev*: *id est* (Latin), that is; that is to say.

-ie *suffix, forming nouns* a variant of **-y**^{2}: *hippie* • *nightie* • *movie*.

if *conj* **1** in the event that; on condition that; supposing that. **2** although; even though: *very enjoyable, if overpriced.* **3** whenever: *She jumps if the phone rings.* **4** whether. **5** (*usu* **if only**) used to express a wish. **6** used to make a polite request or suggestion: *if you wouldn't mind waiting.* **7** used in exclamations, to express surprise or annoyance: *Well, if it isn't John!* ▸ *noun* **1** a condition or supposition: *ifs and buts.* **2** an uncertainty. [Anglo-Saxon *gif*]

iffy *adj* (*-ier, -iest*) *informal* uncertain; dubious. [20c]

igloo *noun* a dome-shaped Inuit house built with blocks of hard snow. [19c: from Inuit *iglu* house]

igneous *adj* **1** relating to or like fire. **2** *geol* of a rock: formed by the solidification of molten **magma**. [17c: from Latin *igneus*, from *ignis* fire]

ignite *verb* **1** to set fire to something or heat it to the point of combustion. **2** *intr* to catch fire. **3** to excite (feelings, emotions, etc). ▪ **ignitable** *or* **ignitible** *adj*. [17c: from Latin *ignire* to set on fire]

ignition *noun* **1** *chem* the point at which combustion begins. **2** (*usu* **the ignition**) a system that produces the spark which ignites the mixture of fuel and air in an **internal-combustion engine**. **3** an act or the means or process of igniting something.

ignoble *adj* **1** dishonourable; mean. **2** of humble or low birth; not noble. ▪ **ignobly** *adv.* [15c: French, from Latin *ignobilis*]

ignominy /ˈɪgnəmɪnɪ/ *noun* (**-*ies***) **1** public shame, disgrace or dishonour. **2** dishonourable conduct. ▪ **ignominious** /ɪgnəˈmɪnɪəs/ *adj.* [16c: from Latin *ignominia*]

ignoramus *noun* an ignorant or unintelligent person. [17c: from Latin *ignoramus* we do not know]

ignorant *adj* **1** knowing very little; uneducated. **2** (*usu* **ignorant of sth**) knowing little or nothing about it. **3** rude; ill-mannered. ▪ **ignorance** *noun.* ▪ **ignorantly** *adv.* [14c: from Latin *ignorare* not to know]

ignore *verb* to take no notice of someone or something. [19c: from Latin *ignorare* not to know]

iguana *noun* (***iguanas*** *or* ***iguana***) a large lizard with a crest of spines along its back. [16c: Spanish, from Carib (a native S American language) *iwana*]

ikon see **icon**

il- *prefix* a form of **in-** used before words beginning in *l*: *illegible*.

ileum *noun* (***ilea***) *anatomy* the lowest part of the small intestine. [17c: from Latin *ilia* groin or guts]

ilex /ˈaɪlɛks/ *noun, botany* a shrub or tree of the genus that includes **holly**. [14c: Latin]

ilium *noun* (***ilia***) *anatomy* one of the bones that form the upper part of the pelvis. [18c: from Latin *ilia* groin]

ilk *noun* type; kind; class. [Anglo-Saxon *ilca* same]
IDIOMS **of that ilk** *Scot* of the place of the same name: *Macdonald of that ilk (ie Macdonald of Macdonald).*

I'll *contraction* I will or I shall.

ill *adj* (***worse, worst***; *informal* ***iller, illest***) **1** unwell. **2** of health: not good. **3** bad; harmful: *ill effects*. **4** hostile; unfriendly: *ill feeling*. **5** causing or heralding bad luck: *an ill omen*. **6** of manners: incorrect; improper. ▸ *adv* (***worse, worst***) **1** badly; wrongly: *ill-fitting*. **2** harshly; unfavourably: *speak ill of someone*. **3** not easily; with difficulty: *ill able to afford the money.* ▸ *noun* **1** evil; trouble: *the ills of modern society.* **2** an injury or misfortune. [15c: from Norse *illr*]
IDIOMS **ill at ease** uneasy; uncomfortable; embarrassed.

ill-advised *adj* foolish; done, or doing things, with little thought or consideration. ▪ **ill-advisedly** *adv.*

ill-bred *adj* badly brought up or educated; rude. ▪ **ill-breeding** *noun.*

ill-considered *adj* not well planned.

ill-disposed *adj* (*esp* **ill-disposed towards sb** *or* **sth**) unfriendly; unsympathetic.

illegal *adj* **1** not legal. **2** not authorized by law. ▪ **illegality** /ɪlɪˈgalɪtɪ/ ▸ *noun* (**-*ies***). ▪ **illegally** *adv.* [17c: from Latin *illegalis*]

illegible *adj* difficult or impossible to read. ▪ **illegibility** *noun.* ▪ **illegibly** *adv.* [17c]

illegitimate *adj* **1** born of unmarried parents. **2** of a birth: happening outside marriage. **3** unacceptable or not allowed; illegal. **4** *logic* not properly reasoned. **5** improper. ▪ **illegitimacy** *noun.* [16c]

ill-equipped *adj* poorly provided with the necessary tools, skills, etc.

ill fame *noun* a bad reputation; notoriety.

ill-fated *adj* ending in or bringing bad luck or ruin.

ill-favoured *adj* unattractive.

ill-founded *adj* without sound basis or reason.

ill-gotten *adj* obtained dishonestly.

illiberal *adj* **1** narrow-minded; prejudiced. **2** not generous. **3** uncultured; unrefined. ▪ **illiberality** *noun.* [16c: from Latin *illiberalis* mean or ignoble]

illicit *adj* not permitted by law, rule or social custom. [17c: from Latin *illicitus*]

ill-informed *adj* **1** lacking knowledge or information. **2** made without the relevant or necessary information.

illiterate *adj* **1** unable to read and write. **2** uneducated; ignorant of some subject. ▸ *noun* an illiterate person. ▪ **illiteracy** *noun.* [16c: from Latin *illiteratus*]

ill-judged *adj* done without proper consideration.

ill-mannered *adj* rude.

ill-natured *adj* spiteful; mean; surly.

illness *noun* **1** a disease. **2** the state of being ill.

illogical *adj* **1** not based on careful reasoning. **2** against the principles of logic. ▪ **illogicality** *noun.* ▪ **illogically** *adv.* [16c]

ill-omened *or* **ill-starred** *adj* likely to end badly; unlucky; doomed.

ill-tempered *adj* bad-tempered; surly.

ill-timed *adj* said or done at an unsuitable time.

ill-treat *verb* to abuse; to maltreat. ▪ **ill-treatment** *noun.*

illuminance *noun, physics* (SI unit **lux**) the luminous **flux** on a given surface per unit area. Also called **illumination**.

illuminate *verb* **1** to light something up or make it bright. **2** to decorate something with lights. **3** to decorate (a manuscript) with elaborate designs. **4** to make something clearer and more easily understood. **5** to enlighten someone spiritually or intellectually. ▪ **illuminating** *adj.* ▪ **illuminative** *adj.* [16c: from Latin *illuminare*]

illumination *noun* **1** illuminating or being illuminated. **2** any source of light; lighting. **3** (*usu* **illuminations**) decorative lights hung in streets and towns, eg at times of celebration. **4** the art of decorating manuscripts with elaborate designs and letters. **5** such a design or letter in a manuscript.

illusion *noun* **1** a deceptive or misleading appearance: *an optical illusion*. **2** a false or misleading impression, idea or belief: *under the illusion he worked here.* [14c: from Latin *illusio* deceit]

---

illusion, allusion

Be careful not to use the word **illusion** when you mean **allusion**. An **allusion** is an indirect reference to something:

He makes allusions to his family in most of his books.

---

illusionist *noun* a conjurer who plays tricks, performs optical illusions, etc.

illusive *or* **illusory** *adj* **1** seeming to be or like an illusion. **2** deceptive; unreal. ▪ **illusively** *or* **illusorily** *adv.* ▪ **illusiveness** *or* **illusoriness** *noun.*

illustrate *verb* **1** to provide or create pictures and/or diagrams for (a book, lecture, etc). **2** to make (a statement, etc) clearer by providing examples. **3** to be an example of, or an analogy for, something. ▪ **illustrated** *adj*. ▪ **illustrative** *adj*. ▪ **illustrator** *noun*. [17c: from Latin *illustrare* to light up]

illustration *noun* **1** a picture or diagram. **2** an example. **3** illustrating or being illustrated.

illustrious *adj, rather formal* distinguished; celebrated; noble. [16c: from Latin *illustris* bright or lustrous]

ill will *noun* hostile or unfriendly feeling.

I'm *contraction* I am.

im- *prefix* a form of **in-** used before words beginning in *b, m* and *p*: *imbalance • immature • impartial*.

image *noun* **1** a likeness of a person or thing, esp a portrait or statue. **2** someone or something that closely resembles another: *He's the image of his father.* **3** an idea or picture in the mind. **4** the visual display produced by a television. **5** the impression that people in general have of someone's character, behaviour, etc. **6** a simile or metaphor. **7** *optics* an optical reproduction of a physical object. **8** *physics* a reproduction of an object formed by sound waves or electromagnetic radiation, eg an **ultrasound scan** or **X-ray** photograph. **9** a typical example or embodiment of something. ▸ *verb* **1** to form a likeness or image of something or someone. **2** *med* to produce a pictorial representation of (a body part) using eg X-ray or ultrasound scanning. **3** to form a mental or optical image of something or someone. **4** to portray; to be a typical example of something. ▪ **imaging** *noun*. [13c: from Latin *imago* a likeness]

imagery *noun* (*-ies*) **1** figures of speech in writing, literature, etc that produce a particular effect: *Heaney's use of agricultural imagery.* **2** the making of images, esp in the mind. **3** mental images. **4** images in general. **5** statues, carvings, etc.

imaginary *adj* **1** existing only in the mind or imagination; not real. **2** *maths* consisting of or containing an **imaginary number**.

imaginary number *noun, maths* the square root of a negative number.

imagination *noun* **1** the forming or ability to form mental images of things, people, events, etc that one has not seen or of which one has no direct knowledge. **2** the creative ability of the mind. **3** the ability to cope resourcefully with unexpected events or problems.

imaginative *adj* **1** showing, done with or created by imagination. **2** having a lively imagination.

imagine *verb* **1** to form a mental picture of something: *I can't imagine her wearing a hat.* **2** to see, hear or think something that is not true or does not exist: *You're imagining things.* **3** to think, suppose or guess: *I can't imagine where she is.* **4** *intr* to use the imagination. **5** used as an exclamation of surprise: *Imagine that!* ▪ **imaginable** *adj*. [14c: from Latin *imaginari*]

imaginings *plural noun* things seen or heard that do not exist; fancies or fantasies.

imago /ɪˈmeɪɡoʊ/ *noun* (***imagos*** *or* ***imagines*** /-dʒɪniːz/) a sexually mature adult insect. [18c: Latin, meaning 'likeness']

imam /ɪˈmɑːm/ *Islam noun* **1** a leader of prayers in a mosque. **2** (**Imam**) a title given to various Muslim leaders. [17c: Arabic, meaning 'leader']

imbalance *noun* a lack of balance or proportion; inequality.

imbecile *noun* **1** *old use* someone of very low intelligence. **2** *informal* a fool. ▸ *adj*. ▪ **imbecility** *noun* (*-ies*). [16c: from Latin *imbecillus* feeble or fragile]

imbed a less usual spelling of **embed**

imbibe *verb* **1** *now facetious or formal* to drink, esp alcoholic drinks. **2** *formal or literary* to take in or absorb something (eg ideas). [14c: from Latin *imbibere* to drink in]

imbroglio /ɪmˈbroʊlɪoʊ/ *noun* **1** a confused and complicated situation. **2** a misunderstanding or disagreement. [18c: Italian]

imbue *verb* (***imbued, imbuing***) **1** (*esp* **imbue sb with sth**) to fill or inspire someone, esp with ideals or principles. **2** to soak or saturate something, esp with dye. [16c: from Latin *imbuere* to saturate]

IMF *abbrev* International Monetary Fund.

IMHO *abbrev* in my humble opinion.

imitate *verb* **1** to copy the behaviour, appearance, etc of someone; to mimic someone. **2** to make a copy of something. ▪ **imitable** *adj*. ▪ **imitator** *noun*. [16c: from Latin *imitari*]

imitation *noun* **1** an act of imitating. **2** something that is produced by imitating; a copy or counterfeit. ▸ *adj* sham or artificial: *imitation leather.*

imitative *adj* **1** imitating, copying or mimicking. **2** copying a more expensive or superior-quality original.

immaculate *adj* **1** perfectly clean and neat. **2** free from blemish, flaw or error. **3** free from any moral stain or sin. ▪ **immaculately** *adv*. [15c: from Latin *immaculatus* spotless]

immanent *adj* **1** existing or remaining within something; inherent. **2** of a Supreme Being or power: permanently present throughout the universe everywhere. ▪ **immanence** *noun*. [16c: from medieval Latin *immanere*]

immaterial *adj* **1** not important or relevant. **2** not formed of matter. [14c: from Latin *immaterialis*]

immature *adj* **1** not fully grown or developed; not mature or ripe. **2** not fully developed emotionally or intellectually; childish. ▪ **immaturity** *noun*. [16c: from Latin *immaturus*]

immeasurable *adj* too great to be measured; very great; immense. ▪ **immeasurably** *adv*. [15c]

immediacy *noun* (*-ies*) **1** the quality of being immediate or appealing directly to the emotions, understanding, etc. Also called **immediateness**. **2** an immediate problem, requirement or necessity.

immediate *adj* **1** happening or done at once and without delay. **2** nearest or next in space, time, relationship, etc: *the immediate family.* **3** belonging to the current time; urgent: *deal with the immediate problems first.* **4** having a direct effect: *the immediate cause of death.* [16c: from Latin *immediatus*]

immediately *adv* **1** at once; without delay. **2** without anything between: *immediately next to me.* ▸ *conj* as soon as: *Immediately he arrived, the meeting began.*

immemorial *adj* extending far back in time, beyond anyone's memory or written records. [17c: from Latin *immemorialis*]

immense *adj* **1** very or unusually large or great. **2** *dated, informal* very good; splendid. ▪ **immensely**

adv. ▪ **immenseness** *or* **immensity** *noun* (**-*ies***). [15c: French, from Latin *immensus* immeasurable]

immerse *verb* (*esp* **immerse sth** *or* **sb in sth**) to dip it or them into a liquid completely. ▪ **immersible** *adj.* ▪ **immersion** *noun.* [17c: from Latin *immergere* to dip]

IDIOMS **be immersed in sth** to be occupied, involved or absorbed in it.

immigrant *noun* **1** someone who immigrates or has immigrated. **2** *biol* an animal or plant that becomes established in an area where it was previously not found. ▸ *adj* **1** belonging or relating to immigrants. **2** immigrating or having recently immigrated.

immigrate *verb, intr* to come to a foreign country with the intention of settling in it. ▪ **immigration** *noun* **1** the process of immigrating. *as adj*: *immigration control.* **2** *informal* **a** the immigration checkpoint at an airport, seaport etc; **b** the immigration authorities. [17c: from Latin *immigrare*]

imminent *adj* likely to happen in the near future. ▪ **imminence** *noun.* ▪ **imminently** *adv.* [16c: from Latin *imminere* to project over something]

immiscible ▸ *noun, chem* of liquids, eg oil and water: forming separate layers and not mixing when shaken together. [17c: from Latin *miscere* to mix]

immobile *adj* **1** not able to move or be moved. **2** motionless. ▪ **immobility** *noun.* [14c: French, from Latin *immobilis*]

immobilize *or* **-ise** *verb* to make or keep something or someone immobile. ▪ **immobilization** *noun.*

immoderate *adj* excessive or extreme. [14c: from Latin *immoderatus*]

immodest *adj* **1** shameful; indecent. **2** boastful and conceited; forward. [16c: from Latin *immodestus*]

immolate *verb* to kill or offer as a sacrifice. ▪ **immolation** *noun.* [16c: from Latin *immolare* to sprinkle (a sacrificial victim) with meal before sacrificing it]

immoral *adj* **1** morally wrong or bad. **2** not conforming to the sexual standards of society. **3** unscrupulous; unethical. ▪ **immorality** *noun.* [17c]

immortal *adj* **1** living forever. **2** lasting forever. **3** to be remembered forever. ▸ *noun* **1** someone who will live forever or who will always be remembered. **2** someone, eg an author, whose greatness or genius will be remembered forever. **3** (**the immortals**) the ancient Greek and Roman gods. ▪ **immortality** *noun.* [14c: from Latin *immortalis*]

immortalize *or* **-ise** *verb* **1** to make (a person, etc) famous for ever, eg in a work of art or literature. **2** to make someone immortal. ▪ **immortalization** *noun.*

immovable *or* **immoveable** *adj* **1** impossible to move; not meant to be moved. **2** steadfast; unyielding. **3** incapable of feeling or showing emotion, esp sorrow or pity. **4** *law* of property: not liable to be removed; consisting of land or houses. ▪ **immovability** *noun.* [14c]

immune *adj* **1** (*esp* **immune to sth**) having a natural resistance to or protected by **inoculation** from (a particular disease). **2** (*esp* **immune from sth**) free, exempt or protected from it. **3** (*esp* **immune to sth**) unaffected by or not susceptible to it: *immune to criticism.* **4** *physiol* relating to or concerned with producing immunity: *the immune system.* ▪ **immunity** *noun.* [15c: from Latin *immunis*]

immune response *noun, physiol* the response of the body to a foreign substance, eg a virus.

immune system *noun, physiol* the natural defensive system of an organism that identifies and neutralizes harmful matter within itself.

immunize *or* **-ise** *verb, med* to produce artificial immunity to a disease in someone by injecting them with eg a treated antigen. ▪ **immunization** *noun.*

immunodeficiency *noun, physiol, med* a deficiency or breakdown in the body's ability to fight infection.

immunology *noun* the scientific study of immunity and the defence mechanisms that the body uses to resist infection and disease. ▪ **immunological** *adj.* ▪ **immunologist** *noun.*

immunotherapy *noun* the treatment of disease, esp cancer, by antigens which stimulate the patient's own natural immunity.

immure *verb* **1** to enclose or imprison someone within, or as if within, walls. **2** to shut someone away. [16c: from Latin *immurare*, from *murus* wall]

immutable *adj* **1** unable to be changed. **2** not susceptible to change. ▪ **immutability** *noun.* ▪ **immutably** *adv.* [15c: from Latin *immutabilis*]

IMO *or* **imo** *abbrev* in my opinion (used in text messages and e-mails).

imp *noun* **1** a small mischievous or evil spirit. **2** a mischievous or annoying child. ▪ **impish** *adj.* [Anglo-Saxon *impa* a shoot or offspring]

impact *noun* /'ɪmpakt/ **1** the collision of an object with another object. **2** the force of such a collision. **3** a strong effect or impression. ▸ *verb* /ɪm'pakt/ **1** **a** to press (two objects) together with force; **b** to force (one object) into (another). **2** *intr* to come forcefully into contact with another body or surface, etc. **3** to have an impact or effect on. ▪ **impaction** *noun.* [17c: from Latin *impingere* to strike against]

impacted *adj* **1** of a tooth: unable to come into a normal position because it is firmly wedged between the jawbone and another tooth. **2** of a fracture: with the broken ends of the bone driven into each other.

impair *verb* to damage or weaken something, esp in terms of its quality or strength. ▪ **impairment** *noun.* [14c: from French *empeirer*]

impala /ɪm'pɑːlə/ *noun* (***impalas*** *or* ***impala***) an antelope of S and E Africa. [19c: from Zulu *i-mpala*]

impale *verb* **1** **a** to pierce with, or as if with, a long, pointed object or weapon; **b** to put someone to death by this method. **2** *heraldry* to put (two coats-of-arms) on a shield divided vertically into two. ▪ **impalement** *noun.* [16c: from Latin *impaler*, from *palus* a stake]

impalpable *adj* **1** not able to be felt or perceived by touch. **2** difficult to understand or grasp. ▪ **impalpability** *noun.* ▪ **impalpably** *adv.* [16c: French]

impart *verb* **1** to make (information, knowledge, etc) known. **2** to give or transmit (a particular quality). [15c: from Latin *impartire*]

impartial *adj* fair and unbiased. ▪ **impartiality** *noun.* ▪ **impartially** *adv.* [16c]

impassable *adj* of a road, path, etc: not able to be travelled along. ▪ **impassability** *noun.* [16c]

impasse /'ɪmpas, am'pas; *French* ɛ̃pas/ *noun* a situation with no possible progress or escape. [19c: French, from *passer* to pass]

impassioned *adj* **1** fervent, zealous or animated. **2** deeply moved by emotion.

impassive *adj* **1** incapable of feeling and expressing emotion. **2** showing no feeling or emotion. ▪ **impassively** *adv.* ▪ **impassiveness** *or* **impassivity** *noun.* [17c: from Latin *passivus* susceptible to pain]

impasto *noun, art* in painting and pottery: **a** the technique of laying paint or pigment on thickly; **b** paint applied thickly. [18c: Italian]

impatient *adj* **1** unwilling to wait or delay; lacking patience. **2** (*usu* **impatient of** *or* **with sth** *or* **sb**) intolerant; showing a lack of patience. **3** (*often* **impatient to do** *or* **for sth**) restlessly eager and anxious. ▪ **impatience** *noun.* ▪ **impatiently** *adv.* [14c: French, from Latin *impatiens*]

impeach *verb* **1** *Brit law* to charge someone with a serious crime, esp against the state. **2** *N Am* to accuse (a public or government official) of misconduct while in office. **3** to cast doubt upon (eg a person's honesty). ▪ **impeachable** *adj.* ▪ **impeachment** *noun.* [14c: from French *empecher* to hinder or impede]

impeccable *adj* faultless; perfect; flawless. [16c: from Latin *impeccabilis*]

impecunious *adj* having little or no money. [16c: from Latin *pecunia* money]

impedance /ɪm'piːdəns/ *noun* **1** *elec* (SI unit **ohm**) (symbol **Z**) the effective **resistance** of an electric circuit or component. **2** anything that impedes.

impede *verb* to prevent or delay the start or progress of (an activity, etc); to obstruct or hinder something or someone. [17c: from Latin *impedire*]

impediment *noun* **1** an obstacle or hindrance. **2** (*also* **speech impediment**) a defect in a person's speech, eg a lisp or stutter. [14c: Latin *impedimentum*]

impedimenta *plural noun* objects that impede progress or movement, eg military baggage and equipment, legal obstructions, etc. [16c: Latin *impedimentum* a hindrance]

impel *verb* (***impelled, impelling***) **1** to push, drive or urge something forward. **2** to force or urge someone into action. [15c: from Latin *impellare*]

impend *verb, intr* **1** to be about to happen. **2** of a danger, etc: to be threateningly close. ▪ **impending** *adj.* [16c: from Latin *impendere* to hang over]

impenetrable *adj* **1** incapable of being entered or passed through. **2** not capable of being understood or explained. **3** not capable of receiving or being touched by intellectual ideas and influences: *impenetrable ignorance.* **4** unable to be seen through; gloomy: *impenetrable despair.* [15c: from Latin *impenetrabilis*]

impenitent *adj* not sorry for having done something wrong. ▸ *noun* an unrepentant person; a hardened sinner. ▪ **impenitence** *noun.* [16c: from Latin *impaenitens*]

imperative *adj* **1** absolutely essential; urgent. **2** having or showing authority; commanding: *an imperative manner.* **3** *grammar* (abbrev **imper.**) of the **mood**[2] of a verb: used for giving orders. ▸ *noun* **1** *grammar* a mood of verbs used for giving orders. Compare **indicative**, **conditional**, **subjunctive**. **2** a verb form of this kind. **3** something imperative, esp a command or order. ▪ **imperatively** *adv.* [16c: from Latin *imperativus*, from *imperare* to command]

imperceptible *adj* **1** too small, slight or gradual to be seen, heard, noticed, etc. **2** not able to be perceived by the senses. ▪ **imperceptibly** *adv.* [16c]

imperceptive *or* **impercipient** *adj* having no power to perceive; lacking perception. ▪ **imperceptively** *or* **impercipiently** *adv.* ▪ **imperceptiveness** *or* **impercipience** *noun.* [17c in the form *imperceptive*; 19c in the form *impercipient*]

imperfect *adj* **1** having faults; spoilt. **2** lacking the full number of parts; incomplete or unfinished. **3** *grammar* of the tense of a verb: expressing a continuing state or incomplete action in the past. **4** *music* of a chord, interval, etc: diminished; reduced by a semitone. Compare **perfect.** ▸ *noun, grammar* **a** the imperfect tense; **b** a verb in the imperfect tense. ▪ **imperfection** *noun.* [14c: from French *imparfait* and Latin *imperfectus*]

imperial *adj* **1** relating to an empire, emperor or empress. **2** having supreme authority. **3** commanding; august. **4** regal; magnificent. **5** *Brit* of a non-metric measure or weight, or of the non-metric system: conforming to standards fixed by parliament. ▪ **imperially** *adv.* [14c: from Latin *imperialis*]

imperialism *noun* **1** the power of, or rule by, an emperor or empress. **2** the policy or principle of having or extending control or influence over other nations, eg by conquest, trade or diplomacy. **3** the spirit, character, motivation, etc of empire. ▪ **imperialist** *noun, adj.* ▪ **imperialistic** *adj.*

imperil *verb* (***imperilled, imperilling***; *US* ***imperiled, imperiling***) to endanger. ▪ **imperilment** *noun.* [16c]

imperious *adj* arrogant, haughty and domineering. ▪ **imperiously** *adv.* [16c: from Latin *imperiosus*]

imperishable *adj* not subject to decay; lasting forever. ▪ **imperishability** *noun.* ▪ **imperishably** *adv.* [17c]

impermanent *adj* not lasting or remaining. ▪ **impermanence** *noun.* [17c]

impermeable *adj* of a material, etc: not allowing substances, esp liquids, to pass through it. ▪ **impermeability** *noun.* [17c: from Latin *impermeabilis*]

impermissible *adj* not allowed. [19c]

impersonal *adj* **1** having no reference to any particular person; objective. **2** without or unaffected by personal or human feelings, warmth, sympathy, etc. **3** without personality. **4** *grammar* (abbrev **impers.**) **a** of a verb: used without a subject or with a purely formal one (as in *It's snowing*); **b** of a pronoun: not referring to a particular person; indefinite. ▪ **impersonality** *noun.* ▪ **impersonally** *adv.* [16c: from Latin *impersonalis*]

impersonate *verb* to pretend to be, or copy the behaviour and appearance of, someone, esp in order to entertain or deceive other people. ▪ **impersonation** *noun.* ▪ **impersonator** *noun.* [18c: from Latin *persona* person]

impertinent *adj* disrespectful; impudent. ▪ **impertinence** *noun.* [14c: from Latin *impertinens*]

imperturbable *adj* always calm and unruffled. ▪ **imperturbability** *noun.* ▪ **imperturbably** *adv.* [15c: from Latin *imperturbabilis*]

impervious *adj* (*usu* **impervious to sth**) **1** of a substance or material, etc: not allowing (eg water) to pass through or penetrate it; impermeable. **2** not influenced or affected by it. [17c: from Latin *impervius*]

impetigo /ɪmpɪ'taɪgoʊ/ *noun, pathol* a contagious skin disease characterized by pustules and yellow crusty sores. [14c: Latin, from *impetere* to attack]

impetuous *adj* **1** acting or done hurriedly and without due consideration. **2** moving or acting forcefully or with great energy. ▪ **impetuosity** *noun.* [14c: from Latin *impetuosus*]

impetus *noun* **1** the force or energy with which something moves. **2** a driving force. **3** an incentive or encouragement. [17c: Latin, meaning 'attack' or 'force']

impinge *verb, intr* (*usu* **impinge against** *or* **on sth** *or* **sb**) **1** to interfere with or encroach on it or them. **2** to make an impression on it or them. ▪ **impingement** *noun.* [17c: from Latin *impingere* to force, thrust or drive violently]

impious *adj* lacking respect or proper reverence. ▪ **impiety** *noun* (***-ies***). [16c: from Latin *impius*]

implacable *adj* not able to be calmed, satisfied or placated; unyielding. ▪ **implacability** *noun.* ▪ **implacably** *adv.* [16c: French]

implant *verb* /ɪm'plɑːnt/ **1** to fix or plant something securely; to embed it. **2** to fix or instil (ideas, beliefs, etc) in someone's mind. **3** *surgery* to insert or graft (an object, tissue, etc) into the body. ▶ *noun* /'ɪmplɑːnt/ *surgery* an implanted object, tissue, etc. ▪ **implantation** *noun.* [16c: from French *implanter*]

implausible *adj* not easy to believe; not likely to be true. ▪ **implausibly** *adv.* [17c]

implement *noun* a tool or utensil. ▶ *verb* to carry out, fulfil or perform. ▪ **implementation** *noun.* [15c: from Latin *implementum*]

implicate *verb* **1** to show or suggest that someone is or was involved in eg a crime. **2** to imply. ▪ **implicative** *adj.* [16c: from Latin *implicare* to interweave]

implication *noun* **1** implicating someone or being implicated. **2** implying something or being implied. **3** something that is implied.

implicit *adj* **1** implied but not stated directly. **2** present, although not explicit or immediately discernible: *There was a threat implicit in her words.* **3** unquestioning; complete: *implicit faith.* ▪ **implicitly** *adv.* [16c: from Latin *implicitus* involved or interwoven]

implode *verb, tr & intr* to collapse or make something collapse inwards. [19c: modelled on **explode**]

implore *verb* **1** to entreat or beg someone. **2** (*usu* **implore sb for** *or* **to do sth**) to beg them earnestly for it or to do it. [16c: from Latin *implorare*]

imply *verb* (***-ies, -ied***) **1** to suggest or express something indirectly; to hint at it. **2** to suggest or involve something as a necessary result or consequence: *These privileges imply a heavy responsibility.* [14c: from French *emplier*, from Latin *implicare* to interweave]

imply, infer

Be careful not to use the word **imply** when you mean **infer**. If you **infer** something, you decide it is the case from the facts you have or from what has been said:

I infer from what you are saying that you don't want to get involved.

impolite *adj* rude, disrespectful. ▪ **impolitely** *adv.* ▪ **impoliteness** *noun.* [17c: from Latin *impolitus*]

impolitic *adj* unwise; not to be advised. [16c]

imponderable *adj* having influence or importance that cannot be measured or assessed. ▶ *noun* something imponderable. [18c: from Latin *imponderabilis*]

import *verb* /ɪm'pɔːt/ **1** to bring (goods, etc) into a country from another country. **2** to bring something in from an external source. **3** *comput* to load (a file, text, data, etc) into a program. **4** *formal or old use* to signify, imply or portend. ▶ *noun* /'ɪmpɔːt/ **1** an imported commodity, article, etc. **2** the act or business of importing goods. *as adj*: *import duty.* **3** *formal* importance: *a matter of great import.* **4** *formal or old use* meaning. ▪ **importation** *noun.* ▪ **importer** *noun.* [15c: from Latin *importare*]

important *adj* **1** having great value, influence, significance or effect. **2** having high social rank or status. **3** *rather formal or literary* pompous or pretentious. ▪ **importance** *noun.* ▪ **importantly** *adv.* [16c: French]

importunate *adj, formal* **1** persistent or excessively demanding. **2** extremely urgent or pressing. [15c: from Latin *importunus* inconvenient]

importune *verb, tr & intr, formal* **1** to make persistent and usu annoying requests of someone. **2** to solicit for immoral purposes, eg prostitution. ▪ **importunity** *noun* (***-ies***). [15c: from Latin *importunus* inconvenient]

impose *verb* **1** (*usu* **impose sth on** *or* **upon sb**) to make payment of (a tax, fine, etc) or performance of (a duty) compulsory. **2** (*esp* **impose oneself on** *or* **upon sb**) to force one's opinions, company, etc on them. **3** (*esp* **impose on** *or* **upon sb** *or* **sth**) *intr* to take advantage of them or it; to set unreasonable burdens or tasks on them: *We mustn't impose on your good nature.* **4** (*usu* **impose sth on** *or* **upon sb**) to palm it off on them surreptitiously or dishonestly. [17c: from French *imposer*]

imposing *adj* impressive, esp in size, dignity, handsome appearance, etc.

imposition *noun* **1** the act or process of imposing. **2** an unfair or excessive demand, burden or requirement. **3** a tax or duty.

impossible *adj* **1** not capable of happening, being done, etc. **2** not capable of being true; difficult to believe. **3** *informal* unacceptable, unsuitable or difficult to bear; intolerable. ▪ **impossibility** *noun.* ▪ **impossibly** *adv.* [14c: from Latin *impossibilis*]

impostor *or* **imposter** *noun* someone who pretends to be someone else in order to deceive others. ▪ **imposture** *noun.* [16c: from French *imposteur*]

impotent *adj* **1** powerless; lacking the necessary strength. **2** of an adult male: **a** unable to maintain a sexual erection; **b** unable to have an orgasm. ▪ **impotence** *noun.* [15c: French]

impound *verb* **1** to shut (eg an animal) up in, or as if in, a **pound**[2]. **2** to take legal possession of something; to confiscate it. [16c]

impoverish *verb* **1** to make poor or poorer. **2** to reduce the quality, richness or fertility of something (eg soil). ▪ **impoverished** *adj.* [15c: from French *empovrir*]

impracticable *adj* **1** not able to be done, put into practice, used, etc. **2** not in a suitable condition for use. ▪ **impracticability** *noun.* [17c: see **practice**]

impractical *adj* **1** not effective in actual use. **2** of a person, plan, etc: lacking common sense. ▪ **impracticality** *noun* (***-ies***). [19c]

imprecation *noun, formal or old use* a curse. ▪ **imprecatory** *adj.* [17c: from Latin *imprecari* to pray]

imprecise *adj* inaccurate. ▪ **imprecision** *noun.* [19c]

impregnable *adj* **1** of a city, fortress, etc: not able to be taken by force. **2** not affected by criticism, doubts, etc. ▪ **impregnability** *noun*. [15c: from French *imprenable*]

impregnate *verb* **1** to make (a woman or female animal) pregnant; to fertilize (eg a female cell or plant). **2** to permeate something completely; to saturate it. **3** to fill or imbue something. ▪ **impregnation** *noun*. [16c: from Latin *impraegnare* to fertilize]

impresario *noun* **1** someone who organizes public concerts, etc. **2** the manager of an opera or theatre company. [18c: Italian, meaning 'someone who undertakes business']

impress *verb* /ɪm'prɛs/ **1** to produce a strong and usu favourable impression on someone. **2** (*esp* **impress sth on** *or* **upon sb**) to make it very clear or emphasize it to them. **3** to make or stamp (a mark, pattern, etc) on something by pressure. **4** (*often* **impress sth on** *or* **upon sb**) to fix (a fact, belief, etc) firmly or deeply in their mind or memory. ▸ *noun* /'ɪmprɛs/ **1** the act or process of impressing. **2** something (eg a mark or impression) made by impressing. ▪ **impressible** *adj*. [14c: from Latin *imprimere* to press into or on]

impression *noun* **1** an idea or effect, esp a favourable one, produced in the mind or made on the senses. **2** a vague or uncertain idea, notion or belief: *I got the impression he was lying*. **3** an act or the process of impressing. **4** a mark or stamp produced by, or as if by, pressure. **5** an imitation, often a caricature, of a person, or an imitation of a thing or sound, done for entertainment: *He does impressions of pop stars*. **6** the number of copies of a book, newspaper, etc printed at one time.

impressionable *adj* easily impressed or influenced. ▪ **impressionability** *noun*.

Impressionism *noun* (*sometimes* **impressionism**) in art, music or literature: a 19c style aiming to give a general impression of feelings and events rather than a formal treatment of them. [19c: from Monet's picture *Impression: soleil levant* (Impression: Rising Sun)]

impressionist *noun* **1** (*usu* **Impressionist**) a painter, writer or composer in the style of Impressionism. **2** someone who imitates, or performs impressions of, other people. ▸ *adj* (*usu* **Impressionist**) relating to Impressionism.

impressionistic *adj* based on impressions or feelings rather than facts or knowledge.

impressive *adj* **1** capable of making a deep impression on a person's mind, feelings, etc. **2** producing admiration, wonder or approval. ▪ **impressively** *adv*. [16c]

imprimatur /ɪmprɪ'meɪtə(r), -'mɑːtə(r)/ *noun* **1** permission to print or publish a book, now esp one granted by the Roman Catholic Church. **2** approval; permission. [17c: Latin, meaning 'let it be printed']

imprint *noun* /'ɪmprɪnt/ **1** a mark made by pressure. **2** a permanent effect, eg on the mind. **3** a publisher's name and address, and often the date and place of publication, as printed eg at the bottom of a book's title page. ▸ *verb* /ɪm'prɪnt/ (*usu* **imprint sth on sth**) **1** to mark or print an impression of it on (eg a surface). **2** to fix it firmly in (the mind, etc). **3** *zool* to cause (a young animal) to undergo **imprinting**. [15c: see **print**]

imprinting *noun, zool* the process by which animals learn the appearance, sound or smell of members of their own species, esp parents or suitable mates.

imprison *verb* **1** to put in prison. **2** to confine or restrain as if in a prison. ▪ **imprisonment** *noun*. [13c: from French *emprisoner*]

improbable *adj* **1** unlikely to happen or exist. **2** hard to believe. ▪ **improbability** *noun* (**-ies**). ▪ **improbably** *adv*. [16c: from Latin *improbabilis*]

improbity *noun* (**-ies**) dishonesty; wickedness. [16c: from Latin *improbitas*]

impromptu *adj* made or done without preparation or rehearsal. ▸ *adv* without preparation; spontaneously. [17c: from Latin *in promptu* in readiness]

improper *adj* **1** not conforming to accepted standards of modesty and moral behaviour. **2** not correct; wrong: *improper use of funds*. **3** not suitable: *We consider jeans improper dress for the occasion*. ▪ **improperly** *adv*. [16c: from Latin *improprius*]

improper fraction *noun, maths* a fraction in which the **numerator** has a value equal to or higher than that of the **denominator**, eg $^5/_4$. Compare **proper fraction**.

impropriety *noun* (**-ies**) **1** an improper act. **2** the state of being improper. [17c: from Latin *improprietas*]

improve *verb* **1** *tr & intr* to make or become better or of higher quality or value; to make or cause something to make progress. **2** (*esp* **improve on sth**) to produce something better, or of higher quality or value, than a previous example. **3** to increase the value or beauty of (land or property) by cultivation, building, etc. [17c: from French *emprower*]

improvement *noun* **1** improving or being improved. **2** someone or something considered better than a previous example. **3** something that improves, esp by adding value, beauty, quality, etc: *home improvements*.

improvident *adj* **1** not considering or providing for likely future needs. **2** careless; thoughtless; rash. ▪ **improvidence** *noun*. ▪ **improvidently** *adv*. [16c]

improving *adj* **1** tending to cause improvement. **2** uplifting or instructive, esp in regard to someone's morals.

improvise *verb* **1** *tr & intr* to compose, recite or perform (music, verse, etc) without advance preparation. **2** to make or provide something quickly, without preparation and using whatever materials are to hand. ▪ **improvisation** *noun*. [19c: from French *improviser*]

imprudent *adj* lacking good sense or caution. ▪ **imprudence** *noun*. [14c: from Latin *imprudens*]

impudent *adj* rude, insolent or impertinent. ▪ **impudence** *noun*. [14c: from Latin *impudens*]

impugn /ɪm'pjuːn/ *verb* to call into question or raise doubts about (the honesty, integrity, etc of someone or something). [14c: from French *impugner*]

impulse *noun* **1** a sudden push forwards; a force producing sudden movement forwards. **2** the movement produced by such a force or push. **3** a sudden desire or urge to do something without thinking of the consequences: *bought the dress on impulse*. **4** an instinctive or natural tendency. **5** *physiol* an electrical signal that travels along a nerve fibre. **6** *physics* the force produced when two objects briefly collide with each other. [17c: from Latin *impulsus* pressure]

impulsive *adj* **1** tending or likely to act suddenly and without considering the consequences. **2** done without consideration of consequences. **3** having the power to urge or push forwards, into motion or into action. ▪ **impulsively** *adv.* ▪ **impulsiveness** *noun.*

impunity *noun* freedom or exemption from punishment, injury, loss, etc. [16c: from Latin *impunitas*]

impure *adj* **1** mixed with something else; adulterated or tainted. **2** dirty. **3** immoral; not chaste. **4** *relig* ritually unclean. ▪ **impurity** *noun* (**-ies**). [16c: from Latin *impurus*]

impute *verb* (*usu* **impute sth to sb** *or* **sth**) to regard (something unfavourable or unwelcome) as being brought about by them or it. ▪ **imputable** *adj.* ▪ **imputation** *noun.* [14c: from French *imputer*]

In *symbol, chem* indium.

in *prep* **1** used to express position with regard to what encloses, surrounds or includes someone or something. **2** into. **3** after (a period of time): *Come back in an hour.* **4** during; while: *lost in transit.* **5** used to express arrangement or shape: *in a square.* **6** from; out of something: *one in every eight.* **7** by the medium or means of, or using, something: *in code.* **8** wearing (something). **9** used to describe a state or manner: *in a hurry.* **10** used to state an occupation: *She's in banking.* **11** used to state a purpose: *in memory of his wife.* **12** of some animals: pregnant with (young): *in calf.* ▸ *adv* **1** to or towards the inside; indoors. **2** at home or work: *Is John in?* **3** so as to be added or included: *beat in the eggs.* **4** so as to enclose or conceal: *The fireplace was bricked in.* **5** in or into political power or office: *when the Tories were in.* **6** in or into fashion. **7** in favour: *kept in with the boss.* **8** in certain games: batting. **9** into a proper, required or efficient state: *run a new car in.* **10** of the tide: at its highest point. **11** *in compounds* expressing prolonged activity, esp by many people gathered in one place, originally as a form of protest: *a sit-in.* ▸ *adj* **1** inside; internal; inwards: *the in door.* **2** fashionable: *Orange is the in colour.* **3** *in compounds* used for receiving things coming in: *an in-tray.* **4** *in compounds* shared by a particular group of people: *an in-joke.* [Anglo-Saxon]

IDIOMS **be in for it** *or* **sth** *informal* to be going to experience some trouble or difficulty. **have it in for sb** *informal* to want to make trouble for someone one dislikes. **in as far as** *or* **in so far as ...** (*sometimes written* **insofar as ...**) to the degree that ... **in as much as ...** *or* **inasmuch as ...** because ...; considering that ... **in itself** intrinsically; essentially; considered on its own. **in on sth** *informal* knowing about it; sharing in it. **ins and outs** the complex and detailed facts of a matter; intricacies. **insomuch that** *or* **insomuch as 1** in as much as. **2** to such an extent that. **in that ...** for the reason that ...

in. *abbrev* inch or inches.

in-[1] *prefix* (*also* **il-**, **im-** *and* **ir-**) *signifying* not; lacking: *inhospitable* • *illogical* • *immaturity* • *irrelevance.* [Latin]

in-[2] *prefix* (*also* **il-**, **im-** *and* **ir-**) *signifying* **1** in, on or towards: *immigrant* • *imprison* • *intrude.* **2** used to add emphasis or force: *intumesce.* [Latin *in-* and French *en-* in or into]

-in *suffix, chem, forming nouns, denoting* **1** a neutral substance such as a protein or fat: *albumin* • *lanolin.* **2** an antibiotic or other pharmaceutical drug: *penicillin* • *aspirin.* **3** any of certain enzymes: *pepsin.* [A variant of **-ine**[2]]

-ina *suffix, denoting* a feminized form of a male name, title, etc: *Christina* • *tsarina.* [Italian, Spanish or Latin, modelled on such words as **ballerina**]

inability *noun* the lack of sufficient power, means or ability. [15c]

inaccessible *adj* **1** difficult or impossible to approach, reach or obtain. **2** of a person: difficult to understand; unapproachable. ▪ **inaccessibility** *noun.* [16c]

inaccurate *adj* containing errors. ▪ **inaccuracy** *noun* (**-ies**). ▪ **inaccurately** *adv.*

inaction *noun* lack of action; sluggishness; inactivity.

inactive *adj* **1** taking little or no exercise. **2** no longer operating or functioning. **3** not taking part in or available for duty or operations. **4** *chem* of a substance: showing little or no chemical reactivity. ▪ **inactively** *adv.* ▪ **inactivity** *noun.* [18c]

inadequate *adj* **1** not sufficient or adequate. **2** not competent or capable. ▪ **inadequacy** *noun* (**-ies**).

inadmissible *adj* not allowable or able to be accepted.

inadvertent *adj* **1** not deliberate; unintentional. **2** not paying attention; heedless. ▪ **inadvertently** *adv.* [17c: from Latin *advertere* to direct attention to]

inadvisable *adj* not wise; not advisable.

inalienable *adj* not capable of being taken or given away: *an inalienable right.* [17c]

inane *adj* **1** without meaning or point. **2** silly or senseless. ▪ **inanity** *noun* (**-ies**). [19c: from Latin *inanis* empty]

inanimate *adj* **1** without life; not living. **2** dull; spiritless. ▪ **inanimately** *adv.* ▪ **inanimation** *noun.* [16c]

inapplicable *adj* not applicable or suitable.

inapposite *adj, rather formal* not suitable or apposite; out of place.

inappreciable *adj* too small or slight to be noticed or to be important. [19c]

inappropriate *adj* not suitable or appropriate.

inapt *adj* **1** not apt or appropriate. **2** lacking skill; unqualified. ▪ **inaptitude** *noun.*

inarticulate *adj* **1** unable to express oneself clearly or to speak distinctly. **2** badly expressed; not spoken or pronounced clearly. **3** not jointed or hinged. [17c: from Latin *inarticulatus*]

inasmuch see under **in**

inattentive *adj* not paying attention; neglectful; not attentive. ▪ **inattention** *or* **inattentiveness** *noun.*

inaudible *adj* not loud enough to be heard.

inaugural *adj* **1** officially marking the beginning of something. **2** of a speech, lecture, etc: given by someone on taking office or at their inauguration ceremony. ▸ *noun* an inaugural speech or lecture. [17c: from Latin *inaugurare* to inaugurate]

inaugurate *verb* **1** to place (a person) in office with a formal ceremony. **2** to mark the beginning of (some activity) with a formal ceremony, dedication, etc. ▪ **inauguration** *noun.* [17c: from Latin *inaugurare*]

inauspicious *adj* not promising future success; unlucky.

inboard *adj, adv* esp of a boat's motor or engine: situated inside the hull. Compare **outboard**.

inborn *adj* of an attribute or characteristic: possessed from birth; innate or hereditary. [16c]

inbound *adj* said of a vehicle, flight, carriageway, etc: coming towards its destination; arriving.

in-box *noun, comput* a file for storing incoming e-mail.

inbred *adj* **1** **inborn**. **2** *biol* of a plant or animal: produced by inbreeding.

inbreed *verb* (*past tense & past participle* ***inbred***) *biol* to allow or be involved in reproduction between closely related individuals, esp over several generations. ▪ **inbreeding** *noun*.

in-built *adj* integral; built-in.

Inc. *abbrev, esp US* Incorporated.

Inca *noun, hist* **1** a member of a S American people living in Peru before the Spanish conquest in the 16c, who had a complex civilization and empire. **2** **a** a king or emperor of the Incas; **b** a member of the Incan royal family. *adj* belonging or relating to this people. ▪ **Incan** *adj*. [16c: Spanish, from Quechua *inka* ruler or king]

incalculable *adj* **1** not able to be estimated or reckoned in advance; unpredictable. **2** too great to be measured. ▪ **incalculability** *noun*. ▪ **incalculably** *adv*. [18c]

in camera *adv* in secret; in private. [19c: Latin, meaning 'in a chamber']

incandescent *adj* **1** white-hot; glowing with intense heat. **2** shining brightly; luminous. **3** of a substance: emitting light as a result of being heated to a high temperature. **4** relating to or consisting of light produced by heating a substance to a high temperature. ▪ **incandescence** *noun*. [18c: from Latin *incandescere*]

incantation *noun* **1** a spell. **2** the use of spells and magical formulae. [14c: French]

incapable *adj* **1** lacking the ability, power, character, etc to do it. **2** unable or unfit to do it, esp to look after one's own affairs. [17c: from Latin *incapabilis*]

incapacitate *verb* (*often* **incapacitate sb for sth**) **1** to take away strength, power or ability; to make unfit (eg for work). **2** to disqualify someone legally. [17c]

incapacity *noun* (***-ies***) **1** a lack of the necessary strength, power, ability, etc; inability or disability. **2** legal disqualification. [17c: from French *incapacité*]

incapsulate see **encapsulate**

incarcerate *verb* to shut in or keep in prison. ▪ **incarceration** *noun*. [16c: from Latin *incarcerare*]

incarnate *adj* (*usu placed after a noun*) **1** in bodily, esp human, form: *God incarnate*. **2** personified; typified: *She is laziness incarnate*. ▸ *verb* **1** to give bodily, esp human, form to (a spirit or god). **2** to personify or typify something. [16c: from Latin *incarnatus* made flesh]

incarnation *noun* **1** the bodily form, esp human form, taken by a spirit or god. **2** someone or something that typifies a quality or idea; an embodiment. **3** a period spent in a particular bodily form or state.

incautious *adj* acting or done without thinking; heedless. [18c]

incendiary *adj* **1** relating to the deliberate and illegal burning of property or goods. **2** capable of catching fire and burning readily. **3** causing, or likely to cause, trouble or violence. ▸ *noun* (***-ies***) **1** someone who deliberately and illegally sets fire to buildings or property. **2** (*also* **incendiary bomb**) a device containing a highly inflammable substance, designed to burst into flames on striking its target. [17c: from Latin *incendere* to kindle or set on fire]

incense¹ /ˈɪnsɛns/ *noun* **1** a spice or other substance that gives off a pleasant smell when burned, used esp during religious services. **2** the smell or smoke given off by burning spices, etc. ▸ *verb* **1** to offer incense to (a god). **2** to perfume or fumigate something with incense. [13c: from Latin *incensum* a thing burnt]

incense² /ɪnˈsɛns/ *verb* to make someone very angry. [15c: from Latin *incendere* to set on fire]

incentive *noun* something, such as extra money, that motivates or encourages an action, work, etc. ▸ *adj* serving to motivate or encourage: *an incentive scheme*. [15c: from Latin *incentivus*]

inception *noun* beginning; outset. [15c: from Latin *incipere* to begin]

incessant *adj* going on without stopping; continual. ▪ **incessantly** *adv*. [16c: French]

incest *noun* sexual intercourse between people who are too closely related to be allowed to marry. ▪ **incestuous** *adj*. [13c: from Latin *incestum*]

inch *noun* **1** a unit of length equal to 2.54cm or one twelfth of a foot. **2** *meteorol* the amount of rain or snow that will cover a surface to the depth of one inch. **3** *meteorol* a unit of pressure equal to the amount of atmospheric pressure required to balance the weight of a column of mercury one inch high. **4** (*also* **inches**) a small amount or distance. **5** (**inches**) stature. ▸ *verb, tr & intr* (*esp* **inch along, forward, out**, *etc*) to move or be moved slowly, carefully and by small degrees. [Anglo-Saxon *ynce*]

IDIOMS **every inch** completely; in every way. **inch by inch** *or* **by inches** gradually; by small degrees. **within an inch of sth** very close to or almost as far as it.

inchoate /ɪŋˈkoʊeɪt/ *adj, formal or technical* **1** at the earliest stage of development; just beginning. **2** not fully developed; unfinished; rudimentary. [16c: from Latin *inchoare* to begin]

incidence *noun* **1** the frequency with which something happens or the extent of its influence. **2** *physics* the way in which something moving in a line (eg a ray of light) comes into contact with a surface or plane. **3** the fact or manner of falling on, striking or affecting something. [15c]

incident *noun* **1** an event or occurrence; a relatively minor event or occurrence which might have serious consequences. **2** a brief violent conflict or disturbance. ▸ *adj* **1** belonging naturally to it or being a natural consequence of it. **2** *physics* of light rays, particles, etc: falling on a surface, etc. [15c: French]

incidental *adj* **1** happening, etc by chance in connection with something else, and of secondary or minor importance: *incidental expenses*. **2** occurring or likely to occur as a minor consequence of it. **3** (*usu* **incidental on** *or* **upon sth**) following or depending upon it, or caused by it, as a minor consequence. ▸ *noun* **1** anything that occurs incidentally. **2** (**incidentals**) minor expenses, details, items, etc. ▪ **incidentally** *adv*. [17c]

incidental music *noun* music that accompanies the action of a film, play, etc.

incinerate *verb, tr & intr* to burn to ashes. ▪ **incineration** *noun*. [16c: from Latin *incinerare* to reduce to ashes]

incinerator *noun* a furnace for burning rubbish, etc.

incipient *adj* beginning to exist; in an early stage. [17c: from Latin *incipere* to begin]

incise *verb, esp technical* **1** to cut into, esp precisely with a sharp tool. **2** to engrave (an inscription, stone, etc). [16c: from French *inciser*]

incision *noun* **1** a cut, esp one made by a surgeon. **2** an act of cutting, esp by a surgeon.

incisive *adj* clear and sharp; to the point; acute. ▪ **incisively** *adv.* ▪ **incisiveness** *noun.* [16c: see **incise**]

incisor *noun* in mammals: a sharp chisel-edged tooth in the front of the mouth, used for biting and nibbling.

incite *verb* (*esp* **incite sb to sth**) to stir up or provoke to action, etc. ▪ **incitement** *noun.* [15c: from Latin *incitare* to set in rapid motion]

incivility *noun* (**-*ies***) **1** rudeness. **2** a rude or uncivil act or remark. [17c]

incl. *or* (*sometimes*) **inc.** *abbrev* **1** included. **2** including. **3** inclusive.

inclement /ɪŋ'klɛmənt/ *adj, formal* of weather: stormy or severe. [17c: from Latin *inclemens*]

inclination *noun* **1** (*often* **an inclination for** *or* **towards sth** *or* **to do sth**) a tendency or feeling; a liking, interest or preference. **2** the degree to which an object slopes. **3** see **incline** ▸ *noun.* **4** a bow or nod of (the head, etc). **5** the act of inclining; being inclined.

incline /ɪŋ'klaɪn/ *verb* **1** *tr & intr* (*esp* **incline to** *or* **towards sth**) to lean or make someone lean towards or be disposed towards (a particular opinion or conduct): *He inclined towards radicalism.* **2** *tr & intr* to slope or make something slope. **3** to bow or bend (the head, one's body, etc) forwards or downwards. ▸ *noun* /'ɪŋklaɪn/ a slope; an inclined plane. Also called **inclination.** ▪ **inclined** *adj.* [14c: from Latin *inclinare* to bend towards]

inclose *and* **inclosure** see **enclose** *and* **enclosure**

include *verb* **1** to count, take in or consider something or someone as part of a group. **2** to contain or be made up of something, or to have it as a part of the whole. Opposite of **exclude.** ▪ **including** *prep* which includes. [15c: from Latin *includere* to shut in]

inclusion *noun* **1** including or being included. **2** something that is included.

inclusive *adj* **1** (*usu* **inclusive of sth**) incorporating it; taking it in. **2** counting the items or terms forming the limits. **3** comprehensive; all-embracing.

incognito *adj, adv* keeping one's identity secret, eg by using a disguise and a false name. ▸ *noun* **1** the disguise and false name of a person who wishes to keep their identity secret. **2** someone who is incognito. [17c: Italian, meaning 'unknown']

incognizant *or* **-isant** *adj, formal* not aware of it; not knowing it. ▪ **incognizance** *noun.* [19c]

incoherent *adj* **1** not expressed clearly or logically; difficult to understand. **2** unable to speak clearly and logically. [17c]

income *noun* money received over a period of time as salary or wages, interest or profit. [17c]

incomer *noun* someone who comes to live in a place, not having been born there.

income tax *noun* a tax levied on income, eg salaries and wages.

incoming *adj* **1** coming in; approaching: *the incoming train.* **2** next or following. **3** of an official, politician, etc: coming into office.

incommensurable *adj* (*esp* **incommensurable with sth**) **1** having no common standard or basis and not able to be compared with it. **2** *maths* of a quantity or magnitude: having no common factor with another. ▪ **incommensurability** *noun.* [16c: from Latin *incommensurabilis*]

incommensurate *adj* **1** (*esp* **incommensurate with** *or* **to sth**) out of proportion to it; inadequate for it. **2** **incommensurable.** [17c]

incommode *verb, formal or old use* to cause trouble or inconvenience to someone. [16c: from French *incommoder*]

incommodious *adj, formal* of eg accommodation: inconvenient or uncomfortable; too small. [16c]

incommunicado *adv, adj* not able or allowed to communicate with other people, esp when in solitary confinement. [19c: Spanish]

incomparable *adj* **1** having no equal. **2** not comparable; lacking a basis for comparison.

incompatible *adj* **1** unable to live, work or get on together in harmony. **2** (*often* **incompatible with sth**) not in agreement; inconsistent. **3** of eg drugs: not able to be combined or used together. **4** of eg machines, computer software or hardware, etc: incapable of functioning together. ▪ **incompatibility** *noun.* [16c]

incompetent *adj* **1** lacking the necessary skill, ability or qualifications, esp for a job. **2** not legally qualified or **competent.** ▸ *noun* an incompetent person. ▪ **incompetence** *noun.* ▪ **incompetently** *adv.* [16c]

incomplete *adj* not complete or finished. [14c]

incomprehensible *adj* difficult or impossible to understand. ▪ **incomprehensibility** *noun.* [14c]

inconceivable *adj* **1** unable to be imagined, believed or conceived by the mind. **2** *informal* extremely unlikely. ▪ **inconceivability** *noun.* [17c]

inconclusive *adj* not leading to a definite conclusion, result or decision. ▪ **inconclusiveness** *noun.* [17c]

incongruous *adj* **1** out of place; unsuitable; inappropriate. **2** (*often* **incongruous with** *or* **to sth**) incompatible or out of keeping with it. ▪ **incongruity** *noun* (**-*ies***). [17c: from Latin *incongruus*]

inconsequent *adj* **1** not following logically or reasonably; illogical. **2** irrelevant. **3** (also **inconsequential**) not connected or related. ▪ **inconsequently** *adv.* [16c: from Latin *inconsequens*]

inconsequential *adj* **1** of no importance, value or **consequence. 2** **inconsequent**. [17c: from Latin *inconsequens*]

inconsiderable *adj, often with negatives* not worth considering; small in amount, value, etc: *lent her a not inconsiderable sum.* ▪ **inconsiderably** *adv.* [17c]

inconsiderate *adj* thoughtless, esp in not considering the feelings, rights, etc of others. ▪ **inconsiderateness** *or* **inconsideration** *noun.* [15c]

inconsistent *adj* **1** not in agreement or accordance with it. **2** containing contradictions. **3** not consistent in thought, speech, behaviour, etc; changeable. ▪ **inconsistency** *noun* (**-*ies***). [17c]

inconsolable *adj* not able to be comforted. [16c]

inconsonant *adj* (*esp* **inconsonant with sth**) not agreeing or in harmony with it. [17c]

inconspicuous *adj* not easily noticed; attracting little attention. [17c]

inconstant *adj* **1** having frequently changing feelings; unfaithful. **2** subject to frequent change. ▪ **inconstancy** *noun*. [15c]

incontestable *adj* indisputable; undeniable. [17c]

incontinent *adj* **1** unable to control one's bowels and/or bladder. **2** *formal or old use* unable to control oneself, esp one's sexual desires. ▪ **incontinence** *noun*. [14c: French, from Latin *incontinens*]

incontrovertible *adj* not able to be disputed or doubted. ▪ **incontrovertibly** *adv*. [17c]

inconvenience *noun* **1** trouble or difficulty. **2** something that causes trouble or difficulty. ▸ *verb* to cause trouble or difficulty to someone. ▪ **inconvenient** *adj*. ▪ **inconveniently** *adv*. [16c]

incorporate *verb* /ɪŋˈkɔːpəreɪt/ **1** *tr & intr* to include or contain something, or be included, as part of a whole. **2** *tr & intr* to combine something, or be united thoroughly, in a single mass. **3** to admit someone to membership of a legal corporation. **4** to form (a company or other body) into a legal corporation. **5** *intr* to form a legal corporation. ▸ *adj* /ɪŋˈkɔːpərət/ (*also* **incorporated**) **1** united in one body or as a single whole. **2** forming a legal corporation. ▪ **incorporation** *noun*. [14c: from Latin *incorporare*]

incorporeal *adj* **1** without bodily or material form or substance. **2** spiritual. [16c]

incorrect *adj* **1** not accurate; containing errors or faults. **2** not in accordance with normal or accepted standards; improper. [15c]

incorrigible *adj* of a person, their bad behaviour or a bad habit: not able to be improved, corrected or reformed. ▪ **incorrigibility** *noun*. [14c]

incorruptible *adj* **1** incapable of being bribed or morally corrupted. **2** not liable to decay. ▪ **incorruptibility** *noun*. ▪ **incorruptibly** *adv*. [14c]

increase *verb* /ɪŋˈkriːs/ *tr & intr* to make or become greater in size, intensity or number. ▸ *noun* /ˈɪŋkriːs/ **1** increasing or becoming increased; growth. **2** the amount by which something increases or is increased. ▪ **increasing** *adj*. ▪ **increasingly** *adv*. [14c: from French *encresser*]

incredible *adj* **1** difficult or impossible to believe. **2** *informal* amazing; unusually good. ▪ **incredibility** *noun*. ▪ **incredibly** *adv*. [15c]

incredulous *adj* **1** showing or expressing disbelief. **2** (*often* **incredulous of sth**) unwilling to believe or accept that it is true. ▪ **incredulity** *noun*. ▪ **incredulously** *adv*. [16c]

increment *noun* **1** an increase, esp of one point or level on a scale, eg a regular increase in salary. **2** the amount by which something is increased. **3** *maths* a small positive or negative change in the value of a variable. ▪ **incremental** *adj*. [15c: from Latin *incrementum*]

incriminate *verb* **1** (*sometimes* **incriminate sb in sth**) **a** to show that they were involved in it (esp in a crime); **b** to involve or implicate them (esp in a crime). **2** to charge someone with a crime or fault. ▪ **incriminating** *or* **incriminatory** *adj*. ▪ **incrimination** *noun*. [18c: from Latin *incriminare* to accuse someone of a crime]

incrust see under **encrust**

incubate *verb* **1** *tr & intr* of birds: to hatch (eggs) by sitting on them to keep them warm. **2** to encourage (germs, bacteria, etc) to develop, eg in a culture medium in a laboratory. **3** *intr* of germs, etc: to remain inactive in an organism before the first signs of disease appear. **4** to maintain (a substance) at a constant temperature over a period of time in order to study chemical or biochemical reactions. **5** *tr & intr* to develop slowly or gradually. ▪ **incubation** *noun*. [17c: from Latin *incubare* to lie on]

incubator *noun* **1** *med* a transparent boxlike container in which a premature baby can be nurtured under controlled conditions. **2** a cabinet or room that can be maintained at a constant temperature, used for culturing micro-organisms, hatching eggs, etc.

incubus /ˈɪŋkjʊbəs/ *noun* (***incubuses*** *or* ***incubi*** /-baɪ/) something that oppresses or weighs heavily upon one, esp a nightmare. [13c: Latin, meaning 'nightmare']

inculcate *verb* (*esp* **inculcate sth in** *or* **into** *or* **upon sb**) *rather formal* to teach or fix (ideas, habits, a warning, etc) firmly in their mind by constant repetition. ▪ **inculcation** *noun*. [16c: from Latin *inculcare* to tread something in]

inculpate *verb, formal* to blame someone or show them to be guilty of a crime. ▪ **inculpation** *noun*. ▪ **inculpatory** *adj*. [18c: from Latin *inculpare* to blame]

incumbent *adj, rather formal* **1** (*esp* **incumbent on** *or* **upon sb**) imposed as a duty or responsibility on them: *feel it incumbent upon me to defend him*. **2** currently occupying a specified position or office: *the incumbent bishop*. ▸ *noun* a holder of an office, esp a church office or benefice. ▪ **incumbency** *noun* (*-ies*). [15c: from Latin *incumbere* to lie, lean or press on]

incumbrance see **encumbrance**

incur *verb* (***incurred, incurring***) **1** to bring (something unpleasant) upon oneself. **2** to become liable for (debts, payment of a fine, etc). ▪ **incurrable** *adj*. [16c: from Latin *incurrere* to run into]

incurable *adj* **1** of eg a disease: not curable. **2** of a person: incapable of changing a specified aspect of their character: *an incurable optimist*. ▸ *noun* an incurable person or thing. ▪ **incurably** *adv*. [14c]

incurious *adj* showing no interest; lacking normal curiosity. [16c]

incursion *noun* **1** a brief or sudden attack made into enemy territory. **2** a damaging invasion into or using up of something. **3** the action of leaking or running into something. ▪ **incursive** *adj*. [15c: from Latin *incursio*]

Ind. *abbrev* **1** Independent. **2** India or Indian.

indebted *adj* (*usu* **indebted to sb**) **1** having reason to be grateful or obliged to them. **2** owing them money. ▪ **indebtedness** *noun*. [14c: from French *endetter* to involve someone in debt]

indecent *adj* **1** offensive to accepted standards of morality or sexual behaviour. **2** in bad taste; improper: *He remarried with indecent haste*. ▪ **indecency** *noun* (*-ies*). ▪ **indecently** *adv*. [16c]

indecent assault *noun, law* a sexual attack.

indecipherable *adj* unable to be read, deciphered or understood.

indecisive *adj* **1** not producing a clear or definite decision or result; inconclusive. **2** of a person: unable to make a firm decision; hesitating. ▪ **indecision**

noun. ▪ **indecisively** adv. ▪ **indecisiveness** noun. [18c]

indecorous *adj, formal* in bad taste; improper or unseemly. [17c]

indeed *adv* **1** without any question; in truth. **2** in fact; actually. **3** used for emphasis: *very wet indeed*. ▸ *exclam* expressing irony, surprise, disbelief, disapproval, etc, or simple acknowledgement of a previous remark: *'I'm going whether you like it or not.' 'Indeed?'* [14c: **in** + **deed**]

indefatigable *adj* **1** without tiring; unflagging. **2** never stopping; unremitting. ▪ **indefatigably** *adv*. [16c: French, from Latin *indefatigabilis*]

indefensible *adj* **1** unable to be excused or justified. **2** of an opinion, position, etc: untenable; unable to be defended. **3** *literally* not possible to defend against attack. ▪ **indefensibility** *noun*. ▪ **indefensibly** *adv*. [16c]

indefinable *adj* unable to be clearly or exactly defined or described. ▪ **indefinably** *adv*. [19c]

indefinite *adj* **1** without fixed or exact limits or clearly marked outlines: *off sick for an indefinite period*. **2** uncertain; vague; imprecise: *indefinite about her plans*. **3** *grammar* not referring to a particular person or thing. See also **indefinite article**. ▪ **indefinitely** *adv*. [16c]

indefinite article *noun, grammar* in English *a* or *an*, or any equivalent word in another language. Compare **definite article**.

indehiscent /ɪndɪ'hɪsənt/ *adj, botany* of a fruit: not splitting open to scatter its seeds when mature. Compare **dehiscent**. ▪ **indehiscence** *noun*.

indelible *adj* **1** unable to be removed or rubbed out. **2** designed to make an indelible mark. ▪ **indelibly** *adv*. [16c: from Latin *indelebilis*]

indelicate *adj* **1** tending to embarrass or offend. **2** slightly coarse; rough. ▪ **indelicacy** *noun* (**-ies**). ▪ **indelicately** *adv*. [18c]

indemnify *verb* (**-ies, -ied**) **1** (*esp* **indemnify sb against** *or* **from sth**) to provide them with security or protection against (loss or misfortune). **2** (*usu* **indemnify sb for sth**) to pay them compensation for (esp loss or damage). ▪ **indemnification** *noun*. [17c: from Latin *indemnis* unharmed or without loss]

indemnity *noun* (**-ies**) **1 a** compensation for loss or damage; **b** money paid in compensation. **2** security or protection from loss or damage; insurance. **3** legal exemption from liabilities or penalties. [15c]

indent[1] *verb* /ɪn'dɛnt/ **1** *printing, typing* to begin (a line or paragraph) further in from the margin than the main body of text. **2** to divide (a document drawn up in duplicate in two columns) along a zigzag line. **3** to draw up (a document, deed, etc) in duplicate. **4** *tr & intr, Brit, commerce* to make out a written order (for goods). **5** to indenture someone as an apprentice. **6** to notch (eg a border). ▸ *noun* /'ɪndɛnt/ **1** *Brit, commerce* a written order or official requisition for goods. **2** *printing, typing* an indented line or paragraph. **3** a notch. **4** an indenture. [14c: from Latin *indentare* to make toothlike notches in something]

indent[2] *verb* /ɪn'dɛnt/ to form a dent in something or mark it with dents. ▸ *noun* /'ɪndɛnt/ a hollow, depression or dent. [14c, meaning 'to inlay']

indentation *noun* **1** a cut or notch, often one of a series. **2** a deep, inward curve or recess, eg in a coastline. **3** the act or process of indenting. **4** **indention**.

indention *noun, printing, typing* **1** the indenting of a line or paragraph. **2** the blank space at the beginning of a line caused by indenting a line or paragraph.

indenture *noun* **1** (*usu* **indentures**) a contract binding an apprentice to a master. **2** an indented document, agreement or contract. ▸ *verb, chiefly old use* **1** to bind (eg an apprentice) by indentures. **2** to bind (eg another party) by an indented contract or agreement. [14c]

independent *adj* (*sometimes* **independent of sth** *or* **sb**) **1 a** not under the control or authority of others; **b** of a country, etc: self-governing. **2** not relying on others for financial support, care, help or guidance. **3** thinking and acting for oneself and not under an obligation to others. **4** *maths, etc* not dependent on something else for value, purpose or function. **5** of two or more people or things: not related to or affected by the others. **6** of private income or resources: large enough to make it unnecessary to work for a living: *a man of independent means*. **7** not belonging to a political party. **8** of a school or broadcasting company: not belonging to the state system. ▸ *noun* an independent person or thing. ▪ **independence** *noun*. ▪ **independently** *adv*. [17c]

---

independent
This word is often misspelt. The ending is *ent*. It might help you to remember that the word indepen**dent** contains the word **dent**.

---

independent clause *noun, grammar* a **main clause**.

in-depth *adj* thorough; exhaustive.

indescribable *adj* unable to be put into words, esp because too extreme, too difficult, too vague, too exciting, etc. ▪ **indescribably** *adv*. [18c]

indestructible *adj* not able to be destroyed. [17c]

indeterminable *adj* **1** not able to be fixed, decided or measured. **2** unable to be settled. ▪ **indeterminably** *adv*. [17c: from Latin *indeterminabilis*]

indeterminate *adj* **1** not precisely fixed or settled. **2** doubtful; vague: *an indeterminate outlook*. **3** *maths* of an equation: having more than one variable and an infinite number of possible solutions. **4** *maths, denoting* an expression that has no defined or fixed value or no quantitative meaning, eg 0/0. [17c: from Latin *indeterminatus*]

index *noun* (***indexes*** *or technical* ***indices*** /'ɪndɪsiːz/) **1** an alphabetical list of names, subjects, etc dealt with in a book, with the page numbers on which each item appears. **2** in a library, etc: a catalogue that lists each book, magazine, etc alphabetically and gives details of where it is shelved. **3** anything that points to, identifies or highlights a particular trend or condition. **4** a scale of numbers that shows changes in price, wages, etc: *retail price index*. **5** *maths* an **exponent** (sense 3). **6** *physics* a numerical quantity that indicates the magnitude of an effect: *refractive index*. **7** *comput* a file containing the location of items of data. ▸ *verb* **1** to provide (a book, etc) with an index. **2** to list something in an index. **3** to make something **index-linked**. ▪ **indexation** *noun*. ▪ **indexer** *noun*. [16c: from Latin, meaning 'informer' or 'forefinger']

index finger *noun* the finger next to the thumb. Also called **forefinger**.

index-linked *adj, econ* of prices, wages, rates of interest, etc: rising or falling by the same amount as the cost of living.

Indian *adj* **1** relating to India or the Indian subcontinent, its inhabitants, languages or culture. **2** *chiefly old use* relating to the indigenous peoples of America, their languages or culture. Now **Native American**. ▶ *noun* **1** a citizen or inhabitant of, or person born in, India or the Indian subcontinent, or someone belonging to the same races. **2** *chiefly old use* a **Native American** or someone belonging to one of the indigenous peoples of America. **3** *chiefly old use* any of the Native American languages. **4** *informal* **a** a restaurant that specializes in Asian food, esp curries; **b** a meal in, or a takeaway from, this type of restaurant.

Indian club *noun* one of a pair of heavy bottle-shaped clubs swung to develop the arm muscles.

Indian corn see **maize**

Indian file see **single file**

Indian ink or (*N Amer*) **India ink** *noun* a black ink.

Indian summer *noun* **1** a period of unusually warm weather in late autumn. **2** a period of happiness and success towards the end of someone's life, an era, etc.

India rubber *noun* a **rubber**[1] (sense 2).

Indic *adj* belonging or relating to the Indian branch of the Indo-European languages, which comprises Sanskrit and its modern descendants, Hindi, Gujarati, Urdu, Bengali, Punjabi, Romany, etc. ▶ *noun* this group of languages. [19c: from Latin *Indicus*, from Greek *Indikos* Indian]

indicate *verb* **1** to point out or show. **2** to be a sign or symptom of something. **3** of a gauge, dial, etc: to show something as a reading. **4** to show or state something: *He indicated his consent*. **5** *med, etc* (esp in the passive) to point to something as a treatment: *A course of steroids was indicated*. **6** *intr* to use an **indicator** (sense 2) on a motor vehicle. ▪ **indication** *noun*. [17c: from Latin *indicare* to make known]

indicative *adj* **1** (*also* **indicatory**) (*usu* **indicative of sth**) serving as a sign or indication of it. **2** *grammar* (abbrev **indic.**) **a** of the **mood**[2] of a verb: used to state facts, describe events or ask questions; **b** of a verb, tense, etc: in this mood. ▶ *noun, grammar* **1** the indicative **mood**[2]. Compare **conditional**, **imperative**, **subjunctive**. **2** a verb form of this kind. ▪ **indicatively** *adv*.

indicator *noun* **1** **a** an instrument or gauge that shows the level of temperature, fuel, pressure, etc; **b** a needle or pointer on such a device. **2** a flashing light on a motor vehicle which shows that the vehicle is about to change direction. **3** any sign, condition, situation, etc that shows or indicates something: *an economic indicator*. **4** a board or diagram giving information, eg in a railway station. **5** *chem* a substance (eg **litmus**) that changes colour depending on the pH of a solution. **6** *biol* (*also* **indicator species**) a plant or animal species whose presence or absence indicates the levels of a particular environmental factor in an area.

indices see **index**

indict /ɪn'daɪt/ *verb, law* to accuse someone of, or charge them formally with, a crime, esp in writing. ▪ **indictable** *adj*. [14c: from French *enditer*, and Latin *indicere* to announce]

indictment *noun* **1** a formal written accusation or charge. **2** an act of indicting someone. **3** something that deserves severe criticism or censure, or that serves to criticize or condemn something or someone.

indie *noun, informal* **1** a small independent and usu non-commercial record or film company. **2** a type of music produced predominantly by indie labels. ▶ *adj* produced by small independent companies; not mainstream or commercial: *indie music*. [20c: abbrev of **independent**]

indifferent *adj* **1** (*esp* **indifferent to** *or* **towards sth** *or* **sb**) showing no interest in or concern for it or them. **2** neither good nor bad; average; mediocre. **3** fairly bad; inferior. **4** unimportant. **5** neutral. ▪ **indifference** *noun*. ▪ **indifferently** *adv*. [14c: from Latin *indifferens* not differing, of medium quality]

indigenous *adj* **1** *biol* of plants or animals: belonging naturally to or occurring naturally in a country or area. **2** of a person: born in a region, area, country, etc. [17c: from Latin *indigena* an original inhabitant]

indigent *adj, formal* very poor; needy. ▪ **indigence** *noun* poverty. [15c: French, from Latin *indigens*]

indigestible *adj* **1** difficult or impossible to digest. **2** not easily understood. ▪ **indigestibility** *noun*. [16c: from Latin *indigestibilis*]

indigestion *noun* discomfort or pain in the abdomen or lower region of the chest caused by difficulty in digesting food. [15c: French]

indignant *adj* feeling or showing anger or a sense of having been treated unjustly or wrongly. ▪ **indignantly** *adv*. ▪ **indignation** *noun*. [16c: from Latin *indignari* to consider unworthy]

indignity *noun* (**-*ies***) **1** any act or treatment that makes someone feel shame or humiliation. **2** a feeling of shame, disgrace or dishonour. [16c: from Latin *indignitas*]

indigo *noun* (***indigos*** *or* ***indigoes***) **1** a violet-blue dye. **2** a plant whose leaves yield this dye. **3** the deep violet-blue colour of this dye. ▶ *adj* violet-blue in colour. [16c: Spanish *índigo* or *índico*]

indirect *adj* **1** of a route, line, etc: not direct or straight. **2** not going straight to the point; not straightforward or honest. **3** not directly aimed at or intended: *indirect consequences*. [15c]

indirect object *noun, grammar* a noun, phrase or pronoun that is affected indirectly by the action of a verb, usu standing for the person or thing to whom something is given or for whom something is done. Compare **direct object**.

indirect question *noun* a question reported in indirect speech, as in *They're asking who you are*.

indirect speech *noun, grammar* a speaker's words as reported by another person, eg *We will come* becomes *They said they would come* in indirect speech. Also called **reported speech**. Compare **direct speech**.

indirect tax *noun* a tax levied on goods and services when they are purchased. Compare **direct tax**.

indiscernible *adj* unable to be noticed or recognized as being distinct, esp because too small. [17c]

indiscipline *noun* lack of discipline. [18c]

indiscreet *adj* **1** giving away too many secrets or too much information. **2** not wise or cautious. ▪ **indiscreetly** *adv.* ▪ **indiscretion** *noun.* [15c]

indiscriminate *adj* **1** making no distinctions; not making careful choice or showing discrimination; random. **2** confused; not differentiated. ▪ **indiscriminately** *adv.* ▪ **indiscriminateness** *noun.* [17c]

indispensable *adj* necessary; essential. ▪ **indispensability** *noun.* ▪ **indispensably** *adv.* [17c]

indisposed *adj, rather formal* **1** slightly ill. **2** (*esp* **indisposed to do sth**) reluctant or unwilling to do it. ▪ **indisposition** *noun.* [15c: meaning 'not organized or properly arranged']

indisputable *adj* certainly true; beyond doubt. [16c]

indissoluble *adj* incapable of being dissolved or broken; permanent; lasting. [16c]

indistinct *adj* not clear to a person's eye, ear or mind. ▪ **indistinctly** *adv.* ▪ **indistinctness** *noun.* [16c]

indistinguishable *adj* not able to be distinguished or told apart from something. [17c]

indium *noun, chem* (symbol **In**) a soft, silvery-white metallic element. [19c: from Latin (from the indigo lines in its spectrum)]

individual *adj* **1** intended for or relating to a single person or thing: *jam served in individual portions.* **2** particular to one person; showing or having a particular person's unique qualities or characteristics. **3** separate; single. ▸ *noun* **1** a particular person, animal or thing, esp in contrast to the group to which it belongs: *the rights of the individual.* **2** *informal* a person. ▪ **individually** *adv.* [15c: from Latin *individualis*, from *individuus* indivisible]

individualism *noun* **1** **a** the belief that individual people should lead their lives as they want and should be independent; **b** behaviour governed by this belief. **2** the theory that the state should not control the actions of the individual. **3** self-centredness; egoism. [19c]

individualist *noun* **1** someone who thinks and acts with independence or great individuality. **2** someone who supports individualism. ▸ *adj* (*also* **individualistic**) relating to individualists or individualism.

individuality *noun* (**-ies**) **1** the qualities and character that distinguish one person or thing from others. **2** a separate and distinct existence or identity. [17c]

individualize *or* **-ise** *verb* **1** to make something suitable for a particular person, thing or situation. **2** to give someone or something a distinctive character or personality. ▪ **individualization** *noun.* [17c]

indivisible *adj* **1** not able to be divided or separated. **2** *maths* of a number: not divisible (by a given number) without leaving a remainder. ▸ *noun, maths* an indefinitely small quantity. [14c]

Indo- *combining form, denoting* Indian, or India: *Indo-European.* [From Greek *Indos* Indian]

indoctrinate *verb* to teach (an individual or group) to accept and believe a particular set of beliefs, etc uncritically. ▪ **indoctrination** *noun.* [17c: from Latin *doctrinare* to teach]

Indo-European *adj* relating to the family of languages that are spoken in most of Europe and many parts of Asia, eg French, German, English, Greek, Russian, Hindi and Persian. ▸ *noun* **1** the languages that form this family. **2** (*also* **Proto-Indo-European**) the hypothetical language that all of the languages in the Indo-European family come from.

indolent *adj* lazy; disliking and avoiding work and exercise. ▪ **indolence** *noun.* ▪ **indolently** *adv.* [17c: from Latin *indolens* not suffering pain]

indomitable *adj* unable to be conquered or defeated. ▪ **indomitably** *adv.* [17c]

Indonesian *adj* belonging or relating to Indonesia, a republic in SE Asia comprised of many islands, or to its inhabitants, their languages or culture. ▸ *noun* **1** a citizen or inhabitant of, or person born in, Indonesia. **2** the group of languages spoken in the Malay archipelago, especially the official language (**Bahasa Indonesia**) of the Republic of Indonesia. [19c: from **Indo-** + Greek *nesos* island]

indoor *adj* used, belonging, done, happening, etc inside a building. [18c: from earlier *within-door*]

indoors *adv* in or into a building. [19c]

indorse see **endorse**

indrawn *adj* **1** esp of the breath: drawn or pulled in. **2** of a person: aloof or introspective. [18c]

indubitable *adj* unable to be doubted; certain. ▪ **indubitably** *adv.* [17c: from Latin *indubitabilis*]

induce *verb* **1** to persuade, influence or cause someone to do something. **2** *obstetrics* to initiate or hasten (labour) by artificial means. **3** to make something happen or appear. **4** to produce or transmit (an electromotive force) by **induction**. **5** *logic* to infer (a general conclusion) from particular cases. **6** *biol* to cause (a non-specialized embryonic cell) to become specialized. ▪ **inducible** *adj.* [14c: from Latin *inducere* to lead in]

inducement *noun* something that persuades or influences; an incentive or motive.

induct *verb* **1** to place (eg a priest) formally and often ceremonially in an official position. **2** to initiate someone as a member of eg a society or profession. [14c: from Latin *inducere* to lead in]

inductance *noun, physics* the property of an electric circuit or circuit component that causes an **electromotive force** to be generated in it when a changing current is present.

induction *noun* **1** inducting or being inducted, esp into office. **2** *obstetrics* the initiation of labour by artificial means. **3** *elec* the production of an electric current in a conductor as a result of its close proximity to a varying magnetic field. **4** *elec* magnetization caused by close proximity either to a magnetic field or to the electromagnetic field of a current-carrying conductor. **5** *logic* the forming of a general conclusion from particular cases. Compare **deduction**. ▪ **inductional** *adj.* ▪ **inductive** *adj.*

induction coil *noun, physics* a type of **transformer** that can produce a high-voltage alternating current from a low-voltage direct current source.

induction course *noun* a course of introductory formal instruction given to familiarize a new employee, appointee.

inductor *noun* **1** *elec* a component of an electrical circuit that shows **inductance**. **2** someone or something that inducts.

indulge *verb* **1** *tr & intr* (*esp* **indulge in sth** *or* **indulge sb in sth**) to allow oneself or someone else pleasure or the pleasure of (a specified thing). **2** to allow someone to have or do anything they want. **3** to give in to (a desire, taste, wish, etc) without restraint. **4** *intr, informal* to eat or drink something one should not: *No, I won't indulge. I'm driving.* [17c: from Latin *indulgere* to be kind or indulgent]

indulgence *noun* **1** the state of being indulgent; generosity; favourable or tolerant treatment. **2** an act or the process of indulging a person, desire, etc. **3** a pleasure that is indulged in. **4** *RC Church* a special grant of remission from the punishment that remains due for a sin after it has been absolved. [14c: French]

indulgent *adj* quick or too quick to overlook or forgive faults or gratify the wishes of others; too tolerant or generous. ▪ **indulgently** *adv.* [16c: from Latin *indulgere*]

industrial *adj* **1** relating to or suitable for industry. **2** of a country, city, etc: having highly developed industry.

industrial action *noun, Brit* action taken by workers as a protest, eg a **strike**, **go-slow** or **work to rule**.

industrial espionage *noun* the practice of obtaining or attempting to obtain confidential information about a company's products or activities by underhand or dishonest means.

industrial estate *noun* an area in a town that is developed for industry and business. Also called **trading estate**.

industrialism *noun* a social system in which industry (rather than agriculture) forms the basis of commerce and the economy.

industrialist *noun* someone who owns a large industrial organization or who is involved in its management at a senior level.

industrialize *or* **-ise** *verb, tr & intr* to develop industrially; to introduce industry to (a place). ▪ **industrialization** *noun.*

industrial relations *plural noun* relations between management and workers.

industrial revolution *noun* **1** the rapid development of a country's industry, characterized by a change from small-scale production to increased mechanization and mass production. **2** (**the Industrial Revolution**) *hist* this process in Britain from the last quarter of the 18c, initiated by the mechanization of the textile industries of Lancashire etc.

industrial-strength *adj, sometimes humorous* very powerful; suitable for use in industry rather than in the home: *industrial-strength adhesive • industrial-strength coffee.*

industrial tribunal *noun, business, law* a tribunal set up to hear complaints and make judgements in disputes between employers and employees.

industrious *adj* busy and hard-working. ▪ **industriously** *adv.* ▪ **industriousness** *noun.* [16c: from Latin *industriosus* diligent]

industry *noun* (**-ies**) **1** the business of producing goods. **2** a branch of manufacturing and trade that produces a particular product: *the coal industry.* **3** organized commercial exploitation or use of natural or national assets: *the tourist industry.* **4** hard work or effort. [15c: from Latin *industria* diligence]

-ine[1] *suffix, forming adjectives, signifying* **1** belonging or relating to the specified thing: *Alpine.* **2** like, similar to or consisting of the specified thing: *crystalline.* [From Latin adjectival ending *-inus*]

-ine[2] *suffix, chem, forming nouns, denoting* **1** a basic organic compound containing nitrogen, such as an amino acid or alkaloid: *glutamine.* **2** a **halogen**: *chlorine • fluorine.* **3** a mixture of compounds: *kerosine • benzine.* **4** a feminized form: *heroine.* [French, from Latin feminine adjectival ending *-ina*]

inebriate *verb* /ɪn'iːbrɪeɪt/ **1** to make someone drunk. **2** to exhilarate someone greatly. ▸ *adj* /ɪn'iːbrɪət/ (*now usu* **inebriated**) drunk, esp habitually drunk. ▸ *noun* /ɪn'iːbrɪət/ *formal* someone who is drunk, esp regularly so. ▪ **inebriation** *noun.* [16c: from Latin *inebriare*]

inedible *adj* not fit or suitable to be eaten, eg because poisonous, indigestible or rotten. [19c]

ineffable *adj, esp literary or formal* **1** unable to be described or expressed in words, esp because of size, magnificence, etc. **2** not supposed or not allowed to be said, esp because too sacred. ▪ **ineffably** *adv.* [15c: French, from Latin *ineffabilis*]

ineffective *adj* **1** having no effect; not able or likely to produce a result, or the result or effect intended. **2** not capable of achieving results; inefficient or incompetent. ▪ **ineffectiveness** *noun.* [17c]

ineffectual *adj* **1** not producing a result or the intended result. **2** lacking the ability and confidence needed to achieve results. ▪ **ineffectuality** *or* **ineffectualness** *noun.* ▪ **ineffectually** *adv.* [15c]

inefficacious *adj* not having the desired or intended effect. ▪ **inefficaciously** *adv.* ▪ **inefficacy** *noun.* [17c]

inefficient *adj* lacking the power or skill to do or produce something in the best, most economical, etc way. ▪ **inefficiency** *noun.* ▪ **inefficiently** *adv.* [18c]

inelegant *adj* lacking grace or refinement. ▪ **inelegance** *noun.* ▪ **inelegantly** *adv.* [16c]

ineligible *adj* **1** not qualified to stand for election. **2** not suitable to be chosen. ▪ **ineligibility** *noun.* [18c]

ineluctable *adj, esp literary or formal* unavoidable, irresistible or inescapable. ▪ **ineluctably** *adv.* [17c: from Latin *ineluctabilis*, from *eluctari* to struggle out]

inept *adj* **1** awkward; done without, or not having, skill. **2** not suitable or fitting; out of place. **3** silly; foolish. ▪ **ineptitude** *noun.* [17c: from Latin *ineptus* unsuited]

inequable *adj* **1** not fair or just. **2** changeable; not even or uniform. [18c]

inequality *noun* (**-ies**) **1** a lack of equality, fairness or evenness, or an instance of this. **2** *maths* a statement that the values of two numerical quantities, algebraic expressions, functions, etc are not equal. [15c]

inequitable *adj, rather formal* not fair or just. [17c]

inequity *noun* (**-ies**) *rather formal* **1** an unjust action. **2** lack of fairness or equity. [16c]

inert *adj* **1** *physics* tending to remain in a state of rest or uniform motion in a straight line unless acted upon by an external force. **2** not wanting to move, act or think; indolent; sluggish. **3** *chem* unreactive or showing only a limited ability to react with other chemical elements. [17c: from Latin *iners* unskilled or idle]

inert gas see **noble gas**

inertia *noun* **1** *physics* the tendency of an object to be **inert**. **2** the state of not wanting to move, act or think; indolence; sluggishness. ▪ **inertial** *adj.* [18c]

inescapable *adj* inevitable; unable to be avoided. ▪ **inescapably** *adv.* [18c]

inessential *adj* not necessary. ▸ *noun* an inessential thing. [17c]

inestimable *adj, rather formal* too great, or of too great a value, to be estimated, measured or fully appreciated. ▪ **inestimably** *adv.* [14c]

inevitable *adj* **1** unable to be avoided; certain to happen. **2** *informal* tiresomely regular or predictable. ▸ *noun* (*esp* **the inevitable**) something that is certain to happen and is unavoidable. ▪ **inevitability** *noun.* ▪ **inevitably** *adv.* [15c: from Latin *inevitabilis*]

inexact *adj* not quite correct or true. [19c]

inexcusable *adj* too bad to be excused, justified or tolerated. ▪ **inexcusably** *adv.* [16c]

inexhaustible *adj* **1** of eg a supply: incapable of being used up. **2** tireless; never failing or giving up. [17c]

inexorable *adj* **1** refusing to change opinion, course of action, etc; unrelenting. **2** unable to be altered or avoided. ▪ **inexorably** *adv.* [16c: from Latin *exorare* to prevail upon]

inexpensive *adj* cheap or reasonable in price. [19c]

inexperience *noun* lack of skill or knowledge gained from experience. ▪ **inexperienced** *adj.* [16c]

inexpert *adj* (*often* **inexpert at** *or* **in sth**) unskilled at it. ▪ **inexpertly** *adv.* [15c]

inexplicable *adj* impossible to explain or understand. ▪ **inexplicably** *adv.* [16c]

inexpressible *adj* unable to be expressed or described. ▪ **inexpressibly** *adv.* [17c]

inexpressive *adj* esp of a face: expressing little or no emotion. [17c]

in extremis *adv* **1** at, or as if at, the point of death or ultimate failure. **2** in desperate circumstances; in serious difficulties. [16c: Latin, 'in the last things']

inextricable *adj* **1** of a situation, etc: unable to be escaped from. **2** of a knot, dilemma, etc: unable to be disentangled. ▪ **inextricably** *adv.* [16c]

inf. *abbrev* **1** infantry. **2** inferior. **3** infinitive. **4** information. See also **info. 5** informal.

infallible *adj* **1** of a person: never liable to make a mistake; incapable of error. **2** *RC Church* of the Pope: unable to err when pronouncing officially on dogma. **3** of a plan, method, etc: always, or bound to be, successful or effective. ▪ **infallibility** *noun.* [15c]

infamous *adj* **1** notoriously bad. **2** *formal* vile; disgraceful. ▪ **infamously** *adv.* ▪ **infamy** *noun* (**-ies**). [14c: from Latin *infamosus* (see **famous**)]

infancy *noun* (**-ies**) **1** the state or time of being an infant. **2** an early period of existence, growth and development: *when television was still in its infancy.* **3** *law* **minority** (sense 4). [15c]

infant *noun* **1** a very young child. **2** *Brit* a schoolchild under the age of seven or eight. **3** *law* a **minor** (*noun* sense 1). ▸ *adj* **1** relating to or involving infants: *infant mortality.* **2** at an early stage of development. [14c: from French *enfant*]

infanta /ɪnˈfantə/ *noun, hist* (*often* **Infanta**) a daughter of the reigning monarch of Spain or Portugal who is not heir to the throne, especially the eldest daughter. [17c: Spanish and Portuguese, from Latin *infans* **infant**]

infanticide *noun* **1** the murder of a child. **2** someone who commits this act. **3** the practice of killing newborn children. ▪ **infanticidal** *adj.* [17c]

infantile *adj* **1** relating to infants or infancy. **2** very childish; immature. [17c: from Latin *infantilis*]

infantry *noun* (**-ies**) soldiers trained and equipped to fight on foot. *as adj*: *infantry regiments.* Compare **cavalry.** [16c: from French *infanterie*]

infantryman *noun* a soldier in the infantry.

infarction *noun, pathol* the death of a localized area of tissue as a result of the blocking of its blood supply. [17c: from Latin *infarcire* to block off]

infatuate *verb* to make someone feel passionate, foolish, intense, etc love or admiration. ▪ **infatuated** *adj* (*esp* **infatuated with sb** *or* **sth**) filled with intense love; besotted. ▪ **infatuation** *noun.* [16c: from Latin *infatuare* to make a fool of]

infect *verb* (*often* **infect sth** *or* **sb with sth**) **1** *biol, med, etc* to contaminate (a living organism) with a bacterium, virus, etc and thereby cause disease. **2** to taint or contaminate (eg water, food or air) with a bacterium, pollutant, etc. **3** to pass on a feeling or opinion, esp a negative one, to someone. **4** *comput* to inflict with a **virus** (sense 4). [14c: from Latin *inficere* to spoil or impregnate]

infection *noun* **1** infecting or being infected. **2** *biol, med, etc* the invasion of a human, animal or plant by disease-causing micro-organisms. **3** a disease caused by such micro-organisms. **4** the passing on of feelings, opinions, etc, esp negative ones.

infectious *adj* **1** of a disease: caused by bacteria, viruses or other micro-organisms, and therefore capable of being transmitted through air, water, etc. **2** eg of a person: capable of infecting others; causing infection. **3** of an emotion, opinion, etc: likely to be passed on to others: *Laughter is infectious.*

infectious, contagious

Be careful not to use the word **infectious** when you mean **contagious**. An **infectious** disease can be spread through the air, while a **contagious** disease is spread by touch. However, if you use these words figuratively, describing laughter for example, they mean the same thing.

infective *adj* **infectious** (sense 1).

infelicitous *adj* **1** not happy, fortunate or lucky. **2** not suitable, fitting or apt. [19c]

infer *verb* (***inferred, inferring***) **1** *tr & intr* to conclude or judge from facts, observation and deduction. **2** *informal* to imply or suggest. ▪ **inferable** *or* **inferrable** *adj.* [16c: from Latin *inferre* to bring in]

infer

If you are using formal English, it is best not to use **infer** with meaning 2. Many people who are precise about language think this is wrong:

What are you inferring when you say that?

Use **imply** or **suggest** instead:

What are you implying when you say that?

inference *noun* **1** an act of inferring. **2** something that is inferred. ▪ **inferential** *adj.*

inferior *adj* (*often* **inferior to sth** *or* **sb**) **1** poor or poorer in quality. **2** low or lower in value, rank or status. **3** low or lower in position. **4** of letters or figures: printed or written slightly below the line. ▸ *noun* someone or something that is inferior. ▪ **inferiority** *noun.* [15c: Latin, meaning 'lower']

inferior

Remember that **inferior** does not behave like *better, worse* and the other comparative adjectives. It is followed by *to* rather than *than*:

Modern chemical dyes are usually considered inferior to the natural dyes used in older rugs.

inferiority complex *noun* **1** *psychol* a disorder arising from the conflict between the desire to be noticed and the fear of being shown to be inadequate, characterized by aggressive behaviour or withdrawal. **2** *loosely* a general feeling of inadequacy or worthlessness.

infernal *adj* **1** belonging or relating to the underworld. **2** belonging or relating to hell. **3** wicked; evil; hellish. **4** *informal* extremely annoying, unpleasant, burdensome, etc. [14c: French, from Latin *infernalis*, from *inferus* low]

inferno *noun* **1** (*often* **the Inferno**) hell. **2** a place or situation of horror and confusion. **3** a raging fire. [19c: Italian, from Latin *infernus* hell]

infertile *adj* **1** of soil, etc: lacking the nutrients required to support the growth of crops, etc. **2** unable to produce offspring. ▪ **infertility** *noun*. [16c]

infest *verb* **1** of fleas, lice, etc: to invade and occupy an animal or plant. **2** of someone or something harmful or unpleasant: to exist in large numbers or quantities. ▪ **infestation** *noun*. [15c: from Latin *infestare* to assail or molest]

infidel *noun* **1** someone who rejects a particular religion, esp Christianity or Islam. **2** someone who rejects all religions. ▸ *adj* relating to unbelievers; unbelieving. [15c: from Latin *infidelis* unfaithful]

infidelity *noun* (**-ies**) **1** unfaithfulness, esp of a sexual nature, or an instance of this. **2** lack of belief or faith in a religion. [16c: from Latin *infidelitas* unfaithfulness]

infield *noun* **1** *cricket* **a** the area of the field close to the wicket; **b** the players positioned there. **2** *baseball* **a** the diamond-shaped area of the pitch enclosed by the four bases; **b** the players positioned there. Compare **outfield**. ▪ **infielder** *noun*.

in-fighting *noun* **1** fighting or competition between members of the same group, organization, etc. **2** *boxing* fighting at close quarters. ▪ **in-fighter** *noun*.

infill *noun* (*also* **infilling**) **1** the act of filling or closing gaps, holes, etc. **2** the material used to fill a gap, hole, etc. ▸ *verb* to fill in (a gap, hole, etc). [19c]

infiltrate *verb* **1** of troops, agents, etc: to get into (territory or an organization) secretly to gain influence or information. **2** to filter (eg liquid or gas) slowly through the pores (of a substance). **3** *intr* eg of liquid or gas: to filter in. ▪ **infiltration** *noun*. ▪ **infiltrator** *noun*. [18c]

infinite *adj* **1** having no limits in size, extent, time or space. **2** too great to be measured or counted. **3** very great; vast. **4** *maths* of a number, series, etc: having an unlimited number of elements, digits or terms. **5** all-encompassing; complete: *God in his infinite wisdom*. ▸ *noun* anything that has no limits, boundaries, etc. ▪ **infinitely** *adv*. [14c: see **finite**]

infinitesimal *adj* **1** infinitely small; with a value too close to zero to be measured. **2** *informal* extremely small. ▸ *noun* an infinitesimal amount. ▪ **infinitesimally** *adv*. [19c: from Latin *infinitesimus* 'infiniteth']

infinitive *noun, grammar* (abbrev **inf.**) a verb form that expresses an action but which does not refer to a particular subject or time, in English often used with *to* (eg go in *Tell him to go* • *Let her go*). ▸ *adj* of a verb: having this form. Compare **finite**. [16c: from Latin *infinitivus* unlimited or indefinite]

infinitude *noun* **1** the state or quality of being infinite. **2** an infinite quantity, degree, amount, etc. [17c: from **infinite**, modelled on **magnitude**, etc]

infinity *noun* (**-ies**) **1** space, time, distance or quantity that is without limit or boundaries. **2** *loosely* a quantity, space, time or distance that is too great to be measured. **3** *maths* (symbol ∞) **a** a number that is larger than any **finite** value; **b** the **reciprocal** of zero. **4** the quality or state of being infinite. [14c: from Latin *infinitas*]

infirm *adj* **1** weak or ill, esp from old age. **2** (**the infirm**) weak or ill people. [14c: from Latin *infirmus* weak, fragile, frail]

infirmary *noun* (**-ies**) **1** a hospital. **2** a room or ward, eg in a boarding school, monastery, etc, where the sick and injured are treated. [17c: from Latin *infirmaria*]

infirmity *noun* (**-ies**) **1** the state or quality of being sick, weak or infirm. **2** a disease or illness. [14c]

infix *verb* to fix something firmly in (eg the mind). ▪ **infixation** *noun*. [16c: from Latin *infigere*]

in flagrante delicto /ɪn flə'grantɪ dɪ'lɪktoʊ/ *adv, law* in the very act of committing a crime. Sometimes shortened to **in flagrante**. [18c: Latin, literally 'with the crime blazing']

inflame *verb* **1** to arouse strong or violent emotion in someone or something. **2** to make something more heated or intense; to exacerbate it. **3** *tr & intr* to become or to make (part of the body) red, heated, swollen and painful. [14c: from French *enflammer*]

inflammable *adj* **1** easily set on fire. See also **flammable**. **2** easily excited or angered. ▸ *noun* an inflammable substance or thing. ▪ **inflammability** *noun*. [17c]

inflammation *noun* **1** *pathol* a response of body tissues to injury, infection, etc in which the affected part becomes inflamed. **2** inflaming or being inflamed.

inflammatory *adj* **1** likely to cause strong or violent emotion, esp anger. **2** *pathol* relating to, causing, or caused by, inflammation of part of the body.

inflatable *adj* able to be inflated for use. ▸ *noun* an inflatable object.

inflate *verb* **1** *tr & intr* to swell or cause something to swell or expand with air or gas. **2** *econ* **a** to increase (prices generally) by artificial means; **b** to increase (the volume of money in circulation). Compare **deflate**, **reflate**. **3** to exaggerate the importance or value of something. **4** to raise (the spirits, etc); to elate. [16c: from Latin *inflare* to blow into]

inflation *noun* **1** *econ* a general increase in the level of prices caused by an increase in the amount of money and credit available. See also **deflation**, **reflation**, **stagflation**. **2** *loosely* the rate at which the level of prices is rising. **3** inflating or being inflated. ▪ **inflationary** *adj*.

inflect *verb* **1** **a** *grammar* to change the form of (a word) to show eg tense, number, gender or grammatical case; **b** *intr* of a word, language, etc: to change, or be able to be changed, in this way. **2** to vary the tone or pitch of (the voice, a note, etc). **3** to bend inwards. [15c: from Latin *inflectere* to curve]

inflection *or* **inflexion** *noun* **1** *grammar* **a** the change in the form of a word which shows tense, number, gender, grammatical case, etc; **b** an inflected form of a word; **c** a suffix that is added to a word to form an inflected form, eg *-s*, *-ing*. **2** a change in the tone, pitch, etc of the voice. **3** *geom* a change in a curve from being **convex** to **concave** or vice versa (at the **point of inflection** or **inflection point**). **4** an act of inflecting or state of being inflected. ▪ **inflectional** *adj*. [16c]

inflexible *adj* **1** incapable of being bent. **2** *derog* unyielding; obstinate. **3** unable to be changed. ▪ **inflexibility** *noun*. ▪ **inflexibly** *adv*. [15c]

inflict *verb* (*esp* **inflict sth on sb**) to impose (something unpleasant) on them, or make them suffer it. ▪ **inflictable** *adj*. ▪ **inflicter** *or* **inflictor** *noun*. ▪ **infliction** *noun* **1** an act of inflicting. **2** something that is inflicted. [16c: from Latin *infligere* to strike against]

inflorescence *noun, botany* **1** the flower-head and stem of a flowering plant. **2** any of the various possible arrangements of the flowers on a flowering plant. [18c: from Latin *inflorescere* to begin to blossom]

inflow *noun* **1** the act or process of flowing in. **2** something that flows in. ▪ **inflowing** *noun, adj*.

influence *noun* **1** (*esp* **influence on** *or* **over sb** *or* **sth**) the power that one person or thing has to affect another. **2** a person or thing that has such a power. **3** power resulting from political or social position, wealth, ability, etc. ▸ *verb* **1** to have an effect on (a person, their work, events, etc). **2** to exert influence on someone or something; to persuade. [14c: French, from Latin *influere* to flow into]

IDIOMS **under the influence** *informal* drunk.

influential *adj* **1** having influence or power. **2** (*esp* **influential in sth**) making an important contribution to it. ▪ **influentially** *adv*.

influenza *noun, pathol* a viral infection, with symptoms including headache, fever, a sore throat, catarrh and muscular aches and pains. Commonly shortened to **flu**. [18c: Italian, literally 'influence']

influx *noun* **1** a continual stream or arrival of large numbers of people or things. **2** a flowing in or inflow. [17c: from Latin *influere* to flow in]

info *noun, informal* information. [20c shortening]

infold see **enfold**

inform *verb* **1** *tr & intr*, (*esp* **inform sb about** *or* **of sth**) to tell them about it. **2** *intr* (*often* **inform against** *or* **on sb**) to give incriminating evidence about them to the authorities. **3** *literary or formal* to animate, inspire, or give life to something. **4** *formal* to give an essential quality to something. [14c: from Latin *informare* to give form to or describe]

informal *adj* **1** without ceremony or formality; relaxed and friendly. **2** of language, clothes, etc: suitable for and used in relaxed, everyday situations. ▪ **informality** *noun* (**-*ies***). ▪ **informally** *adv*. [17c]

informant *noun* someone who informs, eg against another person, or who gives information. Compare **informer**. [17c]

information *noun* **1** knowledge gained or given; facts; news. *as adj*: *information desk*. **2** the communicating or receiving of knowledge. [14c: from Latin *informatio* conception of an idea]

information technology *noun, comput* (abbrev **IT**) the use, study or production of technologies such as computer systems, digital electronics and telecommunications to store, process and transmit information.

informative *adj* giving useful or interesting information. ▪ **informatively** *adv*. ▪ **informativeness** *noun*.

informed *adj* **1** esp of a person: having or showing knowledge, esp in being educated and intelligent. **2** *also in compounds* of eg a newspaper article, a guess or estimate, opinion, etc: based on sound information; showing knowledge or experience: *well-informed*.

informer *noun* someone who informs against another, esp to the police.

infra *adv* in books, texts, etc: below; lower down on the page or further on in the book. [18c: Latin, meaning 'below']

infra- *prefix, chiefly technical, forming adjs and nouns, denoting* below, or beneath, a specified thing: *infrared*. [17c: Latin, meaning 'below']

infraction *noun, formal* the breaking of a law, rule, etc. [17c: from Latin *infractio*]

infra dig *adj, informal* beneath one's dignity. [19c: abbrev of Latin *infra dignitatem*]

infrared *or* (*sometimes*) **infra-red** *adj* **1** of electromagnetic radiation: with a wavelength between the red end of the visible spectrum and microwaves and radio waves. **2** relating to, using, producing or sensitive to radiation of this sort: *infrared camera*. ▸ *noun* **1** infrared radiation. **2** the infrared part of the spectrum. [19c]

infrasonic *adj* relating to or having a frequency or frequencies below the range that can normally be heard by the human ear.

infrasound *noun, physics* sound waves with a frequency below the range that can be heard by the human ear. ▪ **infrasonic** *adj*. [20c]

infrastructure *noun* **1** the basic inner structure of a society, organization or system. **2** the roads, railways, bridges, factories, schools, etc needed for a country to function properly. [20c]

infrequent *adj* occurring rarely or occasionally. ▪ **infrequency** *noun*. ▪ **infrequently** *adv*. [16c]

infringe *verb* **1** to break or violate (eg a law or oath). **2** *intr* (*esp* **infringe on** *or* **upon sth**) to encroach or trespass; to interfere with (a person's rights, freedom, etc) in such a way as to limit or reduce them. ▪ **infringement** *noun*. [16c: from Latin *infringere* to break]

infuriate *verb* to make someone very angry. ▪ **infuriating** *adj*. [17c: from Latin *infuriare*]

infuse *verb* **1** *tr & intr* to soak, or cause (eg herbs or tea) to be soaked, in hot water to release flavour or other qualities. **2** (*esp* **infuse sb with sth** *or* **infuse sth into sb**) to inspire them with (a positive feeling, quality, etc). ▪ **infusible** *adj*. [15c: from Latin *infundere* to pour in]

infusion *noun* **1** an act or the process of infusing something. **2** a solution produced by infusing eg herbs or tea.

-ing[1] *suffix, forming nouns* **1** formed from a verb: usually expressing the action of that verb, its result, product or something relating to it, etc: *building* • *driving* • *washing*. **2** formed from a noun: describing something made of, used in, etc the specified thing: *guttering* • *roofing* • *bedding*. **3** formed from an adverb: *offing* • *outing*. [Anglo-Saxon *-ing* or *-ung*]

-ing[2] *suffix* **1** used to form the present participle of verbs, as in *I was only asking* and *saw you walking in the park*. **2** used to form adjectives derived from present participles, eg *charming, terrifying*. [Anglo-Saxon in the form *-ende*]

-ing[3] *suffix, forming nouns, signifying* one belonging to a specified kind, etc or one of the same kind of quality, character, etc: *gelding* • *whiting*. [Anglo-Saxon]

ingenious *adj* showing or having skill, originality and inventive cleverness. ▪ **ingeniously** *adv.* ▪ **ingeniousness** *or* **ingenuity** *noun.* [15c: from Latin *ingenium* common sense or cleverness]

ingenious, ingenuous
Be careful not to use the word **ingenious** when you mean **ingenuous.**
Ingenuous means innocent and childlike:
It is ingenuous to suppose that everything will be all right now.

ingénue /*French* ɛ̃ʒeny/ ▸ *noun* **1** a naive and unsophisticated young woman. **2** an actress playing the role of an ingénue. [19c: French]

ingenuous *adj* innocent and childlike, esp in being frank, honest and incapable of deception. ▪ **ingenuously** *adv.* ▪ **ingenuousness** *noun.* [16c: from Latin *ingenuus* native or freeborn]

ingest *verb, technical* to take (eg food or liquid) into the body. ▪ **ingestible** *adj.* ▪ **ingestion** *noun.* [17c: from Latin *ingerere* to carry something in]

inglorious *adj* **1** bringing shame. **2** *chiefly old use* ordinary; not glorious or noble. [16c]

ingoing *adj* going in; entering.

ingot /ˈɪŋgət/ *noun* a brick-shaped block of metal, esp of gold or silver. [14c: meaning 'a mould for casting metal in']

ingrain *verb* **1** to dye something in a lasting colour. **2** to fix (a dye) firmly in. **3** to firmly instil (a habit, etc). [18c]

ingrained *adj* **1** difficult to remove or wipe off or out. **2** fixed firmly; instilled or rooted deeply. [16c: from *dyed in grain* dyed in the yarn or thread (before manufacture)]

ingratiate *verb* (*esp* **ingratiate oneself with sb**) to gain or try to gain their favour or approval. ▪ **ingratiating** *adj.* [17c: from Italian *ingratiarsi*]

ingratitude *noun* lack of due gratitude. [14c: from Latin *ingratitudo*]

ingredient *noun* a component of a mixture or compound, esp in cooking. [15c: from Latin *ingrediens* going into]

ingress *noun, formal* **1** the act of going in or entering. **2** the power or right to go in or enter. ▪ **ingression** *noun.* [16c: from Latin *ingredior* to go in]

ingrowing *adj* **1** growing inwards, in or into something. **2** esp of a toenail: growing abnormally so that it becomes embedded in the flesh. ▪ **ingrown** *adj.*

inhabit *verb* to live in or occupy (a place). ▪ **inhabitable** *adj* ▪ **inhabitant** *noun.* [14c: from Latin *inhabitare* to live in]

inhalant *noun* a medicinal preparation in the form of a vapour or aerosol, inhaled for its therapeutic effect. ▸ *adj* **1** inhaling; drawing in. **2** of a medicinal preparation: inhaled to treat a respiratory disorder, etc.

inhale *verb* to draw (air, tobacco smoke, etc) into the lungs; to breathe in. ▪ **inhalation** *noun.* [18c: from Latin *inhalare*, from *halare* to breathe out]

inhaler *noun* **1** *med* a small, portable device used for inhaling certain medicinal preparations. **2** someone who inhales eg tobacco smoke.

inharmonious *adj* **1** not sounding well together. **2** not agreeing or going well together; not compatible. [18c]

inhere *verb, intr, formal or technical* of character, a quality, etc: to be an essential or permanent part. [16c: from Latin *inhaerere* to stick in]

inherent *adj* of a quality, etc: existing as an essential, natural or permanent part. ▪ **inherently** *adv.* [16c]

inherit *verb* **1** to receive (money, property, a title, etc) after someone's death. **2** to receive (genetically transmitted characteristics) from the previous generation. **3** *informal* to receive something second-hand from someone. ▪ **inheritable** *adj.* ▪ **inheritor** *noun.* [14c: from French *enheriter*]

inheritance *noun* **1** something (eg money, property, a title, a physical or mental characteristic) that is or may be inherited. **2** the legal right to inherit something. **3 heredity. 4** the act of inheriting.

inheritance tax *noun* in the UK: a tax levied on bequests and inherited property.

inhibit *verb* **1** to make someone feel unable to act freely or spontaneously. **2** to hold back, restrain or prevent (an action, desire, progress, etc). **3** to prohibit or forbid someone from doing something. **4** *chem* to decrease the rate of (a chemical reaction), or to stop it altogether, by means of an **inhibitor** (sense 1). ▪ **inhibited** *adj.* [15c: from Latin *inhibere* to keep back]

inhibition *noun* **1** a feeling of fear or embarrassment which prevents one from acting, thinking, etc freely or spontaneously. **2** inhibiting or being inhibited. **3** something that inhibits, prevents progress, holds back or forbids, etc.

inhibitor *or* **inhibiter** *noun* **1** *chem* a substance that interferes with a chemical or biological process. **2** something that inhibits.

inhospitable *adj* **1** not friendly or welcoming to others, esp in not offering them food, drink, and other home comforts. **2** of a place: offering little shelter, eg from harsh weather; bleak or barren. [16c]

in-house *adv, adj* within a particular company, organization, etc.

inhuman *adj* **1** cruel and unfeeling. **2** not human. [15c]

inhumane *adj* showing no kindness, sympathy or compassion. [16c]

inhumanity *noun* (**-*ies***) **1** brutality; cruelty; lack of feeling or pity. **2** an inhumane action.

inimical *adj, formal* **1** tending to discourage; unfavourable. **2** not friendly; hostile or in opposition. [17c: from Latin *inimicalis*, from *inimicus* enemy]

inimitable *adj* too good, skilful, etc to be satisfactorily imitated by others; unique. [16c]

iniquity *noun* (**-*ies***) **1** an unfair, unjust, wicked or sinful act. **2** wickedness; sinfulness. ▪ **iniquitous** *adj.* [14c: from Latin *iniquitas*]

initial *adj* relating to or at the beginning. ▸ *noun* the first letter of a word, esp of a name: *Write your initials at the bottom.* ▸ *verb* (***initialled, initialling***; (*N Am*) ***initialed, initialing***) to mark or sign something with the initials of one's name. [16c: from Latin *initialis*]

initialize *or* **-ise** *verb, comput* **1** to assign initial values to (variables, eg in a computer program). **2** to return (a device, eg a computer or printer) to its initial state.

initially *adv* **1** at first. **2** as a beginning.

initiate *verb* /ɪ'nɪʃɪeɪt/ **1** to begin (eg a relationship, project, conversation, etc). **2** (*usu* **initiate sb into sth**) to accept (a new member) into a society, organization, etc, esp with secret ceremonies. **3** (*usu* **initiate sb in sth**) to give them instruction in the basics of a skill, science, etc. ▸ *noun* /ɪ'nɪʃɪət/ someone who has recently been or is soon to be initiated. ▪ **initiation** *noun*. [17c: from Latin *initiare* to begin]

initiative *noun* **1** the ability to initiate things, take decisions or act resourcefully. **2** (*esp in* **take the initiative**) a first step or move towards an end or aim. **3** (*esp* **the initiative**) the right or power to begin something. ▸ *adj* serving to begin; introductory. [17c]

initiator *noun* **1** someone who initiates. **2** *chem* a substance that starts a chain reaction. **3** a highly sensitive explosive used in a detonator.

inject *verb* **1** to introduce (a liquid, eg medicine) into the body using a hypodermic syringe. **2** to force (fuel) into an engine. **3** to introduce (a quality, element, etc): *inject a note of optimism.* ▪ **injectable** *adj*. [17c: from Latin *injicere* to throw in]

injection *noun* **1** **a** the introduction of eg medicine into the body with a hypodermic syringe; **b** the liquid itself. **2** the spraying of vaporized fuel into the cylinder of an internal-combustion engine.

injudicious *adj* not wise.

injunction *noun* **1** *law* an official court order that forbids or commands. **2** any authoritative order or warning. [16c: from Latin *injungere* to enjoin]

injure *verb* **1** to do physical harm or damage to someone or something. **2** to harm, spoil or weaken something: *Only his pride was injured.* **3** to do an injustice or wrong to someone. [16c: back-formation from **injury**]

injurious *adj* causing injury or damage.

injury *noun* (**-ies**) **1** **a** physical harm or damage; **b** an instance of this: *did herself an injury playing squash.* **2** a wound: *has a serious head injury.* **3** something that harms, spoils or hurts something: *a cruel injury to her feelings.* **4** *now chiefly law* a wrong or injustice. [14c: from Latin *injuria* a wrong]

injustice *noun* **1** unfairness or lack of justice. **2** an unfair or unjust act. [14c]

IDIOMS **do sb an injustice** to judge them unfairly.

ink *noun* **1** a coloured liquid used for writing, drawing or printing. **2** *biol* a dark liquid ejected by octopus, squid, etc to confuse predators. ▸ *verb* **1** to mark something with ink. **2** to cover (a surface to be printed) with ink. [13c: from French *enque*]

inkblot test see **Rorschach test**

inkjet printer *noun, comput* a printer that produces characters by spraying a fine jet of ink.

inkling *noun* a vague or slight idea or suspicion. [15c: from obsolete *inkle* to utter in a whisper]

inkstand *noun* a small rack for ink bottles and pens.

inkwell *noun* a small container for ink, esp in a desk.

inky *adj* (**-ier, -iest**) **1** covered with ink. **2** like ink; black or very dark. ▪ **inkiness** *noun*.

inlaid see **inlay**

inland *adj* **1** not beside the sea. **2** *esp Brit* not abroad; domestic. ▸ *noun* that part of a country that is not beside the sea. ▸ *adv* in or towards the parts of a country away from the sea. [Anglo-Saxon]

in-laws *plural noun, informal* relatives by marriage, esp one's mother- and father-in-law. [19c]

inlay *verb* (*past tense & past participle* ***inlaid***) **1** to set or embed (eg pieces of wood, metal, etc) flush in another material. **2** to decorate (eg a piece of furniture) by inlaying pieces of coloured wood, ivory, metal, etc in its surface. ▸ *noun* **1** a decoration or design made by inlaying. **2** the pieces used to create an inlaid design. **3** *dentistry* a filling shaped to fit a cavity in a tooth. [16c]

inlet *noun* **1** *geog* a narrow arm of water running inland from a sea coast or lake shore or between two islands. **2** a narrow opening or valve through which a gas or liquid enters a device. **3** *dressmaking* an extra piece of material sewn into a garment to make it larger. [13c: meaning 'letting in']

in-line skates see **Rollerblades**

in loco parentis /ɪn 'loʊkoʊ pə'rɛntɪs/ *adv* in the role or position of a parent. [19c: Latin, literally 'in the place of a parent']

inmate *noun* someone living in or confined to an institution, esp a prison or a hospital. [16c]

in memoriam *prep* in memory of (a specified person). [19c: Latin]

inmost *adj* **innermost**. [Anglo-Saxon as *innemest*]

inn *noun, esp Brit* a public house or small hotel providing food and accommodation. [15c]

innards *plural noun, informal* **1** the inner organs of a person or animal, esp the stomach and intestines. **2** the inner workings of a machine. [19c: a variant of **inwards**]

innate *adj* **1** existing from birth; inherent. **2** natural or instinctive, rather than learnt or acquired. ▪ **innately** *adv*. [15c: from Latin *innatus* inborn]

inner *adj* **1** further in; situated inside, close or closer to the centre. **2** of thoughts, feelings, etc: secret, hidden and profound, or more secret, profound, etc. [Anglo-Saxon *innera*]

inner city *noun* the central area of a city, esp if densely populated and very poor, with bad housing, roads, etc. *as adj*: *inner-city housing.*

inner ear *noun, anatomy* the innermost part of the ear. Compare **middle ear**.

innermost *or* **inmost** *adj* **1** furthest within; closest to the centre. **2** most secret or hidden. [15c]

inning *noun* in a baseball game: any of the nine divisions per game in which each team may bat.

innings *noun* **1** *cricket* **a** a team's or player's turn at batting; **b** the runs scored during such a turn. **2** *Brit* a period during which someone has an opportunity for action or achievement. [18c]

innkeeper *noun, old use* someone who owns or manages an inn.

innocent *adj* **1** free from sin; pure. **2** not guilty, eg of a crime. **3** not causing, or intending to cause, harm or offence: *an innocent remark.* **4** simple and trusting; guileless. **5** lacking, free or deprived of something: *innocent of all knowledge of the event.* ▸ *noun* an innocent person, esp a young child or simple and trusting adult. ▪ **innocence** *noun*. ▪ **innocently** *adv*. [14c: French, from Latin *innocens* harmless]

innocuous *adj* harmless; inoffensive. [16c: from Latin *innocuus*]

innominate bone *noun* either of two bones that form each side of the pelvis. [From Latin *innominatus* unnamed]

innovate *verb, intr* to introduce new ideas, methods, etc. ▪ **innovation** *noun*. ▪ **innovative** *adj*. ▪ **innovator** *noun*. ▪ **innovatory** *adj*. [16c: from Latin *innovare* to renew]

innuendo *noun* (***innuendos*** or ***innuendoes***) **1 a** an indirectly unpleasant, critical or spiteful remark, eg about someone's character; **b** a rude or smutty allusion or insinuation. **2** the act or practice of making such remarks. [17c: Latin, meaning 'by nodding at']

Innuit see **Inuit**

innumerable *adj* too many to be counted; a great many. [14c: from Latin *innumerabilis*]

innumerate *adj* having no understanding of mathematics or science. ▪ **innumeracy** *noun*. [20c: modelled on **illiterate**]

inoculate *verb* **1** *med* to inject a harmless form of an **antigen** into (a person or animal). **2** *biol, etc* to introduce a micro-organism, eg a bacterium or virus, into (a medium) in order to start a **culture**, or into another organism in order to produce antibodies. **3** *literary or old use* to imbue or instil someone, eg with ideas or feelings. ▪ **inoculation** *noun*. [15c: from Latin *inoculare* to implant]

inoculate
This word is often misspelt. It has one *n* and one *c*.

inoffensive *adj* harmless; not objectionable or provocative. [16c]

inoperable *adj, med* of a disease or condition: not able to be treated by surgery. [19c]

inoperative *adj* **1** of a machine, etc: not working or functioning. **2** of rule, etc: having no effect. [17c]

inopportune *adj* not suitable or convenient; badly-timed. [16c: from Latin *inopportunus*]

inordinate *adj* greater than or beyond what is normal or acceptable. [14c: from Latin *inordinatus* unrestrained]

inorganic *adj* **1** not composed of living or formerly living material. **2** not caused by natural growth. **3** not produced or developed naturally. **4** *chem* not containing chains or rings of carbon atoms. [18c]

inorganic chemistry *noun* the branch of chemistry concerned with the properties and reactions of the elements, and of compounds that do not contain chains or rings of carbon atoms. Compare **organic chemistry**.

inpatient *noun* a patient temporarily living in hospital while receiving treatment there. Compare **outpatient**.

input *noun* **1** *comput* the data that is entered into the main memory of a computer. *as adj*: *input device*. **2** something that is put or taken in, eg a contribution to a discussion: *Your input would be valuable at the meeting*. **3** the money, power, materials, labour, etc required to produce something; the power or electrical current put into a machine. **4** an act or process of putting something in. ▸ *verb* to enter (data) into the main memory of a computer. Compare **output**. [18c]

input device *noun, comput* any device used to enter data into memory, such as a **keyboard** or **mouse**.

inquest *noun* **1** a coroner's investigation into an incident, eg a sudden death. **2** *informal, esp facetious* analysis of the result of a game, campaign, etc and discussion of mistakes made. [13c: from French *enqueste*]

inquietude /ɪŋ'kwaɪətʃuːd/ *noun, formal* restlessness or uneasiness. [15c: from Latin *inquietudo*]

inquire *or* **enquire** *verb* **1** *tr & intr* to seek or ask for information. **2** *intr* (*often* **inquire into sth**) to try to discover the facts of (a crime, etc), esp formally. **3** *intr* (**inquire after sb**) to ask about their health or happiness. [13c: from Latin *inquirere*]

inquire, enquire
Both **inquire** and **enquire** are correct, but **inquire** is used more than **enquire**, especially in formal writing such as reports and contexts such as investigations.

inquiring *or* **enquiring** *adj* **1** eager to discover or learn things: *an inquiring mind*. **2** esp of a look: appearing to be asking a question. ▪ **inquiringly** *adv*.

inquiry *or* **enquiry** *noun* (***-ies***) **1** an act or the process of asking for information. **2** (*often* **an inquiry into sth**) an investigation, esp an official or a formal one.

inquiry, enquiry
Both **inquiry** and **enquiry** are correct for meaning 1, asking for information. However, the spelling **inquiry** and not **enquiry** is usually used for meaning 2, a formal investigation.

inquisition *noun* **1** a searching or intensive inquiry or investigation. **2** an official or judicial inquiry. **3** (**the Inquisition**) *hist* in the RC Church between the 13c and 19c: a papal tribunal responsible for discovering, suppressing and punishing heresy and unbelief, notably in Spain (the **Spanish Inquisition**). ▪ **inquisitional** *adj*. [14c: French, from Latin *inquisitio*]

inquisitive *adj* **1** over-eager to find out things, esp about other people's affairs. **2** eager for knowledge or information; curious. ▪ **inquisitively** *adv*. ▪ **inquisitiveness** *noun*. [15c: from Latin *inquisitivus*]

inquisitor *noun, usu derog* someone who carries out an inquisition or inquiry, esp harshly or intensively. [16c]

inquisitorial *adj* **1** relating to or like an inquisitor or inquisition. **2** unnecessarily or offensively curious about other people's affairs. ▪ **inquisitorially** *adv*.

inroad *noun* **1** (*usu* **inroads into sth**) a large or significant using up or consumption of it, or encroachment on it. **2** a hostile attack or raid. [16c]

insane *adj* **1** mad; mentally ill. **2** *informal* esp of actions: extremely foolish; stupid. **3** relating to the mentally ill. ▪ **insanely** *adv*. ▪ **insanity** *noun*. [16c: from Latin *insanus*]

insanitary *adj* so dirty as to be dangerous to health. ▪ **insanitariness** *noun*. [16c]

insatiable /ɪn'seɪʃəbəl/ *adj* not able to be satisfied; extremely greedy. [15c: from Latin *insatiabilis*]

inscribe *verb* **1** to write, print or engrave (words) on (paper, metal, stone, etc). **2** to enter (a name) on a list or in a book; to enrol. **3** (*often* **inscribe sth to sb**) to dedicate or address (a book, etc) to them, usu by writing in the front of it. **4** *geom* to draw (a figure) within another figure so as to touch all or some of its sides or faces. Compare **circumscribe**. [16c: from Latin *scribere* to write in]

inscription *noun* **1** words written, printed or engraved, eg as a dedication in a book or as an epitaph on a gravestone. **2** the act of inscribing, esp of writing a dedication in the front of a book or of entering a name on a list. [15c: from Latin *inscriptio*]

inscrutable *adj* hard to understand or explain; enigmatic. ▪ **inscrutability** *noun*. [15c: from Latin *inscrutabilis*, from *scrutare* to search thoroughly]

insect *noun* **1** *zool* an invertebrate animal, such as a fly, beetle, ant or bee, typically with a segmented body and two pairs of wings. **2** *loosely* any other small invertebrate, eg a spider. **3** *derog* an insignificant or worthless person. [17c: from Latin *insectum*, meaning 'cut' or 'notched' (animal)]

insecticide *noun* any substance used to kill insects. ▪ **insecticidal** *adj*. [19c]

insectivore *noun* **1** an animal or bird that feeds on insects. **2** a plant that traps and digests insects. ▪ **insectivorous** /ɪnsɛk'tɪvərəs/ *adj*. [19c: French, from Latin *insectivorus* insect-eating]

insecure *adj* **1** not firmly fixed; unstable. **2** lacking confidence; anxious about possible loss or danger. **3** under threat or in danger or likely to be so: *insecure jobs*. ▪ **insecurity** *noun* (**-*ies***). [17c: from Latin *insecurus*]

inselberg *noun* (***inselberge*** /-bɜːgə/) *geog* a steep-sided hill rising from a plain, often found in the semi-arid regions of tropical countries. [Early 20c: German, meaning 'hill-island']

inseminate *verb* **1** to introduce **semen** into (a female). **2** *now rather formal or literary* to sow (seeds, ideas, attitudes, etc). ▪ **insemination** *noun*. [17c: from Latin *inseminare* to implant or impregnate]

insensate *adj, formal or literary* **1** not able to perceive physical sensations; not conscious; inanimate. **2** insensitive and unfeeling. **3** having little or no common sense; stupid. [16c]

insensible *adj, formal or literary* **1** not able to feel pain; not conscious. **2** (*usu* **insensible of** *or* **to sth**) unaware of it; not caring about it. **3** incapable of feeling emotion; callous; indifferent. **4** too small or slight to be noticed. ▪ **insensibility** *noun*. [14c]

insensitive *adj* **1** not aware of, or not capable of responding sympathetically or thoughtfully to, other people's feelings, etc. **2** not feeling or reacting to (stimulation, eg touch or light). ▪ **insensitivity** *noun*. [17c]

inseparable *adj* **1** incapable of being separated. **2** unwilling to be apart; constantly together. **3** *grammar* of a prefix, etc: not able to stand as a separate word. ▪ **inseparability** *noun*. ▪ **inseparably** *adv*. [14c]

insert *verb* /ɪn'sɜːt/ **1** to put or fit something inside something else. **2** to introduce (text, words, etc) into the body of other text, words, etc. ▸ *noun* /'ɪnsɜːt/ something inserted, esp a loose sheet in a book or magazine, or piece of material in a garment. ▪ **insertion** *noun*. [16c: from Latin *inserere*]

in-service *adj* carried on while a person is employed.

inset *noun* /'ɪnsɛt/ **1** something set in or inserted, eg a piece of lace or cloth set into a garment, or a page or pages set into a book. **2** a small map or picture put in the corner of a larger one. ▸ *verb* /ɪn'sɛt/ (***inset, insetting***) to put in, add or insert something. [19c]

inshore *adv, adj* in or on water, but near or towards the shore: *inshore shipping*. Compare **offshore**.

inside *noun* **1** the inner side, surface or part of something. Opposite of **outside**. **2** the side of a road nearest to the buildings, pavement, etc (as opposed to the other lane or lanes of traffic). **3** the part of a pavement or path away from the road. **4** *sport* the inside track, or the equivalent part of any racetrack. **5** (**insides**) *informal* the inner organs, esp the stomach and bowels. **6** *informal* a position that gains one the confidence of and otherwise secret information from people in authority: *Those on the inside knew his plans*. ▸ *adj* **1 a** being on, near, towards or from the inside; **b** indoor. **2** *informal* coming from, concerned with, provided by or planned by a person or people within a specific organization or circle: *inside knowledge*. ▸ *adv* **1** to, in or on the inside or interior. **2** indoors. **3** *informal* in or into prison. ▸ *prep* **1** to or on the interior or inner side of something; within. **2** in less than (a specified time). [16c]

inside out *adv* **1** (*also* **outside in**) with the inside surface turned out. **2** *informal* thoroughly; completely.

insider *noun* a member of an organization or group who has access to confidential or exclusive information about it.

insider dealing *or* **insider trading** *noun, finance* the illegal buying and selling of shares by people, eg on the **stock exchange**, who have access to information that has not been made public.

insidious *adj* **1** developing gradually without being noticed but causing great harm. **2** attractive but harmful; treacherous. ▪ **insidiously** *adv*. ▪ **insidiousness** *noun*. [16c: from Latin *insidiosus* cunning]

insight *noun* **1** the ability to gain a relatively rapid, clear and deep understanding of the real, often hidden and usu complex nature of a situation, problem, etc. **2** an instance or example of this. **3** *psychol* awareness of one's own mental or psychological condition, processes, etc. ▪ **insightful** *adj*. [13c: meaning 'discernment']

insignia *singular or plural noun* (***insignia*** *or* ***insignias***) **1** badges or emblems of office, honour or membership. **2** *loosely* the distinguishing marks by which something is known. [17c: Latin, meaning 'badges']

insignificant *adj* **1** of little or no meaning, value or importance. **2** relatively small in size or amount. ▪ **insignificance** *noun*. [17c]

insincere *adj* not genuine; false; hypocritical. ▪ **insincerely** *adv*. ▪ **insincerity** *noun* (**-*ies***). [17c]

insinuate *verb* **1** to suggest or hint (something unpleasant) in an indirect way. **2** to introduce (eg an idea) in an indirect, subtle or devious way. **3** (*esp* **insinuate oneself into sth**) to succeed in gaining (eg acceptance or favour) by gradual, careful and often cunning means. ▪ **insinuation** *noun*. [16c: from Latin *insinuare*]

insipid *adj* **1** having little or no interest or liveliness; boring. **2** having little or no taste or flavour. ▪ **insipidness** *or* **insipidity** *noun*. [17c: from Latin *insipidus*]

insist *verb* **1** *tr & intr* to maintain or assert something firmly. **2** (*usu* **insist on** *or* **upon sth**) to demand it firmly. [16c: from Latin *insistere* to persist]

insistent *adj* **1** making continual forceful demands. **2** demanding attention; compelling. ▪ **insistence** *or* **insistency** *noun*. ▪ **insistently** *adv*.

in situ /ɪn 'sɪtjuː/ *adv* in the natural or original position. [18c: Latin, meaning 'in the place']

insofar as see under **in**

insolation *noun* **1** exposure to the sun's rays. **2** the amount of solar radiation on a surface. [From Latin *insolare*, from *in* in, and *sol* the sun]

insole *noun* an inner sole in a shoe or boot. [19c]

insolent *adj* rude or insulting; showing a lack of respect. ▪ **insolence** *noun*. ▪ **insolently** *adv*. [14c: from Latin *insolens*, literally 'departing from custom']

insoluble *adj* **1** of a substance: not able to be dissolved in a particular solvent (esp water). **2** of a problem or difficulty: not able to be solved or resolved. ▪ **insolubility** *noun*. [14c]

insolvent *adj* **1** not having enough money to pay debts, etc. **2** relating to insolvent people or insolvency. ▪ **insolvency** *noun*. [16c]

insomnia *noun* the chronic inability to sleep or to have enough sleep. ▪ **insomniac** *noun, adj*. [18c: Latin]

insomuch see under **in**

insouciant /ɪn'suːsɪənt; *French* ɛ̃susjɑ̃/ *adj, rather formal or literary* without cares or worries; lighthearted; unconcerned. ▪ **insouciance** *noun*. [19c: French]

inspect *verb* **1** to look at or examine closely, often to find faults or mistakes. **2** to look at or examine (a body of soldiers, etc) officially or ceremonially. ▪ **inspection** *noun*. [17c: from Latin *inspicere* to look into]

inspector *noun* **1** someone whose job is to inspect something. **2** (*often* **Inspector**) *Brit* a police officer below a superintendent and above a sergeant in rank.

inspectorate *noun* **1** a body of inspectors. **2** the office or post of inspector. Also called **inspectorship**.

inspiration *noun* **1** someone or something that inspires; a supposed power that stimulates the mind, esp to artistic activity or creativity. **2** the state of being inspired. **3** a brilliant or inspired idea. **4** *relig* a supposed divine power or influence that leads to the writing of Scripture. **5** *physiol* **a** the act of drawing breath into the lungs; **b** a breath taken in this way. ▪ **inspirational** *adj*.

inspire *verb* **1** (*often* **inspire sb to sth** *or* **to do sth**) to stimulate them into activity, esp into artistic or creative activity. **2** to fill someone with a feeling of confidence, encouragement and exaltation. **3** (*esp* **inspire sb with sth** *or* **inspire sth into sb**) to create (a particular feeling) in them. **4** to be the origin or source of (a poem, piece of music, etc). **5** *relig* of supposed divine power or influence: to guide or instruct someone. **6** *tr & intr* to breathe in (air, etc); to inhale. ▪ **inspired** *adj* so good, skilful, etc as to seem to be the result of inspiration. [14c: from Latin *inspirare* to breathe into]

Inst. *abbrev* **1** Institute. **2** Institution.

inst. *abbrev* instant, ie of or in the current month (see **instant** *adj* sense 4).

instability *noun* lack of physical or mental steadiness or stability. [15c: from Latin *instabilitas*]

install or (*sometimes*) **instal** *verb* (***installed, installing***) **1** to put (equipment, machinery, etc) in place and make it ready for use. **2** to place (a person) in office with a formal ceremony. **3** to place (something, oneself, etc) in a particular position, condition or place. [16c: from Latin *installare*]

installation *noun* **1** the act or process of installing. **2** a piece of equipment, machinery, etc, or a complete system, that has been installed ready for use. **3** a military base. **4** *art* a large-scale work in an art gallery, often involving video or mixed media.

instalment *or* (*US*) **installment** *noun* **1** one of a series of parts into which a debt is divided for payment. **2** one of several parts published, issued, broadcast, etc at regular intervals. [18c: from French *estaler* to fix or set]

instance *noun* **1** an example, esp one of a particular condition or circumstance. **2** a particular stage in a process or a particular situation: *in the first instance*. **3** *formal* request; urging: *at the instance of your partner.* [14c: from Latin *instantia*, from *instare* to be present]

IDIOMS **for instance** for example.

instant *adj* **1** immediate. **2** of food and drink, etc: quickly and easily prepared, esp by reheating or the addition of boiling water. **3** present; current. **4** (abbrev **inst.**) of the current month. **5** *rather formal or old use* urgent; pressing. ▶ *noun* **1** a particular moment in time. **2** a moment: *I'll be there in an instant*. **3** *informal* an instant drink, esp instant coffee. ▪ **instantly** *or* **this instant** *adv* immediately. [14c: French, from Latin *instare* to be present]

instantaneous *adj* done, happening or occurring at once, very quickly or in an instant. [17c: from Latin *instantaneus*]

instate *verb* to install someone (in an official position, etc). ▪ **instatement** *noun*. [17c]

instead *adv* as a substitute or alternative; in place of something or someone. [13c]

instep *noun* **1** the prominent arched middle section of the human foot, between the ankle and the toes. **2** the part of a shoe, sock, etc that covers this. [16c: see **step**]

instigate *verb* **1** to urge someone on or incite them, esp to do something wrong or evil. **2** to set in motion or initiate (eg an inquiry). ▪ **instigation** *noun*. ▪ **instigator** *noun*. [16c: from Latin *instigare* to urge on]

instil *or* (*US*) **instill** *verb* (***instilled, instilling***) (*esp* **instil sth in** *or* **into sb**) to impress, fix or plant (ideas, feelings, etc) slowly or gradually in their mind. ▪ **instillation** *or* **instilment** *noun*. ▪ **instiller** *noun*. [16c: from Latin *instillare* to drip into]

instinct *noun* **1** in animal behaviour: an unlearned and inherited response to a stimulus. **2** in humans: a basic natural drive that urges a person towards a specific goal, such as survival or reproduction. **3** intuition: *Instinct told me not to believe him*. [16c: from Latin *instinctus* prompting]

instinctive *adj* **1** prompted by instinct or intuition. **2** involuntary; automatic. ▪ **instinctively** *adv*.

institute *noun* **1** a society or organization that promotes research, education or a particular cause. **2** a building or group of buildings used by an institute. **3** an established law, principle, rule or custom. **4** (**institutes**) a book of laws or principles. ▶ *verb, rather formal* **1** to set up, establish or organize something: *instituted a trust fund*. **2** to initiate something or cause it to begin: *to institute legal proceedings*. **3** to appoint someone to, or install them in, a position or office. [14c: from Latin *instituere* to establish]

institution *noun* **1** an organization or public body founded for a special purpose, esp for a charitable or educational purpose or as a hospital. **2** a hospital, old people's home, etc, regarded as impersonal or bureaucratic. **3** a custom or tradition; something that is well-established: *the institution of marriage.* **4** *informal* a familiar and well-known object or person. **5** the act of instituting or process of being instituted. ▪ **institutional** *adj* **1** like or typical of an institution, esp in being dull or regimented: *institutional food.* **2** depending on, or originating in, an institution. ▪ **institutionalism** *noun.* [15c: see **institute**]

institutionalize *or* **-ise** *verb* **1** to place someone in an institution. **2** to cause someone to lose their individuality and ability to cope with life by keeping them in (eg a long-stay hospital or prison) for too long. **3** to make something into an institution. [19c]

instruct *verb* **1** **a** to teach or train someone in a subject or skill; **b** (*usu* **instruct sb in sth**) to give them information about or practical knowledge of it. **2** to direct or order, eg someone to do something. **3** *law* to give (a lawyer) the facts concerning a case. **4** *law* to engage (a lawyer) to act in a case. [15c: from Latin *instruere* to equip or train]

instruction *noun* **1** (*often* **instructions**) a direction, order or command: *She's always issuing instructions.* **2** teaching; the act or process of instructing. **3** *comput* a command that activates a specific operation. **4** (**instructions**) guidelines on eg how to operate a piece of equipment. **5** (**instructions**) *law* the information, details, etc of a case, given to a lawyer. ▪ **instructional** *adj.* [15c]

instructive *adj* giving knowledge or information.

instructor *noun* **1** someone who gives instruction: *driving instructor.* **2** *N Am* a college or university teacher ranking below an assistant professor.

instrument *noun* **1** a tool, esp one used for delicate scientific work or measurement. **2** (*also* **musical instrument**) a device used to produce musical sounds. **3** a device that measures, shows and controls speed, temperature, direction, etc. *as adj*: *instrument panel.* **4** a means of achieving or doing something: *She was the instrument of his downfall.* **5** a formal or official legal document. [13c: from Latin *instrumentum* equipment or tool]

instrumental *adj* **1** (*often* **instrumental in** *or* **to sth**) being responsible for it or an important factor in it. **2** of music: performed by or for musical instruments only. **3** relating to or done with an instrument or tool. ▸ *noun* a piece of music for or performed by musical instruments only. [14c: French]

instrumentalist *noun* someone who plays a musical instrument. [19c]

instrumentation *noun* **1** the way in which a piece of music is written or arranged to be played by instruments. **2** the instruments used to play a piece of music. **3** the use, design or provision of instruments or tools.

insubordinate *adj* refusing to take orders or submit to authority. ▪ **insubordination** *noun.* [19c]

insubstantial *adj* **1** not solid, strong or satisfying; flimsy; tenuous: *insubstantial evidence.* **2** not solid or real. ▪ **insubstantially** *adv.* [17c]

insufferable *adj* too unpleasant, annoying, etc to tolerate. ▪ **insufferably** *adv.* [16c]

insufficient *adj* not enough or not adequate. ▪ **insufficiency** *noun.* ▪ **insufficiently** *adv.* [14c: from Latin *insufficiens*]

insular *adj* **1** relating to an island or its inhabitants. **2** narrow-minded; isolated; prejudiced. ▪ **insularity** *noun.* [17c: from Latin *insularis,* from *insula* island]

insulate *verb* **1** to surround (a body, device or space) with a material that prevents or slows down the flow of heat, electricity or sound. **2** to remove or set someone or something apart; to isolate. ▪ **insulation** *noun.* ▪ **insulator** *noun.* [16c: from Latin *insula* island]

insulin *noun* a **hormone** that controls the concentration of sugar in the blood. [20c: from Latin *insula* island]

insult *verb* /ɪn'sʌlt/ **1** to speak rudely or offensively to or about someone or something. **2** to behave in a way that offends or affronts. ▸ *noun* /'ɪnsʌlt/ **1** a rude or offensive remark or action. **2** an affront: *an insult to the intelligence.* **3** *med* **a** injury or damage to the body; **b** a cause of this. [16c: French: from Latin *insultare* to assail]

insuperable *adj* too difficult to be overcome, defeated or dealt with successfully. [14c]

insupportable *adj* **1** intolerable. **2** not justifiable. [16c]

insurance *noun* **1** an agreement by which a company promises to pay a person, etc money in the event of loss, theft, damage to property, injury or death, etc. **2** the contract for such an agreement. Also called **insurance policy**. **3** the protection offered by such a contract. **4** an insurance **premium**. **5** the sum that will be paid according to such an agreement. **6** the business of providing such contracts for clients. *as adj*: *insurance company.* **7** anything done, any measure taken, etc to try to prevent possible loss, disappointment, problems, etc. **8** an act or instance of insuring. [17c]

insure *verb* **1** *tr & intr* to arrange for the payment of an amount of money in the event of the loss or theft of or damage to (property) or injury to or the death of (a person), etc by paying regular amounts of money to an insurance company. **2** to take measures to try to prevent (an event leading to loss, damage, difficulties, etc). ▪ **insurable** *adj.* [15c variant of **ensure**]

insured *adj* **1** covered by insurance. **2** (**the insured**) *law, etc* a person whose life, health or property is covered by insurance.

insurer *noun* (*esp* **the insurer**) *law, etc* a person or company that provides insurance.

insurgence *or* **insurgency** *noun* (***insurgences*** *or* ***insurgencies***) an uprising or rebellion.

insurgent *adj* opposed to and fighting against the government of the country. ▸ *noun* a rebel. [18c: from Latin *insurgere* to rise up]

insurmountable *adj* too difficult to be dealt with; impossible to overcome. [17c]

insurrection *noun* an act of rebellion against authority. [15c: French, from Latin *insurgere* to rise up]

int. *abbrev* **1** interior. **2** internal. **3** (*also* **Int.**) international.

intact *adj* whole; not broken or damaged; untouched. [15c: from Latin *intactus*]

intaglio /ɪn'tɑːlɪoʊ/ *noun* **1** a stone or gem that has a design engraved into its surface. Compare **cameo** (sense 1). **2** **a** the art or process of engraving designs into the surface of objects, esp jewellery; **b** an engraved design. [17c: Italian, from *intagliare* to cut into]

intake *noun* **1** a thing or quantity taken in or accepted. **2 a** a number or the amount taken in; **b** the people, etc taken in. **3** an opening through which liquid or gas (eg air) enters a pipe, engine, etc. **4** an act of taking in.

intangible *adj* **1** not perceptible by touch. **2** difficult for the mind to grasp. **3** of eg a business asset: having value but no physical existence. [17c: from Latin *intangibilis*]

integer *noun* **1** *maths* a positive or negative whole number. **2** any whole or complete entity. [16c: Latin, meaning 'entire']

integral *adj* **1** being a necessary part of a whole. **2** forming a whole; supplied as part of a whole. **3** complete. **4** *maths, denoting* an **integer**. ▸ *noun, maths* the sum of a large number of small quantities, either between definite limits (a **definite integral**) or without limits (an **indefinite integral**). [16c: from Latin *integralis*]

integral calculus *noun, maths* the branch of calculus concerned with finding integrals and applying them to find eg the solution of differential equations. See also **integration**.

integrand /ˈɪntəgrand/ *noun, maths* a function that is to be integrated. [19c: from Latin *integrandus*, from *integrare* to integrate]

integrate *verb* **1** to fit (parts) together to form a whole. **2** *tr & intr* to mix (people) or cause (people) to mix freely with other groups in society, etc. **3** to end racial segregation in something. **4** *maths* **a** to find the integral of (a function or equation); **b** to find the total or mean value of (a variable). [17c: from Latin *integrare* to renew or make whole]

integrated circuit *noun, electronics* a circuit on a chip of semiconductor material, usu silicon.

integration *noun* **1** the process of integrating. **2** *maths* a method used in calculus of determining the sum of a large number of infinitely small quantities, ie finding the integral of a function or variable, used to calculate the area under a curve.

integrity *noun* **1** moral uprightness. **2** the quality or state of being whole and unimpaired. [15c: from Latin *integritas* wholeness]

integument *noun, zool, botany* a protective outer layer of tissue. [17c: from Latin *integumentum*, from *integere* to cover]

intellect *noun* **1** the part of the mind that thinks, reasons and understands. **2** the capacity to use this part of the mind. **3** someone who has great mental ability. [14c: from Latin *intelligere* to understand]

intellectual *adj* **1** involving or appealing to the intellect. **2** having a highly developed ability to think, reason and understand. ▸ *noun* an intellectual person.

intellectual property *noun, law* property, such as trademarks, etc, that is the product of creative work.

intelligence *noun* **1** the ability to use one's mind to solve problems, etc. **2** news or information. **3 a** the gathering of secret information about an enemy; **b** the government department, army personnel, etc responsible for this. [14c: from Latin *intelligentia*, from *intelligere* to understand]

intelligence quotient *noun* (abbrev **IQ**) a measure of a person's intellectual ability.

intelligent *adj* **1** having highly developed mental ability. **2** of a machine, computer, etc: able to vary its behaviour according to the situation. ▪ **intelligently** *adv.*

intelligentsia *noun* (*usu* **the intelligentsia**) the most highly educated and cultured people in a society. [Early 20c: Russian *intelligentsiya*, from Latin *intelligentia* intelligence]

intelligible *adj* able to be understood. ▪ **intelligibility** *noun.* ▪ **intelligibly** *adv.* [14c: from Latin *intelligibilis*]

intemperate *adj* **1** going beyond reasonable limits. **2** habitually drinking too much alcohol. **3** of a climate or region: having extreme and severe temperatures. Compare **temperate.** ▪ **intemperance** *noun.* [15c]

intend *verb* **1** to plan or have in mind as one's purpose or aim. **2** (**intend sth for sb** *or* **sth**) to set it aside or destine it to some person or thing. **3** to mean. [14c: from French *entendre*]

intended *adj* meant; done on purpose or planned. ▸ *noun, informal* someone's future husband or wife.

intense *adj* **1** very great or extreme. **2** feeling or expressing emotion deeply. **3** very deeply felt: *intense happiness.* ▪ **intensely** *adv.* [14c: French]

intensifier *noun, grammar* an adverb or adjective that adds emphasis to or intensifies the word or phrase that follows it, eg *very.* Also called **intensive**.

intensify *verb* (***-ies, -ied***) *tr & intr* to make or become intense or more intense. ▪ **intensification** *noun.*

intensity *noun* (***-ies***) **1** the quality or state of being intense. **2** *physics* the rate per unit area at which power or energy is transmitted, eg loudness or brightness. **3** *chem* the concentration of a solution. **4** *physics* the power per unit area transmitted by a wave. [17c]

intensive *adj* **1** *often in compounds* using, done with or requiring considerable amounts of thought, effort, time, etc within a relatively short period: *labour-intensive.* **2** thorough; intense; concentrated. **3** using large amounts of capital and labour (rather than more land or raw materials) to increase production: *intensive farming.* **4** *grammar* of an adverb or adjective: adding force or emphasis, eg *extremely, quite.* ▸ *noun, grammar* an **intensifier**. ▪ **intensively** *adv.* ▪ **intensiveness** *noun.* [16c: from Latin *intensivus*; see **intense**]

intensive care *noun* **1** the care of critically ill patients who require continuous attention. **2** (*in full* **intensive-care unit**) a hospital unit that provides such care.

intent *noun* **1** an aim, intention or purpose. **2** *law* the purpose of committing a crime: *loitering with intent.* ▸ *adj* **1** (*usu* **intent on** *or* **upon sth**) firmly determined to do it. **2** (*usu* **intent on sth**) having one's attention fixed on it. **3** showing concentration; absorbed: *an intent look.* ▪ **intently** *adv.* ▪ **intentness** *noun.* [13c: from Latin *intentus*, from *intendere* to stretch towards]

IDIOMS **to all intents and purposes** in every important respect; virtually.

intention *noun* **1** an aim or purpose. **2** (**intentions**) *informal* a man's purpose with regard to marrying a particular woman. [14c: from Latin *intendere* to stretch towards]

intentional *adj* said, done, etc on purpose. ▪ **intentionally** *adv.*

inter *verb* (***interred, interring***) to bury (a dead person, etc). [14c: from Latin *interrare*, from *terra* earth]

inter- *prefix, denoting* **1** between or among: *intermingle*. **2** mutual or reciprocal. [Latin, meaning 'among']

interact *verb, intr* to act with or on one another. ▪ **interaction** *noun*. ▪ **interactive** *adj* **1** characterized by interaction. **2** involving or allowing a continuous exchange of information between a computer and its user. ▪ **interactively** *adv*. [18c]

inter alia /ɪntəˈreɪlɪə; *Latin* ˈɪntɛr ˈalɪa/ *adv* among other things. [17c: Latin]

interbreed *verb, tr & intr* **1** to breed within a single family or strain so as to control the appearance of certain characteristics in the offspring. **2** to crossbreed.

intercede *verb, intr* **1** to act as a peacemaker between (two people, groups, etc). **2** (*usu* **intercede for sb**) to make an appeal on their behalf. [17c: from Latin *intercedere* to intervene]

intercept *verb* **1 a** to stop or catch (eg a person, missile, aircraft, etc) on their or its way from one place to another; **b** to prevent (a missile, etc) from arriving at its destination, often by destroying it. **2** *maths* to mark or cut off (a line, plane, curve, etc) with another line, plane, etc that crosses it. **3** of a plant, building, etc: to collect precipitation. ▸ *noun, maths* **1** the part of a line or plane that is cut off by another line or plane crossing it; the distance from the origin to the point where a straight line or a curve crosses one of the axes of a coordinate system. **2** the point at which two figures intersect. ▪ **interception** *noun*. ▪ **interceptive** *adj*. [16c: from Latin *intercipere*]

interceptor *noun* someone or something that intercepts, esp a small light aircraft used to intercept approaching enemy aircraft.

intercession *noun* **1** an act of interceding. **2** *Christianity* a prayer to God on behalf of someone else. [16c: from Latin *intercessio*]

interchange *verb, tr & intr* to change or cause to change places with something or someone. ▸ *noun* **1** an act of interchanging; an exchange. **2** a road junction consisting of roads and bridges designed to prevent streams of traffic from directly crossing one another. ▪ **interchangeability** *noun*. ▪ **interchangeable** *adj*. ▪ **interchangeably** *adv*. [14c]

intercity *adj* between cities.

intercom *noun* an internal system that allows communication within a building, aircraft, ship, etc. [20c: abbrev of **intercommunication**]

intercommunicate *verb, intr* **1** to communicate mutually or together. **2** of adjoining rooms: to have a connecting door. ▪ **intercommunication** *noun*. [16c]

interconnect *verb, tr & intr* to connect (two things) or be connected with one another. ▪ **interconnection** *noun*. [19c]

intercontinental *adj* travelling between or connecting different continents. [19c]

intercostal *adj, anatomy* between the ribs. [16c: from Latin *costa* rib]

intercourse *noun* **1 sexual intercourse**. **2** communication, connection or dealings between people, groups, etc. [15c: from French *entrecours* commerce]

interdenominational *adj* involving (members of) different religious denominations.

interdepartmental *adj* involving (members of) different departments within a single organization, etc.

interdependent *adj* depending on one another. ▪ **interdependence** *noun*. ▪ **interdependently** *adv*.

interdict *noun* /ˈɪntədɪkt/ **1** an official order forbidding someone to do something. **2** *RC Church* a sentence or punishment removing the right to most sacraments (including burial but not communion) from the people of a place or district. **3** *Scots law* an **injunction** (sense 1). ▸ *verb* /ɪntəˈdɪkt/ to place under an interdict; to forbid or prohibit. ▪ **interdiction** *noun*. ▪ **interdictory** *adj*. [13c: from Latin *interdictum* prohibition]

interdisciplinary *adj* involving two or more subjects of study.

interest *noun* **1** the desire to learn or know about someone or something; curiosity. **2** the power to attract attention and curiosity. **3** something that arouses attention and curiosity; a hobby or pastime. **4** a charge for borrowing money or using credit. **5** (*often* **interests**) advantage, benefit or profit, esp financial: *It is in your own interests to be truthful.* **6** a share or claim in a business and its profits, or a legal right to property. **7** (*also* **interest group**) a group of people or organizations with common, esp financial, aims and concerns: *the banking interest*. ▸ *verb* **1** to attract the attention and curiosity of someone. **2** (*often* **interest sb in sth**) to cause them to take a part in or be concerned about some activity. [15c: from Latin *interest* it concerns]

interested *adj* **1** showing concern or having an interest. **2** personally involved; not impartial or disinterested. ▪ **interestedly** *adv*.

interesting *adj* attracting interest; holding the attention. ▪ **interestingly** *adv*.

interest rate *noun, finance* a charge made on borrowed money.

interface *noun* **1** a surface forming a common boundary between two regions, things, etc. **2** a common boundary or meeting-point. **3** *comput* a link between a computer and a peripheral device, such as a printer, or a user. ▸ *verb, tr & intr* to connect (a piece of equipment, etc) with another so as to make them compatible. ▪ **interfacial** *adj*. [19c]

interfacing *noun* a piece of stiff fabric sewn between two layers of material to give shape and firmness.

interfere *verb, intr* **1** (*often* **interfere with** *or* **in sth**) **a** of a person: to meddle with something not considered their business; **b** of a thing: to hinder or adversely affect something else: *The weather is interfering with picture reception.* **2** (**interfere with sb**) *euphem* to assault or molest them sexually. **3** *physics* of sound waves, rays of light, etc: to combine together to cause disturbance or interference. **4** of a horse: to strike a foot against the opposite leg in walking. ▪ **interfering** *adj*. [16c: from French *s'entreferir* to strike each other]

interference *noun* **1** the act or process of interfering. **2** *physics* the interaction between two or more waves of the same frequency. **3** *telecomm* the distortion of transmitted radio or television signals by an external power source.

interferon /ɪntəˈfɪərɒn/ *noun, biochem* any of various proteins that are capable of preventing a virus from multiplying. [20c: from **interfere**]

intergalactic *adj* happening or situated between galaxies.

interim *adj* provisional, temporary. [16c: Latin, meaning 'meanwhile']
IDIOMS **in the interim** in the meantime.

interior *adj* **1** on, of, suitable for, happening or acting in, or coming from the inside; inner: *interior design*. **2** away from the shore or frontier; inland. **3** concerning the domestic or internal affairs of a country. **4** belonging to or existing in the mind or spirit; belonging to the mental or spiritual life. ▸ *noun* **1** an internal or inner part; the inside. **2** the part of a country or continent that is furthest from the coast. **3** the internal or home affairs of a country. **4** a picture or representation of the inside of a room or building, esp with reference to its decoration or style: *a typical southern French interior*. [15c: Latin, comparative of *inter* inward]

interior angle *noun, maths* an angle inside a polygon, at a vertex.

interior decoration *or* **interior design** *noun* **1** the decoration, design and furnishings of a room or building. **2** the designing of the insides of rooms, including selecting colours and furnishings. ▪ **interior decorator** *or* **interior designer** *noun*.

interj *abbrev* interjection.

interject *verb* to say or add abruptly; to interrupt with something. [16c: from Latin *intericere* to insert]

interjection *noun* **1** an exclamation of surprise, sudden disappointment, pain, etc. **2** an act of interjecting.

interlace *verb* **1** *tr & intr* to join by lacing or by crossing over. **2** to mix or blend with something: *a story interlaced with graphic descriptions*. [14c]

interlard *verb* to add foreign words, quotations, unusual phrases, etc to (a speech or piece of writing), esp to do so excessively. [16c]

interlay *verb* to lay (eg layers) between. [17c]

interleaf *noun* (***interleaves***) a usu blank leaf of paper inserted between two leaves of a book.

interleave *verb* to insert interleaves between the pages of a book.

interline[1] *verb* to insert (words) between the lines of (a document, book, etc). ▪ **interlineation** *noun*. [15c]

interline[2] *verb* to put an extra lining between the first lining and the fabric (of a garment), esp for stiffness. ▪ **interlining** *noun*. [15c]

interlink *verb, tr & intr* to join or connect together. [16c]

interlock *verb, tr & intr* to fit, fasten or connect together, esp by the means of teeth or parts which fit into each other. ▸ *noun* a device or mechanism that connects and co-ordinates the functions of the parts or components of eg a machine. ▸ *adj* of a fabric or garment: knitted with closely locking stitches. ▪ **interlocking** *adj*. [17c]

interlocutor *noun* **1** someone who takes part in a conversation or dialogue. **2** *Scots law* **a** *strictly* a judgement coming just short of the final decree; **b** *loosely* any order of the court. ▪ **interlocution** *noun*. [16c: from Latin *interloqui* to speak between]

interlocutory *adj* **1** relating or belonging to conversation or dialogue. **2** *law* of a decree: given provisionally during legal proceedings.

interloper *noun* someone who interferes with other people's affairs, or goes to places where they have no right to be; an intruder. [17c: from Dutch *loopen* to leap]

interlude *noun* **1** a short period of time between two events or a short period of a different activity; a brief distraction. **2** a short break between the acts of a play or opera or between items of music. **3** a short piece of music, or short item of entertainment, played during such a break. **4** a short dramatic or comic piece, formerly often performed during this interval. [14c: from Latin *interludium*, from *ludus* play]

intermarry *verb, intr* **1** of different races, social or religious groups, etc: to become connected by marriage. **2** to marry someone from one's own family. ▪ **intermarriage** *noun*.

intermediary *noun* (***-ies***) **1** someone who mediates between two people or groups, eg to try to settle a dispute or get agreement. **2** any intermediate person or thing.

intermediate /ɪntə'miːdɪət/ *adj* in the middle; placed between two points, stages or extremes. ▸ *noun* **1** an intermediate thing. **2** *chem* a short-lived chemical compound formed during one of the middle stages of a series of chemical reactions. **3** *chem* the precursor of a particular end-product, eg a dye. ▸ *verb* /ɪntə'miːdɪeɪt/ *intr* to act as an intermediary. ▪ **intermediation** *noun*. [17c: from Latin *intermediatus*, from *medius* middle]

interment *noun* burial, esp with appropriate ceremony. [14c]

intermezzo /ɪntə'mɛtsoʊ/ *noun* (***intermezzi*** /-tsiː/ *or* ***intermezzos***) *music* a short instrumental piece usu performed between the sections of a symphonic work, opera or other dramatic musical entertainment. [18c: Italian, from Latin *intermedium* intervening place]

interminable *adj* seemingly without an end, esp because of being extremely dull and tedious. [14c: from Latin *interminabilis*]

intermingle *verb, tr & intr* to mingle or mix together. [15c]

intermission *noun* **1** a short period of time between two things, eg two parts of a film, play, etc. **2** the act of intermitting. [16c: from Latin *intermissio* interruption]

intermittent *adj* happening occasionally; not continuous. ▪ **intermittently** *adv*. [16c: from Latin *intermittere* to interrupt]

intern *verb* **1** /ɪn'tɜːn/ to confine within a country, restricted area or prison, esp during a war. **2** /'ɪntɜːn/ *intr, chiefly US* to train or work as an intern. ▸ *noun* (*also* **interne**) /'ɪntɜːn/ **1** *chiefly US* an advanced student or graduate who gains practical experience by working, eg in a hospital. **2** an inmate. ▪ **internee** *noun*. ▪ **internment** *noun*. ▪ **internship** *noun*. [19c: from French *interne*, from Latin *internus* inward]

internal *adj* **1** on, in, belonging to or suitable for the inside; inner. **2** on, in, belonging to or suitable for the inside of the body. **3** relating to a nation's domestic affairs. **4** for, belonging to or coming from within an organization. **5** relating to the inner nature or feelings or of the mind or soul. ▪ **internally** *adv*. [16c: from Latin *internalis*, from *internus* inward]

internal-combustion engine *noun* an engine that produces power by burning a mixture of fuel and air within an enclosed space.

internalize *or* **-ise** *verb* **1** to make (a type of behaviour, a characteristic, etc) part of one's personality. **2** to keep (an emotion, etc) inside oneself rather than express it. ▪ **internalization** *noun.*

internal rhyme *noun* a rhyme occurring inside a line of verse.

international *adj* involving or affecting two or more nations. ▸ *noun* **1** a sports match or competition between two national teams. **2** (*also* **internationalist**) someone who takes part in, or has taken part in, such a match or competition.

International Date Line *noun* an imaginary line on the Earth's surface running N to S across the middle of the Pacific Ocean, the date in countries to the east of it being one day ahead of the date in countries to the west.

internationalism *noun* the view that the nations of the world should co-operate and work towards greater mutual understanding. ▪ **internationalist** *noun.*

internationalize *or* **-ise** *verb* to make international, esp to bring under the control of two or more countries. ▪ **internationalization** *noun.*

International Monetary Fund *noun* (abbrev **IMF**) an international financial organization set up to promote trade by keeping currencies stable and having a fund of money from which member states may borrow.

International Phonetic Alphabet *noun* (abbrev **IPA**) a system of letters and symbols used to represent the speech sounds of every language.

interne see **intern** (*noun*)

internecine /ɪntə'niːsaɪn/ *adj* **1** of a fight, war, etc: destructive and damaging to both sides. **2** of a conflict or struggle: within a group or organization. [17c: from Latin *internecinus* murderous]

the Internet *noun* a global computer communications network. Often shortened to **the net**. [20c]

Internet service provider *noun* (abbrev **ISP**) a company or organization that provides access to the Internet.

interpersonal *adj* concerning or involving relationships between people.

interphase *noun, biol* the period between successive divisions by **mitosis** of a cell.

interplanetary *adj* **1** relating to the solar system. **2** happening or existing in the space between the planets.

interplay *noun* the action and influence of two or more things on each other.

Interpol *noun* an international organization that allows police forces in different countries to communicate and co-operate with each other. [1950s: from *Inter*national Criminal *Pol*ice Organization]

interpolate *verb* **1** to add (words) to a book or manuscript, esp to make the text misleading or corrupt. **2** to alter (a text) in this way. **3** to interrupt a conversation, a person speaking, etc with (a comment). **4** *maths* to estimate (the value of a function) at a point between values that are already known. ▪ **interpolation** *noun.* [17c: from Latin *interpolare* to refurbish]

interpose *verb* **1** *tr & intr* to put something, or come, between two other things. **2** to interrupt a conversation or argument with (a remark, comment, etc). **3** *intr* to act as mediator; to intervene. ▪ **interposition** *noun.* [16c: from French *interposer*]

interpret *verb* **1** to explain the meaning of (a foreign word, dream, etc). **2** *intr* to act as an interpreter. **3** to consider or understand (behaviour, a remark, etc): *interpreted her silence as disapproval.* **4** to convey one's idea of the meaning of (eg a dramatic role, piece of music) in one's performance. ▪ **interpretable** *adj.* ▪ **interpretation** *noun.* ▪ **interpretative** *or* **interpretive** *adj.* [14c: from Latin *interpretari*]

interpreter *noun* **1** someone who translates foreign speech as the words are spoken and relays the translation orally. **2** *comput* a program that translates a statement written in a high-level language into machine code and then executes it.

interracial *adj* between different races of people.

interregnum *noun* (***interregnums*** *or* ***interregna***) **1** the time between two monarchs' reigns when the throne is unoccupied. **2** the time between rule by one government and rule by the next. **3** any interval or pause in events. [16c: from Latin *regnum* reign]

interrelate *verb, tr & intr* to be in or be brought into a mutually dependent or reciprocal relationship.

interrogate *verb* **1** to question closely and thoroughly. **2** *comput* to transmit a request to a device or program. **3** of a radar set, etc: to send out signals to (a radio beacon) to work out a position. ▪ **interrogation** *noun.* ▪ **interrogator** *noun.* [15c: from Latin *interrogare*]

interrogation mark see **question mark**

interrogative *adj* **1** like a question; asking or seeming to ask a question. **2** *grammar* of an adjective or pronoun: used to introduce a question, eg *what, whom*, etc. ▸ *noun* an interrogative word, sentence or construction. ▪ **interrogatively** *adv.* [16c]

interrogatory *adj* involving or expressing a question. ▸ *noun* (***-ies***) *esp law* a question or inquiry. [16c]

interrupt *verb* **1** *tr & intr* to break into (a conversation or monologue) by asking a question or making a comment. **2** *tr & intr* to make a break in the continuous activity of (an event), or to disturb someone from some action. **3** to destroy (a view, eg of a clear sweep of land) by getting in the way. ▪ **interrupter** *or* **interruptor** *noun* **1** someone who interrupts. **2** *electronics* a device for opening and closing an electric circuit at set intervals and so produce pulses. ▪ **interruption** *noun.* ▪ **interruptive** *adj.* [15c: from Latin *interrumpere* to break apart]

---

interrupt

This word is often misspelt. It has two *r*'s. It might help you to remember the following sentence:

*It's **r**eally **r**ude to inte**rr**upt.*

---

intersect *verb* **1** to divide (lines, an area, etc) by passing or cutting through or across. **2** *intr* esp of lines, roads, etc: to run through or cut across each other. [17c: from Latin *intersecare* to cut through]

intersection *noun* **1** a place where things meet or intersect, esp a road junction. **2** the act of intersecting. **3** *geom* the point or set of points where two or more lines or plane surfaces cross each other. **4** *geom* a set of points common to two or more geometrical figures. **5** *maths* the set of elements formed by the elements common to two or more other sets.

intersex *noun, biol* an individual with characteristics of both sexes. [20c]

interspace *noun* a space between two things. ▸ *verb* to put a space or spaces between. [15c]

intersperse *verb* **1** to scatter or insert something here and there. **2** *intr* to diversify or change slightly with scattered things. ▪ **interspersion** *noun*. [16c: from Latin *interspergere*]

interstate *adj* between two or more states. ▸ *noun, esp US* a major road that crosses a state boundary. [19c]

interstellar *adj* happening or existing in the space between individual stars within galaxies. [17c]

interstice /ɪn'tɜːstɪs/ *noun* a very small gap or space. [17c: from Latin *interstitium*]

intertwine *verb, tr & intr* to twist or be twisted together. [17c]

interval *noun* **1** a period of time between two events. **2** a space or distance between two things. **3** *Brit* a short break between the acts of a play or opera, or between parts of a concert or long film. **4** *music* the difference in pitch between two notes or tones. **5** *maths* a set of real numbers or points between two given numbers or points. [13c: from Latin *intervallum* space between pallisades]

IDIOMS **at intervals 1** here and there; now and then. **2** with a stated distance in time or space between: *at intervals of ten minutes.*

interval training *noun, athletics* alternate fast and slow running, as training for long-distance races.

intervene *verb, intr* **1** (*often* **intervene in sth**) to involve oneself in something which is happening in order to affect the outcome. **2** (*often* **intervene in sth** *or* **between people**) to involve oneself or interfere in a dispute between other people in order to settle it or prevent more serious conflict. **3** to come or occur between two things in place or time. [16c: from Latin *intervenire* to come between]

intervention *noun* an act of intervening, esp in the affairs of other people or countries.

interventionism *noun* the belief that a government should, or should be allowed to, interfere in the economic affairs of the country or in the internal affairs of other countries. ▪ **interventionist** *noun, adj.*

interview *noun* **1** a formal meeting and discussion with someone, esp one at which an employer meets and judges a prospective employee. **2** a conversation or discussion that aims at obtaining information, esp one for broadcasting or publication in which a famous or important person is questioned. ▸ *verb* to hold an interview. ▪ **interviewee** *noun*. ▪ **interviewer** *noun*. [16c: from French *entrevue*]

interweave *verb, tr & intr* to weave or be woven together. [16c]

intestate *law adj* of a person: not having made a valid will before their death. ▸ *noun* someone who dies without making a valid will. ▪ **intestacy** *noun*. [14c: from Latin *intestatus*, from *testari* to make a will]

intestine *noun* the muscular tube-like part of the alimentary canal between the stomach and the anus. ▪ **intestinal** *adj.* [16c: from Latin *intestinus* internal]

intifada /ɪntɪ'fɑːdə/ *noun* **1** (**the Intifada**) the movement by Palestinians against Israeli occupation of the Gaza Strip and West Bank of the Jordan. **2** any large-scale uprising. [20c: Arabic, meaning 'shaking off']

intimacy *noun* (**-ies**) **1** warm close personal friendship. **2** an intimate or personal remark. **3** the state or quality of being intimate.

intimate[1] /'ɪntɪmət/ *adj* **1** marked by or sharing a close and affectionate friendship. **2** very private or personal. **3** of a place: small and quiet with a warm, friendly atmosphere. **4** (*often* **intimate with sb**) sharing a sexual relationship with them. **5** of knowledge: deep and thorough. ▸ *noun* a close friend. ▪ **intimately** *adv.* [17c: from Latin *intimus* innermost]

intimate[2] /'ɪntɪmeɪt/ *verb* **1** to announce or make known. **2** to hint or suggest indirectly. ▪ **intimation** *noun*. [16c: from Latin *intimare*]

intimidate *verb* **1** to coerce, esp with threats. **2** to frighten, scare or overawe. ▪ **intimidation** *noun*. [17c: from Latin *intimidare*, from *timidus* frightened]

into *prep* **1** to or towards the inside or middle of something. **2** against; making contact or colliding with something or someone. **3** used to express a change of state or condition: *get into difficulties.* **4** having reached a certain period of time: *into extra time.* **5** *maths* used to express division: *Four into twenty makes five.* **6** *informal* involved with, interested in or enthusiastic about: *into golf in a big way.* [Anglo-Saxon]

intolerable *adj* too bad, difficult, painful, etc to be put up with. ▪ **intolerably** *adv.* [15c]

intolerant *adj* refusing or unwilling to accept ideas, beliefs, behaviour, etc different from one's own. ▪ **intolerance** *noun*. [18c: from Latin *intolerans*]

intonation *noun* **1** the rise and fall of the pitch of the voice in speech. **2** an act of intoning. **3** the correct pitching of musical notes.

intone *verb, tr & intr* **1** to recite (a prayer, etc) in a solemn monotonous voice or in singing tones. **2** to say something with a particular intonation or tone. [15c: from Latin *intonare* to thunder]

in toto *adv* totally, completely; in sum. [18c: Latin]

intoxicate *verb* **1** to make drunk. **2** to excite or elate. ▪ **intoxicant** *noun, adj.* ▪ **intoxicating** *adj.* ▪ **intoxication** *noun*. [16c: from *intoxicare* to poison]

intra- *prefix, denoting* within; inside; on the inside. [Latin, meaning 'within']

intractable *adj* **1** difficult to control or influence; obstinate. **2** difficult to solve, cure or deal with. ▪ **intractability** *noun*. [16c: from Latin *intractabilis*]

intramural *adj* **1** within or amongst the people in an institution, esp a school, college or university. **2** within the scope of normal studies. ▪ **intramurally** *adv.* [19c: from Latin *murus* wall]

intranet /'ɪntrənɛt/ *noun, comput* a restricted network of computers, eg within a company. [Late 20c: from **intra-** + **net**[1] (*noun* sense 7)]

intransigent *adj* refusing to change or compromise one's beliefs. ▸ *noun* an intransigent person. ▪ **intransigence** *noun*. [18c: from Spanish *intransigente*]

intransitive *adj, grammar* of a verb: not taking or having a direct object. ▸ *noun* such a verb. Compare **absolute, transitive.** ▪ **intransitively** *adv.* [17c: from Latin *intransitivus* not passing over]

intrauterine /ɪntrə'juːtəraɪn/ *adj, med* located or occurring within the uterus. [19c]

intravenous /ɪntrə'viːnəs/ *adj, med* located within or introduced into a vein or veins. ▪ **intravenously** *adv.* [19c]

in-tray *noun, Brit* a tray, eg on a desk, etc, that incoming mail, etc is put in before it is dealt with.

intrench see **entrench**

intrepid *adj* bold and daring; brave. ▪ **intrepidity** *noun*. ▪ **intrepidly** *adv*. [17c: from Latin *intrepidus*]

intricate *adj* full of complicated, interrelating or tangled details or parts and therefore difficult to understand, analyse or sort out. ▪ **intricacy** *noun* (*-ies*). ▪ **intricately** *adv*. [16c: from Latin *intricare* to perplex]

intrigue *noun* /ˈɪntriːg/ **1** secret plotting or underhand scheming. **2** a secret plot or plan. **3** a secret illicit love affair. ▸ *verb* /ɪnˈtriːg/ **1** to arouse the curiosity or interest of someone. **2** *intr* to plot secretly. ▪ **intriguing** *adj*. ▪ **intriguingly** *adv*. [17c: French, from Latin *intricare* to perplex]

intrinsic *adj* being an inherent and essential part of something or someone. ▪ **intrinsically** *adv*. [17c: from Latin *intrinsecus* inwardly]

intro *noun, informal* an introduction, esp to a piece of music. [1920s]

intro- *prefix, denoting* within; into; inwards: *introspection*. [Latin, meaning 'to the inside']

introduce *verb* **1** (*usu* **introduce sb to sb else**) to present them to one another by name. **2** to announce or present (eg a radio or television programme) to an audience. **3** to bring (something) into a place, situation, etc for the first time. **4** to bring into operation, practice or use. **5** to put forward or propose (a possible law or bill) for consideration or approval. **6** (*usu* **introduce sb to sth**) to cause someone to experience or discover something for the first time. **7** to start or preface: *Introduce the play with a brief analysis of the plot*. **8** (*usu* **introduce one thing into another**) to put something into something else. [16c: from Latin *introducere* to lead in]

introduction *noun* **1** the act or process of introducing or process of being introduced. **2** a presentation of one person to another or others. **3** a section at the beginning of a book that explains briefly what it is about, why it was written, etc. **4** a book that outlines the basic principles of a subject. **5** a short passage of music beginning a piece or song, or leading up to a movement. **6** something that has been introduced.

introductory *adj* giving or serving as an introduction; preliminary; given during an initial period.

introit *noun, Christianity* a hymn, psalm or anthem sung at the beginning of a service. [15c: from Latin *introitus* entrance]

introspection *noun* the examination of one's own thoughts, feelings, etc. ▪ **introspective** *adj*. [17c: from Latin *introspicere* to look within]

introvert *noun* **1** *psychol* someone who is more interested in the self and inner feelings than in the outside world and social relationships. **2** someone who tends not to socialize and who is uncommunicative and withdrawn. ▸ *adj* (*also* **introverted**) concerned more with one's own thoughts and feelings than with other people and outside events. Compare **extrovert**. ▪ **introversion** *noun*. ▪ **introverted** *adj*. [17c: from Latin *vertere* to turn]

intrude *verb, tr & intr* (*often* **intrude into** *or* **on sb** *or* **sth**) to force or impose (oneself, one's presence or something) without welcome or invitation. [16c: from Latin *intrudere* to thrust in]

intruder *noun* someone who enters premises secretly or by force, esp in order to commit a crime.

intrusion *noun* **1** an act or process of intruding, esp on someone else's property. **2** *geol* the forcing of molten magma under pressure into pre-existing rock. **3** a mass of igneous rock formed by solidification after being forced into pre-existing rock. [14c: from Latin *intrusio*, from *intrudere* to thrust in]

intrusive *adj* **1** tending to intrude. **2** of rock: formed by **intrusion**. **3** of a speech sound, esp *r*: introduced into a piece of connected speech without etymological justification. ▪ **intrusively** *adv*. ▪ **intrusiveness** *noun*.

intrust see **entrust**

intuit *verb* to know or become aware of something by intuition. ▪ **intuitable** *adj*.

intuition *noun* **1** the power of understanding or realizing something without conscious rational thought or analysis. **2** something understood or realized in this way. **3** immediate instinctive understanding or belief. ▪ **intuitive** *adj*. ▪ **intuitively** *adv*. ▪ **intuitiveness** *noun*. [16c: from Latin *intuitio*, from *tueri* to look]

intumesce /ɪntʃʊˈmɛs/ *verb, intr* to swell up. ▪ **intumescence** *noun*. ▪ **intumescent** *adj*. [18c: from Latin *intumescere*]

Inuit *or* **Innuit** *noun* (*pl* ***Inuit*** *or* ***Innuit***) **1** a member of a people of the Arctic and sub-Arctic regions of Canada, Greenland and Alaska. **2** their language. ▸ *adj* belonging or relating to this people or their language. [19c: Inuit, pl of *inuk* person]

Inuktitut *noun* the Inuit language, especially the variety spoken in the Canadian Arctic. [20c: Inuit, meaning 'the Inuit way', the title of a periodical]

inundate *verb* **1** to overwhelm with water. **2** to swamp: *was inundated with applications for the job*. ▪ **inundation** *noun*. [17c: from Latin *inundare* to flow over]

inure *or* **enure** *verb* (*often* **inure sb to sth**) to accustom them to something unpleasant or unwelcome. ▪ **inurement** *noun*. [15c: from French *en ure* in use]

invade *verb* **1** *tr & intr* to enter (a country) by force with an army. **2** *tr & intr* to attack or overrun: *Angry supporters invaded the pitch*. **3** to interfere with (a person's rights, privacy, etc). ▪ **invader** *noun*. [15c: from Latin *invadere*]

invalid[1] /ˈɪnvəlɪd/ *noun* someone who is constantly ill or who is disabled. ▸ *adj* suitable for or being an invalid. ▸ *verb* **1 a** (*usu* **invalid sb out**) to discharge (a soldier, etc) from service because of illness; **b** (*usu* **invalid sb home**) to send (a soldier, etc) home because of illness. **2** to affect with disease. ▪ **invalidity** *noun*. [17c: from French, from Latin *invalidus* weak]

invalid[2] /ɪnˈvalɪd/ *adj* **1** of a document, agreement, etc: having no legal force. **2** of an argument, reasoning, etc: based on false reasoning or a mistake and therefore not valid, correct or reliable. ▪ **invalidity** *noun*. ▪ **invalidly** *adv*. [17c: from Latin *invalidus* weak]

invalidate *verb* to make (a document, agreement, argument, etc) invalid. ▪ **invalidation** *noun*. [17c]

invaluable *adj* having a value that is too great to be measured.

invariable *adj* not prone to change or alteration. ▪ **invariably** *adv*. [17c: from Latin *invariabilis*]

invariant *noun, maths* a property of a mathematical equation, geometric figure, etc, that is unaltered by a particular procedure. ▶ *adj* invariable.

invasion *noun* **1** invading, or being invaded, eg by a hostile country or by something harmful. **2** an encroachment or violation. **3** *pathol* the spread of a disease within a living organism. **4** *ecol* the spread of a species of plant to where it previously did not grow. ▪ **invasive** *adj*. [16c: from Latin *invasio*, from *invadere* to invade]

invective *noun* **1** sarcastic or abusive language. **2** a denunciation or critical attack using such words. ▶ *adj* characterized by such an attack. [15c: from Latin *invectivus* abusive]

inveigh /ɪn'veɪ/ *verb, intr* (*usu* **inveigh against sb** *or* **sth**) to speak strongly or passionately against them or it, esp in criticism or protest. [16c: from Latin *invehi* to attack with words]

inveigle *verb* (*usu* **inveigle sb into sth**) to trick, deceive or persuade them into doing it. ▪ **inveiglement** *noun*. [16c: from French *enveogler* to blind]

invent *verb* **1** to be the first person to make or use (a machine, game, method, etc). **2** to think or make up (an excuse, false story, etc). ▪ **invention** *noun*. ▪ **inventive** *adj*. ▪ **inventively** *adv*. ▪ **inventiveness** *noun*. ▪ **inventor** *noun*. [16c: from Latin *invenire* to find]

inventory /'ɪnvəntərɪ/ *noun* (**-ies**) **1** a list of the articles, goods, etc in a particular place. **2** the items on such a list. ▶ *verb* (**-ies, -ied**) to make an inventory of (items); to list in an inventory. [16c: from Latin *inventorium* a list of things that have been found]

inverse *adj* **1** opposite or reverse in order, sequence, direction, effect, etc. **2** *maths* of a mathematical operation: opposite in effect or nature to another operation, eg as multiplication is to division. ▶ *noun* **1** a direct opposite. **2** the state of being directly opposite or reversed. **3** *maths* one of two numbers that cancel each other out in a mathematical operation, eg the inverse of 3 in addition is −3, because 3 + -3 = 0. ▪ **inversely** *adv*. [17c: from Latin *inversus*, from *invertere* to invert]

invert *verb* **1** to turn upside down or inside out. **2** to reverse in order, sequence, direction, effect, etc. ▪ **inversion** *noun*. [17c: from Latin *invertere*]

invertebrate *noun, zool* any animal that does not possess a backbone, such as an insect, worm, snail or jellyfish. ▶ *adj* (*also* **invertebral**) **1** relating to an animal without a backbone. **2** having no strength of character. [19c: from Latin *vertebra* spinal joint]

inverted commas see **quotation marks**

invest *verb* **1** *tr & intr* to put (money) into a company or business, eg by buying shares in it, in order to make a profit. **2** *tr & intr* to devote (time, effort, energy, etc) to something. **3** *intr* (**invest in sth**) *informal* to buy it. **4** (*often* **invest sb with sth**) to give them the symbols of power, rights, rank, etc officially. **5** (*usu* **invest sth in sb**) to place power, rank, a quality or feeling, etc in somebody. **6** to clothe or adorn. **7** *military* to besiege (a stronghold). ▪ **investor** *noun*. [16c: from Latin *investire* to clothe]

investigate *verb, tr & intr* to carry out a thorough and detailed inquiry into or examination of something or someone. ▪ **investigation** *noun*. ▪ **investigative** *or* **investigatory** *adj*. ▪ **investigator** *noun*. [16c: from Latin *investigare* to track down]

investigative journalism *noun* journalism involving the investigation and exposure of corruption, crime, inefficiency, etc.

investiture *noun* a formal ceremony giving a rank or office to someone. [14c: from Latin *investitura*]

investment *noun* **1** a sum of money invested. **2** something, such as a business, house, etc in which one invests money, time, effort, etc. **3** the act of investing.

investment trust *noun* a company that, on behalf of its members, holds shares in other companies.

inveterate *adj* **1** of a habit, etc: firmly established. **2** of a person: firmly fixed in a habit by long practice. ▪ **inveterately** *adv*. [16c: from Latin *inveteratus*]

invidious *adj* likely to cause envy, resentment or indignation, esp by being or seeming to be unfair. ▪ **invidiously** *adv*. ▪ **invidiousness** *noun*. [17c: from Latin *invidiosus*, from *invidia* envy]

invigilate *verb, tr & intr, Brit* to keep watch over people sitting an examination, esp to prevent cheating. ▪ **invigilation** *noun*. ▪ **invigilator** *noun*. [16c: from Latin *invigilare* to keep watch over]

invigorate *verb* to give fresh life, energy and health to something or someone; to strengthen or animate. ▪ **invigorating** *adj*. ▪ **invigoration** *noun*. [17c: from Latin *vigor* strength]

invincible *adj* indestructible; unable to be defeated. ▪ **invincibility** *noun*. ▪ **invincibly** *adv*. [15c: from Latin *invincibilis*]

inviolable *adj* not to be broken or violated; sacred. ▪ **inviolability** *noun*. ▪ **inviolably** *adv*. [16c: from Latin *inviolabilis*]

inviolate *adj* not broken, violated or injured. [15c: from Latin *inviolatus* unhurt]

invisible *adj* **1** not able to be seen. **2** unseen. **3** *econ* relating to services (eg insurance, tourism) rather than goods: *invisible exports*. **4** *econ* not shown in regular statements: *invisible assets*. ▶ *noun* an invisible item of trade. ▪ **invisibility** *noun*. ▪ **invisibly** *adv*. [14c]

invitation *noun* **1** a request to a person to come or go somewhere, eg to a party, meal, etc. **2** the form such a request takes, eg written on a card, etc. **3** an act of inviting. **4** encouragement; enticement; inducement.

invite *verb* /ɪn'vaɪt/ **1** to request the presence of someone at one's house, at a party, etc, esp formally or politely. **2** to ask politely or formally for (eg comments, advice, etc). **3** to bring on or encourage (something unwanted or undesirable). **4** to attract or tempt. ▶ *noun* /'ɪnvaɪt/ *informal* an invitation. [16c: from Latin *invitare*]

inviting *adj* attractive or tempting. ▪ **invitingly** *adv*.

in vitro /ɪn 'viːtroʊ/ *adj, adv, biol* of biological processes: performed in an artificial environment created by means of scientific equipment, eg in a test-tube: *in-vitro fertilization*. Compare **in vivo**. [19c: Latin, meaning 'in the glass']

in vivo /ɪn 'viːvoʊ/ *adj, adv* of biological processes: performed within a living organism. Compare **in vitro**. [20c: Latin, meaning 'in a living thing']

invocation *noun* **1** an act or the process of invoking. **2** a prayer calling on God, a saint, etc for blessing or help. **3** an opening prayer at the beginning of a public service or sermon. **4** any appeal to supernatural beings, spirits, etc, such as an appeal to a Muse for inspiration at the beginning of a poem. ▪ **invocatory** /ɪn'vɒkətərɪ/ *adj.* [14c: from Latin *invocatio*]

invoice *noun* a list of goods supplied, delivered with the goods and giving details of price and quantity, usu treated as a request for payment. ▸ *verb* **1** to send an invoice to (a customer). **2** to provide an invoice for (goods). [16c: from French *envoyer* to send]

invoke *verb* **1** to make an appeal to (God, some deity, a Muse, authority, etc) for help, support or inspiration. **2** to appeal to (a law, principle, etc) as an authority or reason for eg one's behaviour. **3** to make an earnest appeal for (help, support, inspiration, etc). **4** to conjure up (a spirit) by reciting a spell. **5** to put (a law, decision, etc) into effect. [15c: from Latin *invocare* to call upon]

involuntary *adj* done without being controlled by the will; not able to be controlled by the will; unintentional. ▪ **involuntarily** *adv.* [16c]

involute *adj* **1** entangled; intricate. **2** *botany* of petals, etc: rolled in at the edges. **3** of shells: curled up in a spiral shape, so that the axis is concealed. ▸ *verb, intr* to become involute or undergo involution. [17c: from Latin *involvere, involutum* to **involve**]

involution *noun* **1** involving or being involved or entangled. **2** *zool* degeneration. **3** *physiol* the shrinking of an organ after its purpose has been served or as a result of ageing.

involve *verb* **1** to require as a necessary part. **2** (*usu* **involve sb in sth**) to cause them to take part or be implicated in it. **3** to have an effect on someone or something. **4** (*often* **involve oneself in sth**) to become emotionally concerned in it. ▪ **involved** *adj* **1** concerned, implicated. **2** complicated. ▪ **involvement** *noun.* [14c: from Latin *involvere* to roll up]

invulnerable *adj* incapable of being hurt, damaged or attacked. ▪ **invulnerability** *noun.*

inward *adj* **1** placed or being within. **2** moving towards the inside. **3** relating or belonging to the mind or soul. ▸ *adv* (*also* **inwards**) **1** towards the inside or the centre. **2** into the mind, inner thoughts or soul. [Anglo-Saxon *inweard*]

inwardly *adv* **1** on the inside; internally. **2** in one's private thoughts; secretly.

inwards see **inward**

iodide *noun* a chemical compound containing iodine and another element or **radical** (*noun* sense 3).

iodine *noun* **1** *chem* (symbol **I**) a non-metallic element consisting of dark-violet crystals that form a violet vapour when heated. **2** (*also* **tincture of iodine**) *med* a solution of iodine in ethanol, used as an antiseptic. [19c: from Greek *ioeides* violet-coloured]

iodize *or* **-ise** *verb* to treat something with iodine, esp common salt so as to provide iodine as a nutritional supplement.

ion *noun, chem* an atom or group of atoms that has acquired a net positive charge as a result of losing one or more electrons, or a net negative charge as a result of gaining one or more electrons. ▪ **ionic** *adj.* [19c: Greek, meaning 'going']

-ion *suffix, forming nouns, denoting* a process, state, result, etc: *completion* • *pollution*. See also **-ation**. [French, from Latin *-io, -ionis*]

ion exchange *noun, chem* a chemical reaction in which ions which have the same charge are exchanged between a solution and a porous granular solid in contact with it.

Ionic *adj* **1** *archit, denoting* an **order** of classical architecture characterized by a style of column with slim and usu fluted shafts and capitals with spiral scrolls. Compare **Corinthian**, **Doric**, **Tuscan**. **2** (*also* **Ionian**) belonging or relating to Ionia, an ancient region of the W coast of Asia Minor, its inhabitants or their dialect of Ancient Greek. ▸ *noun* one of the four main dialects of Ancient Greek, spoken in Ionia. [16c: from Greek *Ionikos*]

ionic bond *noun, chem* a chemical bond formed by the transfer of electrons from one atom to another, resulting in the conversion of neutral atoms to positively and negatively charged ions.

ionize *or* **-ise** *verb, tr & intr, chem* to produce or make something produce ions. ▪ **ionization** *noun.*

ionosphere *noun, meteorol* the upper layer of the Earth's atmosphere, which contains many ions and free electrons produced by the ionizing effects of solar radiation. [20c: from **ion** + **sphere**]

iota /aɪ'oʊtə/ *noun* **1** the ninth letter of the Greek alphabet. **2** a very small amount; a jot: *Nothing she said makes an iota of difference.* [17c: Greek]

IOU *noun* (***IOUs, IOU's***) *informal* a written and signed note that serves as an acknowledgement of a debt. [17c: pronunciation of *I owe you*]

IP *abbrev, comput* Internet protocol. See **TCP/IP**.

IPA *abbrev* International Phonetic Alphabet.

ipecacuanha /ɪpɪkakjʊ'anə/ *or* **ipecac** /'ɪpɪkak/ *noun* **1** a small Latin American shrub. **2** the dried root of this plant prepared as a tincture or syrup, which is used in small doses as an expectorant or as a purgative or emetic. [17c: Portuguese, from Tupí (a native S American language) *ipekaaguene*]

iPod /'aipod/ *noun, trademark* a brand of digital audio player.

ipso facto *adv* by or because of that very fact; thereby. [16c: Latin]

IQ *abbrev* (***IQs, IQ's***) intelligence quotient.

Ir *symbol, chem* iridium.

ir- *prefix* a form of **in-** used before words beginning in *r*: *irrelevant*.

IRA *abbrev* Irish Republican Army, an anti-British paramilitary guerrilla force.

Iranian /ɪ'reɪnɪən; *N Am* aɪ'reɪnɪən/ *adj* **1** belonging or relating to Iran, a republic in SW Asia, or its inhabitants. **2** belonging or relating to the Iranian group of languages. ▸ *noun* **1** a citizen or inhabitant of, or person born in, Iran. **2** a subgroup of the Indo-Iranian branch of the Indo-European family of languages. **3** the language of Iran. Also called **Farsi**.

Iraqi /ɪ'rɑːkɪ, ɪ'rakɪ/ *adj* belonging or relating to Iraq, a republic in SW Asia, or its inhabitants. ▸ *noun* a citizen or inhabitant of, or person born in, Iraq.

irascible *adj* easily made angry; irritable. ▪ **irascibility** *noun.* ▪ **irascibly** *adv.* [16c: from Latin *irascibilis*, from *ira* anger]

irate *adj* very angry; enraged. ▪ **irately** *adv.* ▪ **irateness** *noun.* [19c: from Latin *iratus*, from *ira* anger]

ire *noun, literary* anger. [13c: from Latin *ira* anger]

iridescent *adj* having many bright rainbow-like colours which seem to shimmer and change constantly. ▪ **iridescence** *noun.* ▪ **iridescently** *adv.* [18c: from Greek *iris* rainbow]

iridium *noun, chem* (symbol **Ir**) a silvery metallic element that is resistant to corrosion. [19c: from Greek *iris* rainbow, from the colourful appearance of solutions of its salts]

iris *noun* **1** (***irises,*** *technical* ***irides*** /ˈaɪərɪdiːz/) a plant that has flattened sword-shaped leaves and large brilliantly coloured flowers. **2** *anatomy* an adjustable pigmented ring of muscle lying in front of the lens of the eye, surrounding the pupil. **3** (*in full* **iris diaphragm**) a device consisting of a series of thin overlapping crescent-shaped plates surrounding a central aperture, used to control the amount of light entering an optical instrument. [14c: Greek, meaning 'rainbow']

Irish *adj* **1** belonging or relating to Ireland, its inhabitants, their Celtic language or their dialect of English. **2** (**the Irish**) the people of Ireland. **3** *informal, often offensive* amusingly contradictory or inconsistent; illogical. ▸ *noun* **1** (*in full* **Irish Gaelic**) the Celtic language of Ireland. **2** whiskey made in Ireland. ▪ **Irishman** *and* **Irishwoman** *noun.* [Anglo-Saxon *Iras* people of Ireland]

Irish coffee *noun* coffee with a dash of Irish whiskey served with cream on top. Also called **Gaelic coffee.**

Irish moss see **carrageen**

Irish stew *noun* a stew made from mutton, potatoes and onions.

irk *verb* to annoy or irritate, esp persistently. [16c]

irksome *adj* annoying, irritating or boring.

iron *noun* **1** (symbol **Fe**) a strong hard greyish metallic element that is naturally magnetic. See also **ferric, ferrous. 2** a tool, weapon or other implement made of iron. **3** a triangular, flat-bottomed, now usu electrical, household tool used for smoothing out creases and pressing clothes. **4** *golf* any of various clubs with an angled iron head. **5** a **brand** (sense 4). **6** great physical or mental strength. **7** (**irons**) chains; fetters. ▸ *adj* **1** made of iron. **2** very strong, inflexible, unyielding, etc: *iron determination.* ▸ *verb* **1** to smooth the creases out of or press (eg clothes) with an iron. **2** *intr* of clothing or fabric: to react or respond in the way specified to being ironed: *shiny material which irons badly.* [Anglo-Saxon *isen*]

IDIOMS **have several irons in the fire** to have several commitments. **strike while the iron is hot** to act while the situation is to one's advantage.

PHRASAL VERBS **iron sth out 1** to remove or put right (difficulties, problems, etc) so that progress becomes easier. **2** to remove creases in it by ironing.

Iron Age *noun* the period in history following the Bronze Age and beginning about 1200 BC, when weapons and tools were made of iron.

ironclad *adj* **1** covered with protective iron plates. **2** inflexible; set firm. ▸ *noun, hist* a 19c warship covered with protective iron plates.

Iron Curtain *noun* from 1945 to 1989, a notional barrier between countries in W Europe and the communist countries of E Europe, which hindered trade and communications. [First used by Nazi propaganda minister Goebbels in 1945]

ironic *or* **ironical** *adj* **1** containing, characterized by or expressing irony. **2** of a person: given to frequent use of irony. ▪ **ironically** *adv.*

ironing *noun* **1** clothes and household linen, etc that need to be or have just been ironed. **2** the act or process of ironing.

iron lung *noun* an airtight chamber that covers the body up to the neck and which, by means of varying air pressure, helps the person in it to breathe.

ironmaster *noun* the owner of an ironworks.

ironmonger *noun, Brit* a dealer in articles made of metal, eg tools, locks, etc, and other household hardware. ▪ **ironmongery** *noun.* [14c]

iron pyrites see **pyrite**

iron rations *plural noun* food with a high energy value, carried for emergencies by climbers, walkers, military personnel, etc.

ironstone *noun* hard, white earthenware.

ironware *noun* things made of iron, esp household hardware.

ironwork *noun* **1** articles made of iron, such as gates and railings. **2** (**ironworks**) a factory where iron is smelted.

irony *noun* (**-*ies***) **1** a linguistic device or form of humour that takes its effect from stating the opposite of what is meant. **2** a dramatic device by which information is given to the audience that is not known to all the characters in the drama, or in which words are meant to convey different meanings to the audience and to the characters. Also called **dramatic irony. 3** awkward or perverse circumstances applying to a situation that is in itself satisfactory or desirable. [16c: from Greek *eironeia* dissimulation]

irradiate *verb* **1** *med* to subject (a part of the body) to **irradiation. 2** to preserve food by **irradiation. 3** to shed light on something; to light up. **4** to make bright or clear intellectually or spiritually. [17c: from Latin *irradiare* to shine forth]

irrational *adj* **1** not the result of clear, logical thought. **2** unable to think logically and clearly. **3** *maths* not commensurable with natural numbers. **4** *maths* of a root, expression, etc: involving irrational numbers. ▸ *noun* an irrational number. ▪ **irrationality** *noun.* ▪ **irrationally** *adv.* [15c]

irrational number *noun, maths* a real number that cannot be expressed as a ratio of two integers, eg π. Compare **rational number.**

irreconcilable *adj* **1** not agreeing or able to be brought into agreement; inconsistent; incompatible. **2** hostile and opposed; unwilling to be friendly. ▸ *noun* **1** a hostile or obstinate opponent. **2** any of various opinions, ideas, etc that cannot be brought into agreement. ▪ **irreconcilability** *noun.* ▪ **irreconcilably** *adv.*

irrecoverable *adj* **1** not able to be recovered or regained. **2** not able to be corrected. ▪ **irrecoverably** *adv.*

irredeemable *adj* **1** of a person: too evil to be saved; beyond help. **2** incapable of being recovered, repaired or cured. **3** of shares, etc: unable to be bought back from the shareholder by the issuing company for the sum originally paid. **4** of paper money: unable to be exchanged for coin. ▪ **irredeemably** *adv.*

irreducible *adj* **1** unable to be reduced or made simpler. **2** unable to be brought from one state into another, usu desired, state. ▪ **irreducibly** *adv.*

irrefutable *adj* not able to be denied or proved false. ▪ **irrefutability** *noun.* ▪ **irrefutably** *adv.* [17c]

irregular *adj* **1** not happening or occurring at regular or equal intervals. **2** not smooth, even or balanced. **3** not conforming to rules, custom, accepted or normal behaviour, or to routine. **4** *grammar* of a word: not changing its form (eg to show tenses or plurals) according to the usual patterns in the language. **5** of troops: not belonging to the regular army. ▸ *noun* an irregular soldier. ▪ **irregularity** *noun*. ▪ **irregularly** *adv.* [14c]

irrelevant *adj* not connected with the subject in hand. ▪ **irrelevance** *noun*. ▪ **irrelevantly** *adv.* [18c]

irreligion *noun* **1** lack of religion. **2** lack of respect for or opposition or hostility towards religion. ▪ **irreligious** *adj.* [16c]

irremediable *adj* unable to be cured, corrected or made better. ▪ **irremediably** *adv.* [16c]

irremovable *adj* not able to be removed. ▪ **irremovability** *noun*. ▪ **irremovably** *adv.* [16c]

irreparable *adj* not able to be restored or put right. ▪ **irreparability** *noun*. ▪ **irreparably** *adv.* [15c]

irreplaceable *adj* not able to be replaced, esp because too rare or valuable or of sentimental value. ▪ **irreplaceably** *adv.* [19c]

irrepressible *adj* not able to be controlled, restrained or repressed, esp because of being too lively and full of energy or strength. ▪ **irrepressibility** *noun*. ▪ **irrepressibly** *adv.* [19c]

irreproachable *adj* free from faults; blameless. ▪ **irreproachability** *noun*. ▪ **irreproachably** *adv.* [17c]

irresistible *adj* **1** too strong to be resisted. **2** very attractive or enticing. ▪ **irresistibility** *or* **irresistibleness** *noun*. ▪ **irresistibly** *adv.* [16c: from Latin *irresistibilis*]

irresolute *adj* hesitating or doubtful; not able to take firm decisions. ▪ **irresolutely** *adv.* ▪ **irresoluteness** *or* **irresolution** *noun*. [16c]

irrespective *adj* (*always* **irrespective of sth**) without considering or taking it into account. ▸ *adv, informal* nevertheless; regardless. ▪ **irrespectively** *adv.* [17c]

irresponsible *adj* **1** done without, or showing no, concern for the consequences; reckless; careless. **2** not reliable or trustworthy. ▪ **irresponsibility** *noun*. ▪ **irresponsibly** *adv.* ▪ **irresponsive** *adj* not responding. [17c]

irretrievable *adj* not able to be recovered or put right. ▪ **irretrievability** *noun*. ▪ **irretrievably** *adv.*

irreverent *adj* lacking respect or reverence (eg for things considered sacred or for important people). ▪ **irreverence** *noun*. ▪ **irreverently** *adv.* [15c]

irreversible *adj* **1** not able to be changed back to a former or original state; permanent. **2** not able to be recalled or annulled. ▪ **irreversibility** *or* **irreversibleness** *noun*. ▪ **irreversibly** *adv.* [17c]

irrevocable *adj* unable to be changed, stopped, or undone. ▪ **irrevocability** *noun*. ▪ **irrevocably** *adv.* [14c]

irrigate *verb* **1** to supply (land) with water by channels etc, especially to enable crops to be grown in dry regions. **2** *med* to wash out (the eye, a wound, body cavity, etc), with a flow of water or antiseptic solution. ▪ **irrigation** *noun*. [17c: from Latin *irrigare*]

irritable *adj* **1** easily annoyed, angered or excited. **2** extremely or excessively sensitive. **3** *biol* denoting a living organism that can respond to an external stimulus, such as light, heat or touch. ▪ **irritability** *or* **irritableness** *noun*. ▪ **irritably** *adv.* [17c: see **irritate**]

irritable bowel syndrome *noun, med* inflammation of the mucous membrane of the colon.

irritant *noun* **1** any chemical, physical or biological agent that causes irritation of a tissue, esp inflammation of the skin or eyes. **2** someone or something that causes physical or mental irritation. ▸ *adj* irritating.

irritate *verb* **1** to make someone angry or annoyed. **2** to make (part of the body, an organ, etc) sore and swollen or itchy. **3** *biol* to stimulate (eg an organ) to respond in a characteristic way. ▪ **irritating** *adj*. ▪ **irritatingly** *adv.* ▪ **irritation** *noun*. ▪ **irritative** *adj*. [16c: from Latin *irritare* to incite, provoke or irritate]

irrupt *verb, intr* to burst into or enter (a place, etc) suddenly with speed and violence. ▪ **irruption** *noun*. [19c: from Latin *irrumpere* to break in]

is *present tense of* **be**.

ISA *abbrev* Individual Savings Account.

ischaemia *or* **ischemia** /ɪ'skiːmɪə/ *noun, med* an inadequate flow of blood to a part of the body. [19c: from Greek *ischein* to restrain + *haima* blood]

ISDN *abbrev* integrated services digital network.

-ise see **-ize**

-ish *suffix, forming adjs, signifying* **1** slightly; fairly; having a trace of something specified: *reddish*. **2** like; having the qualities of something specified: *childish*. **3** having as a nationality: *Swedish*. **4** approximately; about: *fiftyish*. [Anglo-Saxon *-isc*]

isinglass /'aɪzɪŋglɑːs/ *noun* **1** gelatine from the dried swim bladders of certain fish, eg sturgeon. **2** thin transparent sheets of **mica** used in furnace and stove doors. [16c]

Islam *noun* **1** the monotheistic religion of the **Muslims**, as revealed by the prophet Muhammad, and set forth in the **Koran**. **2** **a** Muslims collectively; **b** the parts of the world in which Islam is the main or recognized religion. ▪ **Islamic** *adj*. [19c: Arabic, meaning 'surrendering (to God)']

Islamicist *adj* someone who studies Islam, Islamic law or Islamic culture.

Islamist /'ɪzləmɪst/ *n* **1** an **Islamicist**. **2** a person engaged in a political movement seeking to establish a traditional Islamic society. ▸ *adj* of or relating to Islamists.

island *noun* **1** a piece of land, smaller than a continent, that is completely surrounded by water. **2** anything that is like an island, esp in being isolated or detached. **3** (*in full* **traffic island**) a small raised area in the middle of a street on which people may safely stand when crossing the road. **4** *anatomy* a group of cells or a region of tissue detached and differing from surrounding cells or tissues. [Anglo-Saxon *iegland*, with spelling influenced by *isle*]

islander *noun* someone who lives on an island.

isle *noun* an island, esp a small one. [13c: French, from Latin *insula*]

islet *noun* **1** a small island. **2** any small group of cells that has a different nature and structure to the cells surrounding it.

islets of Langerhans *plural noun, anatomy* small groups of cells in the pancreas that control the level of glucose in the blood by secreting **insulin**. [19c: named after the German anatomist Paul Langerhans, who was the first person to describe them]

ism *noun, informal, often derog* a distinctive and formal set of ideas, principles or beliefs. [17c: from **-ism**, regarded as a separate word]

-ism *suffix, forming nouns, denoting* **1** beliefs, ideas, principles, etc: *feminism*. **2** a quality or state: *heroism*. **3** an activity or practice or its result: *criticism*. **4** discrimination or prejudice: *ageism*. **5** an illness or condition: *alcoholism*. **6** a characteristic of a language or variety of language: *regionalism* • *Americanism*. [From Greek *-ismos* or *-isma*]

isn't *contraction* is not.

ISO *abbrev* International Standards Organization.

iso- *combining form, denoting* **1** same; equal. **2** *chem* an isomeric substance. [From Greek *isos* equal]

isobar *noun* a line on a weather chart connecting points that have the same atmospheric pressure. ▪ **isobaric** *adj*. [19c: from Greek *isobares* of equal weight]

isochronal /aɪˈsɒkrənəl/ *or* **isochronous** /aɪˈsɒkrənəs/ *adj* **1** having the same length of time. **2** performed or happening at the same time. **3** happening at equal or regular intervals. [17c: from Greek *isochronos* equal in age or time]

isolate *verb* **1** to separate from others; to cause to be alone. **2** to place in quarantine. **3** to separate or detach, esp to allow closer examination: *isolate the problem*. **4** to separate so as to obtain in a pure or uncombined form. ▶ *noun* someone or something that is isolated. ▪ **isolation** *noun*. [19c: from **isolated**]

isolated *adj* **1** placed or standing alone or apart. **2** separate. **3** solitary. [18c: from Italian *isolato*, from Latin *insula* island]

isolationism *noun* the policy of not joining with other countries in international political and economic affairs. ▪ **isolationist** *noun, adj*.

isomer /ˈaɪsəmə(r)/ *noun* **1** *chem* one of two or more chemical compounds that have the same molecular composition but different three-dimensional structures. **2** *physics* one of two or more atomic nuclei with the same atomic number and mass number, but with different energy states and radioactive properties. ▪ **isomeric** /aɪsəˈmɛrɪk/ *adj*. [19c: from Greek *isomeres* having equal parts]

isometric *adj* **1** having equal size or measurements. **2** of a three-dimensional drawing: having all three axes equally inclined to the surface of the drawing and all lines drawn to scale. **3** *physiol* relating to muscular action that generates tension but does not produce contraction. Compare **isotonic**. **4** relating to **isometrics**. ▪ **isometry** *noun*. [19c]

isometrics *singular or plural noun* a system of physical exercises for strengthening and toning the body in which the muscles are pushed either together or against an immovable object and are not contracted, flexed or made to bend limbs.

isomorph *noun* **1** any object that is similar or identical in structure or shape to another object. **2** *chem* any of two or more substances having the same crystalline structure but differing in chemical composition. **3** *biol* any of two or more individuals that appear similar in form, although they belong to different races or species.

isomorphism *noun* **1** *biol* the apparent similarity of form between individuals belonging to different races or species. **2** *chem* the existence of two or more chemical compounds with the same crystal structure. **3** *maths* a one-to-one correspondence between the elements of two or more sets. ▪ **isomorphic** *or* **isomorphous** *adj*. [19c]

isosceles /aɪˈsɒsəliːz/ *adj* of a triangle: having two sides of equal length. [16c: from **iso-** + Greek *skelos* leg]

isotherm *noun* **1** a line on a weather map connecting places where the temperature is the same at a particular time or for a particular period of time. **2** *physics* a line on a graph linking all places or points having a certain temperature. [19c: from **iso-** + Greek *therme* heat]

isotonic *adj* **1** *chem* denoting a solution that has the same **osmotic pressure** as another solution with which it is being compared. **2** denoting a drink designed to restore the body's levels of minerals and salts after vigorous exercise. **3** *physiol* relating to muscular action that produces contraction, resulting in movement. Compare **isometric**. [19c]

isotope *noun, chem* one of two or more atoms of the same chemical element that contain the same number of protons but different numbers of neutrons in their nuclei. ▪ **isotopic** *adj*. ▪ **isotopically** *adv*. ▪ **isotopy** *noun*. [Early 20c: from **iso-** + Greek *topos* place (ie on the periodic table)]

isotropic *adj* **1** having physical properties that are identical in all directions. **2** tending to show equal growth in all directions. ▪ **isotropy** *noun*. [19c: from **iso-** + Greek *tropos* turn]

ISP *abbrev, comput* Internet service provider.

Israeli *adj* belonging or relating to Israel, a modern state in the Middle East, or its inhabitants. ▶ *noun* a citizen or inhabitant of, or person born in, Israel. [20c]

Israelite *noun, Bible, hist* someone born or living in the ancient kingdom of Israel, esp a person claiming descent from Jacob. ▶ *adj* belonging or relating to the ancient kingdom of Israel or its inhabitants.

issue *noun* **1** the giving out, publishing or making available of something, eg stamps, a magazine, etc. **2** something given out, published or made available. **3** one item in a regular series. **4** a subject for discussion or argument. **5** a result or consequence. **6** *formal* children; offspring. **7** an act of going or flowing out. **8** a way out, outlet or outflow, eg where a stream begins. ▶ *verb* **1** to give or send out, distribute, publish or make available, esp officially or formally. **2** (*usu* **issue sb with sth**) to supply them with the required item. **3** *intr* (*often* **issue forth** *or* **out**) to flow or come out, esp in large quantities. **4** (*usu* **issue in sth**) to end or result in it. **5** *intr* (*often* **issue from sb** *or* **sth**) to come or descend from them or it; to be produced or caused by them or it. [13c: French]

IDIOMS **at issue 1** in dispute or disagreement. **2** under discussion. **force the issue** to act so as to force a decision to be taken. **join** *or* **take issue with sb** to disagree with them. **make an issue of sth** to make it the explicit subject of an argument or disagreement.

-ist *suffix, denoting* **1** a believer in some system, idea or principle: *feminist* • *realist*. **2** someone who carries out some activity or practises some art or profession: *novelist* • *dentist*. [From Greek *-istes*]

isthmus /ˈɪsməs, ˈɪsθməs/ *noun* a narrow strip of land, bounded by water on both sides, that joins two larger areas of land. [16c: Latin, from Greek *isthmos*]

-istic *suffix, forming adjectives and some nouns* corresponding to words formed by **-ist** and **-ism**.

IT *abbrev* information technology.

it *pron* **1** the thing, animal, baby or group already mentioned. **2** the person in question: *Who is it?* **3** used as the subject with impersonal verbs and when describing the weather or distance or telling the time: *It's a bit blustery today.* **4** used as the grammatical subject of a sentence when the real subject comes later, eg *It's very silly to run away.* **5** used to refer to a general situation or state of affairs: *How's it going?* **6** used to emphasize a certain word or phrase in a sentence: *When is it that her train's due?* **7** exactly what is needed, suitable or available: *That's it!* **8** used with many verbs and prepositions as an object with little meaning: *run for it.* ▸ *noun* **1** the person in a children's game who has to oppose all the others, eg by trying to catch them. **2** *old use, informal* sex appeal. [Anglo-Saxon *hit*]

ital. *abbrev* italic.

Italian *adj* belonging or relating to Italy, its inhabitants or their language. ▸ *noun* **1** a citizen or inhabitant of, or person born in, Italy. **2** the official language of Italy, also spoken in parts of Switzerland. **3** *informal* **a** a restaurant that serves Italian food; **b** a meal in one of these restaurants. [15c: from Latin *Italianus*]

Italianate *adj* esp of decoration, architecture or art: done in an Italian style.

italic *adj* **1** of a typeface: containing characters that slope upwards to the right. **2** (**Italic**) belonging or relating to ancient Italy. **3** (**Italic**) denoting a group of Indo-European languages spoken in ancient Italy, including Latin. ▸ *noun* **1** (*usu* **italics**) a typeface with characters that slope upwards to the right. **2** a character written or printed in this typeface. Compare **roman**. **3** the Italic languages. [16c: from Greek *Italikos*]

italicize *or* **-ise** *verb* to print or write in italics; to change (characters, words, etc in normal typeface) to italics. ▪ **italicization** *noun.*

itch *noun* **1** an unpleasant or ticklish irritation on the surface of the skin which makes one want to scratch. **2** *informal* a strong or restless desire. **3** a skin disease or condition that causes a constant unpleasant irritation, esp scabies. ▸ *verb* **1** *intr* to have an itch and want to scratch. **2** *tr & intr* to cause someone to feel an itch. **3** *intr, informal* to feel a strong or restless desire. ▪ **itchiness** *noun.* ▪ **itchy** *adj* (**-ier, -iest**). [Anglo-Saxon *giccan*]

itchy feet *noun, informal* the strong desire to leave, move or travel.

it'd *contraction* **1** it had. **2** it would.

-ite *suffix, forming nouns, signifying* **1** a member of a national, regional, tribal, etc group: *Canaanite.* **2** a follower of or believer in something; a member of a group or faction: *Shiite.* **3** a fossil: *trilobite.* **4** a mineral: *graphite.* **5** a salt of a certain formula: *nitrite.* Compare **-ide**. **6** any of various manufactured substances: *dynamite.* [From Greek *-ites*]

item *noun* **1** a separate object or unit, esp one on a list. **2** a separate piece of information or news. **3** *informal* a couple regarded as having a romantic or sexual relationship. [16c: Latin, meaning 'likewise']

itemize *or* **-ise** *verb* to list (things) separately, eg on a bill. ▪ **itemization** *noun.* ▪ **itemizer** *noun.* [19c]

iterate *verb* to say or do again. ▪ **iteration** *noun.* ▪ **iterative** *adj.* [16c: from Latin *iterare*, from *iterum* again]

itinerant *adj* travelling from place to place, eg on business. ▸ *noun* a person whose work involves going from place to place or who has no fixed address. [16c: from Latin *itinerare* to travel]

itinerary *noun* (**-ies**) **1** a planned route for a journey or trip. **2** a diary or record of a journey. **3** a guidebook. ▸ *adj* belonging or relating to journeys. [15c: ultimately from Latin *iter* journey]

-itis *combining form, denoting* inflammation: *appendicitis.* [From Greek *-itis*]

it'll *contraction* **1** it will. **2** it shall.

its *adj* belonging to it. ▸ *pronoun* the one or ones belonging to it.

---

its, it's

Be careful not to use the spelling **its** when you should use **it's**, and vice versa.

Its means 'belonging to it':

The car is old and its bodywork is rusting.

It's is a short form of 'it is' or 'it has':

It's nice to see you again.

---

it's *contraction* **1** it is. **2** *informal* it has.

itself *pron* **1** the reflexive form of **it**. **2** used for emphasis: *His behaviour itself was bad.* **3** its usual or normal state: *The puppy was soon itself again.* **4** (*also* **by itself**) alone; without help.

itsy-bitsy *or* **itty-bitty** *adj, informal* very small. [20c: a childish rhyming compound based on *little bit*]

ITV *abbrev, Brit* Independent Television.

-ity *suffix, forming nouns, denoting* a state or quality, or an instance of it: *irregularity* • *confidentiality.* [From French *-ité*, from Latin *-itas*]

IUD *abbrev* intrauterine device, a contraceptive device inserted into the womb, which prevents implantation of the fertilized egg. Also called **coil**.

-ium *suffix, forming nouns, signifying* **1** (*also* **-um**) a metallic element: *plutonium.* **2** a group forming positive ions. **3** a biological structure. [Latin, from Greek *-ion*]

I've *contraction* I have.

-ive *suffix, forming adjectives, signifying* a quality, action, tendency, etc: *creative* • *emotive.* [From French *-if*]

IVF *abbrev* in-vitro fertilization.

ivory *noun* (**-ies**) **1** a hard white material that forms the tusks of the elephant, walrus, etc. **2** the creamy-white colour of this substance. **3** an article made from this substance. **4** (**ivories**) *informal* the keys on a piano. ▸ *adj* **1** made of ivory: *ivory statuette.* **2** ivory-coloured, often with the implication of smoothness: *ivory skin.* [13c: from French *ivoire*]

ivory tower *noun* a hypothetical place where the unpleasant realities of life can be ignored.

ivy *noun* (**-ies**) **1** a woody evergreen climbing or trailing plant. **2** any of several other climbing plants, such as poison ivy. [Anglo-Saxon *ifig*]

-ize *or* **-ise** *suffix, forming verbs, signifying* **1** to make or become something specified: *equalize.* **2** to treat or react in a specified way: *criticize.* **3** to engage in a specified activity: *theorize.* ▪ **-ization** *suffix, forming nouns*: *familiarization.* [From Latin *-izare*]

-ize, -ise

Although the ending **-ize** is common in American English, both **-ize** and **-ise** are acceptable endings for many verbs in British English.

Note that there are some verbs you must spell with **-ise**, eg *exercise, supervise* and *comprise*.

There are also some verbs you must spell with **-ize**, eg *capsize, prize* (in the sense 'to value') and *seize*.

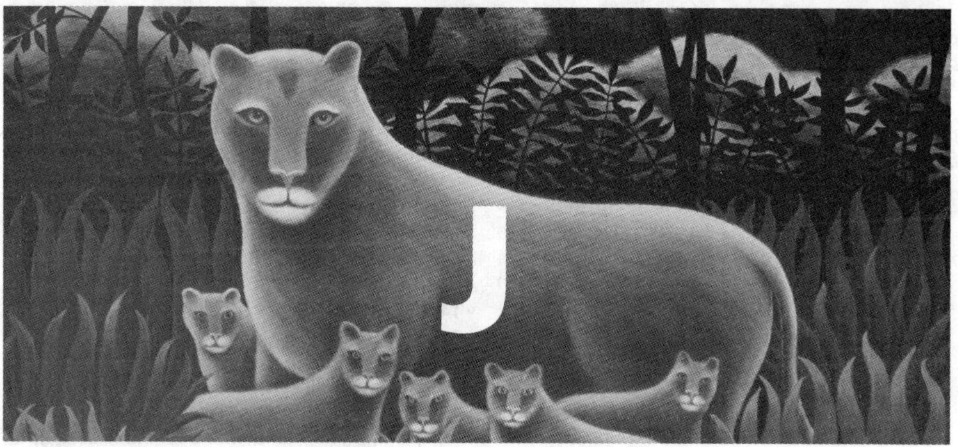

J[1] *or* **j** *noun* (***Js, J's*** *or* ***j's***) the tenth letter of the English alphabet.

J[2] *abbrev* joule.

jab *verb* (***jabbed, jabbing***) (*also* **jab at**) **1** to poke or prod (someone or something). **2** to strike (someone or something) with a short quick punch. ▸ *noun* **1** a poke or prod. **2** *informal* an injection or inoculation: *a tetanus jab*. [19c: variant of Scots *job* to stab or pierce]

jabber *verb, tr & intr* to talk or utter rapidly and indistinctly. ▸ *noun* rapid indistinct speech. ▪ **jabbering** *noun, adj*. [15c: imitating the sound]

jack *noun* **1** a device for raising a heavy weight, such as a car, off the ground. **2** a winch. **3** *elec, telecomm, etc* a socket with two or more terminals into which a **jack plug** can be inserted in order to make or break a circuit or circuits. **4** *cards* the court card of least value, bearing a picture of a page (see **page**[2] *noun* sense 2). Also called **knave**. **5** *bowls* the small white ball that the players aim at. **6** a small national flag flown at the bows of a ship. ▸ *verb* to raise (something) with a jack. [16c]

IDIOMS **every man jack** everybody.

PHRASAL VERBS **jack sth in** *or* **up** *slang* to give it up, or abandon it. **jack up** to increase (prices, etc).

jackal *noun* **1** a carnivorous scavenging mammal, closely related to the dog and wolf, that lives in deserts, grassland and woodland in Asia and Africa. **2** a person who does someone else's dirty work. [17c: from Persian *shagal*]

jackass *noun* **1** a male ass or donkey. **2** *informal* a foolish person. [18c]

jackboot *noun* **1** a tall knee-high military boot. **2** such a boot as a symbol of oppressive military rule. [17c]

jackdaw *noun* a bird of the crow family with black plumage shot with blue on the back and head, and a reputation for stealing bright objects. [16c: from **jack** + old word *daw* jackdaw]

jacket *noun* **1** a short coat, esp a long-sleeved, hip-length one. **2** something worn over the top half of the body: *life jacket*. **3** a **dust jacket**. **4** the skin of an unpeeled cooked potato. [15c: from French *jaquet*]

Jack Frost *noun* a personification of frost.

jackhammer *noun* a hand-held compressed-air drill for rock-drilling.

jack-in-office *noun, Brit, derog* a self-important minor official.

jack-in-the-box *noun* a box containing a doll attached to a spring, which jumps out when the lid is opened.

jackknife *noun* **1** a large pocket knife with a folding blade. **2** a dive in which the body is bent double and then straightened before entering the water. ▸ *verb, intr* of an articulated vehicle: to go out of control in such a way that the trailer swings round against the cab.

jack-of-all-trades *noun* (***jacks-of-all-trades***) someone who turns their hand to a variety of different jobs.

jack plug see **jack** (sense 3)

jackpot *noun* the maximum win, to be made in a lottery, card game, etc. [20c]

IDIOMS **hit the jackpot** *informal* to have a remarkable financial win or stroke of luck.

jack rabbit *noun* a large N American hare with long hind legs and large ears with black tips. [19c]

Jack tar *noun, old use* a sailor.

Jacobean *adj* belonging or relating to the reign of James I of England (also VI of Scotland) (1603–25). ▸ *noun* someone who lived during the reign of James I & VI. [18c: from Latin *Jacobus* James]

Jacobin *noun, hist* **1** a member of a radical political society in the French Revolution, so called from their meeting in the hall of a Jacobin convent. **2** an extremist or radical in politics.

Jacobite *Brit hist, noun* an adherent of the **Jacobites**, supporters of James II, his son or grandson, the Stuart claimants to the British throne. ▸ *adj* relating to the Jacobites. [17c: from Latin *Jacobus* James]

jacquard /ˈdʒakɑːd/ *noun* **1** a piece of equipment consisting of a set of coded perforated cards that can be fitted to a loom to produce a fabric with an intricate woven pattern. **2** (*in full* **jacquard loom**) a loom fitted with this kind of device. **3** fabric produced on this kind of loom. [19c: named after the French inventor of the device, Joseph Marie Jacquard]

Jacuzzi /dʒəˈkuːzɪ/ *noun, trademark* a large bath or pool with underwater jets that massage and invigorate the body. [20c]

jade *noun* **1** *geol* a very hard, green, white, brown or yellow semi-precious stone used to make vases and carved ornaments. **2** the intense green colour of jade. [18c: from Spanish *piedra de ijada* stone of the ribs, from the belief that it helped to cure colic]

jaded *adj* fatigued; dull and bored.

Jaffa *noun* a large oval orange with a particularly thick skin. [19c: named after Jaffa, the Israeli city where this type of orange was first grown]

jag *noun* **1** a sharp projection. **2** *Scots* an injection; an inoculation. ▸ *verb* (***jagged, jagging***) **1** to cut (something) unevenly. **2** to make indentations in (something). ▪ **jaggy** *adj* (***-ier, -iest***).

jagged /ˈdʒagɪd/ *adj* having a rough or sharp uneven edge. ▪ **jaggedness** *noun*.

jaguar *noun* the largest of the American big cats, with a deep yellow or tawny coat covered with black spots. [17c: from Tupí (a native S American language) *jaguara*]

jail *or* **gaol** *noun* prison. ▸ *verb* to imprison. ▪ **jailer, jailor** *or* **gaoler** *noun*. [13c: from French *gaole*]

jailbird *or* **gaolbird** *noun, informal* a person who is, or has been, frequently in prison.

jailbreak *or* **gaolbreak** *noun* an escape, esp by several prisoners, from jail.

Jain *noun* an adherent of **Jainism**, an indigenous religion of India that advocates non-injury to all living things. [19c: from Hindi *jaina* saint]

jalopy *or* **jaloppy** /dʒəˈlɒpɪ/ *noun* (***-ies***) *informal* a worn-out old car. [20c]

jam[1] *noun* a thick sticky food made from fruit boiled with sugar, used as a spread on bread, etc. [18c]

jam[2] *verb* (***jammed, jamming***) **1** *often in passive* to stick or wedge (something) so as to make it immovable. **2** *tr & intr* of machinery, etc: to stick or make it stick and stop working. **3** to push or shove (something); to cram, press or pack. **4** (*also* **jam up**) to fill (eg a street) so full that movement comes to a stop. **5** to cause interference to (a radio signal, etc), esp deliberately. **6** *intr, informal* to play jazz in a **jam session**. [18c: prob an imitation of the actions or its sound]

Jamaican *adj* belonging or relating to Jamaica, an island nation in the Caribbean Sea, or its inhabitants. ▸ *noun* a citizen or inhabitant of, or person born in, Jamaica.

jamb /dʒam/ *noun* the vertical post at the side of a door, window or fireplace. [14c: from French *jambe* leg]

jamboree *noun* **1** a large rally of Scouts, Guides, etc. **2** *informal* a large and lively gathering. [19c: orig US slang]

jammy *adj* (***-ier, -iest***) **1** covered or filled with jam. **2** *informal* of a person: lucky.

jam-packed *adj, informal* packed tight.

jam session *noun, slang* a session of live, esp improvised, jazz or popular music. [20c: see **jam**[2]]

Jan. *abbrev* January.

JANET *abbrev, trademark* Joint Academic Network, a computer network linking UK universities, research bodies, etc, part of **the Internet**.

jangle *verb* **1** *tr & intr* to make or cause (something) to make an irritating, discordant ringing noise. **2** to upset or irritate (a person's nerves). ▸ *noun* an unpleasant dissonant ringing sound. ▪ **jangling** *noun*. [13c: from French *jangler*]

janitor *noun* **1** *N Am, Scot* a caretaker, esp of a school. **2** a doorkeeper. [17c: Latin, from *janua* door]

January *noun* (abbrev **Jan.**) the first month of the year. [14c: from Latin *Januarius mensis* month of the god Janus]

japan *noun* a hard glossy black lacquer, orig from Japan, used to coat wood and metal. ▸ *verb* (***japanned, japanning***) to lacquer (something) with japan. [17c: named after the country]

Japanese *adj* belonging or relating to Japan, its inhabitants or their language. ▸ *noun* **1** a citizen or inhabitant of, or person born in, Japan. **2** the official language of Japan.

jape *noun, old use* a trick, prank or joke. [14c]

japonica *noun* **1** an ornamental, red-flowered shrub which bears round green, white or yellow fruit. **2** the **camellia**. [19c: Latin, meaning 'Japanese']

jar[1] *noun* **1** a wide-mouthed cylindrical container, usu made of glass **2** *informal* a glass of beer. [16c: from French *jarre*]

jar[2] *verb* (***jarred, jarring***) **1** *intr* to have a harsh effect; to grate. **2** *tr & intr* to jolt or vibrate. **3** *intr* (*esp* **jar with**) to clash or conflict (with something). ▸ *noun* a jarring sensation, shock or jolt. [16c: imitating the sound or effect]

jardinière /ʒɑːdɪˈnjɛə(r)/ *noun* an ornamental pot or stand for flowers. [19c: French, feminine of *jardinier* gardener]

jarful *noun* the amount a **jar**[1] can hold.

jargon *noun* **1** the specialized vocabulary of a particular trade, profession, group or activity. **2** *derog* language that uses this type of vocabulary in a pretentious or meaningless way. [14c: French]

jasmine *noun* a shrub or vine whose fragrant flowers are used as a source of jasmine oil in perfumery and also to scent tea. [16c: from Persian *yasmin*]

jasper *noun, geol* a semi-precious gemstone, an impure form of **chalcedony**, used to make jewellery and ornaments. [14c: from Greek *iaspis*]

jaundice *noun, pathol* a condition that turns the skin and the whites of the eyes a yellowish colour, caused by an excess of bile pigments in the blood. [14c: from French *jaunisse*, from *jaune* yellow]

jaundiced *adj* **1** suffering from jaundice. **2** of a person or attitude: bitter or resentful; cynical.

jaunt *noun* a short journey for pleasure. ▸ *verb, intr* to go for a jaunt.

jaunty *adj* (***-ier, -iest***) **1** of someone's manner or personality: breezy and exuberant. **2** of dress, etc: smart; stylish. ▪ **jauntily** *adv*. ▪ **jauntiness** *noun*. [17c: from French *gentil* noble or gentle]

Java /ˈdʒɑːvə/ *noun* **1** a rich variety of coffee. **2** *trademark* a **programming language** designed for the Internet. [19c in sense 1: from the island of Java in Indonesia; 1990s in sense 2]

javelin *noun* **1** a light spear for throwing, either as a weapon or in sport. **2** (**the javelin**) the athletic event of throwing the javelin. [16c: from French *javeline*]

jaw *noun* **1** *zool, biol* in most vertebrates: either of the two bony structures that form the framework of the mouth and in which the teeth are set. See also **mandible, maxilla**. **2** the lower part of the face round the mouth and chin. **3** (**jaws**) the mouth, esp of an animal. **4** (**jaws**) a threshold, esp of something terrifying: *the jaws of death*. **5** (**jaws**) in a machine or tool: a pair of opposing parts used for gripping, crushing, etc. **6** *informal* a long conversation; talk; chatter. ▸ *verb, intr, informal* to chatter, gossip or talk. [14c: from French *joue* cheek]

jawbone *noun, non-technical* the upper or lower bone of the jaw. *Technical equivalents* **mandible** and **maxilla**.

jay *noun* a bird of the crow family which has pinkish-brown plumage and blue, black and white bands on its wings. [14c: from French *jai*]

jaywalk *verb, intr* to cross streets wherever one likes, regardless of traffic signals. ▪ **jaywalker** *noun*. ▪ **jaywalking** *noun*. [20c: orig US, from *jay*, meaning 'fool']

jazz *noun* **1** a type of popular music of Black American origin, with strong catchy rhythms, performed with much improvisation. **2** *informal* talk; nonsense; business, stuff, etc. ▸ *verb* (*usu* **jazz up**) *informal* **1** to enliven or brighten (something). **2** to give (something) a jazzy rhythm. [20c]

jazzy *adj* (**-*ier*, -*iest***) **1** in the style of, or like, jazz. **2** *informal* showy; flashy; stylish. ▪ **jazzily** *adv*.

JCB *noun* a type of mobile excavator used in the building industry, with a hydraulic shovel at the front and a digging arm at the back. [20c: named after *J*oseph *C*yril *B*amford, the British manufacturer]

jealous *adj* (*often* **jealous of sb**) **1** envious (of someone else, their possessions, success, talents, etc). **2** suspicious and resentful (of possible rivals); possessive: *a jealous husband*. **3** anxiously protective (of something one has). **4** caused by jealousy: *a jealous fury*. ▪ **jealously** *adv*. Compare **envious**. [13c: from French *gelos*]

jealousy *noun* (**-*ies***) the emotion of envy or suspicious possessiveness.

jeans *plural noun* casual trousers made esp of denim. [19c: from *jean* a strong cotton from Genoa (French *Gênes*)]

Jeep *noun, trademark* a light military vehicle capable of travelling over rough country. [20c: from *general-purpose vehicle*]

jeer *verb* **1** to mock or deride (a speaker, performer, etc). **2** *intr* (**jeer at sb** *or* **sth**) to laugh unkindly at them or it: *jeered at his accent*. ▸ *noun* a taunt, insult or hoot of derision. ▪ **jeering** *noun, adj*. [16c]

jehad see **jihad**

jejune /dʒɪ'dʒuːn/ *adj, derog* **1** of writing, ideas, etc: dull, unoriginal and empty of imagination. **2** childish; naive. [17c: from Latin *jejunus* hungry or empty]

jejunum /dʒɪ'dʒuːnəm/ *noun, anatomy* in mammals: the part of the **small intestine** between the duodenum and the ileum. [16c: Latin]

Jekyll and Hyde /'dʒɛkɪl ənd haɪd; *US* 'dʒiːkɪl/ *noun* a person with two distinct personalities, one good, the other evil. [19c: from *The Strange Case of Dr Jekyll and Mr Hyde*, a novel by Robert Louis Stevenson]

jell *or* **gel** *verb, intr* **1** to become firm; to set. **2** *informal* to take definite shape. [19c: from **jelly**]

jellied *adj* set in jelly: *jellied eels*.

jelly *noun* (**-*ies***) **1** a wobbly, transparent, fruit-flavoured dessert set with gelatine. **2** a clear jam made by boiling and straining fruit. **3** meat stock or other savoury medium set with gelatine. **4** any jelly-like substance. [14c: from French *gelée*]

jellyfish *noun, zool* any of various marine **coelenterates**, usu having an umbrella-shaped body and tentacles containing stinging cells. [19c in this sense]

jemmy *noun* (**-*ies***) a small crowbar used esp by burglars for forcing open windows, etc. ▸ *verb* (**-*ies*, -*ied***) to force (a door, window, etc) open with a jemmy or similar tool. [19c: from the name *James*]

jenny *noun* (**-*ies***) **1** a name given to the female of certain animals, esp the donkey, ass and wren. **2** a **spinning jenny**. [17c: from the name *Jenny*]

jeopardize *or* **-ise** *verb* to put (something) at risk of harm, loss or destruction: *She jeopardized her chances of passing her exam by doing very little work*.

jeopardy *noun* **1** danger of harm, loss or destruction: *His job was in jeopardy due to the takeover*. **2** *US law* the danger of trial and punishment faced by a person accused on a criminal charge. [14c: from French *jeu parti* a divided or even (ie uncertain) game]

jeremiad *noun, informal* a lengthy and mournful tale of woe. [18c: from French *jérémiade*, from *The Lamentations of Jeremiah* in the Old Testament]

jerk *noun* **1** a quick tug or pull. **2** a sudden movement; a jolt. **3** *derog slang* a useless or idiotic person. ▸ *verb* **1** to pull or tug (something) sharply. **2** *intr* to move with sharp suddenness. [16c]

jerkin *noun* a sleeveless jacket, short coat or close-fitting waistcoat. [16c]

jerky *adj* (**-*ier*, -*iest***) making sudden movements or jerks. ▪ **jerkily** *adv*. ▪ **jerkiness** *noun*.

jerry-built *adj* of a building: cheaply and quickly built. [19c: poss referring to the town of Jericho and the biblical story in which its walls came tumbling down]

jerry can *noun* a flat-sided can used for carrying water, petrol, etc. [20c]

jersey *noun* (**-*eys***) **1** a knitted garment worn on the upper part of the body, pulled on over the head. **2** a fine knitted fabric, usu machine-knitted and slightly stretchy, in cotton, nylon, etc. [16c: named after Jersey in the Channel Islands]

Jerusalem artichoke *noun* **1** a tall plant widely cultivated for its edible tubers. **2** the underground tuber of this plant, with white flesh and knobbly brownish or reddish skin, which can be eaten as a vegetable. [17c: a corruption of Italian *girasole* sunflower]

jest *noun* a joke or prank. ▸ *verb, intr* to make a jest; to joke. [13c: from French *geste* deed]

IDIOMS **in jest** as a joke; not seriously.

jester *noun, hist* a professional clown, employed by a king or noble to amuse the court. [14c]

Jesuit *noun* a member of the Society of Jesus (**the Jesuits**), a male religious order founded in 1540 by Ignatius de Loyola. ▪ **jesuitical** *adj*. [16c: from Latin *Jesuita*, from *Jesus*]

Jesus *noun* Jesus Christ, the central figure of the Christian faith. ▸ *exclam* an exclamation of surprise, anger, etc.

jet[1] *noun, geol* a hard black variety of **lignite** that can be cut and polished, used to make jewellery and ornaments. [14c: from French *jaiet*]

jet[2] *noun* **1** a strong continuous stream of liquid or gas, forced under pressure from a narrow opening. **2** an orifice, nozzle or pipe through which such a stream is forced. **3** any device powered by such a stream of liquid or gas, esp a jet engine. **4** (*also* **jet aircraft**) an aircraft powered by a jet engine. ▸ *verb* (***jetted*, *jetting***) *tr & intr, informal* to travel or transport (something) by jet aircraft. [16c: from French *jeter* to throw]

jet-black *adj* deep glossy black.

jet engine *noun* any engine, esp in an aircraft, that generates all or most of its forward thrust by ejecting a jet of gases formed as a result of fuel combustion.

jet lag *noun* the tiredness and lethargy that result from the body's inability to adjust to the rapid changes of **time zone** that go with high-speed, long-distance air travel. ▪ **jet-lagged** *adj*.

jet propulsion *noun* the forward thrust of a body brought about by means of a force produced by ejection of a jet of gas or liquid to the rear of the body. ▪ **jet-propelled** *adj*.

jetsam *noun* goods jettisoned from a ship and washed up on the shore. Compare **flotsam**. [16c: contracted from **jettison**]

the jet set *singular or plural noun, informal* wealthy people who lead a life of fast travel and expensive enjoyment. ▪ **jet-setter** *noun*. ▪ **jet-setting** *noun, adj*.

jet ski *noun* a powered craft, similar to a motorbike, adapted for skimming across water on a ski-like keel. ▪ **jet-ski** *verb*.

jet stream *noun* **1** *meteorol* a narrow band of high-speed, westerly winds more than 10,000 metres above the earth. **2** the exhaust of a jet engine.

jettison *verb* **1** to throw (cargo) overboard to lighten a ship, aircraft, etc in an emergency. **2** *informal* to abandon, reject or get rid of (someone or something). [15c: from French *getaison*]

jetty *noun* (***-ies***) **1** a stone or wooden landing stage. **2** a stone barrier built out into the sea to protect a harbour from currents and high waves. [15c: from French *jetee*]

Jew *noun* **1** a member of the Hebrew race. **2** someone who practises Judaism. [12c: from French *Juiu*]

jewel *noun* **1** a precious stone. **2** a personal ornament made with precious stones and metals. **3** a gem used in the machinery of a watch. **4** someone or something greatly prized. ▪ **jewelled** *adj*. [13c: from French *joel*]

jeweller *or* (*US*) **jeweler** *noun* a person who deals in, makes or repairs jewellery.

jewellery *or* (*US*) **jewelry** *noun* articles worn for personal adornment, eg bracelets, necklaces and rings.

Jewish *adj* relating or belonging to the Jews or to Judaism.

Jewry *noun, old use* Jews collectively.

Jew's harp *noun* a tiny, lyre-shaped musical instrument held between the teeth, with a narrow metal tongue that is twanged with the finger.

Jezebel *noun, derog* a shamelessly immoral or scheming woman. [16c: named after Ahab's wife in the Old Testament]

jib[1] *noun, naut* a small three-cornered sail in front of the mainsail of a yacht. ▸ *verb* (***jibbed, jibbing***) (**jib at sth**) *intr* of a person: to object to it. [17c]

jib[2] *noun* the projecting arm of a crane from which the lifting gear hangs. [18c: from **gibbet**]

jibe see **gybe**

jiffy *or* **jiff** *noun* (***jiffies*** *or* ***jiffs***) *informal* a moment: *in a jiffy.* [18c]

Jiffy bag *noun, trademark* a padded envelope.

jig *noun* **1** a lively country dance or folk dance. **2** music for such a dance. **3** a jerky movement. **4** *mech* a device that holds a piece of work in position and guides the tools being used on it. ▸ *verb* (***jigged, jigging***) **1** *intr* to dance a jig. **2** *tr & intr* to jerk rapidly up and down.

jigger[1] *noun* **a** a small quantity of alcoholic spirits; **b** a glass for measuring this. [19c]

jigger[2] see **chigger**

jiggery-pokery *noun, informal* trickery or deceit. [19c: from Scots *joukery-pawkery*, from *jouk* to dodge + *pawk* trick]

jiggle *verb, tr & intr* to jump or make (something) jump or jerk about. ▸ *noun* a jiggling movement. [19c]

jigsaw *noun* **1** (*also* **jigsaw puzzle**) a picture, mounted on wood or cardboard and cut into interlocking irregularly shaped pieces, to be fitted together again. **2** a fine-bladed saw for cutting intricate patterns. [19c: **jig** + **saw[2]**]

jihad *or* **jehad** /dʒɪ'hɑːd/ *noun* a holy war, against infidels, fought by Muslims on behalf of Islam. [19c: Arabic, meaning 'struggle']

jilbab /'dʒɪlbab/ *noun* (***jilbabs*** *or* ***jalabib*** /'dʒaləbɪb/) a long outer garment, worn by women in some Islamic communities. [Arabic]

jilt *verb* to leave and abruptly discard (a lover). [17c: contracted from dialect *jillet* a flirt]

Jim Crow Laws *plural noun, hist* a name given to US state laws from the 1890s onwards which segregated blacks from whites in the south in schools, housing, public transport, etc. [A derogatory name for a black person, from a black minstrel song]

jimjams *plural noun* **1** *informal* pyjamas. **2** *informal slang* delirium tremens. [19c]

jingle *noun* **1** a light ringing or clinking sound, eg of small bells, coins, keys, etc. **2** a simple rhyming verse, song or tune, esp one used to advertise a product, etc. ▸ *verb, tr & intr* to make, or cause (something) to make, a ringing or clinking sound. [16c: prob imitating the sound]

jingo *or* **Jingo** *noun* (***jingoes***) a ranting patriot. ▪ **jingoism** *noun* over-enthusiastic or aggressive patriotism. ▪ **jingoist** *noun*. ▪ **jingoistic** *adj*. [19c from a chauvinistic song]

jink *verb* **1** *intr* to dodge. **2** to elude (someone or something). ▸ *noun* a dodge; a jinking movement. [18c: imitating the sudden dodging movement]

jinni, jinnee *or* **djinni** /'dʒɪnɪ/ *or* **djinn** /dʒɪn/ *noun* (*pl* ***jinn*** *or* ***djinn***) in Muslim folklore: a supernatural being able to adopt human or animal form. [19c: Arabic]

jinx *noun* **1** (*usu* **a jinx on sth** *or* **sb**) an evil spell or influence, held responsible for misfortune. **2** someone or something that appears to bring bad luck. ▸ *verb* to bring bad luck to (someone or something). ▪ **jinxed** *adj*. [20c: from Greek *iynx* the wryneck, a bird used in spells; hence a spell or charm]

jitter *informal verb, intr* to behave in an agitated or nervous way. ▸ *noun* (*usu* **the jitters**) an attack of nervousness: *He's got the jitters.* ▪ **jittery** *adj*. [20c: variant of dialect and Scots *chitter* to shiver]

jitterbug *noun, US* an energetic dance like the **jive**, popular in the 1940s. ▸ *verb* (***jitterbugged, jitterbugging***) *intr* to dance the jitterbug. [20c: from **jitter**]

jiu-jitsu see **ju-jitsu**

jive *noun* **1** a lively style of jazz music or swing, popular in the 1950s. **2** the style of dancing done to this music. ▸ *verb, intr* to dance in this style. ▪ **jiver** *noun*.

Jnr *or* **jnr** *abbrev* Junior or junior.

job *noun* **1** a person's regular paid employment. **2** a piece of work. **3** a completed task: *made a good job of the pruning*. **4** a function or responsibility. **5** *informal* a problem; difficulty: *had a job finding it*. **6** a crime, esp a burglary: *an inside job*. **7** an underhand scheme: *a put-up job*. **8** *informal* a surgical operation, usu involving plastic surgery: *a nose job*. [16c]

IDIOMS **do the job** to succeed in doing what is required: *This new lock should do the job*. **just the job** exactly what is required.

job centre *or* **Jobcentre** *noun, Brit* a government office displaying information on available jobs.

job club *or* **Jobclub** *noun, Brit* an association aimed at helping the jobless find work through learning and using the necessary skills of presentation, etc.

jobless *adj* having no paid employment; unemployed. ▸ *noun* (**the jobless**) unemployed people as a group.

job lot *noun* a mixed collection of objects sold as one item at an auction, etc.

Job's comforter /dʒoʊbz/ *noun* a person whose attempts at sympathy have the effect of adding to one's distress. [18c: referring to Job in the Old Testament, whose friends responded to his troubles by reproving him]

Jobseeker's Allowance *noun* (abbreviation **JSA**) *Brit* a means-tested state allowance paid to the unemployed.

job-sharing *noun* the practice of sharing one full-time job between two or more part-time workers.

jock *noun, informal* **1** *US* a male athlete. **2** a jockey. **3** a disc-jockey. **4** a jockstrap. [19c]

jockey *noun* (**-eys**) a rider, esp a professional one, in horse races. ▸ *verb* **1** to ride (a horse) in a race. **2** *tr & intr* to manipulate (someone or something) skilfully or deviously. [16c: diminutive of the personal name *Jock*, meaning 'lad']

IDIOMS **jockey for position** to seek an advantage over rivals, esp unscrupulously.

jockstrap *noun* a garment for supporting the genitals, worn by male athletes. [20c: from dialect *jock* penis]

jocose /dʒəˈkoʊs/ *adj, formal* playful; humorous. ▪ **jocosely** *adv*. ▪ **jocosity** *noun*. [17c: from Latin *jocosus*]

jocular *adj* **1** of a person: given to joking; good-humoured. **2** of a remark, etc: intended as a joke. ▪ **jocularity** *noun*. [17c: from Latin *joculus* a little joke]

jocund /ˈdʒoʊkənd/ *adj, formal* cheerful; merry; good-humoured. ▪ **jocundity** *noun*. ▪ **jocundly** *adv*. [14c: from Latin *jocundus* agreeable]

jodhpurs /ˈdʒɒdpəz/ *plural noun* riding-breeches that are loose-fitting over the buttocks and thighs, and tight-fitting from knee to calf. [19c: named after Jodhpur in India]

jodhpurs
This word is often misspelt. It has an *h* after the *d*. It might help you to remember the hidden **h** for **h**orse.

joey *noun* (**-eys**) **1** *Aust* a young animal, esp a kangaroo. **2** *NZ* an opossum. [19c: from an Australian Aboriginal language]

jog *verb* (***jogged, jogging***) **1** to knock or nudge (someone or something) slightly. **2** **a** to remind (someone); **b** to prompt (a person's memory). **3** *intr* (*also* **jog along** *or* **on**) to progress slowly and steadily; to plod. **4** *intr* to run at a slowish steady pace, esp for exercise. ▸ *noun* **1** a period or spell of jogging: *go for a jog*. **2** a nudge, knock or jolt. ▪ **jogger** *noun*. ▪ **jogging** *noun*. [14c: prob a variant of dialect *shog* to shake]

joggle *verb, tr & intr* to jolt, shake or wobble. ▸ *noun* a shake or jolt. [16c: from **jog**]

jog-trot *noun* an easy pace like that of a horse between walking and trotting. ▸ *verb, intr* to move at such a pace.

john *noun, N Am informal* (*usu* **the john**) a lavatory. [20c: from the name *John*]

johnny *noun* (***-ies***) *Brit informal, old use* a chap; a fellow. [17c: from the familiar name *Johnny*]

joie de vivre /ʒwɑː də ˈviːvrə/ *noun* enthusiasm for living. [19c: French, meaning 'joy of living']

join *verb* **1** to connect, attach, link or unite. **2** *tr & intr* to become a member of (a society, firm, etc). **3** *tr & intr* of roads, rivers, etc: to meet. **4** to come together (with someone or something); to enter the company of (a person or group of people): *joined them for supper*. **5** to take part in (something). **6** to do the same as someone, for the sake of companionship: *Who'll join me in a drink?* ▸ *noun* a seam or joint. [13c: from French *joindre*]

PHRASAL VERBS **join in** to take part. **join up** to enlist as a member of an armed service.

joiner *noun* a craftsman who makes and fits wooden doors, window frames, stairs, shelves, etc. ▪ **joinery** *noun*. [14c]

joint *noun* **1** the place where two or more pieces join. **2** *anatomy* in vertebrates: the point of contact or articulation between two or more bones, together with the ligaments that surround it. **3** a piece of meat, usu containing a bone, for cooking or roasting. **4** *slang* a cheap shabby café, bar or nightclub, etc. **5** *slang* a cannabis cigarette. **6** *geol* a crack in a mass of rock. ▸ *verb* **1** to connect to (something) by joints. **2** to divide (a bird or animal) into, or at, the joints for cooking. ▸ *adj* owned or done, etc in common; shared: *joint responsibility*. ▪ **jointed** *adj*. ▪ **jointly** *adv*. [13c: French]

IDIOMS **out of joint 1** of a bone: dislocated. **2** in disorder.

joint account *noun* a bank account held in the name of two or more people.

joint-stock company *noun* a business whose capital is owned jointly by the shareholders.

joist *noun* any of the beams supporting a floor or ceiling. [14c: from French *giste*]

jojoba /hoʊˈhoʊbə/ *noun* a shrub whose edible seeds contain a waxy oil, used in the manufacture of cosmetics and lubricants. [20c: Mexican Spanish]

joke *noun* **1** a humorous story: *crack a joke*. **2** anything said or done in jest. **3** an amusing situation. **4** *informal* something or someone ludicrous. ▸ *verb, intr* **1** to make jokes. **2** to speak in jest, not in earnest. ▪ **jokey** *adj* (***-ier, -iest***). ▪ **jokingly** *adv*. [17c: from Latin *jocus* joke]

IDIOMS **no joke** *informal* a serious matter.

joker *noun* **1** *cards* an extra card in a pack, usu bearing a picture of a jester, used in certain games. **2** a cheerful person, always full of jokes. **3** *informal* an irresponsible or incompetent person.

jollify *verb* (**-*ies*, -*ied***) to make (something) jolly. ▪ **jollification** *noun*.

jollity *noun* **1** merriment. **2** (**jollities**) festivities.

jolly *adj* (**-*ier*, -*iest***) **1** good-humoured; cheerful. **2** happy; enjoyable; convivial. ▸ *adv, Brit informal* very: *jolly good*. ▸ *verb* (**-*ies*, -*ied***) (**jolly sb** *or* **sth along**) to keep them or it going in a cheerful way. ▪ **jolliness** *noun*. [14c: from French *jolif* pretty or merry]

jolt *verb* **1** *intr* to move along jerkily. **2** to shock (someone) emotionally. ▸ *noun* **1** a jarring shake. **2** an emotional shock. [16c: prob a combination of dialect *jot* and *joll*, both meaning 'to bump']

Jonah *noun* a person who seems to bring bad luck. [17c: named after Jonah in the Old Testament]

jonquil *noun* a small daffodil with fragrant white or yellow flowers. [16c: from French *jonquille*]

josh *verb, tr & intr, informal, orig N Am* to tease.

joss-stick *noun* a stick of dried scented paste, burnt as incense. [19c: from pidgin Chinese *joss* household god]

jostle *verb* **1** *intr* to push and shove. **2** to push against (someone) roughly. **3** *intr* (*usu* **jostle for sth**) to compete aggressively for it. [14c: from **joust**]

jot *noun* (*usu with negatives*) the least bit: *not a jot of sympathy*. ▸ *verb* (***jotted, jotting***) (**jot sth down**) to write it down hastily. [16c: from *iota* the Greek letter *i*, the smallest letter in the Greek alphabet]

jotter *noun* a school notebook for rough work and notes.

jotting *noun* (*usu* **jottings**) something jotted down.

joule /dʒuːl/ *noun, physics* (abbrev **J**) in the SI system: the unit of work and energy. [19c: named after James Joule, British natural philosopher]

journal *noun* **1** a magazine or periodical, eg one dealing with a specialized subject. **2** a diary in which one recounts one's daily activities. [14c: from Latin *diurnalis* daily]

journalese *noun, derog* the language, typically shallow and full of clichés and jargon, typically used in newspapers and magazines. [19c]

journalism *noun* the profession of writing for newspapers and magazines, or for radio and television. ▪ **journalist** *noun*. ▪ **journalistic** *adj*. [19c: from French *journalisme*; see **-ism**]

journey *noun* (**-*eys***) **1** a process of travelling from one place to another. **2** the distance covered by, or time taken for, a journey. ▸ *verb, intr* to make a journey. [13c: from French *journee* day, or a day's travelling]

journeyman *noun* a craftsman qualified in a particular trade and working for an employer.

joust *noun, hist* a contest between two knights on horseback armed with lances. ▸ *verb, intr* to take part in a joust. ▪ **jouster** *noun*. [13c: from French *jouster*]

Jove *noun* **Jupiter**. [14c: from Latin *Jupiter, Jovis* Jupiter]

IDIOMS **by Jove!** *Brit informal, old use* an exclamation expressing surprise or emphasis.

jovial *adj* good-humoured; merry; cheerful. ▪ **joviality** *noun*. ▪ **jovially** *adv*. [16c: from Latin *jovialis* relating to the planet **Jupiter**, believed to be a lucky influence]

jowl[1] *noun* **1** the lower jaw. **2** the cheek. ▪ **jowled** *adj, usu in compounds*: *heavy-jowled*. [16c: from Anglo-Saxon *ceafl* jaw]

jowl[2] *noun* (*usu* **jowls**) in humans: loose flesh under the chin; a pendulous double chin. [16c: from Anglo-Saxon *ceole* throat]

joy *noun* **1** a feeling of happiness; intense gladness. **2** someone or something that causes delight: *She's a joy to live with*. **3** *Brit informal* satisfaction; success: *Any joy at the enquiry desk?* [13c: from French *joie*]

joyful *adj* **1** happy; full of joy. **2** expressing or resulting in joy. ▪ **joyfully** *adv*. ▪ **joyfulness** *noun*.

joyous *adj* filled with, causing or showing joy. ▪ **joyously** *adv*. ▪ **joyousness** *noun*.

joyride *noun* a jaunt, esp a reckless drive in a stolen vehicle. ▸ *verb, intr* to go for such a jaunt. ▪ **joyrider** *noun*. ▪ **joyriding** *noun*. [20c: orig colloquial US]

joystick *noun, informal* **1** the controlling lever of an aircraft, machine etc. **2** *comput* a lever for controlling the movement of an image on a VDU screen.

JP *abbrev* justice of the peace.

JPEG /ˈdʒeɪpɛg/ *abbrev, comput* Joint Photographic Experts Group, a standard image file format.

Jr *or* **jr** *abbrev* Junior or junior: *John Smith, Jr*.

jubilant *adj* showing and expressing triumphant joy; rejoicing. ▪ **jubilantly** *adv*. [17c: from Latin *jubilare* to shout for joy]

jubilation *noun* triumphant rejoicing. [14c: from Latin *jubilatio*]

jubilee *noun* a special anniversary of a significant event, esp the 25th (**silver jubilee**) or 50th (**golden jubilee**). [14c: from French *jubile*]

Judaic *adj* relating to the Jews or Judaism.

Judaism /ˈdʒʊdeɪɪzəm/ *noun* the Jewish religion, based on a belief in one God, or way of life.

Judas *noun* a traitor, esp someone who betrays their friends. [15c: named after Judas Iscariot, who betrayed Jesus]

judder *verb, intr* to jolt, shake, shudder or vibrate. ▸ *noun* an intense jerking motion. [20c: perhaps from **shudder** + **jar**[2]]

judge *noun* **1** a public officer who hears and decides cases in a law court. **2** a person appointed to decide the winner of a contest. **3** someone qualified to assess something; someone who shows discrimination. ▸ *verb* **1** to try (a legal case) in a law court as a judge; to decide (questions of guiltiness, etc). **2** to decide the winner of (a contest). **3** *intr* to act as judge or adjudicator. **4** to assess; to form an opinion about (something or someone). **5** to consider or state (something to be the case), after consideration: *judged her fit to travel*. **6** to criticize (someone or something), esp severely; to condemn. [14c: from French *juge*]

judgement *or* **judgment** *noun* **1** the decision of a judge in a court of law. **2** the act or process of judging. **3** the ability to make wise or sensible decisions; good sense: *I value his judgement*. **4** an opinion: *in my judgement*. [13c: from French *jugement*]

IDIOMS **against one's better judgement** contrary to what one believes to be the sensible course. **pass judgement on sb** *or* **sth** to give an opinion about them.

judgemental *or* **judgmental** *adj* apt to pass judgement, esp to make moral judgements.

judicature /ˈdʒuːdɪkətʃə(r), dʒʊˈdɪ-/ *noun* **1** the administration of justice by legal trial. **2** the office of judge. **3** a body of judges. **4** a court or system of courts. [16c: from Latin *judicatura*]

judicial *adj* relating or referring to a court of law, judges or the decisions of judges. ▪ **judicially** *adv*. [14c: from Latin *judicialis*]

judiciary *noun* (**-*ies***) **1** the branch of government concerned with the legal system and the administration of justice. **2** a country's body of judges. [16c: from Latin *judiciarius* relating to the law courts]

judicious *adj* shrewd, sensible, wise or tactful. ▪ **judiciously** *adv*. [16c: from Latin *judicium* judgement]

judo *noun* a Japanese sport and physical discipline based on unarmed self-defence techniques, developed from **ju-jitsu**. ▪ **judoist** *noun*. [19c: Japanese, from *ju* gentleness + *do* art]

jug *noun* **1** a deep container for liquids, with a handle and a shaped lip for pouring. **2** (*also* **jugful**) the amount a jug holds. **3** *slang* prison.

juggernaut *noun* **1** *Brit informal* a very large articulated lorry. **2** a mighty force sweeping away and destroying everything in its path. [19c: named after the gigantic chariot of the Hindu god, Jagannatha]

juggle *verb* **1** to keep several objects simultaneously in the air by skilful throwing and catching. **2** (*also* **juggle with sth**) to adjust (facts or figures) to create a misleading impression. ▪ **juggler** *noun*. ▪ **juggling** *noun, adj*. [14c: from French *jogler* to act as jester]

jugular *noun, anatomy* (*also* **jugular vein**) any of several veins that carry deoxygenated blood from the head to the heart. [16c: from Latin *jugulum* throat]

juice *noun* **1** the liquid or sap from fruit or vegetables. **2** a natural fluid in the body: *digestive juices*. **3** *slang* power or fuel, esp electricity or petrol. **4** *US slang* alcoholic drink. ▸ *verb* to squeeze juice from (a fruit, etc). [13c: from French *jus*]

juicer *or* **juice extractor** *noun* a device for extracting the juice from fruit and vegetables.

juicy *adj* (**-*ier*, -*iest***) **1** full of juice; rich and succulent. **2** *informal* of gossip: intriguing; spicy. ▪ **juiciness** *noun*.

ju-jitsu *or* **jiu-jitsu** /dʒuːˈdʒɪtsuː/ *noun* a martial art founded on the ancient Japanese system of combat and self-defence without weapons. [19c: from Japanese *ju* gentleness + *jutsu* art]

jujube /ˈdʒuːdʒuːb/ *noun* a soft fruit-flavoured sweet made with gelatine. [14c: from Latin *jujuba*]

jukebox *noun* a coin-operated machine that plays the record or CD one selects. [20c: from Gullah (a W African language) *juke* disorderly + **box**[1] (*noun* sense 3a)]

Jul. *abbrev* July.

julep /ˈdʒuːlɪp/ *noun* **1** a sweet drink, often a medicated one. **2** (*also* **mint julep**) esp in N America: an iced drink of spirits and sugar, flavoured esp with mint. [14c: from Persian *gulab* rosewater]

Julian calendar *noun* the calendar introduced by Julius Caesar in 46 BC, with a year of 365 days and 366 every leap year or centenary year. See also **Gregorian calendar**.

julienne /dʒuːlɪˈɛn/ *noun* a clear soup, with shredded vegetables. ▸ *adj* of vegetables: in thin strips; shredded. [19c: from the French personal name]

July *noun* (abbrev **Jul.**) the seventh month of the year. [13c: from Latin *Julius mensis* month of Julius Caesar]

jumble *verb* **1** to mix or confuse (things or people), physically or mentally. **2** to throw (things) together untidily. ▸ *noun* **1** a confused mass. **2** unwanted possessions collected, or suitable, for a jumble sale. [16c]

jumble sale *noun* a sale of unwanted possessions, eg used clothing, usu to raise money for charity.

jumbo *informal, adj* extra-large. ▸ *noun* a jumbo jet. [18c: prob from the name of an elephant exhibited in London in the 1880s]

jumbo jet *noun, informal* the popular name for a large wide-bodied jet airliner.

jump *verb* **1** *intr* to spring off the ground, pushing off with the feet. **2** *intr* to leap or bound. **3** to get over or across (something) by jumping. **4** to make (esp a horse) leap. **5** *intr* of prices, levels, etc: to rise abruptly. **6** *intr* to make a startled movement. **7** *intr* to twitch, jerk or bounce. **8** *tr & intr* to omit or skip (something): *jump the next chapter*. **9** *informal* to pounce on someone or something. **10** *N Am, informal* to board and travel on (esp a train) without paying. **11** *informal* of a car: to pass through (a red traffic light). ▸ *noun* **1** an act of jumping. **2** an obstacle to be jumped, esp a fence to be jumped by a horse. **3** the height or distance jumped: *a jump of two metres*. **4** a jumping contest: *the long jump*. **5** a sudden rise in amount, cost or value: *a jump in prices*. **6** an abrupt change or move. **7** a startled movement; a start: *gave a jump of surprise*. [16c]

IDIOMS **jump down sb's throat** *informal* to snap at them impatiently. **jump the gun** to get off one's mark too soon; to act prematurely; to take an unfair advantage. **jump the queue** to get ahead of one's turn.

PHRASAL VERBS **jump at sth** to accept it eagerly. **jump on sb** to attack them physically or verbally.

jumped-up *adj, derog, informal* having an inflated view of one's importance; cocky; arrogant.

jumper *noun* **1** a knitted garment for the top half of the body. *N Am equivalent* **sweater**. See also **pullover**. **2** *N Am* a pinafore dress. [19c: from old word *jump* a short coat]

jump jet *noun* a jet aircraft capable of taking off and landing vertically.

jump leads *plural noun* two electrical cables used to start a motor vehicle with a flat battery by connecting them to the charged battery of another vehicle and the flat battery.

jump-start *verb* to start the engine of (a motor vehicle) that has a weak or flat battery by using **jump leads** or by pushing it and engaging the gears while it is moving. See also **bump-start**. ▸ *noun* the act of jump-starting a vehicle.

jumpsuit *noun* a one-piece garment combining trousers and top.

jumpy *adj* (**-*ier*, -*iest***) nervy; anxious.

Jun. *abbrev* **1** June. **2** Junior.

jun. *abbrev* junior.

junction *noun* a place where roads or railway lines meet or cross; an intersection. [18c: from Latin *junctio* joining]

juncture *noun* **1** a joining; a union. **2** a point in time, esp a critical one. [16c: from Latin *junctura* connection]

June *noun* (abbrev **Jun.**) the sixth month of the year. [Anglo-Saxon as *Junius*]

jungle *noun* **1** an area of dense vegetation, esp in a tropical region. **2** a mass of complexities difficult to penetrate: *the jungle of building regulations.* **3** a complex or hostile environment where toughness is needed for survival: *the concrete jungle.* **4** fast rhythmic music characterized by very low bass lines and complex percussion breaks (see **break** *noun* sense 12). [18c: from Hindi *jangal* desert or waste or forest]

junior (abbrev **Jr**, **Jnr**, **jnr**, **Jun.** or **jun.**) *adj* **1 a** low or lower in rank; **b** younger. **2** relating or belonging to, or for, schoolchildren aged between 7 and 11: *junior schools.* **3** used after the name of a person with the same forename as their father. **4** denoting a weight category in boxing, etc that is slightly less than one of the standard categories: *junior welterweight.* ▸ *noun* **1** a person of low or lower rank in a profession, organization, etc. **2** a pupil in a junior school. **3** *N Am, esp US* a third-year college or high-school student. **4** a person younger than the one in question: *She's three years his junior.* **5** (*often* **Junior**) *N Am, esp US* a name used to address or refer to the son of a family. [16c: Latin, meaning 'younger']

juniper *noun* an evergreen coniferous tree or shrub with purple berry-like cones, oils from which are used to flavour gin. [14c: from Latin *juniperus*]

junk[1] *noun, informal* **1** worthless or rejected material; rubbish. **2** nonsense. **3** *slang* narcotic drugs, esp heroin. ▸ *verb, informal* **1** to treat (something) as junk. **2** to discard or abandon (something) as useless. [15c: from *jonke* pieces of old rope]

junk[2] *noun* a flat-bottomed square-sailed boat, with high forecastle and poop, from the Far East. [17c: from Portuguese *junco*]

junket /ˈdʒʌŋkɪt/ *noun* **1** a dessert made from sweetened and curdled milk. **2** a feast or celebration. **3** a trip made by a government official, businessman, etc which they do not pay for themselves. ▸ *verb, intr* to feast, celebrate or make merry. [14c: from French *jonquette* a rush basket]

junk food *noun* food with little nutritional value.

junkie *or* **junky** *noun* (*-ies*) **1** *slang* a drug addict or drug-pusher. **2** *informal* someone who is addicted to something: *a TV junkie.* [20c: from **junk**[1] (*noun* sense 3)]

junk mail *noun* unsolicited mail, such as advertising circulars, etc.

junta /ˈdʒʌntə, ˈhʊnta/ *noun, derog* a group or faction, usu of army officers, in control of a country after a coup d'état. [17c: Spanish, 'meeting' or 'council']

Jupiter *noun, astron* the fifth planet from the Sun, and the largest in the solar system. [13c: named after Jupiter, the chief Roman god]

Jurassic *geol, noun* in the Mesozoic era, the period of geological time between the Triassic and Cretaceous periods, lasting from about 210 to 140 million years ago. ▸ *adj* belonging or relating to this period. [19c: named after the Jura, a limestone mountain range in E France]

juridical *or* **juridic** *adj* relating or referring to the law or the administration of justice. ▪ **juridically** *adv.* [16c: from Latin *juridicus* relating to justice]

jurisdiction *noun* **1** the right or authority to apply laws and administer justice. **2** the district or area over which this authority extends. **3** authority generally. [13c: from Latin *jurisdictio* administration of justice]

jurisprudence *noun* **1** knowledge of or skill in law. **2** a speciality within law: *medical jurisprudence.* [17c: from Latin *jus* law + *prudentia* wisdom]

jurist *noun* **1** an expert in the science of law. **2** *US* a lawyer. [15c: from French *juriste*]

juror *noun* **1** a member of a jury in a court of law. **2** someone who takes an oath.

jury *noun* (*-ies*) **1** a body of people sworn to give an honest verdict on the evidence presented to a court of law on a particular case. **2** a group of people selected to judge a contest. [14c: from French *juree* something sworn]

just[1] *adj* **1** fair; impartial. **2** reasonable; based on justice. **3** deserved. ▪ **justly** *adv.* ▪ **justness** *noun.* [14c: from Latin *justus* just, upright or equitable]

just[2] *adv* **1** exactly; precisely. **2** a short time before: *He had just gone.* **3** at this or that very moment: *was just leaving.* **4** and no earlier, more, etc: *only just enough.* **5** barely; narrowly: *The bullet just missed him.* **6** only; merely; simply: *just a brief note.* **7** *informal* used for emphasis: *That's just not true.* **8** *informal* absolutely: *just marvellous.* [14c: from Latin *justus* right or proper]

IDIOMS **just about** almost: *I'm just about ready.* **just about to do sth** on the point of doing it. **just a minute** *or* **second**, *etc* an instruction to wait a short while. **just now** at this particular moment. **just so 1** a formula of agreement. **2** neat and tidy: *They like everything just so.* **just the same** nevertheless.

justice *noun* **1** the quality of being just; fairness. **2** the quality of being reasonable. **3** the law, or administration of or conformity to the law: *a miscarriage of justice.* **4** (**Justice**) the title of a judge. **5** a justice of the peace. **6** *N Am, esp US* a judge. [Anglo-Saxon as *justise*]**bring sb to justice** to arrest and try them.

justice of the peace *noun* (***justices of the peace***) a person authorized to judge minor criminal cases. Often shortened to **JP**.

justifiable *adj* able to be justified. ▪ **justifiably** *adv.*

justify *verb* (*-ies, -ied*) **1** to prove (something) to be right, just or reasonable. **2** *printing* to arrange (text) so that the margins are even-edged. ▪ **justification** *noun.* [13c: from Latin *justus* just + *facere* to make]

jut *verb* (***jutted, jutting***) *intr* (*also* **jut out**) to stick out; to project. ▪ **jutting** *adj.* [16c: variant of **jet**[2]]

jute *noun* fibre from certain types of tropical bark, used for making sacking, etc. [18c: from Bengali *jhuta*]

juvenile *adj* **1** young; youthful. **2** suitable for young people. **3** *derog* childish; immature. ▸ *noun* a young person. [17c: from Latin *juvenilis* youthful]

juvenile delinquent *noun, dated* a young person who is guilty of an offence, esp vandalism or antisocial behaviour. ▪ **juvenile delinquency** *noun.*

juxtapose *verb* to place (things) side by side. ▪ **juxtaposition** *noun.* [19c: from Latin *juxta* beside]

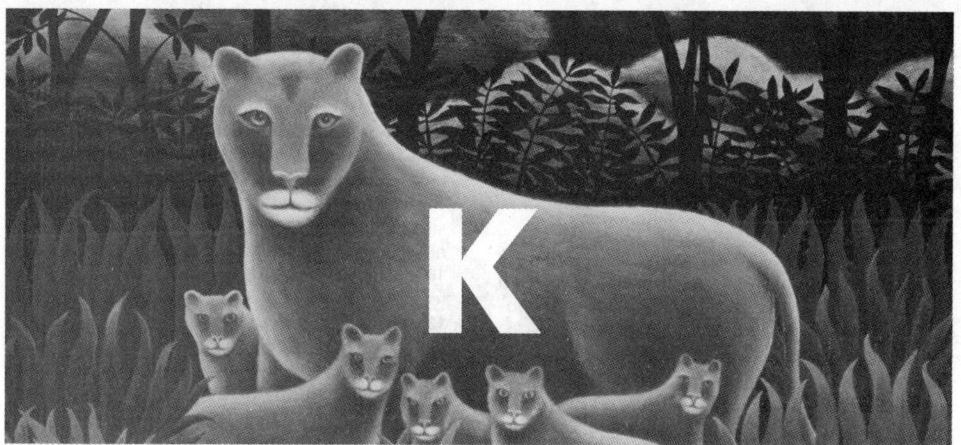

K[1] *or* **k** *noun* (***Ks, K's*** *or* ***k's***) **1** the eleventh letter of the English alphabet. **2** the speech sound represented by this letter.

K[2] *noun* (*pl* ***K***) *informal* **1** one thousand, esp £1000. **2** *comput* a unit of memory equal to 1024 bits, bytes or words. [20c: from **kilo-**]

K[3] *abbrev* **1** *physics* kelvin, the kelvin scale or a degree on the kelvin scale. **2** kilo or kilo-. **3** *comput* kilobyte.

K[4] *symbol* **1** *chem: kalium* (Latin), potassium. **2** *chess* king.

k *abbrev* **1** karat or **carat**. **2** kilo or kilo-.

k *symbol, chem, physics* constant.

kabala, kabbala *or* **kabbalah** see **cabbala**

kadi see **cadi**

kaftan see **caftan**

kagoule see **cagoule**

kai /kaɪ/ *noun, NZ* **1** food. **2** a meal. [19c: Maori]

kail see **kale**

Kaiser /ˈkaɪzə(r)/ *noun, hist* any of the emperors of Germany, Austria or the Holy Roman Empire. [16c: German, from Latin *Caesar*, family name of the earliest Roman emperors]

kakapo /ˈkɑːkəpoʊ/ *noun, zool* a nocturnal flightless parrot, resembling an owl, found only in the rainforests of New Zealand. [19c: from Maori *kaka* parrot + *po* night]

kalashnikov *noun* a type of submachine-gun manufactured in the Soviet Union. [20c: named after its Russian inventor, M T Kalashnikov]

kale *or* **kail** *noun* a variety of cabbage with loose wrinkled or curled leaves that do not form a head. [Anglo-Saxon as *cawl*]

kaleidoscope *noun* **1** an optical toy consisting of long mirrors fixed at an angle to each other inside a tube containing small pieces of coloured plastic, glass or paper, so that multiple reflections produce random regular patterns when the tube is viewed through an eyepiece at one end and rotated or shaken. **2** any colourful and constantly changing scene or succession of events. ▪ **kaleidoscopic** *adj*. [19c: from Greek *kalos* beautiful + *eidos* form + *skopeein* to view]

kalends see **calends**

kalif see **caliph**

kamikaze /kamɪˈkɑːzɪ/ *noun* **1** in World War II: a Japanese plane loaded with explosives that the pilot would deliberately crash into an enemy target. **2** the pilot of this kind of plane. ▸ *adj* **1** relating or referring to such an attack or the pilot concerned. **2** *informal* of exploits, missions, etc: suicidally dangerous. [20c: Japanese, literally 'divine wind']

Kampuchean *adj, hist* belonging or relating to Kampuchea or its inhabitants. ▸ *noun* a citizen or inhabitant of, or person born in, Kampuchea. [1970s: Kampuchea was the name given to Cambodia by the Khmer Rouge government from 1976 to 1989]

kangaroo *noun* a marsupial mammal with a thick tail and large powerful hind legs adapted for leaping, native to Australia, Tasmania and New Guinea. [18c: from *gangurru* in an Australian Aboriginal language]

kangaroo court *noun* a court that has no legal status and which is usu perceived as delivering unfair or biased judgements.

kaolin *or* **kaoline** *noun* a soft white clay used for making fine porcelain, and medicinally to treat diarrhoea and vomiting. Also called **china clay**. [18c: from Chinese *Gaoling*, literally 'high ridge', the name of a mountain where it was mined]

kapellmeister /kəˈpɛlmaɪstə(r)/ *noun* the director of an orchestra or choir, esp in the 18c in the household of a German prince. [19c: from German *Kapelle* chapel or orchestra + *Meister* master]

kapok /ˈkeɪpɒk/ *noun* the light waterproof silky fibres that surround the seeds of certain trees, used for padding and stuffing eg pillows. [18c: from Malay *kapoq* the name of the tree]

kappa *noun* the tenth letter of the Greek alphabet.

kaput /kəˈpʊt/ *adj, informal* ruined; destroyed. [19c: from German *kaputt* broken]

karakul *or* **caracul** /ˈkɑːrəkuːl/ *noun* **1** (*often* **Karakul**) a breed of sheep, native to central Asia, which has coarse black, brown or grey wool. **2** the soft curly fleece of a lamb of this breed. [19c: named after Kara Kul, a lake in central Asia]

karaoke /karɪˈoʊkɪ/ *noun* a form of entertainment in which amateur performers sing pop songs to the accompaniment of pre-recorded music. [20c: Japanese, literally 'empty orchestra']

karat see **carat**

karate /kəˈrɑːtɪ/ *noun* a system of unarmed self-defence, using blows and kicks, now a popular combative sport. [20c: Japanese, literally 'empty hand']

karma *noun, Buddhism, Hinduism* **1** the sum of someone's lifetime's actions, seen as governing their fate in the next life. **2** destiny; fate. **3** *popularly* an aura or quality that is perceived to be given off by someone or something, or by a place. [19c: from Sanskrit *karma* act or deed]

kart *noun, informal* a **go-kart.** ▪ **karting** *noun.* [20c]

kasbah *or* **casbah** /'kazbɑː/ (*sometimes* **Kasbah** *or* **Casbah**) *noun* **1** a castle or fortress in a N African town. **2** the area around it. [18c: from dialect *kasba* fortress]

kauri /'kaʊərɪ/ *noun* **1** (*in full* **kauri pine**) a tall coniferous tree, native to SE Asia and Australasia. **2** (*in full* **kauri gum**) the brownish resin of this tree, used mainly in varnishes and in the manufacture of linoleum. [19c: Maori]

kayak /'kaɪak/ *noun* **1** a sealskin-covered canoe for one person used by the Inuit. **2** a similar craft used in the sport of canoeing. [18c: from Inuit *qayaq*]

kazi /'kɑːzɪ/ *noun, slang* a lavatory. [Early 20c: from Italian *casa* house]

kazoo *noun* a crude wind instrument which makes a buzzing sound when blown. [19c: imitating the sound]

KB *abbrev, comput* kilobyte.

KBE *abbrev* Knight Commander of the Order of the British Empire.

kbit *abbrev, comput* kilobit.

kbyte *abbrev, comput* kilobyte. Usually called **KB**, **K**.

KC *abbrev* King's Counsel.

kc *abbrev* kilocycle.

kcal *abbrev* kilocalorie.

KCB *abbrev* Knight Commander of the Order of the Bath.

kebab *noun* (*in full* **shish kebab**) a dish of small pieces of meat and vegetable grilled on a skewer. Compare **doner kebab**. [17c: from Arabic *kabab* roast meat]

kecks see **keks**

kedge *verb, tr & intr* to manoeuvre by means of a hawser attached to a light anchor. ▸ *noun* a light anchor used for kedging. [17c]

kedgeree *noun, cookery* a European, but esp British, dish, now usu a mixture of rice, fish and eggs. [17c: from Hindi *khichri* a dish of rice and sesame]

keek *Scot & N Eng, noun* a peep. ▸ *verb, intr* to take a peep. [14c: prob from Dutch *kiken* to look]

keel *noun* **1** the timber or metal strut extending from stem to stern along the base of a ship, from which the hull is built up. **2** *zool* the projection of bone from the sternum to which the flight muscles of birds are attached. [14c: from Norse *kjölr*]

IDIOMS **on an even keel** calm and steady.

PHRASAL VERBS **keel over 1** of a ship: to tip over sideways. **2** *informal* to fall over, eg in a faint.

keelhaul *verb* **1** to drag someone under the keel of a ship from one side to the other, as a naval punishment. **2** to rebuke someone severely. [17c]

keelson see **kelson**

keen[1] *adj* **1** eager; willing. **2** of competition or rivalry, etc: fierce. **3** of the wind: bitter. **4** of a blade, etc: sharp. **5** of the mind or senses: quick; acute. **6** of prices: competitive. ▪ **keenness** *noun.* [Anglo-Saxon *cene* fierce]

IDIOMS **keen on sb** *or* **sth** enthusiastic about them or it; fond of them or it.

keen[2] *verb, tr & intr* to lament or mourn in a loud wailing voice. ▸ *noun* a lament for the dead. [19c: from Irish *caoine* lament]

keep *verb* (***kept***) **1** to have; to possess. **2** to continue to have something; not to part with it. **3** to maintain or retain: *keep one's temper.* **4** to store. **5** *tr & intr* to remain or cause something to remain in a certain state, position, place, etc. **6** *intr* to continue or be frequently doing something: *keep smiling.* **7** of a shopkeeper, etc: to have something regularly in stock. **8** to own and look after (an animal, etc): *keep hens.* **9** to own or run (a shop, boarding-house, etc). **10** to look after something: *keep this for me.* **11** *intr* of food: to remain fit to be eaten: *This cake keeps well.* **12** to maintain (a record, diary, accounts, etc). **13** to preserve (a secret). **14** to stick to (a promise or appointment). **15** to celebrate (a festival, etc) in the traditional way; to follow (a custom). **16** to support someone financially. ▸ *noun* **1** the cost of one's food and other daily expenses: *earn one's keep.* **2** the central tower or stronghold in a Norman castle. [Anglo-Saxon *cepan* to guard, observe or watch]

IDIOMS **for keeps** *informal* permanently; for good. **keep to oneself** to avoid the company of others.

PHRASAL VERBS **keep at sth** to persevere at or persist in it. **keep sth back** to conceal information, etc. **keep sb down** to oppress them; to prevent their development or progress, etc. **keep sth down 1** to control or limit (prices, development, etc). **2** to manage not to vomit (food, etc). **keep off sth 1** to avoid (a harmful food, awkward topic, etc). **2** to stay away from it: *Keep off my books!* **keep sb on** to continue to employ them. **keep on at sb** to nag or harass them. **keep to sth** not to leave it: *Keep to the path.* **keep sth up 1** to prevent (eg spirits, morale, etc) from falling. **2** to maintain (a habit, friendship, pace, etc). **3** to maintain (a house, garden, etc) in good condition. **keep up with sb 1** not to be left behind by them. **2** to maintain the pace or standard set by them.

keeper *noun* **1** a person who looks after something, eg a collection in a museum. **2** a person who looks after animals or birds in captivity. **3** a gamekeeper. **4** *informal* a goalkeeper. **5** a wicketkeeper.

keep fit *noun* a series or system of exercises intended to improve the circulation and respiratory system, suppleness and stamina, etc. *as adj*: *keep-fit classes.*

keeping *noun* care or charge.

IDIOMS **in keeping with sth** in harmony with it.

keepsake *noun* something kept in memory of the giver, or of a particular event or place.

kefuffle see **carfuffle**

keg *noun* a small barrel, usu for transporting and storing beer. [17c: from Norse *kaggi*]

keks *or* **kecks** *plural noun, informal* trousers.

kelim see **kilim**

kelp *noun* any large brown seaweed that grows below the low-tide mark. [14c as *culp*]

kelson *or* **keelson** *noun* a timber fixed along a ship's keel for strength. [17c: from German *kielswin* keel swine, ie 'keel timber']

Kelt see **Celt**

kelt *noun* a salmon that has just spawned. [14c]

kelter see **kilter**

Keltic see **Celtic**

kelvin *noun, physics* (abbrev **K**) in the SI system: a unit of thermodynamic or **absolute temperature**. [19c: named after the UK physicist, Lord Kelvin]

Kelvin scale *noun* a thermodynamic temperature scale starting at **absolute zero**.

ken *verb* (***kent*** *or* ***kenned, kenning***) *Scot & N Eng dialect* **1** to know. **2** to understand. ▸ *noun* range of knowledge: *beyond our ken.* [Anglo-Saxon *cennan*]

kendo *noun* a Japanese art of fencing using bamboo staves or sometimes real swords, while observing strict ritual. [20c: Japanese, literally 'sword way']

kennel *noun* **1** a small shelter for a dog. **2** (**kennels**) an establishment where dogs are boarded or bred. ▸ *verb* (***kennelled, kennelling***; *N Am* ***kenneled, kenneling***) to put or keep (an animal) in a kennel. [14c: from Latin *canis* dog]

kepi /'keɪpiː/ *noun* a French military cap with a flat circular crown and horizontal straight-edged peak. [19c: from French *képi*]

kept *past tense, past participle of* **keep**

keratin *noun, biochem* a tough fibrous protein forming the main component of hair, nails, claws, horns, feathers and the dead outer layers of skin cells.

kerb *or* (*esp N Am*) **curb** *noun* **1** the row of stones or concrete edging forming the edge of a pavement. **2** a kerbstone. [17c variant of **curb**]

kerbstone *noun* one of the stones used to form a kerb.

kerchief *noun* a square of cloth or a scarf for wearing over the head or round the neck. [13c: from French *cuevrechief*]

kerfuffle see **carfuffle**

kermes /'kɜːmiːz/ *noun* **1** the dried bodies of the female scale insect used as a red dye. **2** (*also* **kermes oak**) a small evergreen oak tree on which the insects breed. [16c: from Persian and Arabic *qirmiz*]

kernel *noun* **1** the inner part of a seed, eg the edible part of a nut. **2** in cereal plants such as corn: the entire grain or seed. **3** the important, essential part of anything. [Anglo-Saxon *cyrnel*]

kerosine *or* **kerosene** *noun* **1** a combustible oily mixture of hydrocarbons obtained mainly by distillation of petroleum, used as a fuel for jet aircraft, domestic heating systems and lamps, and as a solvent. **2** *N Am* **paraffin**. [19c: from Greek *keros* wax]

kestrel *noun* a small falcon with a long tail and broad pointed wings. [16c as *castrell*]

ketch *noun* a small two-masted sailing boat, the foremast being the taller. [15c as *cache*; related to **catch**]

ketchup *noun, popularly* a thick sauce made from tomatoes, vinegar, spices, etc. [18c: from Malay *kechap*]

ketone *noun, chem* any of a class of organic chemical compounds that are formed by the oxidation of secondary alcohols. [19c: from German *Keton*]

kettle *noun* **1** a container with a spout, lid and handle, for boiling water. **2** a metal container for heating liquids or cooking something in liquid. ▪ **kettleful** *noun*. [Anglo-Saxon *cetel*]

IDIOMS **a different kettle of fish** *informal* an entirely different matter. **a pretty** *or* **fine kettle of fish** *informal* an awkward situation.

kettledrum *noun* a large copper or brass cauldron-shaped drum with a skin stretched over the top, tuned by adjusting screws that alter the tension of the skin. ▪ **kettle-drummer** *noun*.

key[1] *noun* **1** a device for opening or closing a lock, or for winding up, turning, tuning, tightening or loosening. **2** one of a series of buttons or levers pressed to sound the notes on a musical instrument, or to print or display a character on a computer, typewriter, calculator, etc. **3** a system of musical notes related to one another in a scale. **4** pitch, tone or style: *spoke in a low key.* **5** something that provides an answer or solution. **6** a means of achievement: *the key to success.* **7** a table explaining signs and symbols used on a map, etc. **8** a pin or wedge for fixing something. **9** *biol* a taxonomic system for distinguishing similar species. ▸ *adj* centrally important: *key questions.* ▸ *verb* **1** (*also* **key sth in**) to enter (data) into a computer, calculator, etc by means of a keyboard. **2** to lock or fasten something with a key. [Anglo-Saxon *cæg*]

IDIOMS **keyed up** *informal* excited; tense; anxious. **under lock and key 1** safely stored. **2** in prison.

key[2] *or* **cay** /keɪ, kiː/ *noun* a small low island or reef formed of sand, coral, rock or mud, esp one off the coast of Florida. [17c: from Spanish *cayo*]

keyboard *noun* **1** the set of keys on a piano, etc. **2** the bank of keys for operating a typewriter or computer. **3** *music* esp in jazz, rock, etc: an electronic musical instrument with a keyboard. ▸ *verb* **1** *intr* to operate the keyboard of a computer. **2** to set (text) using a computer keyboard. ▪ **keyboarder** *noun*.

keyhole *noun* **1** the hole through which a key is inserted into a lock. **2** any small hole similar to this.

keyhole surgery *noun* a technique that involves internal surgical operations being performed with minimal external excision through a small opening.

key money *noun* a payment in addition to rent, demanded in return for the grant of a tenancy.

keynote *noun* **1** the note on which a musical scale or key is based; the **tonic**. **2** a central theme, principle or controlling thought. ▸ *adj* of fundamental importance.

keypad *noun* a small device with push-button controls, eg a TV remote control unit or a pocket calculator.

key ring *noun* a ring for keeping keys on.

key signature *noun, music* the sharps and flats shown on the stave at the start of a piece of music indicating the key it is to be played in.

keystone *noun, archit* the central supporting stone at the high point of an arch.

keystroke *noun* a single press of a key on a keyboard.

keyword *noun* **1** a word that sums up or gives an indication of the nature of the passage in which it occurs. **2** *comput* a group of letters or numbers that is used to identify a database record.

KG *abbrev* Knight of the Order of the Garter.

kg *abbrev* kilogram or kilograms.

KGB *abbrev*: *Komitet gosudarstvennoi bezopasnosti* (Russian), Committee of State Security, the former Soviet and then Russian secret police. [20c]

khaki /'kɑːkɪ/ *noun* **1** a dull brownish-yellow or brownish-green colour. **2 a** a cloth of this colour; **b** military uniform made of such cloth. [19c: Urdu and Persian, meaning 'dusty']

khalif see **caliph**

Khalsa /'kalsə/ *noun* the order of baptized Sikhs. [18c: Urdu]

khan /kɑːn/ *noun* the title of a ruler or prince in central Asia. ▪ **khanate** *noun*. [14c: related to Turkish *kagan* ruler]

Khmer /kmɛə(r)/ *adj* belonging or relating to the Khmer region of SE Asia, or to Cambodia, a republic in SE Asia, or to their inhabitants, or their language.

▸ *noun* **1** a citizen or inhabitant of, or person born in, the Khmer region or Cambodia. **2** the language spoken there. [19c: the local name for this area and country]

Khmer Rouge /ruːʒ/ *noun, hist* a Communist guerrilla movement formerly active in Cambodia.

kHz *abbrev* kilohertz.

kibble *verb* to grind (cereal, etc) fairly coarsely. [18c]

kibbutz /kɪ'bʊts/ *noun* (***kibbutzim*** /-'siːm/) in Israel: a communal farm or other concern owned and run jointly as a co-operative by its workers. ▪ **kibbutznik** *noun* someone who lives and works on a kibbutz. [20c: from Modern Hebrew *kibbus* a gathering]

kibosh *or* **kybosh** /'kaɪbɒʃ/ *informal, noun* rubbish; nonsense. [19c]

IDIOMS **put the kibosh on sth** to put an end to it; to ruin it.

kick *verb* **1** to hit with the foot. **2** to propel something with the foot: *kicks the ball.* **3** *intr* to strike out or thrust with one or both feet, eg when swimming, struggling, etc. **4** *tr & intr* esp in dancing: to jerk (the leg) vigorously or swing it high. **5** *intr* of a gun, etc: to recoil when fired. **6** *intr* (*sometimes* **kick against sth**) to resist it: *kick against discipline.* **7** to get rid of (a habit, etc). ▸ *noun* **1** a blow or fling with the foot. **2** *dancing, gymnastics, etc* a swing of the leg: *high kicks.* **3** *swimming* any of various leg movements. **4** the recoil of a gun, etc after firing. **5** *informal* a thrill of excitement: *He gets a kick out of violence.* **6** *informal* the powerful effect of certain drugs or strong drink: *That fruit punch has quite a kick.* [14c as *kiken*]

IDIOMS **for kicks** for thrills. **kick in the teeth** *informal* a humiliating snub. **kick the bucket** *informal* to die.

PHRASAL VERBS **kick about** *or* **around** *informal* **1** to lie around unused and neglected: *The old game's kicking around in the attic.* **2** to be idle: *kicking about with his mates.* **kick in** to take effect: *as the effects of the pay freeze kick in commitment decreases.* **kick off 1** to start, or restart, a football game by kicking the ball away from the centre. **2** *informal* (*also* **kick sth off**) to begin a discussion or other activity involving several people. **kick sth off** *informal* to begin (a discussion, etc).

kickback *noun* part of a sum of money received that is paid to someone else for help or favours already received or to come, esp if this is illegally given.

kickboxing *noun* a martial art in which the combatants kick with bare feet and punch with gloved fists.

kick-off *noun* **1** the start or restart of a football match. **2** the first kick in a game of football that starts, or restarts, the match. **3** *informal* the start of anything.

kickstand *noun* a metal device attached to a bicycle or motorcycle, etc, which is kicked down into position to hold the vehicle upright when it is parked.

kick-start *noun* **1** (*also* **kick-starter**) a pedal on a motorcycle that is kicked vigorously downwards to start the engine. **2** the starting of an engine with this pedal. ▸ *verb* **1** to start (a motorcycle) using this pedal. **2** to get something moving; to give an advantageous, and sometimes sudden, impulse to something.

kid[1] *noun* **1** *informal* a child; a young person. **2** a young goat, antelope or other related animal. **3** the smooth soft leather made from the skin of such an animal. ▸ *adj, informal* younger: *my kid sister.* ▸ *verb* (***kidded, kidding***) *intr* of a goat, etc: to give birth. [13c as *kide*]

kid[2] *verb* (***kidded, kidding***) *informal* (*sometimes* **kid sb on** *or* **along**) **1** to fool or deceive them, esp lightheartedly or in fun. **2** *intr* to bluff; to pretend. ▪ **kidder** *noun.* [19c: perhaps from **kid**[1]]

kiddie *or* **kiddy** *noun* (***-ies***) *informal* a small child. [19c: from **kid**[1]]

kid glove *noun* a glove made of kidskin.

IDIOMS **handle sb with kid gloves** to treat them with special care or caution.

kidnap *verb* (***kidnapped, kidnapping***; *N Am* ***kidnaped, kidnaping***) to seize and hold someone prisoner illegally, usu demanding a ransom for their release. ▪ **kidnapper** *noun.* [17c: from **kid**[1] + obsolete *nap* to steal]

kidney *noun* (***-eys***) **1** *anatomy* either of a pair of organs at the back of the abdomen whose function is to remove waste products from the blood, and excrete them from the body in the form of urine. See also **renal**. **2** animal kidneys as food. [14c as *kidenei*]

kidney bean *noun* a dark-red kidney-shaped seed, eaten as a vegetable.

kidney machine *noun, med* a machine that removes toxic waste products, by dialysis, from the blood of someone whose kidneys do not function properly.

kidology *noun, informal* the art of deceiving or bluffing. [20c: **kid**[2] + Greek *logos* word or reason]

kilim *or* **kelim** /kɪ'liːm/ *noun* a woven rug without any pile. [19c: Turkish]

kill *verb* **1** *tr & intr* to cause the death of (an animal or person); to murder; to destroy someone or something. **2** *informal* to cause severe pain to someone: *My feet are killing me.* **3** *informal* to cause something to fail; to put an end to it: *how to kill a conversation.* **4** to defeat (a parliamentary bill); to veto (a proposal). **5** *informal* to deaden (pain, noise, etc). **6** to pass (time), esp aimlessly or wastefully, while waiting for some later event: *killing an hour in the pub before his train left.* **7** *informal, esp ironic* to exhaust or put a strain on someone: *Don't kill yourself doing unpaid overtime.* **8** *informal* to overwhelm someone with admiration, amazement, laughter, etc. ▸ *noun* **1** an act of killing. **2** the prey killed by any creature. **3** game killed. ▪ **killer** *noun* **1** a person or creature that kills. **2** a murderer. [13c as *cullen* or *killen*]

IDIOMS **kill oneself** *informal* to be reduced to helpless laughter: *It was so funny we were absolutely killing ourselves.* **kill two birds with one stone** to accomplish two things by one action.

killer whale *noun* a toothed whale, having a black body with white underparts and white patches on its head, and a narrow triangular dorsal fin similar to that of a shark.

killing *noun* an act of slaying. ▸ *adj, informal* **1** exhausting. **2** highly amusing. **3** deadly; fatal.

IDIOMS **make a killing** *informal* to make a large amount of money, esp from a single transaction.

killjoy *noun* someone who spoils the pleasure of others.

kiln *noun* a heated oven or furnace used for drying timber, grain or hops, or for firing bricks, pottery, etc. [Anglo-Saxon *cyln*]

kilo *noun* (symbol **k**) **1** a **kilogram**. **2** a **kilometre**.

kilo- *combining form* (abbrev **K** *or* **k**) **1** one thousand: *kilogram.* **2** *comput* when describing storage capacity: 1024 (2^{10}). In other contexts in computing it is used in sense 1. [From French]

kilobit *noun* (abbrev **Kbit**) *comput* a measure of computer data or memory, equal to 1024 **bits** (see **bit**[3]).

kilobyte *noun* (abbrev **KB, kbyte** *or* **K**) *comput* a unit of memory equal to 1024 **bytes**.

kilocalorie *noun* (abbrev **kcal**) a metric unit of heat or energy equal to 1000 calories, now replaced by the SI unit **kilojoule**.

kilocycle *noun* (abbrev **kc**) *old use* a **kilohertz**.

kilogram *or* **kilogramme** *noun* (abbrev **kg**) in the SI system: the base unit of measurement of mass, equal to 1000 grams or about 2.205 pounds.

kilohertz *noun* (*pl* ***kilohertz***) (abbrev **kHz**) an SI unit of frequency equal to 1000 **hertz** or 1000 cycles per second, used to measure the frequency of sound and radio waves. Formerly called **kilocycle**.

kilojoule *noun* (abbrev **kJ**) 1000 joules, an SI unit used to measure energy, work and heat, replacing the metric unit **kilocalorie** (1 kj = 0.2388 kcal).

kilolitre *or* (*US*) **kiloliter** *noun* (abbrev **kl**) a unit of measurement of volume, equal to 1000 litres.

kilometre *or* (*US*) **kilometer** *noun* (abbrev **km**) a unit of measurement of distance, equal to 1000 metres or about 0.62 miles. ▪ **kilometric** *adj*.

kiloton *or* **kilotonne** *noun* (abbrev **kt** *or* **kT**) a metric unit of explosive power equivalent to that of 1000 tonnes of TNT.

kilovolt *noun* (abbrev **kV**) an SI unit: 1000 volts.

kilowatt *noun* (abbrev **kW**) an SI unit of electrical power equal to 1000 watts or about 1.34 horsepower.

kilowatt hour *noun* (abbrev **kWh**) a commercial metric unit of electrical energy, based on the **watt**, equal to the energy consumed when an electrical appliance with a power of one kilowatt operates for one hour.

kilt *noun* **1** a pleated tartan knee-length wraparound skirt, traditionally worn by men as part of Scottish Highland dress. **2** any similar garment. [14c: related to Danish *kilte* to tuck up]

kilter *or* **kelter** *noun* good condition. [17c]
IDIOMS **out of kilter** not working properly.

kimono /kɪˈmoʊnoʊ/ *noun* **1** a long, loose, wide-sleeved Japanese garment fastened by a sash at the waist. **2** a dressing-gown, etc, imitating this in style. [19c: Japanese, meaning 'clothing']

kin *noun* **1** one's relatives. **2** people belonging to the same family. ▸ *adj* related: *kin to the duke*. [Anglo-Saxon *cynn*]

kind[1] *noun* **1** a group, class, sort, race or type. **2** a particular variety or a specimen belonging to a specific variety. **3** nature, character or distinguishing quality: *differ in kind*. [Anglo-Saxon *gecynd* nature]
IDIOMS **in kind 1** of payment: in goods instead of money. **2** of repayment or retaliation: in the same form as the treatment received. **kind of** *informal* somewhat; slightly: *kind of old-fashioned*. **nothing of the kind** not at all; completely the reverse. **of a kind 1** of the same sort: *three of a kind*. **2** of doubtful worth: *an explanation of a kind*.

kind[2] *adj* **1** friendly, helpful, generous or considerate. **2** warm; cordial: *kind regards*. ▪ **kindness** *noun*. [Anglo-Saxon *gecynde* in obsolete sense 'natural']

kindergarten *noun* a school for young children, usu those aged between 4 and 6. [19c: German, literally 'children's garden']

kindle *verb, tr & intr* **1** to start or make something, etc start burning. **2** of feelings: to stir or be stirred. ▪ **kindling** *noun* materials for starting a fire, eg dry twigs or leaves, sticks, etc. [13c: related to Norse *kyndill* torch]

kindly *adv* **1** in a kind manner: *She kindly offered me a lift*. **2** please: *Kindly remove your feet from the desk*. ▸ *adj* (***-ier, -iest***) kind, friendly, generous or good-natured. ▪ **kindliness** *noun*.
IDIOMS **look kindly on sb** *or* **sth** to approve of them or it. **not take kindly to sth** to be unwilling to put up with it.

kindred *noun* **1** one's relatives; family. **2** relationship by blood or, less properly, by marriage. ▸ *adj* **1** related. **2** having qualities in common. [Anglo-Saxon *cynred*]

kindred spirit *noun* someone who shares one's tastes, opinions, etc.

kindy *noun* (***-ies***) *Aust & NZ* a kindergarten.

kine *plural noun, old use, esp Bible* cattle. [Anglo-Saxon *cyna* of cows]

kinematics *singular noun, physics* the study of the motion of objects, without consideration of the forces acting on them. ▪ **kinematic** *or* **kinematical** *adj*. [19c: from Greek *kinema* movement]

kinetic *adj* **1** *physics* relating to or producing motion. **2** *chem* relating to the speed of chemical reactions. ▪ **kinetically** *adv*. [19c: from Greek *kinetikos*]

kinetic art *or* **kinetic sculpture** *noun* art and sculpture that has movement as an essential feature.

kinetic energy *noun* (abbrev **KE**) the energy that an object possesses because of its motion.

kinetics *singular noun, physics* the branch of **mechanics** concerned with moving objects, their masses and the forces acting on them. [19c: from **kinetic**]

kinfolk *or* **kinfolks** see **kinsfolk**

king *noun* **1** a male ruler of a nation, esp a hereditary monarch. **2** a ruler or chief. **3** a creature considered supreme in strength, ferocity, etc: *the lion, king of beasts*. **4** a leading or dominant figure in a specified field, eg a wealthy manufacturer or dealer: *the diamond king*. **5** *cards* the court card bearing a picture of a king. **6** *chess* the most important piece, which must be protected from checkmate. **7** *draughts* a piece that, having crossed the board safely, has been crowned (see **crown** *verb* sense 6), and may move both forwards and backwards. ▸ *adj* signifying a large, or the largest, variety of something: *king penguin* • *king prawns*. ▪ **kingly** *adj* (***-ier, -iest***). ▪ **kingship** *noun*. [Anglo-Saxon *cyning*]

kingdom *noun* **1** a region, state or people ruled, or previously ruled, by a king or queen. **2** *biol* any of the divisions corresponding to the highest rank in the classification of plants and animals. **3** the area associated with something: *the kingdom of the imagination*. [Anglo-Saxon *cyningdom*]
IDIOMS **to** *or* **till kingdom come** *informal* **1** into the next world: *blow them all to kingdom come*. **2** until the coming of the next world; for ever: *wait till kingdom come*.

kingfisher *noun* a brightly coloured fish-eating bird with a long pointed bill and short wings. See also **halcyon**. [15c, orig as *kyngys fyschare*]

kingpin *noun* **1** the most important person in an organization, team, etc. **2** *mech* a bolt serving as a pivot. **3** the tallest or most prominently placed pin, such as the front pin in **tenpin bowling**.

king prawn *noun* a large prawn.

King's Bench see **Queen's Bench**

King's Counsel see **Queen's Counsel**

King's English see **Queen's English**

King's evidence see **Queen's evidence**

King's Guide see **Queen's Guide**

King's highway see **Queen's highway**

king-size *or* **king-sized** *adj* of a large or larger-than-standard size.

King's Speech see **Queen's Speech**

kink *noun* **1** a bend or twist in hair or in a string, wire, etc. **2** *informal* an oddness of personality. ▸ *verb, tr & intr* to develop, or cause something to develop, a kink. [17c: prob Dutch, meaning 'a twist in a rope']

kinky *adj* (***-ier, -iest***) **1** *informal* eccentric. **2** of cable, hair, etc: twisted; in loops. ▪ **kinkiness** *noun*. [19c: from **kink**]

kinsfolk, (*N Am*) **kinfolk** *or* **kinfolks** *plural noun* one's relations.

kinship *noun* **1** family relationship. **2** a state of having common properties or characteristics.

kinsman *or* **kinswoman** *noun* a relative.

kiosk *noun* **1** a small booth or stall for the sale of sweets, newspapers, etc. **2** a public telephone box. [17c: from French *kiosque* a stand in a public park]

kip *informal, noun* **1** sleep or a sleep. **2** somewhere to sleep; a bed. ▸ *verb* (***kipped, kipping***) *intr* **1** to sleep. **2** (*also* **kip down**) to go to bed; to doss down. [18c: from Danish *kippe* a hovel]

kipper *noun* a fish, esp a herring, that has been split open, salted and smoked. ▸ *verb* to cure (herring, etc) by salting and smoking. [Anglo-Saxon *cypera* spawning salmon]

kirk *noun, Scot* **1** a church. **2** (**the Kirk**) the Church of Scotland. [Anglo-Saxon *kirke*]

kirsch /kɪəʃ/ *or* **kirschwasser** /ˈkɪəʃvasə(r)/ *noun* a clear liqueur distilled from black cherries. [19c: German *Kirschwasser* cherry water]

kismet *noun* **1** *Islam* the will of Allah. **2** fate or destiny. [19c: from Turkish *qismet* portion, lot or fate]

kiss *verb* **1** to touch someone with the lips, or to press one's lips against them, as a greeting, sign of affection, etc. **2** *intr* to kiss one another on the lips. **3** to express something by kissing: *kissed them goodbye*. **4** *intr* of billiard or snooker balls: to touch each other gently while moving. ▸ *noun* **1** an act of kissing. **2** a gentle touch. ▪ **kissable** *adj*. ▪ **kisser** *noun, slang* the mouth or face. [Anglo-Saxon *cyssan*]

IDIOMS **kiss and make up** to be mutually forgiving and so become reconciled. **kiss sth goodbye** *or* **kiss goodbye to sth** to lose the chance of having it, esp through folly, mismanagement, etc: *we can kiss goodbye to a holiday*.

kiss curl *noun* a flat curl of hair pressed against the cheek or forehead.

kiss of death *noun, informal* someone or something that brings failure or ruin on some enterprise.

kiss of life *noun* **1** **mouth-to-mouth**. *Technical equivalent* **artificial respiration.** **2** a means of restoring vitality.

Kiswahili see **Swahili** (sense 1)

kit[1] *noun* **1** a set of instruments, equipment, etc needed for a purpose, esp one kept in a container. **2** a set of special clothing and personal equipment, eg for a soldier, footballer, etc. **3** a set of parts ready for assembling. ▸ *verb* (***kitted, kitting***) (*also* **kit sb out**) to provide someone with clothes and equipment. [18c: from Dutch *kitte* tankard]

kit[2] *noun* **1** a kitten. **2** the young of various smaller fur-bearing animals, eg the ferret or fox. [16c: shortened form of **kitten**]

kitbag *noun* a soldier's or sailor's bag, usu cylinder-shaped and made of canvas, for holding kit.

kitchen *noun* a room or an area in a building where food is prepared and cooked. [Anglo-Saxon *cycene*]

kitchenette *noun* a small kitchen, or a section of a room serving as a kitchen. [20c]

kitchen garden *noun* a garden, or a section of one, where vegetables, and sometimes fruit, are grown.

kitchenware *noun* pots and pans, cutlery and utensils, etc, that are used in kitchens.

kite *noun* **1** a bird of prey of the hawk family, noted for its long pointed wings, deeply forked tail, and soaring graceful flight. **2** a light frame covered in paper or some other light material, with a long holding string attached to it, for flying in the air for fun, etc. **3** (*also* **box kite**) a more complicated structure built of boxes, sometimes used for carrying recording equipment or a person in the air. **4** *slang* an aircraft. [Anglo-Saxon *cyta*]

Kite mark *or* **kite mark** *noun, Brit* a kite-shaped mark indicating that a manufactured item meets the specifications of the British Standards Institution.

kith *noun* friends. [Anglo-Saxon *cythth*]

IDIOMS **kith and kin** friends and relations.

kitsch /kɪtʃ/ *noun* sentimental, pretentious or vulgar tastelessness in art, design, writing, film-making, etc. ▸ *adj* tastelessly or vulgarly sentimental. ▪ **kitschy** *adj* (***-ier, -iest***). [20c: German]

kitten *noun* **1** a young cat. **2** the young of various other small mammals, eg the rabbit. ▸ *verb, tr & intr* of a cat: to give birth. ▪ **kittenish** *adj* **1** like a kitten; playful. **2** of a woman: affectedly playful; flirtatious. [14c: from Norman French *caton*, diminutive of cat]

kittiwake *noun* a type of gull which has white plumage with dark-grey back and wings, a yellow bill and black legs. [17c: imitating its cry]

kitty[1] *noun* (***-ies***) **1** a fund contributed to jointly, for communal use by a group of people. **2** *cards* a pool of money used in certain games. [19c]

kitty[2] *noun* an affectionate name for a cat or kitten.

kiwi *noun* **1** a nocturnal flightless bird, found in New Zealand, with hair-like brown or grey feathers, a long slender bill and no tail. **2** *informal* a New Zealander. **3** *informal* a kiwi fruit. [19c: Maori]

kiwi fruit *noun* an oval edible fruit with pale-green juicy flesh enclosed by a brown hairy skin. Also called **Chinese gooseberry**. [20c: so called because the fruit was exported from New Zealand]

kJ *abbrev* kilojoule or kilojoules.

kl *abbrev* kilolitre or kilolitres.

klaxon *noun* a loud horn used as a warning signal on ambulances, fire engines, etc. [20c: orig a trade-name for a type of hooter on early cars]

Kleenex *noun* (***Kleenex*** *or* ***Kleenexes***) *trademark* a kind of soft paper tissue used as a handkerchief. [20c]

kleptomania *noun* an irresistible urge to steal, esp objects that are not desired for themselves and are of little monetary value. ▪ **kleptomaniac** *noun, adj.* [19c: from Greek *kleptein* to steal + **-mania**]

klezmer /ˈklɛzmə(r)/ *noun, music* traditional E European Jewish music.

klutz /klʌts/ *noun, US, slang* an idiot; an awkward, stupid person. ▪ **klutzy** *adj* (**-ier, -iest**). [20c: Yiddish]

km *abbrev* kilometre or kilometres.

km/h *abbrev* kilometres per hour.

kn *abbrev, naut* knot (see **knot** *noun* sense 9).

knack *noun* **1** the ability to do something effectively and skilfully. **2** a habit or tendency, esp an intuitive or unconscious one. [14c: prob related to obsolete *knack* a sharp blow or sound]

knacker *noun* a buyer of old horses for slaughter. ▸ *verb, informal* **1** to exhaust: *knackered after the climb.* **2** to break or wear out: *This clock is knackered.* [16c]

knapsack *noun* a hiker's or traveller's bag for food, clothes, etc, traditionally made of canvas or leather, carried on the back or over the shoulder. [17c: from German *knappen* eat + *sack* bag]

knave *noun, old use* **1** *cards* the **jack**. **2** a mischievous young man; a scoundrel. ▪ **knavish** *adj.* [Anglo-Saxon *cnafa* a boy or youth]

knead *verb* **1** to work (dough) with one's fingers and knuckles into a uniform mass. **2** to massage (flesh) with firm finger-movements. [Anglo-Saxon *cnedan*]

knee *noun* **1** in humans: the joint in the middle of the leg where the lower end of the **femur** articulates with the upper end of the **tibia**. **2 a** the corresponding joint in the hind limb of other vertebrates; **b** in a horse's foreleg: the joint corresponding to the wrist. **3** the area surrounding this joint. **4** the lap: *sat with the child on her knee.* **5** the part of a garment covering the knee: *patches on the knee and elbow.* ▸ *verb* (***kneed, kneeing***) to hit, nudge or shove someone or something with the knee. [Anglo-Saxon *cneow*]
IDIOMS **bring sb to their knees** to defeat, prostrate, humiliate or ruin them utterly. **on one's knees 1** kneeling. **2** exhausted. **3** begging.

kneecap *noun* a small plate of bone situated in front of and protecting the knee joint in humans and most other mammals. Also called **patella**. ▸ *verb* to shoot or otherwise damage someone's kneecaps as a form of revenge, torture or unofficial punishment. ▪ **kneecapping** *noun.*

knee-deep *adj, adv* **1** rising or reaching to someone's knees. **2** sunk to the knees: *standing knee-deep in mud.* **3** deeply involved.

knee-high *adj* rising or reaching to the knees.
IDIOMS **knee-high to a grasshopper 1** very young. **2** very small.

knee-jerk *noun* an involuntary kick of the lower leg, caused by a reflex response when the tendon just below the kneecap is tapped sharply. ▸ *adj* of a response or reaction: automatic; predictable.

kneel *verb* (***knelt*** *or* ***kneeled***) *intr* (*often* **kneel down**) to support one's weight on, or lower oneself onto, one's knees. ▪ **kneeler** *noun* a cushion for kneeling on, esp in church. [Anglo-Saxon *cneowlian*]

knee-length *adj* coming down or up as far as the knees: *knee-length skirt.*

knees-up *noun, Brit, informal* a riotous party.

knell *noun* **1** the tolling of a bell announcing a death or funeral. **2** something that signals the end of anything. ▸ *verb* to announce something or summon someone by, or as if by, a tolling bell. [Anglo-Saxon *cnyll*]

knelt *past tense, past participle of* **kneel**

knew *past tense of* **know**

knickerbockers *or* (*US*) **knickers** *plural noun* baggy trousers tied just below the knee or at the ankle. [19c: named after Diedrich Knickerbocker, the pseudonym of the author of Washington Irving's *History of New York*, 1809]

knickers *plural noun* an undergarment with two separate legs or legholes, worn by women and girls, and covering part or all of the lower abdomen and buttocks. [19c: short form of **knickerbockers**]

knick-knack *or* **nick-nack** *noun* a little trinket or ornament. [17c: from *knack* in the obsolete sense 'toy']

knife *noun* (***knives***) a cutting instrument, typically in the form of a blade fitted into a handle or into machinery, and sometimes also used for spreading. ▸ *verb* **1** to cut. **2** to stab or kill with a knife. ▪ **knifing** *noun* the act of attacking and injuring someone using a knife. [Anglo-Saxon *cnif*]

knife edge *noun* the cutting edge of a knife.
IDIOMS **on a knife edge** in a state of extreme uncertainty; at a critical point.

knifepoint *noun* the sharp tip of a knife.
IDIOMS **at knifepoint** under threat of injury from a knife.

knight *noun* **1** a man who has been awarded the highest or second highest class of distinction in any of the four British orders of chivalry. See also **dame**. **2** *hist* in medieval Europe: a man-at-arms of high social status, usu mounted, serving a feudal lord. **3** *hist* the armed champion of a lady, devoted to her service. **4** *chess* a piece shaped like a horse's head. ▸ *verb* to confer a knighthood on someone. ▪ **knighthood** *noun* **1** the rank of a knight, just below that of a baronet, conferring the title 'Sir'. **2** the order of knights. ▪ **knightly** *adj* (**-ier, -iest**). [Anglo-Saxon *cniht* a boy, servant or warrior]

knight commander see **commander**

knight errant *noun* (***knights errant***) *hist* a knight who travelled about in search of daring and chivalrous deeds. ▪ **knight errantry** *noun.*

knit *verb* (***knitted*** *or old use* ***knit, knitting***) **1** *tr & intr* to produce a fabric composed of interlocking loops of yarn, using a pair of **knitting needles** or a **knitting machine**. **2** to make (garments, etc) by this means. **3** to unite something: *The tragedy served to knit them closer together.* **4** *tr & intr* of broken bones: to grow or make them grow together again. **5** to draw (one's brows) together in a frown. ▸ *noun* a fabric or a garment made by knitting. ▪ **knitting** *noun* **1** a garment, etc that is in the process of being knitted. **2** the art or process of producing something knitted. [Anglo-Saxon *cnyttan* in obsolete sense 'to tie']

knitwear *noun* knitted clothing.

knives pl of **knife**

knob *noun* **1** a hard rounded projection. **2** a handle, esp a rounded one, on a door or drawer. **3** a button on mechanical or electrical equipment that is pressed or rotated to operate it. **4** a small roundish lump: *a knob of butter.* ▪ **knobby** *adj* (**-ier, -iest**). [14c: from German *knobbe* a knot in wood]

knobbly *adj* (**-ier, -iest**) covered with or full of knobs.

knobkerrie *noun* a stick with a knob on the end used as a club and missile by S African tribesmen. [19c: from Afrikaans *knopkierie*]

knock *verb* **1** *intr* to tap or rap with the knuckles or some object, esp on a door for admittance. **2** to strike and so push someone or something, esp accidentally. **3** to put someone or something into a specified condition by hitting them or it: *knocked him senseless*. **4** to make by striking: *knocked a hole in the boat*. **5** *tr & intr* (*usu* **knock against** *or* **on** *or* **into sth** *or* **sb**) to strike, bump or bang against it or them. **6** *informal* to find fault with or criticize someone or something. **7** *intr* of an internal-combustion engine: to make a metallic knocking sound caused by a fault. ▸ *noun* **1** an act of knocking. **2** a tap or rap. **3** a push or shove. **4** *informal* a personal misfortune, blow, setback, calamity, etc. **5** in an internal-combustion engine: a metallic knocking sound. **6** *informal* a criticism. [Anglo-Saxon *cnucian*]

IDIOMS **knock sth on the head** *informal* to put an end to it.

PHRASAL VERBS **knock about** *or* **around** *informal* to lie about unused; to be idle: *knocking about the streets*. **knock sb about** *or* **around** *informal* to treat them roughly; to hit or batter them. **knock sb back 1** *informal* to cost them (a specified amount): *knocked me back 500 quid*. **2** to rebuff or reject them; to turn them down. **knock sth back** *informal* to eat or drink it quickly. **knock sth down** *informal* to reduce its price: *knocked these down to a fiver each*. **knock off** *informal* to finish work: *We knock off at 5pm*. **knock sb off** *slang* to kill them. **knock sth off 1** *informal* to produce it or them at speed or in quick succession, apparently quite easily: *knocks off several books a year*. **2** *informal* to deduct (a certain amount): *knocked off £15 for a quick sale*. **knock on** *rugby* to commit the foul of pushing the ball forward with the hand. **knock sb out 1** to make them unconscious, esp by hitting them. **2** *boxing* to make them unconscious or render them incapable of rising in the required time. **3** to defeat them in a knockout competition. **4** *informal* to amaze them; to impress them greatly. See also **knockout**. **knock up** *tennis* to exchange practice shots with one's opponent before a match. **knock sb up** to wake them by knocking. **knock sth up 1** *informal* to make it hurriedly. **2** *cricket* to score (a number of runs).

knockabout *adj* of comedy: boisterous; slapstick.

knock-back *noun* a setback; a rejection or refusal.

knockdown *adj, informal* **1** very low; cheap: *knockdown prices*. **2** of furniture: able to be taken to pieces easily. **3** of an argument: overwhelmingly strong.

knocker *noun* **1** (*also* **doorknocker**) a heavy piece of metal, usu of a decorative shape, fixed to a door by a hinge and used for knocking. **2** someone who knocks.

knock knee *or* (*popularly*) **knock knees** *noun* a condition in which the lower legs curve inwards, causing the knees to touch when the person is standing with their feet slightly apart. ▪ **knock-kneed** *adj*.

knock-on effect *noun* a secondary or indirect effect of some action, etc on one or more indirectly related matters or circumstances.

knockout *noun* **1** *informal* someone or something stunning. **2** a competition in which the defeated teams or competitors are dropped after each round. **3** *boxing, etc* **a** the act of rendering someone unconscious; **b** a blow that renders the opponent or victim unconscious. ▸ *adj* **1** of a competition: in which the losers in each round are eliminated. **2** of a punch, etc: leaving the victim unconscious. **3** *informal* attractive; excellent.

knoll *noun* a small round hill. [Anglo-Saxon *cnoll*]

knot *noun* **1** a join or tie in string, etc made by looping the ends around each other and pulling tight. **2** a bond or uniting link. **3** a coil or bun in the hair. **4** a decoratively tied ribbon, etc. **5** a tangle in hair, string, etc. **6** a difficulty or complexity. **7** a hard mass of wood at the point where a branch has grown out from a tree trunk. **8** a scar on a piece of timber, representing a cross-section through such a mass. **9** (abbrev **kn** *or* **kt**) used in meteorology and in navigation by aircraft and at sea: a unit of speed equal to one nautical mile (1.85km) per hour. **10** a tight feeling, eg in the stomach, caused by nervousness. ▸ *verb* (***knotted, knotting***) **1** to tie something in a knot. **2** *tr & intr* to tangle; to form knots. **3** *intr* eg of the stomach: to become tight with nervousness. ▪ **knotty** *adj* (**-ier, -iest**). [Anglo-Saxon *cnotta*]

IDIOMS **tie sb** *or* **oneself in knots** to bewilder, confuse or perplex them or oneself. **tie the knot** *informal* to get married.

know *verb* (*past tense* ***knew,*** *past participle* ***known***) **1** *tr & intr* (*usu* **know sth** *or* **know of** *or* **about sth**) to be aware of it; to be certain about it. **2** to have learnt and remembered something. **3** to have an understanding or grasp of something. **4** to be familiar with someone or something: *know her well*. **5** to be able to recognize or identify someone or something. **6** to be able to distinguish someone or something, or to tell them apart: *wouldn't know him from Adam*. **7** *intr* to have enough experience or training: *knew not to question him further*. **8** to experience or be subject to something: *has never known poverty*. ▪ **knowable** *adj*. [Anglo-Saxon *cnawan*]

IDIOMS **in the know** *informal* **1** having information not known to most people. **2** initiated. **know better than to do sth** to be wiser, or better instructed, than to do it. **know the ropes** to understand the detail or procedure. **know what's what** to be shrewd, wise or hard to deceive. **know which side one's bread is buttered on** to be fully aware of one's own best interests. **you never know** *informal* it's not impossible; perhaps.

know-all *noun, derog* someone who seems, or claims, to know more than others.

know-how *noun, informal* ability; adroitness; skill.

knowing *adj* **1** shrewd; canny; clever. **2** of a glance, etc: signifying secret awareness. **3** deliberate. ▪ **knowingly** *adv*. ▪ **knowingness** *noun*.

knowledge *noun* **1** the fact of knowing; awareness; understanding. **2** the information one has acquired through learning or experience. **3** learning; the sciences: *a branch of knowledge*. **4** specific information about a subject. [14c as *knouleche*]

IDIOMS **to one's** *or* **to the best of one's knowledge** as far as one knows.

knowledgeable *or* **knowledgable** *adj* well-informed. ▪ **knowledgeably** *adv*.

known *verb, past participle of* **know**. ▸ *adj* **1** widely recognized. **2** identified by the police: *a known thief*.

knuckle *noun* **1** a joint of a finger, esp one that links a finger to the hand. **2** *cookery* the knee or ankle joint of an animal, esp with the surrounding flesh, as food. [14c as *knokel*]
IDIOMS **near the knuckle** *informal* bordering on the indecent.
PHRASAL VERBS **knuckle down to sth** to begin to work hard at it. **knuckle under** *informal* to submit, yield or give way.

knuckle-duster *noun* a set of metal links or other metal device worn over the knuckles as a weapon.

knurl *or* **nurl** *noun* a ridge. ▪ **knurled** *adj.* [17c]

KO *or* **k.o.** *abbrev* **1** kick-off. **2** knockout.

koala /koʊ'ɑːlə/ *noun* an Australian tree-climbing marsupial with thick grey fur and bushy ears that feeds on eucalyptus leaves. [19c: from *gula* in an extinct Australian Aboriginal language]

kohl /koʊl/ *noun* a cosmetic for darkening the eyelids. [18c: from Arabic *koh'l* powdered antimony]

kohlrabi /koʊl'rɑːbɪ/ *noun* (***kohlrabis*** *or* ***kohlrabi***) a variety of cabbage with a short swollen green or purple edible stem. [19c: German]

kola see **cola**

kook *noun, N Am, informal* a crazy or eccentric person. ▪ **kooky** *or* **kookie** *adj* (***-ier, -iest***). [20c]

kookaburra *noun* a large kingfisher, found in Australia and New Guinea and known for its chuckling cry. *Also called* **laughing jackass**. [19c: from Wiradhuri (an Australian Aboriginal language) *gugubarra*]

kopeck, **kopek** *or* **copek** *noun* a coin or unit of currency of Russia, and the former USSR, worth one hundredth of a rouble. [17c: from Russian *kopeika*]

koppie *or* (*S Afr*) **kopje** *noun* a low hill. [19c: from Afrikaans *kopje* a little head]

Koran, **Qoran**, **Quran** *or* **Qur'an** /kɔː'rɑːn, kə'rɑːn/ *noun, Islam* the holy book of Islam. ▪ **Koranic** /-'ranɪk/ *adj.* [17c: from Arabic *qur'an* book]

Korean *adj* of or relating to North or South Korea in E Asia, their people or language. ► *noun* **1** an inhabitant or native of North or South Korea. **2** their language.

korfball *noun* a game similar to basketball, played by two teams, consisting each of six men and six women. [20c: from Dutch *korfbal*]

korma *noun* in Indian cookery: meat or vegetables braised in stock, yoghurt or cream. [19c: Urdu]

KO's *or* **k.o.'s** *pl of* **KO**

kosher /'koʊʃə(r)/ *adj* **1** in accordance with Jewish law. **2** of food: prepared as prescribed by Jewish dietary laws. **3** *informal* legitimate. [19c: Yiddish]

kowtow *verb* **1** *intr* (*usu* **kowtow to sb**) *informal* to defer to them, esp in an over-submissive way. **2** to touch the forehead to the ground in a gesture of submission, orig a Chinese ceremonial custom. ► *noun* an act of kowtowing. [19c: from Chinese *ke tou* to strike the head]

kph *abbrev* kilometres per hour.

Kr *symbol, chem* krypton.

kr *abbrev* **1** krona. **2** krone.

kraal /krɑːl/ *noun* **1** a S African village of huts surrounded by a fence. **2** *S Afr* an enclosure for cattle, sheep, etc. [18c: Afrikaans]

kraft *or* **kraft paper** *noun* a type of strong brown wrapping paper. [20c: German, meaning 'strength']

krans /'krɑːns/, **kranz** *or* **krantz** /krɑːnts/ *noun, S Afr* **1** a crown of rock on a mountain top. **2** a precipice. [18c: Afrikaans]

kremlin *noun* the citadel of a Russian town, esp (**the Kremlin**) that of Moscow. [17c: from Russian *kreml* a citadel]

krill *noun* (*pl* ***krill***) a shrimp-like crustacean that feeds on plankton and lives in enormous swarms. [20c: from Norwegian *kril* small fry or young fish]

krona *noun* (***kronor***) (abbrev **K** *or* **Kr**) the standard unit of currency of Sweden. [19c: Swedish and Icelandic, meaning 'crown']

krone /'kroʊnə/ *noun* (***kroner***) (abbrev **K** *or* **Kr**) the standard unit of currency of Denmark and Norway. [19c: Danish and Norwegian, meaning 'crown']

Krugerrand *or* **krugerrand** /'kruːgərand/ *noun* a S African one-ounce (or 28-gram) gold coin minted only for investment. Also called **rand**. [20c: see **rand**]

krypton *noun* (symbol **Kr**) a colourless odourless tasteless noble gas that is almost inert, used in lasers, fluorescent lamps and discharge tubes. [19c: from Greek *kryptos* hidden or secret]

KT *abbrev* Knight of the Thistle.

Kt *abbrev* kiloton or kilotons.

kt *abbrev* **1** (*also* **kT**) kiloton or kilotons. **2** carat. **3** *naut* knot.

kudos /'kjuːdɒs/ *noun* credit, honour or prestige. [18c: Greek, meaning 'glory']

kudu /'kuːduː/ *noun, zool* a lightly striped African antelope. [18c: from Afrikaans *koedoe*]

Ku Klux Klan *noun* a secret society of White Protestants in the southern USA, formed after the Civil War, and later revived in an attempt to preserve White Protestant supremacy by violent means.

kulak /'kuːlak/ *noun, hist* a relatively wealthy, property-owning Russian peasant. [19c: from Russian, meaning 'fist' or 'tight-fisted person']

kulfi /'kʊlfɪ/ *noun* in Indian cookery: an ice-cream dessert. [Late 20c: Hindi]

kumquat *or* **cumquat** /'kʌmkwɒt/ *noun* **1** a small spiny citrus shrub or tree, native to China. **2** the small orange citrus fruit produced by this plant. [17c: from Cantonese Chinese *kam kwat* golden orange]

kung fu *noun* a Chinese martial art with similarities to karate and judo. [20c: Chinese, meaning 'combat skill']

Kurd *noun* a member of the Islamic people of Kurdistan, a mountainous region of Turkey, Iran and Iraq.

Kurdish *adj* belonging or relating to the Kurds or their language. ► *noun* the language of the Kurds. [19c]

kV *abbrev* kilovolt or kilovolts.

kW *symbol* kilowatt or kilowatts.

Kwanzaa /'kwanzə/ *noun, US* a non-religious seven-day holiday (from 26 December to 2 January) celebrating African-American life, history and culture. [20c: Swahili, literally 'first fruits']

kWh *abbrev* kilowatt hour or kilowatt hours.

kybosh see **kibosh**

kyle *noun, Scot* a channel or sound. [16c: from Gaelic *caoil* a narrow strait]

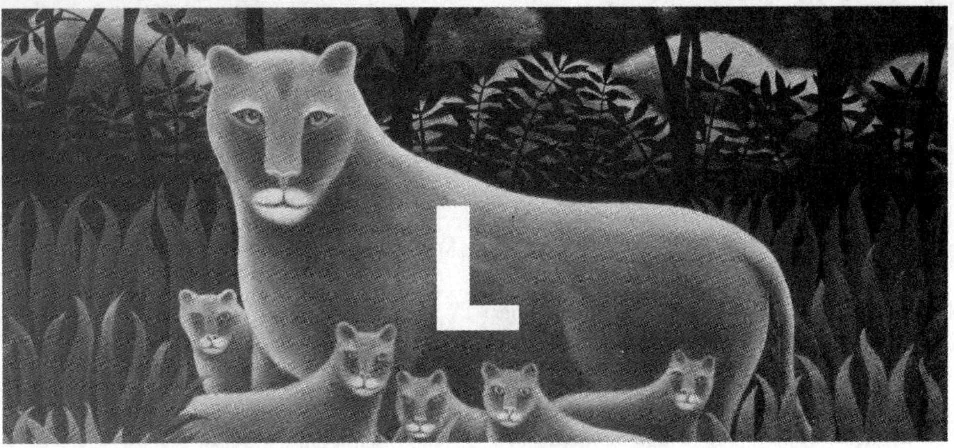

L[1] *or* **l** *noun* (***Ls, L's** or **l's***) **1** the twelfth letter of the English alphabet. **2** something in the shape of an L. **3** the speech sound represented by this letter.

L[2] *abbrev* **1** lake. **2** learner driver. **3** as a clothes size, etc: large. **4** Liberal. **5** licentiate. **6** lira or lire.

L[3] *symbol* the Roman numeral for 50.

l *abbrev* **1** left. **2** length. **3** line. **4** lira or lire. **5** litre or litres.

LA *abbrev* Los Angeles.

La *symbol, chem* lanthanum.

la see **lah**

Lab. *abbrev* Labour.

lab *contraction* short form of **laboratory**.

label *noun* **1** a tag, etc attached to something specifying its contents, etc or how to use it, wash it, etc. **2** a descriptive word or short phrase. **3** a small strip of material on a garment, etc with the name of the maker or designer. **4** a recording company's trademark. **5** *comput* a character or set of characters used to identify an **instruction** by citing it in a particular place in a program. ▸ *verb* (***labelled, labelling** or US **labeled, labeling***) **1** **a** to mark (something) in a specified way with a special tag, sticker, etc; **b** to attach a tag, sticker, etc to (something). **2** to call (someone or some group) by a specified name. [14c: French, meaning 'ribbon']

labial *adj* **1** relating to or beside the lips. **2** *phonetics* of a sound: produced by the active use of one or both lips. ▸ *noun, phonetics* a labial sound. ▪ **labially** *adv.* [16c: from Latin *labium* lip]

labiate *noun, botany* a plant, eg, mint and thyme, where the **corolla** of petals is divided into two lips. ▸ *adj* **1** *botany* referring or relating to this type of plant. **2** *biol* having or resembling lips. [18c: from Latin *labium* lip]

labile /'leɪbaɪl *or* (*esp US*) 'leɪbəl/ *adj* **1** unstable. **2** *chem* of a chemical compound: readily altered by heat etc. [15c: from Latin *labilis*, from *labi* to slip]

labium /'leɪbɪəm/ *noun* (***labia*** /-bɪə/) **1** a lip or lip-like structure. **2** (*usu* **labia**) one section of the two pairs of fleshy folds which form part of the **vulva**. [16c: Latin, meaning 'lip']

laboratory *noun* (***-ies***) a room or building specially equipped for scientific experiments, research, the preparation of drugs, etc. Often shortened to **lab**. [17c: from Latin *laborare* to work]

laborious *adj* of a task, etc: requiring hard work or much effort. ▪ **laboriously** *adv.* [14c: from **labour**]

labour *or* (*N Am*) **labor** *noun* **1** strenuous and prolonged work. **2** (*usu* **labours**) the amount of effort put in to doing something. **3** working people or their productive output regarded collectively. **4** the process of giving birth, esp from the point when the contractions of the uterus begin. **5** (**Labour**) *Brit* the Labour Party. ▸ *verb, intr* **1** to work hard or with difficulty. **2** to progress or move slowly and with difficulty. **3** to spend time and effort achieving something. [14c: from Latin *labor*]

IDIOMS **labour a** *or* **the point** to spend excessive time on one particular subject, etc.

laboured *or* (*N Am*) **labored** *adj* **1** showing signs of effort or difficulty: *laboured breathing*. **2** not natural or spontaneous: *a laboured prose style*.

labourer *or* (*N Am*) **laborer** *noun* someone employed to do heavy, usu unskilled, physical work.

labour exchange *noun, Brit, informal* a former name for a **job centre**.

labour-intensive *adj, econ, geog* of an industry: requiring a large resource of workers for the capital invested, as opposed to machinery etc. Compare **capital-intensive**.

labour of love *noun* (***labours of love***) an undertaking made mainly for personal satisfaction or pleasure rather than for profit or material advantage.

Labour Party *noun* **1** in the UK: a political party traditionally on the left of the political spectrum, founded by members of trades unions and socialist organizations. **2** (*often* **Labor Party**) any similar party in several other countries.

Labrador *noun* a medium-sized retriever dog with a short black or golden coat. [19c: named after Labrador, where the breed was developed]

laburnum *noun* a small tree with hanging clusters of yellow flowers and poisonous seeds. [16c: Latin]

labyrinth /'labɪrɪnθ/ *noun* **1** a network of interconnected, sometimes underground, passages. **2** anything that is complicated, intricate or difficult to negotiate. **3** *anatomy* the complex arrangement of membranous and bony structures in the inner ear of vertebrates. ▪ **labyrinthine** *adj.* [14c: from Greek *labyrinthos*]

lac *noun* a resinous substance produced by certain tropical Asian insects. [16c: from Hindi *lakh* 100,000, because of the vast numbers of insects required for the production of small quantities of the substance]

lace *noun* **1** a delicate material made by knotting, looping or twisting thread into open intricate symmetrical patterns. **2** a string or cord drawn through holes or round hooks and used for fastening shoes, etc. ▸ *verb* **1** *tr & intr* to fasten or be fastened with a lace or laces. **2** to put a lace or laces into (shoes, etc). **3** to flavour, strengthen, adulterate, etc (with alcohol, drugs, poison, etc): *laced the trifle with sherry.* **4** to mark or streak with colour: *a pink sky laced with red.* [13c: from Latin *laqueum* noose]

PHRASAL VERBS **lace sth up** to tighten or fasten shoes, etc with laces.

lacerate *verb* **1** to tear or cut (esp flesh) roughly. **2** to wound or hurt (someone's feelings). ▪ **lacerated** *adj.* ▪ **laceration** *noun.* [16c: from Latin *lacerare* to tear]

lachrymal *or* **lacrimal** /ˈlakrɪməl/ *adj anatomy* referring or relating to tears or the glands that secrete them. [15c: from Latin *lacrima* tear]

lachrymose /ˈlakrɪmoʊs/ *adj, literary* **1** prone to crying. **2** of a novel, play, film, etc: likely to make someone cry. ▪ **lachrymosely** *adv.* [17c: from Latin *lacrima* tear]

lack *noun* a deficiency or want: *a lack of understanding.* ▸ *verb* to be without or to have too little of (something). ▪ **lacking** *adj.* [13c]

lackadaisical /lakəˈdeɪzɪkəl/ *adj* **1** showing little energy, interest, enthusiasm, etc. **2** lazy or idle, esp in a nonchalant way. [18c: from *alack the day,* an obsolete exclamation of surprise, shock, regret, etc]

lackey *noun* (**-eys**) **1** *derog* a grovelling or servile follower. **2** *old use* a male servant, esp a footman or valet. [16c: from French *laquais* a foot soldier]

lacklustre *or* (*US*) **lackluster** *adj* having or showing little energy, enthusiasm, brightness, etc.

laconic *adj* **1** of speech or writing: using few words; neatly concise and to the point. **2** of a person: laconic in speech or writing. ▪ **laconically** *adv.* [16c: from Greek *lakonikos* belonging to Laconia, the inhabitants of which were noted for terse speech]

lacquer *noun* **1** a substance made by dissolving natural or man-made resins in alcohol and used to form a hard, shiny covering on wood and metal. **2** the sap from some trees, used as a varnish for wood. **3 hairspray.** ▸ *verb* to cover with lacquer. ▪ **lacquered** *adj.* [17c]

lacrimal see **lachrymal**

lacrosse *noun* a team game similar to hockey but played with a stick with a netted pocket. [18c: French *la* the + *crosse* hooked stick]

lactate[1] *verb, intr* of mammary glands: to secrete milk. ▪ **lactation** *noun.* [19c: from Latin *lactare* to suckle]

lactate[2] *noun, biochem* a salt or ester of lactic acid. [18c]

lacteal *adj* referring or relating to, or consisting of, milk. ▸ *noun, anatomy* a lymphatic vessel that absorbs the products of digestion of fats in the small intestine. [17c: from Latin *lacteus* milky]

lactic *adj* relating to, derived from or containing milk. [18c: from Latin *lactis* milk]

lactic acid *noun, biochem* an organic acid produced during the souring of milk and in muscle tissue when there is insufficient oxygen available to break down carbohydrates.

lacto- *or* (*before a vowel*) **lact-** *combining form, denoting* milk. [From Latin *lactis* milk]

lactose *noun, biochem* a white crystalline disaccharide sugar found in milk.

lacuna /ləˈkjuːnə/ *noun* (***lacunae*** /-niː/ *or* ***lacunas***) a gap or a space where something is missing, esp in printed text. [17c: Latin, meaning 'hole']

lacy *adj* (**-ier, -iest**) like, made of or trimmed with lace.

lad *noun* **1** a boy or youth. **2** (**the lads**) a group of male friends who regularly socialize together. **3** *Brit* someone who works in a stable, regardless of their age or sex. [14c]

ladder *noun* **1** a piece of equipment used for climbing up or down, consisting of a set of parallel horizontal rungs or steps set between two vertical supports. **2** *chiefly Brit* a long narrow flaw, esp in a stocking, tights or other knitted garment, where a row of stitches has broken. Also called **run**. **3** a hierarchical or graded route of advancement or progress: *climb the social ladder.* ▸ *verb, chiefly Brit* **a** to cause a ladder to appear in (a stocking, etc); **b** *intr* of a stocking, etc: to develop a ladder. [Anglo-Saxon *hlæder*]

laddie *noun, informal* a young boy or lad. [16c]

laddish *adj* of young males or their behaviour: characterized by loud arrogance, vulgarity and sometimes aggression, often brought on by heavy drinking.

lade *verb* (*past tense* ***laded***, *past participle* ***laden***) **1 a** to load cargo on to (a ship); **b** *intr* of a ship: to take cargo on board. **2** to put a burden, esp one of guilt, on (someone). [Anglo-Saxon *hladen* to load or to draw up]

laden *adj* **1** of a ship: loaded with cargo. **2** of a person, an animal, the sky, a vehicle, etc: heavily loaded, weighed down, burdened: *trees laden with fruit.* **3** of a person: oppressed, esp with guilt, worry, etc.

la-di-da *or* **lah-di-dah** *adj, informal* pretentiously snobbish. [19c: an imitation of an affected way of talking]

ladies *singular and plural noun, informal* a women's public lavatory.

lading *noun* the cargo or load that a ship, etc carries.

ladle *noun* a large spoon with a long handle and deep bowl, for serving or transferring liquid. ▸ *verb* to serve or transfer with a ladle. ▪ **ladleful** *noun.* [Anglo-Saxon *hlædel*]

PHRASAL VERBS **ladle sth out** to serve or distribute praise, blame, etc generously or excessively.

lady *noun* (**-ies**) **1** a woman who is regarded as having good manners and elegant or refined behaviour. **2** a polite word for a woman generally. **3** *hist* a woman of the upper classes. **4** (**Lady**) *Brit* a title of honour used for peeresses, wives and daughters of peers and knights, etc. ▸ *adj, now rather dated* of the female gender: **a** used esp for occupations, etc formerly considered to be the domain of men: *a lady doctor;* **b** used esp when the attendant noun fails to signal gender: *went on holiday with his lady friend.* [Anglo-Saxon *hlæfdige*, meaning 'bread-kneader']

ladybird *or* (*N Am*) **ladybug** *noun* a small beetle whose body is usu red or yellow with black spots.

Lady Chapel *noun, chiefly RC Church* a chapel dedicated to the Virgin Mary, usu built behind and to the east of the main altar.

lady-in-waiting *noun* (***ladies-in-waiting***) a woman who attends a queen, princess, etc.

lady-killer *noun, informal* a man who is irresistibly attractive to women.

ladylike *adj* showing attributes, eg, refinement, politeness, etc, appropriate to a lady.

Lady Mayoress *noun* the wife of a **Lord Mayor**.

Ladyship *noun* (*usu* **Your** *or* **Her Ladyship**) a title used to address or refer to peeresses and the wives and daughters of peers and knights, etc.

lady's man *or* **ladies' man** *noun* a man who enjoys and cultivates the company of women.

lady's-slipper *noun* an orchid with a large yellow slipper-like lip.

lag[1] *verb* (***lagged, lagging***) *intr* (*usu* **lag behind**) to move or progress so slowly as to become separated or left behind. ▸ *noun* a delay or the length of a delay. [16c]

lag[2] *verb* (***lagged, lagging***) to cover (a boiler, water pipes, etc) with thick insulating material in order to minimize heat loss. [19c]

lager *noun* a light-coloured effervescent beer. [19c: from German *lagern* to store]

lager lout *noun* a person, esp a youngish male, who, after an extended drinking bout, starts behaving in an aggressive or unruly manner.

laggard *noun* someone or something that lags behind.

lagging *noun* insulating cover for pipes, boilers, etc.

lagoon *noun* a relatively shallow body of water separated from the open sea by a barrier such as a reef or a narrow bank of sand. [17c: from Latin *lacuna* a pool]

lah *or* **la** *noun, music* in **sol-fa** notation: the sixth note of the major scale. [14c: see **sol-fa**]

laid *past tense, past participle of* **lay**[1]

laid-back *adj, informal* relaxed; easy-going.

laid paper *noun* a type of paper that has faint lines running across the surface.

laid-up *adj* of a person: confined to bed because of illness or injury.

lain *past participle of* **lie**[2]

lair *noun* **1** a wild animal's den. **2** *informal* a place of refuge or hiding. [Anglo-Saxon *leger* a bed or lying place]

laird *noun, Scot* someone who owns a large country estate. [15c: a variant of **lord**]

laissez-faire *or* **laisser-faire** /lɛseɪ'fɛə(r)/ *noun* a policy of not interfering in what others are doing. [19c: French]

laity /'leɪɪtɪ/ *noun* (*usu* **the laity**) the people who are not members of a particular profession, esp the clergy. [16c: from **lay**[3]]

lake[1] *noun* a large area of fresh or salt water, surrounded by land. [14c: from Latin *lacus* a vat or pool]

lake[2] *noun* **1** a reddish dye, orig obtained from **lac**, but now more usu obtained from **cochineal**. **2** a dye made by combining animal, vegetable or coal-tar pigment with a metallic oxide or earth. [17c: a variant spelling of **lac**]

lam *verb* (***lammed, lamming***) *slang* to thrash. [16c: from Norse *lemja* to make someone lame]

lama *noun* a Buddhist priest or monk in Tibet and Mongolia. See also **Dalai Lama**. [17c: from Tibetan *blama*]

the Lamb *or* **the Lamb of God** *noun, Christianity* a title given to Christ (John 1.29 and Revelation 17.14, etc) because of the sacrificial nature of his death.

lamb *noun* **1** a young sheep. **2** the flesh of a lamb or sheep used as food. **3** *informal* **a** a quiet and well-behaved child; **b** a kind, gentle, good, sweet, etc person. ▸ *verb, intr* of a ewe: to give birth to a lamb or lambs. [Anglo-Saxon]

IDIOMS **like a lamb to the slaughter** innocently and without resistance.

lambaste *or* **lambast** /lam'bast/ *verb* **1** to beat severely. **2** to criticize or scold severely. [17c: **lam** + **baste**[3]]

lambda *noun* the eleventh letter of the Greek alphabet.

lambent *adj* **1** of a flame or light: flickering over a surface. **2** of eyes, the sky, etc: gently sparkling. **3** of wit, writing style, etc: playfully light and clever. ▪ **lambency** *noun*. [17c: from Latin *lambere* to lick]

lambskin *noun* the skin of a lamb, usu with the wool left on it, used to make slippers, coats, etc. [14c]

lame *adj* **1** not able to walk properly, esp due to an injury or defect. **2** of an excuse, etc: not convincing; weak; ineffective. ▸ *verb* to make lame. ▪ **lamely** *adv*. ▪ **lameness** *noun*. [Anglo-Saxon *lama*]

lamé /'lɑːmeɪ/ *noun* a fabric which has metallic threads, usu gold or silver, woven into it. [20c: French, meaning 'having metal plates or strips']

lamebrain *noun, informal* someone who is considered to be extremely stupid. [20c]

lame duck *noun* someone who depends on the help of others to an excessive extent. [18c]

lamella *noun* (***lamellae*** /-liː/) *biol* **1** a thin sheet or plate of tissue, especially one of the many layers that make up compact bone. **2** any of the thin sheet-like membranes within the **chloroplast**s of plant cells. **3** any of the vertical spore-bearing structures on the underside of the cap of a mushroom or toadstool. [17c: Latin, meaning 'thin layer']

lament *verb, tr & intr* to feel or express regret or sadness. ▸ *noun* **1** an expression of sadness, grief, regret, etc. **2** a poem, song, etc which expresses great grief, esp following someone's death. ▪ **lamentation** *noun*. [16c: from Latin *lamentari* to wail or moan]

lamentable *adj* **1** regrettable, shameful or deplorable. **2** inadequate; useless. ▪ **lamentably** *adv*. [15c]

lamented *adj* of a dead person: sadly missed; mourned for: *her late lamented father.*

lamina *noun* (***laminae*** /'lamɪniː/) a thin plate or layer, esp of bone, rock or metal. [17c: Latin, meaning 'thin plate']

laminate *verb* /'lamɪneɪt/ **1** to beat (a material, esp metal) into thin sheets. **2** to form (a composite material) by bonding or glueing together two or more sheets of that material. **3** to cover or overlay (a surface) with a thin sheet of protective material, eg transparent plastic film. **4** *tr & intr* to separate or be separated into thin layers. ▸ *noun* /'lamɪnət/ a laminated sheet, material, etc. ▸ *adj* /'lamɪnət/ of a material: composed of layers or beaten into thin sheets. ▪ **lamination** *noun*. [17c: from Latin *lamina* thin plate]

Lammas *noun, Christianity* a former church feast day held on 1 August, one of the four **quarter days** in Scotland. [Anglo-Saxon *hlafmæsse*, from *hlaf* loaf + *mæsse* mass]

lamp *noun* **1** a piece of equipment designed to give out light: *an electric lamp • an oil lamp.* **2** any piece of equipment that produces ultraviolet or infrared radiation and which is used in the treatment of certain medical conditions. [12c: from Greek *lampein* to shine]

lampblack *noun* soot obtained from burning carbon and used as a pigment. [15c]

lampoon *noun* an attack, usu in the form of satirical prose or verse, on someone or something. ▸ *verb* to satirize (someone or something). ▪ **lampooner** *or* **lampoonist** *noun*. [17c: from French *lampons* let's booze]

lamppost *noun* a tall post that supports a streetlamp.

lamprey *noun* (**-eys**) *zool* a primitive eel-like fish with a sucker-like mouth. [13c: from French *lampreie*]

lampshade *noun* a shade placed over a lamp or light bulb to soften or direct the light coming from it.

lampshell see **brachiopod**

LAN *abbrev, comput* local area network, a computer network that operates over a small area, such as an office or group of offices.

Lancastrian *noun* **1** someone who comes from or lives in Lancaster or Lancashire. **2** *hist* a supporter of the House of Lancaster in the Wars of the Roses. Compare **Yorkist**. ▸ *adj* relating to Lancaster, the House of Lancaster or Lancashire. [19c]

lance *noun* **1** a long spear used as a cavalry weapon. **2** any similar implement used in hunting, whaling, etc. ▸ *verb* **1** to cut open (a boil, abscess, etc) with a lancet. **2** to pierce with, or as if with, a lance. [13c: from Latin *lancea* a light spear with a leather thong attached]

lance corporal *noun* a British army rank between private and corporal, being the lowest rank of non-commissioned officer.

lanceolate *adj* shaped like a spear-head, tapering at both ends. [18c: from Latin *lanceola* small lance]

lancer *noun, formerly* a cavalry soldier belonging to a regiment armed with lances.

lancet *noun* a small pointed surgical knife which has both edges sharpened. [15c: from French *lancette* a small lance]

lancet arch *noun, archit* a high, narrow, pointed arch.

lancet window *noun, archit* a high, narrow, pointed window.

Lancs. /laŋks/ *abbrev, English county* Lancashire.

land *noun* **1** the solid part of the Earth's surface as opposed to the area covered by water. **2** ground or soil, esp with regard to its use or quality: *farm land*. **3** ground that is used for agriculture. **4** a country, state or region: *native land*. **5** (**lands**) estates. **6** *in compounds* any area of ground that is characterized in a specified way: *gangland* • *hinterland*. ▸ *verb* **1** *tr & intr* to come or bring to rest on the ground or water, or in a particular place, after flight through the air: *The plane landed on time*. **2** *intr* to end up in a specified place or position, esp after a fall, jump, throw, etc. **3** *tr & intr* to end up or cause someone to end up in a certain position or situation, usu unwelcome or unfavourable: *landed themselves in trouble*. **4** to bring on to the land from a ship: *landed the cargo*. **5** to bring (a fish, esp one caught on a line) out of the water. **6** *informal* to be successful in getting (a job, contract, prize, etc). **7** *informal* to give someone (a punch or slap). [Anglo-Saxon]

PHRASAL VERBS **land up** *informal* to come to be in a specified position or situation: *landed up homeless after losing his job*. **land sb with sth** *informal* to give or pass (something unpleasant or unwanted) to them: *landed us with all the bills*.

landau /ˈlandɔː/ *noun* a four-wheeled horse-drawn carriage with a removable front cover and a back cover which folds down. [18c: named after Landau in Germany, where they were first made]

landed *adj* **1** owning land or estates: *landed gentry*. **2** consisting of or derived from land: *landed estates*.

landfall *noun* the first land visible towards the end of a journey by sea or air.

landfill *noun* **1** a site where rubbish is disposed of by burying it under layers of earth. **2** the rubbish that is disposed of in this way. [20c]

land girl *noun, Brit, formerly* a member of the Women's Land Army, who worked on a farm, esp during World Wars I and II.

landing *noun* **1** the act of coming or being put ashore or of returning to the ground. **2** a place for disembarking, esp from a ship. **3** a level part of a staircase either between two flights of steps, or at the very top. [15c]

landing gear *noun* the wheels and supporting structure which allow an aircraft to land and take off.

landing stage *noun* a platform where passengers, cargo, etc from a ship can come ashore.

landing strip *noun* a long narrow stretch of ground where aircraft can take off and land.

landlady *noun* **1** a woman who rents property out to a tenant or tenants. **2** a woman who owns or runs a public house or hotel.

landlocked *adj* of a country or a piece of land: almost or completely enclosed by land.

landlord *noun* **1** a man who rents property out to a tenant or tenants. **2** a man who owns or runs a public house or hotel.

landlubber *noun* someone who has no sailing or sea-going experience.

landmark *noun* **1** a distinctive feature, esp one used by sailors or travellers as an indication of where they are. **2** an event or development of importance, esp one that is significant in the history or progress of something.

landmass *noun* a large area of land unbroken by seas.

land mine *noun* an explosive device that is laid on or near the surface of the ground and which detonates if it is disturbed from above.

landowner *noun* someone who owns land.

landscape *noun* **1** the area and features of land that can be seen in a broad view, esp when they form a particular type of scenery. **2** **a** a painting, drawing, photograph, etc of the countryside; **b** this genre of art. **3** an orientation of a page, illustration, etc that is wider than it is tall or deep. Compare **portrait**. ▸ *verb* to improve the look of (a garden, park, etc) by enhancing the existing natural features or by artificially creating new ones. [17c: from Dutch *land* + *schap* creation]

landscape gardening *noun* the art or practice of laying out a garden, grounds, etc, esp to produce the effect of a natural landscape. ▪ **landscape gardener** *noun*.

landside *noun* the part of an airport accessible to the general public. Compare **airside**.

landslide *noun* **1** (*also* **landslip**) **a** a sudden downward movement of a mass of soil and rock material, esp in mountainous areas; **b** the accumulation of soil and rock material from a landslide. **2** a victory in an election by an overwhelming majority.

lane *noun* **1** a narrow road or street. **2** a subdivision of a road for a single line of traffic. **3** a regular course taken by ships across the sea, or by aircraft through the air: *shipping lane*. **4** a marked subdivision of a running track or swimming pool for one competitor. **5** a division of a bowling alley. [Anglo-Saxon *lanu*]

langouste /lɑ̃ŋ'guːst/ *noun* a saltwater crustacean similar to the lobster but rather smaller and with no claws. Also called **spiny lobster**. [19c: French, related to Latin *locusta* a lobster or locust]

langoustine /lɑ̃ŋgʊ'stiːn/ *noun* a saltwater crustacean similar to the crayfish and rather bigger than the king prawn. [1940s: French diminutive of *langouste*]

language *noun* **1** a formalized system of communication, esp one that uses sounds or written symbols which the majority of a particular community will readily understand. **2** the speech and writing of a particular nation or social group. **3** the faculty of speech. **4** a specified style of speech or verbal expression: *elegant language*. **5** any other way of communicating or expressing meaning: *sign language*. **6** professional or specialized vocabulary: *legal language*. **7** a system of signs and symbols used to write computer programs. [13c: from French *langage*]

languid *adj* **1** lacking in energy or vitality. **2** sluggish; slow-moving. [16c: from Latin *languere* to grow faint]

languish *verb, intr* **1** to spend time in hardship or discomfort. **2** to grow weak; to lose energy or vitality. **3** to pine. ▪ **languishment** *noun*. [14c: see **languid**]

languor /'laŋgə(r)/ *noun* **1** a feeling of dullness or lack of energy. **2** tender softness or sentiment. **3** a stuffy suffocating atmosphere or stillness. ▪ **languorous** *adj*. [14c: from Latin *languere* to grow faint]

lank *adj* **1** long and thin. **2** of hair, etc: long, straight and dull. [Anglo-Saxon *hlanc*]

lanky *adj* (***-ier, -iest***) thin and tall, esp in an awkward and ungainly way. ▪ **lankiness** *noun*. [Anglo-Saxon *hlanc*]

lanolin *noun* a fat that occurs naturally in sheep's wool, used in cosmetics, ointments and soaps, and for treating leather. [19c: from Latin *lana* wool + *oleum* oil]

lantern *noun* **1** a lamp or light contained in a transparent case, usu of glass. **2** the top part of a lighthouse, where the light is kept. **3** a structure, esp on the top of a dome, that admits light and air. [14c: from French *lanterne*]

lantern jaws *plural noun* long thin jaws that give the face a drawn appearance. ▪ **lantern-jawed** *adj*.

lanthanide *noun, chem* any of a group of 15 highly reactive metallic elements with atomic numbers ranging from 57 (lanthanum) to 71 (lutetium). Also called **rare-earth**. [20c: see **lanthanum**]

lanthanum *noun, chem* (symbol **La**) a silvery-white metallic element. [19c: from Greek *lanthanein* to escape notice]

lanugo /lə'njuːgoʊ/ *noun* a covering of soft downy hairs, especially those that cover the body of the human fetus from about 20 weeks and which are shed in the ninth month of gestation. [17c: Latin]

lanyard *noun* **1** a cord for hanging a knife, whistle, etc round the neck, esp as worn by sailors. **2** *naut* a short rope for fastening rigging, etc. [15c: from French *laniere*]

lap[1] *verb* (***lapped, lapping***) **1** usu of an animal: to drink (milk, water, etc) using the tongue. **2** *tr & intr* of water, etc: to wash or flow against (a shore or other surface) with a light splashing sound. ▸ *noun* the sound, act or process of lapping. [Anglo-Saxon *lapian*]

PHRASAL VERBS **lap sth up** to drink or consume it eagerly or greedily.

lap[2] *noun* **1** the front part of the body from the waist to the knees, when in a sitting position. **2** the part of someone's clothing, esp of a skirt or dress, which covers this part of the body. [Anglo-Saxon *læppa*]

lap[3] *noun* **1** one circuit of a racecourse or other track. **2** one section of a journey. **3** a part which overlaps or the amount it overlaps by. ▸ *verb* **1** to get ahead of (another competitor in a race) by one or more laps. **2** to make (something) overlap (something else). **3** *intr* to lie with an overlap. [14c as *lappen* to enfold]

lapdog *noun* a small pet dog. [17c: from **lap**[2]]

lapel /lə'pɛl/ *noun* the part of a collar on a coat or jacket that is folded back towards the shoulders. ▪ **lapelled** *adj*. [18c: a diminutive of **lap**[2]]

lapidary *noun* (***-ies***) someone whose job is to cut and polish gemstones. ▸ *adj* relating to stones. [14c: from Latin *lapis* stone]

lapis lazuli /'lapɪs 'lazjʊliː/ *noun* **1** *geol* a deep-blue mineral used as a gemstone. **2** a bright-blue colour. [14c: Latin, from *lapis* stone + *lazuli* azure]

lap of honour *noun* (***laps of honour***) a ceremonial circuit of a racecourse or sports ground by the winner or winners.

Lapp *noun* **1** (*also* **Laplander**) a member of a mainly nomadic people who live chiefly in the far north of Scandinavia. **2** (*also* **Lappish**) the language spoken by this people. ▸ *adj* referring or relating to this people, their language or their culture. [19c: Swedish, meaning 'lip']

lappet *noun* **1** a small flap or fold in material, a piece of clothing, etc. **2** a piece of loose hanging flesh. [16c: a diminutive of **lap**[2]]

lapse *noun* **1** a slight mistake or failure. **2** a perceived decline in standards of behaviour, etc. **3** a passing of time. **4** *law* the loss of a right or privilege because of failure to renew a claim to it. ▸ *verb, intr* **1** to fail to behave in what is perceived as a proper or morally acceptable way. **2** to turn away from a faith or belief. **3** (*usu* **lapse into sth**) to pass into or return to (a specified state). **4** *law* of a right, privilege, etc: to become invalid because the claim to it has not been renewed. **5** of a membership of a club, society, etc: to become invalid, usu because the fees have not been paid or some other condition has not been met. ▪ **lapsed** *adj*. [16c: from Latin *lapsus* a slip]

laptop *noun* a portable personal computer, small enough to be used on someone's lap. Compare **notebook** (sense 2). [20c: orig *laptop computer*]

lapwing *noun* a crested bird of the plover family. Also called **peewit**. [Anglo-Saxon *hleapewince*]

larceny *noun* (***-ies***) *law, old use* theft of personal property. ▪ **larcenist** *noun*. [15c: from French *larcin*]

larch *noun* **1** a deciduous coniferous tree with rosettes of short needles and egg-shaped cones. **2** the wood of this tree. [16c: from German *Lärche*]

lard *noun* a soft white preparation made from pig fat, used in cooking and baking, ointments and perfumes. ▸ *verb* **1** to coat (meat, etc) in lard. **2** to insert strips of bacon or pork into (lean meat) in order to make it more moist and tender once it is cooked. **3** to sprinkle (a piece of writing, etc) with technical details or over-elaborate words. [15c: from Latin *laridum* bacon fat]

larder *noun* a cool room or cupboard for storing food, orig bacon. [14c: from French *lardier*, from Latin *laridum* bacon fat]

lardon *noun* a strip or cube of fatty bacon or pork used in larding food, and in French salads, etc. [15c]

large *adj* **1** occupying a comparatively big space. **2** comparatively big in size, extent, amount, etc. **3** broad in scope; wide-ranging; comprehensive. **4** generous. ▸ *adv* importantly; prominently: *loom large.* ▪ **largeness** *noun.* [12c: French, from Latin *largus* plentiful]

IDIOMS **as large as life** *informal* in person. **at large 1** of prisoners, etc: free and threatening. **2** in general; as a whole: *people at large.* **3** at length and with full details. **larger than life** exaggerated; flamboyant, impressive.

large intestine *noun* in mammals: the part of the alimentary canal comprising the **caecum**, **colon** and **rectum**. See also **small intestine**.

largely *adv* **1** mainly or chiefly. **2** to a great extent. [13c]

largesse *or* **largess** *noun* **1** generosity. **2** gifts, money, etc given generously. [13c: French, from Latin *largus* plentiful]

largo *music, adv* slowly and with dignity. ▸ *adj* slow and dignified. ▸ *noun* a piece of music to be played in this way. [17c: Italian, meaning 'broad']

lariat *noun* **1** a lasso. **2** a rope used for tethering animals. [19c: from Spanish *la reata* the lasso]

lark[1] *noun* any of various gregarious, brownish birds, esp the skylark. [Anglo-Saxon *lawerce*]

lark[2] *noun, informal* **1** a joke or piece of fun. **2** *Brit informal* a job or activity: *I'm really getting into this gardening lark now.* ▸ *verb, intr* (*usu* **lark about** *or* **around**) *informal* to play or fool about frivolously. [19c]

larkspur *noun* a plant with blue, white or pink flowers, related to the delphinium. [16c]

larva *noun* (***larvae*** /ˈlɑːviː/) *zool* the immature stage in the life cycle of many insects between the egg and pupa stages. ▪ **larval** *adj.* [17c: Latin, meaning 'ghost' or 'mask']

laryngeal /ləˈrɪndʒəl/ *adj* relating to the **larynx**.

laryngitis /larɪnˈdʒaɪtɪs/ *noun* inflammation of the larynx.

larynx /ˈlarɪŋks/ *noun* (***larynges*** /ləˈrɪndʒiːz/ *or* ***larynxes***) in mammals and other higher vertebrates: the expanded upper part of the trachea containing the vocal cords. [16c: Greek]

lasagne *or* **lasagna** /ləˈzanjə/ *noun* **1** pasta in the form of thin flat sheets. **2** a dish made of layers with these sheets alternating with minced beef or vegetables in a tomato sauce and cheese sauce. [18c: Italian; *lasagne* is the plural form and *lasagna* is the singular]

lascivious /ləˈsɪvɪəs/ *adj* **1** of behaviour, thoughts, etc: lewd; lecherous. **2** of poetry, prose, art, etc: causing or inciting lewd or lecherous behaviour, thoughts, etc. [15c: from Latin *lascivus* playful or wanton]

laser *noun* a device that produces a very powerful narrow beam of coherent light of a single wavelength by stimulating the emission of photons from atoms, molecules or ions. [20c: from *l*ight *a*mplification by *s*timulated *e*mission of *r*adiation, modelled on **maser**]

laser disc *noun* a disc on which material is recorded as a series of microscopic pits readable only by laser beam.

laser printer *noun, comput* a type of fast high-quality printer that uses a laser beam to produce text, etc and transfers this to paper.

lash[1] *noun* **1** a stroke or blow, usu made by a whip as a form of punishment. **2** the flexible part of a whip. **3** an eyelash. **4** (**the lash**) punishment by whipping. ▸ *verb* **1** to hit or beat with a lash. **2** *tr & intr* to move suddenly, restlessly, uncontrollably, etc. **3** to attack with harsh scolding words or criticism. **4** *intr* to make a sudden whip-like movement. **5** *tr & intr* of waves or rain: to beat with great force. **6** to urge on as if with a whip. [14c]

PHRASAL VERBS **lash out 1 a** to hit out violently; **b** to speak in a very hostile or aggressive manner. **2** *informal* to spend money extravagantly.

lash[2] *verb, chiefly naut* to fasten with a rope or cord. [17c]

lashing[1] *noun* **1** a beating with a whip. **2** (**lashings**) a generous amount. [15c]

lashing[2] *noun* a rope used for tying things fast. [17c]

lass *noun, Scot & N Eng dialect* a girl or young woman. [14c]

Lassa fever *noun* a viral disease, sometimes fatal, of tropical Africa. [20c: named after Lassa, a village in NE Nigeria where it was first identified]

lassie *noun, Scot & N Eng dialect, informal* a girl. [18c]

lassitude *noun* physical or mental tiredness; a lack of energy and enthusiasm. [16c: from Latin *lassus* weary]

lasso /ləˈsuː/ *noun* (***lassos*** *or* ***lassoes***) a long rope with a sliding noose at one end used for catching cattle, horses, etc. ▸ *verb* (***lassoes, lassoed***) to catch with a lasso. [18c: from Spanish *lazo*]

last[1] *adj* **1** being, coming or occurring at the end of a series or after all others. **2** most recent; happening immediately before the present (week, month, year, etc). **3** only remaining after all the rest have gone or been used up: *gave him her last fiver.* **4** least likely, desirable, suitable, etc: *the last person you'd expect help from.* **5** final: *administered the last rites.* ▸ *adv* **1** most recently: *When did you see her last?* **2** lastly; at the end (of a series of events, etc): *and last she served the coffee.* ▸ *noun* **1** a person or thing that is at the end or behind the rest. **2** (**the last**) the end; a final moment, part, etc: *That's the last of the milk.* **3** (**the last**) the final appearance or mention: *We haven't heard the last of him.* [Anglo-Saxon *latost* latest]

IDIOMS **at last** *or* **at long last** in the end, esp after a long delay. **to the last** until the very end.

last[2] *verb, tr & intr* **1** to take (a specified amount of time) to complete, happen, come to an end, etc. **2**

to be adequate (for someone): *enough water to last us a week*. **3** to be or keep fresh or in good condition: *The bread will only last one more day.* [Anglo-Saxon *læstan*]

last[3] *noun* a foot-shaped piece of wood or metal used in making and repairing shoes, etc. [Anglo-Saxon *læste*]

last-ditch *adj* done as a last resort: *a last-ditch attempt*.

lasting *adj* existing or continuing for a long time or permanently: *had a lasting effect*.

Last Judgement see **Day of Judgement**

lastly *adv* used to introduce the last item or items in a series or list: finally.

last name *noun* a **surname**.

the last post *noun, military* **1** a final bugle call of a series given to signal that it is time to retire at night. **2** a farewell bugle call at military funerals.

the last rites *plural noun, Christianity* the formalized ceremonial acts performed for someone who is dying.

the last straw *noun, informal* a minor inconvenience which, if it occurs after a series of other misfortunes, difficulties, accidents, etc, serves to make the whole situation intolerable.

the Last Supper *noun, Christianity* the final meal Jesus had with his disciples before the Crucifixion.

lat. *abbrev* latitude.

latch *noun* **1** a door catch consisting of a bar which is lowered or raised from its notch by a lever or string. **2** a door lock by which a door may be opened from the inside using a handle, and from the outside by using a key. ▸ *verb, tr & intr* to fasten or be fastened with a latch. [Anglo-Saxon *læccan*]

PHRASAL VERBS **latch on** *informal* to understand. **latch on to sth** *informal* to cling to it, often obsessively.

latchkey child *or* **latchkey kid** *noun* a child who comes home from school while the parent or parents are still out at work.

late *adj* **1** coming, arriving, etc after the expected or usual time. **2 a** far on in the day or night: *late afternoon*; **b** well into the evening or night; **c** *in compounds* occurring towards the end of a specified historical period, etc: *late-Georgian architecture*; **d** written, painted, etc towards the end of someone's life or towards the end of their active career: *a late Picasso*. **3** happening, growing, etc at a relatively advanced time: *Let's go to the late showing*. **4** dead: *his late father*. **5** former: *the late prime minister*. **6** recent: *quite a late model of car*. ▸ *adv* **1** after the expected or usual time: *He arrived late for the meeting*. **2** far on in the day or night: *He arrived late on Thursday.* **3** at an advanced time: *flower late in the season*. **4** recently: *The letter was sent as late as this morning*. **5** formerly, but no longer: *late of Glasgow*. ▪ **lateness** *noun*. [Anglo-Saxon *læt*]

lateen *adj, naut* denoting a triangular sail on a long sloping yard. [18c: from French *voile latine* Latin sail]

lately *adv* in the recent past; not long ago.

latent *adj* **1** of a characteristic, tendency, etc: present or existing in an undeveloped or hidden form. **2** *pathol* of a disease: failing to present or not yet presenting the usual or expected symptoms. ▪ **latency** *noun*. [17c: from Latin *latere* to lie hidden]

latent heat *noun, physics* the amount of heat energy required to change a solid to a liquid, or a liquid to a gas, without a change in temperature.

later *adj* more late. ▸ *adv* at some time after, or in the near future. [16c]

lateral *adj* at, from or relating to a side or the side of something: *lateral fins*. ▪ **laterally** *adv*. [17c: from Latin *lateris* side]

lateral thinking *noun* an indirect or seemingly illogical approach to problem-solving or understanding something.

latest *adj* **1** most recent. **2** (**the latest**) the most recent news, occurrence, fashion, etc. [16c]

IDIOMS **at the latest** not later than a specified time

latex *noun* (***latexes*** *or* ***latices*** /ˈleɪtɪsiːz/) **1** a thick milky juice that is produced by some plants and used commercially, esp in the manufacture of rubber. **2** a synthetic product that has similar properties to rubber. [17c: Latin, meaning 'liquid']

lath /lɑːθ/ *noun* a thin narrow strip of wood, esp one of a series used to support plaster, tiles, slates, etc. [Anglo-Saxon *lætt*]

lathe *noun* a machine tool used to cut, drill or polish a piece of metal, wood or plastic that is rotated against its cutting edge. [17c]

lather /ˈlɑːðə(r)/ *noun* **1** a foam made by mixing water and soap or detergent. **2** foamy sweat, eg, on a horse during strenuous exercise. ▸ *verb* **1** *intr* to form a lather. **2** to cover (something) with lather. ▪ **lathery** *adj*. [Anglo-Saxon *leathor* washing soda]

IDIOMS **in a lather** *informal* extremely agitated.

Latin *noun* **1** the language of ancient Rome and its empire. **2** a person of Italian, Spanish, Portuguese or Latin American extraction. ▸ *adj* **1** relating to, or in, the Latin language. **2** applied to languages derived from Latin, esp Italian, Spanish and Portuguese. **3** of a person: Italian, Spanish, Portuguese or Latin American in origin. **4** passionate or easily excitable: *his Latin temperament*. **5** belonging or relating to the Roman Catholic Church. [Anglo-Saxon: from Latin *Latinus* of Latium]

Latin American *noun* an inhabitant of Latin America, the areas in America where languages such as Spanish and Portuguese are spoken. ▪ **Latin-American** *adj*.

Latino *or* **Latina** *noun* a man or woman respectively, usu a N American, who is of Latin American descent. [20c]

latish *adj, adv* slightly late.

latitude *noun* **1** *geog* angular distance north or south of the equator, measured from 0 degrees at the equator to 90 degrees at the north and south poles. Compare **longitude**. **2** (*usu* **latitudes**) *geog* a region or area thought of in terms of its distance from the equator or its climate: *warm latitudes*. **3** scope for freedom of action or choice. ▪ **latitudinal** *adj*. ▪ **latitudinally** *adv*. [14c: from Latin *latitudo* breadth]

latitudinarian *noun* someone who believes in freedom of choice, thought, action, etc, esp in religious matters. [17c]

latrine *noun* a lavatory, esp in a barracks or camp, etc. [17c: from Latin *lavatrina* a privy]

latte /ˈlɑːteɪ, ˈlateɪ/ *noun* (***lattes***) espresso coffee with frothed hot milk. Also called **caffè latte**. [1990s: from Italian *caffè latte* milk coffee]

latter *adj* **1** nearer the end than the beginning: *the latter part of the holiday.* **2** used when referring to two people or things: mentioned, considered, etc second. [Anglo-Saxon *lætra*]

IDIOMS **the latter** of two people or things: the second one mentioned, considered, etc. Compare **former**.

latter-day *adj* recent or modern.

Latter-day Saints *plural noun* the name that the Mormons prefer to call themselves.

latterly *adv* **1** recently. **2** towards the end. [18c]

lattice *plural noun* **1** (*also* **lattice-work**) an open frame made by crossing narrow strips of wood or metal over each other to form an ornamental pattern and used esp in gates and fences. **2** (*also* **lattice window**) a window with small diamond-shaped panels of glass held in place with strips of lead. **3** *chem* the regular three-dimensional grouping of atoms, ions or molecules that forms the structure of a crystalline solid. ▪ **latticed** *adj.* [14c: from French *latte* lath]

Latvian *adj* belonging or relating to Latvia, its inhabitants, or their language. ▸ *noun* **1** a citizen or inhabitant of, or person born in, Latvia. **2** the official language of Latvia.

laud *formal, verb* **1** to praise. **2** to sing or speak the praises of (someone or something, esp a god). ▸ *noun* praise. See also **lauds**. [14c: from Latin *laudis* praise]

laudable *adj* worthy of praise; commendable. ▪ **laudability** *noun.* ▪ **laudably** *adv.*

laudanum /ˈlɔːdənəm/ *noun* a solution of morphine in alcohol, prepared from raw opium, formerly used to relieve pain, aid sleep, etc. [17c]

laudatory *adj* containing or expressing praise. [16c: from Latin *laudatorius*]

lauds *plural noun, now esp RC Church* the first of the **canonical hours** of the day, when traditional morning prayers and psalms are said and sung. [14c: pl of **laud**]

laugh *verb* **1** *intr* to make spontaneous sounds associated with happiness, amusement, scorn, etc. **2** to express (a feeling, etc) by laughing: *laughed his contempt.* **3** *intr* (**laugh at sb** *or* **sth**) **a** to make fun of or ridicule them or it; **b** to find them or it funny. ▸ *noun* **1** an act or sound of laughing. **2** *informal* someone or something that is good fun, amusing, etc. [Anglo-Saxon *hlæhhan*]

IDIOMS **be laughing** *informal* to be in a very favourable situation. **have the last laugh** *informal* to win or succeed in the end, esp after setbacks; to be finally proved right.

PHRASAL VERBS **laugh sth off** to treat an injury, embarrassment, etc lightly or trivially.

laughable *adj* **1** deserving to be laughed at. **2** absurd; ludicrous. ▪ **laughably** *adv.*

laughing gas *noun* **nitrous oxide**, esp when used as an anaesthetic.

laughing hyena see **hyena**

laughing jackass see **kookaburra**

laughing stock *noun* someone or something that is the object of ridicule, mockery, contempt, etc.

laughter *noun* the act or sound of laughing.

launch[1] *verb* **1** **a** to send (a ship or boat, etc) into the water at the beginning of a voyage; **b** to send (a newly-built ship or boat) into the water for the first time. **2** to send (a spacecraft, missile, etc) into space or into the air. **3** to start (someone or something) off in a specified direction. **4** to bring (a new product) on to the market, esp with promotions and publicity. **5** to begin (an attack, etc). **6** *intr* (**launch into sth**) **a** to begin (an undertaking, etc) with vigour and enthusiasm; **b** to begin (a story or speech, esp a long one). ▸ *noun* **1** the action or an instance of a ship, spacecraft, missile, etc being sent off into the water or into the air. **2** the start of something. ▪ **launcher** *noun.* [15c: from Latin *lanceare* to wield a lance]

launch[2] *noun* a large powerful motorboat. [17c: from Spanish *lancha*]

launching pad *or* **launch pad** *noun* the area or platform for launching a spacecraft or missile, etc.

launder *verb* **1** to wash and iron (clothes, linen, etc). **2** *informal* to transfer (illegally obtained money, etc) to cover up its origins. [14c: from Latin *lavare* to wash]

launderette *or* **laundrette** *noun* a place where clothes can be washed and dried using coin-operated machines. *N Am equivalent* **laundromat**. [20c: orig a trademark]

laundry *noun* (**-ies**) **1** a place where clothes, linen, etc are washed. **2** clothes, linen, etc for washing or newly washed.

laureate *adj* **1** (*often following a noun*) honoured for artistic or intellectual distinction: *poet laureate.* **2** crowned with laurel leaves as a sign of honour or distinction. ▸ *noun* someone honoured for artistic or intellectual achievement, esp a **poet laureate**. [14c: from Latin *laurus* laurel]

laurel *noun* **1** a small evergreen tree with smooth dark shiny leaves. **2** a crown of laurel leaves worn as a symbol of victory or mark of honour. **3** (**laurels**) honour; praise. [14c: from Latin *laurus*]

IDIOMS **look to one's laurels** to beware of losing one's reputation by being outclassed. **rest on one's laurels** to be satisfied with one's past successes and so not bother to achieve anything more.

lava *noun* **1** *geol* **magma** that has erupted from a volcano or fissure. **2** the solid rock that forms as a result of cooling and solidification of this material. [18c: Italian, orig meaning 'a sudden stream of water, caused by rain']

lavatorial *adj* of humour, jokes, etc: rude, esp in making use of references to excrement.

lavatory *noun* (**-ies**) **1** a piece of equipment, usu bowl-shaped with a seat, where urine and faeces are deposited and then flushed away by water into a sewer. **2** a room or building containing one or more of these. [14c: from Latin *lavare* to wash]

lavender *noun* **1** a plant or shrub with sweet-smelling pale bluish-purple flowers. **2** the dried flowers from this plant, used to perfume clothes or linen. **3** a pale bluish-purple colour. **4** a perfume made from the distilled flowers of this plant. Also called **lavender water**. [13c: from Latin *lavendula*]

lavish *adj* **1** spending or giving generously. **2** gorgeous or luxurious: *lavish decoration.* **3** extravagant or excessive. ▸ *verb* to spend (money) or give (praise, etc) freely or generously. ▪ **lavishly** *adv.* [15c: from French *lavasse* deluge of rain]

law *noun* **1** a customary rule recognized as allowing or prohibiting certain actions. **2** a collection of such rules according to which people live or a country or state is governed. **3** the control which such rules exercise: *law and order.* **4** a controlling force: *Their* *word is law.* **5** a collection of laws as a social system or a subject for study. **6** one of a group of rules which set out how certain games, sports, etc should be played. **7** the legal system as a recourse; litigation: *go to law.* **8** a rule in science, philosophy, etc, based on practice or observation, which says that under certain conditions certain things will always happen. [Anglo-Saxon *lagu*]

IDIOMS **the law 1** people who are knowledgeable about law, esp professionally. **2** *informal* the police or a member of the police.

law-abiding *adj* obeying the law.

lawcourt *noun* (*also* **court of law**) a place where people accused of crimes are tried and legal disagreements settled.

lawful *adj* **1** allowed by or according to law. **2** just or rightful. ▪ **lawfully** *adv.*

lawless *adj* **1** ignoring or breaking the law, esp violently. **2** having no laws. ▪ **lawlessness** *noun.*

Law Lord *noun* **1** a peer in the House of Lords who sits in the highest Court of Appeal. **2** *Scot* a judge in the Court of Session.

lawman *noun, US, now chiefly archaic or facetious* a sheriff or policeman.

lawn¹ *noun* an area of smooth mown cultivated grass, esp as part of a garden or park. [18c]

lawn² *noun* fine linen or cotton. [15c]

lawnmower *noun* a machine for cutting grass. [19c]

lawn tennis *noun* **tennis** (sense 1).

lawrencium *noun, chem* (symbol **Lr**) a synthetic radioactive metallic element. [20c: named after the US physicist, Ernest Orlando Lawrence]

lawsuit *noun* an argument or disagreement taken to a court of law to be settled.

lawyer *noun* a person employed in the legal profession, esp a solicitor. [14c]

lax *adj* **1** showing little care or concern over behaviour, morals, etc. **2** loose, slack or flabby. **3** negligent. ▪ **laxity** *noun.* ▪ **laxly** *adv.* [14c: from Latin *laxus* loose]

laxative *adj* inducing movement of the bowels. ▸ *noun* a medicine or food that induces movement of the bowels. [14c: from Latin *laxare* to loosen]

lay¹ *verb* (***laid***) **1** to place (something) on a surface, esp in a horizontal position: *laid the letter on the table.* **2** to put or bring (something) to a stated position or condition: *laid her hand on his arm.* **3** to design, arrange or prepare: *lay plans.* **4** to put plates and cutlery, etc on (a table) ready for a meal. **5** to prepare (a fire) by putting coal, etc in the grate. **6** *tr & intr* of a female bird: to produce (eggs). **7** to present: *laid his case before the court.* **8** to set down as a basis: *laid the ground rules.* **9** to deal with or remove: *lay a fear.* **10** *informal* to place (a bet): *I'll lay 20 quid you can't do it.* ▸ *noun* the way or position in which something is lying: *the lay of the surrounding countryside.* [Anglo-Saxon *lecgan*]

IDIOMS **lay bare** to reveal or explain (a plan or intention that has been kept secret). **lay down one's arms** to surrender or call a truce. **lay down the law** to dictate in a forceful and domineering way. **lay it on thick** *informal* to exaggerate, esp in connection with flattery, praise, etc. **lay one's hands on sb** *or* **sth** *informal* to succeed in getting hold of them or it. **lay oneself open to sth** to expose oneself to criticism or attack. **lay sth on sb 1** to assign or attribute it to them: *laid the blame on his friends.* **2** *informal* to give it to them. **lay sb low** of an illness: to affect them severely. **lay to rest** to bury (a dead body). **lay waste** to destroy or devastate completely.

PHRASAL VERBS **lay sth down 1** to put it on the ground or some other surface. **2** to give it as a deposit, pledge, etc. **3** to give it up or sacrifice it: *lay down one's life.* **4** to formulate or devise: *lay down a plan.* **5** to store (wine) in a cellar. **lay sth in** to get and store a supply of it. **lay into sb** *informal* to attack or scold them severely. **lay sb off** to dismiss (an employee) when there is no work available. See also **lay-off**. **lay off sth** *informal* to stop it. **lay off sb** *informal* to leave them alone. **lay sth on** to provide a supply of it. **lay sb out 1** *informal* to knock them unconscious. **2** to prepare their dead body for burial. **lay sth out 1** to plan and arrange (esp land or natural features). **2** to spread it out or display it. **3** *informal* to spend it. See also **layout**. **lay sb up** *informal* to force them to stay in bed or at home. **lay sth up 1** to keep or store it. **2** to put a ship out of use, esp for repairs.

---

lay, lie

Be careful not to use the verb **lay** when you mean **lie**, and vice versa. Their meanings are close and their forms overlap, since **lay** is also the past of **lie**:

✓ *Many armies began to lay down their arms.*
✓ *Lucy lay on the bed.*
✗ *I got so tired I used to lay down on the bunk.*

Be careful also not to use **laid** instead of **lain**, and vice versa. **Laid** is the past and past participle of **lay**, but **lain** is only the past participle of **lie**:

✓ *He paused, then laid a hand on her shoulder.*
✗ *He had lain the saw aside and was hammering.*
✓ *He had lain on his bed all afternoon.*

---

lay² *past tense of* **lie²**

lay³ *adj* **1** relating to or involving people who are not members of the clergy. **2** not having specialized or professional knowledge of a particular subject. [14c: from Greek *laos* the people]

lay⁴ *noun* a short narrative or lyric poem, esp one that is meant to be sung. [13c]

layabout *noun, informal* a habitually idle person.

lay-by *noun* (***lay-bys***) *Brit* an area off to the side of a road where cars can stop safely.

layer *noun* **1** a thickness or covering, esp one of several on top of each other. **2** *in compounds* someone or something that lays something specified: *bricklayer.* **3** a hen that regularly lays eggs. **4** a shoot from a plant fastened into the soil so that it can take root while still attached to the parent plant. ▸ *verb* **1** to arrange or cut in layers. **2** to produce (a new plant) by preparing a layer from the parent plant. ▪ **layered** *adj.* [16c: from **lay¹**]

layette *noun* a complete set of clothes, blankets, etc for a new baby. [19c: French]

layman, laywoman *or* **layperson** *noun* **1** someone who is not a member of the clergy. **2** someone who does not have specialized or professional knowledge of a particular subject. See also **laity**. [15c: from **lay³**]

lay-off *noun* a dismissal of employees when there is no work available. [19c]

layout *noun* **1** an arrangement or plan of how land, buildings, pages of a book, etc are to be set out. **2**

the things displayed or arranged in this way. **3** the general appearance of a printed page.

laze *verb, intr* (*often* **laze about** *or* **around**) to be idle or lazy. ▸ *noun* a period of time spent lazing. [16c: a back-formation from **lazy**]

lazy *adj* (*-ier, -iest*) **1** disinclined to work or do anything requiring effort. **2** idle. **3** appropriate to idleness. **4** of a river: slow-moving; sluggish. ▪ **lazily** *adv.* ▪ **laziness** *noun.* [16c]

lazybones *noun* (*pl* ***lazybones***) *informal* someone who is lazy.

lb *abbrev* pound or pounds (Latin *libra*).

lbw *or* **l.b.w.** *abbrev, cricket* leg before wicket.

lc *abbrev* **1** *loco citato* (Latin), in the place cited. **2** *printing* lower case.

LCD *abbrev* **1** liquid crystal display. **2** (*also* **lcd**) lowest common denominator.

LCM *or* **lcm** *abbrev* lowest common multiple.

LEA *abbrev, Brit* Local Education Authority.

lea *noun, poetic* a field, meadow or piece of arable or pasture land. [Anglo-Saxon *leah*]

leach *verb* **1** *chem* to wash (a soluble substance) out of (a solid) by allowing a suitable liquid solvent to percolate through it. **2** to make (liquid) seep through (ash, soil, etc), in order to remove substances from that material. [prob Anglo-Saxon *leccan* to water]

lead[1] /liːd/ *verb* (***led***) **1** *tr & intr* to guide by going in front. **2** to precede. **3** to guide or make (someone or something) go in a certain direction by holding or pulling with the hand, etc. **4** to guide. **5** to conduct. **6** to induce. **7** to cause to live or experience. **8** *tr & intr* to direct or be in control of (something). **9** to cause (someone) to act, feel or think in a certain way. **10** to live, pass or experience: *lead a miserable existence.* **11** *tr & intr* to go or take (someone) in a certain direction: *The road leads to the village.* **12** *intr* (**lead to sth**) to result in it. **13** *tr & intr* to be foremost or first; to be the most important or influential in (a group, etc): *They lead the world in engineering.* **14** *intr* (*usu* **lead with** *or* **on**) of a newspaper: to have (a particular story) as its most important article: *The tabloids all lead with the latest scandal.* **15** *tr & intr, cards* to begin a round of cards by playing (the first card, esp of a particular suit). ▸ *noun* **1** an instance of guidance given by leading. **2** the first, leading, or most prominent place; leadership. **3** the amount by which someone or something, etc is in front of others in a race, contest, etc: *had a lead of about a metre.* **4** a strap or chain for leading or holding a dog, etc. **5** an initial clue or piece of information which might help solve a problem, mystery, etc. **6** the principal part in a play, film, etc; the actor playing this role. **7** the most important story in a newspaper. **8** a precedent or example. **9** precedence. **10** an indication. **11** direction. **12** initiative. **13** a wire or conductor taking electricity from a source to an appliance. **14** *cards* the act or right of playing first, the first card played or the turn of someone who plays first. **15** the first player in some team sports and games. [Anglo-Saxon *lædan*]

PHRASAL VERBS **lead off** to begin. **lead sb on 1** to persuade them to go further than intended. **2** to deceive or mislead them.

lead[2] /lɛd/ *noun* **1** (symbol **Pb**) a soft, heavy, bluish-grey, highly toxic metallic element used in building and in the production of numerous alloys. **2** graphite. **3** a thin stick of graphite, or some other coloured substance, used in pencils. **4** a lump of lead used for measuring the depth of the water, esp at sea. **5** (**leads**) a sheet of lead for covering roofs; a roof covered with lead sheets. **6** a lead frame for a small window-pane, eg in stained glass windows. ▸ *verb* **1** to fit or surround with lead. **2** to cover or weight with lead. **3** to set (eg window panes) in lead. **4** *printing* to separate (lines of type) with leading. [Anglo-Saxon]

leaden *adj* **1** made of lead. **2** dull grey in colour. **3** heavy or slow. **4** depressing; dull.

leader *noun* **1** someone or something that leads or guides others. **2** someone who organizes or is in charge of a group. **3 a** *Brit* the principal violinist in an orchestra; **b** *US* an alternative name for a conductor of an orchestra, etc. **4** *Brit* (*also* **leading article**) an article in a newspaper, etc written to express the opinions of the editor. **5** a short blank strip at the beginning and end of a film or tape. **6** a long shoot growing from the stem or branch of a plant. ▪ **leadership** *noun.*

leaderboard *noun, sport, esp golf* a scoreboard that lists the names and scores of the current leaders in a competition.

lead-free see **unleaded**

lead-in /ˈliːd-/ *noun* an introduction, opening, etc.

leading[1] /ˈliːdɪŋ/ *adj* chief; most important. ▸ *noun* guidance; leadership.

leading[2] /ˈlɛdɪŋ/ *noun* **1** *printing* a thin strip of metal used to produce a space between lines of metal type. **2** the vertical distance between the bottom of one line of type and the top of the next in a document.

leading aircraftman *or* **leading aircraftwoman** *noun* a man or woman with the rank above aircraftman or aircraftwoman.

leading lady *or* **leading man** *noun* someone who plays the principal female or male role in a film or play.

leading light *noun* someone who is very important and influential in a particular field or subject.

leading question *noun* a question asked in such a way as to suggest the answer wanted.

lead time *noun* the time between the conception or design of a product, etc and its actual production, completion, etc.

leaf *noun* (***leaves***) **1** an expanded outgrowth, usu green and flattened, from the stem of a green plant, that is the main site of **photosynthesis**. **2** anything like a leaf, such as a scale or a petal. **3** leaves regarded collectively. **4** a single sheet of paper forming two pages in a book. **5** a very thin sheet of metal: *gold leaf.* **6** a hinged or sliding extra part or flap on a table, door, etc. ▸ *verb* **1** of plants: to produce leaves. **2** (**leaf through sth**) to turn the pages of (a book, etc) quickly and cursorily. [Anglo-Saxon *leaf*]

IDIOMS **turn over a new leaf** to begin a new and better way of behaving or working.

leaflet *noun* **1** a single sheet of paper, or several sheets of paper folded together, giving information, advertising products, etc, usu given away free. **2** a small or immature leaf. **3** a division of a compound leaf. ▸ *verb* (***leafleted, leafleting***) *tr & intr* to distribute leaflets.

leaf mould *noun* earth formed from rotted leaves, used as a compost for plants.

leafy *adj* (*-ier, -iest*) **1** having or covered with leaves. **2** shaded by leaves. **3** like a leaf.

league[1] *noun* **1** a union of people, nations, etc formed for the benefit of the members. **2** a group of sports clubs which compete over a period for a championship. **3** a class or group, considered in terms of ability, importance, etc. ▸ *verb, tr & intr* to form or be formed into a league. [15c: from Latin *ligare* to bind]
IDIOMS **in league with sb** acting or planning with them, usu for some underhand purpose.

league[2] *noun, old use* **1** a unit of distance, usu taken to be about 4.8km (3 miles). **2** *naut* a measure, 1/20th of a degree, 3 international nautical miles, 5.556km (3.456 statute miles). [14c: from Latin *leuga*]

league table *noun* **1** a list where people or clubs are placed according to performance or points gained. **2** any grouping where relative success or importance is compared or monitored.

leak *noun* **1 a** an unwanted crack or hole in a container, pipe, etc where liquid or gas can pass in or out; **b** the act or fact of liquid or gas escaping in this way; **c** liquid or gas which has escaped in this way. **2 a** a revelation of secret information, esp when unauthorized; **b** information revealed in this way; **c** someone who reveals information in this way. ▸ *verb* **1 a** *intr* of liquid, gas, etc: to pass accidentally in or out of an unwanted crack or hole; **b** to allow (liquid, gas, etc) to pass accidentally in or out. **2 a** to reveal (secret information) without authorization; **b** *intr* of secret information: to become known. ▪ **leaky** *adj* (*-ier, -iest*). [15c as *leken*: from Norse *leka*]
IDIOMS **have** *or* **take a leak** *slang* to urinate.

leakage *noun* **1** an act or instance of leaking. **2** something that enters or escapes through a leak.

lean[1] *verb* (*leant* or *leaned*) **1** *tr & intr* to slope or be placed in a sloping position. **2** *tr & intr* to rest or be rested against something for support. **3** *intr* (*usu* **lean towards**) to have an inclination to, a preference for or tendency towards. ▸ *noun* **1** an act or condition of leaning. **2** a slope.

lean[2] *adj* **1** of a person or animal: thin. **2** of meat: containing little or no fat. **3** producing very little food, money, etc; unfruitful: *lean years.* ▸ *noun* meat with little or no fat. ▪ **leanness** *noun.* [Anglo-Saxon *hlæne*]

leaning *noun* a liking or preference; tendency.

leant *past tense, past participle* of **lean[1]**

lean-to *noun* (*lean-tos*) a shed or other light construction built against another building or a wall.

leap *verb* (*leapt* or *leaped*) **1** *intr* to jump or spring suddenly or with force. **2** to jump over (something). **3** *intr* of prices: to go up by a large amount suddenly and quickly. ▸ *noun* an act of leaping or jumping. [Anglo-Saxon *hleapan*]
IDIOMS **a leap in the dark** an action, decision, etc whose results cannot be guessed in advance. **by leaps and bounds** extremely rapidly.
PHRASAL VERBS **leap at sth** *informal* to accept it eagerly.

leapfrog *noun* a game in which each player in turn jumps over the back of the stooping player in front. ▸ *verb* (*leapfrogged, leapfrogging*) *tr & intr* **1** to jump over (someone's back) in this way. **2** of two or more people, vehicles, etc: to pass or overtake alternately. [19c]

leap year *noun* a year, occurring once in every four years, of 366 days, with an extra day on 29 February.

learn *verb* (*learnt* or *learned*) **1** *tr & intr* (*often* **learn about** *or* **of sth**) to be or become informed of or to hear of (something). **2** *tr & intr* to gain knowledge of or skill in (something) through study, teaching, instruction or experience. **3** to get to know by heart; to memorize. **4** *non-standard* to teach. ▪ **learner** *noun.* [Anglo-Saxon *leornian*]

learned /ˈlɜːnɪd/ *adj* **1** having great knowledge or learning, esp through years of study. **2** scholarly. **3** (**the learned**) those who have great knowledge.

learning *noun* knowledge gained through study.

learning curve *noun* **1** a graph used in education and research to represent progress. **2** the process of becoming familiar with a subject or activity.

lease *noun* a contract by which the owner of a house, land, etc agrees to let someone else use it for a stated period of time in return for payment. ▸ *verb* **1** of an owner: to allow someone else to use (a house, land, etc) under the terms of a lease. **2** of an occupier: to borrow (a house, land, etc) from the owner under the terms of a lease. ▪ **leaser** *noun* a **lessee**. [13c: from French *lais*]
IDIOMS **a new lease of life** renewed strength or liveliness.

leaseback *noun* an arrangement whereby the seller of a property, land, etc then leases it from the buyer.

leasehold *noun* **1** the holding of land or buildings by lease. **2** the land or buildings held by lease. Compare **freehold**. ▪ **leaseholder** *noun.*

leash *noun* a strip of leather or chain used for leading or holding a dog or other animal. ▸ *verb* **1** to put a leash on (a dog, etc). **2** to control or restrain. [14c: from French *laisser* to let a dog run on a leash]

least *adj* smallest; slightest. ▸ *adv* in the smallest or lowest degree. ▸ *pron* the smallest amount: *I think he has least to offer.* [Anglo-Saxon *læst*]
IDIOMS **at least 1** if nothing else; at any rate. **2** not less than: *at least half an hour late.* **not in the least** *or* **not in the least bit** not at all. **the least** the minimum: *The least you could do is visit from time to time.*

leather *noun* **1** the skin of an animal made smooth by tanning. **2** a small piece of leather for polishing or cleaning. **3** (*usu* **leathers**) clothes made of leather, esp as worn by motorcyclists. ▸ *verb* **1** to cover or polish with leather. **2** *informal or dialect* to thrash. [Anglo-Saxon *lether*]

leatherjacket *noun* a larva of the **cranefly**, which has a greyish-brown leathery skin.

leathery *adj* **1** tough. **2** looking or feeling like leather.

leave[1] *verb* (*left*) **1** *intr* to go away from (someone or somewhere). **2** to allow (something) to remain behind, esp by mistake: *left the keys at home.* **3** to move out of (an area). **4** to abandon. **5** to resign or quit. **6** to allow (someone or something) to be or remain in a particular state etc: *leave the window open.* **7** to deliver to or deposit: *I'll leave the keys with a neighbour.* **8** to cause: *It may leave a scar.* **9** to have as a remainder: *Three minus one leaves two.* **10** to make a gift of in a will: *left all her money to charity.* **11** to be survived by: *leaves a wife and daughter.* **12** to cause (esp food or drink) to remain unfinished: *She left half her dinner.* **13** to hand or turn (something) over to (someone else): *left the driving to her.* [Anglo-Saxon *læfan* to remain]

IDIOMS **leave sb** *or* **sth alone** to allow them or it to remain undisturbed. **leave it out!** *slang* stop it!
PHRASAL VERBS **leave off sth** to stop doing it. **leave sb** *or* **sth out** to exclude or omit them or it.

leave[2] *noun* **1** permission to do something. **2 a** permission to be absent, esp from work or military duties; **b** permitted absence from work or military duties; **c** the length of time this lasts: *a week's leave.* [Anglo-Saxon *leafe* permission]
IDIOMS **on leave** officially absent from work. **take one's leave** *formal, old use* to depart.

leaven /ˈlɛvən/ *noun* **1** a substance, esp yeast, added to dough to make it rise. **2** anything which is an influence and causes change. ▸ *verb* **1** to cause (dough) to rise with leaven. **2** to influence or cause change in (something). [14c: from Latin *levamen* a means of raising]

leaves *pl of* **leaf**

leavings *plural noun, informal* things which are left over; rubbish.

Lebensraum /ˈleɪbənzraʊm/ *noun* (sometimes **lebensraum**) space in which to live and, if necessary, expand. [20c: from German *Lebens* of life + *Raum* space]

lech *noun, slang* **1** a lecherous person. **2** a lecherous act. ▸ *verb* to behave in a lecherous way. [18c: back-formation from **lecher**]

lecher *noun* someone who behaves in a lecherous way. [12c: from French *lechier* to lick]

lecherous *adj* having or showing great sexual desire, esp in ways which are offensive. ▪ **lechery** *noun.*

lecithin /ˈlɛsɪθɪn/ *noun, biochem* an organic chemical compound that is a major component of cell membranes in higher animals and plants, and is used in foods, pharmaceuticals, cosmetics and paints. [19c: from Greek *lekithos* egg-yolk]

lectern *noun* a stand with a sloping surface for holding a book, notes, etc for someone to read from, esp in a church or lecture-hall. [14c: from Latin *legere* to read]

lecture *noun* **1** a formal talk on a particular subject given to an audience. **2** a lesson or period of instruction, esp as delivered at a college or university. **3** a long and tedious scolding or warning. ▸ *verb* **1** *tr & intr* to give or read a lecture or lectures (to a group of people). **2** to scold (someone) at length. **3** to instruct by lectures, esp in a college or university. ▪ **lecturer** *noun.* ▪ **lectureship** *noun.* [14c: from Latin *legere* to read]

LED *abbrev, electronics* light-emitting diode, a semiconductor diode used in the displays of calculators, digital watches, etc.

led *past tense, past participle of* **lead**[1]

LEDC *abbrev* Less Economically Developed Country.

ledge *noun* **1** a narrow horizontal shelf or shelf-like part. **2** a ridge or shelf of rock, esp one on a mountain side or under the sea. [14c: perhaps from *leggen* to lay]

ledger *noun* the chief book of accounts of an office or shop, in which details of all transactions are recorded. [15c: from *leggen* to lay]

ledger line *or* **leger line** *noun, music* a short line added above or below a musical stave on which to mark a note higher or lower than the stave allows.

lee *noun* **1** shelter given by a neighbouring object. **2** the sheltered side, away from the wind. [Anglo-Saxon *hleo* shelter]

leech *noun* **1** an annelid worm with suckers at each end, esp a blood-sucking parasite formerly used medicinally. **2** a person who befriends another in the hope of personal gain. [Anglo-Saxon *læce*]

leek *noun* a long thin vegetable with broad flat leaves and a white base, closely related to the onion, and adopted as the national emblem of Wales. [Anglo-Saxon *leac*]

leer *noun* **1** a lecherous look or grin. **2** a sideways look. ▸ *verb, intr* **1** to look or grin lecherously. **2** to look sideways. [16c: Anglo-Saxon *hleor* face or cheek]

leery *adj* (**-ier, -iest**) wary; suspicious: *leery of going there after dark.*

lees *plural noun* **1** sediment at the bottom of wine bottles, etc. **2** the worst part or parts. [14c: from French *lie*]

leeside *noun, naut* the sheltered side.

leeward *naut, adj, adv* in or towards the direction in which the wind blows. ▸ *noun* the sheltered side.

leeway *noun* **1** scope for freedom of movement or action. **2** *naut* a ship's drift sideways.

left[1] *adj* **1** referring to, relating to, or indicating the side facing west from the point of view of someone or something facing north. **2** relatively liberal, democratic, progressive, innovative in disposition, political outlook, etc. **3** inclined towards socialism or communism. ▸ *adv* on or towards the left side. ▸ *noun* **1** the left side, part, direction, etc. **2** the region to the left side. **3** (**the Left**) **a** people, political parties, etc in favour of socialism; **b** the members of any political party that holds the most progressive, democratic, socialist, radical or actively innovating views. **4** the left hand: *a boxer who leads with his left.* **5** a blow with the left hand. **6** a glove, shoe, etc which fits the left hand or foot. **7** a turning to the left. [Anglo-Saxon *left* weak]

left[2] *past tense, past participle of* **leave**[1]

left-hand *adj* **1** relating to, on or towards the left. **2** done with the left hand.

left-handed *adj* **1** having the left hand stronger and more skilful than the right. **2** for use by left-handed people, or the left hand. **3** awkward; clumsy. **4** of compliments, etc: dubious or ambiguous. **5** anticlockwise. ▪ **left-hander** *noun.*

leftism *noun* principles and policies of the political left. ▪ **leftist** *noun, adj.*

left-luggage *noun* **1** (*in full* **left-luggage office**) in an airport or a railway or coach station: an area with lockers where luggage can be stored for collection at a later time. **2** luggage so stored.

leftover *adj* not used up or not eaten, etc. ▸ *noun* (**leftovers**) food that remains uneaten.

left wing *noun* **1** the members of a political party or group who are most inclined towards a socialist viewpoint. **2** *sport* **a** the extreme left side of a pitch or team in a field game; **b** (*also* **left-winger**) a player playing on this side. **3** the left side of an army. ▪ **left-wing** *adj.*

lefty *noun* (**-ies**) *informal, often derog* **1** a person with socialist leanings. **2** a left-handed person.

leg *noun* **1** one of the limbs on which animals, birds and people walk and stand. **2** an animal's or bird's

leg used as food. **3** the part of a piece of clothing that covers one of these limbs. **4** a long narrow support of a table, chair, etc. **5** one stage in a journey. **6** a section of a competition or lap of a race. **7** *cricket* **a** (*also* **leg side**) the side of the field that is to the left of a right-handed batsman or to the right of a left-handed batsman; **b** a fielder positioned here, eg fine leg, long leg, short leg, square leg. **8** a branch or limb of a forked or jointed object. [13c: from Norse *leggr*]
IDIOMS **leg it** *informal* to walk briskly, to run or dash away. **not have a leg to stand on** *informal* to have no way of excusing behaviour or supporting an argument, etc. **pull sb's leg** *informal* to try to make them believe something which is not true.

legacy *noun* (*-ies*) **1** an amount of property or money left in a will. **2** something handed on or left unfinished by a past owner or predecessor: *a legacy of mismanagement*. [15c: from Latin *legare* to leave by will]

legal *adj* **1** lawful; allowed by the law. **2** referring or relating to the law or lawyers. **3** created by law. ▪ **legally** *adv*. [16c: from Latin *legalis*]

legal aid *noun* financial assistance from public funds for those who cannot afford to pay for legal advice or proceedings. [19c]

legalese *noun* technical legal jargon.

legalism *noun* the tendency to observe the letter or form of the law rather than the spirit. ▪ **legalist** *noun, adj*. ▪ **legalistic** *adj*. [19c: from Latin *legalis*]

legality *noun* (*pl* in sense 2 only *-ies*) **1** the state of being legal; lawfulness. **2** a legal obligation.

legalize *or* **-ise** *verb* to make (something) legal or lawful. ▪ **legalization** *noun*. [18c]

legal tender *noun* currency which, by law, must be accepted in payment of a debt.

legate *noun* an ambassador or representative, esp from the Pope. [12c: from Latin *legare* to send as a deputy]

legatee *noun* the recipient of a legacy.

legation *noun* **1** a diplomatic mission or group of delegates. **2** the official residence of such a mission or group. **3** the office or status of a legate.

legato /lɪ'gɑːtoʊ/ *music, adv* smoothly, with the notes running into each other. ▸ *adj* smooth and flowing. ▸ *noun* **1** a piece of music to be played in this way. **2** a legato style of playing. [19c: Italian *legato* bound]

leg before wicket *or* **leg before** *noun, cricket* (abbrev **lbw**) a way of being given out for having prevented the ball from hitting the wicket with any part of the body other than the hand.

leg break *noun, cricket* **1** a ball that breaks from the leg side towards the off side on pitching. Also called **leg spin**. **2** a ball bowled to have this kind of effect. **3** spin imparted to a ball to achieve this effect.

legend *noun* **1** a traditional story which is popularly regarded as true, but not confirmed as such. **2** such stories collectively. **3** someone famous about whom popularly-believed stories are told. **4** words accompanying a map or picture, etc which explain the symbols used. **5** an inscription on a coin, medal or coat of arms. [14c: from Latin *legenda* things to be read]

legendary *adj* **1** relating to or in the nature of legend. **2** described or spoken about in legend. **3** *informal* very famous. ▪ **legendarily** *adv*.

legerdemain /lɛdʒədə'meɪn/ *noun* **1** skill in deceiving or conjuring with the hands. **2** trickery. [15c: French *léger* light + *de* of + *main* hand]

leger line see **ledger line**

leggings *plural noun* **1** close-fitting stretch coverings for the legs, worn by girls and women. **2** outer and extra protective coverings for the lower legs.

leggy *adj* (*-ier, -iest*) **1** of a woman: having attractively long slim legs. **2** of a plant: having a long stem.

legible *adj* esp of handwriting: clear enough to be read. ▪ **legibly** *adv*. [14c: from Latin *legibilis*]

legion *noun* **1** *hist* a unit in the ancient Roman army, containing between three and six thousand soldiers. **2** a very great number. **3** a military force: *the French Foreign Legion*. ▸ *adj* great in number: *Books on this subject are legion*. ▪ **legionary** *noun, adj*. [13c: from Latin *legere* to choose]

legionnaire *noun* a member of a legion.

Legionnaires' Disease *or* **Legionnaire's Disease** *noun, pathol* a severe and sometimes fatal disease caused by a bacterial infection of the lungs. [20c: named after the outbreak at a convention of the American Legion in 1976]

legislate *verb, intr* to make laws. [18c: back-formation from **legislator**]
IDIOMS **legislate for sth** to make provision for it.

legislation *noun* **1** the process of legislating. **2** a group of laws.

legislative *adj* **1** relating to or concerned with law-making. **2** having the power to make laws: *a legislative assembly*. ▸ *noun* **1** law-making power. **2** a law-making body.

legislator *noun* someone who makes laws, esp a member of a legislative body. ▪ **legislatorial** *adj*. [17c: from Latin *lex* law + *lator*, from *latum* to bring]

legislature *noun* the part of the government which has the power to make laws.

legit /lə'dʒɪt/ *adj, informal* legitimate.

legitimate *adj* /lə'dʒɪtɪmət/ **1** lawful. **2** born to parents who are married to each other. **3** of an argument, conclusion, etc: reasonable or logical. ▸ *verb* /-meɪt/ **1** to make lawful or legitimate. **2** to justify. ▪ **legitimacy** *noun*. ▪ **legitimately** *adv*. ▪ **legitimation** *noun*. [15c: from Latin *legitimare* to declare as lawful]

legitimize *or* **-ise** *verb* **1** to make legitimate. **2** to make (an argument, etc) valid. ▪ **legitimization** *noun*.

legless *adj* **1** *informal* very drunk. **2** having no legs.

Lego *noun, trademark* a toy construction system consisting of small plastic bricks, windows, wheels etc which can be fastened together. [20c: from Danish *lege godt* to play well]

leg-pull *noun, informal* a joking attempt to make someone believe something which is not true.

legroom *noun* the amount of space available for someone's legs while sitting.

leg side see **leg** (*noun* sense 7)

leg spin *noun, cricket* a **leg break**.

legume *noun* **1** any of a family of flowering plants with fruit in the form of a pod, eg pea, bean, lentil. **2** the fruit of such a plant, containing edible seeds rich in protein. **3** an edible seed of this plant. ▪ **leguminous** *adj*. [17c: from Latin *legere* to gather]

legwarmers *plural noun* long footless socks, often worn during exercise or dance practice.

legwork *noun* work that involves a lot of research or travelling around.

lei /leɪ/ *noun* a Polynesian garland of flowers worn round the neck. [19c: Hawaiian]

Leics *abbrev, English county* Leicestershire.

leisure *noun* free time, esp when a person can relax, pursue a hobby, etc. [14c: from Latin *licere* to be permitted]

IDIOMS **at leisure 1** not occupied. **2** without hurrying. **at one's leisure** at a time one finds convenient.

---

leisure

This word is often misspelt. It might help you to remember the following sentence:

*It's our **lei**sure time, so **l**et's **e**njoy **i**t.*

---

leisure centre *noun* a centre providing a wide variety of recreational facilities, esp sporting ones.

leisurely *adj* not hurried; relaxed. ▸ *adv* without hurrying; taking plenty of time. ▪ **leisureliness** *noun.*

leitmotif *or* **leitmotiv** /ˈlaɪtmoʊtiːf/ *noun* a recurring theme, image, etc in a piece of music, novel, etc that is associated with a particular person, idea, feeling, etc. [19c: German *Leitmotiv*]

lemma *noun* (***lemmas*** *or* ***lemmata***) **1** *maths* a proposition, or a premise taken for granted. **2** a heading or outline of an argument in a piece of literary writing. ▪ **lemmatical** *adj.* [16c: Greek, in sense 2, from *lambanein* to take]

lemming *noun* **1** a small rodent which occasionally participates in huge migrations once popularly but erroneously believed to result in mass drownings at sea. **2** someone who blindly follows others on a course to predictable disaster. [16c: Norwegian *lemmen*]

lemon *noun* **1** a small oval citrus fruit with pointed ends and a tough yellow rind enclosing sour-tasting juicy flesh. **2** the small evergreen tree that produces this fruit. **3** a pale yellow colour. **4** *informal* someone or something thought of as worthless, disappointing, unattractive or defective. ▸ *adj* **1** pale yellow in colour. **2** tasting of or flavoured with lemon. ▪ **lemony** *adj.* [15c: from Arabic *lima* citrus fruits]

lemonade *noun* a fizzy or still drink flavoured with or made from lemons.

lemon curd *or* **lemon cheese** *noun* a thick creamy paste made from lemons, sugar, butter and egg.

lemon sole *noun* a European **flatfish** used as food.

lemur *noun* a nocturnal tree-dwelling **primate**, now confined to Madagascar, with large eyes and a long bushy tail. [18c: from Latin *lemures* ghosts]

lend *verb* (***lent***) **1** to allow (someone) to use (something) on the understanding that it (or its equivalent) will be returned. **2** to give (someone) the use of (usu money), esp in return for interest paid on it. **3** to give or add (interest, beauty, etc) to: *The lighting lends a calming atmosphere.* ▪ **lender** *noun.* [Anglo-Saxon *lænan*]

IDIOMS **lend a hand** to help, though not necessarily by using the hands: *Can you lend a hand with working out this sum?* **lend an ear** to listen. **lend itself to sth** to be suitable for (a purpose): *The hall lends itself to staging live bands.*

---

lend, loan

Be careful not to use **lend** when you mean the noun **loan**:

✘ *Will you give me a lend of your bike?*

✓ *Will you give me a loan of your bike?*

---

length *noun* **1** the distance from one end of an object to the other, normally the longest dimension. Compare **breadth**. **2** *often in compounds* the distance something extends. **3** the quality of being long. **4** a long piece of something or a stated amount of something long: *a length of rope.* **5** the extent from end to end of a horse, boat, etc, as a way of measuring one participant's lead over another in a race: *won by two lengths.* **6** (*often* **in length**) a stretch or extent. **7** *swimming* **a** the longer measurement of a swimming pool; **b** this distance swum. **8 a** an extent of time; **b** *phonetics, music* the amount of time a vowel, syllable, note, etc sounds. [Anglo-Saxon *lengthu*]

IDIOMS **at length 1** at last. **2** in great detail.

lengthen *verb, tr & intr* to make or become longer.

lengthways *or* **lengthwise** *adv, adj* in the direction of or according to something's length.

lengthy *adj* (***-ier, -iest***) **1** of great, often excessive, length. **2** of speech, etc: long and tedious. ▪ **lengthily** *adv.* ▪ **lengthiness** *noun.*

lenient *adj* mild and tolerant, esp in punishing; not severe. ▪ **lenience** *or* **leniency** *noun.* ▪ **leniently** *adv.* [17c: from Latin *lenis* soft]

lenity *noun, old use* mildness; mercifulness. [16c: from Latin *lenis* soft]

lens *noun* **1 a** an optical device consisting of a piece of glass, clear plastic, etc curved on one or both sides, used for converging or diverging a beam of light; **b** a contact lens. **2** in a camera: a mechanical equivalent of the lens of an eye which allows the image to fall on the photographer's eye or, when the shutter is open, on the film plane. [17c: Latin, meaning 'lentil' (because of the shape)]

Lent *noun, Christianity* the time, lasting from Ash Wednesday to Easter Sunday, of fasting or abstinence in remembrance of Christ's fast in the wilderness (Matthew 4.2). ▪ **Lenten** *adj.* [Anglo-Saxon *lencten* spring]

lent *past tense, past participle of* **lend**

lentil *noun* **1** a small orange, brown or green seed used as food. **2** a leguminous plant which produces these seeds. [13c: from Latin *lens*]

lento *music, adv* slowly. ▸ *adj* slow. ▸ *noun* a piece of music to be performed in this way. [18c: Italian]

Leo *noun* (*pl* ***Leos*** in sense b) *astrol* **a** the fifth sign of the zodiac; **b** a person born between 21 July and 22 August, under this sign. [11c: Latin, meaning 'lion']

leonine *adj* relating to or like a lion. [14c: from Latin *leo* lion]

leopard *noun* a large member of the cat family of Africa and Asia, with a black-spotted tawny coat or a completely black coat. *Also called* **panther**. [13c: Greek *leon* lion + *pardos* panther]

leopardess *noun* a female leopard.

leotard *noun* a stretchy one-piece tight-fitting garment worn for dancing, exercise, etc. [20c: named after Jules Léotard, a French trapeze artist]

leper *noun* **1** *med* someone who has leprosy. **2** *derog* someone who is avoided, esp on moral grounds. [14c: from Greek *lepros* scaly]

lepidopterist *noun* a person who studies butterflies and moths.

lepidopterous *adj* relating or belonging to the order of insects that includes butterflies and moths. ▪ **lepidopteran** *adj, noun*. [18c: from Greek *lepis* scale + *pteron* wing]

leprechaun *noun, Irish folklore* a small mischievous elf. [17c: from Irish *lú* small + *corp* body]

leprosy *noun* an infectious disease of the skin, mucous membranes and nerves which, before drug treatment was available, often led to severe disfigurement. ▪ **leprous** *adj*. [16c: from Greek *lepros* scaly]

lepton *noun, physics* any of various subatomic particles, including electrons, muons and tau particles, that only participate in weak interactions with other particles. ▪ **leptonic** *adj*. [20c: from Greek *leptos* small or thin]

lesbian *noun* a woman who is sexually attracted to other women. ▸ *adj* for, relating to or referring to lesbians. ▪ **lesbianism** *noun*. [19c: from *Lesbos*, Aegean island, home of the ancient Greek poetess Sappho]

lese-majesty /leɪz'madʒəstɪ/ *noun* an insult to a sovereign; treason. [15c: from Latin *laesa majestas* injured majesty]

lesion *noun* **1** an injury or wound. **2** *pathol* an abnormal change in the structure of an organ or tissue as a result of disease or injury. [15c: from Latin *laedere* to injure]

less *adj* **1** smaller in size, quantity, duration, etc. **2** *informal* fewer in number: *smoke less cigarettes*. ▸ *adv* not so much; to a smaller extent: *exercises less nowadays*. ▸ *pron* a smaller amount or number: *tried to eat less*. ▸ *prep* without; minus: *£100 less the discount*. [Anglo-Saxon *læssa*]

---

less, fewer

Be careful not to use the word **less** when you should use the word **fewer**.

Fewer should be used with the plurals of count nouns:

- ✓ *I might not be so fat if I ate fewer cakes and chocolates.*
- ✗ *Less people are buying videos now that DVDs are coming down in price.*

Less should be used with the plurals of uncount nouns:

- ✓ *I might not be so fat if I ate less chocolate.*

However, you also should use **less** for specific measurements of quantity or amounts of money:

- ✓ *There were less than twelve hours before the big day.*
- ✓ *People who are 65 years of age or less.*

-less *suffix, forming adjs denoting* **1** free from; lacking; without: *painless* • *penniless*. **2** not subject to the action of the specified verb: *dauntless*. [Anglo-Saxon *leas* free from]

lessee *noun* someone granted the use of property by lease.

lessen *verb, tr & intr* to make or become less.

lesser *adj* used in names, esp plant, animal and place names to denote: smaller in size, quantity or importance: *lesser celandine*.

lesson *noun* **1** an amount taught or learned at one time. **2** a period of teaching. **3** (**lessons**) instruction in a particular subject given over a period of time. **4** an experience or example which one should take as a warning or encouragement: *Let that be a lesson to you*. **5** a passage from the Bible read during a church service. [16c: from Latin *lectio* a reading]

lessor *noun* someone who rents out property by lease.

lest *conj, formal or literary* in case: *speak quietly lest they hear us*. [13c: from Anglo-Saxon *thy læs the* the less that]

let[1] *verb* (***let, letting***) **1 a** to allow, permit, or cause: *let her daughter borrow the car*; **b** used in commands, orders, warnings, etc: *let him go*. **2** *Brit* to give the use of (rooms, a building, or land) in return for payment. **3** *maths, philos* used to suggest that a symbol or a hypothesis be understood as something: *Let 'D' be the distance travelled*. ▸ *noun, Brit* **1** the leasing of a property, etc: *got the let of the cottage for £100 a week*. **2** the period of time for which a property, etc is leased: *a two-week let*. [Anglo-Saxon *lætan* to permit]

IDIOMS **let alone** used to link alternatives so that disapproval, surprise, etc is emphasized: *didn't even clear the table let alone do the washing up*. **let fly at sb** to attack them physically or verbally. **let go of sth** to release or stop holding it. **let oneself go 1** to act without restraint. **2** to allow one's appearance or lifestyle, etc to deteriorate. **let sb alone** *or* **let sb be** to avoid disturbing or worrying them. **let sth drop** to make secret information, etc known, esp unintentionally.

PHRASAL VERBS **let sb** *or* **sth down 1** to disappoint or fail to help (someone) at a crucial time. **2** to lower them or it. **3** to allow the air to escape from (something inflated): *let down the tyres*. **4** to make longer: *let the hem down*. **let sb in on sth** *informal* to share a secret, etc with them. **let sb off 1** to allow them to go without punishment, etc. **2** to release them from work, duties, etc. **let sth off 1** to fire (a gun) or explode (a bomb, etc). **2** to release liquid or gas. **let sth out 1** to enlarge it: *let out the waist of the jeans*. **2** to emit (a sound): *let out a horrible scream*. **let up** to stop or to become less strong or violent: *The rain let up at last*.

let[2] *noun, sport* esp in racket games: an obstruction during service that requires the ball, etc to be served again. [19c: Anglo-Saxon *lettan* to hinder]

-let *suffix, signifying* a small or young example: *leaflet* • *piglet*.

let-down *noun* a disappointment.

lethal *adj* causing or enough to cause death. ▪ **lethally** *adv*. [17c: from Latin *let(h)um* death]

lethargy *noun* **1** lack of energy and vitality. **2** *pathol* a state of abnormal drowsiness and inactivity caused by inadequate rest, etc. ▪ **lethargic** *adj*. ▪ **lethargically** *adv*. [14c: from Greek *lethargos* drowsy]

let-out *noun* a chance to escape, avoid keeping an agreement, contract, etc.

let's *contraction* let us, used esp in suggestions: *let's go*.

letter *noun* **1** a conventional written or printed mark, usu part of an alphabet, used to represent a speech sound or sounds. **2** a written or printed message normally sent by post in an envelope. **3** (**the letter**) the strict literal meaning of words, esp in legal documents, or how such words can be interpreted: *according to the letter of the law*. **4** printing type. ▸ *verb* to write or mark letters on. ▪ **lettering** *noun*.

[13c: from Latin *littera* letter of the alphabet]

IDIOMS **to the letter** exactly; in every detail: *followed the instructions to the letter.*

letter box *noun, Brit* **1** a slot in a door through which letters are delivered. **2** a large box, with a slot in the front, for people to post letters. Also called **pillar box, postbox**.

lettered *adj* **1** well educated; literary. **2** marked with letters.

letterhead *noun* **1** a printed heading on notepaper giving a company's or an individual's name, address, etc. **2** a piece of notepaper with this kind of heading.

letter of credit *noun* (***letters of credit***) a letter authorizing a bank, etc to issue a person with credit or money up to a set amount.

letterpress *noun* a technique of printing where ink is applied to raised surfaces and then pressed onto paper.

lettuce *noun* a green plant with large edible leaves used in salads. [13c: from Latin *lac* milk, because of its milky juice]

let-up *noun* end; respite; relief.

leuco- *or* **leuko-** *or* (*before a vowel*) **leuc-** *or* **leuk-** *combining form, denoting* white or colourless. [From Greek *leukos* white]

leucocyte *or* **leukocyte** /ˈluːkəsaɪt/ *noun, anatomy* a white blood cell or **corpuscle.** [19c]

leukaemia *or* (*esp US*) **leukemia** /luˈkiːmɪə/ *noun* a malignant disease which affects the bone marrow and other blood-forming organs, resulting in the overproduction of abnormal white blood cells. [19c]

levee[1] *noun* **1** *US* esp on the Lower Mississippi: the natural embankment of silt and sand that is deposited along the banks of a river or stream during flooding. **2** an artificial embankment constructed along a watercourse. **3** a quay. [18c: from French *levée* raised]

levee[2] *noun, hist* the first official meeting of a sovereign or other high-ranking person after they have risen from bed. [17c: from French *levée*, from *lever* to raise]

level *noun* **1** a horizontal plane or line. **2** a specified height, value or extent. **3** position, status, or importance in a scale of values. **4** a stage or degree of progress. **5** any device for checking whether a surface is horizontal or not: *spirit level*. **6** (**the level**) a flat area of land. **7** a storey of a building. ▸ *adj* (***leveller, levellest***) **1** having a flat smooth even surface. **2** horizontal. **3** having or being at the same height (as something else). **4** having the same standard (as something else); equal. **5** steady; constant; regular. **6** *cookery* of measurements: filled so as to be even with the rim: *3 level tablespoons*. ▸ *verb* (***levelled, levelling***) **1** to make flat, smooth or horizontal. **2** to make equal. **3** to pull down or demolish. **4** (*often* **level sth at sb**) to point (a gun, etc) at them. **5** (*usu* **level sth at** *or* **against sb**) to direct (an accusation, criticism, etc) at them. **6** *intr, informal* to speak honestly with someone: *Let me level with you – I'm leaving the company.* [14c: from Latin *libella* little scale]

IDIOMS **on the level** *slang* honest; genuine.

PHRASAL VERBS **level off** *or* **level sth off** to make or become flat, even, steady, regular, etc. **level out** *or* **level sth out** to make or become level.

level crossing *noun, Brit, Aust & NZ* a place where a road and a railway line, or two railway lines, cross at the same level.

level-headed *adj* sensible; well-balanced.

leveller *noun* someone or something that flattens or makes equal: *Death is the one great leveller.*

level playing field *or* **flat playing field** *noun* equal terms on which to compete.

lever *noun* **1** a simple device for lifting and moving heavy loads, consisting of a rigid bar supported by and pivoting about a **fulcrum** at some point along its length, so that an effort applied at one point can be used to move an object (the load) at another point. **2** a strong bar for moving heavy objects, prising things open, etc. **3** a handle for operating a machine. **4** anything that can be used to gain an advantage. ▸ *verb* to move or open using a lever. [13c: from Latin *levare* to raise]

leverage *noun* **1** the mechanical power or advantage gained through using a lever. **2** the action of a lever. **3** power or advantage.

leveret *noun* a young hare, esp one less than a year old. [16c: from Latin *lepus* hare]

leviathan *or* **Leviathan** /ləˈvaɪəθən/ *noun* **1** *Bible* a sea monster. **2** anything which is large or powerful. [14c: from Hebrew *liwyathan*]

levitate *verb, tr & intr* to float or cause to float in the air, esp by invoking some supernatural power. ▪ **levitation** *noun*. [17c: from Latin *levis* light]

levity *noun* a lack of seriousness; silliness. [16c: from Latin *levis* light]

levy *verb* (***-ies, -ied***) **1** to calculate and then collect (a tax, etc). **2** to raise (an army or the money needed to fund a war). ▸ *noun* (***-ies***) **1** the collection of a tax, etc. **2** the amount of money raised by collecting a tax, etc. **3** the act of raising an army or the money needed to fund a war. **4** soldiers or money collected in preparation for a war. [14c: from Latin *levare* to raise]

lewd *adj* **1** feeling, expressing or designed to stimulate lust. **2** obscene; indecent. ▪ **lewdly** *adv.* ▪ **lewdness** *noun*. [14c: Anglo-Saxon *læwede* unlearned]

lexical *adj* **1** referring or relating to the words in a language. **2** referring or relating to a lexicon. ▪ **lexically** *adv.* [19c: from Greek *lexis* word]

lexicography *noun* the writing, compiling and editing of dictionaries. ▪ **lexicographer** *noun*. [17c: from Greek *lexis* word + *graphein* to write]

lexicology *noun* the study of the history, meaning, form, etc of words.

lexicon *noun* **1** a dictionary, esp one for Arabic, Greek, Hebrew or Syriac. **2** the vocabulary of terms as used in a particular branch of knowledge or by a particular person, group, etc. [17c: Greek, from *lexis* word]

lexis *noun* **1** all the words of a language. **2** the way a piece of writing is expressed in words.

ley /leɪ/ *or* **ley line** *noun* (***leys***) a straight line thought to be the route of a prehistoric road joining prominent features of the landscape. [20c]

LF *abbrev, radio* low frequency.

Li *symbol, chem* lithium.

liability *noun* (***-ies***) **1** the state of being legally liable or responsible for something. **2** a debt or obligation. **3** someone or something one is responsible for. **4** someone or something that is a problem or that causes a problem. **5** a likelihood. **6** a tendency. [18c]

liable *adj* **1** legally bound or responsible. **2** given or inclined: *She is liable to outbursts of temper.* **3** likely. **4** susceptible. [16c: perhaps from French *lier* to bind]

liaise *verb, tr & intr* (*usu* **liaise with** *or* **between**) to communicate with or be in contact with (someone). [20c: back-formation from **liaison**]

liaison *noun* **1** communication or co-operation between individuals or groups. **2** an adulterous or illicit relationship. [17c: from Latin *ligare* to bind]

liana *or* **liane** *noun* a woody climbing plant found mainly in tropical rain forests. [18c: from French]

liar *noun* someone who tells lies. [Anglo-Saxon]

Lib. *abbrev* Liberal.

lib *noun, informal* used esp in the names of movements: short form of **liberation** (see under **liberate**): *gay lib* • *women's lib.*

libation /laɪˈbeɪʃən/ *noun* **1** the pouring out of wine, etc in honour of a god. **2** a drink so poured. **3** *facetious* **a** an alcoholic drink; **b** the act of drinking, esp alcohol. [14c: from Latin *libare* to pour]

libber *noun, informal* someone advocating a specified form of freedom or change: *women's libber.*

Lib Dem *abbrev* Liberal Democrat.

libel *noun* **1** *Brit, law* **a** the publication of a statement in some permanent form (including broadcasting) which has the potential to damage someone's reputation and which is claimed to be false; **b** the act of publishing this kind of statement. **2** **a** any false or potentially damaging description of someone; **b** a depiction, such as a portrait or sculpture, that is unflattering. ▸ *verb* (***libelled, libelling*** *or US* ***libeled, libeling***) **1** *law* to publish a libellous statement about (someone). **2** to accuse wrongly and spitefully. Compare **slander**. ▪ **libellous** *or* (*US*) **libelous** *adj.* [14c: from Latin *libellus* little book]

liberal *adj* **1** given or giving generously, freely or abundantly. **2** tolerant of different opinions; open-minded. **3** lavish; extensive: *poured liberal glasses of wine.* **4** in favour of social and political reform, progressive. **5** (**Liberal**) belonging to the **Liberal Party**. **6** of education: aiming to develop general cultural interests and to broaden the mind, as opposed to being technically or professionally orientated: *a liberal arts student.* **7** free from restraint; not rigorous: *a liberal interpretation.* ▸ *noun* **1** someone who has liberal views, either politically or in general. **2** (**Liberal**) a member or supporter of the **Liberal Party**. ▪ **liberalism** *noun.* ▪ **liberally** *adv.* [14c: from Latin *liber* free]

Liberal Democrat *noun* in the UK: a member or supporter of a political party (the **Liberal Democrats**) slightly to the left of centre. [20c]

liberality *noun* **1** the quality of being generous. **2** the quality of being open-minded and free from prejudice.

liberalize *or* **-ise** *verb, tr & intr* to make or become more liberal or less strict. ▪ **liberalization** *noun.* [18c]

Liberal Party *noun* **1** in the UK: a political party advocating liberal policies and which in 1989, after undergoing a number of changes to its constitution, became the **Liberal Democrats**. **2** any similar political party in other countries. [19c]

liberate *verb, tr & intr* **1** to set free. **2** to free (a country from enemy occupation). **3** to free from accepted moral or social conventions or from traditional gender-based roles. ▪ **liberation** *noun.* ▪ **liberator** *noun.* [17c: from Latin *liberare* to free]

liberated *adj* **1** not bound by traditional ideas about sexuality, morality, etc. **2** freed from enemy occupation.

libertarian *noun* **1** someone who advocates that people should be free to express themselves, their ideas, etc as they like. **2** someone who believes in the doctrine of **free will** and the power of self-determination. ▪ **libertarianism** *noun.* [18c]

libertine *noun, old use* someone who is not bound by the generally accepted codes of morality. ▸ *adj* unrestrained; dissolute; promiscuous. [14c: from Latin *libertus* made free]

liberty *noun* (***-ies***) **1** freedom from captivity, slavery, restrictions, etc. **2** freedom to act and think as one pleases. **3** (*usu* **liberties**) a natural right or privilege. See also **civil liberty**. **4** an action or utterance thought of as over-familiar or presumptuous. [14c: from Latin *liber* free]

IDIOMS **at liberty** **1** free from prison or control; **2** allowed or permitted: *at liberty to use the company car.* **take liberties** **1** to treat someone with too much familiarity; to be too presumptuous or impertinent. **2** to act in an unauthorized way; to be deliberately inaccurate. **take the liberty to** *or* **of** to do or venture to do (something), usu without permission.

libidinous /lɪˈbɪdɪnəs/ *adj* lustful; lewd. ▪ **libidinously** *adv.* [15c: from Latin *libido* desire]

libido /lɪˈbiːdoʊ/ *noun* sexual urge or desire. ▪ **libidinal** *adj.* [20c: Latin, meaning 'desire']

Libra *noun* (*pl* ***Libras*** in sense b) *astrol* **a** the seventh sign of the zodiac. **b** a person born between 23 September and 22 October, under this sign. ▪ **Libran** *adj, noun.* [From Latin *libra* pound weight]

librarian *noun* someone who works in or is in charge of a library. ▪ **librarianship** *noun.*

library *noun* (***-ies***) **1** a room, rooms or building where books, films, records, videos, etc are kept for study, reference, reading or for lending. **2** a collection of books, films, records, videos, etc for public or private use. **3** a group of books published as a series. **4** *comput* a collection of computer programs, software, files, etc. [14c: from Latin *librarium* bookcase]

libretto *noun* (***libretti*** /lɪˈbrɛtiː/ *or* ***librettos***) the words or text of an opera, oratorio, or musical. ▪ **librettist** *noun.* [18c: Italian, meaning 'little book']

Libyan *adj* belonging or relating to Libya or its inhabitants. ▸ *noun* a citizen or inhabitant of, or person born in, Libya.

lice *pl of* **louse**

licence *or* (*US*) **license** *noun* **1** an official document that allows someone to own something, eg, a dog, gun, etc, or that gives permission to do something, eg, use a television set, get married, drive a car, sell alcohol, etc. **2** permission or leave in general. **3** excessive freedom of action or speech. **4** a departure from a rule or convention, esp by writers and artists, for effect: *poetic licence.* [14c: from Latin *licere* to be allowed]

---

licence, license

Be careful not to use the noun spelling **licence** instead of the verb spelling **license**, and vice versa:

The grocer will be licensed to sell alcoholic drinks.
a television licence

Note also that American English uses **licence** for both.

---

license *verb* **1** to give a licence or permit for (something). **2** to give a licence or permit (to someone) to do something such as drive, get married, etc. [14c]

licensee *noun* someone who has been given a licence, esp to sell alcohol.

licentiate *noun* someone who holds a certificate of competence to practise a profession.

licentious *adj* immoral or promiscuous. ▪ **licentiousness** *noun*. [16c: from Latin *licentia* licence]

lichee see **lychee**

lichen /ˈlaɪkən, ˈlɪtʃən/ *noun* a primitive plant form, usu found on rocks, walls or tree trunks. [17c: from Greek *leichen*]

lichgate *or* **lychgate** *noun* a roofed gateway to a churchyard, orig used to shelter a coffin before a funeral. [15c: Anglo-Saxon *lic* corpse + **gate**]

licit *adj* lawful; permitted. [15c: from Latin *licere* to be lawful]

lick *verb* **1** to pass the tongue over in order to moisten, taste or clean. **2** of flames, etc: to flicker over or around. **3** *informal* to defeat. **4** *informal* to beat or hit repeatedly. ▸ *noun* **1** an act of licking with the tongue. **2** *informal* a small amount. **3** *informal* a quick speed: *drove away at some lick*. **4** *informal* a sharp blow. [Anglo-Saxon *liccian*]

IDIOMS **lick into shape** *informal* to make more efficient or satisfactory. **lick one's wounds** to recover after having been thoroughly defeated or humiliated.

licking *noun, informal* **1** a severe thrashing, both physical and figurative. **2** a humiliating defeat.

licorice see **liquorice**

lid *noun* **1** a removable or hinged cover for a pot, box, etc. **2** an eyelid. ▪ **lidded** *adj*. [Anglo-Saxon *hlid*]

IDIOMS **put the lid on it 1** to put an end to something. **2** to be the last in a series of injustices or misfortunes: *and the flat tyre just put the lid on it*.

lido /ˈliːdoʊ/ *noun* **1** a fashionable beach. **2** a public open-air swimming pool. [20c: named after Lido, an island in the Venetian lagoon with a fashionable beach]

lie[1] *noun* **1** a false statement made with the intention of deceiving. **2** anything misleading; a fraud: *live a lie*. ▸ *verb* (***lied, lying***) *intr* **1** to say things that are not true with the intention of deceiving. **2** to give a wrong or false impression: *The camera never lies*. [Anglo-Saxon *lyge*]

IDIOMS **give the lie to** to show (a statement, etc) to be false.

lie[2] *verb* (*past tense* ***lay****, past participle* ***lain****, present participle* ***lying***) *intr* **1** to be in or take on a flat or more or less horizontal position on a supporting surface. **2** to be situated: *The village lies to the west of here*. **3** to stretch or be spread out to view: *The harbour lay before us*. **4** of subjects for discussion: to remain undiscussed: *let matters lie*. **5** **a** to be or remain in a particular state: *lie dormant*; **b** to be buried: *Jim's remains lie in a cemetery in Paris*. **6** (*usu* **lie in sth**) to consist of it or have it as an essential part: *Success lies in hard work*. **7** (**lie with sb**) of a duty or responsibility: to rest with them. ▸ *noun* **1** **a** the way or direction in which something is lying; **b** *golf* the relative position of a ball that has been struck: *Despite finding the rough, he had a good lie*. **2** an animal's or bird's hiding place. [Anglo-Saxon *licgan*]

IDIOMS **lie in wait (for sb** *or* **sth)** to hide before ambushing (them or it). **lie low** to stay quiet or hidden. **take sth lying down** *often with negatives* to accept a rebuke or disappointment, etc meekly and without protest.

PHRASAL VERBS **lie in** to stay in bed later than usual.

---

lie

See the Usage Note at **lay**.

---

lied /liːd; *German* liːt/ *noun* (***lieder*** /ˈliːdə(r)/; *German* /ˈliːdɛə/) a German song for solo voice and piano accompaniment. [19c: German *Lied* song, pl *Lieder*]

lie detector *noun* a machine for measuring changes in someone's blood pressure, pulse, etc, taken as indications that they are giving dishonest replies to questions. *Technical equivalent* **polygraph**.

lie-down *noun* a short rest taken lying down.

liege /liːdʒ/ *adj* **1** of a feudal lord: entitled to receive service, etc from a vassal. **2** of a vassal: bound to give service, etc to a feudal lord. ▸ *noun* **1** (*also* **liege lord**) a feudal superior, lord or sovereign. **2** (*also* **liege man**) a feudal subject or vassal. [13c: French]

lie-in *noun* a longer than usual stay in bed.

lien /liːn/ *noun, law* a right to keep someone's property until a debt has been paid. [16c: French, from Latin *ligare* to bind]

lie of the land *noun* the current state of affairs.

lieu /ljuː, luː/ *noun* **1** (**in lieu**) instead. **2** (**in lieu of**) in place of. [13c: French, meaning 'place']

Lieut *or* **Lieut.** *abbrev* Lieutenant.

lieutenant /lɛfˈtɛnənt; *US* luː-/ *noun* **1** a deputy acting for a superior. **2** an army officer of the rank below captain. **3** a naval officer of the rank below lieutenant commander. **4** *US* a police officer or fireman with the rank immediately below captain. [14c: French, from *lieu* place + *tenant* holding]

lieutenant colonel *noun* **1** an army officer of the rank below colonel. **2** an officer in the US Air Force of the rank below colonel.

lieutenant commander *noun* a naval officer of the rank below commander.

lieutenant general *noun* an army officer of the rank below general.

life *noun* (***lives***) **1** **a** the quality or state which distinguishes living animals and plants from dead ones; **b** collectively, the characteristics which distinguish living animals, plants, etc from inanimate objects, esp the ability to grow, develop and reproduce. **2** **a** the period between birth and death; **b** the period between birth and the present time: *has led a very sheltered life*; **c** the period between the present time and death: *had his life carefully mapped out*. **3** the length of time a thing exists or is able to function: a *long shelf life*. **4** living things in general or as a group: *marine life*. **5** a living thing, esp a human: *many lives lost in war*. **6** a way or manner of living: *leads a very busy life*. **7** *in compounds* a specified aspect of someone's life: *her love-life*. **8** liveliness; energy; high spirits: *full of life*. **9** a source of liveliness, energy or high spirits: *the life and soul of the party*. **10** a written account of someone's life. **11** *informal* a **life sentence**: *got life for murder*. **12** any of a number of chances a player has of remaining in a game: *got to level six without losing a life*. [Anglo-Saxon *lif*]

IDIOMS **for the life of me** despite trying very hard: *For the life of me, I just can't understand what she* *sees in him.* **get a life!** *informal* stop being so petty, boring, conventional, sad, etc. **the life of Riley** *informal* an easy, carefree life. **not on your life!** *informal* certainly not! **to the life** exactly like the original.

life-and-death *adj* extremely serious or critical.

life assurance *or* **life insurance** *noun* an insurance policy that guarantees that a sum of money will be paid to the policyholder when they reach a certain age, or to the policyholder's named dependant(s) if the policyholder dies before that age.

lifebelt *noun* a ring or belt used to support someone who is in danger of drowning.

lifeblood *noun* **1** the blood necessary for life. **2** anything that is an essential part or factor.

lifeboat *noun* **1** a boat for rescuing people who are in trouble at sea. **2** a small boat, often one of several, carried on a larger ship for use in emergencies.

lifebuoy *noun* a float for supporting someone in the water until they are rescued.

life cycle *noun* the sequence of stages through which a living organism passes from the time of fusion of male and female gametes until the same stage in the next generation.

life expectancy *noun* the average length of time for which a person from a particular place might be expected to live.

lifeguard *noun* an expert swimmer employed at a swimming pool or beach to rescue people in danger of drowning.

life jacket *noun* an inflatable sleeveless jacket for supporting someone in the water.

lifeless *adj* **1** dead. **2** unconscious. **3** having no energy or vivacity; dull. ▪ **lifelessly** *adv.* ▪ **lifelessness** *noun.*

lifelike *adj* of a portrait, etc: very like the person or thing represented.

lifeline *noun* **1** a rope for support in dangerous operations or for saving lives. **2** a vital means of communication or support. **3** a line used by a diver for signalling.

lifelong *adj* lasting the whole length of someone's life.

life peer *or* **life peeress** *noun* a peer whose title is not hereditary. ▪ **life peerage** *noun.*

lifer *noun, slang* someone sent to prison for life.

life raft *noun* a raft kept on a ship, for use in emergencies.

lifesaver *noun* someone or something that saves lives, or that saves someone from difficulty.

life sciences *plural noun* the branches of science concerned with the study of living organisms, eg biochemistry, genetics, etc.

life sentence *noun, Brit* a prison sentence that is for the rest of the offender's life, but which is often less than that.

life-size *or* **life-sized** *adj* of a copy, drawing, etc: having the same size as the original.

lifestyle *noun* the particular way a group or individual lives.

life-support *adj* of machines, etc: allowing someone to remain alive, eg in an unfavourable environment such as space, or when seriously ill: *life-support machine* • *life-support system.* ▸ *noun* (*also* **life support machine** *or* **life support**) a machine or system which allows someone to remain alive.

lifetime *noun* **1** the duration of someone's life. **2** *informal* a very long time or what seems like a very long time: *had to wait a lifetime for the bus.*

lift *verb* **1** *tr & intr* to raise or rise to a higher position. **2** to move (esp one's eyes or face) upwards. **3** to take and carry away; to remove. **4** to raise to a better or more agreeable level: *lift one's spirits.* **5** *intr* **a** of cloud, fog, etc: to clear; **b** of winds: to become less strong. **6** to remove or annul: *They will lift the trading restrictions.* **7** to dig up (potatoes, etc). **8** *informal* to plagiarize from someone else's work or from published material. **9** *slang* to arrest. **10** *informal* to steal. ▸ *noun* **1** an act of lifting. **2** lifting power. **3** the upward force of the air on an aircraft, etc. **4** *Brit* a device for moving people and goods between floors of a building. *N Am equivalent* **elevator**. **5** *Brit* a ride in a person's car or other vehicle, often given without payment as a favour. **6** a boost to the spirits or sudden feeling of happiness. [13c: from Norse *lypta*]

lift-off *noun* the vertical launching of a spacecraft or rocket.

lig *verb* (***ligged, ligging***) esp in the media or entertainment industries, to take advantage of invitations to parties or events, product samples, etc that are available only to the privileged few. ▪ **ligger** *noun.* [20c]

ligament *noun* **1** *anatomy* a band of tough connective tissue that holds two bones together at a joint. **2** a bond or tie. [14c: from Latin *ligare* to bind]

ligature *noun* **1** anything that binds or ties. **2** *music* a **slur** (*noun* sense 3b). **3** *printing* a character formed from two or more characters joined together, eg, æ. ▸ *verb* to bind with a ligature. [14c: from Latin *ligare* to bind]

light[1] *noun* **1** a form of electromagnetic radiation that travels freely through space, and can be absorbed and reflected, esp that part of the spectrum which can be seen with the human eye. **2** any source of this, such as the sun, a lamp, a candle, etc. **3** an appearance of brightness; a shine or gleam: *see a light in the distance.* **4** (**the lights**) traffic lights: *turn left at the lights.* **5** the time during the day when it is daylight. **6** dawn. **7** a particular quality or amount of light: *a good light for taking photographs.* **8** a flame or spark for igniting. **9** a means of producing a flame for igniting, such as a match. **10** a way in which something is thought of or regarded: *see the problem in a new light.* **11** a hint, clue or help towards understanding. **12** a glow in the eyes or on the face as a sign of energy, liveliness, happiness or excitement. **13** someone who is well regarded in a particular field: *a leading light.* **14** an opening in a wall that lets in light, such as a window. **15** (**lights**) *formal* someone's mental ability, knowledge or understanding: *act according to your lights.* ▸ *adj* **1** having light; not dark. **2** of a colour: pale; closer to white than black. ▸ *verb* (*past tense & past participle* ***lit*** *or* ***lighted***) **1** to provide light for: *lit the stage.* **2** *tr & intr* to begin to burn or make (something) begin to burn: *light the fire.* **3** to guide or show someone (the way) using a light or torch. **4** *tr & intr* to make or become bright, sparkling with liveliness, happiness or excitement. [Anglo-Saxon *leoht*]

IDIOMS **come to light** to be made known or discovered. **in a good** *or* **bad light** putting a favourable or unfavourable construction on something. **in the light of sth** taking it into consideration. **light at the**

end of the tunnel an indication of success or completion. **see the light 1** to understand something. **2** to have a religious conversion. **see the light of day 1** to be born, discovered or produced. **2** to come to public notice.

PHRASAL VERBS **light up** *informal* to light (a cigarette, etc) and begin smoking.

light[2] *adj* **1** weighing little; easy to lift or carry. **2** low in weight, amount or density: *light rain.* **3** not pressing heavily; gentle: *a light touch.* **4** easy to bear, suffer or do: *light work.* **5** weighing less than is correct or proper. **6** equipped with only hand-held weapons: *light infantry.* **7** without problems, sorrow, etc; cheerful: *a light heart.* **8** graceful and quick; nimble: *a light skip.* **9** not serious or profound, but for amusement only: *light reading.* **10** thoughtless or trivial: *a light remark.* **11** not thinking clearly or seriously; giddy: *a light head.* **12** easily digested: *a light meal.* **13** denoting a weight category in boxing, etc that is slightly below one of the standard categories: *light middleweight.* **14** of cakes, etc: spongy and well risen. **15** (*also* **lite**) of alcoholic drinks: low in alcohol. **16** (*also* **lite**) of food and non-alcoholic drinks: containing little fat and/or sugar. ▸ *adv* **1** in a light manner. **2** with little luggage: *travel light.* ▪ **lightly** *adv.* ▪ **lightness** *noun.* [Anglo-Saxon *leoht*]

IDIOMS **make light of sth** to treat it as unimportant or trivial.

light[3] *verb* (*past tense & past participle* ***lit*** *or* ***lighted***) **1** of birds, etc: to come to rest after flight. **2** (**light on** *or* **upon sth**) to come upon or find it by chance: *suddenly lit upon the idea.* [Anglo-Saxon *lihtan* to alight]

light bulb *noun* an airtight glass bulb with an electric filament which emits visible light when a current is passed through it.

light-emitting diode see **LED**

lighten[1] *verb* **1** *tr & intr* to make or become brighter. **2** to cast light on. **3** *intr* to shine or glow. [14c]

lighten[2] *verb* **1** *tr & intr* to make or become less heavy. **2** *tr & intr* to make or become happier or more cheerful. **3** to make (a problem, unhappy mood, etc) less: *tried to lighten her sadness.* ▪ **lightening** *noun.*

PHRASAL VERBS **lighten up** *informal* **1** to relax. **2** to become less serious, angry, etc.

---

lightening, lightning

Be careful not to use the spelling **lightening** when you mean **lightning**:

thunder and lightning

---

lighter[1] *noun* **1** a device for lighting cigarettes, etc. **2** someone who sets something alight. [16c]

lighter[2] *noun* a large open boat used for transferring goods between ships, or between a ship and a wharf. [15c: from Anglo-Saxon *lihtan* to relieve of a weight]

light-fingered *adj* having a habitual tendency to steal. [16c]

light-footed *adj* nimble; active.

light-headed *adj* having a dizzy feeling in the head, esp one brought on by alcohol or drugs.

light-hearted *adj* **1** of entertainment, etc: not serious; cheerful and amusing. **2** happy and carefree.

lighthouse *noun* a building on the coast with a flashing light to guide ships or warn them of rocks, etc.

light industry *noun* a factory or factories involving the production of smaller goods, eg knitwear, glass, electronics components, etc.

lighting *noun* **1** equipment for providing light. **2** light, usu of a specified kind: *subdued lighting.*

lighting-up time *noun* the time of day when road vehicles must have their lights turned on.

lightning *noun, meteorol* a bright flash of light produced by the discharge of static electricity between or within clouds, or between a cloud and the Earth's surface. ▸ *adj* very quick and sudden: *a lightning dash to catch the bus.*

---

lightning, lightening

Be careful not to use the spelling **lightning** when you mean **lightening**:

The sky started lightening.

I am lightening my hair.

---

lightning conductor *or* **lightning rod** *noun* a metal rod, usu projecting above the roof of a building, designed to divert lightning directly to earth.

lightning strike *noun* an industrial or military strike that happens without warning.

light pen *noun* **1** *comput* a light-sensitive pen-like device that can be used to generate or modify images and move them about on a computer screen by touching the screen with the device. **2** a pen-like device for reading bar codes.

light pollution *noun* an excessive amount of artificial lighting, esp in large cities.

lights *plural noun* the lungs of an animal, used as food. [13c: a specialized use of **light**[2]]

lightship *noun* a ship with a beacon, that acts as a lighthouse.

lightweight *adj* **1** light in weight. **2** *derog* having little importance or authority. **3** belonging to or relating to the lightweight class of boxing, etc. ▸ *noun* **1** a person or thing of little physical weight. **2** *derog* a person or thing having little importance or authority. **3** a class for boxers, wrestlers and weight-lifters of not more than a specified weight, which is 61.2kg (135 lb) in professional boxing, and similar weights in amateur boxing and the other sports. **4** a boxer, etc competing in one of these classes.

light year *noun* the distance travelled by a beam of light in a vacuum in one year, equal to about 9.46 trillion km, used as a unit of measurement for the distances between stars and galaxies.

ligneous *adj* resembling or composed of wood. [17c: from Latin *lignum* wood]

lignify *verb* (***-ies, -ied***) *intr* of the walls of plant cells: to thicken and become woody as a result of the deposition of lignin. ▪ **lignification** *noun.* [19c]

lignin *noun, botany* the substance that cements together the fibres within the cell walls of plants, making them woody and rigid. [19c: from Latin *lignum* wood + *-in*, denoting a neutral substance]

lignite *noun, geol* a soft brown low-grade form of coal, intermediate between peat and bituminous coal. Also called **brown coal**. [19c]

like[1] *adj* **1** similar; resembling: *as like as two peas.* **2** typical of: *It's just like them to forget.* **3** used in asking someone for a description of someone or something: *What's he like?* ▸ *prep* **1** in the same manner as; to the same extent as: *run like a deer.* **2** such as: *animals like cats and dogs.* ▸ *adv, informal* **1** approximately. **2** as it were: *It was magic, like.* ▸ *conj, informal* **1** as if; as though: *It's like I've been here before.* **2** in the same way as: *not pretty like you are.* ▸ *noun, usu preceded by a possessive pronoun*: the counterpart or equal of someone or something: *people of their like.* [Anglo-Saxon *gelic* alike]

IDIOMS **the like a** things of the same kind: *TVs, radios and the like are on the third floor;* **b** *with negatives and in questions* anything similar: *never see the like again.* **the likes of** *usu contemptuous* people or things such as: *wouldn't have much to do with the likes of them.* **like crazy** *or* **mad** *informal* furiously; very much, fast, etc: *drove like crazy.* **more like it a** nearer to what is wanted or required: *A cup of tea? A large brandy would be more like it;* **b** nearer to the truth: *calls her his research assistant but dogsbody is more like it.*

like[2] *verb* **1** to enjoy or be pleased with (something). **2** to be fond of (someone or something). **3** to prefer: *She likes her tea without sugar.* **4** to wish, or wish for: *if you like.* ▸ *noun* (**likes**) things that someone has a preference for: *likes and dislikes.* ▪ **likeable** *or* **likable** *adj.* [Anglo-Saxon *lician* to please]

-like *adj, forming adjectives, signifying* **1** resembling: *catlike.* **2** typical of: *childlike.*

likelihood *or* **likeliness** *noun* probability.

likely *adj* **1** probable. **2** suitable or useful for a particular purpose: *a likely spot for a picnic.* **3** *ironic* credible: *a likely tale.* ▸ *adv* probably.

IDIOMS **not likely** *informal* absolutely not: *Invite him? Not bloody likely!*

like-minded *adj* sharing a similar outlook, opinion, taste, purpose, etc.

liken *verb* to compare or point to the similarities between (two things or people).

likeness *noun* **1** a similarity: *a family likeness.* **2** *formerly* a portrait or formal photograph.

likewise *adv* **1** in the same or a similar manner. **2** also; in addition.

liking *noun* **1** a fondness: *a liking for chocolates.* **2** affection. **3** taste; preference: *Is it to your liking?*

lilac *noun* **1** a small European tree or shrub of the olive family, with white or pale pinkish-purple sweet-smelling flowers. **2** a pale pinkish-purple colour. [17c: from Persian *nilak* bluish, from *nil* blue]

Lilliputian *noun* someone or something very small. ▸ *adj* (*also* **lilliputian**) very small. [18c: from Lilliput, an imaginary country inhabited by tiny people in Swift's *Gulliver's Travels*]

Lilo *or* **Li-lo** *noun, trademark* a type of inflatable mattress. [20c: from **lie**[2] + **low**[1]]

lilt *noun* **1** a light graceful swinging rhythm. **2** a tune, song or voice with such a rhythm. **3** a springing quality in someone's walk. ▸ *verb, intr* to speak, sing or move with a lilt. ▪ **lilting** *adj.* [16c]

lily *noun* (**-ies**) **1** *strictly* a plant with an underground bulb, narrow leaves, and white or brightly coloured flowers, often spotted, with long protruding stamens. **2** *loosely* any of various other plants with flowers superficially resembling those of a lily, eg water lily. [Anglo-Saxon, from Latin *lilium*]

lily-livered *adj* cowardly.

lily-of-the-valley *noun* (***lilies-of-the-valley***) a spring plant with small white bell-shaped flowers that have a sweet smell.

lily pad *noun* a large water lily leaf that sits on top of a pond, etc.

limb[1] *noun* **1** an arm, leg or wing. **2** a projecting part. **3** a main branch on a tree. **4** a spur of a mountain. **5** a branch or section of a larger organization. ▪ **limbless** *adj.* [Anglo-Saxon *lim*]

IDIOMS **out on a limb** exposed or isolated, esp as regards an opinion or attitude.

limb[2] *noun* an edge of the disk of the Sun, Moon or a planet. [15c: from Latin *limbus* border]

limber[1] *adj* flexible and supple. [18c: meaning 'to make supple', perhaps from **limb**[1]]

PHRASAL VERBS **limber up** to stretch and warm up before taking exercise.

limber[2] *noun* the detachable front part of a gun carriage, consisting of an axle, pole and two wheels. ▸ *verb* to attach (a gun) to a limber. [15c: as *lymour*]

limbo[1] *or* **Limbo** *noun* **1** *Christianity* an area between heaven and hell that is believed to be reserved for the unbaptized dead. **2** a place of oblivion or neglect. [14c: from Latin *in limbo* on the border]

IDIOMS **in limbo** in a state of uncertainty or waiting.

limbo[2] *noun* a West Indian dance in which the object is to lean backwards and shuffle under a rope or bar. [20c: from Jamaican English *limba* to bend]

lime[1] *noun* **1** *loosely* **calcium oxide**. **2** *loosely* **slaked lime**. **3** *loosely* **limestone**. **4** **bird-lime**. **5** *dialect* any slimy or gluey substance. ▸ *verb* **1** to cover with lime. **2** to apply ground limestone as a fertilizer to (soil). **3** to trap (usu birds, but sometimes animals) using bird-lime. ▪ **limy** *adj* (***-ier, -iest***). [Anglo-Saxon *lim*]

lime[2] *noun* **1** a small, round or oval, yellowish-green citrus fruit with a sour taste. **2** a small evergreen tree that bears this fruit. **3** the yellowish-green colour of this fruit. [17c: from Spanish *lima* lemon]

lime[3] *noun* (*also* **lime tree**) a deciduous tree or shrub with pendulous clusters of fragrant flowers. Also called **linden**. [17c: from Anglo-Saxon *lind* linden]

limekiln *noun* a kiln for heating limestone to produce lime.

limelight *noun* **1** formerly used in theatres: a bright white light produced by heating a block of lime in a flame. **2** the glare of publicity: *in the limelight.* [19c]

limerick *noun* a humorous poem with five lines rhyming *aabba*, the opening line usu beginning something like: *There was a young lady from ...* [19c: prob from the Irish town of Limerick]

limescale *noun* a type of **scale**[2] (*noun* sense 4) caused by calcium deposits.

limestone *noun, geol* a sedimentary rock composed mainly of **calcium carbonate**.

limewater *noun, chem* an alkaline solution of calcium hydroxide in water.

limey *noun* (**-eys**) *N Am, Aust & NZ slang* **1** a British person. **2** *formerly* a British sailor or ship. [19c: from **lime**[2], because British sailors used to take lime juice to prevent scurvy]

limit *noun* **1** a point, degree, amount or boundary, esp one which cannot or should not be passed. **2** a restriction or boundary. **3** (**the limit**) *informal, sometimes facetious* someone or something that is intolerable or extremely annoying. **4** *maths* in calculus: a value that is approached increasingly closely, but never reached. ▸ *verb* (***limited, limiting***) **1** to be a limit or boundary to. **2** to restrict. ▪ **limitable** *adj.* [14c: from Latin *limes* boundary]

limitation *noun* **1** an act of limiting or the condition of being limited. **2** *law* a specified period within which an action must be brought. **3** (*often* **limitations**) someone's weakness, lack of ability, etc: *know your limitations.*

limited *adj* **1** having a limit or limits. **2** narrow; restricted: *a limited understanding.*

limited company *or* **limited liability company** *noun* a company owned by its shareholders, who have liability for debts, etc only according to the extent of their stake in the company.

limited edition *noun* an edition of a book, art print, etc of which only a certain number of copies are printed or made.

limo /'lɪmoʊ/ *noun, informal* short form of **limousine**.

limousine *noun* a large, luxurious motor car, esp one with a screen separating the driver from the passengers. [20c: French, orig meaning 'a cloak worn by shepherds in Limousin, a province in France']

limp[1] *verb, intr* **1** to walk with an awkward or uneven step, often because one leg is weak or injured. **2** of a damaged ship or aircraft: to move with difficulty. ▸ *noun* the walk of someone who limps. [Anglo-Saxon from *lemp* to happen + *healt* limp]

limp[2] *adj* **1** not stiff or firm; hanging loosely. **2** without energy or vitality; drooping. **3** of a book: with a soft cover. ▪ **limply** *adv.* [18c: prob Scandinavian]

limpet *noun* **1** a marine gastropod mollusc with a conical shell that clings to rock surfaces, etc by a muscular foot. **2** someone who is difficult to get rid of. [Anglo-Saxon, from Latin *lambere* to lick + *petra* a stone]

limpid *adj* **1** of water, eyes, etc: clear; transparent. **2** of speeches, writing, etc: easily understood. ▪ **limpidity** *noun.* [17c: from Latin *lympha* clear liquid]

linage *or* **lineage** /'laɪnɪdʒ/ *noun* **1** the number of lines in a piece of printed matter. **2** *journalism* measurement or payment by the line. [14c: from **line[1]**]

linchpin *noun* **1** a pin-shaped rod passed through an axle to keep a wheel in place. **2** someone or something essential to a business, plan, etc. [14c: from Anglo-Saxon *lynis* axle]

Lincs /lɪŋks/ *abbrev, English county* Lincolnshire.

linctus *noun, Brit* a syrupy medicine taken by mouth to relieve coughs, etc. [17c: Latin, from *lingere* to lick]

linden see under **lime[3]**

line[1] *noun* **1** a long narrow mark, streak or stripe. **2** *often in compounds* a length of thread, rope, wire, etc used for specified purposes: *a washing line* • *mending the telephone lines.* **3** a wrinkle or furrow, esp on the skin. **4** *maths* something that has length but no breadth or thickness. **5** the path which a moving object is considered to leave behind it, having length but no breadth. **6** a row. **7** a row of words or printed or written characters: *a line from Shakespeare.* **8** (**lines**) the words of an actor's part. **9** (*often* **lines**) an outline or shape: *a car of stylish lines.* **10** (**lines**) a punishment at school where a phrase or sentence has to be written out a set number of times. **11** *music* any one of the five horizontal marks forming a musical stave. **12** *music* a series of notes forming a melody. **13** *informal* a short letter or note: *drop him a line.* **14** a series or group of people coming one after the other, esp in the same family or profession: *from a long line of doctors.* **15** a field of activity, interest, study or work: *his line of business.* **16** a course or way of acting, behaving, thinking or reasoning: *think along different lines.* **17** the rules or limits of acceptable behaviour: *overstep the line.* **18** a group or class of goods for sale: *a new line in tonic water.* **19** a production line. **20** one of several white marks outlining a pitch, race-track, etc on a field: *goal line.* **21 a** a single track for trains or trams; **b** a branch or route of a railway system. **22** a route, track or direction of movement: *line of fire.* **23 a** a continuous system, eg of telephone cables, connecting one place with another; **b** a telephone connection: *trying to get a line to Aberdeen;* **c** *in compounds* a telephone number that connects the caller to some kind of special service: *called the ticket line.* **24** a company running regular services of ships, buses or aircraft between two or more places. **25** an arrangement of troops or ships side by side and ready to fight. **26** (*always* **lines**) a connected series of military defences: *behind enemy lines.* **27** *N Am* a **queue** (sense 1). **28** *drug-taking slang* a small amount of powdered drugs, usu cocaine, arranged in a narrow channel, ready to be sniffed. **29** *slang* a remark, usu insincere, that someone uses in the hope of getting some kind of benefit: *He spun her a line.* ▸ *verb* **1** to mark or cover (something) with lines. **2** to form a line along (something): *Crowds lined the streets.* [13c: from Anglo-Saxon *line* rope]

IDIOMS **all along the line** at every point. **bring sb** *or* **sth into line** to make them or it conform. **get a line on sb** *or* **sth** *informal* to get information about them or it. **in line for sth** likely to get it: *in line for promotion.* **in line with sb** *or* **sth** in agreement or harmony with them or it. **lay it on the line** to speak frankly. **lay** *or* **put sth on the line** to risk one's reputation or career over it. **out of line 1** not aligned. **2** impudent. **3** exhibiting unacceptable behaviour.

PHRASAL VERBS **line up** to form a line. **line people** *or* **things up 1** to form them into a line. **2** to align them. **line sth up** to organize it: *lined up a new job.*

line[2] *verb* **1** to cover the inside of (clothes, boxes, curtains, etc) with some other material. **2** to cover as if with a lining: *line the walls with books.* **3** *informal* to fill, esp with large amounts. [14c: Anglo-Saxon *lin* flax]

IDIOMS **line one's pocket** *or* **pockets** to make a profit, esp by dishonest means.

lineage[1] *noun* ancestry, esp when it can be traced from one particular ancestor. [14c: from Latin *linea* **line[1]**]

lineage[2] see **linage**

lineal *adj* **1** of family descent: in a direct line. **2** referring to or transmitted by direct line of descent or legitimate descent. **3** of or in lines. [14c: from Latin *linea* **line[1]**]

lineament *noun* (*usu* **lineaments**) a distinguishing feature, esp on the face. [15c: from Latin *linea* **line[1]**]

linear *adj* **1** referring to, consisting of or like a line or lines. **2** in or of one dimension only. **3** sequential. **4** long and very narrow with parallel sides. ▪ **linearity** *noun.* [17c: from Latin *linearis* of lines]

linear equation *noun, maths* an equation in which none of the variables are raised above the power of one, and which can be shown by a straight line on a graph.

line drawing *noun* a drawing in pen or pencil using lines only.

linen *noun* **1** cloth made from flax. **2** articles, eg, sheets, tablecloths, underclothes, etc, orig made from linen, now more likely to be made from cotton or artificial fibres. ▸ *adj* made of or like linen. [Anglo-Saxon, from *lin* flax]

IDIOMS **wash one's dirty linen in public** to let personal problems and quarrels, often of a sordid nature, become generally known.

line of best fit *noun, maths* a line on a scatter graph between values, showing the best estimate of a linear relationship between them.

line-out *noun, rugby union* a method of restarting play in which the forwards of both teams form two rows facing the touchline and try to catch or deflect the ball when it is thrown in.

line printer *noun* a printer attached to a computer which prints a line at a time rather than a character at a time.

liner[1] *noun* a large passenger ship or aircraft.

liner[2] *noun, often in compounds* something used for lining: *bin-liner.*

liner[3] *noun, often in compounds* colouring used to outline the eyes or the lips: *eye-liner.*

linesman *noun* an official at a boundary line in some sports whose job is to indicate when the ball has gone out of play.

line-up *noun* **1** an arrangement of things or people in line. **2** a list of people selected for a sports team. **3** the artistes appearing in a show. **4** an identity parade.

ling[1] *noun* (***ling*** *or* ***lings***) a long slender edible marine fish, related to the cod. [13c: possibly related to 'long']

ling[2] *noun* same as **heather**. [14c: from Norse *lyng*]

-ling *suffix denoting* **1** a young, small or minor person or thing: *duckling* • *darling*. **2** someone with a specified attribute or position: *weakling* • *underling*.

linger *verb, intr* **1** of sensations: to remain for a long time. **2** to be slow or reluctant to leave. **3** (**linger over sth**) to spend a long time with it or doing it. **4** of someone who is dying: to die very slowly. ▪ **lingering** *noun*. [From Anglo-Saxon *lengan* to lengthen]

lingerie /'lɛ̃ʒərɪ/ *noun* women's underwear and nightclothes. [19c: French, from Latin *linum* flax]

lingo *noun, informal* **1** a language, esp one that is not highly thought of or that is not understood: *doesn't speak the lingo.* **2** the specialized vocabulary of a particular group, profession, etc: *medical lingo.* [17c: from Latin *lingua* tongue or language]

lingua franca *noun* (***lingua francas***) a language, often a simplified form, used as a means of communication amongst the speakers of different languages. [17c: Italian *lingua franca* Frankish language]

lingual *adj* **1** referring or relating to the tongue. **2** relating to speech or language. ▪ **lingually** *adv.* [17c: from Latin *lingua* tongue or language]

linguini *or* **linguine** /lɪŋ'gwiːnɪ/ *plural noun* pasta in long narrow strips like flattened spaghetti. [1940s: Italian plural of *linguina* a little tongue]

linguist *noun* someone skilled in languages or linguistics. [16c: from Latin *lingua* tongue or language]

linguistic *adj* **1** relating to language. **2** relating to linguistics. ▪ **linguistically** *adv.*

linguistics *singular noun* the study of language.

liniment *noun* a thin oily cream applied to the skin to ease muscle pain, etc. [15c: from Latin *linire* to smear]

lining *noun* **1** material used for lining something. **2** an inner covering, eg, of a bodily organ, etc: *stomach lining.*

link *noun* **1** a ring of a chain or in chain-mail. **2** someone or something that connects. **3** a means of communication or travel. ▸ *verb* **1** to connect or join. **2** *intr* to be or become connected. **3** *intr* (*often* **link up**) to be or become connected: *They linked up to satellite TV.* [14c: from Norse *link*]

linkage *noun* **1** an act, method, etc of linking. **2** a chemical bond. **3** *genetics* the association between two or more genes that occur close together on the same chromosome and tend to be inherited together.

linkman *or* **linkwoman** *noun* someone who provides a connection between two parts or items on TV, radio, etc.

links *plural noun* **1** a stretch of more or less flat ground along a shore near the sea. **2** a golf course by the sea. [From Anglo-Saxon *hlinc* ridge]

link-up *noun* a connection or union, esp between military units, broadcasting systems, etc.

linnet *noun* a small brown songbird of the finch family. [11c: from Latin *linum* flax, because it eats flax seeds]

lino /'laɪnoʊ/ *noun, informal* **linoleum**.

linocut *noun* **1** a design cut in relief in linoleum. **2** a print made from this.

linoleum *noun, dated* a smooth hard-wearing covering for floors, made by impregnating a fabric with a mixture of substances such as linseed oil and cork. [19c: from Latin *linum* flax + *oleum* oil]

linseed *noun* a seed of the flax plant. [Anglo-Saxon *linsæd*]

linseed oil *noun* oil extracted from linseed and used in paints, varnishes, enamels, etc. [19c]

lint *noun* **1** linen or cotton with a raised nap on one side, for dressing wounds. **2** fine, very small pieces of wool, cotton, etc; fluff. [14c as *lynt*]

lintel *noun* a horizontal wooden or stone supporting beam over a doorway or window. [14c: from Latin *limes* boundary or border]

Linux /'laɪnʌks/ *noun, comput* a computer operating system similar to **Unix**, but designed for use on personal computers. [Late 20c: from *Linus* + **Unix**, after the Finnish computer programmer Linus Torvalds]

lion *noun* **1** a large member of the cat family, found mainly in Africa, with a tawny coat, a tufted tail, and, in the male, a thick mane. **2** the male of this species, as opposed to the female. **3** someone who is brave. **4** someone who is the centre of public attention. **5** (**the Lion**) **a** *astron* the constellation of **Leo**; **b** *astrol* the sign of the zodiac, **Leo**. [13c: from Latin *leo* lion]

lioness *noun* a female lion.

lionheart *noun* someone who is very brave. ▪ **lionhearted** *adj* very brave or tenacious.

lionize *or* **-ise** *verb* to treat (someone) as a celebrity or hero.

lip *noun* **1** either of the two fleshy parts which form the edge of the mouth. **2** the edge or rim of something: *the lip of the milk jug.* **3** *informal* cheek. [Anglo-Saxon as *lippa*]

lipid *noun, biochem* any of a group of organic compounds, mainly oils and fats, that occur naturally in living organisms, and are generally insoluble in water. [20c: from Greek *lipos* fat + French *-ide*]

lipo- *or* (*before vowels*) **lip-** *combining form, denoting* fat. [From Greek *lipos* fat]

liposome /ˈlɪpousoum, ˈlaɪpou-/ *noun* a naturally-occurring lipid globule in the cytoplasm of a cell. [Early 20c]

liposuction *noun* the removal for cosmetic reasons of excess fat from the body by sucking it out through an incision in the skin. [20c]

lippy *adj*, (**-ier, -iest**) *informal* **1** cheeky. **2** talkative.

lip-read *verb* to make sense of (what someone is saying) by watching the movement of their lips. ▪ **lip-reader** *noun*. ▪ **lip-reading** *noun*.

lip-service *noun* insincere or feigned approval, acceptance, etc.

lipstick *noun* cosmetic colouring for the lips.

liquefy *verb* (**-ies, -ied**) *tr & intr* to make or become liquid. ▪ **liquefaction** *noun*. [15c: from Latin *liquere* to be liquid + *facere* to make]

liqueur /lɪˈkjʊə(r)/ *noun* a potent alcoholic drink, sweetened and highly flavoured, and usu drunk at the end of a meal. [18c: from Latin *liquere* to be liquid]

liquid *noun* **1** a state of matter between **solid** and **gas**, where the volume remains constant, but the shape depends on that of its container. **2** any substance in a water-like state. ► *adj* **1** of a substance: able to flow and change shape. **2** like water in appearance, esp in being clear. **3** flowing and smooth. **4** of assets: able to be easily changed into cash. ▪ **liquidity** *noun*. [14c: from Latin *liquidus* liquid or clear]

liquidate *verb* **1** to bring to an end the trading of (an individual or a company), and have debts and assets calculated. **2** to turn (assets) into cash. **3** to pay off (a debt). **4** to eliminate or kill. ▪ **liquidation** *noun*. ▪ **liquidator** *noun*. [16c: from Latin *liquidare* to make clear]

liquid crystal *noun, chem* an organic compound that flows like a liquid but resembles solid crystalline substances in its optical properties. [19c]

liquid crystal display *noun* (abbrev **LCD**) in digital watches, calculators, etc: a display of numbers or letters produced by applying an electric field across a **liquid crystal** solution sandwiched between two transparent electrodes. [20c]

liquidize *or* **-ise** *verb* **1** to make liquid. **2** to make (food, etc) into a liquid or purée. ▪ **liquidizer** *noun*. [19c]

liquid paraffin *noun* a colourless mineral oil derived from petroleum, used as a lubricant and laxative.

liquor *noun* **1** strong alcoholic, esp distilled, drink. **2** any fluid substance, esp water or liquid produced in cooking. [13c: from Latin *liquere* to be liquid]

liquorice *or* **licorice** *noun* **1** a plant with sweet roots used in confectionery and medicine. **2** a black sticky sweet made from the juice of the roots of this plant. [13c: from Greek *glykys* sweet + *rhiza* root]

lira *noun* **1** (***lire***) the former standard unit of currency of Italy, replaced in 2002 by the euro. **2** (***liras***) the standard unit of currency of Turkey. [17c: Italian, from Latin *libra* pound]

lisle /laɪl/ *noun* fine smooth cotton thread used for making gloves, stockings and underwear. [19c: named after Lisle (Lille), in N France, where it was first made]

LISP /lɪsp/ *noun, comput* a general purpose programming language in which the expressions are represented as lists. [20c: from *list* + processing]

lisp *verb* **1** *intr* to pronounce the sounds of *s* and *z* in the same way as the *th* sounds in *thin* and *this* respectively. **2** to say or pronounce (words, an answer, etc) in this way. ► *noun* a speech defect distinguished by lisping. [Anglo-Saxon *wlisp* lisping]

lissom *or* **lissome** *adj* graceful and supple in shape or movement. [19c: from **lithe** + Anglo-Saxon *-sum*]

list[1] *noun* **1** a series of names, numbers, prices, etc printed out, written down or said one after the other. **2** *comput* an arrangement of data in a file. ► *verb* **1** to make a list of (something). **2** to add (an item, etc) to a list. **3** to include in a list. [From Anglo-Saxon *liste* border]

list[2] *verb, intr* of a ship, etc: to lean over to one side. ► *noun* an act of listing or a listing position. [17c]

listed building *noun* a building which, because of its architectural or historical interest, cannot, by law, be destroyed or changed.

listen *verb, intr* **1** to try to hear. **2** to pay attention to. **3** to follow advice: *I warned him but he wouldn't listen*. ▪ **listener** *noun*.

listeria *noun* a bacterium sometimes found in certain foods, eg chicken and soft cheese, which if not killed in cooking may cause the serious disease **listeriosis**. [20c: named after Joseph Lister, British surgeon and pioneer of antiseptics]

listing *noun* **1** a list. **2** a position in a list. **3** *comput* a printout of a file or a program. **4** (**listings**) a guide to what is currently available in entertainment, eg, on television or radio, or at the cinema, theatre, etc. [17c: from Anglo-Saxon *list*]

listless *adj* tired and lacking energy or interest. ▪ **listlessly** *adv*. [15c: from 13c *list* desire + **-less**]

lists *plural noun, hist* **1** the barriers enclosing an area used for jousting and tournaments. **2** any scene of combat or conflict. [14c: from Anglo-Saxon *liste* a border]

lit *past tense, past participle of* **light**[1], **light**[3]

litany *noun* (**-ies**) **1** *Christianity* a series of prayers or supplications with a response which is repeated several times by the congregation. **2** (**the Litany**) such a series as it appears in the Book of Common Prayer. **3** a long tedious recital or list. [13c: from Greek *litaneia* prayer]

litchi see **lychee**

lite see **light**[2]

liter the *US* spelling of **litre**.

literacy *noun* the ability to read and write. [15c: from **literate**]

literal *adj* **1** of words or a text: following the exact meaning, without allegorical or metaphorical interpretation. **2** of a translation: following the words of the original exactly. **3** true; exact: *the literal truth*. ► *noun, printing* a misprint of one letter. ▪ **literally** *adv*. [15c: from Latin *litera* letter]

literally

The word **literally** is often used to intensify a statement rather than say something is truly or exactly so:

The red carpet was literally out for them.

It is not incorrect to use the word this way, but some

people think it is bad style. However, you should be careful not to create a bizarre or funny effect that you did not intend:

People have been literally beside themselves with frustration.

---

literalism *noun* strict adherence to the literal meaning of words. ▪ **literalist** *noun.*

literary *adj* **1** referring or relating to, or concerned with, literature or writing. **2** of a person: knowing a great deal about canonical literature. **3** of a word: formal; used in literature. [17c: from Latin *litera* letter]

literate *adj* **1** able to read and write. **2** educated. **3** *in compounds* competent and experienced in something specified: *computer-literate.* ▸ *noun* someone who is literate. [15c: from Latin *litera* letter]

literati *plural noun* **1** learned people. **2** people who consider themselves to be knowledgeable about literature. [17c: Latin, from *literatus* literate]

literature *noun* **1** written material, such as novels, poems and plays, that is valued for its language, content, etc. **2** the whole body of written works of a particular country, period in time, subject, etc: *American literature* • *scientific literature.* **3** the art or works produced by a writer. **4** *informal* any printed matter, esp advertising leaflets. [14c: from Latin *litera* letter]

lithe *adj* supple and flexible. [Anglo-Saxon *meaning* 'gentle' or 'soft']

lithium *noun, chem* (symbol **Li**) a soft silvery metallic element. [19c: from Greek *lithos* stone]

litho /ˈlaɪθoʊ/ *noun* **1** a **lithograph**. **2** **lithography**. ▸ *adj* lithographic. ▸ *verb* (***lithos*** *or* ***lithoes, lithoed***) to lithograph.

litho- *or* (*before a vowel*) **lith-** *combining form, denoting* stone. [From Greek *lithos* stone]

lithograph *noun* a picture or print made by lithography. ▸ *verb* to print (images, etc) using lithography. ▪ **lithographic** *adj.* ▪ **lithographically** *adv.* [18c]

lithography *noun* a method of printing using a stone or metal plate which has been treated so that the ink adheres only to the design or image to be printed. ▪ **lithographer** *noun.* [18c: **litho-** + Greek *graphein* to write]

lithophyte *noun, botany* any plant that grows on rocks or stones. ▪ **lithophytic** /-ˈfɪtɪk/ *adj.* [18c]

lithosphere /ˈlɪθoʊsfɪə(r)/ *noun* the rigid outer layer of the earth, consisting of the crust and the outermost layer of the mantle. ▪ **lithospheric** *adj.* [19c]

Lithuanian *adj* belonging or relating to Lithuania, or to its inhabitants, or their language. ▸ *noun* **1** a citizen or inhabitant of, or person born in, Lithuania. **2** the official language of Lithuania.

litigant *noun* someone involved in a lawsuit.

litigate *verb* **1** *intr* to be involved in a lawsuit. **2** to contest (a point, claim, etc) in a lawsuit. ▪ **litigation** *noun.* ▪ **litigator** *noun.* [17c: from Latin *lis* lawsuit + *agere* to do]

litigious /lɪˈtɪdʒəs/ *adj* **1** relating to litigation or lawsuits. **2** inclined to taking legal action over arguments, problems, etc. [14c: from Latin *litigium* quarrel]

litmus *noun, chem* a dye obtained from certain lichens, widely used as an indicator to distinguish between acid solutions, in which it turns red, and alkaline ones, in which it turns blue. [16c: from Norse *litmosi* dyeing-moss]

litmus paper *noun, chem* paper that has been treated with litmus, used to test for acidity and alkalinity.

litmus test *noun* **1** *chem* a chemical test for relative acidity or alkalinity using litmus paper. **2** *informal* a definitive test or trial of something.

litotes /ˈlaɪtoʊtiːz/ *noun, rhetoric* understatement used for effect, esp by negating the opposite, as in *not a little angry* meaning *furious.* Also called **meiosis**. [17c: Greek, meaning 'small']

litre *or* (*US*) **liter** *noun* (abbrev **l**) **1** a unit of measurement of volume, equal to one cubic decimetre (1000 cubic centimetres) or about 1.76 pints. **2** *in compounds, denoting* the capacity of the cylinders of a motor vehicle engine: *a three-litre engine.* [18c: from Greek *litra* pound]

litter *noun* **1** discarded paper, rubbish, etc lying in a public place. **2** a number of animals born to the same mother at the same time: *a litter of five grey kittens.* **3** any scattered or confused collection of objects. **4 a** straw, hay, etc used as bedding for animals; **b** absorbent material put in a tray for an indoor cat to urinate and defecate in. **5** *old use* a framework consisting of cloth stretched tight between two long poles, used to carry sick or wounded people. **6** *old use* a framework consisting of a couch covered by curtains, with poles on either side, for transporting a single passenger. ▸ *verb* **1** to make (something) untidy by spreading litter or objects about. **2** of objects: to lie untidily around (a room, etc). **3** of animals: to give birth to (young). **4** to give bedding litter to (animals). [14c: from French *litiere*]

little *adj* (often having connotations of affection or another emotion and used instead of the more formal *small*) **1** small in size, extent or amount. **2** young; younger: *a little girl* • *her little brother.* **3** small in importance: *a little mishap.* **4** used as a way of detracting from a potentially disparaging implication; not troublesome: *funny little ways.* ▸ adv (***less, least***) not much or at all: *They little understood the implications.* ▸ *pron* not much: *little to be gained from that course of action.* [Anglo-Saxon *lytel*]

IDIOMS **a little** (with a noun such as *bit, while, way* understood but not expressed) **1** a small amount: *do a little to help out.* **2** a short time: *He'll be here in a little.* **3** a short distance: *down the road a little.* **4** a small degree or extent: *run around a little to keep warm.* **little by little** gradually; by degrees. **make little of sth** **1** to treat it as unimportant or trivial. **2** to understand only a little of it. **not a little** very: *He was not a little upset.* **think little of sth** *or* **sb** to have a low opinion of it or them; to disapprove of it or them.

the Little Bear (*Brit*) *or* (*US*) **the Little Dipper** *noun* the constellation Ursa Minor.

little people *plural noun, folklore* fairies, leprechauns, etc. [18c]

littoral *adj* **1** on or near the shore of a sea or lake. **2** of plants or animals: inhabiting the area on or near the shore of a sea or lake. ▸ *noun* the shore or an area of land on a shore or coast. [17c: from Latin *litus* shore]

liturgy *noun* (***-ies***) **1** the standard form of service in a church. **2** the service of Holy Communion in the Eastern Orthodox Church. ▪ **liturgical** *adj.* [16c: from Greek *leitourgia* public service]

live[1] /ˈlɪv/ *verb* **1** *intr* to have life. **2** *intr* to be alive. **3** *intr* to continue to be alive. **4** *intr* to survive or to escape death. **5** *intr* to have a home or dwelling: *We live in a small flat.* **6** (*often* **live on**) to continue or last: *Memories live on.* **7** *intr* to lead life in a certain way: *live well.* **8** (**live off sth** *or* **sb**) to be supported by them or it: *live off the land.* **9** to pass or spend: *live a happy life in the country.* **10** *intr* to enjoy life passionately or to the full: *They really know how to live.* **11** to express (something) through a way of living: *lived a lie.* [Anglo-Saxon *lifian* and *libban*]

IDIOMS **live and let live** *informal* to be tolerant of others and expect toleration in return.

PHRASAL VERBS **live sth down** to carry on living until something in the past has been forgotten or forgiven by other people: *He lived down the shame of his arrest.* **live in** to live in accommodation supplied at one's workplace. **live up to sb** to become as respected as them: *could never live up to his brother.* **live up to sth** to turn out in a manner worthy of them or it: *tried to live up to her parents' expectations.* **live with sth 1** to continue to suffer from or be haunted by the memory of it: *will live with the mistake for the rest of his life.* **2** to put up with it: *He has to live with psoriasis.*

live[2] /laɪv/ *adj* **1** having life; not dead. **2** of a radio or TV broadcast: heard or seen as the event takes place and not from a recording. **3** of a record, video, etc: recorded during a performance. **4** of a wire: connected to a source of electrical power. **5** of coal, etc: still glowing or burning. **6** of a bomb, etc: still capable of exploding. **7** up-to-date; relevant: *tackles live issues.* **8** of a volcano: still liable to erupt. **9** of entertainments: playing to an audience: *a good live band.* **10** *comput* fully operational. ▸ *adv* at, during, or as a live performance: *They had to perform live on stage.* [16c: from **alive**]

liveable *adj* **1** of a house, etc: fit to live in. **2** of life: worth living.

lived-in *adj* **1** of a room, etc: having a comfortable, homely feeling. **2** *informal* of a face: marked by life's experiences.

live-in *adj* **1** living at a workplace: *a live-in nanny.* **2** of a partner: sharing the same home: *a live-in lover.*

livelihood *noun* a means of earning a living. [Anglo-Saxon *lif* life + *lad* course]

livelong /ˈlɪvlɒŋ/ *adj, poetic* of the day or night: complete, in all its pleasant or tedious length. [14c: from *lief* dear + *longe* long]

lively *adj* (**-ier, -iest**) **1** active and full of life, energy and high spirits. **2** brisk. **3** vivid or bright. **4** interesting or stimulating: *a lively debate.* ▪ **liveliness** *noun.* [Anglo-Saxon *liflic*]

liven *verb, tr & intr* (*usu* **liven up**) to make or become lively.

liver[1] *noun* **1** in vertebrates: a large dark red glandular organ whose main function is to regulate the chemical composition of the blood. **2** this organ in certain animals, used as food. **3** a dark reddish-brown colour. [Anglo-Saxon *lifer*]

liver[2] *noun* someone who lives in a specified way: *a riotous liver.*

liverish *adj* **1** *old use* suffering from a disordered liver. **2** disgruntled or irritable. ▪ **liverishness** *noun.*

Liverpudlian *noun* a native or citizen of Liverpool in NW England. ▸ *adj* belonging or related to Liverpool or its inhabitants. [19c: from Liverpool, with *-puddle* facetiously substituted for *-pool* + Latin *-ianus*]

liver salts *plural noun* mineral salts taken to relieve indigestion.

liver spot *noun* a brown mark on the skin, usu appearing in old age.

liverwort *noun* a small spore-bearing plant without a vascular system, closely related to mosses, typically growing in moist shady conditions. [Anglo-Saxon *liferwyrt*]

livery *noun* (**-ies**) **1** a distinctive uniform worn by male servants belonging to a particular household or by the members of a particular trade guild, etc. **2** any distinctive uniform or style, esp as used by companies so that their employees, vehicles, etc can be easily identified. **3** the distinctive colours and decoration used to identify the buses, aircraft, etc operated by a particular company. **4** the feeding, care, stabling and hiring out of horses for money. [14c: from Latin *liberare* to free]

lives *pl of* **life**

livestock *singular or plural noun* domesticated farm animals. [18c]

live wire *noun, informal* someone who is full of energy and enthusiasm.

livid *adj* **1** *informal* extremely angry. **2** having the greyish colour of lead. **3** of a bruise: black and blue. **4** white or very pale. [17c: from Latin *lividus* lead-coloured]

living *adj* **1** having life; alive. **2** currently in existence, use or activity. **3** of a likeness: exact. ▸ *noun* **1** livelihood or means of subsisting. **2** a manner of life: *riotous living.* **3** in the Church of England: a position as a vicar or rector which has an income or property attached to it. **4** (**the living**) people who are alive. [14c: from Anglo-Saxon *lifian, libban*]

living room *noun* a room in a house, etc where people sit and relax.

lizard *noun* a reptile closely related to the snake. [14c: from Latin *lacerta* lizard]

'll *verb, contraction of* **shall** and **will**: *I'll* • *they'll.*

llama *noun* a domesticated hoofed S American mammal kept for its meat, milk and wool, and used as a beast of burden. [17c: Spanish, from Quechua]

lm *symbol, physics* lumen.

lo *exclam, old use* look! see! [Anglo-Saxon *la*]

IDIOMS **lo and behold** *usu facetious* an exclamation used to introduce some startling revelation.

loach *noun* a small edible freshwater fish of the carp family. [14c: from French *loche*]

load *noun* **1** something that is carried or transported. **2 a** an amount that is or can be carried or transported at one time; **b** *in compounds*: *lorryload of bricks.* **3** a burden. **4** a cargo. **5** a specific quantity, varying according to the type of goods. **6** the weight carried by a structure, etc. **7** (**loads**) *informal* a large amount: *loads of time.* **8** something, eg a duty, etc, oppressive or difficult to bear: *a load off my mind.* **9** an amount or number of things to be dealt with at one time. **10** the power carried by an electric circuit. **11** the power output of an engine. **12** the amount of work imposed on or expected of someone: *a heavy teaching load.* **13** a single discharge from a gun. ▸ *verb* **1** to put (cargo, passengers, etc) on (a ship, vehicle, plane, etc). **2** *intr* (*also* **load up**) to take or pick up a load. **3** to fill: *load the dishwasher.* **4** *photog* to put (film) in (a camera). **5** to weigh down or overburden. **6** to be a weight on or burden to someone or something; to oppress. **7** *comput* **a** to put (a disk, computer tape, etc) into a drive, so that it may be used; **b** to transfer (a program or data) into main memory, so that it may be used. See also **download**. **8** to put (ammunition) into (a gun). **9** to give weight or bias to (dice, a roulette wheel, a question, etc). **10** to put a large amount of (paint) on (a paintbrush or canvas). **11** *insurance* to add charges to. **12** to add a substance to (wine, etc). [Anglo-Saxon *lad* course or journey]

load-bearing *adj* of a wall, etc: supporting a structure, carrying a weight.

loaded *adj* **1** carrying a load; with a load in place. **2** of a gun: containing bullets. **3** of a camera: containing film. **4** *informal* very wealthy. **5** *N Am slang* under the influence of alcohol or drugs.

loaded question *noun* a question that is designed to bring out a specific kind of response.

loadline *noun* a **Plimsoll line**.

loadstar see **lodestar**

loadstone see **lodestone**

loaf[1] *noun* (***loaves***) **1** a shaped lump of dough, esp after it has risen and been baked. **2** *in compounds* a quantity of food formed into a regular shape: *meatloaf*. **3** *informal* the head or brains: *Use your loaf*. [Anglo-Saxon *hlaf*]

loaf[2] *verb, intr* (*often* **loaf about** *or* **around**) to loiter or stand about idly. [19c]

loafer *noun* **1** someone who loafs about. **2** a light casual shoe like a moccasin.

loam *noun* **1** a dark fertile easily-worked soil. **2** a mixture basically of moist clay and sand used in making bricks, casting moulds, plastering walls, etc. ▪ **loamy** *adj*. [Anglo-Saxon *lam*]

loan *noun* **1** something lent, esp money lent at interest. **2** an act or the state of lending or being lent. ▸ *verb* to lend (esp money). [13c: from Norse *lan*] IDIOMS **on loan** given as a loan.

loan shark *noun, informal* someone who lends money at exorbitant rates of interest.

loath *or* **loth** /loʊθ/ *adj* unwilling; reluctant: *were loath to admit it*. [Anglo-Saxon *lath* hated]

loath, loathe

Be careful not to use **loath** when you mean the verb **loathe**, and vice versa:

I am loath to criticize him in case it affects his confidence.

I can see they loathe each other.

loathe *verb* **1** to dislike intensely. **2** to find (someone or something) disgusting. [Anglo-Saxon *lathian* to hate]

loathing *noun* intense dislike or disgust.

loathsome *adj* causing intense dislike or disgust.

loaves *pl of* **loaf[1]**

lob *noun* **1** *tennis* a ball hit in a high overhead path. **2** *cricket* a slow high underhand ball. **3** *sport* any high looping ball. ▸ *verb* (***lobbed, lobbing***) **1** to hit, kick or throw (a ball) in this way. **2** to send a high ball over (an opponent): *tried to lob the goalkeeper*. [14c]

lobar *adj* relating to or affecting a lobe, esp in the lungs.

lobate *adj* having lobes.

lobby *noun* (***-ies***) **1** a small entrance hall, passage or waiting room. **2** a common entrance giving access to several flats or apartments. **3** an antechamber of a legislative hall. **4** *Brit* (*also* **division lobby**) either of two corridors in the House of Commons that members pass into when they vote. **5** *Brit* a hall in the House of Commons where members of the public meet politicians. **6** a group of people who try to influence the Government, politicians, legislators, etc to favour their particular cause. **7** the particular cause that such a group tries to promote. ▸ *verb* (***-ies, -ied***) **1** to try to influence (the Government, politicians, legislators, etc) to favour a particular cause. **2** *intr* to frequent a parliamentary lobby in order to influence members or to collect political information. **3** *intr* to conduct a campaign in order to influence public officials. ▪ **lobbyist** *noun*. [16c: from Latin *lobia* covered walk or cloister]

lobe *noun* **1** (*also* **earlobe**) the soft lower part of the outer ear. **2** a division of an organ or gland in the body, esp the lungs, brain or liver. **3** a broad, usu rounded division or projection of a larger object. **4** a division of a leaf. ▪ **lobed** *adj*. [16c: from Greek *lobos* ear lobe]

lobelia *noun* a garden plant with red, white, purple, blue or yellow flowers. [18c: named after Matthias de Lobel, Flemish botanist]

lobotomy *noun* (***-ies***) *surgery* an operation that involves cutting into a lobe of an organ or gland. [20c: from Greek *lobos* earlobe + **-tomy**]

lobster *noun* **1** a large edible marine crustacean with two large pincer-like claws. **2** its flesh used as food. [Anglo-Saxon *loppestre*, related to Latin *locusta* a locust]

lobster pot *noun* a basket for catching lobsters.

local *adj* **1** relating or belonging to a particular place. **2** relating or belonging to someone's home area or neighbourhood. **3** of a train or bus: stopping at all the stations or stops in a neighbourhood or small area. **4** *med* affecting or confined to a small area or part of the body: *a local infection*. ▸ *noun* **1** someone who lives in a particular area. **2** *Brit* someone's nearest and most regularly visited pub. **3** a local bus or train. **4** a local anaesthetic. ▪ **localization** *noun*. ▪ **localize** *or* **-ise** *verb*. ▪ **locally** *adv*. [14c: from Latin *locus* place]

local anaesthetic *noun, med* **a** an injection that anaesthetizes only a small part of the body; **b** the medication used for this.

local authority *noun* the elected local government body in an area.

locale /loʊˈkɑːl/ *noun* a scene of some event or occurrence. [18c: from French *local* local]

local government *noun* government of town or county affairs by a locally elected authority, as distinct from national or central government.

locality *noun* (***-ies***) **1** a district or neighbourhood. **2** the scene of an event. **3** the position of a thing. [17c: from Latin *locus* place]

locate *verb* **1** to set in a particular place or position. **2** to find the exact position of. **3** to establish (something) in a place or position. [17c: from Latin *locatus* placed]

location *noun* **1** a position or situation. **2** the act of locating or process of being located. [16c]

IDIOMS **on location** *cinema* at an authentic site as opposed to in the studio.

loc. cit. *abbrev*: *loco citato* (Latin), in the passage just quoted.

loch /lɒk; *Scot* lɒx/ *noun, Scot* **1** a lake. **2** (*also* **sea loch**) a long narrow arm of the sea surrounded by land on three sides. [14c: Gaelic and Irish]

loci *pl of* **locus**

lock[1] *noun* **1** a mechanical device, usu consisting of a sliding bolt moved by turning a key, dial, etc, that secures a door, lid, machine, etc. **2** an enclosed section of a canal or river in which the water level can be altered by means of gates. **3** a state of being jammed or fixed together, and completely immovable. **4** the part of a gun that explodes the charge. **5** *wrestling* a tight hold which prevents an opponent from moving. **6** the full amount by which the front wheels of a vehicle will turn. **7** (*also* **lock forward**) *rugby* either of the two inside players in the second row of a scrum. ▸ *verb* **1** to fasten (a door, box, etc) with a lock. **2** *intr* of a door, window, etc: to become or have the means of becoming locked. **3** (*also* **lock sth up**) to shut up or secure (a building, etc) by locking all doors and windows. **4** *tr & intr* to jam or make (something) jam. **5** *tr & intr* to fasten or make (something) be fastened so as to prevent movement. ▪ **lockable** *adj*. [Anglo-Saxon]

IDIOMS **lock, stock and barrel** completely; including everything. **under lock and key** securely locked up.

PHRASAL VERBS **lock on** *or* **onto sth** of a radar beam, etc: to track (it) automatically. **lock sb up** to confine them or prevent them from leaving by locking them in.

lock[2] *noun* **1** a section or curl of hair. **2** (**locks**) hair. [Anglo-Saxon *locc*]

locker *noun* a small lockable cupboard for storage, eg, of luggage at a station, clothes and sports equipment at a gym, etc.

locket *noun* a small decorated case for holding a photograph or memento, worn on a chain round the neck. [17c: from French *loquet* latch]

lockout *noun* the exclusion of employees by the management from their place of work during an industrial dispute, as a means of imposing certain conditions.

locksmith *noun* someone who makes and mends locks.

lockup *noun, Brit* **1** a building, etc that can be locked up. **2** a small shop with no living quarters attached.

loco[1] *noun, informal* a locomotive.

loco[2] *adj, slang* crazy. [19c: from Spanish *loco* insane]

locomotion *noun* the power, process or capacity of moving from one place to another. [17c: from Latin *locus* place + *motio* motion]

locomotive *noun* a railway engine driven by steam, electricity or diesel power, used for pulling trains. ▸ *adj* relating to, capable of or causing locomotion. [17c]

locum /ˈloʊkəm/ (*in full* **locum tenens**) /ˈtɛnɛnz/ *noun* (***locums*** *or* ***locum tenentes*** /tɛnˈɛntiːz/) someone who temporarily stands in for someone else, esp in the medical and clerical professions. [15c: from Latin *locus* place + *tenere* to hold]

locus *noun* (***loci*** /ˈloʊsaɪ/) **1** *law* an exact place or location, esp one where some incident has taken place. **2** *maths* the set of points or values that satisfy an equation or a particular set of conditions. **3** *genetics* the position of a particular gene on a chromosome. [18c: Latin]

locust *noun* a grasshopper noted for its tendency to form dense migratory swarms that eat all the vegetation in their path, including crops. [13c: from Latin *locusta* lobster or locust]

locution *noun* **1** a style of speech. **2** an expression, word or phrase. [15c: from Latin *locutio* an utterance]

lode *noun* a thin band of rock containing metallic ore. [Anglo-Saxon *lad* course or journey]

lodestar *or* **loadstar** *noun* **1** a star used as a guide by sailors and astronomers, esp the Pole Star. **2** any guide or guiding principle. [14c: from Anglo-Saxon *lad* course + *steorra* star]

lodestone *or* **loadstone** *noun* **1** a form of magnetite which exhibits polarity, behaving, when freely suspended, as a magnet. **2** a magnet. **3** something that attracts.

lodge *noun* **1** a cottage at the gateway to the grounds of a large house or mansion. **2** a small house in the country orig used by people taking part in field sports: *a hunting lodge*. **3** a porter's room in a university or college, etc. **4 a** the meeting-place of a local branch of certain societies, eg, the **Freemason**s and the Orange Order; **b** the members of a branch of one of these societies. **5** a beaver's nest. ▸ *verb* **1** *intr* to live, usu temporarily, in rented accommodation, esp in someone else's home. **2** *tr & intr* **a** to become or cause (something) to become firmly fixed; **b** of feelings, ideas, thoughts, etc: to become implanted: *The idea was firmly lodged in his mind*. **3 a** to bring (a charge or accusation) against someone; **b** to make (a complaint) officially. **4** to provide with rented accommodation, esp in one's home. **5** (*usu* **lodge sth with sb**) to deposit money or valuables with them, esp for safe-keeping. **6** *intr* (*usu* **lodge in** *or* **with sb**) of power, authority, etc: to be in or under their control: *The power to hire and fire lodges with the board*. [13c: from French *loge* hut]

lodger *noun* someone who rents accommodation in someone else's home, often temporarily.

lodging *noun* **1** (*usu* **lodgings**) a room or rooms rented in someone else's home. **2** temporary accommodation.

loess /ˈloʊɪs/ *noun, geol* a loose quartz-based loam found esp in river basins. [19c: from German *löss* loose]

loft *noun* **1** a room or space under a roof. **2** a gallery in a church or hall: *an organ loft*. **3** a room used for storage, esp one over a stable for storing hay. **4 a** (*also* **pigeon loft**) a room or shed where pigeons are kept; **b** a group of pigeons. **5** *golf* the relative backward slant of the face of a golf club. **6** *golf* **a** a stroke that causes a golf ball to rise up high; **b** the amount of height that a player gives a ball. ▸ *verb* to strike, kick or throw (a ball, etc) high up in the air. [Anglo-Saxon *loft* sky or upper room]

lofty *adj* (**-*ier*, -*iest***) **1** very tall; of great or imposing height. **2** high or noble in character: *lofty thoughts*. **3** haughty or proud. ▪ **loftily** *adv*. ▪ **loftiness** *noun*. [16c: from **loft**]

log *noun* **1 a** a part of a tree trunk or branch that has been cut, esp for firewood; **b** a tree trunk or large branch that has fallen to the ground. **2** a detailed record of events occurring during the voyage of a ship or aircraft, etc. **3** a logbook. **4** *comput* a record eg of all the files accessed, websites visited, etc over a certain period of time. **5** a float, orig made of wood, attached by a line to a ship and used for measuring its speed. ► *verb* (***logged, logging***) **1 a** to record (distances covered, events, etc) in a book or logbook; **b** to record (speed) over a set distance. **2** to cut (trees or branches) into logs. **3** *intr* to cut logs. [14c]

PHRASAL VERBS **log in** *or* **on** *comput* **1** to start a session on a computer system, usu by typing a password. **2** to make a connection with another computer. **log out** *or* **off** *comput* **1** to end a session on a computer system. **2** to close a connection with another computer.

loganberry *noun* **1** a large edible dark red berry. **2** the plant that produces it. [19c: named after Judge J H Logan, who first grew it]

logarithm /'lɒgərɪðəm/ *noun* (*often* **log**) *maths* the power to which a real number, called the **base**[1] (*noun* sense 9), must be raised in order to give another number or variable, eg the logarithm of 100 to the base 10 is 2 (*written* $\log_{10} 100 = 2$). Also called **Napierian logarithm**. See also **antilogarithm**. ▪ **logarithmic** *adj*. [17c: first coined by John Napier, Scottish mathematician, from Greek *logos* word or ratio + *arithmos* number]

logbook *noun* **1** a book containing an official record of the voyage of a ship, aircraft, etc. **2** *Brit, formerly* the registration documents of a motor vehicle, now called **Vehicle Registration Document**.

loggerhead *noun* (*in full* **loggerhead turtle**) a large sea turtle. [16c as *logger* a dialect word meaning 'something heavy and clumsy' + **head**]

IDIOMS **at loggerheads** disagreeing fiercely.

logging *noun* the work of cutting trees and preparing timber. ▪ **logger** *noun*.

logic *noun* **1 a** *philos* the exploration of the validity or otherwise of arguments and reasoning; **b** *maths* the analysis of the principles of reasoning on which mathematical systems are based. **2** the rules or reasoning governing a particular subject or activity: *the logic of the absurd*. **3 a** the extent to which someone's reasoning is sound: *I didn't understand his logic*; **b** the convincing and compelling force of an argument: *The logic for having exams is dubious*; **c** rationalized thinking: *Logic dictated that she shouldn't go*. **4** the way that related events or facts are interconnected. **5** *electronics, computing* the system underlying the design and operation of computers. ▪ **logician** *noun*. [14c: from Greek *logos* word or ratio]

logical *adj* **1** relating or according to logic: *a logical truth*. **2** correctly reasoned or thought out: *a logical conclusion*. **3** able to reason correctly: *a logical mind*. **4** following reasonably or necessarily from facts or events: *the logical choice*. ▪ **logically** *adv*. [16c]

logistics *singular or plural noun* **1** the organizing of everything needed for any large-scale operation. **2** the art of moving and supplying troops and military equipment. ▪ **logistic** *adj*. ▪ **logistical** *adj*. ▪ **logistically** *adv*. [19c: from French *logistique*, from *loger* to **lodge**]

log jam *noun* **1** a blockage of logs being floated down a river. **2** a deadlock.

LOGO *noun, comput* a simple programming language with distinctive graphics.

logo *noun* a small design used as the symbol for a company, etc. [20c: contraction of *logotype*]

-logy *or* **-ology** *combining form, forming nouns, denoting* **1** a science or study: *geology*. **2** writing or speech: *trilogy*. [From Greek *logos* word or reason]

loin *noun* **1** (**loins**) the area of the body stretching from the bottom rib to the pelvis. **2** a cut of meat from the lower back area of an animal. [14c: from French dialect *loigne* a loin of veal]

loincloth *noun* a piece of material worn round the hips.

loiter *verb, intr* **1** to wait around, esp furtively; to skulk. **2** to stand around or pass time doing nothing. [15c: from Dutch *loteren* to wag]

loll *verb, intr* **1** (*often* **loll about**) to lie or sit about lazily; to lounge or sprawl. **2** of the tongue: to hang out. [14c]

lollipop *noun* a boiled sweet on a stick. [18c: from dialect *lolly* tongue + **pop**[1] (sense 2)]

lollipop lady *or* **lollipop man** *noun* someone employed to see that children get across busy roads safely, esp when going to or from school. [20c: from the pole they carry which looks like a **lollipop**]

lollop *verb* (***lolloped, lolloping***) *intr, informal* to bound around, esp with big ungainly strides. [18c: onomatopoeic extension of **loll**]

lolly *noun* (***-ies***) **1** *informal* a **lollipop** or an **ice lolly**. **2** *slang* money. [19c]

Lombard *noun* **1** an inhabitant of Lombardy in Northern Italy, or the dialect of this region. **2** one of the Langobardi, a Germanic tribe which founded a kingdom in Lombardy in 568, and was overthrown by Charlemagne in 774. ► *adj* relating to the Lombards. [14c: from French, from Latin *Langobardus*]

lone *adj* **1** without a partner, spouse or companion: *a lone parent*. **2** only: *the lone car in the car park*. **3** *poetic* of a place: isolated and unfrequented. [14c: from **alone**]

lonely *adj* (***-ier, -iest***) **1** of a person: sad because they have no companions or friends. **2** solitary and without companionship: *a lonely existence*. **3** of a place: isolated and unfrequented: *in a lonely street*. ▪ **loneliness** *noun*.

loner *noun* a person or animal that prefers to be alone.

lonesome *adj* **1** sad and lonely. **2** causing feelings of loneliness.

long[1] *adj* **1 a** measuring a great distance in space from one end to the other; **b** of time: lasting for an extensive period. **2** *often in compounds* **a** measuring a specified amount: *six centimetres long*; **b** lasting a specified time: *a three-hour-long movie*. **3** having a large number of items: *a long list*. **4 a** measuring more than is usual, expected or wanted: *She has really long hair*; **b** lasting a greater time than is usual, expected or wanted: *The breakdown made it a really long journey*. **5** of someone's memory: able to recall things that happened a considerable time ago. **6** having greater length than breadth. **7 a** of a dress or skirt: reaching down to the feet; **b** of trousers: covering the whole of the legs: *Older boys were allowed to wear long trousers*. **8** of a cold drink: large and thirst-quenching. **9** of stocks: bought in large amounts in expectation of a rise in prices. **10 a** *pho-*

netics of a vowel: having the greater of two recognized lengths; **b** of a syllable in verse: stressed. **11** *cricket* of fielders: covering the area near the boundary. ▸ *adv* **1** for, during or by a long period of time: *They had long expected such news.* **2** throughout the whole time: *all night long.* ▸ *noun* **1** a comparatively long time: *won't be there for long.* **2** a syllable that takes a comparatively long time to pronounce. [Anglo-Saxon *lang*]

IDIOMS **as long as** *or* **so long as 1** provided that. **2** while; during the time that. **before long** in the near future; soon. **the long and the short of it** the most important facts in a few words.

long² *verb, intr* (*often* **long for** *or* **to**) to desire very much: *longed to hear from her.* [Anglo-Saxon *langian*]

longboat *noun, formerly* the largest boat carried by a sailing ship.

longbow *noun* a large bow, drawn by hand, used for hunting and as a weapon.

long division *noun, maths* a calculation that involves **division**, where the **divisor** is usu greater than 12 and the working is shown in full.

long-drawn-out *adj* taking too long: *a long-drawn-out argument.*

longevity /lɒn'dʒɛvɪtɪ/ *noun* great length of life. [17c: from Latin *longaevitas*]

long face *noun* a dismal or miserable expression.

longhand *noun* ordinary handwriting as opposed to **shorthand**, typing or word-processing.

long haul *noun* **1** the carrying of cargo or passengers over a long distance. **2** anything requiring great effort or considerable time. ▪ **long-haul** *adj.*

longing *noun* an intense desire or yearning. ▸ *adj* having or exhibiting this feeling: *a longing look.* ▪ **longingly** *adv.*

longitude *noun* the angular distance east or west of the **prime meridian** measured from 0 degrees at this meridian to 180 degrees east or west of it. Compare **latitude**. [14c: from Latin *longus* long]

longitudinal *adj* **1** relating to longitude; measured by longitude. **2** relating to length. **3** lengthways. ▪ **longitudinally** *adv.*

long johns *plural noun, informal* underpants with long legs.

long jump *noun* an athletics event in which competitors take a running start and try to jump as far as possible. ▪ **long-jumper** *noun.*

long-life *adj* of food and drink: treated so that, even without refrigeration, it may be stored for a long time in an unopened container: *long-life milk.*

long-lived *adj* having a long life.

long-playing *adj* (abbrev **LP**) denoting a **record** (*noun* sense 4) where each side lasts approximately 25 minutes.

long-range *adj* **1** of predictions, etc: looking well into the future: *a long-range weather forecast.* **2** of a missile or weapon: able to reach far-off targets.

longship *noun, hist* a long narrow Viking warship with a large squarish sail, which could also be powered by banks of rowers.

longshore *adj* **1** found on or employed along the shore. **2** living on or frequently visiting the shore. [19c: from *alongshore*]

long shot *noun* **1** *informal* **a** a guess, attempt, etc that is unlikely to be successful; **b** a bet made in the knowledge that there is only a slim chance of winning; **c** a participant in a competition, etc generally thought to have little chance of winning: *The horse was a real long shot.* **2** *cinematog* a camera shot that makes viewers feel they are at a considerable distance from the scene. Opposite of **close-up**.

long-sighted *adj* **1** only able to see distant objects clearly. Compare **short-sighted. 2 a** tending to consider what effect actions, etc might have on the future; **b** wise. ▪ **long-sightedness** *noun.*

long-standing *adj* having existed or for a long time.

long-suffering *adj* patiently tolerating difficulties, hardship, unreasonable behaviour, etc.

long-term *adj* of a plan, etc: occurring in or concerning the future.

longtime *adj* of long standing: *a longtime friend.*

long wave *noun* an electromagnetic wave, esp a radio wave, with a wavelength greater than 1000m. Compare **medium wave**, **short wave**.

longways *adv, adj* in the direction of a thing's length.

long-winded *adj* of a speaker or speech: tediously using or having far more words than are necessary. ▪ **long-windedly** *adv.* ▪ **long-windedness** *noun.*

loo *noun, Brit informal* a lavatory. [20c]

loofah *noun* the roughly cylindrical dried inner part of a tropical gourd-like fruit, used as a kind of rough sponge. [19c: from Egyptian Arabic *lufah*]

look *verb* **1** *intr* (*often* **look at sth**) to direct one's sight towards it: *looked out of the window.* **2** *intr* (*often* **look at sth**) to direct one's attention towards it: *look at all the implications.* **3** *intr* (**look to sb** *or* **sth**) to rely on, turn to or refer to them or it: *looked to her for support.* **4** to seem to be; to have the appearance of being: *She looked much younger than she was* • *She looked an absolute sight* • *made him look ridiculous.* **5** *intr* to face or be turned in a specified direction: *The window looks south.* **6** to express by a look: *She was looking daggers at him.* **7** to consider or realize: *Just look what you've done!* **8** *intr* (**look for sb** *or* **sth**) **a** to search for them or it; **b** *informal* to be hoping for it: *He was looking for £100 for the bike.* ▸ *noun* **1 a** an act or the action of looking; a glance or view: *had a look through his photos;* **b** a glance or stare that conveys a particular feeling or emotion: *gave her an impatient look.* **2** (*sometimes* **looks**) the outward appearance of something or someone: *She always has that tired look* • *She didn't like the looks of the restaurant.* **3** (**looks**) beauty; attractiveness. **4** a particular way of dressing, etc, esp one that is different or particularly up-to-date: *went for a punk look.* **5 a** a search: *I'll have another look for that missing CD;* **b** a browse. **6** (*sometimes* **Look here!**) used as an exclamation to call for attention or to express protest: *Look here! What do you think you're doing?* [Anglo-Saxon *locian*]

IDIOMS **by the look** *or* **looks of sb** *or* **sth** *informal* going by appearances: *By the look of him, he's in need of a rest.* **by the look of things** *informal* going by how things stand at the moment: *By the look of things, we won't get this finished today.* **look as if** *or* **as though** to appear to be the case that; to give the impression that: *looks as though she'd seen a ghost.* **look down one's nose at sb** *or* **sth** *informal* to disapprove of them or it; to treat them or it with contempt. **look like** *informal* **1** to seem probable: *looks* *like it will rain.* **2** to appear to be similar to: *looks like her sister.* **3** to seem to be: *He looks like a nice guy.* **look oneself** to seem to be as healthy as usual: *He doesn't quite look himself yet, does he?* **look the part** to appear to be very well suited (to do or be something): *In the yellow lizard costume, he really did look the part.* **look a picture** to be extremely attractive: *The bride looked an absolute picture.* **look right** *or* **straight through sb** *informal* to ignore them on purpose. **look sharp** *informal* to hurry up: *We'd better look sharp if we're going to be there for seven.* **never look back** to continue to make progress or to prosper: *After the operation he never looked back.* **not know where to look** to feel acutely embarrassed.

PHRASAL VERBS **look after sb** *or* **sth** to attend to or take care of them or it. **look back** to think about the past; to reminisce. **look down on** *or* **upon sb** *or* **sth** to consider them or it inferior or contemptible. **look forward to sth** to anticipate it with pleasure. **look in on sb** to visit them briefly. **look into sth** to investigate it. **look on** *or* **upon sb** *or* **sth in a certain way** to think of or consider them or it in that way: *look on it as a bonus • look upon me as a friend.* **look out 1** to keep watch and be careful. **2** used as an exclamation warning of imminent danger. See also **lookout**. **look out sth** to find it by searching: *I'll look out that magazine for you.* **look out for sb** *or* **sth 1** to be alert about finding them or it. **2** *informal* to protect: *He has always looked out for his younger brother.* **look up** to show signs of improving: *The weather's looking up at last.* **look sb up** *informal* to visit or get in touch with them: *I'll look you up when I'm next in town.* **look sth up** to search for an item of information, etc in a reference book, etc. **look up to sb** to respect their behaviour, opinions, etc.

lookalike *noun* someone or something that looks very much like someone or something else.

looker *noun, informal* someone, usu a woman, who is considered attractive.

look-in *noun* **1** a chance of joining in, being included, or doing something: *never gives her a look-in.* **2** a quick informal visit.

looking-glass *noun, old use* a mirror.

lookout *noun* **1** a careful watch. **2** a place from which such a watch can be kept. **3** someone who has to keep watch, eg on board ship. **4** *informal* a personal concern or problem: *That's your lookout.*

look-see *noun, informal* a quick inspection.

loom[1] *noun* a machine that weaves thread into fabric. [Anglo-Saxon *geloma* a tool]

loom[2] *verb, intr* **1** to appear indistinctly and usu in some enlarged or threatening form. **2** of an event: to be imminent, esp in some menacing way. [16c]

loon *noun, N Am* a **diver** (sense 3). [17c]

loony *slang, noun* (***-ies***) someone who is mad. ▸ *adj* (***-ier, -iest***) **1** crazy; mad. **2** overzealous; fanatical: *a loony fringe group.* [19c: shortened from **lunatic**]

loop *noun* **1** a rounded or oval-shaped single coil in a piece of thread, string, rope, chain, etc, formed as it crosses over itself. **2** any similar oval-shaped or U-shaped bend, eg in a river, the path of a planet, etc. **3** a manoeuvre in which an aircraft describes a complete vertical circle in the sky. **4** a strip of magnetic tape or motion-picture film whose ends have been spliced together to form a loop so that the sound or images on it can be continually repeated. **5** *electronics* a closed circuit which a signal can pass round, as, for example, in a **feedback** (sense 3) control system. **6** *comput* a series of instructions in a program that is repeated until a certain condition is met. **7** *maths* a line on a graph which begins and ends at the same point. **8** *physics* a closed curve on a graph. **9** in knitting and crochet: a **stitch**. ▸ *verb* **1** to fasten with or enclose in a loop. **2** to form into a loop or loops. [15c]

IDIOMS **loop the loop** of an aircraft, pilot, etc: to make a vertical loop in the sky.

loophole *noun* a means of escaping or evading a responsibility, duty, obligation, etc without infringing a law, regulation, etc. [16c]

loopy *adj* (***-ier, -iest***) *slang* mad; crazy.

loose *adj* **1** not or no longer tied up or attached to something else; free. **2** of clothes, etc: not tight or close-fitting. **3 a** not held together; not fastened or firmly fixed in place: *Jane kept wiggling her loose tooth;* **b** not packaged: *Get the loose oranges rather than the pre-packed ones.* **4** not tightly-packed or compact: *loose soil.* **5** vague or inexact: *loose translation.* **6** promiscuous; immoral. **7** indiscreet: *loose talk.* **8** *sport* of a ball, etc: in play but not under a player's control. **9** hanging; droopy; baggy. **10** of the bowels: moving frequently and producing softer faeces than is usual. **11** of a cough: producing phlegm easily. ▸ *adv* in an unrestrained way: *The dog can run loose in the park.* ▸ *verb* **1** to release or set free. **2** to unfasten or untie. **3** to make less tight, compact or dense. **4** to relax: *loose one's hold.* **5** to discharge (a gun, bullet, arrow, etc). ▪ **loosely** *adv.* ▪ **looseness** *noun.* [14c: from Norse *lauss*]

IDIOMS **on the loose** free from confinement or control.

---

loose, lose

Be careful not to use the spelling **loose** when you mean **lose**:

Where did you lose your purse?

---

loose box *noun* a part of a stable or horse box where horses are kept untied.

loose end *noun* (*often* **loose ends**) something that has been left unfinished or that has not been explained or decided: *signed the contract after the loose ends had been tied up.*

IDIOMS **at a loose end** lacking something to do.

loose-leaf *adj* of a folder, etc: having clips or rings which open to allow pages to be taken out or put in.

loosen *verb* **1** *tr & intr* (*sometimes* **loosen up** *or* **loosen sth up**) to make or become loose or looser. **2** to free; to cause to become free or freer: *Drink always loosened his tongue.* [14c]

PHRASAL VERBS **loosen up** *informal* to relax or become more relaxed.

loot *verb* **1** *intr* **a** to steal from shops, warehouses, etc, often during or following rioting; **b** to steal from an enemy in wartime. **2** *informal* to steal from: *looted his son's piggy-bank.* ▸ *noun* **1 a** money, goods or supplies stolen from shops, warehouses, etc, esp when taken during or following rioting; **b** money or goods stolen from an enemy in wartime. **2** *slang* money. ▪ **looter** *noun.* [18c: from Hindi *lut*]

lop *verb* (***lopped, lopping***) (*usu* **lop sth off**) **1** to cut off (esp the branches of a tree). **2** to cut away the unnecessary or superfluous parts of (something): *lopped five pages off the article.* [15c]

lope *verb, intr* to run with long bounding steps. ▸ *noun* a bounding leap. [14c: from Norse *hlaupa* to leap]

lop-eared *adj* of animals: having ears that droop. [17c]

lopsided *adj* **1** with one side smaller, lower or lighter than the other. **2** leaning over to one side. [18c]

loquacious *adj* very talkative. ▪ **loquacity** *noun*. [17c: from Latin *loqui* to speak]

lord *noun* **1** a master or ruler. **2** *feudalism* someone who is in a superior position. **3** *chiefly Brit* **a** a man who is a member of the aristocracy; **b** (**Lord**) a title used to address certain members of the aristocracy. **4** (**My Lord** *or* **my lord**) **a** a conventional way for lawyers, barristers, etc to address a judge in court; **b** a formal way of addressing certain members of the clergy and aristocracy. **5** (**Lord** *or* **Our Lord** *or* **the Lord**) *Christianity* a way of addressing or referring to God or Jesus Christ. **6** (**Lord**) *in compounds* forming part of the titles of some high-ranking officials: *Lord Provost* • *Lord Privy Seal*. **7** (**Lord!**) expressing shock, surprise, dismay, etc. [Anglo-Saxon *hlaf* loaf + *ward* keeper]
IDIOMS **lord it over sb** to behave in a condescending or overbearing manner towards them.

Lord Advocate *noun, Scot* see **Attorney General**

Lord Chief Justice *noun, Brit* the head of the Queen's Bench division.

Lord Lieutenant *noun, Brit* the crown representative in a county in England and Wales.

lordly *adj* (**-ier, -iest**) **1** grand or haughty. **2** belonging, relating or suitable to a lord or lords. ▪ **lordliness** *noun*.

Lord Mayor *noun* the title of the mayor of London and the mayors of certain other English cities.

Lord Privy Seal *noun* a senior British cabinet minister without official duties. [15c]

the Lords *singular noun* (**the Lords**) the House of Lords.

Lordship *noun* (**His** *or* **Your Lordship**) **1** a title used to address bishops, judges and all peers except dukes. **2** *facetious* a form of address used to mock someone behaving in a pretentious or overbearing way.

the Lord's Prayer *noun, Christianity* the prayer that begins, 'Our Father, who art in heaven'. Also called **Our Father**.

Lords Spiritual *plural noun, Brit* the English and Welsh Anglican archbishops and bishops entitled to sit in the House of Lords. Compare **Lords Temporal**.

Lords Temporal *plural noun, Brit* all the members of the House of Lords who are not archbishops or bishops. Compare **Lords Spiritual**.

lore *noun* the whole body of knowledge on a particular subject, esp the kind of knowledge that has been enhanced by legends, anecdotes, traditional beliefs, etc: *classical lore*. [Anglo-Saxon *lar*]

lorgnette /lɔːn'jɛt/ *noun* a pair of spectacles that are held up to the eyes using a long handle. [19c: French, from *lorgner* to squint]

lorry *noun* (**-ies**) *Brit* a large road vehicle for transporting heavy loads. [20c]

lose *verb* (**lost**) **1 a** to fail to keep or obtain (something), esp because of a mistake, carelessness, etc: *lost his money through a hole in his pocket*; **b** to stop or begin to stop having (some distinguishing quality, characteristic or property): *She was losing her nerve* • *Despite everything, he hasn't lost his sense of humour*; **c** to become less marked, noticeable, intense, etc in (a specified way): *These roses have lost their scent*. **2 a** to misplace (something), esp temporarily: *I've lost the car keys*; **b** to be unable to find (something); **c** to leave accidentally: *I lost the umbrella at the cinema*. **3 a** to suffer the loss of (usu a close friend or relative) through death; **b** to suffer the loss of (an unborn baby) through miscarriage or stillbirth; **c** to fail to save the life of (esp a patient); **d** to be deprived of (life, possessions, etc), esp in a war, fire, natural disaster, etc: *The village lost half its population in the earthquake*; **e** (**be lost**) to be killed or drowned, esp at sea. **4** to fail to use or get; to miss (an opportunity, etc). **5 a** *tr & intr* to fail to win (a game, vote, proposal, election, battle, bet, etc); **b** to give away; to forfeit: *lost £50 on the horses*. **6 a** to be unable or no longer able to hear, see, understand, etc: *Sorry, I lost what you said when that noisy bus went by*; **b** to confuse or bewilder (someone): *Sorry, you've lost me there*. **7 a** to escape or get away from (someone or something); **b** of a competitor in a race, etc: to leave (the rest of the field, etc) behind. **8** of a clock or watch: to become slow by (a specified amount). [Anglo-Saxon *losian* to be lost]
IDIOMS **lose one's cool** *informal* to become upset. **lose face** to be humiliated or discredited. **lose one's grip** *or* **lose one's grip on sth** to be unable to control or understand things. **lose ground** to slip back or fall behind. **lose one's head** to become angry or irrational. **lose heart** to become discouraged. **lose one's heart (to sb)** to fall in love (with them). **lose one's licence** to be disqualified from driving. **lose one's marbles** *slang* to go completely crazy. **lose one's mind** *or* **reason** to behave irrationally, esp temporarily. **lose one's** *or* **the rag** *Brit informal* to become very angry. **lose sight of sb** *or* **sth 1** to be unable or no longer able to see them or it. **2** to forget or ignore the importance of them or it: *They lost sight of their original aims*. **lose sleep over sth** to worry about it or be preoccupied by it. **lose one's temper** to become angry. **lose one's touch** to forget how to do something or to be less proficient at doing something than one used to be. **lose touch with sb** *or* **sth** to no longer be in contact with them or it. **lose track of sb** *or* **sth** to fail to notice or monitor the passing or progress of them or it. **lose one's voice** to be unable or hardly able to speak, esp due to having a sore throat, a cold or flu. **lose one's** *or* **the way** to stray from one's route by mistake.
PHRASAL VERBS **lose out** *informal* **1** to suffer loss or be at a disadvantage. **2** to fail to get something one wants.

---

lose, loose
Be careful not to use the spelling **lose** when you mean **loose**:
a loose tooth
The dog ran loose in the park.

---

loser *noun* **1** someone or something that is defeated. **2** *informal* someone who is habitually unsuccessful.
IDIOMS **a bad, poor** *or* **good loser** someone who loses in bad, poor or good spirit.

losing *adj* failing; never likely to be successful: *fighting a losing battle*.

loss *noun* **1** an act or instance of losing or being lost: *the loss of his driving licence*. **2** the thing, amount, etc lost: *His loss of hearing was severe.* **3** the disadvantage that results when someone or something goes: *a great loss to the company.* **4 a** the death of a close friend or relative: *He couldn't come to terms with the loss of his mother;* **b** the sadness felt after such a death: *He did his best to console her in her loss.* [Anglo-Saxon]

IDIOMS **at a loss 1** puzzled; uncertain; unable to understand: *Her tantrums left me at a complete loss.* **2** of a selling price, etc: lower than the buying price: *had to sell the house at a loss.* **3** of a company, etc: losing more money than it is making: *trading at a loss.*

loss adjuster *noun, insurance* someone who assesses claims for compensation on behalf of an insurance company.

loss leader *noun, commerce* an item on sale at a loss, as a means of attracting custom for other goods.

lost *past tense, past participle of* **lose**

lost cause *noun* an aim, ideal, person, etc that has no chance of success.

lot *noun* **1** *informal* (*usu* **a lot** *or* **lots**) a large number or amount of something: *an awful lot of work to do: lots of children.* **2 a** (**the lot**) everything; the total; the whole number or amount: *ate the lot;* **b** (**one's lot**) *informal* all one is getting: *That's your lot!* **3** a group of people or things that have something, often a specified attribute or quality, in common: *Get a move on, you lazy lot.* **4 a** a straw, slip of paper, etc that is drawn from a group of similar objects, in order to reach a fair and impartial decision: *draw lots to see who'd go first;* **b** the use of lots to arrive at a decision, choice, etc: *made their selection by lot.* **5** someone's fortune, destiny, plight, etc: *Something must be done to remedy the lot of the homeless.* **6** an item or set of items for sale by auction, usu identified by a number: *Lot 49 looks intriguing.* **7** *N Am* an area of land for a specified purpose: *parking lot.* **8** the area around a film studio used for outside filming. [Anglo-Saxon *hlot* portion or choice]

IDIOMS **a bad lot** a group or person considered to be dishonest, immoral, etc. **cast** *or* **throw in one's lot with sb** to decide to share their fortunes.

loth see **loath**

lotion *noun* any liquid, used either as a medicine or a cosmetic, for healing or cleaning the skin. [15c: from Latin *lavare* to wash]

lottery *noun* (**-ies**) **1** a system for raising money which involves randomly drawing numbered tickets from a drum, etc and giving prizes to those who hold the tickets with the same numbers as the ones that have been picked out. **2** anything thought of as being a matter of chance. [16c: from French *loterie*]

lotto *noun* **1** an earlier name for the game now usu called **bingo**. **2** a name used for various lotteries.

lotus *noun* **1** *Greek myth* a fruit which was thought to produce a state of blissful and dreamy forgetfulness. **2** a water lily sacred to the ancient Egyptians. **3** a water lily traditionally associated with Buddhism and Hinduism. [16c: from Greek *lotos*]

lotus-eater *noun* someone who lives a lazy and indulgent life. [19c]

lotus position *noun, yoga* a seated position with the legs crossed and each foot resting on the opposite thigh.

louche /luːʃ/ *adj* shady, sinister, shifty or disreputable. ▪ **louchely** *adv.* [19c: French, in the sense 'squinting']

loud *adj* **1** making a relatively great sound; noisy. **2** capable of making a relatively great sound: *a loud horn.* **3** emphatic and insistent: *loud complaints.* **4** of colours, clothes, designs, etc: tastelessly bright, garish or gaudy. **5** of a person or their behaviour: aggressively noisy and coarse. ▸ *adv* in a loud manner. ▪ **loudly** *adv.* ▪ **loudness** *noun.* [Anglo-Saxon *hlud*]

loudhailer *noun* a portable device for amplifying the voice.

loudmouth *noun, informal* someone who is very noisy and boastful. ▪ **loud-mouthed** *adj.*

loudspeaker *noun* (*often just* **speaker**) an electronic device that converts electrical signals into audible sound waves.

lough /lɒk; *Irish* lɒx/ *noun, Irish* a **loch**. [14c: Irish Gaelic *loch*]

lounge *verb, intr* **1** to lie, sit, stand, recline etc in a relaxed and comfortable way. **2** to pass the time without doing very much: *He would lounge from morning to night.* ▸ *noun* **1** a sitting-room in a private house. **2** a large room in a public building, such as a hotel, where people can sit and relax. **3** (*also* **departure lounge**) an area or large room in an airport, ferry terminal, etc, where passengers can relax prior to being called to board the aeroplane, ferry, etc. **4** *Brit* (*also* **lounge bar**) the more up-market bar of a pub or hotel. **5** an act or spell of lounging. [16c]

lounger *noun* **1** someone who lounges. **2** an extending chair or lightweight couch for lounging on.

lounge suit *noun, Brit* a man's suit for everyday wear.

lour *or* **lower** *verb, intr* **1** of the sky: to darken or threaten rain or storms. **2** to scowl or look angry or gloomy. ▪ **louring** *adj.* [13c]

louse *noun* **1** (*pl* ***lice***) a wingless parasitic insect infesting human hair and skin. **2** (*pl* ***louses***) *slang* a scornful term of abuse for a person. [Anglo-Saxon *lus*]

PHRASAL VERBS **louse sth up** *slang* to spoil or ruin it.

lousy *adj* (**-ier, -iest**) **1** having lice. **2** *slang* very bad, unpleasant, or disgusting. **3** poor or second-rate.

lout *noun* someone, usu a teenage male, whose behaviour, esp in public, is generally considered unacceptable. ▪ **loutish** *adj.* ▪ **loutishness** *noun.* [16c]

louvre *or* (*N Am*) **louver** /ˈluːvə(r)/ *noun* **1** any one of a set of overlapping slats in a door, etc which let air in but keep rain and light out. **2** a dome-like structure on a roof for letting smoke out and light and air in. ▪ **louvred** *adj.* [14c: from French *lovier*]

lovage *noun* a S European flowering plant used medicinally and for flavouring. [14c: from French *luvesche*]

lovat *noun* **1** a palish dusky green colour. **2** a tweed suit in this colour. ▪ **lovat-green** *adj.* [20c: named after Lovat, a town in the Scottish Highlands famous for producing tweed of this colour]

love *verb* **1** to feel great affection for (someone). **2 a** to enjoy very much: *I love to boogie;* **b** to like very much: *I love chocolate biscuits.* ▸ *noun* **1** a feeling of great affection: *brotherly love.* **2** a strong liking: *a love of the outdoors.* **3** used as an affectionate term of address: *my love.* **4** *tennis, squash, whist, etc* no score. ▪ **lovable** *or* **loveable** *adj.* [Anglo-Saxon *lufu*]

IDIOMS **fall in love with sb** to develop feelings of love and attraction for them. **in love (with sb)** having strong feelings of affection and attraction (for them). **make love to** *or* **with sb 1** to have sexual intercourse with them. **2** *old use* to woo them.

lovebird *noun* **1** a small parrot sometimes kept as a cage bird. **2** (**lovebirds**) lovers who openly display their affection for each other in public.

love child *noun, old use* an illegitimate child.

lovelorn *adj* sad or pining because the love felt for someone else is not returned. [17c]

lovely *adj* (**-ier, -iest**) **1** strikingly attractive; beautiful. **2** *informal* delightful or pleasing. ▸ *noun* (**-ies**) *informal* a pretty woman. [Anglo-Saxon *luflie*]

lovemaking *noun* **1** *formerly* courting. **2** any form of sexual activity. [15c]

lover *noun* **1** someone who is in love with someone else. **2** (**lovers**) two people who are in love with one another or who are sharing a sexual relationship. **3** someone who enjoys or is fond of a specified thing: *a cat lover* • *a lover of fine wine*.

lovesick *adj* **1** infatuated with someone. **2** lovelorn. [16c]

lovey-dovey *adj, informal* of a couple: openly displaying affection, esp in a sentimental way. [19c]

loving *adj* **1** affectionate and caring. **2** *in compounds* enjoying, valuing, cherishing or appreciating a specified thing: *fun-loving*. ▪ **lovingly** *adv*. [15c]

loving cup *noun* a large two-handled drinking cup passed round at the end of a banquet. [19c]

low[1] *adj* **1** of a building, hill, etc: measuring comparatively little from top to bottom. **2** close to the ground, sea-level, the horizon, etc: *low cloud*. **3** of a temperature, volume of water, score, etc: measuring comparatively less than is usual or average: *The river is low*. **4** having little value; not costing very much. **5** of numbers: small. **6** not near the top: *Shopping was low on her list of priorities*. **7** coarse, rude, vulgar, etc. **8** being of humble rank or position. **9** not very advanced; unsophisticated: *Worms are a low form of animal life*. **10** of the neckline of a garment: leaving the neck and upper part of the chest bare. **11** of a sound, note, voice, etc: **a** quiet; soft: *The fridge gives out a low hum*; **b** produced by slow vibrations and having a deep pitch. **12 a** weak; lacking in energy or vitality: *feeling low after the operation*; **b** depressed; dispirited: *feeling low after losing his job*. **13** unfavourable: *a low opinion*. **14** underhanded; unprincipled: *How low can you get?* **15** giving a relatively slow engine speed: *a low gear*. **16** subdued: *low lighting*. **17** not prominent or conspicuous: *keeping a low profile*. **18** of latitudes: near the equator. ▸ *adv* **1** in or to a low position, state or manner: *aimed low and fired* • *brought low by his gambling debts*. **2** in a small quantity or to a small degree. **3** of a sound, etc: **a** quietly; **b** with or in a deep pitch. **4** *in compounds* **a** not measuring much in a specified respect: *low-voltage*; **b** not far off the ground: *low-slung*; **c** deeply: *low-cut*; **d** lowly: *low-born*. ▸ *noun* **1** a depth, position, level, etc which is low or lowest. **2** *meteorol* a **cyclone** (sense 1). ▪ **lowness** *noun*. [12c: from Norse *lagr*]

low[2] *verb, intr* of cattle: to make a gentle mooing sound. ▸ *noun* the gentle mooing sound made by cattle. ▪ **lowing** *noun*. [Anglo-Saxon *hlowan*]

lowbrow *adj* lacking cultural or intellectual values. ▸ *noun* a lowbrow person. Compare **middlebrow**, **highbrow**.

Low Church *noun* a group within the Church of England which puts little value on ceremony, but which stresses evangelical theology. [17c]

the lowdown *noun, informal* information about someone or something: *I've got all the lowdown on their affair*. [20c]

low-down *adj, informal* mean and dishonourable: *a low-down dirty trick*. [16c]

lower[1] *adj* **1** not as high in position, status, height, value, etc: *lower middle class*. **2** of an animal or plant: less highly developed than other species. **3** of part of a river or the land around it: relatively far from the source: *lower Deeside*. **4** in place names: **a** relatively far south; **b** geographically not so high. ▸ *adv* in or to a lower position. ▸ *verb* **1** to lessen or become less in amount, value, status, sound, etc. **2 a** to pull down: *We'd better lower the window*; **b** to cause or allow (something) to come down: *lowered the lifeboat*. **3** to reduce or cause (something) to be reduced: *The rejection lowered his confidence*. [13c]

lower[2] see **lour**

lower case *printing* (abbrev **lc**) *adj* referring or relating to small letters as opposed to capitals. ▸ *noun* a letter or letters of this kind: *a novel written entirely in lower case*. Compare **upper case**.

lower class *noun* a social group that traditionally includes manual workers. ▸ *adj* (**lower-class**) referring or relating to this social group. [18c]

lower house *or* **lower chamber** *noun* in a **bicameral** parliament: usu the larger section, more representative of the population as a whole, such as the House of Commons in the United Kingdom. [16c]

lowest common denominator *noun, maths* (abbrev **LCD** *or* **lcd**) in a group of fractions, the lowest common multiple of all the denominators. See also **common denominator**.

lowest common multiple *noun, maths* (abbrev **LCM** *or* **lcm**) the smallest number into which every member of a group of numbers will divide exactly.

low frequency *noun* a radio frequency between 30 and 300 kilohertz.

low-key *adj* restrained or subdued.

lowland *noun* **1** (*also* **lowlands**) land which is comparatively low-lying and flat. **2** (**the Lowlands**) the less mountainous region of Scotland lying to the south and east of the Highlands. ▸ *adj* (**lowland** *or* **Lowland**) belonging or relating to lowlands or the Scottish Lowlands. ▪ **lowlander** *or* **Lowlander** *noun*. [16c]

low-level language *noun, comput* a programming language in which each instruction represents a single **machine-code** operation. See also **high-level language**.

lowly *adj* (**-ier, -iest**) **1** humble in rank, status or behaviour. **2** simple, modest. ▪ **lowliness** *noun*.

low-pitched *adj* **1** of a sound: low in pitch. **2** of a roof: having a gentle slope.

low profile *noun* a deliberate avoidance of publicity and attention. ▸ *adj* (**low-profile**) **1** unobtrusive; getting little publicity: *low-profile talks*. **2** of car tyres: wider than is usual.

low-tech *adj, informal* not involving the use of the latest technology. [20c: modelled on **high-tech**]

low tide *noun* the tide at its lowest level or the time when this occurs. Also called **low water**.

low-water mark *noun* **1 a** the level that a low tide reaches; **b** a naturally occurring or artificial line that marks this level. **2** the lowest point possible.

loyal *adj* **1** faithful and true. **2** personally devoted to a sovereign, government, leader, friend, partner, etc. **3** expressing or showing loyalty: *the loyal toast to the Queen.* ▪ **loyally** *adv.* [16c: from Latin *legalis* legal]

loyalist *noun* **1** a loyal supporter, esp of a sovereign or an established government. **2** (**Loyalist**) in Northern Ireland: a person in favour of continuing the parliamentary union with Great Britain. Compare **Republican** (*noun* sense 3). ▪ **loyalism** *noun.* [17c]

loyalty *noun* (***-ies***) **1** the state or quality of being loyal. **2** (*often* **loyalties**) a feeling of loyalty or duty: *divided loyalties.* [15c]

loyalty card *noun* a machine-readable plastic card issued by certain retailers, enabling customers to accumulate credits to be redeemed for goods or cash.

lozenge /ˈlɒzɪndʒ/ *noun* **1** a small sweet or tablet, esp one with some kind of medicinal property, which dissolves in the mouth. **2** *maths* a less common term for a **rhombus**. [14c: from French *losenge*]

LP *abbrev* **1** long-playing. **2** long-playing record.

L-plate *noun, Brit* a small square white sign with a red letter *L* on it which, by law, a learner driver must display on the back and front of a car.

Lr *symbol, chem* lawrencium.

LSD *abbrev* lysergic acid diethylamide, an illegal hallucinatory drug. Also called **acid**.

Lt *or* **Lt.** *abbrev* Lieutenant.

Ltd *or* **Ltd.** *abbrev* Limited, as used at the end of the names of limited liability companies.

Lu *symbol, chem* lutetium.

lubricant *noun* oil, grease, etc used to reduce friction. [19c]

lubricate *verb* **1** to coat (engine parts, etc) with oil, grease, etc in order to reduce friction. **2** *intr* to act as a lubricant. ▪ **lubrication** *noun.* [17c: from Latin *lubricare* to make slippery or smooth]

lubricious *adj* **1** lewd. **2** evasive. ▪ **lubricity** *noun.* [17c: from Latin *lubricus* slippery]

lucerne /luˈsɜːn/ *noun, Brit* **alfalfa**. [17c: from French *luzerne*]

lucid *adj* **1** clearly presented and easily understood. **2** not confused, esp in contrast to bouts of insanity or delirium. ▪ **lucidity** *noun.* ▪ **lucidly** *adv.* ▪ **lucidness** *noun.* [16c: from Latin *lucidus* full of light]

Lucifer *noun* Satan; the Devil. [11c: Latin, meaning 'light-bringer']

luck *noun* **1** chance, esp as it is perceived as influencing someone's life at specific times: *luck was on his side.* **2** good fortune. **3** events in life which cannot be controlled and seem to happen by chance: *She's had nothing but bad luck.* ▪ **luckless** *adj.* [15c: from Dutch *luk*]

IDIOMS **down on one's luck** experiencing problems or suffering hardship. **in luck** fortunate. **no such luck** *informal* unfortunately not. **out of luck** unfortunate. **try** *or* **test one's luck** to attempt something without being sure of the outcome. **worse luck** *informal* unfortunately.

lucky *adj* (***-ier, -iest***) **1** having good fortune. **2** bringing good fortune. **3** happening by chance, esp when the outcome is advantageous: *It was lucky the weather was good.* ▪ **luckily** *adv.* [16c]

lucky dip *noun* **1** a chance to rummage around in a tub or container full of shredded paper, sawdust, etc in which prizes have been hidden, and to draw out a prize at random. **2** any process in which a choice is made at random.

lucrative *adj* affording financial gain; profitable. ▪ **lucratively** *adv.* [15c: from Latin *lucrari* to gain]

lucre /ˈluːkə(r)/ *noun, derog* profit or financial gain, esp when it has been obtained in a dishonourable or exploitative way. [14c: from Latin *lucrum* gain]

Luddite *noun* **1** (**the Luddites**) *hist* a group of artisans who, in the early 19c, destroyed machinery, fearing that it threatened their jobs. **2** anyone who opposes new technology. [19c: after Ned Lud or Ludd, who attacked manufacturing equipment]

ludicrous *adj* completely ridiculous or absurd. ▪ **ludicrousness** *noun.* [17c: from Latin *ludere* to play]

ludo *noun, Brit* a board game where counters are moved according to the number shown by each throw of the dice. [19c: Latin, meaning 'I play']

luff *verb* **1** to steer (a ship) closer to the wind. **2** to move (the jib of a crane or derrick) up or down. [13c]

lug[1] *verb* (***lugged, lugging***) to carry, pull or drag with difficulty or effort.

lug[2] *noun* **1** *dialect or informal* an ear. **2 a** a protruding part on something, esp one that acts as a kind of handle; **b** a projecting part on a spade or similar implement. [15c]

luge /luːʒ/ *noun* a light toboggan for either one or two people. ▸ *verb, intr* to travel or race on this type of toboggan. [20c: Swiss dialect]

luggage *noun, Brit* suitcases, bags, etc used when travelling. [16c: from **lug**[1]]

lugger *noun* a small vessel with square sails. [18c]

lugubrious *adj* sad and gloomy; mournful. [17c: Latin *lugere* to mourn]

lugworm *noun* a large marine worm which burrows on seashores and river estuaries and which is often used as fishing bait. [17c: related to **lug**[1]]

lukewarm *adj* **1** of liquids: moderately warm. **2** of interest, support, response, etc: not enthusiastic; indifferent. [14c: from Anglo-Saxon *hleuke* tepid + **warm**]

lull *verb* **1** to soothe or induce a feeling of well-being in (someone): *lulled the baby to sleep.* **2** to allay (suspicions), esp falsely. **3** to deceive (someone): *lulled them into a false sense of security.* ▸ *noun* a period of calm and quiet: *a lull before the storm.* [14c: imitating the sound of quiet singing]

lullaby *noun* (***-ies***) a soft soothing song to help send a child to sleep. [16c: from **lull** + **bye**[2]]

lumbago *noun* chronic pain in the lower region of the back. [17c: Latin *lumbago*, from *lumbus* loin]

lumbar *adj, anatomy* relating to or situated in the region of the lower back. [19c: from Latin *lumbus* loin]

lumbar puncture *noun, med* the withdrawal of spinal fluid through a needle inserted into the lower region of the spine as an aid to diagnosing a disease.

lumber[1] *noun* **1** disused articles of furniture or odds and ends that are no longer used and which have been stored away. **2** *N Am* timber, esp when partly cut up ready for use. ▸ *verb* **1** to fill something with lumber or other useless items. **2** *tr & intr, chiefly N Am* to fell trees and saw the wood into timber. **3** (**lumber sb with sth**) *informal* to burden them with (something unwanted, difficult, etc). [16c]

lumber[2] *verb, intr* to move about heavily and clumsily. ▪ **lumbering** *adj.* [16c]

lumberjack *noun* someone who works at felling trees, sawing them up and moving them. [19c: from **lumber**[1] + *jack* meaning 'man']

lumen *noun* (***lumina*** or ***lumens***) **1** *physics* (symbol **lm**) in the SI system: a unit of measurement of luminous flux. **2** *biol* in living organisms: the space enclosed by the walls of a vessel or tube, eg within a blood vessel or intestine. [19c: Latin, meaning 'light']

luminance *noun* **1** *physics* (symbol **L**) a measure of the brightness of a surface that is radiating or reflecting light, expressed in **candela**s per square metre. **2** the state or quality of radiating or reflecting light. [20c: from Latin *lumen* light]

luminary *noun* (***-ies***) **1** someone who is considered an expert or authority in a particular field. **2** a famous or prominent member of a group. [15c: from Latin *luminarium* a lamp]

luminescence *noun, physics* the emission of light by a substance, usu a solid, in the absence of a rise in temperature. ▪ **luminescent** *adj.* [19c: from Latin *lumen* a light]

luminous *adj* **1** full of or giving out light. **2** *non-technical* glowing in the dark: *a luminous clock face.* **3** *non-technical* of colours: very bright and garish. ▪ **luminosity** *noun* (***-ies***). [15c: from Latin *lumen* a light + -ous]

lump[1] *noun* **1** a small solid mass that has no definite shape: *a lump of coal.* **2** a swelling or tumour. **3** a number of things taken as a single whole. **4** a heavy, dull or awkward person. ▸ *verb* (*often* **lump things together**) to gather (esp dissimilar things) into a group or pile, often without any legitimate reason for doing so. [14c]

IDIOMS **a lump in one's throat** a sensation of tightness in one's throat, usu caused by great emotion.

lump[2] *verb, informal* to put up with (something unpleasant): *like it or lump it.* [19c]

lumpectomy *noun* (***-ies***) *surgery* the removal of a lump from the breast. [20c: from **lump**[1] + **-ectomy**]

lumpish *adj* heavy, dull or awkward.

lump sum *noun* a comparatively large single payment, as opposed to several smaller ones.

lumpy *adj* (***-ier, -iest***) full of lumps. ▪ **lumpiness** *noun.* [18c]

lunacy *noun* (***-ies***) **1** insanity. **2** great foolishness or stupidity; a misguided or misjudged action: *It would be sheer lunacy to do that.* [16c]

lunar *adj* **1** relating to, like or caused by the Moon. **2** for use on the surface of the Moon or in connection with travel to the Moon: *lunar vehicle.* [17c: from Latin *luna* moon]

lunar eclipse see under **eclipse**

lunate /ˈluːneɪt/ *adj, biol* crescent-shaped. [18c: from Latin *luna* moon + **-ate**[1] (sense 3)]

lunatic *adj* **1 a** *formerly* insane; **b** *law* of unsound mind and so not legally responsible for any actions taken. **2** foolish, stupid or wildly eccentric. ▸ *noun* **1** someone who is foolish or highly eccentric. **2 a** *formerly* someone who is considered insane; **b** *law* someone who is deemed lunatic. [13c: from Latin *lunaticus* moonstruck, from *luna* moon]

lunatic fringe *noun* the most extreme, fanatical or eccentric members of any group. [20c]

lunch *noun* a light meal eaten in the middle of the day. ▸ *verb, intr* to eat lunch. [16c]

luncheon *noun* **1** a formal meal served in the middle of the day. **2** *formal* lunch. [16c]

luncheon meat *noun* a type of pre-cooked meat, processed and mixed with cereal. [20c]

luncheon voucher *noun, Brit* (abbrev **LV**) a voucher given by employers to workers for part-payment for food at participating restaurants, etc. [20c]

lung *noun* in the chest cavity of air-breathing vertebrates: one of a pair of large spongy respiratory organs which remove carbon dioxide from the blood and replace it with oxygen. [Anglo-Saxon *lungen*]

lunge *noun* **1** a sudden plunge forwards. **2** *fencing* a sudden thrust with a sword. ▸ *verb, intr* **1** to make a sudden strong or thrusting movement forwards. **2** *fencing* to make a sudden forward movement with a sword. [18c: from French *allonger* to lengthen]

lungfish *noun* a large freshwater fish which, in addition to gills, has either one or two lungs with which it breathes air at the water surface.

lupin *noun* a garden plant with long spikes of brightly coloured flowers. [15c]

lupine *adj* relating to or like a wolf. [17c: from Latin *lupus* wolf]

lupus *noun* (***lupuses*** or ***lupi*** /ˈluːpaɪ/) any of a variety of skin diseases characterized by the formation of ulcers and lesions. [15c: Latin, meaning 'wolf'; so called because of the way it eats away the skin]

lurch[1] *verb, intr* **1** of a person: to stagger unsteadily: *He lurched towards the nearest bar.* **2** of ships, etc: to make a sudden roll to one side. ▸ *noun* **1** an act of staggering: *a lurch for the door.* **2** a sudden roll to one side. [18c]

lurch[2] *noun, cards* a state of play in cribbage, whist, etc where one side or player is being roundly beaten by the other. [16c: from French *lourche* a game which is believed to have been like backgammon, popular in 16c]

IDIOMS **leave sb in the lurch** *informal* to abandon them in a difficult situation.

lurcher *noun, Brit* a cross-bred dog, usu a cross between a greyhound and a collie. [17c: from obsolete *lurch* to lurk]

lure *verb* to tempt or entice, often by the offer of some reward. ▸ *noun* **1** someone or something which tempts, attracts or entices: *left teaching for the lure of more money.* **2** *falconry* a piece of meat attached to a bunch of feathers used for encouraging a hawk, etc to return to its falconer. [14c: from French *luerre* bait]

Lurex *noun, trademark* a type of material or yarn which has a shiny metallic thread running through it.

lurgy or **lurgi** /ˈlɜːgɪ/ *noun* (***-ies***) any unspecified disease or complaint: *the dreaded lurgy.* [20c: popularized in the radio show, *The Goon Show*]

lurid *adj* **1** glaringly bright, esp when the surroundings are dark: *a lurid light in the sky.* **2** horrifying or sensational: *lurid details.* **3** of someone's complexion: pale or wan; having a sickly colour. ▪ **luridly** *adv.* [17c: Latin *luridus* pale-yellow or wan]

lurk *verb* **1** to lie in wait, esp in ambush, with some sinister purpose in mind. **2** to linger unseen or furtively; to be latent: *The idea lurked at the back of his mind.* [14c]

luscious *adj* **1** of a smell, taste, etc: richly sweet; delicious. **2** voluptuously attractive: *luscious lips.* [15c as *lucius*]

lush[1] *adj* **1** of grass, foliage, etc: green and growing abundantly. **2** of fruit, etc: ripe and succulent. **3** luxurious; opulent. [15c as *lusch*, meaning 'slack']

lush[2] *noun, slang* a drunkard or alcoholic. [19c]

lust *noun* **1** strong sexual desire. **2** enthusiasm; relish: *a lust for life.* ▸ *verb, intr* (*usu* **lust after**) to have a strong desire for. ▪ **lustful** *adj.* ▪ **lustfully** *adv.* [Anglo-Saxon, meaning 'desire' or 'appetite']

lustre *or* (*US*) **luster** *noun* **1** the shiny appearance of something in reflected light. **2** shine, brightness or gloss. **3** splendour and glory, on account of beauty or accomplishments, etc. **4** a glaze for pottery that imparts a shiny appearance. ▪ **lustrous** *adj.* [16c: French]

lusty *adj* (**-ier, -iest**) **1** vigorous or loud: *a baby's lusty cries.* **2** strong and healthy. ▪ **lustily** *adv.* [13c]

lute *noun, music* a stringed instrument with a long neck and a pear-shaped body. ▪ **lutenist** *or* **lutanist** *noun.* [14c: from Arabic *al 'ud* the wood]

lutetium /luːˈtiːʃɪəm/ *noun, chem* (symbol **Lu**) a very rare soft silvery metallic element, belonging to the **lanthanide** series. [20c: from Latin *Lutetia*, ancient name of Paris, where it was discovered]

Lutheran *noun* a follower of Martin Luther, German protestant reformer. ▸ *adj* relating to Luther or his teaching. ▪ **Lutheranism** *noun.* [16c]

luv *noun, informal* love.

luvvie *or* **luvvy** *noun* (**-ies**) *Brit, facetious* an actor, esp one who speaks and behaves in an overly pretentious or camp manner.

lux *noun* (**lux**) *physics* the SI unit of illuminance, equal to one **lumen** per square metre. [19c: Latin, meaning 'light']

luxe see **de luxe**

luxuriant *adj* **1** of plants, etc: growing abundantly; lush. **2** of someone's writing, imagination, language, etc: full of metaphors and very elaborate; fanciful and inventive; bombastic. **3** of material things: ornate; overwrought. ▪ **luxuriance** *noun.* ▪ **luxuriantly** *adv.* [16c: from Latin *luxuriare* to grow rank]

luxuriate *verb, intr* **1** to live in great comfort or luxury. **2** (**luxuriate in sth**) to enjoy it greatly or revel in it. [17c: from Latin *luxuriare* to grow rank]

luxurious *adj* **1** expensive and opulent: *a luxurious hotel.* **2** enjoying luxury. ▪ **luxuriously** *adv.* [14c: from Latin *luxus* excess]

luxury *noun* (**-ies**) **1** expensive, rich and extremely comfortable surroundings and possessions. **2** habitual indulgence in or enjoyment of luxurious surroundings. **3** something that is pleasant but not essential. [14c: from Latin *luxus* excess]

-ly *suffix* **1** *forming advs denoting* in a particular way: *cleverly.* **2** *forming adjs and advs denoting* at intervals of; for the duration of: *daily.* **3** *forming adjs denoting* in the manner of; like: *brotherly.* [From Anglo-Saxon *lic* like]

lychee, lichee *or* **litchi** /laɪˈtʃiː/ *noun* a small fruit with sweet white flesh. [16c: from Chinese *lizhi*]

lychgate see **lichgate**

Lycra *noun, trademark* a stretchy fibre or fabric made from lightweight polyurethane and used in the manufacture of sportswear, tights, etc. [20c]

lye *noun* **1** an alkaline solution made by leaching water through wood ash, etc. **2** a strong solution of sodium or potassium hydroxide. [From Anglo-Saxon *leag* to leach]

lying *present participle of* **lie**[1], **lie**[2]

lymph *noun, anatomy* in animals: a colourless fluid that bathes all the tissues and drains into the vessels of the **lymphatic system**, and which contains **lymphocyte**s and antibodies which prevent the spread of infection. ▪ **lymphatic** *adj.* [17c: from Latin *lympha* water]

lymphatic system *noun, anatomy* the network of vessels that transports **lymph** around the body.

lymph node *or* **lymph gland** *noun, anatomy* a small rounded structure that produces antibodies and filters bacteria and foreign bodies from lymph.

lymphocyte *noun* a type of white blood cell present in large numbers in lymphatic tissues, and involved in immune responses. [19c]

lymphoma *noun* (***lymphomas*** *or* ***lymphomata*** /lɪmˈfoʊmətə/) *pathol* any tumour of the lymphatic tissues, esp a malignant tumour of the lymph nodes.

lynch *verb* of a group of people: to execute (someone thought guilty of a crime), usu by hanging, without recourse to the law. ▪ **lynching** *noun.* [19c: named after Captain William Lynch of Virginia]

lynx *noun* (***lynxes*** *or* ***lynx***) a wild cat with yellowish-grey or reddish fur, a stubby tail with a black tip, and tufted ears. [14c: Greek]

lyre *noun* a small U-shaped stringed musical instrument. ▪ **lyrate** *adj.* [13c: from Greek *lyra* lyre]

lyrebird *noun* an Australian bird, so called because the male spreads its tail into a lyre-shaped fan during courtship displays. [19c]

lyric *adj* **1** *poetry* expressing personal, private or individual emotions. **2** having the form of a song; intended for singing, orig to the lyre. **3** referring or relating to the words of songs rather than the music or tunes. ▸ *noun* **1** a short poem or song, usu written in the first person and expressing a particular emotion: *a love lyric.* **2** (**lyrics**) the words of a song. [16c: from Greek *lyra* lyre]

lyrical *adj* **1** lyric; song-like. **2** full of enthusiastic praise: *waxing lyrical.* ▪ **lyrically** *adv.*

lyricism *noun* **1** the state or quality of being lyrical. **2** an affected pouring out of emotions.

lyricist *noun* **1** someone who writes the words to songs. **2** a lyric poet.

-lysis *combining form, denoting* a disintegration; a breaking down: *electrolysis.* [From Greek *lysis* dissolution]

M[1] *or* **m** *noun* (***Ms, M's*** *or* ***m's***) the thirteenth letter of the English alphabet.

M[2] *abbrev* **1** Master. **2** as a clothes size, etc: medium. **3** million. **4** Monsieur. **5** *Brit* Motorway, followed by a number, as in **M1**.

M[3] *symbol,* as a Roman numeral: 1000. [From Latin *mille* 1000]

m *or* **m.** *abbrev* **1** male. **2** married. **3** masculine. **4** metre or metres. **5** mile or miles. **6** million or millions. **7** minute or minutes. **8** month. **9** milli-.

'm *contraction* am: *I'm going.*

MA *abbrev* Master of Arts.

ma *noun, informal* a mother. [19c: shortened from **mama**]

ma'am /mam *or* (*mainly in addressing female royalty*) mɑːm/ *contraction* used as a polite or respectful form of address to a lady: madam.

mac *or* **mack** *noun, informal* short form of **mackintosh**.

macabre /məˈkɑːbrə/ *adj* causing fear or anxiety; ghastly; gruesome. [15c: from French *danse macabre* dance of Death]

macadam *noun, esp US* **1** a road-making material consisting of layers of compacted broken stones, usu bound with tar. **2** a road surface made with this. Compare **tarmacadam**. ▪ **macadamize** *or* **-ise** *verb.* [19c: named after its inventor, Scottish engineer John McAdam]

macadamia *noun* **1** an evergreen tree belonging to a native Australian genus. Sometimes called **macadamia tree**. **2** the round edible oily nut of the macadamia. Also called **macadamia nut**. [20c: named after the Australian chemist, John Macadam]

macaque /məˈkɑːk/ *noun* a type of short-tailed or tailless monkey of Asia and Africa, with large cheek-pouches. [17c: French]

macaroni *noun* (***macaronis*** *or* ***macaronies***) pasta in the form of short narrow tubes. [16c: from Italian *maccaroni*]

macaroon *noun* a sweet cake or biscuit made with sugar, eggs and crushed almonds. [17c: from French *macaron*]

macaw *noun* any of numerous large brilliantly-coloured parrots with long tails and strong beaks, found mainly in the tropical forests of Central and S America. [17c: from Portuguese *macao*]

mace[1] *noun* **1** **a** a ceremonial staff carried by some public officials; **b** someone who carries a mace in a ceremonial procession. Also called **macebearer**. **2** *hist* a heavy club, usu with a spiked metal head, used as a weapon in medieval times. [13c: French meaning 'a large hammer']

mace[2] *noun* a spice made from the layer around the nutmeg seed, dried and ground up. [14c: French]

Macedonian /masəˈdoʊnɪən/ *adj* **1** of or relating to the republic of Macedonia in S Europe, its language or its inhabitants. **2** of or relating to the ancient region of Macedonia, corresponding to parts of modern-day Greece and Bulgaria as well as modern Macedonia. ▸ *noun* **1** a native or citizen of Macedonia. **2** the language of Macedonia.

macerate /ˈmasəreɪt/ *verb, tr & intr, technical* to break up or make something break up or become soft by soaking it. ▪ **maceration** *noun.* [16c: from Latin *macerare* to soak]

Mach see under **Mach number**

machete /məˈʃɛtɪ/ *noun* a long heavy broad-bladed knife used as a weapon or cutting tool. [16c: Spanish]

Machiavellian /makɪəˈvɛlɪən/ *adj* of a person or their conduct, activities, etc: crafty, amoral and opportunist. ▪ **Machiavellianism** *noun.* [16c: from the Italian political philosopher and statesman Niccolo Machiavelli]

machinations *plural noun* a crafty scheme or plot, esp a sinister one. [17c: from Latin *machinari* to invent]

machine *noun* **1** a device with moving parts, and usu powered, designed to perform a particular task: *sewing machine*. **2** a group of people or institutions, or a network of equipment, under a central control: *the party's political machine*. **3** *informal* a motor vehicle, esp a motorcycle. ▸ *verb* to make, shape or cut something with a machine. [16c: French]

machine code *or* **machine language** *noun, comput* a numerical code used for writing instructions in a form that a computer can process. ▪ **machine-code** *adj.*

machine gun *noun* a portable gun that fires a continuous rapid stream of bullets when the trigger is pressed. ▸ *verb* (***-gunned, -gunning***) to shoot at someone or something with a machine gun. [19c]

machine-readable *adj, comput* of data, text, etc: in a form that can be directly processed by a computer.

machinery *noun* (***-ies***) **1** machines in general. **2** the working or moving parts of a machine. **3** the combination of processes, systems or people that keeps anything working, or that produces the desired result.

machine shop *noun* a workshop where items such as metal parts are machined using machine tools.

machine tool *noun* any stationary power-driven machine used to shape or finish metal, wood or plastic parts by cutting, planing, etc.

machinist *noun* **1** someone who operates a machine. **2** someone who makes or repairs machines. **3** a **mechanician**.

machismo /maˈtʃɪzmoʊ, maˈkɪzmoʊ/ *noun, usu derog* exaggerated manliness. [20c: American Spanish]

Mach number /mɑːk, mak/ *noun* (often shortened to **Mach**) *aeronautics* a ratio of the speed of an object (such as an aircraft) to the speed of sound in the same medium. [20c: devised by the Austrian physicist Ernst Mach]

macho /ˈmatʃoʊ/ *adj, often derog* exaggeratedly or aggressively manly. ► *noun* **1** *informal* a macho man. **2 machismo**. [20c: Spanish, meaning 'male']

mack see **mac**

mackerel *noun* (***mackerels*** *or* ***mackerel***) an important food fish with a streamlined body that is blue-green above and silvery below. [14c: from French *maquerel*]

mackintosh *or* **macintosh** *noun* **1** *chiefly Brit* a waterproof raincoat. Often shortened to **mac** or **mack**. **2** a kind of rubberized waterproof material. [19c: named after Charles Macintosh, Scottish chemist]

macramé /məˈkrɑːmeɪ/ *noun* **1** the art of knotting string or coarse thread into patterns. **2** decorative articles made in this way. [19c: French]

macro *noun, comput* a single instruction that brings a set of instructions into operation. Also (and orig) called **macroinstruction**.

macro- *or* (*before a vowel*) **macr-** *combining form, denoting* large, long or large-scale. [From Greek *makros*]

macrobiotics *singular noun* the science of devising diets using whole grains and organically-grown fruit and vegetables. ▪ **macrobiotic** *adj.*

macrocosm *noun* **1** (**the macrocosm**) the universe as a whole. **2** any large or complex system or structure made up of similar smaller systems or structures. Compare **microcosm**. [17c: from French *macrocosme*]

macroeconomics *singular noun* the study of economics on a large scale or in terms of large economic units such as national income, international trade, etc. Compare **microeconomics**. ▪ **macroeconomic** *adj.*

macromolecule *noun, chem* a very large molecule, eg proteins, DNA.

macron *noun* a straight horizontal bar (¯) placed over a letter to show that it is a long or stressed vowel. Compare **breve**. [19c: from Greek *makros* long]

macroscopic *adj, technical* **1** large enough to be seen by the naked eye. Compare **microscopic**. **2** considered in terms of large units or elements.

macula /ˈmakjʊlə/ *noun* (***maculae*** /-liː/) *technical* a spot, discoloured mark or blemish, eg a freckle on the skin. ▪ **macular** *adj.* [15c: Latin]

mad *adj* (***madder, maddest***) **1** mentally disturbed; insane. **2** foolish or senseless; extravagantly carefree. **3** *informal, orig & esp US* (*often* **mad at** *or* **with sb**) very angry; furious. **4** *informal* (*usu* **mad about** *or* **on sth**) extremely enthusiastic; fanatical. **5** marked by extreme confusion, haste or excitement: *a mad dash for the door.* **6** of a dog, etc: infected with rabies. ▪ **madly** *adv* **1** in a mad way. **2** *informal* passionately. ▪ **madness** *noun.* [13c: from Anglo-Saxon *gemæded*]

IDIOMS **go mad 1** to become insane or demented. **2** *informal* to become very angry. **like mad** *informal* frantically; very energetically: *ran like mad for the bus.*

madam *noun* (*pl* in sense 1 ***mesdames*** /meɪdam/ or in other senses ***madams***) **1** a polite form of address to any woman, esp a married or elderly woman or any female customer in a shop, etc, used instead of a name. **2** a form of address to a woman in authority, often prefixed to an official title: *Madam Chairman.* **3** a woman who manages a brothel. **4** *informal, esp Brit* an arrogant or spoiled girl or young woman: *Cheeky little madam!* [13c: from French, orig two words *ma* my + *dame* lady]

Madame /məˈdɑːm, ˈmadəm/ (abbrev **Mme**) *noun* (***Mesdames*** /meɪˈdam/; abbrev **Mmes**) a title equivalent to **Mrs**, used esp of a French or French-speaking woman, usu a married one. Compare **Mademoiselle**.

madcap *adj* foolishly impulsive, wild or reckless. ► *noun* a foolishly impulsive person. [16c, orig meaning 'a madman']

mad cow disease *noun, informal* **BSE**.

madden *verb* to make (a person, etc) mad, esp to enrage them. ▪ **maddening** *adj.* ▪ **maddeningly** *adv.*

madder *noun* **1 a** a plant with yellow flowers and a red root; **b** any related plant. **2** a dark red dye, orig made from the root of this plant. [Anglo-Saxon *mædere*]

made *verb, past tense, past participle of* **make**. ► *adj* **1** (*esp* **made from, in** *or* **of sth**) artificially produced or formed. **2** *in compounds, denoting* produced, constructed or formed in a specified way or place: *handmade.* **3** of a person, etc: whose success or prosperity is certain: *a made man.*

IDIOMS **have it made** *informal* to enjoy, or be assured of, complete success, happiness, etc.

Mademoiselle /madəmwəˈzɛl, madməˈzɛl/ (abbrev **Mlle**) *noun* (***Mesdemoiselles*** /meɪ-/; abbrev **Mlles**) **1** a title equivalent to Miss, used of an unmarried French or French-speaking woman. **2** (**mademoiselle**) a French governess or teacher. Also shortened to **Mamselle** /mamˈzɛl/. [15c: French, orig two words *ma* my + *demoiselle* **damsel**]

made up *adj* **1** of a person: wearing make-up. **2** of a story, etc: not true; invented. **3** *informal* of a person: extremely pleased.

madhouse *noun* **1** *informal* a place of great confusion and noise. **2** *old use* a mental hospital.

madman *or* **madwoman** *noun* **1** an insane person. **2** a very foolish person.

Madonna *noun* **1** (**the Madonna**) *esp RC Church* the Virgin Mary, mother of Christ. **2** (*sometimes* **madonna**) a picture, statue, etc of the Virgin Mary. [16c: Italian, orig two words *ma* my + *donna* lady]

madras *noun* a kind of medium-hot curry. [19c]

madrigal *noun, music* an unaccompanied **part song**, popular in the 16c and 17c. [16c: from Italian *madrigale*]

maelstrom /ˈmeɪlstroʊm/ *noun, esp literary* **1** a place or state of uncontrollable confusion or destruction. **2** a violent whirlpool. [17c: Dutch, meaning 'whirlpool']

maenad /'miːnad/ *noun* **1** *Greek & Roman myth* a female participant in orgies and rites in honour of Bacchus or Dionysus, the god of wine. **2** *literary* a frenzied woman. [16c: from Latin *maenas*]

maestro /'maɪstroʊ/ *noun* (***maestros*** *or* ***maestri*** /-rɪ/) someone who is regarded as being specially gifted in a specified art, esp a distinguished musical composer, conductor, performer or teacher. Often used as a title (**Maestro**). [18c: Italian, literally 'master']

Mae West *noun* an inflatable life jacket. [20c: named after Mae West, an American actress]

Mafia *noun* **1** (**the Mafia**) a secret international criminal organization, originating in Sicily, that controls numerous illegal activities worldwide, esp in Italy and the US. Also called **the Mob**. **2** (*often* **mafia**) any group that exerts a secret and powerful influence, esp one that uses unscrupulous or ruthless criminal methods. [19c: Sicilian Italian, literally 'hostility to the law']

Mafioso *or* (*sometimes*) **mafioso** *noun* (***Mafiosi*** *or* ***Mafiosos***) a member of the Mafia or a mafia.

mag *noun, informal* a **magazine** or periodical.

magazine *noun* **1** a paperback periodical publication, usu a heavily illustrated one, containing articles, stories, etc by various writers. Sometimes shortened to **mag**. **2** *TV, radio* a regular broadcast in which reports are presented on a variety of subjects. **3** in some automatic firearms: a metal container for several cartridges. **4 a** a storeroom for ammunition, explosives, etc; **b** any place, building, etc in which military supplies are stored. **5** *photog* a removable container from which slides are automatically fed through a projector, or film is fed through a movie camera, printer or processor. [16c: French *magasin*]

magenta *adj* dark, purplish-red in colour. ▸ *noun* this colour. [19c: named after Magenta, an Italian town]

maggot *noun* the worm-like larva of various flies, esp that of the housefly. ▪ **maggoty** *adj*. [14c]

magi *or* **Magi** see under **magus**

magic *noun* **1** the supposed art or practice of using the power of supernatural forces, spells, etc to affect people, objects and events. **2** the art or practice of performing entertaining illusions and conjuring tricks. **3** the quality of being wonderful, charming or delightful. **4** a secret or mysterious power over the imagination or will. ▸ *adj* **1** belonging or relating to, used in, or done by, sorcery or conjuring. **2** causing wonderful, startling or mysterious results. **3** *informal* excellent; marvellous; great. *Also as exclam.* ▸ *verb* (***magicked, magicking***) to produce something by using, or as if by using, sorcery or conjuring: *magicked a rabbit out of his hat*. ▪ **magical** *adj*. ▪ **magically** *adv*. [14c: from Greek *magike techne* magic art]

IDIOMS **like magic 1** mysteriously. **2** suddenly and unexpectedly. **3** excellently.

magic carpet *noun* in fairy stories: a carpet that can carry people magically through the air.

magician *noun* **1** an entertainer who performs conjuring tricks, illusions, etc. **2** someone who practises black or white magic, or who uses supernatural powers.

magisterial *adj* **1** belonging or relating to, or administered by, a magistrate. **2** authoritative; dictatorial. ▪ **magisterially** *adv*. [17c: from Latin *magister* master]

magistracy *noun* (***-ies***) **1** the rank or position of a magistrate. **2** (*usu* **the magistracy**) magistrates as a whole. Also called **magistrature**.

magistrate *noun* **1** in England and Wales: a judge who presides in a lower court of law (**Magistrates' Court**), dealing with minor criminal and civil cases. **2** any public official administering the law. [14c: from Latin *magistratus*]

magma *noun* (***magmas*** *or* ***magmata***) *geol* hot molten rock material generated deep within the Earth's crust or mantle. ▪ **magmatic** *adj*. [17c: from Greek, meaning 'a thick ointment']

Magna Carta *noun, hist* the charter obtained by barons from King John of England in 1215, defining a body of law and custom the king should observe. [from Latin, meaning 'great charter']

magnanimous *adj* having or showing admirable generosity of spirit towards another person or people. ▪ **magnanimity** *noun*. [16c: from Latin *magnanimus*]

magnate *noun* someone of high rank or great power, esp in industry. [15c: from Latin *magnus* great]

magnesia *noun, chem* **1** a white light powder, magnesium oxide. **2** *med* magnesium carbonate, as an antacid and laxative. Also called **milk of magnesia**. [14c: named after Magnesia, a mineral-rich region in ancient Greece]

magnesium *noun, chem* (symbol **Mg**) a reactive silvery-grey metallic element that burns with a dazzling white flame. [19c: from **magnesia**]

magnet *noun* **1** a piece of metal, esp a piece of iron, with the power to attract and repel iron. **2** someone or something that attracts: *That rubbish bin is a magnet to flies*. [15c: from Greek *Magnetis lithos* Magnesian stone]

magnetic *adj* **1** belonging to, having the powers of, or operated by a magnet or magnetism. **2** of a metal, etc: able to be made into a magnet. **3** of a person, personality, etc: extremely charming or attractive.

magnetic disk *noun, comput* a flat circular sheet of material coated with a magnetic oxide, used to store programs and data. Often shortened to **disk**.

magnetic field *noun, physics* the region of physical space surrounding a permanent magnet, electromagnetic wave or current-carrying conductor, within which magnetic forces may be detected.

magnetic flux *noun, physics* (SI unit **weber**) a measure of the amount of magnetism, considering both the strength and extent of the **magnetic field**. See also **flux** (*noun* sense 6).

magnetic mine *noun* a mine detonated by a pivoted **magnetic needle** when it detects a magnetic field created by the presence of a large metal object.

magnetic needle *noun* the slim rod or bar in a nautical compass which, because it is magnetized, always points to the north, or in other instruments is used to indicate the direction of a magnetic field.

magnetic north *noun* the direction in which a compass's **magnetic needle** always points.

magnetic pole *noun, geol* either of two points on the Earth's surface to or from which a **magnetic needle** points.

magnetic storm *noun, meteorol* a sudden severe disturbance of the Earth's magnetic field caused by streams of particles from the Sun.

magnetic strip *or* **magnetic stripe** *noun* a dark horizontal strip on the back of a credit card, identity card, etc containing information which can be read electronically.

magnetic tape *noun, electronics* a narrow plastic ribbon, coated on one side with a magnetic material, used to record and store data in audio and video tape recorders and computers.

magnetism *noun* **1** the properties of attraction possessed by magnets. **2** the phenomena connected with magnets. **3** the scientific study of the properties of magnets and magnetic phenomena. **4** strong personal charm.

magnetite *noun, geol* a black, strongly magnetic mineral form of iron oxide, an important ore of iron. See also **lodestone**.

magnetize *or* **-ise** *verb* **1** to make something magnetic. **2** to attract something or someone strongly; to hypnotize or captivate. ▪ **magnetizable** *adj*. ▪ **magnetization** *noun*. ▪ **magnetizer** *noun*.

magneto /mag'niːtoʊ/ *noun, elec* a simple electric generator consisting of a rotating magnet that induces an alternating current in a coil surrounding it, used to provide the spark in the ignition system of petrol engines without batteries, eg in lawnmowers, etc. [Late 19c: short for *magneto-electric generator* or *machine*]

magnetron *noun, physics* a device for generating **microwaves**, developed for use in radar transmitters, and now widely used in microwave ovens. [20c: from **magnet** + **electron**]

magnification *noun* **1** *optics* a measure of the extent to which an image of an object produced by a lens or optical instrument is enlarged or reduced. **2** the action or an instance of magnifying, or the state of being magnified. [17c: see **magnify**]

magnificent *adj* **1** splendidly impressive in size, extent or appearance. **2** *informal* excellent; admirable. ▪ **magnificence** *noun*. ▪ **magnificently** *adv*. [16c: French]

magnify *verb* (*-ies, -ied*) **1** to make something appear larger, eg by using a microscope or telescope. **2** to exaggerate something. **3** *formal, old use* to praise highly; to extol. [14c: from Latin *magnificare*]

magnifying glass *noun* a convex lens, esp a hand-held one, through which objects appear larger.

magniloquent *adj, formal* speaking or spoken in a grand or pompous style. ▪ **magniloquence** *noun*. [17c: from Latin *magnus* great + *loquus* speaking]

magnitude *noun* **1** importance or extent. **2** physical size; largeness. **3** *astron* the degree of brightness of a star. [14c: from Latin *magnitudo*]

magnolia *noun* **1** **a** a tree or shrub with large sweet-smelling usu white or pink flowers; **b** one of its flowers. **2** a very pale, pinkish-white or beige colour. ▸ *adj* having the colour magnolia. [18c: Latin, named after the French botanist Pierre Magnol]

magnox *noun* **a** an aluminium-based alloy containing a small amount of magnesium, from which certain nuclear reactor fuel containers are made; **b** such a container or reactor. [20c: from *magnesium no oxidation*]

magnum *noun* a champagne or wine bottle that holds approximately 1.5 l, ie twice the amount of a standard bottle. [18c: Latin, meaning 'something big']

magnum opus *noun* (***magnum opuses*** *or* ***magna opera***) a great work of art or literature, esp the greatest one produced by a particular artist or writer. [18c: Latin, meaning 'great work']

magpie *noun* **1** a black-and-white bird of the crow family, known for its habit of collecting shiny objects. **2** a person who hoards, steals or collects small objects. [17c]

magus /'meɪgəs/ *noun* (***magi*** /'meɪdʒaɪ/) **1** (*usu* **the Magi**) *Christianity* the three wise men from the east who in tradition brought gifts to the infant Jesus, guided by a star. Also called **the Three Kings** and **the Three Wise Men**. **2** *hist* a sorcerer. **3** *hist* a Persian priest. [14c: from Persian *magus* magician]

Magyar *noun* **1** an individual belonging to the predominant race of people in Hungary. **2** the **Hungarian** language. ▸ *adj* belonging or relating to the Magyars or their language. [18c: the native name]

maharajah *or* **maharaja** *noun, hist* an Indian prince, esp any of the former rulers of the states of India. Also (**Maharajah**) as a title. See also **raja**. [17c: Hindi]

maharani *or* **maharanee** *noun* **1** the wife or widow of a maharajah. **2** a woman of the same rank as a maharajah in her own right. Also (**Maharani**) as a title. See also **rani**. [19c: Hindi]

maharishi *noun* a Hindu religious teacher or spiritual leader. Often (**Maharishi**) as a title. [18c: Hindi]

mahatma *noun* a wise and holy Hindu leader. Often (**Mahatma**) as a title. [19c: Hindi]

Mahdi /'mɑːdiː/ *noun* **1** *Islam* the great leader of the faithful Muslims, who is to appear in the last days. **2** *history* a title of various rebellious leaders. [19c: Arabic, meaning 'divinely guided one']

mah-jong *or* **mah-jongg** *noun* an old game of Chinese origin, usu played by four players using a set of 144 small patterned tiles. [20c: Shanghai Chinese *ma chiang*, meaning 'sparrows']

mahogany *noun* (*-ies*) **1** a tall evergreen tree of tropical Africa and America, grown commercially for timber. **2** the hard attractively-marked wood of this tree. **3** the colour of the wood, a dark reddish-brown. ▸ *adj* **1** made from this wood. **2** dark reddish-brown in colour.

mahout /mə'haʊt/ *noun* someone who drives, trains and looks after elephants. [17c: from Hindi *mahaut*]

maid *noun* **1** a female servant. **2** *literary & old use* an unmarried woman. [13c: a shortened form of **maiden**]

maiden *noun* **1** *literary* a young, unmarried woman. **2** *literary* a virgin. **3** *horse-racing* a horse that has never won a race. **4** *cricket* a **maiden over**. ▸ *adj* **1** first ever: *maiden voyage*. **2** unmarried: *maiden aunt*. ▪ **maidenly** *adj*. [Anglo-Saxon *mægden*]

maidenhair *noun* a fern with delicate, fan-shaped leaves.

maiden name *noun* the surname of a married woman at birth, ie before she married for the first time.

maiden over *noun, cricket* an **over** (*noun* sense 1) from which no runs are scored.

maid of honour *noun* (***maids of honour***) **1** an unmarried female servant of a queen or princess. **2** the principal bridesmaid at a wedding.

maidservant *noun, old use* a female servant.

mail[1] *noun* **1** the postal system. **2** letters, parcels, etc sent by post. **3** a single collection or delivery of letters, etc: *Has the mail arrived yet?* **4** a vehicle carrying letters, etc. **5** short for **electronic mail.** ▸ *verb* **1** *esp N Am* to send (a letter, parcel, etc) by post. **2** to send an e-mail to (someone). [13c: from French *male*]

mail[2] *noun* flexible armour made of small linked metal rings. Also called **chainmail.** ▪ **mailed** *adj.* [14c: from French *maille* a mesh]

mailbag *noun* a large strong bag in which letters, etc are carried.

mailbox *noun* **1** *esp N Am* a public or private letter box or postbox. **2** *comput* in an electronic mail system: a facility that allows computer messages from one user to be stored in the file of another.

mailing list *noun* **1** a list of the names and addresses of people to whom an organization or business, etc regularly sends information, esp advertising material, etc. **2** *comput* a file containing a list of addresses to which an e-mail is to be sent.

mailman *noun, esp N Am* a **postman**.

mailmerge *noun, wordprocessing, comput* a program which produces a series of letters addressed to individuals by merging a file of names and addresses with a file containing the text of the letter.

mail order *noun* a system of buying and selling goods by post. ▸ *adj* (**mail-order**) relating to, bought, sold, sent or operating by mail order: *mail-order catalogue.*

mailshot *noun* **1** an unrequested item sent by post, esp a piece of advertising material. **2** the action or an instance of sending out a batch of such post.

maim *verb* to wound (a person or animal) seriously, esp to disable, mutilate or cripple them. ▪ **maiming** *noun.* [13c: from French *mahaignier* to wound]

main *adj* **1** most important; chief; leading. **2** (**mains**) belonging or relating to the mains (see *noun* senses 1 and 2): *mains supply.* ▸ *noun* **1** (*often* **the mains**) the chief pipe, conduit or cable in a branching system: *not connected to the mains.* **2** (*usu* **the mains**) *chiefly Brit* the network by which power, water, etc is distributed. **3** *old use* great strength, now usu only in the phrase **with might and main**. See under **might**[2]. [Anglo-Saxon *mægen*]

IDIOMS **in the main** mostly; on the whole.

mainbrace *noun, naut* the rope controlling the movement of a ship's mainsail.

main clause *noun, grammar* a clause which can stand alone as a sentence. Also called **independent clause, principal clause.** Compare **subordinate clause.**

main course *noun* the principal, and usu most substantial, course in a meal.

mainframe *noun, comput* a large powerful computer to which several smaller computers can be linked, that is capable of handling very large amounts of data at high speed and can usu run several programs simultaneously. *as adj*: *mainframe computer.*

mainland *noun* (*esp* **the mainland**) a country's principal mass of land, as distinct from a nearby island or islands forming part of the same country. *as adj*: *mainland Britain.* ▪ **mainlander** *noun.*

main line *noun* **1** the principal railway line between two places. **2** *US* a principal route, road, etc. **3** *slang* a major vein. ▸ *adj* **1** (*usu* **mainline**) principal; chief. **2** mainstream.

mainly *adv* chiefly; for the most part; largely.

mainmast /ˈmeɪnməst, -mɑːst/ *noun, naut* the principal mast of a sailing ship, usu the second mast from the prow.

mainsail /ˈmeɪnsəl, ˈmeɪnseɪl/ *noun, naut* the largest and lowest sail on a sailing ship.

mainspring *noun* **1** the chief spring in a watch or clock, or other piece of machinery, that gives it motion. **2** a chief motive, reason or cause.

mainstay *noun* (***-ays***) **1** *naut* a rope stretching forward and down from the top of the **mainmast**. **2** a chief support: *He has been my mainstay during this crisis.*

mainstream *noun* **1** (*usu* **the mainstream**) the chief trend, or direction of development, in any activity, business, movement, etc. **2** the principal current of a river which has tributaries. **3** mainstream jazz (see *adj* sense 3 below). ▸ *adj* **1** belonging or relating to the mainstream. **2** in accordance with what is normal or standard: *takes a mainstream view on this subject.* **3** *jazz* said of swing, etc: belonging or relating to a style that developed between early and modern jazz.

maintain *verb* **1** to continue; to keep something in existence: *must maintain this level of commitment.* **2** to keep something in good condition. **3** to pay the expenses of someone or something: *a duty to maintain his children.* **4** to continue to argue something; to affirm or assert (eg an opinion, one's innocence, etc). ▪ **maintained** *adj, esp in compounds* of a school, etc: financially supported, eg from public funds: *grant-maintained.* [13c: from French *maintenir*, from Latin *manu tenere* to hold in the hand]

maintenance *noun* **1** the process of keeping something in good condition. **2** money paid by one person to support another, as ordered by a court of law, eg money paid to an ex-wife and/or children, following a divorce. See also **alimony.** **3** the process of continuing something or keeping it in existence.

---

maintenance

This word is often misspelt. It might help you to remember the following sentence:

*The **main ten**t is where the d**ance** is held.*

---

maiolica see **majolica**

maisonette *or* **maisonnette** *noun* a flat within a larger house or block, esp one on two floors. *US equivalent* **duplex**. [19c: French diminutive of *maison* house]

maître d'hôtel /meɪtrədoʊˈtɛl/ *noun* the manager or head waiter of a hotel or restaurant. Often (*informal*) shortened to **maître d'** /meɪtrəˈdiː/ (***maîtres d'*** *or* ***maître d's***). [16c: French, meaning 'master of the hotel']

maize *noun* **1** a tall cereal plant, widely grown for its edible yellow grain which grows in large spikes called **corncobs**. Also called *N Am, Aust & NZ* **corn**, **Indian corn**. **2** the grain of this plant, eaten ripe and unripe as a vegetable (**sweetcorn**). [16c: from Spanish *maíz*]

Maj. *abbrev* Major.

majestic *adj* having or showing majesty; stately, dignified or grand in manner, style, appearance, etc.

majesty *noun* (***-ies***) **1** great and impressive dignity, sovereign power or authority, eg the supreme greatness and power of God. **2** splendour; grandeur. **3 His, Her** *or* **Your Majesty** (***Their*** *or* ***Your Majesties***) the title used when speaking of or to a king or queen. [14c: from French *majesté*]

majolica /mə'dʒɒlɪkə/ *or* **maiolica** /mə'jɒ-/ *noun* colourfully glazed or enamelled earthenware, esp that of the early 16c decorated with scenes in the Renaissance style. [16c: from Italian *maiolica*]

major *adj* **1** great, or greater, in number, size, extent, value, importance, etc. **2** *music* **a** of a scale: having two full tones between the first and third notes; **b** of a key, chord, etc: based on such a scale. In all senses compare **minor.** ▸ *noun* **1 a** an army officer of the rank above captain; **b** an officer who is in charge of a military band: *pipe major.* **2** *music* a major key, chord or scale. **3** *esp N Am* **a** a student's main or special subject of study: *English is his major;* **b** a student studying such a subject: *He's a psychology major.* **4** someone who has reached the age of full legal responsibility. Compare **minor** (*noun* sense 1). See also **majority** (sense 4). ▸ *verb, intr* (*always* **major in sth**) *esp US* to specialize in (a particular subject of study). [15c: Latin, comparative of *magnus* great]

major-domo *noun* a chief servant or steward in charge of the management of a household. [16c: from Spanish *mayor-domo*]

majorette *noun* a member of a group of girls who march in parades, performing elaborate displays of baton-twirling, etc. [20c, orig US]

major-general *noun* an army officer of the rank below lieutenant general.

majority *noun* (***-ies***) **1** the greater number; the largest group; the bulk: *The majority of the population is in favour.* **2** the difference between the greater and the lesser number. **3** the winning margin of votes in an election: *a Labour majority of 2549.* **4** the age at which someone legally becomes an adult. See **major** (*noun* sense 4). Compare **minority.** [16c: from French *majorité*]

IDIOMS **in the majority** forming the larger group or greater part.

---

majority

Strictly, sense 1 of **majority** should only be used if you are speaking or writing about things that could be numbered or counted:

✓ *The majority of our customers leave a generous tip.*

✓ *The majority of flowers bloom during this period.*

It should not be used if you are speaking or writing about things that cannot be counted, such as substances and ideas:

✗ *He spent the majority of his working life as a teacher.*

---

make *verb* (***made***) **1** to form, create, manufacture or produce something by combining or shaping materials: *make the tea.* **2** to cause, bring about or create something by one's actions, etc: *He's always making trouble.* **3** to force, induce or cause someone to do something: *He makes me laugh.* **4** (*often* **make sth** *or* **sb into sth**) to cause it or them to change into something else; to transform or convert it or them. **5** to cause something or someone to be, do or become a specified thing: *made me cross.* **6** to be capable of turning or developing into or serving as (a specified thing); to have or develop the appropriate qualities for something: *This box makes a good table.* **7** (*always* **make sb sth**) to appoint them as something: *They made her deputy head.* **8** (*also* **make sb** *or* **sth into sth**) to cause them or it to appear to be, or to represent them or it as being (a specified thing): *Long hair makes her look younger.* **9** to gain, earn or acquire something: *makes £400 a week.* **10** to add up to or amount to something; to constitute: *4 and 4 makes 8* • *The book makes interesting reading.* **11** to calculate, judge or estimate something to be (a specified thing): *I make it three o'clock.* **12** (*always* **make of sth** *or* **sb**) to understand by it or them: *What do you make of their comments?* **13** to arrive at or reach something, or to succeed in doing so: *can't make the party.* **14** to score or win (points, runs, card tricks, etc). **15** to tidy (a bed) after use by smoothing out and tucking in the sheets, rearranging the duvet, etc. **16** to bring about or ensure the success of something; to cap or complete something: *It made my day.* **17** to propose something or propose something to someone: *make me an offer.* **18** to engage in something; to perform, carry out or produce something: *make a speech* • *make a decision.* ▸ *noun* **1** a manufacturer's brand: *What make of car is it?* **2** applied to a physical object, a person's body, etc: structure, type or build; the way in which it is made. ▪ **maker** *noun.* [Anglo-Saxon *macian*]

IDIOMS **make as if** *or* **as though** *or* (*US*) **make like sth** *or* **make like to do sth** to act or behave in a specified way: *She made as if to leave.* **make do** *informal* to manage or get by: *always having to make do.* **make do with sth** *informal* to manage with, or make the best use, of a second or inferior choice. **make do without sth** *informal* to manage without it. **make it** *informal* **1** to be successful: *to make it in show business.* **2** to survive. **make it up to sb** to compensate or repay them for difficulties, inconvenience, etc which they have experienced on one's account, or for kindness, generosity, etc which they have shown to one. Compare **make up to sb** below. **make or break sth** *or* **sb** to be the crucial test that brings it or them either success or failure: *The takeover will either make or break the company.* **on the make** *informal* of a person: seeking a large or illegal personal profit.

PHRASAL VERBS **make away with sb** to kill them. **make for sth** *or* **sb** to go towards it or them, esp rapidly, purposefully or suddenly. **make off** to leave, esp in a hurry or secretly. **make off** *or* **away with sth** *or* **sb** to run off with it or them; to steal or kidnap it or them. **make out 1** *informal* to progress or get along: *How did you make out in the exam?* **2** *informal, chiefly N Am* to manage, succeed or survive: *It's been tough, but we'll make out.* **make out sth** *or* **that sth** to pretend or claim that it is so: *He made out that he was ill.* **make out sth** *or* **make sth out 1** to begin to discern it, esp to see or hear it. **2** to write or fill in a document, etc: *made out a cheque for £20.* **make sth** *or* **sb out to be sth** to portray them, or cause them to seem to be, what they are not: *They made us out to be liars.* **make over sth** *or* **make sth over 1** to transfer ownership of it: *made over my* *shares to her when I retired.* **2** *N Am, esp US* to convert or alter it. See also **makeover**. **make up for sth** to compensate or serve as an apology for it. **make up to sb** *informal* to seek their friendship or favour; to flirt with them. **make up with sb** to resolve a disagreement with someone. **make sth up 1** to fabricate or invent it: *made up the story.* **2** to prepare or assemble it. **3** to constitute it; to be the parts of it: *The three villages together make up a district.* **4** to form the final element in something; to complete it: *another player to make up the team.*

make-believe *noun* pretence, esp playful or innocent imaginings. ▸ *adj* pretended; imaginary.

makeover *noun* **1** a complete change in a person's style of dress, appearance, make-up, hair, etc. **2** a remake or reconstruction. See also **make over sth** under **make**.

Maker *noun* God, the Creator: *go to meet his Maker.*

makeshift *adj* serving as a temporary and less adequate substitute for something: *a makeshift bed.*

make-up *noun* **1 a** cosmetics such as mascara, lipstick, etc applied to the face, esp by women; **b** cosmetics worn by actors to give the required appearance for a part. **2** the combination of characteristics or ingredients that form something, eg a personality or temperament: *Greed is not in his make-up.*

makeweight *noun* a person or thing of little value or importance, included only to make up for a deficiency.

making *noun* the materials or qualities from which something can be made.

IDIOMS **be the making of sb** to ensure their success. **in the making** in the process of being made, formed or developed: *She is a star in the making.*

makings *plural noun*

IDIOMS **have the makings of sth** to have the ability to become a specified thing.

mal- *prefix, denoting* **1** bad or badly: *malformed.* **2** incorrect or incorrectly: *malfunction.* [French]

malachite /'maləkaɪt/ *noun, geol* a bright green copper mineral that is used as a gemstone and as a minor ore of copper. [14c: ultimately from Greek *malakhe* the **mallow** plant, whose leaves are a similar shade of green]

maladjusted *adj* of a person: psychologically unable to deal with everyday situations and relationships. ▪ **maladjustment** *noun.*

maladminister *verb* to manage (eg public affairs) badly, dishonestly or incompetently. ▪ **maladministration** *noun.*

maladroit *adj, rather formal* clumsy; tactless; unskilful. ▪ **maladroitness** *noun.* [17c: French]

malady /'malədɪ/ *noun* (***-ies***) *rather formal or old use* an illness or disease. [13c: French]

malaise *noun* a feeling of uneasiness, discontent, general depression or despondency. [18c: French]

malapropism *noun* **1** the unintentional misuse of a word, usu with comic effect, through confusion with another word that sounds similar but has a different meaning. **2** a word misused in this way. [18c: named after Mrs Malaprop, in Sheridan's play *The Rivals*]

malaria *noun* an infectious disease that produces recurring bouts of fever, caused by the bite of the mosquito. ▪ **malarial** *adj.* [18c: from Italian *mal' aria*, literally 'bad air']

malarkey *or* **malarky** *noun, informal* nonsense; rubbish; absurd behaviour or talk. [20c: orig US]

Malay *noun* (***Malays***) **1** a member of a race of people inhabiting Malaysia, Singapore and Indonesia, formerly known as the Malay Peninsula. **2** the language of this people, the official language of Malaysia. ▸ *adj* belonging or relating to the Malays or their language or countries. Sometimes called **Malayan**. [16c: from Malay *malayu*]

Malaysian *adj* **1** belonging or relating to Malaysia, an independent SE Asian federation of states, or its inhabitants. **2** belonging or relating to the **Malay** Peninsula. ▸ *noun* a citizen or inhabitant of, or person born in, Malaysia. [19c]

malcontent *adj* (*also* **malcontented**) of a person: dissatisfied and inclined to rebel. ▸ *noun* a dissatisfied or rebellious person. [16c: French]

Maldivian *or* **Maldivan** *adj* belonging or relating to the Maldives, a republic consisting of an island archipelago in the Indian Ocean, its inhabitants, or their language. ▸ *noun* **1** a citizen or inhabitant of, or person born in, the Maldives. **2** the official language of the Maldives. [19c]

male *adj* **1** denoting the sex that produces sperm and fertilizes the egg cell produced by the female. **2** denoting the reproductive structure of a plant that produces the male **gamete**. **3** belonging to or characteristic of men; masculine: *male hormones.* **4** for or made up of men or boys: *male college.* **5** *eng* of a piece of machinery, etc: having a projecting part that fits into another part (the **female** *adj* sense 4). ▸ *noun* a male person, animal or plant. ▪ **maleness** *noun.* [14c: from French *masle* or *male*]

male chauvinist *noun* a man who believes in the superiority of men over women. ▪ **male chauvinism** *noun.*

malediction /malɪ'dɪkʃən/ *noun, literary or formal* **1** a curse or defamation. **2** the uttering of a curse. ▪ **maledictory** *adj.* [15c: from Latin *maledictio*]

malefactor /'malɪfaktə(r)/ *noun, literary or formal* a criminal; an evil-doer or wrongdoer. [15c: Latin]

malevolent /mə'lɛvələnt/ *adj* wishing to do evil to others; malicious. ▪ **malevolence** *noun.* ▪ **malevolently** *adv.* [16c: from Latin *malevolens*]

malfeasance *noun, law* wrongdoing; the committing of an unlawful act, esp by a public official. ▪ **malfeasant** *adj.* [17c: from French *malfaisance*]

malformation *noun* **1** the state or condition of being badly or wrongly formed or shaped. **2** a badly or wrongly formed part; a deformity. ▪ **malformed** *adj.*

malfunction *verb, intr* to work imperfectly; to fail to work. ▸ *noun* failure of, or a fault or failure in, the operation of a machine, etc. [20c]

malice /'malɪs/ *noun* the desire or intention to harm or hurt another or others. [13c: French]

malice aforethought *noun, law* a firm intention to commit a crime, esp one against a person, such as murder or serious injury.

malicious *adj* deliberately vicious, spiteful or cruel. ▪ **maliciously** *adv.* [13c: French, from **malice**]

malign /mə'laɪn/ *verb* to say or write bad or unpleasant things about someone, esp falsely or spitefully. ▸ *adj* **1** of a person: evil in nature or influence. **2** of a disease: harmful; malignant. [14c: from Latin *malignus*]

malignant /məˈlɪgnənt/ *adj* **1** of a person: feeling or showing hatred or the desire to do harm to another or others; malicious. **2** *med* **a** denoting any disorder that, if left untreated, may cause death; **b** esp of a cancerous tumour: of a type that, esp if left untreated, destroys the surrounding tissue and may spread elsewhere in the body. Compare **benign**. ▪ **malignancy** *noun* (**-ies**). [16c: from Latin *malignare* to act maliciously]

malinger /məˈlɪŋgə(r)/ *verb, intr* to pretend to be ill, esp in order to avoid having to work. ▪ **malingerer** *noun*. [19c: from French *malingre* sickly]

mall /mɔːl, mal/ *noun* **1** a shopping centre, street or area, etc with shops, that is closed to vehicles. **2** a public promenade, esp one that is broad and tree-lined. [20c: named after *The Mall*, a street in London]

mallard *noun* (***mallard*** *or* ***mallards***) a common wild duck, the male of which has a green head. [14c: from French *mallart* wild drake]

malleable /ˈmalɪəbəl/ *adj* **1** of certain metals and alloys, etc: able to be beaten into a different shape, etc without breaking. **2** eg of a person or personality: easily influenced. ▪ **malleability** *noun*. [14c: French]

mallet *noun* **1** a hammer with a large head, usu made of wood. **2** in croquet, polo, etc: a long-handled wooden hammer used to strike the ball. [15c: from French *maillet*]

mallow *noun* a plant with pink, purple or white flowers. [Anglo-Saxon *mealwe*]

malnourished *adj* suffering from **malnutrition**.

malnutrition *noun, med* a disorder resulting from inadequate food intake, an unbalanced diet or inability to absorb nutrients from food.

malodorous *adj, formal* foul-smelling.

malpractice *noun, law* improper, careless, illegal or unethical professional conduct, eg medical treatment which shows a lack of reasonable skill or care.

malt *noun* **1** *brewing* a mixture, used in brewing, prepared from barley or wheat grains that have been soaked in water, allowed to sprout and then dried in a kiln. **2** **malt whisky**, or another liquor made with malt. ▸ *verb* to make (a grain) into malt. ▪ **malted** *adj*. ▪ **malty** *adj*. [Anglo-Saxon *mealt*]

Maltese *adj* belonging or relating to Malta, an archipelago republic in the central Mediterranean Sea, its inhabitants, or their language. ▸ *noun* (*pl* ***Maltese***) **1** a citizen or inhabitant of, or a person born in, Malta. **2** the official language of Malta. [17c]

Maltese cross *noun* a cross with four arms of equal length that taper towards the centre, each with a V cut into the end.

Malthusian /malˈθjuːzɪən/ *adj* of the theory that the increase of population tends to outstrip that of the means of living and therefore sexual restraint should be exercised. [19c: named after British economist Thomas Malthus]

maltose *noun, biochem* a hard white crystalline sugar that occurs in starch and glycogen, and is composed of two **glucose** molecules linked together. [19c]

maltreat *verb* to treat someone or something roughly or cruelly. ▪ **maltreatment** *noun*. [18c: from French *maltraiter*]

malt whisky *noun* whisky made entirely from malted barley. Often shortened to **malt**.

malversation *noun, formal & rare* corruption in public affairs, eg extortion, bribery, etc. [16c: French]

mam *noun, dialect or informal* mother. [16c: from **mama**]

mama or (*chiefly US*) **mamma** *or* **mammy** *noun* (***mamas, mammas*** *or* ***mammies***) **1** *rather dated* now used chiefly by young children: mother. Often shortened to **ma**, **mam**. **2** *slang, chiefly US* a woman. See also **mom**. [16c: repetition of the sound *ma* often heard in babbling baby-talk]

mamba *noun* a large, poisonous, black or green African snake. [19c: from Zulu *imamba*]

mambo *noun* **1** a rhythmic Latin American dance resembling the **rumba**. **2** a piece of music for this dance. [1940s: American Spanish, prob from Haitian meaning 'voodoo priestess']

Mameluke /ˈmaməluk/ *noun* **1** a member of a military force that formed the ruling class of Egypt from the mid-13c to the early 19c. **2** a slave in a Muslim country, esp white. [From Arabic *mamlûk* a purchased slave]

mammal *noun, zool* any warm-blooded, vertebrate animal characterized by the possession in the female of **mammary gland**s which secrete milk to feed its young, eg a human, whale, etc. ▪ **mammalian** /məmˈeɪlɪən/ *adj*. [19c: from scientific Latin *mammalis* of the breast]

mammary *adj, biol, med* belonging to, of the nature of, or relating to the breasts or other milk-producing glands. [17c: from Latin *mamma* breast]

mammary gland *noun, biol, anatomy* the milk-producing gland of a mammal, eg a woman's breast or a cow's udder.

mammography *noun, med* the process of X-raying the breast (called a **mammograph** *or* **mammogram**), usu in order to detect any abnormal or malignant growths at an early stage.

mammon *noun, chiefly literary or Bible* **1** wealth when considered as the source of evil and immorality. **2** (**Mammon**) the personification of this in the New Testament as a false god, the god of riches. [14c: from Greek *mamonas* or *mammonas*]

mammoth *noun* an extinct shaggy-haired, prehistoric elephant, with long curved tusks. ▸ *adj* huge; giant-sized. [18c: from Russian *mammot* or *mamont*]

mammy see under **mama**

Mamselle see under **Mademoiselle**

man *noun* (***men***) **1** an adult male human being. **2** human beings as a whole or as a genus; the human race: *when man first walked the earth.* Also called **mankind**. **3** any subspecies of, or type of creature belonging to, the human genus *Homo*. **4** a human being; a person: *the right man for the job.* **5** an ordinary employee, worker or member of the armed forces, as distinguished from a manager or officer. **6** an adult male human being displaying typical or expected masculine qualities, such as strength and courage: *Stand up and be a man.* **7** in various board games, eg draughts and chess: one of the movable pieces. **8** *informal* a husband or boyfriend. **9** *informal* used as a form of address to an adult male, in various contexts, eg indicating impatience: *Damn it, man!* **10** *informal* the perfect thing or person, esp for a specified job or purpose: *If you need a good mechanic, David's your man.* ▸ *verb* (***manned, manning***) **1** to provide (eg a ship, industrial plant, fortress, etc) with men, ie workers, operators, defenders, esp male ones. **2** to operate (a piece of equipment, etc) or to make it ready for action: *man the pumps.* ▸ *exclam, informal, esp US* used to intensify a statement that follows it: *Man, is she gorgeous!* ▪ **manned** *adj* of a ship, machine, spacecraft, etc: provided with men, operators, crew, etc. [Anglo-Saxon *mann*]

IDIOMS **man and boy** from childhood to manhood; for all of someone's life. **sort out** *or* **separate the men from the boys** *informal* to serve as a test that will prove someone's ability, calibre, quality, etc or otherwise. **to a man** *slightly formal or old use* without exception.

man-about-town *noun* (***men-about-town***) a fashionable, city-dwelling, socializing man.

manacle *noun* a handcuff; a shackle for the hand or wrist. Compare **fetter**. ▸ *verb* to restrain someone with manacles. [14c: French]

manage *verb* **1** to be in overall control or charge of, or the manager of, something or someone. **2** to deal with something or handle it successfully or competently: *I can manage my own affairs.* **3** *tr & intr* to succeed in doing or producing something: *Can you manage the food if I organize the drink?* **4** to have, or to be able to find, enough room, time, etc for something: *Can you manage another sandwich?* **5** *intr* (*usu* **manage on sth**) to succeed in living on (a specified amount of money, etc). [16c: from Italian *maneggiare* to handle or train (a horse)]

manageable *adj* able to be managed or controlled, esp without much difficulty; governable.

management *noun* **1** the skill or practice of controlling, directing or planning something, esp a commercial enterprise or activity. **2** the managers of a company, etc, as a group. **3** manner of directing, controlling or using something.

manager *noun* (abbrev **Mgr**) **1** someone who manages a commercial enterprise, organization, project, etc. See also **manageress**. **2** someone who manages esp actors, musicians, sportsmen and sportswomen, or a particular team, etc. ▪ **managerial** *adj.*

manageress *noun* a female manager of a business, etc.

---

manageress

Like some other words ending in *-ess* that are used to refer to women, this is now often regarded as old-fashioned and condescending.

---

managing director *noun* (abbrev **MD**) a director in overall charge of an organization and its day-to-day running, often carrying out the decisions of a board of directors. *N Am equivalent* **chief executive officer.**

man-at-arms *noun* (***men-at-arms***) *hist* a soldier, esp a heavily-armed, mounted soldier.

manatee *noun* a large plant-eating marine mammal of the tropical waters of America, Africa and the W Indies. [16c: from Spanish *manatí*]

Mancunian /maŋ'kjuːnɪən, man-/ *noun* a citizen or inhabitant of, or person born in, the city of Manchester in NW England. ▸ *adj* belonging or relating to Manchester. [Early 20c: from Latin *Mancunium* Manchester]

mandala *noun, Buddhism, Hinduism* a pictorial symbol of the universe, usually a circle enclosing images of deities or geometric designs. [Sanskrit]

mandarin *noun* **1** (*also* **mandarin orange**) a small citrus fruit, similar to the tangerine. **2** (**Mandarin** *or* **Mandarin Chinese**) **a** the name given to the form of Chinese spoken in the north, centre and west of China; **b** the official spoken language of China, based on the Beijing variety of this language. **3** a high-ranking official or bureaucrat, esp one who is thought to be outside political control: *at the mercy of the mandarins at Whitehall.* **4** a person of great influence, esp a reactionary or pedantic literary figure. **5** *hist* a senior official belonging to any of the nine ranks of officials under the Chinese Empire. [16c: from Portuguese *mandarim*]

mandate *noun* **1** a right or authorization given to a nation, person, etc to act on behalf of others. **2** (*also* **Mandate**) *hist* **a** a territory administered by a country on behalf of the League of Nations, especially after World War I. Also called **mandated territory**; **b** the power conferred on a country by the League of Nations to administer such a territory. ▸ *verb* **1** to give authority or power to someone or something. **2** to assign (a territory) to a nation under a mandate. [16c: from Latin *mandatum* a thing that is commanded]

mandatory *adj* **1** not allowing any choice; compulsory. **2** referring to the nature of, or containing, a **mandate** or command.

mandible *noun, zool* **1** the lower jaw of a vertebrate. **2** the upper or lower part of a bird's beak. **3** one of a pair of jawlike mouthparts in insects, crustaceans, etc. [16c: from Latin *mandibula*]

mandir *noun* a Hindu or Jain temple. [Hindi]

mandolin *or* **mandoline** *noun* a musical instrument like a small guitar, with eight metal strings tuned in pairs. [18c: from Italian *mandolino*]

mandrake *noun* a plant with purple flowers and a forked root, formerly thought to have magical powers. [14c: from Latin *mandragora*]

mandrel *or* **mandril** *noun, technical* **1** the rotating shaft on a lathe that the object being worked on is fixed to. **2** the axle of a circular saw or grinding wheel. [16c: related to French *mandrin* lathe]

mandrill *noun* a large W African baboon with distinctive red and blue striped markings on its muzzle and hindquarters. [18c]

mane *noun* **1** on a horse, lion or other animal: the long hair growing from and around the neck. **2** on a human: a long, thick head of hair. [Anglo-Saxon *manu*]

maneuver, maneuvered, *etc* the *N Am* spellings of **manoeuvre**, etc.

man Friday *noun* (***man Fridays***) **1** a faithful or devoted manservant or male assistant. **2** a junior male worker given various duties, esp in an office. [19c: after the loyal servant in *Robinson Crusoe* (1719) by Daniel Defoe]

manful *adj* brave and determined. ▪ **manfully** *adv.*

manganese *noun, chem* (symbol **Mn**) a hard brittle pinkish-grey metallic element, widely used to make alloys that are very hard and resistant to wear, eg in railway lines, etc. [17c: from French *manganèse*]

mange /meɪndʒ/ *noun, vet med* a skin disease that affects hairy animals such as cats and dogs, causing itching and loss of hair. ▪ **mangy** *or* **mangey** *adj* (***-ier, -iest***) **1** suffering from mange. **2** *derog* shabby; dirty or scruffy. [15c: from French *mangeue* itch]

mangel-wurzel *or* (*US*) **mangel** *noun* a variety of beet with a large yellow root, used as cattle food. [18c: from German *Mangoldwurzel*]

manger *noun* an open box or trough from which cattle or horses feed. [14c: from French *mangeoire*]

mangetout /mɒndʒ'tuː/ *noun* a variety of garden pea with an edible pod. [20c: from French *mange tout*, literally 'eat-all']

mangle[1] *verb* **1** to damage or destroy something or someone by cutting, crushing, tearing, etc. **2** to spoil, ruin or bungle something. ▪ **mangled** *adj*. [15c: from French *mangler*]

mangle[2] *noun* **1** *dated* a device, usu hand-operated, that consists of two large heavy rotating rollers which have wet laundry fed between them so as to squeeze most of the water out. Also called **wringer**. **2** *esp US* a machine that presses laundry by passing it between two large heated rollers. ▶ *verb* to pass (laundry, etc) through a mangle. [18c: from Dutch *mangel*]

mango *noun* (***mangos*** *or* ***mangoes***) a heavy oblong fruit with a central stone surrounded by sweet, soft juicy orange flesh and a thick, green, yellow or red skin. [16c: from Portuguese *manga*]

mangrove *noun* a tropical evergreen tree that grows in salt marshes and on mudflats, producing aerial roots from its branches that form a dense tangled network.

manhandle *verb* **1** to treat someone or something roughly; to push or shove them or it. **2** to move or transport something using manpower, not machinery.

manhole *noun* an opening large enough to allow a person through, esp one that leads down into a sewer.

manhood *noun* **1** the state of being an adult male. **2** manly qualities.

man-hour *noun* a unit of work equal to the work done by one person in one hour.

manhunt *noun* an intensive and usu large-scale organized search for someone, esp a criminal or fugitive.

mania *noun* **1** *psychol* a mental disorder characterized by great excitement or euphoria and violence. **2** *loosely* (*esp* **a mania for sth**) a great desire or enthusiasm for it; a craze or obsession. [14c: Latin]

-mania *combining form, forming nouns, denoting* **1** *psychol* an abnormal, uncontrollable or obsessive desire for a specified thing: *kleptomania*. **2** a great desire or enthusiasm for a specified thing; a craze: *bibliomania*.

maniac *noun* **1** *informal* a person who behaves wildly. **2** an extremely keen enthusiast: *a video maniac*. [17c]

manic *adj* **1** *psychol* characteristic of, relating to or suffering from **mania** (sense 1). **2** *informal* very energetic or active. ▪ **manically** *adv*. [20c]

manic-depressive *psychiatry, adj* affected by or suffering from an illness which produces alternating phases of extreme elation (**mania** sense 1) and severe depression. ▶ *noun* someone who is suffering from this kind of depression.

manicure *noun* **1** the care and cosmetic treatment of the hands, esp the fingernails. **2** an individual treatment of this kind. Compare **pedicure**. ▶ *verb* to carry out a manicure on (a person or their hands). [19c: from Latin *manus* hand + *cura* care]

manifest *verb, formal* **1** to show or display something clearly. **2** (*usu* **manifest itself**) to reveal or declare itself. **3** to be evidence or proof of something: *an act which manifested his sincerity*. ▶ *adj* easily seen or perceived; obvious: *a manifest lie*. ▶ *noun* **1** a customs document that gives details of a ship or aircraft, its cargo and destination. **2** a passenger list, for an aeroplane, etc. ▪ **manifestation** *noun*. ▪ **manifestly** *adv* obviously; undoubtedly. [14c: from Latin *manifestare*]

manifesto *noun* (***manifestos*** *or* ***manifestoes***) a written public declaration of policies, intentions, opinions or motives, esp one produced by a political party or candidate. [17c: Italian]

manifold *adj, formal or literary* many and various; of many different kinds: *manifold pleasures*. ▶ *noun* (*also* **manifold pipe**) *technical* a pipe with several inlets and outlets. [Anglo-Saxon *manigfeald*]

manikin *or* **mannikin** *noun* **1** a model of the human body, used in teaching art and anatomy, etc. **2** *old use* an abnormally small person; a dwarf. Compare **mannequin**. [16c: Dutch, double diminutive of *man* **man**]

manila *or* **manilla** *noun* (*also* **manila paper** *or* **manilla paper**) a type of thick strong brown paper, orig made from **Manila hemp**. [19c: orig made in the city of Manila in the Philippines]

Manila hemp *noun* the fibre of a Philippine tree.

the man in the street *noun* the ordinary, typical or average man.

manioc *noun* **cassava**. [16c: from Tupí (a native S American language) *mandioca*, the name for the roots of the plant]

manipulate *verb* **1** to handle something, or move or work it with the hands, esp in a skilful way. **2** to control or influence someone or something cleverly and unscrupulously, esp to one's own advantage. **3** to give a false appearance to something, etc: *manipulating the statistics to suit his argument*. ▪ **manipulation** *noun*. ▪ **manipulative** *or* **manipulatory** *adj*. ▪ **manipulator** *noun*. [19c: from Latin *manipulus* handful]

man jack *noun, informal* (*usu* **every man jack**) an individual person.

mankind *noun* **1** the human race as a whole; human beings collectively. **2** human males collectively.

manky *adj* (***-ier, -iest***) *informal or dialect* **1** dirty. **2** of poor quality; shoddy; rotten. [20c: from obsolete Scots *mank* defective]

manly *adj* (***-ier, -iest***) **1** displaying qualities considered admirable in a man, such as strength, determination, courage, etc. **2** considered suitable for or characteristic of a man. ▪ **manliness** *noun*.

man-made *adj* made by or originated by humans: *man-made fibre*.

manna *noun* **1** in the Old Testament: the food miraculously provided by God for the Israelites in the wilderness (Exodus 16:14–36). **2** any unexpected gift or windfall: *manna from heaven*. [Anglo-Saxon]

mannequin *noun* **1** a fashion model, esp a woman, employed to model clothes, etc. **2** a life-size dummy of the human body, used in the making or displaying of clothes. Compare **manikin**. [18c: French]

manner *noun* **1** way; fashion: *an unusual manner of walking*. **2** (*often* **manners**) behaviour towards others: *has a very pleasant manner*. **3** (**manners**) good or polite social behaviour. **4** *formal or dated* kind or kinds: *all manner of things*. [12c: from French *maniere*]

IDIOMS **in a manner of speaking** in a way; to some degree; so to speak. **to the manner born** of a person: naturally suited to a particular occupation, lifestyle, etc.

mannered *adj, formal* **1** *usu derog* unnatural and artificial; affected. **2** *in compounds* having or displaying a specified kind of social behaviour: *bad-mannered*.

mannerism *noun* **1** an individual characteristic, such as a gesture or facial expression. **2** *derog* esp in art or literature: noticeable or excessive use of an individual or mannered style.

mannerly *adj, old use* polite; showing good manners. ▪ **mannerliness** *noun*.

mannish *adj* of a woman: having an appearance or qualities regarded as more typical of a man.

manoeuvre *or* (*N Am*) **maneuver** /mə'nuːvə(r)/ *noun* **1** a movement requiring, or performed with, skill or intelligence. **2** a clever or skilful handling of affairs, often one involving deception or inventiveness. **3** *military, navy* **a** (*usu* **manoeuvres**) a large-scale battle-training exercise by armed forces; **b** a skilful or clever tactical movement of troops or ships, etc. ▸ *verb* **1** *tr & intr* to move something accurately and with skill. **2** *tr & intr* to use ingenuity, and perhaps deceit, in handling something or someone. **3** *intr* to carry out military exercises. **4** *tr & intr* to change the position of (troops or ships, etc). ▪ **manoeuvrability** *noun*. ▪ **manoeuvrable** *adj*. [15c: French]

man of letters *noun* **1** a scholar. **2** an author.

man-of-war *or* **man-o'-war** *noun, hist* an armed sailing ship used as a warship.

manor *noun* **1** (*also* **manor house**) the principal residence on a country estate, often the former home of a medieval lord. **2** *hist* in medieval Europe: an area of land under the control of a lord. **3** *Brit, informal* the area in which a particular person or group, esp a police unit or a criminal, operates. [13c: from French *manoir*]

manpower *noun* the number of available employees or people fit and ready to work.

manqué /'mɒŋkeɪ; *French* mɑ̃ke/ *adj (following its noun) literary* applied to a specified kind of person: having once had the ambition or potential to be that kind of person, without achieving it; unfulfilled: *an artist manqué*. [18c: French, meaning 'having missed']

mansard *noun, archit* (*in full* **mansard roof**) a four-sided roof, each side of which is in two parts, the lower part sloping more steeply. [18c: from French *mansarde*, named after François Mansart, French architect]

manse *noun* esp in Scotland: the house of a religious minister. [15c: from Latin *mansus* dwelling]

manservant *noun* (***menservants***) *old use* a male servant, esp a valet.

mansion *noun* **1** a large house, usu a grand or luxurious one. **2** (**mansions** *or* **Mansions**) *Brit* used eg as the name or address of a residential property: a large building divided into luxury apartments. [14c: French]

manslaughter *noun, law* the crime of **homicide** without **malice aforethought**, eg as a result of gross negligence, provocation or diminished responsibility. *Scot equivalent* **culpable homicide**.

manta *or* **manta ray** *noun* a type of fish, a giant **ray²**, with a broad mouth situated across the front of the head. [18c: Spanish, meaning 'cloak' or 'blanket']

mantel *noun, chiefly old use* a mantelpiece or mantelshelf. [15c: related to **mantle**]

mantelpiece *noun* the ornamental frame around a fireplace, esp the top part which forms a shelf.

mantelshelf *noun* the shelf part of a mantelpiece, over a fireplace.

mantilla /man'tɪlə; *Spanish* man'tiːja/ *noun* a lace or silk scarf worn by women as a covering for the hair and shoulders, esp in Spain and S America. [18c: Spanish, diminutive of *manta* a cloak]

mantis *noun* (***mantises*** *or* ***mantes***) a tropical insect-eating insect that sits in wait for prey with its two front legs raised. Also called **praying mantis**. [17c: Latin]

mantissa *noun, maths* the part of a logarithm comprising the decimal point and the figures following it. [17c: Latin, 'something added']

mantle *noun* **1** a cloak or loose outer garment. **2** *literary* a covering: *a mantle of snow*. **3** *geol* the part of the Earth between the crust and the core. **4** a fireproof mesh around a gas or oil lamp, that glows when the lamp is lit. **5** *literary* a position of responsibility: *The leader's mantle passed to him*. ▸ *verb, literary* to cover, conceal or obscure something or someone: *mantled in darkness*. [13c: from Latin *mantellum*]

man-to-man *adj* esp of personal discussion: open and frank. ▸ *adv* in an open and frank manner; honestly.

mantra *noun* **1** *Hinduism, Buddhism* a sacred phrase, word or sound chanted repeatedly as part of meditation and prayer, as an aid to concentration and the development of spiritual power. **2** *Hinduism* any of the hymns of praise in the Vedas (see **Veda**), the ancient sacred scriptures. [19c: Sanskrit, meaning 'instrument of thought']

manual *adj* **1** belonging or relating to the hand or hands: *manual skill*. **2** using the body, rather than the mind; physical. **3** worked, controlled or operated by hand; not automatic or computer-operated, etc. ▸ *noun* **1** a book of instructions, eg for repairing a car or operating a machine. Also called **handbook**. **2** an organ keyboard or a key played by hand not by foot. ▪ **manually** *adv*. [15c: from Latin *manualis*]

manufacture *verb* **1** to make something from raw materials, esp in large quantities using machinery. **2** to invent or fabricate something. ▸ *noun* **1** the practice, act or process of manufacturing something. **2** anything manufactured. ▪ **manufacturer** *noun*. ▪ **manufacturing** *adj, noun*. [16c: French]

manumit *verb* (***manumitted, manumitting***) *formal* to release (a person) from slavery; to set someone free. ▪ **manumission** *noun*. [15c: from Latin *manumittere* to send from one's hand or control]

manure *noun* any substance, esp animal dung, used on soil as a fertilizer. ▸ *verb* to apply manure to (land, soil, etc); to enrich (soil) with a fertilizing substance. [15c: from French *maynoverer* to work with the hands]

manuscript *noun* (abbrev **MS** *or* **ms.**) **1** an author's handwritten or typed version of a book, play, etc before it has been printed. **2** a book or document written by hand. [16c: from Latin *manuscriptus* written by hand]

Manx *adj* belonging or relating to the Isle of Man, its inhabitants, or their language. [16c: from *Maniske* Manish]

many *adj* (***more, most***) **1** (*sometimes* **a great many** *or* **good many**) consisting of a large number; numerous: *Many teenagers smoke.* **2** (**the many**) the majority or the crowd; ordinary people, not nobility or royalty. ▶ *pronoun* a great number (of people or things): *The sweets were so rich that I couldn't eat many.* See also **more, most**. [Anglo-Saxon *manig*]

Maori /'mɑʊərɪ/ *noun* (*pl* ***Maori*** *or* ***Maoris***) **1** a member of the aboriginal Polynesian people of New Zealand. **2** the language of this people. ▶ *adj* belonging or relating to this people or their language. [9c: a native name]

map *noun* **1** a diagram of any part of the Earth's surface, showing geographical and other features, eg the position of towns and roads. **2** a similar diagram of the surface of the Moon or a planet. **3** a diagram showing the position of the stars in the sky. **4** a diagram of the layout of anything. ▶ *verb* (***mapped, mapping***) **1** to make a map of something. **2** *maths* to place (the elements of a **set**[2] (*noun* sense 2)) in one-to-one correspondence with the elements of another set. ▪ **mapper** *noun.* ▪ **mapping** *noun, chiefly maths.* [16c: from Latin *mappa* a napkin or painted cloth]

IDIOMS **put sth** *or* **sb on the map** *informal* to cause (eg a town, an actor, etc) to become well-known or important.

PHRASAL VERBS **map sth out** to plan (a route, course of action, etc) in detail.

maple *noun* **1** (*also* **maple tree**) a broad-leaved deciduous tree of northern regions whose seeds float by means of wing-like growths. **2** the hard light-coloured wood of these trees. [Anglo-Saxon *mapul*]

maple leaf *noun* the leaf of a maple tree, esp as the national emblem of Canada.

maple syrup *noun, esp N Am* the distinctively flavoured syrup made from the sap of the sugar-maple tree.

maquis /mɑː'kiː/ *noun* (*pl* ***maquis***) **1** a type of thick, shrubby vegetation found in coastal areas of the Mediterranean. **2** (**the maquis** *or* **the Maquis**) *hist* **a** the French resistance movement that fought against German occupying forces during World War II; **b** a member of this movement. [19c: French]

Mar. *abbrev* March.

mar *verb* (***marred, marring***) to spoil something: *The trip was marred by rain.* [Anglo-Saxon *merran*]

marabou *or* **marabout** *noun* (*pl* in sense 1 only ***marabous*** *or* ***marabouts***) **1** a large black-and-white African stork. **2** its feathers, used to decorate clothes. [19c: French]

maraca *noun* a hand-held percussion instrument, usu one of a pair, consisting of a gourd filled with dried beans, pebbles, etc. [19c: from Portuguese *maracá*]

maraschino /marə'ʃiːnoʊ, -'skiːnoʊ/ *noun* a liqueur made from cherries. [18c: Italian]

maraschino cherry *noun* a cherry preserved in **maraschino**, used for decorating cocktails, cakes, etc.

Maratha /mə'rɑːtə/ *noun* a member of a once dominant people of SW India. [From Sanskrit *maharatra* great kingdom]

marathon *noun* **1** (*sometimes* **marathon race**) a long-distance race on foot, usu 42.195km (26ml 385yd). **2** any lengthy and difficult task. ▶ *adj* **1** belonging or relating to a marathon race. **2** requiring or displaying great powers of endurance or stamina: *a marathon effort.* [19c: named after Marathon in Greece, from where a messenger is said to have run to Athens with news of victory over the Persians in 490 BC; the length of the race is based on this distance]

maraud *verb* **1** *intr* to wander in search of people to attack and property to steal or destroy. **2** to plunder (a place). ▪ **marauder** *noun.* ▪ **marauding** *adj, noun.* [18c: from French *marauder* to prowl]

marble *noun* **1 a** *geol* a hard, metamorphic rock, white when pure but usu mottled or streaked; **b** any such rock that can be highly polished, used in building and sculpture. **2** in children's games: a small hard ball, now usu made of glass, but orig made of marble. **3** a work of art, tombstone, tomb, slab or other object made of marble. ▶ *verb* to stain or paint something (esp paper) to resemble marble. ▪ **marbled** *adj.* ▪ **marbling** *noun* **1** a marbled appearance or colouring. **2** the practice or act of staining or painting (esp the endpapers or edges of a book) in imitation of marble. [13c: French]

marbles *singular noun* any of several children's games played with marbles.

IDIOMS **have all**, *or* **lose, one's marbles** to be in full possession of, or to lack, one's mental faculties.

marc *noun* **1** *technical* the leftover skins and stems of grapes used in winemaking. **2** a kind of brandy made from these. [17c: French]

marcasite *noun* **1** *geol* a pale yellow mineral, a compound of iron, formerly used in jewellery and now mined for use in the manufacture of sulphuric acid. **2** a polished gemstone made from this or any similar mineral. [15c: from Latin *marcasita*]

March *noun* (abbrev **Mar.**) the third month of the year. [13c: from French *Marche*]

march[1] *verb* **1** *intr* to walk in a stiff, upright, formal manner, usu at a brisk pace. **2** to make or force someone, esp a soldier or troop of soldiers, to walk in this way. **3** *intr* to walk in a purposeful and determined way: *suddenly marched out of the room.* **4** *intr* to advance or continue, steadily or irresistibly: *events marched on.* ▶ *noun* **1** an act of marching. **2** a distance travelled by marching. **3** a brisk walking pace. **4** a procession of people moving steadily forward. **5** *music* a piece of music written in a marching rhythm. **6** steady and unstoppable progress or movement: *the march of time.* ▪ **marcher** *noun.* [16c: from French *marcher* to walk]

march[2] *noun* **1** a boundary or border. **2** a border district. [13c: from French *marche*]

March hare *noun* a hare during its breeding season in March, noted for its excitable and erratic behaviour: *mad as a March hare.*

marching orders *plural noun* **1** orders to march in a certain way, given to soldiers, etc. **2** *informal* dismissal from a job, house, relationship, etc.

marchioness /ˈmɑːʃənəs/ *noun* **1** the wife or widow of a **marquis**. **2** a woman who holds the rank of marquis in her own right. [16c: from Latin *marchionissa*]

march past *noun, military* a march performed by a body of troops, etc in front of a person, eg the sovereign or a senior officer, who reviews it.

Mardi Gras /ˈmɑːdɪ grɑː; *French* maʀdigʀa/ *noun* **1** **Shrove Tuesday**, a day celebrated with a festival in some places, especially famously in Rio de Janeiro, Brazil. **2** the festival held on this day. [17c: French, literally 'fat Tuesday']

mare[1] *noun* an adult female horse, ass, zebra, etc. [Anglo-Saxon *mere*]

mare[2] /ˈmɑːreɪ/ *noun* (***maria***) *astron* any of numerous large, flat areas on the surface of the Moon or Mars, seen from Earth as dark patches. [18c: Latin, meaning 'sea']

mare's nest *noun* **1** a discovery that proves to be untrue or without value; a hoax. **2** *chiefly US* a disordered or confused place or situation.

marg *or* **marge** *contraction, informal* margarine.

margarine *noun* a food, usu made from vegetable oils with water, flavourings, colourings, vitamins, etc, used as a substitute for butter. [19c: French]

margin *noun* **1** the blank space around a page of writing or print. **2** any edge, border or fringe. **3** an extra amount, eg of time or money, beyond what should strictly be needed: *allow a margin for error.* **4** an amount by which one thing exceeds another: *win by a large margin.* **5** *business* the difference between the selling and buying price of an item; profit. **6** *econ, etc* an upper or lower limit, esp one beyond which it is impossible for a business, etc to exist or operate. [14c: from Latin *margo* a border]

marginal *adj* **1** small and unimportant or insignificant. **2** near to the lower limit; barely sufficient. **3** *chiefly Brit* of a political constituency: whose current MP or other representative was elected by only a small majority of votes at the last election. **4** of a note, mark, design, etc: appearing in the margin of a page of text. **5** in, on, belonging to or relating to a margin. ▸ *noun, chiefly Brit* a marginal constituency or seat. Compare **safe seat**. ▪ **marginality** *noun*. ▪ **marginally** *adv*.

marginalia *plural noun* notes written in the margin or margins of a page, book, etc. Also called **marginal notes**. [19c: from Latin *marginalis* marginal]

marginalize *or* **-ise** *verb* to push something or someone to the edges of anything, in order to reduce its or their effect, relevance, significance, etc. ▪ **marginalization** *noun*. [20c]

maria *pl of* **mare[2]**

marigold *noun* a garden plant with bright orange or yellow flowers and strongly-scented leaves. [14c: from *Mary* (the Virgin Mary) + *gold*]

marijuana *or* **marihuana** /marɪˈwɑːnə/ *noun* **cannabis**.

marimba *noun, music* a type of **xylophone** consisting of a set of hardwood strips which, when struck with hammers, vibrate metal plates underneath. [18c: from Kongo (a W African language)]

marina *noun* a harbour for berthing private pleasure boats, usu with associated facilities provided. [19c: from Italian and Spanish]

marinade *noun, cookery* any liquid mixture, esp a mixture of oil, herbs, spices, vinegar or wine, etc, in which food, esp meat or fish, is soaked before cooking. ▸ *verb, tr & intr* to soak (meat or fish, etc) in a marinade. Also called **marinate**. [17c: French]

marinate *verb* to **marinade** something. [17c: from Italian *marinare*]

marine *adj* **1** belonging to or concerned with the sea: *marine landscape.* **2** inhabiting, found in or obtained from the sea: *marine mammal.* **3** belonging or relating to ships, shipping trade or the navy: *marine insurance.* ▸ *noun* **1** (*often* **Marine**) **a** a soldier trained to serve on land or at sea; **b** a member of the Royal Marines or the US Marine Corps. **2** the merchant or naval ships of a nation collectively. [15c: from Latin *marinus*]

mariner /ˈmarɪnə(r)/ *noun* a seaman. [13c: French]

marionette *noun* a puppet with jointed limbs moved by strings. [17c: French, diminutive of Marion]

marital *adj* belonging or relating to marriage: *marital status.* ▪ **maritally** *adv*. [17c: from Latin *maritalis* married]

maritime *adj* **1** belonging or relating to the sea or ships, sea-trade, etc: *maritime communications.* **2** of plants, etc: living or growing near the sea. **3** of climate: cool in summer and mild in winter, because of the nearness of the sea. [16c: from Latin *maritimus* of the sea]

marjoram *noun* (*in full* **wild marjoram**) a pungent plant used to season food, esp pasta dishes. Also called **oregano**. [14c: French]

mark[1] *noun* **1** a visible blemish, such as a scratch or stain. **2 a** a grade or score awarded according to the proficiency of a student or competitor, etc; **b** a letter, number, or percentage used to denote this: *What mark did you get? Only C+.* **3** a sign or symbol: *a question mark.* **4** an indication or representation: *a mark of respect.* **5** the position from which a competitor starts in a race. See also **on your marks** below. **6** an object or thing to be aimed at or striven for; a target or goal: *It fell wide of the mark.* **7** a required or normal standard: *up to the mark.* **8** an impression, distinguishing characteristic or influence: *Your work bears his mark.* **9** (*often* **Mark**) (abbrev **Mk**) applied esp to vehicles: a type of design; a model or issue: *driving a Jaguar Mark II.* See also **marque**. ▸ *verb* **1** *tr & intr* to spoil something with, or become spoiled by, a mark. **2 a** to read, correct and award (a grade) to a piece of written work, etc; **b** to allot a score to someone or something. **3** to show; to be a sign of something: *events marking a new era.* **4** (*often* **mark sth down**) to make a note of something; to record it. **5** to pay close attention to something: *mark my words.* **6** *sport* to stay close to (an opposing player) in order to try and prevent them from getting or passing the ball. **7** to characterize or label someone or something: *This incident marks him as a criminal.* [Anglo-Saxon *merc* boundary or limit]

IDIOMS **make** *or* **leave one's mark** to make a strong or permanent impression. **mark time 1** to move the feet up and down as if marching, but without going forward. **2** merely to keep things going, without ma-

king progress or speeding up. **off the mark 1** not on target; off the subject or target. **2** of an athlete, etc: getting away from the **mark** (*noun* sense 5) in a race, etc: *slow off the mark*. **on your marks** *or* **mark** *athletics* said to the runners before a race begins: get into your position, ready for the starting command or signal. **up to the mark 1** of work, etc: satisfactory; of a good standard. **2** of a person: fit and well.
PHRASAL VERBS **mark sb down** to give them or their work a lower mark. **mark sth down 1** to reduce its price: *a jacket marked down from £75 to £55*. **2** to note it. **mark sth up** to increase its price; to make a profit for the seller on it. See also **mark-up**.

mark[2] *noun* another name for **Deutschmark**. [Anglo-Saxon *marc*]

marked *adj* **1** obvious or noticeable: *a marked change in her attitude*. **2** of a person: watched with suspicion; selected as the target for an attack: *a marked man*. ▪ **markedly** /ˈmɑːkɪdlɪ/ *adv*.

marker *noun* **1** a pen with a thick point, for writing signs, etc. Also called **marker pen**. **2** anything used to mark the position of something.

market *noun* **1** a gathering of people that takes place periodically, where stalls, etc are set up allowing them to buy and sell a variety of goods or a specified type of goods. **2** a public place, square, building, etc in which this regularly takes place. **3** a particular region, country or section of the population, considered as a potential customer: *the teenage market*. **4** buying and selling; a level of trading: *The market is slow*. **5** opportunity for buying and selling; demand: *no market for these goods*. **6** *esp N Am* a shop or supermarket. ▸ *verb* (***marketed, marketing***) **1** to offer something for sale; to promote (goods, etc). **2** *intr* to trade or deal, esp at a market. **3** *intr, esp US* to shop; to buy provisions. ▪ **marketable** *adj*. [Anglo-Saxon]
IDIOMS **be in the market for sth** to wish to buy it. **on the market** on sale; able to be bought.

marketeer *noun* **1** someone who trades at a market. **2** *econ* someone who is involved with, or who promotes, a particular kind of market: *black marketeer*.

market forces *plural noun* the willingness of customers to buy goods or services that suppliers are willing to offer at a particular price; supply and demand.

market garden *noun* an area of land, usu near a large town or city, that is used commercially to grow produce, esp vegetables, salad crops, etc. ▪ **market gardener** *noun*.

marketing *noun* **1** *business* the techniques or processes by which a product or service is sold, including assessment of its sales potential and responsibility for its promotion, distribution and development. **2** *esp N Am* an act or process of shopping.

market leader *noun, business* **1** a company that sells more goods of a specific type than any other company. **2** a brand of goods that sells more than any other of its kind.

market maker *noun, stock exchange* a broker-dealer, a person or firm combining the jobs of stockbroker and stockjobber.

marketplace *noun* **1** the open space in a town, etc in which a market is held. **2** (**the marketplace**) the commercial world of buying and selling.

market price *noun* the price for which a thing can be sold, and is being sold, at a particular time. Also called **market value**.

market research *noun* analysis of the habits, needs and preferences of customers, often in regard to a particular product. ▪ **market researcher** *noun*.

market town *noun* a town, often at the centre of a farming area, where a market is held regularly, usu on the same day every week.

marking *noun* **1** (*often* **markings**) a distinctive pattern of colours on an animal or plant. **2** the act or process of giving marks (eg to school work) or making marks on something.

marksman *or* **markswoman** *noun* someone who can shoot a gun or other weapon accurately, esp a trained soldier, police officer, etc. ▪ **marksmanship** *noun*. [17c]

mark-up *noun, commerce* an increase in price, esp in determining level of profit. See also **mark sth up** at **mark**[1].

marl *noun, geol* a mixture of clay and limestone. ▪ **marly** *adj*. [14c: from French *marle*]

marlin *noun* (***marlin*** *or* ***marlins***) a large fish found in warm and tropical seas which has a long spear-like upper jaw. Also called **spearfish**. [20c: from **marlinspike**, because of its pointed snout]

marlinspike *or* **marlinespike** *noun, naut* a pointed metal tool for separating the strands of rope to be spliced.

marmalade *noun* jam made from the pulp and rind of any citrus fruit, esp oranges. [16c: from Portuguese *marmelada*]

marmoreal /mɑːˈmɔːrɪəl/ *adj, formal or literary* **1** like marble; cold, smooth, white, etc. **2** made of marble. [18c: from Latin *marmor* marble]

marmoset *noun* a small S American monkey with a long bushy tail and tufts of hair around the head and ears. [14c: from French *marmouset* grotesque figure]

marmot *noun* a stout, coarse-haired, burrowing rodent of Europe, Asia and N America. [17c: from French *marmotte*]

maroon[1] *adj* dark brownish-red or purplish-red in colour. ▸ *noun* this colour. [18c: from French *marron* chestnut]

maroon[2] *verb* **1** to leave someone in isolation in a deserted place, esp on a desert island. **2** to leave someone helpless or without support. [18c: from American Spanish *cimarrón* wild]

marque /mɑːk/ *noun* applied esp to cars: a brand or make. See also **mark**[1] (*noun* sense 9). [20c: French, meaning 'mark' or 'sign']

marquee /mɑːˈkiː/ *noun* a very large tent used for circuses, parties, etc. [17c: coined from **marquise**]

marquess /ˈmɑːkwɪs/ *noun, Brit* a member of the nobility. See also **marquis, marquise**. [16c: from French *marchis*]

marquetry /ˈmɑːkətrɪ/ *noun* (***-ies***) the art or practice of making decorative arrangements or patterns out of pieces of different-coloured woods, ivory, etc, esp set into the surface of wooden furniture. Compare **inlay**. [16c: French]

marquis /ˈmɑːkwɪs; *French* maʀki/ *noun* (***marquis*** *or* ***marquises***) **1** in various European countries: a nobleman next in rank above a count. **2** a **marquess**. See also **marchioness**. [17c]

marquise /mɑːˈkiːz/ *noun* **1** in various European countries: a **marchioness**. **2** a gemstone cut to form a pointed oval. [19c]

marram *or* **marram grass** *noun* a coarse grass that grows on sandy shores, often planted to stop sand erosion. [17c: from Norse *maralmr*]

marriage *noun* **1** the state or relationship of being husband and wife. **2** the act, or legal contract, of becoming husband and wife. **3** the civil or religious ceremony during which this act is performed; a wedding. **4** a joining together; a union. [13c: French]

marriageable *adj* of a woman, or sometimes a man: suitable for marriage, esp in terms of being at a legal age for marriage. ▪ **marriageability** *noun*.

marriage certificate *noun* an official piece of paper showing that two people are legally married.

marriage guidance *noun* professional counselling given to couples with marital or personal problems.

married *adj* **1** having a husband or wife. **2** belonging or relating to the state of marriage: *married life*. **3** (*esp* **married to sth**) closely fixed together; joined, esp inseparably or intimately, to it: *He's married to his work*.

marrow *noun* **1** (*also* **bone marrow**) the soft tissue that fills the internal cavities of bones. **2** (*also* **vegetable marrow**) **a** a plant with large prickly leaves, cultivated worldwide for its large, oblong, edible fruit; **b** the fruit of this plant which has a thick, green or striped skin, and soft white flesh, and is cooked as a vegetable. [Anglo-Saxon *mærg*]

marrowbone *noun* a bone containing edible marrow.

marrowfat *or* **marrowfat pea** *noun* **1** a variety of large, edible pea. **2** the plant that bears it.

marry[1] *verb* (***-ies, -ied***) **1** to take someone as one's husband or wife. **2** of a priest, minister, official, etc: to perform the ceremony of marriage between two people: *My uncle married us*. **3** *intr* to become joined in marriage: *We married last June*. **4** *intr* (*also* **marry sth up**) to fit together, join up, or match (usu two things) correctly. [13c: from French *marier*]

PHRASAL VERBS **marry sb off** (*informal*) to find a husband or wife for them.

marry[2] *exclam, archaic* an expression of surprise or earnest declaration; indeed! [14c: for 'By (the Virgin) Mary!']

Mars *noun, astron* the fourth planet from the Sun, and the nearest planet to the Earth. [14c: named after Mars, the Roman god of war]

marsh *noun* a poorly-drained, low-lying, often flooded area of land, commonly found at the mouths of rivers and alongside ponds and lakes. ▪ **marshy** *adj* (***-ier, -iest***). [Anglo-Saxon *mersc* or *merisc*]

marshal *noun* **1** (*often* **Marshal**) *in compounds* **a** a high-ranking officer in the armed forces: *Air Vice-Marshal*; **b** *Brit* a high-ranking officer of State: *Earl Marshal*. **2** an official who organizes parades etc, or controls crowds at large public events. **3** *US* in some states: a chief police or fire officer. **4** a law-court official with various duties and responsibilities: *judge's marshal*. ▸ *verb* (***marshalled, marshalling***; *US* ***marshaled, marshaling***) **1** to arrange (troops, competitors, facts, etc) in order. **2** to direct, lead or show the way to (a crowd, procession, etc), esp in a formal or precise way. [13c: French from *mareschal*]

marshalling yard *noun* a place where railway wagons are arranged into trains.

marshal of the Royal Air Force *noun, Brit* an officer of highest rank in the Royal Air Force.

marsh fever *noun* **malaria**.

marsh gas *noun* **methane**.

marshland *noun* marshy country.

marshmallow *noun* a spongy, pink or white sweet.

marsh mallow *noun* a pink-flowered plant that grows wild in coastal marshes. [Anglo-Saxon: *merscmealwe*]

marsh marigold *noun* a marsh plant with yellow flowers like large buttercups.

marsupial *noun, zool* a mammal, such as the kangaroo, koala and wombat, in which the young is carried and suckled in an external pouch on the mother's body until it is mature enough to survive independently. ▸ *adj* belonging to or like a marsupial. [17c: from Latin *marsupium* pouch]

mart *noun* a trading place; a market or auction. [15c: from Dutch *markt*]

martello *noun* a small circular fortified tower used for coastal defence. Also called **martello tower**. [19c: from Cape Mortella in Corsica, where such a tower was captured with difficulty by a British fleet in 1794]

marten *noun* **1** a small, tree-dwelling, predatory mammal with a long thin body and a bushy tail. **2** its highly-valued, soft, black or brown fur. [15c: from French *martre*]

martial *adj* belonging or relating to, or suitable for, war or the military; warlike; militant. ▪ **martialism** *noun*. ▪ **martially** *adv*. [14c: French]

martial art *noun* a fighting sport or self-defence technique of Far Eastern origin, eg karate or judo.

martial law *noun* law and order strictly enforced by the military powers, eg when ordinary civil law has broken down during a war, revolution, etc.

Martian *adj* belonging or relating to the planet **Mars**. [14c: from Latin *Martius*]

martin *noun* a small bird of the swallow family, with a square or slightly forked tail. [15c]

martinet *noun, derog* someone who maintains strict discipline. [17c: French, named after Jean Martinet, one of Louis XIV's generals, a stringent drillmaster]

martingale *noun* a strap that is passed between a horse's forelegs and fastened to the girth and to the bit, noseband or reins, used to keep the horse's head down. [16c: French]

martini *noun* a cocktail made of gin and vermouth. [19c: from the name of the Italian wine makers Martini and Rossi]

Martinmas *noun* St Martin's Day, 11 November. [13c]

martyr *noun* **1** someone who chooses to be put to death as an act of witness to their faith, rather than abandon his or her religious beliefs. **2** someone who suffers or dies, esp for their beliefs, or for a particular cause. **3** (*usu* **a martyr to sth**) *informal* someone who suffers greatly on account of something (eg an illness, ailment or misfortune): *She is a martyr to arthritis*. ▸ *verb* to put someone to death as a martyr. ▪ **martyrdom** *noun*. [Anglo-Saxon]

marvel *verb* (***marvelled, marvelling***; *US* ***marveled, marveling***) *intr* (*esp* **marvel at sth**) to be filled with astonishment or wonder. ▸ *noun* an astonishing or wonderful person or thing; a wonder. [14c: from French *merveille*]

marvellous or (*US*) **marvelous** *adj* **1** so wonderful or astonishing as to be almost beyond belief. **2** *informal* excellent; extremely pleasing. ▪ **marvellously** *adv.*

Marxism *noun* the theories of Karl Marx (1818–83), the German economist and political philosopher, stating that the struggle between different social classes is the main influence on political change. ▪ **Marxist** *adj, noun.*

Marxism-Leninism *noun* a distinct variant of **Marxism** formulated by Vladimir Ilyich Lenin (1870–1924), which became the basis of communist ideology. ▪ **Marxist-Leninist** *adj, noun.*

marzipan *noun* a sweet paste made of ground almonds, sugar and egg whites, used to decorate cakes, make sweets, etc. [15c: from Italian *marzapane*]

masala *noun, cookery* **1** a blend of spices ground into a powder or paste used in Indian cookery. **2** a dish using this: *chicken tikka masala*. [18c: Hindi, meaning 'spices']

masc. *abbrev* masculine.

mascara *noun* a cosmetic for darkening, lengthening and thickening the eyelashes, applied with a brush. [19c: Spanish, meaning 'mask']

mascarpone /maskə'pounɪ/ *noun* a soft Italian cream cheese. [20c: Italian]

mascot *noun* a person, animal or thing thought to bring good luck and adopted for this purpose by a person, team, etc. [19c: from French *mascotte*]

masculine *adj* **1** belonging to, typical of, peculiar to or suitable for a man or the male sex; male. **2** of a woman: mannish; unfeminine. **3** *grammar* (abbrev **m.** or **masc.**) in many languages: belonging or referring to one of the **genders** into which nouns and pronouns are divided, ie that which includes most words denoting human and animal males, plus, in many languages, many other words. Compare **feminine**, **neuter**. ▸ *noun, grammar* **a** the masculine gender; **b** a word belonging to this gender. ▪ **masculinity** *noun.* [14c: from Latin *masculinus* male]

maser *noun* a device for increasing the strength of **microwaves**. Compare **laser**. [20c: acronym for *mi*crowave *a*mplification by *s*timulated *e*mission of *r*adiation]

mash *verb* (*also* **mash sth up**) to beat or crush it into a pulpy mass. ▸ *noun* (*pl* in senses 1 and 2 only ***mashes***) **1** a boiled mixture of grain and water used to feed farm animals. **2** a mixture of crushed malt and hot water, used in brewing. **3** any soft or pulpy mass. **4** *informal* mashed potatoes. ▪ **mashed** *adj.* ▪ **masher** *noun.* [Anglo-Saxon *masc-*, used in compounds]

masjid /'mʌsdʒɪd/ *noun, Islam* a mosque. [Arabic]

mask *noun* **1 a** any covering for the face or for part of the face, worn for amusement, protection or as a disguise: *Hallowe'en mask.* **b** a covering for the mouth and nose, such as an **oxygen mask**, or a **surgical mask** worn by surgeons, nurses, etc to reduce the spread of infection. **2** a pretence; anything that disguises the truth, eg false behaviour: *a mask of light-heartedness.* **3** a moulded or sculpted cast of someone's face: *death-mask.* **4** a cosmetic face pack. ▸ *verb* **1** to put a mask on someone or something. **2** to disguise, conceal or cover. **3** to protect something with a mask, or as if with a mask, from some effect or process. [16c: French]

masking tape *noun* sticky tape, used eg in painting to cover the edge of a surface to be left unpainted.

masochism /'masəkɪzəm/ *noun* **1** *psychol* the gaining of pleasure from pain or humiliation inflicted by another person. Compare **sadism.** **2** a tendency to take pleasure in one's own suffering. ▪ **masochist** *noun.* ▪ **masochistic** *adj.* [19c: named after Leopold von Sacher Masoch, Austrian novelist who described cases of it]

mason *noun* **1** a **stonemason**. **2** (**Mason**) a **Freemason**. ▪ **masonic** /mə'sɒnɪk/ ▸ *adj* (*often* **Masonic**) belonging or relating to Freemasons. [13c: from French *masson*]

masonry *noun* **1** the part of a building built by a mason; stonework and brickwork. **2** the craft of a mason.

masque /mɑːsk/ *noun, hist* in English royal courts during the 16c and 17c: a kind of dramatic entertainment performed to music by masked actors. [16c: French]

masquerade /maskə'reɪd/ *noun* **1** a pretence or false show. **2 a** a formal dance at which the guests wear masks and costumes; **b** *chiefly US* any party or gathering to which costumes or disguises are worn. **3** *chiefly US* the costume or disguise worn at a masquerade, etc; fancy dress. ▸ *verb, intr* (*esp* **masquerade as sb** *or* **sth**) **1** to disguise oneself. **2** to pretend to be someone or something else: *masquerading as a vicar.* [16c: from Spanish *mascarada*]

mass[1] *noun* **1** *physics* the amount of matter that an object contains, which is a measure of its **inertia**. **2** a large quantity, usu a shapeless quantity, gathered together; a lump. **3** (*often* **masses**) *informal* a large quantity or number: *He has masses of books.* **4** (*usu* **the mass of sth**) the majority or bulk of it. **5** *technical* a measure of the quantity of matter in a body. **6** (**the masses**) ordinary people; the people as a whole. ▸ *adj* **a** involving a large number of people: *a mass meeting* • *mass murder*; **b** belonging or relating to a mass, or to large quantities or numbers: *mass production.* ▸ *verb, chiefly intr* (*sometimes* **mass together**) to gather or form in a large quantity. See also **amass.** [14c: from French *masser*]

mass[2] *or* **Mass** *noun* **1** *Christianity* in the Roman Catholic and Orthodox Churches: **a** the **Eucharist**, a celebration of **the Last Supper**; **b** the ceremony in which this occurs. See also **High Mass**, **Low Mass.** **2** a part of the text of the Roman Catholic liturgy set to music and sung by a choir or congregation: *a requiem mass.* [Anglo-Saxon *mæsse*]

massacre /'masəkə(r)/ *noun* **1** a cruel and indiscriminate killing of large numbers of people or animals. **2** *informal* in a game, sports match, etc: an overwhelming defeat. ▸ *verb* **1** to kill (people or animals) cruelly, indiscriminately and in large numbers. **2** *informal* to defeat (the opposition or enemy, etc) overwhelmingly. [16c: French]

massage /'masɑːʒ/ *noun* **1** a technique of easing pain or stiffness in the body, esp the muscles, by rubbing, kneading and tapping with the hands. **2** a body treatment using this technique. ▸ *verb* **1** to perform massage on someone. **2** to alter something (esp statistics or other data) to produce a more favourable result. [19c: French]

masseur /ma'sɜː(r)/ *or* **masseuse** /-'sɜːz/ *noun* someone who is trained to carry out massage, esp as their profession. [19c: French]

massif /'masiːf/ *noun, geol* a mountainous plateau that differs from the surrounding lowland, usu composed of rocks that are older and harder. [19c: French]

massive *adj* **1** of physical objects: very big, bulky, solid and heavy. **2** *informal* very large; of great size or power: *a massive explosion*. ▪ **massively** *adv*. ▪ **massiveness** *noun*. [15c: from French *massif*]

mass market *noun, econ* the market for goods that have been mass-produced. ▪ **mass-marketing** *noun*.

mass media see **media**

mass noun *noun, grammar* a noun which cannot be qualified in the singular by the indefinite article and cannot be used in the plural, eg *furniture*. Compare **count noun**.

mass number *noun, chem* the total number of protons and neutrons in the nucleus of an atom.

mass-produce *verb* to produce (goods, etc) in a standard form in great quantities, esp using mechanization. ▪ **mass-produced** *adj*. ▪ **mass production** *noun*.

mass spectrograph *noun, chem, physics* a device used to give precise measurements of the atomic mass units of different isotopes of an element, by passing beams of ions through electric and magnetic fields so that they can be separated according to the ratio of their charge to their mass.

mass spectrometer *noun, chem, physics* a **mass spectrograph** used to measure the relative atomic masses of isotopes of chemical elements, and that uses an electrical detector, as opposed to a photographic plate, to determine the distribution of **ions**. ▪ **mass spectrometry** *noun*.

mast[1] *noun* any upright wooden or metal supporting pole, esp one carrying the sails of a ship, or a radio or television aerial. [Anglo-Saxon *mæst*]

IDIOMS **before the mast** *naut* serving as an apprentice seaman or ordinary sailor.

mast[2] *noun* the nuts of various forest trees, esp beech, oak and chestnut, used as food for pigs. [Anglo-Saxon *mæst*]

mastaba *noun, archaeol* an ancient Egyptian tomb built of brick or stone with sloping sides and a flat roof, having an outer area in which offerings were made, connected to a secret inner room from which a shaft led to an underground burial chamber. [17c: from Arabic *mastabah* bench]

mastectomy *noun* (**-*ies***) *surgery* the surgical removal of a woman's breast. Compare **lumpectomy**. [20c: from Greek *mastos*]

master *noun* **1** someone, esp a man, who commands or controls. **2** the owner, esp a male owner, of a dog, slave, etc. **3** someone with outstanding skill in a particular activity, eg art. **4** a fully qualified craftsman or tradesman, allowed to train and direct others. **5** *rather dated* a male teacher. Compare **mistress** (sense 2). **6** the commanding officer on a merchant ship. **7 a** (**Masters**) a degree of the level above **bachelor** (sense 2): *has a Masters in geophysics*; **b** (**Master**) someone who holds this degree: *Master of Science*. **8** (**Master**) a title for a boy too young to be called **Mr**. ▸ *adj* **1** fully qualified; highly skilled; expert. **2** main; principal: *master bedroom*. **3** controlling: *master switch*. ▸ *verb* **1** to overcome or defeat (eg feelings or an opponent). **2** to become skilled in something. [Anglo-Saxon *mægester*]

masterclass *noun* a lesson, especially in the performing arts, given to talented students by a renowned expert.

masterful *adj* showing the authority, skill or power of a master. ▪ **masterfully** *adv*. ▪ **masterfulness** *noun*.

master key *noun* a key which opens a number of different locks.

masterly *adj* showing the skill of a master.

mastermind *noun* **1** someone who has great intellectual ability. **2** the person responsible for devising a complex scheme or plan. ▸ *verb* to be the mastermind of (a scheme, etc); to originate, think out and direct something.

master of ceremonies *noun* (***masters of ceremonies***) (abbrev **MC**, or *pl* ***MCs***) an announcer, esp one who announces the speakers at a formal dinner or the performers in a stage entertainment.

masterpiece *noun* an extremely skilful piece of work, esp the greatest work of an artist or writer. Sometimes called **masterwork**.

masterstroke *noun* a very clever or well-timed action.

mastery *noun* (**-*ies***) **1** (*usu* **mastery of sth**) great skill or knowledge in it. **2** (*esp* **mastery over sb** *or* **sth**) control over them or it.

masthead *noun* **1** *naut* the top of a ship's mast. **2** *journalism* the title of a newspaper or periodical, and other information such as logo, price and place of publication, printed at the top of its front page.

mastic *noun* **1** a gum obtained from a Mediterranean evergreen tree, used in making varnish. **2** *building* a waterproof, putty-like paste used as a filler. [14c: French]

masticate *verb, tr & intr, formal or technical* to chew (food). ▪ **mastication** *noun*. [17c: from Latin *masticare* to chew]

mastiff *noun* a large powerful short-haired breed of dog. [14c: from French *mastin*]

mastitis *noun* inflammation of a woman's breast or an animal's udder. [19c: Latin]

mastodon *noun* any of several, now extinct, mammals from which elephants are thought to have evolved. [19c: from Greek *mastos* breast + *odontos* tooth, because of the teat-like prominences of its molar teeth]

mastoid *anatomy, adj* like a nipple or breast. ▸ *noun* **1** the raised area of bone behind the ear. **2** *informal* **mastoiditis**. [18c: from Greek *mastoeides* like a breast]

mastoiditis *noun* inflammation of the mastoid air cells.

masturbate *verb, tr & intr* to rub or stroke the genitals of (oneself or someone else). ▪ **masturbation** *noun*. [18c: from Latin *masturbari*]

mat *noun* **1** a flat piece of any carpet-like material, used as a decorative or protective floor-covering, for wiping shoes on to remove dirt, or absorbing impact on landing or falling in gymnastics, etc. **2** a smaller piece of fabric, or a harder material, used under a plate, vase, etc to protect a surface from heat or scratches. ▸ *verb* (***matted, matting***) *tr & intr* to become, or make something become, tangled or interwoven into a dense untidy mass. ▪ **matted** *adj* of hair: tangled. [Anglo-Saxon *matt* or *matte*]

matador *noun* the principal **toreador** who kills the bull in bullfighting. [17c: Spanish]

match[1] *noun* **1** a formal contest or game. **2** (*esp* **a match for sb** *or* **sth**) a person or thing that is similar or identical to, or combines well with, another. **3** a person or thing able to equal, or surpass, another: *met his match.* **4** a partnership or pairing; a suitable partner, eg in marriage. **5** a condition of exact agreement, compatibility or close resemblance, esp between two colours. ▸ *verb* **1** *tr & intr* (*also* **match up** *or* **match sth up**) to combine well; to be well suited, compatible or exactly alike. **2** to set (people or things) in competition; to hold them up in comparison. **3** to be equal to something; to make, produce, perform, etc an equivalent to something: *cannot match, let alone beat, the offer.* ▪ **matching** *adj.* [Anglo-Saxon *gemæcca* a mate or companion]

IDIOMS **be a match for sb** to be as good at something as them; to be as successful, strong, etc as them.

match[2] *noun* **1** a short thin piece of wood or strip of card coated on the tip with a substance that ignites when rubbed against a rough surface. **2** a slow-burning fuse used in cannons, etc. [14c: from French *mesche*]

matchbox *noun* a small cardboard box for holding matches.

matchless *adj* having no equal; superior to all.

matchmaker *noun* someone who tries to arrange romantic partnerships or marriages between people. ▪ **matchmaking** *noun, adj.*

match play *noun, golf* scoring according to holes won and lost rather than the number of strokes taken. Compare **stroke play**.

match point *noun, tennis, etc* the stage in a game at which only one more point is needed by a player to win; the winning point.

matchstick *noun* the stem of a wooden **match**[2] (sense 1). ▸ *adj* **1** very thin, like a matchstick: *matchstick legs.* **2** of figures in a drawing, etc: with limbs represented by single lines: *matchstick men.*

matchwood *noun* **1** wood suitable for making matches. **2** splinters.

mate *noun* **1** an animal's breeding partner. **2** *informal* a person's partner, esp a husband or wife. **3 a** *informal* a companion or friend; **b** used as a form of address, esp to a man: *all right, mate.* **4** *in compounds* a person someone shares something with: *workmate* • *flatmate.* **5** a tradesman's assistant: *plumber's mate.* **6** one of a pair. **7** *naut* any officer below the rank of master on a merchant ship: *first mate.* ▸ *verb* **1** *intr* of animals: to copulate. **2** to bring (male and female animals) together for breeding. **3** *tr & intr* to marry. **4** to join (two things) as a pair. [14c: related to Anglo-Saxon *gemetta* a guest at one's table]

material *noun* **1** any substance out of which something is, or may be, made. **2** cloth; fabric. **3** (**materials**) instruments or tools needed for a particular activity or task. **4** information that provides the substance from which a book, TV programme, etc is prepared. **5** someone who is suitable for a specified occupation, training, etc: *He is management material.* ▸ *adj* **1** relating to or consisting of solid matter, physical objects, etc; not abstract or spiritual: *the material world.* **2** (*usu* **material to sth**) *technical* important; significant; relevant: *facts not material to the discussion.* Compare **immaterial**. ▪ **materially** *adv.* [14c: from Latin *materialis*]

materialism *noun* **1** *often derog* excessive interest in or devotion to material possessions and financial success. **2** *philos* the theory stating that only material things exist, esp denying the existence of a soul or spirit. ▪ **materialist** *noun, adj.* ▪ **materialistic** *adj.*

materialize *or* **-ise** *verb, intr* **1** to become real, visible or tangible; to appear or take shape. **2** *loosely* to become fact; to happen. ▪ **materialization** *noun.* [18c]

matériel /mətɪərɪ'ɛl/ *noun* materials and equipment, esp for an army. [19c: French]

maternal *adj* **1** belonging to, typical of or like a mother. **2** of a relative: related on the mother's side of the family: *my maternal grandfather.* Compare **paternal**. ▪ **maternally** *adv.* [15c: from French *maternel*]

maternity *noun* **1** the state of being or becoming a mother; motherhood. **2** the qualities typical of a mother; motherliness. ▸ *adj* relating to pregnancy or giving birth: *maternity hospital* • *maternity wear.* [17c: from French *maternité*]

matey *or* **maty** *adj* (***matier, matiest***) *informal* friendly or familiar. ▸ *noun* (***mateys*** *or* ***maties***) *informal* usu used in addressing a man: friend; pal.

math *noun, N Am informal* mathematics. *Brit equivalent* **maths**.

mathematical *adj* **1** belonging or relating to, or using, mathematics. **2** of calculations, etc: very exact or accurate. ▪ **mathematically** *adv.*

mathematician *noun* someone who specializes in or studies mathematics.

mathematics *singular noun* the science dealing with measurements, numbers, quantities, and shapes, usu expressed as symbols. [16c: from Greek *mathematike* relating to learning]

maths *singular noun, Brit informal* mathematics. *N Am equivalent* **math**.

matinée *or* **matinee** /'matɪneɪ/ *noun* an afternoon performance of a play or showing of a film. [19c: French, meaning 'morning']

matinée jacket *or* **matinée coat** *noun* a baby's short jacket or coat.

matins *singular or plural noun* **1** *now esp RC Church* the first of the **canonical hours**, orig at midnight, but often now taken together with **lauds**. **2** (*also* **morning prayer**) in the Church of England: the daily morning service. Compare **evensong**. ▪ **matinal** *adj.* [13c: French]

matriarch /'meɪtrɪɑːk/ *noun* the female head of a family, community or tribe. ▪ **matriarchal** *adj.* [17c: from Latin *mater* mother, modelled on **patriarch**]

matriarchy /'meɪtrɪɑːkɪ/ *noun* (***-ies***) a social system in which women are the heads of families or tribes, and property and power passes from mother to daughter. Compare **patriarchy**.

matricide *noun* **1** the act of killing one's own mother. **2** someone who commits this act. [16c: from Latin *matricidium*]

matriculate *verb, intr* to register as a student at a university, college, etc. ▪ **matriculation** *noun.* [16c: French]

matrimony *noun* (**-ies**) *formal* **1** the state of being married. **2** the wedding ceremony. ▪ **matrimonial** *adj*. [14c: from French *matremoyne*]

matrix /ˈmeɪtrɪks/ *noun* (***matrices*** /-trɪsiːz/ *or* ***matrixes***) **1** *maths* a square or rectangular arrangement of symbols or numbers, in rows or columns, used to summarize relationships between different quantities, etc. **2** *geol* the rock in which a mineral or fossil is embedded. **3** *biol* in tissues such as bone and cartilage: the substance in which cells are embedded. **4** *anatomy* the tissue lying beneath the body and root of a fingernail or toenail, and from which it develops. **5** *printing* a mould, esp one from which printing type is produced. [16c: Latin, meaning 'womb']

matron *noun* **1** the former title of the head of the nursing staff in a hospital. Now usu called **senior nursing officer**. **2** a woman in charge of nursing and domestic arrangements in an institution such as a boarding school or old people's home. **3** any dignified, worthy or respectable middle-aged or elderly woman, esp a married one. ▪ **matronly** *adj*. [14c: French *matrone*]

matron of honour *noun* (***matrons of honour***) a married woman who is a bride's chief attendant at a wedding.

matt *or* (*sometimes*) **matte** *adj* eg of paint: having a dull surface without gloss or shine. [17c: from French *mat* a dull colour or unpolished surface]

matter *noun* **1** the substance from which all physical things are made; material. **2** material of a particular kind: *reading matter*. **3** a subject or topic; a concern, affair or question: *it's a matter of money*. **4** content, as distinct from style or form. **5** (*usu* **a matter of sth**) **a** an approximate quantity or amount of (time, etc): *I'll be there in a matter of minutes;* **b** used in saying what is involved or necessary: *It's just a matter of asking her to do it*. **6** (**the matter** *or* **the matter with sb** *or* **sth**) something that is wrong; the trouble or difficulty: *What is the matter?* **7** *med* pus or discharge. ▸ *verb intr* to be important or significant. [13c: French]

IDIOMS **a matter of opinion** something about which different people have different opinions. **as a matter of fact** in fact; actually. **for that matter** used when referring to some alternative or additional possibility, etc: as far as that is concerned. **no matter** it is not important; it makes no difference. **no matter how, what** *or* **where**, *etc* regardless of how or what, etc.

matter-of-fact *adj* calm and straightforward; not excited or emotional. ▪ **matter-of-factly** *adv*.

matting *verb, present participle of* **mat**. ▸ *noun* material of rough woven fibres used for making mats.

mattock *noun* a kind of pickaxe with a blade flattened horizontally at one end, used for breaking up soil, etc. [Anglo-Saxon *mattuc*]

mattress *noun* a large flat fabric-covered pad, now often made of foam rubber or springs, used for sleeping on, by itself or on a supporting frame. [13c: from Arabic *almatrah* a place where anything is thrown]

mature *adj* **1** fully grown or developed. **2** having or showing adult good sense, emotional and social development, etc. **3** of cheese, wine, etc: having a fully developed flavour. **4** of bonds, insurance policies, etc: paying out, or beginning to pay out, money to the holder. ▸ *verb* **1** *tr & intr* to make or become fully developed or adult in outlook. **2** *intr* of a life insurance policy, etc: to begin to produce a return. ▪ **maturation** *noun*. ▪ **maturity** *noun*. [16c: from Latin *maturus* ripe]

maty see **matey**

matzo *noun* **1** unleavened bread. **2** a wafer or cracker made of this, now usu a large, thin, square one, eaten esp during Passover, etc. [19c: from Yiddish *matse*]

maudlin *adj* esp of a drunk person: foolishly sad or sentimental. [14c: from Latin *Magdalena*, in reference to Mary Magdalene who was often portrayed weeping]

maul *verb* **1** to attack someone or something fiercely, usu tearing the flesh. **2** to handle someone or something roughly or clumsily. **3** to subject someone to fierce criticism. ▸ *noun, rugby* a quickly-formed gathering of players from both teams around a player who is holding the ball. [13c: from French *mail*]

maunder *verb, intr* **1** (*also* **maunder on**) to talk in a rambling way; to drivel. **2** to wander about, or behave, in an aimless way. ▪ **maundering** *adj*.

maundy *noun* (**-ies**) the ceremonial distribution of **Maundy money**. [13c: from French *mandé*]

Maundy money *noun, Brit* silver money that is specially minted for the sovereign to distribute on **Maundy Thursday**, the day before Good Friday.

mausoleum /mɔːsəˈlɪəm/ *noun* (***mausoleums*** *or* ***mausolea*** /-lɪə/) a grand or monumental tomb. [16c as *Mausoleum*, meaning specifically the Tomb of *Mausolus*, King of Caria]

mauve /moʊv/ *adj* pale purple in colour. ▸ *noun* this colour. [19c: French]

maverick *noun* **1** *N Am, esp US* an unbranded stray animal, esp a calf. **2** a determinedly independent person; a nonconformist. [19c: named after Samuel Maverick, a Texas cattle-raiser who left his calves unbranded]

maw *noun* the jaws, throat or stomach of a voracious animal. [Anglo-Saxon *maga*]

mawkish *adj* **1** weakly sentimental, maudlin or insipid. **2** sickly or disgusting. ▪ **mawkishly** *adv*. ▪ **mawkishness** *noun*. [17c: from obsolete *mawk* a maggot]

max. *abbrev* maximum.

IDIOMS **max out** *slang* to exhaust the limit of (a credit card, mobile-phone account, etc).

maxi *adj, often in compounds* **1** of a skirt, coat, etc: extra long; full length. **2** extra large. ▸ *noun* a maxi garment. Compare **mini**. [20c: from **maximum**]

maxilla /makˈsɪlə/ *noun* (***maxillae*** /-liː/) *biol* **1** the upper jaw or jawbone in animals. **2** the chewing organ or organs of an insect, just behind the mouth. See also **jaw** (sense 1), **jawbone**. ▪ **maxillary** *adj*. [17c: Latin, meaning 'jaw']

maxim *noun* **1** a saying that expresses a general truth. **2** a general rule or principle. [15c: from Latin *maxima propositio* or *sententia* greatest axiom or opinion]

maximal *adj* belonging or relating to a **maximum**; having the greatest possible size, value, etc.

maximize *or* **-ise** *verb* to make something as high or great, etc as possible. ▪ **maximization** *noun*. [19c: from Latin *maximus* greatest]

maximum (abbrev **max.**) *adj* greatest possible. ▸ *noun* (***maximums*** *or* ***maxima***) **1** the greatest or most; the greatest possible number, quantity, degree, etc. Also (*chiefly US informal*) called **the max**.

2 *geom* in co-ordinate geometry: the point at which the slope of a curve changes from positive to negative. [18c: from Latin *maximus* greatest]

maxwell *noun, physics* (abbrev **mx**) the **cgs unit** of magnetic flux, equal to 10^{-8} weber. [20c: named after James Clerk Maxwell, a Scottish physicist]

May *noun* the fifth month of the year. [13c: from French *Mai*]

may[1] *auxiliary verb* (*past tense* ***might***) **1** used to express permission: *You may go now.* **2** (*sometimes* **may well**) used to express a possibility: *I may come with you if I get this finished.* **3** used to express an offer: *May I help you?* **4** *formal* used to express a wish: *May you prosper!* **5** *formal & old use* used to express purpose or result: *Listen, so that you may learn.* **6** *affected, old use or facetious* used to express a question: *And who may you be?* **7** used to express the idea of 'although': *You may be rich, but you're not happy.* See also **might**[1]. [Anglo-Saxon *mæg*]

IDIOMS **be that as it may** in spite of that. **come what may** whatever happens.

---

may, can

See the Usage Note at **can**.

---

may[2] *noun* **1** the blossom of the **hawthorn** tree. Also called **mayflower**. **2** any variety of hawthorn tree. Also called **may tree**. [16c: from **May**, the month in which it usu blooms]

Maya *noun* **1** a S American people of Central America and Southern Mexico who developed a remarkable pre-Columbian civilization. **2** (*also* **Mayan**) the language of this people. **3** (*also* **Mayan**) a member of this people ▸ *adj* (*also* **Mayan**) of or relating to the Mayas.

maybe *adv* it is possible; perhaps. ▸ *noun* a possibility.

May Day *noun* the first day of May, a national holiday in many countries, on which labour demonstrations are held, and traditionally a day of festivities.

mayday *or* **Mayday** *noun* the international radio distress signal sent out by ships and aircraft. [20c: a phonetic representation of French *m'aider* help me]

mayfly *noun* (***-ies***) a short-lived insect with transparent wings, which appears briefly in spring.

mayhem *noun* **1** a state of great confusion and disorder; chaos. **2** *US & formerly law* the crime of maiming someone. [15c: from French *mahaignier* to wound]

mayn't *contraction, informal* may not.

mayonnaise *noun, cookery* a cold, creamy sauce made of egg yolk, oil, vinegar or lemon juice and seasoning. Sometimes (*informal*) shortened to **mayo**. [19c: French]

mayor *noun* **1** in England, Wales and N Ireland: the head of the local council in a city, town or borough. Compare **provost**. **2** in other countries: the head of any of various communities. ▪ **mayoral** *adj*. [13c: from French *maire*]

mayoress *noun* **1** a mayor's wife. **2** *old use* a female mayor.

maypole *noun* a tall, decorated pole traditionally set up for dancing round on **May Day**.

maze *noun* **1** a confusing network of paths bordered by high walls or hedges, laid out in a garden as a puzzling diversion in which a person might become lost or disorientated. **2** any confusingly complicated system, procedure, etc. [14c: related to **amaze**]

mazel tov /ˈmazəl toʊv, ˈmazəl tov/ *exclam* an expression conveying congratulations or best wishes. [19c: Yiddish, from Hebrew *mazzal tobh* good luck]

mazurka *noun* **1** a lively Polish dance in triple time. **2** a piece of music for this dance. [19c: Polish, meaning 'a woman from Mazovia', a province in Poland]

MB *abbrev, comput* megabyte.

mbar *abbrev* millibar or millibars.

MBE *abbrev* Member of the Order of the British Empire.

Mbit *abbrev, comput* megabit(s).

MC *abbrev* **1** master of ceremonies. **2** *US* Member of Congress.

McCarthyism *noun* the policy of finding people suspected of having links with communism and removing them all from public employment. [20c: named after US senator Joseph R McCarthy]

MD *abbrev* managing director.

Md *symbol, chem* mendelevium.

MDF *abbrev* medium density fibreboard, a strong **fibreboard** used in furniture and house-building.

ME *abbrev* **1** Middle English. **2** *med* myalgic encephalomyelitis.

me[1] *pron* **1** the object form of **I**[2], used by a speaker or writer to refer to himself or herself: *asked me a question.* **2** used for *I* after the verb **be** or when standing alone: *It's only me.* [Anglo-Saxon]

---

me, I

After a preposition, you should always use the word **me** (rather than **I**) as the object:

✓ *between you and me*

✗ *between you and I*

✓ *for John and me*

✗ *for John and I*

If you are not sure, try the phrase without the *you*, and you will see that *between I* and *for I* are wrong.

---

me[2] *or* **mi** *noun, music* in sol-fa notation: the third note of the major scale. [16c: see **sol-fa**]

mea culpa /meɪə ˈkʊlpə/ *exclam, literary or facetious* as an acknowledgement of one's own guilt or mistake: I am to blame. [14c: Latin, literally 'by my fault']

mead[1] *noun* an alcoholic drink made by fermenting honey and water, usu with spices added. [Anglo-Saxon *meodu*]

mead[2] *noun, poetic or old use* a meadow. [Anglo-Saxon *mæd*]

meadow *noun* **1** a low-lying field of grass, used for grazing animals or making hay. **2** any moist, grassy area near a river. [Anglo-Saxon *mædwe*]

meagre *or* (*US*) **meager** *adj* **1** lacking in quality or quantity; inadequate. **2** of a person: thin, esp unhealthily so. ▪ **meagrely** *adv*. ▪ **meagreness** *noun*. [14c: from French *maigre* thin]

meal[1] *noun* **1** an occasion on which food is eaten, eg lunch, supper, dinner, etc. **2** an amount of food eaten on one such occasion. [Anglo-Saxon *mæl*, meaning 'a measure' or 'a portion of time']

IDIOMS **make a meal of sth** *informal* to exaggerate the importance of it.

meal[2] *noun, often in compounds* **1** the edible parts of any grain, usu excluding wheat, ground to a coarse powder: *oatmeal*. **2** any other food substance in ground form: *bone meal*. ▪ **mealy** *adj* (***-ier, -iest***). [Anglo-Saxon *melo*]

meals-on-wheels *singular noun, Brit* a welfare service by which cooked meals are delivered by car, etc to the homes of old or sick people.

meal ticket *noun* **1** *informal* a person or situation that provides a source of income or other means of living. **2** *N Am, esp US* a **luncheon voucher**.

mealy-mouthed *adj, derog* of a person: afraid to speak plainly or openly; not frank or sincere.

mean[1] *verb* (***meant***) **1** to express or intend to express, show or indicate something. **2** to intend something; to have it as a purpose: *didn't mean any harm*. **3** to be serious or sincere about something: *He means what he says*. **4** to be important to the degree specified; to represent something: *Your approval means a lot to me*. **5** to entail something necessarily; to involve or result in it: *War means hardship*. **6** to foretell or portend something: *Cold cloudless evenings mean overnight frost*. [Anglo-Saxon *mænan*]

IDIOMS **be meant for sth** to be destined to it. **mean well** to have good intentions.

mean[2] *adj* **1** not generous. **2** low; despicable. **3** poor; shabby; characterized by inferior quality. **4** *informal, esp N Am* vicious; malicious; bad-tempered. **5** *informal* good; skilful: *plays a mean guitar*. ▪ **meanly** *adv*. ▪ **meanness** *noun*. [Anglo-Saxon *gemæne* low in rank or birth, common]

IDIOMS **no mean sth** *informal* **1** an excellent one: *He's no mean singer*. **2** not an easy one; a very difficult one: *That was no mean feat*.

mean[3] *adj* **1** midway; intermediate. **2** average. ▸ *noun* **1** a midway position or course, etc between two extremes. **2** *maths, stats* a mathematical **average**, in particular: **a** the average value of a set of numbers. Also called **arithmetic mean**; **b** the average value of a set of *n* numbers, also taking into account their frequency, by multiplying each number by the number of times it occurs, summing the resulting values and dividing them by *n*. Also called **weighted mean**; **c** the *n*th root of the product of *n* quantities or numbers, eg the geometric mean of 2 and 3 is the second (square) root of 6. Also called **geometric mean**. Compare **median** (sense 3), **mode** (sense 5). [14c: from French *meien*]

meander /mɪ'andə(r)/ *verb, intr* **1** of a river: to bend and curve. **2** (*also* **meander about**) to wander randomly or aimlessly. ▸ *noun* (*often* **meanders**) **1** a bend, esp in a winding river. **2** a winding course. [16c: from Latin *Maeander*]

meanie *or* **meany** *noun* (***-ies***) *informal* **1** a selfish or ungenerous person. **2** *esp N Am* a malicious or bad-tempered person.

meaning *noun* **1** the sense in which a statement, action, word, etc is intended to be understood. **2** significance, importance or purpose, esp when hidden or special.

meaningful *adj* **1** having meaning; significant. **2** full of significance; expressive. ▪ **meaningfully** *adv*.

meaningless *adj* **1** without meaning or reason. **2** having no importance. **3** having no purpose; pointless. ▪ **meaninglessly** *adv*.

means *singular or plural noun* **1** the instrument or method used to achieve some object. **2** wealth; resources.

IDIOMS **a means to an end** something treated merely as a way of achieving a desired result, considered unimportant in every other respect. **by all means** *rather formal* yes, of course. **by any means** using any available method. **by means of sth** with the help or use of it. **by no means** *or* **not by any means** not at all; definitely not.

means test *noun* an official inquiry into someone's wealth or income to determine their eligibility for financial benefit from the state.

meant *past tense, past participle of* **mean**[1]

meantime *noun* (*esp* **in the meantime**) the time or period in between; the intervening time. ▸ *adv* **meanwhile**.

meanwhile *adv* **1** during the time in between. **2** at the same time.

measles *singular noun* a highly infectious viral disease characterized by fever, a sore throat and a blotchy red rash. See also **German measles**. [14c]

measly *adj* (***-ier, -iest***) **1** *derog, informal* of an amount, value, etc: very small; miserable; paltry. **2** relating to, or suffering from, measles. ▪ **measliness** *noun*.

measurable *adj* **1** able to be measured. **2** noticeable; significant. ▪ **measurably** *adv*.

measure *noun* **1** size, volume, etc determined by comparison with something of known size, etc, usu an instrument graded in standard units. **2** such an instrument for taking a measurement of something. **3** a standard unit of size, etc; a standard amount: *a measure of whisky*. **4** a system of such units: *metric measure*. **5** (*usu* **measures**) an action; a step: *We must take drastic measures*. **6** a limited, or appropriate, amount or extent: *a measure of politeness*. **7** an enactment or bill. **8** *music* time or rhythm; a bar. **9** *poetry* rhythm or metre. ▸ *verb* **1** *tr & intr* (*often* **measure sth up**) to determine the size, volume, etc of, usu with a specially made instrument or by comparing it to something else. **2** *intr* to be a specified size. **3** (*also* **measure off sth** *or* **measure sth off** *or* **out**) to mark or divide something into units of a given size, etc. **4** to set something in competition with something else: *measure his strength against mine*. ▪ **measuring** *noun*. [13c: from Latin *mensura*]

IDIOMS **for good measure** as something extra, or above the minimum necessary.

PHRASAL VERBS **measure up to sth** to reach the required standard; to be adequate.

measured *adj* **1** slow and steady. **2** carefully chosen or considered: *a measured response*. ▪ **measuredly** *adv*.

measurement *noun* **1** (*often* **measurements**) a size, amount, etc determined by measuring: *measurements for the new bedroom carpet*. **2** (*often* **measurements**) the size of a part of the body. **3** the act of measuring. **4** a standard system of measuring.

meat *noun* **1** the flesh of any animal used as food. **2** the basic or most important part; the essence. ▪ **meatless** *adj*. [Anglo-Saxon *mete*]

meatball *noun, cookery* a small ball of minced meat mixed with breadcrumbs and seasonings.

meat loaf *noun* a loaf-shaped food made from chopped or minced meat, seasoning, etc, cooked and usu eaten cold in slices.

meaty *adj* (***-ier, -iest***) **1** full of, or containing, meat. **2** resembling or tasting like meat, esp cooked meat. **3** full of interesting information or ideas.

mecca *or* **Mecca** *noun* any place of outstanding importance or significance to a particular group of people, esp one which they feel they have to visit.

mech. *abbrev* **1** mechanical. **2** mechanics.

mechanic *noun* a skilled worker who repairs, maintains or constructs machinery.

mechanical *adj* **1** belonging to or concerning machines or mechanics. **2** worked by, or performed with, machinery or a mechanism. **3** of an action or movement, etc: done without or not requiring much thought. ▪ **mechanically** *adv.* [15c: from Latin *mechanicus*]

mechanical engineering *noun* the branch of engineering concerned with the design, construction and operation of machines of all types.

mechanician *noun* someone skilled in constructing machines and tools.

mechanics *singular noun* **1** the branch of physics that deals with the motion of bodies and the forces that act on them. **2** the art or science of machine construction. ▸ *plural noun* **1** the system on which something works. **2** *informal* routine procedures.

mechanism *noun* **1** a working part of a machine or its system of working parts. **2** the arrangements and action by which something is produced or achieved; the process. **3** *psychol* an action that serves some purpose, often a subconscious purpose: *laughter is a common defence mechanism.* ▪ **mechanistic** *adj.* [17c: from Latin *mechanismus*]

mechanize *or* **-ise** *verb* **1** to change (the production of something, a procedure, etc) from a manual to a mechanical process. **2** *military* to provide (troops etc) with armoured armed vehicles. ▪ **mechanization** *noun.*

med. *abbrev* **1** medical. **2** medicine. **3** medieval. **4** medium.

medal *noun* a flat piece of metal decorated with a design or inscription and awarded, eg to a soldier, sportsperson, etc, or produced in celebration of a special occasion. ▪ **medallist** *noun, sport* someone who is awarded a medal. [16c: from French *médaille*]

medallion *noun* **1** a large medal-like piece of jewellery, usu worn on a chain. **2** in architecture or on textiles: an oval or circular decorative feature. **3** *cookery* a thin circular cut of meat. [17c: from French *médaillon*]

MEDC *abbrev* More Economically Developed Country.

meddle *verb, intr* **1** (*usu* **meddle in sth**) to interfere in it. **2** (*usu* **meddle with sth**) to tamper with it. ▪ **meddler** *noun.* ▪ **meddlesome** *adj, derog* fond of meddling. ▪ **meddling** *noun, adj.* [14c: from French *medler*]

media *pl of* **medium**. ▸ *singular or plural noun* (*usu* **the media** *or* **the mass media**) the means by which news and information, etc is communicated to the public, usu considered to be TV, radio and the press collectively.

---

media

The word **media** in the sense of newspapers and broadcasting is still used most often as a plural noun, which takes a plural verb:

✓ *The media are sometimes criticized for their focus on violence.*

However, if you want to emphasize the idea of the media as a single unit, you can use the word as a singular noun, which takes a singular verb:

These people have fears which the media has played on over the years.
The media may slant its coverage.

---

mediaeval, **mediaevalism, mediaevalist** a less common spelling of **medieval**, etc.

medial /ˈmiːdɪəl/ *adj, technical* belonging to or situated in the middle; intermediate. ▪ **medially** *adv.* [16c: from Latin *medialis*]

median /ˈmiːdɪən/ *noun* **1** a middle point or part. **2** *geom* a straight line between any **vertex** of a triangle and the centre of the opposite side. **3** *stats* **a** the middle value in a set of numbers or measurements arranged from smallest to largest, eg the median of 1, 5 and 11 is 5; **b** of an even number of measurements: the **average** of the middle two measurements. Compare **mean**[3] (sense 2a), **mode** (sense 5). ▸ *adj* (*also* **medial**) **1** situated in or passing through the middle. **2** *stats* belonging or relating to the median. [16c: from Latin *medianus*]

mediate /ˈmiːdɪeɪt/ *verb, intr* **1 a** to act as the agent seeking to reconcile the two sides in a disagreement; **b** to intervene in or settle (a dispute) in this way. **2** to hold an intermediary position. ▪ **mediation** *noun.* ▪ **mediator** *noun.* [16c: from Latin *mediatus*]

medic *noun, informal* a doctor or medical student.

medical *adj* **1** belonging or relating to doctors or the science or practice of medicine. **2** concerned with medicine, or treatment by medicine, rather than surgery. ▸ *noun* a medical examination to discover a person's physical health. ▪ **medically** *adv.* [17c: from French *médical*]

medical certificate *noun* **1** a certificate outlining a person's state of health, provided by a doctor who has carried out a medical examination on them. **2** a certificate from a doctor stating that a person is, or has been, unfit for work.

Medical Officer *or* **medical officer** *noun* (abbrev **MO**) in the armed services, etc: a doctor in charge of medical treatment.

medicament /məˈdɪkəmənt/ *noun, formal* a medicine. [16c: from Latin *medicamentum*]

medicate *verb* **1** to treat someone with medicine. **2** to add a healing or health-giving substance to something. ▪ **medication** *noun.* [17c: from Latin *medicare* to cure]

medicinal /məˈdɪsɪnəl/ *adj* having healing qualities; used as a medicine. ▪ **medicinally** *adv.*

medicine *noun* **1** any substance used to treat or prevent disease or illness, esp one taken internally. **2** the science or practice of treating or preventing illness, esp using prepared substances rather than surgery. **3** in primitive societies: something regarded as magical or curative. [13c: from French *medecine*]

IDIOMS **have** *or* **get a taste** *or* **dose of one's own medicine** to suffer the same unpleasant treatment that one has given to other people.

medicine man *noun* a person believed to have magic powers, used for healing or sorcery.

medico- *combining form, denoting* medicine or medical matters: *medico-legal.*

medieval *or (less commonly)* **mediaeval** *adj* **1** belonging or relating to, or characteristic of, **the Middle Ages**. **2** *derog, informal* extremely old and primitive. ▪ **medievalist** *noun*. [19c: from Latin *medius* middle + *aevum* age]

mediocre /miːdɪ'oʊkə(r)/ *adj* only ordinary or average; rather inferior. ▪ **mediocrity** /miːdɪ'ɒkrɪtɪ/ *noun* (**-*ies***). [16c: from French *médiocre*]

meditate *verb* **1** *intr* to spend time in deep religious or spiritual thought, often with the mind in a practised state of emptiness. **2** (*often* **meditate about** *or* **on sth**) to think deeply and carefully about something; to reflect upon it. ▪ **meditative** *adj*. [16c: from Latin *meditari* to reflect upon]

meditation *noun* **1** the act or process of meditating. **2** deep thought; contemplation, esp on a spiritual or religious theme.

Mediterranean *adj* **1** in, belonging or relating to the area of the Mediterranean Sea, a large inland sea lying between S Europe, N Africa and SW Asia. **2** characteristic of this area. **3** of a human physical type: of slight to medium stature and with a dark complexion. [16c: from Latin *mediterraneus*]

medium *noun* (*pl* in all senses except 2 and 5 ***mediums*** or, in all senses except 3, ***media***) **1** something by or through which an effect is produced. **2** see **media**. **3** someone through whom the spirits of dead people are said to communicate with the living. **4** *art* a particular category of materials seen as a means of expression, eg watercolours, photography or clay. **5** *comput* (*usu* **media**) any material on which data is recorded, eg magnetic disk. **6** *biol* a **culture medium**. **7** a middle position, condition or course: a *happy medium*. ▸ *adj* **1** intermediate; midway; average. **2** moderate. **3** of meat, esp steak: cooked through so that it is not bloody when cut open. Compare **rare²**, **well-done**. [16c: Latin, from *medius* middle]

medium wave *noun* a radio wave with a wavelength between 200 and 1000 metres. Compare **long wave, short wave**.

medlar *noun* a small brown apple-like fruit eaten only when already decaying. [14c: from French *medler*]

medley *noun* (**-*eys***) **1** a piece of music made up of pieces from other songs, tunes, etc. **2** a mixture or miscellany. **3** a race in stages with each stage a different length or, in swimming, with each stage swum using a different stroke. [15c: from French *medlee*]

medulla /mɛ'dʌlə/ *noun* (***medullae*** /-liː/ *or* ***medullas***) **1** *biol* the central part of an organ or tissue, when this differs in structure or function from the outer layer, eg the pith of a plant stem. **2** *anatomy* the **medulla oblongata**. [17c: Latin, meaning 'pith']

medulla oblongata /mɛ'dʌlə ɒblɒŋ'gɑːtə/ *noun* (***medullae oblongatae*** /-liː -tiː/ *or* ***medulla oblongatas***) *anatomy* in vertebrates: the part of the brain that arises from the spinal cord and forms the lower part of the brainstem. [17c: Latin, meaning 'oblong marrow']

medusa /mə'djuːzə, -sə/ *noun* (***medusas*** *or* ***medusae*** /-siː/) *zool* a free-swimming, disc-shaped or bell-shaped organism with marginal tentacles, being the sexually-reproducing stage in the life cycle of a jellyfish. [18c: from Latin *Medusa*]

meek *adj* **1** having a mild and gentle temperament. **2** submissive. ▪ **meekly** *adv*. [13c: from Norse *mjukr* soft, gentle]

meerkat *noun* any of several species of mongoose-like carnivores native to S Africa. [15c in obsolete sense 'monkey']

meerschaum /'mɪəʃəm, -ʃaʊm/ *noun* **1** a fine, whitish, clay-like mineral. **2** a tobacco pipe with a bowl made of this. [18c: German, from *Meer* sea + *Schaum* foam]

meet¹ *verb* (***met***) **1** *tr & intr* to be introduced to someone for the first time. **2** *tr & intr* **a** (*also* **meet up with sb** *or US* **meet with sb**) to come together with them by chance or by arrangement; **b** of two people, groups, etc: to come together, either by chance or arrangement. **3** to be present at the arrival of (a vehicle, etc): *met the train*. **4** *tr & intr* (*often* **meet with sth**) to come into opposition against it: *My plan met with fierce resistance*. **5** *tr & intr* to join; to come into contact with something: *where the path meets the road*. **6** to satisfy: *meet your requirements*. **7** to pay: *meet costs*. **8** to come into the view, experience or presence of something: *the sight that met my eyes*. **9** (*also* **meet with sth**) to encounter or experience it: *met with disaster*. **10** (*also* **meet with sth**) to receive it: *My suggestions met with approval*. ▸ *noun* **1** the assembly of hounds and huntsmen and huntswomen before a fox hunt begins. **2** a sporting event, esp a series of athletics competitions. [Anglo-Saxon *metan*]

IDIOMS **more than meets the eye** *or* **ear** more complicated, interesting, etc than it first appears or sounds.

meet² *adj, old use* proper, correct or suitable. ▪ **meetly** *adv*. [Anglo-Saxon *gemæte*]

meeting *noun* **1** an act of coming together. **2** an assembly or gathering at a prearranged time, usu to discuss specific topics. **3** a sporting event, esp an athletics or horse-racing event: *race meeting*.

meg *noun, comput* short for **megabyte**.

mega *adj, informal* excellent.

mega- *combining form, denoting* **1** (symbol **M**) a million: *megawatt*. **2** (*also* **megalo-**) large or great. **3** *informal* great: *megastar*. [From Greek *megas, megal-* big]

megabit *noun, comput* a measure of computer data or memory, approximately 2^{20} (one million) bits (abbrev **Mbit**).

megabuck *noun, N Am informal* **1** a million dollars. **2** (*usu* ***megabucks***) a huge sum of money.

megabyte *noun, comput* a unit of storage capacity equal to 2^{20} or 1,048,576 bytes (abbrev **mbyte** *or* **MB**).

megadeath *noun* death of a million people, used as a unit in estimating casualties in nuclear war.

megahertz *noun* (*pl* ***megahertz***) (symbol **MHz**) a unit of frequency equal to one million hertz. Formerly called **megacycle**.

megalith *noun, archaeol* a very large stone, esp one that forms part of a prehistoric monument. See also **cromlech**. ▪ **megalithic** *adj*.

megalo- see under **mega-**

megalomania *noun* **1** *med* a mental condition characterized by an exaggerated sense of power and self-importance. **2** *informal* greed for power. ▪ **megalomaniac** *noun, adj*. [19c]

megaphone *noun* a funnel-shaped device which, when someone speaks into it, amplifies the voice.

megastore *noun* a very large shop, esp any of the large chain stores.

megaton *noun* **1** a unit of measurement of weight, equal to one million tons. **2** a unit of explosive power equal to one million tons of TNT.

meiosis /maɪ'oʊsɪs/ *noun* (***-ses*** /-siːz/) *biol* a type of cell division in which four daughter nuclei are produced, each containing half the number of chromosomes of the parent nucleus and resulting in the formation of male and female **gamete**s. Also called **reduction**. Compare **mitosis**. ▪ **meiotic** /maɪ'ɒtɪk/ *adj*. [20c: from Greek *meion* less]

meitnerium /maɪt'nɛərɪəm/ *noun, chem* (symbol **Mt**) an artificially manufactured radioactive chemical element. [20c: named after the Austrian physicist Lise Meitner]

mela *noun, Hinduism, Sikhism* a festival or fair. [Hindi]

melamine *noun, chem* a white crystalline organic compound used to form artificial resins (**melamine resin**s) that are resistant to heat, water and many chemicals. [19c: from German *Melamin*]

melancholia /mɛlən'koʊlɪə/ *noun, old use* mental depression. [17c: Latin]

melancholy /'mɛlənkɒlɪ, -kəlɪ/ *noun* (***-ies***) **1** a tendency to be gloomy or depressed. **2** prolonged sadness. **3** a sad, pensive state of mind. ▸ *adj* sad; causing or expressing sadness. ▪ **melancholic** /mɛlən'kɒlɪk/ *adj*. [14c: from Greek *melancholia*]

Melanesian *adj* belonging or relating to Melanesia, a group of islands NE of Australia, its inhabitants or their languages. ▸ *noun* **1** a citizen or inhabitant of, or person born in, Melanesia. **2** a group of languages spoken in Melanesia, or one of these languages. [19c: from *melano-* , from Greek *melas, melanos* black, because the dominant race in these islands is dark-skinned]

melange *or* **mélange** /meɪ'lɑːnʒ; *French* melɑ̃ʒ/ *noun* a mixture, esp a varied or confused one. [17c: French]

melanin *noun, physiol, chem* the black or dark brown pigment found to varying degrees in the skin, hair and eyes of humans and animals. [19c]

melanoma *noun* (***melanomas*** *or* ***melanomata***) *med* a cancerous tumour, usu of the skin, that may spread to other parts of the body. [19c: Latin]

meld *verb, tr & intr* to merge or blend. [20c]

melee *or* **mêlée** /'mɛleɪ/ *noun* **1** a riotous brawl involving large numbers of people. **2** any confused or muddled collection. [17c: French *mêlée*]

mellifluous /mɪ'lɪflʊəs/ *or* **mellifluent** /-flʊənt/ *adj* of sounds, speech, etc: having a smooth sweet flowing quality. [15c: from Latin *mel* honey + *fluere* to flow]

mellow *adj* **1** of a person or their character: calm and relaxed with age or experience. **2** of sound, colour, light, etc: soft, rich and pure. **3** of wine, cheese, etc: fully flavoured with age; well matured. **4** of fruit: sweet and ripe. **5** of a person: pleasantly relaxed or warm-hearted through being slightly drunk or affected by a recreational drug. ▸ *verb, tr & intr* to make or become mellow. ▪ **mellowness** *noun*. [15c: perhaps from Anglo-Saxon *mearu* soft or tender]

melodeon *or* **melodion** *noun* **1** a small reed-organ; a harmonium. **2** a kind of accordion. [19c: German *Melodion*]

melodic *adj* **1** relating or belonging to melody. **2** pleasant-sounding; tuneful; melodious. ▪ **melodically** *adv*.

melodious *adj* **1** pleasant to listen to; tuneful. **2** having a recognizable melody. ▪ **melodiousness** *noun*.

melodrama *noun* **1** a play or film containing sensational events, and also usu appealing to the emotions. **2** *derog* excessively dramatic behaviour. ▪ **melodramatic** *adj*. [19c: from French *mélodrame*]

melody *noun* (***-ies***) **1** *music* the sequence of single notes forming the core of a tune. **2** pleasantness of sound; tuneful music. **3** esp in poetry: pleasant arrangement or combination of sounds. [13c: from Greek *melodia*]

melon *noun* **1** any of several plants of the gourd family, cultivated for their fruits. **2** the large rounded edible fruit of any of these plants, which generally have a thick skin, sweet juicy flesh and many seeds. [14c: French]

melt *verb, tr & intr* **1** (*sometimes* **melt down** *or* **melt sth down**) to make or become soft or liquid, esp through the action of heat; to dissolve (something solid). **2** (*often* **melt into sth**) to combine or fuse, or make something combine or fuse with something else, causing a loss of distinctness. **3** (*also* **melt away** *or* **melt sth away**) to disappear or make something disappear or disperse: *support for the scheme melted away.* **4** *informal* to make or become emotionally or romantically tender or submissive: *Her smile melted my heart.* ▸ *noun* **1** the act of melting. **2** the quantity or material melted. ▪ **melting** *noun, adj*. ▪ **meltingly** *adv*. [Anglo-Saxon *meltan*]

IDIOMS **melt in the mouth** of food: to be especially delicious, eg in lightness of texture.

PHRASAL VERBS **melt down** to turn (metal, or metal articles) to a liquid state so that the raw material can be reused.

meltdown *noun, informal* a major disaster or failure.

melting point *noun* (abbrev **mp**) the temperature at which a particular substance changes from a solid to a liquid.

melting pot *noun* a place or situation in which varying beliefs, ideas, cultures, etc come together.

member *noun* **1** someone who belongs to a group or organization. **2** (*often* **Member**) an elected representative of a governing body, eg a Member of Parliament, or of a local council, etc. **3** a part of a whole, esp a limb of an animal or a petal of a plant. **4** a plant or animal belonging to a specific class or group. [13c: from French *membre*]

Member of Parliament *noun* (abbrev **MP**) **1** in the UK: a person elected to represent the people of a **constituency** in the House of Commons. Sometimes shortened to **Member**. **2** (*also* **member of parliament**) a person elected to a legislative assembly in various countries. See also **MEP**.

membership *noun* **1** the state of being a member. **2 a** the members of an organization collectively; **b** the number of members.

membrane *noun* **1** a thin sheet of tissue that lines a body cavity or surrounds a body part, organ, etc. **2** *biol* a thin layer of lipid and protein molecules that forms the boundary between a cell and its surroundings. Also called **cell membrane, plasma membrane.** ▪ **membranous** *adj*. [17c: from Latin *membrana* the skin of the body]

memento *noun* (***mementos*** or ***mementoes***) a thing that serves as a reminder of the past; a souvenir. [15c: Latin]

memento mori /mə'mɛntoʊ 'mɔriː/ *noun* an object intended as a reminder of the inevitability of death. [Latin, literally 'Remember that you must die']

memo *contraction* a short note. [19c: shortened from **memorandum**]

memoir /'mɛmwɑː(r)/ *noun* **1** a written record of events in the past, esp one based on personal experience. **2** (*usu* **memoirs**) a person's written account of his or her own life; an autobiography. [16c: from French *mémoire* memory]

memorabilia *plural noun* souvenirs of people or events. [19c: Latin, meaning 'memorable things']

memorable *adj* worth remembering; easily remembered. [15c: from Latin *memorabilis*]

memorandum *noun* (***memorandums*** or ***memoranda***) **1** a written statement or record, esp one circulated for the attention of colleagues at work. **2** a note of something to be remembered. **3** *law* a brief note of some transaction, recording the terms, etc. [15c: Latin, meaning 'a thing to be remembered']

memorial *noun* a thing that honours or commemorates a person or an event, eg a statue or monument. ▸ *adj* **1** serving to preserve the memory of a person or event: *a memorial fund*. **2** relating to or involving memory. [14c: from Latin *memoriale* reminder]

memorize *or* **-ise** *verb* to learn something thoroughly, so as to be able to reproduce it exactly from memory.

memory *noun* (***-ies***) **1** the ability of the mind to remember. **2** the mind's store of remembered events, impressions, knowledge and ideas. **3** the mental processes of memorizing information, retaining it, and recalling it on demand. **4** any such impression reproduced in the mind: *have no memory of the event*. **5** *comput* the part of a computer that is used to store data and programs. Also called **store**. **6** the limit in the past beyond which one's store of mental impressions does not extend: *not within my memory*. **7** the act of remembering; commemoration: *in memory of old friends*. **8** reputation after death: *Her memory lives on*. [14c: from French *memorie*]

memsahib /'mɛmsɑːɪb/ *noun, formerly* in India: a married European woman. Also used as a polite form of address. [19c: from **ma'am** + **sahib**]

men *pl of* **man**

menace *noun* **1** a source of threatening danger. **2** a threat; a show of hostility. **3** *informal* something or someone that is very annoying. ▸ *verb, tr & intr* to threaten; to show an intention to damage or harm someone. ▪ **menacing** *adj*. [14c: from French]

ménage /meɪ'nɑːʒ; *French* menɑːʒ/ *noun, literary* a household. [13c: French]

ménage à trois /*French* menɑːʒ a trwɑ/ *noun* (***ménages à trois***) an arrangement consisting of three people, esp a husband, a wife and the lover of one of them. [19c: literally 'household of three']

menagerie /mə'nadʒərɪ/ *noun* **a** a collection of wild animals caged for exhibition; **b** the place where they are kept. [18c: from French *ménagerie*]

menarche /mɛ'nɑːkɪ/ *noun, physiol* the first menstruation. [20c: from Greek *men* month + *arche* beginning]

mend *verb* **1** to repair something. **2** *intr* to heal or recover. **3** to improve or correct something: *mend one's ways*. ▸ *noun* on a garment, etc: a repaired part or place. [13c: shortened from **amend**]

IDIOMS **on the mend** getting better, esp in health.

mendacious *adj* lying, or likely to lie. ▪ **mendaciously** *adv*. [17c: from Latin *menitiri* to lie]

mendacity *noun* (***-ies***) *formal* **1** untruthfulness; the tendency to lie. **2** a lie or falsehood.

mendelevium *noun, chem* (symbol **Md**) an artificially produced radioactive metallic element. [20c: named after Dmitri I Mendeleyev, Russian chemist]

mendicant *noun* **1** a monk who is a member of an order that is not allowed to own property and is therefore entirely dependent on charity. **2** *formal* a beggar. ▸ *adj* **1** dependent on charity. **2** *formal* begging. [14c: from Latin *mendicare* to beg]

menfolk *plural noun* men collectively, esp the male members of a particular group, family, etc.

menhir /'mɛnhɪə(r)/ *noun* a prehistoric monument in the form of a single upright standing stone. [19c: French]

menial /'miːnɪəl/ *adj* of work: unskilled, uninteresting and of low status. ▸ *noun, derog* a domestic servant. [15c: French]

meninges /mɛ'nɪndʒiːz/ *plural noun* (*singular* ***meninx*** /'mɛnɪŋks/) *anatomy* the three membranes that cover the brain and spinal cord. ▪ **meningeal** *adj*. [17c: Latin]

meningitis /mɛnɪn'dʒaɪtɪs/ *noun, pathol* inflammation of the **meninges**, usu caused by bacterial or viral infection, the main symptoms being severe headache, fever, stiffness of the neck and aversion to light. [19c]

meniscus /mə'nɪskəs/ *noun* (***meniscuses*** or ***menisci*** /-skaɪ, -saɪ/) **1** *physics* the curved upper surface of a liquid in a partly-filled narrow tube, caused by the effects of surface tension. **2** *anatomy* a crescent-shaped structure, such as the disc of cartilage in the knee joint. **3** *optics* a lens that is convex on one side and concave on the other. [17c: Latin]

menopause *noun* the period in a woman's life, typically between the ages of 45 and 55, when menstruation ceases and pregnancy is no longer possible. Also called **change of life, the change.** ▪ **menopausal** *adj*. [19c: from French *ménopause*]

menorah /mə'nɔːrə/ *noun* a candelabrum with seven branches regarded as a symbol of Judaism. [19c: Hebrew, meaning 'candlestick']

menses /'mɛnsiːz/ *plural noun, biol, med* **1** the fluids discharged from the womb during menstruation. **2** the time of menstruation. [16c: Latin, pl of *mensis* month]

menstrual *adj* relating to or involving menstruation.

menstrual cycle *noun, biol* the cycle during which ovulation and menstruation occurs, happening about once in every 28 days in humans.

menstruate *verb, intr, biol* to discharge blood and other fluids from the womb through the vagina during menstruation. [17c: from Latin *menstruare*]

menstruation *noun, biol* **1** in women of childbearing age: the discharge through the vagina of blood and fragments of mucous membrane, that takes place at approximately monthly intervals if fertilization of an **ovum** has not occurred. **2** the time or occurrence of menstruating.

mensuration *noun* **1** *technical* the application of geometric principles to the calculation of measurements such as length, volume and area. **2** *formal* the process of measuring. [16c: from Latin *mensurare* to measure]

menswear *noun* clothing for men.

-ment *suffix, forming nouns, denoting* **1** a process, action, result or means: *repayment* • *treatment*. **2** a quality, state or condition: *enjoyment* • *merriment*. [From Latin *-mentum*]

mental *adj* **1** belonging or relating to, or done by using, the mind or intelligence: *mental arithmetic*. **2** *old use* belonging to, or suffering from, an illness or illnesses of the mind: *a mental patient*. **3** *informal* foolish; stupid. **4** *informal* ridiculous; unimaginable. ▪ **mentally** *adv.* [15c: French]

mental age *noun, psychol* the age at which an average child would have reached the same stage of mental development as the individual in question: *He is 33, with a mental age of 10.*

mental handicap *noun* a condition in which a person has impaired intellectual abilities, typically with an IQ of less than 70, and suffers from some form of social malfunction due to a congenital condition, brain damage, etc.

mentality *noun* (***-ies***) **1** an outlook; a certain way of thinking. **2** intellectual ability.

menthol *noun* a sharp-smelling substance obtained from peppermint oil, used as a decongestant and a painkiller. ▪ **mentholated** *adj.* [19c: German]

mention *verb* **1** to speak of or make reference to something or someone. **2** to remark on something or someone, usu briefly or indirectly. ▸ *noun* **1** a remark, usu a brief reference: *made no mention of it*. **2** a reference made to an individual's merit in an official report, esp a military one: *a mention in dispatches*. ▪ **mentionable** *adj.* [14c: from Latin *mentio* a calling to mind]

IDIOMS **don't mention it** *informal* no apologies or words of thanks are needed. **not to mention sth** used to introduce (a subject or facts that the speaker is about to mention), usu for emphasis.

mentor *noun* a trusted teacher or adviser. [18c: French]

menu *noun* **1 a** the range of dishes available in a restaurant, etc; **b** a list of these dishes. **2** *comput* a set of options displayed on a computer screen. [19c: French]

menu bar *noun, comput* a bar in a window giving a list of options.

meow, meowed *or* **meowing** see under **miaow**

MEP *abbrev* Member of the European Parliament.

mephitic /mɛˈfɪtɪk/ *adj* of air, an atmosphere, etc: foul-smelling or poisonous. [17c: from Latin *mephitis* a poisonous vapour]

mercantile *adj, formal* belonging or relating to trade or traders; commercial. [17c: French]

mercenary *adj* **1** *derog* excessively concerned with the desire for personal gain, esp money. **2** hired for money. ▸ *noun* (***-ies***) a soldier available for hire by a country or group. [14c: from Latin *mercenarius*]

mercerize *or* **-ise** *verb* to treat a material, esp cotton, with a substance which strengthens it and gives it a silky appearance. ▪ **mercerized** *adj.* [19c: named after John Mercer, an English textile manufacturer who invented the process]

merchandise *noun* commercial goods. ▸ *verb, tr & intr* **1** to trade; to buy and sell. **2** to plan the advertising or supplying of, or the selling campaign for (a product). ▪ **merchandising** *noun.* [13c: from French *marchandise*]

merchant *noun* **1** a trader, esp a wholesale trader. **2** *N Am, esp US & Scot* a shopkeeper. **3** *informal* someone who indulges in a specified activity, esp one that is generally not acceptable or appropriate: *gossip merchant*. ▸ *adj* used for trade; commercial: *merchant ship*. ▪ **merchantable** *adj.* [13c: from French *marchand*]

merchant bank *noun* a bank whose main activities are financing international trade, lending money to industry and assisting in company takeovers, etc. ▪ **merchant banker** *noun.*

merchantman *noun* a ship that carries merchandise; a trading ship. Also called **merchant ship**.

merchant navy *or* **merchant service** *noun* the ships and crews that are employed in a country's commerce.

merciful *adj* showing or exercising mercy; forgiving. ▪ **mercifully** *adv* **1** luckily; thankfully. **2** in a merciful way. ▪ **mercifulness** *noun.*

merciless *adj* without mercy; cruel; pitiless. ▪ **mercilessly** *adv.*

mercurial *adj* **1** relating to or containing mercury. **2** of someone or their personality, mood, etc: lively, active and unpredictable. ▪ **mercurially** *adv.*

mercuric *adj, chem* containing or relating to divalent mercury.

mercurous *adj, chem* containing or relating to monovalent mercury.

mercury *noun* **1** (symbol **Hg**) a dense, silvery-white metallic element, and the only metal that is liquid at room temperature. Also called **quicksilver**. **2** (**Mercury**) *astron* the closest planet to the Sun. [14c: from Latin *Mercurius*, the Roman god Mercury]

mercy *noun* (***-ies***) **1** kindness or forgiveness shown when punishment is possible or justified. **2** an act or circumstance in which these qualities are displayed, esp by God. **3** a tendency to be forgiving. **4** a piece of good luck; a welcome happening: *grateful for small mercies*. [12c: from French *merci*]

IDIOMS **at the mercy of sb** *or* **sth** wholly in their or its power; liable to be harmed by them or it.

mere[1] *adj* nothing more than; no better, more important or useful than: *but he's a mere boy*. ▪ **merely** *adv.* [16c: from Latin *merus* pure, undiluted]

mere[2] *noun, old use, poetic* often in English place names: a lake or pool. [Anglo-Saxon]

meretricious *adj, formal* bright or attractive on the surface, but of no real value. ▪ **meretriciously** *adv.* [17c: from Latin *meretricius*]

merge *verb* **1** *tr & intr* (*often* **merge with sth**) to blend, combine or join with something else. **2** *intr* (**merge into sth**) to become part of it and therefore impossible to distinguish from it. [17c: from Latin *mergere* to plunge]

merger *noun* a joining together, esp of business firms. Also called **amalgamation**.

meridian *noun* **1** *geog* **a** an imaginary line on the Earth's surface passing through the poles at right angles to the equator; a line of longitude; **b** a representation of this, eg on a map. **2** in Chinese medicine: any of several lines or pathways through the body along which life energy flows. ▪ **meridional** *adj* **1** *technical* belonging or relating to, or along, a meridian. **2** *literary* belonging or relating to the south, esp to S Europe. [14c: from Latin *meridianus*]

meringue /məˈraŋ/ *noun* **1** a crisp, cooked mixture of sugar and egg-whites. **2** a cake or dessert made from this, often with a filling of cream. [18c: French]

merino *noun* **1** a type of sheep bred for its long, fine wool. Also called **merino sheep**. **2** fine yarn or fabric made from its wool. *as adj*: *merino shawl*. [18c: Spanish]

merit *noun* **1** worth, excellence or praiseworthiness. **2** (*often* **merits**) a good point or quality: *got the job on his own merits*. ▸ *verb* to deserve; to be worthy of or entitled to something. [13c: from French *merite*]

meritocracy /mɛrɪˈtɒkrəsɪ/ *noun* (**-ies**) a social system based on leadership by people of great talent or intelligence, rather than of wealth or noble birth. ▪ **meritocrat** /ˈmɛrɪtəkrat/ *noun*. ▪ **meritocratic** *adj*.

meritorious *adj, formal* deserving reward or praise; having merit. ▪ **meritoriously** *adv*. [15c]

merlin *noun* a small, dark-coloured falcon with a black-striped tail. [14c: from French *esmerillon*]

Merlot /ˈmɜːləʊ/ *noun* **1** a variety of black grape used in winemaking. **2** a red wine that is produced from, or mainly from, this variety of grape. [19c: French, meaning 'baby blackbird']

mermaid *noun, folklore* a mythical sea creature with a woman's head and upper body and a fish's tail. ▪ **merman** *noun*. [14c: from Anglo-Saxon **mere**[2] + **maid**]

merry *adj* (**-ier, -iest**) **1** cheerful and lively. **2** *informal* slightly drunk. **3** causing or full of laughter. ▪ **merrily** *adv*. ▪ **merriment** *noun*. ▪ **merriness** *noun*. [Anglo-Saxon *myrige*]

merry-go-round *noun* **1** a fairground ride consisting of a revolving platform fitted with rising and falling seats in the form of horses or other figures. Sometimes called **roundabout**. **2** a whirl of activity. [18c]

merrymaking *noun* cheerful celebration; revelry. ▪ **merrymaker** *noun*.

mesa /ˈmeɪsə/ *noun, geol* an isolated, flat-topped hill with at least one steep side or cliff. [18c: Spanish, meaning 'table']

mésalliance /mɛˈzalɪəns; *French* mezaljɑ̃s/ *noun, literary* a marriage to someone of lower social status. [18c: literally 'misalliance']

mescal *noun* **1** a globe-shaped cactus of Mexico and the SW USA, with buttonlike tubercles (called **mescal buttons**) on its stems. Also called **peyote**. **2** a colourless Mexican spirit made from the sap of this and certain other plants. [18c: from Aztec *mexcalli*]

mescaline *or* **mescalin** *noun* a hallucinogenic drug obtained from the **mescal** cactus.

Mesdames see under **Madame**

mesdames see under **madam**

Mesdemoiselles see under **Mademoiselle**

mesh *noun* **1** netting, or a piece of netting made of wire or thread. **2** each of the openings between the threads of a net. **3** (*usu* **meshes**) a network. ▸ *verb, intr* **1** *technical* of the teeth on gear wheels: to engage. **2** (*often* **mesh with sth**) to fit or work together. **3** to become entangled. [16c: from Dutch *maesche*]

mesmerize *or* **-ise** *verb* **1** to grip the attention of someone; to fascinate. **2** *old use* to hypnotize someone. ▪ **mesmerism** *noun*. ▪ **mesmerizing** *adj*.

Mesolithic *or* **mesolithic** *adj* belonging or relating to the middle period of the Stone Age. [19c]

mesomorph *noun* a person of muscular body build. Compare **ectomorph**, **endomorph**. ▪ **mesomorphic** *adj*. [1940s]

meson /ˈmiːzɒn/ *noun, physics* any of a group of unstable, strongly-interacting, elementary particles, with a mass between that of an **electron** and a **nucleon**. [20c]

mesophyll *noun, botany* the tissue between the upper and lower surfaces of a plant leaf. [19c]

mesosphere *noun, meteorol* the layer of the Earth's atmosphere above the **stratosphere** and below the **thermosphere**. ▪ **mesospheric** *adj*.

Mesozoic /mɛsoʊˈzoʊɪk/ *adj* **1** *geol* belonging or relating to the era of geological time between the **Palaeozoic** and **Cenozoic** eras. **2** relating to the rocks formed during this era. [19c: from Greek *mesos* middle + *zoion* animal]

mess *noun* **1** an untidy or dirty state: *The kitchen's in a mess*. **2** a state of disorder or confusion: *The accounts are in a mess*. **3** a badly damaged state. **4** something or someone in a damaged, disordered or confused state: *My hair is a mess*. **5** a communal dining room, esp in the armed forces: *the sergeants' mess*. **6** *old use* a portion of any pulpy food: *a mess of potage*. ▸ *verb* **1** (*often* **mess sth up**) to put or get it into an untidy, dirty, confused or damaged state; to spoil. **2** (*usu* **mess with sth**) to meddle, tinker or interfere in it. **3** (**mess with sb**) *informal* to become involved in argument or conflict with them; to cause them trouble or aggravation. **4** *intr* of soldiers, etc: to eat, or live, together. [13c: French *mes* dish]

PHRASAL VERBS **mess about** *or* **around** *informal* to behave in an annoyingly foolish way. **mess about** *or* **around with sth** to play or tinker with something.

message *noun* **1** a spoken or written communication sent from one person to another. **2** the instructive principle contained within a story, poem, religious teaching, work of art, etc. **3** (*usu* **messages**) *chiefly Scot* household shopping. [13c: French]

IDIOMS **get the message** *informal* to understand.

message board *noun* a **bulletin board**.

message box *noun, comput* a box that appears on a computer screen to give information.

messenger *noun* someone who carries communications between people. [13c: from French *messager*]

messenger RNA *noun, biochem* (abbrev **mRNA**) a molecule of RNA that transports coded genetic instructions for the manufacture of proteins from the **DNA** in the nucleus to a **ribosome**.

Messiah *noun* (*usu* **the Messiah**) **1** *Christianity* Jesus Christ. **2** *Judaism* the king of the Jews still to be sent by God to free his people and restore Israel. **3** someone who sets a country or a people free. ▪ **Messianic** /mɛsɪˈanɪk/ *adj* **1** belonging or relating to, or associated with, a Messiah. **2** relating to any popular or inspirational leader, esp a liberator. [14c from French *Messie*, from Hebrew *mashiah* anointed]

Messieurs *pl of* **Monsieur**

Messrs *pl of* **Mr**

messy *adj* (*-ier, -iest*) **1** involving or making dirt or mess. **2** confused, untidy. ▪ **messily** *adv.* ▪ **messiness** *noun.*

met *past tense, past participle of* **meet**[1]

metabolism /mə'tabəlɪzəm/ *noun, biochem* the sum of all the chemical reactions that occur within the cells of a living organism, including both **anabolism** and **catabolism** of complex organic compounds. ▪ **metabolic** *adj.* [19c: from Greek *metabole* change]

metabolize *or* **-ise** *verb, tr & intr, biochem* to break down complex organic compounds into simpler molecules.

metacarpus *noun* (***metacarpi***) *anatomy* the set of five bones in the human hand between the wrist and the knuckles. See also **carpal**. Compare **metatarsus**. ▪ **metacarpal** *adj.* [19c: Latin]

metal *noun* **1** any of a class of chemical elements with certain shared characteristic properties, most being shiny, malleable, ductile and good conductors of heat and electricity, and all (except **mercury**) being solid at room temperature. **2** road metal, broken rock for making and mending roads. **3** (**metals**) the rails of a railway. ▸ *adj* made of, or mainly of, metal. ▪ **metallic** *adj* **1** made of metal. **2** characteristic of metal, eg in sound or appearance. See also **mettle**. [13c: French]

metalanguage *noun* a language or system of symbols used to discuss another language or symbolic system.

metalloid *noun, chem* a chemical element that has both metallic and non-metallic properties, eg silicon and arsenic.

metallurgy /mɛ'talədʒɪ, 'mɛtəlɜːdʒɪ/ *noun* the scientific study of the nature and properties of metals and their extraction from the ground. ▪ **metallurgic** *or* **metallurgical** *adj.* ▪ **metallurgist** *noun.* [18c: from Latin *metallurgia*]

metalwork *noun* **1** the craft, process or practice of shaping metal and making items of metal. **2** articles made of metal. ▪ **metalworker** *noun.*

metamorphic *adj* **1** relating to **metamorphosis**. **2** *geol* of any of a group of rocks: formed by **metamorphism**.

metamorphism *noun, geol* the transformation of the structure of rock by the action of the Earth's crust.

metamorphose *verb, tr & intr* to undergo or cause something to undergo metamorphosis.

metamorphosis /mɛtə'mɔːfəsɪs/ *noun* (***-ses*** /-siːz/) **1** a change of form, appearance, character, etc; a transformation. **2** *biol* the change of physical form that occurs during the development into adulthood of some creatures, eg butterflies. [16c: from Greek *meta* among, with or beside + *morphe* form]

metaphor *noun* **1** an expression in which the person, action or thing referred to is described as if it really were what it merely resembles, eg a rejection described as 'a slap in the face', or a ferocious person as 'a tiger'. **2** such expressions in general. ▪ **metaphorical** *adj.* ▪ **metaphorically** *adv.* [16c: from Greek *metaphora*]

metaphysical *adj* **1** belonging or relating to **metaphysics**. **2** abstract. **3** supernatural. **4** (*also* **Metaphysical**) of a poet: whose work is seen as belonging to a style termed **metaphysical poetry**. ▸ *noun* a poet writing in this style. ▪ **metaphysically** *adv.*

metaphysical poetry *noun* a term applied to 17c English poetry which makes use of elaborate images, intricate word-play, paradox, etc to express intense feelings and complex ideas. [17c: the term was first applied in a derogatory sense by Dryden and Dr Johnson]

metaphysics *singular noun* **1** the branch of philosophy dealing with the nature of existence and the basic principles of truth and knowledge. **2** *informal* any type of abstract discussion, writing or thinking. [16c: from Greek *ta meta ta physika*, 'the things coming after natural science', from the order of subjects in Aristotle's writings]

metastasis /mɛ'tastəsɪs/ *noun* (***metastases*** /-siːz/) *med* the spread of a disease, esp of a malignant tumour, from one part of the body to another. [17c: Greek, meaning 'change of place']

meta-tag *noun, comput* tags on a web page outlining its subject etc, invisible to the user but which can be found by a browser making particular searches.

metatarsus *noun* (***metatarsi***) *anatomy* the set of five long bones in the human foot between the ankle and the toes. See also **tarsus**. Compare **metacarpus**. ▪ **metatarsal** *adj.* [17c: from Greek *meta* among, with or beside + *tarsos* instep]

metathesis /mɛ'taθəsɪs/ *noun, linguistics* alteration of the normal order of sounds or letters in a word. [17c: from Greek *meta* among, with or beside + **thesis**]

metazoan /mɛtə'zoʊən/ *noun, zool* any multicellular animal that has specialized differentiated body tissues. Compare **protozoan**. ▸ *adj* belonging or relating to the Metazoa. [19c: Latin]

mete *verb, rather formal* (*now always* **mete sth out** *or* **mete out sth**) to give out or dispense something, esp punishment. [Anglo-Saxon *metan*]

meteor *noun, astron* the streak of light seen when a meteoroid enters into the Earth's atmosphere, where it burns up as a result of friction. Also called **shooting star**. [15c: from Latin *meteorum*]

meteoric /miːtɪ'ɒrɪk/ *adj* **1** belonging or relating to meteors. **2** **a** of success, etc: very rapid; very short-lived; **b** like a meteor in terms of brilliance, speed, transience, etc. ▪ **meteorically** *adv.*

meteorite *noun, astron* the remains of a **meteoroid** which has survived burn-up in its passage through the Earth's atmosphere as a **meteor**. ▪ **meteoritic** *adj.*

meteoroid *noun, astron* in interplanetary space: a small, moving, solid object or dust particle, which becomes visible as a **meteorite** or a **meteor** if it enters the Earth's atmosphere.

meteorology *noun* the scientific study of weather and climate over a relatively short period. ▪ **meteorological** *adj.* ▪ **meteorologist** *noun.*

meter[1] *noun* **1** an instrument for measuring and recording, esp quantities of electricity, gas, water, etc used. **2** a parking meter. ▸ *verb* to measure and record (eg electricity) using a meter. [19c: from Greek *metron* a measure]

meter

Be careful not to use the spelling **meter** when you mean **metre**:

The room measured five metres by three.
the poem's metre

meter[2] the *US* spelling of **metre**[1], **metre**[2]

-meter *combining form, forming nouns, denoting* **1** an instrument for measuring: *thermometer.* **2** a line of poetry with a specified number of units of stress, or feet (see **foot** sense 8): *pentameter.* [From Greek *metron* a measure]

meth *noun, slang* short for **methamphetamine**.

methadone *noun* a drug similar to **morphine**, but less addictive, used as a painkiller and as a heroin substitute for drug addicts. [20c: from d*imeth*ylamino-d*iphenyl*-petan*one*]

methamphetamine /mɛθam'fɛtəmiːn/ *noun* a derivative of **amphetamine** with rapid and long-lasting action, used as a stimulant.

methanal *noun, chem* **formaldehyde**.

methane *noun, chem* a colourless odourless flammable gas, belonging to the alkane series of hydrocarbons, used in the manufacture of organic chemicals and hydrogen, and as a cooking and heating fuel (in the form of **natural gas** of which it is the main component). [19c]

methanoic acid see under **formic acid**

methanol *noun, chem* a colourless flammable toxic liquid used as a solvent and antifreeze, and which can be catalytically converted to petrol. Also called **methyl alcohol**. [19c: from **methane**]

methinks *verb* (***methought***) *old use or humorous* it seems to me (that). [Anglo-Saxon *me thyncth*]

method *noun* **1** a way of doing something, esp an ordered set of procedures or an orderly system. **2** good planning; efficient organization. **3** (*often* **methods**) a technique used in a particular activity: *farming methods.* ▪ **methodical** *adj* efficient and orderly; done in an orderly or systematic way. ▪ **methodically** *adv.* [16c: from Greek *methodos*]

Methodist *Christianity, noun* **1** a member of the Methodist Church, a denomination founded by John Wesley as an evangelical movement within the Church of England. **2** a supporter of Methodism. ▸ *adj* belonging or relating to Methodism. ▪ **Methodism** *noun.*

methodology *noun* (**-ies**) **1** the system of methods and principles used in a particular activity, science, etc. **2** the study of method and procedure.

methought *past tense of* **methinks**

meths *singular noun, informal, esp Brit* methylated spirits.

methyl alcohol see under **methanol**

methylate *verb* to mix or impregnate something with methanol.

methylated spirits *or* **methylated spirit** *singular noun* ethanol treated with additives, used as a fuel and solvent.

meticulous *adj* paying, or showing, very careful attention to detail; scrupulously careful. ▪ **meticulously** *adv.* ▪ **meticulousness** *noun.* [19c: from Latin *meticulosus* frightened]

métier /'mɛtɪeɪ; *French* metje/ *noun* **1** a person's business or line of work. **2** the field or subject, etc in which one is especially skilled; one's forte. [18c: French]

metonymy /mɪ'tɒnɪmɪ/ *noun* (***-ies***) *linguistics* the use of a word referring to an element or attribute of something to mean the thing itself, eg *the bottle* for 'the drinking of alcohol' or *the Crown* for 'the sovereign'. [16c: from Greek *metonymia*, literally 'change of name']

metre[1] *or* (*US*) **meter** *noun* (abbrev **m**) in the SI system: the base unit of measurement of length, equal to 100 centimetres or about 39.37 inches (or 1.094 yards). [18c: from French *mètre*]

metre
Be careful not to use the spelling **metre** when you mean **meter**:
The gas man came to read the meter.

metre[2] *or* (*US*) **meter** *noun* **1** *poetry* the arrangement of words and syllables, or feet (see **foot** sense 8), in a rhythmic pattern according to their length and stress; a particular pattern or scheme. **2** *music* **a** the basic pattern or structure of beats; **b** tempo. [Anglo-Saxon *meter*]

metre-kilogram-second system *noun* (abbrev **mks system** *or* **MKS system**) a system of scientific measurement that uses the metre, kilogram and second as its units of length, mass and time respectively.

metric[1] *adj* relating to or based on the **metre**[1] or the metric system. ▪ **metrically** *adv.* [19c: from French *métrique*]

metric[2] see **metrical**

metrical *or* **metric** *adj, technical* **1** in or relating to verse as distinct from prose. **2** belonging or relating to measurement. [15c: from Latin *metricus*]

metricate *verb, tr & intr* to convert (a non-metric measurement, system, etc) to a metric one using units of the metric system. ▪ **metrication** *noun.* Compare **decimalize.** [20c]

metric system *noun* a standard system of measurement, based on **decimal** units, in which each successive multiple of a unit is 10 times larger than the one before it. *Technical equivalent* **SI**.

metro *noun* an urban railway system, usu one that is mostly underground, esp and orig the **Métro**, the system in Paris. [20c: from French *métro*, abbrev of *chemin de fer métropolitain* metropolitan railway]

metronome *noun* a device that indicates musical tempo by means of a ticking pendulum that can be set to move at different speeds. [19c: from Greek *metron* measure + *nomos* rule or law]

metropolis /mə'trɒpəlɪs/ *noun* (***-lises*** /-lɪsɪz/) a large city, esp the capital city of a nation or region. [16c: Latin]

metropolitan *adj* **1** belonging or relating to, typical of, or situated in, a large city. **2** belonging or referring to a country's mainland, as opposed to its overseas territories. ▸ *noun* **1** *Christianity* in the Roman Catholic and Orthodox Churches: a bishop, usu an archbishop, with authority over all the bishops in a province. **2** an inhabitant of a metropolis.

mettle *noun, literary* **1** courage, determination and endurance. **2** character; personal qualities: *show one's mettle.* [16c: orig a variant of **metal**]

IDIOMS **put sb on their mettle** *literary* to encourage or force them to make their best effort.

MeV *abbrev, physics* mega-electron-volt or -volts.

mew *verb, intr* to make the cry of a cat; to **miaow**. ▸ *noun* a cat's cry. [16c: imitating the sound]

mews *singular noun* (***mews*** *or* ***mewses***) **1** a set of stables around a yard or square, esp one converted into residential accommodation or garages. **2** (**Mews**) used in street names.

mezzanine /ˈmɛzəniːn/ *noun, archit* in a building: a small storey between two main floors, usu the ground and first floors. [18c: French]

mezzo /ˈmɛtsoʊ/ *adv, music* moderately, quite or rather, as in **mezzo-forte** rather loud, and **mezzo-piano** rather soft. [19c: Italian, literally 'half']

mezzo-soprano *noun, music* **1** a singing voice with a range between soprano and contralto. **2** a singer with this kind of voice. **3** a musical part for this kind of voice.

mezzotint /ˈmɛtsoʊtɪnt/ *noun, chiefly hist* **1** a method of engraving a copper plate, by polishing and scraping to produce areas of light and shade. **2** a print made from a plate engraved in this way. [17c: from Italian *mezzotinto*]

MF *abbrev, radio* medium frequency.

Mg *symbol, chem* magnesium.

mg *abbrev* milligram or milligrams.

Mgr *abbrev* **1** manager. **2** Monseigneur. **3** (*also* **Monsig.**) Monsignor.

MHz *abbrev* megahertz.

mi[1] see **me**[2]

mi[2] *abbrev* mile or miles.

miaow *or* **meow** /mɪˈaʊ/ *verb, intr* to make the cry of a cat. ▸ *noun* a cat's cry. Also called **mew**. [17c: imitating the sound]

miasma /mɪˈazmə/ *noun* (***miasmata*** *or* ***miasmas***) *literary* **1** a thick foul-smelling vapour. **2** an evil influence or atmosphere. [17c: Latin]

mica /ˈmaɪkə/ *noun, geol* any of a group of silicate minerals that split easily into thin flexible sheets and are used as electrical insulators, **dielectrics**, etc because they are poor conductors of heat and electricity. See also **isinglass**. [18c: from Latin *mica* crumb]

mice *pl of* **mouse**

Michaelmas /ˈmɪkəlməs/ *noun, Christianity* a festival in honour of St Michael the archangel, held on 29 September.

mickey *noun*

IDIOMS **take the mickey** *or* **take the mickey out of sb** *informal* to tease or make fun of them.

mickle *or* **muckle** *archaic or N Eng dialect & Scot, adj* much or great. ▸ *adv* much. ▸ *noun* a great quantity. [Anglo-Saxon *micel*]

micro *noun, informal* **1** a microcomputer or microprocessor. **2** a microwave oven.

micro- *or (sometimes before a vowel)* **micr-** *combining form, denoting* **1** very small: *microchip*. **2** one millionth part; 10^{-6} (symbol μ): *micrometre*. **3** using, used in, or prepared for, microscopy. **4** dealing with minute quantities, objects or values: *microchemistry*. [From Greek *mikros* little]

microbe *noun, loosely* any micro-organism, esp a bacterium that is capable of causing disease. ▪ **microbial** *or* **microbic** *adj*. [19c: French]

microbiology *noun* the branch of biology dealing with the study of micro-organisms.

microchip see under **silicon chip**

microcircuit *noun* an electronic circuit with components formed in one microchip.

microclimate *noun* the climate of a very small area, especially if different from that of a surrounding area. ▪ **microclimatic** *adj*. [20c]

microcode *noun, comput* **1** a **microinstruction**. **2** a sequence of microinstructions.

microcomputer *noun* a small, relatively inexpensive computer designed for use by one person at a time, and containing an entire CPU on a single microchip. Now usu called **personal computer**.

microcosm *noun* **1** any structure or system which contains, in miniature, all the features of the larger structure or system that it is part of. **2** *philos* humankind regarded as a model or epitome of the universe. Compare **macrocosm**. ▪ **microcosmic** *adj*. [15c: French]

microdot *noun* a photograph, eg one taken of secret documents, reduced to the size of a pinhead.

microeconomics *singular noun* the branch of economics concerned with the financial circumstances of individual households, firms, etc, and the way individual elements in an economy (eg specific products) behave.

microelectronics *singular noun* the branch of electronics dealing with the design and use of small-scale electrical circuits or other very small electronic devices.

microfibre *noun* a synthetic, very closely woven fabric.

microfiche /ˈmaɪkrəfiːʃ, -roʊ-/ *noun* (***microfiche*** *or* ***microfiches***) *photog* a flat sheet of film with printed text on it that has been photographically reduced, used for storing library catalogues, newspaper texts, etc. Often shortened to **fiche**. [20c: from French *fiche* a sheet of paper]

microfilm *noun* a length of thin photographic film on which printed material is stored in miniaturized form. ▸ *verb* to record something on microfilm.

microhabitat *noun, biol, ecol* a small area that has different environmental conditions from those of the surrounding area.

microinstruction *noun, comput* a single, simple command that encodes any of the individual steps to be carried out by a computer. See also **microcode**.

microlight *noun* a very lightweight, small-engined aircraft, like a powered hang-glider.

micrometer /maɪˈkrɒmɪtə(r)/ *noun* an instrument of various kinds used for accurately measuring very small distances, thicknesses or angles. ▪ **micrometry** *noun*.

micrometre *or* (*US*) **micrometer** /ˈmaɪkroʊmiːtə(r)/ *noun* in the SI or metric system: a unit of length equal to 10^{-6}m; one millionth of a metre. See also **micron**.

microminiaturize *or* **-ise** *verb* to reduce (scientific or technical equipment, etc, or any part of such equipment) to an extremely small size.

micron *noun* (symbol μ) the former name for the **micrometre**. [19c: Greek]

Micronesian *adj* belonging or relating to Micronesia, a group of small islands in the West Pacific, or specifically to the Federated States of Micronesia, its inhabitants or their languages. ▸ *noun* **1** a citizen or inhabitant of, or person born in, Micronesia. **2** the group of languages spoken in Micronesia. [19c: from **micro-** + Greek *nesos* an island]

micro-organism *noun* any living organism that can only be observed with the aid of a microscope, eg bacteria, viruses, etc.

microphone *noun* an electromagnetic transducer that converts sound waves into electrical signals. Often *(informal)* shortened to **mike**. [17c: meaning 'an instrument for intensifying very small sounds']

microphotography *noun* photography, esp of documents, plans and graphic material, in the form of greatly-reduced images of small area (**microphotographs**) which have to be viewed by magnification or enlarged projection.

microprocessor *noun, comput* a single circuit performing most of the basic functions of a CPU. Also shortened to **micro**.

microscope *noun* an instrument consisting of a system of lenses which produce a magnified image of objects that are too small to be seen with the naked eye. ▪ **microscopy** /maɪˈkrɒskəpɪ/ *noun*.

microscopic *adj* **1** too small to be seen without the aid of a microscope. Compare **macroscopic**. **2** *informal* extremely small. ▪ **microscopically** *adv*.

microsecond *noun* in the SI or metric system: a unit of time equal to one millionth part of a second.

microsurgery *noun, med* any intricate surgical procedure that is performed on very small body structures by means of a powerful microscope and small specialized instruments.

microwave *noun* **1** a form of electromagnetic radiation with wavelengths in the range 1mm to 0.3m (ie between those of **infrared** and **radio waves**), used in radar, communications and cooking. Also called **microwave radiation**. **2** a microwave oven. ▸ *verb* to cook something in a microwave oven.

microwave oven *noun* an electrically operated oven that uses microwaves to cook food more rapidly than is possible in a conventional oven, by causing water molecules within the food to vibrate and generate heat.

micturate *verb, intr, formal* to urinate. ▪ **micturition** *noun*. [19c: from Latin *micturire* to wish to urinate]

mid[1] *adj, often in compounds* (sometimes with hyphen) referring to the middle point or in the middle of something: *mid-March* • *in mid sentence*. [Anglo-Saxon *midd*]

mid[2] *or* **'mid** *prep, poetic* a short form of **amid**.

mid-air *noun* any area or point above the ground: *caught it in mid-air*.

midday *noun* the middle of the day; twelve o'clock.

midden *noun* **1** *chiefly old use or dialect* a rubbish heap; a pile of dung. **2** *informal* an untidy mess. [14c: from Danish *mykdyngja*]

middle *adj* **1** at, or being, a point or position between two others, usu two ends or extremes, and esp the same distance from each. **2** intermediate; neither at the top or at the bottom end of the scale: *middle income*. **3** moderate, not extreme; taken, used, etc as a compromise: *middle ground*. **4** (**Middle**) said especially of languages: belonging to a period coming after the Old period and before the Modern: *Middle English*. ▸ *noun* **1** the middle point, part or position of something: *the middle of the night*. **2** *informal* the waist. [Anglo-Saxon *middel*]

IDIOMS **be in the middle of sth** to be busy with it and likely to remain so for some time.

middle age *noun* the years between youth and old age, usu thought of as between the ages of 40 and 60. ▪ **middle-aged** *adj*.

the Middle Ages *plural noun* in European history: **1** the period (c. 500–1500) between the fall of the Roman Empire in the West and the Renaissance. **2** *sometimes strictly* the period between 1100 and 1500.

middle-age spread *or* **middle-aged spread** *noun* fat around the waist, often regarded as a consequence of reaching middle age.

middlebrow *derog, adj* intended for, or appealing to, people with conventional tastes and average intelligence. ▸ *noun* a middlebrow person. Compare **highbrow, lowbrow**.

middle class *noun* (*esp* **the middle class**) a social class between the working class and the upper class, traditionally thought of as being made up of educated people with professional or business careers. ▸ *adj* (**middle-class**) belonging or relating to, or characteristic of, the middle class.

middle distance *noun* in a painting, photograph, etc: the area between the foreground and the background. ▸ *adj* (**middle-distance**) **1** of an athlete: competing in races of distances of 400, 800 and 1500m. **2** of a race: run over any of these distances.

middle ear *noun, anatomy* in vertebrates: an air-filled cavity that lies between the eardrum and the **inner ear**.

middleman *noun* **1** a dealer who buys goods from a producer or manufacturer and sells them to shopkeepers or to the public. **2** any intermediary.

middle name *noun* **1** a name which comes between a **first name** and a **surname**. **2** a quality or feature for which a person is well-known: *Punctuality is his middle name*.

middle-of-the-road *adj, often derog* **1** eg of politics or opinions: not extreme; moderate. **2** eg of music: **a** of widespread appeal (*abbrev* **MOR**); **b** boringly average or familiar.

middle school *noun, England & Wales* a school for children between the ages of 8 or 9 and 12 or 13.

middle-sized *adj* characterized by being of average or medium size.

middleweight *noun* **1** a class for boxers, wrestlers and weightlifters of not more than a specified weight, which is 73 kg (160 lb) in professional boxing, and similar weights in the other sports. **2** a boxer or wrestler, etc of this weight.

middling *informal, adj* average; moderate; mediocre. ▸ *adv* esp of a person's health: fairly good; moderately: *middling good*. [15c: Scots]

Middx *abbrev, former English county* Middlesex.

midfield *noun, football* the middle area of the pitch, not close to the goal of either team. ▪ **midfielder** *noun*.

midge *noun* a small insect that gathers with others near water, esp one of the kinds that bite people. [Anglo-Saxon *mycge*]

midget *noun* **1** an unusually small person whose limbs and features are of normal proportions. **2** any thing that is smaller than others of its kind. [19c: from **midge**]

midi *noun, informal* a skirt or coat of medium length or medium size. Compare **maxi, mini**. [20c: from **mid**[1]]

midi- *prefix, rather dated* (sometimes without hyphen) *denoting* of medium size or length: *midi-skirt.*

midland *adj* belonging or relating to the central, inland part of a country.

midlife crisis *noun* a period of panic, frustration and feelings of pointlessness, sometimes experienced by a person when they reach middle age and realize that their youth has passed.

midmost *literary, adv* in the very middle. ▸ *adj* nearest the middle. [Anglo-Saxon *midmest*]

midnight *noun* twelve o'clock at night.

midnight sun *noun, astron* a phenomenon that occurs during the summer in the Arctic and Antarctic regions, where the sun remains visible for 24 hours a day.

mid-on *or* **mid-off** *noun, cricket* a fielder in a roughly-horizontal line with, but at a certain distance from, the non-striking batsman, on the on or off side respectively (see **on** *adj* sense 6, **off** *adj* sense 4).

midpoint *noun* a point at or near the middle in distance or time.

midriff *noun* **1** the part of the body between the chest and waist. **2** *anatomy* the **diaphragm**. [Anglo-Saxon *midhrif*]

midshipman *noun, naut* a trainee naval officer, stationed on land.

midships see **amidships**

midst *noun* **1** (*always* **in the midst of sth**) **a** among it or in the centre of it; **b** at the same time as something; during it. **2** (*always* **in sb's midst**) among them or in the same place as them. [15c: from Anglo-Saxon *in middes* amidst]

midstream *noun* the area of water in the middle of a river or stream, away from its banks.
IDIOMS **in midstream** before a sentence, action, etc is finished: *She cut him off in midstream.*

midsummer *noun* the period of time in the middle of summer, or near the **summer solstice**, ie around 21 June in the N hemisphere or 22 December in the S hemisphere. Opposite of **midwinter**.

midterm *noun* **1** the middle of an academic term or term of office, etc. **2** the middle of a particular period of time, esp of a pregnancy.

midway *adj, adv* halfway between two points in distance or time.

midweek *noun* the period of time in the middle of the week, esp Wednesday.

Midwestern *adj* relating to or typical of the US Midwest, the states between the Great Lakes and the upper Mississippi river valley.

mid-wicket *noun, cricket* **1** the area between the stumps on the on side (see **on** *adj* sense 6), roughly midway between the wicket and the boundary. **2** a fielder placed in this area.

midwife *noun* a nurse, esp a female one, trained to assist women in childbirth and to provide care and advice for women before and after childbirth. ▪ **midwifery** /ˈmɪdwɪfərɪ/ *noun.* [14c: from Anglo-Saxon *mid* with + *wif* woman]

midwinter *noun* the period of time in the middle of winter, or near the **winter solstice**, ie around 22 December in the N hemisphere or 21 June in the S hemisphere. Opposite of **midsummer**.

mien /miːn/ *noun, formal or literary* an appearance, expression or manner, esp one that reflects a mood: *her thoughtful mien.* [16c]

miff *verb, intr, informal* (*usu* **miffed at, about** *or* **with sb** *or* **sth**) to be offended. ▪ **miffed** *adj* offended, upset or annoyed. [17c]

might[1] *auxiliary verb* **1** *past tense of* **may**[1]: *He asked if he might be of assistance.* **2** (*sometimes* **might well**) used to express a possibility: *He might win if he tries hard.* **3** used to request permission: *Might I speak to you a moment?* [Anglo-Saxon *miht*]

might[2] *noun* power or strength. [Anglo-Saxon *miht*]
IDIOMS **with might and main** *literary* with great strength; with all one's strength.

mightn't *contraction* might not.

mighty *adj* (**-ier, -iest**) **1** having great strength or power. **2** very large. **3** very great or important. ▸ *adv, N Am, esp US, informal* very: *mighty pretty.* ▪ **mightily** *adv.* ▪ **mightiness** *noun.*

migraine *noun* a throbbing headache that usu affects one side of the head and is often accompanied by nausea or vomiting, and sometimes preceded by visual disturbances. [18c: French]

migrant *noun* a person or animal that migrates. ▸ *adj* regularly moving from one place to another.

migrate *verb, intr* **1** of animals, esp birds: to travel from one region to another at certain times of the year. **2** of people: to leave one place and settle in another, esp another country, often regularly. ▪ **migration** *noun.* ▪ **migratory** *adj.* [17c: from Latin *migrare* to move from one place to another]

mikado *or* (*often*) **Mikado** /mɪˈkɑːdoʊ/ *noun* a title formerly given by foreigners to an emperor of Japan. [18c: Japanese, literally 'exalted gate']

mike *contraction, informal* short for **microphone**.

mil *abbrev, informal* **1** millimetre. **2** millions.

milady *noun* (**-ies**) *dated* a term formerly used to address, or to refer to, a rich English woman, esp an aristocratic one. [19c: French]

milch /mɪltʃ/ *adj* of cattle: producing milk. [Anglo-Saxon *milce*]

mild *adj* **1** gentle in temperament or behaviour. **2** not sharp or strong in flavour or effect. **3** not great or severe. **4** of climate, etc: not characterized by extremes; rather warm. ▸ *noun* (*also* **mild ale**) dark beer less flavoured with hops than **bitter** beer. ▪ **mildly** *adv.* ▪ **mildness** *noun.* [Anglo-Saxon *milde*]
IDIOMS **to put it mildly** to understate the case.

mildew *noun* **a** a parasitic fungus that produces a fine white powdery coating on the surface of infected plants; **b** similar white or grey patches on the surface of paper which has been exposed to damp conditions. ▸ *verb, tr & intr* to affect or become affected by mildew. ▪ **mildewy** *adj.* [Anglo-Saxon *mildeaw*]

mild steel *noun* steel that contains little carbon and is easily worked.

mile *noun* (abbrev **m, m.** *or* **ml**) **1** (abbrev **m, mi** *or* **ml**) in the imperial system: a unit of measurement of distance equal to 1760 yards or about 1.61 kilometres. See also **nautical mile**. **2** a race over this distance, esp a race on foot. **3** *informal* a great distance; a large margin: *missed by a mile.* ▸ *adv* (**miles**) **a** at a great distance: *lives miles away;* **b** *informal* very much: *feel miles better.* [Anglo-Saxon *mil*: orig a

Roman unit of length consisting of 1000 double paces, from Latin *mille passuum* a thousand paces]

mileage *noun* **1** the number of miles travelled or to be travelled. **2 a** the number of miles a motor vehicle will travel on a fixed amount of fuel; **b** the total number of miles a car has done since new, as shown on the mileometer. **3** *informal* use; benefit; advantage: *We can get a lot of mileage out of that story.*

mileometer *or* **milometer** /maɪ'lɒmɪtə(r)/ *noun* in a motor vehicle: an instrument for recording the total number of miles travelled.

milestone *noun* **1** a very important event; a significant point or stage. **2** a stone pillar at a roadside showing distances in miles to various places.

milieu /'miːljɜː/ *noun* (***milieus*** *or* ***milieux***) *literary* a social environment or set of surroundings. [19c: French, meaning 'middle place']

militant *adj* **1** taking, or ready to take, strong or violent action; aggressively active. **2** *formal* engaged in warfare. ▸ *noun* a militant person. ▪ **militancy** *noun.* ▪ **militantly** *adv.* [15c: French]

militarism *noun, often derog* **1** an aggressive readiness to engage in warfare. **2** the vigorous pursuit of military aims and ideals. ▪ **militarist** *noun.* ▪ **militaristic** *adj.*

militarize *or* **-ise** *verb* **1** to provide (a country, body, etc) with a military force. **2** to make something military in nature or character. ▪ **militarization** *noun.*

military *adj* **1** by, for, or belonging or relating to the armed forces or warfare: *military encounter.* **2** characteristic of members of the armed forces: *military bearing.* ▸ *noun* (***-ies***) (*usu* **the military**) the armed forces. ▪ **militarily** *adv.* [16c: from French *militaire*]

military honours *plural noun* a display of respect shown to a dead soldier, etc by fellow soldiers, royalty, etc.

military police *or* **Military Police** *noun* (abbrev **MP**) a police force within an army, enforcing army rules.

militate *verb, intr* (*usu* **militate for** *or* **against sth**) of facts, etc: to have a strong influence or effect: *The evidence militates against your sworn statement.* [17c: from Latin *militare* to serve as a soldier]

militia /mɪ'lɪʃə/ *noun* a civilian fighting force used to supplement a regular army in emergencies. ▪ **militiaman** *noun.* [16c: Latin, meaning 'a military force']

milk *noun* **1** a whitish liquid that is secreted by the **mammary gland**s of female mammals to provide their young with nourishment. **2** the whiteish, milk-like juice or sap of certain plants: *coconut milk.* **3** any preparation that resembles milk: *milk of magnesia.* ▸ *verb* **1** to take milk from (an animal). **2** to extract or draw off a substance (eg venom or sap) from something. **3** *informal* to obtain money, information or any other benefit from someone or something, cleverly or relentlessly; to exploit: *milked the scandal for all it was worth.* **4** *intr* of cattle: to yield milk. ▪ **milker** *noun.* ▪ **milkiness** *noun.* ▪ **milking** *noun.* ▪ **milky** *adj* (***-ier, -iest***). [Anglo-Saxon *milc*]

milk and water *noun, derog* weak, insipid or weakly sentimental speech or writing. [16c in obsolete sense 'the colour of milk and water']

milk chocolate *noun* chocolate containing milk. Compare **plain chocolate**.

milk float *noun, Brit* a vehicle, usu an electrically-powered one, used for delivering milk.

milkmaid *noun* a woman who milks cows, goats, etc.

milkman *noun, Brit* a man who delivers milk to people's houses.

milk of magnesia see under **magnesia**

milk pudding *noun* a dessert made by baking or boiling grain (eg rice or tapioca) in milk, usu with added sugar and flavouring.

milk round *noun* **1** a milkman's regular daily route from house to house. **2** a series of visits made periodically, eg a tour of universities made by representatives of a large company in order to attract or recruit undergraduates.

milkshake *noun* a drink consisting of a mixture of milk, flavouring and sometimes ice cream, whipped together until creamy.

milksop *noun, derog, old use* a weak, effeminate or ineffectual man or youth.

milk tooth *noun* any of a baby's or young mammal's first set of teeth. Also called **baby tooth**.

the Milky Way *noun, astron* **1** *strictly* a band of diffuse light that circles the night sky as seen from Earth, and the billions of stars in the plane of our galaxy which are too faint to be seen individually. **2** the galaxy to which our sun belongs.

mill *noun* **1 a** a large machine that grinds grain into flour; **b** a building containing such a machine: *windmill.* **2** a smaller machine or device for grinding a particular thing: *a pepper mill.* **3** a factory, esp one with one or more large machines that press, roll or otherwise shape something: *a woollen mill.* ▸ *verb* **1** to grind (grain, etc). **2** to shape (eg metal) in a mill. **3** to cut grooves into the edge of (a coin). **4** *intr, informal* (*esp* **mill about** *or* **around**) to move in an aimless or confused manner. ▪ **miller** *noun* someone who owns or operates a mill, esp a grain mill. [Anglo-Saxon *myln*]

IDIOMS **go** *or* **put sb** *or* **sth through the mill** to undergo or make them or it undergo an unpleasant experience or difficult test.

millennium *noun* (***millenniums*** *or* ***millennia***) **1** a period of a thousand years. **2** (**the millennium**) **a** a future period of a thousand years during which some Christians believe Christ will rule the world; **b** a future golden age of worldwide peace and happiness. ▪ **millennial** *adj.* [17c: from Latin *mille* a thousand + *annus* year]

---

millennium

This word is often misspelt. It has two *l*'s and two *n*'s. It might help you to remember the following sentence:

*A mi**ll**e**nn**ium is a **l**ot **l**onger than **n**inety-**n**ine years.*

---

millepede see **millipede**

millesimal /mɪ'lɛsɪməl/ *adj* **1** thousandth. **2** consisting of or relating to thousandths. ▸ *noun* a thousandth part. [18c: from Latin *millesimus*]

millet *noun* a cereal grass which is grown as an important food crop, and also widely used as animal fodder. [15c: French]

milli- *combining form* (abbrev **m**) **1** one thousandth: *milligram* • *millilitre.* **2** one thousand: *millipede.* [From Latin *mille* a thousand]

milliard *noun, old use* a thousand million. Now called **billion**. [18c: French]

millibar *noun, physics, meteorol, etc* (abbrev **mbar**) a unit of atmospheric pressure equal to 10^{-3} (one thousandth) of a bar. See also **bar²**.

milligram *or* **milligramme** *noun* (abbrev **mg**) a unit of measurement of mass, equal to one thousandth of a gram.

millilitre *or* (*US*) **milliliter** *noun* (abbrev **ml**) a unit of measurement of volume, equal to one thousandth of a litre.

millimetre *or* (*US*) **millimeter** *noun* (abbrev **mm**) a unit of measurement of length, equal to one thousandth of a metre.

milliner *noun* someone who makes or sells women's hats. ▪ **millinery** *noun*. [16c: from Milaner, a trader in the fancy goods for which the Italian city of Milan was once famous]

million *noun* (***millions*** or after a number ***million***) **1 a** the cardinal number 10^6; **b** the quantity that this represents, being a thousand thousands. **2** a numeral, figure or symbol representing this, eg *1 000 000*. **3** a set of a million people or things. **4** (*often* **millions**) *informal* a great number: *He's got millions of friends.* ▸ *adj* **1** totalling one million. **2** *informal* very many: *I've told you a million times.* [14c: French]
IDIOMS **one in a million** something or someone very rare of their kind, and therefore very valuable or special.

millionaire *or* **millionairess** *noun* someone whose wealth amounts to a million pounds, dollars, etc or more. [19c: French]

millionth *adj* **1** the last of one million people or things. **2** the millionth position in a sequence of numbers. ▸ *noun* one of one million equal parts.

millipede *or* **millepede** *noun* (***millipedes*** *or* ***millepedes***) a small wormlike creature with a many-jointed body and numerous pairs of legs. [17c: from Latin *millepeda* a woodlouse]

millisecond *noun* (abbrev **ms**) a unit of time equal to one thousandth of a second.

millpond *noun* a pond containing water which is, or used to be, used for driving a mill.
IDIOMS **like** *or* **as calm as a millpond** of a stretch of water: completely smooth and calm.

millstone *noun* **1** either of the large, heavy stones between which grain is ground in a mill. **2** (*esp* **a millstone around sb's neck**) any heavy burden which someone has to bear and which inhibits/slows their progress.

millstream *noun* a stream of water that turns a millwheel.

millwheel *noun* a wheel, esp a waterwheel, used to drive a mill.

milometer see **mileometer**

milord *noun, dated* a term formerly used on the continent to address or refer to a rich English gentleman, esp an aristocrat. [16c: French]

milt *noun* the testis or sperm of a fish. [Anglo-Saxon *milte*]

mime *noun* **1** the theatrical art of conveying meaning without words through gesture, movement and facial expression. **2** a play or dramatic sequence performed in this way. **3** an actor who practises this art. Also called **mime artist**. ▸ *verb, tr & intr* **1** to act or express (feelings, etc) without words through gesture, movement and facial expression. **2** to mouth the words to a song in time with a recording, giving the illusion of singing. [17c: from Latin *mimus*]

mimeograph /ˈmɪmɪəɡrɑːf/ *noun* **1** a machine that produces copies of printed or handwritten material from a stencil. **2** a copy produced in this way. ▸ *verb* to make a copy of something in this way.

mimesis /mɪˈmiːsɪs/ *noun* in art or literature: imitative representation. ▪ **mimetic** *adj* consisting of, showing, or relating to imitation; imitative. [16c: Greek, meaning 'imitation']

mimic *verb* (***mimicked, mimicking***) **1** to imitate someone or something, esp for comic effect. **2** to copy. **3** to simulate. **4** *biol* to resemble something closely, especially as a defence mechanism. ▸ *noun* **1** someone who is skilled at imitating other people, esp in a comic manner. **2** *biol* a plant or animal displaying mimicry. ▸ *adj* **1** imitative. **2** mock or sham. ▪ **mimicry** *noun* (**-*ies***). [16c: from Latin *mimicus* imitative]

mimosa *noun* (***mimosas*** *or* ***mimosae***) a tropical shrub or tree which has leaves that droop when touched, and clusters of flowers, typically yellow ones. [18c: Latin]

Min. *abbrev* **1** Minister. **2** Ministry.

min *noun, informal* a minute.

min. *abbrev* **1** minimum. **2** minute or minutes.

minaret *noun* a tower on or attached to a mosque, with a balcony from which the **muezzin** calls Muslims to prayer. [17c: from Arabic *manarat* lighthouse]

minatory *adj, formal* threatening. [16c: from Latin *minari* to threaten]

mince *verb* **1** to cut or shred something (esp meat) into very small pieces. **2** (*esp* **mince words with sb** *or* **mince one's words**), *chiefly with negatives* to restrain or soften the impact of (one's words, opinion, remarks, etc) when addressing someone: *not one to mince his words.* **3** *intr, usu derog* to walk or speak with affected delicateness. ▸ *noun* minced meat. ▪ **mincer** *noun*. [14c: from French *mincier*]

mincemeat *noun* a spiced mixture of dried fruits, apples, candied peel, etc and often suet, used as a filling for pies.
IDIOMS **make mincemeat of sb** *or* **sth** *informal* to destroy or defeat them or it thoroughly.

mince pie *noun* a pie filled with mincemeat or with minced meat.

mincing *adj, usu derog* of a manner of walking or behaving: over-delicate and affected.

mind *noun* **1** the power of thinking and understanding; the intelligence. **2** the place where thoughts, feelings and creative reasoning exist; the intellect. **3** memory; recollection: *call something to mind.* **4** opinion; judgement: *It's unjust, to my mind.* **5** attention: *keep your mind on the job.* **6** wish; inclination: *I have a mind to go.* **7** a very intelligent person: *great minds agree.* **8** right senses; sanity: *has lost his mind.* ▸ *verb* **1** to look after or care for something or someone: *Stay here and mind the luggage.* **2** *tr & intr* to be upset, concerned or offended by something or someone: *I don't mind the noise.* **3** (*also* **mind out** *or* **mind out for sth**) to be careful or wary (of it): *Mind where you step.* See also *exclam* below. **4** to take notice of or pay attention to something or someone: *Mind your own business.* **5** to take care to control something: *Mind your language.* **6** *tr & intr* to take care to protect something or someone: *Mind your jacket near this wet paint!* ▸ *exclam* (*often* **mind out!**) be careful; watch out!: *Mind! There's a car reversing.* See also *verb* (sense 3) above. [Anglo-Saxon *gemynd*]

IDIOMS **bear sth in mind** to remember or consider it. **do you mind!** an exclamation expressing disagreement or objection. **in one's mind's eye** in one's imagination. **make up one's mind** to come to a decision. **mind you** an expression used when adding a qualification to something already said: *I refuse to go. Mind you, I'd like to be there just to see his face.* **on one's mind** referring to something that is being thought about, considered, worried about, etc. **to my mind** in my opinion.

mind-bending *adj, informal* **1** mind-blowing. **2** mind-boggling.

mind-blowing *adj, informal* **1** very surprising, shocking, or exciting. **2** of a drug: producing a state of hallucination or altered consciousness.

mind-boggling *adj, informal* too difficult, large, strange, etc to imagine or understand; impossible to take in.

minded *adj, in compounds* having the specified kind of mind or attitude: *open-minded • like-minded.*

minder *noun* **1** *in compounds* someone who takes care of or supervises someone or something: *childminder.* **2** *informal* a bodyguard. **3** someone who minds.

mindful *adj* (*usu* **mindful of sth**) keeping it in mind.

mindless *adj* **1** *derog* senseless; done without a reason: *mindless violence.* **2** *derog* needing no effort of mind: *watching mindless rubbish on TV.* **3** (*usu* **mindless of sth**) taking no account of it: *mindless of his responsibilities.* ▪ **mindlessly** *adv.*

mind-numbing *adj, informal* so boring or dull that it seems to deaden the brain. ▪ **mind-numbingly** *adv.*

mind-reader *noun* someone who claims to be able to know other people's thoughts. ▪ **mind-reading** *noun.*

mindset *noun* an attitude or habit of mind, esp a firmly fixed one.

mine[1] *pron* **1** something or someone belonging to, or connected with, me; the thing or things, etc belonging to me: *That coat is mine.* **2** my family or people: *as long as it doesn't affect me or mine.* ▸ *adj, old use, poetic* used in place of **my** before a vowel sound or *h*: *mine host.* [Anglo-Saxon *min*]

mine[2] *noun* **1** an opening or excavation in the ground, used to remove minerals, metal ores, coal, etc, from the Earth's crust. **2** an explosive device that is placed just beneath the ground surface or in water, designed to destroy tanks, ships, etc, when detonated. **3** a rich source: *He's a mine of information.* ▸ *verb* **1** *tr & intr* to dig for (minerals, etc). **2** (*also* **mine somewhere for sth**) to dig (a particular area) in order to extract minerals, etc. **3** to lay exploding mines in (land or water): *The beach has been mined.* ▪ **miner** *noun* someone who mines or works in a mine, esp a coal mine. ▪ **mining** *noun.* [14c: French]

minefield *noun* **1** an area of land or water in which mines (see **mine**[2] *noun* sense 2) have been laid. **2** a subject or situation that presents many problems or dangers, esp hidden ones.

minelayer *noun* a ship or aircraft designed for laying mines.

mineral *noun* **1** *technical* a naturally occurring substance that is inorganic, and has characteristic physical and chemical properties by which it may be identified. **2** *loosely* any substance obtained by mining, including fossil fuels (eg coal, natural gas or petroleum) although they are organic. **3** any inorganic substance, ie one that is neither animal nor vegetable. **4** (**minerals**) see **mineral water**. ▸ *adj* belonging or relating to the nature of a mineral; containing minerals. [14c: from Latin *mineralis* relating to mines]

mineralogy /mɪnəˈralədʒɪ/ *noun* the scientific study of minerals. ▪ **mineralogical** *adj.* ▪ **mineralogist** *noun.*

mineral oil *N Am* see **liquid paraffin**

mineral water *noun* water containing small quantities of dissolved minerals, esp water that occurs naturally in this state at a spring.

minestrone /mɪnəˈstroʊnɪ/ *noun, cookery* a clear soup containing a variety of chunky vegetables and pasta. [19c: Italian, from *minestrare* to serve]

minesweeper *noun* a ship equipped to clear mines from an area. ▪ **minesweeping** *noun.*

mingle *verb* (*often* **mingle with sth** *or* **sb**) **1** *tr & intr* to become or make something become blended or mixed. **2** *intr* to move from person to person at a social engagement, briefly talking to each. [15c: from Anglo-Saxon *mengan* to mix]

mingy /ˈmɪndʒɪ/ *adj* (**-ier, -iest**) *Brit derog, informal* ungenerous; mean; meagre. [20c]

mini *informal, noun* something small or short of its kind, esp a **miniskirt**, or a type of small car. ▸ *adj* small or short of its kind; miniature. [20c]

mini- *prefix, forming nouns, denoting* smaller or shorter than the standard size. Compare **maxi**, **midi-**. [20c: a shortening of **miniature** or **minimum**]

miniature *noun* **1** a small copy, model or breed of anything. **2** a very small painting, esp a portrait on a very small scale. ▸ *adj* minute or small-scale; referring to the nature of a miniature. ▪ **miniaturist** *noun* an artist who paints miniatures. [16c: from Italian *miniatura*]

IDIOMS **in miniature** on a small scale.

---

miniature
This word is often misspelt. There is an *i* before and after the *n*. It might help you to remember the following sentence:
A ***minia****ture is a* ***mini a****rtwork.*

---

miniaturize *or* **-ise** *verb* **1** to make (eg technical equipment) on a small scale. **2** to make something very small. ▪ **miniaturization** *noun.*

minibar *noun* a small refrigerator in a hotel room, stocked with drinks and light snacks.

minibus *noun* a small bus.

minicab *noun* a taxi that is ordered by telephone from a private company, not one that can be stopped in the street.

minicam *noun* a miniature, portable, shoulder-held TV camera, as used in news reporting. [20c]

minicomputer *noun* a medium-sized computer which is more powerful than a **microcomputer**.

minidish *noun* a small satellite dish used to receive **digital television**.

minidisk *noun, comput* a very compact magnetic disk storage medium for microcomputers.

minim *noun* **1** *music* a note half the length of a **semibreve**. Also called **half note**. **2** in the imperial system: a unit of liquid volume, equal to $\frac{1}{60}$ of a fluid drachm (0.06ml). [15c: from Latin *minimus* smallest]

minimal *adj* very little indeed; negligible: *caused minimal damage.* ▪ **minimally** *adv.*

minimalism *noun* esp in art, music and design: the policy of using the minimum means, eg the fewest and simplest elements, to achieve the desired result. ▪ **minimalist** *noun, adj.*

minimize *or* **-ise** *verb* **1** to reduce something to a minimum. **2** to treat something as being of little importance or significance.

minimum *noun* (***minimums*** *or* ***minima***) **1** the lowest possible number, value, quantity or degree. **2** (*sometimes* **a minimum of sth**) the lowest number, value, quantity or degree reached or allowed: *There must be a minimum of three people present.* **3** *geom* in co-ordinate geometry: the point at which the slope of a curve changes from negative to positive. ▸ *adj* **1** relating or referring to the nature of a minimum; lowest possible: *minimum waste.* **2** lowest reached or allowed: *minimum age.* Opposite of **maximum**. [17c: Latin, from *minimus* smallest]

minimum wage *noun* the lowest wage an employer is allowed to pay, by law or union agreement.

minion *noun, derog* an employee or follower, esp one who is fawning or subservient. [16c, orig meaning 'a darling or favourite']

minipill *noun* a low-dose oral contraceptive containing progesterone but no oestrogen.

miniseries *singular noun, TV* a short series of related programmes, esp dramas, usu broadcast over consecutive days or weeks.

miniskirt *noun* a very short skirt, with a hemline well above the knee. Often shortened to **mini**. [20c]

minister *noun* **1** the political head of, or a senior politician with responsibilities in, a government department. **2** a member of the clergy in certain branches of the Christian Church. Compare **priest**. **3** a high-ranking diplomat, esp the next in rank below an ambassador. ▸ *verb, intr, formal* (*esp* **minister to sb**) to provide someone with help or some kind of service; to take care of them. ▪ **ministerial** /mɪnɪˈstɪərɪəl/ *adj.* [13c: French]

ministration *noun, formal* **1** the act or process of ministering. **2** (*usu* **ministrations**) help or service given.

ministry *noun* (***-ies***) **1 a** a government department; **b** the premises it occupies. **2** (**the ministry**) **a** the profession, duties or period of service of a religious minister; **b** religious ministers collectively. **3** the act of ministering.

minivan *noun* a small van with removable seats, used to transport goods or passengers.

mink *noun* (*pl* ***mink***) **1** a European or N American mammal with a slender body, webbed feet and thick fur. **2** the highly valued fur of this animal. **3** a garment made of this fur. [15c: perhaps from Swedish *mänk*]

minneola *noun* an orange-like citrus fruit which is a cross between a grapefruit and a tangerine. [20c: perhaps named after *Mineola* in Texas, USA]

minnow *noun* a small freshwater fish of the carp family. [15c]

Minoan /mɪˈnoʊən/ *adj* belonging or relating to the Bronze Age civilization that flourished in Crete and other Aegean islands from approximately 3000–1100 BC. ▸ *noun* an individual belonging to this civilization. [19c: from *Minos*, a mythological king of Crete]

minor *adj* **1** not as great in importance or size; fairly or relatively small or insignificant: *only a minor problem.* **2** *music* **a** of a scale: having a semitone between the second and third, fifth and sixth, and seventh and eighth notes; **b** of a key, chord, etc: based on such a scale. **3** *Brit, esp formerly* used after the surname of the younger of two brothers attending the same school: junior: *Simcox minor.* **4** of a person: below the age of legal majority or adulthood. ▸ *noun* **1** someone who is below the age of legal majority (see **majority** sense 4). **2** *music* a minor key, chord or scale. **3** *esp US* **a** a student's minor or subsidiary subject of study; **b** a student studying such a subject: *a history minor.* ▸ *verb, esp US* (*always* **minor in sth**) to study a specified minor or subsidiary subject at college or university. Compare **major**. [13c: Latin meaning 'less']

minority *noun* (***-ies***) **1** a small number, or the smaller of two numbers, sections or groups. **2** a group of people who are different, esp in terms of race or religion, from most of the people in a country, region, etc. **3** the state of being the smaller or lesser of two groups: *in a minority.* **4** the state of being below the age of legal majority. Compare **majority**. [16c: from Latin *minoritas*]

minor planet see **asteroid**

minster *noun* a large church or cathedral, esp one that was orig attached to a monastery: *York Minster.* [Anglo-Saxon *mynster*]

minstrel *noun, hist* **1** in the Middle Ages: a travelling singer, musician and reciter of poetry, etc. **2** *formerly* in the USA and Britain: any of a group of white-skinned entertainers made up to look black, who performed song and dance routines superficially of Negro origin. [13c: French]

mint[1] *noun* **1** an aromatic plant with paired leaves and small white or purple flowers, widely grown as a garden herb. **2** *cookery* the pungent-smelling leaves of this plant, used fresh or dried as a flavouring. **3** a sweet flavoured with mint, or with a synthetic substitute for mint. ▪ **minty** *adj* (***-ier, -iest***). [Anglo-Saxon *minte*]

mint[2] *noun* **1** a place where coins are produced under government authority. **2** *informal* a very large sum of money: *must be worth a mint.* ▸ *verb* **1** to manufacture (coins). **2** to invent or coin (a new word, phrase, etc). ▪ **mintage** *noun.* [Anglo-Saxon *mynet*]

IDIOMS **in mint condition** *or* **state** in perfect condition, as if brand new; never or hardly used.

mint julep see **julep** (sense 2)

minuet /mɪnjʊˈɛt/ *noun* **1** a slow formal dance with short steps in triple time, popular in the 17c and 18c. **2** a piece of music for this dance. [17c: from French *menuet*]

minus *prep* **1** with the subtraction of (a specified number): *Eight minus six equals two.* **2** *informal* without: *arrived minus his wife.* ▸ *adj* **1** negative or less than zero. **2** of a student's grade, and placed after the grade: indicating a level slightly below that indicated by the letter: *got a B minus for my essay.* **3** *informal* characterized by being a disadvantage: a *minus point.* ▸ *noun* **1** a sign (–) indicating a negative quantity or that the quantity which follows it is to be subtracted. Also called **minus sign**. **2** *informal* a negative point; a disadvantage. **3** a negative quantity or term. Opposite of **plus**. [15c: Latin, from *minor* less]

minuscule *adj* extremely small.

minuscule
This word is sometimes written as *miniscule*. However, it is strictly correct to spell the word with a *u*.

minute[1] /'mɪnɪt/ *noun* (abbrev **min**) **1** a unit of time equal to 1⁄60 of an hour; 60 seconds. **2** *informal* a short while: *Wait a minute.* **3** a particular point in time: *At that minute the phone rang.* **4** the distance that can be travelled in a minute: *a house five minutes away.* **5** (*usu* **the minutes**) the official written record of what is said at a formal meeting. **6** *geom* (symbol ′) a unit of angular measurement equal to 1⁄60 of a degree; 60 seconds. ▸ *verb* to make an official written record of what is said in (eg a meeting); to take or record something in the minutes of (eg a meeting). [14c: French]
IDIOMS **up to the minute** *or* **up-to-the-minute** very modern, recent or up-to-date; the latest.

minute[2] /maɪ'njuːt/ *adj* **1** very small; tiny. **2** precise; detailed. [15c: from Latin *minutus* small]

minute steak /'mɪnɪt/ *noun* a thin steak, usu beef, that can be cooked quickly.

minutiae /mɪ'njuːʃɪaɪ/ *plural noun* small and often unimportant details. [18c: pl of Latin *minutia* smallness]

minx *noun, humorous or rather dated* a cheeky, playful, sly or flirtatious young woman. [16c]

Miocene /'maɪəsiːn/ *geol, noun* the fourth epoch of the Tertiary period. ▸ *adj* **1** belonging or relating to this epoch. **2** relating to rocks formed during this epoch. [19c: from Greek *meion* smaller]

MIPS *or* **mips** /mɪps/ *abbrev, comput* millions of instructions per second.

miracle *noun* **1** an act or event that breaks the laws of nature, and is therefore thought to be caused by the intervention of God or another supernatural force. **2** *informal* a fortunate happening; an amazing event. **3** *informal* an amazing example or achievement of something: *a miracle of modern technology.* [12c: French]

miraculous *adj* **1** brought about by, relating to, or like a miracle. **2** *informal* wonderful; amazing; amazingly fortunate: *a miraculous escape.* ▪ **miraculously** *adv.*

mirage /'mɪrɑːʒ, mɪ'rɑːʒ/ *noun* **1** an optical illusion that usu resembles a pool of water on the horizon reflecting light from the sky, commonly experienced in deserts, and caused by the refraction of light by very hot air near to the ground. **2** anything illusory or imaginary. [19c: French, from *mirer* to reflect]

mire *noun* **1** deep mud; a boggy area. **2** trouble; difficulty; anything unpleasant and messy. ▸ *verb, tr & intr* to sink, or to make something or someone sink, in a mire. [14c: from Norse *myrr* bog]

mirk see **murk**

mirror *noun* **1** a smooth highly-polished surface, such as glass, coated with a thin layer of metal, such as silver, that reflects an image of what is in front of it. **2** any surface that reflects light. **3** a faithful representation or reflection: *when art is a mirror of life.* ▸ *verb* **1** to represent or depict something faithfully. **2** to reflect something or someone as in a mirror. [14c: French]

mirror image *noun* a reflected image as produced by a mirror, ie one in which the right and left sides are reversed.

mirth *noun* laughter; merriment. ▪ **mirthful** *adj.* ▪ **mirthless** *adj.* [Anglo-Saxon *myrgth*]

mis- *prefix, denoting* **1** wrong or wrongly; bad or badly: *mismanagement* • *misconceived.* **2** a lack or absence of something: *mistrust.* [Anglo-Saxon]

misadventure *noun, formal* **1** an unfortunate happening. **2** *law* an accident, with total absence of negligence or intent to commit crime: *death by misadventure.*

misalign *verb* to align something wrongly. ▪ **misalignment** *noun.*

misalliance *noun, formal* a relationship, esp a marriage, in which the parties are not suited to each other.

misanthrope /'mɪzənθroʊp/ *or* **misanthropist** /mɪz'anθrəpɪst/ *noun* someone who has an irrational hatred or distrust of people in general. ▪ **misanthropic** *adj.* ▪ **misanthropy** *noun.* [16c: from Greek *misos* hatred + *anthropos* man]

misapply *verb* (**-ies, -ied**) **1** to apply something wrongly. **2** to use something unwisely or for the wrong purpose.

misapprehend *verb, formal* to misunderstand something. ▪ **misapprehension** *noun.*

misappropriate *verb, formal, esp law* to put something (eg funds) to a wrong use. ▪ **misappropriation** *noun* embezzlement or theft.

misbegotten *adj* **1** *literary* foolishly planned or thought out; ill-conceived. **2** *old use* illegitimate.

misbehave *verb, intr* to behave badly. ▪ **misbehaviour** *or* (*US*) **misbehavior** *noun.*

misc. *abbrev* miscellaneous.

miscalculate *verb, tr & intr* to calculate or estimate something wrongly. ▪ **miscalculation** *noun.*

miscall *verb* to call by the wrong name.

miscarriage *noun* **1** *med* the expulsion of a fetus from the uterus before it is capable of independent survival, ie at any time up to about the 24th week of pregnancy. Also called **spontaneous abortion**. **2** an act or instance of failure or error.

miscarriage of justice *noun* a failure of a judicial system to do justice in a particular case.

miscarry *verb* (**-ies, -ied**) *intr* **1** of a woman: to have a **miscarriage** (sense 1). **2** *formal* of a plan, etc: to go wrong or fail; to be carried out wrongly or badly.

miscellaneous /mɪsə'leɪnɪəs/ *adj* made up of various kinds; mixed. [17c: from Latin *miscellaneus*]

miscellany /mɪ'sɛlənɪ/ *noun* (**-ies**) a mixture of various kinds. [17c: from Latin *miscellanea*]

mischance *noun* **1** bad luck. **2** an instance of bad luck.

mischief *noun* **1** behaviour that annoys or irritates people but does not mean or cause any serious harm. **2** the desire to behave in this way: *full of mischief.* **3** damage or harm; an injury: *You'll do yourself a mischief.* [14c: from French *meschief* a disaster or bad end]

mischief
This word is often misspelt. The letter *i* comes before the letter e. It might help you to remember the following sentence:
*Causing **h**avoc **i**s **e**xcellent **f**un!*

mischievous /'mɪstʃɪvəs/ *adj* **1** of a child, etc: tending to make mischief. **2** of behaviour: playfully troublesome. **3** *rather dated* of a thing: damaging or harmful. ▪ **mischievously** *adv.*

miscible /ˈmɪsɪbəl/ *adj, formal, chem* of a liquid or liquids: capable of dissolving in each other or mixing with each other. [16c: from Latin *miscibilis* capable of mixing]

misconceive *verb* **1** *tr & intr* (*also* **misconceive of sth**) to have the wrong idea or impression about it; to misunderstand it. **2** to plan or think something out badly. ▪ **misconceived** *adj.*

misconception *noun* a wrong or misguided attitude, opinion or view.

misconduct *noun* improper or unethical behaviour.

misconstrue *verb* to interpret something wrongly or mistakenly.

miscount *verb, tr & intr* to count something wrongly; to miscalculate. ▸ *noun* an act or instance of counting wrongly.

miscreant /ˈmɪskrɪənt/ *noun, literary or old use* a malicious person; a villain or scoundrel. ▸ *adj* villainous or wicked. [14c: from French *mescreant*]

miscue *verb* (***miscueing***) **1** *tr & intr* in billiards, snooker and pool: to hit the **cue ball** wrongly with the cue; to make a miscue. **2** *intr, theatre* to miss one's cue or answer the wrong cue (see **cue**[1], sense 1). ▸ *noun* **1** in billiards, snooker and pool: a stroke in which the cue does not hit the cue ball properly, slips off it or misses it. **2** an error or failure.

misdeed *noun, literary or formal* an example of bad or criminal behaviour; a wrongdoing.

misdemeanour *or* (*N Am*) **misdemeanor** *noun* **1** *formal* a wrongdoing; a misdeed. **2** *old use, law* a crime less serious than a **felony**. [15c: from obsolete *misdemean* to misbehave]

misdiagnose *verb* **1** to diagnose something (eg a disease) wrongly. **2** to wrongly diagnose the condition of (eg a patient). ▪ **misdiagnosis** *noun.*

misdirect *verb, formal* to give wrong directions to someone; to direct, address or instruct something or someone wrongly. ▪ **misdirection** *noun.*

mise-en-scène /miːzɒnˈsɛn; *French* miːzɑ̃sɛn/ ▸ *noun, theatre* **a** the arrangement of the scenery and props; **b** the visual effect such an arrangement has. Also called **stage setting**. [19c: French, literally 'a putting-on-stage']

miser *noun* someone who stores up their wealth and hates to spend any of it. ▪ **miserly** *adj.* [16c: Latin, meaning 'wretched']

miserable *adj* **1** of a person: **a** very unhappy; **b** habitually bad-tempered or depressed. **2** marked by great unhappiness: *a miserable life.* **3** causing unhappiness or discomfort: *miserable weather.* **4** marked by poverty or squalor: *miserable living conditions.* **5** *dialect* ungenerous; mean. ▪ **miserably** *adv.* [16c: from French *misérable*]

misericord /mɪˈzɛrɪkɔːd/ *noun* in a church: a ledge on the underside of a seat in the choir stalls which a standing person can use as a support when the seat is folded up. [14c: from Latin *misericordia* compassion]

misery *noun* (***-ies***) **1** great unhappiness or suffering. **2** a cause of unhappiness: *His biggest misery is the cold.* **3** poverty or squalor: *living in misery.* **4** *informal* a habitually sad or bad-tempered person. [14c: from French *miserie*]

IDIOMS **put sb** *or* **sth out of their misery 1** to relieve them from their physical suffering or their mental anguish. **2** to kill (an animal that is in great pain).

misfire *verb, intr* **1** of a gun, etc: to fail to fire, or to fail to fire properly. **2** of an engine or vehicle: to fail to ignite the fuel at the right time. **3** of a plan, practical joke, etc: to be unsuccessful; to produce the wrong effect. ▸ *noun* an instance of misfiring.

misfit *noun* someone who is not suited to the situation, job, social environment, etc that they are in.

misfortune *noun* **1** bad luck. **2** an unfortunate incident.

misgiving *noun* (*often* **misgivings**) a feeling of uneasiness, doubt or suspicion.

misguided *adj* acting from or showing mistaken ideas or bad judgement. ▪ **misguidedly** *adv.*

mishandle *verb* to deal with something or someone carelessly or without skill.

mishap *noun* an unfortunate accident, esp a minor one; a piece of bad luck. [14c: from obsolete *hap* luck or happening]

mishear *verb* to hear something or someone incorrectly.

mishit *verb* /mɪsˈhɪt/ *sport, etc* to fail to hit (eg a ball) cleanly or accurately. ▸ *noun* /ˈmɪshɪt/ **1** an act of mishitting. **2** a wrongly-hit ball, shot, etc.

mishmash *noun, informal* a jumbled assortment or mixture. [15c: a reduplication of **mash**]

misinform *verb* to give someone incorrect or misleading information. ▪ **misinformation** *noun.*

misinterpret *verb* to understand or explain something incorrectly or misleadingly. ▪ **misinterpretation** *noun.*

misjudge *verb* to judge something or someone wrongly, or to have an unfairly low opinion of them. ▪ **misjudgement** *or* **misjudgment** *noun.*

miskey *verb, comput, etc* to key (esp data) incorrectly.

mislay *verb* to lose something, usu temporarily, esp by forgetting where it was put.

mislead *verb* to cause someone to have a false impression or belief. ▪ **misleading** *adj* likely to mislead.

mismanage *verb* to manage or handle something or someone badly or carelessly. ▪ **mismanagement** *noun.*

mismatch *verb* /mɪsˈmatʃ/ to match (things or people) unsuitably or incorrectly. ▸ *noun* /ˈmɪsmatʃ/ an unsuitable or incorrect match.

misname *verb* **1** to call something or someone by the wrong name. **2** to give something an unsuitable name.

misnomer /mɪsˈnoʊmə(r)/ *noun* **1** a wrong or unsuitable name. **2** the use of an incorrect name or term. [15c: from French *mesnommer* to misname]

misogamy /mɪˈsɒgəmɪ/ *noun* hatred of marriage. ▪ **misogamist** *noun.* [17c: from Greek *misogamos*]

misogyny /mɪˈsɒdʒɪnɪ/ *noun* hatred of women. ▪ **misogynist** *noun.* [17c: from Greek *misogynes*]

misplace *verb* **1** to lose something, usu temporarily, esp by forgetting where it was put. **2** to give (trust, affection, etc) unwisely or inappropriately. **3** to put something in the wrong place or an unsuitable place.

misprint *noun* /ˈmɪsprɪnt/ a mistake in printing, eg an incorrect or damaged character. ▸ *verb* /mɪsˈprɪnt/ to print something wrongly.

mispronounce *verb* to pronounce (a word, etc) incorrectly. ▪ **mispronunciation** *noun.*

misquote *verb* to quote something or someone inaccurately, sometimes with the intention of deceiving.

misread *verb* **1** to read something incorrectly. **2** to misunderstand or misinterpret something.

misrepresent *verb* to represent something or someone falsely, esp to give a false or misleading account or impression of it or them, often intentionally. ▪ **misrepresentation** *noun.*

misrule *noun, formal* **1** bad or unjust government. **2** civil disorder. ▸ *verb* to govern (eg a country) in a disorderly or unjust way.

miss[1] *verb* **1** *tr & intr* to fail to hit or catch something: *missed the ball.* **2** to fail to get on something: *missed my train.* **3** to fail to take advantage of something: *missed your chance.* **4** to feel or regret the absence or loss of someone or something: *I miss you when you're away.* **5** to notice the absence of someone or something. **6** to fail to hear or see something: *missed his last remark.* **7** to refrain from going to (a place or an event): *I'll have to miss the next class.* **8** to avoid or escape (esp a specified danger): *just missed being run over.* ▸ *noun* a failure to hit or catch something, etc. [Anglo-Saxon *missan*]

IDIOMS **give sth a miss** *informal* to avoid it or refrain from it. **miss the boat** *or* **bus** *informal* to miss an opportunity, esp by being too slow to act.

PHRASAL VERBS **miss out** to fail to benefit from something enjoyable or worthwhile, etc: *Buy some now; don't miss out!* **miss sth out** *or* **miss out sth** to fail to include it; to leave it out.

miss[2] *noun* **1** a girl or unmarried woman. **2** (**Miss**) a term used when addressing an unmarried woman (esp in front of her surname). See also **Ms.** [17c: an abbreviation of **mistress**]

missal *noun, RC Church* a book containing all the texts used in the service of mass throughout the year. [14c: from Latin *missale*]

mis-sell *verb, finance* to sell an inappropriate financial product, eg a personal pension. ▪ **mis-selling** *noun.*

misshapen *adj* badly shaped; deformed.

missile *noun* **1** a self-propelled flying bomb. **2** any weapon or object that is thrown or fired. [17c: from Latin *missilis*]

missing *adj* **1** absent; lost; not able to be found. **2** of a soldier, military vehicle, etc: not able to be located, but not known to be dead or destroyed.

IDIOMS **go missing** to disappear, esp unexpectedly and inexplicably.

missing link *noun* (*esp* **the missing link**) **1** any one thing that is needed to complete a series. **2** a hypothetical extinct creature representing a supposed stage of evolutionary development between apes and humans.

mission *noun* **1** a purpose for which a person or group of people is sent. **2 a** a journey made for a scientific, military or religious purpose; **b** a group of people sent on such a journey. **3** a flight with a specific purpose, such as a bombing raid or a task assigned to the crew of a spacecraft. **4** a group of people sent somewhere to have discussions, esp political ones. **5** (*usu* **mission in life**) someone's chosen, designated or assumed purpose in life or vocation. **6** a centre run by a charitable or religious organization, etc to provide a particular service in the community. [16c: from Latin *missionis*]

missionary *noun* (**-ies**) a member of a religious organization seeking to carry out charitable works and religious teaching.

mission statement *noun* a summary of the aims and principles of an organization, drawn up for the supposed benefit of its members and customers.

missive *noun, literary or law, etc* a letter, esp a long or official one. [15c: French]

misspell *verb* to spell something incorrectly. ▪ **misspelling** *noun.*

---

misspell

This word itself is often misspelt. There are two *s*'s in the middle, as the word is formed from the prefix *mis-* and the verb *spell*. It might help you to remember the following sentence:

*Don't **miss** the other **s** out of **misspell**.*

---

misspend *verb* to spend (money, time, etc) foolishly or wastefully.

missus *or* (*sometimes*) **missis** *noun, informal* **1** *humorous* a wife: *Bring the missus.* **2** *old use* a term used to address an adult female stranger. See also **Mrs.** [18c: orig as a spoken form of **mistress**]

missy *noun* (**-ies**) *informal, old use, usu facetious or derog* a term used to address a girl or young woman.

mist *noun* **1** condensed water vapour in the air near the ground; thin fog or low cloud. **2** a mass of tiny droplets of liquid, eg one forced from a pressurized container. **3** condensed water vapour on a surface. **4** *literary* a watery film: *a mist of tears.* ▸ *verb, tr & intr* (*also* **mist up** *or* **over**) to cover or become covered with mist, or as if with mist. ▪ **misty** *adj* (**-ier, -iest**). [Anglo-Saxon]

mistake *noun* **1** an error. **2** a regrettable action. **3** an act of understanding or interpreting something wrongly. ▸ *verb* (*past tense* ***mistook,*** *past participle* ***mistaken***) **1** to misinterpret or misunderstand something: *I mistook your meaning.* **2** to make the wrong choice of something: *He mistook the turning in the fog.* ▪ **mistakable** *adj.* [14c: from Norse *mistaka* to take something wrongly]

IDIOMS **by mistake** accidentally.

mistaken *adj* **1** understood, thought, named, etc wrongly; incorrect: *mistaken identity.* **2** guilty of, or displaying, a failure to understand or interpret correctly: *You are mistaken in saying that he's English.* ▸ *verb, past participle of* **mistake** ▪ **mistakenly** *adv.*

mister *noun* **1** (**Mister**) the full form of the abbrev **Mr.** **2** *informal* a term used when addressing an adult male stranger: *Can I have my ball back please, mister?* [16c: orig a spoken form of **master**]

mistime *verb* **1** to do or say something at a wrong or unsuitable time. **2** *sport* to misjudge the timing of (a stroke, etc) in relation to the speed of an approaching ball.

mistletoe *noun* an evergreen shrub that grows as a parasite on trees and produces clusters of white berries in winter. [Anglo-Saxon *misteltan*]

mistook *past tense of* **mistake**

mistreat *verb* to treat someone or something cruelly or without care. ▪ **mistreatment** *noun.*

mistress *noun* **1** the female lover of a man married to another woman. **2** *rather dated* a female teacher:

She is the French mistress. Compare **master** (sense 5). **3** a woman in a commanding or controlling position; a female head or owner. **4** (*esp* **Mistress**) *formerly* a term used when addressing any woman, esp one in authority. Compare **Mrs.** [14c: French]

mistrial *noun, law* a trial not conducted properly according to the law and declared invalid.

mistrust *verb* to have no trust in, or to be suspicious of, someone or something. ▸ *noun* a lack of trust. ▪ **mistrustful** *adj.* ▪ **mistrustfully** *adv.*

misunderstand *verb, tr & intr* to fail to understand something or someone properly. ▪ **misunderstanding** *noun* **1** a failure to understand properly. **2** a slight disagreement.

misunderstood *verb, past tense, past participle of* **misunderstand.** ▸ *adj* usu of a person: not properly understood or appreciated as regards character, feelings, intentions, purpose, etc.

misuse *noun* /mɪs'juːs/ improper or inappropriate use: *the misuse of funds.* ▸ *verb* /mɪs'juːz/ **1** to put something to improper or inappropriate use. **2** to treat something or someone badly.

mite[1] *noun* a small, often microscopic, animal with a simple rounded body and eight legs. [Anglo-Saxon]

mite[2] *noun* **1** any small person or animal. **2** a small amount of anything, esp of money. [14c: Dutch a small copper coin]

miter the *US* spelling of **mitre**[1], **mitre**[2].

mitigate *verb* to make (pain, anger, etc) less severe. ▪ **mitigating** *adj*: *mitigating circumstances.* ▪ **mitigation** *noun.* [15c: from Latin *mitigare* to calm or soothe]

mitochondrion *noun* (***mitochondria***) *biol* in the cytoplasm of most cells: a specialized oval structure, consisting of a central matrix surrounded by two membranes. ▪ **mitochondrial** *adj.* [20c: from Greek *mitos* thread + *khondrion* granule]

mitosis *noun* (***-ses***) *biol* a type of cell division in which two new nuclei are produced, each containing the same number of chromosomes as the parent nucleus. Compare **meiosis.** [19c: Latin]

mitral valve /'maɪtrəl/ *noun, anatomy* the valve in the heart that allows blood to flow from the left atrium to the left ventricle. [17c: from its resemblance to a bishop's **mitre**]

mitre[1] *or* (*US*) **miter** *noun* the ceremonial headdress of a bishop or abbot, a tall pointed hat with separate front and back sections. [14c: French]

mitre[2] *or* (*US*) **miter** *noun* in joinery, etc: a corner joint between two lengths of wood, etc made by fitting together two 45° sloping surfaces cut into their ends. Also called **mitre joint.** ▸ *verb* to join (two lengths of wood, etc) with a mitre. [17c]

mitt *noun* **1** *informal* a hand: *Keep your mitts off!* **2** *baseball* a large padded leather glove worn by the catcher. **3** a thick loosely-shaped glove designed for a specific purpose: *oven mitt.* **4** a mitten or fingerless glove. [18c: a shortening of **mitten**]

mitten *noun* a glove with one covering for the thumb and a large covering for all the other fingers together. [14c: from French *mitaine*]

mix *verb* **1** (*esp* **mix sth with sth else**, or **mix sth and sth else together** *or* **up together**) to put (things, substances, etc) together or to combine them to form one mass. **2** to prepare or make something by doing this: *mix a cake.* **3** *intr* to blend together to form one mass: *Water and oil do not mix.* **4** *intr* of a person: **a** to meet with people socially; **b** to feel at ease in social situations. **5** to do something at the same time as something else; to combine: *I'm mixing business with pleasure.* **6** to drink (different types of alcoholic drink) on one occasion: *Don't mix your drinks!* **7** *technical* to adjust (separate sound elements, eg the sounds produced by individual musicians) electronically to create an overall balance or particular effect. See also **remix.** ▸ *noun* **1** a collection of people or things mixed together. **2** a collection of ingredients, esp dried ingredients, from which something is prepared: *cake mix.* **3** *technical* in music, broadcasting, cinema, etc: the combined sound or soundtrack, etc produced by mixing various recorded elements. [16c: from Latin *miscere* to mix]

IDIOMS **be mixed up in sth** *or* **with sth** *or* **sb** *informal* to be involved in it or with them, esp when it is something illicit or suspect.

PHRASAL VERBS **mix sth** *or* **sb up 1** to confuse it or them for something else. **2** *informal* to upset or put into a state of confusion: *The divorce really mixed me up.* See also **mixed-up.**

mixed *adj* **1** consisting of different and often opposite kinds of things, elements, characters, etc: *a mixed reaction.* **2** done, used, etc by people of both sexes: *mixed bathing.* **3** mingled or combined by mixing.

mixed bag *noun, informal* a collection of people or things of different kinds, characteristics, standards, backgrounds, etc.

mixed blessing *noun* something which has both advantages and disadvantages.

mixed farming *noun* a combination of **arable** and **livestock** farming.

mixed grill *noun, cookery* a dish of different kinds of grilled meat, often with tomatoes and mushrooms.

mixed marriage *noun* a marriage between people of different races or religions.

mixed metaphor *noun* a combination of two or more metaphors which produces an inconsistent or incongruous mental image, and is often regarded as a stylistic flaw, eg *There are concrete steps in the pipeline.*

mixed number *noun* a number consisting of an integer and a fraction, eg 2½.

mixed-up *adj* **1** mentally or emotionally confused. **2** badly-adjusted socially.

mixer *noun* **1** a machine used for mixing: *a cement mixer.* **2** a soft drink for mixing with alcoholic drinks. **3** *informal* someone considered in terms of their ability to mix socially: *a good mixer.* **4** *electronics* a device which combines two or more input signals into a single output signal.

mixer tap *noun* a tap which can mix the hot and cold water supplies, with one outlet for both hot and cold, and separate controls for adjusting the mix.

mixture *noun* **1** a blend of ingredients prepared for a particular purpose: *cake mixture* • *cough mixture.* **2** a combination: *a mixture of sadness and relief.* **3** the act of mixing. **4** the product of mixing.

mix-up *noun* a confusion or misunderstanding.

mizzenmast *noun, naut* on a ship with three or more masts: the third mast from the front of the ship. Often shortened to **mizzen.** [15c: from Italian *mezzano* middle + **mast**[1]]

Mk *abbrev* mark, a type of design or model, esp of vehicles. See **mark**[1] (*noun* sense 9).

MKS *or* **mks** *abbrev* metre-kilogram-second: *mks unit* • *MKS system.*

ml *abbrev* **1** mile or miles. **2** millilitre or millilitres.

Mlle *abbrev* (***Mlles***) *Mademoiselle* (French), Miss.

mm *abbrev* millimetre or millimetres.

Mme *abbrev* (***Mmes***) *Madame* (French), Mrs.

MMR *abbrev, med* measles, mumps and rubella, a vaccine given to protect children against these diseases.

Mn *symbol, chem* manganese.

mnemonic /nɪ'mɒnɪk/ *noun* a device or form of words, often a short verse, used as a memory-aid. ▸ *adj* serving to help the memory. [18c: from Greek *mnemonikos*]

MO *abbrev* **1** Medical Officer, an army doctor. **2** money order.

Mo *symbol, chem* molybdenum.

mo *noun, chiefly Brit informal* a short while; a moment. [19c: a shortening of **moment**]

moa *noun* an extinct flightless ostrich-like bird of New Zealand. [19c: Maori]

moan *noun* **1** a low prolonged sound expressing sadness, grief or pain. **2** any similar sound, eg made by the wind or an engine. **3** *informal* a complaint or grumble. **4** *informal* someone who complains a lot. ▸ *verb* **1** *intr* to utter or produce a moan. **2** *intr, informal* to complain, esp without good reason. **3** to utter something with a moan or moans. ▪ **moaner** *noun.* ▪ **moaning** *adj, noun.* [13c]

moat *noun* a deep trench, often filled with water, dug round a castle or other fortified position to provide extra defence. [14c: French from *mote* mound]

mob *noun* **1** a large, disorderly crowd. **2** *informal* any group or gang. **3** (**the mob**) *informal* ordinary people; the masses. **4** (**the mob**) an organized gang of criminals, esp the **Mafia**. **5** *Aust, NZ* a large herd or flock. ▸ *verb* (***mobbed, mobbing***) **1** to attack something or someone as a mob. **2** to crowd round someone or something, esp curiously or admiringly. **3** *esp N Am* to crowd into (a building, shop, etc). ▪ **mobbed** *adj, informal* densely crowded; packed. [17c: shortening of Latin *mobile vulgus* fickle masses]

mobie *or* **mobey** *noun, slang* a **mobile phone**.

mobile *adj* **1** able to be moved easily; not fixed. **2** set up inside a vehicle travelling from place to place: *mobile shop.* **3** of a face: that frequently changes expression. **4** moving, or able to move, from one social class to another: *upwardly mobile.* **5** *informal* provided with transport and able to travel. ▸ *noun* **1** a hanging decoration or sculpture, etc made up of parts that are moved around by air currents. **2** *informal* a mobile phone, shop, etc. ▪ **mobility** *noun.* [15c: French]

mobile home *noun* a type of house, similar to a large caravan, which can be towed but is usu kept in one place and connected to the local utilities.

mobile phone *noun* a portable telephone that operates by means of a cellular radio system. Often shortened to **mobile**.

mobilize *or* **-ise** *verb* **1** to organize or prepare something or someone for use, action, etc. **2** **a** to assemble and make (forces, etc) ready for war; **b** *intr* of forces, etc: to assemble and become ready for war. ▪ **mobilization** *noun.*

mobster *noun, slang* a member of a gang or an organized group of criminals, esp the **Mafia**.

moccasin *noun* **1** a deerskin or other soft leather shoe with a continuous sole and heel, as worn by Native Americans. **2** any slipper or shoe in this style. [17c: from Algonquian (a family of Native American languages)]

mocha /'mɒkə/ *noun* **1** a flavouring made from coffee and chocolate. **2** a deep brown colour. **3** dark brown coffee of fine quality. [18c: from *Mocha*, an Arabian port]

mock *verb* **1** *tr & intr* (*also* **mock at sb** *or* **sth**) to speak or behave disparagingly, derisively, or contemptuously towards someone or something. **2** to mimic someone, usu in a way that makes fun of them. **3** *chiefly literary* to make something seem to be impossible or useless; to defy, disappoint or frustrate it, as though showing contempt for it: *Violent winds mocked my attempt to pitch the tent.* ▸ *adj* **1** false; sham: *mock sincerity.* **2** serving as practice for the similar but real or true thing, event, etc which is to come later: *a mock examination.* ▸ *noun, informal* in England and Wales: a mock examination. *Scot equivalent* **prelim.** ▪ **mocking** *adj, noun.* [15c: from French *mocquer* to deride or jeer]

mockers *plural noun*

IDIOMS **put the mockers on sth** *or* **sb** *informal* to spoil or end its or their chances of success.

mockery *noun* (**-*ies***) **1** an imitation, esp a contemptible or insulting one. **2** **a** any ridiculously inadequate person, action or thing; **b** the subject of ridicule or contempt: *make a mockery of someone.* **3** ridicule; contempt. [15c: from French *moquerie*]

mock turtle soup *noun, cookery* soup made in the style of turtle soup, but using a calf's head.

mock-up *noun* **1** a full-size model or replica of something, built for experimental purposes. **2** a rough layout of a printed text or item, showing the size, colours, etc.

mod[1] *adj, informal, dated* short form of **modern**. ▸ *noun* (**Mod**) orig in the 1960s: a follower of a British teenage culture characterized by a liking for smart clothes and motor scooters. Compare **Rocker**. [20c]

mod[2] *or* **Mod** *noun* a Scottish Gaelic literary and musical festival, held annually. [19c: Gaelic]

mod. *abbrev* **1** moderate. **2** *music* moderato. **3** modern.

modal /'moʊdəl/ *adj* **1** *grammar* belonging or relating to, or concerning, **mood**[2] or a mood. **2** of music: using or relating to a particular mode. ▸ *noun, grammar* a verb used as the auxiliary of another verb to express grammatical mood such as condition, possibility and obligation, eg *can, could, may, shall, will, must, ought to.* Also called **modal auxiliary, modal verb**. See also **auxiliary verb**. ▪ **modally** *adv.* [16c: from Latin *modalis*]

modality *noun* (**-*ies***) **1** *music* the quality or characteristic of music as determined by its **mode** (sense 4). **2** *grammar* the modal property of a verb or construction.

mod cons *plural noun, informal* modern household conveniences, eg central heating, washing machine, etc. [20c: abbreviation of *modern conveniences*]

mode *noun* **1** *rather formal* a way of doing something, or of living, acting, etc: *a new mode of transport.* **2** a fashion or style, eg in clothes or art: *the latest mode*. **3** *comput* a method of operation as provided by the software: *print mode*. **4** *music* any of several systems according to which notes in an octave are or were arranged. **5** *stats* the value of greatest frequency in a set of numbers. Compare **mean**[3] (sense 2a), **median** (sense 3). [14c: from Latin *modus* manner or measure]

model *noun* **1** a small-scale representation of something that serves as a guide in constructing the full-scale version. **2** a small-scale replica. *as adj*: *a model railway.* **3** one of several types or designs of manufactured article: *the latest model of car.* **4** a person whose job is to display clothes to potential buyers by wearing them. **5** a person who is the subject of an artist's or photographer's work, etc. **6** a thing from which something else is to be derived; a basis. **7** an excellent example; an example to be copied: *She's a model of loyalty. as adj*: *a model boss.* ▶ *verb* (***modelled, modelling***; *US* ***modeled, modeling***) **1** *tr & intr* to display (clothes) by wearing them. **2** *intr* to work as a model for an artist, photographer, etc. **3** *tr & intr* to make models of something. **4** (*esp* **model sth on sth else**) to plan, build or create it according to a model. [16c: from French *modelle*]

modelling *or* (*US*) **modeling** *noun* **1** the act or activity of making a model or models. **2** the activity or occupation of a person who models clothes.

modem *noun, comput* an electronic device that transmits information from one computer to another along a telephone line, converting digital data into audio signals and back again. [20c: contraction from *mo*dulator + *dem*odulator]

moderate *adj* /ˈmɒdərət/ **1** not extreme; not strong or violent. **2** average; middle rate: *moderate intelligence.* ▶ *noun* /ˈmɒdərət/ someone who holds moderate views, esp on politics. ▶ *verb* /ˈmɒdəreɪt/ **1** *tr & intr* to make or become less extreme, violent or intense. **2** *tr & intr* to control what is published, eg in an Internet newsgroup. **3** *intr* (*also* **moderate over sth**) to act as a moderator in any sense, eg over an assembly. ▪ **moderately** *adv.* [15c: from Latin *moderatus*]

moderation *noun* **1** the quality or state of being moderate. **2** an act of becoming or making something moderate or less extreme. **3** lack of excess; self-control.

moderato /mɒdəˈrɑːtoʊ/ *music, adv, adj* at a restrained and moderate tempo. [18c: Italian]

moderator *noun* **1** *Christianity* in a Presbyterian Church: a minister who presides over a court or assembly. **2** someone who settles disputes. Also called **mediator**. **3** *nuclear physics* a substance used for slowing down neutrons in nuclear reactors. **4** a person or thing that moderates in any other sense.

modern *adj* **1** belonging to the present or to recent times; not old or ancient. **2** of techniques, equipment, etc: involving, using or being the very latest available: *modern transport.* ▶ *noun* a person living in modern times, esp someone who follows the latest trends. ▪ **modernity** *noun.* [16c: from French *moderne*]

modern dance *noun* an expressive style of dance developed in the early 20c, which rejects the stylized movements and structure of classical ballet.

modernism *noun* **1** modern spirit or character. **2** a modern usage, expression or trait. **3** (**Modernism**) in early 20c art, literature, architecture, etc: a movement characterized by the use of unconventional subject matter and style, experimental techniques, etc. ▪ **modernist** *noun, adj.*

modernize *or* **-ise** *verb* **1** to bring something up to modern standards, or adapt it to modern style, conditions, etc. **2** *intr* to switch to more modern methods or techniques. ▪ **modernization** *noun.*

modest *adj* **1** not having or showing pride; humble; not pretentious or showy. **2** not large; moderate: *a modest income.* **3** unassuming; shy or diffident. **4** *old use* esp of clothing: plain and restrained: *a modest dress.* ▪ **modestly** *adv.* ▪ **modesty** *noun* (***-ies***). [16c: from Latin *modestus* moderate]

modicum *noun, formal or facetious* a small amount. [15c: Latin]

modifier *noun* **1** *grammar* a word or phrase that modifies or identifies the meaning of another word, eg *in the green hat* in the phrase *the man in the green hat*, and *vaguely* in the phrase *He was vaguely embarrassed.* **2** a person or thing that modifies in any sense.

modify *verb* (***-ies, -ied***) **1** to change the form or quality of something, usu only slightly. **2** *grammar* to act as a modifier of (a word). **3** to moderate. ▪ **modifiable** *adj.* ▪ **modification** *noun.* [14c: from French *modifier*]

modish /ˈmoʊdɪʃ/ *adj, rather formal* stylish; fashionable. ▪ **modishly** *adv.* ▪ **modishness** *noun.*

modulate *verb* **1** *technical* to alter the tone or volume of (a sound, or one's voice). **2** *formal* to change or alter. **3** *intr* (*often* **modulate to** *or* **into sth**) *music* to pass from one key to another with a linking progression of chords. **4** *radio* to cause modulation of a wave. ▪ **modulator** *noun.* [17c: from Latin *modulari* to regulate]

modulation *noun* **1** the act or process of, or an instance of, modulating something. **2** *technical* in radio transmission: the process whereby the frequency or amplitude, etc of a wave is increased or decreased in response to variations in the signal being transmitted. See also **amplitude modulation, frequency modulation**.

module *noun* **1** a separate self-contained unit that combines with others to form a larger unit, structure or system. **2** in a space vehicle: a separate self-contained part used for a particular purpose: *lunar module.* **3** *education* a set course forming a unit in a training scheme, degree programme, etc. ▪ **modular** *adj.* [16c: French]

modulus *noun* (***moduli***) *maths* the absolute value of a real number, whether positive or negative. [19c: Latin, meaning 'a small measure']

modus operandi /ˈmoʊdəs ɒpəˈrandiː, -daɪ/ *noun* (***modi operandi*** /ˈmodaɪ/) a method of working. [17c: Latin, literally 'way of working']

modus vivendi /ˈmoʊdəs vɪˈvɛndiː, -daɪ/ *noun* (***modi vivendi*** /ˈmodaɪ/) an arrangement by which people or groups in conflict can work or exist together; a compromise. [19c: Latin, meaning 'way of living']

moggy *or* **moggie** *noun* (***-ies***) *Brit informal* a cat, esp an ordinary domestic cat. Often shortened to **mog**. [19c: orig as dialect pet name for a calf]

mogul *noun* **1** an important, powerful, or influential person: *a movie mogul.* **2** (**Mogul**) *hist* a Mongol or

Mongolian, esp one of the followers of Baber, the conqueror of India (1483–1530). Also **Mughal**. [16c: from Persian *Mughul* **Mongol**]

mohair *noun* **1** the long soft hair of the Angora goat. **2** a yarn or fabric made of this, either pure or mixed with wool. See also **angora**. [16c: from Arabic *mukhayyar*]

mohican *noun* a hairstyle popular amongst **punks**, in which the head is partially shaved, leaving a central, front-to-back band of hair, usu coloured and formed into a spiky crest. [20c: the style is associated with the Mohicans, a Native American tribe]

moiety /ˈmɔɪətɪ/ *noun* (*-ies*) *literary or law* a half; one of two parts or divisions. [14c: from French *moité*]

moire /mwɑː(r)/ *noun* a fabric, esp silk, with a pattern of glossy irregular waves. [17c: French]

moiré /ˈmwɑːreɪ/ *adj* of a fabric: having a pattern of glossy irregular waves; watered. ▸ *noun* this pattern on the surface of a fabric or metal. [19c: French]

moist *adj* **1** damp or humid; slightly wet or watery. **2** of a climate: rainy. ▪ **moistness** *noun*. [14c: from French *moiste*]

moisten *verb, tr & intr* to make something moist, or become moist.

moisture *noun* liquid in vapour or spray form, or condensed as droplets.

moisturize *or* **-ise** *verb* **1** to make something less dry; to add moisture to it. **2** *tr & intr* to apply a cosmetic moisturizer to the skin. ▪ **moisturizer** *noun*.

mol *symbol, chem* **mole**[3].

molar *noun* any of the large back teeth in humans and other mammals, used for chewing and grinding. ▸ *adj* belonging or relating to a molar. [17c: from Latin *mola* millstone]

molasses *singular noun* **1** the thickest kind of treacle, left over in the process of refining raw sugar. **2** *N Am* treacle. [16c: from Portuguese *melaço*]

mold, molder, molding, moldy, etc the *N Am* spelling of **mould, moulder, moulding, mouldy,** etc.

mole[1] *noun* **1** a small insectivorous burrowing mammal with velvety greyish-black fur and strong front legs with very broad feet adapted for digging. **2** *informal* a spy who works inside an organization and passes secret information to people outside it. [20c]

mole[2] *noun* a raised or flat, dark, permanent spot on the skin, caused by a concentration of melanin. [Anglo-Saxon *mal*]

mole[3] *noun, chem* (symbol **mol**) the SI unit of amount of substance, equal to the amount of a substance (in grams) that contains as many atoms, molecules, etc, as there are atoms of carbon in 12 grams of the isotope carbon-12. [20c: from German *Mol*]

mole[4] *noun* **1** a pier, causeway or breakwater made of stone. **2** a harbour protected by any of these. [16c: from Latin *moles* mass]

molecule /ˈmɒlɪkjuːl/ *noun* **1** *chem, physics* the smallest particle of an element or compound that can exist independently and participate in a reaction, consisting of two or more atoms bonded together. **2** *loosely* a tiny particle. ▪ **molecular** /məˈlɛkjʊlə(r)/ *adj*. [18c: from French *molécule*]

molehill *noun* a little pile of earth thrown up by a burrowing mole (see **mole**[1]).

mole salamander see under **axolotl**

moleskin *noun* **1** mole's fur. **2 a** a heavy twilled cotton fabric with a short nap. **b** (**moleskins**) trousers made of this fabric.

molest *verb* **1** to attack or interfere with someone sexually. **2** *formal* to attack someone, causing them physical harm. ▪ **molestation** *noun*. ▪ **molester** *noun*. [14c: from Latin *molestare*]

moll *noun, slang, old use* a gangster's girlfriend. [16c: from the female name *Moll*, a diminutive of *Mary*]

mollify *verb* (*-ies, -ied*) **1** to make someone calmer or less angry. **2** to soothe, ease, or soften something (eg someone's anger, etc). ▪ **mollification** *noun*. ▪ **mollifier** *noun*. [16c: from French *mollifier*]

mollusc *noun, zool* an invertebrate animal with a soft unsegmented body, with its upper surface often protected by a hard, chalky shell, eg the snail, mussel, etc. [18c: from Latin *molluscus* softish]

mollycoddle *verb, informal* to treat someone with fussy care and protection. [19c: from Molly, a female name + **coddle**]

molt the *N Am* spelling of **moult**

molten *adj* in a melted state; liquefied: *molten metal*. [14c: an old past participle of **melt**]

molto *adv, adj, music* very; much: *molto allegro*. [19c: Italian]

molybdenum /məˈlɪbdənəm/ *noun, chem* (symbol **Mo**) a hard silvery metallic element that is used as a hardening agent in various alloys, etc. [19c: Latin]

mom, momma *or* **mommy** *noun* (***moms, mommas,*** *or* ***mommies***) *N Am informal* mother. *Brit equivalents* **mum, mummy**.

moment *noun* **1** a short while: *It will only take a moment*. Sometimes shortened to **mo**. **2** a particular point in time: *at that moment*. **3** (**the moment**) the present point, or the right point, in time: *cannot be disturbed at the moment*. **4** *formal* importance or significance: *a literary work of great moment*. **5** *physics* a measure of turning effect, eg the **moment of force** about a point is the product of the force and the perpendicular on its line of action from the point. [14c: from Latin *momentum* movement]

IDIOMS **of the moment** currently very popular, important, fashionable, etc.

momentarily *adv* **1** for a moment: *paused momentarily*. **2** every moment: *kept pausing momentarily*. **3** *N Am* at any moment.

momentary *adj* lasting for only a moment.

moment of truth *noun* a very important or significant point in time, esp one when a person or thing is faced with stark reality or is put to the test.

momentous *adj* describing something of great importance or significance.

momentum *noun* (***momentums*** *or* ***momenta***) **1 a** continuous speed of progress; impetus: *The campaign gained momentum*; **b** the force that an object gains in movement. **2** *physics* the product of the mass and the velocity of a moving object. [17c: Latin, meaning 'movement']

momma *or* **mommy** see under **mom**

Mon. *abbrev* Monday.

mon- see **mono-**

monad *noun* **1** *philos* any self-contained non-physical unit of being, eg God, or a soul. **2** *biol* a single-celled organism. **3** *chem* a univalent element, atom or **radical** (*noun* sense 3). [17c: from Greek *monas* a unit]

monandrous *adj* **1** *botany* having only one stamen in each flower. See also **polyandrous**. **2** *sociol* having or allowing only one husband or male partner at a time. [19c: from Greek *andros* man]

monarch *noun* a king, queen or other non-elected sovereign with a hereditary right to rule. ▪ **monarchic** *or* **monarchical** *adj*. [15c: from Latin *monarcha*]

monarchism *noun* **1** the principles of monarchic government. **2** support for monarchy. ▪ **monarchist** *noun* a supporter of the monarchy.

monarchy *noun* (**-ies**) **1** a form of government in which the head of state is a **monarch**. **2** a country which has this form of government.

monastery *noun* (**-ies**) the home of a community of monks. [15c: from Greek *monasterion*]

monastic *adj* **1** belonging or relating to monasteries, monks or nuns. **2** marked by simplicity and self-discipline, like life in a monastery. ▪ **monasticism** *noun*. [17c: from Latin *monasticus*]

Monday *noun* (abbrev **Mon.**) the second day of the week, and the beginning of the working week. [Anglo-Saxon *monandæg* moon day]

monetarism *noun, econ* the theory or practice of basing an economy on, and curbing inflation by, control of the **money supply** rather than by fiscal policy. Also called **monetarist theory**. ▪ **monetarist** *noun, adj*.

monetary *adj* belonging or relating to, or consisting of, money. [19c: from Latin *monetarius*]

money *noun* (*pl* in sense 1b and 4 ***monies*** *or* ***moneys***) **1 a** coins or banknotes used as a means of buying things; **b** any currency used as **legal tender**. **2** wealth in general. **3** *informal* a rich person; rich people: *marry money*. **4** *commerce, law* (*always* **monies** *or* **moneys**) sums of money. ▪ **moneyed** *or* **monied** *adj*. [13c: from French *moneie*]

IDIOMS **be in the money** *informal* to be wealthy. **for my, our,** *etc* **money** *informal* in my, our, etc opinion. **money for old rope** *informal* money obtained without any effort. **money talks** an expression used to convey the idea that people with money have power and influence over others. **on the money** *US slang* spot-on; exactly right. **put money on sth** *informal* to bet on it. **put one's money where one's mouth is** to support what one has said by risking or investing money, or giving other material or practical help.

moneybags *singular noun, informal* a very rich person.

money-grubber *noun, derog, informal* someone who greedily acquires as much money as possible. ▪ **money-grubbing** *adj, noun*.

moneylender *noun* a person or small business that lends money to people at interest, esp at rates higher than general commercial interest rates. ▪ **moneylending** *noun*.

moneymaker *noun, informal* a project or company, etc that makes, or is expected to make, a large profit. ▪ **moneymaking** *adj, noun*.

money order *noun* a written order for the transfer of money from one person to another, through a post office or bank. See also **postal order**.

money-spinner *noun, informal* an idea or project, etc that brings in large sums of money. ▪ **money-spinning** *adj, noun*.

money supply *noun, econ* the amount of money in circulation in an economy at a given time.

-monger *combining form, forming nouns, denoting* **1** a trader or dealer: *fishmonger*. **2** someone who spreads or promotes something undesirable or evil: *scandalmonger*. [Anglo-Saxon *mangere*]

Mongol *noun, hist* any member of the tribes of central Asia and S Siberia that were united to form an empire under Genghis Khan in 1206.

Mongolian *adj* belonging or relating to Mongolia, a republic in E central Asia, its inhabitants, or their language. ▸ *noun* (*also* **Mongol**) **1** a citizen or inhabitant of, or person born in, Mongolia. **2** the official language of Mongolia.

mongoose *noun* (***mongooses***) a small mammal that preys on snakes, etc, and has a long, slender body, pointed muzzle and a bushy tail. [17c: from Marathi (a language of S India) *mangus*]

mongrel *noun* **1** an animal, esp a dog, of mixed breeding. **2** *derog* a person or thing of mixed origin or nature. ▸ *adj* **1** characterized by being of mixed breeding, origin or nature. **2** neither one thing nor another. [15c]

monied *or* **monies** see under **money**

moniker *noun, slang* a nickname. [19c]

monism *noun, philos* the theory that reality exists in one form only, esp that there is no difference in substance between body and soul. ▪ **monist** *noun*. ▪ **monistic** *adj*. [19c: from Greek *monos* single]

monitor *noun* **1** any instrument designed to check, record or control something on a regular basis. **2** a high-quality screen used in closed-circuit television systems, in TV studios, etc to view the picture being transmitted, etc. **3** the visual display unit of a computer, used to present information to the user. **4** someone whose job is to monitor eg a situation, process, etc. ▸ *verb* to check, record, track or control something on a regular basis; to observe or act as a monitor of something. ▪ **monitorial** *adj*. ▪ **monitorship** *noun*. [16c: from Latin *monere* to warn or advise]

monk *noun* a member of a religious community of men living disciplined austere lives devoted primarily to worship, under vows of poverty, chastity and obedience. [Anglo-Saxon *munuc*]

monkey *noun* (**-eys**) **1** any mammal belonging to the **primate**s other than a human, ape, chimpanzee, gibbon, orang utan or lemur, with a hairy coat, nails instead of claws, and usu tree-dwelling. **2** *informal* a mischievous child. **3** *Brit slang* £500. **4** *US slang* an oppressive burden or habit, esp a drug addiction. ▸ *verb, intr, informal* (*esp* **monkey about** *or* **around with sth**) to play, fool, interfere, etc with it. [16c]

IDIOMS **make a monkey out of sb** *informal* to make them seem ridiculous; to make a fool of them. **not give a monkey's** *slang* not to care at all.

monkey business *noun, informal* mischief; illegal or dubious activities.

monkey nut *noun* a peanut in its shell.

monkey tricks *plural noun, informal* mischief; pranks. *US equivalent* **monkey shines**.

monkey wrench *noun* a spanner-like tool with movable jaws; an adjustable spanner.

mono *informal, noun* **1** monophonic reproduction of sound. **2** a monophonic ringtone. ▸ *adj* **1** short form of **monophonic**. **2** short form of **monounsaturated**.

mono- *or* (*before a vowel*) **mon-** *combining form, denoting* one; single: *monosyllable* • *monoxide.* [From Greek *monos* single]

monochromatic *adj, physics* **a** of light: having only one wavelength; **b** of radiation or oscillation: having a unique or very narrow band of frequency.

monochrome *adj* **1** of visual reproduction: using or having one colour, or in black and white only. **2** esp of painting: using shades of one colour only. **3** lacking any variety or interest; dull or monotonous. ▸ *noun* **1** a monochrome picture, photograph, drawing, etc. **2** representation in monochrome. **3** the art or technique of working in monochrome. [17c: from medieval Latin *monochroma*]

monocle *noun* a lens for correcting the sight in one eye only, held in place between the bones of the cheek and brow. ▪ **monocled** *adj.* [19c: French]

monocline *noun, geol* in rock strata: a fold with one side that dips steeply, after which the strata resume their original direction. ▪ **monoclinal** *adj.* [19c: from Greek *klinein* to cause something to slope]

monocotyledon *noun, botany* a flowering plant with an embryo that has one **cotyledon**, eg daffodil, grasses and palms. Compare **dicotyledon**.

monocracy /mɒˈnɒkrəsɪ/ *noun* (**-ies**) **1** government by one person only. **2** the rule of such a person. **3** a country, state, society, etc that is governed by one person. ▪ **monocrat** *noun.* ▪ **monocratic** *adj.*

monocular *adj* for the use of, or relating to, one eye only.

monoculture *noun* **1** growing the same crop each year on a piece of land, rather than growing different crops in rotation. **2** an area where there is one shared culture, eg a single social or religious culture.

monocyte *noun, biol* the largest type of white blood cell, which has a single, oval or kidney-shaped nucleus and clear cytoplasm. [20c: from German *Monozyt*; see **-cyte**]

monody *noun* (**-ies**) **1** *literary* esp in Greek tragedy: a mournful song or speech performed by a single actor. **2** *music* a song in which the melody is sung by one voice only, with other voices accompanying. ▪ **monodist** *noun.* [17c: from Greek *monoidia*]

monogamy *noun* **1** the state or practice of having only one husband or wife at any one time. Compare **polygamy**. **2** *zool* the state or practice of having only one mate. ▪ **monogamist** *noun.* ▪ **monogamous** *adj.* [17c]

monoglot *noun* a person who only knows and speaks one language. [19c]

monogram *noun* a design composed from letters, usu a person's initials, often used on personal belongings, clothing, etc. [17c]

monograph *noun* a book or essay dealing with one particular subject or a specific aspect of it.

monolingual *adj* **1** of a person: able to speak one language only. **2** expressed in, or dealing with, a single language: *a monolingual dictionary.*

monolith *noun* **1** a single, tall block of stone, esp one shaped like or into a column or pillar. **2** anything resembling one of these in its uniformity, immovability or massiveness. ▪ **monolithic** *adj.* [19c: from French *monolithe*]

monologue *or* (*US*) **monolog** *noun* **1** *theatre, etc* **a** a long speech by one actor in a film or play. See also **soliloquy**; **b** a drama for one actor. **2** *usu derog* any long, uninterrupted piece of speech by one person, esp a tedious or opinionated speech that prevents any conversation. [17c: French, meaning 'a person who likes to talk at length']

monomania *noun, psychol* domination of the mind by a single subject, to an excessive degree. ▪ **monomaniac** *noun, adj.* [19c: from French *monomanie*]

monomer *noun, chem* a simple molecule that can be joined to many others to form a much larger molecule known as a **polymer**. [20c]

monomial *noun, maths* an algebraic expression that consists of one term only. [18c: from **mono-**, modelled on **binomial**]

mononuclear *adj* of a cell: having a single nucleus.

mononucleosis *noun, pathol* a condition, esp infectious mononucleosis, in which an abnormally large number of lymphocytes are present in the blood.

monophonic *adj* of a recording or broadcasting system, record, etc: reproducing sound or records on one channel only. Now usu shortened to **mono**.

monophthong /ˈmɒnəfθɒŋ/ *noun* a single vowel sound. Compare **diphthong**. [17c: from **mono-** + Greek *phthongos* sound]

monoplane *noun* an aeroplane with a single set of wings. Compare **biplane**.

monopolize *or* **-ise** *verb* **1** to have a monopoly or exclusive control of trade in (a commodity or service). **2** to dominate (eg a conversation or a person's attention), while excluding all others. ▪ **monopolization** *noun.*

monopoly *noun* (**-ies**) **1** the right to be, or the fact of being, the only supplier of a specified commodity or service. **2** a business that has such a monopoly. **3** a commodity or service controlled in this way. **4** exclusive possession or control of anything: *You don't have a monopoly on the truth!* [16c: from Latin *monopolium*]

monorail *noun* a railway system in which the trains run on, or are suspended from, a single rail.

monosaccharide *noun, biochem* a simple sugar, eg **glucose** or **fructose**, that cannot be broken down into smaller units.

monoski *noun* a broad single ski on which the skier places both feet. ▪ **monoskiing** *noun.*

monosodium glutamate *noun* (abbrev **MSG**) a white crystalline chemical substance used to enhance the flavour of many processed savoury foods.

monosyllable *noun* a word consisting of only one syllable. ▪ **monosyllabic** *adj.*

monotheism *noun* the belief that there is only one God. ▪ **monotheist** *noun.* ▪ **monotheistic** *adj.* [17c: from Greek *theos* god]

monotone *noun* **1** in speech or sound: a single unvarying tone. **2** a sequence of sounds of the same tone. **3** esp in colour: sameness; lack of variety. ▸ *adj* **1** lacking in variety; unchanging. **2** in monotone. [17c: from Latin *monotonus*]

monotonous *adj* **1** lacking in variety; tediously unchanging. **2** of speech or sound, etc: in one unvaried tone. ▪ **monotonously** *adv.*

monotony *noun* (**-ies**) **1** the quality of being monotonous. **2** routine or dullness or sameness.

monounsaturated *adj* esp of an oil or fat: containing only one double or triple bond per molecule. Also shortened to **mono**. Compare **polyunsaturated**.

monovalent *adj, chem* of an atom of an element: with a valency of one; capable of combining with one atom of hydrogen or its equivalent. Also called **univalent**. ▪ **monovalence** *or* **monovalency** *noun.*

monoxide *noun, chem* a compound that contains one oxygen atom in each molecule.

Monseigneur /mɒn'sɛnjə(r)/ *noun* (***Messeigneurs*** /meɪ'sɛn-/) (abbrev **Mgr** or *pl* **Mgrs**) a title equivalent to *My Lord*, used to address a French man of high rank or birth, eg a prince. [17c: French]

Monsieur /mə'sjɜː(r)/ *noun* (***Messieurs*** /meɪ-'sjɜː(r)s/) **1** (abbrev **M** or *pl* **MM**) a French title equivalent to **Mr**. **2** (**monsieur**) a Frenchman, when not used with a surname. [16c: French]

Monsignor /mɒn'siːnjə(r)/ *noun* (***Monsignors*** *or* ***Monsignori*** /-'njɔːrɪ/) a title given to various high-ranking male members of the Roman Catholic Church (abbrev **Monsig.** *or* **Mgr**). [17c: Italian]

monsoon *noun* **1** esp in India, etc and S Asia: a wind that blows from the NE in winter (the **dry monsoon**) and from the SW in summer (the **wet monsoon**). **2** in India: the heavy rains that accompany the summer monsoon. [16c: from Dutch *monssoen*]

monster *noun* **1** esp in fables and folklore: any large and frightening imaginary creature. **2** a cruel or evil person. **3** any unusually large thing. **4** *old use* a deformed person, animal or plant. ▸ *adj* huge; gigantic: *monster portions*. [14c: from French *monstre*]

monstrance *noun, RC Church* a gold or silver cup in which the **host**[3] is displayed to the congregation during Mass. [16c: French]

monstrosity *noun* (***-ies***) any very ugly or outrageous thing; a monster or freak.

monstrous *adj* **1** like a monster; huge and horrible. **2** outrageous; absurd. **3** extremely cruel; evil. **4** *old use* deformed; abnormal. ▪ **monstrously** *adv.*

montage /mɒn'tɑːʒ/ *noun* **1 a** the process of creating a picture by assembling and piecing together elements from other pictures, photographs, etc, and mounting them on to canvas, etc; **b** a picture made in this way. **2** the process of editing film material. **3** *cinema, TV* a film sequence made up of short clips, or images superimposed, dissolved together, etc, esp one used to condense events that take place over a long period. **4** *cinema, TV* extensive use of changes in camera position to create an impression of movement or action in a filmed scene. See also **mise-en-scène**. [20c: French, from *monter* to mount]

Montenegrin *adj* belonging or relating to Montenegro, a republic in Europe, or its inhabitants. ▸ *noun* a citizen or inhabitant of, or person born in, Montenegro.

month *noun* **1** any of the 12 named divisions of the year, which vary in length between 28 and 31 days. Also called **calendar month**. **2** a period of roughly four weeks or 30 days. **3** the period between identical dates in consecutive months. Also called **calendar month**. [Anglo-Saxon *monath*]

monthly *adj* **1** happening, published, performed, etc once a month. **2** lasting one month. ▸ *adv* once a month. ▸ *noun* (***-ies***) **1** a monthly periodical. **2** *informal* a menstrual period.

monument *noun* **1** something, eg a statue, built to preserve the memory of a person or event. **2** any ancient building or structure preserved for its historical value. **3** *formal* something that serves as clear evidence of something; an excellent example: *This work is a monument to her artistic skill.* **4** *formal* a tombstone. [14c: from Latin *monumentum*]

monumental *adj* **1** like a monument, esp huge and impressive. **2** belonging or relating to, or taking the form of, a monument. **3** *informal* very great; extreme: *monumental arrogance*. ▪ **monumentally** *adv.*

moo *noun* the long low sound made by a cow, ox, etc. ▸ *verb* (***mooed***) *intr* to make this sound. ▪ **mooing** *noun.* [16c: imitating the sound]

mooch *verb, informal* **1** *intr* (*usu* **mooch about** *or* **around**) to wander around aimlessly. **2** *tr & intr* to cadge or scrounge. [19c]

mood[1] *noun* **1** a state of mind at a particular time. **2** (*esp* **the mood**) a suitable or necessary state of mind: *not in the mood for dancing*. **3** a temporary grumpy state of mind: *Now he's gone off in a mood.* **4** an atmosphere: *The mood in the factory is tense.* [Anglo-Saxon *mod* 'mind' or 'feeling']

mood[2] *noun, grammar* each of several forms of a verb, indicating whether the verb is expressing a fact (see **indicative**), a wish, possibility or doubt (see **subjunctive**) or a command (see **imperative**). [16c: orig a variant of **mode**]

moody *adj* (***-ier, -iest***) **1** tending to change mood often. **2** frequently bad-tempered or sulky. ▪ **moodily** *adv.* ▪ **moodiness** *noun.*

moon[1] *noun* **1** (*often* **Moon**) the Earth's natural satellite, illuminated to varying degrees by the Sun depending on its position and often visible in the sky, esp at night. **2** the appearance of the Moon to an observer on Earth, esp in terms of its degree of illumination, eg **half-moon, full moon**. **3** a natural satellite of any planet: *the moons of Jupiter*. **4** *literary or old use* a month. [Anglo-Saxon *mona*]

IDIOMS **over the moon** *informal* thrilled; delighted.

moon[2] *verb, intr* (*usu* **moon about** *or* **around**) to wander around aimlessly; to spend time idly. [20c]

moonbeam *noun* a ray of sunlight reflected from the moon.

moonface *noun* a full, round face. ▪ **moon-faced** *adj.*

moonlight *noun* sunlight reflected by the moon. ▸ *verb, intr, informal* to work at a second job outside the working hours of one's main job, often evading income tax on the extra earnings. ▪ **moonlighter** *noun.* ▪ **moonlighting** *noun.*

moonlit *adj* illuminated by moonlight: *a clear, moonlit night*.

moonshine *noun, informal* **1** foolish talk; nonsense. **2** *chiefly N Am* smuggled or illegally-distilled alcoholic spirit.

moonshot *noun* a launching of an object, craft, etc to orbit or land on the moon.

moonstone *noun, geol* a transparent or opalescent, silvery or bluish **feldspar**, used as a semi-precious gemstone. [17c: so called because it was once thought that its appearance changed with the waxing and waning of the moon]

moonstruck *adj, informal* behaving in an unusually distracted, dazed, or wild way, as if affected by the moon. [17c]

moony *adj* (***-ier, -iest***) *informal* in a dreamy, distracted mood.

Moor *noun* a Muslim belonging to a mixed Arab/Berber race of NW Africa, that conquered the Iberian peninsula in the 8c. ▪ **Moorish** *adj*. [14c: from French *More* or *Maure*, from Latin *Maurus*]

moor[1] *noun* a large area of open, uncultivated upland with an acid peaty soil. [Anglo-Saxon *mor*]

moor[2] *verb* **1** to fasten (a ship or boat) by a rope, cable or anchor. **2** *intr* of a ship, etc: to be fastened in this way. ▪ **moorage** *noun*. [15c as *more*]

moorhen *noun* a small black water bird of the rail family (see **rail**[3]), with a red beak.

mooring *noun* **1** a place where a boat is moored. **2** (**moorings**) the ropes, anchors, etc used to moor a boat.

moorland *noun* a stretch of **moor**[1].

moose *noun* (*pl* ***moose***) a large deer with flat, rounded antlers, found in N America. Also called **elk**. [17c: from Algonquian (a family of Native American languages) *moos*]

moot *verb* to suggest; to bring something up for discussion. ▸ *adj* open to argument; debatable: *a moot point*. [Anglo-Saxon as *mot* assembly]

mop *noun* **1** a tool for washing or wiping floors, consisting of a large sponge or a set of thick threads fixed on to the end of a long handle. **2** a similar smaller tool for washing dishes. **3** *informal* a thick or tangled mass of hair. ▸ *verb* (***mopped, mopping***) **1** to wash or wipe (eg a floor) with a mop. **2** to wipe, dab or clean (eg a sweaty brow). [15c]

PHRASAL VERBS **mop up** *or* **mop sth up 1** to clean something up (eg a spillage) with a mop. **2** *informal* to capture or kill (remaining enemy troops) after a victory. **3** *informal* to deal with or get rid of (anything that remains).

mope *verb, intr* **1** (*esp* **mope about** *or* **around**) to behave in a depressed, sulky or aimless way. **2** to move in a listless, aimless or depressed way. ▸ *noun* **1** a habitually sulky or depressed person. **2** (**the mopes**) low spirits; depression. ▪ **mopy** *adj* (***-ier, -iest***). [16c]

moped /'moʊpɛd/ *noun* a small-engined motorcycle, esp one that is started by using pedals. [20c: a shortening of *mo*tor-assisted *ped*al-cycle]

moppet *noun* a term of affection used to a small child. See also **poppet**. [17c: diminutive of obsolete *mop* rag doll]

moquette /mɒ'kɛt/ *noun* thick velvety material used to make carpets and upholstery. [18c: French]

moraine *noun, geol* a ridge of rock and earth formed by the gradual movement of a glacier down a valley. [18c: French]

moral *adj* **1** belonging or relating to the principles of good and evil, or right and wrong. **2** conforming to what is considered by society to be good, right or proper; ethical. **3** having a psychological rather than a practical effect: *moral support*. **4** considered in terms of psychological effect, rather than outward appearance: *a moral victory.* **5** of a person: capable of distinguishing between right and wrong. ▸ *noun* **1** a principle or practical lesson that can be learned from a story or event. **2** (**morals**) a sense of right and wrong, or a standard of behaviour based on this: *loose morals*. ▪ **morally** *adv*. [14c: from Latin *moralis*]

morale /mə'rɑːl/ *noun* the level of confidence or optimism in a person or group; spirits: *The news boosted morale in the camp.* [18c: French]

moralist *noun* **1** someone who lives according to strict moral principles. **2** someone who tends to lecture others on their low moral standards. ▪ **moralistic** *adj*.

morality *noun* (***-ies***) **1** the quality of being moral. **2** behaviour in relation to accepted moral standards. **3** a particular system of moral standards.

moralize *or* **-ise** *verb* **1** *intr* to write or speak, esp critically, about moral standards. **2** to explain something in terms of morals. **3** to make someone or something moral or more moral. ▪ **moralization** *noun*.

morass *noun* **1** an area of marshy or swampy ground. **2** *literary* a dangerous or confused situation. [17c: from Dutch *moeras*]

moratorium *noun* (***moratoriums*** *or* ***moratoria***) **1** an agreed temporary break in an activity. **2 a** a legally-authorized postponement of payment of a debt for a given time; **b** the period of time authorized for this. [19c: Latin, from *mora* delay]

moray *noun* a sharp-toothed eel of warm coastal waters. [17c: from Portuguese *moreia*]

morbid *adj* **1** displaying an unhealthy interest in unpleasant things, esp death. **2** *med* relating to, or indicating the presence of, disease. ▪ **morbidity** *noun*. ▪ **morbidly** *adv*. [17c: from Latin *morbus* disease]

mordant *adj* sharply sarcastic or critical; biting. ▸ *noun* **1** *chem* a chemical compound, usu a metallic oxide or salt, that is used to fix colour on textiles, etc that cannot be dyed directly. **2** a corrosive substance. ▪ **mordancy** *noun*. [15c: French, literally 'biting']

more (*used as the comparative of* **many** and **much**) *adj* greater; additional: *Don't use more than two bags.* ▸ *adv* **1** used to form the comparative form of many adjectives and most adverbs, esp those of two or more syllables: *a more difficult problem.* **2** to a greater degree; with a greater frequency: *I miss him more than ever.* **3** again: *Do it once more.* ▸ *pronoun* a greater, or additional, number or quantity of people or things: *If we run out, I'll have to order more.* See also **most**. [Anglo-Saxon *mara* greater]

IDIOMS **more and more** increasingly; continuing to increase. **more or less 1** almost: *more or less finished.* **2** roughly: *It'll take two hours, more or less.*

moreish *or* **morish** *adj, Brit informal* esp of a food: so tasty, delicious, etc that one wants to keep eating more of it. [18c]

morel *noun, botany* an edible fungus whose fruiting body has a pale stalk and a ridged egg-shaped head. [17c: from French *morel* dark brown]

morello *noun* a bitter-tasting, dark-red cherry. [17c: from Italian, meaning 'blackish']

moreover *adv, slightly formal or old use* also; besides; and what is more important.

mores /'mɔːreɪz/ *plural noun, formal* social customs that reflect the basic moral and social values of a particular society. [20c: Latin, pl of *mos* custom]

morganatic *adj, technical* of marriage: between a person of high social rank and one of low rank, and allowing neither the lower-ranking person nor any child from the marriage to inherit the title or property of the higher-ranking person. Compare **left-handed**. [18c: from Latin *matrimonium ad morganaticam*, literally 'marriage with a morning gift'; the offering of the gift, after consummation, is the husband's only duty in such a marriage]

morgue /mɔːg/ *noun* **1** a **mortuary**. **2** in a newspaper office, etc: a place where miscellaneous information is stored for reference. [19c: French]

moribund *adj* **1** dying; near the end of existence. **2** lacking strength or vitality. [18c: from Latin *moribundus*]

morish see **moreish**

Mormon *noun* a member of the Church of Jesus Christ of Latter-Day Saints, a religious sect which accepts as scripture both the Bible and the *Book of Mormon*. [18c: named after Mormon, the supposed author of the Book of Mormon]

morn *noun, poetic* morning. [13c: from Anglo-Saxon *morgen*]

mornay or (*sometimes*) **Mornay** *adj* (following its noun) *cookery* served in a cheese sauce: *cod mornay*. [20c]

morning *noun* **1** the part of the day from sunrise to midday, or from midnight to midday. **2** sunrise; dawn. [13c: from *morn*, modelled on **evening**]

morning coat *noun* a man's black or grey **tailcoat** worn as part of morning dress.

morning dress *noun* men's formal dress for the daytime, consisting of morning coat, grey trousers and usu a top hat.

morning prayer see under **matins** (sense 2)

mornings *adv, informal, dialect or US* in the morning, esp on a regular basis: *I don't work mornings*.

morning sickness *noun, informal* nausea and vomiting or both, often experienced during the early stages of pregnancy, frequently in the morning.

morning star *noun* a planet, usu Venus, seen in the eastern sky just before sunrise.

morocco *noun* a type of soft fine goatskin leather. Also called **morocco leather**. [17c: named after Morocco, the country that this leather was orig brought from]

moron *noun* **1** *derog, informal* a very stupid person. **2** *old use, now very offensive* a person with a mild degree of mental handicap. ▪ **moronic** *adj*. [20c: from Greek *moros* foolish]

morose /mə'roʊs/ *adj* silently gloomy or bad-tempered. ▪ **morosely** *adv*. [16c: from Latin *morosus* peevish]

morph *verb, cinematog, comput* in computer graphics: to blend one screen image into another, eg to transform or manipulate an actor's body. ▪ **morphing** *noun*. [20c]

morpheme *noun, linguistics* any of the grammatically or lexically meaningful units forming or underlying a word, not divisible themselves into smaller meaningful units. ▪ **morphemic** *adj*. [19c: from French *morphème*]

morphine *noun* a highly addictive, narcotic drug obtained from opium, used medicinally as a powerful analgesic and as a sedative. Also (*formerly*) called **morphia**. [19c: from German *Morphin*]

morphogenesis *noun, biol* the development of form and structure in a living organism. ▪ **morphogenetic** *adj*. [19c]

morphology *noun* **1** the study of **morphemes** and the rules by which they combine to form words. **2** the scientific study of the structure of plants and animals. ▪ **morphological** *adj*. ▪ **morphologist** *noun*.

the morrow *noun, old use or poetic* **1** the following day. **2** the morning. [13c: see **morn**]

Morse or **Morse code** *noun* a code used for sending messages, each letter of a word being represented as a series of short or long radio signals or flashes of light. [19c: named after Samuel Morse]

morsel *noun* a small piece of something, esp of food. [13c: French, from *mors* a bite]

mortal *adj* **1** esp of human beings: certain to die at some future time. **2** causing or resulting in death: *mortal combat*. **3** extreme: *mortal fear*. **4** characterized by intense hostility; implacable: *mortal enemies*. **5** used for emphasis: conceivable; single: *every mortal thing*. ▸ *noun* a mortal being, esp a human being. ▪ **mortally** *adv*. [14c: from Latin *mortalis*]

mortality *noun* (**-ies**) **1** the state of being mortal. **2** the number of deaths, eg in a war or epidemic; the death-rate. Also called **mortality rate**. **3** death, esp on a broad scale.

mortal sin *noun, RC Church* a serious sin, for which there can be no forgiveness from God. Compare **venial sin**.

mortar *noun* **1** *building* a mixture of sand, water and cement or lime, used to bond bricks or stones. **2** the small heavy dish in which substances are ground with a **pestle**. **3** a type of short-barrelled artillery gun for firing shells over short distances. ▸ *verb* **1** to fix something (esp bricks) in place with mortar. **2** to plaster (eg a wall) with mortar. **3** to bombard (a place, etc) using a mortar. [13c: from French *mortier*]

mortarboard *noun* **1** *building* a flat board used by bricklayers to carry mortar, held horizontally by a handle underneath. **2** a black cap with a hard, square, flat top, worn by academics at formal occasions.

mortgage /'mɔːgɪdʒ/ *noun* **1 a** a legal agreement by which a building society or bank, etc (the **mortgagee**) grants a client (the **mortgagor** or **mortgager**) a loan for the purpose of buying property, ownership of the property being held by the mortgagee until the loan is repaid; **b** the deed that brings such a contract into effect. **2 a** the money borrowed for this; **b** the regular amounts of money repaid. ▸ *verb* to give ownership of (property) as security for a loan. ▪ **mortgageable** *adj*. [14c: French, from *mort* dead + *gage* pledge]

mortician *noun, N Am, esp US* an undertaker. [19c: from Latin *mortis* death]

mortify *verb* (**-ies, -ied**) **1** to make someone feel humiliated or ashamed. **2** *relig* to control (physical desire) through self-discipline or self-inflicted hardship: *mortify the flesh*. **3** *intr, pathol, old use* of a limb, etc: to be affected by gangrene. ▪ **mortification** *noun*. [14c: from French *mortifier*]

mortise lock *noun* a lock fitted into a hole cut in the side edge of a door, rather than on to the door's surface.

mortuary *noun* (**-ies**) a building or room in which dead bodies are laid out for identification or kept until they are buried or cremated. Also called **morgue**. [14c: from Latin adj *mortuarius*]

Mosaic /moʊ'zeɪɪk/ *adj* relating to Moses, the biblical prophet and lawgiver, or to the laws attributed to him: *Mosaic law*. See also **Pentateuch**.

mosaic /moʊ'zeɪɪk/ *noun* **1** a design or piece of work formed by fitting together lots of small pieces of coloured stone, glass, etc. **2** anything that resembles a mosaic or is pieced together in a similar way. [15c: from French *mosaïque*]

mosey *verb, intr* (*usu* **mosey along**) *informal, orig & esp US* to walk in a leisurely way; to saunter. [19c]

Moslem see **Muslim**

mosque *noun* a Muslim place of worship. [15c: from French *mosquée*]

mosquito *noun* (***mosquitos*** *or* ***mosquitoes***) a type of small two-winged insect with thin, feathery antennae, long legs and a slender body, the female of which has piercing mouthparts for sucking blood. [16c: Spanish]

moss *noun* **1** the common name for a type of small spore-bearing plant, typically found growing in dense, spreading clusters in moist shady habitats. **2** *dialect, esp Scot & N Eng* an area of boggy ground. ▪ **mosslike** *adj.* ▪ **mossy** *adj* (***-ier, -iest***). [Anglo-Saxon *mos* in the sense 'bog']

mossie *or* **mozzie** *noun, informal* a mosquito.

most (*used as the superlative of* **many** and **much**) *adj, denoting* the greatest number, amount, etc: *Most people enjoy parties.* ▸ *adv* **1** (*also* **the most**) used to form the superlative of many adjectives and most adverbs, esp those of more than two syllables: *the most difficult problem of all.* **2** (*also* **the most**) to the greatest degree; with the greatest frequency: *I miss him most at Christmas.* **3** extremely: *a most annoying thing.* ▸ *pronoun* the greatest number or quantity, or the majority of people or things: *Most of them are here.* See also **more**. [Anglo-Saxon *mast* or *mæst*]

IDIOMS **at the most** *or* **at most** certainly not more than (a specified number). **for the most part** mostly. **make the most of sth** to take the greatest possible advantage of it.

mostly *adv* **1** mainly; almost completely. **2** usually.

mote *noun* a speck, esp a speck of dust. [Anglo-Saxon *mot*]

motel *noun* a hotel situated near a main road and intended for overnight stops by motorists. [1920s: a blend of *mo*tor ho*tel*]

motet *noun* a short piece of sacred music for several voices. [14c: French diminutive of *mot* word]

moth *noun* the common name for one of many winged insects belonging to the same order as butterflies but generally duller in colour and night-flying. [Anglo-Saxon *moththe*]

mothball *noun* a small ball of camphor or naphthalene that is hung in wardrobes, etc to keep away clothes moths. ▸ *verb* **1** to postpone work on something (eg a project), or to lay it aside, esp for an indefinitely long time. **2** to put (clothes, linen, etc), with mothballs, into a place for long-term storage.

moth-eaten *adj* **1** of cloth, etc: damaged by clothes moths. **2** *informal* old and worn.

mother *noun* **1** a female parent. **2** (*also* **Mother**) as a term of address or a title for: one's female parent or stepmother, foster-mother, etc. See also **ma, mom, mum**[1], **mummy**[1]. **3** the cause or origin; the source from which other things have sprung or developed: *Necessity is the mother of invention.* ▸ *verb* **1** to give birth to or give rise to someone or something. **2** to treat someone with care and protection, esp excessively so. ▪ **motherhood** *noun.* ▪ **motherless** *adj.* ▪ **motherly** *adj.* [Anglo-Saxon *modor*]

IDIOMS **the mother of all sths** *informal* one that is bigger than any other.

motherboard *noun, comput* a **printed circuit board** that can be plugged into the back of a computer, and into which other boards can be slotted to allow the computer to operate various **peripherals**.

mother country *noun* **1** a person's native country. Also called **motherland**. **2** the country that emigrants leave to settle elsewhere.

mother-in-law *noun* (***mothers-in-law***) the mother of one's husband or wife.

mother-of-pearl *noun* a hard shiny iridescent substance made mainly of calcium carbonate, that forms the inner layer of the shell of some molluscs (eg oysters) and is used to make buttons, beads, etc. Also called **nacre**.

mother-to-be *noun* (***mothers-to-be***) a pregnant woman, esp one who is expecting her first child.

mother tongue *noun* one's native language.

motif /moʊ'tiːf/ *noun* **1** on clothing, etc: a single design or symbol. **2** a shape repeated many times within a pattern. Also called **motive**. **3** in the arts: something that is often repeated throughout a work or works, eg a theme in a novel. [19c: French]

motile *adj, biol* of a living organism: capable of independent spontaneous movement. ▪ **motility** *noun.* [19c: from Latin *motus* movement]

motion *noun* **1** the act, state, process or manner of moving. **2** a single movement, esp one made by the body; a gesture or action. **3** the ability to move a part of the body. **4** a proposal for formal discussion at a meeting. **5** *law* an application made to a judge during a court case for an order or ruling to be made. **6** *Brit* **a** an act of discharging faeces from the bowels; **b** (**motions**) faeces. ▸ *verb, tr & intr* (*often* **motion to sb**) to give a signal or direction. ▪ **motionless** *adj.* [14c: from Latin *motio*]

IDIOMS **go through the motions 1** to pretend to do something; to act something out. **2** to perform a task mechanically or half-heartedly. **in motion** moving; operating.

motion picture *noun, N Am, esp US* a cinema film.

motion sickness *noun* travel sickness.

motivate *verb* **1** to be the motive of something or someone. **2** to cause or stimulate (a person) to act; to be the underlying cause of (an action). ▪ **motivation** *noun.*

motive *noun* **1** a reason for, or underlying cause of, action of a certain kind. **2** see **motif** (sense 2). ▸ *adj* causing motion: *motive force.* [14c: from French *motif*]

mot juste /*French* mo ʒyst/ *noun* (***mots justes*** /*French* mo ʒyst/) the word or expression which fits the context most exactly. [20c: from French *le mot juste* the exact word]

motley *adj* **1** made up of many different kinds: *a motley crew.* **2** many-coloured. [14c]

motocross *noun* a form of motorcycle racing in which specially-adapted motorcycles compete across rough terrain. [20c: from *moto*rcycle + *cross*-country]

motor *noun* **1** an engine, esp the **internal-combustion engine** of a vehicle or machine. **2** *informal* a car. **3** a device that converts electrical energy into mechanical energy. ▸ *adj* **1** *anatomy* **a** of a nerve: transmitting impulses from the **central nervous system** to a muscle or gland; **b** of a nerve cell: forming part of such a nerve. **2** *physiol* relating to muscular movement, or the sense of muscular movement. **3** giving or transmitting motion. ▸ *verb, intr* **1** to travel by motor vehicle, esp by private car. **2** *informal* to move or work, etc fast and effectively. ▪ **motoring** *noun*. ▪ **motorist** *noun*. [16c: *motor* Latin a mover]

motorbike *noun, informal* a **motorcycle**.

motorcade *noun* a procession of cars carrying VIPs, esp political figures. [20c: from **motor**, modelled on **cavalcade**]

motor car *noun, old use* a **car**.

motorcycle *noun* any two-wheeled vehicle powered by an internal combustion engine. Also called **motorbike**. ▪ **motorcyclist** *noun*.

motorize *or* **-ise** *verb* to fit a motor or motors to something. ▪ **motorization** *noun*.

motormouth *noun, derog, slang* a person who talks non-stop or too much.

motor neurone *noun, anatomy* a nerve cell that carries impulses from the spinal cord or the brain to an organ such as a muscle or gland.

motor scooter see under **scooter**

motorway *noun, Brit, Aust & NZ* a major road for fast-moving traffic, esp one with three lanes per carriageway and limited access and exit points.

motte and bailey *noun, hist* a type of fortification, orig of earth and timber, consisting of an artificial mound (the **motte**) surrounded by a ditch, with a walled outer court (the **bailey**) adjoining it to one side. [19c: from French *mote* or *motte* mound]

mottled *adj* having a pattern of different coloured blotches or streaks.

motto *noun* (***mottos*** *or* ***mottoes***) **1** **a** a phrase adopted by a person, family, etc as a principle of behaviour; **b** such a phrase appearing on a coat of arms, crest, etc. **2** a printed phrase or verse contained in a paper cracker. **3** a quotation at the beginning of a book or chapter, hinting at what is to follow. [17c: Italian]

mould[1] *or* (*N Am*) **mold** *noun* **1** a fungus that produces an abundant woolly network of thread-like strands which may be white, grey-green or black in colour. **2** a woolly growth of this sort on foods, plants, etc. See also **mildew**. [15c]

mould[2] *or* (*N Am*) **mold** *noun* **1** a hollow, shaped container into which a liquid substance, eg jelly, is poured so that it takes on the container's shape when it cools and sets. **2** nature, character or personality: *We need a leader in the traditional mould.* **3** a framework on which certain manufactured objects are built up. ▸ *verb* **1** to shape something in or using a mould. **2** **a** to shape (a substance) with the hands: *moulded the clay in her hands;* **b** to form something by shaping a substance with the hands: *moulded a pot out of the clay.* **3** *tr & intr* to fit, or make something fit, tightly: *The dress was moulded to her body.* **4** (*esp* **mould sth** *or* **sb into sth**) to exercise a controlling influence over the development of something or someone. [13c: from French *modle*]

mould[3] *or* (*N Am*) **mold** *noun* loose soft soil that is rich in decayed organic matter: *leaf mould.* [Anglo-Saxon *molde*]

moulder *or* (*N Am*) **molder** *verb, intr* (*also* **moulder away**) to become gradually rotten with age; to decay. [16c]

moulding *or* (*N Am*) **molding** *noun* a shaped, decorative strip, esp one made of wood or plaster.

mouldy *or* (*N Am*) **moldy** *adj* (***-ier, -iest***) **1** covered with mould. **2** old and stale. **3** *derog, informal* rotten or bad; a general term of dislike. [14c: from **mould**[1]]

moult *or* (*N Am*) **molt** *verb, intr, zool* of an animal: to shed feathers, hair or skin to make way for a new growth. ▸ *noun* **1** the act or process of moulting. **2** the time taken for this. [14c: from Anglo-Saxon]

mound *noun* **1** any small hill, or bank of earth or rock. **2** a heap or pile. [16c, meaning 'a hedge or other boundary']

mount[1] *verb* **1** *tr & intr* to go up: *mounting the stairs.* **2** *tr & intr* to get up on to (a horse, bicycle, etc). **3** *intr* (*also* **mount up**) to increase in level or intensity: *pressure mounts up.* **4** to put (a picture, etc) in a frame or on a background for display; to hang or put something up on a stand or support. **5** to organize or hold (a campaign, etc). **6** to carry out (an attack, etc); to put something into operation. ▸ *noun* **1** a support or backing on which something is placed for display or use, etc. **2** a horse that is ridden. ▪ **mounted** *adj* **1** of a person, etc: on horseback. **2** of a picture, etc: hung on a wall, or placed in a frame or on a background. [14c: from French *monter*]

mount[2] *noun, chiefly poetic or old use* a mountain. Also **Mount** in place names. [Anglo-Saxon *munt:* from Latin *mons* mountain]

mountain *noun* **1** a very high, steep hill, often one of bare rock. **2** (*also* **mountains of sth**) *informal* a large heap or mass: *a mountain of washing.* **3** a huge surplus of some commodity: *a butter mountain.* ▪ **mountainous** *adj*. [13c: from French *montaigne*]
IDIOMS **make a mountain out of a molehill** to exaggerate the seriousness or importance of some trivial matter.

mountain ash see under **rowan**

mountain bike *noun* a sturdy bicycle with thick, deep-tread tyres and straight handlebars, designed for riding in hilly terrain.

mountaineer *noun* someone who climbs mountains. ▸ *verb, intr* to climb mountains. ▪ **mountaineering** *noun*.

mountain lion see under **puma**

mountain sickness *noun* feelings of nausea, lightheadedness, headache, etc caused by breathing low-oxygen mountain air.

mountainside *noun* the slope of a mountain.

mountebank *noun, literary, derog* **1** *formerly* a medically unqualified person who sold supposed medicines from a public platform; a quack. **2** any person who swindles or deceives. [16c: from Italian *montimbanco* a person who stands up]

mourn *verb* **1** *tr & intr* (*esp* **mourn for** *or* **over sb** *or* **sth**) to feel or show deep sorrow at the death or loss of them or it. **2** *intr* to be in mourning or wear mourning. ▪ **mourner** *noun*. [Anglo-Saxon *murnan*]

mournful *adj* **1** feeling or expressing grief. **2** suggesting sadness or gloom: *mournful music.* ▪ **mournfully** *adv*.

mourning *noun* **1** grief felt or shown over a death. **2** a symbol of grief, esp black clothing or a black armband (a **mourning band**). **3** a period of time during which someone is officially mourning a death.

mouse *noun* (***mice*** or in sense 3 ***mouses***) **1** a small rodent with a grey or brown coat, pointed muzzle, bright eyes and a long hairless tail. **2** *informal* a very shy, quiet or timid person. **3** *comput* an input device which can be moved around on a flat surface, causing a **cursor** (sense 1) to move around the computer screen in response, and which has one or more buttons which are clicked (see **click** *verb* sense 4) to choose one of a number of specified options displayed. ▸ *verb, intr* of an animal, esp a cat: to hunt mice. ▪ **mouser** *noun* a cat that catches mice, or is kept esp for catching mice. [Anglo-Saxon *mus*]

mousemat *or* **mousepad** *noun* a small flat piece of fabric backed with foam rubber, used as a surface on which to move a **mouse** (*noun* sense 3).

mousetrap *noun* **1** a mechanical trap for catching or killing mice. **2** *informal, old use* poor quality cheese.

moussaka /mʊ'sɑːkə/ *noun, cookery* a dish made with minced meat, aubergines, onions, tomatoes, etc, covered with a cheese sauce and baked. [1940s: modern Greek]

mousse *noun* **1** *cookery* **a** a dessert made from a whipped mixture of cream, eggs and flavouring, eaten cold: *strawberry mousse*; **b** a similar but savoury dish, made with meat, fish, etc: *salmon mousse*. **2** (*also* **styling mousse**) a foamy or frothy chemical preparation applied to hair to add body or to make styling easier. [19c: French, literally 'froth' or 'moss']

moustache *or* (*N Am*) **mustache** /mə'stɑːʃ, mʌ'stɑːʃ/ *noun* unshaved hair growing across the top of the upper lip. ▪ **moustached** *adj*. [16c: French]

mousy *or* **mousey** *adj* (**-ier, -iest**) **1** like a mouse, or belonging or relating to a mouse. **2** of hair: light dullish brown in colour. **3** of a person: shy, quiet or timid. ▪ **mousiness** *noun*.

mouth *noun* /maʊθ/ **1** in humans, animals, etc: an opening in the head through which food is taken in and speech or sounds emitted, and containing the teeth, gums, tongue, etc. **2** the lips; the outer visible parts of the mouth. **3** an opening, eg of a bottle. **4** the part of a river that widens to meet the sea. **5** a person considered as a consumer of food: *five mouths to feed*. **6** *derog, informal* boastful talk: *He's all mouth*. **7** *informal* use of language; way of speaking: *a foul mouth*. ▸ *verb* /maʊð/ **1** to form (words) without actually speaking. **2** *tr & intr, derog* to speak (words) pompously or insincerely: *is always mouthing platitudes*. [Anglo-Saxon *muth*]

PHRASAL VERBS **mouth off** *slang, esp US* **1** to express opinions forcefully or loudly. **2** to boast or brag.

mouthful *noun* **1** as much food or drink as fills the mouth or is in one's mouth. **2** a small quantity, esp of food. **3** *informal* a word or phrase that is difficult to pronounce. **4** *informal* an outburst of forceful and often abusive language: *gave me such a mouthful*.

mouth organ see under **harmonica**

mouthpiece *noun* **1** the part of a musical instrument, telephone receiver, tobacco pipe, etc that is held in or against the mouth. **2** a person or publication that is used to express the views of a group.

mouth-to-mouth *adj* of a method of resuscitation: involving someone breathing air directly into the mouth of the person to be revived in order to inflate their lungs. ▸ *noun* mouth-to-mouth resuscitation. Also called **kiss of life**. See also **artificial respiration**.

mouthwash *noun* an antiseptic liquid used for gargling or for rinsing or freshening the mouth.

mouth-watering *adj* **1** of food: having a delicious appearance or smell. **2** *informal* highly desirable.

movable *or* **moveable** *adj* **1** not fixed in one place; portable. **2** *esp Scots law* of property: able to be removed; personal. **3** of a religious festival: taking place on a different date each year: *Easter is a movable feast*.

move *verb* **1** *tr & intr* to change position or make something change position or go from one place to another. **2** *intr* to make progress of any kind: *move towards a political solution*. **3** *chiefly intr* (*often* **move on, out** *or* **away,** *etc*) to change one's place of living, working, operating, etc. **4** to affect someone's feelings or emotions. **5** (*usu* **move sb to do sth**) to prompt them or affect them in such a way that they do it: *What moved him to say that?* **6** *tr & intr* to change the position of (a piece in a board game). **7** *tr & intr, formal* (*usu* **move for** *or* **that sth**) to propose or request it formally, at a meeting, etc. **8** *intr* to spend time; to associate with people: *move in fashionable circles*. **9** *intr, informal* to take action; to become active or busy: *must move on this matter straight away*. **10** *intr, informal* to travel or progress fast: *That bike can really move*. **11** **a** *intr* of the bowels: to be evacuated; **b** to cause (the bowels) to evacuate. ▸ *noun* **1** an act of moving the body; a movement. **2** an act of changing homes or premises: *How did your move go?* **3** *games* **a** an act of moving a piece on the board; **b** a particular player's turn to move a piece. ▪ **mover** *noun*. [13c: from French *movoir*]

IDIOMS **make a move 1** *informal* to start on one's way; to leave. **2** to begin to proceed. **move heaven and earth** to make strenuous efforts to achieve something. **on the move 1** moving from place to place. **2** advancing or making progress.

PHRASAL VERBS **move over** to move so as to make room for someone else.

movement *noun* **1** a process of changing position or going from one point to another. **2** an act or manner of moving: *made a sudden, jerky movement*. **3** an organization, association or group, esp one that promotes a particular cause: *the women's movement*. **4** a general tendency or current of opinion, taste, etc: *a movement towards healthy eating*. **5** *music* a section of a large-scale piece, esp a symphony. **6** (**movements**) a person's actions during a particular time. **7** **a** an act of evacuating the bowels; **b** the waste matter evacuated. **8** the moving parts of a watch or clock.

movie *noun, esp US* **1** a cinema film. *Brit equivalent* **film**. **2** (*esp* **the movies**) cinema films in general. [20c: a shortening of 'moving picture']

moving *adj* **1** having an effect on the emotions; touching; stirring: *a moving story*. **2** in motion; not static: *a moving staircase*. ▪ **movingly** *adv*.

mow *verb* (***mown***) to cut (grass, a lawn, crop, etc) by hand or with a machine. ▪ **mower** *noun*. [Anglo-Saxon *mawan*]

PHRASAL VERBS **mow sb** *or* **sth down** *informal* to kill them or it in large numbers.

mozzarella /mɒtsə'rɛlə/ *noun* a soft, white, Italian curd cheese, esp used as a topping for pizza and in salads. [20c: Italian]

mozzie see **mossie**

MP *abbrev* **1** Member of Parliament. **2** *Eng* Metropolitan Police. **3** Military Police. **4** mounted police.

MPEG /'ɛmpɛg/ *abbrev, comput* Moving Picture Experts Group, a standard for coding audiovisual information.

mpg *abbrev* miles per gallon.

mph *abbrev* miles per hour.

MP3 *abbrev, comput* MPEG-1 Layer 3, a compressed file format that allows fast downloading of audio data from the Internet.

MPV *abbrev* multipurpose vehicle.

Mr /'mɪstə(r)/ *noun* (***Messrs*** /'mɛsəz/) **1** the standard title given to a man, used as a prefix before his surname: *Mr Brown*. **2** a title given to a man who holds one of various official positions, used as a prefix before his designation: *Mr Speaker*. [15c: an abbreviation of **mister**]

mRNA *abbrev, biochem* messenger RNA.

Mrs /'mɪsɪz/ *noun* the standard title given to a married woman, used as a prefix before her surname, or before her full name with either her own or her husband's first name. See also **missus, Ms**. [17c: an abbreviation of **mistress**]

MS *or* **ms.** *abbrev* **1** (***MSS*** *or* ***mss***). manuscript. **2** Master of Surgery. **3** multiple sclerosis.

Ms /məz, mɪz/ *noun* the standard title given to a woman, married or not, used as a prefix before her surname in place of **Mrs** or **Miss**: *Ms Brown*.

ms. *abbrev* **1** see under **MS**. **2** millisecond or milliseconds.

MSc *abbrev* Master of Science.

MSDOS *or* **MS-DOS** /ɛmɛs'dɒs/ *abbrev, trademark, comput* Microsoft disk-operating system. [20c]

MSG *abbrev* **1** monosodium glutamate. **2** (*also* **msg**) message (used in text messages).

MSP *abbrev* Member of the Scottish Parliament.

Mt[1] *abbrev* Mount: *Mt Etna*.

Mt[2] *symbol, chem* meitnerium.

mu *noun* **1** the twelfth letter of the Greek alphabet. **2** *physics, chem, etc* the symbol (μ) for **micro-** (sense 2) and **micron**. See also **muon**.

much *adj, pron* (***more, most***) esp with negatives and in questions: **1** a great amount or quantity of something: *You don't have much luck*. **2** (*only as pronoun*) a great deal; anything of significance or value: *Can you see much?* ▸ *adv* **1** by a great deal: *That looks much prettier*. **2** to a great degree: *don't like her much*. **3** (*often* **much the same**) nearly the same; almost: *Things look much as I left them*. See also **more, most**. [13c: from Anglo-Saxon *mycel*]
IDIOMS **a bit much** *informal* rather more that can be tolerated or accepted: *His constant teasing is a bit much*. **(as) much as** although: *I cannot come, much as I would like to*. **make much of sth** *or* **sb 1** to cherish or take special interest in them or it, or to treat them or it as very important. **2** *with negatives* to find much sense in, or to succeed in understanding, them or it: *couldn't make much of what he was saying*. **not much of a sth** *informal* not a very good example of it; a rather poor one: *I'm not much of a singer*. **not up to much** *informal* of a poor standard; not much good. **too much for sb** more than a match for them.

muchness *noun*
IDIOMS **much of a muchness** *informal* very similar; more or less the same.

mucilage /'mju:sɪlɪdʒ/ *noun, botany* a type of gum-like substance that becomes viscous and slimy when added to water, present in or secreted by various plants. ▪ **mucilaginous** *adj*. [15c: from Latin *mucilago*, literally 'mouldy juice']

muck *noun* **1** *informal* dirt, esp wet or clinging dirt. **2** animal dung; manure. **3** *derog, informal* anything disgusting or of very poor quality: *How can you read that muck?* ▸ *verb* to treat (soil) with manure. [13c]
IDIOMS **make a muck of sth** *informal* to do it badly; to ruin or spoil it.
PHRASAL VERBS **muck about** *or* **around** *informal* to behave foolishly. **muck about** *or* **around with sth** *informal* to interfere, tinker or fiddle about with it. **muck sb about** *or* **around** to treat them inconsiderately; to try their patience. **muck in** *or* **muck in with sb** *informal* to take a share of the work or responsibilities with others. **muck out** *or* **muck sth out** to clear dung from (a farm building, etc) or clear dung from the stall, etc of (animals). **muck sth up** *informal* **1** to do it badly or wrongly; to ruin or spoil it. **2** to make it dirty.

muckle see **mickle**

muckraking *noun, informal* the practice of searching for and exposing scandal, esp about famous people. ▪ **muckraker** *noun*.

mucky *adj* (***-ier, -iest***) *informal* very dirty: *mucky hands*.

mucosa /mju:'koʊsə/ *noun* (***mucosae*** /-si:/) the technical term for **mucous membrane**.

mucous /'mju:kəs/ *adj* consisting of, like or producing **mucus**. ▪ **mucosity** *noun*.

---

mucous, mucus
Be careful not to use the adjective spelling **mucous** when you mean the noun **mucus**.

---

mucous membrane *noun, zool, anatomy* in vertebrates: the moist, mucus-secreting lining of various internal cavities of the body.

mucus /'mju:kəs/ *noun* the thick slimy substance that protects and lubricates the surface of **mucous membranes** and traps bacteria and dust particles. [17c: Latin, meaning 'nasal mucus']

---

mucus, mucous
Be careful not to use the noun spelling **mucus** when you mean the adjective **mucous**.

---

mud *noun* **1** soft, wet earth. **2** *informal* insults; slanderous attacks: *throw mud at someone*. [14c]
IDIOMS **clear as mud** *informal* not at all clear. **my, his,** *etc* **name is mud** *informal* I am, he is, etc disgraced or out of favour.

mudbath *noun* a medical treatment in which the body is covered in mud rich in minerals.

muddle *verb* (*also* **muddle sth** *or* **sb up**) **1** to put it or them into a disordered or confused state. **2 a** to confuse the mind of someone: *You'll muddle him with all those figures*; **b** to confuse (different things) in the mind: *I always muddle their names*. ▸ *noun* a state of disorder or mental confusion. [17c: meaning 'to wallow in mud']
PHRASAL VERBS **muddle along** *informal* to manage or make progress slowly and haphazardly. **muddle through** *informal* to succeed by persevering in spite of difficulties.

muddy *adj* (***-ier, -iest***) **1** covered with or containing mud. **2** of a colour, a liquid, etc: dull, cloudy or dirty. **3** of thoughts, etc: not clear; vague. ▸ *verb* (***-ies, -ied***) to make something muddy, esp to make it unclear or difficult to understand. ▪ **muddiness** *noun*.

mudflap *noun* a flap of rubber, etc fixed behind the wheel of a vehicle to prevent mud, etc being thrown up behind. *N Am equivalent* **splash guard**.

mudflat *noun* (*often* **mudflats**) a relatively flat area of land which is covered by a shallow layer of water at high tide, but not covered at low tide.

mudguard *noun* a curved, metal guard over the upper half of the wheel of a bicycle or motorcycle to keep rain or mud from splashing up.

mud-slinging *noun, informal* the act or process of making slanderous personal attacks or allegations to discredit someone else. ▪ **mud-slinger** *noun*.

muesli *noun* a mixture of crushed grain, nuts and dried fruit, eaten with milk. [20c: Swiss German]

muezzin /mʊ'ɛzɪn/ *noun, Islam* the Muslim official who calls worshippers to prayer, usu from a **minaret**. [16c: from Arabic *mu'adhdhin*]

muff[1] *noun* a wide fur tube which the wearer places their hands inside for warmth. [16c]

muff[2] *informal, verb* **1** to bungle or fluff something. **2** to miss (an opportunity, etc). [19c: orig meaning 'someone who is awkward or bungling at sport']

muffin *noun* **1** *Brit* a small round flat breadlike cake, usu eaten toasted or hot with butter. **2** *N Am* a cup-shaped sweet cake, usu of a specified flavour: *blueberry muffins*. [18c]

muffle *verb* **1** to make something quieter; to suppress (sound). **2** to prevent someone from saying something. ▪ **muffled** *adj*. ▪ **muffler** *noun* **1** a thick scarf. **2** *US* a **silencer**. [15c]

mufti *noun, old use* civilian clothes when worn by people who usu wear a uniform. [19c]

mug[1] *noun* **1** a drinking-vessel with a handle, used without a saucer. **2** a **mugful**. **3** *informal* a face or mouth. **4** *informal* someone who is easily fooled; a dupe. ▶ *verb* (***mugged, mugging***) to attack and rob someone violently or under threat of violence. ▪ **mugger** *noun*. ▪ **mugging** *noun*. [17c]

mug[2] *verb* (***mugged, mugging***) *tr & intr* (*esp* **mug sth up** *or* **mug up on sth**) *informal* to study or revise (a subject, etc) thoroughly, esp for an examination. [19c]

mugful *noun* the amount a mug will hold.

muggins *noun, Brit informal* a foolish person, used esp to describe oneself when one has been taken advantage of by others. [19c]

muggy *adj* (***-ier, -iest***) of the weather: unpleasantly warm and damp; close. ▪ **mugginess** *noun*. [18c: from dialect *mug* drizzle or mist]

Mughal see **mogul** (sense 2)

mugshot *noun, informal, orig US* a photograph of a criminal's face, taken for police records.

mujaheddin, **mujahedin** *or* **mujahadeen** /muːdʒəhə'diːn/ *plural noun* (*usu* **the Mujaheddin**) in Afghanistan, Iran and Pakistan: Muslim fundamentalist guerillas. [20c: from Arabic *mujahidin* fighters of a jihad]

mulberry *noun* (***-ies***) **1** a tree that produces small edible purple berries. **2** such a berry. **3** a dark purple colour. ▶ *adj* **1** belonging or relating to the tree or its berries. **2** having a dark purple colour. [14c: from Latin *marum* the mulberry]

mulch *noun* straw, compost, shredded bark, etc laid on the soil around plants to retain moisture and prevent the growth of weeds. ▶ *verb* to cover (soil, etc) with mulch. [17c: from obsolete *mulch* soft]

mule[1] *noun* **1** the offspring of a male donkey and a female horse. **2** a stubborn person. **3** a cotton-spinning machine that produces yarn on spindles. [Anglo-Saxon *mul*: from Latin *mulus*]

mule[2] *noun* a shoe or slipper with no back part covering the heel. [16c: from French *mules* chilblains]

muleteer *noun* someone whose job is to drive mules.

mulish *adj* stubborn; obstinate. [18c: from **mule**[1] (sense 2)]

mull[1] *verb* (*now always* **mull sth over**) to consider it carefully; to ponder on it. [19c]

mull[2] *verb* to spice, sweeten and warm (wine or beer). ▪ **mulled** *adj*: *mulled wine*. [17c]

mull[3] *noun, Scot* a headland or promontory: *the Mull of Kintyre*. [14c: from Gaelic *maol*]

mullah *noun* a Muslim scholar and adviser in Islamic religion and sacred law. [17c: from Arabic *maula*]

mullet *noun* any of a family of thick-bodied edible marine fish. [15c: from French *mulet*]

mulligatawny *noun, cookery* a thick curry-flavoured meat soup, orig made in E India from chicken stock. [18c: from Tamil *milagu-tannir* pepper-water]

mullion *noun, archit* a vertical bar or post separating the panes or casements of a window. ▪ **mullioned** *adj*. [14c: from French *moinel*]

multi- *or* (*before a vowel*) **mult-** *prefix, denoting* many: *multicoloured*. [From Latin *multus* much]

multi-access see under **multi-user**

multicellular *adj, biol* of an organism etc: having or made up of many cells.

multicoloured *or* (*N Am*) **multicolored** *adj* having many colours.

multicultural *adj* esp of a society, community, etc: made up of, involving or relating to several distinct racial or religious cultures, etc.

multifarious /mʌltɪ'fɛərɪəs/ *adj, formal* consisting of many different kinds; very varied. [16c: from Latin *multifarius* manifold]

multigym *noun* an apparatus consisting of an arrangement of weights and levers, designed for exercising and toning up all the muscles of the body.

multilateral *adj* **1** involving or affecting several people, groups, parties or nations: *a multilateral treaty*. **2** many-sided. [17c]

multilingual *adj* **1** written or expressed in several different languages. **2** of a person: able to speak several different languages.

multimedia *adj* **1** in entertainment, education, etc: involving the use of a combination of different media, eg TV, radio, slides, hi-fi, or visual arts. **2** *comput* of a computer system: able to present and manipulate data in a variety of forms, eg text, graphics and sound, often simultaneously. ▶ *singular noun* a number of different media taken collectively.

multimillionaire *noun* someone whose wealth is valued at several million pounds, dollars, etc.

multinational *adj* esp of a large business company: operating in several different countries. ▶ *noun* a multinational corporation, business or organization.

multiparous /mʌl'tɪpərəs/ *adj, zool* of a mammal: producing several young at one birth. [17c: from Latin *multiparus*]

multipartite *adj* divided into many parts or segments. [18c: from Latin *partitus* divided]

multiple *adj* **1** having, involving or affecting many parts. **2** many, esp more than several. **3** multiplied or repeated. ▸ *noun, maths* a number or expression for which a given number or expression is a **factor** (sense 2), eg 24 is a multiple of 12. See also **lowest common multiple**. [17c: from French]

multiple-choice *adj* of a test, exam or question: giving a list of possible answers from which the candidate has to try to select the correct one.

multiple sclerosis *noun* (abbrev **MS**) a progressive disease of the central nervous system, producing symptoms such as inability to coordinate movements and weakness of the muscles.

multiplex *noun* a large cinema building divided into several smaller cinemas. ▸ *adj, formal* having very many parts; manifold; complex. [16c: Latin, meaning 'of many kinds']

multiplicand *noun, maths* a number to be multiplied by a second number (the **multiplier**). [16c: from Latin *multiplicare* to **multiply**]

multiplication *noun* **1** *maths* **a** an operation in which one number is added to itself as many times as is indicated by a second number, written using the **multiplication sign**; **b** the process of performing this operation. **2** the act or process of multiplying. [14c: French]

multiplication sign *noun, maths* the symbol × used between two numbers to indicate that they are to be multiplied.

multiplication table *noun, maths* a table that lists the products of multiplying pairs of numbers together, esp all pairs from 1 to 12.

multiplicity *noun* (*-ies*) *formal* **1** a great number and variety. **2** the state of being many and various. [16c: from Latin *multiplicitas*]

multiplier *noun* **1** *maths* a number indicating by how many times another number (the **multiplicand**), to which it is attached by a multiplication sign, is to be multiplied. **2** a person or thing that multiplies.

multiply *verb* (*-ies, -ied*) **1** (*esp* **multiply sth by sth**) **a** to add (one number or amount) to itself a specified number of times: *Two multiplied by two equals four*; **b** (*sometimes* **multiply sth and sth together**) to combine (two numbers) by the process of **multiplication**. **2** *intr* to increase in number, esp by breeding. [13c: from French *multiplier*]

multipurpose *adj* having many uses.

multipurpose vehicle *noun* a **people carrier**.

multiracial *adj* for, including, or consisting of, people of many different races. ▪ **multiracialism** *noun*.

multistorey *adj* of a building: having many floors or levels. ▸ *noun, informal* a car park that has several levels.

multitasking *noun, comput* the action of running several processes simultaneously on one system.

multitude *noun* **1** a great number of people or things. **2** (**the multitude**) ordinary people. ▪ **multitudinous** *adj*. [14c: French]

multi-user *adj, comput* of a system: consisting of several terminals linked to a central computer, allowing access by several users at the same time. Also called **multi-access**.

multivalent *adj. chem* of an atom: able to combine with more than one atom of hydrogen. Also called **polyvalent**. ▪ **multivalence** *or* **multivalency** *noun*. [19c]

multivitamin *noun* a pill containing several vitamins, taken as a dietary supplement. [20c]

mum[1] *noun* **1** *informal* a mother. **2** a term used to address or refer to one's own mother. See also **ma**, **mother**, **mummy**[1]. *N Am equivalent* **mom**. [19c: shortened from **mummy**[1]]

mum[2] *adj, informal* silent; not speaking: *keep mum about it*. [14c: imitating a sound produced with closed lips]

IDIOMS **mum's the word!** *informal* an entreaty or warning to someone to keep quiet about something.

mumble *verb, tr & intr* to speak or say something unclearly, esp with the mouth partly closed. ▸ *noun* the sound of unclear, muffled or hushed speech. ▪ **mumbling** *noun, adj*. [14c: from **mum**[2]]

mumbo-jumbo *noun, informal* **1** foolish talk, esp of a religious or spiritual kind. **2** baffling jargon. [18c]

mummer *noun, hist* in medieval England: one of a group of masked actors who visited houses during winter festivals, distributing gifts and performing dances, etc. ▪ **mumming** *noun*. [15c: from French *momeur*]

mummery *noun* (*-ies*) **1** a performance by a group of mummers. **2** *derog* ridiculous or pretentious ceremony.

mummify *verb* (*-ies, -ied*) to preserve (a corpse) as a **mummy**[2]. ▪ **mummification** *noun*. [17c]

mummy[1] *noun* (*-ies*) *chiefly Brit* a child's word for mother. *N Am equivalent* **mommy**. [18c: orig a dialect alteration of **mama**]

mummy[2] *noun* (*-ies*) esp in ancient Egypt: a corpse preserved with embalming spices and bandaged, in preparation for burial. [15c: from French *mumie*]

mumps *singular noun* (*also* **the mumps**) *med* an infectious viral disease causing fever, headache and painful swelling of the salivary glands on one or both sides of the face. [16c: from obsolete *mump* a grimace]

---

mumps

Because this is a singular noun, you should use a singular verb with it:

Mumps is no longer one of the most common childhood illnesses.

---

mumsy *adj* (*-ier, -iest*) *informal* **1** homely; comfy. **2** maternal, in an old-fashioned cosy way. [19c: an affectionate variant of **mum**[1]]

munch *verb, tr & intr* to chew with a steady movement of the jaws, esp noisily. [14c]

mundane *adj* **1** ordinary; dull; everyday. **2** belonging or relating to this world. [15c: from French *mondain*]

mung bean *noun* **1** an E Asian plant that produces beans and beansprouts. **2** the edible green or yellow bean of this plant. [19c: Hindi *mung*]

municipal *adj* belonging or relating to, or controlled by, the local government of a town or region. [16c: from Latin *municipalis*]

municipality *noun* (*-ies*) **1** a town or region that has its own local government. **2** the local government itself. [18c]

munificent *adj, formal* extremely generous. ▪ **munificence** *noun*. [16c: French]

muniments *plural noun, law* official papers that prove ownership. [14c: French]

munitions *plural noun* military equipment, esp ammunition and weapons. [16c: French]

muon /ˈmjuːɒn/ *noun, physics* an elementary particle that behaves like a heavy **electron**, but decays to form an electron and **neutrino.** ▪ **muonic** *adj.* [20c]

mural /ˈmjʊərəl/ *noun* (*also* **mural painting**) a painting that is painted directly on to a wall. ▸ *adj, formal* belonging or relating to, on or attached to, a wall or walls. [15c: from French *muraille*]

murder *noun* **1** the act of unlawfully and intentionally killing a person. **2** *informal* something, or a situation, which causes hardship or difficulty: *The traffic in town was murder today.* ▸ *verb* **1** *tr & intr* to kill someone unlawfully and intentionally. **2** *informal* to punish someone severely or cruelly; to be furious with them: *I'll murder him when he gets home.* **3** *informal* to spoil or ruin something (eg a piece of music), by performing it very badly. **4** *informal* to defeat someone by a huge margin. ▪ **murderer** *noun.* ▪ **murderess** *noun.* [Anglo-Saxon *morthor*]

IDIOMS **scream, shout** *or* **cry blue murder** *informal* to protest loudly or angrily.

murderous *adj* **1** of a person, weapon, etc: intending, intended for, or capable of, causing or committing murder: *a murderous look.* **2** *informal* very unpleasant; causing difficulty. ▪ **murderously** *adv.*

murine /ˈmjʊəraɪn, -rɪn/ *adj* **1** mouselike. **2** *zool* belonging to the mouse family or subfamily. [17c: from Latin *murinus*]

murk *or* (*rarely*) **mirk** *noun* darkness; gloom. [Anglo-Saxon *mirce*]

murky *adj* (**-ier, -iest**) **1** dark; gloomy. **2** of water: dark and dirty. **3** suspiciously vague or unknown; shady: *her murky past.* ▪ **murkily** *adv.* ▪ **murkiness** *noun.*

murmur *noun* **1** a quiet, continuous sound, eg of running water or low voices. **2** anything said in a low, indistinct voice. **3** a complaint, esp a subdued, muttering one. **4** *med* in **auscultation**: an abnormal rustling sound made by the heart, often indicating the presence of disease. ▸ *verb tr & intr* to speak (words) softly and indistinctly. ▪ **murmuring** *noun, adj.* ▪ **murmurous** *adj.* [14c: from French *murmurer*]

murrain /ˈmʌrɪn/ *noun, vet med* any infectious cattle disease, esp foot-and-mouth disease. [14c: from French *morine* a plague]

mus. *abbrev* **1** music. **2** musical.

muscle *noun* **1** an animal tissue composed of bundles of fibres that are capable of contracting to produce movement of part of the body. **2** a body structure or organ composed of this tissue. **3** bodily strength. **4** power or influence of any kind: *financial muscle.* ▸ *verb, informal* (*always* **muscle in on sth**) to force one's way into it. [16c: from Latin *musculus*]

muscle-bound *adj* having over-enlarged muscles that are stiff and difficult to move.

muscleman *noun* a man with very big muscles, esp one employed to intimidate people.

muscular *adj* **1** belonging or relating to, or consisting of, muscle. **2** having well-developed muscles; strong; brawny. ▪ **muscularity** *noun.*

muscular dystrophy *noun, med* a hereditary disease in which there is progressive wasting of certain muscles.

musculature *noun* the arrangement, or degree of development, of muscles in a body or organ.

Muse *noun, Greek myth, also literary, art, etc* any of the nine goddesses of the arts, said to be a source of creative inspiration to all artists, esp poets. [14c: French]

muse *verb* **1** *intr* (*often* **muse on sth**) to reflect or ponder silently. **2** to say something in a reflective way. **3** *intr* to gaze contemplatively. [14c: from French *muser* to loiter or waste time]

museum *noun* a place where objects of artistic, scientific or historical interest are displayed to the public, preserved and studied. [17c: Latin]

museum piece *noun* an article or specimen displayed in a museum, or something fit for this because of its special quality, age or interest.

mush[1] *noun* **1** a soft half-liquid mass of anything. **2** *derog, informal* sloppy sentimentality. [17c]

mush[2] *exclam, N Am* used esp to a team of dogs: go on! go faster! ▸ *verb, intr* to travel on a sledge pulled by dogs. [19c]

mushroom *noun* **1 a** a type of **fungus** which consists of a short white stem supporting an umbrella-shaped cap with numerous spore-bearing gills on the underside. See also **toadstool**. **b** the edible species of such fungi. **2** anything resembling this in shape. ▸ *verb, intr* to develop or increase with alarming speed. [15c: from French *mousseron*]

mushy *adj* (**-ier, -iest**) **1** in a soft half-liquid state; consisting of or like **mush**[1]. **2** sentimental in a sickly way.

music *noun* **1** the art of making sound in a rhythmically organized, harmonious form, either sung or produced with instruments. **2** such sound, esp that produced by instruments. **3 a** any written form or composition in which such sound is expressed; **b** musical forms or compositions collectively. **4** the performance of musical compositions. **5** pleasing or melodic sound. [13c: from French *musique*]

IDIOMS **music to one's ears** news, etc that is particularly welcome.

musical *adj* **1** consisting of, involving, relating to or producing music. **2** pleasant to hear; melodious. **3** of a person: having a talent or aptitude for music. ▸ *noun* a play or film that features singing and dancing. ▪ **musicality** *noun.* ▪ **musically** *adv.*

musical chairs *singular noun* **1** a party game in which the participants walk or run round a decreasing number of chairs while the music plays, and when the music stops, try to grab a chair, with the player left without a seat being eliminated. **2** a series of position-changes involving a number of people.

musical instrument see **instrument**

music hall *noun* **1 variety** (sense 4) entertainment. **2** a theatre in which variety entertainment can be seen.

musician *noun* **1** someone who is skilled in music, esp in performing or composing it. **2** someone who performs or composes music as their profession.

musicology *noun* the academic study of music in all its aspects. ▪ **musicologist** *noun.*

musk *noun* **1** a strong-smelling substance much used in perfumes, secreted by the glands of various animals, esp the male musk deer. **2** any similar synthetic substance. [14c: from French *musc*]

musket *noun, hist* an early rifle-like gun that was loaded through the barrel and fired from the shoulder. ▪ **musketeer** *noun.* [16c: from French *mousquet*]

muskrat *or* **musquash** *noun* **1** a large, N American water rodent, which produces a musky smell. **2** its highly-prized thick brown fur. [17c: from Abnaki (a native N American language) *muskwessu*]

musky *adj* (*-ier, -iest*) containing, or like the smell of, musk. ▪ **muskily** *adv.* ▪ **muskiness** *noun.*

Muslim *or* **Moslem** *noun* a follower of the religion of Islam. ▸ *adj* belonging or relating to Muslims or to Islam. See also **Islam.** [17c: from Arabic *muslim*, literally 'one who submits']

Moslem, Muslim

Both **Moslem** and **Muslim** are used, but **Muslim** is more common and is the preferred spelling.

---

muslin *noun* a fine cotton cloth with a gauze-like appearance. [17c: from French *mousseline*]

muss *verb, N Am, esp US, informal* (*usu* **muss sth up**) to make something (esp clothes or hair) untidy; to mess up or disarrange. [19c]

mussel *noun* an edible marine **bivalve** mollusc that has a bluish-black shell and anchors itself to rocks, etc. [Anglo-Saxon *muscle* or *musle*]

must[1] *auxiliary verb* **1** used to express necessity: *I must earn some extra money.* **2** used to express duty or obligation: *You must help him.* **3** used to express certainty: *You must be Charles.* **4** used to express determination: *I must remember to go to the bank.* **5** used to express probability: *She must be there by now.* **6** used to express inevitability: *We must all die some time.* **7** used to express an invitation or suggestion: *You must come and see us soon.* See also **mustn't.** ▸ *noun* (*always* **a must**) a necessity; something essential: *Fitness is a must in professional sport.* [Anglo-Saxon *moste*]

must[2] *noun* the juice of grapes or other fruit before it is completely fermented to become wine. [Anglo-Saxon: from Latin *mustum vinum* new wine]

mustache the *N Am* spelling of **moustache.**

mustachio /mə'stɑːʃɪoʊ/ *noun* (*often* ***mustachios***) an elaborately curled moustache. ▪ **mustachioed** *adj.* [16c: from Spanish *mostacho*]

mustang *noun* a small wild or half-wild horse native to the plains of the western US. [19c: from Spanish *mestengo* belonging to the *mesta* (graziers' union) + *mostrenco* stray]

mustard *noun* **1** a plant with bright yellow flowers. **2** a hot-tasting paste used as a condiment or seasoning, made from powdered or crushed whole seeds of black or white mustard or both, mixed with water or vinegar. **3** a light yellow or brown colour. ▸ *adj* having a light yellow or brown colour. [13c: from French *moustarde*]

IDIOMS **as keen as mustard** *informal* extremely keen or enthusiastic.

mustard gas *noun* a highly poisonous gas, or the colourless oily liquid of which it is the vapour, that causes severe blistering of the skin, widely used as a **chemical warfare** agent in World War I.

muster *verb* **1** *tr & intr* esp of soldiers: to gather together for duty or inspection, etc. **2** (*also* **muster sth up** *or* **muster up sth**) to summon or gather (eg courage or energy). ▸ *noun* any assembly or gathering, esp of troops for duty or inspection. [14c: from French *mostre*]

IDIOMS **pass muster** to be accepted as satisfactory, eg at an inspection.

mustn't *contraction* must not.

musty *adj* (*-ier, -iest*) **1** mouldy or damp. **2** smelling or tasting stale or old. ▪ **mustiness** *noun.*

mutable *adj* subject to or able to change; variable. ▪ **mutability** *noun.* [14c: from Latin *mutabilis*]

mutagen *noun, biol* a chemical or physical agent that induces or increases the frequency of mutations in living organisms. ▪ **mutagenic** *adj.* [20c: from **mutation**]

mutant *noun* a living organism or cell that carries a specific mutation of a gene which usu causes it to differ from previous generations in one particular characteristic. ▸ *adj* of an organism or cell: carrying or resulting from a mutation. [20c: from Latin *mutantem* changing]

mutate *verb, tr & intr* **1** *biol* to undergo or cause to undergo **mutation** (sense 1). **2** *formal* to change. [19c: back-formation from **mutation**]

mutation *noun* **1** *genetics* in a living organism: a change in the structure of a single gene, the arrangement of genes on a chromosome or the number of chromosomes, which may result in a change in the appearance or behaviour of the organism. **2** *formal* a change of any kind. [14c: from Latin *mutatio*]

mute *adj* **1** of a person: unable to speak; dumb. **2** silent. **3** felt, but not expressed in words: *mute anger.* **4** of a letter in a word: not sounded, like the final e in many English words, eg *bite.* ▸ *noun* **1** *med* someone who is physically unable to speak. **2** *psychol* someone who refuses to speak, eg as a result of psychological trauma. **3** a device that softens or deadens the sound of a musical instrument. **4** an unsounded letter in a word. ▸ *verb* to soften or deaden the sound of (a musical instrument). ▪ **mutely** *adv.* ▪ **muteness** *noun.* [14c: French]

muted *adj* **1** of sound or colour: not loud or harsh; soft. **2** of feelings, etc: mildly expressed; not outspoken: *muted criticism.*

mute swan *noun* the commonest European swan, with pure white plumage and an orange bill.

mutilate *verb* **1** to cause severe injury to (a person or animal), esp by removing a limb or organ. **2** to damage something severely, esp to alter (eg a text, song, etc) beyond recognition. ▪ **mutilation** *noun.* ▪ **mutilator** *noun.* [16c: from Latin *mutilare* to cut off]

mutinous *adj* of a person, soldier, crew, etc: having mutinied or likely to mutiny.

mutiny *noun* (***-ies***) rebellion, or an act of rebellion, against established authority, esp in the armed services. ▸ *verb* (***-ies, -ied***) *intr* to engage in mutiny. ▪ **mutineer** *noun.* [16c: from French *mutin* rebellious]

mutt *noun, slang* **1** a dog, esp a mongrel. **2** a foolish, clumsy person. [20c: shortened from **muttonhead**]

mutter *verb* **1** *tr & intr* to utter (words) in a quiet, barely audible voice. **2** *intr* to grumble or complain, esp in a low voice. ▸ *noun* **1** a soft, barely audible or indistinct tone of voice. **2** a muttered complaint. ▪ **muttering** *noun, adj.* [14c]

mutton *noun* the flesh of an adult sheep, used as food. [13c: from French *moton* sheep]

mutual *adj* **1** felt by each of two or more people about the other or others; reciprocal. **2** to, towards or of each other: *mutual supporters.* **3** *informal* shared by each of two or more; common: *a mutual friend.* ▪ **mutuality** *noun.* ▪ **mutually** *adv.* [15c: from French *mutuel*]

mutualism *noun, biol* a close relationship between two living organisms of different species, that is beneficial to both of them. Compare **commensalism**, **parasitism**. [19c]

muzak see under **piped music**

muzzle *noun* **1** the projecting jaws and nose of an animal, eg a dog. **2** an arrangement of straps fitted round an animal's jaws to prevent it biting. **3** the open end of a gun barrel. ▸ *verb* **1** to put a muzzle on (eg a dog). **2** to prevent someone from speaking or being heard. [15c: from French *musel*]

muzzy *adj* (**-*ier***, **-*iest***) **1** not thinking clearly; confused. **2** blurred; hazy. ▪ **muzzily** *adv.* ▪ **muzziness** *noun.*

MW *abbrev* **1** medium wave. **2** megawatt(s).

mx *abbrev, physics* maxwell, or maxwells.

my *adj* **1** belonging or relating to **me**[1]: *my book.* **2** used with nouns in various exclams: *My goodness!* • *My foot!* **3** used in respectful terms of address such as *my lord.* ▸ *exclam* (*also* **my word**, **my goodness** or, more strongly, **my God**) expressing surprise or amazement: *My, how grown-up you look!* [12c: from Anglo-Saxon *min* genitive of **me**[1]]

myalgia *noun, med* pain in the muscles or a muscle. ▪ **myalgic** *adj.* [19c]

myalgic encephalomyelitis *noun* (abbrev **ME**) a virus-associated debilitating disorder, characterized by extreme fatigue, muscular pain, lack of concentration and depression. Also called **postviral syndrome** and **chronic fatigue syndrome**.

mycelium *noun* (***mycelia***) *biol* in multicellular fungi: a mass or network of thread-like filaments formed when the non-reproductive tissues are growing.

Mycenaean /maɪsə'niːən/ *adj* relating to the ancient Bronze Age civilization in Greece (1500–1100 BC), known from the Homeric poems and from remains at Mycenae and other sites in S Greece. ▸ *noun* an inhabitant of the Mycenaean world.

mycology *noun, biol* the study of fungi. ▪ **mycologist** *noun.* [19c: from Latin *mycologia*]

mycotoxin *noun, biol* any poisonous substance produced by a fungus. [20c]

myelin *noun, zool, anatomy* a soft white substance that forms a thin insulating sheath around the nerve fibres of vertebrates. [19c: German]

myelitis *noun, pathol* **1** inflammation of the spinal cord. **2** inflammation of the bone marrow. [19c: from Greek *myelos* marrow]

myeloma *noun* (***myelomas*** *or* ***myelomata***) *med, pathol* a tumour of the bone marrow. [19c: from Greek *myelos* marrow]

myna *or* **mynah** *noun* a large bird of the starling family which can be taught to imitate human speech. [18c: from Hindi *maina*]

myocardium *noun* (***myocardia***) *anatomy* the muscular tissue of the heart. ▪ **myocardiac** *or* **myocardial** *adj.* [19c]

myopia *noun* short-sightedness, in which rays of light entering the eye are brought to a focus in front of the retina rather than on it, so that distant objects appear blurred. ▪ **myopic** *adj.* [17c: from Greek *myops* short-sighted]

myriad *noun* (*esp* **myriads** *or* **a myriad of sth**) an exceedingly great number. ▸ *adj* numberless; innumerable: *her myriad admirers.* [16c: from Greek *myrias* ten thousand]

myriapod *noun, zool* a crawling, many-legged **arthropod**, eg the centipede or millipede. [19c: from Latin *Myriapoda*]

myrrh /mɜː(r)/ *noun* **1** a type of African and Asian tree and shrub that produces a bitter, brown, aromatic resin. **2** the resin produced by these, used in medicines, perfumes, etc. [Anglo-Saxon *myrra*: from Greek *myrra*]

myrtle *noun* **1** an evergreen shrub with pink or white flowers and dark blue, aromatic berries. **2** any related shrub. [15c: from French *myrtille*]

myself *pron* **1** the reflexive form of **I**[2] (*used instead of me* when the speaker or writer is the object of an action he or she performs): *I burnt myself.* **2** used with *I* or *me*, to add emphasis or to clarify something: *I prefer tea myself.* **3** my normal self: *I am not myself today.* **4** (*also* **by myself**) alone; without any help. [14c: Anglo-Saxon *me seolf*]

mysterious *adj* **1** difficult or impossible to understand or explain; deeply curious. **2** creating, containing or suggesting mystery. ▪ **mysteriously** *adv.*

mystery *noun* (**-*ies***) **1** an event or phenomenon that cannot be, or has not been, explained. **2** someone about whom very little is known. **3** a story about a crime that is difficult to solve. **4** a religious rite, esp the Eucharist. [14c: from Latin *mysterium*]

mystery tour *noun* a round trip to a destination that is not revealed to the travellers in advance.

mystic *noun, relig* someone whose life is devoted to meditation or prayer in an attempt to achieve direct communication with and knowledge of God, regarded as the ultimate reality. ▸ *adj* mystical. [14c: from Greek *mystikos*]

mystical *adj* (*also* **mystic**) **1** *relig* **a** relating to or involving truths about the nature of God and reality revealed only to those people with a spiritually-enlightened mind; esoteric; **b** relating to the mysteries or to mysticism. **2** mysterious. **3** wonderful or awe-inspiring.

mysticism *noun* **1** *relig* the practice of gaining direct communication with God through prayer and meditation. **2** the belief in the existence of a state of reality hidden from ordinary human understanding.

mystify *verb* (**-*ies***, **-*ied***) **1** to puzzle or bewilder. **2** to make something mysterious or obscure. ▪ **mystification** *noun.* [19c: from French *mystifier*]

mystique /mɪ'stiːk/ *noun* a mysterious, distinctive or compelling quality possessed by a person or thing. [19c: French]

myth *noun* **1** an ancient story that deals with gods and heroes, esp one used to explain some natural phenomenon. **2** such stories in general; mythology. **3** a commonly-held, false notion. **4** a non-existent, fictitious person or thing. ▪ **mythical** *adj.* [19c: from Greek *mythos*]

mythology *noun* (**-*ies***) **1** myths in general. **2** a collection of myths, eg about a specific subject. **3** the study of myths. ▪ **mythological** *adj.* [15c: from Greek *mythos* myth]

myxomatosis /mɪksəmə'toʊsɪs/ *noun, vet med, biol* an infectious, usu fatal, viral disease of rabbits, transmitted by fleas and causing the growth of numerous tumours through the body. [20c]

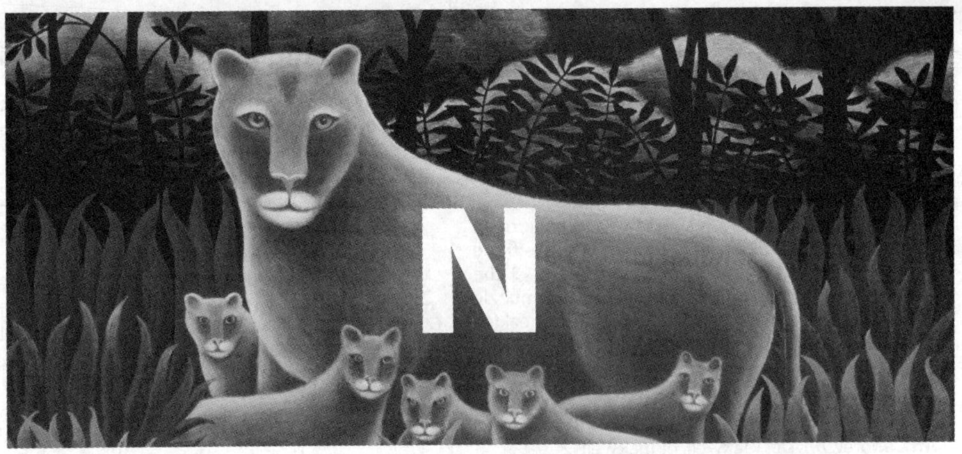

N[1] *or* **n** *noun* (***Ns, N's*** *or* ***n's***) the fourteenth letter of the English alphabet.

N[2] *abbrev* **1** National. **2** Nationalist. **3** New. **4** *physics* newton. **5** North. **6** Northern.

N[3] *symbol* **1** *chess* knight. **2** *chem* nitrogen.

n[1] *noun* **1** *maths* an indefinite number. **2** *colloq* a large number. ▸ *adj* being an indefinite or large number.

n[2] *abbrev* **1** nano-. **2** *grammar* neuter. **3** *physics* neutron. **4** *grammar* nominative. **5** note. **6** *grammar* noun.

'n' *abbrev, colloq* and.

Na *symbol, chem* sodium. [From Latin *natrium*]

n/a *abbrev* not applicable.

naan see **nan**

nab *verb* (***nabbed, nabbing***) *colloq* **1** to catch someone doing wrong. **2** to arrest someone. **3** to grab or take something. [17c]

nabob /'neɪbɒb/ *noun, colloq* a wealthy influential person. [17c: from Urdu *nawwab*]

nacelle /nə'sɛl/ *noun* **1** the basket or gondola of a balloon, airship, etc. **2** a streamlined structure on an aircraft that houses an engine or accommodates crew and passengers, etc. [20c: French, meaning 'a small boat']

nachos *plural noun, cookery* tortilla chips topped with chillis, melted cheese, etc. [20c]

nacre /'neɪkə(r)/ *noun* **mother-of-pearl.** ▪ **nacreous** *adj.* [17c: from Arabic *naqqarah* shell]

nadir /'neɪdɪə(r)/ *noun* **1** *astron* the point on the celestial sphere directly opposite the zenith. **2** the lowest point; the depths, eg of despair or degradation. [15c: from Arabic *nazir-as-samt* opposite the zenith]

naevus *or* (*US*) **nevus** /'niːvəs/ *noun* (***naevi*** /-vaɪ/) a birthmark or mole. [19c: Latin]

naff *adj, slang* **1** of poor quality; worthless. **2** tasteless; vulgar. [20c]
IDIOMS **naff off!** *offensive* go away! get lost!

nag[1] *noun* **1** *derog* a broken-down old horse. **2** a small riding-horse. [15c: meaning 'a riding-horse']

nag[2] *verb* (***nagged, nagging***) **1** (*also* **nag at sb**) *tr & intr* to keep finding fault with them. **2** (*also* **nag at sb**) *intr* to worry them or cause them anxiety. **3** *intr* of pain: to persist. ▸ *noun* someone who nags. ▪ **nagging** *adj.* [19c: from Norse *nagga* to rub, grumble or quarrel]

Nahuatl see **Aztec**

naiad /'naɪad/ *noun* (***naiades*** /-ədiːz/ *or* ***naiads***) *Greek myth* a water nymph. [17c: from Greek *naias*]

nail *noun* **1** the hard structure at the tip of a finger or toe. **2** a metal spike for hammering into something, eg to join two objects together. ▸ *verb* **1** to fasten something with, or as if with, a nail or nails. **2** *colloq* to catch, trap or corner someone. **3** to detect, identify or expose (a lie, etc). [Anglo-Saxon *nægl*]
IDIOMS **a nail in one's** *or* **the coffin 1** an event, experience, etc that shortens one's life. **2** a contributory factor in someone's or something's downfall. **hit the nail on the head 1** to pinpoint a problem or issue exactly. **2** to sum something up precisely. **on the nail** *colloq* immediately.
PHRASAL VERBS **nail sb down** *colloq* to extract a definite decision or promise from them. **nail sth down** to define or identify it clearly.

nail-biting *adj* excitingly full of suspense.

nailfile *noun* a **file**[2] (*noun* sense 2).

nail polish *or* **nail varnish** *noun* lacquer which gives colour and shine to finger- and toenails.

naive *or* **naïve** /naɪ'iːv/ *adj* **1** simple, innocent or unsophisticated. **2** *derog* too trusting; credulous. ▪ **naively** *adv.* ▪ **naivety** /-vətɪ/ *or* **naïveté** /-vəteɪ, naɪ'iːvtɪ/ *noun.* [17c: French, feminine of *naïf*]

naked *adj* **1** wearing no clothes. **2** without fur, feathers or foliage. **3** barren; empty. **4** simple; without decoration. **5** undisguised; blatant or flagrant: *naked greed.* **6** of a light or flame: uncovered; exposed. **7** of the eye: unaided by an optical instrument. **8** *literary* vulnerable; defenceless. ▪ **nakedly** *adv.* ▪ **nakedness** *noun.* [Anglo-Saxon *nacod*]

namby-pamby *adj, derog* **1** feebly sentimental; soppy. **2** prim; over-demure. ▸ *noun* (***-ies***) **1** namby-pamby writing or talk. **2** a namby-pamby person. [18c: from the nickname given to the poet Ambrose Philips]

name *noun* **1** a word or words by which a person, place or thing is identified and referred to. **2** reputation: *get a bad name.* **3** a famous or important person, firm, etc: *the big names in fashion.* ▸ *verb, tr & intr* **1** to give a name to someone or something. **2** to mention or identify someone or something by name. **3** to specify or decide on someone or something. **4** to choose or appoint. [Anglo-Saxon *nama*]
IDIOMS **call sb names** to insult or abuse them verbally. **in all but name** in practice, though not officially. **in name only** officially, but not in practice. **in the name of sb** *or* **sth 1** by their or its authority. **2** on their or its behalf. **3** for their or its sake; using them or it as justification. **make a name for oneself** to become famous. **name names** to identify eg culprits by

name. **the name of the game** *colloq* the essential aspect or aim of some activity. **to one's name** belonging to one.

PHRASAL VERBS **name sb** *or* **sth after** *or* (*N Am*) **for sb else** to give (eg a child or a place) the same name as someone, as an honour or commemoration.

name-dropping *noun, derog* the practice of casually referring to well-known people as if they were friends. ▪ **name-dropper** *noun*. [20c]

nameless *adj* **1** having no name. **2** unidentified. **3** anonymous; undistinguished. **4** too awful to specify.

namely *adv* used to introduce an expansion or explanation of what has just been mentioned.

nameplate *noun* a plate on or beside the door of a room etc, bearing the name, and sometimes occupation, etc, of the occupant.

namesake *noun* someone with the same name as, or named after, another person. [17c]

nan *or* **naan** /nɑːn/ *or* **nan bread** *noun* a slightly leavened Indian and Pakistani bread, baked in a flat round or teardrop shape. [20c: Hindi]

nandrolone /'nandrəloun/ *noun* an anabolic steroid that is illegally used as a performance-enhancing drug by some athletes. [Late 20c: altered from *nor-* an organic compound that is derived from another, *andro-* male, and the suffix *-one*]

nanny *noun* (***-ies***) a children's nurse. ▸ *adj, derog* protective to an intrusive extent. ▸ *verb* (***-ies, -ied***) to overprotect or oversupervise. [18c: from Nanny, a form of Ann]

nanny goat *noun* an adult female goat.

nano- *combining form, denoting* **1** a thousand millionth: *nanosecond*. **2** of microscopic size: *nanoplankton*. [From Greek *nanos* dwarf]

nanometre *or* (*US*) **nanometer** *noun* (abbrev **nm**) a unit of length equal to one thousand millionth of a metre.

nanosecond *noun* (abbrev **ns**) one thousand millionth of a second. [1950s: **nano-** + **second**[2]]

nanotechnology /nanoutɛk'nɒlədʒɪ/ *noun* the manufacture and measuring of objects of tiny dimensions. [Late 20c: **nano-** + **technology**]

nap[1] *noun* a short sleep. ▸ *verb* (***napped, napping***) *intr* to have a nap. [Anglo-Saxon *hnappian*]

IDIOMS **catch sb napping** *colloq* to find them unprepared or off-guard.

nap[2] *noun* a woolly surface on cloth. [15c]

nap[3] *noun* **1** a card game like whist. **2** *horse-racing* a tip that is claimed to be a certainty. ▸ *verb* (***napped, napping***) *horse-racing* to name (a particular horse) as certain to win. [Late 19c: from *napoleon*, the full name of the card game]

napalm /'neɪpɑːm/ *noun* an incendiary agent used in bombs and flamethrowers. ▸ *verb* to attack someone or destroy something with napalm. [20c: from *na*phthenate *palm*itate]

nape *noun* the back of the neck. [14c]

naphtha /'nafθə, 'napθə/ *noun, chem* a flammable liquid distilled from coal or petroleum and used as a solvent. [16c: Greek]

naphthalene *noun, chem* a white crystalline hydrocarbon distilled from coal tar, used eg in mothballs and dyes. [19c]

napkin *noun* (*also* **table napkin**) a piece of cloth or paper for wiping one's mouth and fingers or to protect one's clothing at mealtimes. [15c: diminutive of French *nappe* tablecloth]

nappy *noun* (***-ies***) a pad of disposable material or soft cloth secured round a baby's bottom to absorb urine and faeces. [20c: diminutive of **napkin**]

narcissism *noun* excessive admiration for oneself or one's appearance. ▪ **narcissistic** *adj*. [19c: from *Narkissos*, a youth in Greek mythology who fell in love with his own reflection]

narcissus /nɑː'sɪsəs/ *noun* (***narcissuses*** *or* ***narcissi*** /-saɪ/) a plant similar to the daffodil, with white or yellow flowers. [16c: from Greek *narkissos*]

narco- *or* (*before vowels*) **narc-** *combining form, signifying* **1** numbness or torpor. **2** drugs. [From Greek *narke* numbness]

narcosis *noun* (***-ses***) *pathol* drowsiness, unconsciousness, or other effects produced by a narcotic. [17c: from Greek *narkosis* numbing]

narcotic *noun* **1** a drug which causes numbness, drowsiness and unconsciousness, deadens pain or produces a sense of well-being. **2** *loosely* any addictive or illegal drug. **3** any substance that has a narcotic effect, eg alcohol. ▸ *adj* **1** relating to narcotics or the users of narcotics. **2** relating to **narcosis**. [14c: from Greek *narkotikos* numbing]

nark *noun, slang* **1** a spy or informer working for the police. **2** a habitual grumbler. ▸ *verb, colloq* **1** *tr & intr* to annoy. **2** *intr* to grumble. **3** *intr* to inform or spy, esp for the police. ▪ **narky** *adj* (***-ier, -iest***) *colloq* irritable. [19c: perhaps from Romany *nak* nose]

narrate *verb, tr & intr* **1** to tell (a story). **2** to give a running commentary on (a film, etc). ▪ **narration** *noun*. ▪ **narrator** *noun*. [17c: from Latin *narrare* to relate]

narrative *noun* **1** an account of events. **2** those parts of a book, etc that recount events. ▸ *adj* **1** telling a story; recounting events. **2** relating to the telling of stories. [15c: from Latin *narrativus*, from *narrare* to relate]

narrow *adj* **1** not wide. **2** of interests or experience: restricted; limited. **3** of attitudes or ideas: illiberal, unenlightened or intolerant. **4** of the use of a word: restricted to its precise or original meaning. **5** close; only just achieved, etc: *a narrow escape*. ▸ *noun* **1** a narrow part or place. **2** (**narrows**) a narrow part of a channel, river, etc. ▸ *verb, tr & intr* **1** to make or become narrow. **2** (*also* **narrow sth down**) to reduce or limit (eg a range of possibilities), or be reduced or limited. ▪ **narrowness** *noun*. [Anglo-Saxon *nearu*]

narrowboat *noun* a canal barge.

narrowcast *verb* **1** *tr & intr* to transmit (TV programmes, etc) on a cable system. **2** *intr* to target a particular audience. ▪ **narrowcasting** *noun* **1** cable TV. **2** the production and distribution of material on video tapes, cassettes, etc. [20c: modelled on **broadcast**]

narrowly *adv* **1** only just; barely. **2** with close attention: *eyed him narrowly*. **3** in a narrow or restricted way.

narrow-minded *adj, derog* **1** intolerant. **2** bigoted; prejudiced. ▪ **narrow-mindedness** *noun*.

narrow squeak see under **squeak**

narwhal *noun* an arctic whale, the male of which has a long spiral tusk. [17c: from Danish *narhval*]

NASA /'nasə/ *abbrev* National Aeronautics and Space Administration.

nasal *adj* **1** relating to the nose. **2** pronounced through, or partly through, the nose. **3** of a voice, etc: abnormally or exceptionally full of nasal sounds. ▸ *noun* **1** a nasal sound. **2** a letter representing such a sound. ▪ **nasalize** *or* **-ise** *verb, tr & intr.* ▪ **nasally** *adv.* [17c: from Latin *nasus* nose]

nascent *adj* coming into being; in the early stages of development. ▪ **nascency** *noun.* [17c: from Latin *nasci* to be born]

naso- *combining form, denoting* nose. [From Latin *nasus* nose]

nasturtium /nəˈstɜːʃəm/ *noun* a climbing garden plant with red, orange or yellow trumpet-like flowers. [16c: Latin, meaning 'cress']

nasty *adj* (**-ier, -iest**) **1** unpleasant; disgusting. **2** malicious; ill-natured. **3** worrying; serious: *a nasty wound.* **4** of weather: wet or stormy. ▸ *noun* (**-ies**) someone or something unpleasant, disgusting or offensive: *a video nasty.* ▪ **nastily** *adv.* ▪ **nastiness** *noun.* [14c]

Nat. *abbrev* **1** National. **2** Nationalist.

nat *noun, colloq* a nationalist.

nat. *abbrev* **1** national. **2** native. **3** natural.

natal /ˈneɪtəl/ *adj* connected with birth. [15c: from Latin *natalis*, from *nasci* to be born]

natch /nɑːtʃ/ *adv, slang* of course. [1940s: short for **naturally**]

nation *noun* **1** the people of a single state. **2** a race of people of common descent, history, language, culture, etc. **3** a Native American tribe or federation. ▪ **nationhood** *noun.* [13c: French, from Latin *natio* tribe]

national *adj* **1** belonging to a particular nation. **2** concerning or covering the whole nation. **3** public; general. ▸ *noun* **1** a citizen of a particular nation. **2** a national newspaper. ▪ **nationally** *adv.*

national anthem *noun* a nation's official song.

national debt *noun* the money borrowed by the government of a country and not yet repaid.

national grid *noun* **1** the network of high-voltage electric power lines in Britain. **2** the system of vertical and horizontal lines used in Ordnance Survey maps.

National Health Service *noun, Brit* (abbrev **NHS**) the system set up in 1948 to provide medical treatment for all UK residents free, or at a small charge, paid for mainly by public taxation.

national insurance *noun, Brit* (abbrev **NI**) a system of state insurance to which employers and employees contribute, to provide for the sick, etc.

nationalism *noun* **1** great pride in or loyalty to one's nation; patriotism. **2** extreme or fanatical patriotism. **3** a policy of, or movement aiming at, national unity or independence. ▪ **nationalist** *noun, adj.* ▪ **nationalistic** *adj.*

nationality *noun* (**-ies**) **1** citizenship of a particular nation. **2** a group that has the character of a nation. **3** the racial or national group to which one belongs. **4** national character.

nationalize *or* **-ise** *verb* **1** to bring (eg an industry) under state ownership and control. **2** to make something national. ▪ **nationalization** *noun.*

national park *noun* an area of countryside, usu important for its natural beauty, wildlife, etc, under the ownership and care of the nation.

national service *noun* compulsory service in the armed forces.

nationwide *adj* extending over the whole of a nation. ▸ *adv* over the whole of a nation.

native *adj* **1** being in or belonging to the place of one's upbringing. **2** born a citizen of a particular place: *a native Italian.* **3** inborn or innate: *native wit.* **4** being a person's first language. **5** originating in a particular place: *native to Bali.* **6** belonging to the original inhabitants of a country: *native Balinese music.* **7** natural; in a natural state. ▸ *noun* **1** someone born in a certain place. **2** a plant or animal originating in a particular place. **3** *often derog* an original inhabitant of a place as distinct from later, esp European, settlers. [14c: from Latin *nativus* natural, from *nasci* to be born]

Native American *noun* a member of any of the indigenous peoples of America. ▸ *adj* relating or referring to any of the indigenous peoples of America, the languages they speak, their culture, etc. Also called *(dated)* **American Indian, Indian.** [20c]

native land *noun* the land to which someone belongs by birth.

native speaker *noun* someone who speaks the language in question as their native language.

nativity *noun* (**-ies**) **1** birth, advent or origin. **2** (**Nativity**) **a** the birth of Christ; **b** a picture representing it; **c** Christmas. [14c: from Latin *nativitas* birth]

NATO *or* **Nato** /ˈneɪtoʊ/ *abbrev* North Atlantic Treaty Organization.

natter *colloq, verb, intr* to chat busily. ▸ *noun* an intensive chat. [19c: imitating the sound of chattering]

natterjack *noun, zool* a European toad with a yellow stripe down its spine. [18c]

natty *adj* (**-ier, -iest**) *colloq* **1** of clothes: flashily smart. **2** clever; ingenious. ▪ **nattily** *adv.* [18c: related to **neat**]

natural *adj* **1** normal; unsurprising. **2** instinctive; not learnt. **3** born in one; innate. **4** being such because of inborn qualities. **5** of manner, etc: simple, easy and direct; not artificial. **6** of looks: not, or apparently not, improved on artificially. **7** relating to nature, or to parts of the physical world not made or altered by man: *natural sciences* • *areas of natural beauty.* **8** following the normal course of nature. **9** of materials, products, etc: derived from plants and animals; not manufactured. **10** wild; uncultivated or uncivilized. **11** related by blood: *one's natural parents.* **12** *euphem* **illegitimate. 13** *music* not sharp or flat. ▸ *noun* **1** *colloq* someone with an inborn feel for something. **2** an obvious choice for something. **3** someone or something that is assured of success; a certainty. **4** *music* **a** a sign (♮) indicating a note that is not to be played sharp or flat; **b** such a note. ▪ **naturalness** *noun.* [14c: from Latin *naturalis*, from *natura* nature]

natural-born *adj* native.

natural childbirth *noun* childbirth with as little medical intervention as possible.

natural frequency *noun, physics* the frequency at which an object or system will vibrate freely, in the absence of external forces.

natural gas *noun* a fuel gas found under the ground or sea-bed.

natural history *noun* the study of plants, animals and minerals.

natural increase *noun* the difference between the birth rate and the death rate in a given area.

naturalism *noun* **1** realistic treatment of subjects in art, literature, etc, without idealizing them. **2** the view that rejects supernatural explanations of phenomena, maintaining that all must have natural causes. ▪ **naturalistic** *adj.*

naturalist *noun* **1** someone who studies animal and plant life. **2** a follower of naturalism.

naturalize *or* **-ise** *verb* **1** to confer citizenship on (a foreigner). **2** *tr & intr* of a word of foreign origin: come to be considered as part of a language. **3** to gradually admit (a custom) among established traditions. **4** to make (an introduced species of plant or animal) adapt to the local environment. **5** *intr* of a plant or animal: to adapt to a new environment. **6** to make something natural or lifelike. ▪ **naturalization** *noun.* [16c]

natural language *noun* a language which has evolved naturally, and has not been artificially created.

natural logarithm *noun, maths* a logarithm to the base constant e (2.718…).

naturally *adv* **1** of course; not surprisingly. **2** in accordance with the normal course of things. **3** by nature; as a natural characteristic. **4** by means of a natural process, as opposed to being produced by a man-made process. **5** in a relaxed or normal manner.

natural number *noun, maths* any whole positive number, sometimes including zero.

natural philosophy *noun* physics.

natural resources *plural noun* sources of energy and wealth that occur naturally in the earth.

natural science *noun* the science of nature (including biology, chemistry, geology and physics).

natural selection *noun* the process by which plant and animal species that adapt most successfully to their environment survive, while others die out; the basis for **evolution**.

natural wastage *noun, business* non-replacement of employees that leave or retire, as a means of reducing staffing levels.

nature *noun* **1** (*also* **Nature**) the physical world and the forces that have formed and control it. **2** animal and plant life as distinct from human life. **3** what something is or consists of. **4** a fundamental tendency; essential character; attitude or outlook. **5** a kind, sort or type. [13c: from Latin *natura*]

IDIOMS **in the nature of sth** with the characteristics of it; like it.

nature reserve *noun* an area of land specially managed to preserve the flora and fauna in it.

naturism *noun* nudism. ▪ **naturist** *noun.* [20c]

naturopathy *noun* the promotion of good health and natural healing by diet, exercise, manipulation and hydrotherapy. ▪ **naturopath** *noun.* ▪ **naturopathic** *adj.* [20c]

naught *noun* nothing. [14c: Anglo-Saxon *nawiht*, from *na* no + *wiht* thing]

naught

Be careful not to use the spelling **naught** when you mean **nought**:

The figure for one million has six noughts.

naughty *adj* (**-ier, -iest**) **1** mischievous; disobedient. **2** mildly shocking or indecent; titillating. ▪ **naughtily** *adv.* ▪ **naughtiness** *noun.* [16c: from **naught** in its earlier sense 'wickedness']

nausea /'nɔːzɪə/ *noun* **1** a feeling that one is about to vomit. **2** disgust. [16c: from Greek *nausia* seasickness]

nauseate *verb* **1** to make someone feel nausea. **2** to disgust someone. ▪ **nauseating** *adj.* [17c: from Latin *nauseare* to be seasick]

nauseous *adj* **1** sickening; disgusting. **2** affected by nausea. [17c: from Latin *nauseosus*]

nautical *adj* relating to ships, sailors or navigation. [17c: from Greek *nautikos*, from *nautes* sailor]

nautical mile *noun* a measure of distance traditionally used at sea, equal to about 1.85km.

nautilus *noun* (***nautiluses*** *or* ***nautili***) a sea creature related to the squid and octopus. [17c: from Greek *nautilos* sailor]

naval *adj* relating to a navy or to ships generally. [17c: from Latin *navalis*, from *navis* ship]

nave[1] *noun, archit* the main central part of a church. [17c: from Latin *navis* ship]

nave[2] *noun* the central part of a wheel. [Anglo-Saxon *nafu*]

navel *noun* **1** the small hollow at the point where the umbilical cord was attached to the fetus. **2** the central point of something. [Anglo-Saxon *nafela*]

navigable *adj* **1** able to be sailed along or through. **2** seaworthy. **3** steerable. [16c: from Latin *navigabilis*, from *navigare* to sail]

navigate *verb* **1** *intr* to direct the course of a ship, aircraft or other vehicle. **2** *intr* to find one's way and hold one's course. **3** to steer (a ship or aircraft). **4 a** to manage to sail along or through (a river, channel, etc); **b** to find one's way through, along, over or across something, etc. **5** *intr* of a vehicle passenger: to give the driver directions on the correct route. ▪ **navigator** *noun.* [16c: from Latin *navigare*, from *navis* ship]

navigation *noun* **1** the act, skill or science of navigating. **2** the movement of ships and aircraft. ▪ **navigational** *adj.*

navvy /'navɪ/ *noun* (**-ies**) a labourer, esp one employed in road-building or canal-building. ► *verb* (**-ies, -ied**) *intr* to work as or like a navvy. [19c: from **navigation** in its earlier sense 'canal']

navy /'neɪvɪ/ *noun* (**-ies**) **1** (*often* **the Navy**) **a** the warships of a state, and their personnel; **b** the organization to which they belong. **2** a body or fleet of ships with their crews. **3** (*also* **navy blue**) a dark blue colour. ► *adj* (*also* **navy-blue**) having a navy blue colour. [14c: from French *navie*]

nawab /nə'wɑːb/ *noun, hist* a Muslim ruler or landowner in India. [18c: from Urdu *nawwab*]

nay *exclam, old use or dialect* **1** no. **2** rather; to put it more strongly. ► *noun* **1** the word 'no'. **2** *formal* esp in parliament: **a** someone who casts a negative vote; **b** a vote against: *Nays to the left; ayes to the right.* [12c: from Norse]

Nazarene *adj* belonging to Nazareth. ► *noun* **1** someone from Nazareth. **2** (**the Nazarene**) *hist* Jesus Christ. **3** *hist* a Christian. [13c: from Greek *Nazarenos*]

Nazi /'nɑːtsɪ/ *noun* **1** *hist* a member of the German National Socialist Party, which came to power in Germany in 1933 under Adolf Hitler. **2** *derog colloq* someone with extreme racist and dogmatic opinions. ▪ **Nazism** *noun*. [20c: German contraction of *Nationalsozialist*]

NB *abbrev* (*also* **nb**) *nota bene* (Latin), note well; take note.

Nb *symbol, chem* niobium.

NCO *noun* non-commissioned officer.

Nd *symbol, chem* neodymium.

NE *abbrev* **1** north-east. **2** north-eastern.

Ne *symbol, chem* neon.

Neanderthal /nɪ'andətɑːl/ *adj* **1** denoting a primitive type of man living in Europe during the **palaeolithic** period of the Stone Age. **2** (*sometimes* **neanderthal**) *colloq* primitive. **3** (*sometimes* **neanderthal**) *colloq* extremely old-fashioned and reactionary. [19c: from Neandert(h)al in Germany, where remains were first found]

neap tide *or* **neap** *noun* a tide occurring at the first and last quarters of the moon, when there is the least variation between high and low water. Compare **spring tide**. [Anglo-Saxon *nepflod* neap flood]

near *prep* close to (someone or something). ▸ *adv* **1** close: *came near to hitting her.* **2** *old use or informal* almost; nearly: *She damn near died.* ▸ *adj* **1** being a short distance away; close. **2** closer of two. **3** similar; comparable: *the nearest thing to a screwdriver.* **4** closely related to one. **5** almost amounting to, or almost turning into, the specified thing. ▸ *verb, tr & intr* to approach. ▪ **nearness** *noun*. [Anglo-Saxon, from *neah* nigh and Norse *na* nigh]

nearby *adj, adv* a short distance away; close at hand.

Near East *noun* the Middle East.

nearly *adv* almost. [16c; see **near**]

IDIOMS **not nearly** very far from; nothing like.

near miss *noun* **1** something not quite achieved, eg a shot that almost hits the target. **2** something (eg an air collision) only just avoided.

nearside *noun* the side of a vehicle, horse or team of horses nearer the kerb. *as adj*: *the nearside front tyre.*

near-sighted *adj* short-sighted.

near thing *noun* a narrow escape; a success only just achieved.

neat *adj* **1** tidy; clean; orderly. **2** pleasingly small or regular. **3** elegantly or cleverly simple. **4** skilful or efficient: *Neat work!* **5** *N Am* excellent: *That's neat!* **6** esp of an alcoholic drink: undiluted. ▪ **neatly** *adv*. ▪ **neatness** *noun*. [16c: from French *net* clean or tidy]

neaten *verb* to make something neat and tidy. [16c]

neath *or* **'neath** *prep, dialect or poetry* beneath. [18c: shortened form of older *aneath* or **beneath**]

neb *noun, Scot & N Eng* **1** a beak or bill. **2** the nose. [Anglo-Saxon *nebb* beak or face]

nebula /'nɛbjʊlə/ *noun* (***nebulae*** /-liː/ *or* ***nebulas***) *astron* a luminous or dark patch in space representing a mass of dust or particles. ▪ **nebular** *adj*. [17c: Latin, meaning 'mist']

nebulizer *noun, med* a device with a mouthpiece or face mask, through which a drug is administered as a fine mist. [19c: from *nebulize* to make into mist]

nebulous *adj* vague; lacking distinct shape, form or nature. [19c: from Latin *nebulosus*, from *nebula* mist]

necessarily *adv* as a necessary or inevitable result.

necessary *adj* **1** needed; essential; indispensable. **2** inevitable; inescapable. **3** logically required or unavoidable. **4** of eg an agent: not free. ▸ *noun* (***-ies***) **1** (*usu* **necessaries**) something that is necessary. **2** (**the necessary**) *humorous, informal* **a** money needed for a purpose; **b** action that must be taken. [14c: from Latin *necessarius*, from *necesse* unavoidable]

necessary
This word is often misspelt. It has one *c* and two *s*'s. It might help you to remember the following sentence:
*One **c**ollar and two **s**leeves are ne**c**e**ss**ary on a shirt.*

necessitate *verb* **1** to make something necessary or unavoidable. **2** to compel someone to do something. [17c: from Latin *necessitare*, from *necessitas* necessity]

necessity *noun* (***-ies***) **1** something necessary or essential. **2** circumstances that make something necessary or unavoidable. **3** a pressing need. **4** poverty; want; need. [14c: from Latin *necessitas*]

IDIOMS **of necessity** necessarily; unavoidably.

neck *noun* **1** the part of the body between the head and the shoulders. **2** the part of a garment at or covering the neck. **3** a narrow part; a narrow connecting part. **4** *horse-racing* a head-and-neck's length: *won by a neck.* **5** meat from the neck of an animal. **6** *informal* impudence; boldness. ▸ *verb, tr & intr, slang* to hug and kiss amorously. ▪ **necking** *noun*. [Anglo-Saxon *hnecca*]

IDIOMS **get it in the neck** *informal* to be severely rebuked or punished. **neck and neck** of competitors: exactly level. **up to one's neck in sth** *informal* deeply involved in (*esp* a troublesome situation); busy.

neckband *noun* **1** a band or strip of material sewn round the neck of a garment to finish it or as the base for a collar. **2** a band worn around the neck.

neckerchief *noun* (***neckerchiefs*** *or* ***neckerchieves***) a cloth worn round the neck. [14c: **neck** + **kerchief**]

necklace *noun* a string of beads, chain, etc, worn round the neck as jewellery. [16c: **neck** + **lace**]

necklet *noun* a simple necklace.

neckline *noun* the edge of a garment at the neck, or its shape.

neck of the woods *noun, humorous* a neighbourhood or locality.

necktie *noun, esp US* a man's **tie**.

necro- *or* (*before a vowel*) **necr-** *combining form, denoting* **1** dead. **2** dead body. **3** dead tissue. [From Greek *nekros* a dead body]

necromancy *noun* **1** divination or prophecy through communication with the dead. **2** black magic; sorcery. ▪ **necromancer** *noun*. ▪ **necromantic** *adj*. [14c: from Greek *nekros* corpse + *mantis* prophet]

necropolis /nɛ'krɒpəlɪs/ *noun, archaeol* a cemetery or burial site. [19c: from Greek *nekros* corpse + *polis* city]

necrosis *noun* (***-ses***) *pathol* the death of living tissue or bone, esp where the blood supply has been interrupted. ▪ **necrotic** *adj*. [17c: Greek, from *nekros* corpse]

nectar *noun* **1** a sugary substance produced in flowers, collected by bees to make honey. **2** *Greek myth* the special drink of the gods. **3** any delicious drink. **4** anything delightful to the senses, esp taste or smell. [16c: from Greek *nektar*]

nectarine *noun* a variety of peach with a shiny downless skin. [17c, as *adj* meaning 'like nectar']

née *or* **nee** /neɪ/ *adj* used in giving a married woman's maiden name: born. [18c: French *née*, feminine of *né* born]

need *verb* **1** to lack; to require. **2** *intr* (*also as auxiliary verb*) to be required or obliged to be or do something: *We need to find a replacement.* ▸ *noun* **1** something one requires. **2** (**need of** *or* **for sth**) a condition of lacking or requiring it; an urge or desire. **3** (**need for sth**) necessity or justification for it. [Anglo-Saxon *nead* or *nied*]

IDIOMS **if need** *or* **needs be** if necessary. **in need** needing help or financial support. **needs must** one must do what is necessary, even if it is disagreeable.

needful *adj* necessary. ▸ *noun* (**the needful**) *humorous, informal* **1** whatever action is necessary. **2** money needed for a purpose.

needle *noun* **1** a slender pointed sewing instrument with a hole for the thread. **2** a longer, thicker implement without a hole, for knitting, crocheting, etc. **3 a** a hypodermic syringe; **b** its pointed end. **4** *med* a slender instrument for suturing, dissection, etc. **5** a gramophone **stylus**. **6** the moving pointer on a compass or other instrument. **7** anything slender, sharp and pointed. **8** a pinnacle of rock. **9** an obelisk. **10** a long slender crystal. **11** the needle-shaped leaf of a tree such as the pine or fir. **12** (**the needle**) *informal* **a** provocation; **b** irritation; anger; **c** dislike. ▸ *verb, tr & intr, informal* to provoke or irritate someone, esp deliberately. [Anglo-Saxon *nædl*]

IDIOMS **look for a needle in a haystack** to undertake a hopeless search.

needlepoint *noun* **1** embroidery on canvas. **2** lace made with needles over a paper pattern.

needless *adj* unnecessary. ▪ **needlessly** *adv.*

needlework *noun* sewing and embroidery.

needn't *contraction,* need not.

needy *adj* (**-*ier*, -*iest***) **1** in severe need; poverty-stricken. **2** craving attention or affection.

ne'er *adv, poetic* never.

ne'er-do-well *adj* good-for-nothing. ▸ *noun* an idle irresponsible useless person. [18c]

nefarious /nɪˈfɛərɪəs/ *adj* wicked; evil. ▪ **nefariously** *adv.* [17c: from Latin *nefarius*, from *nefas* a crime]

neg. *abbrev* **1** negative. **2** negatively. **3** negotiable.

negate *verb* **1** to cancel the effect of something. **2** to deny the existence of something. ▪ **negator** *noun.* [17c: from Latin *negare* to deny]

negation *noun* **1** the act of negating. **2** the absence or opposite of something. **3** the denial of the existence of something.

negative *adj* **1** meaning or saying 'no'. **2** unenthusiastic, defeatist or pessimistic. **3** *maths* less than zero. **4** contrary to, or cancelling the effect of, whatever is regarded as positive. **5** *maths* opposite to positive. **6** *elec* having the kind of electric charge produced by an excess of electrons. **7** *photog* of film: having the light and shade of the actual image reversed, or complementary colours in place of actual ones. **8** *biol* away from the source of stimulus. ▸ *noun* **1** a word, statement or grammatical form expressing 'no' or 'not'. **2** a photographic film with a negative image, from which prints are made. ▸ *verb* **1** to reject or veto something. **2** to deny something. **3** to neutralize or cancel out something. ▪ **negativeness** *or* **negativity** *noun.* [16c: from Latin *negativus*, from *negare* to deny]

negative equity *noun, econ* the situation when the market value of property is less than the value of the mortgage on it. [20c]

negative sign *noun* the symbol of subtraction (–).

negativism *noun* a tendency to deny and criticize without offering anything positive. ▪ **negativist** *noun, adj.* ▪ **negativistic** *adj.* [19c]

neglect *verb* **1** not to give proper care and attention to someone or something. **2** to leave (duties, etc) undone. **3** to fail or omit (to do something). ▸ *noun* **1** lack of proper care. **2** a state of disuse or decay. ▪ **neglectful** *adj* inattentive or negligent; undutiful or unconscientious. [16c: from Latin *negligere* to neglect]

négligée *or* **negligee** /ˈnɛglɪʒeɪ/ *noun* a woman's thin light dressing-gown. [20c: from French *négligé* carelessness or undress]

negligent *adj* **1** not giving proper care and attention. **2** careless or offhand. ▪ **negligence** *noun.* ▪ **negligently** *adv.* [14c]

negligible *adj* small or unimportant enough to ignore. [19c: from Latin *negligere* to disregard]

negotiable *adj* **1** open to discussion. **2** able to be got past or through. **3** of a cheque, etc: that can be transferred to another person and exchanged for its value in money.

negotiate *verb* **1** *intr* to confer; to bargain. **2** to bring about (an agreement), or arrange (a treaty, price, etc), by conferring. **3** to pass safely (a hazard on one's way, etc). **4** *informal* to cope with something successfully. ▪ **negotiation** *noun.* ▪ **negotiator** *noun.* [16c: from Latin *negotiari* to trade]

neigh *noun* the cry of a horse. ▸ *verb, intr* to make this cry or a sound like it. [Anglo-Saxon *hnægan*, imitating the sound]

neighbour *or* (*N Am*) **neighbor** *noun* **1** someone near or next door to one. **2** an adjacent territory, person, etc. **3** *old use* a fellow human: *Love your neighbour.* ▪ **neighbouring** *adj* **1** nearby. **2** adjoining. [Anglo-Saxon *neahgebur*, from *neah* near + *gebur* dweller]

neighbourhood *or* (*N Am*) **neighborhood** *noun* **1** a district or locality. **2** the local community. **3** the area near something or someone.

IDIOMS **in the neighbourhood of** approximately.

neighbourhood watch *noun* a crime-prevention scheme under which householders keep a general watch on each other's property and the local streets. [20c]

neighbourly *or* (*N Am*) **neighborly** *adj* friendly, esp to the people around one.

neither *adj, pron* not the one nor the other thing or person: *Neither proposal is acceptable.* • *Neither of the proposals is acceptable.* ▸ *conj* (*used to introduce the first of two or more alternatives*) not: *I neither know nor care.* ▸ *adv* nor; also not: *If you won't, then neither will I.* [Anglo-Saxon *nawther* or *nahwæther*]

IDIOMS **neither here nor there** irrelevant; unimportant.

neither

You can use a singular or plural verb with **neither**, but many people think only the singular verb is correct. Therefore it is best to use a singular verb, especially if you are writing:

Neither likes the idea very much.
Neither should be used with **nor**, not with **or**:
✓ *The police have found neither a witness nor a suspect.*

nelly *noun, old slang* life. [20c: perhaps from 'Nelly Duff', rhyming slang for 'puff', meaning 'life']

nelson *or* **full nelson** *noun, wrestling* a hold in which one passes one's arms under and over one's opponent's from behind, with the palms against the back of their neck. Compare **half nelson**. [19c: from the name of Horatio Nelson]

nematode *noun, zool* a long thin worm, a parasite in plants and animals as well as occurring in soil or sediment. [19c: from Greek *nema* thread + *eidos* form]

nemesis /ˈnɛməsɪs/ *noun* (*-ses* /-siːz/) **1** retribution or just punishment. **2** something that brings this. [16c: from Nemesis, Greek goddess of retribution]

neo- *prefix, denoting* new, or a new form; modern. [From Greek *neos* new]

neoclassical *adj* of artistic or architectural style, esp in the late 18c and early 19c: imitating or adapting the styles of the ancient classical world. ▪ **neoclassicism** *noun*.

neodymium *noun, chem* (symbol **Nd**) a silvery metallic element, one of the rare earth elements. [19c: from *didymium*, a substance once thought to be an element]

Neofascism *noun* a movement attempting to reinstate the policies of **fascism**. ▪ **Neofascist** *noun, adj*.

neolithic *or* **Neolithic** *adj* belonging or relating to the later Stone Age, in Europe lasting from about 4000 to 2400 BC, and characterized by the manufacture of polished stone tools. [19c: from **neo-** + Greek *lithos* stone]

neologism /nɪˈɒlədʒɪzəm/ *noun* **1** a new word or expression. **2** a new meaning acquired by an existing word or expression. [Early 19c: from French *néologisme*]

neon *noun, chem* (symbol **Ne**) an element, a colourless gas that glows red when electricity is passed through it, used eg in illuminated signs. *as adj*: *neon sign*. [Late 19c: Greek, neuter of *neos* new]

neonatal *adj* relating to newly born children. ▪ **neonate** *noun, biol, med* a newly born child. [19c: from Latin *neonatus*]

Neo-Nazi *noun* a supporter of any modern movement advocating the principles of the Nazis. ▪ **Neo-Nazism** *noun*.

neon light *or* **neon lamp** *noun* **1** a neon-filled glass tube used for lighting. **2** *loosely* any similar tubular fluorescent light.

neophyte *noun* **1** a beginner. **2** a new convert to a religious faith. **3** a novice in a religious order. [16c: from Greek *neophytos* newly planted]

Neozoic /niːoʊˈzoʊɪk/ *adj, geol* relating to the period between the **Mesozoic** and the present age. ▸ *noun* this period. [19c]

Nepalese *adj, noun* (*pl* ***Nepalese***) **Nepali**.

Nepali *noun* (*pl* ***Nepali*** *or* ***Nepalis***) **1** a citizen or inhabitant, or person born in Nepal, a kingdom in S Asia. **2** the official language of Nepal. ▸ *adj* belonging or relating to Nepal, its inhabitants or their language. [19c]

nephew *noun* the son of one's brother or sister, or of the brother or sister of one's wife or husband. [13c: from French *neveu*]

nephrite *noun, geol* a hard glistening mineral that occurs in a wide range of colours; **jade**. ▪ **nephritic** *adj*. [18c: from Greek *nephros* kidney]

nephritis /nɪˈfraɪtɪs/ *noun, pathol* inflammation of a kidney. ▪ **nephritic** *adj*. [16c]

nephro- *or* (*before a vowel*) **nephr-** *combining form, denoting* one or both kidneys. [From Greek *nephros* kidney]

ne plus ultra /niː plʌs ˈʌltrə, neː-/ *noun* the uttermost point or perfection of anything. [17c: Latin]

nepotism *noun* the favouring of one's relatives or friends, esp in making official appointments. ▪ **nepotist** *noun*. ▪ **nepotistic** *adj*. [17c: from Latin *nepos* grandson or nephew]

Neptune *noun, astron* the eighth planet from the Sun. [19c: from Latin *Neptunus*, the Roman god Neptune]

neptunium *noun, chem* (symbol **Np**) a metallic element obtained artificially in nuclear reactors during the production of **plutonium**. [20c: named after the planet Neptune]

nerd *or* **nurd** *noun, derog slang* someone foolish or annoying, esp one who is wrapped up in something that is not thought by others to be worthy of such interest. ▪ **nerdy** *adj* (***-ier, -iest***). [20c]

nerve *noun* **1** a cord that carries instructions and information between the brain or spinal cord and other parts of the body. **2** courage; assurance. **3** *informal* cheek; impudence. **4** (**nerves**) *informal* nervousness; tension or stress. **5** (**nerves**) *informal* one's capacity to cope with stress or excitement. **6** *botany* a leaf-vein or rib. ▸ *verb* (*often* **nerve oneself for sth**) to prepare (oneself) for (a challenge or ordeal). [16c: from Latin *nervus*]
IDIOMS **get on sb's nerves** *informal* to annoy them.

nerve agent *noun* a **nerve gas** or similar substance.

nerve cell see under **neurone**

nerve centre *noun* **1** a cluster of nerve cells responsible for a particular bodily function. **2** the centre of control within an organization, etc.

nerve gas *noun* a poisonous gas that acts on the nerves, used as a weapon.

nerveless *adj* **1** lacking feeling or strength; inert. **2** fearless.

nerve-racking *or* **nerve-wracking** *adj* making one feel tense and anxious.

nervous *adj* **1** timid; easily agitated. **2** apprehensive; uneasy. **3** relating to the nerves. **4** consisting of nerves. ▪ **nervously** *adv*. ▪ **nervousness** *noun*. [17c: from Latin *nervosus* sinewy]

nervous breakdown *noun* a mental illness attributed loosely to stress, with intense anxiety, low self-esteem and loss of concentration.

nervous system *noun* the network of communication, represented by the brain, nerves and spinal cord, that controls all one's mental and physical functions.

nervy *adj* (***-ier, -iest***) **1** excitable. **2** nervous.

ness *noun* a headland. [Anglo-Saxon *næs*]

-ness *suffix, forming nouns, denoting* a state, condition or degree of something.

nest *noun* **1** a structure built by birds, rats, wasps, etc in which to lay eggs or give birth to and look after young. **2** a cosy habitation or retreat. **3** a den or haunt, eg of thieves, or secret centre, eg of vice, crime, etc. **4** a brood, swarm, gang, etc. **5** a set of things that fit together: *a nest of tables*. ▶ *verb* **1** *intr* to build and occupy a nest. **2** *tr & intr* to fit things together compactly, esp one inside another. **3** *intr* to go in search of birds' nests. [Anglo-Saxon]

nest egg *noun* **1** a real or artificial egg left in a nest to encourage laying. **2** *informal* a sum of money saved up for the future.

nestle *verb, intr* (*often* **nestle together**, *etc*) to lie or settle snugly. [Anglo-Saxon *nestlian* to make a nest]

nestling *noun* a young bird still unable to fly. [14c: **nest** + **-ling**]

net[1] *noun* **1** an open material made of thread, cord, etc knotted, twisted or woven to form mesh. **2** a piece of this, eg for catching fish, confining hair, dividing a tennis court, etc. **3** a strip of net dividing a tennis or badminton court, etc. **4** *sport* the net-backed goal in hockey, football, etc. **5** (**nets**) *cricket* **a** a practice pitch enclosed in nets; **b** a practice session in nets. **6** a snare or trap. **7** *maths* a flat figure made up of polygons which fold and join to form a polyhedron. **8** (**the Net**) short for **the Internet**. ▶ *adj* made of or like net. ▶ *verb* (***netted, netting***) **1** to catch something in a net. **2** to capture or acquire, as with a net. **3** to cover something with a net. **4** *sport* to hit, kick, etc (a ball) into the net or goal. ▪ **netted** *adj* **1** made into a net. **2** net-like. **3** caught in a net. **4** covered with a net. [Anglo-Saxon *net* or *nett*]

net[2] *adj* **1** of profit: remaining after all expenses, etc have been paid. **2** of weight: excluding the packaging or container. ▶ *verb* (***netted, netting***) to produce, or earn, (an amount) as clear profit. Opposite of **gross**. [14c: French, meaning 'clean']

netball *noun* a game played by teams of women or girls, points being scored for the ball being thrown through a net hanging from a ring at the top of a pole.

nether *adj, literary or old use* lower or under. ▪ **nethermost** *adj* lowest; farthest down. [Anglo-Saxon *nither* down]

nether world *singular noun or* **nether regions** *plural noun* the underworld; hell.

netting *noun* any material with meshes, made by knotting or twisting thread, cord or wire, etc.

nettle *noun* a plant covered with hairs that sting if touched. [Anglo-Saxon *netele*]

IDIOMS **grasp the nettle** to deal boldly with a difficult situation.

nettle rash *noun, non-technical* **urticaria**.

network *noun* **1** any system that resembles a mass of criss-crossing lines. **2** any co-ordinated system involving large numbers of people or branches, etc: *a telecommunications network*. **3** a group of radio or TV stations that broadcast the same programmes at the same time. **4** *comput* a linked set of computers capable of sharing power or storage facilities. ▶ *verb* **1** to broadcast something on a network. **2** *intr* to build or maintain relationships with a network of people for mutual benefit. **3** to link (computer terminals, etc) to operate interactively.

neural *adj* relating to the nerves or nervous system. ▪ **neurally** *adv*. [19c: from Greek *neuron* nerve]

neuralgia *noun, pathol* spasmodic pain originating along the course of a nerve. ▪ **neuralgic** *adj*. [19c]

neuritis /njʊəˈraɪtɪs/ *noun, pathol* inflammation of a nerve or nerves, in some cases with defective functioning of the affected part. [19c]

neuro- *or* (*before a vowel*) **neur-** *combining form, denoting* a nerve or the nervous system: *neurosurgery*.

neurology *noun, med* the study of the **central nervous system**, and the peripheral nerves. ▪ **neurological** *adj*. ▪ **neurologist** *noun*. [17c]

neurone *or* **neuron** *noun, anatomy* a specialized cell that transmits nerve impulses from one part of the body to another. Also called **nerve cell**. [19c: Greek *neuron* nerve]

neurosis *noun* (***-ses***) **1** a mental disorder that causes obsessive fears, depression and unreasonable behaviour. **2** *informal* an anxiety or obsession. [18c]

neurotic *adj* **1** relating to, or suffering from, a neurosis. **2** *informal* overanxious, oversensitive or obsessive. ▶ *noun* someone suffering from a neurosis. [19c]

neurotransmitter *noun, physiol* a chemical released from a nerve fibre by means of which an impulse passes to a muscle or another nerve. [20c]

neut. *abbrev* **1** *grammar* neuter. **2** neutral.

neuter *adj* (abbrev **n.** *or* **neut.**) **1** *grammar* neither **masculine** nor **feminine**. **2** of plants: lacking pistils or stamens. **3** sexually undeveloped or castrated. **4** sexless or apparently sexless. ▶ *noun* **1** *grammar* **a** the neuter gender; **b** a word belonging to this gender. **2** a neuter plant, animal or insect, eg a worker bee or ant. **3** a castrated cat. ▶ *verb* to castrate (an animal). [14c: Latin *neuter* neither]

neutral *adj* **1** not taking sides in a quarrel or war. **2** not belonging or relating to either side: *neutral ground*. **3** of colours: indefinite enough to blend easily with brighter ones. **4** with no strong or noticeable qualities; not distinctive. **5** *elec* with no positive or negative electrical charge. **6** *chem* neither acidic nor alkaline. ▶ *noun* **1** a neutral person or nation, not allied to any side. **2** the disengaged position of an engine's gears, with no power being transmitted to the moving parts. ▪ **neutrality** *noun*. [16c: from Latin *neutralis*, from *neuter* neither]

neutralism *noun* the policy of not entering into alliance with other nations and avoiding taking sides ideologically. ▪ **neutralist** *noun, adj*.

neutralize *or* **-ise** *verb* **1** to cancel out the effect of something. **2** to declare (a country, etc) neutral. [18c]

neutrino *noun, physics* a stable **subatomic** particle that has no electric charge, virtually no mass, and travels at or near the speed of light. [20c: Italian, from *neutro* neutral]

neutron *noun, physics* one of the electrically uncharged particles in the nucleus of an atom. [20c: from Latin *neuter* neither]

neutron bomb *noun* a type of bomb that destroys life by intense radiation, without the blast and heat that destroy buildings. [20c]

neutron star *noun, astron* a star of very small size and very great density.

never *adv* **1** not ever; at no time. **2** not: *I never realized that*. **3** emphatically not: *This will never do*. **4** surely

not: *Those two are never twins!* [Anglo-Saxon *næfre*]
IDIOMS **well I never!** an expression of astonishment.

nevermore *adv, formal or literary* never again.

never-never *noun, informal* the hire-purchase system.

never-never land *noun* (*sometimes* **Never-Never-Land**) an imaginary place or conditions too fortunate to exist in reality. [20c]

nevertheless *adv* in spite of that.

nevus see **naevus**

new *adj* **1** recently made, bought, built, opened, etc. **2** recently discovered. **3** never having existed before; just invented, etc. **4** fresh; additional; supplementary: *a new consignment*. **5** recently arrived, installed, etc. *a new prime minister.* **6** (*chiefly* **new to sb** *or* **sth**) unfamiliar; experienced, or experiencing something, for the first time. **7** of a person: changed physically, mentally or morally for the better. **8** renewed: *gave us new hope.* **9** modern: *the new generation.* **10** used in naming a place after an older one: *New York.* ▸ *adv, usu in compounds* **1** only just; freshly: *new-baked bread.* **2** anew. ▪ **newly** *adv* **1** only just; recently. **2** again; anew: *newly awakened hope.* ▪ **newness** *noun.* [Anglo-Saxon *niwe*]

new blood see **blood** (*noun* sense 5b)

newborn *adj* **1** just or very recently born. **2** of faith, etc: reborn.

new broom *noun* a new person in charge, bent on making sweeping improvements.

newcomer *noun* **1** someone recently arrived. **2** a beginner.

newel *noun* **1** the central spindle round which a spiral stair winds. **2** (*also* **newel post**) a post at the top or bottom of a flight of stairs, supporting the handrail. [14c: from French *nouel* nut kernel]

newfangled *adj* modern, esp objectionably so. [14c: from Anglo-Saxon *newefangel* eager for novelty]

newly-weds *plural noun* a recently married couple.

new moon *noun* **1** the moon when it is visible as a narrow waxing crescent. **2** the time when the moon becomes visible in this form.

new potatoes *plural noun* the first potatoes of the new crop.

news *singular noun* **1** information about recent events, esp as reported in newspapers, on radio or TV, or via the Internet. **2** (**the news**) a radio or TV broadcast report of news. **3** any fresh interesting information. **4** a currently celebrated person, thing or event: *He's big news in America.* [15c, meaning 'new things']
IDIOMS **that's news to me** *informal* I have not heard that before.

news agency *noun* an agency that collects news stories and supplies them to newspapers, etc.

newsagent *noun* a shop, or the proprietor of a shop, that sells newspapers and usu also confectionery, etc.

newscast *noun* a radio or TV broadcast of news items. ▪ **newscaster** *noun.* ▪ **newscasting** *noun.* [20c]

news conference see **press conference**

newsflash *noun* a brief announcement of important news that interrupts a radio or TV broadcast.

newsgroup *noun, comput* a group that exchanges views and information by means of the Internet.

newsletter *noun* a sheet containing news, issued to members of an organization, etc.

newspaper *noun* **1** a daily or weekly publication composed of folded sheets, containing news, advertisements, topical articles, correspondence, etc. **2** the printed paper which makes up such a publication. [17c]

newspeak *noun, ironic* the ambiguous language used by politicians and other persuaders. [20c: from *Newspeak,* a form of English used as an official language in G Orwell's novel *Nineteen Eighty-Four*]

newsprint *noun* **1** the paper on which newspapers are printed. **2** the ink used to print newspapers.

newsreader *noun* a radio or television news announcer.

newsreel *noun* a film of news events, once a regular cinema feature.

newsroom *noun* an office in a newspaper office or broadcasting station where news stories are received and edited.

news stand *noun* a stall or kiosk that sells newspapers and magazines, etc.

newsworthy *adj* interesting or important enough to be reported as news.

newsy *adj* (***-ier, -iest***) full of news, esp gossip.

newt *noun* a small amphibious animal with a long body and tail and short legs. [Anglo-Saxon *efeta; an ewt* came to be understood as *a newt*]

New Testament *noun* the part of the Bible concerned with the teachings of Christ and his earliest followers. Compare **Old Testament**.

newton *noun, physics* (abbrev **N**) in the SI system: a unit of force equivalent to that which gives a one kilogram mass an acceleration of one second every second. [19c: named after Sir Isaac Newton, English scientist]

new town *noun* a town planned and built to relieve congestion in nearby cities.

new wave *noun* an artistic, musical or cultural movement that abandons traditional ideas.

New World *noun* the American continent.

New Year *noun* the first day of the year or the days, usu festive ones, immediately following or preceding it.

next *adj* **1** following in time or order: *next on the list.* **2** following this one: *next week.* **3** adjoining; neighbouring: *in the next compartment.* **4** first, counting from now: *the next person I meet.* ▸ *noun* someone or something that is next. ▸ *adv* **1** immediately after that or this. **2** on the next occasion: *when I next saw her.* **3** following, in order of degree: *Walking is the next best thing to cycling.* [Anglo-Saxon *nehst* the nearest]
IDIOMS **next to sth** *or* **sb 1** beside it or them. **2** after it or them, in order of degree: *Next to swimming, I like dancing.* **3** almost: *wearing next to no clothes.*

next-door *adj* occupying or belonging to the next room, house, shop, etc. ▸ *adv* (**next door**) to or in the next room, house, shop, etc.
IDIOMS **next door to sth** bordering on or very near it.

next of kin *noun* one's closest relative or relatives.

nexus *noun* (***nexus*** *or* ***nexuses***) **1** a connected series or group. **2** a bond or link. [17c: Latin, from *nectere* to bind]

NHS *abbrev* National Health Service.

NI *abbrev* **1** National Insurance. **2** Northern Ireland.

Ni *symbol, chem* nickel.

niacin /ˈnaɪəsɪn/ *or* **nicotinic acid** *noun* **vitamin B_7**. [20c]

nib *noun* **1** the writing-point of a pen, esp a metal one with a divided tip. **2** a point or spike. **3** (**nibs**) crushed coffee or cocoa beans. [16c: meaning 'a bird's beak']

nibble *verb, tr & intr* **1** to take very small bites of something; to eat a little at a time. **2** to bite gently. [16c]

nibs *singular noun* (*usu* **his** *or* **her nibs**) *facetious* a derogatory title for an important or would-be important person. [19c]

nicad *noun* **1** nickel-cadmium. **2** a battery made using nickel-cadmium. [20c]

Nicam /ˈnaɪkam/ *noun* a system by which digital stereo sound signals are transmitted along with the standard TV signal, allowing the viewer to receive sound of CD quality. [20c: *n*ear-*i*nstantaneous *c*ompanded (compressed and expanded) *a*udio *m*ultiplexing]

nice *adj* **1** pleasant; agreeable; respectable. **2** *often ironic* good; satisfactory. **3** *ironic* nasty: *a nice mess.* **4** fine; subtle: *nice distinctions.* **5** exacting; particular: *nice in matters of etiquette.* ▪ **niceness** *noun.* [13c: meaning 'foolish', 'coy' or 'exotic']

IDIOMS **nice and …** *informal* satisfactorily …; commendably …: *nice and firm.*

nicely *adv* **1** in a nice or satisfactory way. **2** precisely; carefully: *judged it nicely.* **3** suitably; effectively: *That will do nicely.*

nicety /ˈnaɪsətɪ/ *noun* (***-ies***) **1** precision. **2** a subtle point of detail.

IDIOMS **to a nicety** exactly.

niche /niːʃ, nɪtʃ/ *noun* **1** a shallow recess in a wall. **2** a position in life in which one feels fulfilled or at ease. **3** a small specialized group identified as a market for a particular range of products or services. *as adj*: *niche marketing.* ▸ *verb* **1** to place something in a niche. **2** to ensconce (oneself). [17c: French, meaning 'nest']

Nick *or* **Old Nick** *noun* the Devil.

nick *noun* **1** a small cut; a notch. **2** *slang* a prison or police station. **3** *slang* state of health or condition: *She's kept the car in good nick.* ▸ *verb* **1** to make a small cut in something. **2** *slang* to arrest (a criminal). **3** *slang* to steal. [16c]

IDIOMS **in the nick of time** just in time.

nickel *noun* **1** *chem* (symbol **Ni**) a greyish-white metallic element used esp in alloys and for plating. **2** an American or Canadian coin worth five cents. ▸ *adj* made of or with nickel. ▸ *verb* (***nickelled, nickelling***; *US* ***nickeled, nickeling***) to plate something with nickel. [18c: from German *Küpfernickel* copper devil, so called by miners mistaking it for copper]

nickelodeon *noun, US old use* **1** an early form of jukebox. **2** a type of Pianola. [20c: **nickel** + **melodeon**]

nickel silver *noun, chem* a silvery alloy of copper, zinc and nickel.

nicker *noun* (*pl* ***nicker***) *old slang* a pound sterling. [20c]

nick-nack see **knick-knack**

nickname *noun* a name given to a person or place in fun, affection or contempt. ▸ *verb* to give a nickname to someone. [15c: from *eke* addition or extra; *an ekename* came to be understood as *a nickname*]

nicotine *noun* a poisonous alkaline substance contained in tobacco. [19c: French, named after J Nicot, French diplomat]

nicotinic acid see **niacin**

niece *noun* the daughter of one's sister or brother, or of the sister or brother of one's husband or wife. [13c: from French]

---

niece

This word is often misspelt. The letter *i* comes before the letter e. It might help you to remember the following sentence:

My ***ni****ece is* ***ni****ce.*

---

niff *noun, slang* a bad smell. ▸ *verb, intr* to smell bad. ▪ **niffy** *adj* (***-ier, -iest***). [19c]

nifty *adj* (***-ier, -iest***) **1** clever; adroit; agile. **2** stylish. ▪ **niftily** *adv.* [19c]

niggardly *adj* **1** stingy; miserly. **2** meagre. ▪ **niggard** *noun* a stingy person. ▪ **niggardliness** *noun.*

niggle *verb, intr* **1** to complain about small or unimportant details. **2** to bother or irritate, esp slightly but continually. ▸ *noun* **1** a slight nagging worry. **2** a small complaint or criticism. ▪ **niggling** *adj.* [19c]

nigh *adv, old use, dialect or poetic* near. [Anglo-Saxon *neah*]

IDIOMS **nigh on** *or* **well nigh** nearly; almost.

night *noun* **1** the time of darkness between sunset and sunrise. **2** the time between going to bed and getting up in the morning. **3** evening: *last night.* **4** nightfall. **5** *poetic* darkness. **6** an evening on which a particular activity takes place: *my aerobics night.* ▸ *adj* **1** belonging to, occurring, or done in the night: *the night hours.* **2** working or on duty at night: *the night shift.* ▪ **nightly** *adj* done or happening at night or every night. ▸ *adv* at night; every night. ▪ **nights** *adv, informal* at night; most nights or every night. [Anglo-Saxon *niht*]

IDIOMS **make a night of it** *informal* to celebrate late into the night.

nightbird *noun* **1** a bird that flies or sings at night. **2** someone who is active or awake at night.

nightcap *noun* **1** a drink, esp an alcoholic one, taken before going to bed. **2** *old use* a cap worn in bed.

nightclass *noun* a class at **night school**.

nightclothes *plural noun* clothes for sleeping in.

nightclub *noun* a club open in the evening and running late into the night for drinking, dancing, entertainment, etc. ▪ **nightclubber** *noun.* ▪ **nightclubbing** *noun.*

nightdress *noun* a loose garment for sleeping in, worn by women and girls.

nightfall *noun* the beginning of night; dusk.

nightgown *noun* a loose garment for sleeping in.

nightie *or* **nighty** *noun* (***nighties***) *informal* a nightdress. [19c]

nightingale *noun* a small brown thrush known for its melodious song, heard esp at night. [Anglo-Saxon *nehtegale*]

nightjar *noun* a nocturnal bird of the swift family that has a harsh discordant cry. [17c: **night** + **jar**[2]]

nightlife *noun* entertainment available in a city or resort, etc, late into the night.

night light *noun* a dim-shining lamp or slow-burning candle that can be left lit all night.

nightmare *noun* **1** a frightening dream. **2** an intensely distressing or frightful experience or situation. ▪ **nightmarish** *adj.* [16c: from Anglo-Saxon *mare* a nightmare-producing monster]

night owl *noun* someone who likes to stay up late at night or who is more alert and active, etc, at night.

night safe *noun* a safe built into the outer wall of a bank, in which to deposit money when the bank is closed.

night school *noun* **1** educational classes held in the evening, esp for those who are at work during the day. **2** an institution providing such classes.

nightshade *noun* any of various wild plants, some with poisonous berries, including **belladonna**. Also called **deadly nightshade**. [Anglo-Saxon *nihtscada*]

night shift *noun* **1** a session of work or duty during the night. **2** the staff working during this period. See also **day shift**.

nightshirt *noun* a loose garment like a long shirt for sleeping in.

nightspot *noun, informal* a nightclub.

night-time *noun* the time of darkness between sunset and sunrise.

night watch *noun* **1** a guard or watch kept at night. **2** someone who is on guard at night. **3** a period of keeping watch at night.

nightwatchman *noun* someone who looks after a public building, industrial premises, etc at night.

nighty see **nightie**

nihilism /ˈnaɪɪlɪzəm/ *noun* **1** the rejection of moral and religious principles. **2** a 19c Russian movement aimed at overturning all social institutions. ▪ **nihilist** *noun*. ▪ **nihilistic** *adj.* [19c: from Latin *nihil* nothing]

-nik *suffix, forming nouns, sometimes derog, denoting* someone concerned with the specified cause, activity, etc: *peacenik*. [20c: from Yiddish, from Slavic]

nil *noun, games, sport, etc* a score of nothing; zero. [19c: from Latin *nihil* nothing]

nimbi *a pl of* **nimbus**

nimble *adj* **1** quick and light in movement; agile. **2** of wits: sharp; alert. ▪ **nimbly** *adv.* [Apparently Anglo-Saxon *næmel* receptive or *numol* quick to learn]

nimbostratus *noun* (***nimbostrati*** /-taiː/) *meteorol* a low dark-coloured layer of cloud bringing rain. [20c]

nimbus *noun* (***nimbuses*** *or* ***nimbi*** /-baiː/) **1** *meteorol* a heavy dark type of cloud bringing rain or snow. **2** a luminous mist or halo surrounding a god or goddess, or a representation of this. [17c: Latin]

NIMBY *or* **Nimby** *noun* not in my back yard: denoting an attitude of being willing to have something happen so long as it does not affect you or your locality. ▪ **nimbyism** *noun*. [1980s: from *not in my back yard*]

nincompoop *noun* a fool; an idiot. [17c]

nine *noun* **1 a** the cardinal number 9; **b** the quantity that this represents, being one more than eight. **2** any symbol for this, eg *9* or *IX*. **3** the age of nine. **4** something, esp a garment or a person, whose size is denoted by the number 9. **5** the ninth hour after midnight or midday: *opens at nine • 9am*. **6** a set or group of nine people or things. ▸ *adj* **1** totalling nine. **2** aged nine. [Anglo-Saxon *nigon*]

IDIOMS **dressed up to the nines** wearing one's best clothes; elaborately dressed.

nine days' wonder *noun* something that grips everyone's attention for a brief time. [16c]

ninefold *adj* **1** equal to nine times as much or many. **2** divided into, or consisting of, nine parts. ▸ *adv* by nine times as much.

ninepins *singular noun* a game similar to skittles, using a wooden ball to knock down nine skittles arranged in a triangle.

nineteen *noun* **1 a** the cardinal number 19; **b** the quantity that this represents, being one more than eighteen, or the sum of ten and nine. **2** any symbol for this, eg *19* or *XIX*. **3** the age of nineteen. **4** something, esp a garment or a person, whose size is denoted by the number 19. **5** a set or group of nineteen people or things. ▸ *adj* **1** totalling nineteen. **2** aged nineteen. ▪ **nineteenth** *adj, noun, adv.* [Anglo-Saxon *nigontiene*]

IDIOMS **talk nineteen to the dozen** to chatter away animatedly.

nineties (often written **90s** *or* **90's**) *plural noun* **1** (**one's nineties**) the period of time between one's ninetieth and hundredth birthdays. **2** (**the nineties**) the range of temperatures between ninety and a hundred degrees. **3** (**the nineties**) the period of time between the ninetieth and hundredth years of a century.

ninety *noun* (***-ies***) **1 a** the cardinal number 90; **b** the quantity that this represents, being one more than eighty-nine, or the product of ten and nine. **2** any symbol for this, eg *90* or *XC*. **3** the age of ninety. **4** a set or group of ninety people or things. ▸ *adj* **1** totalling ninety. **2** aged ninety. See also **nineties**. ▪ **ninetieth** *adj, noun, adv.* [Anglo-Saxon *nigontig*]

ninety- *combining form* **a** *forming adjectives and nouns* with cardinal numbers between *one* and *nine*: *ninety-two*; **b** *forming adjectives and nouns* with ordinal numbers between *first* and *ninth*: *ninety-second*.

ninja *noun* (***ninja*** *or* ***ninjas***) esp in medieval Japan: one of a body of professional assassins trained in martial arts and stealth. [20c: Japanese, from *nin* stealth + *ja* person]

ninny *noun* (***-ies***) a foolish person. [16c]

ninth (often written **9th**) *adj* **1** in counting: **a** next after eighth; **b** last of nine. **2** in ninth position. **3** being one of nine equal parts: *a ninth share*. ▸ *noun* **1** one of nine equal parts. **2** a **fraction** equal to one divided by nine (usu written ⅑). **3** a person coming ninth, eg in a race or exam. **4** (**the ninth**) **a** the ninth day of the month; **b** *golf* the ninth hole. ▸ *adv* ninthly. ▪ **ninthly** *adv* used to introduce the ninth point in a list. [Anglo-Saxon]

niobium *noun, chem* (symbol **Nb**) a relatively unreactive soft greyish-blue metallic element. [19c: from Niobe, in Greek mythology]

nip[1] *verb* (***nipped, nipping***) **1** to pinch or squeeze something or someone sharply. **2** to give a sharp little bite to something. **3** (*often* **nip off sth**) to remove or sever it by pinching or biting. **4** *tr & intr* to sting; to cause smarting. **5** *informal* to go quickly: *nip round to the shop*. ▸ *noun* **1** a pinch or squeeze. **2** a sharp little bite. **3** a sharp biting coldness, or stinging qual-

ity. [14c: from Norse *hnippa* to poke]
IDIOMS **nip sth in the bud** to halt its growth or development at an early stage.

nip[2] *noun* a small quantity of alcoholic spirits. [18c: from Dutch *nippen* to sip]

nip and tuck *informal, noun* a surgical operation carried out for cosmetic reasons. ▸ *adj, adv, N Am* neck and neck.

nipper *noun* **1** the large claw of a crab, lobster, etc. **2** (**nippers**) pincers, tweezers, forceps, or other gripping or severing tool. **3** *old informal use* a small child.

nipple *noun* **1** the deep-coloured pointed projection on a breast. **2** *N Am* the teat on a baby's feeding-bottle. **3** *mech* any small projection with a hole through which a flow is regulated or machine parts lubricated. [16c]

nippy *adj* (**-ier, -iest**) *informal* **1** cold; chilly. **2** quick-moving; nimble. **3** of flavour: pungent or biting. [16c]

nirvana *or* **Nirvana** *noun* **1** *Buddhism, Hinduism* the ultimate state of spiritual tranquillity attained through release from everyday concerns and extinction of individual passions. **2** a place or state of perfect bliss. [19c: Sanskrit, meaning 'extinction']

nit[1] *noun* the egg or young of a louse, found eg in hair. [Anglo-Saxon *hnitu*]

nit[2] *noun, slang* an idiot. [16c: from **nit**[1], influenced by **nitwit**]

nit-picking *noun* petty criticism or fault-finding. ▸ *adj* fussy. ▪ **nit-picker** *noun*. [20c: from **nit**[1]]

nitrate *chem, noun* **1** a salt or ester of **nitric acid**. **2** sodium nitrate or potassium nitrate used as a soil fertilizer. ▸ *verb* **1** to treat something with nitric acid or a nitrate. **2** *tr & intr* to convert something into a nitrate. ▪ **nitration** *noun*. [18c]

nitre *noun, chem* potassium nitrate; saltpetre. [15c: French, from Greek *nitron* sodium carbonate]

nitric *adj, chem* belonging to or containing nitrogen. [18c]

nitric acid *noun, chem* a colourless acid used as an oxidizing agent and for making explosives, fertilizers and dyes.

nitride *noun, chem* a compound of nitrogen with another, metallic, element. [19c]

nitrify *verb* (**-ies, -ied**) *tr & intr, chem* usu of ammonia: to convert or be converted into nitrates or nitrites through the action of bacteria. ▪ **nitrification** *noun*. [19c]

nitrite *noun, chem* a salt or ester of **nitrous acid**. [19c]

nitro- *combining form, chem* **1** made with, or containing, **nitrogen**, **nitric acid** or **nitre**. **2** containing the group $-NO_2$.

nitrogen /ˈnaɪtrədʒən/ *noun* (symbol **N**) *chem* an element, the colourless, odourless and tasteless gas making up four-fifths of the air we breathe. ▪ **nitrogenous** *adj*. [18c: from **nitre** + Greek *-genes* born]

nitroglycerine *or* **nitroglycerin** *noun, chem* an explosive liquid compound used in dynamite. [19c]

nitrous *adj, chem* relating to or containing nitrogen in a low valency. [17c]

nitrous acid *noun, chem* a weak acid occurring only in solution or in nitrite salts.

nitrous oxide *noun, chem* dinitrogen oxide, used as an anaesthetic and popularly known as **laughing gas**.

the nitty-gritty *noun, informal* the fundamental issue or essential part of any matter, situation, etc. [1960s: orig US; perhaps rhyming compound of *grit*]

nitwit *noun* a stupid person. [20c: from German dialect *nit* (variant of *nicht* not) + **wit**[1]]

nm *abbrev* **1** nanometre. **2** nautical mile.

No[1], **No.** *or* **no.** *abbrev* number.

No[2] *symbol, chem* nobelium.

no[1] *exclam* **1** used as a negative reply, expressing denial, refusal or disagreement. **2** *informal* used as a question tag expecting agreement: *It's a deal, no?* **3** used as an astonished rejoinder: *No! You don't say!* ▸ *adv* **1** not any: *no bigger than one's thumb*. **2** used to indicate a negative alternative: not: *willing or no*. ▸ *noun* (***noes***) a negative reply or vote: *The noes have it*. [Anglo-Saxon *na*]
IDIOMS **no more 1** destroyed; dead. **2** never again; not any longer. **not take no for an answer** to continue with an activity in spite of refusals; to insist.

no[2] *adj* **1** not any. **2** certainly not or far from something specified: *He's no fool*. **3** hardly any: *do it in no time*. **4** not allowed: *no smoking*. [Anglo-Saxon *na*]
IDIOMS **no go** *informal* impossible; no good. **no one** no single: *No one candidate is the obvious choice*. **no way** *informal* no; definitely not.

n.o. *abbrev, cricket* not out.

nob[1] *noun, slang* someone of wealth or high social rank. [19c]

nob[2] *noun, slang* the head. [17c: prob from **knob**]

no-ball *noun, cricket, baseball, rounders, etc* a ball bowled in a manner that is not allowed by the rules.

nobble *verb, informal* **1** *horse-racing* to drug or otherwise interfere with (a horse) to stop it winning. **2** to persuade someone by bribes or threats. **3** to obtain something dishonestly. **4** to catch (a criminal). **5** to swindle someone. [19c: possibly from *an hobbler*, later understood as *a nobbler*, meaning 'a person who lames horses']

nobelium *noun, chem* (symbol **No**) a radioactive element produced artificially. [20c: named after the Nobel Institute, Stockholm]

nobility *noun* (**-ies**) **1** the quality of being noble. **2** (**the nobility**) people of noble birth. [15c: from Latin *nobilitas*]

noble *adj* **1** honourable. **2** generous. **3** of high birth or rank. **4** grand, splendid or imposing in appearance. ▸ *noun* a person of noble rank. ▪ **nobly** *adv*. [13c: from Latin *nobilis*]

noble gas *noun, chem* any of the gases helium, neon, argon, krypton, xenon and radon. Also called **inert gas**. [20c]

nobleman *or* **noblewoman** *noun* a member of the nobility.

noble metal *noun* a metal such as gold, silver or platinum that is highly unreactive and so does not easily tarnish.

noblesse oblige /noʊˈblɛs oʊˈbliːʒ/ *noun, usu ironic* it is the duty of the privileged to help the less fortunate. [19c: French, meaning 'nobility obliges']

nobody *pron* no person; no one. ▸ *noun* (**-ies**) someone of no significance.

no-brainer *noun, N Am informal* something that requires no great mental effort.

nock *noun* a notch, or a part carrying a notch, esp on an arrow or a bow.

no-claims bonus *or* **no-claim bonus** *noun* a reduction in the fee one pays for insurance if one has made no claim over a particular period.

nocti- *or* (*before a vowel*) **noct-** *combining form, denoting* night. [From Latin *nox* night]

nocturnal *adj* **1** of animals, etc: active at night. **2** happening at night. **3** belonging or relating to the night. [15c: from Latin *nocturnus*, from *nox* night]

nocturne *noun* **1** *music* a dreamy piece of music, usu for the piano. **2** *art* a night or moonlight scene. [19c: French, from Latin *nocturnus* nocturnal]

nod *verb* (***nodded, nodding***) **1** *tr & intr* to make a brief bowing gesture with (the head) in agreement, greeting, etc. **2** *intr* to let the head droop with sleepiness; to become drowsy. **3** *intr* to make a mistake through momentary loss of concentration. **4** to indicate or direct by nodding. **5** *intr* of flowers, plumes, etc: to sway or bob about. ▸ *noun* a quick bending forward of the head as a gesture of assent, greeting or command. [14c]

IDIOMS **on the nod** *informal* of the passing of a proposal, etc: by general agreement, without the formality of a vote. **the Land of Nod** sleep.

PHRASAL VERBS **nod off** *intr* to fall asleep. **nod sb** *or* **sth through** to pass something without a discussion, vote, etc.

noddle *noun, informal* the head or brain. [15c]

noddy *noun* (**-*ies***) **1** a tropical bird of the tern family, so unafraid of humans as to seem stupid. **2** a simpleton. [16c: perhaps from an obsolete *adj* sense, meaning 'silly']

node *noun* **1** a knob, lump, swelling or knotty mass. **2** *botany* a swelling where a leaf is attached to a stem. **3** *geom* the point where a curve crosses itself. **4** *astron* a point where the orbit of a body intersects the apparent path of the sun or another body. **5** *physics* in a vibrating body: the point of least movement. **6** *comput* a location where processing takes place, eg a computer on a network. ▪ **nodal** *adj*. [17c: from Latin *nodus* knot]

nodule *noun* **1** a small round lump. **2** *botany* a swelling in a root of a leguminous plant, inhabited by bacteria that convert nitrogen to the plant's use. ▪ **nodular** *adj*. [17c: from Latin *nodulus*, diminutive of *nodus* knot]

Noel *or* **Noël** *noun* now only used in Christmas cards and carols, etc: Christmas. Also written **Nowell**. [19c: French, from Latin *natalis* birthday]

no-frills *adj* basic, not elaborate or fancy.

nog *noun* an alcoholic drink made with whipped eggs. [19c]

noggin *noun* **1** a small measure or quantity of alcoholic spirits. **2** a small mug or wooden cup. **3** *informal* one's head. [17c]

no-go area *noun* an area to which normal access is prevented.

noise *noun* **1** a sound. **2** a harsh disagreeable sound; a din. **3** *radio* interference in a signal. **4** *comput* irrelevant or meaningless material appearing in output. **5** something one says as a conventional response, vague indication of inclinations, etc: *make polite noises*. ▸ *verb* (*usu* **noise abroad** *or* **about**) to make something generally known; to spread (a rumour, etc). ▪ **noiseless** *adj*. ▪ **noiselessly** *adv*. [13c: French, from Latin *nausea* seasickness]

noise pollution *noun* an excessive or annoying degree of noise, eg from traffic.

noisette /nwa'zɛt/ *noun* **1** a small piece of meat (usu lamb) cut off the bone and rolled. **2** a nutlike or nut-flavoured sweet. ▸ *adj* flavoured with or containing hazelnuts. [19c: French, meaning 'hazelnut']

noisome *adj* **1** disgusting; offensive; stinking. **2** harmful; poisonous. [14c]

noisy *adj* (***-ier, -iest***) **1** making a lot of noise. **2** full of noise; accompanied by noise. ▪ **noisily** *adv*.

nomad *noun* **1** a member of a people without a permanent home, who travel from place to place seeking food and pasture. **2** a wanderer. ▪ **nomadic** *adj*. [16c: from Greek *nomas*]

no-man's-land *noun* **1** unclaimed land; waste land. **2** neutral territory between opposing armies or between two countries. **3** a state or situation that is neither one thing nor another. [14c]

nom-de-plume *or* **nom de plume** /nɒm də 'pluːm/ *noun* (***noms-de-plume*** *or* ***noms de plume*** /nɒm-/) a pseudonym used by a writer; a pen-name. [19c: from French *nom* name + *de* of + *plume* pen]

nomenclature /noʊ'mɛŋklətʃə(r)/ *noun* **1** a classified system of names, esp in science; terminology. **2** a list or set of names. [17c: from Latin *nomenclatura*]

nominal *adj* **1** in name only; so called, but not actually. **2** very small in comparison to actual cost or value: *a nominal rent*. **3** *grammar* being or relating to a noun. **4** being or relating to a name. **5** *space flight* according to plan. ▸ *noun, grammar* a noun, or a phrase, etc standing as a noun. ▪ **nominally** *adv* **1** in name only. **2** theoretically rather than actually. **3** *grammar* as a noun. [15c: from Latin *nominalis*, from *nomen* name]

nominal value *noun* the stated or face value on a bond, share certificate, etc.

nominate *verb* **1** (*usu* **nominate sb for sth**) to propose them formally as a candidate for election, a job, etc. **2** (*usu* **nominate sb to sth**) to appoint them to (a post or position). **3** to specify formally (eg a date). ▪ **nomination** *noun*. [16c: from Latin *nominare* to name]

nominative *noun, grammar* **1** in certain languages: the form or **case**[2] used to mark the subject of a verb. **2** a noun, etc in this case. ▸ *adj* **1** *grammar* belonging to or in this case. **2** appointed by nomination rather than election. [14c: from Latin *nominativus*, from *nominare* to name]

nominee *noun* **1** someone nominated to, or nominated as a candidate for, a job, position, etc. **2** a person or organization appointed to act on behalf of another. **3** someone on whose life an annuity or lease depends. [17c: from Latin *nominare* to name]

non- *prefix, signifying* **1** not; the opposite of something specified: *non-essential*. **2** *ironic* not deserving the name of something specified: *a non-event*. **3** not belonging to a specified category: *non-fiction*. **4** not having the skill or desire to be, or not participating in, something specified: *non-swimmers* • *non-voting*. **5** rejection, avoidance, or omission of something specified: *non-payment*. **6** not liable to do something specified: *non-shrink*. **7** not requiring a certain treatment: *non-iron*. [From Latin *non* not]

nonage *noun, law* the condition of being under age; one's minority or period of immaturity. [14c: French, from *non* non- + *age* age]

nonagenarian *noun* someone between the ages of 90 and 99 years old. [19c: from Latin *nonagenarius* consisting of ninety]

nonagon *noun, geom* a nine-sided figure. [17c: from Latin *nonus* ninth + Greek *gonia* angle]

non-aligned *adj* not allied to any of the major power blocs in world politics; neutral. ▪ **non-alignment** *noun.*

nonce *noun* (**the nonce**) the present time. [14c: orig *for then ones* for the once, *then once* coming to be understood as *the nonce*]

nonce-word *noun* a word coined for one particular occasion.

nonchalant /ˈnɒnʃələnt/ *adj* calmly or indifferently unconcerned. ▪ **nonchalance** *noun.* ▪ **nonchalantly** *adv.* [18c: French, from *non* not + *chaloir* to matter]

non-combatant *noun* **1** a member of the armed forces whose duties do not include fighting. **2** in time of war: a civilian.

non-commissioned officer *noun* (abbrev **NCO**) an officer such as a corporal or sergeant, appointed from the lower ranks of the armed forces, not by being given a **commission**.

non-committal *adj* avoiding expressing a definite opinion or decision.

non compos mentis *adj, often humorous* not of sound mind. [17c: Latin, meaning 'not in command of one's mind']

nonconformist *noun* **1** someone who refuses to conform to generally accepted practice. **2** (**Nonconformist**) in England: a member of a Protestant Church separated from the Church of England. ▸ *adj* of or relating to nonconformists. ▪ **nonconformity** *noun* **1** refusal to conform to accepted practice. **2** lack of correspondence or agreement between things. [17c]

non-contributory *adj* **1** of a pension scheme: paid for by the employer, without contributions from the employee. **2** of a state benefit: not dependent on the payment of National Insurance contributions.

non-custodial *adj* of a judicial sentence: not involving imprisonment.

non-denominational *adj* **1** not linked with any particular religious denomination. **2** for the use or participation of members of all denominations.

nondescript *adj* with no strongly noticeable characteristics or distinctive features. ▸ *noun* a nondescript person or thing. [17c: meaning 'not previously described']

none[1] /nʌn/ *pron* (*with singular or plural verb*) **1** not any. **2** no one; not any people: *None were as kind as she.* [Anglo-Saxon *nan* not one or no]

IDIOMS **none but** only. **none of** I won't put up with: *None of your cheek!* **none other than sb** *or* **sth** the very person or thing mentioned or thought of. **none the** (*followed by a comparative*) not any: *none the worse for his adventure.* **none the less** *or* **nonetheless** nevertheless; in spite of that. **none too** by no means: *none too clean.*

none[2] /noʊn/ *or* **nones** /noʊnz/ *noun, esp RC Church* the fifth of the **canonical hours**. [18c: from Latin *nona hora* the ninth hour]

nonentity *noun* (**-ies**) **1** *derog* someone of no significance, character, ability, etc. **2** *derog* a thing of no importance. **3** a thing which does not exist. **4** the state of not being. [17c]

nones[1] /noʊnz/ *plural noun* in the Roman calendar: the seventh day of March, May, July and October, and the fifth day of other months. [15c: from Latin *nonae*]

nones[2] see **none**[2]

nonesuch *or* **nonsuch** *noun, literary* a unique, unparalleled or extraordinary thing. [16c]

nonet /noʊˈnɛt/ *noun, music* **1** a composition for nine instruments or voices. **2** a group of nine instrumentalists or singers. [19c: from Italian *nonetto*]

nonetheless see under **none**[1]

non-event *noun* an event that fails to live up to its promise.

non-feasance *noun, law* omission of something which ought to be, or ought to have been, done. [16c: from French *faisance* doing]

non-ferrous *adj* **1** not iron or steel. **2** not containing iron.

non-fiction *noun* literature concerning factual characters or events. ▸ *adj* of a literary work: factual.

non-flammable *adj* not liable to catch fire or burn easily.

non-invasive *adj* of medical treatment: not involving surgery or the insertion of instruments, etc into the patient.

non-negotiable *adj* **1** not open to negotiation. **2** of a cheque, etc: not **negotiable**.

no-no *noun* (***no-nos*** *or* ***no-noes***) *informal* **1** something which must not be done, said, etc. **2** something impossible.

no-nonsense *adj* sensible and straightforward.

nonpareil /nɒnpəˈreɪl/ *adj* having no equal; matchless. ▸ *noun* a person or thing without equal. [16c: French, from *non-* not + *pareil* equal]

nonplus *verb* (***nonplussed, nonplussing***; *US* ***nonplused, nonplusing***) to puzzle; to disconcert. [16c: from Latin *non plus* no further]

non-profit-making *adj* of a business, etc: not organized with the purpose of making a profit.

non-proliferation *noun* lack or limitation of the production or spread of something, esp the policy of limiting the production and ownership of nuclear or chemical weapons.

non-residence *noun* the fact of not (either permanently or for the moment) residing at a place, esp where one's official or social duties might require one to reside or where one is entitled to reside. ▪ **non-resident** *adj, noun.*

nonsense *noun* **1** words or ideas that do not make sense. **2** foolishness; silly behaviour. ▸ *exclam* you're quite wrong. [17c]

IDIOMS **make a nonsense of sth** to destroy the effect of it; to make it pointless.

nonsensical *adj* making no sense; absurd.

non sequitur *noun* **1** an illogical step in an argument. **2** a conclusion that does not follow from the premises. [16c: Latin, literally 'it does not follow']

non-specific *adj* **1** not specific. **2** of a disease: not caused by any specific agent that can be identified.

non-standard *adj* **1** not standard. **2** of language: different to the usage of educated speakers and considered by some to be incorrect.

non-starter *noun* **1** a person, thing or idea, etc that has no chance of success. **2** a horse which, though entered for a race, does not run.

non-stick *adj* of a pan, etc: that has a coating to which food does not stick during cooking.

non-stop *adj* without a stop; continuous. ▸ *adv* without stopping; continuously.

nonsuch see **nonesuch**

non-U *adj, Brit informal* of behaviour, language, etc: not acceptable among the upper classes. Compare **U²**. [20c]

noodle¹ *noun* (*usu* **noodles**) *cookery* a thin strip of pasta made with egg. [18c: from German *Nudel*]

noodle² *noun, informal* **1** a simpleton. **2** *N Am* the head. [18c]

nook *noun* **1** a secluded retreat. **2** a corner or recess. [13c]

IDIOMS **every nook and cranny** absolutely everywhere.

noon *noun* midday; twelve o'clock. [13c: from Latin *nona* (*hora*) the ninth hour]

noonday *noun* midday. ▸ *adj* relating to midday.

no one *or* **no-one** *noun* no person. [17c]

noose *noun* **1** a loop made in the end of a rope, etc, with a sliding knot. **2** any snare or bond. ▸ *verb* to tie or snare someone or something in a noose. [15c: from French *nous*]

nope *exclam, slang* emphatic form of **no¹**.

Nor. *abbrev* **1** Norman. **2** North. **3** Norway. **4** Norwegian.

nor *conj* **1** (*used to introduce alternatives after* **neither**): *He neither knows nor cares.* **2** and not: *It didn't look appetizing, nor was it.* ▸ *adv* not either: *If you won't, nor shall I.* [13c: a contraction of Anglo-Saxon *nother*, from *ne* not + *other* either]

nor' *adj, in compounds, naut* north: *a nor'-wester.*

Nordic *adj* **1** relating or belonging to Scandinavia or its inhabitants. **2** Germanic or Scandinavian in appearance, typically tall, blond and blue-eyed. **3** (**nordic**) denoting a type of competitive skiing with cross-country racing and ski-jumping. [19c: from French *nordique*, from *nord* north]

norm *noun* **1** (**the norm**) a typical pattern or situation. **2** an accepted way of behaving, etc. **3** a standard, eg for achievement in industry: *production norms.* [19c: from Latin *norma* carpenter's square or a rule]

norm. *abbrev* normal.

normal *adj* **1** usual; typical; not extraordinary. **2** mentally or physically sound: *a normal baby.* **3** (**normal to sth**) *geom* perpendicular. ▸ *noun* **1** what is average or usual. **2** *geom* a perpendicular line or plane. ▪ **normality** *or* (*N Am*) **normalcy** *noun.* ▪ **normalization** *noun.* ▪ **normalize** *or* **-ise** *verb.* ▪ **normally** *adv* **1** in an ordinary or natural way. **2** usually. [15c: from Latin *normalis* regulated by a carpenter's square]

Norman *noun* **1** a person from Normandy, esp one of the descendants of the Scandinavian settlers of N France, who then conquered England in 1066. **2** Norman French. ▸ *adj* **1** relating to the Normans, their language, etc, or to Normandy. **2** *archit* signifying or relating to a building style typical in 10c and 11c Normandy and 11c and 12c England, with round arches and heavy massive pillars. [13c: from French *Normant*, from Norse *Northmathr*]

normative *adj* establishing a guiding standard or rules. [19c: from **norm**]

Norse *adj* **1** relating or belonging to ancient or medieval Scandinavia. **2** Norwegian. ▸ *noun* **1** the Germanic language group of Scandinavia. **2** the language of this group used in medieval Norway and its colonies. [16c: perhaps from Dutch *noorsch*]

Norseman *noun* a Scandinavian; a **Viking**.

north *noun* (*also* **North** *or* **the North**) **1** the direction to one's left when one faces the rising sun. **2 magnetic north. 3** one of the four **cardinal point**s of the compass. **4** (*usu* **the North**) any part of the earth, a country or a town, etc lying in the direction of north. **5** (**the North**) the industrialized nations. ▸ *adj* (*also* **North**) **1** in the north; on the side that is on or nearest the north. **2** facing or toward the north. **3** esp of wind: coming from the north. ▸ *adv* in, to or towards the north. [Anglo-Saxon]

Northants *abbrev, English county* Northamptonshire.

northbound *adj* going or leading towards the north.

north-east *noun* (*sometimes* **North-East**) **1** the compass point or direction that is midway between north and east. **2** an area lying in this direction. ▸ *adj* **1** in the north-east. **2** from the direction of the north-east: *a north-east wind.* ▸ *adv* in, to or towards the north-east.

north-easter *or* **nor'-easter** *noun* a strong wind or storm from the north-east.

north-easterly *adj, adv* **1** from the north-east. **2** (*also* **north-eastward**) towards the north-east. ▸ *noun* a wind blowing from the north-east.

north-eastern *adj* **1** belonging to the north-east. **2** in, toward or facing the north-east or that direction.

north-eastward *adj, adv* toward the north-east. ▸ *noun* the region to the north-east. ▪ **north-eastwardly** *adj, adv.* ▪ **north-eastwards** *adv.*

northerly *adj* **1** of a wind, etc: coming from the north. **2** looking or lying, etc towards the north; situated in the north. ▸ *adv* **1** to or towards the north. **2** from the north. ▸ *noun* (**-ies**) a northerly wind.

northern *or* **Northern** *adj* **1** belonging or relating to the **north**. **2** in the north or in the direction toward it. **3** of winds, etc: proceeding from the north. ▪ **northerner** *noun* (*sometimes* **Northerner**) a person who lives in or comes from the north, esp the northern counties of England or the northern states of the USA. ▪ **northernmost** *adj* situated furthest north.

northern hemisphere *noun* the half of the earth that lies to the north of the equator.

the northern lights *plural noun* the **aurora borealis**.

northing *noun, chiefly naut* **1** motion, distance or tendency northward. **2** distance of a heavenly body from the equator northward. **3** difference of **latitude** made by a ship in sailing.

North Pole *or* **north pole** *noun* **1** (*usu* **the North Pole**) the point on the Earth's surface that represents the northern end of its axis. **2** (**north pole**) the north-seeking pole of a magnet.

Northumb *abbrev, English county* Northumberland.

northward *adj* towards the north. ▸ *adv* (*also* **northwards**) towards the north. ▸ *noun* the northward direction, sector, etc. ▪ **northwardly** *adj, adv.*

north-west *noun* (*sometimes* **North-West**) **1** the compass point or direction that is midway between north and west. **2** an area lying in this direction. ▸ *adj* **1** in the north-west. **2** from the direction of the north-west: *a north-west wind*. ▸ *adv* in, to or towards the north-west.

north-wester *noun* a strong wind from the north-west.

north-westerly *adj, adv* **1** from the north-west. **2** (*also* **north-westward**) towards the north-west. ▸ *noun* a wind blowing from the north-west.

north-western *adj* **1** belonging to the north-west. **2** in, towards or facing the north-west or that direction.

north-westward *adj, adv* toward the north-west. ▸ *noun* the region to the north-west. ▪ **north-westwardly** *adj, adv*. ▪ **north-westwards** *adv*.

Norwegian *adj* belonging or relating to Norway, a kingdom in NW Europe in the W part of the Scandinavian peninsula, its inhabitants or their language. ▸ *noun* **1** a citizen or inhabitant of, or person born in, Norway. **2** the language of Norway. [17c: from Latin *Norvegia*, from Norse *northr* north + *vegr* way]

Nos, Nos. *or* **nos** *abbrev* numbers.

nose *noun* **1** the projecting organ above the mouth, with which one smells and breathes. **2** an animal's snout or muzzle. **3** the sense of smell. **4** a scent or aroma, esp a wine's bouquet. **5** the front or projecting part of anything, eg a motor vehicle. **6** the nose as a symbol of inquisitiveness or interference: *poke one's nose into something*. ▸ *verb* **1** *tr & intr* to move carefully forward: *nosed the car out of the yard*. **2** to detect something by smelling. **3** of an animal: to sniff at something or nuzzle it. **4** *intr* (*often* **nose about** *or* **around**) to pry. [Anglo-Saxon *nosu*]

IDIOMS **a nose for sth** a faculty for detecting or recognizing something. **by a nose** by a narrow margin. **cut off one's nose to spite one's face** to act from resentment in a way that can only cause injury to oneself. **get up sb's nose** *informal* to annoy them. **keep one's nose clean** *informal* to avoid doing anything that might get one into trouble. **look down** *or* **turn up one's nose at sth** *or* **sb** to show disdain for it or them. **not see beyond** *or* **further than the end of one's nose** not to see the long-term consequences of one's actions. **on the nose** of bets made in horse-racing: to win only, ie not to come second, etc. **pay through the nose** to pay an exorbitant price. **put sb's nose out of joint** to affront them. **under one's (very) nose** in full view and very obviously in front of one; close at hand.

PHRASAL VERBS **nose sth out** to discover it by prying; to track it down.

nosebag *noun* a food bag for a horse, hung over its head.

nosebleed *noun* a flow of blood from the nose.

nose cone *noun* the cone-shaped cap on the front of a rocket, etc.

nosedive *noun* **1** a steep nose-downward plunge by an aircraft. **2** a sharp plunge or fall. **3** a sudden drop, eg in prices. ▸ *verb, intr* to plunge or fall suddenly. [20c]

nosegay *noun, old use* a posy of flowers. [15c: **nose** + **gay** in the obsolete sense 'ornament']

nose job *noun, informal* plastic surgery performed on the nose in an attempt to improve its appearance. [20c]

nosey see **nosy**

nosh *informal, noun* food. ▸ *verb, intr* to eat. [20c: Yiddish, from German *nascheln* to nibble at something]

no-show *noun* someone who does not arrive for something they have booked and who fails to cancel the booking. [20c: orig US]

nosh-up *noun, Brit informal* a large and satisfying meal.

nostalgia *noun* **1** a yearning for the past. **2** homesickness. ▪ **nostalgic** *adj*. ▪ **nostalgically** *adv*. [18c: from Greek *nostos* homecoming]

nostril *noun* either of the two external openings in the nose. [Anglo-Saxon *nosthyrl*, from *nosu* nose + *thyrel* hole]

nostrum *noun* **1** a patent medicine; a cure-all. **2** a pet solution or remedy, eg one for political ills. [17c: Latin, meaning 'our own (make)']

nosy *or* **nosey** *derog, adj* (***nosier, nosiest***) inquisitive; prying. ▸ *noun* (***nosies*** *or* ***noseys***) a prying person. ▪ **nosiness** *noun*. [Early 20c: from **nose**]

nosy parker *noun, derog, informal* a nosy person; a busybody. [Early 20c]

not *adv* (often shortened to **-n't**) **1** used to make a negative statement, etc. **2** used in place of a negative clause or predicate: *We might be late, but I hope not*. **3** (indicating surprise, an expectation of agreement, etc) surely it is the case that ...: *Haven't you heard?* **4** used to contrast the untrue with the true: *It's a cloud, not a mountain*. **5** barely: *with his face not two inches from mine*. [14c: a variant of **nought**]

IDIOMS **not at all** don't mention it; it's a pleasure. **not just** *or* **not only**, *etc* used to introduce what is usu the lesser of two points, etc: *not just his family, but his wider public*. **not on** *informal* **1** not possible. **2** not morally or socially, etc acceptable.

nota bene /noʊtə 'bɛnɪ/ *verb* (abbrev **NB** *or* **nb**) take note; mark well. [18c: Latin]

notable /'noʊtəbəl/ *adj* **1** worth noting; significant. **2** distinguished. ▸ *noun* a notable person. ▪ **notability** *noun*. ▪ **notably** *adv* as something or someone notable, esp in a list or group: *several people, notably my father*. [14c: from Latin *notabilis*, from *notare* to note or observe]

notary /'noʊtərɪ/ *noun* (**-*ies***) (*in full* **notary public**, *pl* ***notaries public***) a public official with the legal power to draw up and witness official documents, and to administer oaths, etc. [14c: from Latin *notarius* secretary or clerk]

notation *noun* **1** the representation of quantities, numbers, musical sounds or movements, etc by symbols. **2** any set of such symbols. [16c: from Latin *notatio* marking]

notch *noun* **1** a small V-shaped cut or indentation. **2** a nick. **3** *informal* a step or level. ▸ *verb* **1** to cut a notch in something. **2** (*also* **notch something up**) to record something with, or as if with, a notch. **3** (*usu* **notch something up**) to achieve it. **4** to fit (an arrow) to a bowstring. ▪ **notched** *adj*. [16c: from French *oche*, *an oche* coming to be understood as *a notch*]

note *noun* **1** (*often* **notes**) a brief written record made for later reference. **2** a short informal letter. **3** *often in compounds* a brief comment explaining a textual point, etc: *a footnote*. **4** a short account or essay. **5** **a** a banknote; **b** a promissory note. **6** esp in diplomacy: a formal communication. **7** attention; notice: *buildings worthy of note*. **8** distinction; eminence. **9**

music **a** a written symbol indicating the pitch and length of a musical sound; **b** the sound itself; **c** a key on a keyboard instrument. **10** *esp poetic* the call or cry of a bird or animal. **11** an impression conveyed; a hint or touch: *with a note of panic in her voice.* ▸ *verb* **1** (*also* **note sth down**) to write it down. **2** to notice something; to be aware of it. **3** to pay close attention to something. **4** to mention or to remark upon something. **5** *music* to write down (music) in notes. **6** to annotate something. ▪ **noted** *adj* **1** famous; eminent: *noted for his use of colour.* **2** notorious. ▪ **notedly** *adv.* [14c: from Latin *nota* a mark or sign]

IDIOMS **of note 1** well-known; distinguished. **2** significant; worthy of attention. **strike a false note** to act or speak inappropriately. **strike the right note** to act or speak appropriately. **take note** (*often* **take note of sth**) to observe (it) carefully, to pay attention (to it).

notebook *noun* **1** a small book in which to write notes, etc. **2** a small portable computer, smaller than a **laptop**. [16c]

notelet *noun* a folded piece of notepaper.

notepad *noun* a block of writing-paper for making notes on.

notepaper *noun* paper for writing letters on.

noteworthy *adj* worthy of notice; remarkable.

nothing *noun* **1** no thing; not anything. **2 a** zero; **b** the figure 0. **3 a** very little; **b** something of no importance or not very impressive; **c** no difficulty or trouble. **4** an absence of anything. ▸ *adv* not at all: *nothing daunted.* ▪ **nothingness** *noun* **1** the state of being nothing or of not existing. **2** emptiness. **3** worthlessness. **4** a thing of no value. [Anglo-Saxon]

IDIOMS **come to nothing** to fail or peter out. **for nothing 1** free; without payment or personal effort. **2** for no good reason; in vain. **3** *derog* because it is so obvious that you should know: *I'll tell you that for nothing.* **have nothing on sb** *or* **sth 1** *informal* to have no information about them or evidence against them. **2** *informal* to be not nearly as good, beautiful, skilled, etc as them. **have nothing to do with sb** *or* **sth 1** to avoid them. **2** to be unconnected with them. **3** to be of no concern to them. **make nothing of sb** *or* **sth** not to understand them or it. **nothing but** only; merely. **nothing doing** *informal* **1** an expression of refusal. **2** no hope of success. **nothing for it but to** no alternative except to. **nothing if not** primarily, above all, or very: *nothing if not keen.* **nothing much** very little. **nothing short of** *or* **less than sth 1** downright; absolute: *They were nothing less than criminals.* **2** only: *will accept nothing less than an apology.* **nothing to it** *or* **in it** straightforward; easy. **think nothing of sth 1** to regard it as normal or straightforward. **2** to feel no hesitation, guilt or regret about it. **to say nothing of sth** as well as it; not to mention it.

notice *noun* **1** an announcement displayed or delivered publicly. **2** one's attention: *It escaped my notice.* **3 a** a warning or notification given: *will continue until further notice.* **b** warning or notification given before leaving, or dismissing someone from, a job. **4** a review of a performance or book, etc. ▸ *verb* **1** to observe; to become aware of something. **2** to remark on something. **3** to show signs of recognition of someone, etc. **4** to treat someone with polite attention. [15c: French]

IDIOMS **at short notice** with little warning or time for preparation, etc. **take notice of sb** *or* **sth** to pay attention to them or it.

noticeable *adj* easily seen. ▪ **noticeably** *adv.*

notify *verb* (**-ies, -ied**) to tell or to inform. ▪ **notifiable** *adj* of infectious diseases: that must be reported to the public health authorities. ▪ **notification** *noun.* [14c: from Latin *notus* known + *facere* to make]

notion *noun* **1** an impression, conception or understanding. **2** a belief or principle. **3** an inclination, whim or fancy. **4** (**notions**) small items such as pins, needles, threads, etc. ▪ **notional** *adj* **1** existing in imagination only. **2** theoretical. **3** hypothetical. ▪ **notionally** *adv.* [16c: from Latin *notio* an idea]

notochord /ˈnoʊtoʊkɔːd/ *or* **notochordal** /-dəl/ *noun, zool* a flexible rod-like structure, which strengthens and supports the body in the embryos and adults of more primitive animals. [19c: from Greek *notos* + *chorde* a string]

notorious *adj* famous, usu for something disreputable: *a notorious criminal.* ▪ **notoriety** *noun.* ▪ **notoriously** *adv.* [16c: from Latin *notorius* well-known]

not-out *adj, adv, cricket* still in; at the end of the innings without having been put out.

not proven /ˈproʊvən/ *noun, Scots law* a verdict delivered when there is insufficient evidence to convict, resulting in the freedom of the accused.

Notts. *abbrev, English county* Nottinghamshire.

notwithstanding *prep* in spite of. ▸ *adv* in spite of that; however. ▸ *conj* although.

nougat /ˈnuːɡɑː, ˈnʌɡət/ *noun* a chewy sweet containing chopped nuts, cherries, etc. [19c: French]

nought *noun* **1** the figure 0; zero. **2** *old use* nothing; **naught**. [Anglo-Saxon *noht*]

---

nought

Be careful not to use the spelling **nought** when you mean **naught**, as these words have separate meanings in modern English:

All his efforts came to naught.

---

noughts and crosses *singular noun* a game for two players, the aim being to complete a row of three noughts (for one player) or three crosses (for the other) within a framework of nine squares.

noun *noun, grammar* a word used as the name of a person, animal, thing, place or quality. [14c: from Latin *nomen* name]

nourish *verb* **1** to supply someone or something with food. **2 a** to encourage the growth of something; **b** to foster (an idea, etc). ▪ **nourishing** *adj.* ▪ **nourishment** *noun.* [13c: from French *norir*]

nous /nɑʊs/ *noun, informal* common sense; gumption. [18c: Greek, meaning 'mind']

nouveau riche /ˈnuːvoʊ riːʃ/ *noun, derog* (*usu in pl* ***nouveaux riches*** /ˈnuːvoʊ riːʃ/) people who have recently acquired wealth but lack good taste. [19c: French, meaning 'new rich']

nouvelle cuisine /ˈnuːvɛl kwɪˈziːn/ *noun* a simple style of cookery characterized by much use of fresh produce and elegant presentation. [20c: French, meaning 'new cookery']

Nov. *abbrev* November.

nova /ˈnoʊvə/ *noun* (***novae*** /-viː/ *or* ***novas***) *astron* a normally faint star that flares into brightness then fades again. [19c: from Latin *nova stella* new star]

novel¹ *noun* **1** a book-length fictional story. **2** (**the novel**) such writing as a literary genre. ▪ **novelist** *noun.* [15c: from Italian *novella* short story]

novel² *adj* new; original; previously unheard-of. [15c: from Latin *novellus* new]

novelette *noun* a short novel, esp one that is considered trite or sentimental. [19c]

novella *noun* a short story or short novel. [20c: Italian]

novelty *noun* (**-ies**) **1** the quality of being new and intriguing. **2** something new and strange. **3** a small, cheap toy or souvenir. [14c: from French *novelté*]

November *noun* (abbrev **Nov.**) the eleventh month of the year. [13c: Latin, meaning 'the ninth month'; in the Roman calendar the year began in March]

novena /noʊ'viːnə/ *noun, RC Church* a series of special prayers and services held over a period of nine days. [19c: from Latin *noveni* nine each]

novice /'nɒvɪs/ *noun* **1** someone new in anything; a beginner. **2** a probationary member of a religious community. **3** *horse-racing* a horse that has not won a race in a season prior to the current season. **4** a competitor that has not yet won a recognized prize. [14c: from Latin *novicius*, from *novus* new]

noviciate *or* **novitiate** *noun* **1** the period of being a novice, esp in a religious community. **2** the state of being a novice. [17c: from French *noviciat*]

now *adv* **1** at the present time or moment. **2** immediately. **3** in narrative: then: *He now turned from journalism to fiction.* **4** in these circumstances; as things are: *I planned to go, but now I can't.* **5** up to the present: *has now been teaching for 13 years.* **6** used in conversation to accompany explanations, warnings, commands, rebukes, words of comfort, etc: *Now, this is what happened.* • *Careful now!* ▸ *noun* the present time. ▸ *conj* (*also* **now that**) because at last; because at this time: *Now we're all here, we'll begin.* [Anglo-Saxon *nu*]

IDIOMS **just now 1** a moment ago. **2** at this very moment. **now and again** *or* **now and then** sometimes; occasionally. **now for** used in anticipation, or in turning from one thing to another: *Now for some fun!* **now, now! 1** used to comfort someone: *Now, now, don't cry!* **2** (*also* **now then!**) a warning or rebuke: *Now, now! Less noise please!*

nowadays *adv* in these present times. [14c]

Nowell *or* **Nowel** *noun* **Noel**. [14c: French]

nowhere *adv* in or to no place; not anywhere. ▸ *noun* a non-existent place.

IDIOMS **from** *or* **out of nowhere** suddenly and inexplicably: *They appeared from nowhere.* **get nowhere** to make no progress. **in the middle of nowhere** *informal* isolated; remote from towns or cities, etc. **nowhere near** not nearly; by no means: *nowhere near enough.* **nowhere to be found** *or* **seen** lost.

no-win *adj* of a situation: in which one is bound to fail or lose, whatever one does. [20c]

nowt *noun, informal or dialect* nothing. [19c variant of **naught**]

noxious *adj* harmful; poisonous. [17c: from Latin *noxius* harmful]

nozzle *noun* an outlet tube or spout, esp as a fitting attached to the end of a hose, etc. [17c: a diminutive of **nose**]

Np *symbol, chem* neptunium.

NQ *abbrev* in Scotland: National Qualification, a qualification awarded for competence in subjects at any of five different levels.

nr *abbrev* near.

ns *abbrev* nanosecond or nanoseconds.

NSW *abbrev, Aust state* New South Wales.

NT *abbrev* **1** New Testament. **2** *Aust territory* Northern Territory.

-n't *contraction* not.

Nth *abbrev* North.

nth /enθ/ *adj* **1** denoting an indefinite position in a sequence: *to the nth degree.* **2** many times removed from the first; **umpteenth**: *I'm telling you for the nth time.*

nu /njuː/ *noun* the thirteenth letter of the Greek alphabet.

nuance /'njuːɑːns/ *noun* a subtle variation in colour, meaning, expression, etc. [18c: French, meaning 'shade' or 'hue']

the nub *noun* the central and most important issue; the crux. [19c: from German dialect *knubbe*]

nubile /'njuːbaɪl/ *adj* of a young woman: **1** sexually mature. **2** marriageable. **3** physically attractive. [17c: from Latin *nubilis*, from *nubere* to marry]

nuclear /'njuːklɪə(r)/ *adj* **1** having the nature of, or like, a **nucleus**. **2** relating to atoms or their nuclei: *nuclear physics.* **3** relating to or produced by the fission or fusion of atomic nuclei: *nuclear energy.* [19c]

nuclear bomb see **atom bomb**

nuclear energy *noun* energy produced through a nuclear reaction. Also called **atomic energy**.

nuclear family *noun* the basic family unit, mother, father and children.

nuclear fission *noun* a reaction in which an atomic nucleus of a radioactive element splits with simultaneous release of large amounts of energy. [20c]

nuclear fuel *noun* material such as **uranium** or **plutonium** used to produce nuclear energy.

nuclear fusion *noun* a **thermonuclear** reaction in which two atomic nuclei combine with a release of large amounts of energy. [20c]

nuclearize *or* **-ise** *verb* **1** to make something nuclear. **2** to supply or fit something with nuclear weapons. ▪ **nuclearization** *noun.* [20c]

nuclear physics *noun* the study of atomic nuclei, esp relating to the generation of **nuclear energy**.

nuclear power *noun* power, esp electricity, obtained from reactions by **nuclear fission** or **nuclear fusion**. ▪ **nuclear-powered** *adj.*

nuclear reaction *noun* a process of **nuclear fusion** or **nuclear fission**.

nuclear reactor *noun* an apparatus for producing nuclear energy, eg to generate electricity, by means of sustained and controlled **nuclear fission**.

nuclear waste *noun* radioactive waste material.

nuclear weapon *noun* a weapon that derives its destructive force from the energy released during **nuclear fission** or **nuclear fusion**. Also called **atomic weapon**.

nuclear winter *noun* a period without light, heat or growth, predicted as an after-effect of nuclear war.

nuclease /'njuːklɪeɪz/ *noun, biochem* any enzyme that catalyses the splitting of the chain of nucleotides comprising a **nucleic acid**.

nucleate *verb, tr & intr* to form, or form something into, a nucleus. ▸ *adj* having a nucleus. [19c]

nuclei *pl of* **nucleus**

nucleic acid *noun* a complex compound, either **DNA** or **RNA**, found in all living cells. [19c]

nucleo- *combining form, denoting* **1** nuclear. **2** nucleic acid. **3** nucleus.

nucleon *noun, physics* a **proton** or **neutron**. [20c: from **nucleus**]

nucleonics *singular noun* the study of the uses of radioactivity and nuclear energy. [20c]

nucleotide *noun, biochem* an organic compound that forms part of a **DNA** or **RNA** molecule. [20c]

nucleus /ˈnjuːklɪəs/ *noun* (***nuclei*** /ˈnjuːklɪaɪ/) **1** *physics* the central part of an atom, consisting of neutrons and protons. **2** *biol* the central part of a plant or animal cell, containing genetic material. **3** *chem* a stable group of atoms in a molecule acting as a base for the formation of compounds. **4** a core round which things grow or accumulate. [18c: Latin, meaning 'kernel']

nude *adj* **1** wearing no clothes; naked. **2** uncovered; bare. ▸ *noun* **1** a representation of one or more naked figures in painting or sculpture, etc. **2** someone naked. **3** the state of nakedness: *in the nude*. ▪ **nudity** *noun*. [16c: from Latin *nudus* naked]

nudge *verb* **1** to poke or push someone gently, esp with the elbow, to get attention, etc. **2** to give someone a gentle reminder or persuasion. ▸ *noun* a gentle prod. [17c: possibly from Norwegian dialect *nugga* to push or rub]

nudism *noun* the practice of not wearing clothes, as a matter of principle. ▪ **nudist** *noun, adj*.

nugatory /ˈnjuːgətərɪ/ *adj, formal* **1** worthless; trifling; valueless. **2** ineffective; futile. **3** invalid. [17c: from Latin *nugae* trifles]

nugget *noun* **1** a lump, esp of gold. **2** a small piece of something precious: *nuggets of wisdom*. [19c]

nuisance *noun* **1** an annoying or troublesome person, thing or circumstance. **2** *law* something obnoxious to the community or an individual, that is disallowed by law. [15c: French, from *nuire* to injure]

nuke *slang, verb* to attack with nuclear weapons. ▸ *noun* a nuclear weapon. [20c]

null *adj* **1** legally invalid: *declared null and void*. **2** with no significance or value. **3** *maths* of a set: with no members; empty. ▪ **nullity** *noun* **1** the state of being null or void. **2** (***-ies***) something without legal force or validity. **3** lack of existence, force or efficacy. ▪ **nullness** *noun*. [16c: from Latin *nullus* none]

nullify *verb* (***-ies, -ied***) **1** to cause or declare something to be legally invalid. **2** to make something ineffective; to cancel it out. ▪ **nullification** *noun*. [16c: from Latin *nullus* of no account + *facere* to make]

num. *abbrev* **1** number. **2** numeral.

numb *adj* **1** deprived completely, or to some degree, of sensation. **2** too stunned to feel emotion; stupefied: *numb with shock*. ▸ *verb* **1** to make something numb. **2** to deaden something. ▪ **numbly** *adv*. ▪ **numbness** *noun*. [15c with the meaning 'seized', ie with paralysis: from *nim* to take]

number *noun* **1** the system by which things are counted. **2** an arithmetical symbol representing such a quantity, eg *5* or *V*. **3** a numeral or set of numerals identifying something or someone within a series: *telephone numbers*. **4** (with a numeral) the person, animal, vehicle, etc bearing the specified numeral: *Number 2 is pulling ahead*. **5** a single one of a series, eg an issue of a magazine. **6** a quantity of individuals. **7** an act or turn in a programme. **8** a piece of popular music or jazz. **9** *informal* an article or person considered appreciatively: *driving a white sports number*. **10** a group or set: *isn't one of our number*. **11** (**numbers**) numerical superiority: *overwhelmed by sheer weight of numbers*. **12** *grammar* the property of expressing, or classification of word forms into, **singular** and **plural** and, in some languages, **dual** (for two people, things, etc). ▸ *verb* **1** to give a number to something; to mark it with a number. **2** to amount to (a specified number). **3** *tr & intr* to list; to enumerate. **4** *tr & intr* to include or be included: *I number her among my enemies*. ▪ **numberless** *adj* **1** too many to count; innumerable. **2** without a number. [13c: from French *nombre*, from Latin *numerus*]

IDIOMS **by numbers** of a procedure, etc: performed in simple stages. **one's days are numbered** one is soon to die, or come to the end of (eg a job) unpleasantly. **get** *or* **have sb's number** *informal* to understand them; to have them sized up. **one's number is up** *informal* one is due for some unpleasant fate, eg death or ruin. **without number** more than can be counted; countless.

number-cruncher *noun* **1** a computer designed to carry out large quantities of complex numerical calculations. **2** someone who operates such a computer. **3** someone who carries out such calculations in their head. ▪ **number-crunching** *noun*.

number one *noun, informal, ironic* oneself. ▸ *adj* (**number-one**) first; of primary importance: *give it number-one priority*.

number plate *noun* a plate on a motor vehicle bearing its registration number.

number theory *noun* the branch of mathematics concerned with the abstract study of the relationships between, and properties of, positive whole numbers.

number two *noun, informal* second-in-command.

numbskull see **numskull**

numen *noun* (***numina***) a presiding deity. [17c: Latin, meaning 'divinity']

numerable *adj* that may be numbered or counted. ▪ **numerably** *adv*. [16c]

numeral *noun* an arithmetical symbol or group of symbols used to express a number, eg *5* or *V*, *29* or *XXIX*. ▸ *adj* relating to, consisting of, or expressing a number. [16c: from Latin *numerus* number]

numerate *adj* **1** able to perform arithmetical operations. **2** having some understanding of mathematics and science. ▪ **numeracy** /ˈnjuːmərəsɪ/ *noun*. [15c: from Latin *numerus* number, modelled on **literate**]

numeration *noun* **1** the process of counting or numbering. **2** a system of numbering. [15c: from Latin *numerare* to count]

numerator *noun* the number above the line in a fraction. [16c]

numeric *or* **numerical** *adj* relating to, using, or consisting of, numbers. ▪ **numerically** *adv*. [17c]

numerology *noun* the study of numbers as supposed to predict future events or influence human affairs. ▪ **numerological** *adj*. ▪ **numerologist** *noun*. [20c]

numerous *adj* **1** many. **2** containing a large number of people. [16c: from Latin *numerosus*]

numina *pl of* **numen**

numinous *adj* **1** mysterious; awe-inspiring. **2** characterized by the sense of a deity's presence. [17c: from Latin *numen* deity]

numismatics *or* **numismatology** *noun* the study or collecting of coins and medals. ▪ **numismatist** *or* **numismatologist** *noun*. [18c: from Greek *nomisma* coin]

numskull *or* **numbskull** *noun, informal* a stupid person. [18c: **numb** + **skull**]

nun *noun* a member of a female religious order living within a community, in obedience to certain vows. [Anglo-Saxon *nunne*]

nuncio /ˈnʌnsɪoʊ/ *noun* an ambassador from the pope. [16c: from Latin *nuntios* messenger]

nunnery *noun* (*-ies*) a house in which a group of nuns live; a **convent**.

nuptial *adj* **1** relating to marriage. **2** *zool* relating to mating. ▸ *noun* (*usu* **nuptials**) a marriage ceremony. [15c: from Latin *nuptialis*, from *nuptiae* marriage]

nurd see **nerd**

nurl see **knurl**

nurse *noun* **1** someone trained to look after sick, injured or feeble people, esp in hospital. **2** someone, esp a woman, who looks after small children in a household, etc. **3** a worker ant, bee, etc, that tends the young in the colony. ▸ *verb* **1** to look after (sick or injured people) esp in a hospital. **2** *intr* to follow a career as a nurse. **3** *tr & intr* **a** to breastfeed a baby; **b** of a baby: to feed at the breast. **4** to hold something with care: *gave him the bag of meringues to nurse*. **5** to tend something with concern: *was at home nursing a cold*. **6** to encourage or indulge (a feeling) in oneself: *nursing her jealousy*. ▪ **nursing** *adj, noun*. [14c: from French *norrice*]

nurseling see **nursling**

nursemaid *or* **nurserymaid** *noun* a children's nurse in a household.

nursery *noun* (*-ies*) **1 a** a place where children are looked after while their parents are at work, etc; **b** a **nursery school**. **2** a room in a house, etc, set apart for young children and, where appropriate, their nurse or other carer. **3** a place where plants are grown for sale. **4** a place where young animals are reared or tended. **5** a place where the growth of anything is promoted. ▸ *adj* relating or belonging to the nursery or early training. [14c: as *norcery*, meaning 'upbringing' or 'nursing']

nurseryman *noun* someone who grows plants for sale.

nursery nurse *noun* someone trained in the care of babies and young children.

nursery rhyme *noun* a short simple traditional rhyme or song for young children.

nursery school *noun* a school for young children, usu those aged between three and five. Also shortened to **nursery**.

nursery slopes *plural noun, skiing* the lower, more gentle slopes, used for practice by beginners.

nursing home *noun* a small private hospital or home, esp one for old people.

nursling *or* **nurseling** *noun* a young child or animal that is being nursed or fostered. [16c]

nurture *noun* care, nourishment and encouragement given to a growing child, animal or plant. ▸ *verb* **1** to nourish and tend (a growing child, animal or plant). **2** to encourage the development of (a project, feeling, etc). [14c: from French *norriture*]

nut *noun* **1** *popularly* **a** a fruit consisting of a kernel contained in a hard shell, eg a hazelnut or walnut; **b** the kernel itself. **2** *botany* a hard dry **indehiscent** one-seeded fruit. **3** *popularly* a roasted peanut. **4** a small, usu hexagonal, piece of metal with a hole through it, for screwing on the end of a bolt. **5** *informal* a person's head. **6** *informal* (*also* **nutter**) a crazy person. **7** *informal, usu in compounds* an enthusiast: *a football nut*. **8** a small lump: *a nut of butter*. ▸ *verb, informal* (***nutted, nutting***) to butt someone with the head. ▪ **nutter** see *noun* sense 6 above. [Anglo-Saxon *hnutu*]

IDIOMS **a hard** *or* **tough nut to crack** *informal* **1** a difficult problem to solve. **2** an awkward person to deal with. **do one's nut** *informal* to be furious.

nutcase *noun, colloq* a crazy person. [20c]

nutcracker *noun* (*usu* **nutcrackers**) a utensil for cracking nuts.

nuthatch *noun* a bird that feeds on insects, nuts and seeds. [14c: from *note* nut + *hache* (related to **hack**[1], **hatch**[2])]

nutmeg *noun* the hard aromatic seed of the fruit of an E Indian tree, used as a spice. [14c]

nutria *noun* **1** the coypu. **2** its fur. [19c: Spanish, meaning 'otter']

nutrient *noun* any nourishing substance. ▸ *adj* nourishing. [17c: from Latin *nutrire* to nourish]

nutriment *noun* nourishment; food. [16c: from Latin *nutrimentum*]

nutrition *noun* **1** the act or process of nourishing. **2** the study of the body's dietary needs. **3** food. ▪ **nutritional** *adj*. ▪ **nutritionist** *noun*. [16c]

nutritious *adj* nourishing; providing nutrition.

nutritive *adj* **1** nourishing. **2** relating to nutrition.

nuts *adj, informal* insane; crazy.

the nuts and bolts *plural noun, informal* the essential or practical details.

nutshell *noun* the case containing the kernel of a nut.

IDIOMS **in a nutshell** concisely expressed.

nutty *adj* (*-ier, -iest*) **1** full of, or tasting of, nuts. **2** *informal* crazy. ▪ **nuttiness** *noun*.

nux vomica *noun* **1** the seed of an East Indian tree, containing strychnine. **2** the drug made from it. [16c: Latin, meaning 'vomiting nut']

nuzzle *verb, tr & intr* **1** to push or rub someone or something with the nose. **2** (*usu* **nuzzle up to** *or* **against sb**) to snuggle up against them. [17c: from **nose**]

NVQ *abbrev* National Vocational Qualification.

NW *abbrev* **1** north-west. **2** north-western.

NY *abbrev* New York.

nylon *noun* **1** a polymeric amide that can be formed into fibres, bristles or sheets. **2** a yarn or cloth made of nylon. **3** (**nylons**) nylon stockings. [20c: orig a tradename]

nymph *noun* **1** *myth* a goddess that inhabits mountains, water, trees, etc. **2** *poetic* a beautiful young woman. **3** *zool* the immature larval form of certain insects. [14c: from Greek *nymphe* nymph or bride]

NZ *abbrev* New Zealand.

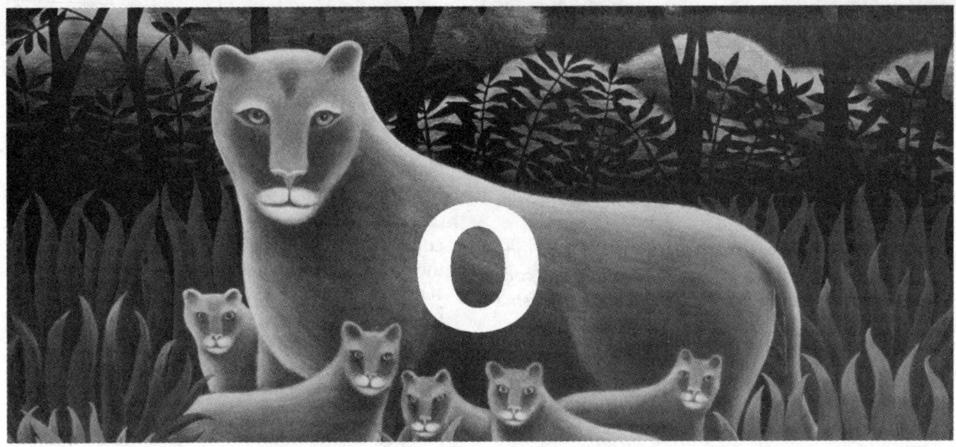

O[1] *or* **o** *noun* (***Oes, Os*** or ***o's***) **1** the fifteenth letter of the English alphabet. **2** the shape of this letter: *formed his mouth into an O.* **3** in telephone, etc jargon: zero; nought.

O[2] *abbrev, formerly*: ordinary, in eg O-level or O-grade.

O[3] *symbol, chem* oxygen.

o' *prep, chiefly archaic & dialect* short form of **of**.

oaf *noun* a stupid, awkward or loutish person. ▪ **oafish** *adj.* [17c: from Norse *alfr* elf]

oak *noun* **1** any tree or shrub which produces acorns, and usu has lobed leaves. **2** the hard durable wood of this tree, widely used in building construction and furniture. [Anglo-Saxon *ac*]

oak-apple *or* **oak-gall** *noun* a round brownish woody gall found on oak trees, produced by the larvae of certain wasps.

oaken *adj, old use* made of oak wood.

oakum *noun* pieces of old, usu tarred, rope untwisted and pulled apart, used to fill small holes and cracks in wooden boats and ships. [Anglo-Saxon *acumba* off-combings]

OAP *abbrev, Brit* old age pensioner.

oar *noun* a long pole with a broad flat blade at one end, used for rowing a boat. [Anglo-Saxon *ar*]
IDIOMS **put** *or* **stick one's oar in** *informal* to interfere or meddle, esp by giving one's unwanted opinion.

oarsman *or* **oarswoman** *noun* a man or woman who rows. ▪ **oarsmanship** *noun.*

oasis *noun* (***oases***) **1** a fertile area in a desert, where water is found and plants grow. **2** any place or period of rest or calm, etc in the middle of hard work, problems or trouble. [20c: Latin]

oast *noun* a kiln for drying hops or, formerly, malt. [Anglo-Saxon *ast* kiln]

oat *noun* **1** a cereal and type of grass cultivated as a food crop. **2** (**oats**) the grains of this plant, used to make porridge, etc, and for feeding livestock. [Anglo-Saxon *ate*]

oatcake *noun* a thin dry savoury biscuit made from oatmeal.

oath *noun* **1** a solemn promise to tell the truth or to be loyal, etc, usu naming God as a witness. **2** swear-word, obscenity or blasphemy. [Anglo-Saxon *ath*]
IDIOMS **on** *or* **under oath 1** having sworn to tell the truth, eg in a court of law. **2** attested by oath. **take an oath** to pledge formally.

oatmeal *noun* **1** meal ground from oats, used to make oatcakes, etc. **2** the pale brownish-yellow flecked colour of oatmeal.

OB *abbrev* outside broadcast.

ob. *abbrev* on tombstones, etc: *obiit* (Latin), he or she died.

obbligato *or* **obligato** /ɒblɪ'gɑːtoʊ/ *music, noun* (***obbligatos*** *or* ***obbligati*** /-tiː/) an accompaniment that forms an essential part of a piece of music, esp one played by a single instrument accompanying a voice. ▸ *adj* played with an obbligato. [18c: Italian, meaning 'obligatory']

obdurate *adj* **1** hard-hearted. **2** stubborn; difficult to influence or change, esp morally. ▪ **obduracy** *noun.* ▪ **obdurately** *adv.* [15c: from Latin *obdurare* to harden]

OBE *abbrev, Brit* Officer of the Order of the British Empire.

obedient *adj* obeying; willing to obey. ▪ **obedience** *noun.* ▪ **obediently** *adv.* [13c: from French *obédient*]

obeisance /oʊ'beɪsəns/ *noun* a bow, act or other expression of obedience or respect. ▪ **obeisant** *adj.* [14c: from French *obéissance*]

obelisk *noun* **1** a tall tapering, usu four-sided, stone pillar with a pyramidal top. **2** an **obelus**. [16c: from Greek *obeliskos* a small spit]

obelus /'ɒbələs/ *noun* (***obeli*** /-laɪ/) *printing* a dagger-shaped mark (†) used esp for referring to footnotes. [14c: Latin]

obese /oʊ'biːs/ *adj* very or abnormally fat. ▪ **obesity** *noun.* [17c: from Latin *obesus* plump]

obey *verb* **1** to do what one is told to do by someone. **2** to carry out (a command). **3** *intr* to do what one is told. [13c: from French *obéir*]

obfuscate *verb* **1** to darken or obscure (something). **2** to make (something) difficult to understand. ▪ **obfuscation** *noun.* ▪ **obfuscatory** *adj.* [16c: from Latin *ob-* completely + *fuscare* to darken]

obituary *noun* (***-ies***) a notice or announcement, esp in a newspaper, of a person's death, often with a short account of their life. ▪ **obituarist** *noun.* [18c: from Latin *obitus* death]

object /'ɒbdʒɪkt, 'ɒbdʒɛkt/ *noun* **1** a material thing that can be seen or touched. **2** an aim or purpose. **3** a person or thing to which action, feelings or thought are directed: *the object of his affections.* **4** *grammar* **a** a noun, noun phrase or pronoun affected by the action of the verb. **b** a noun, noun phrase or pronoun affected by a preposition. See also **subject**

(*noun* sense 6). **5** *philos* a thing which is outside of, and can be perceived by, the mind. **6** *comput* an entity that can be individually manipulated, eg a command button or picture. ▶ *verb* /əb'dʒɛkt/ **1** *intr* (*usu* **object to** *or* **against sth**) to feel or express dislike or disapproval for it. **2** to state something as a ground for disapproval or objection. ▪ **objector** *noun*. [14c: from Latin *objectus* a throwing before]

IDIOMS **no object** not a difficulty or obstacle: *Money's no object.*

objection *noun* **1** the act of objecting. **2** an expression or feeling of disapproval, opposition or dislike, etc. **3** (*often* **objection against** *or* **to sth**) a reason or cause for disapproving, opposing or disliking it, etc.

objectionable *adj* unpleasant; offensive.

objective *adj* **1 a** not depending on, or influenced by, personal opinions or prejudices; **b** relating to external facts, etc as opposed to internal thoughts or feelings. **2** *philos* **a** having existence outside the mind; **b** based on fact or reality. Compare **subjective**. **3** *grammar* of a case or word: **a** indicating the object; **b** in the relation of object to a verb or preposition. ▶ *noun* **1** a thing aimed at or wished for; a goal. **2** something independent of or external to the mind. **3** *grammar* **a** the objective case; **b** a word or form in that case. ▪ **objectival** /ɒbdʒɛk'taɪvəl/ *adj*. ▪ **objectively** *adv*. ▪ **objectivity** *or* **objectiveness** *noun*.

object lesson *noun* an instructive experience or event, etc that provides a practical example of some principle or ideal.

objet d'art /ɒbʒeɪ 'dɑː(r)/ *noun* (***objets d'art*** /ɒbʒeɪ 'dɑː(r)/) a small object of artistic value. [19c: French, meaning 'object of art']

oblate *adj, geom* of something approximately spherical: flattened at the poles, like the Earth. Compare **prolate**. [18c: from Latin *oblatus* lengthened]

oblation *noun* **1** *Christianity* the offering of the bread and wine to God at a Eucharist. **2** a religious or charitable offering. ▪ **oblational** *or* **oblatory** /'ɒblətərɪ/ *adj*. [15c: French]

obligate *verb* **1** to bind or oblige (someone) by contract, duty or moral obligation. **2** to bind (someone) by gratitude. ▶ *adj, biol* of an organism, especially a bacterium: limited to specific functions and by specific conditions. [16c: from Latin *obligare*]

obligation *noun* **1** a moral or legal duty or tie. **2** the binding power of such a duty or tie. **3** a debt of gratitude for a service: *be under obligation to her.*

obligato see **obbligato**

obligatory *adj* **1** legally or morally binding. **2** compulsory.

oblige *verb* **1** to bind (someone) morally or legally; to compel. **2** to bind (someone) by a service or favour. **3** to please or do a favour for (someone): *Please oblige me by leaving at once.* **4** to do something as a favour or contribution for (someone): *obliged us with a song*. [13c: from French *obliger*]

IDIOMS **much obliged** an expression of gratitude.

obliging *adj* ready to help others; courteously helpful. ▪ **obligingly** *adv*.

oblique /ə'bliːk/ *adj* **1** sloping; not vertical or horizontal. **2** *geom* of lines and planes, etc: not at a right angle. **3** not straight or direct; roundabout; underhand. ▶ *noun* **1** an oblique line; a solidus (/). **2** anything that is oblique. ▪ **obliquely** *adv*. ▪ **obliqueness** *or* **obliquity** *noun*. [15c: French]

obliterate *verb* to destroy (something) completely. ▪ **obliteration** *noun*. [16c: from Latin *oblitterare* to blot out or erase]

oblivion *noun* **1** the state or fact of having forgotten or of being unconscious. **2** the state of being forgotten. [14c: from Latin *oblivio* forgetfulness]

oblivious *adj* (*usu* **oblivious of** *or* **to sth**) unaware or forgetful of it. ▪ **obliviousness** *noun*.

oblong *adj* rectangular with adjacent sides of unequal length; with a greater breadth than height. ▶ *noun, non-technical* something that has this shape; a rectangular figure. [15c: from Latin *oblongus*]

obloquy /'ɒbləkwɪ/ *noun* (**-*quies***) **1** abuse, blame or censure. **2** disgrace; loss of honour, good name or reputation. [15c: from Latin *obloquium* contradiction]

obnoxious *adj* offensive; objectionable. ▪ **obnoxiousness** *noun*. [16c: from Latin *obnoxius*]

oboe *noun* (***oboes***) a double-reed treble woodwind instrument with a penetrating tone. ▪ **oboist** *noun*. [18c: Italian]

obscene *adj* **1** offensive to accepted standards of behaviour or morality. **2** *informal* indecent; disgusting. **3** *Brit law* of a publication: tending to cause moral corruption. ▪ **obscenely** *adv*. [16c: Latin *obscenus* ill-omened, foul or indecent]

obscenity /əb'sɛnɪtɪ/ *noun* (**-*ies***) **1** the state or quality of being obscene. **2** an obscene word or act. **3** something that is extremely ugly or offensive.

obscure *adj* **1** dark; dim. **2** not clear; hidden. **3** not well known. **4** difficult to understand. ▶ *verb* **1** to make (something) dark or dim. **2** to overshadow (something). **3** to make (something) difficult to understand. ▪ **obscurity** *noun* (**-*ies***). [14c: from French *obscur*]

obsequies /'ɒbsəkwɪz/ *plural noun* funeral rites. [14c: from Latin *obsequiae*]

obsequious /əb'siːkwɪəs/ *adj* submissively obedient; fawning. ▪ **obsequiously** *adv*. ▪ **obsequiousness** *noun*. [15c: from Latin *obsequiosus* compliant]

observance *noun* **1** the fact or act of obeying rules or keeping customs, etc. **2** a custom or religious rite observed.

observant *adj* quick to notice; perceptive.

observation *noun* **1 a** the act of noticing or watching; **b** the state of being observed or watched. **2** the ability to observe; perception. **3** a remark or comment. **4** the noting of behaviour, symptoms or phenomena, etc as they occur, esp before analysis or diagnosis. **5** the result of such observing. ▪ **observational** *adj*.

observatory *noun* (**-*ies***) a room or building, etc specially equipped for making systematic observations of natural phenomena, esp the stars and other celestial objects visible in the night sky. [17c]

observe *verb* **1** to notice or become conscious of (something). **2** to watch (something) carefully; to pay close attention to it. **3** *tr & intr* to examine and note (behaviour, symptoms or phenomena, etc). **4** to obey, follow or keep (a law, custom or religious rite, etc). **5** *tr & intr* to make (a remark or comment): *observed that he was late again.* ▪ **observable** *adj*. ▪ **observer** *noun*. [14c: from Latin *observare*]

obsess *verb* **1** to occupy (someone's thoughts or mind) completely, persistently or constantly; to preoccupy or haunt: *She is obsessed by football.* **2** *tr & intr* to think or worry constantly (about something). [16c: from Latin *obsidere* to besiege]

obsession *noun* **1** a persistent or dominating thought, idea, feeling, etc. **2** *psychol* a recurring thought, feeling or impulse, generally of an unpleasant nature and with no rational basis, that preoccupies a person against their will and is a source of constant anxiety. **3** the act of obsessing or state of being obsessed. ▪ **obsessional** *adj.* [16c]

obsessive *adj* **1** relating to or resulting from obsession, an obsession or obsessions. **2** of a person: affected by an obsession. ▸ *noun* someone affected or characterized by obsessive behaviour. [20c]

obsidian *noun, geol* a volcanic glass, usu black, but sometimes red or brown in colour, formed by the rapid cooling and solidification of granite magma. [17c: from Latin *obsidianus*, an erroneous form of *(lapis) obsianus*, a stone supposedly found by one Obsius in Ethiopia]

obsolescent *adj* going out of use; becoming out of date. ▪ **obsolescence** *noun.*

obsolete *adj* **1** no longer in use or in practice. **2** out of date; outmoded. **3** *biol* organs, etc: no longer functional or fully developed. [16c: from Latin *obsoletus* worn out]

obstacle *noun* someone or something that obstructs, or hinders or prevents advance. [14c: from Latin *obstaculum*]

obstetrician *noun* a physician who specializes in obstetrics.

obstetrics *singular noun* the branch of medicine and surgery that deals with pregnancy, childbirth and the care of the mother. ▪ **obstetric** *adj.* [19c]

obstinate *adj* **1** refusing to change one's opinion or course of action; stubborn. **2** **a** difficult to defeat or remove; **b** esp of a disease or medical condition, etc: difficult to treat. ▪ **obstinacy** *noun.* ▪ **obstinately** *adv.* [14c: from Latin *obstinare* to persist]

obstreperous *adj* noisy and hard to control; unruly. [16c: from Latin *strepere* to make a noise]

obstruct *verb* **1** to block or close (a passage or opening, etc). **2** to prevent or hinder the movement or progress of (someone or something). **3** to block or impede (a view or line of vision, etc). [16c: from Latin *obstruere*]

obstruction *noun* **1** a thing that obstructs or blocks. **2** the act of obstructing. **3** *sport* an act of hindering or unfairly getting in the way of another player or competitor.

obstructionism *noun* the practice of obstructing parliamentary or legal action. Compare **filibuster**. ▪ **obstructionist** *noun.*

obstructive *adj* causing or designed to cause an obstruction. ▪ **obstructively** *adv.* ▪ **obstructiveness** *noun.*

obtain *verb* **1** to get (something); to become the owner, or come into possession, of (something). **2** *intr* to be established, exist or hold good. ▪ **obtainable** *adj.* [15c: from Latin *obtinere* to lay hold of]

obtrude *verb* **1** *intr* to be or become unpleasantly noticeable or prominent. **2** to push (oneself or one's opinions, etc) forward, esp when they are unwelcome. ▪ **obtrusion** *noun.* [16c: from Latin *obtrudere*]

obtrusive *adj* unpleasantly noticeable or prominent. ▪ **obtrusiveness** *noun.*

obtuse *adj* **1** stupid and slow to understand. **2** *chiefly botany & zool* of eg a leaf or other flat part: blunt; not pointed or sharp; rounded at the tip. **3** *geom* of an angle: greater than 90° and less than 180°. Compare **acute** (*adj* sense 6), **reflex** (*adj* sense 5). ▪ **obtuseness** *noun.* [16c: from Latin *obtundere* to blunt]

obverse *noun* **1** the side of a coin with the head or main design on it. **2** an opposite or counterpart, eg of a fact or truth. [17c: from Latin *obversus* turned against or towards]

obviate *verb* to prevent or remove (a potential difficulty or problem, etc) in advance; to forestall. [16c: from Latin *obviare* to go to meet]

obvious *adj* easily seen or understood. ▸ *noun* (**the obvious**) something which is obvious: *to state the obvious.* ▪ **obviously** *adv.* ▪ **obviousness** *noun.* [16c: from Latin *obvius*]

ocarina *noun* a small simple fluty-toned wind instrument that has an egg-shaped body with fingerholes and a projecting mouthpiece. [19c: Italian, from *oca* goose, so-called because of its shape]

occasion *noun* **1** a particular event or happening, or the time at which it occurs: *met on three occasions.* **2** a special event or celebration. **3** a suitable opportunity or chance. **4** a reason; grounds: *have no occasion to be angry.* ▸ *verb* to cause something; to bring it about, esp incidentally. [14c: from Latin *occasio* opportunity or cause]

IDIOMS **on occasion 1** as the need or opportunity arises. **2** from time to time; occasionally.

occasional *adj* **1** happening irregularly and infrequently. **2** produced on or for a special occasion. ▪ **occasionally** *adv.*

occasional table *noun* a small portable side-table used irregularly and for various purposes.

Occident *noun* (**the Occident**) the countries in the west, esp those in Europe and America regarded as culturally distinct from eastern countries (**the Orient**). ▪ **Occidental** *adj.* [14c: from Latin *occidens* setting, west or sunset]

occipital /ɒk'sɪpɪtəl/ *anatomy, adj* relating to or in the region of the back of the head. ▸ *noun* (*also* **occipital bone**) the bone that forms the back of the skull and part of its base, and encircles the spinal column. [16c: from Latin *occipitalis*]

occiput /'ɒksɪpʌt/ *noun, anatomy* **1** the back of the head or skull. **2** the occipital bone. [14c: Latin, from *ob-* against + *caput* head]

occlude *verb, technical* **1** to block up or cover (an opening or passage). **2** to shut (something) in or out. **3** to cover (an eye) to prevent its use. **4** *chem* of a solid: to absorb (a gas) so that its atoms or molecules occupy the spaces within the lattice structure of the solid. **5** *tr & intr, meteorol* to form or cause to form an **occluded front**. ▪ **occlusion** *noun.* [16c: from Latin *occludere* to shut or close up]

occluded front *noun, meteorol* the final stage in an atmospheric depression, when a cold front catches up with and overtakes a warm front, lifting the warm air mass off the ground. Also called **occlusion**.

occult *adj* **1** involving, using or dealing with that which is magical, mystical or supernatural. **2** beyond ordinary understanding. **3** secret, hidden or esoteric. ▸ *noun* (**the occult**) the knowledge and study of magical, mystical or supernatural things. ▪ **occultism** *noun.* [16c: from Latin *occulere* to hide]

occupancy *noun* (**-ies**) **1** the act or condition of occupying (a house or flat, etc), or the fact of its being occupied. **2** the period of time during which a house, etc is occupied.

occupant *noun* someone who occupies, holds or resides in property, or in a particular position, etc.

occupation *noun* **1** a person's job or profession. **2** an activity that occupies a person's attention or free time, etc. **3** the act of occupying or state of being occupied: *the terrorists' occupation of the embassy.* **4** the act of taking and keeping control of a foreign country by military power. ▪ **occupational** *adj* related to or caused by a person's job. [16c: from Latin *occupatio* seizing]

occupational therapy *noun* a form of rehabilitation in which patients with physical or psychiatric illnesses participate in selected activities that will equip them to function independently in everyday life. ▪ **occupational therapist** *noun.*

occupy *verb* (**-ies, -ied**) **1** to have possession of or live in (a house, etc). **2** to be in or fill (time or space, etc). **3** to take possession of (a town, foreign country, etc) by force. **4** to enter and take possession of (a building, etc) often by force and without authority. **5** to hold (a post or office). ▪ **occupier** *noun* someone who lives in a building, either as a tenant or owner; an occupant. [14c: from Latin *occupare* to seize]

occur *verb* (**occurred, occurring**) *intr* **1** to happen or take place. **2** to be found or exist. **3** (**occur to sb**) to come into their mind, esp unexpectedly or by chance. [15c: from Latin *occurrere* to run towards, to befall]

occurrence *noun* **1** anything that occurs; an event. **2** the act or fact of occurring.

---

occurrence
This word is often misspelt. It has two *c*'s and two *r*'s. It might help you to remember the following sentence:
Crimson cats and red rabbits are rare occurrences.

---

ocean *noun* **1** the continuous expanse of salt water that covers about 70% of the Earth's surface. **2** any one of its five main divisions: the Atlantic, Indian, Pacific, Arctic and Antarctic. **3** the sea. **4** (*often* **oceans**) a very large number, amount or expanse. ▪ **oceanic** *adj.* [13c: from Latin *oceanus*]

oceanarium *noun* (**oceanariums** *or* **oceanaria**) *orig US* a large saltwater aquarium, or an enclosed part of the sea, in which sea creatures are kept for research purposes or for display to the public. [20c]

ocean-going *adj* of a ship, etc: suitable for sailing across oceans.

oceanic crust *noun, geog* that part of the Earth's crust that is normally beneath ocean.

oceanography *noun* the scientific study of the oceans. ▪ **oceanographer** *noun.* ▪ **oceanographic** *or* **oceanographical** *adj.*

ocelot /ˈɒsəlɒt, ˈoʊ-/ *noun* **1** a medium-sized wild cat, found in the forests of Central and S America, that has dark-yellow fur marked with spots and stripes. **2** its fur. [18c: from Nahuatl *ocelotl* jaguar]

och /ɒx/ *exclam, Scot & Irish* expressing surprise, impatience, disagreement, annoyance or regret, etc.

oche /ˈɒkɪ/ *noun, darts* the line, groove or ridge on the floor behind which a player must stand to throw. [20c: perhaps related to Anglo-Saxon *oche* to lop]

ochre /ˈoʊkə(r)/ *or* (*N Am*) **ocher** *noun* **1** a fine earth or clay used as a red, yellow or brown pigment. **2** a pale brownish-yellow colour. ▸ *adj* pale brownish-yellow in colour. [14c: from French *ocre*]

o'clock *adv* after a number from one to twelve: used in specifying the time, indicating the number of hours after midday or midnight: *three o'clock.* [18c: a contraction of *of the clock*]

OCR *abbrev, comput* optical character recognition, reader or reading.

Oct. *abbrev* October.

oct. *abbrev* octavo.

octad *noun* a group, series or set, etc of eight things. [19c: from Greek *oktas* a group of eight]

octagon *noun* a plane figure with eight straight sides and eight angles. ▪ **octagonal** *adj.* [16c: from Latin *octagonum*]

octahedron *or* **octohedron** /ɒktəˈhiːdrən/ *noun* (**octahedra** /-drə/ *or* **octahedrons**) a solid figure with eight plane faces. ▪ **octahedral** *adj.* [16c: from Greek *oktaedron*]

octal *adj* containing or having the number 8 as a basis. [1930s]

octane *noun, chem* a colourless liquid, belonging to the alkane series of hydrocarbons, which is present in petroleum.

octane number *or* **octane rating** *noun* a numerical system for classifying motor fuels according to their resistance to knocking.

octave /ˈɒktɪv, ˈɒkteɪv/ *noun* **1** *music* **a** the range of sound, or the series of notes, between the first and the eighth notes of a major or minor scale, eg from C to the C above; **b** a musical note that is an eighth above or below another. **2** *poetry* **a** a verse or stanza with eight lines; **b** the first eight lines of a sonnet. [14c: from Latin *octavus* eighth]

octavo *noun, printing, publishing* (abbrev **oct.**) **1** a size of page produced by folding a standard-sized sheet of paper three times to give eight leaves. **2** a book or page of this size. [16c: from Latin *in octavo* in an eighth (said of a sheet)]

octet *or* **octette** *noun* **1** any group of eight people or things. **2** *music* **a** a group of eight musicians or singers who perform together; **b** a piece of music written for eight instruments or voices. [19c: from Latin *octo* eight]

October *noun* (abbrev **Oct.**) the tenth month of the year. [Anglo-Saxon]

octogenarian *noun* someone who is 80 years old, or between 80 and 89 years old. ▸ *adj* **1** between 80 and 89 years old. **2** relating to an octogenarian or octogenarians. [19c: from Latin *octogenarius* relating to eighty]

octohedron see **octahedron**

octopus *noun* (**octopuses**) a marine mollusc with a soft rounded body, no external shell, and eight arms with suckers. [18c: Latin]

octuplet *noun* **1** *music* a group of eight notes to be played in the time of six. **2** one of eight children or animals born at one birth.

ocular *adj* relating to or in the region of the eye. [16c: from Latin *ocularis*]

oculist *noun* a specialist in diseases and defects of the eye; an optician or ophthalmologist.

OD[1] /oʊ'diː/ *slang, noun* (***ODs*** *or* ***OD's***) an overdose of drugs. ▸ *verb* (***OD's, OD'd, OD'ing***) *intr* to take a drug overdose. [20c: from *over*dose]

OD[2] *or* **O/D** *abbrev* **1** on demand. **2** overdrawn.

odalisque *or* **odalisk** /'oʊdəlɪsk/ *noun, hist* a female slave or concubine in a harem. [17c: French]

odd *adj* **1** left over when others are put into groups or pairs; remaining. **2** not matching: *odd socks.* **3** not one of a complete set. **4** *maths* of a whole number: not exactly divisible by two. **5** unusual; strange: *an odd face.* ▪ **oddly** *adv* **1** in an odd way or manner. **2** strangely; surprisingly: *Oddly, he refused to stay.* ▪ **oddness** *noun.* [14c: from Norse *oddi* point, triangle or odd number]

IDIOMS **odd man** *or* **odd one out** someone that is set apart or in some way different from others forming a particular group.

oddball *informal, noun* a strange or eccentric person. ▸ *adj* of a thing, a plan or circumstances, etc: eccentric; peculiar.

oddity *noun* (***-ies***) **1** a strange or odd person or thing. **2** an odd quality or characteristic; a peculiarity. **3** the state of being odd or unusual; strangeness.

odd job *noun* (*usu* **odd jobs**) casual or occasional pieces of work, often routine or domestic.

oddment *noun* something left over or remaining from a greater quantity: *oddments of fabric.*

odds *plural noun* **1** the chance or probability, expressed as a ratio, that something will or will not happen: *The odds are 10–1 against.* **2** the difference, expressed as a ratio, between the amount placed as a bet and the money which might be won: *offer odds of 2 to 1.* **3** an advantage that is thought to exist, esp in favour of one competitor over another: *The odds are in her favour.* **4** likelihood: *The odds are he'll be late again.* [16c, orig meaning 'unequal things']

IDIOMS **against all (the) odds** in spite of great difficulty or disadvantage. **at odds** in disagreement or dispute; on bad terms. **over the odds** more than is normal, required or expected, etc.

odds and ends *plural noun, informal* miscellaneous objects or pieces of things, etc, usu of little value or importance.

odds-on *adj* very likely to succeed, win or happen.

ode *noun* a lyric poem, usu a fairly long one, with lines of different lengths and complex rhythms, addressed to a particular person or thing. [16c: from Latin *oda*]

odious *adj* repulsive; extremely unpleasant or offensive. ▪ **odiously** *adv.* ▪ **odiousness** *noun.* [14c: from Latin *odiosus*]

odium *noun* hatred, strong dislike, or disapproval of a person or thing, esp when widespread. [17c: Latin]

odometer /ɒ'dɒmɪtə, oʊ'dɒmɪtə/ *noun, N Am* a device for measuring and displaying the distance travelled by a wheeled vehicle or a person, eg the milometer in a car. ▪ **odometry** *noun.* [18c: from French *odomètre*]

-odon *suffix, forming nouns, indicating* (in the names of animals) some characteristic of the teeth: *mastodon.* [From Greek *odon,* from *odous* tooth]

odontology *noun, anatomy* the study of the structure, development and diseases of the teeth. ▪ **odontologist** *noun.*

odoriferous *adj* with or giving off a smell, usu a sweet or pleasant smell. [15c: from Latin *odorifer*]

odour *or* (*N Am*) **odor** *noun* **1** a distinctive smell; scent. **2** a characteristic or quality. ▪ **odorous** *adj.* ▪ **odourless** *adj.* [13c: from French *odor*]

odyssey /'ɒdɪsɪ/ *noun* a long and adventurous journey or series of wanderings. [19c: from Greek *Odysseia*, the Greek epic poem, the *Odyssey,* attributed to Homer, that describes the adventures and wanderings of Odysseus (Ulysses)]

oecumenic *or* **oecumenical** see **ecumenical**

oedema *or* **edema** /ɪ'diːmə/ *noun* (***oedemata*** /-mətə/ *or* ***oedemas***) *pathol* **1** an abnormal accumulation of fluid within body tissues or body cavities, causing swelling. **2** *botany* an abnormal swelling in a plant caused by an accumulation of water in the tissues. ▪ **oedematous** *adj.* [15c: Latin, from Greek *oidein* to swell]

Oedipus complex /'iːdɪpəs/ *noun, psychoanal* a repressed sexual desire of a son for his mother. ▪ **Oedipal** *or* **oedipal** *adj.* [20c: from Greek *Oidipous,* the name of a legendary king of Thebes, who unwittingly killed his father and married his mother]

oenology /iː'nɒlədʒɪ/ *noun* the study or knowledge of wine. ▪ **oenological** *adj.* ▪ **oenologist** *noun.* [19c: from Greek *oinos* wine]

o'er *prep, adv, poetic or old use* short form of **over.**

oesophagus /ɪː'sɒfəgəs/ *or* (*esp N Am*) **esophagus** *noun* (***oesophagi*** /-gaɪ, -dʒaɪ/) *anatomy* a narrow muscular tube through which food passes from the mouth to the stomach. ▪ **oesophageal** /-fə'dʒɪəl/ *adj.* [14c: Latin]

oestrogen /'iːstrədʒən/ *or* (*N Am*) **estrogen** *noun, biochem* a hormone, produced mainly by the ovaries, that controls the growth and functioning of the female sex organs, and that regulates the menstrual cycle. ▪ **oestrogenic** *adj.* [20c: from **oestrus**]

oestrus /'iːstrəs/ *or* (*N Am*) **estrus** *noun, zool, physiol* a regularly occurring period of sexual receptivity that occurs in most female mammals apart from humans. ▪ **oestrous** *adj.* [19c: from Greek *oistros* a gadfly noted for its frenzy]

of *prep* **1** used to show origin, cause or authorship: *people of Glasgow* • *die of hunger.* **2** belonging to or connected with something or someone. **3** used to specify a component, ingredient or characteristic, etc: *built of bricks* • *a heart of gold.* **4** at a given distance or amount of time from something: *within a minute of arriving.* **5** about; concerning: *tales of Rome.* **6** belonging to or forming a part of something: *most of the story.* **7** existing or happening, etc, at, on, in or during something: *Battle of Hastings.* **8** used with words denoting loss, removal or separation, etc: *cured of cancer.* **9** used to show the connection between a verbal noun and the person or thing that is performing, or that is the object of, the action stated: *the eating of healthy food.* **10** aged: *a boy of twelve.* **11** *N Am, esp US* in giving the time: to; before a stated hour: *a quarter of one.* [Anglo-Saxon]

off *adv* **1** away; at or to a distance. **2** in or into a position which is not attached; separate: *The handle came off.* **3** in or into a state of no longer working or operating; not on: *Turn the radio off.* **4** in or into a state of being stopped or cancelled: *The match was rained off.* **5** in or into a state of sleep: *nodded off.* **6**

to the end, so as to be completely finished: *Finish the work off.* **7** away from work or one's duties: *Take an hour off.* **8** situated as regards money: *well off* • *badly off.* ▸ *adj* **1** of an electrical device: not functioning or operating; disconnected; not on: *The radio was off.* **2** cancelled; not taking place: *The meeting's off.* **3** not good; not up to standard: *an off day.* **4** *cricket* on the side of the field towards which the batsman's feet are pointing, usu the bowler's left. Opposite of **on** (*adj* sense 6). **5** in a restaurant, on a menu, etc: no longer available as a choice: *Peas are off.* **6** esp of food or drink: in a state of decay; gone bad or sour: *The milk was off.* ▸ *prep* **1** from or away from something: *Lift it off the shelf.* **2** removed from or no longer attached to something. **3** opening out of, leading from, or not far from something: *a side street off the main road.* **4** not wanting or no longer attracted by something: *off one's food.* **5** no longer using something, etc: *be off the tablets.* ▸ *noun* **1** (*usu* **the off**) the start, eg of a race or journey: *ready for the off.* **2** *cricket* the side of a field towards which the batsman's feet are pointing, usu the bowler's left. [Anglo-Saxon *of* away]

offal *noun* the heart, brains, liver and kidneys, etc of an animal, used as food. [14c: from *of* off + *fal* fall]

offbeat *adj, informal* unusual; unconventional; eccentric.

off-break *or* **off-spin** *noun, cricket* a ball bowled so as to deviate inwards from the offside spin with which it is bowled.

off-centre *adj* not quite central.

off chance see **on the off chance** at **chance**

off-colour *adj* **1** *Brit* slightly unwell; not in good health. **2** *chiefly N Am* (**off-color**) of humour: rude; smutty.

offcut *noun* a small piece of eg wood or cloth, etc cut off or left over from a larger quantity, esp when making or shaping something.

offence *or* (*chiefly US*) **offense** *noun* **1 a** the breaking of a rule or law, etc; **b** a crime. **2** any cause of anger, annoyance or displeasure. **3** displeasure, annoyance or resentment: *I mean no offence.*

IDIOMS **give offence** to cause displeasure or annoyance. **take offence at sth** to be offended by it.

offend *verb* **1** to make (someone) feel hurt or angry; to insult (them). **2** to be unpleasant or annoying to (someone). **3** *intr* (*usu* **offend against sb** *or* **sth**) to commit a sin or crime against them. ▪ **offender** *noun*. ▪ **offending** *adj*. [14c: from Latin *offendere*]

offensive *adj* **1** giving or likely to give offence; insulting. **2** unpleasant and repulsive, esp to the senses: *an offensive smell.* **3** *sport, military, etc* used for attacking: *offensive weapons.* ▸ *noun* **1** an aggressive action or attitude: *go on the offensive.* **2** an attack. ▪ **offensively** *adv*. ▪ **offensiveness** *noun*. [16c]

offer *verb* **1** to put forward (a gift, payment or suggestion, etc) for acceptance, refusal or consideration. **2** *formal* to provide: *a site offering the best view.* **3** *intr* to state one's willingness (to do something). **4** to present (something) for sale. **5** to provide (an opportunity) (for something): *a job offering rapid promotion.* **6** *intr* to present itself; to occur: *if opportunity offers.* **7** *tr & intr* to propose (a sum of money) as payment (to someone): *offer him £250 for the car.* **8** to present (a prayer or sacrifice) (to God). ▸ *noun* **1** an act of offering. **2** something that is offered, esp an amount of money offered to buy something. [Anglo-Saxon *offrian*]

IDIOMS **on offer** for sale, esp at a reduced price. **under offer** of a property, etc for sale: for which a possible buyer has made an offer, but with the contracts still to be signed.

offering *noun* **1** the act of making an offer. **2** anything offered, esp a gift. **3** a gift of money given to a church, usu during a religious service, used for charity, etc. **4** a sacrifice made to God, a saint or a deity, etc in the course of worship.

offertory *noun* (**-ies**) *Christianity* **1** the offering of bread and wine to God during a Eucharist. **2** an anthem or hymn sung while this is happening. **3** money collected during a church service. [14c: from Latin *offertorium* place of offering]

offhand *or* **offhanded** *adj* casual or careless, often with the result of being rude: *an offhand manner.* ▸ *adv* impromptu: *I can't remember his name offhand.* ▪ **offhandedness** *noun*.

office *noun* **1** the room, set of rooms or building in which the business of a firm is done, or in which a particular kind of business, clerical work, etc is done. **2** a local centre or department of a large business. **3** a position of authority, esp in the government or in public service: *run for office.* **4 a** the length of time for which an official position is held; **b** of a political party: the length of time for which it forms the government: *hold office.* **5** (**Office**) a government department: *the Home Office.* **6** the group of people working in an office. **7** a function or duty. **8** (*usu* **offices**) an act of kindness or service: *through her good offices.* **9** (*often* **Office**) an authorized form of Christian worship or service, esp one for the dead. [13c: from Latin *officium* favour, duty or service]

office-bearer *or* **office-holder** *noun* someone who holds office; someone with an official duty in a society or a church organization, etc.

office boy *or* **office girl** *noun* a young person employed to do minor jobs in an office.

officer *noun* **1** someone in a position of authority and responsibility in the armed forces. **2** someone with an official position in an organization, society or government department. **3** a policeman or policewoman.

official *adj* **1** relating or belonging to an office or position of authority. **2** given or authorized by a person in authority: *an official report.* **3** formal; suitable for or characteristic of a person holding office: *official dinners.* ▪ **officially** *adv*.

officialdom *noun* **1** officials and bureaucrats as a group. **2** excessive devotion to official routine and detail.

officialese *noun* unclear, wordy and pompous language or jargon, thought to be typical of officials or official letters and documents, etc.

official receiver see under **receiver**

officiate *verb, intr* **1 a** to act in an official capacity; **b** to perform official duties, esp at a particular function. **2** to conduct a religious service. ▪ **officiation** *noun*. ▪ **officiator** *noun*. [17c: from Latin *officiare* to serve]

officious *adj* too ready to offer help or advice, etc, esp when it is not wanted. ▪ **officiousness** *noun*. [16c: from Latin *officiosus* obliging or dutiful]

offing *noun, naut* the more distant part of the sea that is visible from the shore.

IDIOMS **in the offing** not far off; likely to happen soon.

off-key *adj, adv* **1** *music* **a** in the wrong key; **b** out of tune. **2** *informal* not quite suitable.

off-licence *noun, Brit* a shop, or a counter in a pub or hotel, that is licensed to sell alcohol to be drunk elsewhere. Compare **on-licence**.

off-limits *adj, esp military* not to be entered; out of bounds. ▸ *adv* (**off limits**) in or into an area that is out of bounds.

offline *adj, comput* of a peripheral device, eg a printer: **1** not connected to the central processing unit, and therefore not controlled by it. **2** not connected; switched off. *as adv*: *went offline at 2 o'clock*. Compare **online**.

offload *verb* **1** *tr & intr* to unload. **2** to get rid of (something, esp something unpleasant or unwanted), etc by passing it on to someone else.

off-peak *adj* of services, eg electricity, etc: used at a time when there is little demand, and therefore usu cheaper: *off-peak travel*.

off-piste *adj* relating to skiing on new unused snow, away from or off the regular runs.

off-putting *adj, informal* **1** disconcerting; distracting. **2** unpleasant; repulsive.

off-road *adj* **1** of vehicle use: not on public roads; esp on rough ground or terrain. **2** of a car, bike or other vehicle: suitable for such use. ▪ **off-roader** *noun*.

off-season *noun* the less popular and less busy period in a particular business or for a particular activity.

offset *noun* /ˈɒfsɛt/ **1** a start; the outset. **2** a side-shoot on a plant, used for developing new plants. **3** *printing* a process in which an image is inked on to a rubber roller which then transfers it to paper, etc. ▸ *verb* /ɒfˈsɛt/ (***-set***, ***-setting***) **1** to counterbalance or compensate for (something): *price rises offset by tax cuts*. **2** to print (something) using an offset process.

offshoot *noun* **1** a shoot growing from a plant's main stem. **2** anything which is a branch of, or has developed or derived from, something else.

offshore *adv, adj* **1** situated in, at, or on the sea, not far from the coast: *offshore industries*. **2** of the wind: blowing away from the coast. Compare **inshore**.

offside *adj, adv, football, rugby, etc* in an illegal position between the ball and the opponents' goal. Compare **onside**. ▸ *noun* the side of a vehicle or horse nearest the centre of the road, in the UK the right side.

off-site *adj, adv* working, happening, etc away from a working site.

off-spin see **off-break**

offspring *noun* (*pl* ***offspring***) **1** a person's child or children. **2** the young of an animal. **3** a result or outcome. [Anglo-Saxon *ofspring*]

off-stage *adj, adv, theatre* not on the stage and so unable to be seen by the audience.

off-the-peg *adj* of clothing: ready to wear.

off-the-shelf *adj* **1** immediately available. **2** ready to use.

off-the-wall *adj, slang* of humour, etc: unorthodox; outlandish.

often *adv* **1** many times; frequently. **2** in many cases. [14c: variant of Anglo-Saxon *ofte*]

IDIOMS **every so often** sometimes.

ogle *verb* **1** to look at or eye (someone) in an amorous or lecherous way. **2** to stare or gape at (something). [17c: perhaps from German *oegeln*]

ogre *or* **ogress** *noun* **1** in fairy stories: a frightening, cruel, ugly giant. **2** a cruel, frightening or ugly person. ▪ **ogreish** *or* **ogrish** *adj*. [18c: French]

oh *exclam* expressing surprise, admiration, pleasure, anger or fear, etc.

ohm *noun* the SI unit of electrical resistance. [19c: named after Georg Simon Ohm, German physicist]

ohmmeter *noun* a device for measuring electrical resistance.

OHMS *abbrev, Brit* On Her (or His) Majesty's Service, often written on mail from government departments.

-oid *suffix, forming nouns and adjectives, signifying* something similar to or with the form of the specified thing: *humanoid* • *factoid* • *rhomboid*. ▪ **-oidal** *suffix, forming adjectives*. [From Greek *eidos* shape]

oik *noun, Brit informal* someone thought of as inferior, esp because of being rude, badly educated or lower class.

oil *noun* **1** any greasy, viscous and usu flammable substance, insoluble in water but soluble in organic compounds, that is derived from animals, plants or mineral deposits, or manufactured artificially, and used as a fuel, lubricant or food. **2 petroleum**. **3 a** (*often* **oils**) **oil paint**; **b** an oil painting. ▸ *verb* to apply oil to (something); to lubricate or treat (something) with oil. [12c: from French *oile*]

IDIOMS **burn the midnight oil** to work or study late into the night. **pour oil on troubled waters** to soothe or calm a person or situation.

oil can *noun* a can for carrying or applying oil.

oilcloth *noun* cloth, often cotton, treated with oil to make it waterproof; oilskin.

oil drum *noun* a cylindrical metal barrel for oil.

oilfield *noun* an area of land or seabed that contains reserves of petroleum, esp one that is already being exploited.

oil-fired *adj* of central heating, etc: using oil as a fuel.

oil paint *noun* paint made by mixing ground pigment with oil, often linseed oil.

oil painting *noun* **1** a picture painted with oil paints. **2** the activity or art of painting in oils.

IDIOMS **no oil painting** *informal* of a person: not very attractive.

oil rig *noun* the complete installation required for drilling oil wells, including the equipment and machinery, etc that it supports.

oilseed rape *noun* a plant with vivid yellow flowers, the seed of which contains large amounts of oil and is used in margarine, cooking oils and some lubricating oils. Often shortened to **rape**.

oilskin *noun* **1** cloth treated with oil to make it waterproof. **2** (*often* **oilskins**) an outer garment made of oilskin.

oil slick *noun* a wide layer of spilled oil floating on the surface of water, often as a result of damage to or discharge from an oil tanker or pipelines, etc.

oil well *noun* a well, usu a vertical one, bored in the ground or seabed to extract mineral oil from underground deposits.

oily *adj* (***-ier***, ***-iest***) **1 a** like oil; greasy; **b** containing or consisting of oil. **2** soaked in or covered with oil. **3**

derog of a person or behaviour, etc: smooth; unctuous; servile and flattering. ▪ **oiliness** *noun*.

oink *noun* a representation of the characteristic grunting noise made by a pig. [20c]

ointment *noun* any greasy or oily semi-solid preparation, usu medicated, that can be applied externally to the skin in order to heal, soothe or protect it. [14c: from French *oignement*]

OK *or* **okay** *informal, adj* all correct; all right; satisfactory: *an okay song*. ▸ *adv* well; satisfactorily. ▸ *exclam* expressing agreement or approval; yes; certainly: *OK! I'll do it!* ▸ *noun* (***OKs, OK's*** *or* ***okays***) approval, sanction or agreement. ▸ *verb* (***OK'd*** *or* ***OK'ed, Ok'ing***; ***okayed, okaying***) to approve or pass (something) as satisfactory. [19c: prob from oll korrect, a facetious spelling of *all correct*]

okapi /oʊˈkɑːpɪ/ *noun* (***okapis*** *or* ***okapi***) a ruminant animal related to the giraffe, but with a shorter neck, and which has a reddish- or blackish-brown coat, with thick irregular horizontal black and white stripes on the hindquarters and upper parts of the legs. [20c: the native name]

okey-doke *or* **okey-dokey** *adv, adj, exclam, informal* OK; fine.

okra *noun* **1** a tall plant that has red and yellow flowers. **2** the edible fruit of this plant, consisting of long green seed pods, used in soups and stews, etc. Also called **gumbo**, **lady's finger**. [18c: from a W African name]

-ol *suffix, forming nouns, denoting* **1 a** substances that are alcohols or compounds analogous to alcohol; **b** substances derived from or related to **phenol**. **2** oils and oil-based substances.

old *adj* (***older*** *or* ***elder, oldest*** *or* ***eldest***) **1** advanced in age; that has existed for a long time; not young. **2** having a stated age: *five years old*. **3** belonging or relating to the end period of a long life or existence: *old age*. **4** worn out or shabby through long use: *old shoes*. **5** no longer in use; out of date; old-fashioned. **6** belonging to the past. **7** former or previous; earliest of two or more things: *went back to see their old house*. **8** of long standing or long existence: *an old member of the society*. **9** with the characteristics, eg experience, maturity or appearance, of age: *be old beyond one's years*. **10** (**Old**) of a language: relating to or denoting its earliest form: *Old English*. **11** *informal, jocular* used in expressions of familiar affection or contempt, etc: *silly old fool*. ▸ *noun* an earlier time: *men of old*. [Anglo-Saxon *eald*]

---

older, elder, oldest, eldest
See the Usage Notes at **elder**[1] and **eldest**.

---

old age *noun* the later part of life.

old age pension *noun* a retirement pension. ▪ **old age pensioner** *noun* (abbrev **OAP**).

old boy *noun* **1** *Brit* a former male pupil of a school. **2** *informal* an elderly man. **3** *informal* an affectionate or familiar form of address to a man.

old country *noun* an immigrant's country of origin.

olden *adj, archaic* former; past: *in olden days*.

Old English see under **Anglo-Saxon**

old-fashioned *adj* **1** belonging to, or in a style common to, some time ago; out of date. **2** of a person: in favour of, or living and acting according to, the habits and moral views of the past.

old flame *noun, informal* a former boyfriend or girlfriend.

old girl *noun* **1** *Brit* a former female pupil of a school. **2** *informal* an elderly woman. **3** *informal* an affectionate or familiar form of address to a girl or woman.

old guard *noun* the original or most conservative members of a society, group or organization.

old hand *noun, informal* **1** an experienced person; an expert. **2** an ex-convict.

old hat *adj, informal* tediously familiar or well known.

oldie *noun, informal* an old person, song or film.

old lady *noun, slang* a person's wife or mother.

old maid *noun, derog, informal* **1** a woman who is not married and is probably unlikely ever to marry; a spinster. **2** a woman or man who is prim and fussy.

old man *noun* **1** *slang* someone's husband or father. **2** *informal* an affectionate form of address for a man or boy, usu only said by a man addressing another man.

old master *noun, art* **1** any of the great European painters from the period stretching from the Renaissance to about 1800. **2** a painting by one of these painters.

Old Nick *noun, informal* the devil.

Old Norse *noun* the old N Germanic language from around 700 to 1350 from which the Scandinavian languages are derived.

old school *noun* a group of people or section of society with traditional or old-fashioned ways of thinking, ideas or beliefs, etc. *as adj* (**old-school**): *old-school attitudes*.

old school tie *noun* **1** a tie with a characteristic pattern or colour worn by former members of a public school. **2** the system by which former members of the same public school do favours for each other.

Old Testament *noun* the first part of the Christian Bible, containing the Hebrew scriptures.

old-time *adj* belonging to or typical of the past; old-fashioned.

old-timer *noun, informal* **1** someone who has been in a job, position or profession, etc, for a long time; a veteran. **2** *US* esp as a form of address: an old man.

old wives' tale *noun* an old belief, superstition or theory considered foolish and unscientific.

old woman *noun, slang* **1** someone's wife or mother. **2** *derog* a person, esp a man, who is timid or fussy.

old-world *adj* belonging to earlier times, esp in being considered quaint or charming: *old-world charm*.

oleaginous /oʊlɪˈadʒɪnəs/ *adj* **1** like or containing oil; oily. **2** producing oil. **3** unctuous; obsequious. [17c: from Latin *oleaginus*]

olfactory *adj* relating to the sense of smell. [17c: from Latin *olfacere* to smell]

oligarchy /ˈɒlɪgɑːkɪ/ *noun* (***-ies***) **1** government by a small group of people. **2** a state or organization governed by a small group of people. **3** a small group of people which forms a government. ▪ **oligarch** *noun*. ▪ **oligarchic** *or* **oligarchical** *adj*. [15c: from Greek *oligarkhia*]

Oligocene /ˈɒlɪgəʊsiːn/ *geol, noun* the third epoch of the Tertiary period. ▸ *adj* relating to this epoch or rocks formed during it. [19c]

oligopoly *noun* (*-ies*) *econ* a situation in which there are few sellers of a particular product or service, and a small number of competitive firms control the market. See also **monopoly**. [19c: from Greek *oligos* little or few, modelled on **monopoly**]

olive *noun* **1** a small evergreen tree cultivated mainly in the Mediterranean region for its fruit and the oil obtained from the fruit. **2** the small green or black oval edible fruit of this tree. **3** the wood of this tree, used to make furniture. **4** (*also* **olive green**) a dull yellowish-green colour like that of unripe olives. ▶ *adj* **1** (*also* **olive-green**) dull yellowish-green in colour. **2** of a complexion: sallow. [13c: French]

olive branch *noun* a sign or gesture that indicates a wish for peace or reconciliation.

olive oil *noun* the pale-yellow oil obtained by pressing ripe olives, used as a cooking and salad oil, and also in soaps, ointments and lubricants.

olivine *noun, geol* any of a group of hard glassy rock-forming silicate minerals, typically olive-green. [18c]

oloroso /ɒlə'rəʊsəʊ/ *noun* a golden-coloured sweet sherry. [19c: Spanish, meaning 'fragrant']

Olympiad *noun* **1** a celebration of the modern Olympic Games. **2** a regular international contest, esp in chess or bridge. [14c]

Olympian *noun* **1** someone who competes in the Olympic Games. **2** *Greek myth* any of the twelve ancient Greek gods thought to live on Mount Olympus in N Greece. ▶ *adj* **1** *Greek myth* relating or belonging to Mount Olympus or to the ancient Greek gods thought to live there. **2** relating or belonging to ancient Olympia, or its inhabitants. **3** godlike, esp in being superior or condescending. [17c: from Greek *Olympios*]

Olympic *adj* **1** relating to the Olympic Games. **2** relating to ancient Olympia. [17c: from Greek *Olympikos*]

Olympic Games *singular or plural noun* **1** *hist* games celebrated every four years at Olympia in Greece, that included athletic, musical and literary competitions. **2** (*also* **the Olympics**) a modern international sports competition held every four years.

Om *or* **Aum** *noun, Hinduism* a sacred syllable intoned as part of Hindu devotion and contemplation.

-oma *suffix* (*-omas or -omata*) *forming nouns, denoting* a tumour or abnormal growth, etc: *carcinoma*. [Greek]

ombudsman *noun* an official appointed to investigate complaints against public authorities, government departments or the people who work for them. [20c: Swedish, meaning 'legal representative' or 'commissioner']

-ome *suffix, forming nouns, denoting* a mass: *rhizome • biome*. [Variant of **-oma**]

omega /'əʊmɪɡə; *US* əʊ'miːɡə/ *noun* **1** the 24th and last letter of the Greek alphabet, pronounced as a long open o. **2** the last of a series; a conclusion. [16c: from Greek *o mega*, literally 'great O']

omelette *or* (*N Am, esp US*) **omelet** *noun, cookery* a dish made of beaten eggs fried in a pan, often with a savoury filling. [17c: French, from *amelette* altered]

omen *noun* **1** a circumstance, phenomenon, etc that is regarded as a sign of a future event, either good or evil. **2** threatening or prophetic character: *bird of ill omen*. [16c: Latin]

omicron /oʊ'maɪkrɒn/ *noun* the 15th letter of the Greek alphabet. [17c: from Greek *o mikron*, literally 'little O']

ominous *adj* threatening; containing a warning of something evil or bad. ▪ **ominously** *adv*. [16c: from Latin *ominosus*]

omission *noun* **1** something that has been left out or neglected. **2** the act of leaving something out or neglecting it. [14c: from Latin *omissio*]

omit *verb* (***omitted, omitting***) **1** to leave (something) out, either by mistake or on purpose. **2** to fail to do (something). [15c: from Latin *omittere*]

omnibus *noun* **1** *old use or formal* a **bus**. **2** (*also* **omnibus book** *or* **omnibus volume**) a book that contains reprints of a number of works by a single author, or several works on the same subject or of a similar type. **3** a TV or radio programme made up of or edited from the preceding week's editions of a particular serial. [19c: Latin, meaning 'for all']

omnipotent /ɒm'nɪpətənt/ *adj* **1** of God or a deity: all-powerful; with infinite power. **2** with very great power or influence. ▪ **omnipotence** *noun*. [14c: from Latin *omnis* all + *potens* able or powerful]

omnipresent *adj* esp of a god: present everywhere at the same time. ▪ **omnipresence** *noun*. [17c]

omniscient /ɒm'nɪsɪənt/ *adj* **1** esp of God: with infinite knowledge or understanding. **2** with very great knowledge; knowing everything. ▪ **omniscience** /-sɪəns/ *noun*. [17c: from Latin *omnis* all + *sciens* knowing]

omnivore *noun* a person or animal that eats any type of food.

omnivorous *adj* **1** eating any type of food, esp both meat and vegetable matter. **2** taking in, reading or using, etc everything. [17c: from Latin *omnivorus*]

on *prep* **1** touching, supported by, attached to, covering, or enclosing: *a chair on the floor: a dog on a lead*. **2** in or into (a vehicle, etc): *got on the bus*. **3** *informal* carried with (a person): *I've got no money on me*. **4** very near to or along the side of something: *a house on the shore*. **5** at or during (a certain day or time, etc): *on Monday*. **6** immediately after, at or before: *He found the letter on his return*. **7** within the (given) limits of something: *a picture on page nine*. **8** about: *a book on Jane Austen*. **9** through contact with or as a result of something: *cut himself on the broken bottle*. **10** in the state or process of something: *on fire • on a journey*. **11** using as a means of transport: *goes to work on the bus*. **12** using as a means or medium: *talk on the telephone*. **13** having as a basis or source: *on good authority*. **14** working for or being a member of something: *on the committee • work on the case*. **15** at the expense of or to the disadvantage of something or someone: *treatment on the National Health • drinks on me*. **16** supported by something: *live on bread and cheese*. **17** regularly taking or using something: *on tranquillizers*. **18** staked as a bet: *put money on a horse*. ▶ *adv* **1** esp of clothes: in or into contact or a state of enclosing, covering, or being worn, etc: *have no clothes on*. **2** ahead, forwards or towards in space or time: *later on*. **3** continuously; without interruption: *keep on about something*. **4** in or into operation or activity: *put the radio on*. ▶ *adj* **1** working, broadcasting or performing: *You're on in two minutes*. **2** taking place: *Which films are on this week?* **3** *informal* possible, practicable or acceptable: *That just isn't on*. **4**

informal talking continuously, esp to complain or nag: *always on at him to try harder.* **5** in favour of a win: *odds of 3 to 4 on.* **6** *cricket* on the side of the field towards which the bat is facing, usu the batsman's left and the bowler's right. Opposite of **off** (*adj* sense 4). [Anglo-Saxon]

IDIOMS **be on to sb** *or* **sth** *informal* **1** to realize their or its importance or intentions. **2** to be in touch with them: *We'll be on to you about the party.* **get on to sb** *informal* to get in touch with them. **on and off** now and then; occasionally. **on and on** continually; at length. **on time** promptly; at the right time.

-on *combining form, denoting* **1** *physics* an elementary particle: *neutron.* **2** *chem* a molecular unit: *codon.*

onager *noun* a variety of wild ass found in central Asia. [14c: from Greek *onagros*]

ONC *abbrev* Ordinary National Certificate.

once *adv* **1 a** a single time: *I'll say this only once;* **b** on one occasion: *They came once.* **2** multiplied by one. **3** at some time in the past; formerly: *lived in London once.* **4** by one degree of relationship: *a cousin once removed.* ▸ *conj* as soon as; when once or if once: *Once you have finished you can go out.* ▸ *noun* one time or occasion: *just this once.* [Anglo-Saxon *anes*, orig meaning 'of one', from *an* one]

IDIOMS **all at once 1** suddenly. **2** all at the same time; simultaneously. **at once 1** immediately; without any delay. **2** all at the same time; simultaneously. **for once** on this one occasion if on no other; as an exception. **once again** *or* **once more** one more time, as before. **once (and) for all** for the last time; now and never again. **once in a while** occasionally; rarely. **once or twice** a few times. **once upon a time** the usual way to begin fairy tales: at an unspecified time in the past.

once-over *noun, informal* **1** a quick, often casual, examination or appraisal: *give the car the once-over.* **2** a violent beating.

oncogene *noun, genetics* a gene that causes a normal cell to develop into a cancerous cell, or to multiply in an uncontrolled manner. [20c]

oncology *noun* the branch of medicine that deals with the study of tumours, esp cancerous ones. ▪ **oncologist** *noun.* [19c]

oncoming *adj* approaching; advancing.

OND *abbrev* Ordinary National Diploma.

one *noun* **1 a** the cardinal number 1; **b** the quantity that this represents, being a single unit. **2** a unity or unit. **3** any symbol for this, eg *1* or *I*. **4** the age of one. **5** the first hour after midnight or midday: *Come at one o'clock • 1pm.* **6** a score of one point. ▸ *adj* **1** being a single unit, number or thing. **2** being a particular person or thing, esp as distinct from another or others of the same kind: *lift one leg and then the other.* **3** being a particular but unspecified instance or example: *visit him one day soon.* **4** being the only such: *the one woman who can beat her.* **5** same; identical: *of one mind.* **6** undivided; forming a single whole: *They sang with one voice.* **7** first: *page one.* **8** *informal* an exceptional example or instance of something: *That was one big fellow.* **9** totalling one. **10** aged one. ▸ *pron* **1** (often referring to a noun already mentioned or implied) an individual person, thing or instance: *buy the blue one.* **2** anybody: *One can't do better than that.* **3** *formal or facetious* I; me: *One doesn't like to pry.* [Anglo-Saxon *an*]

IDIOMS **at one with sb** *or* **sth 1** in complete agreement with them or it. **2** in harmony with them. **for one** as one person: *I for one don't agree.* **one and all** everyone without exception. **one and only** used for emphasis: only. **one another** used as the object of a verb or preposition when an action takes place between two (or more than two) people, etc: *Chris and Pat love one another.* **one by one** one after the other. **one or two** *informal* a few.

one-armed bandit *noun* a fruit machine with a long handle at the side which is pulled down hard to make the machine work. [20c]

one-horse *adj* **1** using a single horse. **2** *informal* small, poor and of little importance: *a one-horse town.*

one-horse race *noun* a race or competition, etc in which one particular competitor or participant is certain to win.

one-liner *noun, informal* a short amusing remark or joke made in a single sentence. [20c]

one-man, **one-woman** *or* **one-person** *adj* consisting of, for or done by one person: *a one-person tent.*

oneness *noun* **1** the state or quality of being one; singleness. **2** agreement. **3** the state of being the same. **4** the state of being unique.

one-off *informal, chiefly Brit, adj* made or happening, etc on one occasion only. ▸ *noun* something that is one-off.

one-on-one see **one-to-one**

one-parent family *noun* a family that consists of a child or children and one parent, the other parent being dead or estranged.

one-person see **one-man**

one-piece *adj* of a garment, esp a swimsuit: made as a single piece. ▸ *noun* a garment, esp a swimsuit, made in such a way. Compare **bikini**.

onerous /ˈoʊnərəs, ˈɒnərəs/ *adj* heavy; difficult to do or bear; oppressive. [14c: from Latin *onerosus*]

oneself *or* **one's self** *pron* **1** the reflexive form of **one** (*pronoun*): *not able to help oneself.* **2** the emphatic form of **one** (*pronoun*): *One hasn't been there oneself.* **3** one's normal self: *not feeling oneself after an operation.*

one-sided *adj* **1** of a competition, etc: with one person or side having a great advantage over the other. **2** seeing, accepting, representing or favouring only one side of a subject or argument, etc; unfair; partial. **3** occurring on or limited to one side only.

one-time *adj* former; past: *one-time lover.*

one-to-one *adj* **1** with one person or thing exactly corresponding to or matching another. **2** in which a person is involved with only one other person: *one-to-one teaching. N Am equivalent* **one-on-one**.

one-track *adj* **1** with only a single track. **2** *informal* of a person's mind: **a** incapable of dealing with more than one subject or activity, etc at a time; **b** obsessed with one idea.

one-two *noun, informal* **1** *boxing* the delivery of a blow with one fist quickly followed by a blow with the other. **2** *football, hockey, etc* a move in which one player passes the ball to another then runs forward to receive the ball as it is immediately passed back again.

one-up *adj, informal* with a particular advantage over someone else.

one-upmanship *noun, informal* the art of gaining psychological, social or professional advantages over other people.

one-way *adj* **1 a** of a road or street, etc: on which traffic is allowed to move in one direction only; **b** relating to or indicating such a traffic system: *one-way sign.* **2** of a feeling or relationship: not reciprocated. **3** *N Am, esp US* of a ticket: valid for travel in one direction only.

one-woman see **one-man**

ongoing *adj* in progress; going on.

onion *noun* **1** a plant belonging to the lily family. **2** the edible bulb of this plant, which consists of white fleshy scales and a pungent oil, surrounded by a brown papery outer layer, and is eaten raw, cooked or pickled. ▪ **oniony** *adj.* [14c: from French *oignon*]
IDIOMS **know one's onions** *informal* to know one's subject or job well.

on-licence *noun* a licence to sell alcoholic drink for consumption on the premises. Compare **off-licence**.

online *adj* **1** *comput* of a peripheral device, eg a printer: connected to and controlled by the central processor of a computer. **2** of a service, etc: run with a direct connection to and interaction with a computer: *online shopping. as adv*: *The telephone banking service went online last year.* Compare **offline**.

onlooker *noun* someone who watches and does not take part; an observer. ▪ **onlooking** *adj.*

only *adj* **1** without any others of the same type. **2** of a person: having no brothers or sisters. **3** *informal* best: *Flying is the only way to travel.* ▸ *adv* **1** not more than; just. **2** alone; solely. **3** not longer ago than; not until: *only a minute ago.* **4** merely; with no other result than: *I arrived only to find he had already left.* ▸ *conj* **1** but; however: *Come if you want to, only don't complain if you're bored.* **2** if it were not for the fact that: *I'd come too, only I know I'd slow you down.* [Anglo-Saxon *anlic*]
IDIOMS **if only** I wish. **only too** very; extremely: *only too ready to help.*

o.n.o. *abbrev* or near offer; or nearest offer.

on-off *adj* of a switch: able to be set to one of only two positions, either 'on' or 'off'.

onomatopoeia /ɒnəmatə'pɪə/ *noun* the formation of words whose sounds imitate the sound or action they represent, eg *hiss, squelch.* ▪ **onomatopoeic** *adj.* [16c: from Greek *onomatopoios*]

onrush *noun* a sudden and strong movement forward.

onscreen *adj,* ▸ *adv* relating to information that is displayed on a TV screen or VDU.

onset *noun* **1** an attack; an assault. **2** a beginning, esp of something unpleasant.

onshore *adv* /ɒn'ʃɔː(r)/ towards, on, or on to the shore. ▸ *adj* /'ɒnʃɔː(r)/ found or occurring on the shore or land.

onside *adj, adv, football, rugby, etc* of a player: in a position where the ball may legally be played; not offside. Also written **on-side**. Compare **offside**.

onslaught *noun* a fierce attack; an onset. [17c: from Dutch *aenslag*]

onto *prep* on to.
IDIOMS **be onto sb** to be suspicious or aware of their (usu underhand) actions.

ontology *noun, philos* the branch of metaphysics that deals with the nature and essence of things or of existence. ▪ **ontologic** *or* **ontological** *adj.* ▪ **ontologically** *adv.* [18c]

onus /'oʊnəs/ *noun* a responsibility or burden: *The onus is on you to prove it.* [17c: Latin, meaning 'burden']

onward *adj* moving forward in place or time; advancing. ▸ *adv* (*also* **onwards**) **1** towards or at a place or time which is advanced or in front; ahead. **2** continuing to move forwards or progress.

onyx *noun, geol* a very hard variety of agate with straight alternating bands of one or more colours, used as a gemstone. [13c: Latin]

oocyte /'oʊəsaɪt/ *noun, biol* a cell that gives rise to an ovum by two meiotic divisions. [19c]

oodles *plural noun, informal* lots; a great quantity: *oodles of money.* [19c]

ooh *exclam* expressing pleasure, surprise, excitement or pain. ▸ *verb* (*often* **ooh and aah**) to make an ooh sound to show surprise or excitement, etc.

oompah *or* **oom-pah** *noun, informal* a common way of representing the deep sound made by a large brass musical instrument, such as a tuba.

oomph *noun, informal* energy; enthusiasm.

oops *exclam, informal* expressing surprise or apology, eg when one makes a mistake.

ooze[1] *verb* **1** *intr* to flow or leak out gently or slowly. **2** *intr* of a substance: to give out moisture. **3** to give out (a liquid, etc) slowly. **4** to overflow with (a quality or feeling); to exude: *oozed charm.* ▸ *noun* a slow gentle leaking or oozing. ▪ **oozy** *adj* (**-ier, -iest**). [Anglo-Saxon *wos* sap or juice]

ooze[2] *noun* mud or slime, esp the kind found on the beds of rivers or lakes. [Anglo-Saxon *wase* marsh]

op *noun, informal* **1** a surgical operation. **2** a military operation. [20c short form]

op. *abbrev* **opus**.

opacity /əʊ'pasɪtɪ/ *noun* **1** opaqueness. **2** the state of having an obscure meaning and being difficult to understand. **3** dullness; obtuseness. [16c: from Latin *opacitas*]

opal *noun, geol* a usu milky-white stone, used as a gemstone, often with characteristic shimmering flashes caused by light reflected from different layers within the stone. [16c: from French *opale*]

opalescent *adj* reflecting different colours as the surrounding light changes, like an opal. ▪ **opalescence** *noun.*

opaque *adj* **1** not allowing light to pass through; not transparent or translucent. **2** difficult to understand; obscure. [15c: from Latin *opacus* dark or shaded]

op. cit. /ɒp 'sɪt/ *abbrev*: *opere citato* (Latin), in the work already quoted; used in footnotes, etc to refer to the last citation that is given.

open *adj* **1 a** of a door or barrier, etc: not closed or locked; **b** of a building or an enclosed space, etc: allowing people or things to go in or out; with its door or gate, etc not closed or locked. **2** of a container, etc: **a** not sealed or covered; **b** with the insides visible: *an open cupboard.* **3** of a space or area of land, etc: not enclosed, confined or restricted: *the open sea.* **4** not covered, guarded or protected: *an open wound.* **5** expanded, spread out or unfolded: *an open newspaper.* **6** of a shop, etc: receiving customers; ready for business. **7** *music* **a** of a string: not stopped by a finger; **b** of a note: played on an open string, or without holes on the instrument being covered. **8** generally known; public. **9** (*usu* **open to sth**) liable or susceptible to it; defenceless against it: *leave oneself open to abuse.* **10** of a competition: not restricted; allowing anyone to compete or take part, esp both amateurs and professionals. **11** free from restraint or restrictions of any kind: *the open fishing season* • *an open marriage* • *the open market.* **12** unprejudiced: *have an open mind.* **13** (*usu* **open to**) amenable to or ready to receive (eg new ideas or impressions): *open to suggestion.* **14** of a person: ready and willing to talk honestly; candid. ▶ *verb* **1** **a** to unfasten or move (eg a door or barrier) to allow access; **b** *intr* of a door or barrier, etc: to become unfastened to allow access. **2** *tr & intr* to become or make (something) become open or more open, eg by removing obstructions, etc. **3** (*also* **open out**) *tr & intr* to spread (something) out or become spread out or unfolded, esp so as to make or become visible. **4** *tr & intr* to start or begin working: *The office opens at nine.* **5** to declare (something) open with an official ceremony: *open the new hospital.* **6** *tr & intr* to begin (something) or start speaking or writing, etc: *opened his talk with a joke.* **7** to arrange (a bank account, etc), usu by making an initial deposit. **8** *tr & intr, cricket* to begin (the batting) for one's team. ▶ *noun* **1** (**the open**) an area of open country; an area not obstructed by buildings, etc. **2** (**the open**) public notice or attention (*esp* **bring something into the open** *or* **out into the open**). **3** (**Open**) *often in compounds* a sports contest which both amateurs and professionals may enter: *the British Open.* ▪ **openly** *adv.* ▪ **openness** *noun.* [Anglo-Saxon]

IDIOMS **open fire** to start shooting. **with open arms** warmly; cordially: *welcomed him with open arms.*

PHRASAL VERBS **open up 1** to open a shop for the day. **2** to start firing. **3** to begin to reveal one's feelings and thoughts or to behave with less restraint.

open air *noun* unenclosed space outdoors. ▶ *adj* (**open-air**) in the open air; outside: *open-air theatre.*

open-and-shut *adj* easily proved, decided or solved: *an open-and-shut case.*

open book *noun* someone who keeps no secrets and is easily understood.

opencast *adj, mining* using or relating to a method in which the substance to be mined is exposed by removing the overlying layers of material, without the need for shafts or tunnels.

open court *noun, law* a court whose proceedings are carried out in public. Compare **in camera**.

open day *noun* a day when members of the public can visit an institution usu closed to them.

open-ended *adj* **1** with an open end or ends. **2** of a question or debate, etc: not limited to strictly 'yes' or 'no' answers; allowing for free expression.

opener *noun* **1** *often in compounds* a device for opening something: *bottle-opener* • *tin-opener.* **2** *cricket* either of the two batsmen who begins the batting for their team. **3** an opening remark, etc.

open fracture see **compound fracture**

open-handed *adj* generous.

open-hearted *adj* **1** honest, direct and hiding nothing; candid. **2** kind; generous.

open-heart surgery *noun* surgery performed on a heart that has been stopped while the blood circulation is maintained by a heart-lung machine.

open house *noun* the state of being willing to welcome visitors at any time: *keep open house.*

opening *noun* **1** the act of making or becoming open. **2** a hole or gap, esp one that can serve as a passageway. **3** a beginning or first stage of something. **4** *theatre* the first performance of a play or opera, etc. **5** an opportunity or chance. **6** a vacancy. **7** *chiefly US* an area of ground in a forest, etc in which there are very few or no trees. *Brit equivalent* **clearing**. ▶ *adj* relating to or forming an opening; first: *opening night at the opera* • *opening batsman.*

open letter *noun* a letter, esp one of protest, addressed to a particular person or organization, etc but intended to be made public, eg through publication in a newspaper or magazine.

open-minded *adj* willing to consider or receive new ideas; unprejudiced. ▪ **open-mindedness** *noun.*

open-plan *adj* of a building or office, etc: with few internal walls and with large undivided rooms.

open prison *noun* a prison which allows prisoners who are considered to be neither dangerous nor violent greater freedom of movement than in normal prisons.

open question *noun* a matter that is undecided.

open season *noun* **1** a specified period of the year in which particular animals, birds or fish, etc may be legally killed for sport. **2** *informal* a period during which there are no restrictions on a particular activity: *It's open season for computer hackers just now.*

open secret *noun* something that is supposedly a secret but that is in fact widely known.

open-source *adj, comput* **1** of software: with its basic code freely available. **2** of programming: using open-source software that can be developed, tested, etc by many programmers working together.

open verdict *noun, law* a verdict given by the coroner's jury at the end of an inquest that death has occurred, but without giving details of whether it was suicide, accidental or murder, etc.

opera[1] *noun* **1** a dramatic work set to music, in which the singers are usu accompanied by an orchestra. **2** operas as an art-form. **3** a company that performs opera. ▪ **operatic** *adj* **1** relating to or like opera. **2** dramatic or overly theatrical; exaggerated. ▪ **operatically** *adv.* [17c: Italian]

opera[2] *pl of* **opus**

opera glasses *plural noun* small binoculars used at the theatre or opera, etc.

opera house *noun* a theatre specially built for the performance of opera.

operand *noun, maths, logic* a quantity on which an **operation** (sense 7) is performed. [19c: from Latin *operandum*]

operate *verb* **1** *intr* to function or work. **2** to make (a machine, etc) function or work; to control the functioning of (something). **3** to manage, control or direct (a business, etc). **4** (*usu* **operate on sb**) *intr* to perform a surgical operation on them. **5** *intr* to perform military, naval or police, etc operations. ▪ **operable** *adj* **1** *med* of a disease or injury, etc: that can be treated by surgery. **2** that can be operated. [17c: from Latin *operari* to work]

operating system *noun, comput* (abbrev **OS**) a software system that controls all the main activities of a computer.

operating theatre *or* **operating room** *noun* the specially equipped room in a hospital, etc where surgical operations are performed.

operation *noun* **1** an act, method or process of working or operating. **2** the state of working or being active: *The factory is not yet in operation.* **3** an activity; something done. **4** an action or series of actions which have a particular effect. **5** *med* any surgical procedure that is performed in order to treat a damaged or diseased part of the body (often shortened to **op**). **6** (*often* **operations**) one of a series of military, naval or police, etc actions, usu involving a large number of people, performed as part of a much larger plan. **7** *maths* a specific procedure, such as addition or multiplication, whereby one numerical value is derived from another value or values. **8** *comput* a series of actions that are specified by a single instruction. [14c: French, meaning 'action' or 'deed']

operational *adj* **1** relating to an operation or operations. **2** able or ready to work or perform an intended function.

operative *adj* **1** working; in action; having an effect. **2** of a word: esp important or significant: *'Must' is the operative word.* **3** relating to a surgical operation. ▸ *noun* **1** a worker, esp one with special skills. **2** *N Am, esp US* a private detective.

operator *noun* **1** someone who operates a machine or apparatus. **2** someone who operates a telephone switchboard, connecting calls, etc. **3** someone who runs a business. **4** *maths* any symbol used to indicate that a particular mathematical operation is to be carried out, eg ×, which shows that two numbers are to be multiplied. **5** *informal* a calculating, shrewd and manipulative person.

operetta *noun* a short light opera, with spoken dialogue and often dancing.

ophthalmia *noun, pathol* inflammation of the eye, esp of the conjunctiva. [16c: from Greek *ophthalmos* eye]

ophthalmic *adj* pertaining or relating to the eye.

ophthalmic optician *noun* an optician qualified both to examine the eyes and test vision, and to prescribe, make and sell glasses or contact lenses. Also called **optometrist** (see under **optometry**).

ophthalmology *noun, med* the study, diagnosis and treatment of diseases and defects of the eye. ▪ **ophthalmologist** *noun.*

ophthalmoscope *noun* a device that is used to examine the interior of the eye, by directing a reflected beam of light through the pupil.

opiate /ˈoʊpɪət/ *noun* **1** a drug containing or derived from opium that depresses the central nervous system, and can be used as a steroid **analgesic**. **2** anything that dulls physical or mental sensation. [16c: from Latin *opiatus*]

opine *verb, formal* to suppose or express (something) as an opinion. [16c: from Latin *opinari* to think]

opinion *noun* **1** a belief or judgement which seems likely to be true, but which is not based on proof. **2** (*usu* **opinion on** *or* **about sth**) what one thinks about it. **3** a professional judgement given by an expert: *medical opinion.* **4** estimation or appreciation: *has a high opinion of himself.* [13c: from Latin *opinio* belief]

opinionated *adj* with very strong opinions that one refuses or is very unwilling to change; stubborn.

opinion poll see under **poll**

opium *noun* a highly addictive narcotic drug extracted from the seed capsules of the **opium poppy**, used in medicine to bring sleep and relieve pain. [14c: from Greek *opion* poppy juice or opium]

opossum *noun* (***opossums*** *or* ***opossum***) **1** a small tree-dwelling American marsupial with thick fur and a hairless prehensile tail. **2** any similar marsupial, native to Australasia. Also called **possum.** [17c: from Algonquian (a family of Native American languages) *opassom*]

opponent *noun* someone who belongs to the opposing side in an argument, contest or battle, etc. [16c: from Latin *opponens* setting before or against]

opportune *adj* **1** of an action: happening at a time which is suitable, proper or correct. **2** of a time: suitable; proper. [15c: from Latin *opportunus*]

opportunist *noun* someone whose actions and opinions are governed by the particular events and circumstances, etc of the moment rather than being based on settled principles. ▸ *adj* referring to such actions or opinions. ▪ **opportunism** *noun.* ▪ **opportunistic** *adj.*

opportunity *noun* (***-ies***) **1** an occasion offering a possibility; a chance. **2** favourable or advantageous conditions. [16c: from Latin *opportunitas*]

opposable *adj* of a digit, esp the thumb: able to be placed in a position so that it faces and can touch the ends of the other digits of the same hand or foot. ▪ **opposability** *noun.*

oppose *verb* **1** to resist or fight against (someone or something) by force or argument. **2** *intr* to compete in a game or contest, etc against another person or team; to act in opposition. ▪ **opposer** *noun.* ▪ **opposing** *adj.* [14c: from Latin *opponere* to set before or against]

IDIOMS **as opposed to** in contrast to; as distinct from.

opposite (abbrev **opp.**) *adj* **1** placed or being on the other side of, or at the other end of, a real or imaginary line or space. **2** facing in a directly different direction: *opposite sides of the coin.* **3** completely or diametrically different. **4** referring to something that is the other of a matching or contrasting pair: *the opposite sex.* **5** *maths* of a side of a triangle: facing a specified angle. ▸ *noun* an opposite person or thing. ▸ *adv* in or into an opposite position: *live opposite.* ▸ *prep* **1** (*also* **opposite to sb** *or* **sth**) in a position across from and facing them or it: *a house opposite the station.* **2** of an actor: in a role which complements that taken by another actor; co-starring with them: *played opposite Olivier.* [14c: from Latin *opponere*]

opposite number *noun* someone with an equivalent position in another company or country.

opposition *noun* **1** the act of fighting against someone or something by force or argument; resistance. **2** the state of being hostile or in conflict. **3** a person or group of people who are opposed to something. **4** (*usu* **the Opposition**) a political party which opposes the party in power. **5** *astron, astrol* the position of a planet or star when it is directly opposite another, esp the Sun, as seen from the Earth.

oppress *verb* **1** to govern with cruelty and injustice. **2** to worry, trouble or make (someone) anxious. **3** to distress or afflict (someone). ▪ **oppression** *noun.* ▪ **oppressor** *noun.* [14c: from Latin *oppressare*]

oppressive *adj* **1** cruel, tyrannical and unjust: *an oppressive regime.* **2** causing worry or mental distress; weighing heavily on the mind. **3** of the weather: heavy, hot and sultry. ▪ **oppressiveness** *noun.*

opprobrium *noun* (*pl* in sense 2 ***opprobria***) **1** public shame, disgrace or loss of favour; infamy. **2** anything that brings such shame or disgrace, etc. ▪ **opprobrious** *adj.* [17c: Latin, from *op-* against + *probrum* reproach or disgrace]

oppugn /əˈpjuːn/ *verb* to call into question; to dispute. [15c: from Latin *oppugnare*]

opt *verb, intr* (*usu* **opt for sth** *or* **to do sth**) to decide between several possibilities; to choose. [19c: from French *opter*]

PHRASAL VERBS **opt in** to choose to take part or participate in something. **opt out 1** to choose not to take part in something. **2** of a school or hospital: to leave local authority control. See also **opt-out**.

optic *adj* relating to the eye or vision. [16c: from Greek *optikos*]

optical *adj* **1** relating to sight or to what one sees. **2** relating to light or optics. **3** of a lens: designed to improve vision. ▪ **optically** *adv.*

optical character reader *noun, comput* (abbrev **OCR**) a light-sensitive device for inputting data directly onto a computer by means of **optical character recognition.**

optical character recognition *noun, comput* (abbrev **OCR**) the scanning, identification and recording of printed characters by a photoelectric device attached to a computer.

optical disk *noun, comput* a disk that can be read from and often written to by a laser.

optical fibre *noun, telecomm* a thin flexible strand of glass used to convey information, eg in the cables for telephones, cable TV, etc. Compare **fibre optics**.

optical illusion *noun* **1** something that has an appearance which deceives the eye. **2** a misunderstanding caused by such a deceptive appearance.

optician *noun* **1** (*also* **dispensing optician**) someone who fits and sells glasses and contact lenses but is not qualified to prescribe them. **2** *loosely* an **ophthalmic optician.** [17c: from French *opticien*]

optic nerve *noun, anatomy* in vertebrates: a cranial nerve, responsible for the sense of vision, which transmits information from the retina of the eye to the visual cortex of the brain.

optics *singular noun, physics* the study of light and its practical applications in a range of devices and systems.

optimal *adj* most favourable; optimum. [19c: from Latin *optimus* best]

optimism *noun* **1** the tendency to take a bright, hopeful view of things and expect the best possible outcome. **2** *philos* the belief that we live in the best of all possible worlds. **3** the theory that good will ultimately triumph over evil. Compare **pessimism**. ▪ **optimist** *noun.* ▪ **optimistic** *adj.* ▪ **optimistically** *adv.* [18c: from French *optimisme*]

optimize *or* **-ise** *verb* **1** to make the most or best of (a particular situation or opportunity, etc). **2** *comput* to prepare or modify (a computer system or program) so as to achieve the greatest possible efficiency. ▪ **optimization** *noun.*

optimum *noun* (***optimums*** *or* ***optima***) the condition, situation, amount or level, etc that is the most favourable or gives the best results. ▸ *adj* best or most favourable. [19c: Latin, neuter of *optimus* best]

option *noun* **1** an act of choosing. **2** that which is or which may be chosen. **3** the power or right to choose: *You have no option.* **4** *commerce* the exclusive right to buy or sell something, eg stocks, at a fixed price and within a specified time-limit. ▸ *verb, chiefly US* **1** to buy or sell (something) under option. **2** to have or grant an option on (something). [16c: from Latin *optio*]

IDIOMS **keep** *or* **leave one's options open** to avoid making a choice or committing oneself to a particular course of action. **soft option** the easiest choice or course of action.

optional *adj* left to choice; not compulsory.

optometry *noun* **1** the science of vision and eyecare. **2** the practice of examining the eyes and vision. **3** the prescription and provision of glasses and contact lenses, etc for the improvement of vision. ▪ **optometrist** *noun* an **ophthalmic optician**. [19c: from Greek *optos* seen]

opt-out *noun* **a** the action or an act of opting out of something; **b** of a school or hospital: the act of leaving local authority control. See also **opt**.

opulent *adj* **1** rich; wealthy. **2** abundant. ▪ **opulence** *noun.* ▪ **opulently** *adv.* [16c: from Latin *opulentus*]

opus *noun* (***opuses*** *or* ***opera***) (abbrev **op.**) an artistic work, esp a musical composition, often used with a number to show the order in which a composer's works were written or catalogued. [18c: Latin, meaning 'work']

or *conj* used to introduce: **1** alternatives: *red or pink.* **2** a synonym or explanation: *a puppy or young dog.* **3** the second part of an indirect question: *Ask her whether she thinks he'll come or not.* **4** because if not; or else: *Run or you'll be late.* [13c: a contraction of **other**]

IDIOMS **or else 1** otherwise. **2** *informal* expressing a threat or warning: *Give it to me or else!* **or so** about; roughly: *been there two hours or so.*

-or *suffix, forming nouns, denoting* a person or thing that performs an action or function: *actor* • *elevator.* [Latin]

oracle *noun* **1** in ancient Greece or Rome: a holy place where a god was believed to give advice and prophecy. **2** a priest or priestess at an oracle, through whom the god was believed to speak. **3** someone who is believed to have great wisdom or be capable of prophesying the future. [14c: from Latin *oraculum*]

oracular /ɒˈrakjʊlə(r)/ *adj* **1** relating to or like an oracle. **2** difficult to interpret; mysterious and ambiguous. **3** prophetic.

oral *adj* **1** spoken; not written. **2** relating to or used in the mouth. **3** of a medicine or drug, etc: taken in through the mouth: *oral contraceptive.* ▸ *noun* a spoken test or examination. ▪ **orally** *adv.* [17c: from Latin *oralis*]

orange *noun* **1** a round citrus fruit with a tough reddish-yellow outer rind or peel filled with sweet or sharp-tasting juicy flesh. **2** the evergreen tree, cultivated in most subtropical regions, that bears this fruit. **3** a reddish-yellow colour like that of the skin of an orange. **4** an orange-flavoured drink. ▸ *adj* **1** orange-coloured. **2** orange-flavoured. ▪ **orangey** *and* **orangish** *adj.* [14c: ultimately from Sanskrit *naranga*]

orangery *noun* (*-ies*) a greenhouse or other building in which orange trees can be grown in cool climates.

orang-utan *or* **orang-outang** *noun* a large tree-dwelling ape, found in tropical forests in Borneo and Sumatra, with long reddish hair and long strong arms. [17c: from Malay *orang* man + *hutan* forest]

oration *noun* a formal or ceremonial public speech delivered in dignified language. [14c: from Latin *oratio*]

orator /'ɒrətə(r)/ *noun* someone who is skilled in persuading, moving or exciting people through public speech.

oratorical /ɒrə'tɒrɪkəl/ *adj* **1** relating to or characteristic of an orator. **2 a** relating to or like **oratory**[2], especially in using rhetoric; **b** given to using oratory. ▪ **oratorically** *adv.* [16c]

oratorio /ɒrə'tɔːrɪoʊ/ *noun* a musical composition, usu based on a biblical or religious theme or story, sung by soloists and a chorus accompanied by an orchestra. [17c: Italian]

oratory[1] /'ɒrətərɪ/ *noun* (*-ies*) a chapel or small place set aside for private prayer. [14c: from Latin *oratorium*]

oratory[2] /'ɒrətərɪ/ *noun* **1** the art of public speaking; rhetoric. **2** rhetorical style or language. [16c: from Latin *ars oratoria* the art of public speaking]

orb *noun* **1** a globe with a cross on top that is decorated with jewels and is carried as part of a monarch's regalia. **2** anything in the shape of a globe or sphere. **3** *poetic* a star, the sun or a planet. **4** *poetic* the eye or eyeball. [16c: from Latin *orbis* a circle]

orbit *noun* **1** *astron* in space: the elliptical path of one celestial body around another, eg the Earth's orbit around the Sun, or of an artificial satellite or spacecraft, etc around a celestial body. **2** *physics* the path of an electron around the nucleus of an atom. **3** a sphere of influence or action. **4** *anatomy* in the skull of vertebrates: one of the two bony hollows in which the eyeball is situated; an eye socket. ▸ *verb* **1** of a celestial body, or a spacecraft, etc: to circle (the Earth or another planet, etc) in space. **2** to put (a spacecraft, etc) into orbit. ▪ **orbiter** *noun* a spacecraft or satellite that orbits a planet but does not land on it. [16c: from Latin *orbitus*]

orbital *adj* **1** relating to or going round in an orbit. **2** of a road: forming a complete circle or loop round a city. ▸ *noun, chem* any region outside the nucleus of an atom or molecule where there is a high probability of finding an electron.

orchard *noun* a garden or piece of land where fruit trees are grown. [Anglo-Saxon *ortgeard*]

orchestra *noun* **1** a large group of instrumentalists who play together as an ensemble. **2** (*also* **orchestra pit**) the part of a theatre or opera house where the musicians sit, usu immediately in front of, or under the front part of, the stage. ▪ **orchestral** *adj.* [16c: Greek]

orchestrate *verb* **1** to arrange, compose or score (a piece of music) for an orchestra. **2** to organize or arrange (elements of a plan or a situation, etc) so as to get the desired or best result. ▪ **orchestration** *noun.* ▪ **orchestrator** *noun.*

orchid *noun* a plant which is best known for its complex and exotic flowers. [19c: from Greek *orchis* testicle, so called because of the shape of its root-tubers]

ordain *verb* **1** *Christianity* to appoint or admit (someone) as priest or vicar, etc. **2** to order, command or decree (something) formally. ▪ **ordainment** *noun.* See also **ordination**. [13c: from Latin *ordinare*]

ordeal *noun* **1** a difficult, painful or testing experience. **2** *hist* a method of trial in which the accused person was subjected to physical danger, survival of which was taken as a sign from God of the person's innocence. [Anglo-Saxon *ordal* judgement]

order *noun* **1** a state in which everything is in its proper place; tidiness. **2** an arrangement of objects according to importance, value or position, etc. **3** a command, instruction or direction. **4** a state of peace and harmony in society, characterized by the absence of crime and the general obeying of laws. **5** the condition of being able to function properly: *in working order.* **6** a social class or rank making up a distinct social group: *the lower orders.* **7** a kind or sort: *of the highest order.* **8** an instruction to a manufacturer, supplier or waiter, etc to provide something. **9** the goods or food, etc supplied. **10** an established system of society: *a new world order.* **11** *biol* in taxonomy: any of the groups into which a **class** (*noun* sense 9) is divided, and which is in turn subdivided into one or more families (see **family** *noun* sense 7). **12** *commerce* a written instruction to pay money. **13** the usual procedure followed at esp official meetings and during debates: *a point of order.* **14** (**Order**) a religious community living according to a particular rule and bound by vows. Also called **religious order. 15** any of the different grades of the Christian ministry. **16** (**orders**) holy orders. **17** the specified form of a religious service: *order of marriage.* **18** (**Order**) a group of people to which new members are admitted as a mark of honour or reward for services to the sovereign or country: *Order of the British Empire.* **19** any of the five classical styles of architecture (Doric, Ionic, Corinthian, Tuscan and Composite) characterized by the way a column and entablature are moulded and decorated. **20** any of the nine ranks of angel (seraph, cherub, dominion, virtue, power, principality, throne, archangel and angel). ▸ *verb* **1** to give a command to (someone). **2** to command (someone) to go to a specified place: *order the regiment to Germany.* **3** to instruct a manufacturer, supplier or waiter, etc to supply or provide (something): *ordered the fish.* **4** to arrange or regulate: *order one's affairs.* **5** *intr* to give a command, request or order, esp to a waiter for food: *ready to order.* [13c: from French *ordre*]

IDIOMS **a tall order** *informal* a difficult or demanding job or task. **in order 1** in accordance with the rules; properly arranged. **2** suitable or appropriate: *Her conduct just isn't in order.* **3** in the correct sequence. **in order that** so that. **in order to do sth** so as to be able to do it. **in the order of** approximately (the number specified). **on order** of goods: having been ordered but not yet supplied. **out of order** not correct, proper or suitable. **to order** according to a customer's particular or personal requirements. **under orders** having been commanded or instructed (to do something).

PHRASAL VERBS **order sb about** *or* **around** to give them orders continually and officiously.

orderly *adj* **1** in good order; well arranged. **2** well behaved; quiet. ▸ *noun* (*-ies*) **1** an attendant, usu without medical training, who does various jobs in a hospital, such as moving patients. **2** *military* a soldier who carries an officer's orders and messages. ▪ **orderliness** *noun*.

ordinal *noun, RC Church* a service book.

ordinal number *noun* a number which shows a position in a sequence, eg *first, second, third*, etc. See also **cardinal number**.

ordinance *noun* a law, order or ruling. [14c: from French *ordenance*]

ordinary *adj* **1** of the usual everyday kind; unexceptional. **2** plain; uninteresting. ▸ *noun* (*-ies*) **1** *law* a judge of ecclesiastical or other causes who acts in his own right, such as a bishop or his deputy. **2** (**Ordinary**) *RC Church* those parts of the Mass which do not vary from day to day. **3** *heraldry* a simple type of armorial charge. ▪ **ordinarily** *adv* usually; normally. [13c: from Latin *ordinarius* orderly, usual]

IDIOMS **out of the ordinary** unusual; strange.

Ordinary level see **O-level**

ordinary seaman *noun* (abbrev **OS**) a sailor of the lowest rank (below an **able seaman**) in the Royal Navy.

ordinary shares *plural noun, stock exchange* shares which form part of the common stock, entitling holders to receive a dividend from the net profits.

ordinate *noun, maths* in coordinate geometry: the second of a pair of numbers (*x* and *y*), known as the *y* coordinate, and which specifies the distance of a point from the horizontal or *x*-axis. See also **abscissa**. [18c: from Latin *ordinatus* ordained]

ordination *noun* the act or ceremony of ordaining a priest or minister of the church.

ordnance *noun* **1** heavy guns and military supplies. **2** the government department responsible for military supplies. [14c]

Ordovician /ɔːdʊ'vɪʃɪən/ *adj, geol* relating to the second period of the Palaeozoic era, during which the first vertebrates (jawless fishes) appeared. [19c: from Latin *Ordovices*, the name of an ancient British tribe in N Wales]

ordure *noun* waste matter from the bowels; excrement. [14c: French]

ore *noun, geol* a solid naturally occurring mineral deposit from which one or more economically valuable substances, esp metals, can be extracted. [Anglo-Saxon *ora* unwrought metal, combined with *ar* brass]

oregano /ɒrɪ'gɑːnoʊ; *US* ə'rɛgənoʊ/ *noun* a sweet-smelling herb, used as a flavouring in cooking. [18c: Spanish and American Spanish]

organ *noun* **1** a part of a body or plant which has a special function, eg a kidney. **2** a musical instrument with a keyboard and pedals, in which sound is produced by air being forced through pipes of different lengths. **3** any similar instrument without pipes, such as one producing sound electronically. **4** a means of spreading information, esp a newspaper or journal of a particular group or organization, etc. [13c: from Latin *organum* instrument]

organdie *or* **organdy** *noun* a very fine stiffened cotton fabric. [19c: from French *organdi*]

organelle /ɔːgə'nɛl/ *noun, biol* in the cell of a living organism: any of various types of membrane-bound structure, each of which has a specialized function. [20c: from Latin *organella*, from *organum* instrument]

organ-grinder *noun* a musician who plays a barrel organ in the streets for money.

organic *adj* **1** *biol* relating to, derived from, or with the characteristics of a living organism. **2** **a** relating to farming practices that avoid the use of synthetic fertilizers and pesticides, etc; **b** relating to food produced in this way. **3** being or formed as an inherent or natural part; fundamental. **4** systematically organized. ▪ **organically** *adv*. [16c: meaning 'serving as an organ']

organic chemistry *noun* the branch of chemistry dealing with compounds which contain carbon, carbon being found in all living things. Compare **inorganic chemistry**.

organic compound *noun, chem* any of the many chemical compounds that, with a few exceptions, contain carbon atoms arranged in chains or rings, together with smaller amounts of (usu) hydrogen and oxygen.

organism *noun* **1** any living structure, such as a plant, animal, fungus or bacterium. **2** any establishment, system or whole made up of parts that depend on each other. [18c]

organist *noun* a person who plays an organ.

organization *or* **-isation** *noun* **1** a group of people formed into a society, union or esp a business. **2** the act of organizing. **3** the state of being organized. **4** the way in which something is organized. ▪ **organizational** *adj*.

organize *or* **-ise** *verb* **1** to give an orderly structure to (something): *organized the books into a neat pile*. **2** to arrange, provide or prepare (something): *organized the tickets*. **3** to form or enrol (people or a person) into a society or organization. **4** *intr* to form a society or organization, esp a trade union. ▪ **organizer** *noun* **1** someone or something that organizes. **2** a **personal organizer**. [15c: from Latin *organizare*]

organophosphate /ɔːganoʊ'fɒsfeɪt/ *noun, chem* any of a group of chemical insecticides.

organza *noun* a very fine stiff dress material made of silk or synthetic fibres. [19c]

orgasm *noun* the climax of sexual excitement, experienced as an intensely pleasurable sensation. ▪ **orgasmic** *adj*. [17c: from Greek *orgasmos* swelling]

orgy *noun* (*-ies*) any act of excessive or frenzied indulgence: *an orgy of shopping*. [16c: from Latin *orgia*]

oriel *noun* **1** a small room or recess with a polygonal bay window, esp one supported on brackets or corbels. **2** (*also* **oriel window**) the window of an oriel. [14c: from French *oriol* gallery]

orient *noun* (**the Orient**) the countries in the east, esp those of E Asia regarded as culturally distinct from western countries (the **Occident**). ▸ *verb* **1** to place (something) in a definite position in relation to the points of the compass or some other fixed or known point. **2** to acquaint (oneself or someone) with one's position or their position relative to points known, or relative to the details of a situation. **3** to position (something) so that it faces east. [14c: from Latin *oriens* rising]

oriental *adj* (*also* **Oriental**) from or relating to the Orient; eastern. ▸ *noun* (*usu* **Oriental**) *often offensive* a person born in the Orient; an Asiatic.

orientate *verb* to orient. [19c]

orientation *noun* **1** the act or an instance of orienting or being oriented. **2** a position relative to a fixed point. **3** a person's position or attitude relative to their situation or circumstances. **4** a meeting giving information or training needed for a new situation.

orienteering *noun* a sport in which contestants race on foot and on skis, etc over an unfamiliar cross-country course, finding their way to official check points using a map and compass. ▪ **orienteer** *verb.* [20c: from Swedish *orientering*]

orifice /ˈɒrɪfɪs/ *noun* a usu small opening or hole, esp one in the body. [16c: from Latin *orificium*]

orig. *abbrev* **1** origin. **2** original. **3** originally.

origami *noun* the Japanese art of folding paper into decorative shapes and figures. [20c: Japanese, from *ori* fold + *kami* paper]

origin *noun* **1** a beginning or starting-point; a source. **2** (*usu* **origins**) a person's family background or ancestry. **3** *maths* in coordinate geometry: the point on a graph where the horizontal *x*-axis and the vertical *y*-axis cross each other, having a value of zero on both axes. [16c: from Latin *origo*]

original *adj* **1** relating to an origin or beginning. **2** existing from the beginning; earliest; first. **3** of an idea or concept, etc: not thought of before; fresh or new. **4** of a person: creative or inventive. **5** being the first form from which copies, reproductions or translations are made; not copied or derived, etc from something else. ▸ *noun* **1** the first example of something, such as a document, photograph or text, etc, which is copied, reproduced or translated to produce others, but which is not itself copied or derived, etc from something else. **2** a work of art or literature that is not a copy or imitation. **3** a person or thing that serves as a model in art or literature. ▪ **originality** *noun.* ▪ **originally** *adv.* [14c]

original sin *noun, Christianity* the supposed innate sinfulness of the human race, inherited from Adam, who disobeyed God.

originate *verb, tr & intr* to bring or come into being; to start. ▪ **origination** *noun.* ▪ **originator** *noun.*

oriole *noun* a songbird with bright yellow and black plumage. [18c: from Latin *oriolus*]

ormolu /ˈɔːməluː/ *noun* a gold-coloured alloy, eg copper, zinc or sometimes tin, that is used to decorate furniture, make ornaments, etc. [18c: from French *or moulu*, literally 'ground gold']

ornament *noun* /ˈɔːnəmənt/ **1** something that decorates or adds grace or beauty to a person or thing. **2** embellishment or decoration. **3** a small, usu decorative object. **4** someone whose talents add honour to the group or company, etc to which they belong. **5** *music* a note or notes that embellish or decorate the melody or harmony but do not belong to it, eg a trill. ▸ *verb* /ɔːnəˈmɛnt/ to decorate (something) with ornaments or serve as an ornament to (something); to adorn. ▪ **ornamental** *adj.* ▪ **ornamentation** *noun.* [18c: from French *ournement*]

ornate *adj* **1** highly or excessively decorated. **2** of language: flowery; using many elaborate words or expressions. ▪ **ornately** *adv.* [15c: from Latin *ornare* to adorn]

ornery *adj, N Am informal* **1** stubborn or cantankerous. **2** contemptible. [19c: variant of **ordinary**]

ornithology *noun* the scientific study of birds and their behaviour. ▪ **ornithological** *adj.* ▪ **ornithologist** *noun.* [17c: from Greek *ornis* bird]

orotund *adj* **1** of the voice: full, loud and grand. **2** of speech or writing: boastful or self-important; pompous. ▪ **orotundity** *noun.* [18c: from Latin *ore rotundo*, meaning 'with rounded mouth']

orphan *noun* a child who has lost both parents. ▸ *verb, usu in passive* to make (a child) an orphan. [15c: from Greek *orphanos* bereft]

orphanage *noun* a home for orphans. [19c]

orrery *noun* (**-ies**) a clockwork model of the Sun and the planets which revolve around it. [18c: named after Charles Boyle, Earl of Orrery, for whom one was made]

orris *noun* **1** an iris which has white flowers and fragrant fleshy rhizomes. **2** (*also* **orrisroot**) the dried sweet-smelling rhizome of this plant, used in perfumes. [16c: a variant of **iris**]

orthocentre *noun, geom* the point of intersection of the three **altitude**s (sense 2) of a triangle.

orthodontics *singular noun, dentistry* the branch of dentistry concerned with the prevention and correction of irregularities in the alignment of the teeth or jaws. ▪ **orthodontist** *noun.* [20c: from Greek *odous* tooth]

orthodox *adj* **1** believing in, living according to, or conforming with established or generally accepted opinions; conventional. **2** (*usu* **Orthodox**) belonging or relating to the **Orthodox Church**. **3** (*usu* **Orthodox**) belonging or relating to the branch of Judaism which keeps to strict traditional interpretations of doctrine and scripture. [16c: from Greek *orthos* straight or correct + *doxa* opinion]

Orthodox Church *noun* a communion of self-governing Christian Churches that recognize the primacy of the Patriarch of Constantinople. Also called **Eastern Orthodox Church**, **Eastern Church**.

orthogonal /ɔːˈθɒgənəl/ *adj* right-angled; perpendicular. ▪ **orthogonally** *adv.* [16c]

orthography *noun* (**-ies**) **1** correct or standard spelling. **2** a particular system of spelling. **3** the study of spelling. ▪ **orthographer** *or* **orthographist** *noun.* [15c: from Latin *ortographia*]

orthopaedics *or* (*US*) **orthopedics** /ɔːθəˈpiːdɪks/ *singular noun, med* the correction by surgery or manipulation, etc of deformities arising from injury or disease of the bones and joints. ▪ **orthopaedic** *adj.* ▪ **orthopaedist** *noun.* [19c: from French *orthopédie*]

-ory[1] *suffix, forming nouns, denoting* a place or object, etc for a specified activity or purpose: *dormitory* • *repository.* [From Latin *-orium, -oria*]

-ory[2] *suffix, forming adjectives and nouns* relating to or involving the action of the verb: *depository* • *signatory.* [From Latin *-orius*]

oryx *noun* (***oryxes*** *or* ***oryx***) any large grazing antelope typically with very long slender horns. [14c: from Greek, meaning 'a stonemason's pick-axe', because of the shape of the animal's horns]

OS *abbrev* **1** *comput* operating system. **2** outsize.

Os *symbol, chem* osmium.

Oscar *noun, trademark* each of a number of gold-plated statuettes awarded annually by the American Academy of Motion Picture Arts and Sciences for outstanding acting or directing, etc in films. Also called **Academy Award**. [1930s: an Academy employee is said to have remarked that the statuette reminded her of her uncle Oscar]

oscillate /ˈɒsɪleɪt/ *verb* **1** *tr & intr* to swing or make (something) swing backwards and forwards like a pendulum. **2** *tr & intr* to vibrate. **3** *intr* to waver between opinions, choices, courses of action, etc. **4** *intr, electronics* of an electrical current: to vary regularly in strength or direction between certain limits. ▪ **oscillation** *noun.* ▪ **oscillator** *noun.* [18c: from Latin *oscillare* to swing]

oscilloscope /əˈsɪləskoʊp/ *noun* a device that measures the rapidly changing values of an oscillating electrical current over time, and that displays the varying electrical signals graphically on the fluorescent screen of a cathode-ray tube. Also called **cathode-ray oscilloscope** (abbrev **CRO**). [20c]

osier /ˈoʊzɪə(r)/ *noun* **1** a species of willow tree or shrub. **2** a flexible branch or twig from this tree. [14c: from French]

-osis *suffix* (*-oses*) *forming nouns, denoting* **1** a condition or process: *hypnosis* • *metamorphosis.* **2** a diseased or disordered state: *neurosis.* [Latin or Greek]

osmiridium *noun, chem* a hard white alloy of osmium and iridium, used to make pen nibs. [19c: from *osm*ium + *iridium*]

osmium *noun, chem* (symbol **Os**) a very hard dense bluish-white metal, the densest known element, used as a catalyst, and as a hardening agent in alloys. [19c: from Greek *osme* smell, because of its unpleasant pungent smell]

osmosis *noun* **1** *chem* the spontaneous movement of a solvent, eg water, through a semipermeable membrane into a more concentrated solution. **2** a gradual, usu unconscious, process of assimilation or absorption of ideas or knowledge, etc. ▪ **osmotic** *adj.* [19c: from Greek *osmos* a push]

osmotic pressure *noun, chem* the pressure that must be applied to a solution to prevent osmosis.

osprey *noun* a large fish-eating bird of prey, with a dark-brown body, white head and legs. [15c: from French *ospres*]

osseous *adj* relating to, like, containing, or formed from bone; bony. [17c: from Latin *osseus*]

ossicle *noun* **1** *anatomy, zool* a small bone, especially any of the three small bones of the middle ear. **2** *zool* a bonelike plate or joint, etc. [16c: from Latin *ossiculum*, diminutive of *os* bone]

ossify *verb* (*-ies, -ied*) **1** *tr & intr* to turn into or make (something) turn into bone or a bonelike substance. **2** *intr* of one's opinions or habits, etc: to become rigid, fixed or inflexible. ▪ **ossification** *noun.* [18c: from French *ossifier*]

ostensible *adj* of reasons, etc: stated or claimed, but not necessarily true; apparent. ▪ **ostensibly** *adv.* [18c: from Latin *ostensibilis*]

ostensive *adj* **1** *logic* directly or manifestly demonstrative. **2** of a definition: giving examples of things to which the defined word properly applies. ▪ **ostensively** *adv.* [16c: from Latin *ostentivus* provable]

ostentation *noun* pretentious display of wealth or knowledge, etc, esp to attract attention or admiration. ▪ **ostentatious** *adj.* ▪ **ostentatiously** *adv.* [15c: from Latin *ostendere* to show]

osteoarthritis *noun, pathol* a chronic disease of bones, in which degeneration of the cartilage overlying the bones at a joint leads to deformity of the bone surface. ▪ **osteoarthritic** *adj.* [19c: from Greek *osteon* bone + **arthritis**]

osteology /ɒstɪˈɒlədʒɪ/ *noun* **1** the branch of human anatomy that deals with the study of bones and the skeleton. **2** (*pl* *-ies*) the structure and arrangement of an animal's bones. ▪ **osteological** *adj.* ▪ **osteologist** *noun.* [17c: from Greek *osteon* bone]

osteomyelitis *noun, pathol* inflammation of bone and bone marrow, caused by infection. [19c]

osteopathy /ɒstɪˈɒpəθɪ/ *noun, med* a system of healing or treatment, mainly involving manipulation of the bones and joints and massage of the muscles, that provides relief for many bone and joint disorders. ▪ **osteopath** *noun.* [19c]

osteoporosis /ɒstɪoʊpɔːˈroʊsɪs/ *noun, pathol* a disease in which the bones become porous, brittle and liable to fracture, owing to loss of calcium. [19c]

ostinato *adj, music* frequently repeated. [19c: Italian, meaning 'obstinate' or 'persistent']

ostler /ˈɒslə(r)/ *noun, hist* someone who attends to horses at an inn. [15c: from **hostel**]

ostracize *or* **-ise** *verb* to exclude (someone) from a group or society, etc. ▪ **ostracism** *noun.* [17c: from Greek *ostrakizein*]

ostrich *noun* (*ostriches* or *ostrich*) **1** the largest living bird, native to Africa, having an extremely long neck and legs, and only two toes on each foot. **2** *informal* someone who refuses to face or accept unpleasant facts. [13c: from French *ostruce*]

Ostrogoth *noun, hist* a member of the Eastern Goths, who established their power in Italy in the 5c and 6c. Compare **Visigoth**. [17c: from Latin *Ostrogothi*, with the first element meaning 'east']

OT *abbrev* Old Testament.

other *adj* **1** remaining from a group of two or more when one or some have been specified already: *Now close the other eye.* **2** different from the one or ones already mentioned, understood or implied: *other people.* **3** additional; further: *need to buy one other thing.* **4** far or opposite: *the other side of the world.* ▸ *pron* **1** **a** another person or thing; **b** (**others**) other people or things. **2** (**others**) further or additional ones: *I'd like to see some others.* **3** (*usu* **the others**) the remaining people or things of a group: *Go with the others.* ▸ *adv* (*usu* **other than**) otherwise; differently: *couldn't do other than hurry home.* ▸ *noun* someone or something considered separate, different, additional to, apart from, etc the rest: *introduced him as his significant other.* ▪ **otherness** *noun.* [Anglo-Saxon]

IDIOMS **every other** each alternate; every second: *see him every other week.* **in other words** this means: *In other words, you won't do it?* **the other day** *or* **week**, *etc* a few days or weeks, etc ago.

other ranks *plural noun, chiefly Brit* members of the armed services who do not hold a commissioned rank.

otherwise *conj* or else; if not. ▸ *adv* **1** in other respects: *He is good at languages but is otherwise not very bright.* **2** in a different way: *couldn't act otherwise than as she did.* **3** under different circumstances: *might otherwise have been late.* ▸ *adj* different: *The truth is otherwise.* [Anglo-Saxon *othre wisan* in other wise or manner]

otherworldly *adj* **1** belonging or relating to, or resembling, a world supposedly inhabited after death.

2 concerned with spiritual or intellectual rather than practical matters. ▪ **otherworldliness** *noun*.

otiose /ˈoʊtɪoʊs/ *adj, formal* futile; serving no useful function. [18c: from Latin *otiosus*]

OTT *abbrev, slang* over the top (see under **over**).

otter *noun* (***otters*** *or* ***otter***) a carnivorous semi-aquatic mammal with a long body covered with short smooth fur, a broad flat head and large webbed hind feet. [Anglo-Saxon *otor* or *ottor*]

Ottoman *adj, hist* relating to the Ottomans or their Empire, which lasted from the 13c until the end of World War I, and was centred in what is now Turkey. ▶ *noun* **1** an inhabitant of the Ottoman Empire; a Turk. **2** (**ottoman**) a long low seat, usu without a back or arms. [16c: from Arabic *Utman* Othman or Osman, the founder of the Ottoman Empire]

oubliette /uːblɪˈɛt/ *noun, hist* a secret dungeon with a single, often concealed, opening at the top. [18c: French, from *oublier* to forget]

ouch *exclam* expressing sudden sharp pain.

ought *auxiliary verb* used to express: **1** duty or obligation: *You ought to help if you can.* **2** advisability: *You ought to see a doctor.* **3** probability or expectation: *She ought to be here soon.* **4** shortcoming or failure: *He ought to have been here hours ago.* **5** enthusiastic desire on the part of the speaker: *You really ought to read this book.* **6** logical consequence: *The answer ought to be 'four'.* [Anglo-Saxon *ahte*, past tense of *agen* to owe]

Ouija /ˈwiːdʒə/ *or* **Ouija board** *noun, trademark* (*also* **ouija**) a board with the letters of the alphabet printed round the edge, used with a glass or other object to spell out messages supposed to be from the dead. [19c: from French *oui* yes + German *ja* yes]

ounce *noun* **1** (abbrev **oz**) in the imperial system: a unit of measurement of weight equal to one sixteenth of a pound or about 28.35 grams. **2** short form of **fluid ounce**. **3** a small amount or quantity. [14c: from French *unce*]

our *adj* **1** relating or belonging to, associated with, or done by us: *our children.* **2** relating or belonging to people in general, or to humanity: *our planet.* **3** *formal* used by a sovereign: my: *our royal will.* [Anglo-Saxon *ure*]

Our Father *noun* **the Lord's Prayer**.

Our Lady *noun, RC Church* the Virgin Mary.

ours *pron* the one or ones belonging to us: *They're ours* • *Ours are better.*

ourselves *pron* **1** reflexive form of *we*; us: *We helped ourselves to cakes.* **2** used for emphasis: we personally; our particular group of people: *We ourselves know nothing about that.* **3** our normal selves: *We can relax and be ourselves.* **4** (*also* **by ourselves**) **a** alone: *went by ourselves;* **b** without anyone else's help: *did it all by ourselves.*

-ous *suffix, forming adjectives, signifying* **1** a particular character, quality or nature: *marvellous* • *venomous.* **2** *chem* an element in its lower valency. [From Latin *-osus*]

oust *verb* to force (someone) out of a position and take their place. [16c: from French *oster* to remove]

out *adv* **1** away from the inside; not in or at a place: *Go out into the garden.* **2** not in one's home or place of work: *I called but you were out.* **3** to or at an end; to or into a state of being completely finished, exhausted, etc: *The milk has run out* • *before the day is out.* **4** aloud: *cried out in surprise.* **5** with care or taking care: *watch out.* **6** in all directions from a central point: *Share out the sweets.* **7** to the fullest extent or amount: *Spread the blanket out.* **8** to public attention or notice; revealed: *The secret is out.* **9** *sport* of a person batting: no longer able to bat, eg because of having the ball caught by an opponent. **10** in or into a state of being removed, omitted or forgotten: *Rub out the mistake.* **11** not to be considered; rejected: *That idea's out.* **12** removed; dislocated: *have a tooth out.* **13** not in authority; not having political power: *voted them out of office.* **14** into unconsciousness: *pass out in the heat.* **15** in error: *Your total is out by three.* **16** *informal* existing: *the best car out.* **17** of a flower: in bloom. **18** of a book: published: *will be out in the autumn.* **19** visible: *the moon's out.* **20** no longer in fashion: *Drainpipes are out, flares are in.* **21** of workers: on strike: *called the miners out.* **22** of a jury: considering its verdict. **23** *old use* of a young woman: introduced into fashionable society. **24** of a tide: at or towards the lowest level of water: *The tide's going out.* ▶ *adj* **1** external. **2** directing or showing direction outwards. ▶ *prep, informal, esp US* out of something: *Get out the car.* ▶ *exclam* expressing: **1** *sport* that the batsman is dismissed. **2** that a radio transmission has finished: *over and out.* ▶ *noun* a way out, a way of escape; an excuse. ▶ *verb* **1** *intr* to become publicly known: *Murder will out.* **2** to make public the homosexuality of (a famous person who has been attempting to keep their homosexuality secret). Compare **come out** (sense 6) at **come**. [Anglo-Saxon *ut*]

IDIOMS **be out for sth** *informal* to be determined to achieve it: *He's just out for revenge.* **out and about** active outside the house, esp after an illness. **out of sth 1** from inside it: *drive out of the garage.* **2** not in or within it: *be out of the house.* **3** having exhausted a supply of it: *we're out of butter.* **4** from among several: *two out of three cats.* **5** from a material: *made out of wood.* **6** because of it: *out of anger.* **7** beyond the range, scope or bounds of it: *out of reach.* **8** excluded from it: *leave him out of the team.* **9** no longer in a stated condition: *out of practice.* **10** at a stated distance from a place: *a mile out of town.* **11** without or so as to be without something: *cheat him out of his money.* **out of date** old-fashioned and no longer of use; obsolete. **out of it 1** *informal* not part of, or wanted in, a group or activity, etc. **2** *slang* unable to behave normally or control oneself, usu because of drink or drugs. **out of pocket** having spent more money than one can afford. **out of the way 1** difficult to reach or arrive at. **2** unusual; uncommon. **out with it!** an exhortation to speak openly.

out- *prefix, denoting* **1** an excelling or surpassing of the specified action: *outrun.* **2** external; separate; from outside: *outhouse.* **3** away from the inside, esp as a result of the specified action: *output.* **4** going away or out of; outward: *outdoor.*

outage /ˈaʊtɪdʒ/ *noun* a period of time during which a power supply fails to operate.

out-and-out *adj* complete; utter; thorough: *an out-and-out liar.*

outback *noun* isolated remote areas of a country, esp in Australia.

outbid *verb* to offer a higher price than (someone else), esp at an auction.

outboard *adj* **1** of a motor or engine: portable and designed to be attached to the outside of a boat's stern. **2** of a boat: equipped with such a motor or engine. ▸ *adv, adj* nearer or towards the outside of a ship or aircraft. ▸ *noun* **1** an outboard motor or engine. **2** a boat equipped with an outboard motor or engine. Compare **inboard**.

outbound *adj* of a vehicle, flight, carriageway, etc: going away from home or a station, etc; departing. Opposite of **inbound**.

outbreak *noun* a sudden beginning or occurrence, usu of something unpleasant, eg a disease.

outbuilding *noun* a building such as a barn, stable, etc that is separate from the main building of a house but within the grounds surrounding it.

outburst *noun* **1** a sudden violent expression of strong emotion. **2** an eruption or explosion.

outcast *noun* **1** someone who has been rejected by their friends or by society. **2** an exile or vagabond.

outclass *verb* **1** to be or become of a much better quality or class than (something else). **2** to defeat (someone) easily.

outcome *noun* the result of some action or situation, etc; consequence.

outcrop *noun* a rock or group of rocks which sticks out above the surface of the ground.

outcry *noun* a widespread and public show of anger or disapproval.

outdated *adj* no longer useful or in fashion.

outdistance *verb* to leave (a competitor) far behind.

outdo *verb* to do much better than (someone or something else); to surpass.

outdoor *adj* **1** done, taking place, situated or for use, etc in the open air: *outdoor pursuits*. **2** preferring to be in the open air or fond of outdoor activities and sport, etc: *an outdoor person*.

outdoors *adv* (*also* **out-of-doors**) in or into the open air; outside a building. ▸ *singular noun* the open air; the world outside buildings: *the great outdoors*.

outer *adj* **1** external; belonging to or for the outside. **2** further from the centre or middle. ▸ *noun, archery* **1** the outermost ring on a target. **2** a shot which hits this. [Anglo-Saxon *uterra*]

outermost *adj* nearest the edge; furthest from the centre; most remote.

outer space *noun* any region of space beyond the Earth's atmosphere.

outface *verb* to stare at (someone) until they look away.

outfall *noun* the mouth of a river or sewer, etc where it flows into the sea; an outlet.

outfield *noun* **1** *cricket* the area of the pitch far from the part where the stumps, etc are laid out. **2** *baseball* the area of the field beyond the diamond-shaped pitch where the bases are laid out. Compare **infield**. ▪ **outfielder** *noun*.

outfit *noun* **1** a set of clothes worn together, esp for a particular occasion. **2** a set of articles, tools or equipment, etc for a particular task. **3** *informal* a group of people working as a single unit or team. ▪ **outfitter** *noun*. [19c]

outflank *verb* **1** *military* to go round the side or sides of (an enemy's position). **2** to get the better of (someone or something), esp by a surprise action.

outflow *noun* **1** a flowing out. **2** anything that flows out. **3** the amount that flows out.

outfox *verb* to get the better of (someone) by being more cunning; to outwit (someone).

outgoing *adj* **1** of a person: friendly and sociable; extrovert. **2** leaving; departing. **3** of an official, politician, etc: about to leave office: *the outgoing president*. ▸ *noun* the act of going out.

outgoings *plural noun* money spent; expenditure.

outgrow *verb* **1** to grow too large for (one's clothes). **2** to become too old for (childish ailments or children's games, etc). **3** to grow larger or faster than (someone or something else).

outgrowth *noun* **1** the act or process of growing out. **2** anything which grows out of something else; a by-product.

outhouse *noun* a building, usu a small one such as a shed, etc built close to a house.

outing *noun* a short pleasure trip or excursion.

outlandish *adj* of appearance, etc: very strange; odd; bizarre. [Anglo-Saxon *utlendisc* foreign]

outlaw *noun* **1** *orig* someone excluded from, and deprived of the protection of, the law. **2** a criminal who is a fugitive from the law. ▸ *verb* **1** to deprive (someone) of the protection of the law; to make them an outlaw. **2** to forbid (something) officially.

outlay *noun* money, or occasionally time, spent on something; expenditure.

outlet *noun* **1** a vent or way out, esp for water or steam. **2** a way of releasing or using energy, talents or strong feeling, etc. Opposite of **inlet**. **3** a market for, or a shop that sells, the goods produced by a particular manufacturer. **4** an electrical power point.

outline *noun* **1** a line that forms or marks the outer edge of an object. **2** a drawing with only the outer lines and no shading. **3** the main points, etc without the details: *an outline of the plot*. **4** (*usu* **outlines**) the most important features of something. ▸ *verb* **1** to draw the outline of (something). **2** to give a brief description of the main features of (something).

outlive *verb* **1** to live longer than (someone or something else). **2** to survive the effects of (a disease, etc).

outlook *noun* **1** a view from a particular place. **2** someone's mental attitude or point of view. **3** a prospect for the future.

outmoded *adj* no longer in fashion; out of date.

outpatient *noun* a patient who receives treatment at a hospital or clinic but does not stay there overnight. Compare **inpatient**.

outpost *noun* **1** *military* a group of soldiers stationed at a distance from the main body. **2** a distant or remote settlement or branch.

outpouring *noun* **1** (*usu* **outpourings**) a powerful show of emotion. **2** an amount that pours out.

output *noun* **1** the quantity or amount of something produced. **2** *comput* data transferred from the main memory of a computer to a disk, tape or output device such as a VDU or printer. **3** the power or energy produced by an electrical component or apparatus. ▸ *adj* concerned with output: *output device*. ▸ *verb, comput* to transfer (data from the main memory of a computer) to a disk or tape, or to an output device. Compare **input**.

outrage *noun* **1** an act of great cruelty or violence. **2** an act which breaks accepted standards of morality, honour and decency. **3** great anger or resentment.

▸ *verb* to insult, shock or anger (someone) greatly. [13c: from French *outrer* to exceed]

outrageous *adj* **1** not moderate in behaviour; extravagant. **2** greatly offensive to accepted standards of morality, honour and decency. **3** *informal* terrible; shocking. ▪ **outrageously** *adv.* [14c]

outrank *verb* to have a higher rank than (someone); to be superior to (them).

outré /ˈuːtreɪ/ *adj* not conventional; eccentric; shocking. [18c: French, from *outrer* to exceed]

outrider *noun* an attendant or guard who rides a horse or motorcycle at the side or ahead of a carriage or car conveying an important person.

outrigger *noun, naut* a beam or framework sticking out from the side of a boat to help balance the vessel and prevent it capsizing.

outright *adv* /ɑʊtˈraɪt/ **1** completely: *be proved outright.* **2** immediately; at once: *killed outright.* **3** openly; honestly: *ask outright.* ▸ *adj* /ˈɑʊtraɪt/ **1** complete: *an outright fool.* **2** clear: *the outright winner.* **3** open; honest: *outright disapproval.*

outset *noun* a beginning or start.

outside *noun* /ˈɑʊtsaɪd/ **1** the outer surface; the external parts. Opposite of **inside**. **2** everything that is not inside or within the bounds or scope of something. **3** the farthest limit. **4** the side of a pavement next to the road. ▸ *adj* /ˈɑʊtsaɪd/ **1** relating to, on or near the outside. **2** not forming part of a group, organization or one's regular job, etc: *outside interests.* **3** unlikely; remote. ▸ *adv* /ɑʊtˈsaɪd/ **1** on or to the outside; outdoors. **2** *slang* not in prison. ▸ *prep* /ɑʊtˈsaɪd/ **1** on or to the outside of something. **2** beyond the limits of something. **3** except; apart from.

IDIOMS **at the outside** at the most.

outside broadcast *noun* (abbrev **OB**) a radio or TV programme that is recorded somewhere other than in a studio.

outsider *noun* **1** someone who is not part of a group, etc or who refuses to accept the general values of society. **2** in a race or contest, etc: a competitor who is not expected to win.

outsize *adj* (*also* **outsized**) (abbrev **os**) over normal or standard size. ▸ *noun* anything, esp a garment, that is larger than standard size.

outskirts *plural noun* the outer parts or area, esp of a town or city.

outsmart *verb, informal* to outwit.

outsource *verb,* of a business, company, etc: **1** to subcontract (work) to another company; to contract (work) out. **2** to buy in (parts for a product) from another company rather than manufacture them. ▪ **outsourcing** *noun.*

outspoken *adj* **1** of a person: saying exactly what they think; frank. **2** of a remark or opinion, etc: candid; frank. ▪ **outspokenness** *noun.*

outstanding *adj* **1** excellent; superior; remarkable. **2** not yet paid or done, etc: *outstanding debts.* ▪ **outstandingly** *adv.*

outstation *noun* a position, post or station in a remote or lonely area far from towns.

outstay *verb* **1** to stay longer than the length of (one's invitation, etc): *outstay one's welcome.* **2** to stay longer than (other people).

outstretch *verb* **1** to stretch or spread out; to expand. **2** to reach or stretch out (esp one's hand); to extend. ▪ **outstretched** *adj.*

outstrip *verb* **1** to go faster than (someone or something else). **2** to leave behind; to surpass.

outtake *noun, cinema, TV* a section of film or tape removed from the final edited version of a motion picture or video.

outvote *verb* to defeat (someone or something) by obtaining more votes.

outward *adj* **1** on or towards the outside. **2** of a journey: away from a place. **3** apparent or seeming: *outward appearances.* ▸ *adv* (*also* **outwards**) towards the outside; in an outward direction. ▪ **outwardly** *adv.*

outweigh *verb* **1** to be greater than (something) in weight. **2** to be greater than (something) in value, importance or influence.

outwit *verb* to get the better of or defeat (someone) by being cleverer or more cunning than they are.

outwith *prep, chiefly Scot* outside; beyond.

outwork *noun* (*usu* **outworks**) a defence work that is outside the main line of fortifications.

outworn *adj* esp of an idea, belief or institution: no longer useful or in fashion; out of date; obsolete.

ouzo /ˈuːzoʊ/ *noun* a Greek alcoholic drink flavoured with aniseed and usu drunk diluted with water. [19c: from modern Greek *ouzon*]

ova *pl of* **ovum**

oval *adj* **1** having the outline of an egg; shaped like an egg. **2** *loosely* elliptical. ▸ *noun* any egg-shaped figure or object. [16c: from Latin *ovalis*]

ovary *noun* (**-ies**) **1** in a female animal: the reproductive organ in which the ova are produced. **2** *botany* the base of the carpel of a flower, which contains the ovules. ▪ **ovarian** *adj.* [17c: from Latin *ovarium*]

ovate *adj* egg-shaped. [18c: from Latin *ovatus* egg-shaped]

ovation *noun* sustained applause or cheering to express approval, etc. [16c: from Latin *ovatio*]

oven *noun* **1** a closed compartment or arched cavity in which substances may be heated, used esp for baking or roasting food, drying clay, etc. **2** a small furnace. [Anglo-Saxon *ofen*]

ovenproof *adj* suitable for use in a hot oven.

oven-ready *adj* of food: prepared beforehand so as to be ready for cooking in the oven immediately.

over *adv* **1** above and across. **2** outwards and downwards: *knock him over.* **3** across a space; to or on the other side: *fly over from Australia.* **4** from one person, side or condition to another: *turn the card over.* **5** through, from beginning to end, usu with concentration: *think it over thoroughly.* **6** again; in repetition: *do it twice over.* **7** at an end: *The game is over.* **8** so as to cover completely: *paper the cracks over.* **9** beyond a limit; in excess (of): *go over budget.* **10** remaining: *left over.* ▸ *prep* **1** in or to a position which is above or higher in place, importance, authority, value or number, etc. **2** above and from one side to another: *fly over the sea.* **3** so as to cover: *flopped over his eyes.* **4** out and down from: *fall over the edge.* **5** throughout the extent of: *read over that page again.* **6** during a specified time or period: *sometime over the weekend.* **7** until after a specified time: *stay over Monday night.* **8** more than: *over a year ago.* **9** concerning; about: *argue over who would pay.* **10** while occupied with something: *chat about it over coffee.* **11** occupying time with something: *spend a day over the preparations.* **12** recovered from the effects of something: *She's over the accident.* **13** by means of something: *hear about it over the radio.* **14** divided by: *Six over three is two.* ▸ *adj* **1** upper; higher. **2** outer. **3** excessive. ▸ *exclam* used during two-way radio conversations: showing that one has finished speaking and expects a reply. ▸ *noun, cricket* **1** a series of six (or *formerly* in Australia eight) balls bowled by the same bowler from the same end of the pitch. **2** play during such a series of balls. [Anglo-Saxon *ofer*]

IDIOMS **over and above sth** in addition to it. **over and over again** repeatedly. **over the top** (abbrev **OTT**) *informal* excessive; exaggerated.

over- *prefix, denoting* **1** excessive or excessively; beyond the desired limit: *overconfident*. **2** above; in a higher position or authority: *oversee*. **3** position or movement above: *overhang*. **4** outer; extra: *overcoat*. **5** movement downwards; away from an upright position: *overturn*. **6** completely: *overwhelm*.

overact *verb, tr & intr* to act (a part) with too much expression or emotion.

overall *noun* /ˈoʊvərɔːl/ **1** *Brit* a coat-like garment worn over ordinary clothes to protect them. **2** (**overalls**) a one-piece garment with trousers to cover the legs, worn to protect clothes. ▸ *adj* /ˈoʊvərɔːl/ **1** including everything: *the overall total*. **2** from end to end: *the overall length*. ▸ *adv* /oʊvərˈɔːl/ as a whole; in general: *quite good, overall*.

overarm *adj, adv* of a ball, esp in cricket: bowled or thrown with the hand and arm raised over and moving round the shoulder.

overawe *verb* to subdue or restrain (someone) by filling them with awe, fear or astonishment.

overbalance *verb, tr & intr* to lose or cause (someone or something) to lose balance and fall.

overbearing *adj* **1** domineering; too powerful and proud. **2** having particularly great importance.

overblown *adj* overdone; excessive.

overboard *adv* over the side of a ship or boat into the water: *fall overboard*.

IDIOMS **go overboard** *informal* to be very or too enthusiastic.

overburden *verb* to give (someone) too much to do, carry or think about.

overcast *adj* of the sky or weather: cloudy.

overcharge *verb* **1** *tr & intr* to charge (someone) too much. **2** to overfill or overload (something).

overcoat *noun* a warm heavy coat.

overcome *verb* **1** to defeat (someone or something); to succeed in a struggle against (them or it). **2** to deal successfully with (something): *overcame his problems*. **3** *intr* to be victorious. **4** to affect (someone) strongly; to overwhelm (them).

overdo *verb* **1** to do (something) too much; to exaggerate. **2** to cook (food) for too long. **3** to use too much of (something).

IDIOMS **overdo it** *or* **things** to work too hard.

overdose *noun* an excessive dose of a drug, etc. ▸ *verb, tr & intr* to take an overdose or give an excessive dose to (someone). See also **OD**[1].

overdraft *noun* **1** a state in which one has taken more money out of one's bank account than was in it. **2** the excess of money taken from one's account over the sum that was in it. [19c]

overdraw *verb, tr & intr* to draw more money from (one's bank account) than is in it. ▪ **overdrawn** *adj*.

overdress *verb, tr & intr* to dress (someone or oneself) in clothes that are too formal, smart or expensive for the occasion.

overdrive *noun* an additional very high gear in a motor vehicle's gearbox, which reduces wear on the engine and saves fuel when travelling at high speeds.

overdue *adj* of bills or work, etc: not yet paid, done or delivered, etc, although the date for doing this has passed.

overestimate *verb* to estimate or judge, etc (something) too highly. ▸ *noun* too high an estimate.

overexpose *verb* **1** to expose (someone) to too much publicity. **2** to expose (photographic film) to too much light. ▪ **overexposure** *noun*.

overflow *verb* **1** to flow over (a brim) or go beyond (the limits or edge of something). **2** *intr* of a container, etc: to be filled so full that the contents spill over or out. **3** (**overflow with sth**) *intr* to be full of it: *was overflowing with gratitude*. ▸ *noun* **1** something that overflows. **2** the act of flowing over. **3** a pipe or outlet for surplus water. **4** an excess or abundance of something.

overgrown *adj* **1** of a garden, etc: dense with plants that have grown too large and thick. **2** grown too large or beyond the normal size.

overhang *verb, tr & intr* to project or hang out over (something). ▸ *noun* **1** a piece of rock or part of a roof, etc that overhangs. **2** the amount by which something overhangs.

overhaul *verb* **1** to examine carefully and repair (something). **2** to overtake. ▸ *noun* a thorough examination and repair.

overhead *adv, adj* above; over one's head. ▸ *noun* (**overheads**) the regular costs of a business, such as rent, wages and electricity.

overhear *verb, tr & intr* to hear (a person or remark, etc) without the speaker knowing.

overheat *verb* **1** to heat (something) excessively. **2** *intr* to become too hot. **3** *econ* to overstimulate (the economy) with the risk of increasing inflation.

overjoyed *adj* very glad; elated.

overkill *noun* action, behaviour or treatment, etc that is far in excess of what is required.

overladen *adj* overloaded.

overlap *verb* **1** of part of an object: to partly cover (another object). **2** *intr* of two parts: to have one part partly covering the other. **3** *intr* of two things: to have something in common; to partly coincide.

overlay *verb* /oʊvəˈleɪ/ to lay (one thing) on or over (another). ▸ *noun* /ˈoʊvə-/ **1** a covering; something that is laid over something else. **2** a layer, eg of gold leaf, applied to something for decoration. **3** *comput* **a** the process by which segments of a large program are brought from backing store for processing, with only those segments currently requiring processing being held in the main store; **b** a segment of a program transferred in this way.

overleaf *adv* on the other side of the page.

overload *verb* **1** to load (something) too heavily. **2** to put too great an electric current through (a circuit). ▸ *noun* too great an electric current flowing through a circuit.

overlook *verb* **1** to give a view of (something) from a higher position: *overlooks the garden*. **2** to fail to see or notice (something). **3** to allow (a mistake or crime, etc) to go unpunished.

overlord *noun* a lord or ruler with supreme power.

overly *adv* too; excessively.

overnice *adj* fussy; critical and hard to please.

overnight *adv* **1** during the night. **2** for the duration of the night. **3** suddenly: *Success came overnight.* ▸ *adj* **1** done or occurring in the night. **2** sudden: *an overnight success.* **3** for use overnight: *an overnight bag.*

overpass see under **flyover**

overplay *verb* **1** to exaggerate or overemphasize (the importance of something). **2** *tr & intr* to exaggerate (an emotion, etc); to act in an exaggerated way. IDIOMS **overplay one's hand** to overestimate or overtax one's talents or assets, etc.

overpopulation *noun, geog* more people in a given area than the natural resources of the area can sustain. ▪ **overpopulated** *adj.*

overpower *verb* **1** to defeat or subdue (someone or something) by greater strength. **2** to weaken or reduce (someone or something) to helplessness. ▪ **overpowering** *adj.*

overproduction *noun* the production of more food, goods, etc than can be sold.

overqualified *adj* with more qualifications or experience than are required for a particular job.

overrate *verb* to value too highly. ▪ **overrated** *adj.*

overreach *verb* **1** to defeat (oneself) by trying to do too much. **2** to strain (oneself) by trying to reach too far.

overreact *verb, intr* to react excessively or too strongly. ▪ **overreaction** *noun.*

override *verb* **1** to ride over; to cross (an area) by riding. **2** to dominate or assume superiority over (someone). **3** to annul something or set it aside. **4** to take manual control of (a normally automatically controlled operation). ▪ **overriding** *adj* dominant; most important.

overrule *verb* **1** to rule against or cancel (esp a previous decision or judgement) by higher authority. **2** to impose a decision on (a person) by higher authority.

overrun *verb* **1** to spread over or through (something); to infest (it): *overrun with weeds.* **2** to occupy an area, country, etc quickly and by force. **3** *tr & intr* to go beyond (a fixed limit).

overseas *adv* in or to a land beyond the sea; abroad: *working overseas.* ▸ *adj* (*also* **oversea**) across or from beyond the sea: *an overseas posting.* ▸ *noun* a foreign country or foreign countries in general.

oversee *verb* to supervise (someone or something). ▪ **overseer** *noun.*

oversew *verb* to sew (two edges) together with close stitches that pass over both edges.

overshadow *verb* **1** to seem much more important than (someone or something else); to outshine (them). **2** to cast a shadow over (something); to make (it) seem more gloomy.

overshoe *noun* a shoe, usu made of rubber or plastic, worn over a normal shoe to protect it.

overshoot *verb* to shoot or go farther than (a target aimed at). ▸ *noun* **1** the action or an act of overshooting. **2** the degree to which something overshoots.

oversight *noun* a mistake or omission, esp one made through a failure to notice something.

oversize *adj* (*also* **oversized**) larger than normal.

oversleep *verb, intr* to sleep longer than one intended.

overspend *verb* **1** to spend in excess of (a specified amount or limit, etc). **2** *intr* to spend too much money; to spend beyond one's means.

overspill *noun, Brit* the people leaving an overcrowded or derelict town area to live elsewhere.

overstate *verb* to state (something) too strongly; to exaggerate. ▪ **overstatement** *noun.*

overstay *verb* to stay longer than the length of (one's invitation, etc): *overstay one's welcome.*

overstep *verb* (*esp* **overstep the mark**) to go beyond (a certain limit, or what is prudent or reasonable).

oversubscribe *verb* to apply for or try to purchase (eg shares, etc) in larger quantities than are available.

overt *adj* not hidden or secret; open; public. ▪ **overtly** *adv.* [14c: from French *ouvert* open]

overtake *verb* **1** *tr & intr, chiefly Brit* to catch up with and go past (a car or a person, etc) moving in the same direction. **2** to draw level with and begin to do better than (someone). **3** to come upon (someone) suddenly or without warning: *overtaken by bad weather.*

overtax *verb* **1** to demand too much tax from (someone). **2** to put too great a strain on (someone).

over-the-counter *adj* of goods, eg drugs and medicines: legally sold directly to the customer.

overthrow *verb* **1** to defeat completely (an established order or a government, etc). **2** to upset or overturn (something). ▸ *noun* the act of overthrowing or state of being overthrown.

overtime *noun* **1** time spent working beyond the regular hours. **2** money paid for this. **3** *sport, N Am* extra time. ▸ *adv* during overtime; in addition to regular hours: *work overtime.*

overtone *noun* **1** (*often* **overtones**) a subtle hint, quality or meaning; a nuance: *political overtones.* **2** *music* a tone that contributes towards a musical sound and adds to its quality.

overture *noun* **1** *music* **a** an orchestral introduction to an opera, oratorio or ballet; **b** a one-movement orchestral composition in a similar style. **2** (*usu* **overtures**) a proposal or offer intended to open a discussion, negotiations or a relationship, etc. [14c: French, meaning 'opening']

overturn *verb* **1** *tr & intr* to turn or cause (something) to be turned over or upside down. **2** to bring down or destroy (a government). **3** to overrule or cancel (a previous legal decision).

overview *noun* a brief general account or description of a subject, etc; a summary.

overweening *adj* **1** of a person: arrogant; conceited. **2** of pride: inflated and excessive. [14c: from Anglo-Saxon *wenan* to think or believe]

overweight *adj* above the desired or usual weight.

overwhelm *verb* **1** to crush mentally; to overpower (a person's emotions or thoughts, etc). **2** to defeat completely by superior force or numbers. **3** to supply or offer (something) in great amounts. ▪ **overwhelming** *adj.* ▪ **overwhelmingly** *adv.*

overwind *verb* to wind (a watch, etc) too far.

overwork *verb* **1** *intr* to work too hard. **2** to make (someone) work too hard. **3** to make too much use of (something). ▸ *noun* excessive work.

overwrite *verb* **1** to write on top of (something else). **2** *comput* to record new information over (existing data), thereby destroying (it).

overwrought *adj* very nervous or excited; over-emotional.

oviduct *noun, anatomy, zool* the tube through which ova are conveyed from the ovary. [18c: from Latin *ovum* egg + **duct**]

oviform *adj* egg-shaped. [17c]

ovine *adj* relating to or characteristic of a sheep or sheep; sheep-like. [19c: from Latin *ovinus*]

oviparous /oʊ'vɪpərəs/ *adj, zool* laying eggs that develop and hatch outside the mother's body. Compare **ovoviviparous**, **viviparous**. [17c]

ovipositor *noun, zool* an egg-laying organ in female insects and some female fishes. [19c: from Latin *ovum* egg + *positor* placer]

ovoid /'oʊvɔɪd/ *adj, chiefly zool & botany* egg-shaped; oval. [19c: from French *ovoïde*]

ovoviviparous /oʊvoʊvɪ'vɪpərəs/ *adj, zool* producing eggs that hatch within the body of the mother. Compare **oviparous**, **viviparous**. [19c]

ovulate *verb, intr, physiol* **1** to release an ovum or egg cell from the ovary. **2** to form or produce ova. ▪ **ovulation** *noun*. [19c: from Latin *ovum* egg]

ovule *noun, botany* in flowering plants: the structure that develops into a seed after fertilization. ▪ **ovular** *adj*. [19c: from Latin *ovulum*]

ovum *noun* (***ova***) **1** *biol* an unfertilized egg or egg cell. **2** *botany* the non-motile female gamete. [18c: Latin, meaning 'egg']

owe *verb* **1** *tr & intr* to be under an obligation to pay (money) (to someone): *owes him £5*. **2** to feel required by duty or gratitude to do or give (someone) (something): *owe you an explanation*. **3** (**owe sth to sb** *or* **sth**) to have or enjoy it as a result of them or it. [Anglo-Saxon *agan* to own]

owing *adj* still to be paid; due.

IDIOMS **owing to sth** because of it; on account of it.

owl *noun* a nocturnal bird of prey with a flat face, large forward-facing eyes and a short hooked beak. ▪ **owlish** *adj*. [Anglo-Saxon *ule*]

owlet *noun* a young or small owl.

own *adj* often used for emphasis: belonging to or for oneself or itself: *my own sister*. ▸ *pron* one belonging (or something belonging) to oneself or itself: *lost his own, so I lent him mine*. ▸ *verb* **1** to have (something) as a possession or property. **2** (*usu* **own to sth**) *intr* to admit or confess to it: *owned to many weaknesses*. ▪ **owner** *noun*. ▪ **ownership** *noun*. [Anglo-Saxon *agen*, past participle of *agan* to possess]

IDIOMS **come into one's own 1** to take possession of one's rights or what is due to one. **2** to have one's abilities or talents, etc duly recognized, or to realize one's potential. **hold one's own** to maintain one's position, esp in spite of difficulty or opposition, etc; not to be defeated. **on one's own 1** alone. **2** without help.

PHRASAL VERBS **own up** *or* **own up to sth** to confess; to admit a wrongdoing, etc.

own goal *noun* **1** *sport* a goal scored by mistake for the opposing side. **2** *informal* an action that turns out to be to the disadvantage of the person who took it.

ox *noun* (***oxen***) an adult castrated bull, used for pulling loads or as a source of meat. [Anglo-Saxon *oxa*]

oxalic acid *noun, chem* a highly poisonous white crystalline solid that occurs in certain plants.

oxbow *noun* (*also* **oxbow lake**) a shallow curved lake on a river's flood plain formed when one of the meanders of the river has been cut off.

Oxbridge *noun, Brit* the universities of Oxford and Cambridge considered together.

oxen *pl of* **ox**

oxidant *noun* **1** *chem* an oxidizing agent. **2** *engineering* a chemical compound, usually one containing oxygen, that is mixed with fuel and burned in the combustion chamber of a rocket. [19c]

oxidation *noun, chem* the process of oxidizing.

oxide *noun, chem* any compound of oxygen and another element. [18c: French, from *ox(ygène)* oxygen + *(ac)ide* acid]

oxidize *or* **-ise** *verb, tr & intr, chem* **1** to undergo, or cause (a substance) to undergo, a chemical reaction with oxygen. **2** to lose or cause (an atom or ion) to lose electrons. **3** to become, or make (something) become, rusty as a result of the formation of a layer of metal oxide. ▪ **oxidization** *noun*. ▪ **oxidizer** *noun*.

oxlip /'ɒkslɪp/ *noun* **1** a naturally occurring hybrid of the common primrose and the cowslip, with deep-yellow flowers. **2** the true oxlip, which has pale-yellow flowers in a one-sided cluster. [Anglo-Saxon *oxanslyppe*, from *oxa* ox + *slyppe* slime]

oxtail *noun* the tail of an ox used as food.

oxyacetylene *noun* a mixture of oxygen and acetylene which burns with an extremely hot flame and is used in torches for cutting and welding metals.

oxygen *noun* (symbol **O**) a colourless odourless tasteless gas, which is an essential requirement of most forms of plant and animal life. [18c: from Greek *oxys* sharp or acid + *gennaein* to generate]

oxygenate *verb* to combine, treat, supply or enrich (eg the blood) with oxygen. ▪ **oxygenation** *noun*.

oxygen mask *noun* a mask-like breathing apparatus that covers the nose and mouth, and is used to supply oxygen on demand, esp in rarefied atmospheres by mountaineers, aircraft passengers, etc.

oxymoron *noun* a rhetorical figure of speech in which contradictory terms are used together, often for emphasis or effect, eg *horribly good*. [17c: from Greek *oxys* sharp + *moros* foolish]

oyez *or* **oyes** /oʊ'jɛz, oʊ'jɛs/ *exclam, hist* a cry for silence and attention, usu shouted three times by an official before a public announcement. [15c: from French *oyez* or *oiez*, meaning 'Hear!' or 'Hear ye!']

oyster *noun* a marine mollusc with a soft fleshy body enclosed by a hinged shell, eaten as food, certain types of which produce pearls. [14c: from French *huistre*]

Oz *or* **Ozzie** *adj, noun, slang* Australian. [20c as *Oss* or *Ossie*: imitating the pronunciation *Aus*tralia(n)]

oz *abbrev* ounce or ounces. [16c: from Italian *onza* ounce]

ozone *noun, chem* a pungent **allotrope** of oxygen formed when an electric spark acts on oxygen. [19c: from Greek *ozein* to smell]

ozone-friendly *adj* of products such as aerosols, etc: free from chemicals, eg chlorofluorocarbons, that deplete the ozone layer.

ozone layer *or* **ozonosphere** *noun* a layer of the upper atmosphere where ozone is formed, which filters harmful ultraviolet radiation from the Sun and prevents it from reaching the Earth.

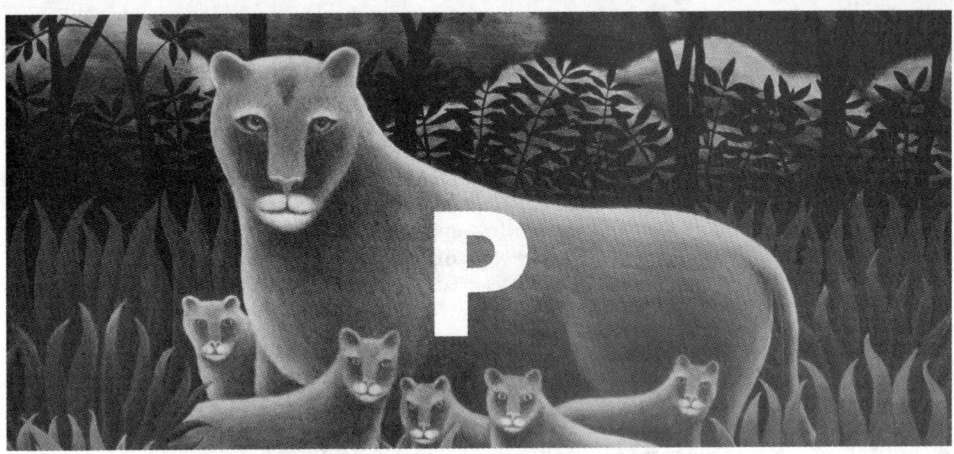

P[1] *or* **p** *noun* (***Ps, P's*** *or* ***p's***) the sixteenth letter of the English alphabet.
IDIOMS **mind one's p's and q's** *informal* to behave with the etiquette suitable to a particular situation.

P[2] *abbrev* as a street sign: parking.

P[3] *symbol* **1** *chess* pawn. **2** *chem* phosphorus.

p *abbrev* **1** page. Also written **pg**. See also **pp**. **2** penny or pence.

PA *abbrev* **1** personal assistant. **2** public-address system.

Pa *symbol* **1** pascal. **2** *chem* protactinium.

pa *noun* a familiar word for **father**. [Early 19c]

p.a. *symbol* per annum.

pace[1] /ˈpeɪs/ *noun* **1** a single step. **2** the distance covered by one step when walking. **3** rate of walking or running, etc: *at a slow pace.* **4** rate of movement or progress: *at your own pace.* **5** any of the gaits used by a horse. ▸ *verb* **1** *tr & intr* (*often* **pace about** *or* **around**) to keep walking about, in a preoccupied or frustrated way. **2** *intr* to walk steadily. **3** to set the pace for (others) in a race, etc. **4** (*often* **pace sth out**) to measure out (a distance) in paces. [14c: from French *pas* step]
IDIOMS **go through** *or* **show one's paces** to demonstrate one's skills at something. **keep pace with sb** to go as fast as them. **put sb through their paces** to test them in some activity. **set the pace** to be ahead of, and so set the rate for, others.

pace[2] /ˈpeɪsiː, ˈpɑːkeɪ/ *prep* with due respect to (someone with whom one is disagreeing). [19c: Latin ablative of *pax* peace or pardon]

pacemaker *noun* **1** *med* an electronic device that stimulates the heart muscle to contract at a specific and regular rate, used to correct weak or irregular heart rhythms. **2** a pacesetter.

pacesetter *noun* a person, horse, vehicle, etc that sets the pace in a race; a leader.

pachyderm /ˈpakɪdɜːm/ *noun* any large thick-skinned non-ruminant mammal, esp the elephant, rhinoceros or hippopotamus. [19c: from Greek *pachys* thick + *derma* skin]

pacific *adj* tending to make peace or keep the peace; peaceful; peaceable. [16c: from Latin *pacificus*, literally 'peacemaking']

pacifier *noun, N Am* a baby's **dummy**.

pacifist *noun* someone who believes that violence is unjustified and refuses to take part in making war. ▪ **pacifism** *noun*. [20c: from French *pacifiste*]

pacify *verb* (***-ies, -ied***) **1** to calm, soothe or appease someone. **2** to restore something to a peaceful condition. ▪ **pacification** *noun*. [17c: from French *pacifier*]

pack[1] *noun* **1** a collection of things tied into a bundle for carrying. **2** a rucksack; a backpack. **3** a set of playing cards, usu 52. **4** a group of animals living and hunting together, eg dogs or wolves. **5** a compact package, eg of equipment for a purpose: *a first-aid pack.* **6** *in compounds* a collection of things of a specified number or for a specified purpose: *a four-pack* • *a party-pack.* **7** *derog* a collection or bunch: *a pack of lies.* **8** a group of Brownie Guides or Cub Scouts. **9** *rugby* the forwards in a team. **10** a medicinal or cosmetic skin preparation: *a face pack.* ▸ *verb* **1** to stow (goods, clothes, etc) compactly in cases, boxes, etc for transport or travel. **2** *intr* to put one's belongings into a suitcase, rucksack, travel bag, etc, ready for a journey: *Have you packed yet?* **3** to put (goods, food, etc) into a container, or to wrap them, ready for sale. **4** (*usu* **pack sth in**) **a** to push and cram it into something that is already quite full; **b** to cram (a great deal of activity) into a limited period. **5** *intr* to be capable of being formed into a compact shape. **6** to fill something tightly or compactly: *The hall was packed.* **7** *tr & intr, N Am informal* to make a habit of carrying (a gun). [13c]
IDIOMS **packed out** of a place: very busy. **send sb packing** *informal* to send them away unceremoniously.
PHRASAL VERBS **pack sb off** to send them off hastily or abruptly. **pack up 1** to stop work, etc at the end of the day or shift, etc. **2** *informal* of machinery, etc: to break down.

pack[2] *verb* to fill (a jury, meeting, etc) illicitly with people one can rely on to support one. [16c, orig in obsolete sense 'to intrigue']

package *noun* **1** something wrapped and secured with string, adhesive tape, etc; a parcel. **2** a case, box or other container for packing goods in. **3** a **package deal**. **4** *comput* a group of related computer programs designed to perform a particular complex task.

package deal *noun* a deal covering a number of related proposals that must be accepted as a whole.

package holiday *or* **package tour** *noun* a holiday or tour for which one pays a fixed price that includes travel, accommodation, meals, etc.

packaging *noun* the wrappers or containers in which goods are packed and presented for sale.

pack animal *noun* an animal, eg a donkey, mule or horse, used to carry luggage or goods for sale.

packet *noun* **1** a wrapper or container made of paper, cardboard or plastic, with its contents: *packet of biscuits*. **2** a small pack or package. **3** a boat that transports mail and also carries cargo and passengers, travelling a regular and fixed route. Also called **packet boat**. **4** *informal* a large sum of money: *cost a packet*. [16c: from French *pacquet*]

pack ice *noun* a large area of free-floating sea ice consisting of pieces that have been driven together to form a solid mass.

packing *noun* **1** materials used for padding or wrapping goods for transport, etc. **2** the act of putting anything into packs or tying it up for transporting or storing.

pact *noun* an agreement reached between two or more parties, states, etc for mutual advantage. [15c: from Latin *pactum* agreement or covenant]

pad[1] *noun* **1** a wad of material used to cushion, protect, shape or clean. **2** a leg-guard for a cricketer, etc. **3** *also in compounds* a quantity of sheets of paper fixed together into a block: *notepad*. **4** a rocket-launching platform. **5** the soft fleshy underside of an animal's paw. **6** *N Am* a large water lily leaf. **7** *slang* the place where someone lives. ▸ *verb* (***padded, padding***) **1** to cover, fill, stuff, cushion or shape something with layers of soft material. **2** (*also* **pad sth out**) *derog* to include unnecessary or irrelevant material in (a piece of writing, speech, etc) for the sake of length. [16c]

pad[2] *verb* (***padded, padding***) **1** *intr* to walk softly or with a quiet or muffled tread. **2** *tr & intr* to tramp along (a road); to travel on foot. [16c: Dutch, meaning 'path']

padding *noun* **1** material for cushioning, shaping or filling. **2** *derog* irrelevant or unnecessary matter in a speech or piece of writing, added to extend it to the desired length.

paddle[1] *verb* **1** *intr* to walk about barefoot in shallow water. **2** to trail or dabble (fingers, etc) in water. ▸ *noun* a spell of paddling: *went for a paddle in the sea*. [16c]

paddle[2] *noun* **1** a short light oar with a blade at one or both ends, used to propel and steer a canoe, kayak, etc. **2** one of the slats fitted round the edge of a paddle wheel or mill wheel. **3** a paddle-shaped instrument for stirring, beating, etc. **4** *US* a small bat, as used in table tennis. ▸ *verb, tr & intr* **1** to propel (a canoe, kayak, etc) with paddles. **2** *intr* (*also* **paddle along**) to move through water using, or as if using, a paddle or paddles.

paddle wheel *noun* a large engine-driven wheel at the side or back of a ship which propels the ship through the water as it turns.

paddock *noun* **1** a small enclosed field for keeping a horse in. **2** *horse-racing* an enclosure beside a race track where horses are saddled and walked round before a race. [16c]

paddy[1] *noun* (**-*ies***) *informal* a fit of rage.

paddy[2] *noun* (**-*ies***) **1** (*also* **paddy field**) a field filled with water in which rice is grown. **2** rice as a growing crop; harvested rice grains that have not been processed in any way. [17c: from Malay *padi*]

padlock *noun* a detachable lock with a U-shaped bar that pivots at one side, so that it can be passed through a ring or chain and locked in position. ▸ *verb* to fasten (a door, cupboard, etc) with a padlock. [15c]

padre /ˈpɑːdreɪ/ *noun* a chaplain in any of the armed services. [16c: Portuguese, Spanish and Italian, meaning 'father']

paean *or* (*US*) **pean** /pɪən/ *noun* a song of triumph, praise or thanksgiving. [16c: from Greek *Paian* the physician of the gods, used as a title for Apollo]

paediatrician *or* (*N Am*) **pediatrician** /piːdɪəˈtrɪʃən/ *noun* a doctor who specializes in the study, diagnosis and treatment of children's diseases.

paediatrics *or* (*N Am*) **pediatrics** /piːdɪˈatrɪks/ *singular noun, med* the branch of medicine concerned with the health and care of children. ▪ **paediatric** *or* (*N Am*) **pediatric** *adj*. [19c]

paedophilia /piːdoʊˈfɪlɪə/ *noun* sexual attraction to children. ▪ **paedophile** *noun*. [From Greek *paid-*, *pais* child]

paella /paɪˈɛlə/ *noun, cookery* a Spanish rice dish of fish or chicken with vegetables and saffron. [19c: Catalan, from Latin *patella* pan]

pagan *adj* **1 a** not Christian, Jewish, or Muslim; **b** belonging or relating to, or following, a religion in which a number of gods are worshipped. **2** without religious belief. ▸ *noun* a pagan person; a heathen. ▪ **paganism** *noun*. [14c: from Latin *paganus* a rustic or villager]

page[1] *noun* (abbrev **p** *or* **pa**, *pl* ***pp***) **1** one side of a leaf in a book, etc. **2** a leaf of a book, etc. **3** *literary* an episode or incident in history, one's life, etc: *a dark page in history*. [16c: French]

page[2] *noun* **1** *hist* a boy attendant serving a knight and training for knighthood. **2** a boy attending the bride at a wedding. **3** a boy who carries messages or luggage, etc in hotels, clubs, etc. ▸ *verb* to summon someone by calling their name out loud, or through a **public-address system** or **pager**. [13c: French, from Italian *paggio*]

pageant /ˈpadʒənt/ *noun* **1** a series of tableaux or dramatic scenes, usu depicting local historical events or other topical matters. **2** any colourful and varied spectacle, esp involving a procession. [14c: from Latin *pagina* page, scene or stage]

pageantry /ˈpadʒəntrɪ/ *noun* splendid display; pomp.

pageboy *noun* **1** a **page**[2] (*noun* sense 2). **2** a smooth jaw-length hairstyle with the ends curled under. *as adj*: *a pageboy cut*.

pager *noun, telecomm* a small individually-worn radio receiver and transmitter that enables its user to receive a signal (typically a 'beep' or a short message) to which they can respond with a phone call, etc to the sender. Also called **bleeper**, **bleep**.

paginate *verb* to give consecutive numbers to the pages of (a text), carried out by a command within a word-processing package, or as part of the printing process, etc. Compare **foliate**. ▪ **pagination** *noun*. [19c: from Latin *pagina* page]

pagoda *noun* **1** a Buddhist shrine or memorial building in India, China and parts of SE Asia, esp in the form of a tall tower with many storeys. **2** an ornamental building imitating this. [17c: from Portuguese *pagode*]

paid *verb, past tense, past participle of* **pay**.
IDIOMS **put paid to sth** to destroy any chances of success in it.

paid-up *adj* of a society member, etc: having paid a membership fee. See **pay up** at **pay**.

pail *noun* a bucket. [Anglo-Saxon *pægel* gill (liquid measure)]

paillasse see **palliasse**

pain *noun* **1** an uncomfortable, distressing or agonizing sensation caused by the stimulation of specialized nerve endings by heat, cold, pressure or other strong stimuli. **2** emotional suffering. **3** *derog informal* an irritating or troublesome person or thing. **4** (**pains**) trouble taken or efforts made in doing something. ▸ *verb, rather formal* to cause distress to someone: *It pained me to see the injured donkey.* [13c: from Latin *poena* punishment]
IDIOMS **on pain of sth** at the risk of incurring it as a punishment. **take pains** to be careful to do something properly; to be thorough over a task, etc.

pained *adj* of an expression, tone of voice, etc: expressing distress or disapproval.

painful *adj* **1** causing pain: *a painful injury.* **2** of part of the body: affected by some injury, etc which causes pain. **3** causing distress: *a painful duty.* **4** laborious and slow: *painful progress.* ▪ **painfully** *adv.*

pain in the neck *noun, slang* **1** an exasperating circumstance. **2** an annoying or tiresome person.

painkiller *noun* any drug or other agent that relieves pain; an **analgesic**.

painless *adj* without pain. ▪ **painlessly** *adv.*

painstaking *adj* conscientious and thorough, ie taking pains or care: *painstaking work.* ▪ **painstakingly** *adv.*

paint *noun* **1** colouring matter, esp in the form of a liquid, which is applied to a surface and dries forming a hard surface. **2** a dried coating of this. **3** *old use* face make-up; cosmetics. ▸ *verb* **1** to apply a coat of paint to (walls, woodwork, etc). **2** to turn something a certain colour by this means: *paint the door yellow.* **3** *tr & intr* to make (pictures) using paint. **4** to depict (a person, place or thing) in paint. **5** to describe (a scene, place or person) as if in paint. **6** *tr & intr, old use* to put make-up on (one's face). [13c: from French *peint*]
IDIOMS **paint the town red** to go out and celebrate something lavishly.

paintball *noun* a game in which players shoot each other with pellets of paint fired from compressed-air guns.

paintbrush *noun* a brush of any kind used for applying paint, eg used by an artist or a decorator.

painter *noun* **1** someone who decorates houses internally or externally with paint. **2** an artist who paints pictures.

painting *noun* **1** a painted picture. **2** the art or process of applying paint to walls, etc. **3** the art of creating pictures in paint.

pair *noun* **1** a set of two identical or corresponding things, eg shoes or gloves, intended for use together. **2** something consisting of two joined and corresponding parts: *a pair of trousers • a pair of scissors.* **3** one of a matching pair: *Where's this earring's pair?* **4** two people associated in a relationship; a couple. **5** two mating animals, birds, fishes, etc. **6** two horses harnessed together: *a coach and pair.* **7** two playing cards of the same denomination. **8** in a parliament: two voters on opposite sides who have an agreement to abstain from voting on a specific motion. ▸ *verb* **1** *tr & intr* (*often* **pair off** *or* **pair sth** *or* **sb off**) to divide into groups of two; to sort out in pairs. **2** *intr* of two opposing voters in a parliament: to agree a **pair** (*noun* sense 8) or to have such an agreement. ▪ **paired** *adj.* [13c: from French *paire* a couple]
IDIOMS **in pairs** in twos.

paisley *or* **paisley pattern** *noun* a design whose characteristic feature is a highly ornate device which looks like a tree cone with a curving point, used mainly on fabrics. [19c: first used on a shawl made in Paisley, Scotland]

pajamas see **pyjamas**

Pakistani *adj* belonging or relating to Pakistan, a republic in S Asia, or to its inhabitants. ▸ *noun* **1** a citizen or inhabitant of, or person born in, Pakistan. **2** an immigrant from, or a person whose ancestors are immigrants from, Pakistan. [1940s]

pakora /pəˈkɔːrə/ *noun* an Indian dish of vegetables, chicken, etc formed into balls, coated in batter and deep-fried. [1950s: Hindi]

pal *informal, noun* a friend; a mate. ▸ *verb* (***palled, palling***) *intr* (*usu* **pal up with sb**) to make friends with them. ▪ **pally** *adj* (***-ier, -iest***). [17c: Romany, meaning 'brother']

palace *noun* **1** the official residence of a sovereign, bishop, archbishop or president. **2** a spacious and magnificent residence or other building; a palatial home. [13c: from French *paleis*]

paladin *noun, hist* **1** any of the 12 peers of Charlemagne's court. **2** a **knight errant**; a champion of a sovereign. [16c: from Italian *paladino*]

palaeo- *or* **paleo-** /palɪoʊ/ *or* (*before a vowel*) **palae-** *or* **pale-** *combining form, denoting* **1** old; ancient. **2** the very distant past. Most of the following forms can be spelt as either *palaeo-* or *paleo-*. [From Greek *palaios* old]

Palaeocene *adj, geol* the earliest epoch of the **Tertiary** period, during which time many reptiles became extinct and mammals became the dominant vertebrates. [19c]

palaeography /palɪˈɒgrəfɪ/ *noun* **1** the study of ancient writing and manuscripts. **2** an ancient handwriting. ▪ **palaeographer** *noun.* [19c]

palaeolithic *or* **Palaeolithic** *adj* relating or belonging to an early period of the Stone Age, extending from about 2.5 million years ago to about 10,000 years ago, characterized by the use by primitive people of tools made of unpolished chipped stone. [19c]

palaeontology *noun, geol* the scientific study of the structure, distribution, environment and evolution of extinct life forms by interpretation of their fossil remains. ▪ **palaeontologist** *noun.* [19c: from **palaeo-** + Greek *onta* being + *logos* word or reason]

Palaeozoic /palɪoʊˈzoʊɪk/ *adj, geol* relating to the era of geological time extending from about 580 million to 250 million years ago, during which time the first vertebrates appeared. [19c: from Greek *zoion* animal]

palamino see **palomino**

palanquin *or* **palankeen** /paləŋˈkiːn/ *noun, hist* a light covered litter used in the Orient. [16c: from Portuguese *palanquim*]

palatable *adj* **1** having a pleasant taste; appetizing. **2** acceptable; agreeable. [17c]

palatal *adj* **1** relating to the palate. **2** *phonetics* of a speech sound: produced by bringing the tongue to or near the hard palate. ▸ *noun, phonetics* a sound produced in this way, eg /j/ as in *yellow* /jɛloʊ/.

palate /'palət/ *noun* **1** the roof of the mouth. **2** the sense of taste. [14c: from Latin *palatum*]

palatial *adj* like a palace in magnificence, spaciousness, etc. [18c: from Latin *palatium* **palace**]

palatine *adj* **1** referring to a palace. **2** having royal privileges or jurisdiction. [15c]

palaver /pə'lɑːvə(r)/ *noun* **1** a long, boring, complicated and seemingly pointless exercise; an unnecessary fuss: *What a palaver!* **2** idle chatter. [18c: from Portuguese *palavra*]

pale[1] *adj* **1** of a person, face, etc: having less colour than normal, eg from illness, fear, shock, etc. **2** of a colour: whitish; closer to white than black; light: *pale-green.* **3** lacking brightness or vividness; subdued: *pale sunlight.* ▸ *verb, intr* **1** to become pale. **2** to fade or become weaker or less significant: *My worries pale by comparison.* ▪ **paleness** *noun.* [13c: from French *palle*]

pale[2] *noun* **1** a wooden or metal post or stake used for making fences. **2** a fence made of these; a boundary fence. See also **paling**. [14c: from Latin *palus* stake]
IDIOMS **beyond the pale** outside the limits of acceptable behaviour; intolerable.

pale- *or* **paleo-** see **palaeo-**

palette /'palət/ *noun* **1** a hand-held board with a thumb-hole, on which an artist mixes colours. **2** the range of colours used by a particular artist, in a particular picture, etc. [17c: French, literally 'small spade']

palette knife *noun* **1** an artist's knife for mixing and applying paint. **2** a round-ended knife used for spreading butter, mixing ingredients, etc.

Pali *noun* the sacred language of the Buddhists of India, closely related to Sanskrit. [18c: from Sanskrit *pali-bhasa*, from *pali* canon + *bhasa* language]

palimpsest *noun* a parchment or other ancient writing surface re-used after the original content has been erased. [17c: from Greek *palin* again + *psaein* to rub smooth]

palindrome *noun* a word or phrase that reads the same backwards and forwards, eg *Hannah*, and *sums are not set as a test on Erasmus*, and (perhaps the first ever palindrome) *Madam, I'm Adam.* ▪ **palindromic** *adj.* [17c: from Greek *palin* back + *dromein* run]

paling *noun* **1** the act of constructing a fence with pales (see **pale[2]** sense 1). **2** a fence of this kind. **3** an upright stake or board in a fence.

palisade *noun* a tall fence of pointed wooden stakes fixed edge to edge, for defence or protection. [16c: from Provençal *palissada*]

pall[1] /pɔːl/ *noun* **1** **a** the cloth that covers a coffin at a funeral; **b** the coffin itself. **2** anything spreading or hanging over: *a pall of smoke.* [Anglo-Saxon *pæll* a covering]

pall[2] /pɔːl/ *verb* **1** *intr* to begin to bore or seem tedious. **2** to cloy; to bore. [14c: a variant of **appal**]

Palladian *adj, archit* in the style of architecture introduced by Andrea Palladio (1518–80). ▪ **Palladianism** *noun.*

palladium *noun, chem* (symbol **Pd**) a soft silvery-white metallic element used as a catalyst, and in gold dental alloys, jewellery, electrical components, and catalytic converters for car exhausts. [Named after the asteroid Pallas]

pall-bearer *noun* one of the people carrying the coffin or walking beside it at a funeral.

pallet[1] *noun* **1** a small wooden platform on which goods can be stacked for lifting and transporting, esp by fork-lift truck. **2** a flat-bladed wooden tool used for shaping pottery. [16c in sense 2: from French *palette* (see **palette**)]

pallet[2] *noun* **1** a straw bed. **2** a small makeshift bed. [14c: from French *paillet* a bundle or heap of straw, from *paille* straw]

palliasse *or* **paillasse** *noun* a straw-filled mattress. [16c: from French *paillasse*, from *paille* straw]

palliate *verb* **1** to ease the symptoms of (a disease) without curing it. **2** to serve to lessen the gravity of (an offence, etc); to mitigate. **3** to reduce the effect of (anything disagreeable). [16c: from Latin *palliare* to cloak]

palliative *noun* anything used to reduce pain or anxiety. ▸ *adj* having the effect of alleviating or reducing pain. [16c: French]

pallid *adj* **1** pale, esp unhealthily so. **2** lacking vigour or conviction. [16c: from Latin *pallidus* pale]

pallor *noun* paleness, esp of complexion. [17c: Latin]

palm[1] *noun* **1** the inner surface of the hand between the wrist and the fingers. **2** the part of a glove covering this. ▸ *verb* to conceal something in the palm of the hand. [14c: French]
IDIOMS **in the palm of one's hand** in one's power; at one's command.
PHRASAL VERBS **palm sth off on sb** *or* **palm sb off with sth** *informal* to give them something unwanted or unwelcome, esp by trickery.

palm[2] *noun* a tropical tree with a woody unbranched trunk bearing a crown of large fan-shaped or feather-shaped leaves. [Anglo-Saxon]

palmate /'palmeɪt/ *or* **palmated** *adj*, **1** *botany* of a leaf: divided into lobes that radiate from a central point, resembling an open hand. **2** *zool* of an animal, especially an aquatic bird: having webbed toes. [18c]

palmetto *noun* (***palmettos*** *or* ***palmettoes***) a small palm tree with fan-shaped leaves. [16c: from Spanish *palmito* small palm]

palmistry *noun* the art of telling someone's fortune by reading the lines on the palm of their hand. Also called **chiromancy**. ▪ **palmist** *noun.* [15c]

palm oil *noun* the oil obtained from the outer pulp of the fruit of some palm trees, used in cooking fats.

Palm Sunday *noun, Christianity* the Sunday before Easter.

palmtop *noun* a portable computer small enough to be held in the hand.

palmy *adj* (***-ier, -iest***) effortlessly successful and prosperous: *one's palmy days.* [17c]

palomino *or* **palamino** *noun* a golden or cream horse, largely of Arab blood, with a white or silver tail and mane. [20c: American Spanish *palomino* dove-like]

palpable *adj* **1** easily detected; obvious. **2** *med* eg of an internal organ: able to be felt. ▪ **palpably** *adv.* [14c: from Latin *palpare* to touch]

palpate *verb, med* to examine (the body or a part of it) by touching or pressing. [19c: from Latin *palpare* to touch]

palpitate *verb, intr* **1** *med* of the heart: to beat abnormally rapidly, eg as a result of physical exertion, fear, emotion or heart disease. **2** to tremble or throb. ▪ **palpitation** *noun*. [17c: from Latin *palpitare* to throb]

palsy /ˈpɔːlzɪ/ *noun* (**-ies**) paralysis, or loss of control or feeling in a part of the body. ▸ *verb* (**-ies, -ied**) to affect someone or something with palsy; to paralyse. [13c: from French *paralisie*]

paltry *adj* (**-ier, -iest**) worthless; trivial; meagre; insignificant or insultingly inadequate. [16c: from German dialect *paltrig* ragged]

pampas grass *noun* a large S American grass bearing silvery-white or pink plume-like panicles. [19c: from Spanish *Pampa* a vast prairie in S America]

pamper *verb* to treat (a person or animal) overindulgently; to cosset or spoil them. [14c]

pamphlet *noun* a booklet or leaflet providing information or dealing with a current topic. [14c: from French *pamphilet*, from the title of the Latin love poem *Pamphilus, seu de Amore*]

pan[1] *noun* **1** a pot, usu made of metal, used for cooking. **2** a panful, the amount a pan will hold. **3** *often in compounds* a vessel, usu shallow, used for domestic, industrial and other purposes: *dustpan* • *bedpan*. **4** the bowl of a lavatory. **5** either of the two dishes on a pair of scales. **6** a shallow hollow in the ground: *a salt pan*. **7** *hist* the hollow part of an old gunlock, that holds the priming. See also **a flash in the pan** at **flash**. ▸ *verb* (**panned, panning**) **1** (*often* **pan for sth**) *tr & intr* to wash (river gravel) in a shallow metal vessel in search of (eg gold). **2** *informal* to criticize something or review (a performance, book, etc) harshly. ▪ **panful** *noun*. [Anglo-Saxon *panne*]

PHRASAL VERBS **pan out 1** to result or turn out. **2** to come to an end; to be exhausted.

pan[2] *verb* (**panned, panning**) *tr & intr* of a film camera, camcorder, etc: to swing round so as to follow a moving object or show a panoramic view. ▸ *noun* a panning movement or shot. [20c: a short form of **panorama**]

pan- *combining form, denoting* **1** all; entire: *panchromatic*. **2** referring to a movement or ideal: to unite (a whole continent, group of people, etc) politically, economically, etc: *pan-Africanism*. [From Greek *pas, pantos* all]

panacea /panəˈsɪə/ *noun* a universal remedy; a cure-all for any ill, problem, etc. [16c: from Greek *panakeia* universal remedy]

panache /pəˈnaʃ/ *noun* flamboyant self-assurance; a grand manner. [19c: French]

panama hat *noun* **1** a lightweight brimmed hat for men made from the plaited leaves of a palm-like Central American tree. **2** a hat in this style. [19c: named after Panama, a state in C America]

panatella *noun* a long slim cigar. [20c: American Spanish, meaning 'a long thin biscuit']

pancake *noun* a thin cake made from a batter of eggs, flour and milk, cooked on both sides in a frying pan or on a griddle. [15c: **pan**[1] + **cake**]

Pancake Day *noun* **Shrove Tuesday**, when pancakes are traditionally eaten.

pancetta /panˈtʃɛtə/ *noun, cookery* an Italian variety of cured pork. [20c: Italian, literally little belly]

panchromatic *adj, photog* of a film: sensitive to all colours. [20c]

pancreas /ˈpaŋkrɪəs/ *noun, anatomy* in vertebrates: a large carrot-shaped gland lying between the duodenum and the spleen, that secretes pancreatic juice serving hormonal and digestive functions. See also **sweetbread**. ▪ **pancreatic** *adj*. [16c: from Greek *pankreas*]

panda *noun* **1** (*also* **giant panda**) a black-and-white bearlike animal, native to China. **2** (*also* **red panda**) a related species, smaller and with reddish brown coat, native to forests of S Asia. [19c: Nepalese]

pandemic *adj, med* describing a widespread epidemic of a disease, one that affects a whole country, continent, etc. [17c: from Greek *pan-* all + *demos* people]

pandemonium *noun* **1** any very disorderly or noisy place or assembly. **2** noise, chaos and confusion. [17c: the capital of Hell in Milton's *Paradise Lost*]

pander *verb* (**pander to sb** *or* **sth**) to indulge or gratify them or their wishes or tastes. [16c: named after Pandarus in Chaucer and Shakespeare]

pandit see under **pundit**

Pandora's box *noun* any source of great and unexpected troubles. [16c: from Pandora, the name of the first woman in Greek mythology, who was given a box by Zeus which was opened against his advice, letting loose all the ills of the world, except for hope which was in the bottom of the box]

p & p *abbrev* postage and packing.

pane *noun* a sheet of glass, esp one fitted into a window or door. [13c: from French *pan* a strip of cloth]

panegyric /panəˈdʒɪrɪk/ *noun* a speech or piece of writing in praise of someone or something; a eulogy. ▪ **panegyric** *or* **panegyrical** *adj*. [17c: from Greek *panegyrikos* fit for a national festival]

panel *noun* **1** a rectangular wooden board forming a section, esp an ornamentally sunken or raised one, of a wall or door. **2** one of several strips of fabric making up a garment. **3** any of the metal sections forming the bodywork of a vehicle. **4** a board bearing the instruments and dials for controlling an aircraft, etc: *control panel*. **5** rectangular divisions on the page of a book, esp for illustrations. **6** a team of people selected to judge a contest, or to participate in a discussion, quiz or other game before an audience. *as adj*: *panel discussion* • *panel game*. **7 a** a list of jurors; **b** the people serving on a jury. ▸ *verb* (**panelled, panelling**; *esp N Am* **paneling, paneled**) to fit (a wall or door) with wooden panels. [13c: French diminutive of *pan* a strip of cloth]

panel-beating *noun* the removal of dents from metal, esp from the bodywork of a vehicle, using a soft-headed hammer. ▪ **panel-beater** *noun*.

panelling *or* (*N Am*) **paneling** *noun* **1** panels covering a wall or part of a wall, usu as decoration. Also called **panel-work**. **2** material for making these.

panellist *or* (*N Am*) **panelist** *noun* a member of a panel of people, esp in a panel game on TV or radio.

pang *noun* a brief but painfully acute feeling of hunger, guilt, remorse, etc: *a pang of guilt*. [16c]

pangolin *noun* a toothless mammal that is covered with large overlapping horny plates and can curl into an armoured ball when threatened by a predator. [18c: from Malay *peng-goling* roller]

panhandle *noun, esp US* a narrow strip of territory stretching out from the main body into another territory, eg part of a state which stretches into another.

panic *noun* a sudden overpowering fear that affects an individual, or esp one that grips a crowd or population. ▶ *verb* (***panicked, panicking***) *tr & intr* to feel panic, or make someone feel panic. ▪ **panicky** *adj.* [17c: from French *panique*]

panicle *noun, botany* a branched flower-head, common in grasses, in which the youngest flowers are at the tip of the flower-stalk. [16c: from Latin *panicula* tuft]

panic-stricken *adj* struck with sudden fear; terrified.

panini /pa'niːnɪ/ *plural noun, cookery* grilled sandwiches. [Late 20c: Italian, plural of *panino* little bread]

panjandrum *noun, humorous* a pompous official. [18c: from 'the Grand Panjandrum', used in a string of nonsense composed by Samuel Foote]

pannier *noun* **1** one of a pair of baskets carried over the back of a donkey or other pack animal. **2** one of a pair of bags carried on either side of the wheel of a bicycle, etc. [13c: from French *panier*]

panoply /'panəplɪ/ *noun* (***-ies***) **1** the full assemblage got together for a ceremony, etc. **2** *hist* a full set of armour and weapons. [17c: from Greek *panoplia* full armour]

panorama *noun* **1** an open and extensive or all-round view, eg of a landscape. **2** a view of something in all its range and variety: *the panorama of history.* ▪ **panoramic** *adj.* [18c: from Greek *pan-* all + *horama* view]

panpipes, Pan pipes *or* **Pan's pipes** *plural noun* a musical instrument, made of reeds of different lengths bound together and played by blowing across their open ends. [19c: named after Pan, the Greek god]

pansy *noun* (***-ies***) a garden plant which has flat flowers with five rounded white, yellow or purple petals. [15c: from French *pensée* thought]

pant *verb* **1** *intr* to breathe in and out with quick, shallow, short gasps as a result of physical exertion. **2** to say something breathlessly. ▶ *noun* a gasping breath. ▪ **panting** *noun, adj.* [15c: from French *pantaisier*]

pantaloons *plural noun* **1** baggy trousers gathered at the ankle. **2** tight-fitting trousers for men with buttons or ribbons below the calf, worn at the turn of the 19c. [16c: from *Pantalone*, a figure from Italian comedy]

pantechnicon *noun* a large furniture-removal van. [19c: from Greek *pan-* all + *techne* art; orig the name of the premises of a London art dealer, which were later used as a furniture warehouse]

panth /pʌnθ/ *noun, Sikhism* the Sikh community.

pantheism *noun* **1** the belief that equates all the matter and forces in the Universe with God. **2** readiness to believe in all or many gods. ▪ **pantheist** *noun.* ▪ **pantheistic** *or* **pantheistical** *adj.* [18c: from Greek *pan-* all + *theos* god]

panthenol *noun, US* **pantothenol**.

pantheon *noun* **1** all the gods of a particular people: *the ancient Greek pantheon.* **2** a temple sacred to all the gods. **3** a building in which the glorious dead of a nation have memorials or are buried. [14c: from Greek *pantheios* of all the gods]

panther *noun* **1** a **leopard**, esp a black one, formerly believed to be a different species. **2** *N Am* a **puma**. [13c: from Latin *panthera*]

panties *plural noun* thin light knickers, mainly for women and children.

pantihose see **panty hose**

pantile *noun, building* a roofing tile with an S-shaped cross section. ▪ **pantiled** *adj.* [17c: **pan**[1] + **tile**]

panto *noun, informal* short form of **pantomime**.

pantograph *noun* **1** a device consisting of jointed rods forming an adjustable parallelogram, for copying maps, plans, etc to any scale. **2** a similarly shaped metal framework on the roof of an electric train, transmitting current from an overhead wire. [18c]

pantomime *noun* **1** a Christmas entertainment usu based on a popular fairy tale, with songs, dancing, comedy acts, etc. *as adj*: *pantomime season.* **2** a farcical or confused situation: *What a pantomime!* [16c: from Greek *pantomimos* a mime actor]

pantothenic acid *noun, biochem* a member of the **vitamin B complex** that is found in many foods, esp cereal grains, egg yolk, liver, yeast and peas. [20c: from Greek *pantothen* from every side, because of its wide occurrence]

pantothenol *noun* a vitamin of the **vitamin B complex**. [20c: see **pantothenic acid**]

pantry *noun* (***-ies***) a small room or cupboard for storing food, cooking utensils, etc; a larder. [13c: from French *paneterie* a place where bread was stored]

pants *plural noun* **1** *Brit* an undergarment worn over the buttocks and genital area; underpants. **2** *N Am* trousers. [19c: orig US, a shortening of **pantaloons**]

panty hose *or* **pantihose** *plural noun, N Am* women's tights.

pap[1] *noun* **1** soft semi-liquid food for babies and sick people. **2** *derog* trivial or worthless reading matter or entertainment. ▪ **pappy** *adj* (***-ier, -iest***). [15c]

pap[2] *noun* **1** *old use* a nipple or teat. **2** *Scot* in place-names: a round conical hill. [13c: from Scandinavian]

papa /pə'pɑː/ *noun, old use or jocular* a child's word for father. [17c: French]

papacy /'peɪpəsɪ/ *noun* (***-ies***) **1** the position, power or period of office of a **pope**. **2** government by popes. [14c: from Latin *papatia*, from *papa* pope]

papal *adj* referring or relating to the **pope** (*noun* sense 1) or the **papacy**. [14c]

papal bull *noun* a **bull**[3].

paparazzo /papə'ratsoʊ/ *noun* (***paparazzi*** /-tsiː/) a newspaper photographer who follows famous people about in the hope of photographing them in unguarded moments. [20c: from the name of the photographer in the film *La Dolce Vita* (1959)]

papaw /pə'pɔː/ *or* **pawpaw** /'pɔːpɔː/ *noun* a large oblong yellow or orange fruit, which has sweet orange flesh and a central cavity filled with black seeds. Sometimes called **papaya**. [15c: Spanish *papaya*]

paper *noun* **1** a material manufactured in thin sheets from pulped wood, rags, or other forms of cellulose, used for writing and printing on, wrapping things, etc. **2** a loose piece of paper, eg a wrapper or printed sheet. **3** other material used for a similar purpose or with a similar appearance, eg **papyrus**, **rice paper**. **4** wallpaper. **5** **a** a newspaper; **b** (**the papers**) newspapers collectively; the press. **6** a set of questions on a certain subject for a written examination. **7** **a** a written article dealing with a certain subject, esp for reading to an audience at a meeting, conference, etc; **b** an essay written eg by a student. **8** (**papers**) personal documents establishing one's identity, nationality, etc. **9** (**papers**) a person's accumulated correspondence, diaries, etc. ▸ *adj* **1** consisting of or made of paper. **2** paper-like, esp thin like paper; papery. **3** on paper. ▸ *verb* **1** to decorate (a wall, a room, etc) with wallpaper: *paper the hall*. **2** to cover something with paper. ▪ **papery** *adj*. [14c: from French *papier*]

IDIOMS **on paper** **1** in theory or in abstract as distinct from practice: *The plans looked good on paper.* **2** in written form: *get one's ideas down on paper.*

PHRASAL VERBS **paper over sth** to conceal or avoid (an awkward fact, mistake, etc).

paperback *noun* a book with a thin flexible paper binding, as opposed to a **hardback**. *as adj*: *a paperback novel.*

paper chase *noun* a cross-country race in which runners follow a trail of dropped shreds of paper.

paper clip *noun* a metal clip formed from bent wire, for holding papers together.

paper hanger *noun* someone who puts up wallpaper.

paperless *adj* using esp electronic means, rather than paper, for recording, etc: *a paperless office.*

paper money *noun* bank notes, as opposed to coins.

paperweight *noun* a heavy, usu ornamental, object kept on a desk for holding papers down.

paperwork *noun* routine written work, eg filling in forms, keeping files, writing letters and reports, etc.

papier-mâché /papɪeɪ'maʃeɪ, papjeɪ-/ *noun* a light hard material consisting of pulped paper mixed with glue, moulded into shape while wet and left to dry, and used to make boxes, jars, jewellery, masks, etc. *as adj*: *a papier-mâché puppet*. [18c: French, literally 'chewed paper']

papilla /pə'pɪlə/ *noun* (***papillae*** /-liː/) *anatomy, biol* **1** a small nipple-like projection from the surface of a structure. **2** a protuberance at the base of a hair, feather, tooth, etc. ▪ **papillary** *adj*. [18c: Latin, diminutive of *papula* pimple]

papoose *noun* a pouch for carrying an infant on one's back. [17c: from Algonquian (a family of Native American languages) *papoos*]

pappadom see **poppadum**

pappy *noun* (***-ies***) *US informal* father; papa.

paprika *noun* a powdered hot spice made from red peppers. [19c: Hungarian]

papyrus /pə'paɪərəs/ *noun* (***papyri*** /pə'paɪəraɪ/ *or* ***papyruses***) **1** a tall plant, common in ancient Egypt. **2** the writing material prepared from the pith of the flowering stems of this plant, used by the ancient Egyptians, Greeks and Romans. **3** an ancient manuscript written on this material. [14c: from Greek *papyros*]

par *noun* **1** a normal level or standard. **2** *golf* the standard number of strokes that a good golfer would take for a certain course or hole. **3** *commerce* (*also* **par of exchange**) the established value of the unit of one national currency against that of another. [17c: Latin, meaning 'equal']

IDIOMS **below** *or* **not up to par** *informal* **1** not up to the usual or required standard. **2** slightly unwell. **par for the course** *informal* only to be expected; typical.

para *noun, informal* a paratrooper. [20c]

parable *noun* a story intended to convey a moral or religious lesson. [14c: from Latin *parabola* comparison]

parabola /pə'rabələ/ *noun, geom* a **conic section** produced when a plane intersects a cone and the plane is parallel to the cone's sloping side. [16c: from Greek *parabole* placing alongside]

paracetamol *noun* **1** a mild analgesic drug, used to relieve pain or to reduce fever. **2** a tablet of this drug. [20c: from *para-acetylaminophenol*]

parachute *noun* **1** an umbrella-shaped apparatus consisting of light fabric, with a harness for attaching to, and slowing the fall of, a person or package dropped from an aircraft. **2** any structure that serves a similar purpose. Also shortened to **chute**. ▸ *verb, tr & intr* to drop from the air by parachute. ▪ **parachutist** *noun*. [18c: French]

parade *noun* **1** a ceremonial procession of people, vehicles, etc. **2** of soldiers, etc: **a** the state of being drawn up in rank for formal marching or inspection; **b** a group or body of soldiers, etc drawn up in this way. **3** a self-advertising display. **4** a row of shops, a shopping street, etc. ▸ *verb* **1** *tr & intr* to walk or make (a body of soldiers, etc) walk or march in procession, eg across a square, etc. **2** to display ostentatiously; to flaunt. [17c: French]

paradigm /'parədaɪm/ *noun* **1** an example, model or pattern. **2** *grammar* **a** a table of the inflected forms of a word serving as a pattern for words of the same declension or conjugation; **b** the words showing a particular pattern. [15c: from Greek *paradeigma* pattern]

paradisaic /parədɪ'seɪɪk/, **paradisaical** /parɪdɪ'zaɪəkəl/, **paradisal** /-'daɪsəl/ *or* **paradisiac** /parɪ'dɪzɪak/ *adj* relating to or resembling paradise.

paradise *noun* **1** heaven. **2** a place of utter bliss or delight. **3** the Garden of Eden. [12c: French]

paradox *noun* **1** a statement that seems to contradict itself, eg *More haste, less speed.* **2** a situation involving apparently contradictory elements. **3** *logic* a proposition that is essentially absurd or leads to an absurd conclusion. ▪ **paradoxical** *adj*. ▪ **paradoxically** *adv*. [16c: from Greek *paradoxos* incredible]

paraffin *noun* **1** a fuel oil obtained from petroleum or coal and used in aircraft, domestic heaters, etc. **2** any of a series of saturated aliphatic hydrocarbons derived from petroleum. Now more commonly called an **alkane**. *N Am equivalent* **kerosene**. [19c: from Latin *parum* little + *affinis* having an affinity, because of its unreactiveness]

paraffin wax *noun, chem* a white tasteless odourless solid, obtained from the distillation of petroleum, used to make candles, polishes, wax crayons, etc.

paragliding *noun* a sport in which the participant is towed through the air by a light aircraft while wearing a modified parachute, then released to glide in the air and eventually drift to the ground. ▪ **paraglider** *noun*. [20c]

paragon *noun* someone who is a model of excellence or perfection. [16c: French]

paragraph *noun* **1** a section of a piece of writing of variable length, starting on a fresh, often indented, line, and dealing with a distinct point or idea. **2** a short report in a newspaper. **3** *music* a musical passage forming a unit. **4** (*also* **paragraph mark**) *printing* a sign (¶), indicating the start of a new paragraph. ▸ *verb* to divide (text) into paragraphs. [16c: from Greek *paragraphe* marked passage]

parakeet *noun* a small brightly-coloured parrot with a long pointed tail. [16c: from French *paroquet* parrot]

parallax *noun* **1** *physics* the apparent change in the position of an object, relative to a distant background, when it is viewed from two different positions. **2** *astron* the angle between two straight lines joining two different observation points to a celestial body, used to measure the distance of stars from the Earth. ▪ **parallactic** *adj*. [16c: from Greek *parallaxis* change or alteration]

parallel *adj* (*often* **parallel to sth**) **1** of lines, planes, etc: the same distance apart at every point; alongside and never meeting or intersecting: *parallel lines*. **2** similar; exactly equivalent; corresponding; analogous: *parallel careers*. ▸ *adv* (*often* **parallel to sth**) alongside and at an unvarying distance from it. ▸ *noun* **1** *geom* a line or plane parallel to another. **2** a corresponding or equivalent instance of something. **3** any of the lines of **latitude** circling the Earth parallel to the equator and representing a particular angular degree of distance from it. Also called **parallel of latitude**. ▸ *verb* (***paralleled, paralleling***) **1** to equal. **2** to correspond to or be equivalent to something. **3** to run parallel to something. [16c: from Greek *parallelos* side by side]

IDIOMS **in parallel 1** of electrical appliances: so coordinated that terminals of the same polarity are connected. **2** simultaneously. **without parallel** unequalled; unprecedented.

parallel
This word is often misspelt. It has two *l*'s in the middle and one at the end. It might help you to remember that par**all**el contains the word **all**.

parallel bars *plural noun* two parallel horizontal rails, fixed to upright posts, used by men for gymnastic exercises and display.

parallelism *noun* **1** the state or fact of being parallel. **2** resemblance in corresponding details. **3** a verse or sentence in which one part is a repetition of another, either in form or meaning.

parallelogram *noun, geom* a two-dimensional four-sided figure in which opposite sides are parallel and equal in length, and opposite angles are equal. [16c: from Greek *parallelogrammon*]

parallel processing *noun, comput* the use of two or more processors simultaneously to carry out a single computing task, each processor being assigned a particular part of the task at any given time.

the Paralympics *noun* a multi-sport competition for people with physical and learning disabilities. ▪ **Paralympic** *adj*. [20c: from *parallel* + *Olympics*]

paralyse *or* (*N Am*) **paralyze** *verb* **1** to affect (a person or bodily part) with paralysis. **2** of fear, etc: to have an immobilizing effect on someone. **3** to disrupt something or bring it to a standstill. [Early 19c]

paralysis *noun* (***-ses***) **1** a temporary or permanent loss of muscular function or sensation in any part of the body, usu caused by nerve damage, eg as a result of disease or injury. **2** a state of immobility; a standstill. [16c: Greek, from *paralyein* to enfeeble]

paralytic *adj* **1** relating to, caused by or suffering from paralysis. **2** *informal* helplessly drunk. ▸ *noun* a person affected by paralysis.

paramedic *noun* a person, esp one trained in emergency medical procedures, whose work supplements and supports that of the medical profession. ▪ **paramedical** *adj*. [20c]

parameter /pə'ramɪtə(r)/ *noun* **1** *maths* a constant or variable that, when altered, affects the form of a mathematical expression in which it appears. **2** a limiting factor that serves to define the scope of a task, project, discussion, etc. [17c: from Latin *parametrum*]

paramilitary *adj* organized like a professional military force and often reinforcing it, but not a professional military force. ▸ *noun* (***-ies***) **1** a group organized in this way. **2** a member of such a group. [20c]

paramount *adj* foremost; supreme; of supreme importance. [16c: from French *par* by + *amont* above]

paramour *noun* a male or female lover. [14c: from French *par amour* by or through love]

paranoia *noun* **1** *psychol* a rare mental disorder, characterized by delusions of persecution by others. **2** a strong, usu irrational, feeling that one is being persecuted by others, resulting in a tendency to be suspicious and distrustful. [19c: Greek, from *para-* beyond + *nous* mind]

paranoid, **paranoiac** /parə'nɔɪak/ *or* **paranoic** /parə'nɔɪk/ *adj* relating to or affected by paranoia. ▸ *noun* a person affected by paranoia.

paranormal *adj* of phenomena, observations, occurrences, etc: beyond the normal scope of scientific explanation, and therefore not possible to explain in terms of current understanding of scientific laws. ▸ *noun* (**the paranormal**) paranormal occurrences. See also **supernatural**. [20c]

parapet *noun* **1** a low wall along the edge of a bridge, balcony, roof, etc. **2** an embankment of earth or sandbags protecting the soldiers in a military trench. [16c: from Italian *parapetto*]

paraphernalia *plural noun, sometimes used as a singular noun* **1** the equipment and accessories associated with a particular activity, etc. **2** personal belongings. [18c: from Greek *parapherna* a bride's personal effects]

paraphrase *noun* a restatement of something using different words, esp in order to clarify; a re-wording or re-phrasing. ▸ *verb* to express something in other words. [16c: French]

paraplegia /parə'pliːdʒɪə/ *noun, med* paralysis of the lower half of the body, usu caused by injury or disease of the spinal cord. ▪ **paraplegic** *adj, noun*. Compare **hemiplegia**, **quadriplegia**. [17c: Greek, meaning 'a one-sided stroke']

parapsychology *noun* the study of mental phenomena, such as telepathy and clairvoyance, that suggest the mind can gain knowledge by means other than the normal perceptual processes. ▪ **parapsychological** *adj*. ▪ **parapsychologist** *noun*. [20c]

pararhyme same as **half-rhyme**

parasite *noun* **1** *biol* a plant or animal that for all or part of its life obtains food and physical protection from a living organism of another species (the **host**[1] *noun* sense 4) which is usually damaged by its presence. **2** *derog* a person who lives at the expense of others, contributing nothing in return. ▪ **parasitic** *or* **parasitical** *adj*. ▪ **parasitically** *adv*. [16c: from Greek *parasitos* someone who lives at another's expense]

parasitism *noun* **1** *biol* a parasitical relationship of two living organisms. Compare **commensalism, mutualism**. **2** the state of being a parasite. **3** the state of being infested with parasites.

parasitology /parəsaɪ'tɒlədʒɪ/ *noun, zool* the scientific study of parasites. ▪ **parasitologist** *noun*. [19c]

parasol *noun* a light umbrella used as a protection against the sun; a sunshade. [17c: from French]

paratroops *plural noun* a division of soldiers trained to parachute from aircraft into enemy territory or a battle zone. ▪ **paratrooper** *noun* a member of such a division. [20c]

paratyphoid *noun, med* an infectious disease, similar to but milder than **typhoid** fever, caused by a bacterium. [20c]

par avion /*French* par avjɔ̃/ *adv* used as a label on mail which is to be sent by aeroplane: by air mail.

parboil *verb* to boil something until it is partially cooked. [15c: from French *parbo(u)illir*, from Latin *perbullire* to boil thoroughly; the meaning has been altered by confusion of *par-* with **part**]

parcel *noun* **1** something wrapped in paper, etc and secured with string or sticky tape; a package. **2** a portion of something, eg of land. **3** a group of people, etc. **4** a lot or portion of goods for sale; a deal or transaction. ▸ *verb* (***parcelled, parcelling***) **1** (*also* **parcel sth up**) to wrap it up in a parcel. **2** (*also* **parcel sth out**) to divide it into portions and share it out. [14c: from French *parcelle*]

parch *verb* **1** to dry something up; to deprive (soil, plants, etc) of water. **2** to make something or someone hot and very dry. **3** to roast (peas) slightly. [14c]

parched *adj* **1** *informal* very thirsty. **2** very dry.

parchment *noun* **1 a** a material formerly used for bookbinding and for writing on, made from goatskin, calfskin or sheepskin; **b** a piece of this, or a manuscript written on it. **2** stiff off-white writing-paper resembling this. ▸ *adj* made of, or resembling, parchment: *parchment paper*. [13c: from French *parchemin*]

pardon *verb* **1** to forgive or excuse someone for a fault or offence: *pardon me for interrupting*. **2** to allow someone who has been sentenced to go without the punishment. **3** *intr* to grant pardon. ▸ *noun* **1** forgiveness. **2** the cancellation of a punishment; remission. ▪ **pardonable** *adj*. [14c: from French *pardonner*]

IDIOMS **pardon me 1** a formula of apology. **2** (also **pardon**) a request to someone to repeat something said.

pare *verb* **1** to trim off (skin, etc) in layers. **2** to cut (fingernails or toenails). **3** to peel (fruit). **4** (*also* **pare sth down**) to reduce (expenses, funding, etc) gradually, in order to economize. [14c: from French *parer*]

parent *noun* **1** a father or mother. **2** the adopter or guardian of a child. **3** an animal or plant that has produced offspring. **4** something from which anything is derived; a source or origin. ▸ *verb, tr & intr* to be or act as a parent; to care for someone or something as a parent. ▪ **parenthood** *noun*. ▪ **parenting** *noun*. [15c: from Latin *parens*, from *parere* to bring forth]

parentage *noun* **1** descent from parents. **2** rank or character derived from one's parents or ancestors. **3** the state or fact of being a parent.

parental *adj* **1** related to or concerning parents. **2** *biol, genetics* denoting the first generation that gives rise to all successive or filial generations. ▪ **parentally** *adv*.

parent company *noun* a business company that owns other, usu smaller, companies.

parenthesis /pə'rɛnθəsɪs/ *noun* (***-ses*** /-siːz/) **1** a word or phrase inserted into a sentence as a comment, usu marked off by brackets or dashes. **2** (**parentheses**) a pair of round brackets ( ), used to enclose such a comment. [16c: Greek, from *tithenai* to place]

parenthetic *or* **parenthetical** *adj* **1** referring to the nature of a parenthesis. **2** using parenthesis. ▪ **parenthetically** *adv*.

par excellence /pɑːr 'ɛksɛlɑ̃s, -ləns/ *adv* in the highest degree; beyond compare. [17c: French, meaning 'as an example of excellence']

pariah /pə'raɪə/ *noun* **1** someone scorned and avoided by others; a social outcast. **2** in S India and Burma: a member of a caste lower than the four Brahmanical castes. [17c: from Tamil *paraiyan* drummer]

parietal /pə'raɪətəl/ *adj, med, anatomy* relating to, or forming, the wall of a bodily cavity, eg the skull: *the parietal bones*. [16c: from Latin *paries* wall]

parish *noun* **1** a district or area served by its own church and priest or minister, usu the established church of that particular area. **2** esp in England: the smallest unit of local government. Also called **civil parish**. **3** the inhabitants of a parish. ▸ *adj* **1** belonging or relating to a parish. **2** employed or supported by the parish. ▪ **parishioner** *noun*. [14c: from French *paroisse*]

parish register *noun* a book in which the christenings, marriages, and deaths in a parish are recorded.

parity *noun* (***-ies***) **1** equality in status, eg in pay. **2** precise equivalence; exact correspondence. **3** *commerce* an established equivalence between a unit of national currency and an amount in another national currency. [16c: from Latin *paritas*, from *par* equal]

park *noun* **1** an area in a town with grass and trees, for public recreation. **2** an area of land kept in its natural condition as a nature reserve, etc. **3** the woodland and pasture forming the estate of a large country house. **4** a place where vehicles can be left temporarily; a **car park**. **5** an area containing a group of buildings housing related enterprises: *a science park • a business park*. **6** *chiefly N Am* a sports field or stadium. **7** (**the park**) *informal* the pitch in use in a football game. ▸ *verb* **1** *tr & intr* **a** to leave (a vehicle) temporarily at the side of the road or in a car park; **b** to manoeuvre (a vehicle) into such a position. **2** *informal* to lay or leave something somewhere temporarily. **3** (**park oneself**) *informal* to sit or install oneself. [13c: from French *parc* enclosure]

parka *noun* **1** a hooded jacket made of skins, worn by the Inuit and Aleut people of the Arctic. **2** a windproof jacket, esp a quilted one with a fur-trimmed hood; an anorak. [18c: Aleut, meaning 'skin or coat']

parkin *or* **perkin** *noun, Scot & N Eng* a moist ginger-flavoured oatmeal cake made with treacle. [18c]

parking lot *noun, N Am* a **car park**.

parking meter *noun* a coin-operated meter in the street beside which a car may be parked for a period.

parking ticket *noun* an official notice of a fine served on a motorist for parking illegally.

parkinsonism *noun, med* an incurable disorder, usu occurring later in life, and characterized by trembling of limbs, rigidity of muscles, a mask-like facial expression, and stooping posture. [19c: named after James Parkinson, English surgeon]

Parkinson's disease *noun, med* the commonest form of **parkinsonism**, caused by degeneration of brain cells. Often shortened to **Parkinson's**. [20c]

Parkinson's law *noun* the maxim that work expands to fill the time available for its completion. [20c: named after C. N. Parkinson, historian and journalist]

parkland *noun* pasture and woodland forming part of a country estate.

parkway *noun, N Am* a broad thoroughfare incorporating grassy areas and lined with trees.

parky *adj* (***-ier, -iest***) *Brit informal* of the weather: somewhat cold; chilly. [19c]

parlance *noun* a particular style or way of using words: *in legal parlance*. [16c: French, from *parler* to talk]

parley *verb, intr* to discuss peace terms, etc with an enemy, esp under truce. ▸ *noun* a meeting with an enemy to discuss peace terms, etc. [16c: from French *parler* to talk]

parliament *noun* **1** the highest law-making assembly of a nation. **2** (**Parliament**) in the UK: the Houses of Commons and Lords. [13c: from French *parlement*]

---

parliament

This word is often misspelt. It has an a in the middle. It might help you to remember the following sentence:

***Liam** is a Member of Par**liam**ent.*

---

parliamentarian *noun* **1** an expert in parliamentary procedure. **2** an experienced parliamentary debater. **3** *hist* during the 17c English Civil War: a supporter of the Parliamentary party against Charles I.

parliamentary *adj* **1** relating to, or issued by, a parliament. **2** of conduct or procedure: in keeping with the rules of parliament.

parlour *or* (*N Am*) **parlor** *noun* **1** *usu in compounds* a shop or commercial premises providing specified goods or services: *an ice-cream parlour* • *funeral parlour*. **2** *dated* a sitting-room for receiving visitors. [13c: from French *parlur*]

parlous *adj, archaic or facetious* precarious; perilous; dire. [14c: a variant of *perilous*]

Parmesan /ˈpɑːməzan/ *noun* a hard dry Italian cheese made from skimmed milk mixed with rennet and saffron. [16c: from Italian *Parmegiano*, 'from Parma']

parochial *adj* **1** *derog* of tastes, attitudes, etc: concerned only with local affairs; narrow, limited or provincial in outlook. **2** referring or relating to a parish. ▪ **parochialism** *or* **parochiality** *noun*. [14c: from Latin *parochialis*]

parody *noun* (***-ies***) **1** a comic or satirical imitation of a work, or the style, of a particular writer, composer, etc. **2** a poor attempt at something; a travesty. ▸ *verb* (***-ies, -ied***) to ridicule something through parody; to mimic satirically. ▪ **parodist** *noun* the author of a parody. [16c: from Greek *paroidia*]

parole *noun* **1 a** the release of a prisoner before the end of their sentence, on promise of good behaviour: *released on parole*. *as adj*: *the parole system*. **b** the duration of this conditional release. **2** the promise of a prisoner so released to behave well. ▸ *verb* to release or place (a prisoner) on parole. ▪ **parolee** *noun*. [17c: from French *parole d'honneur* word of honour]

parotid *adj, anatomy* situated beside or near the ear. ▸ *noun* the **parotid gland**, a salivary gland in front of the ear. [17c: from Greek *parotis*, from *para* beside + *os* ear]

paroxysm *noun* **1** a sudden emotional outburst, eg of rage or laughter. **2** a spasm, convulsion or seizure, eg of coughing or acute pain. **3** a sudden reappearance of or increase in the severity of the symptoms of a disease or disorder. ▪ **paroxysmal** *adj*. [17c: from Greek *paroxysmos* a fit]

parquet /ˈpɑːkeɪ/ *noun* flooring composed of small inlaid blocks of wood arranged in a geometric pattern. ▸ *adj* made of parquet: *parquet floor*. [19c: French, diminutive of *parc* enclosure]

parquetry /ˈpɑːkətrɪ/ *noun* inlaid work in wood arranged in a geometric pattern, used esp to cover floors or to decorate furniture, etc.

parr *noun* (***parr*** *or* ***parrs***) a young salmon aged up to two years, before it becomes a **smolt**. [18c]

parricide *noun* **1** the act of killing one's own parent or near relative. See also **patricide**, **matricide**. **2** someone who commits this act. [16c: French]

parrot *noun* **1** a brightly-coloured bird, native to forests of warmer regions, with a large head and a strong hooked bill. **2** a person who merely imitates or mimics others. ▸ *verb* to repeat or mimic (another's words, etc) unthinkingly. [16c: from French *paroquet*]

parrot-fashion *adv* by mindless, unthinking repetition: *We learnt our tables parrot-fashion.*

parry *verb* (***-ies, -ied***) **1** to fend off (a blow). **2** to sidestep (a question) adeptly. ▸ *noun* (***-ies***) an act of parrying, esp in fencing. [17c: from French *parer* to ward off]

parse *verb, tr & intr* **1** *grammar* to analyse (a sentence) grammatically; to give the part of speech of and explain the grammatical role of (a word). **2** *comput* to analyse (a string of input symbols) in terms of the computing language being used. [16c: from Latin *pars orationis* part of speech]

parsec *noun, astron* a unit of astronomical measurement equal to 3.26 light years or 3.09×10^{13}km. [20c: from **parallax** + **second**[2]]

parsimony *noun* reluctance or extreme care in spending money; meanness. ▪ **parsimonious** *adj*. [15c: from Latin *parsimonia* thrift]

parsley *noun* a plant with finely-divided bright green curly aromatic leaves, used as a culinary herb and as a garnish. [Anglo-Saxon]

parsnip *noun* a plant widely grown for its thick fleshy tap root, eaten as a vegetable. [14c: from Latin *pastinacum*]

parson *noun* **1** a parish priest in the Church of England. **2** any clergyman. [13c: from Latin *persona* parish priest, person, personage or mask]

parsonage *noun* the residence of a parson.

parson's nose *noun, informal* a piece of fatty flesh at the rump of a plucked fowl, esp a turkey or chicken.

part *noun* **1** a portion, piece or bit; some but not all. **2** one of a set of equal divisions or amounts that compose a whole: *five parts cement to two of sand.* **3** an essential piece; a component: *vehicle spare parts.* **4** a section of a book; any of the episodes of a story, etc issued or broadcast as a serial. **5 a** a performer's role in a play, opera, etc; **b** the words, actions, etc belonging to the role. **6** the melody, etc given to a particular instrument or voice in a musical work. **7** one's share, responsibility or duty in something: *do one's part.* **8** (*usu* **parts**) a region: *foreign parts.* **9** (**parts**) talents; abilities: *a man of many parts.* ▸ *verb* **1** to divide; to separate. **2** *intr* to become divided or separated. **3** to separate (eg curtains, combatants, etc). **4** *intr* of more than one person: to leave one another; to go in different directions. **5** *intr* (**part from** *or* **with sb**) to leave them or separate from them. **6** *intr* (**part with sth**) to give it up or hand it over. **7** to put a parting in (hair). **8** *intr* to come or burst apart. ▸ *adj* in part; partial: *part payment.* [13c: from Latin *pars* part]
IDIOMS **be parted from sth** to give it up or hand it over. **for my part** as far as I am concerned. **for the most part 1** usually. **2** mostly or mainly. **in part** partly; not wholly but to some extent. **on the part of sb 1** as done by them. **2** so far as they are concerned. **part and parcel of sth** an essential part of it. **part company with sb** to separate from them. **play a part** to be involved. **take sth in good part** to take no offence at (a criticism, joke, etc). **take part in sth** to participate in it; to share in it. **take sb's part** to support them; to take their side.

partake *verb* (***partook, partaken***) *intr* (*usu* **partake in** *or* **of sth**) **1** to participate in it. **2** to eat or drink. [16c: formed from *partaking*]

parterre /pɑːˈtɛə(r)/ *noun* a formal flower-garden with lawns and paths. [17c: from French *par terre* on the ground]

part exchange *noun* a purchase or sale of new goods made by exchanging used goods for part of the value of the new goods. Compare **trade-in**.

parthenogenesis *noun, biol* in some insects and plants: reproduction without fertilization by the male. ▪ **parthenogenetic** *adj.* [19c: from Greek *parthenos* maiden + **genesis**]

Parthian shot see **parting shot**

partial *adj* **1** incomplete; in part only. **2** (*always* **partial to sth**) having a liking for it. **3** favouring one side or person unfairly; biased. ▪ **partially** *adv* not completely. [15c: from Latin *partialis*, from *pars* part]

partial fraction *noun, maths* one of two or more fractions, with denominators that cannot be factorized, into which a given fraction can be broken down.

partiality *noun* (***-ies***) **1** being partial. **2** favourable bias or prejudice. **3** fondness.

participate *verb, intr* (*often* **participate in sth**) to take part or be involved in it. ▪ **participant** *or* **participator** *noun.* ▪ **participation** *noun.* [16c: from Latin *pars* part + *capere* to take]

participle *noun, grammar* a word formed from a verb, which has adjectival qualities as well as verbal ones. There are two participles in English, the **present participle**, formed with the ending *-ing*, as in *going, swimming* or *shouting*, and the **past participle**, generally ending in *-d, -ed, -t* or *-n*, as in *chased, shouted, kept* and *shown*, but also with irregular forms such as *gone, swum*, etc. ▪ **participial** /pɑːtɪˈsɪpɪəl/ ▸ *adj* having the role of a participle: *participial clause.* [14c: from Latin *participium* a sharing]

particle *noun* **1** a tiny piece; a minute piece of matter. **2** the least bit: *not a particle of sympathy.* **3** *physics* a tiny unit of matter such as a **molecule**, **atom** or **electron**. **4** *grammar* a word which does not have any inflected forms, eg a **preposition**, **conjunction** or **interjection**. **5** *grammar* an **affix**, such as *un-, de-, -fy* and *-ly.* [14c: from Latin *particula*]

particle accelerator *noun, physics* a device that is used to accelerate charged subatomic particles to a high velocity.

particoloured *or* (*N Am*) **particolored** *adj* partly one colour, partly another; variegated. [16c: from French *parti* variegated]

particular *adj* **1** specific; single; individually known or referred to: *that particular day.* **2** especial: *took particular care.* **3** difficult to satisfy; fastidious; exacting: *He's very particular.* **4** exact; detailed. ▸ *noun* **1** a detail. **2** (**particulars**) personal details, eg name, date of birth, etc. [14c: from Latin *particularis*]
IDIOMS **in particular** particularly; especially; specifically; in detail.

particularity *noun* (***-ies***) **1** the quality of being particular. **2** minuteness of detail. **3** (*often* **particularities**) a single instance or case; a detail: *the particularities of the case.*

particularize *or* **-ise** *verb* **1** to specify individually. **2** to give specific examples of something. **3** *intr* to go into detail. [16c: from French *particulariser*]

particularly *adv* **1** more than usually: *particularly good.* **2** specifically; especially: *particularly wanted red.*

parting *noun* **1** the act of taking leave. **2** a divergence or separation: *a parting of the ways.* **3** a line of exposed scalp that divides sections of hair brushed in opposite directions: *a middle parting.* ▸ *adj* referring to, or at the time of, leaving; departing: *a parting comment.*

parting shot *noun* a final hostile remark made on departing. Also called **Parthian shot**. [19c: referring to the practice of the horsemen of ancient Parthia of turning to shoot arrows at enemies following them as they rode off]

partisan *noun* **1** an enthusiastic supporter of a party, person, cause, etc. **2** a member of an armed resistance group in a country occupied by an enemy. ▸ *adj* strongly loyal to one side, esp blindly so; biased. ▪ **partisanship** *noun.* [16c: French, from *parte* **part**]

partition *noun* **1** something which divides an object into parts. **2** a screen or thin wall dividing a room. **3** the dividing of a country into two or more independent states. ▸ *verb* **1** to divide (a country) into independent states. **2** (*also* **partition sth off**) to separate it off with a partition. [16c: from Latin *partitio* division]

partitive *grammar, adj* of a word, form, etc: denoting a part of a whole of what is being described. ▸ *noun* a partitive word or form, eg *some, any, most*. [16c: from Latin *partire* to divide]

partly *adv* in part, or in some parts; to a certain extent, not wholly.

partner *noun* **1** one of two or more people who jointly own or run a business or other enterprise on an equal footing. **2** a person with whom one has a sexual relationship, esp a long-term one. **3** a person one dances with: *dance partner*. **4** a person who is on the same side as oneself in a game of eg bridge, tennis, etc. **5** *biol* an animal or plant that takes part in commensalism or symbiosis. ▸ *verb* to join as a partner with someone; to be the partner of someone. [13c: from *parcener* joint inheritor]

partnership *noun* **1** a relationship in which two or more people or groups operate together as partners. **2** the status of a partner: *offered her a partnership*. **3** a business or other enterprise jointly owned or run by two or more people, etc.

part of speech *noun* (***parts of speech***) *grammar* any of the grammatical classes of words, eg noun, adjective, verb or preposition.

partook *past tense of* **partake**

partridge *noun* (***partridge*** or ***partridges***) a plump ground-dwelling game bird, with brown or grey plumage, unfeathered legs and feet, and a very short tail. [13c: from French *perdriz*]

part song *noun* a song for singing in harmonized parts.

part-time *adj* done, attended, etc during only part of the full working day. ▸ *adv*: *studying part-time*. ▸ *verb* to work on a part-time basis. Compare **full-time**. ▪ **part-timer** *noun*.

parturient *adj, med* **1** referring or relating to childbirth. **2** giving birth or about to give birth. [16c: from Latin *parturire* to give birth]

parturition *noun, med* the process of giving birth; childbirth.

party *noun* (***-ies***) **1** a social gathering, esp of invited guests, for enjoyment or celebration. **2** a group of people involved in a certain activity together: *search party*. **3** (*often* **Party**) an organization, esp a national organization, of people united by a common, esp political, aim. **4** *law* each of the individuals or groups concerned in a contract, agreement, lawsuit, etc: *no third party involved*. *in compounds, as adj*: *third-party insurance*. **5** *old facetious use* a person: *an elderly party*. ▸ *verb* (***-ies, -ied***) *intr, informal* to gather as a group to drink, chat, dance, etc for enjoyment; to have fun. [13c: from French *partie* a part, share, etc]

party line *noun* **1** a telephone line shared by two or more people. **2** the official opinion of a political party on any particular issue.

parvenu *or* **parvenue** /'pɑːvənjuː, -nuː/ *noun* (***parvenus*** *or* ***parvenues***) *derog* respectively a man or woman who has recently acquired wealth but lacks the social refinement sometimes thought necessary to go with it. *as adj*: *a parvenu land developer*. [19c: French, literally 'arrived']

PASCAL /pas'kal/ *noun, comput* a high-level computer programming language used for general programming purposes. [20c: named after Blaise Pascal, French philosopher and scientist]

pascal /'paskəl/ *noun* (symbol **Pa**) in the SI system: a unit of pressure, equal to a force of one newton per square metre. [20c: see **PASCAL**]

Pascal's triangle *noun, stats* a group of numbers arranged to form a triangle in which each number is the sum of the two numbers to its right and left in the line above. [19c: named after Blaise Pascal (see **PASCAL**), who described the triangle in his work]

paschal /'paskəl/ *adj* **1** relating to the Jewish festival of **Passover**. **2** relating to Easter. [15c: from Latin *paschalis*]

pas de deux /pɑː də dɜː/ *noun* (*pl* ***pas de deux***) a dance sequence for two performers. [18c: French, literally 'step for two']

pasha *noun, hist* placed after the name in titles: a high-ranking Turkish official in the Ottoman Empire. [17c: Turkish]

Pashto, Pushto *or* **Pushtu** *noun* **1** one of the official languages of Afghanistan, also spoken in NW Pakistan, an Iranian language of the Indo-European family. **2** a native speaker of this language. [18c: Persian and Afghan]

paso doble /'pasoʊ 'doʊbleɪ/ *noun* (***paso dobles*** *or* ***pasos dobles***) **1** a fast modern ballroom dance, based on a Latin American marching style. **2** the music for this dance usu in duple time. [20c: Spanish *paso* step + *doble* double]

pass *verb* **1** *tr & intr* to come alongside and progress beyond something or someone: *passed her on the stairs*. **2** *intr* to run, flow, progress, etc: *blood passing through our veins*. **3** *tr & intr* (*also* **pass through, into**, *etc* **sth** *or* **pass sth through, into**, *etc* **sth**) to go or make it go, penetrate, etc: *pass through a filter*. **4** (*sometimes* **pass sth round, on**, *etc*) to circulate it; to hand or transfer it from one person to the next in succession. **5** *tr & intr* to move lightly across, over, etc something: *pass a duster over the furniture*. **6** *intr* to move from one state or stage to another. **7** to exceed or surpass: *pass the target*. **8** *tr & intr* of a vehicle: to overtake. **9** **a** *tr & intr* to achieve the required standard in (a test, etc); **b** to award (a student, etc) the marks required for success in a test, etc. **10** *intr* to take place: *what passed between them*. **11** *tr & intr* of time: to go by; to use up (time) in some activity, etc. **12** *tr & intr* (*usu* **pass down** *or* **pass sth down**) to be inherited; to hand it down. **13** *tr & intr, sport* to throw or kick (the ball, etc) to another player in one's team. **14** *tr & intr* to agree to (a proposal or resolution) or be agreed to; to vote (a law) into effect. **15** of a judge or law court: to pronounce (judgement). **16** *intr* (*sometimes* **pass off**) to go away after a while: *Her nausea passed*. **17** *intr* to be accepted, tolerated or ignored: *let it pass*. **18** *intr* to choose not to answer in a quiz, etc or bid in a card game. **19** to make (a comment, etc). **20** to discharge (urine or faeces). ▸ *noun* **1** a route through a gap in a mountain range. **2** an official card or document permitting one to enter somewhere, be absent from duty, etc. **3** a successful result in an examination, but usu without distinction or honours. **4** *sport* a throw, kick, hit, etc to another player in one's team. **5** a state of affairs: *came to a sorry pass*. **6** a decision not to answer in a quiz, etc, or not to bid in a card game. [13c: from

Latin *passus* step or pace]

IDIOMS **come** *or* **be brought to pass** to happen. **pass the time of day** to exchange an ordinary greeting with someone.

PHRASAL VERBS **pass away** *or* **on** *euphem* to die. **pass sth** *or* **sb by** to overlook or ignore them. **pass off** of an arranged event: to take place with the result specified: *The party passed off very well.* **pass oneself off as sb** *or* **sth** to represent oneself as that person or thing: *passed themselves off as students.* **pass sth off** to successfully present (something which is fraudulent). **pass out 1** to faint. **2** to leave a military or police college having successfully completed one's training. **pass over sth** to overlook it; to ignore it. **pass sth up** *informal* to neglect or sacrifice (an opportunity).

passable *adj* **1** barely adequate. **2** *informal* fairly good. **3** of a road, etc: able to be travelled along, crossed, etc.

passage *noun* **1** a route through; a corridor, narrow street, or channel. **2** a tubular vessel in the body. **3** a piece of a text or musical composition of moderate length. **4** the process of passing: *the passage of time.* **5 a** a journey, esp by ship or aeroplane; **b** the cost of such a journey. **6** permission or freedom to pass through a territory, etc. **7** the voting of a law, etc into effect: *passage of the bill.* [13c: French, from *passer* to pass]

passageway *noun* a narrow passage or way, etc, usu with walls on each side; a corridor; an alley.

passbook *noun* a book in which the amounts of money put into and taken out of a building society account, bank account, etc, are recorded.

passé /ˈpaseɪ, ˈpɑːseɪ/ *adj* old-fashioned; outmoded. [18c: French, meaning 'passed']

passenger *noun* **1** a traveller in a vehicle, boat, aeroplane, etc, driven, sailed or piloted by someone else. **2** *derog* someone not doing their share of the work in a joint project, etc. ▸ *adj* relating to, or for, passengers: *passenger train.* [14c: from French *passagier*]

passer-by *noun* (***passers-by***) someone who is walking past a house, shop, incident, etc.

passerine *adj* belonging or relating to the largest order of birds, characterized by a perching habit, and which includes the songbirds. ▸ *noun* any bird belonging to this order. [18c: from Latin *passer* sparrow]

passim *adv* of a word, reference, etc: occurring frequently throughout the literary or academic work in question. [19c: Latin, meaning 'here and there']

passing *adj* **1** lasting only briefly. **2** casual; transitory: *a passing glance.* ▸ *noun* **1** a coming to the end. **2** *euphem* death. [14c: present participle of **pass**]

IDIOMS **in passing** while dealing with something else; casually; by allusion rather than directly.

passion *noun* **1** a violent emotion, eg anger or envy. **2** a fit of anger. **3** sexual love or desire. **4 a** an enthusiasm: *has a passion for bikes;* **b** the subject of great enthusiasm: *Bikes are his passion.* **5** (*usu* **the Passion**) the suffering and death of Christ. [12c: French]

passionate *adj* **1** easily moved to passion; strongly emotional. **2** keen; enthusiastic; intense. ▪ **passionately** *adv.*

passion fruit *noun* the round yellow or purple edible fruit of a tropical plant.

passive *adj* **1** lacking positive or assertive qualities; submissive. **2** lethargic; inert. **3** *gram* **a** denoting or relating to a verbal construction which in English consists of *be* and the **past participle** (see under **participle**), which carries a meaning in which the subject undergoes, rather than performs, the action of the verb, such as *'the letter'* in *The letter was written by John.* Compare **active** (*adj* sense 6); **b** denoting or relating to the verb in such a construction. ▸ *noun, gram* **1** (*also* **passive voice**) the form or forms that a passive verb takes. **2** a passive verb or construction. ▪ **passively** *adv.* ▪ **passivity** *noun.* [14c: from Latin *passivus*]

passive resistance *noun* the use of non-violent means, eg fasting, peaceful demonstration, etc, as a protest.

passive smoking *noun* the involuntary breathing in of tobacco smoke by non-smokers.

passkey *noun* a key designed to open a varied set of locks; a **master key**.

Passover *noun* an annual Jewish festival held in March or April, commemorating the deliverance of the Israelites from bondage in Egypt. Also called **Pesach**. [16c: so called because the angel of death passed over the houses of the Israelites when he killed the first-born of the Egyptians (Exodus 13)]

passport *noun* **1** an official document issued by the government, giving proof of the holder's identity and nationality, and permission to travel abroad with its protection. **2** an asset that guarantees one something, esp a privilege: *A degree is your passport to a good job.* [15c: from French *passeport*]

password *noun* **1** *esp military* a secret word allowing entry to a high-security area or past a checkpoint, etc. **2** *comput* a set of characters personal to a user which they input to gain access to a computer or network.

past *adj* **1** referring to an earlier time; of long ago; bygone. **2** recently ended; just gone by: *the past year.* **3** over; finished. **4** former; previous: *past presidents.* **5** *grammar* of the tense of a verb: indicating an action or condition which took place or began in the past. ▸ *prep* **1** up to and beyond: *went past me.* **2** after in time or age: *past your bedtime.* **3** beyond; farther away than: *the one past the library.* **4** having advanced too far for something: *She's past playing with dolls.* **5** beyond the reach of something: *past help* • *What he did was past belief.* ▸ *adv* **1** so as to pass by: *watched me go past.* **2** ago: *two months past.* ▸ *noun* **1** (*usu* **the past**) **a** the time before the present; **b** events, etc belonging to this time. **2** one's earlier life or career. **3** a disreputable episode or period earlier in one's life: *a woman with a past.* **4** *grammar* **a** the past tense; **b** a verb in the past tense. [14c: an obsolete past participle of **pass**]

IDIOMS **not put it past sb** *informal* to believe them quite liable or disposed to do a certain thing. **past it** *informal* having lost the vigour of one's youth or prime.

pasta *noun* a dough made with flour, water and eggs, shaped into a variety of forms such as spaghetti, macaroni, lasagne, etc. [19c: Italian]

paste *noun* **1** a stiff moist mixture made from a powder, traditionally flour, and water, and used as an adhesive: *wallpaper paste.* **2** a spread for sandwiches, etc made from ground meat or fish, etc. **3** any fine, often sweet, dough-like mixture: *almond paste.* **4** a hard brilliant glass used in making imitation gems. ▸ *verb* **1** to stick something with paste. **2** (*also* **paste sth up**) *printing* to mount (text, illustrations, etc) on a backing as a proof for printing from or photographing, etc. See also **paste-up**. **3** *word-processing* to insert text, etc which has been copied or cut from another part of the document, etc. **4** *informal* to thrash or beat soundly. [14c: French, from Latin *pasta* paste or dough]

pasteboard *noun* stiff board built up from thin sheets of paper glued or pasted together.

pastel *noun* **1** a chalk-like crayon made from ground pigment. **2** a picture drawn with pastels. ▸ *adj* **1** of colours: delicately pale; soft, quiet. **2** drawn with pastels. [17c: French]

pastern *noun* the part of a horse's foot between the hoof and the fetlock. [16c: from French *pasturon*]

paste-up *noun* (***paste-ups***) a set of text, illustrations, etc mounted on a board, prepared for copying or photographing. See also **paste sth up** at **paste**.

pasteurize *or* **-ise** /ˈpɑːstjʊraɪz/ *verb* to partially sterilize (food, esp milk) by heating it to a specific temperature for a short period before rapidly cooling it. ▪ **pasteurization** *noun*. [19c: named after Louis Pasteur, French chemist and bacteriologist]

pastiche /paˈstiːʃ/ *noun* a musical, artistic or literary work in someone else's style, or in a mixture of styles. [19c: French]

pastille *noun* **1** a small fruit-flavoured sweet, sometimes medicated: *fruit pastille*. **2** a cone of fragrant paste, burned as incense, for scenting a room. [17c: French]

pastime *noun* a spare-time pursuit; a hobby. [15c: from **pass** + **time**]

pasting *noun, informal* a thrashing.

past master *noun* an expert; someone who is thoroughly proficient. [18c]

pastor *noun* a member of the clergy, esp in churches other than Anglican and Catholic, with responsibility for a congregation. [14c: Latin, meaning 'shepherd']

pastoral *adj* **1 a** relating to the countryside or country life; **b** of a poem, painting, musical work, etc: depicting the countryside or country life, esp expressing nostalgia for an idealized simple rural existence. **2** relating to a member of the clergy or their work. **3** relating to a shepherd or their work. **4** of land: used for pasture. ▸ *noun* **1** a pastoral poem or painting. **2** *music* a **pastorale**. **3** a letter from a bishop to the clergy and people of the diocese. [15c: from Latin *pastor* shepherd]

pastorale /pastəˈrɑːl/ *noun, music* a musical work that evokes the countryside; a pastoral. [18c: Italian, meaning 'pastoral']

pastoralism *noun, anthropol* a way of life characterized by keeping herds of animals, common in dry, mountainous or severely cold climates not suitable for agriculture.

past participle see under **participle**

past perfect see under **perfect**

pastrami *noun* a smoked highly-seasoned cut of beef. [20c: from Yiddish *pastrame*]

pastry *noun* (***-ies***) **1** dough made with flour, fat and water, used for piecrusts. **2** a sweet baked article made with this; a pie, tart, etc. [16c: from **paste**]

pasturage *noun* **1** an area of land where livestock is allowed to graze. **2** grass for feeding.

pasture *noun* an area of grassland suitable or used for the grazing of livestock. Also called **pastureland**. ▸ *verb* **1** to put (animals) in pasture to graze. **2** *intr* of animals: to graze. [14c: French]

pasty[1] /ˈpastɪ, ˈpɑːstɪ/ *noun* (***-ies***) a pie consisting of pastry folded round a savoury or sweet filling: *Cornish pasty*. [13c: from French *pastée*]

pasty[2] /ˈpeɪstɪ/ *adj* (***-ier, -iest***) **1** like a paste in texture. **2** of the complexion: unhealthily pale. ▪ **pastiness** *noun*. [17c: from **paste**]

pat *verb* (***patted, patting***) **1** to strike (a person or animal) lightly or affectionately with the palm of one's hand. **2** to shape something by striking it lightly with the palm or a flat instrument: *pat it into shape*. ▸ *noun* **1** a light blow, esp an affectionate one, with the palm of the hand. **2** a round flat mass: *a pat of butter*. ▸ *adv* esp of things said: immediately and fluently, as if memorized: *Their answers came too pat*. ▸ *adj* of answers, etc: quickly and easily supplied. [14c]

IDIOMS **a pat on the back** an approving word or gesture. **have** *or* **know sth off pat** to have memorized it and know it perfectly.

patch *noun* **1** a piece of material sewn on or applied, eg to a garment or piece of fabric, etc, so as to cover a hole or reinforce a worn area. **2** a plot of earth: *a vegetable patch*. **3** a pad or cover worn as protection over an injured eye. **4** a small expanse contrasting with its surroundings: *patches of ice*. **5** scrap or shred. **6** *informal* a phase or period of time: *go through a bad patch*. **7** *slang* the area patrolled by a police officer or covered by a particular police station. **8** *comput* a set of instructions added to a program to correct an error. ▸ *verb* **1** to mend (a hole or garment) by sewing a patch or patches on or over it. **2** (*also* **patch sth up**) to repair it hastily and temporarily. See also **patch-up**. **3** *comput* to make a temporary correction in (a program). [14c]

IDIOMS **not a patch on sb** *or* **sth** *informal* not nearly as good as them.

PHRASAL VERBS **patch sth up** *informal* to settle (a quarrel, etc).

patchouli *noun* (***patchoulis*** *or* ***patchoulies***) a shrubby SE Asian plant that yields an aromatic **essential oil** used in perfumery. [19c: from Tamil *pacculi*]

patch-up *noun* (***patch-ups***) a provisional repair.

patchwork *noun* **1** needlework done by sewing together small pieces of contrastingly patterned fabric. **2** a piece of work produced in this way. *as adj*: *a patchwork quilt*. **3** a variegated expanse: *a patchwork of fields*.

patchy *adj* (***-ier, -iest***) **1** forming, or occurring in, patches. **2** covered in patches. **3** uneven or variable in quality: *gave a patchy performance*.

pate *noun, old use or facetious* the head or skull. [14c]

pâté /ˈpateɪ/ *noun* a spread made from ground or chopped meat, fish or vegetables blended with herbs, spices, etc. [20c in this sense: French]

pâté de foie gras see under **foie gras**

patella /pəˈtɛlə/ *noun* (***patellae*** /-ˈtɛliː/ *or* ***patellas***) *anatomy* the **kneecap**. [17c: Latin diminutive of *patina* a **paten** or small dish]

paten /ˈpatən/ *noun, relig* a circular metal plate on which the bread is placed in the celebration of the

Eucharist. [13c: French, from Latin *patina* a wide flat plate or dish]

patent /'peɪtənt, 'patənt/ *noun* **1** an official licence from the government granting a person or business the sole right, for a certain period, to make and sell a particular article. **2** the right so granted. **3** the invention so protected. ▶ *verb* to obtain a patent for (an invention, design, etc). ▶ *adj* **1** very evident: *a patent lie.* **2** concerned with the granting of, or protection by, patents. **3** of a product: made or protected under patent. **4** open for inspection: *letters patent.* ▪ **patentable** *adj.* ▪ **patently** *adv* openly; clearly: *patently obvious.* [14c: from Latin *patens* lying open]

patent leather *noun* leather made glossy by varnishing. [20c]

patent medicine *noun, technical* a patented medicine which is available without prescription.

pater *noun, old use or facetious* father. [14c: Latin]

paterfamilias *noun* (***patresfamilias***) the father as head of the household. [15c: Latin]

paternal *adj* **1** referring, relating, or appropriate to a father: *paternal instincts.* **2** of a relation or ancestor: related on one's father's side: *paternal grandmother.* Compare **maternal**. [17c: from Latin *paternalis*]

paternalism *noun* governmental or managerial benevolence towards its citizens, employees, etc taken to the extreme of overprotectiveness and authoritarianism. ▪ **paternalistic** *adj.* [19c]

paternity *noun* **1** the quality or condition of being a father; fatherhood. **2** the relation of a father to his children. **3** the authorship, source or origin of something. [16c: from Latin *paternitas*]

paternity suit *noun* a lawsuit brought by the mother of a child to establish that a certain man is the father of her child and therefore liable for its support.

paternoster *noun* **1 the Lord's Prayer**. **2** every tenth bead in a rosary at which the Lord's Prayer is repeated. [Anglo-Saxon: from Latin *Pater noster* Our Father]

path *noun* **1** (*also* **pathway**) a track trodden by, or specially surfaced for, walking. **2** the line along which something is travelling: *the path of Jupiter.* **3** a course of action: *the path to ruin.* **4** *comput* the location of a file in terms of a computer's disk drives and directory structure. [Anglo-Saxon *pæth*]

pathetic *adj* **1** moving one to pity; touching, heartrending, poignant or pitiful: *her pathetic sobs.* **2** *derog, informal* hopelessly inadequate. ▪ **pathetically** *adv.* [16c: from Greek *pathetikos* sensitive]

pathetic fallacy *noun* in literature: the transference of human feelings, etc to inanimate things, as in *a frowning landscape.*

pathname *noun, comput* the description of the location of a file in terms of a computer's disk drives and directory structure.

pathogen *noun, pathol* any micro-organism, esp a bacterium or virus, that causes disease in a living organism. ▪ **pathogenic** *adj.* [19c]

pathological *adj* **1** relating to pathology. **2** caused by, or relating to, illness. **3** *informal* compulsive; habitual: *a pathological liar.* ▪ **pathologically** *adv.*

pathology *noun* (***-ies***) **1** the branch of medicine concerned with the study of the nature of diseases. **2** the manifestations, characteristic behaviour, etc of a disease. ▪ **pathologist** *noun.* [17c]

pathos *noun* a quality in a situation, etc, esp in literature, that moves one to pity. [17c: Greek, meaning 'feeling' or 'suffering']

pathway *noun* a **path** (sense 1).

patience *noun* **1** the ability to endure delay, trouble, pain or hardship in a calm and contained way. **2** tolerance and forbearance. **3** perseverance. **4** *cards* a solo game in which the player, in turning each card over, has to fit it into a certain scheme. Also (*US*) called **solitaire**. [13c: French]

patient *adj* having or showing patience. ▶ *noun* a person who is being treated by, or is registered with, a doctor, dentist, etc. ▪ **patiently** *adv.* [14c]

patina *noun* **1** a coating formed on a metal surface by oxidation. **2** a mature shine on wood resulting from continual polishing and handling. **3** any fine finish acquired with age. ▪ **patinated** *adj.* ▪ **patination** *noun.* [18c: Italian, meaning 'coating']

patio *noun* **1** an open paved area beside a house. **2** an inner courtyard in a Spanish or Spanish-American house. [19c: Spanish]

patisserie /pə'tiːsəriː/ *noun* **1** a shop or café selling fancy cakes, sweet pastries, etc in the continental style. **2** such cakes. [18c: French]

patois /'patwɑː/ *noun* (*pl* ***patois***) **1** the local dialect of a region, used usu in informal everyday situations. **2** jargon. [17c: French]

patriarch *noun* **1** the male head of a family or tribe. Compare **matriarch**. **2** in the Eastern Orthodox Church: a high-ranking bishop. **3** in the Roman Catholic Church: the pope. **4** in the Old Testament: any of the ancestors of the human race or of the tribes of Israel, eg Adam, Abraham or Jacob. **5** a venerable old man. ▪ **patriarchal** *adj.* [13c: from Greek *patriarches* a senior bishop, or the father of a family]

patriarchate *noun* the office, authority, or residence of a church patriarch.

patriarchy *noun* (***-ies***) **1** a social system in which a male is head of the family and descent is traced through the male line. **2** a society based on this system. Compare **matriarchy**.

patrician *noun* **1** *hist* a member of the aristocracy of ancient Rome. Compare **plebeian** (sense 1). **2** an aristocrat. **3** someone who is thought of as refined and sophisticated. ▶ *adj* **1** belonging or relating to the aristocracy, esp that of ancient Rome. **2** refined and sophisticated. [15c: from Latin *patricius* having a noble father]

patricide *noun* **1** the act of killing one's own father. **2** someone who kills their own father. [16c: a variant of earlier **parricide**, influenced by Latin *pater* father]

patrimony *noun* (***-ies***) **1** property inherited from one's father or ancestors. **2** something inherited; a heritage. [14c: from Latin *patrimonium*]

patriot *noun* someone who loves and serves their fatherland or country devotedly. ▪ **patriotic** *adj.* ▪ **patriotically** *adv.* ▪ **patriotism** *noun.* [16c: from Greek *patriotes* fellow-countryman]

patrol *verb* (***patrolled, patrolling***) **1** *tr & intr* to make a regular systematic tour of (an area) to maintain security or surveillance. **2** *intr* of a police officer: to be on duty on a beat. ▶ *noun* **1** the act of patrolling: *on patrol.* **2** a person or group of people performing this duty. **3** a body of aircraft, ships, etc carrying out this duty. **4** any of the units of six or so into which a troop of Scouts or Guides is divided. [17c: from French *patrouiller*]

patron *noun* **1** someone who gives financial support and encouragement eg to an artist, the arts, a movement or charity: *a patron of the arts*. **2** a regular customer of a shop, attender at a theatre, etc. ▪ **patronal** /pəˈtroʊnəl/ *adj*. [14c: from Latin *patronus* protector]

patronage *noun* **1** the support given by a patron. **2** regular custom given to a shop, theatre, etc. **3** the power of bestowing, or recommending people for, offices.

patronize *or* **-ise** /ˈpatrənaɪz; *N Am* ˈpeɪtrənaɪz/ *verb* **1** to treat someone condescendingly. **2** to act as a patron towards (an organization, individual, etc). **3** to give custom, esp regularly, to (a shop, theatre, restaurant, etc). ▪ **patronizing** *adj*. ▪ **patronizingly** *adv*.

patron saint *noun* the guardian saint of a country, profession, craft, etc.

patronymic *noun* a name derived from one's father's or other male ancestor's name, usu with a suffix or prefix, as in *Donaldson* or *Macdonald*. [17c: from Greek *pater* father + *onyma* name]

patsy *noun* (**-ies**) *slang, chiefly N Am* an easy victim; a sucker; a scapegoat or fall guy. [20c]

patter[1] *verb, intr* **1** of rain, footsteps, etc: to make a light rapid tapping noise. **2** to move with light rapid footsteps. ▸ *noun* the light rapid tapping of footsteps or rain. [17c: frequentative of **pat**]

patter[2] *noun* **1** the fast persuasive talk of a salesman, or the quick speech of a comedian. **2** the jargon or speech of a particular group or area: *Glasgow patter*. ▸ *verb, tr & intr* to say or speak rapidly or glibly. [14c: from **paternoster**, because of the fast mumbling style in which this prayer and others were recited]

pattern *noun* **1** a model, guide or set of instructions for making something: *a dress pattern*. **2** a decorative design, often consisting of repeated motifs, eg on wallpaper or fabric. **3** a piece, eg of fabric, as a sample. **4** any excellent example suitable for imitation. **5** a coherent series of occurrences or set of features: *a pattern of events*. ▸ *verb* (*usu* **pattern sth on another thing**) to model it on another type, design, etc. [14c: French]

patty *noun* (**-ies**) **1** *N Am* a flat round cake of minced meat, vegetables, etc. **2** a small meat pie. [18c: from French *pâté* **pasty**[1]]

paucity *noun* (**-ies**) smallness of quantity; fewness; a scarcity or lack; dearth. [15c: from Latin *pauci* few]

paunch *noun* a protruding belly, esp in a man. ▪ **paunchy** *adj* (**-ier, -iest**). [14c: from French *panche*]

pauper *noun* **1** a poverty-stricken person. **2** *hist* someone living on charity or publicly provided money. [16c: Latin, meaning 'poor']

pause *noun* **1** a relatively short break in some activity, etc. **2** *music* **a** the prolonging of a note or rest beyond its normal duration; **b** a sign (⌢) indicating this, usu placed above the note, etc. ▸ *verb, intr* **1** to have a break; to stop briefly. **2** to hesitate. [15c: from Latin *pausa*]

IDIOMS **give sb pause** to make them hesitate before acting.

pave *verb* to surface (esp a footpath, but also a street, etc) with stone slabs, cobbles, etc. ▪ **paved** *adj*. [14c: from Latin *pavire* to ram or tread down]

IDIOMS **pave the way for sth** *or* **sb** to prepare for and make way for its introduction or their arrival.

pavement *noun* **1** a raised footpath edging a road, etc, often but not always paved. *N Am equivalent* **sidewalk**. **2** a paved road, area, expanse, etc: *a mosaic pavement*. **3** a road surface; road-surfacing material. [13c: French]

pavilion *noun* **1** a building in a sports ground in which players change their clothes, store equipment, etc. **2** a light temporary building such as a marquee, in which to display exhibits at a trade fair, etc. **3** a summerhouse or ornamental shelter. **4** a large ornamental building for public pleasure and entertainment. **5** a large and elaborate tent. [13c: from French *pavillon*]

paving *noun* **1** stones or slabs used to pave a surface. **2** a paved surface.

Pavlovian *adj, psychol, physiol* **1** relating to the work of the Russian physiologist, Ivan Pavlov (1849–1936), on conditioned reflexes. **2** of reactions, responses, etc: automatic; unthinking. [20c]

paw *noun* **1** the foot, usu clawed, of a four-legged mammal. **2** *informal* a hand, esp when used clumsily. See also **southpaw**. ▸ *verb* **1** to finger or handle something clumsily; to touch or caress someone with unwelcome familiarity. **2** (*also* **paw at sth**) of an animal: to scrape or strike it with a paw. [13c: from French *poue*]

pawn[1] *verb* **1** to deposit (an article of value) with a pawnbroker as a pledge for a sum of money borrowed. **2** to pledge or stake something. ▸ *noun* **1** the condition of being deposited as a pledge: *in pawn* • *at pawn*. **2** an article pledged in this way. [15c: from French *pan* pledge or surety]

pawn[2] *noun* **1** *chess* (symbol **P**) a chess piece of lowest value. **2** a person used and manipulated by others. [14c: from French *poun*]

pawnbroker *noun* someone who lends money in exchange for pawned articles. [17c]

pawnshop *noun* a pawnbroker's place of business.

pawpaw see under **papaw**

pax *noun, formal church use* the kiss of peace. ▸ *exclam, dated informal* truce! let's call a truce! [15c: Latin, meaning 'peace']

pay *verb* (**paid**) **1** *tr & intr* to give (money) to someone in exchange for goods, services, etc. **2** *tr & intr* to settle (a bill, debt, etc). **3** *tr & intr* to give (wages or salary) to an employee. **4** *tr & intr* to make a profit, or make something as profit: *businesses that don't pay*. **5** *tr & intr* to benefit; to be worthwhile: *It pays one to be polite* • *Dishonesty doesn't pay*. **6** *tr & intr* (*also* **pay for sth**) to suffer a penalty on account of it; to be punished for it. **7** **a** to do someone the honour of (a visit or call): *paid her a visit in hospital*; **b** to offer someone (a compliment, one's respects, etc). **8** to give (heed or attention). ▸ *noun* money given or received for work, etc; wages; salary. ▪ **payable** *adj* that can or must be paid: *Make cheques payable to me* • *payable by 31st July*. [13c: from French *paie*]

IDIOMS **in the pay of sb** employed by them. **pay its way** to compensate adequately for initial outlay. **pay one's way** to pay all of one's own debts and living expenses. **put paid to sth** *or* **sb** *informal* to put an end to them; to deal effectively or finally with them. **pay through the nose** to pay a very high price.

PHRASAL VERBS **pay sb back** to revenge oneself on

them. **pay sth back** to return (money owed). **pay off** to have profitable results. See also **payoff**. **pay sth off** to finish paying (a debt, etc). See also **payoff**. **pay sth out 1** to spend or give (money), eg to pay bills, debts, etc. See also **payout**. **2** to release or slacken (a rope, etc) esp by passing it little by little through one's hands. **pay up** *informal* to pay the full amount that is due, esp reluctantly.

pay-as-you-earn *noun* (abbrev **PAYE**) in Britain and New Zealand: a method of collecting income tax from employees by deducting it from their wages or salary.

pay-as-you-go *adj* denoting a service for which the user pays only when the service is used.

payee *noun* someone to whom money is paid or a cheque is made out.

payload *noun* **1** the part of a vehicle's load which earns revenue. **2** the operating equipment carried by a spaceship or satellite. **3** the quantity and strength of the explosive carried by a missile. **4** the quantity of goods, passengers, etc carried by an aircraft. [20c]

paymaster *noun* an official in charge of the payment of wages and salaries.

payment *noun* **1** a sum of money paid. **2** the act of paying or process of being paid. **3** a reward or punishment. [14c]

payoff *noun, informal* **1** a fruitful result; a good return. **2** a bribe. **3** a final settling of accounts. **4** a climax, outcome or final resolution. See also **pay off**, **pay sth off** under **pay**.

payola *noun* **1** a bribe for promoting a product. **2** the practice of giving or receiving such bribes. [20c: from **pay**, modelled on **Pianola**]

payout *noun* **1** the act of paying out money. **2** an amount of money paid out. See also **pay sth out** under **pay**.

pay-per-view *or* **pay-as-you-view** *adj* of satellite TV, cable TV, etc: referring or relating to **pay TV**.

payphone *noun* a telephone that is operated by coins, a phonecard or credit card.

payroll *noun* a register of employees that lists the wage or salary due to each.

payslip *noun* a note of an employee's pay, showing deductions for tax or national insurance, etc.

pazzazz *or* **pazazz** see **pizzazz**

Pb *symbol, chem* lead.

PC *abbrev* **1** personal computer. **2** Police Constable. **3 a** political correctness; **b** politically correct.

pc *abbrev* **1** per cent. **2** *informal* postcard.

pct *abbrev, N Am* per cent.

Pd *symbol, chem* palladium.

pd *abbrev* **1** paid. **2** (*also* **PD**) *physics* potential difference.

PDA *abbrev* personal digital assistant.

PDF *abbrev, comput* Portable Document Format, a file format that allows documents to keep their original appearance when viewed on a different operating system.

PE *abbrev* **1** physical education. **2** *physics* potential energy.

pea *noun* **1** a climbing plant of the pulse family, cultivated for its edible seeds, which are produced in long pods. **2** the round protein-rich seed of this plant, eaten as a vegetable. [17c: a singular form of **pease**, which was spelt *peas* and mistaken for a plural]

peace *noun* **1** freedom from or absence of war. **2** a treaty or agreement ending a war. **3** freedom from or absence of noise, disturbance or disorder; quietness or calm. **4** freedom from mental agitation; serenity: *peace of mind*. **5** *in compounds* usu referring to an organization, person, etc: promoting or advocating peace: *peacemaker* • *peace talks*. [13c: from French *pais*, from Latin *pax* peace]

IDIOMS **at peace 1** not at war; not fighting. **2** in harmony or friendship. **3** in a calm or serene state. **4** freed from earthly worries; dead. **hold one's peace** to remain silent. **keep the peace 1** *law* to preserve law and order. **2** to prevent, or refrain from, fighting or quarrelling. **make peace** to end a war or quarrel, etc.

peaceable *adj* peace-loving; mild; placid. ▪ **peaceably** *adv*.

peaceful *adj* **1** calm and quiet. **2** unworried; serene. **3** free from war, violence, disturbance, disorder, etc.

peacekeeping force *noun* a military force sent into a particular area with the task of preventing fighting between opposing factions.

peacemaker *noun* **1** someone who makes or brings about peace with the enemy. **2** someone who reconciles enemies. ▪ **peacemaking** *noun, adj*.

peace offering *noun* something offered to end a quarrel, or as an apology. [16c]

peace pipe *noun* a **calumet**.

peacetime *noun* periods that are free of war. [16c]

peach[1] *noun* **1** a small deciduous tree, widely cultivated for its edible fruit or for ornament. **2** the large round fruit of this tree, consisting of a hard stone surrounded by sweet juicy yellow flesh and a yellowish-pink velvety skin. **3** the yellowish-pink colour of this fruit. **4** *informal* something delightful: *a peach of a day*. ▸ *adj* yellowish-pink in colour: *a peach blouse*. [15c: from French *pesche*]

peach[2] *verb* (*always* **peach on sb**) *informal* to betray or inform on them, esp on an accomplice. [15c]

peachy *adj* (**-ier, -iest**) **1** coloured like or tasting like a peach. **2** *informal* very good; excellent.

peacock *noun* (***peacock*** *or* ***peacocks***) **1** a large bird, the male of which has a train of green and gold feathers with large spots which it fans showily during courtship. Also called **peafowl**. **2** the male peafowl (the female being the **peahen**). **3** *derog* a vain person. [14c]

pea-green *adj* bright-green or yellowish-green in colour. *Also* (**pea green**) *as noun*.

peak[1] *noun* **1 a** a sharp pointed summit; **b** a pointed mountain or hill. **2** a maximum, eg in consumer use: *Consumption reaches its peak at around 7pm*. **3** a time of maximum achievement, etc: *His peak was in his early twenties*. **4** the front projecting part of a cap. ▸ *adj* referring or relating to the period of highest use or demand: *peak viewing time*. ▸ *verb, intr* **1** to reach a maximum. **2** to reach the height of one's powers or popularity. [16c: prob related to **pike**[2]]

peak[2] *verb, intr* to droop; to look thin or sickly. [16c]

peaked *adj* **1** having a peak or peaks. **2** *in compounds* of a mountain or hill: having a summit with the specified number of peaks: *three-peaked* • *twin-peaked*.

peaky *adj* (**-ier, -iest**) ill-looking; pallid. [19c: related to **peak**[2]]

peal *noun* **1** the ringing of a bell or set of bells. **2** *non-technical* a set of bells, each with a different note. **3** a burst of noise: *a peal of thunder.* ▸ *verb* **1** *intr* to ring or resound. **2** to sound or signal (eg a welcome) by ringing. [14c: from obsolete *apele* **appeal**]

pean see **paean**

peanut *noun* **1** a low-growing plant of the pulse family, widely cultivated for its edible seeds which are produced under the ground in pods. **2** the protein-rich seed of this plant. Also called **groundnut, monkey nut. 3** (**peanuts**) *informal* **a** something small, trivial or unimportant; **b** a paltry amount of money. [19c]

peanut butter *noun* a savoury spread made from ground roasted peanuts.

pear *noun* **1** a deciduous tree, widely cultivated for its edible fruit and ornamental flowers. **2** the edible cone-shaped fruit of this tree, consisting of a core of small seeds surrounded by sweet juicy white pulp. [Anglo-Saxon *peru*: from Latin *pirum* pear]

pearl[1] *noun* **1** a bead of smooth hard lustrous material found inside the shell of certain molluscs, eg oysters, and used as a gem. **2** an artificial imitation of this. **3** (**pearls**) a necklace of pearls: *wearing my pearls.* **4** mother-of-pearl. **5** something resembling a pearl. **6** something valued or precious: *pearls of wisdom.* ▸ *adj* **1** like a pearl in colour or shape. **2** made of or set with pearls or mother-of-pearl. ▸ *verb* **1** to set something with, or as if with, pearls. **2** *intr* to fish for pearls. [14c: from a diminutive of Latin *perna* sea mussel]

pearl[2] see **purl[1]** (*noun* sense 3)

pearl barley *noun* seeds of barley ground into round polished grains, used in soups and stews.

pearl-grey *or* (*chiefly US*) **pearl-gray** *adj* pale bluish-grey in colour. *Also* (**pearl grey**) *as noun.*

pearly *adj* (*-ier, -iest*) **1** like a pearl or pearl; nacreous. **2** covered in pearl.

pearly gates *plural noun, informal* the gates of Heaven. [19c: from the biblical description in Revelation 21:21]

peasant *noun* **1** in poor agricultural societies: a farm worker or small farmer. **2** *derog* a rough unmannerly or culturally ignorant person. ▪ **peasantry** *noun* **1** the peasant class. **2** the condition of being a peasant. [15c: from French *païsant*]

pease *noun* (*pl* ***pease***) *archaic* a pea or pea-plant. [Anglo-Saxon *pise*]

pease pudding *noun* a purée made from split peas.

pea-shooter *noun* a short tube through which to fire dried peas by blowing, used as a toy weapon.

pea-souper *noun, informal* a very thick fog.

peat *noun* **1** a mass of dark-brown or black fibrous plant material, produced by the compression of partially decomposed vegetation, used in compost and in dried form as a fuel. **2** a cut block of this material. ▪ **peaty** *adj* (*-ier, -iest*). [13c: from Anglo-Latin *peta* a peat]

peat moss see **sphagnum**

pebble *noun* a small fragment of rock, esp one worn round and smooth by the action of water. *as adj*: *a pebble beach.* ▸ *verb* to cover with pebbles. ▪ **pebbled** *adj* covered with pebbles. ▪ **pebbly** *adj* (*-ier, -iest*) full of or covered with pebbles. [Anglo-Saxon *papol*]

pebbledash *noun, Brit* a coating for exterior walls of cement or plaster with small stones embedded in it.

pec *noun* (*usu* **pecs**) *informal* a **pectoral muscle**. [20c]

pecan *noun* **1** a deciduous N American tree, widely cultivated for its edible nut. Also called **pecan tree. 2** the oblong reddish-brown edible nut, with a sweet oily kernel, produced by this tree. Also called **pecan nut**. [18c: from Native American]

peccadillo *noun* (***peccadillos*** *or* ***peccadilloes***) a minor misdeed. [16c: from Spanish *pecadillo*, diminutive of *pecado* sin]

peck[1] *verb* **1** (*also* **peck at sth**) of a bird: to strike, nip or pick at it with the beak: *pecked at the bark of the tree.* **2** to poke (a hole) with the beak. **3** to kiss someone or something in a quick or perfunctory way: *pecked her on the cheek.* **4** *intr* (*often* **peck at sth**) **a** to eat (food) in a cursory, inattentive or dainty way, without enjoyment or application; **b** to nit-pick or quibble at it. ▸ *noun* **1** a tap or nip with the beak. **2** a perfunctory kiss. [14c: prob related to **pick[1]**]

peck[2] *noun* **1** in the imperial system: a measure of capacity of dry goods, esp grain, equal to two gallons (9.1 l) or a quarter of a **bushel**. **2** a measuring container holding this quantity. **3** *old use* a large amount: *a peck of troubles.* [13c: from French *pek*]

pecker *noun* **1** something that pecks; a beak. **2** a woodpecker. **3** *informal* spirits; resolve: *keep one's pecker up.*

pecking order *noun* any social hierarchy in animals or humans, or system of ranks and privileges.

peckish *adj* **1** *informal* quite hungry. **2** *US informal* irritable. [18c: from **peck[1]**]

pectin *noun, biochem* a complex carbohydrate that functions as a cement-like material within and between plant cell-walls. It forms a gel at low temperatures and is widely used in jam-making. [19c: from Greek *pektos* congealed]

pectoral *adj* **1** referring or relating to the breast or chest. **2** worn on the breast. ▸ *noun* **1** a pectoral muscle. **2** a pectoral fin. **3** a neck ornament worn covering the chest. **4** armour for the breast of a person or a horse. [15c: from Latin *pectoralis*, from *pectus* chest]

pectoral fin *noun* in fishes: one of a pair of fins situated just behind the gills, used to control the angle of ascent or descent, and for slowing down.

pectoral muscle *noun, anatomy* either of two muscles situated on either side of the top half of the chest.

peculate *verb, tr & intr, formal* to appropriate something dishonestly for one's own use; to embezzle. ▪ **peculation** *noun.* [18c: from Latin *peculari*]

peculiar *adj* **1** strange; odd. **2** (**peculiar to sb** *or* **sth**) exclusively or typically belonging to or associated with them: *habits peculiar to cats.* **3** special; individual: *their own peculiar methods.* **4** especial; particular: *of peculiar interest.* ▪ **peculiarly** *adv.* [16c: from Latin *peculium* private property]

peculiarity *noun* (*-ies*) **1** the quality of being strange or odd. **2** a distinctive feature, characteristic or trait. **3** an eccentricity or idiosyncrasy.

pecuniary *adj* relating to, concerning or consisting of money. [16c: from Latin *pecunia* money]

pedagogue *noun, old derog use* a teacher, esp a strict or pedantic one. ▪ **pedagogic** *adj.* [14c: from Greek *paidagogos* a child's tutor]

pedagogy /ˈpɛdəgɒdʒɪ/ *noun* the science or work of teaching. [17c: from French *pédagogie*]

pedal /ˈpɛdəl/ *noun* a lever operated by the foot, eg on a machine, vehicle or musical instrument. *as adj*: *a pedal bike*. ▸ *verb* (***pedalled, pedalling***; or (*esp N Am*) ***pedaled, pedaling***) *tr & intr* to move or operate by means of a pedal or pedals. ▸ *adj* /ˈpiːdəl/ *zool* referring or relating to the foot or feet. [17c: from Latin *pedalis* of the foot]

pedant *noun, derog* someone who is overconcerned with correctness of detail, esp in academic matters. ▪ **pedantic** *adj*. [16c: from Italian *pedante* teacher]

pedantry *noun* (***-ies***) **1** excessive concern with correctness. **2** a pedantic expression. **3** unnecessary formality.

pedate *adj, biol* footed or foot-like. [18c: from Latin *pedatus* footed]

peddle *verb* **1** *tr & intr* to go from place to place selling (a selection of small goods); to be a pedlar. **2** *informal* to deal illegally in (narcotic drugs). **3** *informal* to publicize and try to win acceptance for (ideas, theories, etc). [16c: a back-formation from **pedlar**]

peddler *noun* **1** the usual *N Am* spelling of **pedlar**. **2** someone who deals illegally in narcotics.

pedestal *noun* the base on which a vase, statue, column, etc is placed or mounted. [16c: from Italian *piedistallo* foot of stall]

IDIOMS **put** *or* **place sb on a pedestal** to admire or revere them extremely; to idolize them.

pedestrian *noun* someone travelling on foot, esp in a street; someone who is walking. ▸ *adj* **1** referring to, or for, pedestrians. **2** dull; unimaginative; uninspired. [18c: from Latin *pedester* on foot]

pedestrianize *or* **-ise** *verb* to convert (a shopping street, etc) into an area for pedestrians only by excluding through-traffic and usu paving over the street. ▪ **pedestrianization** *noun*. [20c in this sense]

pedestrian precinct *noun* a shopping street or similar area from which traffic is excluded.

pediatrician, pediatric *or* **pediatrics** alternative *N Am* spellings of **paediatrician, paediatric, paediatrics**

pedicel *noun* **1** *botany* the stalk of a single flower. **2** *zool* the stalk of an animal organ, eg a crab's eye. [17c: from Latin *pedicelus*, diminutive of *pediculus* a little foot]

pedicure *noun* a medical or cosmetic treatment of the feet and toenails. [19c: from Latin *pes* foot + *curare* to look after]

pedigree *noun* **1** a person's or animal's line of descent, esp if long and distinguished, or proof of pure breeding. **2** a genealogical table showing this; a family tree. [15c: from French *pie de grue* foot of the crane, from its similarity to a branching family tree]

pediment *noun* **1** *archit* a wide triangular gable set over a classical portico or the face of a building. **2** *geol* a gently sloping surface, formed by the erosion of cliffs or steep slopes. ▪ **pedimented** *adj*. [16c: perhaps a corruption of **pyramid**]

pedlar *or* (*chiefly N Am*) **peddler** *noun* someone who peddles. [14c]

pedometer /pɪˈdɒmɪtə(r)/ *noun* a device that measures a distance walked by recording the number of steps taken. [18c: from Latin *pedi-* foot + Greek *metron* measure]

peduncle *noun* **1** *botany* a short stalk, eg one carrying an inflorescence or a single flower-head. **2** *anatomy, pathol* any stalk-like structure. ▪ **peduncular** *or* **pedunculated** *adj*. [18c: from Latin *pedunculus* small foot]

pee *informal, verb* (***peed***) *intr* to urinate. ▸ *noun* **1** an act of urinating. **2** urine. [18c]

peek *verb, intr* (*also* **peek at sth**) to glance briefly and surreptitiously at it; to peep. ▸ *noun* a brief furtive glance. [14c]

peel *verb* **1** to strip the skin or rind off (a fruit or vegetable). **2** *intr* to be able to be peeled: *Grapes don't peel easily.* **3** (*also* **peel sth away** *or* **off**) to strip off (an outer layer). **4** *intr* of a wall or other surface: to shed its outer coating in flaky strips. **5** *intr* of skin, paint or other coverings: to flake off in patches. **6** *intr* of a person or part of the body: to shed skin in flaky layers after sunburn. ▸ *noun* the skin or rind of vegetables or fruit, esp citrus fruit: *candied peel*. ▪ **peeler** *noun* a small knife or device for peeling fruit and vegetables. [From Latin *pilare* to deprive of hair]

PHRASAL VERBS **peel off 1** of an aircraft or vehicle: to veer away from the main group. **2** *informal* to undress.

peelings *plural noun* strips of peel removed from a fruit or vegetable.

peen *or* **pein** *noun* the end of a hammer-head opposite the hammering face. [17c]

peep[1] *verb, intr* **1** (*often* **peep at sth** *or* **sb** *or* **peep out**) to look quickly or covertly, eg through a narrow opening or from a place of concealment; to peek. **2** (*also* **peep out**) to emerge briefly or partially. ▸ *noun* **1** a quick covert look. **2** a first faint glimmering: *at peep of day.* [16c: a variant of **peek**]

peep[2] *noun* **1** the faint high-pitched cry of a baby bird, etc; a cheep. **2** the smallest utterance: *not another peep out of you!* ▸ *verb, intr* **1** of a young bird, etc: to utter a high-pitched cry; to cheep. **2** *informal* to sound or make something sound: *peep the horn.* [15c]

peephole *noun* a hole, crack, aperture, etc through which to peep.

peeping Tom *noun* a man who furtively spies on other people; a voyeur. [19c: named after the tailor who, according to legend, peeped at Lady Godiva as she rode naked through the streets of Coventry]

peepshow *noun* a box with a peephole through which a series of moving pictures, esp erotic ones, can be watched.

peer[1] *noun* **1** a member of the nobility, such as, in Britain, a **duke**, **marquess**, **earl**, **viscount** or **baron**. Compare **aristocrat**, **noble**. **2** a member of the House of Lords, known as either a **life peer** or **life peeress**, a **spiritual peer**, ie a bishop or archbishop, or a **temporal peer**, ie all other members of the House of Lords. **3** someone who is one's equal in age, rank, etc; a contemporary, companion or fellow. *as adj*: *peer group.* [14c: from French *per*]

peer[2] *verb, intr* **1** (*also* **peer at sth** *or* **sb**) to look hard at it or them, esp through narrowed eyes, as if having difficulty in seeing. **2** (*sometimes* **peer out**) *literary* to peep out or emerge briefly or partially. [16c]

peerage *noun* **1** the title or rank of a peer. **2** *singular or plural* the members of the nobility as a group.

peerless *adj* without equal; excelling all. [14c]

peer pressure *noun* compulsion to do or obtain the same things as others in one's peer group.

peer-to-peer *adj, comput* (abbrev **P2P**) denoting a system in which the workload of a network is evenly distributed among the workstations.

peeve *informal, verb* to irritate, annoy or offend. ▸ *noun* a cause of vexation or irritation. ▪ **peeved** *adj.* [20c: a back-formation from **peevish**]

peevish *adj* irritable; cantankerous; inclined to whine or complain. ▪ **peevishly** *adv.* [14c]

peewit /ˈpiːwɪt/ *or* **pewit** /ˈpiːwɪt, ˈpjuːɪt/ *noun* a **lapwing**. [16c: imitating its cry]

peg *noun* **1** a little shaft of wood, metal or plastic shaped for fixing, fastening or marking uses. **2** a coat hook fixed to a wall, etc. **3** a wooden or plastic clip for fastening washing to a line to dry; a clothes peg. **4** a small stake for securing tent ropes, marking a position, boundary, etc. **5** any of several wooden pins on a stringed instrument, which are turned to tune it. **6** a pin for scoring, used eg in cribbage. **7** *informal* a leg. **8** *informal* a **peg leg** (sense 1). **9** *old informal* a drink of spirits. ▸ *verb* (***pegged, pegging***) **1** to insert a peg into something. **2** to fasten something with a peg or pegs. **3** (*sometimes* **peg sth out**) to mark out (ground) with pegs. **4** to set or freeze (prices, incomes, etc) at a certain level. [15c: from Dutch *pegge*]

IDIOMS **a square peg in a round hole** a person who does not fit in well in their environment, job, etc. **off the peg** of clothes: ready to wear; ready-made. **take sb down a peg or two** *informal* to humiliate them; to humble them.

PHRASAL VERBS **peg away at sth** *informal* to work steadily at it. **peg out 1** *informal* to die. **2** to become exhausted.

peg leg *noun, informal* **1** an artificial leg. **2** a person with an artificial leg.

pein see **peen**

pejorative /pəˈdʒɒrətɪv/ *adj* of a word or expression: disapproving, derogatory, disparaging or uncomplimentary. ▸ *noun* a word or affix with derogatory force. [19c: from Latin *peiorare* to make worse]

pelagic /pɪˈladʒɪk/ *adj* **1** *technical* relating to, or carried out on, the deep open sea. **2** *biol* denoting floating plankton and fish, and other organisms that swim freely in the surface waters. Compare **benthos.** ▪ **pelagian** *adj, noun.* [17c: from Greek *pelagos* sea]

pelargonium *noun* a plant with hairy stems, rounded or lobed aromatic leaves, and conspicuous scarlet, pink or white fragrant flowers, often cultivated under the name **geranium**. [19c: from Greek *pelargos* stork, modelled on **geranium**]

pelf *noun, derog* riches; money; lucre. [15c: from French *pelfre* booty]

pelican *noun* (***pelican*** *or* ***pelicans***) a large aquatic bird that has an enormous beak with a pouch below it, and mainly white plumage. [Anglo-Saxon]

pelican crossing *noun* a **pedestrian crossing** with a set of pedestrian-controlled traffic lights. [20c: adapted from *pe*destrian *li*ght-*con*trolled crossing]

pelisse /pɛˈliːs/ *noun, hist* **1** a long mantle of silk, velvet, etc, worn esp by women. **2** a fur or fur-lined garment, esp a military cloak. [18c: French]

pellagra *noun, med* a disease characterized by scaly discoloration of the skin, diarrhoea, vomiting, and psychological disturbances. [19c: Italian]

pellet *noun* **1** a small rounded mass of compressed material, eg paper. **2** a piece of small shot for an airgun, etc. **3** a ball of undigested material regurgitated by an owl or hawk. ▸ *verb* (***pelleted, pelleting***) **1** to form (esp seeds) into pellets by coating them with a substance, eg to aid planting. **2** to bombard someone or something with pellets. [14c: from French *pelote*]

pell-mell *adv* headlong; in confused haste; helter-skelter. ▸ *adj* confusedly mingled; headlong. [16c: from French *pesle-mesle*]

pellucid *adj* **1** transparent. **2** absolutely clear in expression and meaning. ▪ **pellucidity** /pɛluːˈsɪdɪtɪ/ *or* **pellucidness** *noun.* ▪ **pellucidly** *adv.* [17c: from Latin *per* utterly + *lucidus* clear]

pelmet *noun* a strip of fabric or a narrow board fitted along the top of a window to conceal the curtain rail. [20c]

pelota /pɛˈloʊtə/ *noun* a game in which players use their hand or a basket-like device strapped to their wrists to catch and throw a ball against a specially marked wall. [19c: Spanish, meaning 'ball']

pelt[1] *verb* **1** to bombard with missiles: *was pelted with stones.* **2** *intr* to rush along at top speed: *pelting along the motorway.* **3** *intr* (*often* **pelt down**) to rain heavily. ▸ *noun* an act or spell of pelting. [15c]

IDIOMS **at full pelt** as fast as possible.

pelt[2] *noun* **1** the skin of a dead animal, esp with the fur still on it. **2** the coat of a living animal. **3** a hide stripped of hair for tanning. [15c]

pelvic *adj* relating to or in the region of the pelvis.

pelvic girdle *or* **pelvic arch** *noun, zool, anatomy* the posterior limb-girdle of vertebrates, consisting of two hip bones, the **sacrum** and the **coccyx**.

pelvis *noun* (***pelvises*** *or* ***pelves*** /-viːz/) *anatomy* **1** the basin-shaped cavity formed by the bones of the pelvic girdle. **2** the **pelvic girdle**. [17c: Latin, meaning 'basin']

pen[1] *noun* **1** a writing instrument that uses ink. **2** this instrument as a symbol of the writing profession. ▸ *verb* (***penned, penning***) *formal* to compose and write (a letter, poem, etc) with a pen. ▪ **penned** *adj* written; quilled. [14c: from Latin *penna* feather]

pen[2] *noun* **1** a small enclosure, esp for animals. **2** *often in compounds* any small enclosure or area of confinement for the specified purpose: *a playpen.* ▸ *verb* (***penned*** *or* ***pent, penning***) (*often* **pen sb** *or* **sth in** *or* **up**) to enclose or confine them in a pen, or as if in a pen. [Anglo-Saxon *penn*]

pen[3] *noun, N Am informal* a **penitentiary.**

pen[4] *noun* a female swan. [16c]

penal /ˈpiːnəl/ *adj* relating to punishment, esp by law. ▪ **penally** *adv.* [15c: from Latin *poenalis*]

penalize *or* **-ise** *verb* **1** to impose a penalty on someone, for wrongdoing, cheating, breaking a rule, committing a foul in sport, etc. **2** to disadvantage someone. [19c]

penalty *noun* (***-ies***) **1** a punishment, such as imprisonment, a fine, etc, imposed for wrongdoing, breaking a contract or rule, etc. **2** a punishment that one brings on oneself through ill-advised action: *paid the penalty for my error.* **3** *sport* a handicap imposed on a competitor or team for a foul or other infringement of the rules, in team games taking the form of an advantage awarded to the opposing side. [16c: from Latin *poenalitas*]

IDIOMS **under** *or* **on penalty of sth** with liability to the penalty of a particular punishment in case of violation of the law, etc: *swear on penalty of death*.

penalty area *or* **penalty box** *noun, football* an area in front of either goal within which a foul by any player in the defending team is punished by a penalty awarded to the attacking team.

penalty kick *noun* **1** *rugby* a free kick. **2** *football* a free kick at goal from a distance of 12yd (11m), awarded to the attacking team for a foul committed in the **penalty area** by the defending team.

penance *noun* repentance or atonement for an offence or wrongdoing, or an act of repentance: *do penance*. [13c: from French *peneance*]

pence *a pl of* **penny**

penchant /'pɑ̃ʃɑ̃/ *noun* a taste, liking, inclination or tendency: *a penchant for childish pranks*. [17c: French, present participle of *pencher* to lean]

pencil *noun* **1** a writing and drawing instrument consisting of a wooden shaft containing a stick of graphite or other material. *as adj*: *a pencil drawing*. **2** something with a similar function or shape, eg for medical or cosmetic purposes: *an eyebrow pencil*. **3** something long, fine and narrow in shape. *as adj*: *pencil pleats • a pencil torch*. ▶ *verb* (***pencilled, pencilling***; *N Am* ***penciled, penciling***) to write, draw or mark something with a pencil. [15c: from Latin *penicillus* painter's brush]

PHRASAL VERBS **pencil sth** *or* **sb in** to note down a provisional commitment, eg for a meeting, etc, in one's diary, for later confirmation.

pendant *or* (*sometimes*) **pendent** *noun* **1 a** an ornament suspended from a neck chain, necklace, bracelet, etc; **b** a necklace with such an ornament hanging from it. **2** any of several hanging articles, eg an earring, ceiling light, etc. [14c: French, from *pendre* to hang]

pendent *or* (*sometimes*) **pendant** *adj* **1** hanging; suspended; dangling. **2** projecting; jutting; overhanging. **3** undetermined or undecided; pending. [15c: from French *pendant*; see **pendant**]

pending *adj* **1** remaining undecided; waiting to be decided or dealt with. **2** of a patent: about to come into effect. ▶ *prep* until; awaiting; during: *held in prison pending trial*. [17c: from Latin *pendere* to hang]

pendulous *adj* hanging down loosely; drooping; swinging freely. [17c: from Latin *pendulus* hanging]

pendulum *noun* **1** *physics* a weight, suspended from a fixed point, that swings freely back and forth. **2** a swinging lever used to regulate the movement of a clock. **3** anything that undergoes obvious and regular shifts or reversals in direction, attitude, opinion, etc. [17c: Latin, neuter of *pendulus* hanging]

penes *a pl of* **penis**

penetrate *verb* **1** (*also* **penetrate into sth**) to find a way into it; to enter it, esp with difficulty. **2** to gain access into and influence within (a country, organization, market, etc) for political, financial, etc purposes. **3** to find a way through something; to pierce or permeate: *penetrate enemy lines*. **4** *intr* to be understood: *The news didn't penetrate at first*. **5** to see through (a disguise). **6** to fathom, solve, or understand (a mystery). **7** of a man: to insert his penis into the vagina of (a woman) or anus of (a man or a woman). ▪ **penetrative** *adj*. [16c: from Latin *penetrare* to penetrate]

penetrating *adj* **1** of a voice, etc: all too loud and clear; strident. **2** of a person's mind: acute; discerning. **3** of the eyes or of a look: piercing; probing.

penetration *noun* **1** the process of penetrating or being penetrated. **2** mental acuteness; insight.

pen friend *or* **pen pal** *noun* someone, usu living abroad, with whom one corresponds by letter, and whom one may not have met in person.

penguin *noun* a flightless sea bird with a stout body, small almost featherless wings, short legs, bluish-grey or black plumage, and a white belly. [16c: possibly from Welsh *pen* head + *gwyn* white]

penicillin *noun* any of various **antibiotics**, derived from a mould or produced synthetically, that are widely used to treat bacterial infections. [20c: from Latin *penicillus* painter's brush]

peninsula *noun* a piece of land projecting into water from a larger landmass and almost completely surrounded by water. ▪ **peninsular** *adj*. [16c: from Latin *paene* almost + *insula* island]

penis *noun* (***penises*** *or* ***penes*** /'piːniːz/) in higher vertebrates: the male organ of copulation which is used to transfer sperm to the female reproductive tract and also contains the **urethra** through which urine is passed. ▪ **penile** *adj*. [17c: Latin, orig meaning 'tail']

penitent *adj* regretful for wrong one has done, and feeling a desire to reform; repentant. ▶ *noun* **1** a repentant person, esp one doing penance on the instruction of a confessor. **2** *RC Church* a member of one of various orders devoted to penitential exercises, etc. ▪ **penitence** *noun*. [14c: from Latin *paenitens* repentant]

penitential *adj* referring to, showing or constituting penance: *penitential psalms*.

penitentiary *noun* (***-ies***) *N Am* a federal or state prison. Often shortened to **pen**. ▶ *adj* **1** referring or relating to punishment or penance. **2** penal or reformatory. [16c]

penknife *noun* a pocket knife with blades that fold into the handle. [14c: from **pen**[1] (*noun* sense 1), because such a knife was orig used for cutting quills]

penmanship *noun* the ability to write beautifully or well.

pen name *noun* a pseudonym used by a writer. [19c]

pennant *noun* **1** *naut* a dangling line from the masthead, etc, with a block for tackle, etc. **2** *naut* a small narrow triangular flag, used on vessels for identification or signalling. Also called **pennon**. [17c: prob from **pennon** + **pendant**]

pennate *adj, biol* **1** winged; feathered; shaped like a wing. **2** **pinnate**. [18c: from Latin *pennatus* winged]

penne /'pɛneɪ/ *noun* pasta in the form of short thick ridged tubes. [20c: Italian, literally 'quills']

penniless *adj* without money; poverty-stricken. [14c]

pennon *noun* **1** *hist* a long narrow flag with a tapering divided tip, eg borne on his lance by a knight. **2** a **pennant** (sense 2). [14c: from Latin *penna* feather]

penny /'pɛnɪ/ *noun* (***pence*** in senses 1 and 2, or ***pennies***) **1** (*sing* and *pl* abbrev **p**) in the UK: a hundredth part of £1, or a bronze coin having this value. **2** (*sing* and *pl* symbol **d**) in the UK before decimalization in

1971: 1⁄12 of a shilling or 1⁄240 of £1, or a bronze coin having this value. **3** *with negatives* the least quantity of money: *won't cost a penny.* **4** *N Am* one cent, or a coin having this value. **5** /ˈpɛnɪ, pənɪ/ *in compounds* denoting a specified number of pennies (as a value): *a five-penny piece.* [Anglo-Saxon *pening*]

IDIOMS **a pretty penny** *ironic* a huge sum. **spend a penny** *euphem, informal* to urinate. **the penny dropped** *informal* understanding about something finally came. **two a penny** *or* **ten a penny** very common; in abundant supply and of little value.

penny farthing *noun, Brit* an early type of bicycle, dating from the 1860s, with a large front wheel and small back wheel. See also **boneshaker**.

penny-pinching *adj, derog* too careful with one's money; miserly; stingy. ▪ **penny-pincher** *noun.*

penny whistle *noun* a tiny whistle or flageolet.

penology *or* **poenology** /piːˈnɒlədʒɪ/ *noun* the study of crime and punishment. ▪ **penological** *adj.* ▪ **penologist** *noun.* [19c: from Greek *poine* punishment + *logos* word or reason]

pen pal see **pen friend**

pen pusher *noun* a clerk or minor official whose job includes much tedious paperwork. ▪ **pen-pushing** *noun, adj.* [19c: orig *pencil pusher*]

pension /ˈpɛnʃən/ *noun* **1** a government allowance to a retired, disabled or widowed person. **2** a regular payment by an employer to a retired employee. **3** a regular payment from a private pension company to a person who contributed to a pension fund for much of their working life. **4** /*French* pɑ̃sjɔ̃/ a boarding house in continental Europe. ▸ *verb* to grant a pension to (a person). ▪ **pensioner** *noun* someone who is in receipt of a pension. [14c: French]

PHRASAL VERBS **pension sb off** to put them into retirement, or make them redundant, on a pension.

pensionable *adj* entitling one to a pension; entitled to a pension: *of pensionable age.*

pensive *adj* preoccupied with one's thoughts; thoughtful. ▪ **pensively** *adv.* [14c: from French *pensif*, from *penser* to think]

pent *past tense, past participle of* **pen²**. See also **pent-up**.

penta- *or* (*before a vowel*) **pent-** *combining form, denoting* five: *pentatonic.* [From Greek *pente* five]

pentacle *noun* a **pentangle**. [16c: from Latin *pentaculum*]

pentad *noun* **1** a set of five things. **2** a period of five years or five days. [17c: from Greek *pentados* a group of five]

pentagon *noun, geom* a plane figure (see **plane²** *adj* sense 3) with five sides and five angles. ▪ **pentagonal** /pɛnˈtagənl/ *adj.* [16c: from Greek *pente* five + *gonia* angle]

pentagram *noun* **1** a figure in the shape of a star with five points and consisting of five lines. **2** such a figure used as a magic symbol; a **pentacle**. [19c: from Greek *pentagrammos*]

pentahedron *noun* (***pentahedrons*** *or* ***pentahedra***) *geom* a five-faced solid figure. ▪ **pentahedral** *adj.* [18c: compare **polyhedron**]

pentameter /pɛnˈtamɪtə(r)/ *noun, poetry* a line of verse with five metrical feet. [16c: Latin]

pentane *noun, chem* a hydrocarbon of the alkane series with five carbon atoms.

pentangle *noun* a **pentagram** or similar figure or amulet used as a defence against demons. [14c]

pentanoic acid *noun, chem* a colourless acid used in the perfume industry.

Pentateuch /ˈpɛntətjuːk/ *noun* the first five books of the Old Testament. ▪ **Pentateuchal** *adj.* [16c: from Greek *pentateuchos* five-volumed]

pentathlon *noun* an athletic competition comprising five events all of which the contestants must compete in. [18c: from Greek *pente* five + *athlon* contest]

pentatonic *adj, music* of a musical scale: having five notes to the octave. [19c]

pentavalent *adj, chem* of an atom of a chemical element: having a valency of five. Also **quinquevalent**. [19c]

Pentecost *noun, Christianity* a festival on Whit Sunday, the seventh Sunday after Easter, commemorating the descent of the Holy Spirit on the Apostles. [Anglo-Saxon: from Latin *pentecoste*]

Pentecostal *adj* **1** denoting any of several fundamentalist Christian groups that put emphasis on God's gifts through the Holy Spirit, characterized by their literal interpretation of the Bible and informal worship. **2** relating to Pentecost ▪ **Pentecostalism** *noun.* ▪ **Pentecostalist** *noun, adj.*

penthouse *noun* an apartment, esp a luxuriously appointed one, built on to the roof of a tall building. *as adj*: *the penthouse suite.* [20c]

pent-up (*also* **pent up**) *adj* of feelings, energy, etc: repressed or stifled; bursting to be released.

penult *or* **penultima** *noun* the last but one syllable in a word. [16c: from Latin *paenultimus* **penultimate**]

penultimate *adj* last but one. ▸ *noun* **1** the penult. **2** the last but one. [17c: from Latin *paene* almost + *ultimus* last]

penumbra *noun* (***penumbrae*** /pɛˈnʌmbriː/ *or* ***penumbras***) **1** the lighter outer shadow that surrounds the dark central shadow produced by a large unfocused light-source shining on an opaque object. **2** *astron* the lighter area around the edge of a sunspot. ▪ **penumbral** *or* **penumbrous** *adj.* [17c: Latin, from *paene* almost + *umbra* shadow]

penury *noun* extreme poverty. ▪ **penurious** *adj.* [15c: from Latin *penuria* want]

peon *noun* **1** in India and Ceylon: an office messenger; an attendant. **2** in Latin America: a farm labourer. [17c: Spanish]

peony *or* **paeony** /ˈpɪənɪ/ *noun* (**-ies**) a plant with large round red, pink, yellow or white flowers. [Anglo-Saxon: from French *pione*]

people *noun, usu plural* **1** a set or group of persons. **2** men and women in general. **3** a body of persons held together by belief in common origin, speech, culture, political union, or by common leadership, etc. **4 a** (**the people**) ordinary citizens without special rank; the general populace; **b** *in compounds* denoting that the specified thing belongs or relates to the people, general populace, etc: *people-power* • *people-oriented.* **5** (**the people**) voters as a body. **6** subjects or supporters of a monarch, etc. **7** *singular* a nation or race: *a warlike people.* **8** *informal* one's parents, or the wider circle of one's relations. ▸ *verb* **1** to fill or supply (a region, etc) with people; to populate. **2** to inhabit. [14c: from French *poeple*]

IDIOMS **of all people 1** especially; more than anyone else: *You, of all people, should know that.* **2** very strangely or unexpectedly: *chose me, of all people, as spokesperson.*

people carrier *noun* a vehicle with a greater seating capacity than a standard car, used eg for transporting a large family. Also called **people mover, multi-purpose vehicle**.

pep *noun, informal* energy; vitality; go. ▸ *verb* (***pepped, pepping***) (*always* **pep sb** *or* **sth up**) to enliven or invigorate them or it. ▪ **peppy** *adj* (***-ier, -iest***). [20c: a shortening of **pepper**]

peperoni see **pepperoni**

peplum *noun* (***peplums*** *or* ***pepla***) a short skirt-like section attached to the waistline of a dress, blouse or jacket. [17c: from Greek *peplos*]

pepper *noun* **1 a** a climbing shrub, widely cultivated for its small red berries which are dried to form **peppercorns**; **b** a pungent seasoning prepared by grinding the dried berries of this plant. **2 a** a tropical shrub cultivated for its large red, green, yellow or orange edible fruits; **b** the fruit of this plant, eaten raw in salads or cooked as a vegetable. Also called **capsicum, sweet pepper**. ▸ *verb* **1** to bombard something or someone (with missiles). **2** to sprinkle liberally: *The text was peppered with errors.* **3** to season (a dish, etc) with pepper. [Anglo-Saxon *pipor*, from Latin *piper*]

peppercorn *noun* **1** the dried berry of the pepper plant. **2** something nominal or of little value.

peppermill *noun* a device for grinding peppercorns.

peppermint *noun* **1** a species of mint with dark-green leaves and spikes of small purple flowers, widely cultivated for its aromatic oil. **2** a food flavouring prepared from the aromatic oil produced by this plant. **3** a sweet flavoured with peppermint.

pepperoni *or* **peperoni** *noun* a hard, spicy beef and pork sausage. [20c: Italian]

peppery *adj* **1** well seasoned with pepper; tasting of pepper; hot-tasting or pungent. **2** short-tempered; irascible. ▪ **pepperiness** *noun.*

pep pill *noun* a pill containing a stimulant drug. [20c]

pepsin *noun, biochem* in the stomach of vertebrates: a digestive enzyme produced by the gastric glands that catalyses the partial breakdown of dietary protein. [19c: from Greek *pepsis* digestion]

pep talk *noun* a brief talk intended to raise morale for a cause or course of action. [20c]

peptic *adj* **1** referring or relating to digestion. **2** referring or relating to the stomach. **3** referring or relating to pepsin. [17c: from Greek *peptikos* able to digest]

peptide *noun, biochem* a molecule that consists of a relatively short chain of amino acids. [20c: from Greek *pepsis* digestion]

per *prep* **1** out of every: *two per thousand.* **2** for every: *£5 per head.* **3** in every: *60 miles per hour* • *100 accidents per week.* **4** through; by means of: *per post.* [14c: Latin, meaning 'for', 'each', or 'by']

IDIOMS **as per ...** according to ...: *proceed as per instructions.* **as per usual** *informal* as always.

per- *prefix, denoting* **1** *chem* the highest state of oxidation of an element in a compound: *peroxide.* **2** in words derived from Latin: through, beyond, thoroughly or utterly. [Latin, from *per* **per**]

peradventure *adv, archaic* perhaps; by chance. [13c: from French *par aventure* by chance]

perambulate *verb, formal* **1** to walk about (a place). **2** *intr* to stroll around. ▪ **perambulation** *noun.* [16c: from **per** + Latin *ambulare* to walk]

perambulator *noun, formal* a **pram**. [19c]

per annum *adv* (abbrev **p.a.** *or* **per an.**) for each year; yearly; by the year. [17c: Latin]

per capita *adv, adj* for each person: *income per capita.* [Latin, literally 'by heads']

perceive *verb* **1** to observe, notice, or discern. **2** to understand, interpret or view: *how one perceives one's role.* ▪ **perceivable** *adj.* [14c: from French *percever*]

per cent *adv, adj* (symbol **%**) **1** in or for every 100: *Sales are 20 per cent down.* **2** on a scale of 1 to 100: *90 per cent certain.* ▸ *noun* (*usu* **percent**) **1** a percentage or proportion. **2** one part in or on every 100: *half a percent.* [16c: from Latin *per centum* for every hundred]

percentage *noun* **1** an amount, number or rate stated as a proportion of one hundred. **2** a proportion: *a large percentage of students fail.* **3** *informal* commission: *What percentage do you take?* **4** profit; advantage. [18c]

percentile *noun, stats* one of the points or values that divide a collection of statistical data, arranged in order, into 100 equal parts. [19c]

perceptible *adj* able to be perceived; noticeable; detectable. ▪ **perceptibly** *adv.*

perception *noun* **1** *psychol* the process whereby information about one's environment, received by the senses, is organized and interpreted so that it becomes meaningful. **2** one's powers of observation; discernment; insight. **3** one's view or interpretation of something. [17c: from Latin *percipere* to perceive]

perceptive *adj* quick to notice or discern; astute. ▪ **perceptively** *adv.* ▪ **perceptiveness** *noun.*

perch[1] *noun* **1** a branch or other narrow support above ground for a bird to rest or roost on. **2** any place selected, esp temporarily, as a seat. **3** a high position or vantage point. ▸ *verb* **1** *intr* of a bird: to alight and rest on a perch. **2** *intr* to sit, esp insecurely or temporarily. **3** *tr & intr* to sit or place high up. [13c: from French, from Latin *pertica* rod]

perch[2] *noun* a freshwater fish which has a streamlined body and a silvery-white belly. [14c: from Greek *perke*]

perchance *adv, old use* **1** by chance. **2** perhaps. [14c: from French *par chance* by chance]

percipient *adj* perceptive; acutely observant; discerning. ▪ **percipience** *noun.* [17c: from Latin *percipere* to perceive]

percolate *verb* **1** *tr & intr* to undergo or subject (a liquid) to the process of filtering, oozing or trickling. **2** *intr* (*also* **percolate through**) *informal* of news or information: to trickle or spread slowly. **3** *tr & intr* of coffee: to make or be made in a percolator. Sometimes shortened to **perk**. ▪ **percolation** *noun.* [17c: from Latin *percolare* to filter through]

percolator *noun* a pot for making coffee, in which boiling water circulates up through a tube and down through ground coffee beans. [19c]

percussion *noun* **1** the striking of one hard object against another. **2 a** musical instruments played by striking, eg drums, cymbals, xylophone, etc; **b** these instruments collectively as a section of an orchestra.

▪ **percussionist** *noun.* ▪ **percussive** *adj.* [16c: from Latin *percussio* striking]

percussion cap *noun* a metal case containing a material that explodes when struck, formerly used for firing rifles.

per diem /pər ˈdiːɛm/ *adv, adj* for each day; daily; by the day. [16c: Latin]

perdition *noun* everlasting punishment after death; damnation; hell. [14c: from Latin *perditio* ruin]

peregrinate *verb, literary* **1** *intr* to travel, voyage or roam; to wander abroad. **2** to travel through (a place, region, etc). ▪ **peregrination** *noun.* ▪ **peregrinator** *noun.* [16c: from Latin *peregrinari* to roam]

peregrine *noun* a large falcon with greyish-blue plumage on its back and wings and paler underparts. Also called **peregrine falcon**. [14c: from Latin *peregrinus* wandering abroad]

peremptory *adj* **1** of an order: made in expectation of immediate compliance: *a peremptory summons.* **2** of a tone or manner: arrogantly impatient. **3** of a statement, conclusion, etc: allowing no denial or discussion. [16c: from Latin *peremptorius* deadly]

perennial *adj* **1** *botany* referring or relating to a plant that lives for several to many years. See also **annual**, **biennial**. **2** lasting throughout the year. **3** constant; continual. ▸ *noun* a perennial plant. ▪ **perennially** *adv.* [17c: from Latin *perennis*]

perestroika /pɛrəˈstrɔɪkə/ *noun* a restructuring or reorganization, specifically that of the economic and political system of the former USSR instigated by Mikhail Gorbachev in the 1980s. [20c: Russian, meaning 'reconstruction']

perfect *adj* /ˈpɜːfɪkt/ **1** complete in all essential elements. **2** faultless; flawless. **3** excellent; absolutely satisfactory. **4** exact: *a perfect circle.* **5** *informal* absolute; utter: *perfect nonsense.* **6** *grammar* of the tense or aspect of a verb: denoting an action completed at some time in the past or prior to the time spoken of. ▸ *noun* /ˈpɜːfɪkt/ *grammar* **1** the perfect tense, in English formed with the auxiliary verb *have* and the past **participle**, denoting an action completed in the past (**present perfect**, eg *I have written the letter*) or that was or will be completed at the time being spoken of (**past perfect** or **pluperfect**, eg *I had written the letter*; **future perfect**, eg *I will have written the letter*). **2** a verb in a perfect tense. ▸ *verb* /pəˈfɛkt/ **1** to improve something to one's satisfaction: *perfect one's Italian.* **2** to finalize or complete. **3** to develop (a technique, etc) to a reliable standard. ▪ **perfectible** *adj.* [13c: from Latin *perficere* to complete]

perfection *noun* **1** the state of being perfect. **2** the process of making or being made perfect, complete, etc. **3** flawlessness. **4** *informal* an instance of absolute excellence: *The meal was perfection.*
IDIOMS **to perfection** perfectly: *did it to perfection.*

perfectionism *noun* **1** the doctrine that perfection is attainable. **2** an expectation of the very highest standard. ▪ **perfectionist** *adj, noun.*

perfectly *adv* **1** in a perfect way. **2** completely; quite: *a perfectly reasonable reaction.*

perfect number *noun, maths* a number that is equal to the sum of all its factors, eg 6 (because 1 + 2 + 3 = 6).

perfect pitch *noun, music* the ability to recognize a note from its pitch, or spontaneously sing any note with correct pitch. Also called **absolute pitch**.

perfidious *adj* treacherous, double-dealing or disloyal. ▪ **perfidiously** *adv.* ▪ **perfidy** *noun.* [16c: from Latin *perfidus* faithlessness]

perforate *verb* **1** to make a hole or holes in something; to pierce. **2** to make a row of holes in something, for ease of tearing. ▪ **perforation** *noun.* [16c: from Latin *perforare* to pierce]

perforce *adv, chiefly old use* necessarily; inevitably or unavoidably. [14c: from French *par force* by force]

perform *verb* **1** to carry out (a task, job, action, etc); to do or accomplish. **2** to fulfil (a function) or provide (a service, etc). **3** *tr & intr* to act, sing, play, dance, etc (a play, song, piece of music, dance, etc) to entertain an audience. **4** *intr* eg of an engine: to function. **5** *intr* to conduct oneself, esp when presenting oneself for assessment. **6** *intr* of commercial products, shares, etc: to fare in competition. ▪ **performer** *noun.* ▪ **performing** *adj.* [14c: from French *parfournir*]

performance *noun* **1** **a** the performing of a play, part, dance, piece of music, etc before an audience; **b** a dramatic or artistic presentation or entertainment. **2** the act or process of performing a task, etc. **3** a level of achievement, success or, in commerce, profitability. **4** manner or efficiency of functioning. **5** *derog* an instance of outrageous behaviour, esp in public.

performance art *noun* a presentation in which several art forms are combined, such as acting, music, sculpture, photography, etc. ▪ **performance artist** *noun.*

the performing arts *plural noun* the forms of art that require performance to be appreciated, esp music, drama and dance.

perfume *noun* /ˈpɜːfjuːm/ **1** a sweet smell; a scent or fragrance. **2** a fragrant liquid prepared from the extracts of flowers, etc, for applying to the skin or clothes; scent. ▸ *verb* /pəˈfjuːm/ to give a sweet smell to something; to apply perfume to something. ▪ **perfumed** *adj.* ▪ **perfumer** *noun* a maker or seller of perfumes. ▪ **perfumery** *noun* (**-ies**). ▪ **perfumy** *adj.* [16c: from French *parfum*]

perfunctory *adj* done merely as a duty or routine, without genuine care or feeling. ▪ **perfunctorily** *adv.* ▪ **perfunctoriness** *noun.* [16c: from Latin *perfunctorius* slapdash]

perfusion *noun* **1** *biol* the movement of a fluid through a tissue or organ. **2** *med* the deliberate introduction of a fluid into a tissue or organ, usu by injection into a blood vessel. [16c: from Latin *perfusus* poured over]

pergola *noun* an arched framework constructed from slender branches. [17c: Italian]

perhaps *adv* possibly; maybe. [16c: from French *par* by + Norse *happ* fortune or chance]

peri- *prefix, denoting* **1** around: *periscope* • *pericardium.* **2** near: *perinatal* • *perigee.* [From Greek *peri* round or around]

perianth *noun, botany* the outer part of a flower, usu consisting of a circle of petals within a circle of **sepals**. [18c: from Latin *perianthium*]

pericarditis *noun, pathol* inflammation of the pericardium.

pericardium *noun* (***pericardia***) *anatomy* the sac, composed of fibrous tissue, that surrounds the heart. ▪ **pericardiac** *or* **pericardial** *adj.* [16c: Latin]

pericarp *noun, botany* in plants: the wall of a fruit, which develops from the ovary wall after fertilization. [17c: from Latin *pericarpium*]

peridot *noun* a yellowish-green, glassy, silicate mineral, used in jewellery. [14c in the form *peritot*, etc: from French *péridot*]

perigee *noun, astron* the point in the orbit of the Moon or a satellite around the Earth when it is closest to the Earth. Compare **apogee**. [16c: from French *perigée*]

periglacial *adj, geog* of or like a region bordering a glacier.

perihelion *noun* (***perihelia***) *astron* the point in the orbit of a planet round the Sun when it is closest to the Sun. Compare **aphelion**. [17c: from Latin *perihelium*]

peril *noun* **1** grave danger. **2** a hazard. ▪ **perilous** *adj.* ▪ **perilously** *adv.* [13c: from French *péril*]
IDIOMS **at one's peril** at the risk of one's life or safety.

perimeter /pə'rɪmɪtə(r)/ *noun* **1** the boundary of an enclosed area. *as adj*: *a perimeter fence.* **2** *geom* **a** the boundary or circumference of any plane figure; **b** the length of this boundary. ▪ **perimetric** *adj.* [16c: from Greek *perimetros*, from *metros* measure]

perinatal *adj, med* denoting or relating to the period extending from the 28th week of pregnancy to about one month after childbirth. [20c]

perineum /pɛrɪ'nɪəm/ *noun* (***perinea*** /-'nɪə/) *anatomy* the region of the body between the genital organs and the anus. ▪ **perineal** *adj.* [17c: from Latin *perinaeum*]

period *noun* **1** a portion of time. **2** a phase or stage, eg in history, or in a person's life and development, etc. **3** an interval of time at the end of which events recur in the same order. **4** *geol* a unit of geological time that is a subdivision of an **era**. **5** any of the sessions of equal length into which the school day is divided, and to which particular subjects or activities are assigned. **6** *esp N Am* a **full stop**. **7** *informal* added to a statement to emphasize its finality: *You may not go, period.* **8** the periodic discharge of blood during a woman's menstrual cycle. **9** *chem* in the periodic table: any of the seven horizontal rows of chemical elements. **10** *physics* the time interval after which a cyclical phenomenon, eg a wave motion, repeats itself; the reciprocal of the frequency. ▸ *adj* dating from, or designed in the style of, the historical period in question: *period furniture.* [15c: from Greek *periodos* circuit or going round]

periodic *adj* **1** happening at intervals, esp regular intervals. **2** occurring from time to time; occasional. **3** *chem* referring or relating to the periodic table. ▪ **periodicity** *noun.*

periodical *noun* a magazine published weekly, monthly, quarterly, etc. ▸ *adj* **1** referring or relating to such publications. **2** published at more or less regular intervals. **3** periodic. ▪ **periodically** *adv.*

periodic table *noun, chem* a table of all the chemical elements in order of increasing atomic number.

peripatetic /pɛrɪpə'tɛtɪk/ *adj* **1** travelling about from place to place. **2** of a teacher: employed by several schools and so obliged to travel between them. ▸ *noun* a peripatetic teacher. ▪ **peripatetically** *adv.* [16c: from Greek *peripatetikos*]

peripheral /pɛ'rɪfərəl/ *adj* **1** relating or belonging to the outer edge or outer surface: *peripheral nerves.* **2** (**peripheral to sth**) not central to the issue in hand; marginal. **3** *comput* supplementary; auxiliary. **4** relating to the outer edge of the field of vision. ▸ *noun, comput* a device concerned with the input, output or backup storage of data, eg a printer, mouse or disk drive. Also called **peripheral device**.

periphery /pə'rɪfərɪ/ *noun* (***-ies***) **1** the edge or boundary of something. **2** the external surface of something. **3** a surrounding region. [16c: from Greek *periphereia* circumference or surface]

periphrasis /pə'rɪfrəsɪs/ *noun* (***-ses*** /-siːz/) a roundabout way of saying something; circumlocution. ▪ **periphrastic** *adj.* [16c: Latin and Greek]

periscope *noun, optics* a system of prisms or mirrors that enables the user to view objects that are above eye-level or obscured by a closer object, used in submarines, military tanks, etc. [19c: from Greek *periskopeein* to look around]

perish *verb* **1** *intr* to die; to be destroyed or ruined. **2** **a** *intr* of materials: to decay; **b** *tr* to cause (materials) to decay or rot. [13c: from French *perir*]

perishable *adj* of commodities, esp food: liable to rot or go bad quickly.

perished *adj* **1** *informal* feeling the cold severely. **2** of materials such as rubber: weakened and made liable to break or crack by age or exposure.

perishing *adj* **1** *informal* of weather, etc: very cold. **2** *old use, informal* damned, infernal or confounded.

peristalsis /pɛrɪ'stalsɪs/ *noun* (***-ses*** /-siːz/) *physiol* in hollow tubular organs, eg the intestines: the waves of involuntary muscle contractions that force the contents of the tube, eg food, further forward. ▪ **peristaltic** *adj.* [18c: from Greek *peristellein* to contract round]

peritoneum /pɛrɪtə'niːəm/ *noun* (***peritonea*** /-'niːə/ *or* ***peritoneums***) *anatomy* a **serous** membrane that lines the abdominal cavity. ▪ **peritoneal** *adj.* [16c: Latin]

peritonitis /pɛrɪtə'naɪtɪs/ *noun, pathol* inflammation of the peritoneum. [18c]

periwig *noun* a man's wig of the 17c and 18c. [16c: a variant of *peruke*, from French *perruque* head of hair]

periwinkle[1] *noun* a climbing plant with slender trailing stems, oval shiny green leaves, and single bluish-purple flowers. [Anglo-Saxon *perwince*]

periwinkle[2] *noun* a small marine mollusc with a spirally coiled shell, esp the common edible variety, the **winkle**. [16c: prob from Anglo-Saxon *pinewincle*]

perjure *verb* (*now always* **perjure oneself**) to forswear oneself in a court of law, ie lie while under oath; to commit perjury. [15c: from Latin *perjurare*]

perjury /'pɜːdʒərɪ/ *noun* (***-ies***) the crime of lying while under oath in a court of law. ▪ **perjurer** *noun.*

perk[1] *verb, tr & intr* (*always* **perk up**) to become or make (someone) more lively and cheerful. [14c]

perk[2] *noun, informal* a benefit, additional to income, derived from employment, such as the use of a company car, etc. [19c: a shortening of **perquisite**]

perk[3] *verb, tr & intr, informal* to **percolate** (coffee). [20c]

perkin see **parkin**

perky *adj* (*-ier, -iest*) lively and cheerful. ▪ **perkily** *adv.* ▪ **perkiness** *noun.* [19c: from **perk**[1]]

Perl *or* **PERL** *noun, comput* a high-level programming language. [1980s: an acronym of *p*ractical *e*xtraction and *r*eport *l*anguage]

perm[1] *noun* a hair treatment using chemicals that give a long-lasting wave or curl. ▸ *verb* to curl or wave (hair) with a perm. [20c: a shortening of **permanent wave**]

perm[2] *informal, noun* short form of **permutation** (sense 2). ▸ *verb* short form of **permute**. [20c]

permaculture *noun, ecol* an ecologically friendly and self-sustaining system of agriculture. [20c: from *perma*nent + agri*culture*]

permafrost *noun, geol* an area of subsoil or rock that has remained frozen for at least a year, and usu much longer. [20c: from *perma*nent *frost*]

permanent *adj* **1** lasting, or intended to last, indefinitely; not temporary. **2** of a condition, etc: unlikely to alter. ▪ **permanence** *noun.* ▪ **permanently** *adv.* [15c: from Latin *permanere* to remain]

permanent magnet *noun, physics* a magnet that keeps its magnetic properties after the force which magnetized it has been removed.

permanent wave *noun, old use* a **perm**[1]. [20c]

permanent way *noun* a railway track, including the rails, sleepers and stones.

permanganate *noun, chem* any of the salts of **permanganic acid** used as an oxidizing and bleaching agent and disinfectant. [19c]

permeable *adj* of a porous material or membrane: allowing certain liquids or gases to pass through it. ▪ **permeability** *noun.* [15c: from Latin *permeabilis*; see **permeate**]

permeate *verb* (*also* **permeate through sth**) **1** of a liquid or gas: to pass, penetrate or diffuse through (a fine or porous material or a membrane). **2** *tr & intr* of a smell, gas, etc: to spread through a room or other space; to fill or impregnate. ▪ **permeation** *noun.* [17c: from Latin *permeare* to penetrate]

Permian *adj* **1** *geol* relating to the last period of the **Palaeozoic** era, during which reptiles became more abundant. **2** relating to the rocks formed during this period. [19c: named after the Perm region in Russia]

permissible *adj* allowable; permitted.

permission *noun* consent, agreement or authorization. [15c: from Latin *permissio*]

permissive *adj* **1** tolerant; liberal. **2** allowing usu excessive freedom, esp in sexual matters: *the permissive society.* ▪ **permissively** *adv.* ▪ **permissiveness** *noun.*

permit *verb* /pəˈmɪt/ (***permitted, permitting***) **1** to consent to or give permission for something. **2** to give (someone) leave or authorization. **3** to allow someone something: *permitted him access to his children.* **4** (*also* **permit of sth**) *formal* to enable it to happen or take effect; to give scope or opportunity for it: *an outrage that permits of no excuses.* ▸ *noun* /ˈpɜːmɪt/ a document that authorizes something: *a fishing permit*. [15c: from Latin *permittere*]

permutation *noun* **1** *maths* **a** any of several different ways in which a set of objects or numbers can be arranged; **b** any of the resulting combinations. **2** a fixed combination in football pools for selecting the results of matches. Often shortened to **perm**. [14c: from Latin *permutatio*]

permute *or* **permutate** *verb* to rearrange (a set of things) in different orders, esp in every possible order in succession. Also shortened to **perm**. [14c: from Latin *permutare* to change completely]

pernicious *adj* harmful; destructive; deadly. [16c: from Latin *perniciosus* ruinous]

pernicious anaemia *noun, med* a form of anaemia caused by a dietary deficiency of vitamin B_{12}.

pernickety *adj* **1** of a person: overparticular about small details; fussy. **2** of a task: tricky; intricate. [19c: Scots]

peroration *noun* the concluding section of a speech, in which the points made are summed up. [15c: from Latin *peroratio*]

peroxide *noun* **1** *chem* a strong oxidizing agent that releases hydrogen peroxide when treated with acid, used in rocket fuels, antiseptics, disinfectants and bleaches. **2** a solution of hydrogen peroxide used as a bleach for hair and textiles. *as adj*: *a peroxide blonde.* ▸ *verb* to bleach (hair) with hydrogen peroxide. [19c]

perpendicular *adj* **1** vertical; upright; in the direction of gravity. **2** (*also* **perpendicular to sth**) at right angles; forming a right angle with (a particular line or surface). **3** of a cliff, etc: precipitous; steep. **4** (*usu* **Perpendicular**) *archit* referring or relating to the form of English Gothic architecture from late 14c to 16c, characterized by the use of slender vertical lines and vaulting. ▸ *noun* **1** a perpendicular line, position or direction. **2** an instrument for determining the vertical line. ▪ **perpendicularity** *noun.* ▪ **perpendicularly** *adv.* [14c: from Latin *perpendicularis*]

perpetrate *verb* to commit, or be guilty of (a crime, misdeed, error, etc). ▪ **perpetration** *noun.* ▪ **perpetrator** *noun.* [16c: from Latin *perpetrare*]

perpetual *adj* **1** everlasting; eternal; continuous; permanent. **2** continual; continually recurring: *perpetual quarrels.* ▪ **perpetually** *adv.* [14c: from Latin *perpetualis*]

perpetual motion *noun, physics* the motion of a hypothetical machine that continues to operate indefinitely without any external source of energy.

perpetuate *verb* **1** to make something last or continue: *perpetuate a species.* **2** to preserve the memory of (a name, etc). **3** to repeat and pass on (an error, etc). ▪ **perpetuation** *noun.* [16c: from Latin *perpetuare* to make perpetual]

perpetuity *noun* (*-ies*) **1** the state of being perpetual. **2** eternity. **3** duration for an indefinite period. **4** something perpetual, eg an allowance to be paid indefinitely. [15c: from Latin *perpetuitas*]

IDIOMS **in perpetuity** for ever.

perplex *verb* **1** to puzzle, confuse or baffle someone with intricacies or difficulties. **2** to complicate. ▪ **perplexed** *adj.* ▪ **perplexing** *adj.* ▪ **perplexity** *noun* (*-ies*). [16c: from Latin *per-* thoroughly + *plexus* entangled]

per pro see under **pp**

perquisite *noun* **1** a **perk**[2]. **2** a customary tip expected on some occasions. [18c: from Latin *perquisitum* something acquired]

perry *noun* (*-ies*) an alcoholic drink made from fermented pear juice. [14c: from French *peré*]

per se /pɜː seɪ/ *adv* in itself; intrinsically: *not valuable per se.* [16c: Latin, meaning 'through itself']

persecute *verb* **1** to ill-treat, oppress, torment or put to death (a person or people), esp for their religious or political beliefs. **2** to harass, pester or bother someone continually. ▪ **persecution** *noun*. ▪ **persecutor** *noun*. [15c: from Latin *persequi* to pursue or ill-treat]

perseverance *noun* the act or state of persevering; continued effort to achieve something one has begun, despite setbacks.

persevere *verb, intr* (*also* **persevere in** *or* **with sth**) to keep on striving for it; to persist steadily with (an endeavour). [14c: from French *perseverer*]

Persian *adj* relating to ancient Persia or modern Iran, or to their people or language. ▸ *noun* **1** a citizen or inhabitant of, or person born in, ancient Persia or modern Iran. **2** the language of Persia or Iran. See also **Farsi**. **3** a Persian cat. [14c]

Persian cat *noun* a domestic cat with a long silky coat and a bushy tail.

persiflage /ˈpɜːsɪflɑːʒ/ *noun* banter; teasing; flippancy or frivolous talk. [18c: French, from *persifler* to banter]

persimmon *noun* **1** a tall tree, widely cultivated for its hard wood and edible fruits. **2** the plum-like fruit of this tree. [17c: from Algonquian (a family of Native American languages)]

persist *verb, intr* **1** (*also* **persist in** *or* **with sth**) to continue with it in spite of resistance, difficulty, discouragement, etc. **2** of rain, etc: to continue steadily. **3** eg of a mistaken idea: to remain current. **4** to continue to exist. ▪ **persistence** *noun*. [16c: from Latin *persistere* to stand firm]

persistent *adj* **1** continuing with determination in spite of discouragement; dogged; tenacious. **2** constant; unrelenting: *persistent questions*. **3** *zool, botany* of parts of animals and plants, such as horns, hair, leaves, etc: remaining after the time they usu fall off, wither or disappear. ▪ **persistently** *adv*.

person *noun* (***persons*** or in sense 1 also ***people***) **1** an individual human being. **2** the body, often including clothes: *A knife was found hidden on his person*. **3** *grammar* each of the three classes into which pronouns and verb forms fall, **first person** denoting the speaker (or the speaker and others, eg *I* and *we*), **second person** the person addressed (with or without others, eg *you*) and **third person** the person(s) or thing(s) spoken of (eg *she, he, it* or *they*). [13c: from French *persone*]

IDIOMS **in person 1** actually present oneself. **2** doing something oneself.

persona /pəˈsoʊnə/ *noun* (***personae*** /-niː/ *or* ***personas***) **1** a character in fiction, esp in a play or novel. **2** in Jungian psychology: one's character as one presents it to the world, masking one's inner thoughts, feelings, etc. [20c: Latin, meaning 'an actor's mask']

personable *adj* good-looking or likeable.

personage *noun* a well-known, important or distinguished person. [15c: from Latin *personagium*]

persona grata / ˈgrɑːtə/ *noun* (***personae gratae*** /-tiː/) a person who is acceptable, liked or favoured. Compare **persona non grata**. [19c: Latin, meaning 'a welcome person']

personal *adj* **1** of a comment, opinion, etc: coming from someone as an individual, not from a group or organization: *my personal opinion*. **2** done, attended to, etc by the individual person in question, not by a substitute: *give it my personal attention*. **3** relating to oneself in particular: *a personal triumph*. **4** relating to one's private concerns: *details of her personal life*. **5** of remarks: referring, often disparagingly, to an individual's physical or other characteristics. **6** relating to the body: *personal hygiene*. **7** *grammar* indicating **person** (sense 3): *personal pronoun*. [14c: from Latin *personalis*]

personal assistant *noun* (abbrev **PA**) a secretary or administrator, esp one who helps a senior executive.

personal column *noun* a newspaper column or section in which members of the public may place advertisements, enquiries, etc.

personal computer *noun* (abbrev **PC** *or* **pc**) a microcomputer designed for use by one person.

personal digital assistant *noun* (abbrev **PDA**) a hand-held computer with functions to help organize one's diary, finances, etc.

personal identification number see **PIN**

personality *noun* (***-ies***) **1** a person's nature or disposition; the qualities that give one's character individuality. **2** strength or distinctiveness of character: *lots of personality*. **3** a well-known person; a celebrity. [14c: from Latin *personalitas*]

personality cult *noun* excessive adulation of an individual, esp someone in public life.

personalize *or* **-ise** *verb* **1** to mark something distinctively, eg with name, initials, etc, as the property of a particular person. **2** to focus (a discussion, etc) on personalities instead of the matter in hand. **3** to personify. ▪ **personalization** *noun*. [18c]

personally *adv* **1** as far as one is concerned: *Personally, I disapprove*. **2** in person. **3** as a person. **4** as directed against one: *take a remark personally*.

personal organizer *noun* **a** a small loose-leaf folder with sections in which personal notes and information may be kept; **b** an electronic device performing a similar function. Sometimes shortened to **organizer**. Compare **Filofax**.

personal pronoun *noun, grammar* any of the pronouns that represent a person or thing, eg *I, you, she, her, he, it, they, us*.

personal stereo *noun* a small cassette or CD player with earphones, that can be worn attached to a belt or carried in a pocket.

persona non grata /nɒn ˈgrɑːtə/ *noun* (***personae non gratae*** /-tiː/) someone who is not wanted or welcome within a particular group. [20c: Latin, meaning 'unwelcome person']

personate *verb* **1** to play the part of (a character in a play, etc). **2** to impersonate someone, esp with criminal intent. ▪ **personator** *noun*. [16c]

personify *verb* (***-ies, -ied***) **1** in literature, etc: to represent (an abstract quality, etc) as a human being or as having human qualities. **2** of a figure in art, etc: to represent or symbolize (a quality, etc). **3** to embody something in human form; to be the perfect example of it: *She's patience personified*. ▪ **personification** *noun*. [18c: prob from French *personnifier*]

personnel *plural noun* the people employed in a business company, an armed service or other organization. ▸ *singular noun* a department within such an organization that deals with matters concerning employees. *as adj*: *a personnel officer* • *the personnel department*. See also **human resources**. [19c: French, meaning 'personal']

perspective *noun* **1** the observer's view of objects in relation to one another, esp with regard to the way they seem smaller the more distant they are. **2** the representation of this phenomenon in drawing and painting. **3** the balanced or objective view of a situation, in which all its elements assume their due importance. **4** an individual way of regarding a situation, eg one influenced by personal experience or considerations. [14c: from Latin *ars perspectiva* optical science]

Perspex *noun, trademark* polymethylmethacrylate, a tough transparent plastic used to make windshields, visors, etc. *US equivalent* **Plexiglas**.

perspicacious /pɜːspɪ'keɪʃəs/ *adj* shrewd; astute; perceptive or discerning. ▪ **perspicacity** /-'kasɪtɪ/ *noun*. [17c: from Latin *perspicax*]

perspicuous /pə'spɪkjʊəs/ *adj* of speech or writing: clearly expressed and easily understood. ▪ **perspicuity** /pɜːspɪ'kjuːətɪ/ *noun*. [15c: from Latin *perspicuus* transparent or manifest]

perspiration *noun* **1** the secretion of fluid by the sweat glands of the skin, usu in response to heat or physical exertion. **2** the fluid secreted in this way.

perspire *verb, intr* to secrete fluid from the sweat glands of the skin; to sweat. [18c: from Latin *perspirare* to breathe through or sweat]

persuade *verb* **1** (*also* **persuade sb to do sth**) to urge successfully; to prevail on or induce someone. **2** (*often* **persuade sb of sth**) to convince them that it is true, valid, advisable, etc. ▪ **persuadable** *adj*. [16c: from Latin *persuadere*]

persuasion *noun* **1** the act of urging, coaxing or persuading. **2** a creed, conviction, or set of beliefs, esp that of a political group or religious sect.

persuasive *adj* having the power to persuade; convincing or plausible. ▪ **persuasiveness** *noun*.

pert *adj* **1** impudent; cheeky. **2** of clothing or style: jaunty; saucy. ▪ **pertly** *adv*. ▪ **pertness** *noun*. [14c: from French *apert* open]

pertain *verb, intr* (*often* **pertain to sb** *or* **sth**) **1** to concern or relate to them or it; to have to do with them or it. **2** to belong to them or it: *skills pertaining to the job*. **3** to be appropriate; to apply. [14c: from Latin *pertinere*]

pertinacious /pɜːtɪ'neɪʃəs/ *adj* determined in one's purpose; dogged; tenacious. ▪ **pertinacity** /-'nasɪtɪ/ *noun*. [17c: from Latin *pertinax* holding fast]

pertinent *adj* (*also* **pertinent to sb** *or* **sth**) relating to or concerned with them or it; relevant. ▪ **pertinence** *noun*. [14c: from Latin *pertinens* pertaining]

perturb *verb* to make someone anxious, agitated, worried, etc. ▪ **perturbation** *noun*. ▪ **perturbed** *adj*. [14c: from Latin *perturbare* to throw into confusion]

peruse *verb* **1** to read through (a book, magazine, etc) carefully. **2** to browse through something casually. **3** to examine or study (eg someone's face) attentively. ▪ **perusal** *noun*. ▪ **peruser** *noun*. [16c]

Peruvian *adj* belonging or relating to Peru, a republic on the W coast of S America, or its inhabitants. ▸ *noun* a citizen or inhabitant of, or person born in, Peru. [18c]

pervade *verb* to spread or extend throughout something; to affect throughout something; to permeate. ▪ **pervasion** *noun*. ▪ **pervasive** *adj*. [17c: from Latin *pervadere*]

perverse *adj* **1** deliberately departing from what is normal and reasonable. **2** unreasonable; awkward; stubborn or wilful. ▪ **perversely** *adv*. ▪ **perversity** *noun* (**-ies**). [14c: from Latin *perversus*]

perversion *noun* **1** the process of perverting or condition of being perverted. **2** a distortion. **3** a departure from what is normal and reasonable. [14c: from Latin *pervertere*]

pervert *verb* /pə'vɜːt/ **1** to divert something or someone illicitly from what is normal or right: *pervert the course of justice*. **2** to lead someone into evil or unnatural behaviour; to corrupt them. **3** to distort or misinterpret (words, etc). ▸ *noun* /'pɜːvɜːt/ someone who is morally or sexually perverted. [14c: from Latin *pervertere*]

Pesach *or* **Pesah** /'peɪsax/ *noun* **Passover**.

peseta /pə'seɪtə/ *noun* (***peseta*** *or* ***pesetas***) the former standard unit of currency of Spain, replaced in 2002 by the euro. [19c: Spanish, diminutive of *pesa* weight]

pesky *adj* (**-ier, -iest**) *N Am informal* troublesome or infuriating. ▪ **peskily** *adv*. [18c: prob from **pest**]

peso /'peɪsoʊ/ *noun* the standard unit of currency of many Central and S American countries and the Philippines. [16c: Spanish, literally 'weight']

pessary *noun* (**-ies**) a vaginal **suppository**. [14c: from Latin *pessarium*]

pessimism *noun* **1** the tendency to emphasize the gloomiest aspects of anything, and to expect the worst to happen. **2** the belief that this is the worst of all possible worlds, and that evil is triumphing over good. Compare **optimism**. ▪ **pessimist** *noun*. ▪ **pessimistic** *adj*. [18c: from Latin *pessimus* worst + **-ism**]

pest *noun* **1** a living organism, such as an insect, fungus or weed, that has a damaging effect on animal livestock, crop plants or stored produce. **2** *informal* a person or thing that is a constant nuisance. [16c: from Latin *pestis* plague]

pester *verb* **1** to annoy constantly. **2** to harass or hound someone with requests. ▪ **pestering** *adj*. [16c: from French *empestrer* to entangle]

pesticide *noun* any of various chemical compounds, including insecticides, herbicides and fungicides, that are used to kill pests. [20c]

pestilence *noun* **1** a virulent epidemic or contagious disease, such as bubonic plague. **2** anything that is harmful to the morals. [14c: from Latin *pestilentia*]

pestilent *adj* **1** deadly, harmful or destructive. **2** *informal, often facetious* infuriating; troublesome. [15c: from Latin *pestilens*]

pestilential *adj* infuriating; troublesome.

pestle *noun* a club-shaped utensil for pounding, crushing and mixing substances in a **mortar**. [14c: from French *pestel*]

pesto *noun* an Italian sauce made with basil leaves, pine kernels, olive oil, garlic and Parmesan cheese. [1930s: Italian, from *pestato* crushed]

pet[1] *noun* **1** a tame animal or bird kept as a companion. **2** someone's favourite: *the teacher's pet*. **3** a darling or love. **4** a term of endearment. ▸ *adj* **1** kept as a pet: *a pet lamb*. **2** relating to pets or for pets: *pet food*. **3** favourite; own special: *her pet subject*. ▸ *verb* (***petted, petting***) **1** to pat or stroke (an animal, etc). **2** to treat someone indulgently; to make a fuss of them. **3** *intr* of two people: to fondle and caress each other for erotic pleasure. ▪ **petting** *noun.* [16c]

pet[2] *noun* a fit of bad temper or sulks. See also **pettish**. [16c]

petal *noun* **1** *botany* in a flower: one of the modified leaves, often scented and brightly coloured, which in insect-pollinated plants attract passing insects. **2** a term of endearment. [18c: ultimately from Greek *petalon* leaf]

petard *noun, hist* a small bomb for blasting a hole in a wall, door, etc. [16c: from French *pétard* a banger or firecracker]

IDIOMS **hoist with one's own petard** blown up by one's own bomb, ie the victim of one's own trick or cunning; caught in one's own trap.

peter *verb, intr* (*always* **peter out**) to dwindle away to nothing. [19c: orig US mining slang]

Peter Pan *noun* a youthful, boyish or immature man. [20c: the eponymous hero of J M Barrie's play]

pet hate *noun* something that one especially dislikes.

pethidine /'pɛθɪdiːn/ *noun* a mildly sedative pain-relieving drug, widely used in childbirth. [20c]

petiole *noun* **1** *botany* the stalk that attaches a leaf to the stem of a plant. **2** *zool* a stalk-like structure, esp that of the abdomen in wasps, etc. [18c: from Latin *petiolus* little foot]

petit bourgeois /'pɛtɪ bʊə'ʒwɑː, bɔː'ʒwɑː/ *noun* (***petits bourgeois*** /'pɛtɪ/) a member of the lower middle class. Also written **petty bourgeois**. [19c: French, literally 'little citizen']

petite /pə'tiːt/ *adj* of a woman or girl: small and dainty. [18c: French, feminine of *petit* small]

petite bourgeoisie /pə'tiːt bɔːʒwɑː'ziː/ *noun* (***petites bourgeoisies*** /pə'tiːt/) the lower middle class. [Early 20c: French]

petit four /'pɛtɪ fʊə(r), fɔː(r), 'pətɪ/ *noun* (***petits fours*** /fʊəz, fɔːz/) a small sweet biscuit, usu decorated with icing. [19c: French, literally 'little oven']

petition *noun* **1** a formal written request to an authority to take some action, signed by a large number of people. **2** any appeal to a higher authority. **3** *law* an application to a court for some procedure to be set in motion. ▸ *verb, tr & intr* (*also* **petition sb for** *or* **against sth**) to address a petition to them for or against some cause; to make an appeal or request. ▪ **petitionary** *adj.* ▪ **petitioner** *noun.* [15c: French]

petit mal /'peti mal/ *noun, med* a mild form of **epilepsy**, without convulsions. Compare **grand mal**. [19c: French, literally 'little illness']

petits pois /'pɛtɪ pwɑː/ *plural noun* small young green peas. [19c: French, meaning 'little peas']

pet name *noun* a special name used as an endearment.

Petrarchan sonnet *noun* a sonnet with the rhyme scheme *abbaabba cdcdcd.* [Named after Italian poet Francesco Petrarch]

petrel *noun* a small seabird with a hooked bill and external tube-shaped nostrils, esp the storm petrel. [17c]

Petri dish /'piːtrɪ, 'pɛtrɪ / *noun, biol* a shallow circular plate with a flat base and a loosely fitting lid, used for culturing bacteria, etc. [19c: named after Julius R Petri, German bacteriologist]

petrifaction *or* **petrification** *noun, geol* **1** a type of fossilization whereby organic remains are turned into stone as the original tissue is gradually replaced by minerals. **2** the state of being petrified.

petrify *verb* (***-ies, -ied***) **1** to terrify; to paralyse someone with fright. **2** *tr & intr* of organic remains: to turn into stone by the process of petrifaction. **3** *tr & intr* to fix or become fixed in an inflexible mould. [16c: from French *pétrifier*, from Greek *petra* stone]

petrochemical *noun* any organic chemical derived from petroleum or natural gas. ▸ *adj* **1** referring or relating to such chemicals. **2** referring or relating to the petrochemical industry. [20c]

petrodollar *noun* the US dollar as representative of the foreign currency earned by oil-exporting countries. [20c]

petrol *noun* a volatile flammable liquid mixture of hydrocarbons, used as a fuel in most internal combustion engines. Also called (*N Am*) **gasoline**. [19c: from French *petrole*]

petrolatum /pɛtrə'leɪtəm/ *noun* a **paraffin**-base **petroleum** used as a lubricant or medicinally as an ointment. Also called **petroleum jelly**. [19c: Latin, from **petrol**]

petroleum *noun* a naturally occurring oil consisting of a thick dark liquid mixture of hydrocarbons, distillation of which yields a wide range of petrochemicals, eg liquid and gas fuels, asphalt, and raw materials for the manufacture of plastics, solvents, drugs, etc. Compare **petrol**. [16c: Latin, from *petra* rock + *oleum* oil]

petrology *noun, geol* the scientific study of the structure, origin, distribution and history of rocks. ▪ **petrological** *adj.* ▪ **petrologist** *noun.* [19c]

petrol station *noun* a **filling station**.

petticoat *noun* a woman's underskirt. [15c: from **petty** (*adj* sense 1) + **coat**]

pettifogger *noun* **1** a lawyer who deals with unimportant cases, esp somewhat deceitfully or quibblingly. **2** *derog* someone who argues over trivial details; a quibbler. ▪ **pettifog** *verb* (***pettifogged, pettifogging***) *intr* to act as a pettifogger. ▪ **pettifogging** *noun, adj.* [16c: from **petty** + German dialect *voger* arranger]

pettish *adj* peevish; sulky. [16c]

petty *adj* (***-ier, -iest***) **1** being of minor importance; trivial. **2** small-minded or childishly spiteful. **3** referring to a low or subordinate rank. ▪ **pettily** *adv.* ▪ **pettiness** *noun.* [14c: from French *petit* small]

petty cash *noun* money kept for small everyday expenses in an office, etc.

petty officer *noun* a non-commissioned officer in the navy.

petulant *adj* ill-tempered; peevish. ▪ **petulance** *noun.* ▪ **petulantly** *adv.* [16c: French]

petunia *noun* a plant with large funnel-shaped, often striped, flowers in a range of bright colours. [19c: from French *petun* tobacco plant]

pew *noun* **1** one of the long benches with backs used as seating in a church. **2** *informal* a seat: *take a pew.* [15c: from French *puie*]

pewit see **peewit**

pewter *noun* **1** a silvery alloy with a bluish tinge, composed of tin and lead, used to make tableware (eg tankards), jewellery and other decorative objects. **2** articles made of pewter. ▸ *adj* made of pewter: *pewter goblets.* ▪ **pewterer** *noun.* [14c: from French *peutre*]

peyote /peɪ'oʊtɪ, peɪ'oʊteɪ/ *noun* (***peyotes***) **1** the **mescal** cactus, native to N Mexico and the southwest USA. **2** a hallucinogenic substance obtained from the button-like tops of this plant. [19c: from Nahuatl (S American Native language) *peyotl*]

PG *abbrev* as a film classification: parental guidance, ie containing scenes possibly unsuitable for children.

pg. *abbrev* page. See also **p**, **pp**.

pH *or* **pH value** *noun, chem* a measure of the relative acidity or alkalinity of a solution expressed as the logarithm of the reciprocal of the hydrogen-ion concentration of the solution. [20c: a shortening of German *Potenz* power or exponent + *H*, the symbol for hydrogen]

phaeton /'feɪtən/ *noun* an open four-wheeled carriage for one or two horses. [16c: named after Phaeton, who, in Greek mythology, was son of the god Helios and who drove his father's chariot so close to the Earth that he was destroyed by Zeus]

phage *noun, biol* short for **bacteriophage**.

phagocyte /'fagoʊsaɪt/ *noun, biol* a cell, esp a white blood cell, that engulfs and destroys microorganisms and other foreign particles. ▪ **phagocytic** *adj*. [19c]

phalanger *noun* a nocturnal tree-dwelling marsupial, with thick fur, small fox-like ears and large forward-facing eyes. Also called **possum**. [18c: from Greek *phalangion* spider's web, because of its webbed toes]

phalanx /'falaŋks, 'feɪlaŋks/ *noun* (***phalanxes*** *or* ***phalanges*** /-dʒiːz/) **1** *hist* in ancient Greece: a body of infantry in close-packed formation. **2** a solid body of people, esp one representing united support or opposition. [16c: Greek, 'a line of soldiers drawn up for battle']

phallic *adj* relating to or resembling a phallus.

phallus *noun* (***phalluses*** *or* ***phalli***) a penis. [17c: Latin, from Greek *phallos*]

Phanerozoic /fanərə'zoʊɪk/ *adj, geol* relating to the eon consisting of the Palaeozoic, Mesozoic and Cenozoic eras, extending from about 570 million years ago until the present time. [19c: from Greek *phaneros* visible + *zoion* animal]

phantasm *noun* **1** an illusion or fantasy. **2** a ghost or phantom. Also called **phantasma** (***phantasmata***). ▪ **phantasmal** *adj*. [13c: from Greek *phantasma* apparition]

phantasmagoria *noun* a fantastic succession of real or illusory images seen as if in a dream. ▪ **phantasmagoric** *or* **phantasmagorical** *adj*. [19c: perhaps from Greek *phantasma* apparition + *agora* assembly]

phantom *noun* **1** a ghost or spectre. **2** an illusory image or vision. ▸ *adj* **1** referring to the nature of a phantom; spectral. **2** imaginary; fancied; not real: *a phantom pregnancy*. [14c: from French *fantosme*]

Pharaoh /'fɛəroʊ/ *noun* the title of the kings of ancient Eygpt, specifically the god-kings from the time of the New Kingdom (c.1500 BC) onwards. ▪ **Pharaonic** /fɛəreɪ'ɒnɪk/ *adj*. [Anglo-Saxon: from Greek *pharao*]

Pharaoh

This word is often misspelt. It might help you to remember the following sentence:

Pyramids house ancient relics and other historical items.

Pharisee *noun* **1** a member of an ancient Jewish sect whose strict interpretation of the Mosaic law led to an obsessive concern with the rules covering the details of everyday life. **2** *derog* anyone more careful of the outward forms than of the spirit of religion. **3** *derog* a self-righteous or hypocritical person. ▪ **Pharisaic** /farɪ'seɪɪk/ *adj*. [Anglo-Saxon: from Greek *pharisaios*]

pharmaceutical *or* **pharmaceutic** *adj* referring or relating to the preparation of drugs and medicines. [17c: from Latin *pharmaceutics*]

pharmaceutics *singular noun* the preparation and dispensing of drugs and medicine.

pharmacist *noun* someone who is trained and licensed to prepare and dispense drugs and medicines. [19c]

pharmacology *noun* the scientific study of medicines and drugs and their effects and uses. ▪ **pharmacological** *adj*. ▪ **pharmacologist** *noun*. [18c: from Greek *pharmakon* drug + *logos* word or reason]

pharmacopoeia /fɑːməkə'piːə/ *noun, med* an authoritative book that contains a list of drugs, together with details of their properties, uses, side-effects, methods of preparation and recommended dosages. [17c: Latin, from Greek *pharmakopoiia* preparation of drugs]

pharmacy *noun* (***-ies***) **1** the mixing and dispensing of drugs and medicines. **2** a dispensary in a hospital, etc. **3** a pharmacist's or chemist's shop. [14c: from French *farmacie*]

pharyngitis /farɪn'dʒaɪtɪs/ *noun, med* inflammation of the mucous membrane of the pharynx. [19c]

pharynx /'farɪŋks/ *noun* (***pharynxes*** *or* ***pharynges*** /ɪndʒiːz/) **1** *anatomy* in mammals: the part of the alimentary canal that links the mouth and nasal passages with the oesophagus and trachea. **2** the throat. ▪ **pharyngeal** *adj*. [17c: Greek, meaning 'throat']

phase *noun* **1** a stage or period in growth or development. **2** the appearance or aspect of anything at any stage. **3** *astron* any of the different shapes assumed by the illuminated surface of a celestial body, eg the Moon. **4** *physics* the stage that a periodically varying wave has reached at a specific moment, usu in relation to another wave of the same frequency. ▸ *verb* to organize or carry out (changes, etc) in stages. [19c: from Greek *phasis* appearance]

PHRASAL VERBS **phase sth in** *or* **out** to introduce it, or get rid of it, gradually and in stages.

phatic /'fatɪk/ *adj* of spoken language: used for social reasons and to build relationships with other people rather than communicate ideas or facts. [1920: from Greek *phatos* spoken]

PhD *abbrev*: *philosophiae doctor* (Latin), Doctor of Philosophy. See also **DPh**.

pheasant *noun* (***pheasant*** *or* ***pheasants***) a ground-dwelling bird, the male of which is usu brightly coloured and has a long pointed tail. [13c: from French *fesan*]

phenobarbitone *or* (*chiefly N Am*) **phenobarbital** *noun* a hypnotic and sedative drug used to treat insomnia, anxiety and epilepsy. [20c]

phenol *noun, chem* **1** a colourless crystalline toxic solid used in the manufacture of resins, nylon, solvents, explosives, drugs, dyes and perfumes. Also called **carbolic acid**. **2** any member of a group of weakly acidic organic chemical compounds, many of which are used as antiseptics, eg trichlorophenol (TCP). [19c: from *phene*, an old name for benzene]

phenolphthalein *noun, chem* a dye which is colourless in acidic solutions and turns red in alkaline solutions, used as a pH indicator. [19c]

phenomenal *adj* **1** remarkable; extraordinary; abnormal. **2** referring to the nature of a phenomenon. **3** relating to phenomena. ▪ **phenomenally** *adv.* [19c]

phenomenology *noun* **1** the science of observing, or of describing, phenomena. **2** philosophy concerned with the subjective experiences of the self, as opposed to **ontology**. ▪ **phenomenological** *adj.* ▪ **phenomenologist** *noun.* [18c: from **phenomenon** + **-logy**]

phenomenon *noun* (***phenomena***) **1** a happening perceived through the senses, esp something unusual. **2** an extraordinary or abnormal person or thing; a prodigy. **3** a feature of life, social existence, etc: *stress as a work-related phenomenon.* [17c: from Greek *phainomenon* appearing]

---

phenomenon, phenomena

The word **phenomena** is plural. 'A phenomena' is often used, but is not correct:

✗ *A hurricane is a relatively common phenomena.*

✓ *A hurricane is a relatively common phenomenon.*

---

phenotype *noun, genetics* the observable characteristics of an organism, determined by the interaction between its **genotype** and environmental factors. [20c: from German *Phaenotype*]

phenyl /ˈfiːnɪl/ *noun, chem* an organic **radical** (*noun* sense 3) found in benzene, phenol, etc. [19c: from *phene*, an old name for benzene]

pheromone *noun, zool* any chemical substance secreted by an animal which has a specific effect on the behaviour of other members of the same species. [20c: from Greek *pherein* to bear + **hormone**]

phew *exclam* used to express relief, astonishment or exhaustion. [17c: imitating the sound of a whistle]

phi /faɪ/ *noun* the twenty-first letter of the Greek alphabet.

phial *noun* a little medicine bottle. [14c: from Latin *phiala*]

philander *verb, intr* of men: to flirt or have casual love affairs with women; to womanize. ▪ **philanderer** *noun.* [16c: from Greek *philandros*, literally 'fond of men' but misapplied as 'a loving man']

philanthropy /fɪˈlanθrəpɪ/ *noun* a charitable regard for one's fellow human beings, esp in the form of benevolence to those in need. ▪ **philanthropic** /-lən ˈθrɒpɪk/ *adj* benevolent. ▪ **philanthropist** *noun.* [17c: from Greek *philanthropia*, from *phil-* loving + *anthropos* man]

philately /fɪˈlatəlɪ/ *noun* the study and collecting of postage stamps. ▪ **philatelic** /fɪləˈtɛlɪk/ *adj.* ▪ **philatelist** *noun.* [19c: from French *philatélie*]

-phile *or* **-phil** *combining form, forming nouns, denoting* fondness, attraction or loving of the specified thing: *bibliophile.* [From Greek *philos* loving]

philharmonic *adj* used as part of the name of choirs and orchestras: dedicated to music. [19c: from French *philharmonique*]

-philia *combining form, forming nouns, denoting* **1** a tendency towards an abnormal functioning of the specified thing: *haemophilia*. **2** an abnormal liking or love of the specified thing: *paedophilia*.

philippic *noun* a speech making a bitter attack. [16c: from the orations of the Athenian Demosthenes against Philip of Macedon]

philistine *adj* having no interest in or appreciation of art, literature, music, etc, and tending rather towards materialism. ► *noun* **1** a philistine person. **2** in ancient times, one of the inhabitants of south-west Palestine, enemies of the Israelites. ▪ **philistinism** *noun.* [19c]

philology *noun* **1** the study of language, its history and development; the comparative study of related languages; linguistics. **2** the study of literary and non-literary texts, esp older ones. ▪ **philological** *adj.* ▪ **philologist** *noun.* [17c: from Greek *philologia* love of argument, literature or learning]

philosopher *noun* someone who studies philosophy, esp one who develops a particular set of doctrines or theories.

philosopher's stone *noun, hist* a hypothetical substance able to turn any metal into gold, long sought by alchemists. [14c]

philosophical *or* **philosophic** *adj* **1** referring or relating to philosophy or philosophers. **2** calm and dispassionate in the face of adversity; resigned, stoical or patient. ▪ **philosophically** *adv.*

philosophize *or* **-ise** *verb, intr* **1** to form philosophical theories. **2** to reason or speculate in the manner of a philosopher. ▪ **philosophizer** *noun.* [16c]

philosophy *noun* (***-ies***) **1** the search for truth and knowledge concerning the universe, human existence, perception and behaviour, pursued by means of reflection, reasoning and argument. **2** any particular system or set of beliefs established as a result of this. **3** a set of principles that serves as a basis for making judgements and decisions: *one's philosophy of life.* [14c: from Greek *philosophia* love of wisdom]

phlebitis /flɪˈbaɪtɪs/ *noun, pathol* inflammation of the wall of a vein, often resulting in the formation of a blood clot at the affected site. [19c: Latin]

phlegm /flɛm/ *noun* **1** a thick yellowish substance produced by the mucous membrane that lines the air passages, brought up by coughing. **2** calmness or impassiveness; stolidity or sluggishness of temperament. [14c: French, from Greek *phlegma*]

phlegmatic /flɛgˈmatɪk/ *or* **phlegmatical** *adj* **1** of a person: calm; not easily excited. **2** producing or having phlegm. ▪ **phlegmatically** *adv.*

phloem /ˈfloʊəm/ *noun, botany* the plant tissue that is responsible for the transport of sugars and other nutrients from the leaves to all other parts of the plant. See also **xylem**. [19c: German, from Greek *phloios* bark]

phobia *noun* an obsessive and persistent fear of a specific object or situation, eg spiders, open spaces, etc, representing a form of neurosis. ▪ **phobic** *adj.* [18c]

Phoenician *adj* belonging or relating to ancient Phoenicia, a narrow strip of land in the Eastern Mediterranean between the mountains of Lebanon and the sea, or to its people or culture. ► *noun* **1** a member of the Phoenician people. **2** their Semitic language. [14c]

phoenix /ˈfiːnɪks/ *noun* **1** in Arabian legend: a bird which every 500 years sets itself on fire and is reborn from its ashes to live a further 500 years. **2** someone or something of unique excellence or unsurpassable beauty. [Anglo-Saxon *fenix*: from Greek *phoinix*]

phone *or* **'phone** *noun* a telephone. *as adj*: *phone call* • *phone box*. ▸ *verb* (*also* **phone sb up**) *tr & intr* to telephone someone. [19c]

phone book see **telephone directory**

phonecard *noun* a card that can be used to pay for phone calls from public telephones. [20c]

phone-in *noun* a radio or TV programme in which telephoned contributions from listeners or viewers are invited and discussed live by an expert or panel in the studio. [20c]

phoneme *noun, linguistics* the smallest unit of sound in a language that has significance in distinguishing one word from another. ▪ **phonemic** *adj*. [Late 19c: French]

phonemics *singular noun* **1** the study and analysis of phonemes. **2** the system or pattern of phonemes in a language.

phonetic *adj* **1** referring or relating to the sounds of a spoken language. **2** eg of a spelling: intended to represent the pronunciation. **3** denoting a pronunciation scheme using symbols each of which represents one sound only. ▪ **phonetically** *adv*. [19c: from Greek *phonetikos*]

phonetics *singular noun* the branch of linguistics that deals with speech sounds, esp how they are produced and perceived. ▪ **phonetician** /foʊnɪ'tɪʃən/ *noun*. [19c]

phoney *or* (*US*) **phony** *adj* (***-ier, -iest***) not genuine; fake, sham, bogus or insincere. ▸ *noun* (***phoneys*** *or* ***phonies***) someone or something bogus; a fake or humbug. [20c]

phonograph *noun, N Am, old use* a record player. [19c]

phonology *noun* (***-ies***) **1** the study of speech sounds in general, or of those in any particular language. **2** any particular system of speech sounds. ▪ **phonological** *adj*. ▪ **phonologist** *noun*. [18c, orig meaning **phonetics**]

phooey *exclam, informal* an exclamation of scorn, contempt, disbelief, etc. [20c: prob a variant of **phew**]

phosgene /'fɒsdʒiːn/ *noun, chem* a poisonous gas, carbonyl chloride, used in the manufacture of pesticides and dyes. [19c: from Greek *phos* light + *-genes* born, because it was orig produced by exposing carbon monoxide and chlorine to sunlight]

phosphate *noun, chem* any salt or ester of phosphoric acid, found in living organisms and in many minerals, and used in fertilizers, detergents, etc. [18c]

phosphor *noun, chem* any substance that is capable of phosphorescence, used to coat the inner surface of television screens and fluorescent light tubes, and as a brightener in detergents. [17c: from Greek *phosphoros*; see **phosphorus**]

phosphorescence *noun* **1** the emission of light from a substance after it has absorbed energy from a source such as ultraviolet radiation, and which continues for some time after the energy source has been removed. **2** a general term for the emission of light by a substance in the absence of a significant rise in temperature. ▪ **phosphoresce** *verb*. ▪ **phosphorescent** *adj*. [18c]

phosphoric *adj, chem* referring to or containing phosphorus in higher **valency**.

phosphoric acid *noun, chem* a transparent crystalline water-soluble compound used in soft drinks, rust removers, and as a rustproof layer on steel.

phosphorous *adj, chem* referring to or containing phosphorus in lower **valency**.

phosphorus *noun, chem* (symbol **P**) a non-metallic element that exists as several different allotropes, including a whitish-yellow soft waxy solid that ignites spontaneously in air. [17c: from Greek *phosphoros* bringer of light]

photo *noun, informal* a **photograph**. [19c]

photocell see **photoelectric cell**

photochemistry *noun, chem* the branch of chemistry concerned with the study of chemical reactions that only take place in the presence of visible light or ultraviolet radiation, and reactions in which light is produced. ▪ **photochemical** *adj*. ▪ **photochemist** *noun*.

photocopier *noun* a machine that makes copies of printed documents or illustrations by any of various photographic techniques, esp **xerography**.

photocopy *noun* (***-ies***) a photographic copy of a document, drawing, etc. ▸ *verb* (***-ies, -ied***) to make a photographic copy of (a document, etc). [20c]

photoelectric *adj* referring or relating to the electrical effects of light, eg the emission of electrons or a change in resistance. ▪ **photoelectricity** *noun*. [19c]

photoelectric cell *noun* (abbrev **PEC** *or* **pec**) a light-sensitive device that converts light energy into electrical energy, used in light meters, burglar alarms, etc. Also called **photocell**.

photoengraving *noun* a technique for producing metal printing plates on cylinders carrying the image of continuous-tone and half-tone text and illustrations.

photo-essay *noun* an article or book on a particular subject, illustrated with a number of photographs.

photo finish *noun* a race finish in which the runners are so close that the result must be decided by looking at a photograph taken at the finishing line. [20c]

Photofit *or* **photofit** *noun, trademark* **1** a system where photographs are used by the police to build up a likeness of someone to fit a witness's description. **2** a likeness produced in this way. [20c]

photogenic *adj* **1** esp of a person: characterized by the quality of photographing well or looking attractive in photographs. **2** *biol* producing, or produced by, light.

photograph *noun* a permanent record of an image that has been produced on photosensitive film or paper by the process of photography. ▸ *verb, tr & intr* to take a photograph of (a person, thing, etc). [19c]

photographic *adj* **1** relating to or similar to photographs or photography. **2** of memory: retaining images in exact detail. ▪ **photographically** *adv*.

photography *noun* the process of creating an image on light-sensitive film or some other sensitized material using visible light, X-rays, or some other form of radiant energy. ▪ **photographer** *noun*. [19c]

photogravure *noun* **1** a method of engraving in which the design is photographed on to a metal plate, and then etched in. **2** a picture produced in this way. [19c: **photo** + French *gravure* engraving]

photojournalism *noun* journalism consisting mainly of photographs to convey the meaning of the article, with written material playing a small role. ▪ **photojournalist** *noun.* [20c]

photolysis /foʊˈtɒlɪsɪs/ *noun, chem* a chemical reaction in which the breaking of a chemical bond within a molecule of a substance is brought about by exposure to light or ultraviolet radiation. ▪ **photolytic** *adj.* [20c]

photometry /foʊˈtɒmɪtrɪ/ *noun, physics* the measurement of visible light and its rate of flow, which has important applications in photography and lighting design. ▪ **photometric** *adj.* [18c]

photomontage /foʊtoʊmɒnˈtɑːʒ/ *noun* the assembling of selected photographic images, either by mounting cut-out portions of prints on a backing, or by combining several separate negatives during printing. [20c: from French *montage* mounting]

photon *noun, physics* a particle of electromagnetic radiation that travels at the speed of light, used to explain phenomena that require light to behave as particles rather than as waves. [20c]

photophobia *noun, med* a fear of or aversion to light. [18c]

photoreceptor *noun, biol* a cell or group of cells that is sensitive to and responds to light. [20c]

photosensitive *adj* readily stimulated by light or some other form of radiant energy. ▪ **photosensitivity** *noun.* [19c]

photosphere *noun, astron* the outermost visible layer of the Sun, representing the zone from which light is emitted. [19c]

Photostat *noun, trademark* **1** a photographic apparatus for copying documents, drawings, etc. **2** a copy made by this. [20c]

photosynthesis *noun, botany* the process whereby green plants manufacture carbohydrates from carbon dioxide and water, using the light energy from sunlight trapped by the pigment **chlorophyll** in specialized structures known as **chloroplast**s. ▪ **photosynthesize** *or* **-ise** *verb.* ▪ **photosynthetic** *adj.* [19c]

phototaxis *noun, biol* the movement of a cell or motile organism towards or away from a light source. ▪ **phototactic** *adj.* [19c]

phototropism *noun, botany* the growth of the roots or shoots of plants in response to light. [19c]

photovoltaic cell see **solar cell**

phrasal verb *noun, grammar* a phrase consisting of a verb plus an adverb or preposition, or both, frequently with a meaning or meanings that cannot be determined from the meanings of the individual words, eg *let on* or *come up with something.*

phrase *noun* **1** a set of words expressing a single idea, forming part of a sentence though not constituting a **clause** (sense 1). **2** an idiomatic expression: *What is the phrase she used?* **3** manner or style of speech or expression: *ease of phrase.* See also **turn of phrase**. **4** *music* a run of notes making up an individually distinct part of a melody. ▸ *verb* **1** to express; to word something: *He phrased his reply carefully.* **2** *music* to bring out the phrases in (music) as one plays. ▪ **phrasal** *adj.* [16c: from Greek *phrasis* expression]

phrase book *noun* a book that lists words and phrases in a foreign language, esp for the use of visitors to a country where that language is spoken.

phraseology /freɪzɪˈɒlədʒɪ/ *noun* (**-ies**) **1** one's choice of words and way of combining them, in expressing oneself. **2** the language belonging to a particular subject, group, etc: *legal phraseology.* [17c]

phrasing *noun* **1** the wording of a speech or passage. **2** *music* the grouping of the parts, sounds, etc into musical phrases.

phrenetic see **frenetic**

phrenology *noun* the practice, now discredited, of assessing someone's character and aptitudes by examining the shape of their skull. ▪ **phrenological** *adj.* ▪ **phrenologist** *noun.* [19c: from Greek *phren* mind + *logos* word or reason]

phut *noun, informal* the noise of a small explosion. [19c]

IDIOMS **go phut 1** to break down or cease to function. **2** to go wrong.

phylactery *noun* (**-ies**) **1** *Judaism* either of two small boxes containing religious texts worn on the left arm and forehead by Jewish men during prayers. **2** a reminder. **3** a charm or amulet. [14c: from Greek *phylakterion*]

phyllo see **filo**

phylum *noun* (***phyla***) *biol, zool* in taxonomy: any of the major groups, eg *Chordata* (the vertebrates), into which the animal **kingdom** (sense 2) is divided and which in turn is subdivided into one or more **class**es (*noun* sense 9). [19c: from Greek *phylon* race]

physical *adj* **1** relating to the body rather than the mind; bodily: *physical strength.* **2** relating to objects that can be seen or felt; material: *the physical world.* **3** relating to nature or to the laws of nature: *physical features* • *a physical impossibility.* **4** involving bodily contact. **5** relating to **physics**. ▪ **physically** *adv.* [16c: from Latin *physicalis*]

physical education *noun* (abbrev **PE**) instruction in sport and gymnastics.

physical geography *noun* the branch of geography concerned with the study of the earth's natural features, eg mountain ranges, ocean currents, etc.

physical training *noun* (abbrev **PT**) instruction in sport and gymnastics, esp in the army.

physician *noun* **1** in the UK: a registered medical practitioner who specializes in medical as opposed to surgical treatment of diseases and disorders. **2** in other parts of the world: anyone who is legally qualified to practise medicine. [13c: French]

physics *singular noun* the scientific study of the properties and interrelationships of matter, energy, force and motion. ▪ **physicist** *noun.* [16c]

physio *noun, informal* **1** **physiotherapy**. **2** a **physiotherapist**.

physiognomy /fɪzɪˈɒnəmɪ/ *noun* (**-ies**) **1** the face or features, esp when used or seen as a key to someone's personality. **2** the art of judging character from appearance, esp from the face. **3** the general appearance of something, eg the countryside. ▪ **physiognomist** /-ˈɒnəmɪst/ *noun.* [14c: from Latin *phisonomia*]

physiography *noun* physical geography. ▪ **physiographer** *noun.* [19c]

physiology *noun, biol* the branch of biology that is concerned with the internal processes and functions of living organisms, as opposed to their structure. ▪ **physiologic** *or* **physiological** *adj* **1** referring or relating to physiology. **2** referring or relating to the normal functioning of a living organism. ▪ **physiologist** *noun* a scientist who specializes in physiology. [16c: from Latin *physiologia*]

physiotherapy *noun, med* the treatment of injury and disease by external physical methods, such as remedial exercises, manipulation or massage, rather than by drugs or surgery. ▪ **physiotherapist** *noun*. [20c]

physique *noun* the structure of the body with regard to size, shape, proportions and muscular development; the build. [19c: French, orig meaning 'physical', from Greek *physikos* of nature]

pi[1] /paɪ/ *noun* **1** the sixteenth letter of the Greek alphabet. **2** *maths* this symbol (π), representing the ratio of the circumference of a circle to its diameter, in numerical terms 3.14159.

pi[2] see **pie**[2]

pia mater /ˈpaɪə ˈmeɪtə(r)/ *noun, anatomy* the delicate innermost membrane that encloses the brain and spinal cord. [16c: Latin, literally 'tender mother']

pianissimo *music, adv* performed very softly. ▸ *adj* very soft. ▸ *noun* a piece of music to be performed in this way. [18c: Italian, superlative of *piano* quiet]

pianist *noun* someone who plays the piano.

piano[1] *noun* a large musical instrument with a keyboard, the keys being pressed down to operate a set of hammers that strike tautened wires to produce the sound. [19c: short form of **pianoforte**]

piano[2] *music, adv* softly. ▸ *adj* soft. ▸ *noun* a passage of music to be played or performed softly. [17c: Italian]

piano accordion *noun* an **accordion** whose melody is produced by means of a keyboard.

pianoforte /pɪanoʊˈfɔːtɪ/ *noun* the full formal term for a **piano**[1]. [18c: from Italian *piano e forte* soft and loud]

Pianola *noun, trademark* a mechanical piano that is operated automatically. [20c]

piazza /pɪˈatsə/ *noun* **1** a public square in an Italian town. **2** *mainly Brit* a covered walkway. [16c: Italian]

pic *noun* (***pics*** *or* ***pix***) *informal* a photograph or picture. [19c: short for **picture**]

pica /ˈpaɪkə/ *noun, printing* an old type-size, giving about six lines to the inch, approximately 12-point and still used synonymously for that point size. [15c: Latin, referring to a book of ecclesiastical rules for determining dates of religious festivals]

picador *noun, bullfighting* a **toreador** who weakens the bull by wounding it with a lance. [18c: Spanish, from *pica* lance]

picaresque *adj* of a novel, etc: telling of the adventures of a usu likeable rogue in separate, only loosely connected, episodes. [19c: from Spanish *picaro* rogue]

piccalilli *noun* a pickle consisting of mixed vegetables in a mustard sauce. [18c]

piccolo *noun* a small transverse **flute** pitched one octave higher than the standard flute and with a range of about three octaves. [19c: from Italian *flauto piccolo* little flute]

pick[1] *verb* **1** *tr & intr* to choose or select. **2** to detach and gather (flowers from a plant, fruit from a tree, etc). **3** to open (a lock) with a device other than a key, often to gain unauthorized entry. **4** to get, take or extract whatever is of use or value from something: *pick a bone clean* • *pick someone's brains.* **5** to steal money or valuables from (someone's pocket). See also **pickpocket**. **6** to undo; to unpick: *pick a dress to pieces.* **7** to make (a hole) by unpicking. **8** to remove pieces of matter from (one's nose, teeth, a scab, etc) with one's fingernails, etc. **9** *intr* (*often* **pick at sth**) **a** to eat only small quantities of (one's food); **b** to keep pulling at (a scab, etc) with one's fingernails. **10** to provoke (a fight, quarrel, etc) with someone. ▸ *noun* **1** the best of a group: *the pick of the bunch.* **2** one's own preferred selection. ▪ **picker** *noun*. [15c]

IDIOMS **pick and choose** to be over-fussy in one's choice. **pick sb's brains** to ask someone for information, ideas, etc, and then use it as your own. **pick holes in sth** to find fault with it. **pick sb** *or* **sth to pieces** to criticize them or it severely. **pick up the pieces** to have to restore things to normality or make things better after some trouble or disaster.

PHRASAL VERBS **pick on sb 1** to blame them unfairly. **2** to bully them. **pick sb out 1** to select them from a group. **2** to recognize or distinguish them among a group or crowd. **pick up** of a person, a person's health, or a situation: to recover or improve. **pick up** *or* **pick sth up** to resume: *pick up where one left off.* **pick sb up 1** to arrest or seize them. **2** to go and fetch them from where they are waiting. **3** to stop one's vehicle for them and give them a lift. **pick sth up 1** to lift or raise it from a surface, from the ground, etc. **2** to learn or acquire (a habit, skill, language, etc) over a time. **3** to notice or become aware of it: *picked up a faint odour.* **4** to obtain or acquire it casually, by chance, etc: *pick up a bargain* • *pick up an infection.* **5** to go and fetch (something waiting to be collected). **6** *telecomm* to receive (a signal, programme, etc). **7** *informal* to agree to pay (a bill, etc): *pick up the tab.* **pick sb up on sth** to point out their error.

pick[2] *noun* **1** a tool with a long metal head pointed at one or both ends, for breaking ground, rock, ice, etc. **2** a poking or cleaning tool: *a toothpick.* **3** a plectrum. [14c: prob related to **pike**[2]]

pickaback see **piggyback**

pickaxe *noun* a large pick. [14c: from French *picois*]

picket *noun* **1** a person or group of people stationed outside a place of work to persuade other employees not to go in during a strike. **2** a body of soldiers on patrol or sentry duty. **3** a stake fixed in the ground, eg as part of a fence. ▸ *verb* **1** to station pickets or act as a **picket** (*noun* sense 1) at (a factory, etc). **2** to guard or patrol with, or as, a military picket. **3** to fence (an area, etc) with **picket**s (*noun* sense 3). [18c: from French *piquet*, diminutive of *pic* **pick**[2]]

picket line *noun* a line of people acting as pickets (see **picket**, *noun* sense 1) in an industrial dispute.

pickings *plural noun, informal* profits made easily or casually from something: *rich pickings.*

pickle *noun* **1** (*also* **pickles**) a preserve of vegetables, eg onions, cucumber or cauliflower, in vinegar, salt water or a tart sauce. **2** a vegetable preserved in this way. **3** the liquid used for this preserve. **4** *informal* a mess; a quandary; a predicament: *got herself in a terrible pickle.* **5** *informal* a troublesome child. ▸ *verb* to preserve something in vinegar, salt water, etc. [14c: from German *Pekel*]

pickled *adj* **1** preserved in pickle. **2** *informal* drunk.

pick-me-up *noun* **1** a stimulating drink, such as tea, a whisky, etc. **2** anything that revives. [19c]

pickpocket *noun* a thief who steals from people's pockets, usu in crowded areas. [16c]

pick-up *noun* **1** the **stylus** on a record player. **2** a **transducer** on electric musical instruments. **3** a small lorry, truck or van. **4 a** a halt or place to load goods or passengers; **b** the goods or passengers loaded. See also **pick up** at **pick**[1].

picky *adj* (***-ier, -iest***) *informal* choosy or fussy, esp excessively so; difficult to please. [19c: from **pick**[1]]

picnic *noun* **1** an outing on which one takes food for eating in the open air. **2** food taken or eaten in this way. ▸ *verb* (***picnicked, picnicking***) *intr* to have a picnic. ▪ **picnicker** *noun.* [18c: from French *pique-nique*]

IDIOMS **no picnic** *or* **not a picnic** *informal* a disagreeable or difficult job or situation.

pico- *prefix, forming nouns, denoting* a millionth of a millionth part, or 10^{-12}, of the specified unit: *picocurie* • *picosecond.* [Spanish, meaning 'a small quantity']

picot /'piːkoʊ/ *noun* **1** a loop in an ornamental edging. **2** *embroidery* a raised knot. [19c: French, meaning 'point' or 'prick']

Pict *noun* a member of an ancient N British people. ▪ **Pictish** *adj.* [Anglo-Saxon: from Latin *picti* painted men]

pictograph *or* **pictogram** *noun* **1** a picture or symbol that represents a word, as in Chinese writing. **2** a pictorial or diagrammatic representation of values, statistics, etc. ▪ **pictographic** *adj.* ▪ **pictography** *noun.* [19c: from Latin *pictus* painted]

pictorial *adj* relating to, or consisting of, pictures. ▸ *noun* a periodical with a high proportion of pictures as opposed to text. [17c: from Latin *pictor* painter]

picture *noun* **1** a representation of someone or something on a flat surface; a drawing, painting or photograph. **2** someone's portrait. **3** a view; a mental image: *a clear picture of the battle.* **4** a situation or outlook: *a gloomy financial picture.* **5** a person or thing strikingly like another: *She is the picture of her mother.* **6** a visible embodiment: *was the picture of happiness.* **7** an image of beauty: *looks a picture.* **8** the image received on a television screen: *We get a good picture.* **9** a film; a motion picture. **10** (**the pictures**) *informal* the cinema: *went to the pictures last night.* ▸ *verb* **1** to imagine or visualize: *Just picture that settee in our lounge.* **2** to describe something or someone vividly; to depict. **3** to represent or show someone or something in a picture or photograph. [15c: from Latin *pictura* painting]

IDIOMS **get the picture** *informal* to understand something. **in the picture** informed of all the facts, etc.

picture card see **court card**

picture postcard *noun* a postcard with a picture on the front, usu a view of a village, town, landscape, holiday resort, etc. ▸ *adj* (**picture-postcard**) very pretty or quaint. [19c]

picturesque *adj* **1** of places or buildings: charming to look at, esp if rather quaint. **2** of language: **a** colourful, expressive or graphic; **b** *facetious* vivid or strong to the point of being offensive. [18c: from French *pittoresque*]

picture window *noun* a large window with a plate-glass pane, usu affording an extensive view.

piddle *informal, verb, intr* to urinate. ▸ *noun* **1** urine. **2** the act of urinating.

piddling *adj* trivial; trifling: *piddling excuses.* [16c]

pidgin *noun* **1** a type of simplified language used esp for trading purposes between speakers of different languages, commonly used in the East and West Indies, Africa and the Americas. See also **creole**. **2** (*also* **pigeon**) *informal* one's own affair, business or concern. [19c: said to be a Chinese pronunciation of *business*]

pie[1] *noun* a savoury or sweet dish, usu cooked in a container, consisting of a quantity of food with a covering of pastry, a base of pastry, or both. [14c]

IDIOMS **easy as pie** very easy. **pie in the sky** some hoped-for but unguaranteed future prospect.

pie[2] *or* **pi** *noun* **1** *printing* confusedly mixed type. **2** a mixed state; confusion. [17c]

piebald *adj* having contrasting patches of colour, esp black and white. Compare **pied**. ▸ *noun* a horse with black and white markings. [16c: *pie* (an old name for a magpie) + *bald* in the obsolete sense 'with white markings']

piece *noun* **1** a portion of some material; a bit. **2** any of the sections into which something (eg a cake) is divided; a portion taken from a whole. **3** a component part: *a jigsaw piece.* **4** an item in a set. *as adj*: *a 3-piece suite.* **5** an individual member of a class of things represented by a collective noun: *a piece of fruit* • *a piece of clothing.* **6** a specimen or example of something: *a fine piece of Chippendale.* **7** an instance: *a piece of nonsense.* **8** a musical, artistic, literary or dramatic work. **9** an article in a newspaper, etc. **10** a coin: *a 50 pence piece* • *pieces of eight.* **11** one of the tokens or men used in a board game. **12** a cannon or firearm. ▸ *verb* (**piece sth** *or* **things together**) to join it or them together to form a whole. [13c: from French *piece*]

IDIOMS **all in one piece** undamaged, unhurt, intact. **a piece of one's mind** a frank and outspoken reprimand. **go to pieces** *informal* to lose emotional control; to panic. **of a piece with sth** consistent or uniform with it. **say one's piece** to make one's contribution to a discussion.

pièce de résistance /pɪ'ɛs də reɪ'zɪstɑ̃s/ (***pièces de résistance*** /pɪ'ɛs də reɪ'zɪstɑ̃s/) *noun* **1** the best or most impressive item. **2** the main dish of a meal. [19c: French]

piecemeal *adv* a bit at a time. [13c]

piece of cake *noun* something that is easy, simple, etc. [20c]

piecework *noun* work paid for according to the amount done, not the time taken to do it.

pie chart, pie diagram *or* **pie graph** *noun* a diagram used to display statistical data, consisting of a circle divided into sectors, each of which contains one category of information. Compare **bar chart**.

pied *adj* of a bird: having variegated plumage, esp of black and white. [14c]

pied-à-terre /pjeɪda'tɛə(r)/ *noun* (***pieds-à-terre*** /pjeɪda-/) a house or apartment, eg in a city, that one keeps as somewhere to stay on occasional visits there. [20c: French, literally 'foot on the ground']

pie-eyed *adj, informal* drunk. [20c]

pier *noun* **1 a** a structure built of stone, wood or iron, projecting into water for use as a landing stage or breakwater; **b** such a structure used as a promenade with funfair-like sideshows, amusement arcades, etc. **2** a pillar supporting a bridge or arch. **3** the masonry between two openings in the wall of a building. [12c: from Latin *pera*]

pierce *verb* (*also* **pierce through sth**) **1** of a sharp object or a person using one: to make a hole in or through; to puncture; to make (a hole) with something sharp. **2** to penetrate or force a way through or into something: *The wind pierced through her thin clothing.* **3** of light or sound: to burst through (darkness or silence). **4** to affect or touch (someone's heart, soul, etc) keenly or painfully. [13c: from French *percer*]

piercing *adj* **1** referring to something that pierces. **2** penetrating, acute, keen or sharp: *a piercing cry.* ▸ *noun* **body piercing**. ▪ **piercingly** *adv.*

Pierrot *or* **pierrot** /'pɪərou/ *noun* a clown dressed and made up like Pierrot, the traditional male character from French pantomime, with a whitened face, white frilled outfit and pointed hat. [18c: a French name, diminutive of *Pierre* Peter]

pietism *noun* pious feeling or an exaggerated show of piety. ▪ **pietist** *noun.*

piety *noun* **1** dutifulness; devoutness. **2** the quality of being pious, dutiful or religiously devout. **3** sense of duty towards parents, benefactors, etc. [17c: from Latin *pietas* dutifulness or piety]

piezoelectricity /paiːzouɪlɛk'trɪsɪtɪ, piːzou-/ *noun* electricity produced by stretching or compressing quartz crystals and other non-conducting crystals. ▪ **piezoelectric** *adj.* [19c: from Greek *piezein* to press + **electricity**]

piffle *noun, informal* nonsense; rubbish. [19c: from dialect]

piffling *adj, informal* trivial, trifling or petty.

pig *noun* **1** a hoofed omnivorous mammal with a stout heavy bristle-covered body and a protruding flattened snout, kept worldwide for its meat. **2** an abusive term for a person, esp someone greedy, dirty, selfish or brutal. **3** *slang* an unpleasant job or situation. **4** *offensive slang* a policeman. **5** **a** a quantity of metal cast into an oblong mass; **b** the mould into which it is run. ▸ *verb* (***pigged, pigging***) **1** of a pig: to produce young. **2** *tr & intr* of a person: to eat greedily. See also **porcine**. [13c]

IDIOMS **a pig in a poke** *informal* a purchase made without first inspecting it to see whether it is suitable. **make a pig of oneself** *informal* to eat greedily. **make a pig's ear of sth** *informal* to make a mess of it; to botch it.

PHRASAL VERBS **pig out** to eat a large amount with relish and overindulgence; to overeat.

pigeon[1] *noun* **1** a medium-sized bird with a plump body, a rounded tail and dense soft grey, brown or pinkish plumage. **2** *slang* a dupe or simpleton. See also **stool pigeon**. [15c: from French *pijon*]

pigeon[2] see **pidgin** (sense 2)

pigeon-breasted *or* **pigeon-chested** *adj* of humans: having a narrow chest with the breastbone projecting, as a pigeon has.

pigeonhole *noun* **1** any of a set of compartments, eg in a desk or on a wall, for filing letters or papers in. **2** a compartment of the mind or memory. ▸ *verb* **1** to put something into a pigeonhole. **2** to put someone or something mentally into a category, esp too readily or rigidly.

pigeon-toed *adj* of a person: standing and walking with their toes turned in.

piggery *noun* (***-ies***) **1** a place where pigs are bred. **2** *informal* greediness or otherwise disgusting behaviour. [18c]

piggish *adj, derog* greedy, dirty, selfish, mean or ill-mannered. ▪ **piggishness** *noun.*

piggy *or* **piggie** *noun* (***-ies***) a child's diminutive: **a** a pig; a little pig; **b** a toe. ▸ *adj* (***-ier, -iest***) **1** pig-like. **2** of the eyes: small and mean-looking. [18c]

piggyback *or* **pickaback** *noun* a ride on someone's back, with the legs supported by the bearer's arms. ▸ *adj* carried on the back of someone else. ▸ *adv* on the back of someone else. [16c]

piggy bank *noun* a child's pig-shaped china container for saving money in. [20c]

pigheaded *adj* stupidly obstinate. ▪ **pigheadedly** *adv.* ▪ **pigheadedness** *noun.* [17c]

pig-in-the-middle *or* **piggy-in-the-middle** *noun* **1** a game in which one person stands between two others and tries to intercept the ball they are throwing to each other. **2** (***pigs-*** *or* ***piggies-in-the-middle***) any person helplessly caught between two contending parties.

pig iron *noun, metallurgy* an impure form of iron produced by smelting iron in a **blast furnace**. [17c: from **pig** (*noun* sense 5)]

piglet *noun* a young pig.

pigment *noun* **1** any insoluble colouring matter that is used in suspension in water, oil or other liquids to give colour to paint, paper, etc. Compare **dye**. **2** a coloured substance that occurs naturally in living tissues, eg the red blood pigment **haemoglobin**, or **chlorophyll** in the leaves of green plants. ▸ *verb* to colour something with pigment; to dye or stain. ▪ **pigmentary** *or* **pigmented** *adj.* ▪ **pigmentation** *noun.* [14c: from Latin *pigmentum*]

pigmy see **pygmy**

pigskin *noun* leather made from the skin of a pig.

pigsty *noun* (***-ies***) **1** a pen where pigs are kept. **2** *informal* a filthy and disordered place.

pigswill *noun* kitchen or brewery waste for feeding to pigs.

pigtail *noun* a plaited length of hair, esp one of a pair, worn hanging at the sides or back of the head.

pike[1] *noun* (***pike*** *or* ***pikes***) a large predatory freshwater fish with a narrow pointed head and a small number of large teeth in the lower jaw. [14c: from **pike**[2], referring to the shape of its head]

pike[2] *noun* **1** *hist* a weapon like a spear, consisting of a metal point mounted on a long shaft. **2** a point or spike. **3** *N Eng dialect* a sharp-pointed hill or summit. [Anglo-Saxon *pic* point]

pike[3] *noun* **1** a **turnpike**. **2** *US* a main road. [19c]

pike[4] *adj, diving, gymnastics* (*also* **piked**) of a body position: bent sharply at the hips with the legs kept straight at the knees and toes pointed. ▸ *verb, intr* to move into this position. [20c]

pikestaff *noun* the shaft of a **pike**[2].

IDIOMS **plain as a pikestaff** all too obvious.

Pilates /pɪ'lɑːtiːz/ *noun* an exercise system intended to stretch the muscles, improve the posture, etc. [1930s: named after Joseph Pilates, who devised it]

pilau /pɪ'lau/, **pilaf** *or* **pilaff** /pɪ'laf/ *noun* an oriental dish of spiced rice with, or to accompany, chicken, fish, etc. *as adj*: *pilau rice*. [17c: from Persian *pilaw*]

pilchard *noun* a small edible marine fish of the herring family, bluish-green above and silvery below, covered with large scales. [16c]

pile[1] *noun* **1** a number of things lying on top of each other; a quantity of something in a heap or mound. **2** (**a pile** *or* **piles**) *informal* a large quantity. **3** *informal* a fortune: *made a pile on the horses*. **4** a massive or imposing building. **5** a **pyre**. Also called **funeral pile**. **6** a **nuclear reactor**, orig the graphite blocks forming the moderator for the reactor. Also called **atomic pile**. ▸ *verb* **1** *tr & intr* (*usu* **pile up** *or* **pile sth up**) to accumulate into a pile. See also **pile-up**. **2** *intr* (**pile in** *or* **into sth** *or* **pile off, out**, *etc*) to move in a crowd or confused bunch into or off it, etc. [15c: from Latin *pila* a stone pier]

IDIOMS **pile it on** *informal* to exaggerate.

pile[2] *noun* a heavy wooden shaft, stone or concrete pillar, etc driven into the ground as a support for a building, bridge, etc. [Anglo-Saxon *pil*, from Latin *pilum* javelin]

pile[3] *noun* **1** the raised cropped threads that give a soft thick surface to carpeting, velvet, etc. Compare **nap**[2]. **2** soft fine hair, fur, wool, etc. [15c: from Latin *pilus* hair]

pile-driver *noun* a machine for driving piles (see **pile**[2]) into the ground.

piles *plural noun* haemorrhoids. [14c: from Latin *pila* ball]

pile-up *noun* a vehicle collision in which following vehicles also crash, causing a number of collisions. [20c]

pilfer *verb, tr & intr* to steal in small quantities. ▪ **pilferage** *or* **pilfering** *noun* petty theft. ▪ **pilferer** *noun*. [14c: from French *pelfre* booty]

pilgrim *noun* **1** someone who makes a journey to a holy place as an act of reverence. **2** a traveller. ▪ **pilgrimage** *noun*. [12c: from Latin *peregrinus* foreigner or stranger]

Pilipino *noun* the national language of the Philippines, a standardized version of **Tagálog**. ▸ *adj* relating to, or spoken or written in, Pilipino. [20c: from Spanish *Filipino* Philippine]

pill *noun* **1** a small ball or tablet of medicine, for swallowing. **2** something unpleasant that one must accept. **3** (**the pill**) an oral contraceptive, usu one taken by women. [15c: from Latin *pila* ball]

pillage *verb, tr & intr* to plunder or loot. ▸ *noun* **1** the act of pillaging. **2** loot, plunder or booty. ▪ **pillager** *noun*. [14c: from French *piller*]

pillar *noun* **1** a vertical post of wood, stone, metal or concrete serving as a support to a main structure; a column. **2** any slender vertical mass of something, eg of smoke, rock, etc. **3** a strong and reliable supporter of a particular cause or organization: *He is a pillar of the village community*. [13c: from French *piler*]

IDIOMS **from pillar to post** from one place to another, esp moving between these in desperation, frustration, etc.

pillar box see **letter box**

Pillars of Islam *plural noun* the five major Islamic duties, ie the statement of faith, prayer, fasting, giving of alms, and pilgrimage to Mecca.

pillbox *noun* **1** a small round container for pills. **2** *military* a small, usu circular, concrete shelter for use as a lookout post and gun emplacement. **3** a small round flat-topped hat.

pillion *noun* a seat for a passenger on a motorcycle or horse, behind the driver or rider. *as adj*: *a pillion rider* • *the pillion seat*. ▸ *adv* on a pillion: *to ride pillion*. [16c: from Scottish Gaelic *pillinn* or Irish Gaelic *pillín*]

pillock *noun, Brit slang* a stupid or foolish person. [20c: from Norwegian dialect *pillicock* penis]

pillory *noun* (**-ies**) *hist* a wooden frame with holes for the hands and head, into which wrongdoers were locked as a punishment and publicly ridiculed. ▸ *verb* (**-ies, -ied**) **1** to hold someone up to public ridicule. **2** to put someone in a pillory. [13c: from French *pilori*]

pillow *noun* **1** a cushion for the head, esp a large rectangular one on a bed. **2** anything that resembles a pillow in shape, feel or function. [Anglo-Saxon: from Latin *pulvinus* cushion]

pillowcase *or* **pillowslip** *noun* a removable washable cover for a pillow.

pillow talk *noun* confidential conversation with a partner in bed.

pilot *noun* **1** someone who flies an aircraft, hovercraft, spacecraft, etc. **2** someone employed to conduct or steer ships into and out of harbour. **3** someone who is qualified to act as pilot. **4** a guide. ▸ *adj* of a scheme, programme, test, etc: serving as a preliminary test which may be modified before the final version is put into effect; experimental: *a pilot project*. ▸ *verb* **1** to act as pilot to someone. **2** to direct, guide or steer (a project, etc). [16c: from French *pillote*]

pilot light *noun* **1** a small permanent gas flame, eg on a gas cooker, that ignites the main burners when they are turned on. **2** an indicator light on an electrical apparatus showing when it is switched on.

pimento *noun* **1** a small tropical evergreen tree, cultivated mainly in Jamaica. **2** any of the dried unripe berries of this tree which are a source of allspice. Also called **allspice**. **3** the **pimiento**. [17c: altered from Spanish *pimiento*; see **pimiento**]

pi-meson see **pion**

pimiento /pɪmɪˈɛntoʊ/ *noun* **1** a variety of sweet pepper, widely cultivated for its mild-flavoured red fruit. **2** the fruit of this plant, eaten raw or cooked. [19c: Spanish, meaning 'paprika']

pimp *noun* a man who finds customers for a prostitute or a brothel and lives off the earnings. ▸ *verb, intr* to act as a pimp. [17c]

pimpernel *noun* a small sprawling plant, esp the scarlet pimpernel. [15c: from French *pimprenelle*]

pimple *noun* a small raised often pus-containing swelling on the skin; a spot. ▪ **pimply** *adj* (**-ier, -iest**). [15c: from Latin *papula* pimple]

PIN /pɪn/ *abbrev, noun* personal identification number, a multi-digit number used to authorize electronic transactions, such as cash withdrawal from a dispenser at a bank, access to an account via a telephone line, etc. Also called **PIN number**. [20c]

pin *noun* **1** a short slender implement with a sharp point and small round head, usu made of stainless steel, for fastening, attaching, etc, and used esp in dressmaking. **2** *in compounds* a fastening device consisting of or incorporating a slender metal or wire shaft: *hatpin* • *safety pin*. **3** a narrow brooch. **4** *in compounds* any of several cylindrical wooden or metal objects with various functions: *a rolling pin*. **5** a peg. **6** any or either of the cylindrical or square-sectioned legs on an electric plug. **7** a club-shaped object set upright for toppling with a ball: *ten-pin bowling*. **8** the clip on a grenade, that is removed before it is thrown. **9** *golf* the metal shaft of the flag marking a hole. **10** (**pins**) *informal* one's legs: *shaky on my pins*. **11** *old use* the least bit: *doesn't care a pin*. ► *verb* (***pinned, pinning***) **1** to secure with a pin. **2** to make a small hole in something. **3** (**pin sth on sb**) *informal* to put the blame (for a crime or offence) on them. [Anglo-Saxon: from Latin *pinna* point]

IDIOMS **pin one's hopes** *or* **faith on sth** *or* **sb** to rely on or trust in them entirely.

PHRASAL VERBS **pin sb down** to force a commitment or definite expression of opinion from them. **pin sth down** to identify or define it precisely. **pin sth** *or* **sb down** to hold them fast or trap them.

pinafore *noun* **1** an apron, esp one with a bib. Sometimes shortened to **pinny**. **2** (*also* **pinafore dress**) a sleeveless dress for wearing over a blouse, sweater, etc. [17c: from pin + afore, because it was formerly pinned to the front of a dress]

pinball *noun* a game played on a slot machine, in which a small metal ball is propelled by flippers round a course, the score depending on what hazards it avoids and targets it hits; a form of **bagatelle** (sense 1). [20c]

pince-nez /ˈpansneɪ/ *plural noun* spectacles that are held in position by a clip gripping the nose. [19c: French, literally 'pinch nose']

pincers *plural noun* **1** a hinged tool with two claw-like jaws joined by a pivot, used for gripping objects, pulling nails, etc. **2** the modified claw-like appendage of a decapod crustacean, eg a crab or lobster, adapted for grasping. [14c: from French *pincier* to pinch]

pinch *verb* **1** to squeeze or nip the flesh of someone or something, between thumb and finger. **2** to compress or squeeze something painfully. **3** of cold or hunger: to affect someone or something painfully or injuriously. **4** *tr & intr* of tight shoes: to hurt or chafe. **5** *tr & intr, informal* to steal. **6** *intr* of controls, restrictions, shortages, etc: to cause hardship. **7** *intr* to economize: *had to pinch and scrape to get by*. **8** *informal* to arrest someone. ► *noun* **1** an act of pinching; a nip or squeeze. **2** the quantity of something (eg salt) that can be held between thumb and finger. **3** a very small amount. **4** a critical time of difficulty or hardship. [14c: from French *pincier* to pinch]

IDIOMS **at a pinch** *informal* if absolutely necessary. **feel the pinch** *informal* to find life, work, etc difficult because of lack of money.

pinchbeck *noun* a copper-zinc alloy with the appearance of gold, used in cheap jewellery. ► *adj* cheap, artificial, sham, counterfeit or imitation. [18c: named after its inventor Christopher Pinchbeck, English watchmaker]

pinched *adj* of a person's appearance: pale and haggard from tiredness, cold or other discomfort.

pincushion *noun* a pad into which to stick dressmaking pins for convenient storage.

pine[1] *noun* **1** (*also* **pine tree**) an evergreen coniferous tree with narrow needle-like leaves. *as adj*: *pine fragrance*. **2** (*also* **pinewood**) the pale durable wood of this tree, used to make furniture, telegraph poles, paper pulp, etc, and widely used in construction work. *as adj*: *a pine table*. [Anglo-Saxon: from Latin *pinus*]

pine[2] *verb, intr* **1** (*also* **pine for sb** *or* **sth**) to long or yearn for them or it. **2** (*also* **pine away**) to waste away from grief or longing. [Anglo-Saxon *pinian* in obsolete sense 'to torment']

pineal gland *or* **pineal body** /ˈpɪnɪəl/ *noun, anatomy* in vertebrates: a small outgrowth from the roof of the forebrain, which produces hormones. [17c: from French *pinéal*]

pineapple *noun* **1** a tropical S American plant with spiky sword-shaped leaves, widely cultivated for its large edible fruit. **2** the fruit of this plant, which has sweet juicy yellow flesh covered by a yellowish-brown spiny skin. [17c]

pine nut *or* **pine kernel** *noun* the edible oily seed of various species of pine trees.

ping *noun* a sharp ringing sound like that made by plucking a taut wire, lightly striking glass or metal, etc. ► *verb, tr & intr* to make or cause something to make this sound. [19c: imitating the sound]

ping-pong *noun* **table tennis**. Also written **Ping-Pong** (*trademark in US*). [20c: imitating the sound of the ball]

pinhead *noun* **1** the little rounded or flattened head of a pin. **2** something that is very small. **3** *slang* a stupid person. ▪ **pinheaded** *adj*.

pinhole *noun* a tiny hole made by, or as if by, a pin.

pinion[1] *verb* **1** to immobilize someone by holding or binding their arms; to hold or bind (someone's arms). **2** to hold fast or bind. ► *noun* **1** the extreme tip of a bird's wing. **2** a bird's flight feather. [15c: from French *pignon* wing]

pinion[2] *noun* a small cogwheel that engages with a larger wheel or rack. [17c: from French *pignon* cogwheel]

pink[1] *noun* **1** a light or pale-red colour, between red and white. **2** a plant, eg a **carnation**, which has grass-like bluish-green leaves and flowers with five spreading toothed or slightly frilled pink, red, white, purple, yellow, orange or variegated petals. **3** **a** a scarlet hunting coat or its colour; **b** the person wearing it. **4** the highest point; the acme: *in the pink of condition*. ► *adj* **1** having, being or referring to the colour pink. **2** slightly left-wing. ▪ **pinkish** *and* **pinky** *adj* (***-ier, -iest***). ▪ **pinkness** *noun*. [16c]

IDIOMS **in the pink** *informal* in the best of health.

pink[2] *verb* to cut (cloth) with a notched or serrated edge that frays less readily than a straight edge. See also **pinking shears**. [Anglo-Saxon *pyngan* to prick]

pink[3] *verb, intr* of a vehicle engine: to **knock** (*verb* sense 7). [20c: imitating the sound made]

pink eye see **conjunctivitis**

pinkie *or* **pinky** *noun* (***-ies***) *Scot & N Am* the little finger. [19c: from Dutch *pinkje*]

pinking shears *plural noun* scissors with a serrated blade for cutting a zig-zag edge in cloth. See **pink[2]**.

pin money *noun* extra cash earned for spending on oneself, on luxury items, etc.

pinna /ˈpɪnə/ *noun* (***pinnae*** /-niː/) *anatomy* in mammals: the part of the outer ear that projects from the head. [18c: Latin, meaning 'feather' or 'wing']

pinnace /ˈpɪnəs/ *noun* a small boat carried on a larger ship; a ship's boat. [16c: from French *pinace*]

pinnacle *noun* **1** a slender spire crowning a buttress, gable, roof or tower. **2** a rocky peak. **3** a high point of achievement: *the pinnacle of her success.* [14c: from Latin *pinnaculum*]

pinnate *adj, botany* denoting a compound leaf that consists of pairs of leaflets arranged in two rows on either side of a central axis. ▪ **pinnately** *adv.* [18c: from Latin *pinnatus* feathered]

PIN number see under **PIN**

pinny see **pinafore**

pinpoint *verb* to place, define or identify something precisely. [20c]

pinprick *noun* **1** a tiny hole made by, or as if by, a pin. **2** a slight irritation or annoyance.

pins and needles *plural noun* an abnormal tingling sensation in a limb, etc, felt as the flow of blood returns to it after being temporarily obstructed.

pinstripe *noun* **1** a very narrow stripe in cloth. **2** cloth with such stripes. ▪ **pinstriped** *adj* of fabric or garments, esp suits: having pinstripes.

pint *noun* **1** in the UK, in the imperial system: a unit of liquid measure equivalent to ⅛ of a gallon or 20fl oz, equivalent to 0.568 l (liquid or dry). **2** in the US: a unit of liquid measure equivalent to ⅛ of a gallon or 16 US fl oz, equivalent to 0.473 (liquid) and 0.551 l (dry). **3** *informal* a drink of beer of this quantity. [14c: from French *pinte*]

pinta *noun, informal* a pint of milk. [20c: a contraction of *pint of*]

pintle *noun* a bolt or pin, esp one which is turned by something. [Anglo-Saxon *pintel* in original and dialect sense 'penis']

pinto *US, adj* mottled; piebald. ▶ *noun* a piebald horse. [19c: Spanish, meaning 'painted' or 'mottled']

pint-size *or* **pint-sized** *adj, humorous* of a person: very small.

pin tuck *noun* a narrow decorative tuck in a garment.

pin-up *noun* **1** a picture of a pop star or a famous, glamorous or otherwise admirable person that one pins on one's wall. **2** someone whose picture is pinned up in this way. [20c]

pinwheel *noun* **1** a whirling firework; a Catherine wheel. **2** *N Am, esp US* a toy windmill.

Pinyin *noun* a system for writing Chinese using letters of the Roman alphabet. [20c: from Chinese *pinyin* phonetic spelling]

pion *noun, physics* a type of **meson** that is the source of the nuclear force holding protons and neutrons together. Also called **pi-meson**.

pioneer *noun* **1** an explorer of, or settler in, hitherto unknown or wild country. **2** someone who breaks new ground in anything; an innovator. **3** *botany* a plant or species that is characteristically among the first to establish itself on bared ground. ▶ *verb* **1** *intr* to be a pioneer; to be innovative. **2** to explore and open up (a route, etc). **3** to try out, originate or develop (a new technique, etc). [16c: from French *peonier* foot soldier]

pious *adj* **1** religiously devout. **2** dutiful. **3** *derog* ostentatiously virtuous; sanctimonious. ▪ **piously** *adv.* ▪ **piousness** *noun.* [16c: from Latin *pius* dutiful]

pip[1] *noun* the small seed of a fruit such as an apple, pear, orange or grape. ▪ **pipless** *adj.* [18c: shortening of **pippin** (sense 2)]

pip[2] *noun* **1** one of a series of short high-pitched signals on the radio, telephone, etc. **2** (**the pips**) *informal* the six pips broadcast as a time-signal by BBC radio. [20c: imitating the sound]

pip[3] *verb* (***pipped, pipping***) to defeat someone narrowly. [Late 19c: from **pip**[1] or **pip**[4]]

IDIOMS **pipped at the post** *informal* overtaken narrowly in the closing stages of a contest, etc.

pip[4] *noun* **1** one of the emblems or spots on playing-cards, dice or dominoes. **2** *military* in the British army: a star on a uniform indicating rank. **3** on a radar screen: a mark, eg a spot of light, that indicates the presence of an object. [17c]

pip[5] *noun, old use* a disease of fowl. [15c: Dutch]

IDIOMS **give sb the pip** *informal* to irritate them.

pipe[1] *noun* **1** a tubular conveyance for water, gas, oil, etc. **2 a** a little bowl with a hollow stem for smoking tobacco, etc; **b** a quantity of tobacco smoked in one of these. **3** a wind instrument consisting of a simple wooden or metal tube. **4** (**the pipes**) the **bagpipes**. **5** any of the vertical metal tubes through which sound is produced on an organ. **6** a boatswain's whistle. **7** a pipe-like vent forming part of a volcano. **8** a cylindrical quantity of ore, etc. **9** *old use or in compounds* any of the air passages in an animal's body: *the windpipe.* ▶ *verb* **1** to convey (gas, water, oil, etc) through pipes. **2** *tr & intr* to play on a pipe or the pipes: *piped the same tune all evening.* **3** (*also* **pipe sb** *or* **sth in**) to welcome or convey with music from a pipe or the bagpipes: *piped in the haggis.* **4** *tr & intr* of a child: to speak or say in a small shrill voice. **5** *intr* to sing shrilly as a bird does. **6 a** to use a bag with a nozzle in order to force (icing or cream, etc from the bag) into long strings for decorating a cake, dessert, etc; **b** to make (designs, etc) on a cake, etc by this means. **7** *comput* to direct (the output of one program) into another program as its input in order to increase the speed of execution. [Anglo-Saxon: from Latin *pipare* to chirp or play a pipe]

PHRASAL VERBS **pipe down** *informal* to stop talking; to be quiet: *Will you please pipe down!* **pipe up** to speak unexpectedly, breaking a silence, etc.

pipe[2] *noun* **1** a cask or butt of varying capacity, but usu about 105 gallons in Britain (equal to 126 US gallons), used for wine or oil. **2** a measure of this amount. [14c: French, meaning 'cask']

pipeclay *noun* fine white clay for making tobacco pipes and delicate crockery.

piped music *noun* light popular recorded music played continuously through loudspeakers, esp in public places. Also called **muzak** (*trademark*).

pipe dream *noun* a delightful fantasy of the kind indulged in while smoking a pipe, orig one filled with opium. [19c]

pipeline *noun* a series of connected pipes laid underground to carry oil, natural gas, water, etc, across large distances.

IDIOMS **in the pipeline** *informal* under consideration; forthcoming or in preparation.

piper *noun* a player of a pipe or the bagpipes.

pipette *noun* a small laboratory device usu consisting of a narrow tube into which liquid can be sucked and from which it can subsequently be dispensed in known amounts. [19c: French, diminutive of *pipe* pipe]

piping *noun* **1** a length of pipe, or a system or series of pipes conveying water, oil, etc. **2** covered cord forming a decorative edging on upholstery or clothing. **3** strings and knots of icing or cream decorating a cake or dessert. **4** the art of playing a pipe or the bagpipes. ▶ *adj* of a voice: small and shrill.
IDIOMS **piping hot** of food: satisfyingly hot.

pipistrelle *noun* the smallest and most widespread European bat, which has a reddish-brown body and short triangular ears. [18c: from French]

pipit *noun* a small ground-dwelling songbird with a slender body, streaked brown plumage and a long tail. [18c: imitating the sound of its call]

pippin *noun* **1** any of several varieties of eating apple with a green or rosy skin. **2** *obsolete or dialect* the seed or pip of a fruit. [13c: from French *pepin*]

pipsqueak *noun, derog informal* someone or something insignificant or contemptible. [20c]

piquant /ˈpiːkənt/ *adj* **1** having a pleasantly spicy taste or tang. **2** amusing, intriguing, provocative or stimulating. ▪ **piquancy** *noun* the state of being piquant. [16c: French, from *piquer* to prick]

pique /piːk/ *noun* resentment; hurt pride. ▶ *verb* **1** to hurt someone's pride; to offend or nettle them. **2** to arouse (curiosity or interest). **3** to pride (oneself) on something: *piqued himself on his good taste.* [16c: French, from *piquer* to prick]

piqué /ˈpiːkeɪ/ *noun* a stiff corded fabric, esp of cotton. [19c: French, meaning 'pricked']

piquet /pɪˈkɛt, pɪˈkeɪ/ *noun* a card game for two, played with 32 cards. [17c: French]

piracy *noun* (**-ies**) **1** the activity of pirates, such as robbery on the high seas. **2** unauthorized publication or reproduction of copyright material. [16c]

piranha /pɪˈrɑːnə/ *or* **piraña** /pəˈrɑːnjə/ *noun* an extremely aggressive S American freshwater fish, with sharp saw-edged teeth. [19c: Portuguese]

pirate *noun* **1** someone who attacks and robs ships at sea. **2** the ship used by pirates. **3** someone who publishes material without permission from the copyright-holder, or otherwise uses someone else's work illegally. **4** someone who runs a radio station without a licence. ▶ *verb* to publish, reproduce or use (someone else's literary or artistic work, or ideas) without legal permission. ▪ **piratic** *or* **piratical** *adj.* [15c: from Latin *pirata*]

pirouette /pɪrʊˈɛt/ *noun* a spin or twirl executed on tiptoe in dancing. ▶ *verb, intr* to execute a pirouette. [18c: French, orig meaning 'a spinning top']

piscatorial *or* **piscatory** *adj, formal* relating to fish or fishing. [17c: from Latin *piscatorius* fisherman]

Pisces /ˈpaɪsiːz/ *noun, astrol* **a** the twelfth sign of the zodiac; **b** someone born between 20 February and 20 March, under this sign. ▪ **Piscean** *noun, adj.* [14c: Latin, meaning 'fishes']

pisciculture /ˈpɪsɪkʌltʃʊə(r)/ *noun* the rearing of fish by artificial methods or under controlled conditions. ▪ **piscicultural** *adj.* ▪ **pisciculturist** *noun.* [19c: from Latin *piscis* fish]

piscina /pɪˈsiːnə/ *noun* (***piscinae*** /-niː/ *or* ***piscinas***) a stone basin with a drain, found in older churches, in which to empty water used for rinsing the sacred vessels. [18c: from Latin]

piscine /pɪˈsaɪn/ *adj* referring or relating to, or resembling, a fish or fishes. [18c: from Latin *piscis* fish]

pistachio /pɪˈstɑːʃɪoʊ/ *noun* **1** a small deciduous tree with greenish flowers and reddish-brown nut-like fruits containing edible seeds. **2** the edible greenish seed of this tree. [16c: from Italian *pistacchio*]

piste /piːst/ *noun* a ski slope or track of smooth compacted snow. [18c: French, meaning 'race track']

pistil *noun, botany* in a flowering plant: the female reproductive structure. [16c: from Latin *pistillum* pestle]

pistol *noun* a small gun held in one hand when fired. [16c: from French *pistole*]

pistol-whip *verb* to hit someone with a pistol. [20c]

piston *noun* **1** *eng* a cylindrical device that moves up and down in the cylinder of a petrol, diesel or steam engine. **2** a sliding valve on a brass wind instrument. [18c: French]

pit[1] *noun* **1** a big deep hole in the ground. **2** a mine, esp a coalmine. **3** a cavity sunk into the ground from which to inspect vehicle engines, etc. **4** (**the pits**) *motor sport* any of a set of areas beside a racetrack where vehicles can refuel, have wheel changes, etc. **5** an enclosure in which fighting animals or birds are put. **6** **a** the floor of the auditorium in a theatre; **b** the people sitting there. **7** *anatomy* a hollow, indentation or depression, eg the **armpit**. **8** a scar left by a smallpox or acne pustule. **9** (**the pit**) *old use* hell. **10** (**the pits**) *slang* an awful or intolerable situation, person, etc. ▶ *verb* (***pitted, pitting***) **1** (*often* **pit oneself against sb**) to set or match oneself against them in competition. **2** to mark something with scars and holes. [Anglo-Saxon: from Latin *puteus* well]

pit[2] *noun, N Am* the stone in a peach, apricot, plum, etc. ▶ *verb* (***pitted, pitting***) to remove the stone from (a piece of fruit). [19c: from Dutch, meaning 'kernel']

pit-a-pat *noun* **1** a noise of pattering. **2** a succession of light taps. ▶ *adv* with a pattering or tapping noise: *rain falling pit-a-pat.* ▶ *verb* (***pit-a-patted, pit-a-patting***) to make a succession of quick light taps. [16c: imitating the sound]

pitch[1] *verb* **1** to set up (a tent or camp). **2** to throw or fling. **3** *tr & intr* to fall or make someone or something fall heavily forward. **4** *intr* of a ship: to plunge and lift alternately at bow and stern. **5** *tr & intr* of a roof: to slope: *is pitched at a steep angle.* **6** to give a particular musical pitch to (one's voice or a note) in singing or playing, or to set (a song, etc) at a higher or lower level within a possible range: *The tune is pitched too high for me.* **7** to choose a level, eg of difficulty, sophistication, etc at which to present (a talk, etc). **8** **a** *cricket* to bowl (the ball) so that it lands where the batsman can hit it; **b** *golf* to hit (the ball) high and gently, so that it stays where it is on landing; **c** *tr & intr, baseball* of the **pitcher**[2]: to throw the ball overarm or underarm to the person batting. ▶ *noun* **1** the field or area of play in any of several sports. **2** an act or style of pitching or throwing. **3** a degree of intensity; a level: *reached such a pitch of excitement.* **4** **a** the angle of steepness of a slope; **b** such a slope. **5** *music* the degree of highness or lowness of a note that results from the frequency of the vibrations producing it. **6** a street trader's station. **7** a line in sales talk, esp one often made use of. **8** the plunging and rising motion of a ship. ▪ **pitchy** *adj* (***-ier, -iest***). [13c:

as *picchen* to throw or put up]

PHRASAL VERBS **pitch in** *informal* **1** to begin enthusiastically. **2** to join in; to make a contribution. **pitch into sb** *informal* to rebuke or blame them angrily.

pitch² *noun* **1** a thick black sticky substance obtained from coal tar, used for filling ships' seams, etc. **2** any of various bituminous substances. [Anglo-Saxon *pic*]

pitch-black *or* **pitch-dark** *adj* utterly, intensely or unrelievedly black or dark. [16c]

pitchblende *noun, geol* a radioactive glossy brown or black form of uraninite, the main ore of uranium and radium. [18c: from German *Pechblende*]

pitched battle *noun* **1** a prearranged battle between two sides on chosen ground. **2** a fierce dispute or violent confrontation.

pitcher¹ *noun* a large earthenware jug with either one or two handles. ▪ **pitcherful** *noun*. [13c: from French *pichier*]

pitcher² *noun, baseball* the player who throws the ball to the person batting to hit. [19c]

pitchfork *noun* a long-handled fork with two or three sharp prongs, for tossing hay. [15c]

piteous *adj* arousing one's pity; moving, poignant, heartrending or pathetic. ▪ **piteously** *adv.* ▪ **piteousness** *noun*. Compare **pitiable**, **pitiful**. [13c: from French *pitos*]

pitfall *noun* a hidden danger, unsuspected hazard or unforeseen difficulty. [16c in this figurative sense]

pith *noun* **1** the soft white tissue that lies beneath the rind of many citrus fruits, eg orange. **2** *botany* in the stem of many plants: a central cylinder of generally soft tissue. **3** the most important part of an argument, etc. **4** substance, forcefulness or vigour as a quality in writing, etc. [Anglo-Saxon *pitha*]

pithead *noun* the entrance to a mineshaft and the machinery round it. *as adj*: *a pithead ballot*. [19c]

pithy *adj* (*-ier, -iest*) **1** of a saying, comment, etc: brief, forceful and to the point. **2** referring to, resembling or full of pith. ▪ **pithily** *adv.* ▪ **pithiness** *noun*.

pitiable *adj* **1** arousing pity. **2** miserably inadequate; contemptible. [15c]

pitiful *adj* **1** arousing pity; wretched or pathetic: *His clothes were in a pitiful state.* **2** sadly inadequate or ineffective: *a pitiful attempt*. ▪ **pitifully** *adv.* ▪ **pitifulness** *noun*. [15c; 16c in sense 2]

pitiless *adj* showing no pity; merciless, cruel or relentless. ▪ **pitilessly** *adv.*

piton /ˈpiːtɒn/ *noun, mountaineering* a metal peg or spike with an eye for passing a rope through, hammered into a rock face as an aid to climbers. [19c: French, meaning 'ringbolt']

pitstop *noun, motor sport* a pause made at a refuelling **pit¹** (*noun* sense 4) by a racing driver.

pitta *noun* a Middle-Eastern slightly leavened bread, usu in a hollow oval shape that can be filled with other foods. Also called **pitta bread**. [20c: modern Greek, meaning 'cake' or 'pie']

pittance *noun* a meagre allowance or wage. [13c: from French *pietance* ration]

pitter-patter *noun* the sound of pattering. ▸ *adv* with this sound. ▸ *verb, intr* to make such a sound. [15c: imitating the sound]

pituitary *noun* (*-ies*) short form of **pituitary gland**. ▸ *adj* relating to this gland. [19c: from Latin *pituita* phlegm or rheum]

pituitary gland *or* **pituitary body** *noun, physiol* in vertebrates: an endocrine gland at the base of the brain that is responsible for the production of a number of important hormones.

pity *noun* (*-ies*) **1** a feeling of sorrow for the troubles and sufferings of others; compassion. **2** a cause of sorrow or regret. ▸ *verb* (*-ies, -ied*) to feel or show pity for someone or something. ▪ **pitying** *adj.* ▪ **pityingly** *adv.* [13c: from French *pité*]

IDIOMS **have** *or* **take pity on sb** to feel or show pity for them, esp in some practical way.

pivot *noun* **1** a central pin, spindle or pointed shaft round which something revolves, turns, balances or oscillates. **2** someone or something crucial, on which everyone or everything else depends. **3** a centre-half in football or a similarly placed player in other games. ▸ *verb* **1** *intr* (*often* **pivot on sth**) **a** to turn, swivel or revolve; **b** to depend. **2** to mount something on a pivot. [17c: French]

pivotal *adj* **1** constructed as or acting like a pivot. **2** crucially important; critical: *a pivotal moment in our history.*

pix¹ *noun* **pyx**.

pix² *a pl of* **pic**

pixel *noun, electronics* the smallest element of the image displayed on a computer or TV screen, consisting of a single dot which may be illuminated (ie on) or dark (off). [20c: **pix²** + *el*ement]

pixie *or* **pixy** *noun* (*-ies*) *myth* a kind of fairy, traditionally with mischievous tendencies. [17c: orig dialect]

pixilated *or* **pixillated** *adj, chiefly US* **1** bemused or bewildered. **2** mildly eccentric; slightly crazy. **3** *slang* drunk. [19c: from **pixie**, modelled on *titillated*, etc]

pizza *noun* a circle of dough spread with cheese, tomatoes, etc and baked. [20c: Italian]

pizzazz, **pazzazz**, **pizazz** *or* **pazazz** *noun, informal* a quality that is a combination of boldness, vigour, dash and flamboyance. [20c: thought to have been coined by Diana Vreeland, US fashion editor]

pizzeria *noun* a restaurant specializing in pizzas.

pizzicato /pɪtsɪˈkɑːtoʊ/ *music adj, adv* of music for stringed instruments: played using the fingers to pluck the strings. ▸ *noun* **1** a passage of music to be played in this way. **2** the playing or technique of playing a piece by plucking. [19c: Italian, literally 'twitched']

pl. *abbrev* plural.

placable *adj* easily appeased. [15c: from Latin *placabilis*]

placard *noun* a board or stiff card bearing a notice, advertisement, slogan, message of protest, etc, carried or displayed in public. ▸ *verb* **1** to put placards on (a wall, etc). **2** to announce (a forthcoming event, etc) by placard. [15c: French]

placate *verb* to pacify or appease (someone who is angry, etc). ▪ **placation** *noun*. ▪ **placatory** *adj*. [17c: from Latin *placere* to appease]

place *noun* **1** a portion of the earth's surface, particularly one considered as a unit, such as an area, region, district, locality, etc. **2** a geographical area or position, such as a country, city, town, village, etc. **3** a building, room, piece of ground, etc, particularly one assigned to some purpose: *place of business* • *place of worship*. **4** *informal* one's home or lodging: *Let's go to my place.* **5** *in compounds* somewhere with a specified association or function: *one's birthplace* • *a hiding place*. **6** a seat or space, eg at table: *lay three places*. **7** a seat in a theatre, on a train, bus, etc. **8** an area on the surface of something, eg on the body: *point to the sore place*. **9** the customary position of something or someone: *put it back in its place*. **10** a point reached, eg in a conversation, narrative, series of developments, etc: *a good place to stop*. **11** a point in a book, etc, esp where one stopped reading: *made me lose my place*. **12** a position within an order eg of competitors in a contest, a set of priorities, etc: *finished in third place* • *lost his place in the queue*. **13** social or political rank: *know one's place*. **14** a vacancy at an institution, on a committee, in a firm, etc: *a university place*. **15** one's role, function, duty, etc: *It's not my place to tell him*. **16** an open square or a row of houses: *the market place*. **17** *maths* the position of a number in a series, esp of decimals after the point. ▸ *verb* **1** to put, position, etc in a particular place. **2** to submit: *place an order*. **3** to find a place, home, job, publisher, etc for someone. **4** to assign final positions to (contestants, etc): *was placed fourth*. **5** to identify or categorize: *a familiar voice that I couldn't quite place*. **6** *commerce* to find a buyer for (stocks or shares, usu a large quantity of them). **7** to arrange (a bet, loan, etc). **8** *intr, esp N Am* to finish a race or competition (in a specified position or, if unspecified, in second position). [13c: from Anglo-Saxon *plæce* and French *place* an open place or street]

IDIOMS **all over the place** in disorder or confusion. **go places** *informal* **1** to travel. **2** to be successful. **in place** in the correct position. **in place of sth** *or* **sb** instead of it or them. **in places** here and there. **know one's place** to show proper subservience (to someone, an organization, etc). **lose one's place** to falter in following a text, etc; not to know what point has been reached. **out of place 1** not in the correct position. **2** inappropriate. **put** *or* **keep sb in their place** to humble them as they deserve because of their arrogance, conceit, etc. **take one's place** to assume one's usual or rightful position. **take place** to happen, occur, be held, etc. **take the place of sb** *or* **sth** to replace or supersede them or it.

placebo /plə'siːboʊ/ *noun, med* a substance that is administered as a drug but has no medicinal content, either given to a patient for its reassuring and therefore beneficial effect (the **placebo effect**), or used in a clinical trial of a real drug, in which participants who have been given a placebo serve as untreated **control** subjects for comparison with those actually given the drug. [18c: Latin *I shall please*]

placement *noun* **1** the act or process of placing or positioning. **2** the finding of a job or home for someone. **3** a temporary job providing work experience, esp for someone on a training course.

placename *noun* the name of a town, village, hill, lake, etc.

placenta /plə'sɛntə/ *noun* (***placentas*** *or* ***placentae*** /-tiː/) in mammals: a disc-shaped organ attached to the lining of the uterus during pregnancy and through which the embryo obtains nutrients and oxygen. ▪ **placental** *adj*. [17c: Latin]

place setting see **setting** (*noun* sense 2)

placid *adj* calm; tranquil. ▪ **placidity** *or* **placidness** *noun*. ▪ **placidly** *adv*. [17c: from Latin *placidus*]

placket *noun, dressmaking* **1** an opening in a skirt for a pocket or at the fastening. **2** a piece of material sewn behind this. [17c, orig meaning 'breastplate']

plagiarize *or* **-ise** /'pleɪdʒəraɪz/ *verb, tr & intr* to copy (ideas, passages of text, etc) from someone else's work and use them as if they were one's own. ▪ **plagiarism** *noun*. ▪ **plagiarist** *noun*. [18c: from Latin *plagiarius* kidnapper]

plague *noun* **1** *med* **a** any of several epidemic diseases with a high mortality rate; **b** specifically, an infectious epidemic disease of rats and other rodents, caused by a bacterium and transmitted to humans by flea bites, eg **bubonic plague**. **2** an overwhelming intrusion by something unwelcome: *a plague of tourists*. **3** *informal* a nuisance. **4** an affliction regarded as a sign of divine displeasure: *a plague on both your houses*. ▸ *verb* **1** to afflict someone: *plagued by headaches*. **2** to pester someone; to annoy them continually. [14c: from Latin *plaga* blow, disaster or pestilence]

plaice *noun* (*pl* ***plaice***) **1** a flatfish that has a brown upper surface covered with bright orange spots, and is an important food fish. **2** *N Am* any of several related fishes. [13c: from French *plais*]

plaid /plad/ *noun* **1** tartan cloth. **2** a long piece of woollen cloth worn over the shoulder, usu tartan and worn with a kilt as part of Scottish Highland dress. ▸ *adj* with a tartan pattern or in tartan colours: *plaid trousers*. [16c: from Gaelic *plaide* blanket]

Plaid Cymru /plaɪd 'kʌmrɪ/ *noun* in the UK: a nationalist party committed to attaining national status for Wales within the EU. [20c: Welsh *plaid* party + *Cymru* Wales]

plain *adj* **1** all of one colour; unpatterned; undecorated. **2** simple; unsophisticated; without improvement, embellishment or pretensions: *plain food*. **3** obvious; clear. **4** straightforward; direct: *plain language* • *plain dealing*. **5** frank; open. **6** of a person: lacking beauty. **7** sheer; downright: *plain selfishness*. ▸ *noun* **1** a large area of relatively smooth flat land without significant hills or valleys. **2** *knitting* the simpler of two basic stitches, with the wool passed round the front of the needle. See also **purl**[1]. ▸ *adv* utterly; quite: *just plain stupid*. ▪ **plainly** *adv*. ▪ **plainness** *noun*. [13c: French, from Latin *planus* level]

plain chocolate *noun* dark-coloured chocolate made without milk.

plain clothes *plural noun* ordinary clothes worn by police officers on duty, as distinct from a uniform. ▸ *adj* (**plain-clothes** *or* **plain-clothed**) of police officers on duty: wearing ordinary clothes, not uniformed.

plain flour *noun* flour that contains no raising agent.

plain sailing *noun* **1** easy unimpeded progress. **2** *naut* sailing in unobstructed waters.

plainsong *noun* in the medieval Church, and still in the Roman Catholic and some Anglican churches: music for unaccompanied voices, sung in unison. [16c]

plain-spoken *adj* frank to the point of bluntness.

plaint *noun* **1** *poetic* an expression of woe; a lamentation. **2** *law* a written statement of grievance against someone, submitted to a court of law. [13c: from French *plainte*]

plaintiff *noun, law* someone who brings a case against another person in a court of law. See also **defendant**. [14c: from French *plaintif* complaining]

plaintive *adj* mournful-sounding; sad; wistful. ▪ **plaintively** *adv.* [16c: from French *plaintif*]

plait /plat/ *verb* to arrange something (esp hair) by interweaving three or more lengths of it. ▸ *noun* a length of hair or other material interwoven in this way. ▪ **plaited** *adj.* [14c: from French *pleit*]

plan *noun* **1** a thought-out arrangement or method for doing something. **2** (*usu* **plans**) intentions: *What are your plans for today?* **3** a sketch, outline, scheme or set of guidelines. **4** *often in compounds* a large-scale detailed drawing or diagram of a floor of a house, the streets of a town, etc done as though viewed from above: *floor plan* • *street plan.* ▸ *verb* (***planned, planning***) **1** (*also* **plan for sth**) to devise a scheme for it. **2** (*also* **plan for sth**) to make preparations or arrangements for it. **3** *intr* to prepare; to make plans: *plan ahead.* **4** (*also* **plan on sth**) to intend or expect it. **5** to draw up plans for (eg a building); to design. [17c: French, meaning 'ground plan']

Planck's constant *noun, physics* (symbol **h**) a fundamental constant, equal to 6.626×10^{-34} joule seconds, or the energy of a quantum of light divided by its frequency. [20c: named after Max Planck, German physicist]

plane[1] *noun* an **aeroplane**. [20c: short form]

plane[2] *noun* **1** *geom* a flat surface, either real or imaginary, such that a straight line joining any two points lies entirely on it. **2** a level surface. **3** a level or standard: *on a higher intellectual plane.* ▸ *adj* **1** flat; level. **2** having the character of a plane. **3** *maths* lying in one plane: *a plane figure* • *plane geometry.* ▸ *verb, intr* **1** of a boat: to skim over the surface of the water. **2** of a bird: to wheel or soar with the wings motionless. [17c: from Latin *planum* level surface]

plane[3] *noun* a carpenter's tool for smoothing wood by shaving away unevennesses. ▸ *verb* (*also* **plane sth down**) to smooth (a surface, esp wood) with a plane. ▪ **planer** *noun* a tool or machine for planing. [14c: French, from Latin *planare* to smooth]

plane[4] *noun* a large deciduous tree with thin bark which is shed in large flakes, revealing creamy or pink patches on the trunk. Also called **plane tree**. [14c: French, from Latin *platanus*]

plane angle *noun, geom* the two-dimensional angle formed by two lines in a plane figure (see **plane[2]** *adj* sense 3) such as a polygon.

planet *noun* **1** *astron* **a** a celestial body, in orbit around the Sun or another star; **b** one of nine such bodies, Mercury, Venus, Earth, Mars, Jupiter, Saturn, Uranus, Neptune and Pluto, that revolve around the Sun in the solar system. Also called **major planet**. [13c: from French *planète*]

planetarium *noun* (***planetaria*** *or* ***planetariums***) **1** a special projector by means of which the positions and movements of stars and planets can be projected on to a hemispherical domed ceiling in order to simulate the appearance of the night sky to an audience seated below. **2** the building that houses such a projector. [20c: from Latin *planetarius* planetary]

planetary *adj* **1** *astron* **a** relating to or resembling a planet; **b** consisting of or produced by planets; **c** revolving in an orbit. **2** *astrol* under the influence of a planet. **3** erratic.

planetoid *noun, astron* a **minor planet**. [19c]

plangent *adj* of a sound: deep, ringing and mournful. ▪ **plangency** *noun.* ▪ **plangently** *adv.* [19c: from Latin *plangere* to beat or to lament aloud]

planing *present participle of* **plane[2]**, **plane[3]**

plank *noun* **1** a long flat piece of timber thicker than a board. **2** any of the policies forming the platform or programme of a political party. ▸ *verb* to fit or cover something with planks. [14c: from French *planche*]

planking *noun* planks, or a surface, etc constructed of them.

plankton *noun, biol* microscopic animals and plants that passively float or drift with the current in the surface waters of seas and lakes. ▪ **planktonic** *adj.* [19c: from Greek *planktos* wandering]

planner *noun* **1** someone who draws up plans or designs: *a town planner.* **2** a wall calendar showing the whole year, on which holidays, etc can be marked.

planning permission *noun, Brit* permission required from a local authority to erect or convert a building or to change the use of a building or piece of land.

plant *noun* **1** any living organism that is capable of manufacturing carbohydrates by the process of photosynthesis and that typically possesses cell walls containing cellulose. **2** a relatively small organism of this type, eg a herb or shrub as opposed to a tree. **3** the buildings, equipment and machinery used in the manufacturing or production industries, eg a factory, a power station, etc. **4** *informal* something deliberately placed for others to find and be misled by. **5** *informal* a spy placed in an organization in order to gain information, etc. ▸ *verb* **1** to put (seeds or plants) into the ground to grow. **2** (*often* **plant sth out**) to put plants or seeds into (ground, a garden, bed, etc). **3** to introduce (an idea, doubt, etc) into someone's mind. **4** to place something firmly. **5** (*usu* **plant sth on sb**) to give them (a kiss or blow). **6** to post someone as a spy in an office, factory, etc. **7** *informal* to place something deliberately so as to mislead the finder, esp as a means of incriminating an innocent person. [Anglo-Saxon: from Latin *planta* a shoot or sprig]

plantain *noun* **1** a plant belonging to the banana family, widely cultivated for its edible fruit. **2** the green-skinned banana-like edible fruit of this plant, which can be cooked and eaten as a vegetable. [16c: from Spanish *plátano*]

plantation *noun* **1** an estate, esp in the tropics, that specializes in the large-scale production of a single cash crop, eg tea, coffee, cotton or rubber. **2** an area of land planted with a certain kind of tree for commercial purposes: *a conifer plantation.* **3** *hist* a colony. [15c: from Latin *plantatio* a planting]

planter *noun* **1** the owner or manager of a plantation. **2** a device for planting bulbs, etc. **3** a container for house plants.

plaque *noun* **1** a commemorative inscribed tablet fixed to or set into a wall. **2** *dentistry* a thin layer of food debris, bacteria and calcium salts that forms on the surface of teeth and may cause tooth decay. [19c: French]

plasma *noun* **1** *physiol* the colourless liquid component of blood or lymph, in which the blood cells are suspended. **2** *physics* a gas that has been heated to a very high temperature so that most of its atoms or molecules are broken down into free electrons and positive ions. **3** *geol* a bright green **chalcedony**. [18c: Latin]

plasma membrane see **membrane** (sense 2)

plasma screen *or* **plasma display** *noun* a type of screen display for computers, in which electronic signals form illuminated characters on a flat screen.

plaster *noun* **1** a material consisting of lime, sand and water that is applied to walls when soft and dries to form a hard smooth surface. *as adj*: *a plaster wall.* **2** a strip of material, usu with a lint pad and an adhesive backing, that is used for covering and protecting small wounds. Also called **sticking plaster**. **3 plaster of Paris**. ▸ *verb* **1** to apply plaster to (walls, etc). **2** (*usu* **plaster sth with** *or* **on sth**) *informal* to coat or spread thickly. **3** to fix something with some wet or sticky substance: *hair plastered to his skull.* **4** (*often* **plaster sth with sth**) to cover it liberally. ▪ **plasterer** *noun*. ▪ **plastering** *noun*. [Anglo-Saxon: from French *plastre*]

plasterboard *noun* a material consisting of hardened plaster faced on both sides with paper or thin board, used to form or line interior walls.

plaster cast *noun* **1** a copy of an object, eg a sculpture, obtained by pouring a mixture of **plaster of Paris** and water into a mould formed from that object. **2** a covering of plaster of Paris for a broken limb, etc.

plastered *adj* **1** covered with plaster. **2** *informal* drunk; intoxicated.

plaster of Paris *noun* a white powder consisting of a hydrated form of calcium sulphate (**gypsum**), mixed with water to make a paste that sets hard, used for sculpting and for making casts for broken limbs. [15c]

plastic *noun* **1** any of a large number of synthetic materials that can be moulded by heat and/or pressure into a rigid or semi-rigid shape. **2** *informal* a credit card, or credit cards collectively: *Can I pay with plastic?* ▸ *adj* **1** made of plastic. **2** easily moulded or shaped; pliant. **3** easily influenced. **4** *derog* artificial; lacking genuine substance. **5** of money: in the form of, or funded by, a credit card. **6** relating to sculpture and modelling. ▪ **plasticity** *noun*. [17c: from Greek *plastikos* moulded]

plastic arts *plural noun* **a** the art of modelling or shaping in three dimensions, such as ceramics or sculpture; **b** art which is or appears to be three-dimensional.

plastic bullet *noun* a solid plastic cylinder fired by the police to disperse riots, etc.

plastic explosive *noun* an explosive substance that can be moulded by hand, eg Semtex. [20c]

plasticizer *or* **-iser** *noun, chem* an organic compound that is added to a rigid polymer in order to make it flexible and so more easily workable. ▪ **plasticize** *or* **-ise** *verb*. [20c]

plastic surgery *noun, med* the branch of surgery concerned with the repair or reconstruction of deformed or damaged tissue or body parts, the replacement of missing parts, and **cosmetic surgery**. ▪ **plastic surgeon** *noun*.

plate *noun* **1** *also in compounds* a shallow dish, esp one made of earthenware or porcelain, for serving food on: *side plate* • *dinner plate.* **2** **a** a **plateful** (sense 1); **b** a portion served on a plate. **3** (*also* **collection plate**) a shallow vessel in which to take the collection in church. **4** a sheet of metal, glass or other rigid material. **5** *often in compounds* a flat piece of metal, plastic, etc inscribed with a name, etc: *nameplate* • *bookplate.* **6** gold and silver vessels or cutlery. **7** **a** a gold or silver cup as the prize in a horse race, etc; **b** a race or contest for such a prize. **8** a thin coating of gold, silver or tin applied to a base metal. Also called **plating**. **9** an illustration on glossy paper in a book. **10** *photog* a sheet of glass prepared with a light-sensitive coating for receiving an image. **11** **a** a sheet of metal with an image engraved on it; **b** a print taken from one of these. **12** a surface set up with type ready for printing. **13** **a** a rigid plastic fitting to which false teeth are attached; **b** a denture. **14** *geol* any of the rigid sections that make up the Earth's crust. See also **plate tectonics**. **15** *anatomy* a thin flat piece of bone or horn. **16** *baseball* a five-sided white slab at the home base. ▸ *verb* **1** to coat (a base metal) with a thin layer of a precious one. **2** to cover something with metal plates. ▪ **plateful** *noun*. [13c: from French]

IDIOMS **hand** *or* **give sb sth on a plate** *informal* to present them with it without their having to make the least effort. **have a lot** *or* **much on one's plate** *informal* to have a great deal of work, commitments, etc.

plateau /ˈplatoʊ/ *noun* (***plateaux*** /-toʊ/ *or* ***plateaus*** /-toʊz/) **1** *geog* an extensive area of relatively flat high land, usu bounded by steep sides. **2** *econ* a stable unvarying condition of prices, etc after a rise: *The production rate reached a plateau in August.* ▸ *verb, intr* (*sometimes* **plateau out**) to reach a level; to even out. [18c: from French *platel* something flat]

plated *adj* **1** covered with plates of metal. **2** *usu in compounds* covered with a coating of another metal, esp gold or silver.

plateful *noun* **1** the amount a plate can hold. **2** (*usu* **platefuls**) *informal* a great deal; a lot.

plate glass *noun* a high-quality form of glass that has been ground and polished to remove defects, used in shop windows, mirrors, etc.

platelayer *noun* someone who lays and repairs railway lines.

platelet *noun, physiol* in mammalian blood: any of the small disc-shaped cell fragments that are responsible for starting the formation of a blood clot when bleeding occurs. [19c]

platen *noun* **1** in some printing-presses: a plate that pushes the paper against the type. **2** the roller of a typewriter. [15c: from French *platine* metal plate]

plate tectonics *singular noun, geol* a geological theory according to which the Earth's crust is composed of a small number of large plates of solid rock, whose movements in relation to each other are responsible for continental drift. See also **tectonics**. [20c]

platform *noun* **1** a raised floor for speakers, performers, etc. **2** the raised walkway alongside the track at a railway station, giving access to trains. **3** *often in compounds* a floating installation moored to the sea bed, for oil-drilling, marine research, etc: *oil platform* • *production platform.* **4** an open step at the back of some buses, esp older ones, for passengers getting on or off. **5** a very thick rigid sole for a shoe, fashionable particularly in the 1970s. *as adj*: *platform shoes.* **6** the publicly declared principles and intentions of a political party, forming the basis of its policies. [16c: from French *platte forme* flat figure]

plating see **plate** (*noun* sense 8)

platinum *noun, chem* (symbol **Pt**) a silvery-white precious metallic element that does not tarnish or corrode, used to make jewellery, coins, electrical contacts, etc. [19c: Latin]

platinum-blonde *or* **platinum-blond** *adj* of hair: having a silvery fairness. [20c]

platitude *noun* an empty, unoriginal or redundant comment, esp one made as though it were important. ▪ **platitudinous** *adj*. [19c: French, meaning 'flatness', from *plat* flat]

Platonic *adj* **1** belonging or relating to the Greek philosopher Plato. **2** (*usu* **platonic**) of human love: not involving sexual relations. ▪ **platonically** *adv*. [16c]

platoon *noun* **1** *military* a subdivision of a **company**. **2** a squad of people acting in co-operation. [17c: from French *peloton*, diminutive of *pelote* ball]

platter *noun* **1** a large flat dish. **2** *N Am informal* a **record** (*noun* sense 4). [14c: from French *plater*]

platypus *noun* an Australian egg-laying amphibious mammal with dense brown fur, a long flattened toothless snout, webbed feet and a broad flat tail. Also called **duck-billed platypus**. [18c: Latin]

plaudit *noun* (*usu* **plaudits**) a commendation; an expression of praise. [17c: from Latin *plaudite* applaud]

plausible *adj* **1** of an explanation, etc: credible, reasonable or likely. **2** of a person: characterized by having a pleasant and persuasive manner; smooth-tongued or glib. ▪ **plausibility** *noun*. ▪ **plausibly** *adv*. [16c: from Latin *plausibilis* deserving applause]

play *verb* **1** *intr* esp of children: to spend time in recreation, eg dancing about, kicking a ball around, doing things in make-believe, generally having fun, etc. **2** *intr* to pretend for fun; to behave without seriousness. **3** (*also* **play at sth**) to take part in (a recreative pursuit, game, sport, match, round, etc): *We played rounders* • *played at rounders*. **4** (*also* **play against sb**) to compete against them in a game or sport: *St Johnstone played Aberdeen last week*. **5** (**play with sth**) to contemplate (an idea, plan, etc). **6** *intr, informal* to co-operate: *He refuses to play*. **7** *sport* to include someone as a team member: *playing McGuire in goal*. **8** *sport* to hit or kick (the ball), deliver (a shot), etc in a sport. **9** *cards* to use (a card) in the course of a game: *played the three of clubs*. **10** to speculate or gamble on (the stock exchange, etc): *playing the market*. **11** *tr & intr* **a** to act or behave in a certain way: *play it cool* • *not playing fair*; **b** to pretend to be someone or something: *play the dumb blonde*. **12** to act (a particular role): *play host to the delegates*. **13** (*usu* **play in sth**) *tr & intr* to perform a role in (a play): *played Oliver in the school play*. **14** *tr & intr* esp of a pop group: to perform in (a particular place or venue). **15** *intr* of a film, play, etc: to be shown or performed publicly: *playing all next week*. **16** *music* **a** to perform (a specified type of music) on an instrument: *plays jazz on the saxophone*; **b** to perform on (an instrument): *plays the sax*. **17** to turn on (a radio, a tape-recording, etc). **18** *intr* **a** of recorded music, etc: to be heard from a radio, etc; **b** of a radio, etc: to produce sound. **19** *intr* of a fountain: to be in operation. **20** *angling* to allow (a fish) to tire itself by its struggles to get away. ► *noun* **1** recreation; playing games for fun and amusement: *children at play*. **2** the playing of a game, performance in a sport, etc: *rain stopped play*. **3** *informal* behaviour; conduct: *fair play* • *foul play*. **4** a dramatic piece for the stage or a performance of it. **5** fun; jest: *said in play*. **6** range; scope: *give full play to the imagination*. **7** freedom of movement; looseness: *too much play in the steering*. **8** action or interaction: *play of sunlight on water*. **9** use: *bring all one's cunning into play*. ▪ **playable** *adj*. [Anglo-Saxon *plegan*]

IDIOMS **make a play for sth** to try to get (eg someone's attention). **make great play of sth** to emphasize it or stress its importance. **play ball** *informal* to co-operate. **play for time** to delay action or decision in the hope or belief that conditions will become more favourable later. **play hard to get** to make a show of unwillingness to co-operate or lack of interest, with a view to strengthening one's position. **play into the hands of sb** to act so as to give, usu unintentionally, an advantage to them. **play it by ear** to improvise a plan of action to meet the situation as it develops. **play one person off against another** to set them in rivalry, esp for one's own advantage. **play safe** to take no risks. **play with fire** to take foolish risks.

PHRASAL VERBS **play about** *or* **around with sb** to behave irresponsibly towards them, their affections, etc. **play about** *or* **around with sth** to fiddle or meddle with it. **play sb along** to manipulate them, usu for one's own advantage. **play along with sb** to co-operate with them for the time being. **play sth back** to play (a film or sound recording) through immediately after making it. See also **playback**. **play sth down** to represent it as unimportant; to minimize, make light of or discount it. **play off 1** to replay a match, etc after a draw. **2** *golf* to play from the tee. See also **play-off**. **play on sth 1** to exploit (someone's fears, feelings, sympathies, etc) for one's own benefit. **2** to make a pun on it: *played on the two meanings of 'batter'*. **play up 1** *informal* to behave unco-operatively. **2** *informal* to cause one pain or discomfort: *His stomach is playing up again*. **3** *informal* of a machine, etc: to function faultily. **4** to try one's hardest in a game, match, etc. **play sth up** to highlight it or give prominence to it. **play up to sb** to flatter them; to ingratiate oneself with them.

playa /'plɑːjə/ *noun, geog* a basin which becomes a shallow lake after heavy rainfall and dries out again in hot weather. [19c: Spanish, meaning 'shore' or 'beach']

play-act *verb, intr* to behave in an insincere fashion, disguising one's true feelings or intentions. [19c]

playback *noun* a playing back of a sound recording or film. See also **play sth back** at **play**.

playboy *noun* a man of wealth, leisure and frivolous lifestyle.

player *noun* **1** someone who plays. **2** someone who participates in a game or sport, particularly as their profession. **3** *informal* a participant in a particular activity, esp a powerful one: *a major player in the Mafia scene*. **4** a performer on a musical instrument: *a guitar player*. **5** *old use* an actor.

playful *adj* **1** full of fun; frisky. **2** of a remark, etc: humorous. ▪ **playfully** *adv*. ▪ **playfulness** *noun*.

playground *noun* an area for children's recreation, esp one that is part of a school's grounds.

playgroup *noun* an organized group of preschool children that meets for regular supervised play.

playhouse *noun, old use* a theatre.

playing-card *noun* a rectangular card belonging to a **pack**[1] (*noun* sense 3) used in card games. See also **ace, court card**.

playing field *noun* a grassy outdoor area prepared and marked out for playing games on. See also **level playing field**.

playmate *noun* a companion to play with.

play-off *noun* a match or game played to resolve a draw or other undecided contest. See also **play off** at **play**.

play on words *noun* **1** a pun. **2** punning.

playpen *noun* a collapsible frame that when erected forms an enclosure inside which a baby may safely play.

playschool *noun* a **playgroup**, or a school for children between the ages of two and five.

plaything *noun* a toy, or a person or thing treated as if they were a toy.

playtime *noun* a period for recreation, esp a set period for playing out of doors in a school timetable.

playwright *noun* an author of plays.

plaza *noun* a large public square or market place, esp one in a Spanish town. [17c: Spanish]

PLC *or* **plc** *abbrev* public limited company.

plea *noun* **1** an earnest appeal. **2** *law* a statement made in a court of law by or on behalf of the defendant. [13c: from French *plaid* agreement or decision]

plead *verb* (***pleaded*** or *esp N Am & Scot* ***pled***) **1** (*usu* **plead with sb for sth**) to appeal earnestly to them for it: *pleading for mercy.* **2** *intr* of an accused person: to state in a court of law that one is guilty or not guilty: *He pleaded not guilty.* **3** (*also* **plead for sth**) to argue in defence of it: *plead someone's case.* **4** to give something as an excuse: *plead ignorance.* [13c: from French *plaidier*]

pleading *adj* appealing earnestly; imploring. ▸ *noun, law* the act of putting forward or conducting a plea.

pleadings *plural noun, law* the formal statements submitted by defendant and plaintiff in a lawsuit.

pleasant *adj* **1** giving pleasure; enjoyable; agreeable. **2** of a person: friendly; affable. ▪ **pleasantly** *adv.* [14c: from French *plaisant*]

pleasantry *noun* (***-ies***) **1** a remark made for the sake of politeness or friendliness. **2** humour; teasing.

please *verb* **1** *tr & intr* to give satisfaction, pleasure or enjoyment; to be agreeable to someone. **2** (with *it* as subject) *formal* to be the inclination of someone or something: *if it should please you to join us.* **3** *tr & intr* to choose; to like: *Do as you please.* ▸ *adv, exclam* used politely to accompany a request, order, acceptance of an offer, protest, a call for attention, etc. ▪ **pleased** *adj.* ▪ **pleasing** *adj.* [14c: from French *plaisir* to please]

IDIOMS **please oneself** to do as one likes.

pleasurable *adj* enjoyable; pleasant.

pleasure *noun* **1** a feeling of enjoyment or satisfaction. **2** a source of such a feeling: *have the pleasure of your company.* **3** one's will, desire, wish, preference or inclination. **4** recreation; enjoyment. *as adj*: *a pleasure trip.* **5** gratification of a sensual kind: *pleasure and pain.* ▸ *verb, old use* **1** to give pleasure to someone. **2** (*usu* **pleasure in sth**) to take pleasure in it. [14c: from French *plaisir*]

IDIOMS **with pleasure** gladly; willingly; of course.

pleat *noun* a fold sewn or pressed into cloth, etc. ▸ *verb* to make pleats in (cloth, etc). [14c: a variant of **plait**]

pleb *noun, derog* someone who has coarse or vulgar tastes, manners or habits. ▪ **plebby** *adj* (***-ier, -iest***). [19c: a shortening of **plebeian**]

plebeian /plə'biən/ *noun* **1** a member of the common people, esp of ancient Rome. **2** *derog* someone who lacks refinement or culture. ▸ *adj* **1** referring or belonging to the common people. **2** *derog* coarse; vulgar; unrefined. [16c: from Latin *plebeius*, from *plebs* the people]

plebiscite /'plɛbɪsaɪt/ *noun* a vote of all the electors, taken to decide a matter of public importance; a referendum. ▪ **plebiscitary** /-'bɪsɪtrɪ/ *adj.* [16c: from Latin *plebiscitum* a decree of the plebs]

plectrum *noun* (***plectrums*** *or* ***plectra***) a small flat implement of metal, plastic, horn, etc used for plucking the strings of a guitar. [17c: Latin]

pled *a past tense, past participle of* **plead**.

pledge *noun* **1** a solemn promise. **2** something left as security with someone to whom one owes money, etc. **3** something put into pawn. **4** a token or symbol. ▸ *verb* **1** to promise (money, loyalty, etc) to someone. **2** to bind or commit (oneself, etc). **3** to offer or give something as a pledge or guarantee. [14c: from French *plege*]

Pleiocene see **Pliocene**

Pleistocene /'plaɪstoʊsiːn/ *adj, geol* denoting the first epoch of the Quaternary period, which contains the greatest proportion of fossil molluscs of living species and during which modern man evolved. [19c: from Greek *pleistos* most + *kainos* new]

plenary *adj* **1** full; complete: *plenary powers.* **2** of a meeting, assembly, council, etc: to be attended by all members, delegates, etc. Compare **plenum**. [16c: from Latin *plenarius*, from *plenus* full]

plenipotentiary *adj* entrusted with, or conveying, full authority to act on behalf of one's government or other organization. ▸ *noun* (***-ies***) someone, eg an ambassador, invested with such authority. [17c: from Latin *plenus* full + *potentia* power]

plenitude *noun* **1** abundance; profusion. **2** completeness; fullness. [15c: from Latin *plenitudo*]

plenteous *adj, literary* plentiful; abundant. [14c: from French *plentif*]

plentiful *adj* in good supply; copious; abundant. ▪ **plentifully** *adv.* [15c: from **plenty**]

plenty *noun* **1** (*often* **plenty of sth**) a lot: *plenty of folk would agree.* **2** wealth or sufficiency; a sufficient amount: *in times of plenty.* ▸ *pronoun* **1** enough, or more than enough: *That's plenty, thank you.* **2** a lot; many: *I'm sure plenty would agree with me* (ie plenty of folk; many people). ▸ *adv, informal* fully: *That should be plenty wide enough.* [13c: from French *plente*]

plenum *noun* (***plenums*** *or* ***plena***) **1** a meeting attended by all members. Compare **plenary**. **2** *physics* a space completely filled with matter. Opposite of **vacuum**. [17c: Latin, a shortening of *plenum spatium* full space]

pleonasm /'plɪənazəm/ *noun, grammar, rhetoric* **1** the use of more words than are needed to express something. **2** a superfluous word or words. ▪ **pleonastic** *adj.* [16c: from Greek *pleonasmos* superfluity]

plethora /ˈplɛθərə/ *noun* a large or excessive amount. [16c: Latin]

pleura /ˈplʊərə/ *noun* (***pleurae*** /-riː/) *anatomy* in mammals: the double membrane that covers the lungs and lines the chest cavity. ▪ **pleural** *adj.* [17c: Latin, from Greek *pleuron* side or rib]

pleurisy *noun, pathol, med* inflammation of the pleura. ▪ **pleuritic** *adj.* [14c: from French *pleurisie*]

Plexiglas *noun, US trademark* **Perspex**. [20c]

plexus *noun* (***plexus*** *or* ***plexuses***) *anatomy* a network of nerves or blood vessels, eg the **solar plexus** behind the stomach. [17c: Latin, literally 'weaving']

pliable *adj* **1** easily bent; flexible. **2** adaptable or alterable. **3** easily persuaded or influenced. ▪ **pliability** *noun.* [15c: French, from *plier* to fold or bend]

pliant *adj* **1** bending easily; pliable, flexible or supple. **2** easily influenced. ▪ **pliancy** *noun.* [14c: French, from *plier* to fold or bend]

pliers *plural noun* a hinged tool with jaws for gripping small objects, bending or cutting wire, etc. [16c: from **ply**[2]]

plies see **ply**[1], **ply**[2]

plight[1] *noun* a danger, difficulty or situation of hardship that one finds oneself in; a predicament. [14c: from French *pleit*]

plight[2] *verb, old use* to promise something solemnly; to pledge. [Anglo-Saxon *pliht* peril or risk]

IDIOMS **plight one's troth** to pledge oneself in marriage.

plimsoll *or* **plimsole** *noun, old use* a light rubber-soled canvas shoe worn for gymnastics, etc. Also called **gym shoe**. [20c: from the resemblance of the line of the sole to the **Plimsoll line**]

Plimsoll line *or* **Plimsoll mark** *noun* any of several lines painted round a ship's hull showing, for different conditions, the depth to which it may be safely and legally immersed when loaded. [19c: required by the Merchant Shipping Act of 1876, put forward by S. Plimsoll]

plinth *noun* **1** *archit* a square block serving as the base of a column, pillar, etc. **2** a base or pedestal for a statue or other sculpture, or for a vase. [17c: from Latin *plinthus*]

Pliocene *or* **Pleiocene** /ˈplaɪousiːn/ *adj, geol* the last epoch of the Tertiary period, during which the climate became cooler, many mammals became extinct and primates that walked upright appeared. [19c: from Greek *pleion* more + *kainos* new]

PLO *abbrev* Palestine Liberation Organization, an organization of Palestinian groups opposed to Israel.

plod *verb* (***plodded, plodding***) *intr* **1** to walk slowly with a heavy tread. **2** to work slowly, methodically and thoroughly, if without inspiration. ▪ **plodder** *noun.* [16c: an imitation of the sound of a heavy tread]

ploidy *noun* (***-ies***) *biol* the number of complete chromosome sets present in a cell or living organism. [20c]

plonk[1] *informal, noun* the resounding thud made by a heavy object falling. ▸ *verb* **1** to put or place something with a thud or with finality. **2** *intr* to place oneself or to fall with a plonk. ▸ *adv* with a thud: *landed plonk beside her.* [19c: imitating the sound]

plonk[2] *noun, informal* cheap, undistinguished wine. [20c: orig Australian slang]

plonker *noun, slang* a foolish person. [20c]

plop *noun* the sound of a small object dropping into water without a splash. ▸ *verb* (***plopped, plopping***) *tr & intr* to fall or drop with this sound. ▸ *adv* with a plop. [19c: imitating the sound]

plosive *phonetics, adj* of a consonant: made by the sudden release of breath after stoppage. ▸ *noun* a plosive consonant or sound, such as /p/, /t/, /k/, etc. [19c: a shortening of **explosive**]

plot[1] *noun* **1** a secret plan, esp one laid jointly with others, for contriving something illegal or evil; a conspiracy. **2** the story or scheme of a play, film, novel, etc. ▸ *verb* (***plotted, plotting***) **1** *tr & intr* to plan something (esp something illegal or evil), usu with others. **2** to make a plan of something; to mark the course or progress of something. **3** *maths* to mark (a series of individual points) on a graph, or to draw a curve through them. ▪ **plotless** *adj.* ▪ **plotter** *noun.* [16c: from **plot**[2], influenced by French *complot* conspiracy]

plot[2] *noun, often in compounds* a piece of ground for any of various uses: *a vegetable plot*. [Anglo-Saxon]

plough *or* (*N Am*) **plow** /plaʊ/ *noun* **1** a bladed farm implement used to turn over the surface of the soil and bury stubble, weeds, etc, in preparation for the cultivation of a crop. **2** any similar implement, esp a **snowplough**. **3** (**the Plough**) *astron* the seven brightest stars in the constellation Ursa Major. ▸ *verb* **1** (*also* **plough sth up**) to till or turn over (soil, land, etc) with a plough. **2** *intr* to make a furrow or to turn over the surface of the soil with a plough. **3** *intr* (*usu* **plough through sth**) **a** to move through it with a ploughing action; **b** *informal* to make steady but laborious progress with it. **4** *intr* (*usu* **plough into sth**) *informal* of a vehicle or its driver: to crash into it at speed. [Anglo-Saxon *plog* or *ploh*]

PHRASAL VERBS **plough on** *informal* to continue with something although progress is laborious.

ploughman *or* (*N Am*) **plowman** *noun* someone who steers a plough.

ploughman's lunch *noun* a cold meal of bread, cheese, pickle and sometimes meat.

ploughshare *or* (*N Am*) **plowshare** *noun* a blade of a plough. Also called **share**. [14c]

plover *noun* a wading bird with boldly patterned plumage and a short straight bill. [14c: from French *plovier* rain bird]

plow the *N Am* spelling of **plough**

ploy *noun* a stratagem, dodge or manoeuvre to gain an advantage.

PLS *abbrev* please.

pluck *verb* **1** to pull the feathers off (a bird) before cooking it. **2** to pick (flowers or fruit) from a plant or tree. **3** (*often* **pluck sth out**) to remove it by pulling. **4** to shape (the eyebrows) by removing hairs from them. **5** (*often* **pluck at sth**) to pull or tug it. **6** to sound (the strings of a violin, etc) using the fingers or a plectrum. ▸ *noun* **1** courage; guts. **2** a little tug. **3** the heart, liver and lungs of an animal. [Anglo-Saxon *pluccian* to pluck or tear]

IDIOMS **pluck up courage** to strengthen one's resolve for a difficult undertaking, etc.

plucky *adj* (***-ier, -iest***) *informal* courageous; spirited. ▪ **pluckily** *adv.* ▪ **pluckiness** *noun.*

plug *noun* **1** a piece of rubber, plastic, etc shaped to fit a hole as a stopper, eg in a bath or sink. **2** *often in compounds* any device or piece of material for a similar purpose: *earplugs*. **3 a** the plastic or rubber device with metal pins, fitted to the end of the flex of an electrical apparatus, that is pushed into a socket to connect with the power supply; **b** *loosely* the socket or power point: *switch it off at the plug*. **4** *informal* a piece of favourable publicity given to a product, programme, etc, eg on television. **5** a **spark plug**. **6** an accumulation of solidified magma which fills the vent of a volcano. Also called **volcanic plug**. **7** a lump of tobacco for chewing. ▸ *verb* (***plugged, plugging***) **1** (*often* **plug sth up**) to stop or block up (a hole, etc) with something. **2** *informal* to give favourable publicity to (a product, programme, etc), esp repeatedly: *plugged her new book*. **3** *intr* (*usu* **plug away** *or* **along**) *informal* to work or progress steadily. **4** *slang* to shoot someone with a gun. ▪ **plugger** *noun*. [17c: from Dutch *plugge* a bung or peg]

PHRASAL VERBS **plug sth in** to connect (an electrical appliance) to the power supply by an electrical plug.

plug-and-play *adj, comput* of a component, software, etc: able to be used immediately without any complex installation process.

plughole *noun* the hole in a bath or sink through which water flows into the waste-pipe.

plug-in *noun, comput* an additional piece of software that extends an existing one in specific ways.

plug-ugly *informal, adj, derog* of a person: very ugly. ▸ *noun* (***-ies***) *US* a hoodlum; a ruffian. [19c]

plum *noun* **1** a shrub or small tree, cultivated in temperate regions for its edible fruit, or for its ornamental flowers or foliage. **2** the smooth-skinned red, purple, green or yellow fruit of this tree, which has a hard central stone surrounded by sweet juicy flesh, eg damson, greengage. **3** *in compounds* a raisin used in cakes, etc: *plum pudding*. **4** *informal* something especially valued or sought. **5** a deep dark red colour. ▸ *adj* **1** dark red in colour. **2** highly sought-after: *a plum job*. [Anglo-Saxon *plume*]

plumage *noun* a bird's feathers, esp with regard to colour. [15c: French, from *plume* feather]

plumb *noun* a lead weight, usu suspended from a line, used for measuring water depth or for testing a wall, etc for perpendicularity. ▸ *adj* straight, vertical or perpendicular. ▸ *adv* **1** in a straight, vertical or perpendicular way: *drops plumb to the sea bed*. **2** *informal* exactly: *plumb in the middle*. **3** *N Am, esp US informal* utterly: *The guy is plumb crazy*. ▸ *verb* **1** to measure, test, or adjust something using a plumb. **2** to penetrate, probe or understand (a mystery, etc). **3** (*usu* **plumb sth in**) to connect (a water-using appliance) to the water supply or waste pipe. [13c: from French *plomb*]

IDIOMS **out of plumb** not vertical. **plumb the depths of sth** to experience the worst extreme of (a bad feeling, etc): *plumbed the depths of misery*.

plumbago *noun, chem* another name for **graphite**. [18c: Latin, from Pliny's translation of Greek *molybdaina* lead or lead ore]

plumber *noun* someone who fits and repairs water pipes, and water- or gas-using appliances. [14c: from French *plummier*]

plumbing *noun* **1** the system of water and gas pipes in a building, etc. **2** the work of a plumber.

plumbline *noun* a line with a **plumb** attached, used for measuring depth or testing for verticality.

plume *noun* **1** a conspicuous feather of a bird. **2** such a feather, or bunch of feathers, worn as an ornament or crest, represented in a coat of arms, etc. **3** a curling column (of smoke etc). ▸ *verb* **1** of a bird: to clean or preen (itself or its feathers). **2** to decorate with plumes. **3** (*usu* **plume oneself on sth**) to pride or congratulate oneself on it, usu on something trivial. ▪ **plumy** *adj* (***-ier, -iest***). [14c: French]

plummet *verb* (***plummeted, plummeting***) *intr* to fall or drop rapidly; to plunge or hurtle downwards. ▸ *noun* the weight on a plumbline or fishing line. [14c: from French *plommet* ball of lead]

plummy *adj* (***-ier, -iest***) **1** *informal* of a job, etc: desirable; worth having; choice. **2** *derog* of a voice: affectedly or excessively rich and deep. **3** full of plums.

plump[1] *adj* full, rounded or chubby; not unattractively fat. ▸ *verb* (*often* **plump sth up**) to shake (cushions or pillows) to give them their full soft bulk. ▪ **plumply** *adv*. ▪ **plumpness** *noun*. [16c: from Dutch *plomp* blunt]

plump[2] *informal verb* **1** *tr & intr* (*sometimes* **plump down** *or* **plump sth down**) to put down, drop, fall, or sit heavily. **2** *intr* (**plump for sth** *or* **sb**) to decide on or choose it or them; to make a decision in its or their favour. ▸ *noun* a sudden heavy fall or the sound this makes. ▸ *adv* **1** suddenly; with a plump. **2** in a blunt or direct way. ▸ *adj* blunt or direct. [14c: imitating the sound made]

plunder *verb, tr & intr* to steal (valuable goods) or loot (a place), esp with open force during a war; to rob or ransack. ▸ *noun* the goods plundered; loot; booty. ▪ **plunderer** *noun*. [17c: from Dutch *plunderen* to rob of household goods]

plunge *verb* **1** *intr* (*usu* **plunge in** *or* **into sth**) to dive, throw oneself, fall or rush headlong in or into it. **2** *intr* (*usu* **plunge in** *or* **into sth**) to involve oneself rapidly and enthusiastically. **3** to thrust or push something. **4** *tr & intr* to put something or someone into a particular state or condition: *plunged the town into darkness*. **5** to dip something briefly into water or other liquid. **6** *intr* to dip steeply: *The ship plunged and rose*. ▸ *noun* **1** an act of plunging; a dive. **2** *informal* a dip or swim. [14c: from French *plungier*]

IDIOMS **take the plunge** *informal* to commit oneself finally; to take an irreversible decision.

plunger *noun* a rubber suction cup at the end of a long handle, used to clear blocked drains, etc.

plunk *verb* **1** to pluck (the strings of a banjo, etc); to twang. **2** (*often* **plunk sth down**) to drop it, esp suddenly. ▸ *noun* the act of plunking or the sound this makes. [19c: imitating the sound]

pluperfect *grammar, adj* of the tense of a verb: formed in English by the auxiliary verb *had* and a past **participle**, and referring to an action already accomplished at the time of a past action being referred to, as in *They had often gone there before, but this time they lost their way*. ▸ *noun* **a** the pluperfect tense; **b** a verb in the pluperfect tense. [16c: contracted from Latin *plus quam perfectum* more than perfect]

plural *adj* **1** *grammar* denoting or referring to two or more people, things, etc as opposed to only one. **2** consisting of more than one, or of different kinds. ▸ *noun, grammar* a word or form of a word expressing the idea or involvement of two or more people, things, etc. Compare **singular**. ▪ **pluralize** *or* **-ise** *verb*. [14c: from French *plurel*]

pluralism *noun* **1** the existence within a society of a variety of ethnic, cultural and religious groups. **2** the holding of more than one post, esp in the Church. ▪ **pluralist** *noun, adj.* ▪ **pluralistic** *adj.*

plurality *noun* (***-ies***) **1** the state or condition of being plural. **2 pluralism** (sense 2). **3** a large number or variety.

plus *prep* **1** *maths* with the addition of (a specified number): *2 plus 5 equals 7.* **2** in combination with something; with the added factor of (a specified thing): *Bad luck, plus his own obstinacy, cost him his job.* ▸ *adv* after a specified amount: with something more besides: *Helen earns £20,000 plus.* ▸ *adj* **1** denoting the symbol '+': *the plus sign.* **2** mathematically positive; above zero: *plus 3.* **3** advantageous: *a plus factor.* **4** in grades: denoting a slightly higher mark than the letter alone: *B plus.* **5** *physics, elec* electrically positive. ▸ *noun* **1** (*also* **plus sign**) the symbol '+', denoting addition or positive value. **2** *informal* something positive or good; a bonus, advantage, surplus, or extra: *The free crèche was a definite plus.* ▸ *conj, informal* in addition to the fact that. In all senses opposite of **minus**. [17c: Latin, meaning 'more']

plus fours *plural noun* loose breeches gathered below the knee, still occasionally used as golfing wear. [20c: from **plus** + **four**, because four extra inches of fabric are required]

plush *noun* a fabric with a long velvety pile. ▸ *adj* **1** made of plush. **2** *informal* plushy. [16c: from French *pluche*]

plushy *adj* (***-ier, -iest***) *informal* luxurious, opulent, stylish or costly. [20c in this sense]

Pluto *noun, astron* a remote minor planet of the solar system, beyond Neptune. [20c: named after Pluto, the Greek god of the underworld]

plutocracy *noun* (***-ies***) **1** government or domination by the wealthy. **2** a state governed by the wealthy. **3** an influential group whose power is backed by their wealth. [17c: from Greek *ploutos* wealth + **-cracy**]

plutocrat *noun* **1** a member of a plutocracy. **2** *informal* a wealthy person. ▪ **plutocratic** *adj.*

plutonic *adj, geol* relating to coarse-grained igneous rocks that are formed by the slow crystallization of magma deep within the Earth's crust. [19c: from Greek *Plouton* Pluto, the god of the underworld]

plutonium *noun, chem* (symbol **Pu**) a dense highly poisonous silvery-grey radioactive metallic element, whose isotope **plutonium-239** is used as an energy source for nuclear weapons and some nuclear reactors. [20c: named after the planet Pluto]

pluvial *adj* relating to or characterized by rain; rainy. ▸ *noun, geol* a period of prolonged rainfall. [17c: from Latin *pluvia* rain]

ply[1] *noun* (***plies***) **1** thickness of yarn, rope or wood, measured by the number of strands or layers that compose it. **2** a strand or layer. ▸ *adj in compounds* specifying the number of strands or layers involved: *four-ply wool.* [16c: from French *pli* fold]

ply[2] *verb* (***plies, plied***) **1** (*usu* **ply sb with sth**) to keep supplying them with something or making a repeated, often annoying, onslaught on them: *plied them with drinks • plying me with questions.* **2** *tr & intr* (*often* **ply between one place and another**) to travel a route regularly; to go regularly to and fro between destinations. **3** *dated or literary* to work at (a trade). **4** *dated or literary* to use (a tool, etc): *ply one's needle.* ▪ **plier** *noun.* [14c: from **apply**]

plywood *noun* wood which consists of thin layers glued together, widely used in the construction industry. [20c]

PM *abbrev* **1** Postmaster. **2** Paymaster. **3** Prime Minister.

Pm *symbol, chem* promethium.

p.m., pm, P.M. *or* **PM** *abbrev* **1** post meridiem. **2** post mortem.

PMS *abbrev* premenstrual syndrome.

PMT *abbrev* premenstrual tension.

pneumatic /njʊˈmatɪk/ *adj* **1** relating to air or gases. **2** containing or inflated with compressed air: *pneumatic tyres.* See **tyre**. **3** of a tool or piece of machinery: operated or driven by compressed air: *pneumatic drill.* ▪ **pneumatically** *adv.* [17c: from Latin *pneumaticus*]

pneumonia /njʊˈmoʊnɪə/ *noun, pathol* inflammation of one or more lobes of the lungs, usu as a result of bacterial or viral infection. [17c: Latin, from Greek *pneumon* lung]

PO *abbrev* **1** Personnel Officer. **2** Petty Officer. **3** Pilot Officer. **4** Post Office.

Po *symbol, chem* polonium.

po[1] *noun, informal* a chamberpot. [19c: contracted from French *pot de chambre*]

po[2] *or* **p.o.** *abbrev* postal order.

poach[1] *verb, cookery* **1** to cook (an egg without its shell) in or over boiling water. **2** to simmer (fish) in milk or other liquid. [15c: from French *pocher* to pocket (referring to the egg yolk inside the white)]

poach[2] *verb* **1** *tr & intr* to catch (game or fish) illegally on someone else's property. **2** to steal (ideas, etc). **3** to lure away (personnel at a rival business, etc) to work for one. ▪ **poacher** *noun.* [17c: from French *pocher* to gouge]

pock *noun* **1** a small inflamed area on the skin, containing pus, esp one caused by smallpox. **2** a **pockmark**. [Anglo-Saxon *poc*]

pocket *noun* **1** an extra piece sewn into or on to a garment to form a pouch for carrying things in. **2** any container similarly fitted or attached. **3** *in compounds* small enough to be carried in a pocket; smaller than standard: *pocketbook.* **4** one's financial resources: *well beyond my pocket.* **5** a rock cavity filled with ore. **6** in conditions of air turbulence: a place in the atmosphere where the air pressure drops or rises abruptly. **7** an isolated patch or area of something: *pockets of unemployment.* **8** *billiards, etc* any of the holes, with nets or pouches beneath them, situated around the edges of the table and into which balls are potted. ▸ *adj* small enough to be carried in a pocket; smaller than standard: *a pocket calculator.* Also **pocket-size**. ▸ *verb* **1** to put in one's pocket. **2** *informal* to take something dishonestly; to steal it. **3** *billiards, etc* to drive (a ball) into a pocket. ▪ **pocketful** *noun.* [15c: from French *poquet*]
IDIOMS **in one another's pockets** of two people: in close intimacy with, or dependence on, one another. **in** *or* **out of pocket** having gained, or lost, money on a transaction. **in sb's pocket** influenced or controlled by them. **put one's hand in one's pocket** to be willing to contribute money.

pocketbook *noun* **1** *N Am, esp US* a wallet for money and papers. **2** *N Am, esp US* a woman's strapless handbag or purse. **3** a notebook.

pocket knife *noun* a knife with folding blades. Also called **penknife**.

pocket money *noun* **1** *Brit* a weekly allowance given to children by their parents. **2** money carried for occasional expenses.

pockmark *noun* a small pit or hollow in the skin left by a pock, esp one caused by chickenpox or smallpox. ▪ **pockmarked** *adj.*

pod *noun* **1** *botany* **a** the long dry fruit produced by leguminous plants, eg peas and beans, consisting of a seedcase which splits down both sides to release its seeds; **b** the seedcase itself. **2** *aeronautics* in an aeroplane or space vehicle: a detachable container or housing, eg for an engine. [17c]

podcast *verb, tr & intr* to publish (sound files) on the Internet in a form in which they can be downloaded onto a digital audio player. ▸ *noun* a set of files that is published and downloaded in this way. ▪ **podcaster** *noun.* ▪ **podcasting** *noun.* [21c: from **iPod®**, a brand of digital audio player]

podgy *or* **pudgy** *adj* (**-ier, -iest**) *derog* plump or chubby; short and squat. [19c: from dialect *podge* a short fat person]

podiatry /pɒ'daɪətrɪ/ *noun, chiefly N Am* chiropody. ▪ **podiatrist** *noun.* [20c: from Greek *pous* foot + *iatros* doctor]

podium *noun* (***podiums*** *or* ***podia***) a small platform for a public speaker, orchestra conductor, etc. [18c: Latin, meaning 'an elevated place']

poem *noun* **1** a literary composition, typically, but not necessarily, in verse, often with elevated and/or imaginatively expressed content. **2** an object, scene or creation of inspiring beauty. See also **poetry**. [16c: from Greek *poiema* creation, poem]

poenology see **penology**

poesy *noun* (***-ies***) *old use* poetry. [14c]

poet *or* **poetess** *noun* a male or female writer of poems. [13c: from Latin *poeta*]

poetic *or* **poetical** *adj* **1** relating or suitable to poets or poetry. **2** possessing grace, beauty or inspiration suggestive of poetry. **3** written in verse. ▪ **poetically** *adv.*

poetic justice *noun* an occurrence in which evil is punished or good is rewarded in a fitting way.

poetic licence *noun* a poet's or writer's departure from strict fact or standard grammar, for the sake of effect.

poet laureate *noun* (***poets laureate*** *or* ***poet laureates***) in the UK: an officially appointed court poet, commissioned to produce poems for state occasions.

poetry *noun* (***-ies***) **1** the art of composing poems. **2** poems collectively. **3** poetic quality, feeling, beauty or grace. [14c: from Latin *poetria*, from *poeta* poet]

po-faced *adj, derog informal* **1** wearing a disapproving or solemn expression. **2** narrow-minded. [20c]

pogo stick *noun* a spring-mounted pole with a handlebar and foot rests, on which to bounce. [20c]

pogrom *noun* an organized persecution or massacre of a particular group of people, orig that of Jews in 19c Russia. [20c: Russian, meaning 'destruction']

poignant /'pɔɪnjənt/ *adj* **1** painful to the feelings: a *poignant reminder.* **2** deeply moving; full of pathos. **3** of words or expressions: sharp; penetrating. **4** sharp or pungent in smell or taste. ▪ **poignancy** *noun.* ▪ **poignantly** *adv.* [14c: from French *puignant*, from *poindre* to sting]

point *noun* **1** a sharp or tapering end or tip. **2** a dot, eg inserted (either on the line or above it) before a decimal fraction, as in *2.1* or *2·1* (two point one). **3** a punctuation mark, esp a full stop. **4** *geom* a position found by means of coordinates. **5** *often in compounds* a position, place or location: *a look-out point.* **6** a moment: *Sandy lost his temper at that point.* **7** a stage in a process, etc. **8** *in compounds* a stage, temperature, etc: *boiling point.* **9** the right moment for doing something: *She lost courage when it came to the point.* **10** a feature or characteristic. **11** in a statement, argument, etc: a detail, fact or particular used or mentioned. **12** aim or intention: *What is the point of this?* **13** use or value: *There's no point in trying to change her mind.* **14** the significance (of a remark, story, joke, etc). **15** a unit or mark in scoring. **16** any of the 32 directions marked on, or indicated by, a compass. **17** (*often* **points**) an adjustable tapering rail by means of which a train changes lines. **18** *elec* a socket or **power point**. **19** (*usu* **points**) in an internal combustion engine: either of the two electrical contacts which complete the circuit in the distributor. **20** *printing* a unit of type measurement, equal to ¹⁄₁₂ of a **pica**. **21** *cricket* an off-side fielding position at right angles to the batsman. **22** (*usu* **points**) *ballet* **a** the tip of the toe; **b** a block inserted into the toe of a ballet shoe. **23** a headland or promontory. Often in place names: *Lizard Point.* ▸ *verb* **1** to aim something: *The hitman pointed a gun at her.* **2** *tr & intr* **a** to extend (one's finger or a pointed object) towards someone or something, so as to direct attention there; **b** of a sign, etc: to indicate (a certain direction): *a weather vane pointing south.* **3** *intr* to extend or face in a certain direction: *his toes were pointing upward.* **4** *intr* of a gun dog: to stand with the nose turned to where the dead game lies. **5** *often facetious* to direct someone: *Just point me to the grub.* **6** (*usu* **point to sth** *or* **sb**) to indicate or suggest it or them: *It points to one solution.* **7** in dancing, etc: to extend (the toes) to form a point. **8** to fill gaps or cracks in (stonework or brickwork) with cement or mortar. [13c: French, from Latin *punctum* a dot]

IDIOMS **beside the point** irrelevant. **come** *or* **get to the point** to cut out the irrelevancies and say what one wants to say. **in point of fact** actually; in truth. **make a point of doing sth** to be sure of doing it or take care to do it. **make one's point** to state one's opinion forcefully. **on the point of doing sth** about to do it. **score points off sb** to argue cleverly and successfully against them. **to the point** relevant. **up to a point** to a limited degree.

PHRASAL VERBS **point sth out** to indicate or draw attention to it.

point-blank *adj* **1** of a shot: fired at very close range. **2** of a question, refusal, etc: bluntly worded and direct. ▸ *adv* **1** at close range. **2** in a blunt, direct manner: *She refused point-blank.* [16c]

point duty *noun* the task or station of a police officer or traffic warden who is directing traffic.

pointed *adj* **1** having or ending in a point. **2** of a remark, etc: intended for, though not directly addressed to, a particular person. **3** keen or incisive. ▪ **pointedly** *adv.*

pointer *noun* **1** a rod used by a speaker for indicating positions on a wall map, chart, etc. **2** the indicating finger or needle on a measuring instrument. **3** *informal* a suggestion or hint. **4** a gun dog trained to point its muzzle in the direction where the dead game lies.

pointillism /ˈpɔɪntɪlɪzəm, ˈpwan-/ *noun, art* a method of painting by which shapes and colour tones are suggested by means of small dabs of pure colour painted side by side. Also called **Divisionism**. ▪ **pointillist** *noun, adj.* [20c: from French *pointillisme*]

pointing *noun* the cement or mortar filling the gaps between the bricks or stones of a wall.

pointless *adj* **1** without a point. **2** lacking purpose or meaning. ▪ **pointlessly** *adv.*

point of order *noun* (***points of order***) a question raised in an assembly, meeting, etc as to whether the business is being done according to the rules.

point of view *noun* (***points of view***) **1** one's own particular way of looking at or attitude towards something, influenced by personal considerations and experience. **2** the physical position from which one looks at something. **3** the perspective from which a book is written, a film is shot, etc.

point-to-point *noun* a horse race across open country, from landmark to landmark.

poise *noun* **1** self-confidence, calm or composure. **2** grace of posture or carriage. **3** a state of equilibrium, balance or stability, eg between extremes. ▸ *verb* **1** *tr & intr, often in passive* to balance or suspend. **2** *in passive* to be in a state of readiness: *She was poised to take over as leader.* [16c: from French *pois* weight]

poised *adj* **1** of behaviour, etc: calm and dignified. **2** ready for action.

poison *noun* **1** any substance that damages tissues or causes death when injected, absorbed or swallowed by living organisms. **2** any destructive or corrupting influence: *a poison spreading through society.* ▸ *verb* **1** to harm or kill with poison. **2** to put poison into (food, etc). **3** to contaminate or pollute: *rivers poisoned by effluents.* **4** to corrupt or pervert (someone's mind). **5** (*esp* **poison one person against another**) to influence them to be hostile. **6** to harm or spoil in an unpleasant or malicious way: *Jealousy poisoned their relationship.* ▪ **poisoner** *noun.* [13c: from French *puisun*]

poison ivy *noun* a N American woody vine or shrub, all parts of which produce a toxic chemical that causes an itching rash on contact with human skin.

poisonous *adj* **1** liable to cause injury or death if swallowed, inhaled or absorbed by the skin. **2** containing or capable of injecting a poison: *poisonous snakes.* **3** *informal* of a person, remark, etc: malicious. See also **venomous**.

poison-pen letter *noun* a malicious anonymous letter.

poke *verb* **1** (*often* **poke at sth**) to thrust: *Kevin poked at the hole with a stick.* **2** to prod or jab. **3** to make (a hole) by prodding. **4** *tr & intr* to project or make something project: *Her big toe poked through a hole in her sock.* **5** to make (a fire) burn more brightly by stirring it with a poker. **6** *intr* (*esp* **poke about** *or* **around**) to search; to pry or snoop. ▸ *noun* a jab or prod. [14c: Germanic origin]

IDIOMS **poke fun at sb** to tease or laugh at them unkindly. **poke one's nose into sth** *informal* to pry into or interfere in it.

poker[1] *noun* a metal rod for stirring a fire to make it burn better.

poker[2] *noun* a card game in which players bet on the hands they hold, relying on bluff to outwit their opponents. [19c]

poker face *noun* a blank expressionless face that shows no emotion. ▪ **poker-faced** *adj.* [19c: from the practice of experienced poker players who try to reveal nothing about the value of their cards]

poky *adj* (***-ier, -iest***) **1** *informal* of a room, house, etc: small and confined or cramped. **2** *US* slow; dull. ▪ **pokiness** *noun.* [19c: from **poke[1]**]

polar *adj* **1** belonging or relating to the North or South Pole, or the regions round them. **2** relating to or having electric or magnetic poles. **3** having polarity. **4** as different as possible: *polar opposites.* [16c: from Latin *polaris*, from *polus* pole]

polar co-ordinates *noun, maths* co-ordinates that identify a point by the length of a line from the origin to the point (a **radius vector**), and the angle it makes with the origin.

polarity *noun* (***-ies***) **1** the state of having two opposite poles: *magnetic polarity.* **2** the condition of having two properties that are opposite. **3** the tendency to develop differently in different directions along an axis. **4** *physics* the status, whether positive or negative, of the poles of a magnet, the terminals of an electrode, etc: *negative polarity.* **5** the tendency to develop, or be drawn, in opposite directions; oppositeness or an opposite.

polarization *or* **-isation** *noun* **1** *chem* the separation of the positive and negative charges of an atom or molecule, esp by an electric field. **2** *physics* the process whereby waves of electromagnetic radiation, eg light, are restricted to vibration in one direction only.

polarize *or* **-ise** *verb* **1** to give magnetic or electrical polarity to something. **2** *physics* to restrict the vibrations of (electromagnetic waves, eg light) to one direction only by the process of polarization. **3** *tr & intr* of people or opinions: to split according to opposing views.

Polaroid *noun, trademark* a plastic material that polarizes light, used in sunglasses, etc to reduce glare. [20c]

Polaroid camera *noun, trademark* a camera with a special film containing a pod of developing agents which bursts when the film is ejected, producing a finished print within seconds of exposure to daylight.

polder *noun* an area of low-lying land which has been reclaimed from the sea, a river or lake. [17c: from Dutch *polre*]

pole[1] *noun* **1** either of two points representing the north and south ends of the axis about which the Earth rotates, known as the **North Pole** and **South Pole** respectively. **2** a **magnetic pole**. **3** either of the two terminals of a battery. **4** either of two opposite positions in an argument, opinion, etc. [14c: from Latin *polus*]

IDIOMS **poles apart** *informal* widely different; as far apart as it is possible to be.

pole² *noun* a rod, esp one that is cylindrical in section and fixed in the ground as a support.

poleaxe *noun* **1** a short-handled axe with a spike or hammer opposite the blade, used, esp formerly, for slaughtering cattle. **2** *hist* a long-handled battle-axe. ► *verb* to strike, fell or floor (an animal or person) with, or as if with, a poleaxe. [14c: as *pollax*, from **poll** (*noun* sense 4) + **axe**]

polecat *noun* **1** a mammal resembling a large weasel that produces a foul-smelling discharge when alarmed or when marking territory. **2** *N Am, esp US* a skunk. [14c]

polemic /pəˈlɛmɪk/ *noun* **1** a controversial speech or piece of writing that fiercely attacks or defends an idea, opinion, etc. **2** writing or oratory of this sort. **3** someone who argues in this way. ► *adj* (*also* **polemical**) relating to or involving polemics or controversy. ▪ **polemicist** *noun*. [17c: from Greek *polemikos* relating to war]

polemics *singular noun* the art of verbal dispute and debate.

pole position *noun* **1** *motor sport* the position at the inside of the front row of cars at the start of a race. **2** an advantageous position at the start of any contest.

pole vault *noun, athletics* a field event in which athletes attempt to jump over a high horizontal bar with the help of a long flexible pole to haul themselves into the air. ► *verb* (**pole-vault**) *intr* to perform a pole vault or take part in a pole vault competition. ▪ **pole vaulter** *noun*.

police *plural noun* **1** the body of men and women employed by the government of a country to keep order, enforce the law, prevent crime, etc. **2** members of this body. ► *verb* **1** to keep law and order in (an area) using the police, army, etc. **2** to supervise (an operation, etc) to ensure that it is fairly or properly run. [18c: French, from Latin *politia*]

police constable *noun* (abbrev **PC**) a police officer of the lowest rank.

policeman *or* **policewoman** *noun* a male or female member of a police force.

police officer *noun* a member of a police force.

police state *noun* a state with a repressive government that operates through **secret police** to eliminate opposition to it.

police station *noun* the office or headquarters of a local police force.

policy¹ *noun* (***-ies***) a plan of action, usu based on certain principles, decided on by a body or individual. [15c: from French *policie*]

policy² *noun* (***-ies***) **1** an insurance agreement. **2** the document confirming such an agreement. ▪ **policyholder** *noun*. [16c: from French *police*]

polio *noun* short form of **poliomyelitis**.

poliomyelitis /poʊlɪoʊmaɪəˈlaɪtɪs/ *noun, pathol* a viral disease of the brain and spinal cord, which in some cases can result in permanent paralysis. [19c: from Greek *polios* grey + *myelos* marrow + **-itis**]

Polish /ˈpoʊlɪʃ/ *adj* belonging or relating to Poland, a republic in Central Europe, its inhabitants, or their language. ► *noun* the official language of Poland. [17c]

polish /ˈpɒlɪʃ/ *verb* **1** *tr* (*also* **polish sth up**) to make it smooth and glossy by rubbing: *polishing my shoes*. **2** *intr* to become smooth and glossy by rubbing. **3** *tr* (*also* **polish up sth**) to improve or perfect it. **4** *tr* to make cultivated, refined or elegant: *Henrietta polished her vowels before the speech day*. ► *noun* **1** *also in compounds* a substance used for polishing surfaces: *boot polish*. **2** a smooth shiny finish; a gloss. **3** an act of polishing. **4** refinement or elegance. [13c: from French *polir*]

PHRASAL VERBS **polish off sth** *or* **polish sth off** to finish it quickly and completely, esp speedily.

politburo *or* **Politburo** *noun* the supreme policy-making committee of a Communist state or party, esp of the Soviet Union. [20c: from Russian *politbyuro*]

polite *adj* **1** of a person or their actions, etc: well-mannered; considerate towards others; courteous. **2** well-bred, cultivated or refined: *One does not pick one's nose in polite society*. ▪ **politely** *adv*. ▪ **politeness** *noun*. [16c: from Latin *politus* polished]

politic *adj* **1** of a course of action: prudent; wise; shrewd. **2** of a person: cunning; crafty. **3** *old use* political. See also **body politic**. ► *verb* (*also* **politick**) (***politicked, politicking***) *intr, derog* to indulge in politics, esp to strike political bargains or to gain votes for oneself. [15c: from French *politique*]

political *adj* **1** relating or belonging to government or public affairs. **2** relating to **politics**. **3** interested or involved in **politics**. **4** of a course of action: made in the interests of gaining or keeping power. **5** of a map: showing political and social structure rather than physical features. ▪ **politically** *adv*. [16c]

political correctness *noun* (abbrev **PC**) the avoidance of expressions or actions that may be understood to exclude or denigrate certain people or groups of people on the grounds of race, gender, disability, etc. ▪ **politically correct** *adv*.

political party *noun* an organized group of people with the same political aims.

political prisoner *noun* someone imprisoned for their political beliefs, activities, etc, usu because they differ from those of the government.

political science *noun* the study of politics and government, in terms of its principles, methods, etc.

politician *noun* **1** someone engaged in **politics**, esp as a member of parliament. **2** *derog, chiefly US* someone who enters politics for personal power and gain. [16c: see **politic**]

politicize *or* **-ise** *verb* **1** *intr* to take part in political activities or discussion. **2** to give a political nature to something. **3** to make someone aware of or informed about politics. ▪ **politicization** *noun*.

politico *noun* (***politicos*** *or* ***politicoes***) *informal, usu derog* a politician or someone who is keen on politics. [17c: Italian or Spanish]

politics *singular noun* **1** the science or business of government. **2 political science**. **3** a political life as a career: *entered politics in 1961*. ► *singular or plural noun* political activities, wrangling, etc. ► *plural noun* **1** *also in compounds* moves and manoeuvres concerned with the acquisition of power or getting one's way, eg in business: *office politics*. **2** one's political sympathies or principles: *What are your politics?* [16c in sense 1]

polity *noun* (***-ies***) **1** a politically organized body such as a state, church or association. **2** any form of political institution or government. [16c: from Latin *politia*; see **police**]

polka *noun* **1** a lively Bohemian dance usu performed with a partner, which has a pattern of three steps followed by a hop. **2** a piece of music for this dance. ▸ *verb* (***polkaed, polkaing***) *intr* to dance a polka. [19c: Czech]

polka dot *noun* any one of numerous regularly-spaced dots forming a pattern on fabric, etc. *as adj*: *a polka-dot bikini.* [19c]

poll *noun* **1** (**polls**) a political election: *another Tory disaster at the polls.* **2** the voting or votes cast at an election: *a heavy poll.* **3** (*also* **opinion poll**) a survey of public opinion carried out by directly questioning a representative sample of the populace. **4** *old use* the head. ▸ *verb* **1** to win (a number of votes) in an election. **2** to register the votes of (a population). **3** *tr & intr* to cast (one's vote). **4** to conduct an opinion poll among (people, a specified group, etc). **5** to cut off the horns of (cattle). **6** to cut the top off (a tree). [13c: meaning 'the hair of the head']

pollard *noun* **1** a tree whose branches have been cut back, in order to produce a crown of shoots at the top of the trunk. **2** an animal whose horns have been removed. ▸ *verb* to make a pollard of (a tree or animal). [16c: from **poll** (*verb* senses 5, 6)]

pollen *noun* the fine, usu yellow, dust-like powder produced by the **anther**s of flowering plants, and by the male cones of cone-bearing plants. See also **pollinate**. [18c: Latin, meaning 'fine dust']

pollinate *verb, botany* in cone-bearing and flowering plants to transfer pollen from **anther** to **stigma**, or from the male to the female cone in order to achieve fertilization and subsequent development of seed. ▪ **pollination** *noun*. [19c]

polling booth *noun* an enclosed compartment at a polling station in which a voter can mark his or her vote in private.

polling station *noun* the building where voters go to cast their votes during an election.

pollster *noun* someone who organizes and carries out opinion polls.

poll tax *noun* **1** *hist* a fixed tax levied on each adult member of a population. **2** *formerly, informal* the **community charge**. See also **council tax**.

pollutant *noun* any substance or agent that pollutes. ▸ *adj* polluting: *pollutant emissions.*

pollute *verb* **1** to contaminate something with harmful substances or impurities; to cause pollution in something. **2** to corrupt (someone's mind, etc). **3** to defile. ▪ **pollution** *noun*. [14c: from Latin *polluere* to soil or defile]

polo *noun* a game, similar to hockey, played on horseback by two teams of four players, using long-handled mallets to propel the ball along the ground. See also **water polo**. [19c: Balti (a Tibetan dialect), meaning 'ball']

polonaise *noun* **1** a stately Polish marching dance. **2** a piece of music for this dance. [18c: French, feminine of *polonais* Polish]

polo neck *noun* **1** a high close-fitting neckband on a sweater or shirt, which is doubled over. *as adj*: *polo-neck jumper.* **2** a sweater or shirt with such a neck.

polonium *noun, chem* (symbol **Po**) a rare radioactive metallic element that emits **alpha particle**s. [19c: Latin, from *Polonia* Poland, the native country of Marie Curie who discovered it]

polo shirt *noun* a short-sleeved open-necked casual shirt with a collar, esp one made of a knitted cotton fabric.

poltergeist /ˈpoʊltəgaɪst/ *noun* a type of mischievous ghost supposedly responsible for otherwise unaccountable noises and the movement of objects. [19c: German, from *poltern* to make a noise + *Geist* ghost]

poltroon *noun, literary or old use* a despicable coward. [16c: French, from Italian *poltrone* lazybones]

poly *informal, noun* (***polys***) **1** a polyphonic ringtone. **2** a polytechnic. ▸ *adj* **1** polyphonic. **2** polythene: *a poly bag.*

poly- *combining form, denoting* **1** many or much; several: *polytechnic*. **2** *chem* a **polymer**: *polyvinyl*. [Greek, from *polys* many or much]

polyamide *noun, chem* a polymer, eg nylon, formed by the linking of the amino group of one molecule with the carboxyl group of the next. [20c]

polyandrous *adj* **1** *anthropol* having more than one husband at the same time. **2** *botany* of a flower: having many **stamen**s. Compare **monandrous**. [19c: from Greek *aner* man or husband]

polyandry *noun, anthropol* the custom or practice of having more than one husband at the same time. Compare **polygyny**. [18c: from Greek *aner* man or husband]

polychromatic *adj* **1** **polychrome**. **2** of electromagnetic radiation: composed of a number of different wavelengths. [19c]

polychrome *adj* (*also* **polychromatic**) multicoloured. Compare **monochrome**. ▸ *noun* **1** varied colouring. **2** a work of art, esp a statue, in several colours. [19c: from Greek *polychromos*, from Greek *chroma* colour]

polyester *noun* a synthetic resin used to form strong durable crease-resistant artificial fibres, such as Terylene, widely used in textiles for clothing, etc. [20c]

polyethylene see under **polythene**

polygamy /pəˈlɪgəmɪ/ *noun, anthropol* the custom or practice of having more than one husband or wife at the same time. ▪ **polygamist** *noun*. ▪ **polygamous** *adj*. Compare **monogamy**. [16c: from Greek *polygamia*]

polyglot *adj* speaking, using or written in many languages. ▸ *noun* someone who speaks many languages. [17c: from Greek *polyglottos*]

polygon *noun, geom* a plane figure (see **plane**[2] *adj* sense 3) with a number of straight sides, usu more than three, eg a **pentagon** or a **hexagon**. ▪ **polygonal** *adj*. [16c: from Greek *polygonon*]

polygraph *noun, med* a device, sometimes used as a lie-detector, that monitors several body functions simultaneously, eg pulse, blood pressure and conductivity of the skin. [18c]

polygyny *noun, anthropol* the condition or custom of having more than one wife at the same time. Compare **polyandry**. [18c: from Greek *gyne* woman or wife]

polyhedron *noun* (***polyhedrons*** *or* ***polyhedra***) *geom* a solid figure with four or more faces, all of which are polygons, eg a **tetrahedron**. ▪ **polyhedral** *adj*. [16c: Greek, from *hedra* seat, base or face]

polymath *noun* someone who is well educated in a wide variety of subjects. [17c: from Greek *polymathes*]

polymer *noun, chem* a very large molecule consisting of a long chain of **monomer**s linked end to end to form a series of repeating units. ▪ **polymeric** *adj.* ▪ **polymerization** *or* **-isation** *noun.* [19c: from Greek *polymeres* having many parts]

polymorphism *noun* **1** *biol* the occurrence of a living organism in two or more different forms at different stages of its life cycle. **2** *genetics* the occurrence of several genetically determined and distinct forms within a single population, eg the different blood groups in humans. **3** *chem* the occurrence of a chemical substance in two or more different crystalline forms, eg diamond and graphite. ▪ **polymorphic** *or* **polymorphous** *adj.*

Polynesian *adj* belonging or relating to Polynesia, a group of Pacific Islands, its inhabitants, or their language. ▸ *noun* **1** a citizen or inhabitant of Polynesia. **2** the group of languages including Maori and Samoan.

polynomial *maths, adj* of an expression: consisting of a sum of terms each containing a **constant** and one or more **variable**s raised to a power. ▸ *noun* an expression of this sort. [17c]

polyp *noun* **1** *zool* a sessile **coelenterate** with a more or less cylindrical body and a mouth surrounded by tentacles. **2** *pathol* a small abnormal but usu benign growth projecting from a mucous membrane. [16c: from Latin *polypus*]

polypeptide *noun, chem* a peptide in which many amino acids are linked to form a chain. [20c]

polyphone *noun* a letter which can be pronounced or sounded in more than one way, eg the letter *g* in English. [19c in this sense]

polyphonic *adj* **1** having many voices. **2** relating to polyphony. **3** denoting a polyphone.

polyphony /pəˈlɪfənɪ/ *noun* (***-ies***) **1** a style of musical composition in which each part or voice has an independent melodic value. **2** the use of polyphones. [19c: from Greek *polyphonia* diversity of sounds]

polypropylene *or* **polypropene** *noun, chem* a tough white translucent **thermoplastic** used to make fibres, film, rope and moulded articles, eg toys. [20c]

polysaccharide *noun, biochem* a large carbohydrate molecule consisting of many **monosaccharide**s linked together to form long chains, eg starch and cellulose. [19c]

polysemy /pəˈlɪsɪmɪ/ *noun, linguistics* the existence of more than one meaning for a single word, such as *table*. ▪ **polysemous** *adj.* [20c: from Greek adjective *polysemos*]

polystyrene *noun, chem* a tough transparent **thermoplastic** that is a good thermal and electrical insulator, used in packaging, insulation, ceiling tiles, etc. [20c]

polysyllable *noun* a word of three or more syllables. ▪ **polysyllabic** *adj.* [16c]

polytechnic *noun, Brit education, formerly* a college of higher education providing courses in a large range of subjects, esp of a technical or vocational kind. In 1992 the polytechnics became universities. ▸ *adj* relating to technical training. [From Greek *polytechnos* skilled in many arts]

polytheism *noun* belief in or worship of more than one god. ▪ **polytheist** *noun.* ▪ **polytheistic** *adj.* [17c]

polythene *noun* a waxy translucent easily-moulded **thermoplastic**, used in the form of film or sheeting to package food products, clothing, etc, and to make pipes, moulded articles and electrical insulators. Also called **polyethylene**.

polyunsaturated *adj, chem* of a compound, esp a fat or oil: containing two or more double bonds per molecule: *polyunsaturated margarine*. Compare **monounsaturated**. [20c]

polyurethane *noun, chem* a polymer that contains the **urethane** group, and is used in protective coatings, adhesives, paints, etc. [20c]

polyvalent see **multivalent**

polyvinyl chloride *noun, chem* (abbrev **PVC**) a tough white **thermoplastic**, resistant to fire and chemicals and easily dyed and softened, used in pipes and other moulded products, **record**s (*noun* sense 4), food packaging etc.

pom *noun, Aust & NZ derog informal* a short form of **pommy**.

pomace *noun* **a** crushed apples for cider-making; **b** the residue of these or of any similar fruit after pressing. [16c: from Latin *pomum* fruit or apple]

pomade *hist, noun* a perfumed ointment for the hair and scalp. ▸ *verb* to put pomade on (a person's hair, etc). [16c: from French *pommade*]

pomander *noun* **1** a perfumed ball composed of various aromatic substances, orig carried as scent or to ward off infection. **2** a perforated container for this. [15c: from French *pomme d'ambre* apple of amber]

pomegranate *noun* **1** a small deciduous tree or shrub widely cultivated for its edible fruit. **2** the round fruit of this plant, which has tough red or brown skin surrounding a mass of seeds, each of which is enclosed by red juicy edible flesh. [14c: from French *pome grenate*]

pomelo /ˈpɒməloʊ/ *noun* a round yellow citrus fruit, resembling a grapefruit. [19c: from Dutch *pompelmoes* shaddock or grapefruit]

pomfret *or* **pomfret cake** *noun* a disc-shaped liquorice sweet. [19c: from French *Pontfret* Pontefract, where it was orig made]

pommel *noun* **1** the raised front part of a saddle. **2** a rounded knob forming the end of a sword hilt. ▸ *verb* (***pommelled, pommelling***) to pummel. [14c: from French *pomel* knob]

pommy *noun* (***-ies***) *Aust & NZ derog informal* a British, or esp English, person. Often shortened to **pom**. [20c]

pomp *noun* **1** ceremonial grandeur. **2** vain ostentation. [14c: from Latin *pompa* procession]

pompom *or* **pompon** *noun* **1** a ball made of cut wool or other yarn, used as a trimming on clothes, etc. **2** a variety of chrysanthemum with globe-like flowers. [18c: from French *pompon*]

pompous *adj* **1** solemnly self-important. **2** said of language: inappropriately grand and flowery; pretentious. ▪ **pomposity** *noun.* [14c: from Latin *pomposus*]

poncho *noun* an outer garment, orig S American, made of a large piece of cloth with a hole in the middle for the head to go through. [18c: American Spanish]

pond *noun* **1** a small area of still fresh water surrounded by land. **2** *N Am slang* (*usu* **the Pond**) the sea, esp the Atlantic Ocean. [13c: meaning 'enclosure']

ponder *verb, tr & intr* (*often* **ponder on** *or* **over sth**) to consider or contemplate it deeply. [14c: from French *ponderer*]

ponderous *adj* **1** of speech, humour, etc: heavy-handed, laborious, over-solemn or pompous. **2** heavy or cumbersome; lumbering in movement. **3** weighty; important. ▪ **ponderously** *adv*. [14c: from Latin *ponderosus*; see **ponder**]

pone *noun, US* a kind of maize bread. Also called **corn pone**. [17c: Algonquian (a family of Native American languages) *apones*]

pong *informal, noun* a stink; a bad smell. ▸ *verb, intr* to smell badly. ▪ **pongy** *adj* (***-ier, -iest***) stinking; smelly. [20c]

pontiff *noun* a title for the Pope. [17c: from French *pontife*]

pontifical *adj* **1** belonging or relating to a pontiff. **2** *derog* pompously opinionated; dogmatic. [15c]

pontificate *verb* /pɒn'tɪfɪkeɪt/ *intr* **1** to pronounce one's opinion pompously and arrogantly. **2** to perform the duties of a pontiff. ▸ *noun* /pɒn'tɪfɪkət/ the office of a pope. [16c: from Latin *pontificatus* high-priesthood]

pontoon[1] *noun* any of a number of flat-bottomed craft, punts, barges, etc, anchored side by side across a river, to support a temporary bridge or platform. [17c: from French *ponton*]

pontoon[2] *noun, cards* a game in which the object is to collect sets of cards that add up to or close to 21, without going over that total. Also called **twenty-one, vingt-et-un**. [20c]

pontoon bridge *noun* a bridge or platform, etc supported on pontoons.

pony *noun* (***-ies***) **1** any of several small hardy breeds of horse. **2** *Brit slang* a sum of £25. **3** *US slang* a crib or a translation prepared for use in an exam, etc. [17c: from Scots *powney*]

ponytail *noun* a hairstyle in which a person's hair is drawn back and gathered by a band at the back of the head, so that it hangs free like a pony's tail. [20c]

poo see **poop**[3]

pooch *noun, informal* a dog. [20c]

poodle *noun* **1** a breed of lively pet dog of various sizes which has a narrow head with pendulous ears and a long curly coat, often clipped into an elaborate style. **2** *derog* a lackey. [19c: from German *Pudel*, short for *Pudelhund*]

pooh-pooh *verb, informal* to express scorn for (a suggestion, etc). [19c: from **pooh**]

pool[1] *noun* **1** a small area of still water. **2** a puddle; a patch of spilt liquid: *pools of blood*. **3** a swimming pool. **4** a deep part of a stream or river. [Anglo-Saxon *pol*]

pool[2] *noun* **1** *also in compounds* a reserve of money, personnel, vehicles, etc used as a communal resource: *typing pool*. **2** the combined stakes of those betting on something; a jackpot. **3** *commerce* a group of businesses with a common arrangement to maintain high prices, so eliminating competition and preserving profits. **4** a game like **billiards** played with a white cue ball and usu 15 numbered coloured balls, the aim being to shoot specified balls into specified pockets using the cue ball. Compare **snooker**. ▸ *verb* to put (money or other resources) into a common supply for general use. [17c: from French *poule*, literally 'a hen']

the pools *plural noun, Brit* an organized syndicate which involves postal betting on the outcome of football matches. Also called **football pools**.

poop[1] *noun, naut* **1** the raised enclosed part at the stern of old sailing ships. **2** the high deck at the stern of a ship. Also called **poop deck**. [15c: from French *pupe*]

poop[2] *verb, informal* **1** *in passive* to become winded or exhausted: *Sheena was pooped after walking up the hill*. **2** (*also* **poop sb out**) to tire them out; to make them exhausted or winded. [20c]

poop[3] *or* **poo** *slang, noun* faeces. ▸ *verb, intr* to defecate. [18c]

poor *adj* **1** not having sufficient money or means to live comfortably. **2** (**the poor**) poor people in general. **3** (**poor in sth**) not well supplied with it. **4** not good; weak; unsatisfactory: *poor eyesight*. **5** unsatisfactorily small or sparse: *a poor attendance*. **6** used in expressing pity or sympathy: *poor fellow!* ▪ **poorness** *noun*. See also **poverty**. [13c: from French *povre*]

IDIOMS **poor man's** *derog* a substitute of lower quality or price than the specified thing: *This is only lumpfish, poor man's caviare*.

poorhouse *noun, hist* an institution maintained at public expense, for housing the poor; a **workhouse**.

poor law *noun, hist* a law or set of laws concerned with the public support of the poor.

poorly *adv* not well; badly: *I speak French poorly*. ▸ *adj, informal or dialect* unwell: *Do you feel poorly?*

POP *abbrev, comput* **1** point of presence, a point of access to the Internet. **2** post office protocol, the rules controlling the interaction between an e-mail client and server.

pop[1] *noun* **1** a sharp explosive noise, like that of a cork coming out of a bottle. **2** *informal, esp N Am* any sweet non-alcoholic fizzy drink such as ginger beer. ▸ *verb* (***popped, popping***) **1** *tr & intr* to make or cause something to make a pop. **2** *tr & intr* to burst with a pop: *The balloon popped*. **3** (*esp* **pop out** *or* **up**) to spring out or up; to protrude. **4** *intr, informal* to go quickly in a direction specified: *I'll just pop next door for a second*. **5** *informal* to put something somewhere quickly or briefly: *just pop it in the oven*. ▸ *adv* with a pop. [16c: imitating the sound]

IDIOMS **pop the question** *humorous, informal* to propose marriage.

PHRASAL VERBS **pop off** *informal* **1** to leave quickly or suddenly. **2** to die. **pop up** to appear or occur, esp unexpectedly. See also **pop-up**.

pop[2] *noun* (*in full* **pop music**) a type of music, primarily commercial, usu with a strong beat and characterized by its use of electronic equipment such as guitars and keyboards. ▸ *adj* popular: *pop culture*. [19c, as a shortening of 'popular concert']

pop[3] *noun, informal, esp N Am* **1** father; dad. **2** often as a form of address: an elderly man. [19c; see **papa**]

pop. *abbrev* population.

pop art *noun* a form of art drawing deliberately on commonplace material of modern urban life. ▪ **pop artist** *noun*.

popcorn *noun* **1** (*also* **popping corn**) maize grains that puff up and burst open when heated. **2** the edible puffed-up kernels of this grain.

pope *noun* **1** (*often* **Pope**) the Bishop of Rome, the head of the Roman Catholic Church. **2** a priest in the Eastern Orthodox Church. [Anglo-Saxon: from Latin]

popgun *noun* a toy gun that fires a cork or pellet with a pop.

popinjay *noun, old use, derog* a vain or conceited person; a dandy. [16c: from French *papegai* parrot]

poplar *noun* **1** a tall slender deciduous tree found in northern temperate regions, with broad simple leaves which tremble in a slight breeze. **2** the soft fine-grained yellowish wood of this tree. [14c: from French *poplier*]

poplin *noun* a strong cotton cloth with a finely ribbed finish. [18c: from French *popeline*]

pop music see **pop**[2]

poppadum, poppadom *or* **pappadom** *noun* a paper-thin pancake, grilled or fried till crisp, served with Indian dishes. [19c: from Tamil *poppatam*]

popper *noun* **1** someone or something that pops. **2** *informal* a **press stud**. **3** *esp N Am* a container used to make popcorn.

poppet *noun* **1** a term of endearment for someone lovable. **2** in vehicle engines: an unhinged valve that rises and falls in its housing. [14c: an earlier form of **puppet**]

poppy *noun* (**-ies**) a plant with large brightly-coloured bowl-shaped flowers and a fruit in the form of a capsule. [Anglo-Saxon *popig*]

poppycock *noun, informal* nonsense. [19c: from Dutch dialect *pappekak* soft dung]

populace *noun* the body of ordinary citizens; the common people. [16c: French, from Latin *populus* people]

popular *adj* **1** liked or enjoyed by most people. **2** of beliefs, etc: accepted by many people: *a popular misconception*. **3** catering for the tastes and abilities of ordinary people as distinct from specialists, etc: *a popular history of science*. **4** of a person: generally liked and admired. **5** involving the will or preferences of the public in general: *by popular demand*. ▪ **popularity** *noun*. ▪ **popularly** *adv*. [15c: from Latin *popularis*]

popularize *or* **-ise** *verb* **1** to make something popular. **2** to present something in a simple easily understood way, so as to have general appeal. ▪ **popularization** *noun*.

populate *verb* **1** of people, animals or plants: to inhabit or live in (a certain area). **2** to supply (uninhabited places) with inhabitants; to people. [16c: from Latin *populare* to inhabit]

population *noun* **1** all the people living in a particular country, area, etc. **2** the number of people living in a particular area, country, etc. **3** a group of animals or plants of the same species living in a certain area; the total number of these: *the declining elephant population*. **4** *stats* a group that consists of all the possible quantities or values relevant to a statistical study, from which representative samples are taken.

populist *noun* **1** a person who believes in the right and ability of the common people to play a major part in government. **2** a person who studies, supports or attracts the support of the common people. ▸ *adj* of a political cause, programme, etc: appealing to the majority of the people. ▪ **populism** *noun*.

populous *adj* densely inhabited. [15c: from Latin *populosus*]

pop-up *adj* **1** of a picture book, greetings card, etc: having cut-out parts designed to stand upright as the page is opened. **2** of appliances, etc: having a mechanism which causes a component, or the item being prepared, to pop up. See also **pop up** at **pop**[1].

porcelain *noun* **1** a fine white translucent earthenware, orig made in China. *as adj*: *a porcelain dish*. **2** objects made of this. [16c: from French *porcelaine*]

porch *noun* **1** a structure that forms a covered entrance to the doorway of a building. **2** *N Am* a veranda. [13c: from French *porche*]

porcine /ˈpɔːsaɪn/ *adj* relating to or or resembling a pig. [17c: from Latin *porcinus*]

porcupine *noun* a large nocturnal rodent with long black-and-white spikes or quills on the back and sides of its body. [14c: from French *porc d'espine* spiny pig]

pore[1] *noun* **1** a small, usu round opening in the surface of a living organism, eg in the skin, through which fluids, gases and other substances can pass. **2** any tiny cavity or gap, eg in soil or rock. [14c: French, from Latin *porus*]

---

pore, pour

Be careful not to use the spelling **pore** when you mean **pour**:

Sweat was pouring down his face.

---

pore[2] *verb, intr* (*always* **pore over sth**) to study (books, papers, etc) with intense concentration. [13c]

pork *noun* the flesh of a pig used as food. [13c: from French *porc*]

porky *adj* (**-ier, -iest**) **1** resembling pork. **2** *informal* plump.

pornography *noun* books, pictures, films, etc designed to be sexually arousing, often offensive owing to their explicit nature. Often shortened to **porn** *or* **porno**. ▪ **pornographer** *noun*. ▪ **pornographic** *adj*. [19c: from Greek *pornographos* writing about prostitutes]

porous *adj* **1** referring or relating to a material that contains pores or cavities. **2** capable of being permeated by liquids or gases. ▪ **porosity** *noun*. [14c: from Latin *porosus*, from *porus* a pore]

porphyria /ˈpɔːfɪrɪə/ *noun, pathol* any of various disorders of metabolism, characterized by discoloured urine and, in some types, skin photosensitivity. [From Greek *porphyra* purple dye]

porphyry /ˈpɔːfɪrɪ/ *noun, geol* **1** *loosely* any igneous rock that contains large crystals surrounded by much smaller ones. **2** a very hard purple and white rock used in sculpture. ▪ **porphyritic** /pɔːfɪˈrɪtɪk/ *adj*. [14c: from Latin *porphyrites*]

porpoise *noun* **1** a beakless whale, smaller than a dolphin, with a blunt snout. **2** *loosely* a **dolphin**. [14c: from Latin *porcuspiscis*]

porridge *noun* **1** a dish of oatmeal or some other cereal which is boiled in water or milk until it reaches a thick consistency. *N Am equivalent* **oatmeal**. **2** *Brit slang* a jail sentence. [17c: a variant of **pottage**]

porringer *noun* a bowl, with a handle, for soup or porridge. [16c: variation of *potager* soup bowl]

port[1] *noun* **1** a harbour. **2** a town with a harbour. [Anglo-Saxon: from Latin *portus*]

port[2] *noun* the left side of a ship or aircraft. Compare **starboard**. [16c]

port[3] *noun* **1** an opening in a ship's side for loading, etc. **2** a **porthole**. **3** *comput* a socket that connects the **CPU** of a computer to a peripheral device. [Anglo-Saxon: from Latin *porta* gate]

port[4] *noun* a sweet dark-red or tawny fortified wine. [17c: from Oporto, the city in Portugal from where it was orig exported]

portable *adj* **1** easily carried or moved, and usu designed to be so. **2** *comput* of a program: adaptable for use in a variety of systems. ► *noun* a portable radio, television, typewriter, etc. ▪ **portability** *noun*. [14c: French]

portage *noun* **1** an act of carrying. **2** the cost of carrying. **3** the transportation of ships, equipment, etc overland from one waterway to another. **4** the route used for this. ► *verb* to transport (ships, etc) overland. [15c: French, from *porter* to carry]

Portakabin *noun, trademark* a portable structure used as a temporary office, etc. [20c]

portal *noun, formal* an entrance, gateway or doorway, esp an imposing or awesome one. [14c: French]

portcullis *noun, hist* a vertical iron or wooden grating fitted into a town gateway or castle entrance, which was lowered to keep intruders out. [14c: from French *porte coleïce* sliding door or gate]

portend *verb* to warn of (usu something bad); to signify or foreshadow it. [15c: from Latin *portendere* to foreshadow or give a sign]

portent *noun* **1** a prophetic sign; an omen. **2** fateful significance: *an event of grim portent*. **3** a marvel or prodigy. [16c: from Latin *portentum* a sign]

portentous *adj* **1** ominous or fateful; relating to portents. **2** weighty, solemn or pompous. **3** amazing or marvellous. ▪ **portentously** *adv*.

porter[1] *noun* a doorman, caretaker or janitor at a college, office or factory. [13c: from French *portier*]

porter[2] *noun* **1** someone employed to carry luggage or parcels, eg at a railway station. **2** in a hospital: someone employed to move patients when required and to carry out other general duties. **3** a heavy dark-brown beer brewed from malt, formerly reputed to be popular with porters. **4** *N Am* on a train: a sleeping-car attendant. [14c: from French *porteour*]

porterhouse *noun* **1** (*in full* **porterhouse steak**) a choice cut of beef from the back of the sirloin. **2** *formerly* a public house where porter, beer, etc and steaks were served. [18c]

portfolio *noun* **1** a flat case for carrying papers, drawings, photographs, etc. **2** the contents of such a case, as a demonstration of a person's work. **3** *politics* the post of a government minister with responsibility for a specific department. **4** a list of the investments or securities held by an individual, company, etc. [18c: from Italian *portafoglio*]

porthole *noun* **1** an opening, usu a round one, in a ship's side to admit light and air. **2** an opening in a wall through which a gun can be fired. [16c]

portico *noun* (***porticos*** *or* ***porticoes***) *archit* a colonnade forming a porch or covered way alongside a building. [17c: Italian, from Latin *porticus* a porch]

portion *noun* **1** a piece or part of a whole: *divided the cake into 12 equal portions*. **2** a share; a part allotted to one. **3** an individual helping of food. **4** *literary* one's destiny or fate. **5** *law* a woman's dowry. ► *verb* (*now usu* **portion sth out**) to divide it up; to share it out. [13c: from French *porcion*]

portly *adj* (***-ier, -iest***) esp of a man: somewhat stout. [16c: from *port* deportment or bearing]

portmanteau /pɔːt'mantoʊ/ *noun* (***portmanteaus*** *or* ***portmanteaux*** /-toʊz/) a large travelling bag that opens flat in two halves. ► *adj* combining or covering two or more things of the same kind: *portmanteau statistics*. [16c: French, meaning 'cloak carrier']

portmanteau word *noun* a word formed by combining the sense and sound of two words, eg **brunch** (for *breakfast* and *lunch*). Also called **blend**. [19c: orig used by Lewis Carroll, English writer]

portrait *noun* **1** a drawing, painting or photograph of a person, esp of the face only. **2** a written description, film depiction, etc of someone or something: *a portrait of country life*. ► *adj, printing* of a page, illustration, etc: taller than it is wide. Compare **landscape**. [16c: French, from *portraire* to portray]

portraiture *noun* **1** the art or act of making portraits. **2** a portrait, or portraits collectively.

portray *verb* **1** to make a portrait of someone or something. **2** to describe or depict something. **3** to act the part of (a character) in a play, film, etc. ▪ **portrayal** *noun*. [14c: from French *portraire* to represent]

Portuguese /pɔːtʃʊ'giːz/ *adj* belonging or relating to Portugal, its inhabitants or their language. ► *noun* **1** a citizen or inhabitant of, or person born in, Portugal. **2** (**the Portuguese**) the people of Portugal in general. **3** the official language of Portugal. [17c]

pose *noun* **1** a position or attitude of the body: *a relaxed pose*. **2** an artificial way of behaving, adopted for effect: *His punk style is just a pose*. ► *verb* **1** *tr & intr* to take up a position oneself, or position (someone else), for a photograph, portrait, etc. **2** *intr, derog* to behave in an exaggerated or artificial way so as to draw attention to oneself. **3** *intr* (*usu* **pose as sb** *or* **sth**) to pretend to be someone or something that one is not. **4** to ask or put forward (a question). **5** to cause (a problem, etc) or present (a threat, etc). [16c: from French *poser*]

IDIOMS **strike a pose** to adopt a position or attitude, esp a commanding or impressive one.

poser[1] *noun* **1** someone who poses. **2** *derog* someone who tries to impress others by putting on an act and by dressing, behaving, etc so as to be noticed; a poseur. [19c]

poser[2] *noun* a puzzling or perplexing question.

poseur /poʊ'zɜː(r)/ *noun, derog* someone who behaves in an affected or insincere way, esp to impress others. [19c: French, from *poser* to **pose**]

posh *informal, adj* **1** high-quality, expensive, smart or stylish. **2** upper-class. ► *adv* in a way associated with the upper class: *Bert talks posh when he's on the telephone*. [20c: perhaps related to obsolete *posh* a dandy]

posit /'pɒzɪt/ *verb* to lay down or assume something as a basis for discussion; to postulate. ► *noun, philos* a statement made on the assumption that it will be proved valid. [17c: from Latin *ponere* to place]

position *noun* **1** a place where someone or something is: *The mansion was in a fine position overlooking the bay.* **2** the right or proper place: *Volume 2 was out of position.* **3** the relationship of things to one another in space; arrangement. **4** a way of sitting, standing, lying, facing, being held or placed, etc: *an upright position.* **5** *military* a place occupied for strategic purposes. **6** one's opinion or viewpoint. **7** a job or post. **8** rank; status; importance in society: *wealth and position.* **9** the place of a competitor in the finishing order, or at an earlier stage in a contest: *lying in fourth position.* **10** *sport* an allotted place in a team, esp on the pitch or playing-area: *the centre-forward position.* **11** the set of circumstances in which one is placed: *not in a position to help.* ▸ *verb* to place; to put something or someone in position. ▪ **positional** *adj.* [15c: French]

IDIOMS **be in no position to do sth** to have no right to (complain, criticize, etc).

positive *adj* **1** sure; certain; convinced. **2** definite; allowing no doubt: *positive proof of her guilt.* **3** expressing agreement or approval. **4** optimistic: *feeling more positive.* **5** forceful or determined; not tentative. **6** constructive; contributing to progress or improvement; helpful. **7** clear and explicit: *positive directions.* **8** *informal* downright: *a positive scandal.* **9** of the result of a chemical test: confirming the existence of the suspected condition. **10** *maths* of a number or quantity: greater than zero. **11** *physics, elec* having a deficiency of electrons, and so being able to attract them, ie attracted by a negative charge. **12** *photog* of a photographic image: in which light and dark tones and colours correspond to those in the original subject. **13** *grammar* expressing a quality in the simple form, as distinct from the **comparative** or **superlative** forms. Compare **negative**. [14c: from French *positif*]

positive discrimination *noun* the creation of special employment opportunities, etc for those groups or members of society previously disadvantaged or discriminated against.

positive vetting *noun* investigation of the connections and sympathies of a person being considered for a position of trust, eg in the senior civil service.

positivism *noun* a school of philosophy maintaining that knowledge can come only from observable phenomena and positive facts. ▪ **positivist** *noun, adj.*

positron *noun, physics* an **antiparticle** that has the same mass as an electron, and an equal but opposite charge. [20c: a contraction of *positive electron*]

posse /ˈpɒsɪ/ *noun* **1** *N Am, hist* a mounted troop of men at the service of a local sheriff. **2** *informal* any group or band of people, esp friends. [17c: from Latin *posse comitatus* force of the county]

possess *verb* **1** to own. **2** to have something as a feature or quality: *Frances possesses a quick mind.* **3** of an emotion, evil spirit, etc: to occupy and dominate the mind of someone: *What possessed you to behave like that?* ▪ **possessor** *noun.* [15c: from French *possesser*]

possessed *adj* **1** (**possessed of sth**) *formal* owning it; having it: *possessed of great wealth.* **2** *following its noun* controlled or driven by demons, etc: *screaming like a man possessed.*

possession *noun* **1** the condition of possessing something; ownership: *It came into my possession.* **2** the crime of possessing something illegally. **3** occupancy of property: *take possession of the house.* **4** *sport* control of the ball, puck, etc by one or other team in a match. **5** something owned. **6** (**possessions**) one's property or belongings. **7** (**possessions**) *formal* a country's dominions abroad: *foreign possessions.*

---

possession

This word is often misspelt. It has two sets of double *s*. It might help you to remember the following sentence:

I'm in possession of four s's.

---

possessive *adj* **1** relating to possession. **2** of a person or of character: unwilling to share, or allow others to use, things they own: *I'm very possessive about my car.* **3** of a person or of character: inclined to dominate, monopolize and allow no independence to one's wife, husband, child, etc: *a possessive husband.* **4** *grammar* denoting the form or **case**[2] of a noun, pronoun or adjective which shows possession, eg *Kurt's, its, her.* ▸ *noun, grammar* **1** the possessive form or case of a word. **2** a word in the possessive case or in a possessive form. Compare **genitive**. ▪ **possessiveness** *noun.*

possibility *noun* (**-ies**) **1** something that is possible. **2** the state of being possible. **3** a candidate for selection, etc. **4** (**possibilities**) promise or potential: *This idea has definite possibilities.*

possible *adj* **1** achievable; able to be done: *a possible target of 50%.* **2** capable of happening: *the possible outcome.* **3** imaginable; conceivable: *It's possible that he's dead.* ▸ *noun* someone or something potentially selectable or attainable; a possibility. [14c: from Latin *possibilis* that can be done]

possibly *adv* **1** perhaps; maybe. **2** within the limits of possibility: *We'll do all we possibly can.* **3** used for emphasis: at all: *How could you possibly think that?*

possum *noun, informal* **1** an **opossum**. **2** a **phalanger**. [17c]

IDIOMS **play possum** to pretend to be unconscious, asleep or unaware of what is happening.

post[1] *noun* **1** a shaft or rod fixed upright in the ground, as a support or marker, etc. **2** *often in compounds* a vertical timber supporting a horizontal one: *a doorpost.* **3** an upright pole marking the beginning or end of a race track. **4** a **goalpost**. ▸ *verb* **1** (*sometimes* **post sth up**) to put up (a notice, etc) on a post or board, etc for public viewing. **2** to announce the name of someone among others in a published list: *He was posted missing.* [Anglo-Saxon: from Latin *postis* a doorpost]

post[2] *noun* **1** a job: *a teaching post.* **2** a position to which one is assigned for military duty: *never left his post.* **3** *often in compounds* a settlement or establishment, esp one in a remote area: *trading post • military post.* **4** *military* a bugle call summoning soldiers to their quarters at night. See also **the last post**. ▸ *verb* (*usu* **post sb to, at** *or* **in somewhere**) to station them there on duty; to transfer (personnel) to a new location. [16c: from Italian *posto*]

post[3] *noun* (*esp* **the post**) **1** the official system for the delivery of mail. See also **post office**. **2** letters and parcels delivered by this system; mail. **3** a collection of mail, eg from a postbox: *catch the next post.* **4** a delivery of mail: *came by the second post.* **5** a place for mail collection; a postbox or post office: *took it* *to the post.* ▸ *verb* **1** to put (mail) into a postbox; to send something by post. **2** *bookkeeping* **a** to enter (an item) in a ledger; **b** (*now usu* **post up sth**) to update (a ledger). **3** to supply someone with the latest news: *keep us posted.* See also **post**[1] (*verb*). [16c: from French *poste*]

post- *prefix, denoting* **1** after: *postwar* • *postdate.* **2** behind: *postnasal.* [Latin]

postage *noun* the charge for sending a letter, etc through the **post**[3].

postage stamp *noun* a small printed gummed label stuck on a letter, etc indicating that the appropriate postage charge has been paid. Often shortened to **stamp**.

postal *adj* **1** relating or belonging to the **post office** or to delivery of mail. **2** sent by post: *a postal vote.*

postal code see under **postcode**

postal order *noun* (abbrev **po** *or* **p.o.**) a money order available from, and payable by, a post office.

postbag *noun* **1** a mailbag. **2** the letters received by eg a radio or TV programme, magazine or celebrated person, etc.

postbox see **letter box**

postcard *noun* a card for writing messages on, often with a picture on one side, designed for sending through the post without an envelope.

postcode *noun* a code used to identify a postal address, made up of a combination of letters and numerals. Also called **postal code**. *US equivalent* **zip code**. [20c]

postdate *verb* **1** to put a future date on (a cheque, etc). **2** to assign a later date than that previously accepted to (an event, etc). **3** to occur at a later date than (a specified date). [17c]

poster *noun* **1** a large notice or advertisement for public display. **2** a large printed picture. [19c: from **post**[1]]

poste restante /poust 'rɛstɒnt/ *noun* **1** an address on mail indicating that it is to be held at a particular post office until it is collected by the recipient. **2** the department of a post office which deals with such mail. [18c: French, meaning 'post remaining']

posterior *adj* **1 a** placed behind, after or at the back of something; **b** *zool* at or near the hind end; **c** *botany* growing away from the main stem or towards the axis. Compare **anterior**. **2** *formal or old use* coming after in time. ▸ *noun, facetious* the buttocks. [16c: Latin, comparative of *posterus* coming after]

posterity *noun* **1** future generations. **2** one's descendants. [14c: from French *postérité*]

postern *noun, hist* a back door, back gate or private entrance. [13c: from French *posterne*]

poster paint *or* **poster colour** *noun* a water-based paint in an opaque colour. [20c]

postgraduate *noun* a person studying for an advanced degree or qualification after obtaining a first degree. Compare **graduate**. ▸ *adj* relating to such a person or degree: *postgraduate diploma*.

posthaste *adv* with the utmost speed. [16c]

posthumous /'pɒstjʊməs/ *adj* **1** of a work: published after the death of the author, composer, etc. **2** of a child: born after its father's death. **3** coming or occurring after death: *posthumous fame.* ▪ **posthumously** *adv.* [17c: from Latin *postumus* last]

postilion *or* **postillion** *noun, hist* a rider on the nearside horse of one of the pairs of horses drawing a carriage, who, in the absence of a coachman, guides the team. [17c: from French *postillon*]

postimpressionism *or* **Post-Impressionism** *noun, art* an imprecise term used to describe the more progressive forms of painting since c.1880, which developed as a reaction against **Impressionism**, with the aim of conveying the essence of their subjects through a simplification of form. [20c: coined by the art critic Roger Fry]

postman *or* **postwoman** *noun* a man or woman whose job is to deliver mail. *N Am equivalent* **mailman**. [16c, meaning **post**[3] (*noun* sense 6)]

postmark *noun* a mark stamped on mail by the post office, cancelling the stamp and showing the date and place of posting. ▸ *verb* to mark (mail) in this way. Compare **frank**.

postmaster *or* **postmistress** *noun* the man or woman in charge of a local post office.

post meridiem *noun* (abbrev **p.m., pm, P.M.** *or* **PM**) after midday; in the afternoon. [17c: Latin]

post-modernism *noun* a movement in the arts that takes many features of **Modernism** to new, more playful, extremes. ▪ **post-modern** *adj.* ▪ **post-modernist** *noun, adj.* [20c]

postmortem (abbrev **p.m.** *or* **pm**) *noun* **1** (*in full* **postmortem examination**) the dissection and examination of the internal organs of the body after death, in order to determine the cause of death. Also called **autopsy**. **2** *informal* an after-the-event discussion. ▸ *adj* coming or happening after death. [18c: Latin, meaning 'after death']

postnatal *adj* relating to or occurring during the period immediately after childbirth. ▪ **postnatally** *adv.* [19c]

postnatal depression *noun, psychol* a relatively common form of usu mild depression that can affect a mother shortly after giving birth. Also (*informal*) *called* **baby blues**.

post office *noun* **1** a local office that handles postal business, the issuing of various types of licence, etc. **2** (**Post Office**; abbrev **PO**) the government department in charge of postal services.

post-operative *adj* relating to or occurring during the period immediately following a surgical operation.

postpone *verb* to delay or put off something till later. ▪ **postponement** *noun.* [16c: from Latin *postponere*]

postprandial *adj, facetious* following a meal: *a postprandial doze.* [19c]

postscript *noun* (abbrev **PS** *or* **ps**) a message added to a letter as an afterthought, after one's signature. [16c: from Latin *postscribere* to write something after]

postulant *noun* someone who asks or petitions for something, esp a candidate for holy orders or for admission to a religious community. ▪ **postulancy** *noun* (**-ies**). [18c: French]

postulate *verb* /'pɒstjʊleɪt/ **1** to assume or suggest something as the basis for discussion; to take it for granted. **2** to demand; to claim. ▸ *noun* /'pɒstjʊlət/ **1** a stipulation or prerequisite. **2** a position assumed as self-evident. ▪ **postulation** *noun.* [16c: from Latin *postulare* to demand]

posture *noun* **1** the way one holds one's body while standing, sitting or walking. **2** a particular position or attitude of the body. **3** an attitude adopted towards a particular issue, etc. **4** a pose adopted for effect. ▸ *verb* **1** to take up a particular bodily attitude. **2** *intr, derog* to pose, strike attitudes, etc so as to draw attention to oneself. ▪ **postural** *adj*. [17c: French]

postwar *adj* relating or belonging to the period following a war.

posy *noun* (**-*ies***) a small bunch of flowers. [16c: a variant of **poesy**]

pot[1] *noun* **1** a domestic container, usu a deep round one, used as a cooking or serving utensil, or for storage. **2** (*also* **potful**) the amount a pot can hold: *a pot of tea*. **3** *pottery* any handmade container. **4** the pool of accumulated bets in any gambling game. **5** in snooker, billiards, pool, etc: a shot that pockets a ball. **6** a casual shot: *take a pot at something*. **7** a **chamberpot**. **8** a **flowerpot**. **9** (**pots**) *informal* a great deal, esp of money. **10** *informal* a trophy, esp a cup. **11** a **potbelly**. ▸ *verb* (***potted, potting***) **1** to plant something in a plant pot. **2** to preserve (a type of food) in a pot. **3** in snooker, billiards, pool, etc: to shoot (a ball) into a pocket: *couldn't pot the black*. **4 a** *informal* to shoot at (an animal, bird, etc), esp indiscriminately or wildly; **b** to win or secure, esp by shooting: *potted six grouse*. [Anglo-Saxon *pott*]
IDIOMS **go to pot** *informal* to degenerate badly.

pot[2] *noun, informal* **cannabis**. [20c: prob from Mexican Spanish *potiguaya* marijuana leaves]

potable /'poʊtəbəl/ *adj* fit or suitable for drinking. ▪ **potability** *noun*. [16c: French]

potash *noun* a compound of potassium. [17c: from Dutch *potasschen*]

potassium *noun, chem* (symbol **K**) a soft silvery-white metallic element, compounds of which are used in fertilizers, explosives, laboratory reagents, soaps and some types of glass. [19c: from **potash**]

potassium hydroxide *noun, chem* a corrosive white crystalline solid that dissolves to form a strong alkaline solution, used in the manufacture of soft soap and in batteries.

potassium nitrate *noun, chem* a white or transparent highly explosive crystalline solid, used in the manufacture of matches, gunpowder, fertilizers, etc and as a food preservative. Also called **nitre, saltpetre**.

potation *noun, formal or humorous* **1** the act or an instance of drinking. **2** a drink, esp an alcoholic one. **3** a drinking binge. [15c: from French *potacion*]

potato *noun* (***potatoes***) **1** a plant that produces edible **tubers** and is a staple crop of temperate regions worldwide. **2** the starch-rich round or oval tuber of this plant, which is cooked for food. *as adj*: *potato salad*. [16c: from Spanish *patata*]

potato crisp see **crisp** (*noun*)

potbelly *noun* (**-*ies***) *informal* **1** a large overhanging belly. **2** someone who has such a belly. Often shortened to **pot**. ▪ **pot-bellied** *adj*. [18c]

potboiler *noun, derog* an inferior work of literature or art produced by a writer or artist capable of better work, simply to make money and stay in the public view. [19c]

poteen /pɒ'tiːn, pɒ'tʃiːn/ *noun, Irish* illicitly distilled Irish whiskey. [19c: from Irish *poitín* little pot]

potent *adj* **1** strong; effective; powerful. **2** of an argument, etc: persuasive; convincing. **3** of a drug or poison: powerful and swift in effect. **4** of a male: capable of sexual intercourse. Opposite of **impotent**. ▪ **potency** *noun* (**-*ies***) **1** the state of being potent; power. **2** strength or effectiveness, eg of a drug. **3** the capacity for development. [15c: from Latin *potens* able]

potentate *noun, esp hist or literary* a powerful ruler; a monarch. [14c: from Latin *potentatus*]

potential *adj* possible or likely, though as yet not tested or actual: *a potential customer*. ▸ *noun* **1** the range of capabilities that someone or something has; powers or resources not yet developed or made use of: *fulfil your potential*. **2** *physics* the energy required to move a unit of mass, electric charge, etc from an infinite distance to the point in a gravitational or electric field where it is to be measured. ▪ **potentiality** *noun* (**-*ies***). ▪ **potentially** *adv*. [14c: from Latin *potentialis*]

potential difference *noun, physics* (abbrev **pd** *or* **PD**) the **work** (*noun* sense 10) done in moving electric charge between two points in an electrical circuit.

potential energy *noun, physics* (abbrev **PE**) the energy stored by an object by virtue of its position.

potentiometer /pətɛnʃɪ'ɒmɪtə(r)/ *noun, physics* an instrument that measures electric **potential** (*noun* sense 2), used as a volume control in transistor radios. [19c]

pother *noun* a fuss or commotion. [16c]

pot-herb *noun* any plant whose leaves or stems are used in cooking to season or garnish food.

pothole *noun* **1** a roughly circular hole worn in the bedrock of a river as pebbles are swirled around by water eddies. **2** a vertical cave system or deep hole eroded in limestone. **3** a hole worn in a road surface.

potholing *noun* the sport or activity of exploring deep caves and potholes. ▪ **potholer** *noun*. [19c]

potion *noun* a draught of medicine, poison or some magic elixir. [14c: French]

pot luck *noun* whatever happens to be available. *as adj*: *pot-luck supper*.
IDIOMS **take pot luck** to have whatever happens to be available.

pot plant *noun* a plant grown in a pot and usu kept indoors for decoration.

potpourri /poʊ'pʊərɪ/ *noun* **1** a fragrant mixture of dried flowers, leaves, etc placed in containers and used to scent rooms. **2** a medley or mixture. [18c: French, literally 'rotten pot']

pot roast *noun, cookery* a cut of meat braised with a little water in a covered pot.

potsherd /'pɒtʃɜːd/ *noun, archaeol* a fragment of pottery. [14c: from **pot[1]** + Anglo-Saxon *sceard*]

pot shot *noun* **1** an easy shot at close range. **2** a shot made without taking careful aim. [19c]

pottage *noun* a thick soup. [13c: from French *potage* that which is put in a pot]

potted *adj* **1** abridged: *a potted history*. **2** of food: preserved in a pot or jar: *potted meat*. **3** of a plant: growing or grown in a pot: *a potted begonia*.

potter[1] *noun* someone who makes pottery.

potter[2] *verb, intr* **1** (*usu* **potter about**) to busy oneself in a mild way with trifling tasks. **2** (*usu* **potter about** *or* **along**) to progress in an unhurried manner;

to dawdle. ▪ **potterer** *noun.* [18c: from Anglo-Saxon *potian* to thrust]

potter's wheel *noun* an apparatus with a heavy rotating stone platter, on which clay pots can be shaped by hand before firing.

pottery *noun* (**-ies**) **1** containers, pots or other objects of baked clay. **2** the art or craft of making such objects. **3** a factory where such objects are produced commercially. [15c]

potting shed *noun* a shed where garden tools are kept, plants are put into pots, etc.

potty[1] *adj* (**-ier, -iest**) *informal* **1** mad; crazy. **2** (*usu* **potty about sb** *or* **sth**) intensely interested in or keen on them or it. **3** trifling; insignificant. ▪ **pottiness** *noun.* [19c: from **pot**[1]]

potty[2] *noun* (**-ies**) *informal* a child's chamberpot. [20c: diminutive of **pot**[1]]

potty-train *verb* to teach (usu a toddler) to use a potty or the toilet. ▪ **potty-trained** *adj.*

pouch *noun* **1** *chiefly old use* a purse or small bag: *a tobacco pouch.* **2** in marsupials such as the kangaroo: a pocket of skin on the belly, in which the young are carried until they are weaned. **3** a fleshy fold in the cheek of hamsters and other rodents, for storing undigested food. ▸ *verb* **1** to form, or form into, a pouch. **2** *informal* to take possession of something. [14c: from Old French *poche* pocket]

pouffe *or* **pouf** /puːf/ *noun* a firmly stuffed drum-shaped or cube-shaped cushion for use as a low seat. [19c: from French *pouf* something puffed out]

poulterer *noun* a dealer in poultry and game. [17c: from French *pouletier*]

poultice /ˈpoʊltɪs/ *noun, med* a hot, semi-liquid mixture spread on a bandage and applied to the skin to reduce inflammation. [16c: from Latin *pultes*]

poultry *noun* **1** *collective* domesticated birds kept for their eggs or meat, or both, eg chickens, ducks, etc. **2** the meat of such birds. [14c: from French *pouletrie*]

pounce *verb, intr* (*often* **pounce on sth** *or* **sb**) **1** to leap or swoop on (a victim or prey), esp when trying to capture them or it. **2** to seize on it or them; to grab eagerly. ▸ *noun* an act of pouncing. [15c]

pound[1] *noun* **1** (symbol **£**) the standard unit of currency of the UK. Also called **pound sterling**. **2** the English name for the principal currency unit in several other countries, including Egypt. **3** (abbrev **lb**) in the imperial system: a unit of measurement of weight equal to 16 ounces (about 0.45 kilograms) avoirdupois, or 12 ounces (about 0.37 kilograms) troy. [Anglo-Saxon *pund*]

pound[2] *noun* **1** an enclosure where stray animals or illegally parked cars that have been taken into police charge are kept for collection. **2** a place where people are confined. See also **compound**[2]. [Anglo-Saxon]

pound[3] *verb* **1** *tr & intr* (*often* **pound on** *or* **at sth**) to beat or bang it vigorously: *pounding on the door.* **2** *intr* to walk or run with heavy thudding steps. **3** to crush or grind something to a powder. **4** to thump or beat esp with the fists: *pounded him senseless.* **5** of the heart: to beat with heavy thumping pulses, esp through fear, excitement, etc. [Anglo-Saxon *punian*]

poundage *noun* a fee or commission charged per **pound**[1] in weight or money.

-pounder *noun, in compounds, denoting* **1** something weighing a specified number of pounds: *My trout was a three-pounder.* **2** a field gun designed to fire shot weighing a specified number of pounds: *a twenty-four-pounder.*

pound sign *noun* the symbol (**£**) used before a number to designate the **pound**[1] (sense 1).

pound sterling see under **pound**[1]

pour *verb* **1** *tr & intr* to flow or cause something to flow in a downward stream. **2** *tr & intr* of a jug, teapot, etc: to discharge (liquid) in a certain way: *doesn't pour very well.* **3** (*also* **pour sth out**) to serve (a drink, etc) by pouring. **4** *intr* to rain heavily. **5** *intr* (*usu* **pour in** *or* **out**) to come or go in large numbers. **6** *intr* (*also* **pour in** *or* **out**, *etc*) to flow or issue plentifully. **7** *tr* (**pour sth into sth**) to invest eg money, energy, etc liberally into it. ▪ **pourer** *noun.* [14c]

PHRASAL VERBS **pour sth out** to reveal without inhibition: *poured out her feelings.*

---

pour, pore

Be careful not to use the spelling **pour** when you mean **pore**:

He was poring over a book.

---

poussin /*French* pusɛ̃/ *noun* a young chicken killed and eaten at the age of four to six weeks. [20c: French, meaning 'a newly-born chicken']

pout *verb* **1** *tr & intr* to push the lower lip or both lips forward as an indication of sulkiness or seductiveness. **2** *intr* of the lips: to stick out in this way. ▸ *noun* **1** an act of pouting. **2** a pouting expression. [14c]

poverty *noun* **1** the condition of being poor; want. **2** poor quality. **3** inadequacy; deficiency: *poverty of imagination.* [12c: from French *poverte*]

poverty line *noun* the minimum income needed to purchase the basic necessities of life.

poverty-stricken *adj* suffering from poverty.

poverty trap *noun* the inescapable poverty of someone who, in achieving an improvement in income, has their state benefits cut.

POW *abbrev* prisoner of war.

powder *noun* **1** any substance in the form of fine dust-like particles: *talcum powder.* **2** (*also* **face powder**) a cosmetic that is patted on to the skin to give it a soft smooth appearance. **3** **gunpowder**. **4** a dose of medicine in powder form. ▸ *verb* **1** to apply powder to (eg one's face); to sprinkle or cover something with powder. **2** to reduce something to a powder by crushing; to pulverize. ▪ **powdery** *adj.* [13c: from French *poudre*]

powder keg *noun* **1** a barrel of gunpowder. **2** a potentially dangerous or explosive situation.

powder puff *noun* a pad of velvety or fluffy material for patting **powder** (*noun* sense 2) on to the skin.

powder room *noun* a women's cloakroom or toilet in a restaurant, hotel, etc.

power *noun* **1** control and influence exercised over others. **2** strength, vigour, force or effectiveness. **3** *usu in compounds* military strength: *sea power* • *air power.* **4** the physical ability, skill, opportunity or authority to do something. **5** an individual faculty or skill: *the power of speech.* **6** a right, privilege or responsibility: *the power of arrest.* **7** political control. **8** *also in compounds* a state that has an influential role in international affairs: *superpower.* **9** a person or group exercising control or influence. **10** *informal* a great deal: *The rest did her a power of good.* **11** *often in compounds* any form of energy, esp when used as the driving force for a machine: *nuclear power.* **12** *maths* a less technical term for an **exponent** (sense 3). **13** *physics* the rate of doing work or converting energy from one form into another. **14** mechanical or electrical energy, as distinct from manual effort. *as adj*: *power tools.* **15** *optics* a measure of the extent to which a lens, optical instrument or curved mirror can deviate light rays and so magnify an image of an object. ▶ *verb* **1** *also in compounds* to supply something with power: *wind-powered.* **2** *tr & intr, informal* to move or cause something to move with great force, energy or speed. [13c: from French *poer*]

IDIOMS **in power** elected; holding office. **the powers that be** the people who are in control or in authority.

PHRASAL VERBS **power sth up** to recharge its power supply (esp that of a laptop computer) by attaching it to the mains electricity supply.

powerboat *noun* a small boat fitted with a high-powered engine.

power cut *noun* a temporary break or reduction in an electricity supply.

powerful *adj* **1** having great power, strength or vigour. **2** very effective or efficient: *a powerful argument.* ▶ *adv, dialect* extremely: *powerful hot.*

powerhouse *noun* **1** a power station. **2** *informal* a forceful or vigorous person.

powerless *adj* **1** deprived of power or authority. **2** completely unable (to do something).

power of attorney *noun* the right to act for another person in legal and business matters.

power point *noun, Brit* a wall socket where an electrical appliance may be connected to the mains.

power-sharing *noun, politics* an agreement, esp between parties in a coalition, that policy-making, decision-taking, etc will be done jointly.

power station *noun* a building where electricity is generated on a large scale from another form of energy, such as coal, nuclear fuel, moving water, etc.

power steering *or* **power-assisted steering** *noun* in a motor vehicle: a system in which the rotating force exerted on the steering wheel is supplemented by engine power.

powwow *noun* **1** *informal* a meeting for discussion. **2** a meeting of Native Americans. ▶ *verb, intr* to hold a powwow. [17c: from Narragansett *powwaw* priest]

pox *noun* **1** *med, often in compounds* an infectious viral disease that causes a skin rash consisting of pimples containing pus: *chickenpox* • *smallpox.* **2** (*often* **the pox**) a former name for **syphilis**. [16c: a variant of *pocks*, the plural of **pock**]

poxy *adj* (*-ier, -iest*) *Brit informal* worthless, second-rate, trashy. [20c]

pp *abbrev* **1** pages: *pp9–12.* **2** usu written when signing a letter in the absence of the sender: *per procurationem* (Latin), for and on behalf of (the specified person). Also called **per pro. 3** *music* pianissimo.

ppm *abbrev* parts per million.

PPS *abbrev* **1** Parliamentary Private Secretary. **2** (*also* **pps**) *post postscriptum* (Latin), after the postscript, ie an additional postscript.

PR *abbrev* **1** proportional representation. **2** public relations.

Pr *symbol, chem* praseodymium.

practicable *adj* capable of being done, used or successfully carried out; feasible. ▪ **practicability** *noun.* ▪ **practicably** *adv.* [17c: from French *pratiquer* to practise]

practicable, practical

Although both these words mean 'able to be done or used', there is a slight but important difference in the words.

Practicable means 'able to be carried out or used':

We have a plan that is both practicable and cost-efficient.

Practical has the added suggestion of 'sensible or efficient':

We can always depend on her for a practical solution.

practical *adj* **1** concerned with or involving action rather than theory: *put her knowledge to practical use.* **2** effective, or capable of being effective, in actual use. **3** eg of clothes: designed for tough or everyday use; sensibly plain. **4** of a person: **a** sensible and efficient in deciding and acting; **b** good at doing manual jobs. **5** in effect; virtual: *a practical walkover.* ▶ *noun* a practical lesson or examination, eg in a scientific subject. ▪ **practicality** *noun* (*-ies*). [17c: from Greek *praktikos*]

practical joke *noun* a trick or prank which is played on someone, usu making them look silly. ▪ **practical joker** *noun.*

practically *adv* **1** almost; very nearly. **2** in a practical manner.

practice *noun* **1** the process of carrying something out: *put ideas into practice.* **2** a habit, activity, procedure or custom: *Don't make a practice of it!* **3** repeated exercise to improve technique in an art or sport, etc. **4** the business or clientele of a doctor, dentist, lawyer, etc. [16c: from **practise**]

IDIOMS **be in** *or* **out of practice** to have maintained, or failed to maintain, one's skill in an art or sport, etc.

practice, practise

Be careful not to use the noun spelling **practice** instead of the verb spelling **practise**, and vice versa:

She is practising her ballet steps.

ballet practice.

Note that American English uses **practice** for both.

practise *or* (*US*) **practice** *verb* **1** *tr & intr* to do exercises repeatedly in (an art or sport, etc) so as to improve one's performance. **2** to make a habit of something: *practise self-control.* **3** to go in for something as a custom: *tribes that practise bigamy.* **4** to work at or follow (an art or profession, esp medicine or law). **5** to perform (a wrongful act) against someone: *He practised a cruel deception on them.* [15c: from Latin *practicare*]

practised *or* (*US*) **practiced** *adj* (*often* **practised at sth**) skilled; experienced; expert.

practising *or* (*US*) **practicing** *adj* actively engaged in or currently pursuing or observing: *a practising lawyer.* ▶ *noun* an act or the process of doing something for **practice** (sense 3): *Download the program into your computer for practising.*

practitioner *noun* someone who practises an art or profession, esp medicine. See also **general practitioner**. [16c: from French *praticien*]

praesidium see **presidium**

praetor /'pri:tə(r)/ *noun, Roman hist* one of the chief law officers of the state, elected annually, and second to the **consul** in importance. ▪ **praetorian** *adj, noun.* [15c: Latin, meaning 'one who goes before']

pragmatic *adj* **1** concerned with what is practicable, expedient and convenient, rather than with theories and ideals. **2** *philos* relating to pragmatism. [17c: from Latin *pragmaticus*]

pragmatism *noun* **1** a practical matter-of-fact approach to dealing with problems, etc. **2** *philos* a school of thought that assesses the truth of concepts in terms of their practical implications. ▪ **pragmatist** *noun.*

prairie *noun* in N America: a large expanse of flat or rolling natural grassland, usu without trees. [18c: French]

praise *verb* **1** to express admiration or approval of someone or something. **2** to worship or glorify (God) with hymns or thanksgiving, etc. ▸ *noun* **1** the expression of admiration or approval; commendation. **2** worship of God. [13c: from French *preisier*] IDIOMS **sing sb's** *or* **sth's praises** to commend them or it enthusiastically.

praiseworthy *adj* deserving praise; commendable. [16c]

praline /'prɑ:li:n/ *noun* a sweet consisting of nuts in caramelized sugar. [18c: from Marshal Duplessis-Praslin, a French soldier whose cook invented it]

pram *noun* a wheeled baby carriage pushed by someone on foot. [19c: a short form of **perambulator**]

prance *verb, intr* **1** esp of a horse: to walk with lively springing steps. **2** to frisk or skip about. **3** to parade about in a swaggering manner. [14c]

prandial *adj, often facetious* belonging or relating to dinner. See also **postprandial**. [19c: from Latin *prandium* a morning or midday meal]

prang *informal, verb* **1** to crash (a vehicle). **2** to bomb something from the air. ▸ *noun* **1** a vehicle crash. **2** a bombing raid. [20c: orig RAF slang]

prank *noun* a playful trick; a practical joke. ▪ **prankster** *noun.* [16c]

praseodymium /preɪzɪoʊ'dɪmɪəm/ *noun, chem* (symbol **Pr**) a soft silvery metallic element, used in thermoelectric materials, glass, etc. [19c: Latin]

prat *noun, slang* **1** *offensive* a fool; an ineffectual person. **2** the buttocks. [16c]

prate *verb, tr & intr* to talk or utter foolishly; to blab. ▸ *noun* idle chatter. [15c: from Dutch *praeten* to talk]

prattle *verb, tr & intr* to chatter or utter childishly or foolishly. ▸ *noun* childish or foolish chatter. ▪ **prattler** *noun.* [16c: from German *pratelen* to chatter]

prawn *noun* a small edible shrimp-like marine crustacean. [15c]

praxis *noun* (***praxes***) **1** practice as opposed to theory. **2** an example or collection of examples for exercise. **3** accepted practice. [16c: Greek, from *prassein* to do]

pray *verb* (*often* **pray for sth** *or* **sb**) **1** *now usu intr* to address one's god, making earnest requests or giving thanks. **2** *old use, tr & intr* to entreat or implore: *Stop, I pray you!* **3** *tr & intr* to hope desperately. ▸ *exclam, old use* (now often uttered with quaint politeness or cold irony) please, or may I ask: *Pray come in* • *Who asked you, pray?* [13c: from French *preier*]

pray, prey
Be careful not to use the spelling **pray** when you mean **prey**:
The eagle is a bird of prey.

prayer¹ /prɛə(r)/ *noun* **1** an address to one's god, making a request or giving thanks. **2** the activity of praying. **3** an earnest hope, desire or entreaty. [13c: from French *preiere*]

prayer² /preɪə(r)/ *noun* someone who prays.

prayerful *adj* **1** of someone: devout; tending to pray a lot or often. **2** of a speech, etc: imploring.

prayer shawl see **tallith**

praying mantis see under **mantis**

pre- *prefix, denoting* before **a** in time: *pre-war*; **b** in position: *premolar*; **c** in importance: *pre-eminent*. [From Latin *prae-* before]

preach *verb* **1** *tr & intr* to deliver (a sermon) as part of a religious service. **2** (*often* **preach at sb**) to give them advice in a tedious or obtrusive manner. **3** to advise or advocate something. ▪ **preacher** *noun* someone who preaches, esp a minister of religion. [13c: from French *prechier*]

pre-adolescent *adj* **1** belonging or relating to the period immediately preceding adolescence. **2** of a child: at this stage of development. ▸ *noun* a pre-adolescent child. ▪ **pre-adolescence** *noun.*

preamble *noun* an introduction or preface, eg to a speech or document; an opening statement. [14c: from Latin *praeambulare* to walk before]

prearrange *verb* to arrange something in advance. ▪ **prearrangement** *noun.* [18c]

prebend /'prɛbənd/ *noun* **1** an allowance paid out of the revenues of a cathedral or collegiate church to its canons or chapter members. **2** the piece of land, etc which is the source of such revenue. **3** a prebendary. ▪ **prebendal** /prɪ'bɛndəl/ *adj.* [15c: from Latin *praebenda* allowance]

prebendary /'prɛbəndərɪ/ *noun* (***-ies***) **1** a clergyman of a cathedral or collegiate church who is in receipt of a **prebend**. **2** in the Church of England: the honorary holder of a prebend.

Precambrian *geol, adj* **1** relating to the earliest geological era, during which primitive forms of life appeared on earth. **2** relating to the rocks formed during this period. ▸ *noun* (**the Precambrian**) the Precambrian era. [19c: see **Cambrian**]

precancerous *adj* esp of cells: showing early indications of possible malignancy. [Late 19c]

precarious *adj* **1** unsafe; insecure; dangerous. **2** uncertain; chancy. ▪ **precariously** *adv.* [17c: from Latin *precarius* obtained by prayer]

precaution *noun* **1** a measure taken to ensure a satisfactory outcome, or to avoid a risk or danger. **2** caution exercised beforehand. ▪ **precautionary** *adj.* [17c: from Latin *praecautio*]

precede *verb, tr & intr* to go or be before someone or something, in time, order, position, rank or importance. [15c: from Latin *praecedere* to go before]

precedence /'prɛsɪdəns/ *noun* **1** priority. **2** the right to precede others. [16c]

precedent *noun* /'prɛsɪdənt/ **1** a previous incident or legal case, etc that has something in common with one under consideration, serving as a basis for a decision in the present one. **2** the judgement or decision given in such a case.

precentor *noun, relig* someone who leads the singing of a church congregation, or the prayers in a synagogue. [17c: from Latin *praecentor*]

precept *noun* **1** a rule or principle, esp one of a moral kind, that is seen or used as a guide to behaviour. **2** *law* the written warrant of a magistrate. [14c: from Latin *praeceptum*]

preceptor *or* **preceptress** *noun* a teacher or instructor. ▪ **preceptorial** *adj.* [15c: from Latin *praeceptor* an instructor]

precession *noun* **1** *physics* the gradual change in direction of the axis of rotation of a spinning body. **2** *astron* the progressively earlier occurrence of the equinoxes, resulting from the gradual change in direction of the Earth's axis of rotation. Also called **precession of the equinoxes**. **3** the act of preceding. ▪ **precessional** *adj.* [16c: from Latin *praecessio*]

precinct *noun* **1** (*also* **precincts**) the enclosed grounds of a large building, etc: *the cathedral precinct*. **2** (*also* **precincts**) the neighbourhood or environs of a place. **3** a **pedestrian precinct**. **4** *N Am, esp US* **a** any of the districts into which a city is divided for administrative or policing purposes; **b** the police station of one of these districts. [15c: from Latin *praecingere* to surround]

preciosity /prɛʃɪ'ɒsɪtɪ/ *noun* (**-ies**) affectedness or exaggerated refinement in speech or manner. [19c: see **precious**]

precious *adj* **1** valuable. **2** dear; beloved; treasured. **3** *derog* of speech or manner: affected or overprecise. **4** *informal, ironic* **a** confounded: *Him and his precious goldfish!* **b** substantial: *And a precious lot you'd care!* [13c: from Latin *pretiosus* valuable]
IDIOMS **precious few** *or* **little** *informal* almost none.

precious metal *noun* gold, silver or platinum.

precious stone *noun* a gemstone, such as a diamond, ruby, etc, valued for its beauty and rarity, esp with regard to its use in jewellery or ornamentation.

precipice *noun* a steep, vertical or overhanging cliff or rock face. [17c: from Latin *praecipitare* to fall headlong]

precipitate *verb* /prɪ'sɪpɪteɪt/ **1** to cause something or hasten its advent: *precipitated a war*. **2** to throw or plunge: *Jim precipitated himself into the controversy.* **3** *tr & intr, chem* to form or cause something to form a suspension of small solid particles in a solution, as a result of certain chemical reactions. **4** *meteorol* of moisture, etc: to condense and fall as rain, snow, etc. ▸ *adj* /prɪ'sɪpɪtət/ of actions or decisions: recklessly hasty or ill-considered. ▸ *noun* /prɪ'sɪpɪtət/ **1** *chem* a suspension of small solid particles formed in a solution as a result of certain chemical reactions. **2** *meteorol* moisture deposited as rain or snow, etc. [16c: from Latin *praecipitare* to fall or throw headlong]

precipitation *noun* **1** rash haste. **2** *meteorol* water that falls from clouds in the atmosphere to the Earth's surface in the form of rain, snow, etc. **3** the act of precipitating or process of being precipitated. **4** *chem* the formation of a precipitate.

precipitous *adj* **1** dangerously steep. **2** of actions or decisions: rash; precipitate. ▪ **precipitously** *adv.*

précis /'preɪsiː/ *noun* (*pl* ***précis***) a summary of a piece of writing. ▸ *verb* to make a précis of something. [18c: French, meaning 'precise' or 'cut short']

precise *adj* **1** exact; very: *at this precise moment*. **2** clear; detailed: *precise instructions*. **3** accurate: *precise timing*. **4** of someone: careful over details. ▪ **preciseness** *noun.* [16c: from Latin *praecisus* shortened]

precisely *adv* **1** exactly: *began at eight o'clock precisely.* **2** in a precise manner. **3** said in response to a remark: you are quite right.

precision *noun* accuracy. ▸ *adj* designed to operate with minute accuracy: *precision tools.*

preclude *verb* **1** to rule out or eliminate something or make it impossible. **2** (*often* **preclude sb from sth**) to prevent their involvement in it. ▪ **preclusion** *noun.* ▪ **preclusive** *adj.* [17c: from Latin *praecludere* to impede]

precocious *adj* eg of a child: unusually advanced in mental development, speech, behaviour, etc. ▪ **precociously** *adv.* ▪ **precociousness** *or* **precocity** *noun.* [17c: from Latin *praecox* ripening early]

precognition *noun* the supposed ability to foresee events; foreknowledge. ▪ **precognitive** *adj.* [17c: from Latin *praecognitio*]

preconceive *verb* to form (an idea, etc) of something before having direct experience of it. ▪ **preconceived** *adj.* [16c]

preconception *noun* **1** an assumption about something not yet experienced. **2** (*often* **preconceptions**) a prejudice.

precondition *noun* a condition to be satisfied in advance. [19c]

precursor *noun* something that precedes, and is a sign of, an approaching event. ▪ **precursive** *or* **precursory** *adj.* [16c: Latin, from *praecurrere* to run before]

predacious *adj* of animals: predatory. [18c: from Latin *praeda* booty or prey]

predate *verb* **1** to write an earlier date on (a document, cheque, etc). **2** to occur at an earlier date than (a specified date or event). [19c]

predation *noun* the killing and consuming of other animals for survival; the activity of preying. [20c: from Latin *praedari* to plunder]

predator /'prɛdətə(r)/ *noun* **1** any animal that obtains food by catching, usu killing, and eating other animals. **2** *derog* a predatory person. [20c: from Latin *praedator* plunderer]

predatory /'prɛdətərɪ/ *adj* **1** of an animal: obtaining food by catching and eating other animals. **2** of a person: cruelly exploiting the weakness or goodwill of others for personal gain.

predecessor *noun* **1** the person who formerly held a job or position now held by someone else. **2** the previous model, etc of a particular thing or product. **3** an ancestor. [14c: from Latin *praedecessor*]

predestination *noun* **1** the act of predestining or fact of being predestined. **2** *relig* the doctrine that whatever is to happen has been unalterably fixed by God from the beginning of time.

predestine *verb* **1** to determine something beforehand. **2** to ordain or decree by fate. [14c]

predetermine *verb* **1** to decide, settle or fix in advance. **2** to influence, shape or bias something in a certain way. ▪ **predeterminate** *adj.* ▪ **predetermination** *noun.* ▪ **predetermined** *adj.* [17c]

predicable *adj* able to be predicated or affirmed. [16c: from Latin *praedicabilis*; see **predicate**]

predicament *noun* **1** a difficulty, plight or dilemma. **2** *logic* a category. [14c: from Latin *praedicamentum* something asserted]

predicate *noun* /'prɛdɪkət/ **1** *grammar* the word or words in a sentence that make a statement about the subject, usu consisting of a verb and its complement, eg *ran* in *John ran* and *knew exactly what to do* in *The people in charge knew exactly what to do.* **2** *logic* what is stated as a property of the subject of a proposition. ▸ *verb* /'prɛdɪkeɪt/ **1** to assert. **2** to imply; to entail the existence of something. **3** *logic* to state something as a property of the subject of a proposition. **4** (*usu* **predicate on** *or* **upon sth**) to make the viability of (an idea, etc) depend on something else being true: *Their success was predicated on the number of supporters they had.* ▪ **predication** *noun*. [16c: from Latin *praedicare* to assert]

predicative /prɪ'dɪkətɪv/ *adj* **1** *grammar* of an adjective: forming part of a **predicate**, eg 'asleep' in *They were asleep.* Compare **attributive**. **2** relating to predicates. ▪ **predicatively** *adv, grammar* with a predicative function.

predict *verb* to prophesy, foretell or forecast. [17c: from Latin *praedicere* to foretell]

predictable *adj* **1** able to be predicted; easily foreseen. **2** *derog* boringly consistent in behaviour or reactions, etc; unoriginal. ▪ **predictability** *noun*. ▪ **predictably** *adv*.

prediction *noun* **1** the act or art of predicting. **2** something foretold.

predilection *noun* a special liking or preference for something. [18c: from French *prédilection*]

predispose *verb* **1** to incline someone to react in a particular way: *Clear handwriting will predispose the examiners in your favour.* **2** to make someone susceptible to something (esp illness). ▪ **predisposition** *noun*. [17c]

predominant *adj* **1** more numerous, prominent or powerful. **2** more frequent; prevailing. ▪ **predominance** *noun*. ▪ **predominantly** *adv*.

predominate *verb, intr* **1** to be more numerous. **2** to be more noticeable or prominent. **3** to have more influence. [16c]

pre-eclampsia *noun, pathol* a toxic condition which can occur late in pregnancy and which may lead to **eclampsia** if left untreated. [20c]

pre-embryo *noun, biol, med* a human embryo in the first fourteen days after fertilization of an ovum, before **differentiation** (see **differentiate** sense 5). [20c]

pre-eminent *adj* outstanding; better than all others. ▪ **pre-eminence** *noun*. ▪ **pre-eminently** *adv*. [15c: from Latin *praeeminere* to project forwards or stand out before]

pre-empt *verb* **1** to do something ahead of someone else and so make pointless (an action they had planned). **2** to obtain something in advance. [19c: a back-formation from **pre-emption**]

pre-emption *noun* **1** *law* the buying of, or right to buy, property, before others get the chance to do so. **2** the act of pre-empting. [16c: from Latin *prae* before + *emptio* buying]

pre-emptive *adj* **1** having the effect of pre-empting. **2** *military* of an attack: effectively destroying the enemy's weapons before they can be used: *a pre-emptive strike.*

preen *verb* **1** *tr & intr* of a bird: to clean and smooth (feathers, etc) with its beak. **2** of a person: to groom (oneself, hair, clothes, etc), esp in a vain manner.

prefab *noun* a prefabricated building, esp a domestic house. [20c: a shortened form of *prefabricated*]

prefabricate *verb* to manufacture standard sections of (a building) for later quick assembly. [20c]

preface /'prɛfəs/ *noun* **1** an explanatory statement at the beginning of a book. **2** anything of an introductory or preliminary character. ▸ *verb* **1** to provide (a book, etc) with a preface. **2** to introduce or precede something with some preliminary matter. [14c: from French *préface*]

prefatory *adj* **1** relating to a preface. **2** serving as a preface or introduction. **3** introductory. [17c]

prefect *noun* **1** in a school: a senior pupil with minor disciplinary powers. **2** in some countries: the senior official of an administrative district. ▪ **prefectoral** *and* **prefectorial** *adj*. [14c: from Latin *praefectus* an official in charge]

prefecture *noun* **1** the office or term of office of a prefect. **2** the district presided over by a prefect. **3** the official residence of a prefect. See **prefect** (sense 2). [17c]

prefer *verb* (***preferred, preferring***) **1** to like someone or something better than another: *I prefer tea to coffee.* **2** *law* to submit (a charge, accusation, etc) to a court of law for consideration. **3** *formal* to promote someone, esp over their colleagues. [14c: from French *préférer*]

---

prefer

Prefer should be followed by *to*, not *than*:

✓ *He prefers tea to coffee.*

---

preferable *adj* more desirable, suitable or advisable; better. ▪ **preferably** *adv*. [17c]

preference *noun* **1** the preferring of one person, thing, etc to another. **2** one's choice of, or liking for, someone or something particular. **3** favourable consideration. [17c]

IDIOMS **in preference to** rather than.

preferential *adj* bestowing special favours or advantages: *preferential treatment*.

preferment *noun* promotion to a more responsible position. [15c: see **prefer** (sense 3)]

prefigure *verb* **1** to be an advance sign or representation of something that is to come; to foreshadow. **2** to imagine beforehand. ▪ **prefiguration** *noun*. [15c: from Latin *praefigurare*]

prefix *noun* **1** *grammar* an element such as *un-, pre-, non-, de-,* etc which is added to the beginning of a word to create a new word. Compare **affix**, **suffix**. **2** a title such as *Mr, Dr, Ms,* etc used before someone's name. ▸ *verb* **1** to add something as an introduction. **2** *grammar* to attach something as a prefix to a word. **3** to add (a prefix) to something. [17c: **pre-** (sense b) + **fix** (*verb*)]

pregnable *adj* capable of being taken by force; vulnerable. [15c: from French *prenable*]

pregnancy *noun* (***-ies***) *biol* in female mammals, including humans: the period between fertilization or conception and birth, during which a developing embryo is carried in the womb. Also called **gestation**. [16c]

pregnant *adj* **1** of a female mammal, including humans: carrying a child or young in the womb. **2** of a remark or pause, etc: loaded with significance. **3** fruitful in results. ▪ **pregnantly** *adv.* [15c: from Latin *praegnans*]

preheat *verb* to heat (an oven, etc) before use. [19c]

prehensile *adj* denoting a part of an animal that is adapted for grasping, eg the tail of certain vertebrates. [18c: from French *préhensile*]

prehistoric *or* **prehistorical** *adj* **1** belonging or relating to the period before written records. **2** *informal* completely outdated or very old-fashioned. ▪ **prehistorically** *adv.* [19c]

prehistory *noun* the period before written records, classified as encompassing the **Stone Age, Bronze Age** and **Iron Age**. [19c]

prejudge *verb* **1** to form an opinion on (an issue, etc) without having all the relevant facts. **2** to condemn someone unheard. ▪ **prejudgement** *noun.* [16c]

prejudice *noun* **1** a biased opinion, based on insufficient knowledge. **2** hostility, eg towards a particular racial or religious group. **3** *law* harm; detriment; disadvantage: *without prejudice to your parental rights.* ▸ *verb* **1** to make someone feel prejudice; to bias. **2** to harm or endanger. [13c: from French *préjudice*]

prejudicial *adj* **1** causing prejudice. **2** harmful. ▪ **prejudicially** *adv.*

prelacy *noun* (**-ies**) *Christianity* **1** the office of a prelate. **2** the entire body of prelates. **3** administration of the church by prelates.

prelate /ˈprɛlət/ *noun, Christianity* a bishop, abbot or other high-ranking ecclesiastic. ▪ **prelatic** /prɪˈlatɪk/ *and* **prelatical** *adj.* [13c: from French *prélat*]

prelim *noun, informal* **1** in Scotland: any one of a set of school examinations taken before the public ones. **2** the first public examination in certain universities. **3** (**prelims**) *printing* the title page, contents page and other matter preceding the main text of a book. [19c: an abbreviation of *preliminaries*]

preliminary *adj* occurring at the beginning; introductory or preparatory. ▸ *noun* (**-ies**) **1** (*usu* **preliminaries**) something done or said by way of introduction or preparation: *had no time for the usual preliminaries.* **2** a preliminary round in a competition. [17c: from Latin *praeliminaris*]

prelude *noun* **1** *music* an introductory passage or first movement, eg of a fugue or suite. **2** a name sometimes given to a short musical piece or a poetic composition, etc. **3** (*esp* **a prelude to sth**) some event that precedes, and prepares the ground for, something of greater significance. ▸ *verb* **1** *tr & intr* to act as a prelude to something. **2** to introduce something with a prelude. [16c: from Latin *praeludium*]

premarital *adj* belonging to or occurring in the period before marriage. ▪ **premaritally** *adv.* [19c]

premature *adj* **1** *med* of human birth: occurring less than 37 weeks after conception. **2** occurring before the usual or expected time: *premature senility.* **3** of a decision, etc: over-hasty; impulsive. ▪ **prematurely** *adv.* [16c: from Latin *praematurus*]

premedication *noun, med* drugs, usu including a sedative, given to a patient in preparation for a **general anaesthetic** prior to surgery. [20c]

premeditate *verb* to plan; to think something out beforehand. ▪ **premeditated** *adj* esp of a crime: planned beforehand. ▪ **premeditation** *noun.* [16c]

premenstrual *adj* **1** relating to or occurring during the days immediately before a **menstrual** period. **2** of a woman: in the days immediately before a menstrual period. [19c]

premenstrual tension *or* **premenstrual syndrome** *noun* (abbrev **PMT** *or* **PMS**) *med* a group of symptoms associated with hormonal changes and experienced by some women before the onset of menstruation, characterized by fluid retention, headache, depression and irritability. [20c]

premier *adj* **1** first in rank; most important; leading. **2** *Brit* denoting the top division in the football leagues in both England and Wales, and Scotland. **3** first in time; earliest. ▸ *noun* **1** a prime minister. **2** in Australia and Canada: the head of government of a state or province. ▪ **premiership** *noun.* [15c: French, meaning 'first']

première *or* **premiere** /ˈprɛmɪɛə(r)/ *noun* the first public performance of a play or showing of a film. Also called **first night**. ▸ *verb* **1** to present a première of (a film, etc). **2** *intr* of a play, film, etc: to open. [19c: French feminine of *premier* first]

premise *noun* /ˈprɛmɪs/ **1** (*also* **premiss**) something assumed to be true as a basis for stating something further. **2** *logic* either of the propositions introducing a syllogism. ▸ *verb* /prɪˈmaɪz/ to assume or state as a premise. [14c: from French *prémisse*]

premises *plural noun* **1** a building and its grounds, esp as a place of business. **2** *law* **a** the preliminary matter in a document, etc; **b** matters explained or property referred to earlier in the document. [18c]

premium *noun* **1** an amount paid, usu annually, on an insurance agreement. **2** an extra sum added to wages or to interest. **3** a prize. ▸ *adj* finest; exceptional: *premium quality.* [17c: from Latin *praemium* reward]

IDIOMS **be at a premium** to be scarce and greatly in demand.

premolar *noun* any of the teeth between the canine teeth and the molars. ▸ *adj* situated in front of a **molar** tooth. [19c]

premonition *noun* a feeling that something is about to happen, before it actually does; an intuition or presentiment. [16c: from Latin *praemonitio* a forewarning]

prenatal *adj* relating to or occurring during the period before childbirth. ▪ **prenatally** *adv.* Compare **antenatal, postnatal.** [19c]

prenuptial *adj* relating to or occurring during the period before marriage. [19c]

prenuptial agreement *noun* an agreement made between two people who are about to marry, stating how their assets will be divided in the event of a divorce. Often shortened to **pre-nup**.

preoccupation *noun* **1** the state or condition of being preoccupied. **2** something that preoccupies.

preoccupied *adj* **1** lost in thought. **2** (*often* **preoccupied by** *or* **with sth**) having one's attention completely taken up; engrossed. **3** already occupied.

preoccupy *verb* **1** to occupy the attention of someone wholly; to engross or obsess. **2** to occupy or fill something before others. [16c: from Latin *praeoccupare* to seize beforehand]

preordain *verb* to decide or determine beforehand.

prep[1] *noun, informal* **1** short for **preparation** (sense 3). **2** short for **preparatory**: *prep school.*

prep[2] *verb* (***prepped, prepping***) to get (a patient) ready for an operation, etc, esp by giving a sedative.

prep. *abbrev, grammar* preposition.

prepack *verb* to pack (food, etc) before offering it for sale. [20c]

preparation *noun* **1** the process of preparing or being prepared. **2** (*usu* **preparations**) something done by way of preparing or getting ready. **3** *Brit,* chiefly in public schools: school work done out of school hours, done either in school or as **homework**. Often shortened to **prep**. **4** a medicine, cosmetic or other such prepared substance.

preparatory /prə'parətərɪ/ *adj* **1** serving to prepare for something. **2** introductory; preliminary. [15c]

preparatory school *noun* **1** in the UK: a private school for children aged between seven and thirteen, usu preparing them for public school. **2** in the US: a private secondary school, preparing pupils for college. Often shortened to **prep school**. [19c]

prepare *verb* **1** *tr & intr* to make or get ready. **2** to make (a meal). **3** to clean or chop (vegetables or fruit). **4** to get someone or oneself into a fit state to receive a shock, surprise, etc: *We prepared ourselves for bad news.* **5** *intr* to brace oneself (to do something). [15c: from Latin *praeparare*]

prepared *adj* **1** (*usu* **be prepared to do sth**) of a person: to be willing and able: *I'm not prepared to lend any more.* **2** (*usu* **prepared for sth**) expecting it or ready for it: *We were prepared for the worst.*

prepay *verb* to pay for something, esp postage, in advance. ▪ **prepaid** *adj*: *a prepaid envelope.* ▪ **prepayable** *adj.* ▪ **prepayment** *noun.* [19c]

preponderance *noun* **1** the circumstance of predominating. **2** a superior number; a majority. ▪ **preponderant** *adj.* [17c]

preponderate *verb, intr* **1** (*often* **preponderate over sth**) to be more numerous than it; to predominate. **2** to weigh more. [17c: from Latin *ponderare* to weigh]

preposition *noun, grammar* a word, or words, such as *to, from, into, out of,* etc, typically preceding nouns and pronouns, and describing their position, movement, etc in relation to other words in the sentence. ▪ **prepositional** *adj.* [14c: from Latin *praepositio*]

prepossess *verb, rather formal* **1** to charm. **2** to win over; to incline or bias. **3** to preoccupy someone in a specified way. [17c: orig meaning 'to possess beforehand']

prepossessing *adj* attractive; winning.

preposterous *adj* ridiculous, absurd or outrageous. ▪ **preposterously** *adv.* [16c: from Latin *praeposterus* back-to-front]

prepotent *adj* **1** powerfully more influential than others. **2** *biol* of a parent: having an exceptional capacity to pass on hereditary characteristics to the next generation. ▪ **prepotency** *noun.* [17c: from Latin *praepotens,* from *posse* to have power]

preppy *informal, esp N Am, adj* (**-ier, -iest**) of dress sense, etc: neat and conservative. ▸ *noun* (**-ies**) someone who dresses in such a way. [20c]

preprandial *adj, facetious* preceding a meal. [19c]

prep school see **preparatory school**

prepuce /'priːpjuːs/ *noun, anatomy* **1** the fold of skin that covers the top of the penis. Also called **foreskin**. **2** the fold of skin that surrounds the clitoris. [14c: from Latin *praeputium*]

prequel *noun* a book or film produced after one that has been a popular success, but with the story beginning prior to the start of the original story. [20c: from **pre-**, modelled on **sequel**]

Pre-Raphaelite /priː'rafəlaɪt/ *noun* a member of the Pre-Raphaelite Brotherhood, a group (formed in 1848) of artists who advocated a adherence to natural forms and effects. ▸ *adj* relating to or characteristic of the Pre-Raphaelites. [19c, after the Italian master Raphael]

prerecord *verb* to record (a programme for radio or TV) in advance of its scheduled broadcasting time. [20c]

prerequisite *noun* a preliminary requirement that must be satisfied. ▸ *adj* of a condition, etc: required to be satisfied beforehand. [17c]

prerogative /prɪ'rɒgətɪv/ *noun* **1** an exclusive right or privilege arising from one's rank or position. **2** any right or privilege. See also **royal prerogative**. [14c: from Latin *praerogativa* privilege]

Pres. *abbrev* President.

presage /'prɛsɪdʒ/ *verb* **1** to warn of or be a warning sign of something; to foreshadow, forebode or portend. **2** to have a premonition about something. ▸ *noun, formal or literary* **1** a portent, warning or omen. **2** a premonition. [14c: from French *présage*]

presbyter *noun, Christianity* **1** in the early Christian Church: an administrative official with some teaching and priestly duties. **2** in Episcopal Churches: a priest. **3** in Presbyterian Churches: an elder. [16c: Latin]

presbyterian *adj* **1** referring or relating to church administration by presbyters or elders. **2** (*often* **Presbyterian**) designating a Church governed by elders. ▸ *noun* (**Presbyterian**) a member of a Presbyterian Church. [17c]

presbytery *noun, Christianity* (**-ies**) **1** in a Presbyterian Church: an area of local administration. **2** a body of ministers and elders, esp one sitting as a local church court. **3** *archit* the eastern section of a church, beyond the choir. **4** the residence of a Roman Catholic priest. [15c: from French *presbiterie* priest's house]

preschool *adj* denoting or relating to children before they are old enough to attend school: *preschool playgroups.* [20c]

prescience /'prɛsɪəns/ *noun* foreknowledge; foresight. ▪ **prescient** *adj.* [14c: from Latin *praescire* to know beforehand]

prescribe *verb* **1** esp of a doctor: to advise (a medicine) as a remedy, esp by completing a prescription. **2** to recommend officially (eg a text for academic study). **3** to lay down or establish (a duty, penalty, etc) officially. ▪ **prescriber** *noun.* [16c: from Latin *praescribere* to write down beforehand]

---

prescribe, proscribe

Be careful not to use the word **prescribe** when you mean **proscribe**.

If you **proscribe** something, you forbid it:

> *We have proscribed the use of calculators in the exam. Anyone caught with one will instantly fail.*

---

prescript *noun, formal* a law, rule, principle, etc that has been laid down. [16c: from Latin *praescriptum*]

prescription *noun* **1 a** a set of written instructions from a doctor to a pharmacist regarding the preparation and dispensing of a drug, etc for a particular patient. *as adj*: *prescription drugs.* **b** the drug, etc prescribed in this way by a doctor. **2** a set of written instructions for an optician stating the type of lenses required to correct a patient's vision. *as adj*: *prescription sunglasses*. **3** the act of prescribing. [14c: from Latin *praescriptio* an order; see **prescribe**]

prescriptive *adj* **1** authoritative; laying down rules. **2** of a right, etc: established by custom. [18c]

presence *noun* **1** the state or circumstance of being present. **2** someone's company or nearness: *He said so in my presence* • *Your presence is requested.* **3** physical bearing, esp if it is commanding or authoritative: *people with presence*. **4** a being felt to be close by, esp in a supernatural way. **5** a situation or activity demonstrating influence or power in a place: *maintain a military presence in the area*. [14c: French]

presence of mind *noun* the ability to act calmly and sensibly, esp in an emergency.

present[1] /'prɛzənt/ *adj* **1** being at the place or occasion in question. **2** existing, detectable or able to be found. **3** existing now: *the present situation*. **4** now being considered: *the present subject*. **5** *grammar* of the tense of a verb: indicating action that is taking place now, or action that is continuing or habitual, as in *I walk the dog every morning* and *He's going to school*. ▶ *noun* **1** the present time. **2** *grammar* **a** the present tense; **b** a verb in the present tense. [13c: from Latin *praesens*]

present[2] /prɪ'zɛnt/ *verb* **1** to give or award something, esp formally or ceremonially: *presented them with gold medals*. **2** to introduce (a person), esp formally. **3** to introduce or compère (a TV or radio show). **4** to stage (a play), show (a film), etc. **5** to offer something for consideration; to submit. **6** to pose; to set: *shouldn't present any problem*. **7** of an idea: to suggest (itself). **8** to hand over (a cheque) for acceptance or (a bill) for payment. **9** to set out something: *presents her work neatly*. **10** to depict or represent something or someone. **11** to put on (a specified appearance) in public. **12** to offer (one's compliments) formally. **13** to hold (a weapon) in aiming position. [13c: from French *presenter*]

IDIOMS **present arms** to hold a rifle or other weapon vertically in front of one as a salute.

present[3] /'prɛzənt/ *noun* something given; a gift. [13c: French]

presentable *adj* **1** fit to be seen or to appear in company, etc. **2** passable; satisfactory. ▪ **presentability** *noun*. [19c: from **present[2]**]

presentation *noun* **1** the act of presenting. **2** the manner in which something is presented, laid out, explained or advertised. **3** something performed for an audience, eg a play, show or other entertainment. **4** a formal report, usu delivered verbally.

present-day *adj* modern; contemporary.

presenter *noun* someone who introduces a TV or radio programme and provides a linking commentary between items.

presentiment /prɪ'zɛntɪmənt/ *noun* a feeling that something, esp something bad, is about to happen, just before it does. [18c: French, from *pressentir* to sense beforehand]

presently *adv* **1** soon; shortly. **2** *N Am, esp US* at the present time; now.

present participle see under **participle**

present perfect see under **perfect**

preservative *noun* a chemical substance that, when added to food or other perishable material, slows down or prevents its decay. ▶ *adj* having the effect of preserving.

preserve *verb* **1** to save something from loss, damage, decay or deterioration. **2** to treat (food), eg by freezing, smoking, drying, etc, so that it will last. **3** to maintain (eg peace, the status quo, standards, etc). **4** to keep safe from danger or death. ▶ *noun* **1** an area of work or activity that is restricted to certain people: *Politics was once a male preserve*. **2** an area of land or water where creatures are protected for private hunting, shooting or fishing: *game preserve*. **3** a jam, pickle or other form in which fruit or vegetables are preserved by cooking in sugar, salt, vinegar, etc. ▪ **preservation** *noun*. ▪ **preserver** *noun*. [14c: from Latin *praeservare* to guard beforehand]

preset *verb* /priː'sɛt/ to adjust (a piece of electronic equipment, etc) so that it will operate at the required time. ▶ *noun* /'priːsɛt/ a device or facility for presetting. [20c]

preshrink *verb* to shrink (fabric) during manufacture, in order to prevent further shrinkage when it has been made into garments. [20c]

preside *verb, intr* (*often* **preside at** *or* **over sth**) **1** to take the lead at (an event), the chair at (a meeting, etc); to be in charge. **2** to dominate; to be a dominating presence in (a place, etc): *His statue presides over the park*. [17c: from Latin *praesidere* to command]

president *noun* **1** (*often* **President**) the elected head of state in a republic. **2** the chief office-bearer in a society or club. **3** *esp US* the head of a business organization, eg the chairman of a company, governor of a bank, etc. **4** the head of some colleges or other higher-education institutions. ▪ **presidency** *noun* (**-ies**). ▪ **presidential** *adj*. [14c: from Latin *praesidens*]

presidium *or* **praesidium** *noun* (***presidiums*** *or* ***presidia***) (*often with capital*) in a Communist state: a standing executive committee. [20c: from Russian *prezidium*]

press[1] *verb* **1** **a** *tr & intr* to push steadily, esp with the finger: *press the bell*; **b** (*often* **press against** *or* **on** *or* **down on sth**) to push it; to apply pressure to it: *press down on the accelerator*. **2** to hold something firmly against something; to flatten: *pressed her nose against the glass*. **3** to compress or squash. **4** to squeeze (eg someone's hand) affectionately. **5** to preserve (plants) by flattening and drying, eg between the pages of a book. **6** **a** to squeeze (fruit) to extract juice; **b** to extract (juice) from fruit by squeezing. **7** to iron (clothes, etc). **8** to urge or compel someone; to ask them insistently. **9** to insist on something; to urge recognition or discussion of it: *press the point*. **10** *intr* (**press for sth**) to demand it. **11** (**press sth on sb**) to insist on giving it to them. **12** *intr* (*usu* **press on, ahead** *or* **forward**) to hurry on; to continue, esp in spite of difficulties. **13** *law* to bring (charges) officially against someone. **14** to produce (eg a **record** *noun* sense 4) from a mould by a compressing process. ▶ *noun* **1** an act of pressing. **2** any apparatus for pressing, flattening, squeezing, etc. **3** a **printing press**. **4** the process or art of printing. **5** (**the press**) newspapers or journalists in general. **6** newspaper publicity or reviews received by a show, book, etc: *got a poor press*. **7** a crowd: *a press of onlookers*. **8** *Scot* a cupboard. ▶ *adj* belonging or relating to the newspaper industry: *press photographers*. [13c: from French *presser*]

press² *verb* **1** to force (men) into the army or navy. **2** (*esp* **press sth** *or* **sb into service**) to put it or them to use in a way that was not originally intended. [16c: from older *prest* to recruit into military service]

press conference *or* **news conference** *noun* an interview granted to reporters by a politician or other person in the news.

pressed *adj* of a person: under pressure; in a hurry.

pressgang *noun, hist* a gang employed to seize men and force them into the army or navy. ▸ *verb* **1** to force (men) into the army or navy. **2** *facetious* to coerce someone into something.

pressie *or* **prezzie** *noun, informal* a present or gift. [20c: from **present³**]

pressing *adj* urgent: *pressing engagements.* ▸ *noun* in the music industry: a number of records produced from a single mould.

press release *noun* an official statement given to the press by an organization, etc.

press stud *noun* a type of button-like fastener, one part of which is pressed into the other. Also called **popper**.

press-up *noun* an exercise performed face down, raising and lowering the body on the arms while keeping the trunk and legs rigid. [20c]

pressure *noun* **1** *physics* the force exerted on a surface divided by the area of the surface to which it is applied. **2** the act of pressing or process of being pressed. **3** force or coercion; forceful persuasion. **4** urgency; strong demand: *work under pressure.* **5** tension or stress: *the pressures of family life.* ▸ *verb* to try to persuade; to coerce, force or pressurize. [14c: from Latin *pressura*]

pressure cooker *noun* a thick-walled pan with an airtight lid, in which food is cooked at speed by steam under high pressure.

pressure group *noun* a number of people who join together to influence public opinion and government policy on some issue.

pressure point *noun* a point on the body where pressure can be exerted to relieve pain, control the flow of arterial blood, etc.

pressurize *or* **-ise** *verb* **1** to adjust the pressure within (an enclosed compartment such as an aircraft cabin) so that nearly normal atmospheric pressure is constantly maintained. **2** to put pressure on someone or something; to force or coerce. [20c]

prestidigitation *noun* **sleight of hand.** ▪ **prestidigitator** *noun.* [19c: from French *prestidigitateur*]

prestige /prɛˈstiːʒ/ *noun* **1** fame, distinction or reputation due to rank or success. **2** influence; glamour: *a job with prestige.* ▪ **prestigious** /prɛˈstɪdʒəs/ *adj.* [19c: from Latin *praestigiae* sleight of hand or magic tricks]

presto *music, adv* in a very fast manner. ▸ *adj* very fast. ▸ *noun* a piece of music to be played in this way. [17c: Italian, meaning 'quick']

presumably *adv* I suppose; probably.

presume *verb* **1** to suppose (something to be the case) without proof; to take something for granted: *presumed he was dead.* **2** to be bold enough; esp without the proper right or knowledge; to venture: *wouldn't presume to advise the experts.* **3** *intr* (**presume on** *or* **upon sb** *or* **sth**) **a** to rely or count on them or it, esp unduly; **b** to take unfair advantage of (someone's good nature, etc). [14c: from Latin *praesumere* to take in advance]

presumption *noun* **1** something presumed: *The presumption was that her first husband was dead.* **2** grounds or justification for presuming something. **3** inappropriate boldness in one's behaviour towards others; insolence or arrogance. **4** the act of presuming. [13c: from Latin *praesumptio*]

presumptive *adj* **1** presumed rather than absolutely certain. **2** giving grounds for presuming. See also **heir presumptive**.

presumptuous *adj* overbold in behaviour, esp towards others; insolent or arrogant.

presuppose *verb* **1** to take for granted; to assume as true. **2** to require as a necessary condition; to imply the existence of something. ▪ **presupposition** *noun.* [15c]

pretence *or* (*US*) **pretense** *noun* **1** the act of pretending. **2** make-believe. **3** an act someone puts on deliberately to mislead. **4** a claim, esp an unjustified one: *make no pretence to expert knowledge.* **5** show, affectation or ostentation; pretentiousness. **6** (*usu* **pretences**) a misleading declaration of intention: *won their support under false pretences.* **7** show or semblance: *abandoned all pretence of fair play.* [15c: from French *pretensse*]

pretend *verb* **1** *tr & intr* to make believe; to act as if, or give the impression that, something is the case when it is not: *pretend to be asleep.* **2** *tr & intr* to imply or claim falsely: *pretended not to know.* **3** to claim to feel something; to profess something falsely: *pretend friendship towards someone.* **4** *intr* (**pretend to sth**) **a** to claim to have (a skill, etc), esp falsely; **b** *hist* to lay claim, esp doubtful claim, to (eg the throne). ▸ *adj, informal* esp used by or to children: imaginary: *a pretend cave.* [15c: from Latin *praetendere* to stretch forth]

pretender *noun* someone who pretends or pretended to something, esp the throne.

pretension *noun* **1** foolish vanity, self-importance or affectation; pretentiousness. **2** a claim or aspiration: *had no pretensions to elegance.* [17c: see **pretend**]

pretentious *adj* **1** pompous, self-important or foolishly grandiose. **2** phoney or affected. **3** showy; ostentatious. ▪ **pretentiously** *adv.* ▪ **pretentiousness** *noun.* [19c]

preterite /ˈprɛtərɪt/ *grammar, noun* **1** a verb tense that expresses past action, eg *hit, moved, ran.* **2** a verb in this tense. ▸ *adj* denoting this tense. [14c: from Latin *tempus praeteritum* past time]

preternatural *adj* **1** exceeding the normal; uncanny; extraordinary. **2** supernatural. ▪ **preternaturally** *adv.* [16c: from Latin *praeter naturam* beyond nature]

pretext *noun* a false reason given for doing something in order to disguise the real one; an excuse. [16c: from Latin *praetextum*]

prettify *verb* (***-ies, -ied***) to attempt to make something or someone prettier by superficial ornamentation. ▪ **prettification** *noun.* [19c]

pretty *adj* (***-ier, -iest***) **1** usu of a woman or girl: facially attractive, esp in a feminine way. **2** charming to look at; decorative. **3** of music, sound, etc: delicately melodious. **4** neat, elegant or skilful: *a pretty solution.* **5** *ironic* grand; fine: *a pretty mess.* ▸ *adv* fairly; satisfactorily; rather; decidedly. ▪ **prettily** *adv.* ▪ **prettiness** *noun.* [Anglo-Saxon *prættig* astute]

IDIOMS **pretty much** more or less. **pretty nearly** almost. **pretty well** almost; more or less.

pretty-pretty *adj, derog informal* pretty in an over-sweet way.

pretzel *noun* a crisp salted biscuit in the shape of a knot. [19c: German]

prevail *verb, intr* **1** (*often* **prevail over** *or* **against sb** *or* **sth**) to be victorious; to win through: *Common sense prevailed.* **2** to be the common, usual or generally accepted thing. **3** to be predominant. **4** (**prevail on** *or* **upon sb** *or* **sth**) to persuade them or appeal to it. [15c: from Latin *praevalere* to prove superior]

prevailing *adj* most common or frequent.

prevalent /ˈprɛvələnt/ *adj* common; widespread. ▪ **prevalence** *noun.* [16c: see **prevail**]

prevaricate *verb, intr* to avoid stating the truth or coming directly to the point; to behave or speak evasively. ▪ **prevarication** *noun.* ▪ **prevaricator** *noun.* [17c: from Latin *praevaricari* to walk with splayed legs]

prevent *verb* **1** to stop someone from doing something, or something from happening; to hinder. **2** to stop the occurrence of something beforehand or to make it impossible; to avert. ▪ **preventable** *or* **preventible** *adj.* ▪ **prevention** *noun.* [16c: from Latin *praevenire* to anticipate or come before]

preventive *or* **preventative** *adj* **1** tending or intended to prevent or hinder. **2** *med* tending or intended to prevent disease or illness. ▸ *noun* **1** a preventive drug. **2** a precautionary measure. [17c]

preview *noun* **1** an advance view. **2** an advance showing of a film, play, exhibition, etc before it is presented to the general public. ▸ *verb* to show or view (a film, etc) in advance to a select audience. [19c]

previous *adj* **1** earlier: *a previous occasion.* **2** former: *the previous chairman.* **3** prior: *a previous engagement.* **4** *facetious* premature; overprompt or overhasty. **5** (*usu* **previous to sth**) before (an event, etc). ▪ **previously** *adv.* [17c: from Latin *praevius* leading the way]

prey *singular or plural noun* **1** an animal or animals hunted as food by another animal: *in search of prey.* **2** a victim or victims: *easy prey for muggers.* **3** (*usu* **a prey to sth**) someone liable to suffer from (an illness, a bad feeling, etc). ▸ *verb, intr* (*now esp* **prey on** *or* **upon sth** *or* **sb**) **1** of an animal: to hunt or catch (another animal) as food. **2** **a** to bully, exploit or terrorize as victims; **b** to afflict in an obsessive way: *preyed on by anxieties.* [13c: from French *preie*]

prezzie see **pressie**

price *noun* **1** the amount, usu in money, for which a thing is sold or offered. **2** what must be given up or suffered in gaining something. **3** the sum by which someone may be bribed. **4** *betting* odds. ▸ *verb* **1** to fix a price for or mark a price on something. **2** to find out the price of something. [13c: from French *pris*]

IDIOMS **at any price** no matter what it costs, eg in terms of money, sacrifice, etc. **at a price** at great expense. **beyond** *or* **without price** invaluable.

price-fixing *noun, commerce* the fixing of a price by agreement between suppliers. [20c]

priceless *adj* **1** too valuable to have a price; inestimably precious. **2** *informal* hilariously funny.

pricey *or* **pricy** *adj* (**-ier, -iest**) *informal* expensive. [20c]

prick *verb* **1** to pierce slightly with a fine point. **2** to make (a hole) by this means. **3** *tr & intr* to hurt something or someone by this means. **4** *tr & intr* to smart or make something smart: *feel one's eyes pricking.* **5** *tr & intr* (*also* **prick up**) **a** of a dog, horse, etc: to stick (its ears) upright in response to sound; **b** of a dog's, etc ears: to stand erect in this way. **6** to mark out (a pattern) in punctured holes. **7** to trouble: *His conscience must be pricking him.* **8** to plant (seedlings, etc) in an area of soil that has had small holes marked out on it. ▸ *noun* **1** an act of pricking or feeling of being pricked. **2** the pain of this. **3** a puncture made by pricking. [Anglo-Saxon *prica* point]

IDIOMS **prick up one's ears** *informal* to start listening attentively.

prickle *noun* **1** a hard pointed structure growing from the surface of a plant or animal. **2** a pricking sensation. ▸ *verb, tr & intr* to cause, affect something with, or be affected with, a prickling sensation. [Anglo-Saxon *pricel*]

prickly *adj* (**-ier, -iest**) **1** covered with or full of prickles. **2** causing prickling. **3** *informal* of a person: irritable; over-sensitive. **4** of a topic: liable to cause controversy. ▪ **prickliness** *noun.* [16c]

prickly heat *noun* an itchy skin rash caused by blockage of the sweat ducts.

pride *noun* **1** a feeling of pleasure and satisfaction at one's own or another's accomplishments, possessions, etc. **2** the source of this feeling: *That car is my pride and joy.* **3** self-respect; personal dignity. **4** an unjustified assumption of superiority; arrogance. **5** *poetic* the finest state; the prime. **6** the finest item: *the pride of the collection.* **7** a number of lions keeping together as a group. ▸ *verb* (*always* **pride oneself on sth**) to congratulate oneself on account of it. [Anglo-Saxon *pryde*]

IDIOMS **take pride** *or* **take a pride in sth** *or* **sb** **1** to be proud of it or them. **2** to be conscientious about maintaining high standards in (one's work, etc).

pride of place *noun* special prominence; the position of chief importance.

prie-dieu /priːˈdjɜː/ *noun* (***prie-dieux*** *or* ***prie-dieus***) a praying-desk which has a low surface on which to kneel and a support for a book or books. [18c: French, meaning 'pray-God']

priest *noun* **1** **a** in the Roman Catholic and Orthodox Churches: an ordained minister authorized to administer the sacraments; **b** in the Anglican Church: a minister ranking between deacon and bishop. **2** in non-Christian religions: an official who performs sacrifices and other religious rites. ▪ **priestly** *adj.* [Anglo-Saxon *preost*: from Latin *presbyter* elder]

priestess *noun* in non-Christian religions: a female priest.

priesthood *noun* **1** the office of a priest. **2** the role or character of a priest. **3** priests collectively: *members of the priesthood.*

prig *noun* someone who is self-righteously moralistic. ▪ **priggery** *noun.* ▪ **priggish** *adj.* [18c; 16c in obsolete sense 'a tinker']

prim *adj* (***primmer, primmest***) **1** stiffly formal, over-modest or over-proper. **2** prudishly disapproving. ▪ **primly** *adv.* ▪ **primness** *noun.* [17c]

prima ballerina /ˈpriːmə/ *noun* the leading female dancer in a ballet company. [19c: Italian, meaning 'first ballerina']

primacy *noun* (*-ies*) **1** the condition of being first in rank, importance or order. **2** the rank, office or area of jurisdiction of a **primate** of the Church. [14c: from Latin *primatia*]

prima donna /'priːmə 'dɒnə/ *noun* (***prima donnas***) **1** a leading female opera singer. **2** someone difficult to please, esp someone given to tantrums when displeased. [18c: Italian, meaning 'first lady']

primaeval see **primeval**

prima facie /'praɪmə 'feɪʃɪ/ *esp law, adv* at first sight; on the evidence available. ▸ *adj* apparent; based on first impressions: *prima-facie evidence.* [15c: Latin, meaning 'at first sight']

primal *adj* **1** relating to the beginnings of life; original. **2** basic; fundamental. [17c: from Latin *primalis*]

primarily *adv* **1** chiefly; mainly. **2** in the first place; initially. [17c]

primary *adj* **1** first or most important; principal. **2** earliest in order or development. **3** (**Primary**) *geol* **Palaeozoic**. See also **secondary, tertiary. 4** basic; fundamental. **5** at the elementary stage or level. **6** of education, schools, classes etc: for children aged between 5 and 11: *Jane's in primary six.* See also **secondary, tertiary. 7** of a bird's wing feather: outermost and longest. **8** first-hand; direct: *primary sources of information.* ▸ *noun* (*-ies*) **1** something that is first or most important. **2** *US* a preliminary election, esp to select delegates for a presidential election. **3** *Brit informal* a primary school: *attends the local primary.* **4** a bird's primary feather. **5** (**the Primary**) the **Palaeozoic** era. [15c: from Latin *primarius*, from *primus* first]

primary colour *noun* of pigments: the colours red, yellow and blue, which can be combined in various proportions to give all the other colours of the spectrum. [17c]

primary industry *noun* an industry, eg coalmining, concerned with extracting raw materials. Compare **secondary industry, tertiary industry**.

primary school *noun* a school, esp a state one, for pupils aged between 5 and 11.

primate *noun* **1** *zool* any member of an order of mammalian vertebrates which have a large brain, forward-facing eyes, nails instead of claws, and hands with grasping thumbs facing the other digits, eg a human, ape, etc. **2** *Christianity* an archbishop. [13c: from Latin *primas*]

prime *adj* **1** chief; fundamental. **2** the best quality. **3** excellent: *in prime condition.* **4** supremely typical: *a prime example.* **5** having the greatest potential for attracting interest or custom: *prime sites on the high street.* ▸ *noun* the best, most productive or active stage in the life of a person or thing: *cut down in her prime.* ▸ *verb* **1** to prepare something (eg wood for painting) by applying a sealing coat of size, etc, (a gun or explosive device for firing or detonating) by inserting the igniting material, or (a pump for use) by filling it with water, etc. **2** to supply with the necessary facts in advance; to brief. [14c: from Latin *primus* first]

prime meridian *noun, geog* a **meridian** chosen to represent 0, esp that passing through Greenwich, UK, from which other lines of longitude are calculated.

prime minister *noun* (abbrev **PM**) the chief minister of a government. [17c]

prime mover *noun* the force that is most effective in setting something in motion.

prime number *noun, maths* a whole number that can only be divided by itself and 1, eg 3, 5, 7, 11, etc.

primer[1] *noun* a first or introductory book of instruction. [14c: from Latin *primarium*]

primer[2] *noun* **1** any material that is used to provide an initial coating for a surface before it is painted. **2** any device that ignites or detonates an explosive charge. [19c in sense 2]

primeval *or* **primaeval** /praɪ'miːvəl/ *adj* **1** relating or belonging to the Earth's beginnings. **2** primitive. **3** instinctive. [18c: from Latin *primaevus* young]

primitive *adj* **1** relating or belonging to earliest times or the earliest stages of development. **2** simple, rough, crude or rudimentary. **3** *art* simple, naive or unsophisticated in style. **4** *biol* original; belonging to an early stage of development. ▸ *noun* **1** an unsophisticated person or thing. **2 a** a work by an artist in naive style; **b** an artist who produces such a work. ▪ **primitively** *adv*. ▪ **primitiveness** *noun*. [15c: from Latin *primitivus*, meaning 'first of its kind']

primitivism *noun, art* the deliberate rejection of Western techniques and skills in pursuit of stronger effects found, for example, in African tribal or Oceanic art. [19c]

primogeniture *noun* **1** the fact or condition of being the first-born child. **2** the right or principle of succession or inheritance of an eldest son. [17c: from Latin *primogenitura*]

primordial *adj* **1** existing from the beginning; formed earliest: *primordial matter.* **2** *biol* relating to an early stage in growth. [14c: from Latin *primordialis*]

primp *verb, tr & intr* to groom, preen or titivate. [19c: related to **prim**]

primrose *noun* **1** a small plant with a rosette of oval leaves, and long-stalked pale-yellow flowers. **2** (*in full* **primrose yellow**) the pale-yellow colour of these flowers. *as adj*: *a primrose dress.* [15c: from Latin *prima rosa* first rose]

primula *noun* (***primulae*** *or* ***primulas***) a plant with white, pink, purple or yellow flowers with five spreading petals, eg the primrose, cowslip and oxlip. [18c: from Latin *primula veris* first little one of the spring]

Primus *noun, trademark* a portable camping stove fuelled by vaporized oil. Also called **Primus stove**. [20c]

prince *noun* **1** in the UK: the son of a sovereign. **2** a non-reigning male member of a royal or imperial family. **3** a sovereign of a small territory. **4** a nobleman in certain countries. **5** someone or something celebrated or outstanding within a type or class: *the prince of pop.* See also **principality**. [13c: French, from Latin *princeps* leader]

princedom *noun* a **principality**; the estate, jurisdiction, sovereignty or rank of a prince.

princely *adj* **1** characteristic of or suitable for a prince. **2** *often ironic* lavish; generous: *the princely sum of five pence.*

prince regent *noun* (***princes regent***) a prince who rules on behalf of a sovereign who is too ill, young, etc to rule.

princess *noun* **1** the wife or daughter of a prince. **2** the daughter of a sovereign. **3** a non-reigning female member of a royal or imperial family. **4** someone or something that is held in high esteem. [15c]

principal *adj* first in rank or importance; chief; main. ▸ *noun* **1** the head of an educational institution. **2** a leading actor, singer or dancer in a theatrical production. **3** *law* the person on behalf of whom an agent is acting. **4** *law* someone ultimately responsible for fulfilling an obligation. **5** someone who commits or participates in a crime. **6** *commerce* the original sum of money on which interest is paid. **7** *music* the leading player of each section of an orchestra. ▪ **principally** *adv.* [13c: French]

principal, principle
Be careful not to use the spelling **principal** when you mean **principle**:
the principles of chemistry
I declined the invitation as a matter of principle.

principal boy *noun* the part of the young male hero in a pantomime, usu played by a woman.

principal clause see under **main clause**

principality *noun* (*-ies*) **1** a territory ruled by a prince, or one that he derives his title from. **2** (**the Principality**) in the UK: Wales.

principal parts *plural noun, grammar* the main forms of a verb from which all other forms can be deduced, eg in English the infinitive, the past tense and the past participle.

principle *noun* **1** a general truth or assumption from which to argue. **2** a scientific law, esp one that explains a natural phenomenon or the way a machine works. **3** a general rule of morality that guides conduct; the having of or holding to such rules: *a woman of principle*. **4** (**principles**) a set of such rules. **5** a fundamental element or source: *the vital principle*. **6** *chem* a constituent of a substance that gives it its distinctive characteristics. [14c: from Latin *principium* beginning or source]
IDIOMS **in principle** esp of agreement or disagreement to a plan, decision or action: in theory; in general, although not necessarily in a particular case. **on principle** on the grounds of a particular principle of morality or wisdom.

principle, principal
Be careful not to use the spelling **principle** when you mean **principal**:
the principal teacher
paying interest on the principal

principled *adj* holding, or proceeding from, principles, esp high moral principles.

print *verb* **1** to reproduce (text or pictures) on paper with ink, using a printing press or other mechanical means. **2** (*also* **print sth out**) to produce a printed version, eg of computer data. See also **printout**. **3** to publish (a book, article, etc). **4** *tr & intr* to write in separate, as opposed to joined-up, letters. **5** to make (a positive photograph) from a negative. **6** to mark (a shape, pattern, etc) in or on a surface by pressure. **7** to mark designs on (fabric). **8** to fix (a scene) indelibly (on the memory, etc). ▸ *noun* **1** *often in compounds* a mark made on a surface by the pressure of something in contact with it: *pawprint*. **2** a **fingerprint**. **3** hand-done lettering with each letter written separately. **4** mechanically printed text, esp one produced on a printing press: *small print*. **5** a printed publication. **6** a design or picture printed from an engraved wood block or metal plate. **7** a positive photograph made from a negative. **8** a fabric with a printed or stamped design. [13c: from French *priente*]
IDIOMS **be in** *or* **out of print** of a publication: to be currently available, or no longer available, from a publisher.

printed circuit *noun, electronics* an electronic circuit in which circuit components are connected by thin strips of a conducting material that are printed or etched on to the surface of a thin board of insulating material. [20c]

printer *noun* **1** a person or business engaged in printing books, newspapers, etc. **2** a machine that prints, eg photographs. **3** *comput* a type of output device that produces printed copies of text or graphics on to paper.

printing *noun* **1** the art or business of producing books, etc in print. **2** the run of books, etc printed all at one time; an impression. **3** the form of handwriting in which the letters are separately written.

printing press *noun* any of various machines for printing books, newspapers, etc.

printmaker *noun* a worker who produces prints.

printout *noun, comput* output from a computer system in the form of a printed paper copy.

prior[1] *adj* **1** of an engagement: already arranged for the time in question; previous. **2** more urgent or pressing: *a prior claim*. [18c: Latin, meaning 'previous']
IDIOMS **prior to sth** before an event.

prior[2] *noun, Christianity* **1** the head of a community of certain orders of monks and friars. **2** in an abbey: the deputy of the abbot. ▪ **prioress** *noun*. [11c: Latin, meaning 'head' or 'chief']

prioritize *or* **-ise** *verb* to schedule something for immediate or earliest attention. [20c: from **priority**]

priority *noun* (*-ies*) **1** the right to be or go first; precedence or preference. **2** something that must be attended to before anything else. **3** the fact or condition of being earlier. [14c: from Latin *prioritas*]

priory *noun* (*-ies*) *Christianity* a religious house under the supervision of a prior or prioress. [13c]

prise *or* (*US*) **prize** *verb* **1** to lever something open, off, out, etc, usu with some difficulty: *prised open the lid*. **2** to get with difficulty: *prised the truth out of her*. See also **pry**[2]. [17c: French, meaning 'something captured']

prism *noun* **1** *geom* a solid figure in which the two ends are matching parallel polygons (eg triangles or squares) and all other surfaces are parallelograms. **2** *optics* a transparent block, usu of glass and with triangular ends and rectangular sides, that separates a beam of white light into the colours of the visible spectrum. [16c: from Greek *prisma* something sawn]

prismatic *adj* **1** produced by or relating to a prism: *a prismatic compass*. **2** of colour or light: produced or separated by, or as if by, a prism; bright and clear.

prison *noun* **1** a building for the confinement of convicted criminals and certain accused persons awaiting trial. **2** any place of confinement or situation of intolerable restriction. **3** custody; imprisonment. [12c: from French *prisun*]

prisoner *noun* **1** someone who is under arrest or confined in prison. **2** a captive, esp in war.
IDIOMS **take sb prisoner** to capture and hold them as a prisoner.

prisoner of conscience *noun* someone imprisoned for their political beliefs.

prisoner of war *noun* (abbrev **POW**) someone taken prisoner during a war, esp a member of the armed forces.

prissy *adj* (*-ier, -iest*) insipidly prim and prudish. ▪ **prissily** *adv.* [19c: prob from **prim** + **sissy**]

pristine *adj* **1** fresh, clean, unused or untouched. **2** original; unchanged or unspoilt: *still in its pristine state.* **3** former. [16c: from Latin *pristinus* former or early]

privacy *noun* **1 a** freedom from intrusion by the public, esp as a right; **b** someone's right to this: *should respect her privacy.* **2** seclusion; secrecy. [15c in sense 2]

private *adj* **1** not open to, or available for the use of, the general public. **2** of a person: not holding public office. **3** kept secret from others; confidential. **4** relating to someone's personal, as distinct from their professional, life: *a private engagement.* **5** of thoughts or opinions: personal and usu kept to oneself. **6** quiet and reserved by nature. **7** of a place: secluded. **8 a** not coming under the state system of education, healthcare, social welfare, etc; **b** paid for or paying individually by fee, etc. ▸ *noun* **1** a private soldier. **2** (**privates**) *informal* the **private parts**. ▪ **privately** *adv.* [14c: from Latin *privatus* withdrawn from public life]

IDIOMS **in private** not in public; confidentially.

private company *noun* a company with restrictions on the number of shareholders, whose shares may not be offered to the general public.

private detective *or* **private investigator** *noun* someone who is not a member of the police force, engaged to do detective work. Also called **private eye**.

private enterprise *noun* the management and financing of industry, etc by private individuals or companies, not by the state.

privateer *noun, hist* **1** a privately owned ship engaged by a government to seize and plunder an enemy's ships in wartime. **2** (*also* **privateersman**) the commander or a crew member of such a ship. [17c]

private means *or* **private income** *noun* income from investments, etc, not from one's employment.

private member *noun* a member of a legislative body who does not hold a government office.

private parts *plural noun, euphem* the external genitals and excretory organs.

private school *noun* a school run independently by an individual or group, esp for profit.

private sector *noun* that part of a country's economy consisting of privately owned businesses, etc.

privation *noun* the condition of not having, or being deprived of, life's comforts or necessities; a lack of something particular. [14c: from Latin *privatio* deprivation]

privative /ˈprɪvətɪv/ *adj* lacking some quality that is usu, or expected to be, present. [16c: from Latin *privativus*]

privatize *or* **-ise** *verb* to transfer (a state-owned business) to private ownership. ▪ **privatization** *noun.* [20c]

privet *noun* a shrub with glossy lance-shaped dark-green leaves, used esp in garden hedges. [16c]

privilege *noun* **1** a right granted to an individual or a select few, bestowing an advantage not enjoyed by others. **2** advantages and power enjoyed by people of wealth and high social class. **3** an opportunity to do something that brings one delight; a pleasure or honour. ▸ *verb, tr & intr* to grant a right, privilege or special favour to someone or something. ▪ **privileged** *adj.* [12c: from Latin *privilegium* prerogative]

privy *adj* **1** (*usu* **privy to sth**) allowed to share in (secret discussions, etc) or be in the know about secret plans, happenings, etc. **2** *old use* secret; hidden. ▸ *noun* (*-ies*) *old use* a lavatory. [13c: from French *privé* a private thing]

prize[1] *noun* **1** something won in a competition, lottery, etc. **2** a reward given in recognition of excellence. **3** something striven for, or worth striving for. **4** something captured or taken by force, esp a ship in war; a trophy. ▸ *adj* **1** deserving, or having won, a prize: *a prize bull.* **2** highly valued: *her prize possession.* **3** *ironic* perfect; great: *a prize fool.* **4** belonging or relating to, or given as, a prize: *prize money.* ▸ *verb* to value or regard highly. [14c: related to **price** and **praise**]

prize[2] see **prise**

prizefight *noun* a boxing-match fought for a money prize. ▪ **prizefighter** *noun.* [19c: from obsolete *prize* a contest + **fight**]

pro[1] *prep* in favour of something. ▸ *noun* a reason, argument or choice in favour of something. See also **pros and cons**. ▸ *adv, informal* in favour: *thought he would argue pro.* Compare **anti**. [15c: Latin, meaning 'for' or 'on behalf of']

pro[2] *noun, informal* a professional. [19c abbrev]

pro-[1] *prefix, denoting* **1** in favour of (the specified thing); admiring or supporting: *pro-French.* **2** serving in place of (the specified thing); acting for: *proconsul.* [Latin]

pro-[2] *prefix, denoting* before (the specified thing) in time or place; in front: *proboscis.* [Greek and Latin]

proactive *adj* actively initiating change in anticipation of future developments, rather than merely reacting to events as they occur. [20c: from **pro-**[2], modelled on **reactive**]

probability *noun* (*-ies*) **1** the state of being probable; likelihood. **2** something that is probable. **3** *stats* a mathematical expression of the likelihood or chance of a particular event occurring, usu expressed as a fraction or numeral: *a probability of one in four.*

probable *adj* **1** likely to happen: *a probable outcome.* **2** likely to be the case; likely to have happened. **3** of an explanation, etc: likely to be correct; feasible. ▸ *noun* someone or something likely to be selected. ▪ **probably** *adv.* [14c: from Latin *probabilis*]

probate *noun* **1** *law* the process of establishing that a will is valid. **2** an official copy of a will, with the document certifying its validity. [15c: from Latin *probare* to prove]

probation *noun* **1** the system whereby offenders, esp young or first offenders, are allowed their freedom under supervision, on condition of good behaviour. **2** in certain types of employment: a trial period during which a new employee is observed on the job, to confirm whether or not they can do it satisfactorily. ▪ **probationary** *adj.* [19c: from Latin *probatio*]

probationer *noun* someone on probation.

probe *noun* **1** a long, slender and usu metal instrument used by doctors to examine a wound, locate a bullet, etc. **2** a comprehensive investigation. **3** (*also* **space probe**) an unmanned spacecraft designed to study conditions in space, esp around one or more planets or their natural satellites. **4** an act of probing; a poke or prod. ► *verb* (*often* **probe into sth**) **1** to investigate it closely. **2** *tr & intr* to examine it with a probe. **3** *tr & intr* to poke or prod it. [16c: from Latin *proba*]

probity *noun* integrity; honesty. [16c: from Latin *probitas*]

problem *noun* **1** a situation or matter that is difficult to understand or deal with: *a problem with the software* • *He's got a drink problem.* **2** someone or something that is difficult to deal with. **3** a puzzle or mathematical question set for solving. ► *adj* **1** of a child, etc: difficult to deal with, esp in being disruptive or antisocial. **2** of a play, etc: dealing with a moral or social problem. [14c: from Greek *problema* a thing put forward]

IDIOMS **no problem** *informal* **1** said in response to a request, or to thanks: it's a pleasure, no trouble, etc. **2** easily: *found our way, no problem.*

problematic *or* **problematical** *adj* **1** causing problems. **2** uncertain.

proboscis /proʊ'bɒsɪs/ *noun* (***proboscises*** *or* ***proboscides*** /-sɪdiːz/) **1** *zool* the flexible elongated snout of certain animals, eg the elephant. **2** the elongated tubular mouthparts of certain insects, eg the butterfly. [17c: from Greek *proboskis*]

procaryote see **prokaryote**

procedure *noun* **1** the method and order followed in doing something. **2** an established routine for conducting business at a meeting or in a law case. **3** a course of action; a step or measure taken. ▪ **procedural** *adj.* [17c: from Latin *procedere* to advance or proceed]

proceed *verb, intr* **1** *formal* to make one's way: *I proceeded along the road.* **2** (*often* **proceed with sth**) to go on with it; to continue after stopping. **3** to set about a task, etc. **4** *informal* to begin: *proceeded to question her.* **5** (**proceed from sth**) to arise from it. **6** (*often* **proceed against sb**) *law* to take legal action against them. [14c: from Latin *procedere* to advance or proceed]

proceeding *noun* **1** an action; a piece of behaviour. **2** (**proceedings**) a published record of the business done or papers read at a meeting of a society, etc. **3** (**proceedings**) legal action.

proceeds *plural noun* money made by an event, sale, transaction, etc. [17c]

process *noun* **1** a series of operations performed during manufacture, etc. **2** a series of stages which a product, etc passes through, resulting in the development or transformation of it. **3** an operation or procedure: *a slow process.* **4** *anatomy* a projection or outgrowth, esp one on a bone: *the mastoid process.* **5** *law* a writ by which a person or matter is brought into court. **6** any series of changes, esp natural ones: *the aging process.* ► *verb* **1** to put something through the required process; to deal with (eg an application) appropriately. **2** to prepare (agricultural produce) for marketing, eg by canning, bottling or treating it chemically. **3** *comput* to perform operations on (data, etc). [14c: from Latin *processus* progression]

IDIOMS **in the process of sth** in the course of it.

procession *noun* **1** a file of people or vehicles proceeding ceremonially in orderly formation. **2** this kind of succession or sequence. [12c: from Latin *processio* an advance]

processional *adj* relating or belonging to a procession. ► *noun, Christianity* a hymn sung in procession. [15c]

processor *noun* **1** *often in compounds* a machine or person that processes something: *word processor* • *food processor.* **2** *comput* a **central processing unit**.

pro-choice *adj* supporting the right of a woman to have an abortion. Compare **pro-life**. [20c]

proclaim *verb* **1** to announce something publicly. **2** to declare someone to be something: *was proclaimed a traitor.* **3** to attest or prove something all too clearly: *Cigar smoke proclaimed his presence.* ▪ **proclaimer** *noun.* ▪ **proclamation** *noun.* ▪ **proclamatory** *adj.* [14c: from Latin *proclamare* to cry out]

proclivity *noun* (*-ies*) *rather formal* a tendency, liking or preference. [16c: from Latin *proclivitas*]

procrastinate *verb, intr* to put off doing something that should be done straight away. ▪ **procrastination** *noun.* ▪ **procrastinator** *noun.* [16c: from Latin *procrastinare*]

procreate *verb, tr & intr* to produce (offspring); to reproduce. ► *noun.* ▪ **procreation** *noun.* ▪ **procreative** *adj.* ▪ **procreator** *noun.* [16c: from Latin *procreare* to beget]

proctor *noun* in some English universities: an official whose functions include enforcement of discipline. ▪ **proctorial** *adj.* ▪ **proctorship** *noun.* [14c: a contraction of **procurator**]

procurator *noun* an agent with power of attorney in a law court. [13c: from Latin, meaning 'agent' or 'manager']

procurator fiscal *noun, Scot* a district official who combines the roles of coroner and public prosecutor. [16c]

procure *verb* **1** to manage to obtain something or bring it about. **2** *tr & intr* to get (women or girls) to act as prostitutes. ▪ **procurable** *adj.* ▪ **procurement** *noun.* [13c: from Latin *procurare* to take care of]

prod *verb* (***prodded, prodding***) **1** (*often* **prod at sth**) to poke or jab it. **2** to nudge, prompt or spur (a person or animal) into action. ► *noun* **1** a poke, jab or nudge. **2** a reminder. **3** a goad or similar pointed instrument. [16c]

prodigal *adj* **1** heedlessly extravagant or wasteful. **2** (*often* **prodigal of sth**) *formal or old use* lavish in bestowing it; generous. ► *noun* **1** a squanderer, wastrel or spendthrift. **2** (*also* **prodigal son**) a repentant ne'er-do-well or a returned wanderer. ▪ **prodigality** *noun.* ▪ **prodigally** *adv.* [16c: from Latin *prodigus* wasteful]

prodigious *adj* **1** extraordinary or marvellous. **2** enormous; vast. ▪ **prodigiously** *adv.* [16c: from Latin *prodigiosus*; see **prodigy**]

prodigy *noun* (*-ies*) **1** something that causes astonishment; a wonder; an extraordinary phenomenon. **2** someone, esp a child, of extraordinary brilliance or talent. [17c: from Latin *prodigium* something portentous]

produce *verb* /prə'dʒuːs/ **1** to bring out or present something to view. **2** to bear (children, young, leaves, etc). **3** *tr & intr* to yield (crops, fruit, etc). **4** to secrete (a substance), give off (a smell), etc. **5** *tr & intr* to make or manufacture something. **6** to give rise to or prompt (a reaction) from people. **7** to direct (a play), arrange (a radio or television programme) for presentation, or finance and schedule the making of (a film). ▸ *noun* /'prɒdʒuːs/ foodstuffs derived from crops or animal livestock, eg fruit, vegetables, eggs and dairy products. ▪ **producible** *adj.* [15c: from Latin *producere* to bring forth]

producer *noun* a person, organization or thing that produces.

product *noun* **1** something produced, eg through manufacture or agriculture. **2** a result: *the product of much thought.* **3** *maths* the value obtained by multiplying two or more numbers. [15c]

production *noun* **1 a** the act of producing; **b** the process of producing or being produced: *The new model goes into production next year.* **2** the quantity produced or rate of producing it. **3** something created; a literary or artistic work. **4** a particular presentation of a play, opera, ballet, etc. [15c]

production line *noun* **1** a series of activities carried out in sequence as part of a manufacturing process. **2** the workers who carry out these activities.

productive *adj* **1** yielding a lot; fertile; fruitful. **2** useful; profitable: *a productive meeting.* **3** (*usu* **productive of sth**) giving rise to it; resulting in it: *productive of ideas.*

productivity *noun* the rate and efficiency of work, esp in industrial production, etc.

proem /'proʊɛm/ *noun* an introduction, prelude or preface, esp at the beginning of a book. [14c: ultimately from Greek *pro* before + *oime* song]

Prof. *abbrev* Professor.

prof *noun, informal* a professor.

profane *adj* **1** showing disrespect for sacred things; irreverent. **2** not sacred or spiritual; temporal or worldly. **3** esp of language: vulgar; blasphemous. ▸ *verb* **1** to treat (something sacred) irreverently. **2** to violate or defile (what should be respected). ▪ **profanation** *noun.* ▪ **profanity** *noun* (**-*ies***). [14c: from Latin *profanus* outside the temple]

profess *verb* **1** to make an open declaration of (beliefs, etc). **2** to declare adherence to something. **3** to claim or pretend: *profess to be an expert.* Compare **confess.** [14c: from Latin *profiteri* to declare]

professed *adj* **1** self-acknowledged; self-confessed. **2** claimed by oneself; pretended. **3** having taken the vows of a religious order.

profession *noun* **1** an occupation, esp one that requires specialist academic and practical training, eg medicine, teaching, etc. **2** the body of people engaged in a particular one of these. **3** an act of professing; a declaration: *a profession of loyalty.* **4** a declaration of religious belief made upon entering a religious order. [13c: from Latin *professio* a public declaration]

professional *adj* **1** earning a living in the performance, practice or teaching of something that is usu a pastime: *a professional golfer.* **2** belonging to a trained profession. **3** like, appropriate to or having the competence, expertise or conscientiousness of someone with professional training: *did a very professional job.* ▸ *noun* **1** someone who belongs to one of the skilled professions. **2** someone who makes their living in an activity, etc that is also carried on at an amateur level. ▪ **professionalism** *noun.* ▪ **professionally** *adv.*

professor *noun* **1** a teacher of the highest rank in a university; the head of a university department. **2** *N Am, esp US* a university teacher. ▪ **professorial** /prɒfɛ'sɔːrɪəl/ *adj.* ▪ **professorship** *noun.* [14c: Latin, meaning 'public teacher']

proffer *verb* to offer something for someone to accept; to tender. [13c: from French *proffrir*]

proficient *adj* fully trained and competent; expert. ▸ *noun* an expert. ▪ **proficiency** *noun.* [16c: from Latin *proficere* to make progress]

profile *noun* **1 a** a side view of something, esp of a face or head; **b** a representation of this. **2** a brief outline, sketch or assessment. ▸ *verb* **1** to represent in profile. **2** to give a brief outline (of a person, their career, a company, prospects, etc). [17c: from Italian *profilo*]

IDIOMS **in profile** from the side view. **keep a low profile** to maintain a unobtrusive presence.

profit *noun* **1** the money gained from selling something for more than it originally cost. **2** an excess of income over expenses. **3** advantage or benefit. ▸ *verb, intr* (*often* **profit from** *or* **by sth**) to benefit from it. [14c: from Latin *profectus*]

profitable *adj* **1** of a business, etc: making a profit. **2** useful; fruitful. ▪ **profitability** *noun.* [14c]

profiteer *noun* someone who takes advantage of a shortage or other emergency to make exorbitant profits. ▸ *verb, intr* to make profits in such a way. [20c]

profit margin *noun, commerce* the difference between the buying or production price of a product and the selling price. [20c]

profligate /'prɒflɪgət/ *adj* **1** immoral and irresponsible; licentious or dissolute. **2** scandalously extravagant. ▸ *noun* a profligate person. ▪ **profligacy** *noun.* [17c: from Latin *profligare* to strike down]

pro forma *adj, adv* as a matter of form; following a certain procedure. ▸ *noun* (*also* **pro-forma invoice**) an invoice sent in advance of the goods ordered. [16c: Latin, meaning 'for the sake of form']

profound *adj* **1** radical, extensive, far-reaching: *profound changes.* **2** deep; far below the surface. **3** of a feeling: deeply felt or rooted. **4** of comments, etc: showing understanding or penetration. **5** penetrating deeply into knowledge. **6** intense; impenetrable: *profound deafness.* **7** of sleep: deep; sound. ▪ **profoundly** *adv.* ▪ **profundity** *noun.* [14c: from Latin *profundus* deep]

profuse *adj* **1** overflowing; exaggerated; excessive: *profuse apologies.* **2** copious: *profuse bleeding.* ▪ **profusely** *adv.* ▪ **profusion** *or* **profuseness** *noun.* [15c: from Latin *profusus* lavish]

progenitor *noun* **1** an ancestor, forebear or forefather. **2** the founder or originator of a movement, etc. [14c: Latin, from *progignere* to beget]

progeny *noun* (**-*ies***) **1** children; offspring; descendants. **2** a result or conclusion. [13c: from Latin *progenies* offspring]

progesterone *noun, biochem* a steroid sex hormone that prepares the lining of the uterus for implantation of a fertilized egg. [1930s: from *progestin* + *sterol*]

prognosis *noun* (**-*ses***) **1** an informed forecast of developments in any situation. **2** a doctor's prediction regarding the probable course of a disease, disorder or injury. [17c: Greek, meaning 'knowing before']

prognostic *adj* serving as an informed forecast; foretelling. [15c: see **prognosis**]

prognosticate *verb* **1** to foretell. **2** to indicate in advance; to be a sign of something. ▪ **prognostication** *noun*. ▪ **prognosticator** *noun*. [16c: from Latin *prognosticare* to foretell]

programmable *adj* capable of being programmed to perform a task automatically.

programme *or* (*US*) **program** *noun* **1 a** the schedule of proceedings for, and list of participants in, a theatre performance, entertainment, ceremony, etc; **b** a leaflet or booklet describing these. **2** an agenda, plan or schedule. **3** a series of planned projects to be undertaken. **4** a scheduled radio or TV presentation. **5** (*always* **program**) *comput* a set of coded instructions to a computer for the performance of a task or a series of operations, written in a **programming language**. ▸ *verb* **1** to include something in a programme; to schedule. **2** to draw up a programme for something. **3** to set (a computer) by program to perform a set of operations. **4** to prepare a program for a computer. **5** to set (a machine) so as to operate at the required time. **6** to train to respond in a specified way. [18c: from Greek *programma* the order of the day or schedule]

programme music *noun* instrumental music which aims to depict a story or scene.

programmer *noun* someone who writes computer programs (see **programme** *noun* sense 5).

programming language *noun, comput* any system of codes, symbols, rules, etc designed for writing computer programs.

progress *noun* /'proʊgrɛs; *NAm* 'prɒ-/ **1** movement while travelling in any direction. **2** course: *followed the progress of the trial.* **3** movement towards a destination, goal or state of completion: *make slow progress.* **4** advances or development. ▸ *verb* /prə'grɛs/ **1** *intr* to move forwards or onwards; to proceed towards a goal. **2** *intr* to advance or develop. **3** *intr* to improve. **4** to put (something planned) into operation. [15c: from Latin *progredi* to move forward]

IDIOMS **in progress** taking place; in the course of being done.

progression *noun* **1** an act or the process of moving forwards or advancing in stages. **2** improvement. **3** *maths* a sequence of numbers, each of which bears a specific relationship to the preceding term. See **arithmetic progression, geometric progression**.

progressive *adj* **1** advanced in outlook; using or favouring new methods. **2** moving forward or advancing continuously or by stages. **3** of a disease: continuously increasing in severity or complication. **4** of a dance or game: involving changes of partner at intervals. **5** of taxation: increasing as the sum taxed increases. **6** *grammar* of a verbal aspect or tense: expressing continuing action or a continuing state, formed in English with *be* and the present **participle**, as in *I am doing it* and *they will be going*. Also called **continuous**. Compare **perfect**. ▸ *noun* **1** someone with progressive ideas. **2** *grammar* **a** the progressive aspect or tense; **b** a verb in a progressive aspect or tense. ▪ **progressively** *adv*. ▪ **progressivism** *noun*. ▪ **progressivist** *noun, adj*.

progressive rock *or* **prog rock** *noun* a type of rock music featuring complex and often lengthy compositions, with lyrics inspired by science fiction, fantasy and mythology.

prohibit *verb*, **1** to forbid something, esp by law; to ban. **2** to prevent or hinder. [15c: from Latin *prohibere* to prevent]

prohibition *noun* **1** the act of prohibiting or state of being prohibited. **2** a law or decree that prohibits something. **3** a ban by law, especially in the US from 1920 to 1933, on the manufacture and sale of alcoholic drinks. **4** *hist* (**Prohibition**) the period between 1920 and 1933 when the manufacture and sale of alcoholic drinks was prohibited in the USA. ▪ **prohibitionist** *noun*.

prohibitive *or* **prohibitory** *adj* **1** banning; prohibiting. **2** tending to prevent or discourage. **3** of prices, etc: unaffordably high. ▪ **prohibitively** *adv*.

project *noun* /'prɒdʒɛkt/ **1** a plan, scheme or proposal. **2** a research or study assignment. ▸ *verb* /prə'dʒɛkt/ **1** *intr* to jut out; to protrude. **2** to throw something forwards; to propel. **3** to throw (a shadow, image, etc) on to a surface, screen, etc. **4** to propose or plan. **5** to forecast something from present trends and other known data; to extrapolate. **6** to imagine (oneself) in another situation, esp a future one. **7** to cause (a sound, esp the voice) to be heard clearly at some distance. [17c: from Latin *projicere* to throw forward]

projectile *noun* an object designed to be projected by an external force, eg a guided missile, bullet, etc. ▸ *adj* **1** capable of being, or designed to be, hurled. **2** projecting. [17c: from Latin *projectilis*; see **project**]

projection *noun* **1** the act of projecting or process of being projected. **2** something that protrudes from a surface. **3** the process of showing a film or transparencies on a screen. **4** a forecast based on present trends and other known data. **5** *maths* esp on maps: the representation of a solid object, esp part of the Earth's sphere, on a flat surface. **6** *psychol* the reading of one's own emotions and experiences into a particular situation. ▪ **projectionist** *noun* someone who operates a projector. [16c]

projector *noun* an instrument containing a system of lenses that projects an enlarged version of an illuminated still or moving image on to a screen. [19c]

prokaryote *or* **procaryote** *noun, biol* any organism, including all bacteria, in which each cell contains a single DNA molecule coiled in a loop, and not enclosed in a nucleus. See also **eukaryote**. ▪ **prokaryotic** *or* **procaryotic** *adj*. [20c: from **pro-**[2] + Greek *karyon* kernel]

prolapse *pathol, noun* the slipping out of place or falling down of an organ, esp the slipping of the uterus into the vagina. ▸ *verb* of an organ: to slip out of place. [18c: from Latin *prolabi* to slip forward]

prolate *adj, geom* of something approximately spherical: more pointed at the poles. Compare **oblate**. [18c: from Latin *proferre* to enlarge]

prole *noun, adj, derog informal* proletarian. [19c]

proletarian /proʊlə'tɛərɪən/ *adj* relating to the proletariat. ▸ *noun* a member of the proletariat. Compare **patrician**. [17c: from Latin *proletarius* a citizen who has nothing to offer society but his offspring]

proletariat /proʊlə'tɛərɪət/ *noun* **1** the working class, esp unskilled labourers and industrial workers. **2** *hist* in ancient Rome: the lowest class of people. [19c]

pro-life *adj* of a person or an organization: opposing abortion, euthanasia and experimentation on human embryos. Compare **pro-choice.** [20c]

proliferate *verb* **1** *intr* of a plant or animal species: to reproduce rapidly. **2** *intr* to increase in numbers; to multiply. **3** *biol* to reproduce (cells, etc) rapidly. ▪ **proliferation** *noun.* [19c: from Latin *prolifer* bearing offspring]

prolific *adj* **1** abundant in growth; producing plentiful fruit or offspring. **2** of a writer, artist, etc: constantly producing new work. **3** (*often* **prolific of** *or* **in sth**) productive of it; abounding in it. ▪ **prolificacy** *noun.* ▪ **prolifically** *adv.* [17c: from Latin *prolificus*, from *proles* offspring]

prolix *adj* of speech or writing: tediously long-winded; wordy; verbose. ▪ **prolixity** *noun.* [15c: from Latin *prolixus* stretched out]

prologue *noun* **1** *theatre* **a** a speech addressed to the audience at the beginning of a play; **b** the actor delivering it. **2** a preface to a literary work. **3** an event serving as an introduction or prelude. ▸ *verb* to introduce or preface something with a prologue. [13c: from Greek *prologos*, from *logos* discourse]

prolong *verb* to make something longer; to extend or protract. ▪ **prolongation** *noun.* [15c: from Latin *prolongare* to lengthen or extend]

prom *noun, informal* **1** a walkway or promenade. **2** a **promenade concert**. **3** *orig N Am* a formal school or college dance at the end of the academic year. [19c: abbreviation]

promenade *noun* **1** a broad paved walk, esp along a seafront. **2** *facetious* a stately stroll. ▸ *verb* **1** *intr* to stroll in a stately fashion. **2** to walk (the streets, etc). **3** to take someone out for some fresh air; to parade. ▪ **promenader** *noun.* [16c: French, from *promener* to lead forth]

promenade concert *noun* a concert, usu of classical music, at which part of the audience is accommodated in a standing area in which they can move about. [19c]

Promethean *adj* daring and skilfully inventive. [16c: from Prometheus, who, in Greek mythology, dared to steal fire from the gods]

promethium *noun, chem* (symbol **Pm**) a radioactive metallic element that occurs naturally in minute amounts and is manufactured artificially by bombarding neodymium with neutrons. [20c: Latin, named after Prometheus; see **Promethean**]

prominence *noun* **1** the state or quality of being prominent. **2** a prominent point or thing. **3** a projection.

prominent *adj* **1** jutting out; projecting; protruding; bulging. **2** noticeable; conspicuous. **3** leading; notable. [16c: from Latin *prominere* to jut out]

promiscuous *adj* **1** indulging in casual or indiscriminate sexual relations. **2** haphazardly mixed. ▪ **promiscuity** /prɒmɪ'skjuːɪtɪ/ *noun.* ▪ **promiscuously** *adv.* [17c: from Latin *promiscuus* mixed up]

promise *verb* **1** *tr & intr* to give an undertaking (to do or not do something). **2** to undertake to give something to someone: *promised him a treat.* **3** to show signs of bringing something: *clouds that promise rain.* **4** to look likely (to do something): *promises to have a great future.* **5** to assure or warn: *I promise nothing bad will happen.* ▸ *noun* **1** an assurance to give, do or not do something. **2** a sign: *promise of spring in the air.* **3** signs of future excellence. [14c: from Latin *promittere* to send forth]

promised land *noun* **1** *Bible* in the Old Testament: the fertile land promised by God to the Israelites. **2** *Christianity* heaven. **3** any longed-for place of contentment and prosperity.

promising *adj* **1** showing promise; talented; apt. **2** seeming to bode well for the future: *a promising start.*

promissory *adj* containing, relating to or expressing a promise. [17c: from Latin *promissorius*]

promo *noun, informal* something which is used to publicize a product, esp a video for a pop single. [20c: short for **promotional** or **promotion**]

promontory *noun* (**-ies**) a usu hilly part of a coastline that projects into the sea. Also called **headland**. [16c: from Latin *promonturium* mountain ridge]

promote *verb* **1** **a** to raise someone to a more senior position; **b** *sport, esp football* to transfer (a team) to a higher division or league. Compare **relegate** (sense 2). **2** to contribute to something: *Exercise promotes health.* **3** to work for the cause of something: *promote peace.* **4** to publicize; to try to boost the sales of (a product) by advertising. ▪ **promotion** *noun.* ▪ **promotional** *adj.* [14c: from Latin *promovere* to make advance]

promoter *noun* the organizer or financer of a sporting event or other undertaking.

prompt *adj* **1** immediate; quick; punctual. **2** instantly willing; ready; unhesitating. ▸ *adv* punctually. ▸ *noun* **1** something serving as a reminder. **2** *theatre* words supplied by a prompter to an actor. **3** *theatre* a prompter. **4** *comput* a sign on screen indicating that the computer is ready for input. ▸ *verb* **1** to cause, lead or remind someone to do something. **2** to produce or elicit (a reaction or response). **3** *tr & intr* to help (an actor) to remember their next words by supplying the first few. ▪ **promptitude** *noun.* ▪ **promptly** *adv.* ▪ **promptness** *noun.* [14c: from Latin *promptus* ready or quick]

prompter *noun* **1** *theatre* someone positioned offstage to prompt actors if they forget their lines. **2** someone or something that prompts.

promulgate *verb* **1** to make (a decree, etc) effective by means of an official public announcement. **2** to publicize or promote (an idea, theory, etc) widely. ▪ **promulgation** *noun.* ▪ **promulgator** *noun.* [16c: from Latin *promulgare* to make known]

prone *adj* **1** lying flat, esp face downwards. **2** (*often* **prone to sth**) predisposed to it, or liable to suffer from it. *in compounds*: *accident-prone.* **3** inclined or liable to do something. [14c: from Latin *pronus* bent forwards]

prong *noun* **1** a point or spike, esp one on the head of a fork. **2** any pointed projection. [15c]

pronged *adj, in compounds* **1** of a fork, etc: with a specified number of prongs or directions. **2** of an attack, etc: made from a specified number of directions.

pronominal *adj, grammar* referring to or of the nature of a pronoun. [17c: from Latin *pronominalis*]

pronoun *noun, grammar* a word such as *she, him, they, it*, etc used in place of, and to refer to, a noun, phrase, clause, etc. [16c: from Latin *pronomen*]

pronounce *verb* **1** to say or utter (words, sounds, letters, etc); to articulate or enunciate. **2** to declare something officially, formally or authoritatively: *pronounced her innocent*. **3** to pass or deliver (judgement). **4** *intr* (*usu* **pronounce on sth**) to give an opinion or verdict on it. See also **pronunciation**. ▪ **pronounceable** *adj*. [14c: from Latin *pronuntiare* to declaim or pronounce]

pronounced *adj* **1** noticeable; distinct: *a pronounced limp*. **2** spoken; articulated.

pronouncement *noun* **1** a formal announcement. **2** a declaration of opinion; a verdict.

pronto *adv, informal* immediately. [20c: Spanish, meaning 'quick']

pronunciation *noun* **1** the act or a manner of pronouncing words, sounds, letters, etc. **2** the correct way of pronouncing a word, sound, etc in a given language.

proof *noun* **1** evidence, esp conclusive evidence, that something is true or a fact. **2** *law* the accumulated evidence on which a verdict is based. **3** the activity or process of testing or proving. **4** a test, trial or demonstration. **5** *maths* a step-by-step verification of a proposed mathematical statement. **6** *printing* a trial copy of printed text used for examination or correction. **7** a trial print from a photographic negative. **8** a trial impression from an engraved plate. **9** a measure of the alcohol content of a distilled liquid, esp an alcoholic beverage, equal to 49.28% of alcohol by weight. ▸ *adj, esp in compounds* able or designed to withstand, deter or be free from or secure against a specified thing: *proof against storms* • *leakproof*. ▸ *verb* **1** *often in compounds* to make something resistant to or proof against a specified thing: *to dampproof the walls*. **2** to take a proof of (printed material). **3** to proof-read. [13c: from French *preuve*]

proof-read *verb, tr & intr* to read and mark for correction the proofs of (a text, etc). ▪ **proof-reader** *noun*. ▪ **proof-reading** *noun*.

proof spirit *noun* a standard mixture of alcohol and water containing 49.28% alcohol by weight or 57.1% by volume. [18c]

prop[1] *noun* **1** a rigid support, esp a vertical one: *a clothes prop*. **2** a person or thing that one depends on for help or emotional support. **3** (*also* **prop forward**) *rugby* **a** the position at either end of the front row of the scrum; **b** a player in this position. ▸ *verb* (***propped, propping***) **1** (*often* **prop sth up**) to support or hold it upright with, or as if with, a prop. **2** (*usu* **prop against sth**) to lean against it; to put something against something else. **3** to serve as a prop to something. [15c]

prop[2] *noun, informal* (*in full* **property**) *theatre* a portable object or piece of furniture used on stage.

prop[3] *noun, informal* a propeller. [20c]

propaganda *noun* **1** **a** the organized circulation by a political group, etc of doctrine, information, misinformation, rumour or opinion, intended to influence public feeling, raise public awareness, bring about reform, etc; **b** the material circulated in this way. **2** (**Propaganda**) the administrative board of a Roman Catholic Church, responsible for foreign missions and the training of missionaries. ▪ **propagandist** *noun*. [18c: Italian]

propagate *verb* **1** *tr & intr, botany* of a plant: to multiply. **2** *botany* to grow (new plants), either by natural means or artificially. **3** to spread or popularize (ideas, etc). **4** *physics* to transmit energy, eg sound or electromagnetism, over a distance in wave form. ▪ **propagation** *noun*. ▪ **propagator** *noun*. [16c: from Latin *propagare* to grow plants by grafting, etc]

propane *noun, chem* a colourless odourless flammable gas, belonging to the alkane series of hydrocarbons, obtained from petroleum and used as a fuel.

propanone *noun* **acetone**.

propel *verb* (***propelled, propelling***) **1** to drive or push something forward. **2** to steer or send someone or something in a certain direction. [17c: from Latin *propellere* to drive]

propellant *noun* **1** *chem* a compressed inert gas in an aerosol that is used to release the liquid contents as a fine spray when the pressure is released. **2** *eng* the fuel and oxidizer that are burned in a rocket in order to provide thrust. **3** something that propels.

propeller *noun* a device consisting of a revolving hub with radiating blades that produce thrust or power, used to propel aircraft, ships, etc. [18c]

propensity *noun* (***-ies***) a tendency or inclination. [16c: from Latin *propensus* hanging forward]

proper *adj* **1** real; genuine; able to be correctly described as (a specified thing). **2** right; correct. **3** appropriate: *at the proper time*. **4** own; particular; correct: *in its proper place*. **5** socially accepted; respectable. **6** *derog* morally strict; prim. **7** (*usu* **proper to sth**) belonging or appropriate to it; suitable: *the form of address proper to her rank*. **8** used immediately after a noun: strictly so called; itself, excluding others not immediately connected with it: *We are now entering the city proper*. **9** *informal* utter; complete; out-and-out: *a proper idiot*. [13c: from French *propre*]

proper fraction *noun, maths* a fraction in which the **numerator** is less than the **denominator**, eg $\frac{1}{2}$ or $\frac{3}{7}$. Compare **improper fraction**.

properly *adv* **1** suitably; appropriately; correctly. **2** with strict accuracy. **3** fully; thoroughly; completely.

proper noun *or* **proper name** *noun, grammar* the name of a particular person, place or thing, eg *Kurt, Clapham, Internet*.

property *noun* (***-ies***) **1** something someone owns. **2** possessions collectively. **3** the concept of ownership. **4** **a** land or real estate; **b** an item of this. **5** a quality or attribute: *has the property of dissolving easily*. **6** a **prop**[2]. [13c: from French *proprieté*]

prop forward see **prop**[1] (*noun* sense 3)

prophase *noun, biol* in **mitosis** and **meiosis**: the first stage of cell division, during which the chromosomes condense and become discrete. [19c: **pro-**[2] + **phase**]

prophecy *noun* (***-ies***) **1** **a** the interpretation of divine will; **b** the act of revealing such interpretations. **2** **a** the foretelling of the future; **b** something foretold; a prediction. **3** a gift or aptitude for predicting the future. [13c: from French *prophecie*]

prophesy *verb* (***-ies, -ied***) **1** *tr & intr* to foretell (future happenings); to predict. **2** *intr* to utter prophecies; to interpret divine will. [14c: a variant of **prophecy**]

prophet *noun* **1** someone who is able to express the will of God or a god. **2** *Bible* **a** any of the writers of prophecy in the Old Testament; **b** any of the books attributed to them. **3** *Islam* (**the Prophet**) Muhammad. **4** someone who claims to be able to tell what will happen in the future: *a prophet of doom*. **5** a leading advocate of or spokesperson for a movement or cause. ▪ **prophetess** *noun*. [12c: from Greek *prophetes*]

prophetic *adj* **1** foretelling the future. **2** relating or belonging to prophets or prophecy. ▪ **prophetically** *adv*.

prophylactic *adj* guarding against or tending to prevent disease or other mishap. ▶ *noun* **1** a prophylactic drug or device; a precautionary measure. **2** a condom. [16c: from Greek *prophylaktikos*]

propinquity *noun* **1** nearness in place or time. **2** closeness of kinship. [14c: from Latin *propinquitas*]

propitiate /prəˈpɪʃieɪt/ *verb* to appease or placate (an angry or insulted person or god). ▪ **propitiable** *adj*. ▪ **propitiation** *noun*. ▪ **propitiator** *noun*. ▪ **propitiatory** *adj*. [17c: from Latin *propitiare*]

propitious /prəˈpɪʃəs/ *adj* **1** favourable; auspicious; advantageous. **2** (*often* **propitious for** *or* **to sth**) likely to favour or encourage it. ▪ **propitiously** *adv*. [15c: from Latin *propitius* gracious]

proponent *noun* a supporter or advocate of something; someone who argues in favour of their cause. [16c: from Latin *proponere* to propose]

proportion *noun* **1** a comparative part of a total: *a large proportion of the population*. **2** the size of one element or group in relation to the whole or total. **3** the size of one group or component in relation to another: *in a proportion of two parts to one*. **4** the correct balance between parts or elements: *out of proportion*. **5** (**proportions**) size; dimensions: *a garden of large proportions*. **6** *maths* correspondence between the ratios of two pairs of quantities, as expressed in *2 is to 8 as 3 is to 12*. ▶ *verb* to adjust the proportions, or balance the parts, of something. [14c: from Latin *proportio*]

IDIOMS **in proportion to sth 1** in relation to it; in comparison with it. **2** in parallel with it; in correspondence with it; at the same rate.

proportional *adj* **1** corresponding or matching in size, rate, etc. **2** in correct proportion; proportionate. ▶ *noun, maths* a number or quantity in a proportion. ▪ **proportionally** *adv*.

proportional representation *noun* (abbrev **PR**) any electoral system in which the number of representatives each political party has in parliament is in direct proportion to the number of votes it receives. [19c]

proportionate *adj* (**proportionate to sth**) due or in correct proportion. ▪ **proportionately** *adv*.

proposal *noun* **1** the act of proposing something. **2** something proposed or suggested. **3** an offer of marriage. [17c]

propose *verb* **1** to offer (a plan, etc) for consideration; to suggest. **2** to suggest or nominate someone for a position, task, etc. **3** to be the proposer of (the motion in a debate). **4** to intend (to do something): *don't propose to sell*. **5** to suggest (a specified person, topic, etc) as the subject of a toast. **6** *intr* (*often* **propose to sb**) to make them an offer of marriage. ▪ **proposer** *noun*. [14c: from Latin *proponere* to propose]

proposition *noun* **1** a proposal or suggestion. **2** something to be dealt with or undertaken: *an awkward proposition*. **3** *euphem, informal* an invitation to have sexual intercourse. **4** *logic* a form of statement affirming or denying something, that can be true or false; a premise. **5** *maths* a statement of a problem or theorem, esp one that incorporates its solution or proof. ▶ *verb, euphem, informal* to propose sexual intercourse to someone. [14c: from Latin *propositio* a setting forth]

propound *verb* to put forward (an idea or theory, etc) for consideration or discussion. [16c: from Latin *proponere* to propose]

proprietary (abbrev **pty**) *adj* **1** of rights: belonging to an owner or proprietor. **2** suggestive or indicative of ownership. **3** of medicines, etc: marketed under a tradename. **4** *esp Aust, NZ & S Afr* (abbrev **Pty**) of a company etc: privately owned and managed. *UK equivalent* **Ltd.** ▶ *noun* (**-ies**) **1** a body of proprietors. **2** proprietorship. [16c: from Latin *proprietas* ownership]

proprietary name *noun* a **tradename**.

proprietor *or* **proprietress** *noun* an owner, esp of a shop, hotel, business, etc. ▪ **proprietorial** *adj*. ▪ **proprietorship** *noun*. [17c: from **proprietary**]

propriety *noun* (**-ies**) **1** conformity to socially acceptable behaviour, esp between the sexes; modesty or decorum. **2** correctness; moral acceptability. **3** (**proprieties**) accepted standards of conduct. [17c: from French *propriété*]

propulsion *noun* **1** the act of causing something to move forward. **2** *also in compounds* a force exerted against a body which makes it move forward: *jet propulsion*. ▪ **propulsive** *adj*. [18c: from Latin *propulsio*]

pro rata *adv* in proportion; in accordance with a certain rate. [16c: Latin, meaning 'for the rate']

prorogue /proʊˈroʊg/ *verb, formal* **1** to discontinue the meetings of (a legislative assembly) for a time, without dissolving it. **2** *intr* of a legislative assembly: to suspend a session. ▪ **prorogation** *noun*. [15c: from Latin *prorogare* to ask publicly]

prosaic /proʊˈzeɪɪk/ *adj* **1** unpoetic; unimaginative. **2** dull, ordinary and uninteresting. ▪ **prosaically** *adv*. [17c: from Latin *prosaicus*; see **prose**]

pros and cons *plural noun* the various advantages and disadvantages of a course of action, idea, etc. [16c: from **pro**[1] + **con**[2]]

proscenium /proʊˈsiːnɪəm/ *noun* (***prosceniums*** *or* ***proscenia*** /-ə/) *theatre* **1** the part of a stage in front of the curtain. **2** (*also* **proscenium arch**) the arch framing the stage and separating it from the auditorium. [17c: from Greek *proskenion*]

proscribe *verb* **1** to prohibit or condemn something (eg a practice). **2** *hist* to outlaw or exile someone. ▪ **proscription** *noun*. ▪ **proscriptive** *adj*. [16c: from Latin *proscribere* to write in front of]

proscribe, prescribe

Be careful not to use the word **proscribe** when you mean **prescribe**. If you **prescribe** something, you advise it or say that it must happen:

We have prescribed the use of calculators in the exam. Make sure you bring a suitable calculator with you.

prose *noun* **1** the ordinary form of written or spoken language as distinct from verse or poetry. **2** a passage of prose set for translation into a foreign language. **3** dull and uninteresting discussion or speech, etc. [14c: from Latin *prosa oratio* straightforward speech]

prosecute *verb* **1** *tr & intr* to bring a criminal action against someone. **2** *formal* to carry on or carry out something (eg enquiries). ▪ **prosecutable** *adj.* ▪ **prosecutor** *noun.* [15c: from Latin *prosequi* to pursue]

prosecution *noun* **1** the act of prosecuting or process of being prosecuted. **2** the bringing of a criminal action against someone. **3 a** the prosecuting party in a criminal case; **b** the lawyers involved in this. **4** *formal* the process of carrying something out.

proselyte /ˈprɒsəlaɪt/ *noun* a convert, esp a Gentile turning to Judaism. ▪ **proselytism** /ˈprɒsəlɪtɪzəm/ *noun.* [14c: from Greek *proselytos* new arrival or convert]

proselytize *or* **-ise** /ˈprɒsəlɪtaɪz/ *verb, tr & intr* to try to convert someone from one faith to another; to make converts. ▪ **proselytizer** *noun.* [17c]

prosody /ˈprɒsədɪ/ *noun* **1** the study of verse composition, esp poetic metre. **2** (*also* **prosodics** /prəˈsɒdɪks/) the study of rhythm, stress and intonation in speech. ▪ **prosodic** /-ˈsɒdɪk/ *adj.* ▪ **prosodist** *noun.* [15c: from Latin *prosodia* the accent for a syllable]

prospect *noun* /ˈprɒspɛkt/ **1** an expectation of something due or likely to happen. **2** an outlook for the future. **3** (**prospects**) chances of success, improvement, recovery, etc. **4** (**prospects**) opportunities for advancement, promotion, etc: *a job with prospects.* **5** a potentially selectable candidate, team member, etc: *He's a doubtful prospect for Saturday's match.* **6** a potential client or customer. **7** a broad view. ▸ *verb* /prəˈspɛkt/ **1** *tr & intr* to search or explore (an area, region, etc) for gold or other minerals. **2** *intr* to hunt for or look out for (eg a job). [15c: from Latin *prospectus* view]

IDIOMS **in prospect** expected soon.

prospective *adj* likely or expected; future. [18c]

prospector *noun* someone prospecting for oil, gold, etc.

prospectus *noun* **1** a brochure giving information about a school or other institution, esp the courses on offer. **2** a document outlining a proposal for something, eg an issue of shares. [18c: Latin, meaning 'a view']

prosper *verb, intr* **1** of someone: to do well, esp financially. **2** of a business, etc: to thrive or flourish. ▪ **prosperity** *noun.* [15c: from French *prospérer*]

prosperous *adj* wealthy and successful. ▪ **prosperously** *adv.* [15c]

prostate *noun* (*in full* **prostate gland**) *anatomy* in male mammals: a muscular gland around the base of the bladder which produces an alkaline fluid that activates sperm during ejaculation. [17c: from Greek *prostates* one that stands in front]

---

prostate, prostrate

Be careful not to use the word **prostate** when you mean **prostrate**. If you are **prostrate** or **prostrate yourself**, you lie face downwards:

He lay prostrate on the ground.

---

prosthesis /prɒsˈθiːsɪs/ *noun* (**-ses** /-siːz/) *med* an artificial substitute for a part of the body that is missing or non-functional, eg an artificial limb or a pacemaker. ▪ **prosthetic** /-ˈθɛtɪk/ *adj.* [18c: Latin]

prosthetics *singular noun* the branch of surgery concerned with supplying and fitting **prostheses**. [19c]

prostitute *noun* **1** *also in compounds* someone who performs sexual acts or intercourse in return for money. **2** someone who offers their skills or talents, etc for unworthy ends. ▸ *verb* **1** to offer (oneself or someone else) as a prostitute. **2** to put (eg one's talents) to an unworthy use. ▪ **prostitution** *noun.* [16c: from Latin *prostituere* to offer for sale]

prostrate *adj* /ˈprɒstreɪt/ **1** lying face downwards in an attitude of abject submission, humility or adoration. **2** distraught with illness, grief, exhaustion, etc. ▸ *verb* /prɒˈstreɪt/ **1** to throw (oneself) face down in submission or adoration. **2** of exhaustion, illness, grief, etc: to overwhelm someone physically or emotionally. ▪ **prostration** *noun.* [14c: from Latin *prosternere* to throw forwards]

---

prostrate, prostate

Be careful not to use the word **prostrate** when you mean **prostate**. The **prostate** is a gland in the male body:

prostate cancer

---

prosy *adj* (**-ier, -iest**) of speech or writing: **1** proselike. **2** dull and tedious.

prot- see **proto-**

protactinium *noun* (symbol **Pa**) *chem* a white highly toxic radioactive metallic element. [20c]

protagonist *noun* **1** the main character in a play, story, film, etc. **2** any person at the centre of a story or event. **3** *non-standard* a leader or champion of a movement or cause, etc. [17c: from Greek *protagonistes*]

protean /ˈproʊtɪən/ *adj* **1** readily able to change shape or appearance; variable; changeable. **2** esp of a writer, artist, actor, etc: versatile. [16c: from Proteus, the Greek sea god who assumed many shapes]

protease /ˈproʊtɪeɪs/ *noun, biochem* any enzyme that catalyses the breakdown of proteins. [20c: from **protein** + *-ase* (indicating an enzyme)]

protect *verb* **1** to shield someone or something from danger; to guard them or it against injury, destruction, etc; to keep safe. **2** to shield (home industries) from foreign competition by taxing imports. [16c: from Latin *protegere* to cover in front]

protection *noun* **1** the action of protecting or condition of being protected; shelter, refuge, cover, safety or care. **2** something that protects. **3** (*also* **protectionism**) the system of protecting home industries against foreign competition by taxing imports. **4** *informal* **a** the criminal practice of extorting money from shop-owners, etc in return for leaving their premises unharmed; **b** (*also* **protection money**) the money extorted in this way. ▪ **protectionist** *noun.*

protective *adj* **1** giving or designed to give protection: *protective clothing.* **2** inclined or tending to protect. ▸ *noun* **1** something which protects. **2** a condom. ▪ **protectively** *adv.* ▪ **protectiveness** *noun.*

protector *or* **protectress** *noun* **1** someone or something that protects. **2** a patron or benefactor. **3** someone who rules a country during the childhood, absence or incapacity of a sovereign; a regent. ▪ **protectorship** *noun.*

protectorate *noun* **1** the office or period of rule of a protector. **2 a** a protectorship of a weak or backward country assumed by a more powerful one without actual annexation; **b** the territory that is so protected. [17c]

protégé *or* **protégée** /ˈproʊtəʒeɪ/ *noun* a person (male and female respectively) under the guidance, protection, patronage, etc of someone wiser or more important. [18c: from French *protéger* to protect]

protein *noun, biochem* any of thousands of different organic compounds, characteristic of all living organisms, that have large molecules consisting of long chains of amino acids. [19c: from French *protéine*]

pro tempore /proʊ tɛmˈpɔːreɪ/ ▸ *adv, adj* for the time being. Often shortened to **pro tem**. [15c: Latin]

Proterozoic /proʊtəroʊˈzoʊɪk/ *geol adj* **1** relating to the geological era from which the oldest forms of life date. **2** *sometimes* denoting the entire **Precambrian** period. ▸ *noun* (**the Proterozoic**) the Proterozoic era. [20c: from Greek *proteros* earlier + *zoe* life]

protest *verb* /prəˈtɛst/ **1** *intr* to express an objection, disapproval, opposition or disagreement. **2** *N Am, esp US* to challenge or object to (eg a decision or measure). **3** to declare something solemnly, eg in response to an accusation: *protest one's innocence*. ▸ *noun* /ˈproʊtɛst/ **1** a declaration of disapproval or dissent; an objection. **2** an organized public demonstration of disapproval. *as adj*: *a protest march*. **3** the act of protesting. ▪ **protestation** *noun*. ▪ **protester** *or* **protestor** *noun*. [14c: from French *protester*]

IDIOMS **under protest** reluctantly; unwillingly.

Protestant *or* **protestant** *noun* **1** a member of any of the Christian Churches which embraced the principles of the Reformation and, rejecting the authority of the pope, separated from the Roman Catholic Church. **2** a member of any body descended from these. ▸ *adj* relating or belonging to Protestants. ▪ **Protestantism** *noun*. [16c]

protist *noun, biol* any member of the kingdom of unicellular organisms **Protista**, including the protozoans, slime moulds, etc. ▪ **protistic** *adj*. [19c: Greek, from *protistos* very first]

proto- *or before a vowel* **prot-** *combining form, denoting* **1** first; earliest in time: *prototype*. **2** first of a series. [Latin and Greek]

protocol *noun* **1** correct formal or diplomatic etiquette or procedure. **2** a first draft of a diplomatic document, eg one setting out the terms of a treaty. **3** *N Am, esp US* a plan of a scientific experiment or other procedure. **4** *comput* the set of rules controlling the transmission of data between two computers. [16c: from Latin *protocollum*]

proton *noun, physics* any of the positively charged subatomic particles that are found inside the nucleus at the centre of an atom. Compare **neutron**. [20c: Greek, from *protos* first]

protoplasm *noun, biol* the mass of protein material of which cells are composed, consisting of the cytoplasm and usu a nucleus. ▪ **protoplasmic** *adj*. [19c]

prototype *noun* **1** an original model from which later forms are copied, developed or derived. **2** a first working version, eg of a vehicle or aircraft. ▪ **prototypical** *adj*. [17c: from Greek *prototypos* primitive or original]

protozoan /proʊtəˈzoʊən/ *noun* (***protozoa*** /-ˈzoʊə/) a single-celled organism, eg an amoeba. [19c: from **proto-** + Greek *zoion* animal]

protract *verb* **1** to prolong; to cause something to last a long time. **2** to lengthen something out. ▪ **protracted** *adj*. ▪ **protraction** *noun*. [16c: from Latin *protrahere* to drag forth]

protractor *noun, geom* an instrument, usu a transparent plastic semicircle marked in degrees, used to draw and measure angles. [17c]

protrude *verb* **1** *intr* to project; to stick out. **2** to push something out or forward. ▪ **protrusion** *noun*. ▪ **protrusive** *adj*. [17c: from Latin *protrudere* to thrust forward]

protuberant *adj* projecting; bulging; swelling out. ▪ **protuberance** *noun*. [17c: from Latin *protuberare* to swell out]

proud *adj* **1** (*often* **proud of sb** *or* **sth**) feeling satisfaction, delight, etc with one's own or another's accomplishments, possessions, etc. **2** of an event, occasion, etc: arousing justifiable pride: *a proud day*. **3** arrogant; conceited. **4** concerned for one's dignity and self-respect. **5** honoured; gratified; delighted. **6** splendid; imposing; distinguished: *a proud sight*. **7** *technical* projecting slightly from the surrounding surface. ▪ **proudly** *adv*. [Anglo-Saxon *prud*]

IDIOMS **do sb proud** to entertain or treat them grandly.

prove *verb* (*past participle* ***proved*** *or* ***proven***) **1** to show something to be true, correct or a fact. **2** to show something to be (a specified thing): *was proved innocent*. **3** *intr* to be found to be (a specified thing) when tried; to turn out to be the case: *Her advice proved sound*. **4** to show (oneself) to be (of a specified type or quality, etc): *He proved himself reliable*. **5** to show (oneself) capable or daring. **6** *law* to establish the validity of (a will). **7** of dough: to rise when baked. ▪ **provable** *or* **proveable** *adj*. [12c: from French *prover*]

proven *verb, past participle of* **prove**. ▸ *adj* shown to be true, worthy, etc: *of proven ability*.

provenance /ˈprɒvənəns/ *noun* the place of origin (of a work of art, archaeological find, etc). [18c: French]

provender *noun* **1** dry food for livestock. **2** *now usu facetious* food. [14c: from French *provendre*]

proverb *noun* any of a body of well-known neatly-expressed sayings that give advice or express a supposed truth. [14c: from French *proverbe*]

proverbial *adj* **1** belonging or relating to a proverb. **2** referred to in a proverb; traditionally quoted; well known: *turned up like the proverbial bad penny*.

provide *verb* **1** to supply. **2** of a circumstance or situation, etc: to offer (a specified thing): *provide an opportunity*. **3** *intr* (*often* **provide against** *or* **for sth**) to be prepared for (an unexpected contingency, an emergency, etc). **4** *intr* (**provide for sb** *or* **sth**) to support or keep (a dependant, etc), or arrange for the means to do so. ▪ **provider** *noun*. [15c: from Latin *providere* to see ahead]

provided *or* **providing** *conj* on the condition or understanding (that a specified thing happens, etc): *Providing Joe gives me the money, I'll go*.

providence *noun* **1** (**Providence**) God or Nature regarded as an all-seeing protector of the world. **2** the quality of being provident. [14c: French]

provident *adj* **1** having foresight and making provisions for the future. **2** careful and thrifty; frugal.

providential *adj* due to providence; fortunate; lucky; opportune. ▪ **providentially** *adv*.

province *noun* **1** an administrative division of a country. **2** someone's allotted range of duties or field of knowledge or experience, etc. **3** (**the provinces**) the parts of a country away from the capital, typically thought of as culturally backward. [14c: French]

provincial *adj* **1** belonging or relating to a province. **2** relating to the parts of a country away from the capital: *a provincial accent.* **3** *derog* supposedly typical of provinces in being culturally backward, unsophisticated or narrow in outlook: *provincial attitudes.* ▪ **provincialism** *noun.* ▪ **provincially** *adv.* [14c: French]

provision *noun* **1** the act or process of providing. **2** something provided or made available; facilities. **3** preparations; measures taken in advance: *make provision for the future.* **4** (**provisions**) food and other necessities. **5** *law* a condition or requirement; a clause stipulating or enabling something. ▸ *verb* to supply (eg an army, country, boat) with food. [14c: French]

provisional *adj* temporary; for the time being or immediate purposes only; liable to be altered. ▪ **provisionally** *adv.*

proviso /prəˈvaɪzoʊ/ *noun* **1** a condition or stipulation. **2** *law* a clause stating a condition. ▪ **provisory** *adj.* [15c: from Latin *proviso quod* it being provided that]

provitamin *noun, physiol* a substance which is not a vitamin but which is readily transformed into a vitamin within an organism. [Latin *pro* before + **vitamin**]

provocation *noun* **1** the act of provoking or state of being provoked; incitement. **2** a cause of anger, irritation or indignation. [15c: from Latin *provocatio* calling forth or challenge]

provocative *adj* **1** tending or intended to cause anger; deliberately infuriating. **2** arousing or stimulating, esp by design. ▪ **provocatively** *adv.* [17c]

provoke *verb* **1** to annoy or infuriate someone, esp deliberately. **2** to incite or goad. **3** to rouse (someone's anger, etc). **4** to stir up or bring about something: *provoked a storm of protest.* ▪ **provoking** *adj.* ▪ **provokingly** *adv.* [15c: from Latin *provocare* to call forth]

provost *noun* **1** the head of some university colleges. **2** in Scotland: **a** the chief councillor of a district council; **b** *formerly* the chief magistrate of a burgh. [Anglo-Saxon *profost*]

provost marshal *noun* an officer in charge of military police. [16c]

prow *noun* the projecting front part of a ship; the **bow**[3]. [16c: from French *proue*]

prowess *noun* **1** skill; ability; expertise. **2** valour; dauntlessness. [13c: from French *proesse*]

prowl *verb, intr* **1** to go about stealthily, eg in search of prey. **2** *intr* to pace restlessly. ▸ *noun* an act of prowling. ▪ **prowler** *noun.* [14c]

prox. *abbrev* proximo.

proximal *adj, biol* at the near, inner or attached end. Compare **distal**. ▪ **proximally** *adv.* [19c: from Latin *proximus* nearest]

proximate *adj* **1** nearest. **2** immediately before or after in time, place or chronology. ▪ **proximately** *adv.* [16c: from Latin *proximare* to approach]

proximity *noun* (**-*ies***) nearness; closeness in space or time. [15c: from Latin *proximitas*]

proximo *adv* (abbrev **prox.**) used mainly in formal correspondence: in or during the next month. Compare **ultimo**. [19c: from Latin *proximo mense*]

proxy *noun* (**-*ies***) **1 a** a person authorized to act or vote on another's behalf; **b** the agency of such a person. *as adj*: *a proxy vote.* **2 a** the authority to act or vote for someone else; **b** a document granting this. [15c: from Latin *procuratio* procuration]

Prozac /ˈproʊzak/ *noun, trademark* a proprietary name for the antidepressant drug **fluoxetine**.

prude *noun* someone who is, or affects to be, shocked by improper behaviour, mention of sexual matters, etc; a prim or priggish person. ▪ **prudery** *noun.* ▪ **prudish** *adj.* ▪ **prudishness** *noun.* [18c: French, from *prude femme* respectable woman]

prudent *adj* **1** wise or careful in conduct. **2** shrewd or thrifty in planning ahead. **3** wary; discreet. ▪ **prudence** *noun.* [14c: from Latin *prudens*]

prudential *adj, old use* characterized by or exercising careful forethought. ▪ **prudentially** *adv.* [17c]

prune[1] *verb* **1** to cut off (branches, etc) from (a tree or shrub) in order to stimulate its growth, improve the production of fruit or flowers, etc. **2** to cut out (superfluous matter) from (a piece of writing, etc). **3** to cut back on (expenses, etc). ▸ *noun* an act of pruning. ▪ **pruner** *noun.* [15c: from French *proignier*]

prune[2] *noun* **1** a **plum** that has been preserved by drying, which gives it a black wrinkled appearance. **2** *informal* a silly foolish person. [14c: French]

prurient *adj* **1** unhealthily or excessively interested in sexual matters. **2** tending to arouse such unhealthy interest. ▪ **prurience** *noun.* ▪ **pruriently** *adv.* [18c: from Latin *pruriens* itching or lusting after]

Prussian *hist, adj* **1** belonging or relating to Prussia, a former N European state now part of Germany, or its inhabitants. **2** belonging or relating to this state's militaristic tradition. ▸ *noun* a citizen or inhabitant of, or person born in, Prussia. [16c]

pry[1] *verb* (***pries, pried***) *intr* **1** (*also* **pry into sth**) to investigate, esp the personal affairs of others; to nose or snoop. **2** to peer or peep inquisitively. [14c]

pry[2] *verb* (***pries, pried***) *N Am, esp US* to prise. [19c]

PS *abbrev* postscript.

psalm /sɑːm/ *noun* a sacred song, esp one from the Book of Psalms in the Old Testament. [10c: from Latin *psalmus*]

psalmist /ˈsɑːmɪst/ *noun* a composer of psalms.

psalmody /ˈsɑːmədɪ/ *noun* (**-*ies***) **1** the art of singing psalms. **2** a collected body of psalms. [14c: from Greek *psalmos* psalm + *oide* song]

psalter /ˈsɔːltə(r)/ *noun* **1** the Book of Psalms in the Old Testament. **2** a book containing the biblical psalms. [10c: from Latin *psalterium*, from Greek *psalterion* stringed instrument]

psaltery /ˈsɔːltərɪ/ *noun* (**-*ies***) *hist, music* a stringed instrument similar to a **zither**, played by plucking. [14c: see **psalter**]

psephology /sɪˈfɒlədʒɪ/ *noun* the statistical study of elections and voting patterns. ▪ **psephological** *adj.* ▪ **psephologist** *noun.* [20c: from Greek *psephos* a pebble or vote + *logos* word or reason]

pseud /sjuːd, suːd/ *Brit, informal, noun* a pretentious person; a bogus intellectual; a phoney. ▸ *adj* bogus, sham or phoney. [20c: from **pseudo-**]

pseudo *adj, informal* false; sham; phoney.

pseudo- /'sjuːdoʊ, 'suːdoʊ/ *or (before a vowel)* **pseud-** *combining form, forming nouns and adjs, denoting* **1** false; pretending to be something: *pseudo-intellectuals.* **2** deceptively resembling: *pseudo-scientific jargon.* [From Greek *pseudes* false]

pseudonym /'sjuːdənɪm/ *noun* a false or assumed name, esp one used by an author; a pen name or nom de plume. ▪ **pseudonymous** /-'dɒnɪməs/ *adj.* [19c: from **pseudo-** + Greek *onyma* name]

psi[1] /'psaɪ/ *noun* the twenty-third letter of the Greek alphabet.

psi[2] *abbrev* pounds per square inch, a unit of pressure measurement.

psittacosis /sɪtə'koʊsɪs/ *noun, pathol* a contagious disease of birds, esp parrots, that can be transmitted to human beings as pneumonia. [19c: Latin]

psoriasis /sə'raɪəsɪs/ *noun, pathol* a skin disease characterized by red patches covered with white scales. [17c: Latin]

psst *or* **pst** *exclam* used to draw someone's attention quietly or surreptitiously. [20c]

psych *or* **psyche** /saɪk/ *verb, informal* to psychoanalyse someone. [20c]
PHRASAL VERBS **psych sb out** to undermine the confidence of (an opponent, etc). **psych oneself** *or* **sb up** to prepare or steel oneself, or them, for a challenge, etc.

psych- see **psycho-**

psyche /'saɪkɪ/ *noun* the mind or spirit. [17c: Greek, meaning 'breath' or 'life']

psychedelia /saɪkɪ'diːlɪə/ *plural noun* psychedelic items such as posters, paintings, etc collectively or generally. [20c]

psychedelic /saɪkə'dɛlɪk/ *adj* **1 a** of a drug, esp LSD: inducing a state of altered consciousness characterized by an increase in perception, eg of colour, sound, etc, and hallucinations; **b** of an event or experience, etc: resembling such effects; bizarre: *had a psychedelic vision*; **c** belonging or relating to this kind of drug, experience, etc: *the psychedelic 60s.* **2** of perceived phenomena, eg colour, music, etc: startlingly clear and vivid, often with a complex dazzling pattern. ▪ **psychedelically** *adv.* [20c: from **psyche** + Greek *delos* clear]

psychiatry /saɪ'kaɪətrɪ/ *noun* the branch of medicine concerned with the study, diagnosis, treatment and prevention of mental and emotional disorders. ▪ **psychiatric** /saɪkɪ'atrɪk/ *adj.* ▪ **psychiatrist** *noun.* [19c: from **psyche** + Greek *iatros* doctor]

psychic /'saɪkɪk/ *adj* **1** (*also* **psychical**) relating to mental processes or experiences that are not scientifically explainable, eg telepathy. **2** of a person: sensitive to influences that produce such experiences; having mental powers that are not scientifically explainable. ▸ *noun* someone who possesses such powers. [19c: from Greek *psychikos* relating to the **psyche**]

psycho /'saɪkoʊ/ *informal, noun* a psychopath. ▸ *adj* psychopathic. [20c]

psycho- /'saɪkoʊ/ *or (before a vowel)* **psych-** /saɪk/ *combining form, denoting* the mind and its workings. [Greek: see **psyche**]

psychoactive *adj* of a drug: affecting the brain and influencing behaviour. Also called **psychotropic**. [20c]

psychoanalyse *or* (*US*) **psychoanalyze** *verb* to examine or treat someone by psychoanalysis. [20c]

psychoanalysis *noun, psychol* a theory and method of treatment for mental and emotional disorders, which explores the effects of unconscious motivation and conflict on a person's behaviour. ▪ **psychoanalyst** *noun.* ▪ **psychoanalytic** *or* **psychoanalytical** *adj.* [19c: from French *psychoanalyse*]

psychogenic *adj* of symptoms, etc: originating in the mind. [19c]

psychokinesis *noun* the apparent power to move objects, etc by non-physical means. [19c]

psychological *adj* **1** relating or referring to **psychology**. **2** relating or referring to the mind or mental processes. ▪ **psychologically** *adv.*

psychological warfare *noun* the use of propaganda and other methods in wartime to influence enemy opinion and sap enemy morale. [20c]

psychology *noun* (**-ies**) **1** the scientific study of the mind and behaviour of humans and animals. **2** the mental attitudes and associated behaviour characteristic of a certain individual or group. ▪ **psychologist** *noun.* [17c: see **psycho-**]

psychopath *noun* **1** *technical* someone with a personality disorder characterized by extreme callousness, who is liable to behave antisocially or violently in getting their own way, without any feelings of remorse. **2** *informal* someone who is dangerously unstable mentally or emotionally. ▪ **psychopathic** *adj.* ▪ **psychopathically** *adv.* [19c]

psychopathology *noun, med* **1** the scientific study of mental disorders. **2** the symptoms of a mental disorder.

psychosis /saɪ'koʊsɪs/ *noun* (**-ses** /-siːz/) *psychol* one of the two divisions of psychiatric disorders, characterized by a loss of contact with reality, in the form of delusions or hallucinations and belief that only one's own actions are rational. Compare **neurosis**. [19c: from Greek, meaning 'animation']

psychosomatic *adj, med* of physical symptoms or disorders: strongly associated with psychological factors, esp mental stress. [20c]

psychotherapy *noun* the treatment of mental disorders and emotional and behavioural problems by psychological means, rather than by drugs or surgery. ▪ **psychotherapist** *noun.* [19c]

psychotic *adj* relating to or involving a **psychosis**. ▸ *noun* someone suffering from a psychosis.

psychotropic *adj* **psychoactive**. [20c]

PT *abbrev* physical training.

Pt *symbol, chem* platinum.

pt *abbrev* **1** part. **2** pint. **3** point.

PTA *abbrev* Parent-Teacher Association.

ptarmigan /'tɑːmɪgən/ *noun* a mountain-dwelling game bird with white winter plumage. [16c: from Scottish Gaelic *tàrmachan*]

pterodactyl /tɛrə'daktɪl/ *noun* a former name for **pterosaur**. [19c: from Greek *pteron* wing + *daktylos* finger]

pterosaur /'tɛrəsɔː(r)/ *noun* an extinct flying reptile with narrow leathery wings, known from the late Triassic to the end of the Cretaceous period. Formerly called **pterodactyl**. [19c: from Greek *pteron* wing + *sauros* lizard]

PTO *or* **pto** *abbrev* please turn over.

ptomaine /'toʊmeɪn/ *noun, biochem* any of a group of nitrogenous organic compounds, some of which are poisonous, produced during the bacterial decomposition of dead animal and plant matter. [19c: from Italian *ptomaina*]

P2P *abbrev, comput* peer-to-peer.

Pu *symbol, chem* plutonium.

pub *informal, noun* a **public house.** [19c]

puberty *noun, biol* in humans and other primates: the onset of sexual maturity. [14c: from Latin *pubertas* the age of maturity]

pubes /'pjuːbiːz/ *noun* (*pl* ***pubes***) **1** *anatomy* the pubic region of the lower abdomen; the groin. **2** the hair that grows on this part from puberty onward. See also **pubis.** [16c: Latin]

pubescence *noun* **1** the onset of puberty. **2** *biol* a soft downy covering on plants and animals. ▪ **pubescent** *adj.* [17c: French]

pubic *adj* belonging or relating to the pubis or pubes.

pubis *noun* (***pubes*** /'pjuːbiːz/) *anatomy* in most vertebrates: one of the two bones forming the lower front part of each side of the pelvis. [16c: shortened from Latin *os pubis* bone of the pubes]

public *adj* **1** relating to or concerning all the people of a country or community: *public health* • *public opinion.* **2** relating to the organization and administration of a community. **3** provided for the use of the community: *public library* • *public toilet.* **4** well known through exposure in the media: *a famous public figure.* **5** made, done or held, etc openly, for all to see, hear or participate in: *a public inquiry.* **6** known to all: *public knowledge* • *make one's views public.* **7** open to view; not private or secluded: *It's too public here.* **8** provided by or run by central or local government: *under public ownership.* ▸ *singular or plural noun* **1** the people or community. **2** a particular class of people: *the concert-going public.* **3** an author's or performer's, etc audience or group of devotees: *mustn't disappoint my public.* [15c: from Latin *publicus*]

IDIOMS **go public 1** *business* to become a public company. **2** to make something previously private known to everyone. **in public** in the presence of other people. **in the public eye** of a person, etc: well known through media exposure.

---

public

You can use either a singular or plural verb with a collective noun such as **public**. Therefore, if you want to emphasize the public as a single unit, you can use a singular verb:

The public were embarrassed by the national team.

If you want to emphasize the public as a number of individuals, you can use a plural verb:

The public is not as gullible as politicians think.

---

publican *noun, Brit* the keeper of a **public house.** [18c: from Latin *publicanus*]

publication *noun* **1** the act of publishing a printed work; the process of publishing or of being published. **2** a book, magazine, newspaper or other printed and published work. **3** the act of making something known to the public.

public company *or* **public limited company** (abbrev **PLC** *or* **plc**) *noun, business* a company whose shares are available for purchase on the open market by the public. Compare **limited company.**

public convenience *noun* a public toilet.

public domain *noun* the status of a published work which is not, or is no longer, subject to copyright. ▸ *adj* (**public-domain**) of a published work, computer program, etc: not subject to copyright and available to the public free of charge.

public enemy *noun* someone whose behaviour threatens the community, esp a criminal.

public house *noun, Brit* an establishment licensed to sell alcoholic drinks for consumption on the premises. Often shortened to **pub.** [17c]

publicity *noun* **1** advertising or other activity designed to rouse public interest in something. **2** public interest attracted in this way. [18c]

publicize *or* **-ise** *verb* **1** to make something generally or widely known. **2** to advertise. [20c]

public limited company see **public company**

public relations (abbrev **PR**) *singular or plural noun* the process of creating a good relationship between an organization, etc and the public. ▸ *singular noun* the department within an organization that is responsible for this. *as adj*: *public relations officer.* [19c]

public school *noun* **1** in the UK: a secondary school, run independently of the state, financed by endowments and by pupils' fees. **2** in the US: a school run by a public authority. *Brit equivalent* **state school.**

public sector *noun* the part of a country's economy which consists of nationalized industries and of institutions and services run by the state or local authorities.

public servant *noun* an elected or appointed holder of public office; a government employee.

public-spirited *adj* acting from or showing concern for the general good of the whole community.

publish *verb, tr & intr* **1** to prepare, produce and distribute (printed material, computer software, etc) for sale to the public. **2** *tr & intr* of an author: to have (their work) published. **3** to publish the work of (an author). **4** to announce something publicly. ▪ **publishing** *noun.* [14c: from French *publier*]

publisher *noun* **1** a person or company engaged in the business of publishing books, newspapers, software, etc. **2** *N Am* a newspaper proprietor.

puce *noun* a colour between deep purplish-pink and purplish-brown. ▸ *adj* of this colour. [18c: from French *couleur de puce* flea colour]

puck[1] *noun* a goblin or mischievous sprite. ▪ **puckish** *adj.* [Anglo-Saxon *puca*]

puck[2] *noun, sport* a thick disc of hard rubber used in ice hockey instead of a ball. [19c]

pucker *verb, tr & intr* to gather into creases, folds or wrinkles. ▸ *noun* a wrinkle, fold or crease. [16c]

pud *noun, Brit informal* pudding. [18c]

pudding *noun* **1** *often in compounds* any of several sweet or savoury foods usu made with flour and eggs and cooked by steaming, boiling or baking: *rice pudding* • *steak and kidney pudding.* **2 a** any sweet food served as dessert; **b** the dessert course. **3** *in compounds* a type of sausage made with minced meat, spices, blood, etc: *black pudding.* [13c: as *poding* a kind of sausage]

puddle *noun* **1** a small pool, esp one of rainwater on the road. **2** (*also* **puddle clay**) a non-porous watertight material consisting of thoroughly mixed clay, sand and water. ▸ *verb* **1** to make something watertight by means of puddle clay. **2** to knead (clay, sand

and water) to make puddle clay. **3** *metallurgy* to produce (wrought iron) from molten pig by stirring to remove carbon. [14c: prob from Anglo-Saxon *pudd* ditch]

pudenda *plural noun* (*rare singular* ***pudendum***) the external sexual organs, esp those of a woman. [17c: Latin, literally 'things to be ashamed of']

pudgy see **podgy**

puerile /'pjʊəraɪl/ *adj* childish; silly; immature. ▪ **puerility** *noun*. [17c: from Latin *puerilis*, from *puer* boy]

puerperal /pjʊ'ɜːpərəl/ *adj* **1** referring or relating to childbirth. **2** referring or relating to a woman who has just given birth. [18c: from Latin *puerperium* childbirth]

puff *noun* **1 a** a small rush, gust or blast of air or wind, etc; **b** the sound made by it. **2** a small cloud of smoke, dust or steam emitted from something. **3** *informal* breath: *quite out of puff*. **4** an act of inhaling and exhaling smoke from a pipe or cigarette; a drag or draw. **5** *in compounds* a light pastry, often containing a sweet or savoury filling: *jam puffs*. **6** a powder puff. ▸ *verb* **1** *tr & intr* to blow or breathe in small blasts. **2** *intr* of smoke or steam, etc: to emerge in small gusts or blasts. **3** *tr & intr* to inhale and exhale smoke from, or draw at (a cigarette, etc). **4** *intr* of a train or boat, etc: to go along emitting puffs of steam. **5** *intr* to pant, or go along panting: *puffing up the hill*. **6** (*often* **puff sb out**) *informal* to leave them breathless after exertion. **7** *tr & intr* (*also* **puff out** *or* **up**) to swell or cause something to swell. ▪ **puffy** *adj* (***-ier, -iest***). [Anglo-Saxon *pyffan*]

puffin /'pʌfɪn/ *noun* a short stout black-and-white seabird which has a large brightly-coloured parrot-like bill. [14c in the form *poffin*]

puff pastry *noun, cookery* light flaky pastry made with a high proportion of fat.

pug *noun* a small breed of dog with a flattened face with a wrinkled snout and a short curled tail. [18c]

pugilism /'pjuːdʒɪlɪzəm/ *noun, old use or facetious* the art or practice of boxing or prizefighting. ▪ **pugilist** *noun*. [18c: from Latin *pugil* boxer]

pugnacious *adj* given to fighting; quarrelsome, belligerent or combative. ▪ **pugnacity** *noun*. [17c: from Latin *pugnax*]

pug nose *noun* a short upturned nose. ▪ **pug-nosed** *adj*. [18c: from **pug**]

puissance /'pwiːsɑːns/ *noun, showjumping* a competition that tests the horse's ability to jump high fences. [20c]

puissant /'pwiːsɒnt; *US* 'pjuːɪsənt/ *adj, old use, poetic* strong, mighty or powerful. [15c: French]

puke *informal, verb, tr & intr* to vomit. ▸ *noun* **1** vomit. **2** an act of vomiting. **3** *chiefly US* a horrible person. [16c: possibly imitating the sound]

pukka *adj, informal* **1** superior; high-quality. **2** upper-class; well-bred. **3** genuine. [17c: from Hindi *pakka* cooked, firm or ripe]

pulchritude *noun, literary or formal* beauty of face and form. [15c: from Latin *pulchritudo*, beauty]

pull *verb* **1** *tr & intr* to grip something or someone strongly and draw or force it or them towards oneself; to tug or drag. **2** (*also* **pull sth out** *or* **up**) to remove or extract (a cork, tooth, weeds, etc) with this action. **3** to operate (a trigger, lever or switch) with this action. **4** to draw (a trailer, etc). **5** to open or close (curtains or a blind). **6** (*often* **pull sth on sb**) to produce (a weapon) as a threat to them. **7 a** *tr & intr* to row; **b** *intr* (*often* **pull away, off**, *etc*) of a boat: to be rowed or made to move in a particular direction. **8** to draw (beer, etc) from a cask by operating a lever. **9** *intr* **a** of a driver or vehicle: to steer or move (in a specified direction): *pulled right*; **b** of a vehicle or its steering: to go or direct (towards a specified direction), usu because of some defect. **10** *sport* in golf, cricket, snooker, etc: to hit (a ball) so that it veers off its intended course. **11** *intr* of an engine or vehicle: to produce the required propelling power. **12** (*usu* **pull at** *or* **on sth**) to inhale and exhale smoke from (a cigarette, etc); to draw or suck at it. **13** to attract (a crowd, votes, etc). **14** to strain (a muscle or tendon). **15** *printing* to print (a proof). ▸ *noun* **1** an act of pulling. **2** attraction; attracting force. **3** useful influence: *has some pull with the education department*. **4** a drag at a pipe; a swallow of liquor, etc. **5** a tab, etc for pulling. **6** a stroke made with an oar. **7** *printing* a proof. [Anglo-Saxon *pullian* to pluck, draw or pull]

IDIOMS **pull a fast one** to trick or cheat someone. **pull sth apart** *or* **to pieces 1** to rip or tear it; to reduce it to pieces. **2** to criticize it severely. **pull one's punches** to be deliberately less hard-hitting than one might be. **pull the other one** a dismissive expression used by the speaker to indicate that they are not being fooled by what has just been said. **pull sb up short 1** to check someone, often oneself. **2** to take them aback.

PHRASAL VERBS **pull sth back** to withdraw it or make it withdraw or retreat. **pull in 1** of a train: to arrive and halt at a station. **2** of a driver or vehicle: to move to the side of the road. **pull sth off** *informal* to arrange or accomplish it successfully: *pull off a deal*. **pull over** of a driver or vehicle: to move to the side of or off the road and stop. **pull round** *or* **through** to recover from an illness. **pull together** to work together towards a common aim; to co-operate. **pull up** of a driver, vehicle or horse: to stop. **pull sb up** to criticize them or tell them off. **pull sth up** to make (a vehicle or horse) stop.

pull-down menu *noun, comput* a menu on a computer screen viewed by clicking on a button on the toolbar and keeping the mouse pressed down. Compare **drop-down menu**.

pullet *noun* a young female hen in its first laying year. [14c: from French *poulet* chicken]

pulley *noun* a simple mechanism for lifting and lowering weights, consisting of a wheel with a grooved rim over which a rope or belt runs. [14c: from French *polie*]

Pullman *noun* (***Pullmans***) a type of luxurious railway carriage. [19c: after its American originator George M Pullman]

pull-out *noun* **1** a self-contained detachable section of a magazine designed to be kept for reference. **2** a withdrawal from combat or competition, etc.

pullover *noun* a knitted garment pulled on over the head.

pulmonary *adj* **1** belonging or relating to, or affecting, the lungs. **2** having the function of a lung. [18c: from Latin *pulmo* lung]

pulp *noun* **1** the flesh of a fruit or vegetable. **2** a soft wet mass of mashed food or other material. **3** *derog* worthless literature, novels, magazines, etc printed on poor paper. *as adj*: *pulp fiction*. **4** *anatomy* the tissue in the cavity of a tooth, containing nerves. ▸ *verb* **1** *tr & intr* to reduce or be reduced to a pulp. **2** to remove the pulp from (fruit, etc). ▪ **pulpy** *adj* (**-ier, -iest**). [16c: from Latin *pulpa* flesh or fruit pulp]

pulpit *noun* **1** a small enclosed platform in a church, from which the preacher delivers the sermon. **2** (*usu* **the pulpit**) the clergy in general. [14c: from Latin *pulpitum* a stage]

pulsar *noun, astron* in space: a source of electromagnetic radiation emitted in brief regular pulses, mainly at radio frequency, believed to be a rapidly revolving **neutron star**. [20c: from *puls*ating st*ar*]

pulsate *verb, intr* **1** to beat or throb. **2** to contract and expand rhythmically. **3** to vibrate. ▪ **pulsation** *noun*. [18c: from Latin *pulsare* to beat]

pulse¹ *noun* **1** *physiol* the rhythmic beat that can be detected in an artery, as the heart pumps blood around the body. **2** *med, etc* the rate of this beat, often measured as an indicator of a person's state of health. **3** a regular throbbing beat in music. **4** *physics* a signal, eg one of light or electric current, of very short duration. **5** the hum or bustle of a busy place. **6** a thrill of excitement, etc. **7** the attitude or feelings of a group or community at any one time. ▸ *verb* **1** *intr* to throb or pulsate. **2** to drive something by pulses. [14c: from French *pous*]

pulse² *noun* **1** the edible dried seed of a plant belonging to the pea family, eg pea, bean, lentil, etc. **2** any plant that bears this seed. [13c: from French *pols*]

pulverize *or* **-ise** *verb* **1** *tr & intr* to crush or crumble to dust or powder. **2** *informal* to defeat utterly; to annihilate. ▪ **pulverization** *noun*. [16c: from Latin *pulverizare*]

puma *noun* one of the large cats of America, with short brown or reddish fur, found in mountain regions, forests, plains and deserts. Also called **cougar, mountain lion, panther**. [18c: Spanish]

pumice /ˈpʌmɪs/ *noun* (*also* **pumice stone**) *geol* a very light porous white or grey form of solidified lava, used as an abrasive and polishing agent. ▸ *verb* to polish or rub something with pumice. [15c: from French *pomis*]

pummel *verb* (***pummelled, pummelling***) to beat something repeatedly with the fists. [16c: a variant of **pommel**]

pump¹ *noun* a piston-operated or other device for forcing or driving liquids or gases into or out of something, etc. ▸ *verb* **1** *tr & intr* to raise, force or drive (a liquid or gas) out of or into something with a pump. **2** (*usu* **pump sth up**) to inflate (a tyre, etc) with a pump. **3** to force something in large gushes or flowing amounts. **4** to pour (money or other resources) into a project, etc. **5** to force out the contents of (someone's stomach) to rid it of a poison, etc. **6** to try to extract information from someone by persistent questioning. **7** to work something vigorously up and down, as though operating a pump handle. **8** to fire (bullets, etc), often into someone or something: *pumped bullets into her*. [15c: from Dutch *pumpe* pipe]

IDIOMS **pump iron** *informal* to exercise with weights; to go in for weight-training.

pump² *noun* **1** a light dancing shoe. **2** a plain, low-cut flat shoe for women. **3** a **plimsoll**. [16c]

pumpernickel *noun* a dark heavy coarse rye bread. [18c: from German, meaning 'lout']

pumpkin *noun* **1** a trailing or climbing plant which produces yellow flowers and large round fruits at ground level. **2** the fruit of this plant, which contains pulpy flesh and many seeds, enclosed by a hard leathery orange rind. [17c: from French *pompon*]

pun *noun* a form of joke consisting of the use of a word or phrase that can be understood in two different ways, esp one where an association is created between words of similar sound but different meaning. Also called **play on words**. ▸ *verb* (***punned, punning***) *intr* to make a pun. [17c]

punch¹ *verb* **1** *tr & intr* to hit someone or something with the fist. **2** *esp US & Aust* to poke or prod with a stick; to drive (cattle, etc). **3** to prod, poke or strike smartly, esp with a blunt object, the foot, etc. ▸ *noun* **1** a blow with the fist. **2** vigour and effectiveness in speech or writing. [14c: a variant of **pounce**]

punch² *noun* **1** a tool for cutting or piercing holes or notches, or stamping designs, in leather, paper, metal, etc. **2** a tool for driving nail-heads well down into a surface. ▸ *verb* **1** to pierce, notch or stamp something with a punch. **2** *comput, old use* to use a key punch to record (data) on (a card or tape). [15c: shortened from *puncheon* a piercing tool]

punch³ *noun* a drink, usu an alcoholic one, made up of a mixture of other drinks, which can be served either hot or cold. [17c]

punchbag *noun* **1** a heavy stuffed leather bag hanging from the ceiling on a rope, used for boxing practice. **2** someone who is used and abused, either physically or emotionally.

punchball *noun* **1** a leather ball mounted on a flexible stand, used for boxing practice. **2** *US* a ball game similar to baseball. [20c]

punch-drunk *adj* **1** of a boxer: disorientated from repeated blows to the head, with resultant unsteadiness and confusion. **2** dazed from over-intensive work or some other shattering experience. [20c]

punchline *noun* the words that conclude a joke or funny story and contain its point, eg 'We're having another floor built on to our house – but that's another storey'. [20c]

punch-up *noun, informal* a fight. [20c]

punchy *adj* (**-ier, -iest**) of speech or writing: vigorous and effective; forcefully expressed. ▪ **punchily** *adv*. ▪ **punchiness** *noun*.

punctilious *adj* carefully attentive to details of correct, polite or considerate behaviour; making a point of observing a rule or custom. ▪ **punctiliously** *adv*. [17c: from Italian *puntiglio*]

punctual *adj* **1** arriving or happening at the arranged time; not late. **2** of a person: making a habit of arriving on time. ▪ **punctuality** *noun*. ▪ **punctually** *adv*. [17c: from Latin *punctus* point]

punctuate *verb* **1** *tr & intr* to put punctuation marks into (a piece of writing). **2** to interrupt something repeatedly: *Bursts of applause punctuated his speech*. [19c: from Latin *punctuare* to prick or point]

punctuation *noun* **1** a system of conventional marks used in a text to clarify its meaning for the reader, indicating pauses, missing letters, etc. **2 a** the use of such marks; **b** the process of inserting them.

punctuation mark *noun* any of the set of marks such as the **full stop, comma, colon**, etc that in written text conventionally indicate the pauses and intonations that would be used in speech.

puncture *noun* **1** a small hole pierced in something with a sharp point. **2 a** a perforation in an inflated object, esp one in a pneumatic tyre; **b** the resulting flat tyre. ▸ *verb* **1** *tr & intr* to make a puncture in something, or to be punctured. **2** to deflate (someone's pride, self-importance, etc). [14c: from Latin *punctura*]

pundit *noun* **1** an authority or supposed authority on a particular subject, esp one who is regularly consulted. **2** (*also* **pandit**) a Hindu learned in Hindu culture, philosophy and law. [17c: from Hindi *pandit*]

pungent *adj* **1** of a taste or smell: sharp and strong. **2** of remarks or wit, etc: cleverly caustic or biting. **3** of grief or pain: keen or sharp. ▪ **pungency** *noun*. ▪ **pungently** *adv*. [16c: from Latin *pungens* pricking]

punish *verb* **1** to cause (an offender) to suffer for an offence. **2** to impose a penalty for (an offence). **3** *informal* to treat something or someone roughly. **4** to beat or defeat (an opponent, etc) soundly. **5** *informal* to consume large quantities of (eg drink). ▪ **punishable** *adj*. ▪ **punishing** *adj* harsh; severe. [14c: from French *punir*]

punishment *noun* **1** the act of punishing or process of being punished. **2** a method of punishing; a type of penalty. See also **capital punishment**, **corporal punishment**. **3** *informal* rough treatment; suffering or hardship.

punitive /'pjuːnɪtɪv/ *adj* **1** relating to, inflicting or intended to inflict punishment. **2** severe; inflicting hardship. ▪ **punitively** *adv*. [17c]

Punjabi *or* **Panjabi** *adj* belonging or relating to the Punjab, now divided as a state in NW India and a province in E Pakistan, their inhabitants or their language. ▸ *noun* **1** a citizen or inhabitant of, or person born in, Punjab. **2** the language of Punjab, also spoken in parts of India and Pakistan. [19c: Hindi *Panjabi*, from Persian *panj* five + *ab* water, referring to the five rivers which cross the region]

punk *noun* **1** a youth-orientated, anti-establishment movement, at its height in the mid- to late-1970s, which was characterized by aggressive music and dress style, vividly coloured hair and the wearing of cheap utility articles (eg safety pins) as ornament. **2** a follower of punk styles or punk rock. **3** (*in full* **punk rock**) a type of loud aggressive rock music, popular in the mid- to late-1970s. **4** *N Am* a worthless or stupid person. ▸ *adj* **1** relating to or characteristic of punk as a movement. **2** *N Am* worthless; inferior.

punka *or* **punkah** *noun* **1** a fan made from leaf-palm. **2** a large mechanical fan for cooling a room. [17c: from Hindi *pankha* fan]

punnet *noun* a small container for soft fruit. [19c]

punster *noun* someone who makes **puns**, esp habitually.

punt¹ *noun* a long, flat-bottomed open boat with square ends, propelled by a pole pushed against the bed of the river, etc. ▸ *verb* **1** *intr* to travel by or operate a punt. **2** to propel (a punt, etc) with a pole. [Anglo-Saxon]

punt² *noun, rugby* a kick given with the toe of the boot to a ball dropped directly from the hands. ▸ *verb, tr & intr* to kick in this way. [19c]

punt³ *verb, intr* **1** *informal* to bet on horses. **2** *cards* to bet against the bank. ▸ *noun* a gamble or bet. [18c: from French *ponter* to bet]

punter *noun, informal* **1** someone who bets on horses; a gambler. **2** the average consumer, customer or member of the public.

puny *adj* (**-ier, -iest**) **1** small, weak or undersized. **2** feeble or ineffective. [16c: from French *puisné* younger]

pup *noun* **1** a young dog. **2** the young of other animals, eg the seal, wolf and rat. Compare **cub**. ▸ *verb* (***pupped, pupping***) *intr* to give birth to pups. [18c: from **puppy**]

pupa /'pjuːpə/ *noun* (***pupae*** /'pjuːpiː/ *or* ***pupas***) *zool* in the life cycle of certain insects, eg butterflies and moths: the inactive stage during which a larva is transformed into a sexually mature adult while enclosed in a protective case. ▪ **pupal** *adj*. [18c: Latin, meaning 'doll']

pupil¹ *noun* **1** someone who is being taught; a schoolchild or student. **2** someone studying under a particular expert, etc. **3** *Scots law* a girl under the age of 12 or boy under the age of 14, who is in the care of a guardian. [14c: from Latin *pupillus* little boy and *pupilla* little girl]

pupil² *noun, anatomy* in the eye of vertebrates: the dark circular opening in the centre of the **iris** (sense 2), which varies in size, allowing more or less light to pass to the retina. [16c: from Latin *pupilla*]

puppet *noun* **1** a type of doll that can be moved in a number of ways, eg one operated by strings or sticks attached to its limbs, or one designed to fit over the hand and operated by the fingers and thumb. **2** a person, company, country, etc, who is being controlled or manipulated by someone or something else. ▪ **puppeteer** *noun*. [16c: ultimately from Latin *pupa* doll]

puppy *noun* (**-ies**) a young dog. [15c: related to French *poupée* doll]

puppy fat *noun* a temporary plumpness in children that disappears with maturity.

puppy love *noun* romantic love between adolescents, or of an adolescent for an older person. Also called **calf love**.

purblind *adj* **1** nearly blind; dim-sighted. **2** dull-witted; obtuse. [16c]

purchase *verb* **1** to obtain something in return for payment; to buy. **2** to get or achieve something through labour, effort, sacrifice or risk. ▸ *noun* **1** something that has been bought. **2** the act of buying. **3** firmness in holding or gripping; a sure grasp or foothold. **4** *mech* the advantage given by a device such as a pulley or lever. ▪ **purchaser** *noun*. [14c: from French *pourchacier* to seek to obtain]

purdah *noun* in some Muslim and Hindu societies: **1** the seclusion or veiling of women from public view. **2** a curtain or screen used to seclude women. [19c: from Hindi and Urdu *pardah* curtain]

pure *adj* **1** consisting of itself only; unmixed with anything else. **2** unpolluted; uncontaminated; wholesome. **3** virtuous; chaste; free from sin or guilt. **4** utter; sheer: *pure lunacy*. **5** of mathematics or science: dealing with theory and abstractions rather than practical applications. Compare **applied**. **6** of unmixed blood or descent: *pure Manx stock*. **7** of sound, eg a sung note: clear, unwavering and exactly in tune. **8** absolutely true to type or style. ▪ **pureness** *noun*. See also **purity**. [13c: from French *pur*]

pure-bred *adj* of an animal or plant: that is the offspring of parents of the same breed or variety.

purée /ˈpjʊəreɪ/ *cookery, noun* a quantity of fruit, vegetables, meat, fish, game, etc reduced to a smooth pulp by liquidizing or rubbing through a sieve. ▸ *verb* (***puréed, puréeing***) to reduce something to a purée. [18c: from French *purer* to strain]

purely *adv* **1** in a pure way. **2** wholly; entirely. **3** merely.

purgative *noun* **1** a medicine that causes the bowels to empty. **2** something that cleanses or purifies. ▸ *adj* **1** of a medicine, etc: having this effect. Also called **laxative**. **2** of an action, etc: having a purifying, cleansing or cathartic effect. [15c: from Latin *purgare* to clean out]

purgatory *noun* (***-ies***) **1** (**Purgatory**) *chiefly RC Church* a place or state into which the soul passes after death, where it is cleansed of pardonable sins before going to heaven. **2** *humorous, informal* any state of discomfort or suffering. ▪ **purgatorial** *adj*. [13c: from Latin *purgatorium*]

purge *verb* **1 a** to rid (the soul or body) of unwholesome thoughts or substances; **b** to rid (anything) of impurities. **2** to rid (a political party, community, etc) of (undesirable members). **3** *old use* **a** to empty (the bowels), esp by taking a laxative; **b** to make someone empty their bowels, esp by giving them a laxative. **4** *law, relig, etc* to rid (oneself) of guilt by atoning for an offence. **5** *law* to clear (oneself or someone else) of an accusation. ▸ *noun* **1** an act of purging. **2** the process of purging a party or community of undesirable members. **3** *old use* the process of purging the bowels. **4** *old use* a **laxative**. [14c: from Latin *purgare* to cleanse]

purify *verb* (***-ies, -ied***) **1** *tr & intr* to make or become pure. **2** to cleanse something of contaminating or harmful substances. **3** to rid something of intrusive elements. **4** *relig* to free someone from sin or guilt. ▪ **purification** *noun*. ▪ **purifier** *noun*. [14c: from Latin *purificare*]

Purim /ˈpʊərɪm, -ˈriːm/ *noun* the Jewish Feast of Lots, commemorating the rescue of the Jews from a plot to have them massacred. [14c: Hebrew, meaning 'lots']

purism *noun* insistence on the traditional elements of the content and style of a particular subject, esp of language. ▪ **purist** *noun*. [19c]

puritan *noun* **1** (**Puritan**) *hist* in the 16c and 17c: a supporter of the Protestant movement in England and America that sought to rid church worship of ritual. **2** someone of strict, esp over-strict, moral principles. ▸ *adj* **1** (**Puritan**) belonging or relating to the Puritans. **2** characteristic of a puritan. ▪ **puritanical** *adj*. ▪ **puritanism** *noun*. [16c: from Latin *puritas* purity]

purity *noun* **1** the state of being pure or unmixed. **2** freedom from contamination, pollution or unwholesome or intrusive elements. **3** chasteness or innocence. [13c: from Latin *puritas*]

purl[1] *noun* **1** *knitting* a reverse **plain** (*noun* sense 2) stitch. **2** cord made from gold or silver wire. **3** (*also* **pearl**) a decorative looped edging on lace or braid, etc. ▸ *verb* to knit in purl. [16c: from obsolete *pirl* to twist]

purl[2] *verb, intr* **1** to flow with a murmuring sound. **2** to eddy or swirl. [16c]

purlieu /ˈpɜːljuː/ *noun* **1** (*usu* **purlieus**) the surroundings or immediate neighbourhood of a place. **2** (*usu* **purlieus**) someone's usual haunts. **3** *Eng hist* an area of land on the edge of a forest. [15c]

purlin *or* **purline** *noun, building* a roof timber stretching across the principal rafters or between the tops of walls. [15c]

purloin *verb* to steal, filch or pilfer. [16c: from French *purloigner* to remove to a distance]

purple *noun* **1** a colour that is a mixture of blue and red. **2** *hist* a crimson dye obtained from various shellfish. **3** crimson cloth, or a robe made from it, worn eg by emperors and cardinals, symbolic of their authority. **4** (**the purple**) high rank; power. ▸ *adj* **1** purple-coloured. **2** of writing: especially fine in style; over-elaborate; flowery. ▪ **purplish** *and* **purply** *adj*. [Anglo-Saxon: related to Greek *porphyra* a dye-yielding shellfish]

purple patch *noun* **1** a passage in a piece of writing which is over-elaborate and ornate. **2** any period of time characterized by good luck.

purport *verb* /pɜːˈpɔːt/ **1** of a picture, piece of writing, document, etc: to profess by its appearance, etc (to be something): *a manuscript that purports to be written by Camus*. **2** of a piece of writing, or a speech, etc: to convey; to imply (that). ▸ *noun* /ˈpɜːpɔːt/ meaning, significance, point or gist. [15c: from French *purporter* to convey]

purpose *noun* **1** the object or aim in doing something. **2** the function for which something is intended. **3** the intentions, aspirations, aim or goal: *no purpose in life*. **4** determination; resolve: *a woman of purpose*. ▸ *verb* to intend (to do something). ▪ **purposeless** *adj* without purpose; aimless. ▪ **purposely** *adv* intentionally. [13c: from French *pourpos*]
IDIOMS **on purpose** intentionally; deliberately.

purpose-built *adj* designed or made to meet specific requirements.

purposeful *adj* determined; intent; resolute; showing a sense of purpose. ▪ **purposefully** *adv*.

---

purposefully, purposely
Be careful not to use the word **purposefully** when you mean **purposely**.
Purposefully means 'with purpose', and refers to a person's manner or determination:
He stood up and began to pace purposefully round the room.
Purposely means 'on purpose', and refers to a person's intention:
Their estimates had been purposely conservative.

---

purposive *adj* **1** having a clear purpose. **2** purposeful.

purr *verb* **1** *intr* of a cat: to make a soft low vibrating sound associated with contentment. **2** *intr* of a vehicle or machine: to make a sound similar to this, suggestive of good running order. **3** *tr & intr* to express pleasure, or say something, in a tone vibrating with satisfaction. ▸ *noun* a purring sound. [17c: imitating the sound]

purse *noun* **1** a small container carried in the pocket or handbag, for keeping cash, etc in. **2** *N Am* a woman's handbag. **3** funds available for spending; resources. **4** a sum of money offered as a present or prize. ▸ *verb* to draw (the lips) together in disapproval or deep thought. [Anglo-Saxon *purs*]

purser *noun* the ship's officer responsible for keeping the accounts and, on a passenger ship, seeing to the welfare of passengers. [15c]

purse strings *plural noun*

IDIOMS **hold** *or* **control the purse strings** to be in charge of the financial side of things, eg in a family. [15c]

pursuance *noun* the process of pursuing: *in pursuance of his duties.*

pursue *verb* **1** *tr & intr* to follow someone or something in order to overtake, capture or attack them or it, etc; to chase. **2** to proceed along (a course or route). **3** to put effort into achieving (a goal, aim, etc). **4** to occupy oneself with (one's career, etc). **5** to continue with or follow up (investigations or enquiries, etc). ▪ **pursuer** *noun.* [13c: from French *pursuer*]

pursuit *noun* **1** the act of pursuing or chasing. **2** an occupation or hobby. [15c: from French *purseute*]

purulent /ˈpjʊərʊlənt/ *med, etc adj* belonging or relating to, or full of, pus. ▪ **purulence** *noun.* [16c: from Latin *purulentus*]

purvey *verb, tr & intr* to supply (food or provisions, etc) as a business. ▪ **purveyor** *noun.* [13c: from French *purveier*]

purview *noun, formal or technical* **1** scope of responsibility or concern, eg of a court of law. **2** the range of someone's knowledge, experience or activities. [15c: from French *purveu* provided]

pus *noun* the thick, usu yellowish liquid that forms in abscesses or infected wounds. [16c: Latin]

push *verb* **1** (*often* **push against, at** *or* **on sth**) to exert pressure to force it away from one; to press, thrust or shove it. **2** (**push sb** *or* **sth over**) to knock them or it down. **3** to hold (eg a wheelchair, trolley, pram, etc) and move it forward in front of one. **4** *tr & intr* (*often* **push through, in** *or* **past,** *etc*) to force one's way, thrusting aside people or obstacles. **5** *intr* to progress, esp laboriously. **6** to force in a specified direction: *push up prices.* **7** (*often* **push sb into sth**) to coax, urge, persuade or goad them to do it: *pushed me into agreeing.* **8** to pressurize someone (or oneself) into working harder, achieving more, etc. **9** (*usu* **push for sth**) to recommend it strongly; to campaign or press for it. **10** to promote (products) or urge (acceptance of ideas). **11** to sell (drugs) illegally. ▸ *noun* **1** an act of pushing; a thrust or shove. **2** a burst of effort towards achieving something. **3** determination, aggression or drive. [13c: from French *pousser*]

IDIOMS **at a push** *informal* if forced; at a pinch. **be pushed for sth** *informal* to be short of (eg time or money). **be pushing** *informal* to be nearly (a specified age): *She is pushing 30.* **get the push** *informal* to be dismissed from a job, etc; to be rejected by someone. **give sb the push** to dismiss or reject them.

PHRASAL VERBS **push sb around** *or* **about** *informal* **1** to bully them; to treat them roughly. **2** to dictate to them; to order them about. **push off** *or* **along** *informal* to go away. **push on** to continue on one's way or with a task, etc. **push sth through** to force acceptance of (a proposal or bill, etc) by a legislative body, etc.

pushbike *noun, informal* a bicycle propelled by pedals alone.

pushchair *noun* a small folding wheeled chair for a toddler. *N Am equivalent* **stroller**.

pusher *noun, informal* someone who sells illegal drugs.

pushover *noun, informal* **1** someone who is easily defeated or outwitted. **2** a task that is easily accomplished. [20c: US slang]

push-start *verb* to roll (a vehicle) with its handbrake off and gear engaged until the engine begins to turn. ▸ *noun* an instance of doing this. [20c]

pushy *adj* (**-ier, -iest**) *informal* aggressively self-assertive or ambitious. [20c]

pusillanimous /pjuːsɪˈlanɪməs/ *adj* timid, cowardly, weak-spirited or faint-hearted. ▪ **pusillanimity** /-ləˈnɪmətɪ/ *noun.* ▪ **pusillanimously** *adv.* [16c: from Latin *pusillus* very small + *animus* spirit]

puss *noun, informal* a cat. [16c]

pussy *noun* (**-ies**) **1** (*also* **pussycat**) *informal* a cat.

pussyfoot *verb, intr* **1** to behave indecisively. **2** to pad about stealthily. [20c]

pustule *noun* a small inflammation on the skin, containing pus; a pimple. ▪ **pustular** *adj.* [14c: from Latin *pustula*]

put *verb* (*past tense & past participle* **put,** *present participle* **putting**) **1** to place something or someone in or convey them or it to a specified position or situation. **2** to fit: *Put a new lock on the door.* **3** to cause someone or something to be in a specified state: *put him at ease.* **4** to apply. **5** to set or impose: *put a tax on luxuries • put an end to free lunches.* **6** to lay (blame, reliance, emphasis, etc) on something. **7** to set someone to work, etc or apply something to a good purpose, etc. **8** to translate: *Put this into French.* **9** to invest or pour (energy, money or other resources) into something. **10** to classify or categorize something or put it in order: *I put accuracy before speed.* **11** to submit (questions for answering or ideas for considering) to someone; to suggest: *I put it to her that she was lying.* **12** to express something. **13** *informal* to write or say: *don't know what to put.* **14** *athletics* to throw (the shot).

IDIOMS **put it across sb** *or* **put one over on sb** *informal* to trick, deceive or fool them. **put it on** to feign or exaggerate: *said she'd been ill but she was putting it on.* **put sth right** to mend it or make it better.

PHRASAL VERBS **put about** *naut* to turn round; to change course. **put sth about** to spread (a report or rumour). **put sth across** to communicate (ideas, etc) to other people. **put sb away** *informal* **1** to imprison them. **2** to confine them in a mental institution. **put sth away 1** to replace it tidily where it belongs. **2** to save it for future use. **3** *informal* to consume (food or drink), esp in large amounts. **4** *old use* to reject, discard or renounce it. **put sth back 1** to replace it. **2** to postpone (a match or meeting, etc). **3** to adjust (a clock, etc) to an earlier time. **put sb down** to humiliate or snub them. See also **put-down**. **put sth down 1** to lay it on a surface after holding it, etc. **2** to crush (a revolt, etc). **3** to kill (an animal) painlessly, esp when it is suffering. **4** to write it down. **put sth in 1** to fit or install it. **2** to spend (time) working at something: *puts in four hours' violin practice daily.* **3** to submit (a claim, etc). **put in for sth** to apply for it. **put sb off 1** to cancel or postpone an engagement with them. **2** to make them lose concentration; to distract them. **3** to cause them to lose enthusiasm or to feel disgust for something: *was put* *off by its smell.* **put sth off** to postpone (an event or arrangement). **put sb out 1** to inconvenience them. **2** to offend or annoy them. **put sth out 1** to extinguish (a light or fire). **2** to publish (a leaflet, etc). **3** to strain or dislocate (a part of the body). **put sth over** to communicate (an idea, etc) to someone else. **put sb through** to connect them by telephone. **put up** to stay for the night. **put sb up** to give them a bed for the night. **put sth up 1** to build it; to erect it. **2** to raise (prices). **3** to present (a plan, etc). **4** to offer (a house, etc) for sale. **5** to provide (funds) for a project, etc. **6** to show (resistance); to offer (a fight). **put sb** *or* **oneself up for sth** to offer or nominate them, or oneself, as a candidate. **put upon sb** to presume on their good will; to take unfair advantage of them. **put sb up to sth** to urge them to do something they ought not to do. **put up with sb** *or* **sth** to tolerate them or it, esp reluctantly.

putative *adj* supposed; assumed. [15c: from Latin *putativus*, from *putare, putatum* to think]

put-down *noun, informal* a snub or humiliation. See also **put sb down** at **put**.

put-on *adj* of an accent or manner, etc: assumed; pretended.

putrefy *verb* (**-ies, -ied**) *intr* of flesh or other organic matter: to go bad, rot or decay, esp with a foul smell. ▪ **putrefaction** *noun.* [15c: from Latin *putrefacere*]

putrescent *adj* decaying; rotting; putrefying. [18c: from Latin *putrescere* to become rotten]

putrid *adj* **1** of organic matter: decayed; rotten. **2** stinking; foul; disgusting. **3** *informal* repellent; worthless. [16c: from Latin *putridus*]

putsch /pʊtʃ/ *noun* a secretly planned sudden attempt to remove a government from power. [20c: Swiss German, meaning 'knock' or 'thrust']

putt *golf, putting, verb, tr & intr* to send (the ball) gently forward on the green and into or nearer the hole. ▸ *noun* a putting stroke. [17c: orig a form of **put**]

puttee *noun* a long strip of cloth worn by wrapping it around the leg from the ankle to the knee and used as protection or support. [19c: from Hindi *patti* a band]

putter *noun, golf* **1** a club used for putting. **2** someone who putts.

putting *noun* **1** the act of putting a ball towards a hole. **2** a game played on a **putting green** using only putting strokes.

putting green *noun* **1** on a golf course: a smoothly mown patch of grass surrounding a hole. **2** an area of mown turf where **putting** is played.

putty *noun* (**-ies**) a paste of ground chalk and linseed oil, used for fixing glass in window frames, filling holes in wood, etc. Also called **glaziers' putty**. ▸ *verb* (**-ies, -ied**) to fix, coat or fill something with putty. [17c: from French *potée* potful]

put-up job *noun* something dishonestly prearranged to give a false impression.

puzzle *verb* **1** to perplex, mystify, bewilder or baffle. **2** *intr* (*usu* **puzzle about** *or* **over sth**) to brood, ponder, wonder or worry about it. **3** (**puzzle sth out**) to solve it after prolonged thought. ▸ *noun* **1** a baffling problem. **2** a game or toy that takes the form of something for solving. ▪ **puzzlement** *noun.* ▪ **puzzling** *adj.* [16c]

PVC *abbrev* polyvinyl chloride.

pygmy *or* **pigmy** *noun* (**-ies**) **1** (**Pygmy**) a member of one of the unusually short peoples of equatorial Africa. **2** an undersized person; a dwarf. **3** *derog* someone insignificant, esp in a specified field: *an intellectual pygmy.* ▸ *adj* belonging or relating to a small-sized breed: *pygmy hippopotamus.* ▪ **pygmaean** *or* **pygmean** *adj.* [14c: from Greek *pygme* the distance from knuckle to elbow]

pyjamas *or* (*N Am*) **pajamas** *plural noun* **1** a sleeping suit consisting of a loose jacket or top, and trousers. *as adj* (**pyjama**): *pyjama bottoms.* **2** loose-fitting trousers worn by either sex in the East. [19c: from Persian and Hindi *payjamah*]

pylon *noun* a tall steel structure for supporting electric power cables. [Early 20c: Greek, from *pyle* gate]

pyramid *noun* **1** any of the huge ancient Egyptian royal tombs built on a square base, with four sloping triangular sides meeting in a common apex. **2** *geom* a solid of this shape, with a square or triangular base. **3** any structure or pile, etc of similar shape. ▪ **pyramidal** /pɪˈramɪdəl/ *adj.* [16c: from Greek *pyramis*]

pyre *noun* a pile of wood on which a dead body is ceremonially cremated. [17c: from Latin and Greek *pyra* fire]

pyretic /paɪəˈrɛtɪk/ *adj, med* relating to, accompanied by or producing fever. [19c: from Greek *pyretos* fever]

Pyrex *noun, trademark* a type of heat-resistant glass widely used to make laboratory apparatus and cooking utensils. [20c]

pyridoxine *noun* **vitamin B_6**. [20c]

pyrite /ˈpaɪəraɪt/ *noun, geol* the commonest sulphide mineral, used in the production of sulphuric acid. Also called **iron pyrites, fool's gold**.

pyrites /paɪəˈraɪtiːz/ *noun* **1** *geol* **pyrite**. **2** *chem* any of a large class of mineral sulphides: *copper pyrites.* [16c: Latin, meaning 'fire-stone']

pyro- *or* (*before a vowel*) **pyr-** *combining form, forming nouns and adjs, denoting* **1** fire; heat; fever. **2** *chem* an acid or its corresponding salt. [Greek, from *pyr* fire]

pyroclastic *adj, geol* of rocks: formed of fragments thrown out by volcanic action. [19c: from Greek *klastos* broken]

pyromania *noun, psychol* an obsessive urge to set fire to things. ▪ **pyromaniac** *noun.* [19c]

pyrotechnics *singular noun* the art of making fireworks. ▸ *singular or plural noun* **1** a fireworks display. **2** a display of fiery brilliance in speech or music, etc. [18c]

Pyrrhic victory /ˈpɪrɪk/ *noun* a victory won at so great a cost in lives, etc that it can hardly be regarded as a triumph at all. [19c: named after Pyrrhus, king of Epirus in Greece, who won such victories against the Romans in the 3c BC]

Pythagoras' theorem *noun, maths* the theorem that in a right-angled triangle the square of the length of the hypotenuse is equal to the sum of the squares of the lengths of the other two sides. [19c: named after the Greek philosopher and mathematician Pythagoras (6c BC)]

python *noun* a non-venomous egg-laying snake that coils its body around its prey and squeezes it until it suffocates. [19c: named after Python, a monster in Greek mythology killed by the god Apollo]

pyx *noun, Christianity* a container in which the consecrated Communion bread is kept. [14c: from Latin and Greek *pyxis* a small box]

Q[1] *or* **q** *noun* (***Qs, Q's*** *or* ***q's***) the seventeenth letter of the English alphabet.

Q[2] *abbrev* **1** *printing* quarto. **2** Quebec. **3** Queen or Queen's. **4** question.

q *or* **q.** *abbrev* **1** quart. **2** quarter.

qadi see **cadi**

QC *abbrev, law* Queen's Counsel.

QED *abbrev* used esp at the conclusion of a proof of a geometric theorem: *quod erat demonstrandum* /kwɒd ɛrat dɛmən'strandəm/ (Latin), which was the thing that had to be proved.

qi, **chi** *or* **ch'i** /tʃiː/ *noun, Chinese med* the life force that is believed to flow along a network of meridians in a person's body and is vital to their physical and spiritual health. [19c: Chinese, meaning 'breath' or 'energy']

qi gong *or* **chi kung** /tʃiː 'guːŋ/ *noun* a system of exercises for promoting physical and spiritual health by meditation and deep breathing. [1990s: **qi** + Chinese *gong* skill or exercise]

QLD *abbrev, Aust state* Queensland.

Qoran see **Koran**

qq *abbrev, printing* quartos.

qr *abbrev* quarter.

qt *abbrev* quart.

q.t. see **on the quiet** at **quiet**

qua /kweɪ, kwɑː/ *prep* in the capacity of something; in the role of something. [17c: Latin, from *qui* who]

quack[1] *noun* the noise that a duck makes. ▸ *verb, intr* **1** of a duck: to make this noise. **2** to talk in a loud silly voice. [17c: imitating the sound]

quack[2] *noun* **1** someone who practises medicine or who claims to have medical knowledge, but who has no formal training in the subject. **2** *informal, often derog* a term for any doctor or medical practitioner, etc. **3** anyone who pretends to have a knowledge or skill that they do not possess. ▪ **quackery** *noun* (***-ies***). [17c: from Dutch *quacksalver*]

quad[1] *noun, informal* a quadruplet. [Late 19c]

quad[2] *noun, informal* a quadrangle. [19c]

quad[3] *informal, adj* quadraphonic. ▸ *noun* quadraphonics. [1970s]

quadrangle *noun* **1** *geom* a square, rectangle or other four-sided two-dimensional figure. **2** **a** an open rectangular courtyard, esp one that is in the grounds of a college or school, etc; **b** a courtyard of this kind together with the buildings around it. Often shortened to **quad**. ▪ **quadrangular** *adj*. [15c: from Latin *quadrangulum*]

quadrant *noun* **1** *geom* **a** a quarter of the circumference of a circle; **b** a plane figure (see **plane**[2] *adj* sense 3) that is a quarter of a circle, ie an area bounded by two perpendicular radii and the arc between them; **c** a quarter of a sphere, ie a section cut by two planes that intersect at right angles at the centre. **2** any device or mechanical part in the shape of a 90° arc. **3** an instrument that was formerly used in astronomy and navigation and which consists of a graduated 90° arc allowing angular measurements, eg of the stars, to be taken and altitude calculated. ▪ **quadrantal** *adj*. [14c: from Latin *quadrans, quadrantis* a fourth part]

quadraphonic *or* **quadrophonic** *adj* of a stereophonic sound recording or reproduction: using four loudspeakers that are fed by four separate channels. ▪ **quadraphonically** *adv*. ▪ **quadraphonics** *plural noun*. [1960s: from **quadri-**, modelled on **stereophonic**]

quadrate *noun, anatomy, zool* a muscle or bone that has a square or rectangular shape. ▸ *adj, botany* square or almost square in cross-section or face view. ▸ *verb* to make something square. [14c: from Latin *quadrare* to make square]

quadratic *maths, noun* **1** (*in full* **quadratic equation**) an algebraic equation that involves the square, but no higher power, of an unknown quantity or variable. **2** (**quadratics**) the branch of algebra that deals with this type of equation. ▸ *adj* **1** involving the square of an unknown quantity or variable but no higher power. **2** square. [17c]

quadrennial *adj* **1** lasting four years. **2** occurring every four years. [17c: from Latin *quadriennium* a four-year period]

quadri- *or* (*before a vowel*) **quadr-** *combining form, denoting* four. [Latin, from *quattuor* four]

quadriceps *noun* (***quadricepses*** *or* ***quadriceps***) *anatomy* a large four-part muscle that extends the leg, which runs down the front of the thigh. [19c: Latin]

quadrilateral *geom, noun* a two-dimensional figure that has four sides. ▸ *adj* four-sided. [17c]

quadrille *noun* **1** a square dance for four couples, in five or six movements. **2** music for this kind of dance. [18c: French, from Spanish *cuadrilla* a troop]

quadrinomial *maths, adj* said of an algebraic expression: having four terms. ▸ *noun* an algebraic expression of this kind. [18c]

quadripartite *adj* **1** divided into or composed of four parts. **2** of talks or an agreement, etc: involving, concerning or ratified by, etc four parts, groups or nations, etc. [15c: from Latin *partiri* to divide]

quadriplegia *noun, pathol* paralysis that affects both arms and both legs. Compare **hemiplegia**, **paraplegia**. ▪ **quadriplegic** *adj, noun*. [1920s]

quadrophonic see **quadraphonic**

quadruped /ˈkwɒdrupɛd/ *noun* an animal, esp a mammal, that has its four limbs specially adapted for walking. ▸ *adj* four-footed. [17c]

quadruple *adj* **1** four times as great, much or many. **2** made up of four parts or things. **3** *music* of time: having four beats to the bar. ▸ *verb, tr & intr* to make or become four times as great, much or many. [16c: French]

quadruplet *noun* one of four children or animals born to the same mother at the same time. Often shortened to **quad**. [18c: from **quadruple**, modelled on **triplet**]

quadruplicate *adj* /kwɒˈdruːplɪkət/ **1** having four parts which are exactly alike. **2** being one of four identical copies. **3** quadrupled. ▸ *verb* /-keɪt/ to make something quadruple or fourfold. [17c: from Latin *quadruplicare* to multiply by four]

IDIOMS **in quadruplicate** copied four times.

quaff *verb, tr & intr, literary* to drink eagerly or deeply. ▪ **quaffer** *noun*. [16c]

quag *noun* a boggy or marshy place. ▪ **quaggy** *adj* (**-ier, -iest**). [16c]

quagga *noun* an extinct member of the zebra family which had stripes around the head and shoulders, the rest of its body being a yellowish-brown colour. [18c]

quagmire /ˈkwɒgmaɪə(r)/ *noun* **1** an area of soft marshy ground; a bog. **2** a dangerous, difficult or awkward situation. [16c]

quail[1] *noun* (***quail*** *or* ***quails***) a small migratory game bird of the partridge family. [14c: from French *quaille*]

quail[2] *verb, intr* to lose courage; to be apprehensive with fear; to flinch. [15c]

quaint *adj* old-fashioned, strange or unusual, esp in a charming, pretty or dainty, etc way. ▪ **quaintness** *noun*. [18c: from French *cointe*]

quake *verb, intr* **1** of people: to shake or tremble with fear, etc. **2** of a building, etc: to rock or shudder. ▸ *noun, informal* an earthquake. ▪ **quaking** *adj, noun*. [Anglo-Saxon *cwacian*]

Quaker *noun* a member of the Religious Society of Friends, a pacifist Christian organization founded in the 17c by George Fox. ▪ **Quakerism** *noun*. [17c]

quaking ash *noun* another name for the **aspen**.

qualification *noun* **1 a** an official record that one has completed a training or performed satisfactorily in an examination, etc; **b** a document or certificate, etc that confirms this. **2** a skill or ability that fits one for some job, etc. **3** the act, process or fact of qualifying. **4** an addition to a statement, etc that modifies, narrows or restricts its implications; a condition, limitation or modification. [16c: see **qualify**]

qualified *adj* **1** having the necessary competency, ability or attributes, etc (to do something). **2** having completed a training or passed an examination, etc, esp in order to practise a specified profession or occupation, etc. **3** limited, modified or restricted. [16c]

qualify *verb* (**-ies, -ied**) **1** *intr* to complete a training or pass an examination, etc, esp in order to practise a specified profession, occupation, etc. **2 a** (*often* **qualify sb for sth**) to give or provide them with the necessary competency, ability or attributes, etc to do it; **b** to entitle: *that qualifies you to get £10 discount*. **3** *intr* **a** to meet or fulfil the required conditions or guidelines, etc (in order to receive an award or privilege, etc); **b** (*usu* **qualify as sth**) to have the right characteristics to be a specified thing. **4 a** to modify (a statement, document or agreement, etc) in such a way as to restrict, limit or moderate, etc it; **b** to add reservations to something; to tone down or restrict it. **5** *grammar* of a word or phrase, esp an adjectival one: to modify, define or describe (another word or phrase, esp a nominal one). **6** *tr & intr, sport* to proceed or allow someone to proceed to the later stages or rounds, etc (of a competition, etc), usu by doing well in a preliminary round. ▪ **qualifier** *noun*. ▪ **qualifying** *adj, noun*. [16c: from French *qualifier*]

qualitative *adj* relating to, affecting or concerned with distinctions of the quality or standard of something. Compare **quantitative**. [17c]

qualitative analysis *noun, chem* the identification of the different constituents, eg the elements, ions and functioning groups, etc, that are present in a substance. Compare **quantitative analysis**. [19c]

quality *noun* (**-ies**) **1** the degree or extent of excellence of something. **2** general excellence; high standard: *articles of consistent quality*. **3 a** a distinctive or distinguishing talent or attribute, etc; **b** the basic nature of something. **4** *old use* high social status: *families of quality*. ▸ *adj* being of or exhibiting a high quality or standard: *the quality newspapers*. [13c: from French *qualité*]

quality control *noun* a system or the process that involves regular sampling of the output of an industrial process in order to detect any variations in quality. ▪ **quality controller** *noun*.

quality of life *noun* standard of living measured by the social and economic environment, access to amenities, etc.

quality time *noun* a period of time when someone's attention is devoted entirely to someone else, eg a companion or child, without interruptions or distractions.

qualm /kwɑːm/ *noun* **1 a** a sudden feeling of nervousness or apprehension; **b** a feeling of uneasiness about whether a decision or course of action, etc is really for the best; **c** a scruple, misgiving or pang of conscience. **2** a feeling of faintness or nausea. [16c]

quandary *noun* (**-ies**) **1** (*usu* **in a quandary about, over, as to**, *etc* **sth**) a state of indecision, uncertainty, doubt or perplexity. **2** a situation that involves some kind of dilemma or predicament. [16c]

quango *noun* a semi-public administrative body that functions outwith the civil service but which is government-funded and which has its senior appointments made by the government. [1960s: from *qua*si-autonomous *n*on-*g*overnmental *o*rganization]

quanta see under **quantum**

quantify *verb* (**-ies, -ied**) **1** to determine the quantity of something or to measure or express it as a quantity. **2** *logic* to stipulate the extent of (a term or proposition) by using a word such as *all, some*, etc. ▪ **quantifiable** *adj*. ▪ **quantification** *noun*. [19c: from Latin *quantus* how much + *facere* to make]

quantitative *adj* **1** relating to or involving quantity. **2** estimated, or measurable, in terms of quantity. Compare **qualitative**. [16c]

quantitative analysis *noun, chem* the measurement of the amounts of the different constituents that are present in a substance. Compare **qualitative analysis**.

quantity *noun* (**-ies**) **1** the property that things have that allows them to be measured or counted; size or amount. **2** a specified amount or number, etc: *a tiny quantity.* **3** largeness of amount; bulk: *buy in quantity.* **4** (**quantities**) a large amount: *quantities of food.* **5** *maths* a value that may be expressed as a number, or the symbol or figure representing it. [14c: from Latin *quantitas*]

quantity surveyor *noun* a person whose job is to estimate the amount and cost of the various materials and labour, etc that a specified building project will require. [Early 20c]

quantize *or* **quantise** *verb, physics* to form into **quanta** (see under **quantum**). ▪ **quantization** *noun.* [20c]

quantum *noun* (***quanta***) **1 a** an amount or quantity, esp a specified one; **b** a portion, part or share. **2** *physics* **a** the minimal indivisible amount of a specified physical property (eg momentum or electromagnetic radiation energy, etc) that can exist; **b** a unit of this, eg the **photon**. ▸ *adj* **1** concerned with or relating to quanta: *quantum effect.* **2** major, large or impressive but also sudden, unexpected or abrupt, etc. [17c: from Latin, neuter of *quantus* how much]

quantum leap *or* **quantum jump** *noun* **1** a sudden transition; a spectacular advance. **2** *physics* a sudden transition from one quantum state in an atom or molecule to another.

quantum mechanics *singular noun, physics* a mathematical theory that developed from the quantum theory and which is used in the interpretation of the behaviour of particles, especially subatomic ones. [20c]

quantum theory *noun, physics* a theory that is based on the principle that in physical systems, the energy associated with any **quantum** is proportional to the frequency of the radiation.

quarantine *noun* **1** the isolation of people or animals to prevent the spread of any infectious disease that they could be developing. **2** the duration or place of such isolation. ▸ *verb* to put (a person or animal) into quarantine. [17c: from Italian *quarantina* period of 40 days]

quark[1] /kwɔːk, kwɑːk/ *noun, physics* the smallest known bit of matter, being any of a group of subatomic particles which, in different combinations, are thought to make up all protons, neutrons and other hadrons. [1960s in this sense, but first coined by the novelist James Joyce in *Finnegans Wake* (1939)]

quark[2] /kwɑːk/ *noun* a type of low-fat soft cheese that is made from skimmed milk. [1930s: German]

quarrel *noun* **1** an angry disagreement or argument. **2** a cause of such disagreement; a complaint. **3** a break in a friendship; a breach or rupture. ▸ *verb* (***quarrelled, quarrelling***; *US* ***quarreled, quarreling***) *intr* **1** to argue or dispute angrily. **2** to fall out; to disagree and remain on bad terms. **3** (*usu* **quarrel with sb** *or* **sth**) to find fault with them or it. ▪ **quarrelling** *adj, noun.* ▪ **quarrelsome** *adj.* [13c: from Latin *querela*, from *queri* to complain]

quarry[1] *noun* (**-ies**) **1** an open excavation for the purpose of extracting stone or slate for building. **2** a place from which stone, etc can be excavated. ▸ *verb* (**-ies, -ied**) **1** to extract (stone, etc) from a quarry. **2** to excavate a quarry in (land). ▪ **quarrying** *noun.* [15c: from Latin *quadrare* to make (stones) square]

quarry[2] *noun* (**-ies**) **1** an animal or bird that is hunted, esp one that is the usual prey of some other animal or bird. **2** someone or something that is the object of pursuit. [14c: meaning 'the entrails of a deer placed on the hide and given to hunting dogs as a reward']

quarryman *noun* a man who works in a quarry.

quarry tile *noun* an unglazed floor tile.

quart *noun* (abbrev **q** *or* **qt**) **1** in the UK: **a** in the imperial system: a liquid measure equivalent to one quarter of a gallon, two pints (1.136 l) or 40fl oz; **b** a container that holds this amount. **2** in the US: **a** a unit of liquid measure that is equivalent to one quarter of a gallon, two pints (0.946 l) or 32fl oz; **b** a unit of dry measure that is equivalent to two pints (1.101 l), an eighth of a peck or 67.2cu in. [14c: from French *quarte*]

quarter *noun* (abbrev **q** *or* **qr**) **1 a** one of four equal parts that an object or quantity is or can be divided into; **b** (often written ¼) the number one when it is divided by four. **2** any of the three-month divisions of the year, esp one that begins or ends on a **quarter day**. **3** *N Am* **a** 25 cents, ie quarter of a dollar; **b** a coin of this value. **4 a** a period of 15 minutes; **b** a point of time 15 minutes after or before any hour. **5** *astron* **a** a fourth part of the Moon's cycle; **b** either of the two phases of the Moon when half its surface is lit and visible at the point between the first and second and the third and fourth quarters of its cycle. **6** any of the four main compass directions; any direction. **7** a district of a city, etc: *the Spanish quarter.* **8** (*also* **quarters**) a section of the public or society, etc; certain people or a certain person: *no sympathy from that quarter.* **9** (**quarters**) lodgings or accommodation, eg for soldiers and their families: *married quarters.* **10** in the imperial system: **a** a unit of weight equal to a quarter of a hundredweight, ie (*Brit*) 28 lbs or (*US*) 25 lbs; **b** *Brit informal* 4 ozs or a quarter of a pound; **c** *Brit* a unit of measure for grain equal to eight bushels. **11 a** any of the four sections that an animal's or bird's carcass is divided into, each section having a leg or a wing; **b** (**quarters**) *hist* the four similar sections that a human body was divided into, esp after execution for treason. **12** mercy that is shown or offered, eg to a defeated enemy, etc: *give no quarter.* **13** *heraldry* any of the four sections of a shield which are formed by two perpendicular horizontal and vertical lines. **14** *sport, esp Amer football & Aust Rules football* any of the four equal periods that a game is divided into. ▸ *verb* **1** to divide something into quarters. **2 a** to accommodate or billet (troops, etc) in lodgings; **b** esp of military personnel: to be accommodated or billeted in lodgings. **3** *hist* to divide (the body of a hanged traitor, etc) into four parts, each with a limb. **4** *heraldry* **a** to divide (a shield) into quarters using one horizontal and one vertical line; **b** to fill (each quarter of a shield) with bearings. **5** of a hunting dog or a bird of prey: to cross and recross (an area) searching for game. [13c: from French *quartier*]

quarterback *noun, Amer football* a player who directs the attacking play. [19c]

quarter day *noun, Brit* any of the four days when one of the **quarters** (*noun* sense 2) of the year begins or ends. Traditionally they were the days that rent or interest fell due and when tenancies were agreed or renewed. [15c]

quarterdeck *noun, naut* the stern part of a ship's upper deck which is usu reserved for officers. [17c]

quarter final *noun* a match or the round that involves the eight remaining participants or teams in a competition or cup, etc and which precedes the semi-final match or round. [1920s]

quarterlight *noun* in older designs of cars: a small triangular window that pivots open for ventilation. [Late 19c]

quarterly *adj* produced, occurring, published, paid or due, etc once every quarter of a year. ▸ *adv* once every quarter. ▸ *noun* (***-ies***) a quarterly publication. [16c]

quartermaster *noun* **1** an army officer who is responsible for soldiers' accommodation, food and clothing. **2** *naut* (abbrev **QM**) a petty officer who is responsible for navigation and signals. [15c]

quarter note *noun, N Amer, music* a crotchet.

quartet *or* **quartette** *noun* **1** *music* **a** an ensemble of four singers or instrumentalists; **b** a piece of music for four performers. **2** any group or set of four. [18c: from Italian *quartetto*]

quartic *maths, noun* (*in full* **quartic equation**) an algebraic equation that involves an unknown quantity or variable up to the power four, but no higher power. ▸ *adj* involving an unknown quantity or variable up to the power four, but no higher power. [19c: from Latin *quartus* fourth]

quartile *adj, astron* of the aspect of two heavenly bodies: 90° apart. ▸ *noun* **1** *astrol* a quartile aspect between two heavenly bodies. **2** *stats* in a frequency distribution: a value such that one quarter, one half or three quarters of the numbers considered are contained within it. [16c: from Latin *quartilis*, from *quartus* fourth]

quarto *noun* (abbrev **Q**) *printing* **1** a size of paper produced by folding a sheet in half twice to give four leaves or eight pages. **2** a book that has its pages made up of sheets of paper that have been folded in this way and then had the outer folds cut. [16c: from Latin *in quarto* in one fourth]

quartz *noun, geol* a common colourless mineral that is often tinged with impurities that give a wide variety of shades making it suitable as a gemstone. In its pure form, it consists of silica or silicon dioxide. See also **quartzite**. [18c: German]

quartz clock *or* **quartz watch** *noun* a clock or watch that has a mechanism which is controlled by the vibrations of a **quartz crystal**.

quartz crystal *noun* a disc or rod cut from quartz that is ground so that it vibrates at a specified frequency when a suitable electrical signal is applied to it.

quartzite *noun, geol* **1** a highly durable rock that is composed largely or entirely of quartz. **2** a sandstone consisting of grains of quartz cemented together by silica. [19c]

quasar /'kweɪzɑː(r)/ *noun, astron* a highly intense luminous star-like source of light and radio waves that exists thousands of millions of light years outside the Earth's galaxy and which has large red shifts. [20c: from *quasi*-stell*ar* object]

quash *verb* **1** to subdue, crush or suppress, etc (eg a rebellion or protest). **2** to reject (a verdict, etc) as invalid. **3** to annul (a law, etc). [14c: from Latin *quassare* to shake]

quasi- /'kweɪzaɪ/ *combining form, denoting* **1** to some extent; virtually: *a quasi-official role*. **2** seeming or seemingly, but not actually so: *quasi-experts*. [From Latin *quasi* as if]

quaternary *adj* **1** having or consisting of four parts. **2** fourth in a series. **3** (**Quaternary**) *geol* belonging or relating to the most recent period of geological time when humans evolved. **4** *chem* of an atom: bound to four non-hydrogen atoms. ▸ *noun, geol* the Quaternary period or rock system. [15c: from Latin *quaterni* four each]

quatrain *noun, poetry* a verse or poem of four lines which usu rhyme alternately. [16c: French, from *quatre* four]

quatrefoil /'katrəfɔɪl/ *noun* **1** *botany* **a** a flower with four petals; **b** a leaf composed of four lobes or leaflets. **2** *archit* a four-lobed design, esp one that is used in open stonework. [15c: French, from *quatre* four + *foil* leaf]

quattrocento /kwatroʊ'tʃɛntoʊ/ *noun* the 15c, esp with reference to Italian Renaissance art. [17c: Italian, meaning 'four hundred', but taken to mean 'fourteen hundred']

quaver *verb* **1** *intr* of a voice or a musical sound, etc: to be unsteady; to shake or tremble. **2** to say or sing something in a trembling voice. ▸ *noun* **1** *music* a note that lasts half as long as a crotchet and is usu represented in notation by ♪. **2** a tremble in the voice. ▪ **quavering** *adj*. [15c: a blending of **quake** + **waver**]

quay /kiː/ *noun* an artificial structure that projects into the water for the loading and unloading of ships. [17c: from French *kay*]

quayside *noun* the area around a quay, esp the edge along the water.

queasy *adj* (***-ier, -iest***) **1** of a person: feeling slightly sick. **2** of the stomach or digestion: easily upset. **3** of the conscience: readily made uneasy. ▪ **queasily** *adv*. ▪ **queasiness** *noun*. [15c]

Quechua /'kɛtʃwə/ *noun* (*pl* ***Quechua*** *or* ***Quechuas***) **1** a group of native S American peoples that includes the **Incas**, who inhabit Peru and parts of Bolivia, Chile, Colombia and Ecuador. **2** their language, which is widely used in this area as a lingua franca. ▸ *adj* belonging or relating to this group or language. ▪ **Quechuan** *noun, adj*. [19c: Spanish, from Quechua *k'echua* plunderer]

queen *noun* **1** **a** a woman who rules a country, having inherited her position by birth; **b** (*in full* **queen consort**) the wife of a king; **c** (*usu* **Queen**) the title applied to someone who holds either of these positions. **2** a woman, place or thing considered supreme in some way: *queen of people's hearts* • *queen of European cities*. **3** a large fertile female ant, bee or wasp that lays eggs. **4** *chess* a piece that is able to move in any direction, making it the most powerful piece on the board. **5** *cards* any of the four high-ranking face cards that have a picture of a queen on them. ▸ *verb, chess* **a** to advance (a pawn) to the opponent's side of the board and convert it into a queen; **b** *intr* of a pawn: to reach the opponent's side of the board and so be converted into a queen. [Anglo-Saxon *cwene* a woman]

Queen Anne *adj, denoting* a style of English architecture and furniture, etc that was popular in the early 18c. [18c: named after Queen Anne who reigned 1702–14]

queen bee *noun* (*also* **queen**) **1** the fertile female in a beehive. **2** the dominant, superior or controlling woman in an organization or group, etc.

queenly *adj* (**-ier, -iest**) **1** suitable for or appropriate to a queen. **2** majestic; like a queen.

queen mother *noun* the widow of a king who is also the mother of the reigning king or queen.

queen post *noun, archit* in a trussed roof: one of two upright posts that connect the tie-beam to the principal rafters.

Queen's Bench (when the sovereign is a woman) or **King's Bench** (when the sovereign is a man) *noun* (abbrev **QB**) *law* in the UK: a division of the High Court of Justice.

Queensberry Rules *plural noun* **1** the code of rules that govern modern-day boxing. **2** *informal* approved, mannerly, courteous or civilized, etc behaviour, esp in a dispute. [Late 19c: named after Sir John Sholto Douglas, Marquis of Queensberry]

Queen's Counsel (when the sovereign is a woman) or **King's Counsel** (when the sovereign is a man) *noun* (abbrev **QC**) *law* **1** in England and Wales: a senior barrister who is recommended for appointment as Counsel to the Crown. **2** in Scotland: a senior advocate who is recommended for appointment as Counsel to the Crown. Also called **silk**.

Queen's English (when the sovereign is a woman) or **King's English** (when the sovereign is a man) *noun* the standard form of written or spoken Southern British English regarded as most correct or acceptable. [16c]

Queen's evidence (when the sovereign is a woman) or **King's evidence** (when the sovereign is a man) *noun, Brit law* evidence that a participant or accomplice in a crime gives to support the case of the prosecution. *N Am, esp US equivalent* **state's evidence**.

Queen's Guide (when the sovereign is a woman) or **King's Guide** (when the sovereign is a man) *noun, Brit* a **Guide** (*noun* sense 4) who has reached the highest level of proficiency.

Queen's highway (when the sovereign is a woman) or **King's highway** (when the sovereign is a man) *noun, Brit* a public road, regarded as being under royal control.

queen-size *or* **queen-sized** *adj* esp of a bed or other piece of furniture: larger than the usual or normal size but not as large as king-size. [1950s]

Queen's Speech (when the sovereign is a woman) and **King's Speech** (when the sovereign is a man) *noun, Brit* **1** the speech that the reigning monarch makes on the opening of a new session of parliament and which gives details of the government's proposed legislative agenda. **2** a traditional Christmas day broadcast on TV and radio in which the monarch addresses the nation and the Commonwealth.

queer *adj* **1** odd, strange or unusual. **2** *informal* slightly mad. **3** faint or ill. **4** *informal* suspicious; shady. ▸ *verb* to spoil something. ▪ **queerly** *adv.* ▪ **queerness** *noun.* [20c in sense 1; 16c in sense 2]

IDIOMS **in queer street** *Brit, informal* **1** in debt or financial difficulties. **2** in trouble. **queer sb's pitch** *informal* to spoil their plans; to thwart them.

quell *verb* **1 a** to crush or subdue (riots, disturbances or opposition, etc); **b** to force (rebels or rioters, etc) to give in. **2** to suppress, overcome, alleviate or put an end to (unwanted feelings, etc). [Anglo-Saxon *cwellan* to kill]

quench *verb* **1 a** to satisfy (thirst) by drinking; **b** to satisfy (a desire, etc). **2** to extinguish (a fire or light, etc). **3** to damp or crush (ardour, enthusiasm or desire, etc). **4** *metallurgy* to cool (hot metal) rapidly by plunging in cold liquid in order to alter its properties. ▪ **quenching** *adj, noun.* [Anglo-Saxon *acwencan*]

quenelle /kəˈnɛl/ *noun, cookery* an oval or sausage-shaped dumpling made from spiced meat-paste, eg fish, chicken or veal, etc. [19c: French]

quern *noun* **1** a mill, usu consisting of two circular stones (**quernstones**) one on top of the other, used for grinding grain by hand. **2** a small hand mill for grinding pepper or mustard, etc. [Anglo-Saxon *cweorn*]

querulous /ˈkwɛrjʊləs, -rʊləs/ *adj* **1** of someone or their disposition: inclined or ready to complain. **2** of a voice, tone or comment, etc: complaining, grumbling or whining. ▪ **querulously** *adv.* [15c: from Latin *querulus*]

query *noun* (**-ies**) **1** a question, esp one that raises a doubt or objection, etc. **2** a request for information; an inquiry. **3** a less common name for a **question mark**. ▸ *verb* (**-ies, -ied**) **1** to raise a doubt about something. **2** to ask. **3** *chiefly US* to interrogate or question someone. [17c: from Latin imperative *quaere* ask!]

quest *noun* **1** a search or hunt. **2** a journey, esp one undertaken by a medieval knight, that involves searching for something (eg the Holy Grail) or achieving some goal. **3** the object of a search; an aim or goal. ▸ *verb, intr* **1** (*usu* **quest after** *or* **for sth**) to search about; to roam around in search of it. **2** of a dog: to search for game. ▪ **quester** *or* **questor** *noun.* [14c: from Latin *quaerere* to seek]

IDIOMS **in quest of sth** in the process of looking for it.

question *noun* **1 a** a written or spoken sentence that is worded in such a way as to request information or an answer; **b** the interrogative sentence or other form of words in which this is expressed. **2** a doubt or query. **3** a problem or difficulty: *the Northern Ireland question.* **4** a problem set for discussion or solution in an examination paper, etc. **5** an investigation or search for information. **6** a matter, concern or issue: *a question of safety.* ▸ *verb* **1** to ask someone questions; to interrogate them. **2** to raise doubts about something; to query it. ▪ **questioner** *noun.* [13c: from French *questiun*]

IDIOMS **be (only, simply** *or* **just**, *etc*) **a question of sth** to be a situation, case or matter of a specified thing: *It's just a question of time.* **beyond question** not in doubt; beyond doubt. **call sth in** *or* **into question** to suggest reasons for doubting its validity or truth, etc. **in question 1** presently under discussion or being referred to: *was away at the time in question.* **2** in doubt: *Her ability is not in question.* **out of the question** impossible and so not worth considering.

questionable *adj* **1** doubtful; debatable; ambiguous. **2** suspect; disreputable; obscure; shady. ▪ **questionably** *adv.*

questioning *noun* an act or the process of asking a question or questions. ▸ *adj* **1** characterized by doubt or uncertainty; mildly confused: *exchanged questioning looks.* **2** esp of a person's mind: inquisitive; keen to learn. ▪ **questioningly** *adv.*

question mark *noun* **1** the punctuation mark (?) which is used to indicate that the sentence that comes before it is a question. **2** a doubt: *still a question mark over funds.*

questionnaire *noun* **1** a set of questions that has been specially formulated as a means of collecting information and surveying opinions, etc. **2** a document that contains a set of questions of this kind. [Early 20c: French]

---

questionnaire
This word is often misspelt. It has two *n*'s in the middle. It might help you to remember the following sentence:
*There are **no new** questions in this question**n**aire.*

---

queue /kjuː/ *noun* **1** *Brit* a line or file of people or vehicles, etc, esp ones that are waiting for something. *N Am equivalent* **line**. **2** *comput* a list of items, eg programs or data, held in a computer system in the order in which they are to be processed. ▸ *verb, intr* **1** (*also* **queue up**) **a** to form a queue; **b** to stand or wait in a queue. **2** *comput* to line up tasks for a computer to process. [16c: meaning 'a tail': French]

---

queue
This word is often misspelt. It has the sequence of vowels *ueue*. It might help you to remember the following sentence:
*There are **two u**gly **e**lves in the **queue**.*

---

quibble *verb, intr* to argue over trifles; to make petty objections. ▸ *noun* **1** a trifling objection. **2** *old use* a pun. ▪ **quibbling** *adj, noun.* [17c]

quiche /kiːʃ/ *noun* a type of open tart that is usu made with a filling of beaten eggs and cream with various savoury flavourings. [1940s: French]

quick *adj* **1** taking little time. **2** brief. **3** fast; rapid; speedy. **4** not delayed; immediate. **5** intelligent; alert; sharp. **6** of the temper: easily roused to anger. **7** nimble, deft or brisk. **8** not reluctant or slow (to do something); apt, eager or ready: *quick to take offence.* ▸ *adv, informal* rapidly. ▸ *noun* **1** an area of sensitive flesh, esp at the base of the fingernail or toenail. **2** the site where someone's emotions or feelings, etc are supposed to be located: *Her words wounded him to the quick.* **3** (*usu* **the quick**) *old use* those who are alive. ▪ **quickly** *adv.* ▪ **quickness** *noun.* [Anglo-Saxon *cwic* alive]

IDIOMS **be quick** to act immediately.

quicken *verb* **1** *tr & intr* to make or become quicker; to accelerate. **2** to stimulate, rouse or stir (interest or imagination, etc). **3** *intr* **a** of a baby in the womb: to begin to move perceptibly; **b** of a pregnant woman: to begin to feel her baby's movements. ▪ **quickening** *adj, noun.* [14c: meaning 'to give or receive life']

quick-fire *adj* **1** esp of repartee, etc: very rapid. **2** of a gun, etc: able to fire shots in rapid succession.

quick fix *noun* a remedy that has the benefit of being immediate but the drawback of not being very effective.

quick-freeze *verb* to freeze (esp soft fruit such as strawberries) rapidly so that the internal structure is not damaged. ▪ **quick-frozen** *adj.* [1930s]

quickie *noun, informal* **1** something that is dealt with or done rapidly or in a short time. **2** (*also* **a quick one**) a measure of alcohol that is drunk quickly. [1920s: specifically of a quickly-made film]

quicklime see **calcium oxide**

quicksand *noun* **a** loose, wet sand that can suck down anything that lands or falls on it, often swallowing it up completely; **b** an area of this. [15c]

quickset *noun* **1** a living slip or cutting from a plant that is put into the ground with others where they will grow to form a hedge. **2** a hedge that is formed from such slips or cuttings. ▸ *adj* of a hedge: formed from such slips or cuttings. [15c: from **quick**, meaning 'alive', 'living' or 'growing']

quicksilver *noun* **mercury** (sense 1). ▸ *adj* of someone's mind or temper, etc: fast, esp unpredictably so; volatile. [Anglo-Saxon *cwic seolfor*]

quickstep *noun* **1** a fast modern ballroom dance in quadruple time. **2** a piece of music suitable for this kind of dance. ▸ *verb, intr* to dance the quickstep. [19c]

quick-tempered *adj* easily angered; grouchy or irritable.

quickthorn *noun* the **hawthorn**.

quick-witted *adj* **1** having fast reactions. **2** able to grasp or understand situations, etc quickly; clever. ▪ **quick-wittedness** *noun.*

quid[1] *noun* (*pl* ***quid***) *informal* a pound sterling. [17c]

IDIOMS **quids in** well-off; in a profitable or advantageous position.

quid[2] *noun* a bit of tobacco that is kept in the mouth and chewed. [18c: a dialectal variant of **cud**]

quiddity *noun* (***-ies***) **1** the essence of something; the distinctive qualities, etc that make a thing what it is. **2** a quibble; a trifling detail or point. [16c: from Latin *quidditas*]

quid pro quo /kwɪd proʊ 'kwoʊ/ *noun* something that is given or taken in exchange for something else of comparable value or status, etc. [16c: Latin, meaning 'something for something']

quiescent /kwɪ'ɛsənt/ *adj* **1** quiet, silent, at rest or in an inactive state, usu temporarily. **2** *phonetics* of a consonant: not sounded. ▪ **quiescence** *noun.* [17c: from Latin *quiescere* to be quiet]

quiet *adj* **1** **a** making little or no noise; **b** of a sound or voice, etc: soft; not loud. **2** of a place, etc: peaceful; tranquil; without noise or bustle. **3** of someone or their nature or disposition: reserved; unassertive; shy. **4** of the weather or sea, etc: calm. **5** not disturbed by trouble or excitement. **6** without fuss or publicity; informal. **7** of business or trade, etc: not flourishing or busy. **8** secret; private. **9** undisclosed or hidden: *took a quiet satisfaction in his downfall.* **10** enjoyed in peace: *a quiet read.* **11** not showy or gaudy, etc: *quiet tones of beige.* ▸ *noun* **1** absence of, or freedom from, noise or commotion, etc. **2** calm, tranquillity or repose. ▸ *verb, tr & intr* (*usu* **quiet down**) to make or become quiet or calm: *told the class to quiet down.* ▪ **quietly** *adv.* ▪ **quietness** *noun.* [14c: from Latin *quietus*]

IDIOMS **keep quiet about sth** *or* **keep sth quiet** to remain silent or say nothing about it. **on the quiet** (*also* **on the q.t.**) secretly; discreetly.

quiet, quite
Be careful not to use the spelling **quiet** when you mean **quite**:
This sandwich is quite good.

quieten *verb* **1** (*often* **quieten down**) *tr & intr* to make or become quiet. **2** to calm (doubts or fears, etc). [19c]

quietism *noun* **1** a state of calmness and passivity. **2** (**Quietism**) a form of religious mysticism that involves the abandonment of anything connected to the senses in favour of dedication to devotion and contemplation. ▪ **quietist** *noun, adj.*

quietude *noun* quietness; tranquillity. [16c]

quietus /kwaɪ'eɪtəs/ *noun* **1 a** a release from life; death; **b** something that brings about death. **2** release or discharge from debts or duties. [16c: from Latin *quietus est* he is quit, meaning 'he is considered to have discharged his debts']

quiff *noun* a tuft of hair at the front of the head that is brushed up into a crest and which is sometimes made to hang over the forehead. [19c]

quill *noun* **1 a** a large stiff feather from a bird's wing or tail; **b** the hollow base part of this. **2** (*in full* **quill pen**) a pen that is made by sharpening and splitting the end of a feather, esp a goose feather. **3** a porcupine's long spine. [15c]

quilt *noun* **1** a type of bedcover that is made by sewing together two layers of fabric, usu with some kind of soft padding material etc in between them. **2** a bedspread that is made in this way but which tends to be thinner. **3** *loosely* a duvet; a continental quilt. ▸ *verb, tr & intr* **1** to sew (two layers of material, etc) together with a filling in between. **2** to cover or line something with padding. ▪ **quilted** *adj.* ▪ **quilter** *noun.* [13c: from French *cuilte*]

quin *noun, informal* a shortened form of **quintuplet**.

quince *noun* **1** a small Asian tree of the rose family. **2** the acidic hard yellow fruit of this tree, which is used in making jams and jellies, etc. [14c: from the plural of English *quyne* quince]

quincentenary *noun* (*-ies*) **1** a 500th anniversary. **2** a celebration that is held to mark this. ▪ **quincentennial** *adj.* [19c: from Latin *quinque* five + **centenary**]

quincunx *noun* **a** an arrangement in which each of the four corners of a square or rectangle and the point at its centre are all indicated by some object; **b** five objects that are arranged in this way. [17c: Latin, meaning 'five twelfths']

quinine /'kwɪniːn/ *or (esp US)* /'kwaɪnaɪn/ *noun* **1** an alkaloid that is found in the bark of the **cinchona**. **2** *med* a bitter-tasting toxic drug obtained from this alkaloid, formerly taken as a tonic and widely used in treating malaria. [19c: from Spanish *quina* cinchona bark]

quinquagenarian *noun* someone who is aged between 50 and 59. [19c: from Latin *quinquaginta* fifty]

Quinquagesima *noun* (*in full* **Quinquagesima Sunday**) in the Christian calendar: the Sunday before the beginning of Lent. [14c: from Latin *quinquagesima dies* fiftieth day, ie before Easter Day]

quinquennial *adj* **1** lasting for five years. **2** recurring once every five years. [15c: from Latin *quinque* five + *annus* year]

quinquennium *noun* (*quinquennia*) a period of five years. [17c]

quinquereme *noun, hist* a type of ancient Roman or Greek galley ship that had five banks of oars or, possibly, five oarsmen to each oar. [17c: from Latin *quinque* five + *remus* oar]

quinquevalent *adj, chem* alternative for **pentavalent**.

quinsy *noun, pathol* inflammation of the tonsils and the area of the throat round about them, accompanied by the formation of an abscess or abscesses on the tonsils. [14c: from Latin *quinancia*]

quintal *noun* **1** a unit of weight that is equal to a hundredweight, 112 lbs in Britain or 100 lbs in the US. **2** in the metric system: a unit of weight that is equal to 100kg. [15c: French]

quintessence *noun* **1** (*usu* **quintessence of sth**) a perfect example or embodiment of it. **2** the fundamental essential nature of something. **3** *old use* the purest, most concentrated extract of a substance. ▪ **quintessential** *adj.* ▪ **quintessentially** *adv.* [15c: from Latin *quinta essentia* fifth essence]

quintet *or* **quintette** *noun* **1** a group of five singers or musicians. **2** a piece of music for five such performers. **3** any group or set of five. [19c: from French *quintette*]

quintic *noun, maths* (*in full* **quintic equation**) an algebraic equation that involves an unknown quantity or variable up to the power five, but no higher power. ▸ *adj* involving an unknown quantity or variable up to the power five, but no higher power. [19c: from Latin *quintus* fifth]

quintuple *adj* **1** five times as great, much or many. **2** made up of five parts or things. **3** *music* of time: having five beats to the bar. ▸ *verb, tr & intr* to make or become five times as great, much or many. ▸ *noun* an amount that is five times greater than the original or usual, etc amount. [16c: French]

quintuplet *noun* one of five children or animals born to the same mother at the same time. Often shortened to **quin**. [18c: from **quintuple**, modelled on **triplet**]

quintuplicate *adj* /kwɪn'tjuːplɪkət/ **1** having five parts which are exactly alike. **2** being one of five identical copies. **3** quintupled. ▸ *verb* /-plɪkeɪt/ to make something quintuple or fivefold. [17c: from Latin *quintuplicare* to multiply by five]

quip *noun* **1** a witty saying. **2** a sarcastic or wounding remark. ▸ *verb* (***quipped, quipping***) **1** *intr* to make a quip or quips. **2** to answer someone with a quip. ▪ **quipster** *noun.* [16c: from the earlier English *quippy* a quip]

quire *noun* **1** a measure for paper that is equivalent to 25 (formerly 24) sheets and one-twentieth of a **ream**. **2 a** a set of four sheets of parchment or paper folded in half together to form eight leaves; **b** *loosely* any set of folded sheets that is grouped together with other similar ones and bound into book form. [15c: from French *quaier*]

quirk *noun* **1** an odd habit, mannerism or aspect of personality, etc. **2** an odd twist in affairs or turn of events; a strange coincidence. ▪ **quirkiness** *noun.* ▪ **quirky** *adj* (*-ier, -iest*). [16c]

quisling *noun* **1** a traitor. **2** someone who collaborates with an enemy. [1940s: named after the Norwegian Major Vidkun Quisling, a known collaborator with the Germans during their occupation of his country]

quit *verb* (***quitted*** *or* ***quit, quitting***) **1** to leave or depart from (a place, etc). **2** *tr & intr* to leave, give up or resign (a job). **3** to exit (a computer program, application or game, etc). **4** *N Am, esp US, informal* to cease something or doing something. **5** *tr & intr* of a tenant: to move out of rented premises. ▸ *adj* (*usu* **quit of sth**) free or rid of it. [13c: from French *quiter*]

quitch *noun* (*in full* **quitch grass**; *pl* ***quitches***) another name for **couch**[2]. [Anglo-Saxon *cwice*]

quite *adv* **1** completely; entirely: *I quite understand.* • *It's not quite clear what happened.* **2** to a high degree: *quite exceptional.* **3** rather; fairly; to some or a limited degree: *quite a nice day* • *quite enjoyed it.* **4** (*also* **quite so**) used in a reply: I agree, see your point, etc. [14c: from **quit** (*adj*)]

IDIOMS **not quite** hardly; just short of or less than a specified thing. **quite a** *or* **an** a striking, impressive, daunting, challenging, etc: *That was quite a night.* **quite a few** *informal* a reasonably large number of (people or things, etc). **quite another matter** *or* **thing**, *etc* very different. **quite some** a considerably large amount of: *quite some time.* **quite something** very impressive.

---

quite, quiet

Be careful not to use the spelling **quite** when you mean **quiet**:

a quiet village outside the city

---

quits *adj, informal* **1** on an equal footing. **2** even, esp where money is concerned. [15c]

IDIOMS **call it quits** to agree to stop quarrelling or arguing, etc and accept that the outcome is even.

quittance *noun* **1** release from debt or other obligation. **2** a document that acknowledges this.

quitter *noun, informal* **1** someone who gives up too easily. **2** a shirker.

quiver[1] *verb* **1** (*often* **quiver with sth**) *intr* to shake or tremble slightly because of it; to shiver: *Her voice quivered with fear.* **2** *intr* to shake or flutter. **3** of a bird: to make (its wings) vibrate rapidly. ▸ *noun* a tremble or shiver. ▪ **quivering** *adj, noun.* [15c]

quiver[2] *noun* a long narrow case that is used for carrying arrows. [13c: from French *cuivre*]

quixotic /kwɪk'sɒtɪk/ *adj* **1** absurdly generous or chivalrous. **2** naively romantic, idealistic or impractical, etc. ▪ **quixotically** *adv.* [19c: named after the hero of *Don Quixote de la Mancha* (1605), a romantic novel by the Spanish writer Cervantes]

quiz *noun* (***quizzes***) **1** (*also* **quiz show**) an entertainment, eg on radio or TV, in which the knowledge of a panel of contestants is tested through a series of questions. **2** any series of questions as a test of general or specialized knowledge. **3** an interrogation. ▸ *verb* (***quizzes, quizzed, quizzing***) to question or interrogate someone. [18c]

quizmaster *noun* someone who asks the questions and keeps the score, etc in a quiz show. [1940s]

quizzical *adj* of a look or expression, etc: mildly amused or perplexed; mocking; questioning. ▪ **quizzically** *adv.* [19c]

quod *noun, Brit, slang* prison. [18c]

quod erat demonstrandum see under **QED**

quoin /kɔɪn/ *noun* **1** the external angle of a wall or building. **2** a cornerstone. **3** a wedge. [16c: from French *coin*]

quoit /kɔɪt/ *noun* **1** a ring made of metal, rubber or rope used in the game of quoits. **2** (**quoits**) a game that involves throwing these rings at pegs with the aim of encircling them or landing close to them. [15c]

quorate *adj, Brit* of a meeting, etc: attended by or consisting of enough people to form a quorum.

quorum *noun* the fixed minimum number of members of an organization or society, etc who must be present at a meeting for its business to be valid. [17c: Latin, meaning 'of whom', part of the conventional formula used in certain Latin commissions]

quota *noun* **1** the proportional or allocated share or part that is, or that should be, done, paid or contributed, etc out of a total amount, sum, etc. **2** the maximum or prescribed number or quantity that is permitted or required, eg of imported goods, etc. [17c: Latin, from *quota pars* how big a share?]

quotable *adj* worthy of or suitable for quoting.

quotation *noun* **1** a remark or a piece of writing, etc that is quoted. **2** the act or an instance of quoting. **3** *business* an estimated price for a job submitted by a contractor to a client. **4** *stock exchange* an amount that is stated as the current price of a commodity, stock or security, etc. **5** *music* a short extract from one piece that is put into another. [15c]

quotation marks *plural noun* a pair of punctuation marks which can be either single (' ') or double (" "). They are conventionally used to mark the beginning and end of a quoted passage or to indicate the title of an essay, article or song, etc, or are put on either side of a word or phrase to draw the reader's attention to it, eg because it is colloquial, slang, jargon or a new coinage. Also called **inverted commas**.

quote *verb, tr & intr* **1** to cite or offer (someone else or the words or ideas, etc of someone else) to substantiate an argument. **2** to repeat in writing or speech (the exact words, etc of someone else). **3** to cite or repeat (figures or data, etc). **4** *tr & intr* of a contractor: to submit or suggest (a price) for doing a specified job or for buying something: *quoted her £600 as a trade-in.* **5** *stock exchange* to state the price of (a security, commodity or stock, etc). **6** (*usu* **quote sth at sth**) to give (a racehorse) betting odds as specified: *Desert Orchid is quoted at 2/1.* **7 a** to put quotation marks around (a written passage, word or title, etc); **b** (*also* **quote ... unquote**) to indicate (in speech) that a specified part has been said by someone else. ▸ *noun* **1** a quotation. **2** a price quoted. **3** (**quotes**) quotation marks. [14c: from Latin *quotare* to give passages reference numbers]

quoth *verb, old use* said: *"Alas!" quoth he.* [Anglo-Saxon *cwaeth*]

quotidian *adj* **1** everyday; common-place. **2** daily. **3** recurring daily. [14c: from Latin *quotidianus*]

quotient /'kwoʊʃənt/ *noun, maths* the result of a division sum, eg when 72 (the **dividend**) is divided by 12 (the **divisor**), the quotient is 6. [15c: from Latin *quotiens* how often?]

Qur'an *or* **Quran** see **Koran**

qv *or* **q.v.** *abbrev: quod vide* (Latin), which see.

qwerty *or* **QWERTY** *adj* of an English-language typewriter, word processor or other keyboard: having the standard arrangement of keys, ie with the letters *q w e r t y* appearing in that order at the top left of the letters section. [1920s]

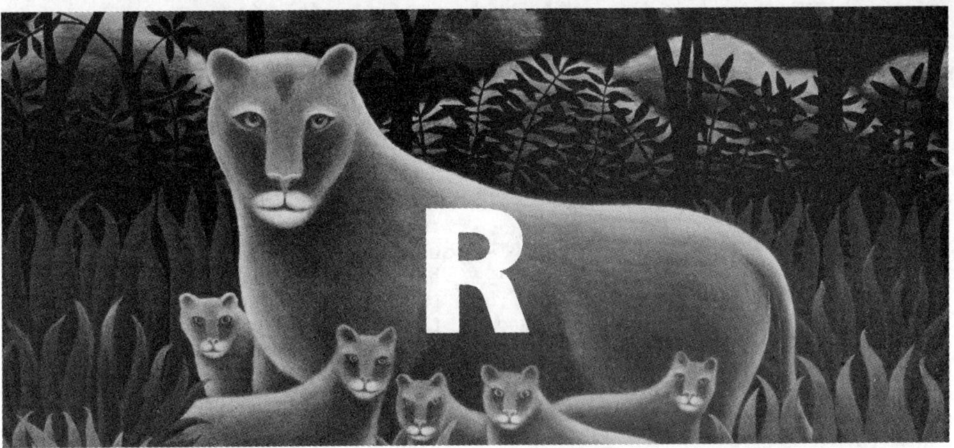

R[1] *or* **r** *noun* (***Rs, R's*** *or* ***r's***) the eighteenth letter of the English alphabet.

R[2] *or* **R.** *abbrev* **1** rand. **2** *physics, electronics* resistance. **3 a** *Regina* (Latin), Queen; **b** *Rex* (Latin), King. **4** River. **5** Röntgen. **6** rupee.

r *or* **r.** *abbrev* **1** radius. **2** right. **3** ruled.

Ra *symbol, chem* radium.

rabbet *noun* a groove cut along the edge of a piece of wood, etc, usu to join with a tongue or projection in a matching piece. ▸ *verb* **1** to cut a rabbet in. **2** to join with a rabbet. [15c: from French *rabattre* to beat down]

rabbi /ˈrabaɪ/ *noun* **1** a Jewish religious leader. **2** a Jewish scholar or teacher of the law. ▪ **rabbinical** /rəˈbɪnɪkəl/ *adj.* [13c: Hebrew, meaning 'my master']

rabbit *noun* **1** a small burrowing herbivorous mammal with long ears and a small stubby tail. **2** its flesh as food. **3** its fur. ▸ *verb, intr* **1** to hunt rabbits. **2** (*usu* **rabbit on** *or* **away**) *informal* to talk at great length, often pointlessly; to chatter. [14c]

rabbit punch *noun* a blow on the back of the neck.

rabble *noun* **1** a noisy disorderly crowd or mob. **2** (**the rabble**) the lowest class of people. [14c in obsolete sense 'a pack of animals']

rabble-rouser *noun* someone who agitates for social or political change. ▪ **rabble-rousing** *adj, noun.* [18c]

rabid *adj* **1** of dogs, etc: suffering from rabies. **2** fanatical; unreasoning. **3** furious. ▪ **rabidity** *or* **rabidness** *noun.* [17c: Latin, from *rabere* to be mad]

rabies *noun* a potentially fatal viral disease affecting mammals, esp dogs, and communicable to humans, causing convulsions and paralysis. Also called **hydrophobia**. [16c: Latin, from *rabere* to be mad]

raccoon *or* **racoon** *noun* (***raccoons*** *or* ***raccoon***) **1** a nocturnal American mammal with characteristic black eye patches. **2** its dense fur. [17c: from Algonquian (a family of Native American languages) *aroughcun*]

race[1] *noun* **1** a contest of speed between runners, cars, etc. **2** (*usu* **the races**) a series of such contests over a fixed course, esp for horses or dogs. **3** any contest, esp to be the first to do or get something: *the space race.* **4** a strong or rapid current of water in the sea or a river. **5** a channel conveying water to and from a mill wheel. ▸ *verb* **1** *intr* to take part in a race. **2** to have a race with. **3** to cause (a horse, car, etc) to race. **4** *intr* (*usu* **race about** *or* **along** *or* **around**) to run or move quickly and energetically. **5** *intr* of an engine, etc: to run too fast. ▪ **racer** *noun.* ▪ **racing** *noun, adj.* [13c: from Norse *ras*]

race[2] *noun* **1** any of the major divisions of humankind distinguished by a particular set of physical characteristics. **2** a nation or similar group of people thought of as distinct from others. **3** (**the human race**) human beings as a group. **4** a group of animals or plants within a species, which have characteristics distinguishing them from other members of that species. [16c: French, from Italian *razza*]

racecourse *or* **racetrack** *noun* a course or track used for racing horses, cars, etc.

racehorse *noun* a horse bred and used for racing.

raceme /raˈsiːm/ *noun, botany* a flower head consisting of individual flowers attached to a main unbranched stem. [18c: from Latin *racemus* bunch of grapes]

race meeting *noun* a series of races, esp horse races, taking place over the same course.

race relations *plural noun* social relations between people of different races living in the same community.

racetrack see **racecourse**

rachitis /rəˈkaɪtɪs/ *noun, med* **rickets**. ▪ **rachitic** /rəˈkɪtɪk/ *adj.* [18c: from Greek *rhachitis* inflammation of the spine]

Rachmanism /ˈrakmənɪzəm/ *noun* exploitation or extortion by a landlord of tenants living in slum conditions. [20c: named after a British property owner, exposed for such conduct in 1963]

racial *adj* **1** relating to a particular race. **2** based on race. ▪ **racialism** *noun.* ▪ **racialist** *noun, adj.*

racism *noun* **1** hatred, rivalry or bad feeling between races. **2** belief in the inherent superiority of a particular race or races over others. **3** discriminatory treatment based on such a belief. ▪ **racist** *noun, adj.* [16c]

rack[1] *noun* **1** a framework with rails, shelves, hooks, etc for holding or storing things. **2** a framework for holding hay, etc from which livestock can feed. **3** a cogged or toothed bar connecting with a cogwheel or pinion for changing the position of something, or converting linear motion into rotary motion, or vice versa. **4** (**the rack**) *hist* a device for torturing people by stretching their bodies. ▸ *verb* **1** to put in a rack. **2** to move or adjust by rack and pinion. **3** *hist* to torture on a rack. **4** to stretch or move forcibly or excessively. **5** to cause pain or suffering to. [14c: from Dutch *rec* shelf, framework]

IDIOMS **on the rack 1** extremely anxious or distressed. **2** of skill, etc: stretched to its limits. **rack one's brains** to think as hard as one can.

rack[2] *noun* destruction. [16c: variant of **wrack**]
IDIOMS **go to rack and ruin** to get into a state of neglect and decay.

rack and pinion *noun* a means of turning rotary motion into linear motion or vice versa by means of a toothed wheel engaging in a rack.

racket[1] *or* **racquet** *noun* a bat with a handle ending in a rounded head with a network of strings used in tennis, badminton, squash, etc. [16c: from French *raquette*, from Arabic *rahat* palm of the hand]

racket[2] *noun* **1** *informal* a loud confused noise or disturbance; a din. **2** a fraudulent or illegal means of making money. **3** *slang* a job or occupation. ▪ **rackety** *adj*. [16c: prob imitating a clattering noise]

racketeer *noun* someone who makes money in an illegal way. ▪ **racketeering** *noun*. [20c]

rackets *singular noun* a game derived from **real tennis** played by two or four players in a four-walled court.

raconteur /rakɒn'tɜː(r)/ *or* **raconteuse** /-'tɜːz/ *noun* a man or woman respectively who tells anecdotes. [19c: French, from *raconter* to relate or tell]

racoon see **raccoon**

racquet see **racket**[1]

racy *adj* (***-ier, -iest***) **1** lively or spirited. **2** slightly indecent; risqué. ▪ **racily** *adv*. ▪ **raciness** *noun*.

rad[1] *noun* (***rad*** *or* ***rads***) *physics* a unit formerly used to measure the amount of ionizing radiation absorbed. [20c: from *r*adiation *a*bsorbed *d*ose]

rad[2] *abbrev* radian.

radar *noun* **1** a system for detecting the presence of ships, aircraft, etc by transmitting short pulses of high-frequency radio waves. **2** the equipment for sending and receiving such radio waves. [20c: from *ra*dio *d*etecting *a*nd *r*anging]

raddle see **ruddle**

raddled *adj* of a person or a person's face: worn out and haggard-looking through debauchery.

radial *adj* **1** spreading out like rays. **2** relating to rays, a radius or radii. **3** along or in the direction of a radius or radii. **4** *anatomy* relating to the **radius**. ▸ *noun* **1** a radiating part. **2** (*in full* **radial-ply tyre**) a tyre with fabric cords laid at right angles to the tread, giving the walls flexibility. ▪ **radially** *adv*. [16c: from Latin *radialis*]

radial symmetry *noun* the arrangement of parts in an object or living organism such that a line drawn through its centre in any direction produces two halves that are mirror images of each other.

radian *noun, geom* (abbrev **rad**) the SI unit of plane angular measurement defined as the angle that is made at the centre of a circle by an arc whose length is equal to the radius of the circle. [19c: from **radius**]

radiant *adj* **1** emitting electromagnetic radiation, eg rays of light or heat. **2** glowing or shining. **3** of a person: beaming with joy, love, hope or health. **4** transmitted by or as radiation. ▸ *noun* **1** a point or object which emits electromagnetic radiation, eg light or heat. **2** *astron* the point in the sky from which meteors appear to radiate outward during a meteor shower. ▪ **radiance** *noun*. ▪ **radiantly** *adv*. [15c: Latin, from *radiare* to radiate]

radiant heat *noun* heat transmitted by electromagnetic radiation.

radiate *verb* **1** to send out rays of light, heat, electromagnetic radiation, etc. **2** *intr* of light, heat, radiation, etc: to be emitted in rays. **3** of a person: to manifestly exhibit (happiness, good health, etc): *radiate vitality*. **4** *tr & intr* to spread or cause (something) to spread out from a central point. ▸ *adj* having rays, radii or a radial structure. [17c: from Latin *radiare* to radiate]

radiation *noun* **1** energy, usu electromagnetic radiation, eg radio waves, microwaves, infrared, visible light, ultraviolet, X-rays, that is emitted from a source and travels in the form of waves or particles through a medium, eg air, or a vacuum. **2** a stream of particles emitted by a radioactive substance.

radiation sickness *noun* illness caused by exposure to high levels of radiation. [20c]

radiator *noun* **1** an apparatus for heating, consisting of a series of pipes through which hot water or hot oil is circulated. **2** an apparatus for heating in which wires are made hot by electricity. **3** an apparatus for cooling an engine, eg in a car, consisting of a series of water-filled tubes and a fan.

radical *adj* **1** concerning or relating to the basic nature or root of something. **2** far-reaching; thoroughgoing: *radical changes*. **3** in favour of or tending to produce reforms. **4** relating to a political, etc group or party in favour of extreme reforms. **5** *med* of treatment: with the purpose of removing the source of a disease: *radical surgery*. **6** *botany* from or relating to the root of a plant. **7** *maths* relating to the root of a number. **8** *linguistics* relating to the roots of words. **9** *slang* excellent, cool, etc: *had a totally radical time*. ▸ *noun* **1** a root or basis in any sense. **2** someone who is a member of a radical political, etc group, or who holds political views. **3** *chem* within a molecule: a group of atoms which remains unchanged during a series of chemical reactions, but is normally incapable of independent existence: *free radical*. **4** *maths* the root of a number. **5** *linguistics* the root of a word. ▪ **radicalism** *noun*. ▪ **radicalize** *or* **-ise** *verb*. ▪ **radically** *adv*. [14c: from Latin *radix* root]

radicchio /ra'diːkɪoʊ/ *noun* a variety of chicory with reddish or purplish leaves used in salads. [20c: Italian, meaning 'chicory']

radices *pl of* **radix**

radicle *noun, botany* **1** the part of a plant embryo which develops into the main root. **2** *anatomy* the rootlike origin of a vein or nerve. [18c: from Latin *radicula* small root]

radii *pl of* **radius**

radio *noun* **1** the use of radio waves to transmit and receive information such as television or radio programmes, telecommunications, and computer data, without connecting wires. **2** a wireless device that receives, and may also transmit, information in this manner. **3** a message or broadcast that is transmitted in this manner. **4** the business or profession of sound broadcasting: *to work in radio*. ▸ *adj* **1** relating to radio. **2** for transmitting by, or transmitted by radio. **3** controlled by radio. ▸ *verb* (***radios, radioed***) **1** to send (a message) to someone by radio. **2** *intr* to broadcast or communicate by radio. [20c: from Latin *radius* spoke, ray]

radio- *combining form, denoting* **1** radio or broadcasting. **2** radioactivity. **3** rays or radiation.

radioactive *adj* relating to or affected by radioactivity.

radioactivity *noun* **1** (*also* **radioactive decay**) the spontaneous disintegration of the nuclei of certain atoms, accompanied by the emission of alpha particles, beta particles or gamma rays. **2** the subatomic particles or radiation emitted during this process.

radio astronomy *noun* **1** astronomical study by means of radar. **2** the study of the radio waves emitted or reflected in space.

radiobiology *noun* the branch of biology concerned with the effects of radiation and radioactive materials on living things.

radiocarbon *noun* a radioactive isotope of carbon, esp carbon-14.

radiocarbon dating *noun* **carbon dating**.

radiochemistry *noun* the branch of chemistry concerned with the study of radioactive elements and their compounds.

radioelement *noun* a **radioisotope**.

radio frequency *noun* a frequency of electromagnetic waves used for radio and television broadcasting.

radio galaxy *noun, astron* a galaxy that is an intense source of cosmic radio waves.

radiogram *noun* **1** a **radiograph** (see under **radiography**). **2** a telegram sent by radio. **3** *old use* an apparatus consisting of a radio and record player.

radiography /reɪdɪ'ɒgrəfɪ/ *noun, med* the examination of the interior of the body by means of recorded images, known as **radiographs**, which are produced by X-rays on photographic film. ▪ **radiographer** *noun*.

radioisotope *noun, physics* a naturally occurring or synthetic radioactive isotope of a chemical element.

radiology /reɪdɪ'ɒlədʒɪ/ *noun* the branch of medicine concerned with the use of **radiation** (eg X-rays) and radioactive isotopes to diagnose and treat diseases. ▪ **radiological** *adj*. ▪ **radiologist** *noun*.

radiophonic /reɪdɪə'fɒnɪk/ *adj* **1** of sound, esp of music: produced electronically. **2** producing electronic music. ▪ **radiophonics** *plural noun*. [19c meaning 'relating to sound produced by radiant energy']

radioscopy /reɪdɪ'ɒskəpɪ/ *noun* the examination of the inside of the body, or of opaque objects, using X-rays. ▪ **radioscopic** /reɪdɪə'skɒpɪk/ *adj*.

radio telephone *noun* a telephone which works by radio waves, used esp in cars and other vehicles.

radio telescope *noun* a large, usu dish-shaped, aerial, together with amplifiers and recording equipment, that is used to study distant stars, galaxies, etc, by detecting the radio waves they emit.

radiotherapy *or* **radiotherapeutics** *noun* the treatment of disease, esp cancer, by X-rays and other forms of radiation. Compare **chemotherapy**.

radio wave *noun, physics* an electromagnetic wave that has a low frequency and a long wavelength, widely used for communication.

radish *noun* a plant of the mustard family, with pungent red-skinned white roots, which are raw in salads. [Anglo-Saxon *rædic*: from Latin *radix* root]

radium *noun, chem* (symbol **Ra**) a silvery-white highly toxic radioactive metallic element, obtained from uranium ores. [19c: from Latin *radius* ray]

radius /'reɪdɪəs/ *noun* (***radii*** /-aɪ/ *or* ***radiuses***) **1** *geom* **a** a straight line running from the centre of a circle or sphere to any point on its circumference; **b** the length of such a line. **2** a radiating line. **3** anything placed like a radius, such as the spoke of a wheel. **4** a distance from a central point, thought of as defining, limiting, etc an area: *houses within a radius of 10km*. **5** *anatomy* **a** the shorter of the two bones in the human forearm, on the thumb side; **b** the equivalent bone in other animals. See also **ulna**. [16c: Latin, meaning 'a rod, spoke or ray']

radix /'reɪdɪks/ *noun* (***radices*** /'reɪdɪsiːz/) **1** a source, root or basis. **2** *maths* the quantity on which a system of numeration or of logarithms, etc is based. [16c: Latin, meaning 'root']

radon /'reɪdɒn/ *noun, chem* (symbol **Rn**) a highly toxic, colourless, extremely dense, radioactive gas that emits alpha particles and is formed by the decay of radium. [20c: from *rad*ium]

RAF *abbrev* Royal Air Force.

raffia *noun* ribbon-like fibre obtained from the leaves of a palm, used for weaving mats, baskets, etc. [19c: a Madagascan word]

raffish *adj* **1** of appearance, dress, behaviour, etc: slightly shady or disreputable, often attractively so; rakish. **2** flashy; vulgar. [19c: from **riff-raff**]

raffle *noun* a **lottery**, often to raise money for charity, in which numbered tickets, which are drawn from a container holding all the numbers sold, win prizes for the holders of the tickets that match the numbers drawn. ▸ *verb* (*also* **raffle off**) to offer in a raffle. [14c: meaning 'a French variety of the game of dice']

raft[1] *noun* **1** a flat structure of logs, timber, etc, fastened together so as to float on water. **2** a flat, floating mass of ice, vegetation, etc. [15c: from Norse *raptr*]

raft[2] *noun* (*often* **raft of**) a large amount or collection.

rafter *noun* a sloping beam supporting a roof. [Anglo-Saxon *ræfter*]

rag[1] *noun* **1** a worn, torn or waste scrap of cloth. **2** a shred, scrap or tiny portion of something. **3** (*usu* **rags**) an old or tattered garment. **4** *informal* a newspaper. [14c: from Anglo-Saxon *raggig* shaggy]

rag[2] *verb* (***ragged, ragging***) **1** to tease. **2** to scold. ▸ *noun* **1** *Brit* a series of stunts and events put on by university or college students to raise money for charity. **2** a prank. [18c]

raga /'rɑːgə/ *noun, music* **1** a traditional pattern of notes in Indian music, around which melodies can be created. **2** a piece of music composed around this pattern. [18c: from Sanskrit *raga*, colour or musical tone]

ragamuffin *noun* **1** a person, usu a child, dressed in rags. **2** **ragga**. [14c: from *Ragamoffyn*, a demon in the poem *Piers Plowman* by William Langland]

rag-and-bone man *noun* someone who collects and deals in old clothes, furniture, etc.

ragbag *noun* **1** a bag for storing rags and scraps of material. **2** *informal* a random or confused collection. **3** *informal* a scruffy untidy person.

rag doll *noun* a doll made from, and often stuffed with, scraps of cloth. [19c]

rage *noun* **1** anger. **2** a passionate outburst, esp of anger. **3** *in compounds* uncontrolled anger or aggression in a particular environment: *air rage*. **4** a violent, stormy action, esp of weather, the sea, etc. **5** an intense desire or passion for something. **6** *infor-*

mal a widespread, usu temporary, fashion or craze. ▸ *verb, intr* **1** to be violently angry. **2** to speak wildly with anger or passion. **3** of the wind, the sea, a battle, etc: to be stormy. ▪ **raging** *adj, noun.* [13c: from French, from Latin *rabies* madness]

IDIOMS **all the rage** *informal* very much in fashion.

ragga *noun* a style of rap music influenced by dance rhythms. Also called **ragamuffin**. [20c: from **ragamuffin** from the scruffy appearance of its exponents]

ragged /ˈragɪd/ *adj* **1** of clothes: old, worn and tattered. **2** of a person: dressed in old, worn, tattered clothing. **3** with a rough and irregular edge; jagged. **4** untidy; straggly. **5** of a performance or ability: uneven; not of consistent quality. ▪ **raggedy** *adj* uneven in quality. [13c: prob from **rag**[1]]

raglan *adj* **1** of a sleeve: attached to a garment by two seams running diagonally from the neck to the armpit. **2** of a garment: having such sleeves. ▸ *noun* an overcoat with the sleeve in one piece with the shoulder. [19c: named after Lord Raglan, British commander in the Crimean War]

ragout /raˈguː/ *noun* a highly seasoned stew of meat and vegetables. ▸ *verb* (***ragouted*** /raˈguːd/, ***ragouting*** /raˈguːɪŋ/) to make a ragout of (meat, etc). [17c: French, from *ragoûter* to revive the appetite]

ragtag *noun* (*usu* **ragtag and bobtail**) the rabble; the common herd. [19c]

ragtime *noun* a type of jazz piano music with a highly syncopated rhythm. [19c: a contraction of **ragged** + **time**]

rag trade *noun, informal* the business of designing, making and selling clothes.

ragworm *noun* a burrowing marine worm, used as bait by fishermen.

raid *noun* **1** a sudden unexpected attack. **2** an air attack. **3** an invasion unauthorized by government. **4** an incursion by police, etc for the purpose of making arrests, or searching for suspected criminals or illicit goods. **5** an onset or onslaught for the purpose of obtaining or suppressing something. **6** *stock exchange slang* the selling of shares by a group of speculators in an attempt to lower share prices. ▸ *verb* **1** to make a raid on (a person, place, etc). **2** *intr* to go on a raid. ▪ **raider** *noun.* [15c Scots, from Anglo-Saxon *rad* incursion]

rail[1] *noun* **1** a bar, usu horizontal and supported by vertical posts. **2** a horizontal bar used to hang things on: *a picture rail.* **3** either of a pair of lengths of metal forming a track for the wheels of a train or other vehicle. **4** the railway as a means of travel or transport: *go by rail.* **5** a horizontal section in panelling or framing. **6** (**the rails**) the fence which forms the inside barrier of a racecourse. ▸ *verb* **1** to provide with rails. **2** (*usu* **rail in** *or* **off**) to enclose or separate (eg a space) within a rail or rails. [13c: from French *reille* iron rod]

IDIOMS **off the rails 1** mad; eccentric. **2** not functioning or behaving normally or properly. **3** disorganized.

rail[2] *verb, intr* (*usu* **rail at** *or* **against**) to complain or criticize abusively or bitterly. [15c: from French *railler* to deride]

rail[3] *noun* a bird with a short neck and wings and long legs, usu found near water. [15c: from French *raale*]

railcar *noun* **1** *US* a railway carriage. **2** a self-propelled railway carriage.

railhead *noun* **1** a railway terminal. **2** the furthest point reached by a railway that is under construction.

railing *noun* **1** fencing or material for building fences. **2** (*often* **railings**) a barrier or ornamental fence, usu of upright iron rods secured by horizontal connections.

raillery *noun* (**-*ies***) **1** good-humoured teasing. **2** an instance of this. [17c: related to **rail**[2]]

railroad *noun, N Am, esp US* a railway. ▸ *verb* to rush or force (someone or something) unfairly (into doing something).

railway *noun* (abbrev **rly**) **1** a track or set of tracks for trains to run on. **2** a system of such tracks, plus all the trains, buildings and people required for it to function. **3** a company responsible for operating such a system. **4** a similar set of tracks for a different type of vehicle: *funicular railway.* [18c]

raiment *noun, archaic, poetic* clothing. [15c: from French *areer* to array]

rain *noun* **1 a** condensed moisture falling as separate water droplets from the atmosphere; **b** a shower; a fall of this. **2** a fall, esp a heavy one, of something: *a rain of bullets.* **3** (**rains**) the season of heavy rainfall in tropical countries. ▸ *verb* **1** *intr* of rain: to fall. **2** *tr & intr* to fall or cause (something) to fall like rain: *rained compliments on her head.* See also **rainy**. [Anglo-Saxon *regn*]

IDIOMS **rain cats and dogs** *informal* to rain very hard. **right as rain** *informal* perfectly all right or in order.

rainbow *noun* **1** an arch of red, orange, yellow, green, blue, indigo and violet seen in the sky when falling raindrops reflect and refract sunlight. **2** a collection or array of bright colours. ▸ *adj* multicoloured like a rainbow. [Anglo-Saxon *regnboga*]

rainbow trout *noun* a large freshwater N American and European trout.

rain check *noun, chiefly N Am* a ticket for future use, given to spectators when a game or sports meeting is cancelled or stopped due to bad weather. [19c]

IDIOMS **take a rain check (on sth)** *informal, orig N Am* to promise to accept (an invitation) at a later date.

raincoat *noun* a waterproof or water-resistant coat.

rainfall *noun* **1** the amount of rain that falls in a certain place over a certain period, measured by depth of water. **2** a shower of rain.

rainforest *noun* forest in tropical regions, which has heavy rainfall.

rainproof *adj* more or less impervious to rain.

rainy *adj* (**-*ier*, -*iest***) characterized by periods of rain or by the presence of much rain: *a rainy afternoon.*

IDIOMS **save** *or* **keep sth for a rainy day** to keep it for a future time of potential need.

raise *verb* **1** to move or lift to a higher position or level. **2** to put in an upright or standing position. **3** to build or erect. **4** to increase the value, amount or strength of something: *raise prices* • *raise one's voice.* **5** to put forward for consideration or discussion: *raise an objection.* **6** to gather together or assemble: *raise an army.* **7** to collect together or obtain (funds, money, etc): *raise money for charity.* **8** to stir up or incite: *raise a protest.* **9** to bring into being; to provoke: *raise a laugh* • *raise the alarm.* **10** to promote to a higher rank. **11** to awaken or arouse from sleep or death. **12** to grow (vegetables, a crop, etc). **13** to bring up or rear (a child, children, etc): *raise a family.* **14** to bring to an end or remove: *raise the siege.* **15** to cause (bread or dough) to rise with yeast. **16** to establish radio contact with. **17** *maths* to increase (a quantity to a given power): *3 raised to the power of 4 is 81.* **18** *cards* to increase a bet. ▶ *noun* **1** an act of raising a bet, etc. **2** *informal, esp N Am* an increase in salary. ▪ **raisable** *or* **raiseable** *adj.* [12c: from Norse *reisa*]

IDIOMS **raise a hand to sb** *or* **sth** to attempt to hit them or it. **raise an eyebrow** *or* **one's eyebrows** to look surprised or shocked. **raise Cain** *or* **the roof** *informal* **1** to make a lot of noise. **2** to be extremely angry. **raise hell** *or* **the devil** *informal* to make a lot of trouble.

---

raise, raze

Be careful not to use the spelling **raise** when you mean **raze**:

A number of villages were razed to the ground.

---

raised beach *noun, geog* an old sea margin above the present water level.

raisin *noun* a dried grape. [13c: French, meaning 'grape']

raison d'être /reɪzɑ̃ 'dɛːtrə/ *noun* (***raisons d'être*** /reɪzɑ̃ 'dɛːtrə/) a purpose or reason that justifies someone's or something's existence. [19c: French, meaning 'reason for being']

raita /raː'iːtə/ *noun* a dish of chopped vegetables, esp cucumber, in yoghurt. [20c: from Hindi *rayta*]

Raj *noun* (*usu* **the Raj**) the British rule of India, 1858–1947. [19c: Hindi, from Sanskrit *rajan* king]

raja *or* **rajah** *noun, hist* an Indian king or prince. [16c: Hindi, from Sanskrit *rajan* king]

rake[1] *noun* **1** a long-handled garden tool with a comb-like part at one end, used for smoothing or breaking up earth, gathering leaves together, etc. **2** any tool with a similar shape or use, eg by a croupier. ▶ *verb* **1** (*usu* **rake up** *or* **together**) to collect, gather or remove with, or as if with, a rake. **2** (*usu* **rake over**) to make smooth with a rake. **3** *intr* to work with, or as if with a rake. **4** *tr & intr* (*often* **rake through**) to search carefully. **5** to sweep gradually along (the length of something), esp with gunfire or one's eyes. **6** to scratch or scrape. [Anglo-Saxon *raca*]

PHRASAL VERBS **rake sth in** *informal* especially of money: to earn or acquire it in large amounts: *must be raking it in!* **rake sth up** *informal* to revive or uncover (something forgotten or lost).

rake[2] *noun, old use* a fashionable man who lives a dissolute and immoral life. ▪ **rakish** *adj.* ▪ **rakishly** *adv.* [17c: from obsolete *rakehell* an utter scoundrel]

rake[3] *noun* **1** a sloping position, esp of a ship's funnel or mast backwards towards the stern, or of a ship's bow or stern in relation to the keel. **2** *theatre* the slope of a stage. **3** the amount by which something slopes. ▶ *verb* **1** to set or construct at a sloping angle. **2** *intr* **a** of a ship's mast or funnel: to slope backwards towards the stern; **b** of a ship's bow or stern: to project out beyond the keel. [17c: perhaps related to German *ragen* to project]

rake-off *noun, informal* a share of the profits, esp when dishonest or illegal.

rallentando *music, adj, adv* (abbrev **rall.**) as a musical direction: becoming gradually slower. ▶ *noun* (***rallentandos, rallentandi***) in a piece of music: a passage to be played in this way. Also called **ritardando** (abbrev **rit.**) [19c: Italian, from *rallentare* to slow down]

rally *verb* (***-ies, -ied***) **1** to come or bring together again after being dispersed. **2** to come or bring together for some common cause or action. **3** *intr* to revive (spirits, strength, abilities, etc) by making an effort. **4** *intr* to recover lost health, fitness, strength, etc, esp after an illness. **5** *intr* of share prices: to increase again after a fall. ▶ *noun* (***-ies***) **1** a reassembling of forces to make a new effort. **2** a mass meeting of people with a common cause or interest. **3** a recovering of lost health, fitness, strength, etc, esp after an illness. **4** *tennis* a series of strokes between players before one of them finally wins the point. **5** a competition to test skill in driving. ▪ **rallier** *noun.* [16c: from French *rallier* to rejoin]

PHRASAL VERBS **rally round sb** to come together to offer support or help them at a time of crisis, etc.

rallycross *noun* motor racing over a course with made-up roads and rough ground.

RAM *abbrev, comput* random access memory, a temporary memory which allows programs to be loaded and run, and data to be changed. Compare **ROM**.

ram *noun* **1** an uncastrated male sheep; a tup. **2** *astrol, astron* (**Ram**) **Aries**. **3** a **battering-ram**. **4** the falling weight of a pile-driver. **5** the striking head of a steam hammer. **6** **a** a piston or plunger operated by hydraulic or other power; **b** a machine with such a piston. ▶ *verb* (***rammed, ramming***) **1** to force (something) down or into position by pushing hard. **2** to strike or crash (something) violently (against, into, etc something or someone): *ram the car into the wall.* ▪ **rammer** *noun.* [Anglo-Saxon *ramm*]

IDIOMS **ram sth down sb's throat** *informal* to force them to believe, accept or listen to a statement, idea, etc by talking about it or repeating it constantly. **ram sth home** to emphasize it forcefully.

Rama *noun, Hinduism* an incarnation of the god **Vishnu**.

Ramadan *or* **Ramadhan** *noun* **1** the ninth month of the Muslim year, during which Muslims fast between sunrise and sunset. **2** the fast itself. [15c: Arabic, from *ramada* to be heated or hot]

ramble *verb, intr* **1** to go for a long walk or walks, esp in the countryside, for pleasure. **2** (*often* **ramble on**) to speak or write, often at length, in an aimless or confused way. ▶ *noun* a walk, usu in the countryside, for pleasure. ▪ **rambler** *noun* **1** someone who rambles. **2** a climbing plant, esp a rose. [17c: prob related to Dutch *rammelen* (of animals) to roam about when on heat]

rambling *noun* walking for pleasure, esp in the countryside. ▶ *adj* **1** wandering; nomadic. **2** of a building, etc: extending without any obvious plan or organization: *a large rambling castle.* **3** of speech, etc: confused, disorganized and often lengthy. **4** of a plant: climbing, trailing or spreading freely: *a rambling rose.*

ramekin /'raməkɪn/ *noun* **1** a small round straight-sided baking dish or mould for a single serving of food. **2** food served in such a dish. [17c: from French *ramequin*]

ramification *noun* **1** an arrangement of branches; a branched structure. **2** a single part or section of a complex subject, plot, situation, etc. **3** (*usu* **ramifications**) a consequence, esp a serious, complicated and unwelcome one. [17c: from Latin *ramus* branch]

ramify *verb* (**-*ies*, -*ied***) to separate or cause to separate into branches or sections.

ramp[1] *noun* **1** a sloping surface between two different levels. **2** a set of movable stairs for entering and leaving an aircraft. **3** a low hump across a road, designed to slow traffic down. ▶ *verb* **1** to provide with a ramp. **2** *intr* to slope from one level to another. **3** *intr* (*often* **ramp around** *or* **about**) to dash about in a wild, violent and threatening way. [18c: from French *ramper* (of an animal) to creep or rear]

ramp[2] *noun, slang* a swindle, esp exploitation to increase the price of a commodity. ▶ *verb* **1** *slang* to rob or swindle. **2** *commerce* (*usu* **ramp up**) to increase greatly (the price of shares, etc), usu dishonestly and for financial advantage. [16c, meaning 'snatch']

rampage *verb* /ram'peɪdʒ/ *intr* to rush about wildly, angrily, violently or excitedly. ▶ *noun* /'rampeɪdʒ/ (*chiefly* **on the rampage**) storming about or behaving wildly and violently in anger, excitement, exuberance, etc. [18c: orig Scottish, prob related to **ramp**[1]]

rampant *adj* **1** uncontrolled; unrestrained: *rampant discrimination*. **2** unchecked: *rampant plant growth*. **3** *heraldry, following its noun* of an animal: in profile and standing erect on the left hind leg with the other legs raised: *lion rampant*. [14c: related to **ramp**[1]]

rampart *noun* **1** a broad mound or wall for defence, usu with a wall or parapet on top. **2** anything which performs such a defensive role. [16c: from French *remparer* to defend, to fortify]

ram-raid *noun* a raid where the front window of a shop or store is smashed with a heavy vehicle and goods are looted. ▪ **ram-raider** *noun*. ▪ **ram-raiding** *noun*.

ramrod *noun* **1** a rod for ramming charge down into, or for cleaning, the barrel of a gun. **2** a strict, stern and inflexible person.

ramshackle *adj* of a building, car, etc: badly made or poorly maintained and so likely to fall down or break down. [19c: from obsolete *ranshackle* to ransack]

ran *past tense of* **run**

ranch *noun* **1** *esp N Am & Aust* **a** an extensive grassland stock farm where sheep, cattle or horses are raised; **b** such a farm including its buildings and the people employed on it. **2** any large farm that specializes in the production of a particular crop or animal: *a mink ranch*. ▶ *verb* to farm on a ranch. ▪ **rancher** *noun*. [19c: from Mexican Spanish *rancho* messroom]

rancid *adj* of stale butter, oil, etc: tasting or smelling rank or sour. ▪ **rancidity** *or* **rancidness** *noun*. [17c: from Latin *rancere* to stink]

rancour *or* (*N Am*) **rancor** *noun* a long-lasting feeling of bitterness, dislike or hatred. ▪ **rancorous** *adj*. [14c: French, from Latin *rancor* rankness]

rand *noun* (***rand*** *or* ***rands***) (abbrev **R**) the standard monetary unit used in South Africa and some neighbouring countries. See also **Krugerrand**. [20c: named after Witwatersrand, a large gold-mining area]

R & B *abbrev* rhythm and blues.

R & D *abbrev* research and development.

random *adj* lacking a definite plan, system or order; haphazard; irregular. ▪ **randomly** *adv*. ▪ **randomness** *noun*. [14c: from French *randir* to gallop]

IDIOMS **at random** without any particular plan, system or purpose; haphazardly: *chosen at random*.

random access *noun, comput* a method of accessing data stored on a disk or in the memory of a computer without having to read any other data stored on the same device, ie the data can be read out of sequence.

random access memory see **RAM**

R & R *abbrev, orig US informal* rest and recreation.

ranee see **rani**

rang *past tense of* **ring**[2]

---

rang, rung

Be careful not to confuse these two forms of the verb **ring**. **Rang** is the past tense:

Ashok rang the bell.

Rung is the past participle, which is used in constructions such as:

Ashok had already rung the bell.

---

range *noun* **1** **a** an area between limits within which things may move, function, etc; **b** the limits forming this area. **2** a number of items, products, etc forming a distinct series. **3** *music* the distance between the lowest and highest notes which may be produced by a musical instrument or a singing voice. **4** the distance to which a gun may be fired or an object thrown. **5** the distance between a weapon and its target. **6** the distance that can be covered by a vehicle without its needing to refuel. **7** an area where shooting may be practised and rockets tested: *firing range*. **8** a group of mountains forming a distinct series or row. **9** *N Am* a large area of open land for grazing livestock. **10** the region over which a plant or animal is distributed. **11** *maths* the set of values that a function or dependent variable may take. **12** *statistics* the difference between the greatest and least values in a set of data. **13** an enclosed kitchen fireplace fitted with a large cooking stove with one or more ovens and a flat top for pans. ▶ *verb* **1** to put in a row or rows. **2** to put (someone, oneself, etc) into a specified category or group. **3** *intr* to vary or change between specified limits. **4** (*usu* **range over** *or* **through**) to roam freely. **5** *intr* to stretch or extend in a specified direction or over a specified area. [13c: French, from *ranger* to place or position]

rangefinder *noun* an instrument which can estimate the distance of an object.

ranger *noun* **1** someone who looks after a royal or national forest or park. **2** *N Am* a soldier who has been specially trained for raiding and combat; a commando. **3** *N Am* a member of a group of armed men who patrol and police a region. **4** (**Ranger** *or* **Ranger Guide**) *Brit* a member of the senior branch of the Guides.

rangy *adj* (**-*ier*, -*iest***) of a person: with long thin limbs and a slender body.

rani *or* **ranee** *noun, hist* **1** an Indian queen or princess. **2** the wife or widow of a **raja**. [17c: Hindi, from Sanskrit *rajni* queen]

rank[1] *noun* **1** a line or row of people or things. **2** a line of soldiers standing side by side. **3** a position of seniority within an organization, society, the armed forces, etc. **4** a distinct class or group, eg according to ability. **5** high social position or status. **6** (**the ranks**) ordinary soldiers, eg privates and corporals, as opposed to officers. **7** *Brit* a place where taxis wait for passengers. **8** *chess* a row of squares along the player's side of a chessboard. Compare **file**[1] (*noun* sense 5). ▸ *verb* **1** to arrange (people or things) in a row or line. **2** *tr & intr* to give or have a particular grade, position or status in relation to others. **3** to have a higher position, status, etc (than someone else). [16c: from French *renc* rank, row]

IDIOMS **close ranks** of a group of people: to keep their solidarity. **pull rank** to use rank or status to achieve something. **the rank and file 1** the ordinary members of an organization or society as opposed to the leaders or principal members. **2** the ordinary soldiers as opposed to the officers.

rank[2] *adj* **1** of eg plants: coarsely overgrown and untidy. **2** offensively strong in smell or taste. **3** bold, open and shocking: *rank disobedience*. **4** complete; utter: *a rank beginner*. [Anglo-Saxon *ranc* proud or overbearing]

rankle *verb, intr* to continue to cause feelings of annoyance or bitterness. [14c: from French *raoncle* or *rancle*, from Latin *dracunculus* a small dragon]

ransack *verb* **1** to search (a house, etc) thoroughly and often destructively. **2** to rob or plunder. ▪ **ransacker** *noun*. [13c: from Norse *rann* house + *skja* to seek]

ransom *noun* money demanded in return for the release of a kidnapped person, or for the return of property, etc. ▸ *verb* to pay, demand or accept a ransom. [14c: from French *ransoun*, from Latin *redemptio* redemption]

IDIOMS **hold sb to ransom 1** to keep them prisoner until a ransom is paid. **2** to blackmail them into agreeing to demands.

rant *verb* **1** *intr* to talk in a loud, angry, pompous way. **2** *tr & intr* to declaim in a loud, self-important, pompous way. ▸ *noun* **1** loud, pompous, empty speech. **2** an angry tirade. ▪ **ranting** *noun, adj*. [16c: from Dutch *ranten* to rave]

rap[1] *noun* **1 a** a quick short tap or blow; **b** the sound made by this. **2** *slang* blame or punishment: *take the rap*. **3** a fast rhythmic monologue recited over a musical backing with a pronounced beat. **4 rap music**. **5** *informal* a conversation. ▸ *verb* (***rapped, rapping***) **1** to strike sharply. **2** *intr* to make a sharp tapping sound. **3** to criticize sharply. **4** *intr, informal* to talk or have a discussion. ▪ **rapper** *noun* a performer of rap music. [14c: prob from Norse]

rap[2] *noun* the least bit: *not care a rap*. [19c: from the name of an 18c Irish counterfeit coin]

rapacious *adj* **1** greedy and grasping, esp for money. **2** of an animal or bird: living by catching prey. ▪ **rapaciously** *adv*. ▪ **rapaciousness** *or* **rapacity** *noun*. [17c: from Latin *rapere* to seize]

rape[1] *noun* **1** the crime of forcing a person, esp a woman, to have sexual intercourse against their will. **2** violation, despoiling or abuse. ▸ *verb* **1** to commit rape on (someone). **2** to violate or despoil (esp a country or place in wartime). ▪ **rapist** *noun*. [14c: from Latin *rapere* to seize]

rape[2] *noun* **oilseed rape**. [14c: from Latin *rapum* turnip]

rapid *adj* **1** moving, acting or happening quickly; fast. **2** requiring or taking only a short time. ▸ *noun* (*usu* **rapids**) a part of a river where the water flows quickly, usu over sharply descending rocks. ▪ **rapidity** *or* **rapidness** *noun*. [17c: from Latin *rapere* to seize]

rapid eye movement *noun, physiol* (abbrev **REM**) quick movements of the eyes behind the closed eyelids during REM sleep.

rapid-fire *adj* fired, asked, etc in quick succession.

rapier /ˈreɪpɪə(r)/ *noun* a long thin sword for thrusting. ▸ *adj* sharp: *rapier wit*. [16c: from French *rapière*]

rapine /ˈrapaɪn/ *noun* plundering; robbery. [15c: from Latin *rapere* to seize]

rapist see under **rape**[1]

rap music *noun* a style of music that has a strong background beat and rhythmic monologues.

rapport /raˈpɔː(r)/ *noun* a feeling of sympathy and understanding; a close emotional bond. [15c: French, from *rapprocher* to bring back]

rapprochement /raˈprɒʃmɑ̃/ *noun* the establishment or renewal of a close, friendly relationship, esp between states. [19c: French, from *rapprocher* to bring back]

rapscallion *noun, old use* a rascal or scamp. [17c: perhaps related to **rascal**]

rapt *adj* **1** enraptured; entranced. **2** completely absorbed. ▪ **raptly** *adv*. [14c: from Latin *rapere* to seize]

raptor *noun* a bird of prey. ▪ **raptorial** *adj*. [17c: Latin, meaning 'plunderer']

rapture *noun* **1** great delight; ecstasy. **2** (**raptures**) great enthusiasm or pleasure: *was in raptures about the concert*. ▪ **rapturous** *adj*. [17c: related to **rapt**]

rare[1] *adj* **1** not done, found or occurring very often; unusual. **2** excellent; unusually good: *a rare old treat*. **3** of a gas, etc: lacking the usual density. ▪ **rarely** *adv*. ▪ **rareness** *noun*. [14c: from Latin *rarus* sparse]

rare[2] *adj* of meat, esp a steak: lightly cooked, and often still bloody. Compare **medium** (*adj* sense 3), **well-done**. [18c: from Anglo-Saxon *hrere* lightly boiled]

rarebit see **Welsh rabbit**

rare earth *noun, chem* **1** a metallic element in the lanthanide series. **2** an oxide of such an element.

rarefied /ˈrɛərɪfaɪd/ *adj* **1** of the air, atmosphere, etc: thin; with a very low oxygen content. **2** refined; select; exclusive: *moves in rarefied circles*.

rarefy /ˈrɛərɪfaɪ/ *verb* (***-ies, -ied***) **1** to make or become rarer, or less dense or solid. **2** to refine or purify. ▪ **rarefaction** *noun*. ▪ **rarefactive** *adj*. [14c: from French *raréfier*, from Latin *rarus* rare + *facere* to make]

rare gas *noun* a **noble gas**.

raring *adj, informal* (**raring to go**) keen and enthusiastic; very willing and ready. [20c: related to **rear**[2]]

rarity *noun* (***-ies***) **1** uncommonness. **2** something valued because it is rare.

rascal *noun* **1** a rogue. **2** a cheeky or mischievous child. ▪ **rascally** *adj*. [14c: from French *rascaille* the rabble]

rase *verb* see **raze**

rash[1] *adj* **1** of an action, etc: **a** overhasty; reckless; **b** done without considering the consequences. **2** of a person: lacking in caution; impetuous. ▪ **rashly** *adv*. ▪ **rashness** *noun*. [14c]

rash[2] *noun* **1** an outbreak of red spots or patches on the skin, usu a symptom of an infectious disease or of a skin allergy. **2** a large number of instances (of something happening) at the same time or in the same place: *a rash of burglaries.* [18c: from French *rasche*, from Latin *radere* to scratch or scrape]

rasher *noun* a thin slice of bacon or ham. [16c]

rasp *noun* **1 a** a coarse, rough file; **b** any tool with a similar surface. **2** a harsh, rough, grating sound or feeling. ▸ *verb* **1** to scrape roughly, esp with a rasp. **2** to grate upon or irritate (eg someone's nerves). **3** to speak or utter in a harsh, grating voice. ▪ **rasping** *adj.* ▪ **raspy** *adj* (**-*ier***, **-*iest***). [16c: from French *rasper* to scrape]

raspberry *noun* (**-*ies***) **1** a cone-shaped berry, usu reddish in colour. **2** a deciduous shrub with thorny canes that is cultivated for these berries. **3 a** a sound expressing disapproval or contempt, made by blowing through the lips. **b** *slang* a refusal or a rebuke. ▸ *adj* **1** having a reddish colour like a raspberry. **2** tasting of or made from raspberries. [17c]

Rastafarian /rastə'fɛərɪən/ *or* **Rastaman** *noun* a follower of an originally West Indian cultural movement, which reveres Haile Selassie (1891–1975), the former Emperor of Ethiopia, as divine. Often shortened to **Rasta**. ▸ *adj* (*also* **Rastafari**) relating to or characteristic of Rastafarians. ▪ **Rastafarianism** *noun.* [1950s: from *Ras Tafari*, the name and title of Haile Selassie]

raster *noun* a set of scanning lines on a television or computer screen, seen as a rectangular patch of light on which the image is reproduced. [Perhaps from Latin *rastrum* rake]

rat *noun* **1** a rodent, similar to a mouse but larger. **2** any of various unrelated but similar rodents, eg the kangaroo rat. **3** *informal* someone who is disloyal to a friend, political party, etc. **4** *informal* a strikebreaker; a blackleg. **5** *informal* a despicable person. ▸ *verb* (***ratted, ratting***) *intr* **1** to hunt or chase rats. **2** (*usu* **rat on**) *informal* to betray, let down or inform on (someone). [Anglo-Saxon *ræt*]

ratafia /ratə'fɪə/ *noun* **1** a liqueur flavoured with fruit kernels and almonds. **2** an almond-flavoured biscuit or small cake. [17c: French]

ratan see **rattan**

rat-a-tat-tat *noun* a sound of knocking on a door. [17c: imitating the sound of a series of knocks]

ratatouille /ratə'tuːɪ/ *noun* a vegetable dish made with tomatoes, peppers, courgettes, aubergines, onions and garlic simmered in olive oil. [19c: French, from *touiller* to stir]

ratchet *noun* **1** a bar which fits into the notches of a toothed wheel causing the wheel to turn in one direction only. **2** (*also* **ratchet-wheel**) a wheel with a toothed rim. **3** the mechanism of such a bar and toothed wheel together. [17c: from French *rochet* a blunt head, eg of a lance]

rate[1] *noun* **1** the number of times something happens, etc within a given period of time; the amount of something considered in relation to, or measured according to, another amount: *a high suicide rate* • *at the rate of 40kph.* **2** a price or charge, often measured per unit: *the rate of pay for the job.* **3** a price or charge fixed according to a standard scale: *rate of exchange.* **4** class or rank: *second-rate.* **5** the speed of movement or change: *rate of progress.* ▸ *verb* **1** to give a value to: *rate him number two in the world.* **2** to be worthy of: *an answer that doesn't rate full marks.* **3** *intr* (*usu* **rate as**) to be placed in a certain class or rank: *rates as the best book on the subject.* [15c: from Latin *reri* to reckon]

IDIOMS **at any rate** in any case; anyway. **at this** *or* **that rate** if this or that is or continues to be the case.

rate[2] *verb* to scold or rebuke severely. [14c]

rateable *or* **ratable** *adj* **1 a** of property: able to have its value assessed for the purpose of payment of **rates**; **b** liable to payment of rates. **2** able to be rated or evaluated.

rateable value *noun* the assessed value of a property, used to calculate the **rates** to be paid on it.

rate-cap *verb* of central government: to set an upper limit on the level of **rates** that can be levied by a local authority. ▪ **rate-capping** *noun.* See also **cap** (*verb* sense 4).

ratepayer *noun, Brit* a person who would have paid, or institution that pays, local **rates**.

rates *plural noun* **1** in the UK: a tax paid by a business, based on the assessed value of property and land owned or leased and collected by a local authority to pay for public services. **2** in the UK until 1990: a tax payable by each household and collected by a local authority to pay for public services based on the assessed value of their property, replaced by **council tax**.

rather *adv* **1 a** more readily; more willingly; **b** in preference: *I'd rather go to the cinema than watch TV.* **2** more truly or correctly: *my parents, or rather my mother and stepfather.* **3** to a limited degree; slightly: *It's rather good.* **4** on the contrary: *She said she'd help me; rather, she just sat around watching TV.* ▸ *exclam* yes indeed; very much: *Would you like a chocolate? Rather!* [Anglo-Saxon *hrathor*]

ratify *verb* (**-*ies***, **-*ied***) to give formal consent to (eg a treaty, agreement, etc), esp by signature. ▪ **ratification** *noun.* [14c: from Latin *ratificare*]

rating *noun* **1** a classification according to order, rank or value. **2** *Brit* an ordinary seaman. **3** an estimated value of a person's position, esp as regards credit. **4** a measure of a TV or radio programme's popularity based on its estimated audience.

ratio *noun* the number or degree of one class of things in relation to another, or between one thing and another, expressed as a proportion. [17c: from Latin *reri* to reckon]

ration *noun* **1** a fixed allowance of food, clothing, petrol, etc, during a time of war or shortage. **2** (**rations**) a daily allowance of food, esp in the army. ▸ *verb* **1** (*often* **ration out**) to distribute or share out (esp something that is in short supply). **2** to restrict (the supply of provisions, etc). [16c: French, from Latin *ratio* reason]

rational *adj* **1** related to or based on reason or logic. **2** able to think, form opinions, make judgements, etc. **3** sensible; reasonable. **4** sane. **5** *maths* of a quantity, ratio, root: able to be expressed as a ratio of whole numbers. ▪ **rationality** *noun.* ▪ **rationally** *adv.* [14c: from Latin *ratio* reason]

rationale /raʃə'nɑːl/ *noun* the underlying principle or reason on which something is based. [17c: from Latin *rationalis* rational]

rationalism *noun* the theory that an individual's actions and beliefs should be based on reason rather than on intuition or the teachings of others. ▪ **rationalist** *noun*. ▪ **rationalistic** *adj*.

rationalize *or* **-ise** *verb* **1** to attribute (something) to sensible, well-thought-out reasons or motives, esp after the event. **2** *intr* to explain one's behaviour, etc in this way. **3** to make something logical or rational. **4** to make (an industry or organization) more efficient and profitable by reorganization to lower costs, etc. **5** *maths* to make (a number) rational, especially by expressing the denominator of a fraction so that it does not contain a root. ▪ **rationalization** *noun*.

rational number *noun, maths* any number that can be expressed as a ratio of two integers, eg $^2/_3$. Compare **irrational number**.

rat race *noun, informal* the fierce, unending competition for success, wealth, etc in business, society, etc.

rattan *or* **ratan** *noun* **1** a climbing palm with very long thin tough stems. **2** a cane made from the stem of this palm. [17c: from Malay *rotan*]

rattle *verb* **1** *intr* to make a series of short sharp hard sounds in quick succession. **2** to cause (eg crockery) to make such a noise. **3** *intr* to move along rapidly, often with a rattling noise. **4** *intr* (*usu* **rattle on**) to chatter thoughtlessly or idly. **5** *informal* to make anxious, nervous or upset. ▸ *noun* **1** a series of short sharp sounds. **2** a baby's toy made of a container filled with small pellets which rattle when it is shaken. **3** a device for making a whirring sound, used esp at football matches. **4** the loose horny structures at the end of a rattlesnake's tail, which produce a rattling sound when vibrated. [14c]
PHRASAL VERBS **rattle sth off** to say, recite or write it rapidly. **rattle through sth** to complete it quickly.

rattler *noun, informal* a rattlesnake.

rattlesnake *noun* a poisonous American snake with a series of dry horny structures at the end of its tail, producing a characteristic rattling sound.

rattling *adj, adv, informal, old use* **1** smart or smartly. **2** brisk or briskly. **3** as a general intensifying word: good or well; very: *told us a rattling good yarn*.

ratty *adj* (**-ier, -iest**) **1** like a rat. **2** *informal* irritable.

raucous *adj* of a sound, esp a voice: hoarse; harsh. ▪ **raucously** *adv*. [18c: from Latin *raucus* hoarse]

raunchy *adj* (**-ier, -iest**) *informal* coarsely or openly sexual; lewd or smutty. ▪ **raunchiness** *noun*. [20c]

ravage *verb, tr & intr* to destroy or cause extensive damage to. ▸ *noun* (*usu* **ravages**) damage or destruction: *the ravages of time*. [17c: from French *ravir* to ravish]

rave *verb* **1** *intr* to talk wildly as if mad or delirious. **2** *intr* (*usu* **rave about** *or* **over**) to talk enthusiastically or passionately about something. ▸ *noun, informal* **1** extravagant praise. **2** a **rave-up**. **3** a gathering in a large warehouse or open-air venue for dancing to dance, etc music. ▸ *adj, informal* extremely enthusiastic: *rave reviews*. [14c]

ravel *verb* (***ravelled, ravelling***; *US* ***raveled, raveling***) **1** *tr & intr* to tangle or become tangled up. **2** (*usu* **ravel out**) **a** to untangle, unravel or untwist; **b** to resolve, explain or make clear. **3** *intr* to fray. ▸ *noun* **1** a tangle or knot. **2** a complication. **3** a loose or broken thread. [16c: perhaps from Dutch *ravelen* to tangle]

raven *noun* a large blue-black bird of the crow family. ▸ *adj* glossy blue-black in colour: *raven hair*. [Anglo-Saxon *hræfn*]

ravenous *adj* **1** extremely hungry or greedy. **2** of hunger, a desire, etc: intensely strong. **3** of an animal, etc: living on prey; predatory. ▪ **ravenously** *adv*. [15c: from *raven* to devour or hunt for food]

raver *noun, informal* **1** someone who leads a full, very lively and often wild social life. **2** someone who attends a **rave** (*noun* sense 3).

rave-up *noun, informal* a lively party or celebration.

ravine /rəˈviːn/ *noun* a deep narrow steep-sided gorge. [15c: from French *ravine* a violent rush (of water)]

raving *verb, present participle of* **rave**. ▸ *adj & adv* **1** frenzied; delirious. **2** *informal* great; extreme: *a raving beauty*. ▸ *noun* (*usu* **ravings**) wild, frenzied or delirious talk.

ravioli *singular or plural noun* small square pasta cases with a savoury filling of meat, cheese, etc. [19c: Italian]

ravish *verb* **1** to overwhelm with joy, delight, etc. **2** to rape. ▪ **ravishing** *adj* delightful; lovely; very attractive.

raw *adj* **1** of meat, vegetables, etc: not cooked. **2** not processed, purified or refined: *raw silk*. **3** of alcoholic spirit: undiluted. **4** of statistics, data, etc: not analysed. **5** of a person: not trained or experienced. **6** of a wound, etc: with a sore, inflamed surface. **7** of the weather: cold and damp. **8** of an edge of material: not finished off and so liable to fray. **9** particularly sensitive: *touched a raw nerve*. [Anglo-Saxon *hreaw*]
IDIOMS **get a raw deal** *informal* get harsh, unfair treatment. **in the raw** in a natural or crude state.

rawboned *adj* lean and gaunt.

rawhide *noun* **1** untanned leather. **2** a whip made from this.

raw material *noun* a substance in its natural state, used as the basis for a manufacturing process.

ray[1] *noun* **1** a narrow beam of light or radioactive particles. **2** a set of lines fanning out from a central point. **3** a small amount (of hope, understanding, etc). [14c: from French *rai*, from Latin *radius* rod]

ray[2] *noun* a cartilaginous fish with a flattened body and extended pectoral fins, eg a stingray, manta ray. [14c: from French *raie*, from Latin *raia*]

ray[3] *or* **re** *noun, music* in sol-fa notation: the second note of the major scale. [14c: see **sol-fa**]

rayon *noun* an artificial fibre or fabrics used to make clothing, conveyor belts, hoses, etc. [20c: from **ray**[1]]

raze *or* **rase** *verb* to destroy (buildings, a town, etc) completely. [16c: from Latin *radere* to scrape]

razor *noun* a sharp-edged instrument used for shaving. ▸ *verb* **1** to use a razor on. **2** to shave or cut, esp closely. [13c: from French *raser* to shave]

razorbill *noun* a seabird with a sharp-edged bill.

razor edge *noun* **1** a very fine sharp edge. **2** *informal* a critical delicately balanced situation.

razor shell *noun* a burrowing marine bivalve with two similar elongated shell valves.

razor wire *noun* thick wire with sharp pieces of metal attached, used for fences, etc.

razzle *noun, slang* a lively spree, outing or party, esp involving a lot of drinking: *out on the razzle*. [20c: from **razzle-dazzle**]

razzle-dazzle *noun, slang* **1** excitement, confusion, dazzling show, etc. **2** a lively spree. [19c: reduplication of **dazzle**]

razzmatazz *noun* **1** razzle-dazzle. **2** humbug. [19c]

Rb *symbol, chem* rubidium.

RC *abbrev* **1** Red Cross. **2** Roman Catholic.

Rd *abbrev* used in street names: Road.

RE *abbrev* religious education.

Re *symbol, chem* rhenium.

re[1] *prep* with regard to; concerning: *re your letter of 18th*. [18c: from Latin *res* thing]

re[2] see **ray**[3]

re- *prefix, denoting* **1** motion backwards or away, withdrawal, reversal, etc: *recede* • *recant*. **2** again, or again and in a different way: *reread* • *rewrite*. [Latin]

're *verb* contraction of **are**[1]: *We're going to Paris*.

reach *verb* **1** to arrive at or get as far as (a place, position, etc). **2** *tr & intr* to be able to touch or get hold of. **3** *tr & intr* to project or extend to a point. **4** *intr* (*usu* **reach across**, **out**, **up**, *etc*) to stretch out one's arm to try to touch or get hold of (something). **5** *informal* to hand or pass: *Can you reach me that CD, please?* **6** to make contact or communicate with, esp by telephone: *I couldn't reach her*. ▸ *noun* **1** the distance one can stretch one's arm, hand, etc: *out of reach*. **2** a distance that can be travelled easily: *within reach of London*. **3** an act of reaching out. **4** range of influence, power, understanding or abilities. **5** (*usu* **reaches**) a section with clear limits, eg part of a river or canal between two bends or locks. **6** (*usu* **reaches**) level or rank: *the upper reaches of government*. [Anglo-Saxon *ræcan*]

react *verb* **1** *intr* **a** (*chiefly* **react to**) to act in response to; **b** *loosely* to act or behave. **2** *intr* (*usu* **react against**) **a** to respond to adversely; **b** to act in a contrary or opposing way. **3** *intr, physics* to exert an equal force in the opposite direction. **4** *tr & intr, chem* to undergo or cause to undergo chemical change produced by a **reagent**. [17c: from Latin *re-agere*, from *agere* to do or act]

reactant *noun, chem* a substance which takes part in a chemical reaction.

reaction *noun* **1** a response to stimulus. **2** an action or change in the opposite direction. **3** a change of opinions, feelings, etc. **4** a response showing how someone feels or thinks. **5** opposition to change, esp political change, reform, etc, and a tendency to revert to a former system, or state of affairs. **6** a physical or psychological effect caused by a drug, allergy, etc. **7** *chem* **a** a chemical process in which the electrons surrounding the nuclei in the atoms of one or more elements or compounds react to form one or more new compounds; **b** chemical change. **8** *physics* a nuclear reaction involving a change in an atomic nucleus. **9** *physics* the force offered by a body that is equal in magnitude but opposite in direction to the force applied to it. [17c: from **react**]

reactionary *adj* of a person or policies: relating to or characterized by opposition to change, and often in favour of reverting to a former system, etc. ▸ *noun* (*-ies*) a reactionary person. [19c]

reactive *adj* showing a reaction; liable to react; sensitive to stimuli.

read /riːd/ *verb* (***read*** /rɛd/) **1** to look at and understand (printed or written words). **2** to speak (words which are printed or written). **3** to learn or gain knowledge of by reading: *read the election results in the newspaper*. **4** *intr* to pass one's leisure time reading, esp for pleasure: *She doesn't read much*. **5** to look at or be able to see (something) and get information: *can't read the clock without my glasses*. **6** to interpret or understand the meaning of: *read a map*. **7** to interpret or understand (signs, marks, etc) without using one's eyes: *read Braille*. **8** *intr* to have a certain wording: *The letter reads as follows*. **9** *tr & intr* to think that (a statement, etc) has a particular meaning: *read it as criticism*. **10** *intr* of writing: to convey meaning in a specified way: *an essay that reads well*. **11** of a dial, instrument, etc: to show a particular measurement: *The barometer reads 'fair'*. **12** to replace (a word, phrase, etc) by another: *for 'three' read 'four'*. **13** to study (a subject) at university. **14** to hear and understand: *Do you read me?* **15** *comput* to retrieve (data) from a storage device. ▸ *noun* **1** a period or act of reading. **2** a book, magazine, etc considered in terms of how readable it is: *a good read*. [Anglo-Saxon *rædan*]

IDIOMS **read between the lines** to perceive a meaning that is not stated. **take sth as read** /rɛd/ to accept or assume it.

PHRASAL VERBS **read sth in** *or* **out** *comput* to transfer data from a disk or other storage device into the main memory of a computer. **read sth out** to read it aloud. **read up on sth** to learn a subject by reading books about it.

reader *noun* **1** someone who reads. **2** (*also* **Reader**) *Brit* a university lecturer of a rank between professor and senior lecturer. **3** someone who reads lessons or prayers in a church. **4** a book containing short texts, used for learning to read or for learning a foreign language: *a German reader*. **5** someone who reads and reports on manuscripts for a publisher. **6** someone who reads and corrects proofs.

readership *noun* **1** the total number of people who read a newspaper, etc. **2** (*also* **Readership**) *Brit* the post of reader in a university.

reading *noun* **1** the action of someone who reads. **2** the ability to read: *his reading is poor*. **3** any book, printed material, etc that can be read. **4** an event at which a play, poetry, etc is read to an audience, often by the author. **5** *Brit politics* any one of the three stages in the passage of a bill through Parliament, when it is respectively introduced, discussed, and reported on by a committee. **6** an understanding or interpretation of something written or said, or of circumstances, etc.

readjust *verb* to alter; to return to a previous condition. ▪ **readjustment** *noun*.

read-only memory see **ROM**

read-out *noun, comput* a record or display of data from the main memory of a computer into an external storage device, eg a disk or tape. Compare **printout**.

read-write head see under **disk drive**

read-write memory *noun, comput* a computer memory which allows data to be both read and changed.

ready *adj* (*-ier, -iest*) **1** prepared and available for use or action. **2** willing; eager: *always ready to help*. **3** prompt; quick, usu too quick: *He's always ready to find fault*. **4** likely or about to: *a plant just ready to flower*. ▸ *noun* (**readies**) *informal* short form of

ready money. ▸ *adv* prepared or made beforehand: *ready cooked meals*. ▸ *verb* (*-ies, -ied*) to make ready; to prepare. ▪ **readily** *adv*. ▪ **readiness** *noun*. [Anglo-Saxon *ræde*]

IDIOMS **at the ready 1** of a gun: aimed and ready to be fired. **2** ready for immediate action. **ready, steady, go** *or* **ready, get set, go** a formulaic expression used to start a race.

ready-made *adj* **1** (*also* **ready-to-wear**) of clothes: made to a standard size, not made-to-measure. **2** convenient; useful: *a ready-made excuse*.

ready money *noun, informal* cash for immediate use. Often shortened to **readies**.

ready reckoner *noun* a book of tables listing standard calculations, used in working out interest, etc.

reafforest *verb* to replant trees in a cleared area of land that was formerly forested. ▪ **reafforestation** *noun*.

reagent /riːˈeɪdʒənt/ *noun, chem* **1** a chemical compound that participates in a chemical reaction. **2** a common laboratory chemical with predictable characteristic reactions. [19c: from Latin *reagere* to **react**]

real[1] /rɪəl/ *adj* **1** actually or physically existing; not imaginary. **2** actual; true: *the real reason*. **3** not imitation; genuine; authentic: *real leather*. **4 a** great, important or serious; **b** deserving to be so called: *a real problem*. **5** *law* consisting of or relating to immovable property, such as land and houses. **6** of income, etc: measured in terms of its buying power rather than its nominal value: *in real terms*. **7** *maths* involving or containing only **real numbers**. ▸ *adv, N Am, Scot* really; very: *real nice*. [15c: from French *réel*, from Latin *res* thing]

IDIOMS **for real** *slang* in reality; seriously.

real[2] /reɪˈɑːl/ *noun* (***reals*** *or* ***reales***) **1** the standard monetary unit of Brazil. **2** *hist* a small silver Spanish or Spanish-American coin. [17c: Spanish, from Latin *regalis* royal]

real ale *noun* ale or beer which is allowed to continue to ferment and mature in the cask after brewing.

realign *verb* **1** to put back into alignment. **2** to regroup politically. ▪ **realignment** *noun*.

realise see **realize**

realism *noun* **1** the tendency to consider, accept or deal with things as they really are. **2** a style in art, literature, etc that represents things in a lifelike way. ▪ **realist** *noun*. [19c: from **real[1]**]

realistic *adj* **1** showing awareness or acceptance of things as they really are. **2** representing things as they actually are; lifelike. **3** based on facts. [19c]

reality *noun* (***-ies***) **1** the state or fact of being real. **2** the real nature of something; the truth. **3** something that is not imaginary. [15c: from French *réalité*, from Latin *realis* **real[1]**]

IDIOMS **in reality** as a fact, often as distinct from a thought or idea; actually.

reality TV *noun* a genre of television programme which takes members of the general public as subjects, presenting their daily lives as if they were soap operas or observing them in artificial situations.

realize *or* **-ise** *verb* **1** to become aware of; to know or understand: *realize the danger*. **2** to accomplish or bring into being: *realize my ambitions*. **3** to make real or appear real. **4** to cause to seem real. **5** to convert (property or goods) into money. **6** to make (a sum of money): *realized £45,000 on the sale of the house*. ▪ **realizable** *adj*. ▪ **realization** *noun*. ▪ **realizer** *noun*. [17c: from **real[1]**]

really *adv* **1** actually; in fact. **2** very: *a really lovely day*. ▸ *exclam* expressing surprise, doubt or mild protest.

realm *noun* **1** a kingdom. **2** a domain, province or region. **3** a field of interest, study or activity. [13c: from French *realme*, from Latin *regalis* royal]

the real McCoy *noun* the genuine article.

real number *noun, maths* any rational or irrational number.

realpolitik /reɪˈɑːlpɒlɪtiːk/ *noun* practical politics based on the realities and necessities of life rather than on moral or ethical ideas. [20c: German, meaning 'politics of realism']

real tennis *noun* an early form of tennis played on a walled indoor court. Compare **lawn tennis**.

real time *noun* the actual time during which an event takes place, esp a period which is analysed by a computer as it happens, the data produced during it being processed as it is generated.

realtone *noun* a ringtone that closely resembles an original sound recording.

realtor *noun, N Am* an estate agent. [20c]

ream *noun* **1** 20 **quire**s of paper. **2** (**reams**) *informal* a large quantity: *wrote reams*. [14c: from French *reame*, from Arabic *rizmah* bale]

reap *verb* **1** to cut or gather (grain, etc); to harvest. **2** to clear (a field) by cutting a crop. **3** to receive (esp an advantage or benefit) as a consequence of one's actions. [Anglo-Saxon *ripan*]

reaper *noun* **1** someone who reaps. **2** a reaping machine. **3** (**the Reaper** *or* **the Grim Reaper**) the personification of death.

rear[1] *noun* **1** the back part; the area at the back. **2** of an army, fleet, etc: the part which is farthest away from the enemy. **3** a position behind or to the back. **4** *informal* the buttocks. ▸ *adj* situated or positioned at the back: *rear window*. [17c]

IDIOMS **bring up the rear** to come last.

rear[2] *verb* **1** to bring up (offspring). **2 a** to breed (animals); **b** to grow (crops). **3** to build or erect something. **4** *intr* (*also* **rear up**) of an animal, esp a horse: to rise up on the hind legs. **5** *intr* to reach a great height, esp in relation to surroundings. **6** to move or hold upwards. [Anglo-Saxon *ræran*]

rear admiral *noun* a naval officer of the rank below vice-admiral.

rearguard *noun* **1** a group of soldiers who protect the rear of an army. **2** a conservative or traditional group in a company, organization, political party, etc. [15c: from French *rereguarde*]

rearguard action *noun* **1** military action undertaken by the rearguard. **2** an effort to prevent or delay defeat, eg, in an argument.

rearm *verb* to arm again, esp with new or improved weapons. ▪ **rearmament** *noun*. [19c]

rearmost *adj* last of all; nearest the back.

rearward *adj* positioned in or at the rear. ▸ *adv* (*also* **rearwards**) **1** towards the back. **2** at the back.

rear-wheel drive *noun* a system in which the driving power is transmitted to the rear wheels of a vehicle.

reason *noun* **1** a justification or motive for an action, belief, etc. **2** an underlying explanation or cause. **3** the power to think, form opinions and judgements, reach logical conclusions, etc. **4** sanity; sound mind: *lose your reason*. ▸ *verb* **1** *intr* to form opinions and judgements, reach logical conclusions, deduce, etc. **2** *intr* (*usu* **reason with sb**) to try to persuade them by means of reasonable or sensible argument. **3** (*usu* **reason sth out**) to think it through or set it out logically. [13c: from French *reisun*, from Latin *reri* to think]

IDIOMS **by reason of sth** because of it; as a consequence of it. **it stands to reason** it is obvious or logical. **within reason** in moderation; within the limits of what is sensible or possible.

reasonable *adj* **1** sensible; rational; showing reason or good judgement. **2** willing to listen to reason or argument. **3** in accordance with reason. **4** fair or just; moderate; not extreme or excessive: *a reasonable price*. **5** satisfactory or equal to what one might expect. ▪ **reasonableness** *noun*. ▪ **reasonably** *adv*.

reasoned *adj* well thought out or argued.

reasoning *noun* **1** the forming of judgements or opinions using reason or careful argument. **2** the act or process of deducing logically from evidence. **3** the opinions or judgements formed, or deductions made, in this way.

reassure *verb* **1** to dispel or alleviate the anxiety or worry of. **2** to confirm (someone) in opinion, etc: *reassured him he was correct*. ▪ **reassurance** *noun*. ▪ **reassuring** *adj*. ▪ **reassuringly** *adv*. [16c]

rebate *noun* /'riːbeɪt/ **1** a refund of part of a sum of money paid. **2** a discount. ▸ *verb* /rɪ'beɪt/ to pay as a rebate. [15c: from French *rabattre* to beat back]

rebel *verb* /rɪ'bɛl/ *intr* (***rebelled, rebelling***) (*often* **rebel against**) **1** to resist or fight against authority or oppressive conditions. **2** to refuse to conform to conventional rules of behaviour, dress, etc. **3** to feel aversion or dislike towards something. ▸ *noun* /'rɛbəl/ someone who rebels. ▪ **rebellion** *noun*. [13c: from French *rebelle*, from Latin *bellum* war]

rebellious *adj* **1** rebelling or having a tendency to rebel. **2** characteristic of a rebel or a rebellion. **3** of a difficulty, problem, etc: refractory; unmanageable.

rebirth *noun* **1 a** a second or new birth; **b** reincarnation. **2** any revival, renaissance or renewal. [19c]

reboot *verb, comput* to restart (a computer), either by pressing a specified combination of keys or by switching it off and on again at the power source, done esp when the computer has crashed or hung.

reborn *adj* **1 a** born again; **b** reincarnated. **2** revived or spiritually renewed. **3** converted to Christianity. See also **born-again**. [16c]

rebound *verb* /rɪ'baʊnd/ *intr* **1** to bounce or spring back after an impact. **2** to recover after a setback. **3** (*also* **rebound on** *or* **upon**) of an action: to have a bad effect (on the person performing the action). ▸ *noun* /'riːbaʊnd/ an instance of rebounding; a recoil. [14c: from French *bondir* to bound]

IDIOMS **on the rebound 1** *informal* while still recovering from or reacting to an emotional shock, esp the ending of a love affair or attachment. **2** while bouncing.

rebrand *verb* to market (a product) using a new brand name or image.

rebuff *noun* **1** a slight or snub. **2** a refusal or rejection, esp of someone's help, advice, etc. ▸ *verb* to give a rebuff to. [16c: from French *rebuffer*, from Italian *buffo* a gust or puff]

rebuke *verb* to let (someone thought to have done wrong) know that the action, behaviour, etc is unacceptable; to reprimand. ▸ *noun* a stern reprimand or reproach. [14c: from French *rebuker*, from *bucher* to beat, strike]

rebus /'riːbəs/ *noun* a puzzle where pictures, etc represent words or syllables in order to form a message or phrase. [17c: from French *rébus*, from Latin *res* thing]

rebut *verb* (***rebutted, rebutting***) **1** to disprove or refute (a charge or claim), esp by offering opposing evidence. **2** to drive back. ▪ **rebuttal** *noun*. [13c: from French *rebouter*, from *boter* to butt]

recalcitrant *adj* not willing to accept authority or discipline. ▪ **recalcitrance** *noun*. [19c: from French *récalcitrant*, from Latin *calx* the heel]

recall *verb* /rɪ'kɔːl/ **1** to call back. **2** to order to return. **3** to bring back by a summons. **4** *US* to remove someone from office by vote. **5** to remember. **6** to cancel or revoke. ▸ *noun* /'riːkɔːl/ **1** an act of recalling. **2** the ability to remember accurately and in detail: *total recall*. [16c]

recant *verb* **1** *intr* to revoke a former declaration, belief, etc. **2** *tr & intr* to withdraw or retract (a statement, belief, etc). ▪ **recantation** *noun*. [16c: from Latin *cantare* to sing]

recap *informal, verb* (***recapped, recapping***) to recapitulate. ▸ *noun* recapitulation.

recapitulate *verb* **1** to go over the chief points of (an argument, statement, etc) again. **2** to summarize. **3** *biol* of an embryo: to repeat (stages in the evolutionary development of its species) during embryonic development. ▪ **recapitulation** *noun*. [16c]

recapture *verb* **1** to capture again. **2** to convey, recreate or re-experience (an image, sensation, etc from the past). ▸ *noun* the act of recapturing or fact of being recaptured. [18c]

recce /'rɛkɪ/ *informal, noun* reconnaissance. ▸ *verb* (***recced*** *or* ***recceed, recceing***) to reconnoitre. [20c]

recede *verb, intr* **1** to go or move back or backwards. **2** to become more distant. **3** to bend or slope backwards. **4 a** of hair: to stop growing above the forehead and at the temples; **b** of a person: to go bald gradually in this way. ▪ **receding** *adj*. [15c: from Latin *cedere* to yield]

receipt /rɪ'siːt/ *noun* **1** a printed or written note acknowledging that money, goods, etc have been received. **2** the act of receiving or being received: *We acknowledge receipt of the goods*. **3** (*usu* **receipts**) money received during a given period of time, esp by a shop or business. ▸ *verb* to mark (a bill) as paid. [14c: from French *receite*, from Latin *recipere* to receive]

---

receipt

This word is often misspelt. It has a silent *p* near the end. It might help you to remember the following sentence:

*I want a rec**eipt** for the **extra I paid them**.*

---

receive *verb* **1** to get, be given or accept (something offered, sent, etc). **2** to experience, undergo or suffer: *receive injuries*. **3** to give attention to or consider: *receive a petition.* **4** to learn of or be informed of: *receive word of their arrival.* **5** to react to in a specified way: *The film was badly received.* **6** to admit or accept (an idea, principle, etc) as true. **7** to be awarded (an honour, etc): *receive the OBE.* **8** to support or bear the weight of something. **9** *tr & intr* to be at home to (guests or visitors). **10** to welcome or greet (guests), esp formally. **11** to permit (someone) to become part of a particular body or group, or to take up a certain position: *be received into the priesthood.* **12** *tr & intr, tennis, badminton* to be the player who returns (the opposing player's service). **13** *tr & intr, Christianity* to participate in communion. **14** *tr & intr, chiefly Brit* to buy or deal in (goods one knows are stolen). **15** to change (radio or television signals) into sounds or pictures. [13c: from French *receivre*, from Latin *capere* to take]

receive
This word is often misspelt. The e comes before the *i*. It might help you to remember that receive follows the rule 'i before e, except after c'.

received *adj* generally accepted: *received wisdom.*

Received Pronunciation *noun* (abbrev **RP**) the form of British English spoken by educated people in Southern England.

receiver *noun* **1** someone or something that receives. **2** an officer who receives taxes. **3** (*in full* **official receiver**) a person appointed by a court to manage property under litigation, or take control of the business of someone who has gone bankrupt or who is certified insane. **4** the part of a telephone held to the ear. **5** the equipment in a telephone, radio or television that changes signals into sounds and pictures, or both. **6** *chiefly Brit* a person who receives stolen goods. [14c]

receivership *noun* **1** (*usu* **in receivership**) the status of a business that is under the control of an official receiver. **2** the office of official receiver.

recent *adj* **1** happening, done, having appeared, etc not long ago. **2** fresh; new. **3** modern. **4** (**Recent**) *geol* **Holocene**. ▪ **recency** *noun*. ▪ **recently** *adv*. [16c: from French *récent*, from Latin *recens* fresh]

receptacle *noun* **1** anything that receives, stores or holds something; a container. **2** *botany* the top of a flower stalk, from which the different flower parts arise. [15c: from Latin *receptaculum* reservoir]

reception *noun* **1** the act of receiving or fact of being received. **2** a response, reaction or welcome; the manner in which a person, information, an idea, etc is received: *a hostile reception.* **3** a formal party or social function to welcome guests, esp after a wedding. **4** the quality of radio or television signals received. **5** an area, office or desk where visitors or clients are welcomed on arrival, eg in a hotel or factory: *ask at reception.* [14c: from Latin *receptio*]

receptionist *noun* someone employed in a hotel, office, surgery, etc to deal with clients, visitors and guests, arrange appointments, etc.

receptive *adj* **1** capable of receiving. **2** able and quick to understand. **3** willing to accept new ideas, suggestions, etc. ▪ **receptively** *adv*. ▪ **receptiveness** *or* **receptivity** *noun*. [16c: from French *réceptif*]

receptor *noun, biol* **1** a cell or body part adapted to respond to external stimuli, eg a sense organ or sensory nerve-ending. **2** the area on the surface of a cell to which a specific antigen, drug or hormone may bind. [15c: Latin]

recess *noun* /rɪ'sɛs, 'riːsɛs/ **1** a space, such as a niche or alcove, set in a wall. **2** part of a room formed by a receding of the wall: *dining recess.* **3** (*often* **recesses**) a hidden, inner or secret place: *the dark recesses of her mind.* **4** a temporary break from work, esp of a law-court, Parliament, etc during a vacation: *summer recess.* **5** *N Am* a short break between school classes. **6** *anatomy* a small indentation or cavity in an organ. ▸ *verb* /rɪ'sɛs/ **1** to put something in a recess. **2** to make a recess in (a wall, etc). **3** *intr* of a law-court, Parliament, etc: to take a break or adjourn. ▪ **recessed** *adj*. [16c: from Latin *recedere* to recede]

recession *noun* **1** the act of receding or state of being set back. **2** a temporary decline in economic activity, trade and prosperity. [17c]

recessive *adj* **1** tending to recede. **2** *biol* denoting a characteristic that is only present when it comes from a gene that is paired with a gene that gives the same characteristic. Compare **dominant**.

recherché /rə'ʃɛəʃeɪ/ *adj* **1** rare, exotic or particularly exquisite. **2** obscure and affected. [17c: French, from *rechercher* to seek out]

recidivism /rɪ'sɪdɪvɪzəm/ *noun* the habit of relapsing into crime. ▪ **recidivist** *noun, adj*. [19c: from French *récidivisme*, from Latin *recidere* to fall back]

recipe *noun* directions for making something, esp for preparing and cooking food, usu consisting of a list of ingredients and instructions point-by-point. [14c: Latin, orig meaning 'take' or 'take it']

recipient *noun* a person or thing that receives something. ▸ *adj* receiving; receptive. [16c: from French *récipient*, from Latin *recipere* to receive]

reciprocal /rɪ'sɪprəkəl/ *adj* **1 a** giving and receiving, or given and received; mutual; **b** complementary. **2** *grammar* of a pronoun: expressing a relationship between two people or things, or mutual action, eg, *one another* in *John and Mary love one another.* ▸ *noun* **1** something that is reciprocal. **2** *maths* the value obtained when 1 is divided by the number concerned, eg, the reciprocal of 4 is $\frac{1}{4}$. [16c: from Latin *reciprocus* alternating]

reciprocate *verb* **1 a** to give and receive mutually; to interchange; **b** to return (affection, love, etc). **2** *intr* of part of a machine: to move backwards and forwards. ▪ **reciprocation** *noun*. [17c: from Latin *reciprocare, reciprocatum*]

reciprocity *noun* (**-ies**) **1** reciprocal action. **2** a mutual exchange of privileges or advantages between countries, trade organizations, businesses, etc. [18c]

recital /rɪ'saɪtəl/ *noun* **1** a public performance of music, usu by a soloist or a small group. **2** a detailed statement or list of something; an enumeration. **3** an act of reciting or repeating something learned or prepared, esp in front of other people. ▪ **recitalist** *noun*. [16c]

recitation *noun* **1** an act or instance of reciting something. **2** something recited or a particular style or quality of reciting something.

recitative /rɛsɪtə'tiːv/ *noun, music* **1** a style of singing resembling speech, used for narrative passages in opera or in oratorio. **2** a passage sung in this way. [17c: from Italian *recitativo*]

recite *verb* **1** to repeat aloud (a poem, etc) from memory, esp before an audience. **2** to make a detailed statement; to list: *recited his grievances.* [15c: from Latin]

reckless *adj* without consideration of the consequences, danger, etc; rash. [Anglo-Saxon *recceleas*]

reckon *verb* **1** (*also* **reckon up**) to calculate, compute or estimate. **2** to regard, consider or class as: *reckon him among my friends.* **3** (*usu* **reckon that**) *informal* to think or suppose: *I reckon it's going to rain.* **4** (*usu* **reckon on sb** *or* **sth**) to rely on or expect them or it: *We reckoned on their support.* [Anglo-Saxon (ge)*recenian* to recount or explain]

IDIOMS **to be reckoned with** of considerable importance or power that is not to be ignored.

reckoner *noun* **1** someone or something that reckons. **2** a **ready reckoner**.

reckoning *noun* **1 a** calculation; counting; **b** estimation; conjecture: *By my reckoning, we must be about eight miles from the town.* **2** an account or bill. **3** a settling of an account, debt, grievance, etc.

reclaim *verb* **1** to seek to regain possession of. **2** to make (land) available for agricultural or commercial use. **3** to recover useful materials from industrial or domestic waste. **4** *old use* to reform or convert (someone) from evil, etc. ▶ *noun* the action of reclaiming something or someone, or the state of being reclaimed. ▪ **reclamation** *noun.* [13c: from French *réclamer*]

recline *verb* **1** *intr* to lean or lie back, esp when resting. **2** to lean or lay (something) in a sloping position. [15c: from French *recliner,* from Latin *reclinare* to lean back]

recluse *noun* **1** someone who lives alone and has little contact with society. **2** a religious devotee who leads a life of seclusion. ▪ **reclusive** *adj.* [13c: from French *reclus,* from Latin *claudere* to shut]

recognition *noun* the act or state of recognizing or being recognized.

recognizance *or* **recognisance** /rɪ'kɒgnɪzəns/ *noun* **1** a legally binding promise made to a magistrate or court to do or not do something specified. **2** money pledged as a guarantee of such a promise being kept.

recognize *or* **-ise** *verb* **1** to identify (a person or thing known or experienced before). **2** to admit or be aware of: *recognized his mistakes.* **3** to show approval of and gratitude for: *recognized her courage with the award of a medal.* **4** to acknowledge the status or legality of (esp a government or state). **5** to accept: *recognize the authority of the court.* ▪ **recognizable** *adj.* [15c: from Latin *cognoscere* to know]

recoil *verb* /rɪ'kɔɪl/ *intr* **1** to spring back or rebound. **2** of a gun: to spring powerfully backwards under the force of being fired. **3** to spring or shrink back, esp in fear, disgust, etc. ▶ *noun* /rɪ'kɔɪl, 'riːkɔɪl/ an act of recoiling. [13c: from French *reculer* to move backwards]

recollect *verb* to recall to memory; to remember, esp with an effort. [16c: from Latin *recolligere* to gather up or collect]

recollection *noun* **1** the act or power of recollecting. **2** a person's memory or the extent of this. **3** something remembered.

recombinant DNA *noun, biol* genetic material produced by joining the DNA of different organisms.

recombination *noun, genetics* the process of rearranging genetic material during the formation of gametes, so that the offspring possesses combinations of genetic characteristics different from those of the parents.

recommend *verb* **1** to suggest as being suitable, acceptable, etc: *recommend a good restaurant.* **2** to make acceptable, desirable or pleasing: *has very little to recommend it.* **3** *tr & intr* to advise as a particular course of action: *recommended he went home.* ▪ **recommendation** *noun.* [14c: from Latin *commendare* to commend]

---

recommend

This word is often misspelt. It has one c and two *m*'s. It might help you to remember the following sentence:

*I re***c***o***mm***end* ***c****ooked* ***m****arsh****m****allows.*

---

recompense *verb* **1** to repay or reward for service, work done, etc. **2** to compensate for loss, injury or hardship suffered. ▶ *noun* **1** repayment or reward. **2** compensation for loss, injury, etc. [15c: from French *récompenser,* from Latin *compensare* to compensate]

reconcile *verb* **1** to put on friendly terms again, esp after a quarrel. **2** to bring (two or more different aims, points of view, etc) into agreement. **3** to agree to accept (an unwelcome fact or situation): *reconciled himself to the fact that his professional career was over.* ▪ **reconciliation** *noun.* [14c: from Latin *reconciliare*]

recondite *adj* **1** of a subject or knowledge: difficult to understand; little known. **2** dealing with profound, abstruse or obscure knowledge. [17c: from Latin *condere* to hide or store]

recondition *verb* to repair or restore (an engine, piece of equipment, etc) to original or good working condition, eg by cleaning or replacing broken parts.

reconnaissance /rɪ'kɒnɪsəns/ *noun* **1** *military* a survey, eg of land or the position of troops, to obtain information about the enemy before advancing. **2** a preliminary survey. Often shortened to **recce**. [19c: French]

reconnoitre *or* (*US*) **reconnoiter** /rɛkə'nɔɪtə(r)/ *verb* to examine or survey (land, enemy troops, etc), esp with a view to military operations etc. Often shortened to **recce**. ▶ *noun* the act of reconnoitring; a reconnaissance. [18c: from French *reconnoître* to examine]

reconsider *verb* to consider (a decision, opinion, etc) again, esp for a possible change or reversal. ▪ **reconsideration** *noun.* [16c]

reconstitute *verb* **1** to restore (esp dried foods or concentrates, by adding water) to the original form or constitution. **2** to form or make up again; to reorganize. ▪ **reconstitution** *noun.* [19c]

reconstruct *verb* **1** to construct or form again; to rebuild. **2** to create a description or idea of (a crime, past event, etc) from the evidence available. **3** to re-enact (an incident, esp a crime). ▪ **reconstruction** *noun.* ▪ **reconstructive** *adj.* [18c]

record *noun* /'rɛkɔːd/ **1** a formal written report or statement of facts, events or information. **2** (*often* **records**) information, facts, etc, collected usu over a fairly long period of time: *dental records.* **3** the state or fact of being recorded: *for the record.* **4** a thin plastic disc used as a recording medium for reproducing music or other sound. **5** esp in sports: a performance which is officially recognized as the best of a particular kind or in a particular class. **6** a description of the history and achievements of a person, institution, company, etc. **7** a list of the crimes a person has been convicted of. **8** *comput* in database systems: a subdivision of a file that can be treated as a single unit of stored information, consisting of a collection of related data or fields, each of which contains a particular item of information, eg a statistic, a piece of text, a name, address, etc. **9** anything that recalls or commemorates past events. ▸ *verb* /rɪˈkɔːd/ **1** to set down in writing or some other permanent form, esp for use in the future. **2** *tr & intr* to register (sound, music, speech, etc) on a record or tape so that it can be listened to in the future. **3** of a dial, instrument, person's face, etc: to show or register (a particular figure, feeling, etc). [13c: from French *recorder*, from Latin *recordari* to remember] IDIOMS **go on record** to make a public statement. **off the record** of information, statements, etc: not intended to be repeated or made public. **on record** officially recorded; publicly known. **set** *or* **put the record straight** to correct a mistake or false impression.

record-breaking *adj* of a performance, an attempt, etc: beating the current **record** (*noun* sense 5).

recorder *noun* **1** a wooden or plastic wind instrument with a tapering mouthpiece and holes which are covered by the player's fingers in various configurations to produce the notes. **2** (*usu* **Recorder**) a solicitor or barrister who sits as a part-time judge in a court. **3** someone who records. **4** a device for recording, esp a tape recorder or video recorder.

recording *noun* **1** the process of registering sounds or images on a record, tape, video, etc. **2** sound or images which have been recorded.

record player *noun* an apparatus which reproduces the sounds recorded on records.

recount *verb* to narrate or tell (a story, etc) in detail. [15c: from French *conter* to tell]

re-count *verb* /riːˈkaʊnt/ to count again. ▸ *noun* /ˈriːkaʊnt/ a second or new counting, esp of votes in an election to check a very close result. [18c]

recoup *verb* **1** to recover or get back (something lost, eg money). **2** to compensate or reimburse someone (eg for something lost). **3** *law* to keep back (something due). [15c: from French *recouper* to cut back]

recourse *noun* **a** an act of turning to someone, or resorting to a particular course of action, for help or protection; **b** a source of help or protection. [14c: from French *recours*, from Latin *recursus* a running back]

recover *verb* **1** to get or find again. **2** *intr* to regain one's good health, spirits or composure. **3** *intr* to regain a former and usu better condition: *The economy recovered slightly last year.* **4** to regain control of: *recover his senses.* **5** *law* to gain (compensation or damages) by legal action. **6** to obtain (a valuable or usable substance) from a by-product or waste product . ▪ **recoverable** *adj.* [14c: from French *recoverer*, from Latin *recuperare* recuperate]

recovery *noun* (**-*ies***) an act, instance or process of recovering, or state of having recovered, in any sense.

recovery position *noun, med* a position of the body on its side with the face tilted slightly upwards, recommended for unconscious or semiconscious patients.

recovery vehicle *noun* a vehicle used to carry away another vehicle that has broken down or been involved in an accident.

recreate *or* **re-create** *verb* to create something again; to reproduce. ▪ **re-creation** *noun.* [16c]

recreation *noun* **1** a pleasant activity. **2** the process of having an enjoyable and often refreshing time. ▪ **recreational** *adj.* [14c]

recrimination *noun* the act of returning an accusation. ▪ **recriminate** *verb.* ▪ **recriminatory** *adj.* [17c: from Latin *criminare* to accuse]

recrudesce *verb* of a disease, troubles, etc: to become active again, after a period of absence. ▪ **recrudescence** *noun.* ▪ **recrudescent** *adj.* [19c: from Latin *crudescere* to grow worse]

recruit *noun* **1** *military* a newly enlisted member of the army, air force, navy, etc. **2** a new member of a society, group, organization, company, etc. ▸ *verb, tr & intr* **1** *military* **a** to enlist (people) as recruits; **b** to raise or reinforce (eg an army) by enlisting recruits. **2** to enrol or obtain new members, employees, etc. ▪ **recruitment** *noun.* [17c: from French *recrute* new growth, from Latin *crescere* to grow]

recta see under **rectum**

rectangle *noun* a four-sided plane figure with opposite sides of equal length and all its angles right angles. ▪ **rectangular** *adj.* [16c: from Latin *rectus* straight + *angulus* angle]

rectifier *noun* **1** someone or something that rectifies. **2** *elec* an electrical device that is used to convert alternating current into direct current.

rectify *verb* (**-*ies*, -*ied***) **1** **a** to put (a mistake, etc) right or correct; **b** to adjust. **2** *chem* to purify (alcohol, etc) by repeated distillation. **3** *elec* to change (alternating current) into direct current. ▪ **rectification** *noun.* [14c: from Latin *rectus* right + *facere* to make]

rectilineal *or* **rectilinear** *adj* **1** in or forming a straight line or straight lines. **2** bounded by straight lines. [17c]

rectitude *noun* **1** correctness of behaviour or judgement. **2** moral integrity. [15c: from Latin *rectitudo*]

recto *noun, printing* **1** the right-hand page of an open book. **2** the front of a sheet of printed paper. Compare **verso**. [19c: from Latin *recto* on the right]

rector *noun* **1** in the Church of England: a clergyman in charge of a parish who would, formerly, have been entitled to receive all the tithes of that parish. **2** in the Roman Catholic Church: a priest in charge of a congregation or a religious house, esp a Jesuit seminary. **3** *US, Scot* in the Protestant Episcopal Church: a clergyman in charge of a congregation. **4** the headmaster of some schools and colleges, esp in Scotland. **5** *Scot* a senior university official elected by and representing the students. ▪ **rectorial** *adj.* ▪ **rectorship** *noun.* [14c: Latin, meaning 'ruler', from *regere* to rule]

rectory *noun* (**-*ies***) the house or residence of a rector.

rectum *noun* (***recta*** *or* ***rectums***) the lower part of the alimentary canal, ending at the anus. ▪ **rectal** *adj.* [16c: from Latin *rectum intestinum* straight intestine, from *rectus* straight]

recumbent *adj* lying down; reclining. [17c: from Latin *recumbere* to recline]

recuperate *verb* **1** *intr* to recover, esp from illness. **2** to recover (health, something lost, etc). ▪ **recupera-**

tion *noun*. ▪ **recuperative** *adj*. [16c: from Latin *recuperare* to recover, from *capere* to take]

recur *verb* (***recurred, recurring***) *intr* **1 a** to happen or come round again; **b** to happen at intervals. **2** of a thought, etc: to come back into one's mind. [15c: from Latin *recurrere* to run back]

recurrent *adj* happening often or regularly. ▪ **recurrence** *noun*. ▪ **recurrently** *adv*.

recursion *noun* **1** a going back; a return. **2** *maths* the repeated application of a function to its own values to produce an infinite series of values. ▪ **recursive** *adj*.

recusant /'rɛkjuzənt/ *noun* **1** *hist* a Roman Catholic who refused to attend Church of England services between c.1570 and c.1790 when this was obligatory. **2** someone who refuses to submit to authority. ▪ **recusance** *or* **recusancy** *noun*. [16c: from Latin *recusare* to refuse, from *causa* a cause]

recycle *verb* to process or treat (waste material, esp paper, glass, etc) for re-use. ▪ **recyclable** *adj*. ▪ **recycling** *noun*.

red *adj* (***redder, reddest***) **1** having the colour of blood, or a colour similar to it. **2** of hair, fur, etc: between a golden brown and a deep reddish-brown colour. **3** of the eyes: bloodshot or with red rims. **4** having a red or flushed face, esp from shame or anger, or from physical exertion. **5** of wine: made with black grapes whose skins colour the wine a deep red. **6** *informal* communist. **7** *chiefly informal* (**Red**) relating to the former USSR; Soviet: *the Red Army*. **8** indicating the most extreme urgency. See **red alert**. ▸ *noun* **1** the colour of blood, or a similar shade. **2** red dye or paint. **3** red material or clothes. **4** the red traffic light, a sign that cars should stop. **5** (*usu* **the red**) the debit side of an account; the state of being in debt, eg, to a bank. Compare **black** (*noun* sense 6). **6** *informal* (*often* **Red**) a communist or socialist. ▪ **reddish** *and* **reddy** *adj* (***-ies, -iest***). ▪ **redness** *noun*. [Anglo-Saxon *read*]

IDIOMS **paint the town red** *informal* to go out to enjoy oneself in a lively, noisy and often drunken way. **see red** *informal* to become angry.

red alert *noun* a state of readiness to deal with imminent crisis or emergency, eg war, natural disaster, etc. Compare **yellow alert**.

red alga *noun* (***red algae***) *botany* any of several **algae** which contain a pigment giving them a pink or reddish colour.

red blood cell *or* **red corpuscle** *noun* a blood cell containing the pigment haemoglobin, which gives the cell its red colour. Also called **erythrocyte**.

red-blooded *adj, informal* full of vitality; manly; virile.

redbreast *noun* a robin.

redbrick *adj* of a British university: established in the late 19c or early 20c.

red card *noun, football* a piece of red card or plastic shown by the referee to a player to indicate that they are being sent off. Compare **yellow card**. ▸ *verb* (**red-card**) of a referee: to show (a player) a red card.

red carpet *noun* special treatment given to an important person.

redcoat *noun* **1** *hist* a British soldier. **2** *Can informal* a member of the Canadian mounted police.

Red Crescent *noun* an organization equivalent to the Red Cross in Muslim countries.

Red Cross *noun* the copyrighted symbol of the international humanitarian organization **the Red Cross**, established to assist those wounded or captured in war and which now carries out extensive humanitarian work.

redcurrant *noun* a widely cultivated European shrub, or its small edible red berry.

redden *verb* **1** to make red or redder. **2** *intr* to become red; to blush.

red dwarf *noun, astron* a cool, faint, old star.

redeem *verb* **1** to buy back. **2** to recover (eg something that has been pawned or mortgaged) by payment or service. **3** to fulfil (a promise). **4** to set free or save (someone) by paying a ransom. **5** to free (someone or oneself) from blame or debt. **6** to free from sin. **7** to make up or compensate for (something bad or wrong). **8** to exchange (tokens, vouchers, etc) for goods. **9** to exchange (bonds, shares, etc) for cash. ▪ **redeemable** *adj*. ▪ **redeeming** *adj* making up for faults or shortcomings: *one of her redeeming features*. [15c: from French *redimer*, from Latin *emere* to buy]

redeemer *noun* **1** someone who redeems. **2** (**the Redeemer**) a name for Jesus Christ.

redemption *noun* **1** the act of redeeming or state of being redeemed. **2** anything which redeems. **3** *Christianity* the freeing of humanity from sin by Christ's death on the Cross. ▪ **redemptive** *adj*. [14c: from Latin *redemptio* buying back]

redeploy *verb* to transfer (soldiers, supplies, etc) to another place or job. ▪ **redeployment** *noun*. [20c]

redevelop *verb* to develop again (esp a run-down urban area). ▪ **redeveloper** *noun*. ▪ **redevelopment** *noun*. [19c]

red-eye *noun* **1** the **rudd**. **2** *US informal* inferior whiskey. **3** *informal* in flash photography: a phenomenon where the pupils of a subject's eyes appear red.

red flag *noun* **1** a symbol of socialism or of revolution. **2** a flag used to warn of danger, defiance, no mercy, or as a signal to stop.

red giant *noun, astron* a large, cool, red star.

red-handed *adj* in the very act of committing a crime or doing something wrong.

redhead *noun* a person, esp a woman, with red hair. ▪ **redheaded** *adj*.

red herring *noun* **1** a herring which has been cured and smoked to a dark reddish colour. **2** a misleading or diverting subject, idea, clue, etc. [19c in sense 2, from the fact that a red herring drawn across a track would put a dog off the scent; 15c in sense 1]

red-hot *adj* **1** of metal, etc: heated until it glows red. **2** feeling or showing passionate or intense emotion or excitement. **3** *informal* feeling or showing great enthusiasm. **4** strongly tipped to win: *a red-hot favourite*. **5** of news, etc: completely up to date.

redid *past tense of* **redo**

red-letter day *noun* a memorable or special day. [18c: from the former custom of marking saints' days in red on calendars]

red light *noun* a red warning light, esp the red traffic light at which vehicles have to stop. ▸ *adj* (**red-light**) *informal* relating to brothels or containing many brothels: *red-light district*.

red meat *noun* dark-coloured meat, eg beef or lamb. Compare **white meat**.

redneck *noun, US derog* in the south-western states: a poor white manual worker.

redo *verb* (***redoes,*** *past tense* ***redid,*** *past participle* ***redone***) **1** to do again or differently. **2** to redecorate (a room, etc). [16c]

redolent *adj* **1** fragrant. **2** (*usu* **redolent of** *or* **with**) **a** smelling strongly; **b** strongly suggestive or reminiscent. ▪ **redolence** *or* **redolency** *noun.* ▪ **redolently** *adv.* [14c: from Latin *redolere* to give off a smell]

redouble *verb* to make or become greater or more intense.

redoubt *noun* a fortification, esp a temporary one defending a pass or hilltop. [17c: from French *redoute,* from Latin *reductus* refuge]

redoubtable *adj* **1** inspiring fear or respect; formidable. **2** brave; valiant. ▪ **redoubtably** *adv.* [14c: from French *redouter* to fear greatly]

redound *verb, intr* **1** (**redound to**) to have a direct, usu beneficial effect on. **2** (*chiefly* **redound on**) to come back to as a consequence. [14c: from French *redonder,* from Latin *redundare* to surge]

redox reaction /'ri:dɔks/ *noun, chem* a chemical reaction in which one of the reacting substances is reduced while the other is oxidized. [20c: from *reduction* + *oxidation*]

red pepper *noun* **1 cayenne** pepper. **2** a red **capsicum** or **sweet pepper**, eaten as a vegetable. Compare **green pepper**.

redress *verb* **1** to set right or compensate for (something wrong). **2** to make even or equal again: *redress the balance.* ▸ *noun* **1** the act of redressing or being redressed. **2** money, etc paid as compensation for loss or wrong done. [14c: from French *redrecier* to straighten]

red shift *noun, astron* an increase in the wavelength of light or other electromagnetic radiation emitted by certain galaxies or quasars.

red spider *or* **red spider mite** *noun* a plant-eating mite that causes severe damage in gardens.

red tape *noun, informal* unnecessary rules and regulations which result in delay; bureaucracy. [18c: from the red tape used to bind official documents]

reduce *verb* **1** *tr & intr* to make or become less, smaller, etc. **2** to change into a worse or less desirable state or form: *reduced her to tears.* **3** *military* to lower the rank, status or grade of: *reduced him to the ranks.* **4** to bring into a state of obedience; to subdue. **5** to make weaker or poorer. **6** to lower (the price of something). **7** *intr* to lose weight by dieting. **8** to convert (a substance) into a simpler form. **9** to simplify. **10** *tr & intr cookery* to thicken (a sauce) by slowly boiling off the excess liquid. **11** *chem* to cause (a substance) to undergo a chemical reaction whereby it gains hydrogen or loses oxygen. ▪ **reducible** *adj.* [14c: from Latin *reducere* to lead back]

reduced circumstances *plural noun* a state of poverty, esp following a time of relative wealth.

reductase *noun, biochem* an enzyme which brings about the reduction of organic compounds. [20c]

reduction *noun* **1** an act, instance or process of reducing; the state of being reduced. **2** the amount by which something is reduced. **3** a copy of a picture, document, etc made on a smaller scale. ▪ **reductive** *adj.*

reductionism *noun* the belief that complex data, phenomena, etc can be explained in terms of something simpler. ▪ **reductionist** *noun, adj.*

redundant *adj* **1** not needed; superfluous. **2** of an employee: no longer needed and therefore dismissed. **3** of a word, phrase, etc: able to be removed without affecting the overall meaning, significance, etc. ▪ **redundancy** *noun* (***-ies***). [17c: from Latin *redundare* to surge]

reduplicate *verb* **1** to repeat, copy or double something. **2** *grammar* to repeat (a word or syllable), often with some minor change, to form a new word, as in *hubble-bubble, riff-raff,* etc. ▪ **reduplication** *noun.* ▪ **reduplicative** *adj.* [16c: from Latin *reduplicare*]

redwood *noun* **1** an extremely tall and long-lived **sequoia**, native to California. **2** its reddish-brown wood.

reebok *or* ***rhebok*** *noun* (***reeboks*** *or* ***reebok***) a S African antelope. [18c: Dutch, meaning 'roebuck']

reed *noun* **1 a** a grass that grows in the margins of streams, lakes and ponds; **b** a stalk of one of these plants used to make thatched roofs, furniture and fencing. **2** a thin piece of cane or metal in certain musical instruments which vibrates and makes a sound when air passes over it. **3** a wind instrument or organ pipe with reeds. [Anglo-Saxon *hreod*]

re-educate *verb* **1** to educate again. **2** to change the beliefs, behaviour, etc of. ▪ **re-education** *noun.*

reedy *adj* (***-ier, -iest***) **1** full of reeds. **2** having a tone like a reed instrument, esp in being thin and piping. **3** thin and weak. ▪ **reediness** *noun.*

reef[1] *noun* a mass of rock, coral, sand, etc that either projects above the surface at low tide, or is permanently covered by shallow water. [16c: from Dutch *rif,* from Norse *rif* a rib]

reef[2] *naut, noun* a part of a sail which may be folded in or let out so as to alter the area of sail exposed to the wind. ▸ *verb* to take in a reef or reefs of (a sail). [14c: from Norse *rif* a rib]

reefer *noun* **1** (*in full* **reefer jacket**) a thick woollen double-breasted jacket. **2** *informal* a cigarette containing marijuana.

reef knot *noun* a knot made by passing one end of a rope over and under the other end, then back over and under it again.

reek *noun* **1** a strong, unpleasant smell. **2** *Scot & N Eng dialect* smoke. ▸ *verb, intr* **1** to give off a strong, usu unpleasant smell. **2** *Scot & N Eng dialect* to give off smoke. **3** (*often* **reek of**) to suggest or hint at (something unpleasant): *a scheme that reeks of corruption.* [Anglo-Saxon *reocan*]

reel *noun* **1** a round wheel-shaped or cylindrical object on which thread, film, fishing lines, etc can be wound. **2** the quantity of film, thread, etc wound on one of these. **3** a device for winding and unwinding a fishing line. **4** a lively Scottish or Irish dance. **5** the music for such a dance. ▸ *verb* **1** to wind something on a reel. **2** (*usu* **reel in** *or* **up**) to pull in or up using a reel: *reel in a fish.* **3** *intr* to stagger or sway; to move unsteadily. **4** *intr* to whirl or appear to move. **5** *intr* to be shaken physically or mentally. **6** *intr* to dance a reel. [Anglo-Saxon *hreol*]

PHRASAL VERBS **reel sth off** to say, repeat or write it rapidly and often with little effort or unthinkingly.

re-entry *noun* (***-ies***) the return of a spacecraft to the Earth's atmosphere.

reeve[1] *noun, hist* **1** the chief magistrate of a town or district. **2** an official who supervises a lord's manor or estate. [Anglo-Saxon *refa*]

reeve[2] *verb* (***rove***) to pass (a rope, etc) through a hole, opening or ring. [17c: from Dutch *reven* to reef]

ref *noun, informal* a sports referee.

refectory *noun* (***-ies***) a dining hall, esp one in a monastery or university. [15c: from Latin *reficere* to refresh]

refectory table *noun* a long narrow dining table.

refer *verb* (***referred, referring***) **1** *intr* (**refer to sth**) **a** to mention or make allusion to it. **b** to look to it for information, facts, etc: *referred to his notes.* **c** to be relevant or relate to it. **2** (**refer sb to sb** *or* **sth**) to direct them to them or it. **3** (**refer sth to sb**) **a** to hand it over to them for consideration: *referred the query to the manager.* **b** to hand it back to the person from whom it came because it is unacceptable. **4** to fail (an examination candidate). [14c: from French *référer*, from Latin *referre* to carry back]

referee *noun* **1** a person to whom reference is made to settle a question, dispute, etc. **2** an umpire or judge, eg of a game or in a dispute. **3** someone who is willing to testify to a person's character, talents and abilities. ▸ *verb* (***refereed***) *tr & intr* to act as a referee in (a game, dispute, etc). [16c]

reference *noun* **1** a mention of or an allusion to something. **2** a direction in a book to another passage or another book where information can be found. **3** a book or passage referred to. **4** the act of referring to a book or passage for information. **5** a written report on a person's character, talents, abilities, etc. **6 a** the providing of facts and information; **b** a source of facts or information. **7** the directing of a person, question, etc to some authority for information, a decision, etc. **8** relation, correspondence or connection: *with reference to your last letter.* **9** a standard for measuring or judging: *a point of reference.* ▸ *verb* **1** to make a reference to something. **2** to provide (a book, etc) with references to other sources. ▪ **referential** *adj.* [16c]

referendum *noun* (***referendums*** *or* ***referenda***) **1** the practice or principle of giving people a chance to state their opinions on a particular matter by voting for or against it. **2** a vote in a referendum. [19c: from Latin *referre* to carry back]

referral *noun* the act of referring someone to someone else, esp the sending of a patient by a GP to a specialist for treatment.

referred pain *noun, med* pain felt in a part of the body other than its actual source.

refill *noun* /ˈriːfɪl/ a new filling for something which has become empty through use; a container for this plus contents. ▸ *verb* /riːˈfɪl/ to fill again. ▪ **refillable** *adj.* [17c]

refine *verb* **1** to make pure by removing dirt, waste substances, etc. **2** *tr & intr* to become or make more elegant, polished or subtle. ▪ **refinable** *adj.*

refined *adj* **1** very polite; well-mannered; elegant. **2** with all the dirt, waste substances, etc removed. **3** improved; polished.

refinement *noun* **1** an act or the process of refining. **2** good manners or good taste; polite speech; elegance. **3** an improvement or perfection. **4** a subtle distinction.

refinery *noun* (***-ies***) a plant where raw materials, esp sugar and oil, are purified. [18c]

refit *verb* /riːˈfɪt/ (***refitted, refitting***) **1** to repair or fit new parts to (esp a ship). **2** *intr* of a ship: to undergo repair or the fitting of new parts. ▸ *noun* /ˈriːfɪt/ the process of refitting or being refitted. ▪ **refitment** *or* **refitting** *noun.* [17c]

reflate *verb* to bring about reflation of (an economy). Compare **inflate, deflate.**

reflation *noun* an increase in economic activity and in the amount of money and credit available, designed to increase industrial production after a period of deflation. See also **deflation**, **inflation**, **stagflation**. ▪ **reflationary** *adj.* [20c: from **re-** + *inflation*]

reflect *verb* **1** *tr & intr* of a surface: to send back (light, heat, sound, etc). **2** *tr & intr* of a mirror, etc: to give an image of (someone or something). **3** *intr* of a sound, image, etc: to be sent back. **4** to have as a cause or be a consequence of. **5** to show or give an idea of. **6** (*also* **reflect on** *or* **upon**) to consider carefully; to contemplate. **7** *intr* (**reflect on** *or* **upon sb**) of an action, etc: to bring about a specified result, attitude, etc: *His behaviour during all the trouble reflects well on him.* [15c: from Latin *reflectere* to bend back]

reflectance *or* **reflecting factor** *noun, physics* the ratio of the intensity of the radiation reflected by a surface to the intensity of radiation incident on that surface.

reflection *or* **reflexion** *noun* **1** the change in direction of a particle or wave, eg the turning back of a ray of light, either when it strikes a smooth surface that it does not penetrate, such as a mirror, or when it reaches the boundary between two media. **2** the act of reflecting. **3** a reflected image. **4** careful and thoughtful consideration; contemplation. **5** *maths* a transformation of a plane around an axis of symmetry in the plane, so that it produces a mirror image on the other side. Compare **enlargement**, **rotation**, **translation**.

reflective *adj* **1** of a person: thoughtful; meditative. **2** of a surface: able to reflect images, light, sound, etc. **3** reflected; resulting from reflection. ▪ **reflectively** *adv.*

reflector *noun* **1** a polished surface that reflects light, heat, etc. **2** a piece of red, white, etc plastic or glass attached to the back, front or spokes of a bicycle which glows when light shines on it. **3** a telescope that uses a mirror to produce images, or the mirror itself.

reflex *noun* **1** (*also* **reflex action**) *physiol* a response to a sensory, physical or chemical stimulus. **2** the ability to respond rapidly to a stimulus. **3 a** reflected light, sound, heat, etc; **b** a reflected image. **4** a sign or expression of something. ▸ *adj* **1** occurring as an automatic response without being thought about. **2** bent or turned backwards. **3** directed back on the source; reflected. **4** of a thought: introspective. **5** *geom* of an angle: greater than 180° and less than 360°. Compare **acute** (*adj* sense 6), **obtuse** (sense 3). [16c: from Latin *reflexus* bent back]

reflex arc *noun, physiol* the simplest functional unit of the nervous system, by which an impulse produces a reflex action.

reflexible *adj* capable of being bent backwards.

reflexive *adj* **1** *grammar* of a pronoun: showing that the object of a verb is the same as the subject, eg in *He cut himself, himself* is a reflexive pronoun. **2** *grammar* of a verb: used with a reflexive pronoun as object, eg, *shave* in *shave oneself.* **3** *physiol* relating to a reflex. ▶ *noun* a reflexive pronoun or verb. ▪ **reflexivity** *noun.*

reflexology *noun* the massaging of the reflex points on the soles of the feet, the hands and the head as a form of therapy. ▪ **reflexologist** *noun.*

reflux *noun, chem* **1** the boiling of a liquid for long periods in a container attached to a condenser, so that the vapour produced condenses and continuously flows back into the container. **2** the condensed vapour involved in this process. ▶ *verb, tr & intr* to boil or be boiled under reflux. [19c: Latin, from *fluxus* flow]

reform *verb* **1** to improve or remove faults from (a person, behaviour, etc). **2** to improve (a law, institution, etc) by making changes or corrections to it. **3** *intr* to give up bad habits; to improve one's behaviour, etc. **4** to stop or abolish (misconduct, an abuse, etc). ▶ *noun* **1** a correction or improvement, esp in some social or political system. **2** improvement in behaviour, morals, etc. ▪ **reformable** *adj.* ▪ **reformative** *adj.* ▪ **reformer** *noun.* [14c: from Latin *reformare* to form again]

re-form *verb, tr & intr* to form again or in a different way. ▪ **re-formation** *noun.* [14c]

reformation /rɛfə'meɪʃən/ *noun* **1** the act or process of reforming or being reformed; improvement; amendment. **2** (**the Reformation**) the great religious and political revolution that took place in Europe in the 16c and resulted in the establishment of the Protestant Churches.

reformatory *noun* (**-ies**) *old use* (*also* **reform school**) a school where young people who had broken the law or who exhibited disruptive behaviour were sent to be reformed. ▶ *adj* with the function or purpose of reforming. [19c]

reformer *noun* someone who advocates or instigates reform, esp of a political or social nature.

reformism *noun, politics* any doctrine or movement that advocates gradual social and political change, rather than revolutionary change. ▪ **reformist** *noun.*

refract *verb* of a medium, eg water, glass: to deflect (a wave of light, sound, etc) when it crosses the boundary between this medium and another at a different angle. ▪ **refraction** *noun.* ▪ **refractive** *adj.* [17c: from Latin *frangere* to break]

refractive index *noun, physics* the ratio of the speed of electromagnetic radiation, esp light, in air or a vacuum to its speed in another medium.

refractor *noun* **1** anything that refracts. **2** a telescope that uses a lens to produce an image or the lens itself.

refractory *adj* **1** difficult to control; stubborn; unmanageable. **2** *med* of a disease: resistant to treatment. **3** of a material: resistant to heat; able to withstand high temperatures without fusing or melting. [17c: from Latin *refractarius* stubborn]

refrain¹ *noun* **1** a phrase or group of lines repeated at the end of each stanza or verse in a poem or song. **2** the music for this. [14c: French, from *refraindre,* from Latin *frangere* to break]

refrain² *verb, intr* (*usu* **refrain from**) to desist, stop or avoid doing (something). [14c: from French *refréner,* from Latin *frenum* a bridle]

refrangible *adj* able to be refracted. ▪ **refrangibility** *noun.* [17c: from Latin *frangere* to break]

refresh *verb* **1** to make fresh again. **2** to make brighter or livelier again. **3** of drink, food, rest, etc: to give renewed strength, energy, enthusiasm, etc to. **4** to revive (someone, oneself, etc) with drink, food, rest, etc. **5** **a** to provide a new supply of; **b** to replenish supplies of. **6** to make cool. **7** to make (one's memory) clearer and stronger by reading or listening to the source of information again. **8** *comput* to update (esp a screen display) with data. [14c: from French *fresche* fresh]

refresher *noun* **1** anything that refreshes, eg, a cold drink. **2** *law* an extra fee paid to counsel during a long case or an adjournment.

refresher course *noun* a course of study or training intended to increase or update previous knowledge.

refreshing *adj* **1** giving new strength, energy and enthusiasm. **2** cooling. **3** particularly pleasing because of being different, unexpected, new, etc: *His attitude was refreshing.* ▪ **refreshingly** *adv.*

refreshment *noun* **1** the act of refreshing or state of being refreshed. **2** anything that refreshes. **3** (**refreshments**) food and drink, esp a light meal.

refrigerant *noun* **1** a fluid that vaporizes at low temperatures and is used in the cooling mechanism of refrigerators. **2** *med* a substance used for reducing fever. ▶ *adj* cooling.

refrigerate *verb* **1** **a** to freeze or make cold; **b** *intr* to become cold. **2** to make or keep (mainly food) cold or frozen to slow down the decay processes. ▪ **refrigeration** *noun.* [16c: from Latin *frigus* cold]

refrigerator *noun* an insulated cabinet or room maintained at a low temperature in order to slow down the decay processes of its contents, esp food. Often shortened to **fridge**.

refuel *verb* **1** to supply (an aircraft, car, etc) with more fuel. **2** *intr* of an aircraft, car, etc: to take on more fuel.

refuge *noun* **1** shelter or protection from danger or trouble. **2** any place, person or thing offering help or shelter. **3** an establishment offering emergency accommodation, protection, support, etc, eg for the homeless, victims of domestic violence, etc. **4** a traffic island for pedestrians. [14c: French, from Latin *fugere* to flee]

refugee *noun* someone who seeks refuge, esp from religious or political persecution, in another country. [17c: from French *réfugier* to take refuge]

refulgent *adj, literary* shining brightly; radiant; beaming. ▪ **refulgence** *noun.* ▪ **refulgently** *adv.* [16c: from Latin *refulgere* to shine brightly]

refund *verb* /rɪ'fʌnd/ to pay (money, etc) back, esp because something bought or a service, etc was faulty, not up to standard, etc. ▶ *noun* /'riːfʌnd/ **1** the paying back of money, etc. **2** money, etc that is paid back. ▪ **refundable** /rɪ'fʌndəbəl/ *adj.* [14c: from Latin *fundere* to pour]

refurbish *verb* **1** to renovate. **2** to redecorate or brighten something up. ▪ **refurbishment** *noun.* [17c]

refusal *noun* **1** an act or instance of refusing. **2** (*usu* **first refusal**) the opportunity to buy, accept or refuse something before it is offered, given, sold, etc to anyone else: *I'll give you first refusal if I decide to sell it.*

refuse[1] /rɪ'fjuːz/ *verb* **1** *tr & intr* to indicate unwillingness. **2** to decline to accept: *refuse the offer of help.* **3** not to allow (someone or something) (access, permission, etc). **4** *tr & intr* of a horse: to stop at a fence and not jump over it. [14c: from French *refuser*]

refuse[2] /'rɛfjuːs/ *noun* **1** rubbish; waste. **2** anything that is thrown away. [15c: from French *refus* rejection]

refute *verb* to prove that (a person, statement, theory, etc) is wrong. ▪ **refutable** *adj.* ▪ **refutation** *noun.* [16c: from Latin *refutare* to drive back or rebut]

---

refute, deny

Be careful not to use the word **refute** when you mean **deny**. If you **deny** something, you say it is wrong without necessarily proving this:

The club denied that an offer had been accepted for the player.

---

regain *verb* **1** to get back again or recover: *regained consciousness.* **2** to get back to (a place, position, etc): *regained her place as the world's number one.*

regal *adj* **1** relating to, like, or suitable for a king or queen. **2** royal. ▪ **regality** *noun.* ▪ **regally** *adv.* [14c: from Latin *regalis* royal, from *rex* king]

regale *verb* **1** (*usu* **regale with**) to amuse (eg with stories, etc). **2** to entertain lavishly. [17c: from French *régaler*, from *gale* pleasure]

regalia *plural noun* **1** the insignia of royalty, eg the crown, sceptre and orb. **2** any ornaments, ceremonial clothes, etc, worn as a sign of importance or authority, eg by a mayor. [16c: Latin, meaning 'things worthy of a king']

regard *verb* **1** to consider in a specified way: *regarded him as a friend.* **2** to esteem or respect: *regarded him highly.* **3 a** to pay attention to or take notice of; **b** to heed. **4** to look attentively or steadily at. **5** to have a connection with or to relate to. ▸ *noun* **1 a** esteem; **b** respect and affection. **2** thought or attention. **3** care or consideration. **4** a gaze or look. **5** connection or relation. **6** (**regards**) **a** greetings; **b** respectful good wishes. [14c: from French *regarder* to look at, from *garder* to guard or keep watch]

IDIOMS **as regards** concerning. **with regard to 1** about or concerning. **2** as concerns.

regarding *prep* about; concerning.

regardless *adv* **1** not thinking or caring about (problems, dangers, etc). **2** nevertheless; in spite of everything. ▸ *adj* (*usu* **regardless of**) taking no notice of.

regatta *noun* a yacht or boat race-meeting. [17c: from Italian *rigatta* a contest]

regency *noun* (**-ies**) **1** (**Regency**) a period when a regent is head of state, eg, in Britain, from 1811–20 or, in France, from 1715–23. **2** government by a regent; any period when a regent rules or ruled. **3** the office of a regent. ▸ *adj* (*also* **Regency**) of art, furniture, etc: belonging to, or in the style prevailing during, the period of the Regency. [15c: from Latin *regere* to rule]

regenerate *verb* /rɪ'dʒɛnəreɪt/ **1** to produce again or anew. **2** *theology* to renew (someone) spiritually. **3** *tr & intr* to make or become morally or spiritually improved. **4** *tr & intr* **a** to develop or give new life or energy to; **b** to be brought back or bring back to life or original strength again. **5** *tr & intr, physiol* to regrow or cause (new tissue) to regrow. ▸ *adj* /-rət/ **1** regenerated, esp morally, spiritually or physically. **2** reformed. ▪ **regeneration** *noun.* ▪ **regenerative** *adj.* ▪ **regenerator** *noun.* [16c: from Latin *regenerare* to bring forth again]

regent *noun* someone who governs a country during a monarch's childhood, absence or illness. ▸ *adj* acting as regent: *Prince regent.* [14c: see **regency**]

reggae *noun* popular music of W Indian origin with a strongly-accented upbeat. [20c: W Indian]

regicide *noun* **1** the act of killing a king. **2** someone who kills a king. [16c: from Latin *rex* king + **-cide**]

regime *or* **régime** /reɪ'ʒiːm/ *noun* **1** a system of government. **2** a particular government or administration. **3** a regimen, esp in medicine. [15c: from French *régime*, from Latin *regimen*]

regimen *noun* **1** *med* a course of treatment, esp of diet and exercise, which is recommended for good health. **2 a** a system of government; **b** rule. [14c: Latin, from *regere* to rule]

regiment *noun* **1** *military* a body of soldiers consisting of several companies, etc and commanded by a colonel. **2** a large number of people or things formed into an organized group. ▸ *verb* **1** to organize or control (people, etc) strictly. **2** *military* to form or group (soldiers, an army, etc) into a regiment or regiments. **3** to group (people or things) in an organized way. ▪ **regimentation** *noun.* [14c: from French, from Latin *regere* to rule]

regimental *adj* belonging or relating to a regiment. ▸ *noun* (**regimentals**) a military uniform, esp that of a particular regiment. ▪ **regimentally** *adv.*

region *noun* **1** an area of the world or of a country, esp when considered geographically, in social or economic terms, etc: *a mountainous region* • *a deprived region of the country.* **2** (**Region**) esp (1973–96) in Scotland: an administrative area. **3** *anatomy* an area of the body, esp when described as being in or near a specified part, organ, etc: *the abdominal region.* **4** an area of activity, interest, study, etc. **5** *maths* a subset of points on a plane or in space, any two of which can be joined by a line that is still inside the region. ▪ **regional** *adj.* ▪ **regionally** *adv.* [14c: from Latin *regio*, from *regere* to rule]

IDIOMS **in the region of** approximately; nearly: *in the region of a hundred pounds.*

register *noun* **1 a** a written list or record of names, events, etc; **b** a book containing such a list. **2** a machine or device which records and lists information, eg a **cash register**. **3** *music* the range of tones produced by the human voice or a musical instrument. **4** *music* **a** an organ stop or stop-knob; **b** the set of pipes controlled by an organ stop. **5** a style of speech or language. **6** *comput* a device for storing small amounts of data. ▸ *verb* **1** to enter (an event, name, etc) in an official register. **2** *intr* to enter one's name and address in a hotel register on arrival. **3** *tr & intr* to enrol formally: *Please register for the conference by Friday.* **4** to send (a letter, parcel, etc) by registered post. **5** of a device: to record and usu show (speed, information, etc) automatically. **6** of a person's face, expression, etc: to show (a particular feeling). **7** *intr, informal* to make an impression on someone, eg by being understood, remembered, etc: *The name didn't register.* [14c: from Latin *regerere* to enter or record]

register office *noun, Brit* an office where records of births, deaths and marriages are kept and where marriages may be performed. Also called **registry office**.

registrar *noun* **1** someone who keeps an official register, esp of births, deaths and marriages. **2** a senior administrator in a university, responsible for student records, enrolment, etc. **3** *Brit* a middle-ranking hospital doctor who is training to become a specialist. ▪ **registrarship** *noun*. [17c: related to **register**]

registration *noun* **1** an act or instance or the process of registering. **2** something registered.

registry *noun* (**-*ies***) **1** an office or place where registers are kept. **2** registration.

regolith *noun, geol* loose material on the earth's surface, including fragments of rock, soil, etc. [Greek *rhegos* a blanket + *lithos* a stone]

regress *verb* /rɪ'grɛs/ **1** *intr* **a** to go back; **b** to return. **2** *intr* to revert to a former state or condition, usu a less desirable or less advanced one. **3** *tr & intr, psychol* to return to an earlier, less advanced stage of development or behaviour. ▸ *noun* /'riːgrɛs/ an act or instance or the process of regressing. [14c: from Latin from *regredi* to return or go back]

regression *noun* **1** an act or instance or the process of regressing. **2** *psychol* a return to an earlier level of functioning, eg an adult's reversion to infantile or adolescent behaviour.

regressive *adj* **1 a** going back; **b** returning. **2** reverting. **3** of taxation: with the rate decreasing as the taxable amount increases. ▪ **regressively** *adv*.

regret *verb* (***regretted, regretting***) **1 a** to feel sorry, repentant, distressed, disappointed, etc about (something one has done or that has happened); **b** to wish that things had been otherwise. **2** to remember (someone or something) with a sense of loss. ▸ *noun* **1 a** a feeling of sorrow, repentance, distress, disappointment, etc; **b** a wish that things had been otherwise. **2** a sense of loss. **3** (**regrets**) a polite expression of sorrow, disappointment, etc, used esp when declining an invitation. [14c: from French *regreter*]

regretful *adj* feeling or displaying regret. ▪ **regretfully** *adv*.

regrettable *adj* unwelcome; unfortunate; serious enough to deserve a reprimand: *a regrettable mistake*.

regular *adj* **1** usual; normal; customary. **2** arranged, occurring, acting, etc in a fixed pattern of predictable or equal intervals of space or time: *at regular intervals*. **3** agreeing with some rule, custom, established practice, etc, and commonly accepted as correct. **4** symmetrical or even. **5** of a geometric figure: having all the faces, sides, angles, etc the same. **6** of bowel movements or menstrual periods: occurring with normal frequency. **7** *orig US* medium-sized: *a regular portion of fries*. **8** *informal* complete; absolute: *a regular little monster*. **9** *grammar* of a noun, verb, etc: following one of the usual patterns of formation, inflection, etc. **10** *military* of troops, the army, etc: belonging to or forming a permanent professional body. **11 a** officially qualified or recognized; **b** professional. **12** *N Am, informal* behaving in a generally acceptable or likeable way: *a regular guy*. ▸ *noun* **1** *military* a soldier in a professional permanent army. **2** *informal* a frequent customer, esp of a pub, bar, shop, etc. ▪ **regularity** *noun*. ▪ **regularization** *noun*. ▪ **regularize** *or* **-ise** *verb*. ▪ **regularly** *adv*. [14c: from French *reguler*, from Latin *regula* rule]

regulate *verb* **1** to control or adjust (the amount of available heat, sound, etc). **2** to control or adjust (a machine) so that it functions correctly. **3** to control or direct (a person, thing, etc) according to a rule or rules. **4** *intr* to make or lay down a rule. ▪ **regulative** /'rɛgjʊlətɪv/ *or* **regulatory** *adj*. ▪ **regulator** *noun*. [17c: from Latin *regula* rule]

regulation *noun* **1** an act or instance or the process or state of regulating or being regulated. **2** a rule or instruction.

regurgitate *verb* **1 a** to pour back; **b** to cast out again. **2** to bring back (food) into the mouth after it has been swallowed. **3** to repeat exactly (something already said or expressed). ▪ **regurgitation** *noun*. [17c: from Latin *regurgitare*]

rehab /'riːhab/ *informal, noun* rehabilitation (see under **rehabilitate**). ▸ *verb* (***rehabbed, rehabbing***) rehabilitate.

rehabilitate *verb* **1** to help (someone who has been ill, etc or a former prisoner) adapt to normal life again. **2** of buildings, etc: to rebuild or restore to good condition. **3** to lift (the reputation of someone or something) to a better status or rank. ▪ **rehabilitation** *noun*. [16c: from Latin *habilitas* skill or ability]

rehash *informal, verb* /riː'haʃ/ to rework or re-use (material which has been used before), but with no significant changes or improvements. ▸ *noun* /'riːhaʃ/ a reworking or re-use of such material. [19c]

rehearsal *noun* **1** an act or instance or the process of rehearsing. **2** a practice session or performance of a play, etc before it is performed in front of an audience.

rehearse *verb* **1** *tr & intr* to practise (a play, piece of music, etc) before performing it in front of an audience. **2** to train (a person) for performing in front of an audience. **3** to give a list of: *rehearsed his grievances*. **4** to repeat or say over again. ▪ **rehearser** *noun*. ▪ **rehearsing** *noun*. [16c: from French *hercier* to harrow]

rehome *verb* to find a new home for (a pet, etc).

rehouse *verb* to provide with new and usu better accommodation or premises. ▪ **rehousing** *noun*. [19c]

rehydrate *verb* **1** *intr* to absorb water again after dehydration. **2** to add water to (a dehydrated substance). ▪ **rehydration** *noun*. [20c]

Reich /raɪk, raɪx/ *noun* (*in full* **the Third Reich**) the name given to the German state during the Nazi regime from 1933 to 1945. [1920s: German, meaning 'kingdom']

Reichstag /'raɪkstɑːg, 'raɪxs-/ *noun* **1** *hist* the lower house of the German parliament. **2** the building in Berlin in which it met, now the home of the German parliament.

reign *noun* **1** the period of time when a king or queen rules. **2** the period during which someone or something rules, is in control or dominates: *reign of terror*. ▸ *verb, intr* **1** to be a ruling king or queen. **2** to prevail, exist or dominate: *silence reigns*. ▪ **reigning** *adj* **1 a** ruling; **b** prevailing. **2** of a winner, champion, etc: currently holding the title of champion, etc. [13c: from French *reigne*, from Latin *regnum* kingdom]

reimburse *verb* **1** to repay (money spent). **2** to pay (a person) money to compensate for or cover (expenses, losses, etc): *will reimburse you your costs.* ▪ **reimbursable** *adj.* ▪ **reimbursement** *noun.* [17c: from Latin *imbursare* to put something into a purse, from *bursa* purse]

rein *noun* **1** (*often* **reins**) the strap, or either of the two halves of the strap, attached to a bridle and used to guide and control a horse. **2** (*usu* **reins**) a device with straps for guiding a small child. **3** any means of controlling, governing or restraining. ▸ *verb* **1** to provide with reins. **2** to guide or control (esp a horse) with reins. **3** (*usu* **rein in**) to stop or restrain with, or as if with, reins. **4** (*usu* **rein in**) *intr* to stop or slow up. **5** (*usu* **rein sth back**) to take measures to stop (eg inflation, costs, etc) from continuing or increasing any further. [13c: from French *resne*, from Latin *tenere* to hold]

IDIOMS **give (a free) rein to sb** *or* **sth** to allow them or it to do as they like. **keep a tight rein on sb** *or* **sth** to keep strict control of them or it.

reincarnation *noun* in some beliefs: the transference of someone's soul after death to another body. ▪ **reincarnate** *verb, adj.* [19c]

reindeer *noun* (***reindeer*** *or* ***reindeers***) a large deer, antlered in both sexes, found in arctic and sub-Arctic regions of Europe and Asia. [14c: from Norse *hreindyri*]

reinforce *verb* **1** to strengthen or give additional support to something. **2** to stress or emphasize: *reinforced his argument*. **3** to make (an army, work force, etc) stronger by providing additional soldiers, weapons, workers, etc. [17c: from French *renforcer*]

reinforced concrete *noun, eng* concrete in which steel bars or wires have been embedded to increase its tensile strength.

reinforcement *noun* **1** an act or instance or the process of reinforcing. **2** anything which reinforces. **3** (*usu* **reinforcements**) soldiers, weapons, workers, etc added to an army, work force, etc to make it stronger.

reinstate *verb* **1** to place in a previous position. **2** to restore (someone) to a position, status or rank formerly held. ▪ **reinstatement** *noun.* [16c]

reiterate *verb* to do or say again or repeatedly. ▪ **reiteration** *noun.* ▪ **reiterative** *adj.* [16c]

reject *verb* /rɪˈdʒɛkt/ **1** to refuse to accept, agree to, admit, believe, etc. **2** to throw away or discard. **3** *med* of the body: to fail to accept (new tissue or an organ from another body). ▸ *noun* /ˈriːdʒɛkt/ **1** someone or something that is rejected. **2** an imperfect article offered for sale at a discount. ▪ **rejectable** *adj.* ▪ **rejection** *noun.* ▪ **rejective** *adj.* ▪ **rejector** *noun.* [15c: from Latin *jacere* to throw]

rejig *verb* (***rejigged, rejigging***) **1** to re-equip or refit (a factory, etc). **2** to rearrange or reorganize (something). [20c]

rejoice *verb* **1** *intr* to feel, show or express great happiness or joy. **2** (*usu* **rejoice that**) to be glad. **3** (**rejoice in sth**) *often ironic* to revel or take delight in it: *rejoices in the name Ben Pink Dandelion.* ▪ **rejoicer** *noun.* ▪ **rejoicingly** *adv.* [14c: from French *réjouir*; see **joy**]

rejoin[1] /rɪˈdʒɔɪn/ *verb* **1 a** to say in reply, esp abruptly or wittily; **b** to retort. **2** *intr, law* to reply to a charge or pleading. ▪ **rejoinder** *noun.* [15c: from French *rejoindre*]

rejoin[2] /riːˈdʒɔɪn/ *verb, tr & intr* to join again.

rejuvenate *verb* to make young again. ▪ **rejuvenation** *noun.* [19c: from Latin *juvenis* young]

relapse *verb, intr* **1** to sink or fall back into a former state or condition, esp one involving evil or bad habits, etc. **2** to become ill again after apparent or partial recovery. ▸ *noun* an act or instance or the process of relapsing into bad habits, etc, or poor health. ▪ **relapser** *noun.* [16c: from Latin *relabi* to slide back]

relate *verb* **1** to tell or narrate (a story, anecdote, etc). **2** to show or form a connection between facts, events, etc: *related his unhappiness to a deprived childhood.* **3** *intr, informal* (**relate to sb**) **a** to get on well with them. **b** to react favourably or sympathetically to them. **4** *intr* (**relate to sth**) **a** to be about it or concerned with it: *I have information that relates to their activities.* **b** to be able to understand it or show some empathy towards it: *I can relate to her angry response.* **5** *intr, law* of a decision, etc: to date back in application; to be valid from a date earlier than that on which it was made. [16c: from Latin *referre* to bring back]

related *adj* **1** belonging to the same family, by birth or marriage. **2** connected. ▪ **relatedness** *noun.*

relation *noun* **1** an act of relating. **2** a telling or narrating. **3** the state or way of being related. **4** a connection or relationship between one person or thing and another. **5** someone who belongs to the same family through birth or marriage. **6** kinship. **7** (**relations**) social, political or personal contact between people, countries, etc. **8** (**relations**) *euphemistic* sexual intercourse.

IDIOMS **in** *or* **with relation to sth** in reference to it; with respect to it.

relational *adj* **1** relating to or expressing relation. **2** *grammar* showing or expressing syntactic relation. **3** *comput* based on interconnected data: *relational database.*

relationship *noun* **1** the state of being related. **2** the state of being related by birth or marriage. **3** the friendship, communications, etc which exist between people, countries, etc. **4** an emotional or sexual affair.

relative *noun* a person who is related to someone else by birth or marriage. ▸ *adj* **1** compared with something else; comparative: *the relative speeds of a car and train.* **2** existing only in relation to something else: *'hot' and 'cold' are relative terms.* **3** (*chiefly* **relative to**) in proportion to: *salary relative to experience.* **4** relevant: *information relative to the problem.* **5** *grammar* **a** of a pronoun or adjective: referring to someone or something that has already been named and attaching a subordinate clause to it, eg *who* in *the children who are playing*, although some clauses of this kind can have the relative word omitted, eg *playing in the park* is a relative clause in *the children playing in the park;* **b** of a clause or phrase: attached to a preceding word, phrase, etc by a relative word such as *which* and *who*, or *whose* in *the man whose cat was lost*. See also **antecedent**. Compare **absolute** (*adj* sense 6a). ▪ **relatively** *adv.* ▪ **relativeness** *noun.* [16c: from Latin *relativus* referring]

relative atomic mass *noun, chem* (*often* **atomic mass**) the ratio of the average mass of one atom of an element to that of one twelfth of the mass of carbon-12, expressed in atomic mass units. Also (*formerly*) called **atomic weight**.

relative error *noun, maths* error expressed as a ratio to the total amount.

relativism *noun, philos* a philosophical position that maintains that there are truths and values, but denies that they are absolute. ▪ **relativist** *noun.* ▪ **relativistic** *adj.* [19c]

relativity *noun* **1** the condition of being relative to and therefore affected by something else. **2** two theories of motion, **special theory of relativity** and **general theory of relativity**, which recognize the dependence of space, time and other physical measurements on the position and motion of the observer who is making the measurements.

relax *verb* **1 a** to make (part of the body, muscles, one's grip, etc) less tense, stiff or rigid; **b** *intr* of muscles, a grip, etc: to become less tense; to become looser or slacker. **2** *tr & intr* to make or become less tense, nervous or worried. **3** *intr* of a person: to become less stiff or formal. **4** *tr & intr* of discipline, rules, etc: to make or become less strict or severe. **5** to lessen the force, strength or intensity of (something): *relaxed his vigilance.* ▪ **relaxed** *adj.* ▪ **relaxing** *adj.* [15c: from Latin *relaxare* to loosen]

relaxant *adj* relating to or causing relaxation. ▸ *noun, med* a drug that causes relaxation of tension or the skeletal muscles. [18c]

relaxation *noun* **1** an act or the process of relaxing or state of being relaxed. **2** recreation. **3** a relaxing activity. **4** *law* partial remission, eg of a punishment.

relay[1] *noun* /'riːleɪ/ **1** a set of workers, supply of materials, etc that replace others doing, or being used for, some task, etc. **2** *old use* a fresh supply of horses, posted at various points along a route, to replace others on a journey. **3** a **relay race**. **4** *electronics* an electrical switching device that, in response to a change in an electric circuit, eg a small change in current, opens or closes one or more contacts in the same or another circuit. **5** *telecomm* a device fitted at regular intervals along TV broadcasting networks, underwater telecommunications cables, etc to amplify weak signals and pass them on from one communication link to the next. **6 a** something which is relayed, esp a signal or broadcast; **b** the act of relaying it. ▸ *verb* /rɪ'leɪ, 'riːleɪ/ **1** to receive and pass on (news, a message, a TV programme, etc). **2** *radio* to rebroadcast (a programme received from another station or source). [15c: from French *relaier* to leave behind, from Latin *laxare* to loosen]

relay[2] *or* **re-lay** /riː'leɪ/ *verb* (***relaid***) to lay again. [16c]

relay race *noun* a race between teams of runners, swimmers, etc in which each member of the team covers part of the total distance to be covered.

release *verb* **1** to free (a prisoner, etc) from captivity. **2** to relieve (someone) of a duty, burden, etc. **3** to loosen one's grip and stop holding something. **4** to make (news, information, etc) known publicly. **5** to offer (a film, recording, book, etc) for sale, performance, etc. **6** to move (a catch, brake, etc) so that it no longer prevents something from moving, operating, etc. **7** to give off or emit (heat, gas, etc). ▸ *noun* **1** an act or the process of releasing or state of being released. **2** an item of news made public, or a document containing this: *press release.* ▪ **releasable** *adj.* ▪ **releaser** *noun.* [13c: from French *relesser*, from Latin *relaxare* to relax]

relegate *verb* **1** to move down to a lower grade, position, status, etc. **2** *sport, esp football* to move (a team) down to a lower league or division. Compare **promote** (sense 1b). **3** to refer (a decision, etc) to someone or something for action to be taken. ▪ **relegation** *noun.* [16c: from Latin *relegare* to send away]

relent *verb, intr* **1** to become less severe or unkind; to soften. **2** to give way and agree to something one initially would not accept. ▪ **relenting** *noun, adj.* [14c: from Latin *lentus* flexible]

relentless *adj* **1 a** without pity; **b** harsh. **2** never stopping: *a relentless fight against crime.* ▪ **relentlessly** *adv.* ▪ **relentlessness** *noun.*

relevant *adj* directly connected with or related to the matter in hand; pertinent. ▪ **relevance** *or* **relevancy** *noun.* ▪ **relevantly** *adv.* [16c: from Latin *relevare* to raise up or relieve]

reliable *adj* **1** dependable; trustworthy. **2** consistent in character, quality, etc. ▪ **reliability** *noun.* ▪ **reliably** *adv.*

reliance *noun* **1** dependability, trust or confidence. **2** the state of relying on someone or something.

relic *noun* **1** a fragment or part of an object left after the rest has decayed: *relics from the stone-age village.* **2** an object valued as a memorial or souvenir of the past. **3** something left from a past time, esp a custom, belief, practice, etc. **4** part of the body of a saint or martyr, or of some object connected with them, preserved as an object of veneration. **5** *informal* **a** an old person; **b** something that is old or old-fashioned. [13c: from Latin *reliquiae* remains]

relict *noun* **1** something surviving in its primitive form. **2** a widow. [16c: from Latin *relinquere, relictum* to leave]

relief *noun* **1** the lessening or removal of pain, worry, oppression, distress, etc or the feeling that comes from this. **2** anything lessening pain, worry, boredom, etc. **3** help, often in the form of money, food, clothing and medicine, given to people in need. **4** someone who takes over a job or task from another person. **5** the freeing of a besieged or endangered town, fortress, etc. **6** *art* a method of sculpture in which figures project from a flat surface. See also **bas-relief**. **7** a clear, sharp outline caused by contrast. [14c: French, from Latin *relevare* to reduce the load]

relief map *noun* a map which shows the variations in the height of the land by shading.

relieve *verb* **1** to lessen or stop (pain, worry, boredom, etc). **2** to remove (a physical or mental burden) (from someone): *relieved her of many responsibilities.* **3** to give help or assistance. **4** to make less monotonous or tedious, esp by providing a contrast. **5** to free or dismiss from a duty or restriction. **6** to take over a job or task from. **7** to come to the help of (a besieged town, fortress, military post, etc). ▪ **relievable** *adj.* ▪ **relieved** *adj.* [14c: from French *relever*, from Latin *levare* to lighten]

IDIOMS **relieve oneself** to urinate or defecate.

relievo /rɪ'liːvoʊ/ *or* **rilievo** /rɪ'ljeɪvoʊ/ *noun, art* **1** relief. **2** a work in relief. **3** appearance of relief. See **relief** (sense 6). [17c: Italian]

religion *noun* **1** a belief in, or the worship of, a god or gods. **2** a particular system of belief or worship, such as Christianity or Judaism. **3** the monastic way of life. [12c: French, from Latin *ligare* to bind]

religiose *adj* excessively or sentimentally religious.

religious *adj* **1** relating to religion. **2 a** following the rules or forms of worship of a particular religion very closely; **b** pious; devout. **3** conscientious. **4** belonging or relating to the monastic way of life. ▶ *noun* (*pl* ***religious***) a person bound by monastic vows, eg a monk or nun. ▪ **religiosity** *noun.* ▪ **religiously** *adv.* ▪ **religiousness** *noun.*

relinquish *verb* **1** to give up or abandon (a belief, task, etc). **2** to release one's hold of (something). **3** to renounce possession or control of (a claim, right, etc). ▪ **relinquishment** *noun.* [15c: from French *relinquir*, from Latin *linquere* to leave]

reliquary /ˈrɛlɪkwərɪ/ *noun* (***-ies***) a container for holy relics. [17c: from French *relique* relic]

relish *verb* **1** to enjoy greatly or with discrimination. **2** to look forward to with great pleasure. ▶ *noun* **1** pleasure; enjoyment. **2 a** a spicy appetizing flavour; **b** a sauce or pickle which adds such a flavour to food. **3** zest, charm, liveliness or gusto. [16c: from French *relaisser* to leave behind or release]

relive *verb* **1** *intr* to live again. **2** to experience again, esp in the imagination. [16c]

relocate *verb* **1** to locate again. **2** *tr & intr* to move (oneself, a business, home, etc) from one place, town, etc to another. ▪ **relocation** *noun.*

reluctance *noun* **1 a** unwillingness; **b** lack of enthusiasm. **2** *physics* (symbol **R**) a measure of the opposition to magnetic flux in a magnetic circuit, analogous to resistance in an electric circuit. [16c: from Latin *reluctari* to resist]

reluctant *adj* unwilling or disinclined: *reluctant to leave.* ▪ **reluctance** *noun.* ▪ **reluctantly** *adv.*

rely *verb* (***-ies, -ied***) (*always* **rely on** *or* **upon**) **1** to depend on or need. **2** to trust. **3** to be certain of. [14c: from French *relier* to bind together]

REM *abbrev* rapid eye movement.

remain *verb, intr* **1** to be left after others, or other parts of the whole, have been used up, taken away, lost, etc. **2 a** to stay behind; **b** to stay in the same place. **3** to stay the same or unchanged; to continue to exist in the same state, condition, etc. **4** to continue to need to be done, shown, dealt with, etc: *That remains to be decided.* [14c: from Latin *remanere* to stay behind]

remainder *noun* **1** what is left after others, or other parts, have gone, been used up, taken away, etc; the rest. **2** *maths* the amount left over when one number cannot be divided exactly by another number. **3** *maths* the amount left when one number is subtracted from another; the difference. **4** the copies of a book left unsold or sold at a reduced price because sales have fallen off. **5** *law* an interest in an estate which comes into effect only if another interest established at the same time comes to an end. ▶ *verb* to sell (copies of a book) at a reduced price because sales have fallen off.

remains *plural noun* **1** what is left after part has been taken away, eaten, destroyed, etc. **2** a dead body. **3** relics.

remake *verb* /riːˈmeɪk/ to make again or in a new way. ▶ *noun* /ˈriːmeɪk/ something that is made again, eg a new version of an existing film. [17c]

remand *verb* to send (an accused person) back into custody to await trial, esp to allow more evidence to be collected. ▶ *noun* an act or the process of remanding someone. [15c: from Latin *mandare* to send word or to command]

IDIOMS **on remand** in custody or on bail awaiting trial.

remark *verb* **1** *tr & intr* to notice and comment on. **2** to make a casual comment. ▶ *noun* **1** a comment, often a casual one. **2** an observation. **3** noteworthiness. [16c: from French *remarquer*]

remarkable *adj* **1** worth mentioning or commenting on. **2** very unusual or extraordinary. ▪ **remarkably** *adv.*

remarry *verb* to marry again, having been married before. ▪ **remarriage** *noun.*

remaster /riːˈmɑːstə(r)/ *verb* to make a new **master** (*noun* sense 9) of (a piece of recorded music).

remedial *adj* **1** affording a remedy. **2** *formerly* relating to or concerning the teaching of children with learning difficulties. ▪ **remedially** *adv.*

remedy *noun* (***-ies***) **1** a drug or treatment which cures or controls a disease. **2** something which solves a problem or gets rid of something undesirable. **3** legal redress. ▶ *verb* (***-ies, -ied***) **1** to cure or control (a disease, etc). **2** to put right or correct (a problem, error, etc). ▪ **remediable** /rɪˈmiːdɪəbəl/ *adj.* [13c: from Latin *mederi* to heal]

remember *verb* **1** to bring from the past to mind. **2** to keep (a fact, idea, etc) in one's mind: *remember to phone.* **3** to reward or make a present to (someone), eg in a will or as a tip. **4** to commemorate. **5** (**remember sb to sb else**) to pass on their good wishes and greetings to the other person. [14c: from French *remembrer*, from Latin *memor* mindful]

remembrance *noun* **1** the act of remembering or being remembered. **2 a** something which reminds a person of something or someone; **b** a souvenir. **3** a memory or recollection: *a dim remembrance of the night's events.*

remind *verb* **1** to cause (someone) to remember (something or to do something): *remind me to speak to him.* **2** to make (someone) think about: *She reminds me of her sister.* [17c]

reminder *noun* **1** something that reminds or is meant to remind: *got a reminder for the gas bill.* **2** a memento.

reminisce *verb, intr* to think, talk or write about things remembered from the past. [16c: from Latin *reminisci* to remember]

reminiscence *noun* **1** the act of thinking, talking or writing about the past. **2** something from the past that is remembered. **3** the process of relating a past event, etc. **4** (*often* **reminiscences**) a written account of things remembered from the past.

reminiscent *adj* **1** (*usu* **reminiscent of**) similar: *a painting reminiscent of Turner.* **2** of a person: often thinking about the past. **3** relating to reminiscence.

remiss *adj* careless; failing to pay enough attention; negligent. [15c: from Latin from *remittere* to loosen]

remission *noun* **1** a lessening in force or effect, esp in the symptoms of a disease such as cancer. **2** a reduction of a prison sentence. **3 a** pardon; **b** forgiveness from sin. **4** the act of remitting or state of being remitted. [13c: from Latin *remissio*]

remit *verb* /rɪˈmɪt/ (***remitted, remitting***) **1** to cancel or refrain from demanding (a debt, punishment, etc). **2** *tr & intr* to make or become loose, slack or relaxed. **3** to send (money) in payment. **4** to refer (a matter for decision, etc) to some other authority. **5** *law* to refer (a case) to a lower court. **6** *intr* of a disease, pain, rain, etc: to become less severe for a period of time. **7** to send or put back into a previous state. **8** of God: to forgive (sins). ▸ *noun* /ˈriːmɪt, rɪˈmɪt/ the authority or terms of reference given to an official, committee, etc in dealing with a matter. ▪ **remittable** *adj*. [14c: from Latin *remittere* to loosen or send back]

remittance *noun* **1** the sending of money in payment. **2** the money sent.

remix *verb* /riːˈmɪks/ to mix again in a different way, esp to mix (a recording) again, changing the balance of the different parts, etc. ▸ *noun* /ˈriːmɪks/ a remixed recording. See also **mix** (*verb* sense 7).

remnant *noun* (*often* **remnants**) **1** a remaining small piece or amount of something larger. **2** a remaining piece of fabric from the end of a roll. **3** a surviving trace or vestige. [14c: from French *remanoir* to remain]

remonstrance *noun* **1** an act of remonstrating. **2** a strong, usu formal, protest.

remonstrate *verb* (*often* **remonstrate with sb**) to protest forcefully (to someone): *remonstrated that they knew nothing about it*. ▪ **remonstration** *noun*. [16c: from Latin *remonstrare* to demonstrate]

remorse *noun* **1** a deep feeling of guilt, regret and bitterness for something wrong or bad. **2** compassion or pity. ▪ **remorseful** *adj*. [14c: from French *remors*, from Latin *mordere* to bite or sting]

remorseless *adj* **1** without remorse. **2** cruel. **3** without respite; relentless. ▪ **remorselessness** *noun*.

remote *adj* **1** far away; distant in time or place. **2** out of the way; far from civilization. **3** operated or controlled from a distance; remote-controlled. **4** *comput* of a computer terminal: located separately from the main processor but having a communication link with it. **5** distantly related or connected. **6** very small, slight or faint: *a remote chance*. **7** aloof or distant. ▸ *noun* **1** *TV & radio, esp US* an outside broadcast. **2** a remote control device, eg for a TV. ▪ **remotely** *adv*. ▪ **remoteness** *noun*. [15c: from Latin *remotus* removed or distant]

remote control *noun* **1** the control of machinery or electrical devices from a distance, by the making or breaking of an electric circuit or by means of radio waves. **2** a battery-operated device for transmitting such waves. ▪ **remote-controlled** *adj*.

remote sensor *noun* a device which scans the Earth and other planets from space in order to collect, and transmit to a central computer, data about them. ▪ **remote sensing** *noun*.

remould *verb* /riːˈmoʊld/ **1** to mould again. **2** to bond new tread onto (an old or worn tyre). ▸ *noun* /ˈriːmoʊld/ a tyre that has had new tread bonded onto it. Also called **retread**. [17c]

remount *verb, tr & intr* **1** to get on or mount again (esp a horse, bicycle, etc). **2** to mount (a picture, etc) again. [14c]

removal *noun* **1** the act or process of removing or state of being removed. **2** the moving of possessions, furniture, etc to a new house.

remove *verb* **1** to move to a different place. **2** to take off (a piece of clothing). **3** to get rid of. **4** to dismiss from a job, position, etc. ▸ *noun* **1** a removal. **2** the degree, usu specified, of difference separating two things: *a government only one remove from tyranny*. **3** *Brit* in some schools: an intermediate form or class. ▪ **removable** *adj*. ▪ **remover** *noun*. [14c: from French *remouvoir*]

removed *adj* **1** separated, distant or remote. **2** usu of cousins: separated by a specified number of generations or degrees of descent: *first cousin once removed*.

remunerate *verb* **1** to recompense. **2** to pay (someone) for services rendered. ▪ **remuneration** *noun*. ▪ **remunerative** *adj*. [16c: from Latin *munus* a gift]

renaissance /rɪˈneɪsəns/ *noun* **1** a rebirth or revival, esp of learning, culture and the arts. **2** (**the Renaissance**) the revival of arts and literature during the 14th-16th centuries or the art, etc produced then. [19c: French, from Latin *renasci* to be born again]

renal /ˈriːnəl/ *adj* relating to the kidneys. [17c: from French *rénal*, from Latin *renes* kidneys]

renascence *noun* rebirth; the fact or process of being born again or into new life. ▪ **renascent** *adj*. [18c: from Latin *renasci* to be born again]

rend *verb* (***rent***) *old use* **1** *tr & intr* to tear (something), esp using force or violence. **2** to tear (hair, clothes, etc) in grief, rage, etc. **3** *tr & intr* to divide or split: *War had rent the country in two*. **4** of a noise: to disturb (the silence, the air, etc) with a loud, piercing sound. [Anglo-Saxon]

render *verb* **1** to cause (something) to be or become: *render things more agreeable*. **2** to give or provide (a service, help, etc). **3** to show (obedience, honour, etc). **4** to pay (money) or perform (a duty), esp in return for something: *render thanks to God*. **5** to give back or return (something). **6** to give in return or exchange. **7** (*also* **render up**) to give up, release or yield: *The grave will never render up its dead*. **8** to translate: *How do you render that in German?* **9** to perform (the role of a character in a play, a piece of music, etc). **10** to portray or reproduce, esp in painting or music. **11** to present or submit for payment, approval, consideration, etc. **12** to cover (brick or stone) with a coat of plaster. **13** **a** to melt (fat), esp to clarify it; **b** to remove (fat) by melting. **14** *law* of a judge or jury: to deliver formally (a judgement or verdict). ▪ **renderer** *noun*. [14c: from French *rendre*]

rendering *noun* **1** an act or instance or the process of rendering something, esp a particular interpretation of a work of music, piece of drama, etc. **2** a coat of plaster or the applying of this. **3** a translation.

rendezvous /ˈrɑ̃deɪvuː, ˈrɒn-/ *noun* (*pl* ***rendezvous*** /-vuːz/) **1** **a** an appointment to meet at a specified time and place; **b** the meeting itself; **c** the place where such a meeting is to be. **2** a place where people generally meet. **3** *space flight* an arranged meeting, and usu docking, of two spacecraft in space. ▸ *verb, intr* **1** to meet at an appointed place or time. **2** of two spacecraft: to meet, and usu dock, in space. [16c: French from *se rendre* to present oneself]

rendition *noun* a performance or interpretation of a piece of music, a dramatic role, etc.

renegade *noun* someone who deserts the religious, political, etc group which they belong to, and joins an enemy or rival group. [15c: from Spanish *renegado*, from Latin *negare* to deny]

renege *or* **renegue** /rɪˈneɪɡ/ *verb* **1** *intr* (*often* **renege on**) to go back on (one's word, a promise, agreement, deal, etc). **2** to renounce (a promise, etc) or desert (a person, faith, etc). **3** *cards* to revoke (*verb* sense 2). [16c: from Latin *negare* to deny]

renew *verb* **1** **a** to make fresh or like new again; **b** to restore to the original condition. **2** **a** to begin to do again; **b** to repeat. **3** *tr & intr* to begin (some activity) again after a break. **4** *tr & intr* to make (a licence, lease, loan, etc) valid for a further period of time. **5** to replenish or replace. ▪ **renewable** *adj*. ▪ **renewal** *noun*.

rennet *noun* a substance that curdles milk, obtained from the stomachs of calves or from some fungi. [15c: related to Anglo-Saxon *gerinnan* to curdle]

renounce *verb* **1** to give up (a claim, title, right, etc), esp formally and publicly. **2** to refuse to recognize or associate with (someone). **3** to give up (a bad habit). ▪ **renouncement** *noun*. ▪ **renouncer** *noun*. [14c: from French *renoncer*, from Latin *renuntiare* to announce]

renovate *verb* **1** to renew or make new again. **2** to restore (esp a building) to a former and better condition. ▪ **renovation** *noun*. ▪ **renovator** *noun*. [16c: from Latin *renovare*]

renown *noun* fame. ▪ **renowned** *adj*. [14c: from French *renomer* to make famous]

rent[1] *noun* money paid periodically to the owner of a property by a tenant in return for the use or occupation of that property. ▸ *verb* **1** to pay rent for (a building, house, flat, etc). **2** (*also* **rent out**) to allow someone the use of (property) in return for payment of rent. **3** *intr* to be hired out for rent. [12c: from French *rente* revenue, from Latin *rendere* to render]

rent[2] *noun, old use* **1** an opening or split made by tearing or rending. **2** a fissure. ▸ *verb, past tense, past participle of* **rend**. [16c]

rental *noun* **1** the act of renting. **2** money paid as rent.

renunciation *noun* **1** an act of renouncing. **2** a formal declaration of renouncing something. **3** self-denial. [14c: from Latin *renuntiare* to proclaim]

rep[1] *noun, informal* a representative, esp a travelling salesperson.

rep[2] see under **repertory**

repair[1] *verb* **1** to restore (something damaged or broken) to good working condition. **2** to put right, heal or make up for (some wrong that has been done). ▸ *noun* **1** an act or the process of repairing. **2** a condition or state: *in good repair*. **3** a part or place that has been mended or repaired. ▪ **repairable** *adj*. ▪ **repairer** *noun*. [14c: from French *reparer*, from Latin *parare* to make ready]

repair[2] *verb, intr* (*usu* **repair to**) *old use* to go or take oneself. [14c: from French *repairer*, from Latin *patria* homeland]

reparation *noun* **1** an act or instance of making up for some wrong that has been done. **2** money paid or something done for this purpose. **3** (*usu* **reparations**) compensation paid after a war by a defeated nation for the damage caused. ▪ **reparable** /ˈrɛpərəbəl/ *adj*. [14c: from French *réparation*, from Latin *reparare* to repair]

repartee *noun* **1** the practice or skill of making spontaneous witty retorts. **2** a quick witty retort. **3** conversation with many such replies. [17c: from French *repartie*, from *repartir* to set out again or to retort]

repast *noun, formal or old use* a meal. [14c: from French *repaistre* to eat a meal, from Latin *pascere* to feed]

repatriate *verb* to send (a refugee, prisoner of war, etc) back to their country of origin. ▪ **repatriation** *noun*. [17c: from Latin *patria* homeland]

repay *verb* **1** to pay back or refund (money). **2** to do or give something (to someone) in return for something they have done or given: *repay his kindness*. ▪ **repayable** *adj*. ▪ **repayment** *noun*.

repeal *verb* to make (a law, etc) no longer valid; to annul (a law, etc). ▸ *noun* the act of repealing (a law, etc). ▪ **repealable** *adj*. [14c: from French *apeler* to appeal]

repeat *verb* **1** to say, do, etc, again or several times. **2** to echo or say again exactly (the words already said by someone else). **3** to tell (something, esp a secret) to someone else. **4** **a** to quote from memory; **b** to recite (a poem, etc). **5** *intr* of food: to be tasted again some time after being swallowed. **6** *intr* to occur again or several times; to recur. **7** (*usu* **repeat itself**) of an event, occurrence, etc: to happen in exactly the same way more than once: *history repeats itself*. **8** *intr* of a gun: to fire several times without being reloaded. **9** *intr* of a clock: to strike the hour or quarter hour. **10** (**repeat oneself**) to say the same thing more than once, esp with the result of being repetitious or tedious. **11** of a TV or radio company: to broadcast (a programme, series, etc) again. ▸ *noun* **1** **a** the act of repeating; **b** a repetition. **2** something that is repeated, esp a television or radio programme which has been broadcast before. **3** *music* **a** a passage in a piece of music that is to be repeated; **b** a sign which marks such a passage. **4** an order for goods, etc that is exactly the same as a previous one. ▸ *adj* second or subsequent: *a repeat showing*. ▪ **repeatable** *adj*. ▪ **repeated** *adj*. ▪ **repeatedly** *adv*. [14c: from French *répéter*]

repeater *noun* **1** someone or something that repeats. **2** a clock that strikes the hour or quarter hour. **3** a gun that can be fired several times without being reloaded. **4** a device for automatically retransmitting a telegraphic message. **5** a device for amplifying the signal in a telephone circuit or a cable.

repel *verb* (***repelled, repelling***) **1** **a** to force or drive back or away; **b** to repulse. **2** *tr & intr* to provoke a feeling of disgust or loathing. **3** to fail to mix with, absorb or be attracted by (something else): *Oil repels water*. **4** to reject or rebuff. ▪ **repeller** *noun*. [15c: from Latin *repellere* to drive back]

repellent *noun* **1** something that drives away or discourages the presence of insects, etc. **2** a substance used to treat fabric so as to make it resistant to water. ▸ *adj* **1** forcing or driving back or away. **2** provoking a feeling of disgust or loathing. ▪ **repellence** *or* **repellency** *noun*. ▪ **repellently** *adv*.

repent *verb* **1** *tr & intr* **a** (*usu* **repent of**) to feel great sorrow or regret for something one has done; **b** to wish (an action, etc) undone. **2** *intr* to feel regret (for the evil or bad things one has done in the past) and change one's behaviour or conduct. ▪ **repentance** *noun*. ▪ **repentant** *adj*. [13c: from French *repentir*]

repercussion *noun* **1** (*usu* **repercussions**) a bad, unforeseen, indirect, etc result or consequence of some action, event, etc. **2** an echo or reverberation. **3** a recoil or repulse after an impact. ▪ **repercussive** *adj.* [16c: from Latin *repercussio*]

repertoire /ˈrɛpətwɑː(r)/ *noun* **1** the list of songs, operas, plays, etc that a singer, performer, group of actors, etc is able or ready to perform. **2** the range or stock of skills, techniques, talents, etc that someone or something has. **3** *comput* the total list of codes and commands that a computer can accept and execute. [19c: from French *répertoire*; see **repertory**]

repertory *noun* (***-ies***) **1** a repertoire, esp of a theatre company. **2** the performance of a repertoire of plays at regular, short intervals. **3** a storehouse or repository. **4** short form of **repertory company**. **5 a** short form of **repertory theatre**; **b** repertory theatres collectively: *worked in repertory for a few years.* Often shortened still further to **rep**. [16c: from Latin *reperire* to discover or find again]

repertory company *noun* a group of actors who perform a series of plays from their repertoire in the course of a season at one theatre.

repertory theatre *noun* a theatre where a repertory company performs its plays.

répétiteur /rɪpɛtɪˈtɜː(r)/ *noun* a coach or tutor, esp one who rehearses opera singers, ballet dancers, etc. [20c: French]

repetition *noun* **1** the act of repeating or being repeated. **2** something that is repeated. **3** a recital from memory, eg of a poem, piece of music, etc. **4** a copy or replica. **5** *music* the ability of a musical instrument to repeat a note quickly. [15c: from French *répétition*]

repetitious *adj* inclined to repetition, esp when tedious, boring, etc. ▪ **repetitiously** *adv.*

repetitive *adj* happening, done, said, etc over and over again. ▪ **repetitively** *adv.*

repetitive strain injury *or* **repetitive stress injury** *noun* (abbrev **RSI**) inflammation of the tendons and joints of the hands and lower arms, caused by repeated performance of identical manual operations such as using a keyboard.

rephrase *verb* to express in different words, esp as a way of improving sense, etc. [19c]

repine *verb, intr* (*usu* **repine at** *or* **against**) **1** to fret. **2** to feel discontented. [16c: from **pine**[2]]

replace *verb* **1** to put back in a previous or proper position. **2** to take the place of or be a substitute for. **3** to supplant. **4** to substitute (a person or thing) in place of (an existing one). ▪ **replaceable** *adj.* [16c]

> **replace**
> Be careful to use the right prepositions with **replace** and **substitute**. If X is put in place of Y, X **replaces** Y or X is **substituted for** Y, and Y is **replaced by** or **replaced with** X.

replacement *noun* **1** the act of replacing something. **2** someone or something that replaces another.

replay *noun* /ˈriːpleɪ/ **1** an act or instance of playing of a game, football match, etc again, usu because there was no clear winner the first time. **2** an act or instance of playing a recording or a recorded incident. ▸ *verb* /riːˈpleɪ/ to play (a tape, recording, football match, etc) again. [19c]

replenish *verb* to fill up or make complete again, esp a supply of something which has been used up. ▪ **replenishment** *noun.* [14c: from French *replenir*, from Latin *plenus* full]

replete *adj* **1** (*often* **replete with**) completely or well supplied. **2** *formal* having eaten enough or more than enough. ▪ **repleteness** *or* **repletion** *noun.* [14c: from Latin *replere* to fill]

replica *noun* **1** an exact copy, esp of a work of art. **2** a facsimile or reproduction. **3** a copy or model, esp a scaled-down one. [19c: Italian, from Latin *replicare* to repeat or fold back]

replicate *verb* /ˈrɪplɪkeɪt/ **1** to make a replica of. **2** to repeat (a scientific experiment). **3** *intr* of a molecule, virus, etc: to make a replica of itself. ▸ *adj* /ˈrɛplɪkət/ **1** *biol* of a leaf, insect's wing, etc: folded back. **2** of a scientific experiment: being a repetition. ▪ **replication** *noun.* [16c: from Latin *replicare* to fold back]

reply *verb* (***-ies, -ied***) **1** *intr* to answer or respond to in words, writing or action. **2** to say or do in response. ▸ *noun* (***-ies***) **1** an answer or response. **2** an act or instance of replying. [14c: from French *replier*, from Latin *replicare* to fold back, reply]

report *noun* **1** a detailed statement, description or account, esp one made after some form of investigation. **2** a detailed and usu formal account of the discussions and decisions of a committee, inquiry or other group of people. **3** an account of news, etc: *a newspaper report.* **4** a statement of a pupil's work and behaviour at school. **5** rumour; general talk. **6** character or reputation. **7** a loud explosive noise, eg of a gun firing. ▸ *verb* **1** to bring back (information, etc) as an answer, news or account: *reported that fighting had broken out.* **2** *intr* to state. **3** (*often* **report on**) to give a formal or official account or description of (findings, information, etc), esp after an investigation. **4** *US* of a committee, etc: to make a formal report on (a bill, etc). **5 a** to give an account of (some matter of news, etc), esp for a newspaper, or TV or radio broadcast; **b** *intr* to act as a newspaper, TV or radio reporter. **6** to make a complaint about someone. **7** *intr* to present oneself at an appointed place or time or to a specified person: *report to reception.* **8** *intr* (*usu* **report to**) to be under (a specified superior): *reports directly to the manager.* **9** *intr* to account for oneself in a particular way: *report sick.* ▪ **reportedly** *adv.* [14c: from French *reporter*, from Latin *reportare* to carry back]

reportage /rɛpɔːˈtɑːʒ/ *noun* **1** journalistic reporting. **2** the style and manner of this kind of reporting.

reported speech see **indirect speech**

reporter *noun* **1** someone who reports, esp for a newspaper, TV or radio. **2** *law* someone whose job is to prepare reports on legal proceedings.

repose[1] *noun* **1** a state of rest, calm or peacefulness. **2** composure. ▸ *verb* **1** *intr* to rest. **2** to lay (oneself, one's head, etc) down to rest. ▪ **reposeful** *adj.* [15c: from French *reposer*, from Latin *repausare* to stop]

repose[2] *verb* to place (confidence, trust, etc) in (someone or something). [15c: from Latin *reponere* to replace, restore, store up]

reposition *verb* **1** to move or put in a new or different place. **2** to alter the position of one's body.

repository *noun* (***-ies***) **1** a storage place or container. **2 a** a place where things are stored for exhibition; **b** a museum. **3** a warehouse. **4** someone or something thought of as a store of information, knowledge, etc. [15c: from Latin *reponere* to replace, to store up]

repossess *verb* of a creditor: to regain possession of (property or goods), esp because the debtor has defaulted on payment. ▪ **repossession** *noun*. [15c]

reprehend *verb* to find fault with; to blame or reprove. ▪ **reprehension** *noun*. [14c: from Latin *reprehendere*]

reprehensible *adj* deserving blame or criticism. ▪ **reprehensibly** *adv*.

represent *verb* **1 a** to serve as a symbol or sign for: *letters represent sounds*; **b** to stand for or correspond to: *A thesis represents years of hard work*. **2** to speak or act on behalf of (someone else). **3 a** to be a good example of; **b** to typify: *What he said represents the feelings of many people*. **4** to present an image of or portray, esp through painting or sculpture. **5** to bring clearly to mind: *a film that represents all the horrors of war*. **6** to describe in a specified way; to attribute a specified character or quality to (someone, something, oneself, etc): *represented themselves as experts*. **7** to show, state or explain: *represent the difficulties forcibly to the committee*. **8** to be an elected member of Parliament for (a constituency). **9** to act out or play the part of on stage. ▪ **representable** *adj*. [14c: from Latin *praesentare* to present]

re-present *verb* to present something again. [16c]

representation *noun* **1** an act or process of representing, or the state or fact of being represented. **2** a person or thing that represents someone or something else. **3 a** an image; **b** a picture or painting. **4** a dramatic performance. **5** (*often* **representations**) a strong statement made to present facts, opinions, complaints or demands. ▪ **representational** *adj*.

representative *adj* **1** representing. **2 a** standing as a good example of something; **b** typical. **3** standing or acting as a deputy for someone. **4** of government: comprised of elected people. ▸ *noun* **1 a** someone who represents someone or something else, esp someone who represents, or sells the goods of, a business or company; **b** someone who acts as a person's agent or who speaks on their behalf. **2** someone who represents a constituency in Parliament. **3** a typical example.

repress *verb* **1 a** to keep (an impulse, a desire to do something, etc) under control; **b** to restrain (an impulse, desire, etc). **2** to put down, esp using force: *repress the insurrection*. **3** *psychol* to exclude (unacceptable thoughts, feelings, etc) from the conscious mind. Compare **suppress**. ▪ **repressible** *adj*. ▪ **repression** *noun*. ▪ **repressive** *adj*. ▪ **repressor** *noun*. [14c: from Latin *reprimere* to press back]

reprieve *verb* **1** to delay or cancel (punishment, esp the execution of a prisoner condemned to death). **2** to give temporary relief or respite from (trouble, difficulty, pain, etc). ▸ *noun* **a** an act or instance or the process of delaying or cancelling a criminal sentence, esp a death sentence; **b** a warrant granting this. [16c: from French *reprendre* to take back]

reprimand *verb* to criticize or rebuke angrily or severely, esp publicly or formally. ▸ *noun* an angry or severe rebuke. [17c: from French *réprimande*, from Latin *premere* to press]

reprint *verb* /riːˈprɪnt/ **1** to print something again. **2** to print more copies of (a book, etc). **3** *intr* of a book, etc: to have more copies printed. ▸ *noun* /ˈriːprɪnt/ **1** the act of reprinting. **2** a copy of a book or any already printed material made by reprinting the original without any changes. **3** the total number of copies made of a reprinted book: *a reprint of 3000*. [16c]

reprisal *noun* revenge or retaliation or an act involving this. [15c: from French *reprisaille*, from Latin *prehendere* to seize]

reprise *music, noun* the repeating of a passage or theme. ▸ *verb* to repeat (an earlier passage or theme). [14c: from French *reprendre* to take back]

repro *informal* short form of **reproduction** (*noun, adj*).

reproach *verb* **a** to express disapproval of, or disappointment with; **b** to blame. ▸ *noun* **1** an act of reproaching. **2** (*often* **reproaches**) a rebuke or expression of disappointment. **3** a cause of disgrace or shame. ▪ **reproachful** *adj*. ▪ **reproachfully** *adv*. [15c: from French *reprochier*]

IDIOMS **beyond reproach** too good to be criticized.

reprobate /ˈrɛprəbeɪt/ *noun* **1** an immoral unprincipled person. **2** *Christianity* someone rejected by God. ▸ *adj* **1** immoral and unprincipled. **2** rejected or condemned. ▸ *verb* **1** to disapprove of or censure. **2** of God: to reject or condemn (a person). ▪ **reprobation** *noun*. [16c: from Latin *probare* to approve]

reproduce *verb* **1** to make or produce again. **2 a** to make or produce a copy or imitation of; **b** to duplicate. **3** *tr & intr* to produce (offspring). [17c]

reproduction *noun* **1** an act or the process of reproducing. **2** a copy or imitation, esp of a work of art. **3** the quality of reproduced sound: *a stereo that gives excellent reproduction*. ▸ *adj* of furniture, etc: made in imitation of an earlier style. ▪ **reproductive** *adj*.

reproof *noun* **1** blame or censure. **2** a rebuke. [14c: from French *reprover* to reprove]

reprove *verb* **1** to rebuke. **2** to blame or condemn for a fault, wrongdoing, etc. ▪ **reprovingly** *adv*. [14c: from French *reprover*]

reptile *noun* **1** *zool* a cold-blooded scaly vertebrate animal, eg, a lizard, snake, tortoise, crocodile, etc. **2** a mean or despicable person. ▪ **reptilian** /rɛpˈtɪlɪən/ *adj, noun*. [14c: from Latin *repere* to creep or crawl]

republic *noun* **1** a form of government without a monarch and in which supreme power is held by the people or their elected representatives, esp one in which the head of state is an elected or nominated president. **2** a state or a governmental unit within a state that forms part of a nation or federation. [16c: from French *république*, from Latin *res* concern or affair + *publicus* public]

republican *adj* **1** relating to or characteristic of a republic. **2** in favour of the republic as a form of government. **3** (**Republican**) belonging or relating to the Republican Party, one of the two chief political parties of the USA. Compare **Democratic** (sense 3). ▸ *noun* **1** someone who favours the republic as a form of government. **2** (**Republican**) a member or supporter of the Republican Party of the USA. Compare **Democrat** (sense 2). **3** (**Republican**) someone who advocates the union of Northern Ireland and the Republic of Ireland. Compare **Loyalist** (sense 2). ▪ **republicanism** *noun*. [17c: from **republic**]

repudiate /rɪˈpjuːdɪeɪt/ *verb* **1** to deny or reject as unfounded: *repudiate the suggestion*. **2** to refuse to recognize or have anything to do with (a person). **3**

to refuse or cease to acknowledge (a debt, etc). ▪ **repudiation** *noun.* [16c: from Latin *repudiare* to put away]

repugnant *adj* distasteful; disgusting. ▪ **repugnance** *noun.* ▪ **repugnantly** *adv.* [14c: from Latin *pugnare* to fight]

repulse *verb* **1** to drive or force back (an enemy, attacking force, etc). **2** to reject (someone's offer of help, kindness, etc) with coldness and discourtesy. **3** to bring on a feeling of disgust, horror or loathing in someone. ▸ *noun* **1** an act or instance of repulsing or state of being repulsed. **2** a cold discourteous rejection. [16c: from Latin *repellere* to drive back]

repulsion *noun* **1** an act or the process of forcing back or of being forced back. **2** a feeling of disgust, horror or loathing. **3** *physics* a force that tends to push two objects further apart, such as that between like electric charges or like magnetic poles.

repulsive *adj* provoking a feeling of disgust, horror or loathing. ▪ **repulsively** *adv.* ▪ **repulsiveness** *noun.*

reputable /ˈrɛpjʊtəbəl/ *adj* well thought of.

reputation *noun* **1** a generally held opinion about someone's abilities, moral character, etc. **2** (*often* **reputation for** *or* **of**) fame or notoriety, esp because of a particular characteristic. **3** a high opinion generally held about someone or something.

repute *verb* to consider (as having some specified quality, etc): *She is reputed to be a fine tennis player.* ▸ *noun* **1** general opinion or impression. **2** reputation. [15c: from French *réputer*]

reputed *adj* **1** supposed. **2** generally considered to be.

request *noun* **1** an act or an instance of asking for something. **2** something asked for. **3** (*usu* **in request**) the state of being asked for or sought after. **4** **a** a letter, etc sent to a radio station, etc asking for a specified song to be played; **b** the song played in response to this. ▸ *verb* to ask for, esp politely or as a favour. [14c: from French *requerre*, from Latin *requirere* to seek for]

IDIOMS **on** *or* **by request** if or when requested.

requiem /ˈrɛkwɪɛm/ *noun* **1** (*also* **Requiem**) *RC Church* **a** a mass for the souls of the dead; **b** a piece of music written for this. **2** any piece of music composed or performed to commemorate the dead. **3** anything that serves as a memorial. [14c: from Latin *requiem* rest]

require *verb* **1** to need or wish to have. **2** to demand, exact or command by authority. **3** to have as a necessary or essential condition for success, fulfilment, etc. [14c: from Latin *quaerere* to seek or search for]

requirement *noun* **1** **a** a need; **b** something that is needed. **2** something that is asked for, essential, ordered, etc. **3** a necessary condition.

requisite /ˈrɛkwɪzɪt/ *adj* **1** required or necessary. **2** indispensable. ▸ *noun* something that is required, necessary or indispensable. [15c: from Latin *requirere* to search for]

requisition *noun* **1** a formal authoritative demand for supplies or the use of something, eg, by the army. **2** an official form on which such a demand is made. ▸ *verb* to demand, take or order (the use of something, etc) by official requisition. [14c: from Latin *requisitio* a searching for]

requite *verb, formal* **1** to make a suitable return in response to (someone's kindness or injury). **2** to repay (someone) for (something). **3** to repay (eg good with good, evil with evil, hate with love, etc). ▪ **requital** *noun.* [16c: from *quite* to pay]

reredos /ˈrɪədɒs/ *noun* an ornamental screen behind an altar. [14c: from French *arere* behind + *dos* back]

reroute *verb* to direct (traffic, aircraft, etc) along an alternative route, eg because of an accident, heavy traffic, bad weather, etc. [20c]

rerun *verb* /riːˈrʌn/ **1** to cause (a race, etc) to be run again or to run (a race, etc) again, eg because of an unclear result, etc. **2** to broadcast (a TV or radio programme or series) for a second or subsequent time. ▸ *noun* /ˈriːrʌn/ **1** a race that is run again. **2** a TV or radio programme or series broadcast for a second or subsequent time. [19c]

rescind *verb* to cancel, annul or revoke (an order, law, custom, etc). ▪ **rescindment** *or* **rescission** *noun.* [16c: from Latin *rescindere* to cut off]

rescue *verb* to save or set free from danger, evil, trouble, captivity, etc. ▸ *noun* an act or an instance or the process of rescuing or being rescued. ▪ **rescuable** *adj.* ▪ **rescuer** *noun.* [14c: from French *rescourre* to shake out or remove, from Latin *quatere* to shake]

research *noun* detailed and careful investigation into some subject or area of study with the aim of discovering and applying new facts or information. ▸ *verb, tr & intr* to do research (on a specified subject, etc). ▪ **researcher** *noun.* [16c: from French *cercher* to seek]

research and development *noun* (abbrev **R&D**) work in a company that concentrates on finding new or improved processes, products, etc and also on the optimum ways of introducing such innovations.

resemblance *noun* **1** likeness or similarity or the degree of likeness or similarity. **2** appearance.

resemble *verb* to be like or similar to (someone or something else), esp in appearance. [14c: from French *ressembler*, from Latin *similis* like]

resent *verb* **1** to take or consider as an insult or an affront. **2** to feel anger, bitterness or ill-will towards or about (someone or something). ▪ **resentful** *adj.* ▪ **resentfully** *adv.* ▪ **resentment** *noun.* [16c: from French *ressentir* to be angry, from Latin *sentire* to feel]

reservation *noun* **1** an act of reserving something for future use. **2** **a** an act of booking or ordering, eg a hotel room, a table in a restaurant, a ticket, etc, in advance; **b** something reserved or booked in advance. **3** (*often* **reservations**) a doubt or objection. **4** a limiting condition, proviso or exception to an agreement, etc. **5** an area of land set aside for a particular purpose, eg for Native Americans. [14c: French]

reserve *verb* **1** to keep back or set aside, eg for a future, special or particular use, etc. **2** to book or order (eg a hotel room, a table in a restaurant, a ticket, etc) in advance. **3** to delay or postpone (a legal judgement, taking a decision, etc). **4** to maintain or secure: *reserve the right to silence.* ▸ *noun* **1** something kept back or set aside, esp for future use or possible need. **2** the state or condition of being reserved or an act of reserving. **3** an area of land set aside for a particular purpose, esp for the protection of wildlife: *a nature reserve.* **4** coolness, distance or restraint of manner; diffidence or reticence. **5** *sport* **a** an extra player or participant who can take another's place if needed;

b (*usu* **the reserves**) the second or B team: *playing for the reserves.* **6** (*also* **reserves**) *military* **a** part of an army or force kept out of immediate action to provide reinforcements when needed; **b** forces in addition to a nation's regular armed services, not usu in service but that may be called upon if necessary; **c** a member of such a force. **7** (*often* **reserves**) *finance* a company's assets, or a country's gold and foreign currency, held at a bank to meet future liabilities. **8** (*usu* **reserves**) a supply of oil, gas, coal, etc, known to be present in a particular region and as yet unexploited. **9** (*usu* **reserves**) extra physical or mental power, energies, stamina, etc that can be drawn upon in a difficult or extreme situation: *reserves of strength.* [14c: from French *réserver,* from Latin *reservare* to keep something back]

IDIOMS **in reserve** unused, but available if necessary.

reserved *adj* **1** kept back, set aside or destined for a particular use or for a particular person. **2** of a hotel room, a table in a restaurant, ticket, etc: booked or ordered in advance. **3** of a person or their manner: cool, distant or restrained; diffident or reticent. [16c: from **reserve**]

reserve price *noun* the lowest price that the owner of something which is being sold by auction is prepared to accept. Also called **floor price**.

reservist *noun, military* a member of a reserve force.

reservoir /ˈrɛzəvwɑː(r)/ *noun* **1** a large natural or artificial lake, or a tank, in which water is collected and stored for public use, irrigation, etc. **2** a chamber in a machine, device, etc where liquid is stored. **3** a supply, eg of information, creativity, etc. **4** a place where fluid or vapour collects. [17c: from French *réserver* to **reserve**]

reservoir
This word is often misspelt. It has an *r* in the middle. It might help you to remember the following sentence:
*The **reservoir** provides a **reserve** of water.*

reset *verb* to set again or differently. [17c]

reshuffle *verb* /riːˈʃʌfəl/ **1** to shuffle (cards) again or differently. **2** to reorganize or redistribute (esp government posts). ▸ *noun* /ˈriːʃʌfəl/ an act of reshuffling: *a cabinet reshuffle.* [19c]

reside *verb, intr* **1** *formal* to live or have one's home (in a place), esp permanently. **2** of power, authority, a particular quality, etc: to rest (with someone) or be attributable (to someone). [15c: from Latin *sedere* to sit]

residence *noun* **1** *formal* a house or dwelling, esp a large, impressive and imposing one. **2 a** an act or an instance of living in a particular place; **b** the period of time someone lives there. [14c: French]

IDIOMS **in residence 1** living in a particular place, esp officially. **2** of a creative writer, artist, etc: working in a particular place for a certain period of time: *The university has an artist in residence.*

residency *noun* (***-ies***) **1** a residence. **2** a band's or singer's regular or permanent engagement at a particular venue. **3** *N Am* **a** the period, after internship, of advanced, specialized medical training for doctors in hospitals; **b** the post held during this period. [16c]

resident *noun* **1** someone who lives permanently in a particular place. **2** a registered guest in a hotel, esp one staying a relatively long time. **3** a non-migratory bird or animal. **4** *med* **a** a doctor who works at and usu lives in a hospital; **b** *N Am* a doctor undergoing advanced or specialized training in a hospital. ▸ *adj* **1** living or dwelling in a particular place, esp permanently or for some length of time. **2** living or required to live in the place where one works. **3** of birds and animals: not migrating. [14c: from Latin *residere* to **reside**]

residential *adj* **1** of a street, an area of a town, etc: containing private houses rather than factories, businesses, etc. **2** requiring residence in the same place as one works or studies: *a residential course.* **3** used as a residence: *a residential home for the elderly.* **4** relating to or connected with residence or residences. ▪ **residentially** *adv.* [17c]

residual *adj* remaining; left over. ▸ *noun* **1** something which remains or is left over as a residue. **2** *stats* the difference between the measured value of a quantity and its theoretical value. ▪ **residually** *adv.* [16c: from **residue**]

residue *noun* **1** what remains or is left over when a part has been taken away, used up, etc. **2** *law* what is left of a dead person's estate after debts and legacies have been paid. **3** *chem* a **residuum**. ▪ **residuary** /rɪˈzɪdjʊərɪ/ *adj.* [14c: from French *résidu,* from Latin *residuus* remaining]

residuum *noun* (***residua***) *chem* a substance remaining after evaporation, combustion or distillation. [17c]

resign *verb* **1** *intr* to give up (a job, an official position, etc). **2** to give up or relinquish (a right, claim, etc). **3** (*usu* **resign oneself to**) to come to accept (a situation, etc) with patience, tolerance, etc. [14c: from French *résigner,* from Latin *resignare* to unseal or cancel]

resignation *noun* **1** an act of resigning from a job, position, etc. **2** a signed notification of intention to resign from a job, etc. **3** uncomplaining acceptance of something unpleasant, inevitable, etc.

resigned *adj* (*often* **resigned to**) prepared to accept something unpleasant, inevitable, etc without complaining. ▪ **resignedly** /rɪˈzaɪnɪdlɪ/ *adv.* [17c]

resilient *adj* **1** of a person: able to recover quickly from, or to deal readily with, illness, sudden unexpected difficulties, hardship, etc. **2** of an object, a material, etc: able to return quickly to its original shape, position, etc. ▪ **resilience** *or* **resiliency** *noun.* ▪ **resiliently** *adv.* [17c: from Latin *resilire* to recoil or leap back]

resin /ˈrɛzɪn/ *noun* **1** a sticky aromatic substance secreted by various plants and trees. Compare **rosin. 2** (*in full* **synthetic resin**) *chem* an organic compound used in the production of plastics, paints, varnishes, textiles, etc. ▸ *verb* to treat with resin. ▪ **resinate** *verb.* ▪ **resinous** *adj.* [14c: from French *resine,* related to Greek *rhetine* resin from a pine]

resist *verb* **1** *tr & intr* to oppose or refuse to comply with. **2** to withstand (something damaging): *a metal which resists corrosion.* **3** to impede: *resisted arrest.* **4** to refrain from or turn down: *can't resist chocolate.* [14c: from Latin *sistere* to stand firm]

resistance *noun* **1** an act or the process of resisting. **2** the ability or power to resist, esp the extent to which damage, etc can be withstood: *resistance is low during the winter months.* **3** *physics* in damped harmonic motion: the ratio of the frictional forces to the speed. **4** *elec* (symbol **R**) a measure of the extent to which a material or an electrical device opposes the flow of an electric current through it. See also **ohm.** **5** a measure of the extent to which a material opposes the flow of heat through it. Compare **conductivity.** **6** an underground organization fighting for the freedom of a country occupied by an enemy force. ▪ **resistant** *adj.* [14c: from French *résistance*]

resistivity *noun, physics* the ability, measured in ohm metres, of a cubic metre of material to oppose the flow of an electric current. [19c]

resistor *noun, elec* a device which introduces a known value of resistance to electrical flow into a circuit.

resit *verb* /riː'sɪt/ *tr & intr* to take (an examination) again, usu after failing or getting a poor grade. ▸ *noun* /'riːsɪt/ an act or instance of taking an examination again or the examination itself. [20c]

resoluble *adj* able to be resolved or analysed. [17c: from Latin *resolvere* to resolve]

resolute *adj* **1** determined; with a fixed purpose or belief. **2** characterized by determination or firmness: *a resolute response.* ▪ **resolutely** *adv.* ▪ **resoluteness** *noun.* [14c: from Latin *resolvere* to resolve]

resolution *noun* **1** an act or instance or the process of making a firm decision. **2** a firm decision. **3** determination or resoluteness. **4** an act or instance or the process of solving a mathematical problem, a difficult question, etc. **5** an answer to a mathematical problem, difficult question, etc. **6** the ability of a television screen, photographic film, etc to reproduce an image in very fine detail. **7** a formal decision, expression of opinion, etc by a group of people, eg at a public meeting. **8** *music* the passing of a chord from discord to concord. **9** an act or the process of separating, eg a chemical compound into its constituent parts or elements. **10** *physics* the ability of a microscope, telescope, etc to distinguish between objects which are very close together. **11** *photog* the ability of an emulsion to produce fine detail in an image. [14c: see **resolute**]

resolve *verb* **1** to decide firmly or make up one's mind. **2** to find an answer to (a problem, question, etc). **3** to take away or dispel (a doubt, difficulty, etc). **4** to bring (an argument, etc) to an end. **5** *tr & intr* to decide, or pass (a resolution), esp formally by vote. **6** of a television screen, photographic film, etc: to produce an image in fine detail. **7** of a microscope, telescope, etc: to distinguish clearly (eg objects which are very close together). **8** *tr & intr, music* of a chord: to pass from discord into concord. **9** to break up or cause to break up into separate or constituent parts or elements. ▸ *noun* **1** determination or firmness of purpose. **2** a firm decision; a resolution. ▪ **resolvable** *adj.* ▪ **resolver** *noun.* [14c: from Latin *solvere* to loosen, dissolve]

resolved *adj* determined; firm in purpose. ▪ **resolvedly** /rɪ'zɒlvɪdlɪ/ *adv.* [15c]

resonance *noun* **1** the quality or state of being resonant. **2** sound produced by sympathetic vibration. **3** *physics* vibration that occurs when an object or system is made to oscillate at its natural frequency. [15c: from Latin *resonare* to resound]

resonant *adj* **1** of sounds: echoing; continuing to sound; resounding. **2** producing echoing sounds: *resonant walls.* **3** full of or intensified by a ringing quality: *a resonant voice.* ▪ **resonantly** *adv.*

resonate *verb, tr & intr* to resound or cause (something) to resound or echo. ▪ **resonator** *noun.*

resort *verb, intr* (*usu* **resort to**) **1** to use (something) as a means of solving a problem, etc. **2** *formal* to frequent (a place), esp habitually or in great numbers. ▸ *noun* **1** a place visited by many people. **2** someone or something used or looked to for help. [14c: from French *sortir* to go out]

IDIOMS **the last resort** the only remaining course of action or means of overcoming a difficulty etc.

resound /rɪ'zaʊnd/ *verb* **1** *intr* of sounds: to ring or echo. **2** *intr* (**resound with** *or* **to**) to reverberate: *The hall resounded to their cheers.* **3** *intr* to be widely known or celebrated: *Her fame resounded throughout the country.* **4** of a place: to make (a sound) echo or ring. [14c: from Latin *resonare* to resound]

resounding *adj* **1** echoing and ringing; reverberating. **2** clear and decisive: *a resounding victory.* [19c]

resource *noun* **1** someone or something that provides a source of help, support, etc when needed. **2** a means of solving difficulties, problems, etc. **3** skill at finding ways of solving difficulties, problems, etc; ingenuity. **4** something useful. **5** (*usu* **resources**) a means of support, esp money or property. **6** (*usu* **resources**) a country's, business's, etc source of wealth or income: *natural resources.* ▸ *verb* to provide with support, usu financial. [17c: from French *ressource*, from Latin *surgere* to rise]

resourceful *adj* skilled in finding ways of overcoming difficulties, solving problems, etc. ▪ **resourcefully** *adv.* ▪ **resourcefulness** *noun.*

respect *noun* **1** admiration; good opinion: *held in great respect.* **2** the state of being honoured, admired or well thought of. **3** (**respect for**) consideration, thoughtfulness or attention: *show no respect for his feelings.* **4** (*often* **respects**) *formal* a polite greeting or expression of admiration, esteem and honour. **5** a particular detail, feature or characteristic: *In what respect are they different?* **6** reference, relation or connection. ▸ *verb* **1** to show or feel high regard for. **2** to show consideration for, or thoughtfulness or attention to: *respect her wishes.* **3** to heed or pay proper attention to (a rule, law, etc). ▪ **respecter** *noun.* [14c: from Latin *respicere* to look back at]

IDIOMS **in respect of** *or* **with respect to sth** with reference to, or in connection with (a particular matter, point, etc). **pay one's last respects to sb** to show respect for someone who has died by attending their funeral. **with respect** *or* **with all due respect** a polite expression indicating disagreement and used before presenting one's own opinion.

respectable *adj* **1** worthy of or deserving respect. **2** having a reasonably good social standing. **3** having a good reputation or character. **4** of behaviour: correct; acceptable; conventional. **5** of a person's appearance: presentable; decent. **6** fairly or relatively good or large: *a respectable turnout.* ▪ **respectability** *noun.* ▪ **respectably** *adv.* [16c]

respectful *adj* having or showing respect. ▪ **respectfully** *adv.* ▪ **respectfulness** *noun.*

respecting *prep* about; concerning. [18c]

respective *adj* belonging to or relating to each person or thing mentioned; particular; separate: *our respective homes.* ▪ **respectively** *adv.* [16c]

respiration *noun* **1** an act or the process of respiring or breathing. **2** a single breath, in and out. **3** (*also* **external respiration**) *physiol* the process in animals and plants in which compounds are broken down to release energy, involving the taking in of oxygen and giving out of carbon dioxide. [15c: from Latin *respirare* to breathe]

respirator *noun* **1** a mask worn over the mouth and nose to prevent poisonous gas, dust, etc being breathed in, or to warm cold air before it is breathed. **2** *med* an apparatus that does a sick or injured person's breathing for them.

respire *verb* **1** *tr & intr* to inhale and exhale (air etc); to breathe. **2** *intr, biochem* to release energy as a result of the breakdown of organic compounds. ▪ **respiratory** /'rɛspɪrətərɪ/ *adj*. [14c: from Latin *respirare* to breathe]

respite *noun* **1** a period of rest or relief from, or a temporary stopping of, something unpleasant, difficult, etc. **2** a temporary delay. **3** *law* temporary suspension of the execution of a criminal; a reprieve. ▸ *verb* to grant a respite to someone; to reprieve. [13c: from French *respit*, from Latin *respectare* to respect]

resplendent *adj* brilliant or splendid in appearance. ▪ **resplendence** *or* **resplendency** *noun*. [15c: from Latin *resplendere* to shine brightly]

respond *verb* **1** *tr & intr* to answer or reply; to say or do in reply. **2** *intr* (*usu* **respond to**) to react favourably or well: *respond to treatment*. **3** *intr, relig* to utter liturgical responses. ▪ **responder** *noun*. [14c: from French *respondre*, from Latin *respondere* to return like for like]

respondent *noun* **1** someone who answers or makes replies. **2** *law* a defendant, esp in a divorce suit. **3** *psychol* a response to a specific stimulus. ▸ *adj* **1** answering; making a reply or response. **2** *psychol* responsive, esp to a specific stimulus. ▪ **respondence** *noun*.

response *noun* **1** an act of responding, replying or reacting. **2** a reply or answer. **3** a reaction: *met with little response*. **4** (*usu* **responses**) *Christianity* an answer or reply, esp one in the form of a short verse which is either sung or spoken, made by the congregation or the choir to something said by the priest or minister during a service. [14c]

responsibility *noun* (*-ies*) **1** the state of being responsible or of having important duties for which one is responsible. **2** something or someone for which one is responsible.

responsible *adj* **1** (*usu* **responsible for** *or* **to**) accountable: *responsible to her immediate superior*. **2** of a job, position, etc: with many important duties. **3** (*often* **responsible for**) being the main or identifiable cause: *Who was responsible for the accident?* **4** of a person: **a** able to be trusted; **b** capable of rational and socially acceptable behaviour: *very responsible for her age*. ▪ **responsibly** *adv*. [16c]

responsive *adj* **1** of a person: ready and quick to react or respond. **2** reacting readily to stimulus. **3** reacting well or favourably: *a disease responsive to drugs*. **4** made as or constituting a response: *a responsive smile*. ▪ **responsively** *adv*. ▪ **responsiveness** *noun*. [14c: from Latin *respondere* to respond]

respray *verb* to spray or paint (esp the bodywork of a vehicle) again, either in the same colour or a different one. ▸ *noun* **1** the action of respraying. **2** the result of respraying. [20c]

rest[1] *noun* **1** a period of relaxation or freedom from work, activity, worry, etc. **2** sleep; repose. **3** calm; tranquillity. **4** a pause from some activity: *stopped half way up the hill for a rest*. **5** death, when seen as repose. **6** a prop or support, eg for a snooker cue, etc. **7** a place or thing which holds or supports. **8** a pause in reading, speaking, etc. **9** *music* **a** an interval of silence in a piece of music: *two bars' rest*; **b** a mark indicating the duration of this. ▸ *verb* **1** *tr & intr* to stop or cause to stop working or moving. **2** *intr* to relax, esp by sleeping or stopping some activity. **3** *tr & intr* to set, place or lie on or against, for support, etc: *rested her arm on the chair*. **4** *intr* to be calm and free from worry. **5** *tr & intr* to give or have as a basis or support: *will rest my argument on practicalities*. **6** *intr* to depend or be based on: *The decision rests with the board*. **7** *intr* to be left without further attention, discussion or action: *Let the matter rest there*. **8** *intr* to lie dead or buried. **9** *intr, euphemistic* of an actor: to be unemployed. [Anglo-Saxon *roest*]
IDIOMS **at rest 1** not moving or working; stationary. **2** free from trouble, worry, etc: *set his mind at rest*. **3** asleep. **4** dead. **lay sb to rest** to bury or inter them.

rest[2] *noun* (*usu* **the rest**) **1** what is left when part of something is taken away, used, finished, etc; the remainder. **2** the others. ▸ *verb, intr* to continue to be; to remain: *rest assured*. [15c: from French *rester*, from Latin *stare* to stand]

restaurant *noun* an establishment where meals may be bought and eaten. [19c: French, from *restaurer* to restore]

restaurant car *noun* a carriage on a train in which meals are served to travellers. Also called **dining car**.

restaurateur /rɛstərə'tɜː(r)/ *noun* an owner or manager of a restaurant.

restful *adj* **1** bringing or giving rest, or producing a sensation of calm, peace and rest. **2** relaxed; at rest. ▪ **restfulness** *noun*.

resting *adj* **1** not moving, working, etc; at rest. **2** *euphemistic* of an actor: unemployed.

restitution *noun* **1** the act of giving something stolen, lost, etc back to its rightful owner. **2** compensation for loss or injury: *ordered to make restitution for the damage*. ▪ **restitutive** *adj*. [13c: from Latin *statuere* to set up]

restive *adj* **1** restless; nervous; uneasy. **2** unwilling to accept control or authority. **3** of a horse: unwilling to move forwards. ▪ **restiveness** *noun*. [17c: from French *restif* inert, from Latin *restare* to remain still or rest]

restless *adj* **1** constantly moving about or fidgeting; unable to stay still or quiet. **2** constantly active or in motion; unceasing. **3** giving no rest; disturbed: *a restless night*. **4** worried, nervous and uneasy. ▪ **restlessly** *adv*. ▪ **restlessness** *noun*.

restoration *noun* **1** an act or instance or the process of restoring or being restored. **2** a model or reconstruction (eg of a ruin, extinct animal, etc). **3** (*usu* **the Restoration**) *hist* the re-establishment of Charles II on the English throne in 1660, or the period of his reign. **4** (*usu* **the Restoration**) *hist* the re-establishment of the Bourbon Dynasty on the French throne in 1814, or the period of its reign. [15c]

restorative *adj* tending or helping to restore or improve health, strength, spirits, etc. ▸ *noun* a restorative food or medicine.

restore *verb* **1** to return (a building, painting, etc) to a former condition by repairing, cleaning, etc. **2** to bring (someone or something) back to a normal or proper state or condition: *be restored to health.* **3** to bring back (a normal, desirable, etc state): *restore discipline.* **4** to return (something lost or stolen) to the rightful owner. **5** to bring or put back to a former and higher status, rank, etc. ▪ **restorable** *adj.* ▪ **restorer** *noun.* [13c: from French *restorer*]

restrain *verb* **1** to prevent (someone, oneself, etc) from doing something. **2** to keep (one's temper, ambition, etc) under control. **3** to confine. ▪ **restrainer** *noun.* [14c: from French *restreindre*, from Latin *restringere* to restrain]

restrained *adj* **1** controlled; able to control one's emotions. **2** showing restraint; without excess. ▪ **restrainedly** *adv.*

restraint *noun* **1** an act or instance of restraining or the state of being restrained. **2** a limit or restriction. **3** the avoidance of exaggeration or excess.

restrict *verb* **1** to keep within certain limits. **2** to limit or regulate; to withhold from general use. ▪ **restricted** *adj.* ▪ **restriction** *noun.* [16c: from Latin *restringere* to restrain]

restrictive *adj* restricting or intended to restrict, esp excessively.

rest room *noun, N Am* a room with lavatories, wash basins and, sometimes, a seating area, eg in a shop, theatre, factory, etc, for the use of the staff or public.

restructuring *noun* the reorganization of a business, company, etc in order to improve efficiency, cut costs, etc, often involving redundancies.

result *noun* **1** an outcome or consequence of something. **2** *informal* (*often* **results**) a positive or favourable outcome or consequence: *His action got results.* **3** a number or quantity obtained by calculation, etc. **4** (**results**) a list of scores, examination outcomes, etc. ► *verb, intr* **1** (*usu* **result from**) to be a consequence or outcome. **2** (*usu* **result in**) to lead (to a specified thing, condition, etc). [15c: from Latin *saltare* to leap]

resultant *adj* resulting. ► *noun, maths, physics* a single force which is the equivalent of two or more forces acting on an object.

resume *verb* **1** *tr & intr* to return to or begin again after an interruption. **2** to take back or return to (a former position, etc): *resume one's seat.* ▪ **resumption** *noun.* [15c: from Latin *resumere* to take up again]

résumé /ˈrɛzjʊmeɪ/ *noun* **1** a summary. **2** *N Am* a curriculum vitae. [19c: French, from *résumer* to resume]

resurface *verb* **1** to put a new surface on (a road, etc). **2** *intr* to reappear. ▪ **resurfacing** *noun.*

resurgence *noun* an act or instance of returning to a state of activity, importance, influence, etc after a period of decline. ▪ **resurgent** *adj.* [19c: from Latin *resurgere* to rise again]

resurrect *verb* **1** to bring (someone) back to life from the dead. **2** to bring (a custom, memory, etc) back.

resurrection *noun* **1** an act or instance or the process of resurrecting. **2** (**the Resurrection**) *Christianity* Christ's rising from the dead. **3** exhumation. [13c: from French *résurrection*, from Latin *resurgere* to rise again]

resuscitate *verb* **1** to bring back to life or consciousness; to revive. **2** *intr* to revive or regain consciousness. ▪ **resuscitation** *noun.* ▪ **resuscitator** *noun.* [16c: from Latin *suscitare* to raise or revive]

retail *noun* /ˈriːteɪl/ the sale of goods, either individually or in small quantities, to customers buying them for personal use. Compare **wholesale.** ► *adj* relating to, concerned with, or engaged in selling such goods. ► *adv* **1** by retail. **2** at a retail price. ► *verb* **1** /ˈriːteɪl/ **a** to sell (goods) in small quantities; **b** *intr* to be sold in small quantities to customers. **2** /riːˈteɪl/ to tell or recount (a story, gossip, etc) in great detail. ▪ **retailer** *noun.* [14c: from French *retailler* to cut off]

retain *verb* **1** to keep or continue to have: *retain a sense of humour.* **2** to be able or continue to hold or contain: *retains moisture.* **3** to keep (facts, information, etc) in one's memory. **4** to hold back or keep in place. **5** to secure the services of (a person, esp a barrister) by paying a preliminary fee. ▪ **retainable** *adj.* ▪ **retainment** *noun.* [14c: from French *retenir*, from Latin *retinere* to hold back]

retainer *noun* **1** someone or something that retains. **2** *hist* a dependant or follower of a person of rank. **3** a domestic servant who has been with a family for a long time. **4** a fee paid to secure professional services, esp of a lawyer or barrister. **5** a reduced rent paid for property while it is not occupied in order to reserve it for future use.

retaining wall *noun* a wall to hold back solid material, such as earth. Also called **revetment**.

retake *verb* /riːˈteɪk/ **1 a** to take again; **b** to take back. **2** to capture (eg, a fortress) again. **3** to sit (an examination) again. **4** to film (eg, a scene) again. ► *noun* /ˈriːteɪk/ **1** the action of retaking something. **2** an examination that someone sits again. **3 a** an act or the process of filming a scene, recording a piece of music, etc again; **b** the scene, recording, etc resulting from this. [17c]

retaliate *verb, intr* to repay an injury, wrong, etc in kind. ▪ **retaliation** *noun.* ▪ **retaliator** *noun.* ▪ **retaliatory** *adj.* [17c: from Latin *talis* such]

retard *verb* to slow down or delay something. ▪ **retardant** *adj, noun.* ▪ **retardation** *or* **retardment** *noun.* [15c: from French *retarder*, from Latin *tardus* slow]

retarded *adj* backward in physical or esp mental development.

retch *verb, intr* to strain as if to vomit, but without actually doing so. ► *noun* an act of retching. [Anglo-Saxon *hræcan*]

retention *noun* **1** the act of retaining something or the state of being retained. **2** the power of retaining or capacity to retain something. **3** the ability to remember experiences and things learnt. [14c: from Latin *retinere* to retain]

retentive *adj* **1** able to retain or keep, esp memories or information. **2** tending to retain (fluid, etc).

rethink *verb* /riːˈθɪŋk/ to think about or consider (a plan, etc) again, usu with a view to changing one's mind about it or reaching a different conclusion. ► *noun* /ˈriːθɪŋk/ an act of rethinking. [18c]

reticent *adj* **1** not saying very much. **2** not willing to communicate; reserved. **3** not communicating everything that is known. ▪ **reticence** *noun.* ▪ **reticently** *adv.* [19c: from Latin *tacere* to be silent]

reticulate *adj* /rɪˈtɪkjʊlɪt/ like a net or network, esp in having lines, veins, etc: *a reticulate leaf.* ► *verb* /rɪˈtɪkjʊleɪt/ *tr & intr* **1** to form or be formed into a network. **2** to mark or be marked with a network of lines, etc. ▪ **reticulation** *noun.* [17c: from Latin *reticulatus* like a net]

reticulum *noun* (***reticula***) **1** *biol* a fine network, especially of fibres, vessels, etc. **2** *zool* the second stomach of a ruminant. [17c: Latin, meaning 'a little net']

retina /ˈrɛtɪnə/ *noun* (***retinas*** *or* ***retinae*** /ˈrɛtɪniː/) the light-sensitive tissue that lines the back of the eyeball. ▪ **retinal** *adj.* [14c: Latin, prob from *rete* a net]

retinol *noun* **vitamin A**. [20c]

retinue *noun* the servants, officials, aides, etc who travel with and attend an important person. [14c: from French *retenir* to retain]

retire *verb* **1** *tr & intr* to stop or make (someone) stop working permanently: *retired at 60.* **2** *intr, formal* to go to bed. **3** *intr, formal* to go away (from or to a place); to leave: *retire to the drawing room.* **4** *tr & intr* to withdraw or make (someone) withdraw from a sporting contest, esp because of injury. **5** *tr & intr* of a military force, etc: to withdraw from a dangerous position. [16c: from French *retirer* to pull back]

retired *adj* **1** no longer working. **2** secluded.

retirement *noun* **1** an act of retiring or the state of being retired from work. **2** seclusion and privacy.

retiring *adj* reserved; not liking to be noticed.

retort[1] *verb* **1** *intr* to make a quick and clever or angry reply. **2** to turn (an argument, criticism, blame, etc) back on the person who first used that argument, criticism, blame, etc. ▸ *noun* **1** a quick and clever or angry reply. **2** an argument, criticism, blame, etc which is turned back on the originator. [16c: from Latin *torquere* to wrench or twist]

retort[2] *noun* **1** a glass vessel with a long neck which curves downwards, used in distilling. **2** *metallurgy* a vessel for heating metals such as iron and carbon to make steel, or for heating coal to produce gas.

retouch *verb* /riːˈtʌtʃ/ to improve or repair (a photograph, negative, painting, etc) by adding extra touches or making small alterations. ▸ *noun* /ˈriːtʌtʃ/ **1** an act of retouching. **2** a photograph, painting, etc that has been retouched. ▪ **retoucher** *noun.* [17c]

retrace *verb* **1** to go back over (a route, path, etc). **2** to trace back to a source or origin: *retrace her roots.* **3** to go over (events, etc) again in one's memory. [17c]

retract *verb* **1** to draw (something, esp an animal's body part, an aircraft's landing gear, etc) in or back. **2** *tr & intr* to withdraw (a statement, claim, charge, etc). ▪ **retractable** *adj.* ▪ **retraction** *noun.* ▪ **retractive** *adj.* [16c: from Latin *trahere* to drag or pull]

retractile *adj* of a cat's, etc claws: able to be drawn in, back or up. ▪ **retractility** *noun.*

retractor *noun* **1** *surgery* an instrument for holding back tissue, skin, an organ, etc from the area being operated on. **2** *anatomy* a muscle that retracts or pulls in a part of the body.

retrain *verb* **1** to teach (a person or animal) new skills. **2** *intr* to learn new skills, esp with a view to finding alternative employment.

retread see **remould**

retreat *verb* **1** *intr* of a military force, army, etc: to move back or away from the enemy or retire after defeat. **2** *intr* to retire or withdraw to a place of safety or seclusion. **3** *intr* to recede; to slope back. ▸ *noun* **1** an act or instance or the process of retreating. **2** *military* a signal to retreat, esp one given on a bugle. **3** a place of privacy, safety or seclusion. **4** **a** a period of retirement or withdrawal from the world, esp for prayer, meditation, study, etc; **b** a place for this. [14c: from French *retret,* from Latin *retrahere* to draw back]

retrench *verb, tr & intr* to economize; to reduce (expenses). ▪ **retrenchment** *noun.* [16c: from French *retrenchier* to cut off or back]

retrial *noun* a second or subsequent trial for the same offence.

retribution *noun* **1** the act of punishing or taking vengeance for sin or wrongdoing. **2** deserved punishment, esp for sin or wrongdoing; vengeance. ▪ **retributive** /rɪˈtrɪbjʊtɪv/ *adj.* ▪ **retributory** *adj.* [14c: from Latin *retribuere* to give back]

retrieve *verb* **1** to get or bring back again. **2** to rescue or save: *retrieve the situation.* **3** *comput* to recover (information) from storage in a computer memory. **4** to remember or recall to mind. **5** *tr & intr* of a dog: to search for and bring back (shot game, or a thrown ball, stick, etc). ▪ **retrievable** *adj.* ▪ **retrieval** *noun.* [15c: from French *retrover*]

retriever *noun* **1** a large dog that can be trained to retrieve game: *a golden retriever.* **2** someone or something that retrieves.

retro *adj* reminiscent of, reverting to, recreating or imitating a style, fashion, etc from the past. [20c]

retro- *prefix, denoting* **1** back or backwards in time or space. **2** behind. [Latin *retro* backwards]

retroactive *adj* applying to or affecting things from a date in the past: *retroactive legislation.* ▪ **retroactively** *adv.* [17c: from Latin *retroagere* to drive back]

retrograde *adj* **1** being, tending towards or causing a worse, less advanced or less desirable state. **2** moving or bending backwards. **3** in a reversed or opposite order. ▸ *verb, intr* **1** to move backwards. **2** to deteriorate or decline. [14c: from Latin *gradi* to go or walk]

retrogress *verb, intr* **1** to go back to an earlier, worse or less advanced condition or state; to deteriorate. **2** to recede or move backwards. ▪ **retrogression** *noun.* ▪ **retrogressive** *adj.* [19c: from Latin *retrogressus* a movement backwards]

retrospect *noun* a survey of what has happened in the past. [17c: from Latin *retrospicere* to look back]
IDIOMS **in retrospect** with the benefit of hindsight; when looking to the past.

retrospection *noun* an act of looking back at the past.

retrospective *adj* **1** of a law, etc: applying to the past as well as to the present and to the future. **2** of an art exhibition, music recital, etc: showing how the work of the artist, composer, etc has developed over their career. **3** inclined to look back on and evaluate past events. ▸ *noun* a retrospective exhibition, etc. ▪ **retrospectively** *adv.*

retroussé /rəˈtruːseɪ/ *adj* of a nose, etc: turned up at the end. [19c: French, from *retrousser* to turn up]

retroversion *noun* the action of turning, or state of being turned, backwards. ▪ **retroverted** *adj.*

retrovirus *noun, biol* a virus with genetic material consisting of RNA which is copied into DNA to allow integration into the host cell's DNA. ▪ **retroviral** *adj.* [20c: from *re*verse *tr*anscriptase (the active enzyme in these viruses) + *-o-* + *virus*]

retsina *noun* a Greek white or rosé wine flavoured with pine resin. [20c: Greek, from *retme* pine resin]

return *verb* **1** *intr* to come or go back again to a former place, state or owner, etc. **2** to give, send, put back, etc in a former position. **3** *intr* to come back to in thought or speech. **4** to repay: *return the compliment*. **5** *tr & intr* to answer or reply. **6** to report or state officially or formally. **7** to earn or produce (profit, interest, etc). **8** to elect as a Member of Parliament. **9** *law* of a jury: to deliver (a verdict). ▶ *noun* **1** an act of coming back from a place, state, etc. **2** an act of returning something, esp to its former place, state, ownership, etc. **3** something returned. **4** profit from work, a business or investment. **5** a statement of income and allowances, used for calculating tax. **6** (*usu* **returns**) a statement of the votes polled in an election. **7** *Brit* (*in full* **return ticket**) a ticket entitling a passenger to travel to a place and back to the starting point. **8** an answer or reply. **9** (*in full* **return key**) **a** a key on a computer or typewriter keyboard that takes the operator from the end of one line to the beginning of the line below; **b** a key on a computer keyboard used for various functions including the loading of software: *Type 'install' and press 'Return'.* ▪ **returnable** *adj*. [14c: from French *retorner*, from Latin *tornare* to turn]

IDIOMS **by return of post** by the next post in the return direction, ie, immediately or as soon as possible. **in return** in exchange; in reply; as compensation. **many happy returns** an expression of good wishes on someone's birthday.

returning officer *noun* an official in charge of running an election in a constituency, counting the votes and declaring the result.

reunion *noun* **1** a meeting of people (eg relatives, friends, former colleagues, etc) who have not met for some time. **2** an act of reuniting or state of being reunited. [17c]

reunite *verb, tr & intr* to bring or come together again after being separated. [15c]

Rev *or* **Revd** *abbrev* Reverend.

rev *noun, informal* **1** (*often* **revs**) the number of revolutions of an engine per minute. **2** an act of revving an engine, etc. ▶ *verb* (***revved, revving***) *informal* (*also* **rev up**) **1** to increase the speed of revolution of (a car engine, etc). **2** *intr* of an engine or vehicle: to run faster. [20c: from **revolution**]

revalue *or* **revaluate** *verb* **1** to make a new valuation of something. **2** to adjust the exchange rate of (a currency), esp making it more valuable with respect to other currencies. Compare **devalue**. [16c]

revamp *verb* to revise, renovate or improve. ▶ *noun* **1** an act of revamping. **2** something that has been revamped. [19c]

reveal[1] *verb* **1** to make (a secret, etc) known. **2** to show or allow to be seen. **3** of a deity: to make known through divine inspiration or by supernatural means. ▪ **revealable** *adj*. ▪ **revealer** *noun*. ▪ **revealingly** *adv*. [14c: from French *reveler*, from Latin *velum* a veil]

reveal[2] *noun, archit* a vertical side surface of a recess in a wall, esp in the opening for a doorway or window. [17c]

reveille /rɪ'valɪ/ *noun* a military wake-up call, usu by a drum or bugle. [17c: from French *réveillez!* wake up!]

revel *verb* (***revelled, revelling***) *intr* **1** (**revel in sth**) to take great delight or luxuriate in it. **2** to have fun in a noisy lively way. ▶ *noun* (*usu* **revels**) an occasion of revelling. ▪ **reveller** *noun*. ▪ **revelry** *noun* (***-ies***). [14c: from French *reveler* to be merry, from Latin *rebellare* to rebel]

Revelation *or* (*popularly*) **Revelations** *singular noun* the last book of the New Testament.

revelation *noun* **1** an act of revealing, showing or disclosing something previously unknown or unexpected. **2** something revealed or disclosed in this way. ▪ **revelational** *adj*. ▪ **revelatory** *adj*. [13c: from Latin *revelatio*, from *revelare* to unveil or reveal]

revenant *noun* someone who returns after a long absence, esp supposedly from the dead. [19c: French, from *revenir* to return]

revenge *noun* **1** malicious injury, harm or wrong done in return for injury, harm or wrong received. **2** something that is done as a means of returning like injury, harm, etc. **3** the desire to do such injury, harm, etc. ▶ *verb* **1** to do similar injury, harm, etc in return for injury, harm, etc received. **2** to take revenge on behalf of oneself or someone else. [14c: from French *revenger*, from Latin *vindicare* to vindicate]

revengeful *adj* keen for or bent on revenge.

revenue *noun* **1** money from a property, shares, etc. **2** **a** money raised by the government of a country or state from taxes, etc; **b** (*often* **Revenue**) a government department responsible for collecting this money. [15c: from French *revenu*]

reverberate *verb* **1** *intr* of a sound, light, heat, etc: to be echoed, repeated or reflected repeatedly. **2** to echo, repeat or reflect (a sound, light, etc) repeatedly. **3** *intr* of a story, scandal, etc: to circulate or be repeated many times. ▪ **reverberant** *adj*. ▪ **reverberation** *noun*. [16c: from Latin *reverberare*]

revere *verb* to feel or show great respect or reverence for. [17c: from Latin *revereri*]

reverence *noun* **1** great respect or veneration, esp that shown to something sacred. **2** a feeling of, or the capacity to feel, such respect. ▶ *verb* to regard with great reverence. [13c: from Latin *reverentia*]

reverend *adj* deserving reverence, esp when used before proper names as a title for members of the clergy. ▶ *noun, informal* a member of the clergy. [15c: from Latin *reverendus* worthy of reverence]

reverent *adj* showing or feeling reverence. [14c]

reverential *adj* reverent or very respectful. ▪ **reverentially** *adv*. [16c]

reverie /'rɛvərɪ/ *noun* **1** a state of dreamy and absent-minded thought. **2** a daydream or absent-minded idea or thought. [14c: French]

revers /rɪ'vɪə(r)/ *noun* (*pl* ***revers***) any part of a garment that is turned back, esp a lapel. [19c: French, meaning 'reverse', from Latin *revertere* to turn back]

reversal *noun* **1** an act of reversing, or the state of being reversed. **2** a change in fortune, esp for the worse. **3** *law* an act of setting aside or overthrowing a legal decision or judgement.

reverse *verb* **1** *tr & intr* to move or make something move backwards or in an opposite direction: *He reversed the car.* **2** to run (a mechanism, piece of machinery, etc) backwards or in the opposite direction from normal. **3** to put or arrange in an opposite position, state, order, etc. **4** to turn (an item of clothing, etc) inside out. **5** to change (a policy, decision, etc) to the exact opposite. **6** *law* to set aside or overthrow (a legal decision, judgement, etc). ▸ *noun* **1** the opposite or contrary of something. **2** a change to an opposite or contrary position, direction, state, etc. **3** the back or rear side of something, eg the back cover of a book. **4** the side of a coin, medal, note, etc that has a secondary design on it. Opposite of **obverse**. **5** a mechanism, esp a car gear, which makes a vehicle, piece of machinery, etc move or operate in a backwards direction. ▪ **reversely** *adv.* ▪ **reversible** *adj.* [14c: from French, from Latin *revertere* to turn back]

reversion *noun* **1** a return to an earlier state, belief, etc. **2** *law* **a** the legal right (eg of an original owner or their heirs) to possess a property again at the end of a certain period, esp when the present owner dies; **b** property to which someone has such a right. **3** insurance which is paid on someone's death. **4** *biol* of individuals, organs, etc: a return to an earlier ancestral, and usu less advanced, type. ▪ **reversional** *adj.* ▪ **reversionary** *adj.* [14c: from Latin *reversio* a turning back]

revert *verb* (*usu* **revert to**) **1** to return (to something in thought or conversation). **2** to return (to a former and usu worse state, practice, way of behaving, etc). **3** *law* of property, etc: to return (to an original owner or their heirs) after belonging temporarily to someone else. [13c: from Latin *revertere* to turn back]

revetment *noun* a **retaining wall**.

review *noun* **1** an act of examining, reviewing or revising, or the state of being examined, reviewed or revised. **2** a general survey of a particular subject, situation, etc. **3** a survey of the past and past events. **4** a critical report of a recent book, play, film, etc, in a newspaper, etc. **5** a magazine or newspaper, or a section of one, with reviews of books, etc and often feature articles on the arts. **6** a second or additional study or consideration of certain facts, events, etc; a re-examination. **7** *military* a formal or official inspection of troops, ships, etc. **8** *law* a re-examination of a case, esp by a superior court. ▸ *verb* **1** to see or view again. **2** to examine or go over, esp critically or formally. **3** to look back on and examine (events in the past). **4** *intr* to write reviews (of books, plays, films, etc), esp professionally. **5** *military* to inspect (troops, ships, etc), esp formally or officially. **6** *law* to re-examine (a case). ▪ **reviewable** *adj.* ▪ **reviewer** *noun.* [16c: from French *revue*]

IDIOMS **in** *or* **under review** undergoing consideration, negotiation, etc.

revile *verb* **1** to abuse or criticize bitterly or scornfully. **2** *intr* to speak scornfully. ▪ **reviler** *noun.* [14c: from French *reviler*, from Latin *vilis* worthless]

revise *verb* **1** to examine or re-examine (eg a text, etc) in order to identify and correct faults, make improvements, etc. **2** *tr & intr* to study or look at (a subject, notes, etc) again, esp in preparation for an examination. **3** to reconsider or amend (eg an opinion, etc). ▸ *noun* **1** an act or the result of revising. **2** *printing* a revised proof that includes corrections made to an earlier proof. ▪ **revisable** *adj.* ▪ **revisal** *noun.* ▪ **reviser** *noun.* ▪ **revisory** *adj.* [16c: from French *reviser*, from Latin *visere* to look at]

revision *noun* **1** an act or the result of revising, or the process of revising. **2** an act or the process of studying a subject or notes on it again, esp in preparation for an examination. **3** a revised book, edition, article, etc. ▪ **revisionary** *adj.* [17c]

revisionism *noun, politics* a policy or practice of revising established political ideas, doctrines, etc. ▪ **revisionist** *noun, adj.* [20c]

revitalize *or* **-ise** *verb* to give new energy to. [19c]

revival *noun* **1** an act or the process of reviving or the state of being revived. **2** a renewed interest, esp in old customs, fashions, styles, etc. **3** a new production or performance, esp of an old play. **4** a period of renewed religious faith and spirituality. **5** a series of evangelistic and often emotional meetings to encourage renewed religious faith. [17c]

revivalism *noun* the promotion of renewed religious faith and spirituality through evangelistic meetings. ▪ **revivalist** *noun.*

revive *verb, tr & intr* **1** to come or bring back to consciousness, strength, health, vitality, etc. **2** to come or bring back into use or fashion, etc. **3** to perform (an old play) again. ▪ **revivable** *adj.* ▪ **reviver** *noun.* [15c: from French *revivre*, from Latin *vivere* to live]

revivify *verb* (***-ies,-ied***) to put new life, vigour, etc into. ▪ **revivification** *noun.* [17c]

revoke *verb* **1** to cancel (a will, agreement, etc). **2** *intr, cards* to fail to follow suit in cards when able to do so. ▸ *noun, cards* an act of revoking. ▪ **revocable** *adj.* ▪ **revocation** /rɛvə'keɪʃən/ *noun.* ▪ **revoker** *noun.* [14c: from Latin *vocare* to call]

revolt *verb* **1** *intr* to rebel or rise up (against a government, authority, etc). **2** *tr & intr* to feel, or provoke a feeling of, disgust, loathing or revulsion. ▸ *noun* a rebellion or uprising against a government, authority, etc. [16c: from French *révolter*]

revolting *adj* **1** causing a feeling of disgust, loathing, etc; nauseating. **2** rising in revolt; rebellious. ▪ **revoltingly** *adv.*

revolution *noun* **1** the overthrow of a government or political system. **2** any complete economic, social, etc change: *the Industrial Revolution*. **3** **a** an act or the process of turning about an axis; **b** a single turn about an axis; **c** the time taken to make one such movement. **4** a cycle of events. ▪ **revolutionism** *noun.* ▪ **revolutionist** *noun.* [14c: from French *révolution*]

revolutionary *adj* **1** relating to or causing a revolution. **2** completely new or different; involving radical change. ▸ *noun* (***-ies***) someone who takes part in or is in favour of a political, social, etc revolution.

revolutionize *or* **-ise** *verb* **1** to bring about revolution, eg, in a country's political system, government, etc. **2** to bring about a great change: *Computers have revolutionized many businesses.* [18c]

revolve *verb* **1** *tr & intr* to move or turn, or cause to move or turn, in a circle around a central point; to rotate. **2** *intr* (*usu* **revolve around** *or* **about**) to have as a centre, focus or main point. **3** *intr* to occur in cycles or at regular intervals. **4** to consider. ▸ *noun, theatre* a section of a stage that can be rotated, providing a means of scene-changing. ▪ **revolvable** *adj.* ▪ **revolving** *adj* **1** able, designed, etc to revolve. **2** recurring at regular intervals. [14c: from Latin *revolvere* to roll back]

revolver *noun* a pistol with a revolving cylinder holding several bullets. [19c]

revue *noun* a humorous theatrical show, that includes songs, sketches, etc. [19c: French, meaning 'review']

revulsion *noun* **1** a feeling of complete disgust, distaste or repugnance. **2** a sudden and often violent change of feeling, esp from love to hate. ▪ **revulsive** *adj.* [16c: from Latin *revulsio*]

reward *noun* **1** something given or received in return for work done, a service rendered, good behaviour, etc. **2** a sum of money offered for finding or helping to find a criminal, stolen or lost property, etc. **3** something given or received in return for a good or evil deed, etc. ▸ *verb* to give as a show of gratitude or in recompense. [13c: from French *reguarder* to regard]

rewarding *adj* giving personal pleasure or satisfaction; worthwhile: *a rewarding job.*

rewind *verb* /riː'waɪnd/ (***rewound***) to wind (thread, tape, film, etc) back. ▸ *noun* /'riːwaɪnd/ **1** the action or process of rewinding. **2** a mechanism for rewinding tape, film, etc. ▪ **rewinder** *noun.* [18c]

rewire *verb* to fit (a house, etc) with new electrical wiring. [20c]

reword *verb* to express in different words.

rework *verb* **1** to work something again. **2** to alter or refashion something in order to use it again. **3** to revise or rewrite something. ▪ **reworking** *noun* **1** the action of working something again, or of altering, revising it, etc. **2** something that is reworked, esp something that is revised or rewritten. [19c]

rewritable *adj, comput* of data: capable of being recorded in the area from which it has been read.

rewrite *verb* /riː'raɪt/ **1** to write something again or in different words. **2** *comput* to retain (data) in an area of store by recording it in the location from which it has been read. ▸ *noun* /'riːraɪt/ **1** the action of rewriting. **2** something that is rewritten.

RF *abbrev* radio frequency.

Rf *symbol, chem* rutherfordium.

Rh[1] *abbrev* rhesus, esp in **Rh factor**.

Rh[2] *symbol, chem* rhodium.

rhapsodize *or* **-ise** *verb, tr & intr* to speak or write with great enthusiasm or emotion. ▪ **rhapsodist** *noun.*

rhapsody *noun* (***-ies***) **1** *music* a piece of music, emotional in character and usu written to suggest a free form or improvisation. **2** an exaggeratedly enthusiastic and highly emotional speech, piece of writing, etc. ▪ **rhapsodic** /rap'sɒdɪk/ *or* **rhapsodical** *adj.* [16c: from Latin *rhapsodia*, from Greek *rhaptein* to sew or work together + *oide* song]

rhea /rɪə/ *noun* a S American flightless bird, like an ostrich but smaller. [19c: Latin, named after *Rhea*, the mother of Zeus in Greek mythology]

rhebok see **reebok**

rhenium *noun, chem* (symbol **Re**) a rare silvery-white metallic element with a very high melting point. [20c: named after the River Rhine (*Rhenus* in Latin)]

rheostat *noun, elec* a device for varying resistance in an electric circuit, used eg in dimming light bulbs, etc. ▪ **rheostatic** *adj.* [19c]

rhesus factor *or* **Rh factor** *noun, med* an **antigen** that is present on the surface of red blood cells of about 84% of the human population, who are said to be **rhesus positive**, and absent in the remaining 16%, who are said to be **rhesus negative**. [20c: named after the rhesus monkey, in which it was first discovered]

rhetoric /'rɛtərɪk/ *noun* **1** the art of using language elegantly, effectively or persuasively. **2** language of this kind, sometimes with overtones of insincerity or exaggeration: *mere rhetoric.* ▪ **rhetorician** /rɛtə'rɪʃən/ *noun.* [14c: from Greek *rhetorike techne* rhetorical art]

rhetorical /rɪ'tɒrɪkəl/ *adj* **1** relating to or using rhetoric. **2** persuasive or insincere in style.

rhetorical question *noun* a question that is asked for effect rather than to gain information. [19c]

rheum /ruːm/ *noun* a watery mucous discharge from the nose or eyes. ▪ **rheumy** *adj.* [14c: from French *reume*, from Greek *rhein* to flow]

rheumatic *adj* **1** relating to, like or caused by rheumatism. **2** affected with rheumatism. ▸ *noun* **1** someone who suffers from rheumatism. **2** (**rheumatics**) *informal* rheumatism or pain caused by it. ▪ **rheumatically** *adv.* [14c: from French *reumatique*, from Greek *rheuma* rheum]

rheumatism *noun* a disease causing painful swelling of the joints, muscles and fibrous tissues. ▪ **rheumatoid** *adj.* [17c: from Latin *rheumatismus*, from Greek *rheuma* rheum]

rheumatology *noun, med* the study of rheumatic diseases. ▪ **rheumatological** *adj.* ▪ **rheumatologist** *noun.* [20c]

rhinestone *noun* an imitation diamond, usu made from glass or plastic. [19c: a translation of French *caillou du Rhin*, 'stone of the Rhine']

rhinitis *noun, med* inflammation of the mucous membrane of the nasal passages. [19c]

rhino *noun* (***rhinos*** *or* ***rhino***) short form of **rhinoceros**.

rhino- *or* (*before a vowel*) **rhin-** *combining form, denoting* the nose. [From Greek *rhis, rhinos* nose]

rhinoceros *noun* (***rhinoceroses*** *or* ***rhinoceros***) a large herbivorous mammal with very thick skin and either one or two horns on its snout. [14c: from Greek *rhinos* nose + *keras* horn]

rhinoplasty *noun* plastic surgery of the nose. Also called (*informal*) **nose job**. ▪ **rhinoplastic** *adj.* [19c]

rhizome *noun, botany* a thick horizontal underground stem which produces both roots and leafy shoots. [19c: from Greek *rhiza* root]

rho /roʊ/ *noun* the seventeenth letter of the Greek alphabet, corresponding to R. [14c]

rhodium *noun, chem* (symbol **Rh**) a hard, silvery-white metallic element, used for making alloys, plating jewellery, etc. [19c: Latin, from Greek *rhodon* rose, from its rose-coloured salts]

rhododendron *noun* (***rhododendrons*** *or* ***rhododendra***) a widely cultivated shrub usu with thick evergreen leaves and large colourful flowers. [17c: from Greek *rhodon* rose + *dendron* tree]

rhomb *noun, geom* a **rhombus**. ▪ **rhombic** *adj.* [16c: from French *rhombe*; see **rhombus**]

rhomboid *noun* a quadrilateral where only the opposite sides and angles are equal. ▸ *adj* (*also* **rhomboidal**) shaped like a rhomboid or rhombus. [16c: from Greek *rhomboeides* shaped like a rhombus]

rhombus /'rɒmbəs/ *noun* (***rhombuses*** *or* ***rhombi*** /-baɪ/) **1** *geom* a quadrilateral with four equal sides and two angles greater than and two angles smaller than a right angle. Also called **rhomb**. **2** a lozenge or diamond shape, or an object with this shape. [16c: Latin, from Greek *rhembein* to spin around]

rhubarb *noun* **1** a plant with large poisonous leaves or its long fleshy edible leafstalks. **2** the roots of a type of rhubarb found in China and Tibet, dried and used as a laxative. **3** *informal* the continuous murmured sound made by actors to give the impression of indistinct background conversation, made esp by constantly repeating the word 'rhubarb'. **4** *informal* nonsense; rubbish. [14c: from Greek *rheon barbaron* foreign rhubarb]

rhumba see **rumba**

rhyme *noun* **1** a pattern of words which have the same final sounds at the ends of lines in a poem. **2** the use of such patterns in poetry, etc. **3** a word which has the same final sound as another: *'Beef' is a rhyme for 'leaf'.* **4** a short poem, verse or jingle written in rhyme. ▸ *verb* **1** *intr* of words: to have the same final sound. **2** to use (a word) as a rhyme for another. **3** *intr* to write using rhymes. **4** to put (a story, etc) into rhyme. ▪ **rhymeless** *adj*. ▪ **rhymer** *noun*. [13c: from French *rimer* to rhyme, from German *Rim* a series or row]

IDIOMS **without rhyme or reason** lacking sense, reason or logic.

rhyme
This word is often misspelt. It might help you to remember the following sentence:
***R**emember **h**ow you **rhy**me.*

rhymester *noun* a poet, esp one who writes simple verses or who is not very talented.

rhyming slang *noun* slang, esp Cockney slang, where one word is replaced by a phrase that rhymes with it, eg *'butcher's hook'* for *'look'*.

rhythm *noun* **1** a regularly repeated pattern, movement, beat, sequence of events, etc. **2 a** the regular arrangement of stress, notes of different lengths, and pauses in a piece of music; **b** a particular pattern of stress, notes, etc in music: *tango rhythm*. **3** a regular arrangement of sounds, and of stressed and unstressed syllables, giving a sense or feeling of movement. **4** ability to sing, speak, move, etc rhythmically. **5** short form of **rhythm section**. [16c: from Latin *rhythmus*, from Greek *rheein* to flow]

rhythm
This word is often misspelt. It might help you to remember the following sentence:
*R**hythm h**elps you **t**o **h**ear **m**usic.*

rhythm and blues *singular noun, music* (abbrev **R & B**) a style of popular music combining blues elements with more lively rhythms.

rhythmic *or* **rhythmical** *adj* **1** relating to rhythm. **2** characterized by rhythm, esp one that is pleasing. **3** regular in beat, pattern, etc. ▪ **rhythmically** *adv*.

rhythm section *noun, music* **1** the instruments in a band or group, eg drums, double bass and piano, whose main function is to supply the rhythm. **2** the players of these instruments.

ria /ˈrɪə/ *noun, geog* a long narrow coastal inlet that gradually decreases in depth and width from its mouth inland. [19c: from Spanish *ría* rivermouth]

rib[1] *noun* **1** in vertebrates: any of the curved paired bones that articulate with the spine, forming the chest wall and protecting the heart, lungs, etc. **2** a cut of meat containing one or more ribs. **3** a part or section of an object or structure that resembles a rib in form or function, eg part of a framework. **4** one of the pieces of wood which curve round and upward from a ship's keel to form the framework of the hull. **5** a rod-like bar which supports and strengthens a layer of fabric, membrane, etc, eg in an umbrella or in the wing of an insect or aircraft. **6** *knitting* alternating plain and purl stitches; a series of ridges produced by these stitches, giving a degree of elasticity to a waistband, wristband, neck, etc of a garment. ▸ *verb* (***ribbed, ribbing***) **1** to provide, support or enclose (an object, structure, etc) with ribs. **2** *knitting* to knit ribs or in ribs. ▪ **ribbed** *adj*. ▪ **ribbing** *noun*. ▪ **ribless** *adj*. [Anglo-Saxon *ribb*]

rib[2] *verb* (***ribbed, ribbing***) *informal* to tease; to mock gently. ▪ **ribbing** *noun*. [20c: perhaps from the verb *rib tickle* to make someone laugh]

ribald /ˈrɪbəld/ *adj* of language, a speaker, humour, etc: humorous in an obscene, vulgar or indecently disrespectful way. ▪ **ribaldry** *noun*. [13c: from French *riber* to lead a licentious life]

riband *or* **ribband** *noun* a ribbon, esp as a prize in sport, etc. [14c: from French *reubon*]

ribbon *noun* **1 a** fine, usu coloured, material such as silk, etc, formed into a long narrow strip or band; **b** a strip of such material used for decorating clothes, tying hair, parcels, etc. **2** a long narrow strip of anything: *hanging in ribbons* • *a typewriter ribbon*. **3** a small strip of coloured cloth, worn to show membership of a team, as a sign of having won an award, medal, etc. [16c: from French *reubon*]

ribbon lake *noun, geog* a long, narrow lake in a depression carved into land by a glacier.

ribcage *noun* the chest wall, formed by the ribs. [20c]

riboflavin *or* **riboflavine** *noun* **vitamin B_2**.

ribonucleic acid *noun, biochem* (abbrev **RNA**) a nucleic acid, present in all living cells, that plays an important part in the synthesis of proteins. Compare **DNA**. [20c]

ribose *noun, biochem* a monosaccharide sugar that is an important component of ribonucleic acid. [19c: German, from *Arabinose* a sugar in gum arabic]

ribosome *noun, biol* in the cytoplasm of a living cell: any of many small particles that are the site of protein manufacture, each consisting of two subunits of different sizes and composed of RNA and protein. [20c]

rice *noun* **1** an important cereal plant of the grass family, native to SE Asia. **2** its edible starchy seeds used as food. ▸ *verb, cookery* to press (eg cooked potatoes) through a coarse sieve to form strands. ▪ **ricer** *noun*. [13c: from French *ris*, from Italian *riso*, from Greek *óryza*]

rice paper *noun* a thin, transparent, edible paper made from the pith of an Asiatic tree, used in baking biscuits and cakes, and also for painting.

rich *adj* **1** having a lot of money, property or possessions. **2** of decoration, furnishings, etc: luxurious, costly and elaborate: *rich clothes*. **3** high in value or quality: *a rich harvest*. **4** (**rich in** *or* **with**) abundant with (esp a natural resource): *rich in minerals*. **5** of soil, a region, etc: very productive. **6** of colour, sound, smell, etc: vivid and intense; deep: *rich red*.

7 a of food: heavily seasoned, strongly flavoured; **b** of food or a diet: containing a lot of fat, oil or dried fruit. **8** of a remark, suggestion, event, etc: ridiculous: *That's rich, coming from you!* **9** of the mixture in an internal combustion engine: with a high proportion of fuel to air. ▪ **richness** *noun*. [Anglo-Saxon *rice* strong or powerful]

riches *plural noun* wealth in general, or a particular form of abundance or wealth: *family riches • architectural riches*. [12c: from French *richesse*]

richly *adv* **1** in a rich way. **2** fully and suitably: *richly deserved*.

ricin /ˈraɪsɪn/ *noun* a highly toxic **albumin** found in the beans of a tropical African plant. [20c: from *Ricinus*, the genus name of the plant that produces it]

rick[1] *noun* a stack or heap, eg of hay, corn, etc, usu made in a regular shape and thatched on top. ▸ *verb* to stack (esp hay, corn, etc). [Anglo-Saxon *hreac*]

rick[2] *verb* to sprain or wrench (one's neck, back, etc). ▸ *noun* a sprain or wrench. [18c]

rickets *singular or plural noun* a disease, esp of children, caused by vitamin D deficiency, characterized by softness and imperfect formation of the bones. *Technical equivalent* **rachitis**. [17c]

rickety *adj* **1** of a construction, piece of furniture, etc: unsteady and likely to collapse; shaky or unstable. **2** of the mind, etc: feeble. **3** suffering from rickets. ▪ **ricketiness** *noun*. [17c]

rickshaw *or* **ricksha** *noun* a small two-wheeled hooded carriage, either drawn by a person on foot, or attached to a bicycle or motorcycle. [19c: shortened from Japanese *jin* a person + *-riki* power + *-sha* a vehicle]

ricochet /ˈrɪkəʃeɪ, -ʃɛt/ *noun* **1** the action, esp of a bullet or other missile, of hitting a surface and then rebounding. **2** a sound or hit made by such an action. ▸ *verb, intr* (***ricocheted*** /-ʃeɪd/ *or* ***ricochetted, ricocheting*** /-ʃeɪɪŋ/ *or* ***ricochetting***) of an object, esp a bullet, projectile, etc: to hit or glance off a surface and rebound. [18c: French]

ricotta *noun* a soft white unsalted Italian curd cheese. [19c: Italian, meaning 'recooked', from Latin *coquere* to cook]

rictus *noun* (***rictus*** *or* ***rictuses***) **1** the gape of an open mouth, esp of a bird's beak. **2** an unnatural fixed grin or grimace. ▪ **rictal** *adj*. [18c: Latin, literally 'open mouth', from *rictus* to gape]

rid *verb* (***rid*** *or* (archaic) ***ridded, ridding***) (**rid of**) to free (someone, oneself, something or somewhere) from (something undesirable or unwanted). [13c: from Norse *rythja* to clear]

riddance *noun* the act of getting rid of something.

IDIOMS **good riddance** a welcome relief from someone or something undesirable or unwanted.

riddle[1] *noun* **1** a short and usu humorous puzzle, often in the form of a question, which can only be solved or understood using ingenuity. **2** a person, thing or fact that is puzzling or difficult to understand. ▸ *verb, intr* to speak enigmatically or in riddles. ▪ **riddler** *noun*. [Anglo-Saxon *rædels*]

riddle[2] *noun* a large coarse sieve for sifting soil, grain, etc. ▸ *verb* **1** to pass through a riddle. **2** (*usu* **riddle with**) to pierce with many holes: *Snipers had riddled the wall with bullets.* **3** (*usu* **riddle with**) to spread through; to fill: *a government department riddled with corruption*. [Anglo-Saxon *hriddel*]

ride *verb* (*past tense* ***rode,*** *past participle* ***ridden***) **1** to sit, usu astride, on and control the movements of (esp a horse, bicycle, motorbike, etc). **2** *intr* to travel or be carried (on a horse, bicycle, etc or in a car, train or other vehicle). **3** *chiefly N Am* to travel on (a vehicle). **4** *intr* to go on horseback, esp regularly. **5** to ride (a horse) in a race. **6** to move across or be carried over (eg the sea, sky, etc): *a ship riding the waves*. **7** of a ship: **a** *intr* to float at anchor; **b** to be attached to (an anchor). **8** *intr* of the moon: to appear to float: *The moon was riding high.* **9** to travel by horse, car, etc: *rode across the desert on camels*. **10** (**ride on sth**) to depend completely upon it: *It all rides on his answer.* **11** to bend before (a blow, punch, etc) to reduce its impact. **12** to infest or dominate: *a cellar ridden with rats • ridden with remorse*. ▸ *noun* **1 a** a journey or certain distance covered on horseback, on a bicycle or in a vehicle; **b** the duration of this: *a long ride home*. **2** a horse, vehicle, etc as a means of transport. **3** an experience or series of events of a specified nature: *a rough ride*. **4** *esp N Am* a **lift** (*noun* sense 5). **5** the type of movement a vehicle, etc gives: *a very smooth ride*. **6** a path or track, esp one through a wood or across an area of countryside, reserved for horseback riding. **7** a fairground machine, such as a rollercoaster or big wheel. [Anglo-Saxon *ridan*]

IDIOMS **ride for a fall** to invite disaster, ridicule, etc by stupid or reckless behaviour. **take sb for a ride** *informal* to trick, cheat or deceive them.

PHRASAL VERBS **ride sth out** to come through (a difficult period, situation, etc) successfully: *ride out the storm*. **ride up** *intr* of clothing, etc: to move gradually out of the correct position.

rider *noun* **1** someone who rides. **2** an object that rests on or astride another. **3** an extra or subsequent clause, etc added to a document as a qualification, amendment, etc. ▪ **riderless** *adj*.

ridge *noun* **1** a strip of ground raised either side of a ploughed furrow. **2** any long narrow raised area on an otherwise flat surface. **3** the top edge of something where two upward sloping surfaces meet, eg on a roof. **4** a long narrow strip of relatively high ground with steep slopes on either side. **5** *meteorol* a long narrow area of high atmospheric pressure, often associated with fine weather and strong breezes. Compare **trough** (sense 4). ▸ *verb, tr & intr* to form or make into ridges. ▪ **ridged** *adj*. ▪ **ridging** *noun*. [Anglo-Saxon *hrycg*]

ridgepole *noun* a horizontal pole at the top of a tent.

ridge tile *noun* a tile shaped to cover the ridge of a roof.

ridgeway *noun* a track along the ridge of a hill.

ridicule *noun* contemptuous mockery or derision. ▸ *verb* to subject or expose (someone or something) to ridicule. [17c: French, from Latin *ridere* to laugh]

ridiculous *adj* **1** deserving or provoking ridicule. **2** absurd or unreasonable: *ridiculous prices*. ▪ **ridiculously** *adv*. ▪ **ridiculousness** *noun*.

riding[1] *noun* **1** the art and practice of riding a horse. **2** a track or path for horseback riding.

riding[2] *noun* **1** any of the three former administrative divisions of Yorkshire, **East Riding**, **North Riding** and **West Riding**. **2** *Can* a political constituency. [Anglo-Saxon as *thriding*, from Norse *thrithjungr* third part]

Riesling /ˈriːslɪŋ, riːz-/ *noun* **1** a dry white wine produced in Germany, Alsace, Austria and elsewhere. **2** the type of vine and grape from which it is made. [19c: German]

rife *adj* **1** very common or numerous. **2** (**rife with**) teeming in (usu something bad or undesirable): *The garden was rife with weeds.* ▪ **rifeness** *noun.* [Anglo-Saxon *ryfe*]

riff *noun, pop music* a short passage of music played repeatedly. ▸ *verb, intr* to play riffs. [20c]

riffle *verb* **1** *tr & intr* (*often* **riffle through**) to turn (pages) rapidly. **2** to shuffle (playing-cards) by dividing the pack into two equal piles and allowing them to fall together more or less alternately. ▸ *noun* an act or instance of riffling. [17c]

riff-raff *noun* worthless, disreputable or undesirable people, esp those considered to be of a low social class; the rabble. [15c: from French *rifler* to spoil + *rafler* to snatch away]

rifle[1] *noun* **1** a large gun with a long barrel with a spiral groove on the inside, usu fired from the shoulder. **2** (*usu* **rifles**) riflemen. ▸ *verb* **1** to cut spiral grooves in (a gun or its barrel). **2** *informal* to hit or kick (a ball, etc) very hard. [17c: from French *rifler* to scratch]

rifle[2] *verb* **1** *tr & intr* (*often* **rifle through**) to search (through a house, safe, drawer, etc). **2** to steal and take away. [14c: from French *rifler* to plunder]

rifleman *noun* a soldier armed with a rifle.

rifling *noun* a pattern of spiral grooves on the inside of the barrel of a gun.

rift *noun* **1** a split or crack, esp one in the earth or in rock. **2** a gap in mist or clouds. **3** a break in previously friendly relations. ▸ *verb* to tear or split apart. ▪ **riftless** *adj.* [13c: from Norse *ript* breaking of an agreement]

rig *verb* (***rigged, rigging***) **1** *naut* to fit (a ship, masts, etc) with ropes, sails and rigging. **2** *aeronautics* to position correctly the various parts and components of (an aircraft, etc). **3** *intr, naut, aeronautics* of a ship, aircraft, etc: to be made ready for use; to be equipped. **4** to control or manipulate for dishonest purposes, or for personal profit or advantage. ▸ *noun* **1** *naut* the particular arrangement of sails, ropes and masts on a ship. **2** an **oil rig**. **3** gear or equipment, esp for a specific task. **4** *N Am* a lorry or truck. [15c]

PHRASAL VERBS **rig sb out 1** to dress them in clothes of a stated or special kind. **2** to provide them with special equipment. **rig sth up** to build or prepare it, esp hastily and with whatever material is available.

rigger *noun* **1** someone who rigs, esp someone who arranges a ship's rigging. **2** someone who works on an oil rig. **3** someone who erects scaffolding, etc. **4** a ship rigged in a particular way.

rigging *noun* the system of ropes, wires, etc which support and control a ship's masts and sails.

right *adj* **1** indicating, relating or referring to, or on, the side facing east from the point of view of someone or something facing north. **2** of a part of the body: on or towards the right side. **3** of an article of clothing, etc: worn on the right hand, foot, etc. **4 a** on, towards or close to an observer's right; **b** on a stage: on or towards the performers' right. **5** of a river bank: on the right side of a person facing downstream. **6** correct; true. **7** of a clock or watch: showing the correct time. **8** suitable; appropriate; proper. **9** most appropriate or favourable. **10** in a correct, proper or satisfactory state or condition. **11** sound or stable: *not in his right mind.* **12** morally correct or good. **13** legally correct or good. **14** on the side of a fabric, garment, etc which is intended to be seen: *turn the dress right side out.* **15** *geom* **a** with an axis perpendicular to the base: *a right angle*; **b** straight. **16** (*also* **Right**) conservative; right-wing. **17** socially acceptable: *know all the right people.* **18** *Brit, informal* complete; utter; real: *a right mess.* ▸ *adv* **1** on or towards the right side. **2** correctly; properly; satisfactorily. **3** exactly or precisely: *It happened right there.* **4** immediately; without delay: *He'll be right over.* **5** completely; absolutely: *It went right out of my mind.* **6** all the way: *went right through him.* **7** of movement, a direction, etc: straight; without deviating from a straight line: *right to the top.* **8** towards or on the right side: *He looked right before crossing the road.* **9** favourably or satisfactorily: *It turned out right in the end.* **10** esp in religious titles: most; very: *right reverend.* **11** *old use or dialect* very; to the full: *be right glad to see her.* ▸ *noun* **1** (*often* **rights**) a power, privilege, title, etc. **2** (*often* **rights**) a just or legal claim. **3** fairness; truth; justice. **4** something that is correct, good or just: *the rights and wrongs of the case.* **5** (*often* **the Right**) the political party, or a group of people within a party, etc which has the most conservative views. **6** the right side, part or direction of something. **7** *boxing* **a** the right hand: *He was lethal with his right*; **b** a punch with the right hand: *He knocked him out with a right.* **8** a glove, shoe, etc worn on the right hand or foot: *Can I try on the right?* **9** (*often* **rights**) *commerce* the privilege given to a company's existing shareholders to buy new shares, usu for less than the market value. **10** (**rights**) the legal permission to print, publish, film, etc a book. ▸ *verb* **1** *tr & intr* to put or come back to the correct or normal, esp upright, position: *They soon righted the boat.* **2** to avenge or compensate for (some wrong done). **3** to correct or rectify. **4** to put in order or return to order. ▸ *exclam* expressing agreement, assent or readiness. ▪ **rightness** *noun.* [Anglo-Saxon *riht, reoht*]

IDIOMS **by right** *or* **rights** rightfully; properly. **do right by sb** to treat them correctly or appropriately, in moral or legal terms. **in the right** with justice, reason, etc on one's side. **put** *or* **set right** *or* **to rights** to make correct or proper. **right away** *or* **now** immediately; at once. **right, left and centre** on all sides; all around.

right angle *noun, geom* an angle of 90°, formed by two lines which are perpendicular to each other. ▪ **right-angled** *adj.*

right arm *noun* a most trusted and reliable helper, etc.

righteous /ˈraɪtʃəs/ *adj* **1** of a person: virtuous, free from sin or guilt. **2** of an action: morally good. **3** justifiable morally: *righteous indignation.* ▪ **righteously** *adv.* ▪ **righteousness** *noun.* [Anglo-Saxon, from *riht* right + *wise* manner]

rightful *adj* **1** having a legally just claim. **2** of property, a privilege, etc: held legally. **3** fair; just; equitable.

right-hand *adj* **1** relating to, on or towards the right. **2** done with the right hand.

right-handed *adj* **1** of a person: using the right hand more easily than the left. **2** of a tool, etc: designed to be used in the right hand. **3** of a blow, etc: done with the right hand. **4** of a screw: fixed by turning clockwise. ▪ **right-handedly** *adv.* ▪ **right-handedness** *noun.*

right-hander *noun* **1** a right-handed person. **2** a punch with the right hand.

right-hand man *or* **right-hand woman** *noun* a valuable, indispensable and trusted assistant.

Right Honourable *noun* a title given to British peers below the rank of marquis, to privy councillors, to present and past cabinet ministers, and to some Lord Mayors and Lord Provosts.

rightism *noun* **1** the political opinions of conservatives or the right. **2** support for and promotion of this. ▪ **rightist** *noun, adj.*

rightly *adv* **1** correctly. **2** justly. **3** fairly; properly. **4** with good reason; justifiably. **5** with certainty.

right-minded *adj* thinking, judging and acting according to principles which are just and sensible.

right of way *noun* (***rights of way***) **1 a** the right of the public to use a path that crosses private property; **b** a path used by this right. **2** the right of one vehicle to proceed before other vehicles coming from different directions.

right-on *slang, adj* **1** excellent. **2** up to date or politically correct. ▸ *exclam* (**right on**) expressing enthusiastic agreement or approval.

rightward *or* **rightwards** *adj, adv* on or towards the right.

right wing *noun* **1** the more conservative members of a group or political party. **2** *sport* **a** the extreme right side of a pitch or team in a field game; **b** (*also* **right-winger**) the member of a team who plays in this position. **3** the right side of an army. ▸ *adj* (**right-wing**) belonging or relating to the right wing.

rigid *adj* **1** completely stiff and inflexible. **2** of a person: strictly and inflexibly adhering to ideas, opinions, rules, etc. ▪ **rigidity** *noun.* ▪ **rigidly** *adv.* ▪ **rigidness** *noun.* [16c: from Latin *rigere* to be stiff]

rigidify *verb* (***-ies, -ied***) to become or make rigid.

rigmarole *noun* **1** an unnecessarily or absurdly long, and often pointless or boring, complicated series of actions, instructions or procedures. **2** a long rambling or confused statement or speech. [18c: from the *Ragman Rolls,* a series of documents in which the Scottish nobles promised allegiance to Edward I of England]

rigor *noun* **1** *med* a sense of chilliness accompanied by shivering, a preliminary symptom of many diseases. **2** a rigid irresponsive state caused by a sudden shock. [14c: Latin, meaning 'numbness' or 'stiffness']

rigor mortis *noun* a stiffening of the body soon after death. [19c: Latin, meaning 'stiffness of death']

rigorous *adj* **1** showing or having rigour; strict; harsh; severe. **2** strictly accurate. ▪ **rigorously** *adv.* ▪ **rigorousness** *noun.*

rigour *or* (*N Am*) **rigor** *noun* **1** stiffness; hardness. **2** strictness or severity of temper, behaviour or judgement. **3** strict enforcement of rules or the law. **4** (*usu* **rigours**) of a particular situation or circumstances, eg of weather or climate: harshness or severity. [14c: from Latin *rigor* stiffness]

rig-out *noun* a set of clothes.

rile *verb* to anger or annoy. [19c: a variant of *roil* to stir up (a liquid)]

rilievo see **relievo**

rill *noun* a small stream or brook. [16c]

rim *noun* **1** a raised edge or border, esp of something curved or circular, eg a cup, spectacles, etc. **2** the outer circular edge of a wheel to which the tyre is attached. ▸ *verb* (***rimmed, rimming***) to form or provide an edge or rim to something; to edge. ▪ **rimless** *adj.* ▪ **rimmed** *adj.* [Anglo-Saxon *rima*]

rime[1] *noun* thick white frost formed esp from cloud or fog. ▸ *verb* to cover with rime. ▪ **rimy** *adj* (***-ier, -iest***). [Anglo-Saxon *hrim*]

rime[2] *archaic* variant of **rhyme**

rind *noun* **1** a thick hard outer layer or covering on fruit, cheese or bacon. **2** the bark of a tree or plant. ▪ **rindless** *adj.* [Anglo-Saxon *rinde*]

rinderpest *noun* a malignant and contagious disease of cattle and other ruminants. [19c: German, from *Rinder* cattle + *Pest* plague]

ring[1] *noun* **1** a small circle of gold, silver, etc, worn on the finger. **2** a circle of metal, wood, plastic, etc, for holding, keeping in place, connecting, hanging, etc. **3** any object, mark or figure which is circular in shape. **4** a circular course or route. **5** a group of people or things arranged in a circle. **6** an enclosed and usu circular area in which circus acts are performed. **7** a square area on a platform, marked off by ropes, where boxers or wrestlers fight. **8** (**the ring**) boxing as a profession. **9** an enclosure for bookmakers at a race-course. **10** at agricultural shows, etc: an enclosure where cattle, horses, etc are paraded or exhibited for auction. **11** a group of people who act together: *a drugs ring* • *a spy ring.* **12** a circular electric element or gas burner on top of a cooker. **13** a circular mark, seen when a tree trunk is examined in section, that represents one year's growth. **14** a segment of a worm, caterpillar, etc. **15** *chemistry* a closed chain of atoms in a molecule. **16** *comput* a computer system suitable for a **LAN**, with several micro-computers or peripheral devices connected by cable in a ring. ▸ *verb* **1** to make, form, draw, etc a ring round (something) or to form into a ring. **2** to cut into rings. **3** to put a ring on (a bird's leg) as a means of identifying it. **4** to fit a ring in (a bull's nose) so that it can be led easily. ▪ **ringed** *adj.* [Anglo-Saxon *hring*]

IDIOMS **make** *or* **run rings round sb** *informal* to beat them or be much better than them.

ring[2] *verb* (*past tense* ***rang,*** *past participle* ***rung***) **1 a** to sound (a bell, etc); **b** *intr* of a bell: to sound. **2 a** to make (a metal object, etc) give a resonant bell-like sound by striking it; **b** *intr* of a metal object, etc: to sound in this way when struck. **3** *intr* of a large building, etc: to resound; to be filled with a particular sound: *The theatre rang with laughter and applause.* **4** *intr* of a sound or noise: to resound; to re-echo: *Applause rang round the theatre.* **5** *intr* (*usu* **ring out**) to make a sudden clear loud sound: *Shots rang out.* **6** *intr* to sound repeatedly; to resound: *Her criticisms rang in his ears.* **7** *intr* of the ears: to be filled with a buzzing, humming or ringing sensation or sound. **8** (*also* **ring up**) *chiefly Brit* to call by telephone. ▸ *noun* **1** an act of ringing a bell. **2** an act or sound of ringing. **3** a clear resonant sound of a bell, etc. **4** *Brit* a telephone call. **5** a suggestion or impression: *a story with a ring of truth about it.* ▪ **ringing** *noun, adj.* ▪ **ringingly** *adv.* [Anglo-Saxon *hringan*]

IDIOMS **ring a bell** to bring to mind a vague memory of having been seen, heard, etc before: *His name rings a bell.* **ring the changes** to vary the way something is done, used, said, etc. **ring the curtain down** *or* **up 1** *theatre* to give the signal for lowering, or raising, the curtain. **2** (*usu* **ring the curtain down** *or* **up on**) *informal* to put an end to, or to begin (a project, relationship, etc).

PHRASAL VERBS **ring sb back** to telephone them again. **ring sb** *or* **sth in** *or* **out** to announce their or its arrival or departure with, or as if with, bell-ringing: *Ring out the old year and ring in the new.* **ring off** to end a telephone call. **ring sth up** to record the price of an item sold, etc on a cash register.

ring binder *noun* a loose-leaf binder with metal rings which can be opened to add or take out pages.

ring circuit *noun, elec* an electrical supply system in which a number of power points are connected forming a closed circuit.

ringer *noun* **1** someone or something that rings a bell, etc. **2** someone who rings the legs of birds. **3** (*also* **dead ringer**) someone or something that is almost identical to another: *He's a dead ringer for Robbie Williams.* **4** *chiefly US* a horse or athlete entered into a race or competition under a false name or other false pretences. **5** *chiefly US informal* an impostor or fake.

ring-fence *noun* **1** a fence that completely encircles an estate. **2** a complete barrier. **3** the compulsory reservation of funds for use within a specific limited sector or department, eg, of a government, company, etc. ▸ *verb* **1** to enclose (an estate) with a ring-fence. **2** to apply a ring-fence to (a sector or department of government or a company).

ringleader *noun* a person who leads or incites a group, esp in wrongdoing.

ringlet *noun* a long spiral curl of hair. ▪ **ringletted** *or* (*US*) **ringleted** *adj.* [16c]

ring main *noun, elec* an electrical supply system in which the power points and the mains are connected in a ring circuit.

ringmaster *noun* a person who presents and is in charge of performances in a circus ring.

ring network *noun, comput* a network that forms a closed loop of connected terminals, eg, a **LAN**.

ring pull *noun* a metal ring on a can, etc, which, when pulled, breaks a seal. ▸ *adj* (**ring-pull**) of a can, etc: with a ring pull attached.

ring road *noun, Brit* a road that bypasses a town centre and so keeps it relatively free of traffic.

ringside *noun* the seating area immediately next to a boxing ring, circus ring, etc.

ringtone *noun* a characteristic sound or tune made by a mobile phone when ringing.

ringworm *noun* a fungal infection, eg athlete's foot, that causes dry, red, itchy patches on the skin. [15c]

rink *noun* **1 a** an area of ice prepared for skating, curling or ice-hockey; **b** a building or enclosure containing this. **2 a** an area of smooth floor for roller-skating; **b** a building or enclosure containing this. **3** *bowls, curling* **a** a strip of grass or ice allotted to a team or set of players in bowling and curling; **b** a team or set of players using such a strip of grass or ice. [14c: orig Scots, perhaps from French *renc* rank or row]

rinse *verb* **1** to wash (soap, detergent, etc) out of (clothes, hair, dishes, etc) with clean water. **2** to remove (traces of dirt, etc) from by dipping in clean water, usu without soap. **3** (*also* **rinse out**) to clean or freshen (a cup, one's mouth, etc) with a swirl of water. ▸ *noun* **1** an act or instance or the process of rinsing. **2** liquid used for rinsing. **3** a temporary tint for the hair. ▪ **rinser** *noun.* [14c: from French *rincer* and *recincier*, perhaps ultimately from Latin *recens* fresh]

riot *noun* **1** a noisy public disturbance or disorder. **2** uncontrolled or wild revelry and feasting. **3** a striking display. **4** *informal* someone or something that is very amusing or entertaining, esp in a wild or boisterous way. ▸ *verb, intr* **1** to take part in a riot. **2** to take part in boisterous revelry. ▪ **rioter** *noun.* [13c: from French *riote* a debate or quarrel]

IDIOMS **read the riot act** *jocular* to give an angry warning. **run riot 1** to act, speak, etc in a wild or unrestrained way: *allowed the children to run riot*. **2** of plants, vegetation, etc: to grow profusely or in an uncontrolled way: *The weeds were running riot*.

riotous *adj* **1** participating in, likely to start, or like, a riot. **2** very active, noisy, cheerful and wild: *a riotous party.* **3** filled with wild revelry, parties, etc: *riotous living*. ▪ **riotously** *adv.*

RIP *abbrev*: *requiescat* (or *requiescant*) *in pace* (Latin), may he, she (or they) rest in peace.

rip *verb* (***ripped, ripping***) **1** *tr & intr* to tear or come apart violently or roughly. **2** *intr, informal* to rush along or move quickly without restraint. **3 a** to make (a hole, etc) by tearing roughly; **b** to make a long ragged tear. **4** (**rip sth off** *or* **out** *or* **up**, *etc*) to remove it quickly and violently. ▸ *noun* **1** a violent or rough tear or split. **2** an unrestrained rush. [15c]

IDIOMS **let rip 1** to speak, behave, etc violently or unrestrainedly. **2** to increase suddenly in speed, volume, etc. **3** to allow (an action, process, etc) to continue in an unrestrained or reckless way.

PHRASAL VERBS **rip sth up** to shred or tear it into pieces: *ripped up his letter.*

riparian /raɪˈpɛərɪən/ *adj* relating to, occurring or living on a river bank. [19c: from Latin *ripa* riverbank]

ripcord *noun* a cord which, when pulled, releases a parachute from its pack.

ripe *adj* **1** of fruit, grain, etc: fully matured and ready to be picked or harvested and eaten. **2** of cheese, wine, etc: having been allowed to age to develop a full flavour. **3** of a flavour or taste, eg that of wine: rich or strong. **4** of a person's age: very advanced. ▪ **ripely** *adv.* ▪ **ripeness** *noun.* [Anglo-Saxon *ripe*]

IDIOMS **ripe for sth** suitable or appropriate for a particular action or purpose: *ripe for reform.*

ripen *verb, tr & intr* to make or become ripe. [16c]

rip-off *noun* **1** an act or instance of stealing, cheating or defrauding. **2** an item which is outrageously overpriced. [20c]

riposte /rɪˈpɒst/ *noun* **1** a quick sharp reply; a retort. **2** *fencing* a quick return thrust after a parry. ▸ *verb, intr* to deliver a riposte. [18c: French, from Italian *rispondere* to respond]

ripping *verb, present participle of* **rip**. ▸ *adj, old Brit slang* splendid; excellent.

ripple *noun* **1** a slight wave or undulation, or a series of these, on the surface of water. **2** a similar wavy appearance or motion in material, hair, etc. **3** of laughter or applause: a sound that rises and falls quickly and gently. **4** a type of ice cream marbled with a coloured flavoured syrup: *raspberry ripple*. ▸ *verb* **1 a** to ruffle or agitate the surface of (water, etc); **b** to mark with ripples, or form ripples in (a surface, material, etc). **2** *intr* to form ripples or move with an undulating motion. **3** *intr* of a sound: to rise and fall quickly and gently. ▪ **ripply** *adj.* [17c]

rip-roaring *adj, informal* wild, noisy and exciting. ▪ **rip-roaringly** *adv.*

ripsaw *noun* a saw for cutting along the grain of timber.

rise *verb* (*past tense* ***rose,*** *past participle* ***risen***) *intr* **1** to get or stand up, from a sitting, etc position. **2** to get up from bed. **3** to move upwards. **4** to increase in size, amount, volume, strength, degree, intensity, etc. **5** of the sun, moon, planets, etc: to appear above the horizon. **6** to stretch or slope upwards. **7** to rebel. **8** to move from a lower position, rank, level, etc to a higher one. **9** to begin or originate: *a river that rises in the mountains.* **10** of a person's spirits: to become more cheerful. **11** of an animal's fur, a person's hair, etc: to become straight and stiff, esp from fear or anger. **12** of a committee, court, parliament, etc: to finish a session; to adjourn. **13** to come back to life. **14** of fish: to come to the surface of the water. **15** of birds: to fly up from the ground, etc. **16** of dough, a cake, etc: to swell up; to increase in volume. **17** to be built. **18** (*usu* **rise to**) to respond (to provocation, criticism, etc). ▸ *noun* **1** an act of rising. **2** an increase in size, amount, volume, strength, status, rank, etc. **3** *Brit* an increase in salary. *US equivalent* **raise**. **4** a piece of rising ground; a slope or hill. **5** a beginning or origin. **6** the vertical height of a step or flight of stairs. [Anglo-Saxon *risan*]

IDIOMS **get** *or* **take a rise out of sb** *informal* to make them angry or upset, esp by teasing or provoking them. **give rise to sth** to cause it or bring it about.

PHRASAL VERBS **rise above sth** to remain unaffected by teasing, provocation, criticism, etc.

riser *noun* **1** someone who gets out of bed, usu at a specified time: *a late riser.* **2** a vertical part between the horizontal steps of a staircase. **3** a vertical pipe on a building, oil rig, etc.

risible *adj* laughable; ludicrous. ▪ **risibility** *noun.* [16c: from Latin *ridere* to laugh]

rising *noun* **1** the act or action of rising. **2** a rebellion. ▸ *adj* **1** moving or sloping upwards; getting higher. **2** approaching greater status or reputation. **3** approaching a specified age: *the rising sevens.*

rising damp *noun, Brit* wetness which rises up through the bricks or stones of a wall.

risk *noun* **1** the chance or possibility of suffering loss, injury, damage, etc; danger. **2** someone or something likely to cause loss, injury, damage, etc. ▸ *verb* **1** to expose (someone or something) to risk. **2** to act in spite of (something unfortunate): *risked being caught.* [17c: from French *risque*]

IDIOMS **at one's own risk** accepting personal responsibility. **at risk 1** in danger. **2** of a child: considered, by a social worker, etc, liable to be abused, neglected, etc. **at the risk of** with the possibility of (some unfortunate consequence): *at the risk of sounding pompous.* **risk one's neck** to do something that puts one's life, job, etc in danger. **run** *or* **take a risk** to act in a certain way despite the risk involved. **run the risk of sth** to risk it; to be in danger of it: *run the risk of being late.*

risky *adj* (***-ier, -iest***) dangerous; likely to cause loss, damage, etc. ▪ **riskily** *adv.* ▪ **riskiness** *noun.* [19c]

risorgimento /rɪsɔːdʒɪˈmɛntoʊ/ *noun* (***risorgimenti*** /-tiː/ *or* ***risorgimentos***) **1** (**Risorgimento**) *hist* the liberation and unification of Italy in the 19th century. **2** a revival; a rebirth. [From Italian meaning 'renewal' or 'renaissance']

risotto *noun* an Italian dish of rice cooked in stock with meat or seafood, onions, tomatoes, etc. [19c: Italian, from *riso* rice]

risqué /ˈrɪskeɪ/ *adj* of a story, joke, etc: rather rude. [19c: French, from *risquer* to risk]

rissole *noun* a small fried cake or ball of chopped meat coated in breadcrumbs. [18c: French]

ritardando see **rallentando**

rite *noun* **1** a formal ceremony or observance, esp a religious one. **2** the required words or actions for such a ceremony. **3** a body of such acts or ceremonies which are characteristic of a particular church. [14c: from Latin *ritus* religious ceremony]

rite of passage *noun* (***rites of passage***) a ritual event or ceremony marking an important transition in a person's life. [20c: from French *rite de passage*]

ritual *noun* **1** a set order or words used in a religious ceremony. **2** a series of actions performed compulsively, regularly, habitually, etc. ▸ *adj* relating to, like or used for religious, social or other rites or ritual. ▪ **ritualize** *or* **-ise** *verb.* ▪ **ritually** *adv.* [16c: from Latin *ritualis*, from *ritus* rite]

ritualism *noun* excessive belief in the importance of, or excessive practice of, ritual. ▪ **ritualist** *noun.* ▪ **ritualistic** *adj.* [19c]

ritzy *adj* (***-ier, -iest***) *informal* **1** very smart and elegant. **2** ostentatiously rich; flashy. ▪ **ritzily** *adv.* ▪ **ritziness** *noun.* [20c: named after the luxury hotels established by Swiss-born hotelier César Ritz]

rival *noun* **1** a person or group of people competing with another. **2** someone or something that is comparable with or equals another in quality, ability, etc. ▸ *verb* (***rivalled, rivalling***; *US* ***rivaled, rivaling***) **1** to try to gain the same objective as; to be in competition with. **2** to try to equal or be better than. **3** to equal or be comparable with, in terms of quality, ability, etc. ▪ **rivalry** *noun* (***-ies***). [16c: from Latin *rivalis*, orig meaning 'someone who uses the same stream as another', from *rivus* a stream]

rive *verb* (*past participle* ***rived*** *or* ***riven***) *poetic, archaic* **1** to tear or tear apart: *a family riven by feuds.* **2** *intr* to split. [13c: from Norse *rifa*]

river *noun* **1** a large permanent body of flowing water, originating at a source, travelling along a fixed course, and emptying into a lake or the sea. **2** an abundant or plentiful stream or flow: *cried rivers • a river of tears.* [13c: from French *rivière*, from Latin *ripa* riverbank]

riverine *adj* relating to or living or situated on or near a river; riparian. [19c]

riverside *noun* a bank of a river or an area of ground along a river.

rivet *noun* a metal pin or bolt for joining pieces of metal, etc. ▸ *verb* **1** to fasten (pieces of metal, etc) with a rivet. **2** to fix securely. **3** to attract and hold (attention, etc). **4** to render motionless, esp with fascination, horror or fear, etc: *I was riveted to the spot.* ▪ **riveter** *noun.* [14c: from French *river* to fasten or clinch]

riveting *adj* fascinating; enthralling.

riviera /rɪvɪ'ɛərə/ *noun* a coastal area with a warm climate, esp the Mediterranean coasts of France and Italy. [18c: Italian, meaning 'coast or shore']

rivulet *noun* a small river or stream. [16c: perhaps from Italian *rivoletto*, from *rivo*, from Latin *rivulus*, from *rivus* a stream]

rms *abbrev* root mean square.

Rn *symbol, chem* radon.

RNA *abbrev, biochem* ribonucleic acid.

roach[1] *noun* (***roaches*** or ***roach***) a silvery freshwater fish of the carp family. [14c: from French *roche*]

roach[2] *noun, informal* **1** *N Am* a cockroach. **2** a butt of a cannabis cigarette. [19c]

road *noun* **1 a** an open way, usu specially surfaced or paved, for people, vehicles or animals to travel on; **b** the part of this designated for the use of vehicles. **2** a route or course: *the road to ruin.* **3** (*usu* **roads**) a relatively sheltered area of water near the shore where ships may be anchored. ▪ **roadless** *adj.* [Anglo-Saxon *rad*, related to **ride**]

IDIOMS **hit the road** to leave; to depart. **one for the road** a final, usu alcoholic, drink before leaving. **on the road** travelling from place to place.

roadblock *noun* a police, army, etc barrier across a road for stopping and checking vehicles and drivers.

road hog *noun, informal* an aggressive, selfish or reckless driver. [19c]

roadholding *noun* the extent to which a vehicle remains stable when turning corners at high speed, in wet conditions, etc.

roadhouse *noun* a public house or inn at the side of a major road.

roadie *noun, informal* a person who helps move and organize the instruments and equipment for a rock or pop group, esp on tour. [20c: shortened form of *road manager*]

road rage *noun* uncontrolled anger or aggression between road users, which usu takes the form of screaming obscenities, making rude gestures, etc, but which can erupt into violence. [20c]

roadshow *noun* **1 a** a touring group of theatrical or musical performers; **b** a show given by such a group. **2 a** a touring disc jockey or radio or TV presenter and their team, equipment, etc; **b** a live broadcast, usu in front of an audience, presented by them from one of a series of venues on the tour. **3 a** a promotional tour by a group or organization to publicize its policies, products, etc; **b** the performances given on such a tour. [20c]

roadside *noun* the ground beside or along a road.

road sign *noun* a sign beside or over a road, motorway, etc, that gives information on routes, speed limits, hazards, traffic systems, etc.

roadstead *noun* same as **road** (sense 3).

roadster *noun* **1** *orig US, old use* an open sports car for two people. **2** a strong bicycle. **3** a horse for riding, or pulling carriages, on roads.

road tax *noun* a former name for **vehicle excise duty**.

road test *noun* **1** a test of a vehicle's performance and roadworthiness. **2** a practical test of a product, etc. ▸ *verb* (**road-test**) **1** to test (a vehicle's roadworthiness). **2** to test out the practicalities, suitability, etc of (a new product, etc).

roadway *noun* the part of a road or street used by traffic. [16c]

roadwork *noun* athletic training, eg for marathons, boxing matches, etc, consisting of running on roads.

roadworks *plural noun* the building or repairing of a road.

roadworthy *adj* of a vehicle: safe to be used on the road. ▪ **roadworthiness** *noun.* [19c]

roam *verb* **1** *intr* to ramble or wander, esp over a large area, with no fixed purpose or direction. **2** to ramble or wander about, over, through, etc (a particular area) in no fixed direction: *roamed the streets.* ▸ *noun* **1** the act of roaming. **2** a ramble. [14c]

roan *adj* of an animal, esp a horse: having a coat whose colour is flecked with many grey or white hairs. ▸ *noun* a roan animal, esp a horse. [16c: French, from Spanish *roano*]

roar *verb* **1** *intr* of a lion or other animal: to give a loud growling cry. **2** of a person: **a** *intr* to give a deep loud cry, esp in anger, pain or exhilaration; **b** to say (something) with a deep loud cry, esp in anger. **3** *intr* to laugh loudly and wildly. **4** *intr* of cannons, busy traffic, wind or waves, a fiercely burning fire, etc: to make a deep loud reverberating sound. **5** to move or be moving very fast and noisily: *traffic roared past.* ▸ *noun* an act or the sound of roaring. [Anglo-Saxon *rarian*]

roaring *noun* an act or the sound of making a loud deep cry. ▸ *adj* **1** uttering or emitting roars. **2** *informal* riotous. **3** *informal* proceeding with great activity or success.

IDIOMS **do a roaring trade** to do very brisk and profitable business. **roaring drunk** *informal* rowdily or boisterously drunk.

roast *verb* **1** to cook (meat, etc) by exposure to dry heat, esp in an oven. **2** to dry and brown (coffee beans, nuts, etc) by exposure to dry heat. **3** *intr* of meat, coffee beans, nuts, etc: to be cooked or dried and made brown by exposure to dry heat. **4** *informal* to warm or heat (oneself or something else) to an extreme or excessive degree: *roast in the sun.* **5** *informal* to criticize severely. ▸ *noun* **1** a piece of meat which has been roasted or is suitable for roasting. **2** *N Am* a party in the open air at which food is roasted and eaten. [13c: from French *rostir*]

roasting *adj* extremely or uncomfortably hot. ▸ *noun* a dose of severe criticism.

rob *verb* (***robbed, robbing***) **1** to steal from (a person or place), esp by force or threats. **2** *intr* to commit robbery. **3** to deprive of something expected as a right or due: *robbed her of her dignity.* ▪ **robber** *noun.* [12c: from French *rober*]

robbery *noun* (***-ies***) an act or instance or the process of robbing, esp theft with threats, force or violence.

robe *noun* **1** (*often* **robes**) a long loose flowing garment, esp the vestment worn on ceremonial occasions by peers, judges, academics, the clergy, etc. **2** a dressing-gown or bathrobe. ▸ *verb* to clothe (oneself or someone else) in a robe or robes. [13c: French, of Germanic origin, related to **rob**, orig meaning 'booty' in the sense of clothes regarded as booty]

robin *noun* **1** (*also* **robin redbreast**) a small brown European thrush with a red breast and white abdomen. **2** a larger N American thrush with a brick-red breast, black and white speckled throat and white rings around its eyes. [16c: a diminutive of the name *Robert*]

robot *noun* **1** esp in science fiction: a machine that vaguely resembles a human being and which can be programmed to carry out tasks. Compare **android**. **2** an automatic machine that can be programmed to perform specific tasks. **3** *informal* someone who works efficiently but who lacks human warmth or sensitivity. ▪ **robotic** *adj*. ▪ **robotize** *or* **-ise** *verb*. [20c: Czech, from Karl Čapek's 1920 play *R.U.R.*, from *robota* forced labour]

robotics *singular noun* the branch of engineering concerned with the design, construction, operation and use of industrial robots.

robust *adj* **1** of a person: strong and healthy. **2** strongly built or constructed. **3** of exercise, etc: requiring strength and energy. **4** of language, humour, etc: rough, earthy, slightly risqué. **5** of wine, food, etc: with a full, rich quality. ▪ **robustly** *adv*. ▪ **robustness** *noun*. [16c: from Latin *robur* an oak or strength]

robusta *noun* **1** a coffee plant widely grown in E Africa. **2** coffee or beans from this plant. [20c]

rock[1] *noun* **1** *geol* a loose or consolidated mass of one or more minerals that forms part of the Earth's crust, eg granite, limestone, etc. **2** a large natural mass of this material. **3** a large stone or boulder. **4** someone or something that provides a firm foundation or support and can be depended upon. **5** *Brit* a hard sweet usu made in the form of long, cylindrical sticks. **6** *slang* a precious stone, esp a diamond. [14c: from French *rocque*]

IDIOMS **on the rocks** *informal* **1** of a marriage: broken down; failed. **2** of an alcoholic drink: served with ice cubes. **3** of a business, etc: in a state of great financial difficulty.

rock[2] *verb* **1** *tr & intr* to sway or make (something) sway gently backwards and forwards or from side to side: *rock the baby to sleep.* **2** *tr & intr* to move or make (something) move or shake violently. **3** *informal* to disturb, upset or shock: *The news rocked the sporting world.* **4** *intr* to dance to or play rock music. ▸ *noun* **1** a rocking movement. **2** (*also* **rock music**) a form of popular music with a very strong beat, usu played on electronic instruments and derived from rock and roll. **3** rock and roll. [Anglo-Saxon *roccian*]

IDIOMS **rock the boat** to destabilize or disturb something, esp unnecessarily or out of spite.

rockabilly *noun* a style of music that combines elements from both rock and roll and hillbilly. [20c]

rock and roll *or* **rock 'n' roll** *noun* **1** a form of popular music originating in the 1950s, deriving from jazz, country and western and blues music, with a lively jive beat and simple melodies. **2** the type of dancing done to this music. ▸ *verb, intr* to dance to or play rock-and-roll music. ▪ **rock and roller** *or* **rock 'n' roller** *noun*. [20c: orig Black slang]

rock bottom *or* **rock-bottom** *noun* **1** bedrock. **2** *informal* the lowest possible level. ▸ *adj, informal* of prices: the lowest possible; unbeatable.

rock cake *noun* a small round bun with a rough surface, containing fruit and spices.

rock crystal *noun* a transparent colourless quartz.

rocker *noun* **1** a curved support on which a chair, cradle, etc rocks. **2** something that rocks on such supports, esp a rocking chair. **3** someone or something that rocks. **4** a device which is operated with a movement from side to side, backwards and forwards, or up and down. **5** (**Rocker**) *Brit* in the 1960s: a member of a teenage movement, typically wearing a leather jacket and riding a motorcycle. Compare **mod**[1] (*noun*). **6** a devotee of rock music or a rock musician.

IDIOMS **off one's rocker** *informal* mad; crazy.

rockery *noun* (**-*ies***) a garden or an area in a garden with large stones placed in the earth, and rock plants growing between them.

rocket[1] *noun* **1** a cylinder containing inflammable material, which, when ignited, is projected through the air, used for signalling, carrying a line to a ship in distress, in a firework display, etc. **2** a projectile or vehicle, esp a space vehicle, that obtains its thrust from a backward jet of hot gases. **3** a missile propelled by a rocket system. **4** *Brit informal* a severe reprimand. ▸ *verb* **1** to propel (a spacecraft, etc) by means of a rocket. **2** *intr* to move, esp upwards, extremely quickly, as if with the speed of a rocket. **3** *intr* of prices, etc: to rise very quickly. **4** to attack with rockets. **5** *Brit informal* to reprimand severely. [17c: from French *roquette*, from Italian *rocca* a distaff, with reference to its shape]

rocket[2] *noun* a Mediterranean salad plant. [16c: from Latin *eruca* a type of herb]

rocketry *noun* the scientific study and use of rockets.

rock garden *noun* a rockery, or a garden containing rockeries.

rocking chair *noun* a chair which rocks backwards and forwards on two curved supports.

rocking horse *noun* a toy horse mounted on two curved supports on which a child can sit and rock backwards and forwards.

rock plant *noun* any plant, esp an alpine, which grows among rocks.

rock salmon *noun* a dogfish, esp when sold as food.

rock salt *noun* common salt occurring as a mass of solid mineral.

rocky[1] *adj* (**-*ier*, -*iest***) **1 a** full of rocks; **b** made of rock; **c** like rock. **2** *informal* full of problems and obstacles. ▪ **rockiness** *noun*. [15c]

rocky[2] *adj* (**-*ier*, -*iest***) shaky; unstable; unsteady. ▪ **rockily** *adv*. ▪ **rockiness** *noun*. [18c]

rococo /rəˈkoukou/ *noun* (*also* **Rococo**) a style of architecture, decoration and furniture-making originating in France in the early 18c, characterized by elaborate ornamentation and asymmetry. ▸ *adj* relating to, or in, this style. [19c: French from *rocaille* rock-work or shell-work]

rod *noun* **1** a long slender stick or bar of wood, metal, etc. **2** a stick or bundle of twigs used to beat people as a punishment. **3** a stick, wand or sceptre carried as a symbol of office or authority. **4** a fishing rod. **5** in surveying: a unit of length equivalent to 5.5yd (5.03m). **6** *anatomy* in the retina of the vertebrate eye: a rod-shaped cell involved in seeing in dim light. Compare **cone** (sense 3). **7** a rod-shaped bacterium. ▪ **rodless** *adj*. ▪ **rodlike** *adj*. [Anglo-Saxon *rodd*]

rode *past tense of* **ride**

rodent *noun, zool* an animal, eg a rat, mouse, squirrel, beaver, etc, with strong, continually growing incisors adapted for gnawing. [19c: from Latin *rodere* to gnaw]

rodeo *noun* **1** a round-up of cattle in order to count or brand them. **2** a place where cattle are assembled for this. **3** a show or contest of skills such as riding, lassoing and animal-handling. [19c: Spanish, from Latin *rotare* to rotate]

roe[1] *noun* **1** (*also* **hard roe**) the mass of mature eggs contained in the ovaries of a female fish. **2** (*also* **soft roe**) the testis of a male fish containing mature sperm. **3** either of these used as food. [15c]

roe[2] *or* **roe deer** *noun* (***roes*** *or* ***roe***) a small European and Asian deer. [Anglo-Saxon *ra* and *rahdeor*]

roentgen *or* **röntgen** /ˈrɜːntjən/ *noun* a former unit for measurement of X-rays or gamma rays. [19c: named after Wilhelm Konrad Roentgen, the German physicist who discovered the rays]

roentgen rays *plural noun* X-rays.

rogan josh /ˈroʊgən dʒɒʃ/ *noun* (***rogan joshes***) in Indian cookery: a dish of curried meat in a tomato-based sauce. [20c: Urdu]

rogation *noun, Christianity* (*usu* **rogations**) solemn supplication. [14c: from Latin *rogare* to ask]

roger *exclam* **1** in radio communications and signalling, etc: message received and understood. **2** *informal* I will; OK: *Roger, will do – see you later.* [20c: from the name *Roger*, representing the letter *R* for *received*]

rogue *noun* **1** a dishonest or unscrupulous person. **2** someone, esp a child, who is playfully mischievous. **3** someone or something, esp a plant, which is not true to its type and is of inferior quality. **4** a horse, person or object that is troublesome and unruly. **5** a vicious wild animal that lives apart from, or has been driven from, its herd. **6** someone or something that has strayed or that is found in an unusual or unexpected place. ▪ **roguery** *noun* (***-ies***). [16c]

rogues' gallery *noun* a collection of photographs of known criminals, kept by the police and used to identify suspects.

roguish *adj* **1** characteristic of a rogue. **2** dishonest; unprincipled. **3** playfully mischievous: *a roguish grin.* ▪ **roguishly** *adv.* [16c]

roister *verb, intr* **1** to enjoy oneself noisily and boisterously. **2** to bluster or swagger. ▪ **roisterer** *noun.* ▪ **roistering** *noun.* ▪ **roisterous** *adj.* [16c: from French *rustre* a ruffian]

role *or* **rôle** *noun* **1** an actor's part or character in a play, film, etc. **2** a function, or a part played or taken on by someone or something in life, business, etc: *in her role as head of the household* • *the role of television in education.* [17c: French, orig meaning 'a roll of parchment on which an actor's part was written']

role model *noun* someone whose character, life, behaviour, etc is taken as a good example to follow.

role-play *or* **role-playing** *noun* assuming and performing of imaginary roles, usu as a method of instruction, training, therapy, etc.

roll *noun* **1** a cylinder or tube formed by rolling up anything flat (such as paper, fabric, etc). **2** a rolled document; a scroll. **3** a small individually-baked portion of bread: *a cheese roll.* **4** a folded piece of pastry or cake with a filling: *swiss roll* • *sausage roll.* **5** a rolled mass of something: *rolls of fat.* **6** an undulation in a surface or of a landscape. **7 a** an official list of names, eg of school pupils, members of a club or people eligible to vote; **b** the total number registered on such a list. **8** an act of rolling. **9** a swaying or rolling movement, eg in walking or dancing, or of a ship. **10** a long low prolonged sound: *a roll of thunder.* **11** (*also* **drum roll**) a series of quick beats on a drum. **12** a complete rotation around its longitudinal axis by an aircraft. **13** a roller or cylinder used to press, shape or apply something. **14 a** an act or bout of rolling: *Sparky had a roll in the sand;* **b** a gymnastic exercise similar to, but less strenuous than, a somersault: *a backward roll.* **15** *informal* money, esp a wad of banknotes. ▸ *verb* **1** *tr & intr* to move or make (something) move by turning over and over, as if on an axis, and often in a specified direction: *rolled the dice.* **2** *tr & intr* to move or make (something) move on wheels, rollers, etc, or in a vehicle with wheels. **3** *intr* (*also* **roll over**) of a person or animal, etc that is lying down: to turn with a rolling movement to face in another direction. **4** *tr & intr* to move or make (something) move or flow gently and steadily. **5** *intr* (*usu* **roll by** *or* **on** *or* **past**, *etc*) of time: to pass or follow steadily and often quickly: *The weeks rolled by.* **6** *intr* to seem to move like or in waves: *a garden rolling down to the river.* **7** *intr* of a ship: to sway or rock gently from side to side. **8** *intr* to walk with a swaying movement: *rolled in drunk at six o'clock.* **9** *tr & intr* to begin to operate or work: *the cameras rolled.* **10** *tr & intr* to move or make (one's eyes) move in a circle, esp in disbelief, despair or amazement. **11** *tr & intr* to form, or form something, into a tube or cylinder by winding or being wound round and round. **12** (*also* **roll up**) **a** to wrap something by rolling: *rolled a spliff;* **b** to curl around: *The hamster rolled up into a ball.* **13** (*also* **roll out**) to spread out or make flat or flatter, esp by pressing and smoothing with something heavy: *rolled out the pastry.* **14** *intr* to make a series of long low rumbling sounds. **15** to pronounce (esp an 'r' sound) with a trill. **16** *slang* to rob someone who is helpless, usu because they are drunk or asleep. **17 a** to make (the credits) appear on a screen; **b** to appear on a screen. **18 a** to make (a car) do a somersault; **b** *intr* of a car: to overturn. ▪ **rolled** *adj.* [14c: from French *rolle*, from Latin *rota* a wheel]

IDIOMS **be rolling in sth** *informal* to have large amounts of it, esp money. **on a roll** *chiefly US, informal* going through a period of continuous good luck or success. **roll on ...** may a specified event, time, etc come soon: *Roll on the holidays.*

PHRASAL VERBS **roll in** to come or arrive in large quantities. **roll over 1** to overturn. **2** see *verb* (sense 3) above. **3** of a jackpot prize, eg in the UK National Lottery: to be carried across to the next week because it has not been won. See also **roll-over**. **roll sth over** *econ* to defer demand for repayment of (a debt, loan, etc) for a further term. See also **roll-over**. **roll up 1** *informal* to arrive. **2** to come in large numbers.

rollbar *noun* a metal bar that strengthens the frame of a vehicle and reduces the danger to its occupants if the vehicle overturns.

roll-call *noun* an act or the process of calling out names from a list at an assembly, meeting, etc to check who is present.

rolled gold *noun* base metal covered with a very thin coating of gold, usu used in inexpensive jewellery.

roller *noun* **1** a cylindrical object or machine used for flattening, crushing, spreading, printing, applying paint, etc. **2** a small cylinder on which hair is rolled to make it curl. **3** a long heavy sea wave.

Rollerblades *plural noun, trademark* a brand of in-line skates, roller skates with wheels set in a single line from front to back along the sole. ▶ *verb* (**roller-blade**) *intr* to move on Rollerblades. ▪ **rollerblading** *noun.*

roller blind *noun* a window blind that wraps around a roller when not in use.

rollercoaster *noun* a raised railway with sharp curves and steep inclines and descents, ridden on for pleasure and excitement at funfairs, etc.

roller skate *noun* a series of wheels attached to a framework which can be fitted onto a shoe, or a shoe with wheels attached to the sole. ▶ *verb* (**roller-skate**) *intr* to move on roller skates. ▪ **roller-skater** *noun.* ▪ **roller-skating** *noun.*

rollick *verb, intr* to behave in a carefree, swaggering, boisterous or playful manner. ▶ *noun* a boisterous romp. ▪ **rollicking** *adj.* [19c]

rollicking *noun, informal* a severe rebuke or scolding. [20c: perhaps a variant of *bollock*]

rolling *adj* **1** of land, countryside, etc: with low, gentle hills and valleys. **2** *informal* extremely wealthy. **3** *informal* staggering with drunkenness. **4** of a contract: subject to review at regular intervals.

rolling mill *noun* **1** a machine for rolling metal into sheets. **2** a factory with such machines.

rolling pin *noun* a cylinder made of wood, pottery, marble, etc for flattening out pastry or dough.

rolling stock *noun* the engines, wagons, coaches, etc used on a railway.

rolling stone *noun* someone who leads a restless or unsettled life.

rollmop *noun* a rolled fillet of raw pickled herring. [20c: from German *Rollmops*, from *rollen* to roll + *Mops* a pug-dog]

rollneck *adj* of a garment: with a high neck which is folded over on itself.

roll-on *noun* **1** a deodorant, etc contained in a bottle with a rotating ball at the top, by means of which the liquid is applied. **2** *Brit* a woman's light elastic corset.

roll-on roll-off *adj* (abbrev **ro-ro**) of a passenger ferry: with entrances at both the front and back of the ship, so that vehicles can be driven on through one entrance and off through the other. ▶ *noun* a ship of this kind.

roll-out *noun* **1** the first public showing of the prototype of an aircraft. **2** the part of an aircraft's landing during which it slows down after touching down.

roll-over *noun* **1** an instance of deferring demand for repayment of a debt, loan, etc for a further term. **2** a jackpot prize which, having not been won in one week, is carried forward to the draw in the following week and added to that week's jackpot.

roll-up *noun, Brit informal* a hand-rolled cigarette.

roly-poly *adj* round and podgy. ▶ *noun* (***-ies***) (*also* **roly-poly pudding**) suet pastry spread with jam and rolled up, then baked or steamed. [19c]

ROM /rɒm/ *abbrev, comput* read-only memory, a storage device which holds data permanently and allows it to be read and used but not changed. Compare **RAM**.

Roman *adj* **1** belonging or relating to modern or ancient Rome, or to the Roman Empire, its history, culture or inhabitants. **2** relating to the Roman Catholic Church. **3** (**roman**) *printing* of type: relating to or indicating the ordinary, upright kind most commonly used for printed material. Compare **italic**. ▶ *noun* **1** an inhabitant of modern or ancient Rome. **2** a Roman Catholic.

roman alphabet *noun* the alphabet developed by the ancient Romans for writing Latin, and now used for most writing in W European languages.

Roman candle *noun* a firework that discharges a succession of flaming sparks. [19c]

Roman Catholic (abbrev **RC**) *adj* belonging or relating to the Roman Catholic Church, the Christian Church which recognizes the pope as its head. ▶ *noun* a member of this Church. Often shortened to **Catholic**. ▪ **Roman Catholicism** *noun.* [17c]

romance *noun* **1** a love affair. **2** sentimentalized or idealized love, valued esp for its beauty, purity and the mutual devotion of the lovers. **3** the atmosphere, feelings or behaviour associated with romantic love. **4** a sentimental account, esp in writing or on film, of a love affair. **5** such writing, films, etc as a group or genre. **6** a fictitious story which deals with imaginary, adventurous and mysterious events, characters, places, etc. **7** a medieval verse narrative dealing with chivalry, highly idealized love and fantastic adventures. **8** (**Romance**) a group of languages, including French, Spanish and Italian, which have developed from Latin. ▶ *adj* (**Romance**) belonging or relating to the languages which have developed from Latin. ▶ *verb* **1** to try to win someone's love. **2** *intr* to talk or write extravagantly, romantically or fantastically. **3** *intr* to lie. ▪ **romancer** *noun.* ▪ **romancing** *noun, adj.* [13c: from French *romans*, from Latin *Romanicus* Roman]

Romanesque *noun* a style of European architecture from the 9c to the 12c, characterized by the use of round arches and massive walls and vaultings. ▶ *adj* in or relating to this style. [18c: French]

Romanian, Rumanian *or* **Roumanian** *adj* belonging or relating to Romania, a republic in SE Europe, its inhabitants or their language. ▶ *noun* **1** a citizen or inhabitant of, or a person born in Romania. **2** the official language of Romania.

Romanize *or* **-ise** *verb* **1** to make (a ceremony, etc) Roman Catholic in character. **2** to convert (someone) to Roman Catholicism. **3** *intr* to become Roman Catholic in character or convert to Roman Catholicism. **4** to transcribe (a language that uses a different writing system) into the roman alphabet. ▪ **Romanization** *noun.* [17c]

Roman nose *noun* a high-bridged or aquiline nose.

Roman numeral *noun* an upper case letter of the roman alphabet used to represent a cardinal number, eg, I = 1, V = 5, X = 10, etc. Compare **Arabic numeral**.

romantic *adj* **1** characterized by or inclined towards sentimental and idealized love. **2** dealing with or suggesting adventure, mystery and sentimentalized love: *romantic fiction*. **3** highly impractical or imaginative. **4** (**Romantic**) of literature, art, music, etc: relating to or in the style of romanticism. ▶ *noun* **1** someone who has a romantic view of love, etc. **2** (**Romantic**) a Romantic poet, writer, artist, composer, etc. ▪ **romantically** *adv.* [17c: from French *romanz* romance]

romanticism *or* **Romanticism** *noun* a late 18c and early 19c movement in the arts with an emphasis on feelings and emotions, often using imagery from nature. ▪ **romanticist** *noun.* [19c]

romanticize *or* **-ise** *verb* **1** to make romantic. **2** *tr & intr* to describe, think of or interpret in an idealized and sometimes misleading way. **3** *intr* to hold or indulge in romantic ideas or act in a romantic way. ▪ **romanticization** *noun*.

Romany *noun* (***-ies***) **1** a Gypsy. **2** the language spoken by Gypsies. ▸ *adj* of or relating to the Romanies, their language or culture. [19c: from Romany *rom* man]

Romeo *noun* **1** an ardent young male lover. **2** a womanizer. [18c: the name of the love-struck hero in Shakespeare's *Romeo and Juliet*]

romp *verb, intr* **1** to play or run about in a lively boisterous way. **2** (*usu* **romp through**) *informal* to complete (a task, etc) quickly and easily. ▸ *noun* **1** an act of romping; boisterous playing or running about. **2** a light-hearted outing or jaunt. **3** a swift pace. [18c]
IDIOMS **romp in** *or* **home** *informal* to win a race, competition, etc quickly and easily.

rompers *plural noun* (*also* **romper suit**) *formerly* a baby's suit, usu one-piece, with short-legged trousers and either a short-sleeved top or a bib top.

rondeau /ˈrɒndoʊ/ *or* **rondel** *noun* (***rondeaux*** /-doʊ, -doʊz/) a poem of 13 or sometimes 10 lines with only two rhymes, and with the first line used as a refrain after the eighth and thirteenth lines. [16c: from French *rond* round]

rondo *noun, music* a piece of music with a recurring principal theme. [18c: Italian, from French *rondeau*; see **rondeau**]

röntgen see **roentgen**

roo *noun, Aust informal* a kangaroo. [20c]

rood *noun* **1** a cross or crucifix, esp a large one set on a beam or screen at the entrance to a church chancel. **2** a former unit of area, equal to a quarter of an acre. [Anglo-Saxon *rod* gallows or cross]

roof *noun* (***roofs*** *or non-standard* ***rooves***) **1 a** the top outside covering of a building; **b** the structure at the top of a building that supports this. **2** a similar top or covering for a vehicle, etc. **3** the interior overhead surface of a room, vault, cave, etc. **4** a dwelling or home: *two families under the same roof.* **5** the top inner surface of something, eg an oven, refrigerator, mouth, etc. ▸ *verb* **1** to cover or provide with a roof. **2** to serve as a roof or shelter for something. ▪ **roofed** *adj*. ▪ **roofless** *adj*. [Anglo-Saxon *hrof*]
IDIOMS **go through the roof** *informal* **1** to become very angry. **2** of a price, etc: to become very expensive. **raise** *or* **hit the roof** *informal* **1** to make a great deal of noise or fuss. **2** to become very angry.

roofer *noun* a person whose job is constructing or repairing roofs.

roofing *noun* **1** materials for building a roof. **2** the roof itself.

roof rack *noun* a frame attached to the roof of a car or other vehicle for carrying luggage, etc.

rooftop *noun* the outside of a roof of a building.
IDIOMS **shout it from the rooftops** to make public something that is better kept quiet.

roof tree *noun* a beam running along a roof's ridge. [15c]

rook[1] *noun* a large, noisy crow-like bird. ▸ *verb, informal* **1** to cheat or defraud, esp at cards. **2** to charge (a customer) an excessively high price. [Anglo-Saxon *hroc*]

rook[2] *noun, chess* a **castle**. [14c: from Persian *rukh*]

rookery *noun* (***-ies***) **1** a colony of rooks. **2** a clump of trees with many rooks' nests. **3** a colony of seals or seabirds, esp penguins. [18c]

rookie *or* **rooky** *noun* (***-ies***) *informal* **1** a new or raw recruit, esp in the police or the army. **2** *sport, chiefly N Am* a new member of a team. [19c]

room *noun* **1** an area within a building enclosed by a ceiling, floor and walls. **2** sufficient or necessary space: *no room for all her books.* **3** all the people present in a room: *The room suddenly became silent.* **4** opportunity, scope or possibility: *room for improvement.* **5** (**rooms**) rented lodgings, esp a set of rooms within a house, etc as an individual unit: *returned to his rooms at Oxford.* ▸ *verb, tr & intr, chiefly N Am* (*also* **room with**) to lodge (with someone); to share a room or rooms. ▪ **-roomed** *adj*. [Anglo-Saxon *rum*]

room and board *US equivalent of* **bed and breakfast**

roommate *noun* a person sharing a room or rooms with another or others.

room service *noun* in a hotel: a facility for guests to order and be served food, drinks, etc in their rooms.

room temperature *noun* the average temperature of a living room, usu about 20°C.

roomy *adj* (***-ier, -iest***) with plenty of room; spacious. ▪ **roominess** *noun*. [16c]

roost *noun* a branch, perch, etc on which a bird perches, esp to rest at night. ▸ *verb, intr* of a bird: to settle on a roost, esp for sleep. [Anglo-Saxon *hrost*]
IDIOMS **come home to roost** of a scheme, etc: to have an unpleasant result for or a bad effect on the originator.

rooster *noun, chiefly N Am* a farmyard cock. [18c]

root[1] *noun* **1** a structure in a plant, usu beneath the soil surface, which anchors the plant in the soil and absorbs water and nutrients. **2** a part by which something, eg a tooth, hair, nail, etc, is attached to or embedded in something larger. **3** a basic cause, source or origin of something: *the root of the problem.* **4** (**roots**) ancestry or family origins, etc: *go back to one's roots.* **5** the basic element in a word to which affixes can be added, eg *love* is the root of *lovable, lovely, lover* and *unloved.* **6** *maths* a factor of a quantity that, when multiplied by itself a specified number of times, produces that quantity, eg 2 is the square root of 4 and the cube root of 8. ▸ *verb* **1** *intr* to grow a root. **2** *intr* to become firmly established. **3** (*usu* **root up** *or* **out**) to dig up by the roots. **4** to fix with or as if with a root. **5** to provide with a root. ▪ **rootlike** *adj*. [Anglo-Saxon *rot*]
IDIOMS **root and branch** thoroughly; completely. **take** *or* **strike root 1** to grow roots. **2** to become firmly settled or established.
PHRASAL VERBS **root sth out** to find, remove or destroy it completely.

root[2] *verb, intr* **1** of pigs: to dig in the earth with the snout in search of food, truffles, etc. **2** *intr* (*usu* **root around** *or* **about**) *informal* to look for by rummaging. **3** (*usu* **root sb** *or* **sth out** *or* **up**) to find and remove them or it. [Anglo-Saxon *wrotan*, from *wrot* snout]

root[3] *verb, intr* (*always* **root for**) *informal* to cheer on, encourage or back (someone or something). [19c]

root beer *noun, N Am, esp US* a fizzy non-alcoholic drink made from plant root extracts.

root canal *noun* a passage through which the nerves and blood vessels of a tooth enter the pulp cavity.

root crop *noun* any plant that is grown mainly for its edible root, tuber or corm, eg carrot, turnip, potato, sugar beet, etc.

root directory *noun, comput* the highest level of **directory** (sense 2), which contains all the others.

rooted *adj* **1** fixed by or as if by roots. **2** firmly established.

rootless *adj* **1** with no roots. **2** with no fixed home; wandering.

root mean square *noun, maths* (abbrev **rms**) the square root of the sum of the squares of a set of quantities divided by the total number of quantities in the set, eg the root mean square of 1, 2, and 3 is the square root of $(1^2 + 2^2 + 3^2)/3$.

rootstock *noun, botany* **1** an underground plant stem that bears buds; a rhizome. **2** a stock onto which another plant has been grafted.

root vegetable *noun* **a** a vegetable, eg a carrot, turnip, etc, with an edible root; **b** the root itself.

rope *noun* **1 a** a strong thick cord made by twisting fibres of hemp, wire, etc together; **b** a length of this. **2** a number of objects, esp pearls or onions, strung together. **3** (**the rope**) **a** a hangman's noose; **b** execution by this means. **4** (**ropes**) the cords that mark off a boxing or wrestling ring, or the boundary of a cricket ground. ▸ *verb* **1** to tie, fasten or bind with rope or as if with rope. **2** (*usu* **rope in** *or* **off**) to enclose, separate or divide with a rope. **3** *mountaineering* to tie (climbers) together with a rope for safety. **4** *chiefly N Am* to catch (an animal) with a rope; to lasso. [Anglo-Saxon *rap*]

IDIOMS **know the ropes** to be thoroughly conversant with a particular thing.

PHRASAL VERBS **rope sb in** *or* **into** to persuade them to take part in some activity.

ropeable *or* **ropable** *adj* **1** able to be roped. **2** *Aust & NZ, slang* of cattle or horses: wild and unmanageable. **3** *Aust & NZ, slang* of a person: extremely or uncontrollably angry. [19c]

ropy *or* **ropey** *adj* (**-ier, -iest**) **1** rope-like. **2** *informal* poor in quality. **3** *informal* slightly unwell.

ro-ro *adj, noun* abbrev for **roll-on roll-off**.

rorqual *noun* a baleen whale with a small dorsal fin near the tail. [19c: French, from Norse *rauthr* red + *hvalr* whale]

Rorschach test /ˈrɔːʃak/ *noun, psychol* a test where a subject is asked to interpret a standard set of inkblots in order to determine intelligence, personality type, mental state, etc. [20c: named after Hermann Rorschach, Swiss psychiatrist]

rosaceous *adj* belonging to the rose family of plants or resembling a rose. [18c: from Latin *rosa* rose]

rosary *noun* (**-ies**) **1** *RC Church* a series of prayers with a set form and order in which five or fifteen decades of Aves are recited. **2** *RC Church* a string of 55 or 165 beads used for counting such prayers. **3** a string of beads used in other religions. [14c: from Latin *rosarium* rose-garden]

rose[1] *noun* **1** a thorny shrub that produces large, often fragrant, flowers and berries known as hips. **2** a flower of this plant. **3** a rose as the national emblem of England. **4** a flowering plant that superficially resembles a rose, eg the Christmas rose. **5** a darkish pink colour. **6** (**roses**) a light-pink, glowing complexion: *put the roses back in one's cheeks.* **7** a perforated nozzle, attached to the end of a hose, watering can, shower-head, etc, so that water comes out in a spray. **8** a circular fitting in a ceiling through which an electric light flex hangs. **9** a circular moulding from which a door handle projects. ▸ *adj* relating to or like a rose or roses, esp in colour, scent or form. ▪ **roselike** *adj.* [Anglo-Saxon, from Latin *rosa* rose]

IDIOMS **under the rose** in confidence; privately. Also called **sub rosa**.

rose[2] *past tense of* **rise**

rosé /ˈroʊzeɪ/ *noun* a pale pink wine. Also called *N Am* **blush**. [19c: French, literally 'pink']

roseate /ˈroʊzɪət/ *adj* **1** like a rose, esp in colour. **2** unrealistically hopeful or cheerful.

rosebud *noun* **1** the bud of a rose. **2** *literary* a pretty young woman. [15c]

rose-coloured *or* **rose-tinted** *adj* **1** pink; rosy. **2** cheerful; overoptimistic.

rosehip *noun* a red berry-like fruit of a rose.

rosemary *noun* a fragrant evergreen shrub with stiff needle-like leaves, used in cookery and perfumery. [15c: from Latin *ros* dew + *marinus* of the sea]

rosette *noun* **1** a badge or decoration made in coloured ribbon to resemble the form of a rose, awarded as a prize, worn to show membership of some group, etc. **2** *archit* a rose-shaped ornament on a wall or other surface. **3** a cluster of leaves radiating from a central point. **4** any rose-shaped structure, arrangement or figure. [18c: French, meaning 'little rose']

rosewater *noun* perfume distilled from roses. [14c]

rosewood *noun* **1** the valuable dark red or purplish wood of any of various tropical trees used in making high quality furniture. **2** a tree from which this wood is obtained. [17c: so called because it is said to smell of roses when newly cut]

Rosh Hashanah *or* **Rosh Hashana** *noun* the Jewish festival of New Year. [18c: Hebrew, from *rosh* head + *hash-shanah* year]

rosin *noun* a clear hard resin, produced by distilling turpentine. ▸ *verb* to rub rosin on (the bow of a violin, etc). [14c variant of **resin**]

roster *noun* a list or roll of people's names, esp one that shows the order in which they are to do various duties, go on leave, etc. ▸ *verb* to put on a roster. [18c: from Dutch *oosten* to roast]

rostrum *noun* (***rostrums*** *or* ***rostra***) **1** a platform for a public speaker, orchestra conductor, etc. **2** a platform in front of an orchestra on which the conductor stands. **3** *zool* **a** a bird's beak; **b** a structure similar to a beak in other animals. [16c: Latin, meaning 'beak-head'. In ancient Rome, the platform for public speaking was decorated with the beak-heads of captured ships]

rosy *adj* (**-ier, -iest**) **1** rose-coloured; pink. **2** of the complexion: with a healthy pink colour; glowing: *rosy cheeks.* **3** filled or decorated with roses. **4** like a rose, esp in fragrance. **5 a** hopeful or optimistic, often overly so: *a rosy view of things;* **b** promising: *The situation looks quite rosy.* ▪ **rosily** *adv.* ▪ **rosiness** *noun.* [14c]

rot *verb* (***rotted, rotting***) **1** *tr & intr* to decay or cause to decay or become putrefied as a result of the activity of bacteria, fungi, etc. **2** *intr* to become corrupt. **3** *intr* to become physically weak, esp through being confined, etc: *left to rot in jail.* ▸ *noun* **1 a** decay; **b** something which has decayed or decomposed. **2** *informal* nonsense; rubbish. ▸ *exclam* expressing contemptuous disagreement. See also **rotten**. [Anglo-Saxon *rotian*]

rota *noun, Brit* a list of duties to be done with the names and order of the people who are to take turns doing them; a roster. [17c: Latin, meaning 'wheel']

rotary *adj* turning on an axis like a wheel. ▸ *noun* (***-ies***) **1** a rotary machine. **2** *N Am* a traffic roundabout. [18c: from Latin *rota* a wheel]

rotate *verb* **1** *tr & intr* to turn or cause (something) to turn about an axis like a wheel; to revolve. **2** to arrange in an ordered sequence. **3** *intr* to change position, take turns in doing something, etc according to an ordered sequence. **4** to grow (different crops) in an ordered sequence on the same ground. ▪ **rotatable** *adj.* [17c: from Latin *rota* wheel]

rotation *noun* **1** the action of rotating or state of being rotated. **2** one complete turn around an axis. **3** *maths* a transformation of a plane with a rotating movement around an axis. Compare **enlargement**, **reflection**, **translation**. **4** a regular and recurring sequence or cycle. ▪ **rotational** *adj.*

rotator *noun* **1** a device that rotates or makes something else rotate. **2** *anatomy* a muscle that enables a limb, etc to rotate. [17c]

rote *noun* (*often* **by rote**) habitual repetition: *learn by rote.*

rotgut *noun, slang* cheap alcoholic drink, esp spirits, of inferior quality. Also called **gutrot**.

rotisserie *noun* **1** a cooking apparatus with a spit on which meat, poultry, etc is cooked by direct heat. **2** a shop or restaurant that sells or serves meat cooked in this way. [19c: from French *rôtir* to roast]

rotor *noun* **1** a rotating part of a machine, esp in an internal-combustion engine. **2** a system of blades providing the force to lift and propel a helicopter. [20c: a variant of **rotator**]

rotten *adj* **1** gone bad, decayed, rotted. **2** falling or fallen to pieces from age, decay, etc. **3** morally corrupt. **4** *informal* miserably unwell: *felt rotten.* **5** *informal* unsatisfactory: *a rotten plan.* **6** *informal* unpleasant; disagreeable: *rotten weather.* ▸ *adv, informal* very much; extremely: *fancied him rotten.* ▪ **rottenly** *adv.* ▪ **rottenness** *noun.* [13c: from Norse *rotinn*]

rotten apple *noun, informal* a corrupt person.

rotten borough *noun, hist* before the Reform Act of 1832: a borough that could elect an MP even though it had few or no inhabitants.

rotter *noun, dated, Brit slang* a thoroughly depraved, worthless or despicable person.

Rottweiler /ˈrɒtvaɪlə(r), -waɪlə(r)/ *noun* a large, powerfully built black-and-tan dog. [20c: named after Rottweil in SW Germany]

rotund *adj* **1** *chiefly botany, zool* round or rounded in form; nearly spherical. **2** of a person, part of the body, etc: plump. **3** of speech, language, etc: impressive or grandiloquent. ▪ **rotundity** *noun.* ▪ **rotundly** *adv.* [15c: from Latin *rota* a wheel]

rotunda *noun* a round, usu domed, building or hall. [17c: from Italian *rotonda* round]

rouble *or* **ruble** *noun* the standard unit of currency in Russia and Belarus. [16c: from Russian *rubl* a silver bar]

roué /ˈruːeɪ/ *noun, old use* a debauched, disreputable man; a rake. [19c: French, meaning 'broken on the wheel'. The name was first applied to the dissolute companions of Philippe, Duke of Orléans, to suggest that they deserved such punishment]

rouge /ruːʒ/ *noun* **1** *old use* a pink or red cosmetic for colouring the cheeks. **2** a fine powder of hydrated ferric oxide used for polishing metal. ▸ *verb* to apply rouge to. [15c: French, meaning 'red']

rough *adj* **1** of a surface or texture: not smooth, even or regular. **2** of ground: covered with stones, tall grass, bushes and/or scrub. **3** of an animal: with shaggy or coarse hair. **4** of a sound: harsh or grating. **5** of a person's character, behaviour, etc: noisy, coarse or violent. **6** of the sea, etc: stormy. **7** requiring hard work or considerable physical effort, or involving great difficulty, tension, etc: *a rough day at work.* **8** hard to bear: *a rough deal.* **9** of a guess, calculation, etc: approximate. **10** not polished or refined: *a rough draft.* **11** *informal* slightly unwell. **12** not well-kept: *a rough area.* ▸ *noun* **1** (**the rough**) rough ground, esp the uncut grass at the side of a golf fairway. **2** the unpleasant or disagreeable side of something: *take the rough with the smooth.* **3** a rough or crude state. **4** a thug or hooligan. ▸ *adv* roughly: *treated her rough.* ▸ *verb* to make rough; to roughen. ▪ **roughness** *noun.* [Anglo-Saxon *ruh*]

IDIOMS **rough it** *informal* to live in a very basic or primitive way, without the comforts one is accustomed to. **sleep rough** to sleep in the open without proper shelter.

PHRASAL VERBS **rough sb up** *informal* to beat them up.

roughage *noun* **dietary fibre**. [19c]

rough-and-ready *adj* **1** quickly prepared and not polished or perfect, but usu good enough for the purpose. **2** of a person: friendly and pleasant but not polite or refined.

rough-and-tumble *noun* disorderly but usu friendly fighting. ▸ *adj* haphazard; disorderly.

roughcast *noun* **1** a mixture of plaster and small stones used to cover the outside walls of buildings. **2** a rough or preliminary model, etc. ▸ *verb* (***roughcast***) to cover (a wall) with roughcast.

rough diamond *noun* **1** an uncut and unpolished diamond. **2** *informal* a good-natured person with rough unrefined manners.

roughen *verb, tr & intr* to make or become rough.

rough-hewn *adj* crude, unpolished, unrefined.

roughhouse *noun, informal* a disturbance or brawl. ▸ *verb* **1** *intr* to create a disturbance; to brawl. **2** to maltreat.

roughly *adv* **1** in a rough way. **2** approximately.

rough ride *noun* a difficult time or experience.

roughshod *adj* of a horse: with shoes that have projecting nails to prevent it slipping.

IDIOMS **ride roughshod over** to behave arrogantly and without regard to other people's feelings, etc.

roulade /rʊˈlɑːd/ *noun* something, usu meat, cooked in the shape of a roll. [18c: French, from *rouler* to roll]

roulette *noun* a gambling game in which a ball is dropped into a revolving wheel, the players betting on which of its small, numbered compartments the ball will come to rest in. [18c: French, from *roue* a wheel]

Roumanian see **Romanian**

round *adj* **1** shaped like, or approximately like, a circle or a ball. **2** not angular; with a curved outline. **3** of a body or part of a body: curved and plump: *a round face.* **4** moving in or forming a circle. **5** of numbers: complete and exact: *a round dozen.* **6** of a number: without a fraction. **7** of a number: approximate; without taking minor amounts into account. **8** of a sum of money: considerable; substantial. **9** of a character in a story or novel: fully and realistically developed. ▸ *adv* **1** in a circular direction or with a circular or revolving movement. **2** in or to the opposite direction, position or opinion: *win someone round.* **3** in, by or along a circuitous or indirect route. **4** on all sides so as to surround: *gather round.* **5** from one person to another successively: *pass it round.* **6** in rotation, so as to return to the starting point: *wait until spring comes round.* **7** from place to place: *drive round.* **8** in circumference: *measures six feet round.* **9** to a particular place, esp someone's home: *come round for supper.* ▸ *prep* **1** on all sides of so as to surround or enclose. **2** so as to move or revolve around a centre or axis and return to the starting point: *run round the field.* **3** *informal* having as a central point or basis: *a story built round her experiences.* **4** from place to place in: *We went round the town shopping.* **5** in all or various directions from somewhere; close to it. **6** so as to pass, or having passed, in a curved course: *drive round the corner.* ▸ *noun* **1** something round, and often flat, in shape. **2 a** movement in a circle; **b** a complete revolution round a circuit or path. **3** a single slice of bread. **4** a sandwich, or two or more sandwiches, made from two slices of bread. **5** a cut of beef across the thigh bone of an animal. **6** *golf* the playing of all 18 holes on a course in a single session. **7** one of a recurring series of events, actions, etc; a session: *a round of talks.* **8** a series of regular activities; a daily routine: *the daily round.* **9** a regular route followed, esp for the sale or delivery of goods: *a milk round.* **10** (*usu* **rounds**) a sequence of visits, usu a regular one, made by a doctor to patients, either in a hospital or their homes. **11** a stage in a competition: *through to the second round.* **12** a single turn by every member of a group of people playing a game, eg in a card game. **13** a single period of play, competition, etc in a group of such periods, eg in boxing, wrestling, etc. **14** a burst of applause or cheering. **15** a single bullet or charge of ammunition. **16** a number of drinks bought at the same time for all the members of a group. **17** *music* an unaccompanied song in which different people all sing the same part continuously but start, and therefore end, at different times. ▸ *verb* **1** *tr & intr* to make or become round. **2** to go round something: *The car rounded the corner.* ▪ **roundness** *noun.* [13c: from French *ront*, from Latin *rota* a wheel]

IDIOMS **go** *or* **make the rounds** of news, information, a cold, etc: **1** to be passed round from person to person; to circulate. **2** to patrol. **in the round 1** with all details shown or considered. **2** *theatre* with the audience seated on at least three, and often four, sides of the stage. **round about 1** on all sides; in a ring surrounding. **2** the other way about. **3** approximately: *round about four o'clock.*

PHRASAL VERBS **round sth down** to lower (a number) to the nearest convenient figure: *round 15.47 down to 15.* **round sth off 1** to make (corners, angles, etc) smooth. **2** to complete: *round off the meal with a brandy.* **round on sb 1** to turn on or attack. **2** to reply or attack verbally. **round sth up 1** to raise (a number) to the nearest convenient figure: *round 15.89 up to 16.* **2** to collect (people, livestock, facts, etc) together. See also **round-up**.

roundabout *noun Brit* **1** a junction of several roads where traffic must travel in the same direction, giving way to vehicles coming from the right, usu round a central traffic island. **2** a **merry-go-round**. ▸ *adj* not direct; circuitous: *a roundabout way of explaining something.*

rounded *adj* **1** curved; not angular. **2** complete; fully developed: *a rounded personality.* **3** *cookery* of measurements: filled so as to be slightly more than level with the rim of the spoon, cup, etc used.

roundel *noun* **1** a small circular window or design. **2** a coloured, round identification disc on a military aircraft. [13c: from French *rondel* a little circle]

roundelay *noun* a simple song with a refrain. [16c: from French *rondel* a little circle]

rounders *noun* **1** a team game with a series of bases, similar to baseball, in which each team sends players in to bat in turn while the other team bowls and fields. **2** (**rounder**) a scoring run made by a batter running a complete circuit, touching all the bases.

Roundhead *noun, hist* a supporter of the parliamentary party against Charles I during the 17c English Civil War. [17c: because of the Puritan custom of wearing closely-cut hair]

roundhouse *noun* a shed with a turntable where locomotive engines are repaired.

roundly *adv* **1** thoroughly: *was roundly defeated.* **2** bluntly: *told him roundly that it wouldn't do.*

round robin *noun* **1** a petition or protest, esp one in which the names are written in a circle to conceal the ringleader. **2** *sport* a tournament in which every competitor plays each of the others in turn.

round-shouldered *adj* having shoulders that bend forward, giving a hunched appearance to the back.

round table *noun* **1** (**Round Table**) an international group formed by business and professional people to do charitable work. **2** a meeting or conference at which the participants meet on equal terms. ▸ *adj* characterized by equality: *round-table talks.* [20c: so called because the table at which King Arthur and his knights sat was round so that no knight should have precedence]

round-the-clock *adj* lasting through the day and night: *round-the-clock surveillance.*

round trip *noun* a trip to a place and back again.

round-up *noun* **1** a systematic gathering together of people or animals. **2** a summary or résumé of facts: *a round-up of the news.*

roundworm *noun* a tiny invertebrate animal with a long slender unsegmented body, mostly parasitic within humans and animals.

rouse *verb* **1** to arouse or awaken (oneself or someone else) from sleep, listlessness or lethargy. **2** *intr* to awaken or become more fully conscious or alert. **3** to excite or provoke: *The injustice of it roused her anger.* **4** *intr* to become excited, provoked, etc. **5** to bring (game) out from cover or a lair. ▪ **rouser** *noun.* [15c: in the sense (of a hawk) 'to ruffle or shake the feathers']

rousing *adj* stirring; exciting.

roustabout *noun* an unskilled labourer, eg on an oil rig or a farm.

rout[1] *verb* to defeat (an army, troops, a sporting team, etc) completely. ▸ *noun* a complete and overwhelming defeat. [13c: from French *route*, from Latin *rupta* a detachment]

rout[2] *verb* **1** *tr & intr* to dig up, esp with the snout. **2** (**rout out** *or* **up**) to find and drive out or fetch by searching. [16c variant of **root**[2]]

route /ruːt; *Brit military & US general* raʊt/ *noun* **1** a way travelled on a regular journey. **2** a particular group of roads followed to get to a place. **3** *N Am* a regular series of calls, eg for the collection or sale of goods; a round. ▸ *verb* (***routeing*** *or* ***routing***) **1** to arrange a route for (a journey, etc). **2** to send by a particular route. [13c: from French *rute*, from Latin *rumpere* to break]

route march *noun* a long and tiring march, esp one for soldiers in training.

router *noun, comput* a device that sends transmitted data, etc by the fastest, most efficient, etc way to its intended destination.

routine *noun* **1** a regular or unvarying series of actions or way of doing things: *a daily routine.* **2** regular or unvarying procedure. **3** a set series of movements or steps in a dance, a skating performance, etc. **4** a comedian's, singer's, etc act. **5** *comput* a program or part of one which performs a specific function. ▸ *adj* **1** unvarying. **2** standard; ordinary: *a routine examination.* **3** done as part of a routine. ▪ **routinely** *adv.* [17c: French, from *route* a regular or customary way]

roux *noun* (*pl* ***roux***) *cookery* a cooked mixture of flour and butter, used to thicken sauces. [19c: French, from *beurre roux*, literally 'brown butter']

rove[1] *verb* **1** *intr* to roam about aimlessly. **2** to wander over or through (a particular area, etc). **3** *intr* of the eyes: to keep looking in different directions. ▸ *noun* the act of roving. ▪ **rover** *noun.* [16c]

rove[2] *past tense, past participle of* **reeve**[2]

roving *adj* **1** wandering; likely to ramble or stray. **2** not confined to one particular place: *roving commission.*

row[1] /roʊ/ *noun* **1** a number of people or things arranged in a line. **2** in a cinema, theatre, etc: a line of seats. **3** a line of plants in a garden: *a row of cabbages.* **4** a street with a continuous line of houses on one or both sides. **5** *maths* a horizontal arrangement of numbers, terms, etc. **6** in knitting: a complete line of stitches. [Anglo-Saxon *raw*]

IDIOMS **in a row 1** forming a row. **2** *informal* in succession: *three telephone calls in a row.*

row[2] /roʊ/ *verb* **1** to move (a boat) through the water using oars. **2** to carry (people, goods, etc) in a rowing boat. **3** *intr* to race in rowing boats for sport. **4** *intr* to compete in a rowing race. ▸ *noun* **1** the action or an act of rowing a boat. **2 a** a period of rowing; **b** a distance of rowing. **3** a trip in a rowing boat. ▪ **rower** *noun.* ▪ **rowing** *noun.* [Anglo-Saxon *rowan*]

row[3] /raʊ/ *noun* **1** a noisy quarrel. **2** a loud unpleasant noise or disturbance. **3** a severe reprimand. ▸ *verb, intr* to quarrel noisily. [18c]

rowan *noun* **1** (*also* **rowan-tree**) a tree of the rose family, with small pinnate leaves. Also called **mountain ash**. **2** (*also* **rowan-berry**) the small red or pink berry-like fruit of this tree. [15c: Scandinavian, related Norwegian *rogn, raun*]

rowboat *noun, N Am* a **rowing boat**.

rowdy *adj* (***-ier, -iest***) loud and disorderly: *a rowdy party.* ▸ *noun* (***-ies***) *informal* a loud, disorderly person. ▪ **rowdily** *adv.* ▪ **rowdiness** *noun.* ▪ **rowdyism** *noun.* [19c]

rowel *noun* a small spiked wheel attached to a spur. [14c: from French *roel* a small wheel, from Latin *rota* a wheel]

rowing boat *noun, Brit* a small boat moved by oars. *N Am equivalent* **rowboat**.

rowlock /ˈrɒlək/ *noun* a device that holds an oar in place and acts as a fulcrum for it. [18c]

royal *adj* **1** relating to or suitable for a king or queen. **2** (*often* **Royal**) under the patronage or in the service of a monarch: *Royal Geographical Society.* **3** regal; magnificent. **4** larger or of better quality, etc than usual. ▸ *noun* (*often* **Royal**) *informal* a member of a royal family. ▪ **royally** *adv.* [14c: from French *roial*, from Latin *regalis* regal, suitable for a king, from *rex* king]

IDIOMS **the Royal We** *or* **the royal we 1** a monarch's use of 'we' instead of 'I' when speaking of himself or herself. **2** *jocular* the use by any individual of 'we' instead of 'I'.

royal assent *noun* in the UK: formal permission given by the sovereign for a parliamentary act to become law.

royal blue *noun* a rich bright deep-coloured blue.

royal icing *noun, cookery* icing made with white of egg, and used esp on rich fruit cakes.

royalist *or* **Royalist** *noun* **1** a supporter of monarchy or of a specified monarchy. **2** *hist* during the 17c English Civil War: a supporter of Charles I. ▸ *adj* relating to royalists. ▪ **royalism** *noun.* [17c]

royal jelly *noun* a rich protein substance secreted by worker bees and fed to very young larvae.

royal prerogative *noun* the right of a monarch, in theory, not restricted in any way, but, in practice, established by custom.

royalty *noun* (***-ies***) **1** the character, state, office or power of a king or queen. **2** members of a royal family or families, either individually or collectively. **3** royal authority. **4** a percentage of the profits from each copy of a book, piece of music, invention, etc that is sold, publicly performed or used, which is paid to the author, composer, inventor, etc. **5** a payment made by companies who mine minerals, oil or gas to the person who owns the land the company is mining or the mineral rights to it. [14c]

royal warrant *noun* an official authorization to a tradesperson to supply goods to a royal household.

rozzer *noun, Brit slang* a policeman. [19c]

RP *abbrev* Received Pronunciation.

rpm *abbrev* revolutions per minute.

RSI *abbrev* repetitive strain or stress injury.

RSVP *abbrev* often written on invitations: *répondez s'il vous plaît* (French), please reply.

RTF *abbrev, comput* Rich Text Format, a standard format for text files.

Rt Hon *abbrev* Right Honourable.

Rt Rev *abbrev* Right Reverend.

RU *abbrev* are you (used in text messages).

Ru *symbol, chem* ruthenium.

rub *verb* (***rubbed, rubbing***) **1** to apply pressure and friction to by moving one's hand or an object backwards and forwards. **2** *intr* (*usu* **rub against**, **on** *or*

along) to move backwards and forwards against, on or along with pressure and friction. **3** (*usu* **rub sth in**) **a** to apply (cream, ointment, polish, etc) to; **b** *cookery* to mix (fat) into flour using the fingertips. **4** to clean, polish, dry, smooth, etc by applying pressure and friction. **5** *tr & intr* to remove or be removed by pressure and friction. **6** *tr & intr* to be sore or cause to be sore through pressure and friction. **7** *tr & intr* to fray by pressure and friction. ▶ *noun* **1** the process or an act of rubbing. **2** an obstacle or difficulty: *It will cost a lot and there's the rub.* [14c]

IDIOMS **rub sb's nose in it** to persist in reminding someone of a fault or mistake they have made. **rub shoulders** to come into social contact. **rub sb up the wrong way** to annoy or irritate them, esp by dealing with them carelessly or tactlessly.

PHRASAL VERBS **rub sth down 1** to rub (one's body, a horse, etc) briskly from head to foot, eg, to dry it. **2** to prepare (a surface) to receive new paint or varnish by rubbing the old paint or varnish off. **3** to become or cause to be smooth by rubbing. **rub sth in** *informal* to insist on talking about or emphasizing (an embarrassing fact or circumstance). **rub off on sb** to have an effect on or be passed to someone by close association: *Some of his bad habits have rubbed off on you.* **rub sb out** *N Am slang* to murder them. **rub sth out** to remove by rubbing, esp with an eraser. **rub sth up 1** to polish it. **2** to refresh one's memory or knowledge of it.

rubato /rʊˈbɑːtoʊ/ *noun, music* (***rubatos*** *or* ***rubati*** /-tiː/) a modified or distorted tempo. [18c: Italian, literally 'robbed', from *rubare* to steal]

rubber[1] *noun* **1** a strong, elastic substance, obtained from the latex of certain plants, esp the rubber tree, or manufactured synthetically. **2** *Brit* a small piece of rubber or plastic for rubbing out pencil or ink marks; an eraser. **3** (**rubbers**) *US* galoshes. ▪ **rubbery** *adj.* [16c: from **rub**]

rubber[2] *noun* **1** *bridge, whist, etc* **a** a match to play for the best of three or sometimes five games; **b** the winning of such a match. **2** *loosely* a session of card-playing. **3** a series of games in any of various sports, such as cricket, tennis, etc. [16c]

rubber band *noun* an **elastic band**.

rubberize *or* **-ise** *verb* to coat or impregnate (a substance, esp a textile) with rubber.

rubberneck *noun, orig US, slang* someone who stares or gapes inquisitively or stupidly. ▶ *verb* **1** *intr* to gape inquisitively or stupidly. **2** to stare at (the aftermath of an accident, etc). [19c]

rubber stamp *noun* **1** a device used to stamp a name, date, etc on books, papers, etc. **2** **a** an act or instance or the process of making an automatic, unthinking, etc agreement or authorization; **b** a person or group doing this. ▶ *verb* (**rubber-stamp**) **1** to mark with a rubber stamp. **2** *informal* to approve or authorize automatically.

rubber tree *noun* a tree that produces a milky white liquid that is used to make rubber.

rubbing *noun* **1** application of friction. **2** an impression or copy made by placing paper over a raised surface and rubbing the paper with crayon, wax, chalk, etc: *a brass rubbing.*

rubbish *noun* **1** waste material; refuse; litter. **2** worthless or useless material or objects. **3** *informal* worthless or absurd talk, writing, etc; nonsense. ▶ *verb, informal* to criticize or dismiss as worthless. ▪ **rubbishy** *adj.* [14c]

rubble *noun* pieces of broken stones, bricks, plaster, etc. ▪ **rubbly** *adj.* [14c]

rubella *noun, med* a viral disease characterized by a pink rash and swelling of the lymph glands. Also called **German measles**. [19c: from Latin *rubeus* red]

Rubicon *or* **rubicon** *noun* a boundary which, once crossed, signifies an irrevocable course of action. [17c: from the name of a stream in NE Italy that separated Julius Caesar's province of Cisalpine Gaul and Italy proper. By crossing the stream with his army in 49 BC Caesar effectively declared war on the Roman republic]

rubicund /ˈruːbɪkənd/ *adj* of the face or complexion: red or rosy; ruddy. [16c: from Latin *rubere* to be red]

rubidium *noun, chem* (symbol **Rb**) a silvery-white, highly reactive metallic element, used in photoelectric cells. [19c: from Latin *rubidus* red, so called because of the two red lines in its spectrum]

ruble see **rouble**

rubric /ˈruːbrɪk/ *noun* **1** a heading, esp one in a book or manuscript, orig one written or underlined in red. **2** *Christianity* a rule or direction for the conduct of divine service, added in red to the liturgy. **3** an authoritative rule or set of rules. [14c: from Latin *rubrica* red ochre]

ruby *noun* (***-ies***) **1** a valuable red gemstone, an impure variety of corundum. **2** a rich deep-red colour. [14c: from Latin *rubinus lapis* red stone]

ruby wedding *noun* a fortieth wedding anniversary.

ruche /ruːʃ/ *noun* a pleated or gathered frill used as a trimming. ▶ *verb* to trim (clothing, etc) with a ruche or ruches. ▪ **ruched** *adj.* ▪ **ruching** *noun.* [19c: French, literally 'beehive']

ruck[1] *noun* **1** a heap or mass of indistinguishable people or things. **2** *rugby* a loose scrum that forms around a ball on the ground. **3** in Australian rules football: the three players who do not have fixed positions but follow the ball about the field. ▶ *verb, intr* to form a ruck or play as a member of the ruck. [13c]

ruck[2] *noun* a wrinkle or crease. ▶ *verb, tr & intr* to wrinkle or crease or become wrinkled or creased. [18c: related to Norse *hrukka*]

rucksack *noun* a bag carried on the back with straps over the shoulders, used esp by climbers and walkers. Also called **backpack**. [19c: from German *Rücken* back + *Sack* sack or bag]

ruckus *noun, orig chiefly N Am* a commotion. [19c]

ruction *noun, informal* **1** a noisy disturbance; uproar. **2** (**ructions**) a noisy and usu unpleasant or violent argument or reaction. [19c]

rudd *noun* a European freshwater fish with yellow sides and reddish fins. [17c]

rudder *noun* **1** a movable flat device fixed vertically to a ship's stern for steering. **2** a movable aerofoil attached to the fin of an aircraft which helps control its horizontal movement. **3** anything that steers or guides. ▪ **rudderless** *adj.* [Anglo-Saxon *rothor*]

ruddle *or* **raddle** *noun* red ochre, used especially to mark sheep. ▶ *verb* to mark (sheep) with ruddle. [16c: from Anglo-Saxon *rudu* redness]

ruddy *adj* (***-ier, -iest***) **1** of the face, complexion, etc: glowing; with a healthy rosy or pink colour. **2** red; reddish. **3** *chiefly Brit, informal* bloody: *ruddy fool.* ▪ **ruddiness** *noun.* [Anglo-Saxon *rudig*]

rude *adj* **1** impolite or discourteous. **2** roughly made: *a rude shelter.* **3** ignorant or primitive. **4** sudden and unpleasant: *a rude awakening.* **5** vigorous; robust: *rude health.* **6** vulgar; indecent: *a rude joke.* ▪ **rudely** *adv.* ▪ **rudeness** *noun.* ▪ **rudery** *noun.* [14c: from French, from Latin *rudis* unwrought, rough]

rudiment *noun* **1** (*usu* **rudiments**) a fundamental fact, rule or skill of a subject: *the rudiments of cooking.* **2** (*usu* **rudiments**) the early and incomplete stage of something. **3** *biol* an organ or part which does not develop fully. [16c: from Latin *rudis* unformed]

rudimentary *adj* **1** basic; fundamental. **2** crude; primitive. **3** *biol* of an organ: **a** primitive or undeveloped; **b** only partially developed. [19c]

rue[1] *verb* (***ruing*** *or* ***rueing***) to wish (something) had not been said, had not happened, etc: *rued the day she ever met him.* [Anglo-Saxon *hreowan*]

rue[2] *noun* a strongly scented evergreen plant with bitter leaves. [14c: from Greek *rhyte*; the symbol of repentance is an allusion to **rue**[1]]

rueful *adj* feeling or showing regret. ▪ **ruefully** *adv.*

ruff[1] *noun* **1** a circular pleated or frilled collar, worn in the late 16c and early 17c, or more recently by the members of some choirs. **2** **a** a fringe or frill of feathers growing on a bird's neck; **b** a similar fringe of hair on an animal's neck. **3** a type of ruffed domestic pigeon. [16c]

ruff[2] *cards, verb, tr & intr* to trump. ▶ *noun* an act of ruffing. [16c: from French *rouffle*, Italian *ronfa*]

ruffian *noun* a coarse, violent, brutal or lawless person. [16c: French, from Italian *ruffiano*]

ruffle *verb* **1** to wrinkle or make uneven. **2** *tr & intr* to make or become irritated, annoyed or discomposed. **3** of a bird: to make (its feathers) erect, usu in anger or display. **4** to gather (lace, linen, etc) into a ruff or ruffle. **5** to flick or turn (pages of a book, etc) hastily. ▶ *noun* **1** a frill of lace, etc worn either round the neck or wrists. **2** an act or instance or the process of ruffling. [13c]

rufous *adj* of a bird or animal: reddish or brownish-red in colour. [18c: from Latin *rufus* red or reddish]

rug *noun* **1** a thick heavy mat or small carpet. **2** a thick blanket or wrap, esp one used for travelling, or as a protective and often waterproof covering for horses. **3** *orig N Am, slang* a toupee or hairpiece. [16c]

IDIOMS **pull the rug (out) from under sb** to leave them without defence, support, etc.

rugby *or* **rugby football** *noun* a team game played with an oval ball which players may pick up and run with and may pass from hand to hand. [19c: named after Rugby, the public school in Warwickshire where the game was first played]

rugged *adj* **1** of landscape, hills, ground, etc: rough, steep and rocky. **2** of facial features: irregular and furrowed. **3** of character: stern, austere and unbending. **4** of manners, etc: unsophisticated; unrefined. **5** involving physical hardships: *a rugged life.* **6** sturdy; robust: *rugged individualism.* **7** of machinery, equipment, etc: strongly or sturdily built to withstand vigorous use. ▪ **ruggedly** *adv.* ▪ **ruggedness** *noun.* [14c]

rugger *noun, informal* **rugby**.

ruin *noun* **1** a broken, destroyed, decayed or collapsed state. **2** (*often* **ruins**) the remains of something which has been broken, destroyed or has decayed or collapsed. **3** **a** complete loss of wealth, social position, power, etc; **b** a person, company, etc that has suffered this; **c** something or someone that causes this. ▶ *verb* **1** to reduce or bring (someone or something) to ruin. **2** to spoil. [14c: from French *ruine*, from Latin *ruere* to tumble down]

IDIOMS **in ruins** of a building, scheme, plan, etc: in a state of ruin; completely wrecked or destroyed.

ruination *noun* **1** an act or the process of ruining. **2** the state of having been ruined.

ruinous *adj* **1** likely to bring about ruin: *ruinous prices.* **2** ruined; decayed; destroyed. ▪ **ruinously** *adv.*

rule *noun* **1** a governing or controlling principle, regulation, etc. **2** **a** government or control; **b** the period during which government or control is exercised. **3** a general principle, standard, guideline or custom: *make it a rule always to be punctual.* **4** *Christianity* the laws and customs which form the basis of a monastic or religious order and are followed by all members of that order: *the Benedictine rule.* **5** a **ruler** (sense 2). **6** *printing* a thin straight line or dash. **7** *law* an order made by a court and judge which applies to a particular case only. ▶ *verb* **1** *tr & intr* to govern; to exercise authority over. **2** to keep control of or restrain. **3** to make an authoritative and usu official or judicial decision. **4** *intr* to be common or prevalent: *chaos ruled.* **5** to draw a straight line. **6** to draw a straight line or a series of parallel lines, eg on paper. [13c: from Latin *regere* to rule]

IDIOMS **as a rule** usually. **be ruled** to take advice. **rule the roost** to be dominant.

PHRASAL VERBS **rule sth out** to leave it out; to preclude it.

rule of thumb *noun* a method of doing something, based on practical experience rather than theory or careful calculation.

ruler *noun* **1** someone, eg a sovereign, who rules or governs. **2** a strip of wood, metal or plastic with straight edges that is marked off in units (usu inches or centimetres), and used for drawing straight lines and measuring.

ruling *noun* an official or authoritative decision. ▶ *adj* **1** governing; controlling. **2** most important or strongest; predominant.

rum[1] *noun* **1** a spirit distilled from fermented sugar-cane juice or from molasses. **2** *N Am* alcoholic liquor in general. [17c]

rum[2] *adj* (***rummer, rummest***) *chiefly Brit, informal* strange; odd; bizarre. [18c]

Rumanian see **Romanian**

rumba *or* **rhumba** *noun* **1** a lively Afro-Cuban dance. **2** **a** a popular ballroom dance derived from this; **b** music for this dance, with a stressed second beat. ▶ *verb, intr* to dance the rumba. [20c: American Spanish]

rum baba see **baba**

rumble *verb* **1** *intr* to make a deep low grumbling sound: *Her stomach rumbled.* **2** *intr* to move with a rumbling noise. **3** *Brit slang* to find out the truth about or see through (someone or something). ▶ *noun* **1** a deep low grumbling sound: *a rumble of thunder.* **2** *N Am slang* a street fight, esp between gangs. [14c]

rumbling *noun* **1** an act or instance of making a rumble. **2** (**rumblings**) early signs or indications: *rumblings of discontent.*

rumbustious *adj, Brit informal* noisy and cheerful; boisterous. [18c]

ruminant *noun* an even-toed hoofed mammal, eg, a cow, sheep, goat, etc that chews the cud and has a complex stomach with four chambers. ► *adj* **1** relating or belonging to this group of mammals. **2** meditative or contemplative. [17c: from Latin *ruminari* to chew the cud]

ruminate *verb* **1** *intr* to chew the cud. **2** *tr & intr* to contemplate. ▪ **rumination** *noun*. ▪ **ruminative** /ˈruːmɪnətɪv/ *adj*. ▪ **ruminatively** *adv*. [16c: from Latin *ruminari* to chew the cud]

rummage *verb* **1** *tr & intr* (*usu* **rummage through**) to search messily through (a collection of things, a cupboard, etc). **2** *intr* (*usu* **rummage about** *or* **around**) to search: *rummage around for a pen*. ► *noun* **1** a search. **2** things found by rummaging. [16c: from French *arrumage* stowing of cargo on a ship]

rummage sale *noun, N Am* a jumble sale.

rummy *noun* a card game in which each player tries to collect sets or sequences of three or more cards. [20c]

rumour *or* (*N Am*) **rumor** *noun* **1** a piece of news or information passed from person to person and which may or may not be true. **2** general talk or gossip; hearsay. ► *verb* to report or spread (news, information, etc) by rumour: *She is rumoured to be leaving.* • *It is rumoured she is leaving.* [14c: French, from Latin *rumor* noise]

rump *noun* **1** the rear part of an animal's or bird's body. **2** a person's buttocks. **3** (*also* **rump steak**) a cut of beef from the rump. **4** a small or inferior remnant. [15c]

rumple *verb, tr & intr* to become or to make (hair, clothes, etc) untidy, creased or wrinkled. ► *noun* a wrinkle or crease. [17c: from Dutch *rompel* wrinkle]

rumpus *noun, informal* a noisy disturbance, fuss, brawl or uproar. [18c]

run *verb* (*past tense* **ran**, *past participle* **run**, *present participle* **running**) **1** *intr* to move so quickly that both or all feet are off the ground together for an instant during part of each step. **2** to cover (a specified distance, etc) by running: *run the marathon*. **3** to perform (an action) as if by running: *run an errand*. **4** *intr* of a vehicle: to move over a surface on, or as if on, wheels. **5** *intr* (*often* **run off**) to flee; to run away. **6** *tr & intr* to move or make (something) move in a specified way or direction or with a specified result: *run the car up the ramp* • *let the dog run free* • *run him out of town*. **7** *tr & intr* (*usu* **run** *or* **run sth along**, **over**, *or* **through**, etc **sth**) to move or cause it to move or pass quickly, lightly or freely in the specified direction: *run your eyes over the report; Excitement ran through the audience*. **8** *intr, chiefly N Am* to stand as a candidate in an election: *is running for governor*. **9** *intr* of water, etc: to flow: *rivers running to the sea*. **10** to make or allow (liquid) to flow: *run cold water into the bath*. **11** *intr* of the nose or eyes: to discharge liquid or mucus. **12** of wax, etc: to melt and flow. **13** *tr & intr* to give out or cause (a tap, container, etc) to give out liquid: *run the tap* • *leave the tap running*. **14** to fill with water: *run a hot bath*. **15** *metallurgy* **a** *tr & intr* to melt or fuse; **b** to form (molten metal) into bars, etc; to cast. **16** *tr & intr* to come to a specified state or condition by, or as if by, flowing or running: *run dry* • *run short of time* • *her blood ran cold*. **17** to be full of or flow with. **18** *tr & intr* to operate or function: *The presses ran all night*. **19** *comput* to execute (a program). **20** *intr* (**run on sth**) of a vehicle: to use (a specified fuel). **21** to organize, manage or be in control of: *runs her own business*. **22** *tr & intr* to continue or cause (something) to continue or extend in a specified direction, for a specified time or distance, or over a specified range: *a road running south* • *colours running from pink to deep red* • *The play ran for ten years*. **23** *intr, law* to continue to have legal force: *a lease with a year still to run*. **24** *informal* to drive (someone or something) in a vehicle: *run you to the station*. **25** *intr* to spread or diffuse: *The colour in his shirt ran*. **26** *intr* to have as wording: *The report runs as follows*. **27** to be affected by or subjected to: *run a high temperature* • *run risks*. **28** *intr* to be inherent or recur frequently: *Blue eyes run in the family*. **29** to own, drive and maintain (a vehicle): *runs a sports car*. **30** to publish: *run the story in the magazine*. **31** to show or broadcast (a programme, film, etc): *run a repeat of the series*. **32** *intr* **a** of stitches: to come undone; **b** of a garment, eg tights: to have some of its stitches come undone and form a ladder. **33** to hunt or track down (an animal): *ran the fox to ground*. **34** to get past or through an obstacle, etc: *run a blockade*. **35** to smuggle or deal illegally in something: *run guns*. **36** *cricket* to score a run by, or as if by, running. ► *noun* **1** an act or instance or the process of running. **2** the distance covered or time taken up by an act of running. **3** a rapid pace quicker than a walk: *break into a run*. **4** a manner of running. **5** a mark, streak, etc made by the flowing of some liquid, eg paint. **6** a trip in a vehicle, esp for pleasure: *a run to the seaside*. **7** a continuous and unbroken period or series of something: *a run of bad luck* • *The play had a run of six weeks*. **8** freedom to move about or come and go as one pleases: *have the run of the house*. **9** a high or urgent demand for (a currency, money, a commodity, etc): *a run on the pound*. **10** a route which is regularly travelled, eg by public transport, or as a delivery round, etc: *a coach on the London to Glasgow run*. **11** a **ladder** (*noun* sense 2). **12** (**the runs**) *informal* diarrhoea. **13** the length of time for which a machine, etc functions or is operated. **14** the quantity produced in a single period of production: *a print run*. **15** *cards* three or more playing-cards in a series or sequence. **16** *cricket* a point scored, usu by a batsman running from one wicket to the other. **17** a unit of scoring in baseball made by the batter successfully completing a circuit of four bases. **18** an enclosure or pen for domestic fowls or animals: *a chicken-run*. [Anglo-Saxon *rinnan*]

IDIOMS **a (good) run for one's money** *informal* **1** fierce competition. **2** enjoyment from an activity.

PHRASAL VERBS **run across** *or* **into sb** to meet them unexpectedly. **run along** *informal* to go away: *Run along – I'm very busy.* **run away** to escape or flee. **run away with sb** to elope with them. **run away** *or* **off with sth 1** to steal it. **2** of someone: to be over-enthusiastic about or carried away by (an idea, etc). **3** to win a (competition, etc) comfortably. **run down** of a clock, battery, etc: to cease to work because of a gradual loss of power. **run sb** *or* **sth down 1** of a vehicle or its driver: to knock them or it to the ground. **2** to speak badly of them or it. **3** to chase or search for them or it until they are found or captured. **run sth down** to allow (eg an operation or business) to be gradually reduced or closed. **run sb in** *informal* to arrest them. **run into sb** *informal* to meet them unexpectedly. **run into sb** *or* **sth** to collide with them or it. **run into sth 1** to suffer from or be beset by (a problem, difficulty, etc): *Our plans quickly ran into problems.* **2** to reach as far as (an amount or quantity): *His debts run into hundreds.* **run sth off** to produce, especially printed material, quickly or promptly. **run off with sth 1** to steal it. **2** to win (a competition, etc) comfortably. **run out** of a supply: to come to an end; to be used up. **run sb out 1** *cricket* to put out (a batsman running towards a wicket) by hitting that wicket with the ball. **2** *chiefly N Am, informal* to force them to leave: *run them out of town.* **run out of sth** to use up a supply of it: *run out of money.* **run out on sb** *informal* to abandon or desert them. **run over 1** to overflow. **2** to go beyond (a limit, etc). **run over** *or* **through sth** to read or perform a piece of music, a script, etc quickly, esp for practice or as a rehearsal. **run sb** *or* **sth over** of a vehicle or driver: to knock them or it down and injure or kill them or it. **run sb through** to pierce them with a sword or similar weapon. **run to sth 1** to have enough money for it: *We can't run to a holiday this year.* **2** of money, resources, etc: to be sufficient for particular needs. **3** of a text: to extend to (a specified extent). **4** to tend towards it: *run to fat.* **run sth up 1** to make (clothing, etc) quickly or promptly. **2** to amass or accumulate (bills, debts, etc). **3** to hoist (a flag). **run up against sb** *or* **sth** to be faced with (an opponent or difficulty).

runabout *noun* a small light car, boat or aircraft.

runaround *noun* a **runabout**.

IDIOMS **give sb the runaround** *informal* to behave repeatedly in a deceptive or evasive way towards them.

runaway *noun* a person or animal that has run away or fled. ▸ *adj* **1** in the process of running away; out of control: *a runaway train.* **2** of a race, victory, etc: easily and convincingly won. **3** done or managed as a result of running away.

run-down *adj* **1** of a person: tired or exhausted; in weakened health. **2** of a building: shabby; dilapidated. ▸ *noun* (**rundown**) **1** a gradual reduction in numbers, size, etc. **2** a brief statement of the main points or items; a summary.

rune *noun* **1** a letter of an early alphabet used by the Germanic peoples between about AD 200 and AD 600, found in inscriptions, etc. **2** a mystical symbol or inscription. ▪ **runic** *adj.* [17c: from Norse *run*]

rung[1] *noun* **1** a step on a ladder. **2** a crosspiece on a chair. [Anglo-Saxon *hrung*]

rung[2] *past participle of* **ring**[2]

---

rung, rang

Be careful not to confuse these two forms of the verb **ring**. **Rung** is the past participle, which is used in constructions such as:

Ashok had already rung the bell.

Rang is the past tense:

Ashok rang the bell.

---

run-in *noun* **1** an approach. **2** *informal* a quarrel.

runnel *noun* **1** a small stream. **2** a gutter. [Anglo-Saxon *rynel*, diminutive of *ryne* a stream]

runner *noun* **1** someone or something that runs. **2** a messenger. **3** a groove or strip along which a drawer, sliding door, curtain, etc slides. **4** either of the strips of metal or wood running the length of a sledge, etc. **5** a blade on an ice skate. **6** in certain plants, eg strawberry: a stem that grows horizontally along the surface of the ground, producing new plants. **7** a long narrow strip of cloth or carpet used to decorate or cover a table, dresser, floor, etc. **8** a **runner bean**. **9** a smuggler: *a drugs runner.*

IDIOMS **do a runner** *slang* to leave a place hastily, esp to leave a shop, restaurant, etc without paying.

runner bean *noun* **1** a climbing plant which produces bright red flowers and long green edible beans. **2** the bean this plant produces.

runner-up *noun* (***runners-up***) **1** a team or competitor that finishes in second place. **2** a team or competitor that finishes close behind the winner.

running *noun* **1** the action of moving quickly. **2** the act of managing, organizing or operating. ▸ *adj* **1** relating to or for running: *running shoes.* **2** done or performed while running, working, etc: *running repairs* • *a running jump.* **3** continuous: *a running dispute.* **4** consecutive: *two days running.* **5** flowing: *running water.* **6** of a wound, etc: giving out pus.

IDIOMS **in** *or* **out of the running** having, or not having, a chance of success. **make** *or* **take up the running** to take the lead or set the pace, eg in a competition, race, etc.

running battle *noun* **1** a military engagement with a constantly changing location. **2** a continuous fight or argument: *a running battle with the Council.*

running knot *noun* a knot that changes the size of a noose as one end of the string, etc is pulled.

running mate *noun, politics* a candidate running for election to a less important post, esp a US vice-presidential candidate.

runny *adj* (***-ier, -iest***) **1** tending to run or flow with liquid. **2** liquid; too watery. **3** of the nose: discharging mucus. [19c]

run-of-the-mill *adj* ordinary; average; not special.

runt *noun* **1** the smallest animal in a litter. **2** an undersized and weak person. [16c]

run-through *noun* a practice or rehearsal.

run time *noun, comput* the time during which a computer program is executed.

run-up *noun* **1** *sport* a run made in preparation for a jump, throw, etc. **2** an approach to something or period of preparation: *the run-up to Christmas.*

runway *noun* **1** a wide hard surface that aircraft take off from and land on. **2** in a theatre, etc: a narrow ramp projecting from a stage into the audience.

rupee *noun* the standard unit of currency in several countries including India and Pakistan. [17c: from Hindi *rupiya*, from Sanskrit *rupya* wrought silver]

rupture *noun* **1 a** a breach; a breaking or bursting; **b** the state of being broken or burst. **2** a breach of harmony or friendly relations. **3** a hernia, esp in the abdominal region. ▸ *verb* **1** to break, tear or burst. **2** to breach or break off (friendly relations). **3** to cause a rupture in (an organ, tissue, etc). **4** *intr* to be affected by a rupture. [15c: from Latin *rumpere* to break]

rural *adj* **1** relating to or suggestive of the country or countryside. **2** pastoral or agricultural. Compare **urban**. [15c: French, from Latin *ruris* the country]

rural dean *noun* in the Church of England: a clergyman with responsibility over a group of parishes.

ruse /ruːz/ *noun* a clever stratagem or plan intended to deceive or trick. [14c: from French *ruser* to retreat]

rush[1] *verb* **1** *intr* to hurry; to move forward or go quickly. **2** to hurry (someone or something) on. **3** to send, transport, etc (someone or something) quickly or urgently: *rushed her to hospital.* **4** to perform or deal with (someone or something) too quickly or hurriedly. **5** *intr* to come, flow, spread, etc quickly and suddenly: *Colour rushed to her cheeks.* **6** to attack (someone or something) suddenly. ▸ *noun* **1** a sudden quick movement, esp forwards. **2** a sudden general movement or migration of people: *a gold rush.* **3** a sound or sensation of rushing. **4** haste; hurry: *in a rush.* **5** a period of great activity. **6** a sudden demand for a commodity. **7** *slang* a feeling of euphoria after taking a drug. ▸ *adj* done, or needing to be done, quickly: *a rush job.* [14c: from French *ruser* to put to flight, from Latin *recusare* to push back]

rush[2] *noun* **1** a densely tufted annual or evergreen perennial plant, typically found in cold wet regions. **2** a stalk or stalk-like leaf of this plant, often used as a material for making baskets, covering floors, etc. **3** rushes as a material. ▪ **rushy** *adj.* [Anglo-Saxon *risc*]

rushes *plural noun, cinematog* the first unedited prints of a scene or scenes. [20c: from **rush**[1]]

rush hour *noun* the period at the beginning or end of a working day when traffic is at its busiest.

rush light *noun* a candle made from the pith of a rush dipped in tallow.

rusk *noun* a piece of bread which has been rebaked, or a hard dry biscuit resembling this, esp as a baby food. [16c: from Spanish or Portuguese *rosca* a twist of bread]

russet *noun* **1** a reddish-brown colour. **2** a variety of apple with a reddish-brown skin. [13c: from French *rousset*, from Latin *russus* red]

Russian *adj* **1** belonging or relating to Russia or its inhabitants. **2** relating to the Russian language. ▸ *noun* **1** a native of Russia. **2** the official language of Russia. [16c: from Latin *Russianus*]

Russian roulette *noun* an act of daring or bravado, esp that of spinning the cylinder of a revolver which is loaded with just one bullet, pointing the revolver at one's own head, and pulling the trigger.

Russo- *combining form, denoting* relating to Russia or (*loosely*) to the former Soviet Union: *a Russo-American treaty.*

rust *noun* **1** a reddish-brown coating that forms on the surface of iron or steel that has been exposed to air and moisture. **2** a similar coating which forms on other metals. **3** the colour of rust, usu a reddish-brown. **4** a fungus disease of cereals, etc, characterized by the appearance of reddish-brown patches on the leaves, etc. ▸ *verb* **1** *tr & intr* to become or cause (something) to become coated with rust. **2** *intr* of a plant: to be affected by rust. **3** *intr* to become weaker, inefficient etc, usu through lack of use. [Anglo-Saxon]

rustic *adj* **1** relating to, characteristic of, or living in the country; rural. **2** simple and unsophisticated. **3** awkward or uncouth. **4** made of rough untrimmed branches: *rustic furniture.* ▸ *noun* a person from, or who lives in, the country, esp one who is thought to be simple and unsophisticated. ▪ **rusticity** /rʌ'stɪsɪtɪ/ *noun.* [15c: from Latin *rus* country]

rusticate *verb* **1** *Brit* to suspend (a student) temporarily from college or university. **2** *intr* to live or go to live in the country. **3** to make rustic. ▪ **rustication** *noun.* [15c: from Latin *rus* country]

rustle *verb* **1** *intr* to make a soft whispering sound like that of dry leaves. **2** *intr* to move with such a sound. **3** to make (something) move with, or make, such a sound: *rustled the newspaper.* **4** *tr & intr, chiefly US* to round up and steal (cattle or horses). **5** *intr, chiefly US informal* to work energetically; to hustle. ▸ *noun* a rustling sound. ▪ **rustler** *noun.* [14c]

PHRASAL VERBS **rustle sth up 1** to gather (people or things) together, esp at short notice: *rustled up a few people to go to the meeting.* **2** to arrange or prepare, esp at short notice.

rustproof *adj* **1** tending not to rust. **2** preventing rusting. ▸ *verb* to make rustproof.

rusty *adj* (***-ier, -iest***) **1** of iron, steel or other metals: covered with rust. **2** of a plant: affected by rust. **3** of a skill, knowledge of a subject, etc: impaired by lack of use or practice: *His French was rusty.* **4** rust-coloured. ▪ **rustily** *adv.* ▪ **rustiness** *noun.*

rut[1] *noun* a deep track or furrow in soft ground, esp one made by wheels. ▸ *verb* (***rutted, rutting***) to furrow (the ground) with ruts. ▪ **rutty** *adj.* [16c]

IDIOMS **in a rut** stuck in a boring or dreary routine.

rut[2] *noun* in male ruminants, eg, deer: a period of sexual excitement. ▸ *verb* (***rutted, rutting***) *intr* of male animals: to be in a period of sexual excitement. [15c: French, from Latin *rugire* to roar]

rutabaga *noun, N Am* a swede. [18c: from a Swedish dialect word *rotabagge*, literally 'root bag']

ruthenium *noun, chem* (symbol **Ru**) a brittle, silvery-white metallic element that occurs in small amounts in some platinum ores. [19c: from Latin *Ruthenia* Russia]

rutherfordium *noun, chem* (symbol **Rf**) an artificially manufactured radioactive metallic element. [20c: named after Ernest Rutherford, New Zealand-born British physicist]

ruthless *adj* without pity; merciless. ▪ **ruthlessly** *adv.* ▪ **ruthlessness** *noun.* [14c: from obsolete *reuthe* pity]

rye *noun* **1 a** a cereal plant similar to barley but with longer, narrower ears; **b** its grain, used for making flour and in the distillation of whiskey, gin, vodka, etc. **2** *esp US* whiskey distilled from fermented rye. **3** *US* **rye bread**: *pastrami on rye.* [Anglo-Saxon *ryge*]

rye bread *noun* any bread made with rye flour.

rye grass *noun* a grass grown for fodder or used for lawns.

S[1] *or* **s** *noun* (***Ss, S's*** *or* ***s's***) **1** the nineteenth letter of the English alphabet. **2** anything shaped like an S.

S[2] *abbrev* **1** Saint. **2** Siemens. **3** South.

S[3] *symbol, chem* sulphur.

s *abbrev* **1** a second or seconds of time. **2** *formerly* in the UK: a shilling or shillings. [From Latin *solidus*]

-s[1] *or* **-es** *suffix* forming the plural of nouns: *dogs* • *churches.*

-s[2] *or* **-es** *suffix* forming the third person singular of the present tense of verbs: *walks* • *misses.*

's[1] *suffix* **1** a word-forming element used to form the possessive: *children's.* **2** a word-forming element used to form the plural of numbers and symbols: *3's, X's.*

's[2] *abbrev* **1** the shortened form of **is**, as in *he's not here.* **2** the shortened form of **has**, as in *she's taken it.* **3** the shortened form of **us**, as in *let's go.*

SA *abbrev, Aust state* South Australia.

Sabbath *noun* a day of the week set aside for religious worship and rest from work, Saturday among Jews and Sunday among most Christians. [Anglo-Saxon: from Hebrew *shabbath* rest]

sabbatical *adj* relating to or being a period of leave usu given to teachers in higher education, esp to study or to undertake a separate and related project. ▸ *noun* a period of sabbatical leave. [17c: from Greek *sabbatikos*]

sable[1] *noun* (***sables*** *or* ***sable***) **1** a small carnivorous mammal, native to Europe and Asia, that is a species of the marten. **2** the thick soft glossy dark brown or black coat of this animal, highly prized as valuable fur. ▸ *adj* made of sable fur. [15c: French]

sable[2] *adj* **1** *poetic* dark. **2** *heraldry* black.

sabot /ˈsaboʊ/ *noun* a wooden clog, or a shoe with a wooden sole, as formerly worn by the French peasantry. [17c: French]

sabotage /ˈsabətɑːʒ/ *noun* **1** deliberate or underhand damage or destruction, esp carried out for military or political reasons. **2** action designed to disrupt any plan or scheme and prevent its achievement. ▸ *verb* to deliberately destroy, damage or disrupt something. ▪ **saboteur** /sabəˈtɜː(r)/ *noun.* [19c: from French *saboter* to ruin through carelessness]

sabre *or* (*US*) **saber** *noun* **1** a curved single-edged cavalry sword. **2** a lightweight sword with a tapering blade used for fencing. [17c: French]

sac *noun, biol* any bag-like part in a plant or animal. [18c: from Latin *saccus* bag]

saccharide *noun, chem* any of a group of carbohydrates consisting of one or more simple sugars, typically having a sweet taste, eg glucose, sucrose. [19c: from Latin *saccharum* sugar]

saccharin /ˈsakərɪn/ *noun* a white crystalline substance used as an artificial sweetener. [19c: from Greek *saccharon* sugar]

saccharine /ˈsakəriːn/ *adj* **1** relating to or containing sugar. **2** over-sentimental or sickly sweet; cloying.

sacerdotal /sasəˈdoʊtəl/ *adj* referring or relating to priests; priestly. [15c: from Latin *sacerdos* priest]

sachet /ˈsaʃeɪ/ *noun* **1** a small sealed packet, usu made of plastic, containing a liquid, cream or powder. **2** a small bag containing pot-pourri or a similar scented substance, used to perfume wardrobes, drawers, etc. [15c: French, diminutive of *sac* bag]

sack[1] *noun* **1** a large bag, esp one made of coarse cloth or paper. **2** the amount a sack will hold; a sackful. **3** (**the sack**) *informal* dismissal from employment. **4** (**the sack**) *slang* bed. ▸ *verb* **1** to put into a sack or sacks. **2** *informal* to dismiss from employment. [Anglo-Saxon *sacc*]

sack[2] *verb* to plunder, pillage and destroy a town. ▸ *noun* the act of sacking a town. [16c: from French *mettre à sac* to put one's loot into a bag; to plunder]

sackbut *noun* an early wind instrument with a slide like a trombone. [16c: from French *saquebute*]

sackcloth *noun* **1** coarse cloth used to make sacks; sacking. **2** a garment made from this, formerly worn in mourning or as a penance.

IDIOMS **sackcloth and ashes** a display of mourning, sorrow or remorse.

sackful *noun* the amount a sack will hold.

sacking *noun* coarse cloth used to make sacks.

sacra *pl of* **sacrum**

sacrament *noun* **1** *Christianity* a religious rite or ceremony, eg marriage or baptism, regarded as a channel to and from God or as a sign of grace. **2** (**Sacrament**) *Christianity* **a** the service of the Eucharist or Holy Communion; **b** the consecrated bread and wine consumed at Holy Communion. ▪ **sacramental** *adj.* [12c: from Latin *sacramentum* an oath]

sacrament of the sick *noun, RC Church* the act of anointing a person who is very ill or badly injured with consecrated oil.

sacred *adj* **1** devoted to a deity, therefore regarded with deep and solemn respect; consecrated. **2** connected with religion or worship: *sacred music.* **3** of rules, etc: not to be challenged, violated or breached in any circumstances. **4** dedicated or appropriate to a saint, deity, etc. [14c: from Latin *sacrare* to worship]

sacred cow *noun, informal* a custom, institution, etc so revered as to be above criticism. [20c: referring to the Hindu doctrine that cows are sacred]

sacrifice *noun* **1** the offering of a slaughtered person or animal on an altar to God or a god. **2** the person or animal slaughtered for such an offering. **3** any offering, symbolic or tangible, made to God or a god. **4** the destruction, surrender, or giving up of something valued for the sake of someone or something else, esp a higher consideration. ▸ *verb* **1** to offer someone or something as a sacrifice to God or a god. **2** to surrender or give up something for the sake of some other person or thing. ▪ **sacrificial** *adj.* [13c: from Latin *sacrificium*]

sacrilege *noun* **1** a profanation or extreme disrespect for something holy or greatly respected. **2** the breaking into a holy or sacred place and stealing from it. ▪ **sacrilegious** *adj.* [13c: from French *sacrilege*]

sacristan *or* **sacrist** *noun* a person responsible for a church's buildings and churchyard; a sexton. [14c: from Latin *sacristanus*]

sacristy *noun* (***-ies***) a room in a church where sacred utensils and vestments are kept; a vestry. [17c: from Latin *sacristia* vestry]

sacrosanct *adj* supremely holy or sacred; inviolable. ▪ **sacrosanctity** *noun.* [17c: from Latin *sacer* holy + *sanctus* hallowed]

sacrum /ˈseɪkrəm/ *noun* (***sacra***) *anatomy* a large triangular bone composed of fused vertebrae, forming the keystone of the pelvic arch in humans. ▪ **sacral** *adj.* [18c: from Latin *os sacrum* holy bone]

SAD *abbrev, psychol* seasonal affective disorder.

sad *adj* (***sadder, saddest***) **1** feeling unhappy or sorrowful. **2** causing unhappiness: *sad news.* **3** expressing or suggesting unhappiness: *sad music.* **4** very bad; deplorable: *a sad state.* **5** *informal* lacking in taste; inspiring ridicule: *He has such sad taste in music.* ▪ **sadly** *adv* **1** in a sad manner; sad to relate. **2** unfortunately. ▪ **sadness** *noun.* [Anglo-Saxon *sæd* weary]

sadden *verb* **1** to make someone sad. **2** *intr* to become sad.

saddle *noun* **1** a leather seat for horseriding, which fits on the horse's back and is secured under its belly. **2** a fixed seat on a bicycle or motorcycle. **3** a pad on the back of a draught animal, used for supporting the load. **4** a butcher's cut of meat including part of the backbone with the ribs. ▸ *verb* **1** to put a saddle on (an animal). **2** *intr* to climb into a saddle. **3** to burden someone with a problem, duty, etc. [Anglo-Saxon *sadol*]

IDIOMS **in the saddle 1** on horseback. **2** in a position of power or control.

saddleback *noun* **1** an animal or bird with a saddle-shaped marking on its back. **2** a hill or mountain with a dip in the middle. ▪ **saddlebacked** *adj.*

saddlebag *noun* a small bag carried at or attached to the saddle of a horse or bicycle.

saddler *noun* a person who makes or sells saddles, harness, and related equipment for horses.

saddlery *noun* (***-ies***) **1** the occupation or profession of a saddler. **2** a saddler's shop or stock-in-trade. **3** a room at a stables, etc for making or storing the saddles, etc.

saddle soap *noun* a type of oily soap used for cleaning and preserving leather.

Sadducee /ˈsadʒʊsiː/ *noun, hist* one of a Jewish priestly and aristocratic sect of traditionalists, who resisted the progressive views of the Pharisees, and who rejected, among other beliefs, that of life after death. [Anglo-Saxon *sadduceas*]

sadhu /ˈsɑːduː/ *noun* a nomadic Hindu holy man, living an austere life. [19c: Sanskrit]

sadism /ˈseɪdɪzəm/ *noun* **1** *psychol* the gaining of pleasure by inflicting pain on others. Compare **masochism**. **2** any infliction of suffering on others for one's own satisfaction. ▪ **sadist** *noun.* ▪ **sadistic** *adj.* [19c: named after Comte (called Marquis) de Sade, French novelist who wrote about this form of pleasure]

SAE *or* **sae** *abbrev* stamped addressed envelope.

safari *noun* an expedition to hunt or observe wild animals, esp in Africa. [19c: Swahili, meaning 'journey']

safari park *noun* a large enclosed area in which wild animals, mostly non-native, roam freely and can be observed by the public from their vehicles.

safe *adj* **1** free from danger or harm. **2** unharmed. **3** giving protection from danger or harm; secure: *a safe place.* **4** not dangerous or harmful: *Is it safe to go out?* **5** involving no risk of loss; assured: *a safe bet.* ▸ *noun* a sturdily constructed cabinet, usu made of metal, in which valuables can be locked away. ▪ **safely** *adv.* ▪ **safeness** *noun.* [15c: from French *sauf*]

safe-conduct *noun* **1** an official permit to pass or travel, esp in wartime, with guarantee of freedom from interference or arrest. **2** a document authorizing this.

safe-deposit *or* **safety-deposit** *noun* a vault, eg in a bank, in which valuables can be locked away.

safeguard *noun* a person, device or arrangement giving protection against danger or harm. ▸ *verb* to protect from harm; to ensure the safety of someone or something.

safekeeping *noun* care and protection; safe custody: *She put her jewellery in the bank for safekeeping.*

safe sex *noun* (***-ies***) sexual activity in which the transmission of disease and viruses, esp HIV, is guarded against.

safety *noun* (***-ies***) **1** the quality or condition of being safe. **2** *Amer football* the most deeply-placed member of the defensive side. Also called **safetyman**. [13c: from French *sauveté*]

safety belt *noun* **1** a seat belt. **2** a strap or belt attaching a workman, etc to a fixed object while carrying out a dangerous operation.

safety catch *noun* any catch to provide protection against something, eg the accidental firing of a gun.

safety curtain *noun* a fireproof curtain between the stage and a theatre audience, lowered to control the spread of fire.

safety-deposit see **safe-deposit**

safety glass *noun* glass that is strengthened to avoid shattering.

safety lamp *noun* a miner's oil lamp designed to prevent ignition of any flammable gases encountered in the mine by covering the flame with a wire gauze. Also called **Davy lamp**.

safety match *noun* a match that only ignites when struck on a specially prepared surface.

safety net *noun* **1** a large net stretched beneath acrobats, tightrope walkers, etc in case they accidentally fall. **2** any precautionary measure or means of protecting against loss or failure.

safety pin *noun* a U-shaped pin with an attached guard to cover the point.

safety razor *noun* a shaving razor with the blade protected by a guard to prevent deep cutting of the skin.

safety valve *noun* **1** a valve in a boiler or pipe system that opens when the pressure exceeds a certain level, and closes again when the pressure drops. **2** an outlet for harmlessly releasing strong emotion.

safflower *noun* a plant with large thistle-like heads of orange-red flowers that yield yellow and red dyes, and seeds that yield **safflower oil**, used in cooking, medicines and paints. [16c: from Dutch *saffloer*]

saffron *noun* **1** a crocus which has lilac flowers with large bright orange stigmas divided into three branches. **2** the dried stigmas of this species, used to dye and flavour food. **3** a bright orange-yellow colour. [13c: from French *safran*]

sag *verb* (***sagged, sagging***) *intr* **1** to bend, sink, or hang down, esp in the middle, under or as if under weight. **2** to hang loosely or bulge downwards; to droop. ▸ *noun* a sagging state or condition. ▪ **saggy** *adj* (***-ier, -iest***). [15c: Norse]

saga *noun* **1** a medieval prose tale of the deeds of legendary Icelandic or Norwegian heroes and events. **2** *informal* any long detailed story or series of events. [18c: Norse]

sagacious *adj, formal* having or showing intelligence and good judgement; wise or discerning. ▪ **sagaciously** *adv.* ▪ **sagacity** *noun.* [17c: from Latin *sagax*]

sage[1] *noun* **1** a shrub with greyish-green aromatic leaves. **2** the leaves of this plant, used in cookery as a seasoning. [14c: from French *sauge*]

sage[2] *noun* someone of great wisdom and knowledge, esp an ancient philosopher. ▸ *adj* extremely wise and prudent. ▪ **sagely** *adv.* [13c: French]

Sagittarius *noun, astrol* **a** the ninth sign of the zodiac, the Archer; **b** a person born between 22 November and 20 December, under this sign. ▪ **Sagittarian** *noun, adj.* [14c: Latin, from *sagitta* arrow]

sago *noun* **1** a starchy grain or powder obtained from the soft pith of the sago palm, a staple food in the tropics, and also widely used in desserts. **2** any of various species of palm that yield this. [16c: from Malay *sagu*]

sahib /ˈsɑːɪb/ *noun* in India: a term of respect used after a man's name, equivalent to 'Mr' or 'Sir', and formerly used on its own to address or refer to a European man. [17c: Arabic, meaning 'lord or friend']

said *verb, past tense, past participle of* **say.** ▸ *adj, often formal* previously or already mentioned: *the said occasion.*

sail *noun* **1** a sheet of canvas, or similar structure, spread to catch the wind as a means of propelling a ship. **2** a trip in a boat or ship with or without sails. **3** a voyage of a specified distance travelled by boat or ship. **4** *naut* a ship with sails. ▸ *verb* **1** *tr & intr* to travel by boat or ship. **2** to control (a boat or ship): *He sailed his ship around the world.* **3** *intr* to depart by boat or ship: *We sail at two-thirty.* **4** to cause (a toy boat, etc) to sail. **5** *intr* (**sail through sth**) *informal* to succeed in it effortlessly. [Anglo-Saxon *segel*]

IDIOMS **sail close to** *or* **near the wind 1** *naut* to keep the boat's bow as close as possible to the direction from which the wind is blowing so that the sails catch as much wind as is safely possible. **2** to come dangerously close to overstepping a limit, eg of good taste or decency. **set sail 1** to begin a journey by boat or ship. **2** to spread the sails.

sailboard *noun* a windsurfing board, like a surfboard with a sail attached, controlled by a hand-held boom. ▪ **sailboarding** *noun.*

sailcloth *noun* **1** strong cloth, such as canvas, used to make sails. **2** heavy cotton cloth used for garments.

sailor *noun* **1** any member of a ship's crew, esp one who is not an officer. **2** someone regarded in terms of ability to tolerate travel on a ship without becoming seasick: *a good sailor.*

sainfoin /ˈseɪnfɔɪn/ *noun* a leguminous plant, widely cultivated as a fodder crop, having bright pink to red flowers veined with purple. [17c: French]

saint *noun* (abbrev **St**) **1** (*often* **Saint**) a person whose profound holiness is formally recognized after death by a Christian Church, and who is declared worthy of everlasting praise. **2** *informal* a very good and kind person. ▪ **sainthood** *noun.* ▪ **saintlike** *adj.* [12c: from Latin *sanctus* holy]

sainted *adj* **1** formally declared a saint. **2** greatly respected or revered; hallowed.

saintly *adj* (***-ier, -iest***) **1** similar to, characteristic of, or befitting a saint. **2** very good or holy. ▪ **saintliness** *noun.*

saint's day *noun* a day in the Church calendar on which a particular saint is honoured and commemorated.

St Valentine's Day *noun* 14 February, a day on which special greetings cards are sent to sweethearts or people to whom one is attracted. See also **valentine**.

Saint Vitus's dance *noun, pathol* chorea.

saithe *noun, Brit* the **coley**. Also called **coalfish**.

sake[1] *noun* **1** benefit or advantage; behalf; account: *for my sake.* **2** purpose; object or aim. [Anglo-Saxon *sacu* lawsuit]

IDIOMS **for the sake of sth** for the purpose of or in order to achieve or assure it: *You should take these exams for the sake of your future.*

sake[2] *or* **saki** /ˈsɑːkɪ/ *noun* a Japanese fermented alcoholic drink made from rice. [17c: Japanese]

Sakti *or* **Shakti** *noun, Hinduism* power, personified by a female deity.

salaam /səˈlɑːm/ *noun* **1** a word used as a greeting in Eastern countries, esp by Muslims. **2** a Muslim greeting or show of respect in the form of a low bow with the palm of the right hand on the forehead. ▸ *verb, tr & intr* to perform the salaam to someone. [17c: from Arabic *salam* peace]

salable see **saleable**

salacious *adj* **1** lecherous or lustful. **2** seeking to arouse sexual desire, esp crudely. ▪ **salaciousness** *noun.* [17c: from Latin *salax* fond of leaping]

salad *noun* a cold dish of vegetables or herbs, either raw or pre-cooked, eaten either on its own or as an accompaniment to a main meal. [15c: from French *salade*]

salad days *plural noun, literary* years of youthful inexperience and carefree innocence.

salamander *noun* **1** a small amphibian resembling a lizard. **2** a mythical reptile or spirit believed to live in fire and be able to quench it with the chill of its body. [14c: from French *salamandre*]

salami *noun* a highly seasoned type of sausage, usu served very thinly sliced. [19c: Italian, pl of *salame*]

sal ammoniac *noun, chem* another name for ammonium chloride. See also **ammonium**.

salaried *adj* **1** having or receiving a salary. **2** of employment: paid by a salary.

salary *noun* (**-ies**) a fixed regular payment, usu made monthly, for esp non-manual work. ▸ *verb* (**-ies, -ied**) to pay a salary to someone. [14c: from French *salaire*]

salat *or* **salah** *noun, Islam* prescribed worship performed five times a day. [Arabic, meaning 'prayer']

sale *noun* **1** the exchange of anything for a specified amount of money. **2** an item sold. **3** a period during which goods in shops, etc are offered at reduced prices. **4** the sale of goods by auction. **5** any event at which certain goods can be bought: *a book sale*. **6** (**sales**) the operations associated with, or the staff responsible for, selling. ▸ *adj* intended for selling, esp at reduced prices or by auction: *sales items*. [Anglo-Saxon *sala*]

IDIOMS **for** *or* **on sale** available for buying.

saleable *or* (*US*) **salable** *adj* **1** suitable for selling. **2** in demand. ▪ **saleability** *noun*.

sale of work *noun* a sale of items made by members of eg a church congregation or association in order to raise money for a charity or other organization.

sale or return *or* **sale and return** *noun* an arrangement by which a retailer may return any unsold goods to the wholesaler.

salesman, **salesgirl**, **saleswoman** *or* **salesperson** *noun* **1** a person who sells goods to customers, esp in a shop. **2** a person representing a company, who often visits people's homes, offices, etc.

salesmanship *noun* the techniques used by a salesman to present goods in an appealing way so as to persuade people to buy them.

sales talk *or* **sales pitch** *noun* persuasive talk used by salespeople.

salicylic acid /salɪˈsɪlɪk/ *noun, chem* a white crystalline solid that occurs naturally in certain plants, used in the manufacture of aspirin, antiseptic ointments, dyes, food preservatives and perfumes. [19c: from Latin *salix* willow]

salient /ˈseɪlɪənt/ *adj* striking; outstanding or prominent. ▸ *noun* a projecting angle, part or section, eg of a fortification or a defensive line of troops. [16c: from Latin *saliens*]

saline /ˈseɪlaɪn/ *adj* **1** of a substance: containing common salt; salty. **2** of medicines: containing or having the nature of the salts of alkali metals and magnesium. ▸ *noun* (*also* **saline solution**) a solution of sodium chloride in water, having the same pH and concentration as body fluids, used in intravenous drips, etc. ▪ **salinity** *noun*. [15c: from Latin *salinus*]

salinization *or* **salination** *noun, geog* the situation of soil becoming too salty, eg because of flooding by sea water.

saliva *noun* a clear liquid produced by the salivary glands of the mouth, that moistens and softens the food and begins the process of digestion. ▪ **salivary** *adj*. [17c: Latin]

salivary gland *noun* a gland that secretes saliva.

salivate *verb, intr* **1** of the salivary glands: to produce a flow of saliva into the mouth in response to the thought or sight of food. **2** to drool. ▪ **salivation** *noun*. [17c: from Latin *salivare*]

sallow *adj* of a person's complexion: being a pale yellowish colour, often through poor health. ▪ **sallowness** *noun*. [Anglo-Saxon *salo* or *salu*]

sally *noun* (**-ies**) **1** a sudden rushing forward or advance of troops to attack besiegers. **2** an excursion or outing. **3** a witty comment or remark. ▸ *verb* (**-ies, -ied**) *intr* **1** of troops: to carry out a sally. **2** *humorous* (*also* **sally forth**) to rush out or surge forward. **3** to set off on an excursion. [16c: from French *saillie*]

salmon /ˈsamən/ *noun* (***salmon*** *or* ***salmons***) **1** a large silvery fish that migrates to freshwater rivers and streams in order to spawn, highly prized as a food and game fish. **2** the reddish-orange flesh of this fish. **3** (*also* **salmon pink**) an orange-pink colour. ▸ *adj* salmon-coloured: *a salmon jumper*. [13c: from French *saumon*]

salmonella /salməˈnɛlə/ *noun* (***salmonellae*** /-liː/ *or* ***salmonellas***) **1** (**Salmonella**) a form of bacteria that can cause food poisoning. **2** food poisoning caused by such bacteria. [Early 20c: named after Daniel E Salmon, US veterinary surgeon]

salon *noun* **1** a reception room, esp in a large house. **2** a social gathering of distinguished people in a fashionable household. **3** a shop or other business establishment where clients are beautified in some way: *a hairdressing salon*. [18c: French]

saloon *noun* **1** *informal* (*in full* **saloon car**) any motor car with two or four doors and an enclosed compartment. **2** a large public cabin or dining room on a passenger ship. **3** (*also* **saloon bar**) a lounge bar; a quieter and more comfortable part of a public house, sometimes separated from it. **4** *N Am, esp US* any bar where alcohol is sold. [18c: from French *salon*]

salsa *noun* **1** rhythmic music of Latin-American origin, containing elements of jazz and rock. **2** a dance performed to this music. **3** *cookery* a spicy Mexican sauce, made with tomatoes, onions, chillies and oil. [19c: Spanish, meaning 'sauce']

salsify *noun* (**-ies**) **1** a plant with a long white cylindrical tap root and large solitary heads of purple flowers. **2** the edible root of this plant, which can be eaten as a vegetable. [17c: from French *salsifis*]

SALT *abbrev* Strategic Arms Limitation Talks (or Treaty).

salt *noun* **1** **sodium chloride**, esp as used to season and preserve food. **2** *chem* a chemical compound that is formed when an acid reacts with a base. **3** liveliness; interest, wit or good sense: *Her opinion added salt to the debate*. **4** (*also* **old salt**) an experienced and usu old sailor. **5** (**salts**) **smelling salts**. ▸ *adj* containing, tasting of or preserved in salt: *salt water* • *salt pork*. ▸ *verb* **1** to season or preserve (food) with salt. **2** to cover (an icy road) with a scattering of salt to melt the ice. **3** to add piquancy, interest or wit to something. ▪ **salted** *adj*. [Anglo-Saxon]

IDIOMS **rub salt in sb's wounds** to add to their discomfort, sorrow, shame, etc. **take sth with a pinch**

of salt to treat a statement or proposition sceptically, or with suspicion and reservation. **the salt of the earth** a consistently reliable or dependable person. **worth one's salt** competent or useful; worthy of respect.

PHRASAL VERBS **salt sth away** to store it up for future use; to hoard it, esp in a miserly way.

saltation *noun* **1** a leaping or jumping. **2** *genetics* a sudden mutation or variation in a species. **3** *geol* the movement of sand and stones on a river bed when they are transported by water, resembling a series of leaps. ▪ **saltatorial, saltatorious** *or* **saltatory** *adj* **1** leaping or jumping. **2** *biol* displaying genetic saltation. [17c: Latin, from *saltare* to jump around]

saltcellar *noun* a container holding salt when used as a condiment.

salt lick *noun* **1** a place to which animals go in order to obtain salt. **2** an object coated in salt, given to pets with a salt deficiency.

salt marsh *noun* an area of land which is usually, or liable to be, flooded with salt water.

saltpetre *or* (*US*) **saltpeter** *noun* potassium nitrate. [16c: from Latin *salpetra* salt of rock]

salty *adj* (***-ier, -iest***) **1** tasting strongly or excessively of, or containing, salt. **2** of humour: sharp or witty; spirited.

salubrious *adj* **1** *formal* promoting health or wellbeing: *a salubrious climate*. **2** decent or respectable; pleasant: *not a very salubrious neighbourhood*. ▪ **salubriousness** *or* **salubrity** *noun*. [16c: from Latin *salubris*]

salutary *adj* **1** beneficial; bringing or containing a timely warning. **2** promoting health and safety; wholesome. [17c: from Latin *salutaris*]

salutation *noun* **1** a word, act, or gesture of greeting. **2** a conventional form of greeting in a letter. ▪ **salutatory** *adj*. [14c: from Latin *salutare* to greet]

salute *verb* **1** to greet with friendly words or a gesture, esp a kiss. **2** to pay tribute to something or someone: *We salute your bravery.* **3** *intr, military* to pay formal respect to someone or something with a set gesture, esp with the right arm. ▸ *noun* **1** a greeting. **2** a military gesture of respect, for a person or an occasion. [14c: from Latin *salutare* to greet]

salvage *noun* **1** the rescue of a ship or its cargo from the danger of destruction or loss. **2** the reward paid by a ship's owner to those involved in saving the ship from destruction or loss. **3** the rescue of any property from fire or other danger. **4** the saving and utilization of waste material. **5** the property salvaged in such situations. ▸ *verb* **1** to rescue (property or a ship) from potential destruction or loss, eg in a fire or shipwreck, or from disposal as waste. **2** to manage to retain (eg one's pride) in adverse circumstances. ▪ **salvageable** *adj*. [17c: from Latin *salvagium*]

salvation *noun* **1** the act of saving someone or something from harm. **2** a person or thing that saves another from harm. **3** *relig* the liberation or saving of man from the influence of sin, and its consequences for his soul. [13c: from Latin *salvatus* saved]

salve *noun* **1** ointment or remedy to heal or soothe: *lip salve*. **2** anything that comforts, consoles or soothes. ▸ *verb* **1** to smear with salve. **2** to ease or comfort: *salve one's conscience*. [Anglo-Saxon *sealf*]

salver *noun* a small ornamented tray, usu of silver, on which something is presented. [17c: from French *salve* a tray for presenting the king's food for tasting]

salvo *noun* (***salvos*** *or* ***salvoes***) a burst of gunfire from several guns firing simultaneously, as a salute or in battle. [17c: from Italian *salva* salute]

sal volatile /sal vɒ'latɪlɪ/ *noun* a former name for ammonium carbonate, esp in a solution used as smelling salts. [17c: Latin, meaning 'volatile salt']

Samaritan *noun* (*in full* **Good Samaritan**) a kind, considerate or helpful person. [Anglo-Saxon]

samarium *noun, chem* (symbol **Sm**) a soft silvery metallic element, used in alloys with cobalt to make strong permanent magnets. [19c: named after Col Samarski, a Russian engineer and mines inspector]

Sama-veda see **Veda**

samba *noun* **1** a lively Brazilian dance in duple time. **2** a piece of music written for this. [19c: Portuguese]

sambuca /sam'buːkə, -'bʊkə/ *noun* a liquorice-flavoured liqueur made from aniseed. [20c: Italian, from Latin *sambucus* elder tree]

same *adj* **1** identical or very similar: *This is the same film we saw last week.* **2** used as emphasis: *He went home the very same day.* **3** unchanged or unvaried: *This town is still the same as ever.* **4** previously mentioned; the actual one in question: *this same man*. ▸ *pronoun* the same person or thing, or the one previously referred to: *She drank whisky, and I drank the same.* ▸ *adv* (**the same**) **1** similarly; likewise: *I feel the same.* **2** *informal* equally: *We love each of you the same.* ▪ **sameness** *noun*. [12c: from Norse *samr*]

IDIOMS **all** *or* **just the same** nevertheless; anyhow. **at the same time** still; however; on the other hand. **be all the same to sb** to make no difference to them. **same here** *informal* an expression of agreement or involvement.

samey *adj, informal* boringly similar or unchanging; monotonous: *I quite like that band, but I think their songs are a bit samey.*

samizdat *noun* **1** in the former Soviet Union: the secret printing and distribution of writings banned by the government. **2** the writings themselves. [1960s: Russian, meaning 'self-published']

samosa *noun* (***samosas*** *or* ***samosa***) a small deep-fried triangular pastry turnover, of Indian origin, filled with spicy meat or vegetables. [1950s: Hindi]

samovar *noun* a Russian water boiler, used for making tea, etc, often elaborately decorated, and traditionally heated by a central pipe filled with charcoal. [19c: Russian, literally 'self-boiler']

sampan *or* **sanpan** *noun* a small Oriental boat with no engine, which is propelled by oars. [17c: Chinese, from *san* three + *ban* plank]

sample *noun* a small portion or part used to represent the quality and nature of others or of a whole. ▸ *adj* used as or serving as a sample. ▸ *verb* **1** to take or try as a sample. **2** to get experience of something: *He has sampled life abroad.* **3** *pop music* **a** to mix a short extract from one recording into a different backing track; **b** to record a sound and program it into a synthesizer which can then reproduce it at the desired pitch. [13c: from French *essample*]

sampler *noun* **1** a collection of samples. **2** *pop music* the equipment used for sampling sound. **3** a piece of embroidery produced as a show or test of skill. ▪ **sampling** *noun*.

samsara *noun* **1** *Hinduism* the world, where the soul passes into other states. **2** *Buddhism* the never-ending cycle of birth, death and rebirth. [Sanskrit *sasara* passing through]

samurai /'samʊraɪ/ *noun* (*pl* ***samurai***) **1** *hist* an aristocratic caste of Japanese warriors. **2** a member of this caste. **3** a samurai's sword; a two-handed sword with a curved blade. [18c: Japanese]

sanatorium *noun* (***sanatoriums*** *or* ***sanatoria***) **1** a hospital for the chronically ill or convalescents. **2** *Brit* a room for sick people in a boarding school, etc. [19c: Latin, from *sanare* to heal]

sanctify *verb* (***-ies, -ied***) **1** to make, consider or show to be sacred or holy. **2** to set aside for sacred use. **3** to free from sin or evil. **4** to declare legitimate or binding in the eyes of the Church: *sanctify a marriage*. ▪ **sanctification** *noun*. [14c: from French *sanctifier*]

sanctimonious *adj* affecting or simulating holiness or virtuousness, esp hypocritically. ▪ **sanctimoniously** *adv*. ▪ **sanctimoniousness** *or* **sanctimony** *noun*. [17c: from Latin *sanctimonia* sanctity]

sanction *noun* **1** official permission or authority. **2** the act of giving permission or authority. **3** aid; support. **4** (*esp* **sanctions**) *politics* an economic or military measure taken by one nation against another as a means of coercion: *trade sanctions*. ▸ *verb* **1** to authorize or confirm formally. **2** to countenance or permit. [16c: from Latin *sanctio*]

sanctity *noun* (***-ies***) **1** the quality of being holy or sacred. **2** purity or godliness; inviolability. [14c: from French *saincteté*]

sanctuary *noun* (***-ies***) **1** a holy or sacred place, eg a church or temple. **2** the most sacred part of a church or temple, eg around an altar. **3** a place providing protection from arrest, persecution or other interference. **4** a place of private refuge or retreat, away from disturbance: *the sanctuary of the garden*. **5** a nature reserve in which animals or plants are protected by law. [14c: from Latin *sanctuarium*]

sanctum *noun* (***sanctums*** *or* ***sancta***) (*esp* **inner sanctum**) **1** a sacred place. **2** a place providing total privacy. [16c: from Latin *sanctum* holy]

sand *noun* **1** *geol* tiny rounded particles or grains of rock, esp quartz. **2** (**sands**) an area of land covered with these particles or grains, such as a seashore or desert. ▸ *adj* **1** made of sand. **2** having the colour of sand, a light brownish-yellow colour. ▸ *verb* **1** to smooth or polish a surface with sandpaper or a sander. **2** to sprinkle, cover or mix with sand. [Anglo-Saxon]

sandal *noun* a type of lightweight shoe consisting of a sole attached to the foot by straps. [14c: from Latin *sandalium*]

sandalwood *noun, botany* **1** an evergreen tree with red bell-shaped flowers. **2** the hard pale fragrant timber obtained from this tree, which is used for ornamental carving and as an ingredient of incense, and also yields an aromatic oil used in perfumes. [16c: from Sanskrit *candana*]

sandbag *noun* a sack filled with sand or earth, used with others to form a protective barrier against gunfire or floods, or used as ballast. ▸ *verb* to barricade or weigh down with sandbags.

sandbank *or* **sandbar** *noun* a bank of sand in a river, river mouth or sea, formed by currents and often above the water level at low tide.

sandblast *verb* to clean or engrave (glass, metal, stone surfaces, etc) with a jet of sand forced from a tube by air or steam pressure. ▪ **sandblasting** *noun*.

sandcastle *noun* a model of a castle made out of wet sand.

sand- dune *noun* a hill or ridge of sand on a beach or in a desert.

sander *noun* a power-driven tool fitted with sandpaper or an abrasive disc, used for sanding wood, etc.

sandman *noun, folklore* a man who supposedly sprinkles magical sand into children's eyes at bedtime to make them sleepy.

sandpaper *noun* abrasive paper with a coating orig of sand, now usu of crushed glass, glued to one side, used for smoothing and polishing surfaces. ▸ *verb* to smooth or polish with sandpaper.

sandshoe *noun* a shoe with a canvas upper and rubber sole; a plimsoll.

sandstone *noun, geol* a sedimentary rock consisting of compacted sand cemented together with clay, silica, etc, widely used in the construction of buildings.

sandwich *noun* a snack consisting of two slices of bread or a roll with a filling of cheese, meat, etc. ▸ *verb* to place, esp with little or no gaps, between two layers. [18c: named after John Montagu, the 4th Earl of Sandwich, who ate such a snack so that he could remain at the gaming-table]

sandwich board *noun* either of two advertising boards supported by straps over the shoulders of their carrier.

sandwich course *noun* an educational course involving alternate periods of academic study and work experience.

sandy *adj* (***-ier, -iest***) **1** covered with or containing sand. **2** having the colour of sand, a light brownish-yellow colour: *sandy hair*. ▪ **sandiness** *noun*.

sane *adj* **1** sound in mind; not mentally impaired. **2** sensible or rational; sound in judgement. ▪ **sanely** *adv*. ▪ **saneness** *noun*. [17c: from Latin *sanus* healthy]

sang *past tense, past participle of* **sing**

sangfroid /sɒŋ'frwɑː/ *noun* calmness or composure; cool-headedness. [18c: French, meaning 'cold blood']

sangha /sʌŋ'gə/ *noun* **1** the Buddhist community. **2** the Buddhist monastic order. [Sanskrit *samgha* community]

sanguinary *adj* **1** bloody; involving much bloodshed. **2** bloodthirsty; taking pleasure in bloodshed. [17c: from Latin *sanguinarius*]

sanguine /'saŋgwɪn/ *adj* **1** cheerful, confident and full of hope. **2** of a complexion: ruddy or flushed. [14c: from Latin *sanguineus*]

Sanhedrin /san'hɛdrɪn, -'hiːdrɪn, 'sanədrɪn/ *or* **Sanhedrim** /-drɪm/ *noun, hist* a Jewish council or court, especially the supreme council and court in Jerusalem. [16c: Hebrew, from Greek *synedrion*]

sanitary *adj* **1** concerned with and promoting hygiene, good health and the prevention of disease. **2** relating to health, esp drainage and sewage disposal. ▪ **sanitarily** *adv*. [19c: from French *sanitaire*]

sanitary towel *or* (*US*) **sanitary napkin** *noun* an absorbent pad worn during menstruation.

sanitation *noun* **1** standards of public hygiene. **2** measures taken to promote and preserve public health, esp through drainage and sewage disposal.

sanitize *or* **-ise** *verb* **1** to make hygienic or sanitary. **2** to make less controversial or more acceptable by removing potentially offensive elements, etc.

sanity *noun* **1** soundness of mind; rationality. **2** good sense and reason. [15c: from Latin *sanitas* health]

sank *past tense, past participle of* **sink**

sanpan see **sampan**

sans /sanz; *French* sɑ̃/ *prep* without.

sansculotte /sanzkjʊ'lɒt, sanzkʊ'lɒt/ *noun* **1** *hist* a nickname for an extreme republican during the French Revolution. **2** an extremist or violent revolutionary. [18c: **sans** + French *culotte* knee breeches]

sanserif *or* **sans serif** /san'sɛrɪf/ *noun, printing* a type in which the letters have no serifs.

Sanskrit *noun* the ancient Indo-European religious and literary language of India. *as adj*: *Sanskrit texts.* [17c: from Sanskrit *samskrta* perfected]

sap[1] *noun* **1** *botany* a vital liquid containing sugars and other nutrients that circulates in plants. **2** energy or vitality. **3** *slang* a weak or easily fooled person. ▸ *verb* (***sapped, sapping***) **1** to drain or extract sap from something. **2** to weaken or exhaust; to drain energy from something. [Anglo-Saxon *sæp*]

sap[2] *noun* a hidden trench by which an attack is made on an enemy position. ▸ *verb* (***sapped, sapping***) **1** *intr* to attack by means of a sap. **2** to undermine or weaken. [16c: from French *sape*]

sapient /'seɪpɪənt/ *adj, formal, often ironic* having or showing good judgement; wise. ▪ **sapience** *noun.* ▪ **sapiently** *adv.* [14c: from Latin *sapientia*]

sapling *noun* a young tree.

saponify *verb* (***-ies, -ied***) *chem* to carry out a process where an alkali is used to convert fats into soap. ▪ **saponification** *noun.* [19c: from French *saponifier*]

sapper *noun* **1** *Brit* a soldier in the Royal Engineers. **2** a soldier responsible for making saps (**sap**[2]).

sapphire /'safaɪə(r)/ *noun* **1** a hard transparent blue stone, prized as a gemstone. **2** the deep blue colour of this stone. ▸ *adj* having the colour of sapphire. [13c: from Latin *sapphirus*, from Greek *sappheiros*, from Sanskrit *sanipriya* dear to the planet Saturn]

sappy *adj* (***-ier, -iest***) **1** of plants: full of sap. **2** full of energy. ▪ **sappiness** *noun.*

saprogenic *or* **saprogenous** *adj, biol* **1** growing on decaying matter. **2** causing or caused by putrefaction or decay. [19c: from Greek *sapros* rotten + *-genic* producing]

saprophyte *noun, biol* a plant, esp a fungus, that feeds on dead and decaying organic matter. ▪ **saprophytic** *adj.* [19c: from Greek *sapros* rotten + *phyton* plant]

saprozoic *adj, biol* said of organisms: feeding on dead or decaying organic matter. [20c: from Greek *sapros* rotten + Greek *zoion* animal]

saraband *or* **sarabande** *noun* **1** a slow formal Spanish dance. **2** a piece of music written for this dance. [17c: from Spanish *zarabanda*]

sarcasm *noun* **1** an often ironical expression of scorn or contempt. **2** the use of such an expression. [16c: from Latin *sarcasmus*]

sarcastic *adj* **1** containing sarcasm. **2** tending to use sarcasm. ▪ **sarcastically** *adv.*

sarcoma *noun* (***sarcomas*** *or* ***sarcomata***) *pathol* a cancerous tumour arising in connective tissue. [17c: from Greek *sarkoma* fleshy growth]

sarcophagus /sɑː'kɒfəgəs/ *noun* (***sarcophagi*** /-gaɪ/ *or* ***sarcophaguses***) a stone coffin or tomb. [17c: from Greek *sarkophagos* flesh-eating]

sardine *noun* (***sardines*** *or* ***sardine***) a young pilchard, an important food fish, commonly tinned in oil. [15c: French]

sardonic *adj* mocking or scornful; sneering. ▪ **sardonically** *adv.* [16c: from French *sardonique*]

sardonyx *noun, geol* a gem variety of **chalcedony** with alternating straight parallel bands of colour, usu white and reddish-brown. [14c: Greek]

sargasso *noun* (***sargassos*** *or* ***sargassoes***) a brown seaweed with branching ribbon-like fronds that floats freely in huge masses. [Early 20c: from Portuguese *sargaço*]

sarge *noun, informal* esp as a form of address: sergeant.

sari *or* **saree** *noun* (***saris*** *or* ***sarees***) a traditional garment of Hindu women, consisting of a single long piece of fabric wound round the waist and draped over one shoulder and sometimes the head. [16c: Hindi]

sarking *noun* a lining for a roof, usu made of wood or felt. [Anglo-Saxon *serc*]

sarky *adj* (***-ier, -iest***) *informal* sarcastic.

sarnie *noun, informal* a sandwich. [1960s: shortened from 'sandwich']

sarong *noun* **1** a Malay garment worn by both sexes, consisting of a long piece of fabric wrapped around the waist or chest. **2** a Western adaptation of this garment, often worn by women as beachwear. [19c: from Malay *sarung*]

SARS /sɑːz/ *abbrev, med* Severe Acute Respiratory Disease, a contagious lung infection, the main symptoms of which are high fever, dry cough, shortness of breath or breathing difficulties. [Early 21c]

sarsaparilla *noun* **1** a climbing tropical American plant with greenish or yellowish flowers. **2** *US* a non-alcoholic drink flavoured with the dried aromatic root of this plant, used as a tonic. [16c: from Spanish *zarzaparilla*]

sartorial *adj* referring or relating to a tailor, tailoring or clothes in general: *sartorial elegance.* ▪ **sartorially** *adv.* [19c: from Latin *sartor* a patcher]

sash[1] *noun* a broad band of cloth, worn round the waist or over the shoulder, orig as part of a uniform. [16c: from Arabic *shash* muslin]

sash[2] *noun* a glazed frame, esp a sliding one, forming a **sash window**. [17c: from French *châssis* frame]

sashay *verb, intr* to walk or move in a gliding or ostentatious way. [19c: an alteration of French *chassé*]

sash cord *noun* a cord attaching a weight to the sash (**sash**[2]) in order to balance it at any height.

sashimi *noun* a Japanese dish of thinly sliced raw fish. [19c: from Japanese *sashi* pierce + *mi* flesh]

sash window *noun* a window consisting of two sashes (**sash**[2]), one of which can slide vertically past the other.

sass *US informal, noun* impertinent talk or behaviour. ▸ *verb, intr* to speak or behave impertinently. ▪ **sassy** *adj* (***-ier, -iest***).

sassafras *noun* **1** a deciduous N American tree with long clusters of greenish-yellow flowers. **2** the aromatic dried bark obtained from the roots of this tree, which yields a pungent oil used in medicines and as a flavouring. [16c: from Spanish *sasafrás*]

Sassenach /'sasənax, -ak/ *noun, Scot, usu derog* an English person. ▸ *adj* English. [18c: from Gaelic *Sasunnach*]

SAT *abbrev, education* **1** in the US: scholastic aptitude test. **2** in the UK: standard assessment task.

Sat. *abbrev* Saturday.

sat *past tense, past participle of* **sit**

Satan *noun* the Devil. [Anglo-Saxon]

satanic *or* **satanical** *adj* **1** referring or relating to Satan. **2** evil; abominable. ▪ **satanically** *adv.*

Satanism *noun* (*also* **satanism**) the worship of Satan. ▪ **Satanist** *noun, adj.*

satchel *noun* a small briefcase-like bag for schoolbooks, often leather, and usu with shoulder straps. [14c: from French *sachel* little bag]

sate *verb* to satisfy (a longing or appetite) to the full or to excess. [Anglo-Saxon *sadian*]

satellite *noun* **1** a celestial body that orbits a much larger celestial body, eg the Moon is a satellite of the Earth. **2** a man-made device launched into space by a rocket, etc, and placed in orbit around a planet, esp the Earth, used for communication, photography, etc. **3** a nation or state dependent, esp economically or politically, on a larger neighbour. [16c: from Latin *satelles* attendant]

---

satellite

This word is often misspelt. It has one *t* and two *l*'s. It might help you to remember the following sentence: ***Tell** me what a sa**tell**ite is.*

---

satellite dish *noun* a saucer-shaped aerial for receiving television signals broadcast by satellite.

satellite TV, satellite television *or* **satellite broadcasting** *noun, telecomm* the broadcasting of television by means of an artificial satellite.

sati see **suttee**

satiable /'seɪʃəbəl/ *adj* able to be satisfied or satiated.

satiate /'seɪʃɪeɪt/ *verb* to gratify fully; to satisfy to excess. ▪ **satiation** *noun.* [15c: from Latin *satiare*]

satiety /sə'taɪətɪ/ *noun* the state of being satiated.

satin *noun* silk or rayon closely woven to produce a shiny finish, showing much of the warp. ▸ *adj* similar to or resembling satin. ▪ **satiny** *adj.* [14c: from *Zaitun*, Arabic name of the Chinese town (prob Quanzhou) where it was orig produced]

satinwood *noun* **1** a shiny light-coloured hardwood used for fine furniture. **2** the tree that yields it.

satire *noun* **1** a literary composition, orig in verse, which holds up follies and vices for criticism, ridicule and scorn. **2** the use of sarcasm, irony, wit, humour, etc in such compositions. **3** satirical writing as a genre. ▪ **satirical** *adj.* ▪ **satirist** *noun.* [16c: from Latin *satira* mixture]

satirize *or* **-ise** *verb* **1** *intr* to write satire. **2** to mock, ridicule or criticize using satire. ▪ **satirization** *noun.*

satisfaction *noun* **1** the act of satisfying, or the state or feeling of being satisfied. **2** something that satisfies. **3** gratification or comfort. **4** compensation for mistreatment or an insult.

satisfactory *adj* **1** adequate or acceptable. **2** giving satisfaction. ▪ **satisfactorily** *adv.*

satisfy *verb* (**-ies, -ied**) **1** *intr* to fulfil the needs, desires or expectations of someone. **2** to give enough to or be enough for someone or something. **3** to meet the requirements or conditions of someone or something. **4** to remove the doubts of someone. ▪ **satisfying** *adj.* [15c: from French *satisfier*]

satrap *noun* a viceroy or governor of an ancient Persian province. [14c: from Greek *satrapes*]

satsuma *noun* **1** a thin-skinned seedless type of mandarin orange. **2** the tree that bears this fruit. [19c: named after *Satsuma*, a former province in Japan]

saturate *verb* **1** to soak. **2** to fill or cover with a large amount of something. **3** to charge (air or vapour) with moisture to the fullest extent possible. **4** *chem* to add a solid, liquid or gas to (a solution) until no more of that substance can be dissolved at a given temperature. [16c: from Latin *saturare*]

saturated *adj* **1** *chem* of a solution: containing as much of a solute as can be dissolved at a particular temperature and pressure. **2** *chem* of a chemical, especially a fat: containing no double bonds between carbon atoms in the molecule, and therefore unable to combine with atoms of other substances. **3** thoroughly wet or soaked.

saturation *noun* **1** the state of being saturated; saturating. **2** *chem* the point at which a solution contains the maximum possible amount of dissolved solid, liquid or gas at a given temperature.

saturation point *noun* **1** a limit beyond which no more can be added. **2** *chem* same as **saturation** (sense 2).

Saturday *noun* (abbrev **Sat.**) the seventh day of the week. [Anglo-Saxon *Sæterndæg* Saturn's day]

Saturn *noun, astron* the sixth planet from the Sun. [Anglo-Saxon]

saturnalia *noun* a scene of rowdy celebration; an orgy. ▪ **saturnalian** *adj.* [16c: Latin *Saturnalia*, the Roman winter festival in honour of the god Saturn]

saturnine *adj* having a grave and gloomy temperament; melancholy in character. [15c]

satyr /'satə(r)/ *noun* **1** *Greek myth* a lecherous woodland god, part man, part goat. **2** a lustful or lecherous man. [14c: from Latin *satyrus*]

sauce *noun* **1** any liquid, often thickened, cooked or served with food. **2** anything that adds relish, interest or excitement. **3** *informal* impertinent language or behaviour; cheek. **4** *US* stewed fruit. [14c: French]

sauce boat *noun* a long shallow container from which sauce is poured over food.

saucepan *noun* a deep cooking pot with a long handle and usu a lid. [17c: so called as it was orig used only for making sauces]

saucer *noun* **1** a shallow round dish, esp one for placing under a cup. **2** anything of a similar shape. [14c: from French *saussiere*]

saucy *adj* (**-ier, -iest**) *informal* **1** similar to or tasting of sauce. **2** impertinent or cheeky; bold or forward. **3** referring to sex, esp in an amusing way: *saucy postcards.* ▪ **saucily** *adv.* ▪ **sauciness** *noun.*

sauerkraut /'saʊəkraʊt/ *noun* a popular German dish, consisting of shredded cabbage pickled in salt water. [17c: German, literally 'sour cabbage']

sauna *noun* **1** a Finnish-style bath where the person is exposed to dry heat, with occasional short blasts of steam created by pouring water on hot coals. **2** a building or room equipped for this. [19c: Finnish]

saunter *verb, intr* to walk, often aimlessly, at a leisurely pace. ▸ *noun* a leisurely walk or stroll. [17c]

saurian *adj, zool* referring or relating to lizards. [19c: from Greek *sauros* lizard]

sausage *noun* **1** a mass of chopped or minced seasoned meat, esp pork or beef, sometimes with fat, cereal, vegetables, etc, and stuffed into a tube of gut. **2** any object of a similar shape. [15c: from French *saussiche*]

sausage dog *noun, informal* a **dachshund**.

sausage roll *noun, Brit* sausage meat baked in a roll of pastry.

sauté /'souteɪ/ *verb* (***sautéed, sautéing*** *or* ***sautéeing***) to fry lightly for a short time. ▸ *noun* a dish of sautéed food. ▸ *adj* fried in this way: *sauté potatoes.* [19c: French, meaning 'tossed']

savage *adj* **1** of animals: untamed or undomesticated. **2** ferocious or furious: *He has a savage temper.* **3** of eg behaviour: uncivilized; coarse. **4** cruel; barbaric. **5** of land: uncultivated; wild and rugged. ▸ *noun* **1** *now offensive* a member of a primitive people. **2** an uncultured, fierce or cruel person. ▸ *verb* to attack ferociously, esp with the teeth, causing severe injury. ▪ **savagely** *adv.* ▪ **savageness** *noun.* [14c: from French *sauvage* wild]

savanna *or* **savannah** *noun* an expanse of level grassland, often dotted with trees and bushes, characteristic esp of Africa. [16c: from Spanish *zavana*]

savant /'savənt or *French* 'savɑ̃/ *or* **savante** /'savənt or *French* 'savɑ̃t/ *noun* a wise and learned man or woman respectively. [18c: French]

save *verb* **1** to rescue, protect or preserve someone or something from danger, evil, loss or failure. **2** to use economically so as to prevent or avoid waste or loss. **3** *intr* (*also* **save up**) to be economical, esp with money: *We're saving up for a holiday abroad next year.* **4** to reserve or store for later use. **5** to spare from potential unpleasantness or inconvenience: *That will save you having to make another trip.* **6** to obviate or prevent. **7** *sport* to prevent (a ball or shot) from reaching the goal; to prevent (a goal) from being scored by the opposing team. **8** *tr & intr, relig* to deliver from the influence or consequences of sin; to act as a saviour. **9** *comput* to transfer (data, the contents of a computer file, etc) onto a disk or tape for storage. ▸ *noun* **1** an act of saving a ball or shot, or of preventing a goal: *He made a great save in that match.* **2** *comput* the saving of data onto a disk or tape. ▸ *prep* (*sometimes* **save for**) except: *We found all the tickets save one.* ▪ **savable** *or* **saveable** *adj.* ▪ **saver** *noun.* [13c: from French *sauver*]

IDIOMS **save one's** *or* **sb's face** to prevent oneself or them from appearing foolish or wrong; to avoid humiliation. **save one's** *or* **sb's skin** *or* **neck** to save one's or their life. **save the day** to prevent something from disaster, failure, etc.

saveloy /'savəlɔɪ/ *noun* a spicy smoked pork sausage. [19c: from French *cervelat*]

saving *verb, present participle of* **save**. ▸ *adj* **1** protecting or preserving. **2** economical or frugal. ▸ *noun* **1** something saved, esp an economy made. **2** anything saved. **3** (**savings**) money set aside for future use.

saving grace *noun* a desirable virtue or feature that compensates for undesirable ones.

saviour *or* (*N Am*) **savior** *noun* **1** a person who saves someone or something else from danger or destruction. **2** (**the Saviour**) *Christianity* Christ. [14c: from French *sauveour*]

savoir-faire /savwɑː'fɛə(r)/ *noun* instinctively knowing exactly what to do and how to do it; expertise. [19c: French, literally 'to know what to do']

savory *noun* (***-ies***) *botany* **1** a plant with paired narrow leaves and loose spikes of two-lipped purplish or white flowers. **2** the leaves of certain species of this plant, used as a culinary herb. [Anglo-Saxon *soetherie*]

savour *or* (*N Am*) **savor** *noun* **1** the characteristic taste or smell of something. **2** a faint but unmistakable quality. ▸ *verb* **1** to taste or smell with relish. **2** to take pleasure in something. **3** to flavour or season. **4** to relish. **5** (*chiefly* **savour of sth**) to show signs of it; to smack of it. ▪ **savourless** *or* (*N Am*) **savorless** *adj.* [13c: from French *savour*]

savoury *or* (*N Am*) **savory** *adj* **1** having a salty, sharp or piquant taste or smell: *a savoury snack.* **2** having a good savour or relish; appetizing. **3** pleasant or attractive, esp morally pleasing or respectable. ▸ *noun* (***-ies***) a savoury course or snack. ▪ **savouriness** *or* (*N Am*) **savoriness** *noun.* [14c: from French *savure*]

savoy *noun* (*in full* **savoy cabbage**) a winter variety of cabbage with a large compact head and wrinkled leaves. [16c: from French *Savoie*, in SE France]

savvy *slang, verb* (***-ies, -ied***) *tr & intr* to know or understand. ▸ *noun* **1** general ability or common sense; shrewdness. **2** skill; know-how. [18c: from Spanish *saber* to know]

saw[1] *past tense of* **see**[1]

saw[2] *noun* any of various toothed cutting tools, either hand-operated or power-driven, used esp for cutting wood. ▸ *verb* (*past participle* ***sawn*** *or* ***sawed***) **1** to cut with, or as if with, a saw. **2** to shape by sawing. **3** *intr* to use a saw. **4** *intr* to make to-and-fro movements, as if using a handsaw. [Anglo-Saxon *sagu*]

sawdust *noun* small particles of wood, made by sawing.

sawmill *noun* a factory in which timber is cut into planks.

sawn-off *or* (*esp US*) **sawed off** *adj* shortened by cutting with a saw: *sawn-off shotgun.*

sawyer /'sɔːjə(r)/ *noun* a person who saws timber, esp in a sawmill.

sax *noun, informal* short for **saxophone**.

Saxon *noun* **1** a member of a Germanic people which conquered Britain in 5c and 6c. **2** any of various Germanic dialects spoken by this people. ▸ *adj* referring or relating to the Saxons, the **Anglo-Saxon**s, their language or culture. [13c: from Latin *Saxones*]

saxophone *noun* a single-reeded wind instrument with a long S-shaped metal body, usu played in jazz and dance bands. Often shortened to **sax**. ▪ **saxophonist** /sak'sɒfənɪst/ *noun.* [19c: named after Adolphe Sax, the Belgian instrument maker who invented it]

say *verb* (***said***) **1** to speak, utter or articulate: *He said he would come.* **2** to express in words: *Say what you* *mean.* **3** to assert or declare; to state as an opinion: *I say we should give it a try.* **4** to suppose: *Say he doesn't come, what do we do then?* **5** to recite or repeat: *say your prayers.* **6** to judge or decide: *It's difficult to say which is best.* **7** to convey information: *She talked for ages but didn't actually say much.* **8** to indicate: *The clock says 10 o'clock.* **9** to report or claim: *Elvis Presley is said by some to be still alive.* **10** *tr & intr* to make a statement; to tell: *I'd rather not say.* ▸ *noun* **1** a chance to express an opinion: *You've had your say.* **2** the right to an opinion; the power to influence a decision: *to have no say in the matter.* ▸ *exclam, N Am, esp US* **1** an expression of surprise, protest or sudden joy. **2** a way of attracting attention. [Anglo-Saxon *secgan*]

IDIOMS **I'll say!** *informal* an expression of wholehearted agreement. **I say!** *esp Brit* an exclamation used for attracting attention, or expressing surprise, protest or sudden joy. **say the word** give the signal or go-ahead: *If you want me to go with you, just say the word.* **that is to say** in other words. **there's no saying** it is impossible to guess or judge: *There's no saying how long she'll take to recover.* **to say nothing of sth** not to mention it: *He wastes all his money on alcohol, to say nothing of all those cigarettes.* **to say the least** at least; without exaggeration: *She is, to say the least, a rather irresponsible person.* **what do you say to?** would you like? how about?: *What do you say to a mug of hot chocolate?* **you can say that again!** *informal* you are absolutely right!

saying *noun* a proverb or maxim.

say-so *noun* **1** an authorized decision. **2** an unsupported claim or assertion.

Sb *symbol, chem* antimony. [From Latin *stibium*]

Sc *symbol, chem* scandium.

scab *noun* **1** a crust of dried blood formed over a healing wound. **2** a contagious skin disease of sheep caused esp by mites, characterized by pustules or scales. **3** a plant disease caused by a fungus, producing crusty spots. **4** *derog, slang* a worker who defies a union's instruction to strike. ▸ *verb* (***scabbed, scabbing***) *intr* **1** (*also* **scab over**) to become covered by a scab. **2** *slang* to work or behave as a scab. [Anglo-Saxon *sceabb*]

scabbard *noun* a sheath, esp for a sword or dagger. [13c: from French *escaubers*]

scabby *adj* (***-ier, -iest***) **1** covered with scabs. **2** *derog, informal* contemptible; worthless. ▪ **scabbiness** *noun.*

scabies /'skeɪbiːz/ *noun, pathol* a contagious skin disease characterized by severe itching, caused by a secretion of the itch mite, which bores under the skin to lay its eggs. [15c: Latin, from *scabere* to scratch]

scabrous /'skeɪbrəs/ *adj* **1** of skin, etc: rough and flaky or scaly; scurfy. **2** bawdy; smutty or indecent. [17c: from Latin *scabrosus*]

scaffold *noun* **1** a temporary framework of metal poles and planks used as a platform from which building repairs or construction can be carried out. **2** any temporary platform. **3** a raised platform for eg performers or spectators. **4** (**the scaffold**) a platform on which a person is executed. [14c: from French *escadafault*]

scaffolding *noun* **1** a temporary scaffold or arrangement of scaffolds. **2** materials used for building scaffolds.

scalar *maths, adj* denoting a quantity that has magnitude but not direction, such as distance, speed and mass. ▸ *noun* a scalar quantity. Compare **vector**. [17c: from Latin *scalaris*]

scald *verb* **1** to injure with hot liquid or steam. **2** to treat with hot water so as to sterilize. **3** to cook or heat to just short of boiling point. ▸ *noun* an injury caused by scalding. ▪ **scalding** *noun, adj.* [13c: from French *escalder*]

scale[1] *noun* **1** a series of markings or divisions at regular intervals, for use in measuring. **2** a system of such markings or divisions. **3** a measuring device with such markings. **4** the relationship between actual size and the size as represented on a model or drawing. **5** *music* **a** a sequence of definite notes; **b** (*usu* **scales**) a succession of these notes performed in ascending or descending order of pitch through one or more octaves. **6** any graded system, eg of employees' salaries. **7** *maths* a numeral system: *logarithmic scale.* **8** extent or level relative to others: *on a grand scale.* ▸ *verb* **1** to climb. **2** (*also* **scale up** and **scale down**) to change something's size according to scale, making it either bigger or smaller than the original. [15c: from Latin *scala* ladder]

IDIOMS **on a large, small,** *etc* **scale** in a great, small, etc way. **to scale** in proportion to the actual dimensions.

scale[2] *noun* **1** any of the small thin plates that provide a protective covering on the skin of fish and reptiles and on the legs of birds. **2** any readily or easily detached flake. **3** tartar on the teeth. **4** a crusty white deposit formed when hard water is heated, esp in kettles. ▸ *verb* **1** to clear something of scales. **2** to remove in thin layers. **3** *intr* to come off in thin layers or flakes. **4** *intr* to become encrusted with scale. ▪ **scaleless** *adj.* ▪ **scaly** *adj* (***-ier, -iest***). [14c: from French *escale* husk]

scale[3] *noun* **1** (**scales**) a device for weighing. **2** the pan, or either of the two pans, of a balance. **3** (**the Scales**) *astron, astrol* same as **Libra**. ▸ *verb* to weigh or weigh up. [13c: from Norse *skal* pan of a balance]

scalene *adj, geom* of a triangle: having each side a different length. [18c: from Greek *skalenos* uneven]

scallion *noun* a spring onion. [14c: from French *escalogne*]

scallop, scollop *or* **escallop** *noun* **1** a marine bivalve mollusc with a strongly ribbed shell consisting of two valves with wavy edges. **2** either of these shells, esp when served filled with food. **3** any of a series of curves forming a wavy edge, eg on fabric. **4** *cookery* an **escalope**. ▸ *verb* to shape (an edge) into scallops or curves. [14c: from French *escalope*]

scallywag *noun, informal* a rascal or scamp; a good-for-nothing. [19c]

scalp *noun* **1** the area of the head covered, or usu covered, by hair. **2** the skin itself on which the hair grows. **3** a piece of this skin with its hair, formerly taken from slain enemies as a trophy, esp by Native Americans. ▸ *verb* **1** to remove the scalp of someone or something. **2** *chiefly US informal* to buy cheaply in order to resell quickly at a profit. [14c: from Norse *skalpr* sheath]

scalpel *noun* a small surgical knife with a thin blade. [18c: from Latin *scalpellum* small knife]

scam *noun, slang* a trick or swindle.

scamp *noun* a cheeky or mischievous person, esp a child. [18c: from French *escamper* to decamp]

scamper *verb, intr* to run or skip about briskly, esp in play. ▸ *noun* an act of scampering.

scampi *plural noun* large prawns. ▸ *singular noun* a dish of these prawns, usu deep-fried in breadcrumbs. [1920s: from pl of Italian *scampo* shrimp]

scan *verb* (***scanned, scanning***) **1** to read through or examine something carefully or critically. **2** to look or glance over something quickly. **3** to examine (all parts or components of something) in a systematic order. **4** to examine (the rhythm of a piece of verse); to analyse (verse) metrically. **5** to recite (verse) so as to bring out or emphasize the metrical structure. **6** *intr* of verse: to conform to the rules of metre or rhythm. **7** *med* to examine (parts, esp internal organs, of the body) using techniques such as ultrasound. **8** *comput* to examine (data) eg on a magnetic disk. ▸ *noun* **1** an act of scanning. **2** a scanning. **3** *med* an image obtained by scanning. [14c: from Latin *scandere* to climb]

scandal *noun* **1** widespread public outrage and loss of reputation. **2** any event or fact causing this. **3** any extremely objectionable fact, situation, person or thing. **4** malicious gossip or slander; a false imputation. ▪ **scandalous** *adj*. [13c: from Latin *scandalum*]

scandalize *or* **-ise** *verb* **1** to give or cause scandal or offence. **2** to shock or outrage.

scandalmonger *noun* someone who spreads or relishes malicious gossip.

Scandinavian *noun* **1** a citizen or inhabitant of, or a person born in, Scandinavia, the area of N Europe consisting of Norway, Sweden, Denmark, and often also including Finland and Iceland. **2** any of the group of N Germanic languages spoken in Scandinavia. ▸ *adj* belonging or relating to Scandinavia, its inhabitants or their languages. [18c]

scandium *noun, chem* (symbol **Sc**) a soft silvery-white metallic element with a pinkish tinge. [19c: named after Scandinavia, where it was discovered]

scanner *noun* **1** *radar* the rotating aerial by which the beam is made to scan an area. **2** *comput* any device capable of recognizing characters, etc, in documents and generating signals corresponding to them, used esp to input text and graphics directly without the need for laborious keying. **3** *med* any device that produces an image of an internal organ, eg in order to locate a tumour.

scansion *noun* **1** the act or practice of scanning poetry. **2** the division of a verse into metrical feet. [17c: from Latin *scansio*]

scant *adj* in short supply; deficient. ▸ *adv* barely; scantily. [14c: from Norse *skamt*]

scanty *adj* (***-ier, -iest***) small or lacking in size or amount; barely enough: *a scanty meal*. ▪ **scantily** *adv*. ▪ **scantiness** *noun*. [17c]

scapegoat *noun* someone made to take the blame or punishment for the errors and mistakes of others. [16c: from **escape** + **goat**, invented by William Tindale, as a translation of the Hebrew *azazel*, incorrectly believed to mean 'the goat that escapes']

scapula /ˈskapjʊlə/ *noun* (***scapulae*** /-liː/ *or* ***scapulas***) *anatomy* the broad flat triangular bone at the back of the shoulder. Also called **shoulder blade**. [16c: Latin]

scapular *adj, anatomy* relating to the scapula. ▸ *noun* a monk's garment which hangs loosely over a habit in front and behind. [Anglo-Saxon]

scar[1] /skɑː/ *noun* **1** a mark left on the skin after a sore or wound has healed. **2** any permanent damaging emotional effect. **3** any mark or blemish. **4** a mark on a plant where a leaf was formerly attached. ▸ *verb* (***scarred, scarring***) *tr & intr* to mark or become marked with a scar. [14c: from French *escare*]

scar[2] *noun* a steep rocky outcrop or crag on the side of a hill or mountain. [14c: from Norse *sker* low reef]

scarab /ˈskarəb/ *noun* **1** a dung beetle, which was regarded as sacred by the ancient Egyptians. **2** an image or carving of the sacred beetle, or a gemstone carved in its shape. [16c: from Latin *scarabaeus*]

scarce *adj* **1** not often found; rare. **2** in short supply. ▸ *adv* scarcely; hardly ever: *We could scarce see it through the mist*. [13c: from French *eschars* niggardly]

IDIOMS **make oneself scarce** *informal* to leave quickly or stay away, often for reasons of tact, etc.

scarcely *adv* **1** only just. **2** hardly ever. **3** not really; not at all: *That is scarcely a reason to hit him*.

scarcity /ˈskɛəsətɪ/ *noun* (***-ies***) **1** a scarce state or fact. **2** a short supply or lack.

scare *verb* **1** *tr & intr* to make or become afraid. **2** to startle. **3** (*usu* **scare sb** *or* **sth away** *or* **off**) to drive them away by frightening them. ▸ *noun* **1** a fright or panic. **2** a sudden, widespread and often unwarranted public alarm: *a bomb scare*. [12c: from Norse *skirra* to avoid]

scarecrow *noun* **1** a device, usu in the shape of a human figure, set up in fields to scare birds. **2** *informal* a shabbily dressed person. [16c]

scaremonger *noun* an alarmist, or someone who causes panic or alarm by initiating or spreading rumours of disaster. ▪ **scaremongering** *noun*.

scarf[1] *noun* (***scarves*** *or* ***scarfs***) a strip or square of fabric, worn around the neck, shoulders or head. [16c: perhaps from French *escarpe* sash or sling]

scarf[2] *noun* a joint made between two ends, esp of timber, cut so as to fit with overlapping, producing the effect of a continuous surface. ▸ *verb* to join by means of a scarf-joint. [15c: from Norse *skarfr*]

scarify *verb* (***-ies, -ied***) **1** *chiefly surgery* to make a number of scratches, shallow cuts, or lacerations in (the skin, etc). **2** to break up the surface of soil with a wire rake, etc, without turning the soil over. **3** to hurt someone with severe criticism. ▪ **scarification** *noun*. [16c: from Latin *scarificare*]

scarlatina *noun, pathol* **scarlet fever**. [19c: from Italian *scarlattina*]

scarlet *noun* a brilliant red colour. [13c: from French *escarlate*]

scarlet fever *noun* an acute infectious disease, caused by bacterial infection, and characterized by fever, sore throat, vomiting and a bright red skin rash.

scarp *noun* **1** the steep side of a hill or rock; an escarpment. **2** *fortification* the inner side of a defensive ditch, nearest to the rampart. [16c: from Italian *scarpa*]

scarper *verb, intr, informal* to run away or escape. [19c: from Italian *scappare* to escape]

SCART plug /skɑːt/ *noun* a plug with 21 pins, used to connect parts of a video or audio system. [20c: acronym from French *Syndicat des Constructeurs des*

Appareils Radiorécepteurs et Téléviseurs, the European syndicate that developed it]

scarves *pl of* **scarf**[1]

scary *adv* (*-ier, -iest*) *informal* causing fear or anxiety; frightening. ▪ **scarily** *adv.* ▪ **scariness** *noun.*

scat[1] *verb* (***scatted, scatting***) *intr, informal* esp as a command: to go away; to run off. [19c: from the noise of a hiss + **cat**, used to drive cats away]

scat[2] *noun* a form of jazz singing consisting of improvised sounds rather than words. ▸ *verb* (***scatted, scatting***) *intr* to sing jazz in this way. [1920s]

scathing *adj* scornfully critical; detrimental: *a scathing attack*. [18c: from Norse *skathe* injury]

scatology *noun* a morbid interest in or preoccupation with the obscene, esp with excrement, or with literature referring to it. ▪ **scatological** *adj.* [19c: from Greek *skor* dung]

scatter *verb* **1** to disperse. **2** to strew, sprinkle or throw around loosely. **3** *tr & intr* to depart or send off in different directions. ▸ *noun* **1** an act of scattering. **2** a quantity of scattered items; a scattering. [12c: a variant of *schateren* to **shatter**]

scatterbrain *noun, informal* a person incapable of organized thought. ▪ **scatterbrained** *adj.* [18c]

scatter graph *or* **diagram** *noun, maths* a graph which shows the distribution of measurements of two random variables, showing them as paired values plotted as points against a set of axes.

scattering *noun* **1** dispersion. **2** something that is scattered. **3** a small amount. **4** *physics* the deflection of photons or particles as a result of collisions with other particles.

scatty *adj* (*-ier, -iest*) *Brit informal* mentally disorganized. [Early 20c: a shortening of *scatterbrained*]

scavenge *verb, tr & intr* to search among waste for (usable items).

scavenger *noun* **1** a person who searches among waste for usable items. **2** an animal that feeds on refuse or decaying flesh. [16: from French *scawage* inspection]

scenario *noun* **1** a rough outline of a dramatic work, film, etc; a synopsis. **2** any hypothetical situation or sequence of events. [19c: Italian]

scene *noun* **1** the setting in which a real or imaginary event takes place. **2** the representation of action on the stage. **3** a division of a play, indicated by the fall of the curtain, a change of place or the entry or exit of an important character. **4** a unit of action in a book or film. **5** any of the pieces making up a stage or film set, or the set as a whole. **6** a landscape, situation or picture of a place or action as seen by someone: *A delightful scene met their eyes.* **7** an embarrassing and unseemly display of emotion in public: *make a scene.* **8** *informal* the publicity, action, etc surrounding a particular activity or profession: *the current music scene.* **9** *informal* a liked or preferred area of interest or activity: *Rock concerts are just not my scene.* [16c: from Latin *scena*]

IDIOMS **behind the scenes 1** out of sight of the audience; backstage. **2** unknown to the public; in private. **set the scene** to describe the background to an event.

scenery *noun* (*-ies*) **1** a picturesque landscape, esp one that is attractively rural. **2** the items making up a stage or film set.

scenic *adj* referring to, being or including attractive natural landscapes: *the scenic route*. [17c: from Latin *scenicus*]

scent *noun* **1** the distinctive smell of a person, animal or plant. **2** a trail of this left behind. **3** a series of clues or findings leading to a major discovery: *The police are on the scent of the drug baron.* **4** perfume. ▸ *verb* **1** to smell; to discover or discern by smell. **2** to sense; to be aware of something by instinct or intuition. **3** *intr* to give out a smell, esp a pleasant one. **4** to perfume. ▪ **scented** *adj* having a smell; fragrant or perfumed. [14c: from French *sentir*]

IDIOMS **put** *or* **throw sb off the scent** to deliberately mislead them.

sceptic *or* (*N Am, esp US*) **skeptic** /ˈskɛptɪk/ *noun* **1** someone with a tendency to disbelieve or doubt the truth or validity of other people's ideas, opinions, etc. **2** someone who questions widely accepted, esp religious, doctrines and beliefs. ▪ **sceptical** *adj.* ▪ **scepticism** *noun.* [16c: from Latin *scepticus*]

---

cynical, sceptical

Be careful not to use the word **sceptical** when you mean **cynical**. A **cynical** person is suspicious of apparently good things and people, whereas a person who is **sceptical** about something is cautious about believing or accepting it.

---

sceptre *noun* a ceremonial staff or baton carried by a monarch as a symbol of sovereignty. ▪ **sceptred** *adj.* [13c: from Latin *sceptrum*]

schadenfreude /ˈʃɑːdənfrɔɪdə/ *noun* malicious pleasure in the misfortunes of others. [19c: German]

schedule *noun* **1** a list of events or activities planned to take place at certain times. **2** the state of an event or activity occurring on time, according to plan: *We are well behind schedule.* ▸ *verb* **1** to plan or arrange something to take place at a certain time. **2** to put something on a schedule. [14c: from Latin *schedula*]

schema /ˈskiːmə/ *noun* (***schemata***) **1** a scheme or plan. **2** a diagrammatic outline or synopsis. [18c: Greek]

schematic *adj* **1** following or involving a particular plan or arrangement. **2** represented by a diagram or plan. ▪ **schematically** *adv.*

schematize *or* **-ise** *verb* to reduce to or represent by a scheme.

scheme *noun* **1** a plan of action. **2** a system or programme: *a pension scheme.* **3** a careful arrangement of different components: *a colour scheme.* **4** a secret plan intended to cause harm or damage. **5** a diagram or table. ▸ *verb, intr* to plan or act secretly and often maliciously. ▪ **schemer** *noun.* ▪ **scheming** *adj, noun.* [16c: Greek]

scherzo /ˈskɛətsoʊ/ *noun* (***scherzos*** *or* ***scherzi*** /-siː/) a lively piece of music, generally the second or third part of a symphony, sonata, etc, replacing the minuet. [19c: Italian, meaning 'joke']

schilling *noun* (abbrev **Sch.**) the former standard unit of currency of Austria, replaced in 2002 by the euro. [18c: German]

schism /ˈskɪzəm/ *noun, relig* a breach or separation from the main group, or into opposing groups. ▪ **schismatic** *adj.* [14c: from Greek *schisma* split]

schist /ʃɪst/ *noun, geol* a coarse-grained metamorphic rock that splits readily into layers. [18c: from French *schiste*]

schistosomiasis /ʃɪstəsoʊ'maɪəsɪs/ *noun, pathol* a tropical disease, transmitted by contaminated water and caused by infestation with **schistosomes**, parasitic flukes which circulate in the blood and may affect other organs. Also called **bilharzia**. [Early 20c: from Greek *schistos* split]

schizo /'skɪtsoʊ/ *informal, noun* a schizophrenic person. ▸ *adj* schizophrenic. [1940s: a shortening of **schizophrenic**]

schizoid /'skɪtsɔɪd/ *adj* displaying some symptoms of schizophrenia, such as introversion or tendency to fantasy, but without a diagnosed mental disorder. ▸ *noun* a schizoid person. [1920s]

schizophrenia /skɪtsə'friːnɪə/ *noun* a severe mental disorder characterized by loss of contact with reality, impairment of thought processes, personality change, loss of emotional responsiveness and social withdrawal. ▪ **schizophrenic** *noun, adj*. [Early 20c: from Greek *schizein* to split + *phren* mind]

schmaltz *noun, informal* extreme or excessive sentimentality, esp in music or other art. ▪ **schmaltzy** *adj* (*-ier, -iest*). [1930s: Yiddish]

schnapps *noun* a strong dry alcoholic spirit, esp Dutch gin distilled from potatoes. [Early 19c: German meaning 'dram of liquor']

schnitzel *noun* a veal cutlet. [19c: German]

scholar *noun* **1** a learned person, esp an academic. **2** a person who studies; a pupil or student. **3** a person receiving a scholarship. ▪ **scholarliness** *noun*. ▪ **scholarly** *adj*. [Anglo-Saxon *scolere*]

scholarship *noun* **1** the achievements or learning of a scholar. **2** a sum of money awarded, usu to an outstanding student, for the purposes of further study.

scholastic *adj* **1** referring or relating to learning institutions, such as schools or universities, and to their teaching and education methods. **2** referring or relating to scholasticism. [16c: from Greek *scholastikos*]

scholasticism *noun* the system of esp moral or religious teaching that dominated W Europe in the Middle Ages, based on the writings of Aristotle and the Church Fathers.

school[1] *noun* **1** a place or institution where education is received, esp primary or secondary education. **2** the building or room used for this purpose. **3** the work of such an institution. **4** the body of students and teachers that occupy such a place. **5** the period of the day or year during which such a place is open to students: *Stay behind after school.* **6** the disciples or adherents of a particular teacher. **7** a group of painters, writers or other artists sharing the same style. **8** any activity or set of surroundings as a provider of experience: *Factories are the schools of life.* ▸ *verb* **1** to educate in a school. **2** to give training or instruction of a particular kind to. **3** to discipline. ▪ **schooling** *noun*. [Anglo-Saxon *scol*]

school[2] *noun* a group of fish, whales or other marine animals swimming together. ▸ *verb, intr* to gather into or move about in a school. [15c: Dutch]

schoolchild *noun* a child, a **schoolboy** or **schoolgirl**, who attends a school.

schoolmarm *noun, informal* **1** *N Am, esp US* a schoolmistress. **2** a prim woman with old-fashioned manners or attitudes. ▪ **schoolmarmish** *adj*.

schoolmaster *or* **schoolmistress** *noun* respectively, a male or female schoolteacher.

schoolteacher *noun* a person who teaches in a school.

school year *noun* the period of generally continual teaching through the year, usu starting in late summer, during which the pupil or student remains in the same class or classes.

schooner *noun* **1** a fast sailing ship with two or more masts, and rigged fore-and-aft. **2** *Brit* a large sherry glass. **3** *N Am, esp US* a large beer glass. [18c: as *skooner* or *scooner*]

schottische /ʃɒ'tiːʃ/ *noun* **1** a German folk dance, similar to a slow polka. **2** the music for such a dance. [19c: from German *der schottische Tanz* the Scottish dance]

schtoom see **shtoom**

sciatic /saɪ'atɪk/ *adj* **1** referring or relating to the hip region. **2** affected by sciatica. [14c: from Latin *sciaticus*]

sciatica /saɪ'atɪkə/ *noun, pathol* pain in the lower back, buttocks and backs of the thighs caused by pressure on the sciatic nerve. [15c: Latin]

science *noun* **1** the systematic observation and classification of natural phenomena in order to learn about them and bring them under general principles and laws. **2** a department or branch of such knowledge or study developed in this way, eg astronomy, genetics, chemistry. **3** any area of knowledge obtained using, or arranged according to, formal principles: *political science.* **4** acquired skill or technique, as opposed to natural ability. ▪ **scientist** *noun*. [14c: from Latin *scientia* knowledge]

science fiction *noun* imaginative fiction presenting a view of life in the future, based on great scientific and technological advances. Often shortened to **sci-fi**.

science park *noun* an industrial research centre, usu attached to a university, set up for the purpose of combining the academic and commercial world.

scientific *adj* **1** referring or relating to, or used in, science. **2** displaying the kind of principled approach characteristic of science. ▪ **scientifically** *adv*.

sci-fi *noun, informal* science fiction.

scimitar *noun* a sword with a short curved single-edged blade, broadest at the point end, used by Turks and Persians. [16c: from Italian *scimitarra*]

scintilla /sɪn'tɪlə/ *noun, literary* a hint or trace; an iota. [17c: Latin, meaning 'spark']

scintillate *verb, intr* **1** to sparkle or emit sparks. **2** to capture attention or impress with one's vitality or wit. ▪ **scintillating** *adj* brilliant or sparkling; full of interest or wit. [17c: from Latin *scintillare*]

scintillation *noun, physics* the emission of a flash of light when alpha, beta or gamma rays strike certain phosphorescent substances.

scion /'saɪən/ *noun* **1** *botany* the detached shoot of a plant inserted into a cut in the outer stem of another plant when making a graft. **2** a descendant or offspring; a younger member of a family. [14c: from French *cion*]

scissors *plural noun* a one-handed cutting device with two long blades pivoted in the middle so the cutting edges close and overlap. [14c: from French *cisoires*]

sclera /'sklɪərə/ *noun* the outermost membrane of the eyeball. Also called **sclerotic**. [19c: from Greek *skleros* hard]

sclerosis /sklə'rousɪs/ *noun* **1** *pathol* abnormal hardening or thickening of an artery or other body part, esp as a result of inflammation or disease. **2** *botany* the hardening of plant tissue by thickening or lignification. [14c]

sclerotic /sklə'rɒtɪk/ *noun, anatomy* in vertebrates: the white fibrous outer layer of the eyeball, which is modified at the front of the eye to form the transparent cornea. Also called **sclera**. ▸ *adj* **1** hard or firm. **2** affected with sclerosis. [16c: from Latin *scleroticus*]

scoff[1] *verb, intr* (*often* **scoff at sb** *or* **sth**) to express scorn or contempt for them; to jeer. ▸ *noun* an expression of scorn; a jeer. ▪ **scoffer** *noun*. ▪ **scoffing** *noun, adj*. [14c: from Danish *scof* mockery]

scoff[2] *verb, tr & intr, informal* to eat (food) rapidly and greedily. [19c: from Scots *scaff* food]

scold *verb* **1** to reprimand or rebuke. **2** *intr* to use strong or offensive language. ▸ *noun, old use* a nagging or quarrelsome person, esp a woman. ▪ **scolding** *noun*. [13c: from Norse *skald*]

scoliosis *noun, pathol* abnormal curvature of the spine. ▪ **scoliotic** *adj*. [18c: from Greek *skolios* bent]

scollop see **scallop**

sconce *noun* a candlestick or lantern fixed by a bracket to a wall, or one with a handle. [14c: from French *esconse*]

scone /skɒn, skoun/ *noun* a small flattish plain cake, sometimes containing dried fruit. [16c: perhaps from Dutch *schoon (brot)* fine (bread)]

scoop *verb* **1** (*also* **scoop sth up**) to lift, dig or remove it with a sweeping circular movement. **2** (*also* **scoop sth out**) to empty or hollow it with such movements. **3** to do better than (rival newspapers) in being the first to publish a story. ▸ *noun* **1** a spoon-like implement for handling or serving food. **2** a hollow shovel or lipped container for lifting loose material. **3** anything of a similar shape. **4** a scooping movement. **5** a quantity scooped. **6** a news story printed by one newspaper in advance of all others. [14c: from Dutch *schoppe* shovel]

scoot *verb, intr, informal* to make off speedily. ▸ *noun* the act of scooting. [18c: from Norse *skjota* to **shoot**]

scooter *noun* **1** a child's toy vehicle consisting of a board on a two-wheeled frame, with tall handlebars connected to the front wheel, propelled by pushing against the ground with one foot. **2** (*in full* **motor scooter**) a small-wheeled motorcycle with a protective front shield curving back to form a support for the feet. [19c: from **scoot**]

scope *noun* **1** the size or range of a subject or topic covered. **2** the aim, intention or purpose of something. **3** the limits within which there is the opportunity to act. **4** range of understanding: *beyond his scope*. [16c: from Italian *scopo*]

scorbutic /skɔː'bjuːtɪk/ *adj, pathol* relating to or suffering from scurvy. [17c: from Latin *scorbuticus*]

scorch *verb* **1** *tr & intr* to burn or be burned slightly or superficially. **2** to dry up, parch or wither. **3** to injure with severe criticism or scorn. ▸ *noun* **1** an act of scorching. **2** a scorched area or burn. **3** a mark made by scorching. ▪ **scorcher** *noun, informal* an extremely hot day. ▪ **scorching** *adj, informal* **1** of the weather: very hot. **2** of a criticism, etc: harsh. [15c: from Norse *skorpna* to shrivel]

score *noun* **1** a total number of points gained or achieved eg in a game. **2** an act of gaining or achieving a point, etc. **3** a scratch or shallow cut. **4** a set of twenty: *three score*. **5** (**scores**) very many; lots: *I have scores of letters to write*. **6** *informal* (**the score**) the current situation; the essential facts: *What's the score with your job?* **7** a written or printed copy of music for several parts, set out vertically down the page. **8** the music from a film or play. **9** (**the score**) a reason; grounds: *rejected on the score of expense*. **10** a grievance or grudge: *He has an old score to settle*. **11** a record of amounts owed. ▸ *verb* **1** *tr & intr* to gain or achieve (a point) in a game. **2** *intr* to keep a record of points gained during a game. **3** to make cuts or scratches in the surface of something; to mark (a line) by a shallow cut. **4** to be equivalent to (a number of points): *black king scores three*. **5** *music* to adapt music for instruments or voices other than those orig intended. **6** to compose music for a film or play. **7** *intr* to achieve a rating; to be judged or regarded: *This film scores high for entertainment value*. ▪ **scorer** *noun*. [Anglo-Saxon *scoru*]

IDIOMS **know the score** to know or be aware of the facts of a situation. **on that score** as regards the matter or concern: *She has no worries on that score*. **over the score** *informal* beyond reasonable limits; unfair. **score points off sb** same as **score off sb** below. **settle a score** to repay an old grudge or debt.

PHRASAL VERBS **score off sb** to humiliate them for personal advantage; to get the better of them.

scoreboard *noun* a board on which the score in a game is displayed, altered as the score changes.

scoria /'skɔːrɪə/ *noun* (***scoriae*** /-rɪaɪ/) **1** dross or slag produced from the smelting of metal from its ore. **2** a quantity of cooled lava with steam-holes. [14c: Latin]

scorn *noun* extreme or mocking contempt. ▸ *verb* **1** to treat someone or something with scorn; to express scorn for. **2** to refuse or reject with scorn. ▪ **scorner** *noun*. ▪ **scornful** *adj* contemptuous. ▪ **scornfully** *adv*. [12c: from French *escarn*]

Scorpio *noun, astrol* **a** the eighth sign of the zodiac, the Scorpion; **b** a person born between 23 October and 21 November, under this sign. [14c: Latin for **scorpion**]

scorpion *noun* an invertebrate animal found in hot regions, with eight legs, powerful claw-like pincers and a long thin segmented abdomen or 'tail', bearing a poisonous sting, that is carried arched over its back. [13c: from Latin *scorpio*]

Scot *noun* a native or inhabitant of Scotland. [Anglo-Saxon *Scottas*]

Scot. *abbrev* **1** Scotland. **2** Scottish.

Scotch *adj* of things, esp products: Scottish: *Scotch broth* • *Scotch eggs*. ▸ *noun* Scotch whisky. [17c: from **Scottish**]

scotch *verb* **1** to ruin or hinder eg plans. **2** to reveal (something, esp rumours) to be untrue.

Scotch mist *noun* very fine rain, common in the Scottish Highlands.

scot-free *adj* unpunished or unharmed. [13c: from obsolete *scot* payment or tax]

Scots *adj* **1** Scottish by birth. **2** esp of law and language: Scottish. ▸ *noun* Lowland Scots. ▪ **Scotsman** *and* **Scotswoman** *noun*. [14c: from Scots *Scottis* Scottish]

Scots pine *noun* a coniferous tree, native to Europe and Asia, with a bare reddish trunk, paired bluish-green needles and pointed cones.

Scottish *adj* belonging or relating to Scotland or its inhabitants. [Anglo-Saxon *Scottisc*]

Scottish Certificate of Education *noun* (abbrev **SCE**) in Scottish secondary education: a certificate obtainable at Standard or Higher grades for proficiency in one or more subjects. Compare **CSYS**.

scoundrel *noun* an unprincipled rogue. [16c]

scour[1] *verb* **1** to clean, polish or remove by hard rubbing. **2** to flush clean with a jet or current of water. ▪ **scourer** *noun*. [13c: from French *escurer*]

scour[2] *verb* **1** to make an exhaustive search of (an area). **2** to range over or move quickly over (an area). [14c: from Norse *skur* storm, shower]

scourge /skɜːdʒ/ *noun* **1** a cause of great suffering and affliction, esp to many people. **2** a whip used for punishing. ▸ *verb* **1** to cause suffering to; to afflict. **2** to whip. [13c: from French *escorge*]

Scouse *informal, noun* (***Scouses***) **1** the dialect of English spoken in and around Liverpool. **2** a native or inhabitant of Liverpool. Also called **Scouser**. ▸ *adj* referring or relating to Liverpool, its people or their dialect. [19c: a shortening of *lobscouse* a sailor's stew]

scout *noun* **1** *military* a person or group sent out to observe the enemy and bring back information. **2** (*often* **Scout**, *formerly* **Boy Scout**) a member of the Scout Association. **3** in the US: a member of the **Girl Scouts**, an organization similar to the Guides. **4** a **talent scout**. **5** *informal* a search. ▸ *verb, intr* **1** to act as a scout. **2** (*often* **scout about** *or* **around**) *informal* to make a search. [14c: from French *escouter*]

scow *noun* a large flat-bottomed barge for freight. [18c: from Dutch *schouw*]

scowl *verb, intr* to look disapprovingly, angrily or menacingly. ▸ *noun* a scowling expression. ▪ **scowling** *adj*. [14c: from Danish *skule* to cast down the eyes]

scrabble *verb, intr* **1** to scratch, grope or struggle frantically. **2** to scrawl. ▸ *noun* an act of scrabbling. [16c: from Dutch *schrabben* to scratch]

scrag *noun* **1** the thin part of a neck of mutton or veal, providing poor quality meat. Also **scrag-end**. **2** an unhealthily thin person or animal. **3** *slang* the human neck. ▪ **scraggy** *adj* (***-ier, -iest***) unhealthily thin; scrawny. [16c: perhaps from **crag**]

scram *verb* (***scrammed, scramming***) *intr, informal* often as a command: to go away at once; to be off. [1920s: perhaps from **scramble**]

scramble *verb* **1** *intr* to crawl or climb using hands and feet, esp hurriedly or frantically. **2** *intr* to struggle violently against others: *starving people scrambling to find food.* **3** to cook (eggs) whisked up with milk, butter, etc. **4** to throw or jumble together haphazardly. **5** to rewrite (a message) in code form, for secret transmission. **6** to transmit (a message) in a distorted form intelligible only by means of an electronic scrambler. **7** *intr* of military aircraft or air crew: to take off immediately in response to an emergency. ▸ *noun* **1** an act of scrambling. **2** a dash or struggle to beat others in getting something. **3** a walk or hike over rough ground. **4** an immediate take-off in an emergency. **5** a cross-country motor car or motorcycle race. ▪ **scrambling** *adj, noun*. [16c: from dialect *scramb* to rake together with the hands]

scrambler *noun, electronics* a device that modifies radio or telephone signals so that they can only be made intelligible using a special decoding device.

scrap[1] *noun* **1** a small piece; a fragment. **2** waste material, esp metal, for recycling or re-using. **3** (**scraps**) leftover pieces of food. ▸ *verb* (***scrapped, scrapping***) to discard or cease to use; to abandon as unworkable. [14c: from Norse *skrap*]

scrap[2] *informal, noun* a fight or quarrel, usu physical. ▸ *verb* (***scrapped, scrapping***) *intr* to fight or quarrel. [17c: from **scrape**]

scrapbook *noun* a book with blank pages for pasting in cuttings, pictures, etc.

scrape *verb* **1** (*also* **scrape sth along**, **over**, *etc* **sth**) to push or drag (esp a sharp object) along or over (a hard or rough surface). **2** *intr* to move along a surface with a grazing action. **3** to graze (the skin) by a scraping action. **4** to move along (a surface) with a grating sound. **5** *intr* to make a grating sound. **6** (*also* **scrape sth off**) to remove it from or smooth (a surface) with such an action. **7** to make savings through hardship: *We managed to scrape enough for a holiday.* ▸ *noun* **1** an instance, process or act of dragging or grazing. **2** a part damaged or cleaned by scraping. **3** a scraped area in the ground. **4** a graze (of the skin). **5** *informal* a difficult or embarrassing situation or predicament. **6** *informal* a fight or quarrel. ▪ **scraper** *noun*. [Anglo-Saxon *scrapian*]

IDIOMS **bow and scrape** to be over-obsequious. **scrape the bottom of the barrel** to utilize the very last and worst of one's resources, opinions, etc.

PHRASAL VERBS **scrape through** *or* **by** to manage or succeed in doing something narrowly or with difficulty. **scrape sth together** *or* **up** to collect it little by little, usu with difficulty.

scrap heap *noun* **1** a place where unwanted and useless objects, eg old furniture, are collected. **2** the state of being discarded or abandoned: *They consigned the idea to the scrap heap.*

IDIOMS **throw sth** *or* **sb on the scrap heap** to reject or discard it or them as useless.

scrappy *adj* (***-ier, -iest***) fragmentary or disjointed; not uniform or flowing. ▪ **scrappiness** *noun*.

scratch *verb* **1** to draw a sharp or pointed object across (a surface), causing damage or making marks. **2** to make (a mark) by such action. **3** *tr & intr* to rub the skin with the fingernails, esp to relieve itching. **4** to dig or scrape with the claws. **5** (*usu* **scratch sth out** *or* **off**) to erase or cancel it. **6** *intr* to make a grating noise. **7** *intr* to withdraw from a contest, competition, etc. ▸ *noun* **1** an act of scratching. **2** a mark made by scratching. **3** a scratching sound. **4** a superficial wound or minor injury. ▸ *adj* **1** casually or hastily got together; improvised: *a scratch meal.* **2** of a competitor: not given a handicap. ▪ **scratchy** *adj* (***-ier, -iest***). [15c: as *cracche* to scratch]

IDIOMS **come up to scratch** *informal* to meet the required or expected standard (from the former meaning of the line in the ring up to which boxers were led before fighting). **from scratch** from the beginning; without the benefit of any preparation or previous experience. **scratch the surface** to deal only superficially with an issue or problem.

scratchcard *noun* a lottery card covered with a thin opaque film, which is scratched off to reveal symbols or numbers which may correspond to prizes.

scrawl *verb, tr & intr* to write or draw illegibly, untidily or hurriedly. ▸ *noun* untidy or illegible handwriting. ▪ **scrawly** *adj* (**-ier, -iest**). [17c: perhaps connected with **crawl** and **sprawl**]

scrawny *adj* (**-ier, -iest**) unhealthily thin and bony. ▪ **scrawniness** *noun*.

scream *verb* **1** *tr & intr* to cry out in a loud high-pitched voice, as in fear, pain or anger. **2** *intr* to laugh shrilly or uproariously. **3** (*often* **scream at sb**) usu of something unpleasant or garish: to be all too obvious or apparent: *Those colours really scream at you.* ▸ *noun* **1** a sudden loud piercing cry or noise. **2** *informal* an extremely amusing person, thing or event. [Anglo-Saxon *scræmen*]

scree *noun, geol* a sloping mass of loose stones at the base of a cliff or on the face of a mountain, caused by weathering of rock. [18c: from Norse *skritha* landslip]

screech *noun* a harsh, shrill and sudden cry, voice or noise. ▸ *verb* **1** *tr & intr* to utter a screech or make a sound like a screech. **2** to speak in such a way. ▪ **screecher** *noun*. ▪ **screechy** *adj* (**-ier, -iest**). [16c as *scrichen*]

screed *noun* a long and often tedious spoken or written passage. [Anglo-Saxon *screade* shred]

screen *noun* **1** a movable set of foldable hinged panels, used to partition off part of a room for privacy. **2** a single panel used for protection against strong heat or light, or any other outside influence. **3** a **windscreen**. **4** a wire netting placed over windows for keeping out insects. **5** the surface on which the images are formed on a television or computer. **6** a white surface onto which films or slides are projected. **7** (**the screen**) the medium of cinema or television: *She is a star of the stage and the screen.* ▸ *verb* **1** to shelter or conceal. **2** to subject someone to tests in order to discern their ability, reliability, worthiness, etc. **3** to test someone in order to check for the presence of disease. **4** to show or project (a film, programme, etc) at the cinema or on TV. ▪ **screening** *noun*. [14c: from French *escran*]

screenplay *noun* the script of a film, comprising dialogue, stage directions, and details for characters and sets.

screen printing, **screen process** *or* **silk-screen printing** *noun* a stencil technique in which coloured ink is forced through a fine silk or nylon mesh.

screen saver *noun, comput* a program which temporarily blanks out a screen display, or displays a preset pattern, when a computer is switched on but is not in active use.

screen test *noun* a filmed audition to test whether or not an actor or actress is suitable for cinema work.

screenwriter *noun* a writer of screenplays.

screw *noun* **1** a small fastening device consisting of a metal cylinder with a spiral ridge down the shaft and a slot in its head, driven into position in wood, etc by rotation using a screwdriver. **2** any object similar in shape or function. **3** the turn or twist of a screw. **4** *snooker, billiards* a shot in which the cue ball is subjected to sidespin or backspin. **5** *slang* a prison officer. ▸ *verb* **1** to twist (a screw) into place. **2** to push or pull with a twisting action. **3** *informal* to swindle or cheat. **4** *snooker, billiards* to put sidespin or backspin on (the cue ball). [15c: from French *escroue*]
IDIOMS **have a screw loose** *informal* to be slightly mad or crazy. **have one's head screwed on** *or* **screwed on the right way** *informal* to be a sensible person. **put the screws on sb** *informal* to use force or pressure on them.
PHRASAL VERBS **screw sth up** *slang* to bungle it.

screwball *noun, slang, N Am, esp US* a crazy person; an eccentric. ▸ *adj* crazy; eccentric.

screwdriver *noun* a hand-held tool with a metal shaft with a shaped end that fits into the slot, etc on a screw's head, turned repeatedly to twist a screw into position.

screwed-up *adj, slang* of a person: extremely anxious, nervous or psychologically disturbed.

screw-up *noun, slang* **1** a disastrous failure. **2** a person who has messed up (their life, etc).

screwy *adj* (**-ier, -iest**) *informal* crazy; eccentric.

scribble *verb* **1** *tr & intr* to write quickly or untidily; to scrawl. **2** *intr* to draw meaningless lines or shapes absent-mindedly. ▸ *noun* **1** untidy or illegible handwriting; scrawl. **2** meaningless written lines or shapes. ▪ **scribbler** *noun*. [15c: from Latin *scribillare*]

scribe *noun* **1** a person employed to make handwritten copies of documents before printing was invented. **2** in biblical times: a Jewish lawyer or teacher of law. ▸ *verb* to mark or score lines with a scribe or anything similar. [14c: from Latin *scriba*]

scrimmage *or* **scrummage** *noun* **1** a noisy brawl or struggle. **2** *Amer football* play between the opposing teams beginning with the snap and ending when the ball is dead. **3** *rugby* a **scrum** (sense 1). ▸ *verb, intr* to take part in a scrimmage. [15c: a variant of **skirmish**]

scrimp *verb, intr* to live economically; to be frugal or sparing. [18c: related to Swedish and Danish *skrumpen* shrivelled]
IDIOMS **scrimp and save** to be sparing and niggardly, often out of necessity.

scrip *noun* **1** *informal* a doctor's prescription. **2** *commerce* a provisional certificate issued before a formal share certificate is drawn up. [18c: a shortened form of **prescription** and **subscription**]

script *noun* **1** a piece of handwriting. **2** type which imitates handwriting, or vice versa. **3** the printed text of a play, film or broadcast. **4** a set of characters used for writing; an alphabet: *Cyrillic script*. **5** a candidate's examination answer paper. **6** *comput* a list of commands to be executed by a computer. ▸ *verb* to write the script of (a play, film or broadcast). [14c: from Latin *scriptum*]

scripture *or* **Scripture** *noun* **1** the sacred writings of a religion. **2** (*also* **the Scriptures**) the Christian Bible. ▪ **scriptural** *adj*. [13c: from Latin *scriptura*]

scriptwriter *noun* a person who writes scripts. ▪ **scriptwriting** *noun*.

scrofula *noun, pathol* the former name for tuberculosis of the lymph nodes, esp of the neck. ▪ **scrofulous** *adj*. [14c: from Latin *scrofulae*]

scroll *noun* **1** a roll of paper or parchment usu containing an inscription, now only a ceremonial format, eg for academic degrees. **2** an ancient text in this format: *the Dead Sea Scrolls*. **3** a decorative spiral shape, eg carved in stonework or in handwriting. ▸ *verb* **1** to roll or cut into a scroll or scrolls. **2** *tr & intr, comput* (*often* **scroll up** *or* **down**) to move the text displayed on a VDU up or down to bring into view data that cannot all be seen at the same time. [15c as *scrowle*]

Scrooge *noun* a miserly person. [19c: named after Ebenezer Scrooge in *A Christmas Carol* by Dickens]

scrotum *noun* (***scrota*** *or* ***scrotums***) *biol* the sac of skin that encloses the testicles. [16c: Latin]

scrounge *verb* **1** *tr & intr, informal* to get something by asking or begging; to cadge or sponge. **2** *intr* (*often* **scrounge for sth**) to hunt or search around for it. ▪ **scrounger** *noun.* [Early 20c: from dialect *scrunge* to steal]

scrub[1] *verb* (***scrubbed, scrubbing***) **1** *tr & intr* to rub (something) hard in order to remove dirt. **2** to wash or clean by hard rubbing. **3** *informal* to cancel or abandon (plans, etc). ▸ *noun* an act of scrubbing. [14c: from German *schrubben*]

PHRASAL VERBS **scrub up** of a surgeon, etc, before an operation: to wash the hands thoroughly.

scrub[2] *noun* **1** vegetation consisting of stunted trees and evergreen shrubs collectively. **2** (*also* **scrubland**) an area, usu with poor soil or low rainfall, containing such vegetation. ▸ *adj* small or insignificant. [14c: a variant of **shrub**[1]]

scrubber *noun* **1** someone who scrubs. **2** apparatus for filtering out impurities from gas. [19c]

scrubby *adj* (***-ier, -iest***) **1** covered with scrub. **2** of trees, shrubs, etc: stunted. [16c: from **scrub**[2]]

scruff[1] *noun* the back or nape of the neck. [18c: a variant of dialect *scuft*]

scruff[2] *noun, informal* a dirty untidy person.

scruffy *adj* (***-ier, -iest***) shabby and untidy. ▪ **scruffily** *adv.* ▪ **scruffiness** *noun.*

scrum *noun* **1** *rugby* the restarting of play when the players from both teams hunch together and tightly interlock their arms and heads in readiness for the ball being thrown in by the player known as the scrum half. Also called **scrimmage**. **2** *informal* a riotous struggle. [19c: a shortening of **scrummage**]

scrummage see **scrimmage**

scrummy *adj* (***-ier, -iest***) *chiefly Brit informal* delicious; scrumptious. [Early 20c: from **scrumptious**]

scrumptious *adj, informal* **1** delicious. **2** delightful. ▪ **scrumptiously** *adv.* [19c: prob from **sumptuous**]

scrumpy *noun* (***-ies***) strong dry cider with a harsh taste made from small sweet apples. [Early 20c: from dialect *scrump* withered apples]

scrunch *verb* **1** *tr & intr* to crunch or crush, esp with relation to the noise produced. **2** *intr* to make a crunching sound. ▸ *noun* an act or the sound of scrunching. [19c: a variant of **crunch**]

scruple *noun* (*usu* **scruples**) a sense of moral responsibility making one reluctant or unwilling to do wrong: *He has no scruples.* ▸ *verb, intr* to be reluctant or unwilling because of scruples: *I would scruple to steal even if we were starving.* [14c: from Latin *scrupulus* anxiety]

scrupulous *adj* **1** having scruples; being careful to do nothing morally wrong. **2** extremely conscientious and meticulous. ▪ **scrupulously** *adv.*

scrutinize *or* **-ise** *verb* to subject to scrutiny.

scrutiny *noun* (***-ies***) **1** a close, careful and thorough examination or inspection. **2** a penetrating or searching look. [15c: from Latin *scrutinium*]

SCSI /ˈskʌzɪ/ *abbrev, comput* Small Computer Systems Interface, a system that allows communication between a computer and several devices (eg hard disks).

scuba *noun* a device used by skin-divers in **scuba diving**, consisting of one or two cylinders of compressed air connected by a tube to a mouthpiece allowing underwater breathing. [1950s: from self-contained underwater breathing apparatus]

scud *verb* (***scudded, scudding***) *intr* **1** esp of clouds: to sweep quickly and easily across the sky. **2** esp of sailing vessels: to sail swiftly driven by the force of a strong wind. [16c: from German *schudden* to shake]

scuff *verb, tr & intr* **1** to drag (the feet) when walking. **2** to brush, graze or scrape (esp shoes or heels) while walking. ▸ *noun* **1** the act of scuffing. **2** an area worn away by scuffing. [19c: see **scuffle**]

scuffle *noun* a confused fight or struggle. ▸ *verb, intr* to take part in a scuffle. [16c: from Swedish *skuffa* to shove]

scull *noun* **1** either of a pair of short light oars used by one rower. **2** a small light racing boat propelled by one rower using a pair of such oars. **3** a large single oar over the stern of a boat, moved from side to side to propel it forward. **4** an act or spell of sculling. ▸ *verb* to propel with a scull or sculls. ▪ **sculler** *noun.* [14c: as *sculle*]

scullery *noun* (***-ies***) a room attached to the kitchen where basic chores, such as the cleaning of utensils, are carried out. [14c: from French *escuelerie*]

sculpt *verb* **1** *tr & intr* to carve or model. **2** to sculpture. [19c: from French *sculpter*]

sculptor *or* **sculptress** *noun* a person who practises the art of sculpture. [17c: Latin]

sculpture *noun* **1** the art or act of carving or modelling with clay, wood, stone, plaster, etc. **2** a work, or works, of art produced in this way. ▸ *verb* **1** to carve, mould or sculpt. **2** to represent in sculpture. ▪ **sculptural** *adj.* ▪ **sculptured** *adj* **1** carved or engraved. **2** of physical features: fine and regular, like those of figures in classical sculpture. [14c: from Latin *sculptura*]

scum *noun* **1** dirt or waste matter floating on the surface of a liquid, esp in the form of foam or froth. **2** *informal, derog* a worthless or contemptible person or such people. ▸ *verb* (***scummed, scumming***) **1** to remove the scum from (a liquid). **2** *intr* to form or throw up a scum. ▪ **scummy** *adj* (***-ier, -iest***). [13c: from Dutch *schum* foam]

scupper[1] *verb* **1** *informal* to ruin or put an end to (a plan, an idea, etc). **2** to deliberately sink (a ship).

scupper[2] *noun* (*usu* **scuppers**) *naut* a hole or pipe in a ship's side through which water is drained off the deck. [15c: from *skopper*, perhaps related to **scoop**]

scurf *noun* **1** small flakes of dead skin, esp **dandruff**. **2** any flaking or peeling substance. ▪ **scurfiness** *noun.* ▪ **scurfy** *adj* (***-ier, iest***). [Anglo-Saxon]

scurrilous *adj* indecently insulting or abusive, and unjustly damaging to the reputation. ▪ **scurrility** /skəˈrɪlɪtɪ/ *noun.* [16c: from Latin *scurrilis*]

scurry *verb* (***-ies, -ied***) *intr* to hurry briskly or in a panicky way, scuttle. ▸ *noun* (***-ies***) **1** an act of or the sound of scurrying. **2** a sudden brief gust or fall, eg of wind or snow; a flurry. [16c: from *hurry-scurry*, a reduplication of **hurry**]

scurvy *noun, pathol* a disease caused by dietary deficiency of vitamin C and characterized by swollen bleeding gums, amnesia, bruising and pain in the joints. ▸ *adj* (**-ier, -iest**) vile; contemptible. [Anglo-Saxon *scurf*]

scut *noun* a short tail, esp of a rabbit, hare or deer. [15c: from Norse *skutr* stern]

scuttle[1] *noun* (*in full* **coal scuttle**) a container for holding coal, usu kept near a fire. [Anglo-Saxon *scutel*]

scuttle[2] *verb, intr* to move quickly with haste; to scurry. ▸ *noun* a scuttling pace or movement. [15c: related to **scud**]

scuttle[3] *noun* a lidded opening in a ship's side or deck. ▸ *verb* **1** *naut* to deliberately sink (a ship) by making holes in it or by opening the lids of the scuttles. **2** to ruin or destroy (eg plans). [15c: from French *escoutille* hatchway]

Scylla /'sɪlə/ *noun, Greek myth* a six-headed sea monster situated on a dangerous rock on the Italian side of the Straits of Messina, opposite **Charybdis** /kə'rɪbdɪs/, a whirlpool. [16c: from Greek *Skylla*]
IDIOMS **between Scylla and Charybdis** faced with danger on both sides, so that avoidance of one means exposure to the other.

scythe /saɪð/ *noun* a tool with a wooden handle and a long curved blade set at right angles, for cutting tall crops or grass. ▸ *verb* to cut with a scythe. [Anglo-Saxon *sithe*]

SDI *abbrev* Strategic Defense Initiative, a proposal made by US President Ronald Reagan in 1983 for developing defensive weapons based in space.

SDLP *abbrev* in Northern Ireland: Social Democratic and Labour Party, a political party aiming to represent the Catholic population.

SE *abbrev* south-east or south-eastern.

Se *symbol, chem* selenium.

sea *noun* **1** (*usu* **the sea**) the large expanse of salt water covering the greater part of the Earth's surface. **2** any geographical division of this, eg the Mediterranean Sea. **3** an area of this with reference to its calmness or turbulence: *choppy seas.* **4** a large inland saltwater lake, eg the Dead Sea. **5** anything resembling the sea in its seemingly limitless mass or expanse: *a sea of paperwork.* **6** a vast expanse or crowd: *a sea of worshippers.* [Anglo-Saxon *sæ*]
IDIOMS **all at sea** completely disorganized or at a loss. **at sea 1** away from land; in a ship on the sea or ocean. **2** completely disorganized or bewildered. **go to sea** to become a sailor. **put** *or* **put out to sea** to start a journey by sea.

sea anchor *noun* a floating device dragged by a moving ship to slow it down or prevent it drifting off course.

sea anemone *noun* a marine invertebrate with a round brightly-coloured body and stinging tentacles.

sea arch *noun, geog* an arch of rock formed at the meeting of two caves that have been eroded into rock by the sea.

seabed *noun* the bottom or floor of the sea.

seaboard *noun* a coast; the boundary between land and sea.

seaborgium /siː'bɔːgɪəm/ *noun, chem* (symbol **Sg**) an artificially manufactured transuranic radioactive chemical element. [20c: named after the US atomic scientist Glen Theodore Seaborg]

sea change *noun* a complete change or transformation.

sea dog *noun* an old or experienced sailor.

seafaring *adj* travelling by or working at sea. ▪ **seafarer** *noun* a person who travels by sea; a sailor.

sea floor *noun* the bottom of the sea.

sea-floor spreading *noun* the forming of new crust on the sea floor when tectonic plates under the sea move apart, and the gap fills with magma which then cools.

seafood *noun* shellfish and other edible marine fish.

seafront *noun* the side of the land, a town or a building facing the sea.

seagoing *adj* of a ship: suitable for sea travel.

seagull see **gull**

seahorse *noun* a small fish with a prehensile tail and horse-like head, that swims in an upright position.

seal[1] *noun* **1** a piece of wax, lead or other material, attached to a document and stamped with an official mark to show authenticity. **2** such a mark: *the royal seal.* **3** an engraved metal stamp for making such a mark eg on wax. **4** a similar piece of material, with or without an official stamp, for keeping something closed. **5** a piece of rubber or other material serving to keep a joint airtight or watertight. **6** a token or object given, or a gesture made, as a pledge or guarantee. ▸ *verb* **1** to fix a seal to something. **2** to fasten or stamp something with a seal. **3** to decide, settle or confirm: *seal someone's fate.* **4** (*sometimes* **seal sth up**) to make it securely closed, airtight or watertight with a seal. **5** to close, esp permanently. **6** (**seal sth off**) to isolate an area, preventing entry by unauthorized persons. [13c: from French *seel*]
IDIOMS **set one's seal to sth** to authorize, approve or formally endorse it.

seal[2] *noun* **1** a marine mammal with a smooth-skinned or furry streamlined body and limbs modified to form webbed flippers. **2** sealskin. ▸ *verb, intr* to hunt seals. [Anglo-Saxon *seolh*]

sealant *noun* any material used for sealing a gap to prevent the leaking of water, etc.

sea legs *plural noun* **1** the ability to resist seasickness. **2** the ability to walk steadily on the deck of a ship.

sea level *noun* the mean level of the surface of the sea between high and low tides, therefore the point from which land height is measured.

seal of approval *noun, often facetious* official approval.

sealskin *noun* the prepared skin of a furry seal, or an imitation of it.

seam *noun* **1** a join between edges, esp one that has been welded. **2** a similar join where pieces of fabric have been stitched together. **3** *geol* a layer of coal or ore in the earth. **4** a wrinkle or scar, esp as a result of surgical incisions. ▸ *verb* **1** to join edge to edge. **2** to scar or wrinkle. ▪ **seamless** *adj.* [Anglo-Saxon, from *siwian* to sew]

seaman *noun* (***seamen***) a sailor below the rank of officer. ▪ **seamanship** *noun* sailing skills.

seamstress *noun* a woman who sews, esp as a profession.

seamy *adj* (**-ier, -iest**) sordid; disreputable. ▪ **seaminess** *noun.*

séance *or* **seance** /'seɪɑns/ *noun* a meeting at which a person, esp a spiritualist, attempts to contact the spirits of dead people on behalf of other people present. [18c: French, meaning 'sitting']

seaplane *noun* an aeroplane designed to take off from and land on water.

seaport *noun* a coastal town with a port for seagoing ships.

sear *verb* **1** to scorch. **2** to dry out or wither. ▸ *noun* a mark made by scorching. ▪ **searing** *adj* burning or intense: *searing heat*. [Anglo-Saxon *searian* to dry up]

search *verb* **1** *tr & intr* to explore something thoroughly in order to try to find someone or something. **2** to check the clothing or body of someone for concealed objects. **3** to examine closely or scrutinize: *search one's conscience.* **4** to ransack. ▸ *noun* an act of searching. [15c: from French *cerchier*]

searching *adj* seeking to discover the truth by intensive examination or observation: *a searching inquiry.*

searchlight *noun* **1** a lamp and reflector throwing a powerful beam of light for illuminating an area in darkness. **2** the beam of light projected in this way.

search party *noun* a group of people participating in an organized search for a missing person or thing.

search warrant *noun* a legal document authorizing a police officer to search premises.

seashell *noun* the empty shell of a marine invertebrate, esp a mollusc.

seashore *noun* the land immediately adjacent to the sea.

seasick *adj* suffering from nausea caused by the rolling or dipping motion of a ship. ▪ **seasickness** *noun.*

seaside *noun* (*usu* **the seaside**) a coastal area or town, esp a holiday resort.

season *noun* **1** any of the four major periods (**spring**, **summer**, **autumn** and **winter**) into which the year is divided according to changes in weather patterns and other natural phenomena. **2** any period having particular characteristics: *our busy season.* **3** a period of the year during which a particular sport, activity, etc is played or carried out: *holiday season.* **4** a period during which a particular fruit or vegetable is in plentiful supply. **5** any particular period of time. ▸ *verb* **1** to flavour (food) by adding salt, pepper and/or other herbs and spices. **2** to prepare something, esp timber, for use by drying it out. **3** to add interest or liveliness to something. [14c: from French *seson*]
IDIOMS **in season 1** of food, esp fruit and vegetables: readily available, as determined by its growing season. **2** of game animals: legally allowed to be hunted and killed, according to the time of year. **3** of a female animal: ready to mate; on heat. **out of season 1** of food, esp fruit and vegetables: not yet available. **2** of game animals: legally not yet to be hunted.

seasonable *adj* **1** of weather: appropriate to the particular season. **2** occurring at the right time.

---

seasonable, seasonal

Be careful not to use the word **seasonable** when you mean **seasonal**, and vice versa.

Seasonable has the sense of 'appropriate' or 'at the right time':

It can be cold in autumn, so bring seasonable clothes with you.

Seasonal relates more directly to the seasons of the year:

seasonal employment at summer holiday spots
seasonal fruit and vegetables

---

seasonal *adj* available, taking place or occurring only at certain times of the year. ▪ **seasonally** *adv.*

seasonal affective disorder *noun, psychol* (abbrev **SAD**) a pattern of repeated depression during the winter months, thought to be caused by reduction in the hours of daylight.

seasoned *adj* **1** of food: flavoured. **2** matured or conditioned: *seasoned wood.* **3** experienced: *seasoned travellers.*

seasoning *noun* **1** the process by which anything is seasoned. **2** any substance such as salt, pepper, herbs, spices, etc used to season food.

season ticket *noun* a ticket, usu bought at a reduced price, allowing a specified or unlimited number of visits or journeys during a fixed period.

seat *noun* **1** anything designed or intended for sitting on, eg a chair, bench, saddle, etc. **2** the part of it on which a person sits. **3** a place for sitting, eg in a cinema or theatre, esp a reservation for such a place: *We booked early to get the good seats.* **4** the buttocks. **5** the part of a garment covering the buttocks. **6** the base of an object, or any part on which it rests or fits. **7** a parliamentary or local government constituency. **8** a position on a committee or other administrative body. **9** a large country house or mansion. ▸ *verb* **1** to place on a seat. **2** to cause to sit down. **3** to assign a seat to someone, eg at a dinner table. **4** to provide seats for (a specified number of people): *My car seats five.* [13c: from Norse *sæti*]
IDIOMS **by the seat of one's pants** instinctively; by intuition. **take a seat** to sit down.

seat belt *noun* a safety belt that prevents a passenger in a car, aeroplane, etc from being thrown violently forward in the event of an emergency stop, a crash, etc.

seating *noun* **1** the provision of seats. **2** the number, allocation or arrangement of seats, eg in a dining room.

sea urchin *noun* a small **echinoderm** with a spherical or heart-shaped shell covered by protective spines.

sea wall *noun* a wall built to keep out the sea and prevent erosion of land.

seaward *adj* facing or moving towards the sea. ▸ *adv* (*also* **seawards**) towards the sea.

seaweed *noun* **1** *botany* the common name for any of numerous species of marine algae. **2** such plants collectively.

seaworthy *adj* of a ship: fit for a voyage at sea. ▪ **seaworthiness** *noun.*

sebaceous *adj* similar to, characteristic of or secreting sebum. [18c: Latin]

sebaceous gland *noun, anatomy* in mammals: any of the tiny glands in the skin that protect the skin by secretion of **sebum**.

sebum /'siːbəm/ *noun, anatomy* in mammals. the oily substance secreted by the sebaceous glands that lubricates and waterproofs the hair and skin. [18c: Latin, meaning 'grease']

sec[1] *noun, informal* short for **second**[2] (sense 3): *wait a sec.* ▸ *abbrev* **second**[2] (sense 1).

sec[2] *abbrev* secant.

secant /'siːkənt/ *noun* (abbrev **sec**) **1** *geom* a straight line that cuts a curve at one or more places. **2** *maths* for a given angle in a right-angled triangle: the ratio of the length of the hypotenuse to the length of the side adjacent to the angle under consideration; the reciprocal of the cosine of an angle. [16c: from Latin *secans*]

secateurs /sɛkə'tɜːz/ *plural noun* small sharp shears for pruning bushes, etc. [19c: French]

secede *verb, intr* to withdraw formally, eg from a political or religious body or alliance. ▪ **secession** *noun*. [18c: from Latin *secedere* to go apart]

seclude *verb* **1** to keep away or isolate from other contacts, associations or influences. **2** to keep out of view. [15c: from Latin *secludere*]

secluded *adj* **1** protected or away from people and noise; private and quiet. **2** hidden from view.

seclusion *noun* **1** the state of being secluded or the act of secluding. **2** a private place. [17c]

second[1] /'sɛkənd/ (often written **2nd**) *adj* **1** in counting: next after or below the first, in order of sequence or importance. **2** in second position. **3** alternate; other: *every second week*. **4** additional; supplementary: *have a second go*. **5** subordinate; inferior: *second to none*. **6** *music* singing or playing a part in harmony which is subordinate or slightly lower in pitch to another part: *second violin*. ▸ *noun* **1** someone or something next in sequence after the first; someone or something of second class. **2** a person coming second, eg in a race or exam: *He finished a poor second*. **3** (**the second**) **a** the second day of the month; **b** *golf* the second hole. **4** (*also* **second gear**) the second forward gear in a gearbox, eg in a motor vehicle. **5** *education, chiefly Brit* a second-class honours in a university degree, usu graded into first and second divisions. **6** an assistant to a boxer or duellist. **7** *music* the interval between successive notes of the diatonic scale. **8** a flawed or imperfect article sold at reduced price. **9** (**seconds**) *informal* a second helping of food. ▸ *verb* **1** to declare formal support for (a proposal, or the person making it). **2** to give support or encouragement to someone or something. **3** to act as second to (a boxer or duellist). ▸ *adv* secondly. ▪ **secondly** *adv* **1** used to introduce the second point in a list. **2** in the second place; as a second consideration. [13c: from Latin *secundus*]

IDIOMS **second to none** best or supreme; unsurpassed or exceptional.

second[2] /'sɛkənd/ *noun* **1** (abbrev **sec** *or* **s**) a unit of time equal to 1⁄60 of a minute. **2** *geom* (symbol ″) a unit of angular measurement equal to 1⁄3600 of a degree or 1⁄60 of a minute. **3** a moment: *wait a second*. [14c: from Latin *secunda minuta* secondary minute]

second[3] /sə'kɒnd/ *verb* to transfer someone temporarily to a different post, place or duty. ▪ **secondment** *noun*. [Early 19c: from French *en second* in the second rank]

secondary *adj* **1** being of lesser importance than the principal or primary concern; subordinate. **2** developed from something earlier or original: *a secondary infection*. **3** of education: between primary and higher or further, for pupils aged between 11 and 18. **4** *geol* (**Secondary**) relating to the **Mesozoic** era. ▸ *noun* (**-ies**) **1** a subordinate person or thing. **2** a delegate or deputy. **3** (**the Secondary**) the **Mesozoic** era. [14c: from Latin *secundarius*]

secondary colour *noun* a colour obtained by mixing or superimposing two primary colours.

secondary industry *noun* an industry concerned with processing raw materials and producing goods. Compare **primary industry, tertiary industry**.

secondary school *noun* a school, esp a state school, for pupils aged between 11 and 18.

second best *noun* the next after the best. ▸ *adj* (**second-best**): *my second-best suit*.

IDIOMS **come off second best** *informal* to lose; to be beaten by someone.

second childhood *noun* senility or dotage; mental weakness in extreme old age.

second class *noun* the next class or category after the first in quality or worth. ▸ *adj* (**second-class**) **1** referring or relating to the class below the first. **2** being of a poor standard; inferior. **3** of mail: sent at a cheaper rate than first class, therefore taking longer for delivery. ▸ *adv* by second-class mail or transport: *sent it second class*.

Second Coming *noun* the second coming of Christ to Earth on Judgement Day.

second cousin *noun* a child of the first cousin of either parent.

second-degree *adj* **1** *med, denoting* the most serious of the three degrees of burning, with blistering but not permanent damage to the skin. **2** *N Am law, denoting* unlawful killing with intent, but no premeditation.

seconder *noun* a person who seconds (see **second**[1] *verb* sense 1) a proposal or the person making it.

second-guess *verb, tr & intr* to anticipate the future actions or behaviour of someone.

second hand *noun* the pointer on a watch or clock that measures and indicates the time in seconds.

second-hand *adj* **1** previously owned or used by someone else. **2** dealing or trading in second-hand goods. **3** not directly received or obtained, but known through an intermediary: *second-hand information*. ▸ *adv* **1** in a second-hand state: *It's cheaper to buy second-hand*. **2** not directly, but from someone else: *They heard it second-hand*.

second lieutenant *noun* an army or navy officer of the lowest commissioned rank.

secondly *adv* in the second place; as a second consideration.

second nature *noun* a habit so deeply ingrained as to seem an innate part of a person's nature.

second person see under **person**

second-rate *adj* inferior or mediocre.

second sight *noun* the power believed to enable someone to see into the future or to see things happening elsewhere.

second thoughts *plural noun* **1** doubts. **2** a process of reconsideration leading to a different decision being made: *On second thoughts I think I'll stay*.

second wind *noun* a burst of renewed energy.

secrecy *noun* **1** the state or fact of being secret. **2** confidentiality: *I'm sworn to secrecy*. **3** the tendency to keep information secret. [15c: from *secre* secret]

secret *adj* **1** kept hidden or away from the knowledge of others. **2** unknown or unobserved by others: *a secret army*. **3** tending to conceal things from others; private or secretive. **4** guarded against discovery or observation: *a secret location*. ▸ *noun* **1** something not disclosed, or not to be disclosed, to others. **2** an unknown or unrevealed method of achievement: *the secret of eternal youth*. **3** a central but sometimes elusive principle, etc: *the secret of a good marriage*. ▪ **secretly** *adv*. [14c: from Latin *secretus* set apart]

IDIOMS **in secret** secretly; unknown to others. **keep a secret** not to disclose or reveal it.

secret agent *noun* a member of the secret service; a spy.

secretaire *noun* a cabinet which folds out to form a writing desk. Also called **escritoire**. [18c: French, meaning '**secretary**']

secretariat *noun* **1** the administrative department of any council, organization or legislative body. **2** its staff or premises. **3** a secretary's office. [19c: French, from **secretary**]

secretary *noun* (*-ies*) **1** a person employed to perform administrative or clerical tasks for a company or individual. **2** the member of a club or society committee responsible for its correspondence and business records. **3** a senior civil servant assisting a government minister or ambassador. ▪ **secretarial** *adj*. [14c: from Latin *secretarius* person spoken to in confidence]

secretary-general *noun* (*secretaries-general*) the principal administrative official in a large, esp political organization, eg the United Nations.

secrete[1] *verb, biol, zool* of a gland or similar organ: to form and release (a substance). [18c: a shortening of **secretion**]

secrete[2] *verb* to hide away or conceal. [18c: related to **secret**]

secretion *noun* **1** the process whereby glands of the body discharge or release particular substances. **2** any of the substances produced by such glands, eg sweat, saliva, mucus, bile. [17c: from Latin *secernere*]

secretive *adj* inclined to or fond of secrecy; reticent. ▪ **secretively** *adv*. ▪ **secretiveness** *noun*.

secret police *noun* a police force operating in secret to suppress opposition to the government.

secret service *noun* a government department responsible for espionage and national security.

sect *noun* **1** a religious or other group whose views and practices differ from those of an established body or from those of a body from which it has separated. **2** a subdivision of one of the main religious divisions of mankind. [14c: from Latin *secta* a following]

sectarian *adj* **1** referring, relating or belonging to a sect. **2** having, showing or caused by hostility towards those outside one's own group or belonging to a particular group. ▪ **sectarianism** *noun*. [17c]

section *noun* **1** the act or process of cutting. **2** any of the parts into which something is or can be divided or of which it may be composed. **3** *geom* the surface formed when a plane cuts through a solid figure. **4** the act of cutting through a solid figure. **5** a plan or diagram showing a view of an object as if it had been cut through. **6** a smaller part of a document, newspaper, book, etc: *Where's the TV section of the newspaper?* **7** *biol* a thin slice of a specimen of tissue prepared for examination under a microscope. **8** *surgery* the act or process of cutting, or the cut or division made. **9** *US* a land area of one square mile. **10** *NZ* a building plot. ▸ *verb* **1** to divide something into sections. **2** *surgery* to cut a section through something. **3** *med* to issue an order for the compulsory admission of (a mentally ill person) to a psychiatric hospital. [16c: from Latin *secare* to cut]

sectional *adj* **1** made in sections. **2** referring or relating to a particular section. **3** restricted to a particular group or area.

sector *noun* **1** *geom* a portion of a circle bounded by two radii and an arc. **2** a division or section of a nation's economic operations. **3** a part of an area divided up for military purposes. **4** a mathematical measuring instrument consisting of two graduated rules hinged together at one end. [16c: Latin, from *secare* to cut]

secular *adj* **1** relating to the present world rather than to heavenly or spiritual things. **2** not religious or ecclesiastical; civil or lay. **3** of clergy: not bound by vows to a particular monastic or religious order. ▪ **secularize** *or* **-ise** *verb*. [13c: from Latin *saecularis*]

secularism *noun* the view or belief that society's values and standards should not be influenced or controlled by religion or the Church. ▪ **secularist** *noun*.

secure *adj* **1** free from danger; providing safety. **2** free from trouble, worry or uncertainty. **3** firmly fixed or attached. **4** not likely to be lost or taken away: *a secure job*. **5** in custody, usu of the police. ▸ *verb* **1** to fasten or attach firmly. **2** to get or assure possession of something: *She's secured a place on the course*. **3** to make free from danger or risk; to make safe. **4** to contrive to get something. **5** to guarantee. ▪ **securely** *adv*. [16c: from Latin *securus*]

security *noun* (*-ies*) **1** the state of being secure. **2** protection from the possibility of future financial difficulty. **3** protection from physical harm, esp assassination. **4** protection from theft: *Our house has good security*. **5** the staff providing such protection against attack or theft. **6** something given as a guarantee, esp to a creditor giving them the right to recover a debt. **7** (*usu* **securities**) a certificate stating ownership of stocks or shares, or the value represented by such certificates. ▸ *adj* providing security: *security guard*. [15c]

security blanket *noun* **1** a blanket or other familiar piece of cloth carried around by a toddler as a source of comfort and security. **2** any familiar object whose presence provides a sense of security.

sedan *noun, N Am* a saloon car.

sedate *adj* **1** calm and dignified in manner. **2** slow and unexciting. ▸ *verb* to calm or quieten someone by means of a sedative. ▪ **sedately** *adv*. ▪ **sedateness** *noun*. [17c: from Latin *sedatus*]

sedation *noun, med* the act of calming or the state of having been calmed, esp by means of sedatives. [16c]

sedative *noun, med* any agent, esp a drug, that has a calming effect. ▸ *adj* of a drug, etc: having a calming effect. [15c]

sedentary /ˈsɛdəntərɪ/ *adj* **1** of work: involving much sitting. **2** of a person: spending much time sitting; taking little exercise. [16c: from Latin *sedentarius*]

Seder /ˈseɪdə(r)/ *noun, Judaism* the ceremonial meal and its rituals on the first night or first two nights of the Passover. [19c: from Hebrew *sedher* order]

sedge *noun* a plant, resembling grass, which grows in bogs, fens, marshes and other poorly drained areas. ▪ **sedgy** *adj*. [Anglo-Saxon *secg*]

sediment *noun* **1** insoluble solid particles that have settled at the bottom of a liquid in which they were previously suspended. **2** *geol* solid material that has been deposited by the action of gravity, wind, water or ice. ▪ **sedimentary** *adj*. [16c: from Latin *sedimentum*]

sedimentation *noun* **1** *chem* the settling of solid particles from a suspension. **2** the formation of sedimentary rock. [19c]

sedition *noun* public speech, writing or action encouraging public disorder, esp rebellion against the government. ▪ **seditious** *adj*. [14c: from Latin *seditio* a going apart]

seduce *verb* **1** to lure or entice someone into having sexual intercourse. **2** to lead astray; to tempt, esp into wrongdoing. ▪ **seducer** *or* **seductress** *noun*. ▪ **seduction** *noun*. [15c: from Latin *seducere* to lead aside]

seductive *adj* **1** tending or intended to seduce. **2** sexually attractive and charming. **3** tempting; enticing. [18c: from Latin *seductivus*]

sedulous *adj, formal* assiduous and diligent; steadily hardworking. [16c: from Latin *sedulus*]

see[1] *verb* (*past tense* ***saw,*** *past participle* ***seen***) **1** to perceive by the sense operated in the eyes. **2** *intr* to have the power of vision. **3** *tr & intr* to understand or realize: *Don't you see what she's trying to do?* **4** to watch: *We're going to see a play.* **5** to be aware of or know, esp by looking or reading: *I see from your letter that you're married.* **6** *tr & intr* to find out; to learn: *We'll have to see what happens.* **7** to predict; to expect: *We could see what was going to happen.* **8** to meet up with someone; to spend time with someone: *I haven't seen her for ages.* **9** to spend time with someone regularly, esp romantically: *He's been seeing her for quite a while now.* **10** to speak to someone; to consult: *He's asking to see the manager.* **11** to receive as a visitor or client: *The doctor will see you now.* **12** to make sure of something: *See that you lock the door.* **13** to imagine, and often also to regard as likely: *I can't see him agreeing.* **14** to consider: *I see her more as an acquaintance than a friend.* **15** to encounter or experience: *She's seen too much pain in her life.* **16** to be witness to something as a sight or event: *We're now seeing huge wage rises.* **17** to escort: *I'll see you home.* **18** to refer to (the specified page, etc) for information: *see page five.* **19** *intr* (**see to sth**) to attend to it; to take care of it. **20** *cards* to match the bet of someone by staking the same sum: *I'll see you and raise you five.* [Anglo-Saxon *seon*]

IDIOMS **see fit to do sth** to think it appropriate or proper to do it. **see things** to have hallucinations.

PHRASAL VERBS **see about sth** to attend to a matter or concern. **see sb off 1** to accompany them to their place of departure: *saw her off at the airport*. **2** *informal* to get rid of them by force: *saw the burglar off.* **see sb out** to outlive them. **see sth out** to stay until the end of it. **see through sth 1** to discern what is implied by an idea or scheme, etc. **2** to detect or determine the truth underlying a lie: *I saw through your plan straight away.* **see sth through** to participate in it to the end.

see[2] *noun* **1** the office of bishop of a particular diocese. **2** the area under the religious authority of a bishop or archbishop. **3 the Holy See**. [13c: from French *sied*]

seed *noun* (***seeds*** *or* ***seed***) **1** *botany* in flowering and cone-bearing plants: the structure that develops from the ovule after fertilization, and is capable of developing into a new plant. **2** a small hard fruit or part in a fruit; a pip. **3** a source or origin: *the seeds of the plan.* **4** *sport* a seeded player: *He is number one seed.* ▸ *verb* **1** *intr* of a plant: to produce seeds. **2** to sow or plant (seeds). **3** to remove seeds from (eg a fruit). **4** to scatter particles of some substance into (a cloud) in order to induce rainfall, disperse a storm or freezing fog, etc. **5** *sport* to arrange (a tournament) so that high-ranking players only meet each other in the later stages of the contest. ▪ **seeded** *adj* **1** having the seeds removed. **2** bearing or having seeds. **3** sown. **4** *sport* of a tournament player: who has been seeded. ▪ **seedless** *adj*. [Anglo-Saxon *sæd*]

IDIOMS **go** *or* **run to seed 1** *botany* of a plant: to stop flowering prior to the development of seed. **2** *informal* to allow oneself to become unkempt or unhealthy through lack of care.

seedbed *noun* **1** a piece of ground prepared for the planting of seeds. **2** an environment in which something, esp something undesirable, develops.

seedling *noun* a young plant grown from seed.

seed pearl *noun* a tiny pearl.

seedy *adj, informal* (***-ier, -iest***) **1** mildly ill or unwell. **2** shabby; dirty or disreputable: *a seedy club.* ▪ **seediness** *noun*.

seeing *noun* the ability to see; the power of vision. ▸ *conj* (*usu* **seeing that**) given (that); since: *Seeing you are opposed to the plan, I shall not pursue it.*

seek *verb* (***sought***) **1** to look for someone or something. **2** to try to find, get or achieve something. **3** to ask for something: *We sought his advice.* ▪ **seeker** *noun*. [Anglo-Saxon *secan*]

PHRASAL VERBS **seek sb** *or* **sth out** to search intensively for and find them or it.

seem *verb, intr* **1** to appear to the eye; to give the impression of (being): *She seems happy today.* **2** to be apparent; to appear to the mind: *There seems to be no good reason for refusing.* **3** to think or believe oneself (to be, do, etc): *I seem to know you from somewhere.* [12c: from Norse *soemr* fitting]

seeming *adj* apparent; ostensible. ▪ **seemingly** *adv*.

seemly *adj* (***-ier, -iest***) fitting or suitable; becoming.

seen *past participle of* **see**[1]

seep *verb, intr* of a liquid: to escape slowly through, or as if through, a narrow opening. ▪ **seepage** *noun*. [Perhaps from Anglo-Saxon *sipian* to soak]

seer *noun* **1** a person who predicts future events; a clairvoyant. **2** a person of great wisdom and spiritual insight; a prophet.

seersucker *noun* lightweight Indian cotton or linen fabric with a crinkly appearance, often with stripes. [18c: from Persian *shir o shakkar* milk and sugar]

seesaw *noun* **1** a plaything consisting of a plank balanced in the middle, allowing people when seated on the ends to propel each other up and down by pushing off the ground with the feet. **2** the activity of using a seesaw. **3** an alternate up-and-down or back-and-forth movement. ▸ *verb, intr* to move alternately up-and-down or back-and-forth. [17c: a reduplication of **saw**[2], from the sawing action]

seethe *verb, intr* **1** to be extremely agitated or upset, esp with anger. **2** of a liquid: to churn and foam as if boiling. ▪ **seething** *adj*. [Anglo-Saxon *seothan*]

see-through *adj* esp of a fabric or clothing: able to be seen through; transparent or translucent.

segment *noun* /ˈsɛgmənt/ **1** a part, section or portion. **2** *geom* in a circle or ellipse: the region enclosed by an arc and its chord. **3** *zool* in certain animals, eg some worms: each of a number of repeating units of which the body is composed. ▸ *verb* /sɛgˈmɛnt/ to divide into segments. ▪ **segmental** *adj*. ▪ **segmentation** *noun*. [16c: from Latin *segmentum*]

segregate *verb* **1** to set apart or isolate. **2** *intr* to separate out into a group or groups. ▪ **segregation** *noun*. ▪ **segregationist** *noun*. [16c: from Latin *segregare*]

seigneur /sɛnˈjɜː(r)/ *or* **seignior** /ˈseɪnjə(r)/ *noun* a feudal lord, esp in France or French Canada. ▪ **seigneurial** *adj*. [16c: French]

seine /seɪn/ *noun* a large vertical fishing net held underwater by floats and weights, and whose ends are brought together and hauled. ▸ *verb, tr & intr* to catch or fish with a seine. [Anglo-Saxon *segne*]

seismic /ˈsaɪzmɪk/ *adj* relating to or characteristic of earthquakes. [19c: from Greek *seismos* a shaking]

seismograph /ˈsaɪzməgrɑːf/ *noun* an instrument that records earthquake shocks.

seismology /saɪzˈmɒlədʒɪ/ *noun, geol* the scientific study of earthquakes. ▪ **seismological** *or* **seismologic** *adj*. ▪ **seismologist** *noun*. [19c]

seize *verb* **1** to take or grab suddenly, eagerly or forcibly. **2** to take by force; to capture. **3** to affect suddenly and deeply; to overcome: *He was seized by panic*. **4** to take legal possession of someone or something. **5** (*often* **seize on** *or* **upon sth**) to use or exploit it eagerly: *She seized on the idea as soon as it was suggested*. **6** *intr* (*often* **seize up**) **a** of a machine or engine: to become stiff or jammed, esp through overuse or lack of lubrication; **b** of part of the body: to become stiff through over-exertion; **c** of a person: to become overwhelmed eg with nerves, fear, etc: *As soon as I stepped on the stage I just seized up*. [13c: from French *saisir*]

seize
This word is often misspelt. It breaks the 'i before e' rule, and the letter e comes before the letter *i*. It might help you to remember the following sentence:
To ***seize*** *is to* ***s****natch* ***e****agerly* ***in****.*

seizure *noun* **1** the act of seizing. **2** a capture. **3** *pathol* a sudden attack of illness, esp producing spasms as in an epileptic fit.

seldom *adv* rarely. [Anglo-Saxon *seldum*]

select *verb* to choose from several by preference. ▸ *adj* **1** picked out or chosen in preference to others. **2** restricted entrance or membership; exclusive: *She mixes with a very select group*. ▪ **selectness** *noun*. ▪ **selector** *noun*. [16c: from Latin *seligere*]

selection *noun* **1** the act or process of selecting or being selected. **2** a thing or set of things selected. **3** a range from which to select. **4** *biol* the process by which some individuals contribute more offspring than others to the next generation.

selective *adj* **1** tending to select or choose; discriminating: *a selective school*. **2** involving only certain people or things; exclusive. ▪ **selectively** *adv*. ▪ **selectivity** *noun*.

selenium *noun, chem* (symbol **Se**) a metalloid element that is a semiconductor, used in electronic devices, photoelectric cells and photographic exposure meters. [Early 19c: from Greek *selene* moon]

Seleucid /səˈluːsɪd/ *noun* a member of the dynasty that ruled Syria from 312 to 65 BC. ▸ *adj* of or relating to the Seleucid dynasty.

self *noun* (***selves***) **1** personality, or a particular aspect of it. **2** a person's awareness of their own identity; ego. **3** a person as a whole, comprising a combination of characteristics of appearance and behaviour: *He was his usual happy self*. **4** personal interest or advantage. ▸ *pronoun, informal* myself, yourself, himself or herself. ▸ *adj* being of the same material or colour. [Anglo-Saxon *seolf*]

self- *combining form, indicating* **1** by or for oneself; in relation to oneself: *self-doubt* • *self-inflicted*. **2** acting automatically: *self-closing*.

self-absorbed *adj* wrapped up in one's own thoughts or circumstances. ▪ **self-absorption** *noun*.

self-addressed *adj* addressed by the sender for return to themselves.

self-appointed *adj* acting on one's own authority, without the choice or approval of others.

self-assurance *noun* confidence in oneself. ▪ **self-assured** *adj*.

self-catering *adj* of a holiday, accommodation, etc: providing facilities allowing guests and residents to prepare their own meals.

self-centred *adj* interested only in oneself and one's own affairs; selfish.

self-coloured *adj* having the same colour all over.

self-confessed *adj* as openly acknowledged and admitted by oneself: *a self-confessed cheat*.

self-confidence *noun* confidence in or reliance on one's own abilities, sometimes with arrogance; total absence of shyness. ▪ **self-confident** *adj*.

self-conscious *adj* ill at ease in company as a result of irrationally believing oneself to be the subject of observation by others.

self-contained *adj* **1** of accommodation: having no part that is shared with others. **2** needing nothing added; complete in itself.

self-control *noun* the ability to control one's emotions and impulses. ▪ **self-controlled** *adj*.

self-defence *noun* **1** the act or techniques of protecting or defending oneself from physical attack. **2** the act of defending one's own rights or principles.

self-denial *noun* the act or practice of denying one's own needs or desires. ▪ **self-denying** *adj*.

self-determination *noun* **1** the freedom to make one's own decisions without intervention from others. **2** a nation's freedom to decide its own government and political relations.

self-effacing *adj* tending to avoid making others aware of one's presence or achievements out of shyness or modesty. ▪ **self-effacement** *noun*.

self-employed *adj* working for oneself and under one's own control, rather than as an employee. ▪ **self-employment** *noun*.

self-esteem *noun* one's good opinion of oneself.

self-evident *adj* clear or evident enough without need for proof or explanation. ▪ **self-evidently** *adv*.

self-explanatory *or* **self-explaining** *adj* easily understood or obvious; needing no explanation.

self-government *noun* a government run by the people of a nation without any outside control or interference. ▪ **self-governing** *adj.*

self-help *noun* the practice of solving one's own problems using abilities developed in oneself rather than relying on assistance from others.

self-image *noun* one's idea or perception of oneself.

self-important *adj* having an exaggerated sense of one's own importance or worth; arrogant or pompous. ▪ **self-importance** *noun.*

self-imposed *adj* taken voluntarily on oneself; not imposed by others.

self-indulgent *adj* giving in or indulging in one's own whims or desires. ▪ **self-indulgence** *noun.*

self-inflicted *adj* inflicted by oneself on oneself.

self-interest *noun* **1** regard for oneself and one's own interests. **2** one's own personal welfare or advantage. ▪ **self-interested** *adj.*

selfish *adj* **1** concerned only with one's personal welfare, with total disregard to that of others. **2** of an act: revealing such a tendency. ▪ **selfishly** *adv.* ▪ **selfishness** *noun.* [17c]

selfless *adj* **1** tending to consider the welfare of others before one's own; altruistic. **2** of an act: revealing such a tendency. ▪ **selflessness** *noun.* [19c]

self-made *adj* having achieved wealth or success by working one's way up from poverty and obscurity, rather than by advantages acquired by birth.

self-pity *noun* pity for oneself, esp involving excessive moaning about one's misfortunes.

self-pollination *noun, botany* in flowering plants: the transfer of pollen from the anther of the stamen to the stigma of the same flower.

self-possessed *adj* calm, controlled and collected, esp in an emergency. ▪ **self-possession** *noun.*

self-preservation *noun* **1** the protection and care of one's own life. **2** the instinct underlying this.

self-propelled *adj* of a vehicle or craft: having its own means of propulsion.

self-raising *adj* of flour: containing an ingredient to make dough or pastry rise.

self-regard *noun* respect for and interest in oneself.

self-reliant *adj* never needing or seeking help from others; independent. ▪ **self-reliance** *noun.*

self-respect *noun* respect for oneself and one's character, and concern for one's dignity and reputation. ▪ **self-respecting** *adj.*

self-righteous *adj* having too high an opinion of one's own merits, and being intolerant of other people's faults. ▪ **self-righteousness** *noun.*

self-sacrifice *noun* the forgoing of one's own needs, interests or happiness for the sake of others. ▪ **self-sacrificing** *adj.*

selfsame *adj* the very same; identical: *He left that selfsame day.*

self-satisfied *adj* feeling or showing complacent or arrogant satisfaction with oneself or one's achievements. ▪ **self-satisfaction** *noun.*

self-sealing *adj* **1** of an envelope: having two flaps coated with an adhesive so they can be stuck together without being moistened. **2** of a tyre: capable of automatically sealing small punctures.

self-seeking *adj* preoccupied with one's own interests and opportunities for personal advantage. ▸ *noun* the act of self-seeking. ▪ **self-seeker** *noun.*

self-service *noun* a system, esp in a restaurant or petrol station, in which customers serve themselves and pay at a checkout. ▸ *adj* of a restaurant, petrol station, etc: operating such a system.

self-serving *adj* benefiting or seeking to benefit oneself, often to the disadvantage of others.

self-starter *noun* **1** in a vehicle's engine: an automatic electric starting device. **2** *informal* a person with initiative and motivation, therefore requiring little supervision in a job.

self-styled *adj* called or considered so only by oneself: *a self-styled superstar.*

self-sufficient *adj* of a person or thing: able to provide for oneself or itself without outside help. ▪ **self-sufficiency** *noun.*

self-supporting *adj* **1** earning enough money to meet all one's own expenses; self-sufficient. **2** of a structure, plant, etc: needing no additional supports to stay fixed or upright. ▪ **self-support** *noun.*

self-willed *adj* stubbornly or obstinately determined to do or have what one wants, esp to the disadvantage of others. ▪ **self-will** *noun.*

Seljuk /sɛl'juːk/ *noun* **1** a member of any of the Turkish dynasties (11c–13c) descended from the chieftain Seljuq. **2** a Turk subject to the Seljuks. ▪ **Seljuk** *or* **Seljukian** *adj.*

sell *verb* (***sold***) **1** to give something to someone in exchange for money. **2** to have available for buying: *Do you sell batteries?* **3** *intr* to be in demand among customers; to be sold: *This particular style sells well.* **4** to promote the sale of something; to cause to be bought: *The author's name sells the book.* **5** to convince or persuade someone to acquire or agree to something, esp by emphasizing its merits or advantages: *It was difficult to sell them the idea.* **6** to lose or betray (eg one's principles) in the process of getting something, esp something dishonourable. ▸ *noun* **1** the act or process of selling. **2** the style of persuasion used in selling: *the hard sell.* ▪ **seller** *noun.* [Anglo-Saxon *sellan* to hand over]

IDIOMS **sell sb down the river** *informal* to betray them. **sell sb, sth** *or* **oneself short** *informal* to understate their good qualities; to belittle them. **sold on sth** *informal* convinced or enthusiastic about it.

PHRASAL VERBS **sell sth off** to dispose of remaining goods by selling them quickly and cheaply. **sell out of sth** to sell one's entire stock of it. **sell out to sb** to betray one's principles or associates to another party: *He sold out to the opposition.* **sell up** to sell one's house or business, usu because of debts.

sell-by date *noun* a date stamped on a manufacturer's or distributor's label indicating when goods, esp foods, are considered no longer fit to be sold.

Sellotape *or* **sellotape** *noun, trademark* a form of usu transparent adhesive tape, esp for use on paper. ▸ *verb* to stick using Sellotape. [1940s]

sell-out *noun* an event for which all the tickets have been sold.

selvage *or* **selvedge** *noun* an edge of a length of fabric sewn or woven so as to prevent fraying. ▪ **selvaged** *adj.* [15c: from **self** + **edge**]

selves *pl of* **self**

semantic *adj* **1** referring or relating to meaning, esp of words. **2** referring or relating to semantics. ▪ **semantically** *adv.* [17c: from Greek *semantikos* significant]

semantics *singular noun* the branch of linguistics that deals with the meaning of words.

semaphore *noun* a system of signalling in which flags, or simply the arms, are held in positions that represent individual letters and numbers. ▸ *verb, tr & intr* to signal using semaphore. [Early 19c: French]

semblance *noun* **1** outer appearance, esp when superficial or deceptive. **2** a hint or trace. [13c: from French *sembler* to seem]

semen *noun* a thick whitish liquid carrying spermatozoa, ejaculated from the penis. [14c: Latin, meaning 'seed']

semester *noun* an academic term lasting for half an academic year. [19c: from Latin *semestris* six-monthly]

semi /ˈsɛmɪ; *US* ˈsɛmaɪ/ *noun* **1** *informal* a semi-detached house. **2** a semifinal.

semi- *prefix, denoting* **1** half: *semiquaver*. **2** partly: *semiconscious* • *semi-nude*. **3** occurring twice in the stated period: *semiannual* • *semi-yearly*. Compare **demi-**. [Latin, meaning 'half']

semi-automatic *adj* **1** partially automatic. **2** of a firearm: continuously reloading itself, but only firing one bullet at a time. ▪ **semi-automatically** *adv*.

semibreve *noun, music* the longest note in common use, equal to half a breve, two minims or four crotchets.

semicircle *noun* **1** one half of a circle. **2** an arrangement of anything in this form. ▪ **semicircular** *adj*.

semicolon *noun* a punctuation mark (;) indicating a pause stronger than that marked by a comma but weaker than that marked by a full stop.

semiconductor *noun, electronics* a crystalline material that behaves either as an electrical conductor or as an insulator, eg silicon, which can be used in the form of silicon chips in the integrated circuits of computers, etc. ▪ **semiconducting** *adj*.

semi-detached *adj* of a house: forming part of the same building, with another house on the other side of the shared wall. ▸ *noun* a semi-detached house. Often shortened to **semi**.

semifinal *noun* in competitions, sports tournaments, etc: either of two matches, the winners of which play each other in the final. ▪ **semifinalist** *noun*.

seminal *adj* **1** referring or relating to seed, semen or reproduction in general. **2** referring or relating to the beginnings or early developments of an idea, study, etc. **3** highly original and at the root of a trend or movement: *seminal writings*. [14c: from Latin *seminalis*]

seminar *noun* **1** a group of advanced students working in a specific subject of study under the supervision of a teacher. **2** any meeting set up for the discussion of any topic. [19c: from Latin *seminarium* **seminary**]

seminary *noun* (**-ies**) **1** a college for the training of priests, ministers and rabbis. **2** *old use* a secondary school, esp for girls. ▪ **seminarian** *noun*. [15c: from Latin *seminarium* seed-plot]

semiotics *or* **semiology** *singular noun* the study of human communication, esp the relationship between words and the objects or concepts they represent. ▪ **semiotic** *adj*. [17c: from Greek *semeiotikos*]

semipermeable *adj, biol* denoting a membrane through which only certain molecules can pass.

semi-precious *adj* of a gem: considered less valuable than a precious stone.

semi-professional *adj* **1** of a person: engaging only part-time in a professional activity. **2** of an activity: engaged in only by semi-professionals. ▸ *noun* a semi-professional person.

semiquaver *noun* a musical note equal to half a quaver or one-sixteenth of a semibreve.

semi-skilled *adj* **1** of a job: having or requiring a degree of training less advanced than that needed for specialized work. **2** of a person: possessing such skills.

semi-skimmed *adj* of milk: having had some of the cream skimmed.

Semitic /səˈmɪtɪk/ *noun* any of a group of languages including Hebrew, Arabic and Aramaic, spoken by **Semites**, a group of people said to be descended from Shem, the eldest son of Noah (Genesis 10). ▸ *adj* **1** referring to or speaking any such language. **2** referring or relating to Semites. **3** referring or relating to the Jews; Jewish. [19c: from Greek *Sem* Shem + **-ite**]

semitone *noun, music* **1** half a tone. **2** the interval between adjacent notes on a keyboard instrument, and the smallest interval in a normal musical scale.

semi-tropical *adj* subtropical.

semivowel *noun* **1** a speech sound having the qualities of both a vowel and a consonant. **2** a letter representing such a sound, such as *y* and *w* in English.

semolina *noun* the hard particles of wheat not ground into flour during milling, used for thickening soups, making puddings, etc. [18c: from Italian *semolino*]

Semtex *noun, trademark* a very powerful type of plastic explosive.

Sen. *abbrev* **1** senate. **2** senator. **3** senior.

senate *noun* (*often* **Senate**) in the USA, Australia and other countries: a legislative body, esp the upper chamber of the national assembly. [13c: from Latin *senatus* council]

senator *noun* (*often* **Senator**) a member of a senate. ▪ **senatorial** *adj*.

send *verb* (***sent***) **1** to cause, direct or order to go or be conveyed. **2** (*also* **send sth off**) to dispatch it, esp by post: *I sent the letter yesterday*. **3** *intr* **a** (**send for sb**) to ask or order them to come; to summon them; **b** (**send for sth**) to order it to be brought or delivered. **4** to force or propel: *He sent me flying*. **5** to cause to pass into a specified state: *She sent him into fits of laughter*. **6** to bring about, esp by divine providence: *a plague sent by God*. ▪ **sender** *noun*. [Anglo-Saxon *sendan*]

PHRASAL VERBS **send away** *or* **off for sth** to order (goods) by post. **send sb off** in football, rugby, etc: to order a player to leave the field with no further participation in the game, usu after infringement of the rules. **send sb** *or* **sth up** *Brit informal* to make fun of or parody them.

send-off *noun* a display of good wishes from a gathering of people to a departing person or group.

send-up *noun, Brit informal* a parody or satire.

senescence *noun* **1** the process of growing old. **2** *biol* the changes in a living organism as it ages, eg the production of flowers and fruit in plants.

senescent *adj, formal* **1** growing old; ageing. **2** characteristic of old age. [17c: from Latin *senescere* to grow old]

seneschal /ˈsɛnɪʃəl/ *noun, hist* a steward in charge of the household or estate of a medieval lord or prince. [14c: French, literally 'old servant']

senile *adj* displaying the feebleness and decay of mind or body brought on by old age. ▪ **senility** *noun.* [17c: from Latin *senilis*]

senile dementia *noun* a psychological disorder caused by irreversible degeneration of the brain, usu commencing after late middle age, and characterized by loss of memory and impaired intellectual ability.

senior *adj* **1** older than someone. **2** higher in rank or authority than someone. **3** for or pertaining to schoolchildren over the age of 11. **4** *N Am* referring to final-year college or university students. **5** (**Senior**) older than another person of the same name, esp distinguishing parent from child: *James Smith, Senior.* ▸ *noun* **1** a person who is older or of a higher rank. **2** a pupil in a senior school, or in the senior part of a school. **3** *N Am* a final-year student. [15c: Latin, meaning 'older', comparative of *senex* old]

senior citizen *noun* an elderly person, esp one retired; an old age pensioner.

seniority *noun* **1** the state or fact of being senior. **2** a privileged position earned through long service in a profession or with a company.

senior nursing officer *noun* a **matron** (sense 1).

senior service *noun* (*usu* **the senior service**) the Royal Navy.

senna *noun* **1** a plant native to Africa and Arabia, with leaves divided into oval leaflets, and long clusters of yellow flowers. **2** the dried leaves or pods of these plants, used as a laxative. [16c: from Arabic *sana*]

sensation *noun* **1** an awareness of an external or internal stimulus as a result of its perception by the senses. **2** a physical feeling: *I've a burning sensation in my mouth.* **3** an emotion or general feeling; a thrill: *a sensation of doubt.* **4** a sudden widespread feeling of excitement or shock: *His presence caused quite a sensation.* **5** the cause of such excitement or shock. [17c: from Latin *sensatio*]

sensational *adj* **1** causing or intended to cause strong feelings such as widespread excitement, intense interest or shock. **2** *informal* excellent; marvellous. **3** referring or relating to the senses. ▪ **sensationally** *adv.*

sensationalism *noun* the practice of or methods used in deliberately setting out to cause widespread excitement, intense interest or shock. ▪ **sensationalist** *noun, adj.* ▪ **sensationalistic** *adj.* ▪ **sensationalize** *or* **-ise** *verb.*

sense *noun* **1** any of the five main faculties used by an animal to obtain information about its external or internal environment, namely sight, hearing, smell, taste and touch. **2** an awareness or appreciation of, or an ability to make judgements regarding, some specified thing: *She has a good sense of direction.* **3** (**senses**) soundness of mind; one's wits or reason: *He's lost his senses.* **4** wisdom; practical worth: *There's no sense in doing it now.* **5** a general feeling or emotion, not perceived by any of the five natural powers: *a sense of guilt.* **6** general, overall meaning: *They understood the sense of the poem.* **7** specific meaning: *In what sense do you mean?* ▸ *verb* **1** to detect a stimulus by means of any of the five main senses. **2** to be aware of something by means other than the five main senses: *I sensed that someone was following me.* [14c: from Latin *sensus*]

IDIOMS **bring sb to their senses** to make them recognize the facts; to make them understand that they must rectify their behaviour. **come to one's senses 1** to act sensibly and rationally after a period of foolishness. **2** to regain consciousness. **in a sense** in one respect; in a way. **make sense 1** to be understandable. **2** to be wise, rational or reasonable. **make sense of sth** to understand it; to see the purpose or explanation in it. **take leave of one's senses** to begin behaving unreasonably or irrationally; to go mad.

senseless *adj* **1** unconscious. *as adv*: *He was beaten senseless.* **2** unwise; without good sense or foolish. ▪ **senselessly** *adv.* ▪ **senselessness** *noun.*

sense organ *noun, physiol* an organ, eg the eye, nose or mouth, that is sensitive to a stimulus such as sound or touch.

sensibility *noun* (**-ies**) **1** the ability or capacity to feel or have sensations or emotions. **2** a delicacy of emotional response; sensitivity: *There was a general sensibility to his grief.* **3** (**sensibilities**) feelings that can easily be offended or hurt. [14c: see **sensible**]

sensible *adj* **1** having or showing reasonableness or good judgement; wise. **2** perceptible by the senses. **3** having the power of sensation; sensitive: *sensible to pain.* ▪ **sensibly** *adv.* [14c: from Latin *sensibilis*]

sensitive *adj* **1** feeling or responding readily, strongly or painfully: *sensitive to our feelings.* **2** *biol* responding to a stimulus. **3** easily upset or offended. **4** stimulating much strong feeling or difference of opinion: *sensitive issues.* **5** of documents, etc: not for public discussion or scrutiny as they contain secret or confidential information, eg concerning national security. **6** of scientific instruments: reacting to or recording extremely small changes. **7** *photog* responding to the action of light. ▪ **sensitivity** *noun* (**-ies**). [14c: from Latin *sensitivus*]

sensitize *or* **-ise** *verb* **1** to make sensitive. **2** *photog* to make a plate, film, etc more sensitive to light.

sensor *noun, elec* any of various devices that detect or measure a change in a physical quantity, usu by converting it into an electrical signal, eg smoke detectors, etc. [1950s]

sensory *adj* referring or relating to the senses or sensation. [17c: from Latin *sensorium* brain, seat of the senses]

sensory nerve *adj* a nerve carrying impulses from the sense organs to the brain.

sensual *adj* **1** relating to the senses and the body rather than the mind or the spirit. **2** of pleasures: connected with often undue gratification of the bodily senses. **3** pursuing physical pleasures. [15c: from Latin *sensualis*]

sensuality *noun* **1** the quality of being sensual. **2** indulgence in physical pleasures. [14c: from Latin *sensualitas*]

sensuous *adj* **1** appealing to the senses aesthetically. **2** affected by or pleasing to the senses. **3** aware of what is perceived by the senses. ▪ **sensuously** *adv.* [17c: from Latin *sensus* sense]

sent *past tense, past participle of* **send**

sentence *noun* **1** a sequence of words forming a meaningful grammatical structure that can stand alone as a complete utterance, and which in written English usu begins with a capital letter and ends with a full stop, question mark or exclamation mark. **2** a punishment pronounced by a court or judge; its announcement in court. **3** a judgement, opinion or decision. ▸ *verb* **1** to announce the judgement or sentence to be given to someone. **2** to condemn someone to a punishment. ▪ **sentential** *adj.* [13c: French]

IDIOMS **pass sentence on sb** to announce the punishment to be given to someone.

sententious *adj* **1** fond of using or full of sayings or proverbs; aphoristic. **2** tending to lecture others on morals. [15c: from Latin *sententiosus* full of meaning]

sentient /ˈsɛnʃənt, ˈsɛntɪənt/ *adj* capable of sensation or feeling; conscious or aware of something: *sentient beings.* ▪ **sentience** *noun.* [17c: from Latin *sentiens*]

sentiment *noun* **1** a thought or emotion, esp when expressed. **2** emotional behaviour in general, esp when considered excessive, self-indulgent or insincere. **3** (*often* **sentiments**) an opinion or view. [14c: from Latin *sentimentum*]

sentimental *adj* **1** readily feeling, indulging in or expressing tender emotions or sentiments, esp love, friendship and pity. **2** provoking or designed to provoke such emotions, esp in large measure and without subtlety. **3** closely associated with or moved by fond memories of the past; nostalgic: *objects of sentimental value.* ▪ **sentimentality** *noun.* ▪ **sentimentally** *adv.*

sentimentalize *or* **-ise** *verb* **1** *intr* to behave sentimentally or indulge in sentimentality. **2** to make sentimental.

sentinel *noun* someone posted on guard; a sentry. [16c: from French *sentinelle*]

sentry *noun* (**-*ies***) a person, usu a soldier, posted on guard to control entry or passage. [17c: a shortening of *centronel*, variant of **sentinel**]

sentry box *noun* a small open-fronted shelter for a sentry to use in bad weather.

Sep. *or* **Sept.** *abbrev* September.

sepal *noun, botany* in a flower: one of the modified leaves, usu green but sometimes brightly coloured, that together form the **calyx** which surrounds the petals. [19c: from French *sépale*, coined by N J de Necker, from Greek *skepe* cover]

separable *adj* able to be separated or disjoined. [14c: from Latin *separabilis*]

separate *verb* /ˈsɛpəreɪt/ **1** to take, force or keep apart (from others or each other): *A hedge separates the two fields.* **2** *intr* of a couple: to cease to be together or live together. **3** to disconnect or disunite; to sever. **4** to isolate or seclude: *He should be separated from the others.* **5** (*also* **separate up**) to divide or become divided into parts: *The building is separated up into smaller apartments.* ▸ *adj* /ˈsɛpərət/ **1** separated; divided. **2** distinctly different or individual; unrelated: *That is a separate issue.* **3** physically unattached; isolated. ▸ *noun* /ˈsɛpərət/ (*usu* **separates**) individual items which form a unit and are often purchased separately to mix and match, eg blouse, skirt, etc forming separate parts of an outfit, or units such as a CD player, amplifier, speakers, etc forming a hi-fi system. ▪ **separately** *adv.* ▪ **separateness** *noun.* ▪ **separation** *noun.* [15c: from Latin *separare*]

separate
This word is often misspelt. It has an *a* in the middle. It might help you to remember the following sentence:
*To sep**ar**ate things is to keep them a**par**t.*

separatist *noun* a person who encourages, or takes action to achieve, independence from an established church, federation, organization, etc. ▪ **separatism** *noun.*

Sephardi *noun* a member of the **Sephardim.** ▸ *adj* of the Sephardim.

Sephardim *plural noun* the Spanish and Portuguese Jews (as distinguished from the Ashkenazim, the Polish and German Jews).

sepia *noun* **1** a rich reddish-brown pigment, obtained from a fluid secreted by the cuttlefish. **2** the colour of this pigment. ▸ *adj* sepia-coloured. [16c: Greek, meaning 'cuttlefish']

sepoy *noun, hist* an Indian soldier serving with a European (esp British) army. [17c: from Urdu and Persian *sipahi* horseman]

sepsis *noun* (***sepses***) *med* the presence of disease-causing micro-organisms, esp viruses or bacteria, and their toxins in the body tissues. [19c: Greek, meaning 'putrefaction']

Sept. see **Sep.**

sept *noun* esp in Scotland or Ireland: a clan; a division of a tribe.

septa *pl of* **septum**

September *noun* (abbrev **Sep.** *or* **Sept.**) the ninth month of the year. [Anglo-Saxon: Latin, meaning 'seventh', as it was the seventh month in the original Roman calendar]

septennial *adj* **1** occurring once every seven years. **2** lasting seven years. [17c: from Latin *septem* seven + *annus* year]

septet *noun* **1** a group of seven musicians. **2** a piece of music for seven performers. **3** any group or set of seven. [19c: from Latin *septem* seven]

septic *adj* **1** *med* of a wound: contaminated with pathogenic bacteria. **2** putrefying. [17c: from Greek *septikos*]

septicaemia /sɛptɪˈsiːmɪə/ *noun, pathol* the presence of pathogenic bacteria; blood poisoning. [19c: from Greek *septikos* putrefied + *haima* blood]

septic tank *noun* a tank, usu underground, in which sewage is decomposed by the action of bacteria.

septuagenarian /sɛptʃʊədʒəˈnɛərɪən/ *adj* aged between 70 and 79 years old. ▸ *noun* a septuagenarian person. [18c: from Latin *septuaginta* seventy]

septum *noun* (***septa***) *biol, anatomy* any partition between cavities, eg nostrils, areas of soft tissue, etc. [18c: from Latin *saeptum* fence or enclosure]

septuple *adj* being seven times as much or as many; sevenfold. ▸ *verb, tr & intr* to multiply or increase sevenfold. [17c: from Latin *septuplus*]

septuplet *noun* **1** any of seven children or animals born at one birth to the same mother. **2** *music* a group of seven notes played in four or six time. [19c: from Latin *septuplus*]

sepulchral /sɪˈpʌlkrəl/ *adj* **1** referring or relating to a tomb or burial. **2** suggestive of death or burial; gloomy or funereal.

sepulchre *or* (*US*) **sepulcher** /'sɛpəlkə(r)/ *noun* a tomb or burial vault. ▸ *verb* to bury in a sepulchre; to entomb. [12c: from Latin *sepulcrum*]

sepulture /'sɛpəltʃʊə(r)/ *noun* the act of burial, esp in a sepulchre. [13c: from Latin *sepultura* buried]

sequel *noun* **1** a book, film or play that continues an earlier story. **2** anything that follows on from a previous event, etc. [15c: from Latin *sequela*]

sequence *noun* **1** a series or succession of things in a specific order; the order they follow. **2** a succession of short pieces of action making up a scene in a film. **3** *maths* a set of values or quantities where each one is a fixed amount greater or smaller than its predecessor, as determined by a given rule. **4** *music* the repetition of a melody in higher or lower parts of the scale. [14c: from Latin *sequi* to follow]

sequencing *noun, biochem* **1** (*in full* **protein sequencing**) the process of determining the order of **amino acids** in a protein. **2** (*in full* **gene sequencing**) the process of determining the order of **nucleotides** in DNA or RNA.

sequential *adj* in, having or following a particular order or sequence.

sequester *verb* **1** to set aside or isolate. **2** to set apart. **3** *law* to sequestrate. ▪ **sequestered** *adj* secluded: *a sequestered garden.* [14c: Latin, meaning 'depository']

sequestrate *verb, law* to remove or confiscate (something, esp property) from someone's possession until a dispute or debt has been settled. ▪ **sequestration** *noun.* ▪ **sequestrator** *noun.* [16c: from Latin *sequestrare*]

sequin *noun* a small round shiny disc of foil or plastic, sewn on a garment for decoration. ▪ **sequined** *adj.* [17c: from Italian *zecchino*]

sequoia /sɪ'kwɔɪə/ *noun* either of two species of massive evergreen trees, native to N America, the Californian **redwood** and the **giant sequoia**. [19c: named after Sequoiah, the Cherokee scholar]

seraglio /sə'rɑːlɪoʊ/ *noun* **1** women's quarters in a Muslim house or palace; a harem. **2** *hist* a Turkish palace, esp that of the sultans at Constantinople. [16c: from Italian *serraglio*]

seraph *noun* (***seraphs*** *or* ***seraphim***) an angel of the highest rank. ▪ **seraphic** *adj.* [17c: Hebrew]

Serbian *or* **Serb** *adj* of or relating to the Serbs, an ethnic group in Serbia and the surrounding republics, or their language. ▸ *noun* **1** someone belonging to this group. **2** **Serbo-Croat.**

Serbo-Croat *or* **Serbo-Croatian** *noun* a language spoken in Serbia, Croatia etc.

serenade *noun* **1** a song or piece of music performed at night under a woman's window by her suitor. **2** any musical piece with a gentle tempo suggestive of romance and suitable for such a performance. ▸ *verb* **1** to entertain (a person) with a serenade. **2** *intr* to perform a serenade. [17c: from Italian *serenata*]

serendipity *noun* the state of frequently making lucky or beneficial finds. ▪ **serendipitous** *adj.* [1754: from a former name for Sri Lanka, coined by Horace Walpole from the folk tale *The Three Princes of Serendip*]

serene *adj* **1** of a person: calm and composed; at peace. **2** of a sky: cloudless. ▪ **serenely** *adv.* ▪ **serenity** /sɪ'rɛnətɪ/ *noun.* [16c: from Latin *serenus* clear]

serf *noun* in medieval Europe: a worker in modified slavery, bought and sold with the land on which they worked. ▪ **serfdom** *noun.* [15c: from Latin *servus* slave]

serge *noun* a strong twilled fabric, esp of wool or worsted. ▸ *adj* made of serge. [14c: French]

sergeant *or* **serjeant** *noun* **1** in the armed forces: a non-commissioned officer of the rank next above corporal. **2** in Britain: a police officer of the rank between constable and inspector. [12c: from French *sergent*]

sergeant-at-arms *or* **serjeant-at-arms** *noun* an officer of a court or parliament who is responsible for keeping order.

sergeant-major *noun* a non-commissioned officer of the highest rank in the armed forces.

serial *noun* **1** a story, television programme, etc published or broadcast in regular instalments. **2** a periodical. ▸ *adj* **1** appearing in instalments. **2** forming a series or part of a series. **3** in series; in a row. [19c: from Latin *serialis*]

serial, series
Be careful not to use the word **serial** when you mean **series**. A **series** is a set of separate stories featuring the same characters.

serialism *noun, music* the technique of using a series or succession of related notes as the basis for a musical composition. [1920s]

serialize *or* **-ise** *verb* to publish or broadcast (a story, television programme, etc) in instalments. ▪ **serialization** *noun.*

serial killer *noun* someone who commits a succession of similar murders.

serial number *noun* the individual identification number on each of a series of identical products.

series *noun* (*pl* ***series***) **1** a number of similar, related or identical things arranged or produced in line or in succession. **2** a TV or radio programme in which the same characters appear, or a similar subject is addressed, in regularly broadcast shows. **3** a set of things that differ progressively. **4** *maths* in a sequence of numbers: the sum obtained when each term is added to the previous ones. **5** *physics* an electric circuit whose components are arranged so that the same current passes through each of them in turn. **6** *geol* a group of rocks, fossils or minerals that can be arranged in a natural sequence on the basis of certain properties, eg composition. [17c: Latin, meaning 'chain or row']

series, serial
Be careful not to use the word **series** when you mean **serial**. A **serial** is a single story presented in separate instalments.

serif *noun, printing* a short decorative line or stroke on the end of a printed letter, as opposed to **sanserif**. [19c: perhaps from Dutch *schreef* stroke]

seriocomic /sɪərɪoʊ'kɒmɪk/ *adj* containing both serious and comic elements or qualities.

serious *adj* **1** grave or solemn; not inclined to flippancy or lightness of mood. **2** dealing with important issues: *a serious newspaper.* **3** severe: *a serious accident.* **4** important; significant: *There were serious differences of opinion.* **5** sincere or earnest: *I am serious about doing it.* **6** *informal* notable, renowned or in significant quantities: *serious money.* ▪ **seriously** *adv.* ▪ **seriousness** *noun.* [15c: from Latin *seriosus*]

serjeant see **sergeant**

sermon *noun* **1** a public speech or discourse, esp one forming part of a church service. **2** a lengthy moral or advisory speech, esp a reproving one. [12c: from Latin *sermo* discourse]

serology /sɪəˈrɒlədʒɪ/ *noun, biol* the study of blood serum and its constituents, esp antibodies and antigens. ▪ **serologist** *noun.* [Early 20c]

seropositive *adj* of a person: having blood that is shown by tests to be infected by the specific disease tested for, usu AIDS.

serotonin *noun, physiol* a hormone that transmits impulses in the central nervous system. [1940s]

serous /ˈsɪərəs/ *adj* characteristic of, relating to or containing serum. [16c]

serpent *noun* **1** a snake. **2** a sneaky, treacherous or malicious person. [14c: from Latin *serpens* creeping thing]

serpentine /ˈsɜːpəntaɪn/ *adj* **1** snakelike. **2** winding; full of twists and bends. ▸ *noun, geol* a soft green or white rock-forming mineral derived from magnesium silicates, so called because it is often mottled like a snake's skin. [14c: from Latin *serpentinum*]

serrate *adj* /ˈsɛreɪt/ notched like the blade of a saw. ▸ *verb* /səˈreɪt/ to notch. ▪ **serration** *noun.* [18c: from Latin *serra* saw]

serried *adj* closely packed or grouped together: *soldiers in serried ranks.* [17c: from French *serrer* to put close together]

serum /ˈsɪərəm/ *noun* (***serums*** *or* ***sera***) **1** (*in full* **blood serum**) *anatomy* the yellowish fluid component of blood, which contains specific antibodies and can therefore be used in a vaccine. **2** *botany* the watery part of a plant fluid. [17c: Latin, meaning 'whey']

servant *noun* **1** *old use* a person employed by another to do household or menial work for them. **2** a person who acts for the good of others in any capacity. **3** a **public servant**. [13c: French, meaning 'serving']

serve *verb* **1** to work for someone as a domestic servant; to be in the service of someone. **2** *intr* to be a servant. **3** to work for the benefit of someone; to aid: *He serves the community well.* **4** *tr & intr* to attend to customers in a shop, etc; to provide to customers. **5** *tr & intr* to attend to the needs or requirements of someone: *These shoes have served me well.* **6** (**serve as sth**) to act as or take the place of it: *This box will serve as a chair.* **7** *tr & intr* (*also* **serve up**) to bring, distribute or present (food or drink) to someone: *I'm ready to serve up now.* **8** *intr* to wait at table. **9** to provide with or supply materials. **10** to render service and obedience to someone: *to serve the country.* **11** *intr* to carry out duties as a member of some body or organization: *They serve on a committee.* **12** *intr* to act as a member of the armed forces: *We served in the marines.* **13** to provide specified facilities: *There are trams serving the entire city.* **14** *intr* to have a specific effect or result: *His speech just served to make matters worse.* **15** to undergo as a requirement: *You have to serve an apprenticeship.* **16** *tr & intr* in racket sports: to put (the ball) into play. **17** *law* to deliver or present (a legal document): *serve with a writ.* **18** of a male animal: to copulate with (a female). ▸ *noun* in racket sports: an act of serving. [13c: from Latin *servire* to serve]

IDIOMS **serve one's time** to undergo an apprenticeship or term in office. **serve sb right** *informal* to be the misfortune or punishment that they deserve. **serve time** to undergo a term of imprisonment.

server *noun* **1** a person who serves. **2** in racket sports: the person who serves the ball. **3** in computer networks: a dedicated computer that stores communal files, processes electronic mail, etc. [14c]

service *noun* **1** the condition or occupation of being a servant or someone who serves. **2** work carried out for or on behalf of others: *do someone a service.* **3** the act or manner of serving. **4** use or usefulness: *Your services are no longer required.* **5** a favour or any beneficial act: *Can I be of service?* **6** employment as a member of an organization working to serve or benefit others in some way; such an organization: *the civil service.* **7** the personnel employed in such an organization. **8** assistance given to customers in a shop, restaurant, etc. **9** a facility provided: *British Rail ran an excellent service.* **10** an occasion of worship or other religious ceremony; the words, etc used on such an occasion: *the marriage service.* **11** a complete set of cutlery and crockery: *a dinner service.* **12** (*usu* **services**) the supply eg of water, public transport, etc. **13** a periodic check and sometimes repair of the workings of a vehicle or other machine. **14** in racket sports: the act of putting the ball into play, or the game in which it is a particular player's turn to do so. **15** a **service charge**, eg in a restaurant: *service not included.* **16** (*often* **services**) any of the armed forces. **17** (**services**) a service area. ▸ *verb* **1** to subject (a vehicle, etc) to a periodic check. **2** of a male animal: to mate with (a female). [12c: from Latin *servitium*]

IDIOMS **at sb's service** ready to serve or give assistance to them. **be of service to sb** to help or be useful to them. **in service 1** in use or operation. **2** working as a domestic servant. **out of service** broken; not in operation.

serviceable *adj* **1** capable of being used. **2** able to give long-term use; durable. ▪ **serviceability** *noun.*

service charge *noun* a percentage of a restaurant or hotel bill added on to cover the cost of service.

service flat *noun* a flat where the cost of certain services, eg domestic cleaning, is included in the rent.

service industry *noun* an industry whose business is providing services rather than manufacturing products, eg entertainment, transport, etc.

serviceman *or* **servicewoman** *noun* a member of any of the armed forces.

service station *noun* a petrol station providing facilities for motorists, esp refuelling, car-washing, etc.

serviette *noun* a table napkin. [15c: French]

servile *adj* **1** slavishly respectful or obedient; fawning or submissive. **2** referring or relating to, or suitable for, slaves or servants: *servile tasks.* ▪ **servility** *noun.* [14c: from Latin *servilis*]

serving *noun* a portion of food or drink served at one time; a helping.

servitude *noun* **1** slavery. **2** subjection to irksome or taxing conditions. [15c: from Latin *servitudo*]

servo *adj* denoting a system in which the main mechanism is set in operation by a subsidiary mechanism and is able to develop a force greater than the force communicated to it: *servo brakes*. [Early 20c: from Latin *servus* slave]

sesame /ˈsɛsəmɪ/ *noun* **1** a plant with solitary white flowers, usu marked with purple or yellow. **2** the small edible seeds of this plant, used to garnish and flavour bread, rolls, cakes, confectionery, etc, and as a source of sesame oil. [15c: from Greek *sesamon*]

sessile *adj* **1** of a flower or leaf: attached directly to the plant, rather than by a stalk. **2** of a part of the body: attached directly to the body. **3** of an animal: stationary or immobile. [18c: from Latin *sessilis* low or squat]

session *noun* **1** a meeting of a court, council or parliament, or the period during which such meetings are regularly held. **2** *informal* a period of time spent engaged in any particular activity: *a drinking session*. **3** an academic term or year. **4** the period during which classes are taught. ▪ **sessional** *adj*. [14c: from Latin *sessio* a sitting]

IDIOMS **in session** of a court, committee, etc: conducting or engaged in a meeting.

sestet *noun* **1** the last six lines of a sonnet. **2** *music* a **sextet**. [Early 19c: from Italian *sestettos*]

set[1] *verb* (***set, setting***) **1** to put, place or fix into a specified position or condition: *set them straight*. **2** to array or arrange: *Everything was set out beautifully.* **3** *tr & intr* to make or become solid, rigid, firm or motionless: *The jelly has set*. **4** to fix, establish or settle: *Let's set a date*. **5** to embed: *set firmly in the cement*. **6** to stud, sprinkle or variegate. **7** to regulate. **8** to put into a state of readiness or preparation: *set the table*. **9** to ordain or fix (a procedure, etc). **10** to adjust (a measuring device, eg a clock) to the correct reading. **11** in Scotland and Ireland: to lease or let to a tenant. **12** to put something upon a course or start it off: *set it going*. **13** to incite or direct. **14** to fix (a broken bone) in its normal position for healing. **15** to impose or assign as an exercise or duty: *set a test*. **16** to present or fix as a lead to be followed: *We must set an example*. **17** to place on or against a certain background or surroundings: *diamonds set in a gold bracelet*. **18** to decorate: *She wore a bracelet set with diamonds*. **19** to stir, provoke or force into activity: *That set me thinking*. **20** to treat (hair) when wet so that it stays in the required style when dry. **21** *intr* of the sun or moon: to disappear below the horizon. **22** to put down or advance (a pledge or deposit). **23** *printing* to arrange. **24** to compose or fit music to (words). **25** to place (a novel, film, etc) in a specified period, location, etc: *The Great Gatsby is set in the 1920s*. **26** to put (a hen) on eggs to hatch them. **27** to put (eggs) under a hen for incubation. **28** of a gun dog: **a** to point out (game); **b** *intr* to indicate the location of game by crouching. **29** *tr & intr* of a colour in dyeing: to become, or to make it become, permanent or to prevent it running. ▸ *noun* **1** the act or process of setting or the condition of being set. **2** a setting. **3** form; shape: *the set of his jaw*. **4** habitual or temporary posture, carriage or bearing. **5** *theatre, cinematog* the scenery and props used to create a particular location. **6** **a** the process of setting hair; **b** a hairstyle produced by setting: *a shampoo and set*. ▸ *adj* **1** fixed or rigid; allowing no alterations or variations: *a set menu*. **2** established; unchanging: *He's too set in his ways*. **3** predetermined or conventional: *set phrases*. **4** ready or prepared: *We're all set to go*. **5** about to receive or experience something; due: *We're set for a pay rise*. **6** assigned; prescribed: *These are the set texts for this year*. [Anglo-Saxon *settan*]

IDIOMS **be set on sth** to be determined to do it.

PHRASAL VERBS **set about sb** to attack them. **set about sth** to start or begin it: *They set about digging the garden*. **set sb against sb else** to make them mutually hostile: *They set him against his own family.* **set sth against sth else** to compare or contrast them. **set sth** *or* **sb apart** to separate or put them aside as different, esp superior. **set sth aside 1** to disregard or reject it. **2** to reserve it or put it away for later use. **set sth back 1** to delay or hinder its progress. **2** to cause it to return to a previous and less advanced stage. **3** *slang* to cost (in money): *How much did that set you back?* **set sb down** to allow them to leave or alight from a vehicle at their destination. **set sth down** to record it in writing. **set in** to become firmly established: *We must leave before darkness sets in*. **set off** to start out on a journey. **set sb off** to provoke them into action or behaviour of a specified kind: *He can always set us off laughing*. **set sth off 1** to detonate (an explosive). **2** to show it off to good advantage or enhance its appearance: *The colour of the dress sets off your eyes*. **set on sb** to attack them. **set sb** *or* **sth on sb** to order them to attack: *I'll set the dogs on you!* **set out 1** to begin or embark on a journey. **2** to resolve or intend (to do something): *She set out to cause trouble*. **set sth out 1** to present or explain it: *She set out her proposals plainly.* **2** to lay it out for display. **set to 1** to start working; to apply oneself to a task. **2** to start fighting or arguing. See also **set-to**. **set sb up 1** to put them into a position of guaranteed security: *The inheritance has set him up for life*. **2** to enable them to begin a new career. **3** *slang* to trick them into becoming a target for blame or accusations, or into feeling embarrassed or foolish. See also **set-up**. **set sth up 1** to bring it into being or operation; to establish it: *He set the company up by himself.* **2** to arrange it. **3** to put up or erect something: *Let's set the tents up over here*. See also **set-up**.

set[2] *noun* **1** a group of related people or things, esp of a kind that usu associate, occur or are used together: *The class has two sets of twins*. **2** *maths* a group of objects, or elements, that have at least one characteristic in common, so that it is possible to decide exactly whether a given element does or does not belong to that group, eg the set of even numbers. **3** a complete collection or series of pieces needed for a particular activity: *a chess set*. **4** the songs or tunes performed by a singer or a band at a concert: *They played quite a varied set*. **5** *tennis, darts, etc* a group of games in which the winning player or players have to win a specified number, with a match lasting a certain number of sets. **6** a device for receiving or transmitting television or radio broadcasts. [14c: from French *sette*]

set[3] *or* **sett** *noun* **1** a badger's burrow. **2** a block of stone or wood used in paving. [19c: from **set**[1]]

setback *noun* a delay, check or reversal to progress.

set piece *noun* **1** a carefully prepared musical or literary performance. **2** *sport* a practised sequence of passes, movements, etc taken at free-kick, etc.

set square *noun* a right-angled triangular plate used as an aid for drawing or marking lines and angles.

settee *noun* a long indoor seat with a back and arms, usu able to hold two or more people; a sofa. [18c: a variant of **settle**[2]]

setter *noun* a large sporting dog with a long smooth coat.

setting *noun* **1** **a** a situation or background within or against which action takes place; **b** *theatre, cinematog* the scenery and props used in a single scene. **2** a set of cutlery, crockery and glassware laid out for use by one person. Also called **place setting**. **3** a position in which a machine's controls are set. **4** a mounting for a jewel. **5** the music composed specifically for a song, etc.

settle[1] *verb* **1** *tr & intr* to make or become securely, comfortably or satisfactorily positioned or established. **2** *tr & intr* (*also* **settle on sth**) to come to an agreement about it: *settle an argument* • *settle on a date*. **3** *intr* to come to rest. **4** to subside: *Wait till the dust has settled.* **5** to establish a practice or routine: *You'll soon settle into the job.* **6** *tr & intr* (*also* **settle down** *or* **settle sb down**) to make or become calm, quiet or disciplined after a period of noisy excitement or chaos. **7** to conclude or decide: *Let's settle this matter once and for all.* **8** *tr & intr* to establish or take up a permanent home or residence. **9** *tr & intr* (*also* **settle up**) to pay off or clear (a bill or debt); to settle accounts. **10** *intr* of particles in a liquid: to sink to the bottom or form a scum. **11** to secure by gift or legal act. [Anglo-Saxon *setlan* to place]

PHRASAL VERBS **settle for sth** to accept it as a compromise or instead of something more suitable. **settle in** to adapt to a new living environment. **settle with sb** to come to an agreement or deal with them.

settle[2] *noun* a wooden bench with arms and a solid high back. [Anglo-Saxon *setl*]

settlement *noun* **1** the act of settling or the state of being settled. **2** a recently settled community or colony. **3** an agreement, esp one ending an official dispute. **4** **a** an act of legally transferring ownership of property; **b** the document enforcing this.

settler *noun* someone who settles in a country that is being newly populated.

set-to *noun* **1** *informal* a fight or argument. **2** a fierce contest. See also **set to** at **set**[1].

set-top box *noun* a device that allows a conventional television set to receive a digital signal.

set-up *noun* **1** *informal* an arrangement or set of arrangements. **2** *slang* a trick to make a person unjustly blamed, accused or embarrassed. See also **set sb up, set sth up** at **set**[1].

seven *noun* **1** **a** the cardinal number 7; **b** the quantity that this represents, being one more than six. **2** any symbol for this, eg *7* or *VII*. **3** the age of seven. **4** something, eg a shoe or a person, whose size is denoted by the number 7. **5** the seventh hour after midnight or midday: *Come at seven* • *7 o'clock* • *7pm*. **6** a set or group of seven people or things. ▸ *adj* **1** totalling seven. **2** aged seven. [Anglo-Saxon *seofon*]

the seven deadly sins *plural noun* the sins believed by some Christians to bring damnation, namely pride, covetousness, lust, anger, gluttony, envy and sloth.

sevenfold *adj* **1** equal to seven times as much or as many. **2** divided into, or consisting of, seven parts. ▸ *adv* by seven times as much.

seven seas *plural noun* (*usu* **the Seven Seas**) all the oceans of the world: the Arctic, Antarctic, N Atlantic, S Atlantic, Indian, N Pacific and S Pacific Oceans.

seventeen *noun* **1** **a** the cardinal number 17; **b** the quantity that this represents, being one more than sixteen, or the sum of ten and seven. **2** any symbol for this, eg *17* or *XVII*. **3** the age of seventeen. **4** something whose size is denoted by the number 17. **5** a set or group of seventeen people or things. ▸ *adj* **1** totalling seventeen. **2** aged seventeen. ▪ **seventeenth** *adj, noun, adv.* [Anglo-Saxon *seofontiene*]

seventh (often written **7th**) *adj* **1** in counting: **a** next after sixth; **b** last of seven. **2** in seventh position. **3** being one of seven equal parts: *a seventh share*. ▸ *noun* **1** one of seven equal parts. **2** a **fraction** equal to one divided by seven (usu written 1/7). **3** a person coming seventh, eg in a race or exam: *a respectable seventh*. **4** (**the seventh**) **a** the seventh day of the month; **b** *golf* the seventh hole. **5** *music* (*also* **major seventh**) **a** an interval of a semitone less than an octave; **b** a note at that interval from another. ▸ *adv* seventhly. ▪ **seventhly** *adv* used to introduce the tenth point in a list. [Anglo-Saxon]

seventh heaven *noun* a state of extreme or intense happiness or joy.

seventies (often written **70s** *or* **70's**) *plural noun* **1** (**one's seventies**) the period of time between one's seventieth and eightieth birthdays. **2** (**the seventies**) the range of temperatures between seventy and eighty degrees. **3** (**the seventies**) the period of time between the seventieth and eightieth years of a century: *born in the seventies*.

seventy *noun* (**-*ies***) **1** **a** the cardinal number 70; **b** the quantity that this represents, being one more than sixty-nine, or the product of ten and seven. **2** any symbol for this, eg *70* or *LXX*. **3** the age of seventy. **4** a set or group of seventy people or things. ▸ *adj* **1** totalling seventy. **2** aged seventy. See also **seventies**. ▪ **seventieth** *adj, noun, adv.* [Anglo-Saxon *seofontig*]

seventy- *combining form* **a** *forming adjectives and nouns* with cardinal numbers between *one* and *nine*: *seventy-two*; **b** *forming adjectives and nouns* with ordinal numbers between *first* and *ninth*: *seventy-second*.

sever *verb* **1** to cut off physically. **2** to separate or isolate. **3** to break off or end: *He's completely severed relations with them.* [14c: from French *sevrer*]

several *adj* **1** more than a few, but not a great number: *I had several drinks.* **2** various or assorted: *They were all there with their several backgrounds.* **3** different and distinct; respective: *They went their several ways.* **4** *law* separate; not jointly. ▸ *pronoun* quite a few people or things. [15c: French]

severance pay *noun* compensation paid by an employer to an employee dismissed through no fault of their own.

severe *adj* **1** extreme and difficult to endure; marked by extreme conditions. **2** very strict towards others. **3** suggesting seriousness: *a severe appearance*. **4** having serious consequences: *a severe injury*. **5** conforming to a rigorous standard. ▪ **severity** *noun.* [16c: from Latin *severus*]

sew /sou/ *verb* (*past participle* ***sewed*** *or* ***sewn***) **1** to stitch, attach or repair (esp fabric) with thread, either by hand with a needle or by machine. **2** to make (garments) by stitching pieces of fabric together. **3**

intr to work using a needle and thread, or sewing machine. ▪ **sewer** *noun.* [Anglo-Saxon *siwian*]

PHRASAL VERBS **sew sth up** *slang* to arrange or complete it successfully and satisfactorily.

sewage /ˈsuːɪdʒ/ *noun* any liquid-borne waste matter, esp human excrement, carried away in drains.

sewer /sʊə(r)/ *noun* a large underground pipe that carries away sewage from drains and water from road surfaces. [14c: from French *essever* to drain off]

sewerage /ˈsʊərɪdʒ/ *noun* **1** a system or network of sewers. **2** drainage of sewage and surface water using sewers.

sewing *noun* **1** the act of sewing. **2** something that is being sewn: *I keep my sewing in the basket.*

sewing machine *noun* a machine for sewing, esp an electric one for sewing clothes, etc.

sewn *a past participle of* **sew**

sex *noun* **1** either of the two classes, male and female, into which animals and plants are divided according to their role in reproduction. **2** membership of one of these classes, or the characteristics that determine this. **3** sexual intercourse, or the activities, feelings, desires, etc associated with it. ▸ *adj* **1** referring or relating to sexual matters in general: *sex education.* **2** due to or based on the fact of being male or female: *sex discrimination.* ▸ *verb* to identify or determine the sex of (an animal). [14c: from Latin *sexus*]

sexagenarian *adj* of a person: aged between 60 and 69. ▸ *noun* a person of this age. [18c: from Latin *sexagenarius*]

sex appeal *noun* the power of exciting sexual desire in other people; sexual attractiveness.

sex change *noun* the changing of sex in humans by the surgical alteration or re-forming of the sex organs, and by the use of hormone treatment.

sex chromosome *noun, genetics* any chromosome that carries the genes which determine the sex of an organism.

sexism *noun* contempt shown for or discrimination against a particular sex, usu by men of women, based on prejudice or stereotype. ▪ **sexist** *noun, adj.* [1960s]

sexless *adj* **1** neither male nor female. **2** having no desire to engage in sexual activity. ▪ **sexlessness** *noun.*

sext *noun, now esp RC Church* the fourth of the **canonical hours**. [14c: from Latin *sextus* sixth]

sextant *noun* **1** a device consisting of a small telescope mounted on a graded metal arc, used in navigation and surveying for measuring angular distances. **2** the sixth part of a circle or circumference. [16c: from Latin *sextans* sixth, the arc being one sixth of a full circle]

sextet *noun* **1 a** a group of six singers or musicians; **b** a piece of music for this group. **2** any set of six. [1840s: a variant of *sestet*]

sexton *noun* someone responsible for a church's buildings and churchyard, often also having bell-ringing, grave-digging and other duties. [14c: from **sacristan**]

sextuple *noun* a value or quantity six times as much. ▸ *adj* **1** sixfold. **2** made up of six parts. ▸ *verb, tr & intr* to multiply sixfold. [17c: from Latin *sextuplus*]

sextuplet *noun* **1** any of six children or animals born at the same time to the same mother. **2** *music* a group of six notes performed in the time of four.

sexual *adj* **1** concerned with or suggestive of sex. **2** referring or relating to sexual reproduction involving the fusion of two gametes. **3** concerned with, relating to or according to membership of the male or female sex.

sexual intercourse *noun* the insertion of a man's penis into a woman's vagina, usu with the release of semen into the vagina.

sexuality *noun* a sexual state or condition. [Early 19c]

sexually transmitted infection *noun* (abbrev **STI**) any infection that is transmitted by sexual intercourse.

sexy *adj* (**-ier, -iest**) *informal* **1** of a person: sexually attractive; stimulating or arousing sexual desire. **2** of an object, idea, etc: currently popular or interesting; attractive or tempting: *sexy products.* ▪ **sexily** *adv.* ▪ **sexiness** *noun.*

SF *abbrev* science fiction.

sforzando /sfɔːtˈsandoʊ/ *or* **sforzato** /sfɔːtˈsɑːtoʊ/ *music, adv, adj* played with sudden emphasis. ▸ *noun* a passage played with sudden emphasis. [Early 19c: Italian]

Sg *symbol, chem* seaborgium.

Sgt *abbrev* Sergeant.

sh *exclam* hush; be quiet.

Shabbat *noun* (***Shabbatot***) *Judaism* the Sabbath, beginning at sunset on Friday and ending at nightfall on Saturday. [Hebrew *Shabbath* day of rest]

shabby *adj* (**-ier, -iest**) **1** esp of clothes or furnishings: old and worn; threadbare or dingy. **2** of a person: wearing such clothes; scruffy. **3** of behaviour, conduct, etc: unworthy, discreditable or contemptible. ▪ **shabbily** *adv.* ▪ **shabbiness** *noun.* [Anglo-Saxon *sceabb*]

Shabuoth, Shavuoth *or* **Shavuot** /shaˈvjuːɒθ/ *noun, Judaism* the Jewish Feast of Weeks, celebrated fifty days after the first day of Passover to commemorate the giving of the Law to Moses. [19c: Hebrew, meaning 'weeks']

shack *noun* a crudely built hut or shanty.

shackle *noun* **1** (*usu* **shackles**) a metal ring locked round the ankle or wrist of a prisoner or slave to limit movement, usu one of a pair joined by a chain. **2** (*usu* **shackles**) anything that restricts freedom; a hindrance or constraint. **3** a U-shaped metal loop or staple closed over by a **shackle-bolt**, used for fastening ropes or chains together. **4** the curved movable part of a padlock. ▸ *verb* **1** to restrain with or as if with shackles. **2** to connect or couple. [Anglo-Saxon *sceacul*]

shad *noun* (***shad*** *or* ***shads***) any of various marine fish resembling a large herring but with a deeper body. [Anglo-Saxon *sceadd*]

shade *noun* **1** the blocking or partial blocking out of sunlight, or the relative darkness caused by this. **2** an area from which sunlight has been completely or partially blocked. **3** any device used to modify direct light, eg a lampshade. **4** a device, eg a screen, used as a shield from direct heat, light, etc. **5** *US* a window blind. **6** a dark or shaded area in a drawing or painting. **7** the state of appearing less impressive than something or someone else: *Her singing puts mine in the shade.* **8** a colour, esp one similar to but slightly different from a principal colour: *a lighter shade of blue.* **9** a small amount; a touch: *My house is a shade smaller than that.* **10** (**shades**) *informal* sunglasses. **11**

literary a ghost. ▸ *verb* **1** to block or partially block out sunlight from someone or something. **2** to draw or paint so as to give the impression of shade. [Anglo-Saxon *sceadu*]

shading *noun* in drawing and painting: the representation of areas of shade or shadows.

shadow *noun* **1** a dark shape cast on a surface when an object stands between the surface and the source of light. **2** an area darkened by the blocking out of light. **3** the darker areas of a picture. **4** a slight amount; a hint or trace: *without a shadow of a doubt*. **5** a sense of gloom, trouble or foreboding: *The incident cast a shadow over the proceedings.* **6** a weakened person or thing that has wasted away to almost nothing: *She's a shadow of her former self.* **7** a constant companion. **8** a person following another closely and secretively, esp a spy or detective. ▸ *verb* **1** to put into darkness by blocking out light. **2** to cloud or darken. **3** to follow closely and secretively. ▸ *adj, politics* in the main opposition party: denoting a political counterpart to a member or section of the government: *shadow Chancellor* • *shadow cabinet*. [Anglo-Saxon *sceadwe*]

shadow-boxing *noun* boxing against an imaginary opponent as training. ▪ **shadow-box** *verb*.

shadowy *adj* **1** dark and shady; not clearly visible: a *shadowy figure*. **2** secluded; darkened by shadows. ▪ **shadowiness** *noun*.

shady *adj* (**-*ier*, -*iest***) **1** sheltered or giving shelter from heat or sunlight. **2** *informal* underhand or disreputable, often dishonest or illegal: *a shady character.* **3** shadowy or mysterious; sinister. ▪ **shadiness** *noun*.

shaft *noun* **1** the long straight handle of a weapon or tool. **2** the long straight part or handle of anything. **3** a ray or beam of light. **4** in vehicle engines: a rotating rod that transmits motion. **5** a vertical passageway in a building, esp one through which a lift moves. **6** a well-like excavation or passage, eg into a mine. **7** either of the projecting parts of a cart, etc to which a horse is attached. **8** *archit* the long middle part of a column, between the base and the capital. ▸ *verb, US slang* to dupe, cheat or swindle. [Anglo-Saxon *sceaft*]

shag[1] *noun* **1** a ragged mass of hair. **2** a long coarse pile or nap on fabric. **3** a type of tobacco cut into coarse shreds. [Anglo-Saxon *sceacga*]

shag[2] *noun* a cormorant with glossy dark-green plumage, a long neck, webbed feet and an upright stance. [Anglo-Saxon **shag**[1]]

shaggy *adj* (**-*ier*, -*iest***) **1** of hair, fur, wool, etc: long and coarse; rough and untidy in appearance. **2** having shaggy hair or fur. ▪ **shagginess** *noun*.

shagreen *noun* **1** a coarse granular leather, often dyed green, made from the skin of animals, esp a horse or donkey. **2** the skin of a shark, ray, etc, used as an abrasive. [17c: from French *chagrin*]

shah *noun, hist* a title of the former rulers of Iran and other Eastern countries. [16c: Persian]

shake *verb* (*past tense* ***shook***, *past participle* ***shaken***) **1** to move with quick, often forceful to-and-fro or up-and-down movements. **2** (*also* **shake sth up**) to mix it in this way. **3** to wave violently and threateningly; to brandish: *He shook his fist at them.* **4** *tr & intr* to tremble or make something or someone tremble, totter or shiver. **5** to cause intense shock to; to agitate profoundly: *the accident that shook the nation.* **6** (*also* **shake sb up**) to disturb, unnerve or upset them greatly. **7** to make something or someone waver; to weaken: *The experience shook my confidence.* **8** *intr* to shake hands. **9** *intr, music* to trill. ▸ *noun* **1** an act or the action of shaking. **2** *informal* a very short while; a moment. **3** (**the shakes**) *informal* a fit of uncontrollable trembling. **4** a milk shake. **5** *music* a trill. ▪ **shakeable** *or* **shakable** *adj*. [Anglo-Saxon *sceacan*]

IDIOMS **no great shakes** *informal* not of great importance, ability or worth. **shake a leg** *informal* to hurry up or get moving. **shake one's head** to turn one's head from side to side as a sign of rejection, disagreement, disapproval, denial, etc. **two shakes (of a lamb's tail)** *informal* a very short time.

PHRASAL VERBS **shake sth** *or* **sb off 1** to get rid of it or them; to free oneself from it or them. **2** to escape from it or them. **shake sb up** *informal* to stimulate them into action, esp from a state of lethargy or apathy. See also **shake-up**. **shake sth up 1** to mix it. **2** *informal* to reorganize it thoroughly. See also **shake-up**.

shakedown *noun, informal* a makeshift or temporary bed, orig made by shaking down straw.

shaker *noun* **1** someone or something that shakes. **2** a container from which something, eg salt, is dispensed by shaking. **3** a container in which something, eg a cocktail, is mixed by shaking.

Shakespearean *or* **Shakespearian** *adj* relating to or characteristic of the works of William Shakespeare.

shake-up *or* **shake-out** *noun, informal* a fundamental change, disturbance or reorganization. See also **shake sb up**, **shake sth up** at **shake**.

shaky *adj* (**-*ier*, -*iest***) **1** trembling or inclined to tremble with, or as if with, weakness, fear or illness. **2** *informal* wavering; not solid or secure. **3** disputable or uncertain: *shaky knowledge*. ▪ **shakily** *adv*.

shale *noun, geol* a fine-grained sedimentary rock, easily split into thin layers, formed as a result of the compression of clay, silt or sand by overlying rocks. [Anglo-Saxon *scealu*]

shall *auxiliary verb* expressing: **1** the future tense of other verbs, esp when the subject is *I* or *we*. **2** determination, intention, certainty, and obligation, esp when the subject is *you, he, she, it* or *they*: *They shall succeed.* • *You shall not kill.* **3** a question implying future action, often with the sense of an offer or suggestion, esp when the subject is *I* or *we*: *What shall we do?* • *Shall I give you a hand?* See also **should**, **will**[1]. [Anglo-Saxon *sceal*]

shallot *or* **shalot** /ʃəˈlɒt/ *noun* a small onion, widely used in cooking and for making pickles. [17c: from French *eschalote*]

shallow *adj* **1** having no great depth. **2** not profound or sincere; superficial. ▸ *noun* (*often* **shallows**) a shallow place or part, esp in water. ▪ **shallowness** *noun*. [15c]

sham *adj* false, counterfeit or pretended; insincere. ▸ *verb* (***shammed, shamming***) *tr & intr* to pretend or feign. ▸ *noun* **1** anything not genuine. **2** a person who shams, esp an impostor. [17c: derived from **shame**]

shaman /ˈʃamən/ *noun* a doctor-priest or medicine man or woman using magic to cure illness, make contact with gods and spirits, etc. [17c: Russian]

shamanism /ˈʃamənɪzəm/ *noun* a religion dominated by shamans, based essentially on magic, spiritualism and sorcery. ▪ **shamanist** *noun*.

shamble *verb, intr* (*usu* **shamble along, past**, *etc*) to walk with slow awkward tottering steps. ▸ *noun* a shambling walk or pace. ▪ **shambling** *noun, adj*. [17c: from **shambles**, in allusion to trestle-like legs]

shambles *singular noun* **1** *informal* a confused mess or muddle; a state of total disorder: *The whole event was a shambles.* **2** a meat market. **3** a slaughterhouse. **4** a scene or place of slaughter or carnage. ▪ **shambolic** *adj, informal* totally disorganized; chaotic. [Anglo-Saxon *scamel* stool]

shame *noun* **1** the humiliating feeling of having appeared unfavourably in one's own eyes, or those of others, as a result of one's own offensive or disrespectful actions, or those of an associate. **2** susceptibility to such a feeling or emotion. **3** fear or scorn of incurring or bringing disgrace or dishonour. **4** disgrace or loss of reputation: *He's brought shame on the whole family.* **5** modesty or bashfulness. **6** a regrettable or disappointing event or situation: *It's such a shame that he failed his exam.* ▸ *verb* **1** to make someone feel shame. **2** (*usu* **shame sb into sth**) to provoke them into taking action by inspiring feelings of shame. **3** to bring disgrace on someone or something. [Anglo-Saxon *sceamu*]

IDIOMS **put sb to shame 1** to disgrace them. **2** to make them seem inadequate by comparison. **shame on you, them**, *etc* you, they, etc should be ashamed.

shamefaced *adj* showing shame or embarrassment; abashed. [16c: orig *shamefast* held by shame]

shameful *adj* bringing or deserving shame; disgraceful: *shameful behaviour.* ▪ **shamefully** *adv*. [Anglo-Saxon]

shameless *adj* **1** incapable of feeling shame; showing no shame. **2** carried out or done without shame; brazen or immodest. ▪ **shamelessly** *adv*. [Anglo-Saxon]

shammy *noun* (**-*ies***) *informal* (*in full* **shammy leather**) a chamois leather. [18c: from **chamois**]

shampoo *noun* **1** a soapy liquid for washing the hair and scalp. **2** a similar liquid for cleaning carpets or upholstery. **3** the act or an instance of treating with either liquid. ▸ *verb* (***shampooed***) to wash or clean with shampoo. [18c: from Hindi *champo* squeeze, from *champna* to press]

shamrock *noun* a plant with leaves divided into three rounded leaflets, esp various species of clover, adopted as the national emblem of Ireland. [16c: from Irish Gaelic *seamrog*]

shandy *noun* (**-*ies***) a mixture of beer or lager with lemonade or ginger beer.

shanghai *verb* (***shanghaied, shanghaiing***) *informal* **1** to kidnap and drug or make drunk and send to sea as a sailor. **2** to trick into any unpleasant situation. [19c: named after Shanghai in China, from the former use of this method in recruiting sailors for trips to the East]

shank *noun* **1** the lower leg between the knee and the foot. **2** the same part of the leg in an animal, esp a horse. **3** the main section of the handle of a tool. [Anglo-Saxon *sceanca* leg]

Shanks's pony *or* (*US*) **Shank's mare** *noun, informal* the use of one's own legs as a means of travelling.

shan't *contraction, informal* shall not.

shantung *noun* a plain and usu undyed fabric of wild silk with a rough finish. [19c: named after Shantung (Shandong) province in China where it was orig made]

shanty[1] *noun* (**-*ies***) a roughly built hut or cabin; a shack. [Early 19c: from Canadian French *chantier* woodcutter's cabin]

shanty[2] *noun* (**-*ies***) a rhythmical song with chorus and solo verses, formerly sung by sailors while working together. [19c: from French *chanter* to sing]

shanty town *noun* a town in which poor people live in makeshift or ramshackle housing.

shape *noun* **1** the outline or form of anything. **2** a person's body or figure. **3** a form, person, etc: *I had an assistant in the shape of my brother.* **4** a desired form or condition: *We like to keep in shape.* **5** a general condition: *in bad shape.* **6** an unidentifiable figure; an apparition: *shapes lurking in the dark.* **7** a mould or pattern. **8** a geometric figure. ▸ *verb* **1** to form or fashion; to give a particular form to something. **2** to influence to an important extent: *the event that shaped history.* **3** to devise, determine or develop to suit a particular purpose. [Anglo-Saxon *sceippan*]

IDIOMS **out of shape 1** unfit; in poor physical condition. **2** deformed or disfigured. **take shape 1** to take on a definite form. **2** to finally become recognizable as the desired result of plans or theories.

PHRASAL VERBS **shape up** *informal* **1** to appear to be developing in a particular way: *This project is shaping up well.* **2** to be promising; to progress or develop well. **3** to lose weight; to tone up: *I'm trying to shape up for summer.*

shapeless *adj* **1** having an ill-defined or irregular shape. **2** unattractively shaped. ▪ **shapelessness** *noun*.

shapely *adj* (**-*ier*, -*iest***) having an attractive, well-proportioned shape or figure. ▪ **shapeliness** *noun*.

shape poem *noun* a poem written or printed so that it forms a shape on the page that represents its subject.

shard *noun* a fragment of something brittle, usu glass or pottery. [Anglo-Saxon *sceard*]

share[1] *noun* **1** a part allotted, contributed, or owned by each of several people or groups. **2** a portion, section or division. **3** (*usu* **shares**) the fixed units into which the total wealth of a business company is divided, ownership of which gives the right to receive a portion of the company's profits. ▸ *verb* **1** to have in common. **2** to use something with someone else: *We had to share a book in class.* **3** (*also* **share in sth**) to have joint possession or use of it, or joint responsibility for it, with another or others. **4** (*often* **share sth out**) to divide it into portions and distribute it among several people or groups. ▪ **sharer** *noun*. [Anglo-Saxon *scearu*]

IDIOMS **share and share alike 1** to give everyone their due share. **2** with or in equal shares.

share[2] *noun* a **ploughshare**. [Anglo-Saxon *scear*]

sharecropper *noun, esp US* a tenant farmer who supplies a share of their crops as rent payment. ▪ **sharecrop** *verb* (**-*cropped*, -*cropping***) *intr* to rent and work a farm in this way.

sharefarmer *noun, esp Aust* a tenant farmer who pays a share of the proceeds from the farm as rent.

shareholder *noun* someone who owns shares in a company. ▪ **shareholding** *noun.*

share index *noun* an index showing the movement of shares in companies trading on a stock exchange.

shareware *noun, comput* software readily available for a nominal fee.

sharia /ʃəˈriːə/ *or* **shariat** /ʃəˈriːət/ *noun* the body of Islamic religious law. [19c: from Arabic]

shark *noun* **1** a large, usu fierce, fish with a long body covered with tooth-like scales, and a prominent dorsal fin. **2** *informal* a ruthless or dishonest person, esp one who swindles, exploits or extorts. [16c: perhaps from German *Schurke* scoundrel]

sharkskin *noun* **1** leather made from a shark's skin; shagreen. **2** smooth rayon fabric with a dull sheen.

sharp *adj* **1** having a thin edge or point that cuts or pierces. **2** having a bitter pungent taste. **3** severely or harshly felt; penetrating: *sharp pain.* **4** sudden and acute: *a sharp bend.* **5** abrupt or harsh in speech; sarcastic. **6** easily perceived; clear-cut or well-defined: *a sharp contrast.* **7** keen or perceptive. **8** eager; alert to one's own interests. **9** barely honest; cunning. **10** *informal* stylish: *a sharp dresser.* **11** *music* higher in pitch by a semitone: *C sharp.* Compare **flat**[1] (*adj* sense 11b). **12** *music* slightly too high in pitch. ▸ *noun* **1** *music* a note raised by a semitone, or the sign indicating this (♯). **2** *music* the key producing this note. **3** *informal* a practised cheat; a **sharper**: *a card sharp.* ▸ *adv* **1** punctually; on the dot: *at 9 o'clock sharp.* **2** suddenly: *pulled up sharp.* **3** *music* high or too high in pitch. ▪ **sharply** *adv.* ▪ **sharpness** *noun.* [Anglo-Saxon *scearp*]

sharpen *verb, tr & intr* to make or become sharp. ▪ **sharpener** *noun.*

sharper *noun, informal* a practised cheat. [17c]

sharpish *adj* quite sharp. ▸ *adv* quickly; promptly: *I'd get there sharpish if I were you!*

sharpshooter *noun* an expert marksman. ▪ **sharpshooting** *noun, adj.*

sharp-witted *adj* quick to perceive, act or react; keenly intelligent or alert. ▪ **sharp-wittedly** *adv.*

shatter *verb* **1** *tr & intr* to break into tiny fragments, usu suddenly or with force. **2** to destroy completely; to wreck. **3** to upset greatly. **4** *informal* to tire out or exhaust. ▪ **shattered** *adj, informal* **1** exhausted. **2** extremely upset. ▪ **shattering** *adj.* [14c: see **scatter**]

shatterproof *adj* made to be specially resistant to shattering.

shave *verb* **1** to cut off (hair) from (esp the face) with a razor or shaver. **2** *intr* to remove one's facial hair in this way. **3** to graze the surface of something in passing. ▸ *noun* **1** an act or the process of shaving one's facial hair. **2** a tool for shaving wood. [Anglo-Saxon *sceafan*]

shaver *noun* **1** an electrical device with a moving blade or set of blades for shaving hair. **2** *old use, informal* a young boy.

shaving *noun* **1** the removal of hair with a razor. **2** a thin sliver (esp of wood) taken off with a sharp bladed tool.

Shavuoth see **Shabuoth**

shawl *noun* a large single piece of fabric used to cover the head or shoulders or to wrap a baby. [17c: from Persian *shal*]

she *pron* a female person or animal, or a thing thought of as female (eg a ship), named before or understood from the context. ▸ *noun* a female person or animal. [Anglo-Saxon *seo*]

sheaf *noun* (***sheaves***) **1** a bundle of things tied together, esp reaped corn. **2** a bundle of papers. ▸ *verb* (***sheafed, sheafing***; ***sheaved, sheaving***) **1** to tie up in a bundle. **2** *intr* to make sheaves. [Anglo-Saxon *sceaf*]

shear *verb* (*past participle* ***sheared*** *or* ***shorn***) **1** to clip or cut off something, esp with a large pair of clippers. **2** to cut the fleece off (a sheep). **3** (*usu* **shear sb of sth**) to strip or deprive them of it. **4** *tr & intr, eng, physics* (*also* **shear off**) to subject to a shear. ▸ *noun* **1** the act of shearing. **2** (**shears**) a large pair of clippers, or a scissor-like cutting tool with a pivot or spring. **3** *eng, physics* a force acting parallel to a plane rather than at right angles to it. ▪ **shearer** *noun* someone who shears sheep. [Anglo-Saxon *sceran*]

sheath *noun* **1** a case or covering for the blade of a sword or knife. **2** a condom. **3** (*also* **sheathdress**) a straight tight-fitting dress. **4** *biol* in plants and animals: any protective or encasing structure. [Anglo-Saxon *sceath*]

sheathe *verb* to put into a sheath or case. [14c]

sheathing *noun* something which sheathes; casing.

shebang /ʃɪˈbaŋ/ *noun, orig US slang* an affair or matter; a situation: *the whole shebang.* [1860s: perhaps connected with **shebeen**]

shebeen /ʃəˈbiːn/ *noun* **1** an illicit liquor-shop. **2** in Ireland: illicit and usu home-made alcohol. [18c]

shed[1] *noun* a wooden or metal outbuilding, usu small, sometimes open-fronted, for working in, for storage or for shelter. [Anglo-Saxon *sced*]

shed[2] *verb* (***shed, shedding***) **1** to release or make something flow: *shed tears.* **2** to get rid of or cast off something: *shed a skin.* **3** to allow to flow off: *This fabric sheds water.* [Anglo-Saxon *sceadan*]

IDIOMS **to shed light on sth** to cause (a problem, situation, etc) to become easier to comprehend.

she'd *contraction* **1** she had. **2** she would.

sheen *noun* shine, lustre or radiance; glossiness. [Anglo-Saxon *sciene* beautiful]

sheep *noun* (*pl* ***sheep***) **1** a herbivorous mammal with a stocky body covered with a thick woolly fleece, kept as a farm animal for its meat and wool. **2** a meek person, esp one who follows or obeys unquestioningly, like a sheep in a flock. **3** a member of a congregation, thought of as being looked after by the pastor. [Anglo-Saxon *sceap*]

sheep-dip *noun* **1** a disinfectant insecticidal preparation in a dipping bath, used for washing sheep. **2** the trough or dipping bath for this preparation.

sheepdog *noun* **1** a working dog that is used to guard sheep from wild animals or to assist in herding. **2** any of several breeds of dog orig developed to herd sheep.

sheepish *adj* embarrassed through having done something wrong or foolish. ▪ **sheepishly** *adv.* ▪ **sheepishness** *noun.*

sheepshank *noun* a nautical knot used for shortening a rope.

sheepskin *noun* **1** the skin of a sheep, either with or without the fleece attached to it. **2** a rug or piece of clothing made from this.

sheer[1] *adj* **1** complete; absolute or downright: *sheer madness.* **2** of a cliff, etc: vertical or nearly vertical: *a sheer drop.* **3** eg of a fabric: so thin or fine as to be almost transparent: *sheer tights*. ▸ *adv* **1** completely. **2** vertically or nearly vertically. [12c: possibly from a lost Anglo-Saxon equivalent of Norse *skaerr* bright]

sheer[2] *verb* **1** to make something change course or deviate. **2** *intr* (*usu* **sheer off** *or* **away**) **a** to change course suddenly; to swerve or deviate; **b** to move away, esp to evade someone or something disliked or feared. [17c: partly another spelling of **shear**]

sheet[1] *noun* **1** a large broad rectangular piece of fabric, esp for covering the mattress of a bed. **2** any large wide piece or expanse. **3** a piece of paper, esp if large and rectangular. **4** a pamphlet, broadsheet or newspaper. ▸ *verb* **1** to wrap or cover with or as if with a sheet. **2** to provide with sheets. **3** *intr* of rain, ice, etc: to form in or fall in a sheet. [Anglo-Saxon *scete*]

sheet[2] *noun, naut* a controlling rope attached to the lower corner of a sail. [Anglo-Saxon *sceata* corner]

sheet anchor *noun, naut* an extra anchor for use in an emergency. [15c: orig *shoot-anchor*]

sheeting *noun* fabric used for making sheets. [18c]

sheet lightning *noun* lightning that appears as a broad curtain of light.

sheet music *noun* music written or printed on unbound sheets of paper.

sheikh *or* **sheik** /ʃeɪk/ *noun* **1** the chief of an Arab tribe, village or family. **2** a Muslim leader. ▪ **sheikhdom** *noun*. [16c: from Arabic *shaikh* old man]

sheila *noun, Aust, NZ informal* a woman or girl. [19c]

shelf *noun* (***shelves***) **1** a usu narrow, flat board fixed to a wall or part of a cupboard, bookcase, etc, for storing or laying things on. **2** a ledge of land, rock, etc; a sandbank. [Anglo-Saxon *scylf*]

IDIOMS **on the shelf 1** of a person or thing: too old or worn out to be of any use. **2** of a person, esp a woman: no longer likely to have the opportunity to marry, esp because of being too old.

shelf life *noun* the length of time that a stored product remains usable, edible, etc.

shell *noun* **1** the hard protective structure covering an egg. **2** *zool* the hard protective structure covering the body of certain animals, esp shellfish, snails and tortoises. **3** *botany* the hard protective structure covering the seed or fruit of some plants. **4** the empty covering of eg a shellfish, found on the seashore. **5** any hard protective cover. **6** a round of ammunition for a large-bore gun, eg a mortar. **7** a shotgun cartridge. **8** *comput* a program that acts as a user-friendly interface between an operating system and the user. **9** *chem* one of a series of concentric spheres representing the possible orbits of electrons around the nucleus of an atom. ▸ *verb* **1** to remove the shell from something. **2** to bombard with (eg mortar) shells. [Anglo-Saxon *scell*]

IDIOMS **come out of one's shell** to cease to be shy and become more friendly or sociable.

PHRASAL VERBS **shell out** *or* **shell out for sth** *informal* to pay out (money) or spend (money) on it.

she'll *contraction* **1** she will. **2** she shall.

shellac /ʃəˈlak/ *noun* **1** a yellow or orange resin produced by the lac insect. **2** a solution of this in alcohol, used as a varnish. Also called **shellac varnish**. ▸ *verb* (***shellacked, shellacking***) **1** to coat with shellac. **2** *US informal* to defeat convincingly; to trounce or thrash. [18c: from **shell** + **lac**]

shellfish *noun* (*pl* ***shellfish***) a shelled edible aquatic invertebrate, eg prawn, crab, shrimp, lobster.

shellshock *noun* a psychological disorder caused by prolonged exposure to military combat conditions.

Shelta *noun* a language used by travelling people in Britain and Ireland. [19c: from *Shelru*, possibly a version of Irish *beulra* language]

shelter *noun* **1** protection against weather or danger. **2** a place or structure providing this. **3** a place of refuge, retreat or temporary lodging in distress. ▸ *verb* **1** to protect someone or something from the effects of weather or danger. **2** to give asylum or lodging. **3** *intr* to take cover. [16c: possibly from Anglo-Saxon *scieldtruma*]

sheltered *adj* **1** protected from the effects of weather. **2** protected from the harsh realities and unpleasantnesses of the world: *a sheltered life*.

shelve *verb* **1** to place or store on a shelf. **2** to fit with shelves. **3** to postpone or put aside; to abandon. **4** to remove from active service.

shelves see under **shelf**

shelving *noun* **1** material used for making shelves. **2** shelves collectively.

shenanigans *plural noun, informal* **1** foolish behaviour; nonsense. **2** underhand dealings; trickery. [1850s]

shepherd *noun* **1** someone who looks after, or herds, sheep. **2** *literary* a religious minister or pastor. ▸ *verb* **1** to watch over or herd sheep. **2** to guide or herd (a group or crowd). [Anglo-Saxon *sceaphirde* sheep herd]

shepherdess *noun, old use* a female shepherd.

shepherd's pie *noun* a dish consisting of minced meat baked with mashed potatoes on the top.

sherbet *noun* **1** a fruit-flavoured powder eaten as confectionery, or made into an effervescent drink. **2** *N Am* a kind of water-ice. [17c: Turkish and Persian]

sheriff *noun* **1** in a US county: the chief elected police officer mainly responsible for maintaining peace and order, attending courts, serving processes and executing judgements. **2** in England: the chief officer of the monarch in the shire or county, whose duties are now mainly ceremonial rather than judicial. **3** in Scotland: the chief judge of a sheriff court of a town or region. ▪ **sheriffdom** *noun* **1** the office, term of office or territory under the jurisdiction and authority of a sheriff. **2** in Scotland: one of six divisions of the judicature, made up of sheriff court districts. [Anglo-Saxon *scirgerefa*, from *scir* shire + *gerefa* reeve]

sheriff court *noun* in a Scottish town or region: a court trying all but the most serious crimes.

Sherpa *noun* (***Sherpa or Sherpas***) a member of an E Tibetan people living on the Himalayas. [19c]

sherry *noun* (***-ies***) a fortified wine ranging in colour from pale gold to dark brown. [17c: from *Xeres*, an earlier form of *Jerez*, Spanish town where it was orig produced]

she's *contraction* **1** she is. **2** she has.

Shetland pony *noun* a kind of small sturdy pony with a long thick coat, orig bred in the Shetland Isles.

Shia *or* **Shiah** /ʃɪə/ *singular noun* the branch of Islam which regards Ali, Muhammad's cousin and son-in-law, as his true successor as leader of Islam. Compare **Sunni**. ▸ *noun* (***Shias or Shiahs***) a member of this branch of Islam; a **Shiite**. [17c: Arabic, meaning 'sect']

shiatsu *or* **shiatzu** *noun, med* a Japanese healing massage technique involving the application of pressure, mainly with the hands, to parts of the body distant from the affected region. Also called **acupressure**. [1960s: Japanese, meaning 'finger pressure']

shibboleth *noun* **1** a common saying. **2** a slogan, catch phrase, custom or belief, esp if considered outdated. **3** a peculiarity of speech. **4** a use of a word, phrase or pronunciation that characterizes members of a particular group. [14c: Hebrew, literally meaning 'ear of corn', used in the Old Testament as a test-word by Jephthah and his Gileadites to detect Ephraimites, who could not pronounce *sh*]

shied *past tense, past participle of* **shy**[1], **shy**[2]

shield *noun* **1** a piece of armour consisting of a broad plate, carried to deflect weapons. **2** a protective plate, screen, pad or other guard. **3** any shield-shaped design or object, esp one used as an emblem or coat of arms. **4** a shield-shaped plate or medal presented as a prize. **5** someone or something that protects from danger or harm. ▸ *verb* **1** to protect from danger or harm. **2** to ward off something. [Anglo-Saxon *sceld*]

shies see **shy**[1], **shy**[2]

shift *verb* **1** *tr & intr* to change the position or direction of something; to change position or direction. **2** to transfer, switch or redirect: *shift the blame on to someone else*. **3** in a vehicle: to change (gear). **4** to remove or dislodge someone or something: *Nothing will shift that mark*. **5** *intr, informal* to move quickly. **6** to take appropriate or urgent action. **7** *intr* to manage or get along; to do as one can. ▸ *noun* **1** a change, or change of position. **2** one of a set of consecutive periods into which a 24-hour working day is divided. **3** the group of workers on duty during any one of these periods. **4** *comput* displacement of an ordered set of data to the left or right. **5** a loose, usu straight, dress. [Anglo-Saxon *sciftan* to divide]

shiftless *adj* **1** having no motivation or initiative. **2** inefficient.

shifty *adj* (**-ier, -iest**) **1** of a person or behaviour: sly, shady or dubious; untrustworthy. **2** of a person or behaviour: evasive or tricky.

Shiite /ˈʃiːaɪt/ *noun* a Muslim who is an adherent of **Shia**. ▸ *adj* referring or relating to Shia. ▪ **Shiism** *noun*. [18c]

shilling *noun* **1** in the UK: a monetary unit and coin, before the introduction of decimal currency in 1971, worth one-twentieth of a pound or 12 old pence (12d). **2** the standard unit of currency in Kenya, Tanzania, Uganda and Somalia, equal to 100 cents. [Anglo-Saxon *scilling*]

shilly-shally *verb* (**-ies, -ied**) *intr* to be indecisive; to vacillate. [17c: reduplication of *shall I?*]

shim *noun* a thin washer or slip of metal, wood, plastic, etc used to adjust or fill a gap between machine parts, esp gears. [18c]

shimmer *verb, intr* to shine tremulously and quiveringly with reflected light; to glisten. ▸ *noun* a tremulous or quivering gleam of reflected light. ▪ **shimmery** *adj*. [Anglo-Saxon *scimerian*]

shimmy *noun* (**-ies**) **1** a vivacious body-shaking dance, particularly popular during the 1920s. Also called **shimmy-shake**. **2** vibration in a motor vehicle, esp of the wheels, or an aeroplane. ▸ *verb* (**-ies, -ied**) *intr* **1** to dance the shimmy, or to make similar movements. **2** to vibrate. [Early 20c: from **chemise**]

shin *noun* **1** the bony front part of the leg below the knee. **2** the lower part of a leg of beef. ▸ *verb* (***shinned, shinning***) *tr & intr* (*usu* **shin up**) to climb by gripping with the hands and legs. [Anglo-Saxon *scinu*]

shinbone *noun* the **tibia**.

shindig *noun, informal* **1** a lively party or celebration. **2** a noisy disturbance or row; a commotion. [19c]

shine *verb* (***shone*** or in sense 4 ***shined***) **1** *intr* to give out or reflect light; to beam with a steady radiance. **2** to direct the light from something: *They shone the torch around the room*. **3** to be bright; to glow: *Her face shone with joy*. **4** to make bright and gleaming by polishing. **5** *intr* to be outstandingly impressive in ability; to excel: *She shines at maths*. **6** *intr* to be clear or conspicuous: *Intelligence shines from their faces*. ▸ *noun* **1** shining quality; brightness. **2** an act or process of polishing. [Anglo-Saxon *scinan*]

IDIOMS **take a shine to sb** *informal* to like or fancy them on first acquaintance.

shiner *noun* **1** someone or something that shines. **2** *informal* a black eye.

shingle[1] *noun* **1** a thin rectangular tile, esp made of wood, laid with others in overlapping rows on a roof or wall. **2** these tiles collectively. **3** *US* a small sign hung outside a shop or business premises. **4** a woman's short hairstyle, cut at the back into overlapping layers. ▸ *verb* **1** to tile with shingles. **2** to cut in a shingle. [12c: from Latin *scindula* wooden tile]

shingle[2] *noun, geol* **1** small pebbles that have been worn smooth by water, found esp in a series of parallel ridges on beaches. **2** a beach, bank or bed covered in gravel or stones. ▪ **shingly** *adj*.

shingles *singular noun, med* a disease which produces a series of blisters along the path of the nerve, esp in the area of the waist and ribs. [14c: from Latin *cingulum* belt]

shinty *noun* (**-ies**) **1** a game, orig Scottish, similar to hockey, played by two teams of 12. **2** (*also* **shinty-stick**) the stick used for this game. [18c]

shiny *adj* (**-ier, -iest**) reflecting light; polished to brightness.

ship *noun* **1** a large engine-propelled vessel, intended for sea travel. **2** a large sailing vessel, esp a three-masted, square-rigged sailing vessel. **3** *informal* a spaceship or airship. ▸ *verb* (***shipped, shipping***) **1** to send or transport by ship. **2** to send or transport by land or air. **3** *naut* of a boat: to take in (water, eg waves) over the side. **4** *naut* to bring on board a boat or ship: *ship oars*. **5** to engage for service on board ship. [Anglo-Saxon *scip*]

IDIOMS **when one's ship comes in** *or* **comes home** when one becomes rich.

-ship *suffix, forming nouns, denoting* **1** position, rank or status; *lordship*. **2** a period of office or rule: *chairmanship*. **3** a state or condition: *friendship*. **4** a specified type of skill: *craftsmanship*. **5** a group of individuals having something in common: *membership*. [Anglo-Saxon *-scipe*]

shipboard *noun* the side of a ship. ▸ *adj* occurring or situated on board a ship.

shipbuilder *noun* a person or company that constructs ships. ▪ **shipbuilding** *noun.*

shipmate *noun* a fellow sailor.

shipment *noun* **1** the act or practice of shipping cargo. **2** a cargo or consignment transported, not necessarily by ship.

shipping *noun* **1** the commercial transportation of freight, esp by ship. **2** ships as traffic.

shipshape *adj* in good order; neat and tidy.

shipwreck *noun* **1** the accidental sinking or destruction of a ship. **2** the remains of a sunken or destroyed ship. **3** wreck or ruin; disaster. ▸ *verb* **1** *tr & intr* to be or make someone the victim of a ship's accidental sinking or destruction. **2** to wreck, ruin or destroy (eg plans).

shipwright *noun* a skilled wright or carpenter who builds or repairs (esp wooden) ships.

shipyard *noun* a place where ships are built and repaired.

shire *noun* **1** a county. **2** *Aust* a rural district having its own elected council. **3** a shire horse. [Anglo-Saxon *scir* authority]

shirk *verb* **1** to evade (work, a duty, etc). **2** *intr* to avoid work, duty or responsibility. ▪ **shirker** *noun.* [17c: perhaps from German *Schurke* scoundrel]

shirt *noun* a garment for the upper body, typically with buttons down the front, and usu a fitted collar and cuffs. [Anglo-Saxon *scyrte*]

IDIOMS **keep one's shirt on** *informal* to control one's temper; to remain calm. **put one's shirt on sth** *informal* to bet all one has on it.

shirt tail *noun* the longer flap hanging down at the back of a shirt.

shirtwaister *noun* a woman's tailored dress with a shirt-like bodice. Also called **shirt dress**.

shirty *adj* (**-*ier*, -*iest***) *informal* ill-tempered or irritable; annoyed. [19c]

shish kebab see **kebab**

shiver[1] *verb, intr* **1** to quiver or tremble, eg with fear. **2** to make an involuntary muscular movement in response to the cold. ▸ *noun* **1** an act of shivering; a shivering sensation. **2** (**the shivers**) *informal* a fit of shivering. ▪ **shivery** *adj.* [12c: as *chivere*]

shiver[2] *noun* a splinter or other small fragment. ▸ *verb, tr & intr* to shatter. [12c: as *scifre*]

shoal[1] *noun* **1** a multitude of fish swimming together. **2** a huge crowd or assemblage; a multitude, flock or swarm. ▸ *verb, intr* to gather or move in a shoal; to swarm. [Anglo-Saxon *scolu* a troop]

shoal[2] *noun* **1** an area of shallow water in a river, lake or sea where sediment has accumulated. **2** such an accumulation of sediment, esp one exposed at high tide. ▸ *verb* **1** *tr & intr* to make or become shallow. **2** *intr, naut* to sail into shallow water. ▸ *adj* shallow. [Anglo-Saxon *sceald* shallow]

shock[1] *noun* **1** a strong emotional disturbance, esp a feeling of extreme surprise, outrage or disgust. **2** a cause of such a disturbance. **3** a heavy and violent impact, orig of charging warriors. **4** (*in full* **electric shock**) a convulsion caused by the passage of an electric current through the body. **5** *med* a state of extreme physical collapse, characterized by lowered blood pressure and body temperature and a sweaty pallid skin, occurring as a result of severe burns, drug overdose, extreme emotional disturbance, etc. ▸ *verb* **1** to assail or attack with a shock. **2** to give a shock to someone. **3** to make someone feel extreme surprise, outrage or disgust. **4** *intr* to outrage feelings. [16c: from French *choc*]

shock[2] *noun* a bushy mass of hair. [19c]

shock[3] *noun* a number of sheaves of corn propped up against each other to dry. [14c: as *schokke*]

shock absorber *noun* in a vehicle: a device, such as a coiled spring, that damps vibrations caused by the wheels passing over bumps in the road.

shocker *noun, informal* **1** a very sensational tale. **2** any unpleasant or offensive person or thing.

shocking *adj* **1** giving a shock. **2** extremely surprising, outrageous or disgusting, esp to oversensitive feelings. **3** *informal* deplorably bad: *His handwriting is shocking.* ▪ **shockingly** *adv.* [17c]

shockproof *adj* protected against or resistant to the effects of shock or impact. ▪ **shockproofing** *noun.*

shock tactics *plural noun* any course of action that seeks to achieve its object by means of suddenness and force.

shock therapy *or* **shock treatment** see **electroconvulsive therapy**

shock wave *noun* **1** *physics* an exceptionally intense sound wave, caused by a violent explosion or the movement of an object at a speed greater than that of sound. **2** a feeling of shock which spreads through a community, etc, after some disturbing event: *The mayor's arrest sent a shock wave through the town.*

shoddy *adj* (**-*ier*, -*iest***) of poor quality; carelessly done or made. ▪ **shoddiness** *noun.*

shoe *noun* **1** either of a pair of shaped outer coverings for the feet, esp ones made of leather or other stiff material, usu finishing below the ankle. **2** anything like this in shape or function. **3** a horseshoe. ▸ *verb* (***shod, shoeing***) **1** to provide with shoes. **2** to fit (a horse) with shoes. [Anglo-Saxon *scoh*]

IDIOMS **in sb's shoes** in the same situation as them; in their position: *I wouldn't like to be in his shoes now.*

shoehorn *noun* a curved piece of metal, plastic or (orig) horn, used for levering the heel into a shoe. ▸ *verb* to fit, squeeze or compress into a tight space.

shoelace *noun* a string or cord passed through eyelet holes to fasten a shoe.

shoemaker *noun* someone who makes, though now more often only sells or repairs, shoes and boots.

shoeshine *noun* the act of polishing shoes.

shoestring *noun, N Am, esp US* a shoelace.

IDIOMS **on a shoestring** *informal* with or using a very small or limited amount of money.

shoe tree *noun* a support put inside a shoe to preserve its shape when it is not being worn.

shogun /ˈʃoʊɡʌn, ˈʃoʊɡʊn/ *noun, hist* any of the hereditary military governors who were the effective rulers of Japan from the 12c until 1867. ▪ **shogunal** *adj.* ▪ **shogunate** *noun.* [17c: Japanese, from Chinese *jiangjun* general]

shone *past tense, past participle of* **shine**

shoo *exclam* an expression used to scare or chase away a person or animal. ▸ *verb* (***shooed***) **1** *intr* to cry 'Shoo!'. **2** (*usu* **shoo sb** *or* **sth away** *or* **off**) to chase them away by, or as if by, shouting 'Shoo!'

shook *past tense of* **shake**

shoot *verb* (***shot***) **1** *tr & intr* to fire a gun or other weapon. **2** to fire bullets, arrows or other missiles. **3** to hit, wound or kill with a weapon or missile. **4** to let fly with force: *The geyser shot water high into the air.* **5** to launch or direct forcefully and rapidly: *He shot questions at them.* **6** *tr & intr* to move or make someone or something move or progress quickly: *That last victory shot them to the top of the table.* **7** *tr & intr, sport* to strike (the ball, etc) at goal. **8** *tr & intr* to film (motion pictures), or take photographs of someone or something. **9** *intr* of pain: to dart with a stabbing sensation. **10** *intr* to dart forth or forwards. **11** *intr* to use a bow or gun in practice, competition, hunting, etc: *He likes to shoot regularly.* **12** *slang* to play a game of eg pool or golf; to have as a score at golf: *We could shoot pool at the club later.* ▸ *noun* **1** an act of shooting. **2** a shooting match or party. **3** an outing or expedition to hunt animals with firearms. **4** an area of land within which animals are hunted in this way. **5** the shooting of a film or a photographic modelling session. **6** a new or young plant growth. **7** the sprouting of a plant. [Anglo-Saxon *sceotan*]

IDIOMS **shoot from the hip** *informal* to speak hastily, bluntly or directly, without preparation or concern for the consequences. **shoot oneself in the foot** *informal* to injure or harm one's own interests by ineptitude. **shoot one's mouth off** *informal* to speak freely, indiscreetly or boastfully. **the whole shoot** *or* **shooting-match** *informal* the whole lot.

PHRASAL VERBS **shoot up** to grow or increase extremely quickly: *prices shot up.*

shooter *noun* **1** someone or something that shoots. **2** *informal* a gun.

shooting gallery *noun* a long room fitted out with targets used for practice or amusement with firearms.

shooting star *noun* a **meteor**.

shop *noun* **1** a room or building where goods are sold or services are provided. **2** a place providing specific goods or services: *a barber's shop* • *a betting shop.* **3** a spell of shopping, esp for food or household items. **4** talk about one's own business. ▸ *verb* (***shopped, shopping***) **1** *intr* to visit a shop or shops, esp in order to buy goods. **2** *slang* to betray or inform on someone to the police, etc. [Anglo-Saxon *sceoppa* treasury]

IDIOMS **all over the shop** *informal* scattered everywhere; in numerous places. **set up shop** to establish or open a trading establishment. **shut up shop** *informal* to stop trading, either at the end of the working day or permanently. **talk shop** *informal* to talk about one's work or business, esp in a tedious way.

PHRASAL VERBS **shop around 1** to compare the price and quality of goods in various shops before making a purchase. **2** *informal* to explore the full range of options available before committing oneself to any.

shop assistant *noun* someone serving customers in a shop.

shop floor *noun* **1** the part of a factory or workshop where the manual work is carried out. **2** the workers in a factory, as opposed to the management.

shopkeeper *noun* someone who owns and manages a shop.

shoplift *verb, tr & intr* to steal (goods) from shops. ▪ **shoplifter** *noun.* ▪ **shoplifting** *noun.*

shopper *noun* **1** someone who shops. **2** a shopping bag or basket.

shopping *noun* **1** the act of visiting shops to look at or buy goods. **2** goods bought in shops.

shop-soiled *adj* slightly dirty, faded or spoiled from being used as a display in a shop.

shop steward *noun* a worker elected by others to be an official trade union representative in negotiations with the management.

shop window *noun* **1** a window of a shop in which goods are arranged in a display. **2** any arrangement which displays something to advantage.

shore[1] *noun* **1** a narrow strip of land bordering on the sea, a lake or any other large body of water. **2** land as opposed to the sea. **3** (**shores**) lands; countries: *foreign shores.* ▸ *verb* to set on shore: *shore a boat.* [14c: as *schore*]

shore[2] *noun* a prop. ▸ *verb* (*usu* **shore sth up**) **1** to support it with props. **2** to give support to it; to sustain or strengthen it. ▪ **shoring** *noun* **1** supporting by using props. **2** a set of props. [15c: from Dutch *schore*]

shoreline *noun* the line formed where land meets water.

shorn *a past participle of* **shear**

short *adj* **1** having little physical length; not long. **2** having little height. **3** having little extent or duration; brief; concise: *a short day.* **4** indicating a seemingly short length of time: *For a few short weeks we could enjoy our time together.* **5** of a temper: quickly and easily lost. **6** rudely abrupt; curt: *She was very short with him.* **7** of the memory: tending not to retain things for long. **8** of pastry: crisp and crumbling easily. **9** in short supply; in demand: *We are two tickets short.* **10** *phonetics* of a vowel sound: being the briefer of two possible lengths of vowel. **11** lacking in money: *I'm a bit short at the moment.* ▸ *adv* **1** abruptly; briefly: *stopped short.* **2** on this or the near side: *The dart fell short of the board.* ▸ *noun* **1** something that is short. **2** shortness; abbreviation or summary. **3** *informal* a drink of an alcoholic spirit. **4** a short cinema film shown before the main film. **5** a **short circuit**. ▸ *verb, tr & intr* to **short-circuit**. ▪ **shortness** *noun.* [Anglo-Saxon *sceort*]

IDIOMS **fall short** to be insufficient; to be less than a required, expected or stated amount. **for short** as an abbreviated form: *She gets called Jenny for short.* **in short** concisely stated; in a few words. **in short supply** not available in the required or desired quantity; scarce. **make short work of sb** *or* **sth** to settle or dispose of quickly and thoroughly. **short and sweet** *informal* agreeably brief. **short for sth** an abbreviated form of it: *Jenny is short for Jennifer.* **short of sth** without going as far as it; except it: *We tried every kind of persuasion short of threats.* **short of** *or* **on sth** deficient; lacking in it. **stop short** to come to an abrupt halt or standstill.

shortage *noun* a lack or deficiency.

shortbread *noun* a rich crumbly biscuit made with flour, butter and sugar.

shortcake *noun* **1** shortbread or other crumbly cake. **2** *US* a light cake, prepared in layers with fruit between, served with cream.

short-change *verb* **1** to give (a customer) less than the correct amount of change, either by accident or intentionally. **2** *informal* to treat dishonestly; to cheat.

short circuit *noun, electronics* a connection across an electric circuit with a very low resistance, usu caused accidentally, eg by an insulation failure, which may damage electrical equipment or be a fire hazard. ▸ *verb* (**short-circuit**) **1** to cause a short circuit in something. **2** to provide with a short cut or bypass.

shortcoming *noun* a fault or defect.

shortcrust *adj* of pastry: having a crisp yet crumbly consistency.

short cut *noun* **1** a quicker route between two places. **2** a method that saves time or effort.

shorten *verb, tr & intr* to make or become shorter.

shortening *noun* butter, lard or other fat used for making pastry more crumbly.

shortfall *noun* **1** a failure to reach a desired or expected level or specification. **2** the amount or margin by which something is deficient: *There is a shortfall of £100.*

shorthand *noun* any of various systems of combined strokes and dots representing speech sounds and groups of sounds, used as a fast way of recording speech in writing.

short-handed *adj* understaffed; short of workers.

shorthorn *noun* a breed of beef and dairy cattle with very short horns.

shortlist *noun* (*also* **short leet**) a selection of the best candidates from the total number submitted or nominated, from which the successful candidate will be chosen. ▸ *verb* (**short-list**) to place on a shortlist.

short-lived *adj* living or lasting only for a short time.

shortly *adv* **1** soon; within a short period of time: *He'll arrive shortly.* **2** in a curt or abrupt manner.

short-range *adj* referring or relating to a short distance or length of time: *a short-range telescope.*

shorts *plural noun* trousers extending from the waist to anywhere between the upper thigh and the knee.

short shrift *noun* discourteously brief or disdainful consideration: *Their suggestions were given short shrift.*

IDIOMS **make short shrift of sth** to discard it without due consideration.

short-sighted *adj* **1** of a person: capable of seeing only near objects clearly; affected by **myopia**. Compare **long-sighted**. **2** of a person, plan, etc: lacking or showing a lack of foresight. ▪ **short-sightedness** *noun.*

short-staffed *adj* having a reduced or insufficient staff.

short-tempered *adj* easily made angry.

short-term *adj* **1** concerned only with the near or immediate future. **2** lasting only a short time.

short wave *noun* **1** a radio wave with a wavelength between 10 and 100 metres. **2** *physics* an electromagnetic wave with a wavelength no longer than that of visible light.

shot[1] *noun* **1** an act of shooting or firing a gun. **2** the sound of a gun being fired. **3** small metal pellets collectively, fired in clusters from a **shotgun**. **4** a person considered in terms of their ability to fire a gun accurately: *a good shot.* **5** a photographic exposure. **6** a single piece of filmed action recorded without a break by one camera. **7** *sport* an act or instance of shooting or playing a stroke eg in tennis, snooker, etc. **8** *athletics* a heavy metal ball thrown in the **shot put**. **9** *informal* an attempt: *I'll have a shot at it.* **10** *informal* an injection. **11 a** the flight of a missile; **b** the distance it travels. **12** *informal* a small drink of alcoholic spirit. **13** the launch of a spacecraft, esp a rocket: *moon shot.* [Anglo-Saxon *sceot*]

IDIOMS **a long shot** a bet with little chance of success: *It's a long shot, but I'll have a try.* **like a shot** extremely quickly or without hesitation; eagerly or willingly.

shot[2] *adj* **1** of a fabric: woven with different-coloured threads in the warp and weft so that movement produces the effect of changing colours: *shot silk.* **2** streaked with a different colour. ▸ *verb, past tense, past participle of* **shoot**.

IDIOMS **a shot in the arm** *informal* an uplifting or reviving influence; a boost. **a shot in the dark** a wild guess. **be** *or* **get shot of sb** *or* **sth** *informal* be rid of them or it.

shotgun *noun* a gun with a long, wide, smooth barrel for firing small shot.

shot put *noun, athletics* a field event in which a heavy metal ball is thrown from the shoulder as far as possible. ▪ **shot-putter** *noun.*

should *auxiliary verb* expressing: **1** obligation, duty or recommendation; ought to: *You should brush your teeth regularly.* **2** likelihood or probability: *He should have left by now.* **3** condition: *If she should die before you, what would happen?* **4** *with first person pronouns* a past tense of *shall* in reported speech: *I told them I should be back soon.* **5** statements in clauses with *that*, following expressions of feeling or mood: *It seems odd that we should both have had the same idea.* [Anglo-Saxon *sceolde*]

shoulder *noun* **1** in humans and animals: the part on either side of the body, just below the neck, where the arm or front limb joins the trunk. **2** the part of a garment that covers this. **3** a cut of meat consisting of the animal's upper foreleg. **4** either edge of a road. ▸ *verb* **1** to bear (eg a responsibility). **2** to carry on one's shoulders. **3** to thrust with the shoulder. [Anglo-Saxon *sculdor*]

IDIOMS **a shoulder to cry on** a person to tell one's troubles to. **put one's shoulder to the wheel** *informal* to get down to some hard work; to make a great effort. **rub shoulders with sb** *informal* to meet or associate with them. **shoulder to shoulder** together in friendship or agreement; side by side.

shoulder blade *noun* the **scapula**.

shouldn't *contraction, informal* should not.

shout *noun* **1** a loud cry or call. **2** *informal* a turn to buy a round of drinks. ▸ *verb* **1** *tr & intr* (*also* **shout out**) to utter a loud cry or call. **2** *intr* to speak in raised or angry tones. ▪ **shouter** *noun.* [14c as *schoute*]

PHRASAL VERBS **shout sb down** to force them to give up speaking, or prevent them from being heard, by means of persistent shouting.

shove *verb* **1** *tr & intr* to push or thrust with force. **2** *informal* to place or put, esp roughly: *Just shove it in the bag.* ▸ *noun* a forceful push. [Anglo-Saxon *scufan*]

PHRASAL VERBS **shove off** *informal* to go away.

shovel *noun* **1** a tool with a deep-sided spade-like blade and a handle, for lifting and carrying loose material. **2** a machine, machine part or device with a scooping action. **3** a scoop; a shovelful, the amount a shovel can hold. ▸ *verb* (***shovelled, shovelling***) **1** to lift or carry with, or as if with, a shovel. **2** to rapidly and crudely gather in large quantities: *She shovelled food into her mouth.* [Anglo-Saxon *scofl*]

show *verb* (*past participle* ***shown*** *or* ***showed***) **1** *tr & intr* to make or become visible, known or noticeable: *Does my embarrassment show?* **2** to present to view. **3** to display or exhibit. **4** to prove, indicate or reveal: *This shows us that man evolved from the ape.* **5** to prove oneself or itself to be: *He always shows himself to be such a gentleman.* **6** to teach by demonstrating. **7** to lead, guide or escort: *I'll show you to the door.* **8** to give: *Show him some respect.* **9** to represent or manifest: *The exam results show a marked improvement.* **10** *intr* of a cinema film, theatre production, etc: to be part of a current programme: *Her latest film is now showing at smaller cinemas.* **11** *intr, slang* to appear or arrive: *What time did he show?* ▸ *noun* **1** an act of showing. **2** any form of entertainment or spectacle. **3** an exhibition. **4** a pretence: *a show of friendship.* **5** a sign or indication: *a show of emotion.* **6** *informal* proceedings; affair. **7** *old use, informal* effort; attempt: *a jolly good show.* [Anglo-Saxon *sceawian* to look]

IDIOMS **for show** for the sake of outward appearances; for effect. **on show** on display; available to be seen. **run the show** *informal* to be in charge; to take over or dominate.

PHRASAL VERBS **show off** to display oneself or one's talents precociously, aimed at inviting attention or admiration. See also **show-off**. **show sth off 1** to display it proudly, inviting admiration. **2** to display it to good effect: *The cream rug shows off the red carpet nicely.* **show up 1** *informal* to arrive; to turn up. **2** to be clearly visible. **show sb up** to embarrass them in public.

showbiz *noun, adj, informal* show business.

show business *noun* the entertainment industry, esp light entertainment in film, theatre and television.

showcase *noun* **1** a glass case for displaying objects. **2** any setting in which someone or something is displayed to good advantage.

showdown *noun, informal* a confrontation or fight by which a long-term dispute may be finally settled.

showed *past tense, a past participle of* **show**

shower *noun* **1** a device that produces a spray of water for bathing under, usu while standing. **2** a room or cubicle fitted with such a device or devices. **3** an act or an instance of bathing under such a device. **4** a sudden but short and usu light fall of rain, snow or hail. **5** a fall of drops of any liquid. **6** a sudden (esp heavy) burst or fall: *a shower of abuse.* **7** *N Am* **a** an abundance of wedding gifts, gifts for a baby, etc; **b** a party at which such gifts are presented. **8** *slang* a detestable or worthless person or group of people. ▸ *verb* **1** *tr & intr* to cover, bestow, fall or come abundantly. **2** *intr* to bathe under a shower. **3** *intr* to rain in showers. ▪ **showery** *adj.* [Anglo-Saxon *scur*]

showgirl *noun* a girl who performs in variety entertainments, usu as a dancer or singer.

showing *noun* **1** an act of exhibiting or displaying. **2** a screening of a cinema film. **3** a display of behaviour as evidence of a fact: *On this showing, he certainly won't get the job.*

showjumping *noun* a competitive sport in which riders on horseback take turns to jump a variety of obstacles, usu against the clock. ▪ **showjumper** *noun.*

showman *noun* **1** someone who owns, exhibits or manages a circus, a stall at a fairground, or other entertainment. **2** someone skilled in displaying things, esp personal abilities. ▪ **showmanship** *noun.*

shown *a past participle of* **show**

show-off *noun, informal* someone who shows off to attract attention; an exhibitionist. See also **show off** at **show**.

showpiece *noun* **1** an item on display; an exhibit. **2** an item presented as an excellent example of its type, to be copied or admired.

showroom *noun* a room where examples of goods for sale, esp large and expensive items, are displayed.

show-stopper *noun* an act or performance that is received with great enthusiasm by the audience. ▪ **show-stopping** *adj.*

showy *adj* (***-ier, -iest***) **1** making an impressive or exciting display. **2** attractively and impressively bright; flashy. ▪ **showily** *adv.* ▪ **showiness** *noun.*

shrank *past tense of* **shrink**

shrapnel *noun* **1** a shell, filled with pellets or metal fragments, which explodes shortly before impact. **2** flying fragments of the casing of this or any exploding shell. [Early 19c: named after H Shrapnel, British inventor of the pellet-filled shell]

shred *noun* **1** a thin scrap or strip cut or ripped off. **2** the smallest piece or amount: *There's not a shred of evidence.* ▸ *verb* (***shredded, shredding***) to cut, tear or scrape into shreds. [Anglo-Saxon *screade*]

shredder *noun* a device for shredding eg documents.

shrew *noun* **1** a small nocturnal mammal with velvety fur, small eyes and a pointed snout. **2** a quarrelsome or scolding woman. ▪ **shrewish** *adj.* [Anglo-Saxon *screawa*]

shrewd *adj* possessing or showing keen judgement gained from practical experience; astute. ▪ **shrewdly** *adv.* ▪ **shrewdness** *noun.* [14c: as *shrewed* malicious]

shriek *verb, tr & intr* to cry out with a piercing scream. ▸ *noun* such a piercing cry. [16c: from Norse *skoekja* to screech]

shrift *noun* absolution; confession. See also **short shrift**.

shrike *noun* any of various small perching birds with a powerful slightly hooked beak. [Anglo-Saxon *scric*]

shrill *adj* of a voice, sound, etc: high-pitched and piercing. ▸ *verb* to utter in such a high-pitched manner. ▪ **shrillness** *noun.* [14c: from German *schrell*]

shrimp *noun* **1** a small edible crustacean with a cylindrical semi-transparent body and five pairs of jointed legs. **2** *informal* a very small slight person. ▸ *verb, intr* to fish for shrimps. [14c: from German *schrimpen* to shrink]

shrine *noun* **1** a sacred place of worship. **2** the tomb or monument of a saint or other holy person. **3** any place or thing greatly respected because of its associations. [Anglo-Saxon *scrin*]

shrink *verb* (*past tense* ***shrank*** *or* ***shrunk***, *past participle* ***shrunk*** *or* ***shrunken***) **1** *tr & intr* to make or become smaller in size or extent, esp through exposure to heat, cold or moisture. **2** *tr & intr* to contract or make something contract. **3** *intr* to shrivel or wither. **4** (*often* **shrink from sth**) to move away in horror or disgust; to recoil. **5** (*often* **shrink from sth**) to be reluctant to do it. ▸ *noun* **1** an act of shrinking. **2** *infor-*

mal a psychiatrist. ▪ **shrinkable** *adj.* [Anglo-Saxon *scrincan*]

shrinkage *noun* **1** the act of shrinking. **2** the amount by which something shrinks.

shrinking violet *noun, informal* a shy, hesitant person.

shrink-wrap *verb* to wrap (goods) in clear plastic film that is then shrunk, eg by heating, so that it fits tightly.

shrivel *verb* (***shrivelled, shrivelling***) *tr & intr* (*also* **shrivel up**) to make or become shrunken and wrinkled, esp as a result of drying out. [16c: from Swedish dialect *skryvla* to wrinkle]

Shrops *abbrev, English county* Shropshire.

shroud *noun* **1** a garment or cloth in which a corpse is wrapped. **2** anything that obscures, masks or hides: *shrouds of fog.* ▸ *verb* **1** to wrap in a shroud. **2** to obscure, mask or hide: *proceedings shrouded in secrecy.* [Anglo-Saxon *scrud* garment]

Shrove Tuesday *noun* in the Christian calendar: the day before Ash Wednesday, on which it was customary to confess one's sins. See also **Pancake Day**. [Anglo-Saxon *scrifan* to confess sins]

shrub *noun, botany* a woody plant or bush, without any main trunk, which branches into several main stems at or just below ground level. ▪ **shrubby** *adj.* [Anglo-Saxon *scrybb* scrub]

shrubbery *noun* (***-ies***) **1** a place, esp a part of a garden, where shrubs are grown. **2** a collective name for shrubs. [18c]

shrug *verb* (***shrugged, shrugging***) *tr & intr* to raise up and drop the shoulders briefly as an indication of doubt, indifference, etc. ▸ *noun* an act of shrugging. [14c as *schruggen* to shudder]

PHRASAL VERBS **shrug sth off 1** to get rid of it easily. **2** to dismiss (esp criticism) lightly; to be indifferent.

shrunk see under **shrink**

shrunken *adj* having shrunk or having been shrunk.

shtoom, **schtoom**, **shtum**, **shtumm** *or* **stumm** /ʃtʊm/ *adj, slang* silent; quiet. [1950s: Yiddish]

shudder *verb, intr* to shiver or tremble, esp with fear, cold or disgust. ▸ *noun* **1** such a trembling movement or feeling. **2** a heavy vibration or shaking. ▪ **shuddering** *adj.* [14c: from German *schoderen*]

shuffle *verb* **1** *tr & intr* to move or drag (one's feet) with short quick sliding steps; to walk in this fashion. **2** *intr* to shamble or walk awkwardly. **3** to rearrange or mix up roughly or carelessly: *shuffle papers.* **4** *tr & intr* to jumble up (playing-cards) randomly. ▸ *noun* **1** an act or sound of shuffling. **2** a short quick sliding of the feet in dancing. [16c: from German *schuffeln*]

shufti *or* **shufty** *noun, informal* a look or glance. [1940s: Arabic, literally meaning 'have you seen?']

shun *verb* (***shunned, shunning***) to intentionally avoid someone or something. [Anglo-Saxon *scunian*]

shunt *verb* **1** to move (a train or carriage) from one track to another. **2** to bypass or sidetrack. **3** to get rid of or transfer (eg a task) on to someone else, as an evasion. ▸ *noun* **1** an act of shunting or being shunted. **2** *electronics* a conductor diverting part of an electric current. **3** *informal* a minor collision between vehicles. ▪ **shunter** *noun.* [13c]

shush *exclam* be quiet! ▸ *verb* to make someone or something quiet by, or as if by, saying 'Shush!'

shut *verb* (***shut, shutting***) **1** *tr & intr* to place or move so as to close an opening: *shut the door.* **2** *tr & intr* to close or make something close over, denying access to the contents or inside: *shut the book.* **3** *tr & intr* (*often* **shut up**) not to allow access to something; to forbid entrance into it: *shut up the building.* **4** to fasten or bar; to lock. **5** to bring together the parts or outer parts of something: *I can't shut the clasp.* **6** to confine: *He shuts himself in his room for hours.* **7** to catch or pinch in a fastening: *I shut my finger in the window.* **8** *intr* of a business, etc: to cease to operate at the end of the day. ▸ *adj* **1** not open; closed. **2** made fast; secure. [Anglo-Saxon *scyttan* to bar]

PHRASAL VERBS **shut down** *or* **shut sth down** to stop or make it stop working or operating, either for a time or permanently. **shut sth off** to switch it off; to stop the flow of it. **shut sb** *or* **sth out 1** to prevent them or it entering a room, building, etc. **2** to exclude them or it. **3** to block out (eg light). **shut up** *informal* to stop speaking. **shut sb up 1** *informal* to make them stop speaking; to reduce them to silence. **2** to confine them, usu against their will.

shutdown *noun* a temporary closing of a factory or business.

shuteye *noun, informal* sleep.

shutter *noun* **1** someone or something that shuts. **2** a movable internal or external cover for a window, esp one of a pair of hinged wooden or metal panels. **3** a device in a camera that regulates the opening and closing of the aperture, exposing the film to light. ▸ *verb* to fit or cover (a window) with a shutter or shutters. [16c: from **shut**]

shuttle *noun* **1** *weaving* the device that carries the horizontal thread (the **weft**) backwards and forwards between the vertical threads (the **warp**). **2** the device that carries the lower thread through the loop formed by the upper in a sewing machine. **3** an aircraft, train or bus that runs a frequent service between two places, usu at a relatively short distance from one another. ▸ *verb, tr & intr* to convey or travel in a shuttle. [Anglo-Saxon *scytel* dart]

shuttlecock *noun* a cone of feathers or of feathered plastic attached to a rounded cork, hit backwards and forwards with or badminton rackets. [16c]

shy[1] *adj* **1** of a person: embarrassed or unnerved by the company or attention of others. **2** easily scared; bashful or timid. **3** (**shy of sth**) wary or distrustful of it. **4** warily reluctant. ▸ *verb* (***shies, shied***) *intr* **1** eg of a horse: to jump suddenly aside or back in fear; to be startled. **2** (*usu* **shy away** *or* **off**) to shrink from something or recoil, showing reluctance. ▸ *noun* (***shies***) an act of shying. ▪ **shyly** *adv.* ▪ **shyness** *noun.* [Anglo-Saxon *sceoh* timid]

shy[2] *verb* (***shies, shied***) to fling or throw. ▸ *noun* (***shies***) a fling or throw.

shyster *noun, N Am, esp US, slang* an unscrupulous or disreputable person, esp a lawyer. [19c: prob named after Scheuster, a disreputable US lawyer]

SI *or* **SI unit** *abbrev* Système International d'Unités, the modern scientific system of units, used in the measurement of all physical quantities.

Si *symbol, chem* silicon.

Siamese *adj* of or relating to Siam, now called Thailand, its inhabitants, or their language. ▸ *noun* **1** (*pl* ***Siamese***) a citizen or inhabitant of, or person born in, Siam. **2** the language of Siam. **3** (*pl* ***Siameses***) a Siamese cat.

Siamese cat *noun* a short-haired variety of domestic cat with a triangular face, blue eyes, and a pale coat with darker patches on the ears, face, legs and tail.

Siamese twins *plural noun* twins who are physically joined to each other from birth. Formal name: **conjoined twins**.

sibilant *adj* similar to, having or pronounced with a hissing sound. ▸ *noun, phonetics* a consonant with such a sound, eg *s* and *z*. ▪ **sibilance** *or* **sibilancy** *noun*. [17c: from Latin *sibilare* to hiss]

sibling *noun* a brother or sister. [Anglo-Saxon *sibb* relationship + **-ling**]

sic *adv* a term used in brackets after a word or phrase in a quotation to indicate that it is quoted accurately, even if it appears to be a mistake. [19c: Latin, meaning 'thus' or 'so']

sick *adj* **1** vomiting; feeling the need to vomit. **2** ill; unwell. **3** referring or relating to ill health: *sick pay.* **4** (*often* **sick for sb** *or* **sth**) pining or longing for them or it. **5** (*often* **sick of sb** *or* **sth**) extremely annoyed; disgusted: *I'm sick of your attitude.* **6** (*often* **sick of sb** *or* **sth**) thoroughly weary or fed up with them or it. **7** mentally deranged. **8** of humour, comedy, jokes, etc: exploiting gruesome and morbid subjects in an unpleasant way. ▸ *noun, informal* vomit. ▸ *verb, tr & intr* (*usu* **sick up**) to vomit. [Anglo-Saxon *seoc*]

sick bay *noun* a compartment, eg on board a ship, for sick and wounded people.

sicken *verb* **1** to make someone or something feel like vomiting. **2** to annoy greatly or disgust. **3** *intr* (*usu* **sicken for sth**) to show symptoms of an illness: *I'm sickening for the flu.*

sickening *adj* **1** causing nausea. **2** causing extreme annoyance or disgust. ▪ **sickeningly** *adv.*

sickle *noun* a tool with a short handle and a curved blade for cutting grain crops. [Anglo-Saxon *sicol*]

sick leave *noun* time taken off work as a result of sickness.

sickle-cell anaemia *noun, pathol* a hereditary blood disorder, mainly affecting Black people, in which the red blood cells become sickle-shaped and fragile, and are destroyed by the body's defence system.

sickly *adj* (**-ier, -iest**) **1** susceptible or prone to illness; ailing or feeble. **2** unhealthy-looking; pallid. **3** weakly sentimental; mawkish. ▸ *adv* to an extent that suggests illness: *sickly pale.* ▪ **sickliness** *noun.*

sickness *noun* **1** the condition of being ill; an illness. **2** vomiting. **3** nausea.

sick pay *noun* payment made to a worker who is absent through illness.

side *noun* **1** any of the usu flat or flattish surfaces that form the outer extent of something; any of these surfaces other than the front, back, top or bottom. **2** an edge or border, or the area adjoining this: *My car's at the side of the road.* **3** either of the parts or areas produced when the whole is divided up the middle: *I'll take the left side of the room.* **4** the part of the body between the armpit and hip. **5** the area of space next to someone or something: *He's round the side of the house.* **6** half of a carcass divided along the medial plane: *a side of beef.* **7** either of the broad surfaces of a flat or flattish object: *two sides of a coin.* **8** any of the lines forming a geometric figure. **9** any of the groups or teams, or opposing positions, in a conflict or competition. **10** an aspect: *We've seen a different side to him.* **11** a page: *My essay covered 5 sides.* **12** *Brit informal* a television channel. **13** either of the two playing surfaces of a record or cassette. ▸ *adj* **1** located at the side: *side entrance.* **2** subsidiary or subordinate: *side road.* ▸ *verb* (*usu* **side with sb**) to take on their position or point of view; to join forces with them. [Anglo-Saxon]

IDIOMS **on** *or* **to one side** removed to a position away from the main concern; put aside. **on the side** in addition to or apart from ordinary occupation or income, often dishonest or illegal. **side by side 1** close together. **2** with sides touching. **take sides** to support one particular side in a conflict, argument or dispute.

sideboard *noun* **1** a large piece of furniture, often consisting of shelves or cabinets mounted above drawers or cupboards, for holding plates, ornaments, etc. **2** (**sideboards**) **sideburn**s.

sideburn *noun* (*usu* **sideburns**) the hair that grows on each side of a man's face in front of the ears. [19c: named after US General Burnside, who pioneered the style of leaving this hair unshaven]

sidecar *noun* a small carriage for one or two passengers, attached to the side of a motorcycle.

side drum *noun* a small double-headed drum with snares, usu slung from the drummer's side.

side effect *noun* **1** an additional and usu undesirable effect, esp of a drug, eg nausea, drowsiness. **2** any undesired additional effect.

sidekick *noun, informal* a close or special friend; a partner or deputy.

sideline *noun* **1** a line marking either side boundary of a sports pitch. **2** a business, occupation or trade in addition to regular work.

sidelong *adj, adv* from or to one side; not direct or directly: *a sidelong glance.*

sidereal /saɪˈdɪərɪəl/ *adj* referring or relating to, or determined by the stars. [17c: from Latin *sidus* star]

sideroad *noun* a **byroad**, esp one joining onto a main road.

side-saddle *noun* a horse's saddle designed to enable a woman in a skirt to sit with both legs on the same side. ▸ *adv* sitting in this way.

sideshow *noun* **1** an exhibition or show subordinate to a larger one. **2** any subordinate or incidental activity or event.

sidespin *noun* the spinning of a ball in a sideways direction.

side-splitting *adj* extremely funny; provoking uproarious and hysterical laughter.

sidestep *verb* **1** to avoid by, or as if by, stepping aside: *You're sidestepping the issue.* **2** *intr* to step aside. ▸ *noun* a step taken to one side.

side street *noun* a minor street, esp one leading from a main street.

sidetrack *verb* to divert the attention of away from the matter in hand.

sidewalk *noun, N Am, esp US* a pavement.

sideways *adv, adj* **1** from, to or towards one side. **2** with one side foremost: *We skidded sideways into the hedge.*

siding *noun* a short dead-end railway line on to which trains, wagons, etc can be shunted temporarily from the main line.

sidle *verb, intr* to go or edge along sideways, esp in a cautious, furtive and ingratiating manner. [17c: back-formation from obsolete *sideling* sideways]

SIDS *abbrev* sudden infant death syndrome.

siege *noun* **1** the act or process of surrounding a fort or town with troops, cutting off its supplies and subjecting it to persistent attack with the intention of forcing its surrender. **2** a police operation using similar tactics, eg to force a criminal out of a building. [13c: from French *sege*]
IDIOMS **lay siege to a place** to subject it to a siege.

---

siege
This word is often misspelt. The letter *i* comes before the letter *e*. It might help you to remember the following sentence:
*Stuck **i**nside, **e**veryone **g**ot **e**xcited.*

---

siemens *noun* (abbrev **S**) the SI unit of conductance. [1930s: named after Werner von Siemens, German electrical engineer]

sienna *noun* a pigment obtained from a type of earth with a high clay and iron content, **raw sienna** being the yellowish-brown colour of the natural pigment, and **burnt sienna** being the reddish-brown colour of the roasted pigment. [18c: named after Siena in Italy]

sierra *noun* esp in Spanish-speaking countries and the US: a mountain range, esp when jagged. [17c: Spanish, meaning 'a saw']

siesta *noun* in hot countries: a sleep or rest after the midday meal. [17c: Spanish]

sieve /sɪv/ *noun* a utensil with a meshed or perforated bottom, used for straining solids from liquids or for sifting large particles from smaller ones. ▸ *verb* to strain or sift with a sieve. [Anglo-Saxon *sife*]

sift *verb* **1** to pass through a sieve in order to separate out lumps or larger particles. **2** *tr & intr* to examine closely and discriminatingly: *sift the data* • *sift through the applications*. ▪ **sifter** *noun*. [Anglo-Saxon *siftan*]

sigh *verb* **1** *intr* to release a long deep audible breath, expressive of sadness, longing, tiredness or relief. **2** *intr* to make a similar sound, esp suggesting breakdown or failure: *We heard the engine sigh.* **3** to express with such a sound. ▸ *noun* an act or the sound of sighing. [Anglo-Saxon *sican*]

sight *noun* **1** the power or faculty of seeing; vision. **2** a thing or object seen; view or spectacle: *It's a lovely sight.* **3** someone's field of view or vision, or the opportunity to see things that this provides: *out of sight*. **4** (*usu* **sights**) places, buildings, etc that are particularly interesting or worth seeing: *see the sights of the city.* **5** a device on a firearm through or along which one looks to take aim. **6** a similar device used as a guide to the eye on an optical or other instrument. **7** *informal* a person or thing unpleasant to look at: *He looked a sight without his teeth in.* ▸ *verb* **1** to get a look at or glimpse of someone or something: *She was sighted there at around midnight.* **2** to aim (a firearm) using the sight. [Anglo-Saxon *sihth*]
IDIOMS **a sight for sore eyes** a very welcome sight. **catch sight of sb** *or* **sth** to catch or get a glimpse of them or it. **know sb** *or* **sth by sight** to recognize them only by their appearance; to know who they are. **set one's sights on sth** to decide on it as an ambition or aim.

sighted *adj* having the power of sight; not blind.

sightless *adj* blind. ▪ **sightlessness** *noun*.

sightly *adj* (**-ier, iest**) pleasing to the eye; attractive or appealing.

sight-reading *noun* playing or singing from printed music that one has not previously seen. ▪ **sight-read** *verb*.

sightsee *verb, intr* to visit places of interest, esp as a tourist. ▪ **sightseeing** *noun*. ▪ **sightseer** *noun*.

sigma *noun* the eighteenth letter of the Greek alphabet.

sign *noun* **1** a printed mark with a meaning; a symbol: *a multiplication sign*. **2** *maths* an indication of positive or negative value: *the minus sign*. **3** a gesture expressing a meaning; a signal. **4** an indication: *signs of improvement*. **5** a portent or omen; a miraculous token. **6** a board or panel displaying information for public view. **7** a board or panel displaying a shopkeeper's name, trade, etc. **8** *med* any external evidence or indication of disease, perceptible to an examining doctor, etc. **9** *astrol* any of the twelve parts of the zodiac, bearing the name of, but not coincident with, a constellation. ▸ *verb* **1** *tr & intr* to give a signal or indication. **2** to write a signature on something; to confirm one's assent to something with a signature. **3** to write (one's name) as a signature: *sign a cheque*. **4** *tr & intr* to employ or become employed with the signing of a contract: *Stoke City have signed a new player.* **5** *tr & intr* to communicate using sign language. **6** to cross or make the sign of the cross over (oneself or someone else). [13c: from French *signe*]
PHRASAL VERBS **sign sth away** to give it away or transfer it by signing a legally binding document. **sign in** *or* **out** to record one's arrival or departure, eg at work, by signing one's name. **sign sb in** to allow someone, usu a non-member, official entry to a club, society, etc by signing one's name. **sign off 1** to bring a broadcast to an end. **2** to stop work, etc. **sign on** *informal* **1** to register as unemployed. **2** to return periodically to an unemployment office to sign one's name as a formal declaration that one is still unemployed. **sign up 1** to enrol with an organization, esp the army. **2** to engage oneself for work by signing a contract.

signal *noun* **1** a message in the form of a gesture, light, sound, etc, conveying information or indicating the time for action, often over a distance. **2** (**signals**) the apparatus used to send such a message, eg coloured lights or movable arms or poles on a railway network. **3** an event marking the moment for action to be taken: *Their arrival was a signal for the party to begin.* **4** any set of transmitted electrical impulses received as a sound or image, eg in television; the message conveyed by them. ▸ *verb* (***signalled, signalling***) **1** *tr & intr* to transmit or convey (a message) using signals. **2** to indicate. ▸ *adj* notable: *a signal triumph*. [14c: French]

signal box *noun* the cabin from which signals on a railway line are controlled.

signalman *noun* a controller who works railway signals.

signal-to-noise ratio *noun, electronics* the ratio of the power of a desired electrical signal to the power of the unwanted background noise, usually expressed in decibels.

signatory /ˈsɪgnətrɪ/ *noun* (*-ies*) a person, organization or state that is a party to a contract, treaty or other document. [17c: from Latin *signatorius*]

signature *noun* **1** one's name written by oneself, or a representative symbol, as a formal mark of authorization, etc. **2** an indication of key or time at the beginning of a line of music. **3** a large sheet of paper with printed pages on it, each with a numeral or letter at the bottom, which when folded forms a section of a book. [16c: from Latin *signatura*]

signature tune *noun* a tune used to identify or introduce a specified radio or television programme or performer.

signet *noun* a small seal used for stamping documents, etc. [14c: from Latin *signum* sign]

signet ring *noun* a finger ring carrying a signet.

significance *noun* **1** meaning or importance. **2** the condition or quality of being significant. **3** a value of probability at which a particular hypothesis is held to be contradicted by the results of a statistical test.

significant *adj* **1** important; worth noting or considering. **2** having some meaning; indicating or implying something. ▪ **significantly** *adv.*

signify *verb* (*-ies, -ied*) **1** to be a sign for something or someone; to suggest or mean. **2** to be a symbol of something or someone; to denote. **3** *intr* to be important or significant. [13c: from Latin *significare*]

sign language *noun* any form of communication using gestures to represent words and ideas, esp an official system of hand gestures used by deaf people.

sign of the zodiac see under **zodiac**

signpost *noun* **1** a post supporting a sign that gives information or directions to motorists or pedestrians. **2** an indication or clue. ▸ *verb* **1** to mark (a route) with signposts. **2** to give directions to someone.

Sikh /siːk/ *noun* an adherent of the monotheistic religion established in the 16c by Guru Nanak. ▸ *adj* belonging or relating to the Sikhs, their beliefs or customs. ▪ **Sikhism** *noun.* [18c: Hindi, meaning 'disciple']

silage /ˈsaɪlɪdʒ/ *noun* animal fodder made from forage crops such as grass, maize, etc compressed and preserved by controlled fermentation, eg in a silo.

sild *noun* a young herring. [1920s: Norwegian]

silence *noun* **1** absence of sound or speech. **2** a time of such absence of sound or speech. **3** failure or abstention from communication, disclosing information or secrets, etc. ▸ *verb* to make someone or something stop speaking, making a noise, or giving away information. ▸ *exclam* Be quiet! [13c: from Latin *silere* to be quiet]

silencer *noun* a device fitted to a gun barrel or engine exhaust to reduce or eliminate the noise made.

silent *adj* **1** free from noise; unaccompanied by sound. **2** refraining from speech; not mentioning or divulging something. **3** unspoken but expressed: *silent joy.* **4** not pronounced: *the silent p in pneumonia*. **5** of a cinema film: having no soundtrack. ▪ **silently** *adv.* [16c]

silent partner see **sleeping partner**

silhouette /sɪlʊˈɛt/ *noun* **1** a dark shape or shadow seen against a light background. **2** an outline drawing of an object or esp a person, in profile, usu filled in with black. ▸ *verb* to represent, or make appear, as a silhouette. [18c: named after Etienne de Silhouette, French finance minister]

silica *noun, geol* a hard white or colourless glassy solid that occurs naturally as quartz, sand and flint, and also as silicate compounds, and is used in the manufacture of glasses, glazes and enamels.

silica gel *noun, chem* an absorbent form of silica used as a drying agent, and as a catalyst in many chemical processes.

silicate *noun, chem* a chemical compound containing silicon, oxygen and one or more metals. [19c]

silicon *noun* (symbol **Si**) a non-metallic element that occurs naturally as silicate minerals in clays and rocks, and as silica in sand and quartz, used as a semiconductor to make transistors and silicon chips for the integrated circuits of computers, etc. [Early 19c: from Latin *silex* flint]

---

silicon, silicone
Be careful not to use the spelling **silicon** when you mean **silicone**:
silicon chip
silicone implants

---

silicon carbide *noun, chem* a hard, iridescent, bluish-black, crystalline compound, widely used as an abrasive, in cutting, grinding and polishing instruments. Also called **Carborundum.**

silicon chip *noun, electronics, comput* a very thin piece of silicon or other ductor material, only a few millimetres square, on which all the components of an integrated circuit are arranged. Also called **chip, microchip.**

silicone *noun, chem* a synthetic polymer, used in lubricants, electrical insulators, paints, adhesives and surgical breast implants.

---

silicone, silicon
See the Usage Note at **silicon.**

---

silicosis *noun, pathol* a lung disease caused by prolonged inhalation of dust containing silica. Compare **asbestosis.**

silk *noun* **1** a fine soft fibre produced by the larva of the silkworm. **2** an imitation made by forcing a viscous solution of modified cellulose through small holes. **3** thread or fabric made from such fibres. **4** a garment made from such fabric. **5 a** the silk gown worn by a Queen's or King's Counsel; **b** the rank conferred by this. [Anglo-Saxon *seolc*]

IDIOMS **take silk** of a barrister: to be appointed a Queen's or King's Counsel.

silken *adj, literary* **1** made of silk. **2** as soft or smooth as silk.

silk-screen printing see **screen printing**

silkworm *noun* the caterpillar of the silk moth, which spins a cocoon of unbroken silk thread.

silky *adj* (*-ier, -iest*) **1** soft and shiny like silk. **2** of a person's manner or voice: suave.

sill *noun* **1** the bottom part of the framework around the inside of a window or door. **2** the ledge of wood, stone or metal forming this. [Anglo-Saxon *syll*]

sillabub see **syllabub**

silly *adj* (*-ier, -iest*) **1** not sensible; foolish; trivial or frivolous. **2** *cricket* in a fielding position very near the batsman: *silly mid-on.* ▸ *noun* (*-ies*) *informal* (*also*

silly-billy) a foolish person. ▪ **silliness** *noun*. [Anglo-Saxon *sælig* happy]

silo *noun* **1** a tall round airtight tower for storing green crops and converting them into silage. **2** an underground chamber housing a missile ready for firing. [19c: Spanish]

silt *noun* sedimentary material, finer than sand and coarser than clay, consisting of very small rock fragments or mineral particles, deposited by or suspended in running or still water. ▸ *verb, intr* (*often* **silt up**) to become blocked up with silt. [15c: as *sylt*]

Silurian /sɪˈluərɪən/ *adj, geol* denoting the period of geological time between the **Ordovician** and **Devonian** periods, during which marine life predominated and the first jawed fish and primitive land plants appeared. [18c: from Latin *Silures* an ancient people of S Wales]

silvan see **sylvan**

silver *noun* **1** (symbol **Ag**) an element, a soft white lustrous precious metal that is an excellent conductor of heat and electricity, and is used in jewellery, ornaments, mirrors and coins. **2** coins made of this metal. **3** articles made of or coated with this metal, esp cutlery and other tableware. **4** a silver medal. ▸ *adj* **1** having a whitish-grey colour. **2** denoting a 25th wedding or other anniversary. ▸ *verb* **1** to apply a thin coating of silver; to plate with silver. **2** to give a silvery sheen to something. **3** *intr* to become silvery. ▪ **silvery** *adj*. [Anglo-Saxon *seolfor*]

IDIOMS **born with a silver spoon in one's mouth** born to affluence or wealthy surroundings.

silver birch *noun* a species of birch tree with silvery-white peeling bark.

silverfish *noun* a primitive wingless insect with a tapering body covered with silvery scales, commonly found in houses.

silver jubilee *noun* a 25th anniversary.

silver lining *noun* a positive aspect of an otherwise unpleasant or unfortunate situation.

silver medal *noun* esp in sporting competitions: a medal of silver awarded to the person or team in second place.

silver nitrate *noun, chem* a colourless chemical compound that is light-sensitive, used in photographic film.

silver plate *noun* **1** a thin coating of silver or a silver alloy on a metallic object, eg cutlery. **2** such objects coated with silver. ▪ **silver-plated** *adj*.

silver screen *noun* **1** (**the silver screen**) *informal* the film industry or films in general. **2** the cinema screen.

silverside *noun* a fine cut of beef from the rump, just below the aitchbone.

silversmith *noun* someone who makes or repairs articles made of silver.

silverware *noun* objects, esp cutlery or tableware, made from or coated with silver.

silvery *adj* **1** having the colour or shiny quality of silver. **2** having a pleasantly light ringing sound: *silvery bells*.

silviculture *noun, botany* the cultivation of forest trees, or the management of woodland to produce timber, etc. [19c: from Latin *silva* wood + **culture**]

SIM card /sɪm/ *noun, telecomm* a removable electronic card inside a mobile phone that stores information about the subscriber. [Late 20c: acronym for *S*ubscriber *I*dentification *M*odule]

simian *noun* a monkey or ape. ▸ *adj* belonging or relating to, or resembling, a monkey or ape. [17c: from Latin *simia* ape]

similar *adj* **1** having a close resemblance to something; being of the same kind, but not identical. **2** *geom* exactly corresponding in shape, regardless of size. ▪ **similarity** *noun* (**-ies**). ▪ **similarly** *adv*. [17c: from French *similaire*]

simile /ˈsɪmɪlɪ/ *noun* a figure of speech in which a thing is described by being likened to something, usu using *as* or *like*, as in *eyes sparkling like diamonds*. [14c: Latin]

similitude *noun, formal* resemblance. [14c]

simmer *verb* **1** *tr & intr* to cook or make something cook gently at just below boiling point. **2** *intr* to be close to an outburst of emotion, usu anger. ▸ *noun* a simmering state. [17c: as *simperen*]

PHRASAL VERBS **simmer down** to calm down, esp after a commotion, eg an angry outburst.

simnel *noun* a sweet fruit cake covered with marzipan, traditionally baked at Easter or Mid-Lent. [13c: from Latin *simila* fine flour]

simony /ˈsaɪmənɪ/ *noun* the practice of buying or selling a religious post, benefice or privilege. [13c: from Simon Magus, the Biblical sorcerer who offered money for the power to convey the gift of the Holy Spirit]

simoom *or* **simoon** *noun* a hot suffocating desert wind in Arabia and N Africa. [18c: from Arabic *samum*]

simper *verb* **1** *intr* to smile in a weak affected manner. **2** to express by or while smiling in this way. ▸ *noun* a simpering smile. [16c: from Norwegian *semper* smart]

simple *adj* **1** easy; not difficult. **2** straightforward; not complex or complicated. **3** plain or basic: *a simple outfit*. **4** down-to-earth; unpretentious; honest. **5** *often ironic* foolish; gullible; lacking intelligence: *He's a bit of a simple lad*. **6** plain; straightforward; not altered or adulterated: *the simple facts*. **7** consisting of one thing or element. [13c: French]

simple fraction *noun, maths* a fraction with whole numbers as numerator and denominator.

simple fracture *noun* a fracture of the bone that does not involve an open skin wound. Compare **compound fracture**.

simple interest *noun* interest calculated only on the basic sum initially borrowed. Compare **compound interest**.

simple sentence *noun* a sentence consisting of one **main clause**.

simpleton *noun* a foolish or unintelligent person.

simplicity *noun* a simple state or quality. [14c: from French *simplicite*, from *simple*]

simplify *verb* (**-ies, -ied**) to make something less difficult or complicated; to make it easier to understand. ▪ **simplification** *noun*. [17c: from Latin *simplus* simple + *facere* to make]

simplistic *adj* unrealistically straightforward or uncomplicated. ▪ **simplistically** *adv*.

simply *adv* **1** in a straightforward, uncomplicated manner. **2** just: *It's simply not true*. **3** absolutely: *simply marvellous*. **4** merely: *We simply wanted to help*.

simulate *verb* **1** to convincingly re-create (a set of conditions or a real-life event), esp for the purposes of training. **2** to assume a false appearance of someone or something. **3** to pretend to have, do or feel: *She simulated anger.* ▪ **simulated** *adj.* ▪ **simulation** *noun.* [17c: from Latin *simulare*]

simulator *noun* a device that simulates a system, process or set of conditions, esp in order to test it, or for training purposes: *a flight simulator.*

simultaneous *adj* happening, or carried out, at exactly the same time. ▪ **simultaneously** *adv.* [17c: from Latin *simul* at the same time]

simultaneous equations *plural noun* two or more equations which are satisfied when their variables are given the same values.

sin[1] *noun* **1** an act that breaches a moral and esp a religious law or teaching. **2** the condition of offending a deity by committing a moral offence. **3** an act that offends common standards of morality or decency; an outrage. **4** a great shame. ▸ *verb* (***sinned, sinning***) *intr* to commit a sin. [Anglo-Saxon *synn*]

sin[2] *abbrev* sine (see **sine**[1]).

since *conj* **1** from the time that. **2** seeing that; as; because: *I'm not surprised you failed the exam since you did no work for it.* ▸ *prep* during or throughout the period between now and some earlier stated time: *I've been there several times since it opened.* ▸ *adv* **1** from that time onwards: *I haven't been back since.* **2** ago: *five years since.* [15c: as *sithens*]

sincere *adj* genuine; not pretended or affected. ▪ **sincerely** *adv.* ▪ **sincerity** *noun.* [16c: from Latin *sincerus* clean]

---

sincerely

This word is often misspelt. It might help you to remember that **sincerely** is made up of **since** and **rely**.

---

sine[1] /saɪn/ *noun, trig* (abbrev **sin**) in a right-angled triangle: a **function** (*noun* sense 4) of an angle, defined as the length of the side opposite the angle divided by the length of the hypotenuse. [16c: from Latin *sinus* curve or bay]

sine[2] /'saɪnɪ, 'sɪnɛ/ *prep* without. [Latin]

sinecure /'sɪnɪkjʊə(r)/ *noun* a paid job involving little or no work. [17c: from Latin *sine* without + *cura* care]

sine qua non /'sɪnɛ kwɑː noːn/ *noun* an essential condition or requirement. [16c: Latin, meaning 'without which not']

sinew *noun* **1** a strong piece of fibrous tissue joining a muscle to a bone; a tendon. **2** (**sinews**) physical strength; muscle. ▪ **sinewy** *adj.* [Anglo-Saxon *sinu*]

sine wave *noun, maths* a wave resembling that obtained by plotting a graph of the size of an angle against the value of its sine.

sinful *adj* wicked; involving sin; morally wrong. ▪ **sinfully** *adv.* ▪ **sinfulness** *noun.*

sing *verb* (*past tense* ***sang,*** *past participle* ***sung***) **1** *tr & intr* to utter (words, sounds, etc) in a melodic rhythmic fashion, esp to the accompaniment of music. **2** *intr* to utter such sounds as a profession: *Her mother was a dancer, but she sings.* **3** to make someone or something pass into a particular state with such sound: *The mother sang her baby to sleep.* **4** *intr* to make a sound like a musical voice; to hum, ring or whistle: *The kettle was singing on the stove.* **5** *intr* to suffer a ringing sound: *a loud bang that made their ears sing.* **6** *intr, esp US slang* to inform or confess; to squeal. **7** *intr* of birds, specific insects, etc: to produce calls or sounds. ▪ **singer** *noun.* [Anglo-Saxon *singan*]

PHRASAL VERBS **sing out** to shout or call out.

sing. *abbrev* singular.

singe *verb* (***singeing***) *tr & intr* to burn lightly on the surface; to scorch or become scorched. ▸ *noun* a light surface burn. [Anglo-Saxon *sengan*]

single *adj* **1** comprising only one part; solitary. **2** having no partner; unmarried, esp never having been married. **3** for use by one person only: *a single room.* **4** of a travel ticket: valid for an outward journey only; not return. **5** unique; individual. **6** even one: *Not a single person turned up.* ▸ *noun* **1** (*often* **singles**) a person without a partner, either marital or otherwise. **2** a single room, eg in a guest house. **3** a ticket for an outward journey only. **4** a recording of an individual pop song released for sale, usu with one or more supplementary tracks. **5** *Brit* a pound coin or note. **6** *US* a one-dollar note. **7** *cricket* a hit for one run. ▸ *verb* (*always* **single out**) to pick someone or something from among others. [14c: French]

single-breasted *adj* of a coat or jacket: having only one row of buttons and a slight overlap at the front.

single cream *noun* cream with a low fat content, which does not thicken when beaten.

single-decker *noun* a vehicle, esp a bus, with only one deck. Compare **double-decker**.

single figures *plural noun* the numbers from 1 to 9.

single file *or* **Indian file** *noun* a line of people, animals, etc standing or moving one behind the other.

single-handed *adj, adv* done, carried out etc by oneself, without any help from others. ▪ **single-handedly** *adv.*

single-minded *adj* determinedly pursuing one specific aim or object. ▪ **single-mindedly** *adv.*

single parent *noun* a mother or father bringing up a child alone.

singles *singular noun* in tennis, etc: a match where one player competes against another.

singlet *noun* a sleeveless vest or undershirt. [18c]

singleton *noun* **1** the only playing-card of a particular suit in a hand. **2** a solitary person or thing.

singly *adv* **1** one at a time; individually. **2** alone; by oneself.

singsong *noun* an informal gathering at which friends, etc sing together for pleasure. ▸ *adj* of a speaking voice, etc: having a fluctuating intonation and rhythm.

singular *adj* **1** single; unique. **2** extraordinary; exceptional. **3** strange; odd. **4** *grammar* denoting or referring to one person, thing, etc as opposed to two or more. Compare **plural**. ▸ *noun, grammar* a word or form of a word expressing the idea or involvement of one person, thing, etc as opposed to two or more. ▪ **singularity** *noun* (***-ies***). ▪ **singularly** *adv.* [14c: from Latin *singis*]

Sinhalese *or* **Singhalese** *noun* (*pl* ***Sinhalese***) **1** a member of the majority population of Sri Lanka. **2** their language. ▸ *adj* belonging or relating to this people or their language. [19c: from Sanskrit *Simhala* Sri Lanka]

sinister *adj* **1** suggesting or threatening evil or danger; malign. **2** *heraldry* on the left side of the shield from the bearer's point of view, as opposed to that of the observer. Compare **dexter**. [14c: Latin, meaning 'left', believed by the Romans to be the unlucky side]

sink *verb* (*past tense* ***sank*** *or* ***sunk,*** *past participle* ***sunk***) **1** *tr & intr* to fall or cause to fall and remain below the surface of water, either partially or completely. **2** *intr* to collapse downwardly or inwardly; to fall because of a collapsing base or foundation; to subside. **3** *intr* to be or become inwardly withdrawn or dejected: *My heart sank at the news.* **4** to embed: *They sank the pole into the ground.* **5** to pass steadily (and often dangerously) into a worse level or state: *He sank into depression after her death.* **6** to diminish or decline: *My opinion of him sank after that incident.* **7** to invest (money) heavily: *We sank a lot of money into this project.* **8** *informal* to ruin the plans of someone; to ruin (plans): *We are sunk.* **9** *informal* to drink (esp alcohol) usu quickly: *We sank four beers within the hour.* **10** *informal* to send (a ball) into a pocket in snooker, billiards, etc and into the hole in golf. **11** to excavate (a well, shaft, etc). **12** to let in or insert: *screws sunk into the wall.* **13** to abandon or abolish: *I'll sink the whole organization if I have to.* ▸ *noun* a basin, wall-mounted or in a sink unit, with built-in water supply and drainage, for washing dishes, etc. [Anglo-Saxon *sincan*]

PHRASAL VERBS **sink in 1** *informal* to be fully understood or realized: *The bad news took a few days to sink in.* **2** to penetrate or be absorbed: *Wait for the ink to sink in first.*

sinker *noun* **1** someone who sinks. **2** a weight used to sink something, eg a fishing line.

sinking fund *noun* a fund formed by setting aside income to accumulate at interest to pay off a debt.

sinner *noun* someone who sins or has sinned.

Sinn Fein /ʃɪn feɪn/ *noun* a Republican political movement and party in Ireland. [Irish Gaelic, 'we ourselves']

Sino- *combining form, denoting* Chinese: *Sino-Soviet.* [From Greek *Sinai* Chinese]

Sinology /saɪ'nɒlədʒɪ/ *noun* the study of China in all its aspects, esp cultural and political. ▪ **Sinologist** *noun* an expert in Sinology. [19c]

sinuous *adj* wavy; winding; bending in a supple manner. ▪ **sinuosity** *or* **sinuousness** *noun.* [16c: Latin, from *sinus* curve]

sinus /'saɪnəs/ *noun, anatomy* a cavity or depression filled with air, esp in the bones of mammals. [16c: Latin, meaning 'curve']

sinusitis *noun* inflammation of the lining of the sinuses, esp the nasal ones. [Early 20c]

Sioux /suː/ *noun* (*pl* ***Sioux*** /suː, suːz/) **1** a Native American of a tribe now living in the Dakotas, Minnesota and Montana. **2** any of a group of languages spoken by them. ▸ *adj* of or relating to the Sioux or their languages. [18c: French, a shortening of *Nadoussioux*]

sip *verb* (***sipped, sipping***) *tr & intr* to drink in very small mouthfuls. ▸ *noun* **1** an act of sipping. **2** an amount sipped at one time. [Anglo-Saxon *sypian*]

siphon *or* **syphon** *noun* **1** a tube held in an inverted U-shape that can be used to transfer liquid from one container at a higher level into another at a lower level, used to empty car petrol tanks, etc. **2** (*in full* **soda siphon**) a bottle from which a liquid, esp soda water, is forced by pressure of gas. ▸ *verb* (*usu* **siphon sth off**) **1** to transfer (liquid) from one container to another using such a device. **2** to take (money, funds, etc) slowly and continuously from a store or fund. [17c: Greek, meaning 'pipe']

sir *noun* **1** a polite and respectful address for a man. **2** (**Sir**) a title used before the Christian name of a knight or baronet. [13c: see **sire**]

sire *noun* **1** the father of a horse or other animal. **2** *hist* a term of respect used in addressing a king. ▸ *verb* of an animal: to father (young). [12c: French, from Latin *senior* elder]

siren *noun* **1** a device that gives out a loud wailing noise, usu as a warning signal. **2** an irresistible woman thought capable of ruining men's lives. [14c: from Greek *Seiren*]

Sirius *noun, astron* the brightest star in the night sky (the **Dog Star**) in the constellation Canis Major. [14c: Latin, from Greek *Seiros*]

sirloin *noun* a fine cut of beef from the loin or the upper part of the loin. [16c: from French *surlonge*]

sirocco *noun* in S Europe: a dry hot dusty wind blowing from N Africa, and becoming more moist as it moves further north. [17c: Italian]

sis *noun, informal* short for **sister**.

sisal /'saɪzəl/ *noun* a strong coarse durable yellowish fibre obtained from the leaves of **sisal hemp** or **sisal grass**, used to make ropes, twine, brush bristles, sacking, etc. [19c: named after Sisal, the port in Yucatan in Mexico]

sissy *or* **cissy** *noun* (***-ies***) *derog* a feeble or cowardly male. ▸ *adj* (***-ier, -iest***) having the characteristics of a sissy. [19c: from **sister**]

sister *noun* **1** a female child of the same parents as another. **2** a nun. **3** a senior female nurse, esp one in charge of a ward. **4** a close female associate; a fellow female member of a profession, class or racial group. ▸ *adj* being of the same origin, model or design: *a sister ship.* [Anglo-Saxon *sweostor*]

sisterhood *noun* **1** the state of being a sister or sisters. **2** a religious community of women; a body of nuns. **3** a group of women with common interests or beliefs.

sister-in-law *noun* (***sisters-in-law***) **1** the sister of one's husband or wife. **2** the wife of one's brother.

sisterly *adj* of a woman or her behaviour: like a sister, esp in being kind and affectionate. ▪ **sisterliness** *noun.*

sit *verb* (***sat, sitting***) **1** *intr* to rest the body on the buttocks, with the upper body more or less vertical. **2** of an animal: to position itself on its hindquarters in a similar manner. **3** *intr* of a bird: to perch or lie. **4** *intr* of a bird: to brood. **5** *intr* of an object: to lie, rest or hang: *There are a few cups sitting on the shelf.* **6** *intr* to lie unused: *I've got all my tools sitting in the shed.* **7** *intr* to hold a meeting or other session: *The court sits tomorrow.* **8** *intr* to be a member, taking regular part in meetings: *sit on a committee.* **9** to have a seat, as in parliament. **10** to have a specific position: *The TV sits on this stand.* **11** to take (an examination); to be a candidate for (a degree or other award): *I'm sitting my first exam tomorrow.* **12** to conduct to a seat; to assign a seat to someone: *They sat me next to him.* **13** *intr* to be or exist in a specified comparison or relation: *His smoking sits awkwardly with his being a doctor.* **14** *intr* to pose as an artist's or photographer's model. [Anglo-Saxon *sittan*]

IDIOMS **be sitting pretty** *informal* to be in a very advantageous position. **sit tight 1** to maintain one's position and opinion determinedly. **2** to wait patiently.

PHRASAL VERBS **sit back 1** to sit comfortably, esp with the head and back rested. **2** to observe rather than take an active part, esp when action is needed. **sit in on sth** to be present at it as a visitor or observer, esp without participating. **sit in for sb** to act as a substitute for them. **sit on sth 1** to be a member of it: *sit on a committee.* **2** *informal* to delay taking action over it. **sit sth out** to take no part, esp in a dance or game. **sit up 1** to move oneself from a slouching or lying position into an upright sitting position. **2** to take notice suddenly or show a sudden interest.

sitar *noun* a guitar-like instrument of Indian origin, with a long neck, rounded body and two sets of strings. [19c: Hindi]

sitcom *noun, informal* short for **situation comedy**.

sit-down *noun, informal* a short rest in a seated position. ▸ *adj* **1** of a meal: for which the diners are seated. **2** of a strike: in which the workers occupy the workplace until an agreement is reached.

site *noun* **1** the place where something was, is, or is to be situated: *the site of the museum* • *a Roman site.* **2** an area set aside for a specific activity: *a camping site.* **3** a website. ▸ *verb* to position or situate. [14c: from Latin *situs* position]

sit-in *noun* the occupation of a public building, factory, etc as a form of protest or as a means of applying pressure, esp towards the settling of a dispute.

sitter *noun* **1** a person or animal that sits. **2** a person who poses for an artist or photographer. **3** a babysitter. **4** *in compounds* a person who looks after a house, pet, etc in the absence of its owner: *a flat sitter.*

sitting *verb, present participle of* **sit**. ▸ *noun* **1** the act or state of being seated. **2** a period of continuous activity, usu while sitting or in a similar position: *He wrote it at one sitting.* **3** a turn to eat for any of two or more sections of a group too large to eat all at the same time in the same place, or the period set aside for each turn. **4** a period of posing for an artist or photographer. **5** a session or meeting of an official body. ▸ *adj* **1** currently holding office: *the sitting MP for this constituency.* **2** seated: *a sitting position.*

sitting duck *or* **sitting target** *noun* someone or something in a defenceless or exposed position.

sitting room *noun* a room, esp in a private house, for relaxing in, entertaining visitors, etc.

sitting tenant *noun, Brit* a tenant occupying a property when it changes ownership.

situate *verb* to place in a certain position, context or set of circumstances. [16c: from Latin *situatus*]

situation *noun* **1** a set of circumstances or state of affairs. **2** a place, position or location. **3** a job; employment: *situations vacant.* [15c]

situation comedy *noun* a radio or TV comedy in which the same characters appear in more or less the same surroundings, and which depends for its humour on the behaviour of the characters in particular, sometimes contrived, situations. Often shortened to **sitcom**.

sit-up *noun* a physical exercise in which the body is raised up and over the thighs from a lying position, often with the hands behind the head.

Siva *or* **Shiva** /ˈsiːvə/ *noun, Hinduism* the third god of the **Trimurti**, the destroyer and reproducer.

six *noun* **1 a** the cardinal number 6; **b** the quantity that this represents, being one more than five. **2** any symbol for this, eg 6 or *VI*. **3** the age of six. **4** something, eg a shoe or a person, whose size is denoted by the number 6. **5** the sixth hour after midnight or midday: *Come at six.* • *6 o'clock* • *6pm.* **6** a set or group of six people or things. **7** *cricket* a hit scoring 6 runs. ▸ *adj* **1** totalling six. **2** aged six. [Anglo-Saxon *siex*]

IDIOMS **at sixes and sevens** in a state of total disorder or confusion. **hit** *or* **knock sb for six** *informal* **1** to defeat or ruin them completely. **2** to shock or surprise them completely. **six of one and half a dozen of the other** equal; equally acceptable or unacceptable; the same on both sides. Sometimes shortened to **six and half a dozen**.

sixer *noun* the Cub Scout or Brownie Guide leader of a team of (more or less) six.

sixfold *adj* **1** equal to six times as much or many. **2** divided into, or consisting of, six parts. ▸ *adv* by six times as much.

six-pack *noun* **1** a pack containing six items sold as one unit, esp a pack of six cans of beer. **2** *informal* a set of well-defined abdominal muscles.

sixpence *noun* in Britain: a former small silver coin worth six old pennies (6d), equivalent in value to 2½p.

sixpenny *adj* **1** worth or costing six old pennies. **2** cheap; worthless.

sixteen *noun* **1 a** the cardinal number 16; **b** the quantity that this represents, being one more than fifteen, or the sum of ten and six. **2** any symbol for this, eg *16* or *XVI*. **3** the age of sixteen. **4** something, esp a garment or a person, whose size is denoted by the number 16. **5** a set or group of sixteen people or things. ▸ *adj* **1** totalling sixteen. **2** aged sixteen. ▪ **sixteenth** *adj, noun, adv.* [Anglo-Saxon *siextiene*]

sixth (often written **6th**) *adj* **1** in counting: **a** next after fifth; **b** last of six. **2** in sixth position. **3** being one of six equal parts: *a sixth share.* ▸ *noun* **1** one of six equal parts. **2** a **fraction** equal to one divided by six (usu written ⅙). **3** a person coming sixth, eg in a race or exam: *a respectable sixth.* **4** (**the sixth**) **a** the sixth day of the month; **b** *golf* the sixth hole. **5** *music* **a** the interval between two notes that are six notes apart on a diatonic scale; **b** a note at that interval from another, or a combination of two tones separated by that interval. ▸ *adv* sixthly. ▪ **sixthly** *adv* used to introduce the sixth point in a list. [Anglo-Saxon]

sixth form *noun* in secondary education: the stage in which school subjects are taught to a level that prepares for higher education. ▪ **sixth-former** *noun.*

sixth sense *noun* an unexplained power of intuition by which one is aware of things that are not seen, heard, touched, smelled or tasted.

sixties (often written **60s** *or* **60's**) *plural noun* **1** (**one's sixties**) the period of time between one's sixtieth and seventieth birthdays. **2** (**the sixties**) the range of temperatures between sixty and seventy degrees. **3** (**the sixties**) the period of time between the sixtieth and seventieth years of a century: *born in the 60s.*

sixty *noun* (**-ies**) **1 a** the cardinal number 60; **b** the quantity that this represents, being one more than fifty-nine, or the product of ten and six. **2** any symbol for this, eg *60* or *LX*. **3** the age of sixty. **4** something whose size is denoted by the number 60. **5** a set or group of sixty people or things. ▸ *adj* **1** totalling sixty. **2** aged sixty. See also **sixties**. ▪ **sixtieth** *adj, noun, adv.*

sixty- *combining form* **a** *forming adjectives and nouns* with cardinal numbers between *one* and *nine*: *sixty-two*; **b** *forming adjectives and nouns* with ordinal numbers between *first* and *ninth*: *sixty-second.*

size[1] *noun* **1** length, breadth, height or volume, or a combination of these; the dimensions of something. **2** largeness; magnitude: *We were amazed at its size.* **3** any of a range of graded measurements into which esp garments and shoes are divided. ▸ *verb* **1** to measure something in order to determine size. **2** to sort or arrange something according to size. ▪ **sized** *adj, usu in compounds* having a particular size: *medium-sized.* [13c: from French *sise*]

PHRASAL VERBS **size sb** *or* **sth up 1** to take a mental measurement of them or it. **2** *informal* to mentally judge their or its nature, quality or worth.

size[2] *noun* a weak kind of glue used to stiffen paper and fabric, and to prepare walls for plastering and wallpapering. ▸ *verb* to cover or treat with size. [15c]

sizeable *or* **sizable** *adj* fairly large; being of a considerable size.

sizeism *or* **sizism** *noun* discrimination against overweight people. ▪ **sizeist** *noun, adj.*

sizzle *verb, intr* **1** to make a hissing sound when, or as if when, frying in hot fat. **2** to be extremely hot: *sizzling weather.* **3** *informal* to be in a state of intense emotion, esp anger or excitement. ▸ *noun* a sizzling sound. ▪ **sizzler** *noun.* [17c: imitating the sound]

sjambok /ˈʃambɒk/ *noun* in S Africa: a whip made from dried animal hide. [19c: Afrikaans]

skate[1] *noun* **1** an **ice skate** or **roller skate**. **2** a spell of skating. ▸ *verb, intr* to move around on skates. ▪ **skater** *noun.* ▪ **skating** *noun.* [17c: from Dutch *schaats*]

IDIOMS **get one's skates on** *informal* to hurry up. **skate on thin ice** to risk danger, harm or embarrassment, esp through lack of care or good judgement.

PHRASAL VERBS **skate over sth** to hurry or rush over it: *We'll skate over this next chapter.* **skate round sth** to avoid dealing with something or considering (a difficulty, etc).

skate[2] *noun* (***skate*** *or* ***skates***) a large edible flatfish with a greyish-brown upper surface with black flecks, a long pointed snout, large wing-like pectoral fins and a long slim tail. [14c: from Norse *skata*]

skateboard *noun* a narrow shaped board mounted on sets of small wheels, usu ridden in a standing position. [1960s]

skedaddle *verb, intr, informal* to run away or leave quickly. ▸ *noun* a hurried departure. [19c]

skein *noun* **1** a loosely tied coil of wool or thread. **2** a flock of geese in flight. [15c: from French *escaigne*]

skeletal *adj* **1** similar to or like a skeleton. **2** painfully or extremely thin. **3** existing in outline only.

skeleton *noun* **1** the framework of bones that supports the body of an animal, and to which the muscles are usu attached. **2** the supporting veins of a leaf. **3** an initial basic structure or idea upon or around which anything is built. **4** an outline or framework: *the skeleton of the plot.* **5** *informal* an unhealthily thin person or animal. [16c: Greek]

skeleton in the cupboard *or* (*US*) **skeleton in the closet** *noun* a shameful or slanderous fact concerning oneself or one's family that one tries to keep secret.

skeleton key *noun* a key whose edge is filed in such a way that it can open many different locks.

skeptic, **skeptical** *or* **skepticism** an alternative *N Am* spelling of **sceptic**, *etc*.

skerry *noun* (***-ies***) a reef of rock or a small rocky island. [17c: from Norse *sker*]

sketch *noun* **1** a rough drawing quickly done, esp one without much detail used as a study towards a more finished work. **2** a rough plan. **3** a short account or outline: *She gave us a quick sketch of the story.* **4** any of several short pieces of comedy presented as a programme. ▸ *verb* **1** *tr & intr* to do a rough drawing or drawings of something. **2** to give a rough outline of something. ▪ **sketcher** *noun.* [17c: from Dutch *schets*]

sketchy *adj* (***-ier, -iest***) **1** like a sketch. **2** lacking detail; not complete or substantial. ▪ **sketchily** *adv.*

skew *adj* **1** slanted; oblique; askew. **2** *maths* of lines: not lying in the same plane. **3** *stats* of a curve in the graph of a distribution: not symmetrical about the **mean**[3] (*noun* sense 2b). ▸ *verb, tr & intr* to slant or cause to slant. ▸ *noun* a slanting position; obliquity: *on the skew.* ▪ **skewed** *adj.* ▪ **skewness** *noun.* [14c: from French *eschuer*]

skewbald *adj* of an animal, esp a horse: marked with patches of white and another colour (other than black). ▸ *noun* an animal, esp a horse, with such markings. [17c: from **skew** + *bald* in the obsolete sense 'with white markings']

skewer *noun* a long wooden or metal pin pushed through chunks of meat or vegetables which are to be roasted. ▸ *verb* to fasten or pierce with, or as if with, a skewer. [17c: from dialect *skiver*]

skew-whiff *adj, adv, informal* lying in a slanted position; crooked; awry.

ski *noun* **1** one of a pair of long narrow runners of wood, metal or plastic, upturned at the front and attached to each of a pair of boots or to a vehicle for gliding over snow. **2** a **water-ski**. ▸ *verb* (***skis, skied*** *or* ***ski'd, skiing***) *intr* to move on skis. ▪ **skier** *noun.* ▪ **skiing** *noun.* [18c: from Norse *skith* piece of split wood]

skid *verb* (***skidded, skidding***) **1** *intr* of a vehicle or person: to slip or slide at an angle, esp out of control. **2** to cause a vehicle to slide out of control. ▸ *noun* an instance of skidding. [17c: see **ski**]

IDIOMS **put the skids under sb** *informal* **1** to cause them to hurry. **2** to bring about their downfall.

skidoo *noun* a motorized sledge, fitted with tracks at the rear and steerable skis at the front. ▸ *verb* (***skidooed***) to use a skidoo. [1960s]

skid pan *noun* a special slippery track on which drivers learn to control skidding vehicles.

skid row *or* **skid road** *noun, esp US informal* the poorest or most squalid part of a town where vagrants, drunks, etc live.

skiff *noun* a small light boat. [16c: from French *esquif*]

skilful *or* (*US*) **skillful** *adj* having or showing skill. ▪ **skilfully** *adv.* ▪ **skilfulness** *noun.*

ski lift *noun* a device for carrying skiers, either by towing or on chairs, to the top of a slope so that they can ski down.

skill *noun* **1** expertness; dexterity. **2** a talent, craft or accomplishment, naturally acquired or developed through training. **3** (**skills**) aptitudes and abilities appropriate for a specific job. [12c: from Norse *skil* distinction]

skilled *adj* **1** of people: possessing skills; trained or experienced. **2** of a job: requiring skill or showing the use of skill.

skillet *noun* **1** a small long-handled saucepan. **2** *esp N Am* a frying pan. [15c: from French *escuelete*]

skim *verb* (***skimmed, skimming***) **1** to remove floating matter from the surface of (a liquid). **2** (*often* **skim off**) to take something off by skimming. **3** *tr & intr* to brush or cause something to brush against or glide lightly over (a surface): *He skimmed the table as he went past.* **4** to throw an object over a surface so as to make it bounce: *We skimmed stones on the river.* **5** (*usu* **skim through sth**) **a** to glance through (eg a book); **b** to deal with or discuss it superficially. ▸ *noun* the act or process of skimming. ▪ **skimming** *noun.* [15c: from French *escume* **scum**]

skimmed milk *or* **skim milk** *noun* milk from which all or virtually all the fat has been removed.

skimp *verb* **1** *intr* (*often* **skimp on sth**) to spend, use or give too little or only just enough of it. **2** *intr* to stint or restrict. **3** to carry out hurriedly or recklessly. ▸ *adj* scanty. [19c: perhaps a combination of **scant** + **scrimp**]

skimpy *adj* (**-*ier, -iest***) **1** inadequate; barely enough. **2** of clothes: leaving much of the body uncovered; scanty. ▪ **skimpily** *adv.* ▪ **skimpiness** *noun.* [19c]

skin *noun* **1** the tough flexible waterproof covering of the human or animal body. **2** an animal hide, with or without the fur or hair attached. **3** the outer covering of certain fruits and vegetables. **4** any outer covering or integument: *sausage skin.* **5** complexion: *greasy skin.* **6** a membrane, esp covering internal organs in animals. **7** a semi-solid coating or film on the surface of a liquid. **8** a container for liquids made from an animal hide. ▸ *verb* (***skinned, skinning***) **1** to remove or strip the skin from something. **2** to injure by scraping the skin: *He skinned his elbow when he fell.* **3** *slang* to cheat or swindle. [12c: from Norse *skinn*]
IDIOMS **by the skin of one's teeth** very narrowly; only just. **get under sb's skin** *informal* **1** to greatly annoy and irritate them. **2** to become their consuming passion or obsession. **no skin off one's nose** *informal* not a cause of even slight concern or nuisance to one: *It's no skin off my nose if he decides to resign.*

skin-deep *adj* superficial; shallow or not deeply fixed. ▸ *adv* superficially.

skin diving *noun* underwater swimming with breathing equipment carried on the back, but with no wet suit and no connection to a boat. ▪ **skin-diver** *noun.*

skinflint *noun, informal* a very ungenerous or stingy person.

skin graft *noun, surgery* the transplantation of a piece of skin from one part of the body to another where there has been an injury, esp a burn.

skinhead *noun* a person, esp a white youth and generally one of a gang, with closely cropped hair, tight jeans, heavy boots and anti-establishment attitudes.

skinny *adj* (**-*ier, -iest***) **1** similar to or like skin. **2** of a person or animal: very thin; emaciated. **3** *informal* of a pullover, T-shirt, etc: tight-fitting.

skinny-dip *verb, intr, informal* to go swimming naked. ▪ **skinny-dipping** *noun.*

skint *adj, slang* without money; hard up; broke. [1930s: from *skinned*]

skin-tight *adj* of a piece of clothing: very tight-fitting.

skip[1] *verb* (***skipped, skipping***) **1** *intr* to move along with light springing or hopping steps on alternate feet. **2** *intr* to make jumps over a skipping-rope. **3** to omit, leave out or pass over. **4** *informal* not to attend eg a class in school. **5** to make (a stone) skim over a surface. **6** of a stone: to skim over a surface. ▸ *noun* **1** a skipping movement. **2** the act of omitting or leaving something out. [13c: from Norse *skopa* to run]
IDIOMS **skip it!** *informal* forget it; ignore it.

skip[2] *noun* **1** *Brit* a large metal container for rubbish from eg building work. **2** a lift in a coal mine for raising minerals. [19c: from Norse *skeppa*]

ski pants *plural noun* trousers made from a stretch fabric and kept taut by a band under the foot, orig designed for skiing but often worn as casual wear.

skipper *noun* **1** a ship's captain. **2** the captain of an aeroplane. **3** the captain of a team. ▸ *verb* to act as skipper of something. [14c: from Dutch *schipper* shipper]

skippet *noun* a flat wooden box for protecting a seal on a document. [14c as *skipet*]

skipping *noun* the art or activity of skipping using a skipping-rope.

skipping-rope *noun* a rope swung backwards and forwards or twirled in a circular motion, either by the person skipping or by two others each holding an end, for jumping over as exercise or as a game.

skirl *Scot, noun* the high-pitched sound of bagpipes. ▸ *verb* **1** *intr* to make this sound. **2** *tr & intr* to shriek or sing in a high-pitched manner. [14c: from Norwegian *skrella* crash]

skirmish *noun* a minor fight or dispute. ▸ *verb, intr* to engage in a skirmish. [14c: from French *escarmouche*]

skirt *noun* **1** a woman's or girl's garment that hangs from the waist. **2** the part of a woman's dress, coat, gown, etc from the waist down. **3** any part or attachment resembling a skirt. **4** the flap around the base of a hovercraft containing the air-cushion. Also called **apron**. **5** cut of beef from the rear part of the belly; the midriff. ▸ *verb* **1** to border something. **2** to pass along or around the edge of something. **3** to avoid confronting (eg a problem): *He's just skirting the issue.* **4** *intr* (*usu* **skirt along**, **around**, *etc* **sth**) to be on or pass along the border of something. [13c: from Norse *skyrta* shirt]

skirting-board *noun* the narrow wooden board next to the floor round the walls of a room.

skit *noun* a short satirical piece of writing or drama. [16c: perhaps related to Norse *skjota* to **shoot**]

skittish *adj* **1** lively and playful; spirited. **2** frequently changing mood or opinion; fickle or capricious. **3** of a horse: easily frightened. ▪ **skittishly** *adv.* ▪ **skittishness** *noun.* [15c]

skittle *noun* **1** each of the upright bottle-shaped wooden or plastic targets used in a game of skittles. **2** (**skittles**) a game in which balls are rolled down an alley towards a set of these targets, the object being to knock over as many as possible. [17c: perhaps from Norse *skutill*]

skive *verb, tr & intr, Brit informal* (*also* **skive off**) to evade work or a duty, esp through laziness. ▸ *noun* the act or an instance of skiving: *I chose drama because it's such a skive.* ▪ **skiver** *noun.* ▪ **skiving** *noun.* [19c: from Norse *skifa*]

skivvy *informal, noun* (**-ies**) **1** *derog* a servant, esp a woman, who does unpleasant household jobs. **2** *esp US slang* a man's undervest. **3** (**skivvies**) *esp US slang* men's underpants. **4** *Aust, NZ* a knitted cotton polo-necked sweater. ▸ *verb* (**-ies, -ied**) *intr* to work as, or as if as, a skivvy. [Early 20c]

skua /ˈskjuːə/ *noun* a large predatory gull-like seabird. [17c: from Norse *skufr*]

skulduggery *or* (*N Am, esp US*) **skullduggery** *noun* (**-ies**) unscrupulous, underhand or dishonest behaviour; trickery. [18c: from Scots *sculduddery* unchastity]

skulk *verb, intr* **1** to sneak off out of the way. **2** to hide or lurk, planning mischief. ▪ **skulking** *noun.* [13c: Norse]

skull *noun* **1** the hard cartilaginous or bony framework of the head. **2** *informal, often derog* the head or brain; intelligence: *Can't you get it through your thick skull?* [13c from Norse *skalli*]

skull and crossbones *noun* a representation of a human skull with two femurs arranged like an X underneath, used formerly as a pirate's symbol, now as a symbol of death or danger.

skullcap *noun* a small brimless cap fitting closely on the head. [17c]

skunk *noun* (**skunk** *or* **skunks**) **1** a small American mammal related to the weasel, best known for the foul-smelling liquid which it squirts from musk glands at the base of its tail in order to deter predators. **2** *derog* a despised person. [17c: from Algonquian (a family of Native American languages) *segonku*]

sky *noun* (**skies**) **1** the apparent dome of space over our heads. **2** (**skies**) the heavens. **3** the maximum limit or aim: *Aim for the sky.* ▸ *verb* (**skies, skied**) *cricket* to mishit (a ball) high into the air. [13c: Norse, meaning 'cloud']

IDIOMS **the sky's the limit** there is no upper limit, eg to the amount of money that may be spent, or achievements to be made. **to the skies** in a lavish or extremely enthusiastic manner: *He praised him to the skies.*

skydiving *noun* free-falling from an aircraft, often involving performing manoeuvres in mid-air, with a long delay before the parachute is opened. ▪ **skydiver** *noun.*

sky-high *adj, adv* esp of prices: very high.

skylark *noun* a small lark which inhabits open country and is known for its loud clear warbling song, performed in flight. ▸ *verb, intr, old use* to lark about; to frolic. [17c]

skylight *noun* a window in a roof or ceiling.

skyline *noun* the outline of buildings, hills and trees seen against the sky; the horizon.

skyrocket *noun* a firework that explodes very high in the sky. ▸ *verb, intr* to rise high and fast.

skyscraper *noun* an extremely tall building.

skyward *adj* directed towards the sky. ▸ *adv* (*also* **skywards**) towards the sky.

slab *noun* **1** a thick flat rectangular piece of stone, etc. **2** a thick slice, esp of cake. ▸ *verb* (**slabbed, slabbing**) to pave with concrete slabs. [13c as *sclabbe*]

slack[1] *adj* **1** limp or loose; not pulled or stretched tight. **2** not careful or diligent; remiss. **3** not busy: *Business is a bit slack these days.* **4** of the tide, etc: still; neither ebbing nor flowing. ▸ *adv* in a slack manner; partially. ▸ *noun* **1** a loosely hanging part, esp of a rope. **2** a period of little trade or other activity. ▸ *verb* (*also* **slacken**) (*often* **slack off**) **1** *intr* (*also* **slack off** *or* **up**) to become slower; to slow one's working pace through tiredness or laziness: *Stop slacking!* **2** *tr & intr* to make or become looser. **3** *intr* to become less busy: *work is slackening off for the winter.* [Anglo-Saxon *slæc*]

slack[2] *noun* coal dust or tiny fragments of coal. [15c: from German *Slecke*]

slacken see under **slack[1]** (*verb*)

slacker *noun* an idle person; a shirker.

slacks *plural noun, dated* a type of loose casual trousers, worn by both males and females.

slag[1] *noun* **1** the layer of waste material that forms on the surface of molten metal ore during smelting and refining. **2** waste left over from coal mining. [16c: from German *Slagge*]

slag[2] *verb* (**slagged, slagging**) *slang* (*usu* **slag sb off**) to criticize or deride them harshly or speak disparagingly about them. [1970s: from **slag[1]**]

slag heap *noun* a hill or mound formed from coal-mining waste.

slain *past participle of* **slay**

slake *verb* **1** *literary* to satisfy or quench (thirst, desire or anger). **2** to cause (lime) to crumble by adding water. [Anglo-Saxon *slacian*]

slaked lime *noun* calcium hydroxide, $Ca(OH)_2$, manufactured from lime (calcium oxide), used in the production of cements. Also called **caustic lime**.

slalom *noun* a race, on skis or in canoes, in and out of obstacles on a winding course designed to test tactical skill. [1920s: Norwegian]

slam[1] *verb* (**slammed, slamming**) **1** *tr & intr* to shut loudly and with violence: *She slammed the window shut.* **2** *tr & intr* (*usu* **slam against, down, into**, *etc*) *informal* to make or cause something to make loud heavy contact: *He slammed his books down on the table.* **3** *slang* to criticize severely. ▸ *noun* **1** the act or sound of slamming. **2** a severe criticism. [17c: from Norwegian *slemma*]

slam[2] *noun* short for **grand slam**.

slammer *noun, slang* (**the slammer**) prison.

slander *noun* **1** *law* damaging defamation by spoken words, or by looks or gestures. **2** a false, malicious and damaging spoken statement about a person. **3** the making of such statements. ▸ *verb* to speak about someone in such a way. Compare **libel**. ▪ **slanderer** *noun.* ▪ **slanderous** *adj* **1** of words, reports, etc: characterized by or amounting to slander. **2** of a person: given to using slander. [13c: from French *esclandre*]

slang *noun* very informal words and phrases used by any class, profession or set of people. ▸ *verb* to speak abusively to someone using coarse language. ▪ **slangy** *adj.* [18c]

slanging match *noun, informal* an angry exchange of insults or abuse.

slant *verb* **1** *intr* to be at an angle as opposed to horizontal or vertical; to slope. **2** to turn, strike or fall obliquely or at an angle. **3** to present (information, etc) in a biased way, or for a particular audience or readership. ▸ *noun* **1** a sloping position, surface or line. **2** a point of view or way of looking at a particular thing. ▸ *adj* sloping; lying at an angle. [15c as *slent*]

slantwise *or* **slantways** *adv, adj* at an angle.

slap *noun* **1** a blow with the palm of the hand or anything flat. **2** the sound made by such a blow, or by the impact of one flat surface with another. **3** a snub or rebuke. ▸ *verb* (***slapped, slapping***) **1** to strike with the open hand or anything flat. **2** to bring or send with a slapping sound: *He slapped the newspaper down on the table.* **3** (*often* **slap sth on**) *informal* to apply thickly and carelessly: *She slapped cream on her face.* ▸ *adv, informal* **1** exactly or precisely: *slap in the middle.* **2** heavily or suddenly; with a slap: *He fell slap on his face.* [17c: from German dialect *slapp*]
IDIOMS **a slap in the face** *informal* an insult or rebuff. **a slap on the back** *informal* congratulations. **a slap on the wrist** *informal, often facetious* a mild reprimand.

slap-bang *adv, informal* **1** exactly or precisely: *slap-bang in the middle.* **2** violently; directly and with force: *He drove slap-bang into the wall.*

slapdash *adv* in a careless and hurried manner. ▸ *adj* careless and hurried: *a slapdash piece of work.*

slap-happy *adj, informal* cheerfully carefree or careless; happy-go-lucky.

slapstick *noun* (*in full* **slapstick comedy**) comedy in which the humour is derived from boisterous antics of all kinds. [19c: from a mechanical sound effects device, used to punctuate (comic) stage fights with loud reports]

slap-up *adj, informal* of a meal: lavish; extravagant.

slash *verb* **1** *tr & intr* to make sweeping cuts or cutting strokes, esp repeatedly. **2** to cut by striking violently and often randomly. **3** to make long cuts or gashes in something. **4** *informal* to reduce (prices, etc) suddenly and drastically. ▸ *noun* **1** a sweeping cutting stroke. **2** a long and sometimes deep cut. **3** (*also* **slash mark**) an oblique line (/) in writing or printing; a solidus. [14c: prob from French *esclachier* to break]

slat *noun* a thin strip, esp of wood or metal. ▪ **slatted** *adj.* [14c: from French *esclat*]

slate[1] *noun* **1** *geol* a shiny dark grey metamorphic rock that is easily split into thin flat layers, formed by the compression of clays and shales, and used for roofing and flooring. **2** a roofing tile made of this. **3** *formerly* a piece of this for writing on. **4** a record of credit given to a customer: *put it on my slate.* **5** a dull grey colour. ▸ *verb* to cover (a roof) with slates. ▸ *adj* **1** made of slate. **2** slate-coloured. ▪ **slating** *noun.* ▪ **slaty** *adj.* [14c: from French *esclate*]
IDIOMS **on the slate** on credit. **wipe the slate clean** to enable a person to make a fresh start in a job, relationship, etc by ignoring past mistakes, crimes, etc.

slate[2] *verb, informal* to criticize extremely harshly; to abuse or reprimand. [19c: Norse]

slaughter *noun* **1** the killing of animals, esp for food. **2** cruel and violent murder. **3** the large-scale indiscriminate killing of people or animals. ▸ *verb* **1** to subject to slaughter. **2** *informal* to defeat resoundingly; to trounce: *I was slaughtered at tennis yesterday.* ▪ **slaughterer** *noun.* [13c: from Norse *slatr* butchers' meat]

slaughterhouse *noun* a place where animals are killed for food; an abattoir.

Slav *noun* a member of any of various Central and E European peoples speaking **Slavonic** languages including Russian, Czech, Slovak, Bulgarian, Polish, Serb and Slovenian. ▸ *adj* **1** of or relating to the Slavs. **2 Slavonic**. [14c: from Latin *Sclavus*]

slave *noun* **1** *hist* someone owned by and acting as servant to another, with no personal freedom. **2** a person who is submissive under domination. **3** a person who works extremely hard for another; a drudge. **4** (*also* **a slave to sth**) a person whose life is dominated by a specific activity or thing: *She's a slave to her work.* ▸ *verb, intr* to work like or as a slave; to work hard and ceaselessly. [13c: from French *esclave*, orig meaning a 'Slav']

slave-driver *noun* **1** *hist* someone employed to supervise slaves. **2** *informal* someone who demands very hard work from others.

slaver /ˈslavə(r)/ *noun* spittle running from the mouth. ▸ *verb, intr* **1** to let spittle run from the mouth; to dribble. **2** (*also* **slaver over sb**) to fawn over them, esp lustfully. **3** *informal* to talk nonsense.

slavery *noun* **1** the state of being a slave. **2** the practice of owning slaves. **3** toil or drudgery.

slavish *adj* **1** characteristic of, belonging to or befitting a slave. **2** very closely copied or imitated; unoriginal. ▪ **slavishly** *adv.*

Slavonic *or* **Slavic** *noun* a group of Central and E European languages that includes Russian, Polish, Bulgarian, Czech, Slovak, Croatian, Serbian and Slovenian. ▸ *adj* of or relating to these languages, the peoples speaking them, or their cultures. [17c: see **Slav**]

slaw *noun, N Am* cabbage salad; coleslaw. [19c: from Dutch *sla*]

slay *verb* (*past tense* ***slew,*** *past participle* ***slain***) *tr & intr, archaic or literary* to kill. ▪ **slayer** *noun.* [Anglo-Saxon *slean*]

sleaze *noun, informal* **1** sleaziness. **2** someone of low, esp moral, standards.

sleazy *adj* (***-ier, -iest***) *informal* **1** dirty and neglected-looking. **2** disreputable and considered to be of low standards, esp with regard to morals: *a sleazy bar.* ▪ **sleaziness** *noun* the condition or state of being sleazy. [17c]

sledge *or* **sled** *noun* **1** a vehicle with ski-like runners for travelling over snow, drawn by horses or dogs. **2** a smaller vehicle of a similar design for children, for sliding on the snow; a toboggan. ▸ *verb* (***sledded, sledding***) *intr* **1** to travel by sledge. **2** to play on a sledge. [17c: from Dutch *sleedse*]

sledgehammer *noun* a large heavy hammer swung with both arms. [Anglo-Saxon *slecg*]

sleek *adj* **1** of hair, fur, etc: smooth, soft and glossy. **2** having a well-fed and prosperous appearance. **3** insincerely polite or flattering; slick in manner. ▸ *verb* to smooth (esp hair). ▪ **sleekly** *adv.* ▪ **sleekness** *noun.* [16c: a variant of **slick**]

sleep *noun* **1** a readily reversible state of natural unconsciousness during which the body's functional powers are restored, and physical movements are minimal. **2** a period of such rest. **3** *informal* mucus that collects in the corners of the eyes during such rest. **4** *poetic* death. ▸ *verb* (***slept***) *intr* **1** to rest in a state of sleep. **2** to be motionless, inactive or dormant. **3** (**sleep with sb**) to have sexual relations with them. **4** to provide or contain sleeping accommodation for (the specified number): *The caravan sleeps four.* **5** *informal* to be in a dreamy state, not paying attention, etc. **6** *poetic* to be dead. [Anglo-Saxon *slæp*]

IDIOMS **lose sleep over sth** *informal, usu with negatives* to be worried or preoccupied by it. **put sb** *or* **sth to sleep 1** to anaesthetize them. **2** *euphem* to kill (an animal) painlessly with an injected drug. **sleep on it** to delay taking a decision about it until the following morning in the hope that one might have a better intuitive feel for the best course of action.

PHRASAL VERBS **sleep around** to engage in casual sexual relations. **sleep in** to sleep later than usual in the morning. **sleep sth off** to recover from it by sleeping.

sleeper *noun* **1** someone who sleeps, esp in a specified way: *a heavy sleeper.* **2** any of the horizontal wooden or concrete beams supporting the rails on a railway track. **3 a** a railway carriage providing sleeping accommodation for passengers; **b** a train with such carriages: *took the sleeper to London.* **4** a small gold hoop worn in a pierced ear to prevent the hole from closing up.

sleeping bag *noun* a large quilted sack for sleeping in when camping, etc.

sleeping partner *noun* a business partner who invests money in a business without taking part in its management. Also called **silent partner**.

sleeping pill *noun* a pill which contains a sedative drug that induces sleep.

sleeping policeman *noun, informal* each of a series of low humps built into the surface of a road, intended to slow down motor traffic in residential areas, parks, etc.

sleeping sickness *noun* an infectious disease transmitted by the tsetse fly, so called because the later stages of the disease are characterized by extreme drowsiness, and eventually death.

sleepless *adj* **1** characterized by an inability to sleep: *a sleepless night.* **2** unable to sleep. ▪ **sleeplessly** *adv.* ▪ **sleeplessness** *noun.*

sleepwalking *noun* an act of walking about in one's sleep. Also called **somnambulism**. ▪ **sleepwalker** *noun.*

sleepy *adj* (***-ier, -iest***) **1** feeling the desire or need to sleep; drowsy. **2** suggesting sleep or drowsiness: *sleepy music.* **3** characterized by quietness and a lack of activity: *a sleepy village.* ▪ **sleepily** *adv.* ▪ **sleepiness** *noun.*

sleepyhead *noun, informal* a sleepy person.

sleet *noun* rain mixed with snow and/or hail. ▸ *verb, intr* to rain and snow simultaneously. ▪ **sleety** *adj.* [13c as *slete*]

sleeve *noun* **1** the part of a garment that covers the arm. **2** *eng* a tube, esp of a different metal, fitted inside a metal cylinder or tube, either as protection or to decrease the diameter. **3** the cardboard or paper envelope in which a **record** (*noun* sense 4) is stored. ▪ **sleeveless** *adj*: *a sleeveless dress.* [Anglo-Saxon *slefe*]

IDIOMS **have sth up one's sleeve** have something in secret reserve, possibly for later use. **laugh up one's sleeve** to laugh privately or secretly.

sleigh *esp N Am noun* a large horse-drawn sledge. ▸ *verb, intr* to travel by sleigh. [17c: from Dutch *slee*]

sleight /slaɪt/ *noun* dexterity; cunning or trickery. [13c: from Norse *slægth* cunning]

sleight of hand *noun* the quick and deceptive movement of the hands in magic tricks.

slender *adj* **1** attractively slim. **2** thin or narrow; slight: *by a slender margin.* **3** meagre: *slender means.* ▪ **slenderness** *noun.* [14c as *slendre*]

slept *past tense, past participle of* **sleep**

sleuth /sluːθ/ *informal noun* a detective. ▸ *verb, intr* to work as a detective. [19c: from Norse *sloth* trail]

slew[1] *past tense of* **slay**

slew[2] *or* **slue** *verb, tr & intr* to twist or cause to twist or swing round, esp suddenly and uncontrollably. ▸ *noun* an instance of slewing. [18c]

slice *noun* **1** a thin broad piece, wedge or segment that is cut off. **2** *informal* a share or portion: *a slice of the business.* **3** a kitchen utensil with a broad flat blade for sliding under and lifting solid food, esp fish. **4** a slash or swipe. **5** in golf and tennis: a stroke causing a ball to spin sideways and curve away in a particular direction; the spin itself. ▸ *verb* **1** to cut up into slices. **2** (*also* **slice sth off**) to cut it off as or like a slice: *slice a piece off the end.* **3** *intr* to cut deeply and easily; to move easily and forcefully: *a boat slicing through the water.* **4** *intr* to slash. **5** to strike (a ball) with a slice. ▪ **slicer** *noun.* [14c: from French *esclice*]

slick *adj* **1** dishonestly or slyly clever. **2** glib; smooth-tongued or suave: *a slick operator.* **3** impressively and superficially smart or efficient: *a slick organization.* **4** esp of hair: smooth and glossy; sleek. ▸ *verb* (*usu* **slick sth back** *or* **down**) to smooth (esp hair). ▸ *noun* an **oil slick**. ▪ **slickness** *noun.* [Anglo-Saxon *slician* to smooth]

slicker *noun* **1** a sophisticated city-dweller. **2** a shifty or swindling person.

slide *verb* (***slid***) **1** *tr & intr* to move or cause to move or run smoothly along a surface. **2** *intr* to lose one's footing, esp on a slippery surface; to slip. **3** *tr & intr* to move or place softly and unobtrusively: *slid the letter into his pocket.* **4** *intr* to pass gradually, esp through neglect or laziness; to lapse: *slid back into his old habits.* ▸ *noun* **1** an act or instance of sliding. **2** a polished slippery track, eg on ice. **3** any part of something that glides smoothly, eg the moving part of a trombone. **4** an apparatus for children to play on, usu with a ladder to climb up and a narrow sloping part to slide down; a chute. **5** a small glass plate on which specimens are mounted to be viewed through a microscope. **6** a small transparent photograph viewed in magnified size by means of a projector. **7** a sliding clasp for a girl's or woman's hair. ▪ **slidable** *adj.* ▪ **slider** *noun.* [Anglo-Saxon *slidan*]

slide rule *noun* a hand-held mechanical device used to perform quick numerical calculations.

sliding scale *noun* a scale, eg of fees charged, varying according to changes in conditions, eg unforeseen difficulties in performing the service requested, etc.

slight *adj* **1** small in extent, significance or seriousness: *a slight problem.* **2** slim or slender. **3** lacking solidity, weight or significance; flimsy. ▸ *verb* to insult someone by ignoring or dismissing them abruptly; to snub them. ▸ *noun* an insult by snubbing or showing neglect. ▪ **slightly** *adv* to a small extent; in a small way. ▪ **slightness** *noun*. [Anglo-Saxon *eorthslihtes* close to the ground]

IDIOMS **not in the slightest** not at all.

slim *adj* (***slimmer, slimmest***) **1** of people: attractively thin; slender. **2** characterized by little thickness or width. **3** not great; slight or remote: *a slim chance*. ▸ *verb* (***slimmed, slimming***) *intr* **1** (*sometimes* **slim down**) to make oneself slimmer, esp by diet and/or exercise. **2** to try to lose weight. ▪ **slimmer** *noun*. ▪ **slimming** *noun*. ▪ **slimness** *noun*. [17c: Dutch, meaning 'crafty']

slime *noun* **1** any thin, unpleasantly slippery or gluey, mud-like substance. **2** any mucus-like substance secreted, eg by snails, slugs and certain fishes. ▸ *verb* to smear or cover with slime. [Anglo-Saxon *slim*]

slime mould *noun, biol* any of a class of very simple plants or fungi consisting of a mass of protoplasm, that feeds on dead or decaying plant matter.

slimy *adj* (***-ier, -iest***) **1** similar to, covered with or consisting of slime. **2** *informal* exaggeratedly obedient or attentive; obsequious. ▪ **slimily** *adv*. ▪ **sliminess** *noun*.

sling[1] *noun* **1** a cloth hoop that hangs from the neck to support an injured arm. **2 a** a weapon for hurling stones, consisting of a strap or pouch in which the stone is placed and swung round fast; **b** a catapult. **3** a strap or loop for hoisting, lowering or carrying a weight. ▸ *verb* (***slung***) **1** *informal* to throw, esp with force; to fling. **2** to hang something loosely: *a jacket slung over his shoulder*. **3** to hurl, fling or toss. [13c: from Norse *slyngva* to fling]

IDIOMS **sling one's hook** *slang* to go away.

sling[2] *noun* a drink of alcoholic spirit and water, usu sweetened and flavoured.

slingback *or* **slingback shoe** *noun* a shoe with a strap fastening round the heel.

slingshot *noun, N Am, esp US* a catapult.

slink *verb* (***slunk***) *intr* **1** to go or move sneakingly or ashamedly. **2** to move in a lithe and seductive manner. ▸ *noun* a slinking gait. [Anglo-Saxon *slincan*]

slinky *adj* (***-ier, -iest***) *informal* **1** of clothing: attractively close-fitting: *a slinky dress*. **2** slender. **3** of a person: walking in a slow and seductive manner. ▪ **slinkily** *adv*. ▪ **slinkiness** *noun*.

slip[1] *verb* (***slipped, slipping***) **1** *intr* to lose one's footing and slide accidentally. **2** *intr* (*also* **slip up**) to make a slight mistake inadvertently rather than due to ignorance. See also **slip-up**. **3** *intr* to slide, move or drop accidentally. **4** to place smoothly, quietly or secretively: *She slipped the envelope into her pocket*. **5** *tr & intr* to move or cause to move quietly, smoothly or unobtrusively with a sliding motion: *He slipped into the church in the middle of the service*. **6** to pull free from someone or something smoothly and swiftly; to suddenly escape from them or it: *The name has slipped my mind*. **7** *informal* to give or pass secretly: *She slipped him a fiver*. **8** *intr, informal* to lose one's former skill or expertise, or control of a situation. **9** to dislocate (a spinal disc). ▸ *noun* **1** an instance of losing one's footing and sliding accidentally. **2** a minor and usu inadvertent mistake. **3** a slight error or transgression. **4** an escape. **5** a slight dislocation. **6** a woman's undergarment, worn under a dress or skirt. **7** a loose covering for a pillow. **8** a **slipway**. [13c: from German dialect *slippen*]

IDIOMS **give sb the slip** *informal* to escape from them skilfully or adroitly. **let sth slip 1** to reveal it accidentally. **2** to fail to take advantage of something, esp an opportunity. **slip of the tongue** *or* **pen** a word, phrase, etc said or written in error when something else was intended.

slip[2] *noun* **1** a small strip or piece of paper. **2** a small pre-printed form. **3** a young or exceptionally slender person: *She's just a slip of a girl*. [15c as *slippe*]

slip[3] *noun* a creamy mixture of clay and water used for decorating pottery. [Anglo-Saxon *slipa* paste]

slipcase *noun* a boxlike case for a book or set of books, open on one side and leaving the spine visible.

slipknot *noun* a knot finishing off a noose, and slipping along the cord to adjust the noose's tightness.

slip-on *noun* a shoe or other item of clothing that is easily put on due to having no laces, buttons or other fastenings. *as adj*: *slip-on shoes*.

slipped disc *noun* a dislocation of one of the flat circular plates of cartilage situated between any of the vertebrae, resulting in painful pressure on a spinal nerve.

slipper *noun* a soft loose laceless indoor shoe. [15c: from **slip**[1]]

slippery *adj* **1** so smooth, wet, etc as to cause or allow slipping. **2** difficult to catch or keep hold of; elusive or evasive. **3** unpredictable or untrustworthy: *a slippery character*. ▪ **slipperiness** *noun*.

slippy *adj* (***-ier, -iest***) *informal* of a thing: liable to slip; slippery. ▪ **slippiness** *noun*.

slip road *noun* a road by which vehicles join or leave a motorway.

slipshod *adj* untidy and careless; carelessly done.

slipstream *noun* a stream of air driven back by an aircraft propeller.

slip-up *noun, informal* a minor and usu inadvertent mistake. See also **slip up** at **slip**[1].

slipway *noun* a ramp in a dock or shipyard that slopes into water, for launching boats.

slit *noun* a long narrow cut or opening. ▸ *verb* (***slit, slitting***) **1** to cut a slit in something, esp lengthwise. **2** to cut something into strips. [Anglo-Saxon *slitan* to split]

slither *verb, intr* **1** to slide or slip unsteadily while walking, esp on ice. **2** to move slidingly, like a snake. ▸ *noun* a slithering movement. ▪ **slithery** *adj*. [Anglo-Saxon *slidrian*]

sliver *noun* a long thin piece cut or broken off. ▸ *verb, tr & intr* to break or cut into slivers. [Anglo-Saxon *slifan* to cleave]

slob *informal, noun* a lazy, untidy and slovenly person. ▸ *verb* (***slobbed, slobbing***) *intr* (*usu* **slob about** *or* **around**) to move or behave in a lazy, untidy or slovenly way. ▪ **slobbish** *or* **slobby** *adj* (***-ier, -iest***). [18c: from Irish Gaelic *slab* mud]

slobber *verb, intr* **1** to let saliva run from the mouth; to dribble. **2** (*usu* **slobber over sth**) *informal* to express extreme or excessive enthusiasm or admiration for it. ▸ *noun* dribbled saliva; slaver. ▪ **slobbery** *adj*. [14c: from Dutch *slobberen* to eat or work in a slovenly manner]

sloe *noun* **1** the fruit of the blackthorn bush. **2** the bush itself. [Anglo-Saxon *sla*]

slog *informal, verb* (***slogged, slogging***) **1** to hit hard and wildly. **2** *intr* to labour or toil. ▸ *noun* **1** a hard wild blow or stroke. **2** extremely tiring work. ▪ **slogger** *noun*. [19c: a variant of **slug**[1]]

slogan *noun* a phrase used to identify a group or organization, or to advertise a product. [16c: from Gaelic *sluagh* army + *gairm* cry]

sloop *noun* a single-masted sailing boat with fore-and-aft sails. [17c: from Dutch *sloep*]

slop *verb* (***slopped, slopping***) **1** (*often* **slop about** *or* **around**) *tr & intr* to splash or cause to splash or spill violently. **2** *intr* to walk carelessly in slush or water. ▸ *noun* **1** spilled liquid; a puddle. **2** (**slops**) waste food. **3** (**slops**) semi-liquid food fed to pigs. [Anglo-Saxon *cusloppe* cow dung]

PHRASAL VERBS **slop about** *or* **around** *informal* to move or behave in an untidy or slovenly manner.

slope *noun* **1** a slanting surface; an incline. **2** a position or direction that is neither level nor upright. **3** a specially prepared track for skiing, on the side of a snow-covered hill or mountain. ▸ *verb, intr* **1** to rise or fall at an angle. **2** to be slanted or inclined. ▪ **sloping** *or* **slopy** *adj*. [Anglo-Saxon *aslupan* to slip away]

PHRASAL VERBS **slope off** *informal* to leave stealthily or furtively.

sloppy *adj* (***-ier, -iest***) **1** wet or muddy. **2** watery. **3** over-sentimental. **4** of language, work, etc: inaccurate or careless; shoddy. **5** of clothes: baggy; loose-fitting. ▪ **sloppily** *adv*. ▪ **sloppiness** *noun*.

slosh *verb* **1** *tr & intr* (*often* **slosh about** *or* **around**) to splash or cause to splash or spill noisily. **2** *slang* to hit or strike with a heavy blow. ▸ *noun* **1** the sound of splashing or spilling. **2** slush; a watery mess. **3** *slang* a heavy blow. [Early 19c: a variant of **slush**]

sloshed *adj, informal* drunk; intoxicated.

slot *noun* **1** a long narrow rectangular opening into which something is fitted or inserted. **2** a slit. **3** a (usu regular) time, place or position within a schedule, eg of radio or TV broadcasts, or airport take-offs and landings. ▸ *verb* (***slotted, slotting***) **1** to make a slot in. **2** (*usu* **slot sth in**) to fit or insert it, or place it in a slot. [14c: from French *esclot*]

sloth /sloʊθ/ *noun* **1** a tree-dwelling mammal with long slender limbs and hook-like claws, noted for its very slow movements. **2** the desire to avoid all activity or exertion; laziness; indolence. ▪ **slothful** *adj* lazy; inactive. [Anglo-Saxon *slæwth*]

slot machine *noun* a machine operated by inserting a coin in a slot, eg a fruit machine. [19c]

slouch *verb, intr* to sit, stand or walk with a tired, lazy or drooping posture. ▸ *noun* such a posture. ▪ **slouching** *adj*. [16c: from Norse *slokr* a slouching person]

IDIOMS **no slouch at sth** *informal* of a person: able in some respect: *He's no slouch at cooking.*

slough[1] *noun* **1** /slaʊ/ a mud-filled hollow. **2** /sluː/ *N Am* an area of boggy land; a marsh or mire. **3** /slaʊ/ *literary* a state of deep and gloomy emotion: *a slough of depression*. [Anglo-Saxon *sloh*]

slough[2] /slʌf/ *noun* any outer part of an animal cast off or moulted, esp a snake's dead skin. ▸ *verb* **1** to shed (eg a dead skin). **2** to cast off or dismiss (eg worries). [13c as *sloh*]

Slovak *adj* belonging or relating to Slovakia, a republic in E Europe, its inhabitants, or their language. ▸ *noun* **1** a citizen or inhabitant of, or person born in, Slovakia. **2** the official language of Slovakia. ▪ **Slovakian** *adj, noun*. [19c]

sloven /ˈslʌvən/ *noun* someone who is carelessly or untidily dressed; a person of shoddy appearance. [15c: from Dutch *slof*]

Slovenian *or* **Slovene** *adj* belonging or relating to Slovenia, a republic in SE Europe, its inhabitants or their language. ▸ *noun* **1** a citizen or inhabitant of, or a person born in, Slovenia. **2** the official language of Slovenia. [19c]

slovenly *adj* **1** careless, untidy or dirty in appearance. **2** careless or shoddy in habits or methods of working. ▸ *adv* in a slovenly manner. ▪ **slovenliness** *noun*.

slow *adj* **1** having little speed or pace; not moving fast or swiftly. **2** taking a long time, or longer than usual or expected. **3** of a watch or clock: showing a time earlier than the correct time. **4** of a mind: unable to quickly and easily understand or appreciate. **5** of wit or intellect: dull; unexciting or uninteresting. **6** progressing at a tediously gentle pace: *a slow afternoon.* **7** boring or dull; tedious: *a slow film.* **8** needing much provocation in order to do something: *He's slow to get angry.* **9** of business: slack. **10** of photographic film: needing a relatively long exposure time. ▸ *adv* in a slow manner. ▸ *verb, tr & intr* (*also* **slow down** *or* **up**) to reduce or make something reduce speed, pace or rate of progress. ▪ **slowly** *adv*. ▪ **slowness** *noun*. [Anglo-Saxon *slaw*]

slowcoach *noun, informal* someone who moves or works at a slow pace.

slow motion *noun* in film or television: a speed of movement that is much slower than real-life movement, created by increasing the speed at which the camera records the action.

slow neutron *noun, physics* a neutron with a relatively low energy content, used to initiate various nuclear reactions.

slowworm *noun* a harmless species of legless lizard with a small mouth and a smooth shiny brownish-grey to coppery body. [Anglo-Saxon *slawyrm*; the first part is not related to **slow** but has been assimilated to it]

sludge *noun* **1** soft slimy mud or mire. **2** muddy sediment. **3** sewage. **4** half-melted snow; slush. ▪ **sludgy** *adj* (***-ier, -iest***). [17c: prob from **slush**]

slue see **slew**[2]

slug[1] *noun* a mollusc, similar to a snail, but which has a long fleshy body and little or no shell. [15c: from Norwegian dialect *slugg* a heavy body]

slug[2] *noun* **1** *informal* **a** an irregularly formed bullet; **b** a bullet. **2** *printing* a solid line or section of metal type produced by a composing machine. [17c]

slug[3] *informal, noun* a heavy blow. ▸ *verb* (***slugged, slugging***) to strike with a heavy blow. ▪ **slugger** *noun*. [Early 19c: from **slog**]

slug[4] *noun, esp US informal* a large gulp or mouthful of alcohol, esp spirit. [18c]

sluggard *noun* a habitually lazy or inactive person. [14c: as *slogarde*]

sluggish *adj* **1** unenergetic; habitually lazy or inactive. **2** less lively, active or responsive than usual: *This engine is a bit sluggish.* ▪ **sluggishness** *noun*.

sluice /sluːs/ *noun* **1** a channel or drain for water. **2** (*in full* **sluicegate**) a valve or sliding gate for regulating the flow of water in such a channel. **3** a trough for washing gold or other minerals out of sand, etc. **4**

an act of washing down or rinsing. ▸ *verb* **1** to let out or drain by means of a sluice. **2** to wash down or rinse by throwing water on. [14c: from French *escluse*]

slum *noun* **1** a run-down, dirty and usu overcrowded house. **2** (*often* **slums**) an area or neighbourhood containing such housing. ▸ *verb* (***slummed, slumming***) *intr* to visit an area of slums, esp out of curiosity or for amusement. ▪ **slummy** *adj.* [Early 19c]
IDIOMS **slum it** *informal* to experience conditions that are less affluent than one is used to.

slumber *chiefly poetic, noun* sleep. ▸ *verb, intr* to sleep. [Anglo-Saxon *sluma* chamber]

slump *verb, intr* **1** to drop or sink suddenly and heavily, eg with tiredness: *He slumped into an armchair.* **2** of prices, trade, etc: to decline suddenly and sharply. ▸ *noun* **1** an act or instance of slumping. **2** a serious and usu long-term decline, esp in a nation's economy. ▪ **slumped** *adj.* [17c]

slung *past tense, past participle of* **sling**[1]

slunk *past tense, past participle of* **slink**

slur *verb* (***slurred, slurring***) **1** to pronounce (words) indistinctly. **2** to speak or write about something very disparagingly; to cast aspersions on it. **3** (*often* **slur over sth**) to mention it only briefly or deal with only superficially. **4** *music* to sing or play (notes) as a flowing sequence without pauses. ▸ *noun* **1** a disparaging remark intended to damage a reputation. **2** a slurred word or slurring way of speaking. **3** *music* **a** a flowing pauseless style of singing or playing; **b** the curved line under the notes indicating this style. Also called **ligature.** [17c]

slurp *verb* to eat or drink noisily with a sucking action. ▸ *noun* a slurping sound. [17c: from Dutch *slurpen* to sip audibly]

slurry *noun* (**-*ies***) **1** a semi-fluid mixture, esp watery concrete. **2** liquid manure. [15c: from **slur**]

slush *noun* **1** half-melted snow. **2** any watery half-liquid substance, eg liquid mud. **3** sickly sentimentality. ▪ **slushy** *adj* (**-*ier*, -*iest***). [17c]

slush fund *noun* a fund of money used for dishonest purposes, eg bribery, esp by a political party.

sly *adj* (***slier*** *or* ***slyer; sliest*** *or* ***slyest***) **1** of people: clever; cunning or wily. **2** surreptitious; secretively deceitful or dishonest. **3** playfully mischievous: *a sly smile.* ▪ **slyly** *or* **slily** *adv.* ▪ **slyness** *noun.* [12c: from Norse *slægr*]
IDIOMS **on the sly** *informal* secretly or furtively.

Sm *symbol, chem* samarium.

smack[1] *verb* **1** to slap loudly and smartly, esp with the hand. **2** *tr & intr, informal* to hit loudly and heavily: *Her head smacked against the wall.* **3** to kiss loudly and noisily. **4** to part (the lips) loudly, with relish or in pleasant anticipation: *She smacked her lips at the thought of the meal.* ▸ *noun* **1** an act, or the sound, of smacking. **2** a loud enthusiastic kiss. ▸ *adv, informal* **1** directly and with force: *He drove smack into the tree.* **2** precisely: *smack in the middle.* ▪ **smacking** *noun, adj.* [16c: from Dutch *smacken*]

smack[2] *verb, intr* (*always* **smack of sth**) **1** to have the flavour of it. **2** to have a trace or suggestion of it. ▸ *noun* **1** taste; distinctive flavour. **2** a hint or trace. [Anglo-Saxon *smæc*]

smack[3] *noun* a small single-masted fishing boat. [17c: from Dutch *smak*]

smacker *noun* **1** *informal* a loud enthusiastic kiss. **2** *slang* a pound sterling or a dollar bill.

small *adj* **1** little in size or quantity. **2** little in extent, importance or worth; not great. **3** slender: *of small build.* **4** humble: *small beginnings.* **5** young: *a small child.* **6** minor; insignificant: *a small problem.* **7** of a printed or written letter: lower-case; not capital. **8** humiliated: *feel small.* ▸ *noun* **1** the narrow part, esp of the back. **2** (**smalls**) *informal* underclothes. ▸ *adv* into small pieces. ▪ **smallness** *noun.* [Anglo-Saxon *smæl*]
IDIOMS **feel small** to feel silly, insignificant, ashamed, humiliated, etc.

small beer *noun, informal* something unimportant.

small calorie *noun* a **calorie** (sense 1).

small change *noun* coins of little value.

small claims *plural noun, law* claims for small amounts of money, dealt with through a simpler legal procedure than larger claims.

small fry *singular or plural noun, informal* **1** a person or thing, or people or things, of little importance or influence. **2** young children.

smallholding *noun* an area of cultivated land smaller than an ordinary farm. ▪ **smallholder** *noun.*

small hours *plural noun* (**the small hours**) the hours immediately after midnight.

small intestine *noun, anatomy* in mammals: the part of the intestine whose main function is to digest and absorb food. See also **large intestine**.

small-minded *adj* narrow-minded; petty-minded. ▪ **small-mindedly** *adv.* ▪ **small-mindedness** *noun.*

smallpox *noun, pathol* a highly contagious viral disease, characterized by fever, vomiting, backache and a rash that usu leaves pitted scars (pocks) on the skin.

small print *noun* the details of a contract or other undertaking, often printed very small, esp when considered likely to contain unattractive conditions that the writer of the contract does not want to be noticed.

the small screen *noun* television, as opposed to cinema.

small talk *noun* polite conversation about trivial matters.

small-time *adj* operating on a small scale; unimportant or insignificant.

smarm *verb* **1** *intr, informal* to be exaggeratedly and insincerely flattering; to fawn ingratiatingly. **2** (*often* **smarm sth down**) to smooth or flatten (the hair) with an oily substance. ▸ *noun, informal* exaggerated or insincere flattery. [19c]

smarmy *adj* (**-*ier*, -*iest***) *informal* nauseatingly suave or charming. ▪ **smarmily** *adv.* ▪ **smarminess** *noun.*

smart *adj* **1** neat, trim and well-dressed. **2** clever; witty; astute or shrewd. **3** expensive, sophisticated and fashionable: *a smart hotel.* **4** quick, adept and efficient in business. **5** of pain, etc: sharp and stinging. **6** brisk: *He walked at a smart pace.* **7** *comput* technologically advanced. **8** computer-guided or electronically controlled: *a smart bomb.* **9** *informal* impressive; excellent. ▸ *verb, intr* **1** to feel or be the cause of a sharp stinging pain. **2** to feel or be the cause of acute irritation or distress: *He's still smarting from the insult.* ▸ *noun* a sharp stinging pain. ▸ *adv* in a smart manner. ▪ **smartly** *adv.* ▪ **smartness** *noun.* [Anglo-Saxon *smeortan*]
IDIOMS **look smart** to hurry up.

smart alec *or* **smart aleck** *noun, informal* a person who thinks that they are cleverer than others.

smart card *noun* a plastic card like a bank card, fitted with a microprocessor (including a memory) used in commercial transactions, telecommunications, etc.

smarten *verb, tr & intr* (*usu* **smarten up**) to make or become smarter: *He should smarten up a bit.*

smartypants *singular noun, informal* a know-all.

smash *verb* **1** *tr & intr* to break or shatter violently into pieces; to destroy or be destroyed in this way. **2** *tr & intr* to strike with violence, often causing damage; to burst with great force: *They smashed through the door.* **3** *informal* to break up or ruin completely: *Police have smashed an international drugs ring.* **4** in racket sports: to hit (a ball) with a powerful overhead stroke. **5** to crash (a car). ▸ *noun* **1** an act, or the sound, of smashing. **2** in racket sports: a powerful overhead stroke. **3** *informal* a road traffic accident. **4** *informal* a **smash hit**. ▸ *adv* with a smashing sound. [17c: prob from **smack**[1] and **mash**]

smash-and-grab *adj, informal* of a robbery: carried out by smashing a shop window and snatching the items on display.

smasher *noun, informal* someone or something very much liked or admired.

smash hit *noun, informal* a song, film, play, etc that is an overwhelming success.

smashing *adj, informal* excellent; splendid.

smash-up *noun, informal* a serious road traffic accident.

smattering *noun* **1** a few scraps of superficial knowledge. **2** a small amount scattered around. [16c as *smateren* to rattle]

smear *verb* **1** to spread (something sticky or oily) thickly over (a surface). **2** *tr & intr* to make or become blurred; to smudge. **3** to say or write abusive and damaging things about someone. ▸ *noun* **1** a greasy mark or patch. **2** a damaging criticism or accusation; a slur. **3** an amount of a substance, esp of cervical tissue, placed on a slide for examination under a microscope. **4** *informal* a cervical smear. ▪ **smeary** *adj.* [Anglo-Saxon *smeru* fat, grease]

smear test *noun* a cervical smear.

smell *noun* **1** the sense that allows different odours to be recognized by specialized receptors in the mucous membranes of the nose. **2** the characteristic odour of a particular substance: *It has a strong smell.* **3** an unpleasant odour: *What a smell!* **4** an act of using this sense: *Have a smell of this.* **5** a sense, savour or suggestion of something: *The smell of money always brings him back.* ▸ *verb* (***smelled*** *or* ***smelt***) **1** to recognize (a substance) by its odour. **2** *intr* to give off an unpleasant odour. **3** to give off a specified odour: *the perfume smells flowery.* **4** to be aware of something by intuition: *I smell a government cover-up.* [12c as *smel*]

PHRASAL VERBS **smell sb** *or* **sth out** to track them or it down by smell, or as if by smell.

smelling salts *plural noun* a preparation of ammonium carbonate with a strong sharp odour, used to stimulate a return to consciousness after fainting.

smelly *adj* (***-ier, -iest***) *informal* having a strong or unpleasant smell. ▪ **smelliness** *noun.*

smelt[1] *verb* to process (an ore), esp by melting it, in order to separate out the crude metal. [16c: from German *smelten*]

smelt[2] *noun* (***smelts*** *or* ***smelt***) a small fish of the salmon family, including several edible species, with a slender silvery body and a jutting lower jaw. [Anglo-Saxon *smylt*]

smelt[3] *a past tense & past participle of* **smell**

smelter *noun* an industrial plant where smelting is done. [15c: from **smelt**[1]]

smidgen, **smidgeon** *or* **smidgin** *noun, informal* a very small amount. [19c]

smile *verb* **1** *intr* to turn up the corners of the mouth, often showing the teeth, usu as an expression of pleasure, favour or amusement. **2** to show or communicate with such an expression: *He smiled his agreement.* **3** *intr* (*usu* **smile on sb** *or* **sth**) **a** to show favour towards them. **b** to be a good omen: *The gods are smiling on you today.* ▸ *noun* an act or way of smiling. ▪ **smiler** *noun.* ▪ **smiling** *noun, adj.* ▪ **smilingly** *adv.* [13c: as *smilen*]

smiley *noun, comput slang* a symbol created from characters on a keyboard, eg :-) intended to look like a smiling face, used to indicate irony or pleasure.

smirch *verb* **1** to make dirty; to soil or stain. **2** to damage or sully (a reputation, etc). ▸ *noun* **1** a stain. **2** a smear on a reputation. [15c: from French *esmorcher* to hurt]

smirk *verb* to smile in a self-satisfied, affected or foolish manner. ▸ *noun* such a smile. ▪ **smirking** *adj.* [Anglo-Saxon *smercian*]

smite *verb* (*past tense* ***smote,*** *past participle* ***smitten***) *literary* **1** to strike or beat with a heavy blow or blows. **2** to kill. **3** to afflict. **4** to cause someone to fall immediately and overpoweringly in love: *He could not fail to be smitten by such beauty.* ▪ **smitten** *adj* in love; obsessed. [Anglo-Saxon *smitan* to smear]

smith *noun* **1** *in compounds* a person who makes articles in the specified metal: *silversmith.* **2** a **blacksmith.** **3** *in compounds* a person who makes skilful use of anything: *wordsmith.* [Anglo-Saxon]

smithereens *plural noun, informal* tiny fragments. [19c: from Irish Gaelic *smidirín*]

smithy *noun* (***-ies***) a blacksmith's workshop.

smock *noun* **1** any loose shirt-like garment worn over other clothes for protection esp by artists, etc. **2** a woman's long loose-fitting blouse. **3** *hist* a loose-fitting overall of linen worn by farm-workers. Also called **smock-frock**. [Anglo-Saxon *smoc*]

smocking *noun* honeycomb-patterned stitching used on gathered or tucked material for decoration.

smog *noun* a mixture of smoke and fog, esp in urban or industrial areas, produced by motor vehicle exhaust fumes, the burning of fuels, etc. ▪ **smoggy** *adj* (***-ier, -iest***). [Early 20c: from *smoke* + *fog*]

smoke *noun* **1** a visible cloud given off by a burning substance. **2** a cloud or column of fumes. **3** *informal* the act or process of smoking tobacco: *Got time for a smoke?* **4** *informal* something that can be smoked, such as a cigarette or cigar. **5** (**the Smoke**) see **the Big Smoke**. ▸ *verb* **1** *intr* to give off smoke, visible fumes or vapours. **2** *tr & intr* to inhale and then exhale the smoke from burning tobacco or other substances in a cigarette, cigar, pipe, etc. **3** *tr & intr* to do this frequently, esp as a habit that is hard to break. **4** to preserve or flavour food by exposing it to smoke. [Anglo-Saxon *smoca*]

IDIOMS **go up in smoke 1** to be completely destroyed

by fire. **2** *informal* of plans, etc: to be ruined completely; to come to nothing.

smoke alarm *or* **smoke detector** *noun* a device that gives a loud warning sound on detecting smoke from a fire in a room.

smokeless *adj* of a fuel: giving off little or no smoke when burned, eg coke.

smokeless zone *noun* an area, usu an urban area, where only smokeless fuels may be used.

smoker *noun* someone who smokes tobacco products.

smokescreen *noun* **1** a cloud of smoke used to conceal the movements of troops, etc. **2** anything said or done to hide or deceive.

smoky *adj* (**-ier, -iest**) **1** giving out much or excessive smoke. **2** filled with smoke (esp tobacco smoke). **3** having a smoked flavour. **4** made dirty by smoke.

smolt *noun* a young salmon migrating from fresh water to the sea. [15c: Scots]

smooch *informal, verb, intr* **1** to kiss and cuddle. **2** to dance slowly while in an embrace. [16c: variant of obsolete *smouch* to kiss]

smoochy *adj* (**-ier, -iest**) of music: sentimental and romantic.

smooth *adj* **1** having an even regular surface; not rough, coarse, bumpy or wavy. **2** having few or no lumps; having an even texture or consistency: *smooth sauce.* **3** free from problems or difficulties: *a smooth journey.* **4** characterized by steady movement and a lack of jolts and lurches: *a smooth ferry crossing.* **5** of skin: having no hair, spots, blemishes, etc. **6** extremely charming, esp excessively or insincerely so: *a smooth talker.* **7** *slang* very classy or elegant: *a smooth dresser.* ▸ *verb* **1** (*also* **smooth sth down** *or* **out**) to make it smooth: *She smoothed out the sheets on the bed.* **2** (*often* **smooth over sth**) to cause a difficulty, etc to seem less serious or important. **3** to free from lumps or roughness. **4** (*often* **smooth sth away**) to remove (esp problems) by smoothing; to calm or soothe. **5** to make easier. **6** *intr* to become smooth. ▸ *adv* smoothly. ▸ *noun* **1** the act or process of smoothing. **2** the easy, pleasurable or trouble-free part or aspect (eg of a situation): *take the rough with the smooth.* ▪ **smoothly** *adv.* ▪ **smoothness** *noun.* [Anglo-Saxon *smoth*]

smoothie *or* **smoothy** *noun* (**-ies**) *informal* a person who is very elegant, charming or suave in dress or manner, esp one excessively or insincerely so.

smooth-talking, **smooth-spoken** *or* **smooth-tongued** *adj* **1** exaggeratedly and insincerely flattering. **2** charmingly persuasive. ▪ **smooth-talker** *noun.*

smorgasbord *noun* a Swedish-style buffet of hot and cold savoury dishes. [1920s: Swedish]

smote *past tense of* **smite**

smother *verb* **1** *tr & intr* to kill with or die from lack of air, esp with an obstruction over the mouth and nose; to suffocate. **2** to extinguish (a fire) by cutting off the air supply, eg by throwing a blanket over it. **3** to cover or smear something with a thick layer: *She loved her bread smothered with jam.* **4** to give an oppressive or stifling amount to someone: *She smothered the children with love.* **5** to suppress or contain. [12c: as *smorther*, related to Anglo-Saxon *smorian*]

smoulder *verb, intr* **1** to burn slowly without flame. **2** of emotions: to linger on in a suppressed and often hidden state. **3** of a person: to harbour suppressed and often hidden emotions: *She sat smouldering in the corner.* [14c: as *smolder*]

smudge *noun* **1** a mark or blot caused or spread by rubbing. **2** a faint or blurred shape, eg an object seen from afar. ▸ *verb* **1** to make a smudge on or of something. **2** *intr* to become or cause a smudge: *These pens smudge easily.* ▪ **smudgy** *adj.* [15c: as *smogen*]

smug *adj* (**smugger, smuggest**) arrogantly self-complacent or self-satisfied. ▪ **smugly** *adv.* ▪ **smugness** *noun.* [16c: from German dialect *smuck* neat]

smuggle *verb* **1** to take (goods) into or out of a country secretly and illegally, eg to avoid paying duty. **2** to bring, take or convey secretly, usu breaking a rule or restriction: *He smuggled his notes into the exam.* ▪ **smuggler** *noun.* ▪ **smuggling** *noun.* [17c: from German dialect *smuggeln*]

smut *noun* **1** a speck of dirt, soot, etc. **2** mildly obscene language, jokes, pictures or images. **3** **a** any of a group of parasitic fungi causing a serious disease of cereal crops, and characterized by the appearance of masses of black spores, resembling soot; **b** the disease caused by such a fungus. ▸ *verb* (**smutted, smutting**) **1** to dirty or affect with smut. **2** to become smutty. [16c: as *smotten* to stain]

smutty *adj* (**-ier, -iest**) **1** dirtied by smut. **2** mildly obscene: *a smutty sense of humour.* ▪ **smuttiness** *noun.*

Sn *symbol, chem* tin.

snack *noun* a light meal often taken quickly, or a bite to eat between meals. ▸ *verb, intr* to eat a snack. [14c: perhaps from Dutch *snacken* to snap]

snack bar *or* **snack counter** *noun* a café, kiosk or counter serving snacks.

snaffle *noun* (*in full* **snaffle-bit**) a simple bridle bit for a horse. ▸ *verb* **1** to fit (a horse) with a snaffle. **2** *slang* to take sneakily or without permission; to steal. [16c: from German and Dutch *Snavel* mouth]

snafu *noun, US slang, orig military* chaos. [1940s: from situation normal: all fouled or fucked up]

snag *noun* **1** a problem or drawback. **2** a protruding sharp or jagged edge on which clothes, etc could get caught. **3** a hole or tear in clothes (esp tights, stockings, etc) caused by such catching. **4** a part of a tree submerged in water, hazardous to boats. ▸ *verb* (**snagged, snagging**) to catch or tear on a snag. [16c: from Norse *snagi* peg]

snaggletooth *noun* a broken, irregular or projecting tooth. ▪ **snaggletoothed** *adj.* [Early 19c: from **snag** + **tooth**]

snail *noun* **1** a mollusc similar to a slug, but carrying a coiled or conical shell on its back, into which the whole body can be withdrawn. **2** a sluggish person or animal. [Anglo-Saxon *snæl*]

IDIOMS **at a snail's pace** extremely slowly.

snail mail *noun, comput slang* the ordinary postal service, as opposed to electronic mail.

snake *noun* **1** a limbless carnivorous reptile which has a long narrow body covered with scaly skin, and a forked tongue. **2** any long and flexible or winding thing or shape. **3** a **snake in the grass**. ▸ *verb, intr* to move windingly or follow a winding course. ▪ **snakelike** *adj.* ▪ **snaky** *adj.* [Anglo-Saxon *snaca*]

snake-charmer *noun* a street entertainer who appears to induce snakes to perform rhythmical movements, esp by playing music.

snake in the grass *noun, informal* a treacherous person; a friend revealed to be an enemy.

snap *verb* (***snapped, snapping***) **1** *tr & intr* to break suddenly and cleanly with a sharp cracking noise: *He snapped the stick over his knee.* **2** *tr & intr* to make or cause to make a sharp noise. **3** *tr & intr* to move quickly and forcefully into place with a sharp sound: *The lid snapped shut.* **4** *intr* to speak sharply in sudden irritation. **5** *informal* to take a photograph of someone or something, esp spontaneously and with a hand-held camera. **6** *intr, informal* to lose one's senses or self-control suddenly. ▸ *noun* **1** the act or sound of snapping. **2** *informal* a photograph, esp taken spontaneously and with a hand-held camera. **3** a catch or other fastening that closes with a snapping sound. **4** a sudden bite. **5** a crisp biscuit or savoury. **6** a card game in which all the cards played are collected by the first player to shout 'snap' on spotting a pair of matching cards laid down by consecutive players. ▸ *exclam* **1** the word shouted in the card game (see *noun* sense 6 above). **2** the word used to highlight any matching pairs, circumstances, etc. ▸ *adj* taken or made spontaneously, without long consideration: *a snap decision.* ▸ *adv* with a snapping sound. [15c: from Dutch *snappen*]

IDIOMS **snap one's fingers** to show contempt or defiance. **snap sb's head** *or* **nose off** to answer irritably and rudely. **snap out of it** *informal* to bring oneself out of a state or condition, eg of sulking or depression.

PHRASAL VERBS **snap sb up** to obtain them for employment, as a partner in a relationship, etc: *You'd better move quick or she'll be snapped up.* **snap sth up** to acquire, purchase or seize it eagerly: *He snapped up the opportunity.*

snapdragon see **antirrhinum**

snapper *noun* **1** someone or something that snaps. **2** a deep-bodied food fish, found in tropical seas. **3** *US* a party cracker.

snappy *adj* (***-ier, -iest***) **1** irritable; inclined to snap. **2** smart and fashionable: *a snappy dresser.* **3** lively: *a snappy tempo.* ▪ **snappily** *adv.* ▪ **snappiness** *noun.*

IDIOMS **look snappy!** *or* **make it snappy!** *informal* hurry up!, be quick about it!

snapshot *noun, informal* a photograph, esp one taken spontaneously and with a hand-held camera.

snare *noun* **1** an animal trap, esp one with a string or wire noose to catch the animal's foot. **2** anything that traps or entangles. **3** anything that lures or tempts. **4** (*in full* **snare drum**) a medium-sized drum sitting horizontally, with a set of wires fitted to its underside that rattle sharply when the drum is struck. ▸ *verb* to catch, trap or entangle in, or as if in, a snare. [Anglo-Saxon *sneare*]

snarl[1] *verb* **1** *intr* of an animal: to growl angrily, showing the teeth. **2** *tr & intr* to speak aggressively in anger or irritation. ▸ *noun* **1** an act of snarling. **2** a snarling sound or facial expression.

snarl[2] *noun* a knotted or tangled mass. ▸ *verb, tr & intr* (*also* **snarl sb** *or* **sth up** *or* **snarl up**) to make or become knotted, tangled, confused or congested. [14c: related to **snare**]

snarl-up *noun, informal* any muddled or congested situation, esp a traffic jam.

snatch *verb* **1** to seize or grab suddenly. **2** *intr* to make a sudden grabbing movement. **3** to pull suddenly and forcefully: *She snatched her hand away.* **4** *informal* to take or have as soon as the opportunity arises: *snatch a bite to eat.* ▸ *noun* **1** an act of snatching. **2** a fragment overheard or remembered: *snatches of conversation.* **3** a brief period: *snatches of rest between long shifts.* **4** *informal* a robbery. ▪ **snatcher** *noun.* [13c: as *snacchen*]

snazzy *adj* (***-ier, -iest***) *informal* fashionably and often flashily smart or elegant. ▪ **snazzily** *adv.* [1930s: perhaps from *snappy* + *jazzy*]

sneak *verb* (***sneaked*** *or* (*informal*) ***snuck***) **1** (*often* **sneak away, off, out,** *etc*) *intr* to move, go or depart quietly, furtively and unnoticed. **2** to bring or take secretly, esp breaking a rule or prohibition: *He tried to sneak a look at the letter.* **3** *intr, informal* to inform about someone; to tell tales. ▸ *noun, informal* someone who sneaks; a tell-tale. [Anglo-Saxon *snican* to creep]

sneakers *plural noun, esp US* sports shoes; soft-soled, usu canvas, shoes.

sneaking *adj* **1** of a feeling, etc: slight but not easily suppressed: *a sneaking suspicion.* **2** secret; unrevealed: *a sneaking admiration.* **3** underhand.

sneak thief *noun* a thief who enters premises through unlocked doors or windows, without actually breaking in.

sneaky *adj* (***-ier, -iest***) done or operating with secretive unfairness or dishonesty; underhand. ▪ **sneakily** *adv.* ▪ **sneakiness** *noun.*

sneer *verb* **1** (*often* **sneer at sb** *or* **sth**) *intr* to show scorn or contempt, esp by drawing the top lip up at one side. **2** *intr* to express scorn or contempt. **3** to say scornfully or contemptuously. ▸ *noun* **1** an act of sneering. **2** an expression of scorn or contempt made with a raised lip, or in other ways. [16c]

sneeze *verb, intr* to blow air out through the nose suddenly, violently and involuntarily, esp because of irritation in the nostrils. ▸ *noun* an act or the sound of sneezing. [Anglo-Saxon *fnesan*]

IDIOMS **not to be sneezed at** *informal* not to be disregarded or overlooked lightly.

snib *chiefly Scot, noun* a small bolt or catch for a door or window-sash. ▸ *verb* (***snibbed, snibbing***) to fasten with a snib. [Early 19c: from German *Snibbe* beak]

snick *noun* **1** a small cut; a nick. **2** *cricket* **a** a glancing contact with the edge of the bat; **b** the shot hit in this way. ▸ *verb* **1** to make a small cut in something. **2** *cricket* to hit with a snick. [16c: from Norse *snikka* to whittle]

snicker *verb, intr* to **snigger**. ▸ *noun* a giggle. [17c]

snide *adj* expressing criticism or disapproval in an offensive, sly or malicious manner. [19c]

sniff *verb* **1** to draw in air with the breath through the nose. **2** *intr* to draw up mucus or tears escaping into the nose. **3** (*often* **sniff sth** *or* **sniff at sth**) *tr & intr* to smell it in this way. ▸ *noun* **1** an act or the sound of sniffing. **2** a smell. **3** a small quantity inhaled by the nose. **4** a slight intimation or suspicion. ▪ **sniffer** *noun.* ▪ **sniffing** *noun, adj.* [14c: imitating the sound]

IDIOMS **not to be sniffed at** *informal* not to be disregarded or overlooked lightly.

PHRASAL VERBS **sniff sb** *or* **sth out** to discover or detect them or it by, or as if by, the sense of smell.

sniffer dog *noun* a dog specially trained to search for or locate illicit or dangerous substances by smell.

sniffle *verb, intr* to sniff repeatedly, eg because of having a cold. ▸ *noun* **1** an act or the sound of sniffling. **2** (*also* **the sniffles**) a slight cold. ▪ **sniffly** *adj.*

sniffy *adj* (**-ier, -iest**) *informal* contemptuous or disdainful, or inclined to be so. ▪ **sniffiness** *noun.*

snifter *noun* **1** *slang* a drink of alcohol, esp alcoholic spirit; a tipple or dram. **2** *US* a brandy glass. [19c: from dialect *snift* to sniff]

snigger *verb, intr* to laugh in a stifled or suppressed way, often derisively or mockingly. ▸ *noun* such a laugh. Also called **snicker**. ▪ **sniggering** *noun, adj.* [18c: an imitation of **snicker**]

snip *verb* (***snipped, snipping***) to cut, esp with a single quick action or actions, with scissors. ▸ *noun* **1** an act or the action of snipping. **2** the sound of a stroke of scissors while snipping. **3** a small shred or piece snipped off. **4** a small cut, slit or notch. **5** *informal* a bargain: *It's a snip at £10.* [16c: from Dutch *snippen*]

snipe *noun* (***snipe*** *or* ***snipes***) **1** a wading bird with a long straight bill and relatively short legs. **2** a sniping shot, ie a shot at someone from a hidden position. **3** a quick verbal attack or criticism. ▸ *verb, intr* **1** to shoot snipe for sport. **2** (*often* **snipe at sb**) **a** to shoot at them from a hidden position; **b** to criticize them bad-temperedly. ▪ **sniper** *noun* someone who shoots from a concealed position. ▪ **sniping** *noun.* [14c: from Norse *snipa*]

snippet *noun* a scrap, eg of information, news, etc. [17c: from **snip**]

snitch *slang, noun* an informer. ▸ *verb* **1** *intr* to inform on or betray others. **2** to steal; to pilfer. ▪ **snitcher** *noun.* [18c]

snivel *verb* (***snivelled, snivelling***) *intr* **1** to whine or complain tearfully. **2** to have a runny nose. **3** to sniff or snuffle. ▸ *noun* an act of snivelling. ▪ **sniveller** *noun.* ▪ **snivelly** *adj.* [Anglo-Saxon *snofl* mucus]

snob *noun* **1** someone who places too high a value on social status, treating those higher up the social ladder obsequiously, and those lower down the social ladder with condescension and contempt. **2** someone having similar pretensions as regards specific tastes: *an intellectual snob.* ▪ **snobbery** *noun.* ▪ **snobbish** *adj.* [18c]

snoek see **snook**[1]

snog *slang, verb* (***snogged, snogging***) *intr* to embrace, kiss and cuddle. ▸ *noun* a kiss and cuddle. [1950s]

snood *noun* a decorative pouch of netting or fabric worn by women on the back of the head, keeping the hair in a bundle. [Anglo-Saxon *snod*]

snook[1] *or* **snoek** *noun* (***snook*** *or* ***snooks***; ***snoek***) a marine fish. [17c: from Dutch *snoek* pike]

snook[2] *noun* the gesture of putting the thumb to the nose and waving the fingers as an expression of derision, contempt or defiance. [19c]

IDIOMS **cock a snook at sb** *informal* **1** to make this gesture at them. **2** to express contempt for them.

snooker *noun* **1** a game played with **cues**, 15 red balls, one white cue ball and six balls of other colours, the object being to use the white cue ball to knock the non-white balls in a certain order into any of the six pockets on the corners and sides of a large cloth-covered table, and to gain more points than the opponent. **2** in this game: a position in which the path between the white ball and the target ball is obstructed by another ball. ▸ *verb* **1** in snooker: to force (an opponent) to attempt to hit an obstructed target ball. **2** *informal* to thwart (a person or a plan). [19c]

snoop *verb, intr* to go about sneakingly and inquisitively; to pry. ▸ *noun* **1** an act of snooping. **2** someone who snoops. ▪ **snooper** *noun.* [19c: from Dutch *snoepen* to eat or steal]

snooty *adj* (**-ier, -iest**) *informal* haughty; snobbish. ▪ **snootily** *adv.* ▪ **snootiness** *noun.*

snooze *verb, intr* to sleep lightly; to doze. ▸ *noun* a brief period of light sleeping; a nap. ▪ **snoozy** *adj.* [18c: perhaps a combination of **snore** and **doze**]

snore *verb, intr* to breathe heavily and with a snorting sound while sleeping. ▸ *noun* an act or the sound of snoring. ▪ **snorer** *noun.* [14c: imitating the sound]

snorkel *noun* a rigid tube through which air from above the surface of water can be drawn into the mouth while one is swimming just below the surface. ▸ *verb* (***snorkelled, snorkelling***) *intr* to swim with a snorkel. [1940s: from German *Schnorchel*]

snort *verb* **1** *intr* esp of animals: to force air violently and noisily out through the nostrils; to make a similar noise while taking air in. **2** *tr & intr* to express contempt or anger in this way. ▸ *noun* an act or the sound of snorting. [14c as *snorten*]

snot *noun* **1** mucus of the nose. **2** a contemptible person. [Anglo-Saxon *gesnot*]

snotty *adj* (**-ier, -iest**) *informal* **1** covered or messy with nasal mucus. **2** haughty or stand-offish; having or showing contempt: *a snotty attitude.* **3** *derog* contemptible; worthless: *What a snotty little car!* ▪ **snottily** *adv.* ▪ **snottiness** *noun.*

snout *noun* **1** the projecting nose and mouth parts of certain animals, eg the pig. **2** *informal* the human nose. **3** any projecting part. [13c: from German *Snut*]

snow *noun* **1** precipitation in the form of ice crystals falling to the ground in soft white flakes, or lying on the ground as a soft white mass. **2** a fall of this: *There's been a lot of snow this year.* **3** *informal* a flickering speckled background on a TV or radar screen, caused by interference or a poor signal. ▸ *verb, intr* of snow: to fall. [Anglo-Saxon *snaw*]

IDIOMS **snowed under** overwhelmed with work, etc.

snowball *noun* a small mass of snow pressed hard together, often used for fun as a missile. ▸ *verb, intr* to develop or increase rapidly and uncontrollably.

snowboard *noun* a board resembling a skateboard without wheels, used on snow and guided with movements of the feet and body. ▸ *verb, intr* to ski on a snowboard. ▪ **snowboarding** *noun.*

snowbound *adj* shut in or prevented from travelling because of heavy falls of snow.

snowcap *noun* a cap of snow, as on the polar regions or a mountain-top. ▪ **snowcapped** *adj.*

snowdrift *noun* a bank of snow blown together by the wind.

snowdrop *noun* a plant with small solitary drooping white bell-shaped flowers.

snowfall *noun* **1** a fall of snow. **2** *meteorol* an amount of fallen snow in a given time: *annual snowfall.*

snowflake *noun* any of the single small feathery clumps of crystals of snow.

snowline *noun* the level or height on a mountain above which there is a permanent covering of snow.

snowman *noun* a figure, resembling a person, made from packed snow.

snowmobile *noun* a motorized vehicle, on skis or tracks, designed for travelling on snow.

snowplough *noun* **1** a vehicle or train fitted with a large shovel-like device for clearing snow from roads or railway tracks. **2** *skiing* a position, used for slowing down, in which the tips of the skis are brought together.

snowshoe *noun* either of a pair of racket-like frameworks strapped to the feet for walking over deep snow.

snowstorm *noun* a heavy fall of snow, especially accompanied by a strong wind.

snowy *adj* (*-ier, -iest*) **1** abounding or covered with snow. **2** white like snow. **3** pure.

SNP *abbrev* in the UK: Scottish National Party, a left-of-centre political party committed to Scottish independence.

Snr *or* **snr** *abbrev* senior.

snub *verb* (***snubbed, snubbing***) to insult by openly ignoring, rejecting or otherwise showing contempt. ▸ *noun* an act of snubbing. ▸ *adj* short and flat; blunt. [14c: from Norse *snubba* to scold]

snub nose *noun* a broad flat nose. ▪ **snub-nosed** *adj.*

snuck *a past tense & past participle of* **sneak**

snuff[1] *verb* **1** *intr* to draw in air violently and noisily through the nose. **2** to examine or detect by sniffing. ▸ *noun* **1** a sniff. **2** powdered tobacco for inhaling through the nose. [16c: from Dutch *snuffen* to snuffle]

snuff[2] *verb* **1** (*often* **snuff sth out**) to extinguish (a candle). **2** to snip off the burnt part of the wick of (a candle or lamp). **3** (*usu* **snuff sth out**) to put an end to it: *tried to snuff out all opposition.* ▸ *noun* the burnt part of the wick of a lamp or candle. [14c: as *snoffe*]

IDIOMS **snuff it** *slang* to die.

snuffer *noun* **1** a device with a cap-shaped part for extinguishing candles. **2** (**snuffers**) a device resembling a pair of scissors for removing snuffs from the wicks of candles or oil lamps.

snuffle *verb* **1** *intr* to breathe, esp breathe in, through a partially blocked nose. **2** *tr & intr* to say or speak nasally. **3** *intr* to snivel. ▸ *noun* an act or the sound of snuffling. ▪ **snuffling** *noun, adj.* [16c: see **snuff**[1]]

snug *adj* (***snugger, snuggest***) **1** warm, cosy and comfortable. **2** well protected and sheltered; not exposed: *a snug boat.* **3** compact and comfortably organized: *a snug kitchen.* **4** comfortably off; well provided for: *a snug income.* **5** close-fitting: *a snug dress.* ▸ *noun* a **snuggery**. ▪ **snugly** *adv.* ▪ **snugness** *noun.* [16c: perhaps from Norse *snoggr* short-haired]

snuggery *noun* (*-ies*) *Brit* a small comfortable room or compartment in a pub.

snuggle *verb, intr* **1** (*usu* **snuggle down** *or* **in**) to settle oneself into a position of warmth and comfort. **2** (*sometimes* **snuggle up**) to hug close; to nestle. [17c: from **snug**]

so[1] *adv* **1** to such an extent: *so expensive that nobody buys it.* **2** to this, that, or the same extent; as: *This one is lovely, but that one is not so nice.* **3** extremely: *She is so talented!* **4** in that state or condition: *promised to be faithful, and has remained so.* **5** also; likewise: *She's my friend and so are you.* **6** used to avoid repeating a previous statement: *You've to go upstairs because I said so.* **7** *informal* used to add vehemence to a statement: *I am so not going to his stupid party!* ▸ *conj* **1** therefore; thereafter: *He insulted me, so I hit him.* **2** (*also* **so that ...**) in order that ...: *Give me more time so I can finish it.* ▸ *adj* the case; true: *You think I'm mad, but it's not so.* ▸ *exclam* used to express discovery: *So, that's what you've been doing!* [Anglo-Saxon *swa*]

IDIOMS **and so on** *or* **and so forth** *or* **and so on and so forth** and more of the same; continuing in the same way. **just so** neatly, precisely or perfectly: *with her hair arranged just so.* **or so** approximately: *five or so days ago.* **so as to ...** in order to ...; in such a way as to ... **so be it** used to express acceptance or defiant resignation. **so far so good** everything is fine up to this point. **so much** *or* **many 1** such a lot: *so much work to do!* **2** just; mere: *politicians squabbling like so many children.* **so much for ...** nothing has come of ...; that has disposed of or ruined ...: *So much for all our plans!* **so to speak** *or* **to say** used as an apology for an unfamiliar or slightly inappropriate expression. **so what?** *informal* that is of no importance or consequence at all.

so[2] see **soh**

soak *verb* **1** *tr & intr* to stand or leave to stand in a liquid for some time. **2** to make someone or something thoroughly wet; to drench or saturate. **3** to penetrate or pass through: *The rain soaked through my coat.* **4** (**soak sth up**) to absorb it. ▸ *noun* **1** an act of soaking. **2** a drenching. **3** *informal* a long period of lying in a bath. ▪ **soaking** *noun, adj, adv.* [Anglo-Saxon *socian*]

so-and-so *noun* (***so-and-sos***) *informal* **1** someone whose name one does not know or cannot remember: *He's gone with so-and-so.* **2** a word in place of a vulgar word or oath: *You crafty little so-and-so!*

soap *noun* **1** a cleaning agent consisting of a **fatty acid** that is soluble in water, in the form of a solid block, liquid or powder. **2** *informal* a **soap opera**. ▸ *verb* to apply soap to something. [Anglo-Saxon *sape*]

soapbox *noun* **1** a crate for packing soap. **2** an improvised platform for public speech-making, orig an upturned crate for packing soap.

soap opera *noun* a radio or TV series concerning the domestic and emotional lives and troubles of a regular group of characters. [20c: orig applied to those sponsored in the USA by soap-manufacturing companies]

soapstone *noun* a soft usu grey or brown variety of the mineral talc, widely used for ornamental carvings. See also **French chalk**.

soapy *adj* (***-ier, -iest***) **1** like soap. **2** containing soap. **3** smeared or covered with soap. **4** *informal* like a soap opera.

soar *verb, intr* **1** to rise or fly high into the air. **2** to glide through the air at a high altitude. **3** to rise sharply to a great height or level: *temperatures are soaring.* ▪ **soaring** *noun, adj.* [14c: from French *essorer* to expose to air by raising up]

sob *verb* (***sobbed, sobbing***) **1** *intr* to cry uncontrollably with intermittent gulps for breath. **2** (*often* **sob out**) to say or tell something while crying in this way. ▸ *noun* a gulp for breath between bouts of crying. ▪ **sobbing** *noun, adj.* [12c: imitating the sound]

sober *adj* **1** not at all drunk. **2** serious, solemn or restrained; not frivolous or extravagant. **3** suggesting sedateness or seriousness rather than exuberance or frivolity: *sober colours.* **4** plain; unembellished:

the sober truth. ▸ *verb, tr & intr* **1** (*always* **sober down** *or* **sober sb down**) to become, or make someone, quieter, less excited, etc. **2** (*always* **sober up** *or* **sober sb up**) to become, or make someone, free from the effects of alcohol. ▪ **sobering** *adj* causing someone to become serious or thoughtful: *a sobering thought*. [14c: from Latin *sobrius*]

sobriety *noun* the state of being sober, esp not drunk. [15c: from Latin *sobrietas*]

sobriquet /ˈsoʊbrɪkeɪ/ *or* **soubriquet** /ˈsuːbrɪkeɪ/ *noun, literary* a nickname. [17c: French, meaning 'a chuck under the chin']

sob story *noun, informal* a story of personal misfortune told in order to gain sympathy.

Soc *abbrev* **1** Socialist. **2** Society.

so-called *adj* known or presented as such with the implication that the term is wrongly or inappropriately used: *a panel of so-called experts*.

soccer see under **football**

sociable *adj* **1** fond of the company of others; friendly. **2** characterized by friendliness. [16c: from Latin *sociabilis*]

social *adj* **1** relating to or for people or society as a whole: *social policies*. **2** relating to the organization and behaviour of people in societies or communities: *social studies*. **3** tending or needing to live with others; not solitary: *social creatures*. **4** intended for or promoting friendly gatherings of people: *a social club*. **5** convivial; jovial. ▸ *noun* **1** a social gathering, esp one organized by a club or other group. **2** (**the social**) *informal* social security. ▪ **socially** *adv*. [16c: from Latin *sociare* to unite]

social climber *noun, often derog* someone who seeks to gain higher social status.

socialism *noun* a political doctrine or system which aims to create a classless society by moving ownership of the nation's wealth (land, industries, transport systems, etc) out of private and into public hands. ▪ **socialist** *noun, adj*. [1830s]

socialite *noun* someone who mixes with people of high social status.

socialize *or* **-ise** *verb* **1** *intr* to meet with people on an informal, friendly basis. **2** *intr* to mingle or circulate among guests at a party; to behave sociably. **3** to organize into societies or communities. ▪ **socialization** *noun*.

social sciences *plural noun* the subjects that deal with the organization and behaviour of people in societies and communities, including sociology, anthropology, economics and history.

social security *noun* **1** a system by which each member of society makes regular contributions from their earned income into a common fund, from which payments are made to those who are unemployed, ill, disabled or elderly. **2** a payment or scheme of payments from such a fund.

social services *plural noun* **1** services provided by local or national government for the general welfare of people in society, eg housing, education and health. **2** the public bodies providing these services.

social work *noun* work in any of the services provided by local government for the care of underprivileged people, eg the poor, the aged, people with disabilities, etc. ▪ **social worker** *noun*.

society *noun* (***-ies***) **1** humankind as a whole, or a part of it such as one nation, considered as a single community. **2** a division of humankind with common characteristics, eg of nationality, race or religion. **3** an organized group or association, meeting to share a common interest or activity. **4 a** the rich and fashionable section of the upper class; **b** the social scene of this class section. **5** *formal* company: *He prefers the society of women*. [16c: from French *societé*]

socioeconomic *adj* referring or relating to social and economic aspects of something together.

sociology *noun* the scientific study of the nature, structure and workings of human society. ▪ **sociological** *adj*. ▪ **sociologist** *noun*.

sock[1] *noun* a fabric covering for the foot and ankle, sometimes reaching to or over the knee, worn inside a shoe or boot. [Anglo-Saxon *socc* light shoe]
IDIOMS **pull one's socks up** *informal* to make an effort to do better. **put a sock in it** *slang* to become silent; to be quiet.

sock[2] *slang, verb* to hit with a powerful blow. ▸ *noun* a powerful blow. [17c]
IDIOMS **sock it to sb** *slang* to make a powerful impression on them.

socket *noun* **1** a specially shaped hole or set of holes into which something is inserted or fitted: *an electrical socket*. **2** *anat* a hollow structure into which another part fits. [14c: from French *soket*, a diminutive of *soc*]

Socratic *adj* referring or relating to the Greek philosopher Socrates, his philosophy, or his method of teaching.

sod *noun* **1** a slab of earth with grass growing on it; a turf. **2** *poetic* the ground. ▸ *verb* (***sodded, sodding***) to cover with sods. [15c: from German *Sode*]

soda *noun* **1** a common name given to any of various compounds of sodium in everyday use, eg **sodium carbonate** or **bicarbonate of soda**. **2** *informal* **soda water**. **3** *N Am, esp US* a fizzy soft drink of any kind. [16c: Latin]

soda ash *noun, chem* the common name for the commercial grade of anhydrous **sodium carbonate**.

soda fountain *noun, N Am, esp US* **1** a counter in a shop from which fizzy drinks, ice cream and snacks are served. **2** an apparatus for supplying soda water.

soda lime *noun, chem* a mixture of sodium or potassium hydroxide and calcium oxide.

soda siphon see **siphon** (*noun* sense 2)

soda water *noun* water made fizzy by the addition of carbon dioxide.

sodden *adj* **1** heavy with moisture; saturated; thoroughly soaked. **2** made lifeless or sluggish, esp through excessive consumption of alcohol: *a drink-sodden brain*. [13c: past tense of *sethen* to **seethe**]

sodium *noun, chem* (symbol **Na**) a soft silvery-white metallic element used in alloys. [19c: from **soda**]

sodium bicarbonate *noun, chem* **bicarbonate of soda**.

sodium borate see **borax**

sodium carbonate *noun, chem* a water-soluble white powder or crystalline solid, used as a water softener and food additive, in glass making, photography and in the manufacture of various sodium compounds. Also called **soda**. See also **washing soda, soda ash**.

sodium chloride *noun, chem* a water-soluble white crystalline salt obtained from seawater and deposits of the mineral halite, used since ancient times for seasoning and preserving food.

sodium hydroxide *noun, chem* a white crystalline solid that dissolves in water to form a highly corrosive alkaline solution, and is used in the manufacture of soap, detergents, etc. Also called **caustic soda**, **soda**.

sodium lamp *noun* a street lamp using sodium vapour and giving a yellow light.

Sod's law *noun, slang* a facetious maxim stating that if something can go wrong it will, or that the most inconvenient thing that could happen will happen.

sofa *noun* an upholstered seat with a back and arms, for two or more people. [17c: from Arabic *suffah*]

soft *adj* **1** easily yielding or changing shape when pressed. **2** easily yielding to pressure. **3** easily cut. **4** of fabric, etc: having a smooth surface or texture producing little or no friction. **5** pleasing or soothing to the senses; quiet: *a soft voice.* **6** having little brightness; not glaring or brash: *soft colours.* **7** kind or sympathetic, esp excessively so. **8** not able to endure rough treatment or hardship. **9** lacking strength of character; easily influenced. **10** *informal* weak in the mind; simple: *soft in the head.* **11** of a person: out of training; in an unfit condition. **12** weakly sentimental. **13** of water: low in or free from mineral salts and so lathering easily. **14** tender; loving or affectionate: *soft words.* **15** *phonetics, non-technical* of the consonants *c* and *g*: pronounced as a fricative as in *dance* and *age* respectively, rather than as a stop, as in *can* and *gate*. Compare **hard** (*adj* sense 19). **16** in computer typesetting and word-processing: referring to a space, hyphen or page break that can be automatically removed when its environment changes to make it redundant. ▸ *adv* softly; gently: *speaks soft.* ▪ **softly** *adv.* ▪ **softness** *noun.* [Anglo-Saxon *softe*]

IDIOMS **be** *or* **go soft on sb** *informal* **1** to be lenient towards them. **2** to be infatuated with them.

softball *noun* a game similar to baseball, played with a larger, softer ball which is pitched underarm, as opposed to overarm in baseball.

soft drink *noun* a non-alcoholic drink.

soften *verb, tr & intr* **1** to make or become soft or softer. **2** to make or become less severe. ▪ **softener** *noun* a substance added to another to increase its softness, pliability, etc, such as fabric softener.

PHRASAL VERBS **soften sb up** *informal* to prepare them for an unwelcome or difficult request.

soft focus *noun, photog, cinematog* the deliberate slight blurring of a picture or scene.

soft fruit *plural noun, Brit* small stoneless edible fruit, such as berries, currants, etc.

soft furnishings *plural noun* rugs, curtains, cushion covers and other articles made of fabric.

soft-hearted *adj* kind-hearted and generous; compassionate.

soft landing *noun* **1** a landing by a spacecraft without uncomfortable or damaging impact. **2** the straightforward solution to a problem, esp an economic one.

softly-softly *adj* cautious or careful; delicate: *a softly-softly approach.*

soft option *noun* the easiest of two or several alternative courses of action.

soft palate *noun, anatomy* the fleshy muscular back part of the palate.

soft pedal *noun* a pedal on a piano pressed to make the tone less lingering or ringing. ▸ *verb* (**soft-pedal**) **1** *music* to play (the piano) using the soft pedal. **2** *informal* to tone down, or avoid emphasizing or mentioning something: *The government were soft-pedalling the scheme's disadvantages.*

soft sell *noun* the use of gentle persuasion as a selling technique, rather than heavy-handed pressure. ▸ *adj* referring or relating to this kind of selling technique: *the soft-sell approach.*

soft soap *noun* **1** a semi-liquid soap containing potash. **2** *informal* flattery or blarney. ▸ *verb* (**soft-soap**) *informal* to speak flatteringly to someone.

soft-spoken *adj* **1** having a soft voice, and usu a mild manner. **2** suave or smooth-tongued.

soft spot *noun, informal* a special liking or affection: *has a soft spot for him.*

soft top *noun* a convertible car with a fabric roof.

soft touch *noun, informal* someone easily taken advantage of or persuaded, esp into giving or lending money willingly.

software *noun, comput* the programs that are used in a computer system, and the magnetic disks, tapes, etc, on which they are recorded. Compare **hardware**.

softwood *noun, botany* the wood of a coniferous tree, eg pine, including some woods that are in fact very hard and durable. Compare **hardwood**.

softy *or* **softie** *noun* (*-ies*) *informal* **1** a weakly sentimental, soft-hearted or silly person. **2** someone not able to endure rough treatment or hardship.

soggy *adj* (*-ier, -iest*) **1** thoroughly soaked or wet; saturated. **2** of ground: waterlogged; boggy. ▪ **sogginess** *noun.* [16c: from dialect *sog* bog]

soh, **so** *or* **sol** *noun, music* in sol-fa notation: the fifth note or **dominant** of a major or minor scale. [14c: see **sol-fa**]

soil[1] *noun* **1** the mixture of fragmented rock, plant and animal debris that lies on the surface of the earth. **2** *literary* country; land: *on foreign soil.* [14c: from French *suel*]

soil[2] *verb* **1** to stain or make dirty. **2** to bring discredit on; to sully. ▸ *noun* **1** a spot or stain. **2** dung; sewage. [13c: from French *souil* wallowing-place]

soirée *or* **soiree** /'swɑːreɪ/ *noun* a formal party held in the evening. [19c: French, meaning 'evening']

sojourn /'sɒdʒən, -ʒːn/ *formal, noun* a short stay. ▸ *verb, intr* to stay for a short while. ▪ **sojourner** *noun.* [13c: from French *sojorner*]

sol[1] see **soh**

sol[2] *noun, chem* a type of colloid that consists of small solid particles dispersed in a liquid.

solace /'sɒləs/ *noun* **1** comfort in time of disappointment or sorrow. **2** a source of comfort. ▸ *verb* to provide with such comfort. [13c: from French *solas*]

solar *adj* **1** referring or relating to the Sun. **2** relating to, by or using energy from the Sun's rays: *solar-powered.* [15c: from Latin *solaris*]

solar battery *noun, elec* a battery consisting of a number of solar cells.

solar cell *noun, elec* an electric cell that converts solar energy directly into electricity. Also called **photovoltaic cell**.

solar eclipse see under **eclipse**

solar energy *noun* **1** energy radiated from the Sun, mainly in the form of heat and light. **2** energy derived from the sun's radiation, eg in a solar cell.

solar flare *noun, astron* a sudden release of energy in the vicinity of an active region on the Sun's surface, generally associated with a sunspot.

solarium *noun* (***solariums*** *or* ***solaria***) a room or establishment equipped with sunbeds. [19c: Latin, meaning 'sundial']

solar plexus *noun, anatomy* an area in the abdomen in which there is a concentration of nerves radiating from a central point.

solar system *noun, astron* the Sun and the system of eight major planets, one minor planet, and the asteroids, comets and meteors that revolve around it.

sold *past tense, past participle of* **sell**

solder *noun, eng* an alloy with a low melting point, often containing tin and lead, applied when molten to the joint between two metals to form an airtight seal. ▸ *verb* to join (two pieces of metal) without melting them, by applying a layer of molten alloy to the joint between them and allowing it to cool and solidify. [14c: from French *souldre*]

soldier *noun* **1** a member of a fighting force, esp a national army. **2** a member of an army below officer rank. **3** *informal* (**soldiers**) narrow strips of bread-and-butter or toast, esp for dipping into a soft-boiled egg. ▪ **soldierly** *adj*. [13c: from French *soudier*]

PHRASAL VERBS **soldier on** to continue determinedly in spite of difficulty and discouragement.

soldier of fortune *noun* a mercenary.

sole[1] *noun* **1** the underside of the foot. **2** the underside of a shoe or boot, esp the part not including the heel. **3** the flattish underside of various things. ▸ *verb* to fit (a shoe or boot) with a sole. [14c: French]

sole[2] *noun* (***sole*** *or* ***soles***) an edible flatfish with a slender brown body and both eyes on the left side of the head. [14c: from Latin *solea*]

sole[3] *adj* **1** alone; only. **2** exclusive: *has sole rights to the story.* [14c: from Latin *solus* alone]

solecism /ˈsɒlɪsɪzəm/ *noun* **1** a mistake in the use of language; a breach of syntax, grammar, etc. **2** an instance of bad or incorrect behaviour. ▪ **solecistic** *adj*. [16c: from Greek *soloikismos*]

solely *adv* **1** alone; without others: *solely to blame.* **2** only; excluding all else: *done solely for profit.*

solemn *adj* **1** done, made or carried out in earnest and seriousness: *a solemn vow.* **2** being of a very serious and formal nature; suggesting seriousness: *a solemn occasion.* **3** accompanied or marked by special (esp religious) ceremonies, pomp or gravity. ▪ **solemnly** *adv*. ▪ **solemnness** *noun*. [14c: from French *solempne*]

solemnity *noun* (***-ies***) **1** the state of being solemn. **2** a solemn ceremony. [13c: from Latin *sollemnitas*]

solemnize *or* **-ise** *verb* **1** to perform (esp a marriage) with a formal or religious ceremony. **2** to make something solemn. [14c: from Latin *sollemnis*]

solenoid *noun, physics* a cylindrical coil of wire that produces a magnetic field when an electric current is passed through it. [19c: from French *solénoïde*]

sol-fa *noun* a system of musical notation, either written down or sung, in which the notes of a scale are represented by the syllables *doh, re, mi, fah, soh, la, ti.* Also called **tonic sol-fa**. [16c: from *sol*, a form of **soh**, + **fah**]

solicit *verb, formal* to ask for something, or for something from someone: *solicited me for advice.* ▪ **solicitation** *noun*. ▪ **soliciting** *noun*. [15c: from Latin *solicitare*]

solicitor *noun* **1** in Britain: a lawyer who prepares legal documents, gives legal advice and, in the lower courts only, speaks on behalf of clients. **2** someone who solicits. **3** in N America: someone who canvasses. **4** in N America: someone responsible for legal matters in a town or city.

solicitous *adj* **1** (**solicitous about** *or* **for sb** *or* **sth**) anxious or concerned about them. **2** willing or eager to do something. ▪ **solicitously** *adv*.

solicitude *noun* **1** anxiety or uneasiness of mind. **2** the state of being solicitous.

solid *adj* **1** in a form other than liquid or gas, and resisting changes in shape due to firmly cohering particles. **2** having the same nature or material throughout; uniform or pure: *solid oak.* **3** not hollow; full of material: *a solid chocolate egg.* **4** firmly constructed or attached; not easily breaking or loosening. **5** *geom* having or pertaining to three dimensions. **6** difficult to undermine or destroy; sound: *solid support.* **7** without breaks; continuous: *We waited for four solid hours.* **8** of a character: reliable; sensible. **9** of a character: weighty; worthy of credit: *He has a solid presence.* **10** financially secure. ▸ *noun* **1** a solid substance or body. **2** a state of matter other than **liquid** or **gas**, which keeps a definite shape and in which the constituent molecules or ions are unable to move freely. **3** *geom* a three-dimensional geometric figure. **4** (**solids**) non-liquid food. ▪ **solidity** *noun*. [14c: from Latin *solidus*]

solidarity *noun* (***-ies***) mutual support and unity of interests, aims and actions among members of a group.

solidify *verb* (***-ies, -ied***) *tr & intr* to make or become solid. ▪ **solidification** *noun*.

solid-state *adj, electronics* denoting an electronic device or component, eg a semiconductor or transistor, that functions by the movement of electrons through solids, and contains no heated filaments or vacuums.

solidus *noun* (***solidi*** /ˈsɒlɪdaɪ/) a printed line sloping downwards from right to left, eg separating alternatives, as in *and/or*; a stroke or slash mark. [14c: from Latin *solidus* (*nummus*) a solid (coin)]

solifluxion *or* **solifluction** *noun, geol* the slow movement of soil or scree down a slope resulting from alternate freezing and thawing. [From Latin *solum* soil + *fluxio, fluxonis* flow]

soliloquy *noun* (***-quies***) **1** an act of talking to oneself, esp a speech in a play, etc in which a character reveals thoughts or intentions to the audience by talking aloud. **2** the use of such speeches as a device in drama. ▪ **soliloquize** *or* **-ise** *verb*. [17c: from Latin *solus* alone + *loqui* to speak]

solipsism /ˈsɒlɪpsɪzəm/ *noun, philos* the theory that one's own existence is the only certainty. ▪ **solipsist** *noun, adj*. ▪ **solipsistic** *adj*. [19c: from Latin *solus* alone + *ipse* self]

solitaire *noun* **1** any of several games for one player only, esp one whose object is to eliminate pegs or marbles from a board and leave only one. **2** a single gem in a setting on its own. **3** *N Am, esp US* the card game **patience**. [14c: French]

solitary *adj* **1** single; lone. **2** preferring to be alone; not social. **3** without companions; lonely. **4** remote; secluded. ▸ *noun, informal* solitary confinement. ▪ **solitariness** *noun*. [14c: from Latin *solitarius*]

solitary confinement *noun* imprisonment in a cell by oneself.

solitude *noun* the state of being alone or secluded, esp pleasantly. [14c: from Latin *solitudo*]

solo *noun* (***solos*** *or* ***soli*** /ˈsouliː/) **1** a piece of music, or a passage within it, for a single voice or instrument, with or without accompaniment. **2** any performance in which no other person or instrument participates. **3** (*in full* **solo whist**) a card game based on **whist**, in which various declarations are made and the declarer does not have a partner. ▸ *adj* performed alone, without assistance or accompaniment. ▸ *adv* alone: *fly solo*. ▸ *verb* (***solos, soloed***) *intr* **1** to fly solo. **2** to play a solo. ▪ **soloist** *noun*. [17c: Italian]

so long *or* **so-long** *exclam, informal* goodbye.

solstice *noun* either of the times when the Sun is furthest from the equator: the longest day (**summer solstice**) and the shortest day (**winter solstice**). ▪ **solstitial** *adj*. [13c: from Latin *solstitium* the standing still of the sun]

soluble *adj* **1** denoting a substance that is capable of being dissolved in a liquid. **2** capable of being solved or resolved. [14c: from Latin *solubilis*]

solute *noun, chem* any substance that is dissolved in a **solvent**. [15c: from Latin *solutus*]

solution *noun* **1** the process of finding an answer to a problem or puzzle. **2** the answer sought or found. **3** *chem* a homogeneous mixture consisting of a solid or gas (the **solute**) and the liquid (the **solvent**) in which it is completely dissolved. **4** *maths* in an equation: the value that one or more of the variables must have for that equation to be valid. **5** *geog* the dissolving of rock by chemicals in a sea or river. Also called **corrosion**. [14c: from Latin *solutio*]

solution set *noun, maths* the set of all the values that solve an equation.

solvation *noun, chemistry* the interaction of molecules of a solvent with ions or molecules of a solute. [20c: from **solve**]

solve *verb* **1** to discover the answer to (a puzzle) or a way out of (a problem). **2** to clear up or explain something. ▪ **solvable** *adj*. [15c: from Latin *solvere* to loosen]

solvent *adj* able to pay all one's debts. ▸ *noun, chem* **1** in a solution: the liquid in which a solid or gas is dissolved. **2** a substance which may act in this way, eg for dissolving and removing an unwanted substance such as glue. ▪ **solvency** *noun* the ability to pay one's debts.

Som *abbrev, English county* Somerset.

soma[1] *noun* (***somas*** *or* ***somata***) the body of a plant or animal, excluding the germ cells. [19c: Greek, meaning 'body']

soma[2] *or* **Soma** *noun* **1** an intoxicating plant juice. **2** the plant yielding this juice. [19c: Sanskrit]

Somali *noun* **1** a group of Cushitic-speaking peoples of Somalia and parts of Kenya, Ethiopia and Djibouti. **2** an individual belonging to this group of peoples.

somatic *adj, med, biol* **1** referring or relating to the body, rather than the mind. **2** relating to the body, as opposed to reproduction: *somatic cells*. ▪ **somatically** *adv*. [18c: from Greek *soma*, meaning 'body']

somatotrophin *noun, physiol* a growth hormone. ▪ **somatotrophic** *adj*. [20c]

sombre *adj* **1** sad and serious; grave. **2** dark and gloomy; melancholy. **3** eg of colours: dark; drab. ▪ **sombrely** *adv*. ▪ **sombreness** *noun*. [18c: from French *sombre*]

sombrero *noun* a wide-brimmed straw or felt hat, esp popular in Mexico. [16c: Spanish]

some *adj* **1** signifying an unknown or unspecified amount or number of something: *She owns some shares*. **2** signifying a certain undetermined category: *Some films are better than others*. **3** having an unknown or unspecified nature or identity: *some problem with the engine*. **4** quite a lot of something: *We have been waiting for some time*. **5** at least a little: *Try to feel some enthusiasm*. ▸ *pronoun* **1** certain unspecified things or people: *Some say he should resign*. **2** an unspecified amount or number: *Give him some, too*. ▸ *adv* **1** to an unspecified extent: *play some more*. **2** approximately: *some twenty feet deep*. [Anglo-Saxon *sum*]

-some[1] /-sʌm/ *suffix* **1** *forming adjectives, signifying* **a** inclined to cause or produce: *troublesome*; **b** inviting: *cuddlesome*; **c** tending to do, be or express something: *quarrelsome*. **2** *forming nouns, signifying* a group of the specified number of people or things: *a foursome*. [Anglo-Saxon *-sum*]

-some[2] /-soum/ *suffix, forming nouns, signifying* a body: *chromosome*.

somebody *pron* **1** an unknown or unspecified person; someone. **2** someone of importance: *He always strove to be somebody*.

someday *adv* at an unknown or unspecified time in the future.

somehow *adv* **1** in some way not yet known. **2** for a reason not easy to explain. **3** (*also* **somehow or other**) in any way necessary or possible: *I'll get there somehow or other*.

someone *pron* somebody.

somersault *noun* a leap or roll in which the whole body turns a complete circle forwards or backwards, leading with the head. ▸ *verb, intr* to perform such a leap or roll. [16c: from French *sombre saut*]

something *pron* **1** a thing not known or not stated: *Take something to eat*. **2** an amount or number not known or not stated: *something short of 500 people*. **3** a person or thing of importance: *make something of oneself*. **4** a certain truth or value: *There is something in what you say*. ▸ *adv* to some degree; rather: *The garden looks something like a scrapyard*.

-something *combining form* (combining with *twenty, thirty, forty*, etc) *forming nouns* **a** indicating an unspecified or unknown number greater than or in addition to the combining number, as in *twenty-something*; **b** an individual or a group of people of this age, as in *he's a thirtysomething*, ie between the ages of 30 and 39. [1980s]

sometime *adv* at an unknown or unspecified time in the future or the past: *I'll finish it sometime*. ▸ *adj* former; late: *the sometime king*.

sometimes *adv* occasionally; now and then.

somewhat *adv* rather; a little: *somewhat unsettled*.

somewhere *adv* in or to some place or degree, or at some point, not known or not specified.

somnambulism *noun* sleepwalking. ▪ **somnambulate** *verb*. ▪ **somnambulist** *noun*. [18c: from Latin *somnus* sleep + *ambulare* to walk]

somniferous *or* **somnific** *adj* causing sleep. [17c: from Latin *somnifer*]

somnolent *adj, formal* sleepy or drowsy; causing sleepiness or drowsiness. ▪ **somnolence** *noun*. [15c: from Latin *somnolentia*]

son *noun* **1** a male child or offspring. **2** a male person closely associated with, or seen as developing from, a particular activity or set of circumstances: *a son of the Russian Revolution*. **3** a familiar and sometimes patronizing term of address used to a boy or man. **4** (**the Son**) *Christianity* the second person of the Trinity, Jesus Christ. [Anglo-Saxon *sunu*]

sonar *noun* a system that is used to locate underwater objects by transmitting ultrasound signals and measuring the time taken for their echoes to return from an obstacle. [1940s: from *so*und *n*avigation *a*nd *r*anging]

sonata *noun* a piece of music written in three or more movements for a solo instrument, esp the piano. [17c: Italian, from past participle of *sonare* to sound]

song *noun* **1** a set of words, short poem, etc to be sung, usu with accompanying music. **2** the music to which these words are set. **3** singing: *poetry and song*. **4** the musical call of certain birds. [Anglo-Saxon *sang*]**going for a song** *informal* at a bargain price. **make a song and dance about sth** *informal* to make an unnecessary fuss about it.

songbird *noun* a bird that has a musical call, eg lark, thrush, etc.

songsmith *noun* a composer of songs.

songster *or* **songstress** *noun, old use* a talented singer.

songwriter *noun* someone who composes music and sometimes also the words for songs. ▪ **songwriting** *adj, noun*.

sonic *adj* relating to or using sound or sound waves. [1920s: from Latin *sonus*]

sonic barrier *noun* the technical term for **sound barrier**.

sonic boom *or* **sonic bang** *noun* a loud boom that is heard when an aircraft flying through the Earth's atmosphere reaches supersonic speed, ie when it passes through the sound barrier.

son-in-law *noun* (***sons-in-law***) the husband of one's daughter.

sonnet *noun* a short poem with 14 lines of 10 or 11 syllables each and a regular rhyming pattern. [16c: from Italian *sonetto*]

sonny *noun* a familiar and often condescending term of address used to a boy or man.

sonograph *noun* a device for scanning and recording sound and its component frequencies. [1950s]

sonorous *adj* **1** sounding impressively loud and deep. **2** giving out a deep clear ring or sound when struck: *a sonorous bell*. **3** of language: impressively eloquent. ▪ **sonority** /sə'nɒrɪtɪ/ *noun*. [17c: from Latin *sonare* to sound]

soon *adv* **1** in a short time from now or from a stated time. **2** quickly; with little delay. **3** readily or willingly. [Anglo-Saxon *sona*]

IDIOMS **as soon as ...** at or not before the moment when ...: *will pay you as soon as I receive the goods.*

sooner *adv* **1** earlier than previously thought. **2** preferably: *I'd sooner die than go back there*.

IDIOMS **no sooner said than done** of a request, promise, etc: immediately fulfilled. **no sooner ... than ...** immediately after ... then ...: *No sooner had I mentioned his name than he appeared.* **sooner or later** eventually.

soot *noun* a black powdery substance produced when coal or wood is imperfectly burned; smut. ▪ **sooty** *adj* (***-ier, -iest***). [Anglo-Saxon *sot*]

soothe *verb* **1** to bring relief from (a pain, etc); to allay. **2** to comfort, calm or compose someone. **3** *intr* to have a calming, tranquillizing or relieving effect. ▪ **soothing** *noun, adj*. ▪ **soothingly** *adv*. [Anglo-Saxon *gesothian* to confirm as true]

soother *noun* **1** a person or thing that soothes. **2** a baby's dummy teat.

soothsayer *noun* someone who predicts the future; a seer. [14c: from archaic *sooth* truth + **say**]

sop *noun* **1** (*often* **sops**) a piece of food, esp bread, dipped or soaked in a liquid. **2** something given or done as a bribe or in order to pacify someone. **3** a feeble or spineless person. ▸ *verb* (***sopped, sopping***) *tr & intr* to soak or become soaked. [Anglo-Saxon *sopp*]

sophism *noun* a convincing but false argument or explanation, esp one intended to deceive. ▪ **sophist** *noun*. ▪ **sophistic** *adj*. [14c: from Greek *sophisma* clever device, from *sophia* wisdom]

sophisticate *verb* /sə'fɪstɪkeɪt/ **1** to make sophisticated. **2** to adulterate or falsify an argument; to make sophistic. ▸ *noun* /sə'fɪstɪkət/ a sophisticated person. [14c: from Latin *sophisticare* to adulterate]

sophisticated *adj* **1** having or displaying a broad knowledge and experience of the world and its culture. **2** appealing to or frequented by people with such knowledge and experience. **3** of a person: accustomed to an elegant lifestyle. **4** esp of machines: complex; equipped with the most up-to-date devices: *sophisticated weaponry*. ▪ **sophistication** *noun*.

sophistry *noun* (***-ies***) **1** plausibly deceptive or fallacious reasoning, or an instance of this. **2** the art of reasoning speciously.

sophomore *noun, N Am, esp US* a second-year student at a school or university. [17c: from Greek *sophos* wise + *moros* foolish]

soporific *adj* **1** causing sleep or drowsiness. **2** extremely slow and boring: *a soporific speech*. ▸ *noun* a sleep-inducing drug. [17c: from Latin *sopor* deep sleep + *facere* to make]

sopping *adj, adv* (*also* **sopping wet**) thoroughly wet; soaking.

soppy *adj* (***-ier, -iest***) *informal* weakly sentimental. ▪ **soppily** *adv*. ▪ **soppiness** *noun*. [17c: from **sop**]

soprano *noun* (***sopranos** or **soprani***) **1** a singing voice of the highest pitch for a woman or a boy. **2** a person having this voice pitch. **3** a musical part for such a voice. **4** a musical instrument high or highest in pitch in relation to others in its family. ▸ *adj* referring or relating to a soprano pitch. [18c: Italian]

sorbet /'sɔːbeɪ/ *noun* a water ice. [16c: French]

sorcery *noun* (***-ies***) **1** the art or use of magic, esp black magic that is associated with the power of evil spirits, supernatural forces, etc. **2** an instance of this kind of magic. ▪ **sorcerer** *or* **sorceress** *noun*. [14c: from French *sorcerie* witchcraft]

sordid *adj* **1** repulsively filthy; squalid. **2** morally revolting or degraded; ignoble: *a sordid affair.* ▪ **sordidly** *adv.* ▪ **sordidness** *noun.* [16c: from French *sordide*]

sore *adj* **1** of a wound, injury, part of the body, etc: painful or tender. **2** of a blow, bite, sting, etc: painful or causing physical pain. **3** causing mental anguish, grief or annoyance: *a sore point.* **4** *N Am, esp US* angry or resentful: *got sore at the kids.* **5** severe or urgent: *in sore need of attention.* ▸ *noun* a diseased or injured spot or area, esp an ulcer or boil. ▪ **soreness** *noun.* [Anglo-Saxon *sar*]

sorely *adv* acutely; very much: *I'm sorely tempted.*

sore point *noun* a subject that causes great anger, resentment, etc whenever it is raised.

sorghum *noun* a grass which is related to the sugar cane, grown as a cereal crop and a source of syrup. [16c: from Italian *sorgo*]

sororicide *noun* **1** the act of killing one's own sister. **2** someone who kills their sister. [15c: from Latin *soror* sister + **-cide**]

sorority *noun* (**-ies**) a women's club or society, esp one affiliated to a US university, college or church. Compare **fraternity**. [16c: from Latin *soror* sister]

sorrel *noun* **1** a plant with spear-shaped leaves which give an acid taste. **2** the leaves of this plant, which are used in medicine and in cookery. [15c: from French *sorele*]

sorrow *noun* **1** a feeling of grief or deep sadness, esp one that arises from loss or disappointment. **2** someone or something that is the cause of this. ▸ *verb, intr* to have or express such feeling. ▪ **sorrowful** *adj.* ▪ **sorrowfully** *adv.* [Anglo-Saxon *sorg*]

sorry *adj* (**-ier, -iest**) **1** distressed or full of regret or shame, esp over something that one has done or said, something one feels responsible for, something that has happened, etc: *I'm sorry if I hurt you.* **2** (*usu* **sorry for sb**) full of pity or sympathy. **3** pitifully bad: *in a sorry state.* ▸ *exclam* **1** given as an apology. **2** used when asking for something that has just been said to be repeated. [Anglo-Saxon *sarig* wounded]

sort *noun* **1** a kind, type or class. **2** *informal* a person: *not a bad sort.* ▸ *verb* **1** to arrange into different groups according to some specified criterion. **2** *informal* to fix something or put it back into working order: *tried to sort the car himself.* **3** (*also* **sort out**) *informal* to resolve (a problem, etc): *You caused the problem, so you'd better sort it.* [13c: French]

IDIOMS **a sort of ...** a thing like a ...: *A cafetière is a sort of pot for making coffee.* **nothing of the sort** no such thing: *I did nothing of the sort.* **of a sort** *or* **of sorts** of an inferior or untypical kind: *an author of a sort.* **out of sorts** *informal* **1** slightly unwell. **2** peevish; bad-tempered. **sort of** *informal* rather; in a way; to a certain extent: *feeling sort of embarrassed.*

PHRASAL VERBS **sort sb out 1** *informal* to deal with them firmly and decisively and sometimes violently. **2** to put them right: *A good night's sleep will soon sort you out.* **sort sth out 1** to separate things out from a mixed collection into a group or groups according to their kind. **2** to put things into order; to arrange them systematically or methodically: *sort out your priorities.*

sortie /ˈsɔːtɪ/ *noun* **1** a sudden attack by besieged troops. **2** *informal* a short return trip: *just going on a quick sortie to the shops.* ▸ *verb* (**sortied, sortieing**) *intr* to make a sortie. [17c: French]

SOS *noun* **1** an internationally recognized distress call that consists of these three letters repeatedly transmitted in Morse code. **2** *informal* any call for help. [Early 20c: the three letters were chosen because, in Morse code, they are the easiest to transmit and recognize]

so-so *adj, informal* neither very good nor very bad; passable; middling. ▸ *adv* in an indifferent or unremarkable way. [16c]

sot *noun, old use* someone who is drunk or who habitually drinks a lot of alcohol. ▪ **sottish** *adj.* [16c]

sotto voce /ˈsɒtoʊ ˈvoʊtʃɪ, ˈvoʊtʃeɪ/ *adv* **1** in a quiet voice, so as not to be overheard. **2** *music* very softly. [18c: Italian, meaning 'below the voice']

soubriquet see **sobriquet**

soufflé /ˈsuːfleɪ/ *noun* a light fluffy sweet or savoury dish that is made by gently combining egg yolks and other ingredients with stiffly beaten egg-whites. [19c: French]

sough[1] /sɑʊ, sʌf; *Scot* suːx/ *noun* a sighing, rustling or murmuring sound that is made by the wind blowing through trees, etc. ▸ *verb, intr* usu of the wind: to make this sound: *The wind soughed through the trees.* [Anglo-Saxon *swogan* to move with a rushing sound]

sough[2] /sʌf/ *noun* a small gutter or drain that allows water, sewage, etc to run off. [14c]

sought *past tense, past participle of* **seek**

sought-after *adj* desired; in demand.

souk /suːk/ *noun* an open-air market or marketplace in Muslim countries, esp in N Africa and the Middle East. [19c: from Arabic *suq* marketplace]

soul *noun* **1 a** the spiritual, non-physical part of someone or something which is often regarded as the source of individuality, personality, morality, will, emotions and intellect, and which is widely believed to survive in some form after the death of the body; **b** this entity when thought of as having separated from the body after death, but which still retains its essence of individuality, etc. **2** emotional sensitivity; morality: *a singer with no soul.* **3** the essential nature or an energizing or motivating force (of or behind something): *Brevity is the soul of wit.* **4** *informal* a person or individual: *a kind soul.* **5** (*also* **soul music**) a type of music that has its roots in African American urban rhythm and blues, and which has elements of jazz, gospel, pop, etc. [Anglo-Saxon *sawol*]

soul-destroying *adj* **1** of a job, task, etc: extremely dull, boring or repetitive. **2** of an on-going situation: difficult to tolerate or accept emotionally: *found being unemployed completely soul-destroying.*

soulful *adj* having, expressing, etc deep feelings, esp of sadness. ▪ **soulfully** *adv.* ▪ **soulfulness** *noun.*

soulless *adj* **1** having, showing, etc no emotional sensitivity, morality, etc. **2** of a place: bleak; lifeless. ▪ **soullessly** *adv.* ▪ **soullessness** *noun.*

soul mate *noun* someone who shares the same feelings, ideas, outlook, tastes, etc as someone else.

soul music *noun* see **soul** (sense 5)

soul-searching *noun* the process of critically examining one's own conscience, motives, actions, etc.

sound[1] *noun* **1** *physics* periodic vibrations that are propagated through a medium, eg air, as pressure waves, so that the medium is displaced from its equilibrium state. **2** the noise that is heard as a result of such periodic vibrations. **3** audible quality: *The guitar has a nice sound.* **4** the mental impression created by something heard: *don't like the sound of that.* **5** (*also* **sounds**) *informal* music, esp pop music: *the sounds of the 60s.* ▸ *verb* **1** *tr & intr* to produce or cause to produce a sound: *The bugle sounded as the emperor approached.* **2** *intr* to create an impression in the mind: *sounds like fun.* **3** to pronounce: *doesn't sound his h's.* **4** to announce or signal with a sound: *sound the alarm.* **5** *med* to examine by tapping or listening. See also **sound**[3] (*verb* sense 2). [13c: from French *soner*]

PHRASAL VERBS **sound off** *informal* to state one's opinions, complaints, etc forcefully or angrily.

sound[2] *adj* **1** not damaged or injured; in good condition; healthy: *The kitten was found safe and sound.* **2** **a** sensible; well-founded; reliable: *a sound investment*; **b** of an argument, opinion, etc: well researched or thought through; logical and convincing. **3** acceptable or approved of. **4** severe, hard or thorough: *a sound telling-off.* **5** of sleep: deep and undisturbed. ▸ *adv* deeply: *sound asleep.* ▪ **soundly** *adv.* ▪ **soundness** *noun.* [Anglo-Saxon *gesund*]

sound[3] *verb, tr & intr* **1** to measure the depth of (esp the sea). **2** *med* to examine (a hollow organ, etc) with a probe. See also **sound**[1] (*verb* sense 5). ▸ *noun* a probe for examining hollow organs. [14c: from French *sonder*]

PHRASAL VERBS **sound sb** *or* **sth out** to try to discover or to make a preliminary assessment of (opinions, intentions, etc).

sound[4] *noun* a narrow passage of water that connects two large bodies of water or that separates an island and the mainland; a strait. [Anglo-Saxon *sund*]

sound barrier *noun, non-technical* the increase in drag that an aircraft experiences when it travels close to the speed of sound. Also called **sonic barrier**.

soundbite *noun* a short and succinct statement extracted from a longer speech and quoted on TV or radio or in the press.

soundbox *noun* the hollow body of a violin, guitar, etc.

soundcard *noun, comput* a printed circuit board added to a computer to provide sound.

sound effects *plural noun* artificially produced sounds used in film, broadcasting, theatre, etc.

sounding *noun* **1** **a** the act or process of measuring depth, esp of the sea, eg by using echo; **b** an instance of doing this; **c** (**soundings**) measurements that are taken or recorded when doing this. **2** (*usu* **soundings**) a sampling of opinions or (eg voting) intentions.

sounding board *noun* **a** a means of testing the acceptability or popularity of ideas or opinions; **b** someone or a group that is used for this purpose.

soundtrack *noun* **1** the recorded sound that accompanies a motion picture. **2** a recording of the music from a film, broadcast, etc.

soup *noun* a liquid food that is made by boiling meat, vegetables, grains, etc together in a stock or in water. ▸ *verb* (*usu* **soup up**) *informal* to make changes to a vehicle or its engine in order to increase its speed or power. [16c: from French *soupe* broth]

IDIOMS **in the soup** *slang* in trouble or difficulty.

soupçon /ˈsuːpsɒn/ *noun, often humorous* the slightest amount; a dash. [18c: French, meaning 'suspicion']

soup kitchen *noun* a place where volunteer workers supply free or very cheap food to people in need.

sour *adj* **1** having an acid taste or smell, similar to that of lemon juice or vinegar. **2** rancid or stale because of fermentation: *sour milk.* **3** sullen; miserable; embittered: *a sour expression.* **4** unpleasant, unsuccessful or inharmonious: *The marriage turned sour.* ▸ *verb, tr & intr* to make or become sour. ▪ **soured** *adj*: *soured cream.* ▪ **sourly** *adv.* ▪ **sourness** *noun.* [Anglo-Saxon *sur*]

source *noun* **1** the place, thing, person, circumstance, etc that something begins or develops from; the origin. **2** a spring or place where a river or stream begins. **3** **a** a person, a book or other document that can be used to provide information, evidence, etc; **b** someone or something that acts as an inspiration, model, standard, etc, esp in the realms of creativity. ▸ *verb* to originate in someone or something. [14c: from French *sors*]

IDIOMS **at source** at the point of origin.

source code *noun, comput* a code written by a programmer that usually has to be translated by a compiler before it can be run.

sour cream *noun* cream that has been deliberately made sour by the addition of lactic acid bacteria.

sour grapes *plural noun* a hostile or indifferent attitude towards something or someone, esp when motivated by envy, bitterness, resentment, etc: *He says he wouldn't have taken the job anyway, but that's just sour grapes.*

sourpuss *noun, informal* a habitually sullen or miserable person. [1940s]

souse *verb* **1** to steep or cook something in vinegar or white wine. **2** to pickle. **3** to plunge in a liquid. **4** to make thoroughly wet; to drench. ▸ *noun* **1** an act of sousing. **2** the liquid in which food is soused. **3** *N Am, esp US* any pickled food. ▪ **soused** *adj, slang* drunk. ▪ **sousing** *adj, noun.* [14c: from French *sous*]

soutane /suːˈtɑːn/ *noun, RC Church* a long plain robe or cassock that a priest wears. [19c: French]

south *noun* (*also* **South** *or* **the South**) **1** one of the four main points of the compass which, if a person is facing the rising sun in the N hemisphere, is the direction that lies to their right. **2** the direction that is directly opposite north, ie 180° from the north and 90° from both east and west. **3** (*usu* **the South**) any part of the earth, a country, a town, etc that lies in this direction. ▸ *adj* **1** belonging, referring or relating to, facing or lying in the south. **2** in place names: denoting the southerly part: *South America* • *South Kensington.* **3** esp of wind: coming from the south. ▸ *adv* in, to or towards the south. [Anglo-Saxon *suth*]

southbound *adj* going or leading towards the south.

south-east *noun* (*sometimes* **South-East**) **1** the compass point or direction that is midway between south and east. **2** an area lying in this direction. ▸ *adj* **1** in the south-east. **2** from the direction of the south-east: *a south-east wind.* ▸ *adv* in, to or towards the south-east.

southeaster *noun* a wind, usu a fairly strong one, that blows from the direction of the south-east.

south-easterly *adj, adv* **1** from the south-east. **2** (*also* **south-eastward**) towards the south-east. ▸ *noun* a wind blowing from the south-east.

south-eastern *adj* **1** belonging to the south-east. **2** in, toward or facing the south-east or that direction.

southerly *adj* **1** of a wind, etc: coming from the south. **2** looking or lying, etc towards the south; situated in the south. ▸ *adv* **1** to or towards the south. **2** from the south. ▸ *noun* (**-*ies***) a southerly wind.

southern *or* **Southern** *adj* **1** belonging or relating to the **south**. **2** in the south or in the direction toward it. **3** (**Southern**) belonging, relating or referring to, or in, the southern states of the US: *that epitome of the Southern belle, Scarlett O'Hara.* **4** of winds, etc: proceeding from the south. ▪ **southerner** *noun* (*sometimes* **Southerner**) someone who lives in or comes from the south, esp the southern part of England or of the USA. ▪ **southernmost** *adj* situated farthest south.

southern hemisphere *noun* the half of the earth that lies to the south of the equator.

the southern lights *plural noun* the **aurora australis**.

southpaw *noun, informal* someone whose left hand is more dominant than their right, esp a boxer.

South Pole *or* **south pole** *noun* **1** (*usu* **the South Pole**) the southernmost point of the Earth's axis of rotation, which is in central Antarctica at latitude 90°S and longitude 0°. **2** (**south pole**) the south-seeking pole of a magnet.

southward *adj* towards the south. ▸ *adv* (*also* **southwards**) towards the south. ▸ *noun* the southward direction, sector, etc. ▪ **southwardly** *adj, adv.*

south-west *noun* (*sometimes* **South-West**) **1** the compass point or direction that is midway between south and west. **2** (**the south-west** *or* **the South-West**) an area lying in this direction. ▸ *adj* **1** in the south-west. **2** from the direction of the south-west: *a south-west wind.* ▸ *adv* in, to or towards the south-west.

southwester *noun* **1** a wind that blows from the south-west. **2** a **sou'wester** (sense 1).

south-westerly *adj, adv* **1** from the south-west. **2** (*also* **south-westward**) towards the south-west. ▸ *noun* a wind blowing from the south-west.

south-western *adj* **1** belonging to the **south-west**. **2** in, towards or facing the south-west or that direction.

souvenir *noun* something that is bought, kept or given as a reminder of a place, person, occasion, etc; a memento. [18c: French, meaning 'a memory']

sou'wester *noun* **1** a type of oilskin or waterproof hat that has a large flap at the back and which is usu worn by seamen. **2** a **southwester** (sense 1). [Early 19c: a shortened form of **southwester**]

sovereign *noun* **1** a supreme ruler or head, esp a monarch. **2** a former British gold coin worth £1. ▸ *adj* **1** having supreme power or authority: *a sovereign ruler.* **2** politically independent: *a sovereign state.* **3** outstanding; unrivalled; utmost: *sovereign intelligence.* **4** effective: *a sovereign remedy.* ▪ **sovereignly** *adv.* [13c: from French *soverain*]

sovereign state *noun* an independent state.

sovereignty *noun* (**-*ies***) **1** supreme and independent political power or authority. **2** a politically independent state. **3** self-government.

soviet *noun* **1** any of the councils that made up the local and national governments of the former Soviet Union. **2** (**Soviet**) a citizen or inhabitant of the former Soviet Union. ▸ *adj* (**Soviet**) belonging, relating or referring to the former Soviet Union. [Early 20c: from Russian *sovet* council]

sow[1] /soʊ/ *verb* (***sown*** *or* ***sowed***) *tr & intr* **1** to scatter or place (plant seeds, a crop, etc) on or in the earth, in a plant pot, etc. **2** to plant (a piece of land) with seeds, a crop, etc: *sowed the upper field with barley.* **3** to introduce or arouse: *sowed the seeds of doubt in his mind.* ▪ **sower** *noun.* [Anglo-Saxon *sawan*]

sow[2] /sɑʊ/ *noun* an adult female pig, esp one that has had a litter of piglets. [Anglo-Saxon *sugu*]

soy *noun* **1** (*also* **soy sauce**) a salty dark brown sauce that is made from soya beans which ferment for around six months. **2** **soya**. [17c: from Japanese *sho-yu*]

soya *or* **soy** *noun* **1** a plant of the pulse family, widely cultivated for their edible seeds. **2** (also called **soya bean**) the edible protein-rich seed of this plant, which is used in making soya flour, soya milk, bean curd, etc, and which yields an oil that is used as a cooking oil and in the manufacture of margarine, soap, enamels, paints, varnishes, etc. [17c: Dutch]

sozzled *adj, informal* drunk. [19c: from the obsolete verb *sozzle* to mix or mingle in a sloppy way]

spa *noun* **1** a mineral water spring. **2** a town where such a spring is or was once located. [16c: named after Spa, a town in Belguim]

space *noun* **1** the limitless three-dimensional expanse where all matter exists. **2** a restricted portion of this; room: *no space in the garden for a pool.* **3** an interval of distance; a gap: *sign in the space below.* **4** any of a restricted number of seats, places, etc. **5** a period of time: *within the space of ten minutes.* **6** (*also* **outer space**) all the regions of the Universe that lie beyond the Earth's atmosphere. ▸ *verb* **1** to set or place at intervals: *spaced the interviews over three days.* **2** to separate or divide with a space or spaces, eg in printing, etc. ▪ **spacing** *noun.* [14c: from French *espace*]

space age *noun* (*usu* **the space age**) the present era thought of in terms of being the time when space travel became possible. ▸ *adj* (**space-age**) **1** technologically very advanced. **2** having a futuristic appearance.

space bar *noun* the long key that is usu situated below the character keys on a keyboard, which inserts a space in the text when it is pressed.

space capsule *noun* a small manned or unmanned vehicle that is designed for travelling through space.

spacecraft *noun* a manned or unmanned vehicle that is designed to travel in space.

spaced *adj* **1** (*also* **spaced out**) *informal* being, acting, appearing to be, etc in a dazed, euphoric, stupefied or dreamlike state, esp one that is or seems to be induced by drugs. **2** set, placed, arranged, occurring, etc at intervals.

spaceman *or* **spacewoman** *noun* someone who travels in space. See also **astronaut**.

spaceship *noun* a spacecraft.

space shuttle *noun* a reusable manned spacecraft that takes off like a rocket but lands on a runway like an aircraft.

space station *noun* a large orbiting artificial satellite, where crews of astronauts can live and carry out scientific and technological research in space over periods of weeks or months.

space suit *noun* a sealed and pressurized suit of clothing that is specially designed for space travel.

space-time *or* **space-time continuum** *noun* the three spatial dimensions of length, breadth and height, plus the dimension of time, thought of collectively, which allow an event, particle, etc to be specifically located.

space walk *noun* an instance of manoeuvring or other physical activity by an astronaut outside his spacecraft while in space.

spacial see **spatial**

spacious *adj* having ample room or space; extending over a large area. ▪ **spaciously** *adv.* ▪ **spaciousness** *noun.* [14c: from Latin *spatiosus*]

spade[1] *noun* a long-handled digging tool with a broad metal blade which is designed to be pushed into the ground with the foot. ▸ *verb* to dig or turn over (ground) with a spade. [Anglo-Saxon *spadu*]
IDIOMS **call a spade a spade** to speak frankly.

spade[2] *noun, cards* **a** one of the four suits of playing-card with a black spade-shaped symbol (♠), the others being the **diamond**, **heart** and **club**; **b** a card of this suit: *laid a spade and won the hand*; **c** (**spades**) one of the playing-cards of this suit. [16c: from Italian *spada* a sword]

spadework *noun* hard or boring preparatory work.

spadix /ˈspeɪdɪks/ *noun* (***spadices*** /ˈspeɪdɪsiːz/) *botany* a spike-shaped structure that consists of numerous tiny flowers on a fleshy axis and which is usu enclosed by a **spathe**. [18c: Latin]

spaghetti *noun* **1** a type of pasta that is in the form of long thin solid string-like strands. **2** a dish made from this kind of pasta. [19c: Italian]

spaghetti western *noun* a film set in the American wild west, with an Italian director.

Spam *noun, trademark* a type of tinned processed cold meat, mainly pork, with added spices. [1930s: prob from *spiced ham*]

spam *noun, comput* electronic junk mail. ▸ *verb* (***spammed, spamming***) *tr & intr* to send out electronic junk mail to people. [1990s: from **spam**]

span *noun* **1** the distance, interval, length, etc between two points in space or time. **2** the length between the supports of a bridge, arch, pier, ceiling, etc. **3** the extent to which, or the duration of time for which, someone can concentrate, process information, listen attentively, etc. **4** the maximum distance between the tip of one wing and the tip of the other, eg in birds and planes. **5** a measure of length equal to the distance between the tips of thumb and little finger on an extended hand, which is conventionally taken as 9in (23cm). ▸ *verb* (***spanned, spanning***) **1 a** of a bridge, pier, ceiling, rainbow, etc: to extend across or over, esp in an arched shape: *A rainbow spanned the sky*; **b** to bridge (a river, etc): *spanned the river using logs.* **2** to last: *The feud spanned more than 30 years.* **3** to measure or cover, eg by using an extended hand. [Anglo-Saxon *spann*]

spangle *noun* a small piece of glittering material, esp a sequin. ▸ *verb* **1** to decorate (eg a piece of clothing) with spangles. **2** *intr* to glitter. ▪ **spangled** *adj.* ▪ **spangly** *adj.* [Anglo-Saxon *spang* a clasp]

spaniel *noun* a dog with a wavy coat and long silky ears. [14c: from French *espaigneul* Spanish dog]

Spanish *adj* **1** belonging or relating to Spain or its inhabitants. **2** relating to the Spanish language. ▸ *noun* the official language of Spain and various other countries. [13c]

Spanish fly *noun* a bright-green beetle, whose dried body is used medicinally. [15c: so called because they are particularly abundant in Spain]

Spanish Inquisition see **the Inquisition** under **inquisition**

spank *verb* to smack, usu on the buttocks with the flat of the hand, a slipper, belt, etc. ▸ *noun* such a smack. ▪ **spanked** *adj.* [18c]

spanking[1] *noun* an act or the process of delivering a series of smacks, eg as a punishment to a child.

spanking[2] *informal, adv* absolutely; strikingly: *a spanking new watch.* ▸ *adj* **1** brisk: *a spanking pace.* **2** impressively fine; striking: *a spanking new car.*

spanner *noun* a metal hand tool that has an opening (sometimes an adjustable one) or various sizes of openings at one or both ends and which is used for gripping, tightening or loosening nuts, bolts, etc. *US equivalent* **wrench**. [18c: German]
IDIOMS **throw, put, chuck,** *etc* **a spanner in the works** to frustrate, annoy, irritate, etc, esp by causing a plan, system, etc that is already in place to change.

spar[1] *noun* a strong thick pole of wood or metal, esp one used as a mast or beam on a ship. [14c]

spar[2] *verb* (***sparred, sparring***) *intr* (*often* **spar with sb** *or* **sth**) **1 a** to box, esp in a way that deliberately avoids the exchange of heavy blows, eg for practice; **b** to box against an imaginary opponent, for practice. **2** to engage in light-hearted argument, banter, etc. ▸ *noun* **1** an act or instance of sparring. **2** a light-hearted argument, banter, etc. [15c]

spar[3] *noun* any of various translucent non-metallic minerals that split easily into layers. [16c: German]

spare *adj* **1** kept for occasional use: *the spare room.* **2** kept for use as a replacement: *a spare wheel.* **3** available for use; additional; extra: *a spare seat • spare time.* **4** lean; thin. **5** frugal; scanty. **6** furious or distraught to the point of distraction: *He went spare when he found out I'd borrowed his car.* ▸ *verb* **1** to afford to give, give away or do without: *I can't spare the time.* **2 a** to refrain from harming, punishing, killing or destroying: *spare their feelings*; **b** to avoid causing or bringing on something: *will spare your embarrassment.* **3** to avoid incurring something: *no expense spared.* ▸ *noun* a duplicate kept in reserve for use as a replacement. [Anglo-Saxon *sparian*]
IDIOMS **to spare** left over; surplus to what is required: *I have one cake to spare.*

spare part *noun* a component for a car, machine, etc that is designed to replace an existing identical part that is lost or that has become worn or faulty.

spare rib *noun* a cut of meat, esp pork, that consists of ribs with very little meat on them. [16c: from German *Ribbesper*]

spare tyre *noun* **1** an extra tyre for a motor vehicle, bicycle, etc that can be used to replace a punctured tyre. **2** *informal* a roll of fat just above someone's waist.

sparing *adj* **1** inclined to be economical or frugal, often to the point of inadequacy or meanness: *He was sparing with the chocolate sauce.* **2** restrained, reserved or uncommunicative: *sparing with the truth.* ▪ **sparingly** *adv.*

spark[1] *noun* **1** a tiny red-hot glowing fiery particle that jumps out from some burning material. **2** **a** a flash of light that is produced by a discontinuous electrical discharge flashing across a short gap between two conductors; **b** this kind of electrical discharge, eg in the engine of a motor vehicle, etc where its function is to ignite the explosive mixture. **3** a trace, hint or glimmer: *a spark of recognition.* ▸ *verb* **1** *intr* to emit sparks of fire or electricity. **2** (*usu* **spark sth off**) to stimulate, provoke or start: *The film sparked off great controversy.* [Anglo-Saxon *spærca*]

spark[2] *noun, often ironic* (*usu* **bright spark**) someone who is lively, witty, intelligent, etc: *What bright spark left the oven on?* [16c: orig in the sense of 'a beautiful witty woman']

sparkle *verb, intr* **1** to give off sparks. **2** to shine with tiny points of bright light: *Her eyes sparkled in the moonlight.* **3** of wine, mineral water, etc: to give off bubbles of carbon dioxide; to effervesce. **4** to be impressively lively or witty. ▸ *noun* **1** a point of bright shiny light; an act of sparkling; sparkling appearance. **2** liveliness; vivacity; wit. ▪ **sparkly** *adj.* [12c: from **spark**[1]]

sparkler *noun* **1** a type of small hand-held firework that produces gentle showers of silvery sparks. **2** *informal* a diamond or other impressive jewel.

sparkling *adj* **1** of wine, mineral water, etc: having a fizz that is produced by escaping carbon dioxide. **2** of eyes, gems, etc: having or giving off a sparkle. **3** of a person, their conversation, etc: impressively lively or witty.

spark plug *or* **sparking plug** *noun* a device that discharges a spark between the two electrodes at its end which ignites the mixture of fuel and air in the cylinder.

sparring partner *noun* **1** someone that a boxer practises with. **2** someone whom one can enjoy a lively argument with.

sparrow *noun* a small grey or brown perching bird with a short conical beak. [Anglo-Saxon *spearwa*]

sparse *adj* thinly scattered or dotted about; scanty. ▪ **sparsely** *adv.* ▪ **sparseness** *noun.* [18c: from Latin *sparsus*]

Spartacist *noun, hist* **1** a follower of Spartacus, leader of the slaves that revolted against Rome 73–71 BC. **2** a member of an extreme German communist group that staged an uprising in 1918.

spartan *adj* **1** of living conditions, upbringing, diet, a regime, etc: austere; frugal; harsh and basic. **2** (**Spartan**) relating to or characteristic of ancient Sparta, a city in ancient Greece, its inhabitants, customs, etc. ▸ *noun* **1** someone who shows discipline, courage, endurance, etc. **2** (**Spartan**) a citizen or inhabitant of ancient Sparta. [15c: from Latin *Spartanus*, from Sparta, because the city was noted for its austerity]

spasm *noun* **1** a sudden uncontrollable contraction of a muscle or muscles. **2** a short period of activity; a spell. **3** a sudden burst (of emotion, etc): *spasm of anger.* ▸ *verb* to twitch or go into a spasm. [15c: from Greek *spasmos* contraction]

spasmodic *or* **spasmodical** *adj* **1** being or occurring in, or consisting of, short periods; not constant or regular; intermittent: *spasmodic gunfire.* **2** relating to or consisting of a spasm or spasms. ▪ **spasmodically** *adv.* [17c: from Latin *spasmodicus*]

spastic *noun* someone who suffers from **cerebral palsy**. ▸ *adj* **a** affected by or suffering from cerebral palsy; **b** relating to, affected by, etc a spasm or spasms. [18c: from Latin *spasticus*]

spat[1] *past tense, past participle of* **spit**[1]

spat[2] *informal noun* a trivial or petty fight or quarrel. ▸ *verb* (***spatted, spatting***) *intr* to engage in a trivial or petty fight or quarrel. [Early 19c]

spate *noun* a sudden rush or increased quantity; a burst: *a spate of complaints.* [15c]

IDIOMS **in spate** of a river: in a fast-flowing state that is brought on by flooding or melting snow.

spathe *noun, botany* a large bract that surrounds and protects the inflorescence or **spadix**. [18c: from Latin *spatha*]

spatial *or* **spacial** *adj* belonging, referring or relating to space. ▪ **spatially** *adv.* [19c: from Latin *spatium* space]

spats *plural noun, hist* cloth coverings that go around the ankles and over the tops of shoes, orig to protect against splashes of mud. [Early 19c: an abbreviation of the obsolete *spatterdash* a type of long gaiter for protecting the trousers from mud splashes]

spatter *verb, tr & intr* **1** of mud, etc: to spray, cover, shower or splash in scattered drops or patches: *The muddy water spattered the car.* **2** to cause (mud, etc) to fly in scattered drops or patches: *the wheels of the bike spattered mud everywhere.* ▸ *noun* **1** a quantity spattered; a sprinkling. **2** the act or process of spattering. [16c]

spatula *noun* **1** *cookery* an implement that has a broad, blunt and often flexible blade and which can be used for a variety of purposes. **2** *med* a flat, usu wooden, implement that is used for holding down the tongue during a throat examination, when a throat swab is being taken, etc. [16c: Latin, meaning 'broad blade']

spawn *noun* **1** the jelly-like mass or stream of eggs that amphibians, fish, molluscs, crustaceans, etc lay in water. **2** *derisive* something that is the product of or that is derived from something else and which, because it is not original, is regarded with a degree of contempt: *the spawn of the devil.* ▸ *verb* **1** *intr* of amphibians, fish, etc: to lay eggs. **2** to give rise to something; to lead to something: *The film's success spawned several sequels.* **3** to give birth to someone or something: *They'd spawned three equally useless sons.* [14c: from French *espandre* to shed]

spay *verb* to remove the ovaries from (esp a domestic animal) in order to prevent it from breeding. ▪ **spayed** *adj.* [15c: from French *espeier* to cut with a sword]

speak *verb* (*past tense* ***spoke,*** *past participle* ***spoken***) **1** *tr & intr* **a** to utter words in an ordinary voice, as opposed to shouting, singing, screaming, etc; **b** to talk: *speaks a load of rubbish.* **2** *intr* to have a conversation: *We spoke on the phone.* **3** *intr* to deliver a speech: *spoke about rising urban crime.* **4** to communicate, or be able to communicate, in (a particular language): *He speaks French.* **5** *intr* to convey meaning: *Actions speak louder than words.* [Anglo-Saxon *specan*]

IDIOMS **so to speak** in a way; as it were: *had a bit of a tiff, so to speak.* **speak for itself** to have an obvious meaning; to need no further explanation or comment. **speak one's mind** to say what one thinks boldly, defiantly, without restraint, etc. **speak volumes** to be or act as a significant factor: *His aggressive response to the question spoke volumes.*

PHRASAL VERBS **speak for 1** to give an opinion on behalf of (another or others). **2** to articulate in either spoken or written words the commonly held feelings, beliefs, views, opinions, etc of (others). **speak out 1** to speak openly; to state one's views forcefully. **2** to speak more loudly. **speak up** *intr* **1** to speak more loudly. **2** to make something known: *If you've any objections, speak up now.* **speak up for sb** *or* **sth 1** to vouch for or defend them or it. **2** to represent them or it.

speakeasy *noun* (**-*ies***) *informal* a bar or other place where alcohol was sold illicitly, esp one that operated when the US prohibition laws were in force.

speaker *noun* **1** someone who speaks, esp someone who gives a formal speech. **2** a shortened form of **loudspeaker**. **3** (*usu* **the Speaker**) the person who presides over debate in a law-making assembly such as the House of Commons.

speaking *noun* an act, instance or the process of saying something. ▸ *adj* **1** able to produce speech: *speaking clock.* **2** from or with regard to a specified point of view: *Roughly speaking, the total cost will be about £100.*

IDIOMS **be on speaking terms** to be sufficiently friendly or familiar to hold a conversation.

spear¹ *noun* a weapon that consists of a long pole with a hard sharp point, usu a metal one, and which is thrown from the shoulder (eg at prey, fish or an enemy). ▸ *verb* to pierce with a spear or something similar to a spear. [Anglo-Saxon *spere*]

spear² *noun* a spiky plant shoot, such as a blade of grass, an asparagus or broccoli shoot, etc. [Early 19c: from **spire**]

spearfish see **marlin**

spearhead *noun* **1** the leading part or member of an attacking force. **2** the tip of a spear. ▸ *verb* to lead (a movement, campaign, attack, etc). [15c]

spearmint *noun* **1** a plant of the mint family with lance-shaped aromatic leaves and spikes of purple flowers. **2** the aromatic oil obtained from its leaves used as a flavouring in confectionery, toothpaste, etc. [16c: so named because of the shape of its leaves]

spec *noun, informal* a commercial venture. [18c: a shortened form of **speculation**]

IDIOMS **on spec** as a speculation or gamble, in the hope of success: *wrote on spec, asking for a job.*

special *adj* **1** distinct from, and usu better than, others of the same or a similar kind; exceptional: *a special occasion.* **2** designed for a particular purpose: *You can get a special program to do that.* **3** not ordinary or common: *special circumstances.* **4** particular; great: *make a special effort.* ▸ *noun* **1** something that is special, eg an extra edition of a newspaper, etc, an extra train that is put on over and above the timetabled ones, an item offered at a low price, a dish on a menu, etc. **2** a special person, such as a member of the special police constabulary: *The specials were drafted in to control the fans.* ▪ **specially** *adv.* ▪ **specialness** *noun.* [13c: from Latin *specialis* individual or particular]

specially, especially

Be careful not to use the word **specially** when you mean **especially**.

Especially means 'above all':

I like making cakes, especially for birthdays.

Specially means 'for a special purpose':

I made this cake specially for your birthday.

special constable *noun* a member of a reserve police force who can be drafted in when necessary, eg in times of national emergency, etc.

special delivery *noun* a delivery of post, etc outside normal delivery times.

special effects *plural noun, cinematog* **1** techniques, such as those that involve computer-generated imagery, lighting, manipulation of film or sound, etc used to contribute to the illusion in films, TV programmes, etc. **2** the resulting impact or illusion that these techniques produce.

specialist *noun* **1** someone whose work, interest or expertise is concentrated on a particular subject. **2** a doctor who is trained in specific diseases, diseases and conditions of particular parts of the body, etc: *a heart specialist.*

speciality *or* (*chiefly US*) **specialty** *noun* (**-*ies***) **1** something such as a particular area of interest, a distinctive quality, a specified product, etc that a company, individual, etc has special knowledge of or that they excel in studying, teaching, writing about, producing, etc *The restaurant's speciality is seafood.* **2** a special feature, skill, characteristic, service, etc.

specialize *or* **-ise** *verb* **1** (*also* **specialize in sth**) to be or become an expert in a particular activity, field of study, etc. **2** of an organism, body part, etc: to adapt or become adapted for a specified purpose or to particular surroundings. ▪ **specialization** *noun.*

special licence *noun* a licence that allows a marriage to take place outwith the normal hours or at short notice and usu without the normal legal formalities.

specialty *noun* (**-*ies***) *chiefly US* a **speciality**. [15c: from French *especialte*]

speciation *noun, biol* the formation of new species.

specie /ˈspiːʃiː/ *noun* money in the form of coins as opposed to notes. [16c: Latin, meaning 'in kind']

IDIOMS **in specie 1** in kind. **2** in coin.

species *noun* (*pl* ***species***) **1 a** *biol* any of the groups into which a **genus** (sense 1) is divided, the main criterion for grouping being that all the members should be capable of interbreeding and producing fertile offspring; **b** *biol* the members of one of these units of classification thought of collectively. **2** (*usu* **species of**) a kind or type. [16c: Latin, meaning 'kind, appearance']

specific *adj* **1** particular; exact; precisely identified. **2** precise in meaning; not vague. ▸ *noun* **1** (*usu* **specifics**) a specific detail, factor or feature, eg of a plan, scheme, etc. **2** a drug that is used to treat one particular disease, condition, etc. ▪ **specifically** *adv.* ▪ **specificity** /spɛsɪˈfɪsɪtɪ/ *noun.* [17c: from Latin *species* kind + *-ficus*]

specification *noun* **1 a** (*often* **specifications**) a detailed description of the methods, materials, dimensions, quantities, etc that are used in the construction, manufacture, building, planning, etc of something; **b** the standard, quality, etc of the construction, manufacture, etc of something: *Volvos are built to high safety specifications.* **2** an act or instance or the process of specifying. [17c: from **specify**]

specify *verb* (**-ies, -ied**) **1** to refer to, name or identify precisely: *The report does not specify who was to blame.* **2** (*usu* **specify that**) to state as a condition or requirement: *The contract specified that the invoice must be paid.* [13c: from French *specifier*]

specimen *noun* **1** a sample or example of something, esp one that will be studied or put in a collection. **2** *med* a sample of blood, urine, tissue, etc that is taken so that tests can be carried out on it. **3** *informal* a person of a specified kind: *an ugly specimen.* [17c: Latin]

specious *adj* superficially or apparently convincing, sound or just, but really false, flawed or lacking in sincerity: *specious arguments.* [14c: from Latin *speciosus* fair or beautiful]

speck *noun* **1** a small spot, stain or mark. **2** a particle or tiny piece of something: *a speck of dirt on your shirt.* ▶ *verb* to mark with specks: *a blue carpet specked with grey.* [Anglo-Saxon *specca*]

speckle *noun* a little spot, esp one of several on a different-coloured background, eg on a bird's egg, etc. ▶ *verb* to mark with speckles. ▪ **speckled** *adj.* [15c: from Dutch *speckel*]

specs *plural noun, informal* a shortened form of **spectacles**.

spectacle *noun* **1** something that can be seen; a sight, esp one that is impressive, wonderful, ridiculous, etc: *The roses make a lovely spectacle.* **2** a display or exhibition, esp one that is put on for entertaining the public. **3** someone or something that attracts attention. [14c: from Latin *spectaculum*]

IDIOMS **make a spectacle of oneself** to behave in a way that attracts attention, esp ridicule or scorn.

spectacles *plural noun* a frame that holds two lenses designed to correct defective vision, and which has two legs that hook over the ears.

spectacular *adj* **1** impressively striking to see or watch. **2** remarkable; dramatic; huge. ▶ *noun* a spectacular show or display, esp one with lavish costumes, sets, music, etc: *an old-fashioned musical spectacular.* ▪ **spectacularly** *adv.* [17c: from Latin *spectaculum*]

spectate *verb, intr* to be a spectator.

spectator *noun* someone who watches an event or incident. [16c: Latin, from *spectare* to look]

spectra *pl of* **spectrum**

spectral *adj* **1** relating to or like a spectre or ghost. **2** relating to, produced by or like a **spectrum**.

spectre *or* (*US*) **specter** *noun* **1** a ghost or an apparition. **2** a haunting fear; the threat of something unpleasant: *The spectre of famine was never far away.* [17c: French]

spectrometer *noun* a device that is designed to produce spectra, esp one that can measure wavelength, energy and intensity. ▪ **spectrometry** *noun.*

spectroscope *noun, chem* an optical device that is used to produce a spectrum for a particular chemical compound, allowing the spectrum to be observed and analysed in order to identify the compound, determine its structure, etc.

spectrum *noun* (***spectra*** *or* ***spectrums***) **1** *physics* (*in full* **visible spectrum**) the band of colours (red, orange, yellow, green, blue, indigo and violet) that is produced when white light is split into its constituent wavelengths by passing it through a prism. **2** a continuous band or a series of lines representing the wavelengths or frequencies of electromagnetic radiation (eg visible light, X-rays, radio waves) emitted or absorbed by a particular substance. **3** any full range: *the whole spectrum of human emotions.* [17c: Latin, meaning 'appearance']

speculate *verb, intr* **1** (*often* **speculate on** *or* **about sth**) to consider the circumstances or possibilities regarding it, usu without coming to a definite conclusion. **2** to engage in risky financial transactions, usu in the hope of making a quick profit. ▪ **speculation** *noun.* ▪ **speculator** *noun.* [16c: from Latin *speculari* to look out]

speculative *adj* **1 a** of a theory, etc: involving guesswork; **b** of a person: tending to come to conclusions that have little or no foundation. **2** of an investment, business venture: risky. ▪ **speculatively** *adv.*

speculum *noun* (***specula*** *or* ***speculums***) **1** *optics* a mirror with a reflective surface usu of polished metal, esp one that forms part of a telescope. **2** *med* a device that is used to enlarge the opening of a body cavity so that the interior may be inspected. [16c: Latin, meaning 'mirror']

sped *past tense, past participle of* **speed**

speech *noun* **1** the act or an instance of speaking; the ability to speak. **2** a way of speaking: *slurred speech.* **3** something that is spoken. **4** spoken language, esp that of a particular group, region, etc: *Doric speech.* **5** a talk that is addressed to an audience. [Anglo-Saxon *sprec*]

speechify *verb* (**-ies, -ied**) *intr, informal* to make a speech or speeches, esp of a tedious nature.

speech impediment see **impediment**

speechless *adj* **1** *often euphem* temporarily unable to speak, because of surprise, shock, emotion, etc. **2** not able to speak at all. ▪ **speechlessness** *noun.*

speech therapy *noun* the treatment of people with speech and language disorders. ▪ **speech therapist** *noun.*

speed *noun* **1** rate of movement or action, esp distance travelled per unit of time. **2** quickness; rapidity: *with speed.* **3** a gear setting on a vehicle: *a five-speed gearbox.* **4** a photographic film's sensitivity to light. **5** *drug-taking slang* an **amphetamine.** ▶ *verb, intr* **1** (***sped***) to move quickly. **2** (***speeded***) to drive at a speed higher than the legal limit. [Anglo-Saxon *sped*]

IDIOMS **at speed** quickly.

PHRASAL VERBS **speed up** *or* **speed sth up** to increase in speed or make it increase in speed.

speedboat *noun* a motor boat that has an engine designed to make it capable of high speeds.

speed dating *noun* the practice of attending an organized social event during which people have a series of short meetings with potential romantic partners.

speeding *noun* **1** an act, instance or the process of going fast. **2** an act, instance or the process of going faster than the designated speed limit. ▸ *adj* moving, acting, etc fast: *a speeding car.*

speed limit *noun* the designated maximum speed a vehicle may legally travel at on a given stretch of road.

speedo *noun, informal* a **speedometer**.

speed of light *noun, physics* the constant and universal speed, 2.99792458108 metres per second, at which electromagnetic waves travel through a vacuum.

speedometer *noun* (often shortened to **speedo**) a device which indicates the speed that a motor vehicle is travelling at, and which often incorporates an odometer that displays the total mileage. Also (*informal) called* **the clock**.

speed trap *noun* a stretch of road where police monitor the speed of vehicles, often with electronic equipment.

speedway *noun* **1** the sport or pastime of racing round a cinder track on lightweight motorcycles. **2** the track that is used for this. **3** *N Am* a racetrack for cars. **4** *N Am* a highway where vehicles are allowed to travel fast.

speedwell *noun* a plant with small bluish (or occasionally white) four-petalled flowers.

speedy *adj* (**-*ier*, -*iest***) fast; prompt; without delay. ▪ **speedily** *adv.* ▪ **speediness** *noun.*

speleology *or* **spelaeology** *noun* **1** the scientific study of caves. **2** the activity or pastime of exploring caves. ▪ **speleological** *adj.* ▪ **speleologist** *noun.* [19c: from French *spéléologie*]

spell[1] *verb* (***spelt*** *or* ***spelled***) **1** to write or name (the constituent letters of a word or words) in their correct order. **2** of letters: to form (a word) when written in sequence: *I T spells 'it'.* **3** to indicate something clearly: *His angry expression spelt trouble.* ▪ **speller** *noun.* [13c: from French *espeller*]

PHRASAL VERBS **spell sth out 1** to read, write or speak (the constituent letters of a word) one by one. **2** to explain something clearly and in detail.

spell[2] *noun* **1** a set of words which, esp when spoken, is believed to have magical power, often of an evil nature: *a magic spell.* **2** any strong attracting influence; a fascination: *found the spell of her personality incredibly powerful.* [Anglo-Saxon, meaning 'narrative']

IDIOMS **cast a spell (on** *or* **upon sb)** to direct the words of a spell (towards them), esp in the hope that something bad will happen. **under a spell** held by the influence of a spell that has been cast. **under someone's spell** captivated by their influence.

spell[3] *noun* **1** (*often* **for a spell** *or* **a spell of**) a period or bout of illness, work, weather, etc often of a specified kind: *hope this spell of sunshine continues.* **2** *now chiefly Aust, NZ & N Eng dialect* an interval or short break from work. ▸ *verb, now chiefly Aust, NZ & N Eng dialect* **1** to replace or relieve someone at work. **2** *intr* to take an interval or short break from work. [Anglo-Saxon *spelian* to act for another]

spellbinding *adj* captivating, enchanting, entrancing or fascinating. ▪ **spellbindingly** *adv.* ▪ **spellbound** *adj.* [Early 19c]

spellcheck *word-processing, noun* (*also* **spellchecker**) a program that checks the operator's spelling against a store of words in a word-processor's database. ▸ *verb* to run a spellcheck program.

spellican see **spillikin**

spelling *noun* **1** the ability to spell: *His spelling is awful.* **2** a way a word is spelt: *an American spelling.*

spelt *past tense, past participle of* **spell[1]**

spelunker *noun* someone who takes part in the sport or activity of exploring caves; a potholer. ▪ **spelunking** *noun.* [1940s: from Latin *spelunca*]

spend *verb* (***spent***) **1** *tr & intr* (*often* **spend on**) to pay out (money, etc) eg on buying something new, for a service, repair, etc. **2** to use or devote (eg time, energy, effort, etc): *spent hours trying to fix the car.* **3** to use up completely; to exhaust: *Her anger soon spends itself.* ▸ *noun* an act or the process of spending (esp money): *went on a massive spend after winning the Lottery.* ▪ **spender** *noun.* ▪ **spending** *noun.* ▪ **spent** *adj* used up; exhausted: *a spent match.* [Anglo-Saxon *spendan*]

spendthrift *noun* someone who spends money freely, extravagantly and often wastefully.

sperm *noun* **1** a **spermatozoon**. **2** **semen**. [14c: from Greek *sperma* seed]

spermaceti /spɜːməˈsiːtɪ/ *noun* a white translucent waxy substance obtained from the snout of the sperm whale, formerly used for making candles, soap, cosmetics, etc. [15c: Latin]

spermatogenesis *noun, zool* the formation and development of sperm in the testes. ▪ **spermatogenetic** *adj.*

spermatophyte *or* **spermophyte** *noun, botany* any seed-bearing plant. ▪ **spermatophytic** *adj.* [19c]

spermatozoid *noun, botany* in certain plants: a mature male sex cell.

spermatozoon /spɜːmətoʊˈzoʊɒn/ *noun* (***spermatozoa*** /-ˈzoʊə/) *zool* in male animals: the small male gamete that locates, penetrates and fertilizes the female gamete. Often shortened to **sperm**. [19c: from Greek *sperma* seed + *zoion* animal]

spermicide *noun* a substance that can kill sperm and which is used in conjunction with various methods of barrier contraception, eg the condom and the diaphragm. ▪ **spermicidal** *adj.*

spew *verb, tr & intr* **1** to vomit. **2** to pour or cause to pour or stream out. ▸ *noun* vomit. [Anglo-Saxon *spiowan* to spit]

sphagnum *noun* (***sphagna***) a moss that grows on temperate boggy or marshy ground, and which forms peat when it decays. Also called **bog moss, peat moss**. [18c: from Greek *sphagnos* moss]

sphere *noun* **1** *maths* a round three-dimensional figure where all points on the surface are an equal distance from the centre. **2** a globe or ball. **3** a field of activity: *Rugby's not really my sphere.* **4** a class or circle within society: *We don't move in the same sphere any more.* [13c: from French *espere*]

sphere of influence *noun* the range or extent over which a place or person is dominant.

spherical *adj* having or being in the shape of a sphere.

spheroid *noun, geom* a figure or body characterized by having, or being in, almost the shape of a sphere.

sphincter *noun, anatomy* a ring of muscle that, when it contracts, closes the entrance to a cavity in the body. ▪ **sphincteral** *adj.* [16c: from Greek *sphingein* to hold tight]

sphinx *noun* **1** (*also* **Sphinx**) any stone carving or other representation in the form of a human head and lion's body, esp the huge recumbent statue near the Egyptian pyramids at Giza. **2** a mysterious or enigmatic person. ▪ **sphinxlike** *adj*. [14c: Latin]

spice *noun* **1** an aromatic or pungent substance, such as pepper, ginger, nutmeg, etc that is derived from plants and used for flavouring food, eg in sauces, curries, etc, and for drinks such as punch. **2** such substances collectively. **3** something that adds interest or enjoyment: *Variety is the spice of life*. ▸ *verb* **1** to flavour with spice. **2** (*also* **spice up**) to add interest or enjoyment to something. [13c: from French *espice*]

spick and span *adj* neat, clean and tidy. [17c: a shortened form of the obsolete *spick and span new*]

spicy *or* **spicey** *adj* (*-ier, -iest*) **1** flavoured with or tasting or smelling of spices; pungent; piquant. **2** *informal* characterized by, or suggestive of, scandal, sensation, impropriety, bad taste, etc: *Got any spicy gossip?* ▪ **spicily** *adv*. ▪ **spiciness** *noun*.

spider *noun* **1** any of numerous species of invertebrate animals that have eight legs and two main body parts, many of which produce silk and spin webs to trap their prey. **2** a snooker rest which has long legs so that it can be used to arch over a ball. **3** *comput* a program that performs automatic searches on the Internet. [Anglo-Saxon *spithra*]

spidery *adj* **1** thin and straggly: *spidery handwriting*. **2** full of spiders.

spiel /ʃpiːl, spiːl/ *noun, informal* a long rambling, often implausible, story, esp one that contains an excuse, one that the speaker hopes will divert attention from something else or one given as sales patter. [Late 19c: German, meaning 'play' or 'a game']

spiffing *adj, Brit old informal use* excellent; splendid.

spigot *noun* **1** a peg or plug, esp one that is used for stopping the vent hole in a cask or barrel. **2 a** *US* a tap; **b** a tap for controlling the flow of liquid, eg in a cask, pipe, etc. [14c]

spike[1] *noun* **1 a** any thin sharp point; **b** a pointed piece of metal, eg one of several on railings. **2** (**spikes**) a pair of running-shoes with spiked soles. **3** a large metal nail. ▸ *verb* **1** to strike, pierce or impale with a pointed object. **2** *informal* **a** to make (a drink) stronger by adding alcohol or extra alcohol; **b** to lace (a drink) with a drug. ▪ **spiked** *adj*. ▪ **spiky** *adj* (*-ier, -iest*). [Anglo-Saxon *spicing*]

spike[2] *noun, botany* a pointed flower head which consists of a cluster of small individual flowers growing together around, or along one side of, an axis, with the youngest flowers at the tip. [16c: from Latin *spica* ear of corn]

spill[1] *verb* (***spilt*** *or* ***spilled***) **1** *tr & intr* to run or flow or cause (a liquid, etc) to run or flow out from a container, esp accidentally. **2** *intr* to come or go in large crowds, esp quickly: *The spectators spilled onto the pitch*. **3** to shed (blood). ▸ *noun* **1** an act of spilling. **2** *informal* a fall, esp from a vehicle or horse. [Anglo-Saxon *spillan*]

IDIOMS **spill the beans** *informal* to reveal confidential information, either inadvertently or deliberately.

spill[2] *noun* a thin strip of wood or twisted paper for lighting a fire, candle, pipe, etc. [Early 19c]

spillage *noun* **1** the act or process of spilling. **2** something that is spilt or an amount spilt.

spillikin, **spilikin** *or* **spellican** *noun* **1** a small thin strip of wood, bone, etc. **2** (**spillikins**) a game where lots of these strips are heaped together and the object is to try and take one after another from the pile without disturbing the others. [18c: a diminutive of **spill**[2]]

spin *verb* (***spun, spinning***) **1** *tr & intr* to rotate or cause to rotate repeatedly, esp quickly: *We spun a coin to see who would go first*. **2** *intr* (*usu* **spin round**) to turn around, esp quickly or unexpectedly. **3** to draw out and twist (fibres, etc) into thread. **4** of spiders, silkworms, etc: to construct (a web, cocoon, etc) from the silky thread they produce. **5 a** to bowl, throw, kick, strike, etc (a ball) so that it rotates while moving forward, causing a change in the expected direction or speed; **b** of a ball, etc: to be delivered in this way. **6** *intr* of someone's head, etc: to have a disorientated sensation, esp one that is brought on by excitement, amazement, drugs or alcohol, etc. **7** to dry (washing) in a spin dryer. ▸ *noun* **1** an act or process of spinning or a spinning motion. **2** rotation in a ball thrown, struck, etc. **3** a nose-first spiral descent in an aircraft, esp one that is out of control. Also called **tailspin**. **4** *informal* a short trip in a vehicle, for pleasure. **5** of information, a news report, etc, esp that is of a political nature: a favourable bias: *The PR department will put a spin on it*. ▪ **spinning** *noun, adj*. [Anglo-Saxon *spinnan*]

IDIOMS **spin a yarn, tale**, *etc* to tell a story, esp a long improbable one.

spina bifida /ˈspaɪnə ˈbɪfɪdə/ *noun, pathol* a condition existing from birth in which there is a protrusion of the spinal column through the backbone, often causing permanent paralysis. [18c: Latin]

spinach *noun* **1** a plant that is widely cultivated for its edible leaves. **2** the young dark green crinkly or flat edible leaves of this plant which are cooked and eaten as a vegetable or used raw in salads. [16c: from French *espinache* spinach]

spinal *adj* belonging, relating or referring to the **spine**.

spinal column *noun* the spine.

spinal cord *noun* a cord-like structure of nerve tissue that is enclosed and protected by the spinal column and which connects the brain to nerves in all other parts of the body.

spin bowler *noun, cricket* a bowler whose technique involves importing variations to the flight and/or **spin** (*noun* sense 2) of the ball.

spindle *noun* **1** a rod with a notched or tapered end that is designed for twisting the fibres in hand-spinning and which is the place where the spun thread is wound. **2** a pin or axis which turns, or around which something else turns. [Anglo-Saxon *spinel*]

spindly *adj* (*-ier, -iest*) *informal* long, thin and, often, frail-looking.

spin doctor *noun, informal* someone, esp in politics, who tries to influence public opinion by putting a favourable bias on information when it is presented to the public or to the media. [1980s]

spindrift *noun* spray that is blown from the crests of waves. [17c: orig a Scots variation of the obsolete *spoondrift*, from *spoon* to be blown by the wind + **drift**]

spin-dry *verb* (***spin-dried*** *or* ***spun-dry, spin-drying*** *or* ***spinning-dry***) to partly dry (wet laundry) in a spin dryer.

spin dryer *or* **spin drier** *noun* an electrically powered machine, either part of a washing machine or free-standing, that takes some of the water out of wet laundry by spinning it at high speed in a revolving drum.

spine *noun* **1** in vertebrates: the flexible bony structure that surrounds and protects the spinal cord. **2** the narrow middle section in the cover of a book that hides the part where the pages are glued or stitched. **3** in certain plants and animals, eg cacti, hedgehogs, etc: one of many sharply pointed structures that protect the plant or animal against predators. [15c: from French *espine*]

spine-chiller *noun* a frightening story, thought, etc. ▪ **spine-chilling** *adj.*

spineless *adj* **1** invertebrate. **2** *informal* of a person, their attitude, behaviour, etc: lacking courage or strength of character. ▪ **spinelessly** *adv.*

spinet *noun* a musical instrument like a small harpsichord. [17c: from French *espinette*]

spinnaker *noun* a large triangular sail set at the front of a yacht. [Late 19c]

spinner *noun* **1** someone or something that spins. **2** an angler's lure that has a projecting wing which makes it spin in the water when the line is pulled. **3** *cricket* **a** a spin bowler; **b** a ball that is bowled with spin.

spinneret *noun, zool* in spiders, silkworms, etc: a small tubular organ that produces the silky thread that they use in making webs, cocoons, etc.

spinney *noun* a small wood or thicket, esp one that has a prickly undergrowth. [16c: from French *espinei* a place full of thorns and brambles]

spinning jenny *noun* a type of early spinning machine that has several spindles.

spinning wheel *noun* a machine with a spindle driven by a wheel operated either by hand or by the foot and used, esp in the home, for spinning thread or yarn.

spin-off *noun* **1** a side-effect or by-product, esp one that is beneficial or valuable. **2** something that comes about because of the success of an earlier product or idea, eg a television series derived from a successful film.

spinster *noun* a woman, esp one who is middle-aged or older, who has never been married. ▪ **spinsterhood** *noun.* ▪ **spinsterish** *adj.* [14c as *spinnestere*, a woman who spins thread]

spiny *adj* (**-ier, -iest**) **1** of plants or animals: covered with spines; prickly. **2** troublesome; difficult to deal with: *a spiny problem.*

spiny lobster *noun* a langouste.

spiracle /ˈspaɪrəkəl/ *noun, zool* a hole or aperture used for respiration in certain insects and fishes, whales, etc. [17c: from Latin *spiraculum*]

spiral *noun* **1** the pattern that is made by a line winding outwards from a central point in circles or near-circles of regularly increasing size. **2** a curve or course that makes this kind of a pattern. **3** a gradual but continuous rise or fall, eg of prices, wages, etc. ▸ *adj* being in or having the shape or nature of a spiral: *a spiral staircase.* ▸ *verb* (***spiralled, spiralling***; *or* (*US*) ***spiraled, spiraling***) *intr* **1** to follow a spiral course or pattern. **2** esp of prices, wages, etc: to go up or down, usu quickly: *Prices were spiralling out of control.* ▪ **spirally** *adv.* [16c: from Latin *spiralis*]

spire *noun* a tall thin structure tapering upwards to a point, esp the top of a tower on a church roof. [Anglo-Saxon *spir* shoot or sprout]

spirit *noun* **1** the animating or vitalizing essence or force that motivates, invigorates or energizes someone or something. **2** this force as an independent part of a person, widely believed to survive the body after death. **3** a supernatural being without a body: *Evil spirits haunted the house.* **4** (**the Spirit**) see **the Holy Ghost**. **5 a** temperament, frame of mind, etc, usu of a specified kind: *She always had a very independent spirit;* **b** the dominant or prevalent mood, attitude, etc: *public spirit;* **c** the characteristic essence, nature, etc of something: *the spirit of Christmas.* **6** a distilled alcoholic drink, eg whisky, brandy, gin, etc. ▸ *verb* (*usu* **spirit sth** *or* **sb away** *or* **off**) to carry or convey them mysteriously or magically. [13c: from French *espirit*]

IDIOMS **in good** *or* **high,** *etc* **spirits** in a happy, contented, etc mood. **in spirit** as a presence that is perceived to be there: *I'll be with you in spirit, if not in person.*

spirited *adj* **1** full of courage or liveliness. **2** *in compounds* having or showing a specified kind of spirit, mood, attitude, etc: *high-spirited.*

spirit gum *noun* a quick-drying sticky substance that is esp used, eg by actors, for securing false facial hair.

spirit lamp *noun* a lamp that burns methylated or other spirit as opposed to oil.

spirit level *noun* a device used for testing that horizontal or vertical surfaces are level, made up of a flat bar into which is set a liquid-filled glass tube with a large air bubble which lies between two markings on the tube when laid on or against a level surface.

spiritual *adj* **1** belonging, referring or relating to the spirit or soul rather than to the body or to physical things. **2** belonging, referring or relating to religion; sacred, holy or divine. **3 a** belonging, referring or relating to, or arising from, the mind or intellect; **b** highly refined in thought, feelings, etc. **4** belonging, referring or relating to spirits, ghosts, etc: *the spiritual world.* ▸ *noun* (*also* **Negro spiritual**) a type of religious song that is characterized by voice harmonies and which developed from the communal singing traditions of African American people in the southern states of the USA. ▪ **spirituality** *noun.* ▪ **spiritually** *adv.* [13c: from Latin *spiritualis*]

spiritualism *noun* the belief that it is possible to have communication with the spirits of dead people, eg through a **medium** (*noun* sense 3), a **Ouija** board, etc. ▪ **spiritualist** *noun.* ▪ **spiritualistic** *adj.*

spirituous *adj* having a high alcohol content.

spirograph *noun, med* a device for measuring and recording breathing movements. [19c: from Greek *speira* a coil]

spirogyra /spaɪərouˈdʒaɪərə/ *noun* a green alga with filaments containing spiralling chloroplasts, found either floating or fixed to stones in ponds and streams. [Late 19c: from Greek *speira* a coil + *gyros* circle]

spirt see **spurt**

spit[1] *verb* (**spat** *or* (*US*) **spit, spitting**) **1 a** *tr & intr* to expel (saliva or phlegm) from the mouth; **b** *intr* to do this as a gesture of contempt: *spat in his face.* **2** (*also* **spit out**) to eject (eg food) forcefully out of the mouth. **3** of a fire, fat or oil in a pan, etc: to throw off (a spark of hot coal, oil, etc) in a spurt or spurts. **4** to speak or utter with contempt, hate, violence, etc. **5** *intr* of rain or snow: to fall in light intermittent drops or flakes. ▸ *noun* **1** spittle; a blob of saliva or phlegm that has been spat from the mouth. **2** an act of spitting. ▪ **spitting** *noun, adj.* [Anglo-Saxon *spittan*]

IDIOMS **spit it out** *informal* to say what one has been hesitating to say: *Come on, spit it out! Are you saying I'm a liar?* **the spit** *or* **very spit** *informal* an exact likeness; a spitting image: *She's the very spit of her mother.*

spit² *noun* **1** a long thin metal rod on which meat is skewered and held over a fire or in an oven for roasting. **2** *geography* a long stretch of sand running into the sea from the mainland. [Anglo-Saxon *spitu*]

spit and polish *noun, informal, often derog* exceptional cleanliness, tidiness, correctness, etc.

spite *noun* **1** the desire to intentionally and maliciously hurt or offend. **2** an instance of this; a grudge. ▸ *verb, chiefly used in the infinitive form*: to annoy, offend, etc: *did it to spite him.* [14c: from French *despit*]

IDIOMS **in spite of** regardless; notwithstanding: *decided to go in spite of the rain.*

spiteful *adj* motivated by spite; vengeful; malicious. ▪ **spitefully** *adv.* ▪ **spitefulness** *noun.*

spitfire *noun* someone who has a quick or fiery temper, esp a woman or girl. [17c]

spitting image *noun, informal* an exact likeness.

spittle *noun* saliva, esp when it has been spat from the mouth; spit. [Anglo-Saxon *spatl*]

spittoon *noun* a container for spitting into.

spiv *noun, informal* a man who sells, deals in, or is otherwise involved in the trading of, illicit, black-market or stolen goods, and who is usu dressed in a very flashy way. [1930s]

splash *verb* **1 a** to make (a liquid or semi-liquid substance) fly around or land in drops; **b** *intr* of a liquid or semi-liquid substance: to fly around or land in drops. **2** to make something wet or dirty (with drops of liquid or semi-liquid): *The bus splashed them with mud.* **3** to print or display something boldly: *The photograph was splashed across the front page.* ▸ *noun* **1** a sound of splashing. **2** an amount splashed. **3** an irregular spot or patch: *splashes of colour.* **4** *informal* a small amount of liquid; a dash: *tea with just a splash of milk.* ▪ **splashing** *noun, adj.* [18c: from Anglo-Saxon *plasc*]

IDIOMS **make a splash** to attract a great deal of attention, esp deliberately or with outrageous behaviour.

PHRASAL VERBS **splash out** *or* **splash out on sth** *informal* to spend a lot of money, esp extravagantly or ostentatiously.

splash guard *N Am* **mudflap**.

splat *noun* the sound made by a soft wet object striking a surface. ▸ *adv* with this sound: *She gave him a custard pie splat in the face.* ▸ *verb* (***splatted, splatting***) to hit, fall, land, etc with a splat. [Late 19c: a shortened form of **splatter**]

splatter *verb* **1** *tr & intr* to make something dirty with lots of small scattered drops. **2** of water, mud, etc: to wet or dirty: *The mud splattered him from head to toe.* ▸ *noun* a splash or spattering, eg of colour, mud, etc. [18c]

splay *verb* to spread (eg the fingers). [14c: from **display**]

splay foot *noun* a foot that turns outwards, esp one that is broad and flat. ▪ **splay-footed** *adj.*

spleen *noun* **1** a delicate organ located beneath the diaphragm on the left side, and which destroys red blood cells that are no longer functional. **2** bad temper; anger: *vented his spleen by punching the wall.* [13c: from French *esplen*]

splendid *adj* **1** very good; excellent. **2** magnificent; impressively grand or sumptuous. ▪ **splendidly** *adv.* [17c: from Latin *splendidus* shining or brilliant]

splendiferous *adj, now informal, humorous* splendid. [15c: from Latin *splendorifer* carrying brightness]

splendour *or* (*N Am*) **splendor** *noun* magnificence, opulence or grandeur. [15c: from French *esplendur*]

splenetic *adj* bad-tempered; spiteful; full of spleen.

splice *verb* **1** to join (two pieces of rope) by weaving the strands of one into the other. **2** to join (two pieces of timber, etc) by overlapping and securing the ends. **3** to join the neatened ends of (two pieces of film, magnetic tape, wire, etc) using solder, adhesive, etc. ▸ *noun* a join made in one of these ways. [16c: from Dutch *splissen*]

IDIOMS **get spliced** *informal* to get married.

splint *noun* a piece of rigid material that is strapped to a broken limb, etc to hold it in position while the bone heals. ▸ *verb* to bind or hold (a broken limb, etc) in position using a splint. [13c: from Dutch *splinte*]

splinter *noun* **1** a small thin sharp piece that has broken off a hard substance, eg wood or glass. **2** a fragment of an exploded shell, etc. ▸ *verb, tr & intr* **1** to break into splinters. **2** of a group, political party, etc: to divide or become divided: *The party splintered over green issues.* ▪ **splintery** *adj.* [14c: Dutch]

splinter group *noun* a small group, esp a political one, that is formed by individuals who have broken away from the main group, esp because of some disagreement, eg over policy, principles, etc.

split *verb* (***split, splitting***) **1** *tr & intr* to divide or break or cause to divide or break apart or into, usu two, pieces, esp lengthways. **2** to divide or share, money, etc. **3** (*also* **split up**) *tr & intr* **a** to divide or separate into smaller amounts, groups, parts, etc; **b** to divide or separate or cause to divide or separate, eg because of disagreement, disharmony, etc: *European policy split the party.* **4** *intr* (*usu* **split away** *or* **split off**) to separate from or break away from; to diverge: *The road splits off to the right.* **5** *intr, informal* to go away or leave: *Let's split and go back for a drink.* ▸ *noun* **1 a** an act or the process of separating or dividing; **b** a division, esp of money, etc: *a two-way split on the Lottery winnings.* **2** a lengthways break or crack. **3** a separation or division through disagreement. **4** a dessert that consists of fruit, esp a banana, sliced open and topped with cream and/or ice cream, sauce, nuts, etc. **5** (**the splits**) an acrobatic leap or drop to the floor so that the legs form a straight line and each leg is at right angles to the torso. ▸ *adj* divided, esp in two. [16c: from Dutch *splitten* to cleave]

IDIOMS **split hairs** to make or argue about fine and trivial distinctions. **split one's sides** *informal* to laugh uncontrollably.

split infinitive *noun, grammar* an **infinitive** that has an adverb or other word coming in between *to* and the verb, as in *to really believe, to boldly go*, etc.

split infinitive
Some people claim that a split infinitive is incorrect grammar. However, this is a 'rule' that was borrowed from Latin grammar, and it is not necessary to apply the rule to English.
It is acceptable to use a split infinitive when the rhythm and meaning of the sentence call for it:
He was never one to idly beat about the bush.
Some modifying words like *only* and *really* have to come between *to* and the verb to convey the right meaning, and this also makes the split infinitive acceptable:
Part of a personnel officer's job is to really get to know all the staff.

split personality *noun, psychol* a condition in which two or more distinct personalities or types of behaviour co-exist in or are displayed by a single person.

split second *noun* a fraction of a second: *In a split second she was gone.*

splitting *adj* **1** of a headache: very painful; severe. **2** of a head: gripped by severe pain: *My head is absolutely splitting.*

splodge *or* **splotch** *noun* a large splash, stain or patch. ▸ *verb, tr & intr* to mark with splodges

splosh *noun, verb, informal* **splash**.

splurge *noun* **1** an ostentatious display. **2** a bout of extravagance, eg a spending spree. ▸ *verb, tr & intr* to spend extravagantly or ostentatiously.

splutter *verb* **1** *intr* to put or throw out drops of liquid, bits of food, sparks, etc with spitting sounds. **2** *intr* to make intermittent noises or movements, esp as a sign of something being wrong: *The car spluttered to a halt.* **3** *tr & intr* to speak or say haltingly or incoherently, eg through embarrassment: *could only splutter that he didn't know the answer.* ▸ *noun* the act or noise of spluttering. ▪ **spluttering** *adj, noun.* [17c]

spoil *verb* (***spoilt*** *or* ***spoiled***) **1** to impair, ruin or make useless or valueless. **2** to mar or make less enjoyable: *The contrived ending spoiled the film.* **3** to harm (eg, the character of a child) by overindulgence: *She is spoiling that boy – he never has to do anything for himself.* **4** *intr* of food: to become unfit to eat. ▸ *noun* (*always* **spoils**) **1** possessions taken by force; plunder: *the spoils of war.* **2** any benefits or rewards: a *company car – just one of the spoils of the new job.* [13c: from French *espoillier*]
IDIOMS **be spoiled** *or* **spoilt for choice** to have so many options or alternatives that it is hard to decide which to choose. **be spoiling for sth** to seek out (a fight, argument, etc) eagerly.

spoilage *noun* **1** decay or deterioration of food. **2** waste, esp waste paper caused by bad printing.

spoiler *noun* **1** a flap on an aircraft wing that is used for increasing drag and so assists in its descent by reducing the air speed. **2** a fixed horizontal structure on a car that is designed to put pressure on the wheels and so increase its roadholding capacity, esp at high speeds. **3** someone or something that spoils.

spoilsport *noun, informal* someone who mars or detracts from the fun or enjoyment of others, esp by refusing to join in.

spoilt *past tense, past participle of* **spoil**

spoke[1] *past tense of* **speak**

spoke[2] *noun* **1** any of the radiating rods or bars that fan out from the hub of a wheel and attach it to the the rim. **2** a rung of a ladder. [Anglo-Saxon *spaca*]
IDIOMS **put a spoke in sb's wheel** to upset their plans, esp intentionally or maliciously.

spoken *adj* **1** uttered or expressed in speech. **2** *in compounds* speaking in a specified way: *well-spoken.* ▸ *verb, past participle of* **speak**.
IDIOMS **be spoken for** of someone: to be married, engaged or in a steady relationship.

spokesperson *noun* someone, a **spokesman** or **spokeswoman**, who is appointed to speak on behalf of other people, a specified group, a government, business, etc.

spoliation *noun* an act, instance or the process of robbing, plundering, etc. [14c: from Latin *spoliare* to spoil]

spondee *noun, prosody* a metrical foot of two long syllables or two stressed syllables and which in English verse tends to suggest weariness, depression, slowness, etc. [14c: from Latin *spondeus*]

spondulicks /spɒn'dju:lɪks/ *plural noun, informal, chiefly US* money; cash. [19c]

sponge *noun* **1** an aquatic, usu marine, invertebrate animal that attaches itself to a solid object such as a rock and consists of a large cluster of cells supported by an often porous skeleton. **2** **a** a piece of the soft porous skeleton of this animal which is capable of holding comparatively large amounts of water and which remains soft when wet, making it particularly suitable for washing, bathing, cleaning, etc; **b** a piece of similarly absorbent synthetic material that is used in the same way. **3** sponge cake or pudding. **4** a wipe with a cloth or sponge in order to clean something: *gave the baby's face a quick sponge.* **5** *informal* someone who regularly drinks a lot. ▸ *verb* **1** (*also* **sponge sth down**) to wash or clean it with a cloth or sponge and water. **2** to mop up. **3** (*usu* **sponge off** *or* **on sb**) *informal* to borrow money, etc from them, often without any intention of paying it back. [Anglo-Saxon]

sponger *noun, informal* someone who survives by habitually imposing on other people, expecting them to pay for things, etc.

spongy *adj* (***-ier, -iest***) soft and springy, and perhaps absorbent, like a sponge. ▪ **sponginess** *noun.*

sponsor *noun* **1** a person or organization that finances an event or broadcast in return for advertising. **2** **a** someone who promises a sum of money to a participant in a forthcoming fund-raising event; **b** a company that provides backing for a sporting team or individual, in return for the team or individual displaying the company's name or logo on their shirts. **3** someone who offers to be responsible for another, esp in acting as a godparent. ▸ *verb* to act as a sponsor for someone or something. ▪ **sponsored** *adj*: a *sponsored walk.* ▪ **sponsorship** *noun.* [17c: from Latin *spondere* to promise solemnly]

spontaneity /spɒntə'neɪɪtɪ/ *noun* natural or unrestrained reaction.

spontaneous *adj* **1** unplanned and voluntary or instinctive, not provoked or invited by others. **2** occurring naturally or by itself, not caused or influenced from outside. [17c: from Latin *sponte* of one's own accord]

spontaneous combustion *noun* an act or instance or the process of a substance or body catching fire as a result of heat that is generated within it, as opposed to heat applied from outside.

spoof *informal, noun* **1** a satirical imitation; a parody. **2** a light-hearted hoax or trick. ▸ *verb* to parody; to play a hoax. [Late 19c: coined by the British comedian, A Roberts, to designate a hoaxing game]

spook *informal, noun* **1** a ghost. **2** *N Am* a spy. ▸ *verb* **1** to frighten or startle. **2** to haunt. **3** to make someone feel nervous or uneasy. ▪ **spookish** *adj*. [Early 19c: from German *Spok* a ghost]

spooky *adj* (***-ier, -iest***) *informal* **1** uncanny; eerie. **2** suggestive of ghosts or the supernatural. ▪ **spookily** *adv*. ▪ **spookiness** *noun*.

spool *noun* a small cylinder, usu with a hole down the centre and with extended rims at either end, on which thread, photographic film, tape, etc is wound; a reel. [14c: from German dialect *Spole* a reel]

spoon *noun* **1** a metal, wooden or plastic utensil that has a handle with a round or oval shallow bowl-like part at one end and which is used for eating, serving or stirring food. **2** the amount a spoon will hold. ▸ *verb* **1** to lift or transfer (food) with a spoon. **2** *intr, old use* to kiss and cuddle. [Anglo-Saxon *spon*]

IDIOMS **be born with a silver spoon in one's mouth** to be born into a family with wealth and/or high social standing.

spoonerism *noun* an accidental slip of the tongue where the positions of the first sounds in a pair of words are reversed, such as *par cark* for *car park*, and which often results in an unintentionally comic or ambiguous expression. [Late 19c: named after Rev. W A Spooner, an English clergyman, whose nervous disposition led him to make such slips]

spoon-feed *verb* **1** to feed (eg a baby) with a spoon. **2** to supply someone with everything they need or require, so that any effort on their part is unnecessary.

spoonful *noun* **1** the amount a spoon will hold. **2** a small amount or number.

spoor *noun* the track or scent left by an animal. [19c: Afrikaans]

sporadic *adj* occurring from time to time, at irregular intervals; intermittent. ▪ **sporadically** *adv*. [17c: from Greek *sporados* scattered]

spore *noun* one of the tiny reproductive bodies produced in vast quantities by certain micro-organisms and non-flowering plants, and which are capable of developing into new individuals. [19c: from Greek *spora* seed]

sporran *noun* a pouch that is traditionally worn hanging from a belt in front of the kilt in Scottish Highland dress and which is usu made of leather or fur. [Early 19c: from Gaelic *sporan* purse]

sport *noun* **1 a** an activity, pastime, competition, etc that usu involves a degree of physical exertion, and which people take part in for exercise and/or pleasure; **b** such activities collectively: *enjoys watching sport on TV.* See also **sports**. **2** good-humoured fun: *It was just meant to be a bit of sport.* **3** *informal* **a** someone who is thought of as being fair-minded, generous, easy-going, etc: *Be a sport and lend me your car*; **b** someone who behaves in a specified way, esp with regard to winning or losing: *Even when he loses, he's a good sport*; **c** *Aust, NZ* a form of address that is esp used between men: *How's it going, sport?* ▸ *verb* **1** to wear or display, esp proudly: *She sported a small tattoo.* **2** *biol* to vary from, or produce a variation from, the parent stock. [15c: a shortened form of **disport**]

sporting *adj* **1** belonging, referring or relating to sport: *sporting dogs.* **2** of someone, their behaviour, attitude, nature, etc: characterized by fairness, generosity, etc: *It was sporting of him to lend me the car.* **3** keen or willing to gamble or take a risk: *I'm not a sporting man, but I like a bet on the Grand National.* ▪ **sportingly** *adv*.

sporting chance *noun* (*usu* **a sporting chance**) a reasonable possibility of success.

sportive *adj* playful. ▪ **sportively** *adv*. ▪ **sportiveness** *noun*.

sports *Brit, singular noun* in schools and colleges: a day or afternoon that each year is dedicated to competitive sport, esp athletics: *Parents may attend the school sports.* ▸ *adj* **1** belonging, referring or relating to sport: *sports pavilion.* **2** used in or suitable for sport: *sports holdall.* **3** casual: *sports jacket.*

sports car *noun* a small fast car, usu a two-seater, often with a low-slung body.

sports jacket *noun* a man's jacket, often one made from tweed, that is meant for casual wear. Also called *N Am, Aust & NZ* **sports coat**.

sportsman *noun* **1** a male sportsperson. **2** someone who plays fair, sticks to the rules and accepts defeat without any rancour or bitterness. ▪ **sportsmanlike** *adj*. ▪ **sportsmanship** *noun*.

sportswear *noun* clothes that are designed for or suitable for sport or for wearing casually.

sportswoman *noun* a female sportsperson.

sport utility vehicle *noun* a four-wheel-drive vehicle.

sporty *adj* (***-ier, -iest***) **1** habitually taking part in sport, or being esp fond of, good at, etc sport. **2** of clothes: casual; suitable for wearing when playing a sport. **3** of a car: looking, performing or handling like a sports car. ▪ **sportily** *adv*. ▪ **sportiness** *noun*.

spot *noun* **1** a small mark or stain. **2** a drop of liquid. **3** a small amount, esp of liquid. **4** an eruption on the skin; a pimple. **5** a place: *found a secluded spot.* **6** *informal* a small amount of work: *did a spot of ironing.* **7** a place or period in a schedule or programme: *a five-minute comedy spot.* **8** *informal* a spotlight. ▸ *verb* (***spotted, spotting***) **1** to mark with spots. **2** to see; to catch sight of something. **3** *usu in compounds* to watch for and record the sighting of (eg trains, planes, etc). **4** to search for (new talent). **5** *intr* of rain: to fall lightly. ▪ **spotting** *noun*. ▪ **-spotting** *noun, in compounds*: *trainspotting*. [12c: from Norse *spotti* small bit]

IDIOMS **in a spot** *informal* in trouble or difficulty. **knock spots off sb** *or* **sth** *informal* to be overwhelmingly better than them. **on the spot 1** immediately and often without warning: *Motorists caught speeding are fined on the spot.* **2** at the scene of some notable event. **3** in an awkward situation, esp one requiring immediate action or response: *put someone on the spot.*

spot check *noun* an inspection made at random and without warning. ▸ *verb* (**spot-check**) to carry out a random check: *The police were spot-checking for worn tyres.*

spotless *adj* **1** absolutely clean. **2** unblemished: *a spotless working record.* ▪ **spotlessly** *adv.* ▪ **spotlessness** *noun.*

spotlight *noun* **1** a concentrated circle of light that can be directed onto a small area, esp of a theatre stage. **2** a lamp that casts this kind of light. ▸ *verb* (***spotlit*** *or* ***spotlighted***) **1** to illuminate with a spotlight. **2** to direct attention to something; to highlight. [Early 20c]

IDIOMS **be in the spotlight** to have the attention of others, the media, etc focused on (one or someone).

spot-on *adj, Brit informal* precisely what is required; excellent; very accurate.

spotted *adj* **1** patterned or covered with spots. **2** stained; marked: *a tie spotted with tomato sauce.*

spotter *noun, usu in compounds* someone who watches for and records the sighting of trains, planes, etc. ▪ **spotting** *noun.*

spotty *adj* (***-ier, -iest***) **1** marked with a pattern of spots. **2** of someone's skin: covered in blemishes, pimples, etc. ▪ **spottiness** *noun.*

spot-weld *verb* to join metal with single circular welds. ▸ *noun* a weld that is made in this way.

spouse *noun* a husband or wife. [13c: from Latin *sponsus*]

spout *noun* **1** a projecting tube or lip, eg on a kettle, teapot, fountain, etc, that allows liquid to pass through or through which it can be poured. **2** a jet or stream of liquid, eg from a fountain or a whale's blowhole. ▸ *verb* **1** *tr & intr* to flow or make something flow out in a jet or stream. **2** *tr & intr* to speak or say, esp at length and boringly. **3** *intr* of a whale: to squirt air through a blowhole. [14c]

IDIOMS **up the spout** *slang* ruined or damaged beyond repair; no longer a possibility.

sprain *verb* to injure (a joint) by the sudden overstretching or tearing of a ligament or ligaments. ▸ *noun* such an injury, usu causing painful swelling. [17c]

sprang *past tense of* **spring**

sprat *noun* a small edible fish of the herring family. [Anglo-Saxon *sprot*]

sprawl *verb, intr* **1** to sit or lie lazily, esp with the arms and legs spread out wide. **2** to fall in an ungainly way. **3** to spread or extend in an irregular, straggling or untidy way. ▸ *noun* **1** a sprawling position. **2** a straggling expansion, esp one that is unregulated, uncontrolled, etc: *an urban sprawl.* [Anglo-Saxon *spreawlian* to move convulsively]

spray[1] *noun* **1** a fine mist of small flying drops of liquid. **2** a liquid designed to be applied as a mist: *body spray.* **3** a device for dispensing a liquid as a mist; an atomizer or aerosol. **4** a shower of small flying objects: *a spray of pellets.* ▸ *verb* **1** to squirt (a liquid) in the form of a mist. **2** to apply a liquid in the form of a spray to something. **3** to subject someone or something to a heavy burst: *sprayed the car with bullets.* [17c: from Dutch *sprayen*]

spray[2] *noun* **1 a** a small branch of a tree or plant which has delicate leaves and flowers growing on it; **b** any decoration that is an imitation of this. **2** a small bouquet of flowers. [13c]

spray gun *noun* a container with a trigger-operated aerosol attached, for dispensing liquid, eg paint, in spray form.

spray-paint *noun* paint that is applied using an aerosol, etc. ▸ *verb* to cover something in paint, using an aerosol, etc. ▪ **spray-painting** *noun.*

spread *verb* (*past tense, past participle* ***spread***) **1** *tr & intr* to apply, or be capable of being applied, in a smooth coating over a surface: *spread the butter on the toast.* **2** (*also* **spread out** *or* **spread sth out**) to extend or make it extend or scatter, often more widely or more thinly. **3** (*also* **spread sth out**) to open it out or unfold it, esp to its full extent: *spread the sheet on the bed.* **4** *tr & intr* to transmit or be transmitted or distributed: *Rumours began to spread.* ▸ *noun* **1** the act, process or extent of spreading. **2** a food in paste form, for spreading on bread, etc. **3 a** *originally* a pair of facing pages in a newspaper or magazine; **b** *loosely* an article in a newspaper or magazine *a huge spread on Madonna.* **4** *informal* a lavish meal. **5 a** *N Am* a farm and its lands, usu one given over to cattle-rearing; **b** a large house with extensive grounds. **6** *informal* increased fatness around the waist and hips: *middle-age spread.* **7** a cover, esp for a bed. ▪ **spreader** *noun.* [Anglo-Saxon *sprædan*]

IDIOMS **spread like wildfire** of gossip, news, etc: to become widely known very quickly. **spread one's wings** to attempt to broaden one's experience.

spread betting *noun* a form of gambling in which people stake money on whether the numerical outcome of an event will be higher or lower than a stated amount.

spread-eagle *adj* (*also* **spread-eagled**) in a position where the arms and legs are stretched out away from the body.

spreadsheet *noun, comput* a program that displays data in a grid, allowing various kinds of calculation, projection, etc.

spree *noun* a period of fun, extravagance or excess, esp one that involves spending a lot of money or drinking a lot of alcohol: *a spending spree.* [19c]

sprig *noun* a small shoot or twig. [14c]

sprightly *adj* (***-ier, -iest***) lively; vivacious; quick-moving and spirited. ▪ **sprightliness** *noun.* [16c: from *spright*, a variant spelling of **sprite**]

spring *verb* (*past tense* ***sprang*** *or* (*US*) ***sprung,*** *past participle* ***sprung***) **1** *intr* to leap with a sudden quick launching action. **2** *intr* to move suddenly and swiftly, esp from a stationary position: *sprang into action.* **3** to set off (a trap, etc) suddenly. **4** to fit (eg a mattress) with springs. **5** (*also* **spring sth on sb**) to present or reveal something suddenly and unexpectedly: *sprang the idea on me without warning.* **6** *slang* to engineer the escape of (a prisoner) from jail. **7** *intr* (**spring from somewhere**) to develop or originate from (a place, etc): *an idea that had sprung from one of his students.* ▸ *noun* **1** a metal coil that can be stretched or compressed, and which will return to its original shape when the pull or pressure is released. **2** any place where water emerges from under ground. **3** (*also* **Spring**) the season between winter and summer, when most plants begin to grow. **4** a sudden vigorous leap. **5 a** the ability of a material to return rapidly to its original shape after a distorting force, such as stretching, bending or compression, has been removed: *The elastic has lost its spring;* **b** a lively bouncing or jaunty quality: *a spring in his step.* [Anglo-Saxon *springan*]

IDIOMS **spring a leak** of a boat, bucket, etc: to develop a hole so that water can flow in or out. **spring to mind** to come into someone's thoughts immediately or suddenly.

springboard *noun* **1** **a** a long narrow pliable board that projects over a swimming pool and which is used in diving to give extra lift; **b** a similar but shorter board that is used in gymnastics and which is placed in front of a piece of apparatus to give extra height and impetus. **2** anything that serves to get things moving.

springbok *noun* (***springbok*** *or* ***springboks***) **1** (*also* **springbuck**) a type of South African antelope that is renowned for its high springing leap when it runs. **2** (**Springbok**) a nickname for a member of a S African sporting team, esp their national rugby union side. [18c: Afrikaans]

spring chicken *noun* a very young chicken valued for its tender flesh.

IDIOMS **no spring chicken** no longer young.

spring-clean *verb, tr & intr* to clean and tidy (a house) thoroughly, esp at the end of the winter. ▸ *noun* an act of doing this. ▪ **spring-cleaning** *noun.*

spring onion *noun* an immature onion that is picked when it is just a tiny white bulb with long thin green shoots, and which is usu eaten raw in salads.

spring roll *noun* a type of deep-fried folded Chinese pancake that can have a variety of savoury fillings.

spring tide *noun* a tidal pattern that occurs twice a month when the Moon is full and again when it is new. Compare **neap tide**.

springtime *or* **springtide** *noun* the season of spring.

springy *adj* (***-ier, -iest***) having the ability to readily spring back to the original shape when any pressure that has been exerted is released; bouncy; elastic; resilient. ▪ **springily** *adv.* ▪ **springiness** *noun.*

sprinkle *verb* **1** to scatter in, or cover with a scattering of, tiny drops or particles. **2** to arrange or distribute in a thin scattering: *The hillside was sprinkled with houses.* ▸ *noun* **1** an act of sprinkling. **2** a very small amount. [Anglo-Saxon *sprengan* to sprinkle]

sprinkler *noun* a person or device that sprinkles, esp one that sprinkles water over plants, a lawn, etc or one for extinguishing fires.

sprinkler system *noun* an arrangement of overhead water pipes and nozzles for extinguishing fires and which is automatically set off by any substantial increase in temperature.

sprinkling *noun* a small amount of something, esp when it is thinly scattered.

sprint *noun* **1** *athletics* a race at high speed over a short distance. **2** a burst of speed at a particular point, usu the end, of a long race, eg in athletics, cycling, horse-racing, etc. **3** a fast run. ▸ *verb, tr & intr* to run at full speed. [18c: from Norse *spretta* to jump up]

sprinter *noun* **1** an athlete, cyclist, etc who sprints. **2** a small bus or train that travels short distances.

sprit *noun* a small diagonal spar used to spread a sail. [Anglo-Saxon *spreot* pole]

sprite *noun* **1** *folklore* a playful fairy; an elf or imp. **2** a number of **pixels** that can be moved around a screen in a group, eg those representing a figure in a computer game. [14c: from French *esprit* spirit]

spritzer *noun* a drink of white wine and soda water. [1960s: from German *spritzen* to spray]

sprocket *noun* **1** any of a set of teeth on the rim of a driving wheel, eg fitting into the links of a chain or the holes on a strip of film. **2** (*also* **sprocket wheel**) a wheel with sprockets. [16c]

sprog *noun, slang* a child.

sprout *verb* **1** *tr & intr* to develop (a new growth, eg of leaves or hair). **2** (*also* **sprout up**) to grow or develop; to spring up: *Cybercafés are sprouting up everywhere.* ▸ *noun* **1** a new growth; a shoot or bud. **2** a shortened form of **Brussels sprout**. [Anglo-Saxon *sprutan*]

spruce[1] *noun* **1** an evergreen pyramid-shaped tree which has needle-like leaves. **2** the valuable white-grained timber of this tree. [17c: from *Pruce*, an obsolete name for Prussia]

spruce[2] *adj* neat and smart, esp in appearance and dress. ▸ *verb* (*usu* **spruce up**) to make oneself, someone or something neat and tidy. [16c]

sprung *adj* fitted with a spring or springs. ▸ *verb, past tense, past participle of* **spring**.

spry *adj* **1** lively; active. **2** light on one's feet; nimble. ▪ **spryly** *adv.* ▪ **spryness** *noun.*

spud *noun* **1** *informal* a potato. **2** a small, narrow spade.

spume *noun* foam or froth, esp on the sea. ▸ *verb, tr & intr* to foam or froth. ▪ **spumy** *adj.* [14c: from Latin *spuma*]

spun *adj* **1** formed or made by a spinning process: *spun gold.* **2** *in compounds*: *home-spun.* ▸ *verb, past tense, past participle of* **spin**.

spunk *noun, informal* courage; mettle. ▪ **spunky** *adj* (***-ier, -iest***). [18c]

spur *noun* **1** a device with a spiky metal wheel, fitted to the heel of a horse-rider's boot, which is used for pressing into the horse's side to make it go faster. **2** anything that urges or encourages greater effort or progress. **3** a spike or pointed part, eg on a cock's leg. **4** a ridge of high land that projects out into a valley. ▸ *verb* (***spurred, spurring***) **1** (*often* **spur sb** *or* **sth on**) to urge or encourage them or it: *The crowd spurred their team to victory.* **2** to press with spurs. **3** to hurry up. [Anglo-Saxon *spura*]

IDIOMS **earn** *or* **win one's spurs** *formerly* to prove oneself worthy of a knighthood through acts of bravery. **on the spur of the moment** suddenly; on an impulse.

spurge *noun* a plant which produces a bitter, often poisonous, milky juice that was formerly used as a laxative. [14c: from French *espurge*]

spurious *adj* false, counterfeit or untrue, esp when superficially seeming to be genuine. ▪ **spuriously** *adv.* ▪ **spuriousness** *noun.* [17c: from Latin *spurius* illegitimate, false]

spurn *verb* to reject (eg a person's love) scornfully. ▸ *noun* an act or instance of spurning. ▪ **spurned** *adj.* ▪ **spurning** *adj, noun.* [Anglo-Saxon *spurnan*]

spurt *or* **spirt** *verb, tr & intr* to flow out or make something flow out in a sudden sharp jet. ▸ *noun* **1** a jet of liquid that suddenly gushes out. **2** a short spell of intensified activity or increased speed: *Business tends to come in spurts.* [16c]

spurtle *or* **spirtle** *noun, Scot* a wooden stick used for stirring porridge, soup, etc. [16c]

sputter same as **splutter**. [16c: imitating the sound]

sputum *noun* (***sputa***) a mixture of saliva and mucus. Also called **phlegm**. [17c: Latin, meaning 'spit']

spy *noun* (***spies***) **1** someone who is employed by a government or organization to gather information about political enemies, competitors, etc. **2** someone who observes others in secret. ▸ *verb* (***spies, spied***) **1** *intr* to act or be employed as a spy. **2** *intr* (**spy on sb** *or* **sth**) to keep a secret watch on them or it. **3** to catch sight of someone or something; to spot. [13c: from French *espier*]

spyglass *noun* a small hand-held telescope.

spyhole *noun* a peephole.

spyware *noun, comput* software that gathers information about a computer user and transmits it to another user.

Sq. *or* **sqn** *abbrev* squadron.

sq *abbrev* **1** square. **2** (**Sq.**) in addresses: Square.

SQL *abbrev, comput* structured query language, a standard programming language used to access information from databases.

squab *noun* **1** a young unfledged bird, esp a pigeon. **2** a short fat person. ▸ *adj* **1** of a bird: newly hatched and unfledged. **2** of a person: short and fat. ▪ **squabby** *adj* (***-ier, -iest***). [17c]

squabble *verb, intr* to quarrel noisily, esp about something trivial. ▸ *noun* a noisy quarrel, esp a petty one. ▪ **squabbler** *noun*. [17c]

squad *noun* **1** a small group of soldiers, often twelve, who do drill formation together or who work together. **2** any group of people who work together in some specified field: *the drug squad*. **3** a set of players from which a sporting team is selected. [17c: from French *escouade*]

squaddy *or* **squaddie** *noun* (***-ies***) *slang* an ordinary soldier; a private.

squadron *noun* the principal unit of an air force. [16c: from Italian *squadrone* a group of soldiers in square formation]

squadron leader *noun* an officer in the Royal Air Force who is in charge of a squadron and who ranks below wing commander.

squalid *adj* **1** esp of places to live: disgustingly filthy and neglected. **2** morally repulsive; sordid: *squalid gossip*. See also **squalor**. [16c: from Latin *squalidus*]

squall¹ *noun, meteorol* a sudden or short-lived violent gust of wind, usu accompanied by rain or sleet. ▪ **squally** *adj*. [18c]

squall² *verb, tr & intr* to yell. [17c]

squalor *noun* the condition or quality of being disgustingly filthy. [16c: Latin, meaning 'dirtiness']

squander *verb* to use up (money, time, etc) wastefully. ▪ **squanderer** *noun*. [16c]

square *noun* **1** a two-dimensional figure with four sides of equal length and four right angles. **2** anything shaped like this. **3** an open space in a town, usu roughly square in shape, and the buildings that surround it. **4** an L-shaped or T-shaped instrument which is used for measuring angles, drawing straight lines, etc. **5** the number that is formed when a number is multiplied by itself. **6** *informal, old use* someone who has traditional or old-fashioned values, tastes, ideas, etc. ▸ *adj* **1** shaped like a square or, sometimes, like a cube. **2** used with a defining measurement to denote the area of something: *The area of a rectangle whose sides are 2 feet by 3 feet would be 6 square feet*. **3** angular; less rounded than normal: *a square jaw*. **4** measuring almost the same in breadth as in length or height. **5** fair; honest: *a square deal*. **6** of debts: completely paid off: *now we're square*. **7** set at right angles. **8** *informal, old use* having traditional or old-fashioned values, tastes, ideas, etc. ▸ *verb* **1** to make square in shape, esp to make right-angled. **2** to multiply (a number) by itself. **3** to pay off or settle (a debt). **4** to make the scores level in (a match). **5** to mark with a pattern of squares. ▸ *adv* **1** solidly and directly: *hit me square on the jaw*. **2** fairly; honestly. ▪ **squarely** *adv*. ▪ **squareness** *noun*. [13c: from French *esquarre* to square]

IDIOMS **all square** *informal* **1** equal. **2** not in debt; with each side owing nothing. **a square peg in a round hole** someone or something that cannot or does not perform their or its function very well; a misfit. **square with sth** to agree or correspond with it. **square sth with sb** to get their approval or permission for it.

PHRASAL VERBS **square up** to settle a bill, etc. **square up to sb** to prepare to fight them. **square up to sth** to prepare to tackle it, esp in a brave way.

square-bashing *noun, slang* military drill on a barracks square.

square bracket *noun* either of a pair of characters ([ ]), chiefly used in mathematical notation or to contain special information, eg comment by an editor of a text.

square dance *chiefly N Am, noun* any of various folk dances that are performed by couples in a square formation. ▸ *verb* (**square-dance**) *intr* to take part in this type of dance. ▪ **square-dancing** *noun*.

square deal *noun, informal* an arrangement or transaction that is considered to be fair and honest by all the parties involved.

square meal *noun* a good nourishing meal.

square number *noun, maths* an integer, such as 1, 4, 9, 16, 25, etc, that is the square of another integer.

square-rigged *adj* of a sailing ship: fitted with large square sails set at right angles to the length of the ship.

square root *noun, maths* a number or quantity that when multiplied by itself gives one particular number, eg 2 is the square root of 4, and 3 is the square root of 9.

squash¹ *verb* **1** to crush or flatten by pressing or squeezing. **2** *tr & intr* to force someone or something into a confined space: *managed to squash everything into one bag*. **3** to suppress or put down (eg a rebellion). **4** to force someone into silence with a cutting reply. ▸ *noun* **1** a concentrated fruit syrup, or a drink made by diluting this. **2** a crushed or crowded state. **3 a squash rackets; b squash tennis. 4 a** an act or the process of squashing something; **b** the sound of something being squashed. [17c: from French *esquasser* to crush]

squash² *noun, N Am, esp US* **1** any of various trailing plants widely cultivated for their marrow-like gourds. **2** the fruit of any of these plants which can be cooked and used as a vegetable. [17c: from Narragansett (a native N American language) *askutasquash*]

squash rackets *or* **squash racquets** *singular noun* a game for either two or four players who use small-headed rackets to hit a little rubber ball around an indoor court with three solid walls and a back wall that is usu glass. Often shortened to **squash**.

squash tennis *noun* a game similar to **squash rackets** but played with larger rackets and an inflated ball. Often shortened to **squash**.

squashy *adj* (**-*ier*, -*iest***) soft and easily squashed.

squat *verb* (***squatted, squatting***) *intr* **1** to take up, or be sitting in, a low position with the knees fully bent and the weight on the soles of the feet. **2** usu of homeless people: to occupy an empty building without legal right. ▸ *noun* **1** a squatting position. **2 a** a building or part of a building that is unlawfully occupied; **b** the unlawful occupation of such a building. ▸ *adj* short and broad or fat. [13c: from French *esquatir* to crush]

squatter *noun* someone who unlawfully occupies a building, usu an empty one.

squaw *noun, offensive* a Native American woman or wife. [17c: from Massachusett (a native N American language) *squa* woman]

squawk *noun* **1** a loud harsh screeching noise, esp one made by a bird, eg a parrot. **2** a loud protest or complaint. ▸ *verb, intr* **1** to make a loud harsh screeching noise. **2** to complain loudly. ▪ **squawker** *noun*. [19c: imitating the sound]

squeak *noun* **1** a short high-pitched cry or sound, like that made by a mouse or a rusty gate. **2** (*also* **narrow squeak**) a narrow escape; a victory or success achieved by the slimmest of margins. ▸ *verb* **1** *tr & intr* to utter a squeak or with a squeak. **2** *intr* (**squeak through sth**) to succeed in it by a very narrow margin. ▪ **squeaker** *noun*. [14c: imitating the sound]

squeaky *adj* (**-*ier*, -*iest***) characterized by squeaks or tending to squeak: *a squeaky voice*. ▪ **squeakily** *adv*. ▪ **squeakiness** *noun*.

squeaky clean *adj, informal* **1** spotlessly clean. **2** virtuous, above reproach or criticism, but often with an implication that this impression is superficial or for show. [1970s: orig used of newly-washed hair, which squeaks when it is being rinsed]

squeal *noun* **1** a long high-pitched noise, cry or yelp, like that of a pig, a child, etc. **2** a screeching sound: *the squeal of brakes*. ▸ *verb* **1** *tr & intr* to utter a squeal or with a squeal. **2** *intr, informal* to inform on someone or to report an incident to the police or other authority. **3** *intr* to complain or protest loudly. [14c: imitating the sound]

squealer *noun* **1** someone or something that squeals. **2** a bird or animal that squeals, esp a piglet. **3** *informal* an informer.

squeamish *adj* **1** slightly nauseous; easily made nauseous. **2** easily offended. ▪ **squeamishness** *noun*. [15c: from French *escoymous*]

squeegee *noun* a device with a rubber blade for scraping water off a surface, eg a window, windscreen, vinyl floor, etc. [Early 20c: derived from **squeeze**]

squeeze *verb* **1** to grasp or embrace tightly. **2** to press forcefully, esp from at least two sides. **3** to press or crush so as to extract (liquid, juice, toothpaste, etc). **4** to press gently, esp as an indication of affection, reassurance, etc: *squeezed his hand*. **5** *tr & intr* to force or be forced into or through a confined space: *Ten of us squeezed into a phone box*. **6** to put under financial pressure: *squeezed his elderly mother for money*. **7** (*usu* **squeeze sth out of sb**) to extract it, esp by exerting some form of pressure: *They eventually squeezed a confession out of him*. ▸ *noun* **1** an act of squeezing. **2** a crowded or crushed state. **3** an amount (of fruit juice, etc) that is obtained by squeezing: *a squeeze of lemon*. **4** a restriction, esp on spending or borrowing money. [Anglo-Saxon *cwysan* to press]

IDIOMS **put the squeeze on sb** *informal* to pressurize them into paying something.

squeeze-box *noun, informal* an accordion or concertina.

squeezy *adj* of a bottle, container, etc: soft and flexible so that its contents can be squeezed out.

squelch *noun* a loud gurgling or sucking sound made by contact with a thick sticky substance, eg wet mud. ▸ *verb, intr* **1** to walk through wet ground or with water in one's shoes and so make this sound. **2** to make this sound. ▪ **squelchy** *adj* (**-*ier*, -*iest***). [17c: imitating the sound]

squib *noun* **1** a small firework that jumps around on the ground before exploding. **2** a satirical criticism or attack; a lampoon. [16c]

squid *noun* (***squid*** *or* ***squids***) **1** a marine mollusc related to the octopus and cuttlefish, which has a torpedo-shaped body, eight sucker-bearing arms and two longer tentacles. **2** the flesh of this animal used as food. [17c]

squidge *verb* to squash; to squeeze together; to squelch.

squidgy *adj* (**-*ier*, -*iest***) soft, pliant and sometimes soggy.

squiffy *adj* (**-*ier*, -*iest***) *old use* slightly drunk; tipsy.

squiggle *noun* a wavy scribbled line. ▪ **squiggly** *adj* (**-*ier*, -*iest***). [Early 19c]

squillion *noun* (***squillions*** or after a number ***squillion***) *informal* a very large number. [1980s: an arbitrary formation, modelled on **million** and **billion**]

squint *noun* **1** *non-technical* the condition of having one or both eyes set slightly off-centre, preventing parallel vision. Also called **strabismus**. **2** *informal* a quick look; a peep. ▸ *verb, intr* **1** to be affected by a squint. **2** to look with eyes half-closed; to peer. ▸ *adj* **1** having a squint. **2** *informal* not being properly straight or centred. ▸ *adv, informal* in a way or manner that is not properly straight or centred: *hung the picture squint*. ▪ **squinting** *noun, adj*. [16c]

squint-eyed *adj* affected by **strabismus**.

squire *noun* **1** *hist* in England and Ireland: an owner of a large area of rural land, esp the chief landowner in a district. **2** *feudalism* a young man of good family who ranked next to a knight and who would attend upon him. **3** *informal* a term of address esp used between men. [13c: see **esquire**]

squirm *verb, intr* **1** to wriggle along. **2** to feel or show embarrassment, shame, nervousness, etc often with slight wriggling movements of the body. ▸ *noun* a writhing or wriggling movement. ▪ **squirmy** *adj*. [17c]

squirrel *noun* a rodent that has a bushy tail, beady eyes and tufty ears, and usu lives in trees. ▸ *verb* (***squirrelled, squirrelling*** *or* (*chiefly US*) ***squirreled, squirreling***) (*often* **squirrel away** *or* **squirrel up**) to store or put away something for future use. [14c: from Greek *skiouros*]

squirt *verb* **1 a** to shoot (a liquid, etc) out in a narrow jet; **b** *intr* of a liquid, etc: to shoot out in a narrow jet: *Paint squirted everywhere*. **2** *intr* to press the nozzle, trigger, etc of a container, etc so that liquid comes shooting out of it. **3** to cover something with a liquid: *squirted the table with polish.* ▸ *noun* **1 a** an act or instance of squirting; **b** an amount of liquid squirted. **2** *informal* a small, insignificant or despicable person, esp one who behaves arrogantly. [15c: imitating the sound]

squish *noun* a gentle splashing or squelching sound. ▸ *verb* **1** *intr* to make this sound; to move with this sound. **2** to crush (eg an insect, etc). ▪ **squishy** *adj* (***-ier, -iest***). [17c: imitating the sound]

squit *noun, informal* **1** an insignificant person. **2** nonsense. **3** (**the squits**) *informal* diarrhoea.

Sr[1] *abbrev* **1** used after a name: Senior. **2** Señor. **3** Sir. **4** Sister.

Sr[2] *symbol, chem* strontium.

sr *symbol, geom* steradian.

SS *abbrev Schutzstaffel,* Hitler's bodyguard of elite police which later formed military units in Nazi Germany.

St *abbrev* **1** Saint. For entries using the abbrev *St*, see under **saint**. **2** in addresses: Street.

st *abbrev* stone (the imperial unit of weight).

stab *verb* (***stabbed, stabbing***) **1 a** to wound or pierce with a sharp or pointed instrument or weapon; **b** of a sharp instrument, etc: to wound or pierce; **c** to push (a sharp implement) into (someone or something). **2** (*often* **stab at sth**) to make a quick thrusting movement with something sharp at something. ▸ *noun* **1** an act of stabbing. **2** a stabbing sensation: *felt a sudden stab of pain.* ▪ **stabber** *noun.* [14c]

IDIOMS **have** *or* **make a stab at sth** to try to do it; to try to answer: *I didn't really know the answer, but at least I made a stab at it.* **stab in the back** a devious or unscrupulous act of betrayal. **stab sb in the back** to betray them in a devious manner. **stab in the dark** an uninformed guess.

stabbing *noun* an act or the action or process of using a sharp implement to cut, wound, etc. ▸ *adj* **1** of a pain: sharp and sudden. **2** of a remark, etc: hurtful.

stability *noun* the state or quality of being stable. [15c: from Latin *stabilitas*]

stabilize *or* **-ise** *verb, tr & intr* to make or become stable or more stable. ▪ **stabilization** *noun.*

stabilizer *or* **-iser** *noun* **1** one or more aerofoils used to give stability to an aircraft. **2** a device used to reduce rolling and pitching of a ship. **3** either of the two small wheels fitted to the back of a child's bicycle to give it added stability, and which can be removed after the child has mastered riding it. **4** a substance that encourages food ingredients that would not otherwise mix well to remain together, eg as used in salad cream to prevent the separation of oil droplets.

stable[1] *adj* **1** firmly balanced or fixed; not likely to wobble or fall over. **2** firmly established; not likely to be abolished, overthrown or destroyed: *a stable government* • *a stable relationship.* **3 a** regular or constant; not erratic or changing; under control: *The patient's condition is stable*; **b** of someone or their disposition, judgement, etc: not fickle, moody, impulsive, etc. [13c: from Latin *stabilis*]

stable[2] *noun* **1** a building where horses are kept. **2** a place where horses are bred and trained. **3** *informal* a number of people or things with a common background or origin, eg a number of athletes trained by the same coach, a number of recording artistes whose work is distributed by the same record label, etc. ▸ *verb* to put (a horse) into or back into its stable. ▪ **stabling** *noun.* [14c: from Latin *stabulum* standing room]

staccato /stəˈkɑːtoʊ/ *music, adv* in a short, abrupt manner. ▸ *adj* short and abrupt. [18c: Italian]

stack *noun* **1** a large pile. **2** a large pile of hay or straw. **3** (*sometimes* **stacks**) *informal* a large amount: *stacks of money.* **4** a large industrial chimney. **5** a hi-fi system where the individual components, such as the turntable, CD player, cassette deck, amplifier, etc are placed on top of each other. **6** *chiefly N Am* an exhaust pipe on a truck that sticks up behind the driver's cab, rather than coming out at the back of the vehicle. ▸ *verb* **1** (*also* **stack things up**) to arrange them in a stack or stacks. **2** to arrange (circumstances, etc) to favour or disadvantage a particular person. **3** to arrange (aircraft that are waiting to land) into a queue in which each circles the airport at a different altitude. **4** to fill something: *stacked the fridge with goodies.* ▪ **stacker** *noun.* [14c: from Norse *stakkr* haystack]

stacked *adj* **1** gathered into a pile. **2** filled or brimming (with a large amount or a large quantity). **3** *comput* of an operation or task: put into a queue of similar tasks to wait until the computer is free to process it: *a backlog of stacked printing jobs.* **4** of cards, odds, etc: weighted or biased (in a specified direction): *The odds were stacked in our favour.*

stadium *noun* (***stadiums*** *or* ***stadia***) a large sports arena in which the spectators' seats are arranged in rising tiers. [19c: from Greek *stadion*]

staff *noun* (*pl* in senses 1–3 ***staffs***, in senses 4–6 ***staffs*** *or* ***staves***) **1 a** the total number of employees working in an organization; **b** the employees working for or assisting a manager. **2** the teachers, lecturers, etc of a school, college, university, etc as distinct from the students. **3** *military* the officers assisting a senior commander. *as adj*: *staff sergeant.* **4** any stick or rod, esp one that is carried in the hand as a sign of authority, dignity, etc. **5** (*also* **flagstaff**) a pole that a flag is hung from. **6** *music* a set of lines and spaces on which music is written. Also called **stave**. ▸ *verb* to provide (an establishment) with staff. [Anglo-Saxon *staf*]

---

staff

You can use either a singular or plural verb with a collective noun such as **staff**. If you are thinking of the staff as a single unit, use a singular verb:

The staff is 60 per cent female.

If you are thinking of the staff as a number of individuals, use a plural verb:

The staff are very helpful.

---

staff nurse *noun* a qualified nurse of the rank below **sister**.

Staffs *abbrev, English county* Staffordshire.

staff sergeant *noun, military* the senior sergeant in an army company. Often shortened to **staff**.

stag *noun* an adult male deer, esp a red deer. [Anglo-Saxon *stagga*]

stage *noun* **1** a platform on which a performance takes place, esp one in a theatre. **2** any raised area or platform. **3** the scene of a specified event: *a battle stage.* **4** any of several distinct and successive periods: *the planning stage*. **5** (**the stage**) the theatre as a profession or art form. **6 a** a part of a journey or route: *The last stage of the trip entails a short bus ride*; **b** *Brit* a major stop on a bus route, esp one that involves a change in ticket prices. Also called **fare stage**. **7** *informal* a stagecoach. ▸ *verb* **1** to present a performance of (a play). **2** to organize and put on something or set it in motion: *It was a huge undertaking to stage the festival.* **3** to prearrange something to happen in a particular way; to engineer: *tried to stage her colleague's downfall.* [13c: from French *estage* storey or tier]

IDIOMS **hold the stage** to contrive to be the centre of attention. **in** *or* **by stages** gradually. **take the stage 1** to begin to act, perform, etc. **2** to come forward to speak to an assembled audience.

stagecoach *noun, formerly* a large horse-drawn coach carrying passengers and mail on a regular fixed route.

stage door *noun* the back or side entrance to a theatre.

stage fright *noun* nervousness felt by an actor or other performer or speaker when about to appear in front of an audience, esp for the first time.

stagehand *noun* someone who is responsible for moving scenery and props in a theatre.

stage-manage *verb* **1** to be the stage manager of (a play). **2** to prearrange for something to happen in a certain way, in order to create a particular effect. ▪ **stage-management** *noun*. ▪ **stage manager** *noun*.

stage name *noun* a name assumed by an actor, performer, etc.

stage-struck *adj* filled with awe of the theatre, esp in having an overwhelming desire to become an actor.

stage whisper *noun* **1** an actor's loud whisper that is intended to be heard by the audience. **2** any loud whisper that is intended to be heard by people other than the person addressed.

stagey see **stagy**

stagflation *noun* inflation in an economy without the expected growth in employment or demand for goods. [1960s: a blend of *stagnation* + *inflation*]

stagger *verb* **1** *intr* to walk or move unsteadily. **2** *informal* to cause extreme shock or surprise to someone. **3** to arrange (a series of things) so that they take place or begin at different times. ▸ *noun* the action or an act of staggering. [16c: from Norse *stakra* to push]

staggering *adj* amazing; shockingly surprising: *a staggering response to the appeal.* ▪ **staggeringly** *adv*.

staggers *singular noun* **1** a disease of the brain in horses and cattle that causes them to stagger. **2** (*often* **the staggers**) giddiness.

staging *noun* scaffolding, esp the horizontal planks used for walking on; any temporary platform.

stagnant *adj* **1** of water: not flowing; dirty and foul-smelling because of a lack of movement. **2** not moving or developing; dull and inactive: *a stagnant market.* ▪ **stagnance** *or* **stagnancy** *noun*. ▪ **stagnantly** *adv*. [17c: from Latin *stagnum* pond]

stagnate *verb, intr* to be or become stagnant. ▪ **stagnation** *noun*. [17c: from Latin *stagnare* to stagnate]

stag night *or* **stag party** *noun* a night out for men only, esp one held to celebrate the end of bachelorhood of a man about to get married. Compare **hen party**.

stagy *or* **stagey** *adj*, *N Am, esp US* (**-ier, -iest**) theatrical; artificial or affectedly pretentious.

staid *adj* serious or sober in character or manner, esp to the point of being dull. ▪ **staidness** *noun*. [16c: an obsolete past participle of **stay**[1]]

stain *verb* **1** to make or become marked or discoloured, often permanently. **2** to change the colour of (eg wood) by applying a liquid chemical. **3** to tarnish or become tarnished: *The affair stained his previously good name.* ▸ *noun* **1** a mark or discoloration. **2** a liquid chemical applied (eg to wood) to bring about a change of colour. **3** a cause of shame or dishonour: *a stain on his reputation.* [14c: from English *steynen* to paint]

stained glass *noun* decorative glass that has been coloured by a chemical process, and which is used esp in mosaics in church windows.

stainless steel *noun* a type of steel that contains a high percentage of chromium, making it resistant to rusting.

stair *noun* **1** any of a set of indoor steps connecting the floors of a building. **2** (*also* **stairs**) a set of these. [Anglo-Saxon *stæger*]

staircase *noun* a set of stairs, often including the stairwell.

stairway *noun* a way into a building or part of a building that involves going up a staircase.

stairwell *noun* **1** the vertical shaft containing a staircase. **2** the floor area at the foot of a flight of stairs.

stake[1] *noun* **1** a stick or post, usu with one pointed end, that is knocked into the ground as a support, eg for a young tree or a fence. **2** (**the stake**) *formerly* a post that is set into materials for a bonfire and which a person is tied to before being burned alive as a punishment. ▸ *verb* to support or fasten to the ground with a stake. [Anglo-Saxon *staca*]

IDIOMS **stake a claim** to assert or establish a right or ownership, esp to a piece of land.

PHRASAL VERBS **stake sth out 1** to mark the boundary of (a piece of land) with stakes, esp as a way of declaring ownership of it. **2** to keep (a building, etc) under surveillance. See also **stakeout**.

stake[2] *noun* **1** a sum of money risked in betting. **2** an interest, esp a financial one: *have a stake in the project's success.* **3** (**stakes**) **a** a prize, esp in horse racing, where the horses' owners put up the money that is to be won; **b** a race of this kind; **c** a specified area or sphere, esp one where there is pressure to appear to succeed: *It all depends on how he fares in the promotion stakes.* ▸ *verb* **1** to risk, esp as a bet. **2** to support, esp financially: *staked the enterprise to the tune of £100 000.* [16c]

IDIOMS **at stake** at risk; in danger.

stakeholder *noun* **1** someone who holds the wager when a number of people place a bet together. **2** someone who has an interest or a **stake**[2] (*noun* sense 2) in something, especially an enterprise, business, etc. *as adj*: *stakeholder economy.* ▪ **stakeholding** *noun*.

stakeout *noun, informal* **1** an act or period of surveillance of a person, building, etc, usu carried out by the police or a private detective. **2** the house, etc where this kind of surveillance takes place.

stalactite *noun* an icicle-like mass of calcium carbonate that hangs from the roof of a cave, etc, and which is formed by water continuously dripping through and partially dissolving limestone rock. [17c: from Greek *stalaktos* a dripping]

stalagmite *noun* a spiky mass of calcium carbonate that sticks up from the floor of a cave, etc, and which is formed by water containing limestone that drips from a stalactite. [17c: from Greek *stalagma* a drop]

stale *adj* **1** of food: past its best because it has been kept too long; not fresh. **2** of air: not fresh; musty. **3** of words, phrases, ideas, etc: overused and no longer interesting or original. **4** of someone: lacking in energy because of overfamiliarity, boredom, etc with the job in hand. **5** of news, gossip, etc: out-of-date. [14c]

stalemate *noun* **1** *chess* a position where either player cannot make a move without putting their king in check and which results in a draw. **2** a position in any contest or dispute where no progress can be made and no winner can emerge; a deadlock: *The staff and management had reached a stalemate over pay and conditions.* [18c]

stalk[1] *noun* **1** *botany* **a** the main stem of a plant; **b** a stem that attaches a leaf, flower or fruit to the plant. **2** any slender connecting part. [14c]

stalk[2] *verb* **1** to hunt, follow, or approach stealthily. **2** *intr* to walk or stride stiffly, proudly, disdainfully, etc: *stalked out of the meeting*. **3** to pervade, penetrate or spread over (a place): *Fear stalked the neighbourhood.* ▸ *noun* **1** an act or the process of stalking. **2** a striding way of walking. ▪ **stalking** *noun, adj*. [Anglo-Saxon *bistealcian* to move stealthily]

stalker *noun* **1** someone who stalks, esp game. **2** someone who follows another person, often with a sinister purpose.

stalking-horse *noun* a person or thing that is used to conceal real intentions, esp a planned attack; a pretext.

stall[1] *noun* **1** a compartment in a cowshed, stable, etc for housing a single animal. **2** a stand, often with a canopy, set up temporarily in a marketplace, bazaar, fête, etc for the selling of goods. **3** (**stalls**) the seats on the ground floor of a theatre or cinema. ▸ *verb* **1** *tr & intr* **a** of a motor vehicle or its engine: to cut out or make it cut out unintentionally; **b** to come, bring or be brought to a standstill: *Plans for the expansion had stalled.* **2** *chiefly US* to stick or to make something stick in snow, mud, etc. [Anglo-Saxon *steall* a standing place]

stall[2] *verb* **1** to delay. **2** *intr* to do something in order to delay something else; to be evasive: *Quit stalling and answer the question.* ▸ *noun* an act of stalling; a delaying tactic. [16c: from obsolete *stale*, a decoy]

IDIOMS **stall for time** to hold off doing something in the hope that things will change in one's favour.

stallion *noun* an uncastrated adult male horse, esp one kept for breeding. [14c: from French *estalon* stallion]

stalwart /ˈstɔːlwət/ *adj* **1** strong and sturdy. **2** unwavering in commitment and support; reliable. ▸ *noun* a long-standing and committed supporter, esp a political one: *the stalwarts of the right*. [Anglo-Saxon *stælwierthe* serviceable]

stamen *noun* (***stamens*** *or* ***stamina*** /ˈstamɪnə/) *botany* in flowering plants: the male reproductive structure where the pollen grains are produced. [17c: Latin, meaning 'warp' or 'thread']

stamina *noun* energy and staying power, esp of the kind that is needed to tackle and withstand prolonged exertion. [18: the Latin pl of **stamen**]

stammer *verb, tr & intr* to speak or say something in a faltering or hesitant way, often by repeating words or parts of words, usu because of heightened emotion or a pathological disorder that affects the speech organs or the nervous system. ▸ *noun* a speech disorder that is characterized by this kind of faltering or hesitancy. ▪ **stammerer** *noun*. ▪ **stammering** *adj, noun*. [Anglo-Saxon *stamerian*]

stamp *verb* **1** *tr & intr* to bring (the foot) down with force: *stamped her feet in rage.* **2** *intr* to walk with a heavy tread. **3** **a** to imprint or impress (a mark or design); **b** to imprint or impress something with a mark or design, esp to show it has official approval or that the appropriate duty, fee, etc has been paid. **4** to fix or mark deeply: *The event was stamped on his memory.* **5** to fix a postage or other stamp on something. ▸ *noun* **1** **a** a small piece of gummed paper bearing an official mark and indicating that a tax or fee has been paid, esp a **postage stamp**; **b** a similar piece of gummed paper that is given away free, eg by petrol stations, and which can be collected until the requisite number of them, when they can be exchanged for a gift. **2** **a** a device for stamping a mark or design; **b** the mark or design that is stamped on something. **3** a characteristic mark or sign: *The crime bears the stamp of a professional.* **4** an act or the process of stamping with the foot. ▪ **stamper** *noun*. ▪ **stamping** *adj, noun*. [Anglo-Saxon *stampian*]

IDIOMS **stamp of approval** an endorsement, either in physical or figurative terms.

PHRASAL VERBS **stamp sth out 1** to put out (a fire) by stamping on it. **2** to put an end to (an activity or practice, esp an illicit one): *tried to stamp out the use of drugs.* **3** to eradicate (a disease): *Smallpox has now been stamped out.*

stamp collecting *noun* an informal term for **philately**.

stamp duty *or* **stamp tax** *noun* a tax that is incurred when certain legal documents, eg those transferring ownership of property, are drawn up.

stampede *noun* **1** a sudden dash made by a group of startled animals, esp when they all go charging off in the same direction. **2** an excited or hysterical rush by a crowd of people. ▸ *verb, tr & intr* to rush or make (animals or people) rush in a herd or crowd. [19c: from Spanish *estampida* a stamping]

stamping-ground *noun* someone's usual or favourite haunt or meeting place. [18c: orig said of the place a wild animal habitually returns to]

stance *noun* **1** point of view; a specified attitude towards something. **2** **a** the position that the body of a person or an animal takes up: *She has a very upright stance*; **b** a position or manner of standing, eg when preparing to play a stroke in sport. [19c: from Latin *stare* to stand]

stanch see **staunch[2]**

stanchion /ˈstanʃən/ *noun* an upright beam or pole that functions as a support. [14c: from French *estanchon*]

stand *verb* (***stood***) **1** *intr* to be in, remain in or move into an upright position supported by the legs or a base. **2** *tr & intr* to place or situate, or be placed or situated in a specified position: *stood the vase on the table.* **3** *intr* to be a specified height: *The tower stands 300 feet tall.* **4** to tolerate or put up with someone or something: *How can you stand that awful noise?* **5** *intr* to be in a specified state or condition: *I stand corrected.* **6** *intr* to be in a position (to do something): *We stand to make a lot of money.* **7** *intr* to continue to apply or be valid: *The decision stands.* **8** to withstand or survive something: *stood the test of time.* ▸ *noun* **1** a base on which something sits or is supported. **2** a stall that goods or services for sale are displayed on. **3 a** a structure at a sports ground, etc which has sitting or standing accommodation for spectators; **b** (**the stand**) a witness box. **4** a rack, frame, etc where coats, hats, umbrellas, etc may be hung. **5** an opinion, attitude or course of action that is adopted resolutely: *took a stand against animal testing.* **6** *cricket* a partnership between batsmen, expressed in terms of the time it lasts or the number of runs scored. **7** an act of resisting attack. [Anglo-Saxon *standan*]

IDIOMS **make a stand** to adopt a determined attitude (against or towards something): *made a stand for higher pay.* **stand at** *or* **to attention** to assume a very erect posture. **stand guard** to keep a lookout for danger, an enemy, etc. **stand on one's own feet** *or* **own two feet** to be or become independent. **stand one's ground** to maintain a position resolutely; to refuse to give in. **stand to reason** to be the logical or obvious assumption to make. **stand trial** to go through the usual legal processes in order to establish guilt or innocence. **take the stand** to enter a witness box and give evidence.

PHRASAL VERBS **stand by 1** to be in a state of readiness to act. **2** to look on without taking the required or expected action: *just stood by and never offered to help.* See also **stand-by**. **stand by sb** to give them loyalty or support, esp when they are in difficulty. **stand down** to resign, esp in favour of someone else. **stand for sth 1** to be in favour of promoting it. **2** of a symbol, letter, device, etc: to represent, mean or signify something: *The red ribbon stands for AIDS awareness.* **3** to tolerate or allow it. **stand in for sb** to act as a substitute for them. See also **stand-in**. **stand off** to keep at a distance. **stand out** to be noticeable or prominent. **stand to** to be ready (to start work, etc). **stand up 1** to assume a standing position. **2** to prove to be valid on examination: *an argument that will stand up in court.* See also **stand-up**. **stand sb up** *informal* to fail to keep an appointment or date with them. **stand up for sb 1** to back them in a dispute, argument, etc. **2** *chiefly US* to act as best man or be a witness at their wedding: *Andy asked Bobby if he would stand up for him.* **stand up for sth** to support it. **stand up to sb** to face or resist them. **stand up to sth** to withstand it (eg hard wear or criticism).

stand-alone *adj* esp of a computer: able to work independently of a network or other system.

standard *noun* **1** an established or accepted model: *Size 14 is the standard for British women.* **2** something that functions as a model of excellence for other similar things to be compared to, measured or judged against: *the standard by which all other dictionaries will be measured.* **3** (*often* **standards**) **a** a degree or level of excellence, value, quality, etc: *Standards of living have fallen;* **b** a principle, eg of morality, integrity, etc: *moral standards.* **4** a flag or other emblem, esp one carried on a pole: *the royal standard.* See also **standard-bearer**. **5** an upright pole or support. **6** an authorized model of a unit of measurement or weight. ▸ *adj* **1** having features that are generally accepted as normal or expected; typical; average; unexceptional: *A month's notice is standard practice.* **2** accepted as supremely authoritative: *the standard text of Shakespeare.* **3** of language: accepted as correct by educated native speakers. [12c: from French *estandart* a gathering place for soldiers]

standard-bearer *noun* **1** someone who carries a flag. **2** the leader of a movement or cause.

Standard English *noun* the variety of English thought of as being spoken by educated people, generally accepted as the correct form and understood by most people.

standard gauge *noun* a railway system where the tracks are 4ft 8½ins (1.435m) apart.

Standard grade *noun, Scot* **1** an examination taken in the fourth year of secondary school and designed to test pupils' ability to apply what they have been taught in practical ways as well as having a written component. **2 a** a subject that is taken at this level; **b** a pass in a subject at this level.

standardize *or* **-ise** *verb* to make (all the examples of something) conform in size, shape, etc. ▪ **standardization** *noun.*

standard lamp *noun* a lamp at the top of a pole which has a base that sits on the floor.

stand-by *noun* (***stand-by's*** *or* ***stand-bys***) **1 a** a state of readiness to act, eg in an emergency; **b** a person or thing that takes on this kind of role. **2 a** of air travel: a system of allocating spare seats to passengers who do not have reservations, after all the booked seats have been taken; **b** a ticket that has been allocated in this way.

IDIOMS **on stand-by** ready and prepared to do something if necessary: *The emergency team were on stand-by.*

stand-in *noun* a deputy or substitute.

standing *noun* **1** position, status, or reputation. **2** the length of time something has been in existence, someone has been doing something, etc: *a professor of long standing.* ▸ *adj* **1** done, taken, etc in or from a standing position: *a standing ovation.* **2** permanent; regularly used: *a standing order.*

standing joke *noun* a subject that causes hilarity, derision or jeering whenever it is mentioned.

standing order *noun* **1** *finance* an instruction from an account-holder to a bank to make fixed payments from the account to a third party at regular intervals. Compare **direct debit**. **2** (**standing orders**) regulations that govern the procedures that a legislative assembly adopts.

standing wave *noun, physics* a wave that results from interference between waves of the same wavelength that are travelling in opposite directions. Also called **stationary wave**.

stand-off *noun* a stalemate or the condition of being in stalemate.

stand-offish *adj* unfriendly or aloof.

standpipe *noun* a vertical pipe leading from a water supply, esp one that provides an emergency supply in the street when household water is cut off.

standpoint *noun* a point of view.

standstill *noun* a complete stop, with no progress being made at all.

stand-up *adj* **1** in a standing position. **2** of a verbal fight as well as a physical one: earnest; passionate; fervent. **3** of a comedian: performing solo in front of a live audience.

stank *past tense of* **stink**

stanza *noun* a verse in poetry. [16c: Italian, meaning 'stopping place']

stapes /ˈsteɪpiːz/ *noun* (***stapes***) *anatomy* a small stirrup-shaped bone in the middle ear. Also called **stirrup bone**. [17c: Latin, meaning 'stirrup']

staphylococcus /stafɪloʊˈkɒkəs/ *noun* (***staphylococci*** /-ˈkɒksaɪ/) *biol* any of several bacteria that form in clusters on the skin and mucous membranes, some of which can cause boils and abscesses. [19c: from Greek *staphyle* bunch of grapes + *kokkos* a grain or berry, referring to their shape]

staple[1] *noun* a squared-off U-shaped wire fastener for holding sheets of paper together and which is forced through the paper from a special device that has several of these loaded into it. ▸ *verb* to fasten or attach with a staple or staples. [Anglo-Saxon *stapol* post or support]

staple[2] *adj* **1** principal; main: *staple foods*. **2** of a traded article, industry, etc of a specified individual, company, region, country, etc: rated and established as being of prime economic importance: *Shipbuilding was once one of our staple industries*. ▸ *noun* **1** an economically important food, product, ingredient, industry, export, etc. **2** a major constituent of a particular community's diet. [15c: from Dutch *stapel* shop or warehouse]

staple gun *noun* a hand-held tool that fires staples into a surface.

stapler *noun* a device for driving staples through paper.

star *noun* **1 a** any celestial body that can be seen in a clear night sky as a twinkling white light, which consists of a sphere of gaseous material which generates heat and light energy by means of nuclear fusion reactions deep within its interior; **b** used more loosely to refer to: any planet, comet or meteor, as well as any of these bodies. **2** a representation of such a body in the form of a figure with five or more radiating points, often used as a symbol of rank or excellence, as an award, etc. **3 a** a celebrity, esp in the world of entertainment or sport: *a film star*; **b** someone or something that is distinguished or thought well of in a specified field: *Her brilliant paper made her the star of the conference*. **4** (**the stars**) **a** the planets regarded as an influence on people's fortunes: *believed his fate was in the stars*; **b** a horoscope: *According to my stars, I'm going to win the Lottery*. **5** an asterisk. ▸ *verb* (***starred, starring***) **1** *tr & intr* to feature someone as a principal performer or to appear in (a film, TV programme, theatre production, etc) as a principal performer. **2** to decorate something with stars. **3** to asterisk. ▪ **starless** *adj*. [Anglo-Saxon *steorra*]

IDIOMS **see stars** to see spots of light before one's eyes, esp as a result of a heavy blow to the head.

starboard *noun* the right side of a ship or aircraft as you look towards the front of it. ▸ *adj, adv* relating to, on or towards the right side. Compare **port[2]**. [Anglo-Saxon *steorbord* steering board]

starch *noun* **1 a** *biochem* a carbohydrate that occurs in all green plants, where it serves as an energy store; **b** the fine white powder form of this substance that is extracted from potatoes and cereals and which is widely used in the food industry; **c** a preparation of this substance used to stiffen fabrics and to make paper. **2** stiffness of manner; over-formality. ▸ *verb* to stiffen with starch. ▪ **starched** *adj*. ▪ **starcher** *noun*. [Anglo-Saxon *stercan* to stiffen]

starchy *adj* (***-ier, -iest***) **1** like or containing starch. **2** of someone's manner, etc: over-formal; solemn and prudish. ▪ **starchily** *adv*. ▪ **starchiness** *noun*.

star-crossed *adj, literary* ill-fated; doomed never to be happy because the stars are in inauspicious positions.

stardom *noun* the state of being a celebrity.

stardust *noun* an imaginary dust that blinds someone's eyes to reality and fills their mind with romantic illusions.

stare *verb, intr* of someone or their eyes: to look with a fixed gaze. ▸ *noun* **1** an act of staring. **2** a fixed gaze. [Anglo-Saxon *starian*]

IDIOMS **be staring sb in the face** of a solution, etc: to be readily apparent, but unnoticed.

PHRASAL VERBS **stare sb out** *or* **down** to stare more fixedly at (someone staring back), causing them to look away.

starfish *noun* the popular name for a star-shaped marine invertebrate animal.

star fruit *noun* a smooth-skinned yellow fruit, star-shaped in cross-section, which is produced by the **carambola**, a SE Asian tree.

stargaze *verb, intr* **1** to study the stars. **2** *informal* to daydream. ▪ **stargazer** *noun*. ▪ **stargazing** *noun, adj*.

stark *adj* **1** barren or severely bare; harsh or simple: a *stark landscape*. **2** plain; unembellished: *the stark truth*. **3** utter; downright: *an act of stark stupidity*. ▸ *adv* utterly; completely: *stark staring bonkers*. [Anglo-Saxon *stearc* hard or strong]

starkers *adj, informal* stark-naked.

stark-naked *adj* without any clothes on at all. [Anglo-Saxon *steort* tail + *nacod* naked]

starlet *noun* a young film actress, esp one who is thought to have the potential to become a star of the future.

starlight *noun* the light from the stars.

starling *noun* a small common gregarious songbird which has dark glossy speckled feathers and a short tail. [Anglo-Saxon *stærling*]

starlit *adj* lit by the stars.

starry *adj* (***-ier, -iest***) **1** relating to or like a star or the stars; filled or decorated with stars. **2** shining brightly.

starry-eyed *adj* naively idealistic or optimistic.

starship *noun* in science fiction: a vehicle for interstellar travel.

star-spangled *adj* decorated with stars.

star-studded *adj* **1** *informal* of the cast of a film, theatre production, etc: featuring many well-known performers. **2** covered with stars.

start *verb* **1** *tr & intr* to begin; to bring or come into being. **2** *intr* (**start with sth**) to have it at the beginning: *The book starts with a gruesome murder*. **3** *tr & intr* to set or be set in motion, or put or be put into a working state: *She started the car.* **4** to establish or set up: *started his own business.* **5** to initiate or get going; to cause or set off: *Harry started the quarrel.* **6** *intr* to begin a journey: *started for home at midday.* **7** *intr* to flinch or shrink back suddenly and sharply, eg in fear or surprise. **8** *intr, informal* to begin to behave in an annoying way, eg by picking a quarrel, making a noise, fighting, raising a disagreeable subject, etc: *Come on, don't start.* ▸ *noun* **1** the first or early part. **2** a beginning, origin or cause. **3** the time or place at which something starts: *made an early start.* **4** an advantage given or held at the beginning of a race or other contest: *gave her a two metre start.* **5** sudden flinching or shrinking back. [Anglo-Saxon *styrten*]

IDIOMS **for a start** as an initial consideration; in the first place.

PHRASAL VERBS **start off** *or* **out 1** to be initially: *The film starts off in black and white.* **2** to begin a journey, etc. **start sth off 1** to be the cause of it: *Anger over the tax started the riots off.* **2** to begin it. **start on sb** to become suddenly and violently hostile towards them; to turn on them. **start up** *or* **start sth up 1** of a car, engine, etc: to run or get it running. **2** to establish it; to put it into action: *The mums started up their own playgroup.*

starter *noun* **1** an official who gives the signal for a race to begin. **2** any of the competitors, horses, greyhounds, etc that assemble for the start of a race. **3** (*also* **starter motor**) an electric motor that is used to start the engine of a motor vehicle. **4** the first course of a meal.

IDIOMS **for starters** *informal* in the first place; for a start.

startle *verb, tr & intr* to be or cause someone or something to be slightly shocked or surprised, often with an attendant jump or twitch. ▪ **startled** *adj.* ▪ **startling** *adj.* [Anglo-Saxon *steartlian* to stumble or struggle]

starve *verb* **1** *tr & intr* **a** to die or cause someone or something to die because of a long-term lack of food; **b** to suffer or cause someone or something to suffer because of a long-term lack of food. **2** *intr, informal* to be very hungry. **3** to deprive someone or something of something that is vital: *starved the project of funds.* ▪ **starvation** *noun.* ▪ **starving** *adj, noun.* [Anglo-Saxon *steorfan* to die]

starveling *noun* someone or something that looks weak and undernourished. ▸ *adj* less than adequate: *starveling wages.*

stash *slang, verb* to put into a hiding place. ▸ *noun* a hidden supply or store of something, or its hiding place. [18c]

stat *abbrev* (*usu* **stats**) *informal* statistic.

state *noun* **1** the condition, eg of health, appearance, emotions, etc that someone or something is in at a particular time. **2** a territory governed by a single political body; a nation. **3** any of a number of locally governed areas making up a nation or federation under the ultimate control of a central government, as in the US. **4** (**the States**) the United States of America. **5** (*also* **State** *or* **the State**) the political entity of a nation, including the government and all its apparatus, eg the civil service and the armed forces. **6** *informal* **a** an emotionally agitated condition: *He was in a right state;* **b** a confused or untidy condition: *What a state your room's in!* ▸ *verb* **1** to express clearly, either in written or spoken form; to affirm or assert. **2** to specify. [13c: from Latin *status*]

IDIOMS **lie in state** of a dead person: to be ceremonially displayed to the public before burial.

stateless *adj* having no nationality or citizenship.

stately *adj* (**-ier, -iest**) noble, dignified and impressive in appearance or manner. ▪ **stateliness** *noun.*

stately home *noun* a large grand old house, esp one that is open to the public.

statement *noun* **1** a thing stated, esp a formal written or spoken declaration: *made a statement to the press.* **2 a** a record of finances, esp one sent by a bank to an account-holder detailing the transactions within a particular period; **b** an account that gives details of the costs of materials, services, etc and the amount that is due to be paid. **3** the act of stating.

state of play *noun* the situation at a specified moment: *What's the state of play with this project?*

state of the art *noun* the current level of advancement achieved by the most modern, up-to-date technology or thinking in a particular field. *as adj* (**state-of-the-art**): *state-of-the-art technology.*

stateroom *noun* **1** a large room in a palace, etc that is used for ceremonial occasions. **2** a large private cabin on a ship.

state school *noun* a school that is state-funded and where the education is free.

state's evidence see **Queen's evidence**

statesman *or* **stateswoman** *noun* an experienced and distinguished politician. See also **elder statesman.** ▪ **statesmanlike** *adj.* ▪ **statesmanship** *noun.*

static *adj* (*also* **statical**) **1** not moving; stationary. **2** fixed; not portable. **3** relating to statics. Compare **dynamic**. **4** characteristic of or relating to TV or radio interference. ▸ *noun* **1** (*in full* **static electricity**) an accumulation of electric charges that remain at rest instead of moving to form a flow of current, eg electricity produced by friction between two materials such as hair and a plastic comb. **2** a sharp crackling or hissing sound that interferes with radio and television signals, and which is caused by static electricity or atmospheric disturbance. [16c: from Greek *statikos* causing to stand]

statics *singular noun* the branch of mechanics that deals with the action of balanced forces on bodies such that they remain at rest or in unaccelerated motion. Compare **dynamics**.

station *noun* **1** a place where trains or buses regularly stop so that people can get off and on, goods can be loaded and unloaded, etc. **2** a local headquarters or depot, eg of a police force, etc. **3** a building equipped for some particular purpose: *a power station* • *a petrol station.* **4 a** a radio or TV channel; **b** the building or organization that broadcasts particular radio or TV programmes. **5** a position in a specified structure, organization, etc: *ideas above his station.* **6** someone's calling, profession, etc. **7** a post or place of duty. **8** *Aust & NZ* a large farm that specializes in rearing sheep or cattle. ▸ *verb* to assign or appoint to a post or place of duty. [14c: from Latin *statio*]

stationary *adj* not moving; still. [15c: from Latin *stationarius* belonging to a military station]

stationary, stationery

Be careful not to use the spelling **stationary** when you mean **stationery.** It might help you to remember that there is an e in **le**tters and in station**e**ry, but if you are station**a**ry you are st**a**nding still.

stationary wave *noun, physics* a **standing wave**.

stationer *noun* a person or shop that sells stationery. [14c: from Latin *stationarius* a person with a regular standing place]

stationery *noun* paper, envelopes, pens and other writing materials. [18c]

stationery, stationary
See the Usage Note at **stationary**.

station house *noun, US* a police or fire station.

stationmaster *noun* the official who is in charge of a railway station.

station wagon *noun, N Am, esp US* an **estate car**.

statistic *noun* a specified piece of information or data. ▪ **statistical** *adj*. ▪ **statistically** *adv*.

statistician *noun* someone who collects, analyses, prepares, etc statistics.

statistics *plural noun* (*sometimes* **stats**) items of related information that have been collected, collated, interpreted, analysed and presented to show particular trends. ► *singular noun* the branch of mathematics concerned with drawing inferences from numerical data, based on probability theory, esp in so far as conclusions can be made on the basis of an appropriate sample from a population. [18c: from German *Statistik* study of political facts and figures]

statuary *noun* statues collectively. ► *adj* belonging or referring to statues or to the sculpting of them. [16c: from Latin *statua* a statue]

statue *noun* **1** a sculpted, moulded or cast figure, esp of a person or animal, usu life-size or larger. **2** (**statues**) a children's game in which the object is to stand as still as possible when the music stops. Also called **musical statues**. [14c: from Latin *statua*]

statuesque /statʃʊ'ɛsk/ *adj* of someone's appearance: tall and well-proportioned; dignified and imposing.

statuette *noun* a small statue.

stature *noun* **1** the height of a person, animal, tree, etc. **2** greatness; eminence; importance. **3** the level of achievement someone has attained. [14c: from Latin *statura*]

status *noun* **1** rank or position in relation to others, within society, an organization, etc: *social status*. **2** legal standing, eg with regard to adulthood, marriage, citizenship, etc. **3** a high degree or level of importance; prestige: *Her huge salary reflects the status of the job*. [17c: Latin, from *stare* to stand]

status quo *noun* (*usu* **the status quo**) the existing situation at a given moment. [19c: Latin, meaning 'the state in which']

status symbol *noun* a possession or privilege that represents, wealth, high social standing, etc.

statute *noun* **1 a** a law made by the legislative assembly of a country and recorded in a formal document; **b** the formal document where such a law is recorded. **2** a permanent rule drawn up by an organization, esp one that governs its internal workings or the conduct of its members. [13c: from Latin *statutum* decree]

statute law *noun* law in the form of statutes, as distinct from **case law**.

statutory *adj* **1** required or prescribed by law or a rule. **2** usual or regular, as if prescribed by law.

staunch[1] *adj* **1** loyal; trusty; steadfast. **2** watertight. ▪ **staunchly** *adv*. ▪ **staunchness** *noun*. [15c: from French *estanche* watertight]

staunch[2] *verb* to stop the flow of (something, such as blood from a wound). [13c: from French *estanchier*]

stave *noun* **1** any of the vertical wooden strips that are joined together to form a barrel, tub, boat hull, etc. **2** *music* a **staff** (*noun* sense 6). **3** a verse of a poem or song. ► *verb* (***staved*** *or* ***stove***) **1** (*often* **stave in**) **a** to smash (a hole, etc in something): *The door was staved in*; **b** to break (a stave or the staves of a barrel or boat). **2** (in this sense *past tense* only ***staved***) (*often* **stave off**) **a** to delay the onset of something: *tried to stave off his downfall by calling an election*; **b** to ward off something: *staved her hunger with an apple*. [14c: a back-formation from **staves**, a pl of **staff**]

staves see **staff**

stay[1] *verb* **1** *intr* to remain in the same place or condition, without moving or changing. **2 a** *intr* to reside temporarily, eg as a guest; **b** *Scot, intr* to live permanently: *She's stayed in Edinburgh all her life*. ► *noun* **1** a period of temporary residence; a visit. **2** a suspension of legal proceedings or a postponement of a legally enforceable punishment: *grant a stay of execution*. [15c: from Latin *stare* to stand]

IDIOMS **stay put** *informal* to remain in the same place. **stay the course** to have the stamina for something demanding.

PHRASAL VERBS **stay over** *informal* to spend the night. **stay up** to remain out of bed, esp beyond one's usual bedtime.

stay[2] *noun* **1** a prop or support. **2** (**stays**) a corset stiffened with strips of bone or metal. [16c: from French *estaye*]

stay[3] *noun* a rope or cable that is used for anchoring something, eg a flagpole, mast, etc, and to keep it upright. [Anglo-Saxon *stæg*]

staying power *noun* stamina; endurance.

stead *noun* (*usu* **in sb's stead**) in place of them. [Anglo-Saxon *stede* place]

IDIOMS **stand sb in good stead** to prove useful to them.

steadfast *adj* firm; resolute; determinedly unwavering. ▪ **steadfastly** *adv*. ▪ **steadfastness** *noun*. [Anglo-Saxon *stede* place + *fæst* fixed]

steady *adj* (***-ier, -iest***) **1** firmly fixed or balanced; not wobbling. **2** regular; constant; unvarying: *a steady job*. **3** stable; not easily disrupted or undermined. **4** having a serious or sober character. **5** continuous: *a steady stream*. ► *verb* (***-ies, -ied***) *tr & intr* to make or become steady or steadier. ► *adv* in a steady manner: *steady as she goes*. ► *exclam* (*also* **steady on!** *or* **steady up!**) used to urge someone to be careful or restrained. ▪ **steadily** *adv*. ▪ **steadiness** *noun*. [16c: from **stead**]

IDIOMS **go steady with sb** *informal* to have a steady romantic relationship with them. **go steady with sth** *informal* to use it sparingly.

steady-state theory *noun, astron* in cosmology: a theory, now generally discredited, that hypothesizes that the universe has always existed and that it is constantly expanding with the continuous creation of matter. Compare **Big Bang**.

steak *noun* **1 a** a fine quality beef for frying or grilling; **b** a thick slice of this, often with a specifying term before or after it to indicate which part of the animal it has come from or how it is served: *fillet steak.* **2** beef that is cut into chunks and used for stewing or braising. **3** a thick slice of any meat or fish: *salmon steaks.* [15c: from Norse *steik* roast]

steakhouse *noun* a restaurant that specializes in serving steaks.

steak knife *noun* a table knife with a serrated edge that is used for eating steaks.

steal *verb* (*past tense* **stole,** *past participle* **stolen**) **1** *tr & intr* to take away (another person's property) without permission or legal right, esp secretly. **2** to obtain something by cleverness or trickery: *steal a kiss.* **3** fraudulently to present (another person's work, ideas, etc) as one's own. **4** *intr* (*often* **steal away**) to go stealthily: *stole down to the basement.* ▸ *noun, informal* **1** a bargain; something that can be easily obtained: *The silk shirt was a steal at £25.* **2** *N Am, esp US* an act of stealing. [Anglo-Saxon *stelan*]

IDIOMS **steal a bye** *cricket* to score a run without the batsman having touched the ball with either his bat or hand. **steal sb's thunder** to divert attention and praise away from someone by presenting or using the same idea, plan, etc before they have an opportunity to do so. **steal the show** to attract the most applause, attention, publicity, admiration, etc.

stealth *noun* **1** softness and quietness of movement in order to avoid being noticed. **2** secretive or deceitful behaviour. [13c: from **steal**]

stealthy *adj* (**-*ier,* -*iest***) acting or done with stealth; furtive. ▪ **stealthily** *adv.* ▪ **stealthiness** *noun.*

steam *noun* **1 a** the colourless gas formed by vaporizing water at 100°C; **b** any similar vapour, esp one that is produced when an **aqueous** liquid is heated. **2** *informal* power, energy or speed: *I haven't got the steam to climb any further.* ▸ *adj* **a** powered by steam: *a steam generator;* **b** using steam: *a steam iron.* ▸ *verb* **1** *intr* to give off steam. **2** to cook, etc using steam. **3** *intr* to move under the power of steam. **4** *intr, informal* to go at speed: *steamed up the road to catch the bus.* [Anglo-Saxon]

IDIOMS **be** *or* **get steamed up** *or* **all steamed up** *informal* to be very angry or excited. **full steam ahead** forward as fast as possible or with as much energy, enthusiasm, gusto, etc as possible. **get up steam** of the boiler of a steam ship, locomotive, etc: to be in the process of heating up. **let off steam** to release bottled-up energy or emotions, eg anger. **run out of steam** to become depleted of energy, power, enthusiasm, etc. **under one's own steam** unassisted by anyone else.

PHRASAL VERBS **steam up** of a transparent or reflective surface: to become clouded by tiny water droplets formed from condensed steam: *His glasses steamed up.*

steamboat *or* **steamship** *noun* a vessel that is driven by steam.

steam engine *noun* **1** an engine that is powered by steam from a boiler that is heated by a furnace. **2** a steam locomotive engine.

steamer *noun* **1** a ship whose engines are powered by steam. **2** a two-tier pot in which food in the upper tier is cooked by the action of steam from water heated in the lower tier.

steamroller *noun* a large vehicle, orig and still often steam-driven, that has huge heavy solid metal cylinders for wheels so that when it is driven over newly made roads it smooths, flattens and compacts the surface. ▸ *verb, informal* **1** to use overpowering force or persuasion to secure the speedy movement or progress of something. **2** (*often* **steamroller sb into sth**) to make them do it, using force or forceful persuasion to overcome their resistance or reluctance.

steamy *adj* (**-*ier,* -*iest***) **1** full of, clouded by, emitting, etc steam. **2** *informal* salacious; sexy; erotic. ▪ **steamily** *adv.*

stearate *noun, chem* a salt or ester of stearic acid. [19c]

stearic acid *noun, chem* a colourless fatty acid, commonly found in animal fats and used as a lubricant and in pharmaceutical products, soap, etc. [19c]

steatite /ˈstiːətaɪt/ *noun* another name for **soapstone**. [17c]

steed *noun* a horse, esp one that is lively and bold. [Anglo-Saxon *steda* stallion]

steel *noun* **1** an iron alloy that contains small amounts of carbon and, in some cases, additional elements. **2** a rough-surfaced rod, made of this alloy, that knives are sharpened on by hand. **3** esp of someone, their character, determination, etc: hardness, strength, etc: *a man of steel.* ▸ *verb* (*usu* **steel oneself**) to harden oneself or prepare oneself emotionally, esp for something unpleasant or unwelcome. [Anglo-Saxon *style*]

steel band *noun* a group, orig in the W Indies, who play music on oil or petrol drums which have had the tops specially beaten so that striking different areas produces different notes.

steel wool *noun* thin strands of steel in a woolly mass that is used for polishing and scouring.

steelworks *singular or plural noun* a factory where steel is manufactured. ▪ **steelworker** *noun.*

steely *adj* (**-*ier,* -*iest***) cold, hard and unyielding: *a steely gaze.* ▪ **steeliness** *noun.*

steelyard *noun* a type of weighing machine that has one short arm that the object to be weighed is put onto and another longer graduated arm which has a single weight on it which is pushed along the arm until the balance is established.

steep[1] *adj* **1** sloping sharply. **2** *informal* of a price, rate, etc: unreasonably high. **3** *informal* of a story or a version of events: hard to believe. ▪ **steeply** *adv.* ▪ **steepness** *noun.* [Anglo-Saxon *steap*]

steep[2] *verb, tr & intr* to soak something thoroughly in liquid. [14c: from English *stepen*]

IDIOMS **be steeped in sth** to be deeply involved in it: *a castle steeped in history.*

steepen *verb, tr & intr* to make or become steep or steeper.

steeple *noun* **1** a tower, esp one with a spire, that forms part of a church or temple. **2** the spire itself. ▪ **steepled** *adj.* [Anglo-Saxon *stepel*]

steeplechase *noun* **1** a horse race round a course with hurdles, usu in the form of hedges. **2** a track running race where athletes have to jump hurdles and, usu, a water jump. ▸ *verb, intr* to take part in a steeplechase. ▪ **steeplechaser** *noun.* ▪ **steeplechasing** *noun.* [18c: so called because the orig horse races were run across country from one village to the next with a church steeple marking the end of the race]

steeplejack *noun* a person whose job is to construct and repair steeples and tall chimneys. [19c]

steer[1] *verb* **1** *tr & intr* to guide or control the direction of (a vehicle or vessel) using a steering wheel, rudder, etc. **2** *intr* **a** to tend towards a specified direction: *This car steers to the right*; **b** to move in a specified way: *This car steers badly.* **3** to guide or encourage (someone, a conversation, etc) to move in a specified direction: *steered the conversation round to the subject of money.* ▪ **steering** *noun.* [Anglo-Saxon *styran*]

IDIOMS **steer clear of sb** *or* **sth** *informal* to avoid them or it.

steer[2] *noun* a young castrated bull or male ox. [Anglo-Saxon *steor*]

steerage *noun* **1** *old use* the cheapest accommodation on board a passenger ship, traditionally near the rudder. **2** an act or the practice of steering.

steering column *noun* in a motor vehicle: the shaft that has the steering wheel at one end and which connects up to the steering gear at the other.

steering committee *noun* a committee that decides on the nature and order of topics to be discussed by a parliament, etc.

steering wheel *noun* a wheel that is turned by hand to direct the wheels of a vehicle or the rudder of a vessel.

stegosaurus *noun* a large herbivorous dinosaur of the late Jurassic and early Cretaceous periods, having a small head, a high domed back with a double row of large vertical bony plates, short front legs and a long tail. [19c: from Greek *stegos* roof + *saurus* lizard]

stein /staɪn; *German* ʃtaɪn/ *noun* a large metal or earthenware beer mug, often with a hinged lid. [19c: German, meaning 'stone']

stele /'stiːlɪ, 'stiːl/ *noun* (***stelae*** /'stiːliː/) an ancient stone pillar or upright slab, usu carved or engraved. [19c: Greek, meaning 'a standing stone']

stellar *adj* **1** referring or relating to or resembling a star or stars. **2** referring or relating to the famous. [17c: from Latin *stella* star]

stem[1] *noun* **1** **a** the central part of a plant that grows upward from its root; **b** the part that connects a leaf, flower or fruit to a branch. **2** any long slender part, eg of a written letter or musical note, of a wine glass, etc. **3** *linguistics* the base form of a word that inflections are added to; for example *love* is the stem of *loved, lover, lovely, unloved*, etc and of *luvvie*, despite the distortion of the spelling. ▸ *verb* (***stemmed, stemming***) *intr* (**stem from sth** *or* **sb**) to originate or derive from it or them. [Anglo-Saxon *stemn*]

stem[2] *verb* (***stemmed, stemming***) to stop (the flow of something). [15c: from Norse *stemma*]

stem cell *noun, biol* an undifferentiated cell that can develop into a cell with a specific function.

stench *noun* a strong and extremely unpleasant smell. [Anglo-Saxon *stenc* a smell, either pleasant or unpleasant]

stencil *noun* **1** a card or plate that has shapes cut out of it to form a pattern, letter, etc and which is put onto a surface, eg paper, a wall, etc, and ink or paint applied so that the cut-out design is transferred to the surface. **2** the design that is produced using this technique. ▸ *verb* (***stencilled, stencilling*** *or* (*US*) ***stenciled, stenciling***) **1** to mark or decorate (a surface) using a stencil. **2** to produce (a design, letter, etc) using a stencil. ▪ **stenciller** *noun.* ▪ **stencilling** *noun.* [15c: from French *estinceller*]

Stenograph *noun, trademark* a kind of typewriter that produces shorthand, used eg for producing courtroom transcripts. ▪ **stenographer** *noun.* ▪ **stenography** *noun.*

stent *noun, med* a device fitted inside a part of the body, eg a heart valve, to keep it open. [1960s in this sense; late 19c as a dental device devised by the English dentist C R Stent]

stentorian *adj, literary* of a voice: loud and strong. [17c: named after Stentor, a Greek herald in the Trojan War who had a voice as loud as 50 men (*Iliad* 5.783–5)]

step *noun* **1** a single complete action of lifting then placing down the foot in walking or running. **2** the distance covered in the course of such an action. **3** a movement of the foot (usu one of a pattern of movements) in dancing. **4** a single action or measure that is taken in proceeding towards an end or goal: *a step in the right direction.* **5** (*often* **steps**) **a** a single (often outdoor) stair, or any stair-like support used to climb up or down; **b** a **stepladder**; **c** a rung on a ladder. **6** the sound or mark of a foot being laid on the ground, etc in walking. **7** a degree or stage in a scale or series: *moved up a step on the payscale.* **8** a way of walking; gait: *always has a bouncy step.* ▸ *verb* (***stepped, stepping***) **1** *intr* to move by lifting up each foot alternately and setting it down in a different place. **2** *intr* to go or come on foot: *Step right this way.* **3** to perform (a dance). **4** to arrange in such a way as to avoid overlap. ▪ **stepper** *noun.* [Anglo-Saxon *steppe*]

IDIOMS **in step 1** walking, marching, etc in time with others or with the music. **2** in harmony, unison, agreement, etc with another or others. **out of step 1** not walking, marching, etc in time with others or with the music. **2** not in harmony, unison, agreement, etc with another or others. **step by step** gradually. **step into sth** to enter into it or become involved in it, esp easily or casually: *stepped into a high-flying job.* **step on it** *informal* to hurry up. **step out of line** to behave in an inappropriate way; to disobey or offend, esp in a minor way. **take steps to** to take action in order to. **watch one's step 1** to walk with careful steps in order to avoid danger, etc. **2** to proceed with caution, taking care not to anger, offend, etc others.

PHRASAL VERBS **step down** to resign from a position of authority. **step in 1** to take up a position or role as a substitute or replacement. **2** to intervene in an argument. **step out 1** to walk quickly and confidently with long strides. **2** *informal* to go out socially. **step up** to increase the rate, intensity, etc of something.

step- *combining form, indicating* a family relationship that is through marriage or partnership as opposed to a blood relationship. [Anglo-Saxon *steop* orphan]

stepbrother *or* **stepsister** *noun* a son or daughter of someone's step-parent.

stepchild, stepdaughter *or* **stepson** *noun* a child of someone's spouse or partner who is the offspring of a previous relationship.

stepfather *noun* a husband or partner of a person's mother who is not that person's biological father.

stepladder *noun* a short ladder with flat steps made free-standing by means of a supporting frame attached by a hinge at the ladder's top where there is usu a platform to stand on.

stepmother *noun* a wife or partner of a person's father who is not that person's biological mother.

step-parent *noun* a stepfather or stepmother.

steppe *noun* an extensive dry grassy and usu treeless plain, esp one found in SE Europe and Asia extending east from the Ukraine through to the Manchurian plains of China. [17c: from Russian *step* lowland]

stepping-stone *noun* **1** a large stone that has a surface which is above the water level of a stream, etc and which can be used for crossing over to the other side. **2** something that functions as a means of progress: *thought of the job as a stepping-stone to better things.*

stepson see under **stepchild**

-ster *suffix, forming nouns, denoting* someone who is characterized by some specified trait, activity, membership of a group, etc: *youngster.*

steradian *noun* (abbrev **sr**) *geom* the SI unit that is used for measuring solid (three-dimensional) angles. [19c: from Greek *stereos* solid + **radian**]

stereo *noun* **1** stereophonic reproduction of sound. **2** a VD player, cassette player, hi-fi system, etc that gives a stereophonic reproduction of sound. ► *adj* a shortened form of **stereophonic**. [1950s: from Greek *stereos* solid]

stereochemistry *noun, chem* the study of the three-dimensional arrangement of atoms within molecules. ▪ **stereochemical** *adj.* ▪ **stereochemist** *noun.* [19c: from Greek *stereos* solid]

stereoisomer *noun, chem* an isomer that has the same chemical composition, molecular weight and structure but a different spacial arrangement of atoms as another. ▪ **stereoisomeric** *adj.* [19c]

stereophonic *adj* of a system for reproducing or broadcasting sound: using two or more independent sound channels leading to separate loudspeakers, in order to simulate the depth and separation of different sounds that would be experienced at a live performance. Often shortened to **stereo**. ▪ **stereophonically** *adv.* ▪ **stereophony** /stɛrɪ'ɒfənɪ/ *noun.* [1920s]

stereoscope *noun* a binocular instrument that presents a slightly different view of the same object to each eye thus producing an apparently 3-D image. ▪ **stereoscopic** *adj.* [19c]

stereotype *noun* **a** an overgeneralized and preconceived idea or impression of what characterizes someone or something, esp one that does not allow for any individuality or variation; **b** someone or something that conforms to such an idea, etc. ► *verb* to attribute overgeneralized and preconceived characteristics to someone or something. ▪ **stereotyped** *adj.* ▪ **stereotypical** *adj.* ▪ **stereotypically** *adv.* [18c: from Greek *stereos* solid + Latin *typus* bas relief]

sterile *adj* **1** biologically incapable of producing offspring, fruit or seeds. **2** free of germs. **3** producing no results; having no new ideas; lacking the usual attributes, qualities, etc. ▪ **sterility** *noun.* [16c: from Latin *sterilis* barren]

sterilize *or* **-ise** *verb* **1** to make something germ-free. **2** to make someone or something infertile. ▪ **sterilization** *noun.* ▪ **sterilizer** *noun.*

sterling *noun* British money. ► *adj* **1** good quality; worthy; reliable: *gave a sterling performance.* **2** of silver: conforming to the official level of purity, which is set at a minimum of 92.5 per cent. **3** authentic; genuine. [Anglo-Saxon *steorra* star, from the markings on early Norman pennies]

stern[1] *adj* **1** extremely strict; authoritarian. **2** harsh, severe or rigorous. **3** unpleasantly serious or unfriendly in appearance or nature. ▪ **sternly** *adv.* ▪ **sternness** *noun.* [Anglo-Saxon *styrne*]

stern[2] *noun* the rear of a ship or boat. [13c: from Norse *stjorn* steering]

sternum *noun* (***sternums*** *or* ***sterna***) *anatomy* in humans: the broad vertical bone in the chest that the ribs and collarbone are attached to. Also called **breastbone**. ▪ **sternal** *adj.* [17c: from Greek *sternon* chest]

sternutation *noun, formal* an act of sneezing; a sneeze. [16c: from Latin *sternuere* to sneeze]

steroid *noun* **1** *biochem* any of a large group of fat-soluble organic compounds that have a complex molecular structure (17-carbon-atom, four-linked ring system), and which are important both physiologically and pharmacologically. **2** *med* a class of drug containing such a compound. See **anabolic steroid**. [1930s]

sterol *noun, biochem* any of a group of colourless waxy solid **steroid** alcohols that are found in plants, animals and fungi, eg cholesterol. [Early 20c: a shortening of chole*sterol*, ergo*sterol*, etc]

stertorous *adj, formal* of breathing: noisy; with a snoring sound. [19c: from Latin *stertere* to snore]

stet *noun* a conventionalized direction given in the margin of a manuscript or other text to indicate that something which has been changed or marked for deletion is to be retained in its original form after all. ► *verb* (***stetted, stetting***) to put this kind of mark on a manuscript, etc. [18c: Latin, meaning 'let it stand']

stethoscope *noun, med* an instrument that consists of a small concave disc that has hollow tubes attached to it and which, when it is placed on the body, carries sounds. [19c: from Greek *stethos* chest + *skopeein* to view]

Stetson *noun, trademark* a man's broad-brimmed felt hat with a high crown, which is indented at the top and is esp worn by cowboys. [19c: named after the American hat-maker, John Stetson, who designed the hat]

stevedore /'stiːvədɔː(r)/ *noun* a person whose job is to load and unload ships; a docker. [18c: from Spanish *estibador*]

stew *verb* **1** *tr & intr* to cook (esp meat) by long simmering. **2** **a** to cause (tea) to become bitter and over-strong by letting it brew for too long; **b** *intr* of tea: to become bitter and over-strong because it has been left brewing for too long. **3** *intr, informal* to be in a state of worry or agitation. ► *noun* **1** a dish of food, esp a mixture of meat and vegetables, that has been cooked by stewing. **2** *informal* a state of worry or agitation. [18c: from French *estuve* a sweat room]

steward *noun* **1** someone whose job is to look after the needs of passengers on a ship or aircraft. See also **flight attendant**. **2** someone whose duties include supervising crowd movements during sporting events, gigs, etc. **3** someone whose job is to oversee the catering arrangements, etc in a hotel or club. **4** *esp hist* someone whose job is to manage another person's property and affairs, eg on a country estate. ▸ *verb* to serve as a steward of something. ▪ **stewardship** *noun*. [Anglo-Saxon *stigweard* hall-keeper]

stewardess *noun* a female steward on a ship, aircraft, etc. See also **flight attendant**.

stewed *adj* **1** of meat, vegetables, fruit, etc: cooked by stewing: *stewed prunes*. **2** of tea: bitter and over-strong because it has been brewed for too long. **3** *informal* drunk.

STI *abbrev* sexually transmitted infection.

stick[1] *noun* **1** a twig or thin branch of a tree. **2** **a** any long thin piece of wood; **b** *in compounds* a shaped piece of wood or other material which has a designated purpose: *a hockey stick* • *the gear stick*. **3** a long thin piece of anything: *a stick of rock*. **4** a piece of furniture, esp when it is one of few. **5** *informal* verbal abuse, criticism or mockery. **6** (**the sticks**) *informal* a rural area that is considered remote or unsophisticated. **7** *informal* a person: *a funny old stick*. ▸ *verb* to support (a plant) using a stick or sticks. [Anglo-Saxon *sticca*]

IDIOMS **get hold of the wrong end of the stick** to misunderstand a situation, a statement, etc. **give sb stick** to criticize or punish them. **up sticks** *informal* to move away, esp without warning.

stick[2] *verb* (*past tense, past participle* ***stuck***) **1** to push or thrust (esp something long and thin or pointed). **2** to fasten by piercing with a pin or other sharp object: *stick it up with drawing pins*. **3** *tr & intr* to fix, or be or stay fixed, with an adhesive. **4** *intr* to remain persistently: *an episode that sticks in my mind*. **5** *tr & intr* to make or be unable to move: *The car got stuck in the snow*. **6** to confine: *stuck in the house all day*. **7** *informal* to place or put: *just stick it on the table*. **8** *informal* to bear or tolerate: *could not stick it any longer*. **9** to cause to be at a loss; to baffle: *He's never stuck for something to say*. [Anglo-Saxon *stician*]

IDIOMS **stick in one's throat** *informal* to be extremely difficult to say or accept, usu for reasons of principle. **stick one's neck out** *or* **stick one's neck out for sb** *or* **sth** to put oneself in a dangerous or tricky position for them or it. **stick one's nose in** *or* **into sth** to interfere or pry, or to interfere with it or pry into it, esp when it is none of one's business. **stick out a mile** *or* **stick out like a sore thumb** to be glaringly obvious. **stick to one's guns** to be adamant.

PHRASAL VERBS **stick around** *informal* to remain or linger. **stick by sb** *or* **sth** to remain loyal or supportive towards them or it: *She sticks by him no matter what he does*. **stick out 1** to project or protrude. **2** to be obvious or noticeable; to stand out. **3** to endure. **stick out for sth** to continue to insist on it; to refuse to yield. **stick to sth 1** to remain faithful to it, eg a promise: *stuck to the same story throughout the questioning*. **2** to keep to it, eg a matter under discussion without digressing. **stick up for sb** *or* **oneself** to speak or act in their or one's own defence.

sticker *noun* **1** an adhesive label or small poster, card etc. **2** someone or something that sticks.

sticking plaster see **plaster** (*noun* sense 2)

sticking point *noun* deadlock.

stick insect *noun* a tropical insect with a long slender body and legs that are camouflaged to look like twigs.

stick-in-the-mud *noun, informal* someone who is opposed to anything new or adventurous and is therefore seen as boring and dull.

stickleback *noun* a small spiny-backed fish. [Anglo-Saxon *sticel* prick + **back**]

stickler *noun* (*usu* **a stickler for sth**) someone who fastidiously insists on something. [Anglo-Saxon *stihtan* to set in order]

sticky *adj* (***-ier, -iest***) **1** covered with something that is tacky or gluey. **2** able or likely to stick to other surfaces. **3** of the weather: warm and humid; muggy. **4** *informal* of a situation, etc: difficult; awkward; unpleasant. ▪ **stickiness** *noun*.

IDIOMS **come to** *or* **meet a sticky end** *informal* to suffer an unpleasant end or death.

sticky wicket *noun, informal* a difficult or awkward situation.

stiff *adj* **1** not easily bent or folded; rigid. **2** of limbs, joints, etc: lacking suppleness; not moving or bending easily. **3** of a punishment, etc: harsh; severe. **4** of a task, etc: difficult; arduous. **5** of a wind: blowing strongly. **6** of someone or their manner: not natural and relaxed; over-formal. **7** thick in consistency; viscous. **8** *informal* of an alcoholic drink: not diluted or only lightly diluted; strong. **9** of a price: excessively high. ▸ *adv, informal* to an extreme degree: *scared stiff*. ▸ *noun, slang* a corpse. ▪ **stiffly** *adv*. ▪ **stiffness** *noun*. [Anglo-Saxon *stif*]

stiffen *verb* **1** *tr & intr* to make or become stiff or stiffer. **2** *intr* to become nervous or tense.

stiff-necked *adj* arrogantly obstinate.

stifle *verb* **1** **a** to suppress (a feeling or action): *stifled a laugh*; **b** to conceal: *stifled the truth*. **2** *tr & intr* to experience or cause to experience difficulty in breathing, esp because of heat and lack of air. **3** to kill or nearly kill by stopping the breathing; to smother. **4** to stamp out: *Police stifled the riot*. [14c]

stifling *adj* **1** unpleasantly hot or airless. **2** overly oppressive. ▪ **stiflingly** *adv*.

stigma *noun* **1** shame or social disgrace. **2** *botany* in a flowering plant: the sticky surface that receives pollen and which is situated at the tip of the **style**. **3** *zool* any of a variety of pigmented markings or spots, eg on the wings of certain butterflies. [16c: Greek, meaning 'brand']

stigmata *plural noun, Christianity* marks that are said to have appeared on the bodies of certain holy people and are thought to resemble Christ's crucifixion wounds. ▪ **stigmatic** *or* **stigmatist** *noun* someone marked by stigmata. [17c: Greek pl of **stigma**]

stigmatize *or* **-ise** *verb* to describe, regard, single out, etc someone as bad, shameful, etc.

stile *noun* a step, or set of steps, that is incorporated into a fence or wall so that people can cross but animals cannot. [Anglo-Saxon *stigel*]

stiletto *noun* **1** (*in full* **stiletto heel**) a high thin heel on a woman's shoe. **2** *informal* a shoe with such a heel. **3** a dagger with a narrow tapering blade. [1950s: Italian]

still[1] *adj* **1** motionless; inactive; silent. **2** quiet and calm; tranquil. **3** of a drink: not having escaping bubbles of carbon dioxide. ▸ *adv* **1** continuing as before, now or at some future time: *Do you still live in Edinburgh?* **2** up to the present time, or the time in question; yet: *I still don't understand*. **3** even then; nevertheless: *knows the dangers but still continues* *to smoke*. **4** quietly and without movement: *sit still*. **5** to a greater degree; even: *older still*. ▸ *verb* **1** *tr & intr* to make or become still, silent, etc. **2** to calm, appease, or put an end to something. ▸ *noun* **1** stillness; tranquillity: *the still of the countryside*. **2** a photograph, esp of an actor in, or a scene from, a cinema film, used for publicity purposes. ▪ **stillness** *noun*. [Anglo-Saxon *stille*]

still² *noun* an apparatus for the distillation of alcoholic spirit. [16c: from **still¹** (*verb* sense 1)]

stillbirth *noun* **1** the birth of a dead baby or fetus. **2** a baby or fetus that is dead at birth.

stillborn *adj* **1** of a baby or fetus: dead when born. **2** of a project, etc: doomed from the start.

still life *noun* **1** a painting, drawing or photograph of an object or objects, eg a bowl of fruit, rather than of a living thing. **2** this kind of art or photography.

still room *noun* **1** a room where distilling is carried out. **2** a housekeeper's pantry in a large house.

stilt *noun* **1** either of a pair of long poles that have supports for the feet part of the way up so that someone can walk around supported high above the ground. **2** any of a set of props on which a building, jetty, etc is supported above ground or water level. [14c: English *stilte* a plough handle]

stilted *adj* **1** of language: unnatural-sounding and over-formal. **2** laboured or jarring; not flowing: *a stilted conversation*. [17c: from **stilt**]

Stilton /ˈstɪltən/ *noun, trademark* either of two strong white English cheeses, one of which has blue veins. [18c: named after Stilton, Cambridgeshire]

stimulant *noun* **1** any substance, such as a drug, that produces an increase in the activity of a particular body organ or function, eg caffeine, nicotine, amphetamines. **2** anything that causes an increase in excitement, activity, interest, etc.

stimulate *verb* **1** to cause physical activity, or increased activity, in (eg an organ of the body). **2** to initiate or get going. **3** to excite or arouse the senses of someone; to animate or invigorate them. **4** to create interest and enthusiasm in someone or something. ▪ **stimulation** *noun*. [16c: from Latin *stimulare* to stimulate]

stimulating *adj* exciting; invigorating.

stimulus /ˈstɪmjʊləs/ *noun* (***stimuli*** /-aɪ/) **1** something that acts as an incentive, inspiration, provocation, etc. **2** something, such as a drug, heat, light, etc, that causes a specific response in a cell, tissue, organ, etc. [17c: Latin, meaning 'a goad']

sting *noun* **1** a defensive puncturing organ that is found in certain animals and plants, which can inject poison or venom. **2** the injection of poison from an animal or plant. **3** a painful wound resulting from the sting of an animal or plant. **4** any sharp tingling pain. **5** anything that is hurtful, eg a vicious insult: *felt the sting of her wicked words*. **6** *slang* a trick, swindle or robbery. ▸ *verb* (*past tense, past participle* ***stung***) **1** to pierce, poison or wound with a sting. **2** *intr* to produce a sharp tingling pain. **3** *slang* to cheat, swindle or rob; to cheat by overcharging: *stung him for 50 quid*. [Anglo-Saxon *stingan* to pierce]

IDIOMS **a sting in the tail** an unexpected turn of events, irony, unpleasantness, etc.

stinging nettle *noun* a **nettle**.

stingray *noun* a **ray²** with a long whip-like tail tipped with spikes that are capable of inflicting severe wounds.

stingy /ˈstɪndʒɪ/ *adj* (***-ier, -iest***) ungenerous; mean; miserly. ▪ **stingily** *adv*. ▪ **stinginess** *noun*. [17c]

stink *noun* **1** a strong and very unpleasant smell. **2** *informal* an angry complaint or outraged reaction; a fuss. ▸ *verb* (*past tense* ***stank*** *or* ***stunk***, *past participle* ***stunk***) **1** *intr* to give off an offensive smell. **2** *intr, informal* to be contemptibly bad or unpleasant: *The idea of going with Harry stinks*. ▪ **stinky** *adj* (***-ier, -iest***). [Anglo-Saxon *stincan* to smell]

IDIOMS **kick up, raise** *or* **make a stink** to cause trouble, esp disagreeably and in public.

PHRASAL VERBS **stink out** *or* **up** to fill (a room, etc) with an offensive smell.

stinker *noun, informal* **1** a very difficult task, question, etc. **2** someone who behaves in a dishonest, cheating or otherwise unscrupulous unpleasant way.

stinking *adj* **1** offensively smelly. **2** *informal* very unpleasant, disgusting, etc. ▸ *adv, informal* extremely; disgustingly: *stinking rich*.

stint *verb* (**stint on**) to be mean or grudging in giving or supplying something: *Don't stint on the chocolate sauce*. ▸ *noun* **1** an allotted amount of work or a fixed time for it: *a twelve hour stint*. **2** a turn: *did his stint yesterday*. [Anglo-Saxon *styntan* to dull]

IDIOMS **without stint** liberally; unreservedly.

stipend /ˈstaɪpɛnd/ *noun* a salary or allowance, now esp one that is paid to a member of the clergy. ▪ **stipendiary** *adj*. [15c: from Latin *stipendium* tax]

stipple *verb* to paint, engrave or draw something in dots or dabs as distinct from using lines or masses of colour. ▸ *noun* a painting, engraving, drawing, etc that has been produced using this technique. ▪ **stippled** *adj*. [17c: from Dutch *stippelen*]

stipulate *verb* in a contract, agreement, etc: to specify as a necessary condition. ▪ **stipulation** *noun*. [17c]

stir¹ *verb* (***stirred, stirring***) **1** to mix or agitate (a liquid or semi-liquid substance) by repeated circular strokes with a spoon or other utensil. **2** to arouse the emotions of someone; to move them. **3** to make or cause to make a slight or single movement: *she stirred in her sleep*. **4** *intr* to get up after sleeping; to become active after resting. **5** to rouse (oneself) to action. **6** to evoke something: *The photos stirred happy memories*. **7** *intr, informal* to make trouble. ▸ *noun* **1** an act of stirring a liquid, etc. **2** an excited reaction; a commotion. [Anglo-Saxon *styrian*]

PHRASAL VERBS **stir up sth** to cause or provoke (eg trouble).

stir² *noun, slang* prison. [19c]

stir-crazy *adj, orig N Am slang* emotionally disturbed through long confinement, esp in prison.

stir-fry *verb* to cook (small pieces of meat or vegetables or a mixture of both) lightly by brisk frying in a wok or large frying pan on a high heat with only a little oil. ▸ *noun* a dish of food that has been cooked in this way.

stirrer *noun* **1** someone or something that stirs. **2** *informal* someone who enjoys making trouble or who deliberately goes about making trouble.

stirring *adj* **1** arousing strong emotions. **2** lively.

stirrup *noun* **1** either of a pair of leather or metal loops suspended from straps attached to a horse's saddle, which are used as footrests for the rider. **2** any strap or loop that supports or passes under the foot: *ski-pants with stirrups.* [Anglo-Saxon *stigrap*]

stirrup cup *noun* an alcoholic drink that is given to someone, orig a rider, who is about to leave, esp someone who is going on a hunt.

stirrup pump *noun* a portable hand-operated pump that draws water from a bucket, etc, and which is used in fighting small fires.

stitch *noun* **1** a single interlinking loop of thread or yarn in sewing or knitting. **2** a complete movement of the needle or needles to create such a loop. **3** a sharp ache in the side resulting from physical exertion. **4** *non-technical* a **suture**. ▶ *verb* (*sometimes* **stitch sth up**) **1** to join, close, decorate, etc with stitches. **2** to sew. **3** *non-technical* to close a cut, wound, etc with stitches. ▪ **stitcher** *noun*. [Anglo-Saxon *stice* prick]

IDIOMS **in stitches** *informal* helpless with laughter. **without a stitch** *or* **not a stitch** *informal* without any clothing or no clothing at all.

PHRASAL VERBS **stitch sb up** *slang* **1** to incriminate, trick, betray or double-cross them. **2** to swindle or overcharge them.

stoat *noun* a small flesh-eating mammal that has a long slender body and reddish-brown fur with white underparts, although in northern regions the fur turns white in winter, and the animal is then known as the **ermine**. [15c as *stote*]

stochastic /stoʊˈkastɪk/ *adj, stats* random. ▪ **stochastically** *adv*. [20c in this sense; 17c, meaning 'pertaining to conjecture': from GreeK *stokhazesthai* to aim at]

stocious *or* **stotious** *adj, informal* drunk. [1930s]

stock *noun* **1** (*sometimes* **stocks**) goods or raw material that a shop, factory, warehouse, etc has on the premises at a given time. **2** a supply kept in reserve: *an impressive stock of fine wine.* **3** equipment or raw material in use. **4** liquid in which meat or vegetables have been cooked and which can then be used as a base for soup, a sauce, etc. **5** the shaped wooden or plastic part of a rifle or similar gun that the user rests against their shoulder. **6** farm animals; livestock. **7** the money raised by a company through the selling of shares. **8** the total shares issued by a particular company or held by an individual shareholder. **9** a group of shares bought or sold as a unit. **10** ancestry; descent: *of peasant stock.* **11** any of various Mediterranean plants of the wallflower family that are cultivated for their bright flowers. **12** (**the stocks**) *formerly* a wooden device that was used for securing offenders who were held by the head and wrists or by the wrists and ankles, so that they could be displayed for public ridicule as a punishment. **13** reputation; standing. ▶ *adj* **1** being of a standard type, size, etc, constantly in demand and always kept in stock. **2** of a phrase, etc: much used, esp so overused as to be meaningless. ▶ *verb* **1** to keep a supply for sale. **2** to provide with a supply: *stocked the drinks cabinet with expensive brandies.* [Anglo-Saxon *stocc* stick]

IDIOMS **out of** *or* **in stock** not currently, or currently, held for sale on the premises. **take stock** to make an inventory of all stock held on the premises at a particular time. **take stock of sth** to make an overall assessment of one's circumstances, etc.

PHRASAL VERBS **stock up on sth** to acquire or accumulate a large supply of it.

stockade *noun* a defensive fence or enclosure that is built of upright tall heavy posts. [17c: from Spanish *estacada*]

stockbroker *noun* someone whose profession is to buy and sell stocks and shares on behalf of customers in return for a fee. Often shortened to **broker**.

stock car *noun* a car that has been specially strengthened and modified for competing in a kind of track racing where deliberate ramming and colliding are allowed.

stock exchange *noun* **1 a** a market where the trading of stocks and shares by professional dealers on behalf of customers goes on; **b** a building where this type of trading is done. **2** (*usu* **the stock exchange**) the level of prices in this type of market or the amount of activity that this type of market generates.

stocking *noun* either of a pair of close-fitting coverings for women's legs which are made of fine semi-transparent nylon or silk. [16c: from **stock**]

IDIOMS **in stockinged feet** without shoes.

stock-in-trade *noun* **1** something that is seen as fundamental to a particular trade or activity. **2** all the goods that a shopkeeper, etc has for sale.

stockist *noun* a person or shop that stocks a particular item or brand.

stockman *noun* **1** someone whose job is keeping, rearing, etc farm animals, esp cattle. **2** *US* a **storeman**.

stock market *noun* the **stock exchange**.

stockpile *noun* a reserve supply that has been accumulated. ▶ *verb* to accumulate a large reserve supply.

stockroom *noun* a storeroom, esp in a shop.

stock-still *adj, adv* completely motionless.

stocktaking *noun* **1** the process of making a detailed inventory and valuation of all the goods, raw materials, etc that are held on the premises of a shop, factory, etc at a particular time. **2** the process of making an overall assessment eg of the present situation with regard to one's future prospects, etc.

stocky *adj* (**-ier, -iest**) of a person or animal: broad, strong-looking and usu not very tall. ▪ **stockily** *adv*. ▪ **stockiness** *noun*.

stockyard *noun* a large yard or enclosure that is usu sectioned off into pens, where livestock are kept temporarily, eg before being auctioned.

stodge *noun* food that is heavy, filling and, usu, fairly tasteless. ▶ *verb* to stuff with food. [17c]

stodgy *adj* (**-ier, -iest**) **1** of food: heavy and filling but usu fairly tasteless and unappetizing. **2** of someone, their attitude, conversation, etc: boringly conventional or serious. ▪ **stodginess** *noun*. [19c; orig meaning 'thick', 'glutinous' or 'muddy']

stoic /ˈstoʊɪk/ *noun* **1** someone who can repress emotions and show patient resignation under difficult circumstances. **2** (**Stoic**) *philos* a member of the Greek school of philosophy that was founded by Zeno around 300 BC. See also **stoicism**. [14c: from Greek *Stoa Poikile* Painted Porch, the name of the place in Athens where Zeno taught]

stoical *adj* **1** accepting misfortune uncomplainingly. **2** indifferent to both pain and pleasure.

stoicism /ˈstoʊɪsɪzəm/ *noun* **1 a** brave or patient acceptance of suffering and misfortune; **b** repression of emotion. **2** (**Stoicism**) the philosophy of the Stoics which was characterized by an emphasis on the development of self-sufficiency in the individual, whose duty was to conform only to the dictates of natural order to which all people belonged equally. [14c: from **stoic**]

stoke *verb* **1** to put coal or other fuel on (eg a fire, the furnace of a boiler). **2** to arouse or intensify (eg passion or enthusiasm). [17c: from Dutch *stoken* to feed (a fire)]

stoker *noun* someone whose job is to stoke a furnace, esp on a steamship or steam train.

stole[1] *noun* a woman's scarf-like garment, often made of fur, that is worn around the shoulders. [Anglo-Saxon]

stole[2] *past tense of* **steal**

stolen *past participle of* **steal**

stolid *adj* showing little or no interest or emotion; impassive. ▪ **stolidity** *noun.* ▪ **stolidly** *adv.* ▪ **stolidness** *noun.* [17c: from Latin *stolidus* dull]

stoma /ˈstoumə/ *noun* (***stomata*** /ˈstoumətə/) **1** *botany* one of many tiny pores that are found on the stems and leaves of vascular plants, where water loss from the plant and gaseous exchange between plant tissue and the atmosphere take place. **2** *biol* any small opening or pore in the surface of a living organism. [17c: Greek, meaning 'mouth']

stomach *noun* **1** in the alimentary canal of vertebrates: a large sac-like organ where food is temporarily stored until it is partially digested. **2** *loosely* the area around the abdomen; the belly. ▸ *verb* **1** *informal* to bear or put up with: *can't stomach his arrogance.* **2** to be able to eat, drink or digest easily: *find red meat very hard to stomach.* [14c: from Greek *stomachos*]

IDIOMS **have the stomach for sth** *informal* to have the inclination, desire, courage, determination, etc for it: *has the stomach for dangerous sports.*

stomacher *noun, hist* an ornate covering, worn by women, for the chest and abdomen that was often decorated with jewels, worn on the front of the bodice. [15c, when it was a garment worn by both men and women]

stomachful *noun* **1** the amount a stomach can hold. **2** an amount that is greater than can be tolerated: *had an absolute stomachful of your lies.*

stomach pump *noun* an apparatus that includes a long tube which is inserted down the throat and into the stomach, used medically for sucking out the contents of the stomach, esp in cases of drug overdosing and other forms of suspected poisoning.

stomata see under **stoma**

stomp *verb, intr* to stamp or tread heavily. [19c: orig a US dialectal variant of **stamp**]

stone *noun* (***stones*** or in sense 7 ***stone***) **1** the hard solid material that rocks are made of. **2 a** a small fragment of rock, eg a pebble; **b** anything that resembles this: *hailstone.* **3** *usu in compounds* a shaped piece of stone that has a designated purpose, eg paving stone, milestone, tombstone, etc. **4** a gemstone. **5** the hard woody middle part of some fruits, eg peach, nectarine, plum, etc, which contains the seed. **6** a hard mass that sometimes forms in the gall bladder, kidney, etc, which often causes pain and which often requires surgical removal. **7** a UK measure of weight equal to 14 pounds or 6.35 kilograms. **8** a dull light grey colour. ▸ *verb* **1** to pelt with stones as a punishment. **2** to remove the stone from (fruit). ▸ *adv, in compounds* completely: *stone-cold.* [Anglo-Saxon *stan*]

IDIOMS **a stone's throw** *informal* a short distance. **leave no stone unturned** to try all the possibilities imaginable or make every possible effort.

Stone Age *noun* the period in human history when tools and weapons were made of stone. *as adj* (**Stone-age** *or* **stone-age**) **a** from or relating to this period: *Stone-age remains;* **b** old-fashioned: *stone-age technology.*

stone circle *noun, archaeol* any of many circular or near-circular rings of standing stones that are found throughout N Europe, which date from the late Neolithic and Early Bronze Ages and whose exact function is unknown.

stone-cold *adj* completely cold.

IDIOMS **stone-cold sober** absolutely sober.

stoned *adj, slang* **1** in a state of drug-induced euphoria. **2** of a fruit: with the stone removed.

stone-deaf *adj* unable to hear at all.

stoneground *adj* of flour: produced by grinding between millstones.

stonemason *noun* someone who is skilled in shaping stone for building work. ▪ **stonemasonry** *noun.*

stonewall *verb* **1** *tr & intr* to hold up progress, esp in parliament, intentionally, eg by obstructing discussion, giving long irrelevant speeches, etc. **2** *intr, cricket* of a batsman: to bat extremely defensively.

stoneware *noun* a type of hard coarse pottery made from clay that has a high proportion of silica, sand or flint in it.

stonewashed *adj* of new clothes or a fabric, esp denim: having a faded and worn appearance because of the abrasive action of the small pieces of pumice stone that they have been washed with.

stonework *noun* **1** a structure or building part that has been made out of stone. **2** the process of working in stone.

stonking *adj, informal* excellent. ▸ *adv* extremely: *a stonking big cup of coffee.* [1980s]

stony *or* **stoney** *adj* (***-ier, -iest***) **1** covered with stones. **2** relating to or resembling stone or stones. **3** unfriendly; unfeeling; callous: *a stony expression.* **4 a** fixed: *a stony stare;* **b** unrelenting: *a stony silence.* ▪ **stonily** *adv.*

stony-broke *adj, Brit informal* absolutely without money; penniless.

stood *past tense, past participle of* **stand**

stooge *noun* **1** a performer whose function is to provide a comedian with opportunities for making jokes and who is often also the butt of the jokes. **2** an assistant, esp one who is given unpleasant tasks or who is exploited in some way. ▸ *verb, intr* to act as a stooge for someone. [Early 20c]

stool *noun* **1** a simple seat without a back. **2** a footstool. **3** faeces. [Anglo-Saxon *stol*]

stool pigeon *noun* a police informer.

stoop[1] *verb, intr* **1** (*sometimes* **stoop down**) to bend the upper body forward and down. **2** to walk with head and shoulders bent forward. **3** (*often* **stoop to sth**) **a** to degrade oneself to do it: *How could you stoop to shoplifting?;* **b** to deign or condescend to do it. ▸ *noun* **1** a bent posture: *walks with a stoop.* **2**

a downward swoop. ▪ **stooped** *adj* bent. [Anglo-Saxon *stupian*]

stoop[2] *noun, N Am, esp US* an open platform, usu a wooden one, with steps leading up to it that runs along the front of a house and sometimes round the sides as well. [18c: from Dutch *stoep*]

stoop[3] an alternative spelling of **stoup**

stop *verb* (***stopped, stopping***) **1** *tr & intr* to bring or come to rest, a standstill or an end; to cease or cause to cease moving, operating or progressing. **2** to prevent. **3** to withhold or keep something back. **4** to block, plug or close something. **5** to instruct a bank not to honour (a cheque). **6** *intr, informal* to stay or reside temporarily: *stopped the night with friends.* **7** *music* to adjust the vibrating length of (a string) by pressing down with a finger. ▸ *noun* **1** an act of stopping. **2** a regular stopping place, eg on a bus route. **3** the state of being stopped; a standstill. **4** a device that prevents further movement: *a door stop.* **5** a temporary stay, esp when it is en route for somewhere else. **6** a **full stop**. **7** **a** a set of organ pipes that have a uniform tone; **b** a knob that allows the pipes to be brought into and out of use. **8** *phonetics* any consonant sound that is made by the sudden release of air that has built up behind the lips, teeth, tongue, etc. [Anglo-Saxon *stoppian*]

IDIOMS **pull out all the stops** to try one's best. **put a stop to sth** to cause it to end, esp abruptly. **stop at nothing** to be prepared to do anything, no matter how unscrupulous, in order to achieve an aim, outcome, etc.

PHRASAL VERBS **stop off, in** *or* **by** to visit, esp on the way to somewhere else. See also **stop-off**. **stop over** to make a break in a journey. See also **stop-off**.

stopcock *noun* a valve that controls the flow of liquid, gas, steam, etc in a pipe and which is usu operated by an external lever or handle.

stopgap *noun* a temporary substitute.

stop-off *or* **stop-over** *noun* a brief or temporary stop during a longer journey.

stoppage *noun* **1** an act of stopping or the state of being stopped. **2** an amount deducted from wages. **3** an organized withdrawal of labour, eg as in a strike.

stopper *noun* a cork, plug or bung.

stop press *noun* late news that can be placed in a specially reserved space of a newspaper even after printing has begun.

stopwatch *noun* a watch that is used for accurately recording the elapsed time in races, etc.

storage *noun* **1** the act of storing or the state of being stored. **2** space reserved for storing things. **3** *comput* the act or process of storing information in a computer's memory. [17c: from **store**]

storage capacity *noun, comput* the maximum amount that can be held in a memory system.

storage device *noun, comput* any piece of equipment, such as a disk, that data can be stored on.

storage heater *noun* a device that encloses a stack of bricks which accumulate and store heat (usu generated from overnight off-peak electricity) which is then slowly released by convection during the daytime.

storax /ˈstɔːraks/ *noun* **1** any of several tropical or subtropical trees which have clusters of white showy flowers. **2** a resin obtained from these trees which smells of vanilla and which was formerly used in medicine and perfumery. [14c]

store *noun* **1** a supply, usu one that is kept in reserve for use in the future. **2** **a** *Brit* a shop, esp a large one that is part of a chain: *department store*; **b** *N Am, esp US* a small grocery, often also selling a wide variety of other goods. **3** (*also* **stores**) a place where stocks or supplies are kept, eg a warehouse. **4** a computer's **memory**. ▸ *verb* **1** (*also* **store away** *or* **store up**) to put aside for future use. **2** to put something, eg furniture, into a warehouse for temporary safekeeping. **3** to put something into a computer's memory. ▪ **stored** *adj.* [13c: from Latin *instaurare* to set up or restore]

IDIOMS **in store 1** kept in reserve; ready to be supplied. **2** destined to happen; imminent: *a surprise in store.* **set** *or* **lay store** *or* **great store by sth** to value it highly.

store card *noun* a credit card that is issued by a department store for exclusive use in that store or any of its branches. Also called **charge card**.

storehouse *noun* a place where things are stored.

storekeeper *noun, N Am, esp US* a person whose job is to look after a store or shop, keep track of supplies, order new stock, etc.

storeman *noun* a person whose job is to look after and monitor goods, etc that are kept in store.

storeroom *noun* **1** a room that is used for keeping thing in. **2** space for storing things.

storey *or* (*N Am, esp US*) **story** *noun* (***storeys*** *or* ***stories***) a level, floor or tier of a building. [14c]

stork *noun* a large wading bird that has long legs, a long bill and neck, and usu black and white plumage. [Anglo-Saxon *storc*]

storm *noun* **1** an outbreak of violent weather, with severe winds and heavy falls of rain, hail or snow that is often accompanied by thunder and lightning. **2** a violent reaction, outburst or show of feeling: *a storm of protest.* **3** a furious burst, eg of gunfire or applause. ▸ *verb* **1** *intr* **a** to go or come loudly and angrily: *stormed out of the meeting*; **b** to come or go forcefully: *stormed through the defence to score.* **2** to say or shout something angrily: *stormed abuse at him.* **3** *military* to make a sudden violent attack on something: *stormed the embassy.* ▪ **storming** *noun, adj.* [Anglo-Saxon *storm*]

IDIOMS **a storm in a teacup** *informal* a big fuss about something unimportant. **take sb** *or* **sth by storm 1** to enthral or captivate them or it totally and instantly. **2** *military* to capture them or it by storming.

storm cloud *noun* **1** a big heavy dark-looking cloud that signals the approach of bad weather. **2** something that is seen as a bad omen.

storm door *noun* an extra outer door that gives added protection in bad weather.

stormtrooper *noun* **a** *hist* a member of the **SA**, a paramilitary wing of the Nazi Party; **b** a member of a group of troops trained to make sudden attacks.

stormy *adj* (***-ier, -iest***) **1** affected by storms or high winds. **2** of a person or their temperament, etc or of circumstances, etc: characterized by violence, passion, emotion, etc; unpredictable: *a stormy relationship.* ▪ **stormily** *adv.* ▪ **storminess** *noun.*

story[1] *noun* (***-ies***) **1** a written or spoken description of an event or series of events which can be real or imaginary. **2** the plot of a novel, play, film, etc. See also

storyline. **3** an incident, event, etc that has the potential to be interesting, amusing, etc. **4** a news article. **5** *informal* a lie. [13c: from French *estorie*]

IDIOMS **cut a long story short** to omit the finer details when telling something.

story² see **storey**

storyboard *noun* a series of sketches, photos, etc that shows the order of the camera shots etc in the shooting of a film.

storybook *noun* a book that contains a tale or a collection of tales, esp one for children.

storyline *noun* the plot of a novel, play or film.

story-teller *noun* **1** someone who tells stories, esp someone who does this in conversation habitually or exceptionally well. **2** *informal* a liar.

stotious see **stocious**

stoup *or* **stoop** /stuːp/ *noun* a basin for holy water. [18c: from Norse *staup* beaker]

stout *adj* **1** of someone: well-built; fattish. **2** hard-wearing; robust. **3** courageous; steadfastly reliable. ▶ *noun* dark beer that has a strong malt flavour. ▪ **stoutly** *adv*. ▪ **stoutness** *noun*. [14c: from French *estout*]

stout-hearted *adj* courageous; steadfastly reliable. ▪ **stout-heartedly** *adv*. ▪ **stout-heartedness** *noun*.

stove¹ *noun* **1** a domestic cooker. **2** any cooking or heating apparatus, eg an industrial kiln. [Anglo-Saxon *stofa* hot air bath]

stove² see **stave**

stovepipe *noun* **1** a metal funnel that takes smoke away from a stove. **2** (*in full* **stovepipe hat**) a tall cylindrical silk dress hat worn by men.

stow *verb* (*often* **stow sth away**) to pack or store it, esp out of sight. [Anglo-Saxon *stow* a place]

PHRASAL VERBS **stow away** to hide on a ship, aircraft or vehicle in the hope of travelling free.

stowage *noun* **1** a place, charge, space, etc for stowing things. **2** the act or an instance of stowing.

stowaway *noun* someone who hides on a ship, aeroplane, etc in the hope of being able to get to the destination undetected.

strabismus *noun, med* the technical term for a **squint** of the eye, which is caused by a muscular defect that prevents parallel vision. [17c: from Greek *strabos* squinting]

straddle *verb* **1** to have one leg or part on either side of something or someone: *straddled the horse*. **2** *informal* **a** to adopt a neutral or non-committal attitude towards something; **b** to seem to be in favour of or see the advantage of both sides of something at once. ▶ *noun* **1** an act of straddling. **2** a stance or attitude that is non-committal. [16c: related to **stride**]

strafe *verb* to attack someone or something with heavy machine-gun fire from a low-flying aircraft. [1915: from German *strafen* to punish]

straggle *verb, intr* **1** to grow or spread untidily. **2** to lag behind or stray from the main group or path, etc. ▪ **straggler** *noun*. ▪ **straggly** *adj* (**-ier, -iest**). [14c]

straight *adj* **1** not curved, bent, curly or wavy, etc: *straight hair*. **2** without deviations or detours; direct: *a straight road*. **3** level; horizontal; not sloping, leaning, or twisted: *Is the picture straight?* **4** frank; open; direct: *a straight answer*. **5** respectable; legitimate; not dishonest or criminal: *a straight deal*. **6** neat; tidy; in good order. **7** successive; in a row: *won three straight sets*. **8** of a drink, esp alcoholic: undiluted; neat. **9** having all debts and favours paid back. **10** not comic; serious. **11** *informal* conventional in tastes and opinions. **12** *informal* heterosexual. ▶ *adv* **1** in or into a level, upright, etc position or posture: *Is the picture hung straight?* **2** following an undeviating course; directly: *went straight home*. **3** immediately: *I'll come round straight after work*. **4** honestly; frankly: *told him straight that it was over*. **5** seriously: *played the part straight*. ▶ *noun* **1** a straight line or part, eg of a race track. **2** *informal* a heterosexual person. ▪ **straightness** *noun*. [Anglo-Saxon *streht*]

IDIOMS **go straight** *informal* to stop taking part in criminal activities and live an honest life. **straight away** immediately. **straight off** without thinking, researching, etc: *couldn't say straight off*. **straight out** without any equivocation; bluntly: *asked her straight out if she was seeing someone else*. **straight up** *informal* honestly; really. **the straight and narrow** the honest, respectable, sober, etc way of life or behaving.

straight, strait

Be careful not to use the spelling **straight** when you mean **strait**:

Much of the world's oil is transported through the Strait of Hormuz.

They found themselves in dire financial straits.

straightedge *noun* a strip or stick that is used for testing the straightness of something or for drawing straight lines.

straighten *verb, tr & intr* **1** to make or become straight. **2** (*sometimes* **straighten out sth**) to resolve, disentangle, make something less complicated or put it into order. **3** *intr* (*often* **straighten up**) to stand upright, esp after bending down.

straight face *noun* an unsmiling expression which is usu hiding the desire to laugh.

straightforward *adj* **1** without difficulties or complications; simple. **2** honest and frank. ▪ **straightforwardly** *adv*. ▪ **straightforwardness** *noun*.

straight man *noun* a comedian's stooge.

strain¹ *verb* **1** to injure or weaken (oneself or a part of one's body) through overexertion. **2** *intr* to make violent efforts. **3** to make extreme use of or demands on something. **4** to pass something through or pour something into a sieve or colander. **5** (*often* **strain sth off**) to remove it by the use of a sieve or colander. **6** to stretch or draw it tight. **7** (*usu* **strain at sth**) to tug it forcefully. **8** *intr* to feel or show reluctance or disgust; to balk. ▶ *noun* **1** an injury caused by overexertion, esp a wrenching of the muscles. **2** an act of forceful mental or physical perseverance or effort: *Talking to her is such a strain*. **3** the fatigue resulting from such an effort. **4** mental tension; stress. **5** *physics* a measure of the deformation of an object when it is subjected to stress which is equal to the change in dimension, eg change in length, divided by the original dimension, eg original length. **6** (*also* **strains**) a melody or tune, or a snatch of one: *the strains of distant pipes*. **7** one's tone in speech or writing. ▪ **straining** *adj, noun*. [13c: from French *estraindre*]

strain² *noun* **1** a group of animals (esp farm livestock) or plants (esp crops) that is maintained by inbreeding, etc so that particular characteristics can be retained. **2** an inherited trait: *a strain of madness in the family*. [Anglo-Saxon *streon* a begetting]

strained *adj* **1** of an action, way of talking, someone's manner, etc: not natural or easy; forced. **2** of an atmosphere, relations, etc: not friendly or relaxed; tense.

strainer *noun* a small sieve or colander.

strait *noun* **1** (*often* **straits**) a narrow strip of water that links two larger areas of ocean or sea. **2** (**straits**) difficulty; hardship: *dire straits.* [13c: from French *estreit*]

strait, straight
Be careful not to use the spelling **strait** when you mean **straight**:
a straight road
I'll come round straight after work.

straiten *verb* **1** to distress, esp financially. **2** to restrict. ▪ **straitened** *adj*: *found themselves in straitened circumstances.* [17c: from **strait**]

straitjacket *noun* **1** a jacket which has very long sleeves that can be crossed over the chest and tied behind the back, used for restraining someone who has violent tendencies. **2** anything that prevents freedom of development or expression.

strait-laced *adj* of someone, their attitude, opinions, etc: strictly correct in moral behaviour and attitudes; prudish.

strand[1] *verb* **1** to run (a ship) aground. **2** to leave someone in a helpless position, eg without transport. ▸ *noun, literary* a shore or beach. [Anglo-Saxon *strand* seashore]

strand[2] *noun* **1** a single thread, fibre, length of hair, etc, either alone or twisted or plaited with others to form a rope, cord or braid. **2** a single element or component part. [15c]

stranded *adj* **1** left without any money, means of transport, etc. **2** driven ashore, aground, etc.

strange *adj* **1** not known or experienced before. **2** unfamiliar or alien. **3** not usual, ordinary or predictable. **4** difficult to explain or understand; odd. ▪ **strangely** *adv.* ▪ **strangeness** *noun.* [13c: from French *estrange*]

stranger *noun* **1** someone whom one does not know. **2** someone who comes from a different place, home town, family, etc.
IDIOMS **a stranger to sth** someone who is unfamiliar with or inexperienced in something: *no stranger to trouble.*

strangle *verb* **1** to kill or attempt to kill by squeezing the throat with the hands, a cord, etc. **2** to hold back or suppress (eg a scream or laughter). **3** to hinder or stop (the development or expression of something): *The job strangled her creativity.* ▪ **strangler** *noun.* [14c: from French *estrangler*]

stranglehold *noun* **1** a choking hold in wrestling. **2** a position of total control; a severely repressive influence.

strangulate *verb* **1** *med* to press or squeeze so as to stop the flow of blood or air. **2** to **strangle**. ▪ **strangulation** *noun.* [17c: related to **strangle**]

strap *noun* **1** a narrow strip of leather or fabric which can be used for hanging something from, carrying or fastening something, etc. **2** (*also* **shoulder strap**) either of a pair of strips of fabric by which a garment hangs from the shoulders. **3 a** a leather belt that is used for giving a beating as punishment; **b** (**the strap**) a beating of this kind, formerly used in some schools: *got the strap for being cheeky.* **4** a loop that hangs down on a bus or train to provide a hand-hold for a standing passenger. ▸ *verb* (***strapped, strapping***) **1** (*also* **strap up**) to fasten or bind something with a strap or straps. **2** to beat something with a strap. ▪ **strapless** *adj.* [16c: a dialect form of **strop**[1]]

straphanger *noun, informal* **1** a standing passenger on a bus, train, etc, esp one who holds onto a strap. **2** a commuter who uses public transport.

strapped *adj* short of money.
IDIOMS **strapped for sth** in dire need of it, esp money, staff, etc.

strapping *adj* tall and strong-looking.

strappy *adj* of shoes, clothes, etc: distinguished by having lots of straps: *a pair of strappy sandals.*

strata see **stratum**

stratagem *noun* a trick or plan, esp one for deceiving an enemy or gaining an advantage. [15c: from Greek *strategema* an act of generalship]

strategic /strəˈtiːdʒɪk/ *adj* **1** characteristic of or relating to strategy or a strategy. **2** of weapons: designed for a direct long-range attack on an enemy's homeland, rather than for close-range battlefield use. ▪ **strategically** *adv.* [19c: from French *strategique*]

strategy *noun* (***-ies***) **1** the process of, or skill in, planning and conducting a military campaign. **2** a long-term plan for future success or development. ▪ **strategist** *noun.* [17c: from French *stratégie*]

strath *noun, Scot* a broad flat valley with a river running through it. [16c: from Gaelic *srath*]

strathspey *noun* **1** a Scottish folk dance that has a similar format to the reel but with slower, more gliding steps. **2** a piece of music for this kind of dance. [17c: named after Strathspey, in Scotland]

strati *pl of* **stratum**

stratify *verb* (***-ies, -ied***) **1** *geol* to deposit (rock) in layers or strata. **2** to classify or arrange things into different grades, levels or social classes. ▪ **stratification** *noun.* ▪ **stratified** *adj*: *stratified rock* • *a highly stratified society.* [17c: from Latin *stratum* something laid down + *facere* to make]

stratocumulus /stratoʊˈkjuːmjʊləs/ *noun* (***stratocumuli*** /-laɪ/) *meteorol* a cloud that occurs as a large globular or rolled mass. [19c: from Latin *strato-* + **cumulus**]

stratosphere *noun, meteorol* the layer of the Earth's atmosphere that extends from about 12km to about 50km above the Earth's surface, contains the ozone layer, and is situated above the **troposphere** and below the **mesosphere**. ▪ **stratospheric** *adj.*

stratovolcano *noun* a **composite volcano**.

stratum /ˈstrɑːtəm/ *noun* (***strata*** /-tə/) **1** a layer of sedimentary rock. **2** a layer of cells in living tissue. **3** a layer of the atmosphere or the ocean. **4** a level, grade or social class. [16c: Latin, meaning 'something spread']

stratus /ˈstreɪtəs/ *noun* (***strati*** /-taiː/) *meteorol* a wide horizontal sheet of low grey layered cloud. [Early 20c: Latin, from *sternere* to spread]

straw *noun* **1** the parts of cereal crops that remain after threshing, which may be ploughed back into the soil, burned as stubble or used as litter or feed for animals, for thatching and weaving into hats, baskets, etc. **2** a single stalk of dried grass or cereal crop. **3** a thin hollow tube for sucking up a drink. **4** a pale yellow colour. ▪ **strawlike** *adj.* [Anglo-Saxon *streaw*]

IDIOMS **clutch** *or* **grasp at straws** to resort to an alternative option, remedy, etc in desperation, even though it is unlikely to succeed. **draw straws** to decide on something by the chance picking of straws, one of which is significantly longer or shorter than the rest. **draw, get, pick,** *etc* **the short straw** to be the person chosen from a group to carry out an unpleasant task, duty, etc.

strawberry *noun* (***-ies***) **1** a juicy red fruit which consists of tiny pips embedded in the surface. **2** the flavour or colour of this fruit. [Anglo-Saxon *streawberige*]

strawberry blonde *adj* of hair: reddish-blonde. ▸ *noun* a woman who has hair of this colour.

strawberry mark *noun* a reddish birthmark.

straw poll *or* **straw vote** *noun* an unofficial vote, esp taken on the spot among a small number of people, to get some idea of general opinion on a specified issue.

stray *verb, intr* **1** to wander away from the right path or place, usu unintentionally. **2** to move away unintentionally from the main or current topic in thought, speech or writing: *He usually strays a bit from the main topic during a lecture.* **3** to depart from the accepted or required pattern of behaviour, living, etc. ▸ *noun* an ownerless or lost pet, farm animal, etc. ▸ *adj* **1** of a pet, etc: homeless; ownerless; lost. **2** not the result of a regular or intended process; random; casual: *stray gunfire.* [13c: from French *estraier* to wander]

streak *noun* **1** a long irregular stripe or band. **2** a flash of lightning. **3** an element or characteristic: *a cowardly streak.* **4** a short period; a spell: *a streak of bad luck.* **5** *informal* a naked dash through a public place. ▸ *verb* **1** to mark with a streak or streaks. **2** *intr* to move at great speed; to dash. **3** *intr, informal* to dash naked through a public place. ▪ **streaked** *adj.* [Anglo-Saxon *strica* stroke]

streaker *noun, informal* someone who makes a naked dash in public.

streaky *adj* (***-ier, -iest***) **1** marked with streaks. **2** of bacon: with alternate layers of fat and meat.

stream *noun* **1** a very narrow river; a brook, burn or rivulet. **2** any constant flow of liquid: *streams of tears.* **3** anything that moves continuously in a line or mass: *a stream of traffic.* **4** an uninterrupted and unrelenting burst or succession, eg of insults: *a stream of questions.* **5** general direction, trend or tendency. **6** *Brit, education* any of several groups that pupils in some schools are allocated to, so that those of a broadly similar ability can be taught together. ▸ *verb* **1** *intr* to flow or move continuously and in large quantities or numbers. **2** *intr* to float or trail in the wind. **3** *Brit* to divide (pupils) into streams. [Anglo-Saxon *stream*]

streamer *noun* **1** a long paper ribbon used to decorate a room. **2** a roll of coloured paper that uncoils when thrown. **3** a long thin flag.

streamline *verb* to make streamlined or more streamlined.

streamlined *adj* **1** of a vehicle, aircraft, or vessel: shaped so as to move smoothly and efficiently with minimum resistance to air or water. **2** of an organization, process, etc: extremely efficient, with little or no waste of resources, excess staff, etc.

stream of consciousness *noun* **1** *psychol* the non-stop and often random flow of thoughts, emotions, etc that continuously bombard the waking mind. **2** a narrative technique that attempts to simulate this, eg by discarding conventional syntax and linking apparently unconnected thoughts. [1890s: first coined by the American psychologist, William James]

street *noun* **1** (*also* in addresses **Street**) a public road with pavements and buildings at the side or sides, esp one in a town. **2** the road and the buildings together. **3** the area between the opposite pavements that is used by traffic. **4** the people in the buildings or on the pavements: *tell the whole street.* ▸ *adj* relating to, happening on, etc a street or streets: *a street map.* [Anglo-Saxon *stræt*]

IDIOMS **be right up** *or* **up sb's street** *informal* to be ideally suited to them. **streets ahead of sb** *or* **sth** *informal* much more advanced than or superior to them.

streetcar *noun, N Am, esp US* a tram.

street cred *noun, informal* (*in full* **street credibility**) approval of those in tune with modern urban culture.

streetlamp *or* **streetlight** *noun* a light, usu one of a series, at the top of a lamppost that lights up the road for motorists and pedestrians at night.

street value *noun* the price something, such as illegal drugs, stolen goods, etc, is likely to go for when it is sold to the person who will use it.

streetwise *adj, informal* **1** experienced in and well able to survive the ruthlessness of modern urban life, esp in areas such as drugs, crime, etc. **2** cynical.

strength *noun* **1** the quality or degree of being physically or mentally strong. **2** the ability to withstand pressure or force. **3** degree or intensity, eg of emotion or light. **4** potency, eg of a drug or alcoholic drink. **5** forcefulness of an argument. **6** a highly valued quality or asset. **7** the number of people, etc needed or normally expected in a group, esp in comparison to those actually present or available: *with the workforce only at half strength.* [Anglo-Saxon *strengthu*]

IDIOMS **go from strength to strength** to achieve a series of successes, each surpassing the last. **on the strength of sth** on the basis of it; judging by it.

strengthen *verb, tr & intr* to make or become strong or stronger.

strenuous *adj* **1** characterized by the need for or the use of great effort or energy. **2** performed with great effort or energy and therefore very tiring. ▪ **strenuously** *adv.* [16c: from Latin *strenuus* brisk]

streptococcus /strɛptoʊˈkɒkəs/ *noun* (***streptococci*** /-ˈkɒksaɪ/) any of several species of bacterium that cause conditions such as scarlet fever and throat infections. ▪ **streptococcal** *or* **streptococcic** *adj.* [19c: from Greek *streptos* twisted + *kokkos* berry]

streptomycin *noun* an antibiotic used to treat various bacterial infections. [1940s: from Greek *streptos* twisted + *mykes* fungus]

stress *noun* **1** physical or mental overexertion. **2** importance, emphasis or weight laid on or attached to something: *The stress was on speed not quality.* **3** the comparatively greater amount of force that is used in the pronunciation of a particular syllable: *The stress is on the first syllable.* **4** *physics* the force that is exerted per unit area on a body causing it to change its dimensions. ▸ *verb* **1** to emphasize or attach importance to something. **2** to pronounce (a sound, word, etc) with emphasis. ▪ **stressed** *adj.* ▪ **stressful** *adj.* ▪ **stressless** *adj.* [14c: shortened form of **distress**]

PHRASAL VERBS **stress sb out** to put them under severe mental, emotional, etc pressure.

stressed-out *adj* debilitated or afflicted by emotional, nervous or mental tension.

stretch *verb* **1** *tr & intr* to make or become temporarily or permanently longer or wider by pulling or drawing out. **2** *intr* to extend in space or time. **3** *tr & intr* to straighten and extend the body or part of the body, eg when waking or reaching out. **4** *tr & intr* to make or become tight or taut. **5** *intr* to lie at full length. **6** *intr* to be extendable without breaking. **7** *tr & intr* to last or make something last longer through economical use. **8** (*also* **stretch out**) to prolong or last. **9** to make extreme demands on or severely test (eg resources or physical abilities): *The course stretched even the brightest students.* **10** to exaggerate (the truth, a story, etc). ▸ *noun* **1** an act of stretching, esp (a part of) the body. **2** a period of time; a spell. **3** an expanse, eg of land or water. **4** capacity to extend or expand. **5** *horse-racing* a straight part on a race-track or course, esp the part that leads up to the finishing line. **6** *informal* a difficult task or test: *a bit of a stretch to get there by six.* **7** *slang* a term of imprisonment: *did a three year stretch for robbery.* [Anglo-Saxon *streccan*]

IDIOMS **at a stretch 1** continuously; without interruption. **2** with difficulty. **stretch a point 1** to agree to something not strictly in keeping with the rules; to bend the rules. **2** to exaggerate. **stretch one's legs** to take a short walk to invigorate oneself after inactivity.

stretcher *noun* **1** a device that is used for carrying a sick or wounded person in a lying position. **2** something that stretches. ▸ *verb* to carry someone on a stretcher. [15c: from **stretch**]

stretcher-bearer *noun* someone who carries a stretcher.

stretch limo *noun, N Am* an elongated and very luxurious car.

stretchy *adj* (**-ier, -iest**) of materials, clothes, etc: having the ability or tendency to stretch.

strew *verb* (*past participle* ***strewed*** *or* ***strewn***) **1** to scatter untidily: *Papers were strewn across the floor.* **2** to cover with an untidy scattering: *The floor was strewn with papers.* [Anglo-Saxon *streowian*]

stria /ˈstraɪə/ *noun* (***striae*** /ˈstraɪiː/) *geol, biol* any of a series of parallel grooves in rock, or furrows or streaks of colour in plants and animals. [17c: Latin, meaning 'a furrow']

striated *adj* marked with striae; striped.

striation *noun* **1** the patterning of striae. **2** the condition of having striae.

stricken *adj, often in compounds* **1** deeply affected, esp by grief, sorrow, panic, etc: *horror-stricken.* **2** afflicted by or suffering from disease, sickness, injury, etc: *a typhoid-stricken community.* [14c: as the *past participle* of **strike**]

strict *adj* **1** demanding obedience or close observance of rules; severe. **2** observing rules or practices very closely: *strict Catholics.* **3** exact; precise: *in the strict sense of the word.* **4** meant or designated to be closely obeyed: *strict instructions.* **5** complete: *in the strictest confidence.* ▪ **strictly** *adv.* ▪ **strictness** *noun.* [16c: from Latin *strictus*]

stricture *noun* a severe criticism. [14c: from Latin *strictura* tightening]

stride *noun* **1** a single long step in walking. **2** the length of such a step. **3** a way of walking in long steps. **4** (*usu* **strides**) a measure of progress or development: *make great strides.* **5** a rhythm, eg in working, playing a game, etc that someone or something aims for or settles into: *soon got into his stride.* **6** (**strides**) *chiefly Aust slang* trousers. ▸ *verb* (*past tense* ***strode,*** *past participle* ***stridden***) **1** *intr* to walk with long steps. **2** *intr* to take a long step. **3** to step or extend over something: *easily strode the puddle.* [Anglo-Saxon *stridan*]

IDIOMS **take sth in one's stride** to achieve it or cope with it effortlessly, as if part of a regular routine.

strident *adj* **1** of a sound, esp a voice: loud and harsh. **2** loudly assertive: *a strident clamour for reforms.* ▪ **stridency** *noun.* [17c: from Latin *stridere* to creak]

strife *noun* **1** bitter conflict or fighting. **2** *informal* trouble of any sort; hassle. [13c: from French *estrif*]

strike *verb* (*past tense, past participle* ***struck***) **1** to hit someone or something; to give a blow to them. **2** to come or bring into heavy contact with someone or something: *The car struck the lamppost.* **3** to make a particular impression on someone: *They struck me as a strange couple.* **4** to come into one's mind; to occur to someone: *It struck me as strange.* **5** to cause (a match) to ignite through friction. **6** *tr & intr* of a clock: to indicate the time, eg on the hour, half-hour, quarter-hour, with chimes, etc. **7** *intr* to happen suddenly: *Disaster struck.* **8** *intr* to make a sudden attack. **9** to afflict someone suddenly; to cause to become by affliction: *The news struck him dumb.* **10** to introduce or inject suddenly: *The thought struck terror into them.* **11** to arrive at or settle (eg a bargain or a balance): *struck a fair deal for the car.* **12** to find a source of (eg oil, gold, etc). **13** *intr* to stop working as part of a collective protest against an employer, working conditions, pay, etc: *The factory has been striking for two weeks.* **14** to dismantle (a camp). **15** to make (a coin) by stamping metal. **16** to adopt (a posture or attitude). **17** *tr & intr* to draw (a line) in order to cross something out. ▸ *noun* **1** an act of hitting or dealing a blow. **2** a situation where a labour force refuses to work in order to protest against an employer, working conditions, pay, etc in the hope that, by doing this, their demands will be met. **3** a prolonged refusal to engage in a regular or expected activity, such as eating, in order to make some kind of a protest: *went on hunger strike.* **4** a military attack, esp one that is carried out by aircraft: *a pre-emptive strike on the ground troops.* **5** a discovery of a source, eg of gold, oil, etc. **6** *cricket* the position of being the batsman bowled at: *take strike.* **7** *baseball* a ball that the batter has taken a swing at but missed. [Anglo-Saxon *strican*]

IDIOMS **on strike** taking part in an industrial or other strike. **strike it lucky** *or* **rich** to enjoy luck or become rich suddenly and unexpectedly.

PHRASAL VERBS **strike back** to retaliate. **strike sb off 1** to remove (the name of a member of a professional body, eg a lawyer, doctor, accountant, etc) from the appropriate register, esp because of misconduct. **2** to remove (someone's name from an official list, register, etc). **strike sth out** to draw a line through (eg a name, etc) in order to to show a cancellation, removal, deletion, etc. **strike out for sth** to head towards it, esp in a determined way. **strike up** of a band, etc: to begin to play. **strike sth up** to start (eg a conversation, friendship, etc).

strike-breaker *noun* someone who continues to work while others **strike** (*verb* sense 13), or who is brought in to do the job of a striking worker.

striker *noun* **1** someone who takes part in a strike. **2** *football* a player who has an attacking role.

striking *adj* **1** impressive; arresting; attractive, esp in an unconventional way. **2** noticeable; marked: *a striking omission*. **3** on strike.

IDIOMS **be** *or* **come within striking distance** to be close, possible, achievable, etc.

string *noun* **1** thin cord, or a piece of this. **2** any of a set of pieces of stretched wire, catgut or other material that can vibrate to produce sound in various musical instruments such as the guitar, violin, piano, etc. **3** (**strings**) **a** the orchestral instruments in which sound is produced in this way, usu the violins, violas, cellos and double basses collectively; **b** the players of these instruments. **4** a group of similar things: *a string of racehorses*. **5** a series or succession: *a string of disasters*. **6** *comput* a group of characters that a computer can handle as a single unit. **7** one of several pieces of taut gut, etc that are used in sports rackets. **8** a set of things that are threaded together, eg beads, pearls, etc. **9** any cord-like thing. ▸ *verb* (***strung***) **1** to fit or provide with a string or strings. **2** (*often* **string sth up**) to hang, stretch or tie it with string. See also **strung-up**. **3** to thread (eg beads) onto a string. **4** to extend something in a string: *strung the onions*. [Anglo-Saxon *streng*]

IDIOMS **no strings attached** of eg an offer: having no undesirable conditions or limitations. **pull strings** *informal* to use one's influence, or relationships with influential people, to get something done.

PHRASAL VERBS **string sb along** to keep them in a state of deception or false hope. **string sb up** *informal* to kill them by hanging.

stringed *adj* of a musical instrument: having strings.

stringent /ˈstrɪndʒənt/ *adj* **1** of rules, terms, etc: severe; rigorous; strictly enforced. **2** marked by a lack of money. ▪ **stringency** *noun*. ▪ **stringently** *adv*. [17c: from Latin *stringere* to draw together]

stringer *noun* **1** a horizontal beam in a framework. **2** a journalist employed part-time to cover a particular town or area. **3** someone or something that strings.

string quartet *noun* a musical ensemble that is made up of two violins, a cello and a viola.

stringy *adj* (***-ier, -iest***) **1** like string, esp thin and thread-like. **2** of meat or other food: full of chewy fibres.

strip[1] *verb* (***stripped, stripping***) **1** to remove (a covering, etc) by peeling or pulling it off: *strip the beds*. **2** (*sometimes* **strip sth off**) to remove (the surface or contents of something): *stripped the varnish • stripped off the wallpaper*. **3** **a** to remove (the clothing) from someone: *They stripped him, then flogged him*; **b** *intr* (*also* **strip off**) *informal* to take one's clothes off. **4** (*also* **strip sth down**) to take it to pieces; to dismantle it: *stripped the engine*. **5** (*usu* **strip sb of sth**) to take it away from them: *stripped her of her dignity*. **6** *informal* to rob: *Burglars had stripped the place clean*. ▸ *noun* an act of undressing. ▪ **stripped** *adj*: *stripped pine*. ▪ **stripping** *noun*. [Anglo-Saxon *strypan*]

strip[2] *noun* **1** a long narrow, usu flat, piece of material, paper, land, etc. **2** *sport* lightweight distinctive clothing that is worn by a team: *Aberdeen's home strip is red*. [15c: from German *Strippe* a strap]

IDIOMS **tear strips off sb** to reprimand them severely and often angrily.

strip cartoon *noun* a sequence of drawings, eg in a newspaper, magazine, etc, that tell a comic or adventure story. Also called **comic strip**.

stripe *noun* **1** a band of colour. **2** a chevron or coloured band on a uniform that indicates rank. ▸ *verb* to mark with stripes. [15c: Dutch]

strip light *or* **strip lighting** *noun* a light or lighting that is given off by tube-shaped **fluorescent lights**.

stripling *noun, literary* a boy or youth.

stripper *noun* **1** *informal* a striptease artiste. **2** **a** a substance or appliance for removing paint, varnish, etc; **b** *in compounds*: *paint-stripper*.

strip search *noun* a thorough and often intimate search of someone's naked body, by police, customs officials, etc checking for concealed or smuggled items, esp drugs. ▸ *verb* (**strip-search**) to carry out a strip search on a suspect.

striptease *noun* a type of show where a performer slowly and gradually takes their clothes off one by one.

stripy *adj* (***-ier, -iest***) marked with stripes; striped.

strive *verb, intr* (*past tense* ***strove,*** *past participle* ***striven***) **1** to try extremely hard; to struggle: *will strive to be the best in Scotland*. **2** (**strive against sth**) to fight against it: *strove against his addiction*. [13c: from French *estriver* to quarrel]

strobe *noun* short form of **strobe lighting** or **stroboscope**. [1940s: from Greek *strobos* whirling round]

strobe lighting *noun* a type of powerful rapidly flashing light which creates an effect of jerky movement when it is directed on moving bodies.

stroboscope *noun* an instrument that uses a flashing light to measure or set the speed of rotating shafts, propellers, etc and which, when the speed of the light is equal to that of the rotating object, makes the object appear to be stationary. ▪ **stroboscopic** *adj*. [19c: from Greek *strobos* whirling + *skopeein* to view]

strode *past tense of* **stride**

stroganoff *noun, cookery* a dish that is traditionally made with strips of sautéed fillet steak, onions and mushrooms, cooked in a creamy white wine sauce. Also called **beef stroganoff**. [1930s: named after the 19c Russian diplomat, Count Paul Stroganov]

stroke *noun* **1** **a** any act or way of striking; **b** a blow. **2** *sport* **a** an act of striking a ball: *took six strokes at the par four*; **b** the way a ball is struck: *a well-timed ground stroke*. **3** a single movement with a pen, paintbrush, etc, or the line or daub produced. **4** **a** a single complete movement in a repeated series, as in swimming or rowing; **b** *usu in compounds* a particular named style of swimming: *backstroke*. **5** the total linear distance travelled by a piston in the cylinder of an engine. **6** **a** the action of a clock, etc striking, or the sound of this; **b** the time indicated or which would be indicated by a clock striking: *out the door on the stroke of five*. **7** a gentle caress or other touching movement, eg when patting a dog, etc. **8** a sloping line used to separate alternatives in writing or print. Also called **solidus. 9** *pathol* a sudden interruption to the supply of blood to the brain that results in loss of consciousness, often with accompanying paralysis of one side of the body and loss of speech, caused by bleeding from an artery, tissue blockage of an artery or a blood clot. **10** *informal* the least amount of work: *hasn't done a stroke all day.* ▸ *verb* **1** to caress in kindness or affection, often repeatedly. **2** to strike (a ball) smoothly and with seeming effortlessness. ▪ **stroking** *adj, noun.* [Anglo-Saxon *strac*]

IDIOMS **at a stroke** with a single action. **a stroke of sth** a significant or impressive instance of it, esp of genius or luck.

stroke play *noun, golf* a method of scoring that involves counting up the number of strokes taken at all 18 holes so that the player with the lower or lowest score wins. Compare **match play**.

stroll *verb, intr* to walk in a slow leisurely way. ▸ *noun* a leisurely walk. [17c]

stroller *noun* **1** someone who strolls. **2** *N Am* a pushchair.

stroma *noun* (***stromata***) *anatomy* the supporting framework of a body part, organ, blood corpuscle or cell. ▪ **stromatic** *or* **stromatous** *adj.* [19c: Latin, meaning 'a bed covering']

strong *adj* **1** exerting or capable of great force or power. **2** able to withstand rough treatment; robust. **3** of views, etc: firmly held or boldly expressed. **4** of taste, light, etc: sharply felt or experienced; powerful. **5** of coffee, alcoholic drink, etc: relatively undiluted with water or other liquid; concentrated. **6** of an argument, etc: having much force; convincing. **7** of language: bold or straightforward; rude or offensive. **8** of prices, values, etc: steady or rising: *a strong dollar.* **9** of a group: made up of about the specified number: *a gang fifty strong.* **10** of a colour: deep and intense. **11** of a wind: blowing hard. **12** impressive: *a strong candidate for the job.* **13** characterized by ability, stamina, good technique, etc: *a strong swimmer.* **14** of an urge, desire, feeling, etc: intense; powerful; overwhelming: *a strong feeling of distrust.* ▪ **strongly** *adv.* [Anglo-Saxon *strang*]

IDIOMS **come on strong** *informal* to be highly persuasive or assertive, often in a way that others might find disconcerting. **going strong** *informal* flourishing; thriving: *He's still going strong at 95.*

strongarm *adj, informal* **1** aggressively forceful. **2** making use of physical violence or threats.

strongbox *noun* a safe, or other sturdy, usu lockable, box for storing money or valuables in.

stronghold *noun* **1** a fortified place of defence, eg a castle. **2** a place where there is strong support (eg for a political party): *a Labour stronghold.*

strong interaction *or* **strong force** *noun, physics* a transfer of energy between **baryons** and **mesons** that is completed in about 10^{-23} seconds.

strong point *noun* something that someone is especially good at: *Maths was never my strong point.*

strongroom *noun* a room that is designed to be difficult to get into or out of so that valuables, prisoners, etc can be held for safekeeping.

strontium *noun, chem* (symbol **Sr**) a soft silvery-white highly reactive metallic element that is a good conductor of electricity. [Early 19c: named after Strontian, the name of the parish in Argyllshire, Scotland, where it was discovered]

strop[1] *noun* a strip of coarse leather or other abrasive material that is used for sharpening razors. ▸ *verb* (***stropped, stropping***) to sharpen (a razor) on a strop. [Anglo-Saxon]

strop[2] *noun* a bad temper, when the person concerned is awkward to deal with: *went off in a strop.* [Back formation from **stroppy**]

stroppy *adj* (***-ier, -iest***) *informal* quarrelsome, bad-tempered and awkward to deal with. ▪ **stroppily** *adv.* [1950s: prob from **obstreperous**]

strove *past tense of* **strive**

struck *verb, past tense, past participle of* **strike**.

IDIOMS **struck on sb** *or* **sth** *informal* infatuated with them or it; enthusiastic about them or it.

structural *adj* belonging or relating to structure or a basic structure or framework. ▪ **structurally** *adv.*

structural formula *noun, chem* a formula that shows the exact arrangement of the atoms within a molecule of a chemical compound.

structuralism *noun* an approach to various areas of study, eg literary criticism and linguistics, which seeks to identify underlying patterns or structures, esp as they might reflect patterns of behaviour or thought in society. ▪ **structuralist** *noun, adj.*

structure *noun* **1** the way in which the parts of a thing are arranged or organized. **2** a thing built or constructed from many smaller parts. **3** a building. ▸ *verb* to put into an organized form or arrangement. [15c: from Latin *structura*]

strudel /ˈstruːdəl; *German* ˈʃtrudəl/ *noun* a baked roll of thin pastry with a filling of fruit, esp apple. [19c: German, meaning 'whirlpool', from the way the pastry is rolled]

struggle *verb, intr* **1** to strive vigorously or make a strenuous effort under difficult conditions. **2** to make one's way with great difficulty. **3** to fight or contend. **4** to move the body around violently, eg in an attempt to get free. ▸ *noun* **1** an act of struggling. **2** a task requiring strenuous effort. **3** a fight or contest. ▪ **struggling** *noun, adj.* [14c]

strum *verb* (***strummed, strumming***) *tr & intr* to play (a stringed musical instrument, such as a guitar, or a tune on it) with sweeps of the fingers or thumb rather than with precise plucking. ▸ *noun* an act or bout of strumming. [18c: a word based on **thrum**, imitating the sound made]

strung *verb, past tense, past participle of* **string**. ▸ *adj* **1** of a musical instrument: fitted with strings. **2** *in compounds* of a person or animal: characterized by a specified type of temperament: *highly-strung.*

strung-up *adj, informal* tense; nervous.

strut *verb* (***strutted, strutting***) *intr* to walk in a proud or self-important way. ▸ *noun* **1** a strutting way of walking. **2** a bar or rod whose function is to support weight or take pressure; a prop. [Anglo-Saxon *strutian*]

strychnine /ˈstrɪkniːn/ *noun* a deadly poison that is obtained from the seeds of a tropical Indian tree and which can be used medicinally in small quantities as a nerve or appetite stimulant. [19c: from Greek *strychnos* nightshade]

stub *noun* **1** a short piece of something that remains when the rest of it has been used up, eg a pencil, etc. **2** the part of a cheque, ticket, receipt, etc that the holder retains as a record, proof of purchase, etc. ▸ *verb* (***stubbed, stubbing***) **1** to accidentally bump the end of (one's toe) against a hard surface. **2** (*usu* **stub out**) to extinguish (eg a cigarette) by pressing the end against a surface. [Anglo-Saxon *stubb*]

stubble *noun* **1** the mass of short stalks left in the ground after a crop has been harvested. **2** a short early growth of beard. [13c: from French *estuble*]

stubborn *adj* **1** resolutely or unreasonably unwilling to change one's opinions, ways, plans, etc; obstinate. **2** determined; unyielding. **3** difficult to treat, remove, deal with, etc: *stubborn stains.* ▪ **stubbornly** *adv.* ▪ **stubbornness** *noun.* [14c]

stubby *adj* (***-ier, -iest***) **1** short and broad or thick-set. **2** small and worn down: *a stubby pencil.* ▸ *noun* (***-ies***) *Aust informal* a small squat bottle of beer or the beer contained in such a bottle. ▪ **stubbiness** *noun.*

stucco *noun* (***stuccos*** *or* ***stuccoes***) **1** a fine plaster that is used for coating indoor walls and ceilings and for forming decorative cornices, mouldings, etc. **2** a rougher kind of plaster or cement used for coating outside walls. ▸ *verb* (***stuccos*** *or* ***stuccoes, stuccoed***) to coat with or mould out of stucco. ▪ **stuccoed** *or* **stucco'd** *adj.* [16c: Italian]

stuck *adj* **1** unable to give an answer, reason, etc. **2** unable to move. ▸ *verb, past tense, past participle of* **stick**[2].

IDIOMS **be stuck for sth** *informal* to be in need of it or at a loss for it. **stuck on sb** *informal* fond of or infatuated with them.

stuck-up *adj, informal* snobbish; conceited.

stud[1] *noun* **1** a rivet-like metal peg that is fitted on to a surface, eg of a garment, for decoration. **2** any of several peg-like projections on the sole of a sports boot or shoe that give added grip, when playing football, hockey, etc. **3** a type of small plain earring or nose-ring. **4** a fastener consisting of two small discs on either end of a short bar or shank, eg for fixing a collar to a shirt. **5** a short form of **press stud**. ▸ *verb* (***studded, studding***) to fasten or decorate with a stud or studs. [Anglo-Saxon *studu* post]

stud[2] *noun* **1** a male animal, esp a horse, kept for breeding. **2** (*also* **stud farm**) a place where animals, esp horses, are bred. **3** a collection of animals kept for breeding. [Anglo-Saxon *stod*]

student *noun* someone who is following a formal course of study, esp in higher or further education, although the word is now often applied to secondary school pupils too. *as adj: a student nurse.* [14c: from French *estudiant*]

studied *adj* **1** of an attitude, expression, etc: carefully practised or thought through and adopted or produced for effect; unspontaneous and affected. **2** carefully considered: *gave a studied report.*

studio *noun* **1** the workroom of an artist or photographer. **2** a room in which music recordings, or TV or radio programmes, are made. **3** **a** a company that produces films; **b** the premises where films are produced. [Early 19c: Italian, meaning 'study']

studio flat *noun* a small flat with one main room with open-plan living, eating and sleeping areas.

studious *adj* **1** characterized by a serious hard-working approach, esp to study. **2** carefully attentive. ▪ **studiously** *adv.* ▪ **studiousness** *noun.*

study *verb* (***-ies, -ied***) **1** *tr & intr* to set one's mind to acquiring knowledge and understanding, esp by reading, research, etc. **2** to take an educational course in (a subject): *studied French to A level.* **3** to look at or examine closely, or think about carefully: *studied her face.* ▸ *noun* (***-ies***) **1** the act or process of studying. **2** (**studies**) work done in the process of acquiring knowledge: *having to work interfered with her studies.* **3** a careful and detailed examination or consideration: *undertook a careful study of the problem.* **4** a work of art produced for the sake of practice, or in preparation for a more complex or detailed work. **5** a piece of music intended to exercise and develop the player's technique. **6** a private room where quiet work or study is carried out. [13c: from French *estudie*]

stuff *noun* **1** **a** any material or substance: *the stuff that dreams are made of;* **b** something that is suitable for, relates to, or is characterized by whatever is specified: *kids' stuff.* **2** movable belongings: *I'll just get my stuff.* **3** the characteristics that define someone, esp positive ones: *made of stronger stuff.* ▸ *verb* **1** to cram or thrust: *stuffed the clothes in the wardrobe.* **2** to fill to capacity; to overfill. **3** to put something away: *stuffed the letter in the drawer.* **4** to fill the hollow or hollowed-out part of something (eg a chicken, pepper, etc) with a mixture of other foods. **5** to fill out the disembodied skin of (an animal, bird, fish, etc) to recreate its living shape. See **taxidermy**. **6** to feed (oneself) greedily: *stuffed himself until he felt sick.* **7** (*also* **stuff up**) to block or clog something, eg a hole, the nose with mucus, etc. **8** *slang* to defeat someone convincingly. [14c: from French *estoffe*]

IDIOMS **do one's stuff** *informal* **1** to display one's talent or skill. **2** to perform the task that one is required to do: *You're always good at the music round – so go on, do your stuff.* **know one's stuff** *informal* to have a thorough understanding of the specific subject that one is concerned or involved with.

stuffed *adj* **1** of a food: having a filling: *stuffed aubergines.* **2** of a dead animal, bird, fish, etc: having had its internal body parts replaced by stuffing: *a stuffed tiger.* **3** of a toy, cushion, etc: filled with soft stuffing: *cuddled her stuffed kitten.* **4** (*also* **stuffed-up**) of the nose: blocked with mucus.

stuffed shirt *noun* a conservative or pompous person.

stuffing *noun* **1** any material that children's toys, cushions, animal skins, etc are filled with. **2** *cookery* any mixture which is used as a filling for poultry, vegetables, etc.

IDIOMS **knock the stuffing out of sb** to deprive them rapidly of strength, force, etc.

stuffy *adj* (***-ier, -iest***) **1** of a room, atmosphere, etc: lacking fresh, cool air; badly ventilated. **2** of someone or their attitude, etc: boringly formal, conventional or unadventurous; pompous. ▪ **stuffiness** *noun.*

stultify *verb* (***-ies, -ied***) **1** to cause something to be useless, worthless, futile, etc. **2** to dull the mind of someone, eg with tedious tasks. ▪ **stultification** *noun.* [18c: from Latin *stultus* foolish + *facere* to make]

stumble *verb, intr* **1** to lose one's balance and trip forwards after accidentally catching or misplacing one's foot. **2** to walk unsteadily. **3** to speak with frequent hesitations and mistakes. **4** to make a mistake in speech or action. **5** (**stumble across, into** *or* **upon**

sth) to arrive at, find, come across, etc it by chance. ▸ *noun* an act of stumbling. [14c as *stomble*]

stumbling-block *noun* **1** an obstacle or difficulty. **2** a cause of failure or faltering.

stumm see under **shtoom**

stump *noun* **1** the part of a felled or fallen tree that is left in the ground. **2** the short part of anything, eg a limb, that is left after the larger part has been removed, used up, etc: *a little stump of a pencil.* **3** *cricket* **a** any of the three thin vertical wooden posts that form the wicket; **b** (**stumps**) the whole wicket, including the bails. ▸ *verb* **1** to baffle or perplex. **2** *intr* to walk stiffly and unsteadily, or heavily and noisily. **3** *cricket* of a fielder, esp a wicketkeeper: to dismiss (a batsman or batswoman) by disturbing the wicket with the ball while they are away from the crease. **4** *intr, N Am, esp US* to go round making political speeches. [14c: from *stumpen* to stumble]

IDIOMS **on the stump** *N Am, esp US* busy with political campaigning, esp by going round delivering speeches.

PHRASAL VERBS **stump up** *informal* to pay.

stumpy *adj* (*-ier, -iest*) short and thick.

stun *verb* (*stunned, stunning*) **1** to make someone unconscious, eg by a blow to the head. **2** to make someone unable to speak or think clearly, eg through shock. **3** *informal* to impress someone greatly; to astound them. ▸ *noun* the act of stunning or state of being stunned. [13c: from French *estoner* to astonish]

stung *past tense, past participle of* **sting**

stunk *past tense, past participle of* **stink**

stunner *noun, informal* someone or something that is extraordinarily beautiful, attractive, etc.

stunning *adj, informal* **1** extraordinarily beautiful, attractive, etc. **2** extremely impressive. ▪ **stunningly** *adv.*

stunt[1] *verb* to curtail the growth or development of (a plant, animal, someone's mind, a business project, etc) to its full potential: *Lack of water stunted the plants.* ▸ *noun* **1** an instance of growth or development being curtailed or a state of curtailed growth or development. **2** an animal or plant whose growth or development has been curtailed. ▪ **stunted** *adj.* [Anglo-Saxon *stunt* dull or stupid]

stunt[2] *noun* **1** a daring act or spectacular event that is intended to show off talent or attract publicity. **2** a dangerous or acrobatic feat that is performed as part of the action of a film or television programme.

stuntman *or* **stuntwoman** *noun* someone who performs stunts, esp someone whose job is to act as a stand-in for a film actor.

stupefaction *noun* **1** stunned surprise, astonishment, etc. **2** the act of stupefying or state of being stupefied; numbness.

stupefy *verb* (*-ies, -ied*) **1** to stun with amazement, fear, confusion or bewilderment. **2** to make someone senseless, eg with drugs or alcohol. [17c: from Latin *stupere* to be stunned + *facere* to make]

stupendous *adj* **1** astounding. **2** *informal* astoundingly huge or excellent. ▪ **stupendously** *adv.* [17c: from Latin *stupere* to be stunned]

stupid *adj* **1** having or showing a lack of common sense, comprehension, perception, etc: *a stupid mistake.* **2** slow to understand; dull-witted. **3** *informal* silly; trivial; unimportant; ridiculous; boring: *a stupid quarrel.* ▪ **stupidly** *adv.* [16c: from Latin *stupidus* senseless]

stupidity *noun* (*-ies*) **1** a stupid state or condition; extreme foolishness. **2** a stupid action, comment, etc.

stupor *noun* **1** a state of unconsciousness or near-unconsciousness, esp one caused by drugs, alcohol, etc. **2** *informal* a daze, esp one brought on by shock, lack of sleep, sadness, etc. ▪ **stuporous** *adj.* [14c: Latin]

sturdy *adj* (*-ier, -iest*) **1** of limbs, etc: thick and strong-looking. **2** strongly built; robust. **3** healthy; vigorous; hardy. ▪ **sturdiness** *noun.* [14c: from French *estourdi* stunned]

sturgeon *noun* a large long-snouted fish which is used as food and valued as the source of true caviar. [13c: from French *esturgeon*]

stutter *verb, tr & intr* to speak or say something in a faltering or hesitant way, often by repeating parts of words, esp the first consonant, usu because of indecision, heightened emotion or some pathological disorder that affects the speech organs or the nervous system. ▸ *noun* a way of speaking that is characterized by this kind of faltering or hesitancy. ▪ **stuttering** *adj, noun.* [16c: from earlier *stutten* to stutter]

sty[1] *noun* (*sties*) **1** a pen where pigs are kept. **2** any filthy or disgusting place. ▸ *verb* (*sties, stied*) to put or keep (a pig, etc) in a sty. [Anglo-Saxon *stig* pen or hall]

sty[2] *or* **stye** *noun* (*sties or styes*) an inflamed swelling on the eyelid at the base of the lash. [15c: from Anglo-Saxon *stigan* to rise]

Stygian /ˈstɪdʒɪən/ *adj, literary* dark and gloomy. [16c: from Latin *Stygius*, from Greek *Stygios*, from *Styx*, the river in Hades in Greek mythology]

style *noun* **1** a manner or way of doing something, eg writing, speaking, etc. **2** a distinctive manner that characterizes a particular author, painter, film-maker, etc. **3** kind; type; make. **4** a striking quality, often elegance or lavishness, that is considered desirable or admirable: *She dresses with style.* **5** the state of being fashionable: *gone out of style.* **6** *botany* in flowers: the part of the **carpel** that connects the **stigma** to the **ovary** (sense 2). ▸ *verb* **1** to design, shape, groom, etc something in a particular way. **2** to name or designate someone: *styled himself an expert.* [13c: from Latin *stilus* writing tool or literary style]

stylish *adj* elegant; fashionable. ▪ **stylishly** *adv.* ▪ **stylishness** *noun.*

stylist *noun* **1** a trained hairdresser. **2** a writer, artist, etc who pays a lot of attention to style.

stylistic *adj* relating to artistic or literary style: *stylistic analysis.*▪ **stylistically** *adv.*

stylized *adj* conventionalized and unnaturalistic: *Cubism is a highly stylized art form.*

stylus *noun* (*styluses or styli*) **a** a hard pointed device at the tip of the arm of a record player, which picks up the sound from a record's grooves; **b** the cutting tool that is used to produce the grooves in a record. [17c: from Latin *stilus* a stake or pointed writing implement]

stymie *verb* (*stymieing or stymying*) to prevent, thwart, hinder or frustrate: *Plans for expansion were stymied by cash-flow problems.* ▸ *noun* **1** *golf, formerly* a situation on the green where an opponent's ball blocks the path between one's own ball and the hole, and which is no longer current because of a change in the rules which now allow for the use of markers. **2** any tricky or obstructed situation. ▪ **stymied** *adj.* [19c]

styptic *med, adj* of a drug or other substance: having the effect of stopping, slowing down or preventing bleeding: *a styptic pencil.* ▸ *noun* a drug or other substance that has this type of effect. [14c: from Greek *styptikos*]

suave /swɑːv/ *adj* of someone, esp a man, or their manner, attitude, etc: polite, charming and sophisticated, esp in an insincere way. ▪ **suavely** *adv.* ▪ **suaveness** *noun.* [19c: from Latin *suavis* sweet]

sub *informal, noun* **1** a submarine. **2** a substitute player. **3** a small loan; an advance payment, eg from someone's wages to help them subsist. **4** a subeditor. **5** (*usu* **subs**) a subscription fee. ▸ *verb* (***subbed, subbing***) **1** *intr* to act as a substitute. **2** *tr & intr* to subedit or work as a subeditor. **3** to lend (esp a small amount of money): *Can you sub me a quid till tomorrow?* [17c]

sub- *prefix, meaning*: **1** under or below: *subaqua*. **2** secondary; lower in rank or importance: *sublieutenant*. **3** only slightly; imperfectly; less than: *subhuman*. **4** a part or division of the specified thing: *subcommittee*. See also **sur-**[2]. [Latin, meaning 'under' or 'near']

subaltern /ˈsʌbəltən/ *noun* **a** any army officer below the rank of captain; **b** someone of inferior status, rank, etc. [16c: from Latin *subalternus*]

subaqua *adj* belonging, relating or referring to underwater activities: *subaqua diving*.

subatomic *adj* **1** smaller than an atom: *subatomic particle.* **2** relating to an atom; existing or occurring in an atom.

subatomic particle *noun, physics* a general term for any particle that is smaller than an atom, eg an **electron**, **neutron**, **proton**, **neutrino**, **quark**[1] or **meson**.

subclavian *or* **subclavicular** *adj, anatomy* below the **clavicle**.

subconscious *noun, psychoanal* the part of the mind where memories, associations, experiences, feelings, etc are stored and from which such things can be retrieved to the level of conscious awareness. ▸ *adj* denoting mental processes which a person is not fully aware of. ▪ **subconsciously** *adv.*

subcontinent *noun* a large part of a continent that is distinctive in some way, eg by its shape, culture, etc: *the Indian subcontinent*.

subcontract *noun* /sʌbˈkɒntrakt/ a secondary contract where the person or company that is initially hired to do a job then hires another to carry out the work. ▸ *verb* /sʌbkənˈtrakt/ (*also* **subcontract out**) to employ (a worker) or pass on (work) under the terms of a subcontract. ▪ **subcontractor** *noun.*

subculture *noun* **1** a group within a society, esp one seen as an underclass, whose members share the same, often unconventional, beliefs, tastes, activities, etc. **2** *biol* of bacteria, etc: a **culture** (*noun* sense 5) that is derived from another. ▪ **subcultural** *adj.*

subcutaneous /sʌbkjuˈteɪnɪəs/ *adj, med* situated, used, introduced, etc under the skin.

subdirectory *noun* (**-ies**) *comput* a directory of files that is contained within another directory.

subdivide *verb* to divide (esp something that is already divided) into even smaller parts. ▪ **subdivision** *noun.*

subdominant *noun, music* the note that comes immediately below the **dominant** in a scale.

subduction *noun* the process of one part of the Earth's crust moving underneath another. [Latin *sub* + *ducere, ductum* to lead, take]

subdue *verb* **1** to overpower and bring under control. **2** to suppress or conquer (feelings, an enemy, etc). [14c: from Latin *subducere* to remove]

subdued *adj* **1** of lighting, colour, noise, etc: not intense, bright, harsh, loud, etc; toned down. **2** of a person: quiet, shy, restrained or in low spirits.

subedit *verb, tr & intr* to prepare (copy) for the ultimate sanction of the editor-in-chief, esp on a newspaper.

subeditor *noun* someone whose job is to select and prepare material, eg articles, etc in a newspaper or magazine, for printing.

subglacial *adjective, geog* at the base or bottom of a glacier.

subheading *or* **subhead** *noun* a subordinate title in a book, chapter, article, etc.

subhuman *adj* **1** relating or referring to animals that are just below humans on the evolutionary scale. **2** of a person or their behaviour, attitude, etc: barbaric; lacking in intelligence.

subject *noun* /ˈsʌbdʒɪkt/ **1 a** a matter, topic, person, etc that is under discussion or consideration or that features as the major theme in a book, film, play, etc; **b** the person that a biography is written about. **2** an area of learning that forms a course of study. **3** someone or something that an artist, sculptor, photographer, etc chooses to represent. **4** someone who undergoes an experiment, operation, form of treatment, hypnosis, psychoanalysis, etc. **5** someone who is ruled by a monarch, government, etc; a citizen: *a British subject*. **6** *grammar* a word, phrase or clause which indicates the person or thing that performs the action of an active verb or that receives the action of a passive verb, eg *The doctor* is the subject in *The doctor saw us*, and *We* is the subject in *We were seen by the doctor.* See also **object** (*noun* sense 4). ▸ *adj* /ˈsʌbdʒɪkt/ **1** (*often* **subject to sth**) **a** liable; showing a tendency; prone: *subject to huge mood swings*; **b** exposed; open: *left himself subject to ridicule*; **c** conditional upon something. **2** dependent; ruled by a monarch or government: *a subject nation.* ▸ *adv* /ˈsʌbdʒɪkt/ (*always* **subject to**) conditionally upon something: *You may go, subject to your parents' permission.* ▸ *verb* /səbˈdʒɛkt/ **1** (*usu* **subject sb** *or* **sth to sth**) to cause them or it to undergo or experience something unwelcome, unpleasant, etc: *subjected them to years of abuse.* **2** to make (a person, a people, nation, etc) subordinate to or under the control of another. [13c: from Latin *subjectus* or thrown under, inferior]

subjection *noun* an act of domination; the state of being dominated: *the subjection of women*.

subjective *adj* **1** based on personal opinion, thoughts, feelings, etc; not impartial. Compare **objective**. **2** *grammar* indicating or referring to the subject of a verb; nominative. ▪ **subjectively** *adv.*

subject matter *noun* the main topic, theme, etc of a book, publication, talk, etc.

sub judice /sʌb 'dʒuːdɪsɪ/ *adj* of a court case: under judicial consideration and therefore not to be publicly discussed or remarked on. [17c: Latin, meaning 'under a judge']

subjugate *verb* **1** esp of one country, people, nation, etc in regard to another: to dominate them; to bring them under control: *As a nation, the Poles have often been subjugated.* **2** to make someone obedient or submissive. ▪ **subjugation** *noun.* [15c: from Latin **sub-** + *jugum* yoke]

subjunctive *grammar adj* of the mood of a verb: used in English for denoting the conditional or hypothetical (eg 'If he *were* in hospital, I would certainly visit him' or 'If I *were* you') or the mandatory (eg 'I insist he *leave* now'), although in other languages it has a wider application. ▸ *noun* **1** the subjunctive mood. **2** a verb in this mood. Compare **indicative**, **conditional**, **imperative**. [16c: from Latin *subjungere* to subjoin]

sublet *verb, tr & intr* to rent out (property one is renting from someone else) to another person. ▪ **subletter** *noun.* ▪ **subletting** *noun.*

sublieutenant *noun* a naval officer, esp in the British Navy, who is immediately below lieutenant in rank.

sublimate *verb, psychol* to channel a morally or socially unacceptable impulse towards something else, esp something creative, that is considered more appropriate. ▸ *noun, chem* the solid product formed after **sublimation**. [16c: from Latin *sublimare* to elevate or exalt]

sublimation *noun* **1** the channelling of a morally or socially unacceptable impulse towards something else, esp some form of creativity, that is considered more appropriate. **2** *chem* the process whereby a solid forms a vapour without appearing in the liquid, ie intermediate, state.

sublime *adj* **1** of someone: displaying the highest or noblest nature, esp in terms of their morality, intellect, etc. **2** of something in nature or art: overwhelmingly great; supreme; awe-inspiring. **3** *loosely* unsurpassed. ▸ *noun* (**the sublime**) the ultimate or ideal example or instance. ▸ *verb, tr & intr, chem* of a substance: to change from a solid to a vapour without passing through the liquid state. ▪ **sublimely** *adv.* ▪ **sublimity** *noun.* [14c: from Latin *sublimis* in a high position]

subliminal *adj* existing in, resulting from, or targeting the area of the mind that is below the threshold of ordinary awareness: *subliminal advertising.* ▪ **subliminally** *adv.*

submachine-gun *noun* a portable machine-gun that can be fired from the shoulder or hip.

submarine *noun* a vessel, esp a military one, that is designed for underwater travel. ▸ *adj* **1** of plants, animals, etc: living under the sea. **2** used, fixed in place, etc underwater: *North Sea submarine piping.* ▪ **submariner** *noun.*

submerge *or* **submerse** *verb* **1** *tr & intr* to plunge or sink or cause to plunge or sink under the surface of water or other liquid. **2** to overwhelm someone, eg with too much work. ▪ **submersion** *noun.*

submersible *adj* of a vessel: designed to operate under water. ▸ *noun* a submersible vessel; a submarine.

submission *noun* **1** an act of submitting. **2** something, eg a plan, proposal, idea, view, etc, is put forward for consideration or approval. **3** readiness or willingness to surrender. [15c: from Latin *submittere* to submit]

submissive *adj* willing or tending to submit; meek; obedient. ▪ **submissively** *adv.* ▪ **submissiveness** *noun.*

submit *verb* (***submitted, submitting***) **1** *intr* (*also* **submit to sb**) to surrender; to give in, esp to the wishes or control of another person; to stop resisting them. **2** *tr & intr* to offer (oneself) as a subject for an experiment, treatment, etc. **3 a** to offer, suggest or present (eg a proposal) for formal consideration by others; **b** to hand in (eg an essay or other piece of written work) for marking, correction, etc. [14c: from Latin *submittere*]

submucosa *noun, anatomy* the layer of tissue below a mucous membrane. ▪ **submucosal** *or* ▪ **submucous** *adj.*

subnormal *adj* esp of someone's level of intelligence: lower than normal.

subordinate *adj* /sə'bɔːdɪnət/ (*often* **subordinate to sb**) lower in rank, importance, etc; secondary. ▸ *noun* /sə'bɔːdɪnət/ someone or something that is characterized by being lower or secondary in rank, status, importance, etc. ▸ *verb* /sə'bɔːdɪneɪt/ **1** to regard or treat someone as being lower or secondary in rank, status, importance, etc; to put someone into this kind of position. **2** to cause or force someone or something to become dependent, subservient, etc. ▪ **subordination** *noun.* [15c: from **sub-** (sense 2) + Latin *ordo* rank]

subordinate clause *noun, grammar* a **clause** which cannot stand on its own as an independent sentence and which functions in a sentence in the same way as a noun, adjective or adverb, eg 'The book *that you gave me for Christmas* was fascinating' or '*What you see* is *what you get*'. Compare **main clause**.

suborn *verb* to persuade someone to commit perjury, a crime or other wrongful act, eg by bribing them. [16c: from Latin *sub* secretly + *ornare* to equip]

subplot *noun* a minor storyline that runs parallel to the main plot in a novel, film, play, opera, etc.

subpoena /sə'piːnə, səb'piːnə/ *noun* a legal document that orders someone to appear in a court of law at a specified time; a summons. ▸ *verb* (***subpoenaed*** *or* ***subpoena'd***) to serve with a subpoena. [15c: from Latin *sub poena* under penalty]

sub-post office *noun, Brit* a small post office that offers fewer services than a main post office and which is usu part of a general shop.

sub rosa *adv* in secret. [17c: Latin]

subroutine *noun, comput* a self-contained part of a computer program which performs a specific task and which can be called up at any time during the running of the main program.

subscribe *verb* **1** *tr & intr* to contribute or undertake to contribute (a sum of money), esp on a regular basis. **2** (*usu* **subscribe to sth**) to undertake to receive (regular issues of a magazine, etc) in return for payment. **3** (*usu* **subscribe to sth**) to agree with or believe in (a theory, idea, etc): *subscribes to classical Marxism.* ▪ **subscriber** *noun.* [15c: from **sub-** (sense 1) + Latin *scribere* to write]

subscript *printing, adj* of a character, esp one in chemistry and maths: set below the level of the line, eg the number 2 in H_2O. ▶ *noun* a character that is in this position.

subscription *noun* **1 a** an act or instance of subscribing; **b** a payment made in subscribing. **2** *Brit* a set fee for membership of a society, club, etc. **3 a** an agreement to take a magazine, etc, usu for a specified number of issues; **b** the money paid for this.

subsequent *adj* (*also* **subsequent to sth**) happening after or following. ▪ **subsequently** *adv.* [15c: from Latin *sub* near + *sequi* to follow]

subservient *adj* **1** ready or eager to submit to the wishes of others, often excessively so. **2** (*usu* **subservient to sth**) functioning as a means to an end. **3** (*usu* **subservient to sb** *or* **sth**) a less common term for **subordinate** (*adj*). ▪ **subservience** *or* **subserviency** *noun.* [17c: from **sub-** (sense 2) + Latin *servire* to serve]

subset *noun, maths* a set (see **set²** sense 2) that forms one part of a larger set, eg *set X* is said to be a subset of a *set Y* if all the members of *set X* can be included in *set Y.*

subside *verb, intr* **1** of land, buildings, etc: to sink to a lower level; to settle. **2** of noise, feelings, wind, a storm, etc: to become less loud or intense; to die down. ▪ **subsidence** /ˈsʌbsɪdəns, səbˈsaɪdəns/ *noun* the sinking of land, buildings, etc to a lower level. [17c: from **sub-** (sense 1) + Latin *sidere* to settle]

subsidiarity /sʌbsɪdɪˈarɪtɪ/ *noun* the principle that a central governing body will permit its member states, local government, etc to have control over those issues, decisions, etc that are deemed more appropriate to the local level.

subsidiary *adj* **1** of secondary importance; subordinate. **2** serving as an addition or supplement; auxiliary. ▶ *noun* (**-ies**) **1** a subsidiary person or thing. **2** (*sometimes* **subsidiary of sth**) a company controlled by another, usu larger, company or organization. [16c: from Latin *subsidium* auxilliary force]

subsidize *or* **-ise** *verb* **1** to provide or support with a subsidy. **2** to pay a proportion of the cost of (a thing supplied) in order to reduce the price paid by the customer: *The company subsidized the meals in the canteen.*

subsidy *noun* (**-ies**) **1** a sum of money given, eg by a government to an industry, to help with running costs or to keep product prices low. **2** financial aid of this kind. [14c: from French *subside*]

subsist *verb, intr* (*usu* **subsist on sth**) to live or manage to stay alive by means of it. ▪ **subsistence** *noun.* [16c: from Latin *subsistere* to stand still or firm]

subsistence farming *noun* a type of farming in which almost all the produce is used to feed and support the farmer's family, leaving little or no surplus for selling.

subsoil *noun, geol* the layer of soil that lies beneath the **topsoil**.

subsonic *adj* relating to, being or travelling at speeds below the speed of sound.

subspecies *noun, biol* in the taxonomy of plants, animals, etc: a subdivision of a species which, because of geographical isolation, displays some differences from others in the species.

substance *noun* **1** the matter or material that a thing is made of. **2** a particular kind of matter with a definable quality: *a sticky substance.* **3** the essence or basic meaning of something spoken or written. **4** touchable reality; tangibility: *Ghosts have no substance.* **5** solid quality or worth: *food with no substance.* **6** foundation; truth: *no substance in the rumours.* **7** wealth and influence: *woman of substance.* [13c: from Latin *substantia*]

IDIOMS **in substance** in actual fact.

substantial *adj* **1** considerable in amount, extent, importance, etc. **2** of real value or worth. **3** of food: nourishing. **4** solidly built. **5** existing as a touchable thing; material; corporeal. **6** belonging or relating to something's basic nature or essence; essential. ▪ **substantially** *adv.*

substantiate *verb* to prove or support something; to confirm the truth or validity of something. ▪ **substantiation** *noun.*

substantive *adj* **1** having or displaying significant importance, value, validity, etc. **2** belonging or relating to the essential nature of something. **3** *grammar* expressing existence. ▶ *noun, grammar* a noun or any linguistic unit that functions as a noun. [15c: from Latin *substantivus*]

substitute *noun* someone or something that takes the place of, or is used instead of, another. ▶ *verb* (*usu* **substitute sth for sth else**) to use or bring something into use as an alternative, replacement, etc for something else. ▪ **substitution** *noun.* [15c: from **sub-** (sense 1) + Latin *statuere* to set]

---

substitute

Be careful to use the right prepositions with **substitute** and **replace**. If X is put in place of Y, X is **substituted for** Y or **replaces** Y, and Y is **replaced by** or **replaced with** X.

---

substrate *noun* **1** *biol* the material or medium (eg soil, rock, etc) that a living organism, such as a plant, bacterium, etc, grows on or is attached to. **2** *biochem* the substance that an enzyme acts on during a biochemical reaction. **3** **substratum**.

substratum *noun* (***substrata***) **1** an underlying layer. **2** a foundation or foundation material. **3** a layer of soil or rock that lies just below the surface. [17c: from Latin *substernere*]

substructure *noun, archit* the part of a building or other construction that supports the framework.

subsume *verb* to include (an example, instance, idea, etc) in or regard it as part of a larger, more general group, category, rule, principle, etc. [19c: from **sub-** (sense 1) + Latin *sumere* to take]

subtenant *noun* someone who rents or leases a property from someone who already holds a lease for that property. ▪ **subtenancy** *noun* (**-ies**).

subtend *verb, geom* of the line opposite a specified angle in a triangle or the chord of an arc: to be opposite and bounding. [16c: from **sub-** (sense 1) + Latin *tendere* to stretch]

subterfuge *noun* a trick or deception that evades, conceals or obscures: *a clever subterfuge.* [16c: from Latin *subter-* secretly + *fugere* to flee]

subterranean *adj* **1** situated, existing, operating, etc underground. **2** hidden; operating, working, etc in secret. [17c: from **sub-** (sense 1) + Latin *terra* earth]

subtext *noun* **1** the implied message that the author, director, painter, etc of a play, film, book, picture, etc creates at a level below that of plot, character, language, image, etc. **2** anything implied but not explicitly stated in ordinary speech or writing.

subtitle *noun* **1** (*usu* **subtitles**) a printed translation of the dialogue of a foreign film that appears bit by bit at the bottom of the frame. **2** a subordinate title that usu expands on or explains the main title. ▸ *verb* to give a subtitle to (a literary work, film, etc).

subtle /ˈsʌtəl/ *adj* **1** not straightforwardly or obviously stated or displayed. **2** of distinctions, etc: difficult to appreciate or perceive. **3** of a smell, flavour, colour, etc: delicate; understated. **4** capable of making fine distinctions: *a subtle mind.* ▪ **subtly** *adv.* [14c: from French *soutil*]

subtlety /ˈsʌtəltɪ/ *noun* (*-ies*) **1** the state or quality of being subtle. **2** a subtle point or argument; subtle behaviour. **3** a fine distinction.

subtotal *noun* the amount that a column of figures adds up to and which forms part of a larger total.

subtract *verb* to take (one number, quantity, etc) away from another; to deduct. ▪ **subtraction** *noun.* [16c: from Latin *sub* away + *trahere* to draw]

subtropics *plural noun* the areas of the world that lie between the tropics and the temperate zone. ▪ **subtropical** *or* **subtropic** *adj.*

suburb *noun* **1** a residential district that lies on the edge of a town or city. **2** (**the suburbs**) the outlying districts of a city thought of collectively. ▪ **suburban** *adj.* [14c: from Latin *sub* near + *urbs* city]

suburbia *noun* the suburbs and its inhabitants and way of life thought of collectively, esp in terms of being characterized by conventional uniformity, lacking sophistication, etc.

subvention *noun* a grant or subsidy, esp a government one. [15c: from French *subvencion*]

subversion *noun* **1** an act or instance of overthrowing a rule, law, government, etc. **2** the act or practice of subverting (usu a government).

subversive *adj* of a person, action, thinking, etc: characterized by a likelihood or tendency to undermine authority. ▸ *noun* someone who is subversive; a revolutionary. ▪ **subversively** *adv.* ▪ **subversiveness** *noun.*

subvert *verb* to undermine or overthrow (esp eg a government or other legally established body). [14c: from Latin *subvertere* to overturn]

subway *noun* **1** an underground passage or tunnel that pedestrians or vehicles can use for crossing under a road, railway, river, etc. **2** *chiefly N Am, esp US* an underground railway.

subzero *adj* below zero degrees.

succeed *verb* **1** *intr* to achieve an aim or purpose. **2** *intr* to develop or turn out as planned. **3** *intr* (*also* **succeed in sth**) to do well in a particular area or field: *succeeded in getting four A's.* **4** to come next after (something); to follow. **5** *tr & intr* (*also* **succeed to sb** *or* **sth**) to take up a position, etc, following on from someone else: *The Queen succeeded her father • She succeeded to the throne.* [14c: from Latin *succedere* to go after]

---

succeed

This word is often misspelt. It has a two *c*'s in the middle, and ends in *eed*. It might help you to remember the following sentence:

Two **c***'s and two* **e***'s will help you suc***cee***d.*

---

success *noun* **1** the quality of succeeding or the state of having succeeded. **2** any favourable development or outcome. **3** someone who attains fame, power, wealth, etc or is judged favourably by others: *became an overnight success.* **4** something that turns out well or that is judged favourably by others.

successful *adj* **1** achieving or resulting in the required outcome. **2** prosperous, flourishing: *a successful business.* ▪ **successfully** *adv.*

succession *noun* **1 a** a series of people or things that come, happen, etc one after the other; **b** the process or an instance of this. **2 a** the right or order by which one person or thing succeeds another; **b** the process or act of doing this. **3** *ecol* the process in which types of plant or animal communities sequentially replace one another until a stable community becomes established.

IDIOMS **in succession** one after the other. **in quick succession** quickly one after the other.

successive *adj* immediately following another or each other. ▪ **successively** *adv.*

successor *noun* someone who follows another, esp someone who takes over another's job, title, etc.

succinct /səkˈsɪŋkt/ *adj* of someone or of the way they write or speak: brief, precise and to the point; concise. ▪ **succinctly** *adv.* ▪ **succinctness** *noun.* [15c: from Latin *succinctus*]

succour *or* (*N Am*) **succor** /ˈsʌkə(r)/ *formal, noun* **1** help or relief in time of distress or need. **2** someone or something that gives this kind of help. ▸ *verb* to give help or relief to someone or something. [13c: from French *succure*]

succulent *adj* **1** full of juice; juicy; tender and tasty. **2** *botany* of a plant: characterized by having thick fleshy leaves or stems. **3** *informal* attractive; inviting. ▸ *noun, botany* a plant that is specially adapted to living in arid conditions by having thick fleshy leaves or stems or both, which allow it to store water. ▪ **succulence** *or* **succulency** *noun.* [17c: from Latin *succulentus*]

succumb *verb, intr* (*often* **succumb to sth**) **1** to give in to (eg pressure, temptation, desire, etc): *succumbed to her charms.* **2** to fall victim to or to die of (something, esp a disease, old age, etc). [15c: from Latin *cumbere* to lie down]

such *adj* **1** of that kind, or of the same or a similar kind: *You cannot reason with such a person.* **2** so great; of a more extreme type, degree, extent, etc than is usual, normal, etc: *You're such a good friend.* **3** of a type, degree, extent, etc that has already been indicated, spoken about, etc: *I did no such thing.* ▸ *pronoun* a person or thing, or people or things, like that or those which have just been mentioned; suchlike: *chimps, gorillas and such.* [Anglo-Saxon *swilc*]

IDIOMS **as such** as is usu thought of, described, etc: *There's no spare bed as such, but you can use the sofa.* **such as** for example.

such-and-such *adj* of a particular but unspecified kind. ▸ *pronoun* a person or thing of this kind.

suchlike *pron* things of the same kind: *went to the chemist for soap, toothpaste and suchlike.* ▸ *adj* of the same kind: *soap, toothpaste and suchlike things.*

suck *verb* **1** *tr & intr* to draw (liquid) into the mouth. **2** to draw liquid from (eg a juicy fruit) with the mouth. **3** (*also* **suck sth in** *or* **up**) to draw in by suction or an action similar to suction: *the roots sucked up the water.* **4** to rub (eg one's thumb, etc) with the tongue and inside of the mouth, using an action similar to sucking in liquids. **5** to draw the flavour from (eg a sweet) with squeezing and rolling movements inside the mouth. **6** to take milk (from a breast or udder) with the mouth. **7** *intr, N Am slang* to be contemptible or contemptibly bad: *That movie sucks!* ▸ *noun* an act or bout of sucking. [Anglo-Saxon *sucan*]

PHRASAL VERBS **suck sb into sth** to drag them into it: *sucked him into the world of politics.* **suck up to sb** *informal* to flatter them or be obsequious to them in order to gain favour.

sucker *noun* **1** someone or something that sucks. **2** *informal* someone who is gullible or who can be easily deceived or taken advantage of. **3** (*usu* **sucker for sth**) *informal* someone who finds a specified type of thing or person irresistible: *a sucker for chocolate ice cream.* **4** *zool* a specially adapted organ that helps an insect, sea creature, etc adhere to surfaces by suction so that it can feed, move, etc. **5** a rubber cup-shaped device that is designed to adhere to a surface by creating a vacuum. **6** *botany* a shoot that sprouts from the parent stem or root. ▸ *verb* **1** to remove the suckers (from a plant). **2** *informal* to deceive, cheat, trick or fool: *suckered him out of £50.*

suckle *verb* **1** to feed (a baby or young mammal) with milk from the nipple or udder. **2** *tr & intr* to suck milk from (a nipple or udder). ▪ **suckler** *noun.* [15c]

suckling *noun* **1** a baby or young animal that is still being fed with its mother's milk. **2** the process of feeding a baby or young animal with its mother's milk.

sucrose /ˈsuːkrous/ *noun, biochem* a white soluble crystalline sugar. [19c: from French *sucre* sugar]

suction *noun* **1** an act, an instance or the process of sucking. **2 a** the production of an adhering or sucking force that is created by a difference or reduction in air pressure; **b** the amount of force that this creates. [17c: from Latin *sugere* to suck]

suction pump *noun* a pumping device for raising water, etc.

Sudanese *adj* belonging or relating to Sudan in NE Africa, or its inhabitants. ▸ *noun* (*pl* ***Sudanese***) a citizen or inhabitant of, or a person born in, Sudan.

sudden *adj* happening or done quickly, without warning or unexpectedly. ▪ **suddenly** *adv.* ▪ **suddenness** *noun.* [14c: from French *soudain*]

IDIOMS **all of a sudden** without any warning.

sudden death *noun* a method of deciding a tied game, contest, quiz, etc by declaring the winner to be the first player or team to score, answer correctly, etc during a period of extra time or in a set of extra questions, etc.

sudden infant death syndrome ▸ *noun* (abbrev **SIDS**) ▸ *med* the sudden unexpected death of an apparently healthy baby without any identifiable cause. Also (*non-technical*) **cot death**.

Sudoku *or* **Su Doku** /suˈdoukuː/ *noun* a type of puzzle in which numbers must be entered into a square grid in such a way that no number is repeated in any row, column or internal square. [Japanese *su* number + *doku* singular]

sudorific /suːdəˈrɪfɪk/ *med, adj* of a drug: causing sweating. ▸ *noun* a drug, remedy or substance that causes sweating. [17c: from Latin *sudor* sweat + *facere* to make]

suds *plural noun* **1** (*also* **soap-suds**) a mass of bubbles produced on water when soap or other detergent is dissolved. **2** water that has detergent in it. [16c: perhaps from Dutch *sudse*, meaning 'marsh' or 'bog']

sue *verb* **1** *tr & intr* to take legal proceedings against (a person or company). **2** *intr* (*usu* **sue for sth**) to make a claim for it. [13c: from French *sivre*]

suede /sweɪd/ *noun* a soft leather, where the flesh side is rubbed or brushed so that it has a velvety finish. [19c: from French *gants de Suède*, gloves from Sweden]

suet *noun* hard fat from around the kidneys of sheep or cattle, used for making pastry, puddings, etc. [14c: from Latin *sebum* fat]

Suff. *abbrev, English county* Suffolk.

suffer *verb* **1** *tr & intr* to undergo or endure (physical or mental pain or other unpleasantness). **2** *intr* to deteriorate (as a result of something). **3** to tolerate: *doesn't suffer fools gladly.* **4** *old use* to allow: *Suffer the little children to come unto me.* ▪ **sufferable** *adj.* ▪ **sufferer** *noun.* ▪ **suffering** *noun.* [13c: from Latin *sufferre* to endure]

sufferance *noun* consent that is understood to be given through the lack of objection.

IDIOMS **on sufferance** with reluctant toleration.

suffice *verb* **1** *intr* to be adequate, sufficient, good enough, etc for a particular purpose. **2** to satisfy. [14c: from Latin *sufficere*]

sufficient *adj* enough; adequate. ▪ **sufficiency** *noun.* ▪ **sufficiently** *adv.* [14c: from Latin *sufficere* to supply]

suffix *noun* **1** *grammar* a word-forming element that can be added to the end of a word or to the base form of a word, eg as a grammatical inflection such as *-ed* or *-s* in *walked* and *monkeys*. Compare **affix**, **prefix**. **2** *maths* an **index** that is placed below the other figures in an equation, etc, eg the *n* in x_n. Also called **subscript**. ▸ *verb* **1** *grammar* to attach something as a suffix to a word. **2** to add (a suffix) to something. ▪ **suffixation** *noun.* [18c: from Latin *suffixus* fixed underneath]

suffocate *verb* **1** *tr & intr* to kill or be killed by a lack of air, eg because the air passages are blocked. **2** *intr* to experience difficulty in breathing because of heat and lack of air; to stifle. **3** to subject to an oppressive amount of something. ▪ **suffocating** *adj*: *suffocating heat.* ▪ **suffocation** *noun.* [16c: from Latin *suffocare*]

suffragan *noun* (*in full* **suffragan bishop** *or* **bishop suffragan**) a bishop considered as subordinate to an archbishop or metropolitan. [14c: French]

suffrage *noun* the right to vote in political elections: *fought for universal suffrage.* ▪ **suffragist** *noun.* [13c: from Latin *suffragium* a voting tablet, pebble, etc]

suffragette *noun* a woman who is in favour of or who campaigns for women having the same voting rights as men, esp one who acted militantly for this in Britain in the early years of the 20th century.

suffuse *verb* (*often* **be suffused with sth**) to be covered or spread over or throughout with (colour, light, liquid, etc): *The sky was suffused with red.* ▪ **suffusion** *noun.* [16c: from Latin *suffundere*]

sugar *noun* **1** a white crystalline carbohydrate that is soluble in water, typically having a sweet taste and widely used as a sweetener in confectionery, desserts, soft drinks, etc. **2** the common name for **sucrose**. **3** a measure of sugar: *takes three sugars in his tea.* **4** *informal* a term of endearment. ▸ *verb* **1** to sweeten something with sugar. **2** to sprinkle or coat something with sugar. ▪ **sugaring** *noun*. [13c: from French *sucre*]

IDIOMS **sugar the pill** to make something unpleasant easier to deal with or accept.

sugar beet *noun* a variety of beet that is widely cultivated for its large white conical root, which is an important source of sugar.

sugar candy *noun* **1** large crystals of sugar that are chiefly used for sweetening coffee, etc. **2** *N Am* confectionery. Often shortened to **candy**.

sugar cane *noun* a tall tropical grass which resembles bamboo and is a main source of sugar.

sugared *adj* **1** sugar-coated; candied. **2** containing sugar.

sugar loaf *noun* refined sugar that is moulded into a conical shape. Also called **loaf sugar**.

sugar-lump *or* **sugar-cube** *noun* a compressed cube of sugar that is used for sweetening tea, coffee, etc and feeding to horses.

sugary *adj* **1** like sugar in taste or appearance. **2** containing much or too much sugar. **3** *informal* exaggeratedly or insincerely pleasant or affectionate; cloying

suggest *verb* **1** (*often* **suggest that sth**) to put forward as a possibility or recommendation. **2** to create an impression of something; to evoke it: *a painting that suggests the artist's anguish*. **3** to give a hint of something: *an expression that suggests guilt*. [16c: from Latin *suggerere* to put under]

suggestible *adj* **1** easily influenced by suggestions made by others. **2** capable of being suggested. ▪ **suggestibility** *noun*.

suggestion *noun* **1 a** something that is suggested; a proposal, plan, recommendation, etc; **b** the act of suggesting. **2** a hint or trace: *delicately flavoured with just a suggestion of coriander*. **3 a** the creation of a belief or impulse in the mind; **b** the process by which an idea, belief, etc can be instilled in the mind of a hypnotized person.

suggestive *adj* **1** (*often* **suggestive of sth**) causing one to think of it; creating an impression of it. **2** capable of a tacitly erotic or provocative interpretation. ▪ **suggestively** *adv*. ▪ **suggestiveness** *noun*.

suicidal *adj* **1** involving or indicating suicide. **2** characterized by behaviour that might result in suicide or ruin; irresponsibly rash or self-destructive. **3** of a person: inclined or likely to commit suicide. ▪ **suicidally** *adv*.

suicide *noun* **1** the act or an instance of killing oneself deliberately, usu in the phrase **commit suicide**. **2** someone who deliberately kills or tries to kill himself or herself. **3** ruin or downfall, esp when it is unintentional: *The minister's speech was political suicide*. [17c: from Latin *sui* of oneself + **-cide**]

suing *present participle of* **sue**

suit *noun* **1** a set of clothes designed to be worn together, usu made from the same or contrasting material and which consists of a jacket and either trousers or a skirt and sometimes a waistcoat. **2** *often in compounds* an outfit worn on specified occasions or for a specified activity: *wet suit* • *suit of armour*. **3** any of the four groups (clubs, diamonds, hearts or spades) that a pack of playing-cards is divided into. **4** a legal action taken against someone; a lawsuit. **5** *disparaging* a businessman. ▶ *verb* **1** *tr & intr* to be acceptable to or what is required by someone. **2** to be appropriate to, in harmony with, or attractive to someone or something. ▪ **suited** *adj*. [13c: from French *sieute* a set of things]

IDIOMS **follow suit** to do the same as someone else has done. **suit oneself** to do what one wants to do, esp without considering others.

suitable *adj* appropriate, fitting, proper, agreeable, etc. ▪ **suitability** *noun*. ▪ **suitableness** *noun*. ▪ **suitably** *adv*.

suitcase *noun* a stiffened portable travelling case that is used for carrying clothes.

suite /swiːt/ *noun* **1** a set of rooms forming a self-contained unit within a larger building, esp a hotel: *bridal suite*. **2** a set of matching furniture, etc: *three-piece suite*. **3** *music* a set of instrumental movements in related keys. [17c: from French *sieute* a set of things]

suiting *noun* material that is used for making suits of clothes.

suitor *noun* **1** *old use* a man who woos a woman, esp with the intention of asking her to marry him. **2** someone who sues; a plaintiff. [14c: see **suit**]

Sukkoth /ˈsʊkout/ *noun* a Jewish harvest festival commemorating the period when the Israelites lived in tents in the desert during the Exodus from Egypt. Also called **Feast of Tabernacles**. [Hebrew, meaning 'tents or huts']

sulk *verb, intr* to be silent, grumpy, unsociable, etc, esp because of some petty resentment, a feeling of being hard done by, etc. ▶ *noun* (*also* **the sulks**) a bout of sulking. [18c]

sulky *adj* (***-ier, -iest***) inclined to moodiness, esp when taking the form of grumpy silence, resentful unsociability, etc. ▪ **sulkily** *adv*. ▪ **sulkiness** *noun*. [18c: prob from Anglo-Saxon *aseolcan* to slack or be slow]

sullen *adj* **1** silently and stubbornly angry, serious, morose, moody or unsociable. **2** of skies, etc: heavy and dismal. ▪ **sullenly** *adv*. ▪ **sullenness** *noun*. [16c]

sully *verb* (***-ies, -ied***) **1** to tarnish or mar (a reputation, etc). **2** *now chiefly literary* to dirty something. ▪ **sullied** *adj*. [16c]

sulpha *or* (*US*) **sulfa** *noun* any synthetic drug that is derived from sulphanilamide.

sulphate *or* (*US*) **sulfate** *noun* a salt or ester of sulphuric acid.

sulphide *or* (*US*) **sulfide** *noun* a compound that contains sulphur and another element.

sulphite *or* (*US*) **sulfite** *noun* a salt or ester of sulphurous acid.

sulphonamide *or* (*US*) **sulfonamide** *noun, chem* **1** an amide of a sulphonic acid. **2** *med* any of a group of drugs containing such a compound that prevent the growth of bacteria.

sulphur *or* (*US*) **sulfur** *noun, chem* (symbol **S**) a yellow solid non-metallic element that is used in the vulcanization of rubber and the manufacture of sulphuric acid, fungicides, insecticides, gunpowder, matches, fertilizers and sulphonamide drugs. Also (*old use*) *called* **brimstone**. ▶ *verb* to treat or fumigate using sulphur. ▪ **sulphuric** /sʌlˈfjʊərɪk/ *adj*. [14c: from Latin *sulfur*]

sulphurate *or* (*US*) **sulfurate** /ˈsʌlfjʊəreɪt/ *verb* to combine or treat with sulphur, eg in bleaching processes. Also called **sulphurize**.

sulphur dioxide *noun, chem* a colourless, pungent-smelling, toxic gas, used as a food preservative, fumigant and solvent, and also in metal refining, paper pulping and the manufacture of sulphuric acid.

sulphuric acid *or* (*US*) **sulfuric acid** *noun, chem* a colourless odourless oily liquid that is widely used in the manufacture of organic chemicals, fertilizers, explosives, detergents, paints, and dyes.

sulphurize *or* **-ise** *or* (*US*) **sulfurize** /ˈsʌlfjʊəraɪz/ *verb* to **sulphurate**.

sulphurous *or* (*US*) **sulfurous** /ˈsʌlfərəs/ *adj* **1** relating to, like, or containing sulphur. **2** having a yellow colour like sulphur.

sulphurous acid *or* (*US*) **sulfurous acid** /sʌlˈfjʊərəs/ *noun, chem* a colourless weakly acidic solution of **sulphur dioxide** in water, that acts as a reducing agent and is used as a bleach, antiseptic and preservative.

sultan *noun* the ruler of any of various Muslim countries. ▪ **sultanate** *noun*. [16c: Arabic, meaning 'king or sovereign']

sultana *noun* **1 a** a pale seedless raisin that is used in making cakes, puddings, etc; **b** the grape that this type of dried fruit comes from. **2** the wife, concubine, mother, sister or daughter of a sultan.

sultry *adj* (***-ier, -iest***) **1** of the weather: hot and humid; close. **2** characterized by a sensual, passionate or suggestive appearance, manner, etc. [16c: from obsolete *sulter* to swelter]

sum *noun* **1** the total that is arrived at when two or more numbers, quantities, ideas, feelings, etc are added together. **2** an amount of money, often a specified or particular one: *the grand sum of 50p*. **3 a** an arithmetical calculation, esp of a basic kind; **b** (**sums**) *informal* arithmetic. ▸ *verb* (***summed, summing***) to calculate the sum of something. [13c: from French *summe*]

IDIOMS **in sum** briefly; to sum up.

PHRASAL VERBS **sum up 1** to summarize before finishing a speech, argument, etc. **2** of a judge: to review the main points of a case for the jury before they retire to consider their verdict. See also **summing-up**. **sum up sb** *or* **sth 1** to express or embody the complete character or nature of them or it: *That kind of pettiness just sums her up*. **2** to make a quick assessment of (a person, situation, etc).

Sumatran *adj* belonging or relating to Sumatra, a mountainous island in W Indonesia, its inhabitants or their language. ▸ *noun* **1** a citizen or inhabitant of, or a person born in, Sumatra. **2** the language of Sumatra. [18c]

Sumerian *adj* belonging or relating to Sumer, a district of the ancient civilization of Babylonia in Mesopotania, its inhabitants or their language. ▸ *noun* **1** a citizen or inhabitant of, or a person born in, Sumer. **2** the extinct language of Sumer. [19c]

summarize *or* **-ise** *verb* to make, present or be a summary of something; to state it concisely.

summary *noun* (***-ies***) a short account that outlines or picks out the main points. ▸ *adj* done or performed quickly and without the usual attention to details or formalities. ▪ **summarily** *adv*: *The case was summarily dismissed*. [15c: from Latin *summarius* summary]

summation *noun* **1** the process of finding the sum; addition. **2** a summary or summing-up. [18c: from Latin *summare* to sum up]

summer *noun* **1** (*also* **Summer**) the warmest season of the year, between spring and autumn. **2** the warm sunny weather that is associated with summer: *a beautiful summer's day*. **3** *literary* a time of greatest energy, happiness, etc; a heyday: *in the summer of her life*. ▪ **summery** *adj*. [Anglo-Saxon *sumer*]

summerhouse *noun* any small building or shelter in a park or garden where people can sit during warm weather and which provides some shade.

summer school *noun, Brit* a course of study held during the summer vacation.

summer solstice *noun* the longest day of the year in either hemisphere, either 21 June for the N hemisphere, or 22 December for the S hemisphere.

summertime *noun* the season of summer.

summing-up *noun* a review of the main points, esp of a legal case by the judge before the members of the jury retire to consider their verdict.

summit *noun* **1** the highest point of a mountain or hill. **2** the highest possible level of achievement or development, eg in a career. **3** a meeting, conference, etc between heads of government or other senior officials, esp when it involves discussion of something of international significance. [15c: from French *sommette*]

summon *verb* **1** to order someone to come or appear, eg in a court of law as a witness, defendant, etc. **2** to order or request someone to do something; to call someone to something; to ask for something: *had to summon help*. **3** (*often* **summon up sth**) to gather or muster (eg one's strength or energy): *summoned up the nerve to tell him*. [13c: from Latin *summonere* to warn secretly]

summons *noun* (***summonses***) **1** a written order that legally obliges someone to attend a court of law at a specified time. **2** any authoritative order that requests someone to attend a meeting, etc or to do something specified. ▸ *verb, law* to serve someone with a summons. [13c: from French *sumunse*]

sumo *noun* a style of traditional Japanese wrestling where contestants of great bulk try to force an opponent out of the unroped ring or to make them touch the floor with any part of their body other than the soles of the feet. [19c: Japanese]

sump *noun* **1** a small depression inside a vehicle's engine that acts as a reservoir so that lubricating oil can drain into it. **2** any pit into which liquid drains or is poured. [17c: from Dutch *somp* a marsh]

sumptuary *adj* **1** relating to or regulating expense. **2** of a law, etc: controlling extravagance. [17c: from Latin *sumptuarius*]

sumptuous *adj* wildly expensive; extravagantly luxurious. ▪ **sumptuosity** *or* **sumptuousness** *noun*. ▪ **sumptuously** *adv*. [15c: from Latin *sumptuosus*]

sum total *noun* the complete or final total.

Sun. *abbrev* Sunday.

sun *noun* **1** (**the Sun**) the star that the planets revolve around and which gives out the heat and light energy necessary to enable living organisms to survive on Earth. **2** the heat and light of this star. **3** any star with a system of planets revolving around it. **4** someone or something that is regarded as a source of radiance, warmth, glory, etc. ▸ *verb* (***sunned, sunning***) to expose (something or oneself) to the sun's rays. ▪ **sunless** *adj*. [Anglo-Saxon *sunne*]

IDIOMS **catch the sun** to sunburn or tan in the sun. **under the sun** anywhere on earth.

sunbathe *verb, intr* to expose one's body to the sun in order to get a suntan. ▪ **sunbather** *noun*. ▪ **sunbathing** *noun*.

sunbeam *noun* a ray of sunlight.

sunbed *noun* **1** a device that has sun-lamps fitted above and often beneath a transparent screen and which someone can lie on in order to artificially tan the whole body. **2** a **sun-lounger**.

sunblock *noun* a lotion, cream, etc that completely or almost completely protects the skin from the harmful effects of the sun's rays.

sunburn *noun* soreness and reddening of the skin caused by overexposure to the sun's rays. ▪ **sunburnt** *or* **sunburned** *adj*.

sundae /'sʌndeɪ/ *noun* a portion of ice cream topped with fruit, nuts, syrup, etc.

Sunday *noun* (abbrev **Sun.**) the first day of the week and for most Christians the day of worship and rest. [Anglo-Saxon *sunnandæg* day of the Sun]

IDIOMS **a month of Sundays** a very long time.

Sunday best *noun, jocular* one's best clothes, formerly these considered the most suitable for wearing to church.

Sunday school *noun* a class for the religious instruction of children that is held on Sundays.

sundeck *noun* **1** an upper open deck on a passenger ship where people can sit in the sun. **2** *N Am, Aust* a balcony or veranda that gets the sun.

sundew *noun, botany* an insectivorous plant that grows in bogs, and which has leaves that are covered with long sticky hairs so that it can trap insects.

sundial *noun* an instrument that uses sunlight to tell the time, by the changing position of the shadow that a vertical arm casts on a horizontal plate with graded markings that indicate the hours.

sundown *noun* sunset.

sundress *noun* a light sleeveless low-cut dress that is usu held up by narrow shoulder-straps.

sun-dried *adj* dried or preserved by exposure to the sun rather than by artificial heating and therefore retaining more flavour: *sun-dried tomatoes*.

sundry *adj* various; assorted; miscellaneous; several. ▸ *noun* (**sundries**) various small unspecified items; oddments. [Anglo-Saxon *syndrig*]

IDIOMS **all and sundry** everybody.

sunfish *noun* a large rounded marine fish.

sunflower *noun* a tall plant which produces large flattened circular flowerheads with closely-packed seeds (which yield **sunflower oil**) in the middle and yellow petals radiating outwards.

sung *past participle of* **sing**

sunglasses *plural noun* spectacles that have tinted lenses, which are worn to protect the eyes from sunlight. Also (*informal*) *called* **shades** (see **shade** *noun* sense 10).

sunk *past participle of* **sink**

sunken *adj* **1** situated or fitted at a lower level than the surrounding area: *a sunken bath*. **2** submerged in water: *sunken treasure*. **3** of eyes, cheeks, etc: abnormally fallen in, gaunt or hollow, eg because of ill health, old age, etc. [14c: a past participle of **sink**]

sun-kissed *adj* having been warmed, bronzed, ripened, etc by the sun: *sun-kissed skin*.

sun-lamp *noun* an electric lamp that emits rays, esp ultraviolet rays, that are similar to natural sunlight and which is used therapeutically and for artificially tanning the skin.

sunlight *noun* light from the sun. ▪ **sunlit** *adj*.

sun lounge *or US* **sun parlor** *noun* a room with large windows for letting in maximum sunlight.

sun-lounger *noun, Brit* a lightweight plastic sunbathing seat that can often be adjusted to a variety of positions and which usu supports the whole body. Also called **sunbed**.

Sunni /'sʊnɪ, 'sʌnɪ/ *singular noun* the more orthodox of the two main branches of the Islamic religion. Compare **Shia**. ▸ *noun* (***Sunni*** *or* ***Sunnis***) a Muslim of this branch of Islam. Also called **Sunnite**. ▪ **Sunnism** *noun*. [17c: from Arabic *sunnah* rule]

sunny *adj* (***-ier, -iest***) **1** of a day, the weather, etc: characterized by long spells of sunshine or sunlight. **2** of a place, etc: exposed to, lit or warmed by plenty of sunshine: *a lovely sunny room*. **3** cheerful; good-humoured. ▪ **sunnily** *adv*. ▪ **sunniness** *noun*.

sunrise *noun* **1** the sun's appearance above the horizon in the morning. **2** the time of day when this happens.

sunrise industry *noun* any new and rapidly expanding industry, esp one that involves computing, electronics, etc.

sunroof *noun* a transparent panel in the roof of a car that lets sunlight in and can usu open for ventilation.

sunscreen *noun* a preparation that protects the skin and minimizes the possibility of sunburn because it blocks out some or most of the sun's harmful rays.

sunset *noun* **1** the sun's disappearance below the horizon in the evening. **2** the time of day when this happens.

sunshade *noun* **1** a type of umbrella that is used as protection in strong sunshine. **2** an awning.

sunshine *noun* **1** the light or heat of the sun. **2** fair weather, with the sun shining brightly. **3** an informal term of address, often used as part of a greeting or in a mockingly condescending or scolding tone.

sunspot *noun* **1** *astron* a relatively dark cool patch on the Sun's surface. **2** *informal* a holiday resort that is renowned for its sunny weather.

sunstroke *noun* a condition of collapse brought on by overexposure to the sun and sometimes accompanied by fever.

suntan *noun* a browning of the skin through exposure to the sun or a sun-lamp. Often shortened to **tan**.

suntrap *noun, Brit* a sheltered sunny place.

sun-up *noun, US* sunrise.

sup[1] *verb* (***supped, supping***) to drink in small mouthfuls. ▸ *noun* a small quantity of something liquid; a sip. [Anglo-Saxon *supan*]

sup[2] *verb* (***supped, supping***) *old use* (*often* **sup off** *or* **on sth**) to eat supper; to eat for supper. [13c: from French *soper* to take supper]

super *adj, informal* extremely good; excellent; wonderful. ▸ *exclam* excellent! ▸ *noun* **1** something of superior quality or grade, eg petrol. **2** *informal* a short form of **superintendent**. **3** *informal* a **supernumerary**, esp an extra in the theatre or on a film set. [19c: Latin, meaning 'above']

super- *prefix, forming adjs, nouns and verbs, denoting* **1** great or extreme in size or degree: *supermarket*. **2** above, beyond or over: *superscript*. **3** higher or more outstanding than usual: *superhero*. Compare **hyper-**. [Latin, meaning 'above, on top of, beyond, besides, in addition']

superable /'suːprəbəl/ *adj* of a problem, difficulty, obstacle, etc: able to be overcome; surmountable.

superabundant *adj* excessively or very plentiful. ▪ **superabundance** *noun*.

superannuated *adj* **1** of a post, vacancy, job, etc: with a pension as an integral part of the employment package. **2** made to retire and given a pension; pensioned off. **3** old and no longer fit for use. [17c: from Latin *annus* year]

superannuation *noun* **1** an amount that is regularly deducted from someone's wages as a contribution to a company pension. **2** the pension someone receives when they retire. **3** retirement: *took early superannuation*.

superb *adj* **1** *informal* outstandingly excellent. **2** magnificent; majestic; highly impressive. ▪ **superbly** *adv*. [16c: from Latin *superbus* proud]

supercharge *verb* **1** to increase the power and performance of (a vehicle engine). **2** (*usu* **supercharge with sth**) to charge or fill (eg an atmosphere, a remark) with an intense amount of an emotion, etc.

supercharger *noun, eng* a device that is used to increase the amount of air taken into the cylinder of an internal combustion engine, in order to burn the fuel more rapidly and so increase the power output.

supercilious *adj* arrogantly disdainful or contemptuous; self-importantly judgemental. ▪ **superciliousness** *noun*. [16c: from Latin *super cilium* eyebrow]

superconductivity *noun, physics* the property of having no electrical resistance that is displayed by many metals and alloys at temperatures close to absolute zero, and that other substances, such as ceramics, display at higher temperatures. ▪ **superconductor** *noun*. [20c]

superego *noun, psychoanal* that aspect of the psyche where someone's moral standards are internalized and which acts as an often subconscious check on the ego. Compare **ego**, **id**.

supererogation /suːpərɛrə'geɪʃən/ *noun* doing more than duty, circumstances, etc require. ▪ **supererogatory** /-ɪ'rɒgətərɪ/ *adj*. [16c: from Latin *erogare* to pay out]

superficial *adj* **1** belonging or relating to, or on or near, the surface: *a superficial wound*. **2** not thorough or in-depth; cursory: *a superficial understanding*. **3** only apparent; not real or genuine: *a superficial attempt to apologize*. **4** lacking the capacity for sincere emotion or serious thought; shallow: *a superficial person*. ▪ **superficiality** *noun* (***-ies***). ▪ **superficially** *adv*. [14c: from Latin *superficies* surface]

superfluity *noun* (***-ies***) **1** the state or fact of being superfluous. **2** something that is superfluous. **3** excess.

superfluous /sʊ'pɜːflʊəs/ *adj* more than is needed or wanted. ▪ **superfluously** *adv*. ▪ **superfluousness** *noun*. [15c: from Latin *superfluus* overflowing]

superglue *noun* a type of quick-acting extra strong adhesive. ▸ *verb* to bond something with superglue.

supergrass *noun, slang* someone who gives the police so much information that a large number of arrests follow, often in return for the informer's own immunity or so that they will face lesser charges.

superhero *noun* a character in a film, novel, cartoon, comic, etc that has extraordinary powers, esp for saving the world from disaster.

super high frequency *noun, radio* (abbrev **SHF**) a radio frequency in the range 3,000 to 30,000MHz.

superhighway *noun, US* **1** a wide road, with at least two carriageways going in either direction, that is meant for fast-moving traffic. **2** (*in full* **information superhighway**) electronic telecommunication systems collectively such as telephone links, cable and satellite TV, and computer networks, esp **the Internet**, over which information in digital forms can be transferred rapidly.

superhuman *adj* beyond ordinary human power, ability, knowledge, etc.

superimpose *verb* to lay or set (one thing) on top of another. ▪ **superimposed** *adj*.

superintend *verb, tr & intr* to look after and manage someone or something; to supervise. [17c: from Latin *superintendere*]

superintendent *noun* **1 a** *Brit* a police officer above the rank of chief inspector. Often shortened to **super**; **b** *US* a high ranking police officer, esp a chief of police. **2** someone whose job is to look after and manage, eg a department, a group of workers, etc. **3** *N Am* someone whose job is to act as caretaker of a building.

superior *adj* (*often* **superior to sb** *or* **sth**) **1** better in some way. **2** higher in rank or position: *reported him to his superior officer*. **3** of high quality. **4** arrogant; self-important. **5** *printing* of a character: set above the level of the line; superscript. ▸ *noun* **1** someone who is of higher rank or position. **2** the head of a religious community. [14c: Latin, literally 'higher']

superiority *noun* the condition of being better, higher, greater than someone or something else.

superlative /sʊ'pɜːlətɪv/ *adj* **1** *grammar* of adjectives or adverbs: expressing the highest degree of a particular quality, eg *nicest, best, most beautiful*. **2** superior to all others; supreme. ▸ *noun, grammar* **1** a superlative adjective or adverb. **2** the superlative form of a word. Compare **positive**, **comparative** (sense 4). ▪ **superlatively** *adv*. ▪ **superlativeness** *noun*. [14c: from Latin *superlativus*]

superman *noun* **1** *philos* an ideal man as he will have evolved in the future. **2** a man who appears to have superhuman powers.

supermarket *noun* a large self-service store that sells food, household goods, etc.

supermodel *noun* an extremely highly-paid, usu female, fashion model.

supernatural *adj* belonging or relating to or being phenomena that cannot be explained by the laws of nature or physics. ▸ *noun* (**the supernatural**) the world of unexplained phenomena. [16c: from Latin *supernaturalis*]

supernova /suːpə'noʊvə/ *noun* (***supernovae*** /-viː/ *or* ***supernovas***) *astron* a vast stellar explosion which takes a few days to complete and which results in the star becoming temporarily millions of times brighter than it was.

supernumerary *adj* additional to the normal or required number; extra. ▸ *noun* (***-ies***) **1** someone or something that is extra or surplus to requirements. **2** an actor who does not have a speaking part. Often shortened to **super** (*noun* sense 3). **3** someone who is not part of the regular staff, but who can be called on to work or serve when necessary. [17c: from Latin *supernumerarius* soldiers added to a legion]

superordinate *adj* of higher grade, status, importance, etc. ▸ *noun* someone or something that is of higher grade, status, importance, etc.

superoxide *noun, chem* **1** a chemical compound that contains the negatively charged O_2 ion. **2** an oxide that reacts with hydrogen ions to form hydrogen peroxide and oxygen.

superphosphate *noun, chem* the most important type of phosphate fertilizer, made by treating calcium phosphate with sulphuric acid.

superpower *noun* a nation or state that has outstanding political, economic or military influence, esp the USA or the former USSR.

superscript *printing, adj* of a character: set above the level of the line that the other characters sit on, eg the number 2 in 10^2. ▸ *noun* a superscript character. [19c: from Latin *super* above + *scribere* to write]

supersede *verb* **1** to take the place of (something, esp something outdated or no longer valid): *DVD-ROMs will supersede videos.* **2** to adopt, appoint or promote in favour of another. [15c: from Latin *super* above + *sedere* to sit]

supersonic *adj* **1** faster than the speed of sound. **2** of aircraft: able to travel at supersonic speeds. ▪ **supersonically** *adv.*

superstar *noun* an internationally famous celebrity, esp from the world of film, popular music or sport. ▪ **superstardom** *noun.*

superstition *noun* **1** belief in an influence that certain (esp commonplace) objects, actions or occurrences have on events, people's lives, etc. **2** a particular opinion or practice based on such belief. ▪ **superstitious** *adj.* ▪ **superstitiously** *adv.* ▪ **superstitiousness** *noun.* [15c: from Latin *superstitio*]

superstore *noun* **1** a very large supermarket that often sells clothes, etc as well as food and household goods and which is usu sited away from the centre of town. **2** a very large store that sells a specified type of goods such as DIY products, electrical products, furniture, etc.

superstructure *noun* **1** a building thought of in terms of it being above its foundations. **2** anything that is based on or built above another, usu more important, part, eg those parts of a ship above the main deck.

supertanker *noun* a large ship for transporting oil or other liquid.

supertax *noun, informal* a surtax.

supervene *verb, intr* to occur as an interruption to some process, esp unexpectedly. ▪ **supervention** *noun.* [17c: from Latin *supervenire*]

supervise *verb* **1** to be in overall charge of (employees, etc). **2** to oversee (a task, project, etc). ▪ **supervision** *noun.* ▪ **supervisor** *noun.* ▪ **supervisory** *adj.* [16c: from Latin *supervidere*]

supine /'suːpaɪn/ *adj* **1** lying on one's back. **2** lazy. [16c: from Latin *supinus* lying face up]

supper *noun* an evening meal, esp a light one. [13c: from French *soper* supper]

supplant *verb* to take the place of someone, often by force or unfair means. [13c: from Latin *supplantare* to trip up]

supple *adj* of a person, their joints, a material, etc: bending easily; flexible. ▪ **supplely** *adv.* ▪ **suppleness** *noun.* [13c: French]

supplement *noun* **1** something that is added to make something else complete or that makes up a deficiency: *vitamin supplement*. **2** an extra section added to a book to give additional information or to correct previous errors. **3 a** a separate part that comes with a newspaper, esp a Sunday one; **b** a separate part that comes with a magazine, esp one that covers a specific topic. **4** an additional charge for a specified service, etc. **5** *maths* the amount by which an angle or arc is less than 180°. ▸ *verb* (*often* **supplement by** *or* **with sth**) to add to something; to make up a lack of something. ▪ **supplementary** *adj.* [14c: from Latin *supplementum* a filling up]

supplementary angles *plural noun, geom* a pair of angles whose sum is 180°. Compare **conjugate angles, complementary angles.**

supplicate *verb, tr & intr* **1** (*usu* **supplicate for sth**) to humbly and earnestly request it. **2** (*usu* **supplicate sb for sth**) to humbly and earnestly request them for it. ▪ **supplicant** *noun.* ▪ **supplicating** *adj.* ▪ **supplication** *noun.* [15c: from Latin *supplicare* to kneel]

supply *verb* (**-ies, -ied**) **a** to provide or furnish (something believed to be necessary): *I'll supply the wine if you bring some beers;* **b** (*also* **supply sb with sth**) to provide or furnish them with it: *The garden supplied them with all their vegetables.* ▸ *noun* (**-ies**) **1** an act or instance of providing. **2** an amount provided, esp regularly. **3** an amount that can be drawn from and used; a stock. **4** (**supplies**) necessary food, equipment, etc that is stored, gathered, taken on a journey, etc. **5** a source, eg of water, electricity, gas, etc: *cut off their gas supply.* **6** *econ* the total amount of a commodity that is produced and available for sale. Compare **demand** (*noun* sense 4). ▪ **supplier** *noun.* [14c: from French *soupleer*]

support *verb* **1** to keep something upright or in place. **2** to keep from falling. **3** to bear the weight of someone or something. **4** to give active approval, encouragement, money, etc to (an institution, belief, theory, etc); to advocate something. **5** to provide someone or something with the means necessary for living or existing: *She supports a large family.* **6** to maintain a loyal and active interest in the fortunes of (a particular sport or team). **7** to reinforce the accuracy or validity of (eg a theory, claim, etc): *The evidence supports the prosecution's case.* **8** to speak in favour of (a proposal, etc). **9** to play a part subordinate to (a leading actor). **10** to perform before (the main item in a concert, show, etc). **11** *comput* of a computer, an operating system, etc: to allow for the use of (a specified language, program, etc). **12** to bear or tolerate something. ▸ *noun* **1** the act of supporting; the state of being supported. **2** someone or something that supports. **3** someone or something that helps, comforts, etc. **4** a group, singer, film, etc that accompanies or comes on before the main attraction. ▪ **supportable** *adj.* ▪ **supporting** *adj, noun.* [14c: from French *supporter* to convey]

supporter *noun* someone who gives a specified institution such as a sport, a team, a political party, etc their active backing, etc: *football supporters.*

support group *noun* **1** a collection of people who get together voluntarily with the aim of helping each other overcome a trauma, difficulty, disease, etc.

supportive *adj* providing support, esp active approval, encouragement, backing, etc.

suppose *verb* **1** to consider something likely, even when there is a lack of tangible evidence for it to be so. **2** to think, believe, agree, etc reluctantly, unwillingly (that something could be true). **3** to assume, often wrongly: *He supposed she wouldn't find out.* **4** of a theory, proposition, policy, etc: to require (some vital factor or assumption) to be the case before it can work, be valid, etc: *Your idea for expansion supposes more money to be available.* [14c: from French *supposer*]

supposed *adj* generally believed to be so or true, but considered doubtful by the speaker: *couldn't find him at his supposed address.* ▪ **supposedly** *adv.*

IDIOMS **be supposed to be** *or* **do sth** to be expected or allowed to be or do it: *You were supposed to be here an hour ago.*

supposition *noun* **1** the act of supposing. **2** something that is supposed; a mere possibility or assumption. **3** conjecture.

suppositious *adj* based on supposition; hypothetical.

suppository *noun* (**-ies**) *med* a soluble preparation of medicine that remains solid at room temperature, but which dissolves when it is inserted into the rectum or vagina, where its active ingredients are then released. [14c: from Latin *suppositorium*]

suppress *verb* **1** to hold back or restrain (feelings, laughter, a yawn, etc). **2** to put a stop to something. **3** to crush (eg a rebellion). **4** to prevent (information, news, etc) from being broadcast, from circulating or from otherwise being made known. **5** to moderate or eliminate (interference) in an electrical device. ▪ **suppressed** *adj.* ▪ **suppression** *noun.* [14c: from Latin *supprimere* to restrain]

suppressant *noun* a substance that suppresses or restrains, eg a drug that suppresses the appetite.

suppurate *verb, intr* of a wound, boil, ulcer, etc: to gather and release pus; to fester; to come to a head. ▪ **suppuration** *noun.* [16c: from Latin *suppurare*]

supra- *prefix, denoting* above or beyond: *supranational.* [Latin, meaning 'above']

supremacy *noun* **1** supreme power or authority. **2** the state or quality of being supreme.

supreme *adj* **1** highest in rank, power, importance, etc; greatest: *the Supreme Court.* **2** most excellent; best: *a supreme effort.* **3** greatest in degree; utmost: *supreme stupidity.* ▪ **supremely** *adv.* [16c: from Latin *supremus* highest]

Supreme Court *or* **supreme court** *noun* **1** in the USA: the highest Federal court, with jurisdiction over all lower courts. **2** the highest court in a number of nations and states.

supremo *noun, informal* **1** a supreme head or leader. **2** a boss. [1930s: from Spanish *generalissimo supremo* supreme general]

Supt. *abbrev* Superintendent.

sur-[1] *prefix, signifying* over, above or beyond: *surreal.* [From French *sur*]

sur-[2] *prefix* a form of **sub-** that is used before some words beginning with *r*: *surrogate.*

sura *or* **surah** *noun* a chapter of the Koran. [From Arabic, meaning 'step']

surcharge *noun* **1** an extra charge, often as a penalty for late payment of a bill. **2** an amount over a permitted load. ▸ *verb* **1** to impose a surcharge on someone. **2** to overload something. ▪ **surcharged** *adj.* ▪ **surcharger** *noun.* [15c: from French *surcharger*]

surd *maths, adj* of a number: unable to be expressed in finite terms; irrational. ▸ *noun* an **irrational number**. [16c: from Latin *surdus* deaf]

sure *adj* **1** confident beyond doubt in one's belief or knowledge; convinced: *felt sure he'd picked up the keys.* **2** undoubtedly true or accurate: *a sure sign.* **3** reliably stable or secure: *on a sure footing.* ▸ *adv, informal* certainly; of course. ▪ **sureness** *noun.* [14c: from French *sur*]

IDIOMS **be** *or* **feel sure** *or* **very, so,** *etc* **sure of oneself** to act in a very self-confident way. **be sure to** to be guaranteed or certain to (happen, etc): *Whenever we plan a picnic it's sure to rain.* **for sure** *informal* definitely; undoubtedly. **make sure** to take the necessary action to remove all doubt or risk. **sure enough** *informal* in fact; as was expected. **to be sure** certainly; admittedly.

sure-fire *adj, informal* destined to succeed.

sure-footed *adj* **1** not stumbling or likely to stumble. **2** not making, or not likely to make, mistakes

surely *adv* **1** without doubt; certainly. **2** used in questions and exclamations: to express incredulous disbelief: *Surely you knew he was just joking?*

IDIOMS **slowly but surely** slowly and steadily.

surety /ˈʃʊərətɪ/ *noun* (**-ies**) **1** someone who agrees to become legally responsible for another person's behaviour, debts, etc. **2** security, usu in the form of a sum of money, against loss, damage, etc or as a guarantee that a promise will be kept, eg that someone will turn up at court when they are supposed to. [14c: from French *surte*]

surf *noun* **1** the sea as it breaks against the shore, a reef, etc. **2** the foam produced by breaking waves. **3** an act or instance of surfing. ▸ *verb* **1** *intr* to take part in a sport or recreation where the object is to stand or lie on a long narrow board, try to catch the crest of a wave and ride it to the shore. **2** to browse through (the Internet) randomly. ▪ **surfer** *noun* **1** someone who goes surfing. **2** someone who browses on the Internet. ▪ **surfing** *noun* **1** the sport or recreation of riding a surfboard on the crests of large breaking waves. **2** browsing on the Internet. [17c]

surface *noun* **1 a** the upper or outer side of anything, often with regard to texture or appearance; **b** the size or area of such a side. **2** the upper level of a body or container of liquid or of the land. **3** the external appearance of something, as opposed to its underlying reality: *On the surface everything seems fine.* **4** *maths* a geometric figure that is two-dimensional, having length and breadth but no depth. ▸ *verb* **1** *intr* to rise to the surface of a liquid. **2** *intr* to become apparent; to come to light: *The scandal first surfaced in the press.* **3** *intr, informal* to get out of bed: *never surfaces till the afternoon.* **4** to give the desired finish or texture to the surface of something. [17c: French]

IDIOMS **come to the surface** to become known, esp after having been hidden. **scratch the surface 1** to begin to have a superficial understanding of or effect on something: *measures that only scratch the surface of the drugs problem.* **2** to begin to investigate: *You only need to scratch the surface to discover the sleaze.*

surface mail *noun* mail that is sent overland or by ship, as distinct from **airmail**.

surface tension *noun, physics* the film-like tension on the surface of a liquid that is caused by the cohesion of its particles, which has the effect of minimizing its surface area.

surfactant *noun, chem* any soluble substance, such as a detergent, emulsifier, etc, that reduces the surface tension of a liquid. [20c: from *surface* + *active*]

surfboard *noun* a long narrow fibreglass board that a surfer stands or lies on. ▸ *verb* to ride on a surfboard. ▪ **surfboarder** *noun.* ▪ **surfboarding** *noun.*

surfeit /'sɜːfɪt/ *noun* **1** (*usu* **surfeit of sth**) an excess. **2** the stuffed or sickened feeling that results from any excess, esp overeating. ▸ *verb* to indulge, esp in an excess of food or drink, until stuffed or disgusted. [13c: from French *surfait* excess]

surge *noun* **1** a sudden powerful mass movement of a crowd, esp forward. **2** a sudden sharp increase, eg in prices, electrical current, etc. **3** a sudden, often uncontrolled, rush of emotion: *felt a surge of indignation.* **4** a rising and falling of a large area of sea. ▸ *verb, intr* **1** of the sea, waves, etc: to move up and down or swell with force. **2** of a crowd, etc: to move forward in a mass. **3** (*also* **surge up**) of an emotion, etc: to rise up suddenly and often uncontrollably: *Sorrow surged up inside him.* **4** of prices, electricity, etc: to increase, esp suddenly. [15c: from Latin *surgere* to rise]

surgeon *noun* a person who is professionally qualified to practise surgery. [14c: from French *surgien*]

surgery *noun* (**-ies**) **1** the branch of medicine that is concerned with treating disease, disorder or injury by cutting into the patient's body to operate directly on or remove the affected part. **2** the performance or an instance of this type of treatment: *The surgery took 10 hours.* **3** *Brit* **a** the place where a doctor, dentist, etc sees their patients and carries out treatment; **b** the time when they are available for consultation. **4** *Brit* a time when a professional person such as an MP, lawyer, accountant, etc can be consulted, usu free of charge. [14c: from French *surgerie*]

surgical *adj* belonging or relating to, involving, caused by, used in, or by means of surgery: *surgical instruments.* ▪ **surgically** *adv.*

surgical spirit *noun* methylated spirit which is used for cleaning wounds and sterilizing medical equipment.

Surinamese *adj* belonging or relating to Surinam, a republic on the NE Atlantic coast of S America, its inhabitants or their language. ▸ *noun* (*pl* ***Surinamese***) a citizen, inhabitant of, or person born in, Surinam. [20c]

surly *adj* (**-ier, -iest**) grumpily bad-tempered; abrupt and impolite in manner or speech. ▪ **surliness** *noun.* [16c: from the obsolete *sirly,* meaning 'haughty']

surmise *verb* to conclude something from the information available, esp when the information is incomplete or insubstantial. ▸ *noun* a conclusion drawn from such information. [15c: from French *surmettre* to accuse]

surmount *verb* **1** to overcome (problems, obstacles, etc). **2** to be set on top of something; to crown. ▪ **surmountable** *adj.* [14c: from French *surmonter*]

surname *noun* a family name or last name, as opposed to a forename or Christian name. Also called **last name.** [14c: from French *sur-* + **name** (*noun* sense 1)]

surpass *verb* **1** to go or be beyond in degree or extent; to exceed. **2** to be better than: *a holiday that surpassed all expectations.* [16c: from French *surpasser* to pass over]

surplice *noun* a loose wide-sleeved white linen garment that is worn ceremonially by members of the clergy and choir singers over their robes. [13c: from French *sourpeliz*]

surplus *noun* **1** an amount that exceeds the amount required or used; an amount that is left over after requirements have been met. **2** *commerce* the amount by which a company's income is greater than expenditure. ▸ *adj* left over after needs have been met; extra. [14c: French]

IDIOMS **surplus to requirements 1** extra; in excess of what is needed. **2** *euphem* no longer needed.

surprise *noun* **1** a sudden, unexpected, astounding, amazing, etc event, factor, gift, etc. **2** a feeling of mental disorientation caused by something of this nature. **3 a** the act of catching someone unawares or off-guard; **b** the process of being caught unawares or off-guard. ▸ *verb* **1** to cause someone to experience surprise by presenting them with or subjecting them to something unexpected, amazing, etc: *surprised her with a kiss.* **2** to come upon something or someone unexpectedly or catch unawares. **3** to capture or attack with a sudden unexpected manoeuvre. ▪ **surprised** *adj.* ▪ **surprising** *adj.* ▪ **surprisingly** *adv.* [15c: French]

IDIOMS **take sb by surprise** to catch them unawares or off-guard.

surreal *adj* **1** dreamlike; very odd or bizarre. **2** being in the style of Surrealism.

surrealism *noun* (*sometimes* **Surrealism**) a movement in art and literature that sprang up between the first and second World Wars, and whose most prominent aim was to allow the artist's or writer's unconscious to be expressed with complete creative freedom. ▪ **surrealist** *adj, noun.* ▪ **surrealistic** *adj.* [Early 20c: from French *surréalisme*]

surrender *verb* **1** *intr* to admit defeat by giving oneself up to an enemy; to yield. **2** to give or hand over someone or something, either voluntarily or under duress: *weapons surrendered under the arms amnesty.* **3** to lose or give up something: *surrendered all hope of being rescued.* **4** *intr* (**surrender to sth**) to allow oneself to be influenced or overcome by a desire or emotion; to give in to it: *He surrendered to her beauty.* ▸ *noun* an act, instance or the process of surrendering. [15c: from French *surrendre*]

surreptitious *adj* secret, sneaky, clandestine, underhand. [15c: from Latin *subreptitius*]

surrogate *noun* someone or something that takes the place of or is substituted for another. ▪ **surrogacy** *noun.* [17c: from Latin *subrogare* to substitute]

surrogate mother *noun* a woman who carries and gives birth to a baby on behalf of another woman.

surround *verb* to extend all around; to encircle. ▸ *noun* a border or edge, or an ornamental structure fitted round this. ▪ **surrounding** *adj.* [17c: from French *suronder* to overflow or abound]

surroundings *plural noun* the places and/or things that are usu round about someone or something; environment: *rural surroundings.*

surtax *noun* **1** an additional tax, esp one that is levied on incomes above a certain level. **2** an additional tax on something that already has a tax or duty levied on it. ▸ *verb* to levy such a tax on someone or something. [19c: from French *surtaxe*]

surtitle *or* (*esp US*) **supertitle** *noun* any of a sequence of captions that are projected onto a screen to the side of, or above, the stage during a foreign-language opera or play and which give a running translation of the libretto or dialogue as it is performed. ▸ *verb* to provide captions of this kind.

surveillance *noun* (*often* **under surveillance** *or* **under the surveillance of sb** *or* **sth**) a close watch over something (eg for security purposes) or someone (eg a suspected criminal). [19c: French]

survey *verb* /sɜːˈveɪ/ **1** to look at or examine at length or in detail, in order to get a general view. **2** to examine (a building) in order to assess its condition or value, esp on behalf of a prospective owner, mortgage lender, etc. **3** to measure land heights and distances in (an area) for the purposes of drawing a detailed map, plan, description, etc. **4** to canvass (public opinion) and make a statistical assessment of the replies. ▸ *noun* /ˈsɜːveɪ/ **1** a detailed examination or investigation, eg to find out public opinion or customer preference. **2** an inspection of a building to assess condition or value. **3** **a** the collecting of land measurements for map-making purposes, etc; **b** the map, plan, report, etc that is drawn up after this has been done. ▪ **surveying** *noun*. [14c: from French *surveoir*]

surveyor *noun* **1** a person who is professionally qualified to survey land, buildings, etc. See also **quantity surveyor**. **2** someone whose job is to canvass public opinion and make a statistical assessment of the replies.

survival *noun* **1** of an individual: the fact of continuing to live, esp after some risk that might have prevented this. **2** something, such as an old custom, etc, that continues to be practised: *It's a survival from Victorian times.*

IDIOMS **survival of the fittest** *non-technical* the process or result of **natural selection**.

survive *verb* **1** *tr & intr* **a** to remain alive, esp despite (some risk that might prevent this): *the only one to survive the tragedy*; **b** *informal* to come or get through (something arduous or unpleasant): *It was a tough course, but I survived it.* **2** to live on after the death of someone: *survived her husband by 10 years.* **3** *intr* to remain alive or in existence: *How do they survive on such a small income?* ▪ **surviving** *adj, noun*. ▪ **survivor** *noun*. [15c: from French *sourvivre*]

sus see **suss**

susceptibility *noun* (**-ies**) **1** the state or quality of being susceptible. **2** **a** the capacity or ability to feel emotions; **b** (**susceptibilities**) feelings; sensibilities.

susceptible *adj* **1** (**susceptible to sth**) prone to being, or likely to be, affected by it, eg bad temper, etc: *always been susceptible to colds.* **2** capable of being affected by strong feelings, esp of love. **3** (**susceptible to sth**) capable of being influenced by something, eg persuasion. [17c: from Latin *suscipere* to take up]

sushi /ˈsuːʃɪ/ *noun* a Japanese dish of small rolls or balls of cold boiled rice topped with egg, raw fish or vegetables. [19c: Japanese, meaning 'it is sour']

suspect *verb* /səˈspɛkt/ **1** to consider or believe likely. **2** to think (a particular person) possibly or probably guilty of a crime or other wrongdoing. **3** to doubt the truth or genuineness of someone or something. ▸ *noun* /ˈsʌspɛkt/ someone who is suspected of committing a crime, etc. ▸ *adj* /ˈsʌspɛkt/ thought to be possibly false, untrue or dangerous; dubious: *His excuse sounds pretty suspect to me.* [14c: from Latin *suspicere* to look up to or admire]

suspend *verb* **1** to hang or hang up something. **2** to bring a halt to something, esp temporarily: *Services are suspended due to flooding.* **3** to remove someone from a job, a team, etc temporarily, as punishment or during an investigation of a possible misdemeanour. [13c: from Latin *suspendere* to hang secretly]

suspended animation *noun* a state in which a body's main functions are temporarily slowed down to an absolute minimum, eg in hibernation.

suspended sentence *noun* a judicial sentence that is deferred for a set time during which the offender is required to be of good behaviour.

suspenders *plural noun* **1** elasticated straps that can be attached to the top of a stocking or sock to hold it in place. **2** *N Am* braces for holding up trousers.

suspense *noun* **1** a state of nervous or excited tension or uncertainty. **2** tension or excitedness, esp as brought on by an eager desire to know the outcome of something. [15c: from French *suspens*]

IDIOMS **keep sb in suspense** to deliberately delay telling them something.

suspension *noun* **1** the act of suspending or the state of being suspended. **2** a temporary exclusion from an official position, work, school, college, etc, esp while allegations of misconduct are being investigated. **3** a temporary cessation: *suspension of hostilities.* **4** a system of springs and shock absorbers that connects the axles of a vehicle to the chassis and absorbs some of the unwanted vibrations transmitted from the road surface. **5** a liquid or gas that contains small insoluble solid particles which are more or less evenly dispersed throughout it.

suspension bridge *noun* a bridge that has a road or rail surface hanging from vertical cables which are themselves attached to thicker cables stretched between towers.

suspicion *noun* **1** an act, instance or feeling of suspecting. **2** a belief or opinion that is based on very little evidence. **3** a slight quantity; a trace. [14c: from French *suspecioun*]

IDIOMS **above suspicion** too highly respected to be suspected of a crime or wrongdoing. **on suspicion** as a suspect: *held on suspicion of murder.* **under suspicion** suspected of a crime or wrongdoing.

suspicious *adj* **1** inclined to suspect guilt, wrongdoing, etc: *a suspicious nature.* **2** inviting or arousing suspicion; dubious: *found the body in suspicious circumstances.* ▪ **suspiciously** *adv*. ▪ **suspiciousness** *noun*. [14c: from French *suspecious*]

suss *or* **sus** *slang, verb* (***sussed, sussing***) **1** to discover, assess or establish something, esp by investigation or intuition: *soon sussed how the video worked.* **2** to suspect something. [1930s: a shortened form of **suspect** or **suspicion**]

PHRASAL VERBS **suss sb** *or* **sth out** **1** to investigate, inspect or examine: *sussed out the nightlife.* **2** to work out or understand: *couldn't suss out his motives.*

sustain *verb* **1** to keep going. **2** to withstand, tolerate or endure: *can sustain impacts even at high speed.* **3**

to bolster, strengthen or encourage: *had a whisky to sustain his nerves.* **4** to suffer or undergo (eg an injury, loss, defeat, etc). **5** to declare that an objection in court is valid. **6** to support, ratify, back up (an argument, claim, etc). **7** to maintain or provide for something: *couldn't sustain her family on such a low salary.* ▪ **sustained** *adj.* ▪ **sustaining** *adj, noun.* [13c: from French *sustenir*]

sustainable *adj* **1** capable of being sustained. **2** of economic development, population growth, renewable resources, etc: capable of being maintained at a set level. ▪ **sustainability** *noun.*

sustenance *noun* **1 a** something, eg food or drink, that nourishes the body or that keeps up energy or spirits; **b** the action or an instance of nourishment. **2** something that maintains, supports or provides a livelihood. [13c: from French *sustenaunce*]

sutra /ˈsuːtrə/ *or* **sutta** *noun* **1** *Hinduism* a book of sayings on rituals, philosophy, etc. **2** *Buddhism* a group of writings including the sermons of Buddha. [Sanskrit, meaning 'thread' or 'rule']

suttee *or* **sati** /ˈsʌtiː/ *noun* **1** a former Hindu custom in which a widow would sacrifice herself by being burned alive on her husband's funeral pyre. **2** a Hindu woman who sacrificed herself in this way. [18c: from Sanskrit *sati* faithful wife]

suture /ˈsuːtʃə(r)/ *noun* **a** a stitch that joins the edges of a wound, surgical incision, etc together; **b** the joining of such edges together; ▸ *verb* to sew up (a wound, surgical incision, etc). [16c: French]

SUV *abbrev* sport utility vehicle.

suzerain *noun* **1** a nation, state or ruler that exercises some control over another state but which allows it to retain its own ruler or government. **2** a feudal lord. ▪ **suzerainty** *noun.* [Early 19c: French]

svelte *adj* slim or slender, esp in a graceful or attractive way. [Early 19c: French]

SW *abbrev* **1** short wave. **2** south-west, or south-western.

swab *noun* **a** a piece of cotton wool, gauze, etc that is used for cleaning wounds, applying antiseptics, taking a medical specimen, etc; **b** a medical specimen, eg of some bodily fluid, etc, that is taken for examination or testing. ▸ *verb* (***swabbed, swabbing***) **1** to clean (a wound) with, or as if with, a swab. **2** to mop something (eg a wound, a ship's deck, etc). [17c: from Dutch *zwabberen* to mop]

swaddle *verb* to wrap (a baby) in swaddling-clothes. [Anglo-Saxon *swathel* bandage]

swaddling-clothes *plural noun, hist* strips of cloth wrapped round a newborn baby.

swag *noun* **1** *slang* stolen goods. **2** *Aust* a traveller's pack or rolled bundle of possessions.

swagger *verb, intr* to walk with an air of self-importance. ▸ *noun* **1** a swaggering way of walking or behaving. **2** *informal* the quality of being showily fashionable or smart. ▪ **swaggering** *noun, adj.* [18c]

swagger-stick *noun* a type of short cane that is carried by a military officer.

swagman *or* **swaggie** *noun, Aust* someone, esp an itinerant workman, who travels about on foot and who carries their belongings in a swag.

Swahili /swəˈhiːlɪ, swɑː-/ *noun* **1** a language that is widely spoken in E Africa both as a mother tongue and as a second language. Also called **Kiswahili**. **2** (*pl* ***Swahilis*** *or* ***Swahili***) a member of a people who speak this language. ▸ *adj* belonging or relating to this language or people. [19c: Swahili, meaning 'pertaining to the coast', from Arabic *sahil* coast]

swain *noun, old use, poetic* **1** a country youth. **2** a young male lover or suitor. [Anglo-Saxon *swan*]

swallow[1] *verb* **1** to perform a muscular movement to make (food or drink) go from the mouth, down the oesophagus and into the stomach. **2** *intr* to move the muscles of the throat involuntarily, esp as a sign of emotional distress. **3** (*also* **swallow sth up**) to engulf or absorb it. **4** to stifle or repress (eg pride, tears, etc). **5** to accept or endure (eg an insult, affront, etc) meekly and without retaliation. **6** *informal* to believe gullibly or unquestioningly. ▸ *noun* **1** an act of swallowing. **2** an amount swallowed at one time. [Anglo-Saxon *swelgan*]

IDIOMS **swallow one's pride** to behave humbly and do something which one would otherwise be reluctant to do. **swallow one's words** to retract what one has said previously.

swallow[2] *noun* a small migratory insect-eating bird that has long pointed wings and a long forked tail. [Anglo-Saxon *swalwe*]

swallow dive *noun* a dive during which the arms are held out to the side, at shoulder level, until just above the level of the water when they are pulled in to the sides and the diver enters the water head first.

swallowtail *noun* **1** a large colourful butterfly that has the back wings extended into slender tails. **2** a tail that is forked like a swallow's.

swam *past tense of* **swim**

swami /ˈswɑːmɪ/ *noun* (***swamis*** *or* ***swamies***) an honorific title for a Hindu male religious teacher. [18c: from Hindi *svami* lord or master]

swamp *noun* an area of land that is permanently waterlogged. ▸ *verb* **1** to overwhelm or inundate. **2** to cause (a boat) to fill with water. **3** to flood. ▪ **swampy** *adj* (***-ier, -iest***). [17c]

swan *noun* a large, generally white, graceful aquatic bird with a long slender elegant neck, powerful wings and webbed feet. See also **cob**, **pen**[4], **cygnet**. ▸ *verb* (***swanned, swanning***) *intr, informal* (*usu* **swan off**, **around**, **about**, *etc*) to spend time idly; to wander aimlessly or gracefully. [Anglo-Saxon]

swank *informal, verb, intr* to boast or show off. ▸ *noun* flashiness; boastfulness. ▪ **swanky** *adj* (***-ier, -iest***) flashy, flamboyant, elaborate, fashionable, etc. [19c]

swan song *noun* the last performance or piece of work that a musician, artist, etc gives before their death or retirement.

swap *or* **swop** *verb* (***swapped, swapping; swopped, swopping***) *tr & intr* to exchange or trade (something or someone) for another. ▸ *noun* **1** an exchange or trading. **2** something that is exchanged or traded. [13c: as *swappen*, to strike or to shake hands on a bargain]

sward *noun* a large, usu grassy, area of land. [Anglo-Saxon *sweard* skin]

swarm[1] *noun* **1** a large group of flying bees, led by a queen, that have left their hive in order to set up a new home. **2** any large group of insects or other small creatures, esp ones that are on the move. **3** a crowd of people, esp one that is on the move or that is in chaos. ▸ *verb, intr* to gather, move, go, etc in a swarm. ▪ **swarming** *adj, noun.* [Anglo-Saxon *swearm*]

swarm[2] *verb, tr & intr* (*often* **swarm up sth**) to climb (esp a rope or tree) by clasping with the hands and knees or feet. [16c]

swarthy *adj* (**-ier, -iest**) having a dark complexion. ▪ **swarthiness** *noun.* [16c: from Anglo-Saxon *sweart* dark or black]

swash *verb* **1** to move about in water making a splashing noise. **2** of water: to pour or move with a splashing noise. ▸ *noun* **1** a forward current, such as one caused by an incoming wave. Compare **backwash**. **2** a watery splashing noise. [16c]

swashbuckler *noun* **1** a daring and flamboyant adventurer. **2** a type of highly stylized film, novel, etc that portrays exciting scenes of adventure, usu in a romanticized historical setting, such as feudalism, piracy, etc, and which usu features scenes of flamboyant swordsmanship. ▪ **swashbuckling** *adj.* [16c]

swastika *noun* **1** an ancient religious symbol, representing the sun and good luck. **2** a plain cross with arms of equal length which are bent at right angles, usu clockwise, at or close to their mid point, used as the adopted badge of the former German Nazi Party. [19c: from Sanskrit *svastika*]

swat[1] *verb* (***swatted, swatting***) to hit (esp a fly) with a heavy slapping blow. ▸ *noun* a heavy slap or blow. ▪ **swatter** *noun* a device for swatting flies with, usu consisting of a long thin handle and a wide flat flexible head. [18c: a US, Scottish and Northern English variant of *squat*]

swat[2] see **swot**

swatch *noun* **1** a small sample, esp of fabric but also of wallpaper, carpet, etc. **2** (*also* **swatchbook**) a collection of samples (esp of fabric) bound together to form a sort of book.

swath /swɔːθ/ *or* **swathe** /sweɪð/ *noun* (***swaths*** *or* ***swathes***) **1** **a** a strip of grass, corn, etc cut by a scythe, mower or harvester; **b** the width of this strip; **c** the cut grass, corn, etc left in such a strip. **2** a broad strip, esp of land. [Anglo-Saxon *swæth* track]

swathe *verb* to bind or wrap someone or something in strips or bands of cloth or fabric, eg bandages. ▸ *noun* a wrapping, esp a strip of cloth or fabric; a bandage. [Anglo-Saxon *swathian*]

sway *verb* **1** *tr & intr* to swing, or make something swing, backwards and forwards or from side to side, esp slowly and smoothly. **2** *tr & intr* to lean or bend, or make something lean or bend, to one side or in one direction. **3** to persuade someone to take a particular view or decision, or dissuade them from a course of action. **4** *intr* (*usu* **sway towards sth**) to incline towards a particular opinion. **5** *intr* to waver between two opinions or decisions. ▸ *noun* **1** a swaying motion. **2** control or influence. [15c: perhaps from Norse *sveigja* to bend]

IDIOMS **hold sway** to have authority or influence.

Swazi *noun* (*pl* ***Swazi*** *or* ***Swazis***) **1** a Bantu-speaking agricultural and pastoral people living in Swaziland, a kingdom in SE Africa, and in adjacent parts of southern Africa. **2** an individual belonging to this people. **3** their language. ▸ *adj* belonging or relating to this people or their language. [19c: from the name of Mswazi, a 19c Swazi king]

swear *verb* (*past tense* ***swore,*** *past participle* ***sworn***) **1** *intr* to use indecent or blasphemous language. **2** to assert something solemnly or earnestly, sometimes with an oath. **3** to promise solemnly, usu by taking an oath. **4** to take (an oath). **5** *intr* (**swear by sb** *or* **sth**) *colloq* to have or put complete trust in it (eg a certain product or remedy) or them (eg a doctor or therapist). ▸ *noun* an act of swearing. ▪ **swearing** *noun.* [Anglo-Saxon *swerian*]

IDIOMS **swear blind** *informal* to assert emphatically.

PHRASAL VERBS **swear sb in** to introduce them formally into a post, or into the witness box, by requesting them to take an oath. **swear off sth** *informal* to promise to renounce it or give it up.

swear-word *noun* a word regarded as obscene or blasphemous.

sweat *noun* **1** the salty liquid produced actively by the sweat glands and given out through the pores of the skin, esp in response to great heat, physical exertion, nervousness or fear. **2** the state, or a period, of giving off such moisture. **3** *informal* any activity that causes the body to give off such moisture. **4** *informal* any laborious activity. **5** *esp N Am informal* a **sweatshirt**. **6** (**sweats**) *esp N Am informal* **a** **sweat pants**; **b** a **sweatsuit**. ▸ *verb, intr* (***sweated*** *or* ***sweat***) **1** to give out sweat through the pores of the skin. **2** *informal* to be nervous, anxious or afraid. ▪ **sweaty** *adj* (**-ier, -iest**). [Anglo-Saxon *swætan*]

IDIOMS **in a sweat** *or* **in a cold sweat** *informal* in a worried or anxious state. **no sweat!** *slang* that presents no problems. **sweat blood** *informal* **1** to work extremely hard. **2** to be in a state of great anxiety. **sweat it out** *informal* to endure a difficult situation to the end, esp to wait for a long time in nervous anticipation.

PHRASAL VERBS **sweat sth off** to remove (weight, fat, etc) by exercise that makes one sweat.

sweatband *noun* a strip of elasticated fabric worn around the wrist or head to absorb sweat when playing sports.

sweater *noun* a knitted jersey or pullover, orig of a kind often worn before and after hard exercise.

sweat gland *noun* any of the minute curled tubes of the skin's **epidermis** which actively secrete sweat.

sweatshirt *noun* a long-sleeved jersey of a thick soft cotton fabric, usu fleecy on the inside.

sweatshop *noun* a workshop or factory where employees work for long hours with poor pay and conditions.

sweatsuit *noun* a loose-fitting suit of sweatshirt and trousers.

Swede *noun* a native or inhabitant of Sweden.

swede *noun* **1** a plant widely cultivated for its edible root. **2** the swollen edible root of this plant, which has orange-yellow or whitish flesh and a purple, yellow or white skin, and can be cooked and eaten as a vegetable. [19c: from *Swede*; the plant was introduced from Sweden in the late 18c]

Swedish *adj* **1** belonging or relating to Sweden, a kingdom in N Europe, its inhabitants or their language. **2** (**the Swedish**) the citizens or inhabitants of or people born in, Sweden; Swedes. ▸ *noun* the official language of Sweden and one of the two official languages of Finland.

sweep *verb* (*past tense, past participle* ***swept***) **1** to clean (a room, a floor, etc) with a brush or broom. **2** to remove (dirt, dust, etc) with a brush or broom. **3** (*usu* **sweep sth aside** *or* **away**) to dismiss (ideas, suggestions, etc) or remove (problems, errors, etc): *She swept aside their objections.* **4** (*often* **sweep sb**

or **sth away, off, past**, *etc*) to take, carry or push them suddenly and with irresistible force: *The current swept the boat through the narrows.* **5** (*often* **sweep sb** *or* **sth off, up,** *etc*) to lift, gather or clear with a forceful scooping or brushing movement: *He swept the child into his arms.* **6** *tr & intr* (*often* **sweep in, out**, *etc*) to move, pass or spread smoothly and swiftly, or strongly, or uncontrollably: *Strong winds were sweeping in from the sea.* **7** *intr* to walk, esp with garments flowing, impressively, arrogantly, angrily, etc: *She swept across the room in her robes.* **8** *tr & intr* to pass quickly over, making light contact: *Her dress swept the floor.* **9** *intr* of emotions, etc: to affect suddenly and overpoweringly: *She felt a chill sweep over her.* **10** to have a decisive electoral win: *expecting to sweep the country in next week's elections.* **11** to cast or direct (eg one's gaze) with a scanning movement. **12** to make extensive searches over (an area, esp the sea) for mines, ships, etc. ▸ *noun* **1** an act of sweeping. **2** a sweeping movement or action. **3** a sweeping line, eg of a road, or broad sweeping stretch, eg of landscape. **4** the range or area over which something moves, esp in a curving or circular path. **5** *informal* a sweepstake. **6** *informal* a chimney-sweep. [Anglo-Saxon *swapan*]

IDIOMS **a clean sweep** the winning of all prizes, awards, political seats, etc. **sweep sb off their feet** to have a strong or sudden effect on their emotions, usu causing them to fall in love. **sweep sth under the carpet** to hide or ignore something (esp unwelcome facts, difficulties, etc).

sweeper *noun* **1** someone who sweeps. **2** a device or machine used for sweeping. **3** *football* a player covering the whole area behind a line of defenders.

sweeping *adj* **1** of a search, change, etc: wide-ranging and thorough. **2** of a statement: too generalized; indiscriminate. **3** of a victory, etc: impressive; decisive. ▪ **sweepingly** *adv* **1** with a sweeping gesture. **2** indiscriminately; comprehensively.

sweepstake *noun* **1** a system of gambling in which the prize money is the sum of the stakes of all those betting. **2** a horse race in which the owner of the winning horse receives sums of money put up by the owners of all the other horses. Also (*N Am*) called **sweepstakes.**

sweet *adj* **1** tasting like sugar; not sour, salty or bitter. **2** pleasing to any of the senses, esp smell and hearing. **3** likeable; charming. **4** of wine: having some taste of sugar or fruit; not dry. **5** *informal* (*usu* **sweet on sb**) fond of them; infatuated with them. **6** of air or water: fresh and untainted. ▸ *noun* **1** any small sugar-based confection that is sucked or chewed. **2** a pudding or dessert. ▸ *adv* sweetly. ▪ **sweetly** *adv.* [Anglo-Saxon *swete*]

sweet-and-sour *adj* cooked in a sauce that includes both sugar and vinegar or lemon juice. ▸ *noun* a sweet-and-sour dish.

sweetbread *noun* the pancreas or thymus of a young animal, esp a calf, used as food.

sweet chestnut see **chestnut**

sweetcorn *noun* kernels of a variety of maize eaten young while still sweet.

sweeten *verb* **1** to make (food) sweet or sweeter. **2** (*also* **sweeten sb up**) *informal* to make them more agreeable or amenable, eg by flattery or bribery. **3** *informal* to make (eg an offer) more acceptable or inviting, by making changes or additions.

sweetener *noun* **1** a substance used for sweetening food, esp one other than sugar. **2** *informal* an inducement, usu illicit, added to an offer to make it more attractive, esp a bribe.

sweetheart *noun* **a** a person one is in love with; **b** used as a term of endearment.

sweetie *noun, informal* **1** a sweet. **2** (*also* **sweetie-pie**) a term of endearment. **3** a lovable person.

sweetmeal *adj* of biscuits: made of sweetened wholemeal.

sweetmeat *noun, old use* any small sugar-based confection or cake.

sweetness *noun* the state, or degree, of being sweet.

IDIOMS **sweetness and light** *informal* mildness, amiability and reasonableness.

sweet nothings *plural noun* the endearments that people in love say to each other.

sweet pea *noun* a climbing plant that has brightly coloured butterfly-shaped flowers.

sweet pepper *noun* **1** a tropical American plant, widely cultivated for its edible fruit. **2** the hollow edible fruit of this plant, which can be eaten when red (or orange or yellow) and ripe or when green and unripe. Also called **capsicum**.

sweet potato *noun* **1** a plant with trailing or climbing stems and large purple funnel-shaped flowers. **2** the swollen edible root of this plant, which has sweet-tasting flesh surrounded by a red or purplish skin, and can be cooked and eaten as a vegetable.

sweet talk *noun, informal* words, often flattery, intended to coax or persuade. ▸ *verb* (**sweet-talk**) *informal* to coax or persuade, or to try to do so, eg with flattering words.

sweet tooth *noun* a fondness for sweet foods.

swell *verb* (*past participle* ***swollen*** *or* ***swelled***) **1** *tr & intr* to become, or make something, bigger or fatter through injury or infection, or by filling with liquid or air. **2** *tr & intr* to increase or make something increase in number, size or intensity. **3** *intr* to become visibly filled with emotion, esp pride. **4** *intr* of the sea: to rise and fall in smooth masses without forming individual waves. **5** *intr* of a sound: to become louder and then die away. ▸ *noun* **1** a heaving of the sea without waves. **2** an increase in number, size or intensity. **3** an increase in volume of sound or music, followed by a dying away. **4** *old informal* someone who dresses smartly and fashionably. **5** *music* **a** an increase in the volume of sound, followed by a dying away; **b** a device in organs and some harpsichords for increasing and decreasing the volume of sound. **6** a broad rounded hill; a piece of smoothly rising ground. ▸ *adj, exclam, chiefly N Am informal* excellent. ▪ **swelling** *noun* an area of the body that is temporarily swollen as a result of injury or infection. [Anglo-Saxon *swellan*]

swelter *verb, intr* to sweat heavily or feel extremely or oppressively hot. ▸ *noun* a sweltering feeling or state; sweltering weather. ▪ **sweltering** *adj* of the weather: extremely or oppressively hot.

swept *past tense, past participle of* **sweep**

swerve *verb, intr* to turn or move aside suddenly and sharply, eg to avoid a collision. ▸ *noun* an act of swerving; a swerving movement. [14c]

swift *adj* **1** fast-moving; able to move fast. **2** done, given, etc quickly or promptly. **3** acting promptly:

His friends were swift to defend him. ▸ *adv* swiftly. ▸ *noun* a small fast-flying bird that has dark brown or grey plumage, long narrow pointed wings and a forked tail. ▪ **swiftly** *adv.* ▪ **swiftness** *noun.* [Anglo-Saxon *swift*]

swig *informal, verb* (***swigged, swigging***) *tr & intr* to drink in gulps, esp from a bottle. ▸ *noun* a large gulp. [17c]

swill *verb* **1** (*also* **swill sth out**) to rinse something by splashing water round or over it. **2** *informal* to drink (esp alcohol) greedily. ▸ *noun* **1** any mushy mixture of scraps fed to pigs. **2** disgusting food or drink. [Anglo-Saxon *swilian* to wash]

swim *verb* (*past tense* ***swam,*** *past participle* ***swum, swimming***) **1** *intr* to propel oneself through water by moving the arms and legs or (in fish) the tail and fins. **2** to cover (a distance) or cross (a stretch of water) in this way: *swim the Channel.* **3** *intr* to float. **4** *intr* to be affected by dizziness: *His head was swimming.* **5** *intr* to move or appear to move about in waves or whirls. ▸ *noun* **1** a spell of swimming. **2** the general flow of events. ▪ **swimmer** *noun.* ▪ **swimming** *noun.* [Anglo-Saxon *swimman*]

IDIOMS **in the swim** *informal* up to date with, and often involved in, what is going on around one.

swim bladder *noun, zool* an internal structure in a fish that can be filled with air and control the buoyancy of the fish in the water. Also called **air bladder**.

swimming bath *noun* or **swimming baths** *plural noun* a swimming pool, usu indoors.

swimming costume *noun* a swimsuit.

swimmingly *adv, informal* smoothly and successfully.

swimming pool *noun* an artificial pool for swimming in.

swimsuit *noun* a garment worn for swimming.

swindle *verb* to cheat or trick someone in order to obtain money from them; to obtain (money, etc) by cheating or trickery. ▸ *noun* an act of swindling. ▪ **swindler** *noun.* [18c: from German *Schwindler* someone who plans extravagant schemes, a cheat]

swine *noun* (***swine*** in sense 1 or ***swines*** in sense 2) **1** a pig. **2** a despicable person. [Anglo-Saxon *swin*]

swineherd *noun, old use* someone who looks after pigs.

swing *verb* (*past tense, past participle* ***swung***) **1** *tr & intr* to move in a curving motion, pivoting from a fixed point: *The door swung shut behind her.* **2** *tr & intr* to move or make something move or turn with a sweeping or curving movement or movements: *swung himself into the saddle.* **3** *tr & intr* to turn or make something turn around a central axis: *She swung round, surprised.* **4** *intr* to undergo, often suddenly or sharply, a change or changes of opinion, mood, fortune or direction: *He swung between extremes of mood.* **5** (*also* **swing sb round**) to persuade them to have a certain opinion: *That should swing them round to our way of thinking.* **6** *informal* to arrange or fix; to achieve the successful outcome of something: *just needs a couple of free gifts to swing the sale.* **7 a** *informal* to determine or settle the outcome of (eg an election in which voters were initially undecided); **b** *intr* of an electorate's voting pattern: to change in favour of a particular party: *The vote has swung decisively to the Green Party.* **8** *tr & intr* (*often* **swing at sb** *or* **sth**) **a** to attempt to hit or make a hit with a curving movement of a bat, etc: *swung wildly at the ball;* **b** *informal* to attempt to punch someone or make (a punch) with a curving arm movement: *He swung a frustrated punch at the goalkeeper.* **9** *intr, informal* of a social function, etc: to be lively and exciting. **10** *intr, informal* to enjoy oneself with vigour and enthusiasm. **11** *intr, informal* to be hanged. **12** *tr & intr, music* to perform or be performed as swing (see *noun* sense 7 below). ▸ *noun* **1** a seat suspended from a frame or branch for a child (or sometimes an adult) to swing on. **2** a change, usu a sudden and sharp change, eg in mood, support, success, etc. **3** a swinging stroke with a golf club, cricket bat, etc; the technique of a golfer. **4** a punch made with a curving movement. **5** an act, manner or spell of swinging. **6** a swinging movement. **7** *music* jazz or jazz-like dance music with a simple regular rhythm, popularized by bands in the 1930s. **8** *cricket* a curving movement of a bowled ball. **9** a change in the voting pattern of the electorate in a particular constituency, at a particular election, etc: *a swing of 40% to Labour.* ▸ *adj* able to swing: *a swing mirror.* [Anglo-Saxon *swingan*]

IDIOMS **in full swing** *or* **into full swing** at, or to, the height of liveliness. **swing into action** to begin to move or act, esp decisively or enthusiastically. **swings and roundabouts** *informal* a situation in which advantages and disadvantages, or successes and failures, are equal.

swing bridge *noun* a bridge that swings open to let boats through.

swingeing /ˈswɪndʒɪŋ/ *adj* hard to bear; severe, extensive. [Anglo-Saxon *swengan* to shake]

swinging *adj* **1** moving or turning with a swing. **2** *informal old use* lively and exciting.

swipe *verb* **1** to hit with a heavy sweeping blow. **2** (*usu* **swipe at sb** *or* **sth**) to try to hit them or it. **3** *informal* to steal. **4** to pass (a swipe card) through a device that electronically interprets the information encoded on the card. ▸ *noun* a heavy sweeping blow. [Anglo-Saxon *swipian* to beat]

swirl *verb, tr & intr* to flow or cause to flow or move with a whirling or circling motion. ▸ *noun* **1** a whirling or circling motion. **2** a curling circling shape. ▪ **swirling** *adj.* [15c: prob from Scandinavian]

swish[1] *verb, tr & intr* to move with a rustling, hissing or whooshing sound. ▸ *noun* a rustling, hissing or whooshing sound, or movement causing such a sound. [18c: imitating the sound]

swish[2] *adj, informal* smart and stylish. [19c: prob from **swish**[1]]

Swiss *adj* belonging or relating to Switzerland, a republic in central Europe, to its inhabitants, or to the German, French or Italian dialects spoken by them. ▸ *noun* (*pl* ***Swiss***) **1** a native or citizen of, or person born in, Switzerland. **2** any of the dialects of German, French or Italian spoken in Switzerland. [16c: from French *suisse*]

Swiss roll *noun* a cylindrical cake made by rolling up a thin slab of sponge spread with jam or cream.

switch *noun* **1** a manually operated or automatic device that is used to open or close an electric circuit. **2** a change. **3** an exchange or change-over, esp one involving a deception. **4** a long flexible twig or cane, esp one used for corporal punishment; a stroke with such a twig or cane. **5** *N Am* a set of railway points. ▸ *verb* **1** *tr & intr* to exchange (one thing or person for another), esp quickly and without notice in order to deceive. **2** *tr & intr* to transfer or change over (eg to a different system). [16c: prob from Dutch *swijch* a branch]

IDIOMS **switched on** *informal* well informed or aware.

PHRASAL VERBS **switch off** *informal* to stop paying attention. **switch sth off** to turn (an appliance) off by means of a switch. **switch sth on 1** to turn (an appliance) on by means of a switch. **2** *informal* to bring on (eg charm or tears) at will in order to create the required effect.

switchback *noun* **1** a road with many twists and turns and upward and downward slopes. **2** a rollercoaster.

switchboard *noun* a board on which incoming telephone calls are connected manually or electronically.

swivel *noun* a joint between two parts enabling one part to turn or pivot freely and independently of the other. ▸ *verb* (***swivelled, swivelling***) *tr & intr* to turn or pivot on a swivel or as if on a swivel. [Anglo-Saxon *swifan* to turn round]

swizz *noun, informal* a thing that, in reality, is disappointingly inferior to what was cheatingly promised. [Early 20c: a shortening of *swizzle*]

swizzle-stick *noun* a thin stick used to stir cocktails and other drinks.

swollen *past participle of* **swell**

swollen head *noun* conceitedness; excessive pride at one's own ability or achievements.

swoon *verb* **1** *intr* to faint, esp from overexcitement. **2** (*often* **swoon over sb** *or* **sth**) to go into raptures about them or it. ▸ *noun* an act of swooning. [14c]

swoop *verb, intr* **1** to fly down with a fast sweeping movement. **2** to make a sudden forceful attack; to pounce. **3** (*usu* **swoop at sb** *or* **sth**) to make a sudden and quick attempt to seize or get hold of them or it. ▸ *noun* **1** an act of swooping. **2** a swooping movement or feeling. [Anglo-Saxon *swapan* to sweep]

IDIOMS **in one fell swoop** in one complete decisive action; all at one time.

swoosh *noun* the noise of a rush of air or water, or any noise resembling this. ▸ *verb, intr* to make or move with such a noise. [19c: prob imitating the sound made]

swop see **swap**

sword *noun* **1** a weapon like a large long knife, with a blade sharpened on one or both edges and usu ending in a point. **2** (**the sword**) violence or destruction, esp in war. **3** anything similar to a sword in shape, such as the long pointed upper jaw of a swordfish. [Anglo-Saxon *sweord*]

IDIOMS **cross swords with sb** to encounter them as an opponent; to argue or fight with them.

sword dance *noun* a dance, usu by a solo dancer, with steps over a cross formed by two swords or one sword and its scabbard laid on the ground.

swordfish *noun* a large marine fish with an upper jaw prolonged into a long flat sword-shaped snout.

sword of Damocles / 'daməkliːz/ *noun, literary* any imminent danger or disaster. [18c: from the story of Damocles in classical mythology, who was forced to sit through a feast with a sword hanging by a single hair above his head in order that he should understand how precarious life is]

swordplay *noun* the activity or art of fencing.

swordsman *noun* a man skilled in fighting with a sword. ▪ **swordsmanship** *noun.*

swordstick *noun* a hollow walking-stick containing a short sword or dagger.

swore *past tense of* **swear**

sworn *verb, past participle of* **swear**. ▸ *adj* confirmed by, or as if by, having taken an oath: *sworn enemies.*

swot *or* **swat** *informal, verb* (***swotted, swotting***; ***swatted, swatting***) *tr & intr* **1** to study hard and seriously. **2** (*also* **swot sth up**) to study it intensively, esp at the last minute, ie just before an exam. ▸ *noun* someone who studies hard, esp single-mindedly or in order to impress a teacher. ▪ **swotting** *noun.* [19c: a variant of **sweat**]

swum *past participle of* **swim**

swung *past tense, past participle of* **swing**

sybarite /'sɪbəraɪt/ *noun* someone devoted to a life of luxury and pleasure. ▪ **sybaritic** *adj* luxurious. [16c: orig an inhabitant of Sybaris, an ancient Greek city in S Italy, noted for its luxury]

sycamore *noun* **1** a large tree with dark green leaves divided into five toothed lobes, yellowish flowers borne in long pendulous spikes, and two-winged fruits. **2** *N Am* any of various plane trees native to America. **3** the wood of any of these trees, used for furniture-making, etc. [13c: from Greek *sykomoros*]

sycophant *noun* someone who flatters in a servile way; a crawler. ▪ **sycophancy** *noun* the behaviour of a sycophant; flattery. ▪ **sycophantic** *adj.* [16c: from Greek *sykophantes* informer or swindler]

syllabic *adj* relating to syllables or the division of words into syllables.

syllabify *verb* (***-ies, -ied***) to divide (a word) into syllables. ▪ **syllabification** *noun.*

syllable *noun* **1** a segment of a spoken word consisting of one sound or of two or more sounds said as a single unit of speech (*segment* has two syllables; *consisting* has three syllables). **2** the slightest word or sound: *He hardly uttered a syllable all evening.* [14c: from Greek *syllabe*, literally 'something that is held or taken together']

IDIOMS **in words of one syllable** in simple language; frankly; plainly.

syllabub *or* **sillabub** *noun* a frothy dessert made with a mixture of cream or milk and wine.

syllabus *noun* (***syllabuses*** *or* ***syllabi***) a series of topics prescribed for a course of study. [17c: from a misreading of Latin *sittybas*]

syllogism *noun* an argument in which a conclusion, whether valid or invalid, is drawn from two independent statements using logic, as in *All dogs are animals, foxhounds are dogs, therefore foxhounds are animals.* See also **logic**, **fallacy**. ▪ **syllogistic** *adj.* [14c: from Greek *syllogismos* a reasoning together]

sylph *noun* **1** in folklore: a spirit of the air. **2** a slender graceful woman or girl. [17c: a word created in the 16c by Paracelsus, a Swiss alchemist]

sylvan *or* **silvan** *adj, literary* relating to woods or woodland; wooded. [16c: from Latin *silva* a wood]

symbiont *noun, biol* either of two organisms in a symbiotic relationship.

symbiosis *noun* (***-ses***) **1** *biol* a close association between two organisms of different species, usu to the benefit of both partners, and often essential for mutual survival. **2** *psychol* a mutually beneficial relationship between two people dependent on each other. ▪ **symbiotic** *adj*. [19c: from Greek *syn* together + *bios* life]

symbol *noun* **1** a thing that represents or stands for another, usu something concrete or material representing an idea or emotion, eg the colour red representing danger. **2** a letter or sign used to represent a quantity, idea, object, operation, etc, such as the £ used to represent pound sterling. ▪ **symbolic** *or* **symbolical** *adj* **1** being a symbol of something; representing or standing for something. **2** relating to symbols or their use. ▪ **symbolically** *adv*. [16c: from Greek *symbolon* token]

symbolism *noun* **1** the use of symbols, esp to express ideas or emotions in literature, cinema, etc. **2** a system of symbols. **3** (*usu* **Symbolism**) a 19th-century movement in art and literature which made extensive use of symbols to indicate or evoke emotions or ideas. ▪ **symbolist** *noun* an artist or writer who uses symbolism.

symbolize *or* **-ise** *verb* **1** to be a symbol of something; to stand for something. **2** to represent something by means of a symbol or symbols.

symmetry *noun* (*-ies*) **1** exact similarity between two parts or halves, as if one were a mirror image of the other. **2** the arrangement of parts in pleasing proportion to each other; also, the aesthetic satisfaction derived from this. ▪ **symmetrical** *adj*. [16c: from Greek *syn* together + *metron* measure]

sympathetic *adj* **1** (*often* **sympathetic to sb** *or* **sth**) feeling or expressing sympathy for them. **2** amiable, esp because of being kind-hearted. **3** acting or done out of sympathy; showing sympathy. **4** in keeping with one's mood or feelings; agreeable.

sympathize *or* **-ise** *verb, intr* **1** (*often* **sympathize with sb**) to feel or express sympathy for them. **2** (*often* **sympathize with sb** *or* **sth**) to support or be in agreement with them. ▪ **sympathizer** *noun*.

sympathy *noun* (*-ies*) **1** (*often* **sympathy for** *or* **with sb**) an understanding of and feeling for the sadness or suffering of others, often shown in expressions of sorrow or pity. **2** (*often* **sympathies**) loyal or approving support for, or agreement with, an organization or belief. **3** affection between people resulting from their understanding of each other's personalities. [16c: from Greek *syn* with + *pathos* suffering]

symphonic poem *noun, music* a large orchestral composition with the movements run together.

symphony *noun* (*-ies*) **1** a long musical work divided into several movements, played by a full orchestra. **2** an instrumental passage in a musical work which consists mostly of singing. **3** *literary* a pleasing combination of parts, eg shapes or colours. **4** a symphony orchestra. ▪ **symphonic** *adj*. [13c: from Greek *syn* together + *phone* sound]

symphony orchestra *noun* a large orchestra capable of playing large-scale orchestral music.

symposium *noun* (***symposia*** *or* ***symposiums***) **1** a conference held to discuss a particular subject, esp an academic subject. **2** a collection of essays by different writers on a single topic. [18c: from Greek *symposion* a drinking-party with intellectual discussion]

symptom *noun* **1** *med* an indication of the presence of a disease or disorder, esp something perceived by the patient and not outwardly visible, eg pain, nausea, etc. **2** an indication of the existence of a, usu unwelcome, state or condition: *The increase in crime is a symptom of moral decline*. [14c: from Greek *symptoma* happening, attribute]

symptomatic *adj* **1** (*often* **symptomatic of sth**) being a symptom of it; indicative of it. **2** belonging or relating to a symptom or symptoms. ▪ **symptomatically** *adv*.

synagogue *noun* a Jewish place of worship and religious instruction. [12c: from Greek *synagoge* assembly]

synapse *noun, anatomy* in the nervous system: a minute gap across which nerve impulses are transmitted from one neurone to another. [19c: from Greek *synapsis* contact or junction]

synapsis *noun* (***synapses***) *biol* the pairing of paternal and maternal chromosomes during **meiosis**. ▪ **synaptic** *adj*. [19c: Greek, meaning 'contact']

synch *or* **sync** /sɪŋk/ *informal, noun* synchronization, esp of sound and picture in film and television. ▸ *verb* to synchronize.

synchromesh *noun* a gear system which matches the speeds of the gear wheels before they are engaged, avoiding shock and noise in gear-changing. [20c: a shortening of *synchronized mesh*]

synchronize *or* **-ise** *verb* **1** *tr & intr* to happen or cause to happen, move or operate in exact time with (something else or each other). **2** to project (a film), or broadcast (a TV programme), so that the action, actors' lip movements, etc precisely match the sounds or words heard. **3** to set (clocks or watches) so that they all show exactly the same time. ▪ **synchronization** *noun*. [17c: from Greek *syn* together + *chronos* time]

synchronized swimming *noun* a sport in which a swimmer or group of swimmers performs a sequence of gymnastic and balletic movements in time to music.

synchronous *adj* occurring at the same time; recurring with the same frequency. ▪ **synchrony** *noun*.

syncline *noun, geol* a large generally U-shaped fold in the stratified rocks of the Earth's crust. [19c: from Greek *syn* together + *klinein* to cause to lean]

syncopate *verb, music* to alter (rhythm) by putting the stress on beats not usu stressed. ▪ **syncopation** *noun*.

syncope /'sɪŋkəpɪ/ *noun* **1** *med* a sudden temporary loss of consciousness; a faint. **2** *linguistics* the dropping of a letter or syllable in the middle of a word, eg in *o'er*, the poetic version of *over*. [16c: from Greek *synkope* a cutting short]

syndic *noun* someone who represents a university, company or other body in business or legal matters. [17c: from Greek *syndikos* advocate]

syndicate *noun* /'sɪndɪkət/ **1** any association of people or groups working together on a single project. **2** a group of business organizations jointly managing or financing a single venture. **3** an association of criminals organizing widespread illegal activities. **4** an agency selling journalists' material to a number of newspapers for publication at the same time. ▸ *verb* /-keɪt/ **1** to form into a syndicate. **2** **a** to sell (an article, photograph, etc) for publication by a number of newspapers; **b** in the US: to sell (a programme) for broadcasting by a number of TV stations. ▪ **syndication** *noun.* [17c: from French *syndicat*]

syndrome *noun* **1** a group of signs or symptoms whose appearance together usu indicates the presence of a particular disease or disorder. **2** a pattern or series of events, observed qualities, etc characteristic of a particular problem or condition. [16c: from Greek *syndrome* a running together]

synecdoche /sɪˈnɛkdəkɪ/ *noun* a figure of speech in which a part of something is used to refer to or denote the whole thing, or the whole to refer to or denote a part, eg the use of *wiser heads* to mean *wiser people*. [15c: from Greek *synekdoche* a receiving together]

synergy *or* **synergism** *noun* **1** an increased effectiveness achieved by a number of people working together. **2** *med* the phenomenon in which the combined action of two or more compounds, esp drugs or hormones, is greater than the sum of the individual effects of each compound. [19c: from Greek *synergia* co-operation]

synod *noun* **a** a local or national council of members of the clergy; **b** a meeting of this. [14c: from Greek *synodos* meeting]

synonym *noun* a word having the same, or very nearly the same, meaning as another. ▪ **synonymous** *adj* (*often* **synonymous with sth**) **1** having the same meaning. **2** very closely associated in the mind: *For some, football is synonymous with hooliganism.* ▪ **synonymy** *noun.* [16c: from Greek *syn* with + *onyma*, a variant form of *onoma* name]

synopsis /sɪˈnɒpsɪs/ *noun* (**-ses** /-siːz/) a brief outline, eg of the plot of a book; a summary. ▪ **synoptic** *adj* being or like a synopsis; giving or taking an overall view. [17c: from Greek *syn* together + *opsis* view]

synovia /sɪˈnoʊvɪə, saɪ-/ *noun* the transparent liquid that lubricates a joint. Also called **synovial fluid**.

syntax *noun* **1 a** the positioning of words in a sentence and their relationship to each other; **b** the grammatical rules governing this. **2** the branch of linguistics that is concerned with the study of such rules. **3** *comput* rules for combining the elements of a programming language. ▪ **syntactic** *or* **syntactical** *adj.* ▪ **syntactically** *adv.* [17c: from Greek *syn* together + *tassein* to put in order]

synthesis /ˈsɪnθəsɪs/ *noun* (**-ses** /-siːz/) **1** the process of putting together separate parts to form a complex whole. **2** the result of such a process. **3** *chem* any process whereby a complex chemical compound is formed from simpler compounds or elements, esp via a series of chemical reactions. [18c: from Greek *syn* together + *thesis* a placing]

synthesize *or* **-ise** *verb* **1** to combine (simple parts) to form (a complex whole). **2** *chem* to form (a compound, product, etc) by a process of synthesis.

synthesizer *or* **-iser** *noun, music* an instrument that produces sound electronically, esp one able to produce the sounds of other instruments.

synthetic *adj* **1** referring or relating to, or produced by, chemical synthesis; not naturally produced; man-made. **2** not sincere; sham. ▸ *noun* a synthetic substance. ▪ **synthetically** *adv.* [18c: from Greek *synthetikos* skilled at putting together]

syphilis *noun, med* a sexually transmitted infection characterized by painless ulcers on the genitals, fever and a faint red rash. ▪ **syphilitic** *adj, noun.* [17c: named after Syphilus, the infected hero of a 16c Latin poem]

syphon see **siphon**

Syrian *adj* belonging or relating to Syria, a republic in the Middle East, to its inhabitants. ▸ *noun* a native or citizen of, or person born in, Syria.

syringe *noun* **1** a medical instrument for injecting or drawing off liquid, consisting of a hollow cylinder with a plunger inside and a thin hollow needle attached. **2** a similar device used in gardening, cooking, etc. ▸ *verb* to clean, spray or inject using a syringe. [15c: from Greek *syrinx* tube]

syrup *noun* **1** a sweet, sticky, almost saturated solution of sugar, eg golden syrup. **2** a solution of sugar in water used to preserve canned fruit. **3** any sugar-flavoured liquid medicine. **4** *informal* exaggerated sentimentality or pleasantness of manner. ▪ **syrupy** *adj* **1** the consistency of or like syrup. **2** excessively sentimental. [14c: from Arabic *sharab* a drink]

system *noun* **1** a set of interconnected or interrelated parts forming a complex whole: *the transport system.* **2** an arrangement of mechanical, electrical or electronic parts functioning as a unit: *a stereo system.* **3** a way of working; a method or arrangement of organization or classification: *a more efficient filing system.* **4** efficiency of organization; methodicalness; orderliness: *You need to get some system into your exam revision.* **5** one's mind or body regarded as a set of interconnected parts: *get the anger out of your system.* **6** (**the system**) society, or the network of institutions that control it, usu regarded as an oppressive force. **7** *geol* the basic unit of classification of rock strata formed during a single period of geological time, ranking above **series** (sense 6) and characterized by its fossil content. **8** an interrelated body of doctrines or theories; a full view of some branch of knowledge. [17c: from Greek *systema*]

systematic *adj* **1** making use of, or carried out according to, a clearly worked-out plan or method. **2** methodical. ▪ **systematically** *adv.*

systematics *singular noun* the scientific study of the classification of living things into a hierarchy of groups which emphasizes their natural interrelationships.

systematize *or* **-ise** *verb* to organize or arrange in a methodical way. ▪ **systematization** *noun.*

Système International d'Unités see **SI**

systemic *adj* **1** *biol* referring or relating to a whole organism. **2** *med* relating to or affecting the whole body. ▪ **systemically** *adv.*

systems analysis *noun, comput* the detailed analysis of some human task in order to determine whether and how it can be computerized.

systole /ˈsɪstəlɪ/ *noun, med* contraction of the heart muscle, during which blood is pumped from the ventricle into the arteries. See also **diastole**. ▪ **systolic** /sɪˈstɒlɪk/ *adj.* [16c: Greek]

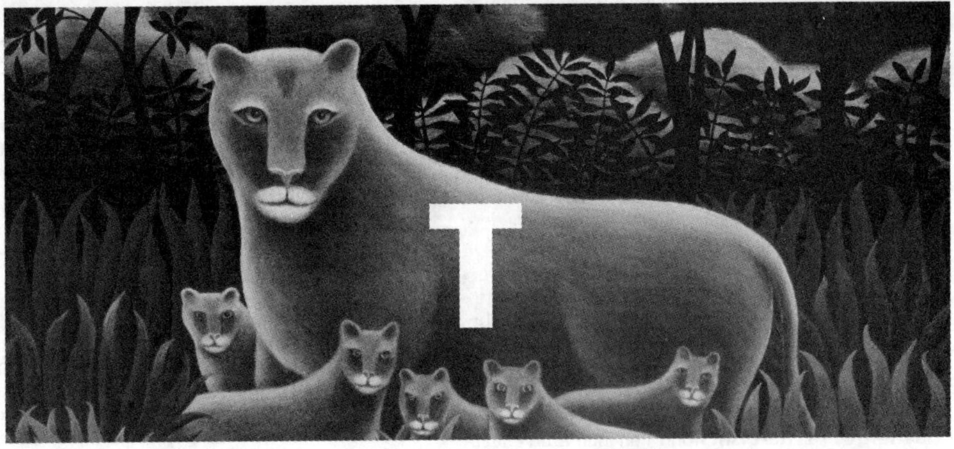

T[1] *or* **t** *noun* (***Ts, T's*** *or* ***t's***) the twentieth letter of the English alphabet.

IDIOMS **to a T** exactly; perfectly well.

T[2] *abbrev, physics* tesla.

T[3] *symbol, chem* tritium.

t *abbrev* ton.

TA *abbrev* Territorial Army.

Ta *symbol, chem* tantalum.

ta *exclam, Brit informal* thank you. [18c: imitating a young child's pronunciation]

tab[1] *noun* **1** a small flap, tag, strip of material, etc attached to something, for hanging it up, opening, holding or identifying it, etc. **2** *chiefly US* a bill, eg, in a bar, restaurant, etc. **3** *chiefly US* a price; cost. **4** a stage curtain or a loop from which it hangs. ▸ *verb* (***tabbed, tabbing***) to fix a tab to. [19c: prob orig a dialect word]

IDIOMS **keep tabs on** *informal* to keep a close watch or check on. **pick up the tab** to pay the bill.

tab[2] *noun* a key on a typewriter or word processor keyboard which sets and then automatically finds the position of margins and columns. Also called **tabulator**. [20c: an abbreviation of **tabulator**]

tabard *noun* **1** a short loose sleeveless jacket or tunic, worn esp by a medieval knight or by a herald. **2** a woman's or girl's sleeveless or short-sleeved tunic or overgarment. [13c: from French *tabart*]

Tabasco *noun, trademark* a spicy sauce made from a pungent type of red pepper. [19c: named after Tabasco, a river and state in Mexico]

tabbouleh /tə'buːleɪ/ *noun* a Mediterranean salad made with cracked wheat and vegetables. [20c: from Arabic *tabbula*]

tabby *noun* (***-ies***) **1** (*also* **tabby cat**) a grey or brown cat with darker stripes. **2** a kind of silk with irregular wavy shiny markings. [17c: from French *tabis*, from *Al-Attabiyah* in Baghdad where the silk was first made]

tabernacle *noun* **1** the tent carried by the Israelites across the desert during the Exodus. **2** *RC Church* a receptacle where the consecrated bread and wine are kept. **3** a place of worship of certain nonconformist Christian denominations. [13c: from Latin *tabernaculum* tent]

tabla *noun* a pair of small drums played with the hands in Indian music. [19c: Hindi, from Arabic *tabl*]

table *noun* **1** a piece of furniture consisting of a flat horizontal surface supported by one or more legs. **2** the people sitting at a table. **3** the food served at a particular table or in a particular house: *keeps a good table*. **4** a group of words or figures, etc arranged in columns and rows. **5** a **multiplication table**: *learn your tables*. ▸ *verb* **1** *Brit* to put forward for discussion. **2** *N Am* to postpone discussion of (a bill, etc) indefinitely. [Anglo-Saxon *tabule*: from Latin *tabula* board or tablet]

IDIOMS **on the table** under discussion. **turn the tables on sb** to reverse a situation so that they are at a disadvantage where they had an advantage.

tableau /'tabloʊ; *French* tablo/ *noun* (***tableaux*** /-bloʊz; *French* tablo/) **1** a picture or pictorial representation of a group or scene. **2** *theatre* a moment or scene in which the action is frozen for dramatic effect. [17c: French, from *tablel* diminutive of *table* **table**]

tablecloth *noun* a cloth for covering a table, esp during meals.

table d'hôte /tɑːbəl 'doʊt; *French* tablədot/ *noun* (***tables d'hôte*** /'tɑːbəlz; *French* tablədot/) a meal or menu with a set number of choices and a set number of courses offered for a fixed price. Compare **à la carte**. [17c: French, literally 'host's table']

tableland *noun* a broad high plain or a plateau.

tablespoon *noun* **1** a large spoon used for measuring and serving food. **2** the amount a tablespoon can hold. ▪ **tablespoonful** *noun*.

tablet *noun* **1** a small solid measured amount of a medicine or drug. **2** a solid flat piece of something, eg, soap. **3** a slab of stone or wood on which an inscription may be carved. [14c: from Latin *tabula* board]

table tennis *noun* a game based on tennis played indoors on a table with small bats and a light hollow ball. Also called **ping-pong**.

tableware *noun* dishes, plates and cutlery, etc collectively for use at table.

tabloid *noun* a newspaper with relatively small pages, usu having an informal and often sensationalist style and many photographs. ▸ *adj* relating to this type of newspaper or this style of journalism: *the tabloid press* • *tabloid television*. Compare **broadsheet**. [20c: orig a trademark for medicines produced in tablet form]

taboo *or* **tabu** *noun* **1** something which is forbidden or disapproved of for religious reasons or by social custom. **2** a system in which certain actions, etc are forbidden. ▸ *adj* forbidden or prohibited as being a taboo. [18c: from Tongan *tabu*]

tabor /'teɪbə(r)/ *noun* a small drum, often accompanying a pipe or fife. [13c: from French *tabour*]

tabular *adj* arranged in systematic columns or lists. [17c: from Latin *tabula* board]

tabulate *verb* to arrange (information) in tabular form. ▪ **tabulation** *noun*. [18c: from Latin *tabula* a board]

tabulator *noun* a **tab**[2].

tachism *or* **tachisme** /'taʃɪzəm/ *noun, art* a movement in mid-20c abstract painting in which paint was laid on in thick patches intended to be interesting in themselves, irrespective of whether a motif was represented. See also **action painting**. ▪ **tachist** *or* **tachiste** *noun, adj*. [1950s: from French *tache* blob (of paint)]

tachograph *noun* a device which keeps a record of a vehicle's speed, esp a lorry, and the time it takes to cover a particular distance. [20c: from Greek *tachos* speed]

tachometer /ta'kɒmətə(r)/ *noun* a device which measures speed, esp that of an engine in revolutions per minute. [19c: from Greek *tachos* speed]

tacit /'tasɪt/ *adj* **1** silent; unspoken. **2** understood but not actually stated. [17c: from Latin *tacere* to be silent]

taciturn /'tasɪtɜːn/ *adj* saying little; quiet and uncommunicative. ▪ **taciturnity** *noun*. [18c: from Latin *tacere* to be silent]

tack[1] *noun* **1** a short nail with a sharp point and a broad flat head. **2** *NAm* a drawing pin. **3** a long loose temporary stitch. **4** a sailing ship's course, esp when taking advantage of winds from different directions. **5** a direction, course of action or policy: *to try a different tack*. ▶ *verb* **1** to fasten with a tack or tacks. **2** to sew with long loose temporary stitches. **3** (*also* **tack sth on**) to attach or add it as a supplement. **4** *intr* to use the wind direction to one's advantage when sailing. **5** *naut* to change the tack of (a ship) to the opposite one. [13c as *tak* a fastening]

tack[2] *noun* a horse's riding harness, saddle and bridle, etc. [20c: shortened from **tackle**]

tackle *noun* **1** *sport* an act of trying to get the ball away from an opposing player. **2** the equipment needed for a particular sport or occupation. **3** a system of ropes and pulleys for lifting heavy objects. **4** the ropes and rigging on a ship. ▶ *verb* **1** to grasp or seize and struggle with. **2** to question (someone) (about a disputed, etc issue): *tackled him about the missing money*. **3** to try to deal with or solve (a problem). **4** *tr & intr, sport* to try to get the ball from (an opposing player). [13c as *takel* gear]

tacky[1] *adj* (**-ier, -iest**) slightly sticky. ▪ **tackiness** *noun*. [18c]

tacky[2] *adj* (**-ier, -iest**) *informal* **1** shabby; shoddy. **2** vulgar; in bad taste. ▪ **tackiness** *noun*. [19c; orig *US* meaning 'a weak or inferior quality horse']

taco *noun* a rolled or folded tortilla with a filling, usu of meat. [20c: Mexican Spanish]

tact *noun* **1** an awareness of the best or most considerate way to deal with others so as to avoid offence, upset, antagonism or resentment. **2** skill or judgement in handling difficult situations; diplomacy. ▪ **tactful** *adj*. ▪ **tactless** *adj*. [17c: from Latin *tangere* to touch]

tactic *noun* a tactical manoeuvre. [18c]

tactical *adj* **1** relating to or forming tactics. **2** skilful; well planned and well executed. **3** of a bomb or missile, etc: used to support other military operations.

tactics *singular or plural noun* **1** the art of employing and manoeuvring troops to win or gain an advantage over the enemy. **2** plans, procedures, etc used in doing or achieving something. ▪ **tactician** *noun*. [17c: from Greek *taktikos* concerning arrangement]

tactile *adj* **1** belonging or relating to, or having, a sense of touch. **2** perceptible to the sense of touch. [17c: from Latin *tangere* to touch]

tad *noun, informal* a small amount: *just a tad of milk in my tea*. [19c: perhaps shortened from **tadpole**]

tadpole *noun* the larval stage of an amphibian, often initially having the appearance of just a head and a tail. [15c: from *tadde* toad + *pol* head]

taekwondo *or* **tae kwon do** *noun* a Korean martial art. [20c: Korean *tae* kick + *kwon* fist + *do* method]

taffeta *noun* a stiff woven silk or silk-like material. [14c: from Persian *taftan* to twist]

taffrail *noun, naut* a rail round a ship's stern. [19c: from Dutch *tafereel* panel]

tag[1] *noun* **1** a label attached to something and carrying information, eg, washing instructions, price, destination, etc. **2** an electronic device such as a bracelet or anklet which transmits radio signals and is used to supervise the movements of a prisoner or offender outside prison. **3** *comput* a marker giving summarized information which applies to the text following it. **4** a metal or plastic point on the end of a shoelace or cord. **5** a trite or common quotation used esp for effect. ▶ *verb* (***tagged, tagging***) **1** to put a tag or tags on. **2** (*usu* **tag along** *or* **on**) *intr* to follow or accompany, esp when uninvited. [15c]

tag[2] *noun* a children's chasing game. Also called **tig**. ▶ *verb* (***tagged, tagging***) to catch or touch in, or as if in, the game of tag. [18c]

Tagálog /tə'gɑːlɒg/ *noun* a language spoken on the island of Luzon in the Philippines. ▶ *adj* belonging or relating to, or spoken or written in, Tagálog. [Early 19c]

tagliatelle /taljə'tɛlɪ/ *noun* pasta in the form of long narrow ribbons. [19c: Italian, from *tagliare* to cut]

tahini *noun* a thick paste made from ground sesame seeds. [1950s: Arabic, from *tahana* to grind]

Tahitian /tə'hiːʃən/ *adj* belonging or relating to Tahiti, the largest island of French Polynesia in the S Pacific Ocean, or to its inhabitants or their language. ▶ *noun* **1** a citizen or inhabitant of, or person born in, Tahiti. **2** the official language of Tahiti. [19c]

t'ai chi /taɪ tʃiː/ *noun* a Chinese system of exercise and self-defence involving extremely slow and controlled movements. [20c: Chinese *t'ai chi chu'an*, meaning 'great art of boxing']

taiga /'taɪgə/ *noun, geog* the large area of predominantly coniferous forest located south of the arctic tundra regions. Also called **boreal forest**.

tail[1] *noun* **1** the part of an animal's body that projects from the lower or rear end. **2** the feathers that project from the rear of a bird's body. **3** anything which has a similar form, function or position as a creature's tail: *shirt tail*. **4** a lower, last or rear part: *the tail of the storm*. **5** the rear part of an aircraft. **6** *astron* the trail of luminous particles following a comet. **7** (**tails**) the reverse side of a coin, that side which does not bear a portrait or head. Compare **heads** at **head** (*noun* sense 21). **8** (**tails**) a **tailcoat**. **9** (**tails**) evening dress for men, usu including a tailcoat and white bow tie. **10** *informal* someone who follows and keeps a constant watch on someone else. ▸ *verb* **1** to remove the stalks (from fruit or vegetables). **2** to follow and watch very closely. ▪ **tailless** *adj.* [Anglo-Saxon *tægel*]

IDIOMS **turn tail** to turn round and run away. **with one's tail between one's legs** completely defeated or humiliated.

PHRASAL VERBS **tail away** *or* **off** to become gradually less, smaller or weaker.

tail² *law, noun* the limitation of who may inherit property to one person and that person's heirs, or to some other particular class of heirs. ▸ *adj* limited in this way. [15c: from French *taillier* to cut]

tailback *noun* a long queue of traffic stretching back from an accident or roadworks, etc.

tailboard *noun* a hinged or removable flap at the rear of a lorry, etc.

tailcoat *noun* a man's formal black jacket with a long divided tapering tail.

tail end *noun* the very end or last part.

tailgate *noun* **1** a door which opens upwards at the back of an estate car or hatchback. **2** *N Am* a **tailboard**.

tail-light *noun* a light, usu red, on the back of a car, train or bicycle, etc.

tailor *noun* someone whose job is making suits, jackets, trousers, etc to measure, esp for men. ▸ *verb* **1** *tr & intr* to make (garments) so that they fit well. **2** to make suitable for particular or special circumstances. **3** *intr* to work as a tailor. [13c: from Latin *taliare* to cut]

tailored *adj* of clothes: well-made or fitting the wearer exactly.

tailor-made *adj* **1** of clothes: made by a tailor to fit a particular person. **2** perfectly suited or adapted for a particular purpose.

tailplane *noun* a small horizontal wing at the rear of an aircraft.

tailspin *noun* **1** a spinning movement made by an aircraft, either because it is out of the pilot's control or one done as part of a display of aeronautical skills. **2** *informal* a state of great agitation.

tail wind *noun* a wind blowing in the same direction as a ship or aircraft, etc is travelling.

taint *verb* **1** *tr & intr* to affect or be affected by pollution, putrefaction or contamination. **2** to contaminate morally. **3** to affect or spoil slightly. ▸ *noun* **1** a spot, mark or trace of decay, contamination, infection or something bad or evil. **2** a corrupt or decayed condition. ▪ **tainted** *adj.* [16c: from Latin *tingere* to dye]

take *verb* (*past tense* ***took,*** *past participle* ***taken***) **1** to reach out for and grasp, lift or pull, etc: *take a book from the shelf.* **2** to carry, conduct or lead to another place. **3** to do or perform: *take a walk • take revenge.* **4** to get, receive, occupy, obtain, rent or buy. **5** to agree to have or accept: *take advice • take office.* **6** to accept as true or valid: *take her word for it.* **7** to adopt or commit oneself to: *take a wife • take a decision.* **8** to endure or put up with: *cannot take his arrogance.* **9** to need or require: *It will take all day to finish.* **10** to use (eg a bus or train) as a means of transport. **11** to make a written note, etc of: *take the minutes of the meeting.* **12** to photograph: *take a few colour slides • Shall I take you standing by the bridge?* **13** to study or teach (a subject, etc). **14** to remove, use or borrow without permission. **15** to proceed to occupy: *take a seat.* **16** to come or derive from: *a quotation taken from Shakespeare.* **17** to have room to hold or strength to support, etc: *The shelf won't take any more books.* **18** to consider as an example. **19** to consider or think of in a particular way, sometimes mistakenly: *took her to be a teacher • Do you take me for a fool?* **20** to capture or win. **21** to charm and delight: *was very taken with the little cottage.* **22** to eat or drink: *take medicine • I don't take sugar in coffee.* **23** to conduct or lead: *This road will take you to the station.* **24** to be in charge or control of: *take the meeting.* **25** to react to or receive (news, etc) in a specified way. **26** to feel: *takes pride in her work.* **27** *intr* (**take to sb** *or* **sth**) to develop a liking for them or it. **28** to derive (help or refuge, etc): *takes refuge in his religion.* **29** *intr* (**take to sth**) to turn to it as a remedy or for refuge: *After the break-up, he took to drink.* **30** *intr* (**take to sth**) to begin to do it regularly. **31** to subtract or remove. **32** to make use of; to select (a route, etc): *took the first road on the left.* **33** to deal with or consider: *take the first two questions together.* **34** *intr* to have or produce the expected or desired effect: *The vaccination didn't take.* **35** *intr* of seeds, etc: to begin to send out roots and grow. **36** to measure: *take a temperature.* **37** *intr* to become suddenly (ill, etc). **38** to understand: *I take him to mean he isn't coming.* ▸ *noun* **1** a scene filmed or a piece of music recorded, etc in a single, uninterrupted period. **2** an amount or number (eg, of caught fish) taken at one time. **3** the amount of money taken in a shop or business, etc over a particular period of time: *the day's take.* [Anglo-Saxon *tacan*]

IDIOMS **take it out of sb** *informal* to exhaust their strength or energy. **take it out on sb** *informal* to vent one's anger or frustration on them, esp when they do not deserve it. **take it upon oneself** to assume responsibility.

PHRASAL VERBS **take after** to resemble in appearance or character. **take against** to dislike immediately. **take sb apart** to criticize or defeat them severely. **take sth apart** to separate it into pieces or components. **take sb back 1** to make them remember the past. **2** to resume relations with (a former partner, lover, etc) after an estrangement. **take sth back 1** to withdraw or retract (a statement or promise). **2** to regain possession of it. **3** to return (something bought from a shop) for an exchange or refund. **take sth down 1** to make a written note or record of it. **2** to demolish or dismantle it. **3** to lower it. **take sb in 1** to include them. **2** to give them accommodation or shelter. **3** to deceive or cheat them. **take sth in 1** to include it. **2** to understand and remember it. **3** to make (a piece of clothing) smaller. **4** to do (paid work of a specified kind) in one's home: *take in washing.* **5** to include a visit to (a place). **take off 1** of an aircraft or its passengers: to leave the ground. **2** *informal* to depart or set out. **3** *informal* of a scheme or product, etc: to become popular and successful and expand quickly. **take sb off** to imitate or mimic them, esp for comic effect. **take sth off 1** to remove: *took off his jacket.* **2** to deduct: *took two pounds off the price.* **3** to spend a period of time away from work on holiday, resting, etc: *took two days off.* **take sb on 1** to give them employment. **2** to challenge or compete with them: *We took them on at snooker.* **take sth on 1** to agree to do or undertake it. **2** to acquire (a new meaning, quality or appearance, etc). **3** of an aircraft, ship, etc: to admit (new passengers) or put (a new supply of fuel or cargo, etc) on board. **take sb out 1** to go out with them or escort them in public. **2** *slang* to kill, defeat or destroy them. **take sth out 1** to remove or extract it. **2** to obtain it on application: *take out a warrant*. **take over** to assume control, management or ownership of (a business, etc). **take sth up 1** to lift or raise it. **2** to use or occupy (space or time). **3** to become interested in (a sport, hobby, etc): *take up the violin*. **4** to shorten (a piece of clothing). **5** to resume (a story or account, etc) after a pause. **6** to assume or adopt: *take up residence*. **7** to accept (an offer). **take sb up on sth 1** to accept their offer, proposal or challenge, etc. **2** to discuss (a point or issue) first raised by them. **take up with sb** to become friendly with them; to begin to associate with them. **take sth up with sb** to discuss it with them.

takeaway *noun* **1** a cooked meal prepared and bought in a restaurant but taken away and eaten somewhere else. **2** a restaurant which provides such meals. ▸ *adj* **1** said of cooked food: prepared in a shop or restaurant for the customer to take away. **2** of a shop or restaurant: preparing such meals.

take-home pay *noun* the salary actually received after deductions for tax, etc.

take-off *noun* **1** an act or instance or the process of an aircraft leaving the ground. **2** an act of mimicking.

takeover *noun* an act of assuming control (esp of a business or company).

taker *noun* someone who takes or accepts an offer, etc.

takings *plural noun* the amount of money taken at a concert or in a shop, etc; receipts.

talc *noun* **1** *geol* a mineral form of magnesium silicate. **2 talcum**. [16c: from Persian *talk*]

talcum *noun* (*in full* **talcum powder**) a fine, often perfumed, powder made from purified talc, used on the body. ▸ *verb* to coat with a dusting of this.

tale *noun* **1** a story or narrative. **2** a false or malicious story or piece of gossip; a lie. [Anglo-Saxon *talu*]

talent *noun* **1** a special or innate skill, aptitude or ability. **2** high general or mental ability. **3** a person or people with such skill or ability. **4** *informal* attractive people thought of as potential romantic partners. **5** *hist* an ancient measure of weight and unit of currency. ▪ **talented** *adj*. [Anglo-Saxon *talente*, from Greek *talanton* sum of money]

talent scout *or* **talent spotter** *noun* someone whose job is to find and recruit talented people.

talisman *noun* a small object, such as a stone, supposed to have magic powers to protect its owner from evil, bring good luck or work magic. ▪ **talismanic** *adj*. [17c: from Greek *telesma* rite or consecrated object]

talk *verb* **1** *intr* to express ideas, etc by spoken words, or by sign language, etc. **2** to discuss: *Let's talk business*. **3** *intr* to use or be able to use speech: *could talk at an early age*. **4** to utter: *Don't talk nonsense!* **5** *intr* to gossip. **6** *intr* to give away secret information. **7** to use (a language): *can't talk Dutch*. **8** to get into a certain state by talking: *talked themselves hoarse*. **9** *intr* to have influence: *Money talks*. **10** *intr* to give a talk or lecture: *Our speaker will talk on potholing*. ▸ *noun* **1** a conversation or discussion. **2** (*often* **talks**) a formal discussion or series of negotiations. **3** an informal lecture. **4** gossip or rumour, or the subject of it: *the talk of the town*. **5** fruitless or impractical discussion or boasting: *His threats are just talk*. ▪ **talker** *noun*. [13c]

IDIOMS **now you're talking** *informal* now you are saying something I want to hear. **you can** *or* **can't talk** *informal* you are in no position to criticize or disagree.

PHRASAL VERBS **talk back** to answer rudely, impudently or boldly. **talk sb down 1** to silence them by speaking more loudly or aggressively. **2** to help (a pilot or aircraft) to land by sending instructions over the radio. **talk down to sb** to talk patronizingly or condescendingly to them. **talk sb into** *or* **out of sth** to persuade them to do or not to do it. **talk sth out 1** to resolve (a problem or difference of opinion) by discussion. **2** *Brit* to defeat (a bill or motion in parliament) by prolonging discussion of it until there is not enough time left to vote on it. **talk sth over** to discuss it thoroughly. **talk sb round** to bring them to another way of thinking by talking persuasively.

talkative *adj* fond of talking a lot; chatty.

talkie *noun, dated informal* a cinema film with sound. [20c: orig US, shortened from *talking movie*]

talking-point *noun* a subject for discussion.

talking-to *noun, informal* a ticking-off or reproof.

talk show *noun, esp N Am* a **chat show**.

tall *adj* **1** above average height. **2** having a specified height: *six feet tall*. **3** higher than others or than expected: *a tall tree*. **4** difficult to believe; extravagant: *a tall story*. **5** difficult or demanding: *a tall order*. [15c, prob from Anglo-Saxon *getæl* swift or ready]

tallboy *noun* a tall chest of drawers, consisting of an upper section standing on a larger lower one. [18c]

tallith *noun* (***talliths*** *or* ***tallithim***) a shawl worn by Jewish men, especially for prayer. Also called **prayer shawl**.[17c: Hebrew]

tallow *noun* hard animal fat melted down and used to make candles, soap, etc. [14c]

tally *noun* (***-ies***) **1** a reckoning up (of work done, debts, or the score in a game). **2** *hist* a stick in which notches were cut to show debts and accounts. **3** a distinguishing or identifying mark or label. **4** a corresponding part. **5** a mark representing a score or number. ▸ *verb* (***-ies, -ied***) **1** *intr* to agree, correspond or match: *Our results don't tally*. **2** to count or mark (a number or score, etc) on, or as if on, a tally. [15c: from Latin *talea* stick]

tally-ho *exclam* a cry to the hounds at a hunt when a fox has been sighted. [18c: perhaps from French *taïnaut*, a hunting cry]

Talmud *noun, Judaism* the body of Jewish civil and canon law. ▪ **Talmudic** *or* **Talmudical** *adj*. ▪ **Talmudist** *noun*. [16c: Hebrew, meaning 'instruction']

talon *noun* a hooked claw, esp of a bird of prey. [14c: from Latin *talus* heel or ankle]

talus[1] *noun* (***tali*** /-laɪ/) the ankle-bone. [17c: Latin, meaning 'ankle']

talus[2] *noun* a scree formed from frost-shattered rocks. [From French, originally from Latin *talutium* a slope]

tamarind *noun* the fruit of a tropical evergreen tree, the acidic pulp of which is used medicinally and as a flavouring. [16c: from Arabic *tamr-hindi* Indian date]

tamarisk *noun* an evergreen shrub or small tree with tiny scale-like leaves and small pink or white flowers. [15c: from Latin *tamariscus*]

tambour *noun* **1** a drum. **2 a** an embroidery frame for holding fabric taut while stitches are sewn; **b** embroidery done on this. [15c: French, meaning 'drum']

tambourine *noun* a musical instrument consisting of a circular frame with a skin stretched over it and small jingling metal discs along the rim, struck with the hand or shaken. [16c: from French *tambour* drum]

tame *adj* **1** of animals: living or working with people. **2** of land, etc: cultivated. **3** docile, meek and submissive. **4** dull and unexciting. ▸ *verb* **1** to make (an animal) used to living or working with people. **2** to make meek and humble. ▪ **tamer** *noun.* [Anglo-Saxon *tam*]

Tamil *noun* **1** a group of peoples living in S India and Sri Lanka. **2** an individual belonging to this group of peoples. **3** their language. ▸ *adj* belonging or relating to this group or their language. [18c]

tammy *noun* (***-ies***) a tam-o'-shanter.

tam-o'-shanter *noun, Scot* a flat round cloth or woollen cap which fits tightly round the brows. [19c: named after the hero of Robert Burns's poem]

tamp *verb* to pack or ram down hard. [19c]

tamper *verb, intr* (*usu* **tamper with**) **1** to interfere or meddle, esp in a harmful way. **2** to attempt to corrupt or influence, esp by bribery. [16c: a form of **temper**]

tampon *noun* a plug of absorbent material inserted into a cavity or wound to absorb blood and other secretions, esp one for use in the vagina during menstruation. [19c: French, from *tapon* a plug of cloth]

tan[1] *noun* **1** a **suntan**. **2** a tawny-brown colour. **3** oak bark or other material, used esp for tanning hides. ▸ *adj* tawny-brown in colour. ▸ *verb* (***tanned, tanning***) **1** *tr & intr* to make or become brown by exposure to ultraviolet light. **2** to convert (hide) into leather. **3** *informal* to beat or thrash. ▪ **tanned** *adj.* ▪ **tanning** *noun.* [Anglo-Saxon, from Latin *tannum* oak bark]

tan[2] *abbrev, maths* tangent.

tandem *noun* **1** a bicycle or tricycle for two people. **2** a carriage-drawn tandem. **3** any two people or things which follow one behind the other. ▸ *adv* one behind the other, esp on a bicycle, or with two horses harnessed one behind the other. [18c: a pun on Latin *tandem*, meaning 'at length' or 'at last']

tandoori *adj* cooked over charcoal in a clay oven: *tandoori chicken.* [20c: from Hindi *tandoor* clay oven]

tang *noun* **1** a strong or sharp taste, flavour or smell. **2** a trace or hint. **3** a projecting part of a knife, chisel, etc that fits into the handle. ▪ **tangy** *adj* (***-ier, -iest***). [15c: from Norse *tange* point]

tanga *noun* underpants which have no material at the sides other than the waistband. [20c: Portuguese, from Kimbundu (an Angolan language) *ntanga* loincloth]

tangent *noun* **1** *geom* a straight or curved line or a curved surface that touches a curve, but does not pass through it. **2** (abbrev **tan**) *trig* a **function** (*noun* sense 4) of an angle in a right-angled triangle, defined as the length of the side opposite the angle divided by the length of the side adjacent to it. [16c: from Latin *tangere* to touch]

tangential *adj* **1** belonging or relating to, or along a tangent. **2** not of central importance; peripheral. ▪ **tangentially** *adv.*

tangerine *noun* **1** a small edible citrus fruit, similar to an orange. **2** a reddish-orange colour. [19c: named after Tangier, a port on the Moroccan coast]

tangible *adj* **1** able to be felt by touch. **2** able to be grasped by the mind. **3** real or definite; material. ▪ **tangibility** *noun.* ▪ **tangibly** *adv.* [16c: from Latin *tangere* to touch]

tangle *noun* **1** an untidy and confused or knotted state or mass, eg, of hair or fibres. **2** a confused or complicated state or situation. ▸ *verb* **1 a** *intr* of hair, fibres, etc: to become untidy, knotted and confused; **b** to cause (hair, fibres, etc) to get into this state. **2** (*usu* **tangle with**) *informal* to become involved (esp in conflict, or an argument). ▪ **tangled** *adj.* [14c]

tango *noun* **1** a Latin-American dance with stylized body positions and long pauses. **2** a piece of music composed for this dance. ▸ *verb* (***tangos*** *or* ***tangoes, tangoed***) *intr* to perform this dance. [20c: American Spanish]

tank *noun* **1** a large container for holding, storing or transporting liquids or gas. **2** the amount a tank can hold. **3** a heavy steel-covered vehicle armed with guns and which moves on Caterpillar tracks. ▪ **tankful** *noun.* [17c: from Gujarati (an Indian language) *tankh* reservoir]

tankard *noun* a large beer mug, sometimes with a hinged lid. [14c]

tanker *noun* **1** a ship or large lorry which transports liquid in bulk. **2** an aircraft which transports fuel. [20c]

tannery *noun* (***-ies***) a place where hides are tanned.

tannic *adj* relating to or containing tannin. [19c]

tannin *noun* any of several substances obtained from certain tree barks, etc used in tanning leather, and which also occur in red wine and tea. Also called **tannic acid**.

Tannoy *noun, trademark* a public address system used in railway stations, etc. [20c]

tansy *noun* (***-ies***) a plant with yellow flowers and aromatic leaves. [15c: from Greek *athanasia* immortality]

tantalize *or* **-ise** *verb* to tease or torment, esp by offering but then withholding an object, etc that is much desired. ▪ **tantalizing** *adj.* [16c: from Tantalus, a mythological king who was condemned to stand in water which receded each time he stooped to drink it, overhung by grapes that drew back when he tried to reach them]

tantalum *noun, chem* (symbol **Ta**) a hard bluish-grey metallic element with a high melting point that is used esp in making dental and surgical instruments. [19c: named after Tantalus, see **tantalize**]

tantalus *noun* a case for holding decanters of alcoholic drink so that they are visible but locked up. [19c: named after Tantalus, see **tantalize**]

tantamount *adj* (*always* **tantamount to**) producing the same effect or result as; equivalent to. [17c: from Italian *tanto montare* to amount to as much]

tantrum *noun* an outburst of childish or petulant bad temper. [18c]

Taoiseach /ˈtiːʃək, -ʃəx/ *noun* the prime minister of the Republic of Ireland. [1930s: Irish Gaelic, meaning 'leader']

Taoism *noun* **1** a Chinese philosophical system based on the teachings of Laozi (c.6c BC) and others, that advocates a life of simplicity and non-interference with the natural course of events. **2** a religion supposedly based on this system of philosophy, but also including magic, alchemy and the worship of many gods. ▪ **Taoist** *noun, adj*. [19c: from Chinese *dao* way]

tap[1] *noun* **1** a quick or light touch, knock or blow, or the sound made by this. **2** tap-dancing. **3** a piece of metal attached to the sole and heel of a tap-dancing shoe. ▸ *verb* (***tapped, tapping***) **1** *tr & intr* to strike or knock lightly, and often audibly. **2** (*also* **tap out**) to produce by tapping: *tap out a message*. [13c: from French *taper*]

tap[2] *noun* **1** a device attached to a pipe, barrel, etc for controlling the flow of liquid or gas. **2 a** a concealed receiver for listening to and recording private telephone conversations; **b** an act of attaching such a receiver. **3** the withdrawal of fluid, eg, from a body cavity: *spinal tap*. **4** a screw for cutting an internal thread. ▸ *verb* (***tapped, tapping***) **1** to get liquid from (a barrel or a cavity in the body, etc) using a tap or tap-like device. **2** to let out (liquid) by opening a tap or tap-like device. **3** to get sap from (a tree) by cutting into it. **4** to attach a concealed receiver to (a telephone, etc). **5** to start using (a source, supply, etc). **6** *informal* to obtain (money, etc) from: *tapped his mum for £10*. [Anglo-Saxon *tæppa*]

IDIOMS **on tap 1** of beer: stored in casks from which it is served. **2** ready and available for immediate use.

tapas /ˈtapəs/ *plural noun* savoury snacks, orig of a Spanish style. [20c: from Spanish *tapa*, literally 'cover' or 'lid']

tap dance *noun* a dance performed wearing shoes with metal attached to the soles and toes so that the dancer's rhythmical steps can be heard clearly. ▸ *verb* (**tap-dance**) *intr* to perform a tap dance. ▪ **tap-dancer** *noun*. ▪ **tap-dancing** *noun*. [20c]

tape *noun* **1** a narrow strip of cloth used for tying, fastening, etc. **2** (*also* **magnetic tape**) a strip of thin plastic or metal used for recording sounds or images: *video tape*. **3** an audio or video recording. **4** (*also* **adhesive tape**) a strip of thin paper or plastic with a sticky surface, used for fastening or sticking, etc. **5** a string, strip of paper or ribbon stretched above the finishing line on a race track. **6** a tape measure. ▸ *verb* **1** to fasten, tie or seal with tape. **2** *tr & intr* to record (sounds or images) on magnetic tape. [Anglo-Saxon *tæppe*]

IDIOMS **have sth** *or* **sb taped** *informal* to understand it or them, or be able to deal with it or them.

tape deck *noun* a device for recording and playing audio tapes, often part of an integrated sound system.

tape measure *noun* a strip of cloth or flexible metal marked off in inches and feet, centimetres and metres, etc, used for measuring length.

taper *noun* **1** a long thin candle. **2** a waxed wick for lighting candles, fires, etc. **3** a lessening of diameter or width towards one end. ▸ *verb, tr & intr* (*also* **taper off**) **1** to make or become narrower towards one end. **2** to make or become gradually less. [Anglo-Saxon *tapor*]

tape recorder *noun* a machine for recording and playing back sounds on magnetic tape. ▪ **tape-recording** *noun*. [20c]

tapestry *noun* (**-ies**) **1** a thick woven textile with an ornamental design, often a picture, used for curtains, wall-hangings, chair coverings, etc. **2** embroidery, or an embroidery, imitating this. [15c: from French *tapisserie* carpeting]

tapeworm *noun* a parasitic segmented flatworm living in the intestines of vertebrates. [18c]

tapioca *noun* hard white grains of starch from the root of the cassava plant, used for puddings. [18c: from Tupí (a native S American language) *tipioca* juice squeezed out]

tappet *noun, mech* a lever or projection that transmits motion from one part of a machine to another. [18c: from **tap**[1]]

taproom *noun* a bar that serves alcoholic drinks, esp beer direct from casks. [18c]

taproot *noun* a long tapering main root of some plants. [17c]

tar[1] *noun* **1** a dark sticky pungent distillation of coal, wood, etc, used in road construction, etc. **2** a similar substance, esp the residue formed from burning tobacco. ▸ *verb* (***tarred, tarring***) to cover with tar. ▪ **tarry** *adj*. [Anglo-Saxon *teoru*]

IDIOMS **tar and feather** to cover with tar and then feathers as a punishment. **tarred with the same brush** possessing the same faults.

tar[2] *noun, old informal* a sailor. [17c: perhaps an abbreviation of *tarpaulin*, an old nickname for a seaman]

taramasalata /tarəməsəˈlɑːtə/ *noun* a creamy pink pâté made from smoked fish roe, olive oil and garlic. [20c: Greek, from *taramus* roe + *salata* salad]

tarantella *noun* **1** a lively country dance from S Italy. **2** a piece of music for it. [18c: Italian]

tarantula *noun* **1** a large European spider. **2** a very large tropical spider with long hairy legs. [16c: from Italian *tarantola*, from Taranto in S Italy]

tarboosh *noun* a hat similar to a fez. [18c: from Arabic *tarbush*]

tardy *adj* (**-ier, -iest**) **1** slow to move, progress or grow; sluggish. **2** slower to arrive or happen than expected. ▪ **tardiness** *noun*. [15c: from Latin *tardus* slow]

tare[1] *noun* **1 vetch**. **2** (*usu* **tares**) in the Bible: a weed which grows in cornfields. [14c]

tare[2] *noun* (abbrev **t**) **1** the weight of the wrapping-paper or container in which goods are packed. **2** an allowance made for this. **3** the weight of a vehicle without its fuel, cargo or passengers. [15c: from Arabic *tarhah* that which is thrown away]

target *noun* **1** an object aimed at in shooting practice, etc, esp a flat round board marked with concentric circles. **2** any object or area fired or aimed at. **3** someone or something that is the object of ridicule, criticism, abuse, etc. **4** something aimed for; a goal. ▸ *verb* (***targeted, targeting***) **1** to direct or aim. **2** to make (a person, place or thing) a target or the object of an attack. [14c: from French *targe* shield]

tariff *noun* **1** a list of fixed prices. **2 a** a duty to be paid on a particular class of imports or exports; **b** a list of such duties. [16c: from Arabic *tarif* explanation]

tarmac *noun* **1** *trademark* tarmacadam. **2** a surface covered with tarmac, esp an airport runway. ▸ *verb* (***tarmacked, tarmacking***) to apply tarmacadam to. [20c]

tarmacadam *or* **Tarmacadam** *noun, trademark* a mixture of small stones bound together with tar, used to make road surfaces, etc. [19c: from **tar**[1] + *macadam*, named after John McAdam, Scottish engineer]

tarn *noun* a small mountain lake. [14c: from Norse *tjörn*]

tarnish *verb* **1 a** to make (metal) dull and discoloured; **b** *intr* of metal: to become dull, esp through the action of air or dirt. **2** to spoil or damage (a reputation, etc). ▸ *noun* **1** a loss of shine, reputation, etc. **2** a discoloured or dull film. [16c: from French *ternir* to dull]

taro /'tɑːroʊ/ *noun* a tropical plant with an edible rootstock. [18c: Polynesian]

tarot /'taroʊ/ *noun* **1** a pack of 78 playing-cards, now used mainly in fortune-telling. **2** any of the 22 trump cards in this pack, which are decorated with allegorical pictures. [16c: French, from Italian *tarocco*]

tarpaulin *noun* **1** heavy canvas waterproofed with tar, etc. **2** a sheet of this material. [17c: from **tar**[1] + **pall**[1]]

tarragon *noun* a bushy plant whose leaves are used to season vinegar and as a flavouring in salads, etc. [16c: from Arabic *tarkhun*]

tarry /'tarɪ/ *verb* (*-ies, -ied*) *intr* **1** to linger or stay in a place. **2** to be slow or late in doing something, etc. [14c]

tarsal *anatomy, adj* relating to the bones of the tarsus. ▸ *noun* any of the bones of the tarsus.

tarsus *noun* (***tarsi***) **1** the bones forming the upper part of the human foot and ankle. **2** the corresponding part in other mammals, in birds, and in some insects and amphibians. [17c: Latin, from Greek *tarsos* the flat of the foot, or the eyelid]

tart[1] *adj* **1** sharp or sour in taste. **2** of a remark, etc: brief and sarcastic; cutting. [Anglo-Saxon *teart* rough]

tart[2] *noun* a pastry case, esp one without a top, with a sweet or savoury filling. [13c: from French *tarte*]

tartan *noun* **1** a distinctive checked pattern, esp one peculiar to a specified Scottish clan. **2** woollen cloth or a garment woven with such a design. [16c]

Tartar *or* **Tatar** *noun* **1 a** *hist* a group of peoples, including Mongols and Turks, which overran Asia and parts of Europe in the Middle Ages; **b** a group of peoples related to the Turks now living especially in the republic of Tatarstan, Uzbekistan, Turkmenistan and W Siberia. **2** an individual belonging to these groups or peoples. **3** their language. ▸ *adj* belonging or relating to these groups or their language. [14c: ultimately from Persian *Tatar*]

tartar[1] *noun* **1** a hard deposit that forms on the teeth. **2** a deposit that forms a hard brownish-red crust on the insides of wine casks during fermentation. [14c: from Greek *tartaron*]

tartar[2] *noun* a fierce, ill-tempered, etc person. [17c: from **Tartar**]

tartaric acid *noun, chem* an organic acid that occurs naturally in many fruits. [19c]

tartar sauce *or* **tartare sauce** *noun* mayonnaise with chopped pickles, capers, etc, often served with fish. [19c: from French *sauce tartare*]

tartrazine *noun* a yellow powder used as an artificial colouring in foods, drugs and cosmetics. [19c: from **tartar**[1]]

TAS *abbrev, Aust state* Tasmania.

task *noun* **1** a piece of work to be done. **2** an unpleasant or difficult job; a chore. ▸ *verb* to overburden; to stretch (someone's capabilities, etc). [13c: from Latin *taxa* tax]

IDIOMS **take sb to task** to scold or criticize them.

taskbar *noun, comput* an area on a computer screen displaying details of all programs currently running.

task force *noun* **1** *military* a temporary grouping of different units that undertake a specific mission. **2** any similar grouping of people for a specific purpose.

taskmaster *noun* someone who sets and supervises the work of others, esp strictly.

tassel *noun* **1** a decorative bunch of dangling threads, etc attached to a curtain, cushion, hat, etc. **2** a tassel-like flower head on some plants. [13c: French]

taste *verb* **1** *tr & intr* to perceive the flavour of (food, drink, etc) in the mouth. **2** to try or test (a food or drink) by having a small amount. **3** to be aware of or recognize the flavour of (something). **4** (**taste of sth**) to have a specified flavour: *tastes of vanilla*. **5** to eat or drink, esp in small quantities or with enjoyment: *I hadn't tasted food for days*. **6** to experience: *taste defeat*. ▸ *noun* **1 a** the particular sensation produced when food, drink, etc is in the mouth; **b** the sense by which this is detected. **2** the quality or flavour of a food, drink, etc as perceived by this sense: *dislike the taste of onions*. **3** an act of tasting or a small quantity of food or drink tasted. **4** a first, usu brief, experience of something: *a taste of what was to come*. **5** the quality or flavour of something: *the sweet taste of victory*. **6** a liking or preference: *a taste for exotic holidays*. **7** ability to judge and appreciate what is suitable, fine, elegant or beautiful: *a joke in poor taste*. [13c: from French *taster* to touch]

taste bud *noun* a sensory organ on the surface of the tongue by which tastes are perceived. [19c]

tasteful *adj* showing, or done with, good judgement or taste. ▪ **tastefully** *adv*.

tasteless *adj* **1** lacking flavour. **2** showing, or done with, a lack of good judgement or taste. ▪ **tastelessly** *adv*.

taster *noun* **1** someone whose job is to taste and judge the quality of food or drink. **2** a sample of something.

tasty *adj* (*-ier, -iest*) **1** having a good, esp savoury, flavour. **2** *informal* interesting or attractive. [17c: from **taste**]

tat *noun, Brit informal* rubbish or junk. [19c: compare **tatter**]

ta-ta *exclam, Brit informal* goodbye. [19c]

tatter *noun* (*usu* **tatters**) a torn ragged shred of cloth, paper, etc. [14c: from Norse *torturr* rag]

IDIOMS **in tatters 1** of clothes: in a torn and ragged condition. **2** of an argument, theory, relationship, etc: completely destroyed.

tattered *adj* ragged or torn.

tattie *noun, Scot* a potato. [18c]

tatting *noun* **1** delicate knotted lace made from sewing-thread and worked by hand with a small shuttle. **2** the process of making such lace. [19c]

tattle *noun* idle chatter or gossip. ▸ *verb* **1** *intr* to chat or gossip idly. **2** to utter (words) in idle chatter. ▪ **tattler** *noun*. [15c: from Dutch *tatelen*]

tattoo[1] *verb* (***tattooed***) to mark (a coloured design, etc) on (a person or a part of the body) by pricking the skin and putting in indelible dyes. ▸ *noun* a design tattooed on the skin. ▪ **tattooer** *or* **tattooist** *noun*. [18c: from Tahitian *tatau*]

tattoo[2] *noun* **1** a signal by drum or bugle calling soldiers to quarters, esp in the evening. **2** an outdoor military display. **3** a rhythmic beating or drumming. [17c: from Dutch *taptoe* shut the taps (of the barrels)]

tatty *adj* (***-ier, -iest***) *informal* shabby and untidy. [16c: prob from **tatter**]

tau /taʊ/ *noun* the nineteenth letter of the Greek alphabet.

taught *past tense, past participle of* **teach**

taunt *verb* to tease, say unpleasant things to, or jeer at in a cruel and hurtful way. ▸ *noun* a cruel, unpleasant and often hurtful or provoking remark. [16c]

taupe /toʊp/ *noun* a brownish-grey colour. [20c: French, meaning 'mole']

Taurus *noun, astrol* **a** the second sign of the zodiac; **b** a person born between 21 April and 20 May, under this sign. ▪ **Taurean** *noun, adj*. [14c: Latin, meaning 'bull']

taut *adj* **1** pulled or stretched tight. **2** showing nervous strain or anxiety. [14c as *taught*]

tauten *verb, tr & intr* to make or become taut. [19c]

tautology *noun* (***-ies***) the use of words which repeat the meaning of words already used, as in *I myself personally am a vegetarian*. ▪ **tautological** *or* **tautologous** *adj*. [16c: from Greek *tauto* same + *legein* to say]

tavern *noun* an inn or public house. [13c: from Latin *taberna* shed]

tawdry *adj* (***-ier, -iest***) cheap, gaudy and of poor quality. ▪ **tawdriness** *noun*. [16c: from *St Audrey lace* lace sold at fairs held on the feast day of St Audrey]

tawny *noun* a yellowish-brown colour. ▸ *adj* (***-ier, -iest***) yellowish-brown. [14c: from French *tané*]

tax *noun* **1** a compulsory contribution to state revenue levied on people's salaries, property, the sale of goods and services, etc. **2** a strain, burden or heavy demand. ▸ *verb* **1** to impose a tax on (a person, goods, etc) or take tax from (a salary, etc). **2** to put a strain on, or make a heavy demand on. **3** (**tax with**) *formal* to accuse (someone) of (a wrongdoing, etc). ▪ **taxable** *adj*. ▪ **taxing** *adj*. [13c: from Latin *taxare* to appraise]

taxation *noun* the levying or payment of taxes.

tax-deductible *adj* of expenses, etc: eligible for deduction from taxable income.

tax haven *noun* a country or state with a relatively low rate of taxation making it an attractive place for wealthy people to live.

taxi *noun* (***taxis*** *or* ***taxies***) a car which may be hired along with its driver to carry passengers on usu short town journeys. ▸ *verb* (***taxis*** *or* ***taxies, taxiing*** *or* ***taxying***) **a** *intr* of an aircraft: to move slowly along the ground before take-off or after landing; **b** to make (an aircraft) move in this way. [20c: a shortening of *taximeter cab*]

taxidermy *noun* the art of preparing, stuffing and mounting the skins of dead animals, birds, etc so that they present a lifelike appearance. ▪ **taxidermist** *noun*. [19c: from Greek *taxis* arrangement + *derma* skin]

taxis *noun* (***taxes***) *biol* the movement of a single cell in response to an external stimulus from a specific direction. [18c: Greek, meaning 'arrangement']

taxonomy *noun* (***-ies***) **1** the science of classification, eg, of animals, plants, fossils, languages, etc. **2** a particular scheme of classification. ▪ **taxonomic** *adj*. [19c: from Greek *taxis* arrangement]

taxpayer *noun* someone who pays or is liable for tax.

tax return *noun* a yearly statement of income, from which the amount due in tax is calculated.

tax year *noun* a **financial year**.

TB *abbrev* tuberculosis.

Tb *symbol, chem* terbium.

T-bone steak *noun* a large beef steak with a T-shaped bone.

tbsp *abbrev* tablespoon, or tablespoonful.

Tc *symbol, chem* technetium.

TCP *abbrev*, **1** *comput* Transmission Control Protocol. See **TCP/IP**. **2** *trademark* trichlorophenylmethyliodosalicyl, an antiseptic and disinfectant.

TCP/IP *abbrev, comput* Transmission Control Protocol/Internet Protocol, rules controlling how data is sent on the Internet.

Te *symbol, chem* tellurium.

te *or* **ti** /tiː/ *noun, music* in sol-fa notation: the seventh note of the major scale. [19c: earlier *si*, from Italian]

tea *noun* **1 a** (*in full* **tea plant**) a small evergreen tree or shrub cultivated for its leaves; **b** its dried leaves; **c** a drink made by infusing these with boiling water. **2** a similar drink made from the leaves or flowers of other plants: *peppermint tea*. **3** (*also* **afternoon tea**) a light afternoon meal with tea, sandwiches, cakes, etc. **4** *Brit* **a** a cooked meal served early in the evening; **b** a main evening meal. See also **high tea**. [17c: from Min Chinese *te*]

tea bag *noun* a small bag or sachet of tea, which is infused in boiling water.

teacake *noun, Brit* a currant bun, usu eaten toasted.

teach *verb* (***taught***) **1** to give knowledge to (an individual, class, etc). **2** *tr & intr* to give lessons in (a subject), esp as a professional. **3** to make (someone) learn or understand, esp by example, experience or punishment. **4** to force home the desirability or otherwise of a particular action or behaviour, etc: *That'll teach you to be more polite*. ▪ **teachable** *adj*. [Anglo-Saxon *tæcan*]

IDIOMS **teach sb a lesson** to demonstrate and reinforce their mistake.

teacher *noun* someone whose job is to teach, esp in a school.

tea chest *noun* a light wooden box in which tea is packed for export.

teaching *noun* **1** the work or profession of a teacher. **2** (*often* **teachings**) something that is taught, esp guidance or doctrine.

tea cosy *noun* (***-ies***) a cover to keep a teapot warm.

teacup *noun* a medium-sized cup for drinking tea.

tea dance *noun* a dance, usu held in the afternoon, at which tea is served. [20c]

teak *noun* **1** a large deciduous tropical tree. **2** the heavy yellowish-brown durable wood of this tree, used in furniture-making, etc. [17c: from Malayalam *tekka*]

teal *noun* (***teals*** *or* ***teal***) **1** a small freshwater duck. **2** a dark greenish-blue colour. [14c]

tea leaf *noun* a leaf or part of a leaf of the tea plant.

team *noun* **1** a group of people who form one side in a game. **2** a group of people working together. **3** two or more animals working together, esp in harness. ▸ *verb* **1** *tr & intr* (*usu* **team up with**) to form a team for some common action. **2** to harness (horses or oxen, etc) together. **3** (*also* **team up**) to match (clothes, etc). [Anglo-Saxon, meaning 'child-bearing' or 'offspring']

---

team

You can use either a singular or plural verb with a collective noun such as **team**. Therefore, if you want to emphasize the team as a single unit, you can use a singular verb:

A team was sent to help with the rescue effort.

If you want to emphasize the team as a number of individuals, you can use a plural verb:

The Greycoats team were brilliant at everything.

---

teamster *noun* **1** a driver of a team of animals. **2** *N Am, esp US* a lorry-driver. [18c]

teamwork *noun* co-operation between those who are working together on a task.

teapot *noun* a pot with a spout and handle used for making and pouring tea.

tear[1] /tɪə(r)/ *noun* **1** a drop of clear saline liquid, secreted by a gland, moistening and cleaning the eyeball, or flowing in response to irritation, emotion, etc. **2** any pear-shaped drop or blob. [Anglo-Saxon]
IDIOMS **in tears** crying; weeping.

tear[2] /tɛə(r)/ *verb* (*past tense* ***tore***, *past participle* ***torn***) **1** to pull or rip apart by force; to pull violently or with tearing movements. **2** to make (a hole, etc) by pulling or ripping. **3** *intr* to come apart; to be pulled or ripped apart: *material that tears easily.* **4** to disrupt or divide: *a family torn by feuding.* **5** *intr* to rush; to move with speed or force. ▸ *noun* **1** a hole or other damage caused by tearing. **2** an act of tearing. **3** damage: *wear and tear.* [Anglo-Saxon *teran*]
IDIOMS **tear one's hair out** to be in despair with impatience and frustration.
PHRASAL VERBS **tear sb apart** to cause them severe suffering or distress. **tear sb away** to remove or take them by force; to force or persuade them to leave. **tear sth down** to pull it down or demolish it using force. **tear into sb** to attack them physically or verbally. **tear sth up** to tear it into pieces, esp to destroy it.

tearaway /ˈtɛərəweɪ/ *noun, Brit informal* an undisciplined and reckless young person.

teardrop *noun* **1** a single tear. **2** anything with a similar shape.

tearful *adj* **1** inclined to cry or weep. **2** with much crying or weeping; covered with tears. **3** causing tears to be shed; sad. ▪ **tearfully** *adv.* [16c]

tear gas *noun* a gas which causes stinging blinding tears, and temporary loss of sight, used in the control of riots and in warfare, etc.

tearing *adj* furious; overwhelming: *a tearing hurry.*

tear-jerker *noun, informal* a sentimental play, film or book, etc intended to make people cry. [20c]

tearoom and **teashop** *noun* a restaurant where tea, coffee and cakes, etc are served.

tease *verb* **1** to annoy or irritate deliberately or unkindly. **2** to laugh at or make fun of playfully. **3** to comb (wool, flax or hair, etc) to remove tangles and open out the fibres. **4** to raise a nap on (cloth), esp with teasels. ▸ *noun* someone or something that teases. [Anglo-Saxon *tæsan* to card]
PHRASAL VERBS **tease sth out** to clarify (an obscure point) by discussion, etc.

teasel, **teazel** *or* **teazle** *noun* **1** a plant with flower heads surrounded by curved prickly bracts. **2** one of its dried flower heads, or a similar artificial substitute, used for raising the nap on cloth. ▸ *verb* to produce a nap on (cloth). [Anglo-Saxon *tæsel*]

teaser *noun* **1** a puzzle or tricky problem. **2** a person who enjoys teasing.

teaspoon *noun* **1** a small spoon for use with a teacup. **2** the amount a teaspoon can hold. ▪ **teaspoonful** *noun.*

teat *noun* **1** a nipple, esp of an animal. **2** a piece of rubber, etc shaped like a nipple, esp one attached to a baby's feeding bottle and through which milk is sucked. [13c: from French *tete*]

tea towel *noun* a towel for drying washed dishes, etc.

tech *noun, informal* **1** a technical college. **2** technology. [20c]

tech. *abbrev* **1** technical. **2** technology.

technetium /tɛkˈniːʃɪəm/ *noun, chem* (symbol **Tc**) an artificially produced radioactive metallic element. [20c: Latin, from Greek *technetos* artificial]

technical *adj* **1** relating to a practical skill or applied science, esp those sciences useful to industry. **2** relating to a particular subject or requiring knowledge of a particular subject to be understood. **3** according to a strict interpretation of the law or rules. **4** belonging or relating to, or showing a quality of, technique. ▪ **technically** *adv.* [17c]

technical college *noun* a college of further education that teaches practical skills and applied sciences. [19c]

technical drawing *noun* drawing of plans, machinery, electrical circuits, etc done with compasses and rulers.

technicality *noun* (***-ies***) **1** a technical detail or term. **2** a usu trivial detail arising from a strict interpretation of a law or rules. **3** the state of being technical.

technician *noun* **1** someone specialized or skilled in a practical art or science. **2** someone employed to do practical work in a laboratory.

Technicolor *noun, trademark* a process of producing colour cinema film by placing several copies of a scene, each one produced using different colour filters, on top of each other. [20c]

technique *noun* **1** proficiency or skill in the practical or formal aspects of something, eg painting, music, etc. **2** mechanical or practical skill or method: *the techniques of film-making.* **3** a way of achieving a purpose skilfully; a knack. [19c: from Greek *techne* art or skill]

techno *noun* a style of dance music that makes use of electronic effects over a frenzied rhythm, and produces fast, but often unmelodic, sounds.

technocracy *noun* (***-ies***) the government of a country or management of an industry by technical experts. ▪ **technocrat** *noun.* ▪ **technocratic** *adj.* [20c]

technology *noun* (**-ies**) **1** the practical use of scientific knowledge in industry and everyday life. **2** practical sciences as a group. **3** the technical skills and achievements of a particular time in history, of a civilization or a group of people. ▪ **technological** *adj.* ▪ **technologist** *noun.* [17c: from Greek *techne* art or skill]

technophobe *noun* someone who dislikes or fears, and usu tries to avoid using, technology. ▪ **technophobia** *noun.* ▪ **technophobic** *adj.* [20c]

tectonics *singular noun, geol* the study of the Earth's crust and the forces which change it. See also **plate tectonics**. [19c: from Greek *tekton* builder]

teddy[1] *noun* (**-ies**) (*in full* **teddy bear**) a stuffed toy bear. [20c: from 'Teddy', the pet-name of Theodore Roosevelt, who was well known as a bear hunter]

teddy[2] *noun* (**-ies**) a woman's one-piece undergarment consisting of a chemise and panties. [20c: possibly from **teddy**[1]]

tedious *adj* tiresomely long; monotonous. [15c: from Latin *taedium* weariness]

tedium *noun* tediousness; boredom. [17c: from Latin *taedium* weariness]

tee[1] *noun* a phonetic spelling for the letter *T.*

tee[2] *noun, golf* **1** a small area of level ground at the start of each hole where the initial shot towards a green is taken. **2** a small peg, etc used to support a ball when this shot is taken. ▸ *verb* (**teed**) **1** (*often* **tee up**) to place a golf ball on a tee ready to be played. **2** (**tee off**) to play a first shot at the start of a golf hole. [17c]

tee-hee *or* **te-hee** *exclam* expressing amusement or mirth. ▸ *noun* a laugh or giggle. ▸ *verb* (**tee-heed**) *intr* to laugh, esp in a derisive way. [14c: imitating the sound]

teem[1] *verb, intr* **1** (*usu* **teem with**) to be full of or abound in: *a resort teeming with tourists.* **2** to be present in large numbers; to be plentiful: *Fish teem in this river.* [Anglo-Saxon *teman* to give birth]

teem[2] *verb, intr* (*usu* **teem down**) of water, esp rain: to pour in torrents. [15c: from Norse *toema* to empty]

teen *noun* **1** (**teens**) the years of a person's life between the ages of 13 and 19. **2** (**teens**) the numbers from 13 to 19. **3** *informal* a teenager. ▸ *adj* for or relating to teenagers. [Anglo-Saxon *tien* ten]

-teen *suffix* used to form the numbers between 13 and 19. [Anglo-Saxon]

teenage *adj* **1** (*also* **teenaged**) between the ages of 13 and 19. **2** relating to or suitable for someone of this age. ▪ **teenager** *noun.* [20c]

teeny *adj* (**-ier, -iest**) *informal* tiny. [19c: from **tiny**]

teenybopper *noun, informal* a young teenage girl who enthusiastically follows the latest trends. [20c]

teeny-weeny *adj, informal* very tiny. [19c]

teepee see **tepee**

tee shirt see **T-shirt**

teeter *verb, intr* **1** to stand or move unsteadily; to wobble. **2** to hesitate or waver. [19c as *titeren*]

teeth *pl of* **tooth**

teethe *verb, intr* to develop or cut teeth, esp milk teeth. ▪ **teething** *noun.* [14c]

teething troubles *plural noun* initial problems with something, usu regarded as temporary and able to be overcome.

teetotal *adj* abstaining completely from alcoholic drink. ▪ **teetotaller** *noun.* [19c: prob connected with 'total abstinence (from alcohol)']

TEFL /'tɛfəl/ *abbrev* Teaching English as a Foreign Language.

Teflon *noun, trademark* for polytetrafluoroethylene, a tough thermoplastic used to coat cooking utensils. [20c]

te-hee see **tee-hee**

tel *abbrev* telephone, or telephone number.

tele- *combining form, denoting* **1** at, over, or to, a distance: *telegram.* **2** television: *teletext.* **3** telephone: *telesales.* [Greek, meaning 'far']

telebanking *noun* a system which enables banking transactions to be carried out by means of a telecommunications network. [20c]

telecast *verb, tr & intr* to broadcast by TV. ▸ *noun* a TV broadcast. ▪ **telecaster** *noun.* [20c]

telecommunication *noun* **1** communication over a distance using cable, telephone, broadcasting, telegraph, fax, e-mail, etc. **2** (**telecommunications**) the branch of technology dealing with these ways of communicating. [20c]

teleconference *noun* a conference between people in two or more locations using video, audio and/or computer links. ▪ **teleconferencing** *noun.* [20c]

telegram *noun, formerly* a message sent by telegraph and delivered in printed form. [19c: **tele-** (sense 1) + Greek *gramma* letter]

telegraph *noun* a system of, or instrument for, sending messages or information over a distance, esp by sending electrical impulses along a wire. ▸ *verb* **1** *tr & intr* to send (a message) (to someone) by telegraph. **2** to give a warning of. **3** *intr* to signal. ▪ **telegrapher** /tə'lɛgrəfə(r)/ *or* **telegraphist** /tə'lɛgrəfɪst/ *noun.* ▪ **telegraphic** *adj.* [18c: from French *télé* **tele-** (sense 1) + *graphe* **-graph**]

telegraphy *noun* the science or practice of sending messages by telegraph. [18c]

telekinesis *noun* **1** the moving of objects at a distance without using physical contact, eg, by will-power. **2** the apparent ability to do this. ▪ **telekinetic** *adj.* [19c]

telemarketing *noun* the marketing of goods and services by telephoning prospective clients. [20c]

telemeter /tə'lɛmɪtə(r)/ *noun* an instrument for taking recorded measurements, readings, etc obtained in one place and sending them to a remote location, usu by electrical or radio signals. ▸ *verb* to record and transmit (data) in this way. ▪ **telemetric** /-'mɛtrɪk/ *adj.* ▪ **telemetry** *noun.* [19c]

teleology *noun* the doctrine that the universe and all phenomena and natural processes are directed towards a goal or are designed according to some purpose. ▪ **teleological** *adj.* ▪ **teleologist** *noun.* [18c: from Greek *telos* end]

telepathy /tə'lɛpəθɪ/ *noun* the apparent communication of thoughts directly from one person's mind to another's without using any of the five known senses. ▪ **telepathic** /tɛlɪ'paθɪk/ *adj.* ▪ **telepathically** *adv.* [19c]

telephone *noun* **1** an instrument for transmitting speech in the form of electrical signals or radio waves. **2** the system of communication that uses such instruments. ▸ *verb* **1** to seek or establish contact and speak to (someone) by telephone. **2** to send (a message, etc) by telephone. **3** *intr* to make a telephone call. Often shortened to **phone**. ▪ **telephonic** *adj*. [19c]

IDIOMS **on the telephone 1** connected to the telephone system. **2** talking to someone by telephone.

telephone box, **telephone booth** *or* **telephone kiosk** *noun* a small enclosed or partly-enclosed compartment with a telephone for public use.

telephone directory *or* **telephone book** *noun* a book with the names, addresses and telephone numbers of telephone subscribers in a particular area. Also called **phone book**.

telephone exchange see **exchange**

telephone number *noun* **1** a combination of digits which identifies a particular telephone and can be dialled to make a connection with it. **2** (*usu* **telephone numbers**) *informal* of a salary, sales figures, etc: a number with several digits that represents very large amount, esp of money.

telephonist /tə'lɛfənɪst/ *noun* a telephone switchboard operator.

telephony /tə'lɛfənɪ/ *noun* the use telephones. [19c]

telephoto lens *noun* a camera lens which produces magnified images of distant or small objects.

teleprinter *noun* an apparatus with a keyboard which types messages as they are received by telegraph and transmits them as they are typed. [20c]

Teleprompter *noun, trademark* a device which allows a speaker to read a script while apparently looking into a TV camera. [20c]

telesales *singular and plural noun* the selling of goods or services by telephone. [20c]

telescope *noun* **1** an optical instrument with a powerful magnifying lens or mirror that makes distant objects appear larger. **2** a **radio telescope**. ▸ *verb* **1** *intr* to be in the form of several cylinders which slide out of or into each other for opening and closing. **2** *tr & intr* to collapse part within part. **3** *tr & intr* to crush or compress, or become crushed or compressed, under impact. ▪ **telescopic** *adj*. [17c: see **tele-** (sense 1) + Greek *skopeein* to view]

teleshopping *noun* the purchase of goods, using a telephone or computer link. [20c]

teletext *noun* a non-interactive news and information service that is produced and regularly updated by a TV company, and able to be viewed on a TV set with a suitable receiver and decoder. [20c]

telethon *noun* a TV programme, usu a day-long one, broadcast to raise money for charity. [20c: from **tele-** (sense 2) and modelled on **marathon**]

televise *verb* to broadcast by television.

television *noun* (abbrev **TV**) **1** an electronic system that converts moving images and sound into electrical signals, which are then transmitted to a distant receiver that converts these signals back to images and sound: *digital TV.* **2** (*also* **television set**) a device with a picture tube and loudspeakers that is used to receive picture and sound signals transmitted in this way. **3** television broadcasting in general: *works in television*. ▪ **televisual** *adj*. [20c: **tele-** (sense 1) + **vision**]

teleworking *noun* working at a distance using an electronic communication link with an office. ▪ **teleworker** *noun*. [20c]

telex *or* **Telex** *noun* **1** an international telecommunications network that uses teleprinters and radio and satellite links to enable subscribers to the network to send messages to and receive messages from each other, often linking several receivers simultaneously. **2** a teleprinter used in such a network. **3** a message received or sent by such a network. ▸ *verb, tr & intr* to send (messages) or communicate by telex. [20c: from *tele*printer + exchange]

tell *verb* (***told***) **1** *tr & intr* to relate (something) in speech or writing (to someone): *told him what happened.* **2** to command or instruct: *told her not to go* • *told me how to fix it.* **3** to express in words: *tell lies.* **4** *tr & intr* to discover or distinguish: *You can tell it by its smell.* **5** (*usu* **tell on**) *informal* to inform against: *I'll tell the teacher on you.* **6** to make known or give away: *promised not to tell.* **7** (*also* **tell on**) *intr* of an ordeal, etc: to have a noticeable effect: *The strain had begun to tell.* **8** *tr & intr* to know or recognize definitely: *I can never tell when he's lying.* **9** to assure: *I'm telling you, that's exactly what he said.* **10** (*usu* **tell against**) *intr* of evidence, circumstances, etc: to have an influence, effect, etc. **11** to count (votes, banknotes, etc). [Anglo-Saxon *tellan*]

IDIOMS **you're telling me!** *informal* an exclamation of agreement.

PHRASAL VERBS **tell sb** *or* **sth apart** to distinguish between them: *can't tell the twins apart*. **tell sb off** to scold or reprimand them.

teller *noun* **1** someone who tells, esp stories. **2** a bank employee who receives money from and pays it out to members of the public. **3** someone who counts votes.

telling *adj* producing a great or marked effect. [19c]

telling-off *noun* a mild scolding.

telltale *noun* someone who spreads gossip, esp about the private affairs or misdeeds of others. ▸ *adj* revealing or indicating: *telltale signs*. [16c]

tellurium *noun, chem* (symbol **Te**) a brittle silvery-white element obtained from gold, silver and copper ores. [19c: Latin, from *tellus* earth]

telly *noun* (**-*ies***) *informal* **1** television. **2** a television set. [20c]

telophase *noun, biol* the final stage of cell division, resulting in the production of two daughter nuclei. [19c: from Greek *telos* end]

temerity *noun* **1** rashness or impetuosity. **2** boldness or impudence. [15c: from Latin *temeritas*]

temp *noun* a temporary employee, esp in an office. ▸ *verb, intr* to work as a temp. [20c: short for **temporary**]

temper *noun* **1** a characteristic state of mind; mood or humour: *have an even temper.* **2** a state of calm; composure; self-control: *lose one's temper.* **3** a state of uncontrolled anger: *in a temper.* **4** a tendency to have fits of uncontrolled anger: *She has quite a temper.* **5** the degree of hardness and toughness of metal or glass. ▸ *verb* **1** to soften or make less severe: *temper firmness with understanding.* **2** to bring (metal, clay, etc) to the desired consistency. [Anglo-Saxon *temprian*: from Latin *temperare* to mix in due proportion]

tempera *noun* **1** a method of painting using an emulsion, eg, powdered pigment mixed with egg yolks and water. **2** this emulsion or a painting produced using it. [19c: from Italian *pingere a tempera* to paint in distemper]

temperament *noun* **1** someone's natural character or disposition. **2** a creative or emotional personality. [15c: from Latin *temperamentum* a mixing]

temperamental *adj* **1** given to or showing extreme mood changes. **2** of a machine, etc: not working reliably or consistently. **3** relating to, or caused by, temperament. ▪ **temperamentally** *adv.*

temperance *noun* **1** moderation or self-restraint, esp in controlling one's appetite or desires. **2** moderation in drinking, or complete abstinence from, alcohol. [14c: from Latin *temperantia* moderation or sobriety]

temperate *adj* **1** moderate and self-restrained, esp in appetite, consumption of alcoholic drink, and behaviour. **2** not excessive; moderate. **3** of a climate or region: characterized by mild temperatures. **4** located between the tropics and the polar circles. [14c: from Latin *temperatus*]

temperature *noun* **1** the degree of hotness or coldness of an object, body, medium, eg, air or water, etc as measured by a thermometer. **2** *informal* a body temperature above normal: *He was running a temperature.* [16c: from Latin *temperatura* proportion]

temperature
This word is often misspelt. It might help you to remember the following sentence:
You might lose your ***temper*** *at high* ***temper****atures.*

tempest *noun* a violent storm with very strong winds. [13c: from Latin *tempestas* 'season' or 'storm']

tempestuous *adj* **1** relating to or like a tempest; very stormy. **2** of a person or behaviour, etc: violently emotional; passionate: *a tempestuous love affair.* [15c]

tempi *pl of* **tempo**

template *noun* **1** a piece of metal, plastic or wood cut in a particular shape and used as a pattern when cutting out material, drawing, etc. **2** any model from which others are produced, eg a document. **3** *biol* the coded instructions carried by a molecule for the formation of a new molecule of the same type. [17c: from Latin *templum* small piece of timber]

temple[1] *noun* a building in which people, usu non-Christians, worship or which is believed to be the dwelling place of a god or gods. [Anglo-Saxon *templ*: from Latin *templum*]

temple[2] *noun* the flat part at either side of the head in front of the ears. [14c: French, from Latin *tempus*]

tempo /ˈtɛmpoʊ/ *noun* (***tempos*** *or* ***tempi*** /-piː/) **1** the speed at which a piece of music should be or is played. **2** rate or speed. [18c: Italian, from Latin *tempus* time]

temporal *adj* **1** relating to time. **2** relating to worldly or secular life rather than to religious or spiritual life. **3** *grammar* relating to tense or the expression of time. ▪ **temporally** *adv.* [14c: from Latin *tempus* time]

temporary *adj* lasting, acting or used etc for a limited period of time only. ▪ **temporarily** *adv.* ▪ **temporariness** *noun.* [16c: from Latin *temporarius*]

temporize *or* **-ise** *verb, intr* **1** to avoid taking a decision, etc to gain time and perhaps win a compromise. **2** to adapt to circumstances or to what an occasion requires. [16c: from Latin *tempus* time]

tempt *verb* **1** to seek to persuade (someone) to do something wrong, foolish, etc. **2** to attract or allure. **3** to risk provoking, esp by doing something foolhardy: *tempt fate.* ▪ **tempter** *noun.* ▪ **temptress** *noun.* [13c: from Latin *temptare* to probe or test]

temptation *noun* **1** an act of tempting or the state of being tempted. **2** something that tempts.

tempting *adj* attractive; inviting; enticing. ▪ **temptingly** *adv.*

ten *noun* **1 a** the cardinal number 10; **b** the quantity that this represents, being one more than nine. **2** any symbol for this, eg *10* or *X*. **3** the age of ten. **4** something, esp a garment or a person, whose size is denoted by the number 10. **5** the tenth hour after midnight or midday: *Come at ten • 10 o'clock • 10pm.* **6** a set or group of ten people or things. ▸ *adj* **1** totalling ten. **2** aged ten. [Anglo-Saxon]

tenable *adj* **1** able to be believed, upheld or maintained. **2** of a post or office: only to be held or occupied for a specified period or by a specified person. ▪ **tenability** *noun.* [16c: from Latin *tenere* to hold]

tenacious *adj* **1** holding or sticking firmly. **2** determined. **3** of memory: retaining information extremely well. ▪ **tenacity** *noun.* [17c: from Latin *tenere* to hold]

tenancy *noun* (***-ies***) **1** the status of being a tenant or the property rented by a tenant. **2** the period during which property or land is held by a tenant.

tenant *noun* **1** someone who rents property or land. **2** an occupant. [14c: French, from Latin *tenere* to hold]

tench *noun* (***tench*** *or* ***tenches***) a European freshwater fish of the carp family. [14c: from French *tenche*, from Latin *tinca*]

Ten Commandments *plural noun* ten rules for living by given to Moses by God, as described in the Old Testament Book of Exodus.

tend[1] *verb* **1** to take care of or look after. **2** to wait on, serve at, manage, etc: *tend bar.* **3** (**tend to**) to attend to. [14c: variant of **attend**]

tend[2] *verb, intr* **1** (*usu* **tend to**) to be inclined to: *He tends to be late.* **2** to move slightly, lean or slope (in a specified direction). [14c: from Latin *tendere* to stretch]

tendency *noun* (***-ies***) **1** a likelihood of acting or thinking, or an inclination to act or think, in a particular way. **2** a general course, trend or drift. **3** a faction or group within a political party, etc. [17c]

tendentious *adj* characterized by a particular bias, tendency or underlying purpose.

tender[1] *adj* **1** soft and delicate; fragile. **2** of meat: easily chewed or cut. **3** easily damaged or grieved; sensitive: *a tender heart.* **4** easily hurt when touched, esp because of having been hurt before. **5** loving and gentle: *tender words.* **6** youthful and vulnerable: *of tender years.* ▪ **tenderly** *adv.* [13c: from French *tendre*]

tender[2] *verb* **1** to offer or present (an apology, resignation, etc). **2** (*usu* **tender for**) to make a formal offer (to do work or supply goods) at a stated amount of money, etc. ▸ *noun* a formal offer, usu in writing, to do work or supply goods for a stated amount of money and within a stated period of time. [16c: from Latin *tendere* to stretch]

tender[3] *noun* **1** a person who looks after something or someone: *bartender.* **2** a small boat which carries stores or passengers to and from a larger boat. **3** a wagon carrying fuel and water and attached to a steam locomotive.

tenderfoot *noun* (***tenderfeet*** *or* ***tenderfoots***) an inexperienced newcomer or beginner. [19c]

tenderize *or* **-ise** *verb* to make tender, esp to make (meat) tender by pounding, marinading, etc. [20c]

tendinitis *or* **tendonitis** *noun, med* inflammation of a tendon. [20c]

tendon *noun* a cord of strong fibrous tissue that joins a muscle to a bone or some other structure. [16c: from Latin *tenere* to hold]

tendril *noun* a long shoot-like extension that some climbing plants use for attaching themselves to objects for support. ▪ **tendrilled** *adj.* [16c]

tenement *noun* **1** a large building divided into several self-contained flats or apartments. **2** a self-contained flat or room within such a building. [14c: from Latin *tenere* to hold]

tenet *noun* a belief, opinion or doctrine. [17c: Latin, meaning 'he or she holds']

tenfold *adj* **1** equal to ten times as much or many. **2** divided into, or consisting of, ten parts. ▸ *adv* by ten times as much.

tenner *noun, informal* **1** a £10 note. **2** *US* a $10 bill. [19c]

tennis *noun* **1** (*also* **lawn tennis**) a game in which two players or two pairs of players use rackets to hit a ball across a net on a rectangular grass, clay or cement court. **2** **real tennis**. [14c: from French *tenetz* hold!]

tennis elbow *noun* painful inflammation of the elbow caused by playing tennis, or overwork. [19c]

tenon *noun* a projection at the end of a piece of wood, etc, formed to fit into a socket in another piece of wood, etc. [15c: French, from *tenir* to hold]

tenor *noun* **1** **a** a singing voice of the highest normal range for an adult man; **b** a singer who has this voice. **2** an instrument, eg, a viola, recorder or saxophone, with a similar range. **3** music written for a voice or instrument with such a range. **4** the general course or meaning of something written or spoken. [13c: from Latin *tenere* to hold]

tenpin bowling *noun* a game in which ten skittles are set up at the end of an alley and a ball is rolled at them with the aim of knocking as many down as possible.

tense[1] *noun, grammar* a form or set of forms of a verb showing the time of its action in relation to the time of speaking and whether that action is completed or not. [13c: from Latin *tempus* time]

tense[2] *adj* **1** suffering, etc emotional, nervous or mental strain. **2** tightly stretched; taut. ▸ *verb, tr & intr* (*also* **tense up**) to make or become tense. ▪ **tensely** *adv.* ▪ **tenseness** *noun.* [17c: from Latin *tendere* to stretch]

tensile *adj* **1** able to be stretched. **2** relating to or involving stretching or tension. ▪ **tensility** *noun.* [17c: from Latin *tensilis*]

tensile strength *noun, physics* a measure of the ability of a material to resist tension, equal to the minimum stress needed to break it.

tension *noun* **1** an act of stretching, the state of being stretched or the degree to which something is stretched. **2** mental or emotional strain. **3** strained relations or underlying hostility between people, countries, etc. **4** *physics* a force which causes a body to be stretched or elongated. **5** *physics* **electromotive force**. ▸ *verb* to subject to tension. [16c: from Latin *tendere* to stretch]

tent *noun* **1** a movable canvas, etc shelter supported by poles or a frame and fastened to the ground with ropes and pegs. **2** something resembling a tent in form or function: *an oxygen tent*. [13c: from Latin *tendere* to stretch]

tentacle *noun* a long thin flexible appendage growing near the mouth of many invertebrates, eg, the sea anemone, octopus, etc, used for feeling, grasping, moving, etc. ▪ **tentacled** *adj.* [17c: from Latin *tentaculum*]

tentative *adj* **1** not finalized or completed; provisional. **2** uncertain; hesitant; cautious. ▪ **tentatively** *adv.* ▪ **tentativeness** *noun.* [16c: from Latin *tentare* to try]

tenterhook *noun* one of a series of hooks on a frame used for drying cloth. [15c]

IDIOMS **on tenterhooks** in a state of impatient suspense or anxiety.

tenth (often written **10th**) *adj* **1** in counting: **a** next after ninth; **b** last of ten. **2** in tenth position. **3** being one of ten equal parts: *a tenth share*. ▸ *noun* **1** one of ten equal parts. **2** a **fraction** equal to one divided by ten (usu written ⅒). **3** a person coming tenth, eg, in a race, exam, etc: *He finished a respectable tenth*. **4** (**the tenth**) **a** the tenth day of the month; **b** *golf* the tenth hole. **5** *music* **a** an interval of an octave and a third; **b** a note at that interval from another. ▸ *adv* tenthly. ▪ **tenthly** *adv* used to introduce the tenth point in a list. [Anglo-Saxon]

tenuous *adj* **1** slight; with little strength or substance. **2** thin; slim. [16c: from Latin *tenuis* thin]

tenure *noun* **1** the holding of an office, position or property. **2** the length of time an office, position or property is held. **3** the holding of a position, esp a university teaching job, for a guaranteed length of time or permanently. **4** the conditions by which an office, position or property is held. [15c: from Latin *tenere* to hold]

tepee *or* **teepee** /ˈtiːpiː/ *noun* a conical tent formed by skins stretched over a frame of poles, used by some Native Americans. [19c: from Dakota *tipi* dwelling]

tepid *adj* **1** slightly or only just warm. **2** unenthusiastic. ▪ **tepidity** *noun.* [14c: from Latin *tepere* to be warm]

tequila /təˈkiːlə/ *noun* a Mexican alcoholic spirit obtained from the agave plant. [19c: named after Tequila, a district in Mexico where it is produced]

tera- *prefix, denoting* in the SI system: 10^{12}: *terawatt*. [From Greek *teras* monster]

terabyte *noun, comput* a unit of storage capacity equal to 2^{40} or 1,099,511,627,776 bytes.

teratoid *adj, biol* resembling a monster. [19c: from Greek]

terbium *noun, chem* (symbol **Tb**) a silvery metallic element of the **lanthanide** series, used in semiconductor devices and phosphors. [19c: Latin, from *Ytterby* in Sweden, where it was discovered]

terce *or* **tierce** *noun* the third of the **canonical hours**. [14c: from Latin *tertia pars* third part]

tercentenary *or* **tercentennial** *noun* a three-hundredth anniversary or the celebration of this. ▸ *adj* relating to a period of three hundred years. [19c]

teredo /tɛ'riːdoʊ/ *noun* (***teredos*** *or* ***teredines*** /tɛ'riːdɪniːz/) a bivalve mollusc which bores into wooden ships, etc. [14c: from Greek *teredon* boring worm]

term *noun* **1** a word or expression, esp one used with a precise meaning in a specialized field. **2** (**terms**) language used; a particular way of speaking: *in no uncertain terms.* **3** a limited or clearly defined period of time: *term of office.* **4** the end of a particular time, esp of pregnancy when the baby is about to be born. **5** (**terms**) a relationship between people or countries: *be on good terms.* **6** (**terms**) the rules or conditions of an agreement: *terms of sale.* **7** (**terms**) fixed charges for work or a service. **8** one of the divisions into which an academic year is divided. **9** the time during which a court is in session. **10** *maths* a quantity which is joined to another by either addition or subtraction. **11** *maths* one quantity in a series or sequence. **12** *logic* a word or expression which may be a subject or a predicate of a proposition. ▸ *verb* to name or call. [13c: from Latin *terminus* boundary]

IDIOMS **come to terms with 1** to come to an agreement or understanding with. **2** to find a way of living with or tolerating (some personal trouble or difficulty). **in terms of** in relation to.

termagant *noun* a scolding, brawling and overbearing woman. [17c: from French *Tervagan*, a deity depicted in morality plays as scolding and overbearing]

terminable *adj* able to come or be brought to an end. [15c: from Latin *terminus* boundary]

terminal *adj* **1** of an illness: causing death; fatal. **2** of a patient: suffering from an illness which will cause death. **3** *informal* extreme; acute: *terminal laziness.* **4** forming or occurring at an end, boundary or terminus. ▸ *noun* **1** an arrival and departure building at an airport. **2** a large station at the end of a railway line or for long-distance buses and coaches. **3** a point in an electric circuit or electrical device at which the current leaves or enters it, or by which it may be connected to another device. **4** a device consisting usu of a keyboard and VDU, which connects with a remote computer. **5** an installation at the end of a pipeline or at a port where oil is stored and from where it is distributed. ▪ **terminally** *adv.* [15c: from Latin *terminus* boundary]

terminate *verb* **1** *tr & intr* to bring or come to an end. **2** to end (a pregnancy) artificially and before the fetus is viable. ▪ **termination** *noun.* [16c: from Latin *terminare* to set a limit to]

terminology *noun* (**-ies**) the words and phrases used in a particular field. ▪ **terminological** *adj.* ▪ **terminologist** *noun.* [19c: from Latin *terminus* term]

terminus /'tɜːmɪnəs/ *noun* (***termini*** /-naɪ/ *or* ***terminuses***) **a** the end of a railway line or bus route, usu with a station; **b** the station at this point. [16c: Latin, meaning 'boundary' or 'limit']

termite *noun* an ant-like insect of mainly tropical areas, some of which cause damage to trees and buildings, etc. [18c: from Latin *termes* a white ant]

tern *noun* a sea-bird, related to the gull, with a long forked tail. [17c: from Danish *terne*]

ternary *adj* **1** containing three parts. **2** *maths* of a number system: using three as a base. [15c: from Latin *ternarius* consisting of three]

terpsichorean /tɜːpsɪkə'rɪən/ *adj* relating to dancing. [19c: from Terpsichore, the Muse of song and dance, from Greek *terpein* to enjoy + *choros* dance]

terrace *noun* **1** each of a series of raised level earth banks on a hillside used for cultivation. **2** *Brit* a row of usu identical and connected houses. **3** a raised level paved area by the side of a house. **4** (*usu* **terraces**) open areas rising in tiers round a sports ground, where spectators stand. ▸ *verb* to form into a terrace or terraces. [16c: from Latin *terra* earth]

terracotta *noun* **1** an unglazed brownish-orange earthenware used for pottery, roof tiles, etc. **2** a brownish-orange colour. ▸ *adj* made of, or having the colour of, terracotta. [18c: Italian, meaning 'baked earth']

terra firma *noun* dry land as opposed to water or air; solid ground. [17c: Latin, meaning 'firm land']

terrain *noun* a stretch of land, esp with regard to its physical features or as a battle area. [18c: ultimately from Latin *terrenus*, from *terra* earth]

terrapin *noun* a small freshwater turtle. [17c: from a Native American language]

terrarium *noun* (***terraria*** *or* ***terrariums***) **1** a container in which small land animals are kept. **2** a large, globe-shaped, sealed jar in which plants are grown. [19c: from Latin *terra* earth, modelled on **aquarium**]

terrazzo /tɛ'ratsoʊ/ *noun* a mosaic covering for concrete floors consisting of marble chips set in cement and then polished. [20c: Italian, meaning 'terrace']

terrestrial *adj* **1** relating to dry land or to the Earth. **2** denoting animals or plants that live on dry land. **3** belonging or relating to this world; mundane. **4** of broadcast signals: sent by a land transmitter as opposed to satellite. ▸ *noun* an inhabitant of the Earth. [15c: from Latin *terra* earth]

terrible *adj* **1** *informal* very bad: *a terrible singer.* **2** *informal* very great; extreme: *a terrible gossip.* **3** causing great fear. **4** causing suffering or hardship: *a terrible struggle.* **5** *informal* **a** ill: *have flu and feel terrible;* **b** regretful: *feel terrible about what I said.* ▪ **terribly** *adv.* [15c: from Latin *terrere* to frighten]

terrier *noun* a breed of small dog orig bred to hunt animals in burrows. [15c: from French *chien terrier* dog of the earth]

terrific *adj* **1** *informal* marvellous; excellent. **2** *informal* very great or powerful: *a terrific storm.* **3** very frightening; terrifying. [17c: from Latin *terrificus* frightful]

terrify *verb* (**-ies, -ied**) to make very frightened; to fill with terror. ▪ **terrified** *adj.* ▪ **terrifying** *adj.* [16c: from Latin *terrificare*]

terrine /tɛ'riːn/ *noun* **1** an earthenware dish in which food may be cooked and served. **2** food cooked or served in such a dish. [18c: earlier form of **tureen**]

territorial *adj* **1** relating to a territory. **2** limited or restricted to a particular area or district. **3** of birds and animals: likely to establish and defend their own territory. ▸ *noun* (**Territorial**) *Brit* a member of the **Territorial Army**. ▪ **territoriality** *noun.* [17c]

Territorial Army (abbrev **TA**) *noun* in the UK: a fully trained volunteer force intended to provide back-up to the regular army in cases of emergency.

territorial waters *plural noun* the area of sea surrounding a state which is considered to belong to that state.

territory *noun* (*-ies*) **1** a stretch of land; a region. **2** the land under the control of a ruler, government or state. **3** an area of knowledge, interest or activity. **4** an area or district in which a travelling salesman or distributor operates. **5** an area which a bird or animal treats as its own and defends against others of the same species. **6** (*often* **Territory**) part of a country with an organized government but without the full rights of a state. [15c: from Latin *territorium* the land round a town]

terror *noun* **1** very great fear or dread. **2** someone or something which causes such fear. **3** *informal* a troublesome or mischievous person, esp a child. [14c: from Latin *terrere* to frighten]

terrorism *noun* the systematic use of violence and intimidation to force a government or community, etc to act in a certain way or accept certain demands. ▪ **terrorist** *noun, adj.* [18c]

terrorize *or* **-ise** *verb* **1** to frighten greatly. **2** to use terrorism against. [19c]

terry *noun* (*-ies*) an absorbent fabric with uncut loops on one side, used esp for towels. ▸ *adj* made of this fabric: *terry towelling*. [18c]

terse *adj* **1** brief and concise; succinct. **2** abrupt and rude; curt. ▪ **tersely** *adv.* ▪ **terseness** *noun.* [17c: from Latin *tergere* to wipe]

tertiary /ˈtɜːʃərɪ/ *adj* **1** third in order, degree, importance, etc. **2** denoting the extraction of petroleum by high-pressure pumping into rock structures. **3** (**Tertiary**) *geol* relating to the first period of the Cenozoic era. ▸ *noun* (**Tertiary**) this geological period. [17c: from Latin *tertius* third]

tertiary industry *noun* an industry concerned with providing services rather than extraction or processing of raw materials. Compare **primary industry, secondary industry**.

Terylene *noun, trademark* a light tough synthetic fabric of polyester fibres. [20c]

TESL *abbrev* Teaching English as a Second Language.

tesla *noun, physics* (abbrev **T**) in the SI system: a unit of magnetic flux density, defined as a magnetic flux of one weber per square metre. [1950s: named after US physicist Nikola Tesla]

tessellate *verb* **1** to form into or mark like a mosaic, esp with tesserae or checks. **2** *intr* of a number of identical shapes: to fit together exactly, leaving no spaces. ▪ **tessellated** *adj.* ▪ **tessellation** *noun.* [18c: from Latin *tessella* small square piece of stone]

tessera /ˈtɛsərə/ *noun* (*tesserae* /-riː/) a square piece of stone or glass, etc used in mosaics. [17c: Latin, from Greek *tesseres* four]

test[1] *noun* **1 a** a critical examination or trial of qualities, abilities, etc; **b** something used as the basis for this: *a test of strength*. **2** a short minor examination, esp in school. **3** *sport* a **test match**. **4** *chem* anything used to distinguish, detect or identify a substance; a reagent. ▸ *verb* **1** to examine, esp by trial. **2** *tr & intr* to examine (a substance) to discover whether another substance is present or not. **3** *intr* to achieve a stated result in a test: *tested negative for the virus*. ▪ **testable** *adj.* [14c: from Latin *testum* earthenware pot]

test[2] *noun, biol* a hard outer covering or shell of certain invertebrates. [19c: from Latin *testa* tile]

testa *noun* /ˈtɛstə/ (*testae* /-tiː/) *biol* the hard outer covering of a seed. [18c: Latin, meaning 'shell']

testament *noun* **1 a** a written statement of someone's wishes, esp of what they want to be done with their property after death; **b** a will: *her last will and testament*. **2** proof, evidence or a tribute: *a testament to her hard work*. **3** a covenant between God and humankind. **4** (**Testament**) either of the two main divisions of the Bible, the Old Testament and the New Testament. ▪ **testamentary** *adj.* [14c: from Latin *testis* witness]

testate *law, adj* having made and left a valid will. ▸ *noun* a testate person, esp at the time of death. [15c: from Latin *testari* to make a will]

testator *noun, law* someone who leaves a will at death. [14c: Latin]

testatrix /tɛˈsteɪtrɪks/ *noun* (*testatrixes* or *testatrices* /-trɪsiːz/) *law* a female testator. [16c: Latin]

test case *noun, law* a case whose outcome will serve as a precedent for all similar cases in the future.

tester *noun* **1** someone who tests. **2** something used for testing, esp a sample of a cosmetic, etc in a shop.

testicle *noun* a testis. ▪ **testicular** *adj.* [15c: from Latin *testiculus*, diminutive of **testis**]

testify *verb* (*-ies, -ied*) **1** *intr* to give evidence in court. **2** (*often* **testify to**) to serve as evidence or proof (of something). **3** *intr* to make a solemn declaration (eg of one's faith). [14c: from Latin *testis* witness]

testimonial *noun* **1** a letter or certificate giving details of a person's character, conduct and qualifications. **2** a gift presented as a sign of respect or as a tribute to personal qualities or services. **3** *sport* a match or series of matches held in honour of a player, who receives all the proceeds.

testimony *noun* (*-ies*) **1** a statement made under oath, esp in a law court. **2** evidence: *testimony to her intelligence*. **3** a declaration of truth or fact. [14c: from Latin *testimonium*, from *testis* witness]

testing *noun* the assessment of an individual level of knowledge or skill, etc. ▸ *adj* **1** troublesome; difficult: *a testing time*. **2** mentally taxing: *a testing question*.

testis *noun* (*testes*) *anatomy* in male animals: either of the two reproductive glands that produce sperm. [18c: Latin, meaning 'witness (of virility)']

test match *noun* in various sports, esp cricket: a match forming one of a series played between two international teams. Often shortened to **test**.

testosterone *noun, physiol* the main male sex hormone, a steroid secreted primarily by the testes. [20c]

test pilot *noun* a pilot who tests new aircraft by flying them.

test tube *noun* a thin glass tube closed at one end, used in chemical tests or experiments.

test-tube baby *noun, informal* a baby produced by in-vitro fertilization. [20c]

testy *adj* (*-ier, -iest*) irritable; bad-tempered; touchy. ▪ **testily** *adv.* ▪ **testiness** *noun.* [14c: from French *testif* headstrong]

tetanus *noun* an infectious and potentially fatal disease whose main symptoms are fever and painful muscle spasms. Also called **lockjaw**. [14c: from Greek *teinein* to stretch]

tetchy *adj* (*-ier, -iest*) irritable; peevish. ▪ **tetchily** *adv*. ▪ **tetchiness** *noun*. [16c]

tête-à-tête /teɪtə'teɪt, tɛtə'tɛt/ *noun* a private conversation between two people. ▸ *adj* private; intimate. ▸ *adv* intimately. [17c: French, literally 'head to head']

tether *noun* a rope, etc for tying an animal to a post or confining it to a particular spot. ▸ *verb* to tie or restrain with a tether. [14c: from Norse *tjothr*]

IDIOMS **at the end of one's tether** having reached the limit of one's patience, mental resources, etc.

tetra- *or* (*before a vowel*) **tetr-** *combining form, denoting* four. [Greek, meaning 'four']

tetrachloromethane *noun, chem* a toxic colourless pungent liquid, formerly used as a solvent and a dry-cleaning reagent.

tetragon *noun, geom* a plane figure with four angles and four sides. ▪ **tetragonal** /tɛ'tragənəl/ *adj*. [17c: from Greek *tetragonon*]

tetrahedron /tɛtrə'hiːdrən/ *noun* (***tetrahedra*** *or* ***tetrahedrons***) *geom* a solid figure with four triangular plane faces. ▪ **tetrahedral** *adj*. [16c: from Greek *tetraedron*]

tetrameter /tɛ'tramɪtə(r)/ *noun, poetry* a line of verse with four metrical feet. [17c: from Greek *tetrametros*]

tetraplegia see **quadriplegia**

tetrapod *noun, zool* an animal with four feet. [19c: from Greek *tetrapous* four-footed]

tetravalent *adj, chem* of an atom: able to combine with four atoms of hydrogen. [19c: from Latin *valere* to be worth]

Teutonic /tʃʊ'tɒnɪk/ *adj* **1** belonging or relating to the Germanic languages or peoples speaking these languages. **2** German.

Tex-Mex *adj* of food, music, etc: typically Mexican, but with Texan elements. [20c: from *Texan* + *Mexican*]

text *noun* **1** the main body of printed words in a book as opposed to the notes and illustrations, etc. **2** the actual words of an author or piece of written work as opposed to commentary on them. **3** a short passage from the Bible taken as the starting-point for a sermon or quoted in authority. **4** a theme or subject. **5** a book, novel or play, etc that forms part of a course of study: *a set text*. **6** *comput* the words written or displayed on a VDU. **7** a text message. **8** a textbook. ▸ *verb tr & intr* to send a text message (to). ▪ **texter** *noun*. ▪ **texting** *noun*. [14c: from Latin *texere* to weave]

textbook *noun* a book that contains the standard principles and information of a subject. ▸ *adj* conforming or as if conforming to the guidance of a textbook; exemplary: *textbook accountancy*.

textile *noun* **1** a cloth or fabric made by weaving or knitting. **2** fibre or yarn, etc suitable for weaving into cloth. ▸ *adj* **1** relating to manufacturing cloth. **2** woven; suitable for being woven into cloth. [17c: from Latin *texere* to weave]

text message *noun* a short message, often using abbreviations, typed and sent by means of a mobile phone. Often shortened to **text**. ▪ **text messaging** *noun*.

textual *adj* relating to, found in, or based on, a text or texts. ▪ **textually** *adv*.

texture *noun* **1** the way a surface feels. **2** the feel or appearance of cloth, etc, caused by the way it is woven, etc. **3** the structure of a substance as formed by the size and arrangement of the smaller particles which form it. ▸ *verb* to give a particular texture to (food, fabric, etc). ▪ **textural** *adj*. [15c: from Latin *texere* to weave]

Th *symbol, chem* thorium.

Th. *abbrev* Thursday.

-th[1] *or* **-eth** *suffix* forming ordinal numbers and fractions from cardinal numbers: *fourth* • *one fiftieth*. [Anglo-Saxon *-tha* or *-the*]

-th[2] *suffix, forming nouns, signifying* an action or process, or a state or condition: *growth* • *filth* • *width*. [Anglo-Saxon *-thu*, *-tho* or *-th*]

Thai /taɪ/ *adj* belonging or relating to Thailand, a kingdom in SE Asia, its inhabitants or their language. ▸ *noun* (***Thai*** *or* ***Thais***) **1** a citizen or inhabitant of, or person born in, Thailand. **2** the official language of Thailand. [20c]

thalamus *noun* (***thalami***) *anatomy* in the forebrain of vertebrates: either of two masses of grey matter that relay sensory nerve impulses to the cerebral cortex. [18c: Latin, from Greek *thalamos* inner room]

thalidomide *noun* a drug formerly used as a sedative but withdrawn in 1961 because it was found to cause malformation of the fetus if taken by the mother in early pregnancy. [20c]

thallium *noun, chem* (symbol **Tl**) a soft bluish-white metallic element. [19c: from Greek *thallos* a green shoot, because of the bright green line in its spectrum]

thallus *noun* (*pl* ***thalluses*** *or* ***thalli*** /'θalaɪ/) *biol* in fungi, lichens and seaweeds: a flattened and sometimes branched structure that is not differentiated into stems, leaves and roots. ▪ **thalloid** *adj*.

than *conj* **1** used to introduce the second part of a comparison, or that part which is taken as the basis of a comparison: *He's better than me*. **2** used to introduce the second, and usu less desirable or rejected, option in a statement of alternatives: *would rather walk than drive*. **3** except; other than: *left with no alternative than to resign*. ▸ *prep* in comparison with: *someone older than him*. [Anglo-Saxon *thonne*]

---

than what

See the Usage Note at **what**.

---

thane *noun, hist* **1** in Anglo-Saxon England: a man holding land from the king or some other superior in exchange for military service. **2** in medieval Scotland: a man holding land from a Scottish king, but not in return for military service; a Scottish feudal lord. [Anglo-Saxon *thegn*]

thank *verb* **1** to express gratitude to: *thanked him for his help*. **2** to hold responsible for something: *has only himself to thank for the mess*. ▸ *noun* (*usu* **thanks**) **1** gratitude or an expression of gratitude: *to express my thanks*. **2** thank you. [Anglo-Saxon *thancian*]

IDIOMS **thank God** *or* **goodness** *or* **heavens**, *etc* an expression of relief. **thanks to** as a result of; because of: *Thanks to Amy, we missed the train*. **thank you** a polite expression acknowledging a gift, help or offer.

thankful *adj* grateful; relieved and happy. ▪ **thankfully** *adv.* ▪ **thankfulness** *noun.*

thankless *adj* bringing no thanks, pleasure or profit. ▪ **thanklessly** *adv.* ▪ **thanklessness** *noun.* [16c]

thanksgiving *noun* **1** a formal act of giving thanks, esp to God. **2** (**Thanksgiving** *or* **Thanksgiving Day**) *N Am* a public holiday for giving thanks, occurring on the fourth Thursday in November in the USA and the second Monday in October in Canada.

thankyou *noun* an instance of thanking, or something that expresses thanks: *some flowers as a thankyou.* ▸ *adj* (**thank-you**) expressing thanks: *a thank-you card.*

that *adj* (*pl* ***those***) **1** indicating the thing, person or idea already mentioned, specified or understood: *There's that girl I was telling you about.* **2** indicating someone or something that is farther away or is in contrast: *not this book, but that one.* ▸ *pronoun* (*pl* ***those***) **1** the person, thing or idea just mentioned, already spoken of or understood: *When did that happen?* **2** a relatively distant or more distant person, thing or idea. ▸ *pronoun* used instead of *which, who* or *whom,* to introduce a relative clause which defines, distinguishes or restricts the person or thing mentioned in the preceding clause: *All the children that were late received detention.* ▸ *conj* used to introduce a noun clause, or a clause showing reason, purpose, consequence or a result or expressing a wish or desire: *He spoke so quickly that I couldn't understand • Oh, that the day would never end!* ▸ *adv* **1** to the degree or extent shown or understood: *won't reach that far.* **2** *informal or dialect* to such a degree that; so: *He's that mean he never buys a round.* [Anglo-Saxon *thæt*]

IDIOMS **all that** *informal* very: *not all that good.* **that's that** that is the end of the matter.

that, which, who, whom

It is acceptable, even in formal English, to use the relative pronoun **that** in sentences such as *The man that I met happened to be Ken's uncle* or *I had a car that just wouldn't start in the mornings.*

It is not necessary to replace **that** with 'who', 'whom' or 'which'.

thatch *noun* **1** a roof covering of straw or reeds, etc. **2** something resembling this, esp a thick head of hair. ▸ *verb, tr & intr* to cover (a roof or building) with thatch. ▪ **thatcher** *noun.* [Anglo-Saxon *theccan*]

thaw *verb* **1 a** *intr* of snow, ice, frozen food, etc: to melt; **b** to make (snow, ice, frozen food, etc) melt. **2** *intr* of the weather: to be warm enough to begin to melt snow and ice: *It's beginning to thaw.* **3** *tr & intr, informal* to make or become less stiff and numb with cold: *Come and thaw out by the fire.* **4** *tr & intr, informal* to make or become more friendly or relaxed. ▸ *noun* **1** an act or the process of thawing. **2** a period of weather warm enough to begin to thaw ice and snow. [Anglo-Saxon *thawian*]

the *definite article* **1** used to refer to a particular person or thing, or group of people or things, already mentioned, implied or known: *Pass me the CD.* Compare **a**[1]. **2** used to refer to a unique person or thing: *the Pope.* **3** used before a singular noun to denote all the members of a group or class: *a history of the novel.* **4 a** used before an adjective to denote a specified thing: *the paranormal;* **b** used before an adjective to denote collectively people or things who have the specified attribute, etc: *the poor.* **5** used before certain titles and proper names. **6** used before an adjective or noun describing an identified person: *Robert the Bruce.* **7** used after a preposition to refer to a unit of quantity or time, etc: *a car which does forty miles to the gallon • paid by the hour.* **8** *informal* my; our: *I'd better check with the wife.* ▸ *adv* **1** used before comparative adjectives or adverbs to indicate (by) so much or (by) how much: *the sooner the better.* **2** used before superlative adjectives and adverbs to indicate an amount beyond all others: *like this book the best.* [Anglo-Saxon, meaning 'who', 'which' or 'that']

theatre *or* (*US*) **theater** *noun* **1** a building or outside area specially designed for the performance of plays, operas, etc. **2** a large room with seats rising in tiers, for lectures, etc. **3** (*also* **the theatre**) the writing and production of plays in general or the world and profession of actors and theatre companies. **4** *Brit* a specially equipped room in a hospital where surgery is performed. **5** a scene of action or place where events take place: *theatre of war.* **6** *N Am* a cinema. [14c: from Greek *theaesthai* to see]

theatrical *adj* **1** relating to theatres or acting. **2** of behaviour or a gesture, etc: done only for effect; artificial and exaggerated. ▸ *noun* (**theatricals**) **1** dramatic performances. **2** insincere or exaggerated behaviour: *Less of the theatricals, please!* ▪ **theatricality** *noun.*

thee *pron* the objective form of **thou**[1]. [Anglo-Saxon]

theft *noun* an act or instance or the process of stealing. [Anglo-Saxon *thiefth*]

their *adj* **1** belonging or relating to them: *their opinion.* **2** his or her: *Has everyone got their books?* [12c: from Norse *thierra*]

their, there, they're

Be careful not to use the spelling **their** when you mean **there**:

There, people can do as they please.

Also be aware of the spelling **they're**, the short form of 'they are':

They're moving their desks over there.

theirs *pron* a person or thing that belongs to them: *That's theirs.*

theism /ˈθiːɪzəm/ *noun* the belief in the existence of God or a god, esp one revealed supernaturally to humans. ▪ **theist** *noun.* ▪ **theistic** *adj.* [17c: from Greek *theos* god]

them *pron* **1** the objective form of **they**: *met them.* **2** *informal or dialect* those: *Them's the best, I reckon.* **3** *informal* him or her. **4** *old use* themselves. [12c: from Norse *thiem*]

theme *noun* **1** a subject of a discussion, speech or piece of writing, etc. **2** *music* a short melody in a piece of music which is developed and repeated with variations. **3** a repeated or recurring image or idea in literature or art. **4** a brief essay or written exercise. ▪ **thematic** *adj.* ▪ **thematically** *adv.* [13c: from Greek *thema*]

theme park *noun* a large amusement park in which all of the rides and attractions are based on a particular theme, eg, outer space.

theme song *or* **theme tune** *noun* a song or melody that is played at the beginning and end of a film or a

TV or radio programme, or which is associated with a particular person, character, etc.

themselves *pron* **1** the reflexive form of **them**: *helped themselves.* **2** used for emphasis: *They, themselves, are to blame.* **3** their normal selves: *not feeling themselves today.* **4** *informal* himself or herself: *Nobody needs to blame themselves.*

then *adv* **1** at that time. **2** soon or immediately after that: *I looked at him, then turned away.* **3** in that case; that being so; as a necessary consequence: *What would we do then?* • *If you're tired, then you should rest.* **4** also; in addition: *Then there's the cost to take into account.* **5** used to continue a narrative after a break or digression. **6** used esp at the end of questions which ask for an explanation, opinion, etc, or which ask for or assume agreement: *Your mind is made up, then?* ▸ *noun* that time: *But, until then, I think you should stay away.* ▸ *adj* being or acting at that time: *the then Prime Minister.* [Anglo-Saxon *thonne*]

thence *adv, old use or formal* **1** from that place or time. **2** from that cause; therefore. [13c: from Anglo-Saxon *thanon* thence]

thenceforth *or* **thenceforward** *adv, old use or formal* from that time or place forwards.

theo- *combining form, denoting* belonging or relating to God or a god. [From Greek *theos* god]

theocracy *noun* (*-ies*) **1** government by a deity or by priests representing a deity. **2** a state ruled in this way. ▪ **theocrat** *noun.* ▪ **theocratic** *adj.* [17c]

theodolite *noun, surveying* an instrument for measuring horizontal and vertical angles. [16c: from Latin *theodelitus*]

theology *noun* (*-ies*) **1** the study of God, religious belief and revelation. **2** a particular system of theology and religion. ▪ **theologian** *noun.* ▪ **theological** *adj.* [14c]

theorem *noun* a scientific or mathematical statement which makes certain assumptions in order to explain observed phenomena, and which has been proved to be correct. [16c: from Greek *theorema*]

theoretical *or* **theoretic** *adj* **1** concerned with or based on theory rather than practical knowledge or experience. **2** existing in theory only; hypothetical. **3** dealing with theory only; speculative. ▪ **theoretically** *adv.*

theoretician *noun* someone who specializes in or is concerned with the theoretical aspects of a subject rather than its practical use. [19c]

theorize *or* **-ise** *verb, intr* to devise theories; to speculate. ▪ **theorist** *noun.* [17c]

theory *noun* (*-ies*) **1** a series of ideas and general principles that seek to explain some aspect of the world: *theory of relativity.* **2** an idea or explanation which has not yet been proved; a conjecture: *My theory is he's jealous!* **3** the general and usu abstract principles or ideas of a subject: *theory of music.* **4 a** an ideal, hypothetical or abstract situation; **b** ideal, hypothetical or abstract reasoning: *a good idea in theory.* [16c: from Greek *theoreein* to view]

theosophy *noun* (*-ies*) a religious philosophy based on the belief that a knowledge of God can be achieved through intuition, mysticism and divine inspiration, esp a modern movement which combines this with elements from Hinduism and Buddhism. ▪ **theosophic** /θɪə'sɒfɪk/ *adj.* ▪ **theosophically** *adv.* ▪ **theosophist** *noun.* [17c: from **theo-** + Greek *sophia* wisdom]

therapeutic /θɛrə'pjuːtɪk/ *adj* **1** relating to, concerning or contributing to healing or curing disease, etc. **2** bringing a feeling of general wellbeing. ▪ **therapeutically** *adv.* [17c: from Greek *therapeuein* to take care of or heal]

therapeutics *singular noun* the branch of medicine concerned with the treatment and curing of diseases.

therapy *noun* (*-ies*) the treatment of physical, social, psychiatric and psychological diseases and disorders by means other than surgery or drugs. ▪ **therapist** *noun.* [19c]

there /ðɛə(r)/ *adv* **1** at, in or to a place or position: *You can sit there.* **2** at that point in speech, a piece of writing or a performance, etc: *Don't stop there.* **3** in that respect: *I agree with him there.* **4** used to begin a sentence when the subject of the verb follows the verb instead of coming before it: *There are no mistakes in this.* **5** used at the beginning of a sentence to emphasize or call attention to that sentence: *There goes the last bus.* **6** used after a noun for emphasis: *That book there is the one you need.* **7** *informal or dialect* used between a noun and *this* or *that*, etc for emphasis: *that there tractor.* ▸ *noun* that place or point. ▸ *exclam* **1** used to express satisfaction, approval, triumph or encouragement, etc: *There! I knew he would come.* **2** used to express sympathy or comfort, etc: *There, there! He's just not worth it.* [Anglo-Saxon *thær*]

IDIOMS **there and then** at that very time and on that very spot.

---

there, their, they're

Be careful not to use the spelling **there** when you mean **their**:

They can do what they like in their own home.

Also be aware of the spelling **they're**, the short form of 'they are':

They're moving their desks over there.

---

thereabouts *or* **thereabout** *adv* near that place, number, amount, degree or time.

thereafter *adv, formal* from that time onwards.

thereby *adv, formal* **1** by that means. **2** in consequence.

therefore *adv* for that reason; as a consequence.

therein *adv, formal* in or into that place, circumstance, etc.

thereof *adv, formal* belonging or relating to, or from, that or it.

thereon *adv, formal* on or on to that or it.

there's *contraction* there is.

---

there's

If you are using formal English, don't use **there's** if you are going to refer to a plural:

✗ *There's many things we still have to do.*

✓ *There are many things we still have to do.*

However, if you are talking about a quantity as a single amount **there's** is correct:

✓ *There's seventy pence for your bus fare.*

You should also use **there's** when you are listing individual people or things:

✓ *'What shall we have for dinner?' 'Well, there's chicken and fish in the freezer, and pasta and quiche in the fridge.'*

---

thereto *adv, formal* to that or it; in addition.

thereunder *adv, formal* under that or it.

thereupon *adv, formal* **1** on that matter or point. **2** immediately after it or that.

therm *noun* a unit of heat equal to 1.055×10^8 joules, used to measure the amount of gas supplied. [20c: from Greek *therme* heat]

thermal *adj* **1** relating to, caused by or producing heat. **2** of clothing: designed to prevent the loss of heat from the body. ▸ *noun* **1** a rising current of warm air, used by birds, gliders, etc to move upwards. **2** (**thermals**) thermal clothing, esp underwear. [18c]

thermal imaging *noun* the visualization of people, objects, etc by detecting and processing the infrared energy they emit.

thermionic valve *noun, electronics* a vacuum tube that emits electrons from an electrically heated cathode into a vacuum, formerly widely used in amplifiers, switches and other electrical devices.

thermistor *noun, physics* a device with an electrical resistance that decreases rapidly as its temperature rises, used in electronic circuits for measuring or controlling temperature. [20c: a contraction of *thermal resistor*]

thermo- *prefix, denoting* heat. [From Greek *therme* heat]

thermocouple *noun* a device for measuring temperature, consisting of two different metallic conductors welded together at their ends to form a loop. [19c]

thermodynamics *singular noun, physics* the branch of physics concerned with the relationship between heat and other forms of energy, esp mechanical energy, and the behaviour of physical systems in which temperature is an important factor. ▪ **thermodynamic** *adj.* [19c]

thermoelectricity *noun* an electric current generated by a difference in temperature in an electric circuit. ▪ **thermoelectric** *adj.* [19c]

thermometer *noun* an instrument for measuring temperature, often consisting of a sealed glass tube filled with a liquid, eg, mercury or alcohol, which expands as the temperature increases and contracts as it decreases. [17c]

thermonuclear *adj* using or showing nuclear reactions which can only be produced at extremely high temperatures: *thermonuclear weapons.* [20c]

thermonuclear bomb see **hydrogen bomb**

thermopile *noun, physics* a device consisting of several **thermocouple**s connected together, used to measure the intensity of thermal radiation.

thermoplastic *noun, chem* a polymer that can be repeatedly softened and hardened, without any appreciable change in its properties, by heating and cooling it. ▸ *adj* denoting such a material. [19c]

Thermos *or* **Thermos flask** *noun, trademark* a kind of **vacuum flask**. [20c: Greek, meaning 'hot']

thermosetting *adj* of plastics: becoming permanently hard after a single melting and moulding. [20c]

thermosphere *noun, meteorol* the layer of the Earth's atmosphere situated above the mesosphere. ▪ **thermospheric** *adj.* [20c: from **thermo-**]

thermostat *noun* a device used to maintain the temperature of a system at a constant preset level, or which activates some other device when the temperature reaches a certain level. ▪ **thermostatic** *adj.* [19c: from **thermo-** + Greek *states* causing to stand]

thesaurus /θɪ'sɔːrəs/ *noun* (***thesauruses*** *or* ***thesauri*** /-raɪ/) a book which lists words and their synonyms according to sense. [18c: Latin, from Greek *thesauros* treasury]

these *pl of* **this**

thesis /'θiːsɪs/ *noun* (***-ses*** /-siːz/) **1** a long written dissertation or report, esp one based on original research and presented for an advanced university degree. **2** an idea or proposition to be supported or upheld in argument. **3** an unproved statement put forward as a basis for argument. [16c: Greek, meaning 'a setting down']

thespian *adj* belonging or relating to tragedy, or to drama and the theatre in general. ▸ *noun, facetious* an actor or actress. [17c: from Thespis, a Greek poet and reputed father of Greek tragedy]

theta /'θiːtə/ *noun* the eighth letter of the Greek alphabet.

they *pron* **1** the people, animals or things already spoken about, being indicated, or known from the context. **2** people in general. **3** people in authority. **4** *informal* he or she: *Anyone can help if they want.* [12c: from Norse *their*]

they'd *contraction* **1** they had. **2** they would.

they'll *contraction* **1** they will. **2** they shall.

they're *contraction* they are.

they've *contraction* they have.

thiamine *or* **thiamin** *noun* **vitamin B_1**. [20c]

thick *adj* **1** having a relatively large distance between opposite sides. **2** having a specified distance between opposite sides: *one inch thick.* **3** having a large diameter: *a thick rope.* **4** of a line or handwriting, etc: broad. **5** of a liquid: containing a lot of solid matter: *thick soup.* **6** having many single units placed very close together; dense: *thick hair.* **7** difficult to see through: *thick fog.* **8** of speech: not clear. **9** of an accent: marked; pronounced. **10** *informal* of a person: stupid; dull. **11** *informal* friendly or intimate: *He is very thick with the new manager.* **12** *informal* unfair: *That's a bit thick!* ▸ *adv* thickly. ▸ *noun* **1** (**the thick**) the busiest, most active or most intense part: *in the thick of the fighting.* **2** the thickest part of anything. ▪ **thickly** *adv.* [Anglo-Saxon *thicce*]

IDIOMS **as thick as thieves** very friendly. **thick and fast** frequently and in large numbers. **through thick and thin** in spite of any difficulties.

thicken *verb* **1** *tr & intr* to make or become thick or thicker. **2** *intr* to become more complicated: *The plot thickens.* [15c]

thickening *noun* **1** something used to thicken liquid. **2** the process of making or becoming thicker. **3** a thickened part.

thicket *noun* a dense mass of bushes and trees. [Anglo-Saxon *thiccet*]

thickhead *noun, informal* a stupid person. ▪ **thickheaded** *adj.* ▪ **thickheadedness** *noun.* [19c]

thickness *noun* **1** the state, quality or degree of being thick. **2** a layer. **3** the thick part of something.

thickset *adj* **1** heavily built; having a thick, short body. **2** growing or planted close together.

thick-skinned *adj* not easily hurt by criticism or insults; not sensitive.

thief *noun* (***thieves***) a person who steals, esp secretly and usu without violence. [Anglo-Saxon *theof*]

thieve *verb, tr & intr* to steal or be a thief. ▪ **thievery** *noun*. ▪ **thieving** *adj*. [Anglo-Saxon *theofian*]

thigh *noun* the part of the leg between the knee and hip in humans, or the corresponding part in animals. [Anglo-Saxon *theoh*]

thigh bone *noun* the **femur**.

thimble *noun* a cap worn on the finger to protect it and push the needle when sewing. [Anglo-Saxon *thymel* orig meaning 'a covering for the thumb']

thimbleful *noun* the amount a thimble will hold, esp used for a very small quantity of liquid.

thin *adj* (***thinner, thinnest***) **1** having a relatively short distance between opposite sides. **2** having a relatively small diameter: *thin string*. **3** of a line or handwriting, etc: narrow or fine. **4** of a person or animal: not fat; lean. **5** of a liquid: containing very little solid matter. **6** set far apart; sparse: *thin hair*. **7** having a very low oxygen content: *thin air*. **8** weak; lacking in body: *thin blood*. **9** not convincing or believable: *a thin disguise*. **10** *informal* difficult; uncomfortable; unpleasant: *have a thin time of it*. ▸ *adv* thinly. ▸ *verb* (***thinned, thinning***) *tr & intr* (*often* **thin out**) to make or become thin, thinner, sparser or less dense. [Anglo-Saxon *thynne*]

thine *old use or dialect, also relig, pron* something which belongs to **thee**. *adj* (sometimes used before a vowel instead of *thy*) belonging or relating to **thee**. [Anglo-Saxon *thin*]

thing *noun* **1** an object, esp an inanimate one. **2** an object that cannot, need not or should not be named. **3** a fact, quality or idea, etc that can be thought about or referred to. **4** an event, affair or circumstance: *Things are getting out of hand*. **5** a quality: *Generosity is a great thing*. **6** *informal* a person or animal, esp when thought of as an object of pity: *Poor thing!* **7** a preoccupation, obsession or interest: *She's got a real thing about Brad Pitt!* **8** what is needed or required: *It's just the thing*. **9** an aim: *The thing is to do better next time*. **10** (**things**) personal belongings: *I'll just get my things*. **11** (**things**) affairs in general: *So, how are things?* [Anglo-Saxon]

thingummy, thingamy, thingummyjig *or* **thingummybob** *noun* (***thingummies,*** etc) *informal* someone or something whose name is unknown, forgotten or deliberately not used. [18c]

think *verb* (***thought***) **1** *tr & intr* **a** to have or form ideas in the mind; **b** to have as a thought in one's mind. **2** *tr & intr* to consider, judge or believe: *I thought you were kidding! • They think of themselves as great singers*. **3** *tr & intr* to intend or plan; to form an idea of: *think about going to London • think no harm*. **4** *tr & intr* to imagine, expect or suspect: *I didn't think there would be any trouble*. **5** to keep in mind; to consider: *think of the children first*. **6** *tr & intr* **a** to remember: *couldn't think of his name*; **b** to consider: *I didn't think to tell her*. **7** to form or have an idea: *think of a plan*. **8** to bring into a specified condition by thinking: *tried to think himself thin*. ▸ *noun, informal* an act of thinking ▪ **thinker** *noun*. [Anglo-Saxon *thencan*]

IDIOMS **think better of sth** *or* **sb 1** to change one's mind about it or them on further thought. **2** to think that it or they would not be so bad as to do something wrong: *I thought better of him than that*. **think little of sth** *or* **not think much of sth** to have a very low opinion of it. **think twice** to hesitate before doing something; to decide in the end not to do it.

PHRASAL VERBS **think sth over** to consider all the advantages and disadvantages of (an action or decision, etc). **think sth through** to think carefully about all the possible consequences of (a plan or idea, etc). **think sth up** to invent or devise it.

thinking *noun* **1** the act of using one's mind to produce thoughts. **2** opinion or judgement: *What is your thinking on this?* ▸ *adj* of people: using or able to use the mind intelligently and constructively.

think tank *noun, informal* a group of experts who research an area to find solutions to problems and think up new ideas. [20c]

thinner *noun* a liquid such as turpentine that is added to paint or varnish to dilute it.

thin-skinned *adj* sensitive; easily hurt or upset.

third (often written **3rd**) *adj* **1** in counting: **a** next after second; **b** last of three. **2** in third position. **3** being one of three equal parts: *a third share*. ▸ *noun* **1** one of three equal parts. **2** a **fraction** equal to one divided by three (usu written ⅓). **3** a person coming third, eg in a race or exam. **4** (**the third**) **a** the third day of the month; **b** *golf* the third hole. **5** (*also* **third gear**) the gear which is one faster than second in a gearbox, eg in a motor vehicle. **6** *education, chiefly Brit* third-class honours in a university degree. **7** *music* **a** an interval of three notes along the diatonic scale; **b** a note at that interval from another. ▸ *adv* thirdly. ▪ **thirdly** *adv* used to introduce the third point in a list. [Anglo-Saxon *thridda*]

third class *noun* **1** the class or rank next (esp in quality) after second. **2** (*also* **third**) a third-class honours degree from a university. ▸ *adj* (**third-class**) belonging or relating to the third class of anything.

third degree *noun* (**the third degree**) prolonged and intensive interrogation, usu involving physical and mental intimidation. ▸ *adj* (**third-degree**) *med* denoting the most serious of the three degrees of burning, with damage to the lower layers of skin tissue. [20c]

third estate see **estate** (sense 2)

third party *noun, law* someone who is indirectly involved, or involved by chance, in a legal action or contract, etc. ▸ *adj* (**third-party**) of insurance: covering damage done by or injury done to someone other than the insured.

third person see under **person**

third-rate *adj* inferior; substandard.

Third World *noun, now sometimes offensive* the developing or underdeveloped countries in Africa, Asia and Latin America. Also called **Developing World**. [20c]

thirst *noun* **1** a need to drink, or the feeling of dryness in the mouth that this causes. **2** a strong and eager desire or longing: *a thirst for knowledge*. ▸ *verb, intr* to have a great desire or long for. [Anglo-Saxon *thyrstan*]

thirsty *adj* (***-ier, -iest***) **1** needing or wanting to drink. **2** eager or longing. **3** causing thirst.

thirteen *noun* **1** **a** the cardinal number 13; **b** the quantity that represents this, being one more than twelve, or the sum of ten and three. **2** any symbol for this, eg *13* or *XIII*. **3** the age of thirteen. **4** something, eg a shoe or a person, whose size is denoted by the number 13. **5** **a** a set or group of thirteen people or things; **b** *rugby league* a team of players. ▸ *adj*

1 totalling thirteen. **2** aged thirteen. ▪ **thirteenth** *adj, noun, adv.* [Anglo-Saxon *threotine*]

thirties (often written **30s** *or* **30's**) *plural noun* **1** (**one's thirties**) the period of time between one's thirtieth and fortieth birthdays. **2** (**the thirties**) the range of temperatures between thirty and forty degrees. **3** (**the thirties**) the period of time between the thirtieth and fortieth years of a century: *born in the 30s.*

thirty *noun* (**-*ies***) **1 a** the cardinal number 30; **b** the quantity that this represents, being one more than twenty-nine, or the product of ten and three. **2** any symbol for this, eg *30* or *XXX*. **3** the age of thirty. **4** something, eg a garment or person, whose size is denoted by the number 30. **5** a set or group of thirty people or things. ▶ *adj* **1** totalling thirty. **2** aged thirty. See also **thirties**. ▪ **thirtieth** *adj, noun, adv.* [Anglo-Saxon *thritig*]

thirty- *combining form* **a** *forming adjectives and nouns* with cardinal numbers between *one* and *nine*: *thirty-two*; **b** *forming adjectives and nouns* with ordinal numbers between *first* and *ninth*: *thirty-second.*

this *pron* (***these***) **1** a person, animal, thing or idea already mentioned, about to be mentioned, indicated or otherwise understood from the context. **2** a person, animal, thing or idea which is nearby, esp which is closer to the speaker than someone or something else. **3** the present time or place. **4** an action, event or circumstance: *What do you think of this?* ▶ *adj* **1** being the person, animal, thing or idea which is nearby, esp closer than someone or something else: *this book or that one.* **2** being the person, animal, thing or idea just mentioned, about to be mentioned, indicated or otherwise understood. **3** relating to today, or time in the recent past ending today: *this morning* • *I've been ill these last few days.* **4** *informal* denoting a person, animal, thing, etc not yet mentioned: *then I had this bright idea.* ▶ *adv* to this degree or extent: *I didn't think it would be this easy.* [Anglo-Saxon *thes*]
IDIOMS **this and that** *informal* various minor unspecified actions or objects, etc.

thistle *noun* **1** a plant with prickly leaves and usu globular purple, red or white flower heads. **2** this plant as the national emblem of Scotland. [Anglo-Saxon]

thistledown *noun* the light fluffy hairs attached to thistle seeds.

thither *adv, old use, literary or formal* to or towards that place. [Anglo-Saxon *thider*]

tho' *or* **tho** *conj, adv* short for **though**.

thole *or* **tholepin** *noun* either one of a pair of pins in the side of a boat to keep an oar in place. [Anglo-Saxon]

thong *noun* **1** a narrow strip of leather used for fastening, etc. **2** a type of skimpy undergarment or bathing costume, similar to a G-string. **3** (**thongs**) *N Am, NZ, Austral* flip-flops. [Anglo-Saxon *thwang*]

thorax *noun* (***thoraxes*** *or* ***thoraces*** /ˈθɔːrəsiːz/) *anatomy, zool* in humans and other vertebrates: the part of the body between the neck and abdomen; the chest. ▪ **thoracal** *or* **thoracic** *adj.* [14c: Latin and Greek, meaning 'breastplate']

thorium *noun, chem* (symbol **Th**) a silvery-grey radioactive metallic element used in X-ray tubes, sunlamps, etc. [19c: named after Thor, the Norse god of thunder]

thorn *noun* **1** a hard sharp point sticking out from the stem or branch of certain plants. **2** a shrub bearing thorns. **3** a constant irritation or annoyance: *a thorn in one's side.* [Anglo-Saxon]

thorny *adj* (**-*ier*, -*iest***) **1** full of or covered with thorns. **2** difficult; causing trouble or problems.

thorough *adj* **1** of a person: extremely careful and attending to every detail. **2** of a task, etc: carried out with great care and great attention to detail. **3** complete; absolute: *a thorough waste of time.* ▪ **thoroughly** *adv.* [Anglo-Saxon *thurh*]

thoroughbred *noun* **1** an animal, esp a horse, bred from the best specimens carefully developed by selective breeding over many years. **2** (**Thoroughbred**) a breed of racehorse descended from English mares and Arab stallions. **3** a racehorse belonging to this breed. ▶ *adj* **1** of an animal, esp a horse: bred from the best specimens; pure-bred. **2** (**Thoroughbred**) relating to a Thoroughbred. [18c]

thoroughfare *noun* **1** a public road or street. **2 a** a road or path that is open at both ends; **b** the right of passage through this. [14c]

thoroughgoing *adj* **1** extremely thorough. **2** utter; out-and-out: *a thoroughgoing villain.* [19c]

those *pl of* **that**

thou[1] /ðaʊ/ *pron, old use or dialect, also relig* you (singular). [Anglo-Saxon *thu*]

thou[2] /θaʊ/ *noun* (***thous*** *or* ***thou***) **1** *informal* a thousand. **2** one thousandth of an inch. [19c]

though *conj* **1** (*often* **even though**) despite the fact that: *I ate it up though I didn't like it.* **2** if or even if: *I wouldn't marry him though he was the richest man in the world.* **3** and yet; but: *We like the new car, though not as much as the old one.* ▶ *adv* however; nevertheless. Sometimes shortened to **tho'** *or* **tho**. [Anglo-Saxon *theah*: from Norse *tho*]
IDIOMS **as though** as if: *It's as though I've known him all my life.*

thought *noun* **1** an idea, concept or opinion. **2** an act or the process of thinking. **3** serious and careful consideration: *I'll give some thought to the problem.* **4** the faculty or power of reasoning. **5** intellectual ideas which are typical of a particular place, time or group, etc: *recent scientific thought.* **6** intention, expectation or hope: *no thoughts of retiring yet.* ▶ *verb, past tense & past participle of* **think**. [Anglo-Saxon *thoht*]

thoughtful *adj* **1** thinking deeply; reflective. **2** showing careful thought: *a thoughtful reply.* **3** considerate. ▪ **thoughtfully** *adv.* ▪ **thoughtfulness** *noun.* [13c]

thoughtless *adj* **1** inconsiderate. **2** showing a lack of careful thought; rash. ▪ **thoughtlessly** *adv.* ▪ **thoughtlessness** *noun.* [16c]

thousand *noun* (***thousands*** *or after a number* ***thousand***) **1 a** the number 1000; **b** the quantity that this represents, being the product of ten and one hundred. **2** any symbol for this, eg *1000* or *M*. **3** a set of a thousand people or things. **4** (**thousands**) *informal* a large but indefinite number: *thousands of people.* ▶ *adj* totalling one thousand. [Anglo-Saxon *thusend*]

thousandth *adj* **1** the last of one thousand people or things. **2** the thousandth position in a sequence of numbers. ▶ *noun* one of one thousand equal parts.

thrall *noun* **1** (*often* **a thrall to**) a slave or captive. **2** (*often* **in thrall**) a state of being in slavery or captivation: *held in thrall by her beauty.* [Anglo-Saxon *thræl*]

thrash *verb* **1** to beat soundly, esp with blows or a whip. **2** to defeat thoroughly or decisively. **3** *intr* to move around violently or wildly. **4** *tr & intr* to thresh (corn, etc). ▸ *noun* **1** an act of thrashing. **2** *informal* a party. **3** (*also* **thrash music**) *informal* a form of popular music combining elements of punk and heavy metal. ▪ **thrashing** *noun.* [Anglo-Saxon *therscan*] PHRASAL VERBS **thrash sth out** to discuss (a problem, etc) thoroughly to try to come to a solution.

thread *noun* **1** a strand of silk, cotton, wool, etc for sewing. **2** a naturally formed strand of fibre, such as that spun by a spider. **3** anything like a thread in length, narrowness, continuity, etc. **4** the projecting spiral ridge round a screw or bolt, or in a nut. **5** a connecting element or theme in a story or argument, etc: *I lost the thread of what he was saying.* **6** (**threads**) *informal* clothes, esp when flashy. ▸ *verb* **1** to pass a thread through the eye of (a needle). **2** (*usu* **thread through**) to pass (tape, film, etc) (into or through something). **3** to put (beads, etc) on a string, etc. **4** *tr & intr* to make (one's way): *threaded my way through the crowd.* **5** to provide (a bolt, etc) with a screw thread. [Anglo-Saxon]

threadbare *adj* **1** of material or clothes: worn thin; shabby. **2** of a person: wearing such clothes. **3** of a word, excuse, etc: commonly used and meaningless; hackneyed; feeble. [14c]

threadworm *noun* a parasitic worm living in the human large intestine.

threat *noun* **1** a warning of impending hurt or punishment. **2** a sign that something dangerous or unpleasant is or may be about to happen. **3** a person or thing seen as dangerous. [Anglo-Saxon, meaning 'affliction']

threaten *verb* **1** to make or be a threat to. **2** to warn. **3** *intr* of something unpleasant or dangerous: to seem likely to happen: *The storm threatened all day.* ▪ **threatening** *adj.* ▪ **threateningly** *adv.* [13c]

three *noun* **1 a** the cardinal number 3; **b** the quantity that this represents, being one more than two. **2** any symbol for this, eg *3* or *III*. **3** the age of three. **4** something, eg a shoe or a person, whose size is denoted by the number 3. **5** the third hour after midnight or midday: *Come at three • 3 o'clock • 3pm.* **6** a set or group of three people or things. ▸ *adj* **1** totalling three. **2** aged three. [Anglo-Saxon *thrie*]

three-dimensional *adj* having or appearing to have three dimensions, ie, height, width and depth. Often shortened to **three-D** *or* **3-D**.

threefold *adj* **1** equal to three times as much or many. **2** divided into, or consisting of, three parts. ▸ *adv* by three times as much.

Three Kings see **magus**

three-legged race *noun* a race run between pairs of runners who have their adjacent legs tied together.

three-line whip *noun, Brit politics* a written notice, underlined three times to indicate its importance, telling politicians that they must attend a vote in parliament and vote in line with their party. [20c as *three-lined whip*]

three-ply *noun* something with three layers or strands bound together, esp wood or wool. ▸ *adj* having three layers or strands.

three-point turn *noun* a manoeuvre, usu done in three movements, in which a driver turns a motor vehicle using forward and reverse gears, to face in the opposite direction.

three-quarter *adj* consisting of three-quarters of the full amount, length, etc.

threescore *noun, adj, archaic* sixty. [14c: see **score** (*noun* sense 4)]

threesome *noun* **1** a group of three. **2** a game, esp a round of golf, played by three people.

Three Wise Men see **Magus**

threnody *noun* (***threnodies***) a song or ode of lamentation, esp for a person's death. ▪ **threnodic** *adj.* ▪ **threnodist** *noun.* [17c: from Greek *threnos* lament + *oide* song]

threonine *noun, biochem* an amino acid essential for growth. [20c: changed from Greek *erythros* red]

thresh *verb* **1** *tr & intr* to separate grain or seeds from (corn, etc) by beating. **2** to beat or strike. [Anglo-Saxon *therscan*]

thresher *noun* **1** a person or machine that threshes corn, etc. **2** a large shark with a long whip-like tail.

threshold *noun* **1** a piece of wood or stone forming the bottom of a doorway. **2** any doorway or entrance. **3** a starting-point: *on the threshold of a new career.* **4** the point, stage, level, etc at which something will happen or come into effect, etc: *a tax threshold.* **5** *biol* the point below which there is no response to a stimulus: *a low pain threshold.* [Anglo-Saxon *thersan* to tread]

threw *past tense of* **throw**

thrice *adv, old use or literary* **1** three times. **2** three times as much. **3** greatly; highly: *thrice blessed.* [Anglo-Saxon *thriwa*]

thrift *noun* **1** careful spending, use or management of resources, esp money. **2** a wild seaside plant with narrow bluish-green leaves and pink flowers. ▪ **thriftless** *adj.* [16c: Norse, meaning 'prosperity']

thrifty *adj* (***-ier, -iest***) showing thrift; economical; frugal. ▪ **thriftily** *adv.* ▪ **thriftiness** *noun.*

thrill *verb* **1** *tr & intr* to feel or cause to feel exhilaration. **2** *tr & intr* to vibrate or quiver. **3** *intr* of a feeling: to pass quickly with a glowing or tingling sensation: *Excitement thrilled through her.* ▸ *noun* **1** a sudden tingling feeling of excitement, happiness or pleasure. **2** something causing this. **3** a shivering or trembling feeling. ▪ **thrilling** *adj.* [Anglo-Saxon *thyrlian* to pierce]

thriller *noun* **1** an exciting novel, play, film, etc, usu involving crime, espionage or adventure. **2** an exciting situation or event: *The cup final was a real thriller.*

thrips *noun* (*pl* ***thrips***) a minute black insect, which feeds by sucking sap from plants, and causes damage to crops. [18c: Greek, meaning 'woodworm']

thrive *verb* (*past tense* ***throve*** *or* ***thrived****, past participle* ***thriven*** *or* ***thrived***) *intr* **1** to grow strong and healthy. **2** to prosper or be successful, esp financially. [13c: from Norse *thrifa* to grasp]

thro' *or* **thro** *prep, adv, adj* short for **through**.

throat *noun* **1** the top part of the windpipe or gullet. **2** the front part of the neck. **3** something similar to a throat, esp a narrow passageway or opening. [Anglo-Saxon]

IDIOMS **cut one's own throat** to cause one's own ruin or downfall. **ram sth down sb's throat** to force them to listen to or pay attention to it.

throaty *adj* (*-ier, -iest*) **1** of a voice: deep and hoarse; husky. **2** *informal* indicating a sore throat: *feeling a bit throaty.* **3** coming from the throat.

throb *verb* (*throbbed, throbbing*) *intr* **1** to beat, esp with unusual force. **2** to beat or vibrate with a strong regular rhythm. ▸ *noun* a regular beat; pulse. [14c: prob imitating the sound]

throe *noun* (*usu* **throes**) a violent pang or spasm, esp during childbirth or before death. [Anglo-Saxon: from *throwian* to suffer]

IDIOMS **in the throes of** busy with, involved in or suffering under: *in the throes of doing the ironing* • *in the throes of the storm.*

thrombosis /θrɒm'boʊsɪs/ *noun* (*-ses* /-siːz/) an abnormal congealing of the blood within a blood vessel, causing a blood clot. [18c: Greek, meaning 'curdling']

throne *noun* **1** a ceremonial chair of a monarch, bishop, etc. **2** the office or power of the sovereign: *come to the throne.* **3** *relig* in the traditional medieval hierarchy of nine ranks of angels: an angel of the third-highest rank. [13c: from Greek *thronos* seat]

throng *noun* a crowd of people or things, esp in a small space; a multitude. ▸ *verb* **1** to crowd or fill: *people thronging the streets.* **2** *intr* to move in a crowd; to come together in great numbers: *The audience thronged into the theatre.* [Anglo-Saxon *gethrang*]

throttle *noun* **a** a valve regulating the amount of fuel, steam, etc supplied to an engine; **b** a pedal or lever controlling this. ▸ *verb* **1** to injure or kill by choking or strangling. **2** to prevent (something from being said, etc). **3** to control the flow of (fuel, steam, etc to an engine) using a valve. [14c: perhaps from **throat**]

through *or* (*US*) **thru** *prep* **1** going from one side or end of something to the other: *a road through the village.* **2** all over: *searched through the house.* **3** from the beginning to the end of: *read through the magazine.* **4** *N Am* up to and including: *Tuesday through Thursday.* **5** because of: *lost his job through his own stupidity.* **6** by way, means, or agency of: *related through marriage.* ▸ *adv* **1** into and out of; from one side or end to the other: *go straight through.* **2** from the beginning to the end. **3** into a position of having completed, esp successfully: *sat the exam again and got through.* **4** to the core; completely: *soaked through.* ▸ *adj* **1** of a journey, route, train or ticket, etc: going or allowing one to go all the way to one's destination without requiring a change of line or train, etc or a new ticket. **2** of traffic: passing straight through an area or town, etc without stopping. **3** going from one surface, side or end to another: *a through road.* Sometimes shortened to **thro'** *or* **thro.** [Anglo-Saxon *thurh*]

IDIOMS **be through with sb** to have no more to do with them. **be through with sth** to have finished or completed it. **put through** to connect by telephone: *I'll put you through to that extension.* **through and through** completely.

throughout *prep* **1** in all parts of: *decorated throughout the house.* **2** during the whole of: *chattered throughout the film.* ▸ *adv* **1** in every part; everywhere: *a house with carpets throughout.* **2** during the whole time: *remain friends throughout.*

throughput *noun* the amount of material put through a process, esp a computer or manufacturing process.

throve *a past tense of* **thrive**

throw *verb* (*past tense* **threw,** *past participle* **thrown**) **1** *tr & intr* to propel or hurl through the air with force. **2** to move or hurl into a specified position. **3** to put into a specified condition: *threw them into confusion.* **4** to direct, cast or emit: *a candle throwing shadows on the wall* • *throw a glance.* **5** *informal* to puzzle or confuse. **6** of a horse: to make (its rider) fall off. **7** *wrestling, judo* to bring (an opponent) to the ground. **8** to move (a switch or lever) so as to operate a mechanism. **9** to make (pottery) on a potter's wheel. **10** *informal* to lose (a contest) deliberately, esp in return for a bribe. **11 a** *tr & intr* to roll (dice) on to a flat surface; **b** to obtain (a specified number) by throwing dice. **12** to have or suffer: *throw a tantrum.* **13** to give (a party). **14** to deliver (a punch). **15** (**throw sth on** *or* **off**) to put on or remove (clothing) hurriedly. **16** to cause (one's voice) to appear to come from elsewhere. ▸ *noun* **1** an act of throwing or instance of being thrown. **2** a distance thrown. **3** *informal* an article, item, turn, etc: *sell them at £2 a throw.* **4** a decorative fabric covering a piece of furniture, etc. [Anglo-Saxon *thrawan* to twist]

PHRASAL VERBS **throw sth away 1** to discard it or get rid of it. **2** to fail to take advantage of it. **throw sth in 1** to include or add it as a gift or as part of a deal at no extra cost. **2** to contribute (a remark) to a discussion, esp casually. **3** *sport* to return (the ball) to play by throwing it in from the sideline. **throw off 1** to get rid of it: *throw off a cold.* **2** to write or say it in an offhand or careless way. **throw out 1** to expel: *threw the troublemakers out.* **2** to confuse or disconcert: *was thrown out by his attitude.* **3** to get rid of: *threw the old newspapers out.* **throw sb over** to leave or abandon (esp a lover). **throw sth together** to construct it hurriedly or temporarily. **throw up** *informal* to vomit. **throw sth up 1** to give it up or abandon it. **2** to build or erect it hurriedly. **3** to bring up (eg a meal) by vomiting.

throwaway *adj* **1** meant to be thrown away after use. **2** said or done casually or carelessly.

throwback *noun* someone or something that shows or reverts to earlier or ancestral characteristics.

throw-in *noun, sport* in football, basketball, etc: an act of throwing the ball back into play from a sideline.

thru see **through**

thrum *verb* (*thrummed, thrumming*) **1** *tr & intr* to strum idly on (a stringed instrument). **2** *intr* to drum or tap with the fingers. **3** *intr* to hum monotonously. ▸ *noun* repetitive strumming, or the sound of this. [16c: imitating the sound]

thrush[1] *noun* a songbird, typically with brown feathers and a spotted chest. [Anglo-Saxon *thrysce*]

thrush[2] *noun* **1** a fungal infection causing white blisters in the mouth, throat and lips. **2** a similar infection in the vagina. [17c]

thrust *verb* (*thrust*) **1** to push suddenly and violently. **2** (*usu* **thrust on** *or* **upon**) to force (someone) to accept (something). **3** to make (one's way) forcibly. ▸ *noun* **1** a sudden or violent movement forward; a push or lunge. **2** *aeronautics* the force produced by a jet or rocket engine that propels an aircraft or rocket forward. **3** an attack or lunge with a pointed weapon; a stab. **4** a military or verbal attack. **5** the main theme, message or gist, eg, of an argument. [12c: from Norse *thrysta*]

thud *noun* a dull sound like something heavy falling to the ground. ▸ *verb* (***thudded, thudding***) *intr* to move or fall with a thud. [Anglo-Saxon *thyddan* to strike]

thug *noun* a violent or brutal person. ▪ **thuggery** *noun*. ▪ **thuggish** *adj*. [19c: from Hindi *thag* 'thief' or 'cheat']

thulium /'θuːlɪəm, 'θjuː-/ *noun, chem* (symbol **Tm**) a soft silvery-white metallic element of the lanthanide series. [19c: from Latin *Thule*, a northern region thought to be the most northerly in the world]

thumb *noun* **1** in humans: the opposable digit on the inner side of the hand, set lower than the other four digits. **2** a part of a glove or mitten covering this. **3** in other animals: the digit corresponding to the human thumb. ▸ *verb* **1** (*often* **thumb through**) *tr & intr* to turn the pages of (a book or magazine, etc) and glance at the contents. **2** to smudge or wear away with the thumb. **3** (*also* **thumb a lift** *or* **ride**) *tr & intr* to hitchhike: *thumbed to London*. [Anglo-Saxon *thuma*]

IDIOMS **all (fingers and) thumbs** awkward and clumsy. **thumb one's nose** to cock a snook (see under **snook**[2]). **thumbs down** a sign indicating failure, rejection or disapproval. **thumbs up** a sign indicating success, best wishes for success, satisfaction or approval. **under sb's thumb** completely controlled or dominated by them.

thumb index *noun* a series of notches, each with a letter or word in them, cut into the outer edges of the pages of a book, etc to enable quick reference. [20c]

thumb nail *noun* **1** the nail on the thumb. **2** *comput* (*also* **thumbnail**) a small version of a picture or layout. ▸ *adj* brief and concise: *a thumb-nail sketch*.

thumbscrew *noun, hist* an instrument of torture which crushes the thumbs.

thump *noun* a heavy blow, or the dull sound of a blow. ▸ *verb* **1** *tr & intr* to beat or strike with dull-sounding heavy blows. **2** *intr* to throb or beat violently. **3** (*often* **thump out**) to play (a tune), esp on a piano, by pounding heavily on the keys. **4** to move with heavy pounding steps. [16c: imitating the sound]

thumping *informal, adj* very big: *a thumping lie*. ▸ *adv* very: *a pair of thumping great boots*. [16c]

thunder *noun* **1** a deep rumbling or loud cracking sound heard soon after a flash of lightning. **2** a loud deep rumbling noise. ▸ *verb* **1** *intr* of thunder: to sound or rumble. **2** *intr* to make a noise like thunder while moving: *tanks thundering over a bridge*. **3** to say or utter in a loud, often aggressive, voice. ▪ **thundery** *adj*. [Anglo-Saxon *thunor*]

thunderbolt *noun* **1** a flash of lightning coming simultaneously with a crash of thunder. **2** a sudden and unexpected event. **3** a supposed destructive stone or missile, etc falling to earth in a flash of lightning.

thunderclap *noun* **1** a sudden crash of thunder. **2** something startling or unexpected.

thundercloud *noun* a large cloud charged with electricity which produces thunder and lightning.

thundering *informal, adj* very great: *a thundering idiot*. ▸ *adv* very: *a thundering great error*. [16c]

thunderous *adj* **1** like thunder, esp in being very loud: *thunderous applause*. **2** threatening or violent. [16c]

thunderstorm *noun* a storm with thunder and lightning, usu accompanied by heavy rain.

thunderstruck *adj* overcome by surprise; astonished.

Thur. *or* **Thurs.** *abbrev* Thursday.

thurible see **censer**

Thursday *noun* (abbrev **Th.**, **Thur.** *or* **Thurs.**) the fifth day of the week. [Anglo-Saxon *thunresdæg* the day of Thunor (the god of thunder)]

thus *adv* **1** in the way or manner shown or mentioned; in this manner. **2** to this degree, amount or distance: *thus far*. **3** therefore; accordingly. [Anglo-Saxon]

thwack *noun* a blow with something flat, or the noise of this. ▸ *verb* to strike with such a noise. [16c: imitating the sound]

thwart *verb* to prevent or hinder (someone or something). ▸ *noun* a seat for a rower that lies across a boat. [13c: from Norse *thvert* across]

THX *or* **thx** *abbrev* thanks (used in text messages).

thy *adj, old use or dialect, also relig* belonging or relating to **thee**. [12c: from **thine**]

thyme /taɪm/ *noun* a herb or shrub with aromatic leaves used to season food. [14c: from Greek *thymon*]

thymine /'θaɪmiːn/ *noun, biochem* a **pyrimidine** derivative, which is one of the four bases found in the **nucleic acid** DNA. See also **adenine**, **cytosine**, **guanine**. [Late 19c: from Greek *thymos* thymus gland]

thymol *noun* a compound obtained from thyme and used as an antiseptic. [19c]

thymus /'θaɪməs/ *noun* (***thymuses*** *or* ***thymi*** /-maɪ/) (*in full* **thymus gland**) in vertebrates: a gland in the chest controlling the development of lymphatic tissue. [17c: Latin, from Greek *thymos*]

thyroid *noun* (*in full* **thyroid gland**) in vertebrates: a gland in the neck that secretes hormones which control growth, development and metabolic rate. [18c: from Greek *thyreoeides* shield-shaped]

Ti *symbol, chem* titanium.

ti see **te**

tiara *noun* **1** a woman's jewelled head-ornament. **2** a three-tiered crown worn by a pope. [16c: Latin, from Greek]

Tibetan /tɪ'bɛtən/ *adj* belonging or relating to Tibet, an autonomous region in SW China, or to its inhabitants or their language. ▸ *noun* **1** a citizen or inhabitant of, or person born in, Tibet. **2** the official language of Tibet. [18c]

tibia *noun* (***tibias*** *or* ***tibiae*** /'tɪbɪiː/) **1** the inner and usu larger of the two human leg bones between the knee and ankle. **2** the corresponding bone in other vertebrates. Compare **fibula**. ▪ **tibial** *adj*. [18c: Latin, meaning 'shinbone']

tic *noun* a habitual nervous involuntary movement or twitch of a muscle, esp of the face. [19c: French]

tick[1] *noun* **1** a regular tapping or clicking sound, such as that made by a watch or clock. **2** *Brit informal* a moment: *Wait a tick.* **3** a small mark, usu a downward-sloping line with the bottom part bent upwards, used to show that something is correct, to mark off items on a list once they are dealt with, etc. ▸ *verb* **1** *intr* of a clock, etc: to make a tick or ticks. **2** *intr* of time: to pass steadily. **3** to mark with a written tick. **4** (*often* **tick off**) to mark (an item on a list, etc) with a tick, eg, when checking. [15c *tek* a little touch]

IDIOMS **what makes sb tick** *informal* their underlying character and motivation.

PHRASAL VERBS **tick sb off** *informal* to scold them. **tick over 1** to function or work quietly and smoothly at a relatively gentle or moderate rate. **2** of an engine: to idle.

tick[2] *noun* **1** a bloodsucking arachnid living on the skin of dogs, cattle, etc. **2** a bloodsucking fly living on the skin of sheep, birds, etc. [Anglo-Saxon *ticia*]

tick[3] *noun* **1** a strong cover of a mattress, bolster, etc. **2** short for **ticking**. [15c: from Greek *theke* case]

tick[4] *noun, Brit informal* credit: *buy it on tick.* [17c: a shortening of **ticket**]

ticker *noun, informal* the heart.

ticker tape *noun* **1** continuous paper tape with messages, esp up-to-date share prices, printed by a telegraph instrument. **2** this type of paper thrown from windows into the streets to welcome a famous person.

ticket *noun* **1** a card, etc entitling the holder to travel on a bus, train, etc, or to be admitted to a theatre, cinema, sports match, etc, or to use a library, etc. **2** an official notice stating that a traffic offence, eg, speeding or illegal parking, has been committed. **3** a tag or label showing the price, size, etc of the item to which it is attached. **4** *N Am* a list of candidates put up for election by a political party. **5** the policies of a particular political party: *ran on the Republican ticket.* **6** *informal* exactly what is required or best: *just the ticket.* ▸ *verb* to give or attach a ticket or label to. [17c: from French *estiquier* to attach or stick]

ticket tout see **tout** (*noun* sense 1)

ticking *noun* a strong coarse, usu striped, cotton fabric used to cover mattresses, bolsters, etc.

ticking-off *noun, Brit informal* a mild scolding.

tickle *verb* **1** to touch (a person or body part) lightly and provoke a tingling or light prickling sensation, laughter, jerky movements, etc. **2** *intr* of a part of the body: to feel a tingling or light prickling sensation. **3** *informal* to amuse or entertain. ▸ *noun* **1** an act of tickling. **2** a tingling or light prickling sensation. [14c]

IDIOMS **tickled pink** *or* **tickled to death** *informal* very pleased or amused. **tickle sb's fancy** to attract or amuse them in some way.

ticklish *adj* **1** sensitive to tickling. **2** of a problem, etc: needing careful handling.

tidal *adj* relating to or affected by tides. ▪ **tidally** *adv.*

tidal wave *noun* **1** an unusually large ocean wave. **2** a widespread show of feeling, etc: *a tidal wave of protest.*

tiddler *noun, Brit informal* **1** a small fish, esp a stickleback or a minnow. **2** a small person or thing. [19c: perhaps from *tittlebat* a childish form of **stickleback** and influenced by **tiddly**[2]]

tiddly[1] *adj* (**-ier, -iest**) *Brit informal* slightly drunk. [19c]

tiddly[2] *noun* (**-ier, -iest**) *Brit informal* little. [19c]

tiddlywinks *singular noun* a game in which players try to flick small flat discs into a cup using larger discs. [19c: perhaps related to **tiddly**[1]]

tide *noun* **1** the twice-daily rise and fall of the water level in the oceans and seas. **2** the level of water, esp the sea, as affected by this: *high tide.* **3** a sudden or marked trend: *tide of public opinion.* **4** *in compounds* a time or season, esp of some festival: *Whitsuntide.* ▸ *verb, intr* to drift with or be carried on the tide. [Anglo-Saxon *tid*]

PHRASAL VERBS **tide sb over** to help them to deal with a problem, a difficult situation, etc: *Here's some money to tide you over.*

tidemark *noun* **1** a mark showing the highest level that the tide has reached or usu reaches. **2** *Brit informal* **a** a scummy ring round a bath indicating where the water had come up to; **b** a mark on the skin indicating the difference between a washed area and an unwashed one.

tidings *plural noun, old use* news. [Anglo-Saxon *tidung*]

tidy *adj* (**-ier, -iest**) **1** neat and in good order. **2** methodical. **3** *informal* large; considerable: *a tidy sum of money.* ▸ *noun* (**-ies**) **1** *often in compounds* a receptacle for keeping odds and ends in: *a sink-tidy* • *a desk-tidy.* **2** an act or the process of tidying: *gave the room a quick tidy.* **3** *esp US* an ornamental cover for a chair-back. ▸ *verb* (**-ies, -ied**) (*also* **tidy away** *or* **up**) to make neat: *tidied up the toys* • *tidied her hair.* ▪ **tidily** *adv.* ▪ **tidiness** *noun.* [14c: meaning 'timely']

tie *verb* (***tied, tying***) **1** (*also* **tie up**) to fasten with a string, ribbon, rope, etc. **2 a** to make (string, ribbon, etc) into a bow or knot; **b** to make (a bow or knot) in. **3** to be fastened in a specified way: *a dress that ties at the back.* **4** (*usu* **tie with**) *intr* to have the same score or final position as (another competitor or entrant) in a game or contest, etc. **5** to limit or restrict. **6** *music* **a** to mark (notes of the same pitch) with a curved line showing that they are to be played as a continuous sound rather than individually; **b** to play (notes of the same pitch) in this way. ▸ *noun* **1** a narrow strip of material worn, esp by men, round the neck under a shirt collar and tied in a knot or bow at the front. **2** a strip of ribbon, rope, cord or chain, etc for binding and fastening. **3** something that limits or restricts. **4** a link or bond: *ties of friendship.* **5 a** a match or competition, etc in which the result is an equal score for both sides; **b** the score or result achieved. **6** *Brit* a game or match to be played, esp in a knockout competition: *The third round ties were all postponed.* **7** a rod or beam holding parts of a structure together. **8** *music* a curved line above two or more notes of the same pitch showing that they are to be played as a continuous sound rather than individually. [Anglo-Saxon *tiegan*]

PHRASAL VERBS **tie in** *or* **up with sth** to be in or be brought into connection with it; to correspond or be made to correspond with it. **tie up** to moor or dock. **tie sb** *or* **sth up 1** to keep them busy. **2** to block or restrict their movement or progress.

tie-break *or* **tie-breaker** *noun* an extra game, series of games, question, etc to decide a drawn match, etc.

tied cottage *noun, Brit* a cottage occupied by a tenant during the period that they are employed by its owner.

tied house *noun, Brit* a public house which may only sell the beer of a particular brewery.

tie-dye *noun* a technique of dyeing fabrics in which parts of the fabric are tied tightly to stop them absorbing the dye, so that a swirly pattern is produced. ▸ *verb* to dye like this. [20c]

tie-in *noun* **1** a connection or link. **2** something presented at the same time as something else, eg a book published to coincide with a TV programme.

tie-pin *noun* an ornamental pin fixed to a tie to hold it in place.

tier /tɪə(r)/ *noun* a level, rank, row, etc, esp one of several positioned one above another to form a structure: *a wedding cake with three tiers* • *tiers of seats*. [16c: from French *tire* sequence]

tierce see **terce**

tiff *noun* a slight petty quarrel. [18c]

tiffin *noun, Anglo-Indian* a light midday meal. [18c: from obsolete *tiff* to sip]

tig see under **tag**[2]

tiger *noun* **1** a large carnivorous Asian member of the cat family with a fawn or reddish coat, with black or brownish-black transverse stripes. See also **tigress**. **2** a fierce cruel person. [13c: from French *tigre*, from Greek *tigris*]

tight *adj* **1** fitting very or too closely. **2** stretched so as not to be loose; tense; taut. **3** fixed or held firmly in place: *a tight knot*. **4** *usu in compounds* preventing the passage of air, water, etc: *watertight*. **5** difficult or awkward: *in a tight spot*. **6** strictly and carefully controlled. **7** of a contest or match: closely or evenly fought. **8** of a schedule or timetable, etc: not allowing much time. **9** *informal* mean; miserly: *He's so tight with his money*. **10** *informal* drunk. **11** of money or some commodity: in short supply; difficult to obtain. ▸ *adv* tightly; soundly; completely: *sleep tight*. ▪ **tightly** *adv*. ▪ **tightness** *noun*. [14c: from Norse *thettr*]

tighten *verb, tr & intr* to make or become tight or tighter. [18c]

IDIOMS **tighten one's belt** *informal* to live more economically.

tight-fisted *adj* mean with money, etc.

tight-knit *or* **tightly-knit** *adj* closely organized or united: *a tight-knit family*.

tight-lipped *adj* saying or revealing nothing.

tightrope *noun* a tightly stretched rope or wire on which acrobats perform.

tights *plural noun* a close-fitting garment covering the feet, legs and body up to the waist, worn esp by women, dancers, acrobats, etc.

tigress *noun* **1** a female tiger. **2** a fierce or passionate woman.

tike another spelling of **tyke**

tikka *adj* of meat in Indian cookery: having been marinated in yoghurt and spices. [20c: Hindi]

tilde /ˈtɪldə/ *noun* a mark (~) placed over *n* in Spanish to show that it is pronounced *ny* and over *a* and *o* in Portuguese to show they are nasalized. [19c: Spanish, from Latin *titulus* **title**]

tile *noun* **1** a flat thin slab of fired clay, or a similar one of cork or linoleum, used to cover roofs, floors and walls, etc. **2** a small flat rectangular piece used in some games. ▸ *verb* to cover with tiles. ▪ **tiler** *noun*. ▪ **tiling** *noun*. [Anglo-Saxon *tigele*: from Latin *tegere* to cover]

IDIOMS **on the tiles** having a wild social time.

till[1] *prep* up to the time of: *wait till tomorrow*. ▸ *conj* up to the time when: *go on till you reach the station*. See also **until**. [Anglo-Saxon *til*]

till[2] *noun* a container or drawer where money taken from customers is put, now usu part of a **cash register**. [15c: meaning 'a drawer for valuables']

till[3] *verb* to prepare and cultivate (soil or land) for the growing of crops. [Anglo-Saxon *tilian* to strive]

tillage *noun* **1** the preparing and cultivating of land for crops. **2** land which has been tilled.

tiller *noun* a lever used to turn the rudder of a boat. [14c: from French *telier* weaver's beam]

tilt *verb* **1** *tr & intr* to slope or cause to slope. **2** (*often* **tilt at**) *intr* to charge or attack. **3** *intr* to fight on horseback with a lance; to joust. ▸ *noun* **1** a sloping position or angle. **2** an act of tilting. **3** a joust. [Anglo-Saxon *tealt* tottering]

IDIOMS **at full tilt** at full speed or with full force.

tilth *noun* **1** cultivation. **2** the condition of tilled soil. [Anglo-Saxon *tilthe*]

timber *noun* **1** wood, esp when prepared for or used in building or carpentry. **2** trees suitable for this. **3** a wooden beam in the framework, esp of a ship or house. ▸ *exclam* a warning cry that a tree has been cut and is about to fall. ▪ **timbering** *noun*. [Anglo-Saxon]

timbered *adj* **1** built completely or partly of wood. **2** of land: covered with trees; wooded.

timbre /ˈtambə(r)/ *noun* the distinctive quality of the tone produced by a musical instrument or voice, as opposed to pitch and loudness. [19c: French, meaning 'bell', from Greek *tympanon* drum]

time *noun* **1** the continuous passing and succession of minutes, days and years, etc. **2** a particular point in time expressed in hours and minutes, or days, months and years, as shown on a clock, watch, calendar, etc. **3** a specified system for reckoning or expressing time: *Eastern European Time*. **4** (*also* **times**) a point or period of time: *at the time of her marriage* • *olden times*. **5** *in compounds* a period of time allocated to an activity, etc: *playtime* • *lunchtime*. **6** an unspecified interval or period: *stayed there for a time*. **7** one of a number or series of occasions or repeated actions: *been to Spain three times*. **8** a period or occasion of a specified kind: *a good time* • *hard times*. **9** a particular period being considered, esp the present. **10** *informal* a prison sentence: *do time*. **11** an apprenticeship: *served her time and became a motor mechanic*. **12** the point at which something, eg, a match, game, etc, ends or must end. **13** *Brit* the time when a public house must close. **14** *music* a specified rhythm or speed: *waltz time*. ▸ *verb* **1** to measure the time taken by (an event or journey, etc). **2** to arrange, set or choose the time for (a journey, meeting, etc). **3** *tr & intr* to keep or beat or cause to keep or beat time. [Anglo-Saxon *tima*]

IDIOMS **against time** with as much speed as possible. **ahead of time** earlier than expected or necessary. **all in good time** in due course; soon enough. **all the time** continually. **at times** occasionally; sometimes. **behind time** late. **behind the times** out of date; old-fashioned. **for the time being** meanwhile; for the moment. **from time to time** occasionally; sometimes. **have no time for sb** *or* **sth** to have no interest in or patience with them or it; to despise them or it. **have the time of one's life** to enjoy oneself very much. **in good time** early. **in no time** very quickly. **in one's own time 1** in one's spare time when not at work. **2** at the speed one prefers. **in time** early enough. **in time with sb** *or* **sth** at the same speed or rhythm as them or it. **keep time 1** to correctly follow the required rhythm of a piece of music. **2** of a watch or clock: to function accurately. **kill time** to pass time aimlessly. **make good time** to travel as quickly as, or more quickly than, expected or hoped. **no time at all** *informal* a very short time. **on time** at the right time; not late. **pass the time of day** to exchange greetings and have a brief casual conversation. **take one's time** to work, etc as slowly as one wishes. **time and time again** again and again; repeatedly.

time-and-motion study *noun* an examination and assessment of the way work is done in a factory, etc with a view to increasing efficiency.

time bomb *noun* a bomb that has been set to explode at a particular preset time.

time capsule *noun* a box containing objects chosen as typical of the current age, buried or otherwise preserved for discovery in the future.

time-consuming *adj* taking up a lot of time.

time-honoured *adj* respected and upheld because of custom or tradition.

timekeeper *noun* **1** someone who records time, eg, as worked by employees or taken by a competitor in a game, etc. **2** a clock, watch, or person thought of in terms of accuracy or punctuality: *a good timekeeper.* ▪ **timekeeping** *noun.* [17c: meaning 'timepiece']

timeless *adj* **1** not belonging to or typical of any particular time or date. **2** unaffected by time; ageless; eternal. ▪ **timelessly** *adv.* ▪ **timelessness** *noun.*

timely *adj* (***-ier, -iest***) coming at the right or a suitable moment; opportune. ▪ **timeliness** *noun.*

time out *noun, N Am* **1** a brief pause or period of rest. **2** *sport* a short break during a match, etc for discussion of tactics or for rest, etc.

timepiece *noun* an instrument for keeping time, such as a watch or clock.

timer *noun* a device like a clock which switches an appliance on or off at preset times, or which makes a sound when a set amount of time has passed.

times *prep* expressing multiplication: *three times two makes six.*

timescale *noun* the time envisaged for the completion of a particular project or stage of a project.

time-served *adj* having completed an apprenticeship; fully trained: *a time-served electrician.*

timeserver *noun* someone who changes their behaviour or opinions to fit those held by people in general or by someone in authority. [16c]

time-sharing *noun* **1** a scheme whereby someone buys the right to use a holiday home for the same specified period each year for an agreed number of years. **2** *comput* a system which allows many users with individual terminals to use a single computer at the same time.

time signature *noun, music* a sign, usu placed after a clef, indicating rhythm.

timetable *noun* **1** a list of the departure and arrival times of trains, buses, etc. **2** a plan showing the order of events, esp of classes in a school. ▸ *verb* to arrange or include in a timetable; to schedule or plan.

timeworn *adj* worn out through long use; old.

time zone *noun* any one of the 24 more or less parallel sections into which the world is divided longitudinally, with all places within a given zone having the same standard time. [20c]

timid *adj* easily frightened or alarmed; nervous; shy. ▪ **timidity** *noun.* [16c: from Latin *timidus*]

timing *noun* the regulating and co-ordinating of actions, events, etc to achieve the best possible effect.

timorous *adj* very timid; frightened. ▪ **timorousness** *noun.* [15c: ultimately from Latin *timere* to fear]

timpani *or* **tympani** /ˈtɪmpənɪ/ *plural noun* a set of two or three kettledrums. ▪ **timpanist** *or* **tympanist** *noun.* [16c: Italian, pl of *timpano*]

tin *noun* **1** *chem* (symbol **Sn**) a soft silvery-white metallic element used in alloys, eg, bronze, pewter and solder, and forming tin plate. **2** an airtight metal container for storing food: *a biscuit tin.* **3** a sealed container for preserving food: *a tin of baked beans.* ▸ *verb* (***tinned, tinning***) to pack (food) in a tin. ▪ **tinned** *adj.* [Anglo-Saxon]

tincture *noun* **1** a slight flavour, trace or addition. **2** a slight trace of colour; hue; tinge. **3** a solution of a drug in alcohol for medicinal use. [14c: from Latin *tinctura* dyeing]

tinder *noun* dry material, esp wood, which is easily set alight and can be used as kindling. [Anglo-Saxon]

tinderbox *noun, hist* a box containing tinder, a flint and steel for striking a spark to light a fire.

tine *noun* a slender prong, eg, of a comb, fork or antler. [Anglo-Saxon *tind*]

tinfoil *noun* aluminium or other metal in the form of thin, paper-like sheets, used esp for wrapping food.

ting *noun* a tinkling sound, eg, made by a small bell. ▸ *verb, tr & intr* to produce or cause to produce this sound. [15c: imitating the sound]

tinge *noun* **1** a trace or slight amount of colour. **2** a trace or hint of (a quality, feeling, etc). ▸ *verb* **1** to give a slight colour to. **2** to give a trace or hint of a feeling or quality, etc to. [15c: from Latin *tingere* to colour]

tingle *verb, tr & intr* to feel or cause to feel a prickling or slightly stinging sensation, eg, due to cold, embarrassment, etc. ▸ *noun* a prickling or slightly stinging sensation. ▪ **tingling** *adj.* [14c: perhaps a variant of **tinkle**]

tin god *noun* **1** a self-important pompous person. **2** someone or something held in excessively or unjustifiably high esteem.

tinker *noun* **1** a travelling mender of pots, pans and other household utensils. **2** *informal* a mischievous or impish person, esp a child. ▸ *verb, intr* to work in an unskilled way, esp in trying to make minor adjustments or improvements: *tinkering with that old car.* [13c]

tinkle *verb, tr & intr* to make or cause to make a succession of jingling sounds. ▸ *noun* **1** a jingling sound. **2** *Brit informal* a telephone call: *I'll give you a tinkle tomorrow.* ▪ **tinkly** *adj.* [14c: imitating the sound]

tinnitus *noun, med* an abnormal and sometimes constant ringing, buzzing or whistling, etc noise in the ears, not caused by any external sound. [19c: from Latin *tinnire* to ring]

tinny *adj* (***-ier, -iest***) **1** relating to or resembling tin. **2** flimsy and insubstantial: *a tinny old car.* **3** of sound: thin and high-pitched. ▸ *noun* (***-ies***) *Aust slang* a can of beer.

tin-opener *noun* a device for opening tins of food.

tin plate *noun* thin sheet iron or steel coated with tin. ▸ *verb* (**tin-plate**) to cover with a layer of tin.

tinpot *adj, Brit informal* cheap or poor quality; paltry or contemptible: *tinpot dictator.* [19c]

tinsel *noun* **1** a long decorative strip of glittering metal threads, used esp at Christmas. **2** something which is cheap and gaudy. ▸ *adj* relating to or resembling tinsel. ▪ **tinselly** *adj.* [16c: from French *estincele* a spark]

tinsmith *noun* a worker in tin and tin plate.

tint *noun* **1** a variety or slightly different shade of a colour, esp one made lighter by adding white. **2** a pale or faint colour. **3** a hair dye. ▸ *verb* to give a tint to (hair, etc); to colour slightly. [18c: from Latin *tingere* to colour]

tintinnabulation *noun* a ringing of bells. [19c: from Latin *tintinnabulum* a tinkling bell]

tiny *adj* (***-ier, -iest***) very small. [16c]

-tion *suffix, forming nouns, signifying* action, result, condition or state, etc: *exploration* • *condemnation.* [From Latin *-tionem*]

tip[1] *noun* **1** an end or furthermost point of something: *the tips of her fingers.* **2** a small piece forming an end or point: *a rubber tip on a walking-stick.* **3** a top or summit. **4** a leaf bud of tea. ▸ *verb* (***tipped, tipping***) to put or form a tip on. [15c: from Norse *typpa*]
IDIOMS **on the tip of one's tongue** about to be said, but not able to be because not quite remembered.

tip[2] *verb* (***tipped, tipping***) **1** *tr & intr* to lean or cause to lean. **2** (*also* **tip out**) to empty (from a container, etc): *tipped the dirty water out of the bucket.* **3** *Brit* to dump (rubbish). ▸ *noun* **1** a place for tipping rubbish, etc. **2** *informal* a very untidy place. [14c: meaning 'to overturn']

tip[3] *noun* **1** money given to a servant or waiter, etc in return for service done well. **2** a piece of useful information. **3** a piece of inside information, eg, the name of a horse likely to win a race. ▸ *verb* (***tipped, tipping***) to give a tip to. [17c: perhaps a special use of **tip[4]**]
PHRASAL VERBS **tip sb off** to give them a piece of useful or secret information.

tip[4] *noun* a light blow or tap. ▸ *verb* (***tipped, tipping***) to hit or strike lightly. [15c]
IDIOMS **tip the balance** to make the critical difference.

tip-off *noun* a piece of useful or secret information, or the disclosing of this. [20c]

tip of the iceberg *noun* a small part of something much bigger, most of which is still to be discovered or dealt with.

tippet *noun* **1** a woman's shoulder-cape made from fur or cloth. **2** a long band of cloth or fur worn by some of the clergy. [14c: prob from **tip[1]**]

tipple *informal, verb, tr & intr* to drink (alcohol) regularly, esp in relatively small amounts. ▸ *noun* alcoholic drink. ▪ **tippler** *noun.* [15c]

tipster *noun* someone who gives tips, esp as to which horses to bet on. [19c]

tipsy *adj, informal* (***-ier, -iest***) slightly drunk. ▪ **tipsily** *adv.* ▪ **tipsiness** *noun.* [16c: prob from **tip[2]**]

tiptoe *verb* (***tiptoed, tiptoeing***) *intr* to walk quietly or stealthily on the tips of the toes. ▸ *noun* (*often* **tiptoes**) the tips of the toes. ▸ *adv* (*usu* **on tiptoe**) on the tips of the toes. [14c as *noun*; 17c as *verb*]

tip-top *informal, adj, adv* excellent; first-class. ▸ *noun* the very best; the height of excellence. [18c]

tirade *noun* a long angry speech, harangue or denunciation. [19c: French, meaning 'a long speech']

tire[1] *verb* **1** *tr & intr* to make or become physically or mentally weary. **2** (**tire of**) to lose patience with or become bored with. [Anglo-Saxon *teorian*]

tire[2] *noun* the *US* spelling of **tyre.** [15c]

tired *adj* **1** wearied; exhausted. **2** lacking freshness or showing the effects of time and wear: *tired, lazy prose.* ▪ **tiredly** *adv.* ▪ **tiredness** *noun.*
IDIOMS **be tired of** to have had enough of.

tireless *adj* never becoming weary or exhausted. ▪ **tirelessly** *adv.* [16c]

tiresome *adj* troublesome and irritating; annoying; tedious. [16c]

'tis *contraction, old use or poetic* it is.

tissue *noun* **1** a group of plant or animal cells with a similar structure and particular function: *muscle tissue.* **2** thin soft disposable paper used as a handkerchief or as toilet paper or a piece of this. **3** (*also* **tissue paper**) fine thin soft paper, used for wrapping, etc. **4** an interwoven mass or collection: *a tissue of lies.* [14c: from French *tissu* woven cloth]

tissue culture *noun, biol* **1** the growth of isolated plant or animal cells, tissues or organs under controlled conditions. **2** the tissue grown.

tit[1] *noun* a small songbird. [16c]

tit[2] *noun* a blow or injury. [16c]
IDIOMS **tit for tat** blow for blow; with repayment of an injury by an injury.

titan *noun* someone or something of very great strength, size, intellect or importance. [19c: named after the Titans, in Greek mythology, a family of giants]

titanic *adj* having great strength or size; gigantic. [18c]

titanium /tɪˈteɪnɪəm/ *noun, chem* (symbol **Ti**) a silvery-white metallic element used in making alloys for components of aircraft, missiles, etc. [18c: see **titan**]

titbit *noun* a choice or small tasty morsel of something, eg, food or gossip. [17c]

titchy *adj* (***-ier, -iest***) *Brit informal* very small.

tithe *noun* **1** (*often* **tithes**) *hist* a tenth part of someone's annual income or produce, paid as a tax to support the church or clergy. **2** a tenth part. ▸ *verb* **1** to demand a tithe or tithes from. **2** *tr & intr* to pay a tithe or tithes. ▪ **tithable** *adj.* [Anglo-Saxon *teotha*]

Titian /ˈtɪʃən/ *adj* of a bright reddish-gold colour: *Titian hair.* [19c: named after the painter Tiziano Vecellio]

titillate *verb* **1** to excite, esp in a mildly erotic way. **2** to tickle. ▪ **titillating** *adj.* ▪ **titillation** *noun.* [17c: from Latin *titillare* to tickle]

titivate *verb, tr & intr, informal* to smarten up or put the finishing touches to. ▪ **titivation** *noun.* [19c: from earlier *tidivate*, from **tidy**, modelled on **elevate**, **renovate**, etc]

title *noun* **1** the distinguishing name of a book, play, work of art, piece of music, etc. **2** an often descriptive heading, eg, of a chapter in a book or a legal document. **3** a word used before someone's name to show acquired or inherited rank, an honour, occupation, marital status, etc. **4** (**titles**) written material on film giving credits or dialogue, etc. **5** *law* a right to the possession or ownership of property. **6** *sport* a championship: *St Johnstone won the title.* **7** a book or publication. ▸ *verb* to give a title to. [13c: from Latin *titulus*]

titled *adj* having a title of nobility or rank.

title deed *noun* a document that proves legal ownership, esp of real property.

title role *noun* the name of the character in a play, film, etc that gives it its title, eg, King Lear.

titrate /ˈtaɪtreɪt/ *verb, chem* to determine the concentration of (a chemical substance in a solution) by adding measured amounts of another solution of known concentration. ▪ **titration** *noun*. [19c: from French *titre* title]

titre *noun* **1** *chem* the concentration of a solution as determined by titration. **2** *biol* the concentration of a virus present in a suspension. **3** the concentration of an antibody in a sample of serum.

titter *informal, verb, intr* to giggle or snigger in a stifled way. ▸ *noun* an instance or noise of this. [17c: imitating the sound]

tittle *noun* a very small insignificant amount. [14c: from Latin *titulus* title]

tittle-tattle *noun* idle or petty gossip or chatter. ▸ *verb, intr* to gossip or chatter idly. [16c]

titular *adj* **1** having the title of an office or position, but none of the authority or duties. **2** relating to a title. [17c: from Latin *titulus* title]

tizzy *or* **tizz** *noun* (***tizzies*** *or* ***tizzes***) *informal* a nervous highly excited or confused state: *got into a tizzy.* [20c]

T-junction *noun* a junction at which one road meets another at a right angle but does not cross it. [20c]

Tl *symbol, chem* thallium.

TLC *abbrev, informal* tender loving care.

Tm *symbol, chem* thulium.

TNT *abbrev* trinitrotoluene.

to *prep* **1** towards; in the direction of, or with the destination of somewhere or something: *go to the shop.* **2** used to express as a resulting condition, aim or purpose: *boil the fruit to a pulp • to my surprise.* **3** as far as; until: *from beginning to end • bears the scars to this day.* **4** used to introduce the indirect object of a verb: *He sent it to us.* **5** used to express addition: *add one to ten.* **6** used to express attachment, connection, contact or possession: *put his ear to the door.* **7** before the hour of: *ten minutes to three.* **8** used to express response or reaction to a situation or event, etc: *rise to the occasion • dance to the music.* **9** used to express comparison or proportion: *won by two goals to one • second to none.* **10** used before an infinitive or instead of a complete infinitive: *He asked her to stay, but she didn't want to.* ▸ *adv* **1** in or into a nearly closed position: *pulled the window to.* **2** back into consciousness: *He came to a few minutes later.* **3** near at hand. **4** in the direction required: *hove to.* [Anglo-Saxon]

IDIOMS **to and fro** backwards and forwards.

toad *noun* **1** a tailless amphibian, with a short squat head and body, and moist skin which may contain poison glands. **2** an obnoxious or repellent person. [Anglo-Saxon *tade*]

toad-in-the-hole *noun, Brit* a dish of sausages cooked in batter. [18c]

toadstool *noun* a fungus with a stalk and a spore-bearing cap, most varieties of which are poisonous or inedible. See also **mushroom**. [14c]

toady *noun* (***-ies***) someone who flatters someone else, does everything they want and hangs on their every word; a sycophant. ▸ *verb* (***-ies, -ied***) *tr & intr* (**toady to sb**) to flatter them and behave obsequiously towards them. ▪ **toadyism** *noun*. [19c: shortened from *toadeater*, an assistant to a charlatan, who would pretend to eat poisonous toads so that his master could show his expertise in ridding the body of poison]

toast *verb* **1** **a** to make (bread, cheese, a marshmallow, etc) brown by exposing to direct heat; **b** *intr* to become brown in this way. **2** *tr & intr* to make or become warm by being exposed to heat. **3** to drink ceremonially in honour of or to the health or future success of (someone or something). ▸ *noun* **1** bread which has been browned by exposure to direct heat. **2** **a** an act of toasting someone, etc; **b** someone who is the subject of a toast. **3** a highly regarded person or thing: *Her singing is the toast of the festival.* **4** a wish conveyed when toasting someone. [14c: ultimately from Latin *torrere* to parch]

toaster *noun* an electric machine for toasting bread.

toastie *noun, informal* a toasted sandwich.

toastmaster *or* **toastmistress** *noun* a man or woman who proposes the toasts at a ceremonial dinner.

tobacco *noun* (***tobaccos*** *or* ***tobaccoes***) **1** a plant with very large leaves. **2** the dried nicotine-containing leaves of some varieties of this plant, used in making cigarettes, cigars, pipe tobacco and snuff. [16c: from Spanish *tabaco*]

tobacconist *noun* a person or shop selling tobacco, cigarettes, cigars and pipes, etc.

-to-be *adj, in compounds* future; soon to become: a *bride-to-be.*

toboggan *noun* a long light sledge for riding over snow and ice. ▸ *verb, intr* to ride on a toboggan. [19c: from Canadian French *tabaganne*]

toby jug *noun* a jug in the shape of a stout man wearing a three-cornered hat. Often shortened to **toby**. [19c: from the name Toby]

toccata /tɒˈkɑːtə/ *noun* a piece of music for a keyboard instrument intended to show off the performer's skill. [18c: Italian, from Latin *toccare* to touch]

tocopherol /tɒˈkɒfərɒl/ *noun* **vitamin E**. [20c: from Greek *tokos* offspring + *pherein* to bear]

tocsin *noun* an alarm bell or warning signal. [16c: French, from Provençal *tocar* to touch + *senh* signal]

tod *noun, Brit informal.*

IDIOMS **on one's tod** alone.

today *noun* **1** this day. **2** the present time. ▸ *adv* **1** on or during this day. **2** nowadays; at the present time: *It doesn't happen much today.* [Anglo-Saxon *to dæg*]

toddle *verb, intr* **1** to walk with unsteady steps, as or like a young child. **2** *informal* to take a casual walk. **3** (*usu* **toddle off**) *informal* to leave; to depart. ▸ *noun* **1** a toddling walk. **2** *informal* a casual walk or stroll. [16c]

toddler *noun* a child who is just beginning, or has just learned, to walk. [18c]

toddy *noun* (**-*ies***) an alcoholic drink with added sugar, hot water, lemon juice and sometimes spices. [17c: from Hindi *tari*, from *tar* palm]

to-do *noun, informal* a fuss or commotion. [16c]

toe *noun* **1 a** one of the five digits at the end of the human foot; **b** a corresponding digit in an animal. **2** a part of a shoe, sock, etc covering the toes. **3** the lower end of a tool, area of land, etc. ▸ *verb* (***toed, toeing***) to kick, strike or touch with the toes. [Anglo-Saxon *ta*]

IDIOMS **on one's toes** alert and ready for action. **toe the line** *informal* to act according to the rules.

toecap *noun* a reinforced covering on the toe of a boot or shoe.

toehold *noun* **1** a place where toes can grip, eg, when climbing. **2** a start or small beginning: *got a toehold in the web designing business.*

toenail *noun* a nail covering the tip of a toe.

toerag *noun, Brit informal* **1** a rascal. **2** a despicable or contemptible person. [19c: orig meaning 'beggar', from the rags wrapped around beggars' feet]

toff *noun, Brit slang* an upper-class and usu smartly dressed person. [19c: perhaps from *tuft* a titled undergraduate, from the gold tassel which was formerly worn on the cap]

toffee *noun* **1** a sticky sweet, made by boiling sugar and butter. **2** a piece of this. [19c: from earlier *taffy*]

toffee-nosed *adj, Brit informal* snobbish; stuck-up.

tofu *noun* a curd made from soya beans. [19c: Japanese, from Chinese *dou fu* rotten beans]

tog[1] *noun* (**togs**) clothes. [18c: a shortening of the obsolete slang *togemans* coat]

tog[2] *noun* a unit for measuring the warmth of fabrics, clothes, duvets, etc. [20c: perhaps from **tog**[1]]

toga /'toʊɡə/ *noun, hist* an ancient Roman's loose outer garment. ▪ **togaed** *or* **toga'd** *adj.* [16c: Latin]

together *adv* **1** with someone or something else; in company: *travel together.* **2** at the same time: *all arrived together.* **3** so as to be in contact, joined or united. **4** by action with one or more other people: *Together we managed to persuade him.* **5** in or into one place: *gather together.* **6** continuously; at a time: *for hours together.* **7** *informal* into a proper or suitable order or state of being organized: *get things together.* ▸ *adj, informal* well organized; competent. [Anglo-Saxon *to gæthere*]

IDIOMS **together with sb** *or* **sth** as well or in addition to them or it.

togetherness *noun* a feeling of closeness, mutual understanding, and of belonging together.

toggle *noun* **1** a fastening, eg, for garments, consisting of a small bar passed through a loop. **2** a pin, bar or crosspiece placed through a link in a chain or a loop in a rope, etc to prevent the chain or rope, etc from slipping. **3** *comput* a keyboard command which allows the user to switch between one mode and another. ▸ *verb* **1** to provide or fasten (something) with a toggle. **2** *comput* to use a toggle to switch between one mode and another. [18c: orig a nautical term]

toil *verb, intr* **1** to work long and hard. **2** to make progress or move forwards with great difficulty or effort. ▸ *noun* long hard work. [16c: from French *toiler* to contend]

toilet *noun* **1** a **lavatory**. **2** (*also* **toilette**) the process of washing, dressing, arranging one's hair. [16c: from French *toilette* a little cloth]

toilet paper *or* **toilet tissue** *noun* paper used for cleaning oneself after urination and defecation.

toiletry *noun* (**-*ies***) an article or cosmetic used when washing, arranging the hair, making up, etc.

toilet water *noun* a light perfume similar to **eau de Cologne**.

toilsome *adj* involving long hard work. [16c]

token *noun* **1** a mark, sign or distinctive feature. **2** something serving as a reminder, etc: *a token of my esteem.* **3** a voucher worth a specified amount that can be exchanged for goods to the same value: *book token.* **4** a small coin-like piece of metal or plastic, used instead of money, eg, in a gambling machine. ▸ *adj* **1** nominal; of no real value: *token gesture.* **2** present, included, etc only for the sake of appearances: *a token woman.* [Anglo-Saxon *tacen*]

IDIOMS **by the same token** also; in addition; for the same reason.

tokenism *noun* the principle or practice of doing no more than the minimum in a particular area, in pretence that one is committed to it, eg, employing one black person in a company to avoid charges of racism. [20c; see **token** (*adj*)]

told *past tense & past participle of* **tell**

tolerable *adj* **1** able to be endured. **2** fairly good. ▪ **tolerably** *adv.*

tolerance *noun* **1** the ability to be fair towards and accepting of other people's beliefs or opinions. **2** the ability to resist or endure pain or hardship. **3** *med* someone's ability to adapt to the effects of a prescribed or illegal drug, so that increasingly larger doses are required to produce the same effect. **4** *biol* lack of reactivity to an **antigen** that would normally cause an immune response. **5** *biol* the ability of a plant or animal to survive extreme conditions, eg drought or low temperature.

tolerant *adj* **1** tolerating the beliefs and opinions of others. **2** capable of enduring unfavourable conditions, etc. **3** indulgent; permissive. ▪ **tolerantly** *adv.*

tolerate *verb* **1** to endure. **2** to be able to resist the effects of (a drug). **3** to treat fairly and accept. ▪ **toleration** *noun.* [16c: from Latin *tolerare, toleratum*]

toll[1] *verb* **1** *tr & intr* to ring (a bell) with slow measured strokes. **2** of a bell: to announce, signal or summon by ringing with slow measured strokes. ▸ *noun* an act or the sound of tolling. [15c]

toll[2] *noun* **1** a fee or tax paid for the use of something, eg, a bridge, road, etc. **2** a cost, eg, in damage, injury, lives lost, esp in a war, disaster, etc. [Anglo-Saxon]

tollbridge *noun* a bridge at which a toll is charged.

tollgate *noun* a gate or barrier across a road or bridge which is not lifted until travellers have paid the toll.

tolu /'toʊljuː/ *noun* a sweet-smelling balsam obtained from a S American tree, used in the manufacture of medicine and perfume. [17c: named after Santiago de Tolu, Columbia]

toluene /'tɒljʊiːn/ *noun, chem* a colourless flammable liquid derived from benzene and used in the manufacture of explosives, etc. [19c]

tom *noun* a male of various animals, esp a male cat. [18c: short form of the name Thomas]

tomahawk *noun* a small axe used as a weapon by some Native Americans. [17c: from Algonquian (a family of Native American languages) *tamahaac*]

tomato *noun* (***tomatoes***) **1** a round fleshy red, orange or yellow fruit, eaten raw, in salads, etc, or cooked. **2** a plant of the nightshade family producing this fruit. [17c: from Nahuatl *tomatl*]

tomb /tuːm/ *noun* **1** a chamber or vault for a dead body. **2** a hole cut in the earth or rock for a dead body. **3** (**the tomb**) *poetic* death. [13c: from Greek *tymbos*]

tombola *noun* a lottery in which winning tickets are drawn from a revolving drum. [19c: from Italian *tombolare* to tumble]

tombolo *noun* a bar of sand or gravel connecting an island with another or with the mainland. [From Italian, from Latin *tumulus* mound]

tomboy *noun* a girl who dresses or behaves in a boyish way. ▪ **tomboyish** *adj.* [16c]

tombstone *noun* an ornamental stone placed over a grave, often having the dead person's name, dates, etc engraved on it.

tomcat *noun* a male cat.

tome *noun* a large, heavy and usu learned book. [16c: French, from Greek *tomos* slice]

tomfool *noun* an absolute fool. [14c]

tomfoolery *noun* (***-ies***) **1** stupid or foolish behaviour; nonsense. **2** an instance of this. [19c]

Tommy *noun* (***-ies***) *informal* a private in the British army. [19c: from Tommy Atkins, the name used on specimens of official forms]

tommygun *noun* a type of submachine-gun. [20c: named after J T Thompson, its American inventor]

tomography *noun, med* a diagnostic scanning technique, often referred to as a CT (computed tomography) or CAT (computer-aided tomography) scan, giving clear images of internal structures in a single plane of a body tissue. [20c: from Greek *tomos* cut]

tomorrow *noun* **1** the day after today. **2** the future. ▸ *adv* **1** on the day after today. **2** in the future. [Anglo-Saxon *to morgen*]

tomtit *noun* a tit, esp a blue tit. [18c]

tom-tom *noun* a tall drum, usu with a small head, which is beaten with the hands. [17c: from Hindi *tam-tam*, imitating the sound]

-tomy *combining form* (***-tomies***) *forming nouns, denoting* **1** removal by surgery: *appendectomy.* **2** a surgical incision: *laparotomy.* **3** a cutting up: *anatomy.* **4** a division into parts: *dichotomy.* [From Greek *temnein* to cut]

ton *noun* **1** (*in full* **long ton**) *Brit* a unit of weight equal to 2240 lb (approximately 1016.06kg). **2** (*in full* **short ton**) *N Am* a unit of weight equal to 2000 lb (approximately 907.2kg). **3** (*in full* **metric ton**) a unit of weight equal to 1000kg (approximately 2204.6 lb). Also called **tonne. 4** (*in full* **displacement ton**) a unit used to measure the amount of water a ship displaces, equal to 2240 lb or 35 cubic feet of seawater. **5** (*in full* **register ton**) a unit used to measure a ship's internal capacity, equal to 100 cubic feet. **6** (*in full* **freight ton**) a unit for measuring the space taken up by cargo, equal to 40 cubic feet. **7** (*usu* **tons**) *informal* a lot. **8** *informal* a speed, score or sum, etc of 100. See also **tonnage.** [14c: a variant of **tun**]

tonal *adj* belonging or relating to tone or tonality.

tonality *noun* (***-ies***) **1** *music* the organization of all of the notes and chords of a piece of music in relation to a single tonic. **2** the colour scheme and tones used in a painting, etc.

tone *noun* **1** a musical or vocal sound with reference to its quality and pitch. **2** *music* a sound that has a definite pitch. **3** a quality or character of the voice expressing a particular feeling or mood, etc. **4** the general character or style of spoken or written expression. **5** *music* the interval between, or equivalent to that between, the first two notes of the major scale. **6** high quality, style or character: *His coarse jokes lowered the tone of the meeting.* **7** the quality, tint or shade of a colour. **8** the harmony or general effect of colours. **9** firmness of the body, a bodily organ or muscle. ▸ *verb* **1** (*also* **tone in**) *intr* to fit in well; to harmonize. **2** to give tone or the correct tone to. **3** *intr* to take on a tone or quality. ▪ **toneless** *adj.* [14c: from Greek *tonos* tension]

PHRASAL VERBS **tone down** to become or make softer or less harsh in tone, colour or force, etc. **tone up** to become or make (muscles or the body) stronger, firmer, etc.

tone-deaf *adj* unable to distinguish accurately between notes of different pitch. [19c]

tonepad *noun, comput* an electronic device allowing data to be input into a central computer from a distance, usu via a telephone link. [20c]

tone poem *noun* a continuous orchestral piece based on a story or a descriptive theme. [20c]

toner *noun* **1** something that tones. **2** a lotion for toning the skin. **3** a fine, coloured powder used in printers and photocopiers.

tong *noun* a Chinese guild or secret society, esp one involved in organized crime. [19c: from Chinese *tong* meeting hall]

tongs *plural noun* **1** a tool, consisting of two joined arms, used for holding and lifting. **2 curling tongs.** [Anglo-Saxon *tang*]

tongue *noun* **1** a fleshy muscular organ in the mouth, used for tasting, licking and swallowing and, in humans, speech. **2** the tongue of some animals, eg, the ox and sheep, used as food. **3** the ability to speak. **4** a particular language. **5** a particular manner of speaking: *a sharp tongue.* **6** anything like a tongue in shape: *the tongue of a shoe* • *a tongue of flame.* **7** a narrow strip of land that reaches out into water. **8** the clapper in a bell. **9** a projecting strip along the side of a board that fits into a groove in another. [Anglo-Saxon *tunge*]

IDIOMS **hold one's tongue** to say nothing. **lose one's tongue** to be left speechless with shock or horror, etc. **speak in tongues** *relig* to speak in an unknown language or a language one has never learned. **tongue in cheek** with ironic, insincere or humorous intention.

tongue-tied *adj* unable to speak, esp because of shyness or embarrassment. [16c]

tongue-twister *noun* a phrase or sentence that is difficult to say quickly. [20c]

tonguing *noun, music* a way of playing a wind instrument that involves using the tongue to open and block the passage of air.

tonic *noun* **1** a medicine that increases or revives strength, energy and general wellbeing. **2** anything that is refreshing or invigorating. **3 tonic water. 4**

music the first note of a scale, the note on which a key is based. ▸ *adj* **1** increasing strength, energy and wellbeing. **2** *music* belonging or relating to the tonic scale. [17c: from Greek *tonikos*]

tonic sol-fa see **sol-fa**

tonic water *noun* a carbonated soft drink flavoured with quinine.

tonight *noun* the night of this present day. ▸ *adv* on or during the night of the present day. [Anglo-Saxon *to niht*]

tonnage *noun* **1** the space available in a ship for carrying cargo, measured in tons. **2** a duty on cargo by the ton. [14c: orig a tax or duty levied on each *tun* of wine carried by a ship]

tonne see **ton** (sense 2)

tonsil *noun* either of two lumps of lymphatic tissue at the back of the mouth. ▪ **tonsillar** *adj*. [17c: from Latin *tonsillae* (plural)]

tonsillitis *noun* inflammation of the tonsils.

tonsorial *adj, often facetious* belonging or relating to barbers or hairdressing. [19c: from Latin *tondere* to clip or shave]

tonsure *noun* **1** the act of shaving the crown or the entire head, esp of a person about to enter the priesthood or a monastic order. **2** a patch or head so shaved. ▸ *verb* to shave the head of. ▪ **tonsured** *adj*. [14c: from Latin *tondere* to clip or shave]

too *adv* **1** to a greater extent or more than is required, desirable or suitable: *too many things to do*. **2** in addition; as well; also: *loves Keats and likes Shelley too*. **3** what is more; indeed: *They need a good holiday, and they'll get one, too!* **4** extremely: *You're too generous!* [Anglo-Saxon: a stressed form of **to**]

took *past tense of* **take**

tool *noun* **1** an implement, esp one used by hand, for cutting or digging, etc, such as a spade or hammer, etc. **2** the cutting part of a **machine tool**. **3** a thing used in or necessary to a particular trade or profession: *Words are the tools of a journalist's trade*. **4** someone who is used or manipulated by another. ▸ *verb* **1** to work or engrave (stone, leather, etc) using tools. **2** *tr & intr* (*also* **tool up** *or* **tool sth up**) to equip it. [Anglo-Saxon *tol*]

toolbar *noun, comput* a bar with a list of utilities, features, functions, etc, which usually appears at the top of the window when running an application.

toot *noun* a quick sharp blast of a trumpet, whistle or horn, etc. ▸ *verb, tr & intr* to sound or cause (a trumpet or horn, etc) to sound with a quick sharp blast. [16c: imitating the sound]

tooth *noun* (***teeth***) **1** in vertebrates: any of the hard structures, usu embedded in the upper and lower jaw bones, used for biting and chewing food. **2** anything like a tooth in shape, arrangement, function, etc: *the teeth of a comb* • *a cog with many teeth*. **3** an appetite or liking: *a sweet tooth*. **4** (**teeth**) enough power or force to be effective. ▸ *verb* **1** to provide with teeth. **2** *intr* of cogs: to interlock. [Anglo-Saxon *toth*]

IDIOMS **get one's teeth into sth** to tackle or deal with it vigorously or eagerly, etc. **in the teeth of sth** against it; in opposition to it. **long in the tooth** *informal* old. **set sb's teeth on edge 1** to cause them a sharp pain in the teeth, eg, when they eat something very cold. **2** to cause them to wince. **3** to irritate them severely. **tooth and nail** fiercely and with all one's strength.

toothache *noun* pain in a tooth, usu as a result of decay.

toothbrush *noun* a brush for cleaning the teeth.

toothpaste *noun* a paste for cleaning the teeth.

toothpick *noun* a small sharp piece of wood or plastic, etc for removing food stuck between the teeth.

toothsome *adj* appetizing; delicious; attractive. [16c]

toothy *adj* (**-*ier*, -*iest***) showing or having a lot of teeth, esp large prominent ones: *a toothy grin*. [16c]

tootle *verb, intr* **1** to toot gently or continuously. **2** *informal* to go about casually, esp by car. ▸ *noun* an act or sound of tootling. [19c]

top[1] *noun* **1** the highest part, point or level of anything. **2 a** the highest or most important rank or position; **b** the person holding this. **3** the upper edge or surface of something. **4** a lid or piece for covering the top of something. **5** a garment for covering the upper half of the body, esp a woman's body. **6** the highest or loudest degree or pitch: *the top of one's voice*. **7** (**the tops**) *informal* the very best person or thing. **8 top gear**. ▸ *adj* at or being the highest or most important. ▸ *verb* (***topped, topping***) **1** to cover or form the top of, esp as a finishing or decorative touch. **2** to remove the top of (a plant, fruit, etc). **3** to rise above or be better than. **4** to reach the top of (a hill, etc). **5** *slang* **a** to kill, esp by hanging; **b** (**top oneself**) to commit suicide. **6** *golf* to hit the upper half of (the ball). [Anglo-Saxon]

IDIOMS **on top of sth 1** in control of it. **2** in addition to it. **3** very close to it. **top the bill** to head the list of performers in a show, as the main attraction.

PHRASAL VERBS **top sth off** to put a finishing or decorative touch to it. **top sb** *or* **sth up 1** to refill (someone's glass or a container, etc that has been partly emptied). **2** to provide money to bring (a grant, wage or money supply, etc) to the required or desirable total.

top[2] *noun* a wooden or metal toy which spins on a pointed base. [Anglo-Saxon]

IDIOMS **sleep like a top** to sleep very soundly.

topaz /'toupaz/ *noun* an aluminium silicate mineral, the pale yellow variety of which is used as a gemstone. [13c: from Greek *topazos*]

top brass *noun, informal* the highest-ranking officers or personnel, esp in the military.

topcoat *noun* an overcoat.

top dog *noun, informal* the most important or powerful person in a group.

top drawer *noun, informal* high social position or origin. ▸ *adj* (**top-drawer**) of the highest quality.

top-dressing *noun* **1** manure or fertilizer spread on soil as opposed to being ploughed or dug in. **2** an application of this. ▪ **top-dress** *verb*. [18c]

topee see **topi**

top-flight *adj* of the best or highest quality. [20c]

top gear *noun, Brit* the highest gear in a motor car, bike, etc. Often shortened to **top**.

top hat *noun* a tall cylindrical men's hat worn as part of formal dress.

top-heavy *adj* **1** disproportionately heavy in the upper part in comparison with the lower. **2** of a company or administration, etc: employing too many senior staff in proportion to junior staff.

topi *or* **topee** /ˈtoʊpɪ/ *noun* a lightweight hat, shaped like a helmet, worn in hot countries as protection against the sun. [19c: Hindi, meaning 'hat']

topiary /ˈtoʊpɪərɪ/ *noun* the art of cutting trees, bushes and hedges into ornamental shapes. ▪ **topiarist** *noun.* [16c: from Latin *topia* landscape gardening]

topic *noun* a subject or theme for a book, film, discussion, etc. [16c: from Greek *ta topika*, the title of a work by Aristotle on reasoning from general considerations]

topical *adj* relating to matters of current interest. ▪ **topicality** *noun.*

topic sentence *noun* a sentence conveying the main idea contained in a paragraph of text.

topknot *noun* **1** *esp hist* a knot of ribbons, etc worn on the top of the head as decoration. **2** a tuft of hair, growing on top of the head. [17c]

topless *adj* **1** of a woman: with her breasts exposed. **2** of a place: where women go topless: *topless beaches.*

topmast *noun, naut* the second mast, usually directly above the lower mast. [15c]

topmost *adj* the very highest of all.

top-notch *adj, informal* the very best quality; superb. [20c]

topography *noun* (**-ies**) **1** a description, map representation, etc of the natural and constructed features of a landscape. **2** such features collectively. ▪ **topographer** *noun.* ▪ **topographic** *or* **topographical** *adj.* [15c: from Greek *topos* place + *graphein* to describe]

topology *noun* the branch of geometry concerned with those properties of a geometrical figure that remain unchanged even when the figure is deformed by bending, stretching or twisting, etc. ▪ **topological** *adj.* [17c: from Greek *topos* place + *logos* word or reason]

topping *noun* something that forms a covering or garnish for food: *cheese topping.*

topple *verb, tr & intr* **1** (*also* **topple over**) to fall, or cause to fall, by overbalancing. **2** to overthrow or be overthrown. [16c: from **top**[1]]

topsail /ˈtɒpseɪl; *naut* -səl/ *noun* a square sail set across the topmast. [14c]

top-secret *adj* very secret, esp officially classified as such.

topside *noun* **1** a lean cut of beef from the rump. **2** the side of a ship above the waterline. ▸ *adj, adv* on deck.

topsoil *noun* the uppermost layer of soil, rich in organic matter, where most plant roots develop. Opposite of **subsoil.**

topspin *noun* a spin given to a ball to make it travel higher, further or faster.

topsy-turvy *adj, adv* **1** upside down. **2** in confusion. [16c: perhaps from **top**[1] + obsolete *terve* to turn over]

toque /toʊk/ *noun* a small close-fitting brimless hat worn by women. [16c: French]

tor *noun* a tower-like rocky peak. [Anglo-Saxon *torr*]

Torah *noun, Judaism* **1** the **Pentateuch. 2** the scroll on which this is written. **3** the whole body of Jewish literature and law, both written and oral. [16c: Hebrew, meaning 'instruction']

torch *noun* **1** *Brit* a small portable battery-powered light. **2** a piece of wood or bundle of cloth, etc set alight and used as a source of light. **3** any source of heat, light or enlightenment, etc. ▸ *verb, informal, esp N Am* to set fire to deliberately. [13c: from French *torche*]

IDIOMS **carry a torch for sb** to feel love, esp unrequited love, for them.

tore *past tense of* **tear**[2]

toreador /ˈtɒrɪədɔː(r)/ *noun* a bullfighter, esp one on horseback. See also **matador, picador.** [17c: Spanish, from *torear* to bait a bull]

torment *noun* /ˈtɔːmɛnt/ **1** great pain, suffering or anxiety. **2** something causing this. ▸ *verb* /tɔːˈmɛnt/ **1** to cause great pain, suffering or anxiety to. **2** to pester or harass. ▪ **tormentor** *noun.* [13c: from Latin *tormentum*]

torn *verb, past participle of* **tear**[2].

tornado *noun* (***tornadoes***) a violently destructive storm characterized by a funnel-shaped rotating column of air. ▪ **tornadic** *adj.* [16c: altered from Spanish *tronada* 'thunderstorm']

torpedo *noun* (***torpedoes*** *or* ***torpedos***) **1** a long self-propelling underwater missile which explodes on impact with its target. **2** a similar device dropped from the air. ▸ *verb* (***torpedoes, torpedoed***) **1** to attack with torpedoes. **2** to wreck or make (a plan, etc) ineffectual. [16c: Latin, meaning 'numbness' or 'electric ray']

torpid *adj* **1** sluggish and dull; lacking energy. **2** unable to move or feel; numb. **3** of a hibernating animal: dormant. ▪ **torpidity** *noun.* [17c: from Latin *torpidus*]

torpor *noun* the state of being torpid. [17c: Latin]

torque /tɔːk/ *noun* **1** *hist* a necklace made of metal twisted into a band, worn by the ancient Britons and Gauls. **2** *physics* force multiplied by the perpendicular distance from a point about which it causes rotation, measured in newton-metres. [19c: from Latin *torquere* to twist]

torrent *noun* **1** a great rushing stream or downpour of water or lava, etc. **2** a violent or strong flow (of questions, abuse, etc). ▪ **torrential** *adj.* [17c: from Latin *torrens* boiling]

torrid *adj* **1** of the weather: so hot and dry as to scorch the land. **2** of land: scorched and parched by extremely hot dry weather. **3** of language, a relationship, etc: passionate; intensely emotional. [16c: from Latin *torridus*]

torsion *noun* twisting by applying force to one end while the other is held firm or twisted in the opposite direction. ▪ **torsional** *adj.* [16c: from Latin *torquere* to twist]

torso *noun* **1** the main part of the human body, without the limbs and head; the trunk. **2** a nude statue of this. [18c: Italian, from Latin *thyrsos* stalk]

tort *noun, law* any wrongful act, other than breach of contract, for which an action for damages or compensation may be brought. [14c: from Latin *tortum* wrong]

torte /tɔːt, ˈtɔːtə/ *noun* (***torten*** *or* ***tortes***) a rich sweet cake or pastry, often garnished or filled with fruit, nuts, cream or chocolate, etc. [18c: German]

tortellini /tɔːtəˈliːnɪ/ *plural noun* small pasta cases, often in the shape of rings, stuffed with various fillings, eg meat, cheese or vegetables. [Early 20c: Italian, diminutive plural of *tortello* cake]

tortilla /tɔːˈtiːjə/ *noun* a thin round Mexican maize cake. [17c: Spanish, diminutive of *torta* cake]

tortoise *noun* a slow-moving reptile with a high domed shell into which the head, short scaly legs and tail can be withdrawn for safety. [14c: from Latin *tortuca*]

tortoiseshell *noun* **1** the brown and yellow mottled shell of a sea turtle, used in making combs, jewellery, etc. **2** a butterfly with mottled orange or red and brown or black wings. **3** a domestic cat with a mottled orange and creamy-brown coat. ▶ *adj* made of or mottled like tortoiseshell.

tortuous *adj* **1** full of twists and turns. **2** devious or involved. [15c: from Latin *torquere* to twist]

tortuous, torturous
Be careful not to use the word **tortuous** when you mean **torturous. Torturous** means 'like or involving torture':
There was a torturous wait for the results of the scan.

torture *noun* **1** the infliction of severe pain or mental suffering, esp as a punishment or as a means of persuasion. **2 a** great physical or mental suffering; **b** a cause of this. ▶ *verb* **1** to subject to torture. **2** to cause to experience great physical or mental suffering. **3** to force out of position. ▪ **torturous** *adj.* ▪ **torturously** *adv.* [16c: from Latin *tortura* torment]

torturous, tortuous
Be careful not to use the word **torturous** when you mean **tortuous. Tortuous** means 'full of twists and turns':
a tortuous route over the mountains, with a number of sharp bends

torus *noun* **1** *physics* a circular ring with a D-shaped cross-section used to contain plasma in nuclear fission reactors. **2** *maths* a solid curved surface with a hole in it, resembling a doughnut, obtained by rotating a circle about an axis lying in the same plane as the circle. **3** *botany* the receptacle of a flower. ▪ **toric** *adj.* [16c: Latin, meaning 'bulge' or 'swelling']

Tory *noun* (**-ies**) **1** a member or supporter of the British Conservative Party. **2** *hist* a member or supporter of a major English political party from the 17c to mid-19c, superseded by the Conservative Party. Compare **Whig**. ▶ *adj* **1** relating to or supporting the Tories. **2** Conservative. ▪ **Toryism** *noun.* [17c: from Irish Gaelic *tóraí* 'bandit' or 'outlaw']

tosh *noun, informal* twaddle; nonsense. [19c]

toss *verb* **1** to throw up into the air. **2** to throw away casually or carelessly. **3** *intr* to move restlessly or from side to side repeatedly. **4** *tr & intr* to be thrown or cause to be thrown from side to side repeatedly and violently: *a ship tossed by the storm.* **5** to jerk (the head). **6** *tr & intr* **a** (*also* **toss up**) to throw (a spinning coin) into the air and guess which side will land facing up, as a way of making a decision or settling a dispute; **b** to settle (with someone) by tossing a coin: *toss you for the last cake.* **7** to coat (food, esp salad) with oil or a dressing, etc by gently mixing or turning it. **8** of a horse, etc: to throw (its rider). **9** of an animal: to throw (a person) into the air with its horns. **10** to discuss or consider (ideas, etc) in casual debate. ▶ *noun* **1** an act or an instance of tossing. **2** *slang* the slightest amount: *not give a toss.* [16c]
IDIOMS **argue the toss** to dispute a decision.
PHRASAL VERBS **toss sth off 1** to drink it quickly, esp in a single swallow. **2** to produce it quickly and easily.

toss-up *noun* **1** *informal* an even chance or risk; something doubtful. **2** an act of tossing a coin.

tot[1] *noun* **1** a small child; a toddler. **2** a small amount of spirits: *a tot of whisky.* [18c]

tot[2] *verb* (***totted, totting***) (*esp* **tot up**) **1** to add together. **2** *intr* of money, etc: to increase. [18c: an abbrev of **total**]

total *adj* whole; complete. ▶ *noun* the whole or complete amount. ▶ *verb* (***totalled, totalling***; *US* ***totaled, totaling***) **1** *tr & intr* to amount to (a specified sum): *The figures totalled 385.* **2** (*also* **total up**) to add (figures, etc) up to produce a total. ▪ **totally** *adv.* [14c: from Latin *totus* all]

total eclipse *noun, astron* an eclipse where all of the Sun or Moon is covered.

totalitarian *adj* belonging or relating to a system of government by a single party which allows no opposition and which demands complete obedience to the State. ▶ *noun* someone in favour of such a system. ▪ **totalitarianism** *noun.* [20c]

totality *noun* (**-ies**) **1** completeness. **2** the time when an eclipse is total.

tote *verb, informal* to carry, drag or wear (esp something heavy). [17c]

totem *noun* **1** in Native American culture: a natural object, esp an animal, used as the badge or sign of a tribe or an individual. **2** an image or representation of this. [18c: from Ojibwa (a Native American language)]

totem pole *noun* **1** in Native American culture: a large wooden pole that has totems carved and painted on it. **2** *informal* a hierarchical system: *the social totem pole.*

totter *verb, intr* **1** to walk or move unsteadily, shakily or weakly. **2** to sway or tremble as if about to fall. **3** of a system of government, etc: to be on the verge of collapse. ▪ **tottery** *adj.* [12c: meaning 'to swing']

toucan /ˈtuːkən, -kan/ *noun* a tropical bird with a huge beak and brightly coloured feathers. [16c: from Tupí (a native S American language) *tucana*]

touch *verb* **1** to bring (a hand, etc) into contact with something. **2 a** *tr & intr* to be in physical contact or come into physical contact with, esp lightly; **b** to bring together in close physical contact: *They touched hands.* **3** *often with negatives* **a** to injure, harm or hurt: *I never touched him!* **b** to interfere with, move, disturb, etc: *Who's been touching my things?* **c** to have dealings with, be associated with or be a party to: *wouldn't touch that kind of job;* **d** to make use of: *He never touches alcohol;* **e** to use (eg money, etc): *I don't touch the money in that account;* **f** to approach in excellence; to be as good as; to compare to: *Nobody can touch her at chess.* **4** to concern or affect; to make a difference to: *It's a matter that touches us all.* **5** (*usu* **touch on** *or* **upon**) to deal with (a matter, subject, etc), esp in passing or not very thoroughly. **6** to affect with pity, sympathy, gratitude, quiet pleasure, etc: *The story of his sad life touched her heart.* **7** to reach or go as far as, esp temporarily: *The temperature touched 100.* **8 a** (*usu* **touch with**) to tinge, taint, mark, modify, etc slightly or delicately: *The sky was touched with pink • a love* *that's touched with sorrow;* **b** to make a usu slight, sometimes harmful, impression, effect, etc on: *Frost had touched the early crop.* **9** (*often* **touch sb for sth**) *slang* to ask them for and receive (money, esp a specified amount, as a loan or gift): *touched him for 50 quid.* ▸ *noun* **1** an act of touching or the sensation of being touched. **2** the sense by which the existence, nature, texture and quality of objects can be perceived through physical contact with the hands, etc. **3** the particular texture and qualities of an object, etc: *the silky touch of the fabric against her skin.* **4** a small amount, quantity, distance, etc; a trace or hint: *move it left a touch.* **5** a slight attack (of an illness, etc): *a touch of the flu.* **6** a slight stroke or mark. **7** a detail which adds to or complements the general pleasing effect or appearance: *The flowers were an elegant touch.* **8** a distinctive or characteristic style or manner: *need the expert's touch.* **9** a musician's individual manner or technique of touching or striking the keys of a keyboard instrument or strings of a string instrument to produce a good tone. **10** an artist's or writer's individual style or manner of working. **11** the ability to respond or behave with sensitivity and sympathy: *have a wonderful touch with animals.* **12** *sport* in rugby, etc: the ground outside the touchlines. **13** *slang* an act of asking for and receiving money from someone as a gift or loan. **14** *slang* someone who can be persuaded to give or lend money: *a soft touch.* **15** a test with, or as if with, a touchstone. [13c: from French *tuchier*]

IDIOMS **in touch (with) 1** in contact, communication, etc (with): *We still keep in touch although we haven't seen each other for 20 years.* **2** up to date: *keeps in touch with the latest news.* **3** aware or conscious (of): *in touch with her inner self.* **lose touch (with) 1** to be no longer in contact, communication, etc (with): *lost touch with them after they moved house.* **2** to be no longer familiar (with) or well-informed (about): *lost touch with what's happening.* **out of touch (with) 1** not in contact, communication, etc (with): *been out of touch with his brother for years.* **2** not up to date (with): *out of touch with the new technology.*

PHRASAL VERBS **touch down 1** of an aircraft, spacecraft, etc: to land. **2** *rugby* to carry the ball over the goal-line and touch the ground with it. **touch sth off 1** to cause it to explode, eg, by putting a match to it. **2** to cause it to begin; to trigger it: *Police brutality touched off the riots.* **touch on** to verge towards: *That touches on the surreal.* **touch up** (*usu* **touch up sth**) to improve it by adding small details, correcting or hiding minor faults, etc: *touched up the painting.*

touch and go *adj* very uncertain in outcome; risky: *It was touch and go whether she'd survive.*

touchdown *noun* **1** an act or instance or the process of an aircraft or spacecraft making contact with the ground when landing. **2** *Amer football* an act or instance or the process of carrying the ball over the touchline and hitting the ground with it to score.

touché /tuːˈʃeɪ/ *exclam* **1** *fencing* an acknowledgement of a hit. **2** a good-humoured acknowledgement of the validity of a point that is made either in an argument or in retaliation. [20c: French, meaning 'touched']

touched *adj* **1** having a feeling of pity, sympathy, quiet pleasure, etc. **2** *informal* slightly mad.

touching *adj* causing feelings of pity or sympathy; moving. ▸ *prep, old use* concerning; pertaining to.

touchline *noun, sport, esp football & rugby* either of the two lines that mark the side boundaries of the pitch.

touch pad *noun, comput* a small input device, used eg with a laptop, operated by touching different areas on its surface.

touchpaper *noun* paper steeped in saltpetre and used for lighting fireworks or firing gunpowder.

touch screen *noun, comput* a type of computer screen that doubles as an input device, operated by pressing it with a finger.

touchstone *noun* **1** a hard black flint-like stone that is used for testing the purity and quality of gold and silver alloys. **2** a test or standard for judging the quality of something.

touch-type *verb, intr* to use a typewriter without looking at the keyboard. ▪ **touch-typist** *noun.* [20c]

touchy *adj* (**-ier, -iest**) *informal* **1** easily annoyed or offended. **2** needing to be handled or dealt with with care and tact: *a touchy subject.*

tough *adj* **1** strong and durable; not easily cut, broken, torn or worn out. **2** of food, esp meat: difficult to chew. **3** of a person, animal, etc: strong and fit and able to endure hardship. **4** difficult to deal with or overcome; testing: *a tough decision.* **5** severe and determined; unyielding; resolute: *a tough customer.* **6** rough and violent; criminal: *a tough area.* **7** *informal* unlucky; unjust; unpleasant: *The divorce was tough on the kids.* ▸ *noun* a rough violent person, esp a bully or criminal. ▸ *adv, informal* aggressively; in a macho way: *acts tough when he's with his mates.* ▪ **toughish** *adj.* ▪ **toughly** *adv.* ▪ **toughness** *noun.* [Anglo-Saxon *toh*]

toughen *verb, tr & intr* (*also* **toughen up**) to become or cause to become tough or tougher. [16c]

toupee /ˈtuːpeɪ/ *noun* a small wig or hairpiece, usu worn by men to cover a bald patch. [18c: from French *toupet* tuft of hair]

tour *noun* **1** an extended journey with stops at various places of interest. **2** a visit round a particular place: *a tour of the cathedral.* **3** a journey with frequent stops for business or professional engagements, eg, by a theatre company, sports team, rock band, etc. **4 a** an official period of duty or military service, esp abroad: *did a tour of duty in Germany;* **b** the time spent on this. ▸ *verb, tr & intr* **1** to travel round (a place). **2** of a theatre company, band, performer, etc: to travel from place to place giving performances. ▪ **touring** *adj, noun.* [13c: from Greek *tornos* tool for making circles]

IDIOMS **on tour** of a theatre company, band, performer, sports team, etc: playing at a series of venues.

tour de force /tʊə də fɔːs/ (***tours de force*** /tʊə-/) ▸ *noun* a feat of strength or skill; an outstanding performance or effort. [19c: French, meaning 'a feat of strength']

tourism *noun* **1** the practice of travelling to and visiting places for pleasure and relaxation. **2** the industry that is involved in offering services for tourists. [19c]

tourist *noun* **1** someone who travels for pleasure and relaxation; a holidaymaker. **2** a member of a sports team visiting from abroad. ▸ *adj* relating or referring to or suitable for people on holiday: *tourist resort.*

tourist class *noun* the cheapest kind of passenger accommodation on a ship, aircraft, etc.

touristy *adj, usu derog* designed for, appealing to, frequented by or full of tourists.

tourmaline *noun* a mineral found in granites and gneisses and used as a gemstone. [18c: from Sinhalese *tormalliya* cornelian]

tournament *noun* **1** a competition, eg, in tennis or chess, that involves many players taking part in heats for a championship. **2** *hist* (*also* **tourney**) in the Middle Ages: **a** a competition with jousting contests; **b** a meeting for this. [13c: from French *torneiement*]

tournedos /'tʊənədoʊ/ *noun* (***tournedos*** /-doʊz/) a small round thick cut of beef fillet. [19c: French]

tourniquet /'tʊənɪkeɪ, 'tɔː-/ *noun* an emergency compression device for stopping the flow of blood through an artery. [17c: French, from *tourner* to turn]

tour operator *noun* a person or firm that organizes holidays for customers.

tousle /'taʊzəl/ *verb* **1** to make (esp hair) untidy. **2** to tangle. ▸ *noun* a tousled mass. ▪ **tousled** *adj.* [15c: from obsolete *touse* to handle roughly]

tout /taʊt/ *verb* **1** *intr* (*usu* **tout for**) to solicit custom, support, etc persistently: *tout for trade.* **2** to solicit the custom of (someone) or for (something). **3** *intr* to spy on racehorses in training to gain information about their condition and likely future performance. ▸ *noun* **1** (*in full* **ticket tout**) someone who buys up large numbers of tickets for a popular sporting event, concert, etc and sells them on at inflated prices. **2** someone who touts. ▪ **touter** *noun.* [15c: from *tuten* to peep out]

tow[1] /toʊ/ *verb* **1** to pull (a ship, car, caravan, etc) along by rope, chain, cable, etc. **2** to pull (someone or something) behind one. ▸ *noun* an act or the process of towing; the state of being towed. ▪ **towage** *noun.* [Anglo-Saxon *togian*]

IDIOMS **in tow 1** of a vehicle: being towed. **2** following or accompanying as a companion or escort: *She arrived late with several men in tow.* **on tow** of a vehicle: being towed. **under tow** of a vessel: being towed.

tow[2] /toʊ, taʊ/ *noun* coarse, short or broken fibres of flax, hemp or jute prepared for spinning. [Anglo-Saxon]

towards *or* **toward** *prep* **1** in the direction of: *turn towards him.* **2** in relation or regard to: *showed no respect toward her boss.* **3** as a contribution to: *donated £1000 towards the costs.* **4** near; just before: *towards midnight*. [Anglo-Saxon *toweard* future]

tow bar /toʊ/ *noun* a device fitted to the back of a car, etc enabling it to tow a trailer, caravan, etc.

towel *noun* **1** a piece of absorbent cloth, etc used for drying the body, dishes, etc: *a bath towel • a tea towel • a paper towel.* **2** *Brit, dated* a **sanitary towel.** ▸ *verb* (***towelled, towelling***; *US* ***toweled, toweling***) to rub, wipe or dry with a towel. [13c: from French *toaille*]

towelling *noun* a highly absorbent material formed from many uncut loops of cotton, etc.

tower *noun* **1 a** a tall narrow structure forming part of a larger, lower building, eg a church; **b** a similar freestanding structure: *a control tower.* **2** a fortress, esp with one or more towers: *the Tower of London.* ▸ *verb, intr* (*usu* **tower above** *or* **over**) to reach a great height, or be vastly superior or considerably taller. [Anglo-Saxon *torr*]

tower block *noun, Brit* a very tall building comprised of many residential flats or offices.

towering *adj* **1** reaching a great height; very tall or elevated: *towering mountains.* **2** of rage, fury, a storm, the sea, etc: intense; violent. **3** very impressive, important or lofty: *a towering intellect*.

tower of strength *noun* someone who is a great help or support.

tow-headed /taʊ-/ *adj* with very fair hair or tousled hair.

town *noun* **1** an urban area smaller than a city but larger than a village. **2** the central shopping or business area in a neighbourhood: *went into town to buy new shoes.* **3** the principal town in an area, or the capital city of a country, regarded as a destination. **4** the people living in a town or a city: *The whole town turned out*. [Anglo-Saxon *tun* enclosure or manor]

IDIOMS **go to town** *informal* to act, work, etc very thoroughly or with great enthusiasm, etc. **on the town** *informal* enjoying the entertainments offered by a town, esp its restaurants, clubs and bars.

town clerk *noun, Brit hist* until 1974, someone who served as secretary, chief administrator and legal advisor to a town council. [14c]

town council *noun* the elected governing body of a town. ▪ **town councillor** *noun.* [17c]

town crier *noun, hist* someone whose job was to make public announcements in the streets. [17c]

townee *or* **townie** *noun, informal, often derog* someone who lives in a town, esp as opposed to someone who lives in the countryside. [19c]

town hall *noun* the building where the official business of a town's administration is carried out.

town house *noun* **1** a terraced house, esp a fashionable one. **2** someone's house in town as opposed to their country one.

township *noun* **1** *S Afr* an urban area that was formerly set aside for non-white citizens. **2** *N Am* a subdivision of a county that has some corporate powers over local administration. **3** *N Am* an area of land or district that is six miles square and that contains 36 sections. **4** *Aust* a small town or settlement. [Anglo-Saxon]

towpath *noun* a path that runs alongside a canal or river where a horse can walk while towing a barge.

toxaemia *or* (*US*) **toxemia** /tɒk'siːmɪə/ *noun, med* **1** blood poisoning. **2** a complication in some pregnancies characterized by a sudden increase in the mother's blood pressure. ▪ **toxaemic** *adj.* [19c: from Latin *toxicum* poison (see **toxic**) + *haima* blood]

toxic *adj* **1** poisonous. **2** relating or referring to, characteristic of or caused by, a poison or toxin. ▪ **toxically** *adv.* ▪ **toxicity** *noun.* [17c: from Latin *toxicum* poison]

toxicology *noun* the scientific study of poisons. ▪ **toxicological** *adj.* ▪ **toxicologist** *noun.* [19c: from French *toxicologie*]

toxin *noun* a poison produced by a micro-organism. [19c: see **toxic**]

toxoid *noun* a toxin that has been treated so that it is no longer poisonous, but still stimulates the production of antibodies.

toy *noun* **1** an object for someone, esp a child, to play with. **2** *often derog* something, esp a gadget, that is intended to be, or that is thought of as being, for amusement or pleasure rather than practical use. **3** something which is very small, esp a dwarf breed or variety of dog. ▸ *adj* imitation, esp of something that adults use: *a toy gun.* ▸ *verb, intr* (*usu* **toy with**) **1** to flirt or trifle: *toyed with the idea of getting a new car.* **2** to move (something) in an idle, distracted, etc way: *toying with his food.* [16c: from *toye* dalliance]

trace[1] *noun* **1** a mark or sign that some person, animal or thing has been in a particular place. **2** a track or footprint. **3** a very small amount that can only just be detected: *found traces of cocaine.* **4** a tracing. **5** a line marked by the moving pen of a recording instrument. **6** a visible line on a cathode-ray tube showing the path of a moving spot. ▸ *verb* **1** to track and discover by, or as if by, following clues, a trail, etc. **2** to follow step by step: *trace the development of medicine.* **3** to make a copy of (a drawing, design, etc) by covering it with a sheet of semi-transparent paper and drawing over the visible lines. **4** to outline or sketch (an idea, plan, etc). **5** to investigate and discover the cause, origin, etc of: *traced her family back to Tudor times.* ▪ **traceable** *adj.* [14c: from French *tracier*]

trace[2] *noun* either of the two ropes, chains or straps by which an animal, esp a horse, pulls a carriage, cart, etc. [13c: French, from *trais*]

trace element *noun* **1** a chemical element that is only found in very small amounts. **2** a chemical element that living organisms require only in very small amounts for normal growth, etc.

tracer *noun* **1 a** someone whose job is to trace, eg, architectural, civil engineering, etc drawings; **b** a device that traces. **2** a bullet, shell, etc which leaves a smoke-trail behind it so that its flight path can be seen. **3** a substance, esp a radioactive element, whose course through the body, or effect on it, can be observed.

tracery *noun* (***-ies***) **1** ornamental open stonework, esp in the top part of a Gothic window. **2** a finely patterned decoration or design.

trachea /trəˈkɪə/ *noun* (***tracheae*** /-ˈkiːi/) **1** an air tube extending from the larynx to the lungs. *Non-technical equivalent* **windpipe**. **2** *zool* in insects and arthropods: any of the openings on the surface of the body where air is absorbed into the blood and tissues. **3** *botany* any fluid-conducting vessel or duct in the woody tissue of plants. See also **phloem**, **xylem**. [15c: from Greek *tracheia arteria* rough artery]

tracheotomy /trakɪˈɒtəmɪ/ *noun* a surgical incision into the trachea to make an alternative airway when normal breathing is not possible, or an operation to do this. [18c]

tracing *noun* **1** a copy of a drawing, etc that is made on semi-transparent paper. **2** an act, instance or the process of making such a copy.

tracing-paper *noun* thin semi-transparent paper designed to be used for tracing drawings, etc.

track *noun* **1 a** a mark or series of marks or footprints, etc left behind: *a tyre track;* **b** a course of action, thought, etc taken: *followed in her mother's tracks and studied medicine.* **2** a rough path: *a track through the woods.* **3** a specially prepared course: *a race track.* **4** the branch of athletics that comprises all the running events. **5** a railway line: *leaves on the track.* **6** a length of railing that a curtain, spotlight, etc moves along. **7 a** the groove cut in a **record** (*noun* sense 4) by the recording instrument; **b** an individual song, etc on an album, CD, cassette, etc; **c** one of several paths on magnetic recording tape that receives information from a single input channel; **d** one of a series of parallel paths on magnetic recording tape that contains a single sequence of signals; **e** a **soundtrack**; **f** *comput* an area on the surface of a magnetic disk where data can be stored and which is created during the process of formatting. **8** a line, path or course of travel, passage or movement: *followed the track of the storm.* **9** a line or course of thought, reasoning, etc: *couldn't follow the track of his argument.* **10** a predetermined line of travel of an aircraft. **11** a continuous band that tanks, mechanical diggers, etc have instead of individual tyres. ▸ *verb* **1** to follow (marks, footprints, etc left behind). **2** to follow and usu plot the course of (a spacecraft, satellite, etc) by radar. **3** *intr* (*often* **track in**, **out** *or* **back**) of a television or film camera or its operator: to move, esp in such a way as to follow a moving subject, always keeping them or it in focus. **4** of a stylus or laser beam: to extract information from (a recording medium, eg, a vinyl record or a CD). **5** *intr* of a vehicle's rear wheels: to run exactly in the course of the front wheels. [15c: from French *trac*]

IDIOMS **keep** *or* **lose track of sth** *or* **sb** to keep, or fail to keep, oneself informed about the progress, whereabouts, etc of them or it: *lost all track of time.* **make tracks** *informal* to leave; to set out. **off the beaten track** away from busy roads and therefore difficult to access or find. **on the right** *or* **wrong track** pursuing the right or wrong line of inquiry.

PHRASAL VERBS **track sb** *or* **sth down** to search for and find them or it after following clues, etc: *managed to track down the address.*

track and field *noun* the branch of athletics that comprises all the running and jumping events plus the hammer, discus, javelin, shot put, etc.

trackball *or* **trackerball** *noun, comput* a ball mounted in a small box that is linked to a computer terminal and which can be rotated with the palm to move a cursor correspondingly on a screen.

tracker dog *noun* a dog that is specially trained to search for missing people, criminals, etc.

tracking *noun* **1** an act or process of adding pre-recorded music to a motion picture as opposed to having a soundtrack of specially commissioned music. **2** *elec eng* leakage of current between two insulated points caused by moisture, dirt, etc.

track record *noun, informal* someone's performance, achievements, etc in the past: *Her CV shows an impressive track record.*

track shoe *noun* a running shoe with a spiked sole.

tracksuit *noun* a loose suit worn by athletes, footballers, etc when exercising, or warming up, etc.

tract[1] *noun* **1** an area of land, usu of indefinite extent: *large tracts of wilderness.* **2** a system in the body with a specified function: *the digestive tract.* [15c: from Latin *tractus* a drawing out]

tract[2] *noun* a short essay or pamphlet, esp on religion, politics, etc and intended as propaganda. [15c: from Latin *tractatus* a handling or discussion]

tractable *adj* **1** of a person, etc: easily managed, controlled, etc; docile. **2** of a material, etc: pliant. ▪ **tractability** *noun.* [15c: from Latin *tractare* to handle]

traction *noun* **1** the action or process of pulling. **2** the state of being pulled or the force used in pulling. **3**

med a treatment involving steady pulling on a muscle, limb, etc using a series of pulleys and weights: *had her leg in traction for six weeks.* **4** the grip of a wheel, tyre, etc on a road surface, rail track, etc. **5** the rolling of large rocks along a river bed. [17c: from Latin *tractio*]

traction engine *noun* a heavy steam-powered vehicle that was formerly used for pulling heavy loads, eg, farm machinery. [19c]

tractor *noun* **1** a motor vehicle for pulling farm machinery, heavy loads, etc. **2** a **traction engine**. [20c: Latin, from *trahere* to draw or drag]

trade *noun* **1 a** an act or instance or the process of buying and selling; **b** buying and selling generally: *foreign trade.* **2 a** a job, etc that involves skilled work, esp as opposed to professional or unskilled work: *left school at 16 to learn a trade;* **b** the people and businesses that are involved in such work: *the building trade.* **3 a** business and commerce, esp as opposed to a profession or the owning of landed property; **b** the people involved in this. **4** customers: *the lunch-time trade.* **5** business at a specified time, for a specified market or of a specified nature: *the tourist trade.* **6** (**trades**) the trade winds. ▸ *verb* **1** *intr* to buy and sell; to engage in trading: *trades in securities.* **2 a** to exchange (one commodity) for another; **b** to exchange (blows, insults, etc); **c** *informal* to swap. **3** *intr* (**trade on sth**) to take unfair advantage of it: *traded on his sister's popularity.* ▪ **trader** *noun.* [14c: orig meaning 'a course or path']
PHRASAL VERBS **trade sth off** to give it in exchange for something else, usu as a compromise.

trade deficit *or* **trade gap** *noun* the amount by which a country's imports outstrip its exports.

trade-in *noun* something, esp a used car, etc, given in part exchange for another.

trademark *noun* **1** (*in full* **registered trademark**) a name, word or symbol, esp one that is officially registered and protected by law, with which a company or individual identifies goods made or sold by them. **2** a distinguishing characteristic or feature. [16c]

tradename *noun* **1** a name that is given to an article or product, or a group of these, by the trade which produces them. **2** a name that a company or individual does business under. [19c]

trade-off *noun* a balance or compromise that is struck, esp between two desirable but incompatible things, situations, etc.

trade price *noun* a wholesale cost that a retailer pays for goods.

trade secret *noun* an ingredient, technique, etc that a company or individual will not divulge. [19c]

tradesman, **tradeswoman** *or* **tradesperson** *noun* **1** someone who is engaged in trading, eg, a shopkeeper. **2** someone who follows a skilled trade, eg, a plumber, electrician, etc.

trade union *or* **trades union** *noun* an organization for the employees of a specified profession, trade, etc that exists to protect members' interests and improve pay, working conditions, etc. ▪ **trade unionism** *noun.* ▪ **trade unionist** *noun.* [19c]

trade wind *noun* a wind that blows continually towards the equator from the north-east and south-east and which, in the N hemisphere, is deflected westwards by the eastward rotation of the earth. [17c]

tradition *noun* **1 a** a doctrine, belief, custom, story, etc passed on from generation to generation, esp orally or by example; **b** the action or process of handing down something in this way. **2** a particular body of doctrines, beliefs, customs, etc. **3** *informal* an established, standard or usual practice or custom. **4** the continuous development of a body of artistic, etc principles or conventions: *a film in the tradition of the American road movie.* [15c: from Latin *traditio* handing over]

traditional *adj* belonging, relating or referring to, based on or derived from tradition: *morris dancers in their traditional costumes.* ▪ **traditionally** *adv.*

traditionalist *noun* someone who subscribes to tradition, esp in a slavish way. ▸ *adj* relating to, involving, etc tradition. ▪ **traditionalism** *noun.*

traduce *verb* to say or write unpleasant things about (someone or something). ▪ **traducement** *noun.* ▪ **traducer** *noun.* [16c: from Latin *traducere* to disgrace]

traffic *noun* **1** the vehicles that are moving along a route. **2** the movement of vehicles, passengers, etc along a route. **3** illegal or dishonest trade: *the traffic of cocaine.* **4** trade; commerce. **5** the transporting of goods or people on a railway, air or sea route, etc. **6** the goods or people transported along a route. **7** communication between groups or individuals. ▸ *verb* (***trafficked, trafficking***) **1** (*usu* **traffic in**) to deal or trade in, esp illegally or dishonestly. **2** to deal in. ▪ **trafficker** *noun.* [16c: from French *traffique*]

traffic calming *noun* the intentional curbing of the speed of road vehicles by having humps, bends, narrowed passing places, etc on roads.

traffic cone *noun* a large plastic cone used for guiding diverted traffic, etc.

traffic island see under **island**

traffic jam *noun* a queue of vehicles that are at a standstill, eg, because of overcrowded roads, an accident, roadworks, etc.

traffic lights *plural noun* a system of red, amber and green lights controlling traffic at road junctions, pedestrian crossings, etc.

traffic warden *noun, Brit* someone whose job is controlling traffic flow and putting parking tickets on vehicles that infringe parking restrictions, etc.

tragedian /trəˈdʒiːdɪən/ *noun* **1** an actor specializing in tragic roles. **2** a writer of tragedies. [14c]

tragedienne /trədʒiːdɪˈɛn/ *noun* an actress specializing in tragic roles.

tragedy *noun* (***-ies***) **1** a serious catastrophe, accident, natural disaster, etc. **2** *informal* a sad, disappointing, etc event: *an absolute tragedy when Aberdeen lost that goal.* **3 a** a serious play, film, opera, etc portraying tragic events and with an unhappy ending; **b** such plays, etc as a group or genre. **4** *loosely* any sad play, film, book, etc. [14c: from Greek *tragos* goat + *oide* song]

tragic *or* **tragical** *adj* **1** very sad; intensely distressing. **2** *theatre* belonging, referring or relating to or in the style of tragedy. ▪ **tragically** *adv.* [16c]

tragicomedy *noun* (***-ies***) **1** a play, film, event, etc that includes a mixture of both tragedy and comedy. **2** such plays, etc as a group or genre. ▪ **tragicomic** *or* **tragicomical** *adj.* [16c: from Latin *tragicomoedia*]

trail *verb* **1** *tr & intr* to drag or be dragged loosely along the ground or other surface. **2** *tr & intr* to walk or move along slowly and wearily. **3** to drag (a limb, etc) esp slowly and wearily. **4** *tr & intr* to fall or lag behind in a race, contest, etc: *trailed their opponents by 20 points.* **5** to follow the track or footsteps of. **6** *tr & intr* **a** of a plant or plant part: to grow so long that it droops over or along a surface towards the ground; **b** to encourage (a plant or plant part) to grow in this way. **7** to advertise (a forthcoming programme, film, etc) by showing chosen extracts, etc. ▸ *noun* **1** a track, series of marks, footprints, etc left by a passing person, animal or thing, esp one followed in hunting. **2** a rough path or track through a wild or mountainous area. **3** something that drags or is drawn behind. [14c, meaning 'to drag behind']

PHRASAL VERBS **trail away** *or* **off** of a voice, etc: to become fainter.

trailblazer *noun* **1** someone who makes inroads into new territory; a pioneer. **2** an innovator in a particular field or activity. ▪ **trailblazing** *noun, adj.*

trailer *noun* **1** a cart that can be hooked up behind a car, etc and used for carrying small loads, transporting small boats, etc. **2** the rear section of an articulated lorry. **3** *N Am* a mobile home or caravan. **4** *cinema, TV, radio* a promotional preview of a forthcoming film, programme, etc made up of short extracts, etc. **5** someone or something that trails behind. [19c]

train *noun* **1 a** a string of railway carriages or wagons with a locomotive; **b** *loosely* a locomotive. **2** a back part of a long dress or robe that trails behind the wearer. **3** the attendants following or accompanying an important person. **4** a connected series of animals, events, actions, ideas, thoughts, etc: *a camel train* • *interrupted my train of thought.* ▸ *verb* **1** to teach or prepare (a person or animal) through instruction, practice, exercises, etc. **2** *intr* to be taught through instruction, practice, exercises, etc: *trained as a nurse.* **3** (*usu* **train for**) to prepare (for a performance, eg, in a sport) through practice, exercise, diet, etc. **4** to point or aim (eg a gun) at or focus (eg a telescope) on (a particular object, etc). **5** to make (a plant, tree, etc) grow in a particular direction: *train the ivy along the wall.* ▪ **trainable** *adj.* [14c: from French *trahiner* to drag]

trainee *noun* someone who is in the process of being trained.

trainer *noun* **1** someone who trains racehorses, athletes, etc. **2** (**trainers**) *Brit* running shoes without spikes, often worn as casual shoes. *N Am equivalent* **sneaker**.

training *noun* an act or the process of preparing or being prepared for something, or of being taught or learning a particular skill: *go into training for the marathon.*

train-spotter *noun* **1** someone whose hobby is noting the numbers of railway locomotives, etc. **2** someone who is overly concerned with trivial details, etc. ▪ **train-spotting** *noun.*

traipse *verb* **1** *intr* to walk or trudge along idly or wearily: *traipsed round the shops.* **2** to wander aimlessly: *traipsing the streets.* ▸ *noun* a long tiring walk. [16c]

trait *noun* an identifying feature or quality, esp of someone's character. [16c: French]

traitor *noun* **1** someone who betrays their country, sovereign, government, etc. **2** someone who betrays a trust. ▪ **traitorous** *adj.* [13c: from French *traitre*]

trajectory *noun* (**-ies**) **1** *physics* the curved path that a moving object describes, eg, when it is projected into the air or when it is subjected to a given force, etc. **2** *geom* a curve that passes through a set of given points, etc at a constant angle. [17c: from Latin *trajectorius* casting over]

tram *noun* an electrically-powered passenger vehicle that runs on rails laid in the streets. [16c: from German *Traam* shaft]

tramline *noun* **1** (*usu* **tramlines**) either of a pair of rails that form the track for trams to run on. **2** the route that a tram takes. **3** (**tramlines**) *informal* **a** the parallel lines at the sides of tennis and badminton courts; **b** the parallel lines at the back of a badminton court. [19c]

trammel *noun* **1** (*usu* **trammels**) something that hinders or prevents free action or movement: *trapped by the trammels of convention.* **2** a triple dragnet for catching fish. ▸ *verb* (***trammelled, trammelling***; *US* ***trammeled, trammeling***) to hinder or catch with or as if with trammels. [15c: from French *tramail* a triple-meshed net]

tramp *verb* **1** *intr* to walk with firm heavy footsteps. **2** *intr* to make a journey on foot, esp heavily or wearily: *tramp over the hills.* **3** to walk heavily and wearily on or through: *tramp the streets.* **4** to walk (a specified distance) heavily and wearily: *tramp six miles across the open moor.* **5** to tread or trample. ▸ *noun* **1** someone who has no fixed home or job. **2** a long, tiring walk. **3** the sound of heavy rhythmic footsteps. **4** *slang* a promiscuous or immoral woman. [14c]

trample *verb, tr & intr* **1** to tread heavily. **2** (*also* **trample on** *or* **over**) to crush underfoot: *trampled grapes* • *trampled on the flowers.* **3** (*also* **trample on** *or* **over**) to treat (someone or their feelings, etc) roughly, dismissively or with contempt. [14c: from **tramp**]

trampoline *noun* a piece of gymnastic equipment that consists of a sheet of tightly stretched canvas, etc attached to a framework by strong springs and used for jumping on, performing somersaults, etc. ▸ *verb, intr* to jump, turn somersaults, etc on a trampoline. ▪ **trampolinist** *noun.*

trance *noun* **1** a sleep-like or half-conscious state in which the ability to react to stimuli is temporarily lost. **2** a dazed or absorbed state. **3** a state, usu self-induced, in which religious or mystical ecstasy is experienced. **4** the state that a medium claims to enter to make contact with the dead. [14c: from French *transe*]

tranche /trɑːnʃ/ *noun* **1** a part, piece or division. **2** *econ* **a** an instalment of a loan; **b** part of a block of shares. [16c: French, from *trancher* to cut]

trannie *or* **tranny** *noun* (**-ies**) *Brit informal* a transistor radio.

tranquil *adj* serenely quiet or peaceful; undisturbed. ▪ **tranquillity** *or* (*US*) **tranquility** *noun.* ▪ **tranquilly** *adv.* [17c: from Latin *tranquillus* quiet]

tranquillize, -ise *or* (*US*) **tranquilize** *verb* to make or become calm, esp by administering a drug.

tranquillizer, -iser *or* (*US*) **tranquilizer** *noun* a drug that has a tranquillizing effect.

trans. *abbrev* **1** transitive. **2** translated. **3** translation.

trans- *prefix, forming words, denoting* **1** across; beyond: *transatlantic*. **2** on, to or towards the other side of. **3** through. **4** into another state or place: *transform*. [Latin, meaning 'across']

transact *verb* to conduct or carry out (business). [16c: from Latin *transigere* to drive through]

transactinide *adj, chem* referring or relating to radioactive elements with atomic numbers higher than the **actinide** series. ▸ *noun* such an element.

transaction *noun* **1** a business deal, etc that is settled or is in the process of being settled. **2** (**transactions**) the published reports of papers read, decisions taken, etc at a meeting of a learned society together with the records of any discussions arising from such a meeting.

transalpine *adj* beyond or stretching across the Alps. [16c: from Latin *transalpinus*]

transatlantic *adj* **1** crossing, or designed for or capable of crossing, the Atlantic. **2 a** beyond the Atlantic; **b** *N Am* European; **c** *Brit* American.

transceiver *noun* a piece of radio equipment designed to transmit and receive signals. [20c]

transcend *verb* **1** to be beyond the limits, scope, range, etc of: *transcends the bounds of human decency*. **2** to surpass or excel. **3** to overcome or surmount: *transcend all difficulties*. [16c: from Latin *transcendere*]

transcendent *adj* **1** excellent; surpassing others of the same or similar kind. **2** beyond ordinary human knowledge or experience. **3** of a deity, etc: existing outside the material or created world. ▪ **transcendence** *noun*.

transcendental *adj* **1** going beyond usual human knowledge or experience. **2** supernatural or mystical. **3** vague, abstract or abstruse.

transcendentalism *noun* a philosophical system concerned with what is constant, innate and a priori, independent of and a necessary prerequisite to experience.

transcendental meditation *noun* a method of meditating that involves silent repetition of a mantra to promote spiritual and mental wellbeing. [20c]

transcribe *verb* **1** to write out (a text) in full, eg from notes. **2** to copy (a text) from one place to another: *transcribed the poem into her album*. **3** to write out (a spoken text). **4** to transliterate. **5** *music* to arrange (a piece of music) for an instrument or voice that it was not orig composed for. **6** *comput* to transfer (data) from one computer storage device to another. ▪ **transcriber** *noun*. [16c: from Latin *transcribere*]

transcript *noun* a written, typed or printed copy, esp a legal record of court proceedings. [13c: from Latin *transcriptum*]

transcription *noun* **1** an act or the process of transcribing. **2** something transcribed. [16c: Latin, from *transcriptio*]

transducer *noun* any device that converts energy from one form to another, eg, a loudspeaker, where electrical energy is converted into sound waves. [20c: from Latin *transducere* to transfer]

transept *noun* in a church with a cross-shaped floor plan: either of two arms at right angles to the nave. [16c: from **trans-** (sense 1) + Latin *saeptum* enclosure]

transfer *verb* /trans'fɜː(r), trɑːns-/ (***transferred, transferring***) **1** *tr & intr* to move from one place, person, group, etc to another. **2** *intr* to change from one vehicle, line, passenger system, etc to another while travelling. **3** *law* to hand over (a title, rights, property, etc) to someone else by means of a legal document. **4** to transpose (a design, etc) from one surface to another. **5** *Brit* **a** *intr* of a professional footballer, etc: to change clubs; **b** of a football club, manager, etc: to arrange for (a player) to go to another club. ▸ *noun* /'transfɜː(r), 'trɑːns-/ **1** an act, instance or the process of transferring or the state of being transferred: *asked for a transfer to another department*. **2** *Brit* a design or picture that can be transferred from one surface to another. **3** someone or something that is transferred. **4** *law* **a** an act of handing over (eg, the legal right to property, etc) from one person to another; **b** any document which records this. **5** *N Am* a ticket that allows a passenger to continue a journey on another route, etc. ▪ **transferable** *or* **transferrable** *adj*. ▪ **transference** *noun*. [14c: from Latin *ferre* to carry or bear]

transfer RNA *noun, biol* (abbrev **tRNA**) a small RNA molecule that links a specific amino acid with messenger RNA so it can be used in protein synthesis. [20c]

transfiguration *noun* **1** a change in appearance, esp one that involves something becoming more beautiful, glorious, exalted, etc. **2** (**Transfiguration**) *Christianity* **a** the radiant change in Christ's appearance described in Matthew 17.2 and Mark 9.2–3; **b** a church festival held on 6 August to commemorate this. [14c]

transfigure *verb* to change or cause to change in appearance, esp in becoming more beautiful, glorious, exalted, etc. [13c: from Latin *transfigurare* to change shape]

transfix *verb* **1** to immobilize through surprise, fear, horror, etc. **2** to pierce with a pointed weapon, etc. [16c: from Latin *transfigere* to pierce through]

transform *verb* **1 a** to change in appearance, nature, function, etc, often completely and dramatically: *Some paint transformed the room*; **b** *intr* to undergo such a change. **2** *elec* to change the voltage or type of (a current). [14c: from Latin *transformare*]

transformation *noun* **1** an act or instance or the process of transforming or being transformed. **2** *maths* an operation, eg a mapping one, that changes a set of elements or variables into another set with the same value, magnitude, etc. ▪ **transformational** *adj*. [15c: from Latin]

transformer *noun, elec* an electromagnetic device designed to transfer electrical energy from one alternating current circuit to another, with an increase or decrease in voltage.

transfuse *verb* **1** *med* **a** to transfer (blood or plasma) from one person or animal to another; **b** to treat (a person or animal) with a transfusion of blood or other fluid. **2** to permeate: *Pink and orange patterns transfused the dawn sky*. [15c: from Latin *transfundere* to pour out]

transfusion *noun, med* (*in full* **blood transfusion**) the process of introducing blood, plasma, etc into the bloodstream of a person or animal.

transgress *verb* **1** to break, breach or violate (divine law, a rule, etc). **2** to go beyond or overstep (a limit or boundary). ▪ **transgression** *noun*. ▪ **transgressor** *noun*. [16c: from Latin *transgredi* to step across]

transient *adj* lasting, staying, visiting, etc for only a short time; passing quickly. ▸ *noun* a temporary resident, worker, etc. ▪ **transience** *or* **transiency** *noun*. [17c: from Latin *transire* to cross over]

transistor *noun* **1** *electronics* a semiconductor device that has three or more electrodes, acting as a switch, amplifier or detector of electric current. **2** (*in full* **transistor radio**) a small portable radio that has transistors instead of valves and tubes. [20c: from *transfer* + *resistor*]

transistorize *or* **-ise** *verb* to design or fit with a transistor or transistors rather than valves. ▪ **transistorization** *noun*. ▪ **transistorized** *adj*. [20c]

transit *noun* **1** an act or the process of carrying or moving goods, passengers, etc from one place to another. **2** a route or passage. **3** *astron* **a** the passage of a heavenly body across a meridian; **b** the passage of a smaller heavenly body across a larger one. [15c: from Latin *transire* to go across]

transition *noun* **1** a change or passage from one condition, state, subject, place, etc to another. **2** *archit* the gradual change from one style to another, esp from Norman to Early English. ▪ **transitional** *or* **transitionary** *adj*. [16c: from Latin *transitio* a going across]

transition element *noun, chem* in the periodic table: any of a group of metallic elements, eg copper, cobalt, iron, etc, that tend to show variable valency. Also called **transition metal**.

transitive *adj, grammar* of a verb: taking a direct object, eg *make* in *They make lots of money.* ▪ **transitively** *adv*. ▪ **transitivity** *noun*. [16c: from Latin *transitivus*]

transitory *adj* short-lived; lasting only for a short time. [14c: from Latin *transitorius* having a passage]

translate *verb* **1 a** to express (a word, speech, written text, etc) in another language. **b** *intr* to do this, esp as a profession. **2** *intr* of a written text, etc: to be able to be expressed in another language, format, etc: *Poetry doesn't always translate well.* **3** to put or express (an idea, etc) in other, usu simpler, terms. **4** to interpret: *translated her expression as contempt*. **5** *tr & intr* to convert or be converted into: *need to translate their ideas into reality* • *The price translates as roughly £50.* **6** *tr & intr* to change or move from one state, condition, person, place, etc to another. ▪ **translatable** *adj*. [13c: from Latin *transferre* to carry across]

translation *noun* **1** a word, speech, written text, etc that has been put into one language from another. **2** an act or instance or the process of translating. **3** *maths* a transformation with a sliding movement but no turning. Compare **enlargement**, **reflection**, **rotation**. **4** *genetics* in living cells: the organization of amino acids into a sequence to form proteins. ▪ **translational** *adj*.

translator *noun* **1** someone whose job is to translate texts, speeches, etc from one language to another. **2** a machine that translates from one language into another. **3** *comput* a program that converts source code into machine code.

transliterate *verb* to replace (the characters of a word, etc) with the nearest equivalent characters of another alphabet. ▪ **transliteration** *noun*. [19c: from Latin *litera* letter]

translucent *adj* **1** allowing light to pass diffusely. **2** clear. ▪ **translucence** *or* **translucency** *noun*. [16c: from Latin *lucere* to shine]

transmigrate *verb, intr* **1** of a soul: to pass into another body at or just after death. **2** to move from one home to another. ▪ **transmigration** *noun*. [17c: from Latin *transmigrare* to migrate]

transmission *noun* **1** an act or the process of transmitting or the state of being transmitted. **2** something that is transmitted, esp a radio or TV broadcast. **3** the system of parts in a motor vehicle that transfers power from the engine to the wheels. ▪ **transmissional** *adj*. [17c: from Latin *transmissio* sending across]

transmit *verb* (***transmitted, transmitting***) **1** to pass or hand on (esp a message, a genetic characteristic, an inheritance, or an infection or disease). **2** to convey (emotion, etc). **3** *tr & intr* **a** to send out (signals) by radio waves; **b** to broadcast (a radio or television programme). ▪ **transmissible** *adj*. ▪ **transmissive** *adj*. ▪ **transmittable** *adj*. ▪ **transmittal** *noun*. [14c: from Latin *transmittere* to send across]

transmitter *noun* **1** someone or something that transmits. **2** the equipment that transmits the signals in radio and TV broadcasting.

transmogrify *verb* (***-ies, -ied***) *humorous* to transform, esp in a surprising or bizarre way. ▪ **transmogrification** *noun*. [17c]

transmutation *noun* **1** the act or an instance or the process of transmuting; a change of form. **2** *physics* the changing of one element into another by nuclear bombardment or irradiation as opposed to spontaneous decay. **3** *alchemy* the changing of a base metal into gold or silver. ▪ **transmutational** *adj*.

transmute *verb* **1** to change the form, substance or nature of. **2** to change (one chemical element) into another. **3** *alchemy* to change (base metal) into gold or silver. [15c: from Latin *transmutare* to change condition]

transnational *adj* extending beyond national boundaries or being of concern to more than one nation. ▸ *noun* a company that has interests in more than one country.

transom *noun* **1** a horizontal bar of wood or stone across a window or the top of a door. **2** a lintel. **3** (*in full* **transom window**) a small window over the lintel of a door or larger window. ▪ **transomed** *adj*. [14c]

transparency *noun* (***-ies***) **1** the quality or state of being transparent. **2** a small photograph on glass or rigid plastic mounted in a frame, to be viewed using a slide projector. **3** a picture, print, etc on glass or other translucent background that can be seen when a light is shone behind it.

transparent *adj* **1** able to be seen through. **2** of a motive, etc: easily understood or recognized; obvious; evident. **3** of an excuse, pretence, disguise, etc: easily seen through. **4** of a person, their character, etc: frank and open; candid. ▪ **transparently** *adv*. [15c: from Latin *parere* to appear]

transpire *verb* **1** *intr* of a secret, etc: to become known; to come to light. **2** *intr, loosely* to happen. **3** *tr & intr, botany* of a plant: to release water vapour. ▪ **transpiration** *noun*. [16c: from Latin *spirare* to breathe]

transplant *verb* /trans'plɑːnt/ **1** to take (living skin, tissue, an organ, etc) from someone and use it as an implant, either at another site in the donor's own body or in the body of another person. **2** to move (esp a growing plant) from one place to another. ▸ *noun* /'trans-/ **1** *surgery* an operation which involves transplanting an organ, etc. **2** an organ, plant, etc which has been transplanted or is ready to be transplanted. ▪ **transplantation** *noun*. [15c: from Latin *transplantare*]

transponder *noun* a radio and radar device that receives a signal and then sends out its own signal in response. [20c: from *trans*mit + res*pond*]

transport *verb* /trans'pɔːt/ **1** to carry (goods, passengers, etc) from one place to another. **2** *hist* to send (a criminal) to a penal colony overseas. **3** to affect strongly or deeply: *was transported with grief.* ▸ *noun* /'transpɔːt/ **1** a system or business for taking people, goods, etc from place to place: *public transport*. **2** a means of getting or being transported from place to place. **3** (*often* **transports**) strong emotion, esp of pleasure. **4** a ship, aircraft, lorry, etc used to carry soldiers or military equipment and stores. ▪ **transportable** *adj*. [15c: from Latin *transportare* to carry across]

transportation *noun* **1** an act of transporting or the process of being transported. **2** a means of being transported; transport. **3** *hist* a form of punishment where convicted criminals were sent to overseas penal colonies. **4** *geog* the collection and deposition of material by rivers.

transport café *noun, Brit* an inexpensive roadside restaurant for long-distance lorry drivers.

transporter *noun* a vehicle that carries other vehicles, large pieces of machinery, etc by road.

transpose *verb* **1** to cause (two or more things, letters, words, etc) to change places. **2** to change the position of (an item) in a sequence or series. **3** *music* to perform or rewrite (notes, a piece of music, etc) in a different key. ▪ **transposition** *noun*. [14c: from French *poser* to put]

transputer *noun, comput* a chip capable of all the functions of a microprocessor, including memory, designed for parallel processing rather than sequential processing. [20c: from *trans*istor + com*puter*]

transsexual *noun* **1** someone who is anatomically of one sex but who adopts the characteristics, behaviour, etc usu perceived as typical of the opposite sex. **2** someone who has had medical, hormonal and/or surgical treatment to alter their physical features so that they more closely resemble those of the opposite sex. ▸ *adj* relating or referring to a transsexual. ▪ **transsexualism** *noun*. ▪ **transsexuality** *noun*. [20c]

transship *verb, tr & intr* to transfer from one ship or form of transport to another. ▪ **transshipment** *noun*. [18c]

transubstantiation *noun* **1** an act or the process of changing, or changing something, into something else. **2** *Christianity* esp in the Roman Catholic Church: **a** the conversion of consecrated Eucharistic bread and wine into the body and blood of Christ; **b** the doctrine which states that this happens. [14c]

transuranic /tranzjʊ'ranɪk/ *adj, chem* of an element: having an atomic number greater than that of uranium. [20c]

transversal *noun, geom* a line that cuts a set of other lines.

transverse *adj* placed, lying, built, etc in a crosswise direction. ▪ **transversely** *adv*. [17: from Latin *vertere* to turn]

transvestite *noun* someone, esp a man, who dresses in clothes that are conventionally thought of as being exclusive to people of the opposite sex. ▪ **transvestism** *noun*. [20c: from Latin *vestire* to dress]

trap *noun* **1** a device or hole, usu baited, for catching animals, sometimes killing them in the process. **2** a plan or trick for surprising someone into speech or action, or catching them unawares: *a speed trap*. **3** a trapdoor. **4** a bend in a pipe, esp a drainpipe, which fills with liquid to stop foul gases passing up the pipe. **5** a light, two-wheeled carriage which is usu pulled by a single horse. **6** a device for throwing a ball or clay pigeon into the air. **7** one of the box-like compartments that are set along the starting line of a greyhound race-track where the dogs wait before being released at the beginning of a race. **8** *golf* a bunker or other hazard. **9** *slang* the mouth. **10** (**traps**) *jazz slang* drums or other percussion instruments. ▸ *verb* (***trapped, trapping***) **1** to catch (an animal) in a trap. **2** to catch (someone) out or unawares, esp with a trick. **3** to set traps in (a place). **4** to stop and hold in or as if in a trap. [Anglo-Saxon *treppe*]

trapdoor *noun* a small door or opening in a floor, ceiling, etc that is usu set flush with its surface.

trapeze *noun* a swing-like apparatus consisting of a short horizontal bar hanging on two ropes, used by gymnasts and acrobats. [19c: French, from Latin *trapezium* trapezium]

trapezium *noun* (***trapeziums*** *or* ***trapezia***) **1** *Brit* a four-sided geometric figure that has one pair of its opposite sides parallel. **2** *N Am* a four-sided geometric figure that has no parallel sides. **3** any four-sided geometric figure that is not a parallelogram. ▪ **trapezial** *adj*. [16c: Latin, from Greek *trapeza* table]

trapezius /trə'piːzɪəs/ *noun* (***trapeziuses*** *or* ***-trapezii*** /-zɪaɪ/) either of a pair of large flat triangular muscles that extend over the back of the neck and the shoulders. [18c: from the trapezium shape they form as a pair]

trapezoid *noun* **1** *Brit* a four-sided geometric figure that has no sides parallel. **2** *N Am* a four-sided geometric figure that has one pair of its opposite sides parallel. ▪ **trapezoidal** *adj*. [16c: from Greek *trapeza* table]

trapper *noun* someone who traps wild animals, usu with the intention of selling their fur.

trappings *plural noun* **1** ornamental accessories denoting office, status, etc: *the trappings of office*. **2** a horse's ceremonial or ornamental harness. [16c: from French *drap* cloth]

Trappist *noun* a branch of Cistercian monks, founded in La Trappe in Normandy, who observe a severe rule which includes a vow of silence. ▸ *adj* belonging or relating to this branch.

traps *plural noun, Brit* personal luggage. [19c: from French *drap* cloth]

trash *noun* **1** **a** rubbish; waste material or objects; **b** *chiefly US* domestic waste. **2** nonsense. **3** a worthless, contemptible, etc person or people: *white trash*. **4** **a** a worthless object or worthless objects; **b** art, literature, cinema, music, etc perceived as having no merit. ▸ *verb* **1** *informal* to wreck. **2** *informal* **a** to expose as worthless; **b** to give (a film, novel, play, performance, etc) a very adverse review. ▪ **trashy** *adj* (**-ier, -iest**). [16c]

trashcan *noun, US* a dustbin.

trattoria /tratəˈriːə/ *noun* (***trattorias*** *or* ***trattorie*** /-eɪ/) an informal Italian restaurant. [19c: Italian, from *trattore* host]

trauma *noun* (***traumas*** *or* ***traumata***) **1** *med* **a** a severe physical injury or wound; **b** a state of shock brought on by this. **2 a** a severe emotional shock that may have long-term effects on behaviour or personality; **b** the condition that can result from this type of emotional shock. **3** *loosely* any event, situation, etc that is stressful, emotionally upsetting, etc. ▪ **traumatize** *or* **-ise** *verb*. [17c: Greek, meaning 'wound']

traumatic *adj* **1** relating to, resulting from or causing trauma. **2** *informal* distressing; emotionally upsetting. ▪ **traumatically** *adv*.

travail *noun* **1** painful or extremely hard work or labour. **2** the pain of childbirth; labour. ▸ *verb, intr* **1** to do hard work. **2** to undergo pain, esp in childbirth. [13c: French, meaning 'painful effort']

travel *verb* (***travelled, travelling***; *US* ***traveled, traveling***) **1** *tr & intr* to go from place to place; to make a journey: *travelled the world* • *travelled through France*. **2** to journey across (a stated distance). **3** *intr* to be capable of withstanding a journey, esp a long one: *not a wine that travels well*. **4** *intr* to journey from place to place as a sales representative. **5** *intr* to move: *Light travels in a straight line*. **6** *intr* to move or pass deliberately, systematically, steadily, etc: *Her eyes travelled over the horizon*. **7** *intr* of machinery: to move along a fixed course. **8** *intr, informal* to move quickly. ▸ *noun* **1** an act or the process of travelling. **2** (*usu* **travels**) a journey or tour, esp abroad. **3** the range, distance, speed, etc of the motion of a machine or a machine part. [14c: from **travail**]

travel agency *noun* a business that makes arrangements for travellers, holidaymakers, etc. ▪ **travel agent** *noun*.

traveller *noun* **1** someone who travels. **2** *old use* a travelling salesman. **3** *Brit informal* a Gypsy.

traveller's cheque *noun* a cheque for a fixed sum that the bearer signs and can then exchange for currency, goods or services in another country.

travelogue *noun* a film, article, talk, etc about travel.

traverse *verb* **1** to go or lie across or through. **2** to examine or consider (a subject, problem, etc) carefully and thoroughly. ▸ *noun* **1** an act or the process of crossing or traversing. **2** a path or passage across eg a rock face or slope. **3** something that lies across. **4** a sideways movement. ▪ **traversal** *noun*. [14c: from French *traverser*]

travesty *noun* (**-*ies***) a ridiculous or crude distortion; a mockery or caricature: *a travesty of justice*. ▸ *verb* (**-*ies*, -*ied***) to make or be a travesty of. [17c: from French *travestir* to disguise]

trawl *noun* **1** (*in full* **trawl-net**) a large bag-shaped net with a wide mouth, used for catching fish at sea. **2** a wide-ranging or extensive search: *a trawl through the library catalogue*. ▸ *verb, tr & intr* **1** to fish (the sea, an area of sea, etc) using a trawl-net. **2** to search through (a large number of things, people, etc) thoroughly: *had to trawl through hundreds of applications*. [16c: prob from Dutch *traghelen* to drag]

trawler *noun* **1** a fishing-boat used in trawling. **2** someone who trawls.

tray *noun* a flat piece of wood, metal, plastic, etc, usu with a small raised edge, used for carrying dishes, etc. [Anglo-Saxon *trig*]

treacherous *adj* **1** of someone, their conduct, etc: not to be trusted; ready or likely to betray. **2** hazardous or dangerous; unreliable or untrustworthy: *Black ice made the roads treacherous*. ▪ **treacherously** *adv*. [14c]

treachery *noun* (**-*ies***) **1** deceit, betrayal, cheating or treason. **2** an act or instance of this. [13c: from French *trechier* to cheat]

treacle *noun* **1** the thick dark sticky liquid that remains after the crystallization and removal of sugar from extracts of sugar cane or sugar beet. **2** molasses. **3** cloying sentimentality. ▪ **treacly** *adj*. [14c: from Greek *theriake antidotos* an antidote to the bites of wild beasts]

tread *verb* (*past tense* ***trod***, *past participle* ***trodden*** *or* ***trod***) **1** *intr* (*usu* **tread on**) to walk or step: *trod on the cat's tail*. **2** to step or walk on, over or along: *trod the primrose path*. **3** to crush or press (into the ground, etc) with a foot or feet: *treading ash into the carpet*. **4** to wear or form (a path, hole, etc) by walking. **5** to perform by walking. **6** *intr* to suppress or treat cruelly. **7** of a male bird: to copulate with (a female bird). ▸ *noun* **1** a manner, style or sound of walking. **2** an act of treading. **3** the horizontal part of a stair. **4** a mark made by treading; a footprint or track. **5 a** the thick, grooved and patterned surface of a tyre that grips the road and disperses rain water; **b** the depth of this surface. [Anglo-Saxon *tredan*]
IDIOMS **tread on sb's toes 1** to encroach on their sphere of influence, etc. **2** to offend them. **tread water** to keep oneself afloat and upright in water by making a treading movement with the legs and a circular movement with the hands and arms.

treadle *noun* a foot pedal that can be pushed back and forward in a rhythmic motion and so produce the momentum to drive a machine, eg, a sewing machine. [Anglo-Saxon *tredel* the step of a stair]

treadmill *noun* **1** an apparatus for producing motion that consists of a large wheel turned by people or animals treading on steps inside or around it. **2** a similar piece of equipment used for exercising. **3** a monotonous and dreary routine.

treason *noun* **1** (*in full* **high treason**) disloyalty to or betrayal of one's country, sovereign or government. **2** any betrayal of trust or act of disloyalty. ▪ **treasonable** *adj*. ▪ **treasonous** *adj*. [13c: from French *traison*, from Latin *traditio* a handing over]

treasure *noun* **1** wealth and riches, esp in the form of gold, silver, precious stones and jewels, etc which have been accumulated over a period of time and which can be hoarded. **2** anything of great value. **3** *informal* someone who is loved and valued, esp as a helper, friend, etc. ▸ *verb* **1** to value greatly or think of as very precious: *treasured him as a friend*. **2** (*usu* **treasure up**) to preserve or collect for future use or as valuable: *treasured up all his old school photographs*. ▪ **treasured** *adj*. [12c: from French *tresor* treasure]

treasure hunt *noun* **1** a game where the object is to find a prize by solving a series of clues about its hiding place. **2** a hunt for treasure.

treasurer *noun* **1** a person in a club, society, etc who is in charge of the money and accounts. **2** an official who is responsible for public money, eg, in a local council.

treasure-trove *noun* **1** *law* something valuable found hidden and of unknown ownership and therefore deemed to be the property of the Crown. **2** anything of value, esp something that unexpectedly gives pleasure. [12c: from French *tresor* treasure + *trover* to find]

treasury *noun* (**-ies**) **1** (**Treasury**) **a** the government department in charge of a country's finances, esp the planning and implementation of expenditure policies, the collection of taxes, etc; **b** the officials who comprise this department; **c** the place where the money that this department collects is kept. **2** the income or funds of a state, government, organization, etc. [13c: from French *tresor* treasure]

treat *verb* **1** to deal with or behave towards (someone or something) in a specified manner: *treat it as a joke*. **2** to care for or deal with (a person, illness, injury, etc) medically. **3** to put (something) through a process, etc: *treat the wood with creosote*. **4** to provide with (food, drink, entertainment, a gift, etc) at one's own expense: *I'll treat you to lunch*. **5** *tr & intr* (*often* **treat of**) to discuss. **6** *intr* (*usu* **treat with**) to negotiate. ▸ *noun* **1** an outing, meal, present, etc that one person treats another to. **2** a source of pleasure or enjoyment, esp when unexpected. ▪ **treatable** *adj*. [13c: from French *traitier*, from Latin *trahere* to draw or drag]

IDIOMS **a treat** *informal, sometimes ironic* very good or well: *He looked a treat in his kilt*.

treatise /'triːtɪz, -tɪs/ *noun* a formal piece of writing that deals systematically and in depth with a subject. [14c: from French *traitier* to treat]

treatment *noun* **1** the medical or surgical care given to cure an illness or injury. **2** an act or the manner or process of dealing with someone or something: *rough treatment*. **3** a way of presenting something, esp in literature, music, art, etc: *his sympathetic treatment of his women characters*.

treaty *noun* (**-ies**) **1** a formal agreement between states or governments. **2** an agreement between two parties or individuals. [14c: from French *traité*; see **treat**]

treble *noun* **1** something that is three times as much or as many. **2** *music* **a** a soprano; **b** someone, esp a boy, who has a soprano singing voice; **c** a part written for this type of voice; **d** an instrument that has a similar range; **e** in a family of instruments: the member that has the highest range. **3** a high-pitched voice or sound. **4** the higher part of the sound frequency range of a radio, record, etc. **5** *betting* a bet on three horses from three different races where the original stake money plus any winnings from the first race goes on the horse from the second race, after which, if the second horse wins, the total is laid on the horse from the third race. **6 a** *darts* the narrow inner ring of a dartboard, where scores are triple the number that is shown on the outside of the board; **b** a dart that hits the board in this area. **7** *sport* esp in football: the winning of three championships, cups, titles, etc in a single season. ▸ *adj* **1** three times as much or as many; threefold; triple. **2** belonging, relating or referring to, being or having a treble voice. **3** of a voice: high-pitched. ▸ *adv* with a treble voice: *sing treble*. ▸ *verb, tr & intr* to make or become three times as much or as many. ▪ **trebly** *adv*. [14c: French, from Latin *triplus* triple]

treble chance *noun, Brit* a type of football pool where winnings are paid out on the basis of how accurately punters can predict the number of draws, home wins and away wins.

treble clef *noun, music* in musical notation: a sign (𝄞) at the beginning of a piece of written music placing the note G (a fifth above middle C) on the second line of the staff.

tree *noun* **1** *botany* **a** a tall woody perennial plant that typically has one main stem or trunk and which, unlike a shrub, usu only begins to branch at some distance from the ground; **b** in extended use: any plant, eg, the banana, plantain, palm, etc, that has a single non-woody stem which grows to a considerable height. **2** a **family tree**. **3 a** a frame or support: *shoe tree*; **b** a branched structure that things can be hung on: *a mug tree*. ▪ **treeless** *adj*. [Anglo-Saxon *treow*]

tree fern *noun* a tropical fern with a tall thick woody stem.

tree of knowledge *noun* **1** *Bible* the tree in the garden of Eden that bore the forbidden fruit (Gen 2.9). **2** a figurative expression for knowledge in general.

tree surgery *noun* the treatment and preservation of diseased or damaged trees. ▪ **tree surgeon** *noun*.

treetop *noun* the upper leaves and branches of a tree.

trefoil /'trɛfɔɪl/ *noun* **1** a leaf which is divided into three sections. **2** a plant with such leaves, eg, clover: *bird's-foot trefoil*. **3** something with three lobes or sections, esp a carved ornament or decoration in a tracery window. ▸ *adj* having three lobes or divided into three parts. [15c: from Latin *folium* leaf]

trek *verb* (***trekked, trekking***) *intr* **1** to make a long hard journey. **2** *S Afr* **a** *hist* to make a journey by ox-wagon; **b** of an ox: to pull a load. ▸ *noun* **1** a long hard journey: *It's a bit of a trek to the shops*. **2** *S Afr* a journey by ox-wagon. [19c: from Afrikaans, from Dutch *trekken* to draw (a vehicle or load)]

trellis *noun* (*in full* **trellis-work**) an open lattice framework, usu fixed to a wall, for supporting or training climbing plants, fruit trees, etc. [14c: from French *trelis*]

trematode *noun* a parasitic flatworm living in the gut of animals and humans. ▪ **trematoid** *adj*. [19c: from Greek *trematodes* perforated]

tremble *verb, intr* **1** to shake or shudder involuntarily, eg, with cold, fear, weakness, etc. **2** to quiver or vibrate: *The harebells trembled in the wind*. **3** to feel great fear or anxiety: *trembled at the thought of going for another interview*. ▸ *noun* a trembling movement or state. ▪ **trembling** *adj*. [14c: from French *trembler*]

tremendous *adj* **1** *informal* extraordinary, very good, remarkable, enormous, etc: *a tremendous relief*. **2** awe-inspiring; terrible: *an accident involving a tremendous loss of lives*. ▪ **tremendously** *adv*. [17c: from Latin *tremendus* fearful, terrible]

tremolo *noun, music* **1** a trembling effect achieved by rapidly repeating a note or notes, or by quickly alternating notes. **2** a similar effect in singing. **3** **a** a device in an organ used for producing a tremolo; **b** (*in full* **tremolo arm**) a lever on an electric guitar used to produce this effect. Compare **vibrato**. [18c: Italian, meaning 'trembling']

tremor *noun* **1** a shaking or quivering: *couldn't disguise the tremor in his voice.* **2** (*in full* **earth tremor**) a minor earthquake. **3** a thrill of fear or pleasure. ► *verb, intr* to shake. [14c: French, from Latin *tremere* to tremble]

tremulous *adj* **1** quivering, esp with fear, worry, nervousness, excitement, etc. **2** of someone's disposition, etc: shy, retiring, fearful, anxious, etc. **3** of a drawn line, writing, etc: produced by a shaky or hesitant hand. ▪ **tremulously** *adv.* [17c: from Latin *tremulus* trembling]

trench *noun* **1** a long narrow ditch in the ground. **2** *military* **a** a large-scale version of this where the earth thrown up by the excavations is used to form a parapet to protect soldiers from enemy fire, shells, etc and which often incorporates rudimentary living quarters; **b** (**trenches**) a series of these that forms a defensive system. **3** a long narrow steep-sided depression in the floor of an ocean. [14c: from French *trenche* a cut]

trenchant *adj* **1** incisive; penetrating: *a trenchant mind.* **2** forthright; vigorous: *a trenchant policy to improve efficiency.* **3** *poetic* cutting; keen. ▪ **trenchancy** *noun.* [14c: from French *trencher* to cut]

trench coat *noun* **1** a long loose raincoat, usu double-breasted and with a belt. **2** a military overcoat.

trencher *noun, hist* a wooden platter or board for serving food. [14c: from French *trencher* to cut]

trencherman *noun* someone who eats well.

trend *noun* **1** a general direction or tendency. **2** the current general movement in fashion, style, taste, etc. ► *verb, intr* to turn or have a tendency to turn in a specified direction. [Anglo-Saxon *trendan*]

trendsetter *noun* someone who starts off a fashion.

trendy *adj* (***-ier, -iest***) *Brit, informal* **1** of someone: following the latest fashions. **2** of clothes, music, clubs, bars, etc: fashionable at a particular time. ► *noun* (***-ies***) someone who is, or who tries to be, trendy.

trepidation *noun* nervousness or apprehension. [17c: from Latin *trepidare* to be agitated or alarmed]

trespass *verb, intr* **1** (*usu* **trespass on** *or* **upon**) to make an unlawful or unwarranted entry (on someone else's property). **2** (*usu* **trespass on**) to intrude (on someone's time, privacy, rights, etc). **3** *old use* to sin. ► *noun* **1** an act or the process of entering someone else's property without the right or permission to do so. **2** an intrusion into someone's time, privacy, etc. **3** *old use* a sin. ▪ **trespasser** *noun.* [13c: from French *trespas* passing across]

tress *noun* **1** a long lock or plait of hair. **2** (**tresses**) a woman's or girl's long hair. [13c: from French *tresse*]

trestle *noun* **1** a supporting framework with a horizontal beam the end of which rests on a pair of legs which slope outwards, used with a board on top to form a table. **2** (*in full* **trestle-table**) a table that consists of a board or boards supported by trestles. [14c: from French *trestel*]

trews *plural noun, Brit* trousers, esp close-fitting, tartan ones. [16c: from Irish *trius* and Gaelic *triubhas*]

tri- *combining form, denoting* three or three times: *triangle* • *tri-weekly.* [From Latin and Greek *tri*, a form of Latin *tres* and Greek *treis* three]

triad *noun* **1** a group of three people or things, esp a chord consisting of three notes. **2** (*also* **Triad**) **a** a Chinese secret society, esp of the kind that operate in foreign countries and are involved in organized crime, etc. **b** a member of such a society. ▪ **triadic** *adj.* [16c: from Greek *trias* group of three]

trial *noun* **1** a legal process in which someone who stands accused of a crime or misdemeanour is judged in a court of law. **2** an act or the process of trying or testing. **3** trouble, worry or vexation, or a cause of this: *Her son is a great trial to her.* **4** *sport* a preliminary test of the skill, fitness, etc of a player, athlete, etc, esp one to decide whether they should be offered a job, team place, etc. **5** a test of a vehicle's performance held esp over rough ground or a demanding course. **6** a competition, usu over rough ground, to test skills in handling high-performance cars or motorcycles. **7** (*usu* **trials**) a competition in which the skills of animals are tested: *sheepdog trials.* **8** an attempt. ► *verb* (***trialled, trialling***; *US* ***trialed, trialing***) *tr & intr* to put (a new product, etc) to the test. [16c: French]

IDIOMS **on trial 1** in the process of undergoing legal action in court: *on trial for murder.* **2** in the process of undergoing tests or examination before being permanently accepted or approved. **trial and error** the process of trying various methods, alternatives, etc until a correct or suitable one is found.

trial run *noun* a test of a new product, etc, esp to assess effectiveness, potential, etc prior to an official launch.

triangle *noun* **1** *geom* a plane figure with three sides and three internal angles. **2** anything of a similar shape. **3** a simple musical percussion instrument made from a metal bar which has been bent into a triangular shape with one corner left open and which is played by striking it with a small metal hammer. **4** an emotional relationship or love affair that involves three people. ▪ **triangular** *adj.* [14c: from Latin *triangulus* three-cornered]

triangulate *verb* **1** to mark off (an area of land) into a network of triangular sections with a view to making a survey. **2** to survey and map (a triangularly divided area of land). ▪ **triangulation** *noun.*

Triassic *geol, adj* belonging, relating or referring to the earliest period of the Mesozoic era, when the first dinosaurs, large sea reptiles and small mammals appeared. ► *noun* this period of time. [19c: from Latin *trias* **triad**, because the period is divisible into three distinct sections]

triathlon *noun* an athletic contest of three events, usu swimming, running and cycling. ▪ **triathlete** *noun.* [20c: from **tri-** and modelled on **decathlon**]

triatomic *adj, chem* having three atoms in the molecule. ▪ **triatomically** *adv.* [19c]

tribalism *noun* **1** the system of tribes as a way of organizing society. **2** the feeling of belonging to a tribe.

tribe *noun* **1** an organized, usu hierarchical, group of people, families, clans, etc who share ancestral, social, cultural, linguistic, religious, economic, etc ties. **2** a large group with a shared interest, profession, etc: *a tribe of protesters.* **3** *biol* a subdivision of a family of plants or animals, made up of several related genera. ▪ **tribal** *adj.* [13c: from Latin *tribus*]

tribesman *or* **tribeswoman** *noun* a man or woman who belongs to a tribe.

tribulation *noun* **1** great sorrow, trouble, affliction, misery, etc. **2** a cause or source of this. [13c: from Latin *tribulatio*]

tribunal *noun* **1** a court of justice. **2** *Brit* a board of people appointed to look into a specified matter and to adjudicate on it: *took her case to the rent tribunal.* **3** a seat or bench in a court for a judge or judges. [16c: Latin, from *tribunus* head of a tribe]

tribune *noun* **1** *hist* **a** (*in full* **tribune of the people**) a high official elected by the ordinary people of ancient Rome to defend their rights; **b** (*in full* **military tribune**) a leader of a Roman legion. **2** a champion or defender of the rights of the common people. [14c: from Latin *tribunus* head of a tribe]

tributary *noun* (**-ies**) **1** a stream or river that flows into a larger river or a lake. **2** *hist* a person or nation that pays tribute to another. ▸ *adj* **1** of a stream or river: flowing into a larger river or a lake. **2** *hist* **a** paid or owed as tribute; **b** of a speech, prayer, gift, etc: paying tribute. [14c: from Latin *tribuere* to assign, give or pay]

tribute *noun* **1** a speech, gift, etc given as an expression of praise, thanks, admiration, affection, etc. **2** a sign or evidence of something valuable, effective, worthy of praise, etc; a testimony: *Her success was a tribute to all her hard work.* **3** *hist* a sum of money regularly paid by one nation or ruler to another in return for protection, etc or as an acknowledgement of submission, etc. [14c: from Latin *tribuere* to assign]

trice *noun* a moment. [15c: from Dutch *trijsen* to pull, hoist or haul]

triceps *noun* (**tricepses** *or* **triceps**) a muscle that is attached in three places, esp the large muscle at the back of the upper arm. [16c: from Latin *caput* head]

trichinosis /trɪkɪˈnɪʊsɪs/ *noun, med* a disease that is caused by entry of a roundworm into the digestive system, the main symptoms of which are nausea, diarrhoea, fever and pain in the muscles. [19c: from Greek *trichinos* of hair]

trichology /trɪˈkɒlɪdʒɪ/ *noun* the scientific study of the hair and its diseases. ▪ **trichologist** *noun.* [19c: from Greek *trichos* hair]

trick *noun* **1** something done or said to cheat, deceive, fool or humiliate someone. **2** a deceptive appearance, esp one caused by the light; an illusion. **3** a mischievous act or plan; a prank or joke. **4** a clever or skilful act or feat which astonishes, puzzles or amuses. **5** a peculiar habit or mannerism: *He has a trick of always saying inappropriate things.* **6** a special technique or knack: *a trick of the trade.* **7** a feat of skill which can be learned. **8** the cards played in one round of a card game and which are won by one of the players. **9** *slang* a prostitute's client. ▸ *verb* **1** to cheat, deceive or defraud. **2** (**trick into** *or* **out of**) to persuade or cheat by: *tricked her into believing him • tricked the old woman out of her savings.* ▪ **trickery** *noun.* [15c: from Norman French *trique*]

IDIOMS **do the trick** *informal* to do or be what is necessary to achieve the required result. **how's tricks?** *informal* a casual greeting.

PHRASAL VERBS **trick out** *or* **up** to dress or decorate in a fancy way.

trickle *verb, tr & intr* **1** to flow or cause to flow in a thin slow stream or drops. **2** to move, come or go slowly and gradually. ▸ *noun* a slow stream, flow or movement. [14c: orig said of tears]

trick or treat *noun, chiefly N Am* the children's practice of dressing up on Hallowe'en to call at people's houses for small gifts, threatening to play a trick on them if they are not given one.

trickster *noun* someone who deceives, cheats or plays tricks.

tricky *adj* (**-ier, -iest**) **1** difficult to handle or do; needing skill and care. **2** inclined to trickery; sly; deceitful. **3** resourceful; adroit. ▪ **trickily** *adv.* ▪ **trickiness** *noun.*

tricolour *or* (*N Am*) **tricolor** *noun* /ˈtrɪkələ(r)/ a three-coloured flag, esp one with three bands of equal size in three different colours, eg, the French flag. ▸ *adj* /ˈtraɪkʌlə(r)/ having or being of three different colours. ▪ **tricoloured** *adj.* [18c: from Latin *tricolor*]

tricycle *noun* a pedal-driven vehicle with two wheels at the back and one at the front. Often shortened to **trike**. ▪ **tricyclist** *noun.* [19c: French, from Greek *kuklos* circle]

trident *noun, hist* a spear with three prongs. [16c: from Latin *tridens* three-toothed]

tried *verb, past tense, past participle of* **try**.

triennial *adj* **1** happening once every three years. **2** lasting for three years. ▸ *noun* **1** a period of three years. **2** an event that recurs every three years. ▪ **triennially** *adv.* [17c: from Latin *triennium* a span of three years]

triennium *noun* (**trienniums** *or* **triennia**) a period of three years. [19c]

trier *noun* **1** someone who perseveres at something, esp something they have little talent or aptitude for. **2** someone who tries out food. [14c: from **try** (*verb*)]

trifle *noun* **1** something of little or no value. **2** a very small amount. **3** *Brit* a dessert of sponge-cake soaked in sherry, topped with jelly and fruit, and then custard and whipped cream. ▸ *verb* (*usu* **trifle with**) **a** to treat (someone, their feelings, etc) frivolously, insensitively or with a lack of seriousness or respect; **b** to talk or think about (a proposition, idea, project, etc) idly or not very seriously. [13c: from French *trufe* mockery, deceit]

IDIOMS **a trifle** slightly, rather; to a small extent: *He's a trifle upset.*

trifling *adj* **1** unimportant; trivial. **2** frivolous. ▪ **triflingly** *adv.*

trifoliate *adj* of a compound leaf: made up of three leaflets. [18c: from Latin *foliatus* leaved]

trigger *noun* **1** a small lever which, when squeezed and released, sets a mechanism going, esp one that fires a gun. **2** something that starts off a train of events, reactions, etc. ▸ *verb* **1** (*also* **trigger off**) to start (a train of events, reactions, etc) in motion. **2** to fire or set off (a gun, detonator, etc). [17c: from Dutch *trekker* a trigger, from *trekken* to pull]

triggerfish *noun* a tropical marine fish whose second dorsal fin can depress the spines on the first fin.

trigger-happy *adj, informal* liable to shoot a gun, etc, or to go into a rage, with little provocation. [20c]

triglyceride *noun, chem* any of a large number of chemical compounds that are present in most fats and oils and which consist of a glycerol molecule combined with three acid radicals. [19c]

trigonometric function *noun, maths* a function of an angle that is defined by the relationship between the angles and sides in a right-angled triangle, eg sine, cosine, tangent, secant, cosecant, cotangent.

trigonometry *noun, maths* the branch of mathematics concerned with the relationships between the sides and angles of triangles. ▪ **trigonometric** *or* **trigonometrical** *adj.* [17c: from Greek *trigonon* triangle + *metron* measure]

trike see under **tricycle**

trilateral *adj* **1** three-sided. **2** of talks, an agreement, treaty, etc: involving three parties, nations, countries, etc. [17c: from Latin *latus* side]

trilby *noun* (**-ies**) *Brit* a soft felt hat with an indented crown and narrow brim. [19c: named after the heroine of George du Maurier's novel *Trilby*]

trilingual *adj* **1** of someone: able to speak three languages fluently. **2** written or spoken in three languages. ▪ **trilingualism** *noun.* [19c: from Latin *lingua* tongue]

trill *noun* **1** *music* a sound produced by repeatedly playing or singing a note and a note above in rapid succession. **2** a warbling sound made by a songbird. **3** a consonant sound, esp an 'r', made by rapidly vibrating the tongue. ▶ *verb, tr & intr* to play, sing, pronounce, etc with a trill. [17c: from Italian *trillare* to quaver or warble]

trillion *noun* (*pl* ***trillion***) **a** *chiefly N Am* a million million (10^{12}). *Brit equivalent* **billion**. **b** *chiefly Brit* a million million million (10^{18}). *N Am equivalent* **quintillion**. ▪ **trillionth** *adj, noun.* [17c: French, modelled on **billion**]

trilobite /'traɪləbaɪt/ *noun* an extinct marine arthropod with a flat oval body divided lengthwise into three lobes, or the fossilized remains of one of these animals. ▪ **trilobitic** *adj.* [19c: from Greek *trilobos* three-lobed]

trilogy *noun* (**-ies**) a group of three related plays, novels, poems, operas, etc. [17c: from Greek *trilogia*, from *logos* word, reason]

trim *verb* (***trimmed, trimming***) **1** to make (hair, etc) neat and tidy, esp by clipping. **2** (*also* **trim away, from** *or* **off**) to remove by, or as if by, cutting: *trim hundreds of pounds off the cost.* **3** to make less by, or as if by, cutting: *trim costs.* **4** to decorate with ribbons, lace, ornaments, etc: *trimmed the dress with pink velvet.* **5** to adjust the balance of (a ship, submarine or aircraft) by moving its cargo, ballast, etc. **6** to arrange (a ship's sails) to suit the weather conditions. **7** *intr* to hold a neutral or middle course between two opposing individuals or groups. **8** *intr* to adjust one's behaviour to suit current trends or opinions, esp for self-advancement. ▶ *noun* **1 a** a neatening haircut; **b** an act or the process of giving or having this type of haircut. **2** proper order or condition: *in good trim.* **3** material, ornaments, etc used as decoration. **4** the upholstery, internal and external colour schemes, and chrome and leather accessories, etc of a car. ▶ *adj* (***trimmer, trimmest***) **1** in good order; neat and tidy. **2** slim. [Anglo-Saxon *trymian* to strengthen]

trimaran /'traɪməran/ *noun* a boat that has three hulls side by side. [20c: from **tri-** (sense 1) + *catamaran*]

trimer /'traɪmə(r)/ *noun, chem* a substance whose molecules are formed from three molecules of a **monomer**. ▪ **trimeric** /traɪ'mɛrɪk/ *adj.* [20c: from Greek *meros* part]

trimester /trɪ'mɛstə(r)/ *noun* a period of three months, esp one of the three such periods of human gestation or a period of roughly three months forming an academic term. [19c: from Latin *trimestris* lasting three months]

trimming *noun* **1** decorative ribbon, lace, etc: *a tablecloth with lace trimming.* **2** (**trimmings**) **a** the traditional or usual accompaniments of a meal or specified dish: *turkey with all the trimmings;* **b** the expected accessories, perks, etc that come with something: *an executive post with all the trimmings – company car, private health scheme, etc.*

Trimurti /trɪ'mʊətɪ/ *noun* (sometimes **trimurti**) the Hindu gods, Brahma, Shiva and Vishnu, representing creation, preservation and destruction. [19c: from Sanskrit *tri* three + *murti* shape]

trinitrotoluene /traɪnaɪtroʊ'tɒljʊiːn/ *or* **trinitrotoluol** /-'tɒljʊɒl/ *noun, chem* a highly explosive yellow crystalline solid that is used as an explosive and in certain photographic chemicals and dyes. Often shortened to **TNT**. [20c]

trinity *noun* (**-ies**) **1** the state of being three. **2** a group of three. **3** (**Trinity**) *Christianity* the unity of the Father, Son and Holy Spirit in a single Godhead. [13c: from Latin *trinitas*]

trinket *noun* a small ornament, piece of jewellery, etc of little value. ▪ **trinketry** *noun.* [16c]

trio *noun* **1** a group or set of three. **2** *music* **a** a group of three instruments, players or singers; **b** a piece of music composed for such a group. **3** *music* a contrastive central section of a minuet, scherzo or march. [18c: French, from Italian *tre* three, influenced by **duo**]

trioxide *noun, chem* an oxide that contains three atoms of oxygen.

trip *verb* (***tripped, tripping***) **1** *tr & intr* (*also* **trip over** *or* **up**) to stumble or cause to stumble. **2** *tr & intr* (*also* **trip up**) to make or cause to make a mistake. **3** to catch (someone) out, eg, in a fault or mistake. **4** *intr* (*often* **trip along**) to walk, skip or dance with short light steps. **5** *intr* to move or flow smoothly and easily: *words tripping off the tongue.* **6** *intr* to take a trip or excursion. **7** *intr, informal* to experience the hallucinatory effects of a drug, esp LSD. **8** *tr & intr* to activate or cause (a device or mechanism) to be activated, esp suddenly. ▶ *noun* **1 a** a short journey or excursion, esp for pleasure; **b** a journey of any length. **2** a stumble; an act or the process of accidentally catching the foot. **3** a short light step or skip. **4** a part or catch that can be struck in order to activate a mechanism. **5** an error or blunder. **6** *informal* a hallucinatory experience, esp one that is brought on by taking a drug, eg, LSD: *a bad trip.* [15c: from French *triper* to strike with the foot, to dance]
IDIOMS **trip the light fantastic** *jocular* to dance.

tripartite *adj* **1** divided into or composed of three parts. **2** of talks, an agreement, etc: involving, concerning, ratified by, etc three parts, groups, people, etc. [15c: from Latin *tripartitus* in three parts]

tripe *noun* **1** parts of the stomach of a cow or sheep, used as food. **2** *informal* nonsense; rubbish. [14c: French, meaning 'the entrails of an animal']

triple *adj* **1** three times as great, as much or as many. **2** made up of three parts or things. **3** *music* having three beats to the bar. ▸ *verb, tr & intr* to make or become three times as great, as much or as many. ▸ *noun* **1 a** an amount that is three times greater than the original, usual, etc amount; **b** a measure (of spirits) that is three times greater than a single measure. **2** a group or series of three. ▪ **triply** *adv.* [14c: French, from Latin *triplus* threefold]

triple crown *noun* **1** *Brit* the winning of three important events, races, etc in the same season, esp in horse-racing and rugby union. **2** the Pope's tiara.

triple jump *noun* an athletic event that involves doing a hop, followed by a skip and then a jump.

triple point *noun, physics* the temperature and pressure at which the solid, liquid and vapour phases of a particular substance, or of any combinations of these phases (eg two solids and a liquid) can co-exist in equilibrium.

triplet *noun* **1** one of three children or animals born to the same mother at one birth. **2** a group or set of three, esp three notes played in the time usu taken by two. [18c: from **triple**, modelled on **doublet**]

triple time *noun* musical time with three beats to the bar.

triplicate *adj* /ˈtrɪplɪkət/ **1** having three parts which are exactly alike. **2** being one of three identical copies. **3** tripled. ▸ *noun* /ˈtrɪplɪkət/ any of three identical copies or parts. ▸ *verb* /ˈtrɪplɪkeɪt/ **1** to make three copies of. **2** to multiply by three. ▪ **triplication** *noun.* [15c: from Latin *triplicare, triplicatum* to triple]

triploid *biol, adj* of an organism or cell: with three times the **haploid** number of chromosomes. ▸ *noun* a triploid organism or cell. [20c: from Greek *triplous* threefold]

tripod *noun* **1** a three-legged stand or support, eg for a camera, etc. **2** a stool, table, etc with three legs or feet. [17c: from Greek *tripous* three-footed]

tripper *noun* **1** *Brit* someone who goes on a journey for pleasure; a tourist: *day trippers.* **2** *informal* someone who experiences the hallucinatory effects of a drug, eg LSD.

triptych /ˈtrɪptɪk/ *noun* a picture or carving that covers three joined panels to form a single work of art, often used as an altarpiece. See also **diptych**. [18c: from Greek *triptychos*]

trip-wire *noun* a hidden wire that sets off a mechanism, eg, of an alarm, bomb, etc, when someone trips over it.

trireme /ˈtraɪəriːm/ *noun* an ancient galley with three banks of rowers on each side, which was principally used as a warship. [17c: from Latin *remus* oar]

trite *adj* of a remark, phrase, etc: having no meaning or effectiveness because of overuse. [16c: from Latin *tritus* worn, common]

tritium *noun, chem* (symbol **T**) a radioactive isotope of hydrogen that has two neutrons as well as one proton in its nucleus, used in fusion reactors. [20c: from Greek *tritos* third]

triumph *noun* **1** a great or notable victory, success, achievement, etc. **2** the joy or feeling of elation that is felt after winning a great victory, etc. ▸ *verb, intr* **1** (*also* **triumph over**) to win a victory or be successful; to prevail. **2** to rejoice in a feeling of triumph; to exult. ▪ **triumphal** *adj.* [14c: from Latin *triumphus*]

triumphant *adj* **1** having won a victory or achieved success. **2** exultant; feeling or showing great joy or elation because of a victory, achievement, etc.

triumvir /traɪˈʌmvɪə(r)/ *noun* (***triumviri*** /-raɪ/ *or* ***triumvirs***) **1** someone who shares an official position, power, authority, etc equally with two other people. **2** *Roman hist* someone who is part of a triumvirate. [16c: Latin, from *triumviri* of three men]

triumvirate /traɪˈʌmvərɪt/ *noun* a group of three people who share an official position, power, authority, etc equally. ▪ **triumviral** *adj.* [16c: orig, in ancient Rome, the coalition between Caesar, Pompey and Crassus]

trivalent *adj, chem* of an atom: able to combine with three atoms of hydrogen. ▪ **trivalence** *or* **trivalency** *noun.* [19c: from Latin *valere* to be worth]

trivet *noun* a three-legged stand or bracket for standing a hot dish, pot, etc on. [Anglo-Saxon *trefet*]

trivia *plural noun* unimportant or petty matters or details. [20c: Latin]

trivial *adj* **1** having or being of very little importance or value. **2** of a person: only interested in unimportant things; frivolous. **3** commonplace; ordinary. ▪ **triviality** *noun* (***-ies***). ▪ **trivially** *adv.* [15c: from Latin *trivialis* commonplace]

trivialize *or* **-ise** *verb* to make or treat as unimportant, worthless, etc. ▪ **trivialization** *noun.* [19c]

-trix *suffix* (***-trices*** *or* ***-trixes***) *esp law, denoting* a feminine agent corresponding to the masculine *-tor*, eg *executor, executrix.*

trochee /ˈtroʊkiː/ *noun, prosody* a metrical foot of one long or stressed syllable followed by one short or unstressed one. ▪ **trochaic** *adj.* [16c: from Greek *trochaios pous* running foot]

trochoid *noun, geom* the curve traced by a point on the radius, but not on the circumference, of a circle as the circle rolls along a straight line. Compare **cycloid**. ▪ **trochoidal** *adj.* [18c: from Greek *trochoeides* circular]

trod *verb, past tense, past participle of* **tread**

trodden *past participle of* **tread**

troglodyte *noun* **1** someone who lives in a cave, esp in prehistoric times. **2** *informal* someone who has little to do with the outside world and has become eccentric and out of touch. ▪ **troglodytic** *adj.* [16c: from Greek *trogle* a hole + *dyein* to creep into]

troika *noun* **1 a** a Russian vehicle drawn by three horses abreast; **b** a team of three horses harnessed abreast. **2** any group of three people working as a team. [19c: Russian]

Trojan *noun* **1** *hist* a citizen or inhabitant of ancient Troy in Asia Minor. **2** someone who works, fights, etc extremely hard or courageously. ▸ *adj* belonging or relating to ancient Troy or its citizens. [14c: from Latin *Troianus*]

Trojan Horse *noun* **1** *hist* a hollow wooden horse that the Greeks used to infiltrate Troy. **2** someone or something that undermines an organization, etc, from within. **3** *comput* a program that contains hidden instructions that can lead to the destruction or corruption of data but which, unlike a virus, does not replicate itself. [16c]

troll[1] *noun, folklore* an ugly, evil-tempered, human-like creature that can take the form of either a dwarf or a giant. [19c: Norse and Swedish]

troll[2] *verb, tr & intr* to fish by trailing bait on a line through water. ▶ *noun* the bait used in trolling, or a line holding this. [14c: from *trollen* to roll or stroll]

trolley *noun* **1** *Brit* a small cart or basket on wheels for conveying luggage, shopping, etc. **2** *Brit* a small wheeled table for conveying food, crockery, etc. **3** a wheeled stretcher for transporting patients in hospital. **4** *Brit* a small wagon or truck running on rails. **5** a **trolley wheel**. **6** *Brit* a **trolley bus**. **7** *N Am* a **trolley car**. [19c: prob from **troll**[2]]
IDIOMS **off one's trolley** *informal* daft; crazy.

trolley bus *noun* a public transport vehicle powered from overhead electric wires.

trolley car *noun, N Am* a public transport vehicle that runs on rails like a tram and is powered by overhead electric wires.

trolley wheel *noun* a small grooved wheel which collects current from an overhead electric wire and transmits it down a pole to power the vehicle underneath.

trombone *noun* a large brass instrument with a sliding tube or a person playing this, esp in an orchestra. ▪ **trombonist** *noun*. [18c: Italian, from *tromba* trumpet]

trompe l'oeil /trɒmp ˈlɜːj/ *noun* (***trompe l'oeils***) a painting or decoration which gives an illusion of reality. [19c: French, meaning 'deceives the eye']

troop *noun* **1** (**troops**) armed forces; soldiers. **2** a group or collection, esp of people or animals. **3** a division of a cavalry or armoured squadron. **4** a large group of Scouts divided into patrols. ▶ *verb, intr* (*usu* **troop along**, **off**, **in**, etc) to move as a group. [16c: from Latin *troppus* a flock]
IDIOMS **troop the colour** *Brit* to parade a regiment's flag ceremonially.

trooper *noun* **1** a private soldier, esp one in a cavalry or armoured unit. **2** a cavalry soldier's horse. **3** *esp US* a policeman mounted on a horse or motorcycle. **4** *Brit* a troop-ship.

trope *noun* a word or expression used figuratively, eg, a metaphor. [16c: from Latin *tropus* a figure of speech]

trophic *adj* relating to nutrition. [From Greek *trophe* food]

trophy *noun* (**-*ies***) **1** a cup, medal, plate, etc awarded as a prize for victory or success in a contest, esp in sport. **2** something which is kept in memory of a victory or success, eg, in hunting. ▶ *adj* of a person's partner, spouse, etc: elevating the person's status or adding something to the way other people perceive them: *a trophy wife*. [16c: from Greek from *trope* a turning, defeat]

tropic *noun* **1** either of two lines of latitude that encircle the earth at 23° 27′ north (**tropic of Cancer**) and 23° 27′ south (**tropic of Capricorn**) of the equator. **2** (**the Tropics**) the parts of the earth that lie between these two circles. ▶ *adj* **tropical**. [14c: from Greek *tropikos* relating to the apparent turning of the sun at a solstice]

tropical *adj* **1** relating to or originating in the tropics: *tropical fish* • *tropical fruit*. **2** of climate: very hot and wet. **3** located between the tropics of Cancer and Capricorn. ▪ **tropically** *adv*.

tropism *noun, biol* the change of direction of an organism, esp a plant or plant part, in response to an external stimulus such as gravity, light or heat. [19c: from Greek *tropos* a turn]

troposphere *noun, meteorol* the lowest layer of the Earth's atmosphere, which extends from the Earth's surface to a height of about 8km over the Poles and rising to about 17km, characterized by having temperatures that decrease as the height increases. ▪ **tropospheric** *adj*. [20c: from Greek *tropos* turn]

trot *verb* (***trotted, trotting***) **1** *intr* of a horse: to move at a steady, fairly fast pace, in a bouncy kind of walk. **2** to make (a horse) move in this way. **3** *intr* to move or proceed at a steady, fairly brisk pace. ▶ *noun* **1** the pace at which a horse, rider, etc moves when trotting. **2** an act or the process of trotting. **3** (**the trots**) *informal* a euphemistic name for an ongoing bout of diarrhoea. [13c: from French *troter*]
IDIOMS **on the trot** *informal* **1** one after the other. **2** continually moving about; busy.
PHRASAL VERBS **trot sth out** *informal* to produce (a story, article, etc), esp without much thought or effort: *trots out the same boring lectures every year.*

troth /troʊθ/ *noun, old use* faith or fidelity. [Anglo-Saxon *treowth* truth]
IDIOMS **plight one's troth** to make a solemn promise, esp in betrothal or marriage.

trotter *noun* **1 a** a pig's foot; **b** (*usu* **pigs' trotters**) pigs' feet used as food. **2** a horse trained to trot in harness.

troubadour /ˈtruːbədʊə(r), -dɔː(r)/ *noun* **1** *hist* one of a group of lyric poets in S France and N Italy during the 11–13c who wrote, usu in Provençal, about a highly idealized form of love. **2** a poet or singer, esp one whose topic is love. [18c: French, from Provençal *trobar* to find, invent or compose in verse]

trouble *noun* **1 a** distress, worry or concern; **b** a cause of this. **2** bother or effort, or a cause of this: *go to a lot of trouble* • *The dog was no trouble.* **3** a problem or difficulty: *Your trouble is that you're too generous.* **4** (*usu* **troubles**) public disturbances and unrest. **5 a** illness or weakness: *heart trouble*; **b** malfunction; failure: *engine trouble.* ▶ *verb* **1** to cause distress, worry, concern, anger, sadness, etc to: *What's troubling you?* **2** to cause physical distress or discomfort to: *His weak knee always troubled him.* **3** used esp in polite requests: to put (someone) to the inconvenience of (doing, saying, etc something): *Could I trouble you to open the window a little?* **4** *intr* to make any effort or take pains: *He didn't even trouble to tell me what had happened.* **5** to disturb or agitate (eg the surface of water). ▪ **troubled** *adj*. [13c: from French *trubler*, from Latin *turbidus* full of confusion, disturbed]
IDIOMS **in trouble** in difficulties, esp because of doing something wrong or illegal.

troublemaker *noun* someone who continually, and usu deliberately, causes trouble, worry, problems, etc to others.

troubleshoot *verb* **1 a** to trace and mend a fault (in machinery, etc); **b** to identify and solve problems. **2** to mediate (in disputes, etc). ▪ **troubleshooter** *noun*. ▪ **troubleshooting** *noun, adj*. [20c: orig applied to the tracing of faults in telegraph or telephone wires]

troublesome *adj* slightly worrying, annoying, difficult, etc. ▪ **troublesomely** *adv*.

trouble spot *noun* a place where unrest, conflict, etc flares up, esp frequently or on a regular basis.

trough /trɒf/ *noun* **1** a long narrow open container that animal feed or water is put into. **2** a channel, drain or gutter. **3** a long narrow hollow between the crests of two waves. **4** *meteorol* a long narrow area of low atmospheric pressure. Compare **ridge** (sense 5). **5** a low point, eg, in an economic recession, etc. [Anglo-Saxon *trog*]

trounce *verb* to beat or defeat completely; to thrash. ▪ **trouncing** *noun.* [16c]

troupe *noun* a group or company of performers. [19c: French, from Latin *troppus* troop]

trouper *noun* **1** a member of a troupe. **2** an experienced, hard-working and loyal colleague.

trousers *plural noun* an outer garment for the lower part of the body, reaching from the waist and covering each leg separately, usu down to the ankle. *as adj* (**trouser**): *a trouser press.* [16c: from Irish *trius* and Scottish Gaelic *triubhas* trews, and influenced by 'drawers']

trouser suit *noun* a woman's suit, consisting of a jacket and trousers.

trousseau /ˈtruːsoʊ/ *noun* (***trousseaux*** /ˈtruːsoʊ/ *or* ***trousseaus*** /-soʊz/) clothes, linen, etc that a woman who is engaged to be married collects and keeps for her wedding and married life. [19c: French, meaning 'a little bundle']

trout *noun* (***trout*** *or* ***trouts***) **1** a freshwater fish of the salmon family, highly valued as food and by anglers. **2** *derog* an unpleasant, interfering old person, usu a woman. [Anglo-Saxon *truht*]

trowel *noun* **1** a small hand-held tool with a flat blade for applying and spreading mortar, plaster, etc. **2** a similar tool with a blade that is slightly curved in on itself for potting plants, etc. [14c: from French *truel*]

troy *noun* (*in full* **troy weight**) a system of weights used for precious metals and gemstones in which there are 12 ounces or 5760 grains to the pound. [14c: from Troyes, in France]

truant *noun* someone who stays away from school or work without good reason or without permission. ▸ *verb, intr* to be a truant. ▪ **truancy** *noun.* [13c: French, related to Welsh *truan* a wretch]

IDIOMS **play truant** to stay away from school without good reason and without permission.

truce *noun* **1** an agreement to stop fighting, usu temporarily. **2** a temporary break in fighting, hostilities, feuding, etc. [14c: from Anglo-Saxon *treow* truth]

truck[1] *noun* **1** *Brit* an open railway wagon for carrying goods. **2** *chiefly N Am* a lorry. **3** a frame with four or more wheels that supports a railway carriage. **4** any wheeled vehicle, trolley or cart for moving heavy goods. ▸ *verb* **1 a** to put on or into a truck; **b** to transport by truck. **2** *intr, chiefly N Am* to work as a truck driver. ▪ **trucker** *noun, N Am.* [17c]

truck[2] *noun* **1** exchange of goods; commercial dealings. **2** *informal* odds and ends: *Clear all the marbles and other truck off the floor.* [13c: from French *troquer* to exchange]

IDIOMS **have no truck with sb** *or* **sth** to avoid or refuse to have anything to do with them or it.

truckle *noun* (*in full* **truckle-bed**) a low bed, usu on wheels, that can be stored away under a larger bed. ▸ *verb, intr* to submit or give in passively or weakly. [14c: from Greek *trochileia* a system of pulleys]

truculent /ˈtrʌkjʊlənt/ *adj* aggressively defiant, quarrelsome or discourteous. ▪ **truculence** *noun.* ▪ **truculently** *adv.* [16c: from Latin *truculentus*]

trudge *verb* **1** *intr* (*usu* **trudge through**, **along**, **over**, *etc*) to walk with slow and weary steps: *trudged through the snow.* **2** to cover (a stated distance, etc) slowly and wearily *trudged three miles to the nearest shops.* ▸ *noun* a long and tiring walk. [16c]

true *adj* **1** agreeing with fact or reality; not false or wrong. **2** real; genuine; properly so called: *The spider is not a true insect.* **3** accurate or exact: *The photograph doesn't give a true idea of the size of the building.* **4** faithful; loyal: *a true friend • be true to one's word.* **5** conforming to a standard, pattern, type or expectation: *behaved true to type.* **6** in the correct position; well-fitting; accurately adjusted. **7** of a compass bearing: measured according to the Earth's axis and not magnetic north. **8** honest; sincere: *twelve good men and true.* ▸ *adv* **1** certainly: *True, she isn't very happy here.* **2** truthfully. **3** faithfully. **4** honestly. **5** accurately or precisely. **6** accurately in tune: *sing true.* **7** conforming to ancestral type: *breed true.* [Anglo-Saxon *treow*]

IDIOMS **come true** of a dream, hope, wish, etc: to happen in reality; to be fulfilled. **out of true** not in the correct position; not straight or properly balanced.

true-blue *Brit, adj* extremely loyal; staunchly orthodox. ▸ *noun* (**true blue**) someone of this type, esp a supporter of the Conservative Party or the Royal Family.

true north *noun* the direction of the north pole, as opposed to **magnetic north**.

truffle *noun* **1** a fungus that grows underground and is considered a delicacy. **2** a type of chocolate sweet with a centre made with cream, butter, chocolate and often flavoured with rum, etc. [16c: French]

trug *noun, Brit* a shallow rectangular basket with a handle, for carrying flowers, fruit, vegetables, small garden tools, etc. [16c]

truism *noun* a statement that is so obviously true that it requires no discussion; a platitude. ▪ **truistic** *adj.* [18c]

truly *adv* **1** really: *Truly, I have no idea.* **2** genuinely; honestly: *truly sorry.* **3** faithfully. **4** accurately; exactly. **5** properly; rightly.

trump[1] *noun* **1 a** (**trumps**) the suit of cards that is declared to be of a higher value than any other suit; **b** (*also* **trump card**) a card of this suit. **2** (*usu* **trump card**) a secret advantage. **3** *informal* a helpful, reliable, fine, etc person. ▸ *verb* **1 a** to defeat (an ordinary card, a trick with no trumps or an opponent) by playing a trump; **b** *intr* to lay a trump card when an opponent has led with another suit. **2** to win a surprising victory or advantage over (a person, plan, idea, etc). [16c: a variant of **triumph**]

IDIOMS **come up** *or* **turn up trumps** *informal* **1** to be unexpectedly useful or helpful in difficult circumstances. **2** to turn out to be better than expected.

trump[2] *noun, old use, poetic* a trumpet blast. [13c: from French *trompe* trumpet]

trumped-up *adj* of evidence, an accusation, etc: invented or made up; false.

trumpery *noun* (***-ies***) **1** flashy but worthless articles. **2** rubbish. ▸ *adj* flashy but worthless. [15c: from French *tromper* to deceive]

trumpet *noun* **1 a** a brass instrument with a narrow tube and flared bell and a set of valves, or a person playing this, esp in an orchestra; **b** a similar but simpler instrument used, esp by the military, for signalling, fanfares, etc. **2** the corona of a daffodil. **3** any conical device designed to amplify sound, eg, an ear trumpet. **4** the loud cry of an elephant. ▸ *verb* **1** *intr* of an elephant: to make a loud cry. **2** *intr* to blow a trumpet. **3** to make known or proclaim loudly. ▪ **trumpeter** *noun.* [13c: from French *trompette*]
IDIOMS **blow one's own trumpet** to boast about one's own skills, achievements, etc.

truncate *verb* to cut a part from (a tree, word, piece of writing, etc), esp in order to shorten: *truncated his lecture.* [15c: from Latin *truncare* to shorten]

truncheon *noun* a short thick heavy stick that police officers carry, used in self-defence or for subduing the unruly, etc. [14c: from French *tronchon* stump]

trundle *verb, tr & intr* to move or roll, or cause to move or roll, heavily and clumsily. ▸ *noun* an act or the process of trundling. [Anglo-Saxon *trendel*]

trunk *noun* **1** the main stem of a tree without the branches and roots. **2** the body of a person or animal, discounting the head and limbs. **3** the main part of anything. **4** a large rigid chest, usu with a hinged lid, for storing or transporting clothes, personal items, etc. **5** *N Am* the boot of a car. **6** the long, muscular nose of an elephant. **7** (**trunks**) men's close-fitting shorts or pants worn esp for swimming. [15c: from Latin *truncus* a main stem of a tree]

trunk road *noun* a main road between large towns.

truss *noun* **1** a framework supporting a roof, bridge, etc. **2** a belt, bandage, etc worn to support a hernia. **3** a bundle of hay or straw. **4** a cluster of flowers or fruit. ▸ *verb* **1** (*often* **truss up**) to tie up or bind tightly. **2** to tie up the legs of (a pig, rabbit, etc), or the wings and legs of (a chicken, etc), before cooking. **3** to support (a roof, bridge, etc) with a truss. [13c: from French *trousser*]

trust *noun* **1** belief or confidence in, or reliance on, the truth, goodness, character, power, ability, etc of someone or something. **2** charge or care: *The child was placed in my trust.* **3** the state of being responsible for the conscientious performance of some task: *be in a position of trust.* **4** a task assigned to someone in the belief that they will perform it well and conscientiously. **5** credit: *put it on trust.* **6** an arrangement by which money or property is managed by one person for the benefit of someone else. **7** the amount of money or property managed by one person for the benefit of another. **8** a group of business firms working together to control the market in a particular commodity, beat down competition, and maximize profits. ▸ *verb* **1** *tr & intr* to have confidence or faith in; to depend or rely on: *We can trust her to do a good job.* **2** (*usu* **trust with**) to allow (someone) to use or do (something) in the belief that they will behave responsibly, honestly, etc: *I wouldn't trust him with your new car.* **3** to give (someone or something) into the care of (someone): *trusted the children to their grandfather.* **4** *tr & intr* to be confident; to hope or suppose: *I trust you had a good journey.* ▪ **trustable** *adj.* [13c: from Norse *traust*]

trustee *noun* **1** someone who manages money or property for someone else. **2** a member of a group of people managing the affairs and business of a company or institution. ▪ **trusteeship** *noun.*

trustful *adj* **1** having confidence or trust in others. **2** lacking in suspicion.

trust fund *noun* money or property held in trust.

trustworthy *adj* able to be trusted or depended on; reliable. ▪ **trustworthiness** *noun.*

trusty *adj* (**-ier, -iest**) *old use* **1** able to be trusted or depended on: *my trusty sword.* **2** loyal: *a trusty servant.* ▸ *noun* (**-ies**) a trusted person, esp a convict who is granted special privileges for good behaviour.

truth *noun* **1** the quality or state of being true, genuine or factual. **2** the state of being truthful; sincerity; honesty. **3** that which is true. **4** that which is established or generally accepted as true: *scientific truths.* **5** strict adherence to an original or standard. [Anglo-Saxon *treowth*]

truthful *adj* **1** of a person: telling the truth. **2** true; realistic. ▪ **truthfully** *adv.* ▪ **truthfulness** *noun.*

try *verb* (**tries, tried**) **1** *tr & intr* to attempt or make an effort; to seek to attain or achieve. **2** (*also* **try out**) to test or experiment with in order to make an assessment of value, quality, etc. **3 a** to conduct the legal trial of: *tried him for murder;* **b** to examine all the evidence of and decide (a case) in a law court. **4** to exert strain or stress on: *try the limits of his patience.* ▸ *noun* (**-ies**) **1** an attempt or effort. **2** *rugby* an act of carrying the ball over the opponent's goal line and touching it down on the ground. [13c: from Latin *triare* to sift or pick out]
IDIOMS **try it on** *Brit informal* to attempt to deceive someone, or to test their patience or tolerance.
PHRASAL VERBS **try sth on** to put on (clothes, shoes, etc) in order to check the fit, appearance, etc. **try out** to go, eg, to a football, rugby, hockey, etc team, and have trials in the hope of being asked to join the team.

try to
In formal speech and writing, you should use **try to** rather than **try and**:
✗ *Try and remember what he looked like.*
✓ *Try to remember what he looked like.*

trying *adj* causing strain or anxiety; stretching one's patience to the limit.

tryst *old use or literary, noun* **1** an arrangement to meet someone, esp a lover. **2** the meeting itself. **3** (*also* **trysting-place**) a place where such a meeting takes place. ▸ *verb, intr* (*usu* **tryst with**) to arrange a tryst. [14c: from French *triste* a hunter's waiting-place]

tsar, **tzar** *or* **czar** /zɑː(r), tsɑː(r)/ *noun, hist* the title of the former emperors of Russia. ▪ **tsarism** *noun.* ▪ **tsarist** *noun, adj.* [16c: Russian, from Latin *Caesar* the family name of the earliest Roman emperors]

tsarina, **tzarina** *or* **czarina** /zɑːˈriːnə, tsɑː-/ *noun, hist* the title of a former Russian empress. [18c]

tsetse /ˈtsɛtsɪ/ *noun* (*in full* **tsetse fly**) an African fly that feeds on human and animal blood and can transmit several dangerous diseases. [19c: the Tswana (a southern African language) name for this fly]

T-shirt *or* **tee shirt** *noun* a short-sleeved collarless top, usu made from knitted cotton. [20c: so called because of its shape when laid out flat]

tsp *abbrev* teaspoon or teaspoonful.

T-square *noun* a T-shaped ruler for drawing and testing right angles.

tsunami /tsʊˈnɑːmɪ/ *noun* a fast-moving and often very destructive wave caused by movement in the

Earth's surface, eg, a volcanic eruption, landslide, etc. [19c: Japanese, from *tsu* harbour + *nami* wave]

TT *abbrev* **1** **a** teetotal; **b** teetotaller. **2** Tourist Trophy (annual motorcycle races held on the Isle of Man).

Tuareg /'twɑːrɛg/ *noun* **1** **a** a nomadic people who live in the western and central Sahara; **b** someone who belongs to this people. **2** the Berber language spoken by this people. ▸ *adj* belonging or relating to this people or their language. [19c: the native name for this people, their language, etc]

tub *noun* **1** a large, low container for holding water, growing plants, etc. **2** a small container for cream, ice cream, yoghurt, margarine, etc. **3** a **tubful**. **4** (*also* **bathtub**) a bath. **5** *informal* a slow-moving boat. ▪ **tubful** *noun*. [14c: from English *tubbe*]

tuba /'tʃuːbə/ *noun* a bass brass instrument with valves and a wide bell that points upwards, or a person playing this, esp in an orchestra. [19c: Latin and Italian *tuba*, orig a straight Roman war trumpet]

tubby *adj* (***-ier, -iest***) *informal* of a person: plump; podgy. ▪ **tubbiness** *noun*. [19c: from **tub**]

tube *noun* **1** a long hollow flexible or rigid cylinder for holding or conveying air, liquids, etc. **2** a similar structure in the body of an animal or plant: *bronchial tubes*. **3** a squeezable, approximately cylindrical container containing a paste, a semi-liquid substance, etc: *a tube of toothpaste*. **4** *Brit* **a** an underground railway system, esp the London one; **b** (*in full* **tube train**) an underground train. **5** **a** a cathode ray tube; **b** *informal* a television set. **6** *N Am* a thermionic valve. **7** *surfing* a rounded hollow formed by a breaking wave: *tried to shoot the tube*. **8** *informal* an extremely stupid person. ▸ *verb* **1** to fit with a tube or tubes. **2** to enclose in a tube. ▪ **tubeless** *adj*. [17c: from Latin *tubus* pipe]

IDIOMS **go down the tubes** *informal* to fail dismally.

tuber *noun, botany* **1** a swollen underground stem or rhizome, such as that of the potato, with buds that are capable of developing into a new plant. **2** a similar structure formed from a root, eg, of a dahlia, but without buds. [17c: Latin *tuber* a swelling]

tubercle *noun* **1** a small round swelling or lump on a bone, etc. **2** a small round swelling in an organ, esp one in the lung which is characteristic of tuberculosis. [16c: from Latin *tuberculum* small swelling]

tubercular *adj* affected by or suffering from tuberculosis.

tuberculin *noun* a sterile liquid preparation extracted from a culture of the bacillus which causes tuberculosis, used to test for the disease.

tuberculosis *noun* (abbrev **TB**) an infectious diseases of humans and animals caused by the tubercle bacillus and characterized by the formation of tubercles, esp on the lungs. [19c: from Latin *tuberculum* small swelling]

tuberous *or* **tuberose** *adj* **1** having tubers. **2** relating to or like a tuber.

tubful *noun* the amount a tub will hold.

tubing *noun* **1** a length of tube or a system of tubes. **2** material that tubes can be made from.

tub-thumper *noun, informal* a passionate or ranting public speaker. ▪ **tub-thumping** *adj, noun*.

tubular *adj* **1** made or consisting of tubes or tube-shaped pieces. **2** shaped like a tube.

tubule *noun* a small tube in the body of an animal or plant. [17c: from Latin *tubulus*, a diminutive of *tubus*]

tuck *verb* **1** (*usu* **tuck in**, **into**, **under**, **up**, *etc*) to push or fold into a specified position: *tucked the note into the envelope*. **2** to make a tuck or tucks in (a piece of material, clothing, etc). **3** to carry out a cosmetic operation to tighten a flabby part, smooth out wrinkles or remove fat. ▸ *noun* **1** a flat pleat or fold sewn into a garment or piece of material. **2** *Brit informal* food, esp sweets, cakes, etc, eaten as snacks. **3** a cosmetic operation to tighten a flabby part, smooth out wrinkles or remove fat: *had a tummy tuck*. See also **nip and tuck**. [Anglo-Saxon *tucian* to disturb]

PHRASAL VERBS **tuck sth away** *informal* **1** to eat (large quantities of food), esp heartily and with enjoyment. **2** to store or conceal, esp in a place that is difficult to find: *Their cottage was tucked away from prying eyes*. **tuck in** *or* **into** *informal* to eat heartily or greedily: *tucked into a huge plate of chips*. **tuck sb in** *or* **up** *informal* to put them to bed by pulling up the covers, duvet, etc snugly.

tucker[1] *noun* **1** *hist* a piece of material, lace, etc that is drawn or fastened over the bodice of a low-cut dress. **2** *informal* food. [15c: from **tuck**]

IDIOMS **best bib and tucker** *informal* best clothes.

tucker[2] *verb* (*usu* **tucker out**) to tire. ▪ **tuckered-out** *adj*. [19c: from **tuck**]

tuck shop *noun, Brit* a small shop that sells sweets, cakes, pastries, etc in or near a school.

Tue. *or* **Tues.** *abbrev* Tuesday.

Tuesday *noun* (abbrev **Tue.** *or* **Tues.**) the third day of the week. [Anglo-Saxon *Tiwesdaeg* Tiw's day, from Tiw, the Teutonic god of war]

tufa *noun, geol* a white spongy porous rock that forms in areas around springs, streams, etc. [18c: Latin *tofus* soft stone]

tuff *noun* rock that is largely composed of fine volcanic fragments and dust. [16c: from Latin *tofus* soft stone]

tuffet *noun* **1** a small grassy mound. **2** a low seat. [16c: a variant of **tuft**]

tuft *noun* a small bunch or clump of grass, hair, feathers, wool, etc attached at the base or growing together. ▪ **tufted** *adj*. ▪ **tufty** *adj* (***-ier, -iest***). [14c]

tug *verb* (***tugged, tugging***) *tr & intr* **1** (*also* **tug at** *or* **on**) to pull sharply or strongly: *a dog tugging at the lead*. **2** to tow (a ship, barge, oil platform, etc) with a tugboat. ▸ *noun* **1** **a** a strong sharp pull; **b** a sharp or sudden pang of emotion. **2** a hard struggle. **3** (*in full* **tugboat**) a small boat with a very powerful engine, for towing larger ships, barges, oil platforms, etc. [13c: from Anglo-Saxon *teon* to tow]

tug-of-love *noun* (***tugs-of-love***) *Brit informal* a dispute over the guardianship of a child.

tug-of-war *noun* (***tugs-of-war***) **1** a contest in which two people or teams pull at opposite ends of a rope and try to haul their opponents over a centre line. **2** any hard struggle between two opposing sides.

tuition *noun* teaching or instruction, esp when paid for: *driving tuition*. [16c in this sense; 13c, meaning 'custody or care': from Latin *tuitio* guardianship]

tulip *noun* **1** a spring-flowering bulbous plant that produces a single cup-shaped flower on a long stem. **2** a flower of this plant. [16c: from the Turkish pronunciation of Persian *dulband* turban]

tulle /tjuːl, tuːl/ *noun* a delicate thin netted silk for making veils, dresses, hats, etc. [19c: named after the town of Tulle in SW France]

tum *noun, Brit informal* the stomach. [19c: a short form of **tummy**]

tumble *verb* **1** *tr & intr* (*often* **tumble down, over**, etc) to fall or cause to fall headlong, esp suddenly or clumsily. **2** *intr* to fall or collapse suddenly, esp in value or amount. **3** *tr & intr* (*often* **tumble about, around**, etc) to roll helplessly or haphazardly: *The kids tumbled around in the garden.* **4** *intr* to perform as an acrobat, esp turning somersaults. **5** *intr* to move in a confused hasty way: *tumble out of the car.* **6** (*also* **tumble to**) *informal* to understand or realize, esp suddenly: *tumbled to their intentions.* ▸ *noun* **1** a fall. **2** a somersault. **3** a confused or untidy state or heap. [Anglo-Saxon *tumbian*]

tumbledown *adj* of a building, etc: falling to pieces.

tumble-dryer *or* **tumble-drier** *noun* an electrically powered machine that dries wet laundry by tumbling it around in a current of warm air. ▪ **tumble-dry** *verb.*

tumbler *noun* **1 a** a flat-bottomed drinking cup without a stem or handle, usu of glass or plastic; **b** (*also* **tumblerful**) the amount this holds: *a tumbler of milk.* **2** an acrobat, esp one who performs somersaults. **3** the part of a lock which holds the bolt until it is moved by a key.

tumbleweed *noun* bushy plants that grow in arid areas and snap off above the root when dead and dry so that they roll about in the wind. [19c]

tumbrel *or* **tumbril** *noun, hist* a two-wheeled cart used during the French Revolution to take people who had been sentenced to death to the guillotine. [15c: from French *tomberel*]

tumescent /tjʊ'mɛsənt/ *adj* swollen or becoming swollen. ▪ **tumescence** *noun.* [19c: from Latin *tumescere* to begin to swell up]

tumid *adj* **1** of an organ or body part: swollen, esp abnormally so. **2** of writing, speech, etc: bombastic; inflated. ▪ **tumidity** *noun.* [16c: from Latin *tumere* to swell]

tummy *noun* (***-ies***) *informal* the stomach. [19c: a childish pronunciation of **stomach**]

tumour *or* (*N Am*) **tumor** *noun* an abnormal growth of benign or malignant cells that develops in, or on the surface of, normal body tissue. ▪ **tumorous** *adj.* [16c: from Latin *tumere* to swell]

tumult *noun* **1** a great or confused noise; an uproar. **2** a violent or angry commotion or disturbance. **3** a state of extreme confusion, agitation, etc: *a mind in tumult.* [15c: from Latin *tumultus* commotion]

tumultuous *adj* **1** noisy and enthusiastic: *arrived to a tumultuous welcome.* **2** disorderly; unruly. **3** agitated.

tumulus *noun* (***tumuli***) *archaeol* an ancient burial mound or barrow. [17c: Latin, from *tumere* to swell]

tun *noun* a large cask for holding beer or wine. [Anglo-Saxon *tunne*]

tuna *noun* (***tuna*** *or* ***tunas***) **1** a large marine fish that lives in warm and tropical seas, related to the mackerel. Also called **tunny**. **2** (*in full* **tuna fish**) its flesh used as food. [19c]

tundra *noun* a vast relatively flat treeless zone lying to the south of the polar ice cap in America and Eurasia with permanently frozen subsoil. [19c: the Lapp name for this kind of region]

tune *noun* **1** a pleasing succession of musical notes; a melody. **2** the correct, or a standard, musical pitch. ▸ *verb* **1** *tr & intr* (*also* **tune up**) to adjust (a musical instrument or its keys or strings, etc) to the correct or a standard pitch. **2 a** to adjust (a radio, TV, video recorder, etc) so that it can pick up signals from a specified frequency or station; **b** *intr* (*usu* **tune in to**) to have a radio adjusted to receive (a specified signal, station, DJ, etc) and listen to (it or them): *She tunes in to Radio 4 in the mornings.* **3** to adjust (an engine, machine, etc) so that it runs properly and efficiently. ▪ **tuner** *noun.* [14c: a variant of **tone**]

IDIOMS **call the tune** *informal* to be in charge. **change one's tune** to change one's attitude, opinions, approach or way of talking. **in tune 1** of a voice or musical instrument: having or producing the correct or a required pitch: *sing in tune.* **2** having the same pitch as other instruments or voices: *The two guitars are not in tune.* **in tune with sb** *or* **sth** being aware of and able to relate to them or it: *in tune with public opinion.* **out of tune 1** not having or producing the correct or a required pitch. **2** not having the same pitch as other instruments or voices. **out of tune with sb** *or* **sth** not being aware of and able to relate to them or it: *completely out of tune with the latest technology.* **to the tune of** *informal* to the (considerable) sum or total of: *had to shell out to the tune of 500 quid for the car repairs.*

tuneful *adj* **1** having a clear, pleasant, etc tune; melodious. **2** full of music.

tuneless *adj* lacking a good, pleasant, etc tune; not melodious.

tungsten *noun, chem* (symbol **W**) a very hard silvery-white metallic element used in the manufacture of filaments of light bulbs, X-ray tubes and TV sets, and in alloying steel. Also called **wolfram**. [18c: Swedish, from *tung* heavy + *sten* stone]

tunic *noun* **1** a close-fitting, usu belted jacket, often forming part of the uniform, eg, of the military, police, security, etc services. **2** a loose garment, often sleeveless, that covers the upper body, usu coming down as far as the hip or knee, worn in ancient Greece and Rome, or by men in the Middle Ages, etc. [Anglo-Saxon, from Latin *tunica* a tunic]

tuning fork *noun* a small device used for tuning musical instruments and testing acoustics, etc, consisting of a stem with two prongs at the top, which, when made to vibrate, produce a specified musical note. [18c: invented by the English trumpeter John Shore]

tunnel *noun* **1** a constructed passage through or under a hill, river, road, etc, allowing access for pedestrians, vehicles, trains, etc. **2** an underground passage that a mole, etc digs. ▸ *verb* (***tunnelled, tunnelling***; (*US*) ***tunneled, tunneling***) **1** *intr* (**tunnel through, under**, etc) to make a tunnel through, under, etc (a hill, river, road, etc). **2** to make (one's way) by digging a tunnel. [15c: from French *tonel* cask]

tunnel vision *noun* **1** a medical condition in which objects on the periphery of the field of vision are unable to be seen. **2 a** the inability or unwillingness to consider other opinions, viewpoints, etc; **b** single-minded determination.

tunny *noun* (***-ies***) (*in full* **tunny-fish**) *esp Brit* tuna. [16c: from French *thon* tuna]

tup *Brit, noun* a ram. [14c]

Tupí /tuː'piː, 'tuːpiː/ *noun* (***Tupí*** *or* ***Tupís***) **1** a group of Native American peoples who live in the Amazon basin. **2** an individual who belongs to one of these peoples. **3** the language of these peoples. ▸ *adj* belonging or relating to these peoples or their language. ▪ **Tupían** *adj, noun.* [19c]

tuppence, **tuppenny** see **twopence**, **twopenny**

turban *noun* **1** a headdress worn esp by Muslim and Sikh men and formed by wrapping a length of cloth around the head or a cap. **2** a woman's hat that looks similar to this. ▪ **turbaned** *adj.* [16c: prob a Turkish pronunciation of *dulband*, the Persian name for this kind of headdress]

turbid *adj* **1** of liquid, etc: cloudy; not clear. **2** of writing, the construction of an argument, etc: confused; disordered; unclear. ▪ **turbidity** *noun.* [17c: from Latin *turba* a crowd]

turbine *noun* a power-generating machine with a rotating wheel driven by water, steam, gas, etc. [19c: French, from Latin *turbo* whirlwind]

turbo *noun* **1** a short form of **turbocharger**. **2** *informal* a car fitted with a turbocharger.

turbocharger *noun* a supercharger driven by a turbine which is itself powered by the exhaust gases of the engine. ▪ **turbocharged** *adj.*

turbofan *noun* **1** a jet engine driven by a gas turbine that increases thrust. **2** an aircraft powered by this kind of engine.

turbojet *noun* **1** (*in full* **turbojet engine**) a type of gas turbine that uses exhaust gases to provide the propulsive thrust. **2** an aircraft powered by this kind of engine.

turboprop *noun* **1** a jet engine in which the turbine drives a propeller. **2** an aircraft powered by this kind of engine.

turbot *noun* (***turbot*** *or* ***turbots***) a large flatfish with bony tubercles instead of scales and eyes on the left side of its head and which is highly valued as food. [13c: from French *tourbout*]

turbulence *noun* **1** a disturbed, wild or unruly state. **2** stormy weather caused by disturbances in atmospheric pressure. **3** **a** irregularity in the flow movement of a liquid or gas, eg, across an aircraft wing, etc; **b** the jolting or bumpy effect of this. [16c: from Latin *turbulentia* agitation]

turbulent *adj* **1** violently disturbed; wild; unruly: *She's had a turbulent life.* **2** stormy. **3** causing disturbance or unrest.

tureen *noun* a large deep dish with a cover that food, esp soup or vegetables, is served from at table. [18c: from French *terrine* a large circular earthen dish]

turf *noun* (***turfs*** *or* ***turves***) **1** **a** the surface of an area of grassland that consists of a layer of grass, weeds, matted roots, etc plus the surrounding earth; **b** a square piece that has been cut from this. **2** a slab of peat used as fuel. **3** (**the turf**) horseracing, a racecourse or the racing world generally. ▸ *verb* to cover (an area of land, garden, etc) with turf. [Anglo-Saxon *tyrf*]

PHRASAL VERBS **turf out** *Brit informal* to throw out.

turf accountant *noun, Brit* a **bookmaker**.

turf war *noun, informal* a dispute over the right to operate within a particular territory.

turgid *adj* **1** swollen; inflated or distended. **2** of language: pompous. ▪ **turgidity** *noun.* [17c: from Latin *turgere* to swell]

Turk *noun* **1** **a** a citizen or inhabitant of, or someone born in, the modern state of Turkey, a republic that straddles SE Europe and W Asia; **b** a citizen or inhabitant of, or someone born in, the former **Ottoman** Empire. **2** someone who speaks a Turkic language. **3** *derog* a wild or unmanageable person. [16c: Persian and Arabic]

turkey *noun* **1** a large gamebird with dark plumage, a bald blue or red head with red wattles and, in the male, a fanlike tail. **2** its flesh used as food, particularly at Christmas, Easter, Thanksgiving, etc. **3** *N Am informal* a stupid or inept person. **4** *N Am informal* a play, film, etc that is a complete failure. [16c: orig applied to a guinea fowl imported from Turkey]

IDIOMS **talk turkey** *N Am informal* **1** to talk bluntly or frankly. **2** to talk business.

Turkic *noun* the family of languages that includes Turkish, Tatar, Uzbek, etc. ▸ *adj* belonging or relating to this family of languages or the people who speak them. [19c]

Turkish *adj* belonging or relating to Turkey, its people, language, etc. ▸ *noun* the official language of Turkey. [16c]

Turkish bath *noun* **1** a type of bath that is taken in a room filled with hot steam or air to induce sweating and which is followed by washing, massaging and finally a cold shower. **2** the room, rooms or building where this takes place. [17c]

Turkish delight *noun* a sticky jelly-like cube-shaped sweet usually flavoured with rosewater and dusted with icing sugar. [19c]

turmeric *noun* **1** an E Indian plant of the ginger family. **2** its aromatic underground stem, dried and powdered, and used as a spice and as a yellow dye. [16c]

turmoil *noun* wild confusion, agitation or disorder; upheaval. [16c]

turn *verb* **1** *tr & intr* to move or go round in a circle or with a circular movement: *turned the key and opened the door.* **2** *tr & intr* to change or cause to change position so that a different side or part comes to the top, front, etc: *turn the pages slowly* • *turn to face the sun.* **3** to put into a specified position by, or as if by, inverting; to tip out: *turned the dough on to the table.* **4** *intr* to change direction or take a new direction: *turn left at the corner.* **5** *tr & intr* to direct, aim or point, or be directed, aimed or pointed: *turned his thoughts to the problems at work.* **6** *tr & intr* to become or cause to become: *Fame turned him into a real show-off* • *love which turned to hate.* **7** *tr & intr* of milk, etc: to make or become sour. **8** to shape using a lathe or potter's wheel. **9** to perform with a rotating movement: *turn somersaults.* **10** *intr* to move or swing around a point or pivot: *a gate turning on its hinge* • *turn on one's heels.* **11** to become or pass (in age or time): *turned forty this year.* **12** to appeal to or have recourse to (someone or something) for help, support, relief, etc: *turned to drink after the divorce.* **13** *tr & intr* **a** of the stomach: to feel nausea or queasiness; **b** to cause (the stomach) to become nauseous or queasy: *That scene is enough to turn your stomach.* **14** *intr* of the tide: to begin to flow in the opposite direction. **15** to make (a profit, etc). ▸ *noun* **1** an act, instance or the process of turning; a complete or partial rotation: *a turn of the wheel.* **2** a change of direction, course or position: *The road takes a turn to the right.* **3** a point or place where a change of direction occurs: *The house is just past the turn in the road.* **4** a direction, tendency or trend: *the twists* *and turns of the saga*. **5** a change in nature, character, condition, course, etc: *an unfortunate turn of events.* **6** an opportunity or duty that comes to each of several people in rotation or succession: *her turn to bat.* **7** inclination or tendency: *a pessimistic turn of mind.* **8** a distinctive style or manner: *a blunt turn of phrase.* **9** an act or service of a specified kind, usu good or malicious: *always doing good turns for others.* **10** *informal* a sudden feeling of illness, nervousness, shock, faintness, etc: *gave her quite a turn.* **11** a short walk or ride: *went for a turn round the garden.* **12 a** each of a series of short acts or performances, eg, in a circus or variety theatre; **b** a performer who does one of these acts. **13** a single coil or twist of rope, wire, etc. **14** *music* an ornament in which the principal note is preceded by that next above it and followed by that next below it. **15** *golf* the place on the course or the stage of play after the ninth hole when the players start heading back to the clubhouse: *They were all square at the turn.* ▪ **turner** *noun.* [Anglo-Saxon *turnian* and 13c French *torner*]

IDIOMS **at every turn** everywhere, at every stage; continually. **in turn** *or* **by turns** one after the other in an orderly or prearranged manner: *The children will be examined in turn.* **on the turn 1** of the tide: starting to change direction. **2** of milk: on the point of going sour. **out of turn 1** out of the correct order or at the wrong time: *played his shot out of turn.* **2** inappropriately, discourteously, etc: *He apologized for speaking out of turn.* **to a turn** to exactly the right degree; to perfection: *The steak was done to a turn.* **turn (and turn) about** one after the other; each taking a turn. **turn sb's head** to make them conceited, smug, snobbish, etc. **turn in one's grave** of a dead person: to be thought certain to have been distressed or offended, had they been alive, by circumstances such as those now in question. **turn sb** *or* **sth loose** to set them or it free. **turn one's ankle** to twist it or strain it slightly. **turn one's back on sb** *or* **sth 1** to leave them or it for good. **2** to have no more to do with them or it. **turn one's hand to sth** to undertake a task, etc or have the ability for it: *She's very talented and can turn her hand to most things.* **turn the other cheek** to refuse to engage in any form of retaliation. **turn tail** to flee. **turn the tide** to cause a change or reversal, in events, thinking, etc.

PHRASAL VERBS **turn about** to move so as to face a different direction. **turn against sb** to become hostile or unfriendly towards them. **turn sb away** to send them away. **turn sth away** to reject it: *turned away his pleas for leniency.* **turn sb** *or* **sth down** to refuse or reject them: *turned him down at the interview.* **turn sth down 1** to reduce (something or the level of light, noise, etc produced by something). **2** to fold down or back: *turned down the bedclothes.* **turn in** *informal* to go to bed. **turn sb** *or* **sth in** to hand (someone or something) over, esp to someone in authority: *turned in the wallet he found to the police.* **turn sth in** to give, achieve, etc (a specified kind of performance, score, etc). **turn off** to leave a straight course or a main road: *The car turned off at the lights.* **turn sb off** *informal* to make (someone) feel dislike or disgust, or to lose interest: *The violent scenes really turned me off.* **turn on sb** *or* **sth 1** to attack them or it physically or verbally, usu suddenly or violently: *The dogs turned on each other.* **2** to depend on them or it: *The whole argument turns on a single point.* **turn sb on** *informal* to make them feel excitement, pleasure, interest, etc. **turn out 1** to happen or prove: *She turned out to be right.* **2** to finally be: *It turned out all right in the end.* **3** to gather or assemble, for a public meeting, event, etc: *Hundreds of people turned out to vote.* **4** *informal* to get out of bed. **turn sb out 1** to send away; to expel: *turned the troublemakers out of the club.* **2** to dress, equip, groom, etc: *He always turns the kids out nicely.* **3** to bend, fold, incline, etc outwards. **turn sth out 1** to switch off (a light, etc). **2** to make, manufacture, etc (usu specified quantities of goods or produce): *They turn out around 50 cars a week.* **3** *Brit* to empty, clear, etc: *The police made him turn out his pockets.* **turn over 1** to roll over when in a lying position. **2** of an engine: to start running at low speed. **turn sb over** *informal* to surrender or transfer them (to another person, an authority, etc): *turned the thief over to the police.* **turn sth over 1** to start (an engine) running at low speed. **2** to turn it so that a hidden or reverse side becomes visible or faces upwards: *turn over the page.* **3** to consider, esp thoughtfully, carefully, etc: *turned over his proposal in her mind.* **4** *slang* to rob it: *turned over the local shop.* **5** to handle or do business at (a specified amount): *The business turns over five million pounds per year.* **turn round 1** to turn to face in the opposite direction: *Peter, turn round and pay attention.* **2** of a loaded vehicle, ship, etc: to arrive, be unloaded, loaded with new cargo, passengers, etc and depart again: *The ship turned round in two hours.* **3** to adopt a different policy, opinion, etc. **turn sth round** to receive and deal with or process (a matter, the arrival of loaded vehicles, etc) in a specified manner, time, etc: *We're able to turn an order round in an hour* • *The ship was turned round in two hours.* **turn up 1** to appear or arrive: *Hardly anyone turned up for the match.* **2** to be found, esp by accident or unexpectedly: *The kitten turned up safe and well.* **turn sth up 1** to increase (the flow, intensity, strength, volume, etc, eg, of sound, light, etc produced by a machine): *turned up the music.* **2** to shorten (clothing or a hem). **3** to discover or reveal it.

turnabout *noun* **1** an act of turning to face the opposite way. **2** a complete change or reversal of direction, opinion, policy, etc.

turnaround *noun* **1 a** an act or the operation of processing something, eg, through a manufacturing procedure; **b** the time that this takes. **2 a** an act or the operation of unloading and reloading a vehicle or ship; **b** the time that this takes. **3** a **turnabout** (sense 2).

turncoat *noun* someone who turns against or leaves his or her political party, principles, etc and joins the opposing side.

turning *noun* **1** a place where one road branches off from another. **2** a road which branches off from another. **3** an act or the process of using a lathe to form curves in wood, metal, etc. **4** (**turnings**) the shavings that come from an object as it is turned on a lathe.

turning circle *noun* the smallest possible circle in which a vehicle can turn round.

turning point *noun* **1** a time, place, event at which there is a significant change or something crucial happens: *Her promotion was the turning point in her career.* **2** *maths* a maximum or minimum point on a graph.

turnip *noun* **1** a plant of the cabbage family. **2** its root used as a vegetable or for animal fodder. [16c]

turnkey *noun, hist* someone who keeps the keys in a prison; a gaoler.

turn-off *noun* **1** a road that branches off from a main road. **2** *informal* someone or something that causes dislike, disgust or revulsion.

turn of phrase *noun* (***turns of phrase***) a way of talking, esp when it is distinctive.

turn-on *noun, informal* someone or something that causes excitement or interest.

turn-out *noun* **1** the number of people who collectively attend a meeting, celebration, event, etc: *a poor turn-out at the match.* **2** the number of people voting in an election. **3** an outfit or set of clothes or equipment. **4** the quantity of goods produced or on display.

turnover *noun* **1** the total value of sales in a business during a certain time. **2** the rate at which stock is sold and replenished. **3** the rate at which money, workers, etc pass through a business: *They pay low wages so there is a high staff turnover.* **4** *biol* the formation, wearing away and replacement of body constituents, eg bone. **5** a small pastry with a fruit or jam filling: *a yummy apple turnover.*

turnpike *noun* **1** *hist* **a** a tollgate or barrier; **b** a road that has a toll system. **2** *N Am* a motorway where drivers must pay a toll. [15c]

turnstile *noun* a gate that allows only one person to pass through at a time, used esp for controlling admissions, eg, at a football ground, etc.

turntable *noun* **1** a revolving platform on a record player where records are placed. **2** a revolving platform used for turning railway engines and other vehicles.

turn-up *noun, Brit* the bottom of a trouser-leg folded back on itself.

IDIOMS **a turn-up for the books** an unexpected and usu pleasant surprise.

turpentine *noun* **1** a thick oily resin obtained from certain trees, eg, pines. **2** a clear oil distilled from this resin and used in many commercial products, esp solvents, paint thinners, and in medicine. Often shortened to **turps**. [14c: from Latin *terebinthina*]

turpitude *noun, formal* vileness; depravity: *moral turpitude.* [15c: from Latin *turpitudo*]

turquoise *noun* **1** an opaque semi-precious stone that comes in varying shades of greenish-blue or light blue. **2** its greenish-blue colour. ▸ *adj* greenish-blue in colour. [14c: from French *pierre turquoise* Turkish stone]

turret *noun* **1** a small tower projecting from a wall of a castle, etc. **2** (*in full* **gun-turret**) a small revolving structure on a warship, tank, etc with a gun mounted on it. **3** a part in a lathe that holds the cutting tools and which can be rotated so that the required tool can be selected. ▪ **turreted** *adj.* [14c: from French *tourette*, a diminutive of *tour* a tower]

turtle *noun* **1** a marine or freshwater reptile with a bony shell enclosing its body and which has flippers or webbed toes. **2** its flesh used as food. **3** *comput* a type of cursor that is moved around in on-screen drawing and plotting. [17c: from Latin *tortuca* a tortoise]

IDIOMS **turn turtle** of a boat, etc: to capsize.

turtledove *noun* a wild dove noted for its soft cooing and for the affection shown to its mate. [14c]

turtle-neck *noun* a round close-fitting neckline coming about a third of the way up the neck. [19c]

turves see **turf**

Tuscan *adj* **1** belonging or relating to Tuscany in central Italy, or to its inhabitants or their language. **2** *archit* denoting the simplest of the orders of classical architecture. ▸ *noun* a citizen or inhabitant of, or someone born in, Tuscany. Compare **Corinthian**, **Doric** and **Ionic**. [16c: from Latin *Tuscanus* belonging to the Tusci, the Etruscans]

tusk *noun* one of a pair of long, curved, pointed teeth which project from the mouth area of certain animals, eg, the elephant, walrus, etc. [Anglo-Saxon *tusc*]

tussle *noun* a verbal or physical struggle or fight. ▸ *verb, intr* to engage in a tussle. [15c: from Scots and N English *touse* to pull or shake about]

tussock *noun* a clump of grass or other vegetation. ▪ **tussocky** *adj.* [16c]

tut *or* **tut-tut** *exclam* expressing mild disapproval, annoyance or rebuke. ▸ *verb* (***tutted, tutting***) *intr* to express this by saying 'tut' or 'tut-tut'. [16c: imitating the sound]

tutelage /ˈtjuːtɪlɪdʒ/ *noun* **1** the state or office of being a guardian. **2** the state of being under the care of a guardian. **3** tuition or instruction, esp as given by a tutor. [17c: from Latin *tutela* guardianship]

tutelary /ˈtjuːtɪlərɪ/ *adj* **1** having the power or role of a guardian. **2** belonging or relating to a guardian. **3** giving protection. [17c: from Latin *tutelaris* guardian]

tutor *noun* **1** a university or college teacher who teaches undergraduate students individually or in small groups, or who is responsible for the general welfare and progress of a certain number of students. **2** a private teacher: *my piano tutor.* **3** *Brit* an instruction book. ▸ *verb, tr & intr* **1** to act or work as a tutor to. **2** to discipline. ▪ **tutorship** *noun.* [14c: Latin, meaning 'a watcher']

tutorial *noun* **1** a period of instruction when a university or college tutor and an individual student or small group of students meet, usu to discuss an assignment, lectures, etc. **2** a printed or on-screen lesson that a learner works through at their own pace, eg, one that teaches the user how to use a computing program: *found the Windows tutorials really useful.* ▸ *adj* belonging or relating to a tutor or tuition by a tutor: *forgot his tutorial exercise.* [18c: from Latin *tutor* a watcher]

tutti /ˈtʊtɪ/ *music, adv* with all the instruments and singers together. ▸ *noun* a passage to be played or sung by all the instruments and singers together. [18c: Italian, pl of *tutto* all]

tutti-frutti *noun* an ice cream or other sweet that contains or is flavoured with mixed fruits. [19c: Italian, meaning 'all fruits']

tut-tut see **tut**

tutu *noun* a very short protruding skirt consisting of layers of stiffened net frills and worn by female ballet dancers. [20c: French, from *cucu*, a diminutive of *cul* the buttocks]

tuxedo /tʌkˈsiːdoʊ/ *noun* (***tuxedos*** *or* ***tuxedoes***) *chiefly N Am* **1** a **dinner jacket**. **2** an evening suit with a dinner jacket. Often shortened to **tux**. [19c: named after a country club at Tuxedo Park, New York]

TV *abbrev* television.

twaddle *noun, informal* nonsense. [18c]

twain *noun, adj, old use* two. [Anglo-Saxon *twegen*, from *twa* two]

twang *noun* **1** a sharp ringing sound like that produced by plucking a tightly-stretched string or wire. **2** a nasal quality or tone of voice. ▸ *verb, tr & intr* **1** to make or cause to make a twang. **2** to play (a musical instrument or a tune) casually, informally, etc. ▪ **twangy** *adj* (**-ier, -iest**). [16c: imitating the sound]

tweak *verb* **1** to get hold of and pull or twist with a sudden jerk. **2** to make fine adjustments to (eg a computer program, an engine, etc). ▸ *noun* an act or instance, or the process, of tweaking. [17c]

twee *adj, Brit informal, disparaging* affectedly or pretentiously pretty, sweet, cute, quaint, etc. [20c: from *tweet*, a childish pronunciation of **sweet**]

tweed *noun* **1** a thick roughish woollen cloth, usu with coloured flecks: *Harris tweed*. **2** (**tweeds**) clothes made of this material. [19c: orig a tradename which was a misreading of Scots *tweel* meaning 'twill']

tweedy *adj* (**-ier, -iest**) **1** relating to or like tweed. **2** relating to or typical of people who enjoy outdoor country activities and who are conventionally thought of as wearing tweed clothes. ▪ **tweediness** *noun*.

tweet *noun* a melodious chirping sound made by a small bird. ▸ *verb, intr* to chirp melodiously. [19c: imitating the sound]

tweeter *noun, electronics* a loudspeaker that is designed to reproduce high-frequency sounds. Compare **woofer**. [20c]

tweezers *plural noun* a small pair of pincers for pulling out individual hairs, holding small objects, etc. [16c: from obsolete *tweeze*, a surgeon's case of instruments]

twelfth (often written **12th**) *adj* **1** in counting: **a** next after eleventh; **b** last of twelve. **2** in twelfth position. **3** being one of twelve equal parts: *a twelfth share*. ▸ *noun* **1** one of twelve equal parts. **2** a **fraction** equal to one divided by twelve (usu written ⅟12). **3** a person coming twelfth, eg in a race or exam: *finished a poor twelfth*. **4** (**the twelfth**) **a** the twelfth day of the month: *I don't get paid till the twelfth*; **b** *golf* the twelfth hole: *scored a double bogey at the twelfth*. **5** *music* **a** an interval of an **octave** and a **fifth** (*noun* sense 5); **b** a note at that interval from another. [Anglo-Saxon *twelfta*]

Twelfth Night *noun* the evening before the twelfth day after Christmas (5 January) or the evening of the day itself (6 January).

twelve *noun* **1** **a** the cardinal number 12; **b** the quantity that this represents, being one more than eleven. **2** any symbol for this, eg *12* or *XII*. **3** the age of twelve. **4** something, esp a garment or a person, whose size is denoted by the number 12. **5** (*also* **12 o'clock, 12am** *or* **12pm**) midnight or midday: *stopped at twelve for lunch*. **6** a set or group of twelve people or things. **7** (written **12**) *Brit* a film that is classified as suitable for people aged twelve or over. ▸ *adj* **1** totalling twelve. **2** aged twelve. [Anglo-Saxon *twelf*]

twelvemonth *noun, old use* a year.

twelve-tone *adj, music* belonging or relating to music based on a pattern formed from the 12 notes of the **chromatic scale**.

twenties (often written **20s** *or* **20's**) *plural noun* **1** (**one's twenties**) the period of time between one's twentieth and thirtieth birthdays. **2** (**the twenties**) the range of temperatures between twenty and thirty degrees. **3** (**the twenties**) the period of time between the twentieth and thirtieth years of a century: *the roaring twenties*.

twenty *noun* (**-ies**) **1** **a** the cardinal number 20; **b** the quantity that this represents, being one more than 19, or the product of ten and two. **2** any symbol for this, eg *20* or *XX*. **3** the age of twenty. **4** something, esp a garment or a person, whose size is denoted by the number twenty. **5** a banknote worth twenty pounds. ▸ *adj* **1** totalling twenty. **2** aged twenty. See also **twenties**. ▪ **twentieth** *adj, noun, adv*. [Anglo-Saxon *twentig*]

twenty- *combining form* **a** *forming adjectives and nouns* with cardinal numbers between *one* and *nine*: *twenty-two*; **b** *forming adjectives and nouns* with ordinal numbers between *first* and *ninth*: *twenty-second*.

twenty-four-seven (usually written **24–7**) *adv, informal* all the time. [1990s: from *twenty-four* hours a day and *seven* days a week]

twenty-twenty (often written **20/20**) *adj* **1** of someone's vision: normal. **2** of perception or hindsight: sharp and insightful.

twerp *or* **twirp** *noun, informal* a contemptible person.

twice *adv* **1** two times: *Twice two is four*. **2** on two occasions. **3** double in amount or quantity: *twice as much*. [Anglo-Saxon *twiges*]

twiddle *verb* **1** to twist round and round: *twiddle the knob on the radio*. **2** to play with or twist round and round idly: *twiddling her hair*. ▸ *noun* **1** an act of twiddling. **2** a curly mark or ornamentation. [16c]

IDIOMS **twiddle one's thumbs** to have nothing to do.

twig[1] *noun* a small shoot or branch of a tree, bush, etc. ▪ **twiggy** *adj* (**-ier, -iest**). [Anglo-Saxon]

twig[2] *verb* (***twigged, twigging***) *tr & intr, Brit informal* to understand (a joke, situation, etc), esp suddenly. [18c: from Irish Gaelic *tuigim* I understand]

twilight *noun* **1** a faint diffused light in the sky when the sun is just below the horizon, esp just after sunset. **2** the time of day when this occurs. **3** partial darkness. **4** a period or state of decline: *the twilight of his life*. [Anglo-Saxon *twi* two + light]

twilight zone *noun* **1** a decaying area of a city or town. **2** an indefinite or intermediate state or position.

twill *noun* a strong fabric woven to give a surface pattern of parallel diagonal ridges. [Anglo-Saxon *twilic* woven of double thread]

twin *noun* **1** either of two people or animals that are born at the same time to the same mother. **2** either of two people or things that are very like each other or closely associated with each other. **3** (**the Twins**) the constellation **Gemini**. ▸ *adj* being twins or one of a pair or consisting of very similar or closely connected parts. ▸ *verb* (***twinned, twinning***) **1** *tr & intr* to bring or come together closely or intimately. **2** to link (a town) with a counterpart in another country to encourage cultural, social, etc exchanges. [Anglo-Saxon *twinn*]

twin bed *noun* one of a pair of matching single beds.

twine *noun* **1** strong string or cord of twisted cotton, hemp, etc. **2** a coil or twist. **3** an act of twisting or clasping. ▸ *verb* **1** to twist together; to interweave. **2** to form by twisting or interweaving. **3** *tr & intr* to twist or coil round. [Anglo-Saxon *twin* double or twisted thread]

twinge *noun* **1** a sudden sharp stabbing or shooting pain. **2** a sudden sharp pang of emotional pain, bad conscience, etc. [Anglo-Saxon *twengan* to pinch]

twinkle *verb* **1** *intr* of a star, etc: to shine with a bright, flickering light. **2** *intr* of the eyes: to shine or sparkle with amusement, mischief, etc. **3** to give off (light) with a flicker. ▸ *noun* **1** a gleam or sparkle in the eyes. **2** a flicker or glimmer of light. **3** an act of twinkling. ▪ **twinkly** *adj* (**-ier, -iest**). [Anglo-Saxon *twinclian*]
IDIOMS **in the twinkling of an eye** in a very short time.

twinset *noun, Brit* a woman's matching sweater and cardigan.

twin town *noun* a town which is linked to another town abroad.

twirl *verb, tr & intr* to turn, spin or twist round: *twirled across the dance floor.* ▸ *noun* **1** an act of twirling: *did a twirl to show off her new dress.* **2** a curly mark or ornament, eg, a flourish made with a pen. ▪ **twirler** *noun.* ▪ **twirly** *adj* (**-ier, -iest**). [16c: from *twist* + *whirl*]

twirp see **twerp**

twist *verb* **1** *tr & intr* to wind or turn round, esp by moving only a single part or by moving different parts in opposite directions: *twist the knob • He twisted round in his seat.* **2** *intr* to follow a winding course: *The road twists through the mountains.* **3** to force or wrench out of the correct shape or position with a sharp turning movement: *twisted his ankle as he fell.* **4** to distort: *twisted his face into an ugly sneer • twisted her words.* ▸ *noun* **1** an act or the process of twisting. **2** something that is formed by twisting or being twisted. **3** a turn or coil; a bend. **4** a sharp turning movement which pulls something out of shape; a wrench. **5** an unexpected event, development or change, eg, of direction: *a twist in the plot.* **6** a distortion of form, nature or meaning. **7** an eccentricity or perversion. **8** **a** a twisted roll of bread; **b** a twisted roll of tobacco; **c** a curl of citrus peel used to flavour a drink: *served with a twist of lemon.* **9** (**the twist**) a 1960s dance which involves making twisting movements of the legs and hips. ▪ **twisty** *adj* (**-ier, -iest**). [14c: from English *twisten* to divide]
IDIOMS **round the twist** *informal* mad; crazy. **twist sb's arm** *informal* to persuade them, usu by applying moral pressure.

twisted *adj* **1** full of twists; coiled or distorted: *a tree with knarled and twisted branches.* **2** *informal* of someone or their mind: emotionally disturbed or perverted.

twister *noun* **1** *Brit informal* a dishonest or deceiving person; a swindler. **2** *N Am informal* a tornado.

twit *noun, informal* a fool or idiot. [20c]

twitch *verb* **1** to move or cause to move with a spasm or jerk: *My eye has been twitching all day.* **2** to pull or pluck sharply or jerkily. ▸ *noun* **1** a sudden spasm or jerk. **2** a sharp pang, eg, of pain, conscience, etc. [12c]

twitcher *noun, informal* a bird-watcher whose aim is to spot as many rare birds as possible.

twitchy *adj* (**-ier, -iest**) **1** *informal* nervous, anxious or restless: *a twitchy smile • feeling twitchy about the interview.* **2** characterized by twitching: *a twitchy eye.* ▪ **twitchily** *adv.*

twitter *noun* **1** a light repeated chirping sound made esp by small birds. **2** *informal* a nervous or excited state: *go all of a twitter.* ▸ *verb* **1** *intr* to make a light repeated chirping sound. **2** to say or utter with such a chirping sound. **3** (*also* **twitter on** *or* **away**) to talk rapidly and often trivially. ▪ **twitterer** *noun.* ▪ **twittery** *adj.* [14c: imitating the sound]

'twixt *prep, old use* a shortened form of **betwixt.**

two *noun* **1** **a** the cardinal number 2; **b** the quantity that this represents, being one more than one. **2** any symbol for this, eg *2* or *II.* **3** the age of two. **4** something, such as a size, that is denoted by the number 2. **5** the second hour after midnight or midday: *The meeting is at two • 2 o'clock • 2pm.* **6** a set or group of two people or things. ▸ *adj* **1** totalling two. **2** aged two. [Anglo-Saxon *twa*]
IDIOMS **put two and two together** to come to a conclusion, usu an obvious one, from the available evidence. **that makes two of us** the same is true of me.

two-bit *adj, orig N Am informal* cheap; petty; small-time.

two-dimensional *adj* **1** having, or appearing to have, breadth and length but no depth. **2** *disparaging* having little depth or substance.

two-edged *adj* **1** double-edged. **2** having both advantageous and disadvantageous functions, side-effects, outcomes, etc.

two-faced *adj* deceitful; hypocritical; insincere.

twofold *adj* **1** twice as much or as many. **2** divided into, or consisting of, two parts. ▸ *adv* by twice as much.

two-handed *adj* **1** having, needing or being meant for two hands or two people: *a two-handed saw.* **2** able to use both hands equally well.

two-horse race *noun* a contest in which only two entrants have a realistic chance of winning.

twopence *noun, Brit* **1** /ˈtʌpəns/ (*also* **tuppence**) the sum of two pence, esp before the introduction of decimal coinage. **2** /tuːˈpɛns/ a decimal coin of the value of two pence.
IDIOMS **not care** *or* **give tuppence** (/ˈtʌpəns/) *informal* not to care at all: *don't give tuppence for what you think.*

twopenny *or* **tuppenny** /ˈtʌpənɪ/ *adj, Brit* **1** worth or costing twopence. **2** *informal* cheap; worthless.

two-piece *adj* of a suit, bathing costume, etc: consisting of two matching or complementary pieces or parts. ▸ *noun* a two-piece suit, etc.

two-ply *adj* consisting of two strands or layers: *two-ply wool • two-ply wood.* ▸ *noun* (**-ies**) knitting wool consisting of two strands twisted together or wood consisting of two layers glued together.

two-sided *adj* **1** having two sides which differ from each other. **2** controversial; having two aspects.

twosome *noun* **1** a game, dance, etc for two people. **2** a pair of people together.

two-step *noun* **1** a ballroom dance in duple time. **2** a piece of music for such a dance.

two-stroke *adj* of an internal-combustion engine: taking one upward movement and one downward movement of the piston to complete the power cycle. ▸ *noun* an engine that works in this way.

two-time *verb, tr & intr, informal* **1** to deceive or be unfaithful to (a husband, wife, lover, etc). **2** to swindle or double-cross. ▪ **two-timing** *adj, noun.* [20c]

two-tone *adj* having two colours or two sounds: *a car with a two-tone trim* • *a two-tone alarm.*

two-way *adj* **1** of a street, etc: having traffic moving in both directions. **2** of a radio, etc: able to send and receive messages. **3** of a switch, wiring, etc: designed so that the electricity can be switched on or off from either of two points. **4** of a mirror: designed so that one side is like a normal mirror but with the other side allowing someone to see through without being observed.

TXT *abbrev* text (used in text messages).

-ty[1] *suffix, forming nouns, denoting* quality or condition: *safety* • *certainty.*

-ty[2] *suffix, denoting* tens: *ninety.*

tycoon *noun* a business magnate. [19c: from Japanese *taikun* great prince]

tying *present participle of* **tie**

tyke *noun* **1** a dog, esp a mongrel. **2** *Brit informal* a rough or coarse person. **3** *Brit informal* a small child, esp a naughty one. [14c: from Norse *tik* a bitch]

tympani see **timpani**

tympanic membrane see **eardrum**

tympanum /ˈtɪmpənəm/ *noun* (***tympana*** /-nə/ *or* ***tympanums***) **1** *anatomy* the middle ear. **2** *archit* a recessed usu triangular face of a pediment. **3** *archit* **a** the area between the lintel of a doorway or window and an arch over it; **b** a carving on this area. **4** a drum or the skin of a drum. [17c: Latin, from Greek *tympanon* a drum]

type *noun* **1** a class or group of people, animals or things that share similar characteristics. **2** the general character, nature or form of a particular class or group; a kind or sort. **3** *informal* a person, esp of a specified kind: *the silent type* • *He's not really my type.* **4** a person, animal or thing that is a characteristic example of its group or class. **5** *printing* **a** a small metal block with a raised letter or character on one surface that is used for printing; **b** a set of such blocks; **c** a set of such blocks that give printing of a specified kind: *italic type.* **6** printed letters, characters, words, etc: *a leaflet with bold red type.* ▶ *verb* **1** *tr & intr* to use a typewriter or word processor (to produce words, text, etc): *Can you type?* • *typed a letter.* **2** to be a characteristic example or type of something; to typify. **3 a** *biol* to allocate (an animal, plant, etc) to a type; **b** *med* to classify: *typed the blood sample for cross-matching.* [15c: from Greek *typos* a blow or impression]

typecast *verb* to put (an actor or actress) regularly in the same kind of part.

typeface *noun, printing* **1** a set of letters, characters, etc of a specified design or style. **2** the part of the type that is inked or the impression this leaves.

typescript *noun* a typewritten document, manuscript or copy.

typeset *verb* (***typeset, typesetting***) *printing* to arrange (type) or set (a page, etc) in type ready for printing. ▪ **typesetter** *noun.*

typewriter *noun* a machine with keys that the user strikes to produce characters on paper. ▪ **typewritten** *adj.*

typhoid *noun* **1** (*in full* **typhoid fever**) *med* a bacterial infection characterized by fever, a rash of red spots on the front of the body, abdominal pain and sometimes delirium. **2** a similar infection in animals. ▪ **typhoidal** *adj.* [19c: so called because the fever was thought to be related to **typhus**]

typhoon *noun* a cyclonic tropical storm of the NW Pacific, west of the International Date Line. Compare **hurricane**. [16c: from Chinese *da feng* great wind]

typhus *noun, med* an infectious disease caused by parasitic micro-organisms and transmitted to humans by lice carried by rodents, characterized by fever, severe headache, a rash and delirium. [18c: Latin, from Greek *typhos* smoke or stupour]

typical *adj* **1** having or showing the usual features, traits, etc, or being a characteristic or representative example: *We take in about £1000 on a typical day.* **2 a** (*often* **typical of**) displaying the usual or expected behaviour, attitude, etc: *It's typical of him to be late;* **b** an exclamation expressing disdain, frustration, etc: *Typical! It always rains when we plan a picnic.* **3** *biol* belonging or relating to, or being a representative or characteristic specimen or type. ▪ **typicality** *noun.* ▪ **typically** *adv.* [17c: from Latin *typicalis*]

typify *verb* (*-ies, -ied*) **1** to be an excellent or characteristic example of. **2** to represent by a type or symbol; to symbolize. [17c: from Latin *typus* + *facere* to make]

typist *noun* **1** someone whose job is to type. **2** someone who types: *I'm not a very fast typist.*

typo *noun, informal* **1** a typographical error. **2** a typographer. [19c: a contraction]

typography *noun* **1** the art or occupation of setting type and arranging texts for printing. **2** the style and general appearance of printed matter. ▪ **typographer** *noun.* ▪ **typographic** *or* **typographical** *adj.* ▪ **typographically** *adv.* [17c: from French *typographie*]

tyrannical *adj* **1** relating to or like a tyrant. **2** oppressive; despotic. ▪ **tyrannically** *adv.*

tyrannize *or* **-ise** *verb, tr & intr* to rule or treat in a cruel, unjust and oppressive way. [16c: from Latin *tyrannizare* to act like a tyrant]

tyrannosaurus *or* **tyrannosaur** *noun* a huge flesh-eating dinosaur that walked on its hind legs and which had relatively small clawlike front legs. [20c: from Greek *tyrannos* tyrant + *sauros* lizard]

tyranny *noun* (*-ies*) **1** the use of cruelty, injustice, oppression, etc to enforce authority or power. **2 a** absolute, cruel and oppressive government by a single tyrant or group of tyrannical people; **b** a state under such government; **c** a period when this kind of government rules. **3** a cruel, unjust or oppressive act. [14c: from French *tyrannie*]

tyrant *noun* **1** a cruel, unjust and oppressive ruler with absolute power. **2** someone who uses authority or power cruelly and unjustly. [13c: French, from Greek *tyrannos* a tyrant]

tyre *or* (*US*) **tire** *noun* **1** a rubber ring around the outside edge of a wheel, eg, on a bicycle, pram, etc. **2** a similar hollow structure with an inner tube filled with compressed air on the wheel of a car, lorry, etc. [18c: a variant of *tire* a headdress, from **attire**]

tyro *noun* a novice or beginner. [17c: from Latin *tiro* a young soldier, a recruit]

tzar, tzarina see **tsar, tsarina**

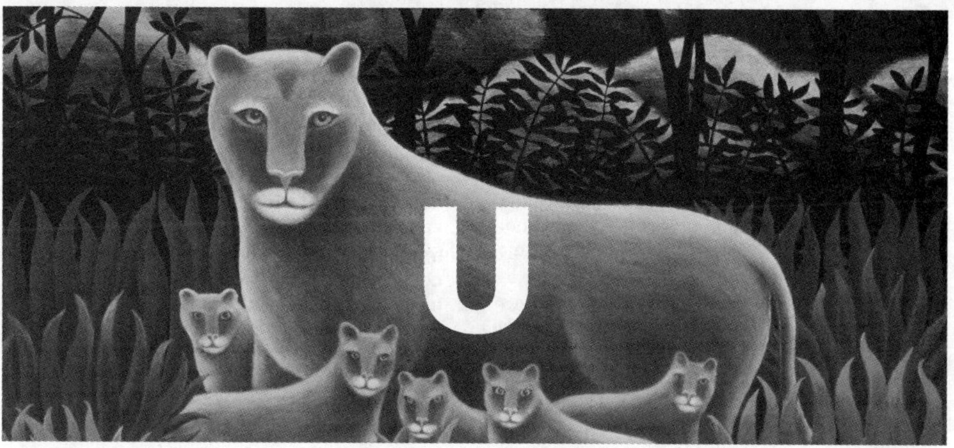

U[1] *or* **u** *noun* (***Us, U's*** *or* ***u's***) **1** the twenty-first letter of the English alphabet. **2** anything shaped like the letter U.

U[2] *adj, Brit informal* esp of language: typical of or acceptable to the upper classes. Compare **non-U**.

U[3] *abbrev, Brit* universal, denoting a film designated as suitable for people of all ages.

U[4] *symbol, chem* uranium.

uber- *or* (*Ger*) **Über-** *prefix, denoting* **1** an exceptional type: *ubercelebrity.* **2** an archetypal example: *uber-Scot*. [From German *Über*, meaning 'over']

ubiquitous /jʊ'bɪkwɪtəs/ *adj* existing, found or seeming to be found everywhere at the same time; omnipresent. ▪ **ubiquitously** *adv.* ▪ **ubiquity** *noun.* [19c: from Latin *ubique* everywhere]

U-boat *noun* a German submarine, used esp in World Wars I and II. [20c: from German *Unterseeboot*, literally 'undersea-boat']

UCAS /'juːkas/ *abbrev* in the UK: Universities and Colleges Admissions Service, an organization which administers entry to universities and colleges.

udder *noun* in certain mammals, eg cows, goats, etc: the bag-like structure, with two or more teats, containing the mammary glands that secrete milk. [Anglo-Saxon *uder*]

UEFA /juː'eɪfə/ *abbrev* Union of European Football Associations.

UFO *or* **ufo** /'juːfoʊ/ *noun* an unidentified flying object. [20c]

ufology /jʊ'fɒlədʒɪ/ *noun* the study of UFOs. ▪ **ufologist** *noun.*

Ugandan *adj* belonging or relating to Uganda, a republic in E Africa, or its inhabitants. ▸ *noun* a citizen or inhabitant of, or person born in, Uganda.

ugh /ʌx, ʌg, ɜːx, ɜːg/ *exclam* expressing dislike or disgust. [18c]

Ugli *noun, trademark* (***Uglis*** *or* ***Uglies***) a large juicy citrus fruit with a thick wrinkled yellow-red skin, that is a cross between a grapefruit, a Seville orange and a tangerine. [20c: from *ugly*, because of the fruit's appearance]

ugly *adj* (***-ier, -iest***) **1** unpleasant to look at; extremely unattractive. **2** morally repulsive or offensive. **3** threatening, or involving danger or violence: *an ugly situation.* **4** angry; bad-tempered: *an ugly mood.* ▪ **ugliness** *noun.* [13c: from Norse *uggligr* to be feared]

ugly duckling *noun* someone or something, initially thought ugly or worthless, that later turns out to be outstandingly beautiful or highly valued. [19c: from *The Ugly Duckling*, the title of a story by Hans Christian Andersen]

UHF *abbrev, radio* ultrahigh frequency.

UHT *abbrev* ultra-heat-treated.

UK *abbrev* United Kingdom.

ukase /jʊ'keɪz/ *noun* **1** a command issued by a supreme ruler, esp the Tsar in Imperial Russia. **2** any arbitrary command. [18c: from Russian *ukaz* order]

Ukrainian *adj* belonging or relating to Ukraine, its inhabitants or their language. ▸ *noun* **1** a citizen or inhabitant of, or person born in, Ukraine. **2** the official language of Ukraine. [19c: from an obsolete Russian word *ukraina* frontier regions]

ukulele *or* **ukelele** /jʊkə'leɪlɪ/ *noun* a small guitar, usu with four strings. [19c: Hawaiian, 'jumping flea']

ulcer *noun* **1** *pathol* a persistent open sore on the surface of the skin or of the mucous membranes lining a body cavity. **2** a source of evil or corruption. ▪ **ulcered** *adj.* ▪ **ulcerous** *adj.* [14c: from Latin *ulcus*]

ulcerate *verb, tr & intr* to form or cause an ulcer on or in a part of the body. ▪ **ulceration** *noun.* ▪ **ulcerative** *adj.*

-ule /-juːl/ *suffix, forming nouns, denoting* a diminutive; smallness: *nodule* • *globule.* [From Latin *-ulus* a diminutive suffix]

-ulent /-jʊlənt/ *suffix, forming adjectives, denoting* full of; with much: *fraudulent.* ▪ **-ulence** *suffix, forming nouns.* [From Latin suffix *-ulentus*]

ulna *noun* (***ulnae*** /'ʌlniː/ *or* ***ulnas***) *anatomy* **1** the thinner and longer of the two bones of the human forearm. Compare **radius** (sense 5). **2** the corresponding bone in the front limb or wing of other vertebrates. ▪ **ulnar** *adj*: *ulnar nerve.* [16c: Latin, meaning 'elbow' or 'arm']

ulster *noun* a man's loose heavy double-breasted overcoat, often worn with a belt. [19c: named after Ulster in Northern Ireland]

Ulsterman *or* **Ulsterwoman** *noun* a citizen or inhabitant of, or person born in, Ulster.

ult. *abbrev* ultimo.

ulterior /ʌl'tɪərɪə(r)/ *adj* of motives, etc: beyond or other than what is apparent or admitted. [17c: Latin, meaning 'further' or 'more distant']

ultimate *adj* **1** last or final in a series or process. **2** most important; greatest possible. **3** fundamental; basic. **4** *informal* best; most advanced. ▸ *noun* **1** the final point; the end or conclusion. **2** (**the ultimate**) *informal* the best; the most advanced of its kind:

the ultimate in computer technology. ▪ **ultimately** *adv* in the end; finally. [17c: from Latin *ultimus* last]

ultimatum *noun* (***ultimatums*** *or* ***ultimata***) **1** in a dispute, negotiations, etc: a final statement from one of the parties involved to another, declaring an intention to take hostile action unless specified conditions are fulfilled. **2** any final terms, demand, etc. [18c: Latin neuter of *ultimatus* **ultimate**]

ultimo *adj* (abbrev **ult.**) used mainly in formal correspondence: of or during last month: *your letter of the tenth ultimo.* Compare **proximo**. [17c: from Latin *ultimus* last]

ultra *adj* of a person or party: holding extreme opinions, esp in political matters. ▸ *noun* someone who holds extreme opinions. [19c: orig meaning 'ultra-royalist']

ultra- *prefix, denoting* **1** beyond in place, range or limit: *ultra-microscopic*. **2** extreme or extremely: *ultra-modern.* [From Latin *ultra* beyond]

ultra-heat-treated *adj* (abbrev **UHT**) of milk, etc: sterilized by exposure to very high temperatures, and thus with its shelf life increased.

ultrahigh frequency *noun* (abbrev **UHF**) a radio frequency between 300 and 3000MHz.

ultramarine *noun* **1** a deep-blue pigment used in paints, orig made by grinding lapis lazuli. **2** the colour of this pigment. ▸ *adj* of the colour ultramarine. [16c: from Latin *ultramarinus*, from *ultra* beyond + *mare* sea]

ultramontane *adj* **1** situated or relating to an area beyond a mountain range, esp the Alps. **2** *RC Church* relating or belonging to a faction which is in favour of supreme papal authority on doctrinal matters. ▸ *noun* **1** someone who lives beyond a mountain range, esp the Alps. **2** *RC Church* a member of the ultramontane faction. [16c: from Latin *ultramontanus*]

ultrasonic *adj* relating to or producing ultrasound. Compare **infrasonic**, **supersonic**, **subsonic**. ▪ **ultrasonically** *adv.* [20c]

ultrasonics *singular noun* the branch of physics that deals with the study of ultrasound. [20c]

ultrasound *noun* sound consisting of waves with frequencies higher than 20,000Hz, widely used in medical diagnosis, in sonar systems, for cleaning industrial tools, and for detecting flaws and impurities in metals. [20c]

ultrasound scan *noun* a medical examination of an internal part, esp a fetus, by directing ultrasound waves through it to produce an image on a screen.

ultraviolet *adj* (abbrev **UV**) **1** denoting electromagnetic radiation with wavelengths in the range 4 to 400nm, ie in the region between violet light and X-rays. **2** relating to or involving ultraviolet radiation or its use. ▸ *noun* the ultraviolet part of the spectrum. [19c]

ultra vires /ˈʌltrə ˈvaɪəriːz/ *adv, adj, law* beyond the powers or legal authority of a person, corporation, etc. [18c: Latin, meaning 'beyond the powers or strength']

ululate /ˈjuːljʊleɪt, ˈʌl-/ *verb, intr* to howl, wail or screech. ▪ **ululant** *adj.* ▪ **ululation** *noun.* [17c: from Latin *ululare* to howl]

umbel *noun, botany* a flower head in which a cluster of flowers with stalks of equal length arise from the same point on the main stem. [16c: from Latin *umbella* sunshade]

umbelliferous *adj, botany* denoting or belonging to plants which typically have flowers arranged in umbels. [17c: from Latin *umbella* (see **umbel**) + *ferre* to carry or bear]

umber *noun* **1** a dark yellowish-brown earthy mineral containing oxides of iron and manganese, used to make pigments. **2** any of these pigments or the brownish colours produced by them. ▸ *adj* referring to the colour of umber; dark brown. [16c: from French *terre d'ombre* or Italian *terra di ombra* shadow earth]

umbilical *adj* relating to the umbilicus or the umbilical cord.

umbilical cord *noun* **1** a long flexible tube-like organ by which a fetus is attached to the placenta and through which it receives nourishment. **2** any cable, tube, servicing line, etc through which essential supplies are conveyed, eg the lifeline that connects astronauts to their spacecraft during a space walk.

umbilicus *noun* (***umbilici*** /ʌmˈbɪlɪsaɪ/ *or* ***umbilicuses***) *anatomy* **1** the navel. **2** *biol* a small depression or navel-like hole such as that at the base of a shell. [17c: Latin, meaning 'navel']

umble pie *noun* **humble pie**

umbles *plural noun, archaic* the entrails (the liver, heart, lungs, etc) of an animal, esp a deer. [14c: from French *nombles*]

umbra *noun* (***umbrae*** /ˈʌmbriː/ *or* ***umbras***) **1** *astron* the shadow cast by the moon on the earth during an eclipse of the sun. **2** the darker inner part of a sunspot. ▪ **umbral** *adj.* [17c: Latin, meaning 'shade' or 'shadow']

umbrage *noun* (*esp* **give** *or* **take umbrage**) annoyance; offence. [15c: from French *ombrage*]

umbrella *noun* **1** a device carried to give shelter from rain, etc, consisting of a rounded fabric canopy supported on a lightweight, usu metal, collapsible framework of ribs fitted around a central stick or handle. **2** *military* a protective screen or shield of fighter aircraft or gunfire. **3** *US military slang* a parachute. **4** something, such as an organization, that provides protection or overall cover for a number of others. ▸ *adj* **1** referring to something that covers or protects a number of things: *an umbrella organization.* **2** of a word, term, etc: general; covering several meanings or ideas. [17c: from Italian *ombrella*]

umlaut /ˈʊmlaʊt/ *noun* in Germanic languages: **1** a change in the pronunciation of a vowel under the influence of a front vowel in a following syllable (esp in a suffix). **2** a mark consisting of two dots placed above a vowel (eg ö or ä) that undergoes or has undergone this change. [19c: German, from *um* around + *Laut* sound]

umma *or* **ummah** /ˈʊmə/ *noun, Islam* the body of Muslim believers considered as one community. [From Arabic meaning 'people', 'community']

umpire *noun* **1** an impartial person who supervises play in various sports, eg cricket and tennis, enforcing the rules and deciding disputes. **2** someone who judges or decides a dispute or deadlock; an arbitrator. ▸ *verb, tr & intr* to act as umpire in a match, dispute, etc. [15c: from French *nompere*, from *non-* not + *per, pair* peer or equal]

umpteen *adj, informal* very many; innumerable: *I've told you umpteen times!* ▪ **umpteenth** *noun, adj.* [20c: from earlier *umpty* a great deal + *-teen*]

UN *abbrev* United Nations.

un- *prefix* **1** *added to adjs, nouns and advs, denoting* the opposite of the base word; not. **2** *added to verbs, denoting* **a** reversal of an action, process or state: *uncurl* • *unharness*; **b** an intensification of the base word: *unloosen*. **3** *added to nouns, forming verbs, chiefly archaic, denoting* release or removal from or deprivation of: *ungarter* • *unfrock*. [Anglo-Saxon]

unable *adj* (*chiefly* **unable to do sth**) not able; not having sufficient strength, skill or authority (to do something). [14c]

unaccompanied *adj* **1** not accompanied; not escorted or attended. **2** *music* without instrumental accompaniment. [16c]

unaccomplished *adj* **1** not accomplished; not achieved or completed. **2** of a person: without social or intellectual accomplishments. [16c]

unaccountable *adj* **1** impossible to explain. **2** of a person: difficult to make out; puzzling in character. **3** not answerable or accountable. ▪ **unaccountably** *adv.* [17c]

unaccounted *adj* (*usu* **unaccounted for**) **1** unexplained. **2** not included in an account.

unaccustomed *adj* **1** not usual or customary; unfamiliar. **2** (*usu* **unaccustomed to sth**) not used or accustomed to it. [16c]

unadopted *adj* of a road, etc: not maintained, repaired, etc by a local authority. [17c]

unadulterated *adj* **1** pure; not mixed with anything else. **2** sheer; complete. [17c]

unadvised *adj* **1** not advised; without advice. **2** unwise; ill-advised. ▪ **unadvisedly** *adv.* ▪ **unadvisedness** *noun.* [14c]

unaffected *adj* **1** sincere or genuine, not affected; free from pretentiousness. **2** not affected or influenced. ▪ **unaffectedly** *adv.* [16c]

unalienable *adj* **inalienable**.

unalloyed *adj* **1** not alloyed; pure. **2** of joy, pleasure, etc: pure; sheer; not mixed with feelings of sadness or anxiety. [17c]

unanimous /jʊˈnanɪməs/ *adj* **1** all in complete agreement; of one mind. **2** of an opinion, decision, etc: shared or arrived at by all, with none disagreeing. ▪ **unanimity** *noun.* ▪ **unanimously** *adv.* [17c: from Latin *unanimus*]

unannounced *adj* not announced; unexpectedly or without warning. [18c]

unapproachable *adj* **1** out of reach; inaccessible. **2** with a manner that discourages familiarity; aloof; unfriendly. ▪ **unapproachably** *adv.* [16c]

unapt *adj* **1** (*usu* **unapt for sth**) not fitted for it; unsuitable. **2** lacking in aptitude; slow. ▪ **unaptly** *adv.* ▪ **unaptness** *noun.* [14c]

unarmed *adj* not armed; without weapons. [13c]

unassailable *adj* **1** not able to be assailed or attacked. **2** not able to be challenged or denied. ▪ **unassailably** *adv.* [16c]

unassuming *adj* modest or unpretentious. ▪ **unassumingly** *adv.* [18c]

unattached *adj* **1** not attached, associated or connected, esp to a particular group, organization, etc. **2** not in a steady romantic relationship. [18c]

unattended *adj* **1** not accompanied or watched over. **2** (*often* **unattended to**) not listened to or paid attention. [17c]

unavailing *adj* of efforts, etc: futile; of no avail. ▪ **unavailingly** *adv.* [17c]

unavoidable *adj* not able to be avoided; inevitable. ▪ **unavoidably** *adv.* [16c]

unaware *adj* with no knowledge (of something); not aware or conscious (of it). ▸ *adv* unawares. ▪ **unawareness** *noun.* [16c]

unawares *adv* **1** unexpectedly; by surprise. **2** without knowing or realizing; inadvertently. [16c]

unbalance *verb* **1** to throw someone or something off balance. **2** to upset someone's mental balance; to derange them. ▸ *noun* lack of balance or (mental) stability. [19c]

unbalanced *adj* **1** not in a state of physical balance. **2** lacking mental balance; deranged. **3** eg of a view or judgement: lacking impartiality; biased. **4** *bookkeeping* not adjusted so as to show balance of debtor and creditor. [17c]

unbearable *adj* not bearable; unendurable. ▪ **unbearably** *adv.* [15c]

unbeatable *adj* not able to be beaten or defeated; unsurpassable. [19c]

unbeaten *adj* not beaten, esp not defeated or surpassed. [13c]

unbecoming *adj* (*also* **unbecoming for** *or* **to sb**) **1** not becoming; not suited to the wearer or showing them to advantage. **2** of behaviour, etc: not appropriate or fitting; unseemly. [16c]

unbeknown *or* **unbeknownst** *adv* (*usu* **unbeknown** *or* **unbeknownst to sb**) unknown to them; without their knowledge. [17c]

unbelievable *adj* **1** too unusual or unexpected to be believed. **2** *informal* remarkable; astonishing. ▪ **unbelievably** *adv.* [16c]

unbeliever *noun* someone who does not believe, esp in a particular religion. [16c]

unbend *verb, tr & intr* **1** to relax (one's mind, behaviour, etc) from stiffness or formality; to make or become affable. **2** to straighten or release something from a bent or curved position. [13c]

unbending *adj* **1** not bending; unyielding or inflexible. **2** strict or severe. [17c]

unbiased *or* **unbiassed** *adj* not biased; unprejudiced or impartial. [17c]

unbidden *adj* **1** not commanded or ordered; spontaneous or voluntary. **2** not invited or solicited. [Anglo-Saxon]

unblinking *adj* without blinking; not showing emotion, esp fear. ▪ **unblinkingly** *adv.* [20c]

unblushing *adj* **1** not blushing. **2** unashamed; shameless or brazen. ▪ **unblushingly** *adv.* [16c]

unbolt *verb* to unfasten or open (a door, etc) by undoing or drawing back a bolt. [15c]

unbolted[1] *adj* not fastened with a bolt or bolts. [16c]

unbolted[2] *adj* of grain, flour, etc: not sifted; coarse. [16c]

unborn *adj* of a baby: not yet born; still in the womb. [Anglo-Saxon]

unbosom *verb* **1** to reveal or confess something. **2** *intr* (*often* **unbosom oneself**) to speak openly about what is on one's mind; to free oneself of worries or troubles by talking about them. [16c]

unbound *adj* **1** not bound or restrained. **2** loose; not tied or fastened with a band, etc. **3** of a book: without binding. [Anglo-Saxon]

unbounded *adj* **1** without bounds or limits. **2** unchecked; unrestrained. ▪ **unboundedly** *adv.* [16c]

unbowed *adj* **1** not bowed or bent. **2** not conquered or forced to yield. [14c]

unbridled *adj* **1** of a horse: not wearing a bridle. **2** said of speech, emotion, etc: fully and freely felt or expressed; unrestrained.

unbroken *adj* **1** not broken; intact. **2** uninterrupted; continuous or undisturbed. **3** undaunted; not subdued in spirit or health. **4** of a horse or other animal: not broken in; untamed. **5** of a (sporting) record: not surpassed. ▪ **unbrokenly** *adv.* [13c]

unburden *verb* **1** to remove a load or burden from someone or something. **2** (*often* **unburden oneself**) to relieve (oneself or one's mind) of worries, secrets, etc by confessing them to another person. [16c]

uncalled-for *adj* of a remark, etc: not warranted or deserved, esp unjustifiably rude or aggressive.

uncanny *adj* **1** weird, strange or mysterious, esp in an unsettling or uneasy way. **2** eg of skill or ability: beyond what is considered normal for an ordinary human. ▪ **uncannily** *adv.* ▪ **uncanniness** *noun.* [19c]

unceasing *adj* not ceasing; never-ending. [14c]

unceremonious *adj* **1** without ceremony; informal. **2** with no regard for politeness or dignity; direct and abrupt. ▪ **unceremoniously** *adv.* [16c]

uncertain *adj* **1** not sure, certain or confident. **2** not definitely known or decided. **3** not to be depended upon. **4** likely to change. ▪ **uncertainly** *adv.* ▪ **uncertainty** *noun* (**-ies**) **1** the state or condition of being uncertain. **2** something that is uncertain. [14c]
IDIOMS **in no uncertain terms** **1** unambiguously. **2** strongly; emphatically.

unchain *verb* **1** to release something from a chain or chains; to set free. **2** to remove the chain from something. [16c]

uncharted *adj* **1** of territory, etc: **a** not fully explored or mapped in detail; **b** not shown on a map or chart. **2** of a non-physical area, a subject area, etc: not yet examined or fully investigated. [19c]

unchartered *adj* **1** not holding or provided with a charter. **2** unauthorized. [19c]

unchecked *adj* **1** not restrained. **2** not checked or verified. [15c]

unchristian *adj* **1** of a person, community, etc: not Christian. **2** not in accordance with the principles or spirit of Christianity; uncharitable or uncaring. [16c]

uncial /ˈʌnsɪəl/ *adj* of a form of writing: in large rounded letters with flowing strokes, of a kind used in ancient manuscripts. ► *noun* **1** an uncial letter or form of writing. **2** a manuscript written in uncials. [17c: from Latin *uncia* a twelfth part or inch]

uncivil *adj* discourteous; rude or impolite. [16c]

uncivilized *or* **-ised** *adj* **1** of a people, tribe, etc: not civilized. **2** uncultured; rough. [17c]

unclassified *adj* **1** not classified. **2** of information: not classified as secret. [19c]

uncle *noun* **1** the brother or brother-in-law of a father or mother. **2** the husband of an aunt. **3** *informal* a form of address used by a child to a male friend of their parents. **4** *slang* a pawnbroker. See also **avuncular.** [13c: from French *oncle, uncle*]

unclean *adj* **1** morally or spiritually impure. **2** of an animal: regarded for religious reasons as impure and unfit to be used as food. **3** not clean; dirty or foul. [Anglo-Saxon]

Uncle Sam *noun, informal* the United States, its government or its people. [19c: perhaps a humorous interpretation of the letters *US*]

unclog *verb* to free something from an obstruction; to unblock it. [17c]

unclothe *verb* **1** to remove the clothes from someone. **2** to uncover or reveal something. [14c]

uncoil *verb, tr & intr* to untwist or unwind something, or to become untwisted. [18c]

uncomfortable *adj* **1** not comfortable. **2** feeling, involving or causing discomfort or unease. ▪ **uncomfortably** *adv.*

uncommitted *adj* not bound or pledged to support any particular party, policy, action, etc. [19c]

uncommon *adj* **1** rare or unusual. **2** remarkably great; extreme. ▪ **uncommonly** *adv* in an uncommon way or to an uncommon degree; unusually. [17c]

uncommunicative *adj* not communicative; not inclined to talk, express opinions, etc. [17c]

uncomplicated *adj* not complicated; straightforward. [18c]

uncompromising *adj* **1** unwilling to compromise or submit. **2** sheer; out-and-out. ▪ **uncompromisingly** *adv.* [19c]

unconcerned *adj* **1** lacking concern or interest; indifferent. **2** not anxious; untroubled. ▪ **unconcernedly** /ʌnkənˈsɜːnɪdlɪ/ *adv.* [17c]

unconditional *adj* **1** not conditional; with no conditions or limits imposed. **2** complete or absolute. ▪ **unconditionally** *adv.* [17c]

unconscionable /ʌnˈkɒnʃənəbəl/ *adj* **1** of a person, behaviour, etc: without conscience; unscrupulous. **2** outrageous; unthinkable. **3** unreasonably excessive. ▪ **unconscionably** *adv.* [16c]

unconscious *adj* **1** of a person or animal: in a state of insensibility, characterized by loss of awareness of the external environment, and inability to respond to sensory stimuli. **2** of an action, behaviour, etc: characterized by lack of awareness; unintentional; not deliberate. **3** *psychol* relating to or produced by the unconscious. ► *noun* (**the unconscious**) *psychol* in psychoanalysis: the part of the mind that contains memories, thoughts and feelings of which one is not consciously aware, but which may be manifested as dreams, psychosomatic symptoms or certain patterns of behaviour. ▪ **unconsciously** *adv.* ▪ **unconsciousness** *noun.* [18c]

unconstitutional *adj* not allowed by or consistent with a nation's constitution. ▪ **unconstitutionally** *adv.* [18c]

unconventional *adj* not conventional; not conforming to the normal or accepted standards, rules, etc; unusual. ▪ **unconventionally** *adv.* [19c]

uncoordinated *adj* **1** not coordinated. **2** eg of a person's movements: lacking co-ordination; clumsy or awkward. [19c]

uncork *verb* **1** to remove the cork from (a bottle, etc). **2** *informal* to release (eg emotion) from a pent-up state. [18c]

uncountable *adj* **1** not able to be counted; innumerable. **2** *grammar* of a noun: that cannot be used with the indefinite article or form a plural.

uncounted *adj* **1** not counted. **2** not able to be counted; innumerable. [15c]

uncouple *verb* **1** to undo the coupling of, or between (two or more things); to disconnect or release. **2** *intr* to become unfastened or disconnected.

uncouth *adj* coarse or awkward in behaviour, manners or language; uncultured or lacking refinement. ▪ **uncouthness** *noun*. [Anglo-Saxon *uncuth* unfamiliar (eg with social graces)]

uncover *verb* **1** to remove the cover or top from something. **2** to reveal or expose something.

uncovered *adj* **1** not covered; bare; revealed or exposed. **2** not protected by insurance.

uncrowned *adj* **1** of a monarch: not yet crowned. **2** with a specified status but not a formal title; denoting an acknowledged master or expert in something: *the uncrowned king of swindlers*.

unction *noun* **1** *Christianity* **a** the act of ceremonially anointing a person with oil; **b** the oil used. **2** ointment of any kind. **3** anything that soothes, such as words or thoughts. [14c: from Latin *unctio*]

unctuous *adj* **1** insincerely and excessively charming. **2** oily; greasy. ▪ **unctuously** *adv*. [14c]

uncut *adj* **1** not cut. **2** of a book: **a** with the pages not (yet) cut open; **b** with the margins untrimmed. **3** of a book, film, etc: with no parts cut out; unabridged. **4** of a gemstone, esp a diamond: not cut into a regular shape.

undaunted *adj* not daunted; not discouraged or put off. ▪ **undauntedly** *adv*.

undead *adj* **1** eg of a vampire, zombie, etc: supposedly dead but still able to move around, etc. **2** (**the undead**) those who are undead. [15c]

undecided *adj* **1** of a problem, question, etc: not (yet) decided; not settled. **2** of a person: not (yet) having decided or not able to decide; hesitating or irresolute. ▪ **undecidedly** *adv*. [16c]

undeniable *adj* **1** not able to be denied; unquestionably or obviously true. **2** clearly and indisputably excellent. ▪ **undeniably** *adv*. [16c]

under *prep* **1** **a** below or beneath something but not in contact with it: *under the table*; **b** below or beneath something and in contact with it: *under the book*. **2** at the foot of: *under the column*. **3** less than; short of: *under 10 per cent*. **4** lower in rank than. **5** during the reign or administration of: *under Queen Elizabeth II*. **6** subjected to, receiving or sustaining: *under consideration* • *under pressure*. **7** in the category or classification of. **8** known by: *goes under the name of*. **9** according to: *under the terms of the agreement*. **10** in view of; because of: *under the circumstances*. **11** propelled by: *under sail*. **12** of a field: planted with (a particular crop). **13** *astrol* within the influence of (a sign of the zodiac). ▸ *adv* **1** in or to a lower place, position or rank. **2** into a state of unconsciousness. ▸ *adj* lower. [Anglo-Saxon]

IDIOMS **under way** **1** of a process, activity, project, etc: in progress. **2** *naut* of a vessel: in motion.

under- *combining form* forming words meaning: **1** beneath or below: *underfoot*. **2** too little in quantity or degree: *underexposed* • *underpaid*. **3** lower in rank or importance: *under-secretary*. **4** less than: *underbid*. **5** less or lower than expectations or potential: *underdeveloped*.

underachieve *verb, intr* to be less successful than expected, esp academically; to fail to fulfil one's potential. ▪ **underachiever** *noun*. [20c]

underactivity *noun* reduced or insufficient activity. ▪ **underactive** *adj*. [20c]

under-age *adj* **1** of a person: below an age required by law; too young: *At seventeen he was under-age*. **2** of an activity, etc: carried on by an under-age person: *under-age drinking*.

underarm *adj* **1** of a style of bowling in sports, esp cricket, or of a service in tennis, etc: performed with the arm kept below the level of the shoulder. **2** eg of a bag, case, etc: placed or held under the arm. **3** relating to or for the armpit. ▸ *adv* with an underarm style or action. ▸ *noun* the armpit. [19c]

underbelly *noun* **1** the part of an animal's belly that faces or is nearest the ground. **2** (*also* **soft underbelly**) any unprotected part vulnerable to attack. [17c]

undercarriage *noun* **1** the landing gear of an aircraft, including wheels, shock absorbers, etc, used to take the impact on landing and support the aircraft on the ground. **2** the supporting framework or chassis of a carriage or vehicle.

undercharge *verb* **1** to charge someone too little money. **2** to put an insufficient charge in (eg an electrical circuit or explosive device). [17c]

underclass *noun* a subordinate social class, esp a class of people disadvantaged in society through poverty, unemployment, etc. [20c]

undercliff *noun* a terrace formed from material that has fallen from a cliff. [19c]

underclothes *plural noun* (*also* **underclothing**) **underwear**. [19c]

undercoat *noun* **1** **a** a layer of paint applied as preparation for the top or finishing coat; **b** the kind of paint used. **2** **underfur**. ▸ *verb* to apply an undercoat to (a surface). [17c]

undercook *verb* to cook (food) insufficiently or for too short a time. [19c]

undercover *adj* working, carried out, etc in secret: *an undercover agent*. ▸ *adv* in secret: *working undercover for the secret police*. [20c]

undercurrent *noun* **1** an unseen current under the (often still) surface of a body of water. **2** an underlying trend or body of opinion, esp if different from the one generally perceived. [17c]

undercut *verb* /ʌndəˈkʌt/ **1** to offer goods or services at a lower price than (a competitor). **2** to cut away the underside of something. **3** *sport* to apply backspin to (a ball). ▸ *noun* /ˈʌndəkʌt/ **1** a part that is cut away underneath. **2** the underside of a sirloin, ie the fillet.

underdeveloped *adj* **1** insufficiently developed; immature or undersized. **2** of a country: with resources inadequately used, a low standard of living and, usu, also lacking capital and social organization to advance. **3** *photog* not sufficiently developed to produce a normal image. [19c]

underdo *verb* to do something incompletely or inadequately, esp to cook (food) insufficiently or (too) lightly. ▪ **underdone** *adj*. [18c]

underdog *noun* **1** the competitor in a contest, etc who is considered unlikely to win. **2** anyone in adversity. [19c]

underdress *verb* to dress too plainly or with insufficient formality for a particular occasion. ▪ **underdressed** *adj.*

underemphasize *or* **-ise** *verb* to emphasize something insufficiently. ▪ **underemphasis** *noun.* [20c]

underemployed *adj* **1** given less work than could realistically be done. **2** given work that fails to make good use of the skills possessed.

underemployment *noun* **1** insufficient use of something. **2** a situation where too large a part of a labour force is unemployed.

underestimate *verb* /ʌndər'ɛstɪmeɪt/ to make too low an estimate of (someone's or something's value, capacity, extent, etc). ▸ *noun* /ʌndər'ɛstɪmət/ an estimate that is too low. ▪ **underestimation** *noun.* [19c]

underexpose *verb, photog* to expose (a film, plate or paper) for too little time or to too little light, resulting in a darkened photograph. ▪ **underexposure** *noun.* [19c]

underfeed *verb* to give (a person or animal) too little food. [17c]

underfloor *adj* situated, operating, etc beneath the floor: *underfloor heating.* [19c]

underfoot *adv* **1** beneath the foot or feet; on the ground. **2** *informal* in the way; always present and causing inconvenience.

underfund *verb* to provide (an organization, public service, etc) with insufficient funding to carry out all the planned activities. ▪ **underfunding** *noun.* [20c]

underfur *noun* a layer of short dense fur that grows under the longer outer layer of an animal's fur or coat. [19c]

undergarment *noun* any garment worn under other clothes, esp an item of underwear. [16c]

undergo *verb* to endure, experience or be subjected to something. [Anglo-Saxon *undergan*]

undergraduate *noun* someone studying for a first degree in a higher education establishment. Sometimes shortened to **undergrad**. [17c]

underground *noun* /'ʌndəgrɑʊnd/ **1** (*often* **the underground**; *also* **Underground**) a system of electric trains running in tunnels below ground. **2** a secret paramilitary organization fighting a government or occupying force. **3** any artistic movement seeking to challenge or overturn established views and practices. ▸ *adj* /'ʌndəgrɑʊnd/ **1** existing or operating below the surface of the ground: *an underground station.* **2** referring or relating to any political or artistic underground: *underground music.* ▸ *adv* /ʌndə 'grɑʊnd/ **1** to a position below ground level. **2** into hiding: *went underground.*

undergrowth *noun* a thick growth of shrubs and bushes among trees. [17c]

underhand *adj* **1** secretively deceitful or dishonest; sly. **2** *sport* **underarm**. ▸ *adv* in an underhand way. [16c]

underhanded *adv* /ʌndə'handɪd/ **underhand.** ▸ *adj* /'ʌndəhandɪd/ **1 underhand. 2** short of workers; undermanned. [19c]

underlay *verb* /ʌndə'leɪ/ to lay underneath something, or support or provide with something laid underneath. ▸ *noun* /'ʌndəleɪ/ a thing laid underneath another, esp felt or rubber matting laid under a carpet for protection.

underlie *verb* **1** to lie underneath something. **2** to be the hidden cause or meaning of (an attitude, event, etc), beneath what is apparent, visible or superficial.

underline *verb* **1** to draw a line under (eg a word or piece of text). **2** to emphasize. [16c]

underling *noun, derog* a subordinate.

underlying *adj* **1** lying under or beneath. **2** present though not immediately obvious: *his underlying intentions.* **3** fundamental: *the underlying causes.*

undermanned *adj* provided with too few workers; understaffed.

undermentioned *adj* mentioned or named below or later in the text. [17c]

undermine *verb* **1** to weaken or destroy something, esp gradually and imperceptibly: *undermined his confidence.* **2** to dig or wear away the base or foundation of (land, cliffs, etc). **3** to tunnel or dig beneath (a wall, etc). ▪ **undermining** *adj, noun.*

underneath *prep, adv* beneath or below; under. ▸ *adj* lower. ▸ *noun* a lower or downward-facing part or surface. [Anglo-Saxon *underneothan*, from **under** + *neothan* below]

undernourished *adj* insufficiently nourished; living on less food than is necessary for normal health and growth. ▪ **undernourishment** *noun.* [20c]

underpaid *adj* not paid sufficiently; paid less than is due. [19c]

underpants *plural noun* a man's undergarment covering the body from the waist or hips to (esp the tops of) the thighs. [20c]

underpart *noun* (*usu* **underparts**) the lower side, esp the underside, or part of the underside, of an animal, bird, etc. [17c]

underpass *noun, orig US* **1** a tunnel for pedestrians under a road or railway; a subway. **2** a road or railway passing under another.

underpay *verb* to pay less than is required or deserved. ▪ **underpayment** *noun.* [19c]

underperform *verb* **1** *intr* **a** to perform less well than expected; **b** of an investment: to be less profitable than expected. **2 a** to perform less well than (another); **b** of an investment: to be less profitable than (another investment). ▪ **underperformance** *noun.* [20c]

underpin *verb* **1** to support (a structure) from beneath, usu temporarily, with brickwork or a prop. **2** to support or corroborate. ▪ **underpinning** *noun.* [16c]

underplay *verb* **1** *tr & intr* to underact; to perform (a role) in a deliberately restrained or understated way. **2** to understate or play down the importance of something. [19c]

underpopulated *adj* with a very low population, or insufficient population to fully exploit the natural resources of an area.

underprivileged *adj* **1** deprived of the basic living standards and rights enjoyed by most people in society. **2** (**the underprivileged**) underprivileged people in general or as a group.

underquote *verb* **1** to quote a lower price than (another person). **2** to quote a lower price (for goods, services, etc) than that quoted by others. [19c]

underrate *verb* to rate or assess something at a lower worth or value than it deserves; to have too low an opinion of something. [16c]

underrepresented *adj* esp of a minority social group or a specified type or specimen: not present in sufficient numbers, eg to accurately reflect opinions, statistics, etc.

underscore *verb* **1** to score or draw a line under something. **2** to stress or emphasize something. ▸ *noun* a line inserted or drawn under a piece of text. [18c]

undersea *adj* situated or lying below the surface of the sea. ▸ *adv* below the sea or the surface of the sea. [17c]

underseal *noun* /ˈʌndəsiːl/ an anti-rusting substance painted onto the underside of a motor vehicle. ▸ *verb* /ʌndəˈsiːl/ to apply such a substance to (a vehicle) in order to seal the metal for protection. [20c]

under-secretary *noun* a junior minister or senior civil servant in a government department. [17c]

undersell *verb* **1** to sell goods or services at a lower price than (a competitor). **2** to sell (goods, etc) at less than their real value or for less than the usual price. ▪ **underseller** *noun*. [17c]

undershirt *noun, chiefly N Am* a vest. [17c]

undershoot *verb* **1** of an aircraft: to land short of (a runway). **2** to fall short of (a target, etc). [17c]

underside *noun* the downward-facing side or surface. [17c]

undersigned *adj* whose names are signed below: *we, the undersigned…* [17c]

undersized *adj* referring to something of less than the usual size. [18c]

underskirt *noun* a thin skirt-like undergarment worn under a dress or skirt; a petticoat. [19c]

underslung *adj* **1** suspended or supported from above. **2** of a vehicle chassis: extending below the axles. [20c]

understaffed *adj* of a business, organization, etc: provided with too few members of staff. ▪ **understaffing** *noun*. [19c]

understand *verb* **1** to grasp the meaning of (a subject, words, a person, a language, etc): *I've never understood trigonometry* • *Do you understand Polish?* **2** to make out the significance, cause, etc of something: *I don't understand what all the fuss is about.* **3** to have sympathetic awareness of someone or something: *I fully understand your point of view.* **4** to infer from the available information: *Did he really get the sack? I understood that he'd resigned.* ▪ **understandable** *adj*. ▪ **understandably** *adv*. [Anglo-Saxon]

understanding *noun* **1** the act of understanding or the ability to understand. **2** someone's perception or interpretation of information received. **3** an informal agreement. **4** a sympathetic harmony of viewpoints. **5** a condition agreed upon: *on the understanding that you stay for six months.* ▸ *adj* sympathetic to, or keenly aware of, the feelings and opinions of others.

understate *verb* **1** to describe something as being less or more moderate than is really the case. **2** to express something in very restrained or moderate terms, often for ironic or dramatic effect. ▪ **understatement** *noun*. [19c]

understated *adj* **1** referring to something that understates. **2** of clothes, someone's appearance, etc: effective through simplicity; not overembellished or showy. [20c]

understeer *verb, intr* of a motor vehicle: to have a tendency to turn less sharply than it should. ▸ *noun* a tendency in a motor vehicle to understeer.

understood *adj* **1** implied but not expressed or stated. **2** realized without being, or needing to be, openly stated. ▸ *verb, past tense, past participle of* **understand**.

understudy *verb* **1** to study or prepare (a role or part) so as to be able to replace the actor or actress who usu plays that part, in case of absence, etc. **2** *tr & intr* to act as understudy to (an actor or actress). ▸ *noun* (***-ies***) **1** an actor or actress who understudies a role. **2** any person who is trained to replace another in case of absence, etc.

undersubscribed *adj* of a share issue, etc: not having enough people prepared to subscribe to it.

undertake *verb* **1** to accept (a duty, responsibility or task). **2** to promise or agree.

undertaker *noun* a person whose job is to organize funerals and prepare the bodies of the dead for burial or cremation.

undertaking *noun* **1** a duty, responsibility or task undertaken. **2** a promise or guarantee. **3** the work of an undertaker. **4 a** using the nearside lane to pass a slow-moving vehicle; **b** an instance of this.

under-the-counter *adj* of goods: obtained or sold illicitly, surreptitiously, etc.

underthings *plural noun* underclothes, esp a woman's or girl's. [19c]

undertone *noun* **1** a quiet tone of voice. **2** an underlying quality, emotion or atmosphere. **3** a subdued sound or shade of a colour. [18c]

undertow *noun* an undercurrent in the sea that flows in the opposite direction to the surface current. [19c]

undervalue *verb* **1** to place too low a value on something. **2** to appreciate something insufficiently. ▪ **undervaluation** *noun*. [16c]

underwater *adj* situated, carried out, happening, etc under the surface of the water. ▸ *adv* below the surface of the water.

underwear *noun* clothes, eg bras, pants, etc, worn under shirts, trousers, dresses and skirts, etc, and usu next to the skin. [19c]

underweight *noun* /ˈʌndəweɪt/ lack or insufficiency of weight. ▸ *adj* /ʌndəˈweɪt/ **1** lacking in weight; not heavy enough. **2** of a person: weighing less than is normal or healthy for their height, build, etc. [17c]

underwhelm *verb, jocular* to fail to impress or make any impact on someone. [20c: modelled on **overwhelm**]

underwing *noun* the hindwing of an insect.

underwired *adj* of a bra: with a thin band of wire under each cup.

underworld *noun* **1** *myth* a world imagined to lie beneath the earth's surface, the home of the souls of the dead. **2** a hidden sphere of life or stratum of society, etc, esp the world of criminals and organized crime. [17c]

underwrite *verb* **1** to write (words, figures, etc) beneath other written matter. **2** to agree to finance (a commercial venture) and accept the loss in the event of failure. **3** to agree to buy, or find a buyer for, left-over shares from (a sale of shares to the public). **4** to issue (an insurance policy), accepting the risk involved. ▪ **underwriter** *noun.*

undesigned *adj* not meant; unintentional.

undesirable *adj* not desirable; unpleasant or objectionable in some way. ▸ *noun* someone or something that is considered undesirable. [17c]

undies /ˈʌndɪz/ *plural noun, informal* items of underwear, esp women's bras, pants, etc. [20c: from *underwear* or *underclothes*, etc]

undigested *adj* **1** not digested. **2** of information, etc: not properly considered or thought through.

undiluted *adj* **1** not diluted. **2** complete; utter: *told a pack of undiluted lies.*

undine /ˈʌndiːn/ *noun* a nymph; a female water spirit. [17c: from Latin *unda* a wave]

undo *verb* (*undoes, past tense* ***undid,*** *past participle* ***undone***) **1** *tr & intr* to open, unfasten or untie (something). **2** to cancel or reverse the doing of something, or its effect or result; to annul. **3** *facetious or literary* to bring about the downfall or ruin of someone or something. [Anglo-Saxon *undon*]

undoing *noun* **1** the act or action of unfastening, untying, opening etc. **2** **a** downfall or ruin; **b** the cause of it.

undone[1] *adj* not done; not achieved; unfinished or incomplete. [14c]

undone[2] *adj* **1** unfastened, untied, etc. **2** reversed; annulled. **3** destroyed; ruined: *I am undone!*

undoubted *adj* beyond doubt or question; clear; evident. ▪ **undoubtedly** *adv.* [15c]

undreamed *or* **undreamt** *adj* (*usu* **undreamed-of** *or* **undreamt-of**) not even imagined or dreamed of, esp thought never to be likely or possible. [17c]

undress *verb* **1** to take the clothes off oneself (or another person). **2** *intr* to take one's clothes off. ▸ *noun* **1** nakedness, or near-nakedness: *walked out of the bathroom in a state of undress.* **2** casual or informal dress. **3** *military* ordinary uniform as opposed to full military dress. [16c]

undressed *adj* **1** of stone, animal hide, etc: not treated, prepared or processed for use. **2** of food, esp salad: without a dressing. **3** not wearing clothes; partially or completely naked. **4** *military* not wearing formal dress or full dress uniform.

undue *adj* **1** unjustifiable; improper. **2** inappropriately or unjustifiably great; excessive: *undue criticism.* ▪ **unduly** *adv* **1** unjustifiably. **2** excessively. [14c]

undulant *or* **undulating** *adj* rising and falling like waves. [19c: from **undulate**]

undulate *verb* **1** *tr & intr* to move or to make something move in or like waves. **2** *tr & intr* to have or to give something a wavy surface, form, etc. ▪ **undulatory** *adj.* [17c: from Latin *unda* a wave]

undulation *noun* **1** the action of undulating. **2** a wave-like motion or form. **3** waviness. **4** a wave.

undying *adj* referring to something that does not die; everlasting; eternal. [14c]

unearned *adj* not deserved or merited. [13c]

unearned income *noun* income, such as dividends and interest earned on savings or from property, that is not remuneration for work done.

unearth *verb* **1** to dig something up out of the ground. **2** to discover something by investigation, or by searching or rummaging. [15c]

unearthly *adj* **1** not of this earth; heavenly or sublime. **2** supernatural; weird; mysterious. **3** *informal* ridiculous or outrageous, esp outrageously early: *at an unearthly hour.* ▪ **unearthliness** *noun.* [17c]

unease *noun* discomfort or apprehension.

uneasy *adj* (**-ier, -iest**) **1** nervous, anxious or unsettled; ill at ease. **2** unlikely to prove lasting; unstable. **3** causing anxiety; unsettling. ▪ **uneasily** *adv.* ▪ **uneasiness** *noun.* [13c]

uneconomic *adj* not economic; not in accordance with sound economic principles, esp unprofitable. [20c]

uneconomical *adj* not economical; wasteful. [19c]

unemployable *adj* unable or unfit for paid employment. ▸ *noun* someone who is unemployable. [19c]

unemployed *adj* **1** without paid employment; jobless. **2** not in use or not made use of. **3** (**the unemployed**) unemployed people in general or as a group. [17c]

unemployment *noun* **1** the state or condition of being unemployed. **2** the number or percentage of unemployed people in a particular region, country, etc. [19c]

unenforceable *adj* of a law, contract, etc: not able to be enforced, esp legally. [19c]

unenviable *adj* not to be envied; not provoking envy, esp because unpleasant or disagreeable: *an unenviable task.* [17c]

unequal *adj* **1** not equal in quantity, value, rank, size, etc. **2** of a contest, etc: not evenly matched or balanced. **3** (*usu* **unequal to sth**) unable to carry it out, deal with it, etc; inadequate. ▪ **unequally** *adv.* [16c]

unequalled *adj* without equal; not matched by any other; supreme.

unequivocal *adj* clearly stated or expressed; unambiguous. ▪ **unequivocally** *adv.* [18c]

unerring *adj* **1** not missing the mark or target; sure or certain. **2** consistently true or accurate; never making an error. ▪ **unerringly** *adv.* [17c]

UNESCO /juːˈnɛskoʊ/ *abbrev* United Nations Educational, Scientific and Cultural Organization.

uneven *adj* **1** of a surface, etc: not smooth or flat; bumpy. **2** of a contest: with contestants or sides poorly matched; unequal. **3** not equal; not matched or corresponding. ▪ **unevenly** *adv.* ▪ **unevenness** *noun.* [Anglo-Saxon *unefen*]

uneventful *adj* during which nothing interesting or out of the ordinary happens; uninteresting or routine. ▪ **uneventfully** *adv.* ▪ **uneventfulness** *noun.* [19c]

unexceptionable *adj* impossible to criticize or object to; completely satisfactory, suitable, etc. ▪ **unexceptionably** *adv.* [17c]

unexceptional *adj* **1** not admitting or forming an exception. **2** ordinary; run-of-the-mill. ▪ **unexceptionally** *adv.* [18c]

unexpected *adj* not expected; surprising. ▪ **unexpectedly** *adv.* ▪ **unexpectedness** *noun.* [16c]

unfailing *adj* **1** remaining constant; never weakening or failing. **2** continuous. **3** certain; sure. ▪ **unfailingly** *adv.* [14c]

unfair *adj* **1** not fair or just; inequitable. **2** involving deceit or dishonesty. ▪ **unfairly** *adv.* ▪ **unfairness** *noun.* [17c; Anglo-Saxon *unfæger*, meaning 'not pleasing to the eye' or 'ugly']

unfaithful *adj* **1** not faithful to a sexual partner, usu by having a sexual relationship with someone else. **2** not loyal. **3** not true to a promise. ▪ **unfaithfully** *adv.* ▪ **unfaithfulness** *noun.* [14c]

unfamiliar *adj* **1** not (already or previously) known, experienced, etc. **2** strange; unusual. **3** (*usu* **unfamiliar with sth**) of a person: not familiar or well acquainted with it. ▪ **unfamiliarity** *noun.* [16c]

unfasten *verb* **1** to undo or release something from a fastening. **2** *intr* to open or become loose. ▪ **unfastened** *adj* **1** released from fastening. **2** not fastened; loose. [13c]

unfathomable *adj* **1** unable to be understood or fathomed; incomprehensible. **2** too deep or vast to measure or fathom. ▪ **unfathomably** *adv.* ▪ **unfathomed** *adj* **1** unsounded; of unknown depth or meaning. **2** not fully explored or understood. [17c]

unfavourable *or* (*N Am*) **unfavorable** *adj* **1** not favourable; adverse or inauspicious. **2** of features, appearance, etc: ill-favoured; disagreeable or unattractive. ▪ **unfavourably** *adv.* [16c]

unfazed *adj, informal* not fazed; not disconcerted or perturbed. [19c: orig US]

unfeeling *adj* **1** without physical feeling or sensation. **2** unsympathetic; hard-hearted. ▪ **unfeelingly** *adv.* [Anglo-Saxon]

unfettered *adj* not controlled or restrained. [17c]

unfit *adj* **1** (*often* **unfit for** *or* **to** *or* **to do sth**) of a person: not suitably qualified for it; not good enough; incompetent. **2** (*often* **unfit for sth**) of a thing: not suitable or appropriate for it. **3** not fit; not in good physical condition. ▪ **unfitness** *noun.* [16c]

unfitted *adj* **1** not adapted or suited (for, to or to do something). **2** not equipped with fittings.

unflappable *adj, informal* never becoming agitated, flustered or alarmed; always remaining calm under pressure. ▪ **unflappability** *noun.* [20c]

unfledged *adj* **1** of a bird: not yet fledged; not yet having developed adult flight feathers. **2** young and inexperienced. [16c]

unflinching *adj* not flinching; showing a fearless determination in the face of danger or difficulty. ▪ **unflinchingly** *adv.* [18c]

unfold *verb* **1** to open out the folds of something; to spread it out. **2** *intr* to open out or be spread out. **3** to reveal (a mystery, idea, etc); to make something clear. **4** *intr* to develop or be revealed gradually. [Anglo-Saxon]

unforced *adj* **1** not compelled. **2** natural.

unfortunate *adj* **1** unlucky; suffering misfortune or ill-luck. **2** resulting from or constituting bad luck: *an unfortunate injury.* **3** regrettable. ▸ *noun* an unfortunate person. ▪ **unfortunately** *adv* **1** in an unfortunate way; unluckily. **2** it's unfortunate that …; I'm sorry to say …: *Unfortunately he can't come.* [16c]

unfounded *adj* of allegations, ideas, rumours, etc: not based on fact; without foundation. [17c]

unfreeze *verb* **1** *tr & intr* to thaw or cause something to thaw. **2** to free (eg prices, wages or funds) from a restriction or control imposed, eg by a government.

unfriendly *adj* **1** not friendly; somewhat hostile. **2** not favourable. ▪ **unfriendliness** *noun.* [15c]

unfrock *verb* to defrock; to deprive (someone in holy orders) of ecclesiastical office or function. [17c]

unfurl *verb, tr & intr* to open, spread out or unroll something from a rolled-up or tied-up state. [17c]

unfurnished *adj* esp of a rented property: lacking furniture.

ungainly *adj* (**-ier, -iest**) awkward and ungraceful in movement; clumsy. ▪ **ungainliness** *noun.* [17c: from obsolete *gainly* graceful]

ungodly *adj* **1** wicked or sinful; irreligious. **2** *informal* outrageous, esp outrageously early: *at an ungodly hour.* ▪ **ungodliness** *noun.* [16c]

ungovernable *adj* esp of a person's temper, etc: uncontrollable; not able to be restrained. ▪ **ungovernability** *noun.* [17c]

unguarded *adj* **1** without guard; unprotected. **2** of speech, behaviour, etc: **a** showing a lack of caution or alertness; **b** revealing. ▪ **unguardedly** *adv.* ▪ **unguardedness** *noun.* [16c]

unguent /ˈʌŋgwənt/ *noun* ointment or salve. [15c: from Latin *unguentum*]

ungulate /ˈʌŋgjʊlət/ *adj, chiefly zool* **1** with the form of a hoof; hoof-shaped. **2** of a mammal: hoofed. ▸ *noun* a hoofed mammal. [19c: from Latin *ungula* hoof or claw]

unhallowed *adj* **1** of ground, etc: not formally hallowed or consecrated. **2** not of a hallowed character; unholy. [Anglo-Saxon]

unhand *verb, archaic or jocular* to let go of someone; to take one's hands off them. [17c]

unhappy *adj* (**-ier, -iest**) **1** sad; in low spirits; miserable. **2** bringing sadness; unfortunate: *an unhappy ending to the film.* **3** inappropriate; infelicitous: *an unhappy choice of words.* ▪ **unhappily** *adv.* ▪ **unhappiness** *noun.* [14c]

unhealthy *adj* (**-ier, -iest**) **1** not conducive to health; harmful. **2** suffering from, or showing evidence of, ill health. **3** flouting or corrupting moral standards. **4** causing or likely to cause anxiety or worry; psychologically damaging: *an unhealthy attitude.* **5** *informal* dangerous to life. ▪ **unhealthily** *adv.* ▪ **unhealthiness** *noun.* [16c]

unheard *adj* **1** not heard; not perceived with the ear. **2** not listened to; not heeded; ignored. [14c]

unheard-of *adj* **1** not known to have ever happened or been done before; unprecedented. **2** not at all famous; unknown: *an unheard-of comedian.*

unhinge *verb* **1** **a** to remove (a door, etc) from its hinges; **b** to remove the hinges from (a door, etc). **2** to unbalance or derange (a person or a person's mind). ▪ **unhinged** *adj.* [17c]

unholy *adj* **1** not holy or sacred. **2** wicked; sinful; irreligious. **3** *informal* outrageous; dreadful. ▪ **unholiness** *noun.* [Anglo-Saxon *unhalig*]

unhook *verb* **1** to remove or free something from a hook or hooks. **2** to unfasten the hook or hooks of (eg a dress or other garment). **3** *intr* to unfasten or become unfastened. [17c]

unhorse *verb* **1** to throw or force (a rider) off a horse. **2** *archaic* to overthrow or dislodge (a person), eg from a position of power. **3** to unharness a horse or horses from a horse-drawn vehicle, etc. [14c]

uni *noun, informal* short form of **university**.

uni- *combining form, signifying* one; a single: *unidirectional.* [From Latin *unus* one]

Uniat *or* **Uniate** *adj* belonging, referring or relating to any Church in eastern Europe and the Near East that acknowledges papal supremacy but retains its own customs, practices, liturgy, etc. ▸ *noun* a member of such a Church. ▪ **Uniatism** *noun*. [19c: from Russian *uniyat*]

unicameral *adj* of a parliamentary system: with only one law-making body or chamber. [19c: from Latin *camera* a chamber or room]

UNICEF /ˈjuːnɪsɛf/ *abbrev* **1** United Nations Children's Fund. **2** *formerly* United Nations International Children's Emergency Fund.

unicellular *adj, biol* of organisms or structures, eg bacteria, protozoa and many spores: consisting of a single cell. [19c]

unicorn *noun* a mythical animal in the form of a horse (usu a white one) with a long straight spiralled horn growing from its forehead. [13c: from French *unicorne*]

unicycle *noun* a cycle consisting of a single wheel with a seat and pedals attached, used esp by acrobats in performances, etc. ▪ **unicyclist** *noun*. [19c]

unidentified *adj* **1** not identified. **2** too strange to identify. ▪ **unidentifiable** *adj*. [19c]

unidirectional *adj* with movement or operating in one direction only. [19c]

unifiable see under **unify**

unification *noun* **1** an act or the process of unifying or uniting. **2** the state of being unified: *The unification of East and West Germany took place in 1990.* ▪ **unificatory** *adj*. [19c]

uniform *noun* **1** distinctive clothing, always of the same colour, cut, etc, worn by all members of a particular organization or profession, eg by schoolchildren or soldiers. **2** a single set of such clothing. **3** the recognizable appearance, or a distinctive feature or way of dressing, that is typical of a particular group of people. ▸ *adj* **1** unchanging or unvarying in form, nature or appearance; always the same, regardless of changes in circumstances, etc. **2** alike all over or throughout. **3** with the same form, character, etc as another or others; alike or like. **4** forming part of a military or other uniform. ▸ *verb* **1** to make (several people or things) uniform or alike. **2** to fit out or provide (a number of soldiers, etc) with uniforms. ▪ **uniformed** *adj* wearing a uniform. ▪ **uniformly** *adv*. ▪ **uniformness** *noun*. [16c: from French *uniforme*]

uniformity *noun* **1** the state or fact of being uniform; conformity or similarity between several things, constituent parts, etc; sameness. **2** monotony; lack of variation. [15c]

unify *verb* (**-ies, -ied**) to bring (two or more things) together to form a single unit or whole; to unite. ▪ **unifiable** *adj*. [16c: from French *unifier*]

unilateral *adj* **1** occurring on, affecting or involving one side only. **2** affecting, involving or done by only one person or group among several: *unilateral disarmament*. ▪ **unilaterally** *adv*. [19c: see **lateral**]

unilateralism *noun* a policy or the practice of unilateral action, esp of unilateral nuclear disarmament. ▪ **unilateralist** *noun* a supporter or advocate of unilateralism. *adj* relating to or involving unilateralism. [20c]

unimpeachable *adj* indisputably reliable or honest; impossible to blame, find fault with, etc. ▪ **unimpeachably** *adv*. [18c]

uninflected *adj* **1** *grammar* of a language, word, etc: not characterized by **inflection** (sense 1). **2** *music* not modulated.

uninstall *or (sometimes)* **uninstal** *verb* (***uninstalled, uninstalling***) to take (something) out of position or use: *Uninstall the program from your computer when you're finished.*

uninterested *adj* not interested; indifferent. ▪ **uninterestedly** *adv*. See also **disinterested**. [18c]

uninteresting *adj* boring; not able to raise, or capable of raising, any interest. ▪ **uninterestingly** *adv*.

union *noun* **1 a** the action or an act of uniting two or more things; **b** the state of being united. **2** a united whole. **3** *formal* **a** marriage; the state of wedlock; **b** sexual intercourse. **4** an association, confederation, etc of people or groups for a common (esp political) purpose. **5** agreement or harmony. **6** a league or association, esp a **trade union**. **7** a device that connects one thing with another, esp a connecting part for pipes, etc. **8** (*also* **Union**) **a** an organization concerned with the interests and welfare of the students in a college, university, etc; **b** the building that houses such an organization. **9** a textile fabric made from more than one kind of fibre. **10** *maths* (symbol P) **a** a **set²** (sense 2) comprising all the members (but no others) of two or more smaller sets; **b** the operation of forming such a set. See also **intersection** (sense 5). **11** (**the Union**) the collection of northern US states that fought against the south in the American Civil War. [15c: from French]

unionism *or* **Unionism** *noun* **1** advocacy of combination into one body for the purposes of social or political organization. **2** *US* advocacy of or adherence to union between the States. **3** advocacy of or adherence to the principles of the former Unionist Party of Great Britain and Ireland or of any party advocating the continued political union of Great Britain and Northern Ireland. **4** advocacy of or support for continued political union between Scotland, England and Wales. **5** adherence to the principles and practices of trade unions. ▪ **unionist** *or* **Unionist** *noun, adj*. [19c]

unionize *or* **-ise** *verb* **1** to organize (a workforce) into a trade union or trade unions. **2** *intr* to join or constitute a trade union. ▪ **unionization** *noun*. [19c]

Union Jack *noun* (*also* **Union flag**) the national flag of the United Kingdom, combining the crosses of St Andrew, St George and St Patrick.

unique *adj* **1** sole or solitary; of which there is only one. **2** referring to something that is the only one of its kind; without equal; unparalleled, esp in excellence. **3** (*usu* **unique to sb** *or* **sth**) referring to something that belongs solely to, or is associated solely with, them or it. **4** *informal, loosely* extremely unusual; excellent. ▪ **uniquely** *adv*. ▪ **uniqueness** *noun*. [17c: from French]

---

unique

The word **unique** strictly refers to something that is the only one of its kind. Try not to use words such as *more, most* and *very* with **unique** when you are writing or speaking to people who are precise about language:

✗ *It is a fairly unique experience.*

---

unisex *adj* suited to, for use by, or to be worn by, both men and women: *a unisex sauna*. [20c]

unisexual *adj* **1** relating to or restricted to one sex only. **2** *botany, zool* of certain organisms: with either male or female reproductive organs but not both. **3** unisex. ▪ **unisexually** *adv.* [19c]

unison *noun* **1** *music* the interval between two notes of the same pitch, or which are one or more octaves apart. **2** the state of acting all in the same way at the same time. **3** (*usu* **in unison**) complete agreement. [16c: from Latin *unus* one + *sonus* sound]

unit *noun* **1** a single item or element regarded as the smallest subdivision of a whole; a single person or thing. **2** a set of mechanical or electrical parts, or a group of workers, performing a specific function within a larger construction or organization. **3** a standard measure of a physical quantity, such as time or distance, specified multiples of which are used to express its size, eg an **SI** unit. **4** any whole number less than 10. **5** any subdivision of a military force. **6 a** an item of furniture that combines with others to form a set; **b** a set of such items. **7** a standard measure used to calculate alcohol intake. **8** *finance* the smallest measure of investment in a **unit trust**. [16c: from Latin *unus* one]

Unitarian *noun* a member of a religious group orig comprising Christians who believed God to be a single entity rather than a Trinity, now including members holding a broad spectrum of beliefs. ▸ *adj* relating to or characteristic of Unitarians. ▪ **Unitarianism** *noun.* [17c]

unitary *adj* **1** relating to, characterized by or based on unity. **2** referring or relating to the nature of a unit; individual. **3** relating to a unit or units. [19c]

unit cost *noun* the actual cost of producing one item.

unite *verb* **1** *tr & intr* to make or become a single unit or whole. **2** *tr & intr* to bring or come together in a common purpose or belief. **3** to have or exhibit (features, qualities, etc) in combination. **4** *tr & intr* to join in marriage. ▪ **unitive** *adj.* [15c: from Latin *unire* to join together]

united *adj* **1** referring to something that is or has been united; joined together or combined. **2** relating or pertaining to, or resulting from, two or more people or things in union or combination. **3** (*usu* **United**) often in the names of churches, societies, etc and in the names of football clubs: made up of or resulting from the union of two or more parts: *Dundee United.* [16c]

United Kingdom *noun* (*in full* **United Kingdom of Great Britain and Northern Ireland**) (abbrev **UK**) since 1922: the official title for the kingdom comprising England, Wales, Scotland and Northern Ireland.

United Nations *singular or plural noun* (abbrev **UN**) an association of independent states formed in 1945 to promote peace and international co-operation.

United States *singular or plural noun* (*in full* **United States of America**) (abbrev **US** *or* **USA**) a federal republic mostly in N America, comprising 50 states and the District of Columbia. Often shortened to **the States**.

unit fraction *noun, maths* a fraction whose numerator is 1 and whose denominator is an integer that is not 0, eg ⅕.

unitholder *noun* someone who holds a unit of securities in a **unit trust**.

unit price *noun* the price per unit of goods supplied.

unit trust *noun* **1** an investment scheme in which clients' money is invested in various companies, with the combined shares purchased divided into units which are allocated in multiples to each client according to the individual amount invested. **2** a financial organization operating such a scheme.

unit vector *noun, maths* a vector with the magnitude 1.

unity *noun* (**-ies**) **1** the state or quality of being one; oneness. **2** a single unified whole. **3** the act, state or quality of forming a single unified whole from two or more parts. **4** agreement; harmony; concord. **5** *maths* the number or numeral 1. [13c: from French *unité*]

Univ. *abbrev* University.

univalent *adj, chem* **monovalent**. ▪ **univalence** *or* **univalency** *noun.* [19c]

univalve *zool, adj* **1** with one valve or shell. **2** of a mollusc: with a shell that is in one piece, lacking a hinge as in a **bivalve**. ▸ *noun* **1** an undivided shell. **2** a mollusc whose shell is composed of a single piece. [17c]

universal *adj* **1** relating to the universe. **2** relating to, typical of, affecting, etc the whole world or all people. **3** relating to, typical of, affecting, etc all the people or things in a particular group. **4** *informal* widespread; general: *won universal approval.* **5** (abbrev **U**) in film classification: suitable for everyone. ▸ *noun* **1** something that is universal. **2** *philos* a general term or concept, or the nature or type signified by such a term. ▪ **universality** *noun.* ▪ **universally** *adv.* [14c: from French *universel* or Latin *universalis*]

universal indicator *noun, chem* a mixture of several chemical indicators, used to measure the pH of a solution.

universalize *or* **-ise** *verb* **1** to make something universal. **2** to bring something into universal use. ▪ **universalization** *noun.* [17c]

universal joint *or* **universal coupling** *noun* a joint or coupling, esp between two rotating shafts, that allows movement in all directions.

universe *noun* **1** *astron* **a** (**the Universe**) all existing space, energy and matter; the cosmos; **b** a star system; a galaxy. **2** the world; all people. [16c: from French *univers,* from Latin *universum* the whole world]

university *noun* (**-ies**) **1** a higher education institution with the authority to award degrees and usu having research facilities. **2** the buildings, staff or students of such an institution. Sometimes (*informal*) *shortened to* **uni**. [14c: from French *université*]

Unix /ˈjuːnɪks/ *noun, trademark, comput* a type of operating system designed to handle large file transfers and allow multi-user access of data. [20c]

unkempt *adj* **1** of hair: uncombed. **2** of general appearance: untidy; dishevelled. [18c: a variant of earlier *unkembed*]

unkind *adj* unsympathetic, cruel or harsh. ▪ **unkindly** *adv.* ▪ **unkindness** *noun.* [14c]

unknowing *adj* **1** not knowing; ignorant. **2** (*often* **unknowing of sth**) ignorant or unaware of it. ▪ **unknowingly** *adv.* [14c]

unknown *adj* **1** not known; unfamiliar. **2** not at all famous. ▸ *noun* **1** an unknown person or thing. **2** (*usu* **the unknown**) something that is unknown, undiscovered, unexplored, etc. [13c]

unknown quantity *noun* a person or thing whose precise identity, nature or influence is not known or cannot be predicted.

unlace *verb* **1** to undo or loosen the lace or laces of (shoes, etc). **2** to unfasten or remove garments, etc from (oneself or someone else) by undoing the laces or lacing. [14c]

unlawful assembly *noun, law* a meeting of three or more people that is considered likely to cause a breach of the peace or endanger the public.

unleaded *adj* (*also* **lead-free**) of petrol: free from lead additives, eg antiknocking agents. [17c]

unlearn *verb* **1** to try actively to forget something learned; to rid the memory of it. **2** to free oneself from (eg an acquired habit). [15c]

unlearned[1] /ʌn'lɜːnɪd/ *adj* not well educated; uneducated.

unlearned[2] /ʌn'lɜːnd/ *or* **unlearnt** /ʌn'lɜːnt/ *adj* **1** of a lesson, etc: not learnt. **2** of a skill, etc: not acquired by learning; instinctive; innate.

unleash *verb* **1** to release (eg a dog) from a leash. **2** to release or give free expression to (eg anger). [17c]

unleavened /ʌn'lɛvənd/ *adj* of bread: not leavened; made without yeast. [16c]

unless *conj* if not; except when; except if: *Unless you come in now you won't get any tea.* [15c as the prepositional phrase *on less*, meaning 'on a lesser footing or on a lower condition (than)']

unlettered *adj* **1** uneducated. **2** illiterate. [14c]

unlike *prep* **1** different from: *Unlike her, he's going shopping today.* **2** not typical or characteristic of: *It's unlike her to be late.* ▸ *adj* not like or alike; different; dissimilar. ▪ **unlikeness** *noun.* [13c]

unlikely *adj* **1** not expected or likely to happen. **2** not obviously suitable; improbable. **3** probably untrue; implausible. ▪ **unlikeliness** *or* **unlikelihood** *noun.* [14c]

unlimited *adj* **1** not limited or restricted. **2** *loosely* very great or numerous. [15c]

unlined[1] *adj* free from or not marked with lines: *a youthful unlined face* • *unlined paper.* [19c]

unlined[2] *adj* of a garment, etc: without any lining.

unlisted *adj* **1** not entered on a list. **2** *stock exchange* of securities: not dealt in on the Stock Exchange. **3** of a telephone number: ex-directory. [17c]

unlit *adj* not lit; without lights or lighting. [19c]

unload *verb* **1** *tr & intr* to remove (a load or cargo) from (a vehicle, ship, etc). **2** to relieve (oneself or one's mind) of troubles or anxieties by telling them to another. **3** to remove the charge of ammunition from (a gun) without firing it. **4** to dispose or get rid of (something undesirable). ▪ **unloader** *noun.* [16c]

unlock *verb* **1** to undo the lock of (a door, etc). **2** to free someone or something from being locked up. **3** to release or reveal (eg emotions, etc): *The accident unlocked bad memories.* [15c]

unloose *or* **unloosen** *verb* to set free; to release. [14c]

unlucky *adj* (**-ier, -iest**) **1** bringing, resulting from or constituting bad luck. **2** having, or tending to have, bad luck. **3** regrettable. ▪ **unluckily** *adv.* ▪ **unluckiness** *noun.* [16c]

unmade *adj* **1** not yet made. **2** of a bed: with bedclothes not arranged neatly. **3** of a road: with no proper surface (eg of tarmac).

unmake *verb* to cancel or destroy the (esp beneficial) effect of something. [15c]

unman *verb, old use, literary* **1** to cause someone to lose self-control, esp to overcome with emotion. **2** to deprive someone of their virility; to emasculate. ▪ **unmanned** *adj.* [16c]

unmanly *adj* **1** not manly; not virile or masculine. **2** weak or cowardly. ▪ **unmanliness** *noun.* [15c]

unmanned *adj* esp of a vehicle or spacecraft: without personnel or a crew, esp controlled remotely or automatically; not manned.

unmannerly *adj* ill-mannered; impolite. ▪ **unmannerliness** *noun.* [14c]

unmapped *adj* **1** not appearing on a geographical or chromosome map. **2** unexplored; untried: *entering unmapped territory.*

unmask *verb, tr & intr* **1** to remove a mask or disguise from (oneself or someone else). **2** to reveal the true identity or nature of (oneself or someone else). [16c]

unmentionable *adj* not fit to be mentioned or talked about, esp because considered indecent. ▸ *noun* **1** (**unmentionables**) *humorous* underwear. **2** (*often* **unmentionables**) someone or something that cannot or should not be mentioned. [19c]

unmerciful *adj* **1** merciless; not merciful. **2** unpleasantly great or extreme. ▪ **unmercifully** *adv.* [15c]

unmet *adj* of a target, quota, etc: not achieved.

unmissable *adj* of a TV programme, film, etc: too good to be missed. [20c]

unmistakable *or* **unmistakeable** *adj* too easily recognizable to be mistaken for anything or anyone else; certain; unambiguous. ▪ **unmistakably** *or* **unmistakeably** *adv.* [17c]

unmitigated *adj* **1** not lessened or made less severe. **2** unqualified; absolute; out-and-out: *an unmitigated disaster.* ▪ **unmitigatedly** *adv.*

unmoral *adj* not moral; with no relation to morality; amoral. ▪ **unmorality** *noun.* [19c]

unmoved *adj* **1** still in the same place. **2** not persuaded. **3** not affected by emotion; calm. [14c]

unmoving *adj* **1** still; stationary. **2** lacking the power to affect the emotions.

unnatural *adj* **1** contrary to the way things usually happen in nature. **2** abnormal. **3** intensely evil or cruel. **4** insincere; affected. ▪ **unnaturally** *adv.*

unnecessary *adj* **1** not necessary. **2** more than is expected or required: *spoke with unnecessary caution.* ▪ **unnecessarily** *adv.* [16c]

unnerve *verb* **1** to deprive of strength; to weaken. **2** to deprive someone of courage or confidence. ▪ **unnervingly** *adv.* [17c]

unnumbered *adj* **1** too numerous to be counted; innumerable. **2** not marked with or given a number.

UNO *abbrev* United Nations Organization.

unoccupied *adj* **1** not doing any work or engaged in any activity; idle. **2** of a building, etc: without occupants or inhabitants; empty. **3** of a country, region, etc: not occupied by foreign troops.

unofficial *adj* **1** not officially authorized or confirmed. **2** not official or formal in character. **3** of a strike: not called or sanctioned by the strikers' trade union. ▪ **unofficially** *adv.* [18c]

unorganized *or* **-ised** *adj* **1** not organized; not brought into an organized state or form. **2** of a workforce: not formed into or represented by a trade union. [17c]

unpack *verb* **1** to take something out of a packed state. **2** to empty (eg a suitcase, bag, etc) of packed contents. **3** *comput* to **unzip** (sense 3). [15c]

unpalatable *adj* **1** of food, drink, etc: not having a pleasant taste. **2** of a suggestion, idea, film scene, etc: unacceptable; distasteful.

unparalleled *adj* so remarkable as to have no equal or parallel. [16c]

unparliamentary *adj* not in accordance with the established procedures by which, or with the spirit in which, a parliament is conducted. [17c]

unpick *verb* **1** to undo (stitches). **2** to take (a sewn or knitted article, seam, etc) to pieces by undoing the stitching.

unpin *verb* **1** to remove a pin or pins from something. **2** *tr & intr* to undo or unfasten by removing pins.

unplaced *adj* eg of a racehorse, greyhound, athlete, etc: not one of the first three to finish a race.

unplanned *adj* **1** not planned or scheduled: *made an unplanned stopover in Paris.* **2** of a pregnancy: accidental.

unplayable *adj* **1** not able to be played. **2** *sport* of a ball: impossible to hit, kick, return, etc.

unpleasant *adj* not pleasant; disagreeable. ▪ **unpleasantly** *adv.* ▪ **unpleasantness** *noun.*

unplug *verb* **1** to unblock or unstop (something that is plugged or blocked). **2** to disconnect (an electrical appliance) by removing its plug from a socket. [18c]

unplumbed *adj* **1** of a building, etc: without plumbing. **2** unfathomed; unsounded. **3** not fully understood. [17c]

unpolished *adj* **1** not polished. **2** unrefined; not cultured or sophisticated.

unpopular *adj* not popular; not popular or liked by an individual or by people in general. ▪ **unpopularity** *noun.* [17c]

unpractical *adj* with no practical skills; not good at practical tasks. Compare **impractical.** ▪ **unpracticality** *noun.* ▪ **unpractically** *adv.* [17c]

unpractised *or* (*US*) **unpracticed** *adj* **1** with little or no practice, experience or skill. **2** not, or not yet, put into practice. [16c]

unprecedented *adj* **1** without precedent; not known to have ever happened before. **2** unparalleled. [17c]

unprejudiced *adj* free from prejudice; impartial. [17c]

unprepossessing *adj* **1** unappealing; unattractive. **2** not creating a good impression. [19c]

unprincipled *adj* without or showing a lack of moral principles. [17c]

unprintable *adj* not fit to be printed, esp because of being obscene or libellous. [19c]

unprofessional *adj* not in accordance with the rules governing, or the standards of conduct expected of, members of a particular profession. ▪ **unprofessionally** *adv.* [19c]

UNPROFOR *or* **Unprofor** /ˈʌnprəfɔː(r)/ *abbrev* United Nations Protection Force.

unprotected *adj* **1** not protected. **2** of an act of sexual intercourse: performed without a condom.

unputdownable *adj, informal* of a book: so absorbing that it proves difficult to stop reading it. [20c]

unqualified *adj* **1** not having any formal qualifications; lacking the formal qualifications required for a particular job, etc. **2** not limited or moderated in any way. **3** absolute; out-and-out: *an unqualified success.* **4** not competent. [16c]

unquestionable *adj* beyond doubt or question. ▪ **unquestionably** *adv.* [17c]

unquestioned *adj* **1** not questioned or interrogated. **2** not examined or inquired into. **3** not called into question; undisputed. [17c]

unquestioning *adj* not arguing or protesting; done, accepted, etc without argument, protest or thought. ▪ **unquestioningly** *adv.* [19c]

unquiet *adj, literary* **1** anxious; ill at ease; restless. **2** characterized by disturbance or disorder. ▪ **unquietness** *noun.*

unquote *verb* to indicate (in speech) the end of something that was said by someone else. [20c]

unravel *verb* **1** to separate out the strands of (a knitted or woven fabric). **2** to take something out of a tangled state. **3** to explain or make clear (something confusing or obscure, a mystery, etc). **4** *intr* to become unravelled. [17c]

unread *adj* **1** of a book, etc: not having been read. **2** of a person: not well-read; not educated or instructed through reading.

unreadable *adj* **1** too difficult or tedious to read. **2** illegible. **3** of facial expression, a remark, etc: uninterpretable. [19c]

unready *adj* **1** not ready. **2** not acting quickly; hesitant. ▪ **unreadily** *adv.* ▪ **unreadiness** *noun.*

unreal *adj* **1** not real; illusory or imaginary. **2** *informal* **a** exceptionally strange; incredible; **b** amazing; excellent. ▪ **unreality** *noun.*

unreasonable *adj* **1** not influenced by, based on, or in accordance with reason or good sense. **2** immoderate; beyond what is reasonable or fair. ▪ **unreasonableness** *noun.* ▪ **unreasonably** *adv.*

unreasoning *adj* not reasoning; showing lack of reasoning; irrational. ▪ **unreasoningly** *adv.* [18c]

unregenerate *adj* **1** not regenerate; unrepentant; unreformed. **2** adhering obstinately to one's own opinions. ▪ **unregeneracy** *noun.* ▪ **unregenerately** *adv.* [16c]

unreleased *adj* **1** not released. **2** of a film, music recording, etc: not having had a public showing.

unrelenting *adj* **1** refusing to change viewpoint or a chosen course of action. **2** not softened by feelings of mercy or pity. **3** constant; relentless; never stopping. ▪ **unrelentingly** *adv.* [16c]

unremitting *adj* **1** not easing off or abating. **2** constant; never stopping. ▪ **unremittingly** *adv.* [18c]

unrequited *adj* esp of love: not returned. [16c]

unreserved *adj* **1** not booked or reserved. **2** open and sociable in manner; showing no shyness or reserve. **3** not moderated or limited; unqualified. ▪ **unreservedly** *adv.* [16c]

unrest *noun* **1** a state of (esp public) discontent bordering on riotousness. **2** anxiety; unease.

unrighteous *adj* **1** sinful or wicked. **2** not right or fair; unjust. ▪ **unrighteously** *adv.* ▪ **unrighteousness** *noun.* [Anglo-Saxon]

unripe *adj* **1** not (yet) fully developed; not matured. **2** of fruit, etc: not (yet) ready to be harvested or eaten; not ripe. [Anglo-Saxon]

unrivalled *or* (*US*) **unrivaled** *adj* far better than any other; unequalled. [16c]

unroll *verb* **1** to open something out from a rolled state. **2** *intr* to become unrolled. **3** *tr & intr* to become or make something visible or known; to unfold gradually.

unruffled *adj* **1** of a surface: smooth or still. **2** of a person: not agitated or flustered. [17c]

unruly *adj* (**-*ier*, -*iest***) disobedient or disorderly, esp habitually. ▪ **unruliness** *noun.*

unsaddle *verb* **1** to take the saddle off (a horse). **2** to throw (a rider) from a horse; to unhorse.

unsafe *adj* **1** not safe or secure; dangerous. **2** of a verdict, conclusion or decision: based on insufficient or suspect evidence. [16c]

unsaid *adj* not said, expressed, spoken, etc, esp when it might have been or should have been. See also **unsay**. [Anglo-Saxon]

unsaturated *adj, chem* **1** of an organic chemical compound: containing at least one double or triple bond between its carbon atoms, eg unsaturated fats. **2** of a solution: not containing the maximum amount of a solid or gas that can be dissolved in it. [18c]

unsavoury *or* (*N Am*) **unsavory** *adj* unpleasant or distasteful; offensive. ▪ **unsavouriness** *or* (*N Am*) **unsavoriness** *noun.*

unsay *verb* (***unsaid***) to take back or withdraw (something said). See also **unsaid.** [15c]

unscathed *adj* **1** not harmed or injured. **2** without harm, injury or damage.

unschooled *adj* **1** not educated. **2** not skilled or trained in a specified field or area.

unscramble *verb* **1** to interpret (a coded or scrambled message). **2** to take something out of a jumbled state and put it in order. **unscrambler** *noun.* [20c]

unscrew *verb* **1** to remove or loosen something by taking out a screw or screws, or with a twisting or screwing action. **2** to loosen (a screw or lid). **3** *intr* to be removed or loosened by turning a screw or screws. **4** *intr* of a screw or lid: to be loosened or removed by a turning action. [17c]

unscripted *adj* of a speech, etc: made or delivered without a prepared script. [20c]

unscrupulous *adj* without scruples or moral principles. ▪ **unscrupulously** *adv.* [19c]

unsealed *adj* not sealed; not closed, marked, etc with a seal.

unseasonable *adj* **1** (*also* **unseasonal**) esp of the weather: not appropriate to the time of year. **2** coming at a bad time; inopportune. ▪ **unseasonably** *adv.*

unseasoned *adj* **1** of food: without seasonings. **2** not matured: *unseasoned timber.* **3** not habituated through time or experience. [16c]

unseat *verb* **1** of a horse: to throw or knock (its rider) off. **2** to remove someone from an official post or position, esp from a parliamentary seat.

unseeded *adj, sport, esp tennis* not placed among the top players in the preliminary rounds of a tournament. [20c]

unseemly *adj* (**-*ier*, -*iest***) not seemly; not becoming or fitting, esp because of being indecent. ▪ **unseemliness** *noun.*

unseen *adj* **1** not seen or noticed. **2** of a text for translation: not seen or prepared in advance. ► *noun* **1** an unseen text for translation in an examination. **2** the translation of such a text.

unselfish *adj* **1** having or showing concern for others. **2** generous. ▪ **unselfishly** *adv.* ▪ **unselfishness** *noun.* [17c]

unsettle *verb* **1** to make someone ill at ease; to disturb them. **2** *intr* to become unsettled. [16c]

unsettled *adj* **1** lacking stability. **2** frequently changing or moving from place to place. **3** undecided or unresolved. **4** of the weather: changeable; unpredictable. **5** not relaxed or at ease. **6** of a debt: unpaid. [16c]

unsheathe *verb* to draw (esp a sword, knife, etc) from a sheath.

unsightly *adj* (**-*ier*, -*iest***) not pleasant to look at; ugly. ▪ **unsightliness** *noun.*

unskilled *adj* not having or requiring any special skill or training: *unskilled jobs.*

unsociable *adj* **1** of a person: disliking or avoiding the company of other people. **2** not conducive to social intercourse. ▪ **unsociably** *adv.* [16c]

unsocial *adj* **1** annoying, or likely to annoy, other people; antisocial. **2** of working hours: falling outside the normal working day. [18c]

unsophisticated *adj* **1** not experienced or worldly; naive. **2** free from insincerity or artificiality. **3** lacking refinement or complexity; basic. [17c]

unsound *adj* **1** not reliable; not based on sound reasoning: *an unsound argument.* **2** not firm or solid. ▪ **unsoundness** *noun.* **of unsound mind** mentally ill; insane.

unsparing *adj* **1** giving generously or liberally. **2** showing no mercy; unrelenting. ▪ **unsparingly** *adv.* [16c]

unspeakable *adj* **1** not able to be expressed in words; indescribable. **2** too bad, wicked or obscene to be spoken about. ▪ **unspeakably** *adv.*

unsteady *adj* **1** not secure or firm. **2** of behaviour, character, etc: not steady or constant; erratic. **3** of movement, a manner of walking, etc: unsure or precarious. ▪ **unsteadily** *adv.* ▪ **unsteadiness** *noun.* [16c]

unstoppable *adj* unable to be stopped or prevented. ▪ **unstoppably** *adv.* [19c]

unstreamed *adj* of schoolchildren: not divided into classes according to ability. [20c]

unstring *verb* **1** to relax or remove the string or strings of (a bow, a musical instrument, etc). **2** to detach or remove (eg beads, etc) from a string. **3** to weaken (a person, a person's nerves, etc) emotionally. **4** *intr* of the nerves: to relax or weaken. [16c]

unstructured *adj* without any formal structure or organization. [20c]

unstrung *adj* **1** of a stringed instrument: with strings removed. **2** unnerved. See also **unstring**.

unstuck *adj* loosened or released from a stuck state. IDIOMS **come unstuck** *informal* of a person, plan, etc: to suffer a setback; to go wrong. See also **unstick**.

unstudied *adj* not affected; natural and spontaneous.

unsubstantial *adj* **1** with no basis or foundation in fact. **2** without material substance. **3** lacking strength or firmness.

unsung *adj* **1** of someone, an achievement, etc: not praised or recognized: *an unsung hero.* **2** not (yet) sung.

unsuspected *adj* **1** not suspected; not under suspicion. **2** not known or supposed to exist. [15c]

unswerving *adj* not deviating from a belief or aim; steadfast. ▪ **unswervingly** *adv.* [17c]

untangle *verb* **1** to disentangle something; to free something from a tangled state. **2** to clear something of confusion.

untaught *adj* **1** without education or instruction; ignorant. **2** not acquired through instruction; innate or spontaneous.

untenable *adj* of an opinion, theory, argument, etc: not able to be maintained or justified. [17c]

unthinkable *adj* **1** too unusual to be likely; inconceivable. **2** too unpleasant to think about.

unthinking *adj* **1** inconsiderate; thoughtless. **2** careless. ▪ **unthinkingly** *adv.* [17c]

untidy *adj* (**-*ier*, -*iest***) not tidy; messy or disordered. ▪ **untidily** *adv.* ▪ **untidiness** *noun.*

untie *verb* **1** to undo (a knot, parcel, etc) from a tied state. **2** *intr* of a knot, etc: to come unfastened. **3** to remove the constraints on something; to set something free. [Anglo-Saxon]

until *prep* **1** up to the time of: *worked until 8.* **2** up to the time of reaching (a place); as far as: *slept until Paris.* **3** *with negatives* before: *not until Wednesday.* ▸ *conj* **1** up to the time that: *He waited until she emerged with the money.* **2** *with negatives* before: *not until I say so.* [13c as *untille*; see **till**[1]]

untimely *adj* **1** happening before the proper or expected time: *an untimely death.* **2** coming at an inappropriate or inconvenient time. ▪ **untimeliness** *noun.*

unto *prep, archaic or literary* to.

untold *adj* **1** not told. **2** too severe to be described. **3** too many to be counted.

untouchable *adj* **1** not to be touched or handled. **2** discouraging physical contact. **3** above the law. **4** unable to be matched; unrivalled. ▸ *noun* **1** an untouchable person or thing. **2** *formerly* in India: a member of the lowest social class or caste whose touch was regarded by members of higher castes as a contamination. [16c]

untoward *adj* **1** inconvenient; unfortunate. **2** adverse; unfavourable. **3** difficult to manage; unruly or intractable. **4** unseemly; improper. [16c]

untrue *adj* **1** not true. **2** not accurate. **3** unfaithful. ▪ **untruly** *adv.* [Anglo-Saxon]

untruth *noun* **1** the fact or quality of being untrue. **2** something that is untrue; a lie.

untruthful *adj* not truthful; lying or untrue. ▪ **untruthfully** *adv.* ▪ **untruthfulness** *noun.*

untuned *adj* **1** not tuned. **2** not in tune; discordant. **3** of an electronic device, eg a radio, etc: not tuned to one particular frequency.

untutored *adj* **1** uneducated; untaught. **2** unsophisticated. [16c]

unused *adj* **1** /ʌn'juːzd/ brand new; never used. **2** /ʌn'juːst/ (*always* **unused to sth**) not used or accustomed to it.

unusual *adj* not usual; uncommon; rare. ▪ **unusually** *adv.* [16c]

unutterable *adj* so extreme or intense as to be impossible to express in words. ▪ **unutterably** *adv.* [16c]

unvarnished *adj* **1** of an account, report, etc: not exaggerated or embellished. **2** not covered with varnish. [17c]

unveil *verb* **1** to remove a veil from (one's own or someone else's face). **2** to remove a curtain or other covering from (a plaque, monument, etc) as part of a formal opening ceremony. **3** to reveal something or make it known for the first time. ▪ **unveiling** *noun* **1** the action or an act of removing a veil. **2** the ceremony of opening or presenting something new for the first time.

unversed *adj* (*usu* **unversed in sth**) not experienced in it. [17c]

unvoiced *adj* **1** not spoken. **2** *phonetics* of a sound: pronounced without vibrating the vocal cords, like 'p'; voiceless.

unwaged *adj* **1** of work: unpaid. **2** of a person: **a** not in paid employment; out of work; **b** doing unpaid work. [16c]

unwarranted *adj* **1** not warranted; not justified. **2** not authorized. [16c]

unwary *adj* not wary; careless or incautious; not aware of possible danger. ▪ **unwarily** *adv.* ▪ **unwariness** *noun.* [16c]

unwashed *adj* not washed; not clean.

IDIOMS **the great unwashed** *informal, jocular* the lower classes; the masses.

unwell *adj* not well; ill.

unwholesome *adj* **1** not conducive to physical or moral health; harmful. **2** of a person: of dubious character or morals. **3** diseased; not healthy. **4** of food: of poor quality.

unwieldy *adj* **1** of an object: large and awkward to carry or manage; cumbersome. **2** of a person: clumsy; not graceful in movement; ungainly.

---

unwieldy

This word is often misspelt. The letter *i* comes before the letter e. It might help you to remember the following sentence:

*Something that is unw**ie**l**dy** **i**sn't **e**asily **l**ifted.*

---

unwilling *adj* **1** reluctant; loath. **2** done, said, etc reluctantly. ▪ **unwillingly** *adv.* ▪ **unwillingness** *noun.* [Anglo-Saxon]

unwind *verb* **1** to undo, slacken, untwist, etc something that has been wound or coiled up. **2** *intr* of something that has been wound or coiled up: to come undone, to slacken, untwist, etc. **3** *tr & intr, informal* to make or become relaxed.

unwise *adj* not prudent; ill-advised; foolish. ▪ **unwisely** *adv.* [Anglo-Saxon]

unwished *adj* (*usu* **unwished for**) **1** unwelcome; uninvited. **2** not wanted or desired. [16c]

unwitting *adj* **1** not realizing or being aware. **2** done without being realized or intended. ▪ **unwittingly** *adv.* [Anglo-Saxon: see **wit**[2]]

unwonted /ʌn'woʊntɪd/ *adj* not usual or habitual. ▪ **unwontedly** *adv.* [16c]

IDIOMS **unwonted to sth** not used to it.

unworldly *adj* **1** not relating or belonging to this world; otherworldly. **2** not concerned with material things. **3** unsophisticated; naive. ▪ **unworldliness** *noun*. [18c]

unworthy *adj* **1** (*often* **unworthy of sth**) not deserving or worthy of it. **2** (*often* **unworthy of sb** *or* **sth**) not worthy or befitting to (a person's character, etc). **3** without worth; of little or no merit or value. **4** of treatment, etc: not warranted; worse than is deserved. ▪ **unworthily** *adv*. ▪ **unworthiness** *noun*.

unwound *past tense, past participle of* **unwind**

unwrap *verb* **1** to remove the wrapping or covering from something; to open something by removing its wrapping. **2** *intr* of something that is wrapped: to become unwrapped; to have the covering come off.

unwritten *adj* **1** not recorded in writing or print. **2** of a rule or law: not formally enforceable, but traditionally accepted and followed.

unzip *verb* **1** to unfasten or open (a garment, etc) by undoing a zip. **2** *intr* to open or come apart by means of a zip. **3** (*also* **unpack**) *comput* to convert (data that has been compressed in order to save storage space) into a less compressed form. [20c]

up *prep* at or to a higher position on, or a position further along: *climbed up the stairs* • *walking up the road*. ▸ *adv* **1** at or to a higher position or level: *lift it up* • *turn up the volume* • *prices went up*. **2** at or to a place higher up, or a more northerly place. **3** in or to a more erect position: *stood up*. **4** fully or completely: *use up* • *eat up*. **5** into the state of being gathered together: *saved up for it* • *parcel up the presents*. **6** in or to a place of storage or lodging: *put them up for the night*. **7** out of bed: *got up*. **8** to or towards: *travelling up to London* • *walked up to him*. **9** *formal* to or at university: *up at Oxford*. ▸ *adj* (***upper, uppermost*** *or* ***upmost***) **1** placed in, or moving or directed to, a higher position. **2** out of bed: *He's not up yet*. **3** having an advantage; ahead: *two goals up*. **4** appearing in court: *up before the judge*. **5** of the sun: visible above the horizon. **6** relating to or providing (esp rail) transport to, rather than away from, a major place, esp London: *the up train* • *the up line*. ▸ *verb* (***upped, upping***) **1** to raise or increase something: *upped the price*. **2** *intr, informal* to start boldly or unexpectedly saying or doing something; to get up (and do something): *He upped and left her*. ▸ *noun* **1** a success or advantage. **2** a spell of good luck or prosperity. [Anglo-Saxon *up* or *upp*]

IDIOMS **it's all up with sb** *informal* there is no hope for them. **not up to much** *informal* not good at all; no good. **on the up-and-up** *informal* **1** steadily becoming more successful. **2** honest; on the level. **something's up** something is wrong or amiss. **up against sb** *or* **sth 1** situated or pressed close against them. **2** facing the difficulties, etc associated with them; having to cope with them. **up for sth 1** presented or offered for (eg discussion or sale). **2** under consideration for (a job or post). **3** prepared and eager to do it: *We're going out clubbing. Are you up for it, too?* **up to sb** their responsibility; dependent on them: *It's up to you*. **up to sth 1** immersed or embedded as far as: *up to his eyes in work*. **2** capable of; equal to: *Are you up to meeting them?* **3** thinking about doing or engaged in doing: *What are you up to?* **4** as good as: *not up to his usual standard*. **5** as many or as much as: *up to two weeks*. **up to the minute** completely up to date. **what's up?** what's the matter?, what's wrong?

up- *prefix, signifying* up, upper or upward.

up-and-coming *adj* beginning to become successful or well known.

up-and-over *adj* of a door, etc: raised to a horizontal position when opened.

upbeat *adj, informal* cheerful; optimistic. ▸ *noun, music* **1** an unstressed beat, esp the last in a bar and so coming before the downbeat. **2** the upward gesture by a conductor which marks this. [19c]

upbraid *verb* to scold or reproach someone. ▪ **upbraiding** *noun*. [Anglo-Saxon *upbregdan*: see **braid**]

upbringing *noun* the all-round instruction and education of a child, which influences their character and values. [16c]

upchuck *verb, N Am slang* to vomit. ▸ *noun* vomit. [20c]

upcoming *adj, informal, esp N Am* forthcoming; approaching.

up-country *noun* the inland part or regions of a country. ▸ *adj, adv* to or in the regions away from the coast; inland. [17c]

update *verb* /ʌp'deɪt/ to make or bring something or someone up to date. ▸ *noun* /'ʌpdeɪt/ **1** an act of updating. **2** something that is updated. [20c: orig US]

up-end *verb* **1** *tr & intr* to turn or place something, or become turned or placed, upside down. **2** to put something into disorder or disarray. [19c]

upfront *adj, informal* (*also* **up-front**) **1** candid; open. **2** of money: paid in advance. ▸ *adv* (*also* **up front**) **1** candidly; openly. **2** of money or a payment: in advance. [20c]

upgrade *verb* /ʌp'greɪd/ **1** to promote someone. **2** to improve the quality of (machinery, equipment, a computer or its memory, etc), esp by adding or replacing features, components, etc. ▸ *noun* /'ʌpgreɪd/ **1** *N Am* an upward slope; an incline. **2** an act or the process of upgrading something. **3** an upgraded version of something, eg a piece of machinery or equipment. ▸ *adv, N Am* uphill. [19c: orig US]

upheaval *noun* **1** a change or disturbance that brings about great disruption. **2** *geol* see **uplift** (*noun* sense 4). [19c]

uphill *adj* **1** sloping upwards; ascending. **2** of a task, etc: requiring great and sustained effort; arduous. ▸ *adv* **1** up a slope. **2** against problems or difficulties. ▸ *noun* an upward slope; an ascent or incline. [16c]

uphold *verb* **1** to support (an action), defend (a right) or maintain (the law), esp against opposition. **2** to declare (eg a court judgement or verdict) to be correct or just; to confirm. **3** to hold something up; to support it. ▪ **upholder** *noun*. [13c]

upholster *verb* to fit (chairs, sofas, etc) with upholstery. ▪ **upholstered** *adj*. [19c: orig US, a back-formation from **upholsterer**]

upholsterer *noun* a person who upholsters furniture, esp as their profession. [17c: from obsolete *upholster* a maker of or dealer in furniture]

upholstery *noun* **1** the springs, stuffing and covers of a chair or sofa. **2** the work of an upholsterer. [17c]

upkeep *noun* **1** the task or process of keeping something in good order or condition; maintenance. **2** the cost of doing this. [19c]

upland *noun* (*often* **uplands**) a high or hilly region. ▸ *adj* relating to or situated in such a region. [16c]

uplift *verb* /ʌp'lɪft/ **1** to lift something up; to raise it. **2** to fill (a person or people) with an invigorating happiness, optimism or awareness of the spiritual nature of things. **3** *Scot, chiefly formal* to pick up; to collect. ▸ *noun* /ˈʌplɪft/ **1** the action or result of lifting up. **2** a morally or spiritually uplifting influence, result or effect. **3** support given by a garment, esp a bra, that raises part of the body, esp the breasts. **4** (*also* **upheaval**) *geol* the process or result of land being raised, eg as in a period of mountain-building. ▪ **uplifting** *adj* cheering; inspiring with hope. [14c]

uplighter *or* **uplight** *noun* a type of lamp or wall light placed or designed so as to throw light upwards. [20c]

upload *verb, tr & intr, comput* to send (data, files, etc) from one computer to another, eg by means of a telephone line and modem. [20c]

up-market *adj* relating to or suitable for the more expensive end of the market; high in price, quality or prestige: *lives in an up-market area of town.* [20c]

upmost see **uppermost**

upon *prep* on or on to. [12c]

upped *past tense, past participle of* **up**

upper *adj* **1** higher; situated above. **2** high or higher in rank or status. **3** (*with capital* when part of a name) upstream, farther inland or situated to the north. **4** (*with capital* when part of a name) *geol, archaeol* designating a younger or late part or division, deposit, system, etc, or the period during which it was formed or deposited. ▸ *noun* **1** the part of a shoe above the sole. **2** the higher of two people, objects, etc. **3** *slang* a drug that induces euphoria. [14c: comparative of **up**]

IDIOMS **on one's uppers** *informal* extremely short of money; destitute.

upper case *printing, adj* (abbrev **u.c.**) referring or relating to capital letters, as opposed to small letters. Compare **lower case**. ▸ *noun* a letter or letters of this kind: *wrote the sign all in upper case.*

upper chamber see **upper house**

upper class *noun* the highest social class; the aristocracy. *as adj* (**upper-class**): *upper-class etiquette.*

upper crust *noun, informal* the upper class.

uppercut *noun* a forceful upward blow with the fist, usu under the chin. ▸ *verb, tr & intr* to hit someone with an uppercut.

upper hand *noun* (*usu* **the upper hand**) a position of advantage or dominance.

upper house *or* **upper chamber** *noun* (*often* **Upper House** and **Upper Chamber**) the higher but normally smaller part of a two-chamber (bicameral) parliament.

uppermost *or* **upmost** *adj, adv* at, in or into the highest or most prominent position. [15c: superlative forms of **up**]

upping *present participle of* **up**

uppish *adj* **1** arrogant or snobbish. **2** pretentious. ▪ **uppishly** *adv.* ▪ **uppishness** *noun.* [18c: from **up** + **-ish**]

uppity *adj, informal* self-important; arrogant; uppish. ▪ **uppitiness** *noun.* [19c: from **up**]

upright *adj* **1** standing straight up; erect or vertical. **2** possessing integrity or moral correctness. ▸ *adv* into an upright position. ▸ *noun* **1** a vertical (usu supporting) post or pole. **2** an **upright piano**. ▪ **uprightness** *noun.* [Anglo-Saxon *upriht*]

upright piano *noun* a piano with strings arranged vertically in a case above the keyboard. Compare **grand piano**.

uprising *noun* a rebellion or revolt. [16c]

uproar *noun* an outbreak of noisy and boisterous behaviour, esp angry protest. [16c: from Dutch *oproer*, from *oproeren* to stir up]

uproarious *adj* **1** making, or characterized by, an uproar. **2** of laughter: loud and unrestrained. **3** provoking such laughter; very funny. ▪ **uproariously** *adv.* [19c]

uproot *verb* **1** to displace (a person or people) from their usual surroundings or home: *Many Bosnians were uprooted by the war.* **2** to pull (a plant) out of the ground completely, with the root attached. **3** to eradicate or destroy something completely. **4** to move away from a usual location or home: *uprooted and moved to the country.* [16c]

ups and downs *plural noun* **1** rises and falls. **2** spells of alternating success and failure; changes of fortune.

upscale *adj, US informal* pertaining to or designed to appeal to the wealthier in society; up-market. [20c]

upset *verb* /ʌpˈsɛt/ **1** to disturb or distress someone emotionally. **2** to ruin or spoil (eg plans, etc). **3** to disturb the proper balance or function of (a person's stomach or digestion). **4** to disturb something's normal balance or stability. **5** *tr & intr* to knock something over or overturn. ▸ *noun* /ˈʌpsɛt/ **1** a disturbance or disorder, eg of plans, the digestion, etc. **2** an unexpected result or outcome, eg of a contest. ▸ *adj* **1** /ʌpˈsɛt/ emotionally distressed, angry or offended, etc. **2** /ʌpˈsɛt, ˈʌpsɛt/ disturbed: *an upset stomach.* ▪ **upsetting** *adj.*

upset price *noun* the lowest price acceptable for something that is for sale, and the price at which bidding starts at an auction; a reserve price.

upshot *noun* (*often* **the upshot**) the final outcome or ultimate effect. [16c]

upside *noun* **1** the upper part or side of anything. **2** *informal* a positive or favourable aspect.

upside down *adj* (*also* **upside-down**) **1** with the top part at the bottom; upturned or inverted. **2** *informal* in complete confusion or disorder. ▸ *adv* **1** in an inverted way or manner: *Why does buttered toast always fall upside down on the floor?* **2** in a completely confused or disordered way. [14c as *up so doun* or *upsedoun*]

upsides *adv* (*usu* **upsides with sb**) *Brit informal* even with them, esp through revenge or retaliation. [18c]

upsilon /ˈʌpsɪlɒn/ *noun* the twentieth letter of the Greek alphabet. [17c: from Greek *u psilon* simple or slender *u*]

upstage *adv* /ʌpˈsteɪdʒ/ **1** on, at or towards the back of a theatre stage. **2** *informal* in an arrogant or haughty manner. ▸ *adj* /ˈʌpsteɪdʒ/ **1** situated, occurring at or towards, or relating to, the back of a theatre stage. **2** *slang* arrogant or haughty. ▸ *verb* /ʌpˈsteɪdʒ/ **1** of an actor: to move upstage and force (another actor) to turn their back to the audience. **2** *informal* to direct attention away from someone on to oneself; to outshine them. [19c]

upstairs *adv* /ʌpˈstɛəz/ **1** up the stairs; to or on an upper floor or floors of a house, etc. **2** *informal* to or in a senior or more senior position. ▸ *adj* /ˈʌpstɛəz/ (*also* **upstair**) on or relating to an upper floor or floors. ▸ *noun* /ʌpˈstɛəz/ an upper floor or the upper floors of a building, esp the part of a house above the ground floor. [16c]

upstanding *adj* **1** standing up. **2** of a person: honest; respectable; trustworthy: *an upstanding member of society.* **3** with a healthily erect posture; vigorous; upright. [Anglo-Saxon]

upstart *noun, derog* someone who has suddenly acquired wealth or risen to a position of power or importance, esp one who is considered arrogant. ▸ *adj* belonging or relating to someone who is an upstart; typical or characteristic of an upstart. [16c]

upstate *US, adv* /ʌpˈsteɪt/ in, to or towards the part of a state remotest from, and usu to the north of, the principal city of the state. ▸ *adj* /ˈʌpsteɪt/ in, relating to, or characteristic of this part of a state. ▸ *noun* /ˈʌpsteɪt/ the remoter, and usu northern, part of a state. ▪ **upstater** *noun.* [20c]

upstream *adv* /ʌpˈstriːm/ towards the source of a river or stream and against the current. ▸ *adj* /ˈʌpstriːm/ situated towards the source of a river or stream. [17c]

upsurge *noun* a sudden sharp rise or increase; a surging up. ▪ **upsurgence** *noun*: *an upsurgence of neofascism in central Europe.* [20c]

upswing *noun* **1** *econ* a recovery in the trade cycle or a period during which this occurs. **2** a swing or movement upwards, or a period of improvement. [20c]

uptake *noun* **1** an act of lifting up. **2** the act of taking up something on offer, or the extent of this. [19c]
IDIOMS **quick** *or* **slow on the uptake** *informal* quick or slow to understand or realize something.

up-tempo *or* **uptempo** *adj, adv, music* with or at a fast tempo. [20c]

upthrow *noun* **1** an uplift; a raising up. **2** *geol* (*also* **upthrust**) **a** the upward movement of the relatively raised strata on one side of a fault; **b** the extent of this movement. [19c]

upthrust *noun* **1** an upward thrust or push. **2** *geol* **a** the action or an instance of thrusting up, esp by volcanic action; **b** an **upthrow** (sense 2). **3** *physics* the upward force exerted by a liquid that makes an object float. [19c]

uptight *adj, informal* **1** nervous; anxious; tense. **2** angry; irritated. **3** strait-laced; conventional. [20c]

up to date *or* **up-to-date** *adj* **1** containing all the latest information. **2** following the latest trends.

uptown *chiefly N Am, adv* in, into or towards the part of a town or city that is away from the centre, usu the more prosperous or residential area. ▸ *adj* situated in, relating, or belonging to or characteristic of this part of a town or city. ▸ *noun* the uptown part of a town or city. ▪ **uptowner** *noun.* [19c]

upturn *noun* /ˈʌptɜːn/ **1** an upheaval. **2** an increase in (esp economic) activity; an upward trend. ▸ *verb* /ʌpˈtɜːn/ **1** to turn something over, up or upside down. **2** *intr* to turn or curve upwards. ▪ **upturned** *adj.*

upward *adv* (*usu* **upwards**) to or towards a higher place, a more important or senior position, or an earlier era. ▸ *adj* moving or directed upwards, to a higher position, etc. ▪ **upwardly** *adv.* [Anglo-Saxon *upweard*]
IDIOMS **upwards of** more than: *upwards of a thousand people.*

upwardly mobile *adj* moving, or in a position to move, into a higher social class or income bracket. ▪ **upward mobility** *noun.*

upwind *adv* /ʌpˈwɪnd/ **1** against the direction of the wind; into the wind. **2** in front in terms of wind direction; with the wind carrying one's scent towards eg an animal one is stalking. ▸ *adj* /ˈʌpwɪnd/ going against or exposed to the wind. [19c]

uranium *noun, chem* (symbol **U**) a dense silvery-white radioactive metallic element chiefly used to produce nuclear energy. ▪ **uranic** *adj.* [18c: named after the planet Uranus]

Uranus /ˈjʊərənəs/ *noun, astron* the seventh planet from the Sun. [19c: from Latin *Uranus*, from Greek *Ouranos*, literally 'the sky']

urban *adj* **1** relating or belonging to, constituting, or characteristic of a city or town: *the urban landscape.* **2** living in a city or town: *an urban fox.* Compare **rural**. [17c: from Latin *urbanus*, from *urbs* city]

urbane *adj* **1** with refined manners; suave; courteous. **2** sophisticated; civilized; elegant. ▪ **urbanely** *adv.* [16c: from French *urbain* or from Latin *urbanus* of the town]

urbanism *noun* **1** the urban way of life. **2** the study of this. ▪ **urbanist** *noun.* [19c]

urbanity *noun* (**-ies**) **1** the quality of being **urbane**; refinement or elegance of manner, etc. **2** urban life. [16c: from French *urbanité*]

urbanize *or* **-ise** *verb* to make (an area) less rural and more town-like. ▪ **urbanization** *noun.* [19c]

urban renewal *or* **urban regeneration** *noun* the clearing and redevelopment of slums, etc, in large cities and towns.

urchin *noun* **1** a mischievous child. **2** a dirty raggedly dressed child. **3** a **sea urchin**. **4** *archaic* a hedgehog. ▸ *adj* relating to or like an urchin. [14c: from French *herichon* hedgehog]

Urdu *noun* an Indo-Aryan language, the official literary language of Pakistan, also spoken in Bangladesh and among Muslims in India. [18c: from Persian and Urdu *(zaban i) urdu* (language of) the camp]

-ure /-jʊə(r)/ *suffix, forming nouns, denoting* **1** an action, process or result: *seizure.* **2** official position: *prefecture.* **3** a collective group: *legislature.* [French, from Latin *-ura*]

urea /jʊəˈrɪə/ *noun, biochem* a compound, white and crystalline when purified, formed during amino-acid breakdown in the liver of mammals, and excreted in the urine. ▪ **ureal** *or* **ureic** *adj.* [19c: from French *urée*]

ureter /jʊəˈriːtə(r)/ *noun, anatomy* one of the two tubes through which urine is carried from the kidneys to the bladder. ▪ **ureteral** *or* **ureteric** /jʊərɪˈtɛrɪk/ *adj.* [16c: from French *uretère* or Latin *ureter*]

urethane /ˈjʊərəθeɪn/ *noun* **1** *chem* a crystalline amide used eg in pesticides and formerly as an anaesthetic. **2** short form of **polyurethane**. [19c: from **urea** + **ethyl**]

urethra /jʊəˈriːθrə/ *noun* (***urethras*** *or* ***urethrae*** /-riː/) *anatomy* the tube through which urine passes from the bladder out of the body and which, in males, also conveys semen. ▪ **urethral** *adj.* [17c: from Greek *ourethra*]

urethritis /jʊərɪˈθraɪtɪs/ *noun, med* inflammation of the urethra. ▪ **urethritic** /-ˈθrɪtɪk/ *adj.* [19c]

urge *verb* **1** (*also* **urge sb on**) to persuade someone forcefully or incite them (to do something). **2** to beg or entreat someone (to do something). **3 a** (*usu* **urge that**) to earnestly advise or recommend that; **b** (*usu*

urge sth) to earnestly recommend it: *urged prudence.* **4** to drive or hurry (onwards, forwards, etc). ▶ *noun* a strong impulse, desire or motivation (to do something). [16c: from Latin *urgere*]

urgent *adj* **1** requiring or demanding immediate attention, action, etc; pressing. **2** of a request, etc: forcefully and earnestly made. ▪ **urgency** *noun.* ▪ **urgently** *adv.* [15c: French, from Latin *urgere* to urge]

uric /ˈjʊərɪk/ *adj* relating to, present in, or derived from, urine. [18c]

uric acid *noun, biochem* an organic acid, a product of protein metabolism, present in urine and blood.

urinal *noun* **1** any receptacle or sanitary fitting, esp one attached to a wall, designed for men to urinate into. **2** a vessel for urine, esp one for use by an incontinent or bedridden person. [19c: French]

urinary *adj* **1** relating to urine or the passing of urine. **2** containing or contained in urine. **3** relating to or affecting the organs and structures that excrete and discharge urine. [16c: from Latin *urina* urine]

urinate *verb, intr* to discharge urine. ▪ **urination** *noun.* [16c]

urine *noun* the yellowish slightly acidic liquid consisting mainly of water and containing urea, uric acid, and other nitrogenous waste products filtered from the blood by the kidneys. ▪ **urinous** *adj.* [14c: French, from Latin *urina*]

urinogenital /jʊərɪnoʊˈdʒɛnɪtəl/ *or* **urogenital** /jʊəroʊ-/ *adj* relating to, or affecting, both the urinary and genital functions or organs. [19c]

urn *noun* **1** a vase or vessel with a rounded body, usu a small narrow neck and a base or foot. **2** such a vase used to contain the ashes of a dead person. **3** a large cylindrical metal container with a tap and an internal heating element, used for heating water or making large quantities of tea or coffee. [14c: from Latin *urna*, from *urere* to burn]

urogenital see **urinogenital**

urology /jʊəˈrɒlədʒɪ/ *noun, med* the branch of medicine that deals with the study and treatment of diseases and disorders of the male and female urinary tracts, and of the male genital tract. ▪ **urologic** *or* **urological** *adj.* ▪ **urologist** *noun.* [19c]

ursine *adj* **1** belonging, relating or referring to a bear or bears. **2** bearlike. [16c: from Latin *ursinus*]

urticaria *noun, med* an allergic skin reaction with raised red or white itchy patches. Also called **nettle rash, hives.** ▪ **urticarial** *adj.* [18c]

urus see **aurochs**

US *abbrev* **1** Under-Secretary. **2** United States.

us *pron* **1** the speaker or writer together with another person or other people; the object form of *we*: *asked us the way* • *give it to us.* **2** all or any people; one: *Computers can help us to work more efficiently.* **3** *informal* **a** me: *Give us a hand;* **b** ourselves: *We'll make us a pile of dough.* **4** *formal* used by monarchs, etc: me. [Anglo-Saxon]

---

us, we

Be careful to use the word **us** (rather than **we**) as an object:

✓ *This is a busy time of year for us farmers.*
✗ *This is a busy time of year for we farmers.*

USA *abbrev* **1** United States of America. **2** United States Army.

usable *or* **useable** *adj* able to be used. ▪ **usability** *noun.*

USAF *abbrev* United States Air Force.

usage *noun* **1** the act or way of using, or fact of being used; use; employment. **2** custom or practice. **3 a** the way that the vocabulary, constructions, etc of a language are actually used in practice; **b** an example of this. **4** the amount or quantity of use, or the rate at which something is used. [14c: from French]

USB *abbrev, comput* Universal Serial Bus, a fast versatile interface between a computer and peripheral devices.

use *verb* /juːz/ **1** to put to a particular purpose. **2** to consume; to take something as fuel. **3** to treat someone as a means to benefit oneself; to exploit them. **4** *slang* to take (eg drugs or alcohol) regularly. **5** *old use* to behave (well or badly) towards someone. ▶ *noun* /juːs/ **1** the act of using. **2** the state of being (able to be) used: *go out of use* • *not in use.* **3** a practical purpose a thing can be put to. **4** the quality of serving a practical purpose: *It's no use complaining* • *Is this spanner any use?* **5** the ability or power to use something (eg a limb): *lost the use of her leg.* **6** the length of time a thing is, will be or has remained serviceable: *should give you plenty of use.* **7** the habit of using; custom. [13c: from French *user*]

IDIOMS **used to sth** *or* **sb** *or* **to doing** *or* **being sth** accustomed to it or them, or to doing or being it: *The puppies haven't got used to us yet.*

PHRASAL VERBS **use sth up 1** to exhaust supplies, etc. **2** to finish off an amount left over.

used /juːzd/ *adj* not new; second-hand: *a used car.*

used to /ˈjuːstə/ *auxiliary verb* used with other verbs to express habitual actions or states that took place in the past: *They used to be friends, but they aren't anymore* • *He didn't use to be so grumpy.*

---

used to

Many people are uncertain about what is the correct negative form of **used to.** The following examples are all acceptable:

✓ *He used not to do it.*
✓ *He usedn't to do it.*
✓ *He didn't use to do it.*

The following are considered incorrect:

✗ *He usen't to do it.*
✗ *He didn't used to do it.*

---

useful *adj* **1** able to be used advantageously; serving a helpful purpose; able to be put to various purposes. **2** *informal* skilled or proficient: *Booth put in a useful performance for Aberdeen.* ▪ **usefully** *adv.* ▪ **usefulness** *noun.* [16c]

IDIOMS **come in useful** to prove to be useful.

useless *adj* **1** serving no practical purpose. **2** (*often* **useless at sth**) *informal* not at all proficient: *useless at maths.* ▪ **uselessly** *adv.* ▪ **uselessness** *noun.* [16c]

user *noun* **1** someone who uses a specified facility such as a leisure centre, a computer network, etc. **2** someone who regularly takes a specified drug.

user-friendly *adj* esp of a computer system: designed to be easy or pleasant to use, or easy to follow: *user-friendly software.* ▪ **user-friendliness** *noun.*

username *or* **user ID** *noun, comput* the name or code by which a person or group is identified when gaining access to a computer network.

U-shaped valley *noun* a **glacial trough.**

usher *noun* **1 a** someone whose job is to show people to their seats, eg in a theatre, cinema, etc; **b** someone whose function is to direct wedding guests to their seats in church, and to look after them generally. **2** an official in a court of law who guards the door and maintains order. **3** an official who escorts, or introduces people to, dignitaries on ceremonial occasions. ▸ *verb* **1** (*usu* **usher sb in** *or* **out**) to conduct or escort them, eg into or out of a room. **2** (*usu* **usher sth in**) *formal or literary* to be a portent of it; to herald it. [14c: from French *ussier*]

usherette *noun* a woman who shows people to their seats in a theatre or cinema. [20c: see **usher**]

USSR *abbrev, hist* Union of Soviet Socialist Republics.

usual *adj* done, happening, etc most often; customary: *took the usual route to work.* ▸ *noun* **1** something which is usual, customary, etc. **2** (*usu* **the** *or* **my usual**) *informal* the thing regularly requested, done, etc, esp the drink that someone regularly or most often orders. ▪ **usually** *adv* ordinarily; normally. ▪ **usualness** *noun.* [14c: French, from Latin *usus* use]
IDIOMS **as usual** as regularly happens.

usurer /ˈjuːʒərə(r)/ *noun* someone who lends money, esp one who charges exorbitant rates of interest. [13c: see **usury**]

usurp /jʊˈzɜːp/ *verb* **1** to take possession of (eg land) or assume (eg power, authority, etc) by force, without right or unjustly. **2** to encroach on something (eg someone else's rights, sphere of interest, etc). ▪ **usurpation** *noun.* ▪ **usurper** *noun.* [14c: from French *usurper*]

usury /ˈjuːʒərɪ/ *noun* (***-ies***) **1** the practice of lending money at an unfairly or illegally high rate of interest. **2** such a rate of interest. [14c: from Latin *usuria*, from *usus* **use**]

utensil *noun* an implement or tool, esp one for everyday or domestic use: *cooking utensils.* [14c: from French *utensile*, from Latin *utensilis* 'fit for use' or 'useful']

uterine *adj* **1** *med* relating to, in the region of or affecting the uterus. See also **intrauterine**. **2** of siblings: born of the same mother but different fathers. [15c: French, from Latin *uterus* **uterus**]

uterus /ˈjuːtərəs/ *noun* (***uteri*** /-raɪ/) *technical* the **womb**. [17c: Latin]

utilitarian *adj* **1** intended to be useful rather than beautiful. **2** concerned too much with usefulness and not enough with beauty; strictly functional. **3** relating to or characterized by utilitarianism. ▸ *noun* a believer in utilitarianism. [18c: from **utility**]

utilitarianism *noun, ethics* a set of values based on the belief that an action is morally right if it benefits the majority of people. [19c]

utility *noun* (***-ies***) **1** usefulness; practicality. **2** something that is useful. **3** *econ* the ability of a commodity to satisfy human needs or wants. **4** a company which provides a supply eg of gas, water or electricity, or other service, for a community. Also called **public utility**. **5** *comput* a program designed to carry out a routine function. ▸ *adj* **1** designed for usefulness or practicality, rather than beauty. **2** of a breed of dog: orig bred to serve a practical purpose. [14c: from French *utilité*]

utility room *noun* a room where things such as a washing machine, freezer, etc are kept.

utilize *or* **-ise** *verb* to make practical use of something; to use it. ▪ **utilizable** *adj.* ▪ **utilization** *noun.* [19c: from French *utiliser*]

utmost *adj* **1** greatest possible in degree, number or amount: *of the utmost urgency.* **2** furthest or most remote in position. ▸ *noun* **1** (*often* **the utmost**) the greatest possible amount, degree or extent. **2** the best or greatest, eg in terms of power, ability, etc: *tried his utmost to win.* [Anglo-Saxon *utemest*, from *ute* out + double superlative suffix *-m-est*]

Utopia *or* **utopia** *noun* any imaginary place, state or society of idealized perfection. [16c: Latin, meaning 'no-place', from Greek *ou* not + *topos* a place; the title of a book by Sir Thomas More]

Utopian *or* **utopian** *adj* relating to Utopia, to a utopia or to some unrealistically ideal place, society, etc. ▸ *noun* **1** an inhabitant of Utopia. **2** someone who advocates idealistic or impracticable social reforms. ▪ **Utopianism** *noun.* [16c]

utter[1] *verb* **1** to give audible vocal expression to (an emotion, etc); to emit (a sound) with the voice: *uttered a piercing cry.* **2** to speak or say; to express something in words. **3** *law* to put (counterfeit money) into circulation. ▪ **utterable** *adj.* ▪ **utterer** *noun.* [14c: from Dutch *uteren* to show or make known]

utter[2] *adj* complete; total; absolute: *utter disbelief.* ▪ **utterly** *adv.* ▪ **utterness** *noun.* [15c: from Anglo-Saxon *uterra* outer, comparative of *ut* out]

utterance *noun* **1** the act of uttering or expressing something with the voice. **2** the ability to utter; the power of speech. **3** a person's manner of speaking. **4** something that is uttered or expressed.

uttermost *adj, noun* **utmost**.

U-turn *noun* **1** a manoeuvre in which a vehicle is turned to face the other way in a single continuous movement, the turn making the shape of a U. **2** a complete reversal of direction, eg of policy.

UUP *abbrev* in Northern Ireland: Ulster Unionist Party, a political party advocating the continued political union of Great Britain and Northern Ireland.

UV *abbrev* ultraviolet.

UV-A *or* **UVA** *abbrev* ultraviolet A, ultraviolet radiation with a range of 320–380 nanometres.

UV-B *or* **UVB** *abbrev* ultraviolet B, ultraviolet radiation with a range of 280–320 nanometres.

uvula /ˈjuːvjʊlə/ *noun* (***uvulas*** *or* ***uvulae*** /-liː/) *anatomy* the small fleshy part of the soft palate that hangs over the back of the tongue at the entrance to the throat. ▪ **uvular** *adj.* [14c: Latin, literally 'small grape']

uxorial /ʌkˈsɔːrɪəl/ *adj* **1** relating or pertaining to a wife or wives. **2** **uxorious**. [19c: from Latin *uxor* wife]

uxoricide /ʌkˈsɔːrɪsaɪd/ *noun* **1** a man who kills his wife. **2** the act of killing one's wife. ▪ **uxoricidal** *adj.* [19c: from Latin *uxor* wife + **-cide**]

uxorious /ʌkˈsɔːrɪəs/ *adj* excessively or submissively fond of one's wife. ▪ **uxoriously** *adv.* ▪ **uxoriousness** *noun.* [16c: from Latin *uxoriosus*, from *uxor* wife]

Uzbek /ˈʊzbɛk, ˈʌz-/ *noun* (***Uzbek*** *or* ***Uzbeks***) **1 a** a member of a Turkic people of central Asia; **b** a citizen or inhabitant of, or person born in, Uzbekistan, a republic in central Asia. **2** the official language of Uzbekistan. ▸ *adj* belonging or relating to the republic, its inhabitants, or their language. [17c]

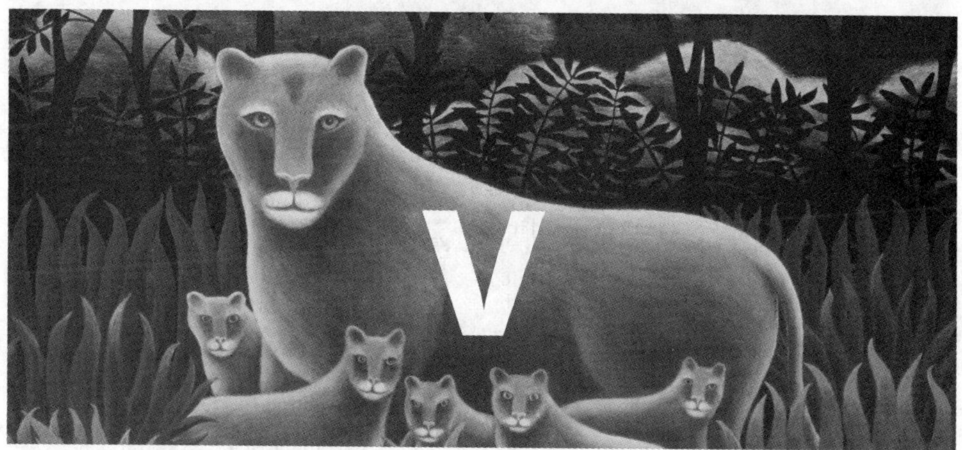

V[1] *or* **v** *noun* (***Vs, V's*** *or* ***v's***) **1** the twenty-second letter of the English alphabet. **2** *also in compounds* an object or mark shaped liked the letter V: *V-sign*. See also **vee**.

V[2] *abbrev* **1** victory. **2** volt.

V[3] *symbol* **1** *chem* vanadium. **2** the Roman numeral for 5.

v *or* **v.** *abbrev* **1** velocity. **2** versus. **3** very. **4** *vide* (Latin), see, refer to. **5** volume.

vac *noun, informal* short for **vacation**.

vacancy *noun* (***-ies***) **1** the state of being vacant; emptiness. **2** an unoccupied job or post. **3** an unoccupied room in a hotel or guesthouse.

vacant *adj* **1** empty or unoccupied. **2** having, showing or suggesting an absence of thought, concentration or intelligence. **3** of a period of time: not assigned to any particular activity. ▪ **vacantly** *adv.* [13c: from Latin *vacare* to be empty]

vacate *verb* **1** to make something empty; to empty something out. **2** *tr & intr* to leave or cease to occupy (a house or an official position). [17c: from Latin *vacare* to be empty]

vacation *noun* **1** *N Am, esp US* a holiday. **2** a holiday between terms at a university, college or court of law. ▸ *verb, intr, N Am, esp US* to take a holiday. [14c: from French]

vaccinate *verb* to administer to a person or an animal a vaccine that gives immunity from a disease; to **inoculate.** ▪ **vaccination** *noun.*

vaccine *noun* **1** *med* a preparation containing killed or weakened (attenuated) bacteria or viruses, or serum containing specific antibodies, used in vaccination to confer temporary or permanent immunity to a bacterial or viral disease by stimulating the body to produce antibodies to a specific bacterium or virus. **2** *comput* a piece of software designed to detect and remove computer viruses (see **virus** sense 4) from a floppy disk, program, etc. [18c: from *viriolae vaccinae* cowpox, the title of a paper (1798) by E Jenner]

vacillate /ˈvasɪleɪt/ *verb, intr* to change opinions or decisions frequently; to waver. ▪ **vacillation** *noun.* [16c: from Latin *vacillare*]

vacuity *noun* (***-ies***) **1** the state or quality of being vacuous. **2** a foolish thought or idea.

vacuole /ˈvakjʊoʊl/ *noun, biol* a space within the cytoplasm of a living cell that is filled with air or liquid. ▪ **vacuolar** *adj.* [19c: French, meaning 'little vacuum']

vacuous *adj* **1** unintelligent; stupid; inane. **2** of a look or expression: blank; conveying no feeling or meaning. **3** empty. **4** having no meaning or purpose. [17c: from Latin *vacuus* empty]

vacuum *noun* (***vacuums*** *or technical* ***vacua***) **1** a space from which all matter has been removed. **2** a space from which all or almost all air or other gas has been removed. **3** a feeling or state of emptiness. **4** a condition of isolation from outside influences. **5** *informal* a **vacuum cleaner.** ▸ *adj* relating to, containing or operating by means of a vacuum: *a vacuum pump.* ▸ *verb, tr & intr, informal* to clean with a vacuum cleaner. [16c: from Latin *vacuus* empty]

vacuum cleaner *noun* an electrically powered cleaning device that lifts dust and dirt by suction. See also **Hoover.** [20c]

vacuum flask *noun* a container for preserving the temperature of liquids, esp drinks, consisting of a double-skinned bottle with a vacuum sealed between the layers, fitted inside a protective metal or plastic container. See also **Thermos.** [20c]

vacuum-packed *adj* esp of food: sealed in a container from which most of the air has been removed. [20c]

vacuum tube *noun, elec* an electron tube containing an electrically heated electrode (the **cathode**) that emits electrons which flow through a vacuum to a second electrode (the **anode**). Also called **valve.**

vagabond *noun* someone with no fixed home who lives an unsettled wandering life, esp someone regarded as lazy or worthless. ▸ *adj* wandering. [15c: French]

vagary /ˈveɪgərɪ/ *noun* (***-ies***) an unpredictable and erratic act or turn of events. [16c: from Latin *vagari* to wander]

vagina /vəˈdʒaɪnə/ *noun* (***vaginas*** *or* ***vaginae*** /-niː/) in the reproductive system of most female mammals: the muscular canal that leads from the cervix of the uterus to the exterior of the body. ▪ **vaginal** *adj.* [17c: Latin, meaning 'sheath']

vagrant /ˈveɪgrənt/ *noun* someone who has no permanent home or place of work. ▸ *adj* wandering. ▪ **vagrancy** *noun.* [15c: prob from French *wakerant* roaming]

vague *adj* **1** indistinct or imprecise. **2** thinking, expressing or remembering without clarity or precision. ▪ **vaguely** *adv.* ▪ **vagueness** *noun.* [16c: from Latin *vagus* wandering]

vain *adj* **1** having too much pride in one's appearance, achievements or possessions. **2** having no useful effect or result. ▪ **vainly** *adv.* [13c: from French]
IDIOMS **in vain** without success; fruitlessly.

vainglory *noun, literary* extreme boastfulness; excessive pride in oneself. ▪ **vainglorious** *adj.* [13c: from French *vaine gloire*]

valance /ˈvaləns/ *noun* a decorative strip of fabric hung over a curtain rail or round the frame of a bed. [15c: possibly from French *valer* to descend]

vale *noun, literary* a **valley**. [13c: from French *val*, from Latin *vallis*]

valediction /valɪˈdɪkʃən/ *noun* **1** the act of saying farewell; a farewell. **2** a valedictory speech, etc. ▪ **valedictory** *adj.* [17c: from Latin *vale* farewell + *dicere* to say]

valency /ˈveɪlənsɪ/ *or* (*esp N Am*) **valence** *noun* (***valencies***; ***valences***) *chem* a positive or negative whole number that denotes the combining power of an atom of a particular element, equal to the number of hydrogen atoms or their equivalent with which it could combine to form a compound. [Late 19c: from Latin *valentia* strength or capacity]

valentine *noun* **1** a card or other message given, often anonymously, as a token of love or affection on **St Valentine's Day**. **2** the person it is given to. [14c]

valerian /vəˈlɪərɪən, vəˈlɛərɪən/ *noun* **a** a small flowering plant with pink tubular flowers and rhizome roots; **b** a sedative drug derived from the root. [14c: from Latin *valeriana herba*]

valet /ˈvaleɪ, ˈvalɪt/ *noun* **1** a man's personal servant, who attends to his clothes, dressing, etc. **2** a man who carries out similar duties in a hotel. ▸ *verb* (***valeted, valeting***) **1** *intr* to work as a valet. **2** to clean the body-work and interior of (a car) as a service. [16c: French, related to **varlet**]

valetudinarian /valɪtʃuːdɪˈnɛərɪən/ *adj, formal* **1** relating to or suffering from a long-term or chronic illness. **2** anxious about one's health. ▸ *noun* a valetudinarian person. [18c: from Latin *valetudo* state of health]

Valhalla *noun, Norse myth* the palace of bliss where the souls of slain heroes feast for eternity with Odin, the supreme creator. [18c: from Norse *valr* the slain + *höll* hall]

valiant *adj* outstandingly brave and heroic. ▪ **valiantly** *adv.* [14c: from French *vailant*]

valid *adj* **1** of an argument, objection, etc: **a** based on truth or sound reasoning; **b** well-grounded; having some force. **2** of a ticket or official document: **a** legally acceptable for use: *a valid passport*; **b** not having reached its expiry date: *The ticket is still valid.* **3** of a contract: drawn up according to proper legal procedure. ▪ **validity** *noun.* [16c: from Latin *validus* strong]

validate *verb* **1** to make (a document, a ticket, etc) valid, eg by marking it with an official stamp. **2** to confirm the validity of something. ▪ **validation** *noun.*

valise /vəˈliːz; *N Am* vəˈliːs/ *noun, now chiefly N Am, esp US* a small overnight case or bag. [17c: French, meaning 'suitcase']

Valium *noun, trademark* **diazepam**, a type of tranquillizing drug. [20c]

valley *noun* a long flat area of land, usu containing a river or stream, flanked on both sides by higher land, eg hills or mountains. [13c: from French *valee*]

valour *or* (*N Am*) **valor** *noun* courage or bravery, esp in battle. ▪ **valorous** *adj.* [15c: French]

valuable *adj* having considerable value or usefulness. ▸ *noun* (*usu* **valuables**) personal possessions of high financial or other value.

---

valuable
This word is often misspelt. It has no e in the middle. It might help you to remember the following sentence:
*Unusual **a**ntiques are often val**ua**ble.*

---

valuation *noun* **1** an assessment of the monetary value of something, esp from an expert or authority. **2** the value arrived at.

value *noun* **1** worth in monetary terms. **2** the quality of being useful or desirable; the degree of usefulness or desirability. **3** the exact amount of a variable quantity in a particular case. **4** the quality of being a fair exchange: *value for money.* **5** (**values**) moral principles or standards. **6** *maths* a quantity represented by a symbol or set of symbols. **7** *music* the duration of a note or rest. ▸ *verb* **1** to consider something to be of a certain value, esp a high value. **2** to assess the value of something. ▪ **valued** *adj.* ▪ **valueless** *adj.* ▪ **valuer** *noun.* [14c: French]

value-added tax *noun, Brit* (abbrev **VAT**) a tax on goods and services sold which is calculated on the difference between the cost of raw materials and production, and the market value of the final product. [20c]

value judgement *noun* an assessment of worth based on personal opinion rather than objective fact.

valvate *adj* **1** with a valve or valves. **2** *biol* using valves. **3** *biol* meeting at the edges without overlapping.

valve *noun* **1** **a** any device that regulates the flow of a liquid or gas through a pipe by opening or closing an aperture; **b** any such device that allows flow in one direction only. **2** *anatomy* in certain tubular organs: a flap of membranous tissue that allows flow of a body fluid, such as blood, in one direction only. **3** any of a set of finger-operated devices that control the flow of air through some brass musical instruments producing different notes. **4** *zool* either half of the hinged shell of a bivalve mollusc such as a cockle or clam. [14c: from Latin *valva* folding door]

valvular *adj* **1** having valves. **2** functioning as a valve.

vamoose *verb, intr, N Am, esp US slang* to depart hurriedly; to clear off. *as exclam*: *Vamoose!* [19c: from Spanish *vamos* let us go]

vamp[1] *informal, noun* a woman who flaunts her charm, esp in order to exploit men. ▸ *verb* **1** to seduce (a man) with intent to exploit him. **2** *intr* to behave like a vamp. [20c: a shortening of **vampire**]

vamp[2] *noun* the part of a shoe or boot that covers the toes. ▸ *verb* to improvise (a musical accompaniment). See also **revamp**. [13c: from French *avanpié* forefoot]
PHRASAL VERBS **vamp sth up** to refurbish it or do it up.

vampire *noun* **1** a dead person who supposedly rises from the grave at night to suck the blood of the living. **2** someone who ruthlessly exploits others. **3** a **vampire bat**. [18c: French, from Hungarian *vampir*]

vampire bat *noun* a bat native to Central and S America that pierces the skin of animals and humans with its sharp teeth and sucks their blood.

van[1] *noun* **1** a commercial road vehicle with luggage space at the rear, lighter than a lorry. **2** (*also* **luggage van**) *Brit* a railway carriage in which luggage and parcels are carried. [19c: a shortening of **caravan**]

van[2] *noun* **1** a vanguard. **2** the forefront: *in the van of progress.* [17c: a shortening of **vanguard**]

vanadium *noun, chem* (symbol **V**) a soft silvery-grey metallic element that is used to increase the toughness and shock resistance of steel alloys. [19c: named after *Vanadis*, a name of the Norse goddess Freyja]

Vandal *noun, hist* a member of a Germanic people who overran Gaul, Spain, N Africa and Rome in the 4c–5c, destroying churches, manuscripts, etc in the process. ▸ *adj* relating to the Vandals. [16c: from Latin *Vandalus*, the name given to these people]

vandal *noun* someone who wantonly damages or destroys personal and public property. ▪ **vandalism** *noun.* [17c: from **Vandal**]

vandalize *or* **-ise** *verb* to inflict wilful and senseless damage on (property, etc).

Van de Graaff generator *noun, physics* a very high-voltage electrostatic generator, using a high-speed belt to accumulate charge in a large metal globe. [20c: named after Robert J Van de Graaff, US physicist]

van der Waals' force /van də wɑːlz, vɑːlz/ *noun, physics* any of the weak attractive forces between atoms or molecules. [19c: named after Johannes Diderik van der Waals, Dutch physicist]

vandyke *or* **Vandyke** *noun* **1** (*in full* **vandyke collar**) a broad collar with the edge cut into deep points. **2** (*in full* **vandyke beard**) a short pointed beard. [18c: named after Sir Anthony Van Dyck]

vane *noun* **1** a **weathervane**. **2** each of the blades of a windmill, propeller or revolving fan. [15c: from obsolete *fane* flag or weathercock]

vanguard *noun* **1** the part of a military force that advances first. **2 a** a person or group that leads the way, esp by setting standards or forming opinion; **b** a leading position: *in the vanguard of discovery.* [15c: from French *avant-garde* advance guard]

vanilla *noun* **1 a** a Mexican climbing orchid having large fragrant white or yellow flowers followed by pod-like fruits; **b** (*in full* **vanilla pod**) its fruit. **2** a flavouring substance obtained from the pod, used in ice cream, chocolate and other foods. ▸ *adj* **1** flavoured with or like vanilla. **2** *informal* ordinary; plain. [17c: from Spanish *vainilla* small pod]

vanish *verb, intr* **1** to disappear suddenly. **2** to cease to exist; to die out. [14c: from Latin *evanescere*]

vanishing point *noun* the point at which parallel lines extending into the distance appear to meet.

vanity *noun* (*-ies*) **1** the quality of being vain or conceited. **2** a thing one is conceited about. **3** futility or worthlessness. [13c: from Latin *vanitas*]

vanity case *noun* a woman's small case for cosmetics.

vanity unit *noun* a piece of furniture combining a dressing table and washbasin.

vanquish *verb, literary* to defeat or overcome someone. [14c: from Latin *vincere* to conquer]

vantage point *noun* a position affording a clear overall view or prospect.

vapid /ˈvapɪd/ *adj* dull; uninteresting; insipid. ▪ **vapidity** *noun.* [17c: from Latin *vapidus* flat-tasting]

vaporize *or* **-ise** *verb* **1** to convert something into vapour. **2** *intr* to become vapour. ▪ **vaporization** *noun.*

vapour *or* (*N Am*) **vapor** *noun* **1** a substance in the form of a mist, fume or smoke, esp one coming off from a solid or liquid. **2** *chem* a gas that can be condensed to a liquid by pressure alone, without being cooled, consisting of atoms or molecules, dispersed in the air, that have evaporated from the surface of a substance that normally exists in the form of a liquid or solid: *water vapour.* **3** (**the vapours**) *old use* a feeling of depression, or of faintness, formerly thought to be caused by gases in the stomach. [14c: from Latin *vapor* steam]

vapour pressure *noun, physics* the pressure exerted by the atoms or molecules of a vapour with its liquid or solid form.

variable *adj* **1** referring to something that varies or tends to vary; not steady or regular; changeable. **2** referring to something that can be varied or altered. ▸ *noun* **1** a thing that can vary unpredictably in nature or degree. **2** a factor which may change or be changed by another. **3** *maths* in an algebraic expression or equation: a symbol, usu a letter, for which one or more quantities or values may be substituted. ▪ **variability** *noun.* ▪ **variably** *adv.* [14c: French]

variance *noun* **1** the state of being different or inconsistent. **2** *stats* the square of the **standard deviation** (ie the mean of the squared deviations of a number of observations from their mean). [14c: from Latin *varientia* difference]

IDIOMS **at variance with sth** in disagreement or conflict with it.

variant *noun* **1** a form of a thing that varies from another form, eg one of several permissible spellings of a word. **2** an example that differs from a standard. ▸ *adj* **1** different. **2** differing from a standard.

variation *noun* **1** the act or process of varying or changing. **2** something that varies from a standard. **3** the extent to which something varies from a standard or changes. **4** a passage of music in which the main melody is repeated with some, usu only slight, changes. **5** *biol* differences in characteristics, eg size or colouring, between members of the same species. [14c: French]

varicella *noun, med* chickenpox. [18c]

varicoloured *or* (*N Am*) **varicolored** *adj* having different colours in different parts.

varicose *adj, pathol* **1** of a superficial vein: abnormally swollen and twisted so that it produces a raised and often painful knot on the skin surface, usu of the legs. **2** of an ulcer: formed as a result of the development of varicose veins. [18c: from Latin *varicosus*]

varied *adj* having variety; diverse.

variegate *verb* to alter the appearance of something, esp with patches of colours. ▪ **variegation** *noun.* [17c: from Latin *variegatus*]

variegated *adj, botany* of leaves or flowers: marked with patches of two or more colours.

variety *noun* (*-ies*) **1** any of various types of the same thing; a kind or sort. **2** the quality of departing from a fixed pattern or routine; diversity. **3** a plant or animal differing from another in certain characteristics, but not enough to be classed as a separate species. **4** a form of theatrical entertainment consisting of a succession of acts of different kinds. *as adj*: *a variety* *show*. Compare **vaudeville**. [16c: from Latin *varietas* difference or diversity]

varifocals *plural noun* a pair of glasses with **varifocal** lenses, whose variable focal lengths allow a wide range of focusing distances. Compare **bifocals**.

various *adj* **1** several different: *worked for various companies*. **2** different; disparate; diverse: *Their interests are many and various*. ▪ **variously** *adv*. [16c: from Latin *varius* changing]

varlet *noun, old use* **1** a menial servant. **2** a rascal or rogue. [15c: French]

varmint *noun, N Am, esp US slang* a troublesome animal or person. [16c: a variant form of **vermin**]

varna /ˈvɜrnə, ˈvɑrnə/ *noun, Hinduism* any of the four main divisions of Hindu society, within which there are castes. [From Sanskrit, meaning 'class']

varnish *noun* **1** an oil-based liquid containing resin, painted on a surface such as wood to give a hard transparent and often glossy finish. **2** any liquid providing a similar finish: *nail varnish*. **3** a superficial attractiveness or impressiveness, esp masking underlying shoddiness or inadequacy; a gloss. ▸ *verb* **1** to apply varnish to something. **2** to make something superficially appealing or impressive. [14c: from French *vernis*]

varsity *noun* (**-ies**) *informal* **1** *Brit* a university, esp with reference to sport. **2** *N Am* the principal team representing a college in a sport. [19c: a colloquial abbreviation of **university**]

vary *verb* (***-ies, -ied***) **1** *intr* to change, or be of different kinds, esp according to different circumstances. **2** *tr & intr* to make or become less regular or uniform and more diverse. ▪ **varying** *noun, adj*. [15c: from Latin *variare* to vary]

vas /vas/ *noun* (***vasa*** /ˈveɪsə/) *anatomy, biol* a vessel, tube or duct carrying liquid. [16c: from Latin *vas* vessel]

vascular *adj, biol* **1** relating to the blood vessels of animals or the sap-conducting tissues (**xylem** and **phloem**) of plants. **2** composed of or provided with such vessels. [17c: from Latin *vasculum*]

vas deferens /vas ˈdɛfərɛnz/ *noun* (***vasa deferentia*** /ˈveɪzə dɛfəˈrɛnʃɪə/) *biol* the duct from each testicle that carries spermatozoa to the penis. [16c: from Latin *deferre* to carry away]

vase /vɑːz; *US* veɪz/ *noun* an ornamental glass or pottery container, esp one for holding cut flowers. [17c: French, from Latin *vas* vessel]

vasectomy *noun* (***-ies***) *med* a surgical operation involving the tying and cutting of the **vas deferens** as a means of sterilization. [19c: from Latin *vas* **vas** + **-ectomy**]

Vaseline *noun, trademark* an ointment consisting mainly of **petrolatum**. [19c]

vassal *noun* **1** *feudalism* someone acting as a servant to, and fighting on behalf of, a medieval lord in return for land or protection or both. **2** a person or nation dependent on or subservient to another. ▪ **vassalage** *noun*. [13c: from Latin *vassus* servant]

vast *adj* **1** extremely great in size, extent or amount. **2** *informal* considerable; appreciable: *a vast difference*. ▪ **vastly** *adv*. ▪ **vastness** *noun*. [16c: from Latin *vastus* desolate or huge]

VAT *or* **Vat** *abbrev, Brit* **value-added tax**.

vat *noun* a large barrel or tank for storing or holding liquids. [Anglo-Saxon *fæt*]

Vatican *noun* (*usu* **the Vatican**) **1** a collection of buildings on Vatican Hill in Rome, including the palace and official residence of the pope. **2** the authority of the pope. [16c: from Latin *Mons Vaticanus* Vatican Hill]

vaudeville *noun, N Am, esp US* **1** variety entertainment (see **variety** sense 4). **2** a music hall. [18c: French]

vault[1] *noun* **1** an arched roof or ceiling, esp in a church. **2** an underground chamber used for storage or as a burial tomb. **3** a wine cellar. **4** a fortified room for storing valuables, eg in a bank. [14c: from French *voute*]

vault[2] *verb, tr & intr* to spring or leap over something, esp assisted by the hands or a pole. ▸ *noun* an act of vaulting. [16c: from French *voulter*]

vaulting[1] *noun* a series of vaults (see **vault**[1] sense 1) considered collectively.

vaulting[2] *adj* esp referring to ambition or pride: excessive or immoderate.

vaunt *verb, tr & intr* to boast or behave boastfully about something. ▸ *noun* a boast. [14c: from Latin *vanitare*]

VB *abbrev, comput* Visual Basic.

VC *abbrev* **1** vice-chancellor. **2** Victoria Cross.

VCR *abbrev* video cassette recorder.

VDU *abbrev* visual display unit.

've *contraction* (usu after pronouns) have: *they've*.

veal *noun* the flesh of a calf, used as food. [14c: from French *veel*]

vector *noun* **1** *maths* a quantity which has both magnitude and direction, eg force, velocity, or acceleration. Compare **scalar**. **2** *aeronautics* the course of an aircraft or missile. **3** *med* any agent, such as an insect, that is capable of transferring a **pathogen** from one organism to another. **4** *biol* in genetic engineering: a vehicle used to transfer DNA from one organism to another to make **recombinant DNA**. [18c: Latin, meaning 'carrier']

Veda /ˈveɪdə/ *noun* any one, or all of, four ancient holy books of the Hindus consisting of the **Rig-veda, Sama-veda**, **Yajur-veda** and **Athara-veda**. ▪ **Vedic** *adj*. ▪ **Vedist** *noun*. [18c: Sanskrit, meaning 'knowledge']

Vedanta *noun* a system of Hindu philosophy founded on the **Veda**. ▪ **Vedantic** *adj*. [18c: Sanskrit, from *veda* **Veda** + *anta* end]

vee *noun* **1** a representation of the twenty-second letter of the English alphabet, V. **2** an object or mark shaped like the letter V. **3** *sometimes in compounds* shaped like the letter V: *vee-neck*. See also **V**[1].

veer *verb, intr* **1** to move abruptly in a different direction: *The car veered off the road into the ditch*. **2** of the wind: to change direction clockwise in the northern hemisphere and anticlockwise in the southern. **3** *naut* to change course, esp away from the wind. ▸ *noun* a change of direction. [16c: from French *virer* to turn]

veg /vɛdʒ/ *noun* (*pl* ***veg***) *informal* a vegetable or vegetables: *meat and two veg*. [19c: short for **vegetable**]

vegan /ˈviːɡən/ *noun* someone who does not eat meat, fish, dairy products or any foods containing animal fats or extracts, often also avoiding using wool, leather and other animal-based substances. ▸ *adj* **1** referring to or for vegans. **2** of a meal or diet:

excluding such foods. ▪ **veganism** *noun*. [20c: from *vegetarian*]

vegeburger *noun* a flat cake resembling and served like a hamburger, made with vegetables, soy beans, etc instead of meat. [20c]

vegetable *noun* **1 a** a plant or any of its parts, other than fruits and seeds, that is used for food, eg roots, tubers, stems or leaves; **b** the edible part of such a plant. **2** *offensive, informal* a person almost totally incapable of any physical or mental activity because of severe brain damage. ▸ *adj* for, relating to, or composed of vegetables. [14c: from Latin *vegetabilis*]

vegetable marrow see **marrow**

vegetable oil *noun* an oil obtained from a plant, used esp in cooking and cosmetics.

vegetable oyster see **salsify**

vegetal *adj* consisting of or relating to vegetables or to plant life in general. [14c: from Latin *vegetalis*]

vegetarian *noun* someone who does not eat meat or fish. ▸ *adj* **1** referring to or for vegetarians. **2** denoting food or a diet that contains no meat or fish. ▪ **vegetarianism** *noun*. [19c: from **vegetable**]

vegetate *verb, intr* of a person: to live a dull inactive life. [17c: from Latin *vegetare* to animate]

vegetation *noun, botany* **1** a collective term for plants. **2** the plants of a particular area.

vegetative *adj* **1** referring to plants or vegetation. **2** *biol* denoting asexual reproduction in plants or animals, as in bulbs, corms, yeasts, etc. **3** *botany* denoting a phase of plant growth as opposed to reproduction. **4** *biol* denoting unconscious or involuntary bodily functions as resembling the process of vegetable growth.

veggie *or* **vegie** *noun, informal* **1** a vegetarian. **2** a vegetable. Also written **veggy**.

vehement *adj* expressed with strong feeling or firm conviction; forceful; emphatic. ▪ **vehemence** *noun*. ▪ **vehemently** *adv*. [15c: from Latin *vehemens* eager]

vehicle *noun* **1** a conveyance for transporting people or things, esp a self-powered one. **2** someone or something used as a means of communicating ideas or opinions: *newspapers as vehicles for political propaganda*. **3** *med* a neutral substance in which a drug is mixed in order to be administered, eg a syrup. **4** a substance in which a pigment is transferred to a surface as paint, eg oil. ▪ **vehicular** *adj*. [17c: from Latin *vehere* to carry]

vehicle excise duty *noun* a tax, usually paid annually, that is levied on motor vehicles that use public roads. Formerly called **road tax**.

veil *noun* **1** a fabric covering for a woman's head or face, forming part of traditional dress in some societies. **2** a covering of fine netting for a woman's head, which may be attached to a hat or headdress. **3** the hoodlike part of a nun's habit. **4** anything that covers or obscures something: *a veil of secrecy*. ▸ *verb* **1** to cover something, or cover the face of someone, with a veil. **2** to disguise or obscure something: *veiled his threats in pleasantries*. ▪ **veiled** *adj*: *veiled criticism*. [13c: from French *veile*]

IDIOMS **take the veil** to become a nun.

vein *noun* **1** *anatomy* a blood vessel that carries deoxygenated blood back towards the heart. **2** *anatomy, loosely* any blood vessel. **3** a thin sheet-like deposit of one or more minerals, eg quartz, deposited in a fracture or joint in the surrounding rock. **4** a streak of different colour, eg in cheese. **5** in a leaf: any of a large number of thin branching tubes containing the vascular tissues. **6** in an insect: any of the tubes that stiffen and support the membranous structure of the wings. **7** a mood or tone: *written in a sarcastic vein*. **8** a distinct characteristic present throughout; a streak. ▪ **veined** *adj*. ▪ **veiny** *adj*. [14c: from French *veine*]

Velcro *noun, trademark* a fastening material consisting of two nylon surfaces, one of tiny hooks, the other of thin fibres, which bond tightly when pressed together but are easily pulled apart. [20c: from French *velours croché* hooked velvet]

veld *or* **veldt** /fɛlt, vɛlt/ *noun* a wide grassy plain with few or no trees, esp in S Africa. [18c: Dutch, meaning 'field']

vellum *noun* **1** a fine kind of parchment, orig made from calfskin. **2** a manuscript written on such parchment. **3** thick cream-coloured writing-paper resembling such parchment. [15c: from French *velin*]

velocipede /vəˈlɒsɪpiːd/ *noun, hist* an early form of bicycle propelled by pushing of the rider's feet along the ground. [19c: from French *vélocipède*]

velocity *noun* (**-ies**) **1** *technical* rate of motion, ie distance per unit of time, in a particular direction. **2** *loosely* speed. [16c: from Latin *velocitas*, from *velox* swift]

velour *or* **velours** /vəˈlʊə(r)/ *noun* any fabric with a velvet-like pile, used esp for upholstery. *as adj*: *a velour dressing gown*. [18c: from French *velours* **velvet**]

velvet *noun* **1** a fabric with a very short soft closely woven pile on one side. **2** the soft skin that covers the growing antlers of deer and is rubbed off as they mature. ▸ *adj* **1** made of velvet. **2** soft or smooth like velvet. ▪ **velvety** *adj*. [14c: from Latin *velvettum*]

velveteen *noun* cotton fabric with a velvet-like pile. *as adj*: *a velveteen dress*. [18c]

vena cava /ˈviːnə ˈkeɪvə/ *noun* (***venae cavae*** /-niː -viː/) *anatomy* either of the two large veins, the **superior vena cava** and the **inferior vena cava**, that carry deoxygenated blood to the right **atrium** of the heart. [16c: Latin, meaning 'hollow vein']

venal /ˈviːnəl/ *adj* **1** of a person: willing to be persuaded by corrupt means, esp bribery. **2** of behaviour: dishonest; corrupt. ▪ **venality** *noun*. [17c: from Latin *venum* goods for sale]

vend *verb* to sell or offer (esp small wares) for sale. [17c: from Latin *vendere* to sell]

vendetta *noun* **1** a bitter feud in which the family of a murdered person takes revenge by killing the murderer or one of their relatives. **2** any long-standing bitter feud or quarrel. [19c: Italian]

vending machine *noun* a coin-operated machine that dispenses small articles such as snacks and cigarettes. [19c]

vendor *noun, law* a seller, esp of property.

veneer *noun* **1** a thin layer of a fine material, esp wood, fixed to the surface of an inferior material to give an attractive finish. **2** a false or misleading external appearance, esp of a favourable quality: *a veneer of respectability*. [18c: from German *furnieren*]

venerable *adj* **1** deserving respect, esp on account of age or religious association. **2** (**Venerable**) **a** in the Church of England: given as a title to an archdeacon; **b** *RC Church* given as a title to a person due to be declared a saint. [15c: from Latin *venerabilis*]

venerate *verb* to regard someone or something with deep respect or awe. ▪ **veneration** *noun*. [17c: from Latin *venerari* to adore or revere]

venereal *adj* **1** of a disease or infection: transmitted by sexual intercourse. **2** relating to, resulting from, or for the treatment of such diseases. [15c: from Latin *Venus* Roman goddess of love]

Venetian *adj* relating or belonging to Venice. ▸ *noun* a citizen or inhabitant of, or person born in, Venice. [15c: from Latin *Venetia* Venice]

Venetian blind *noun* a window blind consisting of horizontal slats strung together, one beneath the other, and tilted to let in or shut out light. [19c]

Venezuelan *adj* belonging or relating to Venezuela, a republic in South America, or its inhabitants. ▸ *noun* a citizen or inhabitant of, or person born in, Venezuela.

vengeance *noun* punishment inflicted as a revenge; retribution. [13c: French]

IDIOMS **with a vengeance 1** forcefully or violently. **2** to a great degree.

vengeful *adj* **1** eager for revenge. **2** carried out in revenge. [16c: from obsolete *venge* to avenge]

venial sin /ˈviːnɪəl/ *noun* a sin that is pardonable or excusable. Compare **mortal sin**. [13c: from Latin *venialis* pardonable]

venison *noun* the flesh of a deer, used as food. [13c: from French *venaison*]

Venn diagram *noun, maths* a diagram that is used to illustrate the relationships between mathematical sets, which are denoted by circles. [19c: named after John Venn, British logician]

venom *noun* **1** a poisonous liquid that some creatures, including scorpions and certain snakes, inject in a bite or sting. **2** spitefulness. ▪ **venomous** *adj*. [13c: from French *venim*]

venous /ˈviːnəs/ *adj* relating to or contained in veins. [17c: from Latin *vena* vein]

vent[1] *noun* a slit in a garment, esp upwards from the hem at the back, for style or ease of movement. [15c: from French *fente* slit]

vent[2] *noun* **1** an opening that allows air, gas or liquid into or out of a confined space. **2** the passage inside a volcano through which lava and gases escape. **3** *biol* the anus of a bird or other small animal. **4** a chimney flue. ▸ *verb* **1** to make a vent in something. **2** to let something in or out through a vent. **3** to release and express (esp emotion) freely: *vented his frustration by shaking his fists*. [16c: from French *éventer* to expose to air]

ventilate *verb* **1** to allow fresh air to circulate throughout (a room, building, etc). **2** to cause (blood) to take up oxygen. **3** to supply air to (the lungs). **4** to expose (an idea, etc) to public examination or discussion. ▪ **ventilation** *noun*. [15c: from Latin *ventilare* to fan]

ventilator *noun* **1** a device that circulates or draws in fresh air. **2** a machine that ventilates the lungs of a person whose respiratory system is damaged.

ventral *adj* **1** denoting the lower surface of an animal that walks on four legs, of any invertebrate, or of a structure such as a leaf or wing. **2** denoting the front surface of the body of an animal that walks upright, eg a human being. **3** denoting a structure that is situated on or just beneath such a surface. Compare **dorsal**. ▪ **ventrally** *adv*. [18c: from Latin *venter*]

ventral fin *noun* either of the paired fins on the belly of a fish.

ventricle *noun, anatomy* **1** in mammals: either of the two lower chambers of the heart which have thick muscular walls. **2** in vertebrates: a cavity within the brain, connecting it to the spinal cord. ▪ **ventricular** *adj*. [14c: from Latin *ventriculus*]

ventriloquism *noun* the art of speaking in a way that makes the sound appear to come from elsewhere, esp a dummy's mouth. ▪ **ventriloquist** *noun*. [18c: from Latin *venter* abdomen + *loqui* to speak]

venture *noun* **1** an exercise or operation involving danger or uncertainty. **2** a business project, esp one involving risk or speculation. **3** an enterprise attempted. ▸ *verb* **1** *tr & intr* to be so bold as to; to dare: *ventured to criticize the chairman*. **2** to put forward or present (a suggestion, etc) in the face of possible opposition: *ventured a different opinion*. **3** to expose someone or something to danger or chance; to risk. [15c: shortening of **adventure**]

venture capital *noun* money supplied by individual investors or business organizations for a new business enterprise. Also called **risk capital**. [20c]

Venture Scout *noun* a member of the senior branch of the Scout movement, for 16- to 20-year-olds. [20c]

venturesome *adj* **1** prepared to take risks; enterprising. **2** involving danger; risky.

venue *noun* **1** the chosen location for a sports event, a concert or other entertainment. **2** a meeting-place. [19c: from Latin *venire* to come]

venule *noun, biol* **1** a branch of a vein in an insect's wing. **2** any of the small blood vessels that join up to form veins. [19c: from Latin *venula*, diminutive of *vena* vein]

Venus *noun, astron* the second planet from the Sun. [Anglo-Saxon, from the Latin name of the goddess of love]

Venus flytrap *noun* an insectivorous plant with leaves consisting of two parts hinged together which shut when an insect touches the inner surface of the leaf, trapping the insect.

veracious *adj, formal* truthful. [17c]

veracity *noun, formal* truthfulness. [17c: from Latin *verax*]

veranda *or* **verandah** *noun* a sheltered terrace attached to a building. [18c: from Hindi *varanda*]

verb *noun* a word or group of words that belongs to a grammatical class denoting an action, experience, occurrence or state, eg *do, feel, happen, love*. See also **auxiliary verb**. [14c: from Latin *verbum* word]

verbal *adj* **1** relating to or consisting of words: *verbal abuse*. **2** spoken, not written: *verbal communication*. **3** *grammar* relating to or derived from a verb or verbs. **4** literal; word-for-word. **5** talkative; articulate. ▪ **verbally** *adv*.

verbalism *noun* excessive attention paid to words used, rather than to ideas expressed, esp in literary criticism; literalism. ▪ **verbalist** *noun*.

verbalize *or* **-ise** *verb* **1** to express (ideas, thoughts, etc) in words. **2** *intr* to use too many words; to be verbose. **3** to turn (any word) into a verb. ▪ **verbalization** *noun*.

verbal noun *noun* a form of a verb that functions as a noun, eg '*to err* is human' and '*swimming* keeps you fit'. Compare **gerund**.

verbatim /vɜːˈbeɪtɪm/ *adj, adv* using exactly the same words; word-for-word. [15c: Latin]

verbena *noun* a plant with fragrant white, pink, red or purplish tubular flowers, used in herbal medicine and cosmetics. [16c: Latin, meaning 'sacred bough']

verbiage *noun* **1** the use of language that is wordy or needlessly complicated. **2** such language. [18c: from French *verbeier* to chatter]

verbose *adj* using or containing too many words; boringly or irritatingly long-winded. ▪ **verbosity** /vɜːˈbɒsɪtɪ/ *noun*. [17c: from Latin *verbosus*]

verdant *adj* **1** covered with lush green grass or vegetation. **2** of a rich green colour. **3** naive or unsophisticated; gullible; green. [16c: from French *verdeant*]

verdict *noun* **1** a decision arrived at by a jury in a court of law. **2** any decision, opinion or judgement. [13c: from Latin *veredictum* truly said]

verdigris /ˈvɜːdɪgriː, -griːs/ *noun, chem* a bluish-green coating of basic copper salts that forms as a result of corrosion when copper, brass or bronze surfaces are exposed to air and moisture for long periods. [14c: from French *verd de Grece* green of Greece]

verdure *noun, literary* **1** lush green vegetation. **2** the rich greenness of such vegetation. [14c: from French *verd* green]

Verey light see **Very light**

verge[1] *noun* **1** a limit, boundary or border. **2** a strip of grass bordering a road. **3** a point or stage immediately beyond or after which something exists or occurs: *on the verge of tears*. ► *verb, intr* (**verge on sth**) to be close to being or becoming something specified: *enthusiasm verging on obsession*. [16c: French, from Latin *virga* rod]

verge[2] *verb, intr* to slope or incline in a specified direction. Compare **converge**, **diverge**. [17c: from Latin *vergere* to bend]

verger *noun* **1** chiefly in the Church of England: a church official who assists the minister and acts as caretaker. **2** chiefly in the Church of England: an official who carries the ceremonial staff of a bishop or other dignitary. [15c: from Latin *virga* rod]

verify *verb* (***-ies, -ied***) **1** to check or confirm the truth or accuracy of something. **2** to assert or prove the truth of something. ▪ **verifiable** *adj*. ▪ **verification** *noun*. [14c: from Latin *verus* true]

verily *adv, old use* truly; really. [13c: related to **very**]

verisimilitude *noun, formal* **1** the appearance of being real or true. **2** a statement or proposition that sounds true but may not be. [17c: from French]

veritable *adj, formal* accurately described as such; real: *a veritable genius!* ▪ **veritably** *adv*. [15c: French, from Latin *verus* true]

verity *noun* (***-ies***) **1** a true statement, esp one of fundamental wisdom or importance; a maxim. **2** truthfulness. [14c: from French *vérité*]

vermicelli /vɜːmɪˈtʃɛlɪ/ *noun* **1** pasta in very thin strands, thinner than spaghetti. **2** (*also* **chocolate vermicelli**) tiny splinters of chocolate used for decorating cakes, etc. [17c: Italian, meaning 'little worms']

vermiform *adj* like a worm; worm-shaped. [18c]

vermiform appendix *noun, anatomy* a small blind tube leading off the **caecum**, part of the large intestine. Usually shortened to **appendix**.

vermilion *noun* **1** a bright scarlet colour. **2** a pigment of this colour consisting of sulphide of mercury; cinnabar. ► *adj* referring to or having this colour. [13c: from French *vermeillon*]

vermin *singular or plural noun* **1** a collective name for wild animals that spread disease or generally cause a nuisance, esp rats and other rodents. **2** detestable people. ▪ **verminous** *adj*. [14c: from Latin *vermis* worm]

vermouth /ˈvɜːməθ/ *noun* an alcoholic drink consisting of wine flavoured with aromatic herbs, orig wormwood. [19c: French]

vernacular *noun* (*usu* **the vernacular**) **1** the native language of a country or people, as opposed to a foreign language that is also in use. **2** the form of a language as commonly spoken, as opposed to the formal language. **3** the language or jargon of a particular group. ► *adj* **1** referring to or in the vernacular. **2** local; native: *vernacular architecture*. [17c: from Latin *vernaculus* native]

vernal *adj* relating to or happening in spring. [16c: from Latin *vernus* referring to spring]

vernier /ˈvɜːnɪə(r)/ *noun* a small sliding device on some measuring instruments, eg barometers and theodolites, used to measure fractions of units. [18c: named after Pierre Vernier, French mathematician]

veronica *noun* a plant of the foxglove family, with small blue, pink or white flowers, including the **speedwell**. [16c: Latin, from the name Veronica]

verruca /vəˈruːkə/ *noun* (***verrucas*** *or* ***verrucae*** /-ˈruːseɪ *or* -ˈruːkiː/) **1** *pathol* a wart, esp one on the sole of the foot. **2** *botany* a wartlike growth. [16c: Latin, meaning 'wart']

---

verruca

This word is often misspelt. It has two *r*'s in the middle and one c at the end. It might help you to remember the following sentence:

*You can get a ve**rr**u**c**a by **r**unning **r**ound **u**nder **c**over.*

---

versatile *adj* **1** adapting easily to different tasks. **2** having numerous uses or abilities. ▪ **versatility** *noun*. [17c: from Latin *versatilis*, from *vertere* to turn]

verse *noun* **1** a division of a poem; a stanza. **2** poetry, as opposed to prose. **3** a poem. **4** a division of a song. **5** any of the numbered subdivisions of the chapters of the Bible. [Anglo-Saxon *fers*]

versed *adj* (*always* **versed in sth**) familiar with it or skilled in it: *well versed in chemistry*.

versify *verb* (***-ies, -ied***) **1** *intr* to write poetry. **2** to express something as, or turn it into, a poem. ▪ **versification** *noun*. ▪ **versifier** *noun*. [14c: from Latin *versificare* to put into verse]

version *noun* any of several types or forms in which a thing exists or is available, eg a particular edition or translation of a book, or one person's account of an incident. [16c: from Latin *versio*]

verso *noun, printing* **1** the back of a loose sheet of printed paper. **2** the left-hand page of two open pages. Compare **recto**. [19c: Latin, from *verso folio* turned leaf]

versus *prep* **1** in a contest or lawsuit: against. **2** (*abbrev* **vs, v**) *informal* in comparison to. [15c: Latin]

vertebra /ˈvɜːtəbrə/ *noun* (***vertebrae*** /-breɪ, -briː/) *anatomy* in vertebrates: any of the small bones or cartilaginous segments that form the backbone. ▪ **vertebral** *adj*. [17c: Latin, from *vertere* to turn]

vertebrate *noun, zool* any animal, including fish, amphibians, reptiles, birds and mammals, that has a backbone. ▸ *adj* having a backbone. [19c]

vertex /ˈvɜːtɛks/ *noun* (***vertexes*** *or* ***vertices*** /-tɪsiːz/) **1** the highest point; the peak or summit. **2** *geom* **a** the point opposite the base of a geometric figure, eg the pointed tip of a cone; **b** the point where the two sides forming an angle meet in a **polygon**, or where three or more surfaces meet in a **polyhedron**; **c** the intersection of a curve with its axis. [16c: Latin, meaning 'summit' or 'whirlpool']

vertical *adj* **1** perpendicular to the horizon; upright. **2** running from top to bottom, not side to side. **3** referring to a vertex or at a vertex. **4** relating to, involving or running through all levels within a hierarchy, all stages of a process, etc, rather than just one. ▸ *noun* a vertical line or direction. ▪ **vertically** *adv.*

vertical angles *or* **vertically opposite angles** *plural noun, maths* a pair of opposite, equal angles formed by intersecting lines.

vertiginous *adj* **1** so high or whirling as to bring on vertigo; dizzying. **2** relating to vertigo.

vertigo *noun* a whirling sensation felt when the sense of balance is disturbed; dizziness; giddiness. [16c: Latin, meaning 'turning']

vervain *noun* a wild **verbena** with small white, lilac or purple flowers borne in long slender spikes. [14c: from French *vervaine*]

verve *noun* great liveliness or enthusiasm. [17c: French, meaning 'loquaciousness']

very *adv* **1** to a high degree or extent: *very kind.* **2** (used with *own, same* and with superlative adjectives) absolutely; truly: *my very own room* • *the very same day* • *my very best effort.* ▸ *adj* (*used for emphasis*) **1** absolute: *the very top.* **2** precise; actual: *this very minute.* **3** most suitable: *That's the very tool for the job.* **4** mere: *shocked by the very thought.* [13c: from French *veri*]

IDIOMS **not very** not at all; the opposite of. **very good** *or* **very well** expressions of consent and approval.

very high frequency *noun* (abbrev **VHF**) **1** a band of radio frequencies between 30 and 300MHz. **2** a radio frequency lying between these frequencies.

Very light *or* **Verey light** *noun* a coloured flare fired from a pistol, as a signal or to illuminate an area. [20c: invented by E W Very, US naval officer]

very low frequency *noun* (abbrev **VLF**) **1** a band of radio frequencies between 3 and 30kHz. **2** a radio frequency lying between these frequencies.

Vesak *or* **Wesak** /ˈvɛsaːk/ *noun* the most widely celebrated Buddhist festival, held in May to commemorate the birth, enlightenment and death of Buddha. [1920s: from Sanskrit *vaisakha* the name of a month]

vesicle *noun* **1** *biol* any small sac or cavity, esp one filled with fluid, within the cytoplasm of a living cell. **2** *med* a small blister. [16c: from Latin *vesicula* bladder or blister]

vespers *singular noun* **1** *now esp RC Church* the sixth of the **canonical hours**, taking place towards evening. **2** an evening service in some Christian Churches; evensong. [17c: from Latin *vesper* evening]

vessel *noun* **1** a container, esp for liquid. **2** a ship or large boat. **3** a tube or duct carrying liquid, eg blood or sap, in animals and plants. [13c: French, from Latin *vascellum* small vessel]

vest *noun* **1** an undergarment for the top half of the body. **2** *US, Aust* a waistcoat. ▸ *verb* (*usu* **vest sth in sb** *or* **sb with sth**) to give or bestow legally or officially: *by the power vested in me.* [15c: from French *vestir*]

vestal *adj* virginal; chaste. ▸ *noun* **1** a chaste woman, esp a nun. **2** a **vestal virgin**. [15c: from Latin *vestalis* of Vesta, the Roman goddess of the hearth and home]

vestal virgin *noun, hist* in ancient Rome: one of the patrician virgins consecrated to the goddess Vesta, who kept the sacred fire burning on her altar.

vested *adj, law* usu of property or money held in trust: recognized as belonging to a person, although not perhaps available to them until some future date.

vested interest *noun* an interest a person has in the fortunes of a particular system or institution because that person is directly affected or closely associated.

vestibule *noun* an entrance hall. [17c: from Latin *vestibulum* entrance court]

vestige /ˈvɛstɪdʒ/ *noun* **1** a slight amount; a hint or shred. **2** *biol* a small functionless part in an animal or plant, once a fully developed organ in ancestors. ▪ **vestigial** /vəˈstɪdʒɪəl/ *adj.* [17c: from Latin *vestigium* footprint]

vestment *noun* **1** a garment worn ceremonially by members of the clergy and church choir. **2** any ceremonial robe. [13c: from Latin *vestimentum*]

vestry *noun* (***-ies***) a room in a church where the vestments are kept, often also used for meetings, Sunday school classes, etc. [14c: prob from French *vestiarie*]

vet[1] *noun* short for **veterinary surgeon**. ▸ *verb* (***vetted, vetting***) to check someone for suitability or reliability. See also **positive vetting**. [19c]

vet[2] *noun, informal N Am, esp US* short for **veteran**: *a war vet.* [19c]

vetch *noun* a climbing plant of the pea family with blue or purple flowers, the pods of which are often used as fodder. Also called **tare**. [14c: from French *veche*]

veteran *noun* **1** someone with many years of experience in a particular activity. **2** an old and experienced member of the armed forces. **3** *N Am, esp US* an ex-serviceman or -woman. [16c: from Latin *veteranus* old]

veteran car *noun* a very old motor car, specifically one made before 1905. Compare **vintage car**.

veterinary *adj* concerned with diseases of animals. [18c: from Latin *veterinarius*]

veterinary surgeon *or* (*N Am*) **veterinarian** *noun* a person qualified to treat diseases of animals.

veto /ˈviːtoʊ/ *noun* (***vetoes***) **1 a** the right to formally reject a proposal or forbid an action, eg in a law-making assembly; **b** the act of using such a right. **2** *informal* any refusal of permission. ▸ *verb* (***vetoes, vetoed***) **1** to formally and authoritatively reject. **2** *loosely* to forbid. [17c: from Latin *veto* I forbid]

vex *verb* **1** to annoy or irritate someone. **2** to worry someone. ▪ **vexation** *noun.* ▪ **vexing** *adj.* [15c: from Latin *vexare* to shake or annoy]

vexatious *adj* vexing; annoying; troublesome.

vexed *adj* **1** annoyed; angry; troubled. **2** of an issue, etc: much discussed or debated: *vexed question.*

VHF *abbrev, radio* very high frequency.

VHS *abbrev* video home system, a video cassette recording system.

via *prep* by way of or by means of; through: *travelled from Edinburgh to London via York* • *sent it via head office*. [18c: Latin, meaning 'way']

viable *adj* **1** of a plan, etc: having a chance of success; feasible; practicable. **2** of a plant, etc: able to exist or grow in particular conditions. **3** of a fetus or baby: able to survive independently outside the womb. ▪ **viability** *noun*. [19c: French]

viaduct *noun* a bridge-like structure of stone arches supporting a road or railway across a valley, etc. [19c: from Latin *via* way + *ducere* to lead]

Viagra /vaɪˈagrə/ *noun, trademark* a proprietary drug used to treat impotence. [1990s]

vial see **phial**

viands *plural noun, formal* items of food; provisions. [14c: from French *viande* food]

viaticum *noun* (***viaticums*** *or* ***viatica***) *RC Church* the Eucharist given to a dying person. [16c: Latin, from *via* way]

vibes *plural noun* **1** (*also* **vibe** *singular noun, informal*) feelings, sensations or an atmosphere experienced or communicated: *bad vibes in the room* • *got a really bad vibe from her.* Also (*in full*) **vibrations**. **2** the **vibraphone**. [20c]

vibrant *adj* **1** extremely lively or exciting; strikingly animated or energetic. **2** of a colour: strong and bright. **3** vibrating. ▪ **vibrancy** *noun*. [16c: from Latin *vibrare*]

vibraphone *noun, music, esp jazz* a percussion instrument with pitched keys set over tuned resonating tubes and electrically driven rotating metal discs which produce a vibrato effect. ▪ **vibraphonist** *noun*. [20c: from **vibrate** + Greek *phone* 'sound' or 'voice']

vibrate *verb* **1** *tr & intr* to move a short distance back and forth very rapidly. **2** *intr* to ring or resound when struck. **3** *intr* to shake or tremble. **4** *intr* to swing back and forth; to oscillate. ▪ **vibratory** *adj*. [17c: from Latin *vibrare* to tremble]

vibration *noun* **1** a vibrating motion. **2 a** a single movement back and forth in vibrating; **b** *sometimes* a half of this period, ie either of the back or forward movements. **3** (**vibrations**) *informal* **vibes**. [Late 19c]

vibrato /vɪˈbrɑːtoʊ/ *noun, music* a faint trembling effect in singing or the playing of string and wind instruments, achieved by vibrating the throat muscles or the fingers. Compare **tremolo**. [19c: Italian, from Latin *vibratus* vibrated]

vibrator *noun* any device that produces a vibrating motion.

VIC *abbrev, Aust state* Victoria.

vicar *noun* **1** in the Church of England: the minister of a parish. **2** *RC Church* a bishop's deputy. [13c: from French *vicaire*]

vicarage *noun* a vicar's residence or benefice.

vicar-general *noun, RC Church* an official who assists a bishop in administrative matters.

vicarious /vɪˈkɛərɪəs/ *adj* **1** experienced not directly but through witnessing the experience of another person: *vicarious pleasure in seeing his children learn*. **2** undergone on behalf of someone else. **3** standing in for another. **4** of authority, etc: delegated to someone else. [17c: from Latin *vicarius* substituted]

vice[1] *or* (*N Am*) **vise** *noun* a tool with heavy movable metal jaws, usu fixed to a bench, for gripping an object being worked on. [15c: French *vis* screw]

vice[2] /vaɪs/ *noun* **1** a habit or activity considered immoral, evil or depraved, esp involving prostitution or drugs. **2** such activities collectively. **3** a bad habit; a fault in one's character. [13c: French, from Latin *vitium* blemish]

vice- *combining form, denoting* next in rank to; acting as deputy for: *vice-admiral* • *vice-president*. [17c]

vice-admiral *noun* an officer in the navy.

vice-chancellor *noun* the deputy chancellor of a British university, responsible for administrative duties.

vicegerent /vaɪsˈdʒɛrənt/ *noun* someone appointed to act in place of a superior. ▸ *adj* acting in this capacity. [16c: from *vice* by turn + Latin *gerere* to manage]

vice-president *noun* **1** a president's deputy or assistant. **2** an officer next below the president.

viceregal *adj* relating to a viceroy.

viceroy *noun* a governor of a province or colony ruling in the name of, and with the authority of, a monarch or national government. [16c: French, from *roi* king]

vice squad *noun* a branch of the police force that investigates crimes relating to **vice**[2].

vice versa *adj* the other way round: *from me to you and vice versa*. [17c: Latin, meaning 'the position being reversed']

vicinity *noun* (***-ies***) **1** a neighbourhood. **2** the area immediately surrounding a place. **3** the condition of being close; nearness. [16c: from Latin *vicinus* neighbour]

vicious *adj* **1** violent or ferocious. **2** spiteful or malicious. **3** extremely severe or harsh. ▪ **viciously** *adv*. ▪ **viciousness** *noun*. [14c: from Latin *vitiosus* faulty]

vicious circle *noun* a situation in which any attempt to resolve a problem creates others which in turn recreate the first one.

vicissitude *noun* an unpredictable change of fortune or circumstance. ▪ **vicissitudinous** *adj*. [16c: from Latin *vicissim* by turns]

victim *noun* **1** a person or animal subjected to death, suffering, ill-treatment or trickery. **2** a person or animal killed in a sacrifice or ritual. [15c: from Latin *victima* beast for sacrifice]

victimize *or* **-ise** *verb* to single someone or something out for hostile, unfair or vindictive treatment. ▪ **victimization** *noun*.

victor *noun* the winner or winning side in a war or contest. [14c: Latin, from *vincere* to conquer]

victoria *noun* a large oval red and yellow variety of plum with a sweet flavour. Also called **victoria plum**. [19c: named after Queen Victoria]

Victoria Cross *noun* (abbrev **VC**) the highest decoration in recognition of outstanding bravery in battle awarded to British and Commonwealth armed forces. [19c: established by Queen Victoria]

Victorian *adj* **1** relating to or characteristic of Queen Victoria or her reign (1837–1901). **2** of attitudes or values: **a** typical of the strictness or conventionality associated with this period; **b** typical of the hypocrisy and bigotry often thought to underlie these values. ▸ *noun* someone who lived during this period. [19c]

Victoriana *or* **victoriana** *plural noun* objects from the Victorian period in Britain, esp bric-à-brac.

victorious *adj* **1** having won a war or contest: *the victorious army*. **2** referring to, marking or representing a victory: *a victorious outcome*. ▪ **victoriously** *adv*.

victory *noun* (**-ies**) **1** success against an opponent in a war or contest. **2** an occurrence of this. [14c: from Latin *victoria*]

victual /ˈvɪtəl/ *verb* (***victualled, victualling***; *US* ***victualed, victualing***) **1** to supply with victuals. **2** *intr* to obtain supplies. **3** *intr* of animals: to eat victuals. See also **victuals**. ▪ **victualler** *or* (*US*) **victualer** *noun*.

victuals /ˈvɪtəlz/ *plural noun* (*occasionally* **victual**) food; provisions. [14c: from Latin *victualis*]

vicuña *or* **vicuna** /vɪˈkuːnjə/ *noun* a ruminant mammal, resembling a **llama** but smaller, with a light-brown coat and a yellowish-red bib. [17c: Spanish]

vide /ˈvaɪdiː/ *verb* (abbrev **vid.**) used as an instruction in a text: refer to or see, eg a particular page-number or section. [16c: Latin, imperative sing of *videre* to see]

videlicet see **viz.**

video *noun* **1** short for **video cassette**. **2** short for **video cassette recorder**. **3** a film or programme pre-recorded on video cassette. **4** the process of recording, reproducing or broadcasting of visual, esp televised, images on magnetic tape. ▸ *adj* relating to the process of or equipment for recording by video. ▸ *verb* (***videos, videoed***) to make a video cassette recording of (a TV programme, a film, etc). [20c: Latin, from *videre* to see]

video camera *noun, photog* a portable camera that records moving visual images directly on to videotape, which can then be played back on a video cassette recorder and viewed on the screen of a television receiver. Compare **camcorder**. [20c]

video cassette *noun* a cassette containing videotape, for use in a video cassette recorder.

video cassette recorder *noun* (abbrev **VCR**) a machine for recording and playing back TV broadcasts, and playing prerecorded tapes of motion pictures.

videoconference *noun* a discussion between people in different locations using electronically linked telephones and video screens. ▪ **videoconferencing** *noun*. [1970s]

video game *noun* any electronically operated game involving the manipulation of images produced by a computer program on a visual display unit, such as a computer screen, a TV screen, etc. [20c]

videophone *noun* a communication device like a telephone which also transmits a visual image. [20c]

video RAM *or* **VRAM** *noun, comput* video random access memory, a part of a computer's memory in which data controlling the visual display is stored.

video recorder *noun* a **video cassette recorder**.

videotape *noun* magnetic tape on which visual images and sound can be recorded.

vie *verb* (***vying***) *intr* (*often* **vie with sb for sth**) to compete or struggle with them for some gain or advantage. [16c: from French *envier* to challenge or invite]

Viet Cong *or* **Vietcong** *noun, hist* a member of the South Vietnamese communist guerrilla army in the Vietnam war of the 1960s and 1970s. [From Vietnamese *Viet Nam Cong San* Vietnamese Communist]

Vietnamese *noun* **1** (*pl* ***Vietnamese***) a citizen or inhabitant of, or person born in, Vietnam. **2** the language of Vietnam. ▸ *adj* belonging or relating to Vietnam, its people or their language.

view *noun* **1** an act or opportunity of seeing without obstruction: *a good view of the stage*. **2** something, esp a landscape, seen from a particular point: *a magnificent view from the summit*. **3** a range or field of vision: *out of view*. **4** a scene recorded in photograph or picture form. **5** a description or impression: *The book gives a view of life in Roman times*. **6** an opinion; a point of view. **7** a way of considering or understanding something: *a short-term view of the situation*. ▸ *verb* **1** to see or look at something. **2** to inspect or examine something: *viewed the house that was for sale*. **3** to consider or regard something. **4** *tr & intr* to watch (a programme) on TV; to watch TV. ▪ **viewer** *noun*. [15c: from French *veue* saw]
IDIOMS **in view of sth** taking account of it. **on view** displayed for all to see or inspect. **take a dim view of sth** to regard it disapprovingly or unfavourably. **with a view to sth** with the intention of achieving it.

viewdata *noun* a system by which computerized information can be displayed on a TV screen by means of a telephone link with a computer source.

viewfinder *noun* a device forming part of a camera that shows the area covered by the lens.

viewing *noun* an act or opportunity of seeing or inspecting something, eg a house for sale.

viewpoint *noun* **1 a** an interpretation of facts received; **b** an opinion or point of view; a standpoint. **2** a location which is particularly good for admiring scenery.

vigil *noun* **1** a period of staying awake, usu to guard or watch over a person or thing. **2** a stationary, peaceful demonstration for a specific cause. **3** the day before a major religious festival, traditionally spent in prayer. [13c: from Latin *vigila*]

vigilance *noun* the state of being watchful or observant. [16c: from Latin *vigilare* to keep awake]

vigilant *adj* ready for possible trouble or danger; alert; watchful. ▪ **vigilantly** *adv*.

vigilante /vɪdʒɪˈlantɪ/ *noun* **1** a member of an organization looking after the interests of a group threatened in some way, especially a self-appointed and unofficial policeman. **2** in the US: a member of a **vigilance committee**, an unauthorized body which exercises powers of arrest, punishment, etc. [19c: from Spanish, meaning 'vigilant']

vignette /viːnˈjɛt/ *noun* **1** a decorative design on a book's title page, traditionally of vine leaves. **2** a photographic portrait with the background deliberately faded. **3** a short literary essay, esp one describing a person's character. [19c: French, meaning 'little vine']

vigorous *adj* **1** strong and active. **2** forceful; energetic: *a vigorous approach to life*. ▪ **vigorously** *adv*.

vigour *or* (*N Am*) **vigor** *noun* **1** great strength and energy of body or mind. **2** liveliness or forcefulness of action. **3** in plants, etc: healthy growth. [14c: from Latin *vigor*]

Viking *or* **viking** *noun* any of the Scandinavian seafaring peoples who raided and settled in much of NW Europe between the 8c and 11c. *as adj*: *a Viking ship*. See also **Norseman**. [19c: from Norse *vikingr*]

vile *adj* **1** morally evil or wicked. **2** physically repulsive; disgusting. **3** *informal* extremely bad or unpleasant. ▪ **vilely** *adv*. ▪ **vileness** *noun*. [13c: from French *vil*]

vilify *verb* (**-ies, -ied**) to say insulting or abusive things about someone or something. ▪ **vilification** *noun*. [16c: from Latin *vilificare* to make worthless or base]

villa *noun* **1** a country residence. **2** a holiday home, esp one abroad. [17c: Latin, meaning 'country house']

village *noun* **1** a group of houses, shops and other buildings, smaller than a town and larger than a hamlet, esp in or near the countryside. **2** the people living in it, regarded as a community: *The village has started to gossip.* ▪ **villager** *noun.* [14c: French]

villain *noun* **1** the principal wicked character in a story. **2** any violent, wicked or unscrupulous person. **3** *informal* a criminal. [14c: orig meaning 'a rustic', from French *vilein* serf]

villainous *adj* like or worthy of a villain.

villainy *noun* (**-*ies***) **1** wicked or vile behaviour. **2** an act of this kind.

villein /'vɪlən/ *noun, hist, feudalism* a peasant worker bound to a lord and showing allegiance to him. ▪ **villeinage** *noun.* [14c: from French *vilein* serf]

villus *noun* (***villi***) **1** *anatomy* any of many tiny finger-like projections that line the inside of the small intestine and absorb the products of digestion. **2** *botany* a long soft hair. ▪ **villous** *adj.* [18c: Latin, meaning 'shaggy hair']

vim *noun, informal* energy; liveliness. [19c: perhaps from Latin *vis* force]

vinaigrette /vɪneɪ'grɛt/ *noun* (*also* **vinaigrette sauce**) a salad dressing made by mixing oil, vinegar and seasonings. [19c: French, from *vinaigre* vinegar]

vindaloo *noun* a hot Indian curry, usu made with meat, poultry or fish. [19c: prob from Portuguese *vin d'alho* wine and garlic sauce]

vindicate *verb* **1** to clear someone of blame or criticism. **2** to show something to have been worthwhile or justified. **3** to maintain or uphold (a point of view, cause, etc). ▪ **vindication** *noun.* [17c: from Latin *vindicare*]

vindictive *adj* **1** feeling or showing spite or hatred. **2** seeking revenge. [17c: from Latin *vindicta* vengeance]

vine *noun* **1** a woody climbing plant that produces grapes. **2** any climbing or trailing plant, including ivy. [13c: from French *vigne*]

vinegar *noun* **1** a sour liquid produced by the fermentation of alcoholic beverages such as cider or wine, used as a condiment and preservative. **2** bad temper or peevishness. [13c: from French *vinaigre* sour wine]

vineyard /'vɪnjəd/ *noun* a plantation of grape-bearing vines, esp for wine-making.

vingt-et-un /*French* vɛ̃teœ̃/ *noun, cards* **pontoon**[2]. [18c: French, meaning 'twenty-one']

viniculture *noun* the cultivation of grapes for wine-making. [19c: from Latin *vinum* wine + **culture**]

vino /'viːnoʊ/ *noun, slang* wine, esp of poor quality. [20c in this sense: Spanish and Italian, meaning 'wine']

vinous /'vaɪnəs/ *adj* **1** belonging or relating to, or resembling, wine. **2** caused by or indicative of an excess of wine: *a vinous complexion.* [17c: from Latin *vinosus*]

vintage *noun* **1** the grape-harvest of a particular year. **2** the wine produced from a year's harvest. **3** the time of year when grapes are harvested. **4** a particular period of origin, esp when regarded as productive: *literature of a postwar vintage.* ▸ *adj* **1** of wine: good quality and from a specified year. **2** typical of someone's best work or most characteristic behaviour: *That remark was vintage Churchill.* [15c: from Norman French]

vintage car *noun, Brit* an old motor car, specifically one built between 1919 and 1930. Compare **veteran car**.

vintner *noun, formal* a wine-merchant. [15c: from French *vinetier*]

vinyl /'vaɪnɪl/ *noun* **1** any of a group of tough plastics manufactured in various forms, eg paint additives and carpet fibres. **2** *informal* plastic records (see **record** *noun* sense 4) regarded collectively, as distinct from cassettes and CDs. ▸ *as adj*: *a vinyl record.* [19c: from Latin *vinum* wine + Greek *hyle* matter]

viol /'vaɪəl/ *noun* a Renaissance stringed musical instrument played with a bow. [15c: from French *vielle*]

viola[1] /vɪ'oʊlə/ *noun* a musical instrument of the violin family, larger than the violin and lower in pitch. [18c: Italian and Spanish]

viola[2] /'vaɪələ/ *noun* any of various plants native to temperate regions, including the violet and pansy. [18c: Latin, meaning 'violet']

violate *verb* **1** to disregard or break (a law, agreement or oath). **2** to treat (something sacred or private) with disrespect. **3** to disturb or disrupt (eg a person's privacy). **4** to rape or sexually abuse someone. ▪ **violation** *noun.* [15c: from Latin *violare* to treat violently]

violence *noun* **1** the state or quality of being violent. **2** violent behaviour. [13c: from Latin *violentus*, from *vis* force]

violent *adj* **1** marked by or using extreme physical force. **2** using or involving the use of such force to cause physical harm. **3** impulsively aggressive and unrestrained in nature or behaviour. **4** intense; extreme: *They took a violent dislike to me.* ▪ **violently** *adv.*

violet *noun* **1** a plant with large purple, blue or white petals. **2** a bluish-purple colour. ▸ *adj* violet-coloured. [14c: from French *violette*]

violin *noun* a four-stringed musical instrument, which is usu held with one end under the chin and played with a bow. See also **fiddle** (*noun* sense 1). ▪ **violinist** *noun.* [16c: from Italian *violino* little viol]

violist *noun* someone who plays the viol or viola.

violoncello /vaɪələn'tʃɛloʊ/ *noun, formal* a **cello**. ▪ **violoncellist** *noun.* [18c: Italian, diminutive of *violone* double bass viol]

VIP *abbrev* very important person.

viper *noun* **1** a poisonous snake with long fangs through which venom is injected into the prey. **2** an **adder**. **3** a treacherous or spiteful person. [16c: from Latin *vipera*]

virago /vɪ'rɑːgoʊ/ *noun* (***viragoes*** *or* ***viragos***) *literary* a loudly fierce or abusive woman. [11c: Latin, meaning 'manlike woman']

viral /'vaɪərəl/ *adj* belonging or relating to or caused by a virus.

virgin *noun* **1** a person, esp a woman, who has never had sexual intercourse. **2** (**the Virgin**) *RC Church* a name for Mary, the mother of Jesus Christ. ▸ *adj* **1** never having had sexual intercourse; chaste. **2** in its original state; never having been used. [13c: from Latin *virgo* maiden]

virginal[1] *adj* **1** belonging or relating or appropriate to a virgin. **2** in a state of virginity.

virginal[2] *noun* a keyboard instrument, used in the 16c and 17c, like a small harpsichord but with strings set at right angles to the keys. [16c: perhaps so called because it was mostly played by young women]

Virgin Birth *noun, Christianity* the birth of Christ to the Virgin Mary, regarded as an act of God.

Virginia creeper *noun* a N American climbing-plant whose foliage turns bright red in autumn.

virginity *noun* the state of being a virgin.

Virgo *noun* (*pl* in sense b ***Virgos***) *astrol* **a** the sixth sign of the zodiac; **b** a person born between 23 August and 22 September, under this sign. ▪ **Virgoan** *noun, adj*. [14c: Latin, meaning 'virgin']

virile *adj* displaying or requiring qualities regarded as typically masculine, esp physical strength. ▪ **virility** *noun*. [15c: from Latin *virilis*, from *vir* man]

virology *noun, med* the branch of microbiology concerned with the study of viruses and viral diseases. ▪ **virological** *adj*. ▪ **virologist** *noun*.

virtual *adj* **1** being so in effect or in practice, but not in name: *a virtual state of war*. **2** nearly so; almost but not quite: *the virtual collapse of the steel industry*. **3** *comput, slang* referring or relating to interaction, connection, use, etc via **the Internet**: *pay by virtual money*. **4** *comput* of memory or storage: appearing to be internal but actually transferred a segment at a time as required from (and to) back-up storage into (and out of) the smaller internal memory. [17c in sense 1: from Latin *virtualis*]

virtually *adv* **1** in practice, though not strictly speaking: *was virtually in charge of us*. **2** almost; nearly: *The war is virtually over.*

virtual reality *noun* (abbrev **VR**) a computer simulation of a real or artificial environment that gives the user the impression of actually being within the environment and interacting with it, eg by way of a special visor and special gloves which are worn by the user.

virtue *noun* **1** a quality regarded as morally good. **2** moral goodness; righteousness. **3** an admirable quality or desirable feature: *The virtue of this one is its long life*. **4** virginity, esp in women. [13c: from French *vertu*]

IDIOMS **by virtue of sth** because of it; on account of it.

virtuoso *noun* **1** someone with remarkable artistic skill, esp a brilliant musical performer. *as adj*: *a virtuoso performance*. **2** someone with a great knowledge or collection of fine art. ▪ **virtuosity** *noun*. [17c: Italian, meaning 'skilful']

virtuous *adj* **1** possessing or showing virtue; morally sound. **2** esp of a woman: chaste. ▪ **virtuously** *adv*.

virulent /ˈvɪrʊlənt, ˈvɪrjʊ-/ *adj* **1** of a disease: having a rapidly harmful effect. **2** of a disease or the organism causing it: extremely infectious. **3** of a substance: highly poisonous. **4** bitterly hostile. ▪ **virulence** *noun*. [14c: from Latin *virulentus* venomous]

virus *noun* **1** an infectious particle, only visible under an electron microscope, that invades the cells of animals, plants and bacteria, and can only survive and reproduce within such cells. **2** the organism that causes and transmits an infectious disease. **3** *loosely* a disease caused by such an organism. **4** (*in full* **computer virus**) a self-replicating program that attaches to a computer system and when activated can corrupt or destroy data stored on the hard disk. [16c: Latin, meaning 'slimy liquid']

visa *noun* a permit stamped into a passport, or a similar document, allowing the holder to enter or leave the country that issues it. [19c: French]

visage /ˈvɪzɪdʒ/ *noun, literary* **1** the face. **2** the usual expression of a face; a countenance. [14c: French]

vis-à-vis /viːzɑːˈviː/ *prep* in relation to something or someone. [18c: French, from Latin *visus* face]

viscera /ˈvɪsərə/ *plural noun, anatomy* the internal organs of the body, esp those found in the abdominal cavity. [17c: Latin, pl of *viscus* internal organ]

visceral /ˈvɪsərəl/ *adj* **1** belonging or relating to the viscera. **2** belonging or relating to the feelings, esp the basic human instincts as distinct from the intellect.

viscid /ˈvɪsɪd/ *adj* glutinous; sticky. [17c: from Latin *viscum* bird-lime]

viscose *noun* **1** cellulose in a viscous state, able to be made into thread. **2** **rayon** made from such thread. [19c]

viscosity *noun* (***-ies***) **1** a measure of the resistance of a fluid to flow, caused by internal friction. **2** a quantity expressing this, measured in units of **pascal** or **poise**.

viscount /ˈvaɪkaʊnt/ *noun* a member of the British nobility ranked below an earl and above a baron. ▪ **viscountcy** *noun* (***-ies***). [14c: from French *visconte*]

viscountess /ˈvaɪkaʊntɪs/ *noun* **1** the wife or widow of a viscount. **2** a woman of the rank of viscount in her own right.

viscous *adj* **1** with a thick semi-liquid consistency; not flowing easily. **2** of liquid: sticky. [14c: from Latin *viscosus* sticky]

vise the *N Am* spelling of **vice**[1]

Vishnu *noun, Hinduism* a Hindu god, regarded by some worshippers as the saviour. [18c: Sanskrit]

visibility *noun* (***-ies***) **1** the state or fact of being visible. **2** the range in which one can see clearly in given conditions of light and weather: *visibility down to 20 yards*.

visible *adj* **1** able to be seen. **2** able to be realized or perceived; apparent: *his visible discomfort*. **3** *econ* relating to actual goods rather than services. ▪ **visibly** *adv*. [14c: from Latin *visibilis*, from *videre* to see]

visible horizon see **horizon**

visible spectrum *noun, physics* the range of wavelengths of electromagnetic radiation that can be seen by the human eye, ie visible light.

Visigoth *noun, hist* a member of the Western Goths, who formed settlements in France and Spain in the 5c and whose kingdom in Spain lasted until the 8c. Compare **Ostrogoth**. [17c: from Latin *Visigothus*, with the first element perhaps meaning 'west']

vision *noun* **1** the ability or faculty of perceiving with the eye; sight. **2** an image conjured up vividly in the imagination. **3** the ability to perceive what is likely, and plan wisely for it; foresight. **4** an image communicated supernaturally, esp by God; an apparition. **5** **a** the picture on a TV screen; **b** the quality of such a picture. **6** someone or something of overwhelming beauty: *a vision in pink*. [13c: from Latin *visio* sight]

visionary *adj* **1** showing great foresight or imagination. **2** possible only in the imagination; fanciful. **3** capable of seeing supernatural images or apparitions. ▸ *noun* (***-ies***) a visionary person.

visit *verb* **1** *tr & intr* to go or come to see (a person or place) socially or professionally. **2** *tr & intr* to go or come to stay with someone temporarily. **3** (*usu* **visit sth on sb**) to inflict (harm or punishment) on them. **4** (*usu* **visit sb with sth**) *old use* to afflict or trouble them. **5** *N Am informal* (*usu* **visit with sb**) to have a chat with them. ▸ *noun* **1** an act of visiting; a social or professional call. **2** a temporary stay. **3** a sightseeing excursion. [13c: from Latin *visitare*]

visitant *noun* **1** *relig* a person appearing in a supernatural vision; an apparition. **2** a **visitor** (sense 2).

visitation *noun* **1** an official visit or inspection. **2** an event regarded as a divine punishment or reward. **3** an instance of seeing a supernatural vision.

visiting card *noun* a card with one's name, address, etc printed on it, which is left instead of a formal visit. *N Am equivalent* **calling card**.

visitor *noun* **1** someone who visits a person or place. **2** (*also* **visitant**) a migratory bird present in a place for a time: *winter visitors*.

visor *or* **vizor** /ˈvaɪzə(r)/ *noun* **1** the movable part of a helmet, covering the face. **2** a flap at the top of a vehicle's windscreen that can be lowered to shield the driver's eyes from the sun's rays. **3** a peaked shield that is worn on the head to protect the eyes from the sun's rays. [14c: from French *viser*, from *vis* face]

vista *noun* **1** a view into the distance. **2** a mental vision extending over a lengthy period of time into the future or past. [17c: Italian, meaning 'view']

visual *adj* **1** relating to or received through sight or vision: *a visual image*. **2** creating vivid mental images: *visual poetry*. ▪ **visually** *adv*. [15c: from Latin *visualis*, from *visus* sight]

visual aid *noun* a picture, film or other visual material used as an aid to teaching or presenting information.

Visual Basic *noun, comput* (abbrev **VB**) a form of the programming language BASIC, widely used in creating graphics and software.

visual display unit *noun* (abbrev **VDU**) a screen on which information from a computer is displayed.

visualize *or* **-ise** *verb* to form a clear mental image of someone or something. ▪ **visualization** *noun*.

vital *adj* **1** relating to or essential for life: *the vital organs*. **2** determining life or death, or success or failure: *a vital error*. **3** essential; of the greatest importance. **4** full of life; energetic. ▸ *noun* (**vitals**) the vital organs, including the brain, heart and lungs. ▪ **vitally** *adv*. [14c: from Latin *vitalis*, from *vita* life]

vital capacity *noun, physiol* the amount of air that can be expelled from the lungs after taking the deepest breath possible.

vitality *noun* **1** liveliness and energy. **2** the state of being alive; the ability to stay alive.

vitalize *or* **-ise** *verb* to fill someone with life or energy. ▪ **vitalization** *noun*.

vital statistics *plural noun* **1** statistics concerning births, marriages, deaths and other matters relating to population. **2** *informal* a woman's bust, waist and hip measurements.

vitamin *noun* any of various organic compounds that occur in small amounts in many foods, are also manufactured synthetically and are essential in small amounts for the normal growth and functioning of the body. [20c: from Latin *vita* life + **amine**]

vitamin A *noun* a vitamin found in liver, fish oils, dairy products and egg yolk, required for normal growth and correct functioning of the eyes. Also called **retinol**.

vitamin B_1 *noun* a member of the vitamin B complex found in yeast, wheat germ, peas, beans and green vegetables, a deficiency of which causes **beriberi**. Also called **thiamine**. Previously called **aneurin**.

vitamin B_2 *noun* a member of the vitamin B complex, found in eg yeast, liver and green vegetables, which is required to promote growth in children. Also called **riboflavin, riboflavine**.

vitamin B_6 *noun* a member of the vitamin B complex found in milk, eggs, liver, cereal grains, yeast and fresh vegetables, required for the metabolism of amino acids. Also called **pyridoxine**.

vitamin B_7 *noun* a member of the vitamin B complex found in liver, yeast extracts, cereals, peas and beans, essential for human nutrition and prevention of **pellagra**. Also called **nicotinic acid, niacin**.

vitamin B_{12} *noun* a member of the vitamin B complex found in eggs, milk and liver, and required for the formation of red blood cells (and hence prevention of pernicious anaemia). Also called **cyanocobalamin**.

vitamin B complex *noun* any of a group of closely interrelated, but distinctly different, vitamins found in yeast, liver and wheat germ, and referred to either by individual B numbers, eg **vitamin B_1, vitamin B_2**, or by specific names, eg thiamine, riboflavin.

vitamin C *noun* a vitamin found in fresh fruits, esp citrus fruits and blackcurrants, potatoes and green vegetables, required for the maintenance of healthy bones, cartilage and teeth. Also called **ascorbic acid**.

vitamin D *noun* a complex of vitamin D_2 (**calciferol**), provitamin D_2 (**ergosterol**) and vitamin D_3 (**cholecalciferol**), found in fish liver oils, egg yolk and milk, and required for the deposition of adequate amounts of calcium and phosphates in the bones (and hence to prevent **rickets**) and teeth.

vitamin E *noun* a vitamin found in wholemeal flour, wheat germ and green vegetables, and which may be required for maintenance of the structure of cell membranes. Also called **tocopherol**.

vitamin H *noun* **biotin**.

vitamin K *noun* either of two fat-soluble organic compounds (vitamins K_1 and K_2) found in green leafy vegetables, and also manufactured by bacteria in the intestines, necessary for blood clotting.

vitamin P *noun* **bioflavonoid**.

vitiate /ˈvɪʃɪeɪt/ *verb* **1** to impair the quality or effectiveness of (eg an argument); to make something faulty or defective. **2** to make (eg a legal contract) invalid. ▪ **vitiation** *noun*. [16c: from Latin *vitiare*]

viticulture *noun* the cultivation of grapes for making wine; viniculture. [19c: from Latin *vitis* vine + **culture**]

vitreous *adj* **1** relating to or consisting of glass. **2** like glass in hardness, sheen or transparency: *vitreous china*. [17c: from Latin *vitreus*]

vitreous humour *noun, anatomy* a gelatinous substance inside the eye, between the lens and the retina. Compare **aqueous humour**.

vitrify *verb* (**-ies, -ied**) *tr & intr* to make into or become glass or something like glass, esp by heating. ▪ **vitrification** *noun*. [16c: from French *vitrifier*]

vitriol *noun* **1** concentrated sulphuric acid. **2** extremely bitter or hateful speech or criticism. [14c: from Latin *vitriolum*]

vitriolic *adj* extremely bitter or hateful.

vituperate /vɪ'tʃuːpəreɪt/ *verb* **1** to attack someone with abusive criticism or disapproval. **2** *intr* to use abusive language. ▪ **vituperation** *noun*. ▪ **vituperative** *adj*. [16c: from Latin *vituperare* to blame]

viva[1] /'viːvə/ *exclam* long live (someone or something named): *viva Rodriguez!* [17c: Spanish and Italian, meaning 'live']

viva[2] /'vaɪvə/ *noun* a **viva voce**. ▶ *verb* (***vivaed, vivaing***) to examine someone orally. [19c: Latin, shortened from **viva voce**]

vivace /vɪ'vɑːtʃɪ/ *music, adv* in a lively manner. ▶ *adj* lively. [17c: Italian]

vivacious *adj* attractively lively and animated. ▪ **vivacity** *noun*. [17c: from Latin *vivax* lively]

vivarium *noun* (***vivariums*** *or* ***vivaria***) any place or enclosure in which live animals are kept, esp under natural conditions. [16c: Latin, from *vivere* to live]

viva voce /'vaɪvə 'voʊtʃɪ/ *adv* in speech; orally. ▶ *noun* an oral examination, usu for an academic qualification. Often shortened to **viva**. [16c: Latin, meaning 'by the living voice']

vivid *adj* **1** of a colour: strong and bright. **2** creating or providing a clear and immediate mental picture: *gave a vivid account of the incident*. ▪ **vividly** *adv*. ▪ **vividness** *noun*. [17c: from Latin *vividus* lively]

vivify *verb* (***-ies, -ied***) **1** to give something life. **2** to make something more vivid or startling. ▪ **vivification** *noun*. [16c: from French *vivifier*]

viviparous /vɪ'vɪpərəs, vaɪ-/ *adj, zool* of an animal: giving birth to live young, as in humans and most other mammals. Compare **oviparous, ovoviviparous**. [17c: from Latin *vivus* alive + *parere* to produce]

vivisection *noun* the practice of dissecting living animals for experimental purposes. ▪ **vivisectionist** *noun*. [18c: from Latin *vivus* living + *secare* to cut]

vixen *noun* **1** a female fox. **2** a fierce or spiteful woman. [Anglo-Saxon *fyxen*]

viz. *adv* (*in full* **videlicet** /vɪ'deɪlɪsɛt/) used esp in writing: namely; that is. [16c: Latin]

vizier /vɪ'zɪə(r)/ *noun* a high-ranking government official in some Muslim countries. [16c: from Turkish *vezir*]

vizor see **visor**

VLF *abbrev, radio* very low frequency.

V-neck *noun* **1** the open neck of a garment cut or formed to a point at the front. **2** a garment, esp a pullover, with such a neck.

vocab *noun, informal* vocabulary.

vocabulary *noun* (***-ies***) **1** the words used in speaking or writing a particular language. **2** the words, or range of words, known to or used by a particular person or group. **3** a list of words with translations in another language alongside. [16c: from Latin *vocabularius*]

vocal *adj* **1** relating to or produced by the voice. **2** expressing opinions or criticism freely and forcefully: *She was very vocal in her support for the homeless.* **3** *phonetics* voiced. ▶ *noun* (**vocals**) the parts of a musical composition that are sung, as distinct from the instrumental accompaniment. ▪ **vocally** *adv*. [14c: from Latin *vocalis*, from *vox* voice]

vocal cords *plural noun, anatomy* in mammals: the two folds of tissue within the larynx that vibrate and produce sound when air is expelled from the lungs.

vocalist *noun* a singer, esp in a pop group or jazz band.

vocalize *or* **-ise** *verb* **1** to utter or produce something with the voice. **2** to express in words; to articulate. ▪ **vocalization** *noun*.

vocation *noun* **1** a particular occupation or profession, esp one regarded as needing dedication and skill. **2** a feeling of being especially suited for a particular type of work. **3** *relig* a divine calling to adopt a religious life or perform good works. ▪ **vocational** *adj*. [15c: from Latin *vocare* to call]

vocative *grammar, noun* **1** in some languages, eg Latin and Greek: the form or **case**[2] of a noun, pronoun or adjective used when a person or thing is addressed directly. **2** a noun, etc in this case. ▶ *adj* belonging to or in this case. [15c: from Latin *vocare* to call]

vociferate *verb, tr & intr, formal* **1** to exclaim loudly and forcefully. **2** to shout or cry in a loud voice; to bawl. [17c: from Latin *vociferari*]

vociferous *adj* **1** loud and forceful, esp in expressing opinions. **2** noisy. ▪ **vociferously** *adv*.

vodka *noun* a clear alcoholic spirit of Russian origin, traditionally made from rye, but sometimes from potatoes. [19c: Russian, literally 'little water']

vogue *noun* (*usu* **the vogue**) the current fashion or trend in any sphere. ▪ **voguish** *adj*. [16c: French, meaning 'fashion' or 'rowing']

voice *noun* **1** a sound produced by the vocal organs and uttered through the mouth, esp by humans in speech or song. **2** the ability to speak; the power of speech: *lost his voice*. **3** a way of speaking or singing peculiar to each individual: *couldn't recognize the voice*. **4** a tone of speech reflecting a particular emotion: *in a nervous voice*. **5** the sound of someone speaking: *heard a voice*. **6** the ability to sing, esp to sing well: *has a lovely voice*. **7** expression in the form of spoken words: *gave voice to their feelings*. **8** a means or medium of expression or communication: *newspapers as the voice of the people*. **9** *grammar* the status or function of a verb in being either **active** or **passive**. ▶ *verb* **1** to express something in speech: *He voiced his disapproval.* **2** *phonetics* to pronounce (a sound) with a vibration of the vocal cords. [13c: from French *vois*, from Latin *vox*]

voice box *noun, informal* the larynx.

voiced *adj* **1** expressed in speech. **2** *phonetics* pronounced with a vibration of the vocal cords, as in *z, d, b*.

voiceless *adj* **1** without a voice. **2** *phonetics* produced without vibration of the vocal cords, as in *s, t, p*.

voice mail *or* **voicemail** *noun* a system by which telephone messages can be stored in a central location and listened to by the addressee later.

voice-over *noun* the voice of an unseen narrator in a film, TV advertisement or programme, etc. [20c]

void *adj* **1** not valid or legally binding: *declared the contract null and void*. **2** containing nothing; empty or unoccupied. **3** (*usu* **void of sth**) lacking in it: *void of humour*. ▶ *noun* **1** an empty space. **2** a feeling of absence or emptiness strongly felt. ▶ *verb* **1** to make empty or clear. **2** to invalidate or nullify. **3** to empty (the bladder or bowels). [13c: from French *voide* empty]

voile /vɔɪl, vwɑːl/ *noun* a thin semi-transparent fabric. [19c: French, meaning 'veil']

vol. *or* **vol** *abbrev* **1** volume. **2** volunteer. **3** voluntary.

volatile *adj* **1** changing quickly from a solid or liquid into a vapour. **2** easily becoming angry or violent. **3** of a situation, etc: liable to change quickly, esp verging on violence. **4** *comput* of a memory: not able to retain data after the power supply has been cut off. ▪ **volatility** *noun.* [17c: from Latin *volatilis*]

volatile oil see **essential oil**

vol-au-vent /ˈvɒloʊvɑ̃/ *noun* a small round puff-pastry case with a savoury filling. [19c: French, literally 'flight in the wind']

volcanic *adj* **1** relating to or produced by a volcano or volcanoes. **2** easily erupting into anger or violence: *a volcanic temper.*

volcano *noun* (***volcanoes***) a vent in the Earth's crust through which **magma** is or has previously been forced out onto the surface, usu taking the form of a conical hill due to the build-up of solidified lava. [17c: Italian, from Latin *Vulcanus* Roman god of fire]

vole *noun* a small rodent related to the lemming, with a small tail, blunt snout and smaller eyes and ears. [19c: orig *vole-mouse*]

volition *noun* the act of willing or choosing; the exercising of one's will: *She did it of her own volition.* ▪ **volitional** *adj.* [17c: French, from Latin *volitio*]

volley *noun* **1 a** a firing of several guns or other weapons simultaneously; **b** the bullets, missiles, etc discharged. **2** an aggressive outburst, esp of criticism or insults. **3** *sport* a striking of the ball before it bounces. ▸ *verb* **1** *tr & intr* to fire (weapons) in a volley. **2** *tr & intr, sport* to strike (a ball) before it bounces. **3** to utter (words, oaths, etc) in an aggressive outburst. [16c: from French *volée*]

volleyball *noun, sport* a game for two teams of six players each, in which a large ball is volleyed back and forth over a high net with the hands.

volt *noun* (symbol **V**) in the SI system: a unit of electric potential, the difference in potential that will carry a current of one ampere across a resistance of one ohm. [19c: named after the Italian physicist Alessandro Volta]

voltage *noun, elec* potential difference expressed as a number of volts.

voltaic cell see **primary cell**

volte-face /vɒltˈfɑːs/ *noun* a sudden and complete reversal of opinion or policy. [19c: French]

voltmeter *noun, elec* an instrument that measures electromotive force in volts.

voluble *adj* **1** speaking or spoken insistently or with ease. **2** tending to talk at great length. ▪ **volubility** *noun.* ▪ **volubly** *adv.* [16c: from Latin *volubilis*]

volume *noun* **1** the amount of three-dimensional space occupied by an object, gas or liquid. **2 a** loudness of sound; **b** the control that adjusts it on a radio, hi-fi system, etc. **3** a book, whether complete in itself or one of several forming a larger work. **4** an amount or quantity, esp when large: *the volume of traffic.* [14c: from French, from Latin *volumen* 'roll' or 'scroll']

volumetric analysis *noun, chem* a method of chemical analysis in which the concentration of a solution of known volume is determined.

voluminous *adj* **1** of clothing: flowing out; ample. **2** of writing: enough to fill many volumes. ▪ **voluminously** *adv.* [17c: from Latin *voluminosus*]

voluntary *adj* **1** done or acting by free choice, not by compulsion. **2** working with no expectation of being paid or otherwise rewarded. **3** of work: unpaid. **4** of an organization: staffed by unpaid workers; supported by donations of money freely given. **5** of a movement, muscle or limb: produced or controlled by the will. **6** spontaneous; carried out without any persuasion. ▸ *noun* (***-ies***) a piece of music, usu for an organ, played before, during or after a church service. ▪ **voluntarily** *adv.* [14c: from Latin *voluntarius*]

volunteer *verb* **1** *tr & intr* (*often* **volunteer for sth**) to offer one's help or services freely, without being persuaded or forced. **2** *intr* to go into military service by choice, without being conscripted. **3** to give (information, etc) unasked. **4** *informal* to assign someone to perform a task or give help without first asking them: *I'm volunteering you for playground duty.* ▸ *noun* **1** someone who volunteers. **2** someone carrying out voluntary work. **3** a member of a non-professional army of voluntary soldiers. [17c: from French *voluntaire*]

voluptuary *noun* (***-ies***) someone addicted to luxury and sensual pleasures. ▸ *adj* promoting or characterized by luxury and sensual pleasures. [17c: from Latin *voluptas* pleasure]

voluptuous *adj* **1** relating to or suggestive of sensual pleasure. **2** of a woman: full-figured and attractive; curvaceous. ▪ **voluptuously** *adv.* ▪ **voluptuousness** *noun.* [14c: from Latin *voluptas* pleasure]

volute *noun* a spiral. [17c: from Latin *volvere* to roll]

vomit *verb* **1** *tr & intr* to eject the contents of the stomach forcefully through the mouth through a reflex action; to be sick. **2** to emit or throw something out with force or violence. ▸ *noun* the contents of the stomach ejected during the process of vomiting. [14c: from Latin *vomere*]

voodoo *noun* **1** witchcraft of a type orig practised by the Black peoples of the West Indies and southern US. **2** the beliefs and practices of the religious cult that developed it, including serpent-worship and human sacrifice. [19c: from *vodu* (in various W African languages) spirit or demon]

voracious *adj* **1** eating or craving food in large quantities. **2** extremely eager in some respect: *a voracious reader.* ▪ **voraciously** *adv.* ▪ **voracity** *noun.* [17c: from Latin *vorare* to devour]

vortex /ˈvɔːtɛks/ *noun* (***vortexes*** *or* ***vortices*** /-tɪsiːz/) **1** a whirlpool or whirlwind; any whirling mass or motion. **2** a situation or activity into which all surrounding people or things are helplessly drawn. ▪ **vortical** *adj.* [17c: Latin, meaning 'a whirlpool']

votary *noun* (***-ies***) **1** someone bound by solemn vows to a religious life. **2** someone dedicated to a particular cause or activity. [16c: from Latin *vovere* to vow]

vote *noun* **1** a formal indication of choice or opinion, eg in an election or debate. **2** the right to express a choice or opinion, esp in a national election. **3** a choice or opinion expressed formally, eg by a show of hands, a mark on a list of options, etc: *a vote in favour of the motion.* **4** the support given by a certain sector of the population, or to a particular candidate or group, in this way: *He'll attract the middle-class vote.* ▸ *verb* **1** *intr* to cast or register a vote: *Have* *you voted yet?* • *I voted against the proposal.* **2** to decide, state, grant or bring about something by a majority of votes: *They voted that the tax be abolished* • *voted to accept the proposal.* **3** (**vote sb in**) to appoint them by voting; to elect them: *voted the Green candidate in.* **4** *informal* to declare or pronounce by general consent: *The show was voted a success.* **5** *informal* to propose or suggest something: *I vote that we go for a swim.* ▪ **voter** *noun.* [14c: from Latin *votum* wish]

PHRASAL VERBS **vote sb** *or* **sth down** to defeat them or it by voting.

votive *adj, relig* done or given in thanks to a deity, or to fulfil a vow or promise. [16c: from Latin *votivus*]

vouch *verb* **1** *intr* (*usu* **vouch for sb** *or* **sth**) to give a firm assurance or guarantee of their authenticity, trustworthiness, etc. **2** to give (evidence) in support of a statement, assertion, etc. [16c: from French *voucher* to call upon to defend]

voucher *noun* **1** a ticket or paper serving as proof, eg of the purchase or receipt of goods. **2** *esp in compounds* a ticket worth a specific amount of money, exchangeable for goods or services up to the same value: *gift voucher.*

vouchsafe *verb, tr & intr, literary* **1** to agree or condescend to do, give, grant or allow. **2** (*usu* **vouchsafe to do sth**) to condescend to do it. [14c]

vow *noun* **1** a solemn and binding promise. **2** (*often* **vows**) a solemn or formal promise of fidelity or affection: *marriage vows.* ▸ *verb, tr & intr* to promise or declare solemnly, or threaten emphatically; to swear. [13c: from French *vou*]

vowel *noun* **1** any speech-sound made with an open mouth and no contact between mouth, lips, teeth or tongue. **2** a letter of the alphabet, used alone or in combination, representing such a sound, in English, eg *a, e, i, o, u, ai, oa* and in some words *y.* Compare **consonant**. [14c: from French *vouel*]

vox pop *noun* **1** popular opinion derived from comments given informally by members of the public. **2** an interview in which such opinions are expressed. [20c: shortened from **vox populi**]

vox populi /vɒks ˈpɒpjʊliː, -laɪ/ *noun* public opinion. [16c: Latin, meaning 'voice of the people']

voyage *noun* **1** a long journey to a distant place. **2** a journey into space. ▸ *verb, intr* to go on a voyage. ▪ **voyager** *noun.* [13c: from French *voiage*]

voyeur /vwaːˈjɜː(r)/ *noun* someone who derives gratification from furtively watching others. ▪ **voyeurism** *noun.* ▪ **voyeuristic** *adj.* [20c: French, from *voir* to see]

VR *abbrev* virtual reality.

VRAM see **video RAM**

vs *or* **vs.** *abbrev* versus.

VSO *abbrev* Voluntary Service Overseas, a British organization that promotes voluntary work, mainly by young people, in developing countries.

VSOP *abbrev* very special old pale, a port, sherry or brandy between 20 and 25 years old.

VTOL /ˈviːtɒl/ *noun* **1** a system that allows an aircraft to take off and land vertically. **2** an aircraft that is fitted with this system. [20c: from *v*ertical *t*ake-*o*ff and *l*anding]

VTR *abbrev* videotape recorder.

vulcanite *noun* hard black vulcanized rubber.

vulcanize *or* **-ise** *verb* to treat natural or artificial rubber with various concentrations of sulphur or sulphur compounds at high temperatures for specific times, so as to harden it and increase its elasticity. ▪ **vulcanization** *noun.* [19c: from Latin *Vulcanus* Roman god of fire]

vulgar *adj* **1** marked by a lack of politeness or social or cultural refinement; coarse. **2** belonging or relating to the form of a language commonly spoken, rather than formal or literary language; vernacular. ▪ **vulgarly** *adv.* [15c: from Latin *vulgaris*]

vulgar fraction *noun* a fraction expressed in the form of a numerator above a denominator, rather than in decimal form. Compare **decimal fraction**.

vulgarian *noun* a vulgar person, esp one who is rich.

vulgarism *noun* **1** a vulgar expression in speech. **2** an example of vulgar behaviour.

vulgarity *noun* (**-ies**) **1** coarseness in speech or behaviour. **2** an instance of it.

vulgarize *or* **-ise** *verb* **1** to make something vulgar. **2** to make something common or popular, or spoil it in this way. ▪ **vulgarization** *noun.*

Vulgate *noun* a Latin version of the Bible prepared mainly by St Jerome in the 4c. [17c: from Latin *vulgata (editio)* popular (edition) (of the Bible)]

vulnerable *adj* **1** easily hurt or harmed physically or emotionally. **2** easily tempted or persuaded. **3** (*often* **vulnerable to sth** *or* **sb**) unprotected against physical or verbal attack from them. **4** *bridge* of a side that has won a game towards the rubber: liable to increased bonuses or penalties. ▪ **vulnerability** *noun* (**-ies**). ▪ **vulnerably** *adv.* [17c: from Latin *vulnerabilis*]

vulpine *adj* **1** belonging or relating to, or resembling, a fox. **2** *formal* cunning. [17c: from Latin *vulpes* fox]

vulture *noun* **1** a large bird with a bare head and a strongly curved beak, which feeds on carrion. **2** someone who exploits the downfall or death of another. [14c: from French *voltour*]

vulva *noun, anatomy* the two pairs of labia surrounding the opening to the vagina; the external female genitals. [16c: Latin, meaning 'wrapping' or 'womb']

vying *present participle of* **vie**

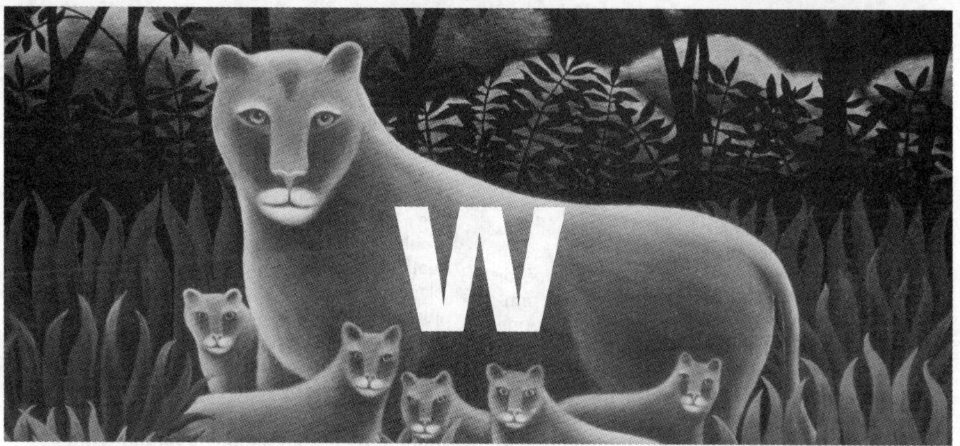

W[1] *or* **w** *noun* (***Ws, W's*** *or* ***w's***) the twenty-third letter of the English alphabet.

W[2] *symbol, chem* tungsten (or wolfram).

W[3] *abbrev* **1** watt. **2** West. **3** Western.

w *abbrev* **1** week. **2** weight. **3** *cricket* wicket. **4** wide. **5** width. **6** with.

WA *abbrev, Aust state* Western Australia.

wacko *informal, adj* mad or crazy; eccentric. ▸ *noun* a mad, crazy or eccentric person. [20c: from **wacky**]

wacky *or* **whacky** *adj* (***-ier, -iest***) *informal, orig N Am, esp US* mad or crazy; eccentric. ▪ **wackiness** *noun*. [20c: dialect, meaning 'left-handed' and 'fool']

wad /wɒd/ *noun* **1** a compressed mass of soft material used for packing or stuffing, etc. **2** a compact roll or bundle of banknotes, etc. [16c: from Latin *wadda*]

wadding *noun* material used as padding or stuffing.

waddle /ˈwɒdəl/ *verb, intr* to sway from side to side in walking. ▸ *noun* the act of waddling. [14c]

wade *verb* **1** *tr & intr* to walk through (something, esp deep water, which does not allow easy movement of the feet). **2** *intr* (*usu* **wade through sth**) to make one's way laboriously through it: *wading through legal documents.* [Anglo-Saxon *wadan* to go]

PHRASAL VERBS **wade in** to involve oneself unhesitatingly and enthusiastically in a task, etc.

wader *noun* **1** any long-legged bird that wades in marshes, or along the shores of rivers, lakes or seas. **2** (**waders**) thigh-high waterproof boots used by anglers.

wadi *or* **wady** /ˈwɒdɪ/ *noun* (***wadies***) a rocky river bed in N Africa and Arabia, dry except during the rains. [19c: Arabic]

wafer *noun* **1** a thin light finely layered kind of biscuit, served eg with ice cream. **2** *Christianity* a thin disc of unleavened bread or rice paper served to communicants at Holy Communion. **3** *comput* a thin disc of silicon from which chips are cut. [14c: Dutch]

waffle[1] *noun, cookery* a light-textured cake made of batter, with a distinctive grid-like surface pattern. [18c: from Dutch *wafel*]

waffle[2] *informal, verb, intr* (*also* **waffle on**) to talk or write at length but to little purpose. ▸ *noun* talk or writing of this kind. [19c: orig Scots and N England dialect]

waft *verb, tr & intr* to float or make (something) float or drift gently, esp through the air. ▸ *noun* **1** the action of wafting. **2** a whiff, eg of perfume. [16c: back formation from obsolete *wafter* escort vessel]

wag *verb* (***wagged, wagging***) **1** *tr & intr* to wave (something) to and fro vigorously. **2** *intr* of the tongue, chin or beard: to move in light or gossiping chatter. **3** *slang* to play truant: *wagged school.* ▸ *noun* **1** a wagging movement. **2** a habitual joker or a wit. ▪ **waggish** *adj*. [Anglo-Saxon *wagian*]

wage *verb* to engage in or fight (a war or battle). ▸ *noun* (*often* **wages**) a regular, esp daily or weekly rather than monthly, payment from an employer to an employee. [14c: from French *wagier* to pledge]

wager *noun* **1** a bet on the result of something. **2** the act of making such a bet. ▸ *verb, tr & intr* to bet; to stake (something) in a bet. [14c: from French *wagier* to pledge]

waggle *verb, tr & intr* to move or make (something) move to and fro. [16c: from **wag**]

wagon *or* **waggon** *noun* **1** a four-wheeled vehicle, often horse-drawn, used esp for carrying loads; a cart. **2** an open truck or closed van for carrying railway freight. **3** *informal* a car, esp an estate car. ▪ **wagoner** *noun*. [16c: from Dutch *wagen*]

IDIOMS **on the wagon** *informal* temporarily abstaining from alcohol.

wagon-lit /*French* vagɔ̃li/ *noun* (***wagon-lits*** /-li/) a sleeping-carriage on a continental train.

wagtail *noun* a bird, so called because of the constant wagging motion of its long tail.

wahine /wɑːˈhiːnɪ/ *noun* (*pl* ***wahine***) a Maori woman. [19c: Maori]

waif *noun* **1** an orphaned, abandoned or homeless child. **2** any pathetically undernourished-looking person. ▪ **waif-like** *adj*. [14c: French, prob from Norse *veif* any flapping or waving thing]

wail *noun* **1** a prolonged and high-pitched mournful or complaining cry. **2** any sound resembling this. ▸ *verb* **1** *tr & intr* to make, or utter (something) with, such a cry. **2** *intr* of a siren, etc: to make a similar noise. [14c]

wain *noun, usu poetic* an open wagon, esp for hay or other agricultural produce. [Anglo-Saxon *wægen*]

wainscot *noun* wooden panelling or boarding covering the lower part of the walls of a room. ▪ **wainscoting** *or* **wainscotting** *noun*. [14c: from Dutch *wagen-schot* wagon partition]

waist *noun* **1** the narrow part of the human body between the ribs and hips. **2** the part of a garment that covers this. [Anglo-Saxon *wæstm* form or figure]

waistband *noun* the reinforced strip of cloth on a skirt, trousers, etc that fits round the waist.

waistcoat *noun* a close-fitting sleeveless garment, usu waist-length, worn esp by men under a jacket. *N Am equivalent* **vest**.

waistline *noun* **1** the line marking the waist. **2** the measurement of a waist.

wait *verb* **1** to be or remain in a particular place in readiness. **2** *intr* (*often* **wait for sth**) to delay action or remain in a certain place in expectation of, or readiness for, it. **3** *intr* of a task, etc: to remain temporarily undealt with: *That can wait*. **4** to postpone action for (a period of time). **5** *intr* (*often* **wait on sb**) to serve (them) as a waiter or waitress. **6** (**wait on sb**) to act as a servant or attendant to them. [12c: from French *waitier* or *guaitier*]
IDIOMS **lie in wait** *or* **lay wait** to be in hiding ready to surprise or ambush someone.
PHRASAL VERBS **wait up** *US* to slow down or wait: *Wait up, I can't run that fast*. **wait up for sb** to delay going to bed at night waiting for their arrival or return.

waiter *or* **waitress** *noun* a man or woman who serves people with food at a hotel, restaurant, etc.

waiting list *noun* a list of people waiting for something currently unavailable, eg surgery.

waiting room *noun* a room for people to wait in, eg at a doctor's surgery.

waive *verb, law* to refrain from insisting upon (something); to voluntarily give up (a claim or right, etc). [13c: from French *weyver* to abandon]

waiver *noun* **1** the act or an instance of waiving. **2** a written statement formally confirming this.

wake[1] *verb* (***woke, woken***) *tr & intr* **1** (*also* **wake** (**sb**) **up**) **a** to rouse (them) or be roused from sleep; **b** to stir or be stirred out of a state of inactivity or lethargy, etc. **2** (*often* **wake up** *or* **wake sb up to sth**) to become or make (them) aware of a fact or situation, etc. ► *noun* a watch or vigil kept beside a corpse. [Anglo-Saxon *wacan* to become awake]

wake[2] *noun* a trail of disturbed water left by a ship, or of disturbed air left by an aircraft. [16c: from Norse *vök* a hole or channel in the ice]
IDIOMS **in the wake of sb** *or* **sth** coming after them or it; resulting from them or it.

wakeful *adj* **1** not asleep or unable to sleep. **2** of a night: sleepless. **3** vigilant or alert. ▪ **wakefulness** *noun*.

waken *verb, tr & intr* **1** to rouse (someone) or be roused from sleep. **2** to rouse (someone) or be roused from inactivity or lethargy. [Anglo-Saxon *wæcnan*]

wake-up call *noun* **1** a prearranged telephone call informing someone that it is time to get up. **2** *informal* something that makes a person aware that a situation is unsatisfactory, dangerous or difficult.

waking hours *plural noun* the part of the day during which one is normally awake.

walk *verb* **1** *intr* to go on foot, moving one's feet alternately and always having one foot on the ground. **2** to go about (the streets or countryside, etc) on foot; to ramble. **3** to lead, accompany or support (someone who is on foot). **4** to take (a dog) out for exercise. **5** *intr, informal* to disappear or go away; to be stolen: *my pen has walked*. ► *noun* **1** the motion or pace of walking. **2** an outing or journey on foot, esp for exercise. **3** a distance walked or for walking. **4** a person's distinctive manner of walking. **5** a route for walking. **6** a path, esp a broad one; a promenade. ▪ **walker** *noun*. [Anglo-Saxon *wealcan*]
IDIOMS **walk all over sb** *informal* **1** to take advantage of them. **2** to defeat them easily. **walk on air** to feel euphoric and light-hearted.
PHRASAL VERBS **walk into sth 1** to collide or meet with (eg a joke, trap) unexpectedly. **2** to involve oneself in trouble or difficulty through one's own unwariness. **walk out 1** of factory workers, etc: to leave the workplace in a body, in declaration of a strike. **2** to depart abruptly, esp in protest. **walk out on sb** to abandon or desert them.

walkabout *noun* a casual stroll through a crowd of ordinary people by a celebrity, esp a member of the royal family or a politician, etc.

walkies *plural noun, informal* a walk for a dog.

walkie-talkie *noun, informal* a portable two-way radio carried by police, etc.

walking-stick *noun* **1** a stick or cane used for support or balance in walking. **2** *US* a **stick insect**.

walk-on *adj* of a part in a play or opera, etc: not involving any speaking or singing.

walkout *noun* a sudden departure, esp of a workforce in declaration of a strike.

walkover *noun, informal* an easy victory.

walkway *noun* a paved path or passage for pedestrians.

wall /wɔːl/ *noun* **1** a solid vertical brick or stone construction serving as a barrier, division, protection, etc. **2** the vertical side of a building or room. **3** something similar to or suggestive of a wall: *a wall of fire*. **4** *biol* **a** an outer covering, eg of a cell; **b** the side of a hollow organ or cavity. **5** an insurmountable barrier such as that experienced physically and psychologically by long-distance runners. ► *verb* **1** to surround (something) with, or as if with, a wall. **2** to fortify (something) with, or as if with, a wall. **3** (*usu* **wall sth off** *or* **in**) to separate or enclose it with a wall. **4** (**wall sth** *or* **sb up**) **a** to block (an opening) with a wall or bricks; **b** to confine (someone) behind a wall, as a form of imprisonment or torture. ▪ **walled** *adj*. [Anglo-Saxon *weall*]
IDIOMS **have one's back to the wall** to be in a difficult or desperate situation. **up the wall** *informal* angry; crazy or mad.

wallaby *noun* (***wallabies*** *or* ***wallaby***) a marsupial of the kangaroo family, native to Australia and Tasmania. [18c: from Aboriginal *wolaba*]

wallah *or* **walla** *noun, Anglo-Indian, in compounds* a person who performs a specified task: *the tea wallah*. [18c: from Hindi *-wala* an adjectival suffix]

wall bars *plural noun* a series of horizontal wooden bars supported by uprights lining the walls of a gymnasium.

wallet *noun* **1** a flat folding case, often made of leather, for holding banknotes, credit cards, etc. **2** any of various kinds of folders for holding papers, etc. [14c]

walleye *noun* an eye that squints away from the nose, so that an abnormal amount of the white shows. ▪ **walleyed** *adj*. [16c: from Norse *wagleygr*]

wallflower *noun* **1** a sweet-smelling plant with yellow, orange or red flowers, widely cultivated as an ornamental garden plant. **2** *informal* someone who sits all evening at the edge of the dance floor, waiting in vain to be asked to dance.

wallies *pl of* **wally**

Walloon /wɒ'luːn/ *noun* **1** a member of the French-speaking population of S Belgium. **2** their language, a dialect of French. ▸ *adj* relating to or belonging to the Walloons. [16c: from French *Wallon*, literally 'foreigner']

wallop *informal, verb* **1** to hit or strike (someone or something) vigorously. **2** to defeat or thrash (someone or something) soundly. ▸ *noun* **1** a hit or a thrashing. **2** a powerful impression. [14c: from French *waloper* to gallop]

walloping *noun* a thrashing. ▸ *adj* great; whopping.

wallow *verb, intr* (*often* **wallow in sth**) **1** to lie or roll about (in water or mud, etc). **2** to revel or luxuriate (in admiration, etc). **3** to indulge excessively (in self-pity, etc). ▸ *noun* **1** the act of wallowing. **2** the place, or the dirt, in which an animal wallows. [Anglo-Saxon *wealwian*]

wallpaper *noun* paper, often coloured or patterned, used to decorate interior walls and ceilings. ▸ *verb* to cover (walls) or the walls of (a room) with wallpaper.

wall-to-wall *adj* of carpeting: covering the entire floor of a room.

wally *noun* (*-ies*) *Brit, informal* an ineffectual, stupid or foolish person. [20c: from the name *Walter*]

walnut *noun* **1** a deciduous tree, cultivated for its timber and edible nut. **2** the round nut yielded by this tree. **3** the hard durable golden brown wood of this tree, highly prized for furniture-making, etc. [Anglo-Saxon *wealhhnutu* foreign nut]

walrus *noun* (***walruses*** *or* ***walrus***) a large carnivorous marine mammal related to the seal, with thick wrinkled skin, webbed flippers and two long tusks. [17c: Dutch, meaning literally 'whale-horse']

walrus moustache *noun* a thick drooping moustache.

waltz *noun* **1** a slow or fast ballroom dance in triple time, in which the dancers spin round the room. **2** a piece of music for this dance or in this style. ▸ *verb, intr* **1** to dance a waltz. **2** (*often* **waltz in** *or* **off**) *informal* to go or move with vivacity and easy confidence: *She just waltzed in and took over.* [18c: from German *Walzer*]

wampum /'wɒmpəm, 'wɔː-/ *noun, hist* shells strung together for use as money among the Native Americans. [17c: a shortening of Algonquian (a family of Native American languages) *wampumpeag* white string of beads]

WAN *abbrev, comput* wide area network, a computer network that operates over a wide area and is therefore normally dependent on telephone lines or other long-distance links rather than cables. Compare **LAN**.

wan /wɒn/ *adj* (***wanner, wannest***) pale and pinched-looking, esp from illness, exhaustion or grief. ▪ **wanly** *adv.* [Anglo-Saxon *wann* dusky or lurid]

wand *noun* **1** a slender rod used by magicians, conjurors and fairies, etc for performing magic. **2** a conductor's baton. **3** a device, similar to a pen, for reading bar codes. [12c: from Norse *vöndr* shoot]

wander *verb* **1** to walk, move or travel about, with no particular destination; to ramble. **2** to stray or deviate, eg from the right path, or from the point of an argument, etc. **3** of thoughts, etc: to flit randomly. ▸ *noun* a ramble or stroll. ▪ **wanderer** *noun.* ▪ **wandering** *noun, adj.* [Anglo-Saxon *wandrian*]

wanderlust *noun* an urge to rove or travel. [19c: German]

wane *verb, intr* **1** of the moon: to appear to grow narrower as the sun illuminates less of its surface. **2** to decline in glory, power or influence, etc. ▸ *noun* the process of waning or declining. ▪ **waning** *adj.* [Anglo-Saxon *wanian* to lessen]

IDIOMS **on the wane** decreasing or declining.

wangle *verb, informal* **1** to contrive or obtain something by persuasiveness. **2** to manipulate something. [19c: perhaps from **waggle** + dialect *wankle* wavering]

wannabe *or* **wannabee** /'wɒnəbiː/ *noun, informal* someone who aspires to be something or who admires and imitates the appearance, mannerisms and habits, etc of another person. ▸ *adj* aspiring: *a wannabe rock star.* [20c: a shortening of *want to be*]

want *verb* **1** to feel a need or desire for (something). **2** to need to be dealt with in a specified way: *The bin wants emptying.* **3** *informal* ought; need: *You want to take more care.* **4** (*often* **want for sth**) to feel the lack of it: *That kid wants for nothing.* **5** to require the presence of (someone or something): *You are wanted next door.* ▸ *noun* **1** a need or requirement. **2** a lack: *a want of discretion.* **3** a state of need; destitution. [12c: from Norse *vanta* to be lacking]

IDIOMS **for want of sth** in the absence of it. **in want of sth** needing it.

---

want, wont

Be careful not to use the spelling **want** when you mean **wont**:

She had many of the failings she was wont to criticize in other people.

---

wanted *adj* **1** needed or desired. **2** of a person: being sought by the police on suspicion of having committed a crime, etc.

wanting *adj* **1** missing; lacking. **2** not up to requirements: *has been found wanting.*

wanton *adj* **1** thoughtlessly and needlessly cruel. **2** motiveless: *wanton destruction.* **3** immoral; lewd or licentious. ▸ *noun, old use* an immoral person, esp a woman. [Anglo-Saxon *wan-* not + *togen* disciplined]

WAP *abbrev* Wireless Application Protocol, a system that enables the Internet to be accessed on a mobile phone.

wapiti /'wɒpɪtɪ/ *noun* (***wapiti*** *or* ***wapitis***) a type of large N American deer. Also (*N Am*) called **elk**. [19c: Shawnee, meaning 'white deer']

War. *abbrev, English county* Warwickshire.

war *noun* **1** an open state of armed conflict, esp between nations. **2** a particular armed conflict. **3** a conflict between states, or between parties within a state. See also **civil war**. **4** any long-continued struggle or campaign. **5** fierce rivalry or competition, eg in business. ▸ *verb* (***warred, warring***) *intr* **1** to fight wars. **2** to be in conflict. [12c: from German *Werra* quarrel]

IDIOMS **have been in the wars** *informal* to have, or show signs of having, sustained injuries.

warble *verb, tr & intr* **1** of a bird: to sing melodiously. **2** of a person: to sing in a high tremulous voice; to trill. [14c: from French *werbler*]

warbler *noun* a small songbird with dull green, brown or grey upper plumage, and a slender pointed bill.

war crime *noun* a crime committed during a war, esp ill-treatment of prisoners or massacre of civilians, etc. ▪ **war criminal** *noun.*

war cry *noun* **1** a cry used to rally or encourage troops, or as a signal for charging. **2** a slogan or watchword.

ward *noun* **1** a room in a hospital with beds for patients. **2** the patients in a ward collectively. **3** any of the areas into which a town, etc is divided for administration or elections. **4** care or guardianship; custody. **5** *law* someone, esp a minor, under the protection of a guardian or court. ▸ *verb* (*usu* **ward off**) to keep (trouble, hunger or disease, etc) away. [Anglo-Saxon *weard* protector]

-ward see **-wards**

warden *noun* **1** someone in charge of a hostel, student residence or old people's home, etc. **2** *in compounds* a public official responsible in any of various ways for maintaining order: *traffic warden* • *game warden.* **3** *N Am* the officer in charge of a prison. [13c: from French *wardein*]

warder *or* **wardress** *noun* **1** *Brit* a prison officer. **2** a man or woman who guards someone or something. [14c: from French *warder* to guard]

wardrobe *noun* **1** a tall cupboard in which clothes are kept. **2** a personal stock of garments and accessories. **3** the stock of costumes belonging to a theatrical company. [14c: from French *garderobe*]

wardrobe mistress *or* **wardrobe master** *noun* the woman or man in charge of the costumes of a theatrical company, or of an individual actor.

wardroom *noun* the officers' quarters on board a warship.

-wards *or* **-ward** *combining form, denoting* direction: *backwards* • *toward.* [Anglo-Saxon *-weardes*]

ware *noun* **1** *in compounds* manufactured goods of a specified material or for a specified use: *kitchenware.* **2** a particular type of pottery. **3** (**wares**) goods for sale. [Anglo-Saxon *waru*]

warehouse *noun* **1** a large building or room for storing goods. **2** a large, usu wholesale, shop.

warfare *noun* **1** the activity or process of waging or engaging in war. **2** armed or violent conflict.

war game *noun* **1** a mock battle or military exercise that provides training in tactics, etc. **2** an elaborate game in which players use model soldiers, etc to enact historical or imaginary battles.

warhead *noun* the front part of a missile or torpedo etc that contains the explosives.

warhorse *noun* **1** *hist* a powerful horse on which a knight rode into battle. **2** an old soldier or politician.

warlike *adj* **1** fond of fighting; aggressive or belligerent. **2** relating to war; military.

warlock *noun* a wizard, male magician or sorcerer. [Anglo-Saxon *warloga* a breaker of an agreement]

warlord *noun* a powerful military leader.

warm *adj* **1** moderately, comfortably or pleasantly hot. **2** of clothes, blankets, etc: providing and preserving heat. **3** of a person: kind-hearted and affectionate. **4** of an environment, etc: welcoming and congenial. **5** enthusiastic; whole-hearted. **6** of a colour: suggestive of comfortable heat, typically containing red or yellow. **7** in a game, etc: close to guessing correctly or finding the thing sought. ▸ *verb* **1** *tr & intr* (*also* **warm up**) to make or become warm or warmer. **2** (*usu* **warm to sth**) to gain in enthusiasm for (a task) as one performs it. **3** *intr* (*usu* **warm to sb**) to gain in affection or approval for them. **4** *tr & intr* (*usu* **warm up** *or* **warm sth up**) **a** to re-heat (food); **b** of a party, etc: to become or make it livelier; **c** of an engine: to reach an efficient working temperature. ▪ **warmly** *adv.* [Anglo-Saxon *wearm*]

PHRASAL VERBS **warm up** to exercise the body gently in preparation for a strenuous work-out or race, etc.

warm-blooded *adj* **1** *zool* of an animal: capable of maintaining its internal body temperature at a relatively constant level, independent of fluctuations in the temperature of its environment. **2** of a person: passionate, impulsive or ardent.

war memorial *noun* a monument erected to commemorate members of the armed forces, esp those from a particular locality, who died in war.

warm front *noun, meteorol* the edge of a mass of warm air advancing against a mass of cold air.

warm-hearted *adj* kind, affectionate and generous; sympathetic.

warmonger *noun* someone who tries to precipitate war, or who generates enthusiasm for it.

warmth *noun* **1** the condition of being warm. **2** affection or kind-heartedness.

warm-up *noun* the act of gently exercising the body in preparation for a strenuous work-out or race, etc.

warn *verb* **1** (*usu* **warn sb of** *or* **about**) to make them aware of (possible or approaching danger or difficulty). **2** to advise (someone) strongly. **3** to rebuke or admonish (someone), with the threat of punishment for a repetition of the offence. **4** (*often* **warn sb against sb** *or* **sth**) to caution them about them or it. **5** (**warn sb off**) to order them to go or keep away, often with threats. [Anglo-Saxon *wearnian*]

warning *noun* **1** a caution against danger, etc. **2** something that happens, or is said or done, that serves to warn against this. ▸ *adj* intended or serving to warn: *a warning shot.*

warp *verb, tr & intr* **1** to become or cause (something) to become twisted out of shape through the shrinking and expanding effects of damp or heat, etc. **2** to become or make (something) distorted, corrupted or perverted. ▸ *noun* **1** the state or fact of being warped. **2** an unevenness or twist in wood, etc. **3** a distorted or abnormal twist in personality, etc. **4** a shift or displacement in a continuous dimension, esp time. **5** *weaving* the set of threads stretched lengthways in a loom, under and over which the widthways set of threads (the **weft** or **woof²**) are passed. ▪ **warped** *adj.* [Anglo-Saxon *weorpan* to throw]

warpaint *noun* **1** paint put on the face and body by peoples when going to war, esp Native Americans. **2** *informal* a woman's make-up.

warpath *noun* a route taken by people, esp Native Americans, going to war.

IDIOMS **on the warpath** *informal* **a** in angry pursuit; **b** in an angry mood.

warrant *noun* **1** a written legal authorization for doing something, eg for searching property. **2** a certificate such as a licence, voucher or receipt, that authorizes, guarantees or confirms something. ▸ *verb* **1** to justify (something). **2** to guarantee (goods, etc) as being of the specified quality or quantity. [13c: from French *warant*]

warrantable *adj* **1** that may be permitted; justifiable. **2** said of deer: being of sufficient age to be hunted. ▪ **warrantably** *adv.* [16c]

warrant officer *noun* (abbrev **WO**) in the armed services: an officer ranked between a commissioned and non-commissioned officer.

warrantor *or* **warranter** *noun, law* someone who gives a warrant or warranty.

warranty *noun* (***-ies***) an assurance of the quality of goods being sold, usu with an acceptance of responsibility for repairs during an initial period of use. See also **guarantee**. [14c]

warren *noun* **1** an underground labyrinth of interconnecting rabbit burrows. **2** an overcrowded dwelling or district. **3** any maze of passages. [14c: from French *warenne*]

warrior *noun* **1** a skilled fighting man, esp one belonging to earlier times. **2** any distinguished soldier or veteran. [13c: from French *werreieor*]

Warsaw Pact *noun, hist* a military alliance of East European countries formed in 1955 and disbanded in 1991.

warship *noun* a ship armed with guns, etc for use in naval battles.

wart *noun* a small and usu hard benign growth, transmitted by a virus, found on the skin, esp of the fingers, hands and face. ▪ **warty** *adj.* [Anglo-Saxon *wearte*]

IDIOMS **warts and all** *informal* with any blemishes or defects showing and accepted.

warthog *noun* a large wild pig with wart-like lumps on its face, a bristly mane and two pairs of curving tusks.

wartime *noun* a period during which a war is going on.

Warwicks. *abbrev, English county* Warwickshire.

wary /ˈwɛərɪ/ *adj* (***-ier, -iest***) **1** alert, vigilant or cautious; on one's guard. **2** distrustful or apprehensive. **3** (*often* **wary of sth** *or* **sb**) suspicious of it or them. ▪ **warily** *adv.* ▪ **wariness** *noun.* [Anglo-Saxon *wær* to beware]

was *past tense of* **be**

wash *verb* **1** to cleanse (someone or something) with water or other liquid, and usu soap or detergent. **2** *intr* to cleanse (oneself, or one's hands and face) with water, etc. **3** *intr* of a fabric or dye: to withstand washing without change or damage. **4** (*also* **wash off** *or* **out**) **a** *tr* to remove (a stain, dirt, etc) esp by using soap and water; **b** *intr* of a stain, dirt, etc: to be removed in this way. **5** *tr & intr* of an animal: to lick (itself or its young, etc) clean. **6** of a river, the sea, waves, etc: to flow against or over (a place or land feature, etc). **7** of flowing water: to erode or gouge out (a channel, etc) in the landscape. **8** to apply a thin layer of metal, paint etc to. **9** *intr, informal* to stand the test; to bear investigation: *That excuse just won't wash.* ▸ *noun* **1** the process of washing or being washed. **2** this process undertaken by a laundry. **3** a quantity of clothes, etc for washing, or just washed. **4** the breaking of waves against something; the sound of this. **5** the rough water or disturbed air left by a ship or aircraft. **6** *often in compounds* a lotion or other preparation for cleansing or washing: *facewash.* **7** *art* a thin application of watercolour. ▪ **washable** *adj.* [Anglo-Saxon *wæscan*]

IDIOMS **come out in the wash** *informal* to turn out satisfactorily, or become known, in the end.

PHRASAL VERBS **wash sth down 1** to wash it from top to bottom. **2** to ease (a pill) down one's throat, or accompany or follow (food), with a drink. **wash up** to wash (the dishes and cutlery) after a meal.

washbasin *or* **washhand basin** *noun* a shallow sink in which to wash one's face and hands.

washed-out *adj* **1** *informal* of a person: worn out and pale; lacking in energy. **2** of the colour in a fabric: faded by, or as if by, washing.

washed-up *adj* **1** *informal* of a person: exhausted; lacking in energy. **2** *slang* done for; at the end of one's resources. **3** of plans, etc: having come to nothing. **4** (*esp* **all washed-up**) *slang* finished; unsuccessful.

washer *noun* **1** someone who washes. **2** a washing machine. **3** a flat ring of rubber or metal for keeping a joint or nut secure.

washer-dryer *or* **washer-drier** *noun* a washing machine with a tumble-dryer built in.

washerwoman *or* **washerman** *noun, hist* a man or woman paid to wash clothes.

washing *noun* **1** the act of cleansing, wetting or coating with liquid. **2** clothes to be, or which have just been, washed.

washing line *noun* a **clothesline**.

washing machine *noun* a machine for washing clothes and bed linen, etc.

washing powder *or* **washing liquid** *noun* a powdered or liquid detergent for washing fabrics.

washing soda *noun* **sodium carbonate** crystals used, dissolved in water, for washing and cleaning.

washing-up *noun* **1** the washing of dishes and cutlery, etc after a meal. **2** dishes and cutlery, etc for washing.

washout *noun* **1** *informal* a flop or failure. **2** *informal* a useless person. **3** a rained-off event, eg a sports match.

washroom *noun, N Am* a lavatory.

washstand *noun, hist* a small table in a bedroom designed to hold a jug and basin for washing one's hands and face.

washy *adj* (***-ier, -iest***) *informal* **1** of a drink: watery or weak, usu excessively so. **2** feeble; lacking liveliness or vigour. **3** of colours: faded-looking or pallid. [16c]

wasn't *contraction* was not.

WASP *or* **Wasp** *noun, US, often derog* a white person representing the most privileged class in US society. [20c: from *W*hite *A*nglo-*S*axon *P*rotestant]

wasp *noun* a common stinging insect with a slender black-and-yellow striped body. [Anglo-Saxon *wæsp*]

waspish *adj* sharp-tongued; caustic or venomous.

wasp waist *noun* a slender waist. ▪ **wasp-waisted** *adj.*

wassail /ˈwɒseɪl/ *noun, old use* **1** a festive bout of drinking. **2** a toast made at such an occasion. **3** a liquor with which such toasts were made, esp an ale made with roasted apple, sugar and nutmeg. ▸ *verb* **1** to hold a wassail. **2** to go from house to house at Christmas singing carols and festive songs. [13c: from Norse *ves heill* be in good health]

wastage *noun* **1** the process of wasting; loss through wasting. **2** the amount lost through wasting. **3** (*esp* **natural wastage**) reduction of staff through retirement or resignation, as distinct from dismissal or redundancy.

waste *verb* **1** to use or spend (something) purposelessly or extravagantly; to squander. **2** *intr* to be used to no, or little, purpose or effect. **3** to fail to use, make the best of or take advantage of (an opportunity, etc). **4** to throw away (something unused or uneaten, etc). **5** (*also* **waste away**) *tr & intr* to lose or cause (someone) to lose flesh or strength. **6** *chiefly US, slang* to attack, kill or murder (someone). **7** to treat (something) as waste material. ▸ *adj* **1** rejected as useless, unneeded or excess to requirements. **2** of ground: lying unused, uninhabited or uncultivated. **3** *physiol* denoting material excreted from the body, usu in the urine or faeces. ▸ *noun* **1** the act or an instance of wasting, or the condition of being wasted. **2** failure to take advantage of something: *a waste of talent*. **3** material that is no longer needed in its present form and must be processed, eg nuclear waste. **4** refuse; rubbish. **5** *physiol* matter excreted from the body. **6** a devastated or barren region. **7** (*often* **wastes**) a vast tract of uncultivated land or expanse of ocean, etc. [12c: from French *wast*]

IDIOMS **go** *or* **run to waste** to be wasted. **lay sth waste** to devastate it.

wasteful *adj* causing waste; extravagant.

wasteland *noun* **1** a desolate and barren region. **2** a place or point in time that is culturally, intellectually and spiritually empty.

waste paper *noun* used paper discarded as rubbish.

waster *noun* **1** an idler, good-for-nothing or wastrel. **2** a person or thing that wastes.

wastrel /ˈweɪstrəl/ *noun* an idle spendthrift; a good-for-nothing. [19c]

wat *noun* a Thai Buddhist temple or monastery. [19c: from Sanskrit *vata* enclosed ground]

watch *verb* **1** *tr & intr* to look at or focus one's attention on (someone or something) that is moving or doing something, etc. **2** *tr & intr* to pass time looking at or observing (TV, a programme, etc). **3** to keep track of, follow or monitor (developments, progress, etc). **4** *intr* to keep vigil; to remain awake or on the alert. **5** (*also* **watch for**) **a** to await one's chance; to be on the alert to take advantage of (an opportunity); **b** to look out for or guard against (something). **6** to pay proper attention to (something): *watch where you're going!* ▸ *noun* **1** a small timepiece, usu worn strapped to the wrist or on a chain in the waistcoat pocket or attached to clothing. **2** the activity or duty of watching or guarding. **3** a wake; a vigil kept beside a corpse. **4** *naut* any of the four-hour shifts during which particular crew members are on duty. [Anglo-Saxon *wæccan* or *wacian* to watch]

IDIOMS **keep a watch on sth** *or* **sb** to keep it or them under observation. **on the watch for sth** seeking or looking out for it. **watch it!** be careful! **watch one's step 1** to step or advance with care. **2** *informal* to act cautiously or warily; to take care not to arouse suspicion or cause offence, etc.

PHRASAL VERBS **watch out** to be careful. **watch out for sth** *or* **sb** to be on one's guard against it or them; to look out for it or them. **watch over sb** *or* **sth** to guard, look after or tend to them or it.

watchable *adj, informal* of an entertainment, esp a TV programme: enjoyable and interesting to watch.

watchdog *noun* **1** a dog kept to guard premises, etc. **2** a person or organization that guards against unacceptable standards, inefficiency or illegality, etc.

watchful *adj* alert, vigilant and wary. ▪ **watchfully** *adv*. ▪ **watchfulness** *noun*.

watchman *noun* (*also* **nightwatchman**) a man employed to guard premises at night.

watchnight *noun* in Protestant Churches: **1** the night of Christmas Eve or New Year's Eve. **2** (*in full* **watchnight service**) a church service lasting through midnight on these nights.

watchtower *noun* a tower from which a sentry keeps watch.

watchword *noun* a catch phrase or slogan that encapsulates the principles of a party or profession, etc.

water *noun* **1** a colourless odourless tasteless liquid that freezes to form ice at 0°C and boils to form steam at 100°C, at normal atmospheric pressure. **2** (*also* **waters**) an expanse of this, with varying degrees of impurity; a sea, lake or river, etc. **3** the surface of a body of water. **4** (**waters**) the sea round a country's coasts, considered part of its territory: *in British waters*. **5** the level or state of the tide: *high water • low water*. **6** *physiol* any of several fluids secreted by the body, esp urine, sweat, tears, etc. **7** (**waters**) the amniotic fluid that surrounds the fetus in the womb. **8** any liquid that resembles or contains water, eg rain. **9** a dose of water given to a plant or animal. **10** *finance* an increase in a company's stock issue without an increase in assets to back it up. ▸ *verb* **1** to wet, soak or sprinkle (something) with water. **2** to irrigate (land). **3** (*also* **water sth down**) to dilute (wine, etc). **4** *intr* of the mouth: to produce saliva in response to a stimulus activated by the expectation of food. **5** *intr* of the eyes: to fill with tears in response to irritation. **6** **a** *tr* to let (animals) drink; **b** *intr* of animals: to drink: *fed and watered*. **7** to wet (plants) with water. **8** *finance* to increase (the debt of a company) by issuing new stock without a corresponding increase in assets. ▪ **waterless** *adj*. [Anglo-Saxon *wæter*]

IDIOMS **hold water** of an explanation, etc: to be valid. **in deep water** in trouble, danger or difficulty. **like a fish out of water** ill at ease; uncomfortable in a particular environment. **like water off a duck's back** of a rebuke or scolding, etc: having no effect at all; making no impression. **water under the bridge** experiences that are past and done with.

PHRASAL VERBS **water sth down** to reduce the impact of it; to make it less controversial or offensive. See also **watered-down**.

waterbed *noun* a waterproof mattress filled with water.

water biscuit *noun* a thin crisp plain biscuit made from water and flour, usu eaten with cheese, etc.

water buffalo *noun* the common domestic buffalo, native to India, Sri Lanka and SE Asia, which has large ridged horns that curve backwards.

water cannon *noun* a hosepipe that sends out a powerful jet of water, used for dispersing crowds.

water chestnut *noun* **1** an aquatic plant which produces white flowers and triangular woody fruits. **2** **a** a sedge, grown in China, that produces edible tubers; **b** the tuber of this plant, eaten as a vegetable, esp in Chinese and Japanese cuisine.

water closet *noun* (abbrev **WC**) **1** a lavatory whose pan is mechanically flushed with water. **2** a small room containing such a lavatory.

watercolour *or* (*N Am*) **watercolor** *noun* **1** paint thinned with water rather than oil. **2** a painting done using such paint.

water-cooled *adj* of an engine, etc: cooled by circulating water.

watercourse *noun* **1** a stream, river or canal. **2** the bed or channel along which any of these flow.

watercress *noun* **1** a plant with hollow creeping stems and dark-green leaves divided into several pairs of oval leaflets, that grows in watery regions. **2** its sharp-tasting leaves used in salads and soups, etc.

water cycle *noun, geog* the continuous cycle in which water evaporates from the sea into the atmosphere, where it later condenses and falls back to the land as rain, snow, etc, when it either evaporates straight back into the atmosphere or runs back into the sea by rivers.

water-diviner *noun* someone who detects, or attempts to detect, underground sources of water, usu with a **divining rod**.

watered-down *adj* **1** very diluted. **2** modified or attenuated; reduced in force or vigour.

waterfall *noun* a sudden interruption in the course of a river or stream where water falls more or less vertically, eg over the edge of a plateau.

waterfowl *singular noun* a bird that lives on or near water, esp a swimming bird such as a duck or swan. ▸ *plural noun* swimming birds collectively.

waterfront *noun* the buildings or part of a town lying along the edge of a river, lake or sea.

water gate *noun* **1** a floodgate. **2** a gate that opens into a river or other watercourse.

waterhole *noun* (*also* **watering hole**) a pool or spring in a dried-up or desert area, where animals can drink.

water ice *noun* sweetened fruit juice or purée frozen and served as a dessert; a sorbet.

watering can *noun* a container with a handle and spout used for watering plants.

watering hole *noun* **1** a waterhole. **2** *slang* a public house.

watering place *noun* **1** a place where animals may obtain water. **2** *hist* a spa or other resort where people go to drink mineral water or bathe.

water jump *noun* in a steeplechase, etc: a jump over a water-filled ditch or pool, etc.

water level *noun* **1** the height reached by the surface of a body of still water. **2** a waterline.

water lily *noun* an aquatic plant with large flat circular leaves and white, pink, red or yellow flowers that float on the surface of still or very slow-moving water.

waterline *noun* the level reached by the water on the hull of a floating vessel when under different conditions of loading.

waterlogged *adj* **1** saturated with water. **2** of a boat: so filled or saturated with water as to be unmanageable.

Waterloo *noun* the challenge that finally defeats someone. [19c: named after the battle of Waterloo where Napoleon was finally defeated in 1815]

water main *noun* a large underground pipe that carries a public water supply.

watermark *noun* **1** the limit reached by the sea at high or low tide; a waterline. **2** a manufacturer's distinctive mark in paper, visible only when the paper is held up to the light.

water meadow *noun* a meadow kept fertile by periodic flooding from a stream.

watermelon *noun* a large round fruit with a hard leathery green skin and sweet juicy pink or red flesh containing many black seeds.

watermill *noun* a mill whose machinery is driven by a waterwheel.

water pistol *noun* a toy pistol that fires squirts of water.

water pollution *noun, ecol* the contamination of any body of water with industrial waste, sewage and other materials considered to be detrimental to living organisms.

water polo *noun* a seven-a-side ball game for swimmers, in which the object is to score goals by propelling the ball into the opposing team's goal.

water power *noun* the power generated by moving water used to drive machinery either directly or indirectly, eg turbines for generating hydroelectricity.

waterproof *adj* impenetrable by water; treated or coated so as to resist water: *a waterproof anorak*. ▸ *verb* to treat (fabric, etc) so as to make it waterproof. ▸ *noun* a waterproof outer garment.

water rat *noun* **1** *Brit* any of various unrelated small rat-like rodents that live near water, esp the **water vole**. **2** *US* the **muskrat**.

water rate *noun* a charge made for the use of the public water supply.

water-repellent *adj* of a fabric, etc: treated so as not to absorb water.

water-resistant *adj* resistant to penetration by water.

watershed *noun* **1** the line that separates two river basins. **2** a crucial point after which events take a different turn.

waterside *noun* the edge of a river, lake or sea.

water-ski *noun* a ski on which to glide over water, towed by a powered boat. ▸ *verb, intr* to travel on water skis. ▪ **water-skier** *noun*. ▪ **water-skiing** *noun*.

water softener *noun* a substance or device used in water to remove minerals, esp calcium, that cause hardness and prevent lathering.

water-soluble *adj* able to be dissolved in water.

water sports *plural noun* sports practised on or in the water, eg swimming and water-skiing, etc.

waterspout *noun, meteorol* a tornado that occurs over open water, mainly in the tropics, and consists of a rotating column of water and spray.

water table *noun, geol* the level below which porous rocks are saturated with water.

watertight *adj* **1** so well sealed as to be impenetrable by water. **2** of an argument, etc: without any apparent flaw, weakness or ambiguity, etc; completely sound.

water tower *noun* a tower that supports an elevated water tank, from which water can be distributed at uniform pressure.

water vapour *noun* water in the form of an air dispersion, esp where evaporation has occurred at a temperature below boiling point.

water vole *noun* a species of vole which burrows into the banks of streams and ponds.

waterway *noun* a navigable channel, eg a canal or river, used by ships or smaller boats for travel or transport.

waterwheel *noun* a wheel that is turned by the force of flowing or falling water on blades or buckets around its rim.

waterwings *plural noun* an inflatable device that supports the chest, or a pair of inflatable armbands, used by people learning to swim.

waterworks *noun* **1** *singular* an installation where water is purified and stored for distribution to an area. **2** *plural, euphem* one's bladder and urinary system. **3** *plural, facetious* tears; weeping.
IDIOMS **turn on the waterworks** to start crying or weeping.

watery *adj* (**-*ier*, -*iest***) **1** relating to, consisting of or containing water. **2** containing too much water; over-diluted; weak or thin. **3** of eyes: moist; inclined to water.

watt *noun* (symbol **W**) *physics* in the SI system: a unit of power, defined as the power that gives rise to the production of energy at the rate of one joule per second. [19c: named after James Watt, the Scottish engineer]

wattage *noun* an amount of electrical power expressed in watts.

wattle *noun* **1** rods or branches, etc forming eg a framework for a wall, fences or roofs, esp when interwoven. **2** a loose fold of skin hanging from the throat of certain birds and lizards. **3** an Australian acacia tree with leaves divided into numerous tiny leaflets, and many tiny yellow flowers. [Anglo-Saxon]

wattle and daub *noun* wattle plastered with mud or clay, used as a building material.

wave *verb* **1** *intr* to move (one's hand) to and fro in greeting, farewell or as a signal. **2** to hold up and move (some other object) in this way for this purpose. **3** *tr & intr* to move or make (something) move or sway to and fro. **4** (*esp* **wave sb on** *or* **through**) to direct them with a gesture of the hand. **5** *intr* of hair: to have a gentle curl or curls. **6** to put a gentle curl into (hair) by artificial means. ▶ *noun* **1** any of a series of moving ridges on the surface of the sea or some other body of water. **2** an act of waving the hand, etc. **3** *physics* a regularly repeated disturbance or displacement in a medium, eg water or air. **4** any of the circles of disturbance moving outwards from the site of a shock, such as an earthquake. **5** a loose soft curl, or series of such curls, in the hair. **6** a surge or sudden feeling of an emotion or a physical symptom. **7** a sudden increase in something: *a heat wave.* **8** an advancing body of people. **9** any of a series of curves in an upward-and-downward curving line or outline. [Anglo-Saxon *wafian* to wave]
IDIOMS **make waves** to create a disturbance or cause trouble, etc; to aggravate a situation.

waveband *noun, radio* a range of frequencies in the electromagnetic spectrum occupied by radio or TV broadcasting transmission of a particular type.

wavelength *noun, physics* **1** the distance between two successive peaks or two successive troughs of a wave. **2** the length of the radio wave used by a particular broadcasting station.
IDIOMS **on the same wavelength** of two or more people: speaking or thinking in a way that is mutually compatible.

waver *verb, intr* **1** to move to and fro. **2** to falter, lessen or weaken, etc. **3** to hesitate through indecision. **4** of the voice: to become unsteady through emotion, etc. ▪ **wavering** *adj.* [14c: from Norse *vafra* to flicker]

wavy *adj* (**-*ier*, -*iest***) **1** of hair: full of waves. **2** of a line or outline: curving alternately upwards and downwards.

wax[1] *noun* **1** *chem* any of various fatty substances of plant, animal or mineral origin that are typically shiny, have a low melting point, are easily moulded when warm, and are insoluble in water. **2** beeswax. **3** sealing wax. **4** the sticky yellowish matter that forms in the ears. ▶ *verb* **1** to use or apply a natural or mineral wax on (something), eg prior to polishing. **2** to remove hair from (a part of the body) by coating with wax, which is then peeled off, removing the hair at the roots. ▪ **waxy** *adj* (**-*ier*, -*iest***). [Anglo-Saxon *weax*]

wax[2] *verb, intr* **1** of the moon: to appear larger as more of its surface is illuminated by the sun. **2** to increase in size, strength or power. **3** *facetious* to become (eloquent or lyrical) in one's description of something. [Anglo-Saxon *weaxan* to grow]
IDIOMS **wax and wane** to increase and decrease in alternating sequence.

waxcloth *noun, old use* **1 oilcloth**. **2 linoleum**.

waxen *adj* **1** made of or covered with wax. **2** resembling wax. **3** easily impressed or penetrated like wax.

wax paper *noun* paper covered with a thin layer of white wax to make it waterproof.

waxwork *noun* **1** a lifelike wax model, esp of a famous person. **2** (**waxworks**) an exhibition of these.

way *noun* **1** **a** a route, entrance or exit, etc that provides passage or access somewhere; **b** the passage or access provided. **2** the route, road or direction taken for a particular journey. **3** (**Way**) used in street names. **4** *often in compounds* a direction or means of motion: *a waterway.* **5** an established position: *the wrong way up.* **6** a distance in space or time: *a little way ahead.* **7** one's district: *if you're round our way.* **8** the route or path ahead; room to move or progress. **9** a means. **10** a distinctive manner or style. **11** a method. **12** (**ways**) customs or rituals. **13** a characteristic piece of behaviour. **14** a mental approach: *different ways of looking at it.* **15** a respect: *correct in some ways.* **16** an alternative course, possibility or choice, etc. **17** a state or condition. **18** progress; forward motion: *made their way through the crowds.* **19** *naut* headway; progress through the water: *made little way that day.* ▶ *adv, informal* far; a long way: *met way back in the 60s.* [Anglo-Saxon *weg*]
IDIOMS **by the way** incidentally; let me mention while I remember. **by way of** as a form or means of: *He grinned by way of apology.* **get** *or* **have one's own way** to do, get or have what one wants, often as opposed to what others want. **give way 1** to collapse or subside. **2** to fail or break down under pressure, etc. **3** to yield to persuasion or pressure. **go out of one's way** to make special efforts; to do more than is needed. **have it both ways** to benefit from

two actions, situations or arguments, etc, each of which excludes the possibility or validity, etc of the others. **in a way** from a certain viewpoint; to some extent. **make one's way 1** to go purposefully. **2** to progress or prosper: *making her way in life.* **no way** *slang* absolutely not. **out of the way 1** situated so as not to hinder or obstruct anyone. **2** remote; in the middle of nowhere. **under way** in motion; progressing.

waybill *noun* a list that gives details of goods or passengers being carried by a public vehicle.

wayfarer *noun, old use or poetic* a traveller, esp on foot. ▪ **wayfaring** *noun, adj.*

waylay *verb* **1** to lie in wait for and ambush (someone). **2** to wait for and delay (someone) with conversation.

way of life *noun* a style or conditions of living; the living of one's life according to certain principles.

way-out *adj, slang* **1** excitingly unusual, exotic or new. **2** *dated* excellent.

ways and means *plural noun* **1** methods for obtaining funds to carry on a government. **2** methods and resources for carrying out and fulfilling any purpose.

wayside *noun* the edge of a road, or the area to the side of it. ► *adj* growing, situated or lying near the edge of roads.

IDIOMS **fall by the wayside** to fail or give up in one's attempt to do something; to drop out.

wayward *adj* undisciplined or self-willed; headstrong, wilful or rebellious. ▪ **waywardness** *noun.*

Wb *symbol* weber.

WC *abbrev* (***WCs*** *or* ***WC's***) water closet.

we *pron,* used as the subject of a verb: **1** to refer to oneself in company with another or others: *We went to a party last night.* **2** to refer to people in general: *the times we live in.* **3** used by a royal person, and by writers and editors in formal use: to refer to themselves or the authority they represent. **4** *patronizing* to mean 'you': *How are we feeling today?* [Anglo-Saxon]

---

we, us

Be careful to use the word **us** (rather than **we**) as an object:

✓ *This is a busy time of year for us farmers.*

✗ *This is a busy time of year for we farmers.*

---

weak *adj* **1** lacking physical strength. **2** lacking in moral or mental force. **3** not able to support or sustain a great weight. **4** not functioning effectively. **5** liable to give way. **6** lacking power. **7** *commerce* dropping in value. **8** too easily influenced or led by others. **9** yielding too easily to temptation. **10** lacking full flavour. **11** of an argument: unsound or unconvincing. ▪ **weakly** *adv.* [13c: from Norse *veikr*]

weaken *verb, tr & intr* to make or become weaker.

weak-kneed *adj, informal* cowardly; feeble.

weakling *noun* **1** a sickly or physically weak person or animal. **2** someone weak in a certain respect: *a moral weakling.*

weakness *noun* **1** the condition of being weak. **2** a fault or failing; a shortcoming. **3** (*often* **a weakness for sth**) a particular, usu indulgent, liking for it.

weak point, weak side *or* **weak spot** *noun* **1** the point in which someone is most easily influenced or liable to temptation. **2** a side or point in anything at which it is susceptible to error or attack, etc.

weak-willed *adj* lacking a strong will; easily tempted.

weal[1] *noun* a long raised reddened mark on the skin caused eg by a slash with a whip or sword. [19c: from Anglo-Saxon *walu* ridge]

weal[2] *noun, old use* welfare or wellbeing. [Anglo-Saxon *wela* wealth or bliss]

wealth *noun* **1** riches, valuables and property, or the possession of them. **2** abundance of resources: *the country's mineral wealth.* **3** a large quantity: *a wealth of examples.* [Anglo-Saxon *wela* wealth or bliss]

wealthy *adj* (***-ier, -iest***) **1** possessing riches and property; rich or prosperous. **2** (**wealthy in sth**) well supplied with it; rich in it.

wean *verb* **1** to accustom (a baby or young mammal) to taking food other than its mother's milk. **2** to gradually break someone of a bad habit, etc: *how to wean him off sweets.* [Anglo-Saxon *wenian* to accustom]

weapon *noun* **1** an instrument or device used to kill or injure people, usu in a war or fight. **2** something one can use to get the better of others: *Patience is our best weapon.* [Anglo-Saxon *wæpen*]

weaponry *noun* (***-ies***) weapons collectively.

wear *verb* (***wore, worn***) **1** to be dressed in (something), or have (it) on one's body. **2** to have (one's hair or beard, etc) cut a certain length or in a certain style. **3** to have (a certain expression). **4** *intr* of a carpet or garment: to become thin or threadbare through use. **5** to make (a hole or bare patch, etc) in something through heavy use. **6** *intr* to bear intensive use; to last in use. **7** *informal* to accept (an excuse or story, etc) or tolerate (a situation, etc). **8** to tire: *worn to a frazzle.* ► *noun* **1** the act of wearing or state of being worn. **2** clothes suitable for a specified purpose, person or occasion, etc: *evening wear.* **3** the amount or type of use that clothing or carpeting, etc gets: *subjected to heavy wear.* **4** damage caused through use. See also **wear and tear**. ▪ **wearer** *noun.* [Anglo-Saxon *werian*]

IDIOMS **wearing thin 1** becoming thin or threadbare. **2** of an excuse, etc: becoming unconvincing or ineffective through overuse.

PHRASAL VERBS **wear sb down** to tire or overcome them, esp with persistent objections or demands. **wear off** of a feeling or pain, etc: to become less intense; to disappear gradually. **wear out** *or* **wear sth out** to become unusable or make it unusable through use. See also **worn out**. **wear sb out** to tire them completely; to exhaust them.

wear and tear *noun* damage sustained in the course of continual or normal use. See also **wear** (*noun* sense 4).

wearing *adj* exhausting or tiring.

wearisome *adj* tiring, tedious or frustrating.

weary *adj* (***-ier, -iest***) **1** tired out; exhausted. **2** (*usu* **weary of sth**) tired by it; fed up with it. **3** tiring, dreary or irksome; wearing. ► *verb* (***-ies, -ied***) **1** *tr & intr* to make or become weary. **2** (*usu* **weary of sth**) *intr* to get tired of it. ▪ **wearily** *adv.* ▪ **weariness** *noun.* [Anglo-Saxon *werig*]

weasel *noun* **1** a small carnivorous mammal with a slender body, short legs and reddish-brown fur with white underparts. **2** *informal* a treacherous or sly person. ► *verb* (***weaselled, weaselling***; *US* ***weaseled, weaseling***) to equivocate. [Anglo-Saxon *wesle*]

PHRASAL VERBS **weasel out** *informal* to extricate oneself or circumvent an obligation or responsibility etc, esp indefensibly.

weather *noun* the atmospheric conditions in any area at any time, with regard to sun, cloud, temperature, wind and rain, etc. ▸ *verb* **1** *tr & intr* to expose or be exposed to the effects of wind, sun and rain, etc; to alter or be altered in colour, texture and shape, etc through such exposure. **2** to come safely through (a storm or difficult situation). [Anglo-Saxon *weder*]
IDIOMS **make heavy weather of sth** to make its progress unnecessarily slow and difficult. **under the weather** *informal* not in good health; slightly unwell.

weatherbeaten *or* **weather-worn** *adj* **1** of the skin or face: tanned or lined by exposure to sun and wind. **2** worn or damaged by exposure to the weather.

weatherboard *noun* any of a series of overlapping horizontal boards covering an exterior wall. ▸ *verb* to fit (something) with such boards or planks. ▪ **weatherboarding** *noun*.

weathercock *noun* a weathervane in the form of a farmyard cock.

weather eye *noun* **1** the eye as the means by which someone forecasts the weather. **2** an eye watchful for developments.

weathering *noun, geol* an alteration in the form, colour, texture or composition of rocks as a result of exposure to wind, rain, humidity, extremes of temperature, etc.

weatherman, **weathergirl** *or* **weatherlady** *noun, informal* a man or woman who presents the weather forecast on radio or television.

weatherproof *adj* designed or treated so as to keep out wind and rain. ▸ *verb* to make (something) weatherproof.

weathervane *noun* a revolving arrow that turns to point in the direction of the wind, having a fixed base with arms for each of the four compass points, mounted eg on a church spire. See also **weathercock**.

weather-worn see **weatherbeaten**

weave[1] *verb* (***wove, woven***) **1** *tr & intr* to make (cloth or tapestry) in a loom, passing threads under and over the threads of a fixed warp; to interlace (threads) in this way. **2** to depict (something) by weaving. **3** to construct (a basket, fence, etc) by passing flexible strips in and out between fixed canes, etc; to make (something) by interlacing or intertwining. **4** to devise (a story or plot, etc). **5** of a spider: to weave or spin (a web). ▸ *noun* the pattern, compactness or texture of the weaving in a fabric. ▪ **weaver** *noun*. [Anglo-Saxon *wefian*]

weave[2] *verb, intr* to move to and fro, or wind in and out. [16c]
IDIOMS **get weaving** *informal* to get busy; to hurry.

web *noun* **1** a network of slender threads constructed by a spider to trap insects. **2** a membrane that connects the toes of a swimming bird or animal. **3** any intricate network: *a web of lies*. **4** (**the Web**) short for **World Wide Web**. *as adj*: *a Web page* • *a Web browser*. ▪ **webbed** *adj*. [Anglo-Saxon *webb*]

webbing *noun* strong jute or nylon fabric woven into strips for use as belts, straps and supporting bands in upholstery.

webcam /ˈwɛbkam/ *noun* a small digital video camera attached to a computer that can be used to send images across the Internet. [1990s]

webcast /ˈwɛbkɑːst/ *noun* a programme broadcast live over the Internet. ▸ *verb, tr & intr* to broadcast over the Internet. [1990s]

web design *noun* the design and creation of websites. ▪ **web designer** *noun*.

weber /ˈveɪbə(r)/ *noun, physics* (symbol **Wb**) in the SI system: a unit of magnetic flux (the total size of a magnetic field). [19c: named after Wilhelm Weber, German physicist]

web-footed *or* **web-toed** *adj* of swimming birds, etc: having webbed feet.

weblog see **blog**

webmaster *noun* a person who creates, manages or maintains a website.

website *noun* a person or organization's location on the **World Wide Web**. [1990s]

Wed. *or* **Weds.** *abbrev* Wednesday.

wed *verb* (***wedded*** *or* ***wed, wedding***) **1** *tr & intr, old use* to marry. **2** *old use* to join (someone) in marriage. **3** (*usu* **wed one thing to** *or* **with another**) to unite or combine them: *wed firmness with compassion*. [Anglo-Saxon *weddian* to promise or marry]

we'd *contraction of* we had, we would or we should.

wedded *adj* **1** married. **2** referring or relating to marriage.
IDIOMS **wedded to** devoted or committed to (a principle or activity, etc).

wedding *noun* **1** a marriage ceremony, or the ceremony together with the associated celebrations. **2** *in compounds* any of the notable anniversaries of a marriage, eg *silver wedding*. [Anglo-Saxon *weddung*]

wedding breakfast *noun* the celebratory meal served after a wedding ceremony and before the newly married couple leave for their honeymoon.

wedding ring *noun* a plain ring, esp a gold one, worn as an indication of married status.

wedge *noun* **1** a piece of solid wood, metal or other material, tapering to a thin edge, that is driven into eg wood to split it, pushed into a narrow gap between moving parts to immobilize them, or used to hold a door open, etc. **2** anything shaped like a wedge, usu cut from something circular. **3** a shoe heel in the form of a wedge, tapering towards the sole. **4** *golf* a club with a steeply angled wedge-shaped head for lofting the ball. ▸ *verb* **1** to fix or immobilize (something) in position with, or as if with, a wedge. **2** to thrust, insert or squeeze, or be pushed or squeezed like a wedge: *wedged herself into the corner*. [Anglo-Saxon *wecg*]
IDIOMS **the thin end of the wedge** something that looks like the small beginning of a significant, usu unwanted, development.

wedlock *noun* the condition of being married; marriage. [Anglo-Saxon *wedlac*]

Wednesday *noun* (abbrev **Wed.** *or* **Weds.**) the fourth day of the week. [Anglo-Saxon *Wodnes dæg* the day of Woden, the chief god of the Germanic peoples]

wee[1] *adj* (***weer, weest***) *esp Scot* small; tiny. [Anglo-Saxon *wæg* weight]

wee[2] *or* **wee-wee** *informal, verb* (***wees, weed***) *intr* to urinate. ▸ *noun* **1** an act of urinating. **2** urine. [20c]

weed *noun* **1** any plant growing where it is not wanted, esp one that is thought to hinder the growth of cultivated plants such as crops or garden plants. **2** *derog* a skinny, feeble or ineffectual man. **3** *slang* marijuana. **4** (**the weed**) *slang* tobacco. ▸ *verb* **1** *tr & intr* to uproot weeds from (a garden or flowerbed, etc). **2** (*also* **weed out**) to identify and eliminate (those who are unwanted) from an organization or other group. ▪ **weeding** *noun*. [Anglo-Saxon *weod*]

weedkiller *noun* a substance, usu a chemical preparation, used to kill weeds.

weedy *adj* (**-ier, -iest**) **1** overrun with weeds. **2** *derog* of a person: having a weak or lanky build.

week *noun* **1** a sequence of seven consecutive days, usu beginning on Sunday. **2** any period of seven consecutive days. **3** (*also* **working week**) the working days of the week, as distinct from the **weekend**. **4** the period worked per week: *works a 45-hour week*. **5** (**weeks**) an indefinitely long period of time: *I haven't seen you for weeks!* ▸ *adv* by a period of seven days before or after a specified day: *We leave Tuesday week*. [Anglo-Saxon *wice*]

weekday *noun* any day except Sunday, or except Saturday and Sunday.

weekend *noun* the period from Friday evening to Sunday night.

weekly *adj* occurring, produced or issued every week, or once a week. ▸ *adv* **1** every week. **2** once a week. ▸ *noun* (**-ies**) a magazine or newspaper published once a week.

weeknight *noun* the evening or night of a weekday.

weeny *adj* (**-ier, -iest**) *informal* very small; tiny. [18c: a combination of **wee**[1] + **tiny** or **teeny**]

weep *verb* (**wept**) **1** *intr* to shed tears as an expression of grief or other emotion. **2** to express (something) while, or by, weeping: *She wept her goodbyes*. **3** *tr & intr* of a wound, etc: to exude matter; to ooze. ▸ *noun* a bout of weeping. [Anglo-Saxon *wepan*]

weeping willow *noun* an ornamental Chinese willow with long drooping branches.

weepy *or* **weepie** *adj* (**-ier, -iest**) **1** tearful. **2** of a film or novel, etc: poignant or sentimental. ▸ *noun* (**-ies**) *informal* a film or novel, etc of this kind.

weer, **weest** see **wee**[1]

weevil *noun* **1** a beetle with an elongated proboscis, which can damage fruit, grain, nuts and trees. **2** any insect that damages stored grain. [Anglo-Saxon *wifel*]

wee-wee see **wee**[2]

weft *noun, weaving* **1** the threads that are passed over and under the fixed threads of the warp in a loom. **2** the thread carried by the shuttle (also called **woof**). [Anglo-Saxon]

weigh *verb* **1** to measure the weight of (something). **2** *tr & intr* to have (a certain weight). **3** (*often* **weigh sth out**) to measure out a specific weight of it. **4** (*often* **weigh up**) to consider or assess (facts or possibilities, etc). **5** *intr* (**weigh with sb**) to impress them favourably. **6** *intr* (*usu* **weigh on** *or* **upon sb**) to oppress them. **7** to raise (the anchor) of a ship before sailing. [Anglo-Saxon *wegan*]

PHRASAL VERBS **weigh sb down** to burden, overload or oppress them. **weigh in** of a wrestler or boxer before a fight, or of a jockey after a race: to be weighed officially. **weigh in with sth** *informal* to contribute (a comment, etc) to a discussion.

---

weigh

This word is often misspelt. It might help you to remember the following sentence:

*We w**eigh** **e**verything **i**n **g**rams **h**ere.*

---

weighbridge *noun* an apparatus for weighing vehicles with their loads, consisting of a metal plate set into a road surface and connected to a weighing device.

weigh-in *noun* the official weighing of a wrestler, boxer or jockey.

weight *noun* **1** the heaviness of something; the amount that it weighs. **2** *physics* the gravitational force, measured in **newton**s, acting on a body. Compare **mass**[1]. **3** any system of units for measuring and expressing weight. **4** a piece of metal of a standard weight, against which to measure the weight of other objects. **5** a heavy load. **6** *athletics* a heavy object for lifting, throwing or tossing. **7** (**weights**) weightlifting or weight-training. **8** a standard amount that a boxer, etc should weigh. **9** a mental burden. **10** strength or significance in terms of amount. **11** influence, authority or credibility. ▸ *verb* **1** to add weight to (something), eg to restrict movement. **2** (*often* **weight sth down**) to hold it down in this way. **3** to burden or oppress (someone). **4** to organize (something) so as to have an unevenness or bias: *a tax system weighted in favour of the wealthy*. [Anglo-Saxon *wiht*]

IDIOMS **pull one's weight** to do one's full share of work, etc. **throw one's weight about** *informal* to behave in an arrogant or domineering manner.

---

weight

This word is often misspelt. It might help you to remember the following sentence:

*We w**eigh** **e**verything **i**n **g**rams **h**ere **t**oday.*

---

weighting *noun* a supplement to a salary, usu to compensate for high living costs: *London weighting*. [20c]

weightless *adj* **1** weighing nothing or almost nothing. **2** of an astronaut, etc in space: not subject to the Earth's gravity, so able to float freely. ▪ **weightlessness** *noun*.

weightlifting *noun* a sport in which competitors lift, or attempt to lift, a barbell which is made increasingly heavier. ▪ **weightlifter** *noun*.

weight-training *noun* muscle-strengthening exercises performed with the aid of adjustable weights and pulleys.

weighty *adj* (**-ier, -iest**) **1** heavy. **2** important or significant; having much influence. **3** grave; worrying.

weir *noun* **1** a shallow dam constructed across a river to control its flow. **2** a fence of stakes built across a river or stream to catch fish. [Anglo-Saxon *wer* enclosure]

weird *adj* **1** eerie or supernatural; uncanny. **2** strange or bizarre. **3** *informal* odd or eccentric. ▪ **weirdly** *adv*. ▪ **weirdness** *noun*. [Anglo-Saxon *wyrd* fate]

weirdo *noun* (**weirdos** *or* **weirdoes**) *derog, informal* someone who behaves or dresses bizarrely or oddly.

welch see **welsh**

welcome *verb* **1** to receive (a guest or visitor, etc) with a warm greeting or kind hospitality. **2** to invite (suggestions or contributions, etc). ▸ *exclam* expressing pleasure on receiving someone. ▸ *noun* **1** the act of welcoming. **2** a reception: *a cool welcome.* ▸ *adj* **1** warmly received. **2** gladly permitted or encouraged (to do or keep something). **3** much appreciated. ▪ **welcoming** *adj*. [Anglo-Saxon *wilcuma* a welcome guest]

IDIOMS **outstay one's welcome** to stay too long. **you're welcome!** used in response to thanks: not at all; it's a pleasure.

weld *verb* **1** *eng* to join (two pieces of metal) by heating them to melting point and fusing them together, or by applying pressure alone, producing a stronger joint than soldering. **2** to unite or blend (two or more things) together firmly. ▸ *noun* a joint between two metals formed by welding. ▪ **welder** *or* **weldor** *noun*. [16c: a past participle of obsolete *well* to melt or weld]

welfare *noun* **1** the health, comfort, happiness and general wellbeing of a person or group, etc. **2** social work concerned with helping those in need, eg the very poor. Also called **welfare work**. **3** financial support given to those in need. [14c: from **well**[1] + **fare**]

welfare state *noun* a system in which the government uses tax revenue to look after citizens' welfare, with the provision of free healthcare, old-age pensions and financial support for the disabled or unemployed.

well[1] *adv* (***better, best***) **1** competently; skilfully. **2** satisfactorily. **3** kindly or favourably. **4** thoroughly, properly or carefully. **5** fully or adequately. **6** intimately: *don't know her well.* **7** successfully; prosperously. **8** attractively. **9** by a long way: *well past midnight*. **10** justifiably: *can't very well ignore him.* **11** conceivably; quite possibly: *may well be right*. **12** understandably: *if she objects, as well she may.* **13** very much: *well worth doing.* ▸ *adj* (***better, best***) **1** healthy. **2** in a satisfactory state. ▸ *exclam* **1** used enquiringly in expectation of a response or explanation, etc. **2** used variously in conversation, eg to resume a narrative, preface a reply, express surprise, indignation or doubt, etc. [Anglo-Saxon *wel*]

IDIOMS **all very well** *informal* used as an objecting response to a consoling remark: satisfactory or acceptable but only up to a point: *It's all very well to criticize.* **as well 1** too; in addition. **2** (*also* **just as well**) for all the difference it makes: *I may as well tell you.* **3** (*also* **just as well**) a good thing; lucky: *It was just as well you came when you did.* **as well as …** in addition to … **well off 1** wealthy; financially comfortable. **2** fortunate; successful.

---

well

If you are using a compound such as **well intentioned** or **well prepared**, you should spell it with a hyphen if it comes before the noun:

a well-intentioned person
a well-prepared meal

If it comes after a verb such as **be**, you should not have a hyphen in the compound:

They were well intentioned.
The meal was well prepared.

Idiomatic expressions such as **well-heeled** are usually spelt with a hyphen no matter their position:

a well-heeled group of people
The group were well-heeled.

---

well[2] *noun* a lined shaft that is sunk from ground level to a considerable depth below ground in order to obtain a supply of water, oil or gas, etc. ▸ *verb, intr* (*often* **well up**) of a liquid: to spring, flow or flood to the surface. [Anglo-Saxon *wella*]

we'll *contraction* we will; we shall.

well-adjusted *adj* **1** emotionally and psychologically sound. **2** having a good adjustment.

well-advised *adj* sensible; prudent.

well-appointed *adj* of a house, etc: well furnished or equipped.

well-balanced *adj* **1** satisfactorily proportioned. **2** sane, sensible and stable.

well-behaved *adj* behaving with good manners or due propriety.

wellbeing *noun* the state of being healthy and contented, etc; welfare.

well-born *adj* descended from an aristocratic family.

well-bred *adj* having good manners; showing good breeding.

well-built *adj* **1** strongly built. **2** of a person: with a muscular or well-proportioned body.

well-connected *adj* having influential or aristocratic friends and relations.

well-disposed *adj* inclined to be friendly, agreeable or sympathetic.

well-done *adj* of food, esp beef: thoroughly cooked. Compare **medium** (*adj* sense 3), **rare**[2].

well-earned *adj* thoroughly deserved or merited: *a well-earned break.*

well-established *adj* of a company or habit, etc: deep-seated; strongly or permanently founded.

well-founded *adj* of suspicions, etc: justified; based on good grounds: *a well-founded belief.*

well-groomed *adj* of a person: with a smart and neat appearance.

well-grounded *adj* **1** of an argument, etc: soundly based; well founded. **2** (*usu* **well grounded in sth**) having had a good basic education or training in it.

wellhead *noun* **1** the source of a stream; a spring. **2** an origin or source.

well-heeled *adj, informal* prosperous; wealthy.

well-informed *adj* **1** having reliable information on something particular. **2** full of varied knowledge.

wellington *or* **wellington boot** *noun* a waterproof rubber or plastic boot loosely covering the foot and calf. Also (*old use*) called **gumboot**. [19c: named after the first Duke of Wellington]

well-intentioned *adj* having or showing good intentions, but often having an unfortunate effect.

well-known *adj* **1** esp of a person: familiar or famous; celebrated. **2** fully known or understood.

well-made *adj* **1** cleverly and competently made, produced, constructed, etc. **2** of a person or animal: strongly built; well proportioned.

well-mannered *adj* polite; courteous.

well-meaning *or* **well-meant** *adj* having good intentions.

well-nigh *adv* almost; nearly.

well-oiled *adj* **1** *informal* drunk. **2** smoothly mechanical from thorough practice.

well-placed *adj* **1** in a good or favourable position for some purpose. **2** holding a position senior or intimate enough to gain information, etc.

well-preserved *adj* youthful in appearance; showing few signs of age.

well-read *adj* having read and learnt much.

well-rounded *adj* **1** pleasantly plump. **2** having had a balanced upbringing and a broad education.

well-spoken *adj* having a courteous, fluent and usu refined way of speaking.

wellspring *noun* **1** a spring or fountain. **2** any rich or bountiful source. [Anglo-Saxon]

well-thumbed *adj* of a book: showing marks of repeated use and handling.

well-timed *adj* timely or judicious; opportune: *a well-timed comment*.

well-to-do *adj* wealthy; financially comfortable.

well-travelled *adj* having travelled often and to many different locations.

well-trodden *adj* often followed or walked along; much used or frequented.

well-versed *adj* thoroughly trained; knowledgeable.

well-wisher *noun* someone concerned for another's welfare.

well-worn *adj* **1** much worn or used; showing signs of wear. **2** of an expression, etc: overfamiliar from frequent use.

welly *or* **wellie** *noun* (**-ies**) *informal* a **wellington**.
IDIOMS **give it (some) welly** *slang* to put a great deal of effort or energy into something.

Welsh *noun* **1** a citizen or inhabitant of, or someone born in, Wales. **2** the official Celtic language of Wales. ▸ *adj* belonging or referring to Wales, its inhabitants or their language. [Anglo-Saxon *welisc*]

welsh *or* **welch** *verb* **1** *intr* (*usu* **welsh on**) to fail to pay (one's debts) or fulfil (one's obligations). **2** *intr* (*usu* **welsh on sb**) to fail to keep one's promise to them. **3** to cheat in such a way. ▪ **welsher** *noun*. [19c]

Welshman *or* **Welshwoman** *noun* a man or woman from Wales.

Welsh rabbit *or* **Welsh rarebit** *noun* a dish consisting of melted cheese, usu with butter, ale and seasoning mixed in, served on toast. Also called **rarebit**.

welt *noun* **1** a reinforcing band or border fastened to an edge, eg the ribbing at the waist of a knitted garment. **2** a **weal**[1] raised by a lash or blow. [15c as *welte* or *walt*]

welter *noun* a confused mass. [13c: from Dutch *welteren*]

welterweight *noun* **1** a class for boxers and wrestlers of not more than a specified weight, which is 66.7kg (114 lb) in professional boxing, and similar but different weights in amateur boxing and wrestling. **2** a boxer or wrestler of this weight.

wen *noun, pathol* a sebaceous cyst on the skin, usu of the scalp. [Anglo-Saxon *wenn* a swelling or wart]

wench *noun* **1** *facetious* a girl; a woman. **2** a servant girl. [Anglo-Saxon *wencel* a child]

wend *verb, archaic or literary* to go or direct (one's course). [Anglo-Saxon *wendan*]
IDIOMS **wend one's way** to go steadily and purposefully on a route or journey.

Wensleydale *noun* a white crumbly variety of cheese. [19c: named after Wensleydale, North Yorkshire]

went *past tense of* **go**

wept *past tense, past participle of* **weep**

were *past tense of* **be**

we're *contraction* we are.

weren't *contraction* were not.

werewolf /ˈwɛəwʊlf/ *noun, folklore* someone who is changed, or changes at free will, into a wolf, usu at full moon. [Anglo-Saxon *werwulf* man-wolf]

Wesak see **Vesak**

west *noun* **1** the quarter of the sky in which the sun sets. **2** one of the four **cardinal points** of the compass. **3** any part of the earth, a country or town, etc lying in the direction of the west. **4** (**the West**) **a** the countries of Europe and N America, in contrast to those of Asia; **b** *old use* the non-communist bloc as distinct from the communist or former communist countries of the East. ▸ *adj* **1** in the west; on the side that is on or nearer the west. **2** of a wind: situated towards or blowing from the west. ▸ *adv* towards the west. [Anglo-Saxon]

westbound *adj* going or leading towards the west.

the West Country *noun* the SW counties of England, namely Somerset, Devon and Cornwall.

westerly *adj* **1** of a wind: coming from the west. **2** looking, lying, etc towards the west. ▸ *adv* to or towards the west. ▸ *noun* (**-ies**) a westerly wind.

western *adj* **1** situated in, directed towards or belonging to the west or the West. **2** (**Western**) belonging to **the West**. ▸ *noun* (**Western**) a film or novel featuring cowboys in the west of the USA, esp during the 19c. ▪ **westerner** *or* **Westerner** *noun* someone who lives in or comes from the west of anywhere, esp the western part of the USA. ▪ **westernmost** *adj*.

westernize *or* **-ise** *verb* to make or become like the people of Europe and America in customs, or like their institutions, practices or ideas. ▪ **westernization** *noun*.

West Indian *adj* belonging or relating to the West Indies. ▸ *noun* a citizen or inhabitant of, or someone born in, the West Indies.

Westminster *noun* the British parliament. [20c: named after the London borough where the Houses of Parliament are situated]

westward *adv* (*also* **westwards**) towards the west. ▸ *adj* towards the west.

wet *adj* (***wetter, wettest***) **1** covered or soaked in water or other liquid. **2** of the weather: rainy. **3** of paint, cement or varnish, etc: not yet dried. **4** *derog slang* of a person: feeble; ineffectual. ▸ *noun* **1** moisture. **2** rainy weather: *Don't stay outside in the wet!* **3** *derog, slang* a feeble ineffectual person. **4** *informal* in politics: a moderate Conservative. ▸ *verb* (***wet** or **wetted, wetting***) **1** to make (someone or something) wet. **2** to urinate involuntarily on (something). ▪ **wetly** *adv*. ▪ **wetness** *noun*. [Anglo-Saxon *wæt*]
IDIOMS **wet behind the ears** *informal* immature or inexperienced. **wet oneself 1** to make oneself wet by urinating inadvertently. **2** to be so excited or frightened, etc as to be on the point of urinating inadvertently.

wet blanket *noun* a dreary and pessimistic person who dampens the enthusiasm of others.

wet dream *noun* a dream that causes the involuntary ejaculation of semen.

wether *noun* a castrated ram. [Anglo-Saxon]

wetland *noun* (*often* **wetlands**) a region of marshy land.

wet nurse *noun* a woman employed to breastfeed another's baby.

wet rot *noun* a form of decay in timber caused by certain fungi which develop in wood that is alternately wet and dry. Compare **dry rot**.

wet suit *noun* a tight-fitting rubber suit that is permeable by water, but conserves body heat, worn by divers and canoeists, etc.

we've *contraction* we have.

whack *informal, verb* to hit (something or someone) sharply and resoundingly. ► *noun* **1** a sharp resounding blow. **2** the sound of this. **3** one's share of the profits, etc: *haven't had their whack yet*. [18c: imitating the sound]

IDIOMS **have a whack at sth** to try it; to have a go at it. **out of whack** *esp Aust & US* out of order. **top, full** *or* **the full whack** the highest price, wage or rate, etc.

whacked *adj, informal* exhausted; worn out.

whacking *informal, noun* a beating. ► *adj* enormous. ► *adv* extremely.

whacky see **wacky**

whale *noun* (***whale*** *or* ***whales***) a large marine mammal which has a torpedo-shaped body, and a blowhole on the top of the head for breathing. ► *verb, intr* to hunt whales. ▪ **whaling** *noun*. [Anglo-Saxon *hwæl*]

IDIOMS **a whale of a ...** *informal* a hugely enjoyable (time or evening, etc).

whalebone *noun* the light flexible horny substance consisting of the baleen plates in toothless whales, used esp formerly for stiffening corsets, etc.

whaler *noun* a person or ship engaged in hunting and killing whales.

wham *noun* a resounding noise made by a hard blow. ► *verb* (***whammed, whamming***) **1** to hit or make (something) hit with a wham. **2** to crash or bang: *The car whammed into the back of the truck*. ► *as exclam & adv*: *He ran, wham!, into the glass door.* [18c: imitating the sound]

whammy *noun* (***-ies***) *orig US informal* **1** an unfortunate or malevolent influence. **2** a stunning or powerful blow, or (*usu* **double whammy**) two such blows. [20c, meaning a spell cast by someone's evil eye (a *double whammy* being one cast by both eyes): from US cartoon strip *Li'l Abner*]

wharf *noun* (***wharfs*** *or* ***wharves***) a landing stage built along a waterfront for loading and unloading vessels. [Anglo-Saxon *hwearf* bank or shore]

what *adj, pron* **1** used in questions, indirect questions and statements, identifying, or seeking to identify or classify, a thing or person: *What street are we in?* **2** used in exclamations expressing surprise, sympathy or other emotions: *What! You didn't pass?* **3** used as a relative pronoun or adjective: that or those which; whatever; anything that: *It is just what I thought.* **4** used to introduce a suggestion or new information: *I know what – let's go to the zoo!* **5** used to ask for a repetition or confirmation of something said: *What? I didn't catch what you said.* ► *adv* used in questions, indirect questions and statements: to how great an extent or degree?: *What does that matter?* [Anglo-Saxon *hwæt*]

IDIOMS **so what?** *or* **what of it?** *informal* why is that important? **what ... for?** for what reason ...? to what purpose ...?: *What did you do that for?* **what's up?** what's the matter? is something wrong? **what's with ...?** *informal* what's the matter with ...?

what

In a sentence such as 'What we need is colouring pencils and paper', the verb should be singular:

✗ *What we need are colouring pencils and paper.*

✓ *What we need is colouring pencils and paper.*

Also, be careful not to add **what** after **than** where it is not necessary:

✗ *He can play faster than what I can.*

✓ *He can play faster than I can.*

It is not correct to use **what** after nouns and pronouns:

✗ *It was the shock what killed him.*

✓ *It was the shock that killed him.*

whatever *pron, adj* **1** (*also* **what ever**) used as an emphatic form of **what**: *Whatever shall I do?* **2** anything: *Take whatever you want.* **3** no matter what: *I must finish, whatever happens.* **4** *with negatives* at all: *has nothing whatever to do with you.* **5** *informal* some or other: *has disappeared, for whatever reason.* **6** used to express uncertainty: *a didgeridoo, whatever that is.*

IDIOMS **... or whatever** *informal* ... or some such thing: *Use tape, glue or whatever.*

whatnot *noun, informal* and other similar things: *cakes, bread and whatnot.*

whatsoever *adj, pron* **1** *old use or literary* whatever; what. **2** *with negatives* at all: *none whatsoever.*

wheat *noun* **1** a cereal grass. **2** the grain of this plant, which provides flour, etc. [Anglo-Saxon *hwæte*]

wheatear *noun* a small songbird which has a conspicuous white rump. [16c]

wheaten *adj* made of wheat flour or grain.

wheat germ *noun* the vitamin-rich germ or embryo of wheat, present in the grain.

wheatmeal *noun* wheat flour containing most of the powdered whole grain (bran and germ).

wheedle *verb* **1** *tr & intr* to coax or cajole (someone); to persuade (them) by flattery. **2** (**wheedle sth out of sb**) **a** to obtain it from them by coaxing. **b** to cheat them of it by cajolery. ▪ **wheedler** *noun*. [17c]

wheel *noun* **1** a circular object or frame rotating on an axle, used eg for moving a vehicle along the ground. **2** such an object serving as part of a machine or mechanism. **3** an object similar to or functioning like a wheel, eg a spinning-wheel. **4** (**wheels**) *informal* a motor vehicle for personal use. **5** a disc or drum on the results of whose random spin bets are made: *a roulette wheel.* **6** any progression that appears to go round in a circle. ► *verb* **1** to fit (something) with a wheel or wheels. **2** to push (a wheeled vehicle or conveyance) or to push (someone or something) in or on it: *He wheeled the bike outside.* **3** to make (something) move in a circular course. **4** *intr* (*usu* **wheel about** *or* **round**) to turn round suddenly; to pivot on one's heel. [Anglo-Saxon *hweol*]

IDIOMS **at** *or* **behind the wheel 1** in the driver's seat of a car, boat, etc. **2** in charge. **wheel and deal** to engage in tough business dealing or bargaining.

wheelbarrow *noun* a hand-pushed cart with a wheel in front and two handles and legs at the rear.

wheelbase *noun* the distance between the front and rear axles of a vehicle.

wheelchair *noun* a chair with wheels in which invalids or disabled people can be conveyed or convey themselves.

wheel clamp *noun* a locking device fitted to the wheel or wheels of an illegally parked vehicle in order to immobilize it, and removed only after the payment of a fine. ▪ **wheel clamping** *noun*. [20c]

wheelhouse *noun* the shelter on a ship's bridge in which the steering-gear is housed.

wheelie *noun, Brit* a trick performed on a motorbike or bicycle in which the front wheel is lifted off the ground, either while stationary or in motion.

wheelie bin *or* **wheely bin** *noun, Brit* a large dustbin in a wheeled frame. [20c]

wheel spin *noun* the rotation of the wheels of a vehicle as a result of reduced road-surface frictional force, causing a spin without any forward movement of the vehicle.

wheelwright *noun* a craftsman who makes and repairs wheels and wheeled carriages.

wheeze *verb, intr* to breathe in a laboured way with a gasping or rasping noise. ▸ *noun* **1** a wheezing breath or sound. **2** *informal* a clever scheme. ▪ **wheezy** *adj*. [15c: from Norse *hvæza* to hiss]

whelk *noun* a large marine snail with a pointed spirally-coiled shell. [Anglo-Saxon *weoloc*]

whelp *noun* **1** the young of a dog or wolf. **2** an impudent boy or youth. ▸ *verb, intr* to give birth to puppies or cubs. [Anglo-Saxon *hwelp*]

when *adv* used in questions, indirect questions and statements: at what time?; during what period? ▸ *conj* **1** at the time, or during the period, that. **2** as soon as. **3** at any time that; whenever. **4** at which time. **5** in spite of the fact that; considering that: *Why just watch when you could be dancing?* ▸ *pron* **1** what or which time: *They stayed talking, until when I can't say.* **2** used as a relative pronoun: at, during, etc which time: *an era when life was harder.* [Anglo-Saxon *hwænne*]

whence *old use, formal or literary, adv, conj* **1** used in questions, indirect questions and statements: from what place?; from which place: *enquired whence they had come.* **2** used esp in statements: from what cause or circumstance: *can't explain whence the mistake arose.* **3** to the place from which: *returned whence they had come.* [13c as *hwannes*]

whenever *conj* **1** at any or every time that: *gets furious whenever he doesn't get his way.* **2** if ever; no matter when: *I'll be here whenever you need me.* ▸ *adv* **1** an emphatic form of **when**: *Whenever could I have said that?* **2** used to indicate that one does not know when: *at Pentecost, whenever that is.*

where *adv* used in questions, indirect questions and statements: **1** in, at or to which place; in what direction: *Where is she going?* **2** in what respect: *showed me where I'd gone wrong.* **3** from what source: *Where did you get that?* ▸ *pron* what place?: *Where have you come from?* ▸ *conj* **1** in, at or to the, or any, place that: *went where he pleased.* **2** in any case in which: *keep families together where possible.* **3** the aspect or respect in which: *That's where you are wrong.* [Anglo-Saxon *hwær*]

whereabouts *adv* where or roughly where? ▸ *singular or plural noun* the (rough) position of a person or thing.

whereas *conj* but, by contrast: *I'm a pessimist, whereas my husband is an optimist.*

whereby *pron* by means of which.

wherefore *conj, adv, formal, old use or law* for what reason? ▸ *noun* a reason: *the whys and wherefores.*

wherein *formal, old use or law, adv, conj* in what place?; in what respect?: *Wherein is the justification?* ▸ *pron* in which place or thing.

whereof *pron, formal or old use* of which; of what: *the circumstances whereof I told you.*

whereon *pron, formal or old use* on which; on what?

whereupon *conj* at which point; in consequence of which.

wherever *pron* any or every place that: *I'll take it to wherever you like.* ▸ *conj* **1** in, at or to whatever place: *They were welcomed wherever they went.* **2** no matter where: *I won't lose touch, wherever I go.* ▸ *adv* **1** an emphatic form of **where**: *Wherever can they be?* **2** used to indicate that one does not know where: *the Round House, wherever that is.*

wherewithal *pron, old use* with which. ▸ *noun* (**the wherewithal**) the means or necessary resources, esp money.

whet *verb* (***whetted, whetting***) **1** to sharpen (a bladed tool) by rubbing it against stone, etc. **2** to arouse or intensify (someone's appetite, interest or desire). ▪ **whetter** *noun*. [Anglo-Saxon *hwettan*]

whether *conj* **1** used to introduce an indirect question: *asked whether it was raining.* **2** used in constructions involving alternative possibilities: *was uncertain whether he liked her or not.* **3** (*also* **whether or not**) used to state the certainty of something, whichever of two circumstances applies: *promised to marry her, whether or not his parents agreed.* [Anglo-Saxon *hwæther*]

whetstone *noun* a stone for sharpening bladed tools. [Anglo-Saxon *hwetstan*]

whew *exclam, informal* expressing relief or amazement.

whey /weɪ/ *noun* the watery content of milk, separated from the curd in making cheese and junket, etc. Compare **curd**. [Anglo-Saxon *hwæg*]

which *adj, pron* **1** used in questions, indirect questions and statements to identify or specify a thing or person, usu from a known set or group: *can't decide which book is better: Which did you choose?* **2** used to introduce a defining or identifying relative clause: *animals which hibernate.* **3** used to introduce a commenting clause, used chiefly in reference to things or ideas rather than people: *The house, which lies back from the road, is painted red.* **4** used in a relative clause, meaning 'any that': *Take which books you want.* [Anglo-Saxon *hwilc*]

which, that, who, whom

It is acceptable, even in formal English, to use the relative pronoun **that** in sentences such as *The man that I met happened to be Ken's uncle* or *I had a car that just wouldn't start in the mornings.*

It is not necessary to replace **that** with *who, whom* or *which.*

whichever *pron, adj* **1** the one or ones that; any that: *Take whichever is suitable.* **2** according to which: *at 10.00 or 10.30, whichever is more convenient.* **3** no matter which: *I'll be satisfied, whichever you choose.*

4 used to express uncertainty: *It's in the 'To Do' folder, whichever that is.*

whiff *noun* **1** a puff or slight rush of air or smoke, etc. **2** a hint or trace: *at the first whiff of scandal.* ▪ **whiffy** *adj* (**-ier, -iest**). [16c: imitating the sound]

Whig *hist, noun* a member of one of the main British political parties that emerged 1679–80, superseded in 1830 by the **Liberal Party**. Compare **Tory**. ▸ *adj* composed of, referring or relating to the Whigs. ▪ **Whiggism** *noun.* [17c: prob from *whiggamore*, the name for a 17c Scottish Presbyterian rebel]

while *conj* **1** at the same time as: *She held the bowl while I stirred.* **2** for as long as; for the whole time that: *guards us while we sleep.* **3** during the time that: *happened while we were abroad.* **4** whereas: *He likes camping, while she prefers sailing.* ▸ *adv* at or during which: *all the months while I was ill.* ▸ *noun* a space or lapse of time: *after a while.* ▸ *verb* (*often* **while away**) to pass (time or hours, etc) in a leisurely or undemanding way. [Anglo-Saxon *hwil*]

IDIOMS **worth (one's) while** worth one's time and trouble.

whilst *conj* **while**.

whim *noun* a sudden fanciful idea; a caprice. [17c: shortened from *whim-wham* a toy]

whimper *verb* **1** *intr* to cry feebly or plaintively. **2** to say (something) plaintively. **3** to say (something) in a whining or querulous manner. ▸ *noun* a feebly plaintive cry. [16c: imitating the sound]

whimsical *adj* **1** delicately fanciful or playful. **2** odd, weird or fantastic. ▪ **whimsically** *adv.*

whimsy *or* **whimsey** *noun* (***whimsies*** *or* ***whimseys***) **1** quaint or fanciful humour. **2** a whim. ▸ *adj* (**-ier, -iest**) quaint or odd. [17c]

whin *noun* **gorse**. [15c]

whine *verb, intr* **1** to whimper. **2** to complain peevishly or querulously. ▸ *noun* **1** a whimper. **2** a continuous shrill or high-pitched noise. **3** an affected, thin and ingratiating nasal tone of voice. ▪ **whining** *noun, adj.* [Anglo-Saxon *hwinan*]

whinge *informal, verb* (***whingeing***) *intr* to complain irritably; to whine. ▸ *noun* a peevish complaint. ▪ **whinger** *noun.* [Anglo-Saxon *hwinsian* to whine]

whinny *verb* (**-ies, -ied**) *intr* of a horse: to neigh softly. ▸ *noun* (**-ies**) a gentle neigh. [16c: imitating the sound]

whip *noun* **1** a lash with a handle for driving animals or punishing people. **2** a stroke administered by, or as if by, such a lash. **3** a whipping action or motion. **4** *politics* a member of a parliamentary party responsible for members' discipline, and for their attendance to vote on important issues. **5** *politics* a notice sent to members by a party whip requiring their attendance for a vote, urgency being indicated (*in compounds*) by the number of underlinings: *a three-line whip.* **6** a dessert of any of various flavours made with beaten egg-whites or cream. ▸ *verb* (***whipped, whipping***) **1** to strike or thrash with a whip. **2** to punish (someone) with lashes or smacking. **3** to lash (someone or something) with the action or force of a whip: *a sharp wind whipped their faces.* **4** *tr & intr* to move or make (something) move with a sudden or whip-like motion: *the branch whipped back.* **5** (*usu* **whip sth off** *or* **out,** *etc*) to take or snatch it: *whipped out a revolver.* **6** to rouse, goad, drive or force into a certain state: *whipped the crowd into a fury.* **7** *informal* to steal. **8** to beat (egg-whites or cream, etc) until stiff or frothy. **9** *informal* to outdo, outwit or defeat. ▪ **whipping** *noun, adj.* [13c]

PHRASAL VERBS **whip sth up 1** to arouse (support, enthusiasm or other feelings) for something. **2** to prepare (a meal, etc) at short notice.

whip hand *noun* (*often* **the whip hand**) the advantage in a situation.

whiplash *noun* **1** the springy end of a whip. **2** the lash of a whip, or the motion it represents. **3** (*also* **whiplash injury**) a popular term for a neck injury caused by the sudden jerking back of the head and neck, esp as a result of a motor vehicle collision.

whipper-in *noun* (***whippers-in***) an assistant to a huntsman, who controls the hounds.

whippersnapper *noun, informal* an insignificant and cheeky young lad or any lowly person who behaves impudently.

whippet *noun* a small slender breed of dog, resembling a greyhound. [17c]

whipping boy *noun* someone who is blamed for the faults and shortcomings of others.

whip-round *noun, informal* a collection of money made, often hastily, among a group of people.

whipstock *noun* the rod or handle of a whip.

whir see **whirr**

whirl *verb* **1** *intr* to spin or revolve rapidly. **2** *tr & intr* to move with a rapid circling or spiralling motion. **3** *intr* of the head: to feel dizzy from excitement, etc. ▸ *noun* **1** a circling or spiralling movement or pattern. **2** a round of intense activity. **3** a dizzy or confused state: *a whirl of emotion.* [13c: from Norse *hvirfla* to turn]

IDIOMS **give sth a whirl** *informal* to try it out.

whirligig *noun* **1** a spinning toy, esp a top. **2** a merry-go-round. **3** anything that revolves rapidly. [15c]

whirlpool *noun* a violent circular eddy of water that occurs in a river or sea at a point where several strong opposing currents converge.

whirlwind *noun* **1** a violently spiralling column of air over land or sea. **2** anything that moves in a similarly rapid and usu destructive way. ▸ *adj* referring or relating to anything that develops rapidly or violently: *a whirlwind courtship.*

whirr *or* **whir** *noun* a rapid drawn-out whirling, humming or vibratory sound. ▸ *verb* **1** *intr* to turn or spin with a whirring noise. **2** to make (something) move with this sound. [14c]

whisk *verb* **1** to transport (someone or something) rapidly: *was whisked into hospital.* **2** to move (something) with a brisk waving motion. **3** to beat (egg-whites or cream, etc) until stiff. ▸ *noun* **1** a whisking movement or action. **2** a hand-held implement for whisking egg-whites or cream, etc. [14c]

whisker *noun* **1** any of the long coarse hairs that grow round the mouth of a cat or mouse, etc. **2** (**whiskers**) a man's beard. **3** the tiniest possible margin: *won by a whisker.* ▪ **whiskered** *or* **whiskery** *adj.* [15c]

whisky *or* (*Irish & N Am, esp US*) **whiskey** *noun* (***whiskies*** *or* ***whiskeys***) an alcoholic spirit distilled from a fermented mash of cereal grains, eg barley, wheat or rye. [18c: from Gaelic *uisge beatha*, literally 'water of life']

whisper *verb* **1** *tr & intr* to speak or say (something) quietly, breathing rather than voicing the words. **2** *intr* of a breeze, etc: to make a rustling sound in leaves, etc. ▸ *noun* **1** a whispered level of speech. **2** (*often* **whispers**) a rumour or hint; whispered gossip. **3** a soft rustling sound. ▪ **whispering** *noun*. [Anglo-Saxon *hwisprian*]

whist *noun* a card game, usu for two pairs of players, in which the object is to take a majority of 13 tricks, each trick over six scoring one point. [17c: altered from its earlier form *whisk*]

whist drive *noun* a gathering for playing **whist**, with a change of partner after every four games.

whistle *noun* **1 a** a shrill sound produced through pursed lips or through the teeth, used to signal or to express surprise, etc; **b** the act of making this sound. **2** any of several similar sounds, eg the call of a bird or the shrill sigh of the wind. **3** a small hand-held device used for making a similar sound, used esp as a signal. **4** any of several devices which produce a similar sound by the use of steam, eg a kettle. ▸ *verb* **1** *tr & intr* **a** to produce (a tune, etc) by passing air through a narrow constriction in the mouth, esp through pursed lips; **b** to signal (something) by doing this or by blowing a whistle. **2** *tr & intr* to blow or play on a whistle. **3** *intr* of a kettle or locomotive: to emit a whistling sound. **4** *intr* of the wind: to make a shrill sound. **5** *tr & intr* of a bird: to sing. **6** *intr* (*usu* **whistle for sth**) *informal* to expect it in vain. [Anglo-Saxon *hwistlian* to whistle]

IDIOMS **blow the whistle on** *informal* **1** to expose (someone or their illegal or dishonest practices) to the authorities. **2** to declare (something) to be illegal. **wet one's whistle** *informal* to have a drink; to quench one's thirst. **whistle in the dark** to do something (eg whistle or talk brightly) to quell or deny one's fear.

whistle-stop *adj* **1** of a politician's tour: with a number of short stops being made, orig at railway stations, to deliver an electioneering address or a **whistle-stop speech** to local communities. **2** of any tour: very rapid, with a number of brief stops.

Whit *noun* Whitsuntide. ▸ *adj* related or belonging to Whitsuntide.

whit *noun, with negatives* the least bit; the smallest particle imaginable: *not a whit worse*. [15c: a variant of *wight* creature]

white *adj* **1** having the colour of snow, the colour that reflects all light. **2** (*often* **White**) **a** of people: belonging to one of the pale-skinned races; **b** referring or relating to such people. **3** abnormally pale, eg from shock or illness. **4** eg of a rabbit or mouse: albino. **5** of hair: lacking pigment, as in old age. **6** of a variety of anything, eg grapes: pale-coloured, as distinct from darker types. **7** of wine: made from white grapes or from skinned black grapes. **8 a** of flour: having had the bran and wheat germ removed; **b** of bread: made with white flour. **9** of coffee or tea: with milk or cream added. ▸ *noun* **1** the colour of snow. **2** white colour or colouring matter, eg paint. **3** white clothes. **4** (*often* **White**) a white person. **5** (*in full* **egg-white**) the clear fluid surrounding the yolk of an egg; albumen. **6** the white part of the eyeball, surrounding the iris. **7** (**whites**) **a** household linen; **b** white clothes, eg as worn for cricket or tennis. ▪ **whiteness** *noun*. ▪ **whitish** *and* **whitey** *adj*. [Anglo-Saxon *hwit*]

whitebait *noun* (*pl* ***whitebait***) the young of any of various silvery fishes, esp herrings and sprats, often fried and eaten whole.

white blood cell *or* **white corpuscle** *noun* a colourless blood cell containing a nucleus, whose main functions are to engulf invading micro-organisms and foreign particles, to produce antibodies, or to remove cell debris from sites of injury and infection. Also called **leucocyte**.

whiteboard *noun* **1** a board with a white plastic surface for writing on using felt-tipped pens, used esp in teaching, presentations, etc. **2** a large white screen, linked to a computer, upon which objects can be inserted, manipulated, etc using eg touch or an electronic pen.

white-collar *adj* referring to or denoting a class of workers, eg clerks or other professions, who are not engaged in manual labour. Compare **blue-collar**.

white dwarf *noun, astron* a small dense hot star that has reached the last stage of its life.

white elephant *noun* a possession or piece of property that is useless or unwanted, esp one that is inconvenient or expensive to keep.

white feather *noun* a symbol of cowardice.

IDIOMS **show the white feather** to behave in a cowardly fashion.

white fish *noun* a general name for edible sea fish, including whiting, cod, sole, haddock and halibut.

white flag *noun* the signal used for offering surrender or requesting a truce.

whitefly *noun* (***-ies***) a small sap-sucking bug, whose body and wings are covered with a white powder.

White Friar *or* **white friar** *noun* a member of the Carmelite order of monks.

white frost see **hoarfrost**

white gold *noun* a pale lustrous alloy of gold containing platinum, palladium, nickel or silver, giving it a white colour.

white goods *plural noun* large kitchen appliances such as washing machines, refrigerators, dishwashers and cookers, traditionally white in colour. Compare **brown goods**.

white heat *noun* **1** the energy contained in a metal, etc such that white light is emitted. **2** *informal* an extremely intense state of enthusiasm, activity or excitement: *the white heat of technology*.

white hope *noun* someone of whom great achievements and successes are expected.

white horse *noun* (*often* **white horses**) a wave with a white crest, seen esp on a choppy sea.

white-hot *adj* **1** of a metal, etc: so hot that white light is emitted. **2** intense; passionate.

white-knuckle *adj, informal* causing or designed to cause extreme fear or anxiety: *a white-knuckle roller-coaster ride*.

white lie *noun* a forgivable lie, esp one told to avoid hurting someone's feelings.

white light *noun* light, such as that of the sun, that contains all the wavelengths in the visible range of the spectrum.

white matter *noun, anatomy* pale fibrous nerve tissue in the brain and spinal cord. Compare **grey matter** (sense 1).

white meat *noun* pale-coloured meat, eg chicken or veal. Compare **red meat**.

whiten *verb, tr & intr* to make or become white or whiter; to bleach. ▪ **whitener** *noun*.

white noise *noun* sound waves that contain a large number of frequencies of roughly equal intensity.

white-out *noun* a phenomenon in snowy weather when the overcast sky blends imperceptibly with the white landscape to give poor visibility. [20c: modelled on **blackout**]

white paper *noun* (*also* **White Paper**) in the UK: a government policy statement printed on white paper, issued for the information of parliament. Compare **green paper**.

white pepper *noun* light-coloured pepper made from peppercorns with the dark outer husk removed.

white sauce *noun* a thick sauce made from flour, fat and a liquid such as milk or stock.

white slave *noun* a girl or woman held against her will, and forced into prostitution. ▪ **white slavery** *noun*.

white spirit *noun* a colourless liquid distilled from petroleum, and used as a solvent and thinner for paints and varnishes.

whitethorn *noun* the **hawthorn**.

white tie *noun* **1** a white bow tie worn as part of men's formal evening dress. **2** formal evening dress for men.

whitewash *noun* **1** (*also* **limewash**) a mixture of lime and water, used to give a white coating to walls, esp outside walls. **2** measures taken to cover up a disreputable affair or to clear a stained reputation, etc. ▸ *verb* **1** (*also* **limewash**) to coat (something) with whitewash. **2** to clean up or conceal (eg a disreputable affair). **3** *informal* in a game: to beat (the opponent) so decisively that they fail to score at all. [16c]

white water *noun* the foaming water as in rapids.

whitewood *noun* unstained wood; wood prepared for staining.

whither *old use or poetic, adv* to what place?: *Whither did they go?* ▸ *conj, pron* towards which place: *Some miles away lay London, whither they journeyed.* [Anglo-Saxon *hwider*]

whiting /'waɪtɪŋ/ *noun* (*pl* ***whiting***) a small edible fish related to the cod, native to the waters of northern Europe. [15c as *hwitling*: so called because of its white colour]

whitlow *noun* an inflammation of the finger or toe, esp near the nail. [14c as *whitflawe* white flaw]

Whitsun *or* **Whitsuntide** *noun* in the Christian Church: the week beginning with Whit Sunday, particularly the first three days. ▸ *adj* relating to, or observed at, Whitsuntide. [13c]

Whit Sunday *or* **Whitsunday** *noun* **Pentecost** (sense 1). [Anglo-Saxon *hwita sunnandæg* white Sunday, because traditionally those newly baptized wore white robes]

whittle *verb* **1** to cut, carve or pare (a stick or piece of wood, etc) with a knife. **2** to shape or fashion (something) by this means. **3** (*usu* **whittle sth away** *or* **down**) to wear it away or reduce it gradually. [Anglo-Saxon *thwitan* to cut]

whizz *or* **whiz** *verb, intr* **1** to fly through the air, esp with a whistling or hissing noise. **2** to move rapidly. ▸ *noun* **1** a whistling or hissing sound. **2** *informal* someone with an exceptional and usu specific talent for something; an expert. [16c: imitating the sound]

whizz kid, **whiz kid** *or* **wiz kid** *noun, informal* someone who achieves success quickly and early, through ability, inventiveness, or ambition.

WHO *abbrev* World Health Organization.

who *pron* **1** used in questions, indirect questions and statements: which or what person; which or what people: *Who is at the door?* • *asked who he had seen.* **2** used as a relative pronoun to introduce a defining clause: *the boy who was on the train.* **3** used as a relative pronoun to add a commenting clause: *Julius Caesar, who was murdered in 44* BC. [Anglo-Saxon *hwa*]

---

who, whom

The basic rule is to use **who** as the subject of a sentence or clause and **whom** as the object:

✘ *Whom came in first?*

✓ *Who came in first?*

Use **whom** in formal speech and writing instead of the more informal **who**:

My aunt, whom I love dearly, is in hospital. [formal]

My aunt, who I love dearly, is in hospital. [informal]

Use **whom** instead of **who** when it comes after a preposition:

✘ *The lady to who he was speaking is his aunt.*

✓ *The lady to whom he was speaking is his aunt.*

---

whoa *exclam* a command to stop, esp to a horse.

who'd *contraction* **1** who would. **2** who had.

whodunit *or* **whodunnit** *noun, informal* a detective novel or play, etc; a mystery. [20c: from *who done it?*, a non-standard form of *who did it?*]

whoever *pron* **1** used in questions, indirect questions and statements as an emphatic form of **who** or **whom**: *Whoever is that at the door?* • *ask whoever you like.* **2** no matter who: *I don't want to see them, whoever they are.* **3** used to indicate that one does not know who: *St Fiacre, whoever he was.*

whole *noun* **1** all the constituents or components of something: *the whole of the time.* **2** something complete in itself, esp something consisting of integrated parts. ▸ *adj* comprising all of something; no less than the whole; entire: *The whole street heard you.* ▸ *adv* **1** *informal* completely; altogether; wholly: *found a whole new approach.* **2** in one piece: *swallowed it whole.* **3** unbroken: *only two cups left whole.* ▪ **wholeness** *noun*. [Anglo-Saxon *hal* healthy]
IDIOMS **on the whole** considering everything.

wholefood *noun* (*sometimes* **wholefoods**) food that is processed as little as possible.

wholehearted *adj* sincere and enthusiastic. ▪ **wholeheartedly** *adv*.

wholemeal *or* **wholewheat** *adj* **1** of flour: made from the entire wheat grain. **2** of bread: made from wholemeal flour.

whole number *noun, maths* an integral number, being one without fractions.

wholesale *noun* the sale of goods in large quantities to a retailer. ▸ *adj, adv* **1** buying and selling, or concerned with buying and selling in this way. Compare **retail**. **2** on a huge scale and without discrimination: *wholesale destruction.* ▪ **wholesaler** *noun*. [15c]

wholesome *adj* **1** attractively healthy. **2** promoting health: *wholesome food.* **3** *old use* morally beneficial. [13c]

wholly /'hoʊllɪ/ *adv* completely; altogether: *not wholly satisfied.*

whom *pron* used as the object of a verb or preposition (but often replaced by **who**, esp in less formal usage): **1** in seeking to identify a person: *To whom are you referring?* **2** as a relative pronoun in a defining clause: *I am looking for the man whom I met earlier.* **3** used as a relative pronoun to introduce a commenting clause: *The man, whom I met earlier, has left.* [Anglo-Saxon *hwam*]

whom, who
See the Usage Note at **who**.

whomever *pron, formal or old use* used as the object of a verb or preposition to mean 'any person or people that': *I will write to whomever they appoint.* Also **whomsoever**.

whoop *noun* a loud cry of delight, joy or triumph, etc. ▸ *verb, tr & intr* to utter or say (something) with a whoop. [14c]

IDIOMS **whoop it up** *informal* to celebrate noisily.

whoopee *exclam* /wʊ'piː/ expressing exuberant delight. ▸ *noun* /'wʊpiː/ **1** exuberant delight or excitement. **2** a cry indicating this. [19c]

whooping cough *noun, pathol* a highly contagious disease that mainly affects children, characterized by bouts of violent coughing followed by a sharp drawing in of the breath which produces a 'whooping' sound. *Technical equivalent* **pertussis**.

whoops *or* **whoops-a-daisy** *exclam* expressing surprise, concern or apology, eg when one has a slight accident, makes an error, etc.

whoosh *or* **woosh** *noun* the sound of, or like that made by, something passing rapidly through the air. ▸ *verb* to move with or make such a sound. [20c: imitating the sound]

whopper *noun, informal* **1** anything very large of its kind. **2** a blatant lie.

whopping *informal, adj* huge; enormous; unusually large. ▸ *noun* a thrashing.

whorl /wɔːl/ *noun* **1** *botany* a **corolla**. **2** *zool* one complete coil in the spiral shell of a mollusc, the number of which indicates the shell's age. **3** a type of fingerprint in which there is a spiral arrangement of the ridges on the skin. **4** any type of convolution. [Anglo-Saxon *hwyrfel*]

who's *contraction* **1** who is. **2** who has.

who's, whose
Be careful not to use the spelling **who's**, the short form of 'who is' or 'who has', when you mean **whose**, and vice versa:
Who's at the door?
Whose boots are these?

whose *pron, adj* **1** used in questions, indirect questions and statements: belonging to which person or people: *Whose is this jacket?* **2** used as a relative adjective to introduce a defining clause: of whom or which: *buildings whose foundations are sinking.* **3** used as a relative adjective to add a commenting clause: *my parents, without whose help I could not have succeeded.* **4** used as a relative adjective, meaning 'whoever's' or 'whichever's': *Take whose advice you will.*

whose
Whose can be used to mean both 'of whom' and 'of which':
the boy whose father is a policeman
the book whose pages are torn

whosoever *pron, formal or old use* used in statements: **whoever**.

why *adv* used in questions, indirect questions and statements: for what reason. ▸ *conj* for, or because of, which: *no reason why I should get involved.* ▸ *exclam* expressing surprise, indignation, impatience or recognition, etc: *Why, you little monster!* ▸ *noun* see **the whys and wherefores**. [Anglo-Saxon *hwi*]

the whys and wherefores *plural noun* all the reasons.

WI *abbrev* **1** West Indies. **2** in the UK: Women's Institute.

wick *noun* the twisted string running up through a candle or lamp and projecting at the top, that burns when lit and draws up the wax or inflammable liquid into the flame. [Anglo-Saxon *weoce*]

wicked *adj* **1** evil or sinful; immoral. **2** mischievous, playful or roguish. **3** *slang* excellent or cool; admirable. **4** *informal* bad: *wicked weather.* ▪ **wickedly** *adv.* ▪ **wickedness** *noun.* [13c: from Anglo-Saxon *wicca* wizard]

wicker *adj* of a fence or basket, etc: made of interwoven twigs, canes or rushes, etc. [14c: Scandinavian]

wickerwork *noun* articles made from wicker; basketwork of any kind.

wicket *noun, cricket* **a** a row of three small wooden posts stuck upright in the ground behind either crease; **b** the playing area between these; **c** a batsman's dismissal by the bowler: *45 runs for two wickets.* [13c: from French *wiket*]

wicketkeeper *noun, cricket* the fielder who stands immediately behind the wicket.

wide *adj* **1** large in extent from side to side. **2** measuring a specified amount from side to side: *three feet wide.* **3** of the eyes: open to the fullest extent. **4** of a range or selection, etc: covering a great variety: *There's a wide choice of films on.* **5** extensive; widespread: *wide support.* ▸ *adv* **1** to the fullest extent: *with the door wide open.* **2** off the mark: *His aim went wide.* ▸ *noun, cricket* a ball bowled out of the batsman's reach. ▪ **widely** *adv.* ▪ **wideness** *noun.* [Anglo-Saxon *wid*]

wide-angle lens *noun, photog, cinematog* a camera lens with an angle of 60° or more and a short focal length, which takes pictures that cover a wider area than a normal lens, but with some distortion.

wideband *adj* another name for **broadband**.

wide boy *noun, informal* a shrewd but dishonest operator, esp in business undertakings.

wide-eyed *adj* **1** showing great surprise. **2** naive.

widen *verb, tr & intr* to make, or become, wide or wider.

wide-ranging *adj* of interests, discussions, etc: covering a large variety of subjects or topics.

widespread *adj* **1** extending over a wide area. **2** affecting or involving large numbers of people.

widgeon see **wigeon**

widget *noun* **1** a device attached to the bottom of cans of draught beer so that when it is poured it has a proper head. **2** a gadget; any small manufactured item or component. [20c: perhaps an alteration of **gadget**]

widow *noun* a woman whose husband is dead and who has not remarried. ▸ *verb* to leave or make (someone) a widow or widower. ▪ **widowhood** *noun.* [Anglo-Saxon *widewe*]

widower *noun* a man whose wife is dead and who has not remarried.

width *noun* **1** extent from side to side; breadth. **2** the distance from side to side across a swimming pool: *swam ten widths.*

wield *verb* **1** to brandish or use (a tool or weapon, etc). **2** to have or exert (power, authority or influence, etc). [Anglo-Saxon *wieldan* to control]

wife *noun* (***wives***) the woman to whom a man is married; a married woman. ▪ **wifely** *adj.* [Anglo-Saxon *wif*]

wig[1] *noun* an artificial covering of natural or synthetic hair for the head. [17c: a short form of **periwig**]

wig[2] *verb* (***wigged, wigging***) *informal* to scold (someone) severely. ▪ **wigging** *noun* a scolding. [17c]

wigeon *or* **widgeon** *noun* (***wigeon*** *or* ***wigeons***; ***widgeon*** *or* ***widgeons***) a freshwater duck with long pointed wings and a wedge-shaped tail. [16c: from French *vigeon*]

wiggle *verb, tr & intr, informal* to move or cause (something) to move, esp jerkily, from side to side or up and down. ▸ *noun* **1** a wiggling motion. **2** a line, eg one drawn by a pen or pencil, with a twist or bend in it. ▪ **wiggly** *adj* (***-ier, -iest***). [13c: from Dutch *wiggelen* to totter]

wigwam *noun* a domed Native American dwelling made of a framework of arched poles covered with skins, bark or mats. [17c: from Abenaki (a native N American language) *wikewam* house]

wiki /ˈwɪkɪ *or* ˈwiːkɪ/ *noun* a type of computer software that enables any user of a website to edit and restructure its contents. [Coined by Ward Cunningham, creator of the software, from Hawaiian *wiki wiki* very quick]

wilco *exclam* in signalling and telecommunications, etc: expressing compliance or acknowledgement of instructions. [20c: from 'I *will comply*']

wild *adj* **1** of animals: untamed or undomesticated; not dependent on humans. **2** of plants: growing in a natural uncultivated state. **3** of country: desolate, rugged or uninhabitable. **4** of peoples: savage; uncivilized. **5** unrestrained; uncontrolled: *wild fury.* **6** frantically excited. **7** distraught: *wild with grief.* **8** dishevelled; disordered: *wild attire.* **9** of the eyes: staring; distracted or scared-looking. **10** of a guess: very approximate, or quite random. **11** *informal* furious; extremely angry. **12** *slang* enjoyable; terrific. ▸ *noun* **1** (**the wild**) a wild animal's or plant's natural environment or life in it: *returned the cub to the wild.* **2** (**wilds**) lonely, sparsely inhabited regions away from the city. ▪ **wildly** *adv.* ▪ **wildness** *noun.* [Anglo-Saxon *wilde*]

IDIOMS **run wild 1** of a garden or plants: to revert to a wild, overgrown and uncultivated state. **2** of children, animals, etc: to live a life of freedom, with little discipline or control.

wild boar *noun* a wild pig of Europe, NW Africa and S Asia, with prominent tusks.

wild card *noun* **1** someone allowed to compete in a sports event, despite lacking the usual or stipulated qualifications. **2** *comput* a symbol, eg an asterisk, that can be used to represent any character or set of characters in a certain position, in order to identify text strings with variable contents.

wildcat *noun* (***wildcats*** *or* ***wildcat***) **1** an undomesticated cat of Europe and Asia, which has a longer stouter body and longer legs than the domestic cat, and a thick bushy tail. **2** a short-tempered, fierce and aggressive person. ▸ *adj* of a business scheme: financially unsound or risky; speculative.

wild dog *noun* any of several wild species of dog, esp the **dingo**.

wildebeest /ˈwɪldəbiːst, ˈvɪl-/ *noun* (***wildebeest*** *or* ***wildebeests***) the **gnu**. [19c: Afrikaans]

wilderness *noun* **1** an uncultivated or uninhabited region. **2** an overgrown tangle of weeds, etc. **3** a large confused or confusing assemblage. **4** *politics* the state of being without office or influence after playing a leading role. [13c: from Anglo-Saxon *wilddeoren* of wild beasts]

wildfire *noun* a highly flammable liquid originally used in warfare.

IDIOMS **spread like wildfire** of disease or rumour, etc: to spread rapidly and extensively.

wildfowl *singular or plural noun* a game bird or game birds.

wild-goose chase *noun* a search that is bound to be unsuccessful and fruitless.

wild hyacinth *noun* the **bluebell**.

wildlife *noun* wild animals, birds and plants.

wild rice *noun* a tall aquatic grass that yields rice-like seeds.

Wild West *or* **the Wild West** *noun, hist* the part of the US west of the Mississippi, settled during the 19c and legendary for the adventures of its cattlemen and the struggle to gain territory from the Native American population.

wile *noun* **1** (**wiles**) charming personal ways. **2** a cunning trick. ▸ *verb* to lure or entice. [Anglo-Saxon *wil*]

wilful *or* (*US*) **willful** *adj* **1** deliberate; intentional. **2** headstrong, obstinate or self-willed. ▪ **wilfully** *adv.* ▪ **wilfulness** *noun.* [Anglo-Saxon]

will[1] *auxiliary verb* expressing or indicating: **1** the future tense of other verbs, esp when the subject is *you, he, she, it* or *they*: *They will no doubt succeed.* **2** intention or determination, when the subject is *I* or *we*: *We will not give in.* **3** a request: *Will you please shut the door?* **4** a command: *You will apologize to your mother immediately!* **5** ability or possibility: *The table will seat ten.* **6** readiness or willingness: *Any of our branches will exchange the goods.* **7** invitations: *Will you have a coffee?* **8** what is bound to be the case: *The experienced teacher will know when a child is unhappy.* **9** what applies in certain circumstances: *An unemployed youth living at home will not receive housing benefit.* **10** an assumption or probability: *That will be Vernon at the door.* **11** choice or desire: *Make what you will of that.* See also **shall**, **won't**, **would**. [Anglo-Saxon *wyllan*]

will[2] *noun* **1** the power of conscious decision and deliberate choice of action: *free will.* **2** one's own preferences, or one's determination in effecting them: *against my will.* **3** desire or determination: *the will to live.* **4** a wish or desire. **5 a** instructions for the disposal of a person's property, etc after death; **b** the document containing these. ▸ *verb* **1** to try to compel (someone) by, or as if by, exerting one's will: *willed herself to keep going.* **2** *formal* to desire or require that (something) be done, etc: *Her Majesty wills it.* **3** to bequeath (something) in one's will.

[Anglo-Saxon *willa*]
IDIOMS **at will** as and when one wishes.

the willies *plural noun, informal* the creeps; a feeling of anxiety or unease. [19c]

willing *adj* **1** ready, glad or not disinclined to do something. **2** eager and co-operative. ▪ **willingly** *adv*. ▪ **willingness** *noun*.

will-o'-the-wisp *noun* (***wills-o'-the-wisp*** *or* ***will-o'-the-wisps***) **1** a light sometimes seen over marshes, caused by the combustion of marsh gas. Also called **ignis fatuus**. **2** any elusive or deceptive person or thing. [17c: literally 'Will of the torch', from *Will*, short for the name William + **wisp**]

willow *noun* **1** a deciduous tree or shrub that generally grows near water, and has slender flexible branches. **2** the wood of this tree, which is used to make cricket bats and furniture. [Anglo-Saxon *welig*]

willow herb *noun* a plant with narrow leaves, and usu pink, rose-purple or white flowers.

willow pattern *noun* a design used on pottery, usu in blue on a white background, showing a Chinese landscape with a willow tree, bridge and figures.

willowy *adj* of a person: slender and graceful.

willpower *noun* the determination, persistence and self-discipline needed to accomplish something.

willy-nilly *adv* whether one wishes or not; regardless. [17c: orig *will I, nill I*, meaning 'will I, will I not']

wilt *verb, intr* **1** *botany* of a plant organ or tissue: to droop or become limp because there is insufficient water to maintain the individual cells in a turgid state. **2** to droop from fatigue or heat. **3** to lose courage or confidence. [17c: a variant of *wilk* to wither]

Wilts. *abbrev, English county* Wiltshire.

wily /'waɪlɪ/ *adj* (***-ier, -iest***) cunning; crafty or devious. ▪ **wiliness** *noun*. [13c: from **wile**]

WIMP /wɪmp/ *abbrev, comput* windows, icons, menus (or mouse), printer, a user-friendly computer interface which allows the user to operate system commands by clicking on symbols on the screen instead of typing out codes. [20c]

wimp *informal, noun* a feeble person. ▸ *verb, intr* (*always* **wimp out**) to back out (of doing something) through feebleness. ▪ **wimpish** *or* **wimpy** *adj* (***-ier, -iest***). [20c]

wimple *noun* a veil folded around the head, neck and cheeks worn as part of a nun's dress. [Anglo-Saxon *wimpel* neck-covering]

win *verb* (***won, winning***) **1** *tr & intr* to be victorious or come first in (a contest, race or bet, etc). **2** *tr & intr* to beat an opponent or rivals in (a competition, war, conflict or election, etc). **3** to compete or fight for, and obtain (a victory or prize, etc). **4** to obtain (something) by struggle or effort. **5** to earn and receive or obtain (something). ▸ *noun, informal* a victory or success. ▪ **winnable** *adj*. [Anglo-Saxon *winnan*]
PHRASAL VERBS **win sb over** *or* **round** to persuade them over to one's side or opinion.

wince *verb, intr* to shrink back, start or grimace, eg in pain or anticipation of it; to flinch. ▸ *noun* a start or grimace in reaction to pain, etc. [13c: from French *wencier* or *guenchier*]

winch *noun* **1** a reel or roller round which a rope or chain is wound for hoisting or hauling heavy loads. **2** a crank or handle for setting a wheel, axle or machinery in motion. ▸ *verb* to hoist or haul (something or someone) with a winch. [Anglo-Saxon *wince*]

wind[1] /wɪnd/ *noun* **1** the movement of air across the Earth's surface as a result of differences in atmospheric pressure between one location and another. **2** a current of air produced artificially, by a fan, etc. **3** an influence that seems to pervade events: *a wind of change*. **4** one's breath or breath supply: *short of wind*. **5** gas built up in the intestines; flatulence. **6** empty, pompous or trivial talk. ▸ *verb* **1** to deprive (someone) of breath temporarily, eg by a punch or fall. **2** to burp (a baby). [Anglo-Saxon]
IDIOMS **break wind** to discharge intestinal gas through the anus. **get wind of sth** to have one's suspicions aroused or hear a rumour about it, esp something unfavourable or unwelcome. **like the wind** swiftly. **put the wind up sb** *informal* to make them nervous, anxious or alarmed.

wind[2] /waɪnd/ *verb* (***wound*** /waʊnd/) **1** (*often* **wind round**) *tr & intr* to wrap or coil, or be wrapped or coiled. **2** *tr & intr* to move or cause (something) to move with many twists and turns. **3** (*also* **wind sth up**) to tighten the spring of (a clock, watch or other clockwork device) by turning a knob or key. ▸ *noun* **1** an act of winding or the state of being wound. **2** a turn, coil or twist. [Anglo-Saxon *windan*]
PHRASAL VERBS **wind down 1** of a clock or clockwork device: to slow down and stop working. **2** of a person: to begin to relax, esp after a spell of tension or stress. **wind sth down** to reduce the resources and activities of (a business or enterprise). **wind up** *informal* to end up: *He wound up in jail*. **wind sb up 1** to make them tense, nervous or excited. **2** *informal* to taunt or tease them. See also **wind-up**. **wind sth up** to conclude or close down a business or enterprise.

windbag *noun, informal* an excessively talkative person who communicates little of any value.

windbreak *noun* a barrier, eg in the form of a screen, fence or line of trees, that provides protection from the wind.

windcheater *noun* a windproof jacket with tightly fitting cuffs, neck and waistband.

windchill *noun, meteorol* the extra chill given to air temperature by the wind.

wind cone see **windsock**

windfall *noun* **1** a fruit, esp an apple, blown down from its tree. **2** an unexpected or sudden financial gain or other piece of good fortune.

wind farm *noun* a concentration of wind-driven turbines generating electricity.

wind gauge *noun* an **anemometer**.

winding-sheet /'waɪndɪŋ-/ *noun* a sheet for wrapping a corpse in; a shroud.

wind instrument *noun* a musical instrument such as a clarinet, flute or trumpet, played by blowing air, esp the breath, through it.

windjammer /'wɪnddʒamə(r)/ *noun, hist* a large fast merchant sailing-ship.

windlass /'wɪndləs/ *noun* a drum-shaped axle round which a rope or chain is wound for hauling or hoisting weights. [14c: from Norse *windass*]

windmill *noun* **1** a mechanical device operated by wind-driven sails that revolve about a fixed shaft, used for grinding grain, pumping water and generating electricity. **2** a toy with a set of plastic or paper sails, mounted on a stick, that revolve in the wind. [13c]

window *noun* **1** an opening in a wall to look through, or let in light and air, consisting of a wooden or metal frame fitted with panes of glass; a pane. **2** the frame itself. **3** the area immediately behind a shop's window, in which goods on sale are displayed. **4** a gap in a schedule, etc available for some purpose. **5** an opening in the front of an envelope, allowing the address written on the letter inside to be visible. **6** *comput* an enclosed rectangular area displayed on the VDU of a computer, which can be used as an independent screen. [13c: from Norse *windauga* literally 'wind eye']

window box *noun* a box fitted along an exterior window ledge, for growing plants in.

window-dressing *noun* **1** the art of arranging goods in a shop window. **2** the art or practice of giving something superficial appeal by skilful presentation. ▪ **window-dresser** *noun.*

window ledge see **windowsill**

windowpane *noun* a sheet of glass set in a window.

window seat *noun* **1** a seat placed in the recess of a window. **2** on a train or aeroplane, etc: a seat next to a window.

window-shopping *noun* the activity of looking at goods in shop windows without buying them.

windowsill *or* **window ledge** *noun* the interior or exterior ledge that runs along the bottom of a window.

windpipe *noun, anatomy* the **trachea**.

windpower *noun* a renewable energy source derived from winds in the Earth's atmosphere, used to generate electricity.

windscreen *noun* the large sheet of curved glass at the front of the motor vehicle. *N Am equivalent* **windshield**.

windscreen-wiper *noun* a device fitted to the windscreen of a motor vehicle, consisting of a rubber blade on an arm which moves in an arc, to keep the windscreen clear of rain, snow, etc.

windsock *or* **wind cone** *noun* an open-ended cone of fabric flying from a mast, eg at an airport, which shows the direction and speed of the wind.

windsurfing *noun* the sport of riding the waves on a sailboard; sailboarding. ▪ **windsurfer** *noun.* [20c: from US trademark Windsurfer, a sailboard]

windswept *adj* **1** exposed to strong winds. **2** dishevelled from exposure to the wind.

wind tunnel *noun, aeronautics* an experimental chamber in which fans blow a controlled stream of air past stationary models of aircraft, cars or trains, etc or their components, in order to test their aerodynamic properties.

wind-up /'waɪndʌp/ *noun* the taunting or teasing of someone, eg the playing of a practical joke on them, or a joke, etc used in this.

windward *noun* the side of a boat, etc facing the wind. ▸ *adj* on this side.

windy *adj* (***-ier, -iest***) **1** exposed to, or characterized by, strong wind. **2** suffering from, producing or produced by flatulence. **3** *informal* of speech or writing: long-winded or pompous. **4** *informal* nervous.

wine *noun* **1** an alcoholic drink made from fermented grape juice. **2** a similar drink made from other fruits or plants, etc. **3** the dark-red colour of red wine. [Anglo-Saxon *win*]

IDIOMS **wine and dine** to partake of, or treat (someone) to, a meal, usu accompanied by wine.

wine bar *noun* a bar which specializes in the selling of wine and often food.

wine cellar *noun* **1** a cellar in which to store wines. **2** the stock of wine stored there.

wine cooler *noun* an ice-filled receptacle for cooling wine in bottles, ready for serving.

wine glass *noun* a drinking-glass typically consisting of a small bowl on a stem with a flared base.

winery *noun* (***-ies***) *chiefly US* a place where wine is prepared and stored. [19c]

wine vinegar *noun* vinegar made from wine, as opposed to malt.

wing *noun* **1** one of the two modified front limbs of a bird or bat that are adapted for flight. **2** one of two or more membranous outgrowths that project from either side of the body of an insect enabling it to fly. **3** one of the flattened structures that project from either side of an aircraft body. **4** any of the corner sections of a vehicle body, forming covers for the wheels. **5** a part of a building projecting from the central or main section: *the west wing*. **6** *sport* in football and hockey, etc: **a** either edge of the pitch; **b** the player at either extreme of the forward line. **7** (**wings**) *theatre* the area at each side of a stage, where performers wait to enter, out of sight of the audience. **8** a group with its own distinct views and character, within a political party or other body. See also **left wing**, **right wing**. ▸ *verb* **1** to make (one's way) by flying, or with speed. **2** to wound (a bird) in the wing or (a person) in the arm or shoulder; to wound (someone or something) superficially. **3** *poetic* to fly or skim lightly (over something). ▪ **winged** *adj.* ▪ **wingless** *adj.* [12c: from Norse *vængre*]

IDIOMS **on the wing** flying. **spread one's wings 1** to use one's potential fully. **2** to escape from a confining environment in order to do this. **under sb's wing** under their protection or guidance.

wing chair *noun* an armchair that has a high back with projections on both sides.

wing collar *noun* a stiff collar worn upright with the points turned down.

wing commander *noun* an officer in the air force.

winger /'wɪŋə(r)/ *noun, sport* in football and hockey, etc: a player in wing position.

wing mirror *noun* a rear-view mirror attached to the side of a motor vehicle.

wing nut *noun* a metal nut easily turned on a bolt by the finger and thumb by means of its flattened projections. Also called **butterfly nut**.

wingspan *noun* the distance from tip to tip of the wings of an aircraft, or of a bird's wings when outstretched.

wink *verb, tr & intr* **1** to shut an eye briefly as an informal or cheeky gesture or greeting. **2** of lights and stars, etc: to flicker or twinkle. ▸ *noun* **1** an act of winking. **2** a quick flicker of light. **3** a short spell of something, esp sleep. See also **forty winks**. [Anglo-Saxon *wincian*]

IDIOMS **tip sb the wink** *informal* to give them a useful hint or valuable information, etc, esp in confidence.

winkle *noun* a small edible snail-shaped shellfish; a periwinkle. ▸ *verb* (*always* **winkle sth out**) to force or prise it out. [16c: from **periwinkle**[2]]

winkle-picker *noun, informal* a shoe or boot with a long narrow pointed toe.

winner *noun* **1** a person, animal or vehicle, etc that wins a contest or race. **2** someone or something that is or seems destined to be a success.

winning *adj* **1** attractive or charming; persuasive. **2** securing victory. ▸ *noun* (**winnings**) money or prizes won, esp in gambling. ▪ **winningly** *adv.*

winnow *verb* **1** to separate (chaff) from (grain) by blowing a current of air through it. **2** to sift (evidence, etc). ▪ **winnower** *noun.* [Anglo-Saxon *windwian*]

wino /ˈwaɪnoʊ/ *noun, slang* someone, esp a down-and-out, addicted to cheap wine; an alcoholic.

winsome *adj* charming; captivating. [Anglo-Saxon *wynsum* joyous]

winter *noun* (*also* **Winter**) the coldest season of the year, coming between autumn and spring. ▸ *adj* **1** referring, relating or belonging to winter: *a winter dish.* **2** of plants, crops and fruit, etc: sown in autumn so as to be reaped in the following winter. ▸ *verb, intr* to spend the winter in a specified place, usu other than one's normal home. ▪ **wintertime** *noun.* [Anglo-Saxon]

wintergreen *noun* **1** an evergreen plant with oval leaves and drooping bell-shaped pink or white flowers. **2** (*in full* **oil of wintergreen**) the aromatic oil obtained from this plant, used medicinally or as a flavouring.

winter solstice *noun* the shortest day of the year, when the sun reaches its lowest point in the N hemisphere (usu 21 December).

winter sports *plural noun* open-air sports held on snow or ice, such as skiing and ice-skating.

wintry *or* **wintery** *adj* (**-ier, -iest**) **1** of weather, etc: characteristic of winter. **2** unfriendly, cold or hostile. [Anglo-Saxon wintrig]

wipe *verb* **1** to clean or dry (something) with a cloth, etc. **2** (**wipe sth away, off, out** *or* **up**) to remove it by wiping. **3** *comput, etc* **a** to clear (magnetic tape or a disk) of its contents; **b** to erase (data) from a disk or magnetic tape. **4** to remove or get rid of (something): *wiped the incident from his memory.* **5** *Aust, informal* to discard (a person, idea or proposition, etc). ▸ *noun* **1** the act of cleaning something by rubbing. **2** a piece of fabric or tissue, usu specially treated, for wiping and cleaning, eg wounds. [Anglo-Saxon *wipian*]

PHRASAL VERBS **wipe sb out** *slang* to kill or murder them. **wipe sth out 1** to get rid of it. **2** to destroy or obliterate it.

wipeout *noun, informal* a complete failure or disaster; total destruction.

wiper *noun* a **windscreen-wiper**.

wire *noun* **1** metal drawn out into a narrow flexible strand. **2** a length of this, usu wrapped in insulating material, used for carrying an electric current. **3** *telecomm* a cable that connects one point with another. **4** *old use* a telegram or telegraph. ▸ *verb* **1 a** to send a telegram to (someone); **b** to send (a message) by telegram. **2** (*also* **wire up**) to fit or connect up (an electrical apparatus or system, etc) with wires. **3** to fasten or secure (something) with wire. [Anglo-Saxon *wir*]

IDIOMS **get one's wires crossed** to misunderstand or be confused about something.

wire brush *noun* a brush with wire bristles, for cleaning dirt off suede shoes and rust off metal, etc.

wired *adj, slang* highly-strung; stressed-out.

wire-haired *adj* of a breed of dog: with a coarse, wiry coat.

wireless *noun, old use* a radio.

wire netting *noun* wires twisted into a network for use as fencing, etc.

wiretap *verb* to tap (a telephone) or the telephone of (a person).

wire wool *noun* a mass of fine wire used for scouring.

wireworm *noun* a hard-bodied worm-like beetle larva, which lives in soil where it is extremely destructive to plant roots.

wiring *noun* the arrangement of wires that connects the individual components of electric circuits into an operating system, eg the mains wiring of a house.

wiry *adj* (**-ier, -iest**) **1** of a person: of slight build, but strong and agile. **2** resembling wire. ▪ **wiriness** *noun.*

wisdom *noun* **1** the quality of being wise. **2** the ability to make sensible judgements and decisions, esp on the basis of one's knowledge and experience. **3** learning; knowledge. [Anglo-Saxon]

wisdom tooth *noun* in humans: any of the last four molar teeth to come through, appearing at the back of each side of the upper and lower jaw.

wise[1] *adj* **1** having or showing wisdom; prudent; sensible. **2** learned or knowledgeable. **3** astute, shrewd or sagacious. **4** *in compounds* knowing the ways of something: *streetwise* • *worldly-wise.* ▪ **wisely** *adv.* [Anglo-Saxon *wis*]

IDIOMS **be wise to sth** *informal* to be aware of or informed about it. **none the wiser** knowing no more than before.

PHRASAL VERBS **wise up to sb** *or* **sth** *informal* to find out the facts about them or it.

wise[2] *noun, old use* way: *in no wise to blame.* [Anglo-Saxon, meaning 'manner']

-wise *combining form, denoting* **1** direction or manner: *clockwise* • *otherwise.* **2** respect or relevance: *money-wise* • *business-wise.* [From **wise**[2]]

wiseacre *noun, derog* someone who assumes an air of superior wisdom. [16c: from Dutch *wijsegghter* soothsayer]

wisecrack *noun* a smart, clever or knowing remark. ▸ *verb, intr* to make a wisecrack. [20c]

wise guy *noun, informal* someone who is full of smart and cocky comments; a know-all.

wish *verb* **1** to want; to have a desire. **2** to desire, esp vainly or helplessly (that something were the case). **3** to express a desire for (luck, success, happiness, etc) to come to (someone). **4** to say (good afternoon, etc) to (someone). ▸ *noun* **1** a desire. **2** (*usu* **wishes**) what one wants to be done, etc. **3** (**wishes**) a hope expressed for someone's welfare: *best wishes.* [Anglo-Saxon *wyscan*]

wishbone *noun* a V-shaped bone in the breast of poultry. [19c]

wishful *adj* **1** having a desire or wish. **2** eager.

wishful thinking *noun* an overoptimistic expectation that something will happen, arising from one's desire that it should.

wishy-washy *adj* **1** pale and insipid; bland. **2** watery; weak.

wisp *noun* **1** a strand; a thin fine tuft or shred. **2** something slight or insubstantial. ▪ **wispy** *adj* (**-ier, -iest**). [14c]

wist see **wit²**

wisteria *or* **wistaria** *noun* a climbing shrub with long pendulous clusters of lilac, violet or white flowers. [19c: named after Caspar Wistar, the American anatomist]

wistful *adj* sadly or vainly yearning. ▪ **wistfully** *adv.* ▪ **wistfulness** *noun.* [18c]

wit¹ *noun* **1** the ability to express oneself amusingly; humour. **2** someone who has this ability. **3** humorous speech or writing. **4** (*also* **wits**) common sense or intelligence or resourcefulness: *Will he have the wit to phone?* [Anglo-Saxon, meaning 'mind' or 'thought']

IDIOMS **at one's wits' end** *informal* reduced to despair; completely at a loss. **have** *or* **keep one's wits about one** to be, or stay, alert. **live by one's wits** to live by cunning. **scared, frightened,** *etc* **out of one's wits** extremely scared, frightened, etc.

wit² *verb* (*first and third person present tense* **wot,** *past tense & past participle* **wist,** *present participle* **witting**) *archaic* to know how; to discern. [Anglo-Saxon *witan* to know]

IDIOMS **to wit** *law* that is to say; namely.

witch *noun* **1** someone, esp a woman, supposed to have magical powers used usu, but not always, malevolently. **2** a frighteningly ugly or wicked old woman or hag. ▪ **witchlike** *adj.* [Anglo-Saxon *wicca*]

witchcraft *noun* **1** magic or sorcery of the kind practised by witches. **2** the use of this.

witch doctor *noun* a member of a tribal society who is believed to have magical powers, and to be able to use them to cure or harm people.

witch elm see **wych-elm**

witch hazel *or* **wych hazel** *noun* **1** a N American shrub with narrow-petalled yellow flowers. **2** an astringent lotion produced from the bark of this shrub, used to treat bruises, etc. [Anglo-Saxon *wice*]

witch hunt *noun* a concerted campaign against an individual or group believed to hold views or to be acting in ways harmful to society.

with *prep* **1** in the company of (someone): *went with her.* **2** used after verbs of partnering, co-operating, associating, etc: *danced with him.* **3** used after verbs of mixing: *mingled with the crowd.* **4** by means of; using: *raised it with a crowbar.* **5** used after verbs of covering, filling, etc: *plastered with mud.* **6** used after verbs of providing: *equipped with firearms.* **7** as a result of (something): *shaking with fear.* **8** in the same direction as (something): *drift with the current.* **9** used after verbs of conflict: *quarrelled with her brother.* **10** used after verbs of agreeing, disagreeing, and comparing: *compared with last year.* **11** used in describing (someone or something): *a man with a limp.* **12** in or under the specified circumstances: *I can't go abroad with my mother so ill.* **13** regarding: *What shall we do with this?* • *can't do a thing with my hair.* **14** loyal to or supporting (someone or something): *We're with you all the way.* [Anglo-Saxon]

withdraw *verb* (**withdrew, withdrawn**) **1** *intr* to move somewhere else, esp more private: *withdrew into her bedroom.* **2** *intr* to leave; to go away: *We tactfully withdrew.* **3 a** *intr* of troops: to move back or retreat; **b** to order (troops, etc) to retreat. **4** to take (money) from a bank account for use. **5** *tr & intr* to back out or pull (something) out of an activity or contest, etc. **6** to take back (a comment) that one regrets making. **7** *intr* to become uncommunicative or unresponsive. [13c]

withdrawal *noun* **1** the act or process of withdrawing. **2** (*usu* **make a withdrawal**) a removal of funds from a bank account. **3** *med* the breaking of an addiction to drugs, etc, with associated physical and psychological symptoms. **4** a retreat into silence and self-absorption.

withdrawn *adj* of a person or their manner, etc: unresponsive, shy or reserved.

wither *verb* **1 a** *intr* of plants: to fade, dry up and die; **b** to cause (a plant) to do this. **2** (*sometimes* **wither away**) *tr & intr* to fade or make (something) fade and disappear. **3** *tr & intr* to shrivel or make (something) shrivel and decay. **4** to humble or disconcert (someone) with a glaring or scornful, etc expression. ▪ **withered** *adj.* [13c: possibly a variant of **weather**]

withers *plural noun* the ridge between the shoulder blades of a horse. [16c]

withhold *verb* **1** to refuse to give or grant (something): *withheld evidence.* **2** to hold back (something): *withholding payment.*

within *prep* **1** inside; enclosed by something: *within these four walls.* **2** not outside the limits of (something); not beyond: *within sight.* **3** in less than (a certain time or distance): *finished within a week.* ▸ *adv* **1** inside: *apply within.* **2** *old use* indoors: *There is someone within.* [Anglo-Saxon *withinnan*]

without *prep* **1** not having the company of (someone): *She went home without him.* **2** deprived of (someone or something): *He can't live without her.* **3** not having (something): *a blue sky without a cloud.* **4** lacking (something): *books without covers.* **5** not (behaving as expected or in a particular way): *answered without smiling* • *did it without being told.* **6** not giving or showing, etc (something): *complied without a murmur.* **7** free from (something): *admitted it without shame.* **8** not having (something required); in neglect of (a usual procedure): *entered without permission.* **9** not using; not having the help of (something): *found our way without a map.* **10** if it had not been for (someone or something): *would have died without their help.* ▸ *adv, old use* outside: *He is without.* [Anglo-Saxon *withutan*]

withstand *verb* **1** to maintain one's position or stance against (someone or something). **2** to resist or brave (something): *withstood his insults.* [Anglo-Saxon]

witless *adj* **1** stupid or brainless; lacking wit, sense or wisdom. **2** crazy. [Anglo-Saxon *witleas*, from **wit¹**]

witness *noun* **1** someone who sees, and can therefore give a direct account of, an event or occurrence, etc. **2** someone who gives evidence in a court of law. **3** someone who adds their own signature to confirm the authenticity of a signature just put on a document, etc. **4** proof or evidence of anything. ▸ *verb* **1** to be present as an observer at (an event or occurrence, etc). **2** to add one's own signature to confirm the authenticity of (a signature on a document, etc). **3** *intr* to give evidence. **4** of a period or place, or of a person: to be the setting for, or to live through, (certain events). [Anglo-Saxon *witnes*]

IDIOMS **bear witness to sth 1** to be evidence of it. **2** to give confirmation of it. **be witness to sth** to be in a position to observe it.

witness box *or* **witness stand** *noun* the enclosed stand from which a witness gives evidence in a court of law.

witter *verb, intr* (*usu* **witter on**) to talk or mutter ceaselessly and ineffectually. [19c: prob a variant of *whitter* to chatter]

witticism *noun* a witty remark or comment.

wittingly *adv* consciously; deliberately.

witty *adj* (**-ier, -iest**) able to express oneself cleverly and amusingly. ▪ **wittily** *adv.* [Anglo-Saxon, from **wit**[1]]

wives *pl of* **wife**

wizard *noun* **1** someone, esp a man, supposed to have magic powers; a magician or sorcerer. **2** *dated, informal* (*often* **a wizard at** *or* **with sth**) someone extraordinarily skilled in a particular way. ▪ **wizardry** *noun.* [15c as *wisard*, from *wis* **wise**[1]]

wizened *adj* shrivelled or wrinkled, esp with age. [Anglo-Saxon *wisnian* to dry up]

wiz kid see **whizz kid**

WMD *abbrev* weapon(s) of mass destruction.

woad *noun* **1** a plant whose leaves yield a blue dye. **2** this dye, used by the ancient Britons to paint their bodies. [Anglo-Saxon *wad*]

wobble *verb* **1** *tr & intr* to rock or make (something) rock, sway or shake unsteadily. **2** *intr* to move or advance in this manner: *wobbled down the street*. **3** *intr* of the voice: to be unsteady. ▸ *noun* a wobbling, rocking or swaying motion. [17c: from German *wabbeln*]

wobbly *adj* (**-ier, -iest**) unsteady; shaky; inclined to wobble. ▸ *noun* (**-ies**) *informal* a fit of anger.

wodge *noun, informal* a large lump, wad or chunk. [20c: a variant of **wedge**]

woe *noun* **1** grief; misery. **2** (*often* **woes**) affliction; calamity. [Anglo-Saxon *wa*]

IDIOMS **woe betide ...** *old use, facetious* may evil befall, or evil will befall (whoever offends or acts in some specified way): *Woe betide anyone who disturbs him.*

woebegone *adj* dismal-looking; showing sorrow. [14c: from *begone* surrounded]

woeful *adj* **1** mournful; sorrowful. **2** causing woe: *a woeful story.* **3** disgraceful; pitiful: *a woeful lack of interest*. ▪ **woefully** *adv.* ▪ **woefulness** *noun.*

woggle *noun* a ring, usu of leather or plastic, through which Cubs, Scouts and Guides, etc thread their neckerchiefs. [20c]

wok *noun* a large metal bowl-shaped pan used in Chinese cookery. [20c: Cantonese Chinese]

woke *past tense of* **wake**[1]

woken *past participle of* **wake**[1]

wold *noun* a tract of open rolling upland. [Anglo-Saxon *wald* or *weald* forest]

wolf *noun* (***wolves***) a carnivorous mammal belonging to the dog family which hunts in packs. ▸ *verb* (*usu* **wolf sth down**) *informal* to gobble it quickly and greedily. [Anglo-Saxon]

IDIOMS **cry wolf** to give a false alarm, usu repeatedly.

wolfhound *noun* a large domestic dog, such as the Irish wolfhound.

wolfram *noun, chem* **tungsten**. [18c: German]

wolf whistle *noun* a loud whistle used as an expression of admiration for a person's appearance. ▸ *verb* (**wolf-whistle**) to whistle in this way. [20c]

wolverine *or* **wolverene** *noun* a large carnivorous animal of the weasel family, which inhabits forests in N America and Eurasia. Also called **glutton**. [16c as *wolvering*: from **wolf**]

wolves *pl of* **wolf**

woman *noun* (***women***) **1** an adult human female. **2** women generally; the female sex. **3** *informal* someone's wife or girlfriend. **4** *old use* a female servant or domestic daily help. **5** *old use* a female attendant to a queen, etc. ▸ *adj* female: *a woman doctor.* ▪ **womanhood** *noun.* [Anglo-Saxon *wifman*]

womanish *adj* of a man, his behaviour or appearance: effeminate; unmanly.

womanize *or* **-ise** *verb, intr* of a man: to pursue and have casual affairs with women. ▪ **womanizer** *noun.*

womankind *noun* (*also* **womanhood**) women generally; the female sex.

womanly *adj* (**-ier, -iest**) **1** having characteristics specific to a woman; feminine. **2** considered natural or suitable to a woman. ▪ **womanliness** *noun.*

womb *noun, anatomy* the organ in female mammals in which the young develop after conception and remain till birth. *Technical equivalent* **uterus**. [Anglo-Saxon *wamb*]

wombat *noun* a nocturnal Australian marsupial, with a compact body, short legs, a large flat head and no tail. [18c: from Aboriginal *wambat*]

women *pl of* **woman**

womenfolk *plural noun* **1** women generally. **2** the female members of a family or society.

women's liberation *noun* (*also with caps*) a movement started by women, aimed at freeing them from the disadvantages they suffer in a male-dominated society. Often shortened to **women's lib.**

won *past tense, past participle of* **win**

wonder *noun* **1** the state of mind produced by something extraordinary, new or unexpected; amazement or awe. **2** something that is a cause of awe, amazement or bafflement; a marvel or prodigy. ▸ *adj* notable for accomplishing marvels: *a wonder drug.* ▸ *verb* **1** *tr & intr* to be curious: *wondering where you'd gone.* **2** (**wonder at someone** *or* **sth**) to be amazed or surprised by them or it: *I wonder at you sometimes!* **3** used politely to introduce requests: *I wonder if you could help me?* ▪ **wonderment** *noun.* [Anglo-Saxon *wundor*]

IDIOMS **do** *or* **work wonders** to achieve marvellous results. **no** *or* **small wonder** it is hardly surprising.

wonderful *adj* **1** arousing wonder; extraordinary. **2** excellent; splendid. ▪ **wonderfully** *adv.*

wonderland *noun* **1** an imaginary place full of marvels. **2** a scene of strange unearthly beauty.

wondrous *adj* wonderful, strange or awesome.

wonky *adj* (**-ier, -iest**) *Brit informal* **1** unsound, unsteady or wobbly. **2** crooked or awry; uneven. ▪ **wonkily** *adv.* ▪ **wonkiness** *noun.* [20c: a variant of dialect *wanky*]

wont /woʊnt/ *chiefly formal, literary or old use, adj* habitually inclined; accustomed: *He is wont to retire to bed early.* ▸ *noun* a habit that one has: *It was her wont to rise early.* ▸ *verb, tr & intr* (***wont*** *or* ***wonts, wont*** *or* ***wonted***) to become or make (someone) become accustomed. [Anglo-Saxon *gewunod* accustomed]

won't *contraction* will not.

wonted *adj* customary.

woo *verb* (***wooed***) **1** *old use* of a man: to try to win the love and affection of (a woman) esp in the hope of marrying her. **2** to try to win the support of (someone): *woo the voters.* ▪ **wooing** *noun, adj.* [Anglo-Saxon *wogian*]

wood *noun* **1** *botany* the hard tissue beneath the bark, that forms the bulk of woody trees and shrubs. **2** this material used for building timber, fencing and furniture-making, etc. **3** (*also* **woods**) an expanse of growing trees. **4** firewood. **5** *golf* a club with a head traditionally made of wood, now usu of metal, used for driving the ball long distances. ▸ *adj* made of, or using, wood. ▸ *verb* to cover (land, etc) with trees. ▪ **wooded** *adj.* [Anglo-Saxon *wudu*]

woodbine *noun* honeysuckle.

woodcarving *noun* **1** the process of carving in wood. **2** an object or decoration carved in wood.

woodchip *noun* **1** a chip of wood. **2** (*in full* **woodchip paper**) paper incorporating chips of wood for texture, used for decorating walls.

woodchuck *noun* a N American marmot. Also called **groundhog**.

woodcock *noun* a long-billed game bird.

woodcut *noun* **1** a design cut into a wooden block. **2** a print taken from this.

woodcutter *noun* **1** someone who fells trees and chops wood. **2** someone who makes woodcuts.

wooden *adj* **1** made of or resembling wood. **2** of an actor, performance, etc: stiff, unnatural and inhibited; lacking expression and liveliness. **3** clumsy or awkward. **4** esp of a facial expression: blank; expressionless. ▪ **woodenly** *adv.*

wooden spoon *noun* a booby prize. [19c]

woodland *noun* (*also* **woodlands**) an area of land planted with relatively short trees that are more widely spaced than those in a forest.

woodlouse *noun* a crustacean with a grey oval plated body, found in damp places.

woodman *or* **woodsman** *noun* **1** a woodcutter. **2** a forest officer.

woodpecker *noun* a tree-dwelling bird which has a straight pointed chisel-like bill that is used to bore into tree bark in search of insects and to drill nesting holes.

woodpigeon *noun* a common pigeon that lives in woods, with a white marking round its neck.

wood pulp *noun* wood fibres that have been chemically and mechanically pulped for papermaking.

woodruff *noun* a sweet-smelling plant with small white flowers and whorled leaves. [Anglo-Saxon *wuduroffe*]

woodsman see **woodman**

wood stain *noun* a substance for staining wood.

woodwind *noun* **1** the wind instruments in an orchestra, including the flute, oboe, clarinet and bassoon. **2** **a** the section of the orchestra composed of these; **b** (*also* **woodwinds**) the players of these.

woodwork *noun* **1** the art of making things out of wood; carpentry. **2** the wooden parts of any structure.

IDIOMS **crawl out from the woodwork** of someone or something undesirable: to make themselves or their presence known.

woodworm *noun* (***woodworm*** *or* ***woodworms***) **1** the larva of any of several beetles, that bores into wood. **2** the condition of wood caused by this.

woody *adj* (***-ier, -iest***) **1** of countryside: wooded; covered in trees. **2** resembling, developing into, or composed of wood: *plants with woody stems.* **3** similar to wood in texture, smell or taste, etc. ▪ **woodiness** *noun.*

woof[1] /wʊf/ *noun* the sound of, or an imitation of, a dog's bark. ▸ *verb, intr* to give a bark. [19c]

woof[2] /wuːf/ *noun, weaving* **1** the weft. **2** the texture of a fabric. [Anglo-Saxon *owef*, later *oof*, with *w* added by association with **weft** and **warp**]

woofer /ˈwʊfə(r)/ *noun, electronics* a large loudspeaker for reproducing low-frequency sounds. Compare **tweeter**.

wool *noun* **1** the soft wavy hair of sheep and certain other animals. **2** this hair spun into yarn for knitting or weaving. **3** fabric or clothing woven or knitted from this yarn. ▸ *adj* **1** made of wool. **2** relating to wool or its production. [Anglo-Saxon *wull*]

IDIOMS **pull the wool over sb's eyes** *informal* to deceive them.

wool-gathering *noun* absent-minded daydreaming.

woollen *or* (*US*) **woolen** *adj* **1** made of or relating to wool. **2** producing, or dealing in, goods made of wool. ▸ *noun* (*often* **woollens**) a woollen, esp knitted, garment.

woolly *or* (*US*) **wooly** *adj* (***-ier, -iest***) **1** made of, similar to, or covered with wool or wool-like fibres, etc; fluffy and soft. **2** vague and muddled; lacking in clarity: *woolly-minded* • *woolly argument.* ▸ *noun* (***-ies***) *informal* a woollen, usu knitted garment. ▪ **woolliness** *noun.*

woolshed *noun, Aust, NZ* a large shed for shearing sheep and baling wool.

woosh see **whoosh**

woozy *adj* (***-ier, -iest***) *informal* **1** having blurred senses, due to drink or drugs, etc. **2** confused; dizzy. [19c: perhaps a combination of *woolly* and *dizzy*]

Worcs *abbrev, English county* Worcestershire.

word *noun* **1** the smallest unit of spoken or written language that can be used independently, usu separated off by spaces in writing and printing. **2** a brief conversation on a particular matter. **3** any brief statement, message or communication: *a word of caution.* **4** news or notice: *any word of Jane?* **5** a rumour: *The word is he's bankrupt.* **6** one's solemn promise. **7** an order: *expects her word to be obeyed.* **8** a word given as a signal for action: *Wait till I give the word.* **9** what someone says or said: *remembered her mother's words.* **10** (**words**) language as a means of communication: *impossible to convey in words.* **11** (**words**) an argument or heated discussion; verbal contention: *We had words when he returned.* **12** (**words**) **a** the lyrics of a song, etc; **b** the speeches an actor must learn for a particular part. **13** (**the**

Word) *Christianity* the teachings contained in the Bible. **14** *comput* **a** a group of bits or bytes that can be processed as a single unit by a computer, the size of a word varying according to the size of the computer; **b** in word-processing: any group of characters separated from other such groups by spaces or punctuation, whether or not it is a real word. ▶ *verb* to express (something) in carefully chosen words. [Anglo-Saxon]

IDIOMS **have words with sb** *informal* to quarrel with them. **in a word** briefly; in short. **in other words** saying the same thing in a different way. **my word** *or* **upon my word** an exclamation of surprise. **say the word** to give one's consent or approval for some action to proceed. **take sb at their word** to take their offer or suggestion, etc literally. **take sb's word for it** to accept what they say as true, without verification. **the last word 1** the final, esp conclusive, remark or comment in an argument. **2** the most up-to-date design or model, or most recent advance in something. **3** the finest example of eg a particular quality, etc: *the last word in good taste*. **word for word** of a statement, etc: repeated in exactly the same words, or translated into exactly corresponding words; verbatim.

word-blindness *noun* **1 alexia**. **2 dyslexia**. ▪ **word-blind** *adj*.

wordgame *noun* any game or puzzle in which words are constructed or deciphered, etc.

wording *noun* **1** the choice and arrangement of words used to express something. **2** the words used in this arrangement.

word of honour *noun* a promise or assurance that cannot be broken without disgrace.

word of mouth *noun* spoken, as opposed to written, communication.

word-perfect *adj* **1** able to repeat something accurately from memory. **2** of a recitation, etc: faultless.

word processor *noun* (abbrev **WP**) *comput* a computer application dedicated completely to the input, processing, storage and retrieval of text. ▪ **word-processing** *noun*.

word wrapping *or* **wordwrap** *noun, comput* in word-processing: a facility that ensures that a word which is too long to fit into the end of a line of text is automatically put to the start of the following line.

wordy *adj* (***-ier, -iest***) using or containing too many words; long-winded, esp pompously so.

wore *past tense of* **wear**

work *noun* **1** physical or mental effort made in order to achieve or make something, eg labour, study, research, etc. **2** employment: *out of work*. **3** one's place of employment: *He leaves work at 4.30*. **4** tasks to be done: *She often brings work home with her*. ▶ *in compounds: housework*. **5** the product of mental or physical labour: *His work has improved: a lifetime's work*. **6** a manner of working, or **workmanship**. **7 a** any literary, artistic, musical, or dramatic composition or creation; **b** (**works**) the entire collection of such material by an artist, composer or author, etc. **8** anything done, managed, made or achieved, etc; an activity carried out for some purpose: *works of charity*. **9** (**the works**) *informal* everything possible, available or going; the whole lot: *She has a headache, fever, cold – the works!* **10** *physics* the transfer of energy that occurs when force is exerted on a body to move it, measured in **joules**. ▶ *adj* relating to, or suitable for, etc work: *work clothes*. ▶ *verb* **1** *intr* to do work; to exert oneself mentally or physically; to toil, labour or study. **2** *tr & intr* to be employed or have a job. **3** to impose tasks on (someone): *She works her staff hard*. **4** *tr & intr* to operate, esp satisfactorily: *Does this radio work?* **5** *intr* of a plan or idea, etc: to be successful or effective. **6** *intr* to function in a particular way: *That's not how life works*. **7** to cultivate (land). **8** to extract materials from (a mine). **9** *informal* to manipulate (a system or rules, etc) to one's advantage. **10** *intr* (**work on sb**) *informal* to use one's powers of persuasion on them. **11** *intr* (**work on sth**) **a** to try to perfect or improve it. **b** to use it as a basis for one's decisions and actions: *worked the nail out of the wall*. **12** *tr & intr* to make (one's way), or shift or make (something) shift gradually: *worked through the crowd*. ▪ **workless** *adj*. [Anglo-Saxon *weorc*]

PHRASAL VERBS **work sth off** to get rid of (energy or the effects of a heavy meal) by energetic activity. **work out 1** to be successfully achieved or resolved: *It'll all work out in the end*. **2** to perform a set of energetic physical exercises: *She's working out at the gym*. **work sth out** to solve it; to sort or reason it out. **work sb over** *slang* to beat them up. **work sb up** to excite or agitate them. **work sth up** to summon up (an appetite, enthusiasm or energy, etc). **work up to sth** to approach (a difficult task or objective) by gradual stages.

workable *adj* **1** of a scheme, etc: able to be carried out. **2** of a material or mineral source, etc: able to be worked.

workaday *adj* **1** ordinary or mundane; commonplace. **2** suitable for a working day; practical or everyday.

workaholic *noun, informal* someone addicted to work. [20c: from **work**, modelled on **alcoholic**]

workbench *noun* a table, usu a purpose-built one, at which a mechanic, craftsman, etc works.

workbook *noun* **1** a book of exercises, often with spaces included for the answers. **2** a book containing a record of jobs undertaken, in progress or completed.

workday see **working day**

worker *noun* **1** someone who works. **2** someone employed in manual work. **3** an employee as opposed to an employer. **4** a female social insect, eg a honey bee or ant, that is sterile and whose sole function is to maintain the colony and forage for food. Compare **queen** (sense 3), **drone** (sense 2).

work ethic *noun* the general attitude towards work, esp one which places a high moral value on hard work.

workforce *noun* **1** the number of workers engaged in a particular industry, factory, etc. **2** the total number of workers potentially available.

workhorse *noun* **1** a horse used for labouring purposes rather than for recreation or racing, etc. **2** a person, machine, etc that carries out arduous work.

workhouse *noun, hist* an institution where the poor were housed and given work to do.

working *noun* **1** (*also* **workings**) the operation or mode of operation of something. **2** (**workings**) excavations at a mine or quarry. ▶ *adj* **1** of a period of time: devoted to work, or denoting that part that is devoted to work. **2** adequate for one's purposes: *a working knowledge of French.*

working capital *noun* money used to keep a business, etc going.

working class *noun* the wage-earning section of the population, employed esp in manual labour. *as adj* (**working-class**): *a working-class hero.*

working day *or* (*N Am*) **workday** *noun* **1** a day on which people go to work as usual. **2** the part of the day during which work is done.

working lunch *noun* a lunch arranged as an alternative to a formal meeting for the discussion of business.

working party *noun* a group of people appointed to investigate and report on something.

working week *or* (*N Am*) **workweek** *noun* **1** the period in the week during which work is normally done. **2** any week in which such work is done, esp as opposed to eg holidays.

workload *noun* the amount of work to be done by a person or machine, esp in a specified time.

workman *noun* a man employed to do manual work.

workmanlike *adj* suitable to, or characteristic of, a good or skilful workman.

workmanship *noun* the degree of expertise or skill shown in making something, or of the refinement of finish in the finished product.

workmate *noun, informal* someone who works with another or others in their place of work; a fellow-worker.

work of art *noun* **1** a painting or sculpture of high quality. **2** anything constructed or composed with obvious skill and elegance.

workout *noun* a session of physical exercise.

worksheet *noun* **1** a paper or form detailing work being planned or already in operation. **2** a sheet of paper used esp by students for roughly calculating or solving problems.

workshop *noun* **1** a room or building where construction and repairs are carried out. **2 a** a course of study or work, esp of an experimental or creative kind, for a group of people on a particular project: *a theatre workshop*; **b** the people participating in such a course.

workshy *adj, informal* lazy; inclined to avoid work.

workstation *noun* an area in an office, etc where one person works, esp at a computer terminal.

work surface *or* **worktop** *noun* a flat surface along the top of kitchen installations for the preparation of food, etc.

work to rule *verb, intr* of workers: to scrupulously observe all the regulations for the express purpose of slowing down work, as a form of industrial action. ▪ **work-to-rule** *noun.*

workweek see **working week**

world *noun* **1** the Earth. **2** the people inhabiting the Earth; humankind: *tell the world.* **3** any other planet or potentially habitable heavenly body. **4** human affairs: *the present state of the world.* **5** (*also* **World**) a group of countries characterized in a certain way: *the Third World.* **6** (*also* **World**) the people of a particular period, and their culture: *the Ancient World.* **7** a state of existence: *in this world or the next.* **8** someone's individual way of life or range of experience: *He's in a world of his own.* **9** an atmosphere or environment: *enter a world of make-believe.* **10** a particular area of activity: *the world of politics.* **11** a class of living things: *the insect world.* **12** *informal* a great deal; a lot: *did her a world of good* • *We are worlds apart.* ▸ *adj* relating to, affecting, or important throughout, the whole world. [Anglo-Saxon *weorold*]

IDIOMS **be** *or* **mean all the world to sb** to be important or precious to them. **the best of both worlds** the benefits of both alternatives with the drawbacks of neither. **bring into the world** to give birth to or deliver (a baby). **come into the world** to be born. **for all the world as if ...** exactly as if ... **in the world** used for emphasis: *without a care in the world.* **not for the world** not for anything. **on top of the world** *informal* supremely happy. **out of this world** *informal* extraordinarily fine; marvellous. **think the world of sb** to love or admire them immensely.

world-class *adj* being among or competing against those of the highest standard in the world.

World Cup *noun, esp football* an international competition, taking place every four years, in which teams from several countries in the world compete.

world-famous *adj* well known throughout the world.

worldly *adj* (**-ier, -iest**) **1** relating to this world; material, as opposed to spiritual or eternal: *worldly possessions.* **2** over-concerned with possessions, money, luxuries, etc; materialistic. **3** shrewd about the ways of the world; sophisticated in outlook. ▪ **worldliness** *noun.*

worldly-wise *adj* knowledgeable about life; having the wisdom of those experienced in, and affected by, the ways of the world.

world music *noun* popular folk music originating in non-western, esp African, cultures.

World Series *noun, baseball* a set of annual championship matches played in the US.

world-shaking *or* **world-shattering** *adj, informal* extremely important or significant; momentous.

World War I, the Great War *or* **the First World War** *noun* the war (1914–18) in which the Central Powers (Germany, Austria-Hungary, Turkey and Bulgaria) were defeated by the Allies (Britain, France, Italy, Russia and later the US).

World War II *or* **the Second World War** *noun* the war (1939–45) in which the Axis Powers (Germany, Italy and Japan) were defeated by the Allies (mainly Britain and countries of the British Commonwealth, the US and the then USSR).

worldweary *adj* tired of the world; bored with life.

worldwide *adj, adv* extending or known throughout the world.

World Wide Web *noun* (abbrev **WWW**) a network of **hypermedia** files containing **hyperlink**s from one file to another over **the Internet**, which allows the user to browse files containing related information from all over the world.

WORM *abbrev, comput* write once read many, a CD system that allows the user to store their own data, and then read it as often as they wish.

worm *noun* **1** *zool* a small soft-bodied limbless invertebrate that is characteristically long and slender. **2** any superficially similar but unrelated animal, eg the larva of certain insects. **3** a mean, contemptible, weak or worthless person. **4** *mech* the spiral thread of a screw. **5** (**worms**) *pathol* any disease characterized by the presence of parasitic worms in the intestines of humans or animals. **6** *comput* an unauthorized computer program, differing from a virus in that it is an independent program rather than a piece of coding, designed to sabotage a computer system, esp by reproducing itself throughout a computer network. ▸ *verb* **1** (*also* **worm out**) to extract (information, etc) little by little: *wormed the secret out of them.* **2** to treat (an animal that has worms) esp to rid it of these. [Anglo-Saxon *wyrm*]

IDIOMS **worm one's way** to wriggle or manoeuvre oneself gradually: *wormed their way to the front.*

wormcast *noun* a coiled heap of sand or earth excreted by a burrowing earthworm or lugworm.

wormhole *noun* a hole left by a burrowing grub, in eg furniture, books or fruit.

wormwood *noun* a bitter-tasting herb from which the flavouring for absinthe is obtained. [Anglo-Saxon *wermod*]

wormy *adj* (**-ier, -iest**) infested by worms.

worn *adj* **1** haggard with weariness. **2** showing signs of deterioration through long use or wear. **3** exhausted.

worn out *adj* **1** damaged or rendered useless by wear. **2** extremely weary; exhausted.

worrisome *adj* **1** causing worry; perturbing or vexing. **2** of a person: inclined to worry.

worry *verb* (**-ies, -ied**) **1** *intr* to be anxious; to fret. **2** to make (someone) anxious. **3** to bother, pester or harass (someone). **4** of a dog: to chase and bite (sheep, etc). **5** (*often* **worry at**) to try to solve (a problem, etc). ▸ *noun* (**-ies**) **1** a state of anxiety. **2** a cause of anxiety. ▪ **worrier** *noun.* [Anglo-Saxon *wyrgan* to strangle]

worry beads *plural noun* a string of beads for fiddling with, as a means of relieving mental tension.

worse *adj* **1** more bad. **2** more ill. **3** more grave, serious or acute. **4** inferior in standard. ▸ *noun* something worse: *Worse was to follow.* ▸ *adv* less well; more badly: *He's doing worse at school.* [Anglo-Saxon *wyrsa*, the adjective form used as a comparative of **bad**]

IDIOMS **none the worse for ...** unharmed by (an accident or bad experience, etc). **the worse for wear 1** worn or shabby from use. **2** in poor condition. **3** drunk. **worse off** in a worse situation, esp financially.

worsen *verb, tr & intr* to make or become worse.

worship *verb* (**worshipped, worshipping**) **1** *tr & intr* to honour (God or a god) with praise, prayer, hymns, etc. **2** to love or admire (someone or something), esp blindly; to idolize (them or it). **3** to glorify or exalt (material things, eg money). ▸ *noun* **1 a** the activity of worshipping; **b** the worship itself. **2** a religious service in which God or a god is honoured: *morning worship.* **3** the title used to address or refer to a mayor or magistrate, usu in the form of **His** *or* **Her Worship** *or* **Your Worship**. ▪ **worshipper** *noun.* [Anglo-Saxon *weorthscipe*, meaning 'worthship']

worshipful *adj* full of or showing reverence or adoration.

worst *adj* **1** most bad, awful or unpleasant, etc. **2** most grave, severe, acute or dire. **3** most inferior; lowest in standard. ▸ *noun* **1** the worst thing, part or possibility. **2** the most advanced degree of badness. ▸ *adv* most severely; most badly. ▸ *verb* to defeat (someone); to get the better of (them). [Anglo-Saxon *wyrst*, the adjective form used as a superlative of **bad** and **ill**]

worsted /ˈwɜːstɪd/ *noun* **1** a fine strong twisted yarn spun out from long combed wool. **2** fabric woven from this. [13c: named after Worstead, a village in Norfolk]

wort *noun* **1** *in compounds* a plant: *liverwort.* **2** *brewing* a dilute solution or infusion of malt, fermented to make beer and whisky. [Anglo-Saxon *wyrt* plant or root]

worth *noun* **1** value, importance or usefulness. **2** financial value. **3** the quantity of anything that can be bought for a certain sum, accomplished in a certain time, etc. ▸ *adj* **1** having a value of a specified amount. **2** *informal* having money and property to a specified value. **3** justifying, deserving or warranting something: *worth consideration.* [Anglo-Saxon *weorth*]

worthless *adj* **1** having no value or significance. **2** having no merit or virtue; useless. ▪ **worthlessness** *noun.*

worthwhile *adj* **1** worth the time, money or energy expended. **2** useful, beneficial or rewarding.

worthy *adj* (**-ier, -iest**) admirable, excellent or deserving. ▸ *noun* (**-ies**) **1** *often patronizing* an esteemed person; a dignitary. **2** someone of notable and eminent worth. ▪ **worthily** *adv.* ▪ **worthiness** *noun.*

IDIOMS **worthy of sb** suitable or appropriate for them. **worthy of sth** deserving it.

wot see under **wit**[2]

would *auxiliary verb*, used: **1** in reported speech, as the past tense of **will**[1]: *said she would leave at 10.* **2** to indicate willingness, readiness, or ability: *was asked to help, but wouldn't.* **3** to indicate habitual action: *would always telephone at six.* **4** to express frustration at some happening: *It would rain, just as we're setting out.* **5** to make polite invitations, offers or requests: *Would you ring her back?* **6** in politely expressing and seeking opinions: *Would you not agree?* [Anglo-Saxon *wolde*, past tense of *wyllan*]

would-be *adj* hoping, aspiring or professing to be a specified thing: *a would-be actor.*

wouldn't *contraction* would not.

wound[1] *past tense, past participle of* **wind**[2]

wound[2] /wuːnd/ *noun* **1** any local injury to living tissue of a human, animal or plant, caused by an external physical means such as cutting, crushing or tearing. **2** an injury caused to pride, feelings or reputation, etc. ▸ *verb, tr & intr* **1** to inflict a wound on (a person, creature or limb, etc). **2** to injure (feelings, etc). ▪ **wounding** *noun, adj.* [Anglo-Saxon *wund*]

wove *past tense of* **weave**[1]

woven *past participle of* **weave**[1]

wow *informal, exclam* an exclamation of astonishment, admiration or wonder. ▸ *noun* a huge success. ▸ *verb* to impress or amaze hugely. [19c: orig Scots]

wowser *noun, Aust, slang* **1** a puritanical person who interferes with the pleasures of others. **2** a teetotaller. [20c: from English dialect *wow*, meaning 'to complain']

WP *abbrev* **1** word-processing. **2** word processor.

WPC *abbrev* Woman Police Constable.

wpm *abbrev* words per minute.

wrack *noun* **1** a type of seaweed, esp one of the large brown varieties, floating in the sea or cast up on the beach. **2** destruction or devastation. **3** a wreck or wreckage. [14c: from Dutch or German *Wrak*]

wraith *noun* **1** a ghost; a spectre. **2** any apparition, esp of a living person, believed to appear shortly before their death. ▪ **wraithlike** *adj*. [16c: orig Scots]

wrangle *verb, intr* to quarrel, argue or debate noisily or bitterly. ▸ *noun* **1** the act of disputing noisily. **2** a bitter dispute. [14c: from German *wrangeln*]

wrap *verb* (***wrapped, wrapping***) **1** to fold or wind (something) round (someone or something). **2** (*also* **wrap sth up**) to cover or enfold it with cloth, paper etc. **3** *intr* (**wrap round**) *comput* of text on a screen: to start a new line automatically as soon as the last character space on the previous line is filled. ▸ *noun* **1** a warm garment, esp a shawl or stole for the shoulders. **2** a protective covering. **3** a wrapper. **4** *cinematog, TV* the completion of filming or recording, or the end of a session of filming or recording. [14c]

IDIOMS **keep sth under wraps** *informal* to keep it secret.

PHRASAL VERBS **wrap up 1** to dress warmly: *Wrap up warm before you leave!* **2** *slang* to be quiet. **wrap sth up** *informal* to finish it off or settle it finally.

wraparound *or* **wrapround** *adj* (*also* **wrapover**) of clothing, eg a skirt or blouse: designed to wrap round with one edge overlapping the other and usu tied. ▸ *noun, comput* on a VDU: the automatic division of input into lines.

wrapper *noun* **1** someone or something that wraps. **2** a paper or Cellophane cover round a packet or sweet, etc.

wrapping *noun* (*usu* **wrappings**) any of various types of cover, wrapper or packing material.

wrasse *noun* (***wrasses*** *or* ***wrasse***) a brightly coloured sea fish with powerful teeth. [17c: from Cornish *wrach*]

wrath /rɒθ/ *noun* violent anger; resentment or indignation. ▪ **wrathful** *adj*. [Anglo-Saxon *wræththo*]

wreak *verb* **1** (*esp* **wreak havoc**) to cause (damage or chaos, etc) on a disastrous scale. **2** to take (vengeance) ruthlessly (on someone). [Anglo-Saxon *wrecan*]

wreath *noun* **1** a ring-shaped garland of flowers and foliage placed on a grave or memorial as a tribute. **2** a similar garland hung up as a decoration, eg at Christmas. **3** (*usu* **wreaths**) a ring, curl or spiral of smoke, mist, etc. [Anglo-Saxon *writha* something coiled]

wreathe *verb* **1** to hang or encircle (something) with flowers, etc. **2** of smoke, mist, etc: to cover or surround (something).

wreck *noun* **1** the destruction, esp accidental, of a ship at sea. **2** a hopelessly damaged sunken or grounded ship. **3** a crashed aircraft or a ruined vehicle. **4** *informal* someone in a pitiful state of fitness or mental health. ▸ *verb* **1** to break or destroy (something). **2** to spoil (plans, hopes, a holiday, relationship, etc). **3** to cause the wreck of (a ship, etc). [13c from Danish *wræce*]

wreckage *noun* the remains of things that have been wrecked.

wrecker *noun* **1** someone or something that wrecks. **2** someone who criminally ruins anything. **3** *hist* someone who deliberately causes a wreck in order to plunder the wreckage. **4** *N Am* a person or business whose job is to demolish buildings or vehicles, etc. **5** *N Am* a breakdown vehicle.

Wren *noun* **1** a member of the Women's Royal Naval Service. **2** (**the Wrens**) the service itself. [20c: from the initials **WRNS**]

wren *noun* a very small songbird with short wings and a short erect tail. [Anglo-Saxon *wrenna*]

wrench *verb* **1** (*often* **wrench off** *or* **out**) to pull or twist (something) violently. **2** to sprain (an ankle, etc). **3** to twist or distort (a meaning). ▸ *noun* **1** an act or instance of wrenching. **2** a violent pull or twist. **3** an adjustable spanner-like tool for gripping and turning nuts and bolts, etc. **4** a painful parting or separation. [Anglo-Saxon *wrencan*]

wrest *verb* **1** to turn or twist (something). **2** to pull or wrench (something) away, esp from someone else's grasp or possession. **3** to extract (a statement or promise, etc) with difficulty. [Anglo-Saxon *wræstan*]

wrestle *verb* **1** *tr & intr* **a** to fight by trying to grip, throw and pinion one's opponent; **b** to force (someone) into some position in this way; **c** to do this as a sport. **2** (*usu* **wrestle with**) to apply oneself keenly to (something). ▪ **wrestler** *noun*. [Anglo-Saxon *wrestlian*]

wrestling *noun* **1** the activity of wrestlers. **2** the sport or exercise, governed by certain fixed rules, in which two people **wrestle** (*verb* sense 1).

wretch *noun* **1** a miserable, unfortunate and pitiful person. **2** a worthless and despicable person. [Anglo-Saxon *wrecca*]

wretched *adj* **1** pitiable. **2** miserable, unhappy, distressed or distraught. **3** inferior or poor; humble or lowly. **4** infuriating. ▪ **wretchedly** *adv*. ▪ **wretchedness** *noun*.

wright *noun usu in compounds* a maker, creator or repairer, usually of a specified thing: *playwright* • *shipwright*. [Anglo-Saxon *wryhta*]

wriggle *verb, tr & intr* **1** to twist to and fro. **2** to make (one's way) by this means. **3** to move, advance or make (one's way) sinuously or deviously. **4** (**wriggle out of sth**) to manage cleverly to evade or escape from (an awkward situation or disagreeable obligation, etc). ▸ *noun* a wriggling action or motion. [15c: from German *wriggeln*]

wring *verb* (***wrung***) **1** (*also* **wring out**) to force liquid from (something) by twisting or squeezing. **2** to force (information or a consent, etc) from someone. **3** to break (the neck) of a bird, etc by twisting. **4** to keep clasping and twisting (one's hands) in distress or agitation. **5** to crush (someone's hand) in one's own, by way of greeting. **6** to tear at (the heart as the supposed seat of the emotions). [Anglo-Saxon *wringan*]

IDIOMS **wringing wet** soaking wet; saturated.

wringer *noun, hist* a machine with two rollers for squeezing water out of wet clothes.

wrinkle *noun* **1** a crease or line in the skin, esp of the face, appearing with advancing age. **2** a slight crease or ridge in any surface. **3** a minor problem or difficulty to be smoothed out. ▸ *verb, tr & intr* to develop or make (something) develop wrinkles. ▪ **wrinkly** *adj* (***-ier, -iest***). [Anglo-Saxon *wrinclian* to wind round]

wrist *noun* **1** *anatomy* in terrestrial vertebrates: the joint between the forearm and the hand. *Technical* *equivalent* **carpus**. **2** the part of a sleeve that covers this. [Anglo-Saxon]

writ *noun* a legal document by which someone is summoned, or required to do or refrain from doing something. [Anglo-Saxon]

write *verb* (*past tense* ***wrote,*** *past participle* ***written***) **1** *tr & intr* (*also* **write sth down**) to mark or produce (letters, symbols, numbers, words, etc) on a surface, esp paper, usu using a pen or pencil. **2 a** to compose or create (a book, music, etc) in manuscript, typescript or on computer, etc; **b** to be the author or composer of (a book or music, etc). **3** *intr* to compose novels or contribute articles to newspapers, etc, esp as a living. **4** to make or fill in (a document or form, etc). **5** *tr & intr* to compose (a letter, etc): *I must write to him.* **6** to say or express in a letter, article or book, etc. **7** to underwrite (an insurance policy). **8** to fill (pages or sheets, etc) with writing. **9** to display clearly: *Guilt was written all over his face.* **10** *comput* to transfer (data) to a memory or storage device. [Anglo-Saxon *writan*]

PHRASAL VERBS **write off** to write and send a letter of request: *I wrote off for a catalogue.* **write sth off 1** to damage (a vehicle in a crash) beyond repair. **2** to cancel (a debt). **3** to discontinue (a project, etc) because it is likely to fail. **4** to dismiss (something) as being of no importance. **write sth out 1** to write it in full; to copy or transcribe it. **2** to remove a character or scene from a film or serial, etc. **write sth up 1** to write or rewrite it in a final form. **2** to bring (a diary or accounts, etc) up to date. **3** to write about it or review it, esp approvingly.

write-off *noun* something that is written off, esp a motor vehicle involved in an accident.

writer *noun* **1** someone who writes, esp as a living; an author. **2** someone who has written a particular thing. [Anglo-Saxon]

write-up *noun* a written or published account, esp a review in a newspaper or magazine, etc. [19c]

writhe *verb, intr* **1** to twist violently, esp in pain or discomfort; to squirm. **2** *informal* to feel painfully embarrassed or humiliated. ▸ *noun* the action of writhing; a twist or contortion. [Anglo-Saxon *writhan* to twist]

writing *noun* **1** written or printed words. **2** handwriting. **3 a** a literary composition; **b** the art or activity of literary composition. **4** (*usu* **writings**) literary work. **5** a form of script: *Chinese writing.*

IDIOMS **in writing** of a promise or other commitment: in written form, esp as being firm proof of intention, etc.

written *adj* expressed in writing, and so undeniable: *written consent.* ▸ *verb, past participle of* **write**.

WRNS *abbrev* Women's Royal Naval Service. See also **Wren**.

wrong *adj* **1** not correct. **2** mistaken. **3** not appropriate or suitable. **4** not good or sensible; unjustifiable. **5** morally bad; wicked. **6** defective or faulty. **7** amiss; causing trouble, pain, etc. **8** of one side of a fabric or garment, etc: intended as the inner or unseen side. ▸ *adv* **1** incorrectly. **2** improperly; badly. ▸ *noun* **1** whatever is not right or just. **2** any injury done to someone else. ▸ *verb* **1** to treat (someone) unjustly; to do wrong to (someone). **2** to judge unfairly. **3** to deprive (someone) of some right; to defraud. ▪ **wrongly** *adv.* [Anglo-Saxon *wrang*]

IDIOMS **get out of bed on the wrong side** to get up in the morning in a bad mood. **go wrong 1** of plans, etc: to fail to go as intended. **2** to make an error. **3** of a mechanical device: to stop functioning properly. **in the wrong** guilty of an error or injustice.

wrongdoing *noun* evil or wicked action or behaviour. ▪ **wrongdoer** *noun.*

wrongfoot *verb* **1** *tennis, etc* to catch (one's opponent) off balance by making an unpredictable shot, etc to a point away from the direction in which they are moving or preparing to move. **2** to contrive to place (an opponent in a dispute, etc) at a tactical or moral disadvantage; to disconcert them.

wrongful *adj* unlawful; unjust. ▪ **wrongfully** *adv.*

wrong-headed *adj* obstinate and stubborn, adhering wilfully to wrong principles and/or policy.

wrote *past tense of* **write**

wroth *adj, old use* angry. [Anglo-Saxon *wrath*]

wrought /rɔːt/ *adj* of metal: beaten into shape with tools. [13c: an old *past participle* of **work**]

wrought iron *noun* a malleable form of iron with a very low carbon content. *as adj* (**wrought-iron**): *wrought-iron railings.*

wrung *past tense, past participle of* **wring**

WRVS *abbrev* Women's Royal Voluntary Service, a service assisting government departments, local authorities and other voluntary bodies in carrying out welfare work for the community.

wry *adj* **1** eg of a smile: slightly mocking or bitter; ironic. **2** of a facial expression: with the features distorted or twisted into a grimace, in reaction to a bitter taste, etc. **3** of humour: dry. ▪ **wryly** *adv.* ▪ **wryness** *noun.* [Anglo-Saxon *wrigian* to turn or twist]

wrybill *noun* a New Zealand bird related to the plover, with a bill that bends sideways which it uses to obtain food from under stones.

wryneck *noun* a small woodpecker which twists its head to look over its shoulder when alarmed.

wt *abbrev* weight.

wuss /wʊs/ *or* **wussy** *noun* (***wusses*** *or* ***wussies***) *N Am, slang* a weakling; a feeble person. ▪ **wussy** *adj* (***-ier, -iest***).

WWW *or* (*in Web addresses*) **www** *abbrev* World Wide Web.

wych-elm *or* **witch elm** *noun* a tree of the elm family, native to N Europe and Asia. [Anglo-Saxon *wice* a tree with pliant branches]

wych hazel see **witch hazel**

WYSIWYG *or* **wysiwyg** /ˈwɪzɪwɪg/ *abbrev, comput* what you see is what you get, indicating that the type and characters appearing on screen are as they will appear on the printout.

X^{1} *or* **x** *noun* (***Xs, X's*** *or* ***x's***) **1** the twenty-fourth letter of the English alphabet. **2** anything shaped like an X. **3** an unknown or unnamed person.

X^{2} *symbol* **1** *maths* (*usu* **x**) an unknown quantity; the first of a pair or group of unknown quantities. See also **Y**^{3}, **Z**^{2}. **2** the Roman numeral for 10. **3** a film classified as suitable for people over the age of 17 (in the USA) or 18 (in the UK; now replaced by '18'). **4** a mark used: **a** to symbolize a kiss; **b** to indicate an error; **c** as the signature of an illiterate person, etc.

xanthene /ˈzanθiːn/ *noun, chem* a white or yellowish crystalline compound, used as a fungicide and as a source of various dyes. [20c]

x-axis *noun, maths* in a graph: the horizontal axis along which one of a set of **co-ordinate**s (*noun* sense 2) is plotted. Compare **y-axis**, **z-axis**.

X-chromosome *noun, biol* the sex chromosome that when present as one half of an identical pair determines the female sex in most animals, including humans. See also **Y-chromosome**.

Xe *symbol, chem* xenon.

xenolith *noun, geol* a piece of foreign material that occurs within a body of igneous rock. [20c]

xenon /ˈzɛnɒn, ˈziːnɒn/ *noun, chem* (symbol **Xe**) an element, a colourless odourless inert gas used in fluorescent lamps, photographic flash tubes, and lasers. [19c: from Greek *xenos* stranger]

xenophobia *noun* intense fear or dislike of foreigners or strangers. ▪ **xenophobe** *noun*. ▪ **xenophobic** *adj*. [20c]

xerography /zɪəˈrɒgrəfɪ/ *noun* an electrostatic printing process used to make photocopies of printed documents or illustrations. ▪ **xerographic** *adj*. [20c]

xerophyte /ˈzɪəroʊfaɪt/ *noun* a desert plant, eg a cactus, adapted to grow in conditions where water is scarce. [19c]

Xerox /ˈzɪərɒks/ *noun, trademark* **1** a type of xerographic process. **2** a copying-machine using this process. **3** a photocopy made by such a process. ▶ *verb* (*usu* **xerox**) to photocopy something using this process. [20c: see **xerography**]

Xhosa /ˈkoʊsə, -zə, ˈhoʊ-/ *noun* (***Xhosa*** *or* ***Xhosas***) **1** a group of Bantu-speaking peoples of the Transkei and Ciskei, S Africa. **2** an individual belonging to this group of peoples. **3** their language. ▶ *adj* belonging or relating to this group or their language. ▪ **Xhosan** *adj*.

xi /ksaɪ/ *noun* the fourteenth letter of the Greek alphabet.

x-intercept *noun, maths* the point at which a line cuts the x-axis.

Xmas /ˈɛksməs, ˈkrɪsməs/ *noun, informal* Christmas. [18c: from X = chi, letter of the Greek alphabet, and the first letter of *Christos*, the Greek form of *Christ*]

XML *abbrev, comput* extensible mark-up language, text formatting instructions designed to aid data searching and the formatting of results.

X-ray *noun* **1** an electromagnetic ray which can pass through many substances that are opaque to light, producing on photographic film an image of the object passed through. **2** a photograph taken using X-rays. **3** a medical examination using X-rays. ▶ *verb* to take a photograph of something using X-rays. [1890s: **X**^{2} (called X because at the time of their discovery in 1895, the nature of the rays was unknown) + **ray**^{1}]

X-ray diffraction *noun, chem* the characteristic interference pattern produced when X-rays are passed through a crystal, often used to determine the arrangement of atoms within crystals.

xylem /ˈzaɪləm/ *noun, botany* the woody tissue that transports water and mineral nutrients from the roots to all other parts of a plant, and also provides structural support. See also **phloem**. [19c: from Greek *xylon* wood]

xylene /ˈzaɪliːn/ *or* **xylol** /ˈzaɪlɒl/ *noun, chem* a colourless liquid hydrocarbon obtained from coal tar, etc, and used as a solvent and in the preparation of specimens for microscopy and the manufacture of organic chemical compounds. [19c]

xylophone /ˈzaɪloʊfoʊn/ *noun* a musical instrument consisting of a series of wooden or sometimes metal bars of different lengths, played by being struck by wooden hammers. ▪ **xylophonist** /zaɪˈlɒfənɪst/ *noun*. [19c]

Y^{1} *or* **y** *noun* (***Ys, Y's*** *or* ***y's***) **1** the twenty-fifth letter of the English alphabet. **2** anything shaped like the letter Y: *Y-junction*.

Y^{2} *abbrev* yen.

Y^{3} *symbol* **1** *chem* yttrium. **2** *maths* (*usu* **y**) the second of two or three unknown quantities. See also **X**^{2}, **Z**^{2}.

-y[1] *suffix, forming adjs* (**-ier, -iest**) *signifying* full of; characterized by; having the quality of; keen on, etc: *spotty* • *shiny* • *horsey.* [From Anglo-Saxon -*ig*]

-y[2] *or* **-ey** *suffix, forming nouns* (*pl* **-ies**) *indicating* **1** a diminutive or term of affection: *doggy.* **2** someone or something with a specified characteristic: *fatty.* [Originally Scots, used in familiar forms of names]

-y[3] *suffix, forming nouns* (*pl* **-ies**) *signifying* **1** a quality or state: *jealousy* • *modesty.* **2** an action: *entreaty* • *expiry.* [From French -*ie*]

yacht /jɒt/ *noun* a boat or small ship, usu with sails and often with an engine, built for racing or cruising. ▪ **yachting** *noun, adj.* [16c: from Dutch *jachtschip* chasing ship]

---

yacht
This word is often misspelt. It might help you to remember the following sentence:
*Yes, **a**ll **c**raft **h**ave **t**riangular sails.*

---

yachtsman *or* **yachtswoman** *noun* a person who sails a yacht.

yack *or* **yak** *derog slang, exclam* imitating the sound of persistent annoying chatter. ▶ *verb* (***yacked, yacking; yakked, yakking***) *intr* to talk at length and often foolishly or annoyingly. ▶ *noun* persistent, foolish or annoying chatter. [20c]

yackety-yak *exclam, verb, noun* **yack**.

yah *exclam* **1** expressing scorn or contempt. **2** *informal* often attributed to an upper-class or affected speaker: yes.

yahoo[1] /jɑːˈhuː/ *noun* a lout or ruffian. [18c: named after the brutish characters that looked like humans in Swift's *Gulliver's Travels*]

yahoo[2] /jɑːˈhuː, jəˈhuː/ *exclam* expressing happiness, excitement, etc.

Yajur-veda see **Veda**

yak[1] *noun* (***yaks*** *or* ***yak***) a large ox-like Tibetan mammal with a thick shaggy black coat and large upward-curving horns. [18c: from Tibetan *gyag*]

yak[2] see **yack**

yakked *and* **yakking** see under **yack**

Yale lock *noun, trademark* a type of lock operated by a flat key with a notched upper edge (a **Yale key**). [19c: named after Linus Yale, US locksmith]

yam *noun* **1** a climbing plant cultivated in tropical regions for its edible tubers. **2** the thick starchy tuber of this plant. **3** *N Am* a sweet potato. [17c: from Portuguese *inhame*]

yammer *verb* **1** *intr* to complain whiningly. **2** *intr* to talk loudly and at length. **3** to say something, esp as a complaint, loudly and at length. ▶ *noun* the act or sound of yammering. [15c as *yamer*: from Anglo-Saxon *geomrian*]

yang see under **yin**

Yank *noun, informal* a person from the US. [18c: short form of **Yankee**]

yank *informal, noun* a sudden sharp pull. ▶ *verb, tr & intr* to pull suddenly and sharply. [19c: orig US]

Yankee *noun* **1** *Brit informal* a person from the US. **2** *N Am, esp US* a person from New England or from any of the northern states of America. [18c: perhaps from Dutch *Jan Kees* John Cheese, the nickname given by the New York Dutch to the British settlers in Connecticut]

yap *verb* (***yapped, yapping***) *intr* **1** eg, of a small dog: to give a high-pitched bark. **2** *derog, informal* of a person: to talk continually in a shrill voice, often about trivial matters. ▶ *noun* a short high-pitched bark. ▪ **yappy** *adj* (**-ier, -iest**). [17c: imitating the sound]

yard[1] *noun* **1** (abbrev **yd**) in the imperial system: a unit of measurement of length equal to three feet or about 0.9144 metres. **2** *naut* a long beam hung on a mast, from which to hang a sail. [Anglo-Saxon *gierd* rod]

yard[2] *noun* **1** *often in compounds* an area of enclosed ground associated with a building. **2** an area of enclosed ground used for a special industrial purpose. **3** *N Am* a garden. [Anglo-Saxon *geard* fence or enclosure]

yardarm *noun, naut* either of the tapering end-sections of a **yard**[1] (sense 2).

yardstick *noun* **1** a standard for comparison. **2** a stick exactly one **yard**[1] long, used for measuring.

yarmulka *or* **yarmulke** /ˈjɑːməlkə/ *noun* a skullcap worn by Jewish men. [20c: Yiddish]

yarn *noun* **1** thread spun from wool, cotton, etc. **2** a story or tale, often a lengthy and incredible one. **3** *informal* a lie. [Anglo-Saxon *gearn*]
IDIOMS **spin sb a yarn** *informal* to tell them a long or untruthful story.

yarrow *noun* a creeping plant, formerly used widely in herbal medicine, with finely divided aromatic leaves and white or pink flower heads in dense flat-topped clusters. [Anglo-Saxon *gearwe*]

yashmak *noun* a veil worn by Muslim women that covers the face below the eyes. [19c: from Arabic *yashmaq*]

yaw *verb, intr* **1** of a ship: to move temporarily from, or fail to keep to, the direct line of its course. **2** of an aircraft: to deviate horizontally from the direct line of its course. ▶ *noun* an act of yawing. [16c]

yawl *noun* **1** a type of small sailing-boat, esp one with two masts. **2** a ship's small boat. [17c: from Dutch *jol*]

yawn *verb, intr* **1** to open one's mouth wide and take a deep involuntary breath when tired or bored. **2** of a hole, gap, etc: to be or become wide open. ▶ *noun* **1** an act or an instance of yawning. **2** *informal* a boring or tiresome event, person, etc. [Anglo-Saxon *ganian* to yawn, and *geonian* to gape widely]

yawning *adj* of a hole, etc: wide; large.

yaws *singular noun, pathol* an infectious skin disease of tropical countries, characterized by red ulcerating sores. [17c]

y-axis *noun, maths* in a graph: the vertical axis along which one of a set of **co-ordinate**s (*noun* sense 2) is plotted. Compare **x-axis, z-axis.**

Yb *symbol, chem* ytterbium.

Y-chromosome *noun, biol* the smaller of the two sex chromosomes, whose presence determines the male sex in most animals. See also **X-chromosome**.

yd *abbrev* yard or yards.

ye[1] *pron, archaic or dialect* you (pl). [Anglo-Saxon ge]

ye[2] *definite article, old or affected use* the: *Ye Olde Englishe Tea Shoppe.* [15c: from the use of *y* by medieval printers as a substitute for the old letter *Þ*]

yea /jeɪ/ *formal or old use, exclam* yes. ▶ *noun* **a** a yes; **b** a person who has voted or is voting yes. [Anglo-Saxon *gea*]

yeah /jɛ, jɛə/ *exclam, informal* yes.

year *noun* **1 a** the period of time the Earth takes to go once round the Sun, about 365¼ days; **b** the equivalent time for any other planet. **2** (*also* **calendar year**) the period between 1 January and 31 December, 365 days in a normal year, 366 days in a leap year. **3** any period of twelve months. **4** a period of less than 12 months during which some activity is carried on: *an academic year.* **5** a period of study at school, college, etc over an academic year: *She's in third year now.* **6** students at a particular stage in their studies, considered as a group: *had a meeting with the third year this morning.* See also **years**. [Anglo-Saxon *gear*]

IDIOMS **year in, year out** happening, done, etc every year, with tedious regularity.

yearbook *noun* a book of information updated and published every year, esp one that records the events, etc of the previous year.

yearling *noun* **a** an animal that is a year old; **b** a racehorse during the calendar year following the 1 January after its birth. ▸ *adj* of an animal: one-year-old.

yearlong *adj* lasting all year.

yearly *adj* **1** happening, etc every year. **2** valid for one year. ▸ *adv* every year.

yearn *verb, intr* **1** (**yearn for** *or* **after sth** *or* **to do sth**) to feel a great desire for it; to long for it. **2** to feel compassion. ▪ **yearning** *noun, adj.* ▪ **yearningly** *adv.* [Anglo-Saxon *giernan* to desire]

year-round *adj* open all year; lasting throughout the year.

years *plural noun* **1** age: *He is wise for his years.* **2** *informal* a very long time: *She's been coming for years.* **3** some period of time in the past or future: *in years gone by.*

yeast *noun* any of various single-celled fungi that are capable of fermenting carbohydrates, widely used in the brewing and baking industries. [Anglo-Saxon *gist*]

yeasty *adj* (**-ier, -iest**) **1** consisting, tasting or smelling of yeast. **2** frothy. **3** trivial.

yell *noun* a loud shout or cry. ▸ *verb, tr & intr* to shout or cry out. [Anglo-Saxon *gellan*]

yellow *adj* **1** of the colour of gold, butter, egg-yolk, a lemon, etc. **2** *derog, informal* cowardly. **3** *often offensive* when used as a term of racial description: having a yellow or yellowish skin. ▸ *noun* **1** any shade of the colour of gold, butter, egg-yolk, etc. **2** something, eg material or paint, that is yellow in colour. ▸ *verb, tr & intr* to make or become yellow. ▪ **yellowish** *and* **yellowy** *adj.* ▪ **yellowness** *noun.* [Anglo-Saxon *geolu*]

yellow alert *noun* a security alert one stage less serious than a **red alert**.

yellow-belly *noun, slang* a coward. ▪ **yellow-bellied** *adj.*

yellow card *noun, football* a yellow-coloured card shown by the referee as a warning to a player being cautioned for a serious violation of the rules. Compare **red card**.

yellow fever *noun, pathol* an acute viral disease of tropical America and W Africa, transmitted by the bite of a mosquito and causing high fever, jaundice and haemorrhaging.

yellowhammer *noun* a large brightly-coloured bunting with a yellow head and underparts.

yellow jersey *noun* in the Tour de France cycle race: any of the jerseys awarded to and worn in turn by each winner of a stage.

Yellow Pages *plural noun, trademark* a telephone directory, or a section of one, printed on yellow paper, in which entries are classified according to the nature of the trade or profession of the individuals or companies listed and the services they offer.

yellow streak *noun* a tendency to cowardice.

yelp *verb, intr* of a dog, etc: to give a sharp sudden cry. ▸ *noun* such a cry. [Anglo-Saxon *gielpan* to boast]

yen[1] *noun* (*pl* **yen**) (abbrev **Y**) the standard unit of currency of Japan. [19c: from Japanese *en*]

yen[2] *informal, noun* a desire. ▸ *verb* (**yenned, yenning**) *intr* (*usu* **yen for sth**) to feel a longing or craving for it. [19c: from Cantonese Chinese *yan* craving]

yeoman /ˈjoʊmən/ *noun* (**yeomen**) **1** *hist* a farmer who owned and worked his own land. **2** *military* a member of the **yeomanry** (sense 2). [14c: perhaps from earlier *yongman* young man]

yeoman of the guard *noun* a member of the oldest corps of the British sovereign's personal bodyguard. Also called **beefeater**.

yeomanry /ˈjoʊmənrɪ/ *noun* (**-ies**) **1** *hist* the class of land-owning farmers. **2** a former volunteer cavalry force formed in the 18c.

yep *exclam, informal* yes.

yes *exclam* used to express agreement or consent. ▸ *noun* (**yesses**) an expression of agreement or consent. [Anglo-Saxon *gese* or *gise*, from *gea* or *ge* yea + *si* let it be]

yeshiva /jəˈʃiːvə/ *noun* (**yeshivas** *or* **yeshivoth** /-vɒt/) *Judaism* **1** a school for the study of the **Talmud**. **2** a seminary for the training of rabbis. **3** an orthodox Jewish elementary school. [19c: from Hebrew *yeshibhah* a sitting]

yes-man *noun, derog* someone who always agrees with the opinions and follows the suggestions of a superior, employer, etc, esp to curry favour with them.

yesses *pl* of **yes**

yesterday *noun* **1** the day before today. **2** *often in pl* the recent past. ▸ *adv* **1** on the day before today. **2** in the recent past. [Anglo-Saxon *giestran dæg*]

yesteryear *noun, literary* **1** the past in general. **2** last year.

yet *adv* **1** (*also* **as yet**) up till now or then; by now or by that time: *He had not yet arrived.* **2** at this time; now: *You can't leave yet.* **3** at some time in the future; before the matter is finished; still: *She may yet make a success of it.* **4** (used for emphasis with *another, more,* or a comparative) even; still: *yet bigger problems: yet another mistake.* ▸ *conj* but; however; nevertheless. [Anglo-Saxon *giet*]

IDIOMS **yet again** once more.

yeti *noun* an ape-like creature supposed to live in the Himalayas. Also called **abominable snowman**. [20c: from Tibetan]

yew *noun* **1** a cone-bearing evergreen tree with reddish-brown flaky bark and narrow leaves. **2** the hard close-grained reddish-brown wood of this tree. [Anglo-Saxon *iw*]

Y-fronts *plural noun* men's or boys' underpants with a Y-shaped front seam.

YHA *abbrev* Youth Hostels Association.

Yiddish *noun* a language spoken by many Jews, based on medieval German, with elements from **Hebrew** and several other, esp **Slavonic**, languages. ▸ *adj* consisting of, or spoken or written in, this language. [19c: from German *jüdisch* Jewish]

yield *verb* **1** to produce (an animal product such as meat or milk, or a crop). **2** *finance* to give or produce (interest, etc): *Shares yield dividends.* **3** to produce (a specified quantity of a natural or financial product). **4** *tr & intr* to give up or give in; to surrender. **5** *intr* to break or give way under force or pressure. ▸ *noun* **1** the amount produced. **2** the total amount of a product produced by an animal or plant, or harvested from a certain area of cultivated land. **3** *finance* the return from an investment or tax. [Anglo-Saxon *gieldan* to pay]

yielding *adj* **1** submissive. **2** flexible. **3** able or tending to give way.

yin *noun* in traditional Chinese philosophy, religion, medicine, etc: one of the two opposing and complementary principles, being the negative, feminine, dark, cold and passive element or force (as opposed to the positive, masculine, light, warm and active **yang**). [17c: Chinese *yin* dark, and *yang* bright]

y-intercept *noun, maths* the point at which a line cuts the y-axis.

yippee *exclam, informal* expressing excitement, delight, etc.

-yl *suffix, chem, forming nouns, denoting* a radical or group: *methyl.* [From Greek *hyle* matter]

YMCA *abbrev* Young Men's Christian Association, a charity providing accommodation and other services, orig for young men and boys, but increasingly now for both sexes. Compare **YWCA**. ▸ *noun* a hostel run by the YMCA.

-yne *suffix, chem, forming nouns, denoting* an organic compound that contains a triple bond: *alkyne.* [Altered from **-ine**[2]]

yo *exclam* **1** used to call someone's attention. **2** used as a greeting. **3** *esp US* used in answer to a call: present; here. [15c as a call to hounds]

yob *or* **yobbo** *noun, slang* a bad-mannered aggressive young person (usu male); a lout or hooligan. ▪ **yobbish** *adj.* ▪ **yobbishness** *noun.* [19c: back-slang for *boy*]

yodel *verb* (***yodelled, yodelling****; US* ***yodeled, yodeling***) *tr & intr* to sing (a melody, etc), changing frequently from a normal to a falsetto voice and back again. ▸ *noun* an act of yodelling. ▪ **yodeller** *noun.* ▪ **yodelling** *noun.* [19c: from German dialect *jodeln*]

yoga *noun* **1** a system of Hindu philosophy showing how to free the soul from reincarnation and reunite it with God. **2** any of several systems of physical and mental discipline based on this, esp (in western countries) a particular system of physical exercises. ▪ **yogic** *adj.* [19c: Sanskrit, meaning 'union']

yoghurt, yogurt *or* **yoghourt** *noun* a type of semi-liquid food made from fermented milk, often flavoured with fruit. [17c: Turkish]

yogi *or* **yogin** *noun* a person who practises the **yoga** philosophy. [17c as *loggue*: Hindi]

yogini *noun* a female yogi. [19c: Sanskrit]

yoke *noun* **1** a wooden frame placed over the necks of oxen to hold them together when they are pulling a plough, cart, etc. **2** a frame placed across a person's shoulders, for carrying buckets. **3** something oppressive; a great burden: *the yoke of slavery.* **4** *dressmaking, etc* the part of a garment that fits over the shoulders and round the neck. **5** a pair of animals, esp oxen. ▸ *verb* (*always* **yoke sth to another** *or* **yoke two things together**) **1** to join them under or with a **yoke** (sense 1). **2** to join or unite them. [Anglo-Saxon *geoc*]

---

yoke, yolk

Be careful not to use the spelling **yoke** when you mean **yolk**:

Use the yolks of two eggs.

---

yokel /ˈjoʊkəl/ *noun, derog* an unsophisticated person from the country, usually a male. [19c]

yolk *noun* **1** in the eggs of birds and some reptiles: the yellow spherical mass of nutritive material. **2** *cookery, etc* this yellow part of an egg, as distinct from the **white** (sense 4). [Anglo-Saxon *geolca*]

---

yolk, yoke

Be careful not to use the spelling **yolk** when you mean **yoke**:

the yoke of slavery
a plough yoked to a horse

Yom Kippur *noun* an annual Jewish religious festival devoted to repentance for past sins, and celebrated with fasting and prayer. Also called **Day of Atonement**. [19c: Hebrew *yom* day + *kippur* atonement]

yon *adj, literary or dialect* that or those: *Do you see yon fellow?* [Anglo-Saxon *geon*]

yonder *adv* in or at that place over there. ▸ *adj* situated over there. [13c]

IDIOMS **the wide blue yonder** the far distance.

yonks *noun, informal* a long time.

yoo-hoo *exclam, informal* used to attract someone's attention.

yore *or* **days of yore** *noun, literary or archaic* times past or long ago. [Anglo-Saxon *geara* formerly]

yorker *noun, cricket* a ball pitched to a point directly under the bat. [19c: prob from the name Yorkshire]

Yorkie *or* **yorkie** *noun* a Yorkshire terrier.

Yorkist *hist, noun* a supporter of the House of York in the Wars of the Roses. Compare **Lancastrian.** ▸ *adj* relating to the House of York.

Yorks. *abbrev, English county* Yorkshire.

Yorkshire pudding *noun* a baked pudding of unsweetened batter, esp and traditionally cooked and served with roast beef. [18c: named after Yorkshire in England]

Yorkshire terrier *noun* a very small terrier with a long straight coat of fine brown and bluish-grey hair that reaches the ground, and large erect ears. Often shortened to **Yorkie**.

Yoruba *noun* (***Yoruba*** *or* ***Yorubas***) **1** a group of peoples of SW Nigeria and Benin, W Africa. **2** an individual belonging to this group of peoples. **3** their language. ▸ *adj* belonging or relating to this group or their language. [19c: native name]

you *pron* **1** the person or people, etc spoken or written to, with or without others: *When are you all coming to visit us?* **2** any or every person: *You don't often see that nowadays.* [Anglo-Saxon *eow*]

you'd *contraction* **1** you would. **2** you had.

you'll *contraction* **1** you will. **2** you shall.

young *adj* **1** in the first part of life, growth, development, etc; not old. **2** (**the young**) young people in general. **3** usu of animals or birds: their offspring: *Some birds feed their young on insects.* **4** (**Young**) used in titles of subsections of political parties or other organizations which are run by and for younger members, and hence also applied to the younger members themselves: *He's a Young Conservative.* **5** in the early stages: *The night is young.* [Anglo-Saxon *geong*]

IDIOMS **with young** of animals: pregnant.

young blood *noun* new people with fresh ideas.

young offender *noun, Brit* a lawbreaker aged between 16 and 21.

young offender institution *noun, Brit* (abbrev **YOI**) an establishment for the detention of **young offenders** who are given custodial sentences.

youngster *noun, informal* a young person.

your *adj* **1** belonging to you. **2** *informal, often derog* usual; ordinary; typical: *Your politicians nowadays have no principles.* [Anglo-Saxon *eower*]

your, you're

Be careful not to use the spelling **your** when you mean **you're**, the short form of 'you are', and vice versa:

What are your names?

You're going to be late.

you're *contraction* you are.

Your Highness see under **highness** (sense 1)

Your Holiness see under **holiness** (sense 2)

Your Honour see under **Honour**

yours *pron* **1** something belonging to you. **2** (*also* **yours faithfully, sincerely** *or* **truly**) conventional expressions written before a signature at the end of a letter.

IDIOMS **of yours** (a specified thing, relation, etc) belonging to you: *that book of yours.*

yourself *pron* (***yourselves***) **1** the reflexive form of **you**. **2** used for emphasis: *you yourself* • *Are you coming yourself?* **3** your normal self: *don't seem yourself this morning.* **4** (*also* **by yourself**) alone; without help: *Can you reach it yourself?*

yours truly *pron, informal* used to refer to oneself, esp with irony or affected condescension: *Then yours truly had to go and fetch it.*

Your Worship see under **worship**

youth *singular noun* **1** the state, quality or fact of being young. **2** the early part of life, often specifically that between childhood and adulthood. **3** the enthusiasm, rashness, etc associated with people in this period of life. **4** (***youths***) a boy or young man. **5** (*singular or plural noun*) young people in general: *The youth of today expect too much.*

youth club *noun* a place or organization providing leisure activities for young people.

youth court *noun, Brit* a court at which **young offenders** are tried.

youthful *adj* **1** young, esp in manner or appearance. **2** of someone who is not young: young-looking, or having the energy, enthusiasm, etc of a young person. ▪ **youthfulness** *noun.*

youth hostel *noun* a hostel providing simple overnight accommodation, esp one that belongs to the Youth Hostels Association.

you've *contraction* you have.

yowl *verb, intr* esp of an animal: to howl or cry sadly. ▸ *noun* such a howl. ▪ **yowling** *noun.* [14c as *yuhel*]

yo-yo *noun* a toy consisting of a pair of wooden, metal or plastic discs joined at their centre, and with a piece of string attached, the toy being repeatedly made to unwind from the string by the force of its weight and rewind by its momentum. ▸ *verb* (***yo-yos, yo-yoed***) *intr* to rise and fall repeatedly; to fluctuate repeatedly in any way. [20c: originally a trademark: apparently Filipino, applied to a similar device, but literally meaning 'come come']

yr *abbrev* **1** year. **2** younger. **3** your.

yrs *abbrev* years.

ytterbium /ɪ'tɜːbɪəm/ *noun, chem* (symbol **Yb**) a soft silvery lustrous metallic element belonging to the **lanthanide** series, used in lasers, and for making steel and other alloys. [19c: named after Ytterby, a quarry in Sweden where it was discovered]

yttrium /'ɪtrɪəm/ *noun, chem* (symbol **Y**) a silvery-grey metallic element used in alloys to make superconductors and strong permanent magnets. [19c: from the same source as **ytterbium**]

yuan /jʊ'ɑːn/ *noun* (*pl* ***yuan***) the standard unit of currency of the People's Republic of China. [20c (the unit was introduced in 1914): Chinese, literally 'round thing']

yucca *noun* a tropical and subtropical American plant with a short thick trunk, stiff narrow sword-shaped leaves and waxy white bell-shaped flowers. [16c as *yuca*, meaning 'cassava': from Carib (a native S American language)]

yuck *or* **yuk** *informal, noun* a disgusting mess; filth. ▸ *exclam* expressing disgust or distaste. ▪ **yucky** *or* **yukky** *adj* (**-*ier*, -*iest***).

Yugoslav *adj* belonging or relating to Yugoslavia, a former country in SE Europe, or its inhabitants. ▸ *noun* a citizen or inhabitant of, or person born in, Yugoslavia. ▪ **Yugoslavian** *adj, noun.*

Yule *noun, old, literary & dialect* **1** Christmas. **2** (*also* **Yuletide**) the Christmas period. [Anglo-Saxon *geol*]

yummy *adj* (**-*ier*, -*iest***) *informal* delicious. [20c: from **yum-yum**]

yum-yum *exclam* expressing delight at or appreciative anticipation of something, esp delicious food. [19c: imitating the sound of the jaws opening and closing]

yuppie *or* **yuppy** *noun* (**-*ies***) *derog, informal* an ambitious young professional person working in a city job. ▪ **yuppiedom** *noun.* [20c: from *y*oung *u*rban *p*rofessional, or *y*oung *u*pwardly-mobile *p*rofessional]

yuppify *verb* (**-*ies*, -*ied***) **1** to alter (usu a place) so as to conform to yuppie taste. **2** to turn someone into a yuppie. ▪ **yuppification** *noun.*

YWCA *abbrev* Young Women's Christian Association. Compare **YMCA**. ▸ *noun* a hostel run by the YWCA.

Z[1] *or* **z** *noun* (***Zs, Z's*** *or* ***z's***) the twenty-sixth and last letter of the English alphabet.

Z[2] *symbol, maths* (*usu* **z**) the third of three unknown quantities. See also **X**[2], **Y**[3].

Z[3] *symbol,* **1** *chem* atomic number. **2** *physics* impedance.

z see **Z**[1], **Z**[2]

zabaglione /zabal'jounɪ/ *noun, cookery* a dessert made from egg-yolks, sugar and wine (usu Marsala), whisked together over a gentle heat. [19c: Italian]

Zairean /zɑː'ɪərɪən/ *adj* belonging or relating to Zaire, a republic in central Africa, or its inhabitants. ▸ *noun* a citizen or inhabitant of, or person born in, Zaire. [20c]

zakat /za'kɑːt/ *or* **zakah** *noun, Islam* a tax of 2½ per cent payable by Muslims on certain kinds of property, with the money raised being devoted to charitable causes. [19c: Persian, from Arabic *zakah*]

Zambian *adj* belonging or relating to Zambia or its inhabitants. ▸ *noun* a citizen or inhabitant of, or person born in, Zambia.

zany /'zeɪnɪ/ *adj* (***-ier, -iest***) amusingly crazy. ▪ **zanily** *adv.* ▪ **zaniness** *noun.* [16c, meaning 'a clown's stooge']

zap *verb* (***zapped, zapping***) *informal* **1** to hit, destroy or shoot something, esp suddenly. **2** to delete all the data in (a file) or from (the main memory of a computer). **3** *intr* to change TV channels frequently using a remote-control device. **4** *tr & intr* to move quickly or suddenly. ▪ **zapping** *noun.* [20c: imitation of the sound]

zapper *noun, informal* a **remote control** (sense 2) for a TV, DVD player or video recorder.

z-axis *noun, maths* in 3-dimensional graphs: the vertical axis at right angles to the **x-axis** and **y-axis**, along which one of a set of **co-ordinate**s (*noun* sense 2) is plotted.

zeal *noun* great, and sometimes excessive, enthusiasm or keenness. [14c: from Greek *zelos*]

zealot /'zɛlət/ *noun, often derog* a single-minded and determined supporter of a political cause, religion, etc. ▪ **zealotry** *noun.* [13c: from Greek *zelotes*]

zealous /'zɛləs/ *adj* enthusiastic; keen. ▪ **zealously** *adv.* ▪ **zealousness** *noun.* [16c: from medieval Latin *zelosus*]

zebra *noun* (***zebras** or **zebra***) a stocky black-and-white striped African mammal with a stubby mane, related to the horse. [16c: from an African language]

zebra crossing *noun, Brit* a pedestrian crossing marked by black and white stripes on the road. See also **pelican crossing**. [20c]

zed *noun, Brit* **1** the name of the letter Z. *N Am equivalent* **zee**. **2** (**zeds**) *slang* sleep. [15c: from French *zède*]

zee *noun, N Am* the name of the letter Z.

Zeitgeist /'zaɪtgaɪst/ *noun* (*also* **zeitgeist**) the spirit of the age; the attitudes of a specific period. [19c: German]

Zen *noun* a school of Buddhism that stresses the personal experience of enlightenment based on a simple way of life, close to nature, and simple methods of meditation. [18c: Japanese]

zenith *noun* **1** *astron* the point on the celestial sphere diametrically opposite the **nadir** and directly above the observer. Also called **vertex**. **2** the highest point. [14c: ultimately from Arabic *samt-ar-ras* direction of the head]

zephyr /'zɛfə(r)/ *noun, literary* a light gentle breeze. [Anglo-Saxon as *zefferus*: from Greek *Zephyros* the west wind]

zeppelin *or* **Zeppelin** *noun* a cigar-shaped airship.

zero *noun* **1** the number, figure or symbol 0. **2** the point on a scale that is taken as the base from which measurements may be made: *5 degrees below zero.* See also **absolute zero**. **3** zero hour. ▸ *adj* **1** being of no measurable size. **2** *informal* not any; no: *She has zero confidence.* ▸ *verb* (***zeroes, zeroed***) to set or adjust something to zero. [17c: from French *zéro*]

PHRASAL VERBS **zero in on sth** to aim for it; to move towards it.

zero hour *noun* the exact time fixed for something to happen.

zero-rate *verb* to assess (goods, etc) at a zero rate of VAT.

zest *noun* **1** keen enjoyment; enthusiasm. **2** something that adds to one's enjoyment of something. **3** *cookery* the coloured outer layer of the peel of an orange or lemon, or the oil contained in it, used for flavouring. **4** piquancy; agreeably sharp flavour. ▪ **zestful** *adj.* ▪ **zesty** *adj* (***-ier, -iest***). [17c: from French *zeste*]

zeta /'ziːtə/ *noun* the sixth letter of the Greek alphabet.

zeugma /'zjuːgmə/ *noun, gram* a figure of speech in which a word is applied to two nouns although strictly it is appropriate to only one of them, or it has a different sense with each, as in *weeping eyes and hearts*. [16c: Greek, meaning 'yoking together']

ziff *noun, Aust & NZ, slang* a beard. [20c]

zigzag *noun* **1** (*usu* **zigzags**) two or more sharp bends to alternate sides in a path, etc. **2** a path, road, etc with a number of such bends. ▸ *adj* **1** having sharp bends to alternate sides. **2** bent from side to side alternately. ▸ *verb* (***zigzagged, zigzagging***) *intr* to move in a zigzag direction. ▸ *adv* in a zigzag direction or manner. [18c: French]

zilch *noun, slang* nothing. [20c]

zillion *noun, informal* a very large but unspecified number. [20c: modelled on **million**, **billion**, etc]

Zimbabwean /zɪm'bɑːbwɪən/ *adj* belonging or relating to Zimbabwe (formerly Southern Rhodesia and later Rhodesia), a republic in SE Africa, or its inhabitants. ▸ *noun* a citizen or inhabitant of, or person born in, Zimbabwe.

Zimmer *or* **Zimmer frame** *noun, trademark* a tubular metal frame, used as a support for walking by the disabled or infirm. [20c: the name of the original manufacturer]

zinc *noun, chem* (symbol **Zn**) a brittle bluish-white metallic element used in dry batteries and various alloys, and as a corrosion-resistant coating to galvanize steel. [17c: from German *Zink*]

zinc ointment *noun* a soothing antiseptic ointment composed of a mixture of zinc oxide and a suitable base such as lanolin or petroleum jelly.

zinc oxide *noun* a white crystalline solid, widely used as an antiseptic and astringent in skin ointments, and as a pigment in paints.

zing *noun* **1** a short high-pitched humming sound, eg that made by a bullet or vibrating string. **2** *informal* zest or vitality. ▸ *verb, intr* to move very quickly, esp while making a high-pitched hum. ▪ **zingy** *adj* (***-ier, -iest***) *informal* full of zest; lively. [20c: imitating the sound]

zinnia *noun* a plant, native to Mexico and S America, with whorled or opposite leaves and brightly coloured daisy-like flower heads. [18c: named after J G Zinn, German botanist]

Zionism *noun* the movement which worked for the establishment of a national homeland in Palestine for Jews and now supports the state of Israel. ▪ **Zionist** *noun, adj.* [19c: from Zion, one of the hills in Jerusalem, and hence allusively Jerusalem itself]

zip[1] *noun* **1** a **zip fastener**. *N Am equivalent* **zipper**. **2** *informal* energy; vitality. **3** a whizzing sound. ► *verb* (***zipped, zipping***) **1** *tr & intr* (*also* **zip up**) to fasten, or be fastened, with a zip fastener. **2** *intr* to make, or move with, a whizzing sound. **3** *comput* to convert (a file, etc) into a compressed form in order to save storage space. [19c: imitating the sound it makes]

zip[2] *noun, US slang* zero; nothing. [20c]

zip code *noun* in the US: a postal code consisting of a five- or nine-figure number. *Brit equivalent* **postcode**. [20c: from *Z*one *I*mprovement *P*lan]

Zip disk *noun, comput, trademark* a floppy disk with a very high capacity on which data is stored in compressed form.

Zip drive *noun, comput, trademark* a specialized hard drive used to compress data.

zip fastener *noun* a device for fastening clothes, etc, in which two rows of metal or nylon teeth are made to fit into each other when a sliding tab is pulled along them.

zipper *N Am, noun* a zip fastener. ► *verb* to fasten with a zipper.

zippy *adj* (***-ier, -iest***) *informal* lively; quick.

zircon *noun, geol* a hard mineral form of zirconium silicate, which is the main ore of zirconium, and occurs in colourless varieties that are used as semi-precious gemstones. [18c: orig from Persian *zargun* golden]

zirconium *noun, chem* (symbol **Zr**) a silvery-grey metallic element that is resistant to corrosion and absorbs neutrons, used in certain alloys and as a coating for fuel rods in nuclear reactors. [19c: from **zircon**]

zit *noun, slang* a pimple.

zither *noun* a musical instrument consisting of a flat wooden soundbox, one section of which has frets on it, over which strings are stretched. [19c: German]

Zl. *abbrev* zloty or zlotys.

zloty /ˈzlɒtɪ/ *noun* (***zloty*** *or* ***zlotys***) the standard unit of currency of Poland. [20c: Polish]

Zn *symbol, chem* zinc.

zodiac *noun* **1** (**the zodiac**) *astron* the band of sky that extends 8° on either side of the Sun's **ecliptic**, divided into 12 equal parts, each of which once contained one of the zodiacal constellations, though some no longer do. **2** *astrol* a chart or diagram (usu a circular one), representing this band of sky and the **signs of the zodiac** contained within it. ▪ **zodiacal** /zoʊˈdaɪəkəl/ *adj.* [14c: from French *zodiaque*]

zombie *or* **zombi** *noun* (***zombies*** *or* ***zombis***) **1** *derog, informal* a slow-moving, stupid, unresponsive or apathetic person. **2** a corpse brought to life again by magic. [19c: from Kongo (a W African language) *zumbi* fetish]

zone *noun* **1** an area or region of a country, town, etc, esp one marked out for a special purpose or by a particular feature. **2** *geog* any of the five horizontal bands into which the Earth's surface is divided by the Arctic Circle, the Tropic of Cancer, the Tropic of Capricorn and the Antarctic Circle. ► *verb* **1** (*also* **zone sth off**) to divide it into zones; to mark it as a zone. **2** to assign to a particular zone. ▪ **zonal** *adj.* [15c: from Greek *zone* girdle]

zonk *verb, informal* to hit with a sharp or firm impact. [20c: imitating the sound of the impact]

PHRASAL VERBS **zonk out** *tr & intr* to collapse or make someone collapse into unconsciousness or in exhaustion.

zoo *noun* a garden or park where wild animals are kept for the purpose of study, breeding of rare species for conservation, etc, and where they are usually on show to the public. [19c: a shortening of **zoological garden**]

zoological garden *noun, formal* a **zoo**.

zoology /zʊˈɒlədʒɪ, zoʊ-/ *noun* the scientific study of animals, including their structure, function, behaviour, ecology, evolution and classification. ▪ **zoological** *adj.* ▪ **zoologist** *noun.* [17c]

zoom *verb* **1** *tr & intr* (*often* **zoom over, past**, *etc*) to move or cause something to move very quickly, making a loud low-pitched buzzing noise. **2** *intr* (*usu* **zoom off**, *etc*) to move very quickly. **3** *intr* to increase quickly: *Prices have zoomed in the past year.* ► *noun* the act or sound of zooming. [19c, meaning 'to make a buzzing noise', but soon transferring its meaning from the sound made by bees to their speed of movement]

PHRASAL VERBS **zoom in on sb** *or* **sth** of a camera or its operator: to close up on somebody or something using a zoom lens.

zoom lens *noun* a type of camera lens which can be used to make a distant object appear gradually closer or further away.

zoophyte /ˈzoʊəfaɪt/ *noun, zool* any of various invertebrate animals which resemble plants, such as sponges, corals and sea anemones. [17c]

zooplankton *noun, zool* drifting or floating microscopic animals. ▪ **zooplanktonic** *adj.* [20c]

Zoroastrianism *noun* an ancient religion of Persian origin founded or reformed by Zoroaster (c.630–c.553 BC), which teaches the existence of two continuously opposed divine beings, one good and the other evil. ▪ **Zoroastrian** *noun, adj.*

zounds *exclam, archaic* used in oaths, etc: expressing astonishment or annoyance. [17c: from *God's wounds*]

Zr *symbol* zirconium.

zucchini /zʊˈkiːnɪ/ *noun* (***zucchini*** *or* ***zucchinis***) *esp N Am & Aust* a courgette. [20c: Italian]

Zulu *noun* (***Zulu*** *or* ***Zulus***) **1** a Bantu people of S Africa. **2** an individual belonging to this people. **3** their language. ► *adj* belonging or relating to this people or their language. [19c]

zygote *noun, biol* the cell that is formed as a result of the fertilization of a female gamete by a male gamete. ▪ **zygotic** *adj.* [19c: from Greek *zygon* yoke]

PLACES, PEOPLE and EVENTS

PLACES

PEOPLE

EVENTS

PLACES

AFGHANISTAN

Official name Islamic Republic of Afghanistan
Capital Kabul
Population 31 057 000 (2006 estimate)
Nationality Afghan
Languages Dari, Pashto
Main religion Islam
Currency 1 Afghani = 100 puls
Internet .af

A landlocked republic in south-central Asia, centred on the Hindu Kush mountain range, with fertile valleys to the north-west, arid uplands in the south and desert in the south-west.

ALBANIA

Official name Republic of Albania
Capital Tirana
Population 3 582 000 (2006 estimate)
Nationality Albanian
Language Albanian
Main religion Islam (with significant minorities practising Christianity or unaffiliated)
Currency 1 Lek (plural Lekë) = 100 qindarka
Internet .al

A republic in the western part of the Balkan Peninsula. Much of the country is mountainous and relatively inaccessible; the majority of the population lives in the low-lying west.

ALGERIA

Official name People's Democratic Republic of Algeria
Capital Algiers
Population 32 930 000 (2006 estimate)
Nationality Algerian
Languages Arabic, Tamazight; French is also spoken
Main religion Islam
Currency 1 Algerian Dinar = 100 centimes
Internet .dz

A republic in north Africa, comprising a densely-populated coastal plain backed by mountains, with the Sahara Desert to the south.

ANDORRA

Official name Principality of Andorra; also known as The Valleys of Andorra
Capital Andorra la Vella
Population 71 201 (2006 estimate)
Nationality Andorran
Language Catalan; French and Spanish are also spoken
Main religion Christianity
Currency 1 Euro = 100 cents
Internet .ad

A mountainous, semi-independent, neutral state on the southern slopes of the central Pyrenees, occupying two valleys of the River Valira.

ANGOLA

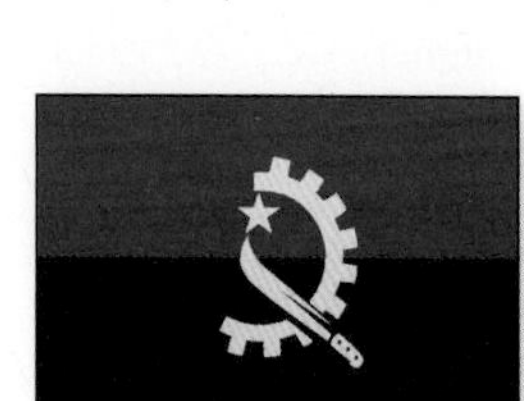

Official name Republic of Angola
Capital Luanda
Population 12 127 000 (2006 estimate)
Nationality Angolan
Language Portuguese; many Bantu languages are also spoken
Main religion Christianity (with significant minority practising traditional beliefs)
Currency 1 Kwanza = 100 lwei
Internet .ao

A republic in south-west Africa comprising a narrow coastal plain which widens in the north towards the Congo Delta and rises to a high inland plateau.

ANTIGUA AND BARBUDA

Official name State of Antigua and Barbuda
Capital St John's
Population 69 100 (2006 estimate)
Nationality Antiguan, Barbudan
Language English
Main religion Christianity
Currency 1 East Caribbean Dollar = 100 cents
Internet .ag

An independent group of three tropical islands (Antigua, Barbuda and the uninhabited Redonda) in the eastern Caribbean Sea; Antigua is mainly hilly, while Barbuda is a flat, coral island with a large lagoon on its western side.

ARGENTINA

Official name Argentine Republic
Capital Buenos Aires
Population 39 922 000 (2006 estimate)
Nationality Argentine, Argentinian
Language Spanish
Main religion Christianity
Currency 1 Argentine Peso = 100 centavos
Internet .ar

A republic in south-eastern South America; the Andes stretch north to south with the *pampa* – a grassy, treeless plain – to the east, and arid steppes to the south.

ARMENIA

Official name Republic of Armenia
Capital Yerevan
Population 2 976 000 (2006 estimate)
Nationality Armenian
Language Armenian; Russian is also spoken
Main religion Christianity
Currency 1 Armenian Dram = 100 lumas
Internet .am

A mountainous, landlocked republic in south-west Asia, crossed by the mountain range of the Lesser Caucasus in the north, with plateaux to the south-west.

AUSTRALIA

Official name Commonwealth of Australia
Capital Canberra
Population 20 264 000 (2006 estimate)
Nationality Australian
Language English; Aboriginal languages are also spoken
Main religion Christianity (with significant minorities practising other religions or unaffiliated)
Currency 1 Australian Dollar = 100 cents
Internet .au

An independent country situated in the southern hemisphere; the largest island in the world, it consists largely of plains and plateaux covered with dry, barren desert, and a mountainous eastern coastline. Population is concentrated in temperate coastal lowlands and valleys in the east and south-west. The Great Barrier Reef lies off the north-east coast, and the island of Tasmania to the south-east.

Australia also possesses Norfolk Island, Christmas Island, the Heard and McDonald Islands, the Cocos (Keeling) Islands, the Coral Sea Islands and the Ashmore and Cartier Islands.

AUSTRIA

Official name	Republic of Austria
Capital	Vienna
Population	8 193 000 (2006 estimate)
Nationality	Austrian
Language	German; Slovene, Croatian and Hungarian are also spoken
Main religion	Christianity
Currency	1 Euro = 100 cents
Internet	.at

A republic in central Europe; situated at the eastern end of the Alps, it is landlocked and almost entirely mountainous.

AZERBAIJAN

Official name	Azerbaijani Republic
Capital	Baku
Population	7 962 000 (2006 estimate)
Nationality	Azerbaijani
Language	Azeri
Main religion	Islam
Currency	1 Azerbaijani Manat (AZM) = 100 gopik
Internet	.az

A republic in south-west Asia crossed by the mountain ranges of the Greater Caucasus in the north and the Lesser Caucasus in the south-west, separated by the plain of the River Kura.

THE BAHAMAS

Official name	Commonwealth of the Bahamas
Capital	Nassau
Population	304 000 (2006 estimate)
Nationality	Bahamian
Language	English
Main religion	Christianity
Currency	1 Bahamian Dollar = 100 cents
Internet	.bs

An independent archipelago of around 700 low-lying coralline limestone islands and over 2,000 keys, extending south-east from the coast of Florida.

BAHRAIN

Official name	Kingdom of Bahrain
Capital	Manama
Population	699 000 (2006 estimate)
Nationality	Bahraini
Language	Arabic
Main religion	Islam
Currency	1 Bahraini Dinar = 1, 000 fils
Internet	.bh

A monarchy in the Arabian Gulf comprising an archipelago of 35 islands; the main island of Bahrain is largely bare and infertile, though helped by many major drainage schemes.

BANGLADESH

Official name	People's Republic of Bangladesh
Capital	Dhaka (formerly known as Dacca)
Population	147 365 000 (2006 estimate)
Nationality	Bangladeshi
Languages	Bangla (Bengali), English
Main religion	Islam (with significant Hindu minority)
Currency	1 Taka = 100 paisha
Internet	.bd

An Asian republic lying between the foothills of the Himalayas and the Indian Ocean, comprising a vast, low-lying alluvial plain cut by a network of rivers and marshes, with hilly regions to the south-east.

BARBADOS

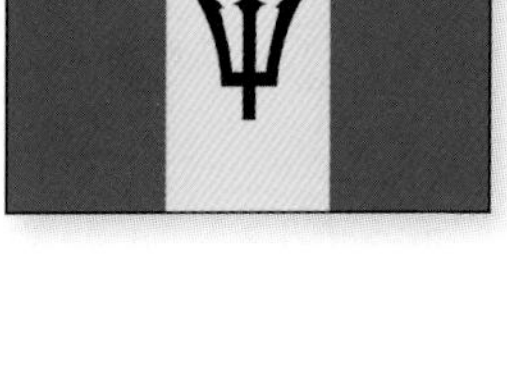

Official name	Barbados
Capital	Bridgetown
Population	280 000 (2006 estimate)
Nationality	Barbadian or (informal) Bajan
Language	English
Main religion	Christianity (with significant minorities practising other religions or unaffiliated)
Currency	1 Barbados Dollar = 100 cents
Internet	.bb

An independent state, the easternmost of the Caribbean Islands, triangular in shape and ringed by a coral reef.

BELARUS

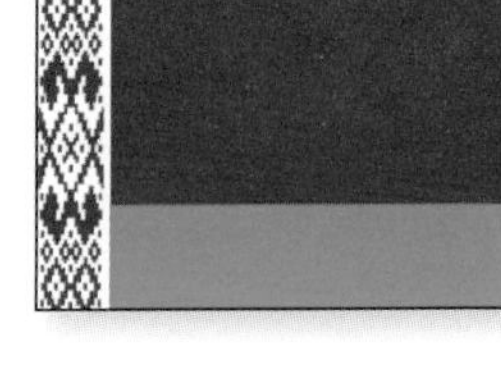

Official name	Republic of Belarus
Capital	Minsk
Population	10 293 000 (2006 estimate)
Nationality	Belarussian
Languages	Belarussian, Russian
Main religion	Christianity (with significant minorities practising other religions)
Currency	1 Belarussian Rouble = 100 kopeks
Internet	.by

A republic in eastern Europe, largely flat, with low hills in the north-west and approximately 11,000 lakes; one third of the country is covered by forests.

BELGIUM

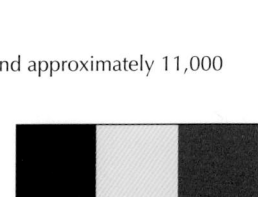

Official name	Kingdom of Belgium
Capital	Brussels
Population	10 379 000 (2006 estimate)
Nationality	Belgian
Languages	Flemish, French, German (mainly on the eastern border)
Main religion	Christianity (with significant minority unaffiliated)
Currency	1 Euro = 100 cents
Internet	.be

A kingdom in north-western Europe, comprising mostly low-lying fertile agricultural land, with a dune-fringed North Sea coastline to the west and some hills in the south-east. The main rivers are linked by a network of canals.

BELIZE

Official name	Belize
Capital	Belmopan
Population	288 000 (2006 estimate)
Nationality	Belizean
Language	English; Spanish and local Mayan, Carib and Creole languages are also spoken
Main religion	Christianity
Currency	1 Belize Dollar = 100 cents
Internet	.bz

An independent state in Central America, with an extensive coastal plain, swampy in the north, and more fertile in the south where it is backed by the Maya Mountains.

BENIN

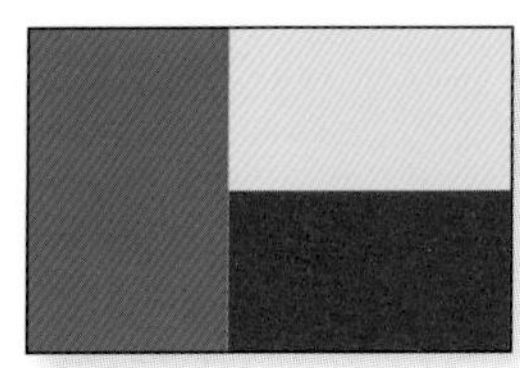

Official name	Republic of Benin
Capital	Porto Novo (administrative and constitutional), Cotonou (economic and seat of government)
Population	7 863 000 (2006 estimate)
Nationality	Beninese
Language	French; local languages are also spoken
Main religion	Traditional beliefs (with significant Christian and Muslim minorities)

Currency 1 CFA Franc = 100 centimes
Internet .bj

A republic in West Africa which rises from a sandy coast with lagoons, to low-lying plains, then to a savannah plateau backed by the Atakora Mountains in the north-west.

BHUTAN

Official name Kingdom of Bhutan
Capital Thimphu
Population 2 280 000 (2006 estimate)
Nationality Bhutanese
Language Dzongkha
Main religion Buddhism (with significant Hindu minority)
Currency 1 Ngultrum = 100 chetrum; the Indian rupee is also used
Internet .bt

A small state in the eastern Himalayas, with forested mountain ridges and fertile valleys descending to low foothills in the south, and many rivers which flow to meet the River Brahmaputra.

BOLIVIA

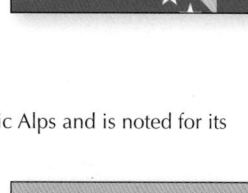

Official name Republic of Bolivia
Capital La Paz (administrative), Sucre (official and legislative)
Population 8 989 000 (2006 estimate)
Nationality Bolivian
Languages Spanish, Quechua, Aymará
Main religion Christianity
Currency 1 Boliviano = 100 centavos
Internet .bo

A landlocked republic in western central South America, dominated in the west by two parallel ranges of the Andes Mountains separated by the Altiplano Plateau. To the north and east, varied lowland habitats include tropical rainforest and savannah.

BOSNIA AND HERZEGOVINA

Official name Republic of Bosnia and Herzegovina; also known as Bosnia-Herzegovina
Capital Sarajevo
Population 4 499 000 (2006 estimate)
Nationality Bosnian, Herzegovinian
Languages Bosnian, Serbian, Croatian
Main religions Christianity, Islam
Currency 1 Convertible Mark = 100 pfennige
Internet .ba

A mountainous republic in central Europe which includes part of the Dinaric Alps and is noted for its limestone gorges.

BOTSWANA

Official name Republic of Botswana
Capital Gaborone
Population 1 640 000 (2006 estimate)
Nationality Motswana (singular noun), Batswana (plural noun), Tswana (adjective)
Languages Setswana, English; local languages are also spoken
Main religions Traditional beliefs, Christianity
Currency 1 Pula = 100 thebe
Internet .bw

A landlocked republic in southern Africa, with 84% of the land covered by the Kalahari Desert; the rich Okavango River delta lies in the north-west, and the population is concentrated in the fertile east, bordered by the River Limpopo.

BRAZIL

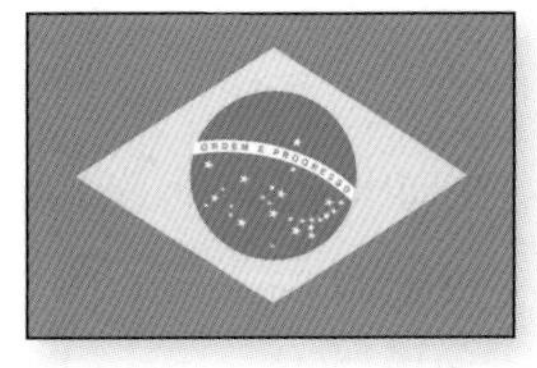

Official name	Federative Republic of Brazil
Capital	Brasília
Population	188 078 000 (2006 estimate)
Nationality	Brazilian
Language	Portuguese
Main religion	Christianity
Currency	1 Brazilian Real = 100 centavos
Internet	.br

A republic in eastern and central South America, with the low-lying Amazon basin in the north covered in dense rainforest and drained by rivers that carry one-fifth of the earth's running water. In the drier, more temperate south, the terrain is characterized by mountain ranges and plateaux which drop down to narrow coastal plains.

BRUNEI DARUSSALAM

Official name	Negara Brunei Darussalam
Capital	Bandar Seri Begawan
Population	379 000 (2006 estimate)
Nationality	Bruneian
Language	Malay; English and Chinese are spoken widely
Main religion	Islam (with significant minorities practising Buddhism, Christianity, traditional beliefs or other religions)
Currency	1 Brunei Dollar = 100 cents
Internet	.bn

A state on the north-west coast of Borneo, south-eastern Asia, comprising a swampy coastal plain rising through foothills to a mountainous region on the Malaysian border. Equatorial rainforest covers 75% of the state, which is divided into two by the Limbang River Valley.

BULGARIA

Official name	Republic of Bulgaria
Capital	Sofia
Population	7 385 000 (2006 estimate)
Nationality	Bulgarian
Language	Bulgarian
Main religion	Christianity (with significant Muslim minority)
Currency	1 Bulgarian Lev = 100 stotinki
Internet	.bg

A republic in the east of the Balkan Peninsula, crossed west to east by the Balkan Mountains, with narrow lowlands stretching south from the River Danube.

BURKINA FASO

Official name	Burkina Faso
Capital	Ouagadougou
Population	13 903 000 (2006 estimate)
Nationality	Burkinabé
Language	French; many local languages are also spoken
Main religions	Traditional beliefs, Islam (with significant Christian minority)
Currency	1 CFA Franc = 100 centimes
Internet	.bf

A landlocked republic in west Africa, with a low-lying plateau falling away to wooded savannahs in the south, and semi-desert in the north.

BURMA See **MYANMAR**

BURUNDI

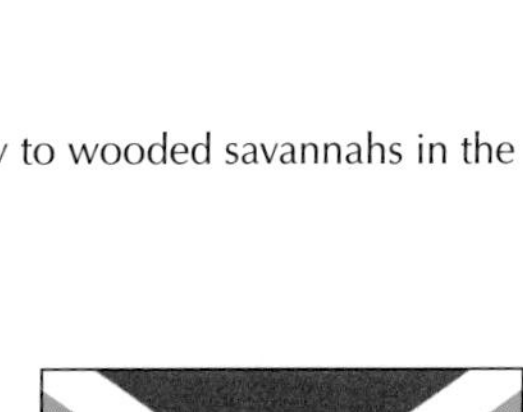

Official name	Republic of Burundi
Capital	Bujumbura
Population	8 090 000 (2006 estimate)
Nationality	Burundian
Languages	French, Kirundi; Swahili is also spoken

Main religion	Christianity (with significant minority practising traditional beliefs)
Currency	1 Burundi Franc = 100 centimes
Internet	.bi

A small landlocked republic in central Africa which lies across the Nile–Congo watershed.

CAMBODIA

Official name	Kingdom of Cambodia
Capital	Phnom Penh
Population	13 881 000 (2006 estimate)
Nationality	Cambodian
Language	Khmer; French is also widely spoken
Main religion	Buddhism
Currency	1 Riel = 100 sen
Internet	.kh

A republic in south-east Asia, surrounding the Tonlé Sap Lake on the Cambodian Plain; the highest land lies in the south-west, where the Cardamom Mountains stretch across the border with Thailand.

CAMEROON

Official name	Republic of Cameroon
Capital	Yaoundé
Population	17 341 000 (2006 estimate)
Nationality	Cameroonian
Languages	French, English; many local languages are also spoken
Main religion	Christianity (with significant minorities practising Islam or traditional beliefs)
Currency	1 CFA Franc = 100 centimes
Internet	.cm

A republic in west Africa with equatorial forest on the coastal plain rising to a central plateau; the west is forested and mountainous, with savannah and semi-desert in the north towards Lake Chad.

CANADA

Official name	Canada
Capital	Ottawa
Population	33 099 000 (2006 estimate)
Nationality	Canadian
Languages	English, French
Main religion	Christianity (with significant minority unaffiliated)
Currency	1 Canadian Dollar = 100 cents
Internet	.ca

An independent country in North America, heavily forested, with plateaux prevalent in the east and centre. The Canadian shield (a craton) dominates the north-east, and is bordered by flat prairies to the south and west. The rugged, heavily-indented western coastline is bordered by mountain ranges including the Rocky and Coast mountains.

CAPE VERDE

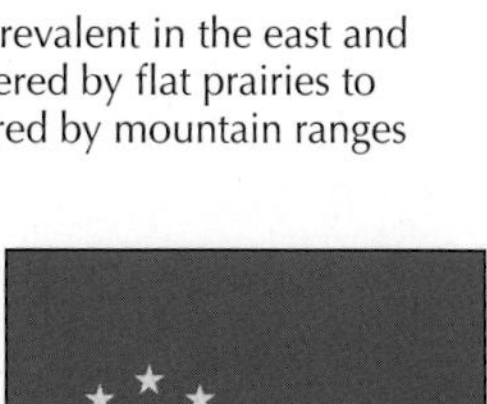

Official name	Republic of Cape Verde
Capital	Praia
Population	421 000 (2006 estimate)
Nationality	Cape Verdean
Language	Portuguese; Crioulo, a Creole language, is widely spoken
Main religion	Christianity
Currency	1 Cape Verde Escudo = 100 centavos
Internet	.cv

A group of mountainous islands of volcanic origin in the Atlantic Ocean, off the west coast of Africa. Coastal plains are semi-desert; savannah or thin forest lies on the mountains; fine, sandy beaches are found on most islands.

CENTRAL AFRICAN REPUBLIC

Official name Central African Republic (CAR)
Capital Bangui
Population 4 303 000 (2006 estimate)
Nationality Central African
Languages French, Sango, tribal languages
Main religion Christianity (with significant minorities practising Islam, traditional beliefs or unaffiliated)
Currency 1 CFA Franc = 100 centimes
Internet .cf

A republic in central Africa situated on a plateau which forms the watershed between the Chad and Congo river basins; the highest ground is in the north-east and north-west.

CHAD

Official name Republic of Chad
Capital N'Djamena (also Ndjamena)
Population 9 944 000 (2006 estimate)
Nationality Chadian
Languages French, Arabic; many local languages are also spoken
Main religion Islam (with significant minorities practising Christianity or traditional beliefs)
Currency 1 CFA Franc = 100 centimes
Internet .td

A landlocked republic in north central Africa, comprising a mostly arid, semi-desert plateau covered with desert scrub or steppe vegetation at the edge of the Sahara Desert. Lake Chad lies in the south-west, with most people living in the tropical south.

CHILE

Official name Republic of Chile
Capital Santiago
Population 16 134 000 (2006 estimate)
Nationality Chilean
Language Spanish
Main religion Christianity (with significant minority unaffiliated)
Currency 1 Chilean Peso = 100 centavos
Internet .cl

A republic in south-western South America, comprising a narrow coastal belt stretching 4 000km from north to south; a fertile central valley lies between the Andean mountains to the east and a coastal range to the west. The Atacama Desert lies in the far north-west; in the south, forests give way to glaciers, fjords and lakes.

CHINA

Official name People's Republic of China (PRC)
Capital Beijing (formerly known as Peking)
Population 1 313 974 000 (2006 estimate)
Nationality Chinese
Languages Standard Chinese (Putong-hua) or Mandarin, also Yue (Cantonese), Wu, Minbei, Minnan, Xiang, Gan, Hakka; minority languages
Main religion Unaffiliated (with significant minorities practising Chinese folk religion, Buddhism or other religions)
Currency 1 Renminbi Yuan = 10 jiao = 100 fen
Internet .cn

A state in central and eastern Asia, which also claims the island of Taiwan. Over two-thirds of the land is sparsely populated, comprising upland hill, mountain and plateau. The highest mountains are in the west at the plateau of Tibet, to the north and east of which the land descends to desert or semi-desert. The southern plains and east coast, with rich, fertile soil, are heavily populated.

China possesses the Special Administrative Regions of Hong Kong and Macau and occupies the Paracel Islands in the South China Sea.

COLOMBIA

Official name Republic of Colombia
Capital Bogotá
Population 43 953 000 (2006 estimate)
Nationality Colombian
Language Spanish
Main religion Christianity
Currency 1 Colombian Peso = 100 centavos
Internet .co

A republic in the north-west of South America, with both Caribbean and Pacific coastlines and several island possessions. In the west the Andes dominate, branching into three ranges, dividing narrow coastal plains from forested Amazon basin lowlands; over half the country is covered in Amazonian rainforest.

COMOROS

Official name Union of the Comoros
Capital Moroni
Population 691 000 (2006 estimate)
Nationality Comoran
Languages French, Arabic; Shikomoro, or Comoran, a local Arabic-Swahili dialect, is also spoken
Main religion Islam (with significant Christian minority)
Currency 1 Comoran Franc = 100 centimes
Internet .km

A group of three volcanic islands, Grand Comore, Anjouan and Mohéli, at the northern end of the Mozambique Channel, with interiors varying from steep mountains to low hills.

CONGO

Official name Republic of Congo; also known as Congo (Brazzaville) or Congo Brazzaville
Capital Brazzaville
Population 3 702 000 (2006 estimate)
Nationality Congolese, Congo
Languages French, Kituba, Lingala
Main religions Christianity, traditional beliefs
Currency 1 CFA Franc = 100 centimes
Internet .cg

A central African republic, whose short Atlantic coastline fringes a broad mangrove plain that rises to an inland mountain ridge, beyond which the land is sparsely populated, dominated by dense grassland, mangrove and forest.

CONGO, DEMOCRATIC REPUBLIC OF

Official name Democratic Republic of Congo (DR Congo, DRC or DROC); also known as Congo (Kinshasa) or Congo-Kinshasa
Capital Kinshasa
Population 62 660 000 (2006 estimate)
Nationality Congolese, Congo
Languages French, Kikongo, Lingala, Swahili, Tshiluba
Main religion Christianity (with significant minorities practising Islam or traditional beliefs)
Currency 1 Congolese Franc = 100 centimes
Internet .cd

A central African republic which rises in the east from the fertile, low-lying drainage basin of the River Congo to a densely-forested plateau. The eastern border is bounded by volcanic mountains marking the western edge of the Great Rift Valley.

COSTA RICA

Official name Republic of Costa Rica
Capital San José
Population 4 075 000 (2006 estimate)
Nationality Costa Rican
Language Spanish
Main religion Christianity
Currency 1 Costa Rican Colón = 100 céntimos
Internet .cr

A republic in Central America, with both Pacific and Caribbean coastlines bordered by swampy terrain which rises to tropical forest, volcanic mountain ranges and plateaux.

CÔTE D'IVOIRE

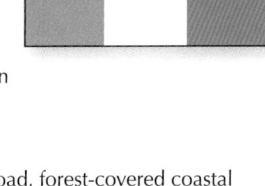

Official name Republic of Côte d'Ivoire
Capital Yamoussoukro (official), Abidjan (administrative and economic)
Population 17 655 000 (2006 estimate)
Nationality Ivorian
Language French; many local languages are also spoken
Main religions Islam, traditional beliefs (with significant Christian minority)
Currency 1 CFA Franc = 100 centimes
Internet .ci

A republic in west Africa with sandy beaches and lagoons backed by a broad, forest-covered coastal plain, rising to upland savannah in the north.

CROATIA

Official name Republic of Croatia
Capital Zagreb
Population 4 495 000 (2006 estimate)
Nationality Croatian
Language Croatian
Main religion Christianity
Currency 1 Kuna = 100 lipa
Internet .hr

A republic in eastern Europe, with islands on the Adriatic coast and mountainous inland terrain which includes fertile plains.

CUBA

Official name Republic of Cuba
Capital Havana
Population 11 383 000 (2006 estimate)
Nationality Cuban
Language Spanish
Main religions Unaffiliated, Christianity
Currency 1 Cuban Peso = 100 centavos
Internet .cu

An island republic in the Caribbean comprising the island of Cuba, Isla de la Juventud and around 1,600 islets and cays. The heavily indented coastline of the main island is low and marshy in the south and steep and rocky in the north; the terrain is mostly flat, with wide, fertile valleys and plains.

CYPRUS

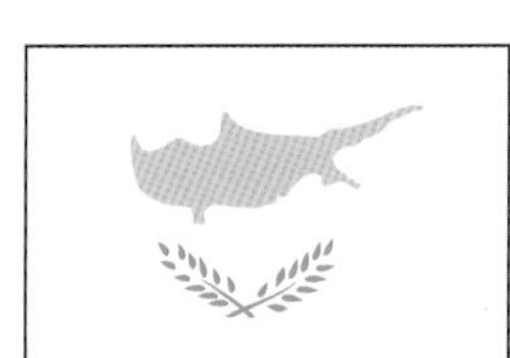

Official name Republic of Cyprus
Capital Nicosia
Population 784 000 (2006 estimate)
Nationality Cypriot
Languages Greek, Turkish; English is also widely spoken
Main religion Christianity (with significant minority practising Islam)
Currency 1 Cyprus Pound = 100 cents; Turkish lira are used in the northern part under Turkish occupation
Internet .cy

An island republic in the north-east Mediterranean with an indented coastline and several long, sandy beaches. Mountain ranges extend along the north coast and in the south west, with a fertile central plain.

CZECH REPUBLIC

Official name	Czech Republic
Capital	Prague
Population	10 235 000 (2006 estimate)
Nationality	Czech
Language	Czech
Main religions	Christianity, unaffiliated
Currency	1 Koruna = 100 haléřù
Internet	.cz

A landlocked republic in eastern Europe, richly wooded with many lakes and rivers and the western range of the Carpathian mountains rising in the east.

DENMARK

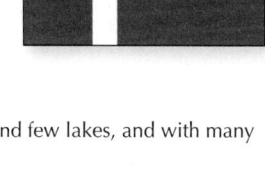

Official name	Kingdom of Denmark
Capital	Copenhagen
Population	5 451 000 (2006 estimate)
Nationality	Dane, Danish
Language	Danish
Main religion	Christianity
Currency	1 Danish Krone = 100 øre
Internet	.dk

A kingdom in northern Europe, uniformly low-lying, with no large rivers and few lakes, and with many lagoons and fjords on the shoreline.

The Faroe Islands and Greenland are Danish self-governing territories.

DJIBOUTI

Official name	Republic of Djibouti
Capital	Djibouti
Population	486 000 (2006 estimate)
Nationality	Djiboutian
Languages	Arabic, French, Somali, Afar
Main religion	Islam
Currency	1 Djibouti Franc = 100 centimes
Internet	.dj

A republic in north-east Africa, comprising a series of plateaux dropping down from mountains to flat, low-lying rocky desert. The Gulf of Tadjoura, which juts deep into the country, is bordered by a fertile coastal strip.

DOMINICA

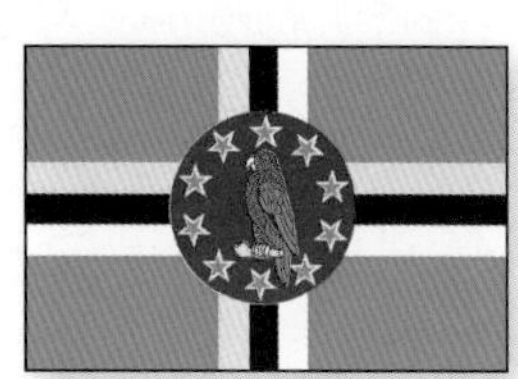

Official name	Commonwealth of Dominica
Capital	Roseau
Population	69 000 (2006 estimate)
Nationality	Dominican
Language	English; French Creole is also spoken
Main religion	Christianity
Currency	1 East Caribbean Dollar = 100 cents
Internet	.dm

An independent republic in the Windward Islands, in the east Caribbean Sea with a deeply-indented coastline, many fumaroles – volcanic holes emitting gases – and sulphur springs, and forestry covering 67% of its area.

DOMINICAN REPUBLIC

Official name	Dominican Republic (DR)
Capital	Santo Domingo
Population	9 184 000 (2006 estimate)
Nationality	Dominican
Language	Spanish

Main religion Christianity
Currency 1 Dominican Peso = 100 centavos
Internet .do

A republic of the West Indies, comprising the eastern two-thirds of the island of Hispaniola. It is crossed by the heavily wooded Cordillera Central mountain range and has a wide coastal plain to the east.

EAST TIMOR

Official name Democratic Republic of Timor-Leste
Capital Dili
Population 1 063 000 (2006 estimate)
Nationality Timorese
Languages Portuguese, Tetum; English and Indonesian are also spoken
Main religion Christianity
Currency 1 US dollar = 100 cents
Internet .tp

A mountainous republic in south-east Asia occupying the eastern half of the island of Timor, the enclave of Oecusse in the west, and the smaller islands of Pulau Atauro and Jaco.

ECUADOR

Official name Republic of Ecuador
Capital Quito
Population 13 547 000 (2006 estimate)
Nationality Ecuadorean or Ecuadorian
Language Spanish; Quechua is also spoken
Main religion Christianity
Currency 1 US dollar = 100 cents
Internet .ec

A republic straddling the equator in the north-west of South America, which also comprises the Galápagos Islands. In the west, coastal plains rise through rolling hills to the Andes mountains, which descend to densely forested alluvial plains in the east.

EGYPT

Official name Arab Republic of Egypt
Capital Cairo
Population 78 887 000 (2006 estimate)
Nationality Egyptian
Language Arabic; English and French are widely spoken
Main religion Islam (with significant Christian minority)
Currency 1 Egyptian Pound = 100 piastres
Internet .eg

A republic in north-east Africa, dominated by desert terrain; 90% of the population lives on the flood plains of the River Nile, which flows north to its delta on the Mediterranean coast.

EL SALVADOR

Official name Republic of El Salvador
Capital San Salvador
Population 6 822 000 (2006 estimate)
Nationality Salvadoran
Language Spanish
Main religion Christianity
Currency 1 El Salvador Colón = 100 centavos/1 US Dollar = 100 cents
Internet .sv

A small, mountainous and volcanic Central American republic, with a narrow coastal belt in the south rising through upland valleys and plateaux to mountains in the north.

EQUATORIAL GUINEA

Official name	Republic of Equatorial Guinea
Capital	Malabo
Population	540 000 (2006 estimate)
Nationality	Equatorial Guinean or Equatoguinean
Languages	Spanish, French; pidgin English and Fang are also spoken
Main religion	Christianity
Currency	1 CFA Franc = 100 centimes
Internet	.gq

A republic in western central Africa, comprising a mainland area and several islands in the Gulf of Guinea. The mainland rises sharply from a narrow coast of mangrove swamps towards the heavily forested African plateau.

ERITREA

Official name	State of Eritrea
Capital	Asmara
Population	4 787 000 (2006 estimate)
Nationality	Eritrean
Languages	Arabic, Tigrinya; English is widely spoken
Main religions	Islam, Christianity
Currency	1 Nakfa = 100 cents
Internet	.er

A country in north-east Africa, with an arid, narrow, low-lying coastal plain on the Red Sea, rising to an inland plateau.

ESTONIA

Official name	Republic of Estonia
Capital	Tallinn
Population	1 324 000 (2006 estimate)
Nationality	Estonian
Language	Estonian
Main religion	Christianity
Currency	1 Kroon = 100 sents
Internet	.ee

A republic in eastern Europe consisting of fairly flat, forested terrain and over 1,500 lakes, with many islands on the coast.

ETHIOPIA

Official name	Federal Democratic Republic of Ethiopia
Capital	Addis Ababa
Population	74 778 000 (2006 estimate)
Nationality	Ethiopian
Language	Amharic; 70 local languages are also spoken
Main religions	Christianity, Islam (with significant minority practising traditional beliefs)
Currency	1 Ethiopian Birr = 100 cents
Internet	.et

A landlocked republic in north-east Africa, dominated by a mountainous central plateau split diagonally by the Great Rift Valley and bordered to the north and east by semi-arid lowlands.

FIJI

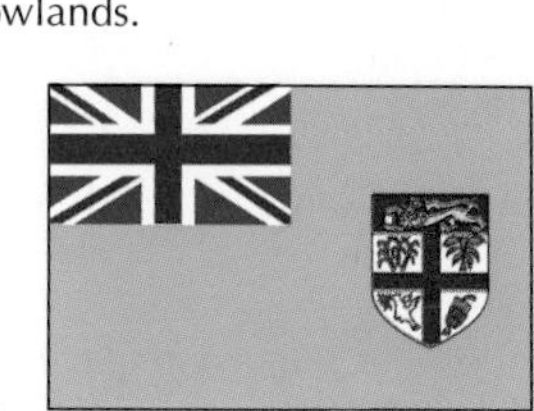

Official name	Republic of the Fiji Islands
Capital	Suva
Population	846 000 (2006 estimate)
Nationality	Fijian
Languages	English, Fijian, Hindi
Main religions	Christianity, Hinduism (with significant minorities practising Islam, Sikhism and others)
Currency	1 Fiji Dollar = 100 cents
Internet	.fj

An independent republic comprising 844 islands and islets in the south-west Pacific Ocean; the larger islands are generally mountainous while the smaller islands consist of limestone with little vegetation. There is tropical forest in the south-east, and an extensive coral reef (Great Sea Reef) along the western fringe.

FINLAND

Official name	Republic of Finland
Capital	Helsinki
Population	5 231 000 (2006 estimate)
Nationality	Finnish
Languages	Finnish, Swedish
Main religion	Christianity
Currency	1 Euro = 100 cents
Internet	.fi

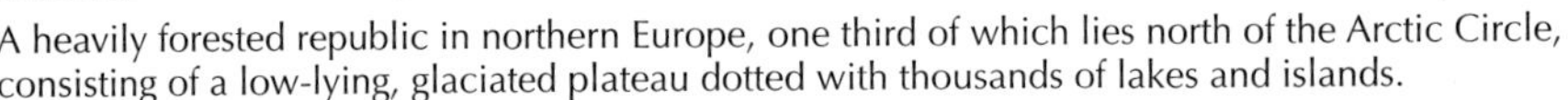

A heavily forested republic in northern Europe, one third of which lies north of the Arctic Circle, consisting of a low-lying, glaciated plateau dotted with thousands of lakes and islands.

FRANCE

Official name	French Republic
Capital	Paris
Population	60 876 000 (2006 estimate)
Nationality	French
Language	French
Main religion	Christianity (with significant minorities practising Islam or unaffiliated)
Currency	1 Euro = 100 cents
Internet	.fr

A republic in western Europe, comprising low and medium-sized hills and plateaux deeply cut by rivers, and bounded to the south and east by the mountain ranges of the Alps and the Pyrenees.

French Guiana, Guadeloupe, Martinique and Réunion are French Overseas departments; French Polynesia, New Caledonia, the French Southern and Antarctic Territories and the Wallis and Futuna Islands are French Overseas Territories; French Territorial Collectivities are Mayotte and St Pierre and Miquelon.

GABON

Official name	Gabonese Republic
Capital	Libreville
Population	1 425 000 (2006 estimate)
Nationality	Gabonese
Language	French; local languages are widely spoken
Main religion	Christianity
Currency	1 CFA Franc = 100 centimes
Internet	.ga

A republic in west equatorial Africa, with lagoons and estuaries on the coast, rising towards the African central plateau.

THE GAMBIA

Official name	Republic of the Gambia
Capital	Banjul
Population	1 641 000 (2006 estimate)
Nationality	Gambian
Language	English; Mandinka, Fula and Wolof are also spoken
Main religion	Islam
Currency	1 Dalasi = 100 butut
Internet	.gm

A republic situated in west Africa consisting of a narrow, flat strip of land stretching 300km along the River Gambia.

GEORGIA

Official name	Georgia
Capital	T'bilisi or Tbilisi
Population	4 661 000 (2006 estimate)
Nationality	Georgian
Languages	Georgian, Russian; Abkhaz is an official language in the region of Abkhazia
Main religion	Christianity (with significant Muslim minority)
Currency	1 Lari = 100 tetri
Internet	.ge

A republic in eastern Europe bordered by the Greater Caucasus to the north and the Lesser Caucasus to the south, with forest covering around 39% of the land.

GERMANY

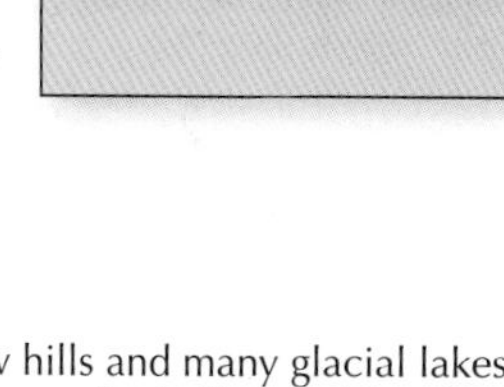

Official name	Federal Republic of Germany
Capital	Berlin
Population	82 422 000 (2006 estimate)
Nationality	German
Language	German; Sorbian (a Slavic language) is spoken by a few
Main religion	Christianity (with significant minorities practising other religions or unaffiliated)
Currency	1 Euro = 100 cents
Internet	.de

A republic in western Europe comprising a fertile, low-lying plain with low hills and many glacial lakes in the north, and central uplands rising in the south to several mountain ranges, including the Bavarian Alps.

GHANA

Official name	Republic of Ghana
Capital	Accra
Population	22 410 000 (2006 estimate)
Nationality	Ghanaian
Language	English; almost 50 African languages are also spoken
Main religion	Christianity (with significant minorities practising traditional beliefs, Islam or other religions)
Currency	1 Cedi = 100 pesewas
Internet	.gh

A republic in west Africa, with a coastline of sandbanks and lagoons backed by low-lying plains, leading to rainforest-covered plateaux in the west and the River Volta basin in the east.

GREECE

Official name	Hellenic Republic
Capital	Athens
Population	10 688 000 (2006 estimate)
Nationality	Greek
Language	Greek
Main religion	Christianity
Currency	1 Euro = 100 cents
Internet	.gr

A mountainous republic in south-eastern Europe, consisting of a large area of mainland linked to the Peloponnese peninsula in the south by the Isthmus of Corinth, and over 1,400 islands.

GRENADA

Official name	State of Grenada
Capital	St George's
Population	89 700 (2006 estimate)
Nationality	Grenadian or Grenadan
Language	English
Main religion	Christianity (with significant minorities practising other religions)

Currency 1 East Caribbean Dollar = 100 cents

Internet .gd

An independent constitutional monarchy in the West Indies comprising the island of Grenada and the South Grenadines, an arc of small islands extending north to St Vincent. Granada island is of volcanic origin, with a ridge of mountains along its entire length.

GUATEMALA

Official name Republic of Guatemala

Capital Guatemala City

Population 12 293 000 (2006 estimate)

Nationality Guatemalan

Language Spanish; many indigenous languages are also spoken

Main religion Christianity

Currency 1 Quetzal = 100 centavos

Internet .gt

The northernmost of the central American republics, consisting of a narrow Pacific coastal plain in the south, rising to extensive, heavily forested mountains (some of which are volcanic), and low undulating tableland in the north.

GUINEA

Official name Republic of Guinea

Capital Conakry

Population 9 690 000 (2006 estimate)

Nationality Guinean

Language French is the official language; eight local languages are also widely spoken

Main religion Islam (with significant minorities practising Christianity or traditional beliefs)

Currency 1 Guinea Franc = 100 centimes

Internet .gn

A republic in west Africa with mangrove forests on the coast, rising to a forested and cultivated coastal plain backed by highlands, and savannah plains in the south-east.

GUINEA-BISSAU

Official name Republic of Guinea-Bissau

Capital Bissau

Population 1 442 000 (2006 estimate)

Nationality Guinea-Bissauan

Languages Portuguese, Guinean Creole (Crioulo); many African languages are also spoken

Main religions Traditional beliefs, Islam

Currency 1 CFA Franc = 100 centimes

Internet .gw

A low-lying republic in west Africa with savannah-covered plateaux in the south and east, and an indented coast with islands and mangrove-lined estuaries backed by forested coastal plains.

GUYANA

Official name Co-operative Republic of Guyana

Capital Georgetown

Population 767 200 (2006 estimate)

Nationality Guyanese

Language English; Hindi, Urdu and local dialects are also spoken

Main religions Christianity, Hinduism (with significant Muslim minority)

Currency 1 Guyana Dollar = 100 cents

Internet .gy

A republic on the northern coast of South America, heavily forested, with grass-covered savannah in the hinterland and a low-lying coastal plain protected by sea defences, canals and dams.

HAITI

Official name	Republic of Haiti
Capital	Port-au-Prince
Population	8 308 000 (2006 estimate)
Nationality	Haitian
Languages	French, Creole
Main religion	Christianity, traditional beliefs
Currency	1 Gourde = 100 centimes
Internet	.ht

A republic in the West Indies occupying the western third of the island of Hispaniola, consisting of two mountainous peninsulas separated by a deep structural depression.

HONDURAS

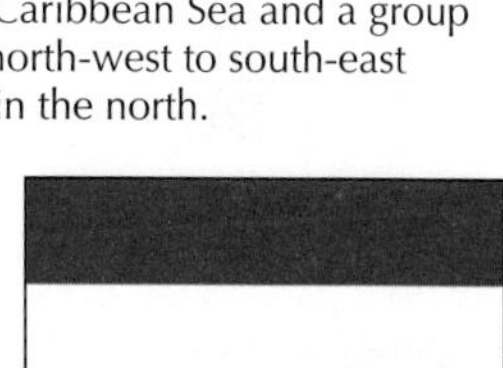

Official name	Republic of Honduras
Capital	Tegucigalpa
Population	7 326 000 (2006 estimate)
Nationality	Honduran
Language	Spanish; English and local dialects are also spoken
Main religion	Christianity
Currency	1 Lempira = 100 centavos
Internet	.hn

A republic in Central America which also comprises the Bay Islands in the Caribbean Sea and a group of around 300 islands in the Gulf of Fonseca. Forested mountains running north-west to south-east separate the Pacific coast in the south from the longer Caribbean coastline in the north.

HUNGARY

Official name	Republic of Hungary
Capital	Budapest
Population	9 981 000 (2006 estimate)
Nationality	Hungarian
Language	Magyar (Hungarian)
Main religion	Christianity (with significant minority unaffiliated)
Currency	1 Forint = 100 fillér
Internet	.hu

A landlocked republic in central Europe, situated between the Alps and the Carpathian Mountains and drained by the River Danube, which separates the Great Plain in the east from the hillier west.

ICELAND

Official name	Republic of Iceland
Capital	Reykjavík
Population	299 400 (2006 estimate)
Nationality	Icelandic
Language	Icelandic
Main religion	Christianity
Currency	1 Iceland Króna = 100 aurar
Internet	.is

An island state lying between the northern Atlantic Ocean and the Arctic Ocean, with much of the land area covered with large snowfields and glaciers. There are many geysers, several active volcanoes and a heavily indented coastline with many long fjords.

INDIA

Official name	Republic of India
Capital	New Delhi
Population	1 095 352 000 (2005 estimate)
Nationality	Indian
Languages	Hindi, English and 17 other official languages; many other languages and dialects spoken
Main religion	Hinduism (with significant minorities practising Islam, Sikhism and Christianity)
Currency	1 Indian Rupee = 100 paise
Internet	.in

A federal republic in southern Asia, bordered to the north by the Himalayas, with fertile agricultural land mainly in the east and along the coastal plains. The north is drained and irrigated by the Ganges and its tributaries; the drier Deccan plateau in the south is bordered by the Eastern and Western Ghats mountain ranges.

INDONESIA

Official name	Republic of Indonesia
Capital	Jakarta
Population	222 781 000 (2005 estimate)
Nationality	Indonesian
Language	Bahasa Indonesia; English, Dutch and Javanese are also widely spoken, as well as 300 regional languages
Main religion	Islam
Currency	1 Rupiah = 100 sen
Internet	.id

A republic in south-east Asia comprising the world's largest island group, totalling over 13,000 islands and islets, around half of which are inhabited.

IRAN

Official name	Islamic Republic of Iran
Capital	Tehran
Population	68 688 000 (2006 estimate)
Nationality	Iranian
Languages	Farsi (Persian), with several minority languages spoken
Main religion	Islam
Currency	1 Iranian Rial = 100 dinars
Internet	.ir

A republic in south-west Asia consisting of a vast arid central plateau with many salt and sand basins, rimmed by mountain ranges that lead down to narrow coastal lowlands.

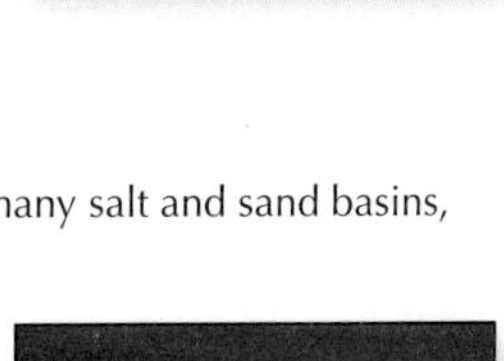

IRAQ

Official name	Republic of Iraq
Capital	Baghdad
Population	26 783 000 (2006 estimate)
Nationality	Iraqi
Language	Arabic; Kurdish is also spoken
Main religion	Islam
Currency	1 Iraqi Dinar = 1,000 fils
Internet	.iq

A republic in south-west Asia, comprising the vast alluvial tract of the Tigris–Euphrates lowland, with mountains in the north and desert in other areas.

IRELAND

Official name	Ireland
Capital	Dublin
Population	4 062 000 (2006 estimate)
Nationality	Irish
Languages	English, with Irish also spoken, mostly in the west
Main religion	Christianity
Currency	1 Euro = 100 cents
Internet	.ie

A republic occupying southern, central and north-western Ireland, with hills and mountains lining the coast; peaty lowlands in the centre and east are drained by slow-moving rivers.

ISRAEL

Official name	State of Israel
Capital	Tel Aviv-Jaffa; Israel claims Jerusalem as its capital, but this is not recognized internationally
Population	6 352 000 (2006 estimate)
Nationality	Israeli

Languages	Hebrew, Arabic
Main religion	Judaism (with significant Muslim minority)
Currency	1 New Israeli Shekel = 100 agorot
Internet	.il

A democratic republic in the Middle East, with a fertile coastal plain and a mountainous interior which drops below sea level in the Jordan–Red Sea Rift Valley; the Negev Desert in the south occupies over half the country's area.

Gaza and parts of the West Bank are autonomous areas under Palestinian control; see **Palestinian autonomous areas**.

ITALY

Official name	Italian Republic
Capital	Rome
Population	58 133 000 (2006 estimate)
Nationality	Italian
Language	Italian; German, French and Slovene are also spoken in some parts
Main religion	Christianity (with significant minority unaffiliated)
Currency	1 Euro = 100 cents
Internet	.it

A republic in southern Europe, comprising a peninsula extending south into the Mediterranean Sea, with Sicily, Sardinia and some smaller islands. In the north, the Alps form an arc above the extensive, fertile plain of the Po valley; the Appenines form the backbone of the peninsula north to south, and are surrounded by hills, plateaux and alluvial plains.

JAMAICA

Official name	Jamaica
Capital	Kingston
Population	2 758 000 (2006 estimate)
Nationality	Jamaican
Language	English; Jamaican Creole is also spoken
Main religion	Christianity (with significant minorities practising other religions or unaffiliated)
Currency	1 Jamaican Dollar = 100 cents
Internet	.jm

An island nation of the West Indies in the Caribbean Sea, mountainous and rugged particularly in the east, with plateaux in the centre and west, and coastal alluvial plains.

JAPAN

Official name	Japan
Capital	Tokyo
Population	127 464 000 (2006 estimate)
Nationality	Japanese
Language	Japanese
Main religions	Shintoism, Buddhism (with significant minorities practising other religions)
Currency	1 Yen = 100 sen
Internet	.jp

An island state off the east coast of Asia, comprising the four large islands of Hokkaido, Honshu, Kyushu and Shikoku, and thousands of smaller islands. The main islands comprise heavily forested, mountainous terrain with many volcanoes, falling to coastal uplands and plains.

JORDAN

Official name	Hashemite Kingdom of Jordan
Capital	Amman
Population	5 907 000 (2006 estimate)
Nationality	Jordanian
Language	Arabic
Main religion	Islam
Currency	1 Jordanian Dinar = 1,000 fils
Internet	.jo

A kingdom in the Middle East, with the Red Sea–Jordan rift valley running north-south, the lowest point of which is at the Dead Sea; sides of the rift rise through undulating hills to the Syrian desert in the east.

KAZAKHSTAN

Official name	Republic of Kazakhstan
Capital	Astana
Population	15 233 000 (2006 estimate)
Nationality	Kazakhstani
Languages	Kazakh, Russian
Main religions	Islam, Christianity
Currency	1 Tenge = 100 tyjyn
Internet	.kz

A republic in western Asia, with central steppes giving way to high plains in the north and desert in the south, and with mountain ranges in the east and south-east.

KENYA

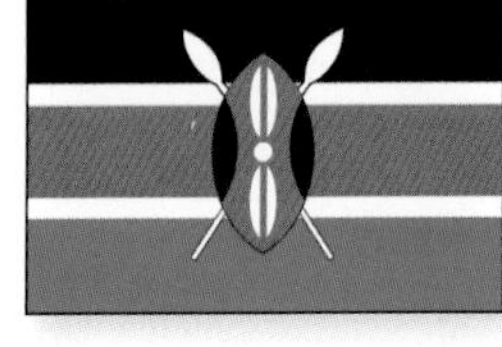

Official name	Republic of Kenya
Capital	Nairobi
Population	34 708 000 (2006 estimate)
Nationality	Kenyan
Languages	English, Swahili; many tribal languages spoken
Main religion	Christianity (with significant minority practising traditional beliefs)
Currency	1 Kenyan Shilling = 100 cents
Internet	.ke

A republic in east Africa crossed by the equator with sparsely populated arid semi-desert in the north and north-east; the population is concentrated in the cooler areas around the high volcanic massifs of the south-west.

KIRIBATI

Official name	Republic of Kiribati
Capital	Tarawa
Population	105 400 (2006 estimate)
Nationality	I-Kiribati
Languages	English, I-Kiribati
Main religion	Christianity
Currency	1 Australian Dollar = 100 cents
Internet	.ki

An island nation comprising three main groups of low-lying coral atolls (33 islands) scattered over 3, 000, 000 sq km of the central Pacific.

KOREA, NORTH

Official name	Democratic People's Republic of Korea (DPRK)
Capital	Pyongyang
Population	23 113 000 (2005 estimate)
Nationality	North Korean
Language	Korean
Main religion	Unaffiliated (with significant minorities practising traditional beliefs or Chondogyo, a nationalist religious movement)
Currency	1 North Korean Won = 100 chon
Internet	.kp

A state in eastern Asia, in the northern half of the Korean Peninsula, comprising heavily forested mountains in the north descending to foothills in the south, and coastal plains in the east and west.

KOREA, SOUTH

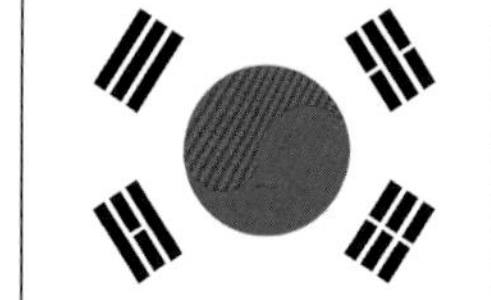

Official name	Republic of Korea (ROK)
Capital	Seoul
Population	48 847 000 (2006 estimate)
Nationality	South Korean
Language	Korean
Main religions	Christianity, Buddhism

Currency	1 Won = 100 jeon
Internet	.kr

A republic in eastern Asia occupying the southern half of the Korean Peninsula and about 3,000 islands off its west and south coasts. The Taebaek Sanmaek mountain range runs north to south along the east coast, and descends through a series of ridges to broad, undulating coastal lowlands.

KUWAIT

Official name	State of Kuwait
Capital	Kuwait City
Population	2 418 000 (2006 estimate)
Nationality	Kuwaiti
Language	Arabic; English is also widely spoken
Main religion	Islam (with significant minorities practising other religions)
Currency	1 Kuwaiti Dinar = 1,000 fils
Internet	.kw

An independent state at the head of the Arabian Gulf, consisting of the mainland and nine offshore islands; the terrain is flat or gently undulating, generally stony with sparse vegetation.

KYRGYZSTAN

Official name	Kyrgyz Republic
Capital	Bishkek
Population	5 214 000 (2006 estimate)
Nationality	Kyrgyz
Languages	Kyrgyz, Russian
Main religion	Islam (with significant Christian minority)
Currency	1 Som = 100 tyjyn
Internet	.kg

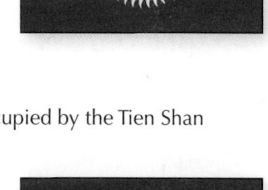

A mountainous, landlocked republic in north-east central Asia, largely occupied by the Tien Shan Mountains.

LAOS

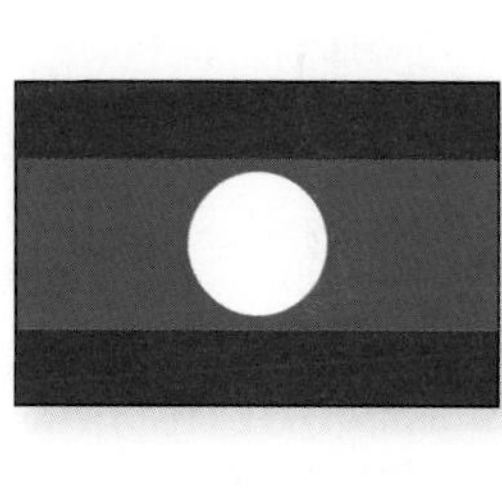

Official name	Lao People's Democratic Republic
Capital	Vientiane
Population	6 368 000 (2006 estimate)
Nationality	Lao or Laotian
Language	Lao
Main religion	Buddhism
Currency	1 Kip = 100 at
Internet	.la

A landlocked republic on the Indochinese Peninsula in south-east Asia, with dense jungle and rugged mountains in the east. The densely populated Mekong River valley follows much of the west frontier with Thailand.

LATVIA

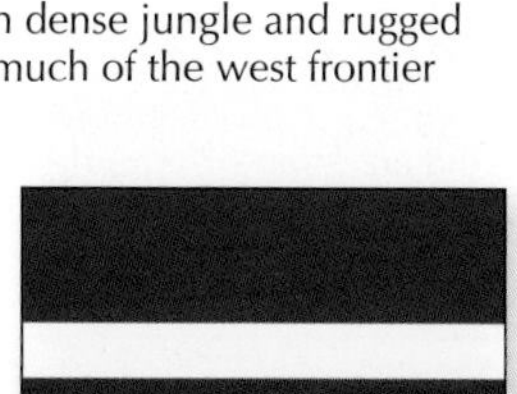

Official name	Republic of Latvia
Capital	Riga
Population	2 290 000 (2005 estimate)
Nationality	Latvian
Language	Latvian
Main religion	Christianity
Currency	1 Lat = 100 santims
Internet	.lv

A republic in north-eastern Europe, comprising a flat, glaciated area largely covered with forests and pastures. The north-west coastline is indented by the Gulf of Riga.

LEBANON

Official name	Republic of Lebanon
Capital	Beirut
Population	3 874 000 (2006 estimate)
Nationality	Lebanese

Languages	Arabic, French; English and Armenian are also spoken
Main religion	Islam (with significant Christian minority)
Currency	1 Lebanese Pound = 100 piastres
Internet	.lb

A republic on the eastern coast of the Mediterranean Sea, with a narrow coastal plain rising to the Lebanon Mountains, which, with the Anti-Lebanon mountain range in the east, frame the fertile El Beqaa plateau.

LESOTHO

Official name	Kingdom of Lesotho
Capital	Maseru
Population	2 022 000 (2006 estimate)
Nationality	Mosotho (singular), Basotho (plural)
Languages	Sesotho, English; Zulu and Xhosa are also spoken
Main religion	Christianity
Currency	1 Loti (plural Maloti) = 100 lisente; the South African Rand is also used
Internet	.ls

A mountainous, landlocked African kingdom completely bounded by South Africa.

LIBERIA

Official name	Republic of Liberia
Capital	Monrovia
Population	3 042 000 (2006 estimate)
Nationality	Liberian
Language	English; many local languages are also spoken
Main religion	Christianity (with significant minorities practising Islam, traditional beliefs or other religions)
Currency	1 Liberian Dollar = 100 cents
Internet	.lr

A tropical republic in west Africa; a narrow coastal plain with lagoons, beaches, and mangrove marshes rises through rolling plateaux with grasslands and forest up to the Nimba Mountains.

LIBYA

Official name	Great Socialist People's Libyan Arab Jamahiriya
Capital	Tripoli
Population	5 901 000 (2006 estimate)
Nationality	Libyan
Language	Arabic
Main religion	Islam
Currency	1 Libyan Dinar = 1,000 dirhams
Internet	.ly

A north African state bordering on the Mediterranean Sea. The land consists mainly of low-lying Saharan desert or semi-desert, sparsely populated except for around infrequent oases; most of the population is concentrated along the less arid east and west coasts bordering the Gulf of Sirte.

LIECHTENSTEIN

Official name	Principality of Liechtenstein
Capital	Vaduz
Population	34 000 (2006 estimate)
Nationality	Liechtensteiner, Liechtenstein
Language	German, mostly spoken in a dialectal form
Main religion	Christianity (with significant minorities practising other religions)
Currency	1 Swiss Franc = 100 centimes = 100 rappen
Internet	.li

A small independent alpine principality in central Europe, bounded to the west by the River Rhine, its valley occupying around 40% of the country; much of the rest consists of forested mountains.

LITHUANIA

Official name	Republic of Lithuania
Capital	Vilnius
Population	3 586 000 (2006 estimate)
Nationality	Lithuanian
Language	Lithuanian
Main religion	Christianity
Currency	1 Litas = 100 centas
Internet	.lt

A republic in north-eastern Europe, with a glaciated landscape of hilly farmland and forest dotted with lakes and plains.

LUXEMBOURG

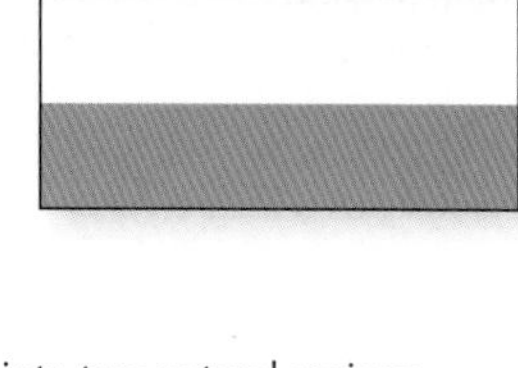

Official name	Grand Duchy of Luxembourg
Capital	Luxembourg
Population	459 500 (2006 estimate)
Nationality	Luxembourger, Luxembourg
Languages	French, German, Lëtzebuergesch
Main religion	Christianity
Currency	1 Euro = 100 cents
Internet	.lu

An independent constitutional monarchy in north-western Europe divided into two natural regions: Ösling in the north, consisting of forests and steep-sided valleys; and flatter, more fertile Gutland in the south.

MACEDONIA

Official name	Former Yugoslav Republic of Macedonia (FYRM or FYR Macedonia; international name); Republic of Macedonia (local name)
Capital	Skopje
Population	2 050 000 (2006 estimate)
Nationality	Macedonian
Languages	Macedonian, Albanian
Main religions	Christianity, Islam
Currency	1 Denar = 100 deni
Internet	.mk

A landlocked, mountainous republic in southern Europe, covered with deep river basins and valleys and bisected by the River Vardar.

MADAGASCAR

Official name	Republic of Madagascar
Capital	Antananarivo
Population	18 595 000 (2006 estimate)
Nationality	Malagasy
Languages	Malagasy, French
Main religions	Traditional beliefs, Christianity
Currency	1 Ariary = 5 Iraimbilanja
Internet	.mg

An island republic in the Indian Ocean, separated from east Africa by the Mozambique Channel. A ridge of high plateaux, some topped with volcanoes, runs north to south; to the east, steep cliffs drop down through tropical forest to a narrow coastal plain, while in the drier west the terrain makes a terraced descent through savannah to the coast.

MALAWI

Official name	Republic of Malawi
Capital	Lilongwe
Population	13 014 000 (2006 estimate)
Nationality	Malawian
Languages	English, Chichewa
Main religion	Christianity (with significant minorities practising Islam or traditional beliefs)

Currency	1 Kwacha = 100 tambala
Internet	.mw

A landlocked republic in south-eastern Africa, bordered to the east by Lake Nyasa (Lake Malawi) which lies in the Great Rift Valley. High plateaux cover the north and centre of the country with uneven, low-lying terrain in the south.

MALAYSIA

Official name	Federation of Malaysia
Capital	Kuala Lumpur (official), Putrajaya (administrative and seat of government)
Population	24 386 000 (2006 estimate)
Nationality	Malaysian
Language	Bahasa Malaysia (Malay); Chinese, English, Tamil and local languages are also spoken
Main religion	Islam (with significant minorities practising Buddhism, Chinese folk religion, Hinduism or Christianity)
Currency	1 Malaysian Ringgit = 100 sen
Internet	.my

An independent federation of states in south-east Asia comprising mainland Peninsular Malaysia, and Sarawak and Sabah on the northern coast of Borneo. The mainland peninsula is mountainous and mostly covered with tropical rainforest and mangrove swamp with narrow coastal plains; Sarawak has a narrow, swampy coastal belt and a mountainous interior; Sabah has a deeply indented coastline and a narrow coastal plain, rising sharply into mountains.

MALDIVES

Official name	Republic of Maldives
Capital	Malé
Population	359 000 (2006 estimate)
Nationality	Maldivian
Language	Dhivehi; English is widely spoken
Main religion	Islam
Currency	1 Rufiyaa = 100 laari
Internet	.mv

A republic in the Indian Ocean consisting of an archipelago of 1,190 small, low-lying islands with sandy beaches fringed with coconut palms, fewer than 200 of which are inhabited.

MALI

Official name	Republic of Mali
Capital	Bamako
Population	13 717 000 (2006 estimate)
Nationality	Malian
Language	French; Bambara and other local languages are widely spoken
Main religion	Islam (with a significant minority practising traditional beliefs)
Currency	1 CFA Franc = 100 centimes
Internet	.ml

A landlocked republic in west Africa on the fringe of the Sahara, with featureless desert land in the north and mainly savannah in the south.

MALTA

Official name	Republic of Malta
Capital	Valletta
Population	400 200 (2006 estimate)
Nationality	Maltese
Languages	English, Maltese; there are many Arabic words in the local vocabulary
Main religion	Christianity
Currency	1 Maltese Lira = 100 cents = 1,000 mils
Internet	.mt

An archipelago republic in the central Mediterranean Sea, generally low-lying with no rivers or mountains and a well-indented coastline.

MARSHALL ISLANDS

Official name	Republic of the Marshall Islands (RMI)
Capital	Majuro
Population	60 600 (2006 estimate)
Nationality	Marshallese
Languages	Marshallese, English
Main religion	Christianity
Currency	1 US Dollar = 100 cents
Internet	.mh

An independent archipelago republic in the central Pacific Ocean comprising low-lying coral limestone and sand islands, atolls and reefs, with few natural resources.

MAURITANIA

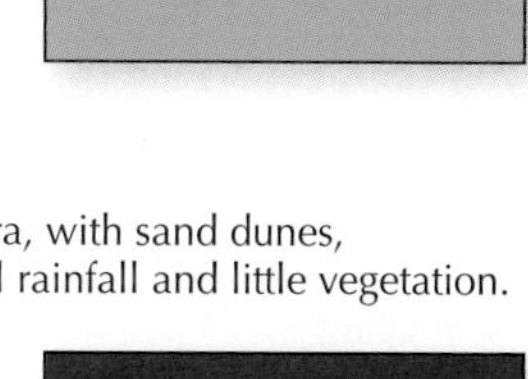

Official name	Islamic Republic of Mauritania
Capital	Nouakchott
Population	3 177 000 (2006 estimate)
Nationality	Mauritanian
Language	Arabic; French is also widely spoken
Main religion	Islam
Currency	1 Ouguiya = 5 khoums
Internet	.mr

A republic in north-west Africa, two thirds of which is located in the Sahara, with sand dunes, mountainous plateaux and occasional oases. The coastal area has minimal rainfall and little vegetation.

MAURITIUS

Official name	Republic of Mauritius
Capital	Port Louis
Population	1 241 000 (2006 estimate)
Nationality	Mauritian
Languages	English, French; Creole is also spoken
Main religion	Hinduism (with significant Christian and Muslim minorities)
Currency	1 Mauritius Rupee = 100 cents
Internet	.mu

A small island nation in the Indian Ocean. The main island of Mauritius is volcanic, comprising a central plateau with a dry, lowland coast bordered by wooded savannah, mangrove swamps and bamboo; it is surrounded by coral reefs enclosing lagoons.

MEXICO

Official name	United Mexican States
Capital	Mexico City
Population	107 449 000 (2006 estimate)
Nationality	Mexican
Language	Spanish; Native American languages are also spoken
Main religion	Christianity
Currency	1 Mexican Peso = 100 centavos
Internet	.mx

A federal republic in the south of North America, bisected by the Tropic of Cancer with narrow coastal plains rising steeply to a central plateau, volcanic peaks to the south, and Yucatán peninsula lowlands in the south-east.

MICRONESIA

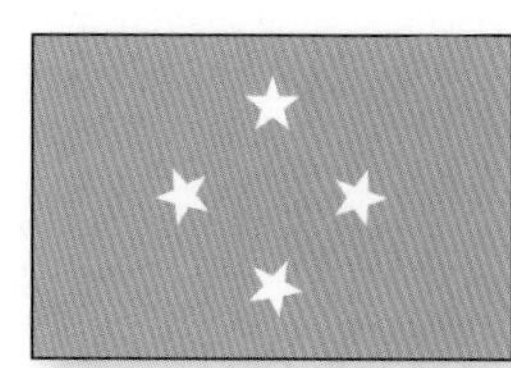

Official name	Federated States of Micronesia (FSM)
Capital	Palikir (on Pohnpei)
Population	108 000 (2006 estimate)
Nationality	Micronesian; also Chuukese, Kosraen, Pohnpeian, Yapese
Language	English; eight major indigenous languages are also spoken
Main religion	Christianity

Currency	1 US Dollar = 100 cents
Internet	.fm

A republic in the western Pacific Ocean consisting of a group of 607 geologically diverse islands divided into four states.

MOLDOVA

Official name	Republic of Moldova
Capital	Chisinau
Population	4 467 000 (2006 estimate)
Nationality	Moldovan
Language	Moldovan
Main religion	Christianity
Currency	1 Moldovan Leu = 100 bani
Internet	.md

A hilly, landlocked republic in eastern Europe, with a temperate continental climate and fertile alluvial plains making it ideal for agriculture.

MONACO

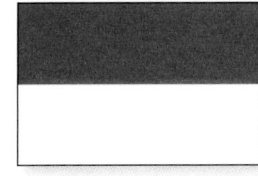

Official name	Principality of Monaco
Capital	Monaco
Population	32 500 (2006 estimate)
Nationality	Monégasque or Monacan
Language	French
Main religion	Christianity
Currency	1 Euro = 100 cents
Internet	.mc

A small principality on the Mediterranean Riviera, close to the Italian frontier with France; hilly, rugged and rocky, it is almost entirely urban.

MONGOLIA

Official name	State of Mongolia
Capital	Ulan Bator
Population	2 832 000 (2006 estimate)
Nationality	Mongolian
Language	Khalkha Mongolian
Main religion	Buddhism
Currency	1 Tugrik = 100 möngö
Internet	.mn

A mountainous, landlocked republic in eastern central Asia with massifs in the west, and lowland plains and arid grasslands in the south forming part of the Gobi Desert.

MONTENEGRO

Official name	Republic of Montenegro
Capital	Podgorica
Population	620 000 (2003 census)
Nationality	Montenegrin
Languages	Serbian, Albanian
Main religions	Christianity, Islam
Currency	1 Euro = 100 cents (adopted unilaterally)
Internet	.me

A mountainous republic in south-eastern Europe with a narrow coastal plain backed by limestone plateaux rising to high mountain ranges dotted with canyons and lakes. Much of the land is covered with forests, pastureland and meadows.

MOROCCO

Official name	Kingdom of Morocco
Capital	Rabat
Population	33 241 000 (2006 estimate)
Nationality	Moroccan
Language	Arabic; Berber and French are also spoken
Main religion	Islam

Currency	1 Moroccan Dirham = 100 centimes
Internet	.ma

A kingdom in north Africa comprising a broad coastal plain rising to a plateau backed by the Atlas Mountains; plains and valleys in the south join the Sahara Desert.

MOZAMBIQUE

Official name	Republic of Mozambique
Capital	Maputo
Population	19 889 000 (2006 estimate)
Nationality	Mozambican
Language	Portuguese; Swahili and other African languages are widely spoken
Main religion	Traditional beliefs (with significant Christian and Muslim minorities)
Currency	1 Metical = 100 centavos
Internet	.mz

A republic in south-eastern Africa. In the south low hills of volcanic origin descend to a low-lying, broad coastal plain with sandy beaches and mangroves; to the north the coastline is more rugged, with savannah plateaux inland.

MYANMAR (BURMA)

Official name	Union of Myanmar; still often referred to internationally as Burma
Capital	Yangon (formerly known as Rangoon, historic capital), Naypyidaw (administrative)
Population	52 000 000 (2006 estimate)
Nationality	Burmese or Myanmarese
Language	Burmese; several minority languages are also spoken
Main religion	Buddhism
Currency	1 Kyat = 100 pyas
Internet	.mm

A densely forested republic in south-east Asia, bordered in the north, east and west by mountains which descend in a series of ridges and valleys to the central Irrawaddy River delta.

NAMIBIA

Official name	Republic of Namibia
Capital	Windhoek
Population	2 044 000 (2006 estimate)
Nationality	Namibian
Language	English; Afrikaans, German and local languages are also widely spoken
Main religion	Christianity (with significant minority practising traditional beliefs)
Currency	1 Namibian Dollar = 100 cents; the South African Rand is also used
Internet	.na

A republic in south-western Africa; the Namib Desert runs along the Atlantic Ocean coast and rises to an inland plateau backed by the Kalahari Desert to the east and south.

NAURU

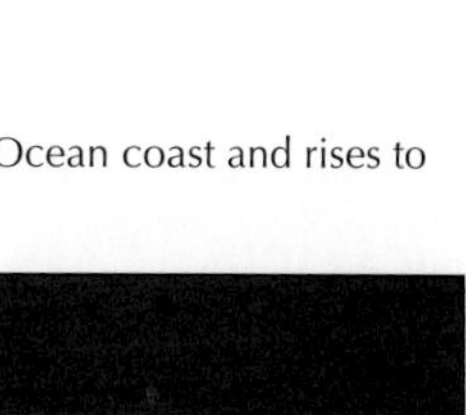

Official name	Republic of Nauru
Capital	There is no capital as such, but government offices are situated in Yaren District
Population	13 300 (2006 estimate)
Nationality	Nauruan
Language	Nauruan; English is also widely understood
Main religion	Christianity
Currency	1 Australian Dollar = 100 cents
Internet	.nr

An independent republic formed by a small, isolated island in the west-central Pacific Ocean, with sandy beaches rising to a fertile coastal belt and a central inland plateau composed largely of phosphate-bearing rocks.

NEPAL

Official name	Kingdom of Nepal
Capital	Kathmandu
Population	28 287 000 (2006 estimate)
Nationality	Nepalese
Language	Nepali; around 70 local dialects and languages are also spoken
Main religion	Hinduism
Currency	1 Nepalese Rupee = 100 paise/pice
Internet	.np

A landlocked independent kingdom lying along the southern slopes of the Himalayas in central Asia, rising steeply from the Ganges Basin, with the highest point at Mount Everest.

THE NETHERLANDS

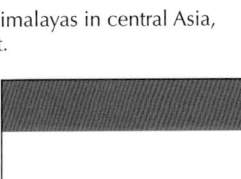

Official name	Kingdom of the Netherlands; often known as Holland
Capital	Amsterdam, The Hague (seat of government)
Population	16 491 000 (2006 estimate)
Nationality	Dutch
Languages	Dutch, Frisian; English is widely spoken
Main religion	Christianity (with significant minority unaffiliated)
Currency	1 Euro = 100 cents
Internet	.nl

A maritime kingdom in north-western Europe, generally low and flat, with approximately one-quarter of the land below sea level, including much of the coast, which is protected by dunes and artificial dykes.

Aruba is a Netherlands overseas territory; Curacao and St Maarten are associated states that were formerly within the Netherlands Antilles, disbanded in 2007.

NEW ZEALAND

Official name	New Zealand (NZ)
Capital	Wellington
Population	4 076 000 (2005 estimate)
Nationality	New Zealand, Kiwi (informal)
Languages	English, Maori
Main religion	Christianity (with significant minorities practising other religions)
Currency	1 New Zealand Dollar = 100 cents
Internet	.nz

An independent state in the Pacific Ocean comprising two principal islands (North and South Islands), Stewart Island, and several minor islands. North Island is mountainous in the centre, with many hot springs; beyond the Cook Strait, South Island is mountainous for its whole length, with many glaciers and mountain lakes.

New Zealand also possesses the self-governing territories of the Cook Islands and Niue, and the non-self-governing territories of Tokelau and the Ross Dependency.

NICARAGUA

Official name	Republic of Nicaragua
Capital	Managua
Population	5 483 000 (2005 census)
Nationality	Nicaraguan
Language	Spanish; English and local languages in Caribbean coastal areas
Main religion	Christianity
Currency	1 Córdoba = 100 centavos = 10 reales
Internet	.ni

The largest of the Central American republics; the interior, particularly the west, is very mountainous, with a narrow Pacific coastal plain and fertile valleys enclosing two large lakes. In the east, rolling uplands and forested plains fall to the wider coastal plain of the Caribbean Sea.

NIGER

Official name	Republic of Niger
Capital	Niamey
Population	12 525 000 (2006 estimate)
Nationality	Nigerien
Language	French; Hausa and Djerma are widely spoken
Main religion	Islam (with significant minorities practising Christianity or traditional beliefs)
Currency	1 CFA Franc = 100 centimes
Internet	.ne

A landlocked republic in west Africa, lying on a high plateau on the southern fringe of the Sahara Desert. With deserts in the east, centre and north, most of the population is concentrated in the Niger valley in the south-west, or towards Lake Chad in the south-east.

NIGERIA

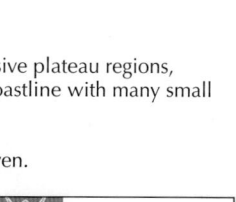

Official name	Federal Republic of Nigeria
Capital	Abuja
Population	139 900 000 (2006 estimate)
Nationality	Nigerian
Language	English; Hausa, Yoruba, Edo and Igbo are also spoken
Main religions	Islam, Christianity (with significant minority practising traditional beliefs)
Currency	1 Naira = 100 kobo
Internet	.ng

A republic in west Africa, with a densely populated coastal strip dominated by the River Niger delta, backed by tropical rainforest and oil palm bush. A dry central plateau of open woodland and savannah extends to the edge of the Sahara Desert in the far north.

NORWAY

Official name	Kingdom of Norway
Capital	Oslo
Population	4 611 000 (2006 estimate)
Nationality	Norwegian
Language	Norwegian, in the varieties of Bokmål and Nynorsk
Main religion	Christianity (with significant minorities practising other religions or unaffiliated)
Currency	1 Norwegian Krone = 100 øre
Internet	.no

A kingdom in north-west Europe with many high mountain ranges and extensive plateau regions, particularly in the south-west and centre, numerous lakes, and an irregular coastline with many small islands and long deep fjords.

Norway also possesses Bouvet Island and the islands of Svalbard and Jan Mayen.

OMAN

Official name	Sultanate of Oman
Capital	Muscat
Population	3 102 000 (2006 estimate)
Nationality	Omani
Language	Arabic
Main religion	Islam (with significant Hindu minority)
Currency	1 Omani Rial = 1,000 baisas
Internet	.om

An independent state in the extreme south-eastern corner of the Arabian Peninsula, comprising a vast desert plain with mountain ranges on the north and south-east coasts, where much of the population is concentrated.

PAKISTAN

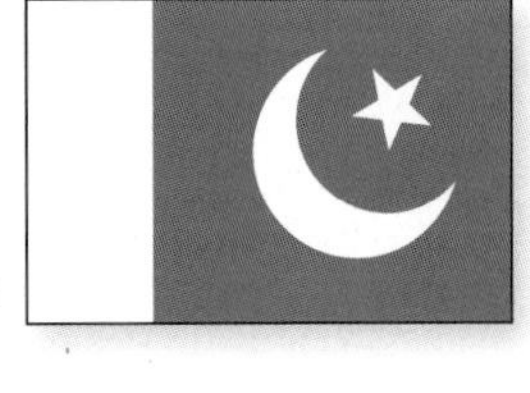

Official name	Islamic Republic of Pakistan
Capital	Islamabad
Population	165 803 000 (2006 estimate)
Nationality	Pakistani
Language	Urdu; English and several local languages are also spoken
Main religion	Islam
Currency	1 Pakistan Rupee = 100 paisa
Internet	.pk

An Asian state bounded to the north and west by mountains. Largely centred on the alluvial flood plain of the River Indus, the terrain comprises mostly flat plateaux and low-lying plains, with some arid desert in the north.

PALAU

Official name	Republic of Palau
Capital	Melekeok
Population	20 600 (2006 estimate)
Nationality	Palauan
Languages	Palauan, English
Main religions	Christianity, traditional beliefs
Currency	1 US Dollar = 100 cents
Internet	.pw

A group of around 350 small islands and islets in the west Pacific Ocean, often surrounded by coral reefs, with terrain varying from the mountainous main island of Babelthuap to low-lying coral islands.

PALESTINIAN AUTONOMOUS AREAS

Capital	Gaza City
Population	3 888 757 (2006 estimate)
Nationality	Palestinian
Language	Arabic; Hebrew and English are also spoken
Religion	Islam (with significant minorities practising Judaism, Christianity or other religions)
Currency	1 Jordanian Dinar = 1 000 fils, 1 New Israeli Shekel = 100 agorot
Internet	.ps

Autonomous areas of Israel, comprising the West Bank in the east, which is bounded to the north, west and south by Israel, and to the east by Jordan and the Dead Sea; and Gaza in the south-west, which is bounded to the east and south-east by Israel, to the south-west by Egypt, and to the west and north-west by the Mediterranean Sea.

PANAMA

Official name	Republic of Panama
Capital	Panama City
Population	3 191 000 (2006 estimate)
Nationality	Panamanian
Language	Spanish
Main religion	Christianity
Currency	1 Balboa = 100 centésimos; the US dollar is also used
Internet	.pa

A republic occupying a strategic position at the south-eastern end of the isthmus of Central America, and controlling the Panama Canal which links the Pacific Ocean, via the Caribbean Sea, to the Atlantic. The terrain is mostly mountainous, with areas of dense tropical forest and fertile coastal plains.

PAPUA NEW GUINEA

Official name	Independent State of Papua New Guinea (PNG)
Capital	Port Moresby
Population	5 670 000 (2006 estimate)
Nationality	Papua New Guinean
Language	Pidgin English; approximately 800 other languages are spoken

Main religions Christianity, traditional beliefs
Currency 1 Kina = 100 toea
Internet .pg

An independent island group in the south-west Pacific Ocean, comprising the eastern half of the island of New Guinea which is mainly covered with tropical rainforest, has a complex mountain system and coastal mangrove swamps; and several smaller islands which are also mountainous and mostly volcanic.

PARAGUAY

Official name	Republic of Paraguay
Capital	Asunción
Population	6 506 000 (2006 estimate)
Nationality	Paraguayan
Languages	Spanish, Guaraní
Main religion	Christianity
Currency	1 Guaraní = 100 céntimos
Internet	.py

A low-lying, landlocked country in central South America, divided into two regions by the River Paraguay; the west comprises mostly cattle country or scrub forest; the east is generally more fertile.

PERU

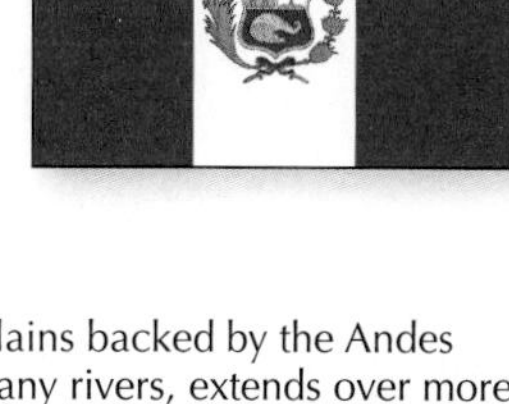

Official name	Republic of Peru
Capital	Lima
Population	28 303 000 (2006 estimate)
Nationality	Peruvian
Languages	Spanish, Quechua; Aymará is also widely spoken
Main religion	Christianity
Currency	1 Nuevo Sol = 100 céntimos
Internet	.pe

A republic on the west coast of South America, with narrow, arid coastal plains backed by the Andes Mountains. To the north and east the forested Amazon basin, drained by many rivers, extends over more than half the country.

PHILIPPINES

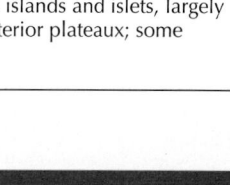

Official name	Republic of the Philippines
Capital	Manila
Population	89 469 000 (2006 estimate)
Nationality	Filipino (masculine), Filipina (feminine), Philippine
Languages	Filipino, English; Spanish, Arabic and many local dialects are also spoken
Main religion	Christianity
Currency	1 Philippine Peso = 100 centavos
Internet	.ph

A republic in south-east Asia consisting of an archipelago of more than 7,100 islands and islets, largely mountainous and heavily forested, with narrow coastal margins and broad interior plateaux; some islands are ringed by coral reefs.

POLAND

Official name	Republic of Poland
Capital	Warsaw
Population	38 537 000 (2006 estimate)
Nationality	Pole, Polish
Language	Polish
Main religion	Christianity
Currency	1 Zloty = 100 groszy
Internet	.pl

A republic in central Europe, mostly part of the great European plain, with a flat Baltic coastline dotted with lagoons, backed by lowlands with numerous lakes. Beyond the Polish plateau in the south lie the Carpathian and Sudetes Mountains.

PORTUGAL

Official name	Portuguese Republic
Capital	Lisbon
Population	10 606 000 (2006 estimate)
Nationality	Portuguese
Language	Portuguese; Mirandese is co-official in Miranda do Douro municipality
Main religion	Christianity
Currency	1 Euro = 100 cents
Internet	.pt

A country in south-western Europe on the western side of the Iberian Peninsula comprising narrow coastal plains rising to the extensive Meseta plateau, and mountain ranges in the north.

Portugal also possesses the Azores and Madeira.

QATAR

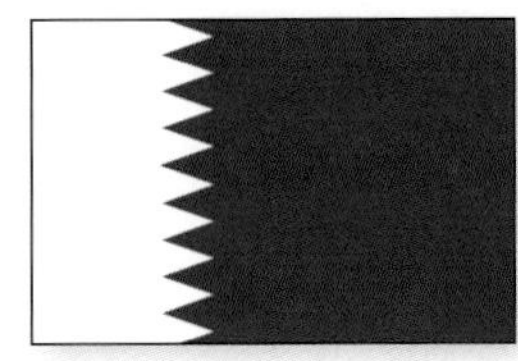

Official name	State of Qatar
Capital	Doha
Population	885 300 (2006 estimate)
Nationality	Qatari
Language	Arabic
Main religion	Islam
Currency	1 Qatari Riyal = 100 dirhams
Internet	.qa

A low-lying state on the east coast of the Arabian Peninsula comprising the Qatar Peninsula, which slopes gently from the Dukhān Heights to the east shore, and numerous small offshore islands and coral reefs.

ROMANIA

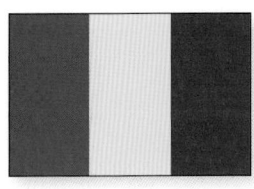

Official name	Romania
Capital	Bucharest
Population	22 303 000 (2006 estimate)
Nationality	Romanian
Language	Romanian; Hungarian, German and other languages are widely spoken
Main religion	Christianity
Currency	1 Leu = 100 bani
Internet	.ro

A republic in south-eastern Europe, dominated by the Carpathian Mountains which surround the plateaux of Transylvania; a rich arable area is situated in the south, on the Romanian Plain.

RUSSIA

Official name	Russian Federation
Capital	Moscow
Population	142 893 000 (2005 estimate)
Nationality	Russian
Language	Russian
Main religion	Christianity (with significant minorities practising Islam or other religions)
Currency	1 Russian Rouble = 100 kopeks
Internet	.ru

A republic occupying much of eastern Europe and northern Asia, forming the largest country in the world. Vast plains dominate in the west, with mountain ranges in the south and east; the Ural Mountains run north to south and separate the East European Plain in the west from the West Siberian Lowlands in the east. There are over 20,000 lakes.

RWANDA

Official name	Republic of Rwanda
Capital	Kigali
Population	8 648 000 (2006 estimate)
Nationality	Rwandan
Languages	English, French, Kinyarwanda; Swahili is widely used in commerce

Main religion	Christianity (with significant minorities practising Islam, traditional beliefs or other religions)
Currency	1 Rwanda Franc = 100 centimes
Internet	.rw

A small, landlocked republic in central Africa, situated at a relatively high altitude which moderates the tropical equatorial climate.

ST KITTS AND NEVIS

Official name	Federation of St Kitts and Nevis; also known as St Christopher and Nevis
Capital	Basseterre
Population	39 100 (2006 estimate)
Nationality	Kittitian, Nevisian
Language	English
Main religion	Christianity (with significant minorities practising other religions)
Currency	1 East Caribbean Dollar = 100 cents
Internet	.kn

An independent state in the North Leeward Islands in the eastern Caribbean Sea, comprising the islands of St Kitts, Nevis and Sombrero.

ST LUCIA

Official name	St Lucia
Capital	Castries
Population	168 000 (2006 estimate)
Nationality	St Lucian
Language	English; French patois is also spoken
Main religion	Christianity
Currency	1 East Caribbean Dollar = 100 cents
Internet	.lc

An independent state and the second-largest of the Windward Islands, situated in the eastern Caribbean Sea. The island has a mountainous centre, with the twin volcanic peaks of Gros and Petit Piton rising steeply from the sea on the south-west coast.

ST VINCENT AND THE GRENADINES

Official name	St Vincent and the Grenadines
Capital	Kingstown
Population	118 000 (2006 estimate)
Nationality	St Vincentian or Vincentian
Language	English; French patois is also spoken
Main religion	Christianity (with significant minorities practising other religions)
Currency	1 East Caribbean Dollar = 100 cents
Internet	.vc

An island country in the Windward Islands, situated in the eastern Caribbean Sea comprising the volcanic island of St Vincent and the northern Grenadine Islands.

SAMOA

Official name	Independent State of Samoa
Capital	Apia
Population	177 000 (2006 estimate)
Nationality	Samoan
Languages	Samoan, English
Main religion	Christianity
Currency	1 Tala = 100 sene
Internet	.ws

An island nation in the south-west Pacific Ocean, comprising two large volcanic islands and several smaller islets. The terrain is mountainous and covered with thick tropical vegetation; there are several coral reefs along the coast.

SAN MARINO

Official name	Republic of San Marino
Capital	San Marino
Population	29 000 (2006 estimate)
Nationality	Sammarinese
Language	Italian
Main religion	Christianity
Currency	1 Euro = 100 cents
Internet	.sm

A small, ruggedly mountainous republic completely surrounded by central Italy, centred on the limestone ridges of Mount Titano.

SÃO TOMÉ AND PRÍNCIPE

Official name	Democratic Republic of São Tomé and Príncipe
Capital	São Tomé
Population	193 000 (2006 estimate)
Nationality	São Toméan, Santoméan
Language	Portuguese
Main religion	Christianity (with significant minorities practising other religions)
Currency	1 Dobra = 100 céntimos
Internet	.st

An equatorial island republic in the Gulf of Guinea off the coast of west Africa comprising two mountainous main islands of volcanic origin, and several small islets.

SAUDI ARABIA

Official name	Kingdom of Saudi Arabia
Capital	Riyadh
Population	27 020 000 (2006 estimate)
Nationality	Saudi or Saudi Arabian
Language	Arabic
Main religion	Islam
Currency	1 Saudi Riyal = 20 qursh = 100 halala
Internet	.sa

A kingdom comprising about four-fifths of the Arabian Peninsula with a varied terrain: the Red Sea coastal plain is bounded to the east by mountains; the Arabian Peninsula slopes north and east to the oil-rich Al Hasa plain on the Arabian Gulf; there are large areas of sand desert in the interior and numerous salt flats in the eastern lowlands.

SENEGAL

Official name	Republic of Senegal
Capital	Dakar
Population	11 987 000 (2006 estimate)
Nationality	Senegalese
Languages	French, Wolof
Main religion	Islam
Currency	1 CFA Franc = 100 centimes
Internet	.sn

A republic in west Africa, with a coastline characterized by dunes, mangrove forests and mudbanks; forests in the south give way to an extensive low-lying basin of savannah and semi-desert vegetation to the north.

SERBIA

Official name	Republic of Serbia
Capital	Belgrade
Population	7 500 000 (2002 estimate)
Nationality	Serbian
Language	Serbian
Main religions	Christianity, Islam
Currency	1 Serbian Dinar = 100 paras (the Euro is used in the province of Kosovo)
Internet	.rs

A landlocked republic in south-eastern Europe with a varied terrain consisting of low-lying, heavily cultivated fertile plains stretching southwards from the Danube towards the rugged mountains of the south and east.

SEYCHELLES

Official name	Republic of Seychelles
Capital	Victoria
Population	81 500 (2006 estimate)
Nationality	Seychellois
Language	Creole; French and English are spoken
Main religion	Christianity
Currency	1 Seychelles Rupee = 100 cents
Internet	.sc

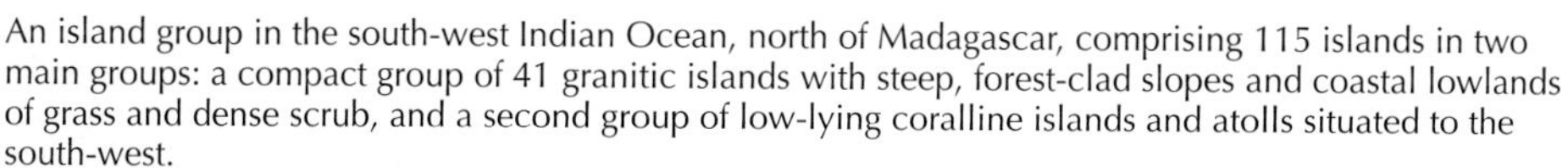

An island group in the south-west Indian Ocean, north of Madagascar, comprising 115 islands in two main groups: a compact group of 41 granitic islands with steep, forest-clad slopes and coastal lowlands of grass and dense scrub, and a second group of low-lying coralline islands and atolls situated to the south-west.

SIERRA LEONE

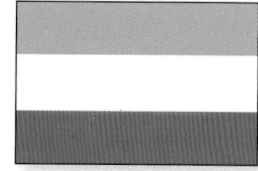

Official name	Republic of Sierra Leone
Capital	Freetown
Population	6 005 000 (2006 estimate)
Nationality	Sierra Leonean
Languages	English, Mende, Temnel; Krio (a Creole language) is also widely spoken
Main religions	Traditional beliefs, Islam (with significant Christian minority)
Currency	1 Leone = 100 cents
Internet	.sl

A republic in west Africa, comprising a coastal plain backed by mangrove swamps rising to forested plateaux with mountains in the north-east.

SINGAPORE

Official name	Republic of Singapore
Capital	Singapore
Population	4 492 000 (2006 estimate)
Nationality	Singaporean, Singapore
Languages	English, Chinese (Mandarin), Malay, Tamil; other Chinese dialects are also spoken
Main religions	Buddhism, traditional beliefs, unaffiliated, Islam, Taoism
Currency	1 Singapore Dollar = 1 Ringgit = 100 cents
Internet	.sg

A republic at the southern tip of the Malay Peninsula, south-east Asia, consisting of the island of Singapore (linked to Malaysia by a causeway) and about 50 adjacent islets.

SLOVAKIA

Official name	Republic of Slovakia (or the Slovak Republic)
Capital	Bratislava
Population	5 439 000 (2006 estimate)
Nationality	Slovak
Language	Slovak
Main religions	Christianity, unaffiliated
Currency	1 Slovak Koruna = 100 haliers
Internet	.sk

A landlocked and mountainous republic in eastern Europe, with the Carpathian mountains extending in the north and fertile lowlands in the south.

SLOVENIA

Official name	Republic of Slovenia
Capital	Ljubljana
Population	2 010 000 (2006 estimate)
Nationality	Slovene, Slovenian
Language	Slovene
Main religion	Christianity (with significant minorities practising other religions)
Currency	1 Euro = 100 cents
Internet	.si

A mountainous and heavily forested republic in central Europe.

SOLOMON ISLANDS

Official name	Solomon Islands
Capital	Honiara
Population	552 400 (2006 estimate)
Nationality	Solomon Islander (noun)
Language	English; pidgin English and Melanesian dialects are also spoken
Main religion	Christianity
Currency	1 Solomon Islands Dollar = 100 cents
Internet	.sb

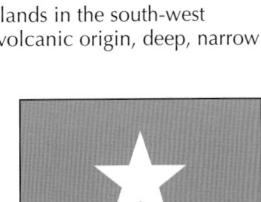

An independent country consisting of an archipelago of several hundred islands in the south-west Pacific Ocean; the larger islands have forested mountain ranges of mainly volcanic origin, deep, narrow valleys, and coastal belts lined with coconut palms.

SOMALIA

Official name	Somalia
Capital	Mogadishu
Population	8 228 000 (2005 estimate)
Nationality	Somali
Languages	Somali, Arabic; English and Italian are also widely spoken
Main religion	Islam
Currency	1 Somali Shilling = 100 cents
Internet	.so

A north-east African republic occupying the eastern Horn of Africa, where a dry coastal plain broadens to the south and rises inland to a plateau; in the north, forested mountains tower above the Gulf of Aden.

SOUTH AFRICA

Official name	Republic of South Africa (RSA)
Capital	Pretoria (administrative), Bloemfontein (judicial), Cape Town (legislative)
Population	44 188 000 (2006 estimate)
Nationality	South African
Languages	Eleven official languages: Afrikaans, English, IsiNdebele, IsiXosa, IsiZulu, Sepedi, Sosetho, SiSwati, Setswana, Tshivenda, Xitsonga
Main religions	Christianity, traditional beliefs
Currency	1 Rand = 100 cents
Internet	.za

A republic occupying the southern extremity of the African plateau, fringed by fold mountains and a lowland coastal margin; the northern interior comprises the Kalahari Basin, scrub grassland and arid desert.

SPAIN

Official name	Kingdom of Spain
Capital	Madrid
Population	40 398 000 (2006 estimate)
Nationality	Spanish

Language Spanish (Castilian); Catalan, Galician (Gallego) and Basque (Euskera) are also spoken in certain regions
Main religion Christianity
Currency 1 Euro = 100 cents
Internet .es

A country in south-western Europe consisting largely of a vast, furrowed central plateau (the Meseta), crossed by mountains ranges and river valleys.

Spain also possesses the Balearic Islands and the Canary Islands.

SRI LANKA

Official name Democratic Socialist Republic of Sri Lanka
Capital Colombo (commercial), Sri Jayawardenepura Kotte (administrative)
Population 20 222 000 (2006 estimate)
Nationality Sri Lankan
Languages Sinhala, Tamil
Main religions Buddhism, Hinduism (with significant Christian and Muslim minorities)
Currency 1 Sri Lanka Rupee = 100 cents
Internet .lk

A pear-shaped, tropical island state situated off the south-east coast of India consisting of plateaux and hills surrounding the south-central uplands. The coastal plain is fringed by sandy beaches and lagoons, and nearly half the island is covered by tropical monsoon forest or open woodland.

SUDAN

Official name Republic of Sudan
Capital Khartoum
Population 41 236 000 (2006 estimate)
Nationality Sudanese
Language Arabic; English is spoken in some regions
Main religion Islam (with significant minorities practising traditional beliefs or Christianity)
Currency 1 Sudanese Dinar = 10 pounds
Internet .sd

A north-east African republic, the largest country on the African continent, astride the middle reaches of the River Nile. The land is mostly flat, with the Nubian Highlands in the east rising above the Red Sea, and mountains along the borders.

SURINAME

Official name Republic of Suriname
Capital Paramaribo
Population 439 000 (2006 estimate)
Nationality Surinamese
Language Dutch; English, Hindi, Javanese and Sranang Tongo are also spoken
Main religions Christianity, Hinduism, Islam
Currency 1 Suriname Dollar = 100 cents
Internet .sr

A republic in north-eastern South America with diverse natural regions ranging from swamp-covered coastal lowlands through savannah to mountainous uplands and dense tropical forest.

SWAZILAND

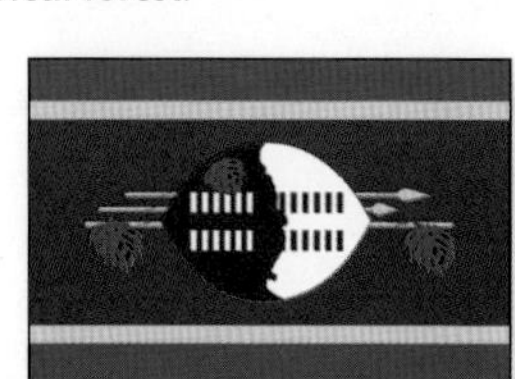

Official name Kingdom of Swaziland
Capital Mbabane (administrative), Lobamba (legislative)
Population 1 136 000 (2006 estimate)
Nationality Swazi
Languages English, Siswati
Main religions Christianity, traditional beliefs
Currency 1 Lilangeni (plural Emalangeni) = 100 cents
Internet .sz

A small monarchy in south-east Africa comprising the mountainous Highveld in the west, the more populated Middleveld in the centre and the rolling, bush-covered Lowveld in the east.

SWEDEN

Official name	Kingdom of Sweden
Capital	Stockholm
Population	9 016 000 (2006 estimate)
Nationality	Swedish
Language	Swedish
Main religion	Christianity
Currency	1 Swedish Krona = 100 øre
Internet	.se

A constitutional monarchy in northern Europe occupying the eastern side of the Scandinavian Peninsula; heavily forested, with a large amount of inland water and many coastal islands, there are mountain ranges in the west along much of the border with Denmark.

SWITZERLAND

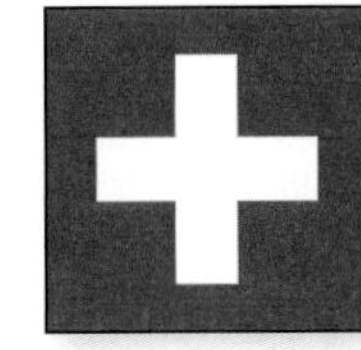

Official name	Swiss Confederation
Capital	Berne
Population	7 524 000 (2006 estimate)
Nationality	Swiss
Languages	German, French, Italian and Romansch
Main religion	Christianity (with significant minority unaffiliated)
Currency	1 Swiss Franc = 100 centimes = 100 rappen
Internet	.ch

A mountainous, landlocked European republic; the Alps run roughly east to west in the south of the country; the central Swiss Plateau is fringed by hills, valleys and large lakes.

SYRIA

Official name	Syrian Arab Republic
Capital	Damascus
Population	18 881 000 (2006 estimate)
Nationality	Syrian
Language	Arabic
Main religion	Islam (with significant Christian minority)
Currency	1 Syrian Pound = 100 piastres
Internet	.sy

A republic in the Middle East, with a narrow Mediterranean coastal plain backed by the Jabal al Nusayriyah Mountains, and open steppe and desert to the east.

TAIWAN

Official name	Republic of China; also sometimes known as Chinese Taipei
Capital	T'aipei
Population	23 036 000 (2006 estimate)
Nationality	Taiwanese, Chinese
Languages	Mandarin Chinese, Taiwanese
Main religions	Chinese folk religion, Buddhism
Currency	1 New Taiwan Dollar = 100 cents
Internet	.tw

An island republic consisting of Taiwan Island and several smaller islands lying south-east of China; a mountain range covering two-thirds of Taiwan Island runs north to south, with low-lying land mainly in the west.

TAJIKISTAN

Official name	Republic of Tajikistan
Capital	Dushanbe
Population	7 321 000 (2006 estimate)
Nationality	Tajik or Tadzhik, Tajikistani
Languages	Tajik, Uzbek, Russian
Main religion	Islam (with significant minorities practising other religions)
Currency	1 Somoni = 100 dirams

Internet	.tj

A republic in south-eastern central Asia, with mountain ranges covering over 90% of the land.

TANZANIA

Official name	United Republic of Tanzania
Capital	Dodoma (political), Dar es Salaam (commercial)
Population	37 445 000 (2006 estimate)
Nationality	Tanzanian
Languages	Kiswahili, English; local languages are also spoken
Main religions	Christianity, Islam, traditional beliefs
Currency	1 Tanzanian Shilling = 100 cents
Internet	.tz

An east African republic consisting of the mainland region of Tanganyika and the island group of Zanzibar; on the mainland a vast central plateau with high grasslands and mountain ranges rises from a narrow coastal plain. The extinct volcano Mount Kilimanjaro, Africa's highest mountain, is in the north, with the extensive Serengeti plain lying to its west.

THAILAND

Official name	Kingdom of Thailand
Capital	Bangkok
Population	64 631 000 (2006 estimate)
Nationality	Thai
Language	Thai
Main religion	Buddhism
Currency	1 Baht = 100 satang
Internet	.th

A kingdom in south-east Asia comprising a central agricultural region, a large north-eastern plateau with extensive mountains to the north, low-lying areas of tropical rainforest in the south and mangrove-forested coastal islands.

TOGO

Official name	Republic of Togo (also Togolese Republic)
Capital	Lomé
Population	5 549 000 (2006 estimate)
Nationality	Togolese
Language	French; many local languages are also spoken
Main religion	Traditional beliefs (with significant Christian and Muslim minorities)
Currency	1 CFA Franc = 100 centimes
Internet	.tg

A republic in west Africa which rises from the lagoon coast of the Gulf of Guinea, past low-lying plains to the Atakora Mountains, which run north-east to south-west across the north of the country.

TONGA

Official name	Kingdom of Tonga; also sometimes known as the Friendly Islands
Capital	Nuku'alofa
Population	114 700 (2006 estimate)
Nationality	Tongan
Languages	English, Tongan
Main religion	Christianity (with significant minorities practising other religions)
Currency	1 Pa'anga = 100 seniti
Internet	.to

An independent group of 169 islands, 36 of which are inhabited, in the south-west Pacific Ocean.

TRINIDAD AND TOBAGO

Official name Republic of Trinidad and Tobago
Capital Port of Spain
Population 1 100 000 (2006 estimate)
Nationality Trinidadian, Tobagonian
Language English
Main religion Christianity (with significant Hindu minority)
Currency 1 Trinidad and Tobago Dollar = 100 cents
Internet .tt

A republic comprising the two southernmost islands of the Lesser Antilles chain in the south-east Caribbean Sea. The majority of the population is based on Trinidad, which is roughly rectangular in shape and comprises low-lying land crossed by three mountain ranges with coastal mangrove swamps.

TUNISIA

Official name Republic of Tunisia
Capital Tunis
Population 10 175 000 (2006 estimate)
Nationality Tunisian
Language Arabic; French is also spoken
Main religion Islam
Currency 1 Tunisian Dinar = 1,000 millimes
Internet .tn

A north African republic with the Northern Tell and High Tell Atlas Mountains in the north and dry, sandy uplands in the south, stretching to the Sahara Desert.

TURKEY

Official name Republic of Turkey
Capital Ankara
Population 70 414 000 (2006 estimate)
Nationality Turkish
Language Turkish
Main religion Islam
Currency 1 new Turkish Lira = 100 new kurus
Internet .tr

A mountainous republic lying partly in Europe and partly in Asia; the Pontic and Taurus mountain ranges surround the central Anatolian plain, which rises from the alluvial plains of the Aegean sea in the west to the Armenian massif in the east.

TURKMENISTAN

Official name Republic of Turkmenistan
Capital Ashgabat
Population 5 043 000 (2006 estimate)
Nationality Turkmen
Languages Turkmen, Russian, Uzbek
Main religion Islam (with significant Christian minority)
Currency 1 Manat = 100 tennesi
Internet .tm

A republic in south-west central Asia, generally low-lying with hills in the south; around 80% of the land is covered by desert.

TUVALU

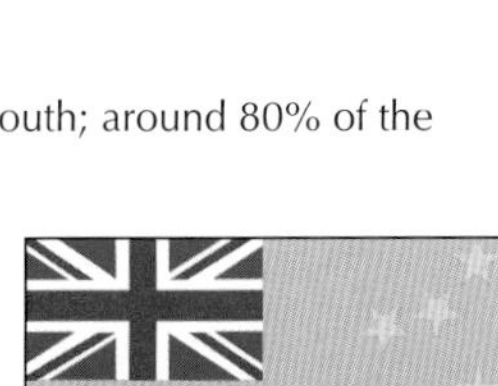

Official name Tuvalu
Capital Fongafale, Funafuti atoll
Population 11 800 (2006 estimate)
Nationality Tuvaluan
Languages Tuvaluan, English
Main religion Christianity
Currency 1 Australian Dollar = 100 cents
Internet .tv

An independent island group in the south-west Pacific, comprising nine extremely low-lying coral atolls running north-west to south-east in a chain 580km long.

UGANDA

Official name Republic of Uganda
Capital Kampala
Population 28 196 000 (2006 estimate)
Nationality Ugandan
Language English; Swahili and other languages are also spoken
Main religion Christianity (with significant minorities practising traditional beliefs or Islam)
Currency 1 Uganda Shilling = 100 cents
Internet .ug

A landlocked east African republic, situated largely on a high plateau dotted with mountain ranges. Much of the terrain is covered with savannah, and the population is concentrated in the fertile Lake Victoria basin.

UKRAINE

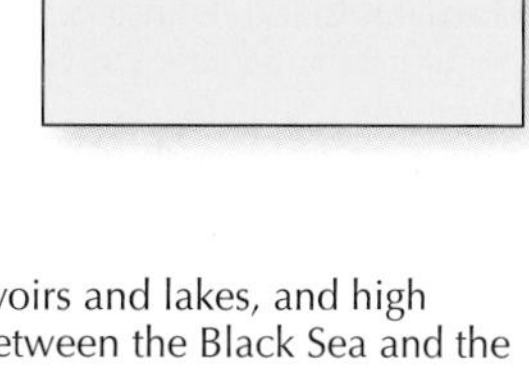

Official name Ukraine
Capital Kiev
Population 47 425 000 (2005 estimate)
Nationality Ukrainian
Languages Ukrainian, Russian
Main religion Christianity
Currency 1 Hryvnia = 100 kopiykas
Internet .ua

A republic in eastern Europe, covered largely by steppes, with many reservoirs and lakes, and high elevations in the west, south and south-east. The Crimean peninsula lies between the Black Sea and the Sea of Asov.

UNITED ARAB EMIRATES

Official name United Arab Emirates (UAE)
Capital Abu Dhabi
Population 4 496 000 (2005 estimate)
Nationality Emirati
Languages Arabic, English
Main religion Islam
Currency 1 UAE Dirham = 100 fils
Internet .ae

A federation in the eastern central Arabian Peninsula comprising seven internally self-governing emirates: Abu Dhabi, Ajman, Dubai, Fujairah, Ras al-Khaimah, Sharjah and Umm al-Qaiwain. Salt marshes predominate on the coast, with barren desert and gravel plain inland.

UNITED KINGDOM

Official name United Kingdom of Great Britain and Northern Ireland (UK)
Capital London
Population 59 668 000 (2005 estimate)
Nationality British
Language English; Welsh and Gaelic are also spoken
Main religion Christianity (with significant minorities unaffiliated or practising other religions)
Currency 1 Pound Sterling = 100 pence
Internet .uk

A kingdom in western Europe, comprising England, Scotland, Wales and Northern Ireland. England comprises largely undulating lowland, with more mountainous regions in Scotland, Wales and Northern Ireland.

The Channel Islands and Isle of Man are British islands. The dependent territories of the UK are: Anguilla, Bermuda, British Antarctic Territory, British Indian Ocean Territory, the British Virgin Islands, the Cayman Islands, the Falkland Islands, Gibraltar, Montserrat, the Pitcairn Islands, St Helena, South Georgia, South Sandwich Island and the Turks and Caicos Islands.

UNITED STATES OF AMERICA

Official name United States of America (USA)
Capital Washington, DC
Population 298 444 000 (2006 estimate)
Nationality American
Language English; there is a sizeable Spanish-speaking minority
Main religion Christianity (with significant minority unaffiliated)
Currency 1 US Dollar = 100 cents
Internet .us

A federal republic in North America with a wide variety of landscape: the East Atlantic coastal plain is backed by the Appalachian Mountains from the Great Lakes in the north to Alabama in the south, from where the land forms plains broadening out towards the Gulf of Mexico and into the Florida Peninsula; to the west, the Gulf Plains stretch north to meet the higher Great Plains in the Mississippi–Missouri basin; further west, the Rocky Mountains, comprising a series of ranges running north to south, tower above high plateaux and river basins.

American Samoa, Guam, the Northern Mariana Islands and the US Virgin Islands are non-self-governing territories. Puerto Rico is an associated commonwealth. The USA also possesses Baker Island, Howland Island, Johnston Atoll, Kingman Reef, Midway Island, Palmyra Atoll and Wake Island in the North Pacific Ocean, Jarvis Island in the South Pacific Ocean and Navassa Island in the Caribbean Sea, all largely uninhabited.

URUGUAY

Official name Eastern Republic of Uruguay
Capital Montevideo
Population 3 432 000 (2006 estimate)
Nationality Uruguayan
Language Spanish; Portunol or Brazilero, a mix of Portuguese and Spanish, is also spoken on the Brazilian border
Main religion Christianity (with significant minorities practising other religions or unaffiliated)
Currency 1 Uruguayan Peso = 100 centésimos
Internet .uy

A republic in eastern South America with grass-covered plains in the south rising north to a high sandy plateau bordering Brazil.

UZBEKISTAN

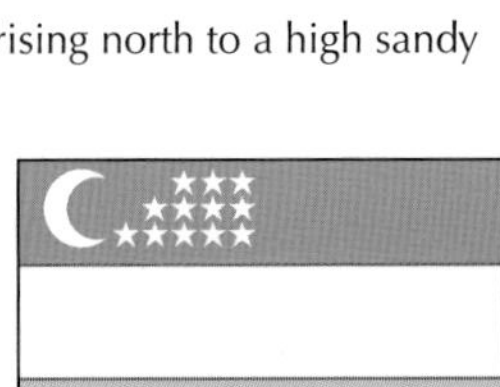

Official name Republic of Uzbekistan
Capital Tashkent
Population 27 307 000 (2006 estimate)
Nationality Uzbek
Language Uzbek; Russian, Tajik and Kazakh are also spoken
Main religion Islam (with significant minorities practising Christianity or other religions)
Currency 1 Uzbekistan Sum = 100 tiyin
Internet .uz

A landlocked republic in central and northern central Asia, dominated by arid, desert terrain, with a large area occupied by the Kyzyl-Kum desert.

VANUATU

Official name Republic of Vanuatu
Capital Port-Vila
Population 209 000 (2006 estimate)
Nationality Ni-Vanuatu
Languages Bislama, English, French; many Melanesian languages are also spoken
Main religion Christianity (with significant minorities practising other religions)
Currency 1 Vatu = 100 centimes
Internet .vu

An independent republic comprising an irregular Y-shaped island chain in the south-west Pacific Ocean; the islands are mainly volcanic, rugged and densely forested, with with narrow strips of cultivated land on the coast and raised coral beaches fringed by reefs.

VATICAN

Official name	Vatican City State; also known as the Holy See
Capital	Vatican City
Population	932 (2006 estimate)
Languages	Latin, Italian
Main religion	Christianity
Currency	1 Euro = 100 cents
Internet	.va

A papal sovereign state, the smallest independent state in the world. Landlocked, urban and entirely enclosed within the Italian city of Rome, it is a World Heritage Site and includes St Peter's Basilica and the Vatican Palace.

VENEZUELA

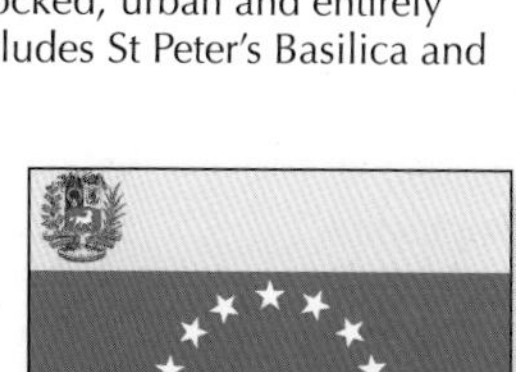

Official name	Bolivarian Republic of Venezuela
Capital	Caracas
Population	25 730 000 (2006 estimate)
Nationality	Venezuelan
Language	Spanish; indigenous languages are also spoken
Main religion	Christianity
Currency	1 Bolívar = 100 céntimos
Internet	.ve

A republic on the northern coast of South America; the Guiana Highlands in the south-east cover over half the country; the Venezuelan Highlands lie in the west and separate the coast from the interior. There are lowlands in the valley around the Orinoco River, which runs through the centre of the country.

VIETNAM

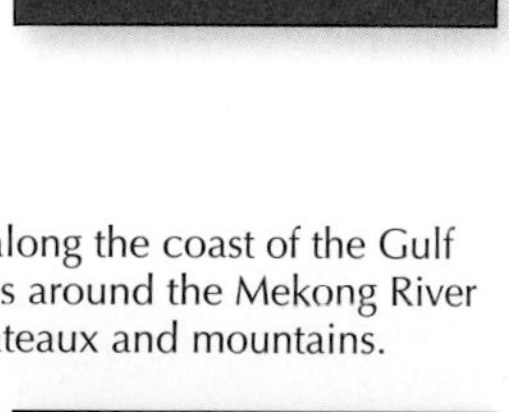

Official name	Socialist Republic of Vietnam (SRV)
Capital	Hanoi
Population	84 403 000 (2006 estimate)
Nationality	Vietnamese
Language	Vietnamese
Main religion	Buddhism (with significant minorities practising other religions or unaffiliated)
Currency	1 Dông = 10 hào = 100 xu
Internet	.vn

An independent socialist state in south-east Asia, occupying a narrow strip along the coast of the Gulf of Tongking and the South China Sea; the fertile and densely populated areas around the Mekong River Delta in the south and the Red River Valley to the north are separated by plateaux and mountains.

WESTERN SAHARA

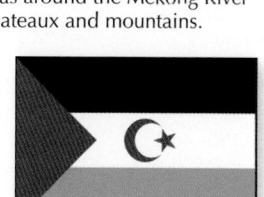

Official name	Saharawi Arab Democratic Republic; Saharan Arab Democratic Republic
Capital	El Aaiún
Population	341 000 (2005 estimate)
Nationality	Sahrawi, Sahraoui; Sahrawian, Sahraouian
Language	Arabic; French, Berber and Spanish are also spoken
Main religion	Islam
Currency	1 Moroccan Dirham = 100 centimes
Internet	.eh

A disputed non-self-governing territory in north-west Africa, administered by Morocco, with low, flat desert terrain composed principally of plains and low plateaux with sparse desert vegetation.

YEMEN

Official name	Republic of Yemen
Capital	Sana'a
Population	21 456 000 (2006 estimate)
Nationality	Yemeni
Language	Arabic
Main religion	Islam
Currency	1 Yemeni Rial = 100 fils
Internet	.ye

A republic in the south of the Arabian Peninsula with a narrow desert plain bordering the Red Sea which rises abruptly to mountains in the west. To the north, a plateau merges with the gravel plains and sand of the Rub al Khali Basin.

ZAMBIA

Official name	Republic of Zambia
Capital	Lusaka
Population	11 502 000 (2006 estimate)
Nationality	Zambian
Language	English; local languages are also spoken
Main religion	Christianity (with significant minority practising traditional beliefs)
Currency	1 Kwacha = 100 ngwee
Internet	.zm

A landlocked republic in southern Africa which occupies a high plateau drained by the Zambezi River and its tribuataries.

ZIMBABWE

Official name	Republic of Zimbabwe
Capital	Harare
Population	12 237 000 (2006 estimate)
Nationality	Zimbabwean
Language	English; Shona, Sindebele and other local languages are also spoken
Main religions	Christianity, traditional beliefs (with significant minorities practising other religions)
Currency	1 Zimbabwe Dollar = 100 cents
Internet	.zw

A landlocked republic in southern Africa, comprising high, wooded plateaux and savannahs which drop towards the Zambezi River in the north and the Limpopo River in the south.

CONTINENTS

Continent	Area	% of total land mass
Africa	30 293 000 sq km (11 696 000 sq mi)	20.2%
Antarctica	13 975 000 sq km (5 396 000 sq mi)	9.3%
Asia	44 493 000 sq km (17 179 000 sq mi)	29.6%
Australia and Oceania[1]	8 945 000 sq km (3 454 000 sq mi)	5.9%
Europe[2]	10 245 000 sq km (3 956 000 sq mi)	6.8%
North America	24 454 000 sq km (9 442 000 sq mi)	16.3%
South America	17 838 000 sq km (6 887 000 sq mi)	11.9%

[1] *The land mass of Australia plus the wider continental area.*
[2] *Including the former western USSR.*

OCEANS

Ocean	Area	Average depth
Arctic	14 056 000 sq km (5 427 000 sq mi)	1 330 m (4 400 ft)
Atlantic	76 762 000 sq km (29 638 000 sq mi)	3 700 m (12 100 ft)
Indian	68 556 000 sq km (26 469 000 sq mi)	3 900 m (12 800 ft)
Pacific	155 557 000 sq km (60 061 000 sq mi)	4 300 m (14 100 ft)
Southern	20 327 000 sq km (7 848 000 sq mi)	4 500 m (14 800 ft)

LARGEST COUNTRIES

Country	Area
Russia	17 075 400 sq km (6 591 104 sq mi)
Canada	9 970 610 sq km (3 848 655 sq mi)
China	9 597 000 sq km (3 704 000 sq mi)
United States of America	9 160 454 sq km (3 535 935 sq mi)
Brazil	8 511 965 sq km (3 285 618 sq mi)
Australia	7 692 300 sq km (2 969 228 sq mi)
Argentina	3 761 274 sq km (1 451 852 sq mi)
India	3 166 829 sq km (1 222 396 sq mi)
Kazakhstan	2 717 300 sq km (1 048 878 sq mi)
Sudan	2 504 530 sq km (966 749 sq mi)

SMALLEST COUNTRIES

Country	Area
Vatican	0.4 sq km (0.2 sq mi)
Monaco	1.9 sq km (0.75 sq mi)
Nauru	21 sq km (8 sq mi)
Tuvalu	26 sq km (10 sq mi)
San Marino	61 sq km (24 sq mi)
Liechtenstein	160 sq km (62 sq mi)
Marshall Islands	180 sq km (70 sq mi)
St Kitts and Nevis	269 sq km (104 sq mi)
Maldives	300 sq km (120 sq mi)
Malta	316 sq km (122 sq mi)

LARGEST ISLANDS

Island	Area
Australia[1]	7 692 300 sq km (2 970 000 sq mi)
Greenland	2 175 600 sq km (840 000 sq mi)
New Guinea	790 000 sq km (305 000 sq mi)
Borneo	737 000 sq km (285 000 sq mi)
Madagascar	587 000 sq km (226 600 sq mi)
Baffin	507 000 sq km (195 800 sq mi)
Sumatra	425 000 sq km (164 100 sq mi)
Honshu (Hondo)	228 000 sq km (88 000 sq mi)
Great Britain	219 000 sq km (84 600 sq mi)
Victoria, Canada	217 300 sq km (83 900 sq mi)

[1] *Sometimes discounted, considered as a continent.*

HIGHEST MOUNTAINS

Mountain[1]	Location	Height
Everest	China/Nepal	8 850 m (29 040 ft)
K2 (Qogir)	Jammu-Kashmir[2]/China	8 610 m (28 250 ft)
Kanchenjunga	India/Nepal	8 590 m (28 170 ft)
Lhotse	China/Nepal	8 500 m (27 890 ft)
Kanchenjunga South Peak	India/Nepal	8 470 m (27 800 ft)
Makalu I	China/Nepal	8 470 m (27 800 ft)
Kanchenjunga West Peak	India/Nepal	8 420 m (27 620 ft)
Lhotse East Peak	China/Nepal	8 380 m (27 500 ft)
Dhaulagiri	Nepal	8 170 m (26 810 ft)
Cho Oyu	China/Nepal	8 150 m (26 750 ft)

[1] *Mt and similar designations have not been included in the name.*
[2] *Jammu-Kashmir is a disputed region on the border of India and Pakistan.*

LONGEST MOUNTAIN RANGES

Mountain range	Location	Length
Andes	South America	7 200 km (4 500 mi)
Rocky Mountains	North America	4 800 km (3 000 mi)
Himalaya–Karakoram–Hindu Kush	Asia	3 800 km (2 400 mi)
Great Dividing Range	Australia	3 600 km (2 250 mi)
Trans-Antarctic Mountains	Antarctica	3 500 km (2 200 mi)
Atlantic Coast Range South	America	3 000 km (1 900 mi)

LARGEST SEAS

Sea	Area
Coral Sea	4 791 000 sq km (1 850 000 sq mi)
Arabian Sea	3 863 000 sq km (1 492 000 sq mi)
South China (Nan) Sea	3 685 000 sq km (1 423 000 sq mi)
Mediterranean Sea	2 516 000 sq km (971 000 sq mi)
Bering Sea	2 304 000 sq km (890 000 sq mi)
Bay of Bengal	2 172 000 sq km (839 000 sq mi)
Sea of Okhotsk	1 590 000 sq km (614 000 sq mi)
Gulf of Mexico	1 543 000 sq km (596 000 sq mi)
Gulf of Guinea	1 533 000 sq km (592 000 sq mi)
Barents Sea	1 405 000 sq km (542 000 sq mi)

LONGEST RIVERS

River	Outflow	Length
Nile–Kagera–Ruvuvu–Ruvusu–Luvironza	Mediterranean Sea (Egypt)	6 690 km (4 160 mi)
Amazon–Ucayali–Tambo–Ene–Apurimac	Atlantic Ocean (Brazil)	6 570 km (4 080 mi)
Mississippi–Missouri–Jefferson–Beaverhead–Red Rock	Gulf of Mexico (USA)	6 020 km (3 740 mi)
Chang Jiang (Yangtze)	East China Sea (China)	5 980 km (3 720 mi)
Yenisey–Angara–Selenga–Ider	Kara Sea (Russia)	5 870 km (3 650 mi)
Amur–Argun–Kerulen	Tartar Strait (Russia)	5 780 km (3 590 mi)
Ob–Irtysh	Gulf of Ob, Kara Sea (Russia)	5 410 km (3 360 mi)
Plata–Parana–Grande	Atlantic Ocean (Argentina/Uruguay)	4 880 km (3 030 mi)
Huang He (Yellow)	Yellow Sea (China)	4 840 km (3 010 mi)
Congo–Lualaba	South Atlantic Ocean (Angola/ Democratic Republic of Congo)	4 630 km (2 880 mi)

HIGHEST WATERFALLS

Waterfall	Total height	Height of tallest drop	Location
Angel Falls	979 m (3 212 ft)	807 m (2 648 ft)	Venezuela
Tugela Falls	948 m (3 110 ft)	411 m (1 350 ft)	South Africa
Tres Hermanas (Three Sisters)	914 m (3 000 ft)	—	Peru
Olo'upena Falls	900 m (2 953 ft)	—	Hawaii, USA
Vinnufossen	860 m (2 822 ft)	420 m (1 378 ft)	Norway
Baläifossen	850 m (2 788 ft)	452 m (1 482 ft)	Norway
Pu'uka'oku Falls	840 m (2 756 ft)	—	Hawaii, USA
Browne Falls	836 m (2 744 ft)	244 m (800 ft)	New Zealand
Strupenfossen	820 m (2 690 ft)	—	Norway
Ramnefjellsfossen (Utigardsfossen)	818 m (2 685 ft)	600 m (1 968 ft)	Norway

LARGEST LAKES

Lake	Location	Area
Caspian Sea	Iran/Russia/Turkmenistan/Kazakhstan/Azerbaijan	371 000 sq km (143 240 sq mi)[1]
Superior	USA/Canada	82 260 sq km (31 760 sq mi)[2]
Aral Sea	Uzbekistan/Kazakhstan	64 500 sq km (24 900 sq mi)[1]
Victoria	East Africa	62 940 sq km (24 300 sq mi)
Huron	USA/Canada	59 580 sq km (23 000 sq mi)[2]
Michigan	USA	58 020 sq km (22 400 sq mi)
Tanganyika	East Africa	32 000 sq km (12 360 sq mi)
Baikal	Russia	31 500 sq km (12 160 sq mi)
Great Bear	Canada	31 330 sq km (12 100 sq mi)
Great Slave	Canada	28 570 sq km (11 030 sq mi)

[1] *Salt lakes.*

[2] *Average of areas given by Canada and USA.*

LARGEST DESERTS

Desert	Location	Area[1]
Sahara	north Africa	8 600 000 sq km (3 320 000 sq mi)
Arabian	south-west Asia	2 330 000 sq km (900 000 sq mi)
Gobi	Mongolia and north-east China	1 166 000 sq km (450 000 sq mi)
Patagonian	Argentina	673 000 sq km (260 000 sq mi)
Great Victoria	south-west Australia	647 000 sq km (250 000 sq mi)
Great Basin	south-west USA	492 000 sq km (190 000 sq mi)
Chihuahuan	Mexico	450 000 sq km (174 000 sq mi)
Great Sandy	south-west Australia	400 000 sq km (154 000 sq mi)
Sonoran	south-west USA	310 000 sq km (120 000 sq mi)
Kyzyl Kum	Kazakhstan	300 000 sq km (116 000 sq mi)

[1] *Desert areas are very approximate, because clear physical boundaries may not occur.*

120°
60°
0°
RUS. FED.
Beaufort Sea
Yukon
Alaska (U.S.A.)
Great Bear Lake
Great Slave Lake
Gulf of Alaska
CANADA
Hudson Bay
Saskatchewan
Nelson
L. Winnipeg
Baffin Bay
Labrador Sea
Greenland (Den.)
Greenland Sea
Svalbard
Jan Mayen (Norw.)
Arctic Circle
ICELAND
Reykjavík
Faroe Is. (Den.)
NORWAY
Oslo
SWEDEN
Stockholm
North Sea
DENMARK
København
LITHUANIA
UNITED KINGDOM
IRELAND
London
NETH.
Berlin
POLAND
BELG.
GERMANY
LUX.
CZ. R.
SLOVAKIA
Paris
FRANCE
SWITZ.
AUSTRIA
HUNG.
SL.
CR.
B&H
S&M
ITALY
Roma
ALB.
GRE.
Athina
Missouri
L. Superior
L. Michigan
L. Huron
Montréal
Ottawa
St Lawrence
UNITED STATES OF AMERICA
Chicago
L. Erie
L. Ontario
New York
Washington
Colorado
Mississippi
Rio Grande
Los Angeles
St-Pierre-et-Miquelon (Fr.)
Azores (Port.)
PORTUGAL
Lisboa
Madrid
SPAIN
Bermuda (U.K.)
Rabat
Alger
Tunis
MALTA
TUNISIA
Tripoli
Madeira (Port.)
MOROCCO
Tropic of Cancer
MEXICO
Gulf of Mexico
Atlantic Ocean
Islas Canarias (Sp.)
Nassau
THE BAHAMAS
La Habana
CUBA
ALGERIA
LIBYA
WESTERN SAHARA
Sahara
México
DOMINICAN REP.
Puerto Rico (U.S.A.)
JAMAICA
HAITI
BELIZE
Port-au-Prince
Santo Domingo
ST KITTS & NEVIS
ANTIGUA & BARBUDA
Guadeloupe (Fr.)
DOMINICA
Martinique (Fr.)
ST LUCIA
ST VINCENT & THE GRENADINES
BARBADOS
GRENADA
TRINIDAD & TOBAGO
Port of Spain
Caribbean Sea
GUATEMALA
Guatemala
HONDURAS
San Salvador
EL SALVADOR
NICARAGUA
Managua
San José
COSTA RICA
Panamá
PANAMA
Caracas
VENEZUELA
Georgetown
Paramaribo
GUYANA
SURINAME
Fr. Guiana
Bogotá
COLOMBIA
Île Clipperton (Fr.)
MAURITANIA
Nouakchott
MALI
NIGER
CHAD
CAPE VERDE
Dakar
SENEGAL
Banjul
THE GAMBIA
Bissau
GUINEA BIS.
GUINEA
Conakry
Freetown
SIERRA LEONE
Monrovia
LIBERIA
Yamoussoukro
Bamako
BURKINA
Niamey
Ndjamena
BENIN
TOGO
NIGERIA
Abuja
CÔTE D'IVOIRE
GHANA
Porto-Novo
Accra
Lomé
CENTRAL AFRICAN REP.
Bangui
CAMEROON
Yaoundé
EQ. G.
SÃO TOMÉ & PRINCIPE
Libreville
GABON
CONGO
Brazzaville
Kinshasa
Equator
Islas Galápagos (Ec.)
Quito
EQUADOR
Amazonas
Amazonia
PERU
Ascension (U.K.)
Luanda
ANGOLA
Pacific Ocean
BRAZIL
Lima
Brasília
St Helena (U.K.)
La Paz
BOLIVIA
Sucre
NAMIBIA
Windhoek
PARAGUAY
Asunción
Rio de Janeiro
São Paulo
Tropic of Capricorn
CHILE
Isla Sala y Gómez (Chile)
Isla de Pascua (Easter Island) (Chile)
Paraná
URUGUAY
Montevideo
Buenos Aires
Santiago
Archipiélago Juan Fernández (Chile)
ARGENTINA
Atlantic Ocean
Tristan da Cunha (U.K.)
SOUTH AFRICA
Cape Town
Falkland Is. (U.K.)
South Georgia (U.K.)
Bouvetøya (Norw.)
capital city
other major city
Antarctic Circle

Arctic Ocean
Barents Sea
Siberia
RUSSIAN FEDERATION
Moskva
Volga
Ob'
Yenisey
Lena
Amur
O. Baykal
Sea of Okhotsk
Chukchi Sea
Alaska (U.S.A.)
CANADA
Bering Sea
Aleutian Is. (U.S.A.)
Kuril'skiye Ostrova (Rus. Fed.)
Astana
KAZAKHSTAN
O. Balkhash
Ulaanbaatar
MONGOLIA
Caspian Sea
Aral Sea
UZBEKISTAN
Toshkent
Bishkek
KYRGYZSTAN
TAJIKISTAN
Dushanbe
GEORGIA
ARMENIA
AZERB.
TURKMENISTAN
Ashgabat
CHINA
Beijing
NORTH KOREA
P'yŏngyang
Sŏul
SOUTH KOREA
JAPAN
Tōkyō
Tehrān
Baghdād
IRAQ
IRAN
Kābul
AFGHANISTAN
Islāmābād
Indus
Tibet
Huang He
Shanghai
Chang Jiang
East China Sea
Midway Is. (U.S.A.)
KUWAIT
PAKISTAN
Ganga
NEPAL
BHUT.
New Delhi
SAUDI ARABIA
Ar Riyāḍ
BAHR.
QATAR
U.A.E.
Masqaṭ
OMAN
Dhaka
BANGLADESH
Kolkata
INDIA
Mumbai
Mekong
T'aipei
TAIWAN
MYANMAR
LAOS
Ha Nôi
Viangchan
Yangon
THAILAND
VIETNAM
Bangkok
CAMBODIA
Phnum Pénh
South China Sea
Arabian Sea
Bay of Bengal
Ṣan'ā'
YEMEN
Asmara
DJIBOUTI
Ādīs Ābeba
Suquṭrā (Y.)
Philippine Sea
Manila
PHILIPPINES
Northern Mariana Islands (U.S.A.)
Wake I. (U.S.A.)
Guam (U.S.A.)
FEDERATED STATES OF MICRONESIA
MARSHALL IS.
PALAU
SRI LANKA
Sri Jayewardenepura Kotte
SOMALIA
Muqdisho
MALDIVES
Kuala Lumpur
Putrajaya
MALAYSIA
BRUNEI
Singapore
SINGAPORE
Celebes Sea
Pacific Ocean
NAURU
KIRIBATI
SEYCHELLES
INDONESIA
Jakarta
PAPUA NEW GUINEA
Port Moresby
SOLOMON IS.
Honiara
TUVALU
COMOROS
Mayotte (Fr.)
Indian Ocean
Cocos Is. (Austr.)
Christmas I. (Aust.)
Wallis & Futuna Is. (Fr.)
Antananarivo
MADAGASCAR
MAURITIUS
Réunion (Fr.)
Coral Sea
VANUATU
Port Vila
FIJI
Suva
AUSTRALIA
Nouvelle-Calédonie (Fr.)
Darling
Murray
Sydney
Canberra
Kermadec Is. (N.Z.)
Île Amsterdam (Fr.)
Île St-Paul (Fr.)
Îles Crozet (Fr.)
Îles Kerguélen (Fr.)
Heard I. (Aust.)
Tasmania
Tasman Sea
NEW ZEALAND
Wellington
Chatham Is. (N.Z.)
Bounty Is. (N.Z.)
Antipodes I. (N.Z.)
Macquarie I. (Aust.)
Auckland I. (N.Z.)
Campbell I. (N.Z.)
Antarctica
60°
120°
180°

AFRICA

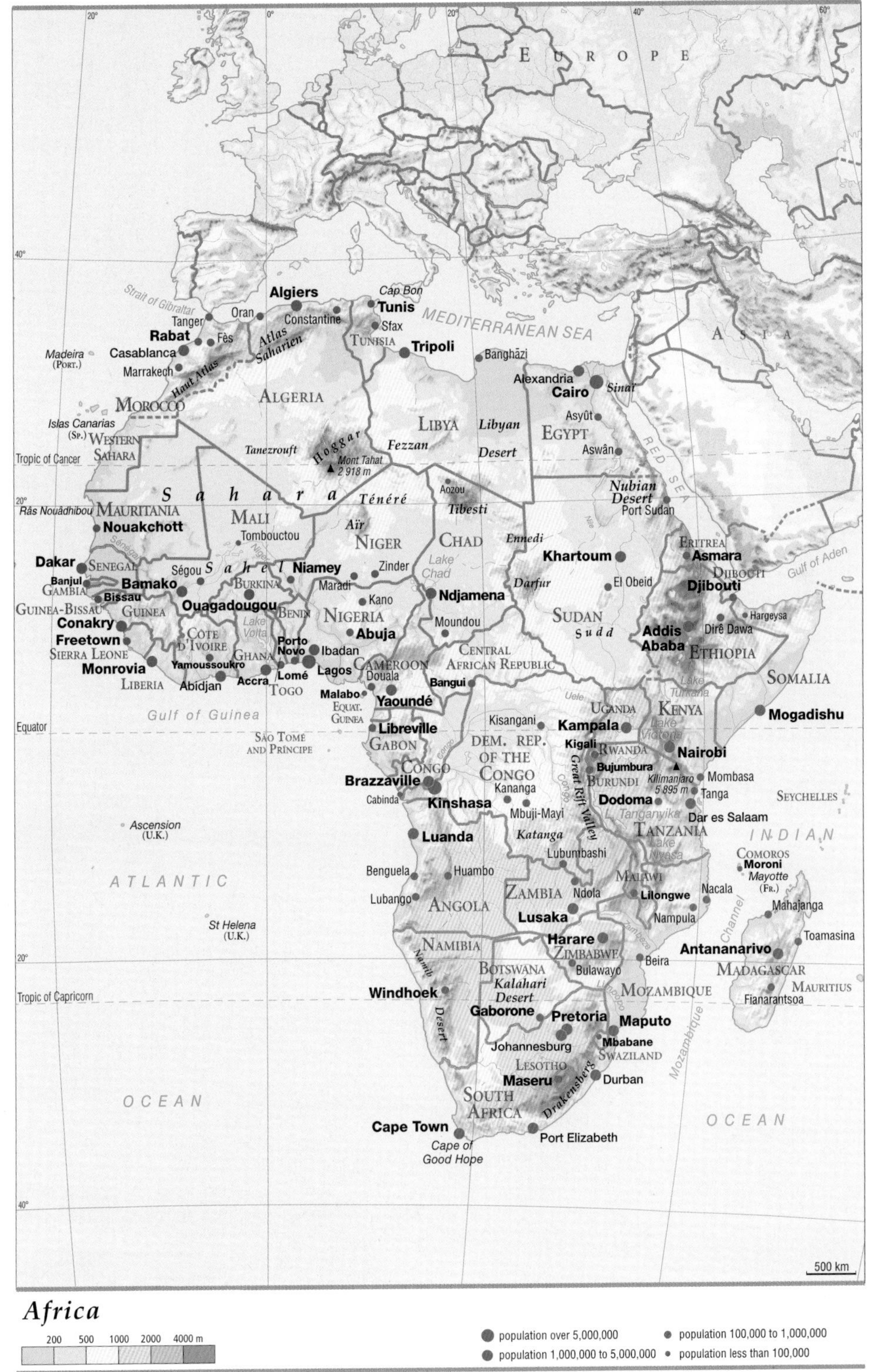

Africa

200	500	1000	2000	4000 m

- ● population over 5,000,000
- ● population 1,000,000 to 5,000,000
- • population 100,000 to 1,000,000
- • population less than 100,000

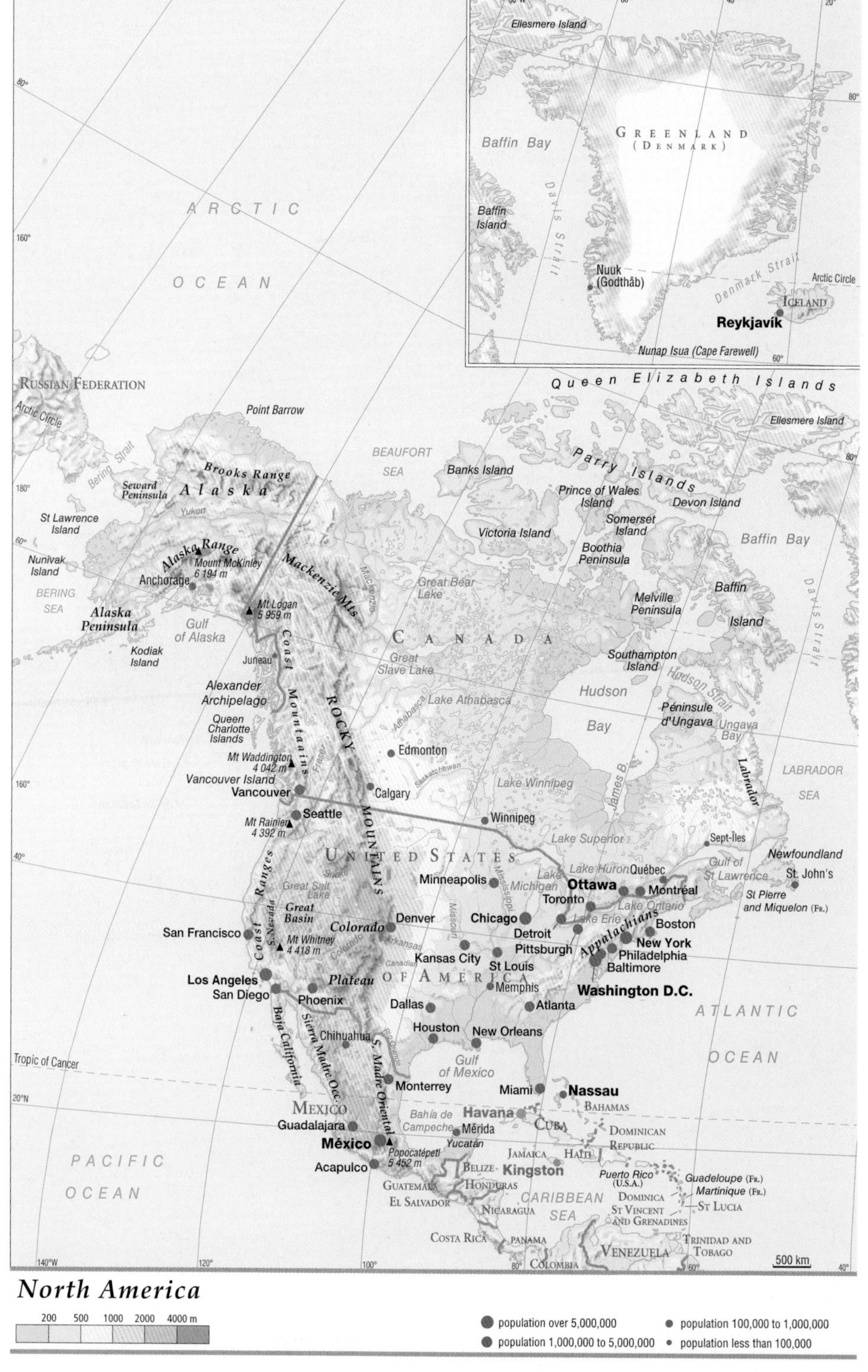
Ellesmere Island
Baffin Bay
GREENLAND
(DENMARK)
Davis Strait
Baffin Island
Nuuk (Godthåb)
Denmark Strait
Arctic Circle
ICELAND
Reykjavík
Nunap Isua (Cape Farewell)
ARCTIC
OCEAN
RUSSIAN FEDERATION
Arctic Circle
Point Barrow
Queen Elizabeth Islands
Ellesmere Island
BEAUFORT SEA
Banks Island
Parry Islands
Prince of Wales Island
Devon Island
Bering Strait
Seward Peninsula
Brooks Range
Alaska
Yukon
St Lawrence Island
Victoria Island
Somerset Island
Boothia Peninsula
Baffin Bay
Nunivak Island
Alaska Range
Mount McKinley 6 194 m
Anchorage
Mackenzie Mts
Mackenzie
Great Bear Lake
Melville Peninsula
Baffin Island
BERING SEA
Alaska Peninsula
Mt Logan 5 959 m
Gulf of Alaska
Kodiak Island
Juneau
Coast Mountains
CANADA
Great Slave Lake
Southampton Island
Hudson Strait
Alexander Archipelago
Queen Charlotte Islands
ROCKY MOUNTAINS
Lake Athabasca
Athabasca
Hudson Bay
Péninsule d'Ungava
Ungava Bay
Edmonton
Mt Waddington 4 042 m
Fraser
Saskatchewan
James B.
Labrador
LABRADOR SEA
Vancouver Island
Vancouver
Calgary
Lake Winnipeg
Mt Rainier 4 392 m
Seattle
Winnipeg
Lake Superior
Sept-Îles
Coast Ranges
Sierra Nevada
UNITED STATES OF AMERICA
Snake
Great Salt Lake
Great Basin
Minneapolis
Mississippi
Lake Michigan
Lake Huron
Ottawa
Québec
Montréal
Toronto
Lake Ontario
Lake Erie
Gulf of St Lawrence
Newfoundland
St. John's
St Pierre and Miquelon (FR.)
Colorado Plateau
Colorado
Denver
Missouri
Chicago
Detroit
Appalachians
Boston
San Francisco
Mt Whitney 4 418 m
Arkansas
Kansas City
Pittsburgh
New York
Philadelphia
Baltimore
Canadian
St Louis
Memphis
Los Angeles
San Diego
Phoenix
Washington D.C.
ATLANTIC
OCEAN
Dallas
Atlanta
Baja California
Sierra Madre Occ.
Chihuahua
Rio Grande
S. Madre Oriental
Houston
New Orleans
Gulf of Mexico
Tropic of Cancer
Monterrey
Miami
Nassau
BAHAMAS
MEXICO
Bahía de Campeche
Havana
Mérida
CUBA
Guadalajara
DOMINICAN REPUBLIC
México
Yucatán
Popocatépetl 5 452 m
JAMAICA
HAITI
Kingston
BELIZE
Acapulco
PACIFIC
OCEAN
Puerto Rico (U.S.A.)
Guadeloupe (FR.)
Martinique (FR.)
GUATEMALA
HONDURAS
EL SALVADOR
NICARAGUA
CARIBBEAN SEA
DOMINICA
ST LUCIA
ST VINCENT AND GRENADINES
COSTA RICA
PANAMA
VENEZUELA
TRINIDAD AND TOBAGO
COLOMBIA
500 km
North America
200 500 1000 2000 4000 m
population over 5,000,000
population 1,000,000 to 5,000,000
population 100,000 to 1,000,000
population less than 100,000

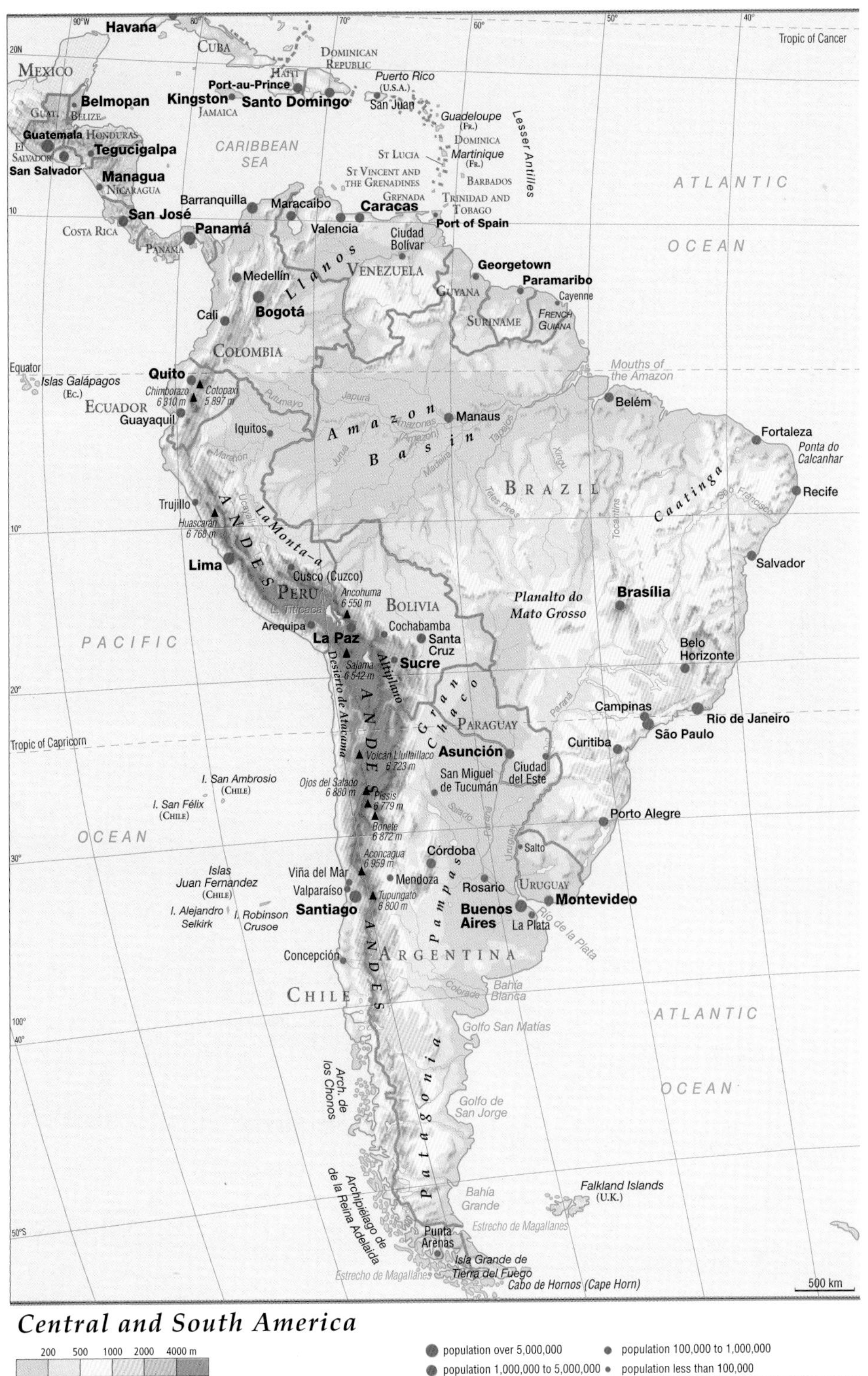

Central and South America

200 500 1000 2000 4000 m

● population over 5,000,000
● population 1,000,000 to 5,000,000
• population 100,000 to 1,000,000
• population less than 100,000

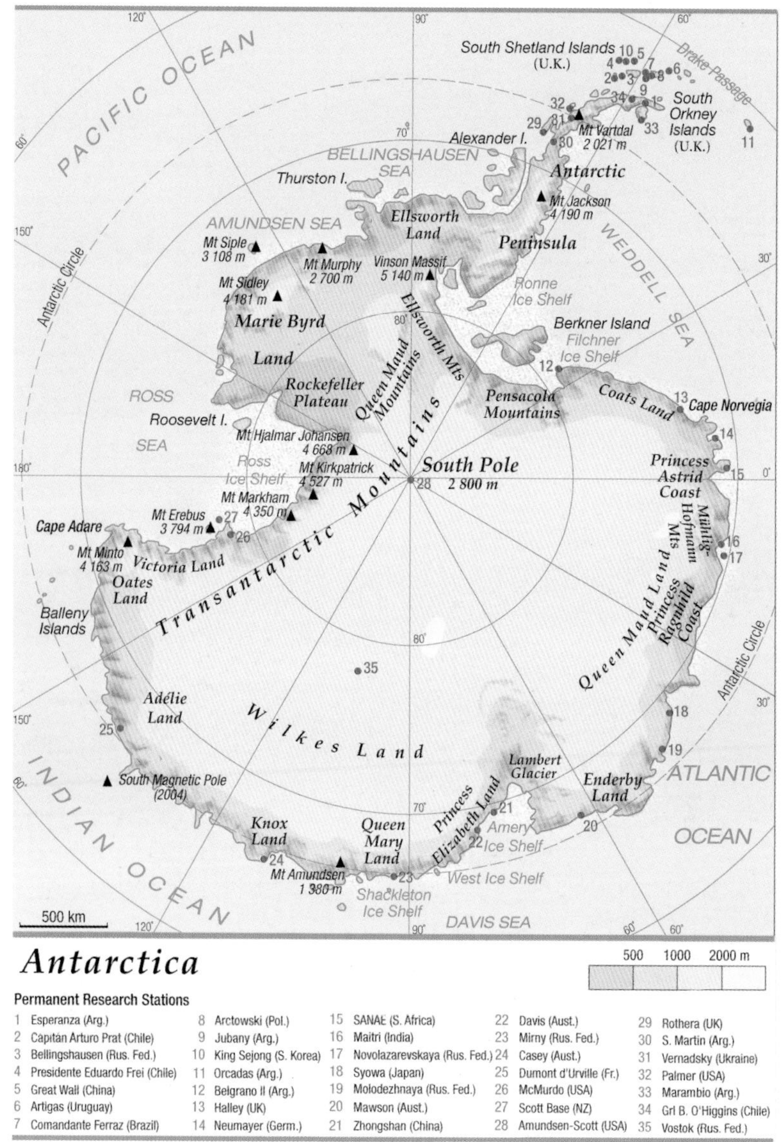
PACIFIC OCEAN
South Shetland Islands (U.K.)
Drake Passage
South Orkney Islands (U.K.)
Alexander I.
Mt Vartdal 2 021 m
BELLINGSHAUSEN SEA
Thurston I.
Antarctic Peninsula
Mt Jackson 4 190 m
AMUNDSEN SEA
Ellsworth Land
Mt Siple 3 108 m
Mt Murphy 2 700 m
Vinson Massif 5 140 m
Mt Sidley 4 181 m
Marie Byrd Land
Ellsworth Mts
WEDDELL SEA
Ronne Ice Shelf
Berkner Island
Filchner Ice Shelf
Antarctic Circle
Rockefeller Plateau
Queen Maud Mountains
Pensacola Mountains
Coats Land
Cape Norvegia
ROSS SEA
Roosevelt I.
Mt Hjalmar Johansen 4 668 m
Ross Ice Shelf
Mt Kirkpatrick 4 527 m
South Pole 2 800 m
Princess Astrid Coast
Mt Markham 4 350 m
Mt Erebus 3 794 m
Cape Adare
Mt Minto 4 163 m
Victoria Land
Oates Land
Transantarctic Mountains
Mühlig-Hofmann Mts
Queen Maud Land
Princess Ragnhild Coast
Balleny Islands
Adélie Land
Wilkes Land
South Magnetic Pole (2004)
Lambert Glacier
Enderby Land
ATLANTIC OCEAN
INDIAN OCEAN
Princess Elizabeth Land
Amery Ice Shelf
Knox Land
Queen Mary Land
Mt Amundsen 1 380 m
West Ice Shelf
Shackleton Ice Shelf
DAVIS SEA
500 km
Antarctica
500 1000 2000 m
Permanent Research Stations
1 Esperanza (Arg.)
2 Capitán Arturo Prat (Chile)
3 Bellingshausen (Rus. Fed.)
4 Presidente Eduardo Frei (Chile)
5 Great Wall (China)
6 Artigas (Uruguay)
7 Comandante Ferraz (Brazil)
8 Arctowski (Pol.)
9 Jubany (Arg.)
10 King Sejong (S. Korea)
11 Orcadas (Arg.)
12 Belgrano II (Arg.)
13 Halley (UK)
14 Neumayer (Germ.)
15 SANAE (S. Africa)
16 Maitri (India)
17 Novolazarevskaya (Rus. Fed.)
18 Syowa (Japan)
19 Molodezhnaya (Rus. Fed.)
20 Mawson (Aust.)
21 Zhongshan (China)
22 Davis (Aust.)
23 Mirny (Rus. Fed.)
24 Casey (Aust.)
25 Dumont d'Urville (Fr.)
26 McMurdo (USA)
27 Scott Base (NZ)
28 Amundsen-Scott (USA)
29 Rothera (UK)
30 S. Martin (Arg.)
31 Vernadsky (Ukraine)
32 Palmer (USA)
33 Marambio (Arg.)
34 Grl B. O'Higgins (Chile)
35 Vostok (Rus. Fed.)

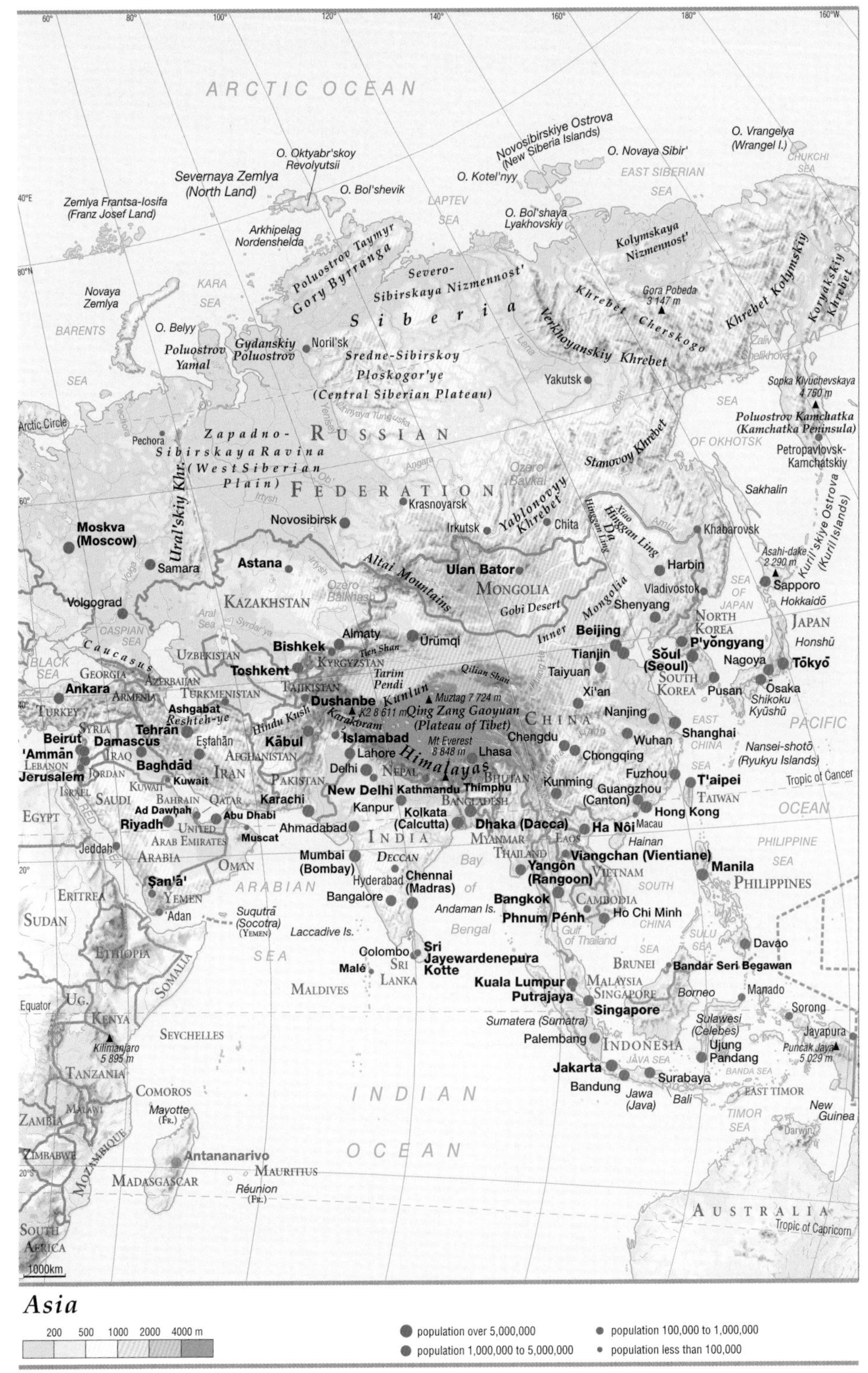

Asia

200 500 1000 2000 4000 m

- population over 5,000,000
- population 1,000,000 to 5,000,000
- population 100,000 to 1,000,000
- population less than 100,000

INDONESIA
EAST TIMOR
ARAFURA SEA
TIMOR SEA
PAPUA NEW GUINEA
INDIAN OCEAN
Joseph Bonaparte Gulf
Arnhem Land
Darwin
Gulf of Carpentaria
Cape York Peninsula
PACIFIC OCEAN
CORAL SEA ISLANDS TERRITORY (AUST.)
CORAL SEA
Great Barrier Reef
Kimberley Plateau
Barkly Plateau
NORTHERN TERRITORY
Tanami Desert
Great Sandy Desert
Great Dividing Range
Hamersley Range
Gibson Desert
Macdonnell Ranges
QUEENSLAND
WESTERN AUSTRALIA
Simpson Desert
Sturt Stony Desert
Great Victoria Desert
SOUTH AUSTRALIA
NEW SOUTH WALES
Brisbane
Gold Coast
Nullarbor Plain
Perth
Adelaide
Sydney
CANBERRA
A.C.T.
VICTORIA
Melbourne
Great Australian Bight
INDIAN OCEAN
TASMAN SEA
TASMANIA
Hobart
300 km

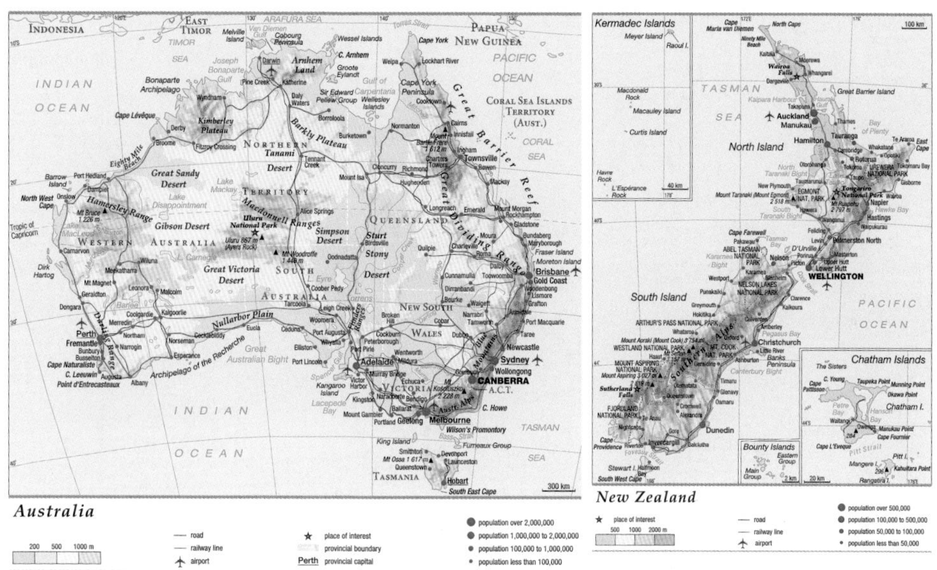

Australia

200 500 1000 m

— road · — railway line · airport · ★ place of interest · provincial boundary · Perth provincial capital

● population over 2,000,000 · ● population 1,000,000 to 2,000,000 · ● population 100,000 to 1,000,000 · • population less than 100,000

Kermadec Islands
North Cape
100 km
TASMAN SEA
Auckland
Manukau
Hamilton
North Island
PACIFIC OCEAN
WELLINGTON
South Island
Christchurch
Dunedin
Chatham Islands
Chatham I.
Bounty Islands
40 km
20 km

New Zealand

★ place of interest · 500 1000 2000 m · — road · — railway line · airport

● population over 500,000 · ● population 100,000 to 500,000 · ● population 50,000 to 100,000 · • population less than 50,000

Nansei-shotō (Ryuku Is.) (Jap.)
Ogasawara-shotō (Bonin Is.) (Jap.)
Tropic of Cancer
Kazan-rettō (Volcano I.) (Jap.)
Minamitori (Jap.)
Hawaiian Islands (U.S.A.)
Kauai
Honolulu
Oahu
Hilo
Hawaii
Northern Mariana Islands (U.S.A.)
Wake I. (U.S.A.)
International Date Line
Johnston (U.S.A.)
PHILIPPINE SEA
MARSHALL ISLANDS
Bikini
Guam (U.S.A.)
PACIFIC OCEAN
Yap
PALIKIR
Ratak Chain
Ralik Chain
Line Islands
KOROR
Caroline Is.
DELAP-ULIGA-DJARRIT
Palmyra (U.S.A.)
Teraina
Tabuaeran (Fanning I.)
Kiritimati (Christmas I.)
PALAU
FEDERATED STATES OF MICRONESIA
Tarawa
YAREN
BAIRIKI
Equator
Jayapura
PAPUA NEW GUINEA
Bismarck Archipelago
NAURU
Banaba
Gilbert Islands
KIRIBATI
Phoenix Is.
Malden I.
Starbuck I.
INDONESIA
New Guinea
Rabaul
New Britain
SOLOMON ISLANDS
TUVALU
Îles Marquises
Aru
Arafura Sea
Guadalcanal
HONIARA
Funafuti
Tokelau (N.Z.)
Penrhyn
Taiohae
Atuona
PORT MORESBY
Louisiade Archipelago
San Cristobal
Sta Cruz Is.
VAIAKU
Wallis & Futuna Is. (Fr.)
SAMOA
APIA
American Samoa (U.S.A.)
Fatatogo
Nassau
Caroline I. (Millennium I.)
French Polynesia (Fr.)
Darwin
VANUATU
Espiritu Santo
PORT VILA
Vanua Levu
Viti Levu
SUVA
TONGA
Cook Is. (N.Z.)
Archipel de la Société
Tahiti
Papeete
Cairns
Great Barrier Reef
Mt Dalrymple 1 277 m
Nouvelle-Calédonie (Fr.)
Nouméa
FIJI
NUKU'ALOFA
Niue (N.Z.)
Rarotonga
Mururoa
Tropic of Capricorn
Îles Australes
Îles Gambier
Pitcairn I. (U.K.)
Kermadec Is. (N.Z.)
Norfolk I. (Aust.)
Brisbane
AUSTRALIA
700 km

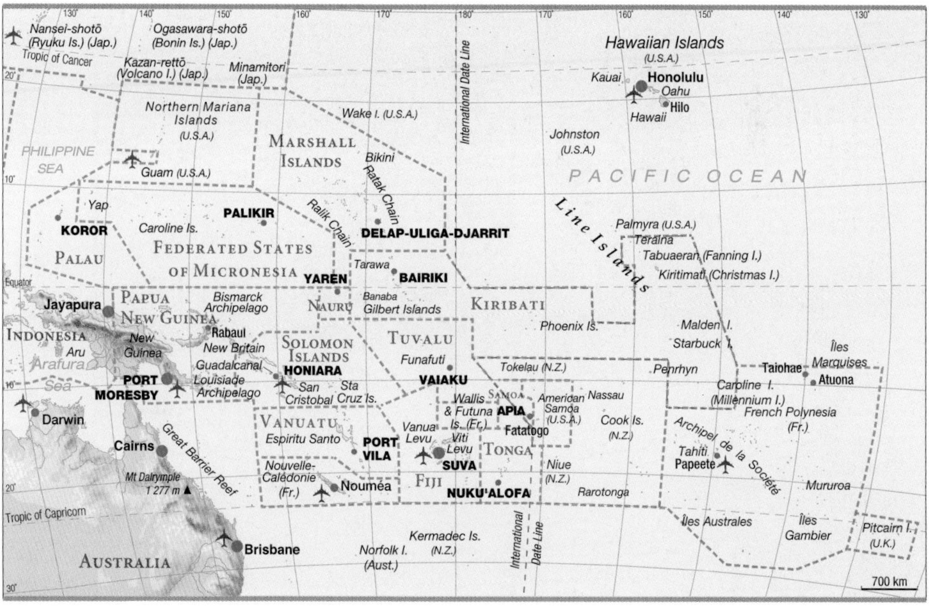

Oceania

0 200 400 600 1000 m

airport

● population over 100,000
● population 50,000 to 100,000
• population less than 50,000

Greenland (Den.)
Denmark Strait
Iceland
Reykjavík
Hvannadalshnúkur 2 119 m
Norwegian Sea
Faroe Islands (Den.)
Shetland Is
Orkney Is
Outer Hebrides
British Isles
United Kingdom
Glasgow
Belfast
Liverpool
Dublin
Ireland
Birmingham
London
English Channel
Atlantic Ocean
Azores (Port.)
Madeira (Port.)
Nordkapp
Lofoten
Lappland
Norway
Bergen
Oslo
Sweden
Stockholm
Göteborg
Gulf of Bothnia
Finland
Helsinki
Gulf of Finland
Tallinn
Estonia
Latvia
Rīga
Lithuania
Vilnius
North Sea
København (Copenhagen)
Denmark
Baltic Sea
Gdansk
Poland
Warszawa (Warsaw)
Kraków
Berlin
Germany
Amsterdam
Neth.
Brussels
Belg.
Lux.
Lille
Frankfurt
München (Munich)
Praha (Prague)
Czech Rep.
Slovakia
Bratislava
Wien (Vienna)
Austria
Budapest
Hungary
Paris
France
Nantes
Bay of Biscay
Bordeaux
Lyon
Toulouse
Mt Blanc 4 808 m
Bern
Switz.
Milano (Milan)
Italy
Marseille
Corse
Sardegna
Ljubljana
Slov.
Zagreb
Croat.
Bosnia-H.
Sarajevo
Belgrade
Ser. & Mont.
Romania
Bucharest
Bulgaria
Sofia
Skopje
Mac.
Tiranë
Albania
Roma (Rome)
Napoli (Naples)
Tyrrhenian Sea
Palermo
Sicilia
Etna 3345 m
Ionian Sea
Valletta
Malta
Greece
Olympos 2 917 m
Aegean Sea
Athina (Athens)
Kriti
Cabo Fisterra
Porto
Portugal
Lisboa (Lisbon)
Cabo de São Vicente
Sevilla
Spain
Madrid
Bilbao
Andorra
Pyrenees
Barcelona
Valencia
Islas Baleares
Mulhacén 3 478 m
Gibraltar (U.K.)
Tanger
Casablanca
Rabat
Morocco
Oran
Alger
Algeria
Tunis
Tunisia
Mediterranean Sea
Tripoli
Libya
Egypt
Cairo
Barents Sea
Kol'skiy Poluostrov (Kola Peninsula)
Beloye More
Arkhangel'sk
O. Kolguyev
O. Onezhskoye (L. Onega)
Ladozhskoye O. (L. Ladoga)
Sankt-Peterburg (St Petersburg)
Russian Federation
Moskva (Moscow)
Nizhniy Novgorod
Sredne-Russkaya Vozvyshennost'
Minsk
Belarus
Kyiv (Kiev)
Ukraine
Dnipropetrov'sk
Moldova
Chişinău
Sea of Azov
Crimea
Rostov-na-Donu
Volgograd
Black Sea
İstanbul
Ankara
Turkey
Adana
İzmir
Lefkosia
Cyprus
Beirut
Lebanon
Israel
Jerusalem
'Ammān
Jordan
Damascus
Syria
Baghdād
Iraq
Saudi Arabia
Kuwait
Georgia
T'bilisi
Yerevan
Armenia
Azerbaijan
Baki
Mt Ararat 5 165 m
Elbrus 5 642 m
Caucasus
Caspian Sea
Prikaspiyskaya Nizmennost' (Caspian Lowland)
Ural'skiy Khrebet (Ural Mountains)
Chelyabinsk
Omsk
Kazakhstan
Aral Sea
Uzbekistan
Turkmenistan
Ashgabat
Tehrān
Esfahān
Iran
Afghanistan
Kandahār
Pakistan
Zapadno (West) Sibirskaya (Siberian) Ravnina (Plain)
Arctic Circle
500 km
Europe
200
500
1000
2000
4000 m
population over 5,000,000
population 1,000,000 to 5,000,000
population 100,000 to 1,000,000
population less than 100,000

PEOPLE

Abelard or **Abailard, Peter** 1079–1142
French philosopher and scholar
Abelard taught at the cathedral school of Notre Dame in Paris, where he became tutor to Héloïse, a 17-year-old girl. They fell passionately in love, but when their affair was discovered, Héloïse's relatives took their revenge on Abelard by castrating him. Abelard later became a monk, and Héloïse a nun. In his final years Abelard retired to the monastery of Cluny. Among his important theological works is *Sic et non* ('Yes and No'), and he and Héloïse are also famous for their letters to each other.

Adam, Robert 1728–92
Scottish architect
He was architect of the king's works, and with his brother James he succeeded in transforming the prevailing, very formal Palladian fashion with a series of romantically elegant variations on classical originals. Surviving examples of their work are Home House in London's Portland Square, Lansdowne House, Derby House, Register House in Edinburgh, the Old Quad of Edinburgh University, and the oval staircase in Culzean Castle, Ayrshire.

Adams, Ansel Easton 1902–84
US photographer
His work is notable for his broad landscapes of the western USA, especially of Yosemite National Park, California, in the 1930s. He established the photographic department of the California School of Fine Art in San Francisco and was a prolific writer and lecturer, always stressing the importance of image quality at every stage of a photographer's work. His publications included *Taos Pueblo* (1930) and *Born Free and Equal* (1944).

Aeschylus c.525–c.456BC
Greek tragic dramatist
Out of some 60 plays ascribed to him, only seven survive: the *Persians*, the *Seven against Thebes*, the *Prometheus Bound*, the *Suppliants*, and the *Oresteia*, which comprises three plays about the murder of Agamemnon, the leader of the Greeks in the Trojan War, and its consequences. He was the first great writer of tragedy and is credited with devising its classical form and presentation.

Akbar the Great, *originally* **Jalal-ud-Din Muhammad Akbar** 1542–1605
Mogul Emperor of India
He succeeded his father, Humayun, in 1556. He soon gained control of the whole of India north of the Vindhya Mountains, and during his reign encouraged science, literature and the arts. He also abolished slavery (1582) and put a stop to the practice of forced suttee (the burning of a widow along with her dead husband). Though himself illiterate, his enlightened, original mind presided over a government that was to be a model for the future Mogul Empire.

Akhenaten and **Nefertiti** 14th century BC
Egyptian king and queen
Akhenaten (also spelt Akhenaton) was the name assumed by Amenhotep IV. Six years into his reign (1379–62BC) he renounced the worship of the old gods and introduced a cult of the sun (Aten). He also built a new capital at Amarna (Akhetaten), and encouraged new developments in the arts. He was married to Nefertiti (Nofretete), who is thought to have been an Asian princess. One of their daughters was married to **Tutankhamun**.

Akihito 1933–
Emperor of Japan
The eldest son of **Hirohito**, in 1959 he married Michiko Shoda, the daughter of a flour company president, who thus became the first non-aristocrat to enter the imperial family. When he became emperor in 1989, the new Heisei ('Achievement of Universal Peace') era commenced.

Albert, Prince 1819–61
Prince consort to Queen Victoria of Great Britain
He was the younger son of the Duke of Saxe-Coburg-Gotha and in 1840 married his first cousin, Queen **Victoria**, a marriage that became a lifelong love-match. In 1857 he was given the title Prince Consort, but public misgivings because of his German connections limited his political influence. He planned and managed the Great Exhibition of 1851, whose profits enabled the building of the Royal Albert Hall (1871). His death led to a long period of seclusion by his widow.

Alcibiades c.450–404BC
Athenian statesman
A member of the powerful Alcmaeonid family of Athens, he was brought up in the house of the statesman **Pericles**. The philosopher **Socrates** also had a considerable influence over him. Alcibiades jointly led the expedition against Syracuse in 415BC, but later fled to Sparta and contributed substantially to the Athenians' defeat in 413BC. He rejoined the Athenian side in 412BC, and directed Athenian operations in the eastern Aegean, where he won several notable victories. He was assassinated in 404BC.

Alcott, Louisa M(ay) 1832–88
US writer
Originally a nurse, in 1868 she achieved enormous success with *Little Women*, which drew on her own home experiences and became a children's classic. A second volume, *Good Wives*, appeared in 1869, followed by *An Old Fashioned Girl* (1870), *Little Men* (1871) and *Jo's Boys* (1886). She also wrote adult novels and was involved in women's suffrage and other reform movements.

Aldrin, Buzz (Edwin Eugene) 1930–
US astronaut

Buzz Aldrin

He was an air force pilot in the Korean War and became an astronaut in 1963. He set a space-walking record in 1966 during the flight of Gemini 12, and during the 1969 expedition in Apollo 11 with **Neil Armstrong** and Michael Collins he became the second man to set foot on the Moon.

Alexander the Great 356–323BC
King of Macedonia
The son of Philip II, King of Macedonia, he was educated by teachers including **Aristotle**. At the age of just 16 he commanded the left wing of the Mace-donian army against an alliance of Greek cities at Chaeronea, and played a decisive part in securing victory in the battle. He became king aged 19, and after a series of victories defeated the Persians at Granicus (334BC) and Issus (333BC). Alexander marched on through Syria and Palestine and was welcomed in Egypt as a liberator from the Persians. He founded Alexandria in 331BC. In 326BC Alexander proceeded to the conquest of India, but at the River Hyphasis (Beas), his army refused to go on any further and he was forced to begin the return march. At Babylon he was taken ill and died. In later antiquity, Alexander was viewed by some as a ruthless conqueror and destroyer, and by others as a far-sighted statesman pursuing a civilizing mission for the world.

Alexander VI See **Borgia, Rodrigo**

Alfred, *called* **Alfred the Great** 849–99
Anglo-Saxon King of Wessex
The youngest son of King Æthelwulf, in 871 he succeeded his brother Ethelred I as king. Alfred defeated the Danes at Edington, Wiltshire (878), captured London (886), and made a treaty formalizing the partition of England, with a significant portion (the Danelaw) under Viking rule. He promoted education in Anglo-Saxon, fostered all the arts, and inspired the production of the *Anglo-Saxon Chronicle*. He himself translated Latin books into Anglo-Saxon.

Alhazen, *Latinized name of* **Abu 'Ali al-Hasan ibn al-Haytham** c.965–c.1040
Arab mathematician
He wrote a work on optics giving the first account of atmospheric refraction and reflection from curved surfaces, and the construction of the eye. He constructed spherical and parabolic mirrors, and it was said that he spent a period of his life feigning madness to escape a boast he had made that he could prevent the flooding of the Nile. In later life he wrote on mathematics and geometry.

Ali, Muhammad, *formerly* **Cassius Marcellus Clay** 1942–
US boxer
He won the world heavyweight title in 1964 by defeating Sonny Liston, then in the same year joined The Nation of Islam (known as the Black Muslims), a movement that favoured black separatism and rejected Christianity as a tool of oppressive whites, and changed his name from Cassius Clay to Muhammad Ali. He refused military service in 1967, for which he was sentenced to prison, but was able to return to professional boxing in 1970. He lost to Joe Frazier in 1971, but later defeated him and regained his title by beating George Foreman. He retired in 1981. In 1996, Ali, showing visible signs of Parkinson's Disease, made an emotionally-charged public appearance at the Olympic Games in Atlanta, Georgia.

Allen, Woody, *originally* **Allen Stewart Konigsberg** 1935–
US screenwriter, actor, director, and short-story writer
He launched his career as a comedian in clubs and on television, and his early comic films, based on the self-deprecating nervousness of his stand-up character, included *Take the Money and Run* (1969), *Bananas* (1971) and *Love and Death* (1975). After *Annie Hall* (1977, three Academy Awards) and *Manhattan* (1979), his films took on a more serious and structured aspect, as in *Stardust Memories* (1980), *Hannah and Her Sisters* (1986, Academy Award), *Crimes and Misdemeanours* (1989), *Mighty Aphrodite* (1995) and *Everyone Says I Love You* (1996).

Alvarez, Luis Walter 1911–88
US experimental physicist
He developed bubble-chamber techniques in order to carry out a range of experiments in which a large number of subatomic particles were identified, and these results ultimately led to the quark model and his award of the Nobel Prize for physics in 1968. With his geologist son Walter he studied the catastrophe which killed the dinosaurs, deducing that its cause was the impact of an asteroid or comet hitting Earth.

Amin (Dada), Idi 1925–2003
Ugandan soldier and politician
Born of a peasant family, he rose rapidly to become Commander-in-Chief of the army and air force (1966). In 1971 he staged a coup, dissolving parliament and establishing a military dictatorship. He expelled 500 Israeli citizens and all Ugandan Asians with British passports, seized foreign-owned businesses and estates, and ordered the killing of thousands of his opponents. His attempt to annex the Kagera area of Tanzania (1978) gave Tanzanian President Nyerere the opportunity to send his troops into Uganda. Amin was deposed within six months (1979) and settled in Saudi Arabia in 1980.

Ampère, André Marie 1775–1836
French mathematician and physicist
Ampère contributed to a number of fields, but is best known for laying the foundations of the science of electrodynamics through his work. His name is given to the basic SI unit of electric current, the ampere or amp.

Amundsen, Roald Engelbreth Gravning 1872–1928
Norwegian explorer
He undertook numerous explorations of the Northwest Passage and North Polar regions and reached the South Pole in December 1911, one month ahead of Captain **Robert Scott**. In 1926 he flew the airship *Norge* from Spitsbergen to Alaska across the North Pole with Lincoln Ellsworth and Umberto Nobile. He disappeared in 1928 when searching by plane for Nobile, whose airship had gone missing.

Anderson, Elizabeth Garrett 1836–1917
English physician
She was the first English woman doctor. In 1866 she established a dispensary for women in London (later renamed the Elizabeth Garrett Anderson Hospital), where she instituted medical courses for women. In

1908 she was elected Mayor of Aldeburgh – the first woman mayor in England. Her sister was the suffragette **Millicent Fawcett**.

Angelou, Maya, (Marguerite Annie), *née* **Johnson** 1928–
US writer
After a traumatic childhood she worked as a dancer, singer and actor, and in the 1960s she was involved in Black struggles in the USA before spending several years in Ghana as editor of *African Review*. Her multi-volume autobiography, commencing with *I Know Why the Caged Bird Sings* (1969), is characterized by optimism in adversity, humour and homespun philosophy. She has published several volumes of verse, and teaches widely. In 1993 she published a collection of personal reflections, *Wouldn't take nothing for my journey now*, and in the same year she read her poem 'On the Pulse of Morning' at President Clinton's inauguration.

Ångström, Anders Jonas 1814–74
Swedish physicist
He wrote on heat, magnetism, and especially optics; the angstrom unit, for measuring wavelengths of light, is named after him. He studied the solar spectrum, and measured the wavelengths of around 1,000 dark lines (known as Fraunhofer lines) crossing the spectrum.

Anne 1665–1714
Queen of Great Britain and Ireland
She was the second daughter of the Duke of York (later **James VII and II**). When he was overthrown in the 'Glorious Revolution' of 1688, she supported the accession of her sister Mary II and her brother-in-law **William III**), but later she was drawn into intrigues for the restoration of her father or the succession of his son, James Stuart, the Old Pretender. In 1701, however, after the death of her own son, she signed the Act of Settlement designating the Hanoverian descendants of **James VI and I** as her successors, and in 1702 she succeeded William III on the throne. Her reign saw the union of the parliaments of Scotland and England in 1707 and the War of the Spanish Succession (1701–13).

Anselm, St 1033–1109
Italian theologian and philosopher
After being an abbot in Normandy, he was appointed Archbishop of Canterbury in 1093. A follower of **Augustine**, he was a major figure in early scholastic philosophy, remembered especially for his ontological proof for the existence of God: if God is 'something than which nothing greater can be conceived' and anything that exists in reality is by nature greater than anything that exists only in the mind, God must exist in reality, for otherwise he would not be 'the greatest conceivable being'. He was canonized, possibly in 1163.

Antony, Mark, *also known as* **Marcus Antonius** c.83–30BC
Roman politician and soldier
He became consul with Julius Caesar in 44. After Caesar's assassination he agreed to share power with **Augustus** and Lepidus, and helped to defeat Brutus and Cassius at Philippi (42BC). After meeting and being captivated by **Cleopatra**, Queen of Egypt, he fell out with Augustus, whose sister he had married. Augustus declared war on Cleopatra in 32BC, and in the naval engagement of Actium (31BC) Antony and Cleopatra were defeated. Antony returned to Egypt where he committed suicide.

Aquinas, St Thomas 1225–74
Italian philosopher and theologian
A thinker whose writings exercised enormous intellectual authority throughout the Church, he was the first among the metaphysical philosophers of the 13th century to stress the importance of sense perception and the foundations of human knowledge. Through his commentaries he made **Aristotle**'s thought available and acceptable in the Christian West. His *Summa Theologiae* (1266–73) includes his famous 'five proofs of the existence of God'.

Arafat, Yasser, *real name* **Mohammed Abed Ar'ouf Arafat** 1929–2004
Palestinian resistance leader
He co-founded the Palestinian Al Fatah resistance group in 1956, and in the 1970s became leader of the Palestine Liberation Organization (PLO). In 1993 Arafat and the Prime Minister of Israel **Yitzhak Rabin** negotiated a peace agreement at the White House, and together with Israel's Foreign Minister Shimon Peres were jointly awarded the Nobel Prize for peace in 1994. The same year, Arafat returned to the occupied territories as head of a Palestinian state.

Arbus, Diane, *née* **Nemerov** 1923–71
US photographer
A rebel against the social norms of her privileged background and her work in conventional fashion photography, her aim was to portray people 'without their masks', and she became famous in the 1960s for her ironic studies of both the wealthy and the deprived classes. After years of increasing depression, she committed suicide.

Archimedes c.287–212BC
Greek mathematician
One of the greatest creative geniuses of ancient times, he discovered the formulae for the areas and volumes of spheres, cylinders, parabolas, and other plane and solid figures. The methods he used anticipated the theories of integration to be developed 1,800 years later. He also founded the science of hydrostatics, studying the equilibrium of floating bodies of various shapes. He is remembered for the story that he discovered the Archimedes principle (that is, the principle of upthrust on a floating body) whilst in the bath and subsequently ran into the street with a cry of 'Eureka!' ('I have found it!').

Aristophanes c.448–c.385BC
Greek comic dramatist
Aristophanes wrote some 50 plays, but only eleven survive; among the best known are *The Birds* (414BC), *Lysistrata* (411BC) and *The Frogs* (405BC). The objects of his often savage satire are social and intellectual pretension, and his plots show a genius for comic and often outrageous invention.

Aristotle 384–322BC
Greek philosopher and scientist
A highly important and influential figure in the history of Western thought, he was first a pupil then a teacher at **Plato**'s Academy in Athens, and in 335BC he founded his own school (the Lyceum). His vast output of writings covered many fields of knowledge:

logic, metaphysics, ethics, politics, rhetoric, poetry, biology, zoology, physics and psychology. Amongst his beliefs were that the Earth is the centre of the eternal universe; that everything beneath the orbit of the Moon was composed of earth, air, fire and water; and that everything above the orbit of the Moon was composed of ether.

Armstrong, Lance 1971–
US cyclist
He turned professional in 1992 and within a year was ranked fifth in the world. He won legs in the Tour de France in 1993 and 1995 but in 1996 was diagnosed with advanced cancer. Declared clear of cancer in 1997, he became the second American (after Greg LeMond) to win the Tour de France, winning it in 1999. He went on to win the Tour de France and win it every year until 2005, when he retired from the sport.

Armstrong, Louis (Daniel), *popularly known as* **Satchmo (from Satchelmouth)** or **Pops** 1901–71
US jazz trumpeter and singer
Brought up in extreme poverty, he learned to play the cornet and developed into the first major jazz virtuoso. After working with King Oliver and Kid Ory he formed the 'Hot Five' and 'Hot Seven' studio groups with numbers such as 'Gut Bucket Blues' (1925) and 'Struttin' With Some Barbecue' (1927). His use of 'scat singing' (imitating an instrument with the voice) started a vogue in jazz. Armstrong made the first of many overseas tours in 1933, and appeared in more than 50 films as a musician and entertainer.

Armstrong, Neil Alden 1930–
US astronaut
A fighter pilot in Korea and later a civilian test pilot, in 1962 he was chosen as an astronaut and in 1969, with **Buzz Aldrin** and Michael Collins, he set out in Apollo 11 on a successful Moon-landing expedition. On 20 July 1969 Armstrong and Aldrin became, in that order, the first men to set foot on the Moon. Armstrong later taught aerospace engineering.

Arnold, Eve 1913–
US photojournalist
The first woman to photograph for the agency Magnum Photos, she travelled to the USSR five times from 1965, to Afghanistan and Egypt (1967–71), and to China (1979). She is well known for her photography of women, the poor and the elderly as well as celebrities such as **Marilyn Monroe**.

Arnold, Matthew 1822–88
English poet and critic
From 1857 to 1867 he was Professor of Poetry at Oxford. He made his mark with *Poems: A New Edition* (1853–4), which contained 'The Scholar Gipsy' and 'Sohrab and Rustum', and with *New Poems* (1867), which contained 'Dover Beach'. He published several distinguished works of criticism.

Asquith, H(erbert) H(enry), 1st Earl of Oxford and Asquith 1852–1928
English statesman
He was Liberal MP for East Fife (1886–1918). He became Home Secretary (1892–5) and Chancellor of the Exchequer (1905–8), then Prime Minister in April 1908. His social reforms included the introduction of old-age pensions, but he found himself in conflict with the House of Lords, and was also confronted by the suffragette movement, the threat of civil war over Home Rule for Ireland, and the international crises which led to World War I. In May 1915 he formed and headed a war coalition but was ousted in December 1916 by supporters of **Lloyd George** and some Conservatives; he led the Independent Liberals, who rejected this coalition. He was recognized as Liberal leader again between 1923 and 1926.

Astaire, Fred, *professional name of* **Frederick Austerlitz** 1899–1987
US actor, dancer and singer
He rose to stardom on Broadway in specially written shows like *Lady Be Good* (1924) and *Funny Face* (1927), then went to Hollywood where he worked notably with Ginger Rogers. His many films include *Top Hat* (1935) and *Easter Parade* (1948). He then turned to straight acting, and received a special Academy Award in 1949. A hardworking perfectionist who made his dancing appear effortless, he revolutionized the film musical.

Aston, Francis William 1877–1945
English physicist
He was noted for his work on isotopes, and invented the mass spectrograph in 1919, with which he investigated the isotopic structures of elements and for which he won the Nobel Prize for chemistry in 1922.

Atahualpa c.1502–1533
Last Emperor of the Incas
On the death of his father he ruled the northern half of the Inca Empire, the Kingdom of Quito, and in 1532 overthrew his elder brother, Huáscar, who ruled Peru from the city of Cuzco. Brave, ambitious, and popular with his troops, he was captured in 1532 by the Spaniards led by Francisco Pizarro. Although a vast ransom was paid for his release, Atahualpa was found guilty of treason and strangled.

Atatürk, Mustapha Kemal, *originally* **Mustafa Kemal** 1881–1938
Turkish general and statesman
During World War I he became a general and fought against the British in the Dardanelles. He drove the Greeks from Anatolia (1919–22), and in 1922 formally abolished the Ottoman Sultanate. In 1923 Turkey was declared a secular republic, with Kemal as president (1923–38). The focus of a strong personality cult, he launched a programme intended to transform Turkey from an absolute monarchy into a modern republic. His reforms included the political emancipation of women (1934) and the introduction of the Latin alphabet. In 1935 he took the name Atatürk (Father of the Turks).

Atget, (Jean) Eugène (Auguste) 1857–1927
French photographer
He worked as a sailor and actor before turning to photography, in which he was self-taught. Shunning modern methods, he continued to use gelatin dry-plate negatives and printing-out paper in order to achieve the extreme contrasts in light and dark that characterize his powerful, poetic photographs of Parisian scenes.

Attenborough, Sir David Frederick 1926–
English naturalist and broadcaster
The younger brother of film-maker **Richard Attenbor-**

ough, he joined the BBC in 1952, and from 1965 to 1968 he was Controller of BBC2 and subsequently director of programmes (1969–72). His nature-documentary series include *Life on Earth* (1979), *The Living Planet* (1984) and *The Life of Birds* (1998). He has written extensively on wildlife subjects.

Attenborough (of Richmond upon Thames), Richard Samuel Attenborough, Baron 1923–
English film actor, producer and director
At first typecast as weak and cowardly youths, he played the thug Pinkie in *Brighton Rock* on stage (1943) and on film (1947). He developed into a skilful character actor, and was actor–producer of several feature films in the 1960s before turning director on *O What a Lovely War!* (1969). His later films as director include *Gandhi* (1982), *Cry Freedom* (1987), *Shadowlands* (1993) and *In Love and War* (1996). He is the brother of Sir **David Attenborough**.

Attila c.406–453AD
King of the Huns
Called the Scourge of God, in 434 he became king of the Huns in Asia, who ranged from the north of the Caspian to the Danube. He soon had dominion over many peoples, so that his rule extended over Germany and Scythia from the Rhine to the frontiers of China. When Attila invaded Gaul in 451, he met defeat, but he later invaded Italy (452), Rome itself being saved only by huge bribes. Attila died the night after his marriage to a princess of Burgundy, Ildeco, and the Hun Empire decayed. His death, in a pool of blood in bed, led to stories of vengeance and murder by his bride.

Attlee, Clement Richard Attlee, 1st Earl 1883–1967
English Labour statesman
After service in World War I, in which he was wounded, he entered parliament in 1922 and became Deputy Leader of the Opposition (1931–5) and then Leader (1935). He was Deputy Prime Minister (1942–5) in Churchill's War Cabinet, then Prime Minister after the 1945 Labour victory. Under his government he carried through a vigorous programme of nationalization and reform, in which the National Health Service was introduced and independence was granted to India (1947) and Burma (1948).

Auden, W(ystan) H(ugh) 1907–73
US poet and essayist
His first volume of *Poems* (1930) was accepted for publication by **T S Eliot**. In the 1930s he wrote passionately on social problems of the time from a far-left standpoint, and during the Spanish Civil War he went to Spain as a civilian in support of the Republican side. He also collaborated with Christopher Isherwood in three plays – *The Dog Beneath the Skin* (1935), *The Ascent of F6* (1936) and *On the Frontier* (1938). A master of verse form in volumes such as *Homage to Clio* (1960), his influence as a poet has been immense.

Augustine of Hippo, St, *originally* **Aurelius Augustinus** AD354–430
Doctor of the Church
Born in Numidia, Africa, he had been involved with a number of religions, but finally converted to Christianity while studying in Italy. He was ordained a priest in AD391, and in AD396 became Bishop of Hippo, North Africa. He was a prolific writer and much of his work is marked by personal spiritual struggle. His *Confessions* (AD397) is a classic of world literature as well as an original work of philosophy. *De Civitate Dei* (AD413–26, 'The City of God'), a work of 22 books, is an influential vindication of Christianity, and *De Trinitate* ('The Trinity') is an exposition of the doctrine of the Trinity. Central to his beliefs were the corruption of human nature through the fall of Man, the consequent slavery of the human will, and predestination.

Augustus, (Gaius Julius Caesar) Octavianus 63BC–AD14
The first Roman emperor
Originally known as Gaius Octavius, he later received the name Augustus (meaning 'sacred', 'venerable'). After Caesar's assassination (March 44BC), Augustus joined **Mark Antony** and Lepidus in forming a triumvirate. He declared war against **Cleopatra**, whom Antony had joined in 37BC, and after his naval victory at Actium (31BC) became the sole ruler of the Roman world. At home and abroad the declared policy of Augustus was one of national revival and restoration of traditional Roman values. Abroad, he pursued a policy of imperial conquest. He was succeeded by his stepson **Tiberius**.

Aung San Suu Kyi 1945–
Burmese political leader
The daughter of Burmese nationalist hero General Aung San, she lived for many years in the UK but returned to Burma in 1988, where she co-founded the National League for Democracy and became its General Secretary. The government had introduced martial law and imprisonment without trial, and banned public meetings, but she gathered numerous supporters. As a result, she was held under house arrest until 1995, only to be held again in 2000–2 and from 2003 onwards. She was awarded the Nobel Peace Prize in 1991.

Aung San Suu Kyi

Aurangzeb 1618–1707
Mogul Emperor of India
The third son of Emperor Shah Jahan, during his reign (1659–1707) the empire remained outwardly prosperous, but his puritanical and narrow outlook alienated the various communities of the empire, particularly the Hindus. Opposed by his own rebellious sons and by the Mahratha Empire in the south, he died a fugitive.

Austen, Jane 1775–1817
English novelist
The daughter of a country rector, her characteristic subject was the closely observed and often ironically depicted morals and mores of country life, for example in *Sense and Sensibility* (1811), *Pride and Prejudice* (1813), *Mansfield Park* (1814), *Emma* (1816), and *Persuasion* (1818). *Northanger Abbey* ridiculed the contemporary taste for Gothic fiction. Her own letters, although carefully edited by her sister Cassandra after her death, are one of the few revealing documentary sources about her life.

Avicenna, *Arabic name* **Abū 'Alī al-Ḥusayn ibn 'Abd Allāh ibn Sīnā** 980–1037
Persian philosopher and physician
He was renowned for his prodigious learning, becoming physician to several sultans, and for some time vizier (a government official) in Hamadan. He was one of the main interpreters of **Aristotle** to the Islamic world, and was the author of some 200 works on science, religion and philosophy. His medical textbook, the *Canon of Medicine*, long remained a standard work.

Avogadro, (Lorenzo Romano) Amedeo Carlo 1776–1856
Italian physicist and chemist
He published widely on physics and chemistry and, in 1811, he formulated the famous hypothesis that equal volumes of all gases contain equal numbers of molecules when at the same temperature and pressure (Avogadro's law). The hypothesis was practically ignored for around 50 years but gained universal acceptance in the 1880s.

Babbage, Charles 1791–1871
English mathematician
He spent most of his life attempting to build two calculating machines, the 'difference engine', which was designed to calculate tables of logarithms and similar functions by repeated addition performed by trains of gear wheels, and the 'analytical engine', which could be programmed by punched cards to perform many different computations. This latter idea can now be seen as the essential idea behind today's electronic computer.

Babur 1483–1530
First Mogul Emperor of India
A descendant of **Genghis Khan**, he won his most decisive victory at Panipat, north of Delhi (1526), and founded the Mogul Empire. As well as being a distinguished soldier, he was also a poet and diarist, with interests in architecture, gardens and music. Himself a Muslim, he initiated the policy of toleration towards non-Muslims that became a hallmark of the Mogul Empire at its height.

Baby Doc See **Duvalier, Jean-Claude**

Bacall, Lauren, *originally* **Betty Perske** 1924–
US film actress
Husky-voiced and graceful, she appeared as tough, sophisticated and cynical as her frequent co-star **Humphrey Bogart**, whom she married in 1945. They co-starred in such thrillers as *The Big Sleep* (1946), *Dark Passage* (1947) and *Key Largo* (1948), and she displayed a gift for light comedy in *How To Marry a Millionaire* (1953). After Bogart's death in 1957, she turned increasingly to the theatre. Later film appearances include *Murder On The Orient Express* (1974) and *The Mirror Has Two Faces* (1996).

Bach, Johann Sebastian 1685–1750
German composer
He held various positions as organist and composer and his last appointment, from 1723 until his death, was as a cantor in Leipzig. Bach wrote a huge amount of music in many forms. Among his best-known pieces are the Brandenburg Concertos, the two passions (*St John Passion* and *St Matthew Passion*), the *Mass in B Minor*, the *Christmas Oratorio*, and the works for keyboard *The Well-tempered Clavier* and the 30 'Goldberg Variations'. Bach transformed the conventional structure of preludes and fugues. His work stands midway between the old and the new, his main achievement being his remarkable development of polyphony (music with two or more melodic parts).

19th-century portrait of Johann Sebastian Bach

Bacon, Francis 1909–92
British artist
He first made a major impact in 1945 with his *Three Figures at the Base of a Crucifixion*. His subjects are often blurred and gory figures imprisoned in unspecific, architectural settings, which frequently evoke atmospheres of terror and angst. A technical perfectionist, Bacon destroyed a great deal of his prolific output. He is widely regarded as Britain's most important postwar artist.

Bacon, Roger c.1214–1292
English philosopher and scientist
He wrote commentaries on **Aristotle**'s *Physics* and *Metaphysics*, and became known as *Doctor Mirabilis* ('Wonderful Teacher'). His *Opus Majus* ('Greater Work') along with two other works, is a summary of all his learning. In 1277 his writings were condemned by the Franciscans, whose order he had joined, and he was imprisoned until shortly before his death. He published some remarkable speculations about lighter-than-air flying machines, mechanical transport on land and sea, the circumnavigation of the globe, and the construction of microscopes and telescopes, as well as many works on mathematics, philosophy and logic, the importance of which was only recognized in later centuries.

Baez, Joan 1941–
US folk-singer and civil-rights campaigner
Her strong, pure soprano was one of the major voices of the folk revival of the 1960s. She broadened her traditional and ballad repertoire to include songs by

contemporary writers like **Bob Dylan** (with whom she had a much-publicized relationship), and was writing her own songs by the end of the decade. She has been active in the civil rights and peace movements, and has continued to combine humanitarian work with music.

Bailey, David Royston 1938–
English photographer
He became an assistant fashion photographer and by 1960 was working with *Vogue*, where his eye for striking photographs made his name. Capturing the spirit of the 1960s with his photographs of cultural icons such as **Mick Jagger** and Catherine Deneuve (the second of his four wives), he became as famous as many of his subjects. In later years he has continued to photograph the famous and has also become known for his nude studies.

Baird, John Logie 1888–1946
Scottish electrical engineer and television pioneer
His researches into television began in the early 1920s, and in 1926 he gave the first demonstration of a television image. His 30-line mechanically scanned system was adopted by the BBC in 1929. Other areas of research initiated by Baird in the 1920s included radar and infrared television ('Noctovision'). He continued his research up to the time of his death and succeeded in producing three-dimensional and coloured images (1944).

Baker, Dame Janet Abbott 1933–
English mezzo-soprano
She made her debut in 1956, and during the 1960s had an extensive operatic career, specializing in early Italian opera and the works of **Benjamin Britten**. Also a concert performer, she was a noted interpreter of **Mahler** and **Elgar**.

Balanchine, George, *originally* **Georgi Melitonovich Balanchivadze** 1904–83
US choreographer
Born in St Petersburg, he formed his own small company whose innovations were frowned on by the theatre authorities. During a European tour in 1924, he defected to the West. His ballets *Apollo* (1928) and *The Prodigal Son* (1929) are regarded as his masterpieces of that period. He later became a major force in American ballet and created over 90 works of great variety, ranging from the theatrical *Nutcracker* (1954) to the abstract *Agon* (1957). Balanchine was also a successful musical-comedy and film choreographer.

Baldwin (of Bewdley), Stanley Baldwin, 1st Earl 1867–1947
English Conservative politician and Prime Minister
An MP in 1906, he unexpectedly succeeded Bonar Law as Prime Minister in 1923. His period of office included the General Strike (1926) and was interrupted by the **Ramsay MacDonald** Coalition government (1931–5), in which he served as Lord President of the Council. He was noted for his reluctance to rearm Britain's defences, and criticism of his failure to recognize the threat from Nazi Germany brought his resignation in 1937.

Ball, John d.1381
English rebel
Born in St Albans, Hertfordshire, he was an excommunicated priest who was executed as one of the leaders in the Peasants' Revolt of 1381, led by **Wat Tyler**.

Ballard, J(ames) G(raham) 1930–
British fiction writer
His early novels such as *The Drowned World* (1962) and *The Drought* offer a view of the world beset by catastrophe. Later, more experimental works include *The Atrocity Exhibition* (1970) and *Crash* (1973, filmed 1996). *Empire of the Sun* (1984), a mainstream autobiographical novel, was shortlisted for the Booker Prize. Other works include *Super-Cannes* (2000) and *Kingdom Come* (2006).

Baltimore, David 1938–
US microbiologist
In 1970 he discovered the enzyme which can transcribe RNA into DNA, and which allows scientists to manipulate the genetic code. His research into the connection between viruses and cancer earned him the 1975 Nobel Prize for physiology or medicine, jointly with Renato Dulbecco and Howard Temin.

Balzac, Honoré de 1799–1850
French novelist
He conceived the idea of the *Comédie humaine* (1842–8), a complete picture of modern civilization. Among the masterpieces which form part of this vast scheme are *Père Goriot* (1835), *Lost Illusions* (1837–43), *Sons of the Soil* (1855) and *Eugénie Grandet* (1833). In 20 years he wrote 85 novels, or more than 4 per year.

Banks, Sir Joseph 1744–1820
English botanist
In 1766 he made a voyage to Newfoundland collecting plants, and between 1768 and 1771 accompanied Captain **James Cook**'s expedition round the world. In 1778 he was elected president of the Royal Society, an office which he held for 41 years. The colony of New South Wales owed its origin mainly to him. His name is commemorated in the *Banksia* genus of shrubs and small trees.

Bannister, Sir Roger Gilbert 1929–
English athlete and neurologist
He was the first man to break the 'four-minute mile', at an athletics meeting at Iffley Road, Oxford, in 1954, with a time of 3 minutes 59.4 seconds. He later had a distinguished medical career.

Banting, Sir Frederick Grant 1891–1941
Canadian physiologist
Working under John Macleod on secretions of the pancreas, in 1921 he discovered (with his assistant **Charles H Best**) the hormone insulin, still the principal remedy for diabetes. For this discovery he was jointly awarded the Nobel Prize for physiology or medicine in 1923 with Macleod; he shared the prize money with Best.

Barbarossa See **Frederick I, Barbarossa**

Bardot, Brigitte, *originally* **Camille Javal** 1934–
French film actress
She was a ballet student and model until her role in *And God Created Woman* (1956) established her reputation as an international sex symbol. Her many screen credits include *The Truth* (1960) and *Viva Maria* (1965), whilst *A Very Private Affair* (1962) was an autobiographical depiction of a young woman

trapped by the demands of her stardom. Since retiring from film-making she has become closely concerned with animal welfare and the cause of endangered animal species.

Barenboim, Daniel 1942–
Argentine-born Israeli pianist and conductor
A noted interpreter of **Mozart** and **Beethoven**, he has worked with the Orchestre de Paris (1975–89), the Chicago Symphony Orchestra (1991 onwards), and the Deutsche Staatsoper, Berlin (1992 onwards). He married the cellist **Jacqueline du Pré** in 1967, and became an Israeli citizen.

Daniel Barenboim

Bar Kokhba, Simon, *also spelt* **Cochba** or **Kochbas** d.135AD
Jewish leader in Palestine
He led a rebellion of Jews in Judea from AD132, in response to the founding of a Roman colony in Jerusalem, with a temple of Jupiter on the ruins of their own temple. It was suppressed by the Roman Emperor **Hadrian** with ruthless severity, and Simon Bar Kokhba was killed at the Battle of Bethar. In 1960 some of his letters were found in caves near the Dead Sea.

Barnard, Christiaan Neethling 1922–2001
South African surgeon
In Cape Town in December 1967 he performed the first successful human heart transplant. The recipient, Louis Washkansky, died of pneumonia 18 days later, but a second patient, Philip Blaiberg, operated on in January 1968, survived for 594 days.

Barrow, Clyde 1909–34
US thief and murderer
He was the partner of **Bonnie Parker**, with whom he committed a number of murders, and with whom he was shot dead at a police roadblock in Louisiana in May 1934. Their end was predicted by Parker in a poem, variously called *The Story of Bonnie and Clyde* and *The Story of Suicide Sal*.

Barry, Sir Charles 1795–1860
English architect
Among the buildings he designed are the Manchester Athenaeum (1836), the Travellers' Club (1831) and the Reform Club (1837) in London's Pall Mall, and the new Palace of Westminster (1840). His work showed the influence of the Italian Renaissance.

Bartholdi, (Frédéric) Auguste 1834–1904
French sculptor
He specialized in enormous monuments, such as the red sandstone *Lion of Belfort* (1880, Belfort, in Alsace) and the colossal bronze *Statue of Liberty* on Bedloe's Island, New York Harbour. Unveiled in 1886, it was a present to the USA from the French Republic.

Bartók, Béla 1881–1945
Hungarian composer
Bartók was one of the foremost composers of the first half of the 20th century. Among his works are the opera *Duke Bluebeard's Castle*, the ballets *The Wooden Prince* and *The Miraculous Mandarin*, two violin concertos and three piano concertos, chamber music including six string quartets, and an important corpus of piano music. He was inspired most of all by Hungarian folk songs. In 1939, he left Hungary and settled in the USA.

Basie, Count (William) 1904–84
US jazz pianist, organist and bandleader
One of the most significant big-band leaders of the swing era and beyond, he founded the world-famous Count Basie Orchestra, which toured widely and with whom he made numerous film and television appearances. During his 50-year career he employed some of the most eminent swing musicians. Among his most popular compositions are 'One O'Clock Jump' and 'Jumpin' at the Woodside'.

Beardsley, Aubrey Vincent 1872–98
English illustrator
He became famous by his fantastic posters and illustrations for Thomas Malory's *Morte d'Arthur*, **Oscar Wilde**'s *Salome*, **Alexander Pope**'s *Rape of the Lock* and **Ben Jonson**'s *Volpone*, as well as for the *Yellow Book* magazine (1894–6) and his own *Book of Fifty Drawings*. Most were in black and white, and in a highly individualistic asymmetrical style. With Wilde he is regarded as leader of the European school of the 1890s known as the Decadents.

Beaufort, Sir Francis 1774–1857
British naval officer and hydrographer
After active service in the Royal Navy, in which he held three commands and was dangerously wounded, he was hydrographer to the navy from 1829 to 1855, devising the Beaufort scale of wind force and a system of weather registration. He was promoted to rear admiral in 1846.

Beauvoir, Simone de 1908–86
French socialist, feminist and writer

Simone de Beauvoir

A pioneer of modern feminism, her most popular and influential work *The Second Sex* (1949) was a study of women's social situation and historical predicament. She contributed with her lifelong companion

Jean-Paul Sartre to the existentialist philosophical movement of the mid-20th century, and her more autobiographical writings and novels include *Les Mandarins* (1954), *Memoirs of a Dutiful Daughter* (1958) and *All Said and Done* (1972).

Beaverbrook, Max (William Maxwell Aitken), 1st Baron 1879–1964
British newspaper magnate and politician
After making a fortune out of Canadian cement mills, he went to Great Britain in 1910, entered parliament (1911–16), and in 1919 plunged into journalism, taking over the *Daily Express* and making it into the most widely read daily newspaper in the world. He also founded the *Sunday Express* (1921) and in 1929 he bought the *Evening Standard*. In World War II **Churchill** successfully harnessed Beaverbrook's dynamic administrative powers to the production of much-needed aircraft.

Beckenbauer, Franz 1945–
German footballer
Nicknamed 'the Kaiser', and a dynamic force in West German football as player, coach, manager and administrator, among his many achievements he captained the West German national side to the World Cup triumph of 1974 and won three successive European Cup winner's medals with Bayern Munich (1974–6). He coached the West German team to victory in the World Cup in 1990. After a spell as coach at Bayern Munich, he became the club's president in 1994, and in 1998 he became the vice-president of Germany's football association.

Becket, Thomas (à) 1118–70
English saint and martyr, Archbishop of Canterbury
In 1155 he became Chancellor, the first Englishman since the Norman Conquest who had filled any high office. When he was created Archbishop of Canterbury in 1162 he championed the rights of the Church against the king, Henry II. In the dispute that followed, Henry's wish to be rid of 'this turbulent priest' led to Becket's murder in Canterbury Cathedral in 1170. Becket was made a saint in 1173 and Henry did public penance at his tomb in 1174. In 1220 his bones were transferred to a shrine in the Trinity chapel, Canterbury, which was the place of pilgrimage described by **Chaucer** in the *Canterbury Tales*.

Beckett, Samuel Barclay 1906–89
Irish writer and playwright
From 1932 he lived mostly in France and was, for a time, secretary to **James Joyce**. His early poetry and first two novels, *Murphy* (1938) and *Watt* (1953), were written in English, but many subsequent works first appeared in French, among them the trilogy *Molloy*, *Malone Dies* and *The Unnameable*, and the plays *Waiting for Godot* (1953) and *End Game* (1957). *Godot* best shows Beckett's view of human existence, with its sense of the pointlessness of all hopes, philosophies, and endeavours, but with its many sudden flashes of humour. His later works include *Happy Days* (1961) and *Not I* (1973). He was awarded the 1969 Nobel Prize for literature.

Becquerel, Antoine Henri 1852–1908
French physicist
During his studies of uranium salt, he accidentally left a sample that had not been exposed to light on top of a photographic plate, and noticed later that the plate had a faint image of the sample. He concluded that these Becquerel rays were a property of atoms, thus discovering radioactivity and prompting the beginning of the nuclear age. His work led to the discovery of radium by **Marie** and **Pierre Curie** and he subsequently shared with them the 1903 Nobel Prize for physics.

Bede or **Baeda, St**, *also called* **the Venerable Bede** c.673–735
Anglo-Saxon scholar, theologian and historian
He lived as a monk at Jarrow for most of his life, where he wrote lives of saints, lives of abbots, hymns, epigrams, works on chronology, grammar and physical science, commentaries on the Old and New Testaments, and translated the Gospel of St John into Anglo-Saxon. His greatest work was his Latin *Ecclesiastical History of the English People*, which he finished in 731, and is the single most valuable source for early English history.

Beethoven, Ludwig van 1770–1827
German composer
An infant prodigy, his influence on the Romantic movement in music and on succeeding generations of musicians has been immense. Among his principal works are his nine symphonies, the opera *Fidelio*, the *Razumovsky* Quartets, the *Archduke* Trio, the *Diabelli* Variations, the late string quartets and the Mass in D (*Missa Solemnis*). According to the accounts of contemporaries he was badly dressed, unhygienic, argumentative and arrogant. The last decade of his life, in which he was completely deaf, saw his most extraordinary musical achievements.

Begin, Menachem 1913–92
Israeli statesman
A committed Zionist and military leader, he entered politics and became the leader of the Likud Front, a right-of-centre nationalist party which ousted the Israel Labour Party in 1977. He was re-elected prime minister in the national elections of 1981. Throughout his life he was a man of hardline views concerning the Arabs, but in the late 1970s he sought a peaceful settlement with the Egyptians, notably at Camp David in 1978. In 1978 he and President **Sadat** of Egypt were jointly awarded the Nobel Prize for peace.

Bell, Alexander Graham 1847–1922
US inventor
After working as an elocution teacher, he began experimenting with various sound-related devices, and on 5 June 1875 he produced the first intelligible telephonic transmission with a message to his assistant. He patented the telephone in 1876, and formed the Bell Telephone Company in 1877. In 1880 he established the Volta Laboratory, and continued to invent various devices.

Bell Burnell, (Susan) Jocelyn, *née* **Bell** 1943–
Northern Irish radio astronomer
She was co-discoverer with Antony Hewish of the first pulsar, a type of rapidly rotating highly-dense star, in 1967. She later joined the staff of the Royal Observatory, Edinburgh, and became the manager of their **James Clerk Maxwell** Telescope on Hawaii. In 1991 she was appointed Professor of Physics at the Open University, and was Dean of Science at the University of Bath from 2001 until 2004. She was also President of the Royal Astronomical Society (2002–4).

Bellini, Giovanni c.1430–1516
Venetian painter
One of a family of painters, he became the greatest Venetian artist of his time. Among his chief contributions to Italian art was his successful use of figures with landscape backgrounds, and his naturalistic treatment of light. Almost all his pictures are religious and he remains best known for a long series of Madonnas.

Belloc, (Joseph) Hilaire (Pierre) 1870–1953
British writer and poet
A Liberal MP (1906–10), he is best known for his nonsensical verse for children, *The Bad Child's Book of Beasts* (1896) and the *Cautionary Tales* (1907). His other books include *The Servile State* (1912), *Napoleon* (1932) and *The Great Heresies* (1938). He was an energetic supporter of the Roman Catholic Church.

Ben-Gurion, David, *originally* **David Gruen** 1886–1973
Israeli statesman
He led the Israeli Labour Party from its formation in 1930 and moulded it into the main party during British rule. He became Prime Minister after independence (1948–53), when he was responsible for Israel absorbing large numbers of refugees from Europe and Arab countries. He was Prime Minister again from 1955 to 1963.

Bentham, Jeremy 1748–1832
English philosopher and social reformer
He is best known as a pioneer of the ethical system of utilitarianism in his works *A Fragment on Government* (1776) and *Introduction to the Principles of Morals and Legislation* (1789), which argued that the aim of all actions and legislation should be 'the greatest happiness of the greatest number'. He also founded University College London, where his clothed skeleton can still be seen.

Bergman, (Ernst) Ingmar 1918–
Swedish film and stage director and writer
His early films include the tender *Smiles of a Summer Night* (1955) and the sombre *The Seventh Seal* (1957), which became a cult for art-cinema audiences. Preoccupied with guilt, emotional repression and death, his later masterpieces include *Shame* (1968), *Cries and Whispers* (1972) and the British–Norwegian co-production *Autumn Sonata* (1978). *Fanny and Alexander* (1982) is an unexpectedly life-affirming story which includes elements from his own childhood.

Bergman, Ingrid 1915–82
Swedish film and stage actress
She became an immensely popular romantic star in such films as *Casablanca* (1942), *For Whom the Bell Tolls* (1943), *Gaslight* (1944), *Spellbound* (1945) and *Notorious* (1946, with **Cary Grant**). Despite attempts at unsympathetic parts, the characteristics she most compellingly conveyed were goodness and stoicism in the face of suffering. After a period working in Italy her later films include *Anastasia*, *The Inn of the Sixth Happiness* (1958) and **Ingmar Bergman**'s *Autumn Sonata* (1978).

Berlin, Irving, *originally* **Israel Baline** 1888–1989
US composer
After working in musical comedy and films in the 1920s and 1930s, in 1939 he wrote 'God Bless America', which achieved worldwide popularity in World War II and has become America's unofficial national anthem. The 1940s saw him at the peak of his career, with the hit musical *Annie Get Your Gun* (1946) and a stream of songs such as 'Anything You Can Do', 'There's No Business Like Show Business' and the enduring 'White Christmas'. In all, he wrote the words and music for more than 900 songs.

Berlioz, (Louis) Hector 1803–69
French composer
One of the founders of 19th-century programme music, he is best known for works such as the *Symphonie fantastique* (1830), the dramatic symphony *Romeo and Juliet* (1839), the cantata *The Damnation of Faust* (1846), and his operas *The Trojans* (1856–8) and *Béatrice et Bénédict* (1860–2).

Bernini, Gian Lorenzo 1598–1680
Italian sculptor, architect and painter
The dominant figure of the Baroque period in Rome, he produced masterpieces such as the altar canopy for St Peter's, the fountain of the four river gods in the middle of the Piazza Navona, and the Cornaro Chapel in the Church of Santa Maria della Vittoria, which features *The Ecstasy of Saint Theresa*. His last work was on the tomb of Alexander VII in St Peter's and the small Jesuit Church of Sant'Andrea al Quirinale.

Bernoulli, Jean or **Johann** 1667–1748
Swiss mathematician
Born in Basle, the younger brother of Jacques Bernoulli, he wrote on differential equations and founded a dynasty of mathematicians which continued for two generations. He was employed by the Marquis de l'Hospital to help him write the first textbook on differential calculus.

Bernstein, Leonard 1918–90
US conductor, pianist and composer
His compositions include three symphonies, a television opera, a mass, a ballet, and many choral works and songs, but he is best known for his two musical comedies *On the Town* (1944) and *West Side Story* (1957), and for his concerts for young people.

Berry, Chuck (Charles Edward Anderson) 1926–
US rock singer
He served three years in a reform school for armed robbery (1944–7) before moving to Chicago in 1955 and launching his professional career. With songs such as 'School Days' (1957), 'Rock And Roll Music' (1957) and 'Johnny B Goode' (1958), he appealed to teenagers of all races. His influence is evident in much of the Beatles' and the Rolling Stones' work.

Berzelius, Jöns Jacob 1779–1848
Swedish chemist
Although active in many areas of chemistry, his greatest achievement was his contribution to atomic theory. Drawing on the work of **Antoine Lavoisier** and others, he devised a table of atomic weights using oxygen as a base, inventing the modern system of chemical symbols. As a result of the poverty of his early years, he had to improvise much of his apparatus, and some of his innovations are still standard laboratory equipment, eg wash bottles, filter paper and rubber tubing.

Besant, Sir Walter 1836–1901
English novelist and social reformer
He is best known for his novels advocating social reform, such as *All Sorts and Conditions of Men* (1882) and *Children of Gibeon* (1886), describing conditions in the slums of the East End of London, which resulted in the establishment of the People's Palace, London (1887), for popular recreation.

Best, Charles Herbert 1899–1978
Canadian physiologist
As a research student in 1921 he helped **Frederick Banting** to isolate the hormone insulin, used in the treatment of diabetes. He later discovered choline (a vitamin that prevents liver damage) and histaminase (the enzyme that breaks down histamine), introduced the use of the anticoagulant heparin, and continued to work on insulin.

Best, George 1946–2005
Northern Irish footballer
Considered the greatest individual footballing talent ever produced by Northern Ireland, he was the leading scorer for Manchester United in the Football League First Division in 1967–8, and in 1968 won a European Cup medal and the title of European Footballer of the Year. However, he became increasingly unable to cope with the pressure of top-class football, and his career fell into decline in the 1970s. Alcohol-related problems eventually contributed to his death.

Bethe, Hans Albrecht 1906–2005
US physicist
In 1939 he proposed the first detailed theory for the generation of energy by stars through a series of nuclear reactions, and during World War II he was director of theoretical physics for the Manhattan atomic bomb project based at Los Alamos. He was awarded the 1967 Nobel Prize for physics.

Betjeman, Sir John 1906–84
English poet, broadcaster and writer on architecture
A popular poet at variance with literary modernism, he became a much-loved poet laureate. His collections include *Continual Dew: A Little Book of Bourgeois Verse* (1937), *Old Lights for New Chancels* (1940), *New Bats in Old Belfries* (1945), *A Few Late Chrysanthemums* (1954) and *Summoned by Bells* (1960). His passionate interest in architecture (especially of Victorian churches) led to the publication of a number of books, including *Ghastly Good Taste* (1933).

Beveridge, William Henry Beveridge, 1st Baron 1879–1963
British economist, administrator and social reformer
He was the author of the *Report on Social Insurance and Allied Services* (1942), known as 'The Beveridge Report', a comprehensive scheme of social insurance covering the whole community without income limit. Published at the height of World War II, it provided the basis for the creation of the welfare state.

Bevin, Ernest 1881–1951
English Labour politician
The pioneer of modern trade unionism, he was a skilled negotiator. He built up the gigantic National Transport and General Workers' Union from 32 separate unions and became its general secretary (1921–40). In 1940 he became Minister of Labour and National Service in **Churchill**'s coalition government, and was a significant member of the War Cabinet. As Foreign Secretary in **Clement Attlee**'s Labour government (1945–51) he was responsible for the satisfactory conclusion of peace treaties with south-east European countries and with Italy. However, he failed to settle the dispute over Palestine, which he handed over to the United Nations.

Bhaskara II *also known as* **Bhaskara the Learned** 1114–c.1185
Indian mathematician and astronomer
He was the leading mathematician of the 12th century, and his teachings on calculus and astronomy were unmatched for many centuries. He was the first to write a book containing a full and systematic use of the decimal number system.

Bhutto, Benazir 1953–
Pakistani politician, the first modern-day woman leader of a Muslim nation
The daughter of the former Prime Minister Zulfikar Ali Bhutto, after the military coup led by General Mohammed Zia ul-Haq, in which her father was executed (1979), she became the leader of the opposition Pakistan People's Party. In 1988 she was elected Prime Minister. In her first term, she achieved an uneasy compromise with the army and improved relations with India, but in 1990 her government was removed from office by presidential decree, and she was accused of corruption. She was returned to power in the elections of 1993. Defeated in the 1997 election, she was later sentenced to five years' imprisonment for corruption, disqualified from politics and sent into exile.

Benazir Bhutto

Billy the Kid See **Bonney, William H**

Bismarck, Prince Otto Edward Leopold von, Duke of Lauenburg 1815–98
Prusso-German statesman
He became Prime Minister in 1862. A national hero during struggles such as the 'Seven Weeks' War' between Prussia and Austria, he further unified German feeling during the Franco-Prussian War (1870–1). He became the first Chancellor of the new German Empire in 1871, and his reign was marked by universal suffrage, codification of the law, nationalization of the Prussian railways, repeated increase of the army, and various attempts to combat socialism. To counteract Russia and France, in 1879 he formed the Austro-German Treaty of Alliance, which Italy

joined in 1886. The phrase 'man of blood and iron', used in a speech in 1862, earned him the nickname 'the Iron Chancellor'.

Bizet, Georges, *originally* **Alexandre Césare Léopold** 1838–75
French composer
Although he won the Prix de Rome, a scholarship for arts students, with *Doctor Miracle* in 1857, his efforts to achieve a reputation as an operatic composer with such works as *The Pearl-Fishers* (1863) and *The Fair Maid of Perth* (1867) were largely unsuccessful during his lifetime. His reputation now largely rests on these works and on the four-act opera *Carmen*, completed just before his death.

Black, Joseph 1728–99
Scottish chemist
With his discovery of 'fixed air' (carbon dioxide) he was the first person to realize that there are gases distinct from atmospheric air. Between 1756 and 1761 he evolved the theory on which his scientific fame chiefly rests, that of 'latent heat' – the heat required to change solid to liquid, or liquid to gas, without change of temperature.

Blair, Tony (Anthony Charles Lynton) 1953–
British Labour politician
After working as a barrister he was elected to parliament as Labour MP for Sedgefield in 1983 and achieved success as opposition Home Affairs spokesman in 1992 by promoting law and order, traditionally a Conservative interest. In 1994 he succeeded John Smith as Leader of the Labour Party and instituted a series of reforms to streamline and modernize the Labour Party. In 1997 Labour's landslide win in the general election made Blair Prime Minister, the third youngest to take office. He was re-elected in 2001 and 2005, but in 2006 he announced he would leave his position before September 2007. He is married to the barrister Cherie Booth.

Blake, William 1757–1827
English poet, painter, engraver and mystic
An artist of great visionary power, he produced many 'illuminated books' in which the text is interwoven with his designs. Such books include *Songs of Innocence* (1789) and *Songs of Experience* (1794), collections of delicate lyrics; and mystical, prophetic and epic works such as the *Book of Thel* (1789) and *The Marriage of Heaven and Hell* (1793). His finest artistic work is to be found in the 21 *Illustrations to the Book of Job* (1826), completed when he was almost 70. Blake's poetry was used as a basis for many musical compositions, notably *Jerusalem*, set by Hubert Parry.

Blériot, Louis 1872–1936
French aviator
He made the first flight across the English Channel (25 July 1909) from Baraques to Dover in a small 24-hp monoplane. He later became an aircraft manufacturer.

Blücher, Gebhard Leberecht von, Prince of Wahlstadt, *known as* **Marshal Forward** 1742–1819
Prussian field marshal
One of the most formidable foes of **Napoleon**, he had victories at the Katzbach and at Leipzig, and on 31 March 1814 entered Paris. After Napoleon's return in 1815, Blücher assumed the general command; he suffered a severe defeat at Ligny, but completed **Wellington**'s victory at the Battle of Waterloo (1815) by his timely appearance on the field.

Blyton, Enid Mary 1897–1968
English children's writer
She began writing her many children's stories in the late 1930s, with such characters as Noddy, the Famous Five, and the Secret Seven. Although she always considered her stories highly educational and moral in tone, she has recently been criticized for racism, sexism and snobbishness. She published over 600 books, and is one of the most translated British authors.

Boadicea See **Boudicca**

Boethius, Anicius Manlius Severinus c.475–524AD
Roman philosopher and politician
Born of a patrician Roman family, he produced numerous translations and commentaries that became standard textbooks on logic in medieval Europe. He was made consul in AD510 during the Gothic occupation of Rome and later Chief Minister, but in AD523 he was accused of treason and imprisoned in Pavia, and was executed the following year. It was during his imprisonment that he wrote the famous *The Consolation of Philosophy*.

Bogarde, Sir Dirk, *originally* **Derek Jules Ulric Niven van den Bogaerde** 1921–99
English actor and novelist
After service in World War II, he was signed to a long-term contract with Rank Films, spending many years playing small-time crooks, military heroes and romantic or light comedy roles, as in *Doctor in the House* (1954). Ambitious to tackle more challenging material, he took on leading roles in films such as *The Servant* (1963), in which he played a sinister valet. Later roles in European cinema, often subtly portraying decadence and ambiguity, include *Death in Venice* (1971).

Bogart, Humphrey DeForest 1899–1957
US film actor
After an early film career mainly in gangster roles, notably *Angels With Dirty Faces* (1938), he achieved stardom with leading parts in *The Maltese Falcon* (1941), *Casablanca* (1942, with **Ingrid Bergman**) and *To Have and Have Not* (1944), which also marked the début of Lauren Bacall, his fourth wife. Over the next 15 years he created an enduring screen persona, cynical but heroic, abrasive, romantic and stubbornly faithful to his own code of ethics, as in *The Big Sleep* (1946) and *Key Largo* (1948). Other classic films include *The African Queen* (1951) and *The Caine Mutiny* (1954).

Bohr, Niels Henrik David 1885–1962
Danish physicist
He greatly extended the theory of atomic structure when he explained the spectrum of hydrogen by means of **Ernest Rutherford**'s atomic model and the quantum theories of **Albert Einstein** and **Max Planck** (1913). During World War II he assisted atom bomb research in the USA; later, in Copenhagen, he developed the liquid drop model of the nucleus. He was awarded the Nobel Prize for physics in 1922. His son, Aage Niels Bohr, won the 1975 Nobel Prize for physics.

Bolívar, Simón, *known as* **the Liberator** 1783–1830
South American revolutionary leader
Born of a noble Venezuelan family, he became dictator of western Venezuela, and after many years fighting the Spaniards, became president of the new republic of Colombia (comprising modern Venezuela, Colombia and, from 1822, Ecuador) in 1819. In 1824 he joined with other rebel leaders to drive the Spaniards out of Peru, and Upper Peru was renamed Bolivia in his honour. In 1829 Venezuela separated itself from Colombia, and Bolívar resigned in 1830. His ideal of a federation of all Spanish-speaking South American states has continued to exert a lively influence.

Bonney, William H, *also known as* **Billy the Kid** 1859–81
US outlaw
He killed his first man at the age of 12, and in 1876 began a series of crimes and killings in the American south-west and Mexico. Two years later he gathered a band of followers and began rustling cattle. He had killed 21 men, one for each year of his life, when he was finally tracked down and shot in Fort Sumner, New Mexico.

Bonnie and Clyde See **Barrow, Clyde** and **Parker, Bonnie**

Boole, George 1815–64
English mathematician and logician
He is best remembered for his *Mathematical Analysis of Logic* (1847) and *Laws of Thought* (1854), in which he employed mathematical symbolism to express logical relations, thus becoming an outstanding pioneer of modern symbolic logic. Boolean algebra is particularly useful in the design of circuits and computers.

Borg, Björn Rune 1956–
Swedish tennis player
He was Wimbledon junior champion at 16, and became the dominant player in world tennis in the 1970s. In 1976 he won the first of his record five consecutive Wimbledon singles titles (1976–80). He also won the Italian championship twice and the French Open six times between 1974 and 1981. His Wimbledon reign ended in 1981 when he lost in the final to **John McEnroe**.

Björn Borg

Borgia, Rodrigo, *later* **Alexander VI** 1431–1503
Spanish nobleman and pope
In 1455 he was made a cardinal and in 1492, having secured the position by flagrant bribery, he was elevated to pope, taking the name Alexander VI. Borgia endeavoured to break the power of the Italian princes and take their possessions for the benefit of his own family. He divided the New World between Spain and Portugal and introduced the censorship of books. The nobles Cesare Borgia and Lucrezia Borgia, both of whom became notorious as ambitious, murderous public figures, were among his children.

Borromini, Francesco 1599–1667
Italian Baroque architect and sculptor
Considered one of the great Baroque architects, he spent all his working life in Rome, where he was associated with his great rival **Gian Bernini** in the Palazzo Berberini (1620–31) and the Baldacchino in St Peter's (1631–3). His own chief buildings were the San Carlo alle Quattro Fontane (1641), Sant'Ivo alla Sapienza (1660), Sant'Andrea delle Fratte (1653–65), and the oratorio of San Filippo Neri (1650).

Bosch, Hieronymus, *real name* **Jerome van Aken** c.1450–1516
Dutch painter
He was named after the town in which he was born, 's-Hertogenbosch in northern Brabant, and he probably spent the whole of his life there. He is famous for his bizarre, nightmarish visions on religious themes, featuring monstrous creatures and scenes of torment, which can be partly traced to devotional woodcuts of the period. His greatest masterpiece is probably *The Garden of Earthly Delights*, a triptych (a three-panelled painting) showing the descent of the Earth into sin.

Boswell, James 1740–95
Scottish writer and biographer of Dr Johnson
He first met Dr **Samuel Johnson** in 1763, and his masterpiece, the *Life of Samuel Johnson* (1791), gives a vivid contemporary insight into the Doctor's character and conversation. Boswell himself lived a life of high adventure, touring Europe extensively and meeting great figures such as **Voltaire** and **Jean Jacques Rousseau**, and pursuing many love affairs. In 1773 Boswell took Dr Johnson on a memorable journey to the Hebrides, later publishing *The Journal of the Tour of the Hebrides* (1785).

Botham, Ian Terence 1955–
English cricketer
An extremely talented all-rounder, he played for England in 102 Test matches, took 383 wickets, and scored 5,200 runs. His performances in 1981 helped bring about victory in the Test series against Australia. He has led successful charity fund-raising campaigns such as his walk from John o' Groats to Land's End and his re-enactment of **Hannibal**'s crossing of the Alps.

Botticelli, Sandro, *originally* **Alessandro Filipepi** 1445–1510
Florentine painter
He produced mostly religious works but is best known for his treatment of mythological subjects such as *The Birth of Venus* (c.1482–4) and the *Primavera* (c.1478). During the Victorian period his work became a source of inspiration for the Pre-Raphaelite movement and art nouveau.

Boudicca, *incorrectly called* **Boadicea** d.61 AD
British warrior-queen
She was queen of the native tribe of Iceni (of Norfolk,

Suffolk and part of Cambridgeshire). Her husband, Prasutagus, an ally of Rome, had made the Emperor **Nero** his co-heir, but when he died (AD60) the Romans annexed all the Iceni territory. According to the Roman historian **Tacitus**, Boudicca was flogged and her daughters raped. The Iceni rebelled, led by Boudicca, and destroyed Colchester, London and St Albans, killing up to 70,000 Romans. The Roman counter-attack overwhelmed the Iceni, and Boudicca herself is said to have taken poison.

Bourgeois, Louise 1911–
US sculptor
Born in Paris, she emigrated to the USA in 1938. She started as a painter but turned to wood-carving, and in the 1960s she started working with stone and metal, creating abstract sculptures which suggest figures, or parts of figures, such as *Labyrinthine Tower* (1963). Her work became increasingly fantastical in the 1970s, and in the 1980s and 1990s commented on ideas of femininity, as in her *Spiders* (1995), a collection of large metal spiders spiked with knitting needles.

Bourke-White, Margaret, *originally* **Margaret White** 1906–71
US photojournalist
A pioneer of the photo-essay, one of her notable early achievements was her 70 photographs for *You Have Seen Their Faces* (1937), a study of rural poverty in the southern USA. She covered World War II for *Life* magazine and was the first woman photographer to be attached to the US armed forces, producing outstanding reports of the Siege of Moscow (1941) and the opening of the concentration camps (1944). After the war, she recorded the troubles in India, Pakistan and South Africa, and was an official UN war correspondent during the Korean War.

Bowie, David, *real name* **David Robert Jones** 1947–
English rock singer
After the success of the single 'Space Oddity' (1969), his career blossomed throughout the 1970s as he adopted a range of extreme stage images to suit a variety of musical styles and concepts. He had a UK number one in 1980 with 'Ashes to Ashes', and again in 1983 with the more commercial 'Let's Dance'. His albums have included *Hunky Dory* (1971), *The Rise And Fall Of Ziggy Stardust And The Spiders From Mars* (1972), *Diamond Dogs* (1974), *Heroes* (1977), *Scary Monsters (and Super Creeps)* (1980) and *Let's Dance* (1983). He has also acted on stage and in films, including *The Man Who Fell To Earth* (1976), *Merry Christmas Mr Lawrence* (1983) and *Labyrinth* (1986).

Boycott, Geoffrey 1940–
English cricketer
The most celebrated batsman in postwar English cricket, he played 108 times for England between 1964 and 1982, and scored more than 150 first-class centuries. He later became a commentator, noted for his forthright views.

Boyle, Robert 1627–91
Irish physicist and chemist
He is probably best known for Boyle's law, which states that the volume of a given mass of gas will increase in direct proportion to a decrease in its pressure, as long as the temperature remains constant. One of the founders of the Royal Society, his assistant was **Robert Hooke**, with whom he conducted various researches concerning air, vacuum, combustion and respiration. In 1661 he published *The Sceptical Chemist*, in which he rejected the traditional theory that all matter was composed of four elements, and defined an element as a substance that cannot be reduced to other, simpler substances or produced by combining simpler substances.

Bradman, Sir Don(ald George) 1908–2001
Australian cricketer
He is regarded as the greatest batsman in the history of the game. A prodigious scorer, he made the largest number of centuries in Tests against England, and holds the record for the highest Australian Test score against England (334 at Leeds in 1930). His batting average in Test matches was an astonishing 99.94 runs per innings.

Bragg, Sir William Henry 1862–1942
English physicist
From 1912 he worked with his son, Lawrence Bragg, on determining the atomic structure of crystals, and their efforts won them a joint Nobel Prize for physics in 1915 – the only father–son partnership to share this honour. During World War I he directed research on submarine detection.

Brahe, Tycho or **Tyge** 1546–1601
Danish astronomer
In 1572 he carefully observed a new star (the supernova now known as Tycho's star) in the constellation of Cassiopeia, a significant observation which made his name. He was later assisted in his work by **Johannes Kepler**. Brahe did not subscribe to **Copernicus**'s theory of a system of planets revolving round the sun, but his data allowed Kepler to prove that Copernicus was essentially correct. Gifted but hot-tempered, Brahe lost most of his nose in a duel at the age of 19, and wore a false silver nose for the rest of his life. He is considered the greatest pre-telescope observer.

Brahms, Johannes 1833–97
German composer
Prolific in all fields except opera, he produced chamber music, songs, piano sonatas, symphonies, choral works such as the *German Requiem* (first performed in 1869) and orchestral works such as the *Academic Festival Overture* (1880). Among his lifelong friends were **Franz Liszt** and **Robert Schumann**, whose enthusiasm for Brahms's early works helped to establish his reputation. He never married, and after 1863, when he settled in Vienna, his life was uneventful except for occasional public appearances in Austria and Germany at which he played his own works.

Brancusi, Constantin 1876–1957
Romanian sculptor
One of the great pioneers of modernism in sculpture, his piece *The Kiss* (1901–21, various versions) was the most abstract work of the period, representing two block-like figures. His *Sleeping Muse* (1910) was the first of his many characteristic, highly-polished, egg-shaped carvings. *The Prodigal Son* (1925) shows the influence of African sculpture.

Brando, Marlon 1924–2004
US film and stage actor
He made his New York debut in 1943 and appeared

in several plays before achieving fame as Stanley Kowalski in the film version of **Tennessee Williams**'s *A Streetcar Named Desire* (1951). He also played roles in films such as *The Wild One* (1953), *Mutiny on the Bounty* (1962), *Last Tango in Paris* (1972) and *Apocalypse Now* (1977). He won an Academy Award for *On the Waterfront* (1954) but refused to accept a second for *The Godfather* (1972), in protest against the film industry's treatment of Native Americans. He returned to film after an absence of eight years in the anti-apartheid drama *A Dry White Season* (1989).

Bream, Julian Alexander 1933–
English guitarist and lutenist
A protégé of Spanish guitarist Andrés Segovia, he formed the Julian Bream Consort in 1961. Many works have been specially written for him, by **Benjamin Britten** and others.

Brecht, (Eugen) Bertolt Friedrich 1898–1956
German playwright and poet
He is considered by many to be Germany's greatest dramatist. His reputation was established by *The Threepenny Opera* (1928), an adaptation of John Gay's *Beggar's Opera*, with music by **Kurt Weill**. A Marxist, Brecht regarded his plays as social experiments. They include *Mother Courage and her Children* (1941), *The Good Person of Setzuan* (1943), *The Caucasian Chalk Circle* (1947) and *The Resistible Rise of Arturo Ui* (1957). All underlined the moral that, however much the intellect may be oppressed, the truth will come out. Brecht lived for a time in Hollywood before returning to East Germany.

Brezhnev, Leonid Ilyich 1906–82
Soviet statesman
After working as a propaganda chief, in 1964 he replaced **Nikita Khrushchev** as General Secretary of the Communist Party. The Brezhnev era saw the USSR establish itself as a military and political superpower, extending its influence in Africa and Asia. At home, however, it was a period of caution and, during the 1970s, of economic stagnation.

Leonid Brezhnev

Brian c.926–1014
King of Ireland
Known as 'Brian Boroimhe' or 'Boru' ('Brian of the tribute'), he became chief of Dál Cais (Dalkey) in 976, and after much fighting he made himself King of Leinster (984). After further campaigns in all parts of the country, his rule was acknowledged over the whole of Ireland (1002). He was killed after defeating the Vikings at Clontarf, near Dublin.

Britten (of Aldeburgh), (Edward) Benjamin Britten, Baron 1913–76
English composer
Often considered to be Britain's greatest 20th-century composer, he produced works in all genres, but is best known for operas such as *Peter Grimes* (1945) and *Billy Budd* (1951), his Violin Concerto (1939), the *Sinfonia da Requiem* (1940), *The Young-Person's Guide to the Orchestra* (1946), and the three suites for solo cello (1964, 1967, 1972). Britten had a special genius in writing with simplicity while retaining artistic and dramatic effectiveness. In 1948 he founded the annual Aldeburgh Festival.

Brønsted, Johannes Nicolaus 1879–1947
Danish physical chemist
Most of his contributions to physical chemistry concerned the behaviour of solutions. He is known for a novel and valuable definition of acids and bases, the Brønsted–Lowry definition, which defines an acid as a substance with a tendency to lose a proton, and a base as a substance that tends to gain a proton.

Brontë, Anne, *pseudonym* **Acton Bell** 1820–49
English writer
She worked as a governess, and wrote two novels, *Agnes Grey* (1845) and *The Tenant of Wildfell Hall* (1848). These are generally regarded as lesser works than those of her sisters, although *Wildfell Hall*, with its controversial subject matter and questioning of the status of married women, had a certain success.

Brontë, Charlotte, *pseudonym* **Currer Bell** 1816–55
English writer
She worked for a time as a teacher and governess, and wrote four complete novels: *The Professor* (published in 1857 after her death), *Jane Eyre* (1847), which was her greatest success, *Shirley* (1849) and *Villette* (1853). After the deaths of her brother and two sisters she married her clergyman father's curate, Arthur Bell Nicholls, in 1854. She died in pregnancy the following year, leaving the fragment of another novel, *Emma*.

Brontë, Emily Jane, *pseudonym* **Ellis Bell** 1818–48
English writer
Emily, like her sisters, worked as a governess. Her single novel, *Wuthering Heights* (1847), is an intense and powerful tale of love and revenge set in the remote wilds of 18th-century Yorkshire; it has much in common with Greek tragedy, and no real counterpart in English literature.

Brook, Peter Stephen Paul 1925–
English theatre and film director
In a prolific career he has worked on many productions in Great Britain, Europe, the USA, Africa and Asia, and has been director at the Royal Opera House, the Royal Shakespeare Company and the National Theatre. His films include *The Beggar's Opera* (1952), *Lord of the Flies* (1962), *Marat/Sade* (1967), *King Lear* (1969) and *Meetings With Remarkable Men* (1979). Among his most famous productions is a nine-hour adaptation of *The Mahabharata*, one of the great Sanskrit epics of ancient India, which toured the world.

Brooke, Rupert Chawner 1887–1915
English poet
He was educated at King's College, Cambridge. His first collection of verse, *Poems*, appeared in 1911, and he also contributed to the first and second volumes of the periodical *Georgian Poetry*. Five war sonnets were published in 1915 and brought him great public recognition, which was increased by *1914 and Other Poems*, published in 1915, after his death. He died a commissioned naval officer on the Greek island of Skyros on his way to the Dardanelles campaign, and was buried there.

Brown, Lancelot, *also known as* **Capability Brown** 1715–83
English landscape gardener
He established a purely English style of garden layout, using simple means to produce natural effects, as in the gardens of Blenheim, Kew, Stowe, Warwick Castle, Chatsworth, and others. He got his nickname from telling clients that their gardens had great 'capabilities'.

Brown, Robert 1773–1858
Scottish botanist
Appointed naturalist to Matthew Flinders's coastal survey of Australia in 1801–5, he brought back nearly 4,000 species of plants for classification. He is renowned for his investigation into the reproduction of plants and for being the first to note that, in general, living cells contain a nucleus. In 1827 he first observed the movement of fine particles in a liquid, which was named 'Brownian movement'.

Browning, Elizabeth Barrett 1806–61
English poet
In her teens she damaged her spine, and was an invalid for a long time. *Poems* (1844) contained 'The Cry of the Children', an outburst against the employment of young children in factories. In 1845 she met **Robert Browning**, and married him the following year. They settled in Italy, where they became the centre of a literary circle. Her other works include *Aurora Leigh* (1856), *Sonnets from the Portuguese* (published in the *Poems* of 1850), *Last Poems* (1851), and several accomplished translations of classical literature.

Browning, Robert 1812–89
English poet
Browning's chief achievement was developing the narrative poem, to which he brought a new psychological insight: famous examples include 'The Pied Piper of Hamelin' (1845), 'Fra Lippo Lippi', 'Childe Roland to the Dark Tower Came' and 'Andrea del Sarto' (all 1855). He also wrote several plays, among them *Pippa Passes* (1841). From 1846 he was married to **Elizabeth Barrett Browning**, and settled with her in Italy. After the death of his wife (1861) he moved to London and wrote *The Ring and the Book* (1868–9).

Bruce, Robert, *later* **Robert I,** *commonly known as* **Robert the Bruce** 1274–1329
King of Scotland
Around 1297 he joined the Scottish revolt under **William Wallace** and in 1306, after much fighting against English and Scottish rivals, was crowned king. Two defeats in 1306 forced him to go into hiding, probably to Rathlin Island off the north coast of Ireland where, tradition has it, he was inspired to renew his attempts to defeat the English when he watched the repeated attempts of a spider to spin a web. His victory (24 June 1314) at Bannockburn, near Stirling, over a larger English army, left him in control of Scotland. The Declaration of Arbroath, a letter composed in 1320 by his chancellor, finally persuaded the Pope to recognize Robert as king in 1323. He was succeeded by his son David II.

Brueghel Pieter, the Elder, *also called* **'Peasant' Brueghel** c.1520–1569
Flemish artist
He was born in the village of Bruegel, near Breda. An early influence on his work was **Hieronymus Bosch**, and later he went to Italy. His work was highly regarded, particularly by **Rubens**, but his reputation went into decline until the beginning of the 20th century. His pictures, often commentaries derived from everyday sayings and proverbs, mainly depict earthy peasants engaging in all sorts of activities against a backdrop of well-observed landscape. This genre reached its highest expression in his later works, *The Blind Leading the Blind* (1568), *The Peasant Wedding* (1568) and *The Peasant Dance* (1568).

Brunel, Isambard Kingdom 1806–59
English engineer and inventor
He was employed by his father, the famous engineer Marc Isambard Brunel, and helped to plan the Thames Tunnel, and in 1829–31 he planned the Clifton Suspension Bridge (completed in 1864). He designed the *Great Western* (1838), the first steamship built to cross the Atlantic Ocean, and the *Great Eastern*, until 1899 the largest vessel ever built. In 1833 he was appointed engineer to the Great Western Railway.

Brunelleschi, *properly* **Filippo di Ser Brunellesco** 1377–1446
Italian architect, goldsmith and sculptor
He began as a goldsmith and later designed the dome of the cathedral in Florence: erected between 1420 and 1461, it is (measured diametrically) the largest in the world. Other well-known buildings by him in Florence include the churches Santo Spirito and San Lorenzo, and the Foundling Hospital. He was one of the figures responsible for the development of the Renaissance style in Florence, and is also noted for his innovative use of perspective.

Brüning, Heinrich 1885–1970
German politician
He became in 1929 leader of the predominantly Catholic Centre Party and then Chancellor (1930–2). Faced with the problems of economic depression, he attempted to rule by decree, but was eventually forced out of office by **Paul von Hindenburg** to make way for the more conservative Franz von Papen.

Buchan, John, 1st Baron Tweedsmuir 1875–1940
Scottish writer and statesman
After serving in World War I he became an MP and later a peer and Governor-General of Canada. His strength as a writer was for fast-moving adventure stories, which include *Prester John* (1910), *Huntingtower* (1922) and *Witch Wood* (1927). He became best known, however, for his spy thrillers featuring Richard Hannay: *The Thirty-Nine Steps* (1915), *Greenmantle* (1916), *The Three Hostages* (1924), and others.

Buddha ('the enlightened one') c.563–c.483BC
The title of Prince Siddhartha Gautama, the founder of Buddhism
Born into a royal family in Nepal, when he was about 30 years old he left the luxuries of the court, and after six years of extreme poverty achieved enlightenment when sitting beneath a banyan tree near Buddh Gaya in Bihar. For the next 40 years he taught, gaining many disciples and followers. His system retained many aspects of Hinduism, the keynote of it being that 'Nirvana', or spiritual tranquillity, is to be attained by devotion to certain rules: only then can release from the cycle of death and rebirth be achieved. After dominating India, Buddhism began to decline there in the 7th and 8th centuries, but spread to Tibet, Sri Lanka, Myanmar, Thailand, China and Japan, where it is still popular.

Bunsen, Robert Wilhelm 1811–99
German chemist and physicist
He was a talented experimentalist and inventor, although the 'Bunsen burner' for which he is best known is a modification of something developed in England by **Michael Faraday**. He shared the discovery of spectrum analysis, in 1859, with Gustav Kirchhoff. This facilitated the discovery of new elements, including caesium and rubidium.

Bunyan, John 1628–88
English writer and preacher
In 1660 he was arrested while preaching without licence in a farmhouse near Ampthill, and during his twelve years' imprisonment in Bedford county jail he wrote numerous religious works. During a second, shorter period in jail he wrote the first part of *The Pilgrim's Progress* (1678), the religious allegory for which he is best known. The second part followed in 1684. Bunyan later became a pastor at Bedford.

Burke, Edmund 1729–97
Irish statesman and philosopher
One of the foremost of all British political thinkers, he trained as a lawyer and entered politics on the side of the Whig Party, becoming Secretary for Ireland in 1765. He was famous for his eloquence, and was known chiefly for his support for the American colonies and his opposition to the French revolution. Among his best-known writings are his *Vindication of Natural Society* (1756) and his *Reflections on the Revolution in France* (1790).

Burke, William 1792–1829
Irish murderer
With his partner William Hare he committed a series of murders in Edinburgh, supplying the bodies for dissection to Dr Robert Knox, an anatomist. Hare gave evidence in court against Burke, and probably died some time in the 1860s, while Burke was hanged.

Burnett, Frances Hodgson, *née* **Frances Eliza Hodgson** 1849–1924
US novelist
Her first literary success was *That Lass o' Lowrie's* (1877), and later works include plays, her most popular story *Little Lord Fauntleroy* (1886), the autobiographical *The One I Knew Best of All* (1893), *The Little Princess* (1905) and *The Secret Garden* (1909), still one of the best-loved classics of children's literature.

Burns, Robert 1759–96
Scottish poet and songwriter
Commonly regarded as the national poet of Scotland, he produced a huge number of poems celebrating love, lust and country life, and was a prolific collector and re-writer of songs such as 'John Anderson My Jo', 'A Red Red Rose' and 'Auld Lang Syne'. *Poems, Chiefly in the Scottish Dialect* (1786) featured many of his best-known works, among them 'Address to the Deil', 'To a Louse' and 'Address to a Haggis'. In 1790 he wrote his long narrative poem 'Tam o'Shanter'. He is also renowned for his many romantic adventures in Scotland and abroad, and Burns Suppers, with a traditional meal of haggis, are held annually worldwide on his birthday (25 January).

Burrell, Sir William 1861–1958
Scottish shipowner and art collector
The son of a shipping agent, he entered his father's business at the age of 15. During his lifetime he accumulated a magnificent collection of 8,000 works of art from all over the world, including modern French paintings, which he gave in 1944 to the city of Glasgow, and which is now known as the Burrell Collection.

Burton, Richard, *originally* **Richard Walter Jenkins** 1925–84
Welsh stage and film actor
His first Hollywood film was *My Cousin Rachel* (1952), which was followed by films including *The Robe* (1953), *Cleopatra* (1963), *The Spy Who Came in from the Cold* (1965), *Who's Afraid of Virginia Woolf* (1968), *Where Eagles Dare* (1969) and *Equus* (1977). In 1954 he was the narrator in the famous radio production of **Dylan Thomas**'s *Under Milk Wood*. He had two well-publicized marriages to **Elizabeth Taylor**.

Bush, George W(alker) 1946–
43rd President of the USA
The son of George Bush, 41st US President, his early career was in the oil industry. He became Governor of Texas in 1994 and was elected president in the 2000 and 2004 elections. In contrast to the Clinton years, his policies were notably right of centre. As a president with little experience in foreign affairs, most commentators anticipated a withdrawal of the USA from the world stage, but in 2001, following terrorist attacks on New York and Washington, Bush was plunged into the international arena and became committed to military action in Afghanistan and Iraq.

Byron (of Rochdale), George Gordon Noel Byron, 6th Baron *known as* **Lord Byron** 1788–1824
English poet
In 1798 he gained his title on the death of his great-uncle. After several years of travel in Europe, he produced the poetry collection *Childe Harold's Pilgrimage* (1812), which became widely popular. Later works include *Beppo* (1818), *A Vision of Judgment* (1822) and the satirical *Don Juan* (1819–24). The lover of numerous women, in 1815 he married an heiress, Anne Isabella Milbanke, who left him in 1816 after the birth of a daughter, Ada (later Countess of **Lovelace**). In 1823 he joined Greek insurgents who had risen against the Turks in the Greek War of independence, and he died of marsh fever at Missolonghi. A friend of many of the Romantic poets, he gave to

Europe the concept of the 'Byronic hero', passionate but with dark character flaws.

Cabot, John, *originally* **Giovanni Caboto** c.1450–c.1500
Italian navigator and explorer, the discoverer of mainland North America
Born in Genoa, he moved to England around 1490. In 1497, under the patronage of King Henry VII, he sailed from Bristol with two ships in search of a route to Asia, accompanied by his three sons. On 24 June, after 52 days at sea, he sighted land (probably Cape Breton Island, Nova Scotia), and claimed North America for England.

Cabot, Sebastian 1474–1557
Venetian navigator and cartographer
He is thought to have sailed with his father, **John Cabot**, on expeditions in search of the Northwest Passage to Asia. As pilot-major for Emperor Charles V he explored the coast of Brazil and the River Plate in 1526, but after a failed attempt at colonization he was imprisoned and banished for two years to Africa. In 1544 he published an engraved map of the world.

Cadbury, George 1839–1922
English Quaker businessman and social reformer
With his brother Richard Cadbury he built the Cadbury's cocoa business into a highly successful firm. In 1894, guided by his Quaker and liberal principles, he established for his workers the model village of Bournville, near Birmingham, which was a prototype for modern methods of housing and town planning. He also founded education and welfare trusts and campaigned actively for social reform.

Caedmon 7th century
Anglo-Saxon poet
He is the earliest Christian English poet known by name. According to **Bede**, he was an uneducated herdsman who in his old age received a divine call in a dream to sing of the Creation. He then became a monk at Whitby, where he turned other biblical themes into poetry. The original hymn of the Creation, only nine lines long, is the only surviving poem that can be attributed to him with any certainty.

Caesar, (Gaius) Julius 100 or 102–44BC
Roman general, statesman and dictator
In his early career Caesar extended Roman power to most of Gaul, and vividly described his campaigns in his *Commentaries*. He invaded Britain in 55BC and 54BC , but with limited success. He made his bid for absolute power in 49BC, famously crossing the Rubicon, the boundary between Cisalpine Gaul (the area of Gaul south of the Alps) and Italy, and after defeating **Pompey** was appointed dictator. **Cleopatra** became his mistress in 47BC. At the height of his power he was assassinated on the Ides (15th) of March. The conspirators, mostly aristocrats led by politicians Brutus and Cassius, believed that they were striking a blow for the restoration of republican freedom, but they merely succeeded in plunging the Roman world into a fresh round of civil wars. As a general, if not as a statesman, he ranks among the greatest in history.

Cage, John 1912–92
US composer
One of the 20th century's most influential avant-garde composers, his pieces, such as *4′ 33″* (1952) which is silent throughout and *Radio Music* (1956), for one to eight radios, challenge traditional ideas about what music is. He carried on a lifelong collaboration with choreographer Merce Cunningham. He was an authority on mushrooms.

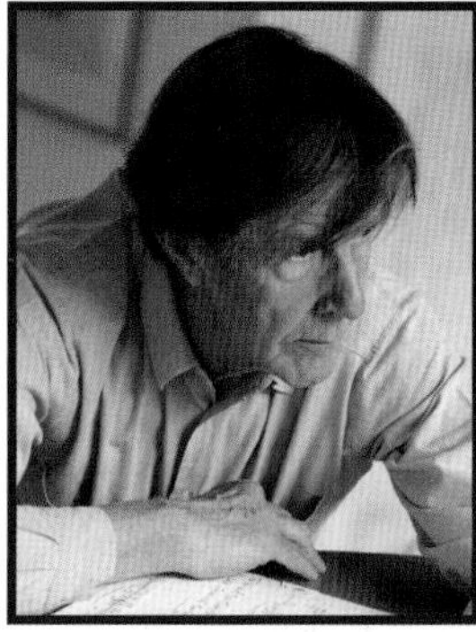

John Cage

Cagney, James Francis 1899–1986
US film actor
He made his film debut in *Sinner's Holiday* (1930), and his performance as the gangster in *The Public Enemy* (1931) brought him stardom. Subsequent films, not always in tough-guy roles, included *Angels with Dirty Faces* (1938), *The Roaring Twenties* (1939), *Yankee Doodle Dandy* (1942; Academy Award), *White Heat* (1949), *One, Two, Three* (1961) and *Ragtime* (1981).

Caine, Sir Michael, *originally* **Maurice Micklewhite** 1933–
English film actor
He won attention for his performance as an aristocratic officer in *Zulu* (1963), and his stardom continued with roles in *The Ipcress File* (1965), *Alfie* (1966), *The Italian Job* (1969) and *Get Carter* (1971). A prolific performer, his reputation for professionalism has withstood his appearance in several inferior films and he has enhanced superior material like *Sleuth* (1972) and *Educating Rita* (1983). He won an Academy Award for *Hannah and Her Sisters* (1986) and again for *The Cider House Rules* (1999).

Caligula, *properly* **Gaius Julius Caesar Germanicus** AD12–41
Roman emperor
After succeeding **Tiberius** in AD37, he banished or murdered most of his own family (excepting his uncle **Claudius** and sister Drusilla), executed and confiscated the property of many citizens of Rome, and awarded himself extravagant honours, hoping to be made a god. His brief but traumatic reign ended when he was assassinated.

Callas, Maria, *stage name of* **Maria Meneghini**, *née* **Kalogeropoulos** 1923–77
US soprano
One of the greatest of all sopranos, the fierce but truthful drama of her performances, her tumultuous personal life (including a long relationship with **Aristotle Onassis**), and her exceptional beauty all added to her fascination in the mind of the public. Driven perhaps too hard, her voice began to fail early, and she gave her last operatic performance at Covent Garden in 1965.

Calloway, Cab(ell) 1907–94
US jazz bandleader and singer
He became a national figure when his band succeeded **Duke Ellington**'s at Harlem's Cotton Club in 1931, and had hits that year with the songs 'Minnie The Moocher' (his signature tune) and 'Kicking The Gong Around', both containing streetwise drug references. His scat-style catchphrases and flamboyant presentation remained characteristic throughout a long career, in which he also acted in stage musicals and in films.

Calvin, John 1509–64
French theologian
One of the most important religious reformers of the 16th century, Calvin spent his early years preaching throughout France. He settled in Geneva in 1542, where he succeeded in controlling virtually all the affairs of the city and the social and religious life of its citizens. Calvin's contribution to Protestantism was twofold: he gave a system to its doctrine and organized its ecclesiastical discipline. His commentaries cover most of the Old Testament and the whole of the New (except the Revelation). In 1559 he founded a theological academy at Geneva that later became the university.

Calvin, Melvin 1911–97
US chemist
He is known for discovering the Calvin cycle which enables plants to convert carbon dioxide and water into organic compounds, and was awarded the Nobel Prize for chemistry in 1961.

Camus, Albert 1913–60
French writer
He was active in the French Resistance during World War II, and later became co-editor with **Jean-Paul Sartre** of the left-wing newspaper *Combat*. A key figure in the existentialist philosophical movement, his novels include *The Outsider* (1942), *The Myth of Sisyphus* (1942), *The Rebel* (1951), *The Plague* (1947), *The Fall* (1956), and an unfinished autobiographical novel, *The First Man* (English translation 1995), published after his death in a car accident. He also wrote several plays and was awarded the 1957 Nobel Prize for literature.

Canaletto, *properly* **Giovanni Antonio Canal** 1697–1768
Italian painter
He is known for his dramatic and picturesque views of Venice, which became immensely popular with foreign visitors and brought him great commercial success. Between 1746 and 1756 he worked in England, where his views of London and elsewhere also proved popular. His nephew and pupil Bernardo Bellotto became known as Canaletto the Younger.

Canute, *also known as* **Cnut the Great** or **Knut Sveinsson** c.995–1035
King of England, Denmark and Norway
The son of Svein I Haraldsson, 'Fork-Beard', in 1015 he challenged **Ethelred II**, the Unready, and had gained all of England by 1016. He inherited the throne of Denmark from his brother (1018) and also seized the throne of Norway in 1030. The story of his apparent attempt to turn back the tide has been misunderstood: in fact, he was trying to demonstrate to his courtiers that only God could control the tide, not man. When he died, his Anglo-Scandinavian Empire quickly disintegrated.

Capote, Truman 1924–84
US writer
Other Voices, Other Rooms (1948), his first novel, revealed his talent for sympathetic description of small-town life in the deep South. *The Grass Harp* (1951) was a fantasy performed against a background of the Alabama of his childhood. Other works are *Breakfast at Tiffany's* (1958), which became a highly successful film, *In Cold Blood* (1966), described by the author as a 'non-fiction novel' about a murder in Kansas, *Music for Chameleons* (1980) and *Answered Prayers* (extracts published 1975).

Caratacus or **Caractacus** or **Caradoc** fl.40–52AD
British chieftain
The son of the chieftain Cymbeline of the Catuvellauni tribe, he fought against the Romans (AD43–50), but was eventually defeated. His wife and daughters were captured, his brothers surrendered, and he himself was handed over by Cartimandua, queen of the Brigantes tribe. He was taken to Rome (AD51), and exhibited in triumph by the Emperor **Claudius**, but according to the Roman historian **Tacitus** his forceful speech gained him a pardon.

Caravaggio, *properly* **Michelangelo Merisi da Caravaggio** 1571–1610
Italian painter
Born in Caravaggio, near Bergamo, he trained in Milan, but moved to Rome in the 1590s. The *Life of Saint Matthew* cycle in the Contarelli Chapel of the church of San Luigi dei Francesi and the *Conversion of Saint Paul* and the *Crucifixion of Saint Peter* in the Cerasi Chapel of Santa Maria del Popolo, both in Rome, incorporate highly original, strongly lit, intensely realistic figures emerging dramatically from dark shadow. His work was often controversial as he used models off the street for biblical characters. In 1606 he fled Rome after killing a man in a brawl, and spent the rest of his life wandering between Naples, Sicily and Malta. He is widely regarded as the greatest Italian painter of the 17th century.

Carlyle, Thomas 1795–1881
Scottish historian and essayist
One of the most influential of Victorian writers, his first major work on social philosophy was *Sartor Resartus, The French Revolution* (1837) and *Past and Present* (1843). Carlyle also helped to introduce German Romantic literature to a British audience with his translations of **Goethe** and other authors.

Carnegie, Andrew 1835–1919
US industrialist and philanthropist
He was born in Dunfermline, Scotland, the son of a weaver who emigrated to Pittsburgh, USA, in 1848. In 1865 he founded his first company, which grew into the largest iron and steel works in the USA. He later gave over £70 million to good causes, including public libraries throughout the USA and Great Britain, the Pittsburgh Carnegie Institute, the Washington Carnegie Institution, and substantial gifts to Scottish and US universities. Besides an autobiography (1920), he wrote philosophical essays including *The Gospel of Wealth* (1889) and *Problems of Today* (1908).

Carnot, (Nicolas Léonard) Sadi 1796–1832
French physicist
After studying engineering, from 1819 he concentrated on scientific research. In his sole published work, he was the first to analyse the working cycle and efficiency of the steam engine according to scientific principles, and arrived at an early form of the second law of thermodynamics. His work laid the foundation for that of **William Kelvin**, **James Joule** and others.

Caro, Sir Anthony 1924–
English sculptor
After working with Sir **Henry Moore**, he developed his characteristic abstract style, typically involving large pieces of metal welded together and painted in primary colours, for example *Early One Morning* (1962). In his later work he has made reference to the traditions of the classical West and of India.

Carroll, Lewis, *pseudonym of* **Charles Lutwidge Dodgson** 1832–98
English children's writer
A lecturer in mathematics at Oxford, his most famous book, *Alice's Adventures in Wonderland* (1865), was written for Alice Liddell and her sisters, the daughters of the Dean of his college. A sequel, *Through the Looking-Glass and What Alice Found There*, appeared in 1871. They were illustrated by John Tenniel, and their characters, the Cheshire Cat, the White Rabbit, the March Hare and others, have since become known, enjoyed and studied worldwide. His other works include *The Hunting of the Snark* (1876) and *Sylvie and Bruno* (2 volumes, 1889 and 1893). He was also a pioneer photographer, and took many portraits, particularly of young girls.

Carson, Rachel Louise 1907–64
US naturalist and science writer
She became well known with *The Sea Around Us* (1951), which warned of the increasing danger of large-scale marine pollution, and the hard-hitting *Silent Spring* (1962), which directed public concern to the problems caused by pesticides and their effect on wildlife. The resulting controls on their use owe much to her work, which also contributed to the growing conservationist movement.

Carter, Jimmy (James Earl) 1924–
39th President of the USA
He served in the US navy until 1953, when he took over the family peanut business and other business enterprises. After becoming Governor of Georgia (1970–4) he was elected president in 1976. Liked for his air of informality, honesty and religious fervour, and his reforming stance on energy, health, civil rights and defence issues, he achieved a notable success in 1978 brokering the Camp David Accords between Israel and Egypt, but his popularity plummeted in 1979–80 as a result of the seizure of US embassy hostages in Iran. He was defeated by the Republican **Ronald Reagan** in the 1980 election. He has since worked as a prolific human-rights campaigner.

Cartier-Bresson, Henri 1908–2004
French photographer and artist
After working with the film director Jean Renoir, and fighting with the Resistance during World War II, he co-founded the independent photographic agency Magnum Photos. He worked only in black-and-white, concerning himself exclusively with capturing spontaneous moments illustrating contemporary life. In the mid-1970s he gave up photography, and returned to painting and drawing.

Henri Cartier-Bresson

Cartwright, John 1740–1824
English reformer
The brother of Edmund Cartwright, inventor of the power loom, he is known as 'the Father of Reform'. He served in the navy (1758–70), but after supporting the colonists against the British government in the American War of Independence he wrote about politics, advocating annual elections for parliament, the secret ballot, and votes for all men. He afterwards took up reform in farming, abolition of slavery, and the national defences.

Caruso, Enrico 1873–1921
Italian tenor
Born the 18th of 20 children, he made his first professional appearance in *Faust* (1895), then went to London (1902) and New York (1903). The great power and musical purity of his voice, combined with his acting ability, won him recognition as one of the finest tenors of all time.

Cash, Johnny (J R) 1932–2003
American country music singer, songwriter and guitarist
A complex and often deeply troubled personality, he became the best-known performer in country music in the 1960s, and helped spread it to a huge new audience. The success of his single 'I Walk The Line' established his style, and he was nicknamed, for his dress and demeanour, 'The Man In Black'.

Castro (Ruz), Fidel 1927–
Cuban revolutionary
A revolutionary from a young age, after several attempts to depose President Fulgencio Batista, in 1958 Castro mounted a successful coup and became Prime Minister. He proclaimed a 'Marxist–Leninist programme' and set about far-reaching reforms in agriculture, industry, and education. His routing of the US-backed Bay of Pigs invasion (1961) was balanced by consequent dependence on communist (mainly Soviet) aid and the near-disaster of the 1962 missile crisis, when the USA demanded that the USSR remove its missile installations from Cuba. After undergoing bowel surgery in 2006, he passed control of the government to his brother and vice-president, Raul.

Catherine II, the Great 1729–96
Empress of Russia from 1762
Born a Prussian princess, in 1745 she married Peter,

heir to the Russian throne, but the marriage was unhappy. Catherine became notorious for her love affairs, and after Peter's accession in 1762 (as Paul III) they lived separately; later Peter was dethroned and murdered, probably with Catherine's knowledge, and Catherine was made empress. Under her rule the dominions and power of Russia rapidly increased, but internal politics was marked by court intrigue and the suppression of any dissent. Catherine was renowned for her intelligence and learning, and corresponded throughout her life with **Voltaire**.

Cavendish, Henry 1731–1810
English natural philosopher and chemist
His family's wealth enabled him to devote his life entirely to scientific pursuits. Among his achievements, he discovered hydrogen, and demonstrated that it was the lightest of all the gases. He worked out that hydrogen and oxygen combined to produce water, which could not therefore be an element. The famous 'Cavendish experiment' enabled him to measure the mean density of the Earth.

Ceauşescu, Nicolae 1918–89
Romanian politician
In 1965 he succeeded as Communist Party leader. Under his leadership, Romania became increasingly independent of the USSR and pursued its own foreign policy, for which Ceauşescu was praised by many Western governments. In internal affairs he put in place a strong personality cult and appointed family members to public office. He ruthlessly forced national minorities to adopt Romanian culture, and replaced traditional villages by collectives of concrete apartments. In 1989 he was deposed and shot with his wife, Elena.

Celsius, Anders 1701–44
Swedish astronomer
He described the Celsius temperature scale in 1742 before the Swedish Academy of Sciences. Two fixed points had been chosen: one (0 degrees) at the boiling point of water, the other (100 degrees) at the melting point of ice. A few years after his death, colleagues at Uppsala began to use the familiar version of this centigrade scale, in which 100 degrees is the boiling point.

Cervantes (Saavedra), Miguel de 1547–1616
Spanish writer, author of Don Quixote
After service as a soldier, he began writing. His first efforts were only moderately successful, but *Don Quixote*, the first part of which came out in Madrid in early 1605, was immediately popular. Though it seems to be one of the most carelessly written of all great books, *Don Quixote* is widely regarded as the precursor of the modern novel, as well as a great comic epic in its own right. Cervantes's other works include various short tales, poetry and plays.

Cézanne, Paul 1839–1906
French painter
A leading figure in Post-Impressionism and the development of modern art, his main early influence was **Camille Pissarro**, who brought him into the realm of Impressionism. In his mature work he emphasized the underlying forms of nature ('the cylinder, the sphere and the cone'), and so became the forerunner of the Cubism movement in painting. Among his most famous paintings are *The Card Players* (1890–2), *Man in a Straw Hat* (c.1871), his self-portrait of 1869, *Rocky Landscape in Aix* (c.1887), *The Gardener* (c.1906) and *The Old Woman with Beads* (c.1897–8).

Chain, Sir Ernst Boris 1906–79
British biochemist
After work including a study of snake venom, he encountered Sir **Alexander Fleming**'s paper on penicillin (1929), discovered that penicillin was not an enzyme but a new small molecule, and greatly improved its purification. Fleming, Chain and Florey later shared the 1945 Nobel Prize for physiology or medicine.

Chamberlain, (Arthur) Neville 1869–1940
English statesman
The son of the politician Joseph Chamberlain, he was a Conservative MP from 1918, and became Prime Minister in 1937. For the sake of peace, and with the country unprepared for war, he chose initially to follow a policy of appeasement of Italy and Germany and signed the 1938 Munich Agreement, claiming to have found 'peace in our time'. Having pressed on with rearmament in the meantime, he declared war in 1939. After criticism of his war leadership, in 1940 he was replaced by **Winston Churchill**.

Chandragupta I or **Sandracottus** c.350–c.250BC
Hindu Emperor
The founder of the Mauryan Empire, he is considered the greatest emperor of India. He conquered the Magadha kingdom and eventually controlled much of India. In c.300BC he defeated the Macedonian king Seleucus I Nicator, and won the territories in the north of India previously held by Alexander the Great. The Greek historian Megasthenes was later sent to his court by Seleucus I Nicator, and here he gathered information for his work *Indica* (from which much of the information about India in this period comes).

Chanel, Coco (Gabrielle) 1883–1971
French fashion designer
She began to revolutionize women's fashions during the 1920s, when, for the first time in a century, women were liberated from the restriction of corsets. The combination of simple elegance and comfort in her designs gave them immediate appeal, and many of the features she introduced, such as the 'little black dress', have retained their popularity. She is also famous for her perfume, Chanel No.5.

Chaplin, Charlie (Sir Charles Spencer) 1889–1977
English film actor and director
Born in London, by the age of eight he was a seasoned stage performer, and went to Hollywood in 1914. He quickly became the foremost star of the silent era, adopting the bowler hat, out-turned feet, moustache and walking-cane which became his trademarks in films such as *The Kid* (1920), *The Gold Rush* (1924) and *Shoulder Arms* (1918), and increasingly turned to writing, directing and producing. Later films with sound included *Modern Times* (1936), *The Great Dictator* (1940) and *Limelight* (1952).

Charlemagne ('Charles the Great'), *Latin* **Carolus Magnus** 747–814
King of the Franks and Christian Emperor of the West
In 771 he became sole ruler of the Franks. The first years of his reign were spent subduing and Christian-

izing neighbouring kingdoms, notably the Saxons to the north-east, the Lombards of northern Italy and the Moors in Spain. In 800 he entered Italy to support the Pope, who crowned him Emperor of the Romans. The remaining years of his reign were spent in consolidating his vast empire, which reached from the Ebro in northern Spain to the Elbe. He was in some ways an enlightened ruler, promoting education, architecture and the arts, but his empire did not survive long after his death. Charlemagne and his followers are the central figures in much of the period's literature.

Charlie, Bonnie Prince See **Stuart, Prince Charles Edward**

Charles, Jacques-Alexandre-César 1746–1823
French experimental physicist
He made himself an expert in popular scientific display, taking part in the first manned ascent in a hydrogen balloon in Paris in December 1783. He invented a megascope (for projecting an enlarged image), a hydrometer and a goniometer (for measuring angles of crystals). He also formulated Charles's Law which relates the volume of a gas at constant pressure to its absolute temperature.

Charles, Ray, *originally* **Ray Charles Robinson** 1930–2004
US singer and pianist
He was blind from the age of five and orphaned at 15. With 'I've got a Woman' (1955) he established an influential new style of rhythm and blues which introduced elements of gospel music. 'Hit the Road Jack' (1961) and 'Unchain my Heart' (1962) were further hits.

Charles I 1600–49
King of Great Britain and Ireland
The son of **James VI and I**, he succeeded to the throne in 1625. From 1628 his Catholic wife, Henrietta Maria of France, came to exercise growing influence over the affairs of state, and after Charles dissolved three parliaments in the first four years of his reign, he ruled without one for twelve years. Hostility towards some of his policies forced him to recall parliament in 1640, and he was compelled to approve the Act of Attainment, by which parliament could not be dissolved without its consent. In 1642 his arrival in the House of Commons to supervise the arrest of five MPs made civil war inevitable. After three years of fighting, the war effectively came to an end with defeat at the Battle of Naseby, but the king finally surrendered at Newark on 5 May 1646. In 1647 he escaped to the Isle of Wight, but he was soon recaptured and returned to stand trial. His refusals to plead were interpreted as a silent confession, and in January 1649 he was beheaded. Two of his three sons were eventually to take the throne, as **Charles II** and **James VII and II**.

Charles II, *called* **the Merry Monarch** 1630–85
King of Great Britain and Ireland
He was the son of **Charles I** and the years of his reign are known in English history as the Restoration Period. When his father was executed in 1649, and after losing the Battle of Worcester to the forces of **Oliver Cromwell**, Charles fled to France and the Netherlands. As a result of successful negotiations in 1659 to restore the monarchy, he returned to England in 1660. His failure to produce an heir compelled him to consent to the marriage in 1677 of his Protestant niece Mary (the future Mary II) to William of Orange (the future **William III**), and anti-Catholicism returned after a fabricated account of a 'Popish plot' to murder the king. In the next three years the future of the Stuart Dynasty was uncertain, with the Whigs favouring the exclusion of Charles's brother (the future **James VII and II**) and the Tories opposed to any change to the succession. The Tories and Charles won the day, and effectively excluded the Whigs from power.

Charlton, Bobby (Sir Robert) 1937–
English footballer
He played with Manchester United throughout his career (1954–73), and captained the team to victory in the 1968 European Cup. He played 106 games for England between 1957 and 1973, scoring a record 49 goals, and was a member of the England side that won the World Cup in 1966. After a brief spell of management with Preston North End, he turned to running highly successful coaching schools. He is the younger brother of the footballer Jack Charlton.

Chaucer, Geoffrey c.1345–1400
English poet
In 1359 he served in the Hundred Years' War in France, and from 1368 he travelled abroad on the king's service; he later became a high-ranking customs officer. His greatest work, probably begun in the late 1380s, was *The Canterbury Tales*, some 17,000 lines of verse and prose recounting the tales told by a group of pilgrims on their journey to Canterbury. His other work includes *The Parliament of Fowls*, *Troilus and Criseyde* and *The Legend of Good Women*. Chaucer was the first great English poet, and he established the southern English dialect as the literary language of England.

Chekhov, Anton Pavlovich 1860–1904
Russian writer
The author of numerous short stories and some of the best-loved plays of world theatre, he originally qualified as a doctor. His stories, which have influenced many writers, include such masterpieces as 'Ward Number Six', 'The Duel' and 'The Grasshopper', and his plays include *The Seagull*, *Uncle Vanya*, *The Cherry Orchard* and *The Three Sisters*. His work often depicts the lives of sensitive, hopeful, struggling people, at the mercy of forces almost always too strong for them.

Chiang Kai-shek (Jiang Jieshi) 1887–1975
Chinese general and politician
He fought for **Sun Yat-sen** in the 1911 revolution. In 1926 he commanded the army which aimed to unify China, a task which he completed by 1928. He consolidated the Guomindang (nationalist) regime, and opposed Japan, but in 1948 communist forces overwhelmed his government and he was forced to withdraw to Formosa (Taiwan). There he set up a new Chinese national government, aided by the USA.

Chomsky, (Avram) Noam 1928–
US linguist and political activist
His grammatical theories developed out of his interest in logic and mathematics, and he tends to believe that language ability is built into the mind before birth. Among his major works on linguistic theory are *Aspects of the Theory of Syntax* (1965) and *Language and Mind* (1968). Politically radical, he has been an outspoken opponent of American foreign policy in

books such as *At War with Asia* (1970) and *Powers and Prospects* (1996).

Chopin, Frédéric François 1810–49
Polish composer and pianist
Strongly influenced by Slavonic folk music (notably the mazurka, a lively Polish dance) Chopin wrote mainly for the piano. His numerous compositions include 50 mazurkas, 25 preludes, 19 nocturnes, 13 waltzes, 3 sonatas, 2 piano concertos, and a funeral march. In 1836 he was introduced to the writer **George Sand** by **Franz Liszt**, and lived with her from 1838 to 1847. He died from tuberculosis.

Christ See **Jesus Christ**

Christie, Dame Agatha Mary Clarissa, *née* **Miller** 1890–1976
English writer
She wrote more than 70 classic detective novels, including those featuring the popular characters Hercule Poirot, a Belgian detective, and Miss Jane Marple, a village spinster. Among her stage plays is *The Mousetrap*, which continued its record-breaking run in London from 1952 into the 21st century. Her best-known novels are *The Mysterious Affair at Styles* (1920), the first featuring Poirot, *The Murder of Roger Ackroyd* (1926), *Murder at the Vicarage* (1930), introducing Miss Marple, *Murder on the Orient Express* (1934) and *Death on the Nile* (1937). She also wrote under the pen name Mary Westmacott.

Churchill, Sir Winston Leonard Spencer 1874–1965
English statesman
He served in the army, and in 1900 he entered parliament as a Conservative MP, but joined the Liberal majority in 1906. He was Secretary of State for War and Air from 1919 to 1921, but then found himself out of favour, and his warnings of the rising Nazi threat were unheeded. However, in 1940, **Neville Chamberlain** stepped down and Churchill became Prime Minister of the coalition that was to see the country through the war years. He was an accomplished speaker, able to convince the people that even in the blackest moments Britain would be victorious. He drew an initially reluctant American people into the battle, and masterminded the strategy adopted for the Battle of Britain and the North African campaign. He was defeated in the general election of 1945, but became Prime Minister again in 1951, before giving up the leadership in 1955, aged 81.

Sir Winston Churchill

Cicero, Marcus Tullius 106–43BC
Roman orator, statesman and man-of-letters
He was born into a wealthy provincial family, and became a senator and supporter of **Pompey** the Great. A gifted orator and politician, his suppression of the conspiracy of Catiline earned him the title 'father of his country'. He wrote several works on rhetoric and philosophy, and is best known for his essays *On Old Age*, *On Friendship* and *On Duty*. His letters are an important resource for historians. He was murdered by soldiers of **Mark Antony**.

Cid, El, *properly* **Rodrigo** or **Ruy Díaz de Vivar** or **Bivar**, *also called* **El Campeador** c.1043–1099
Spanish hero
Both soldier of fortune and patriot, he was constantly fighting. In 1081 he was banished and served both Spaniards and Moors. He besieged and captured Valencia from the Moors (1093–4) and became its ruler. The favourite hero of Spain, he has inspired many legends, poems, and ballads, as well as Corneille's *Le Cid* (1636). 'El Cid' means 'the Lord'.

Clapton, Eric 1945–
English rock and blues guitarist
One of the most significant white performers of black music, particularly the blues, he began his recording career with The Yardbirds before forming the enormously influential trio Cream. Later work as a solo artist established his middle of the road style. The tragic death of his four-year-old son is commemorated in one of his most successful songs, 'Tears In Heaven' (1992). In 1994, he returned to a straight blues idiom on his *From The Cradle* project.

Clare, John 1793–1864
English peasant poet
He had little education, and served for a time as a soldier. In 1817 he published *Proposals for Publishing a Collection of Trifles in Verse* at his own expense, but got no subscribers. It led, however, to the publication of his *Poems Descriptive of Rural Life* (1820), which were well received. His other published works were *Village Minstrel* (1821), *The Shepherd's Calendar* (1827) and *Rural Muse* (1835). He lived in poverty, became insane, and died in an asylum.

Claudel, Camille 1864–1943
French sculptor
Sister of the poet Paul Claudel, she decided to become a sculptor at an early age and in 1884 was introduced to **Auguste Rodin**. She became his student, model and mistress, and produced skilfully executed works such as *The Waltz* (1895). After a fiery relationship, Claudel and Rodin parted company in 1898, but she continued to sculpt, and briefly achieved great renown (c.1900). Her later life was dogged by mental illness.

Claudius I, *full name* **Tiberius Claudius Drusus Nero Germanicus** 10BC–AD54
Fourth Roman emperor
He was the nephew of the Emperor **Tiberius**. After surviving **Caligula**'s reign, and despite physical disabilities including a limp and a stutter, he became emperor in AD41. His period of rule was marked by an expansion of the Roman Empire, notably the conquest of Britain. His third wife, Valeria Messalina, was notorious for her many lovers, and he finally had her executed (AD48). He next married his niece,

Agrippina, who persuaded him to adopt **Nero**, her son by an earlier husband. Agrippina is believed to have poisoned Claudius with a dish of mushrooms.

Clay, Cassius See **Ali, Muhammad**

Clemenceau, Georges Eugène Benjamin 1841–1929
French statesman
Initially leader of the radicals (on the extreme Left), as Prime Minister (1906–9 and 1917–20) his determination spurred France to make the effort to pursue victory in World War I. He presided at the Paris Peace Conference (1919). Nicknamed 'the Tiger' for the ferocity of his attacks on his political opponents, he was equally renowned for his journalism, and notably campaigned for the release of Alfred Dreyfus, who had been transported after being wrongly accused of passing confidential documents to a foreign government.

Cleopatra 69–30BC
Queen of Egypt
The last of the Macedonian dynasty of the Ptolemies, she was supported in her claim to the throne by **Julius Caesar**, who became her lover and probably the father of her child Caesarion. After Caesar's death she became the lover of **Mark Antony**, also bearing him children. War was declared against Cleopatra by **Augustus**, and after the Battle of Actium (31BC), Antony and Cleopatra fled to Egypt. Antony, misled by a false report of Cleopatra's death, committed suicide by falling on his sword, and Cleopatra took her own life, it is said by causing an asp (the Egyptian symbol of royalty) to bite her breast.

Clive (of Plassey), Robert Clive, Baron, *also called* **Clive of India** 1725–74
English general and colonial administrator
After joining the East India Company, he fought against French and Indian forces in India, achieving his greatest victory at Plassey (1757). For three years he was sole ruler of Bengal. In 1761 he entered the British parliament, and in 1762 was made Baron Clive of Plassey. He was sent to India again in 1764 as Governor and Commander-in-Chief of Bengal, but on his return to England in 1767 he was caught up in controversy over his handling of the East India Company's affairs, and committed suicide soon afterwards.

Cobbett, William 1763–1835
English writer and champion of the poor
His best-known work is probably *Rural Rides* (1830), a picture of a vanishing rural world, but he wrote some 40 or more other books on various political and moral themes. By turns a journalist, bookshop owner, farmer, English teacher and MP for Oldham, he lived for much of his life in the USA. He was an uncompromising champion of political and social reform, and spent two years in Newgate Prison, London (1810–12), for his opposition to flogging in the army.

Cobden, Richard, *known as* **the Apostle of Free Trade** 1804–65
English economist and politician
He became an MP in 1841 and was a major force in the abolition of the Corn Laws (import taxes on cheap foreign grain) in 1846. He is also remembered for opposing Britain's involvement in the Crimean War (1853–6).

Cocteau, (Clement Eugène) Jean 1889–1963
French poet, playwright and film director
A friend and supporter of **Picasso**, **Stravinsky**, Giorgio de Chirico and the group of young French composers known as Les Six, he was an actor, director, scenario writer, novelist, critic and artist in the modernist vein. Significant works are novels such as *Les Enfants terribles* (1929) and plays such as *Orpheus* (1926). His films include *The Blood of a Poet* (1930) and *Beauty and the Beast* (1945).

Cohen, Leonard Norman 1934–
Canadian poet, novelist and singer
His novels include *The Favorite Game* (1963) and *Beautiful Losers* (1966). The first of his many albums as a singer-songwriter, noted for their bleak quality, was *The Songs of Leonard Cohen*, which appeared in 1968, the same year as his *Selected Poems*.

Cole, Nat 'King', *originally* **Nathaniel Adams Coles** 1919–65
US singer and pianist
He played the organ in his father's church before embarking on a career as a jazz pianist in the 1930s. His King Cole Trio (1939–51) made its first hit record, 'Straighten Up and Fly Right', in 1943. Remembered mainly as a vocalist, Cole's mellow, caressing voice produced a series of hit ballads, including 'Mona Lisa' (1950) and 'Unforgettable' (1951). He began acting in films in 1943, and became the first black American to host his own television show in 1956, but was subject to racist harassment when he bought a house in the Beverly Hills area.

Coleridge, Samuel Taylor 1772–1834
English poet
One of the founders of the Romantic movement in poetry, he studied for the Church and served briefly in the army. With his friend **William Wordsworth**, in 1798 he published *Lyrical Ballads*, a ground-breaking and enormously influential reaction against artificiality in poetry, which included his poem 'The Rime of the Ancient Mariner'. Opium addiction and marital breakdown limited his output in later years. In 1810 he settled in London, and in 1816 he published *Christabel and other poems*, which included the fragment 'Kubla Khan'. Among his prose is the collection *Biographia Literaria* (1817), and he published translations of **Schiller**.

Collins, Wilkie (William) 1824–89
English novelist
An early writer of novels dealing with mystery, suspense, crime and detection, his best work was written in the 1860s when he produced *The Woman in White* (1860), *No Name* (1862), *Armadale* (1866) and *The Moonstone* (1868). Perhaps because of his poor health and opium addiction, his later novels were less successful.

Coltrane, John William 1926–67
US jazz saxophonist and composer
One of the most influential jazz performers of his era, he worked with **Miles Davis** in the 1950s before going on to develop his so-called 'sheets of sound' style, as in *Giant Steps* (1959). Other important recordings include *A Love Supreme* (1964).

Columbus, Christopher 1451–1506
Genoese explorer
Hoping to reach India by a westward route, and

financed by Ferdinand and Isabella of Castile, in August 1492 he set sail in command of three ships, reaching land on 12 October (probably Watling's Island in the Bahamas). He later visited Cuba and Hispaniola (Haiti) and returned to Spain on 15 March 1493. He made several later voyages resulting in the establishment of various colonies and the discovery of the South American mainland. His last great voyage (1502–4) was along the south side of the Gulf of Mexico. He died at Valladolid in Spain.

Confucius, *Latin for* **Kongfuzi (K'ung-fu-tzu, 'the Master K'ung')** 551–479BC
Chinese philosopher
Originally a high-ranking government official, after quarrels at court he became a teacher and writer. In the *Analects* and other works Confucius emerges as a great moral teacher who tried to replace the old religious rituals with moral values as the basis of social and political order. In his Way (*dao*) he emphasized the practical virtues of benevolence (*ren*), fairness (*shu*), respect and personal effort. Confucianism became the state religion of China, which, until recently, it remained.

Congreve, William 1670–1729
English dramatist and poet
One of the most successful playwrights of the Restoration era, his comedies include *The Old Bachelor* and *The Double Dealer* (both 1693), though his best-known play is *Love for Love* (1695). In 1697 his only tragedy, *The Mourning Bride*, appeared, best remembered for the quotations 'music hath charms to soothe a savage breast' and 'nor hell a fury like a woman scorned' (often misquoted as 'hell hath no fury like a woman scorned').

Connery, Sir Sean Thomas 1930–
Scottish film actor
After an early career working as a milkman and small-time actor, he was cast as secret agent James Bond in *Dr. No* (1962) and became an international star. He played the role on seven occasions until *Never Say Never Again* (1983). Other notable film roles include an army rebel in *The Hill* (1965), a detective-monk in *The Name of The Rose* (1986) and an Irish US policeman in *The Untouchables* (1987).

Conrad, Joseph, *originally* **Józef Teodor Konrad Nalecz Korzeniowski** 1857–1924
British novelist
Born of Polish parents, in 1878 he joined an English merchant ship and became a British citizen in 1884. His experiences at sea inspired much of his writing. His first novel was *Almayer's Folly* (1894), followed by *An Outcast of the Islands* (1896), *Lord Jim* (1900), *Heart of Darkness* (1902), *Nostromo* (1904), *The Secret Agent* (1907) and others. Works such as his semi-autobiographical *The Mirror of the Sea* (1906) and his *Personal Record* (1912) testify to his high artistic aims.

Constable, John 1776–1837
English landscape painter
His landscape work expressed his profound love of the country, and his interest in the effects of changing light and the movement of clouds across the sky. In 1824 he had a success with *The Haywain* (1821) in the Paris Salon, a great annual exhibition of works by living artists, and in 1825 at Lille with his *White Horse*. His later years were saddened by bereavements, ill health and depression, but he worked steadily, though his landscapes were frequently unsold. Other well-known works include *View on the Stour* (1819) and *Salisbury Cathedral* (1823).

Constantine I, *known as* **Constantine the Great**, *properly* **Flavius Valerius Aurelius Constantinus** c.274–337AD
Roman emperor
In AD306 he succeeded his father, Constantius Chlorus, as emperor of the West, and political complications increased until in AD308 there were six emperors. Constantine defeated one, Maxentius, on three occasions; afterwards he converted to Christianity, and gave civil rights to Christians throughout the empire. Later he became sole emperor of the West, and in AD323 defeated Licinius, emperor of the East, to become sole ruler of the Roman world. He chose Byzantium (modern day Istanbul) for his capital, and gave it the name of Constantinople ('City of Constantine'). Christianity became a state religion in AD324, and in AD325 the Nicene Creed, the most widely accepted Christian creed, was adopted.

Cook, James 1728–79
English navigator
His first important expedition was in command of the *Endeavour* for the Royal Society expedition to the Pacific, to observe the transit of Venus across the Sun (1768–71). On his return, he sailed around New Zealand and charted the east coast of Australia, which he claimed for Great Britain. On later voyages of discovery from 1772 he sailed around Antarctica, visited Tahiti and the New Hebrides, discovered New Caledonia and other island groups, and surveyed the west coast of North America, reaching Hawaii in January 1779, where he was killed in a quarrel with the islanders. Cook did more than any other navigator to add to our knowledge of the Pacific and the Southern Ocean.

Coolidge, (John) Calvin 1872–1933
30th President of the USA
Vice-President from 1921 to 1923, he succeeded as President on **Warren G Harding**'s death (1923), and was re-elected in 1924. Known for his cautious temperament, he was chiefly interested in building up the US economy and not greatly concerned with foreign policy, though his administration did see the signing of the Dawes Plan to reduce the reparations demanded from Germany after World War I, and the Kellogg–Briand Pact outlawing war as an instrument of foreign policy.

Copernicus, Nicolaus, *Latin name of* **Mikojaj Kopernik** 1473–1543
Polish astronomer
A mathematician, he pondered deeply on what he considered the unsatisfactory description of the world by **Ptolemy**, which had the Earth as the stationary centre of the universe, and became converted to the idea of a universe with the Sun at its centre. This was set out in his book *The Revolutions of the Celestial Spheres* (1543), in which the Earth is merely one of the planets, revolving around the Sun and rotating on its axis. The first printed copy of Copernicus's treatise, a work which fundamentally altered man's vision of the universe, reached its author on his death bed. It was later banned by the Catholic Church, and remained on the list of forbidden books until 1835.

Copland, Aaron 1900–90
US composer
A series of early works influenced by **Igor Stravinsky** and employing jazz idioms was followed by compositions which drew on US tradition and folk music. Of these, the ballets *Billy the Kid* (1938) and *Appalachian Spring* (1944), and *A Lincoln Portrait* (1942), for orator and orchestra, are typical. As well as ballets and film scores, he composed two operas and three symphonies. He wrote one of his best-known pieces of music, *Fanfare for the Common Man*, in 1942.

Cortés or **Cortéz, Hernán** or **Hernando** 1485–1547
Spanish conquistador and conqueror of Mexico
After taking part in the expedition to conquer Cuba in 1511, in 1518 he commanded an expedition into modern Mexico. With the assistance of local peoples, on 8 November 1519 he reached the capital, Tenochtitlán, and imprisoned the Aztec king Montezuma II. After many fierce battles Tenochtitlán was destroyed and Mexico City founded in its place; Montezuma was killed. In 1522 Cortés was appointed Governor and Captain-General of New Spain. He returned permanently to Spain in 1540.

Coulomb, Charles Augustin de 1736–1806
French physicist
His experiments on mechanical resistance resulted in 'Coulomb's law' concerning the relationship between friction and normal pressure (1779), and he became known for the torsion balance for measuring the force of magnetic and electrical attraction (1784–5). The unit of quantity of electrical charge is named after him.

Cousteau, Jacques Yves 1910–97
French naval officer and underwater explorer
He was partly responsible for the invention of the aqualung diving apparatus (1943), and in 1950 became commander of the oceanographic research ship *Calypso*, from which he made the first underwater film. His other achievements include developing the bathyscaphe (an underwater observation vessel) and promoting the Conshelf programme of 1962–5, which investigated the possibilities of undersea living. He is best known for the popularization of marine biology with his many films.

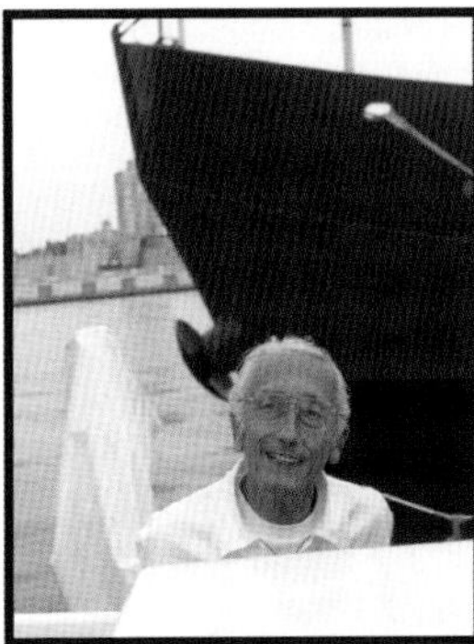
Jacques Cousteau

Coverdale, Miles 1488–1568
English Protestant reformer and biblical scholar
In 1535 he published in Zurich, Switzerland, the first translation of the whole Bible into English, with a dedication to **Henry VIII**. Many of the finest phrases in the Authorized Version of 1611 are directly due to Coverdale. His later translations include the 'Great Bible' of 1539.

Coward, Sir Noël Peirce 1899–1973
English actor, playwright and composer
His first play, *I'll Leave It to You* (1920), was followed by many successes, including *Hay Fever* (1925), *Private Lives* (1930), *Blithe Spirit* (1941) and *This Happy Breed* (1943), all showing his satirical humour and gift for witty dialogue. He was a gifted singer and wrote the music for most of his works, including his play *Cavalcade* (1931), and for a series of revues, including *Words and Music* (1932) with its 'Mad Dogs and Englishmen'. He produced several films based on his own scripts, among them *In Which We Serve* (1942) and *Brief Encounter* (1945).

Cranmer, Thomas 1489–1556
English priest
He was consecrated Archbishop of Canterbury in 1533 and became a loyal supporter of **Henry VIII**, assisting him in his divorces from Catherine of Aragon and Anne of Cleves. After Henry's death in 1547 he compiled Edward VI's Book of Common Prayer and was a major force in the development of Anglican Protestantism. As a supporter of the Protestant Lady Jane Grey in her claim to the English throne, he was sent to the Tower of London by the Catholic queen Mary I, and with the bishops **Hugh Latimer** and Nicholas Ridley was burnt at the stake.

Crawford, Joan, *originally* **Lucille Le Sueur** 1906–77
US film actress
Hugely successful during the 1920s and 1930s in films such as *Untamed* (1929) and *Dancing Lady* (1933), she achieved success in later life cast in the roles of older women beset by emotional problems, as in *Mildred Pierce* (1945, Academy Award) and *Whatever Happened to Baby Jane?* (1962). Her adopted daughter Christina wrote a scathing attack on her in her book *Mommie Dearest* (1978), which was later made into a film.

Crazy Horse, *Sioux name* **Ta-Sunko-Witko** c.1849–77
Sioux Chief
Born in South Dakota and regarded as the foremost Sioux military leader, he defeated General **George Custer** at the Battle of Little Big Horn (1876) with a combined force of Sioux and Cheyenne tribes. He and his followers surrendered the following year, and he died in custody in Fort Robinson, Nebraska.

Crick, Francis Harry Compton 1916–2004
English molecular biologist
In the early 1950s, in Cambridge, he met **James Watson** and together they worked on the structure of DNA, publishing in 1953 their model of a molecule with a double helix. With Watson and **Maurice Wilkins** he was awarded the Nobel Prize for physiology or medicine in 1962. He later researched the visual systems of mammals, and the connections between brain and mind.

Crippen, Hawley Harvey 1862–1910
US murderer
He poisoned his wife, Cora Turner, an unsuccessful opera singer and music hall performer, after falling in love with his secretary, Ethel le Neve. He dissected

the body, burned the bones, and buried the remains in the cellar. Panicking, he and Ethel fled, boarding an Atlantic liner as Mr and Master Robinson. The suspicious captain, who had read police reports of their disappearance, contacted Scotland Yard by radiotelegraphy (the first use of radio for police purposes), the couple were arrested and tried, and Crippen was executed.

Cromwell, Oliver 1599–1658
English soldier and statesman
He fought against **Charles I** at the battles of Edgehill (1642), Gainsborough (1643) and Marston Moor (1644), and commanded the army that won a decisive victory over the king's forces at Naseby on 14 June 1645. After the king's execution on 30 January 1649 Cromwell proclaimed a Commonwealth, with himself at its head. He suppressed Irish resistance by massacring the Catholic garrisons at Drogheda and Wexford, and defeated the supporters of **Charles II**. Later taking the title of Lord Protector, he named his son, Richard Cromwell, his successor. However on his death Richard proved a weak leader, and the monarchy was restored in 1660.

Crosby, Bing, *originally* **Harry Lillis Crosby** 1904–77
US singer and film actor
From the 1930s onwards his distinctive crooning style made him a top attraction on radio, and later on television. He was one of the greatest sellers of records of the 20th century, and his version of 'White Christmas' sold over 30 million copies. Consistently among the most popular pre-war film stars, he won an Academy Award for *Going My Way* (1944). Later notable films include *The Bells of St Mary's* (1945), *Blue Skies* (1946), *White Christmas* (1954) and *High Society* (1956).

Cruyff, Johan 1947–
Dutch footballer
One of the great European forwards of his time, with Ajax Amsterdam he won three European Cup medals in succession and was European Footballer of the Year in 1971, 1973 and 1974. In 1974 he was captain of the Dutch side which lost to West Germany in the final of the World Cup. He went on to become a successful manager of Ajax Amsterdam and FC Barcelona.

Curie, Marie, *originally* **Maria**, *née* **Skłodowska** 1867–1934
Polish-born French physicist
With her husband **Pierre Curie** she worked on magnetism and radioactivity (a term she coined in 1898), and discovered the elements radium and polonium, which she named after her native Poland. They were jointly awarded the Nobel Prize for physics in 1903, with **Antoine Henri Becquerel**. She isolated pure radium in 1910, and received the 1911 Nobel Prize for chemistry. During World War I she developed radiography and afterwards became director of the research department at the newly established Radium Institute in Paris (1918–34). She died of leukaemia, probably caused by her long exposure to radioactivity.

Curie, Pierre 1859–1906
French physicist
With his brother Jacques, he discovered piezoelectricity in 1880. From 1898 he worked with his wife **Marie Curie** on radioactivity, and together with **Antoine Henri Becquerel** they were awarded the Nobel Prize for physics in 1903. He made other important studies of magnetism.

Custer, George Armstrong 1839–76
US soldier
He served with distinction throughout the American Civil War (1861–5), becoming a brigadier general at the age of 23. In 1876 he was ordered to lead a campaign against an alliance of Cheyenne and Sioux tribes organized by **Sitting Bull**, **Crazy Horse** and other chiefs. When he discovered them in the valley of the Little Big Horn River (in present-day Montana), Custer attacked (25 June 1876) without waiting for reinforcements. He and his central unit of some 260 soldiers were surrounded and killed to the last man, an event that became known as 'Custer's Last Stand'.

Cynewulf c.700–c.800
Anglo-Saxon poet and scholar
He came from Mercia (a kingdom in what is now the English Midlands) or Northumberland. The works attributed to him are now restricted to four poems which have his name worked into their inscriptions: *The Ascension of Christ* and *Elene* in the *Exeter Book*, and *St Juliana* and *The Fates of the Apostles* in the *Vercelli Book*.

da Gama, Vasco See **Gama, Vasco da**

Dahl, Roald 1916–90
British author
Born in Wales of Norwegian parents, his first short stories, collected as *Over to You* (1946), were based on his wartime experiences in the RAF. Later collections for adults include *Someone Like You* (1954) and *Kiss Kiss* (1960); his sole novel for adults was *My Uncle Oswald* (1979). His books for children were hugely successful (though some people disapproved of their rudeness and violence). They include *Charlie and the Chocolate Factory* (1964), *James and the Giant Peach* (1961), *Fantastic Mr Fox* (1970), *The BFG* (1982) and *Matilda* (1988). He wrote the screenplays for *You Only Live Twice* (1967) and *Chitty Chitty Bang Bang* (1968). A number of his stories were adapted for television as *Tales of the Unexpected*.

Dalai Lama, *originally* **Tenzin Gyatso** 1935–
Spiritual and political leader of Tibet
Born into a peasant family, he was designated the 14th Dalai Lama in 1937, but in 1950 and 1959 was forced into exile by the Chinese authorities. A revered figure in his homeland, and highly respected throughout the world, the Dalai Lama has continually rejected Chinese overtures to return home as a figurehead, seeking instead full independence for Tibet. In 1988 he modified this position, and proposed the creation of a self-governing Tibet in association with China. The following year he was awarded the 1989 Nobel Prize for peace in recognition of his commitment to the non-violent liberation of his homeland.

Dalí, Salvador, *properly* **Salvador Felipe Jacinto Dalí y Domenech** 1904–89
Spanish artist
A principal figure in the surrealist movement, he made a study of abnormal psychology and dream symbolism, and represented objects with realism in harsh sunburnt landscapes he remembered from his Spanish boyhood. His best-known paintings are

probably *The Persistence of Memory* (1931, also known as the *Limp Watches*), *Soft Construction with Boiled Beans: Premonition of Civil War* (1936), *Swans Reflecting Elephants* (1937), *Sleep* (1937) and *Christ of St John of the Cross* (1951). He also collaborated with the film-maker Luis Buñuel on the films *Un Chien Andalou* (1928) and *L'Age d'Or* (1930). In 1940 he settled in the USA. His publications include *The Secret Life of Salvador Dalí* (1942).

Salvador Dalí

Dalton, John 1766–1844
English chemist and natural philosopher
He began teaching at the age of 12. His atomic theory recognized that all matter is made up of combinations of atoms, the atoms of each element being identical. He concluded that atoms could be neither created nor destroyed, and that chemical reactions take place through the rearrangement of atoms. Also important were his studies showing that in a mixture of gases each gas exerts the same pressure as it would if it were the only gas present in the given volume (Dalton's law). In 1794 he described colour blindness (now also called Daltonism).

d'Annunzio, Gabriele 1863–1938
Italian writer, adventurer and political leader
One of the most important Italian literary figures of the late 19th and early 20th centuries, his work includes the poetry collection *In Early Spring* (1879), the trilogy of novels *Romances of the Rose* (1890s) and the plays *La Gioconda* (1899), *Francesca da Rimini* (1901) and *The Daughter of Jorio* (1904). In politics he was equally important: he urged Italian entry into World War I and served as a soldier, sailor and airman. In 1919 he seized and held the disputed port of Fiume, on the coast of Yugoslavia, and ruled as dictator until he was removed by the Italian government in 1920. He became a strong supporter of the Fascist Party under **Mussolini**.

Dante Alighieri 1265–1321
Italian poet
After serving as a soldier and filling various public offices on behalf of his native city, Florence, he wrote his best-known work, the *Divine Comedy*, begun around 1307. It narrates a journey through Hell and Purgatory, guided by **Virgil**, and finally to Paradise, guided by Beatrice, the woman he had fallen in love with while she was still a young girl. The poem established Italian as a literary language. Other works include the fragment *The Banquet*, the *De Monarchia* and the *Canzoniere*, a collection of short poems.

Darwin, Charles Robert 1809–82
English naturalist
The grandson of the writer Erasmus Darwin, in 1831 he was appointed naturalist on a five-year cruise on board the HMS *Beagle*, during which he visited the Galapagos Islands and formulated his ideas of the evolution of species. From 1842 he lived at Downe, Kent, but delayed publication of his evolutionary ideas until 1859, when the impending publication of similar work by **Alfred Wallace** forced his hand. His book, which set out evolution in detail for the first time, was *The Origin of Species by Means of Natural Selection*. Later works include *The Descent of Man and Selection in Relation to Sex* (1871), which related humans to the ancestors of the orang-utan, chimpanzee and gorilla.

David, *Hebrew* **'beloved'** 11th century BC
King of Israel
His success as a warrior against the Philistines (the inhabitants of south-west Palestine), especially in killing Goliath, the giant, aroused King Saul's jealousy, and he was forced to flee. However, after Saul's death he became King of all Israel. He united the many tribes of Israel, and extended his territory from Egypt to the Euphrates, though the later part of his reign was troubled by attempted revolutions by his sons Absalom and Adonijah. He was succeeded by **Solomon**, his son. He is traditionally the author of several of the Psalms and the ancestor of **Jesus Christ**.

da Vinci, Leonardo See **Leonardo da Vinci**

Davis, Bette (Ruth Elizabeth) 1908–89
US film actress
Her first Hollywood success was in *The Man Who Played God* (1932), and her numerous leading roles included *Of Human Bondage* (1934) and *Dangerous* (1935, Academy Award), which established her as a major star for the next three decades. Highly dedicated, she brought an emotional honesty even to unpromising dramas. She received great critical acclaim for her role in *Whatever Happened to Baby Jane?* (1962); later film appearances also included *Death on the Nile* (1979). She wrote several volumes of autobiography.

Davis, Miles Dewey, III 1926–91
US jazz trumpeter and bandleader
After a classical training he began performing in the New York clubs where the bebop style was emerging, and at 19 he became a member of the **Charlie Parker** Quintet. His later, understated recordings inspired the 'cool jazz' school. In the late 1950s he introduced an approach which broke away from the principles previously accepted in jazz, and his subsequent bands featured electronic instruments and synthesizers as well as rock-style rhythms. His best known album is *Kind of Blue* (1959).

Davy, Sir Humphry 1778–1829
English chemist
One of the greatest of all scientific experimenters, his *Researches, Chemical and Physical* (1799) led to his being appointed lecturer in chemistry at the Royal Institution (1801). He discovered the metals sodium and potassium, as well as barium, strontium, calcium and magnesium, demonstrated the anaesthetic effect of laughing gas (nitrous oxide), and proved that diamond is a form of carbon. **Michael Faraday** was

his assistant and valet. He invented the safety lamp (1815, the 'Davy lamp') which enabled greater coal production as deeper, more gaseous seams could be mined with less risk of explosion.

Day, Doris, *originally* **Doris Kappelhoff** 1924–
US singer and film actress
She made her film debut in *Romance on the High Seas* (1948), and her sunny personality, singing talent and girl-next-door image enlivened many musicals of the 1950s. More satisfying material followed with *Calamity Jane* (1953), *Love Me or Leave Me* (1955) and *The Pajama Game* (1957). The popularity of the comedy *Pillow Talk* (1959) earned her a further career as a comedy actress, often partnered by Rock Hudson. A top-selling recording artist, she also appeared on television in *The Doris Day Show* from 1968 to 1973.

Dean, Christopher 1958–
English ice-skater
He formed a skating partnership with **Jayne Torvill** in 1975, and they were six times British champions (1978–83). They won the Grand Slam of World, Olympic and European ice-dance titles in 1984, with a haunting interpretation of **Ravel**'s 'Bolero'.

Dean, James Byron 1931–55
US film actor
He gained overnight success in the film *East of Eden* (1955), and then starred in only two more films, *Rebel Without a Cause* (1955) and *Giant* (released 1956), before he was killed in a car crash. In just over a year he had become a cult figure, and remains an icon of youthful rebellion and self-assertion.

de Beauvoir, Simone See **Beauvoir, Simone de**

Debussy, (Achille-)Claude 1862–1918
French composer
He first won fame with the experimental *Prélude à l'après-midi d'un faune*, evoked by Stéphane Mallarmé's poem, and further added to his reputation with his operatic setting of *Pelléas et Mélisande* (first performed 1902). His intensely individual compositions explored new and original avenues of musical expression, and were often described as 'musical Impressionism'. He extended his range to orchestral music in *La Mer* (1905) and other pieces, and in his later period composed much chamber music.

Defoe, Daniel 1660–1731
English writer and adventurer
After serving as a soldier and being imprisoned for publishing his satire *The Shortest Way with the Dissenters* (1702), he founded a newspaper, *The Review* (1704–13), and undertook various secret commissions for the government. In 1719–20, at the age of nearly 60, he published his best-known book, *Robinson Crusoe*. His other major fictions include *Journal of the Plague Year* (1722), *Moll Flanders* (1722) and *Roxana* (1724). A writer of astonishing versatility, he published more than 250 works in all.

Degas, (Hilaire Germain) Edgar 1834–1917
French artist
Influenced by Impressionism, Japanese woodcuts and photography, many of his paintings and pastels featured dancers and women dressing or bathing. His best-known works include *Rehearsal of the Ballet* (c.1874), *Dancer Lacing her Shoe* (c.1878), *Dancer at the Bar* and *Cotton-brokers Office* (1873). In later life, because of failing sight, he concentrated on sculpture.

de Gaulle, Charles André Joseph Marie 1890–1970
French general and President
He served as an army officer in World War I, and after Germany's invasion of France in 1939 sought refuge in England to found the Free French Army and lead the French Resistance. He returned to Paris in 1944 and served in various posts before becoming the first president of the Fifth Republic in 1958. In 1959–60 he granted self-government to all French African colonies (including Algeria, which finally achieved independence in 1962), and at home consolidated France's growing international importance, developing a nuclear weapons programme and blocking Great Britain's attempts in 1962 and 1967 to enter the European Economic Community. He was re-elected in 1965 and 1968.

Charles de Gaulle

de la Mare, Walter John 1873–1956
English poet and novelist
A popular writer with adults and children, he produced novels, poetry and short stories. His works include the prose romance *Henry Brocken* (1904), the children's story *The Three Mulla Mulgars* (1910), the novel of the occult *The Return* (1910), the collection of poetry *The Listeners* (1912), the fantasy novel *Memoirs of a Midget* (1921), and short stories in *On the Edge* (1930).

del Sarto, Andrea See **Sarto, Andrea del**

De Mille, Cecil B(lount) 1881–1959
US film producer and director
With Samuel Goldwyn he founded Paramount Films and established Hollywood as a suitable place for shooting the first US feature film, *The Squaw Man* (1914). With the Gloria Swanson comedy *Male and Female* (1919), he became the most 'advanced' of US film directors. His box-office spectacles included *The Ten Commandments* (1923), *King of Kings* (1927), *The Plainsman* (1936), *Reap the Wild Wind* (1942) and *The Greatest Show on Earth* (1952, Academy Award). He also organized the first commercial passenger airline service in the USA in 1917.

Democritus c.460–c.370BC
Greek philosopher
He was one of the most prolific and influential of ancient authors, publishing many works on ethics, physics, mathematics, cosmology and music, but only fragments of his writings (on ethics) survive.

He is best known for his physical speculations, and in particular for the atomic theory he developed, whereby the world consists of an infinite number of everlasting atoms. He was supposedly known as 'the laughing philosopher' in the ancient world because of his wry amusement at human weaknesses.

de Montfort, Simon See **Montfort, Simon V de, Earl of Leicester**

Demosthenes 384–322BC
Athenian orator and statesman
Up to the age of 30 he wrote speeches for others, and gained a reputation as a lawyer. He embarked on his political career around 351BC, when the Greek cities were under threat from Philip II of Macedonia; Demosthenes advocated a policy of total resistance. Philip's attack on the northern state of Olynthus gave occasion to the *Olynthiacs* (349BC), which, with the orations against Philip called the *Philippics* (351BC, 334BC and 341BC), are Demosthenes' greatest speeches. However, war broke out again in 340BC, and Athens was totally defeated. In 323BC Philip's son and heir **Alexander the Great**, from whom Demosthenes had escaped into exile, died, and he was recalled to head another unsuccessful revolt against the Macedonian rulers. After the revolt Demosthenes was sentenced to death, but took poison.

Deng Xiaoping (Teng Hsiao-p'ing), *originally* **Deng Xixian** 1904–97
Chinese Communist politician
He became associated with **Mao Zedong** in the 1920s and served as a political commissar during the civil war (1937–49). By 1978 he had become the dominant figure in Chinese politics, and introduced a new economic modernization programme, attempting to create a 'socialism with Chinese characteristics'. His reputation was tarnished when he sanctioned the army's massacre of around 3,000 unarmed pro-democracy demonstrators in Tiananmen Square, Beijing (Peking), in June 1989.

De Niro, Robert 1943–
US film actor
An actor noted for the often tough authenticity of his characterizations, his films made with director Martin Scorsese include *Taxi Driver* (1976) and *Raging Bull* (1980), for which he won a Best Actor Academy Award. Others include *The Deer Hunter* (1978), *Awakenings* (1990), *Cape Fear* (1991), *Casino* (1995), *Heat* (1995), *Sleepers* (1996), *Ronin* (1998) and *Analyze This* (1999). He made his directorial debut with *The Bronx Tale* (1994).

Robert De Niro in *Taxi Driver*

Depardieu, Gérard 1948–
French film actor
One of the most versatile and skilled actors of his generation, able to combine strength and gentleness, he has appeared in many films, including *Danton* (1982), *The Return of Martin Guerre* (1982), *Jean De Florette* (1986), *Cyrano de Bergerac* (1990), *Green Card* (1990) and *The Man in the Iron Mask* (1998). He has also worked as a director.

Derrida, Jacques 1930–2004
French philosopher
His work spans literary criticism, psychoanalysis and linguistics as well as philosophy, and he founded the school of literary criticism known as 'deconstruction', which questions the ability of language to represent reality. Among his works are the influential *Speech and Phenomena* (1967), *Of Grammatology* (1967) and *Writing and Difference* (1967). His later publications include *Truth in Painting* (1978) and *Aporias* (1994).

Descartes, René 1596–1650
French philosopher and mathematician
Usually regarded as the father of modern philosophy, he attempted to reconstruct the whole subject into a unified system modelled on an entirely rational basis. The *Discourse on Method* (1637), the *Meditations on First Philosophy* (1641) and the *Principles of Philosophy* (1644) set out his fundamental doctrines, including the first unmistakably true proposition, *je pense, donc je suis* or *cogito ergo sum* ('I think, therefore I am'), and the idea of God as the absolutely perfect Being. He also made important contributions to astronomy and mathematics, determining that the position of a point can be defined by co-ordinates.

de Valera, Éamon 1882–1975
Irish statesman
One of the key figures in the Irish movement for independence from Britain, he took part in the Easter Rising of 1916 and won a massive electoral victory for his Sinn Féin Party in 1918. As President and Prime Minister he severed most of the remaining constitutional links with Britain, and introduced a new constitution (1937) under which his title as prime minister was altered to *Taoiseach*. In international affairs he supported Irish neutrality.

Diaz or **Dias, Bartolomeu** c.1450–1500
Portuguese navigator and explorer
In 1486 King John II of Portugal gave him the command of two vessels to follow up discoveries already made on the west coast of Africa. Driven by a violent storm, he sailed round the southern extremity of Africa, the Cape of Good Hope, without immediately realizing the fact. This discovery of the southernmost point of Africa opened the route to India.

Dickens, Charles John Huffam 1812–70
English writer
The most widely known English writer after **Shakespeare**, his novels are a vivid portrayal of social life in Victorian England. He spent his early childhood in poverty before finding work as a journalist, using the pen-name 'Boz', and his first book was *Sketches by Boz* (1833–6). Later novels, which usually appeared as serial instalments in magazines, included *The Pickwick Papers* (1836), *Oliver Twist* (1837–9), *Nicholas Nickleby* (1838–9), *The Old Curiosity Shop* (1840–1), *Barnaby Rudge* (1841), *Martin Chuzzlewit*

(1843), *Dombey and Son* (1846–8), *David Copperfield* (1849–50), *Bleak House* (1852–3), *Hard Times* (1854), *Little Dorrit* (1855–7), *A Tale of Two Cities* (1859), *Great Expectations* (1860–1) and *The Mystery of Edwin Drood* (1870, unfinished).

Dickinson, Emily Elizabeth 1830–86
US poet
At the age of 23 she withdrew from most social contacts and lived a secluded life in Amherst, Massachusetts, writing over 1,700 poems. Apart from several poems published anonymously, her work remained unknown and unpublished until after her death, when her sister Lavinia brought out three highly praised volumes (1890, 1891, 1896). Her lyrics, which show great originality both in thought and in form, have had considerable influence on modern poetry.

Dietrich, Marlene, *originally* **Maria Magdalena Von Losch** 1901–92
US film actress and cabaret performer
Her performance as the temptress Lola in Germany's first sound film *The Blue Angel* (1930) brought her international attention and a Hollywood contract. Her sensual personality was used to great effect in later films such as *Blonde Venus* (1932), *The Devil Is a Woman* (1935), *Destry Rides Again* (1939) and *A Foreign Affair* (1948). After World War II she pursued a career as an international singer and cabaret star, but later became increasingly reclusive.

Disney, Walt(er Elias) 1901–66
US artist and film producer
He worked as a commercial artist before producing animated cartoons, his most famous character being Mickey Mouse. Among his early successes was the first full-length coloured cartoon film, *Snow White and the Seven Dwarfs* (1937). This was followed by *Pinocchio* (1940), *Dumbo* (1941) and others. His later achievements include a series of coloured nature films, and family films such as *Mary Poppins* (1964). He opened the family theme park called Disneyland in California in 1955; others have since been built elsewhere.

Disraeli, Benjamin, 1st Earl of Beaconsfield 1804–81
English statesman and novelist
He entered parliament in 1837 and was prime minister briefly in 1868 and again from 1874 to 1880. Much of the 19th century saw him locked in political rivalry with **William Gladstone**. He also wrote several novels, often on political themes, the most famous being *Coningsby* (1844), *Sybil* (1845) and *Tancred* (1847). Disraeli is often credited with the creation of the Conservative Party in its modern form.

Di Stefano, Alfredo 1926–
Argentine footballer and coach
He played international football with Argentina, Colombia and Spain, but his lasting fame rests on his spell with Real Madrid, during which time he played in five European Cup successes. Later he became a coach and took Valencia to the Spanish League Championship in 1971. In 2003 he was named by the Royal Spanish Football Federation as their greatest player.

Doisneau, Robert 1912–94
French photographer
Doisneau worked for several picture magazines, including the mass-circulation *US Life* magazine. A master of humour who could capture life's absurdities on film, he created images that radiated a mixture of satire and warmth and paid homage to the ordinary. *The Kiss* (1950) is perhaps his best-known picture.

Dollfuss, Engelbert 1892–1934
Austrian politician
He became leader of the Christian Socialist Party, and as Austrian Chancellor (1932–4) he suspended parliamentary government, drove the Socialists into revolt and crushed them (February 1934). Purged of its Socialist majority, parliament then granted Dollfuss power to remodel the state, but in July 1934 a Nazi putsch in Vienna ended in his assassination.

Domingo, Placido 1941–
Spanish tenor
One of the world's leading tenors, his successes have included roles in **Puccini**'s *Tosca*, **Verdi**'s *Otello* and **Bizet**'s *Carmen*. In 1990 he performed alongside José Carreras and **Luciano Pavarotti** in the acclaimed 'Three Tenors' concert in Rome, and performed with them on several subsequent occasions.

Donatello, *real name* **Donato di Niccolo** c.1386–1466
Florentine sculptor
One of the most important artists of early Renaissance Italy, he was the first sculptor since classical times to produce works which are independent in themselves and not mere decorations for their architectural settings. Among his best-known works are the bronze equestrian portrait of the military commander known as Gattemelata – the first lifesize equestrian statue since antiquity – the bronze statue of **David** and his version of *Judith and Holofernes*.

Donne, John c.1572–1631
English poet
One of the greatest of the metaphysical poets, and an important influence on later English poetry, he is best known for the passionate and erotic poems *Songs and Sonnets*, his six *Satires* and his *Elegies*. His more purely religious verse includes pieces such as 'Hymne to God, the Father', 'To God My God, in my Sicknesse' and 'The Author's Last Going into Germany'. King **James VI and I** encouraged him to go into the Church (1614), and made him dean of St Paul's in 1621; several of his sermons survive.

Doppler, Christian Johann 1803–53
Austrian physicist
He is best known for his formulation of 'Doppler's principle', which explains the apparent change in the frequency of waves, as of sound or light, when he source of the waves is moving towards or away from an observer. The Doppler effect applies to all forms of electromagnetic radiation and is used in astronomy, where the changing wavelengths of approaching or receding bodies provide important evidence for the concept of an expanding universe.

Dostoevsky, Fyodor Mikhailovich, *also spelt* **Dostoyevsky** 1821–81
Russian novelist
His first published short story was 'Poor Folk', which gained him immediate recognition. From 1849 to 1854 he was imprisoned in Siberia for taking part in socialist politics: *The House of the Dead* (1860) was a result of this experience. Like **Dickens**, Dos-

toevsky's fiction is dark with the suffering caused by poverty and appalling living conditions, crime and the exploitation of children. Second only to those of **Leo Tolstoy**, his novels *Crime and Punishment* (1866), *The Idiot* (1868), *The Devils* (1872) and *The Brothers Karamazov* (1880) have been profoundly influential.

Douglas, Kirk, *originally* **Issur Danielovich** 1916–
US film actor
An ambitious actor, noted for his intensity, he received Best Actor Academy Award nominations for *Champion* (1949), *The Bad and the Beautiful* (1952) and *Lust For Life* (1956), in which he played **Van Gogh**. His numerous films include *Paths of Glory* (1957), *Spartacus* (1960) and *Lonely Are the Brave* (1962). He also worked as a director, and published an autobiography and several novels.

Doyle, Sir Arthur Conan 1859–1930
Scottish writer
He trained as a doctor, but turned to fiction writing, introducing his detective Sherlock Holmes in the novel *A Study in Scarlet* (1887). *The Adventures of Sherlock Holmes* were serialized in the *Strand Magazine* (1891–3) and published as books under such titles as *The Sign of Four* (1890) and *The Hound of the Baskervilles* (1902). His historical romances, *Micah Clarke* (1887), *The White Company* (1890), *Brigadier Gerard* (1896) and others, were less successful. He also wrote on spiritualism, to which he became a convert in later life.

Drake, Sir Francis c.1540–1596
English adventurer
His early career was spent in various voyages of discovery and plunder, and in 1580 he became the first Englishman to sail around the world. In the autumn of 1585 he sailed against the Spanish Indies and, with a licence from Queen **Elizabeth I**, plundered Hispaniola, Cartagena and the coast of Florida, bringing home the 190 dispirited Virginian colonists, with tobacco and potatoes. Early in 1587 he pillaged Cadiz, and in 1588 took a leading part in harassing the Spanish Armada as it passed through the English Channel. He died while on an expedition to the West Indies.

16th-century portrait of Sir Francis Drake

Dryden, John 1631–1700
English poet
One of the dominant figures of 17th-century English poetry and criticism, he became poet laureate in 1668. In a varied career he produced critical works such as the *Essay of Dramatic Poesy* (1668), satirical and didactic poems such as *Absalom and Achitophel* (1681), *Religio Laici* (1682) and *The Hind and the Panther*, and plays such as *All for Love* (1677). At the Revolution of 1688 he lost the poet laureateship and took up translation to earn a living. His final work, published in 1699, was *Fables, Ancient and Modern*.

Dubček, Alexander 1921–92
Czechoslovak statesman
He joined the Communist Party in 1939, fought as a Slovak patriot against the Nazis (1944–5), and gradually rose in the party hierarchy until in 1968 he became First Secretary. However, his policy of liberalization during the 'Prague Spring' led in August 1968 to the occupation of Czechoslovakia by Warsaw Pact forces, and he spent much of the 1970s and 1980s working as a clerk in a lumber yard. Following the overthrow of the communist regime in November 1989 he re-entered politics, but died as the result of a car accident.

Dumas, Alexandre, *in full* **Alexandre Dumas Davy de la Pailleterie**, *known as* **Dumas père** 1802–70
French novelist and playwright
At the age of 27, he became famous for his play *Henry III and his Court* (1829), which revolutionized historical drama. His literary output was enormous, and it was as a storyteller on French historical themes that he gained enduring success, with the likes of *The Count of Monte Cristo* (1844–5); *The Three Musketeers* (1844) and its sequels; and *Queen Margot* (1845), about the religious wars of 16th-century France.

Duns Scotus, John, *Latin* **Joannes** c.1265–1308
Scottish philosopher and theologian
He was a Franciscan, and known by contemporaries as 'Doctor Subtilis' for his skill in argument, he rivalled **Thomas Aquinas** as the greatest theologian of the Middle Ages. He saw faith as the necessary foundation of Christian theology, but faith was for him exercised through an act of will and was practical, not theoretical. He also pioneered the doctrine of the Immaculate Conception, that the Virgin Mary was conceived without original sin. His best-known works are his collected lectures.

du Pré, Jacqueline Mary 1945–87
English cellist
Probably the 20th century's most famous cellist, she made her concert debut at the Wigmore Hall aged 16, and subsequently toured internationally. In 1967 she married the pianist **Daniel Barenboim**. After developing multiple sclerosis in 1972 she pursued a teaching career, including giving masterclasses on television.

Dürer, Albrecht 1471–1528
German painter and engraver
One of the greatest artists of the Renaissance in northern Europe, he became court painter to Charles V. His best-known paintings include *Adam and Eve* (1507) and the *Adoration of the Trinity* (1511). As an engraver on metal and a designer of woodcuts he ranks even higher than as a painter: his copperplates, over 100 in number, include the *Small Passion* (16 plates, 1508–13) and the *Knight, Death, and the Devil* (1513), while his woodcuts include the *Apocalypse*, begun in 1498. He may also be regarded as the inventor of etching.

Durrell, Gerald Malcolm 1925–95
English writer and naturalist
His childhood on the Greek island of Corfu in the

1930s inspired the bestselling *My Family and Other Animals* (1956). In his later career he combined writing with zoology, publishing books such as *The Aye-Aye and I* (1992) and making many expeditions and wildlife films. He founded the Jersey Zoological Park in 1959, about which he wrote *The Stationary Ark* (1976), and the Jersey Wildlife Preservation Trust in 1963. He was the brother of writer Lawrence Durrell.

Duvalier, François, *known as* **Papa Doc** 1907–71
Haitian politician
He trained in medicine, and in 1957 was overwhelmingly elected President of Haiti. His rule became increasingly autocratic and murderous, and saw the creation of the brutal civil militia of the so-called Tontons Macoutes. A professed believer in voodoo, he fought off invasions and threatened uprisings with US economic help. He was made President for life in 1964 and was succeeded by his son, **Jean-Claude (Baby Doc) Duvalier**.

Duvalier, Jean-Claude, *known as* **Baby Doc** 1951–
Haitian politician
The son of **François (Papa Doc) Duvalier**, he followed his father into politics. At the age of 20 he became President for life, ruling, as had his father, through a private army. In 1986 he was deposed in a military coup and went into exile in Grasse, in the south of France.

Dvořák, Antonín Leopold 1841–1904
Czech composer
Dvořák's work is basically classical in structure, but characterized by colourful Slavonic motifs. His best-known work is his Ninth Symphony (1893), also known as the New World Symphony, composed in the USA, which contains echoes of American folk music yet retains a distinct Slavonic flavour. Other works include the *Slavonic Dances* (1878), much chamber and piano music, and several operas.

Dyer, Reginald Edward Henry 1864–1927
British general
He was the British commander at an incident that became known as the Amritsar Massacre. Following an assault on a British woman missionary in Amritsar, India, Dyer banned all public meetings, but the order was disobeyed and troops fired into the crowd, killing around 400 people. An official enquiry blamed Dyer and he was forced to resign from the army.

Dylan, Bob, *originally* **Robert Allen Zimmerman** 1941–
US singer and songwriter
He was instrumental in the popular revival of the folk tradition in the early 1960s, with an immediately recognizable, and unconventional, vocal style. Many of his songs, notably 'Blowin' in the Wind' and 'The Times They are a-Changin' were widely performed and imitated. He turned in 1965 to rock and roll with the group which later became The Band; his songs from this period include 'Mr Tambourine Man' and 'Like a Rolling Stone'. Numerous live albums have been issued, and he has appeared in or directed a number of films, including the celebrated documentary *Don't Look Back* (1967). He remains one of the seminal influences on popular songwriting.

Earhart, Amelia Mary 1897–1937
US aviator
She was the first woman to fly the Atlantic Ocean (from Newfoundland to Burry Point, Wales) on 17 June 1928. Although merely a passenger on that initial flight, she later became the first woman to fly solo across the Atlantic (1932) and the first person to fly alone from Hawaii to California (1935). In 1937 she attempted a round-the-world flight, but her plane disappeared in the Pacific somewhere between New Guinea and Howland Island.

Amelia Earhart

Eastwood, Clint 1930–
US actor and director
He found television fame in *Rawhide* (1958–65) and then became an international star with three Italian-made 'spaghetti' westerns beginning with *A Fistful of Dollars* (1964). In the USA his box-office status was confirmed in adventure films and as tough detective *Dirty Harry* (1971). He was actor–director for the first time in the thriller *Play Misty for Me* (1971). Later films include *Pale Rider* (1985), *Bird* (1988), *Unforgiven* (1992), for which he won a Best Director Academy Award, *The Bridges of Madison County* (1995) and *Million Dollar Baby* (2004), for which he won another Best Director Academy Award. From 1986 to 1988 he was Mayor of Carmel in California.

Eddington, Sir Arthur Stanley 1882–1944
English astronomer
In 1916 he proposed that there is a relationship between the mass of a star and its total output of radiation, and suggested that some stars, such as white dwarfs, might be extremely dense. He published these investigations in *Internal Constitution of the Stars* (1926). At the same time he had become deeply interested in **Albert Einstein**'s theory of relativity, and published accounts of it in *Space, Time and Gravitation* (1920) and *Mathematical Theory of Relativity* (1923). He wrote a series of scientific books for general readers.

Eddy, Mary (Morse), *née* **Baker** 1821–1910
US founder of the Christian Science Church
Frequently ill as a young woman, she later turned to faith healing. She developed the spiritual and metaphysical system she called Christian Science while recovering from a severe fall in 1866. In 1879 she founded at Boston the Church of Christ, Scientist, which attracted great numbers of followers.

Edison, Thomas Alva 1847–1931
US inventor and physicist
In 1871 he invented the paper ticker-tape telegraph

for stock exchange prices, which made enough money to fund a career in research. He took out more than 1,000 patents in all, including the gramophone (1877), the incandescent light bulb (1879), and the carbon granule microphone as an improvement for **Alexander Graham Bell**'s telephone. To make possible the widespread use of electric light, he invented a system for generating and distributing electricity and designed the first power plant (1881–2). Amongst his other inventions were a megaphone, a storage battery, the electric valve (1883) and the kinetoscope (1891), an early device for viewing motion pictures. In 1912 he produced the first talking motion pictures. He was the most prolific inventor the world has ever seen.

Edmund II, Ironside c.990–1016
King of the English
The son of **Ethelred II**, the Unready, and half-brother of **Edward the Confessor**, he was lord of most of Mercia (a kingdom in what is now the English Midlands) from 1015. When **Canute** (Knut Sveinsson) invaded England that summer, Edmund was elected king, raised an army, reconquered Wessex and relieved London, but was soon routed by Canute. He agreed to partition the country, but died a few weeks later, leaving Canute as sole ruler.

Edward the Confessor c.1003–1066
King of England and saint
He was the elder son of **Ethelred II**, the Unready, by his wife Emma, and half-brother of **Edmund II, Ironside**. In 1016 the English throne passed to **Canute** (Knut Sveinsson), who married Ethelred's widow, and had a son by her, Hardaknut Knutsson. Edward meanwhile went to Normandy (1016–41) and became very religious, taking a vow of chastity. Hardaknut recalled him to England (1041) and he became king in 1042. He founded Westminster Abbey, where he is buried.

Edward I, *also known as* **Edward Longshanks** and **the Hammer of the Scots** 1239–1307
King of England
The son of Henry III, he became king on his father's death (1272). He annexed north and west Wales and tried to unite England and Scotland, but his insistence on control of Scotland led to the Scottish Wars of Independence. Despite victories such as the defeat of **William Wallace** at Falkirk (1298), Edward could not subdue Scotland, and died on campaign near Carlisle (1307).

Edward III, *called* **Edward of Windsor** 1312–77
King of England
He was the son of Edward II. During his childhood the country was governed by his mother, Isabella, sister of Charles IV of France, and her lover, Roger de Mortimer. Edward later executed Mortimer, banished his mother and assumed full control of the government (1330). Edward spent much of his reign fighting the Scots, and started the Hundred Years War against France. He defeated the French at Crécy (1346) and Poitiers (1356).

Edwards, Robert Geoffrey 1925–
British physiologist
In collaboration with **Patrick Steptoe** he contributed substantially to the successful development of the *in vitro* fertilization ('test-tube babies') programme in Oldham, England. In July 1978 the first healthy 'test-tube baby' was born as a result of their research.

Eichmann, (Karl) Adolf 1906–62
Austrian Nazi war criminal
He became a member of the Nazi Party and organized anti-Jewish activities, particularly their deportation to concentration camps. Captured by US forces in 1945, he escaped from prison some months later, having kept his identity hidden, and in 1950 reached Argentina. He was traced by Israeli agents and in 1960 taken to Israel, condemned for crimes against humanity and executed.

Einstein, Albert 1879–1955
German–Swiss–US mathematical physicist
Albert Einstein ranks with **Galileo Galilei** and Sir **Isaac Newton** as one of the great contributors to the understanding of the universe. He spent his early career as a clerk at the Swiss Patent Office (1902–5), and achieved world fame by his special and general theories of relativity (1905 and 1916), which showed how mass and time change under the influence of very fast speeds, and how adjustments to Newtonian gravitational theory were necessary to account for planetary motion. He won the 1921 Nobel Prize for physics for this work. After Adolf **Hitler**'s rise to power, he left Germany and became a US citizen. In 1939 he helped to initiate the Allied attempt to produce an atomic bomb (called the Manhattan Project); however, after World War II he urged international control of atomic weapons.

Eisenhower, Dwight D(avid), *nicknamed* **Ike** 1890–1969
US general and 34th President of the USA
During World War II he led Allied operations in French North Africa and was Supreme Commander of the 1944 D-Day landings. With the establishment of NATO in 1950 he was made Supreme Commander of the combined land forces, and in 1952 was swept to victory as a Republican in the presidential elections. He was re-elected in 1956. During his presidency the US government was preoccupied with foreign policy and the campaign against communism.

El Cid See **Cid, El**

Elgar, Sir Edward 1857–1934
English composer
The leading figure in English music in the early 20th century, his music often suggests patriotic English themes or evokes the English landscape. Among his works are the *Pomp and Circumstance Marches* (1901), which contain the section known as 'Land of Hope and Glory', as well as the *Enigma Variations* (1899) and the oratorio *The Dream of Gerontius* (1900). Other works include the oratorios *The Apostles* (1903) and *The Kingdom* (1906), two symphonies and concertos for violin and cello.

El Greco See **Greco, El**

Eliot, George, *pseudonym of* **Mary Ann** or **Marian Evans** 1819–80
English writer
A voracious reader, she was well-educated in music and languages and travelled on the Continent. Her first novel, *Adam Bede* (1859), had enormous success. *The Mill on the Floss* (1860), *Silas Marner* (1861), *Romola* (1863) and *Felix Holt* (1866) appeared next. Her first poem, 'The Spanish Gypsy' (1868), was followed by

'Agatha' (1869), 'The Legend of Jubal' (1870) and 'Armgart' (1871), and in 1871–2 appeared *Middlemarch*, generally considered her greatest work. After that came *Daniel Deronda* (1876), her last great novel. Her portrayals of farmers, tradesmen, and the lower middle class, generally of the Midlands, are hardly surpassed in English literature.

Eliot, T(homas) S(tearns) 1888–1965
US-born British poet, critic and dramatist
One of the most important figures of 20th-century English literature, he worked for eight years in a bank before becoming a director of the publishing firm of Faber & Gwyer (later Faber & Faber). His poetry, initially full of gloom and foreboding, but later increasingly religious, includes *The Waste Land* (1922), *The Hollow Men* (1925), and *Four Quartets* (1944). He also wrote a collection of children's verse, *Old Possum's Book of Practical Cats* (1939), critical works such as *The Sacred Wood* (1920), and plays such as *Murder in the Cathedral* (1935), *The Family Reunion* (1939) and *The Cocktail Party* (1950). He was awarded the Nobel Prize for literature in 1948.

Elizabeth I 1533–1603
Queen of England and Ireland from 1558
The daughter of **Henry VIII** and his second wife, Anne Boleyn, she was imprisoned in the Tower of London during the reign of her Catholic half-sister Mary I. On Mary's death in 1558 she became Queen and established the Protestant Church of England, persecuting Catholics and the supporters of **Mary, Queen of Scots**. During her reign Sir **Francis Drake** sailed around the world (1577), Sir **Walter Raleigh** mounted expeditions to the North American coast (1580s), the Great Armada sent by Spain was repelled (1588) and England emerged as a world power. Elizabeth, who never married, was known as the 'Virgin Queen'. On her death the Tudor Dynasty came to an end and the throne passed peacefully to the Stuart **James VI and I**.

16th-century portrait of Elizabeth I

Elizabeth II 1926–
Queen of Great Britain and Northern Ireland, and Head of the Commonwealth
She became Queen Elizabeth II on the death of her father, George VI (1952), and is queen of Great Britain and Northern Ireland, Canada, Australia, New Zealand, and of several other more recently independent countries. Her husband was created Duke of Edinburgh (1947), and styled Prince Philip (1957). They have three sons, Prince Charles, styled the Prince of Wales, Prince Andrew, and Prince Edward and a daughter, Princess Anne, styled the Princess Royal. The Queen has aimed to modernize the monarchy and make it more informal. She shows a strong personal commitment to the Commonwealth as a voluntary association of equal partners.

Ellington, Duke (Edward Kennedy) 1899–1974
US jazz pianist, composer and bandleader
He worked during the 1920s at the Cotton Club in Harlem, developing orchestral jazz as the accompaniment for dance shows. He emerged as one of the most important of all jazz composers, going on to produce around 2,000 works. He led some of the greatest big bands ever assembled, and broke new ground in jazz by writing extended works and suites like *Black, Brown and Beige* (1943) and *The Perfume Suite* (1945). Many of his song-length pieces, such as 'Mood Indigo' and 'Sophisticated Lady', became part of the standard jazz repertoire.

Elton, Charles Sutherland 1900–91
English ecologist
A pioneer of the science of animal ecology, his work led to the recognition of the ability of many animals to counter environmental disadvantage by change of habitats, and to the use of the important concepts of 'food chain' and 'niche' (the status of an organism or species within its community).

Emerson, Ralph Waldo 1803–82
US poet and essayist
An influential figure in 19th century thought, he was one of the chief founders of transcendentalism, and wrote widely on philosophy, religion and social organization. He was known as a powerful orator, and his 'address before the Divinity Class, Cambridge, 1838', produced a great sensation. His books include *The Conduct of Life* (1860), *Society and Solitude* (1870) and *Letters and Social Aims* (1876), as well as several volumes of poetry.

Engels, Friedrich 1820–95
German philosopher and politician
One of the founders of communism, he first met **Karl Marx** at Brussels in 1844 and collaborated with him on the *Communist Manifesto* (1848). After Marx's death in 1883, Engels devoted the remaining years of his life to editing and translating Marx's writings. Among his other works are *Condition of the Working Classes in England in 1844* (1845).

Epstein, Sir Jacob 1880–1959
British sculptor
Born in New York City, a Russian–Polish Jew, he became a British subject in 1907, and his early commissions included 18 nude figures for the façade of the British Medical Association building in the Strand, London (1907–8). These and later primitivist sculptures resulted in great controversy, and accusations of indecency and blasphemy. Among his later work are many impressive bronze portrait heads and two bronze *Madonna and Child* sculptures (1927 and 1950).

Erasmus, Desiderius c.1466–1536
Dutch humanist and scholar
One of the most influential figures of the Renaissance, Erasmus was ordained a priest in 1492, but was later drawn to the humanists. He became strongly critical of the abuses of the Catholic Church, and his writings helped prepare the way for **Martin Luther** and the Reformation; but he also came to oppose

the dogmatic theology of the Reformers and specifically attacked Luther in *De Libero Arbitrio* (1523). He studied and taught throughout Europe, and published many popular works, including *Adages* (1500, 1508) and *In Praise of Folly* (1509).

Eratosthenes c.276–194BC
Greek mathematician, astronomer and geographer
He became the head of the great library at Alexandria and was the most versatile scholar of his time. He measured the circumference of the Earth with considerable accuracy, and in mathematics he invented a method, the 'sieve of Eratosthenes', for listing the prime numbers. He also wrote on geography, chronology and literary criticism, but only fragments of this work remain.

Ernst, Max 1891–1976
German painter and sculptor
After studying philosophy and psychiatry at Bonn, he turned to painting, and in 1918 founded at Cologne the German Dada group. Later, in Paris, he participated in the surrealist movement. He invented the technique of frottage (pencil rubbings on canvas), and settled in the USA in 1941, but returned to France in 1953.

Escher, Maurits Cornelius 1898–1972
Dutch artist
Primarily a printmaker, he created whimsical visual fantasies in lithographs and woodcuts. He often used geometric distortions and tricks of perspective to deceive the eye.

Essex, Robert Devereux, 2nd Earl of 1566/67–1601
Elizabethan soldier and courtier
He served as a soldier in the Netherlands (1585–6), and at court he quickly rose in the favour of Queen **Elizabeth I**. In 1591 he commanded the British forces in alliance with Henry IV of France, and later took part in the capture of Cadiz in Spain (1596), but was largely responsible for the failure of an expedition to the Azores (1597). After quarrelling with Elizabeth she had him imprisoned and, when he was discovered plotting to overthrow her, beheaded.

Ethelred or **Æthelred II**, *wrongly referred to as* **the Unready** c.968–1016
King of England
The son of King Edgar, he was ten when he succeeded to the throne (978). He at first attempted to buy off Viking invaders (hence his Anglo-Saxon nickname of *Unræd*, meaning lack of counsel – mistranslated as Unready – meant as a pun on his name Ethelred, which means good counsel). However, in 1002, he ordered a savage massacre of all Danish settlers. In 1013, beleaguered by the invasion of Svein I Haraldsson of Denmark, he abandoned his throne and fled to Normandy but was recalled in 1014. He was the father of **Edmund II, Ironside** and **Edward the Confessor**.

Euclid fl.300BC
Greek mathematician
He taught in Alexandria, where he appears to have founded a mathematical school. His *Elements* of geometry, in 13 books, is the earliest substantial Greek mathematical treatise to have survived, and is probably better known than any other mathematical book. It covers the geometry of lines in the plane, including **Pythagoras**'s theorem, and goes on to discuss circles, ratio, and the geometry of three dimensions. He wrote other works on geometry, and on astronomy, optics and music.

Euler, Leonhard 1707–83
Swiss mathematician
He published many books and papers on every aspect of pure and applied mathematics, physics and astronomy. His *Introductio in analysin infinitorum* (1748) and later treatises on differential and integral calculus and algebra became standard textbooks, and his notations such as *e* and *i* (the square root of -1) have been used ever since. His powerful memory enabled him to continue mathematical work though nearly blind.

Euripides 484 or 480–406BC
Greek tragic dramatist
Of about 80 of his dramas whose titles are known, 18 survive complete. They include *Medea* (431BC), *Andromache* (425BC), *The Women of Troy* (415BC) and *Orestes* (408BC). *The Bacchae* (405BC) and *Iphigenia in Aulis* (405BC) were put on the Athenian stage only after the author's death. He brought a new style to tragedy and the treatment of traditional mythology, and is notable for highlighting unusual opinions and portraying socially marginal characters. **Sophocles** commented that while he himself showed people as they ought to be, Euripides portrayed them as they are.

Evans, Walker 1903–75
US photographer
From 1935 he began to record the life of rural depression in the southern states, and in 1938 published his *American Photographs*, the first section of which shows members of society and the second its buildings. He later worked for *Fortune* magazine to document the lives of the sharecroppers of the Deep South. Other work includes architectural studies and pictures of people in the New York City subways, published in 1966 as *Many Are Called*.

Fahrenheit, (Gabriel) Daniel 1686–1736
German instrument-maker and physicist
He invented and produced several high-quality meteorological instruments, including a commercially successful mercury thermometer (1714). Using the temperatures of melting ice and of the human body, Fahrenheit devised a temperature scale with these points calibrated at 32 and 96 degrees, and zero fixed at the freezing point of ice and salt. He was the first to show that the boiling point of liquids varies at different atmospheric pressures, and suggested this as a principle for the construction of barometers.

Faraday, Michael 1791–1867
English chemist and physicist
The son of a blacksmith, he was apprenticed to a bookbinder whose books sparked his interest in science. In 1813 he was taken on as **Humphry Davy**'s assistant, accompanying him on a European tour, and in 1827 he succeeded to Davy's chair of chemistry at the Royal Institution. His great life work was the series of *Experimental Researches on Electricity*, published over 40 years, in which he described his many discoveries, including electromagnetic induction (1831) and the laws of electrolysis (1833). He is generally considered the greatest of all experimental physicists.

Fassbinder, Rainer Werner 1946–82
German film director
He made over 40 films, usually political criticisms of contemporary Germany, contrasting personal failure and frustration with the country's superficial economic success, and illustrating the misuse of power. Notable among these were *The Bitter Tears of Petra von Kant* (1972), *Effi Briest* (1974) and *The Marriage of Maria Braun* (1979). Before his death he had completed *Lili Marleen* and *Lola*, two of a planned series of films dealing with recent German history as seen through the eyes of women.

Faulkner, William 1897–1962
US novelist
The lyrical style of novels like *The Sound and the Fury* (1929), *Light in August* (1932), *Absalom, Absalom!* (1936) and *Intruder in the Dust* (1948) account for his reputation as one of the modern masters of the novel. Other titles include *Sartoris* (1929), *The Town* (1957) and *The Mansion* (1959), set, like most of the earlier books, in the imaginary Yoknapatawpha County, and *A Fable* (1954), an ambitious but unsuccessful reworking of Christ's Passion, set on the Western Front. He received the 1949 Nobel Prize for literature.

Fawcett, Dame Millicent, *née* **Garrett** 1847–1929
English suffragette and educational reformer
She campaigned for women's suffrage and higher education for women, but opposed the militancy of the Pankhursts. She was a founder of Newnham College, Cambridge (1871), and was president of the National Union of Women's Suffrage Societies (1897–1919). Among her writings is *The Women's Victory – and After* (1920).

Fawkes, Guy 1570–1606
English conspirator
He developed his fervent Catholicism while still a schoolboy, and in 1604 joined the small group of conspirators, led by Robert Catesby, who devised a plan to blow up the House of Lords during the State Opening. The plot, intended to cause chaos in the country and ultimately aid the restoration of a Catholic monarchy, was supposedly discovered with only hours to spare, and Fawkes and seven other conspirators were hanged, drawn and quartered. In Britain, effigies of him are burnt on 5 November.

Fellini, Federico 1920–93
Italian film director

Federico Fellini

His highly individual films, always from his own scripts, include *The Young and the Passionate* (1953), *The Road* (1954), *The Nights of Cabiria* (1957), *Casanova* (1976), *City of Women* (1980) and *Ginger and Fred* (1986). His most famous and controversial work, *La Dolce Vita* (1960, 'The Sweet Life'), was a cynical portrayal of modern Roman high life.

Fenton, Roger 1819–69
English photographer
He was a founder of the Photographic (later Royal Photographic) Society in 1853, and photographed the royal family at Balmoral and Windsor. In 1855 he went to the Crimea as the world's first accredited war photographer, and it is for this work that he is best known.

Fermat, Pierre de 1601–65
French mathematician
He is best known for his work in number theory, the proofs of many of his discoveries being first published by **Leonhard Euler** a hundred years later. His 'last theorem' was the most famous unsolved problem in mathematics, and it was only finally solved in 1995. His correspondence with **Blaise Pascal** marks the foundation of probability theory. In optics Fermat's principle is that the path taken by a ray of light between two given points is the one in which the light takes the least time.

Fermi, Enrico 1901–54
US nuclear physicist
In 1934 he and his colleagues split the nuclei of uranium atoms by bombarding them with neutrons, thus making an important step in the development of nuclear power and weapons. He was awarded the 1938 Nobel Prize for physics. Fearing for the safety of his Jewish wife, he went straight from the prize presentation in Stockholm to the USA, where he played a prominent part in interesting the US Government in atomic energy, constructed the first US nuclear reactor at Chicago (1942), and produced the first controlled chain reaction. The element fermium is named after him.

Feynman, Richard Phillips 1918–88
US physicist
He worked on the Manhattan atomic bomb project, and after World War II worked on quantum electrodynamics (the application of quantum theory to interactions between electromagnetic radiation and particles). He introduced 'Feynman diagrams', using pictures to describe particle interactions, and was awarded the Nobel Prize jointly with Sin-Itiro Tomonaga and Julian Schwinger in 1965. In his later career he studied the structure of protons and the properties of liquid helium.

Fibonacci, Leonardo, *also called* **Leonardo of Pisa** c.1170–c.1250
Italian mathematician
The first outstanding mathematician of the Middle Ages, he popularized the modern Arabic system of numerals (which originated in India), and illustrated its virtues in his *The Book of Calculation* (1202). His greatest work, the *The Book of Square Numbers* (1225) contains remarkably advanced contributions to number theory. He discovered the 'Fibonacci sequence' of integers in which each number is equal to the sum of the preceding two (1,1,2,3,5,8,...).

Fielding, Henry 1707–54
English novelist
He began his career writing light comedies for the stage and a series of satires attacking Sir **Robert Walpole** and his government. Incensed by the publication of **Samuel Richardson**'s prudish *Pamela*, he ridiculed it in a short novel, *An Apology for the Life of Mrs Shamela Andrews* (1741). In 1742 came *The Adventures of Joseph Andrews and his Friend, Mr Abraham Adams*, which was followed by other novels, including his most famous, *The History of Tom Jones, a Foundling* (1749). He was made a justice of the peace in 1748 and campaigned vigorously against legal corruption, helping to found London's first professional police force, the Bow Street Runners.

Fields, W C, *originally* **William Claude Dukenfield** 1880–1946
US comedian
In his early career he was a highly successful vaudeville entertainer, and made his film debut in *Pool Sharks* (1915). A bulbous nose and gravelly voice enhanced his created persona of a tippling, child-hating misanthrope, continually at odds with the world. The writer and performer of several classic comedies like *The Bank Dick* (1940), *My Little Chickadee* (1940) and *Never Give a Sucker an Even Break* (1941), he also played Micawber in *David Copperfield* (1935).

Fitzgerald, Ella (Jane) 1917–96
US jazz and popular singer
She had her first hit with the novelty song 'A Tisket, A Tasket' in 1938. She then began a lengthy recording and performing career, at first with the Chick Webb orchestra, and then solo or in combination with a lengthy roster of jazz musicians including **Duke Ellington**, **Count Basie** and **Louis Armstrong**. Her mastery of jazz phrasing, rhythm and scat singing was unsurpassed, and among jazz musicians only Louis Armstrong achieved a similar level of global recognition and popularity. She appeared in cameo roles in a handful of films.

Fitzgerald, F(rancis) Scott (Key) 1896–1940
US novelist
He captured the spirit of the 1920s especially in *The Great Gatsby* (1925), his best-known book. Other novels include *This Side of Paradise* (1920), *The Beautiful and Damned* (1922) and *Tender is the Night* (1934). His short stories were equally notable. In keeping with his fiction, which revealed both a fascination with the rich and a moral dismay at their lives, he led the life of a playboy in Europe and the USA, which exhausted both his financial and emotional resources and worsened his wife Zelda's mental illness. He wrote a final, unfinished novel, *The Last Tycoon* (1941).

Flaubert, Gustave 1821–80
French novelist
His best-known novel is *Madame Bovary* (1857), which achieved great success despite being condemned as immoral. His second work, *Salammbô* (1862), was followed by *Sentimental Education* (1869) and *The Temptation of St Anthony* (1874). *Three Tales* (1877) reveals his mastery of the short story. *Bouvard and Pecuchet* (1881) and his correspondence with **George Sand** (1884) were published after his death. He brought to the novel a new awareness of form and structure.

Fleming, Sir Alexander 1881–1955
Scottish bacteriologist
In his research he became the first to use anti-typhoid vaccines on human beings. In 1928 by chance exposure of a culture of *staphylococci* he noticed a curious mould, penicillin, which he found to have unsurpassed antibiotic powers. He had to wait eleven years before the experimentalists **Howard Florey** and **Ernst Chain**, with whom he shared the 1945 Nobel prize for physiology or medicine, perfected a method of producing it.

Flitcroft, Henry 1679–1769
English architect
He designed the London churches of St Giles in the Fields and St John at Hampstead, and he rebuilt parts of Wentworth House in Yorkshire and Woburn Abbey.

Florey (of Adelaide and of Marston in the City of Oxford), Howard Walter Florey, Baron 1898–1968
Australian pathologist
As Professor of Pathology at Oxford in 1935, he worked with the biochemist **Ernst Chain** in purifying the antibiotic penicillin, which had been discovered in 1928 by **Alexander Fleming**. Florey supervised clinical testing of the drug in the USA where it was put into mass production; by the end of World War II it had already saved many lives. Florey was knighted in 1944 and he, Chain and Fleming were jointly awarded the Nobel Prize for physiology or medicine in 1945.

Flynn, Errol, *originally* **Leslie Thomson Flynn** 1909–59
Australian-born US film actor
His first Hollywood film, *Captain Blood* (1935), established him as a hero of historical adventure films, and his good looks and athleticism confirmed him as the greatest Hollywood swashbuckler in such films as *The Charge of the Light Brigade* (1936), *The Adventures of Robin Hood* (1938) and *The Sea Hawk* (1940). His legendary reputation for debauchery eventually affected his career, which was briefly revived by his acclaimed performance as a drunken wastrel in *The Sun Also Rises* (1957).

Fonda, Henry Jaynes 1905–82
US actor
His Hollywood debut in *A Farmer Takes A Wife* (1935) was followed by over 100 films, notably *The Grapes of Wrath* (1940), *The Lady Eve* (1941) and *The Oxbow Incident* (1943), which established him in the role of the honest US folk hero. Later films include *Twelve Angry Men* (1957) and *On Golden Pond* (1981), for which he won an Academy Award. He was married five times, and his children include actors Jane and Peter Fonda.

Fonteyn, Dame Margot, *née* **Margaret Hookham** 1919–91
English ballerina
She rose in the Royal Ballet to become one of the most impressive technicians of the 20th century. She created many roles, among them *The Haunted Ballroom* (1939), *Symphonic Variations* (1946) and *The Fairy Queen* (1946), and her career was enhanced in the 1960s by her acclaimed partnership with **Rudolph Nureyev**. She wrote several books,

as well as a six-part television series, *The Magic of Dance* (1979).

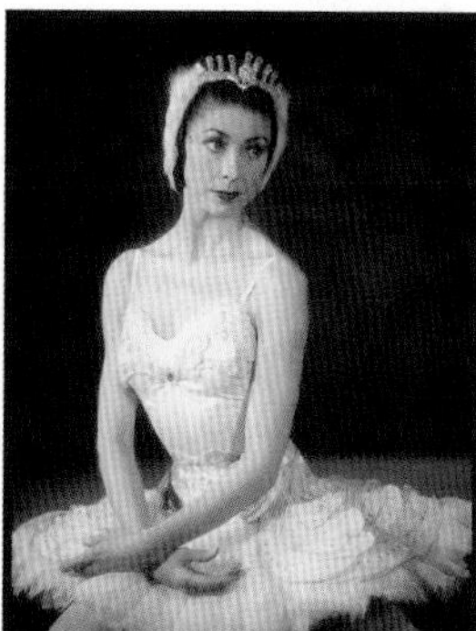

Dame Margot Fonteyn

Ford, Ford Madox, *originally* **Ford Hermann Hueffer** 1873–1939
English novelist, editor and poet
Brought up in Pre-Raphaelite circles, he published his first book when he was only 18. He met **Joseph Conrad** in 1898 and they co-authored various works including *The Inheritors* (1901). He later founded and edited various periodicals which published the early work of many of the century's great writers. He wrote almost 80 books in a hectic career but is best remembered for three novels: *The Fifth Queen* (1906), *The Good Soldier* (1915) and *Parade's End* (1924–8).

Ford, Henry 1863–1947
US car engineer and manufacturer
He produced his first petrol-driven motor car in 1893 and in 1903 founded the Ford Motor Company. He pioneered the modern 'assembly line' mass production techniques for his famous Model T (1908–9), 15 million of which were produced up to 1928. He also branched out into aircraft and tractor manufacture. An eccentric who once declared that 'history is bunk', he preached pacifism during World War I, and paid his employees far more than the standard rate, though he opposed the establishment of labour unions.

Forster, E(dward) M(organ) 1879–1970
English novelist and critic
He was a leading light of the Bloomsbury Group, the literary circle that included **Virginia Woolf**, and early novels such as *Where Angels Fear to Tread* (1905), *A Room with a View* (1908) and *Howards End* (1910) examined pre-1914 English middle-class attitudes and conventions. In 1924 he published his masterpiece, *A Passage to India*, which explored the tragic conflicts of Anglo-Indian life. He also wrote short stories, essays, literary criticism and biography. His novel *Maurice* (written 1913–14) was published posthumously in 1971.

Fossey, Dian 1932–85
US zoologist
In 1963 she went to Africa, where she first encountered gorillas. In 1966 she returned to Tanzania and set up the Karisoke Research Centre in Rwanda in order to study the gorilla population. Her 18-year study is documented in her 1983 book *Gorillas in the Mist* (filmed 1988). Fossey rallied international opposition to the threats posed to the gorillas by poaching and local farming methods. In 1985 she was murdered at the Centre.

Foster (of Thames Bank), Norman Robert Foster, Baron 1935–
English architect
A leading exponent of the 'Hi-Tech' movement in architecture, his designs include the Sainsbury Centre at the University of East Anglia (1978), which uses a steel frame structure; the Hong Kong and Shanghai Bank, Hong Kong (1979–85), acclaimed for its boldly expressive structure; the world's largest airport at Chek Lap Kok, Hong Kong (1998); and the Millennium Bridge, London (2000).

Foucault, Jean Bernard Léon 1819–68
French physicist
He determined the velocity of light by the revolving mirror method, and proved that light travels more slowly in water than in air (1850), which was convincing evidence of the wave nature of light. In 1851, by means of a freely suspended pendulum (Foucault's pendulum), he convincingly demonstrated the rotation of the Earth. In 1852 he constructed the first gyroscope.

Fox, George 1624–91
English religious leader
In 1646 he had a divine revelation that inspired him to preach a gospel of brotherly love, and founded a society, the 'Friends of Truth', later the Society of Friends, or 'Quakers', which embodied it. He experienced much persecution for his beliefs, and in 1656 nearly 1,000 of his followers were in prison. As a writer he will be remembered for his *Journal*, published posthumously in 1694.

Francis of Assisi, St, *originally* **Francesco di Pietro di Bernardone** c.1181–1226
Italian founder of the Franciscan order
The son of a wealthy merchant, he was fond of good living. In c.1205 he was inspired by a dream to live as a hermit and devote himself to the care of the poor and the sick. By 1210 he had a brotherhood of eleven, for which he drew up a rule repudiating all property. In 1212 he also founded the 'Poor Clares', a Franciscan order for women. Francis went to Egypt (1223) and preached in the presence of the sultan, who gave the Franciscan order the privilege they have since enjoyed as guardians of the Holy Sepulchre. On his return to Italy he is said to have received, while praying, the stigmata of the wounds of **Jesus Christ** (1224). His works consist of letters, sermons, ascetic treatises, proverbs and hymns. Many legends about his life centre around his love of animals, and in 1980 he was designated patron saint of ecology.

Franco, Francisco, *in full* **Francisco Paulino Hermenegildo Teódulo Franco Bahamonde** 1892–1975
Spanish general and dictator
In 1936 he joined the conspiracy against the newly elected Popular Front government that led to the Spanish Civil War. He became *generalísimo* of the rebel forces and chief of the authoritarian Nationalist government of Spain that emerged from the war, and oversaw the modernization of the Spanish economy in the 1950s and 1960s. This modernization however finally undermined the political foundations of his police state, and in 1969 he announced that on his death the monarchy he had previously abolished would return.

Frank, Anne 1929–45
German Jewish diarist
After the Nazi occupation of Holland, Anne hid with her family and four others in a specially prepared hiding place in the two upper floors of an office building. There they lived from July 1942 to August 1944, when they were betrayed, sent to Auschwitz and later Bergen–Belsen concentration camps, and died; only her father survived. The lively, moving diary she kept from 14 June 1942 and during her concealment was published in 1947. It has since been published in over 50 languages, and has been dramatized and filmed.

Franklin, Aretha 1942–
US soul singer and pianist
Variously known as 'Lady Soul' and 'the Queen of Soul', she established her name on the gospel circuit before achieving fame as a soul singer and pianist with records such as *I Never Loved A Man The Way I Love You* (1967) and *Lady Soul* (1968). In 1972 she returned to gospel music with her album *Amazing Grace*. Subsequent recordings have included *With Everything I Feel in Me* (1974), *Almighty Fire* (1978), *Get It Right* (1983) and *Jazz to Soul* (1992).

Franklin, Benjamin, *pseudonym* **Richard Saunders** 1706–90
US statesman, diplomat, printer, publisher, inventor and scientist
One of the US founding fathers, he began his career as a printer and publisher, notably of *Poor Richard's Almanac*, but turned to the natural sciences in the 1740s, especially to his famous researches in electricity. He also became active in politics, was a negotiator with Britain before the Revolutionary War, and in 1775 helped draft the Declaration of Independence. In February 1778 he negotiated the signature of a Treaty with the French that was vital to US victory in the war. He remained US Minister in Paris until 1785, and in 1787 was a delegate to the convention which framed the Constitution of the USA. At the age of 83 he invented bifocal eyeglasses.

Franklin, Rosalind Elsie 1920–58
English X-ray crystallographer
In 1951 she began work on DNA at King's College, London, producing X-ray diffraction pictures of DNA which were published in the same issue of *Nature* (1953) in which **James Watson** and **Francis Crick** proposed their model of DNA as a double helix. She died four years before she could be awarded the 1962 Nobel Prize for physiology or medicine jointly with Watson, Crick and **Maurice Wilkins**.

Franz Ferdinand 1863–1914
Archduke of Austria
He was the nephew and heir apparent of Emperor Franz Joseph. On a visit to Sarajevo (now in Bosnia) in 1914 he and his wife Sophie were assassinated by a group of young Serbian nationalists led by Gavrilo Princip. Austria used the incident as a pretext for attacking Serbia, which precipitated World War I.

Frederick I, Barbarossa c.1123–1190
Holy Roman Emperor and King of Germany and Italy
He succeeded as Emperor in 1152. In 1162 his conquest of Milan subdued the rebellious Italian states, but he was defeated at Legnano (1176). He subdued Bavaria, and gained authority over Poland, Hungary, Denmark and Burgundy. In 1189 he led the Third Crusade against **Saladin**, but drowned at Cilicia, a region now in modern Turkey.

16th-century portrait of Frederick I, Barbarossa

Frederick II, *known as* **Frederick the Great** 1712–86
King of Prussia
He became king in 1740. One of his first acts was to attack Austria, precipitating a series of wars by which he gained Upper and Lower Silesia, Polish Prussia and a portion of Great Poland. By the end of his reign the area of Prussia had doubled. He was a prolific writer on political, historical and military subjects, corresponded with **Voltaire** and achieved a high level of proficiency on the flute.

Freud, Sigmund 1856–1939
Austrian neurologist
The founder of psychoanalysis, he used hypnosis as a tool in therapy before developing his technique of 'free association', analysing the thoughts suggested by particular words. In 1900 he published his seminal work, *The Interpretation of Dreams*, arguing that dreams, like neuroses, are disguised manifestations of repressed desires, and produced the further crucial works *The Psychopathology of Everyday Life* (1904), *Totem and Taboo* (1913), *Beyond the Pleasure Principle* (1920) and *The Ego and the Id* (1923). In 1908 he founded the Vienna Psychoanalytical Society, and, in 1910, the International Psychoanalytical Association. Under the Nazi regime psychoanalysis was banned, and in 1938 Freud moved to London, but died the following year.

Frobisher, Sir Martin c.1535–1594
English sailor
In 1576 he set off in search of a Northwest Passage to Cathay (northern China), reached Labrador and discovered Frobisher Bay in the south-east of Baffin Island, Canada. From two expeditions (1577, 1578) he brought back 'black earth' which was supposed to be gold from Frobisher Bay. He commanded a vessel in 1585 in **Francis Drake**'s expedition to the West Indies, and was knighted for his services against the Spanish Armada. He was mortally wounded at the siege of Crozon, near Brest, France.

Frost, Robert Lee 1874–1963
US lyric poet
From 1912 to 1915 he lived in Great Britain, where, encouraged by **Rupert Brooke** and others, he published *A Boy's Will* (1913) and *North of Boston* (1914), which brought him an international reputa-

PEOPLE

tion. Returning to the USA, he continued to write lyric and narrative poetry which drew its characters, background and imagery from rural New England. His volumes of poetry include *West-Running Brook* (1928), *A Witness Tree* (1942) and *In the Clearing* (1962). He was awarded the Pulitzer Prize in 1924, 1931, 1937 and 1943, and he read his poem 'The Gift Outright' at President **John F Kennedy**'s inauguration in 1961.

Fry, Elizabeth, *née* **Gurney** 1780–1845
English Quaker prison reformer
She became a preacher for the Society of Friends in 1810. Visiting Newgate Prison for women in 1813 she found 300 women, with their children, in terrible conditions, and thereafter devoted her life to prison and asylum reform at home and abroad. She also founded hostels for the homeless, as well as charitable societies.

Gable, (William) Clark 1901–60
US film actor
His first Hollywood film was *The Painted Desert*, and after winning an Academy Award for *It Happened One Night* (1934), he was voted 'King of Hollywood' in 1937. His sympathetic, ruggedly masculine and humorous persona made him the perfect Rhett Butler in *Gone With the Wind* (1939), and he remained in demand after World War II in films like *Mogambo* (1953) and *Teacher's Pet* (1958). His last film was *The Misfits* (1961).

Gaddafi or **Qaddafi, Muammar (Muhammad al-)** 1942–
Libyan soldier and political leader
He formed the Free Officers Movement which overthrew the régime of King Idris of Libya in 1969. Gaddafi became chairman of the Revolutionary Command Council and Commander-in-Chief of the Libyan armed forces. As effective head of state, he set about expelling foreigners and closing down British and US military bases. He also encouraged a return to the fundamental principles of Islam. He became President of Libya in 1977. Since then Libya has come into conflict with Chad and the USA, but in more recent times Gaddafi presented a more moderate image, and the USA reopened diplomatic relations with Libya in 2006.

Gagarin, Yuri Alekseyevich 1934–68
Soviet cosmonaut
He joined the Soviet air force in 1957, and in 1961 became the first man to complete a circuit of the Earth in the *Vostok* spaceship satellite. Nominated a Hero of the Soviet Union, he was killed in a plane accident while training.

Gainsborough, Thomas 1727–88
English landscape and portrait painter
One of the greatest English painters of the 18th century, his portraits combine elegance with informality. His early masterpieces include *Mr and Mrs Andrews*, *Blue Boy*, and the great landscapes *The Harvest Wagon* and *The Watering Place*. To his later period belong the character study *Mr Truman*, the luxuriant *Mrs Graham*, *George III*, *Queen Charlotte*, *Mrs Siddons*, *The Morning Walk* and *Cattle Crossing a Bridge*.

Galen, *properly* **Claudius Galenus** c.130–c.201 AD
Greek physician
Friend and physician to the emperor **Marcus Aurelius**, he was also physician to emperors Commodus and Septimius Severus. He wrote many volumes on medical and philosophical subjects, and collated all the medical knowledge of his time. An active experimentalist, he was the first to use the pulse as a diagnostic aid. He was long venerated in the Christian West as the standard authority on medical matters.

Galileo, *properly* **Galileo Galilei** 1564–1642
Italian astronomer, mathematician and natural philosopher
In his early work he observed that all bodies fall at the same rate if air resistance is not present, that a body moving along an inclined plane has a constant acceleration, and that a pendulum has a constant rate of swing. In 1610 he perfected a refracting telescope, which he used to observe, for the first time, the mountains of the Moon, the existence of Jupiter's four satellites, sunspots and other phenomena. His support for the Copernican system, in which the Earth revolves around the Sun, led him to be brought before the Inquisition, and under threat of torture, he recanted. He was finally allowed to live under house arrest, where he continued his researches into the principles of mechanics. He was one of the greatest of all scientific experimenters and observers.

Galsworthy, John 1867–1933
English novelist and playwright
In 1906 he published *The Man of Property*, the first in his celebrated *Forsyte Saga* series – the others being *In Chancery* (1920) and *To Let* (1921). In these novels he describes the life of the affluent middle class which ruled England before World War I. The second cycle of the saga, *A Modern Comedy* (1929), includes *The White Monkey* (1924), *The Silver Spoon* (1926) and *Swan Song* (1928), and examines the plight of the postwar generation. He wrote several other novels and more than 30 plays, and won the Nobel Prize for literature in 1932.

Galvani, Luigi 1737–98
Italian physiologist
He is famous for the discovery of electricity in animals, inspired by his observation that dead frogs suffered convulsions when fixed to an iron fence to dry. He then showed that paroxysms followed if a frog was part of a circuit involving metals, wrongly believing the current source to be in the material of muscle and nerve. Galvani's name lives on in the word 'galvanized', meaning stimulated as if by electricity, and in the galvanometer, used from 1820 to detect electric current.

Gama, Vasco da c.1469–1525
Portuguese navigator
On his most famous voyage he left Lisbon in 1497, and after rounding the Cape of Good Hope, made Malindi (in East Africa) early in the following year. From there he crossed the Indian Ocean and arrived at Calicut, India, in 1498, the first Westerner to sail round the Cape to Asia. He arrived back in Lisbon in 1499. However, 40 other Portuguese left behind were murdered, and to avenge them the king sent out a squadron of 20 ships under da Gama (1502), which founded the colonies of Mozambique and Sofala. In 1524 da Gama became Viceroy of India.

Gandhi, Indira Priyad Arshini 1917–84
Indian politician
The daughter of **Jawaharlal Nehru**, she became in-

creasingly influential in India's Congress Party, and took over as Prime Minister in 1966. In 1975, she was convicted for election malpractices, and in 1977 lost her seat; however, she returned to power as Prime Minister in the 1980 general election, as leader of the new Indian National Congress. She was recognized for her work as a leader of the developing nations, but failed to suppress sectarian violence at home. She was assassinated in 1984 by members of her Sikh bodyguard. This murder provoked a Hindu backlash in Delhi, involving the massacre of 3,000 Sikhs.

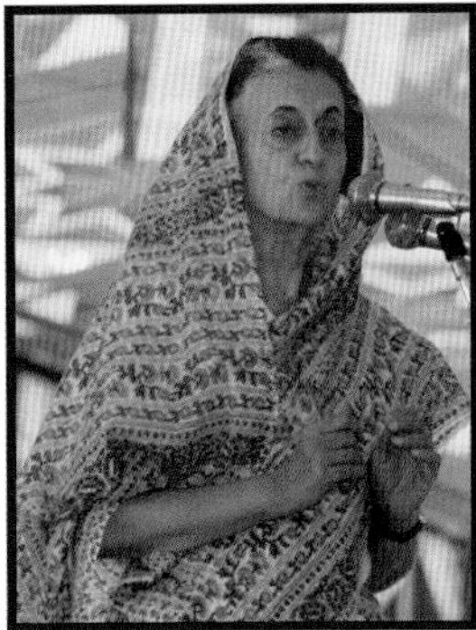

Indira Gandhi

Gandhi, Mahatma ('Great Soul'), *properly* **Mohandâs Karamchand Gandhi** 1869–1948
Indian leader
He studied law in London, and spent over 20 years as a lawyer in South Africa. On his return to India in 1914 he gained control of the Congress Movement and campaigned for Indian independence from Britain, which led to his imprisonment on several occasions. He organized numerous civil disobedience campaigns, and in 1930 led a 200-mile (320km) march to the sea to collect salt in symbolic defiance of the government monopoly on that resource. In May 1947 his efforts for independence bore fruit, but he was assassinated in Delhi by a Hindu fanatic the following year. In his lifetime and afterwards Mahatma ('a great soul') Gandhi was venerated as a moral teacher with a message not only for India but for the world. His publications include the autobiographical *The Story of My Experiment with Truth* (1927–9).

Garbo, Greta, *professional name of* **Greta Lovisa Gustafsson** 1905–90
Swedish-born US film actress
A glamorous star of 1930s films, her first talking role was in *Anna Christie* (1930), and this was followed by her greatest successes, *Queen Christina* (1933), *Anna Karenina* (1935), *Camille* (1936) and *Ninotchka* (1939), a romantic comedy in which she caricatured her own aloof image. She retired from films in 1941 and lived in New York as a total recluse for the rest of her life. She was famous for having said 'I want to be alone.', although she always denied she ever uttered the words.

Garibaldi, Giuseppe 1807–82
Italian revolutionary, soldier and politician
He spent his early career as a soldier fighting in South America, then returned to Italy in 1848 and took part in the government and defence of the Roman Republic, also playing a minor but brilliant part in the 1859 campaign against the Austrians. In 1860 he set sail from Genoa with 1,000 volunteers ('Red Shirts') to assist the rebellion which had broken out in Sicily against the ruling Bourbon Dynasty, and later seized control of the island. He is remembered as the greatest figure of the *Risorgimento*, the period of Italian unification.

Garland, Judy, *originally* **Frances Ethel Gumm** 1922–69
US actress and singer
She became a juvenile film star in *Broadway Melody of 1938* and appeared in several film musicals, among them *The Wizard of Oz* (1939) and *Easter Parade* (1948). Personal appearances confirmed the emotional power of her voice, and in *A Star is Born* (1954) she gave an impressive dramatic performance. Her daughters Liza Minnelli and Lorna Luft have followed in her footsteps as actors and singers.

Gates, Bill (William Henry) 1955–
US computer scientist and businessman
In 1975, at the age of 19, he founded Microsoft Corporation with Paul Allen, and in 1980 they licensed a computer operating system to International Business Machines (IBM) for use in the fledgling personal computer industry. This system (MS-DOS) has been phenomenally successful, and updated versions of it (such as Windows XP) allowed Gates to maintain Microsoft's market dominance. Gates became a billionaire by 1986 and by the turn of the century was estimated to be the world's most wealthy private individual. He has set up several charitable foundations, and among his bestselling books is *Business @ the Speed of Thought* (1999).

Gaudí (i Cornet), Antoni 1852–1926
Spanish architect
The leading exponent of Catalan Modernism (a branch of the art nouveau movement in architecture), he was inspired by a nationalistic search for a romantic medieval past. Strikingly original and ingenious, he designed a number of highly individualistic and unconventional buildings, such as the Palacio Güell (1886–9), the Parque Güell (1900–14), the Casa Batlló (1904–17) and the Casa Milá (1905–9), all in Barcelona. His most celebrated work, the ornate church of the Sagrada Familia in Barcelona, occupied him from 1884 until his death.

Gauguin, (Eugène Henri) Paul 1848–1903
French Post-Impressionist painter
A successful stockbroker in Paris, by 1883 he determined to devote himself entirely to art. He left his Danish wife and five children, and travelled widely, ending his life in Tahiti and the Marquesas Islands, French Polynesia. His works from this latter period include *Why are you angry?* (1896) and *Whence do we come? What are we? Where are we going?* (1898). Gauguin also excelled in wood carvings and wrote an autobiographical novel, *Noa-Noa* (1894–1900). His interest in 'primitivism' influenced almost every school of 20th-century art.

Gauss, (Johann) Carl Friedrich 1777–1855
German mathematician, astronomer and physicist
From a very early age he made many remarkable discoveries in areas such as prime number theory and geometry, and in 1801 published his *Disquisitiones arithmeticae*. The same year he was the first to redis-

cover the asteroid Ceres (found by Giuseppe Piazzi in 1800 and since lost behind the Sun). His other contributions to science include important work in statistics, differential equations, the curvature of surfaces, number theory, magnetism and much else, and he is generally regarded as one of the greatest scientific geniuses of his time.

Gay-Lussac, Joseph Louis 1778–1850
French chemist and physicist
His earliest research work was on the expansion of gases with temperature increases, and he independently discovered the law which in Great Britain is commonly known as **Charles**'s law: that the volume of a given mass of gas will increase as its temperature increases, as long as its pressure remains constant. He also discovered boron, in 1808.

Gehry, Frank 1929–
US–Canadian architect
He became known in the 1960s for his playful, almost surreal designs using inexpensive materials such as chain-link fencing, plywood and raw concrete. His later work includes buildings such as the ING Office Building (1996) in Prague, the Los Angeles Children's Museum (1980) and the American Center (1994) in Paris.

Geiger, Hans Wilhelm 1882–1945
German physicist
With **Ernest Rutherford** he devised a means of detecting alpha particles (1908), and subsequently showed that two alpha particles are emitted in the radioactive decay of uranium. After further important work on radioactivity, he and Walther Müller made improvements to the particle counter, resulting in the modern form of the Geiger counter.

Geldof, Bob 1954–
Irish rock musician and philanthropist
He sang with the rock group the Boomtown Rats (1975–86), and in 1984 established the pop charity 'Band Aid' to help famine-stricken Ethiopia. This raised £8 million through the release of the record 'Do they know it's Christmas?'. In 1985, simultaneous 'Live Aid' charity concerts were held in London and Philadelphia, which raised a further £48 million. Other charitable events followed and Geldof was awarded an honorary knighthood in 1986. In 2005 he organized the 'Live 8' concerts to campaign for third-world debt relief.

Gell-Mann, Murray 1929–
US theoretical physicist
He made a major contribution to the theory of elementary particles and helped develop a system for classifying them. Gell-Mann and George Zweig also introduced the concept of the quark, an elementary particle that comes in six varieties, and for this work he was awarded the Nobel Prize for physics in 1969.

Genghis Khan, *also spelt* **Jingis, Chingis, Chinghiz** or **Chingiz** c.1162–1227
Mongol warrior and ruler
The son of a Mongol chief, he succeeded his father aged 13, and after his first military successes changed his name from Temujin to Genghis Khan, 'Universal Ruler'. He conquered empires stretching from the Black Sea to the Pacific, including huge tracts of modern Russia and China, and organized them into permanent states on which his successors were able to build.

George III, *in full* **George William Frederick** 1738–1820
King of Great Britain and Ireland and of Hanover
In 1760 he succeeded his grandfather, George II, as King of Great Britain and Ireland and Elector of Hanover (King of Hanover from 1815). During his administration, the American colonies declared their independence (4 July 1776), and George's determination to keep them under British control resulted in the Revolutionary War. In 1810 the Princess Amelia, his favourite child, fell dangerously ill, which may have worsened his developing mental illness, although he is now believed to have suffered from porphyria. In 1811 the Prince of Wales was appointed regent, and although the king lived on until January 1820 he did not recover.

Germain, Sophie 1776–1831
French mathematician
She was not admitted, as a woman, to the newly established École Polytechnique in Paris, but in the guise of a male student she submitted a paper which so impressed mathematician Joseph de Lagrange that he became her personal tutor. Among her achievements she gave a more generalized proof of **Pierre de Fermat**'s 'last theorem' than had previously been available, and went on to derive a general mathematical description of the vibrations of curved as well as plane elastic surfaces.

Gershwin, George, *originally* **Jacob Gershvin** 1898–1937
US composer
A composer who successfully fused jazz and popular song, in the 1920s and 1930s he wrote the scores of a series of hit musicals featuring songs such as 'Someone to Watch Over Me', 'Embraceable You' and 'I Got Rhythm'. In 1924 he produced *Rhapsody in Blue*, a concert work in the jazz idiom. This was followed by the *Concerto in F* (1925), *An American in Paris* (1928) and the opera *Porgy and Bess* (1935). Most of his work was written in collaboration with his brother, Ira Gershwin.

Getty, Jean Paul 1892–1976
US oil executive, billionaire and art collector
He made his fortune in the oil business and became one of the richest men in the world, acquiring a huge and extremely valuable art collection. He also developed a legendary reputation for miserliness, installing a pay-telephone for guests in his English mansion. Among his books is the autobiography *As I See It* (1976).

Ghazali, al- 1058–1111
Islamic philosopher, theologian and jurist
In 1091 he was appointed to the position of Professor of Philosophy at Nizamiyah College, Baghdad, but suffered a spiritual crisis which led him to abandon his position for the austere life of a mendicant Sufi (a mystic). His doctrines represent an attempt to reconcile philosophy and Islamic dogma. His main works include *The Intentions of the Philosophers*, *The Deliverance from Error* and the monumental *The Revival of the Religious Sciences*.

Ghiberti, Lorenzo 1378–1455
Italian goldsmith, bronze-caster and sculptor
In 1402 he won a competition to make a pair of bronze doors for the Florence Baptistery. Much of his

life was spent completing this set of doors, and as soon as they were finished in 1424 he was entrusted with the execution of another set (1425–52). He was also responsible for the three bronze figures of the saints Matthew, Stephen and John the Baptist which adorn the exterior of Orsan Michele in Florence. He was also a humanist and scholar and wrote *I commentarii*, a wide ranging history of art.

Giacometti, Alberto 1901–66
Swiss sculptor and painter
He joined the surrealists in 1930, producing many abstract constructions of a symbolic kind, arriving finally at the characteristic 'thin man' bronzes, long spidery statuettes such as *Man Pointing* (1947).

Alberto Giacometti

Gibbon, Lewis Grassic, *pseudonym of* **James Leslie Mitchell** 1901–35
Scottish novelist
His first published book was *Hanno, or the Future of Exploration* (1928), followed by *Stained Radiance* (1930), *The Thirteenth Disciple* (1931), *Three Go Back* (1932) and *The Lost Trumpet* (1932). *Sunset Song*, his greatest achievement, was published in 1932, the first of his books to appear under his pseudonym. It was the first of a trilogy of novels, *A Scots Quair*, on the life of a young girl called Chris Guthrie. The second volume, *Cloud Howe*, appeared in 1933 and the third part, *Grey Granite*, in 1934.

Gide, André Paul Guillaume 1869–1951
French novelist, writer and diarist
His international reputation rests largely on his stylish novels, in which there is a sharp conflict between the spiritual and the physical. They include *The Immoralist* (1902), *Strait is the Gate* (1909) and *Two Symphonies* (1919). His *Journals*, covering the years from 1889 to 1949, are an essential supplement to his autobiography, *If It Die...* (1920–1). He was awarded the Nobel Prize for literature in 1947.

Gielgud, Sir (Arthur) John 1904–2000
English actor and producer
He established his reputation in *The Constant Nymph* (1926), *Hamlet* (1929) and *The Good Companions* (1931), and went on to become one of the leading actors and directors of the 20th century. He appeared in many films, notably as Benjamin Disraeli in *The Prime Minister* (1940) and as conspirator Cassius in *Julius Caesar* (1952). Highly adaptable, he appeared during the 1960s and 1970s in plays by Edward Bond and **Harold Pinter** and in films by directors such as Peter Greenaway. His first autobiography, *Early Stages*, was published as early as 1938.

Gigli, Beniamino 1890–1957
Italian tenor
He made his operatic debut in Amilcare Ponchielli's *La Gioconda* in 1914, and by 1929 had a worldwide reputation. A lyric-dramatic tenor of great natural gifts, he compensated for technical deficiencies and weakness as an actor by the vitality of his singing, and was at his best in the works of **Verdi** and **Puccini**.

Gilbert, Sir W(illiam) S(chwenck) 1836–1911
English parodist and librettist
It is as the librettist of Sir **Arthur Sullivan**'s light operas that he is best remembered. Their famous partnership, which began in 1871, scored its first success with *Trial by Jury*, and later included works such as *HMS Pinafore* (1878), *The Pirates of Penzance* (1879), *The Mikado* (1885) and *The Gondoliers* (1889). Their works were performed from 1881 in the new Savoy Theatre, London, which had been specifically built for them.

Gilbert, William 1544–1603
English physician
He was physician to Queen **Elizabeth I** (1601) and King **James VI and I** (1603). In his *De Magnete* (1600), the first comprehensive scientific work published in England, he established the that the Earth itself is a magnet and theorized that magnetism and electricity were two types of a single force. He was the first to use the terms 'electricity' and 'magnetic pole'.

Gill, (Arthur) Eric (Rowton) 1882–1940
English sculptor, engraver, writer and typographer
A highly influential and individual figurative artist, his sculptures include the *Stations of the Cross* (1913), war memorials up and down Great Britain after World War I, the gigantic figure *Mankind* (1928) and *Prospero and Ariel* (1931). As well as sculpture he also created type designs, such as Perpetua, Bunyan and Gill Sans-serif, and wrote a stream of books including *Art* (1934) and *Autobiography* (1940).

Gillespie, Dizzy (John Birks) 1917–93
US jazz trumpeter, composer and bandleader

Dizzy Gillespie

Along with **Charlie Parker** and others, he was involved in informal jam session experiments in New York that produced the bebop style in the 1940s. In 1945 Gillespie formed the first of his several big bands working in the new idiom. Although he worked intermittently with large orchestras, he is best known as a leader of small bands and as a virtuoso who extended the working range of the trumpet.

Giorgione, *also called* **Giorgio Barbarelli** or **Giorgio del Castelfranco** c.1478–1511
Italian painter
His work, characterized by intense poetic feeling and richness of colouring, includes *The Tempest, The Family of Giorgione, The Three Philosophers* and the *Sleeping Venus*. Giorgione was a great innovator; he created the small intimate easel picture with a new treatment of figures in landscape, aimed at private rather than public collections.

Giotto (di Bondone) c.1267–1337
Italian painter and architect
He was the most innovative artist of his time, and is generally regarded as the founder of the Florentine school. His most important works are the frescoes in the Arena Chapel, Padua, the Navicella mosaic in St Peter's, Rome, the cycle of frescoes depicting scenes from the life of Saint Francis of Assisi, frescoes in the Peruzzi Chapel in the church of Santa Croce, Florence, and the Ognissanti Madonna, now in the Uffizi, Florence. Stylistically he broke with the rigid conventions of Byzantine art, and composed dramatic narratives peopled by realistic and believable figures.

Gladstone, William Ewart 1809–98
English Liberal statesman
The dominant figure of English politics in the second half of the 19th century, he was prime minister four times: 1868–74, 1880–5, 1886 and 1892–4. His rival for much of this time was Benjamin **Disraeli**. He was on famously bad terms with Queen **Victoria**, who said that he always addressed her as if she were a public meeting. During his terms of office he brought in numerous reforms, establishing a national system of education, the beginnings of laws promoting votes for all men, and re-organizing the army and civil service. His foreign policy was concerned chiefly with keeping peace abroad.

Glass, Philip 1937–
US composer
He is much influenced by Far Eastern music, by the melodic repetition found in North African music, and by rock music. The resulting 'minimalist' style gained him a considerable following, especially in such stage works as *Einstein on the Beach* (1976), *Satyagraha* (1980), *Akhnaton* (1984) and *The Voyage* (1992). His other compositions include the film scores for *Hamburger Hill* (1989) and *The Truman Show* (1998), and the operas *Orphee* (1993) and *Monsters of Grace* (1998).

Glendower, Owen, *properly* **Owain Glyndŵr** c.1350–c.1416
Welsh rebel
He quarrelled with a lord over some lands and, unable to obtain redress from **Henry IV**, began a guerrilla campaign against the English lords of the Marches which became a national war of independence. He proclaimed himself Prince of Wales, and in 1402 captured Lord Grey and Sir Edmund Mortimer, both of whom joined him in coalition with Henry Percy (Hotspur). That coalition ended in the Battle of Shrewsbury (1403), won by Henry IV. In 1404 Glendower entered into a treaty with Charles VI of France, who in 1405 sent a force to Wales. Glendower, though often defeated, kept fighting until his death.

Glenn, John Herschel 1921–
US astronaut and politician
In 1957 he completed a record-breaking supersonic flight from Los Angeles to New York. He became an astronaut in 1959, and in 1962 became the first American to orbit the Earth in a three-orbit flight in the Friendship 7 space capsule. From 1975 to 1998 he served as Democratic senator for Ohio, and re-entered space aboard the space shuttle in 1998.

Gluck, Christoph Willibald 1714–87
German composer
In collaboration with the librettist Ranieri Calzabigi, he produced such works as *Orpheus and Eurydice* (1762) and *Alceste* (1767). In the late 1770s, Paris was divided into those who supported Gluck's French opera style and those who supported the traditional Italian style, but Gluck won great accolades with his *Iphigénie en Tauride* (1778), and retired honourably from Paris.

Godard, Jean-Luc 1930–
French film director
He started making short films in 1954 and his first feature film, *Breathless* (1960), established him as a leader of the 'New Wave' cinema. His original use of jump cuts, freeze frames and so on gained him much critical attention, both enthusiastic and otherwise. Other work from the 1960s includes *Pierrot le fou* (1965), *Alphaville* (1965) and *Week-end* (1967). Later feature films include *Slow Motion* (1980), *Detective* (1984), *Woe is Me* (1993), and *Our Music* (2004).

Goebbels or **Göbbels, (Paul) Joseph** 1897–1945
German Nazi politician
An early supporter of Adolf **Hitler**, he led the Nazi Party in Berlin in 1923. When Hitler came to power he was made head of the Ministry of Public Enlightenment and Propaganda. A bitter anti-Semite, he had a gift for oratory which made him a powerful exponent of the more extreme aspects of the Nazi philosophy. By 1943, while Hitler was running the war, Goebbels was virtually running the country. In the Berlin bunker he and his wife committed suicide after they had taken the lives of their six children. His diaries now represent a major historical source.

Goering or **Göring, Hermann Wilhelm** 1893–1946
German Nazi politician
An ace pilot in World War I, he joined the Nazi party in 1922 and next year commanded the **Hitler** storm troopers, the Brownshirts (SA). He founded the Gestapo, set up the concentration camps, and, in the great purge of 30 June 1934 ('night of the long knives'), had his comrades murdered. In 1940 he became economic dictator of Germany and Marshal of the Reich. However, the Battle of Britain, the failure of the 1941 Nazi bombing attacks on Britain, and the mounting Allied air attacks on Germany led to a decline in his prestige. After the war he was tried at Nuremburg, but committed suicide by poison a few hours prior to his intended execution.

Goethe, Johann Wolfgang von 1749–1832
German poet, dramatist, scientist and court official
One of the greatest figures in European literature, his masterpiece is probably his version of *Faust* (1808–32), on which he worked for most of his life. Of his

novels, *The Sorrows of Young Werther* (1774) and the two *Wilhelm Meister* novels (1796–1821) were the most influential on the development of German Romanticism. Other works include *Iphigenie auf Tauris* (1787), *Egmont* (1788) and *Torquato Tasso* (1790). He also took an interest in the sciences, making important contributions in anatomy and botany. He took little part in the political upheavals of his time, although he regarded **Napoleon I** as the saviour of European civilization. His autobiography is *From My Life: Poetry and Truth* (1811–22).

Golding, Sir William Gerald 1911–93
English novelist
He gained international fame with *The Lord of the Flies* (1954), a chronicle of the increasingly malevolent actions of a group of schoolboys shipwrecked on a desert island in the wake of a nuclear war. It was followed by novels including *The Inheritors* (1955), *Free Fall* (1959), *The Spire* (1964), *The Pyramid* (1967), *Rites of Passage* (1980) and *The Paper Men* (1984). He was awarded the Nobel Prize for literature in 1983.

Goldsmith, Oliver 1730–74
Irish playwright, novelist and poet
A writer in several different genres, he worked for many years as a journalist and essayist. He is probably best known for his play *She Stoops to Conquer* (1773). *The Vicar of Wakefield* (1766) secured his reputation as a novelist, and *The Deserted Village* (1770) established him as a poet.

Goodman, Benny (Benjamin David) 1909–86
US clarinettist and bandleader
He formed his own orchestra in New York in 1934 and, thanks to media exposure, became one of the best known leaders of the era with the nickname 'King of Swing'. Hiring top black musicians such as vibraphone player Lionel Hampton, Goodman successfully defied racial taboos of the time. He occasionally performed as a classical player.

Gorbachev, Mikhail Sergeyevich 1931–
Russian statesman

Mikhail Gorbachev

He was promoted to full membership of the politburo in 1980, and succeeded Konstantin Chernenko as party general-secretary in 1985. Under the slogans *glasnost* ('openness') and *perestroika* ('restructuring'), he unveiled a series of liberalizing economic, political and cultural reforms, and signed a nuclear arms control treaty with US President **Ronald Reagan** in 1987. He faced a continuing challenge in **Boris Yeltsin**, who urged more radical reform, and in 1991 he survived a coup staged by conservative elements of the government. Later in the year Gorbachev had no choice but to resign, when the Communist Party was abolished and the Soviet Union disintegrated. He was awarded the Nobel Peace Prize in 1990.

Gormley, Antony Mark David 1950–
English sculptor
He is known chiefly for his sculptures made of moulds from his own body in various poses. After 1990 his bodies expanded into bulbous forms, such as *Still Running* (1990–3). His *Angel of the North* (1997–8), a figure some 20 metres high with a wingspan of 54 metres, was erected in Gateshead, north-east England.

Gould, Glenn 1932–82
Canadian pianist and composer
He toured extensively in the USA and Europe and made many recordings, particularly of works by **Bach** and **Beethoven**. His own work, *A String Quartet*, was premiered in 1956, and his writings were collected together as *The Glenn Gould Reader* (1987).

Goya y Lucientes, Francisco (José) de 1746–1828
Spanish artist
In 1786 he was appointed court painter to the Spanish king, Charles IV, and executed a series of rather unflattering portraits of the Spanish royal family. Other works include *Maja nude* and *Maja clothed* (c.1797–1800). In a series of 82 satirical etchings called *Los Caprichos* issued in 1799, Goya castigated the follies of the court. After the occupation of Spain by Napoleon, he produced an equally sardonic series entitled *The Disasters of War*. His work has influenced virtually every major painter, including **Picasso**.

Grace, W(illiam) G(ilbert) 1848–1915
English cricketer and doctor
He is considered the first genuinely great cricketer of modern times. He scored 2,739 runs in a season in 1871, and in 1876 he scored 344 runs in an innings. He toured Canada and the USA, and twice captained the Test team against Australia. By 1895 he had scored 100 first-class centuries. He took his medical degree in 1879 and had a practice in Bristol, but devoted most of his time to cricket.

Graf, Steffi 1969–
German tennis player
In 1988 she won the Grand Slam of singles titles – the US, French, Australian and Wimbledon – as well as the gold medal at the Seoul Olympics. Her win at Wimbledon the following year confirmed her position as world number one, and other singles wins include the French Open (1987, 1993, 1995–6, 1999), the Australian Open (1989–90, 1994), the US Open (1989, 1993, 1995–6), and the Wimbledon championship (1991–3, 1995–6).

Graham, Martha 1894–1991
US dancer, teacher and choreographer
A pioneer of modern dance, in 1930 she founded the Dance Repertory Theatre, creating works such as *Lamentation* (1930) and *Frontier* (1935). One of her best-known ballets, *Appalachian Spring* (1958, with music by **Aaron Copland**), was a product of her great interest in Native American life and mythology and the early American pioneer spirit, and much of her

work was based on the reinterpretation of ancient myths and historical characters. Her method of dance training has been widely adopted in schools and colleges around the world.

Gram, Hans Christian Joachim 1853–1938
Danish bacteriologist
In 1884 he developed a method of staining bacteria with dyes, an important tool used to identify and classify bacteria and treat infections, and one which is still in use today. The stain divides bacteria into two groups, *Gram-positive* or *Gram-negative*, depending on the structure of their cell walls.

Grant, Cary, *originally* **Archibald Leach** 1904–86
US film actor
Born in Bristol, England, he went to Hollywood in 1928 and made his film debut in *This is the Night* (1932). A suave, debonair performer opposite **Marlene Dietrich** and Mae West, he excelled in sophisticated light comedy, displaying a sense of the ridiculous in films like *Bringing Up Baby* (1938), *His Girl Friday* (1940) and *Arsenic and Old Lace* (1944). He was also notable in **Alfred Hitchcock**'s thrillers, including *Suspicion* (1941) and *North By Northwest* (1959).

Gray, Thomas 1716–71
English poet
Gray is best known for two poems: his 'Ode on a Distant Prospect of Eton College' (1747), and the 'Elegy Written in a Country Churchyard' (1751), which contains some of the best-known lines in English literature. Among other work is his *Pindaric Odes* (1757). He was also Professor of History and Modern Languages at Cambridge.

Greco, El, *properly* **Domenico Theotocopoulos** 1541–1614
Spanish painter
Born in Crete, of Greek descent, he studied in Italy, possibly as a pupil of **Titian**. He settled in Toledo, Spain, about 1577. His paintings feature elongated flame-like figures, strange lighting and colour, and, in his later pictures, almost Impressionist brushwork. The most famous of his paintings is probably the *Burial of Count Orgaz* (1586); others include his *Crucifixion* and *Resurrection* (1604).

Green, Lucinda, *née* **Prior-Palmer** 1953–
British three-day eventer
She won the Badminton Horse Trials a record six times (1973, 1976–7, 1979, 1983–4), and the Burghley Horse Trials in 1977 and 1981. At the European championships she won an individual gold medal in 1975 and 1977, a team gold in 1977, 1985, and 1987, and an individual and team silver in 1983. She was the 1982 world champion on Regal Realm, when she also won a team gold medal.

Greene, (Henry) Graham 1904–91
English writer
His novels, which often fuse comedy and tragedy in a distinctive way, include *Stamboul Train* (1932), *Brighton Rock* (1938), *The Heart of the Matter* (1948) *The Third Man* (1950), *The End of the Affair* (1951), *Our Man in Havana* (1958) and *The Human Factor* (1978). Often heavily influenced by his Catholicism and by a preoccupation with good and evil, Greene himself ironically dismissed his novels as 'entertainments'. He also published numerous travel books, plays, essays, short stories and biographies. He was often cited by his peers as the greatest novelist of his time.

Gregory I, *known as* **Gregory the Great** c.540–604
Pope (from 590) and saint, a Doctor of the Church
As Pope he proved to be a great administrator, and during his period of office the Roman Church underwent a complete overhaul of its ritual and the systematization of its sacred chants, from which arose the Gregorian chant. It was while at Rome that he is said to have seen some Anglo-Saxon youths in the slave-market, and to have been seized with a longing to convert their country to Christianity. He entrusted the mission to convert the English to **Augustine**. In his writings the whole dogmatical system of the modern Church is fully developed.

Gretzky, Wayne 1961–
Canadian ice-hockey player
He has set numerous records, including most goals scored in a season (92 in 1981–2) and most points scored in a National Hockey League career (2,857). Nine times named the NHL's Most Valuable Player (1980–7, 1989), he is nicknamed the Great One and considered the greatest player in the history of the game. He retired in 1999.

Grieg, Edvard Hagerup 1843–1907
Norwegian composer
A strongly national Norwegian composer with an intense awareness of his folk heritage, he is best known for his incidental music for **Ibsen**'s *Peer Gynt* (1876). Apart from his Piano Concerto in A minor, some orchestral suites, three violin sonatas and one quartet, his large-scale output was small, although he wrote many songs.

Grimaldi, Francesco Maria 1618–63
Italian physicist
A Jesuit, among his many contributions to science he verified **Galileo**'s laws of falling bodies, produced a detailed lunar map, discovered diffraction of light, and researched into interference and the behaviour of light travelling through prisms. He was one of the first to out forward a wave theory of light.

Guevara, Che, *properly* **Ernesto Guevara de la Serna** 1928–67
Argentine Communist revolutionary leader
He joined **Fidel Castro**'s revolutionary movement in Mexico (1955), played an important part in the Cuban revolution (1956–9) and afterwards held government posts under Castro. An activist of revolution elsewhere, he left Cuba in 1965 to become a guerrilla leader in South America, and was captured and executed by government troops in Bolivia while trying to foment a revolt. He became an icon for left-wing youth in the 1960s.

Guinness, Sir Alec 1914–2000
English actor
After a stage career and war service in the Royal Navy he began his cinema career in earnest with the Charles **Dickens** adaptations *Great Expectations* (1946) and *Oliver Twist* (1948). Long associated with productions from Ealing Studios, his many comic triumphs include *Kind Hearts and Coronets* (1949) and *The Ladykillers* (1955). He received a Best Actor

Academy Award for *The Bridge on the River Kwai* (1957). His television work included appearances as inscrutable intelligence officer George Smiley in *Tinker, Tailor, Soldier, Spy* (1979) and *Smiley's People* (1982).

Guinness, Sir Benjamin Lee 1798–1868
Irish brewer
He joined the firm of Guinness at an early age, and in 1855 became sole owner. Under him the brand of stout became famous and the business grew into the largest of its kind in the world. He was the first Lord Mayor of Dublin in 1851 and an MP from 1865 to 1868.

Gutenberg, Johannes Gensfleisch 1400–68
German printer, regarded as the inventor of printing
He is said to have invented printing around 1439, although it is probable that simpler forms of printing were practised before that. Apart from his Forty-Two-Line Bible, he is credited with the *Fragment of the Last Judgment* (c.1445), and editions of Aelius Donatus' Latin school grammar.

Haber, Fritz 1868–1934
German physical chemist
In 1904 he began to study the synthesis of ammonia from nitrogen and hydrogen gases, work which led to the large-scale production of ammonia. This was important in maintaining an explosives supply for the German war effort from 1914 to 1918. It also led to Haber receiving the Nobel Prize for chemistry in 1918. This brought about some criticism because he had been involved in the organization of gas warfare.

Hadrian, *in full* **Publius Aelius Hadrianus** AD76–138
Roman emperor
He became prefect of Syria (AD114), and after the emperor Trajan's death was proclaimed emperor by the army (AD117). He spent little of his reign in Rome, and from c.120AD he visited Gaul, Germany, Britain (where he built the wall named after him from the Solway Firth to the Tyne), Spain, Mauretania, Egypt, Asia Minor and Greece. After crushing a major revolt in Judea (AD132–4), he returned to Italy, where he died. Although at times ruthless and tyrannical, he was an able administrator, and among the most intellectual and cultivated of all the Roman emperors.

Hahn, Otto 1879–1968
German radiochemist
His research from 1904 onwards was devoted entirely to the chemistry of the radioactive elements, much of it in collaboration with the Austrian physicist **Lise Meitner**. His best-known research, initially in association with Meitner and later with Fritz Strassmann, led to the discovery of nuclear fission (1938). For this Hahn received the Nobel Prize for chemistry in 1944. Greatly upset that his discovery led to the atomic bombings of Hiroshima and Nagasaki, he became a staunch opponent of nuclear weapons.

Haile Selassie I, *previously* **Prince Ras Tafari Makonnen** 1891–1975
Emperor of Ethiopia
A Christian, he became emperor in 1930, and undertook a programme of westernizing reforms. He settled in England after the Italian conquest of Abyssinia (1935–6), but in 1941 was restored by British forces. In the early 1960s he played a crucial part in the establishment of the Organization of African Unity. Opposition to his reign had existed since 1960, and the disastrous famine of 1973 led to nationwide chaos. In 1974 he was deposed, and suspicion persists about the cause of his death. He is held in reverence by certain groups, notably the Rastafarians.

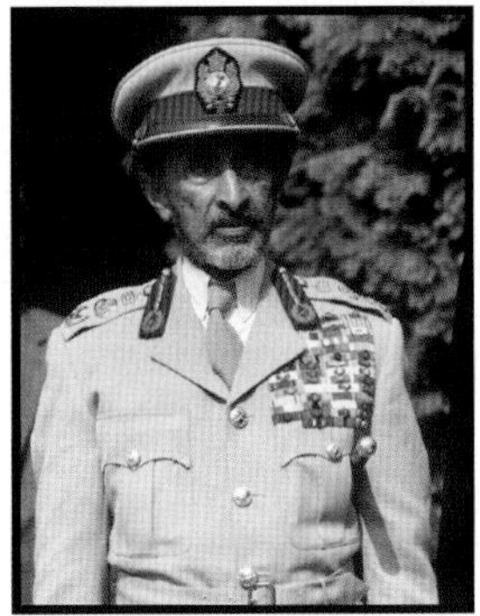

Haile Selassie I

Hall, Sir Peter Reginald Frederick 1930–
English theatre, opera and film director
A dominant force in British theatre since the 1950s, he has been director of the Royal Shakespeare Company, the Covent Garden Opera, the National Theatre and the Glyndebourne Festival. Among his films are *Work is a Four Letter Word* (1968), *Perfect Friday* (1971) and *Akenfield* (1974). In 1988 set up the Peter Hall Company, the inaugural project being his own production of **Tennessee Williams**'s *Orpheus Descending*. He was knighted in 1977.

Halley, Edmond 1656–1742
English astronomer and mathematician
His calculation of the orbits of 24 comets enabled him to predict correctly the return (in 1758, 1835 and 1910) of a comet that had been observed in 1583 (Halley's comet). He was the first to make a complete observation of the transit of Mercury across the sun's disc, and among many other researches he predicted with considerable accuracy the pattern of the solar eclipse that was observed over England in 1715. He also encouraged **Isaac Newton** to write his celebrated *Principia Mathematica* (1687) and paid for its publication himself. In 1720 he became Astronomer Royal.

Hammerstein, Oscar, II 1895–1960
US lyricist and librettist
He formed a famous partnership with **Richard Rodgers** in 1943, and together they produced such classic musicals as *Oklahoma!* (1943), *Carousel* (1945), the Pulitzer Prize-winning *South Pacific* (1949), *The King and I* (1951) and *The Sound of Music* (1959). Hammerstein's sharp dialogue and ability to create dramatic movement through song helped to transform US musical theatre.

Handel, George Frideric, *German (until 1715)* **Georg Friedrich Händel** 1685–1759
German–English composer
Regarded as the greatest composer of his day, he worked chiefly in England, and composed his famous *Water Music* for King George I. His English oratorios

proved to be enormously popular, and include *Saul* (1739), *Israel in Egypt* (1739), and the *Messiah* (1742). His output in total included 46 operas, 32 oratorios, large numbers of cantatas, sacred music, concerti grossi and other orchestral, instrumental and vocal music.

Hannibal, 'the grace of Baal' 247–182BC
Carthaginian soldier
He served under his father Hamilcar and his brother-in-law Hasdrubal, and was elected general after Hasdrubal's death. During the Second Punic War with Rome, in 218BC he surprised the Romans by marching from Spain through southern Gaul, and crossing the Alps into Italy with an army including elephants. After winning a series of victories he was forced to retreat to Africa to meet a Roman invasion. On the conclusion of peace Hannibal devoted himself to political reform, but when the Romans later demanded his surrender, he took poison.

Harald III Sigurdsson, *also called* **Harald Hardraade** or **Hardrada (the Ruthless)** 1015–66
King of Norway
He served as a Viking mercenary, and returned to Norway (1045) to demand, and receive, a half-share in the kingdom from his nephew, Magnus I Olafsson. He became sole king on his nephew's death (1047). He expanded Norway's possessions in Orkney, Shetland and the Hebrides, and after long wars against King Svein II Ulfsson of Denmark, he invaded England (1066) to claim the throne after the death of **Edward the Confessor**. Although he captured York, he was defeated and killed by **Harold II** at Stamford Bridge.

Hardie, (James) Keir 1856–1915
Scottish Labour leader and politician
The first of all Labour candidates, he stood as candidate for the Scottish Labour Party in Mid-Lanark (1888), but was elected for West Ham, South (1892–5), and Merthyr Tydfil (1900–15). In and out of parliament he worked strenuously for socialism and the unemployed. In 1893 he founded the Independent Labour Party, later renamed the Labour Party. A strong pacifist, he opposed the Boer War, and lost his seat in 1915 after opposing Britain's involvement in World War I.

Harding, Warren G(amaliel) 1865–1923
29th President of the USA
He entered politics as a Republican and served as a state senator (1899–1903) and Lieutenant-Governor (1902–6) of Ohio before becoming President (1921–3). He promised a 'return to normalcy' after World War I, and his presidency saw the conclusion of peace treaties with Germany, Austria and Hungary. Politically naive, he had little notion of the real activities of his appointees and advisers until 1923, when he received word that the corrupt schemes of several of his Cabinet members were on the verge of being exposed. This shock probably contributed to his sudden death in San Francisco soon afterwards.

Hardy, Oliver, *originally* **Norvell Hardy Jnr** 1892–1957
US comic actor
He began his career in a travelling minstrel show, entering films in 1913. In 1927 he teamed up with **Stan Laurel**, as Laurel and Hardy; the partnership produced more than 100 comedy films, including silent shorts such as *Leave 'Em Laughing* (1928), *The Finishing Touch* (1928), *Liberty* (1929) and *Big Business* (1929), the sound shorts *Men o' War* (1929), *Perfect Day* (1929) and *The Music Box* (1932), and the feature *Way Out West* (1937). Hardy also made more than 200 films outside the partnership.

Hardy, Thomas 1840–1928
English novelist, poet and dramatist
He first achieved success with the novel *Far From the Madding Crowd* (1874), and went on to produce such enduring classics as *The Return of the Native* (1878), *The Mayor of Casterbridge* (1886), *Tess of the D'Urbervilles* (1891) and *Jude the Obscure* (1895). His marriage was not without difficulties but, ironically, when his wife Emma died in 1912, Hardy was inspired to write some of the most moving love poems in the language. His other poetry expresses his love of rural life.

Harold II c.1022–1066
Anglo-Saxon King of England
In 1053 he succeeded to his father's earldom of Essex and became the right hand of King **Edward the Confessor**. In January 1066 Edward died, and Harold, his nominee, was chosen as king. He defeated **Harald III Sigurdsson** (Harald Hardraade), King of Norway, at Stamford Bridge in September 1066, but four days later Duke William of Normandy landed in the south of England at Pevensey. Harold marched southwards and the two armies met at Senlac, about nine miles from Hastings. On 14 October 1066, the English fought stubbornly all day but were defeated. Harold, the last Anglo-Saxon King of England, was killed; he was supposedly pierced through the eye with an arrow.

Harvey, William 1578–1657
English physician
His celebrated work, *An Anatomical Exercise on the Motion of the Heart and the Blood in Animals*, in which the circulation of the blood was first described, was published in 1628. He was physician to **James VI and I** (from 1618) and **Charles I** (from 1640). He made important contributions to the study of reproduction in animals.

Hawking, Stephen William 1942–
English theoretical physicist
He became Lucasian Professor of Mathematics at Cambridge in 1980, a post famously held by **Isaac Newton**. The theory of black holes, which result when massive stars collapse under their own gravity at the end of their lives, owes much to his mathematical work. His achievements are even more remarkable because from the 1960s he suffered from a highly disabling and progressive neural disease affecting his movement and speech. He has continued to work and produce scientific papers as well as several best-selling popular science books, the first of which, *A Brief History of Time* (1988), explored the various concepts behind modern cosmology.

Hawthorne, Nathaniel 1804–64
US novelist and short-story writer
One of the leading figures of 19th-century American letters, he had an important influence on writers such as **Herman Melville** and **Henry James**. His work includes novels such as *The Scarlet Letter* (1850), *The House of the Seven Gables* (1851), *The Blithedale Romance* (1852), *Tanglewood Tales* (1853) and *The*

Marble Faun (1860). Only belatedly recognized in his own country, his reputation continued to grow in the 20th century.

Haydn, (Franz) Joseph 1732–1809
Austrian composer
He was the most famous composer of his day, and his work is marked by spontaneity, melodiousness, craftsmanship and the expression of both high spirits and gravity. His large output includes 104 symphonies, about 50 concertos, 84 string quartets, 24 stage works, 12 masses, and various chamber, choral, instrumental, and vocal pieces. Examples of these include the 'Salomon' or 'London' Symphonies (Nos 93–104), *The Creation* (1798) and *The Seasons* (1801).

Heaney, Seamus Justin 1939–
Northern Irish poet and critic
One of the greatest modern poets writing in English, he made his debut with *Eleven Poems* (1965). His work in general is redolent of the rural Ireland in which he grew up, and includes the collections *Wintering Out* (1972, much influenced by the outbreak of sectarian violence in Northern Ireland), *North* (1975), *Bog Poems* (1975), *The Spirit Level* (1997), *Electric Light* (2001) and *District and Circle* (2006), for which he won the 2006 T S Eliot Prize for Poetry. He has also written plays and essays. He was awarded the Nobel Prize for literature in 1995.

Seamus Heaney

Hegel, Georg Wilhelm Friedrich 1770–1831
German philosopher
The last and perhaps the most important of the great German idealist philosophers, his first great work *The Phenomenology of Mind* (1807) was followed by *The Science of Logic* (1812 and 1816), in which he set out his famous idea of dialectic, that a thesis (a proposition) generates an antithesis (a counter-proposition), with both superseded by a synthesis (which combines the rational elements of both). In 1817 he produced a compendium of his entire system entitled *Encyclopedia of the Philosophical Sciences, Comprising Logic, Philosophy of Nature and of Mind*, and his later works include the *The Philosophy of Right* (1821). Though his philosophy is difficult and obscure it has been a great influence on later philosophies, including Marxism, Positivism, and existentialism.

Heidegger, Martin 1889–1976
German philosopher
He was a leading figure in the phenomenological movement, but was also much influenced by **Søren Kierkegaard**, and was a key influence on **Jean-Paul Sartre** through his writings on the nature and predicament of human existence, the search for 'authenticity' and the distractions of *Angst* (dread). His major work is the original but almost unreadable *Sein und Zeit* (1927, 'Being and Time').

Heinz, H(enry) J(ohn) 1844–1919
US food manufacturer and packer
In 1876 he became co-founder, with his brother and cousin, of F & J Heinz, a firm producing pickles and other prepared foods. The business was reorganized as the H J Heinz Company in 1888, and he was its president from 1905 to 1919. He invented the advertising slogan '57 Varieties' in 1896.

Heisenberg, Werner Karl 1901–76
German theoretical physicist
In his revolutionary uncertainty principle (1927), he showed that it is impossible to measure with complete accuracy the position and momentum of very small particles (such as electrons) at the same time. This principle and the theory of relativity form the basis of modern physics. Heisenberg was awarded the Nobel Prize for physics in 1932, and in 1958, he and **Wolfgang Pauli** announced the formulation of a unified field theory (a single theory of the workings of all natural phenomena) which, if it were ever established, would remove the uncertainty principle.

Hemingway, Ernest Millar 1899–1961
US writer of novels and short stories
After serving in World War I as an ambulance driver, and being badly wounded, he spent the 1920s in Paris, where he began to write seriously. He first gained widespread critical approval with *In Our Time* (1924), which was followed by a stream of 20th-century classics, among them *A Farewell to Arms* (1929), *Death in the Afternoon* (1932), *For Whom the Bell Tolls* (1940) and *The Old Man and the Sea* (1952). Many myths surround him, and it is said that drinking, brawling, big-game hunting, deep-sea fishing and bullfighting all competed with writing. He won the Pulitzer Prize in 1953 and the Nobel Prize for literature in 1954. However, he suffered from depression and shot himself at his home in Ketchum, Idaho.

Henderson, Arthur 1863–1935
Scottish Labour politician
Several times chairman of the Labour Party (1908–10, 1914–7, 1931–2), he was elected an MP in 1903, served in the coalition cabinets (1915–7), and became Home Secretary (1924) and Foreign Secretary (1929–31) in the first Labour governments. A crusader for disarmament, he was president of the World Disarmament Conference (1932), won the 1934 Nobel Peace Prize, and also helped to establish the League of Nations, the precursor of the United Nations.

Hendrix, Jimi (James Marshall) 1942–70
US rock guitarist and singer
One of rock music's most innovative and influential instrumentalists, he moved to Great Britain in 1966 and formed the Jimi Hendrix Experience. The band's first single, 'Hey Joe', was an immediate British success and his adventurous first album, *Are You Experienced?*, was an unexpected international success which paved the way for other psychedelic and experimental rock acts. The two subsequent albums helped make 1968 his most commercially successful year. However the pressures of success also helped to destroy him, and

he died after mixing barbiturates and alcohol.

Henry, Joseph 1797–1878
US physicist
He discovered electrical induction independently of **Michael Faraday**, constructed the first electromagnetic motor (1829) and also noted the effects of resistance on current, formulated precisely by **Georg Ohm** in 1827. He also introduced a system of weather forecasting based on observations. The SI unit of inductance (the henry) is named after him.

Henry II 1133–89
King of England
Born in France, the grandson of Henry I, in January 1153 he landed in England, and in November was declared the successor of **Stephen**, founding the Angevin or Plantagenet Dynasty of English kings. To help him in restricting the authority of the Church in England he appointed his Chancellor, **Thomas Becket**, as Archbishop of Canterbury, but Becket resisted, and the struggle between them ended with Becket's murder (1170). An able administrator, Henry kept intact an empire stretching from the Scottish border to the Pyrenees until the very last month of his life. He was succeeded by his rebellious son **Richard I, Cœur de Lion**.

Henry IV, *originally* **Henry Bolingbroke** c.1367–1413
First Lancastrian King of England
The son of John of Gaunt, he was surnamed Bolingbroke from his birthplace in Lincolnshire. In 1397 he supported **Richard II** against the Duke of Gloucester, and was created Duke of Hereford, but in 1398 he was banished, and in 1399, when his father died, his estates were declared forfeit to Richard. Henry landed at Ravenspur in Yorkshire and had himself crowned king (1399); four months later Richard died, possibly murdered. During Henry's reign rebellion and lawlessness were rife, but he succeeded in defeating rebellions by **Owen Glendower**, Henry Percy, Earl of Northumberland, and the Earl's son Harry Percy (Hotspur).

Henry V 1387–1422
King of England
The son of **Henry IV**, he was crowned king in 1413. His reign was marked by his attempt to claim the French Crown. In 1415 he took Harfleur, and the same year at Agincourt won against huge odds. Two years later he again invaded France and regained Normandy (1418). By the 'perpetual peace' of Troyes (1420) Henry became Regent of France and was recognized as heir to the French throne. He married the daughter of Charles VI of France, Catherine de Valois, and took his young queen to England to be crowned (1421), but a month later he was recalled to France by news of the defeat of his brother, Thomas, Duke of Clarence and died at Vincennes, leaving his baby son **Henry VI** to succeed him.

Henry VI 1421–71
King of England
He was the son of **Henry V** and became king on the death of his father in 1422. **Edward III**'s third son, Richard, Duke of York, had a better claim to the crown than Henry, and this, as well as Henry's mental instability and weakness, led to the many battles between the rival Houses of York and Lancaster known as the Wars of the Roses. Henry was finally murdered in the Tower of London and the Lancastrian Dynasty came to an end. He was succeeded by the Yorkist Edward IV.

Henry VIII 1491–1547
King of England
The second son of Henry VII, he became king in 1509. His reign was marked by the establishment of the Church of England, which came about as a result of his desire to defy the Catholic Church and divorce his first wife, Catherine of Aragon. His second marriage to Anne Boleyn ended when she was executed for adultery; his third wife, Jane Seymour, died in childbirth; his fourth wife, Anne of Cleves, he divorced; his fifth wife, Catherine Howard, was also executed for adultery; and his sixth, Catherine Parr, survived him. Henry closed all the monasteries in Britain and confiscated their wealth. Among those he executed was his Chancellor, **Thomas More**. His reign, which was also marked by foreign wars, was followed by that of his son by Jane Seymour, Edward VI.

Henryson, Robert c.1425–c.1508
Scottish medieval poet
He is usually designated the 'schoolmaster of Dunfermline', and was certainly a notary in 1478. His work is part of the tradition of the Scottish 'makars' (literary craftsmen), and his best-known poem is the *Testament of Cresseid*, a sequel to **Chaucer**'s *Troilus and Criseyde*.

Hepburn, Audrey, *originally* **Edda Van Heemstra Hepburn-Ruston** 1929–93
Belgian actress
She first appeared on Broadway in *Gigi* (1951), and won a Best Actress Academy Award for *Roman Holiday* (1953). A pencil-slim actress of coltish grace, she had many film successes, including *Funny Face* (1957), *Breakfast At Tiffany's* (1961), *My Fair Lady* (1964) and *Wait Until Dark* (1967). In her later years she travelled extensively as a goodwill ambassador for UNICEF.

Hepburn, Katharine Houghton 1907–2003
US film and stage actress
Noted for her distinctive New England accent, fine bone structure and versatile talent, her many films include *Bringing Up Baby* (1938), *The Philadelphia Story* (1940), *Woman of the Year* (1942), which saw the beginning of a 25-year professional and personal partnership with co-star Spencer Tracy, *Adam's Rib* (1949), *The African Queen* (1951) and *Long Day's Journey Into Night* (1962). She continued to act despite suffering from Parkinson's Disease.

Hepworth, Dame (Jocelyn) Barbara 1903–75
English sculptor

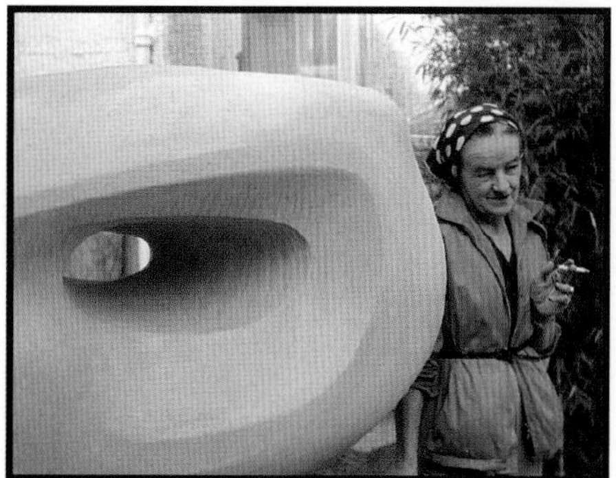

Dame Barbara Hepworth

She was one of the foremost sculptors of her time, notable for the strength and formal discipline of her carving. Until the early 1960s her works were mainly in wood, and she then worked in stone (eg *Three Monoliths*, 1964) and in metal (eg *Four Square (Walk Through)*, 1966). In all this work she developed a distinctive abstract style involving hollows with lengths of wire or string. Her representational paintings and drawings are of equal power.

Herbert, George 1593–1633
English metaphysical poet and clergyman
His connection with the court, and particularly the favour of King **James VI and I**, seemed to point to a worldly career, but in 1630 he took orders and spent his last years as a parish priest of Bemerton, in Wiltshire. Among the greatest of the metaphysical poets, practically all his religious poems are included in *The Temple, Sacred Poems and Private Ejaculations*, posthumously published in 1633. His chief prose work is *A Priest in the Temple* (1652), containing guidance for the country parson.

Herodotus c.485–425BC
Greek historian
He travelled extensively in Asia Minor and the Middle East, Sicily and Lower Italy, collecting historical, geographical, mythological and archaeological material for his great narrative history. He was the first to make the events of the past the subject of research and verification, and **Cicero** and others have called him 'the father of history'.

Herrick, Robert 1591–1674
English poet
Known for his support of the Royalist cause in the Civil War, his writing is mainly collected in *Hesperides: or the Works both Humane and Divine of Robert Herrick Esq* (1648). He was at his best when describing rural rites as in *The Hock Cart* and *Twelfth Night*, and in well-known lyrics such as 'Gather ye rosebuds while ye may' and 'Cherry Ripe'.

Herschel, Sir John Frederick William 1792–1871
English astronomer
The only child of the astronomer Sir **William Herschel**, he re-examined his father's double stars (1821–3) and produced a catalogue which earned him the gold medal of the Royal Astronomical Society (1826). He reviewed his father's great catalogue of nebulae in Slough (1825–33), adding 525 new ones, and went to South Africa to extend the survey to the entire sky. He also made important contributions to chemistry and photography.

Herschel, Sir (Frederick) William, *originally* **Friedrich Wilhelm Herschel** 1738–1822
British astronomer
Born in Hanover, Germany, he moved in 1755 to England where he had a successful career in music before his interest in astronomy began. He built his own telescopes, and in 1781 he discovered the planet Uranus, the first to be found using a telescope. In 1782 King **George III** appointed him his private astronomer. Assisted by his sister Caroline Herschel, his discoveries included two satellites of Uranus (1787) and two of Saturn (1789), but his most important work lay in his studies of the stars. He made a systematic search of nebulae and star clusters, cataloguing more than 800 binary stars and 2,500 nebulae. He was knighted in 1816.

Hertz, Gustav Ludwig 1887–1975
German physicist
With James Franck he showed that atoms would only absorb a fixed amount of energy, and for this work they shared the 1925 Nobel Prize for physics. The results provided data for **Niels Bohr** to develop his theory of atomic structure, and for **Max Planck** to develop his ideas on quantum theory.

Hertz, Heinrich Rudolf 1857–94
German physicist
In 1887 he confirmed **James Clerk Maxwell**'s predictions by his discovery of invisible electromagnetic waves ('Hertzian waves', now known as radio waves) which behave like light waves. Later he was widely honoured for his work on electric waves. The SI unit of frequency, ie the number of times that a cycle occurs per second, was named *hertz* in his honour.

Hesiod c.8th century BC
Greek poet
One of the earliest known Greek poets, he is best known for the didactic peoms *Theogony*, which teaches the origin of the universe and the history of the gods, and *Works and Days*, which deals with the farmer's life and gives a realistic picture of a primitive peasant community.

Hesse, Eva 1936–70
US sculptor
She was born in Hamburg, Germany, into a Jewish family, which emigrated to the USA in 1939. From 1965 she worked in a variety of materials, such as rubber, plastic, string and polythene, creating objects designed to rest on the floor or against a wall or to be suspended from the ceiling, as in *Hang-up* (1965–6). Her unconventional techniques and imaginative work exerted a strong influence on later 'conceptual' artists.

Heston, Charlton, *originally* **Charles Carter** 1924–
US film actor
His major early film successes were the **Cecil B De Mille** films *The Greatest Show on Earth* (1952) and *The Ten Commandments* (1956). He also played the larger-than-life heroes for which his strapping physique suited him in *Ben Hur* (1959, Academy Award) and *El Cid* (1961). Other films include *Touch of Evil* (1958) and *Will Penny* (1967). He has frequently returned to the stage as actor and director and appeared widely on television.

Hideyoshi Toyotomi 1536–98
Japanese soldier
He became the second of the three great historical unifiers of Japan, the others being Nobunaga and Ieyasu Tokugawa. Unusually, he was an ordinary soldier who rose to become Nobunaga's foremost general, and he was later known as 'the Napoleon of Japan'. His law forbade all except samurai to carry swords (1588), and he banned Christianity for political reasons (1597). His armies invaded Korea (1592–8), but withdrew after his death.

Hilda, St 614–80
Anglo-Saxon abbess
In 649 she became abbess of Hartlepool and in 657 founded the monastery at Streaneshalch or Whitby, a double house for nuns and monks, over which she ruled for 22 years. It became an important religious

centre and housed the Synod of Whitby in 664.

Hillary, Sir Edmund Percival 1919–
New Zealand mountaineer and explorer
He joined the 1953 British Everest Expedition, and with the sherpa Tenzing Norgay reached the summit of Mt Everest (at 8,850m/29,030ft) on 29 May 1953. He was knighted for this achievement. He later took part in expeditions all over the world, wrote several books on his adventures, and has raised funds in New Zealand to provide hospitals and schools in the Himalayan region.

Himmler, Heinrich 1900–45
German Nazi leader and chief of police
In 1929 **Hitler** made him head of the SS (*Schutzstaffel*, protective force), which he developed into a powerful party weapon. Inside Germany and later in Nazi war-occupied countries, he unleashed through his Gestapo (secret police) an unmatched system of terror, mass deportation, torture, execution and massacre. In the concentration camps he organized, over six million Jews, Gypsies and other groups were killed. After the attempt on Hitler's life by the army in July 1944, he was made Commander-in-Chief of the home forces, but after his capture by British forces he committed suicide.

Hinault, Bernard, *known as* **Le Blaireau ('the badger')** 1954–
French cyclist
He won the Tour de France five times (1978–9, 1981–2, 1985), a feat matched only by four others: Jacques Anquetil, **Eddy Merckx**, **Miguel Indurain**, and **Lance Armstrong**. He led a protest during the 1978 Tour in which all the riders walked across the finishing line pushing their bikes, complaining about the long days in the saddle.

Hindenburg, Paul Ludwig Hans Anton von Beneckendorff und von 1847–1934
German soldier and statesman
He rose to the rank of general (1903), and at the outbreak of World War I, he and General **Ludendorff** won decisive victories over the Russians; in the summer of 1918 however he was obliged to supervise the retreat of the German armies. A national hero and father figure, he was the second President of the German Republic (1925–34). He defeated **Hitler** in the presidential election of 1932 and Hitler was unable to overthrow constitutional government until Hindenburg's death.

Hipparchos or **Hipparchus** c.180–125BC
Greek astronomer and mathematician
He compiled a catalogue of 850 stars (completed in 129BC) giving their positions in celestial latitude and longitude, the first such catalogue ever to exist. He also estimated the relative distances of the Sun and Moon, improved calculations for the prediction of eclipses, developed a theory of the Sun's motion and measured the unequal durations of the four seasons. Hipparchos was also the first to fix places on the Earth by latitude and longitude.

Hippocrates c.460–377/359BC
Greek physician
Known as the 'father of medicine', and associated with the medical profession's Hippocratic oath, he developed the theory that an imbalance in the four fluids or 'humours' (blood, phlegm, yellow bile and black bile) of the body is the primary cause of disease. His works include *Airs, Waters, Places, Epidemics III, The Sacred Disease* and *Aphorisms* which begins with the famous 'Life is short, the art is long'.

Hirohito 1901–89
Emperor of Japan
The 124th emperor in direct lineage, his reign was marked by rapid militarization and aggressive wars against China (1931–32, 1937–45) and Great Britain and the USA (1941–45), which ended after the two atomic bombs were dropped on Hiroshima and Nagasaki by the USA. Under US occupation, Hirohito in 1946 renounced his legendary divinity and most of his powers to become a democratic constitutional monarch. He was a notable marine biologist.

Hirst, Damien, *originally* **Damien Steven David Brennan** 1965–
English painter and installation artist
One of the most influential artists of his generation, he is best known for his installations in which he employs controversial materials such as blood, maggots, dying butterflies and dead animals. The most famous of these include *The Physical Impossibility of Death in the Mind of Someone Living* (1991), which consists of a tiger shark in a perspex and steel box, and *Mother and Child, Divided* (1993), featuring a cow and a calf, both sliced in half. Hirst was awarded the 1995 Turner Prize.

Hitchcock, Sir Alfred Joseph 1899–1980
English film-maker

Sir Alfred Hitchcock

His early films were made in Britain, and included *The Thirty-Nine Steps* (1935) and *The Lady Vanishes* (1938). By the time he moved to Hollywood in 1939 his work was settled firmly in the area of the suspense thriller, and his first Hollywood film, *Rebecca* (1940), won an Academy Award. Subsequent films starred many of the industry's most celebrated actors and actresses, and included *Spellbound* (1945), *Notorious* (1946), *Rope* (1948), *Dial M for Murder* (1954), *Rear Window* (1955), *Psycho* (1960) and *The Birds* (1963). His films were internationally recognized for their unequalled mastery of suspense and their innovative camerawork, with common themes including murder, deception and mistaken identity.

Hitler, Adolf, *known as* **Der Führer ('The Leader')** 1889–1945
German dictator
After serving in the German army throughout World

War I, he formed the National Socialist German Workers' Party in 1920 and assumed absolute power in 1933. Under the pretext of uniting the German peoples, he invaded Austria and Czechoslovakia in 1938, and his invasion of Poland in 1939 precipitated World War II. In the first years of the war the German forces made spectacular gains, but after suffering defeats at Stalingrad and El Alamein in 1942–3, Germany was overrun and defeated, and Hitler committed suicide. His domestic policy had been one of thorough control of all aspects of German life and the establishment of concentration camps for political opponents and Jews. His *Third Reich*, which was to have endured for ever, ended ingloriously after 12 years in which 30 million people lost their lives. *Mein Kampf* (1925, 'My Struggle') was his political testament.

Hobbes, Thomas 1588–1679
English political philosopher
He saw the world as a mechanical system and sought to apply those laws to human psychology. His chief work was *Leviathan* (1651), which explained the nature and function of the sovereign state, recommending that citizens submit to its power in return for protection under the law. At various times unpopular with the British and French governments, he had fierce enemies among the clergy, who at one time claimed that he was responsible for bringing upon Britain the Plague and the Great Fire of London of 1665–6. His other works included *De Cive* (1642), *De Corpore* (1655), *De Homine* (1658) and *Behemoth: a history of the causes of the Civil Wars of England* (1682).

Hobbs, Jack, *properly* **Sir John Berry Hobbs** 1882–1963
English cricketer
One of England's greatest batsmen, he played for Surrey for 30 years (1905–35). In his first-class career he made 197 centuries, and scored 61,237 runs. An immensely popular figure, he was the first professional English cricketer to be knighted, in 1953.

Ho Chi Minh, *originally* **Nguyen That Thanh** 1890–1969
Vietnamese statesman
He founded the Viet Minh Independence League in 1941, and between 1946 and 1954 directed the successful military operations against the French, becoming Prime Minister (1954–5) and President (1954) of North Vietnam. Re-elected in 1960, with Chinese assistance he was a leading force in the war between North and South. Despite huge US military intervention in support of South Vietnam between 1963 and 1975, Ho Chi Minh's Viet Cong forced a ceasefire in 1973, four years after his death. The civil war continued until 1975, when Saigon fell and was renamed Ho Chi Minh City.

Hockney, David 1937–
English artist
Associated with the Pop Art movement, his early paintings are a mix of artistic styles and fashions, with graffiti-like figures and words, as in *We 2 Boys Together Clinging* (1961). While he was in California (1963–7) he began to develop his celebrated 'swimming-pool' paintings, such as *The Sunbather* (1966). His later work, often double portraits, is more representational, such as *Mr and Mrs Clark and Percy* (1970–1). In 1982 he began a series of photo-collages, and he has also experimented with computer technology and digital inkjet printings.

Hodgkin, Dorothy Mary, *née* **Crowfoot** 1910–94
British crystallographer
Her detailed X-ray analysis of cholesterol was a milestone in crystallography, but an even greater achievement was the determining of the structure of penicillin (1942–5). The discovery of the structure of vitamin B_{12e} (used to fight pernicious anaemia) was another triumph. She was awarded the Nobel Prize for chemistry in 1964, the third woman to receive it (the first two being **Marie Curie** and **Irène Joliot-Curie**) and the first British woman to receive a Nobel science prize.

Hoffman, Dustin 1937–
US actor
He received an Academy Award nomination for his first leading role in *The Graduate* (1967). Similar anti-hero roles followed in *Midnight Cowboy* (1969), *Little Big Man* (1970) and *Marathon Man* (1976). A notorious perfectionist, he has displayed his versatility in such films as *All The President's Men* (1976), *Kramer vs Kramer* (1979, Academy Award), *Tootsie* (1982), *Rain Man* (1988, Academy Award), *Sleepers* (1996) and *Perfume: The Story of a Murderer* (2006).

Hogarth, William 1697–1764
English painter and engraver
He is best known for his paintings and engravings of 'modern moral subjects'. The first of these was *A Harlot's Progress* (1730–1), and was followed by *A Rake's Progress* (1733–5) and his masterpiece, *Marriage à la mode* (1743–5). He then extended his social commentaries to 'men of the lowest rank' by drawing attention to their typical vices in prints such as the *Industry and Idleness* series (1747), *Gin Lane*, and *Beer Street* (1751).

Hokusai, Katsushika 1760–1849
Japanese artist and wood-engraver
He was a master of the Ukiyo-e ('pictures of the floating world') school, which treated commonplace subjects in an expressionist manner. His best-known works are his landscapes, an innovation of the Ukiyo-e movement; they include his *36 Views of Mount Fuji* (c.1826–33). His work greatly influenced the French Impressionists.

Holbein, Hans, the Younger 1497–1543
German painter
One of the most successful portrait painters of his day, he worked throughout northern Europe and became painter to **Henry VIII** (1536). Works executed in his highly detailed style include *Sir Thomas More* (1527), *The Ambassadors* (1533), *Anne of Cleves* (1539) and *Lady with a Squirrel and a Starling* (of uncertain date). He also produced notable woodcuts, including the *Dance of Death* and the *Old Testament* series (issued 1538).

Holiday, Billie, *originally* **Eleanora Fagan** 1915–59
US jazz singer
Her wistful voice and remarkable jazz interpretation of popular songs led to work with such leading musicians as Teddy Wilson and Lester Young, who bestowed her familiar nickname, Lady Day. Her memorable ballads include 'Easy Living' (1937), 'Yesterdays' (1939) and 'God Bless the Child' (1941).

During the 1940s she appeared in several films but by the end of that decade she was falling victim to drug addiction. Her ghost-written autobiography was *Lady Sings The Blues* (1956, filmed 1972).

Holly, Buddy, *originally* **Charles Hardin** 1936–59
US rock singer, songwriter and guitarist
Despite the fact that his recording career lasted less than two years, he is one of the most influential pioneers of rock-and-roll. With his band The Crickets he was the first to use what was to become the standard rock-and-roll line-up of two guitars, bass and drums. He split from The Crickets in 1958, and in 1959 he died when a plane carrying him between concerts crashed. His most popular songs include 'That'll Be The Day', 'Not Fade Away', 'Peggy Sue' and 'Oh Boy'.

Holst, Gustav Theodore, *originally* **Gustav Theodore von Holst** 1874–1934
English composer
He emerged as a major composer with the seven-movement suite *The Planets* (1914–16). Among his other major works are *The Hymn of Jesus* (1917), his comic operas *The Perfect Fool* (1922) and *At the Boar's Head* (1924), and his orchestral tone poem *Egdon Heath* (1927), inspired by **Thomas Hardy**'s *Return of the Native*.

Homer, *Greek* **Homeros** c.8th century BC
Greek epic poet
Homer was regarded in Greek and Roman antiquity as the blind poet who wrote the *Iliad* (dealing with episodes in the Trojan War) and the *Odyssey* (dealing with Odysseus's adventures on his return from Troy). Little is known of the origin of these epics, but some believe that they were developed from orally transmitted poems dated to the 8th century BC, although the *Odyssey* is probably later than the *Iliad*.

Hongwu (Hung-wu), *originally* **Zhu Yuanzhang (Chu Yuan-chang)** 1328–98
Emperor of China and founder of the Ming dynasty
The son of a peasant, he became a leader of the Red Turbans, one of a number of Buddhist and Taoist inspired sects that rose in revolt against the Mongol Yuan Dynasty during the 1340s. In 1356 he captured Nanjing and during the next few years disposed of his rivals to establish his own dynasty, the Ming.

Hooke, Robert 1635–1703
English experimental philosopher and architect
One of the most brilliant and versatile scientists of his day, his major achievements included his *Micrographia* (1665), an account of his microscopic investigations in botany, chemistry and other branches of science. He anticipated the development of the steam engine, formulated the simplest theory of the arch, the balance-spring of watches, constructed the first reflecting telescope, and invented many other scientific instruments. After the Great Fire of London (1666) he designed the new Bethlehem Hospital.

Hooker, John Lee 1920–2001
US blues singer and guitarist
He drew on the raw emotion of early blues styles for his inspiration, set in the characteristic insistent boogie rhythm which most clearly defined his work. His music was very influential on the UK blues boom of the 1960s, but went into relative decline in the 1980s. He bounced back in the 1990s with successful recordings (often with rock star guests) and live performances.

John Lee Hooker

Hoover, Herbert Clark 1874–1964
31st President of the USA
In his early political career he helped initiate such engineering projects as the St Lawrence Seaway and the Boulder (later Hoover) Dam. He won the Presidency as a Republican in 1929. His administration (1929–33) was overshadowed by the Great Depression, and his call for private relief rather than large-scale government programmes, and his reserved, formal demeanour, led to the perception that he lacked compassion for the sufferings of the US people. His popularity plummeted, and the shanty towns that sprang up around the country were called Hoovervilles. He was defeated in his re-election bid by Roosevelt in 1932.

Hoover, William Henry 1849–1932
US industrialist
He ran a tannery business (1870–1907), then bought the patent of an electric cleaning machine from a janitor, James Murray Spangler, and formed the Electric Suction Sweeper Company in 1908 to manufacture and market it throughout the world. The company was renamed Hoover in 1910.

Hope, Bob (Leslie Townes) 1903–2003
US comedian
He began as a vaudeville dancer and comedian, and won fame with a string of hit films, including *The Cat and the Canary* (1939), *My Favourite Blonde* (1942), *The Princess and the Pirate* (1944) and *Paleface* (1948). In partnership with **Bing Crosby** and Dorothy Lamour he appeared in the seven highly successful *Road to ...* comedies (1940–61). During World War II and the Korean and Vietnam wars he spent much time entertaining the troops in the field.

Hopkins, Anthony 1937–
Welsh-born US film and stage actor
Very successful on stage, and a member of the National Theatre company (1966–73), his mastery of timing and technique have allowed him to portray a vast variety of characters. Film appearances include *The Elephant Man* (1980), *The Silence of the Lambs* (1991), *The Remains of the Day* (1993), *Shadowlands* (1993), *Surviving Picasso* (1996) and *The Mask of Zorro* (1998). He made his directorial debut with the film *August* (1995).

Hopkins, Gerard Manley 1844–89
English poet
He was ordained a Jesuit priest in 1877. None of his poems was published in his lifetime, but his friend the poet laureate Robert Bridges brought out a full edition in 1918. His best-known poems include 'The Wreck of the Deutschland' (1876), 'The Windhover' and 'Pied Beauty', in which he used what he called 'sprung rhythm' – a poetic rhythm close to the natural rhythm of speech. His rich, ecstatic use of language, with dense alliteration and internal rhyme, has continued to be highly influential.

Horace, *in full* **Quintus Horatius Flaccus** 65–8BC
Roman poet and satirist
His earliest verses were chiefly satires and lampoons, but some of his first lyrical pieces came to the notice of the statesman Maecenas, a generous patron who is thought to have given Horace a farm in the Sabine Hills. His first book of *Satires* (35BC) was followed by a second, and a small collection of lyrics, the *Epodes* (c.30BC). In 23BC he produced his greatest work, three books of *Odes*, and in about 20BC his *Epistles*. These and other works had a profound influence on poetry and literary criticism in the 17th and 18th centuries.

Houdini, Harry, *originally* **Erich Weiss** 1874–1926
US magician and escape artist
He was born in Budapest, Hungary, and after his family emigrated to the USA he became a trapeze performer. He later gained an international reputation as an escape artist, freeing himself from handcuffs, shackles, and other devices, even while imprisoned in a box underwater or hanging upside-down in mid-air. He was a vigorous campaigner against fraudulent mediums, and was president of the Society of American Magicians. He died from peritonitis following a stomach injury incurred when punched, unprepared, by a member of the public who wanted to test his famous ability to withstand any blow.

Howard, John 1726–90
English philanthropist and reformer
In 1773, as High Sheriff of Bedfordshire, he was appalled by conditions in Bedford gaol, and undertook a tour of British prisons that led to two Acts of Parliament in 1774, one enforcing standards of cleanliness, and the other replacing prisoners' fees for jailers with official salaries. He travelled and wrote widely, and died of typhus contracted while visiting a Russian military hospital in the Crimea. The Howard League for Penal Reform, founded in 1866, was named after him.

Hubble, Edwin Powell 1889–1953
US astronomer
He found that spiral nebulae (cloudy regions in space) are independent stellar systems, and that the Andromeda nebula in particular is very similar to our own Milky Way galaxy. In 1929 he announced his discovery that galaxies recede from us with speeds which increase with their distance. This was the phenomenon of the expansion of the universe, the basis of modern cosmology. The linear relation between speed of recession and distance is known as Hubble's law. The Hubble Space Telescope, launched in 1990, was named in his honour.

Hughes, Howard Robard 1905–76
US millionaire businessman, film producer and director, and aviator
He inherited his father's oil-drilling equipment company at the age of 18, and in 1926 began to involve himself and his profits in Hollywood films. Leaving Hollywood in 1932, he turned his entire attention to designing, building and flying aircraft. He broke most of the world's air speed records (1935–8) then returned to film-making, producing and directing his most controversial film, *The Outlaw* (1943), starring Jane Russell. He later built a revolutionary oversized wooden seaplane, the 'Spruce Goose' (completed 1947). Severely injured in an air crash in 1946, his eccentricity increased, and he eventually became a recluse.

Hughes, Ted (Edward James) 1930–98
English poet
A writer at one with nature, mesmerized by its beauty but not blind to its cruelty and violence, his work includes the collections *The Hawk in the Rain* (1957), *Lupercal* (1960), *Wodwo* (1967), *Crow* (1970) and *Tales from Ovid* (1997). He married the US writer **Sylvia Plath** in 1956, but in 1963 she committed suicide. He edited Plath's collected poems in 1981 and in 1998 published *Birthday Letters*, poems about his relationship with her. Of his books for children, the most remarkable is *The Iron Man* (1968, published in the USA as *The Iron Giant*). He was appointed Poet Laureate in 1984.

Hugo, Victor Marie 1802–85
French poet and writer
A leading figure of the French Romantic movement, his greatest novel, *Les Misérables*, a panoramic piece of social history, appeared in 1862. Other works in a vast output include *Notre Dame de Paris* (1831), later filmed as *The Hunchback of Notre Dame* (1924) and *Toilers of the Sea* (1866). *Songs of the Street and the Forest* (1865) is perhaps his greatest poetic achievement. During the 1840s Hugo became an adherent of republicanism, and his political career was a stormy one. In 1876 however he was made a senator and later buried as a national hero.

Hume, David 1711–76
Scottish philosopher and historian
His first, and most important, work was *A Treatise of Human Nature*, later published as *An Enquiry concerning Human Understanding*, an attempt to introduce the experimental method of reasoning into moral subjects. In politics he challenged the 'social contract' theories of **Thomas Hobbes** and **Jean Jacques Rousseau**, producing works such as *Essays Moral and Political* (1741, 1742), *Dialogues concerning Natural Religion* (written 1750, published 1779) and *Political Discourses* (1752). Hume's atheism brought him into difficulties but he remained a powerful force in literary and court circles. He was a dominant influence on later philosophers.

Huss, John, *also called* **Jan Hus** c.1369–1415
Bohemian religious reformer
In 1398 he began to lecture on theology at Prague, where he was influenced by the writings of **John Wycliffe**. After writing his main work, *De Ecclesia* (1413, 'On the Church'), he was called before a general council at Constance, but he refused to recant and was burned at the stake. The anger of his

PEOPLE

followers in Bohemia (Hussites) led to the Hussite Wars, which lasted until the mid-15th century.

Hussein or **Husain, Saddam** 1937–2006
Iraqi dictator
He became state President of Iraq in 1979 as a member of the leading Ba'ath Party. Ruthless in the pursuit of his objectives, he fought a bitter war against his neighbour, Iran (1980–8), and dealt harshly with Kurdish rebels seeking a degree of autonomy. In July 1990 his army invaded Kuwait, bringing about the first Gulf War in which he was opposed by a UN-backed Allied Force. Hussein's troops surrendered in February 1991 following Operation Desert Storm. The second Gulf War was launched in 2003, mainly by American and British forces seeking chemical, biological or nuclear weapons, none of which were later found. Hussein was arrested later that year and tried for genocide. He was found guilty in 2006 and executed.

Hutton, James 1726–97
Scottish geologist
His work forms the basis of modern geology. In his book *A Theory of the Earth* (1785–99) he demonstrated that the internal heat of the Earth caused intrusions of molten rock into the crust and that granite was the product of the cooling of molten rock. The huge periods of time needed for these processes, far longer than those suggested by traditional Christian doctrine, led him to envisage an Earth with 'no vestige of a beginning and no prospect of an end'.

Huxley, Aldous Leonard 1894–1963
English novelist and essayist
His first novels were *Crome Yellow* (1921) and *Antic Hay* (1923), satires on postwar Great Britain. *Those Barren Leaves* (1925) and *Point Counter Point* (1928) were written in Italy, where he associated with **D H Lawrence**. In 1932, in his most famous novel, *Brave New World*, Huxley depicted a future world in which social control is achieved by the scientific breeding of human beings. His later work tended towards more mystical themes, as in *The Doors of Perception* (1954). He also wrote numerous essays, biographies and other works.

Huygens, Christiaan 1629–93
Dutch physicist
He was, after **Isaac Newton**, the greatest scientist of the second half of the 17th century. In 1655 he discovered the rings and fourth satellite of Saturn, using a refracting telescope he constructed with his brother. He later constructed the pendulum clock, based on the suggestion of **Galileo** (1657), and discovered the laws of collision of elastic bodies at the same time as John Wallis and Sir **Christopher Wren**. In optics he first proposed the wave theory of light, and discovered polarization.

Hypatia c.370–415AD
Greek philosopher
The first notable female astronomer and mathematician, she taught in Alexandria and became head of the philosophical school there. She was the author of commentaries on mathematics and astronomy, though none of these survives. She was renowned for her beauty, eloquence and learning, and drew pupils from all parts of the Greek world, Christian as well as pagan. Cyril, Archbishop of Alexandria, resented her influence and she was murdered by a Christian mob he may have incited to riot.

Ibsen, Henrik 1828–1906
Norwegian dramatist
Generally regarded as the founder of modern prose drama, from the 1870s he began producing the realistic plays for which he is best known, among them *A Doll's House* (1879), *Ghosts* (1881), *An Enemy of the People* (1882), *The Wild Duck* (1884) and *Hedda Gabler* (1890). These plays, concerned with social and political issues, caused a major stir among critics and audiences, not least because Ibsen refused to provide 'happy endings'. His last plays have a strong emphasis on symbolism and the unconscious, as in *The Master Builder* (1892), and *When We Dead Awaken* (1899).

Ignatius Loyola, St, *properly* **Iñigo López de Recalde** 1491–1556
Spanish founder of the Jesuits
He served as a soldier, and was severely injured, but after reading the lives of **Jesus Christ** and the saints renounced military life. In 1534, with St Francis Xavier and four other associates, he founded the Society of Jesus for the spread of Catholic doctrine. He sent out missionaries to Japan, India and Brazil, and founded schools for training the young, and was made a saint in 1622. His *Spiritual Exercises* were a vital work in the training of Jesuits.

Indurain, Miguel 1964–
Spanish cyclist
He became only the fourth cyclist to win five Tours de France (1991–5). As the leader of the Banesto team, he became the richest man in cycle racing and a national hero in Spain. He announced his retirement in 1997.

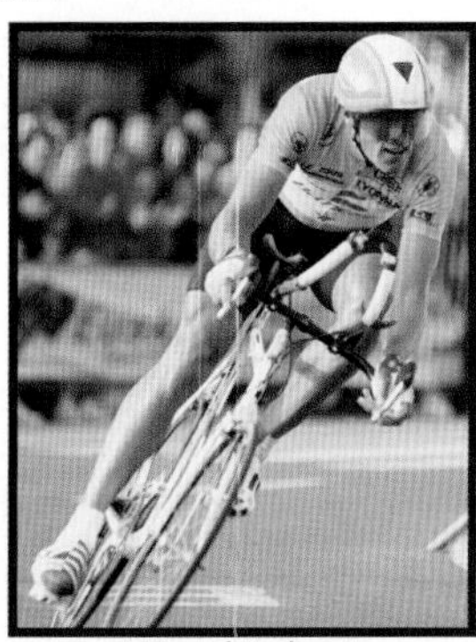
Miguel Indurain

Ionesco, Eugène 1912–94
French playwright
He pioneered a new style of drama that came to be called the Theatre of the Absurd, in which the absurdity of man's condition was mirrored in a dramatic form without a traditional narrative or meaningful dialogue. Many of his plays are in one act: they include *The Bald Prima Donna* (1950) and *The Chairs* (1952). Other plays include *Amédée* (1954) and *Rhinoceros* (1959). He also wrote essays, children's stories and a novel, *The Hermit* (1973).

Issigonis, Sir Alec (Alexander Arnold Constantine) 1906–88
British automobile designer
A period as an enthusiastic sports driver in the 1930s and 1940s familiarized him with all aspects of car design. His greatest successes were the Morris Minor,

launched in 1948 and produced until 1971, and the revolutionary Mini, launched in 1959, a version of which is still in production.

Ivan IV, *known as* **Ivan the Terrible** 1530–84
Tsar of Russia from 1533
The grandson of Ivan III Vasilyevich (Ivan the Great), he assumed power in 1547, becoming the first ruler of Russia to adopt the title of 'tsar'. His reign was characterized by imperial expansion, hostility to the upper nobility and arrests and executions of those who opposed him. Among his greatest crimes was the destruction of the free city of Novgorod in 1570. In a fit of anger in 1581 he accidentally killed his own eldest son, so that the throne passed on his death to his sickly and feeble-minded second son, Fyodor, who ruled from 1584 to 1598.

Jackson, Michael 1958–
US pop singer
As a child he formed part of The Jackson Five with his brothers, Jackie, Tito, Marlon and Jermaine, producing some 16 chart hits in all. His solo album *Off The Wall* produced four hit singles in 1979, and he consolidated his career with *Thriller* (1982), which sold over 40 million copies. Further albums have included *Bad* (1987) and *Invincible* (2001). Having been a celebrity since childhood, he developed a reclusive lifestyle as an adult, and bizarre plastic surgery and controversy over his relationships with young children have added to his notoriety.

Jagger, Sir Mick (Michael Philip) 1943–
English rock singer and songwriter
He is best known as the singer of the Rolling Stones, and was a leading anti-establishment figure in the British pop music of the 1960s. His songwriting partnership with the Rolling Stones's guitarist Keith Richards is one of the most celebrated in rock music. He has also acted in a number of films, and was knighted in 2002.

James VI and I 1566–1625
King of Scotland and of England
The son of **Mary, Queen of Scots**, he was proclaimed King of Scotland as James VI in 1567. During his infancy, power was exercised through a sequence of regents. On the death of **Elizabeth I** of England (1603), James succeeded to the throne of England as great-grandson of James IV's English wife, Margaret Tudor. In England, he was at first well received by his English subjects, although after the failure of the 1605 Gunpowder Plot involving **Guy Fawkes**, severe laws were brought in against Roman Catholics. He was succeeded by his son **Charles I**.

James VII and II 1633–1701
King of Scotland as James VII, and of England and Ireland as James II
The second son of **Charles I**, and brother of **Charles II**, he became king when Charles II died in 1685. A Catholic, his reign was overshadowed by Protestant rebellions, such as that of the Duke of Monmouth in 1685. Eventually the Protestant William, Prince of Orange, James's son-in-law and nephew (the future **William III**), invaded Britain in 1688 and took the throne, and James fled to France. In 1689 James invaded Ireland but was defeated at the Battle of the Boyne (1690). His daughter **Anne** later became queen.

James, Henry 1843–1916
US novelist
A master of the psychological novel, his early works, such as *Daisy Miller* (1879) and *Washington Square* (1880), dealt with the contrast between American and European life. From 1876 he made his home in England, producing novels such as *What Maisie Knew* (1897) and *The Awkward Age* (1899), and reverted to Anglo-American attitudes in final masterpieces including *The Wings of the Dove* (1902) and *The Golden Bowl* (1904). His well-known ghost story, *The Turn of the Screw*, was published in 1898. He also wrote many critical studies, travel sketches and memoirs.

James, Jesse Woodson 1847–82
US Wild West outlaw
He and his brother Frank led a gang of outlaws from 1866. They carried out numerous bank and train robberies over a period of 15 years, until a large price was put on Jesse's head and he was shot by a member of his own gang seeking the reward. Frank gave himself up and after his release lived the rest of his life on the family farm. Jesse became a legendary figure, celebrated in ballads and latterly in Hollywood films.

Jefferson, Thomas 1743–1826
3rd President of the USA
He played a prominent part in the calling of the first Continental Congress in 1774, a meeting of the delegates of the American colonies, and drafted the Declaration of Independence (signed 4 July 1776). He helped to form the Virginia state constitution, and became Governor of Virginia (1779–81) and President in 1801. Among the acts of his presidency were the Louisiana Purchase, the 1803 sale by France to the USA of an area between the Mississippi River and the Rocky Mountains for 15 million dollars, and the prohibition of the slave import trade (1808). In 1809 he retired to his Virginian estate, Monticello, and devoted much time to founding the University of Virginia and designing its campus. He was a gifted architect and wrote numerous books.

Jenner, Edward 1749–1823
English physician, the pioneer of vaccination
In 1796 he vaccinated James Phipps, an eight-year-old boy, with cowpox matter from the hands of Sarah Nelmes, a milkmaid, and soon afterwards inoculated him with smallpox, showing that the boy was protected. The practice of vaccination met with brief opposition, until over 70 principal physicians and surgeons in London signed a declaration of their entire confidence in it, and within five years vaccination was being practised in many parts of the world.

Jesus Christ c.6BC–c.30AD
The central figure of the Christian faith
Our knowledge of the life of Jesus Christ comes almost exclusively from the Gospel accounts and from other early Christian writings. According to these, he was the child of Mary, a woman of Nazareth, Galilee, who was engaged to be married to Joseph, a carpenter. After nearly 18 years of obscurity, he was baptized in the River Jordan by his cousin John the Baptist, and then gathered twelve disciples and began teaching, healing and performing miracles. In Jerusalem, after the Last Supper with his disciples, he was betrayed by Judas Iscariot, handed over to the Romans and

crucified. Three days later he rose from the dead, and stories of the resurrection became the basis for the development of the Christian faith. The name *Jesus* means 'saviour' in Aramaic; *Christ* is a Greek word meaning 'anointed one'.

Joan of Arc, St, *French* **Jeanne d'Arc**, *known as* **the Maid of Orleans** c.1412–1431
French patriot and martyr
The daughter of peasants, at the age of 13 she thought she heard the voices of St Michael, St Catherine and St Margaret bidding her rescue Paris from English domination; after convincing the dauphin (the future Charles VII) of her divine mission, she joined the army assembled at Blois for the relief of Orleans. The English were put to flight, but Joan was later captured, put on trial for heresy and sorcery by a court of the Inquisition, found guilty, and burnt at the stake in Rouen. She was made a saint nearly 500 years later, in 1920.

John, *surnamed* **Lackland** 1167–1216
King of England
John was the youngest son of **Henry II**, and became king in 1199. His oppressive rule led to demands by the barons, clergy, and people that he should keep his oath and restore the laws of Henry I. The army of the barons assembled at Stamford and marched to London; they met the king at Runnymede, and on 15 June 1215 the Great Charter (Magna Carta) was signed. He died during fighting with the French king Louis VIII, and was succeeded by Henry III.

John, Sir Elton Hercules, *originally* **Reginald Kenneth Dwight** 1947–
English pop singer, songwriter and pianist
One of the most successful pop-rock stars of the 1970s onward, the album *Elton John* (1970), which included the single 'Your Song', brought his first solo success. In a prolific career his albums have included *Don't Shoot Me I'm Only The Piano Player* (1973), *A Single Man* (1978) and *Sleeping with the Past* (1989). In the mid-1970s he developed a highly flamboyant stage image. In 1976 he became owner and chairman of Watford Football Club. He was knighted in 1998.

John Paul II, *originally* **Karol Jozef Wojtyła** 1920–2005
Polish pope
He was created cardinal in 1967 and pope in 1978, the first non-Italian pope in 450 years. An outspoken defender of the Church in communist countries, in the 1980s his visits to Poland and his meetings with **Mikhail Gorbachev** were of great assistance in promoting Polish independence, achieved in 1989. In 1995 he took part in historic meetings aimed at discussing relations between the Orthodox and Roman Catholic Churches. He wrote plays and other works, mainly on Christian themes.

Johnson, Amy 1903–41
English aviator
In 1930 she flew solo from England to Australia (the first woman to do so), winning £10,000 from the London *Daily Mail*. In 1931 she flew to Japan via Moscow and back, and in 1932 made a record solo flight to Cape Town in South Africa and back. With her husband James Mollison, she crossed the Atlantic Ocean in a De Havilland biplane in 39 hours (1933). In 1936 she set a new record for a solo flight from London to Cape Town. She died in a flying accident during World War II.

Johnson, Lyndon B(aines), *known as* **L B J** 1908–73
36th President of the USA
After serving in the US navy he became Vice-President under **John F Kennedy** in 1960. After Kennedy's assassination in 1963, he became President. During his administration the Civil Rights Act (1964) and the Voting Rights Act (1965) were passed, making improvements to the position of blacks in the USA, and he also introduced a series of important economic and social welfare reforms. However, the escalation of the war in Vietnam led to active protest and growing personal unpopularity for Johnson, and in 1968 he announced his decision to retire from active politics.

Johnson, Samuel, *known as* **Dr Johnson** 1709–84
English writer, critic, and lexicographer
After working as a schoolteacher and journalist, in 1747 he began his *Dictionary of the English Language*, which was to take him eight years to complete. During this time he also published a long didactic poem, *The Vanity of Human Wishes* (1749), and wrote and edited a bi-weekly periodical, *The Rambler*, which ran for 208 issues (1750–2). Other works include *Rasselas: The Prince of Abyssinia* (1759) and *Lives of the Most Eminent English Poets* (in 10 volumes, 1779–81). In 1763 he met the young Scot **James Boswell**, who became his biographer and recorded the witty conversation for which Johnson is famous.

Joliot-Curie, Frédéric, *originally* **Jean-Frédéric Joliot** 1900–58
French physicist
In 1925 he joined the Radium Institute in Paris under **Marie Curie**, and married Marie's daughter **Irène Joliot-Curie** in 1926. In 1935 he shared with his wife the Nobel Prize for chemistry for making the first artificial radioisotope. He died from cancer, caused by lifelong exposure to radioactivity.

Joliot-Curie, Irène, *née* **Curie** 1897–1956
French physicist
The daughter of **Pierre** and **Marie Curie**, in 1918 she joined her mother at the Radium Institute in Paris, beginning her scientific research in 1921. In 1926 she married **Frédéric Joliot-Curie**, and they collaborated in studies of radioactivity from 1931. In 1933–4 the Joliot-Curies made the first artificial radioisotope, and it was for this work that they were jointly awarded the Nobel Prize for chemistry in 1935. She died from leukaemia due to long periods of exposure to radioactivity.

Jones, Inigo 1573–1652
English architect and stage designer
Regarded as the founder of classical English architecture, he was a lifelong admirer of the architect **Andrea Palladio**, and introduced the Palladian style into England. He also made important contributions to English stage design, introducing the proscenium arch and movable scenery. His buildings include the Queen's House at Greenwich, completed in the 1630s, and the Double Cube room at Wilton (1649–52).

Jonson, Ben(jamin) 1572–1637
English dramatist
A friend and fellow-actor of **Shakespeare**, he was a

successful and influential playwright of the early 17th century. His plays, many with a satirical and comic genius, include *Every Man in his Humour* (1598), *Every Man Out of His Humour* (1599), *Volpone* (1606), *The Silent Woman* (1609), *The Alchemist* (1610) and *Bartholomew Fair* (1614).

Jordan, Michael Jeffrey 1963–
US basketball player
Perhaps the finest all-round player in the history of the game, he set numerous records, including most consecutive seasons leading the league in scoring (from the 1986–7 season through the 1992–3 season). He was named the NBA Most Valuable Player in 1988, 1991, 1992, 1996 and 1998. He spent most of his career with the Chicago Bulls (1984–93, 1995–8).

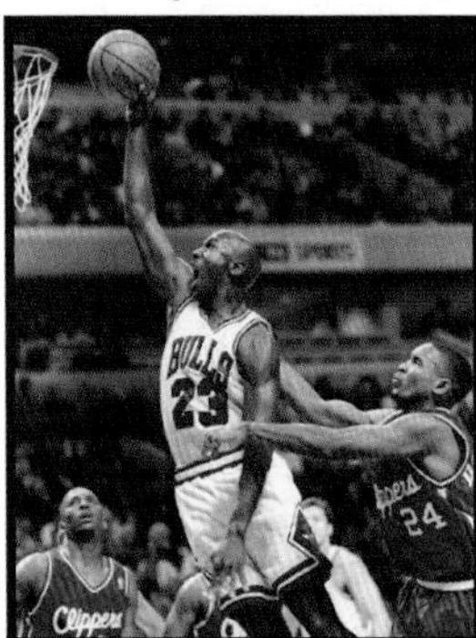

Michael Jordan

Joule, James Prescott 1818–89
English scientist
He is famous for his experiments on heat. He showed through experiment that heat is a form of energy, and determined the amount of mechanical (and later electrical) energy that was needed to produce it. He made many other discoveries. The joule, the SI unit of work or energy, is named after him.

Joyce, James Augustine Aloysius 1882–1941
Irish writer and poet
Joyce was born in Dublin, which provides the setting for most of his writing. His early work, particularly the short story collection *Dubliners* (1914), was immediately acclaimed by fellow writers such as **Ezra Pound**, and it was followed by *A Portrait of the Artist as a Young Man* (1914–15), *Ulysses* (1922) and *Finnegans Wake* (1939), considered three of the greatest novels of the 20th century. His literary experiments, for example his stream-of-consciousness technique, as well as his word play and comedy, exercised a major influence on contemporaries such as **Virginia Woolf** and **Samuel Beckett**.

Julius Caesar See **Caesar, (Gaius) Julius**

Jung, Carl Gustav 1875–1961
Swiss psychiatrist
He became **Sigmund Freud**'s leading collaborator but his independent researches made him increasingly critical of some of Freud's theories. He introduced the concepts of 'introvert' and 'extrovert' personalities, and developed the theory of the 'collective unconscious', that part of the unconscious mind that originates in ancestors' experience. His main works were: *The Psychology of the Unconscious* (1911–12), *Psychology and Religion* (1937), *Psychology and Alchemy* (1944), *The Undiscovered Self* (1957) and his autobiographical *Memories, Dreams, Reflections* (1962).

Juvenal, *in full* **Decimus Junius Juvenalis** c.55–c.140AD
Roman lawyer and satirist
Almost nothing is known of his life except that he lived in Rome, and that he was poor. His 16 verse satires of Roman life and society (c.100–c.128AD) range from savage attacks on the vices and the extravagance of the ruling classes and the precarious makeshift life of their hangers-on, to his hatred of Jews, foreigners and society women.

Kafka, Franz 1883–1924
Austrian novelist
One of the most influential writers of the 20th century, he is best known for short stories such as *Metamorphosis* (1916) and the three unfinished novels *The Trial* (1925), *The Castle* (1926) and *America* (1927), published after his death. These works have been interpreted in many different ways, but all of them tend to portray society as a pointless and irrational organization into which the bewildered individual has strayed. He worked for most of his life as a clerk in an insurance company (1907–23), and died young of a lung disease.

Kandinsky, Wassily, *Russian* **Vasili Vasilyevich Kandinsky** 1866–1944
French painter
Born in Moscow, Russia, he was the originator of abstract painting. After studying law in Moscow, he went to Munich to study art, and at the age of 30, he began painting. A watercolour he produced in 1910 is considered to be the first 'abstract' work of art. In 1912 he published his famous book *On the Spiritual in Art* and in the same year was a co-founder with Franz Marc and **Paul Klee** of the Blaue Reiter Group. From 1920 his paintings were mainly geometric.

Kant, Immanuel 1724–1804
German philosopher
Regarded as one of the great figures in the history of Western thought, Kant exerted an enormous influence on subsequent philosophy, especially the idealism of **Hegel**. His early publications were in the natural sciences, particularly geophysics and astronomy, and he predicted the existence of the planet Uranus before its actual discovery in 1781. His most important works in philosophy are the *Critique of Pure Reason* (1781), the *Critique of Practical Reason* (1788) and the *Critique of Judgement* (1790). He also wrote on political topics, and his *Perpetual Peace* (1795) advocates a world system of free states.

Kapoor, Anish 1954–
British sculptor
Born in Mumbai, India, of Jewish–Indian parentage, he moved to Britain in 1972. He exhibited at the international art exhibition the Venice Biennale in 1990, when he won the Premio Duemila for a young artist. His later work features heavy materials, often stone or polished metal, as in *Turning the World Inside Out* (1995). He was awarded the Turner Prize in 1991.

Karle, Isabella Helen, *née* **Lugoski** 1921–
US chemist and crystallographer
Among the many important chemical structures she has investigated, she co-discovered enkephalin, a

naturally occurring painkiller found in the brain. She has been honoured by scientific academies around the world.

Keaton, Buster (Joseph Francis) 1895–1966
US film comedian
His Hollywood film debut was in *The Butcher Boy* (1917), the start of a prolific career. Famous for his deadpan expression, he starred in and directed such classics as *The Navigator* (1924) and *The General* (1926). His reputation declined with the advent of talking films until the 1950s and 1960s, when many of his silent masterpieces were re-released, and he himself began to appear in character roles in films like *Sunset Boulevard* (1950) and *Limelight* (1952).

Keats, John 1795–1821
English poet
A medical student in London, he took to writing poetry, and became a friend of **Percy Bysshe Shelley**. His most important publication was *Lamia and Other Poems* (1820), which contains pieces such as 'The Eve of St Agnes' and the great odes 'On a Grecian Urn', 'To a Nightingale', 'To Autumn', 'On Melancholy' and 'To Psyche'. In particular, 'The Eve of St Agnes' displays a wealth of sensuous imagery almost unequalled in English poetry. Keats's letters are also greatly admired. He died in Rome of consumption aged 26.

Keller, Helen Adams 1880–1968
US writer
Born in Alabama, USA, she became deaf and blind at 19 months, and was unable to communicate through language until the age of seven, when she was taught to associate words with objects and to read and spell through touch. She later learned to use sign language and to speak, and she graduated from Radcliffe College in 1904. She became a lecturer and crusader for the handicapped and published several books based on her experiences, notably *The Story of My Life* (1902).

Kelly, Gene (Eugene Curran) 1912–96
US actor, dancer, choreographer and film director
An athletic, muscular dancer and choreographer, he revolutionized the screen musical in films like *Cover Girl* (1944), *Anchors Aweigh* (1945), *On The Town* (1949), *An American in Paris* (1951) and *Singin' in the Rain* (1952). He turned to dramatic acting in films like *Marjorie Morningstar* (1958) and *Inherit the Wind* (1960), and directed a number of films, including *Hello Dolly!* (1969).

Kelly, Ned (Edward) 1855–80
Australian bushranger
In 1878 he and his gang ambushed a group of policemen, and Kelly shot three of them. Two bank robberies followed, but the failed hold-up of a train at Glenrowan in Victoria led to the death of three gang members and the capture of Kelly, dressed in his home-made suit of armour. He was hanged in November 1880, and became a folk hero.

Kelvin (of Largs), William Thomson, 1st Baron 1824–1907
Scottish physicist and mathematician
The best-known achievement of his wide-ranging career, in which he brilliantly combined pure and applied science, was probably his proposal of the absolute, or Kelvin, temperature scale in 1848. Among many other achievements he investigated geomagnetism, improved ships' compasses and invented a number of electrical instruments.

Kemal Atatürk, Mustafa See **Atatürk, Mustapha Kemal**

Kennedy, John F(itzgerald) 1917–63
35th President of the USA
He served as a torpedo boat commander in the Pacific during World War II and successfully ran for President in 1960. In domestic policy he is remembered for his attempts to improve civil rights and his decision to begin the Apollo moon landing programme. In foreign policy he faced a number of crises, including the unsuccessful invasion of Cuba at the Bay of Pigs (April 1961), the building of the Berlin Wall (August 1961) and the Cuban Missile Crisis (October 1962). On 22 November 1963, he was assassinated in Dallas, Texas, allegedly by Lee Harvey Oswald, who was himself shot and killed two days later. Kennedy's eloquent idealism and youthful glamour won him much popularity in the USA and abroad.

Kepler, Johannes 1571–1630
German astronomer
His chief interest was the study of the planet Mars, and he found that its movement could not be explained by of the traditional theory of circular planetary orbits. He broke with the tradition of more than 2,000 years by demonstrating that the planets in fact move in elliptical orbits. Kepler's first, second and third laws relate to the areas of these ellipses, and the speeds of the planets as they trace them through space. They were a crucial development of the theories of **Copernicus**.

Kerensky, Aleksandr Fyodorovich 1881–1970
Russian revolutionary leader
In the 1917 Revolution he became Minister of Justice in March, Minister of War in May, and Prime Minister in July in the Provisional Government. Though crushing the military revolt of Lavr Kornilov in August, he found it increasingly difficult to put through moderate reforms, and in October was swept away by the Bolsheviks. The rest of his life was mainly spent in the USA, where he taught and wrote.

Keynes (of Tilton), John Maynard Keynes, 1st Baron 1883–1946
English economist
The most prominent of all 20th-century British economists, his first major publication was *The Economic Consequences of the Peace* (1919), in which he set out his views against the harsh economic terms imposed on Germany after World War I. The unemployment crisis inspired two further important works, *A Treatise on Money* (1930) and the revolutionary *General Theory of Employment, Interest and Money* (1936). His views on a planned economy influenced **Franklin D Roosevelt**'s 'New Deal' administration intended to rescue the US economy. Keynes was also a leading supporter of the arts, particularly theatre and ballet.

Khomeini, Ayatollah Ruhollah, *originally* **Ruholla Hendi** 1900–89
Iranian religious and political leader
A Shiite Muslim who was bitterly opposed to the pro-Western regime of Shah **Muhammad Reza Pahlavi**,

Khomeini took power amid great popular acclaim in 1979 after the collapse of the Shah's government. Under his leadership, Iran underwent an Islamic Revolution in which a return was made to the strict observance of Muslim principles and traditions. His denunciation of US influences led to the storming of the US embassy in Tehran and the holding of 53 US hostages. In 1989 he provoked international controversy by publicly commanding the killing of author Salman Rushdie, after many Muslims claimed his novel *The Satanic Verses* was blasphemous.

Ayatollah Khomeini

Khrushchev, Nikita Sergeyevich 1894–1971
Soviet politician
Joining the Bolshevik Party in 1918, he fought in the Civil War and rose rapidly in the party organization. In World War II he organized guerrilla warfare in the Ukraine, and in 1953, on the death of **Stalin**, he became First Secretary of the All Union Party. Three years later, in a speech that had far-reaching results, he denounced Stalinism and the 'personality cult'. Among the events of his administration were the Hungarian uprising that he crushed (1956) and the failed attempt to install missiles in Cuba (1962). He was deposed in 1964 and forced into retirement, and was replaced by **Leonid Brezhnev**.

Kierkegaard, Søren Aabye 1813–55
Danish philosopher and theologian
Kierkegaard's philosophy represents a strong reaction against the dominant German traditions of the day, and in particular against **Hegel**. His works tend to stress the importance of the individual, and are often written in a literary rather than an academic style. The most important include *Either-Or* (1843), *Fear and Trembling* (1843) and *The Sickness unto Death* (1849). Regarded as one of the founders of existentialism, he achieved real recognition only in the 20th century.

Kim-Il Sung, *originally* **Kim Song-ju** 1912–94
North Korean soldier and political leader
He founded the Korean People's Revolutionary Army in 1932 and led a long struggle against the Japanese. He proclaimed the Democratic People's Republic of Korea (hence North Korea) in 1948 and remained as effective head of state until his death. Kim established a unique personality cult along with an isolationist, Stalinist political–economic system. He was succeeded by his son, Kim Jong Il. In 1998 he was posthumously proclaimed 'Eternal President'.

King, B B, *originally* **Riley B King** 1925–
US blues singer and guitarist
One of the best-known blues performers, his reputation grew considerably in the late 1960s as the blues influence on rock music came to be acknowledged by white audiences. In the late 1970s he became the first blues artist to tour the USSR. Albums released during his prolific recording career have included *Confessin' The Blues* (1966), *Indianola Mississippi Seeds* (1970), *There Must Be A Better World Somewhere* (1981), *Six Silver Strings* (1985), *Blues on the Bayou* (1998) and a collaboration with **Eric Clapton**, *Riding with the King* (2000).

King, Billie Jean, *née* **Moffitt** 1943–
US tennis player
Between 1961 and 1979 she won a then record 20 Wimbledon titles, including the singles in 1966–8, 1972–3, and 1975, and four mixed doubles. She also won 13 US titles (including four singles in 1967, 1971–2, and 1974), four French titles (one singles in 1972), and two Australian titles (one singles in 1968).

King, Martin Luther, Jnr 1929–68
US clergyman, civil-rights leader
Shortly after he had become pastor of the Dexter Avenue Baptist Church in Montgomery, Alabama, the arrest of **Rosa Parks** sparked off the Montgomery bus boycott (1955–6), and King came to national prominence as its eloquent and courageous leader. In 1963 he led the great march on Washington, where he delivered his memorable 'I have a dream' speech. He preached a philosophy of non-violence and passive resistance, and these tactics were successful in bringing about the Civil Rights Act of 1964 and the Voting Rights Act of 1965. In 1964 he also received the Nobel Peace Prize. He was assassinated in Memphis, Tennessee, while on a civil rights mission.

Kingsley, Mary Henrietta 1862–1900
English traveller and writer
In 1893 she made the first of two remarkable journeys to West Africa, where she lived among the native peoples. Returning from her second journey in 1895, she wrote *Travels in West Africa* and *West African Studies* (both 1899). She was subsequently consulted by colonial administrators for her wide understanding of African culture.

Kipling, (Joseph) Rudyard 1865–1936
English writer
He wrote poetry, novels and plays, and is best known for his explorations of the British colonial experience in the late 19th and early 20th centuries. Among his works are the poetry collection *Barrack Room Ballads* (1892), *The Jungle Book* (1894) and *The Second Jungle Book* (1895), which became classics of children's literature, *Kim* (1901), a novel about a child spy, *Stalky and Co* (1899), about his schooldays, and the *Just So Stories* (1902), also for children. Later works include *Puck of Pook's Hill* (1906), *Rewards and Fairies* (1910) and the autobiographical *Something of Myself* (1937). He was awarded the Nobel Prize for literature in 1907.

Kissinger, Henry Alfred 1923–
US politician and diplomat
Born in Fürth, Germany, his family emigrated to the USA in 1938 to escape Nazi persecution of the Jews. He became President **Richard Nixon**'s close adviser (1969), was the main US figure in the negotiations to end the Vietnam War, for which he shared the 1973

Nobel Peace Prize with the Vietnamese statesman Le Duc Tho, and the same year became Secretary of State. He played a major role in the improvement of relations (détente) with both China and the USSR during the early 1970s and in the peace negotiations between the Arabs and Israelis (1973–5).

Klee, Paul 1879–1940
Swiss artist
He was associated with Franz Marc and **Wassily Kandinsky** in the Blaue Reiter group of artists (1911–12). Many of his works were confiscated by the Nazis and 17 of them were included in the 1937 'Degenerate Art' exhibition in Munich. His fantastic, small-scale, mainly abstract pictures gave the effect of inspired doodling, for example the well-known *Twittering Machine*.

Klimt, Gustav 1862–1918
Austrian painter and designer
Under the influence of contemporary movements such as Impressionism, Symbolism and art nouveau, he became a founder and the first president (1898–1903) of the Vienna Secession, a movement dedicated to furthering the avant-garde. His murals for Vienna University (1900–3) were considered indecent and aroused official condemnation. He produced a number of portraits, mainly of women, as well as large allegorical and mythological paintings; typically, these have an elaborate, decorative treatment of the background or clothing.

Knox, John c.1513–1572
Scottish Protestant reformer
He was much influenced by the Protestant reformer **John Calvin** in Geneva. His life was full of conflict, particularly with **Mary, Queen of Scots** in Scotland, and he served time as a prisoner of the French (1547–9). He is known for founding the Church of Scotland on Calvinist lines, and for his book *First Blast of the Trumpet Against the Monstrous Regiment of Women* (1558), which argued against giving women any position of power over men. He also wrote a *History of the Reformation in Scotland* (published 1586).

Knut Sveinsson See **Canute**

Koch, (Heinrich Hermann) Robert 1843–1910
German physician and bacteriologist
Koch discovered the bacillus that is the sole cause of anthrax, publishing his findings in 1876 and 1877, and discovered in 1882 the tubercle bacillus that causes tuberculosis. In 1883 he discovered the cholera bacillus, and in 1890 he produced a drug named tuberculin to prevent the development of tuberculosis. He was awarded the Nobel Prize for physiology or medicine in 1905. His formulation of the essential scientific principles known as 'Koch's postulates' established clinical bacteriology as a medical science in the 1890s.

Korbut, Olga Valentinovna 1956–
Belarussian gymnast
She captivated the world at the 1972 Olympics at Munich with her supple grace, and gave gymnastics a new lease of life as a sport. She won a gold medal as a member of the winning Soviet team, as well as individual golds in the beam and floor exercises and silver for the parallel bars. After retiring, she became a coach.

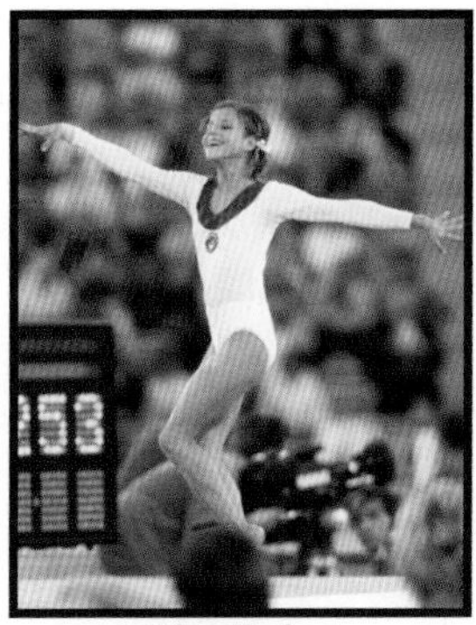
Olga Korbut

Krebs, Sir Hans Adolf 1900–81
British biochemist
In 1932 he described the urea cycle whereby carbon dioxide and ammonia form urea in the liver. Leading on from his earlier work, he described the citric acid cycle (Krebs' cycle) of energy production (c.1943). He carried out numerous other studies, and in 1953 he shared with Fritz Lipmann the Nobel Prize for physiology or medicine.

Kublai Khan, *also spelt* **Kubla** or **Khublai** 1214–94
Great Khan of the Mongols from 1260 and Emperor of China from 1271
Kublai Khan was the grandson of **Genghis Khan**. He completed his grandfather's conquest of northern China, but an attempt to invade Japan ended in disaster. His dominions extended from the Arctic Ocean to the Straits of Malacca, and from Korea to Asia Minor and Hungary. The splendour of his court inspired the writing of **Marco Polo**, who spent 17 years in his service, and later fired the imagination of **Samuel Taylor Coleridge**.

Lamarck, Jean-Baptiste Pierre Antoine de Monet Chevalier de 1744–1829
French naturalist and evolutionist
His early work was mainly in the study of invertebrates, and he originated the distinction between vertebrates and invertebrates. In about 1801 he began to think about the relations and origin of species, expressing his conclusions in his *Zoological Philosophy* (1809), in which he suggested that the characteristics that animals acquire in life can be passed on to their offspring. Lamarck's theory of acquired characteristics was later discredited, but he helped prepare the way for the now accepted theory of evolution.

Landseer, Sir Edwin Henry 1802–73
English animal painter
He began exhibiting at the Royal Academy when only 13 years old. His animal pieces generally expressed some sentiment or idea, but did not lose their correctness and force of draughtsmanship. His *Monarch of the Glen*, depicting a stag in the Scottish Highlands, was exhibited in 1851, and the bronze lions at the foot of Nelson's Monument in Trafalgar Square were modelled by him from 1859 to 1866.

Landsteiner, Karl 1868–1943
US pathologist
Born in Vienna, Austria, he later went to the USA to work in the Rockefeller Institute for Medical Research,

New York City (1922–39). He won the 1930 Nobel Prize for physiology or medicine, especially for his valuable discovery of the four major human blood groups (A, O, B, AB) which he discovered in 1901, and the M and N groups (discovered in 1927). In 1940 he also discovered the rhesus (Rh) factor.

Langland or **Langley, William** c.1332–c.1400
English poet
Educated at the Benedictine school at Malvern, he became a clerk and may have earned a poor living in London from 1362 by singing in a chantry and by copying legal documents. In 1362 he began his famous *Vision of William concerning Piers the Plowman*, a medieval alliterative poem on spiritual pilgrimage.

Laozi (Lao Tzu), *literally* **the old master** 6th century BC
Chinese philosopher and sage
Traditionally the founder of Taoism, he is probably a legendary figure and is represented as the older contemporary of **Confucius**. The *Dao De Jing* (*Tao-Te-Ching*, 'The Book of the Way and its Power'), one of the principal works of Taoism, is traditionally attributed to him although is authorship and date of compilation are not certain. It teaches self-sufficiency, simplicity and detachment.

Larkin, Philip Arthur 1922–85
English poet
One of the best-loved and most accessible of all English poets, he was much concerned with the ordinary tragedies of loss and death in what he perceived as a world without God. He produced only four major collections: *The North Ship* (1945), *The Less Deceived* (1955), *The Whitsun Weddings* (1964) and *High Windows* (1974). His *Collected Poems* was published posthumously in 1988 and became a bestseller. He wrote two novels, *Jill* (1946) and *A Girl in Winter* (1947); his articles on jazz were collected in *All What Jazz?* (1970), and his essays in *Required Writing* (1983).

Latimer, Hugh c.1485–1555
English Protestant reformer
A convert to Protestantism, he was one of the priests appointed to examine the lawfulness of **Henry VIII**'s marriage to Catherine of Aragon. He declared on the King's side, that the marriage could be annulled, and in 1535 he was appointed Bishop of Worcester. Under Mary I he was found guilty of heresy, with Nicholas Ridley and **Thomas Cranmer**, and on 16 October 1555 was burned with Ridley opposite Balliol College, Oxford.

Laurel, Stan, *originally* **Arthur Stanley Jefferson** 1890–1965
US comic actor
Born in Ulverston, in the north of England, he went to the USA in 1910. After gaining his first film part in 1917, he appeared in many of the early silent comedies and teamed up with **Oliver Hardy** in 1927. They made many full-length feature films, including *Bonnie Scotland* (1935) and *Way Out West* (1937), but their best efforts are generally reckoned to be their early shorts (1927–32), one of which, *The Music Box* (1932), won an Academy Award. Their disaster-packed predicaments made them a universally popular comedy duo.

Lavoisier, Antoine Laurent 1743–94
French chemist
A successful experimenter in many fields of science, he is best known for discovering oxygen and demonstrating its importance in respiration, combustion and as a compound with metals. Politically liberal, he saw the great necessity for reform in France but was against revolutionary methods. Despite a lifetime of work for the state, inquiring into the problems of taxation (which he helped to reform), hospitals and prisons, he was guillotined as a collector of taxes.

Lawrence, D(avid) H(erbert) 1885–1930
English novelist, poet and essayist
The son of a miner, he became a schoolmaster, and in 1911, after the success of his first novel, *The White Peacock*, he decided to become a full-time writer. He went on to produce a number of highly original and, at the time, shocking explorations of relationships and marriage, including *Sons and Lovers* (1913), *The Rainbow* (1915), *Women in Love* (1921) and *Lady Chatterley's Lover*, the last of which was not published in the UK in full until after a sensational obscenity trial in 1961. His finest writing probably occurs in his poems, and his *Complete Poems* appeared in 1957. His other writings include vivid travel narratives, essays, plays, works of literary criticism and letters. He was also an accomplished painter.

Lawrence, Ernest Orlando 1901–58
US physicist
In 1929 he constructed the first cyclotron for the production of artificial radioactivity, fundamental to the development of the atomic bomb. He was professor at the University of California at Berkeley from 1930, and in 1936 was appointed first director of the radiation laboratory there. He was awarded the Nobel Prize for physics in 1939.

Lear, Edward 1812–88
English artist, humorist and traveller
He created his famous nonsense limericks and other verse to entertain the grandchildren of his patron, the 13th Earl of Derby. He illustrated these with his own sketches and published them, anonymously, as *A Book of Nonsense* in 1846. Later he published *Nonsense Songs, Stories, Botany, and Alphabets* (1870), *More Nonsense Rhymes* (1871) and *Laughable Lyrics* (1876). He travelled widely in Italy and Greece, making landscape sketches and oil paintings which he published in several travel books.

Leavitt, Henrietta Swan 1868–1921
US astronomer
She was a volunteer research assistant at Harvard College Observatory, Massachusetts, and joined the staff there in 1902, quickly becoming head of the department of photographic photometry. Whilst studying Cepheid stars, which showed some variation in brightness, she noticed that the brighter they were the longer their period of light variation was. By 1912 she had succeeded in showing that the apparent magnitude had a fixed relationship with the period of variation. This simple relationship proved invaluable as the basis for a method of measuring the distance of stars.

Le Corbusier, *pseudonym of* **Charles Édouard Jeanneret** 1887–1965
French architect
An architect whose work has had worldwide in-

fluence on town planning and building design, his first building, based on the technique of the Modulor (a system using standard-sized units, the proportions of which are calculated according to those of the human figure), was the *Unité d'habitation*, Marseilles (1945–50). Among his later projects was the planning of the city of Chandigarh, the new capital of the Punjab. Some of his buildings are raised on stilts or *pilotis*. In the 1920s he designed furniture, especially chairs, which used tubular metal in their construction.

Lee, (Nelle) Harper 1926–
US writer
She was a descendant of **Robert E Lee** and a childhood friend of **Truman Capote**. She won a Pulitzer Prize for fiction (1961) for her only novel, *To Kill a Mockingbird* (1960), which deals with racial injustice in the American South and depicts the characters of a small southern US town through the eyes of a young girl.

Lee, Laurie 1914–97
English poet and writer
He is probably best known for his autobiographical books *Cider With Rosie* (1959), *As I Walked Out One Midsummer Morning* (1969) and *I Can't Stay Long* (1975), which have been widely acclaimed for their evocation of a rural childhood and of life in the numerous countries he visited. He was also an important nature poet whose collections include *The Sun My Monument* (1944), *The Bloom of Candles* (1947) and *My Many-Coated Man* (1955). Other works include *A Rose For Winter* (1955) and *Red Sky at Sunset* (1991).

Lee, Robert E(dward) 1807–70
US soldier
One of the greatest of the Confederate generals in the American Civil War (1861–5), in 1861 he became Commander-in-Chief of the Confederate Army of Virginia. Among his victories were the second Battle of Bull Run (1862) and the Battle of Chancellorsville (1863), but the tide turned against him at the Battle of Gettysburg (1863). In February 1865 Lee became Commander-in-Chief of all of the armies of the South, but the Confederate cause was hopeless at that point and two months later he surrendered his army to Union General **Ulysses S Grant**.

Leeuwenhoek, Antoni van 1632–1723
Dutch amateur scientist
He became skilled in grinding and polishing lenses to inspect cloth fibres. With his microscopes, each made for a specific investigation, he discovered the existence of protozoa in water and bacteria in the tartar of teeth. He also discovered blood corpuscles, blood capillaries, the structure of muscle and the structure of nerves, among many other observations.

Le Fanu, (Joseph) Sheridan 1814–73
Irish novelist and journalist
His novels include *The House by the Churchyard* (1863) and *Uncle Silas* (1864), and many of his short stories are collected in *In a Glass Darkly* (1872). He wrote 14 other works, all preoccupied with the supernatural. His *Poems* appeared after his death in 1896 and *Madam Crowl's Ghost* (1923) was edited by M R James.

Leibniz, Gottfried Wilhelm 1646–1716
German philosopher and mathematician
He made contributions to most areas of mathematics, and in the 1680s both he and **Isaac Newton** independently published systems of calculus. Leibnitz also wrote on history, law and political theory, and his philosophy was the foundation of 18th-century rationalism. His *Theodicy* (1710) was a relatively popular work in theology, expressing his optimism and faith in enlightenment and reason, which **Voltaire** satirized brilliantly in *Candide*. His best-known doctrine is that the world is composed of an infinity of indivisible substances or 'monads', the highest of which is God.

Leibovitz, Annie 1949–
US photographer
Her most famous portraits include a wide variety of politicians, athletes and musicians, among them **Mick Jagger**, **Louis Armstrong**, **Ella Fitzgerald**, and the last portrait ever taken of **John Lennon**. She published *Photographs 1970–90* in 1992 and (with writer Susan Sontag) *Women* in 2000.

Leif the Lucky, *real name* **Leifur heppni Eiríksson** fl.1000
Icelandic explorer
He was the son of explorer Erik the Red. Just before the year 1000 he set sail from Greenland to explore lands to the west, reaching Baffin Land, Labrador, and an area he called 'Vínland' (Wineland) because of the wild grapes he found growing there. Two Icelandic sagas, 'Saga of Eric' and 'Tale of the Greenlanders', tell the story of the Norse discovery and attempted colonization of North America, 500 years before **Christopher Columbus**.

Leigh, Vivien, *originally* **Vivian Mary Hartley** 1913–67
British actress

Vivien Leigh

Her first contract was with film-maker Alexander Korda, playing in *Fire Over England* (1936) with **Laurence Olivier**, whom she later married (1940–60). In Hollywood she played her best-known part, Scarlett O'Hara in *Gone With the Wind* (1939), which won her an Academy Award. Other major film roles were in *Anna Karenina* (1948) and *A Streetcar Named Desire* (1951), which gained her another Academy Award.

Lely, Sir Peter, *originally* **Pieter van der Faes** 1618–80
British painter
A leading painter of popular and often highly sensuous court portraits, his sitters included **Charles I** and **Oliver Cromwell**, and in 1661 he was appointed court

PEOPLE

painter to **Charles II**, for whom he changed his style of painting. His *Windsor Beauties* series is collected at Hampton Court. The 13 Greenwich portraits of *Admirals* are among his most acclaimed works.

Lenin, Vladimir Ilyich, *originally surnamed* **Ulyanov** 1870–1924
Russian revolutionary
A Marxist, he was the leader of the Bolshevik revolutionaries in Tsarist Russia. After the fall of Tsar **Nicholas II** in 1917, he overthrew the shaky provisional government and took supreme power. Lenin inaugurated the 'dictatorship of the proletariat', and for three years he grappled with war and anarchy. His health having been in decline since an assassination attempt in 1918, he died on 21 January 1924, and his body was embalmed in a mausoleum in Red Square, Moscow. He was succeeded by **Stalin**. He was revered in communist countries throughout the 20th century as the founder of Soviet communism.

Lennon, John (Winston) 1940–80
English songwriter, vocalist and rhythm guitarist
He first found fame as a member of the Beatles, one of pop's best-known groups, and with fellow band member **Paul McCartney** he wrote many of their most popular songs, including 'She Loves You' and 'I Want to Hold your Hand'. He pursued a solo career after the group disbanded in 1970. His marriage to Japanese artist Yoko Ono sharpened his social conscience, and their work together produced songs of mild protest such as 'Give Peace a Chance' (1969) and 'Working Class Hero' (1970). His most successful albums were *Imagine* (1971) and *Mind Games* (1973). He was shot dead in New York.

Leonardo da Vinci 1452–1519
Italian painter, sculptor, architect and engineer
Leonardo was the outstanding genius of the Renaissance, with a wide knowledge and understanding far beyond his times of biology, anatomy, physiology and aeronautics; his notebooks, written in mirror writing, contain original remarks on all of these. Few of his painting works have survived, but those that do include the famous *Last Supper* (1498) and the *Mona Lisa* (c.1504). However, there are rich collections of his drawings, and these show that he founded his style on a searching study of nature and, in particular, of light and shade.

Lescot, Pierre c.1510–1578
French Renaissance architect
He was one of the greatest architects of his time. Among his works are the screen of St Germain l'Auxerrois, the Fontaine des Innocents and the Hôtel de Ligneris, all in Paris. His masterpiece was the Louvre, one wing of which he completely rebuilt.

Lewis, Carl (Frederick Carlton) 1961–
US track and field athlete
He won four gold medals at the 1984 Los Angeles Olympics (100m, 200m, 4×100m relay and long jump), and at the 1988 Seoul Olympics he won a gold medal in the long jump and was awarded the 100m gold medal after Ben Johnson was stripped of the title. In 1992 at the Barcelona Olympics he acquired two more golds in the long jump and the 4×100m relay, and in the 1996 Atlanta Olympics he earned the ninth and final gold medal of his career in the long jump, only the fourth Olympian to win as many golds.

Lewis, C(live) S(taples) 1898–1963
British novelist, literary scholar and religious writer
He was a distinguished teacher at Cambridge and won a wide popular audience during World War II for his broadcast talks and his books on religious subjects, notably *The Screwtape Letters* (1940). His series of seven books for children, *The Chronicles of Narnia*, which began with *The Lion, The Witch and The Wardrobe* (1950) and ended with *The Last Battle* (1956), is suffused with Christian allegory and ethics, and remains a children's classic. His most important adult novels are the science-fiction trilogy *Out of the Silent Planet* (1938), *Perelandra* (1939) and *That Hideous Strength* (1945).

Liebknecht, Karl 1871–1919
German barrister, politician and revolutionary
He was a member of the Reichstag from 1912 to 1916, and in World War I he was imprisoned as an independent, anti-militarist social democrat. He was a founder-member with **Rosa Luxemburg** of the German Communist Party in 1918 and led an unsuccessful revolt in Berlin (the 'Spartacus Rising') in January 1919, during which he and Rosa Luxemburg were killed by army officers.

Lincoln, Abraham 1809–65
16th President of the USA
After working as a lawyer, he won election to Congress in 1846, and became well-known for his anti-slavery views. He became President in 1860. His political and oratorical skills were not enough to prevent the American Civil War (1861–5), and after victory by the North he attempted to heal the nation with his Gettysburg Address of 1863, which included the first use of the words 'government of the people, by the people, for the people'. That same year he proclaimed freedom for all slaves, and in 1864 he was re-elected. On Good Friday, 14 April 1865, at Ford's Theatre, Washington, he was shot by John Wilkes Booth, an actor, and he died the next morning. He is remembered particularly for his inspiring speeches and his many statements of the significance of America as a free, democratic nation.

Lindbergh, Charles Augustus 1902–74
US aviator
In May 1927 he made the first non-stop solo transatlantic flight from New York to Paris in a monoplane named *Spirit of St Louis* in 33½ hours. During World War II he advocated US neutrality. His autobiography, *The Spirit of St Louis* (1953), won the Pulitzer Prize in 1954.

Linnaeus, Carolus, *originally* **Carl von Linné** 1707–78
Swedish naturalist and physician
The inventor of the modern scientific nomenclature (naming system) for plants and animals, in which each organism is given a genus and a species name, he had a uniquely influential position in natural history. His major works include his *Systema Naturae* (1735), followed by *Fundamenta Botanica* (1736), *Genera Plantarum* (1737), *Critica Botanica* (1737) and *Species Plantarum* (1753). His manuscripts and collections are kept at the Linnaean Society in London, established in his honour in 1788.

Lippi, Fra Filippo, *called* **Lippo** c.1406–1469
Italian religious painter
His greatest work, on the choir walls of Prato Cathedral, Italy, was begun in 1452. Between 1452 and 1464 he abducted a nun and was released from his monastic vows by the Pope in order to marry her. She was the model for many of his Madonnas and the mother of his son, painter Filippino Lippi. His later works are deeply religious and include the series of *Nativities*. He was immortalized in **Robert Browning**'s poem 'Fra Lippo Lippi' (1855).

Lister, Joseph Lister, 1st Baron 1827–1912
English surgeon
His great work was the introduction of his antiseptic system (1867), a development of the work of **Louis Pasteur**, which revolutionized modern surgery. His early antiseptic work was concerned with the treatment by surgery of compound fractures and tuberculous joints; both conditions would previously have been dealt with by amputation. He worked later in his life on the causes of wound infection.

Liszt, Franz 1811–86
Hungarian composer and pianist
One of the foremost, and most experimental, composers of the Romantic period, his works include twelve symphonic poems, masses, two symphonies, and a large number of piano pieces. He was also renowned as a virtuoso performer on the piano. All his original compositions have a very distinct individuality, and the vocal and piano works of his last years were prophetic of 20th-century developments. His literary works on music include studies of his friend **Frédéric Chopin** and the music of the Gypsies.

Livingstone, David 1813–73
Scottish missionary and traveller
He worked as a missionary for several years in Bechuanaland (now Botswana) and in a series of explorations became the first European to see the Victoria Falls of the Zambezi as well as many other localities. Determined to extend commercial and missionary operations throughout the African interior, he was also firmly against slavery, and his book *The Zambesi and its Tributaries* (1865) was designed to expose the Portuguese slave trade. In 1866 he started from Zanzibar on a Royal Geographical Society expedition to find the sources of the Nile, but was found, very ill, by journalist Henry Morton Stanley, who had been sent to look for him by the *New York Herald* (and to whom is attributed the famous quote, 'Dr Livingstone, I presume?').

Livy, *properly* **Titus Livius** 59BC–AD17
Roman historian
He settled in Rome in about 29BC and was admitted to the court of **Augustus**, but took no part in politics. His history of Rome from its foundation to the death of military leader Nero Claudius Drusus (9BC) comprised 142 books, of which 35 have survived. Livy can be placed in the forefront of Latin writers, and his work was a major influence on subsequent historical writing.

Lloyd, Harold Clayton 1893–1971
US film comedian
His character was that of the shy, sincere, bespectacled boy-next-door, and he developed a reputation for highly demanding stunts in works like *High and Dizzy* (1920) and, most famously, *Safety Last* (1923). He was less successful in the sound era and retired after *Mad Wednesday* in 1947. He published an autobiography, *An American Comedy*, in 1928.

Lloyd-George (of Dwyfor), David Lloyd George, 1st Earl 1863–1945
Welsh Liberal statesman
He entered parliament in 1890, and as Chancellor of the Exchequer from 1908 to 1915 he introduced a number of important reforms, including old age pensions and National Insurance. During World War I he became War Secretary and then Prime Minister (1916–22). By his forceful policy he was, as **Hitler** later said of him, 'the man who won the war'. In 1921 he negotiated and conceded the Irish Free State, a move which was so unpopular with the Conservatives in the government that it led to his downfall, and the downfall of the Liberals as a party at the 1922 election.

Lloyd-Webber, Andrew Lloyd Webber, Baron 1948–
English popular composer
He met lyricist Tim Rice in 1965, and together they wrote the hit musicals *Joseph and the Amazing Technicolor Dreamcoat* (1968), *Jesus Christ Superstar* (1970) and *Evita* (1978). His later successes include *Cats* (1981), *Starlight Express* (1984), *The Phantom of the Opera* (1986), *Aspects of Love* (1989) and *Sunset Boulevard* (1993). He also composed the music for *Whistle Down the Wind* (1996) and *The Beautiful Game* (2000).

Locke, John 1632–1704
English philosopher
Locke's major philosophical work was the *Essay concerning Human Understanding*, published in 1690. The *Essay* is an enquiry into the nature and scope of human reason, seeking to establish that 'all knowledge is founded on and ultimately derives from sense … or sensation'. The work is regarded as the first and probably the most important statement of the British empiricist tradition which led from Locke to George Berkeley and **David Hume**. His other main works were *A Letter concerning Toleration* (1689), *Some Thoughts concerning Education* (1693) and *The Reasonableness of Christianity* (1695).

Longfellow, Henry Wadsworth 1807–82
US poet
His gift of simple, romantic storytelling in verse brought him enduring popularity as a poet. His collection *Ballads* (1841) included 'The Wreck of the Hesperus' and 'The Village Blacksmith', and later successes included *Evangeline* (1847), a tale of the French exiles of Acadia, a former colony in North America, and *The Song of Hiawatha* (1855), which is based on the legends of Native Americans.

Lorenz, Konrad Zacharias 1903–89
Austrian zoologist
He founded, with Nikolaas Tinbergen in the late 1930s, the science of ethology (the study of animal behaviour under natural conditions). In 1935 he published his observations on imprinting in young birds (the discovery for which he is chiefly known), by which hatchlings 'learn' to recognize substitute parents at the earliest stages in life. His books include *Man Meets Dog* (1950) and *On Aggression* (1963). He shared the 1973 Nobel Prize for physiology or medicine with Nikolaas Tinbergen and Karl von Frisch.

Louis XIV, *known as* **Le Roi Soleil ('The Sun King')** 1638–1715
King of France
He came to the throne at the age of five. His reign was notable for its artistic and architectural splendour and for the magnificence of his court at Versailles. His foreign policy was aggressive, especially against the Dutch and Spanish, and despite many victories, the War of the Spanish Succession (1701–14) proved disastrous for France with crushing defeats at Blenheim (1704) and Ramillies (1706). His later policies led to the bloody persecution of Protestants and mass emigration of French Huguenots to Holland and England.

19th-century portrait of Louis XIV

Louis XV, *known as* **le Bien-Aimé ('the Well-Beloved')** 1710–74
King of France
He succeeded his great-grandfather, **Louis XIV**, in 1715, aged five. A popular king, he nevertheless lacked Louis XIV's interest in politics or administration, and his reign was troubled by intrigue at home and a series of military disasters abroad. One particular mistress, Madame de Pompadour, used her position to exert considerable influence over government policy.

Louis XVI 1754–93
King of France
He succeeded his grandfather **Louis XV** in 1774, and was married in 1770 to **Marie Antoinette**, youngest daughter of the Habsburg Empress Maria Theresa. After revolutionary outbreaks in Paris on 12 July 1789, the National Guard of Paris was called out, and on 14 July the people stormed the Bastille prison and the unrest spread to the provinces. Three years later the Republic was proclaimed. In December 1792 the king was brought to trial, and called upon to answer for repeated acts of treason against the Republic. On 20 January 1793 he was executed, ending 1,025 years of monarchy.

Lovelace, (Augusta) Ada, Countess of, *née* **Byron** 1815–52
English writer and mathematician
The daughter of Lord **Byron**, she taught herself geometry, and was educated in astronomy and mathematics. Acquainted with many leading figures of the Victorian era, she owes much of her recent fame to her friendship with **Charles Babbage**, the computer pioneer. She translated and annotated an article on his 'analytical engine' (the precursor of the modern computer), adding many explanatory notes of her own, and this forms an important source on Babbage's work. The high-level universal computer programming language, ADA, was named in her honour.

Lowell, Robert Traill Spence, Jnr 1917–77
US poet
His first collection, *Land of Unlikeness* (1944), contained biographical poems, and his widely acclaimed second volume, *Lord Weary's Castle* (1946), won him the Pulitzer Prize in 1947. *Life Studies* (1959), *For the Union Dead* (1964) and *Near the Ocean* (1967) were also 'confessional' in style. During the Vietnam years, he wrote *Notebook* (1968), and in *The Dolphin* (1973), he made public his personal letters and anxieties.

Lowry, L(aurence) S(tephen) 1887–1976
English painter
While working as a clerk, he trained at Manchester College of Art in the evenings, and from 1915 to 1925 he attended Salford School of Art. He produced numerous pictures of the Lancashire industrial scene, mainly in brilliant whites and greys, often filled with uncommunicative matchstick antlike men and women, in a deliberately naive style. His work is represented in many major collections.

Ludendorff, Erich 1865–1937
German soldier
In 1914, at the beginning of World War I, he was appointed Chief of Staff in East Prussia, and masterminded the annihilation of the Russians at Tannenberg in August of that year. On the Western Front in 1918 he planned the major offensive that nearly won the war for Germany. In 1923 he was a leader in the Munich putsch in which **Hitler** unsuccessfully tried to seize power, but he was acquitted of treason. He was a Nazi member of the Reichstag from 1924 to 1928. Although strongly opposed to Jews, Jesuits and freemasons, in later years he became a pacifist.

Lumière, Auguste Marie Louis Nicolas 1862–1954 and **Louis Jean** 1865–1948
French industrial and physiological chemists
In 1894, after seeing a demonstration of **Thomas Alva Edison**'s kinetoscope, an early form of motion picture viewer which could record movement, Louis determined to invent a method by which moving pictures could be projected. Together the brothers invented the cinematograph, the first machine to project images on a screen, in 1895. The same year they built the first cinema, in Lyons, France, and produced the first film newsreels and the first motion picture in history, *Workers Leaving the Lumière Factory*. After 1900 they worked to improve colour photography, and Auguste also carried out research into cancer, vitamins, and oral vaccination.

Luther, Martin 1483–1546
German religious reformer
As a priest he was appalled by what he saw as the corrupt practices of the Catholic Church, in particular the sale of indulgences (the promised escape from divine punishment after death in return for money). In 1517 he drew up a list of 95 theses on such indulgences, nailing them on the church door at Wittenberg, Germany. Soon afterwards he was summoned to appear before the first Diet at Worms, a general assembly of the Holy Roman Empire, and finally put under house arrest. An enormously influential figure, his work led to the Protestant Reformation. His Bible

translation was hugely successful, and his other writings include *Table-talk*, *Letters* and *Sermons*.

Luxemburg, Rosa 1871–1919
German left-wing revolutionary
Born in Poland, she became a leader of the left-wing movement in Berlin, writing tracts such as *Sozialreform oder Revolution* ('Social Reform or Revolution?'). At the outbreak of World War I she formed, with **Karl Liebknecht**, the Spartakusbund (Spartacus League), later the core of the German Communist Party, and spent most of the war in prison. After her release in 1919 she took part in an unsuccessful uprising, and was murdered with Liebknecht in Berlin.

Lwoff, André Michel 1902–94
French microbiologist
He researched the genetics of bacterial viruses (phage) and showed that when phage enters a bacterial cell, it can protect it against further invasion by the same type of virus. These findings have had important implications for the development of drug resistance and for cancer research. In 1965 Lwoff was awarded the Nobel Prize for physiology or medicine jointly with François Jacob and **Jacques Monod**.

Lyell, Sir Charles 1797–1875
Scottish geologist
Considered one of the founders of modern geology, his interest was primarily in the biological side of geology, and his work had as great a contemporary influence as **Charles Darwin**'s *Origin of Species*. His works include his *Principles of Geology* (1830–3), *The Elements of Geology* (1838) and *The Geological Evidence of the Antiquity of Man* (1863).

Ma, Yo-Yo 1955–
US cellist

Yo-Yo Ma

The son of Chinese professionals in classical music, he became a prodigy on the cello, and moved to New York City with his family at the age of seven. Two years later he made his debut at Carnegie Hall. He has achieved international fame as a cello virtuoso, playing both as a soloist and in chamber music ensembles around the world.

MacArthur, Douglas 1880–1964
US soldier
In 1941 he was appointed commanding general of the US armed forces in the Far East. As World War II developed he carried out a brilliant 'leap-frogging' strategy which enabled him to recapture the Philippine Archipelago from the Japanese, and in 1945, as supreme commander of the Allied powers, he accepted the surrender of Japan, later acting as its *de facto* ruler. When war broke out in Korea in 1950 he became Commander-in-Chief of the UN forces, but after disagreements with President **Truman** he was relieved of his commands. Though a brilliant military leader, he inspired criticism from some for his imperious belief in his own mission.

Macbeth c.1005–1057
King of Scotland
He became king in 1040 when he defeated and killed King Duncan I and drove Duncan's sons, Malcolm and Donald Bán, into exile. He ruled for over a decade, and was killed by Malcolm III, Duncan's son. However, the conventional view of Macbeth as a villainous usurper, a view popularized by Shakespeare's play, has little historical basis. His reign was a period of plenty; he was a friend to the Church and went on pilgrimage to Rome.

MacDiarmid, Hugh, *pseudonym of* **Christopher Murray Grieve** 1892–1978
Scottish poet
A founder-member of the National Party of Scotland (which became the Scottish National Party) in 1928, and intermittently an active communist, he dedicated his life to the regeneration of Scots as a literary language. He is best known for the book-length poem *A Drunk Man Looks at the Thistle* (1926). Other publications include *To Circumjack Cencrastus* (1930), *A Kist o' Whistles* (1947) and *In Memoriam James Joyce* (1955). He wrote numerous essays and two autobiographies.

MacDonald, (James) Ramsay 1866–1937
Scottish Labour statesman
He became leader of the Labour Party in 1911 and from January to November 1924 was Prime Minister of the first Labour government in Britain – a minority government at the mercy of the Liberals. He was Prime Minister again from 1929 to 1931. He met the financial crisis of 1931 by forming a predominantly Conservative 'National' government (opposed by most of his party), which he rebuilt and led from 1931 after a general election. In 1935 **Stanley Baldwin** took over the premiership and MacDonald became Lord President.

Mach, Ernst 1838–1916
Austrian physicist and philosopher
The findings of his experiments have proved of great importance in aeronautical design and the science of projectiles, and his name has been given to the ratio of the speed of flow of a gas to the speed of sound (Mach number) and to the angle of a shock wave to the direction of motion (Mach angle). His writings greatly influenced **Albert Einstein** and laid the foundations of logical positivism, a system much concerned with determining whether or not statements are meaningful.

Machiavelli, Niccolò 1469–1527
Italian statesman, writer and political philosopher
He held high office in Florence but was arrested on a charge of conspiracy, and tortured. Although he was soon released and pardoned, he was obliged to withdraw from public life and devote himself to writing. His masterpiece, *The Prince*, written in 1513, was intended to be a handbook for rulers, and its main theme is that rulers must always be prepared to do

evil if they judge that good will come of it. Machiavelli's admirers have praised him as a political realist, while his critics have denounced him as a dangerous cynic. He also wrote a series of *Discourses* on **Livy** and a treatise on *The Art of War* (published 1521).

Mackintosh, Charles Rennie 1868–1928
Scottish architect, designer and watercolourist
His architectural output, mostly within the Glasgow area, had a very considerable influence on European design and he was both a leader of the 'Glasgow Style', a movement related to art nouveau. His works include the Glasgow School of Art and houses like Hill House in Helensburgh (1903–4). He also designed textiles, furniture and metalwork, and in his later years he turned to painting, producing a series of watercolours, chiefly in France (1923–7).

Madonna, *full name* **Madonna Louise Veronica Ciccone** 1958–
US pop singer and actress
She performed as a singer with a number of rock groups before producing her first hit, *Holiday*, in 1983. Highly ambitious and commercially astute, she made her debut album in the same year which delivered four more US hit singles. Other major recordings include *Like A Virgin* (1984), *Ray of Light* (1998) and *Confessions on a Dance Floor* (2005). Her brash stage persona and striking fashions made her an influential role model. She has starred in a number of films, including *Desperately Seeking Susan* (1985) and *Evita* (1996), and in 2000 she married British film director Guy Ritchie.

Magellan, Ferdinand c.1480–1521
Portuguese navigator
Sailing from Seville on 10 August 1519 with five ships and 270 men, he coasted Patagonia, passing through the strait which bears his name (21 October to 28 November), and reached the ocean which he named the Pacific. He was later killed by local people in the Philippine Islands, but his ship, the *Victoria*, was taken safely back to Spain by the Spanish captain, Juan Sebastian del Cano, on 6 September 1522, to complete the first circumnavigation of the world.

Magritte, René François Ghislain 1898–1967
Belgian surrealist painter
In 1924 he became a leading member of the newly-formed Belgian surrealist group. He made his name with *The Menaced Assassin* (1926) and lived in Paris until 1930. Apart from a brief Impressionist phase in the 1940s, Magritte remained faithful to surrealism, using symbols and recurring dreamlike motifs. His best-known paintings include *The Reckless Sleeper* (1928), *The Red Model* (1935), *The Wind and the Song* (1928–9) and *The Human Condition* (1, 1934; 2, 1935).

Mahler, Gustav 1860–1911
Czech-born Austrian composer
In his lifetime and for many years after, Mahler was known principally as a conductor. More recently, his compositions have gained enormous popularity. His later works consist entirely of songs and symphonies. He wrote nine numbered symphonies, plus the song-symphony *Das Lied von der Erde*, which he did not include in the nine for superstitious reasons – **Beethoven**, **Schubert** and Bruckner having all died after completing nine. In the end, he too left a tenth symphony unfinished. His songs include *Songs on the Death of Children* (1901–4).

Malcolm X, *originally* **Malcolm Little**, *Muslim name* **el-Hajj Malik el-Shabazz** 1925–65
US black nationalist leader
After an adolescence of violence, narcotics and petty crime, while in prison he came under the influence of **Elijah Muhammad**, leader of The Nation of Islam (known as the Black Muslims), a movement that favoured black separatism and rejected Christianity as a tool of oppressive whites. He changed his name, and after his release in 1952 became Muhammad's chief disciple. In 1963 he broke with Muhammad and founded the Organization for Afro-American Unity. In the last year of his life Malcolm announced his conversion to orthodox Islam and put forward the belief in the possible brotherhood between blacks and whites. His extreme stance appealed to many African–Americans in the urban ghettos of the north, but was met with criticism by moderate civil-rights leaders. In 1965 he was killed in Harlem by Black Muslim assassins.

Malpighi, Marcello 1628–94
Italian anatomist
An early pioneer of histology (microscopic anatomy) of both plants and animals, he conducted a remarkable series of studies of the structure of the liver, lungs, skin, spleen, glands and brain. He gave the first full account of an insect, the silkworm moth, and investigated muscular cells.

Malthus, Thomas Robert 1766–1834
English economist and clergyman
In 1798 he published anonymously his *Essay on the Principle of Population*, which maintained that population naturally tends to increase faster than food production, and called for positive action to cut the birth rate. **Charles Darwin** read Malthus in 1838, and was greatly influenced by him, seeing in the struggle for existence a mechanism for producing new species – natural selection.

Mandela, Nelson Rolihlahla 1918–
South African lawyer and statesman
He practised as a lawyer in Johannesburg, and in 1944 he joined the African National Congress (ANC), a black opposition movement. For the next 20 years he directed a campaign of defiance against the South African government and its policy of apartheid. The ANC was banned in 1960, and in 1964 Mandela was sentenced to life imprisonment. From his prison cell, Mandela grew into an international figure and became the focus of an increasingly powerful international campaign for his release, in which his second wife Winnie played a leading part. He was released in February 1990. In 1993 he was awarded the Nobel Peace Prize jointly with South Africa's president F W de Klerk, and from 1994 to 1999 he was South Africa's first black president. His writings include *No Easy Walk to Freedom* (1965) and *Long Walk to Freedom* (1994).

Manet, Édouard 1832–83
French painter
He entered his *Déjeuner sur l'herbe* for the Salon of 1863 but it scandalized the jury with its portrayal of a nude female with clothed male companions, and was rejected. This was followed by the acceptance of his *Olympia* in 1865, but this brought about a similar outcry from the public. In the 1870s he came under

the influence of the Impressionists and, in particular, of **Monet**, and his technique became freer and more spontaneous. His last major work was *Un Bar aux Folies-Bergère* (1881–2).

Mann, Thomas 1875–1955
German novelist
Considered by many to be Germany's greatest 20th-century novelist, he achieved early fame with his family saga *Buddenbrooks* (1901). Further short novels such as *Death in Venice* (1913) dealt with the problem of the artist's salvation, and *The Magic Mountain* (1924) used the story of a sanatorium patient as a symbol of a disintegrating Europe. In 1929 Mann won the Nobel Prize for literature. He was a vocal opponent of fascism, writing on the subject in the novel *Mario and the Magician* (1930). His greatest work is probably *Doktor Faustus* (1947), and his unfinished comic masterpiece was *Confessions of Felix Krull, Confidence Man* (Part I, 1922).

Mao Zedong (Mao Tse-tung) 1893–1976
Chinese Communist leader and first Chairman of the People's Republic
The son of a peasant, he helped found the Chinese Communist Party (CCP) in 1921. Following the 'Long March' (1934–6) of his supporters in retreat from **Chiang Kai-shek**'s Nationalist forces, Mao's communists successfully re-established themselves. They resisted the Japanese between 1937 and 1945, and then defeated the Nationalist regime, proclaiming the People's Republic of China in 1949. He went on to inaugurate the 1958–60 'Great Leap Forward' experiment of rapid agricultural and industrial advance, and the 1966–9 'Cultural Revolution' to deal with political opponents. On his death at the age of 83, there followed a power struggle that was briefly won by the Party members known as 'Gang of Four'.

Maradona, Diego 1960–
Argentinian footballer
He played in Argentina and Spain before joining Napoli in 1984, helping them to their first-ever Italian championship in 1987. He captained the Argentine side to World Cup victory in Mexico in 1986. During the quarter-final against England he illegally punched the ball into the net for his first goal, an action which he subsequently attributed to 'the hand of God', and then went on to score one of the greatest goals of all time, beating five England players in a dribble from the halfway line. He was one of the greatest players of his generation, but in later years his career was marred by repeated suspensions for drug use.

Marconi, Guglielmo, Marchese 1874–1937
Italian physicist and inventor
His first successful experiments in wireless telegraphy were made at Bologna in 1895, and in 1898 he transmitted signals across the English Channel. In 1901 he succeeded in sending signals in Morse code across the Atlantic, from Cornwall, England to St John's, Newfoundland, and the following year he patented the magnetic detector. He later developed short-wave radio equipment, and established a worldwide radio telegraph network for the British government. In the 1930s he was a strong supporter of the Italian Fascist leader Benito **Mussolini**. He shared the 1909 Nobel Prize for physics with Ferdinand Braun.

Marcus Aurelius, *surnamed* **Antoninus**, *originally* **Marcus Annius Verus** AD121–80
Roman emperor and philosopher
He became joint emperor in AD161 and sole emperor in AD169. Peaceful by temperament, he was nevertheless destined to suffer from constant wars throughout his reign. One of the few Roman emperors whose writings have survived, Marcus Aurelius wrote twelve books of *Meditations* which record his innermost thoughts and form a unique document. They show his loneliness, but also that he did not allow himself to be embittered by his experiences of life. After his death he was idealized as the model of the perfect emperor.

Marie Antoinette, *in full* **Josèphe Jeanne Marie Antoinette** 1755–93
Queen of France
Born in Vienna, Austria, she was the fourth daughter of the Empress Maria Theresa and the Emperor Francis I, and in 1770 was married to the Dauphin of France, afterwards **Louis XVI**. She aroused criticism by her frivolity, her extravagance, and her devotion to the interests of Austria, but during the troubled times of the Revolution she acted with dignity and courage. After an attempted escape and imprisonment, and the execution of Louis, she herself was guillotined.

Mark Antony See **Antony, Mark**

Marley, Bob (Robert Nesta) 1945–81
Jamaican singer, guitarist and composer of reggae music

Bob Marley

In 1965, with Peter Tosh (originally Winston Hubert MacIntosh) and Bunny Wailer (originally Neville O'Reilly Livingston), he formed the vocal trio The Wailers. Together they were the first reggae artists to gain international success; Marley later went solo with a series of world tours and became a national hero. A devout Rastafarian, he made reggae popular with white audiences through his warm, expressive voice and his memorable compositions – from the lyrical 'No Woman, No Cry' to the fiercely political 'Exodus' and 'I Shot the Sheriff'.

Marlowe, Christopher 1564–93
English dramatist
With his dramatic tragedies he prepared the way for **Shakespeare**, on whose early work his influence is evident. His first great play, *Tamburlaine the Great*, in two parts, was probably produced in 1587, and *The Tragical History of Dr Faustus* was probably produced soon after *Tamburlaine*. Other plays include *The*

Jew of Malta, produced after 1588, and *Edward II*, produced about 1590. Marlowe probably contributed to Shakespeare's *Henry VI* and *Titus Andronicus*. His poetry includes the well-known 'Come, live with me and be my love', first printed in *The Passionate Pilgrim* (1599). He was fatally stabbed in a tavern brawl.

Marvell, Andrew 1621–78
English metaphysical poet
In 1657 he became John **Milton**'s assistant and two years later, MP for Hull. He wrote several works on politics and government, particularly on religious toleration, but he is best known as the author of lyrics such as 'The Garden' and, most famously, 'To His Coy Mistress'. Most of his poetry was not published until 1681 as *Miscellaneous Poetry*. A subsequent volume was entitled *Poems on Affairs of State* (1689–97).

Marx, Karl 1818–83
German social, political and economic theorist
The founder of Marxist Communism, he wrote, with **Friedrich Engels**, the famous *Communist Manifesto* (1848), a masterpiece of political propaganda which ends with the celebrated rallying-cry: 'The workers have nothing to lose but their chains. They have a world to win. Workers of all lands, unite!' In 1849 he moved with his family to London, where they lived in some poverty, but where he began the researches which produced his major works of economic and political analysis, particularly *Capital* (Volume 1 1867, Volumes 2 & 3 1884, 1894), one of the most influential books of the 19th century. He was buried in Highgate cemetery, London.

Marx Brothers
US family of film comedians
The sons of German immigrants, their names were Julius Henry (Groucho, 1890–1977), Leonard (Chico, 1887–1961), Adolph Arthur (Harpo, 1888–1964) and Herbert (Zeppo, 1901–79). They began their stage career in vaudeville, but their main reputation was made in films such as *Animal Crackers*, *Monkey Business* (both 1932), *Horse Feathers*, *Duck Soup* (both 1933), *A Night at the Opera* (1935) and *A Day at the Races* (1937). Each had a well-defined role: Groucho with his oversized moustache and wisecracks, Chico, the pianist with an individual technique, and Harpo, the dumb clown and harp maestro. Groucho and Harpo wrote several books.

Mary, Queen of Scots 1542–87
Queen of Scotland
The daughter of James V of Scotland, she married the future French king Francis II in 1558 and briefly became Queen of France on his death in 1560. Returning to Scotland she married her cousin, Henry Stewart, Lord Darnley, but after the murder in 1566 of her Italian private secretary, in which Darnley was implicated, they divorced; Darnley later mysteriously died. Subsequently, anti-Catholic pressures in Scotland forced her to abdicate, and, fleeing to England, she found herself a prisoner of **Elizabeth I**. She was implicated in a plot against Elizabeth, and brought to trial and executed. She was the mother of **James VI and I**.

Matisse, Henri (Emile Benoît) 1869–1954
French painter
From his experiments grew the movement dubbed the Fauves ('Wild Beasts') by critics. His most characteristic paintings display a bold use of luminous areas of primary colour, and owe a great deal to oriental influences. In his later years he began working with large paper cut-outs. He also designed the stained glass for the Dominican Chapelle du Rosaire at Vence, Alpes-Maritimes. His works include *Bonheur de vivre* (1906), *L'Escargot* (1953), and *La Liseuse* (1894). He also produced sculpture, and his works in this field include the bronze *The Back I–IV* (1909–30).

Matthews, Sir Stanley 1915–2000
English footballer
First picked for England at the age of 20, he won 54 international caps, spread over 22 years. He continued to play First Division football until after the age of 50, and was knighted in 1965. He later managed Port Vale, and became president of Stoke City Football Club in 1990.

Maxwell, James Clerk, *surname also* **Clerk-Maxwell** 1831–79
Scottish physicist
At the age of 15 he devised a method for drawing oval curves which was published by the Royal Society of Edinburgh. He later did wide-ranging research into areas such as colour perception and colour photography, but is best known for his *Treatise on Electricity and Magnetism* (1873), which treated mathematically **Michael Faraday**'s theory of electrical and magnetic forces and provided the first conclusive evidence that light consisted of electromagnetic waves. His work is considered to have paved the way for **Albert Einstein** and **Max Planck**. He was one of the greatest theoretical physicists the world has known.

Mazarin, Jules, *originally* **Giulio Mazarini** 1602–61
French cleric, diplomat and politician
He entered the service of Louis XIII in 1639 and rose to cardinal. After Louis's death (1643), he retained his authority under the Queen Regent, Anne of Austria, to whom it is said he was married. Blamed by many for the civil wars known as the Frondes (between 1648 and 1653), he twice fled France, and returned to Paris in 1653. His foreign policy was more fruitful: he concluded the Peace of Westphalia (1648) and negotiated the Treaty of the Pyrenees (1659), ending the prolonged Franco-Spanish conflict.

McCarthy, Joseph Raymond 1909–57
US politician
He was elected senator in 1946, and became known in the early 1950s for his accusations that communists had infiltrated the State Department. In 1953 he became chairman of the House Committee on Un-American Activities. Using an aggressive style of cross-examination he brought many innocent citizens to trial, and this kind of anti-communist witch-hunt became known as 'McCarthyism'. His power diminished after he was formally censured for his methods by the Senate in 1954.

McCartney, Sir (James) Paul 1942–
English songwriter, vocalist and bass guitarist
He found fame in the 1960s as a member of the Beatles, one of pop's best-known groups, and with fellow band member **John Lennon** he wrote many of their most popular songs, including 'She Loves You' and 'I Want to Hold Your Hand'. His first solo album was *McCartney* (1970); a second, *Ram* (1971), was recorded with his wife, Linda Eastman. He formed

the group Wings in 1971, releasing *Band on the Run* (1973) and *Venus & Mars* (1975). 'Mull of Kintyre' (1977) was their greatest hit. His autobiographical film *Give My Regards to Broad Street* appeared in 1984. Subsequent albums include *Tripping the Live Fantastic* (1990) and *Driving Rain* (2001). His *Liverpool Oratorio* premiered in 1991, and he wrote a symphony, *Standing Stone*, in 1997.

McClintock, Barbara 1902–92
US geneticist
Her work on the chromosomes of maize provided the ultimate proof of the chromosome theory of heredity. In the 1940s she showed how genes can control other genes, and can be copied from chromosome to chromosome. It was not until the 1970s that her work began to be appreciated, and finally in 1983 she was awarded the Nobel Prize for physiology or medicine.

McEnroe, John Patrick 1959–
US tennis player
He turned professional in 1978, and was runner-up to **Björn Borg** in the 1980 Wimbledon final. He won the Wimbledon title three times (1981, 1983–4), the US Open singles four times (1979–81, 1984), and eight Grand Slam doubles events. He was Grand Prix winner in 1979 and 1984–5, and world championship winner in 1979, 1981 and 1983–4. Throughout his professional career, his outbursts on court resulted in much adverse publicity.

Mehmet II, the Conqueror, *also called* **Mohammed** 1432–81
Sultan of Turkey and founder of the Ottoman Empire
He succeeded his father, Murad II, in 1451, took Constantinople in 1453, and rebuilt it into the prosperous Ottoman capital of Istanbul. This extinguished the Byzantine Empire and gave the Turks their commanding position on the Bosphorus. Checked by János Hunyadi at Belgrade (1456), he nevertheless annexed most of Serbia, all of Greece, and most of the Aegean Islands, took Otranto (1480) and died in a campaign against Persia (Iran).

Mehmet IV 1642–93
Sultan of Turkey
He succeeded his deposed father, Ibrahim I, as a child in 1648. Under Mehmet the Turks suffered defeat by the Austrians (1664) and the Poles (1672–6), but gained Polish Ukraine, which they later lost to Russia (1681). In 1683 under the Grand Vizier Kara Mustafa, they besieged Vienna, which was relieved by King John III Sobieski. After defeat at the second Battle of Mohacs (1687), Mehmet was deposed, and replaced by Süleyman II.

Meir, Golda, *née* **Goldie Mabovich**, *later* **Goldie Myerson** 1898–1978
Israeli politician
Born in Kiev, she settled in Palestine in 1921, where she took up social work and became a leading figure in the Labour movement. She became Israeli ambassador to the Soviet Union (1948–9), Minister of Labour (1949–56), and Foreign Minister (1956–66), and was elected Prime Minister in 1969, but her efforts for peace in the Middle East were halted by the fourth Arab–Israeli War (1973), and she resigned in 1974.

Golda Meir

Meitner, Lise 1878–1968
Austrian physicist
With **Otto Hahn** she discovered the radioactive element protactinium in 1917. In 1938 she fled to Sweden to escape the Nazis, and shortly afterwards Hahn wrote to Meitner about his discovery of radioactive barium. With her nephew Otto Frisch, she proposed that the production of barium was the result of nuclear fission, which was later proved by Frisch. Meitner worked in Sweden until retiring to England in 1960. The element of atomic number 109 is named after her.

Melba, Dame Nellie, *née* **Helen Porter Mitchell** 1861–1931
Australian operatic soprano and pioneer recording artist
She made her operatic debut in Brussels in 1887 as Gilda in **Verdi**'s *Rigoletto*. Her Covent Garden debut was in May 1888, in the title role of Donizetti's *Lucia di Lammermoor*. She soon became a worldwide idol and sang alongside other great singers such as the Italian tenor **Enrico Caruso**. Her first standard records were issued in 1904.

Melville, Herman 1819–91
US novelist, short-story writer and poet
His adventures in the Marquesas and Tahiti inspired his first two books, *Typee* (1846) and *Omoo* (1847). *White Jacket* (1850) drew on his experiences as a seaman on the man-of-war which eventually brought him home. Settling on a farm near Pittsfield, Massachusetts, he wrote his masterpiece, *Moby-Dick* (1851), a novel of vigour and colour about the whaling industry. Later novels include *Pierre* (1852), *The Confidence Man* (1857) and *Billy Budd* (1924), an unfinished novella published posthumously.

Mendel, Gregor Johann 1822–84
Austrian botanist
He was ordained a priest in 1847, and became an abbot in 1868. In the experimental garden of the monastery, he researched the inheritance characteristics of plants. He observed that some characteristics remained constant in every generation, while others remained hidden and became apparent only in later generations, and he coined the terms 'dominant' and 'recessive' to describe these characteristics. His concepts became the basis of modern genetics.

Mendeleev, Dmitri Ivanovich 1834–1907
Russian chemist
In 1869 he organized the elements into a table based

on ascending order of their atomic weight and found that chemically similar elements tended to fall into the same columns. His great achievement was to realize that certain elements still had to be discovered and to leave gaps in the table where he predicted they would fall. He also worked on gases and on aeronautics (he made a solo ascent in a balloon in 1887). The element mendelevium (atomic number 101) is named in his honour.

Mendelssohn(-Bartholdy), (Jakob Ludwig) Felix 1809–47
German composer
He made his first public appearance as a pianist at the age of ten. Within the next few years he composed his Symphony in C minor (1824) and the B minor Quartet (1824–5). His *Midsummer Night's Dream* overture (1826) was an early success, and a tour of Scotland in the summer of 1829 inspired the *Hebrides* overture (1830) and the 'Scotch' Symphony. He produced his oratorio *Elijah* in Birmingham in 1846, one of ten visits to England. His sister's death in 1847 affected him profoundly, and he never recovered.

Menuhin, Yehudi Menuhin, Baron 1916–99
British violinist
He appeared as a soloist with the San Francisco Symphony Orchestra at the age of seven. In 1932 he recorded **Elgar**'s Violin Concerto, conducted by the composer, and subsequently appeared all over the world. During World War II he gave concerts to the troops, and after the war settled in England, beginning to conduct in 1957. In the same year, he set up the annual Gstaad Festival of music (in Switzerland), and in 1963 he founded the Yehudi Menuhin School of Music for musically talented children (in England). He is noted also for raising the profile of Indian music in the West.

Merckx, Eddy, *known as* **the Cannibal** 1945–
Belgian racing cyclist
He won the Tour de France five times (1969–72, and 1974), and now shares the record with Jacques Anquetil, **Bernard Hinault**, **Miguel Indurain** and **Lance Armstrong**. He also won the Tour of Italy five times, and all the major classics, including the Milan–San Remo race seven times. He was the world professional road race champion three times. He won more races (445) and more classics than any other rider before retiring in 1978.

Michelangelo, *in full* **Michelangelo di Lodovico Buonarroti** 1475–1564
Italian sculptor, painter and poet
Michelangelo is often considered the most brilliant representative of the Italian Renaissance, supreme in sculpture and painting, versed in all the learning of his age, and an accomplished poet. His early sculptures include the *Pieta* (1497), now in St Peter's in Rome, and the colossal *David*. Later works in marble include the statue of **Moses** and the monuments to Giuliano and Lorenzo de' Medici in Florence. His best known achievement in painting is undoubtedly the ceiling of the Sistine Chapel (1508–12), also in Rome. In 1537 he began to paint the vast *The Last Judgement*. In 1547 he was appointed architect of St Peter's, and devoted himself to the work until his death.

Mies van der Rohe, Ludwig 1886–1969
US architect
A major figure in 20th-century architecture and a founder of the modern style, he was director of the Bauhaus in Dessau, Germany (1930–3) before World War II, and emigrated to the USA in 1937. He designed two glass apartment towers on Lake Shore Drive in Chicago and collaborated with Philip Johnson on the Seagram Building in New York (1956–58). His other works include the Public Library in Washington, DC (1967), and two art galleries in Berlin (1968).

Mill, John Stuart 1806–73
English philosopher and social reformer
One of the most versatile and influential of all 19th-century British thinkers, he helped to develop the utilitarianism of **Jeremy Bentham**, and campaigned for women's rights (in *The Subjection of Women* of 1869), birth control and religious freedom. The most popular of his works, his essay *On Liberty* (1859), eloquently defends the freedoms of the individual against social and political control. With Bentham he helped found University College London in 1825. Mill's major work was *A System of Logic* (1843), and other works include *Principles of Political Economy* (1848) and *Utilitarianism* (1863). He was elected to parliament in 1865.

Miller, Arthur 1915–2005
US playwright
His first successful play, *All My Sons* (1947), focused on the family of an arms manufacturer and reflected the preoccupation with moral issues that was to characterize his work. His tragedy *Death of a Salesman* (1949) won the Pulitzer Prize and brought him international recognition. *The Crucible* (1953), with its political undertones, is probably his most lasting work. Other works include *A View from the Bridge* (1955), *After the Fall* (1963), *Playing for Time* (1981), *Broken Glass* (1994) and *Mr Peter's Connections* (1998). His marriage to **Marilyn Monroe**, from whom he was divorced in 1961, and his brush with the authorities over early communist sympathies, brought him considerable publicity.

Miller, Henry Valentine 1891–1980
US writer
From 1930 he spent nine years in France, during which time he published *Tropic of Cancer* (1934) and *Tropic of Capricorn* (1938), as well as *Black Spring* (1936). He returned to the USA in 1940 but travelled extensively both at home and abroad before settling in Big Sur, California. Much of his fiction is autobiographical; in his time, however, he became one of the most read US authors. Other important books are *The Colossus of Maroussi* (1941), a travel book, and *The Air-Conditioned Nightmare* (1945), a bleak essay on contemporary USA.

Miller, Lee 1907–77
US photographer
She studied with **Man Ray** in Paris (1929–32) before returning to the USA to run her own photography studio in New York. She was a photographer in London for *Vogue* from 1940, and in 1942 became official war correspondent for the US forces. Her publications include *Grim Glory: Pictures of Britain under Fire* (1941, with E Carter).

Milton, John 1608–74
English poet
His early works included *L'Allegro* and *Il Penseroso*, *Comus* and the pastoral elegy *Lycidas* (1637). On the outbreak of the Civil War in England (1642) he

devoted himself to the cause of the revolution with a series of pamphlets defending civil and religious liberties, among them *Areopagitica, A Speech for the Liberty of Unlicensed Printing* (1644). Although blind from 1652 onwards, he continued to write energetically. After the Restoration of **Charles II**, Milton went into hiding for a short period, and then devoted himself almost wholly to poetry, producing his most famous work, *Paradise Lost* (completed 1665, published 1667), an epic poem dealing with man's relationship to God. Later important works include *Paradise Regained* and *Samson Agonistes* (both 1671).

Miró, Joán 1893–1983
Spanish artist
In 1920 he settled in Paris and came into contact with the artist **Picasso**. Influenced by surrealism he invented a manner of painting using curvilinear, fantastical forms which suggest all kinds of dream-like situations. Eventually, these pictures became almost entirely abstract. His works include *Catalan Landscape* (1923–4) and *Maternity* (1924). He also designed ballet sets, sculptures, murals, and tapestries.

Modigliani, Amedeo 1884–1920
Italian painter and sculptor
He was born in Livorno, Tuscany, and in 1906 moved to Paris. In 1909, impressed by the Romanian sculptor **Constantine Brancusi**, he took to sculpture and produced a number of elongated stone heads in African style. He continued to use this style in his later paintings, with a series of richly-coloured, elongated portraits. In 1918 in Paris he held one of his first one-man shows, which included some very frank nudes; the exhibition was closed for indecency on the first day. It was only after his death from tuberculosis that he obtained recognition.

Moholy-Nagy, László 1895–1946
Hungarian-born US artist and photographer
He produced his first 'photograms' (photographic images made without a camera, by placing objects on photographic paper and exposing it to light) in 1923 and joined the Bauhaus school in 1925. There he began to use a camera and was quickly recognized as a leading avant-garde artist, his work including film-making and typography with photographic illustration. He later taught photography in the USA, and became a US citizen shortly before his death.

Molière, *pseudonym of* **Jean Baptiste Poquelin** 1622–73
French playwright
After early success as an actor and theatrical manager, he began to write the comic plays that made him one of the giants of world theatre. Every year until his death he produced at least one masterpiece, including *The Misanthrope* in 1666, *Tartuffe* in 1667, *The Miser* in 1668 and *The Citizen Turned Gentleman* in 1671. He died of lung disease the night after having acted as the *Invalid* in a performance of his last play, *The Imaginary Invalid*.

Mondrian, Piet, *properly* **Pieter Cornelis Mondriaan**1872–1944
Dutch artist
His work has been a major influence on all purely abstract painters. His early work included a series of paintings, *Trees*; these became increasingly abstract, so that eventually the patterns made become more important than the subject itself. During World War I he discarded the subject altogether and concentrated on constructing grids of simple black lines filled in with primary colours. Later works include more colourful abstracts (such as *Broadway Boogie-Woogie*, 1942–43).

Monet, Claude 1840–1926
French Impressionist painter
In 1874 he exhibited at the first Impressionist Exhibition, and one of his works at this exhibition, *Impression, soleil levant*, gave its name to the movement. He visited and painted extensively in England, Holland and Venice, and spent his career in an attempt to capture the most subtle nuances of colour, atmosphere and light in landscape. Apart from many sea and river scenes, he also produced several series of paintings of subjects under different aspects of light, such as *Haystacks* (1890–1) and *Rouen Cathedral* (1892–5). In his last years he lived and painted at Givenchy, near Paris, where he produced the famous *Waterlilies* series (1899–1906).

Monod, Jacques Lucien 1910–76
French biochemist
Monod worked closely with François Jacob on genetic control mechanisms, and proposed the existence of messenger RNA. They also studied how genes control cellular activity by directing the synthesis of proteins. In 1965 Monod and Jacob shared the Nobel Prize for physiology or medicine with **André Lwoff**.

Monroe, Marilyn, *originally* **Norma Jean Mortenson** 1926–62
US film actress
She first starred as a sexy, beautiful dumb blonde in *How to Marry a Millionaire* and *Gentlemen Prefer Blondes* (both in 1953). She developed her flair for light comedy in Billy Wilder's *The Seven Year Itch* (1955) and *Some Like It Hot* (1959) and also appeared to critical acclaim in *Bus Stop* (1956) and *The Misfits* (1961). Her second husband was the baseball star Joe DiMaggio, and her third the playwright **Arthur Miller**, but she also had a close relationship with **John F Kennedy** and his brother, then Attorney General Robert F Kennedy. She died from an overdose of sleeping pills.

Montfort, Simon V de, Earl of Leicester c.1208–1265
English soldier and politician
He became the leader of the barons who revolted against King Henry III in 1261. De Montfort defeated the king's army at Lewes (1264) and was appointed, with two of his allies, to preside over a parliament in 1265. This, the Model Parliament, was the origin of all modern parliaments. But the barons soon grew dissatisfied with the rule of 'Simon the Righteous' and when hostilities broke out again, his forces were defeated at Evesham and he was killed.

Montgolfier, Joseph Michel 1740–1810 and **Jacques Étienne** 1745–99
French aeronautical inventors
They were the sons of a paper manufacturer. After some preliminary model experiments, they constructed a balloon in 1782 whose bag was lifted by lighting a cauldron of paper beneath it. The world's first manned balloon flight, of 7½ miles (12.1km)

in less than half an hour, at a height of 3,000 feet (915m), carrying two French noblemen, took place in November 1783. Joseph later invented a type of parachute and the widely used hydraulic ram, a device for raising small quantities of water to a considerable height.

Moore, G(eorge) E(dward) 1873–1958
English empiricist philosopher
His works marked an important change of direction in the British empiricist philosophical tradition, emphasizing in particular the intellectual virtues of clarity, precision and honesty, and identifying the analysis of ordinary concepts and arguments as a principal task of philosophy. Moore and **Bertrand Russell**, and later their student **Ludwig Wittgenstein**, were the dominant figures in this tradition in the interwar years. His principal works are *Principia Ethica* (1903) and *Ethics* (1916).

Moore, Henry Spencer 1898–1986
English sculptor
He was born in Yorkshire, the son of a coal miner. He taught sculpture at the Royal College of Art, London (1924–31); from 1931 to 1939 he taught at the Chelsea School of Art. He was an official war artist from 1940 to 1942, and in 1948 he won the International Sculpture prize at the Venice Biennale, an international art exhibition. He is recognized as one of the most original and powerful modern sculptors, producing figures and groups in a style based on the organic forms found in landscape and natural rocks. His principal commissions included the *Madonna and Child* in St Matthew's Church, Northampton (1943–4), the decorative frieze (1952) on the Time-Life building in London, and the massive reclining figures for the UNESCO building in Paris (1958) and the Lincoln Center in New York (1965).

Henry Moore

More, Sir Thomas, St 1478–1535
English politician and scholar
He rose to the position of Lord Chancellor (1529) under **Henry VIII**, and in this position was unusual in the simplicity and virtue of his lifestyle. In 1532 he resigned the chancellorship in protest against Henry's desire to break with the Catholic Church, and his later refusal to recognize any other head of the Church than the Pope led to his sentence for high treason. Still refusing to recant, he was beheaded. He was also an important humanist writer, best known for his Latin *Utopia* (1516). He was made a saint in 1935.

Morris, William 1834–96
English craftsman, poet and socialist
A leading member of the Pre-Raphaelite Brotherhood and the Arts and Crafts movement, he revolutionized the art of house decoration and furniture in England. His literary career began with poems including *The Earthly Paradise* (1868–70), and he developed a passionate interest in the literature of Iceland. His best-known prose works are probably *The Wood beyond the World* (1895) and *The Well at the World's End* (1896). His ideals did much to develop the philosophy of socialism, and in 1884 he formed a Socialist League. In 1890 he founded a publishing house, the Kelmscott Press.

Morrison, Jim (James Douglas), *nicknamed* **the Lizard King** 1943–71
US rock singer and poet
He was the lead singer of The Doors, an important Los Angeles-based rock band of the late 1960s. He combined a poetic intensity with a rebellious nonconformism, but came into conflict with the law, mainly over drugs, but also for outspoken political songs like 'When The Music's Over' or 'Five To One'. He died in Paris in slightly mysterious circumstances, adding fuel to a familiar rock legend, and his grave there became a shrine for fans.

Morrison, Toni, *pen name of* **Chloe Anthony Morrison**, *née* **Wofford** 1931–
US novelist
A writer who explores with rich vocabulary and cold-blooded detail the story of African-Americans in a white-dominated culture, she was awarded the Nobel Prize for literature in 1993. *The Bluest Eye* (1970) focuses on an 11-year-old black girl who feels a sense of inferiority at not having blue eyes; *Sula* (1974) again confronts a generation gap; and *Song of Solomon* (1977) is a merciless study of genteel blacks. Further novels have included *Tar Baby* (1981), *Beloved* (1987), *Jazz* (1992), *Paradise* (1998), and *Love* (2003).

Toni Morrison

Moses, Anna Mary, *known as* **Grandma Moses** 1860–1961
US primitive artist
She was a farmer's wife in Staunton, Virginia, and in New York State, and did embroideries of country scenes. She began to paint at about the age of 75, mainly country scenes remembered from her childhood – 'old, timey things ... all from memory'. From her first show in New York in 1940, she had great popular success in the United States.

Mother Teresa of Calcutta See **Teresa of Calcutta, Mother**

Mozart, (Johann Chrysostom) Wolfgang Amadeus 1756–91
Austrian composer
Mozart could play the keyboard confidently at the age of four, composed his first pieces for it at five, and soon mastered the violin. By 1772 he had written about 25 symphonies (some of which are lost) and his first quartets. He travelled widely but settled finally in Vienna in 1781, and here his reputation as composer and pianist was to reach its peak. His most celebrated works include the three Italian comic operas *The Marriage of Figaro* (1786), *Don Giovanni* (first performed in Prague, 1787), and *Così fan tutte* (1790); the last three symphonies (1788); the serenade *Eine kleine Nachtmusik*; and the Clarinet Quintet. His last works were the opera *The Magic Flute* (1791) and a Requiem, unfinished when he died. He is considered one of the greatest of all musical geniuses.

Mubarak, (Mohammed) Hosni Said 1928–
Egyptian statesman
He was Vice-President under **Anwar Sadat** from 1975 until the latter's assassination in 1981. Mubarak was then declared President and pledged to continue Sadat's domestic and international policies, including firm treatment of Muslim extremists, and the peace process with Israel. In 1995 he survived an assassination attempt by Islamic fundamentalists and was involved in the events leading to the signing of a peace accord between the Palestinian Liberation Organization and Israel. He has been a key figure in both the complex politics of the Middle East and on the world stage.

Muhammad or **Mohammed** c.570–c.632
Arab prophet, and founder of Islam
After he had become increasingly drawn to religious contemplation, he began to receive revelations of the word of Allah. This Qur'an (Koran), or 'reading', commanded that the idols of the shrine should be destroyed and that the rich should give to the poor. By 622 he had a small band of devoted followers but could no longer remain in Mecca; their migration to Yathrib (Medina), called the Hegira, marks the beginning of the Muslim era. By 629 he had taken control of Mecca, and by 630 he had control over all Arabia. He died in 632 in the home of the favourite of his nine wives.

Muhammad, Elijah, *originally* **Elijah Poole** 1897–1975
US religious leader
In 1931 he became an assistant to Wali Farad, the founder of The Nation of Islam (known as the Black Muslims), a movement that favoured black separatism and rejected Christianity as a tool of oppressive whites. On Farad's disappearance in 1934, Elijah Muhammad became the leader of the movement, and by 1962 there were an estimated 250,000 Black Muslims. A split occurred in the Nation of Islam when his disciple **Malcolm X** broke away in 1965, and Malcolm's assassination was allegedly carried out by Black Muslims loyal to Elijah Muhammad.

Munch, Edvard 1863–1944
Norwegian painter
An Expressionist obsessed by themes such as death and love, his most characteristic work is *The Scream* (1893), depicting an anonymous figure on a bridge screaming, with the swirling lines of colour in the painting contributing to the mood of desperation. Other works include many self-portraits (eg *Between the Clock and the Bed*, Oslo, 1940) and various woodcuts and engravings. Munch's work is represented in most major collections, and there is a Munch museum in Oslo.

Murdoch, (Keith) Rupert 1931–
US newspaper publisher
He was born in Melbourne, Australia. When his father died in 1952 he inherited the Adelaide newspaper *The News* and soon made it a success. In 1969 he acquired the *News of the World* and the *Sun* in London. His later acquisitions, which have made him one of the world's most powerful media barons, include *The Times* and *The Sunday Times* in London, the New York *Post* and 20th Century Fox film studios. He also pioneered satellite television with his Sky (now BSkyB) network. His company, News Corporation, continues to expand into new markets, notably China. He has been a US citizen since 1985.

Mussolini, Benito Amilcare Andrea 1883–1945
Italian dictator
In 1919 he founded the Fascist Movement to promote his extreme form of anti-communist nationalism. In 1922 his Blackshirts marched on Rome and formed a government, and in 1925 he took the title *Il Duce* ('the leader'). He launched the conquest of Abyssinia in 1935, which was followed by large-scale intervention in the Spanish Civil War on the side of General **Franco**. Allied with **Hitler**, in 1939 Mussolini annexed Albania but he was increasingly forced to rely on German help. After the allied landings in Sicily in 1942 his supporters turned on him, and he had to be rescued by German paratroops. In 1945 he tried to flee the country but was caught and executed.

Nabokov, Vladimir 1899–1977
US novelist
Born in St Petersburg, Russia, to aristocratic parents, he lived for more than 15 years in Berlin before moving to Paris and finally the USA, where he took citizenship in 1945. He began to write in English and published many short stories and novels, including *Bend Sinister* (1947) and *Pale Fire* (1962). The highly successful, though scandalous, *Lolita* (1955) earned him enough to allow him to devote himself to writing full-time. From 1959 he lived in Montreux in Switzerland. Among 20th-century novelists he is highly regarded for his linguistic ingenuity and dazzling intellect.

Nadir Shah 1688–1747
King of Persia
Originally a brigand leader who expelled the Afghan rulers of Persia (Iran), he was king from 1736. He forced Russia to hand over its Caspian provinces, defeated the Turks, conquered Bahrain, Oman and Afghanistan, and ravaged the north-west of India. His domestic policy led to revolts, especially on religious matters, and he was assassinated at Fathabad.

Nagy, Imre 1895–1958
Hungarian politician
He became Prime Minister in 1953, introducing a 'new course' of milder political and economic control. When the Hungarian Uprising broke out in October

1956, he promised free elections and a Russian military withdrawal. However, when Soviet forces began to suppress the revolution, he was displaced by the Soviet puppet János Kádár and later executed. In 1989, following the overthrow of the communists, he was given a hero's reburial in Budapest.

Nanak, *also known as* **Guru Nanak** 1469–1539
Indian religious leader
The founder of Sikhism, he was a Hindu by birth and belief. He travelled widely to Hindu and Muslim centres where he taught spiritual truth. His doctrine, set out later in the *Guru Granth Sahib*, sought a fusion of Brahmanism and Islam on the grounds that both were monotheistic, although his own ideas leaned towards pantheism.

Nansen, Fridtjof 1861–1930
Norwegian explorer, biologist and oceanographer
His great achievement was the partial accomplishment of his scheme for reaching the North Pole by letting his ship get frozen into the ice north of Siberia and drift with the current towards Greenland. He started in the *Fram*, built for the purpose, in August 1893, and drifted north to 84° 4' in March 1895. There he left the *Fram* and pushed across the ice, reaching the highest latitude till then attained, 86° 14' N, on 7 April. He was awarded the Nobel Peace Prize for Russian relief work in 1922.

Napoleon I, *also called* **Napoleon Bonaparte** 1769–1821
Emperor of France
A Corsican by birth, an artillery officer by training, and initially a supporter of the French Revolution, he soon established himself as the leading French general after his campaign in Italy (1796–7). He overcame political rivals step by step and eventually proclaimed himself emperor on 18 May 1804. By 1807, his military victories against all the major powers of Europe left him ruler of a European empire, though threatened by British naval supremacy. His campaign in Russia, despite his victory at Borodino (1812), was disastrous, and his invasion of Spain and Portugal led to the Peninsular War (1808–14), another drain on his resources. Exiled to the island of Elba after defeat in 1814, he returned to power in the 'Hundred Days' which ended in final defeat at Waterloo (June 18, 1815), and exile on the southern Atlantic island of St Helena.

Nash, John 1752–1835
English architect
He came to the notice of the Prince of Wales (later George IV), and was engaged (1811–25) to plan the layout of the new Regent's Park and its curved terraces. He also laid out Regent Street (1825) to link the Park with Westminster, planned Trafalgar Square and St James's Park, recreated Buckingham Palace from old Buckingham House, designed the Marble Arch which originally stood in front of it (moved to its present site in 1851), and rebuilt Brighton Pavilion in oriental style. He is remembered as one of the greatest town planners.

Nasser, Gamal Abd al- 1918–70
Egyptian statesman
He became dissatisfied with the regime of Egypt's King Farouk, and founded the military junta which led to the regime's downfall in 1952. In 1954 he became President. His nationalization of the Suez Canal in 1956 led to Israel's invasion of the Sinai Peninsula in Egypt, and when Anglo-French forces intervened, Nasser, despite military losses, scored an important political victory. His later attempts to build an Arab empire stretching across North Africa met with only partial success, and the six-day Arab–Israeli War in 1967 led to heavy losses on the Arab side. He died in office, one year before the completion of one of his greatest projects, the Aswan High Dam.

Navratilova, Martina 1956–
US tennis player
She won a record nine singles titles at Wimbledon (1978–9, 1982–7, 1990) and the US Open four times (1983–4, 1986–7) and recorded over 100 tournament successes. She also won the Grand Slam of Australian Open, French Open, Wimbledon and US Open twice. Her impressive number of wins makes her second only to Margaret Smith Court. In 1994, having reached the final at Wimbledon, she retired from regular competitive singles play. Her books include *Martina* (1985) and *Feet of Clay* (1996).

Nefertiti See **Akhenaten**

Nehru, Jawaharlal, *known as* **Pandit ('teacher')** 1889–1964
Indian statesman
In 1929 he was elected president of the Indian National Congress, an office he often held afterwards, and was the leader of the movement's socialist wing. When India achieved independence in 1947, Nehru became its first Prime Minister and Minister of External Affairs. He committed India to a policy of industrialization, to a reorganization of its states on the basis of language, and negotiated with Pakistan over Kashmir. His many works include *India and the World* (1936) and an *Autobiography* (1936). His daughter **Indira Gandhi** was later Prime Minister.

Jawaharlal Nehru

Nelson, Horatio Nelson, Viscount 1758–1805
English admiral
He entered the navy in 1770, and in the course of active service lost his right eye and right arm. In 1798, commanding the *Vanguard*, he defeated the French fleet at the Battle of the Nile. He returned in triumph to Naples, and to a hero's welcome from Emma Hamilton, the wife of the British ambassador in Naples, who became his mistress. At the Battle of Copenhagen in 1801 Nelson disregarded orders and engaged the Danish and Norwegian fleets, and won the battle decisively. In 1805 he won his greatest victory, against the French and Spanish fleets at Trafalgar. He directed the engagement from the

Victory, but was mortally wounded.

Nero AD37–68
Roman emperor
His mother was the wife of the Emperor **Claudius**, after whose death in AD54 Nero became emperor. He soon plunged into debauchery, extravagance and tyranny, and persecuted the Christians, blaming them for the fire that devastated Rome in July AD64. He later rebuilt the city with great magnificence, constructing a splendid palace on the Palatine hill. Nero sought distinction as poet, philosopher, actor, musician and charioteer; as a poet he seems to have had some talent. After the Praetorian Guards (the bodyguards of the Roman emperor) rose against him, he committed suicide.

Newcomen, Thomas 1663–1729
English inventor
A blacksmith by trade, in 1698 he began collaborating with Thomas Savery, who had just patented an atmospheric steam engine for pumping water from mines, and by 1712 he had constructed a practical working engine that was widely used in collieries.

Newman, Paul Leonard 1925–
US film actor
One of the major film actors of his generation, combining masculinity with a rebellious streak, his films include *Cat on a Hot Tin Roof* (1958), *The Hustler* (1961), *Cool Hand Luke* (1967), *Butch Cassidy and the Sundance Kid* (1969), *The Sting* (1973), *The Color of Money* (1986), for which he won an Academy Award, *Blaze* (1989), *Nobody's Fool* (1994), *Twilight* (1998) and *Road to Perdition* (2002). He also directed *Rachel, Rachel* (1968) and *The Glass Menagerie* (1987), among others, and has been active politically in liberal causes and in charity work.

Newton, Helmut 1920–2004
Australian photographer
Born in Berlin, Germany, he emigrated to Australia in 1940 and set up as a freelance photographer in Melbourne. He moved subsequently to Paris and had fashion photographs published in such magazines as *Elle*, *Nova*, *Marie Claire* and *Vogue*. His publications include *White Women* (1976), *Private Property* (1984) and *Naked and Dressed in Hollywood* (1992).

Newton, Sir Isaac 1642–1727
English scientist and mathematician
One of the greatest of all scientific geniuses, Newton first expounded his famous theory of gravitation in his *De Motu Corporum* (1684), which showed that the force of gravity between two bodies, such as the Sun and the Earth, is proportional to their masses and their distance from one another. He described this more completely in his *Principia* (1687), his greatest work, in which he stated his three laws of motion, mathematically relating mass, force and movement. Newton was involved throughout his life in controversies with many other scientists, particularly with **Gottfried Leibniz** over the discovery of calculus. He also devoted much time to the study of alchemy and theology.

Ngo Dinh Diem 1901–63
Vietnamese statesman
He became Minister of the Interior in 1933. Refusing to support **Ho Chi Minh**, he was forced into exile in 1950, but returned to South Vietnam as Prime Minister in 1954, becoming President in 1955. As hostilities with North Vietnam mounted, he was almost wholly dependent on US support for his country's economic and military survival. He was later murdered by dissident army officers.

Nicholas II 1868–1918
Emperor of Russia
The eldest son of Alexander III, he succeeded his father in 1894. His reign was marked by alliance with France, entente with Great Britain, a disastrous war with Japan (1904–5), and the establishment in 1906 of the Duma (parliament). Forced to abdicate in 1917 at the revolution, he was shot with his entire family by the Red Guards in 1918.

Nicklaus, Jack (William), *known as* **the Golden Bear** 1940–
US golfer
His first professional victory was the US Open (1962), a tournament he won a further three times (1967, 1972, 1980). Of the other major competitions, he won the Masters a record six times (1963, 1965–6, 1972, 1975, 1986); the Open championship three times (1966, 1970, 1978); and the US PGA (Professional Golfers' Association) a record-equalling five times (1963, 1971, 1973, 1975, 1980). His total of 20 Major victories (including his two US Amateurs) is also a record, and he is arguably the greatest golfer in history.

Niepce, (Joseph) Nicéphore 1765–1833
French chemist
One of the pioneers of photography, he experimented with a camera obscura to project an image onto a wall, then decided to look for ways of fixing the image automatically. In 1826 he succeeded in making a permanent image using a pewter plate coated with bitumen of Judea, a substance which hardens on exposure to light. This historic negative, which Niepce termed a 'heliograph', is now preserved at the University of Texas.

Nietzsche, Friedrich Wilhelm 1844–1900
German philosopher, scholar and writer
A major influence on many strands of later thought, including existentialism and psychoanalysis, his characteristic themes are the violent opposition to Christian and liberal ethics, the hatred of democratic ideals, the celebration of the *Übermensch* (superman), and the life-affirming 'will to power'. His brilliant, unconventional works, often poetic in form, include *Thus Spake Zarathustra* (1883–92), *Beyond Good and Evil* (1886) and *Ecce Homo* (his autobiography, completed in 1888 but withheld by his sister and not published till 1908). In 1889 he had a complete mental and physical breakdown, and never recovered his sanity.

Nightingale, Florence 1820–1910
English nurse and hospital reformer
After nursing work in London, in the Crimean War she volunteered for duty and took 38 nurses to Scutari (now Üsküdar), Turkey, in 1854. She organized the barracks hospital after the Battle of Inkerman, and by imposing strict discipline and standards of sanitation reduced the hospital mortality rate drastically. She returned to England in 1856 and a fund of £50,000 was raised to enable her to form an institution for the training of nurses at St Thomas's and at King's College Hospital. She devoted many years to the question of

army sanitary reform, to the improvement of nursing and to public health in India. Her main work, *Notes on Nursing* (1859), went through many editions.

Nijinska, Bronislava or **Bronisława** 1891–1972
Russian ballet dancer and choreographer
Nijinska was the sister of **Vaslav Nijinsky**, and she, like her brother, danced with Sergei Diaghilev's Ballets Russes in Paris and London. She became principal choreographer, and among the ballets she created for the company were her masterpieces *Les Noces* (1923) and *Les Biches* (1924). From 1935 she choreographed for many companies in Europe and the USA.

Nijinsky, Vaslav 1890–1950
Russian dancer and choreographer
Considered to be the greatest male dancer of the 20th century, he, like his sister **Bronislava Nijinska**, trained in St Petersburg, and first appeared in ballet at the Maryinski Theatre. As the leading dancer in Sergei Diaghilev's Ballets Russes, which performed in Paris in 1909, he became enormously popular. His choreographic repertoire was small but had two exceptional high points, in **Claude Debussy**'s *L'Après-midi d'un Faune* (1912) and in **Igor Stravinsky**'s *The Rite of Spring* (1913). He was diagnosed a paranoid schizophrenic in 1917.

Nixon, Richard Milhous 1913–94
37th President of the USA

Richard Nixon

He became Vice-President under **Dwight D Eisenhower** in 1953, and won the Presidency in 1968. His administration (1969–74) was marked by continuing controversy over the Vietnam War and his reopening of US relations with the People's Republic of China, and his visit there was the first by a US president. During an official investigation into a break-in in June 1972 at the Democratic National Committee's headquarters in the Watergate building, Washington, Nixon lost credibility with the US people by refusing to hand over tapes of relevant conversations. On 9 August 1974 he resigned, the first US president to do so.

Nobel, Alfred Bernhard 1833–96
Swedish chemist and manufacturer
He was an explosives expert, and in 1866 he invented a safe and manageable form of nitroglycerin, which he called 'dynamite'. Later, he invented smokeless gunpowder, and in 1875 gelignite. On the strength of these inventions, he created an industrial empire which manufactured many of his other inventions, and amassed a huge fortune, much of which he left to endow annual Nobel prizes (first awarded in 1901) for physics, chemistry, physiology or medicine, literature and peace (a sixth prize, for economics, was instituted in his honour in 1969). The synthetic element nobelium was named after him.

Novello, Ivor, *originally* **David Ivor Davies** 1893–1951
Welsh actor, composer, songwriter and dramatist
His song 'Keep the Home Fires Burning' was one of the best known of World War I. He first appeared on the regular stage in London in 1921 and enjoyed great popularity, his most successful and characteristic works being his musical plays such as *Glamorous Night* (1935), *The Dancing Years* (1939) and *King's Rhapsody* (1949). The Ivor Novello Award, presented annually for songwriting, was named in his honour.

Nureyev, Rudolf Hametovich 1938–93
Russian ballet dancer
He became principal dancer for Russia's Kirov Ballet, and while in Paris with them in 1961 he defected and obtained political asylum. An intelligent man with an impressive ability to express emotion through the body, he had many different roles, often appearing with **Margot Fonteyn**; theirs was a partnership which was to transform dance in the West. He also had a successful career as a producer of full-length ballets and was artistic director of the Paris Opera (1983–9). Films in which he appeared include *Swan Lake* (1966) and *Valentino* (1977).

O'Casey, Sean 1884–1964
Irish playwright
His early plays, dealing with low life in Dublin – *Shadow of a Gunman* (1923) and *Juno and the Paycock* (1924) – were written for the Abbey Theatre, Dublin. Later he became more experimental and impressionistic. Other works include *The Plough and the Stars* (1926) and *The Bishop's Bonfire* (1955). He also wrote essays, such as *The Flying Wasp* (1936). His autobiography, begun in 1939 with *I Knock at the Door*, continued through six volumes to *Sunset and Evening Star* (1954).

Occam or **Ockham, William of**, *nicknamed* **the Venerable Inceptor** c.1285–c.1349
English philosopher, theologian and political writer
Perhaps the most influential of later medieval philosophers, he published many works while at Oxford and Avignon, such as the *Summa Logicae* and commentaries on **Aristotle**. He also published several important political treatises. He is best known for his philosophical principle of 'Occam's razor', to the effect that a theory should not propose the existence of anything more than is needed for its explanation.

O'Connell, Daniel, *known as* **the Liberator** 1775–1847
Irish political leader
He was elected MP for County Clare, Ireland, in 1828, but he was prevented from taking his seat until he was re-elected in 1830, after the passing of Catholic Emancipation Bill had allowed Catholics to sit in parliament. He achieved high office in the British government but fiercely opposed British policies in Ireland. In 1840 he founded the Repeal Association for repeal of the 1801 Union with Great Britain, and

in 1841 he was elected Lord Mayor of Dublin. Early in 1844, with his son, O'Connell was imprisoned and fined for conspiracy. After the national trauma of the potato famine, he left Ireland for the last time in January 1847, a broken man, and died in Genoa on his way to Rome.

Offa d.796
King of Mercia
He succeeded his cousin Æthelbald (757), extended his dominion over Kent, Sussex, Wessex and East Anglia, and is thought to have styled himself *rex Anglorum* (king of England) in his charters. To protect his frontiers to the west against the Welsh, he built the great earthwork known as Offa's Dyke, stretching for 70 miles along the Welsh border. He was probably the most powerful English monarch before the 10th century.

Ohm, Georg Simon 1787–1854
German physicist
His 'Ohm's law', describing the relationship between voltage, current and resistance in an electrical circuit, was published in 1827, although neither this nor his other important work sound waves (1843) received immediate recognition. The SI unit of electrical resistance is named after him.

Olivier, Laurence Kerr, Baron Olivier of Brighton 1907–89
English actor, producer and director
He joined the Old Vic Company in 1937 and played all the great Shakespearean roles, while his versatility was underlined by a virtuoso display as a broken-down low comedian in *The Entertainer* (1957). After war service he produced, directed and played in acclaimed films of *Henry V, Hamlet* and *Richard III*. He played memorable roles in several other films, including *Wuthering Heights* (1939), *Rebecca* (1940), *Sleuth* (1972) and *Marathon Man* (1976). His wives included **Vivien Leigh** and Joan Plowright.

Omar Khayyám c.1048–c.1122
Persian poet, mathematician and astronomer
In Samarkand he completed an important work on algebra, and he made the necessary astronomical observations for the reform of the Muslim calendar, collaborating on an observatory in Isfahan. As a poet he had attracted little attention until Edward FitzGerald translated and arranged the collection of *rubaiyat* (four-line poems), attributed to him, into *The Rubáiyát of Omar Khayyám* (first published in 1859).

Onassis, Aristotle Socrates 1906–75
Argentine–Greek ship-owner
He was born in Smyrna, Turkey, but made a fortune in tobacco in Buenos Aires. Buying his first ships in 1932, he built up one of the world's largest independent fleets, and was a pioneer in the construction of supertankers. After a long relationship with **Maria Callas**, in 1968 he married Jacqueline Bouvier Kennedy, widow of US president **John F Kennedy**.

O'Neill, Eugene Gladstone 1888–1953
US playwright
Regarded by many as the USA's finest playwright, his best-known plays are probably *Desire Under the Elms* (1924), a family tragedy set in New England, *Strange Interlude* (1928; Pulitzer Prize), which uses a stream-of-consciousness technique, his trilogy *Mourning Becomes Electra* (1931), set at the end of the American Civil War, *The Iceman Cometh* (first performed in New York 1946), a parable set in a bar, and *Long Day's Journey into Night* (first performed posthumously in 1956, and winner of a Pulitzer Prize in 1957), a family tragedy. He was awarded the Nobel Prize for literature in 1936.

Oppenheimer, (Julius) Robert 1904–67
US nuclear physicist
During World War II he was selected as leader of the atomic bomb project, set up the Los Alamos laboratory and brought together a formidable group of scientists. After the war he became director of the Institute for Advanced Studies at Princeton University and continued to play an important role in US atomic energy policy from 1947, promoting peaceful uses of atomic energy and bitterly opposing development of the hydrogen bomb. In 1953 he was declared a security risk and was forced to retire from political activities.

Orwell, George, *pseudonym of* **Eric Arthur Blair** 1903–50
English novelist and essayist
He served as a soldier in Burma, lived as a tramp, and fought in the Spanish Civil War, and used these experiences for his books *Burmese Days* (1934), *Down and Out in Paris and London* (1933) and *Homage to Catalonia* (1938). Later books include *A Clergyman's Daughter* (1935), *Keep the Aspidistra Flying* (1936) and *The Road to Wigan Pier* (1937). During World War II, he was a war correspondent, and at the end of the war wrote his biting satire of communist ideology, *Animal Farm* (1945). His last major work was the terrifying prophecy *Nineteen Eighty-Four* (1949). His collections of essays include *Inside the Whale* (1940) and *Shooting an Elephant* (1950).

Ovid, *in full* **Publius Ovidius Naso** 43BC–AD17
Roman poet
He had his first literary success with a collection of love poems, the *Loves*, followed by *Heroines*, imaginary love letters from mythological heroines to their lovers. The *Art of Love*, a handbook of seduction, appeared about 1BC, followed by the *Cures for Love*. While writing his *Metamorphoses*, a collection of mythological tales in 15 books, he was banished by **Augustus** (AD8), for some unknown reason, to Tomis (Constanza) on the Black Sea. Other works include the five books of the *Sorrows*.

Owen, Robert 1771–1858
Welsh social and educational reformer
By age 19 he was manager of a cotton mill in Manchester. In 1799 he married the eldest daughter of David Dale, and bought from him the cotton mills and manufacturing village Dale had established at New Lanark in Scotland. Here he established a model community with improved housing and working conditions, and built a school and a village store, the cradle of the co-operative movement. In 1813 he formed New Lanark into a new company with **Jeremy Bentham** and others, but ceased to be manager in 1825 after disagreements with his partners. He organized the Grand National Consolidated Trades Union in 1833, and spent the rest of his life campaigning for various causes, including (later) spiritualism.

Owen, Wilfred 1893–1918
English poet
He trained as a teacher, and served as a soldier throughout World War I, during which he met **Siegfried Sassoon**. He was killed in action a week before the Armistice was signed. Only five of his poems were published while he was alive, and his work was first collected in 1920 by Sassoon. His poetry expresses a horror of the cruelty and waste of war, and individual poems such as 'Dulce et Decorum Est' and 'Anthem for Doomed Youth' have shaped the attitude of many.

Owens, Jesse James Cleveland 1913–80
US athlete
While competing for the Ohio State University team in 1935, he set three world records and equalled another (all within the space of an hour), including a long jump record (26ft 8¼in) which lasted for 25 years. At the 1936 Olympics in Berlin he won four gold medals (100m, 200m, long jump, and 4×100m relay) which it was claimed caused the German Nazi leader, Adolf **Hitler**, to leave the stadium. He is considered the greatest sprinter of his generation.

Pacino, Al(fred James) 1940–
US film actor
He received the first of his numerous Academy Award nominations for *The Godfather* (1972). Drawn to characters on an emotional knife edge, he has made appearances in films such as *Serpico* (1973), *Dog Day Afternoon* (1975), *Scarface* (1983), *Frankie and Johnny* (1991), *Glengarry Glen Ross* (1992), *Heat* (1995) and *Donnie Brasco* (1997). He finally won a Best Actor Academy Award for *Scent of a Woman* (1993) and made his directorial debut with *Looking for Richard* (1996). He has frequently returned to the stage.

Paganini, Niccolò 1782–1840
Italian violinist
He gave his first concert in 1793 (when his father reduced his age by two years in advertisements) and began touring professionally in Italy in 1805. He later toured Europe (1828–31), and his dexterity and technical expertise acquired him an almost legendary reputation. He published six concertos and the celebrated *24 Capricci* (1820).

Paget, Sir James 1814–99
English physician and pathologist
One of the founders of modern pathology, he discovered the cause of trichinosis, and described 'Paget's disease' (an early indication of breast cancer) and 'Paget's disease of bone' (a bone inflammation). He published his *Lectures on Surgical Pathology* and *Clinical Lectures* in 1853.

Pahlavi, Muhammad Reza 1919–80
Shah of Iran
He succeeded on the abdication of his father, Reza Shah Pahlavi, in 1941. His reign was for many years marked by social reforms and a movement away from the old-fashioned despotic concept of the monarchy, but in the later 1970s the economic situation deteriorated and protest at Western-style 'decadence' grew among religious fundamentalists. The Shah, having lost control of the situation, left the country (1979), after which a revolutionary government was formed under Ayatollah **Khomeini**.

Muhammad Reza Pahlavi

Paine, Tom (Thomas) 1737–1809
English radical political writer
One of the 18th century's most passionate and persuasive democrats, he was active in both US and French politics. On the outbreak of the American Revolution (1775–83) he published *Common Sense* (1776), which urged immediate independence. He later served in the continental army and was secretary to the Congress committee on foreign affairs (1777–9). He was a Deputy of the French National Convention from 1792 to 1793. His major works were *The Rights of Man* (1791–2), written in support of the French Revolution and an overthrow of the British monarchy, and *The Age of Reason* (1794–6), a powerful attack on accepted religion.

Palladio, Andrea, *originally* **Andrea di Pietro della Gondola** 1508–80
Italian architect
He developed a modern Italian architectural style based on classical Roman principles, unlike the ornamentation of the Renaissance. This Palladian style was widely imitated all over Europe, in particular by **Inigo Jones** and **Christopher Wren**. Palladio started by remodelling the basilica in Vicenza, and extended his style to villas, palaces and churches, especially in Venice. His *The Four Books of Architecture* (1570) greatly influenced his successors.

Palmer, Samuel 1805–81
English landscape painter and etcher
He produced mainly watercolours in a mystical style derived from his friend **William Blake** (eg *Repose of the Holy Family*, 1824). From 1826 to 1835 he lived in Shoreham, Kent, where he was surrounded by a group of friends who called themselves 'The Ancients'. He was largely forgotten until the mid-20th century, when critics rediscovered his work.

Pankhurst, Emmeline, *née* **Goulden** 1857–1928
English suffragette
In 1889 she founded the Women's Franchise League, and in 1903, with her daughter Christabel, the Women's Social and Political Union, which fought for women's suffrage with violent protest. She was frequently imprisoned and underwent hunger strikes and forcible feeding. She later joined the Conservative Party. Her 40-year campaign reached a peak of success shortly before her death, when the Representation of the People Act of 1928 was finally passed, establishing voting equality for men and women. She had three daughters, Christabel, Sylvia and Adela, all of whom campaigned for various causes.

Papa Doc See **Duvalier, François**

Parker, Bonnie 1911–34
US thief and murderer
She was the partner of **Clyde Barrow**, who she met in 1932 while working as a waitress. Shortly after, when Barrow was convicted of theft and sentenced to two years in jail, Parker smuggled a gun to him and he escaped. With their gang, Parker and Barrow continued to rob and murder until they were shot dead at a police roadblock in Louisiana on 23 May 1934. Their end was predicted by Parker in a poem, variously called *The Story of Bonnie and Clyde* and *The Story of Suicide Sal*.

Parker, Charlie (Charles Christopher), *known as* **Bird** 1920–55
US saxophonist, bandleader and composer
The most influential performer in post-1940s modern jazz, he pioneered the bebop style with trumpeter **Dizzy Gillespie**. The harmonic and rhythmic advances of their music were rightly perceived as a major sea change in jazz. Despite addiction to heroin and alcohol and recurring mental illness, he continued to lead groups, tour and record until the end of his life, and many of his compositions, such as 'Now's The Time' and 'Ornithology', have become standard jazz works.

Parker, Dorothy, *née* **Rothschild** 1893–1967
US wit, short-story writer and journalist
She was born in New Jersey, and her formal education ended in 1908 at the age of 14. She was a voracious reader and decided to make literature her life. In 1916 she sold some of her poetry to the editor of *Vogue*, and was subsequently given an editorial position on the magazine, writing captions for fashion photographs and drawings. She then became drama critic of *Vanity Fair* (1917–20). Although her personal life was turbulent, she was famed for her spontaneous wit, and she has had attributed to her many cruel wisecracks. She was at her most trenchant in stories and book reviews in *The New Yorker*, a magazine whose character she did much to form. She also published poems and sketches. Her poems are included in *Not So Deep as a Well* (1930) and *Enough Rope* (1926), which became a bestseller. Her short stories were collected in *Here Lies* (1936). She also collaborated on several film scripts, including *A Star Is Born* (1937) and *The Little Foxes* (1941).

Parks, Rosa Lee, *née* **McCauley** 1913–2005
US civil-rights activist

Rosa Parks

In December 1955 she was arrested and fined when she refused to give up her seat on a bus to a white man in Montgomery, Alabama, choosing instead to disobey the segregated seating policies common in the South. This incident prompted **Martin Luther King, Jnr** to organize a citywide boycott of the bus company, which resulted in a legal victory. Her refusal to yield her seat is regarded as the beginning of the modern US civil rights movement.

Parnell, Charles Stewart 1846–91
Irish politician
In 1875 he became an MP supporting Home Rule for Ireland, and gained great popularity in Ireland for his work on land reform and Irish parliamentary independence. In 1880 he became chairman of the Irish Parliamentary Party. Always involved in controversy, Parnell was cleared of complicity in the murder of Thomas Henry Burke in 1889, but in the following year was named in a divorce case brought by Captain William Henry O'Shea against his wife Katherine. A decree was granted with costs against Parnell, and he lost support in Ireland. He died suddenly, five months after his marriage to Katherine.

Pascal, Blaise 1623–62
French mathematician, physicist, theologian and scholar
By the age of 11 had worked out for himself in secret the first 23 propositions of **Euclid**, calling straight lines 'bars' and circles 'rounds'. Early experiments with his father, in which he observed how mercury columns fell when carried to higher altitudes, led ultimately to the invention of the barometer, the hydraulic press and the syringe. In 1654 he had the first of two religious revelations and became involved in the theological controversies of the day, attacking the Jesuits in France and fatally undermining their power. His later mathematical work heralded the invention of integral calculus. His work *Pensées* ('Thoughts'), published in 1669, contains profound insights into religious truths coupled with scepticism of rationalist thought and theology.

Pasternak, Boris Leonidovich 1890–1960
Russian lyric poet, novelist and translator
He published three collections of verse between 1917 and 1923, and wrote the political poems collected as *The Year 1905* (1927), on the Bolshevik uprising. He also produced a number of outstanding short stories and translations. He caused a political earthquake with his first novel, *Doctor Zhivago* (1957), which described the Russian revolution from the viewpoint of a disenchanted communist. Expelled by the Soviet Writers' Union, he had to take the step of refusing the 1958 Nobel Prize for literature.

Pasteur, Louis 1822–95
French chemist
The father of modern bacteriology, he pioneered the notion that fermentation is caused by tiny organisms, and introduced the technique of 'pasteurization', a mild and short heat treatment to destroy them. His 'germ theory of disease' maintained that disease was communicable through the spread of micro-organisms, and he demonstrated that sheep and cows 'vaccinated' with the weakened bacilli of anthrax were protected from developing the disease. He also devised preventative treatments for diphtheria, tubercular disease, cholera, yellow fever, plague and rabies.

Paul, St, *also known as* **Saul of Tarsus** d.c.64/68AD
Christian missionary and martyr, the Apostle of the Gentiles
A Pharisee, he took an active part in the persecution of Christians. According to the Acts of the Apostles in the Bible, he was on his way to Damascus when a vision of **Jesus Christ** converted him into an adherent of the new faith. He made three great missionary journeys throughout the Roman world, and addressed his preaching mainly to non-Jews, but was executed under **Nero**, probably at the end of two years' captivity. His writings, in the form of letters, form a large part of the New Testament.

Pauli, Wolfgang 1900–58
Austrian–Swiss theoretical physicist
He is best known for formulating the 'Pauli exclusion principle' (1924), which states that no two electrons in an atom can have identical energy, masses and angular momentums at the same time. This earned him the 1945 Nobel Prize for physics. He also suggested the existence of a low-mass neutral particle (1931), later discovered as the neutrino.

Pauling, Linus Carl 1901–94
US chemist
He did important early work on crystal structures and chemical bonding, and went on to study the structures of proteins and antibodies and the chemical basis of hereditary disease. He advocated the use of vitamin C in combating a wide range of diseases and infections, and his views sometimes generated controversy. He was also controversial for his work in the peace movement and his criticism of nuclear deterrence policy. Pauling was awarded the Nobel Prize for chemistry in 1954 and the Nobel Peace Prize in 1962.

Pavarotti, Luciano 1935–
Italian tenor
His voice and performance are very much in the powerful style of the traditional Italian tenor, and he is also internationally known as a concert performer. He has made many recordings, including joint performances with José Carreras and **Placido Domingo** as 'The Three Tenors'. In 1990, when football's World Cup was held Italy, he recorded the aria *Nessun Dorma* ('None Shall Sleep') from **Puccini**'s *Turandot*, which was used as the theme tune for the event.

Pavlov, Ivan Petrovich 1849–1936
Russian physiologist
His work was concerned with three main areas of physiology: the circulatory system (1874–88), the digestive system (1879–97), and the higher nervous activity including the brain (1902–36). He was awarded the Nobel Prize for physiology or medicine in 1904. His most famous research showed that if a bell is sounded whenever food is presented to a dog, it will eventually begin to salivate when the bell is sounded without food being presented. This he termed a 'conditioned' or acquired reflex.

Paxton, Sir Joseph 1801–65
English gardener and architect
He became superintendent of gardens to the Duke of Devonshire at Chiswick and Chatsworth from 1826, remodelled the gardens and designed a glass and iron conservatory at Chatsworth (1836–40). This became the model for his design of the building for the Great Exhibition of 1851 (it was later re-erected as the Crystal Palace in Sydenham, and destroyed by fire in 1936). He was Liberal MP for Coventry from 1854.

Peake, Mervyn Laurence 1911–68
English writer and artist
He is best known for his Gothic fantasy trilogy *Titus Groan*, *Gormenghast* (1950) and *Titus Alone* (1959). Another novel, *Mr Pye*, appeared in 1953, and his only play, *The Wit to Woo*, in 1957. He published two volumes of verse, *Shapes and Sounds* (1941) and *The Glassblowers* (1950). He illustrated several classics, notably *Treasure Island*, *The Hunting of the Snark* and *The Ancient Mariner*.

Peck, (Eldred) Gregory 1916–2003
US film actor
One of the first major postwar film stars, he portrayed men of action and everyday citizens distinguished by their sense of decency in films such as *Spellbound* (1945), *Twelve O'Clock High* (1949) and *The Gunfighter* (1950). He was nominated five times for an Academy Award, winning Best Actor for his role as a liberal Southern lawyer in *To Kill A Mockingbird* (1962). Later films include *The Omen* (1976), *The Boys from Brazil* (1978) and *Cape Fear* (1991).

Peel, Sir Robert 1788–1850
English statesman and Prime Minister
He entered parliament in 1809 as a Tory. Becoming Home Secretary in 1822, he organized the London police force (the 'Peelers' or 'Bobbies'), and formed a short-lived government from 1834 to 1835. His second government lasted from 1841 to 1846. Much of his career was dominated by debates on the tax on foreign corn, with Peel doing his best to mediate between the various factions. Peel was also a strong opponent of Irish nationalism, and helped to break the power of **Daniel O'Connell**.

Pelé, *pseudonym of* **Edson Arantes do Nascimento** 1940–
Brazilian footballer
In 1958 he won his first World Cup medal, scoring twice in Brazil's win in the final over Sweden. For most of his senior career he played for Santos, and in November 1969 he achieved the staggering mark of 1,000 goals in first-class football. He is considered one of the finest players in the history of the game. His publications include *My Life and the Beautiful Game* (1977) and a novel, *The World Cup Murders* (1988).

Peploe, Samuel John 1871–1935
Scottish artist
He went to Paris in 1911 as an established painter, and later returned to Edinburgh to remodel his style in accordance with the colouring and the analysis of form characterizing the work of **Paul Cézanne**. His later still-life paintings brought him fame as a colourist, and in 1930 he became a leading member of the group known as the Scottish Colourists.

Pepys, Samuel 1633–1703
English diarist and Admiralty official
His celebrated Diary, which ran from 1 January 1660 to 31 May 1669, is interesting both as the personal record (and confessions) of a man with an abounding love of life, and for the vivid picture it gives of contemporary life, including naval administration

PEOPLE

and Court intrigue. The highlights are probably the accounts of the three disasters of the decade – the great plague (1665–6), the great fire of London (1666) and the sailing up the Thames by the Dutch fleet (1665–7). The Diary was written in code, in which form it remained at Magdalene College, Cambridge, until 1825, when it was deciphered and edited.

Pericles c.490–429BC
Athenian statesman
He was elected 15 times to the office of *strategos* (general, but with political functions) between 451BC and his death, and under his rule Athens expanded to become an empire. Athens and Sparta were almost continuously at war during these years, culminating in the Peloponnesian War which broke out in 431BC. Pericles enjoyed the company of the poets and intellectuals of the day, including **Sophocles**, whose personal friend he was. During his rule the Parthenon, the Propylaea, and other buildings on the Acropolis were constructed.

Perlman, Itzhak 1945–
Israeli violinist
The son of Polish immigrants, he moved in 1958 to study at the Juilliard School, New York. He first played on US radio aged 10, at Carnegie Hall in 1963, and in London in 1968. Now one of the most highly acclaimed violinists of his time, he is noted for his brilliant technique and attention to detail.

Perón, (Maria) Eva Duarte De, *known as* **Evita** 1919–52
Argentine popular leader and social reformer
The second wife of **Juan Perón**, she was a radio and stage actress before her marriage to him in 1945. She played a major part in his successful presidential campaign the following year, and became a powerful political influence and mainstay of the government. Meanwhile she used her position to press for women's suffrage, by founding the Peronista Feminist Party in 1949. She was loved by the people, and after her death support for her husband waned. Evita Perón's life story was the theme of a popular musical by **Andrew Lloyd-Webber** and Tim Rice (1978).

Perón, Juan Domingo 1895–1974
Argentine soldier and statesman
A close student of **Benito Mussolini**, he developed a broad base of popular support, helped by his politically astute wife, **Eva Perón**. In 1946 he was elected President, tried to crush all opposition by any means including torture, and sought to modernize and industrialize the economy. In 1955 he was deposed by the army and fled to Spain. Only a year after his dramatic return to power in 1973, Perón died, leaving his office to the vice-president, his third wife, Isabelita Perón.

Pétain, (Henri) Philippe (Omer) 1856–1951
French soldier and statesman
During World War I his defence of Verdun in 1916 made him a national hero. Made Commander-in-Chief in 1917, and facing widespread mutinies following France's disastrous Nivelle offensive, his appeasement policies virtually removed the French army from the war. As Minister for War in 1934, he sponsored the ineffective Maginot Line, and when France collapsed in early 1940, he succeeded as the head of the government, immediately arranging terms with the Germans. His administration at Vichy involved active collaboration with Germany. With the liberation of France (1944) Pétain was brought to trial, his death sentence for treason being commuted to life imprisonment. He died in captivity in 1951.

Peter I, *known as* **the Great** 1672–1725
Tsar and Emperor of Russia
Son of the Tsar Alexis I Mikhailovich, he became emperor in 1721. He was determined to westernize Russia, and in 1703 began the construction of the new city and port of St Petersburg, which was designated as the capital of the empire. In 1712 he married his Lithuanian mistress, Catherine (the future Catherine I). He spent much of his reign fighting the Turks and the Swedes, and enlarged his empire considerably. On his death he had succeeded in making Russia part of the general European state system for the first time in its history, and established it as a major power.

18th-century portrait of Peter I, the Great

Petrarch, Francesco Petrarca 1304–74
Italian poet and scholar
One of the greatest of Renaissance poets, he is best known for his *Canzoniere*, the poems inspired by his unrequited passion for Laura (possibly Laure de Noves, married in 1325, who died, the mother of eleven children, in 1348). His other works include his epic poem *Africa* and his historical work in prose *De Viris Illustribus*, a series of biographies of classical celebrities. The most powerful rulers of the day competed for his presence at their courts. The Petrarchan sonnet is named after him.

Philip II of Spain and I of Portugal 1527–98
King of Spain and of Portugal
The only son of Emperor Charles V, he became King of Spain from 1556. The first of his four wives was Mary I (Mary Tudor) of England, but she died in 1558, four years after the marriage. Philip increasingly identified himself with the Spanish Inquisition, which he saw as useful both for combating heresy and for extending his control over his own dominions, which included Portugal and parts of Italy and the New World. He was involved in constant wars, and in 1588 the great Armada was launched against England, but was destroyed. Philip died two years later, leaving his empire divided, demoralized and economically depressed.

Piaget, Jean 1896–1980
Swiss psychologist
A pioneer in the study of child intelligence, he is best known for his intensive case-study methods of research (using his own children), and for proposing the idea of 'stages' of cognitive development. His

books include *The Child's Conception of the World* (1926), *The Origin of Intelligence in Children* (1936), and *The Early Growth of Logic in the Child* (1958).

Picasso, Pablo 1881–1973
Spanish painter
The dominant figure of early 20th-century French art and a pioneer of Cubism, he moved from Spain to Paris in 1901. His early blue and pink periods, where those colours would dominate his art, gave way in around 1906 to the full-blown Cubist style of *Les Demoiselles d'Avignon* (1906–7), and in later Cubist experiments he used collage, pieces of wood, wire, newspaper and string. The most important canvas of his middle period is probably the immense *Guernica* (1937), which expressed his horror of the bombing of this Basque town during the Spanish Civil War. Picasso worked in a great variety of media; as well as sculpture and painting, he produced constructions in metal, pottery, drawings, engravings, aquatints and lithographs.

Piggott, Lester Keith 1935–
English jockey
Considered the most brilliant jockey since World War II, he was champion jockey in England on eleven occasions. At five feet nine inches, Piggott was known as the 'the Long Fellow', and had to diet rigorously to reach his racing weight. In all he rode 30 Classic winners, including nine Derbies. He later became a trainer, but he was tried for tax irregularities (1987) and sentenced to three years' imprisonment. He successfully resumed his career after his release.

Pine, Courtney 1964–
English jazz saxophonist
He became the figurehead of the so-called British jazz boom of the late 1980s with the success of his debut album, *Journey To The Urge Within* (1986). His early music reflected his interest in soul, reggae and funk, while other projects have concentrated on a more purely defined jazz idiom, as in *Within the Realms of Our Dreams* (1990). A powerful and charismatic performer, he broadened his range still further by incorporating hip-hop DJs in his live act, and on *Modern Day Jazz Stories* (1996).

Pinter, Harold 1930–
English dramatist
His first London production, *The Birthday Party* (1959), received bad reviews, but later successes such as *The Caretaker* (1958, filmed 1963), *The Homecoming* (1965) and *No Man's Land* (1975) led to his recognition as a major force in British theatre. His style tends to use the illogical and inconsequential in everyday talk to induce an atmosphere of menace; later plays often have explicitly political themes. He has written numerous film scripts, including *The French Lieutenant's Woman* (1981) and *The Comfort of Strangers* (1990), and later plays include *Mountain Language* (1988) and *Moonlight* (1993). He won the Nobel Prize for literature in 2005.

Pisano, Giovanni c.1250–c.1320
Italian sculptor and architect
He was the son of **Nicola Pisano**, and worked with him on the pulpit in Siena, on the fountain in Perugia, and then between 1284 and 1286 on a number of impressive, life-size statues for the façade of Siena Cathedral. He also sculpted figures for the entrance to the Baptistery at Pisa, and made a number of free-standing Madonnas. He was one of the great sculptors of his day in the Italian Gothic tradition, and his innovation pointed the way to Renaissance ideals in sculpture.

Pisano, Nicola c.1225–c.1284
Italian sculptor, architect and engineer
His first great work was the sculpted marble panels for the pulpit in the Baptistery in Pisa, finished in 1260. On a second pulpit, for the cathedral at Siena (1268), and on the Fontana Maggiore in Perugia (1278), he collaborated with his son, **Giovanni Pisano**. Although working in a traditional Gothic style, Nicola studied Classical sculpture like the Roman sarcophagi he found in the Campo Santo at Pisa, and incorporated their forms into his own work.

Pissarro, Camille 1830–1903
French Impressionist artist
Pissarro was the leader of the original Impressionists, and the only one to exhibit at all eight of the group's exhibitions in Paris (1874–86). Most of his works were painted in the countryside around Paris. He had considerable influence on **Cézanne** and **Paul Gauguin** at the beginning of their artistic careers. His famous paintings include the *Boulevard Montmartre* by night (1897).

Pitt, William, 1st Earl of Chatham, *known as* **Pitt the Elder** 1708–78
English statesman and orator
He entered parliament in 1735 as a Whig. In 1756 he became Secretary of State in a coalition government, pursuing a vigorous war policy against the French. He was Prime Minister from 1766 to 1768, though dogged during this period by ill health. His second son was **William Pitt, the Younger**.

Pitt, William, *known as* **Pitt the Younger** 1759–1806
English statesman
He was the second son of the Earl of Chatham, **William Pitt, the Elder**. In 1783, at the age of 24, he became Britain's youngest prime minister. He took steps to reduce the national debt, passed the India Act of 1784 to give the government some control of the East India Company, effected the division of Canada between the French and English in 1791, and achieved union with Ireland in 1800. During his second ministry the French were defeated at Trafalgar (1805), and he was hailed as the saviour of Europe. Although he was a popular national figure his private life was comparatively sad and lonely; he had no close friends and did not marry.

Planck, Max Karl Ernst 1858–1947
German theoretical physicist
His work on the law of thermodynamics and black body radiation led him to formulate the quantum theory (1900), which successfully accounted for and predicted certain phenomena which could not be explained by Newtonian theory. **Albert Einstein**'s application of the quantum theory to light (1905) led to the theories of relativity, and in 1913 **Niels Bohr** successfully applied it to the problems of sub-atomic physics. Planck was awarded the Nobel Prize for physics in 1918. In 1930 he was elected president of the Kaiser Wilhelm Institute, but resigned in 1937 in protest against the Nazi regime.

Plath, Sylvia 1932–63
US poet
She studied at Cambridge University in England from 1956, where she met and married **Ted Hughes**. They separated in 1962, a year before Sylvia committed suicide. Writing poetry from early childhood, she published her first volume, *A Winter Ship* (1960), anonymously, but put her name to the second, *The Colossus* (1960). After the birth of her second child she wrote a radio play, *Three Women* (1962), set in a maternity home. Her late poetry was published posthumously in *Ariel* (1965), *Crossing the Water* (1971) and *Winter Trees* (1972). Her only novel, *The Bell Jar* (1963), was published just before her death.

Plato c.428–c.348BC
Greek philosopher
Born into an aristocratic family, he founded the Academy in Athens, which became a famous centre for philosophical, mathematical and scientific research. His works consist of about 30 philosophical dialogues and 13 *Epistles*. The early dialogues feature **Socrates** as a central figure who, in a series of questions and answers, inquires into such problems as the nature of morality, justice and courage. The *Symposium*, *Gorgias*, *Phaedo* and *Republic* are perhaps the most important of the dialogues. The central Platonic doctrine is the Theory of Forms (or Ideas) which contrasts the material things of this world with the Ideas that they reflect. Plato's work had a profound effect on later European political thought. **Aristotle** was one of his pupils.

Plutarch, *Greek* **Ploutarchos** c.46–c.120AD
Greek historian, biographer and philosopher
His surviving writings include his historical works, to which belongs *Parallel Lives,* the work by which he is best known. These are biographies of 23 Greek great politicians and soldiers paired with 23 Roman lives that offer points of similarity and comparison. The less known half of his writings – the *Morals* – are a collection of short treatises on various subjects, including *Ethics*, *Politics*, *History*, *Health*, and *Philosophy*. He occupies a unique place in literature as a recorder of ancient times, and his work is a major source for **Shakespeare**'s Roman plays.

Poe, Edgar Allan 1809–49
US poet and short-story writer
An important influence on science fiction, horror fiction and detective fiction, his short stories, such as 'The Fall of the House of Usher' (1839) and 'The Murders in the Rue Morgue' (one of the first detective stories, published 1841) show genuine originality, and his melodious poems have been admired by **W B Yeats** and others. His best-known poem is probably 'The Raven' (1845), which won him immediate fame but not fortune. In 1836 he married his 13-year-old cousin Virginia Clemm, and after her early death in 1847 he attempted suicide, dying shortly afterwards in a wretched condition in Baltimore.

Poitier, Sidney 1924–
US actor and director
His Hollywood debut was in *No Way Out* (1950), and he gave strong performances in *Cry, the Beloved Country* (1952), *The Blackboard Jungle* (1955) and *The Defiant Ones* (1958). He won an Academy Award for *Lilies of the Field* (1963). Handsome and unassuming, he portrayed noble and intelligent characters in such films as *In the Heat of the Night* (1967) and *Guess Who's Coming to Dinner* (1967). He has also directed a number of comedies and published two autobiographies.

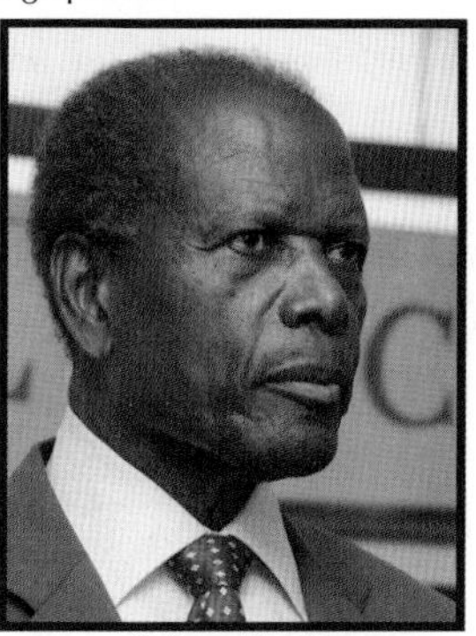
Sidney Poitier

Pollock, (Paul) Jackson 1912–56
US artist
He became the first exponent of tachism or 'action painting' in the USA, producing his first drip paintings in 1947. This technique he continued with increasing violence and often on huge canvases, eg *One*, which is 17ft (5.2km) long. Other striking works include *No. 32*, and the black and white *Echo and Blue Poles*. He was killed in a motor accident.

Polo, Marco 1254–1324
Venetian merchant, traveller and writer
He made his famous journey with his father and uncle to the court of **Kublai Khan** in 1271 arriving in 1275. The emperor took special notice of Marco, and sent him as envoy to Yunnan, northern Burma, Karakorum, Cochin-China and southern India. For three years Marco Polo served as Governor of Yang Chow. The Polos returned in 1295, bringing with them the great wealth they had accumulated. Marco later wrote an account of his travels, *Divisament dou Monde*, one of the most important sources for our knowledge of China and the East before the 19th century.

Pol Pot, *also known as* **Saloth Sar** 1925–98
Cambodian politician
He joined the anti-French resistance movement under **Ho Chi Minh**, and during the 1960s and early 1970s he led the pro-Chinese communist Khmer Rouge in guerrilla activity against the Kampuchean (Cambodian) government. In 1976 he became Prime Minister, and proceeded brutally to introduce an extreme communist regime which resulted in the loss of more than two million lives. The regime was overthrown by Vietnamese troops in January 1979, and Pol Pot took to the resistance struggle once more. In 1997 Pol Pot was arrested by an opposing faction and died whilst under house arrest.

Pompey, *originally* **Gnaeus Pompeius Magnus**, *called* **the Great** 106–48BC
Roman soldier and politician
One of the greatest generals of the Roman world in the 1st century BC, he was a serious rival to **Julius Caesar** and was looked on with much favour by the people and the Senate. He and Caesar, with the plutocrat Crassus, formed the all-powerful 'First Triumvirate'. However, after his allies turned on him, he

suffered a series of setbacks, ending in his final defeat at Pharsalus in 48BC. He then fled to Egypt, where he was murdered.

Pope, Alexander 1688–1744
English poet
At the age of three he suffered his first serious illness and at 12 he was crippled by a tubercular infection of the spine which accounted for his stunted growth (4ft 6in/1.37m). He began writing at an early age. His first successes included *An Essay on Criticism* (1711) and *The Rape of the Lock* (1712), and he went on to produce the satirical masterpieces *The Dunciad* (1728) and *An Essay on Man* (1733–4), among others. His translation of **Homer**'s the *Iliad*, completed in 1720, was an important landmark in such translation.

Porter, Cole 1891–1964
US composer
He created a series of successful musical comedies, including *Anything Goes* (1934) and *DuBarry Was a Lady* (1939), writing both lyrics and music for numerous classics of US popular song, such as 'You Do Something to Me', 'I Get a Kick Out of You', 'You're the Top' and 'Just One of Those Things'. In 1937 he was severely hurt in a riding accident, which left him in permanent pain, but he continued to compose, reaching the height of his success with *Kiss Me Kate* (1948) and *Can-Can* (1953).

Potemkin, Grigori Aleksandrovich 1739–91
Russian soldier and politician
He entered the Russian Horse Guards in 1755, and attracted the notice of **Catherine II**, the Great, by his good looks. In 1774 he became her lover, and directed Russian policy. In charge of the newly acquired lands in the south, he made an able administrator, and constructed a fleet in the Black Sea. He also gained for Russia the Crimea and the north coast of the Black Sea, and he founded Sebastopol, Nikolaev and Yekaterinoslav (Dnipropetrovsk).

Potter, (Helen) Beatrix 1866–1943
English author and illustrator of books for children
She taught herself to draw and paint, and turned to sketching pet animals dressed as human beings in order to amuse younger children. The original version of *The Tale of Peter Rabbit* was published in 1900, and it was followed by *The Tailor of Gloucester* (1902), *The Tale of Squirrel Nutkin* (1903) and many others, which have become classics of children's literature. After her marriage and relocation to the Lake District she devoted herself almost entirely to farming and the National Trust (founded in 1895). Potter wrote with great realism and without sentimentality – the animal world she describes is constantly threatened by deceit, physical harm and death.

Pound, Ezra Weston Loomis 1885–1972
US poet, translator and critic
He lived most of his life in Europe, where he was a friend and collaborator of writers such as **James Joyce** and **T S Eliot**, who regarded him as the motivating force behind 'modern' poetry. *Homage to Sextus Propertius* (1919) and *Hugh Selwyn Mauberley* (1920) are among his most important poems, and his *Cantos* appeared first in 1917, continuing in many instalments. He later became involved with fascist ideas and created resentment by anti-democracy broadcasts from his home in Italy in the early stages of World War II. In addition to poetry, he translated much from Italian, French, Chinese and Japanese.

Poussin, Nicolas 1594–1665
French painter
One of the greatest exponents of 17th-century Baroque painting, Poussin was highly successful in his lifetime. He constructed his historical pictures with great care, and as a result had great influence on the development of the 'History Picture'. His work includes biblical subjects, mythological works and, from his later years, landscape. Among the best known of these are *Cephalus and Aurora* (1630), *The Inspiration of the Poet* (1636), *The Rape of the Sabine Women* (1636–7), *Bacchanalian Festival* (1640), *The Arcadian Shepherds* (1638–9), and *Landscape with the Burial of Phocion* (1648).

Presley, Elvis Aron 1935–77
US popular singer

Elvis Presley

Presley's contribution to popular music sprang from his ability to combine white country and western with black rhythm and blues, the basic formula underpinning rock and roll. His greatest records include 'That's All Right Mama' (1954), 'Heartbreak Hotel' (1956), 'Blue Suede Shoes' (1956), 'Hound Dog' (1956), 'Love Me Tender' (1956), 'All Shook Up' (1957) and 'Jailhouse Rock' (1958), and these, and a string of films, made him the biggest-selling artist in history. Suffering in his last years from ill health caused by obesity and narcotics, he died suddenly in 1977.

Priestley, J(ohn) B(oynton) 1894–1984
English novelist, playwright and critic
His novel *The Good Companions* (1929) gained him wide popularity, and it was followed by other novels including *Angel Pavement* (1930), *Jenny Villiers* (1947) and *The Magicians* (1954). His reputation as a dramatist was established by *Dangerous Corner* (1932), *Time and the Conways* (1937), and other plays on space-time themes, as well as popular comedies and his psychological mystery, *An Inspector Calls* (1947). Priestley was also master of the essay form. *Journey Down the Rainbow* (1955), written with his wife, was a jovial indictment of US life.

Priestley, Joseph 1733–1804
English clergyman and chemist
A dissenting minister, he took up the study of chemistry, and was branded an atheist. His *History of Early Opinions Concerning Jesus Christ* (1786)

was among a number of his works to cause controversy, and his reply to **Edmund Burke**'s *Reflections on the French Revolution* led a Birmingham mob to break into his house and destroy its contents (1791). Priestley was a pioneer in the chemistry of gases, and one of the discoverers of oxygen (building on previous work by **Carl Wilhelm Scheele**).

Prokofiev, Sergei Sergeyevich 1891–1953
Russian composer
One of Russia's greatest 20th-century composers, he lived for much of his early career in the USA and France after falling foul of the Soviet authorities. His works include concertos, symphonies, operas (*The Love for Three Oranges*, *War and Peace*), ballets (*Romeo and Juliet*, *Cinderella*) film scores and a 'children's piece', *Peter and the Wolf*. After returning to the USSR in 1936, he was included among those named by the Communist Party Central Committee in 1948 as composers of music 'marked with formalist perversions' and 'alien to the Soviet people'.

Prost, Alain 1955–
French racing driver
Born in St Chamond, he won his first Grand Prix in 1981. He was world champion four times (1985, 1986, 1989, 1993) and was runner-up four times (1983, 1984, 1988, 1990). In 1987 he surpassed Jackie Stewart's record of 27 Grand Prix wins, thus becoming the most successful driver in the history of the sport until his achievments were eclipsed by those of **Michael Schumacher**. He retired in 1994.

Proust, Marcel 1871–1922
French novelist
His mother's death in 1905, when he was 34 years old, caused him to withdraw from society and shut himself up himself in a soundproof apartment, where he gave himself over entirely to observing his own inner emotional life and writing about it. The result was *Remembrance of Times Past*, a 13-volume series of autobiographical novels, in which no detail escaped his observant eye. Apart from this masterpiece, there was also posthumous publication of an early novel, *Jean Santeuil* (1952) and an extended essay, *By Way of Sainte-Beuve* (1954).

Ptolemy, *Latin* **Claudius Ptolemaeus** c.90–168AD
Egyptian astronomer and geographer
He lived and worked in Alexandria. He corrected and improved the astronomical work of his predecessors to form the Ptolemaic System, with the Earth at the centre of the Universe and heavenly bodies revolving round it; beyond this lay the sphere of the fixed stars. He also compiled geographical catalogues and maps. His Earth-centred view of the universe dominated cosmological thought until swept aside by **Copernicus** in the 16th century.

Puccini, Giacomo (Antonio Domenico Michele Secondo Maria) 1858–1924
Italian composer of operas
Manon Lescaut (1893) was his first great success, but it was eclipsed by *La Bohème* three years later. *Tosca* and *Madame Butterfly* (both 1900) have also remained popular favourites. His last opera, *Turandot*, was left unfinished at his death, and was completed by his friend Franco Alfano. He was, perhaps, the last great representative of the Italian operatic tradition.

Pulitzer, Joseph 1847–1911
US newspaper proprietor
He became a reporter in St Louis, Missouri, in 1865, and began to acquire and revitalize old newspapers, including the *New York World* (1883) which sealed his success. He endowed the Columbia University School of Journalism, and in his will established annual Pulitzer Prizes for literature, drama, music and journalism, which were first awarded in 1917.

Purcell, Henry 1659–95
English composer
The greatest English composer of the Baroque period, his output was prolific. He is credited with six operas, and of these, *Dido and Aeneas* (1689) is now regarded as the first great English opera. He also wrote much harpsichord, vocal and choral music, and sonatas for violins and continuo. Among his work in his official capacity as a royal composer was the music for the coronations of James II (**James VII and II**) and **William III**.

Pushkin, Alexander Sergeyevich 1799–1837
Russian poet and writer
Regarded as Russia's greatest poet, his first success was the romantic poem *Ruslan and Lyudmilla* (1820), which was followed by works such as *The Prisoner of the Caucasus* (1822) and his masterpiece, *Eugene Onegin* (1828), a sophisticated novel in verse. Prolific during his short life, he also wrote essays, short stories, the blank verse historical drama *Boris Godunov* (1825), and, in 1830, the four 'Little Tragedies'. Because of his liberalism he was exiled in 1820 and did not return to Moscow until after the accession of Nicholas I. He died in a duel.

Puskas, Ferenc 1927–2006
Hungarian footballer
He made his debut for Hungary in 1945 and led the celebrated Hungarian side of the 1950s. This team won the Olympic title in 1952, scored a historic victory over England in 1953 and reached the final of the 1954 World Cup, but lost to West Germany. Puskas left Hungary after the Revolution of 1956 and subsequently played for Real Madrid, winning the European Cup in 1960, among other titles.

Puyi (P'u-i), *personal name of* **Xuan Tong (Hsuan T'ung)** 1906–67
Last Emperor of China and the first Emperor of Manchuguo (Manchukuo, Manchuria)
After the revolution of 1912 in China, the young emperor was given a pension and a summer palace near Beijing (Peking). He became known as Henry P'u-i, but in 1932 he was called from private life to be dictator of the Japanese puppet state of Manchuguo and (from 1934) emperor under the name of Kang De (K'ang Te). He was imprisoned by the Russians from 1945 until 1950 and subsequently by the Chinese Communists until 1959. After that he lived as a private citizen in Beijing until his death.

Pythagoras c.580–c.500BC
Greek philosopher, mystic and mathematician
Probably born in Samos, he settled in Croton, a Greek colony in southern Italy, where he attracted followers and established a community. Pythagoras left no writings, and 'Pythagoreanism' was first a way of life rather than a philosophy, emphasizing reincarnation and bodily purification. He is associated with

mathematical discoveries involving the chief musical intervals, the theorem on right-angled triangles which bears his name, and with beliefs about the understanding and representation of the world of nature through numbers. He had a profound influence on **Plato** and on later philosophers, astronomers and mathematicians.

Rabelais, François 1483 or 1494–1553
French monk, physician and satirist
During his monastic life he learned Greek, Hebrew and Arabic, studied all the Latin and French authors whose works he could find, and took an interest in the sciences. In 1532 he became a physician in Lyons, and began the books for which he is best known: *Pantagruel* (1532) and *Gargantua* (1534), in which serious ideas are presented side by side with satirical comment and irreverent mockery. His work was read widely in Europe in the 16th and 17th centuries; it was revived in the 19th century and continues to be admired.

Rabin, Yitzhak or **Itzhak** 1922–95
Israeli soldier and statesman
He rose to become Chief of Staff in 1964, heading the armed forces during the Arab–Israeli Six-Day War of 1967. He then moved into the political arena, becoming Prime Minister from 1974 to 1977. In 1992 he was again Prime Minister of a centre-left government that favoured Palestinian self-government, and granted self-rule to the Palestinians of Gaza and Jericho. In 1994 he signed a peace treaty with Jordan, and the same year he was awarded the Nobel Peace Prize jointly with Shimon Peres and **Yasser Arafat**. Rabin was opposed by hardliners and finally assassinated by a young Israeli extremist.

Rachmaninov or **Rakhmaninov, Sergei Vasilevich** 1873–1943
Russian composer and pianist
An accomplished performer, he played throughout Europe, but after the Russian Revolution he settled in the USA. He wrote operas, orchestral works and songs, but is best known for his piano music, which includes four concertos, the first three of which achieved great popularity. His style epitomizes the lush romanticism of the later 19th century, which is still apparent in *Rhapsody on a Theme of Paganini* (1934) for piano and orchestra, a concert favourite.

Racine, Jean 1639–99
French dramatist and poet
In 1664 his first play, *The Fatal Legacy*, was acted by **Molière**'s company at the Palais Royal. During the following ten years Racine produced his greatest works – *Andromache* (1667), *The Litigants* (1668), *Britannicus* (1669), *Mithridates* (1673), *Achilles; or, Iphigenia in Aulis* (1675), *Phaedre and Hippolytys* (1677), and others. Racine was greatly influenced by Greek drama and adopted its principles as well as taking its subjects (often women). He is regarded, especially in France, as one of the greatest masters of tragic pathos.

Raleigh or **Ralegh, Sir Walter** 1552–1618
English courtier, navigator and poet
He became a favourite of Queen **Elizabeth I** and sent an expedition to America, founding a settlement at Roanoke Island, North Carolina (1585–6). He later introduced tobacco and potatoes into Britain. He was imprisoned in the Tower of London for a secret affair with one of the queen's maids of honour, but after his release in 1595 he explored the coasts of Trinidad, and sailed up the Orinoco. Arrested in 1603 on suspicion of treason, in the Tower he wrote many works, including his *History of the World* (1614). In 1616 he was released to make an expedition to the Orinoco in search of a goldmine, but the mission was a failure, and on his return he was beheaded.

Rambert, Dame Marie, *stage name of* **Cyvia Rambam** 1888–1982
Polish-born British ballet dancer and teacher
A major influence on the development of modern dance, in 1913 she worked in Paris on **Igor Stravinsky**'s *Rite of Spring* with Sergei Diaghilev's Ballets Russes. She moved to London and began to dance and teach, forming a company, the Ballet Club. This became Ballet Rambert in 1935, which has since grown to become one of Great Britain's major touring contemporary dance companies, changing its name again, in 1987, to the Rambert Dance Company.

Rameses II, *known as* **Rameses the Great**, *also spelt* **Ramesses** or **Ramses** 1304–1237BC
Egyptian pharaoh
His reign (c.1292–37BC) marked the last zenith of Egyptian imperial power and is the most renowned in Egyptian history for temple building: he completed the mortuary temple of his father Seti I at Luxor and the hall of the Karnak temple, and built the rock temples of Abu Simbel, dedicating the smaller one to his queen, Nefertari. He is sometimes identified as the Old Testament Pharaoh of the oppression of Jews. His mummy was found at Deir-el-Bahari in 1881.

Raphael, *properly* **Raffaello Santi** or **Sanzio** 1483–1520
Italian painter
One of the greatest artists of the Renaissance, his early work was in Siena and Florence, where he painted the first of his many Madonnas. In 1508 he went to Rome, where he produced the fresco series *The School of Athens*, the *Madonna di Foligno*, the *Isaiah of St Agostino* and many other works. He became architect of St Peter's in 1514; returning to Florence and Bologna he created the *Sistine Madonna*, the *Spasimo*, the *Holy Family* and *St Michael* and numerous other pieces. His fresh colour and perfect rendering of features and expression were a major influence on later artists.

Rasputin, Grigori Efimovich 1871–1916
Russian peasant and self-styled religious 'elder'
He arrived in St Petersburg at a time when mystical religion was fashionable, and obtained an introduction to the royal household. There he quickly gained the confidence of Tsar **Nicholas II** and the Empress Alexandra by his apparent ability to control through hypnosis the bleeding of their haemophiliac son, who was heir to the throne. However, Rasputin's debauchery, and his attempts to appoint his own favourites to positions of power, soon made him powerful enemies, and he was murdered by a group of aristocrats.

Ravel, Maurice 1875–1937
French composer
His first orchestral piece, the overture *Schéhérazade*, had a hostile reception on its first performance in 1899, but he won recognition in the same year with

the *Pavane for a Dead Princess*. The choreographic poem *La Valse*, epitomizing the spirit of Vienna, was staged in 1920, and the opera *The Child and His Spells* in 1925. To this late period also belongs the well-known *Boléro* (1928), originally intended as a miniature ballet. His music is characteristically vivid and dynamic.

Ray, Man, *pseudonym of* **Emanuel Rabinovitch** 1890–1976
US painter, sculptor, photographer and film-maker
A major figure in the development of modernism, he helped to establish the New York Dadaist movement. He experimented with new techniques in painting and photography, moving to Paris, where made surrealist films like *Anemic Cinema* (1924). During the 1930s he published and exhibited many photographs and 'rayographs' (photographic images made without a camera). He returned to the USA in 1940, and taught photography in Los Angeles.

Reagan, Ronald Wilson 1911–2004
40th President of the USA, and former film actor

Ronald Reagan

He starred in 50 films and became interested in politics when serving as president of the Screen Actors' Guild. In 1966 he was elected Governor of California, and became president in 1981. He survived an attempted assassination in 1981 and was re-elected in 1984, serving until 1989. The chief events of his presidency were his summit meetings with Soviet leader **Mikhail Gorbachev**, which led to the scrapping of intermediate nuclear forces, the US invasion of Grenada in 1983 and the 'Iran-Contra Affair' of 1986–7, when members of his administration were involved in selling arms to Iran in order to fund the right-wing Contras of Nicaragua. He had a unique, populist rapport with mainstream America.

Redford, (Charles) Robert 1937–
US film actor and director
Tall, blond and athletic, his good looks and image of integrity made him popular in films including *Butch Cassidy and the Sundance Kid* (1969), *The Sting* (1973) and *Indecent Proposal* (1993). In 1976 he produced and starred in *All The President's Men* and in 1998 directed and starred in *The Horse Whisperer*. He has also directed *Ordinary People* (1980), for which he won an Academy Award, *A River Runs Through It* (1993), *Quiz Show* (1994) and other films.

Redgrave, Sir Steve (Steven Geoffrey) 1962–
English rower
He won his first Olympic gold at Los Angeles in 1984, the beginning of a remarkable Olympic career in which he won five gold medals at successive Games, an unprecedented achievement in world rowing. Nine times world champion, he also won a record three gold medals in the 1986 Commonwealth Games. Redgrave and Matthew Pinsent were world coxless pairs champions four times, Olympic coxless pairs champions twice and won Olympic gold in the coxless pairs in 2000.

Rembrandt, *properly* **Rembrandt Harmensz van Rijn** 1606–69
Dutch painter
The greatest northern European artist of his age, his works include group portraits such as *The Anatomy Lesson of Doctor Tulp* (1632) and *The Night Watch* (1642), biblical subjects such as *Belshazzar's Feast* (c.1636), *Christ and the Woman taken in Adultery* (1644) and *The Return of the Prodigal Son* (c.1669) and a superb series of self-portraits, the first psychological studies in the history of art. His output was enormous: over 600 paintings (including 60 self-portraits), about 300 etchings, and about 2,000 drawings.

Renoir, Pierre-Auguste 1841–1919
French Impressionist artist
In 1882 he exhibited with the Impressionists his important, controversial picture of sunlight filtering through leaves, the *Moulin de la Galette*, dating from 1876. During the next few years (1884–7) he painted a series of *Bathers* in a more cold and classical style. He then returned to hot reds, orange and gold to portray nudes in sunlight, a style which he continued to develop until his death. His other works include *The Umbrellas* (c.1883) and *The Judgement of Paris* (c.1914).

Reynolds, Sir Joshua 1723–92
English portrait painter
After studying in Rome he established himself in London as a fashionable portrait painter. In 1764 he founded the Literary Club of which Dr **Johnson**, **Oliver Goldsmith**, **James Boswell** and **Richard Sheridan** were members. On the establishment of the Royal Academy of Arts (1768) he was elected its first president. In 1784 he became painter to the king, and finished his painting of actress Sarah Siddons as the *Tragic Muse*, a work which exists in several versions. Other works include *Commodore Keppel* (1753) and *Dr Samuel Johnson* (c.1756).

Rhodes, Cecil John 1853–1902
South African statesman
He made a fortune at the Kimberley diamond diggings, where he formed the De Beers Consolidated Mines Company in 1888. Turning to colonial administration, he secured Bechuanaland (later Botswana) as a British protectorate (1884) and later (1889) gained control of the territory later known as Rhodesia. In 1890 he became Prime Minister of Cape Colony, but was forced to resign in the aftermath of the incident known as the Jameson Raid. He took an active part in the Second Boer War (1899–1902). Rhodes founded scholarships at Oxford for Americans, Germans and members of the British Empire (later Commonwealth).

Richard I, *known as* **Cœur de Lion ('the Lion Heart')** 1157–99
King of England
The third son of **Henry II** and Eleanor of Aquitaine, he became King of England in 1189. He spent nearly all of his reign taking part in the crusades. Richard's exploits during the Third Crusade, including his two advances on Jerusalem (which he failed to regain from **Saladin**), his capture of the fortresses in southern Palestine, and his relief of Joppa (now Jaffa, Israel), excited the admiration of Christendom. He suffered a short spell of imprisonment in 1193 at the hands of Holy Roman Emperor Henry VI before being ransomed. He spent the rest of his life campaigning against Philip II of France, and was killed while besieging the castle of Chalus.

Richard II 1367–1400
King of England
The son of Edward the Black Prince, he succeeded his grandfather, **Edward III**, in 1377, at the age of 10, although for a time his uncle John of Gaunt exercised effective control. Richard's reign was characterized by a struggle between his own desire to act independently, and the barons' concern to check his power. The main events of his reign were the Peasants' Revolt of 1381 and continuing war with Scotland. In 1399, John of Gaunt's son Henry Bolingbroke usurped power and was crowned as **Henry IV**. Richard was imprisoned in Pontefract Castle, and died there, probably murdered, early in 1400.

Richard, Sir Cliff, *real name* **Harry Rodger Webb** 1940–
English pop singer
He formed his own band, The Shadows (originally called The Drifters), in 1958. Following the success of 'Living Doll' (1959), The Shadows were hailed as Great Britain's answer to US rock. He made a series of family musical films during the 1960s, including *Expresso Bongo* (1960), *The Young Ones* (1961) and *Summer Holiday* (1962). He was knighted in 1995, and in 1996 he took to the stage, playing the eponymous hero in *Heathcliff*, a musical based upon **Emily Brontë**'s *Wuthering Heights*. In an unusually long pop career, he has had hit singles in every decade from the 1950s to the 2000s.

Richards, Sir Viv (Isaac Vivian Alexander) 1952–
Antiguan cricketer
He has played in the UK for Somerset (1974–86) and Glamorgan (1990–3), and set a world record in 1976 with 1,710 Test runs in the calendar year. His timing, power and range enabled him to score Test cricket's fastest century (off 56 balls) against England in 1986. He was official captain of the West Indies from 1985 to 1991 and holds the West Indies record for the most caps.

Richardson, Samuel 1689–1761
English novelist
His first novel, *Pamela* (1740), 'a series of familiar letters ... published in order to cultivate the Principles of Virtue and Religion', was a huge success, as was his second novel, *Clarissa, Or the History of a Young Lady* (1748). His third novel, *Sir Charles Grandison* (1754), aimed to portray the perfect gentleman, turns on the question of divided love. His work influenced writers such as **Jean Jacques Rousseau**.

Richelieu, Armand Jean Duplessis, Duc de, *known as* **Cardinal Richelieu** 1585–1642
French prelate and statesman
He was made cardinal in 1622. In 1624 he rose to be Minister of State to Louis XIII, and from 1629 he was Chief Minister and effective ruler of France. He directed both France's foreign and its domestic policy, fighting wars against Spain and Germany and for control of Savoy, and seeking alliance with Britain. One of his principal aims was to destroy the political power of the protestant Huguenots. At home the French nobles continually plotted his downfall, but his safety lay in the king's helplessness without him. At the end of his career he had achieved for France a dominating position in Europe. Among his literary works are his *Memoires*.

Richter, Charles Francis 1900–85
US seismologist
With Beno Gutenberg he devised the Richter scale of earthquake strength (1927–35). He played a key role in establishing the southern California seismic array, linked seismographs placed together to be sensitive to the occurrence of earthquakes. He published *Seismicity of the Earth* (1954, with Gutenberg) and *Elementary Seismology* (1958).

Rimbaud, (Jean Nicolas) Arthur 1854–91
French poet
He had written all his major works by the age of 19: the poetry collection *The Drunken Boat* (1871), the prose and verse poems *Les Illuminations* (published later in 1886) and the prose volume *A Season in Hell* (1873). One of his most significant friendships was with the poet Paul Verlaine, who shot and wounded Rimbaud in a drunken quarrel in 1873. Verlaine published *Les Illuminations* to great acclaim as by the 'late Arthur Rimbaud', but Rimbaud was indifferent to its success.

Robert the Bruce See **Bruce, Robert**

Robespierre, Maximilien Marie Isidore de 1758–94
French Revolutionary politician
A lawyer by training, he was elected for Paris to France's assembly, the National Convention, and emerged as leader of a group of extremist assembly members strenuously opposed to the Girondins (moderate politicians), whom he helped to destroy. Robespierre and his extreme group, the Jacobins, supported **Louis XVI**'s execution, which took place on 21 January 1793. His growing autocracy finally spurred his enemies into action, and on 27 July 1794 he was denounced in the Convention and with 21 of his supporters guillotined without trial.

Robinson, Sugar Ray, *originally* **Walker Smith** 1921–89
US boxer
He gained the welterweight title in 1946 and won the middleweight championship five times between 1951 (when he knocked out Jake La Motta) and 1958 (when he defeated Carmen Basilio). He fought 202 professional bouts in his career and lost only 19, most of them when he was over 40.

Robinson, William 1838–1935
Irish gardener and writer
From 1861 he worked at the Royal Botanic Society's gardens at Regent's Park, London. He published 18

books, including *Alpine Flowers for English Gardens* (1870) and *The English Flower Garden* (1883), and founded and edited three horticultural journals: *The Garden* (1872), *Gardening Illustrated* (1879) and *Flora and Sylva* (1903).

Rob Roy, *Gaelic for* **Red Robert**, *properly* **Robert MacGregor** 1671–1734
Scottish outlaw
As a young man he lived quietly grazing sheep, but was forced to raise a private army to protect himself from the activities of outlaws. He then turned to plundering, and became an outlaw in 1712. Legends about him soon developed; they told of his hair's-breadth escapes and of his generosity to the poor. He was arrested in 1727 and sentenced to transportation, but was pardoned. His life was romanticized in Sir **Walter Scott**'s *Rob Roy* (1818).

Rockefeller, John D(avison) 1839–1937
US oil magnate and philanthropist
In 1870 he co-founded the Standard Oil Company, and this eventually gave him control of the US oil trade. He gave over $500 million in support of medical research and to universities and Baptist churches, and in 1913 he established the Rockefeller Foundation. His grandson Nelson Aldrich Rockefeller was Vice-President (1974–7) under Gerald Ford.

Roddick, Anita Lucia 1942–
English businesswoman
In 1976 she founded the Body Shop with her husband Thomas Gordon Roddick, to sell cosmetics made from natural materials. The company went on to establish many stores in the UK and overseas. She lectures on environmental issues and conducts campaigns with Friends of the Earth, and in 1989 she won the UN environmental award. In 1991, she published her autobiography *Body and Soul*.

Anita Roddick

Rodin, (François) Auguste (René) 1840–1917
French sculptor
One of the pioneers of modern sculpture, in 1880 he was commissioned by the French government to produce *The Gate of Hell* for the Musée des Arts Décoratifs, a museum in Paris, and during the next 30 years he was primarily engaged on the 186 figures for these bronze doors. They were never completed, but many of his best-known works were originally conceived as part of the design of the doors, among them *The Kiss* (1898) and *The Thinker* (1904). Other well-known works include *The Burghers of Calais* (1886–95), a nude **Victor Hugo** (1897) and **Honoré de Balzac** in a dressing gown (1898).

Rodgers, Richard 1902–79
US composer
He collaborated with the lyricist Lorenz Hart in a number of musicals including *Babes in Arms* (1937, whose songs included 'The Lady is a Tramp') and *Pal Joey* (1940, which included 'Bewitched, Bothered and Bewildered'). He also worked on a series of hit musicals with **Oscar Hammerstein II**, notably *Oklahoma!* (1943, Pulitzer Prize), *Carousel* (1945), *South Pacific* (1949, Pulitzer Prize), *The King and I* (1951), *The Flower Drum Song* (1958) and *The Sound of Music* (1959).

Röntgen or **Roentgen, Wilhelm Konrad von** 1845–1923
German physicist
At Würzburg in 1895 he discovered the electromagnetic rays which he called X-rays (known now also as Röntgen rays) because of their unknown properties. For his work on them he was awarded the first Nobel Prize for physics in 1901. He also made important contributions to the study of crystals, the specific heat of gases and magnetism.

Roosevelt, Franklin D(elano), *also called* **FDR** 1882–1945
32nd President of the USA
He was a distant cousin of **Theodore Roosevelt**. Stricken by polio and paralysed (1921–3), he was nonetheless elected Governor of New York (1928–32), and President (1932–45). Faced with the Great Depression of 1933, he launched his innovative and successful New Deal programme, an he fostered a new spirit of hope through his optimistic radio 'fireside chats'. On the outbreak of World War II he supported the Allies, and eventually brought the country fully into the conflict after Japan's attack on Pearl Harbor in December 1941. At the end of the war he held meetings with **Churchill** and **Stalin** at Tehran (1943) and Yalta (1945).

Roosevelt, Theodore, *nicknamed* **Teddy** 1858–1919
26th President of the USA
He was Assistant Secretary of the Navy when in 1898 he raised and commanded the volunteer cavalry known as the 'Roughriders' in the Spanish-American War. During his presidency (1901–9) he strengthened the navy, initiated the construction of the Panama Canal, and introduced a 'Square Deal' policy for enforcing anti-trust laws. He received the Nobel Peace Prize in 1906 for his part in the negotiations which ended the Russo-Japanese War. He wrote on US ideals, ranching, hunting and zoology, and was an immensely popular president. He was also a fan of big-game hunting, and the teddy bear is named after him.

Rossetti, Christina Georgina 1830–94
English poet
The sister of **Dante Gabriel Rossetti**, her earliest lyrics were published in the first issue of *The Germ* (1850) under the pseudonym Ellen Alleyne. *Goblin Market* (1862) was her best-known collection. She was a devout Anglican, and her later works include *The Prince's Progress* (1866), *A Pageant and Other Poems* (1881), *Time Flies: A Reading Diary* (1885) and *The Face of the Deep: A Devotional Commentary on the Apocalypse* (1892).

PEOPLE

Rossetti, Dante Gabriel, *properly* **Gabriel Charles Dante Rossetti** 1828–82
English poet, painter and translator
He was the brother of **Christina Rossetti**, and a founder of the Pre-Raphaelite Brotherhood, a group who wanted to return to the principles of Flemish art, away from the style of **Raphael**. Throughout the 1840s he developed his poetry and painting, completing on canvas *The Girlhood of Mary Virgin* (1849) and *Ecce Ancilla Domini* (1850). In 1861 he published *The Early Italian Poets*, which consisted of translations from 60 poets, such as **Dante**. *Ballads and Sonnets* with the sonnet sequence 'The House of Life' and 'The King's Tragedy' appeared in 1881.

Rossini, Gioacchino Antonio 1792–1868
Italian operatic composer
Rossini helped form the early 19th-century Italian operatic style. Many of his works are still much performed, among them *The Barber of Seville* (1816), *Cinderella* (1817) and *The Thieving Magpie* (1817). In 1829 he produced what is arguably his greatest work, *William Tell*. Many of his lively and witty overtures continued to be famous after the operas they were attached to had been forgotten.

Rousseau, Jean Jacques 1712–78
French political philosopher, educationist and author
His most influential works are his *Social Contract* (1764), which, with its slogan 'Liberty, Equality, Fraternity', became the bible of the French Revolution, and his novel *Émile* (1762), which set out his theories of education. This latter work so outraged the political and religious establishment that he had to escape to Switzerland. He moved to England in 1766 where he began writing his *Confessions*, a remarkably frank work published posthumously (1782–9). Other works include his *Discourse on the Origin and Foundations of Inequality Among Men* (1754), in which he argued that man's perfect nature was corrupted by society.

Roux, (Pierre Paul) Émile 1853–1933
French bacteriologist
He became assistant to **Louis Pasteur**, and in 1904 succeeded him as director of the Pasteur Institute. With Pasteur he tested the anthrax vaccine, and contributed much of the early work on the rabies vaccine. He also showed that the symptoms of diphtheria are caused by a lethal toxin produced by the diphtheria bacillus, and successfully tested on patients large quantities of blood serum containing the antitoxin from horses.

Rowntree, Joseph 1836–1925
English Quaker industrialist and reformer
He was the son of Joseph Rowntree, a Quaker grocer. With his brother, Henry Isaac, he became a partner in a cocoa factory in York in 1869, and built up welfare organizations for his employees. He was succeeded as chairman by his son Seebohm Rowntree.

Rubens, Peter Paul 1577–1640
Flemish painter
He was highly successful in his lifetime, and he worked for monarchs such as Philip IV of Spain and Marie de Médicis, Queen of France, for whom he painted 21 large subjects on her life and regency. He also worked actively as a diplomat throughout Europe, in 1629 being appointed envoy to **Charles I** of Great Britain. His triptych *Descent from the Cross* (1611–14) in Antwerp Cathedral is usually regarded as his masterpiece, but he produced a huge number of other works, including landscapes and religious or mythological scenes.

Ruskin, John 1819–1900
English author and art critic
As a young man he met **J M W Turner** and championed his painting in *Modern Painters* (1843–60). Along with *The Seven Lamps of Architecture* (1848) and *The Stones of Venice* (1851–3), this book established him as the major art and social critic of the day. In 1869 he became the first Slade Professor of Fine Art at Oxford. He founded the St George's Guild, a non-profit-making shop in Paddington Street in which members gave a tithe of their fortunes, the John Ruskin School at Camberwell, and the Whitelands College at Chelsea.

Russell, Bertrand Arthur William Russell, 3rd Earl 1872–1970
English philosopher, mathematician and writer
A controversial public figure throughout his long and active life, Russell made important contributions in many areas, including mathematics and logic (in works such as the monumental *Principia Mathematica* of 1910–13), philosophy (in such books as *The Analysis of Mind* of 1921 and the bestselling *History of Western Philosophy* of 1945), and social, moral and religious questions (some of his more celebrated essays were collected in *Why I am not a Christian* in 1957). He was actively involved in politics, and was imprisoned for pacifism in World War I and for his anti-nuclear campaigning in 1961. He was awarded the Nobel Prize for literature in 1950.

Ruth, Babe, *properly* **George Herman Ruth** 1895–1948
US baseball player
He became famous for his powerful hitting with the New York Yankees (1920–34). In 1920 he scored a then-record of 54 home runs, and his 1927 season record of 60 home runs stood until 1961. In all he played in ten World Series, and hit 714 home runs, a record that stood for 30 years until it was surpassed by Hank Aaron in 1974. He ended his career as coach for the Brooklyn Dodgers (1938). He is considered to be one of the greatest players in the history of the game.

Rutherford (of Nelson), Ernest Rutherford, 1st Baron 1871–1937
New Zealand physicist
Known as the 'Father of nuclear physics', he made many basic discoveries and inventions, formulating the theory of atomic disintegration (1898), establishing the nature of alpha particles (1907), and predicting the existence of the neutron (1920). His work essentially led to our current picture of the atom with the mass is concentrated in the nucleus, surrounded by orbiting electrons. He was awarded the Nobel prize for chemistry in 1908. His many works include *Radioactive Transformations* (1906) and *The Newer Alchemy* (1937).

Sabin, Albert Bruce 1906–93
US microbiologist
After working on developing vaccines against dengue fever and Japanese B encephalitis, he became inter-

ested in the polio vaccine and attempted to develop a live vaccine (as opposed to **Jonas Salk**'s killed vaccine). In 1959, as the result of 4.5 million vaccinations, his vaccine was found to be completely safe, and presented a number of advantages over that of Salk.

Sadat, (Muḥammad) Anwar el- 1918–81
Egyptian soldier and politician
In 1952 he was one of the group of officers who carried out the coup deposing King **Farouk I**. He became President of the United Arab Republic (as Egypt was then called) in 1970, and was military Governor-General in the Arab–Israeli war that broke out in 1973. From 1974 he sought diplomatic settlement of the conflict, and was awarded the Nobel Peace Prize after signing the Camp David Accords with **Menachem Begin**. In 1981 he was assassinated by Muslim extremists.

Saladin, *properly* **Salah al-Din al-Ayyubi** 1138–93
Sultan of Egypt and Syria, and founder of a dynasty
In 1171 he made himself sovereign of Egypt, and later took control of Syria and Mesopotamia, and received the homage of the Seljuk princes of Asia Minor. In 1187 he defeated King Guy of Jerusalem and a united Christian army at Hattin near Tiberias, and then captured Jerusalem and almost every fortified place on the Syrian coast. This provoked the Third Crusade. In 1191, **Richard I** defeated Saladin at Arsuf (1191) and obtained a three years' treaty. Saladin died in Damascus. His administration left a legacy of citadels, roads and canals.

Salinger, J(erome) D(avid) 1919–
US novelist and short-story writer
The Catcher in the Rye (1951), his first novel, made him famous, especially among the young. Written in a slick and slangy first-person narrative, disrespectful to adults and authority, it provoked a hostile response from some critics. It was succeeded by works such as *Franny and Zooey* (1961), *Raise High the Roof Beam,* and *Carpenters, Seymour: an Introduction* (both 1963). Notoriously reclusive, publication of a later book, *Hapworth 16, 1924* was postponed in 2000, and apparently cancelled by the author.

Salk, Jonas Edward 1914–95
US virologist
In 1954 he became known worldwide for his work on the 'Salk vaccine' against poliomyelitis, and by the end of 1955 over 7 million doses had been administered. Later the vaccine was superseded by the **Sabin** vaccine, which used a live attenuated strain and could be given orally instead of by injection, but in 1996 the US government advisory committee on immunization recommended reinstating the Salk vaccine to prevent the handful of polio cases contracted each year from the Sabin vaccine itself.

Sampras, Pete 1971–
US tennis player
Five times winner of the US Open (1990, 1993, 1995–6, 2002) and seven times winner of Wimbledon (1993–5, 1997–2000), with 14 Grand Slam Championships in all, he is one of the game's most successful players. He is especially known for his powerful serves.

Sand, George, *pseudonym of* **Amandine Aurore Lucie Dupin, Baronne Dudevant** 1804–76
French novelist
She wrote prolifically in a number of styles: among her best-known work is *Mauprat* (1837), *The Haunted Marsh* (1846), *Francis the Waif,* (1847–8), *Little Fadette* (1849) and *Mademoiselle la Quintinie* (1863). She scandalized bourgeois society for many years with her unconventional ways and her love affairs, and her lovers included **Chopin**. She also wrote the autobiographical *The Story of My Life* (1855) and *He and She* (1859).

Sanger, Frederick 1918–
English biochemist

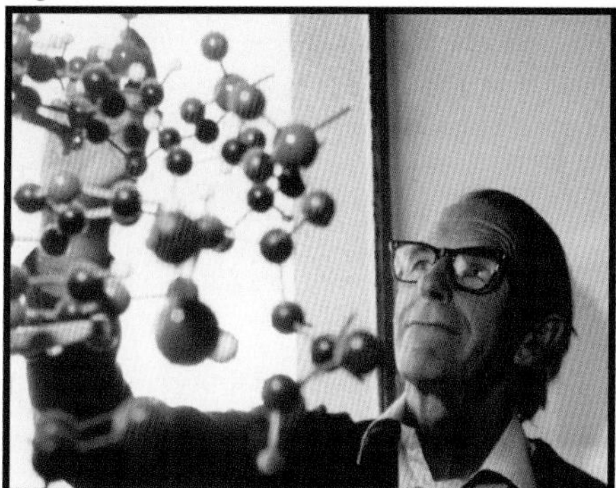

Frederick Sanger

During the 1940s he devised methods of deducing the sequence of amino acids in the hormone insulin. For this he was awarded the Nobel Prize for chemistry in 1958. He then turned to the structure of nucleic acids, working on RNA and DNA, and this work led to the full base sequence of the Epstein–Barr virus by 1984. For this work Sanger shared the 1980 Nobel Prize for chemistry, thereby becoming the first scientist to win two Nobel Prizes in this field.

Śankara c.700–750
Hindu philosopher and theologian
He was the most famous exponent of *Advaita* (the *Vedanta* school of Hindu philosophy), and is the source of the main currents of modern Hindu thought. His thesis was that Brahma (the creator god) alone has true existence, and that the goal of the self is to become one with the Divine. This view was strongly opposed by his successors in the *Bhakti* tradition.

Sargent, John Singer 1856–1925
US painter
Born in Florence, Italy, the son of a US physician, most of his work was executed in England from 1885, where he became the most fashionable and elegant portrait painter of his age. To this period belongs his well-known *Carnation Lily, Lily, Rose* (1885–6). Later work with a Spanish influence includes *Carmencita.* He also painted landscapes, especially in later life, and often in watercolour. He was an official war artist in World War I.

Sarto, Andrea del, *properly* **d'Agnolo** 1486–1531
Italian painter
Many of his most celebrated pictures, including his frescoes for the Church of the Annunciation (1509–14) and his *Madonna of the Harpies* (1517), are in Florence. He was a rapid worker and accurate

draughtsman, displaying a refined feeling for harmonies of colour.

Sartre, Jean-Paul 1905–80
French existentialist philosopher, dramatist and novelist
He taught philosophy at Le Havre, Paris and Berlin (1934–5) and during World War II became a member of the Resistance in Paris. In 1945 he emerged as the most prominent member of the left-wing life of Paris. In 1946, with **Simone de Beauvoir**, he founded and edited the avant-garde monthly *Modern Times*, and then expressed his existentialist doctrines in novels such as *Nausea* (1938), philosophical studies such as *Being and Nothingness* (1943), and plays such as *In Camera* (1944; also known as *No Exit* and *No Way Out*). In 1964 he was awarded the Nobel Prize for literature, but declined it.

Sassoon, Siegfried Louvain 1886–1967
English poet and novelist
He suffered experiences in World War I that made him detest war, a feeling that found fierce expression in *The Old Huntsman* (1917), *Counter-Attack* (1918) and *Satirical Poems* (1926). A semi-fictitious autobiography, *The Complete Memoirs of George Sherston* (1937), had as its first part *Memoirs of a Fox-Hunting Man* (1928), and continued in *Memoirs of an Infantry Officer* (1930) and *Sherston's Progress* (1936). There were several later autobiographical volumes. His later poems are predominantly spiritual, and he became a Roman Catholic in 1957.

Scheele, Carl Wilhelm 1742–86
Swedish chemist
In the 1760s he began to investigate air and fire, and soon came to doubt the received view that substances contain a vital essence which they lose when they burn. He passed on information about his experiments to **Antoine Lavoisier**, who subsequently discovered the true nature of combustion and named the new flammable gas 'oxigine'. Scheele subsequently discovered a great many other substances, including chlorine, copper arsenide (known as 'Scheele's green'), hydrogen sulphide and molybdenum. His investigations were fundamental to the development of organic chemistry.

Schiller, (Johann Christoph) Friedrich (von) 1759–1805
German dramatist, poet and historian
In an energetic career he produced works in many different genres. His first play, *The Robbers* (1781),was an instant success, and was followed by plays such as *Don Carlos* (1787) and the dramatic trilogy *Wallenstein* (1796–9), considered the greatest historical drama in the German language. His poetry includes *Ode to Joy* (c.1788), later set to music by **Beethoven**, and the famous *Song of the Bell* (completed in 1799). He also wrote short stories, journalism, works of history and criticism, and a collection of *Epigrams* (1797) against philistinism and mediocrity in the arts.

Schoenberg, Arnold Franz Walter 1874–1951
Austrian-born composer, conductor and teacher
His search for a new and personal musical style began to show in such works as the first Chamber Symphony (1907) and the second String Quartet (1908), which caused an uproar at their first Vienna performances through their use of dissonance. This developed into the discipline known as the 'twelve-note method', or serialism; its first use was in the Piano Suite Op 25 (1921–3), and it was later adopted by many other composers. Schoenberg was also a talented painter.

Schrödinger, Erwin 1887–1961
Austrian physicist
He originated the science of wave mechanics with his celebrated mathematical equation that describes the wave-like behaviour of subatomic particles. This equation was fundamental to the development of quantum mechanics, and for their work in this area Schrödinger and Paul Dirac shared the 1933 Nobel Prize for physics.

Schubert, Franz Peter 1797–1828
Austrian composer
During a short life lived mostly in poverty, Schubert composed a great number of works of great originality. His contribution to the tradition of German songs is perhaps his most important and influential achievement. His best-known works include the 'Trout' quintet for piano and strings, the Wanderer Fantasy for piano, the *Winter Journey* song cycle, the *moments musicaux* for piano, and several symphonies. His music, even when it is overtly happy, is affected by a underlying sadness.

Schumacher, Michael 1969–
German racing driver
He made a remarkable debut in the 1991 Belgium Grand Prix when he unexpectedly qualified in seventh place, and he joined the Benetton team two weeks later. He won the Formula 1 world championship seven times, in 1994, 1995, 2000, 2001, 2002, 2003 and 2004. In 1996 he signed a $26 million contract with Ferrari. He announced his retirement in 2006 after recording a record 91 Grand Prix wins.

Schumann, Robert Alexander 1810–56
German composer
Schumann was primarily a composer for the piano, for which he produced works of intense poetry and romanticism. Notable among these are the *Abegg Theme and Variations, Papillons, Carnaval, Symphonic Studies, Scenes from Childhood, Kreisleriana, Forest Scenes* and *Album Leaves*. He also wrote many songs and song cycles, following on from Schubert. With the encouragement of his wife Clara he also composed symphonies, concertos and other works. Always mentally unstable, after a suicide attempt he died in an asylum.

Schuschnigg, Kurt von 1897–1977
Austrian statesman
He was elected a Christian Socialist deputy in 1927 and was appointed Minister of Justice (1932) and Minister of Education (1933). After the murder of **Engelbert Dollfuss** in 1934, he succeeded as Chancellor until March 1938, when **Hitler** annexed Austria. Imprisoned by the Nazis, he was liberated by US troops in 1945.

Scott, Robert Falcon 1868–1912
English explorer
In the *Discovery* he commanded the National Antarctic expedition (1901–4) which explored the Ross Sea area, and discovered King Edward VII Land. In 1910, he embarked on a second expedition with the *Terra Nova*, and with a sledge party reached the South Pole on 17 January 1912, only to discover that

the Norwegian expedition under **Roald Amundsen** had beaten them by a month. Delayed by blizzards and sickness, every member of the team eventually perished.

Scott, Sir George Gilbert 1811–78
English architect
He became the leading architect in the Gothic revival, and oversaw the building or restoration of many public buildings. Examples of his work are the Martyrs Memorial at Oxford (1841), the Albert Memorial (1862–3), St Pancras station and hotel in London (1865), Glasgow University (1865) and the chapels of Exeter and St John's Colleges, Oxford.

Scott, Sir Walter 1771–1832
Scottish novelist and poet
His first major work was *The Minstrelsy of the Scottish Border* (volume 1 and 2, 1802; volume 3, 1803), a collection of folk ballads. The *Lay of the Last Minstrel* (1805) grew out of this study, and made him the most popular author of the day. He followed it with a stream of best-selling novels including *Waverley* (1814), *The Bride of Lammermoor* (1819), *Ivanhoe* (1820), *Old Mortality* (1816), *Rob Roy* (1817), *The Heart of Midlothian* (1818), *The Abbot* (1820) and *The Fair Maid of Perth* (1828). His prolific output also included epic poetry such as *Marmion* (1808) and a weighty *Life of Napoleon* (9 volumes, 1827).

Seacole, Mary Jane *née* **Grant** 1805–81
British nurse
She was born in Jamaica, but travelled to London to volunteer as a nurse in the Crimean War. When she was rejected for **Florence Nightingale**'s medical team, possibly because of she was of mixed race, she travelled to the Crimea independently, and there she was lauded for her skills and courage in treating casualties on the field of battle. Always a keen traveller, she wrote about her experiences in her autobiography, *The Wonderful Adventures of Mrs Seacole in Many Lands* (1857).

Segal, George 1924–2000
US sculptor
Beginning as a painter, he turned to sculpture in the later 1950s and is best known for his plaster figures, including *Girl in a Doorway* (1969). Cast from life and usually unpainted, they exist as ghostly presences within the realistic environments he assembled for them. Other works include *The Bowery* (1970) and *The Curtain* (1974).

Selim I, the Grim 1467–1520
Ottoman Sultan of Turkey
In 1512 he dethroned his father, Bayezit II, and caused him, his own brothers, and nephews to be put to death. He declared war against Persia in 1514, and took Diyarbakir and Kurdistan. He later conquered Egypt, Syria and the Hejaz and won control of the holy cities of Mecca and Medina. He introduced new codes of criminal law, expanded trade, refined the recruitment of janissaries (prisoners recruited as soldiers), completed the transfer of government from Edirne to Istanbul, and built a powerful new fleet. He was succeeded by his son, **Süleyman the Magnificent**.

Sellers, Peter 1925–80
English actor and comedian
After a spell as a stand-up comic and impressionist he moved into radio. His meeting with comedian Spike Milligan inspired the *Goon Show*. He starred in a run of successful British comedy films in the 1950s and 60s, including *The Ladykillers* (1955) and *I'm All Right Jack* (1959), and two films with producer and director Stanley Kubrick established his international reputation: *Lolita* (1962) and *Dr Strangelove* (1963). He is perhaps best remembered as the incompetent French detective Inspector Clouseau in a series of films that began with *The Pink Panther* in 1963. He received an Academy Award nomination for *Being There* (1979).

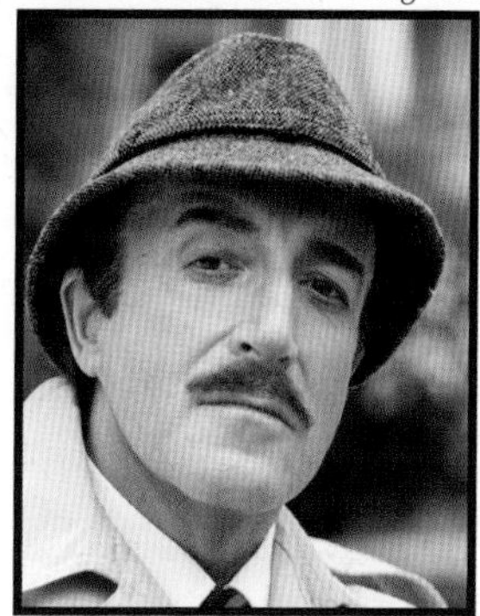

Peter Sellers as Inspector Clouseau

Seneca, Lucius Annaeus, *called* **Seneca the Younger** c.4BC–c.65AD
Roman Stoic philosopher, statesman and tragedian
He began a career in politics and law in Rome in AD31. After a period of banishment he became tutor to the future Emperor **Nero**, enjoyed considerable political influence for a while and was made consul by Nero in AD57. He later withdrew from public life and devoted himself to writing and philosophy. In AD65 he was implicated in the conspiracy of Piso (an attempt to have Nero assassinated) and ordered to commit suicide. The publication in translation of his *Tenne Tragedies* (1581) was important in the evolution of English Elizabethan drama, which took from them the principal division of plays into five acts.

Seurat, Georges Pierre 1859–91
French artist
He developed the technique known as pointillism, in which the whole picture is composed of tiny rectangles of pure colour which merge together when viewed from a distance. He completed only seven canvases in this immensely demanding discipline, including *Sunday Afternoon on the Island of La Grande Jatte* (1884–6) and *The Circus* (1891). His colour theories influenced **Camille Pissarro**, **Degas** and **Renoir**.

Shackleton, Sir Ernest Henry 1874–1922
British explorer
He was an officer under Commander **Robert Scott** in the National Antarctic expedition of 1901–4. In 1908–9, in command of another expedition, he reached a point 97 miles (156.2km) from the South Pole, which was at that time a record. During a further expedition (1914–6), his ship *Endurance* was crushed in the ice. By means of sledges and boats he and his men reached Elephant Island off the coast of Anarctica, from where he and five others made a voyage of 800 miles (1,288km) to South Georgia

and organized relief for those remaining on Elephant Island. He died in South Georgia while on a fourth Antarctic expedition.

Shaftesbury, Anthony Ashley Cooper, 7th Earl of 1801–85
English factory reformer and philanthropist
Educated at Harrow and Christ Church, Oxford, he entered parliament in 1826. As Lord Ashley, he took over the leadership of the factory reform movement in 1832. He piloted successive factory acts (1847, 1850, 1859) through the House of Commons, achieving the ten-hour day and the provision of lodging-houses for the poor (1851). His Coal Mines Act (1842) prohibited underground employment of women and of children under 13. He was a founder, then Chairman for 40 years, of the Ragged Schools Union, a charity which sought to provide education for destitute children. He also assisted **Florence Nightingale** in her schemes for army welfare and took an interest in missionary work.

Shakespeare, William 1564–1616
English playwright, poet and actor
He worked in London and Stratford-upon-Avon as an actor and playwright, becoming the chief playwright of the King's Men under **James VI and I**. His plays, numbering around 36, include *The Taming of the Shrew* (1593), *Romeo and Juliet* (1595), *Henry V* (1598–9), *A Midsummer Night's Dream* (1595), *The Merchant of Venice* (1596–7), *Twelfth Night* (1601), *Julius Caesar* (1599), *Antony and Cleopatra* (1606), *Hamlet* (1600–1), *Othello* (1603–4), *King Lear* (1605–6), *Macbeth* (1606) and *The Tempest* (1611). His recurring themes are those of the universal human experience: love, betrayal, ambition, conflict, age and death, and his poetry and characters have entered the English language and shaped British identity. Shakespeare also wrote a well-known series of sonnets and two long narrative poems, *Venus and Adonis* (1593) and *The Rape of Lucrece* (1594).

Sharon, Ariel 1928–
Israeli general and politician
Prominent in the Arab-Israeli War of Independence (1948) and Sinai Campaign (1956), he became a major-general shortly before the Six-Day War of 1967. He left the army in 1973 but was recalled to fight in the Yom Kippur War. In the same year he helped to form Likud (a coalition of right-wing parties), and was voted into the Knesset, Israel's parliament. As Defence Minister (1981–3) under **Menachem Begin**, Sharon planned Israel's invasion of Lebanon in 1982. He became Prime Minister in 2001, but in 2006 a severe stroke left him in a coma, and he was replaced by Ehud Olmert.

Shaw, George Bernard 1856–1950
Irish dramatist and critic
His numerous plays, many of them masterpieces of 20th-century theatre, include *Mrs Warren's Profession* (1898), *Arms and the Man* (1898), *Caesar and Cleopatra* (1901), *Man and Superman* (1902), *Major Barbara* (1905), *Pygmalion* (1913) and *Saint Joan* (1923). These embrace a wide range of subjects, from politics and statecraft to family life, prostitution and vaccination. A belief in socialism underlay all of his work, and he was a long-standing member of the Fabian Society. His prose works include *The Intelligent Woman's Guide to Socialism and Capitalism* (1928) and *The Black Girl in Search of God* (1932). He was awarded the Nobel Prize for literature in 1925.

Shelley, Mary Wollstonecraft, *née* **Godwin** 1797–1851
English writer
The daughter of writers William Godwin and Mary Wollstonecraft, in 1814 she eloped with **Percy Bysshe Shelley**, and married him as his second wife in 1816. They lived abroad throughout their married life. Her first and most impressive novel was *Frankenstein, or the Modern Prometheus* (1818). After her husband's death in 1822 she returned to England with their son in 1823. Other works include *The Last Man* (1826), *Lodore* (1835) and verse.

Shelley, Percy Bysshe 1792–1822
English lyric poet and writer
A leading figure in the Romantic movement, he was a friend of **Byron** and **Keats**, after whose death he wrote the elegy *Adonais* (1821). His second wife was **Mary Shelley**. Among his best-known works are *Prometheus Unbound*, the major part of which dates to 1819, *The Masque of Anarchy* (1819), 'The Ode to the West Wind', 'To Liberty', 'To A Skylark' (all 1819), *Epipsychidion* (1821) and prose works including *The Defence of Poetry* (1821) and *Essay on the Devil* (1821). In his last years he lived in Italy, and drowned in a boating accident after visiting Byron at Livorno.

Sheridan, Richard Brinsley 1751–1816
Irish dramatist
His first successful play was *The Rivals* of 1775, after which he bought a share in the Drury Lane Theatre. In 1777 he produced his most famous play, *The School for Scandal*, a satirical comedy of manners. *The Critic* (1779), teeming with sparkling wit, was his last dramatic effort, apart from a less successful tragedy, *Pizarro*. In 1780 he was elected MP for Stafford, and became Under-Secretary for Foreign Affairs (1782) and afterwards Secretary to the Treasury (1783). After the Drury Lane theatre burned down in 1809 his financial difficulties grew serious, and he died in poverty.

Shi Huangdi (Shih Huang-ti) c.259–210BC
Chinese emperor and founder of the Qin (Ch'in) Dynasty
The creator of the first unified Chinese empire (221BC), he assumed the title of 'first emperor', and greatly extended and consolidated the empire. He ordered a system of road construction and, using convict labour, he linked together earlier fortifications to make the Great Wall (completed in 214BC). In 1974, excavation of his tomb yielded several thousand terracotta soldiers and horses which had been buried with him.

Shivaji 1627–80
Ruler of the Maratha Empire
He defied the power of the Moguls in Bijapur, and when the Bijapur authorities sent a large army against him (1659), he destroyed it. During the 1660s his power continued to increase and he had himself crowned as raja (1674). The Maratha Empire that he created maintained its independence until 1818.

Shostakovich, Dmitri Dmitriyevich 1906–75
Russian composer
His music was at first highly successful in the Soviet

Union, but the development of a more conservative attitude on the part of the Soviet government, coinciding with his own development of a more experimental outlook, led to official criticism. His second opera, *A Lady Macbeth of Mtsensk* (1930–2), had to be withdrawn after violent press attacks on its failure to observe the principles of 'Soviet realism'. Other work includes 15 symphonies, ballets, operas including *The Nose* (1927–8), concertos, many vocal works, string quartets, a piano quintet, chamber music and songs.

Shute, Nevil, *pseudonym of* **Nevil Shute Norway** 1899–1960
English novelist
He served in World War I and spent his early career in the aeronautical industry building airships. He emigrated to Australia after World War II. His novels include *No Highway* (1948), *A Town Like Alice* (1949), *Round the Bend* (1951), *Beyond the Black Stump* (1956) and *On The Beach* (1957), about an atomic war catastrophe. His success was largely due to his brisk style and his ability to express technical concepts in language understandable to ordinary readers.

Sibelius, Jean Julius Christian 1865–1957
Finnish composer
He abandoned a legal career to study music. He was a passionate nationalist, and wrote a series of symphonic poems (eg *Kullervo*, 1892; *Swan of Tuonela*, 1893) based on episodes in the Finnish oral epic *Kalevala*. His seven symphonies, symphonic poems (notably *En Saga*, 1892, revised 1901; *Finlandia*, 1899; *Tapiola*, 1925–6) and violin concerto have established him as a major 20th-century composer.

Sidney, Sir Philip 1554–86
English poet and patron
A soldier and Governor of Flushing from 1585, he spent his last year in the Netherlands, where he successfully plotted an attack on the town of Axel. He later led an assault on a Spanish convoy, was shot in the thigh and died from the infection, giving rise to the story about his having refused a drink of water on the grounds that another soldier needed it more. His work, none of which was published in his lifetime, includes *Arcadia* (1590), *Astrophel and Stella* (1591) and *A Defence of Poetry* (1595).

Simone, Nina, *professional name of* **Eunice Kathleen Waymon** 1933–2003
US singer, pianist and composer
A gifted pianist, she studied at the Juilliard School in New York City, although she later claimed that her classical ambitions were frustrated by racist attitudes. She became a nightclub singer in Atlantic City and began writing her own highly charged and often overtly political material in the early 1960s. Her first hit was **George Gershwin**'s 'I Loves You, Porgy' in 1959, but later songs such as 'Mississippi Goddam', a response to the race murder of children, were more typical.

Sinatra, Frank (Francis Albert) 1915–98
US singer and film actor
His fine musical phrasing and choice of material made him one of the bestselling recording artists of the 1950s and 1960s as well as a top concert performer into the 1990s. Among his classic recordings (1956–65) are the albums *For Swinging Lovers, Come Fly with Me* and *That's Life*. He made his film debut in 1941, leading to films such as *Anchors Aweigh* (1945), *On The Town* (1949), *From Here to Eternity* (1953) and *Pal Joey* (1957). In a highly publicized private life, he was married on four occasions; his wives included actresses Ava Gardner and Mia Farrow.

Sinclair, Sir Clive Marles 1940–
English electronic engineer and inventor
From 1958 his company, Sinclair Radionics Ltd, developed and successfully marketed a wide range of calculators, miniature television sets and personal computers. He later embarked on the manufacture of a small three-wheeled 'personal transport' vehicle, the C5, powered by rechargeable batteries, but this was widely condemned as unsafe and impractical. In 1992 he unveiled the Zike electric bicycle and in 2004 the folding A-bike.

Sitting Bull, *Indian name* **Tatanka Iyotake** c.1834–90
Native American warrior, Chief of the Dakota Sioux

Sitting Bull

He was a leader in the Sioux War (1876–7), and led the massacre of General **Custer** and his men at the Little Big Horn (1876). He escaped to Canada but surrendered in 1881, and was put into the reservation at Standing Rock. He was featured in Buffalo Bill Cody's Wild West Show (1885), and was killed attempting to evade the police in the Ghost Dance uprising (1890).

Skinner, Burrhus Frederic 1904–90
US psychologist
He was the most consistent and radical proponent of Behaviourism, which sought to explain animal psychology by reference to behaviour rather than mental states, and invented the 'Skinner Box', a chamber containing mechanisms for an animal to operate and an automatic device for presenting rewards. In education, his ideas led to the development of 'programmed learning', a technique which seeks to direct teaching to the needs of each individual and to reinforce learning by regular and immediate feedback. He also wrote fiction, autobiography and philosophy.

Smith, Adam 1723–90
Scottish economist and philosopher
In 1759 he published his *Theory of Moral Sentiments*, and, after travelling abroad, went to London, where he became a member of the club to which **Joshua Reynolds** and **Samuel Johnson** belonged. In 1776

he published his most famous and influential work, *An Inquiry into the Nature and Causes of the Wealth of Nations*, which saw the division of labour as the main ingredient of economic growth, rather than land or money, and emphasized the importance of the free market. His other works include essays on the formation of languages, the history of astronomy, classical physics and logic, and the arts.

Smith, Joseph 1805–44
US religious leader
Regarded as the founder of the Mormons, in 1823 he claimed that an angel had told him of a hidden gospel written on golden plates, and in 1827 the sacred records were apparently delivered into his hands on a hill near Palmyra, New York. This, the so-called *Book of Mormon* (1830), was the founding document of 'the new Church of Jesus Christ of Latter-day Saints', and despite often intense hostility from more orthodox Christians, the new religion rapidly gained converts. Smith was an advocate of polygamy (calling his wives 'spiritual wives'). He was shot dead by a mob.

Smith, Stevie, *pseudonym of* **Florence Margaret Smith** 1902–71
English poet and novelist
Her first novels, *Novel on Yellow Paper* (1936), *Over the Frontier* (1938) and *The Holiday* (1949), were written on the advice of a publicist reacting to her poetry. Meanwhile her reputation as a humorous poet on serious themes was becoming established with *A Good Time Was Had By All* (1937) and *Not Waving but Drowning* (1957). Her poetic style ranged from the childish and whimsical to the deeply religious. She produced a volume of the line-drawings that often accompanied her poems, entitled *Some Are More Human Than Others* (1958).

Smith, W Eugene 1918–78
US photojournalist
He became a war correspondent for *Life* magazine in 1942. Severely wounded at Okinawa in 1945, he did not photograph again until 1947, the year of his famous *The Walk to Paradise Garden* (showing two children walking away towards a sunlit forest clearing). Smith returned to *Life* and produced a series of eloquent photo-essays (eg *Country Doctor*, 1948; *Spanish Village*, 1951). His last great work was a photographic record of a Japanese fishing village suffering the maiming effect of mercury poisoning from factory pollution: *Minimata: Life Sacred and Profane* (1973).

Smollett, Tobias George 1721–71
Scottish novelist
His first novels, *Roderick Random* (1748) and *Peregrine Pickle* (1751), describe the adventures in love and war of an unprincipled hero. In 1753 he settled in Chelsea, editing the new *Critical Review*, which led to his imprisonment for libel in 1760, and writing his *History of England* (3 volumes, 1757–8). *Humphrey Clinker* (1771), which is more kindly in tone and still a favourite, was written in the form of a series of letters from and to members of a party touring England and 'North Britain'.

Snowdon, Antony Charles Robert Armstrong-Jones, 1st Earl of 1930–
English photographer
He was married to HRH Princess Margaret (from 1960 to 1978), and was created Earl of Snowdon in 1961. He became a freelance photojournalist in 1951 and a *Vogue* photographer in 1954. His informal portraits of the famous have often captured unusual facets of character, and he has sympathetically recorded the lives of the disabled, producing documentaries for television on similar themes.

Sobers, Gary, *properly* **Sir Garfield St Auburn Sobers** 1936–
West Indian cricketer
He was born in Bridgetown, Barbados. In 93 Test matches for the West Indies (captain 1965–74), he scored more than 8,000 runs (including 26 centuries), and took 235 wickets and 110 catches. He held the world record for the highest Test innings (365 not out, made at Kingston, Jamaica, in 1958), until Brian Lara made 375 against England in 1994. He was captain of Nottinghamshire from 1968 to 1974.

Socrates 469–399BC
Greek philosopher
He is represented as ugly, snub-nosed and with a paunch. He wrote nothing, founded no school and had no formal disciples, but along with **Plato** and **Aristotle** is one of the three great figures in ancient philosophy. The principal sources for his life are the dialogues of Plato. The 'Socratic method' was to ask for definitions of familiar concepts such as justice, courage and piety, to examine them and then tease out their flaws. Convicted for 'impiety' and 'corrupting the youth', he was tried at the age of 70, and sentenced to die by drinking hemlock.

Solomon c.962–922BC
King of Israel
Solomon was the second son of **David**. According to passages in 1 Kings 1–11 and 2 Chronicles 1–10 of the Bible, Solomon strengthened his army, founded cities, married the Egyptian Pharaoh's daughter, built the temple in Jerusalem, and was famous for his wisdom. Several books of the Bible were later attributed to him, including the Song of Solomon, the Wisdom of Solomon, Proverbs, and some of the Psalms. Among his contacts in the Arabian world was the queen of a country called Sheba, who journeyed to Jerusalem to test the wisdom of Solomon and exchange extravagant gifts.

Solzhenitsyn, Aleksandr Isayevich 1918–
Russian writer
After distinguished service with the Red Army in World War II, he was imprisoned (1945–53) for unfavourable comment on **Stalin**'s conduct of the war. Rehabilitated in 1956, his first novel, *One Day in the Life of Ivan Denisovich* (published 1963 in its English translation) was acclaimed, but his denunciation in 1967 of the strict censorship in Russia led to the banning of his later novels, which included *The Cancer Ward* (1968–9). He was awarded the Nobel Prize for literature in 1970. *The Gulag Archipelago 1918–56*, a factual account of the Stalinist terror, was first published in the West between 1973 and 1975. In 1974 he was deported to West Germany; he later settled in the USA, and in 1994 returned to Russia.

Somerville, Mary, *née* **Fairfax** 1780–1872
Scottish mathematician and astronomer
In 1826 she presented a paper on *The Magnetic Properties of the Violet Rays in the Solar Spectrum* to the Royal Society. In 1831 she published *The*

Mechanism of the Heavens, her account for the general reader of Pierre Simon Laplace's great work *Mécanique Céleste* ('Celestial Mechanics'). This had great success and she wrote several further explanatory works on physics, physical geography and microscopic science. She supported the emancipation and education of women, and Somerville College at Oxford is named after her.

Sondheim, Stephen Joshua 1930–
US composer and lyricist
He wrote the lyrics for **Leonard Bernstein**'s *West Side Story* (1957), and the first show for which he wrote both the music and the lyrics was *A Funny Thing Happened on the Way to the Forum* (1962). Other musicals include *Company* (1970), *Follies* (1971), *A Little Night Music* (1973), *Sunday in the Park with George* (1984) and *Passion* (1994). His musicals are regarded as classics of the genre, the more extraordinary for having been produced in an era when the US musical is generally seen as being in decline.

Sophocles c.496–405BC
Athenian tragedian
One of the great figures of Greek drama, he is said to have written around 130 plays. Seven of the tragedies have survived: *Ajax* (date uncertain), *Antigone* (441BC), *Oedipus Tyrannus* (c.429BC), *Women of Trachis* (c.429), *Electra* (between 418 and 410BC), *Philoctetes* (409BC) and *Oedipus Coloneus* (produced 401BC, after his death). Aristotle based his aesthetic theory of drama on Sophocles' work. A prominent politician, Sophocles was twice elected *strategos* (general) of Athens.

Spark, Dame Muriel Sarah, *née* **Camberg** 1918–2006
Scottish novelist, short-story writer, biographer and poet
She achieved public success with her sixth novel, *The Prime of Miss Jean Brodie* (1961), a portrait of a schoolteacher with advanced ideas who exercises an eerie influence over her select band of pupils on the eve of war in Europe. Other works include *The Ballad of Peckham Rye* (1960), *The Girls of Slender Means* (1963), *The Mandelbaum Gate* (1965) and *A Far Cry from Kensington* (1988). She has also written critical works on the **Brontës**, **Wordsworth** and others.

Spartacus d.71BC
Roman gladiator and rebel
He was a shepherd who became a robber, but was captured and sold to a trainer of gladiators. In 73BC he escaped and built an army of c.90,000 slaves and the dispossessed, with whom he defeated several Roman armies and devastated much of southern Italy. He was defeated by Marcus Licinius Crassus in 71BC, and executed by crucifixion with his followers. The remnants of his army were annihilated by **Pompey**.

Spenser, Edmund c.1552–1599
English poet
His first original work, *The Shepheard's Calender* (1579), heralded the age of Elizabethan poetry. In 1586 he settled at Kilcolman Castle in Cork, where he wrote the *Faerie Queene* and other courtly works. These presentations of the art and thought of the Renaissance were written with an eye to gaining court favour, but despite their popularity did not succeed in gaining the patronage of Queen **Elizabeth I**. Later works include the supreme marriage poem *Epithalamion* (1594), *Colin Clout's Come Home Again* (1595) and *Prothalamion* (1596).

Spielberg, Steven 1946–
US film-maker
A highly praised television film, *Duel* (1971), brought him the opportunity to direct for the cinema, and a succession of hits made him the most commercially successful director ever. His films have included *Jaws* (1975), *Close Encounters of the Third Kind* (1977), *E.T.* (1982), *Raiders of the Lost Ark* (1981), *Poltergeist* (1983), *The Color Purple* (1985), *Back to the Future* (1985), *Who Framed Roger Rabbit?* (1988), *Empire of the Sun* (1988), *Jurassic Park* (1993), *Schindler's List* (1993), *Saving Private Ryan* (1998) and *A.I. Artificial Intelligence* (2001).

Spinoza, Benedict de, *Hebrew* **Baruch** 1632–77
Dutch philosopher and theologian
Regarded as one of the great rationalist thinkers of the 17th century, he was born into a Jewish family that had fled from Portugal to escape Catholic persecution. Condemned by both the Jewish and Christian communities, he made a living grinding and polishing lenses, and died in poverty at an early age. His works include the highly influential *Tractatus Theologico-Politicus* (published anonymously in 1670 and banned in 1674 for its controversial views on the Bible and Christian theology) and the *Ethics* (published posthumously in 1677). His reputation was restored after his death by critics such as **Goethe** and **Coleridge**.

Spitz, Mark (Andrew) 1950–
US swimmer
He earned worldwide fame at the 1972 Olympics by winning seven gold medals, achieving a world record time in each event. He also won two golds in the 1968 Games, and set a total of 26 world records between 1967 and 1972. He turned professional in 1972.

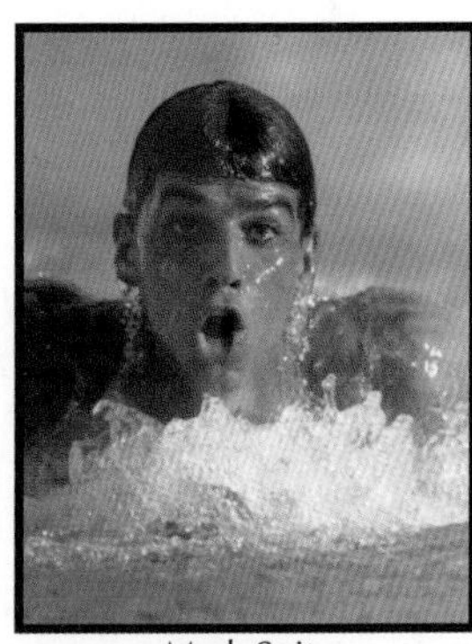
Mark Spitz

Springsteen, Bruce 1949–
US rock singer and guitarist
From the release of his first album he was hailed by critics as the new **Bob Dylan**, although it was not until the release of *Born To Run* (1975) that he met with major commercial success. Later albums included *Darkness On The Edge Of Town* (1978), *The River* (1980), *Nebraska* (1982), *Born In The USA* (1984) and *Human Touch* (1992). By the mid-1980s he was the world's most popular white rock star. In the 1990s he returned to the acoustic style with *The Ghost of Tom Joad* (1995).

PEOPLE

Stalin, Joseph, *originally* **Iosif Vissarionovich Dzhugashvili** 1879–1953
Soviet revolutionary and leader
He took over as leader of the Soviet Union in 1924 after **Lenin**'s death, and engineered **Trotsky**'s downfall in 1928. Among the first victims of his rule were millions of *kulaks*, or property-owning peasants, who were executed or died of famine (1932–3). Stalin also initiated purges of opposition in the Red Army. In 1939 he signed a non-aggression pact with **Hitler**, but the Nazis nevertheless invaded in 1941. After World War II Stalin gained political control of most of Eastern Europe, cutting off Soviet Russia and her satellites behind the 'Iron Curtain'. Stalin's personality cult and the brutal purges of his rule were denounced after his death by **Nikita Khrushchev**.

Stanton, Elizabeth Cady 1815–1902
US social reformer who launched the suffrage movement in the US
Determined to redress the inequality that she discovered in women's legal, political, and industrial rights, in 1848, with Lucretia Mott, she organized the first women's rights convention at Seneca Falls, New York. Stanton joined with Susan B Anthony in 1850, producing the feminist magazine *Revolution* (1868–70) and founding the National Woman Suffrage Movement in 1869. An energetic writer, her autobiography was *Eighty Years and More 1815–1897* (1898).

Steinbeck, John Ernest 1902–68
US novelist
Tortilla Flat (1935), his first major novel, is a faithful picture of the Hispanic people of California, and foreshadows the themes of *The Grapes of Wrath* (1939), a study of the poor in the face of disaster. It led to much-needed reform, and won the 1940 Pulitzer Prize. His other works include *In Dubious Battle* (1935), *Of Mice and Men* (1937), *The Pearl* (1947), *Burning Bright* (1950), *East of Eden* (1952) and *Winter of our Discontent* (1961), as well as the light-hearted *Cannery Row* (1945) and *The Short Reign of Pippin IV* (1957). He won the Nobel Prize for literature in 1962.

Stendhal, *pseudonym of* **Henri Marie Beyle** 1783–1842
French novelist
His masterpieces *Red and Black* (also known as *Scarlet and Black*) and *The Charterhouse of Parma* were published in 1830 and 1839 respectively. The first follows the rise and decline of Julien Sorel, a provincial youth in the France at the time of the Restoration of the Bourbon Dynasty, and the second recounts the fortunes of Fabrice del Dongo at an insignificant Italian court during the same period. They were admired by **Honoré de Balzac**, although neither received great understanding during Stendhal's lifetime. His autobiographical volumes include *Memoirs of an Egotist* (1892).

Stephen c.1097–1154
King of England
He was the grandson of **William the Conqueror**. In 1114 he was given Mortain in Normandy by his uncle, Henry I, and he acquired Boulogne by his marriage. Stephen swore allegiance to Henry's heir, his daughter Matilda (or the Empress Maud), but on Henry's death (1135), Stephen took the crown himself. King David I of Scotland supported Matilda in two invasions, while Stephen antagonized Robert, Earl of Gloucester, an illegitimate son of Henry I. The ensuing civil war brought devastation to parts of the country. In 1141 Matilda imprisoned Stephen and was acknowledged queen; but London rose against her and in November 1141 Stephen regained his liberty and his crown. Matilda's son (**Henry II**) succeeded Stephen, his own son, Eustace, having died (1153).

Stephenson, George 1781–1848
English railway engineer
In 1815 he invented, at the same time as **Humphry Davy**, a colliery safety lamp, the 'Geordie'. In 1814 he constructed his first locomotive, *Blucher*. In 1821 he was appointed engineer for the construction of the Stockton & Darlington mineral railway, opened in September 1825, and in 1826 for the Liverpool & Manchester Railway, opened in September 1830. The previous October had seen the memorable contest of engines at Rainhill, resulting in the triumph of Stephenson's *Rocket* at 30 mph (48.3kph).

Steptoe, Patrick Christopher 1913–88
English gynaecologist and reproduction biologist
One of the pioneers of in *in vitro* fertilization (in which egg cells are fertilized outside the woman's body and then implanted), he worked with **Robert Edwards** from 1968. Ten years later, this work resulted in the birth of a girl, Louise Brown, the first so-called 'test-tube' baby.

Stern, Isaac 1920–2001
US violinist
He made his recital debut in 1935 and his concert debut with the San Francisco Symphony Orchestra in 1936. He played subsequently as soloist and in chamber music throughout the world. The recipient of numerous awards, such as being made a Commander of the French Légion d'Honneur (1989), he was regarded as one of the world's foremost violinists.

Sterne, Laurence 1713–68
Irish novelist
He became a priest in 1738, and in 1759 published the first two volumes of *The Life and Opinions of Tristram Shandy*, with further volumes appearing from 1761 to 1767. Full of playful wit, these broke new ground in the evolution of the novel, and made Sterne a celebrity. *A Sentimental Journey through France and Italy* appeared in 1768, shortly before he died in London of pleurisy. His *Letters from Yorick to Eliza* (1775–9) contain his correspondence with a young married woman to whom he was devoted.

Stevenson, Robert Louis Balfour 1850–94
Scottish writer
His first major works, *Inland Voyage* (1878) and *Travels with a Donkey in the Cévennes* (1879), describe travels in Belgium and northern France. The romantic adventure story *Treasure Island* brought him fame in 1883 and was followed by *Kidnapped* (1886), *Catriona* (1893) and *The Master of Ballantrae* (1889). *The Strange Case of Dr Jekyll and Mr Hyde* (1886) illustrates Stevenson's metaphysical interest in evil. Other works include the unfinished *Weir of Hermiston* (published posthumously in 1896), *A Child's Garden of Verses* (1885) and *The Wrong Box* (1889). His last years were spent in Samoa.

Stewart, James Maitland 1908–97
US film actor
Tall, gangly, and with a distinctive drawl, his first Hollywood films included *Mr. Smith Goes to Washington* (1939) and *Destry Rides Again* (1939). After distinguished service in World War II, he appeared in *It's A Wonderful Life* (1946) and *The Glenn Miller Story* (1953), before developing a more mature image as a tough and resourceful hero in westerns and thrillers such as *Rear Window* (1954), *Vertigo* (1958) and *Anatomy of a Murder* (1959). He won a Best Actor Academy award for *The Philadelphia Story* (1940).

Sting, *pseudonym of* **Gordon Matthew Sumner** 1951–
English singer-songwriter and actor
He was a teacher before winning international fame as a singer-songwriter and bass player with the British rock trio The Police (1977–86). After chart success on both sides of the Atlantic, The Police split and Sting developed his solo career with such bestselling singles as 'An Englishman in New York' (1990) and such albums as *Brand New Day* (1999). He has also appeared in many films, and he is widely known as a campaigner to save Brazilian rainforests and support political prisoners.

Stoker, Bram (Abraham) 1847–1912
Irish writer
He is best remembered for the classic vampire story *Dracula* (1897), and wrote a number of other novels dealing with futuristic and occult themes, including *The Jewel of the Seven Stars* (1903), *The Lady of the Shroud* (1909) and *The Lair of the White Worm* (1911).

Stolypin, Pyotr Arkadevich 1862–1911
Russian statesman
As Prime Minister (1906–11) he introduced a series of agrarian reforms, which had only limited success. In 1907 he suspended the Second Duma (national assembly), and restricted voting rights. He was assassinated in Kiev.

Stowe, Harriet (Elizabeth) Beecher 1811–96
US novelist
She became famous for *Uncle Tom's Cabin* (1852), an anti-slavery novel prompted by the passing of the Fugitive Slave Law in 1850, which provided for the return of slaves who had escaped. Her second anti-slavery novel, *Dred: A Tale of the Dismal Swamp* (1856), also had huge sales. Her other books include *Lady Byron Vindicated* (1870), and further novels, biographies and children's books.

Strauss, Richard 1864–1949
German composer
He began to compose at the age of six, and his first published works date from 1875. His symphonic poems include *Thus Spoke Zarathustra* (1895–6, and *A Hero's Life* (1898). The first of his operas, *Guntram*, was produced at Weimar in 1894 and in the same year he became conductor of the Berlin Philharmonic Orchestra. His operas *Salome* (1905) and *Elektra* (1909), the first of his collaborations with the dramatic poet Hugo von Hofmannsthal, caused sensations, and with Hofmannsthal he went on to compose the popular *Der Rosenkavalier* (1911). His later work led him into difficulties with the Nazi government, but his reputation protected him from serious political reprisal. After the completion of his last opera, *Capriccio*, he turned to instrumental work and song: in 1943 he wrote *Metamorphosen*, an extended piece inspired by the wartime destruction of German cities, and finally a series of small-scale concerto and orchestral works and the valedictory *Four Last Songs* (1948).

Stravinsky, Igor Fyodorovich 1882–1971
Russian-born US composer
A pioneer of the modern movement in music, his first ballet, *The Firebird* (1910) was an instant success. A second ballet, *Petrushka* (1911), consolidated his international reputation, as did *The Rite of Spring* (1913), although there was a riot at its première. Other works include the opera *The Nightingale* (1914), the ballets *Pulcinella* (1920), *Orpheus* (1948) and *Agon* (1957), the opera-oratorio *Oedipus Rex* (1927), and the choral *Symphony of Psalms* (1930). Stravinsky settled in the USA in 1945, where he composed, among other works, *In Memoriam Dylan Thomas* (1954), *Elegy for J.F.K.* (1964) and *Requiem Canticles* (1966).

Stresemann, Gustav 1878–1929
German politician
After World War I he founded and led the German People's Party. He was Chancellor of the new German (Weimar) Republic for a few months in 1923, and in 1925 negotiated the Locarno Pact of mutual security with Aristide Briand of France and Austen Chamberlain of Britain. He secured the entry of Germany into the League of Nations in 1926, and shared with Briand the 1926 Nobel Peace Prize for that year.

Stuart or **Stewart, Prince Charles Edward**, *known as* **the Young Pretender** and **Bonnie Prince Charlie** 1720–88
Claimant to the throne of England and Scotland
Charles Edward Stuart was the elder son of James Francis Stuart, the Old Pretender, and grandson of **James VII and II**. He was born and educated in Rome, where he became the centre of Jacobite hopes. In July 1745 he landed in Scotland and won victories at Prestonpans and Falkirk, but suffered a crushing defeat at the hands of the Duke of Cumberland's troops at Culloden Moor in 1746. The rising was ruthlessly suppressed, and Charles fled to France. He assumed the title of Charles III of Great Britain and retired to Florence, dying in Rome.

Süleyman the Magnificent 1494–1566
Ottoman emperor

16th-century portrait of Süleyman the Magnificent

Süleyman succeeded his father **Selim I** in 1520, and extended the bounds of his empire both to the east and west, capturing Belgrade in 1521 and Rhodes in 1522, and defeating the Hungarians in 1526. His advance to the west was finally checked in 1529 at the gates of Vienna. In the east, he won territory in Persia, and in North Africa he pushed as far as Morocco. At sea he established supremacy in the eastern Mediterranean and Aegean. He was an energetic patron of the arts.

Sullivan, Sir Arthur Seymour 1842–1900
English composer
He is best known for his partnership with **W S Gilbert**, which from 1871 produced the 14 comic 'Savoy' operas, performed from 1881 in the Savoy theatre (which had been built as a showcase for the works). These included *HMS Pinafore* (1878), *The Pirates of Penzance* (1880), *The Mikado* (1885), *The Yeomen of the Guard* (1888) and *The Gondoliers* (1889). Sullivan also composed a *Te Deum* (1872), an opera, *Ivanhoe* (1891), cantatas, ballads and hymn-tunes. His best-known songs include 'Orpheus with his Lute', 'The Lost Chord' and the tune for the hymn 'Onward Christian Soldiers'.

Sun Yat-sen (Sun Yixian) or **Sun Zhongshan (Sun Chung- shan)** 1866–1925
Chinese revolutionary politician
After his first abortive uprising against the Manchus in Guangzhou in 1895, he lived in Japan, the USA and Great Britain. After ten unsuccessful uprisings, engineered by Sun from abroad, he was victorious in the revolution of 1911. In 1923 he was elected President of the Southern Republic. With help from the Russians, Sun reorganized the Kuomintang (the Chinese nationalist people's party) and established the Whampoa Military Academy under **Chiang Kai-shek**, who three years after Sun's death achieved the unification of China. He is acknowledged by all political factions as the father of the Chinese Republic.

Sutherland, Dame Joan 1926–
Australian soprano
She gained international fame in 1959 with her roles in Donizetti's *Lucia di Lammermoor* and **Handel**'s *Samson*. Singing regularly in opera houses and concert halls all over the world, she returned to Australia for a tour with her own company in 1965. She retired from the opera stage in October 1990.

Swift, Jonathan 1667–1745
Anglo-Irish satirist and clergyman
He began publishing satirical works such as the *Battle of the Books* and *A Tale of a Tub* (both 1704). In 1726 he published the world-famous satire *Gulliver's Travels*, directed at politics and religion in general, and culminating in a savage attack on humanity; some have seen the latter as pointing to the author's final mental collapse. His influence, like that of his friend **Alexander Pope**, upheld tradition and Tory values and was directed powerfully against modernity. His poetry and his *Journal to Stella* (1710–13) reflect his quieter and more personal feelings.

Swinburne, Algernon Charles 1837–1909
English poet and critic
Atalanta in Calydon (1865), the first of the series of *Poems and Ballads* (1866), took the public by storm, although the uninhibited and decadent tone of certain passages offended some readers. *Songs before Sunrise* (1871) best expresses his fervent republicanism. A trilogy on **Mary, Queen of Scots** was completed in 1881, and the following year *Tristram of Lyonesse*, an Arthurian romance in rhymed couplets, achieved great success. His *Essays and Studies* (1875) and *Studies in Prose and Poetry* (1894) are his chief contribution to criticism.

Tacitus, *in full* **Publius** or **Gaius Cornelius Tacitus** c.55–120AD
Roman historian
He studied rhetoric in Rome, and rose to eminence as a pleader at the Roman Bar. By AD88 he was praetor and a member of one of the priestly colleges. Under the emperor Nerva he became a consul (AD97). He established a great reputation as an orator, and eleven of Pliny's letters were addressed to him. His major works are the 12-volume *Histories* and *Annals*.

Tamburlaine See **Timur**

Taylor, Dame Elizabeth Rosemond 1932–
US film actress
As a child star she made a number of films including two 'Lassie' stories (1943, 1946), *National Velvet* (1944), and *Little Women* (1949). She was first seen as an adult in *The Father of the Bride* (1950), and her career continued through the 1950s with films including *Cat on a Hot Tin Roof* (1958) and *Suddenly Last Summer* (1959), for both of which she received Academy Award nominations. In 1960 she won her first Academy Award for *Butterfield 8*. She was notable also for her many marriages, and the making of the spectacular epic *Cleopatra* (1962) provided the background to her well-publicized romance with her co-star **Richard Burton**, whom she married for the first time in 1964. She made several films with Burton, including *Who's Afraid of Virginia Woolf?* (1966, Academy Award). After an absence of a few years in the 1980s, she resumed acting, mostly in television. She was created DBE in 2000.

Tchaikovsky, Pyotr Ilyich 1840–93
Russian composer
A composer much loved for his deeply expressive music, his ballets *Swan Lake* (1877), *The Sleeping Beauty* (1890) and *The Nutcracker* (1892) form the core of the classical repertory. He also wrote eleven operas, of which *Eugene Onegin* (1879) and *The Queen of Spades* (1890) are still regularly performed. Other works include six symphonies, of which the last three are the best-known, two piano concertos (a third was left uncompleted), a violin concerto, a number of tone poems including *Romeo and Juliet* (1870), songs and piano pieces. A tempestuous private life and a failed marriage clouded his career, and he is said to have died of cholera from drinking unboiled water.

Te Kanawa, Dame Kiri Janette 1944–
New Zealand soprano
She made her debut in London with the Royal Opera Company in 1970. She has since taken a wide range of leading roles at all the major opera houses and concert halls, and in 1981 sang at the wedding of Charles and Diana, Prince and Princess of Wales. She published *Land of the Long White Cloud* in 1989.

Tennyson, Alfred, 1st Baron Tennyson 1809–92
English poet
His early verse collection *Poems* (1833) contained

'The Lady of Shallott' and 'The Lotus-eaters'. His *Poems* of 1842 established his fame, and in 1850 he produced probably his greatest work, *In Memoriam*, written on the sudden death of his friend Arthur Hallam. In 1850 he became Poet Laureate and was at the height of his popularity. He went on to publish 'The Charge of the Light Brigade' (1854), *Maud: A Monodrama* (1855), *Idylls of the King* (1859), *Locksley Hall Sixty Years After* (1886) and a number of plays. His last poem was the well-known 'Crossing the Bar' (1889).

Teresa of Calcutta, Mother, *originally* **Agnes Gonxha Bojaxhiu** 1910–97
Roman Catholic nun and missionary

Mother Teresa of Calcutta

Born in Yugoslavia of Albanian parents, she went to India in 1928, joined a convent, and in 1948 began working alone in the slums, helping the poor. She was gradually joined by other nuns, and she opened her House for the Dying in 1952. Her religious order, the Order of the Missionaries of Charity, was founded in 1950, and now runs hundreds of charity houses in many countries. In 1957 she founded a leper colony called Shanti Nagar ('Town of Peace') near Asansol in West Bengal. She was awarded the Nobel Peace Prize in 1979.

Tereshkova, Valentina Vladimirovna 1937–
Russian astronaut
The first woman to fly in space, she worked in a textile factory and qualified as a sports parachutist before training as a cosmonaut (1962). She was the solo crew member in the three-day *Vostok 6* flight which was launched from the Tyuratam Space Station in the USSR on 16 June 1963.

Tesla, Nikola 1856–1943
US physicist and electrical engineer
He was born in Serbia. He discovered the principles of alternating current, and developed its use for electricity supply as a more efficient alternative to the prevailing direct current supply. Among his many projects, he improved dynamos and electric motors, and invented devices such as the Tesla coil, a source of high voltage oscillations used for testing. He also predicted wireless communication two years before **Guglielmo Marconi** developed it, and experimented with a wireless communication system.

Thackeray, William Makepeace 1811–63
English novelist
Born in India and educated at Cambridge, he spent much time abroad, especially in Paris, where he worked as a journalist and correspondent. He returned to London in 1837. Despite a troubled family life, he contributed reviews, parodies, sketches and serials to various publications, most famously to *Punch*, in which his work exploited the great theme of English snobbery. His fame was established by the novels that followed – most notably *Vanity Fair* (1847–8), which shows a social climber threading her way through London society, *Pendennis* (1848), the historical novel *Henry Esmond* (3 volumes, 1852) and *The Newcomes* (1853–55).

Thales c.620–c.555BC
Greek natural philosopher and astronomer
He is traditionally the founder of Greek, and therefore European, philosophy, and is important for having proposed the first natural cosmology, identifying water as the original substance and (literally) the basis of the universe. He is said to have predicted accurately a solar eclipse in 585BC, and to have proposed a federation of the Ionian cities of the Aegean.

Thatcher, Margaret Hilda Thatcher, Baroness, *née* **Roberts** 1925–
English Conservative Prime Minister
The MP for Finchley, in 1975 she was elected Leader of the Conservative Party. She became Britain's first woman Prime Minister in 1979 and was re-elected in 1983 and 1987. 'Thatcherism' placed emphasis on the market economy, low inflation, extensive privatization, British independence from Europe, a strong defence policy and the reduction of union power.This last point was confirmed by the failure of a miners' stike (1984–5). In foreign policy she led the recapture of the Falkland Islands from Argentina, formed close links with US President **Ronald Reagan** and was dubbed the 'Iron Lady' in the Soviet Union. Her leadership was finally challenged by rebel Conservative MPs and she was forced to resign in 1990.

Thomas, Dylan Marlais 1914–53
Welsh poet
He established himself with the publication of *Eighteen Poems* in 1934, which was followed by works such as *The Map of Love* (1939), *Portrait of the Artist as a Young Dog* (1940), *The World I Breathe* (1940), *Deaths and Entrances* (1946) and *Adventures in the Skin Trade* (unfinished, published posthumously 1955). From 1944 he worked on a radio 'play for voices' about a Welsh seaside village which became *Under Milk Wood*. He died from chronic alcohol abuse. Praised by critics for his striking rhythms, his original imagery and his technical innovations, his work could also be obscure and difficult.

Thomson, Sir J(oseph) J(ohn), *also called* **JJ** 1856–1940
English physicist, discoverer of the electron
Building on the work of **James Clerk Maxwell** and **Wilhelm Röntgen**, he showed that cathode rays were rapidly-moving particles, and by measuring their speed and charge, he deduced that these 'corpuscles' (electrons) must be nearly 2,000 times smaller in mass than the lightest known atomic particle. This was a key moment in the development of nuclear physics, and he was awarded the Nobel Prize for physics in 1906. Thomson later studied the nature of positive rays (1911) and discovered isotopes.

Tiberius, *in full* **Tiberius Julius Caesar Augustus**, *originally* **Tiberius Claudius Nero** 42BC–AD37
2nd Emperor of Rome
Almost the whole of his first 20 years of adulthood were spent fighting at the borders of the Roman Empire, particularly in Germany. He succeeded his stepfather, the Emperor **Augustus**, in AD14. His rule began well, but was gradually characterized by a growing number of treason trials and executions. In AD26 he retired to the island of Capri, from where he continued to exercise despotic control. He died unmourned and was succeeded by **Caligula**.

Timur, *also called* **Timur the Lame**, *English* **Tamerlane** or **Tamburlaine** 1336–1405
Tartar conqueror
In a series of devastating wars (in which he sustained the wounds which gave him his nickname) he subdued nearly all Persia (from 1392 to 1396), Georgia and the Tartar Empire, and conquered all the states between the River Indus and the lower Ganges. He won Damascus and Syria from the Mameluke sovereigns of Egypt, then defeated the Turks at Ankara (1402). He died while marching to conquer China. His capital, Samarkand, was filled with splendid architectural monuments, covered with brightly coloured mosaics.

Titian, *properly* **Tiziano Vecellio** c.1488–1576
Venetian painter
One of the greatest artists of the Renaissance, he was a pupil of **Giovanni Bellini** and **Giorgione**. His best-known works include his *Sacred and Profane Love* (c.1515), the richly coloured *Bacchus and Ariadne* (1523), the *Presentation of the Virgin* (1534–8), *Ecce Homo* (1543), *Perseus and Andromeda* (c.1556), *Diana and Actaeon* (1559) and *Christ Crowned with Thorns* (c.1570), as well as many portraits. He revolutionized techniques in oil, and his dynamic compositions, in which bright colours are contrasted, have led him to be described as the founder of modern painting.

Tito, *originally* **Josip Broz**, *also called* **Marshal Tito** 1892–1980
Yugoslav leader
He took part in the 1917 Russian Revolution, and in 1928 he was imprisoned in Yugoslavia for conspiring against the regime. In mid-1941 he organized partisan forces against the Germans and Italians, and declared a new Yugoslav Federal Republic in 1945. One-party elections followed, establishing the dominance of the Communist Party, with Tito serving as Prime Minister and, from 1953, as President. After disagreements with **Stalin** he pursued a policy of 'positive neutralism' towards the Soviet Union.

Tolkien, J(ohn) R(onald) R(euel) 1892–1973
British academic and writer
An Oxford professor, he is best known for his fantasy novels of Middle Earth, particularly *The Hobbit* (1937) and *The Lord of the Rings* (3 volumes, 1954–5). His scholarly publications include an edition of *Sir Gawain and the Green Knight* (1925), and studies on **Chaucer** (1934) and *Beowulf* (1937).

Tolstoy, Count Leo Nikolayevich 1828–1910
Russian writer and philosopher
The towering figure of 19th-century Russian literature, after serving in the Crimean War (1853–6) he began his greatest work, *War and Peace* (1863–9), a tale of Russia's struggle against **Napoleon I**. His second major work was *Anna Karenina* (1874–6), in which the passion felt by a married woman for a young army officer has tragic consequences. Later writings include *The Death of Ivan Ilyich* (1886), *The Kreutzer Sonata* (1889) and *Resurrection* (1899). A profound thinker on moral and religious questions, in the last years of his life he gave up his possessions and lived as a peasant.

Torricelli, Evangelista 1608–47
Italian physicist and mathematician
His *Trattato del Moto* (1641) led **Galileo** to invite him to become his literary assistant. He discovered that, because of atmospheric pressure, water will not rise above 33 feet in a suction pump. He demonstrated that this pressure affects the level of mercury in a tube, so giving the first description of a mercury barometer or 'torricellian tube'. He greatly improved both telescopes and microscopes, and published a large number of mathematical papers.

Torvill, Jayne 1957–
English ice-skater
She started skating at the age of 10, and met **Christopher Dean** in 1975. The pair were six times British champions, World ice-dance champions (1981–4), and won the Olympic and European ice-dance titles in 1984. Their highly acclaimed performances included an interpretation of the music from **Ravel**'s *Bolero*.

Toulouse-Lautrec(-Monfa or **Montfa), Henri (Marie Raymond) de** 1864–1901
French painter and lithographer
The child of first cousins, he suffered from bone problems and dwarfism. In 1884 he settled in Montmartre, and his studies of the cabaret stars, the barmaids, the clowns and actors of Montmartre reveal his interest in the human being behind the professional function, as in *The Two Friends* (1894), *Jane Avril dansant* (c.1892) and *La Clownesse Cha-u-Kao* (1895). His revolutionary poster designs were influenced by Japanese woodcuts, which flatten and simplify the subject matter. Other works include *The Bar* (1898) and the *Moulin Rouge* paintings (1894).

Toussaint Louverture, *originally* **François Dominique Toussaint** 1746–1803
Haitian revolutionary leader
Born a slave in Saint Domingue (Haiti since 1804), but freed in 1777, he joined insurgents in 1791, and by 1797 was effective ruler of the former colony. He drove out British and Spanish expeditions, restored order and aimed at independence, but **Napoleon I** sent a new expedition to Saint Domingue and proclaimed the re-establishment of slavery. Toussaint was arrested and died in prison. His surname ('the opening') comes from his bravery in once making a breach in enemy ranks.

Trollope, Anthony 1815–82
English novelist
He first achieved success with *The Warden* (1855), the first of the 'Barchester novels', which also included *Barchester Towers* (1857) and *The Small House at Allington* (1864). The novels are distinguished by their quiet comedy, slow pace and absorbing detail. A second sequence was known as the 'Palliser' novels, which included *Phineas Finn* (1869) and *The Eustace*

Diamonds (1873). He also wrote travel books, biographies, plays, short stories and literary sketches.

Trotsky, Leon, *alias of* **Lev Davidovich Bronstein** 1879–1940
Russian revolutionary
In the abortive 1905 revolution he became President of the St Petersburg Soviet, and later played a major role in the October Revolution. In the Russian Civil War he created the Red Army of 5 million men, but on **Lenin**'s death in 1924 his influence began to decline. **Stalin** ousted him from the politburo, and he was expelled from the USSR in 1929. In 1937, having been sentenced to death in his absence by a Soviet court, he found asylum in Mexico City. There he was assassinated by the Soviet secret police in 1940. His publications remain influential in Marxist circles in the West.

Truman, Harry S 1884–1972
33rd President of the USA
He became President in April 1945 on the death of President **Franklin D Roosevelt**, and was re-elected in 1948. During his presidency he took many historically important decisions, including dropping the first atom bombs on Hiroshima and Nagasaki; making a major change in US policy towards the USSR (the 'Truman Doctrine' of communist containment and support for peoples resisting communism); organizing the Berlin Airlift (1948–9); establishing NATO (1949); and sending US troops to withstand the Communist invasion of South Korea (1950). He also established the CIA.

Turgenev, Ivan Sergeyevich 1818–83
Russian novelist
After graduating from St Petersburg University, he went to Berlin to study philosophy and he mingled with the radical thinkers of the day. He returned to Russia in 1841 to enter the Civil Service, but in 1843 abandoned this to take up literature. In 1850 he wrote his best-known play, *A Month in the Country* (published 1869, staged 1872). *A Sportsman's Sketches* (1852), sympathetic studies of the peasant life, made his reputation. In his greatest novel, *Fathers and Sons* (1867), he portrayed a new generation with its faith in science and a lack of respect for authority. The novel, however, displeased many in his native Russia. Turgenev's popularity slumped at home but rose abroad, particularly in Great Britain, where the book was recognized as a major contribution to literature.

Turing, Alan Mathison 1912–54
English mathematician
In 1936 Turing made an outstanding contribution to the development of computer science, outlining a theoretical 'universal' machine (later called a Turing machine). In World War II he worked in cryptography and on deciphering the German 'Enigma' code, before joining the National Physical Laboratory (1945), where he designed the Automatic Computing Engine (ACE). In 1948 he accepted a post at Manchester University, where he made contributions to the programming of the Manchester Mark I computer and explored the problem of machine intelligence. He committed suicide.

Turner, J(oseph) M(allord) W(illiam) 1775–1851
English painter
One of the great masters of landscape art and of watercolour, he is known for his delicate rendering of light, conveying a mood or impression of a scene. His most famous works include *The Fighting Téméraire* (1839) and *Rain, Steam and Speed* (1844). He also worked on engravings. Turner's revolution in art foreshadowed Impressionism and was championed by **John Ruskin** in *Modern Painters* (1843).

Turpin, Dick (Richard) 1705–39
English robber
He was a butcher's apprentice, smuggler, cattle-thief, housebreaker, highwayman and horse-thief, and was hanged at York for the murder of a keeper of Epping Forest, in south-east England. His famous ride to York on his mare Black Bess, recounted in Harrison Ainsworth's *Rookwood* (1834), is now thought to have been done by 'Swift John Nevison', who in 1676 is said to have robbed a sailor at Gadshill at 4am, and to have established an alibi by reaching York at 7.45pm.

Tutankhamun d.c.1340BC
Egyptian pharaoh of the 18th Dynasty
The son-in-law of **Akhenaten**, he became king at the age of 12 and died at 18. His magnificent tomb at Thebes was discovered in 1922 by Lord Carnarvon and Howard Carter.

Tutu, Desmond Mpilo 1931–
South African Anglican archbishop
He rose rapidly to become Bishop of Lesotho (1976–8) and Archbishop of Cape Town (1986–96). A fierce opponent of apartheid, he repeatedly risked imprisonment for his advocacy of international sanctions against South Africa, although he deplored the use of violence. He was awarded the Nobel Peace Prize in 1984 and chaired the Truth and Reconciliation Commission from 1995 to 1999. His books include *The Rainbow People of God* (1994).

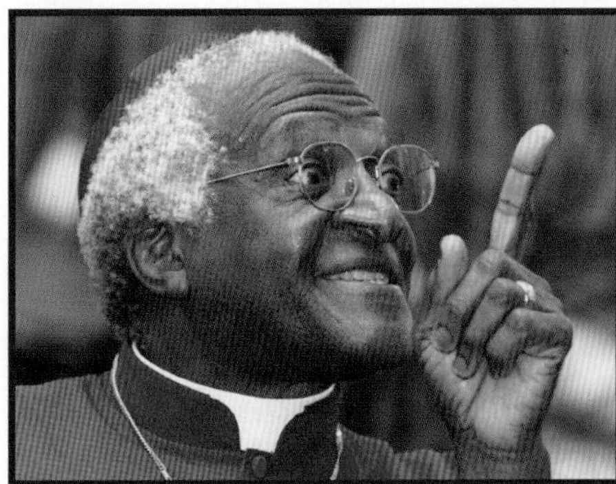
Desmond Tutu

Twain, Mark, *pseudonym of* **Samuel Langhorne Clemens** 1835–1910
US writer
He was first a printer (1847–55), and later a Mississippi river-boat pilot (1857–61). He adopted his pen-name from a well-known call of the man sounding the river in shallow places ('mark twain' meaning 'by the mark two fathoms'). After gaining a reputation as a humourist he published his two great masterpieces, *Tom Sawyer* (1876) and *Huckleberry Finn* (1884), drawn from his own boyhood experiences on the Mississippi frontier. Other works include *The Prince and the Pauper* (1882) and *A Connecticut Yankee in King Arthur's Court* (1889).

Tyler, Wat d.1381
English rebel, leader of the Peasants' Revolt
He was probably a tiler from Essex, chosen by a mob of peasants to be their spokesman after taking Rochester Castle (1381). Under him they moved to Canterbury, Blackheath and London. At a conference with **Richard II** at Smithfield, London, demanding an end to serfdom and greater freedom of labour, blows were exchanged and Tyler was wounded by William Walworth, Mayor of London. Walworth had him dragged out from St Bartholomew's Hospital and beheaded.

Tyndale or **Tindale** or **Hutchins, William** c.1494–1536
English translator of the Bible
He began printing his English New Testament in Cologne, Germany, in 1525, but this had not proceeded beyond the gospels of Matthew and Mark when he was forced to flee to Worms, where he completed his work. He later published his *Pentateuch* (1530–1) and *Jonah* (1531). In 1535 he was arrested in Antwerp, accused of heresy, imprisoned in the Castle of Vilvorde, tried there (1536), and strangled and burned. His other original works were *The Parable of the Wicked Mammon* (1528), *The Obedience of a Christian Man* (1528) and *Practyse of Prelates* (1530).

Valentino, Rudolph, *originally* **Rodolpho Alphonso Guglielmi di Valentina d'Antonguolla** 1895–1926
Italian-born US film actor
His first starring role was as Julio in *The Four Horsemen of the Apocalypse* (1921), in which his dark flashing eyes and erotic movements caused a sensation. Subsequent performances in *The Sheikh* (1921), *Blood and Sand* (1922), *The Eagle* (1925) and *The Son of the Sheikh* (1926) established him as the leading 'screen lover' of the 1920s. He died suddenly in New York of peritonitis at the height of his fame, and his funeral was the occasion of wide public mourning.

Vanbrugh, Sir John 1664–1726
English playwright and baroque architect
A staunch Whig, he became a leading spirit in society life and scored a success with his first comedy, *The Relapse* (1696), followed, again with success, by *The Provok'd Wife* (1697). A natural playwright of the uninhibited Restoration comedy of manners period, he also achieved success as architect of Castle Howard in Yorkshire (1702) and in 1705 was commissioned to design Blenheim Palace at Woodstock.

Van de Graaff, Robert J(emison) 1901–67
US physicist
At Princeton University in 1929 he constructed the first working model of an improved type of electrostatic generator (later to be known as the Van de Graaff generator). The charge was carried to a hollow metal sphere, allowing potentials of over a million volts to be achieved. Van de Graaff later adapted his generator for use as a particle accelerator, and this became a major research tool of atomic and nuclear physicists. The generator was also employed to produce high-energy X-rays, useful in the treatment of cancer.

van der Post, Sir Laurens Jan 1906–96
South African soldier, explorer, writer and philosopher
He served with distinction in World War II in Ethiopia, the Western Desert, Syria and the Far East, where he was captured by the Japanese. He went on to work for the British government on a variety of missions in Africa, and with the Kalahari Bushmen of southern Africa. A sensitive writer with insight, his books include *The Lost World of the Kalahari* (1958), *The Seed and the Sower* (1963, filmed as *Merry Christmas, Mr Lawrence*, 1983), *The Hunter and the Whale* (1967) and *The Voice of the Thunder* (1993).

Van Dyck or **Vandyke, Sir Anthony** 1599–1641
Flemish painter
After travelling throughout Europe painting portraits of royalty, in 1632 he was knighted by **Charles I**, who made him a court painter. His flair for rendering the character of his sitters, always with a hint of flattery and in the most favourable settings, greatly influenced the British school of portraiture in the next century. Among his best portraits are the equestrian portrait of Charles and the three views of Charles's head which served as a model for **Gian Lorenzo Bernini**'s sculpture.

Van Gogh, Vincent Willem 1853–90
Dutch Post-Impressionist painter
After working in England as a teacher, and in Belgium as a travelling preacher, he began painting, supported by his devoted brother Theo. He settled at Arles in the south of France with **Paul Gauguin** and painted *Sunflowers* (1888), *The Chair and the Pipe* (1888) and other works, but after a quarrel with Gauguin he cut off part of his own ear, and in 1890 he shot himself at the scene of his last painting, the *Cornfields with Flight of Birds*. Van Gogh's output included over 800 paintings and 700 drawings. He used colour primarily for its emotive appeal, and profoundly influenced experimenters of 20th-century art.

Velázquez or **Velásquez, Diego de Silva y** 1599–1660
Spanish painter
Considered one of the greatest painters of the 17th century, he achieved lifelong court patronage in 1623 with his equestrian portrait (now lost) of Philip IV. It was during his visit to Italy (1629–31) that his austere, naturalistic style was transformed into the more colourful style apparent in the new type of portrait which he improvised, of the king or his brother, or son, in hunting costume with dog and landscape. He is best remembered for his three late masterpieces, *Maids of Honour* (1656), in which the Infanta, her dwarf and attendants and the artist himself with easel are grouped around a canvas in a large palace room, *The Tapestry Weavers* (c.1657), and *Venus and Cupid*, known as the 'Rokeby Venus' (c.1658), one of the few nudes in Spanish painting.

Verdi, Giuseppe Fortunino Francesco 1813–1901
Italian operatic composer
Nabucco (1842) was his first major success, and *Rigoletto* (1851), *Il Trovatore* (1853) and *La Traviata* (1853) established his position as the leading Italian operatic composer of the day. Later works include *Don Carlos* (1867), *Aïda* (1871), *Otello* (1887) and *Falstaff* (1893). Recurring themes in Verdi's operas include the relationship of father and daughter and of mother and son, and the conflict of political power and human love. His music is characterized by

PEOPLE

intimate tenderness as well as by moments of rousing splendour.

Vermeer, Jan 1632–75
Dutch painter
Most of his works are small, detailed domestic interiors of his own house, every scene perfectly arranged so that everything, material or human, has equal prominence and attention. Fewer than 40 of his paintings are known, including the *Allegory of Painting* (c.1665), *Woman reading a Letter* (c.1662), *Girl with a Pearl Earring* (c.1665), *Woman with a Water Jug* (c.1658–60) and *View of Delft* (c.1660). His importance was only established in the late 19th century.

Verne, Jules 1828–1905
French novelist
His novel *Five Weeks in a Balloon* (1863) struck a new vein of fiction that exaggerated and often anticipated the possibilities of science, and described adventures carried out by means of scientific inventions in exotic places, like submarines and space travel. His best-known books are *A Journey to the Centre of the Earth* (1864), *From the Earth to the Moon* (1865), *Twenty Thousand Leagues Under the Sea* (1869) and *Around the World in Eighty Days* (1873).

Vesalius, Andreas 1514–64
Belgian anatomist
His dissections of human corpses enabled him to point out many errors in traditional medical teachings. For instance, Vesalius insisted he could find no passage for blood through the ventricles of the heart, as **Galen** had assumed. His greatest work, the *On the Structure of the Human Body* (1543), was enriched by magnificent illustrations, and in it many structures are described and drawn for the first time.

Vespucci, Amerigo 1451–1512
Spanish explorer
Although not a navigator or pilot himself, in 1499 he promoted an expedition to the New World commanded by Alonso de Hojeda and sailed there in his own ship, in which he explored the coast of Venezuela. His name (Latinized as 'Americus') was given to the American continents by the young German cartographer Martin Waldseemüller.

Victoria, *in full* **Alexandrina Victoria** 1819–1901
Queen of the United Kingdom of Great Britain and Ireland, and Empress of India
She became queen in 1837 at the age of 18, on the death of her uncle, William IV. She married Prince **Albert** of Saxe-Coburg and Gotha in 1840, and during a happy marriage bore him four sons and five daughters; her son Albert Edward became king as Edward VII. Among the prime ministers she particularly favoured during her long reign was **Disraeli**, who proclaimed her Empress of India in 1876. She oversaw a huge expansion of British industrial strength and foreign power, and brought to the monarchy a highly personal brand of shrewdness and innate political flair.

Virgil or **Vergil**, *full name* **Publius Vergilius Maro** 70–19BC
Roman poet
In the year 37BC his *Eclogues*, ten pastorals modelled on those of Theocritus, were received with great enthusiasm. In 30BC he published the *Georgics*, or *Art of Husbandry*, in four books; they confirmed his position as the foremost poet of the age. The remaining eleven years of his life were devoted to the composition of the *Aeneid*, a great national epic based on the story of Aeneas, legendary founder of the Roman nation. His work has been translated and admired by generations of poets.

Vivaldi, Antonio Lucio 1678–1741
Italian violinist and composer
The twelve concertos of *Harmonic Inspiration* (1712) gave him a European reputation, and *The Four Seasons* (1725), an early example of programme music, was very popular. The composer of many operas, sacred music and over 450 concertos, he developed the solo concerto, but was forgotten for many years after his death. He was also a priest, and known as the 'Red Priest' because of his red hair.

Volta, Alessandro Giuseppe Anastasio, Count 1745–1827
Italian physicist and inventor
His best-known invention was the electrochemical battery, or 'voltaic pile' (1800), which was the first source of continuous or current electricity. He also invented an 'inflammable air' (hydrogen) electric pistol (1777). His name is given to the SI unit of electrical potential difference, the volt.

Voltaire, *pseudonym of* **François Marie Arouet** 1694–1778
French writer
As a young man he was imprisoned twice for controversial attacks on members of the French court, and forced to seek refuge in England. On returning to France he found favour at court, and later went to Berlin at the invitation of **Frederick II, the Great**. He settled in 1755 near Geneva, and there wrote his satirical short story *Candide*, his best-known work. In 1762 he published the first of the anti-religious writings which helped to combat the power of the Catholic Church in France. He was a friend or correspondent of most of the great intellects of the age, and his works and ideas helped to foster the French Revolution.

Vo Nguyen Giap 1912–
Vietnamese military leader
He led the Viet Minh army in revolt against the French, decisively defeating them at Dien Bien Phu in 1954. As Vice-Premier and Defence Minister of North Vietnam, he masterminded the military strategy that forced the US forces to leave South Vietnam (1973) and led to the reunification of Vietnam in 1975. He was a member of the Politburo from 1976 to 1982. He wrote *People's War, People's Army* (1961), which became a textbook for revolutionaries.

Wagner, (Wilhelm) Richard 1813–83
German composer
His first major successes were his operas *Rienzi* (1842) and *The Flying Dutchman* (1843). He was later appointed kapellmeister at Dresden, and there wrote *Tannhäuser* (1845) and early versions of the *Ring* cycle. Later works include *Tristan und Isolde* (1859), *Die Meistersinger* (1868) and *Parsifal* (1882). He founded the now famous theatre at Bayreuth in northern Bavaria, which opened in 1876 with the first complete performance of the *Ring* cycle. One of the most influential of all Romantic composers, Wagner

wrote all his texts himself, and developed the concept of the leitmotif, or repeating thematic phrase. His autobiography is *My Life* (1880).

Waksman, Selman Abraham 1888–1973
US biochemist
From 1915 he worked on the microbial breakdown of organic substances in the soil, work which led to a new classification of microbes (1922) and methods for their scientific cultivation (1932). He discovered the anti-cancer drug actinomycin in 1941, the first anti-tuberculosis drug streptomycin in 1944, and several other antibacterial agents. For these important discoveries he was awarded the Nobel Prize for physiology or medicine in 1952. He also worked extensively on marine bacteria and the enzyme alginase.

Wallace, Alfred Russel 1823–1913
English biologist
A pioneer of the theory of natural selection, he travelled and collected (1848–52) in the Amazon basin and the Malay Archipelago (1854–62). In 1855 he published his paper *On the Law which has Regulated the Introduction of New Species*, and his memoir, sent to **Charles Darwin** in 1858, hastened the publication of Darwin's *The Origin of Species*. In his great *Geographical Distribution of Animals* (1879) and other works, Wallace contributed much to the foundations of zoogeography, the study of the distribution of animals. He was an outspoken advocate of socialism, pacifism, women's rights and other causes.

Wallace, Sir William, *also spelt* **Walays** or **Wallensis** c.1274–1305
Scottish patriot
He was the chief champion of Scotland's independence. Wallace burnt Lanark and defeated **Edward I**'s army at Stirling, and the English were expelled from Scotland. In retaliation Edward invaded Scotland in 1298, meeting Wallace at Falkirk, where the Scots were this time defeated. Wallace eventually escaped to France. He returned in 1303, but in 1305 was arrested and taken to London, where he was condemned and hanged, drawn and quartered.

Walpole, Sir Robert, 1st Earl of Orford 1676–1745
English Whig politician
He rose to power under **George I**, who could not speak English and gave up attending the proceedings of parliament, thereby leaving Walpole considerable freedom as leader of the government. From 1714 Walpole gradually established his supremacy, chairing, on the king's behalf, a small group of ministers which was the forerunner of the present-day cabinet. As a result, he came to be seen as England's first Prime Minister. Walpole's foreign policy was based on a determination to maintain peace. He did not fully recover from the outbreak of the so-called War of Jenkins' Ear with Spain in 1739, which he had opposed, and resigned in 1742.

Warhol, Andy, *originally* **Andrew Warhola** 1928–87
US pop artist and film-maker
He worked as a commercial designer before becoming in 1961 a pioneer of pop art with colourful reproductions of familiar everyday objects (eg *100 Soup Cans* and *Green Coca-Cola Bottles*, 1962). His first films (eg *Sleep*, 1963) endeavoured to eliminate the personality of the film-maker by use of a fixed camera viewpoint without sound. Later productions of his Greenwich Village 'film factory' included *Chelsea Girls* (1967), *Flesh* (1968), *Trash* (1969) and *Dracula* (1974). In the 1970s Warhol turned to portrait painting, as in the ten Mao portraits of 1972.

Andy Warhol

Washington, George 1732–99
1st President of the USA
After an early career spent fighting with the British against the French, on the outbreak of the War of Independence he became Commander-in-Chief of the colonial army (1775), and finally forced the defeat and surrender of the English at Yorktown in 1781. In 1789, after taking an active part in forming a new constitution, he became the first chief-magistrate or president. His two most trusted advisers, **Thomas Jefferson** and Alexander Hamilton, were his Secretary of State and Treasury Secretary respectively. In 1793 Washington was elected to a second term, but retired from the presidency in 1797. The federal capital of the USA was named after him.

Waters, Muddy, *real name* **McKinley Morganfield** 1915–83
US blues singer, composer and guitarist
He was first recorded in a classic Delta blues style in 1941 by Alan Lomax, the folk-music researcher, and moved to Chicago in 1943, where he became the crucial figure in the development of the electric urban blues style. He gained his first national success with 'Rollin' Stone' (1950), and later with his band released singles such as 'I've Got My Mojo Working' (1957) and 'Hoochie Coochie Man' (1954). His earthy, rough-hewn vocals and electrifying guitar work won him a large white audience from the late 1950s.

Watson, James Dewey 1928–
US biologist
While in Cambridge in 1951, Watson worked with **Francis Crick** on the structure of DNA, the biological molecule contained in cells which carries the genetic information. They published their model of a two-stranded helical molecule in 1953. For this work, Watson was awarded the 1962 Nobel Prize for physiology or medicine jointly with Crick and **Maurice Wilkins**. From 1985 until 2002 he was head of the Human Genome Project, aiming to locate all genes in the human body and determine their DNA sequences.

Watson-Watt, Sir Robert Alexander 1892–1973
Scottish physicist
By 1935 he had perfected a short-wave radio wave system called 'RAdio Detection And Ranging', or radar, that was able to locate aeroplanes. He was knighted for his role in the development and introduction of radar in 1942. In 1958 he published *Three Steps to Victory*.

Watt, James 1736–1819
Scottish engineer and inventor
In 1763–4 a model of **Thomas Newcomen**'s steam engine was sent to his workshop for repair. Seeing the defects in the design of the machine, he added a separate steam condenser, which resulted in a much greater efficiency. Manufacture of the new engine (designed to pump water) began, and between 1781 and 1785 he obtained patents for many other improvements. One of his patents described a steam locomotive (1784). The modern scientific unit of power, the watt, is named after him, and horsepower, the original unit of power, was first experimentally determined and used by him in 1783.

Waugh, Evelyn Arthur St John 1903–66
English writer
One of the greatest comic novelists of the 20th century, his first novel *Decline and Fall* (1928) was highly successful. In 1930 he became a Roman Catholic, an event which he regarded as the most important in his life, and in the same year published the satire *Vile Bodies*. His experiences as an officer in World War II inspired the trilogy *Men at Arms* (1952), *Officers and Gentlemen* (1955) and *Unconditional Surrender* (1961). Other books include *Scoop* (1938), *Put Out More Flags* (1942), *Brideshead Revisited* (1945) and *The Loved One* (1947).

Wayne, John, *originally* **Marion Michael Morrison** 1907–79
US film actor
He had a succession of small parts in low-budget films and serials which eventually led to stardom as the Ringo Kid in *Stagecoach* (1939). Known as 'Duke', he went on to make over 80 films in the next 40 years, typically starring in westerns as a tough but warm-hearted gunfighter or lawman, or in war films. He gave notable performances in, among others, *The Searchers* (1956), *True Grit* (1969, Academy Award) and *The Shootist* (1976), his final film and regarded one of his best.

Webster, John c.1580–c.1625
English dramatist
He is best known for his plays *The White Devil* (1612) and *The Duchess of Malfi* (1623), two of the most famous and bloodthirsty examples of Jacobean Revenge Tragedy. The play *A Late Murder of the Son upon the Mother* (1624), unpublished and lost, was written by John Ford and Webster. He was not popular in his own day, but gained stature in the 20th century.

Wegener, Alfred Lothar 1880–1930
German meteorologist and geophysicist
The Origin of Continents and Oceans was first published in 1915, based on his observations that the continents may once have been joined into one huge continent (Pangaea), which later broke up, the fragments drifting apart to form the continents as they are today. The hypothesis remained controversial until the 1960s, when the structure of oceans became understood.

Weill, Kurt 1900–50
US composer
He achieved fame with the music for *The Threepenny Opera*, **Bertolt Brecht**'s modernization of John Gay's *Beggar's Opera*, in 1928. Other works of that time included *The Rise and Fall of the City of Mahagonny* (1927–9) and *The Seven Deadly Sins* (1933), both with Brecht. A refugee from the Nazis, he settled in the USA in 1934. In all his works Weill was influenced by jazz idioms, and his later songs, operas and musical comedies, many of which contain elements of social criticism, are amongst the most impressive written for the American stage.

Welles, (George) Orson 1915–85
US film director and actor
He became a radio producer in 1934 and founded the Mercury Theatre in 1937. His 1938 radio production of **H G Wells**'s *War of the Worlds* was so realistic that it caused panic in the USA. He wrote, produced, directed and acted in *Citizen Kane* (1941), a revolutionary landmark in cinema technique. His later films included *The Magnificent Ambersons* (1942), *Macbeth* (1948), *Othello* (1951), *The Trial* (1962) and *Chimes at Midnight* (1965). As an actor, the most notable of his varied and memorable stage and film performances was as Harry Lime in *The Third Man* (1949).

Wellington, Arthur Wellesley, 1st Duke of, *known as* **the Iron Duke** 1769–1852
Irish-born soldier and statesman
After an early career spent fighting in India, Wellington led forces against **Napoleon I** in the Peninsular War (1808–14), ultimately driving the French out of Spain and Portugal and bringing them to submission at Toulouse in 1814. Created Duke of Wellington and heaped with honours, he was once again summoned to oppose Napoleon after the latter's escape from the island of Elba, where he had been exiled. Wellington routed the French at Waterloo on 18 June 1815. He was later Prime Minister on two occasions: from 1828 to 1830 and briefly in the political crisis of 1834.

Wells, H(erbert) G(eorge) 1866–1946
English novelist, short-story writer and popular historian
He achieved fame as a novelist with *The Time Machine* (1895), which pioneered English science fiction, and followed it with novels such as *The Invisible Man* (1897), *The War of the Worlds* (1898) and *The First Men in the Moon* (1901). He also wrote some of the best-known English comic novels, among them *Kipps* (1905) and *The History of Mr Polly* (1910). His other works include *The Outline of History* (1920), *The Shape of Things to Come* (1933) and the despairing *Mind at the End of its Tether* (1945). *Experiment in Autobiography* (1934) includes a striking self-portrait and studies of friends and contemporaries.

Wesley, Charles 1707–88
English hymnwriter, evangelist and founder of Methodism
The brother of **John Wesley**, in 1729 he formed a small group of fellow students, nicknamed the 'Holy Club' or the 'Oxford Methodists', later joined by John.

After a spiritual experience in 1738, when he found himself 'at peace with God', he became an evangelist and wrote over 5,500 hymns. These include 'Jesu, Lover of My Soul', 'Hark, the Herald Angels Sing' and 'Love Divine, All Loves Excelling'.

Wesley, John 1703–91
English evangelist and founder of Methodism
He became the leader of a small dedicated group which had gathered round his brother **Charles Wesley**, nicknamed the 'Holy Club' or the 'Oxford Methodists'. In the face of opposition from the established Church, in the late 1730s he began preaching to huge crowds in the open air, and made thousands of converts, mostly working people. He also founded charitable institutions at Newcastle and London, and Kingswood School in Bristol. He always regarded Methodism as a movement within the Church of England, and it remained so during his lifetime. Besides an enormous output of hymns, sermons, histories and biographies, he also kept a famous *Journal*.

Weston, Edward 1886–1958
US photographer
He became recognized as a modernist, emphasizing sharp images and precise definition in landscapes, portraits and still life, and pioneered close-up studies of inanimate objects such as shells and vegetables. He produced notable landscapes of the Mohave Desert, and in 1937, with the first-ever award of a Guggenheim Fellowship to a photographer, travelled widely throughout the western states of the USA. Later work included photographic illustrations to an edition of **Walt Whitman**'s *Leaves of Grass*.

Wharton, Edith Newbold, *née* **Jones** c.1861–1937
US novelist and short-story writer
The House of Mirth (1905), a tragedy about a beautiful and sensitive girl who is destroyed by the society her upbringing has designed her to join, established her as a major novelist. Many other works followed, including travel books and volumes of verse, but she is known principally as a witty and satirical observer of society. Her most uncharacteristic novel is *Ethan Frome* (1911), which deals partly with her unhappy marriage. Important later works are *The Age of Innocence* (1920), *The Children* (1928) and *Hudson River Bracketed* (1929). *A Backwards Glance* (1934) is her revealing autobiography.

Whistler, James (Abbott) McNeill 1834–1903
US artist
He became celebrated as a portrait painter in London, and conceived his paintings as experiments in colour harmony and tonal effect; the famous portrait of his mother (1871–2) was originally exhibited as *An Arrangement in Grey and Black*. Other well-known works include *Old Battersea Bridge* (1872–5), and the 'Thames' set of etchings. In 1877 **John Ruskin**'s criticism (he accused Whistler of 'flinging a pot of paint in the public's face') provoked a famous lawsuit in which Whistler was awarded a farthing damages.

Whitman, Walt(er) 1819–92
US poet
In 1855 he published the first edition of *Leaves of Grass*, a collection of poems which constitutes his main work as a writer. Many of the poems in it are now considered American classics, such as the 'Song of Myself', the 'Calamus' sequence, and the elegies 'When Lilacs Last in the Dooryard Bloom'd' and 'O Captain! My Captain!' written in memory of the assassinated US President **Abraham Lincoln**. Whitman included in his verse subjects which, at that time, were considered taboo, and made frequent use of colloquial language.

Whittle, Sir Frank 1907–96
English aeronautical engineer and inventor
He began research into jet propulsion before 1930, while still a student. After long delays, caused partly by official obstruction, his engine was first flown successfully in a Gloster aircraft in May 1941, about two years after the world's first flights of both turbojet and rocket-powered aircraft had taken place in Germany.

Wilberforce, William 1759–1833
English philanthropist and reformer
In 1780 he was elected MP for Hull, and in 1784 for Yorkshire. In 1788 he began a 19-year campaign for the abolition of the slave trade in the British West Indies, which he finally achieved in 1807. He next sought to secure the abolition of the slave trade abroad and the total abolition of slavery itself. However, declining health compelled him in 1825 to retire from parliament. He died one month before the Slavery Abolition Act was passed.

Wilde, Oscar Fingal O'Flahertie Wills 1854–1900
Irish playwright, novelist, essayist, poet and wit
Wilde's literary reputation rests on his plays, which include *Lady Windermere's Fan* (1892), *A Woman of No Importance* (1893), *An Ideal Husband* (1895) and his masterpiece, *The Importance of Being Earnest* (1895). After receiving a note from the Marquis of Queensberry accusing him of being a homosexual, Wilde sued, but lost the case and was imprisoned (1895) for homosexuality. *The Ballad of Reading Gaol* was published in 1898, and *De Profundis*, his bitter reproach to his friend Lord Alfred Douglas, in 1905. Wilde also wrote a novel, *The Picture of Dorian Gray* (1891), as well as literary essays, poetry, short stories and children's stories. He died in Paris.

Wilhelm II 1859–1941
German emperor and King of Prussia
The eldest son of Frederick III, he was Emperor of Germany and King of Prussia from 1888 until 1918. After dismissing **Bismarck** in 1890, a long period of personal rule followed, in which he attempted to strengthen Germany's empire and build up the German navy. After the assassination of the Austrian Archduke **Franz Ferdinand** at Sarajevo in 1914, he tried to avoid war, but political power passed from him to the generals, and during World War I he became a mere figurehead. The defeat of Germany forced him to abdicate and flee the country, and he lived the rest of his life in the Netherlands.

Wilkins, Maurice Hugh Frederick 1916–2004
British physicist
Born in New Zealand, he joined the Medical Research Council's Biophysics Research Unit at King's College London in 1946, becoming director (1970–2) and professor of biophysics (1970–81). **Francis Crick** and **James Watson** deduced their double helix model of DNA from Wilkins and **Rosalind Franklin**'s X-ray data of DNA fibres, and Crick, Watson and Wilkins

PEOPLE

were awarded the 1962 Nobel Prize for physiology or medicine for this work.

William the Conqueror, *also called* **William the Bastard** c.1027/8–87
King of England as William I from 1066
The illegitimate son of Robert, Duke of Normandy, he succeeded his father in 1035. He was the cousin of **Edward the Confessor**, which gave him a claim to the English throne, and he invaded England on 28 September 1066. At the Battle of Hastings (or Senlac) on 14 October 1066, he defeated and killed **Harold II**, and was crowned King of England. In 1086 he ordered the compilation of the Domesday Book, a highly detailed record of property ownership in England. William's rule was successful despite several revolts. He died fighting Philip I of France.

William III, *also called* **William of Orange** 1650–1702
Stadtholder of the Netherlands, and King of Great Britain and Ireland
He was the son of William II of Orange and Mary, eldest daughter of **Charles I** of Great Britain, and raised as a Protestant. In 1672 he was chosen as Stadtholder (head) of the Netherlands, and in 1677 he married Mary, eldest daughter of James, Duke of York (**James VII and II**). When James became King of Scotland and England (1685), his policy of conversion to Catholicism provided William with the opportunity for invading his father-in-law's kingdoms in the name of his wife. James then fled to France, and William and Mary were crowned in February 1689. William's successive defeats of James's supporters effectively ended Jacobite resistance.

Williams, John Christopher 1941–
Australian classical guitarist
A leading international figure on classical guitar, he has been responsible for commissioning a great deal of contemporary compositions for the instrument. He tours widely, giving solo recitals and performing in chamber groups and as soloist with international orchestras, and his extensive repertoire is well represented on records. He has also performed in rock (notably with the group Sky from 1979 to 1984), jazz and folk contexts, and has taken a number of recordings into the pop charts.

Williams, Serena 1981–
US tennis player

Serena and Venus Williams

She and her older sister **Venus Williams** were acknowledged the dominant forces in women's tennis at the beginning of the 21st century. In 1999 she became the first of the sisters to win a Grand Slam title by capturing the US Open singles. She went on to win numerous doubles titles in partnership with Venus, including Olympic gold in 2000, and won the Wimbledon singles title in 2002 and 2003.

Williams, Tennessee, *originally* **Thomas Lanier** 1911–83
US playwright
The Glass Menagerie (1944) introduced him as an important US playwright. He was awarded the Pulitzer Prize in 1948 for *A Streetcar Named Desire*, and again in 1955 for *Cat on a Hot Tin Roof*. He continued with *Suddenly Last Summer* (1958), *Sweet Bird of Youth* (1959) and *The Night of the Iguana* (1961). In addition to his plays, he published the poetry collections *The Summer Belvedere* (1944) and *Winter of Cities* (1956), and short stories, including *It Happened the Day the Sun Rose* (1982). He wrote one novel, *The Roman Spring of Mrs Stone* (1950), and the scripts for several films.

Williams, Venus 1980–
US tennis player
She and her younger sister **Serena Williams** emerged as the leading forces on the women's circuit at the beginning of the 21st century. She reached the final of the US Open in 1997, and her first Grand Slam singles victory came in 2000 when she won the Wimbledon title. She added the US Open and the Olympic singles titles that same year, becoming only the second player to hold the US Open, Olympic and Wimbledon titles simultaneously. Two more Wimbledon singles titles followed in 2001 and 2005.

Wilson, (Thomas) Woodrow 1856–1924
28th President of the USA
He became Governor of New Jersey in 1911 and in 1912 and 1916, as Democratic candidate, he was elected President of the USA. Wilson's administration, ending in tragic failure and physical breakdown, is memorable for the prohibition and women's suffrage amendments to the Constitution, trouble with Mexico, US participation in World War I, his part in the peace conference, his 'fourteen points' plan for peace, which led to the Armistice, his championship of the League of Nations, and the Senate's rejection of the Treaty of Versailles which led to his breakdown. He was awarded the 1919 Nobel Peace Prize.

Witt, Katerina 1965–
German figure skater
She became East German champion in 1982, and won the first of six successive European titles in 1983. She was world champion (1984–5, 1987–8), and Olympic champion in 1984 and 1988.

Wittgenstein, Ludwig Josef Johann 1889–1951
Austrian-born British philosopher
One of the 20th century's most influential philosophers, he served in World War I in the Austrian army and was taken prisoner on the Italian front in 1918. While he was still a prisoner he completed the only work published in his lifetime, the *Tractatus Logico-Philosophicus* (1921), which dealt mainly with problems of language. He later became Professor of Philosophy at Cambridge University, and the work of this second period of his philosophical career is best summarized in the posthumous

Philosophical Investigations (1953).

Wodehouse, Sir P(elham) G(renville) 1881–1975
English novelist
He made his name with *Piccadilly Jim* (1917) and went on to publish over 100 books. He is best known as the creator of Bertie Wooster and his legendary valet, Jeeves, but also gave life to numerous other memorable characters, including Ukridge, Psmith, Mr Mulliner and Lord Emsworth. Noted for his superbly polished comic style and complex plots, his titles include *The Inimitable Jeeves* (1923), *Blandings Castle* (1935) and *The Mating Season* (1949). He also wrote the lyrics for several musical comedies, mainly for the US stage.

Wolsey, Thomas c.1475–1530
English cardinal and politician
The son of a prosperous butcher, he rose to become chaplain to Henry VII. Under **Henry VIII** he was made archbishop of York (1514) and then a cardinal and Lord Chancellor (both 1515), and eventually took charge of much of the country's foreign and domestic policy. He met his downfall over his reluctance to annul the King's marriage to Catherine of Aragon. He was forced to retire to Winchester and arrested on a charge of high treason, and died while journeying from York to London.

Wood, Sir Henry Joseph 1869–1944
English conductor
He founded, with the then manager of the Queen's Hall in London, Robert Newman, the Promenade Concerts, which he conducted annually from 1895 until his death. He composed operettas and an oratorio, *Saint Dorothea* (1889), but his international reputation was gained as conductor of the promenade concerts. In 1938 he published *My Life of Music*.

Woods, Tiger, *real name* **Eldrick Woods** 1975–
US golfer

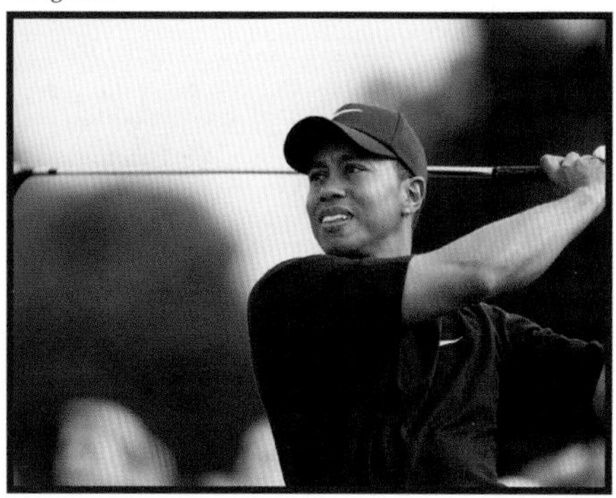

Tiger Woods

Having turned professional in August 1996, he became the first player to record five top-ten finishes in a row on the US Tour. In 1997 he became the youngest and the first black winner of the US Masters. He has continued to win numerous events, including the British Open (2000, 2005, 2006), the United States Open (2000, 2002), the United States PGA Championship (1999, 2000, 2006) and the US Masters (1997, 2001, 2002, 2005).

Woolf, (Adeline) Virginia, *née* **Stephen** 1882–1941
English novelist, critic and essayist
One of the great innovators of the modern novel in English, she and her family and friends formed the nucleus of the literary circle known as the Bloomsbury Group. The three novels on which her reputation chiefly rests were all written within six years: *Mrs Dalloway* (1925), *To the Lighthouse* (1927) and *The Waves* (1931), noted for their impressionistic, stream-of-consciousness style. Other works include *The Voyage Out* (1915), *Jacob's Room* (1922), *Orlando* (1928), the long essay *A Room of One's Own* (1929) and *The Years* (1937). In 1917 she and her husband Leonard formed the Hogarth Press, which published works by other modern writers. She committed suicide by drowning.

Woolworth, Frank Winfield 1852–1919
US businessman
From 1905 he began building a large chain of stores selling cheaply-priced goods, and by the time he died the F W Woolworth company controlled over a thousand stores from their headquarters in the Woolworth building in New York. Woolworth's stores reached Great Britain in 1910, but their main development outside the USA was after the death of their founder.

Wordsworth, William 1770–1850
English poet
His first important publication was *Lyrical Ballads* (1798), which also contained poems by his friend **Samuel Taylor Coleridge**. This revolutionary collection, which began with Coleridge's 'Ancient Mariner' and concluded with Wordsworth's 'Tintern Abbey', was the beginning of the Romantic movement in poetry. Later additions to the volume included the famous *Lucy* poems, and subsequent longer works included *The Prelude* (first published 1850) and *The Excursion* (1814). He became Poet Laureate in 1843.

Wren, Sir Christopher 1632–1723
English architect
Originally a professor of astronomy at Oxford, he helped to lay the foundation of the Royal Society, a learned society for science. From 1663–6 he designed the Sheldonian Theatre at Oxford and the library of Trinity College, Cambridge. The Great Fire of London (1666) presented him with a unique opportunity to redesign the whole city, but his scheme was never implemented. In 1669 he was chosen architect for the new St Paul's, and for more than 50 other churches in place of those destroyed by the fire. He also designed the Royal Exchange Greenwich Observatory, the Ashmolean Museum at Oxford, parts of Westminster Abbey and many other buildings.

Wright, Frank Lloyd 1867–1959
US architect
He became known for low-built prairie-style bungalows, but soon launched into more daring and controversial designs that exploited modern technology and Cubist spatial concepts. His best-known public buildings include the Imperial Hotel in Tokyo (1916–20), the 'Falling Water' weekend retreat at Mill Run, near Pittsburgh in Pennsylvania (1936) and the Guggenheim Museum of Art in New York (1959). He also designed furniture and textiles and is considered one of the outstanding architects of the 20th century.

He wrote an *Autobiography* (1932) and numerous other works.

Wright, Orville 1871–1948 and **Wilbur** 1867–1912
US aviation pioneers
They operated a bicycle shop together and were self-taught inventors, becoming the first to fly in a heavier-than-air machine (17 December 1903), at Kitty Hawk, North Carolina. Encouraged by this, they patented their flying machine and formed an aircraft production company (1909). In 1915 Orville sold his interests in the business in order to devote himself to research.

Wyatt, Sir Thomas 1503–42
English poet and courtier
His is famous for his lyrics and sonnets, and is regarded as the most important of all the English poets who imitated, and then added to, Italian models. The best-known collection of his work was edited by Kenneth Muir (1949, revised edition 1963), who also wrote Wyatt's biography in *Life and Letters* (1963).

Wycliffe, John, *also spelt* **Wycliff, Wyclif, Wicliffe** or **Wiclif** c.1329–1384
English religious reformer
In works such as *De Dominio Divino* (1376) he attacked the power of the Church, later arguing against the whole priestly system and asserting the right of every man to examine the Bible for himself rather than have it interpreted. He began to write in English instead of Latin, and started the first English translation of the Bible, as well as issuing various popular tracts. His followers, known as 'Lollards' (from a Dutch word meaning 'mumblers'), spread his doctrines widely through the country. In 1414 the Council of Constance ordered his bones to be dug up, burned, and cast into the River Swift.

Wyndham, John, *pseudonym of* **John Wyndham Parkes Lucas Beynon Harris** 1903–69
English science-fiction writer
In the late 1920s he began to write science-fiction tales, and in 1951 published his most successful novel, *The Day of the Triffids*. Here, as in his later novels, he is concerned with man's behaviour and moral values when faced with unforeseen and uncontrollable situations. Other novels include: *The Kraken Wakes* (1953), *The Chrysalids* (1955), *The Midwich Cuckoos* (1957), *The Trouble With Lichen* (1960) and *Chocky* (1968). *Consider Her Ways* (1961) and *Seeds of Time* (1969) are collections of short stories.

Yeats, W(illiam) B(utler) 1865–1939
Irish poet
A formative influence on English poetry, his collections, inspired by Irish mythology, mysticism and the occult, include *The Wild Swans at Coole* (1919), *The Tower* (1928) and *The Winding Stair* (1933). He also wrote numerous plays and short stories. In 1889 he met and fell in love with the Irish nationalist Maud Gonne, an event which he described as 'the troubling of my life'; despite repeated offers from him she refused to marry him. He helped found the Irish Literary Theatre in 1899 (later the Abbey Theatre, Dublin), and became a member of the Irish senate in 1922. In 1923 he was awarded the Nobel Prize for literature.

Yeltsin, Boris Nikolayevich 1931–
Russian statesman
He began his career in the construction industry. He joined the Communist Party of the Soviet Union in 1961 and became the Moscow Party chief in 1985. A blunt-talking, hands-on reformer, he played a high-profile part in the resistance against the failed attempt to depose **Mikhail Gorbachev** as President, and in 1990 he was elected President of the Russian Federation. In 1996 he was re-elected, but throughout his presidency he suffered recurring bouts of ill health, and in 1999 he resigned and was replaced by Vladimir Putin.

Zeffirelli, Franco 1923–
Italian stage, opera and film director
His first opera production, *La Cenerentola* (1953), was followed by a brilliant series of productions in Italy and abroad. His stage productions include *Romeo and Juliet* (1960) and *Who's Afraid of Virginia Woolf?* (1964–5). He has also filmed lively and spectacular versions of **Shakespeare** plays, a television version of *Jesus of Nazareth* (1977) and film versions of the operas *La Traviata* (1983) and *Otello* (1986). Recent films include *Jane Eyre* (1996) and *Tea with Mussolini* (1999). He was elected to the Italian senate as a member of the right-wing Forza Italia party in 1994.

Zeno of Citium c.334–c.265BC
Greek philosopher
The founder of Stoicism, he attended **Plato**'s Academy and then set up his own school (c.300BC) in Athens, in the *Stoa poikile* ('painted porch'), which gave the Stoics their name. He had a formative role in the development of Stoicism as a distinctive and coherent philosophy. None of his many treatises survive, but his main contribution seems to have been in the area of ethics. He supposedly committed suicide.

Zinoviev, Grigori Yvseyevich 1883–1936
Russian politician
From 1917 to 1926 he was a leading member of the Soviet government. A letter allegedly written by him to the British Communist Party in 1924 was used in the election campaign to defeat **Ramsay MacDonald**'s first Labour government. In 1927 Zinoviev suffered expulsion, and in 1936 death, having been charged with conspiring to murder Sergei Kirov and **Stalin**. In 1988 he was posthumously declared innocent.

Zola, Émile 1840–1902
French novelist
One of the pioneers of naturalism, his first major novel, *Thérèse Raquin* (1867), is a powerful study of murder and guilt. Later he began the series of novels called *Les Rougon-Macquart*, a collection of some 20 volumes all connected by the appearance of members of a single family. These include *Nana* (1880), *Germinal* (1885), *The Dream* (1888) and *The Beast in Man* (1890). In 1898 Zola espoused the cause of **Alfred Dreyfus**, a French soldier convicted for delivering national defence documents to a foreign government, and confronted the military authorities in his pamphlet *J'accuse* ('I accuse'). He was sentenced to prison, but escaped for a year to England and was welcomed back a hero. He died in Paris, accidentally suffocated by charcoal fumes.

Zoroaster, *Greek form of* **Zarathustra**, *modern form* **Zaradusht**, *originally* **Spitama** c.630–c.553BC
Persian religious leader and prophet
The founder or reformer of Zoroastrianism, he appears as a historical person only in the earliest portion of the *Avesta*, the sacred book of Zoroastrianism. He apparently had visions of Ahura Mazda, a divinity considered to be the creator, which led him to preach against polytheism. The keynote of his system is that the world and history demonstrate the struggle between the creator or good spirit, and the evil principle, the devil, in which at the end good will triumph.

Zwingli, Huldreich or **Ulrich**, *Latin* **Ulricus Zuinglius** 1484–1531
Swiss reformer
Zwingli preached the Reformed doctrines as early as 1516, the year before the appearance of **Martin Luther**'s theses. He regarded original sin as a moral disease rather than as punishable sin or guilt. He maintained that unbaptized infants could achieve salvation, and he believed in the salvation of virtuous heathens. His ideas spread widely over Switzerland, but five Swiss Cantons formed an alliance against him in 1528, and he was killed in a battle at Cappel near Zurich.

EVENTS

PREHISTORY TO c.5000BC

c.4 000 000BC

Primitive hominids (the family comprising man and his ancestors), known as *Australopithecus*, appear in Africa.

c.2 000 000BC

Homo habilis ('skilful man') lives in Africa, hunting small game and using stones as tools.

c.1 500 000BC

Homo erectus ('upright man') emerges in eastern and south-eastern Asia, and spreads to Europe by c.700 000BC. Fire is used for the first time to cook meat.

c.400 000BC

The earliest true human being, *Homo sapiens* ('wise man'), appears in Europe.

c.120 000BC

Neanderthal people live in caves in Europe, using crude flint tools.

c.100 000BC

Cro-Magnon people (*Homo sapiens*) begin to spread from Africa into Asia, and reach Australia by c.50 000BC. They use a wider range of stone tools than their predecessors, as well as other materials, such as wood and bone.

c.30 000BC

North America begins to be populated as people cross from Siberia in Russia to Alaska by a land bridge that is later cut by the Bering Strait.

c.27 000BC

Southern African decorated stone tablets dating from around this time are the first known examples of painting.

c.20 000BC

The last Ice Age is at its height.

In Australia paintings are made on rocks.

c.17 000BC

Cave painting develops, with examples surviving at Lascaux in France, Altamira in Spain and other sites.

c.10 000BC

Farming begins in various parts of the world, notably in the 'Fertile Crescent' in the Middle East.

c.9000BC

Previously nomadic societies begin to make permanent settlements.

Wild cereals are harvested, and dogs, goats and pigs are domesticated.

Human occupation of the Americas extends to the southern extremes of South America.

c.8000BC

Villages built using mud bricks appear in Syria and Palestine in the Middle East.

Jericho, the earliest walled town, is inhabited before 7500BC.

c.7000BC

Sheep and cattle are domesticated in the Near East.

In South America root crops are cultivated, while rice begins to be grown in China.

c.6000BC

The first known pottery and woollen textiles are made in central Turkey.

Lead is smelted.

Farming spreads to south-eastern Europe.

Cattle are used to pull ploughs in the Near East.

c.5000–1BC

c.5000BC

The city of Eridu is founded in Mesopotamia in the Middle East; it is traditionally regarded as the first city. Others soon follow as the Sumerians spread along the valleys of the rivers Tigris and Euphrates.

Civilizations develop in Fayoum and Nubia (southern Egypt and northern Sudan).

The Caribbean islands begin to be settled, probably by groups from South America.

c.4500BC

The Neolithic period (New Stone Age), marked by the building of megalithic (literally 'big stone') monuments, begins in Europe.

The plough is used for the first time in Mesopotamia.

c.4000BC

The plough comes into use in China.

Horses begin to be domesticated in what is now Russia.

c.3700BC

Bronze (an alloy of copper and tin) is invented in Egypt.

c.3500BC

Settlement of the Indus Valley (India and Pakistan) begins.

Farmers on the plateaus of the Andes in South America begin to cultivate potatoes.

The wheel is in use in Mesopotamia, initially for transport but then in making pottery.

c.3400–1100BC

The Minoan civilization (named, in the 20th

century, after the legendary King Minos) is developed in Crete by a non-Greek people. It is noted for the sophistication of its art and architecture, and the enduring mystery of its writing system (now known as Linear A).

3372BC

This is the first year in the calendar of the Maya people of Guatemala and Mexico (based on projection backwards by their astronomers after c.300AD).

c.3200BC

Sumerians invent cuneiform (literally 'wedge-shaped') writing, creating the oldest known written records: tablets setting out the business dealings of temples in the city of Uruk.

c.3100BC

Egypt is unified, apparently for the first time, under a ruler known in legends as Menes.

The building of Stonehenge, a circle of upright stones in south-western England, begins.

c.3000BC

Phoenicians begin to establish trading cities in what are now Lebanon and Syria.

As the climate of much of Africa changes, the Sahara spreads still further southwards, Lake Chad begins to dry up and peoples speaking Bantu languages start their migrations eastwards across the sub-Saharan regions of the continent.

Pictograms, a form of writing in which each sign represents a thing or an idea, come into use in Egypt.

c.2800BC

Sericulture, the cultivation of silkworms, begins in China.

c.2780–2181BC

This is the period of Egyptian history known as the 'Old Kingdom', when the major pyramids were built to house the remains of powerful pharaohs. The period ends with the division of the kingdom among rival 'nomarchs' (local governors).

c.2600BC

Glassware is invented in Egypt.

c.2500BC

The religion of Hinduism originates in northern India.

c.2400BC

The Egyptians send their first known expedition southwards into Nubia, beginning centuries of trade, warfare and cultural exchange.

c.2334BC

Sargon I of Akkad (northern Mesopotamia) establishes the Akkadian Empire, which soon absorbs Sumer (southern Mesopotamia) and lasts until c.2200BC. It is followed by the rise of the city of Ur to a position of dominance, which it maintains until c.1950BC.

c.2300BC

The Bronze Age begins in central Europe.

c.2300–1750BC

Mohenjo-Daro and other planned cities are established in the Indus Valley (in what is now Pakistan).

c.2100BC

The first *ziggurats* (stepped pyramids) are built as centres of worship in the cities of Mesopotamia.

Ziggurat at Ur, modern-day Iraq

c.2040–1786BC

Following the reunification of Egypt, this is the period of the 'Middle Kingdom', marked by expansion southwards into Nubia.

The Baltic peoples (Lithuanians, Latvians and Prussians) begin migrating into Europe from Asia.

The first settlers arrive in New Guinea, probably from south-east Asia.

c.1900–1100BC

The Mycenaean civilization develops in mainland Greece. It writes an early form of Greek.

1894BC

Babylon becomes the centre of the large and powerful First Babylonian Empire, which unites Mesopotamia under its rule until 1595BC when it is overthrown by Hittites from Anatolia (modern-day Turkey).

c.1766–1122BC

The Shang Dynasty rules northern China.

c.1750BC

Hammurabi, ruler of the Babylonian Empire, dies, apparently after 42 years on the throne. His law code, inscribed on a tablet, is the oldest surviving law code in the world.

1567–1085BC

This is the period of the 'New Kingdom' in Egypt, marked by further expansion into Nubia and around the eastern end of the Mediterranean Sea.

1501–1448BC

Under Queen Hatshepsut and Thutmose III, Egypt expands to its greatest extent.

c.1500BC

Peoples later called Aryans invade and settle large areas of what are now northern India and Pakistan.

Settlement of the Pacific islands begins, probably by peoples migrating from east Asia.

1379–1362BC

The pharaoh Akhenaten rules Egypt. He introduces worship of the Sun as a single god.

c.1340BC

The Egyptian pharaoh Tutankhamun, successor to Akhenaten, is buried in a magnificent tomb at Thebes. His burial place remains undiscovered until 1922 when located by Howard Carter and Lord Carnarvon.

Funeral mask of Tutankhamun

c.1300BC

The first settlers arrive in Fiji, Tonga and Samoa.

The Assyrians establish an empire centred on Mesopotamia, rivalling the Hittites to the west and the Egyptians to the south. The Hittites and Egyptians make an alliance in 1269BC.

c.1250BC

A war between Mycenaean Greeks and the Trojans of north-west Anatolia (now in Turkey) ends in the destruction of the city of Troy. This becomes the basis for the legends of the Trojan War that flourish from c.900BC.

c.1200BC

The Chinese inscribe the earliest surviving forms of their written characters on oracle bones, which are animal bones burned so that predictions can be based on the patterns of cracks that result.

c.1200–600BC

The Olmec civilization flourishes in Mexico. It develops astronomy, builds pyramids, makes huge carved heads and takes part in blood sacrifice.

1122BC

At the Battle of Chaoge the Shang Dynasty in China is defeated and replaced by the Chou (Zhou) Dynasty, which, by ruling various parts of China until 256BC, becomes the longest lasting of all the Chinese dynasties.

c.1100BC

Following the collapse of Hittite rule in Anatolia and the eastern Mediterranean, the Assyrians expand their empire, which remains a major power until it collapses in around 612BC.

c.1000BC

The Iron Age starts in southern and central Europe. The use of iron weaponry spreads from Mesopotamia to Egypt and Greece.

The kingdom of Kush establishes control over most of Nubia and begins to challenge Egyptian power over the region.

The Phoenicians in Lebanon develop an alphabet from which the Hebrew, Arabic, Greek, Etruscan, Roman, Cyrillic and many other alphabets are later adapted.

Solomon's Temple, or the First Temple, said to be the first Jewish temple in Jerusalem, is completed.

c.900BC

The city of Sparta is founded by the joining together of a number of villages in the Eurotas river valley.

The Etruscans settle in a region of Italy later known as Etruria.

The blind Greek poet Homer may have lived around this time. Supposedly, he composed the two epic poems that now bear his name – the *Iliad*, presenting episodes of the Trojan War, and the *Odyssey*, describing Odysseus's adventures on his way home from Troy.

c.850BC

The Chavín culture appears in Peru. It is notable for its advances in pottery, metalwork and textiles.

814BC

Phoenician settlers from Tyre in Lebanon found the city of Carthage.

c.800BC

The caste system, dividing the population into rigidly defined groups loosely based on the occupations they have inherited, develops in northern India.

The Eastern Slavs, forebears of the Russians, Belarussians and Ukrainians, start migrating eastwards along the major rivers of the steppes: the Dnieper, the Vistula and the Don.

771–256BC

The era of 'Warring States' sees the disintegration of China, as the empire, still nominally ruled by the Chou (Zhou) Dynasty, is fought over by rival factions.

753BC

According to tradition, Rome is founded by the legendary King Romulus in this year.

750BC

The Nubian rulers of Kush conquer Egypt and found the 25th Dynasty of pharaohs, ruling both lands until 662BC.

c.750–450BC

The Celts (or Gauls, or Gaels) spread from their homeland in central Europe, eventually reaching regions later named after them – Galicia (now in Poland), Gaul (now France), Wales and other parts of the British Isles, and another Galicia (now in Spain).

c.700BC

The Lydians of south-western Anatolia (now in Turkey) develop the earliest known system of coinage.

c.700–200BC

Nomads known as Scythians enter and occupy the lands north of the Black Sea (now southern Russia).

680–669BC

The Assyrian ruler Esarhaddon establishes the capital city of Nineveh, and leads the Assyrian empire to its greatest expansion. In 662BC it conquers Egypt and overthrows the Nubian 25th Dynasty.

c.660BC

Byzantium is founded as a trading centre in north-western Anatolia. It becomes a link between Asia and Europe, is renamed Constantinople in AD330, and since 1930 has been known as Istanbul.

c.630BC

The Persian religious thinker and leader Zoroaster is traditionally said to have been born around this year, probably in what is now Azerbaijan.

c.612–539BC

The rulers of Babylon, having destroyed Nineveh, the capital city of the Assyrian Empire, establish and expand the Second Babylonian Empire by conquering the Kingdom of Judah and the Phoenician cities of Lebanon.

c.600BC

The *Upanishads*, the last section of the Hindu scriptures (the *Vedas*), are composed in the Sanskrit language.

c.580BC

Carthage becomes the dominant power in the western Mediterranean after inflicting a series of defeats on the Greek cities of Sicily.

c.575BC

The Ishtar Gate, a gate to the city of Babylon, is constructed at the order of King Nebuchadrezzar II.

The Ishtar Gate, Babylon

551BC

This is the traditional year of birth of the Chinese philosopher Confucius (d.479BC).

550BC

Cyrus II, the Great (c.600–529BC), founds the first Persian Empire (also called the Achaemenid Empire after the name of the ruling family).

c.540BC

Vardhamana Mahavira, the traditional founder of Jainism (a religion related to Buddhism), is born in India.

539BC

Cyrus II of Persia conquers the Second Babylonian Empire and allows the Jews to return to the former kingdom of Judah.

525BC

Persia conquers Egypt and controls it for most of the following two centuries, despite frequent revolts and three dynasties of native Egyptian pharaohs (28th to 30th dynasties).

515BC

In Jerusalem the Second Temple is completed, having been built to replace Solomon's Temple (the First Temple), which was destroyed by the Babylonians in 586BC.

510BC

After the king of Rome, Lucius Tarquinius Superbus (or Tarquin II), is deposed and expelled, the Senate declares the foundation of the Roman Republic.

c.500BC

Buddhism is founded in northern India by Prince Gautama Siddhartha (c.563–c.483BC), who is said to have become Buddha ('enlightened') through meditation.

490BC

The Athenians and their allies achieve an overwhelming victory over the armies of Darius I of Persia at the Battle of Marathon.

480BC

The attempt of the Persian Emperor Xerxes to conquer Greece is stopped by the victory of the Athenians and their allies in a naval battle at Salamis.

477BC

Athens founds the Delian League, a grouping of allied cities against Persian threats. It effectively becomes an Athenian empire when peace is made with Persia in 448BC.

431–404BC

The Second Peloponnesian War, between the Greek city states of Athens, at the head of the Delian League, and Sparta, joined by other rivals of Athens, ends in victory for Sparta. Sparta then becomes the dominant power in Greece until 371BC, when Thebes becomes the major force.

420BC

The Nabataean Kingdom, the earliest known Arab state, is founded with its capital at Petra (now in Jordan). It lasts until AD106, when it is taken by the Roman Empire, becoming the province of Arabia Petraea.

c.400BC

The Nok culture, noted for its copper, iron and terracotta wares, begins to develop in what is now northern Nigeria.

Carthage achieves control of trade throughout the western Mediterranean after conquering parts of Sicily and beginning colonization of the Spanish coast.

399BC

The philosopher Socrates (b.469BC) is condemned to death for 'corrupting the youth' of Athens. Although no writings by him survive, his influence continues through the writings and teachings of his pupil Plato.

c.396–290BC

Rome gradually conquers Etruria, displacing or assimilating the Etruscans, and the Sabine and Samnite peoples of central Italy.

390BC

Rome's expansion is briefly interrupted as Celts invade Italy and destroy large parts of Rome itself before being driven out.

c.387BC

The Athenian philosopher Plato (c.428–c.348BC), a pupil of Socrates, founds a school known as the Academy, which survives until AD529.

338BC

Philip II, king of Macedonia, completes his conquest of Greece from the north, but is murdered soon after his victory in the Battle of Chaeronea, leaving his new conquests to his son, Alexander, soon to be known as Alexander the Great.

335BC

The philosopher and scientist Aristotle (384–322BC) founds a school in Athens known as the Lyceum.

332BC

Alexander the Great (356–323BC) conquers Egypt and founds the port city of Alexandria.

330BC

Alexander defeats Darius III of Persia (c.381–330BC), ending the Achaemenid Dynasty.

327–325BC

Alexander the Great campaigns in India.

323BC

Alexander dies suddenly in Babylon, perhaps poisoned, and his generals begin to fight over the division of his empire.

321BC

Chandragupta (c.350–250BC) founds the extensive Mauryan Empire in India, and begins India's 'Classical' or 'Golden' Age. It establishes standards of Indian literature, art, architecture and philosophy, and lasts until 185BC.

312–64BC

The Seleucid Dynasty, founded by Seleucus I Nicator (c.358–281BC), rules Anatolia, Syria, Palestine, Mesopotamia and other parts of western Asia, but faces frequent rebellions and divisions.

312–30BC

The regions of south-eastern Europe, North Africa and western Asia conquered by Alexander the Great are divided among three 'Hellenistic' (Greek) empires (Seleucid, Antigonid and Ptolemaic) founded by former generals of Alexander's armies.

306–168BC

The Antigonid Dynasty, founded by Antigonus I, the One-eyed (c.382–301BC), rules Macedonia and Greece.

304–30BC

The Ptolemaic Dynasty, founded by the Macedonian general Ptolemy I (c.367–283BC), rules Egypt and its colonies in North Africa from a new capital, Alexandria.

c.300BC

Two main schools of Buddhism develop: Theravada (found in Sri Lanka, Thailand and Burma) and Mahayana (found in China, Korea, Japan, Mongolia and Tibet).

c.280BC

Celts begin moving into the Balkans and Anatolia (now in Turkey), where the region of Galatia is named after them.

c.273–232BC

The Mauryan emperor Ashoka makes Buddhism

the state religion of India, while giving freedom to other religions.

270BC

The whole of Italy comes under the control of Rome.

264–241BC

Rome and Carthage fight the First Punic War for control of the Mediterranean (the Second is in 218–201BC and the Third in 149–146BC); Rome takes Sicily and Sardinia.

256BC

In China the era of 'Warring States' ends with the decisive victory of Prince Zheng (c.259–210BC), ruler of the state of Ch'in (Qin), over the remnants of the Chou (Zhou) Dynasty.

247BC

Arsaces I rebels against the Seleucid Empire and creates an independent kingdom of Parthia, which grows to rule large parts of Mesopotamia, Persia and Afghanistan until AD224.

246BC

Sri Lanka (Ceylon) is converted to Buddhism.

221BC

The Chinese ruler Zheng, founder of the Ch'in (Qin) Dynasty, creates the first unified Chinese empire, begins the construction of the Great Wall and orders that all Confucian writings be burned. He later becomes known as Shi Huangdi ('first emperor'). After his death in 210BC, he is buried in Xian, the city he founded in north-western China, surrounded with 7,500 life-size terracotta warriors.

Terracotta warriors at the tomb of Shi Huangdi

218–201BC

During the Second Punic War between Rome and Carthage, the Carthaginian general Hannibal (247–182BC) crosses the Alps into Italy with an army whose mounts include elephants. He is defeated, while Rome takes Carthage's territories in what is now eastern Spain.

206BC

In China, Liu Bang (256–195BC) overthrows the Ch'in (Qin) Dynasty and founds the first or Western Han Dynasty.

c.200BC

The kingdom of Axum is established in Ethiopia, and prospers from trading between Egypt and Arabia.

185BC

The Mauryan emperor Brihadratha is murdered and India passes under the control of the Sunga Dynasty.

168BC

Rome conquers Macedonia, expelling the Antigonid Dynasty, and conquers the whole of Greece by 146BC.

149–146BC

The Third Punic War results in the total destruction of Carthage by the Romans and their African allies the Numidians (or Nomads), with the Romans taking control of the whole of the Mediterranean.

136BC

Confucianism becomes the official state ideology in China, due largely to the influence of the scholar and philosopher Dong Zhongshu (c.179–104BC).

73–71BC

Spartacus, a gladiator from Thrace, leads a futile but famous revolt by slaves against Rome.

64BC

Roman armies led by Pompey (106–48BC) conquer the Seleucid Empire (western Asia Minor), and transform Palestine (or Judea) and Syria into provinces of Rome.

60BC

The First Triumvirate – an association of three rulers, namely Pompey, Crassus (c.115–53BC) and Julius Caesar (100/102–44BC) – is formed to rule Rome.

58–50BC

The Roman general Julius Caesar directs the conquest of Gaul (France) from the Celts.

57BC

The kingdom of Silla is established in southern Korea.

46BC

Rome establishes a new city of Carthage near the site of the Phoenician city destroyed in 146BC. It becomes the centre of Roman rule on the coast of North Africa.

Julius Caesar reforms the Roman calendar, imposing the 'Julian' calendar of 365 or 366 days per year, and it is used throughout Europe until 1582.

45BC

Julius Caesar defeats the last of Pompey's supporters in Iberia (modern Spain) and is appointed dictator.

44BC

Julius Caesar is assassinated on the Ides (15th) of March by a group of aristocrats.

43BC

The Roman leaders Mark Antony (c.83–30BC), Octavian (63BC–AD14, the nephew and adopted son of Julius Caesar) and Lepidus (d.13BC) agree to form a second triumvirate.

40BC

A new division of the Roman world is arranged, with Antony taking the east, Octavian the west, and Lepidus having Africa.

37BC

The kingdom of Goguryeo is established in northern Korea and parts of what is now Manchuria in China.

30BC

Egypt becomes a Roman province following the seizure of Alexandria by forces loyal to Octavian. Octavian's rival Mark Antony and Cleopatra, the last ruler of the Ptolemaic Dynasty in Egypt, both commit suicide.

27BC

Octavian becomes emperor of Rome under the name Augustus.

c.4BC

Jesus is born in Bethlehem; his followers believe that he is the Messiah or Christ of Jewish prophecies.

AD1–299

c.1AD

Bantu people begin to migrate to East Africa, taking the knowledge of ironworking with them.

14

Emperor Augustus dies and is succeeded by his stepson Tiberius. This establishes the principle of dynastic succession in Rome, with subsequent emperors chosen from the same family.

25

In China the Han Dynasty moves its capital east from Changan (now Xian) to Luoyang, marking the start of what is now called the Eastern Han Dynasty.

c.30

Jesus is crucified during the reign of the second Roman emperor, Tiberius (42BC–AD37).

41

After displaying signs of mental illness, including allegedly appointing his horse to the Senate, the third Roman emperor, Caligula (b.12), is murdered and replaced by his timid uncle Claudius (10BC–AD54).

43

The Romans, nominally led by Emperor Claudius, invade Britain.

45–8

The Apostles Paul and Barnabas make the first missionary journey to Cyprus, Pisidia, Pamphylia and Lycaonia to convert people to Christianity.

c.50

The first known porcelain is manufactured in China.

60

In southern England Boudicca (Boadicea), Queen of the Iceni, leads an unsuccessful rebellion against Roman rule.

c.60

Mark writes the first of the four Gospels, which together contain virtually all that is known about Jesus.

64

Fire destroys two thirds of Rome. The emperor, Nero, blames the Christians and has many of them, perhaps including their leaders Peter and Paul, put to death.

66–70

The Jews rebel against Roman rule in Judea. Roman armies crush the rebellion, destroy the Second Temple in Jerusalem (built in 515BC), and expel many Jews from the province. This launches the Diaspora, the dispersal of Jews throughout Europe and Asia.

68

A mystical Jewish sect called the Essenes hides its records, the Dead Sea Scrolls, in a cave near Qumran, where they are discovered in 1947.

68–9

The death of the Roman emperor Nero is followed by the 'Year of Four Emperors', as factions of the army put forward rival candidates for emperor.

c.75

Buddhism is introduced into China.

78

The Kushan Empire in northern India and Central Asia reaches the peak of its power and wealth under King Kaniska.

79

Mount Vesuvius in southern Italy erupts, burying the cities of Pompeii and Herculaneum under ashes until their excavation starts in the 18th century.

Cast of a victim of Mount Vesuvius in Pompeii

c.100

The city of Teotihuacán is founded in Mexico. It is originally a religious centre, but goes on to become one of the largest cities in the world.

105

Paper made from tree bark and rags is said to have been invented in China by Zai Lun (c.50–118).

122–8

Hadrian's Wall, running from the Solway Firth to the Tyne, is built under the orders of Roman emperor Hadrian as the northern frontier of Roman Britain and to limit the incursions of northern tribes.

c.130

The astronomer and geographer Ptolemy (c.90–168) completes his *Almagest*, a 'great compendium of astronomy'. His view that the Earth is at the centre of the universe dominates cosmological thought until the work of Nicolaus Copernicus in the 16th century.

c.143

The Antonine Wall, built in southern Scotland to the north of Hadrian's Wall, marks the northernmost boundary of the Roman Empire.

166

Chinese records indicate the arrival of merchants from the Roman Empire.

180

The death of Roman emperor Marcus Aurelius and the accession of his son Commodus (161–92) heralds nearly a century of war and disorder, with a succession of generals being put on the throne by their armies.

184

The Yellow Turban rebellion in China, a peasants' revolt against Emperor Ling Di, weakens the rule of the Han Dynasty.

c.200

The Goths begin migrating from Gotland (now in Sweden) to the lands of the Sarmatians (now in southern Russia).

220

The collapse of the Han Dynasty in China is followed by the era of the 'Three Kingdoms' as the empire is divided, with rival dynasties seeking control of China.

c.224

Ardashir I (d.241) overthrows Ardavan, the last of the Parthian kings, and founds the Sassanid Dynasty, ruling a new Persian Empire. Zoroastrianism becomes the state religion.

c.250

Goths invade the Balkans, the first of many tribes migrating from the East.

The kingdom of Yamato comes to dominate most of Japan.

265–316

The Western Chin (Jin) Dynasty briefly rules most of China, following the chaos of the era of 'Three Kingdoms', but falls to attacks by Xiongnu nomads.

c.265

Bantu-speaking peoples begin to migrate into the southern part of Africa.

c.285

Confucianism reaches Japan from China.

293

The Roman emperor Diocletian (245–313) establishes the tetrarchy ('rule by four'), under which two emperors rule the Roman Empire, each given the title Augustus, and each assisted by a 'Caesar'.

300–599

c.300

In Central America the Maya civilization develops in Mexico and Guatemala, around centres such as Tikal and Palenque.

c.301

The kingdom of Armenia becomes the first officially Christian state.

313

The Roman Emperor Constantine I (c.274–337) gives equality to Christians and ends their persecution, having himself converted to Christianity.

c.320

Chandragupta I founds the Gupta Dynasty in northern India.

325

On the orders of Emperor Constantine I, the first ecumenical council of the Christian Church, held at Nicaea (now Iznik in Turkey), compiles the first version of the Nicene Creed and begins the persecution of heretics. Christianity becomes the official religion of the Roman Empire.

330

Byzantium is refounded as Constantinople, and becomes the capital of the Roman Empire.

350

The kingdom of Axum, which rules most of Ethiopia, conquers the kingdom of Kush in Nubia. Christianity reaches Ethiopia.

c.370

Eastern Europe is invaded by Huns from Central Asia, who push the Goths and others westwards as they advance.

378

At the Battle of Adrianople the Romans are defeated by the Visigoths (western Goths), a Germanic people originally from the coasts of the Baltic Sea.

c.380

Chandragupta II expands the Gupta Empire in northern India, overseeing an era of religious tolerance alongside the flourishing of art, architecture and sculpture.

395

Following the death of Emperor Theodosius I (b.c.343), the Roman Empire is formally split into two parts: the Eastern (or Byzantine) Empire and the Western Empire.

c.400

The highly organized Moche culture becomes well established in Peru. The Moche are skilled builders and produce pottery with pictures of figures and scenes of daily life.

Polynesians reach Easter Island, the location most remote from any other human settlement.

Jewish scholars in Palestine complete the compilation of the Talmud, a book of laws and ethics.

A Chinese Buddhist monk, Fa Xian, makes a pilgrimage to India to find sacred texts. He transmits the rules of monasticism to China, from where they are later taken to Korea and Japan.

410

Rome is sacked by Visigoths led by Alaric I. Roman legions are withdrawn from distant Roman provinces to protect Rome, leaving the provinces more vulnerable to invasion.

429

A Germanic people, the Vandals, invade the Roman province of Carthage in North Africa and rule it as an independent kingdom until 534.

c.450

Angles, Saxons and Jutes from Denmark and north-western Germany begin to invade Britain, while other Saxons begin to migrate to south-eastern Germany.

451–2

Attila, king of the Huns (c.406–53), is defeated when he invades Gaul (France).

455

The Vandals sack Rome, giving their name as a label for deliberately destructive people.

476

Germanic warriors led by Odoacer (433–93) overthrow Emperor Romulus Augustulus and bring the Western Roman Empire to an end. The Byzantine emperor Zeno (r.474–91) claims to be Odoacer's overlord and ruler of both empires, but is ignored.

486

Clovis (465–511), leader of the Salian Dynasty of Franks, overthrows the last Roman governor of Gaul (France) and establishes the Merovingian Dynasty.

493

Theodoric the Great (c.455–526), leader of the Ostrogoths, assassinates Odoacer and takes his place as ruler of large parts of Italy.

510

The Chinese develop block-book printing, in which a wooden block is carved with text, inked and then used to produce multiple copies.

534

Byzantine forces under General Belisarius (505–65) destroy the Vandal kingdom of North Africa and make the region part of the Byzantine Empire.

Franks, under rulers Clovis I, Childebert I and Theudebert I, conquer the Burgundian Kingdom in eastern Gaul (France).

535

The Byzantine emperor Justinian I declares war on the Ostrogoths, claiming Italy, the historic centre of the Western Empire, for the Eastern Empire.

540

The Gupta Dynasty, which rules northern India and parts of central and western India, collapses after attacks by the Hepthalites ('White Huns').

c.550

Nomadic Turks, led by Bumin, invade Central Asia from the east, founding an empire there. They displace the Avars, who move westwards to conquer much of the Danube Valley.

Slavs settle in Bohemia and Moravia (now the Czech Republic), and, under pressure from the invading Avars, cross the Danube to settle the Balkans.

The Hindu ruler Bhavavarman of Chenla conquers the trading kingdom of Funan and founds the first united state of the Khmers (Cambodians).

552

The year it is traditionally believed that Buddhism is brought to Japan by the ruler of Paekche in Korea, and accepted by the emperor Kimmi.

558–61

Clothar I unites the Frankish Kingdom after years of expansion and subjugation. The kingdom becomes divided again after Clothar's death.

563

St Columba founds the monastery at Iona that becomes the mother church of Celtic Christianity in Scotland. Missionary monks from Iona are instrumental in converting the north of England to Christianity.

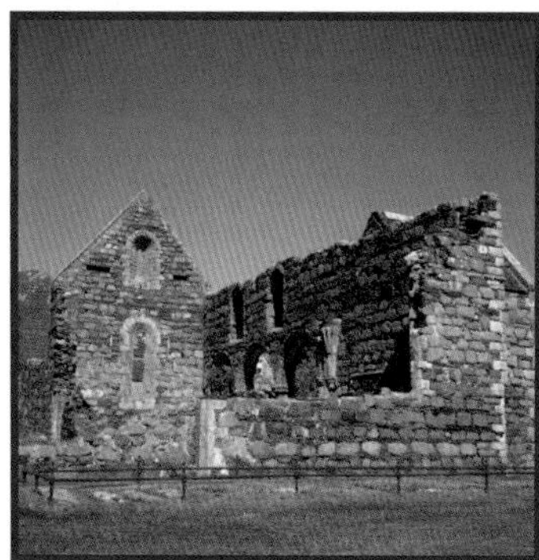

Monastic ruins at Iona

568

Lombards, pushed westwards by the invading Avars, migrate into northern Italy and found a kingdom around the River Po.

c.570

The Prophet Muhammad (d.c.632) is born in Mecca. After his death, his followers establish the line of caliphs ('successors'), leaders who claim authority over all Muslims.

581

Yang Jian overthrows the Northern Chou (Zhou) Dynasty, founds the Sui Dynasty and reunifies China (by 589) after 273 years of division.

590–604

Under Pope Gregory I, the Great (c.540–604), the papacy begins to have power over secular matters in Italy, and alienates the Roman Church from Byzantium. Under him the Church undergoes a complete overhaul of its ritual and the systematization of its sacred chants, giving rise to the Gregorian chant.

594

Buddhism becomes the official religion of Japan, under the influence of Empress Suiko and Prince Shokoto.

597

A mission to convert the English to Christianity, sent by Pope Gregory the Great and led by Augustine (d.c.604), arrives in Kent. Augustine becomes the first Archbishop of Canterbury, and establishes the cathedral there as England's mother church.

600–899

613–19

Chosroes II (d.628), the Sassanid king of Persia, conquers Syria, Palestine, Egypt and parts of Asia Minor, almost defeating the Byzantine Empire.

613–29

Clothar II reunites the kingdom of the Franks.

618

In China the Tang Dynasty, founded by a frontier general, Li Yuan (566–635), replaces the Sui Dynasty and rules until 907.

622

Muhammad makes the Hegira (migration) from Mecca to Medina, 280 miles to the north. This event later marks the beginning of the Islamic calendar.

625–6

Jews are driven from Medina for refusing to accept Islam.

628–33

The Byzantine emperor Heraclius (c.575–641) defeats the Persian Empire and regains lost territories in the East. Under Heraclius, Greek becomes the official language of the empire.

634–51

The second Muslim caliph, Omar (c.581–644), builds up an empire comprising Persia, Syria and the whole of North Africa, conquering lands recently won by the Byzantines and ending the Sassanian Empire. Some of its peoples disperse: the Khazars migrate to what is now southern Russia, the Bulgars to what is now Romania and the Magyars to Ukraine.

643

Arabs take Alexandria, ending Greek rule in Egypt.

645–1192

Japan enters the age of the bureaucratic state, modelled on China.

c.645

King Srong-brtsan-sgam-po of Tibet (c.608–50) introduces Buddhism and orders the creation of a writing system.

c.650

Arab merchants begin to create trading posts on the coast of East Africa, helping to spread Islam as they deal in minerals, cloth and slaves.

The revelations of Muhammad are collected and written down as the Koran.

661

The division within Islam between the Sunni and the Shia begins with a dispute over the succession to the caliphate, the leadership of all Muslims. The Sunni support Mu'Awiyah (c.602–80), who becomes the first caliph of the Umayyad Dynasty and moves the capital to Damascus in Syria; the Shia support the descendants of the fourth caliph, Ali, who is assassinated in this year.

664

In England the Synod of Whitby chooses Roman Christianity over the Celtic Christianity brought to northern England by Irish missionaries.

676–918

After conquering its rivals and repelling a Chinese invasion, the kingdom of Silla unifies most of the Korean peninsula.

c.700

The Serbs are converted to the Eastern or Byzantine form of Christianity, while the Croats, who share a common language and culture, are converted to Western or Roman Christianity.

The kingdom of Ghana in West Africa expands on the basis of trade across the Sahara.

705–15

Caliph al-Walid I (c.668–715) leads the Umayyad Dynasty to the height of its power, including the conquest of Spain.

Chinese influence is reduced in Japan during the Nara Period after the fusion of Shintoism and Buddhism.

711

Iberia (modern Spain and Portugal) is invaded by Muslims from North Africa, who defeat the Visigoths.

712–45

The first Islamic incursions into India begin around the Indus river.

718

The Anglo-Saxon missionary Boniface (c.680–c.754) sets out to convert the tribes of Germany to Christianity.

726

The Byzantine emperor Leo III (c.680–741) forbids the use of icons in public worship, setting off a long-running dispute between Iconoclasts, who reject all images in churches, and Iconodules, who defend their use.

732

The Frankish ruler Charles (c.688–741) defeats Muslim invaders from Iberia at Poitiers. This prevents any more advances in the west.

750

The forces of the Caliph Marwan II of the Umayyad Dynasty are defeated, and he is replaced with Abu al-'Abbas as-Saffah, the first caliph of the 'Abbasid Dynasty.

c.750

The Hindu theologian Śankara (b.c.700) dies. He was the leading exponent of the Vedanta school of philosophy, the source of the main currents of modern Hindu thought.

751

Pepin III, the Short (c.715–68) deposes King Childeric and is anointed the first king of the Franks, founding the Carolingian Dynasty.

The fall of the city of Ravenna to the Lombard king marks the end of Byzantine rule in Italy.

754–75

The caliph Abu-Jafar, under the title al-Mansur ('the victorious'), founds Baghdad, making it the capital of the Islamic Empire instead of Damascus, and fully establishes the Muslim 'Abbasid Dynasty.

771

Charlemagne (747–814), son of Pepin III, becomes sole king of the Franks, ruling much of modern France, the Low Countries and western Germany. In 773–4 he defeats the Lombards, and seizes northern and central Italy, and in 791 conquers the Avars of the Danube Valley.

Bust of Charlemagne

786–809

The reign of Harun al-Rashid marks the height of the 'Abbasid caliphate, which rules an empire stretching from North Africa to Central Asia. He is the caliph who figures in many of the tales of the *Arabian Nights*.

793

Vikings from Scandinavia carry out raids on

northern England, ransacking the monastery on Lindisfarne.

794

The Japanese transfer their capital from Heijo-kyo (now Nara) to Heian-kyo (now Kyoto), an event later taken to mark the start of the Heian Era (794–1185) in Japan.

800

Pope Leo III crowns Charlemagne, the ruler of the Franks, as Emperor of the West, an event later taken to mark the beginning of the Holy Roman Empire. The Carolingian Dynasty later takes its name from Charlemagne.

c.800

Rajput dynasties begin to dominate northern India.

Large and sophisticated Hindu temples begin to be built in eastern India.

802

King Jayavarman II asserts the independence of the Khmers (Cambodians) from their Javanese overlords, founding the Angkor Dynasty.

819–1005

The Samanid Dynasty, based in Bukhara (in modern Uzbekistan), conquers and rules large parts of Persia and Central Asia, and fosters the art and architecture of Samarkand.

c.840

Vikings establish the city of Dublin on the eastern coast of Ireland, and use it as a base from which to extend their power over the surrounding lands. In northern England the Vikings base themselves in York.

843

The Treaty of Verdun divides the Carolingian Empire among three grandsons of Charlemagne, creating the heartlands of modern France and Germany, along with the 'Middle Kingdom' (from the Netherlands south to Burgundy) long disputed between them. Carolingian kings rule Germany until 911 and France until 987.

Kenneth MacAlpin (d.858) begins to rule Picts and Scots as the first king of a united Scotland.

The disruption of the Byzantine Church and Empire by disputes over the use of icons ends with victory for the Iconodules (defenders of icons) over their opponents, the Iconoclasts.

c.850

The West African trading kingdom of Kanem is established near Lake Chad.

c.860

Scandinavian merchants and settlers, known as Rus or Varangians and led by the semi-legendary Rurik, establish the trading city of Novgorod in north-western Russia.

The first Thai kingdom is established, with its capital at Sukhothai.

c.865

Danes invade south-eastern England.

867

The Byzantine emperor Basil I (c.812–86) founds the Macedonian Dynasty.

Photius (c.820–91), Patriarch of Constantinople, separates the Eastern Church from Rome.

868

Ahmad ibn Tulun, a Turk sent by the 'Abbasid caliphate to govern Egypt, effectively makes the country independent, founding the Tulunid Dynasty.

873–876

Byzantine power is re-established in Italy with the conquests of Benevento and Bari.

882

Oleg (d.912) unites Novgorod and Kiev, founding the first Russian state, generally known as Kievan Rus.

886

Alfred the Great, king of Wessex (849–99), makes a treaty with the Viking King Guthrum. England is partitioned, and the Viking realm in the East Midlands, East Anglia and Yorkshire later becomes known as the 'Danelaw'.

888

Charles III ('the Fat') is deposed, and Carolingian power begins to crumble. Smaller kingdoms begin to form in Italy, Germany and France.

896

Vikings settle at the mouth of the River Seine in France, founding Normandy.

c.896

The Magyars, led by Árpád (d.c.907), move westwards out of Ukraine and occupy what is now Hungary.

900–999

c.900

The Maya civilization in Central America begins to decline.

907–60

In China the collapse of the Tang Dynasty is followed by the era of 'Five Dynasties and Ten Kingdoms', a time of renewal of the Empire, but also of social and political turmoil.

909

The Arab Fatimid Dynasty, descended from the

Prophet's daughter Fatima, is established in North Africa.

910

The monastery of Cluny in France is established. From there, religious reform promoting papal control spreads throughout the Western Church.

911

The Viking Rollo (c.860–c.932) is granted the duchy of Normandy in peace talks with French king Charles III (879–929).

918–1392

The Koryo Dynasty replaces the Silla Dynasty as rulers of Korea.

919

The Franks and Saxons place Henry I on the throne of Germany.

927

Athelstan of Wessex (c.895–939) becomes the first king of the English when he takes Northumbria under his control.

930

In Iceland the Althing, believed to be the first national political assembly in the world, meets for the first time.

939

Vietnam, under its ruler Ngo Quyen, achieves lasting independence from China.

944

Igor, ruler of Kievan Rus, makes a treaty with Byzantium, leading to increased Christian influence in Kiev.

945–1055

The Shiite Buyid Dynasty, founded by Ahmad, also known as Mu'izz ad-Dawlah, rules from Baghdad, turning the Sunni 'Abbasid caliphs into mere figureheads.

c.950–c.1160

The Toltecs rule central Mexico from the city of Tula, in what is later seen as a 'golden age' in Mexican history.

955

Otto I of Saxony (912–73), the most powerful ruler in Germany, defeats the Magyars at the Battle of Lechfeld, and brings to an end their attempts to expand beyond Hungary.

960

Axum, the capital of the first Ethiopian state, is destroyed by invading Jewish Falashas.

960–1279

The Sung (Song) Dynasty, founded by General Zhao Guangyin, rules most of China from a new southern capital, Hangzhou.

c.960–1370

The Piast Dynasty, said to have been founded by a former wheelwright named Piast, rules Poland, and introduces Christianity.

961–9

Byzantine army general and emperor Nicephorus Phocas (r.963–9) regains Crete, Aleppo, Cyprus and Cilicia for the Byzantine empire from Arab control.

962

Otto I of Germany is crowned Holy Roman Emperor, and reassembles the empire of Charlemagne, with the exception of France.

c.967

Svyatoslav I, ruler of Kievan Rus, conquers the Khazar Empire to the south, and gains access to the Black Sea.

969

The Fatimids conquer Egypt and build a new capital, Cairo.

975

Géza, ruler of Hungary, leads his people to convert to the Western form of Christianity.

c.975

Arabic numerals are first used in Europe, in al-Andalus (now Spain).

976–1025

The reign of Emperor Basil II sees the height of Byzantine power.

977–1186

The Ghaznavid Dynasty, founded by Sebüktigin, a former slave of Turkic origin, rules an empire that, at its peak, includes Afghanistan, western Persia and northern India.

985

Erik the Red, a Norwegian sailor, founds colonies in Greenland.

987–96

The Capetian Dynasty is established with the reign of Hugh Capet (c.938–96). Later, the Capetian realm expands from the region around Paris to take in most of modern France.

988

Vladimir I (c.956–1015), Grand Prince of Kiev, marries Anna, a sister of the Byzantine emperor Basil II, and is converted to Christianity. The orthodox faith, under the authority of Constantinople, spreads in Russia.

992

The Republic of Venice secures trading rights at Constantinople, and comes to dominate trade between Europe and Asia.

1000–1099

1000

Iceland officially accepts Christianity, while permitting the practice of the old Norse religion in private.

Boleslaw I 'the Brave' is crowned king of Poland (r.992–1025) by the Holy Roman Emperor Otto III, and an archbishopric is created in Poland, confirming its independence.

1000–1099

The feudal system becomes established throughout most of Europe. It involves the granting by kings or princes of portions of land ('fiefs') to nobles and knights, in return for their loyalty; and the farming of the fiefs by tenants and/or serfs, in return for protection.

c.1000

Polynesians begin to settle Aotearoa, the 'Land of the Long White Cloud' (New Zealand).

The people of Kievan Rus are converted to the Eastern or Byzantine form of Christianity.

1001

Hungary is officially converted to Christianity.

1001–26

Mahmud the Great of Ghazni, the first Turkish sultan, leads several campaigns against India.

c.1002

Brian ('Brian Boru') becomes high king of Ireland (d.1014), securing his place as a symbol of Irish independence and power.

1003

Icelanders, including Leif Eriksson, reportedly become some of the first Europeans to reach North America, visiting 'Helluland', 'Markland' and 'Vinland' (probably Baffin Island, Labrador and Newfoundland).

1010

Vietnam is unified by Emperor Le Long Dinh, who makes Hanoi his capital.

1014

At Clontarf, near Dublin, an army of Irishmen and Norse settlers, led by the high king Brian Boru, defeats a largely Danish–Norwegian force, ending the Viking conquests of parts of Ireland.

A Byzantine army led by Emperor Basil II (later called 'the Bulgar slayer') occupies Bulgaria, securing Byzantine rule over the whole of the Balkans until 1185.

1016

Canute or Knut (c.995–1035) becomes king of England after defeating Edmund II, Ironside (b.c.990), who reigns briefly in 1016. Canute then becomes king of Denmark from 1018 and by 1028 has subjugated Norway and some of Sweden.

Canute's fortress at Fyrkat, Denmark

1022

Heretics are burned at Orleans, France, in one of the first instances of the practice.

1025

The city of Srivijaya on Sumatra is destroyed by a Chola invasion from southern India, causing the collapse of Srivijaya's sea-trading empire, and destroying the Malay Empire.

1031

The last Umayyad ruler is deposed, ending the caliphate in Spain. Several Moorish kingdoms are established to replace the caliphate.

1033

The kingdom of Burgundy in south-eastern France is joined with the German Empire.

1035

Sancho III, who expanded his rule in northern Spain and created the kingdoms of Castile and Aragon, as well as holding Navarre, dies.

1040

Seljuk Turks defeat the Ghaznavids, the Turkish rulers of parts of Afghanistan, Persia and India, forcing them to retreat to Lahore.

1050

Bohemia (now in the Czech Republic), Poland and Hungary are declared to be dependent territories of the Western Empire.

c.1050

A Chinese alchemist, Pi Sheng, invents the first movable type for use in printing.

1051

Edward the Confessor (c.1003–1066), king of England, meets William, Duke of Normandy (c.1028–87), and designates him as his heir, laying the foundation for the Norman invasion of 1066.

1054

An East–West Schism divides the Church of Byzantium and other churches later known as 'Orthodox' ('correct') from the Church of Rome, later known as 'Catholic' ('universal'). Their mutual exclusion continues until 1965.

1055

Seljuk Turks establish a sultanate at Baghdad, beginning the mingling of Turkish, Arab and Persian cultures that came to dominate Islamic countries for centuries.

1058

The Almoravids, a Berber dynasty, invade Morocco; they found a new capital at Marrakesh (c.1070).

1066

Harald III (Harald Hardraade or Hardrada) (1015–66), king of Norway, invades northern England but is defeated by King Harold II at Stamford Bridge.

The Norman Conquest of England is led by William, Duke of Normandy, after the defeat and death of Harold II (b.c.1022) at the Battle of Hastings. He becomes William I (William the Conqueror), the first of the Norman kings of England.

1070

After years of fighting, King Vijayabahu of Ceylon takes control, ending 70 years of rule in Ceylon by the Chola Dynasty.

1075

Seljuk Turks take control of Syria and Palestine.

The Investiture Controversy, a conflict between reforming popes and lay rulers over the leadership of Christian societies in western Europe, originates in disputes over the right to invest (appoint) bishops. The controversy abates briefly in 1077, when Emperor Henry IV submits to Pope Gregory VII, but continues until 1122.

c.1080

The Bayeux Tapestry, an embroidered wall-hanging that tells the story of the Norman Conquest, is completed.

Detail from *The Bayeux Tapestry* depicting a scene from the Battle of Hastings

1084

Emperor Henry IV (1050–1106) and the Norman baron Robert Guiscard capture Rome from the papacy, forcing Pope Gregory VII (d.1085) into exile. Henry appoints Clement II to replace him: the first of several antipopes set up by the Holy Roman Empire in opposition to papal power.

1086

William I orders the compilation of the *Domesday Book*, a survey of most of the land in England.

The Almoravids, a Berber dynasty, invade Iberia (modern Spain and Portugal) from north-west Africa.

1090–1

Yusuf ibn-Tashfin takes control of Granada in southern Spain and brings together the Muslim kingdoms in Andalusia, establishing the Almoravid Dynasty in Spain.

1094

Rodrigo Diaz de Bivar, 'El Cid' (c.1043–99), a mercenary fighting for the Muslims, deserts their service to conquer Valencia for himself and rule it until his death. Later legends transformed him into a hero of the *Reconquista*, the gradual expulsion of the Muslims from Spain and Portugal.

1095

Pope Urban II proclaims the First Crusade, in an attempt to regain control over holy sites in Muslim-ruled Palestine, after calls for help from the Byzantine emperor Alexius I Comnenus.

The Seljuk Empire begins to crumble after the death of Seljuk prince Tutush, as rulers from smaller Seljuk clans establish independent principalities in Asia Minor.

1098

The Cistercian Order is founded with the establishment of Citeaux Abbey near Dijon, France. The Cistercians go on to become one of the most powerful bodies in north-western Europe.

1099

European armies on the First Crusade (1095–9) capture Jerusalem, massacre its Jewish and Muslim inhabitants and establish the Kingdom of Jerusalem, which lasts until 1187. They also take the key cities of Edessa and Antioch, and go on to take Acre in 1104.

1100–1199

1100–1199

The Inca Empire comes to dominate the Andes region of South America.

1103

Legislation by Holy Roman Emperor Henry IV declares a peace with the Jews, allowing those forcibly baptized in the First Crusade to return to Judaism.

1106

Henry I (1068–1135), king of England, conquers Normandy from his brother, Robert Curthose (c.1054–1134), at the Battle of Tinchebrai.

c.1113

Work starts on the temple complex of Angkor Wat in Cambodia.

c.1119

The religious and military Order of the Knights Templar is founded to protect Christian pilgrims to the Holy Land.

1126

The Chin people of Manchuria, having helped the Sung (Song) Dynasty rulers of China to defeat invaders from the Liao Kingdom, conquer about one third of China, forcing the Sung to move their capital from Kaifeng in the north to Hangzhou in the south-east. Korea becomes subject, preventing it from forming an alliance with the Sung in the south.

1135

Stephen (c.1097–1154) takes control of England and Normandy after the death of his uncle Henry I, leading to civil war fought against supporters of Henry's daughter the Empress Matilda (or Maud), widow of Emperor Henry V.

1136

In Russia, Novgorod becomes independent from Kiev and survives as a trading republic until 1478.

1138–42

Rivalries between supporters of the popes ('Guelfs') and supporters of the Holy Roman emperors ('Ghibellines') begin to dominate politics in Italy and Germany.

In Germany, Henry the Proud, the Guelf duke of Bavaria and Saxony, refuses to swear allegiance to Conrad (of the rival Hohenstaufen Dynasty) as king of Germany, and civil war breaks out, ending when Conrad gives Saxony and Bavaria separate rulers.

1139

Alfonso I (1110–85) defeats a Muslim army at Ourique and proclaims himself the first king of Portugal at Oporto, securing Portuguese independence from the Kingdom of León (now part of modern Spain).

1144

Geoffrey of Anjou (1113–51) gains control of Normandy, expanding the Angevin Empire.

1147

The Almohad Dynasty overthrows the Almoravid Dynasty in north-west Africa and then in al-Andalus (now Spain).

1147–9

The Second Crusade takes place, its armies comprising mainly the Germans under Conrad III (1093–1152) and the French under Louis VII (c.1120–80). It ends after disastrous campaigns in Syria and Anatolia, and an unsuccessful siege of Damascus.

1152

Eleanor of Aquitaine divorces from King Louis VII of France and marries Henry, then count of much of western France, adding Aquitaine to his lands. He becomes king of England, as Henry II, in 1154.

The reign of the most renowned Hohenstaufen Holy Roman Emperor, Frederick I, Barbarossa (c.1123–1190), begins.

1154

Henry II (1133–89) succeeds Stephen as king of England and Duke of Normandy, founding the Plantagenet Dynasty.

Nicholas Breakspear (c.1100–59) becomes the only Englishman to have held the office of pope, taking the name Adrian (or Hadrian) IV.

1156

Grand Prince Yuri Dolgoruki of Kiev founds the city of Moscow.

c.1156

The Carmelite religious order is founded at Mount Carmel, Palestine. Initially a community of hermits, members of the order are reorganized as mendicant (involved in begging) friars.

1157

King Eric IX of Sweden launches the conquest and conversion to Christianity of Finland, which remains under Swedish rule until 1809.

1157–82

The rise of Denmark begins with the reign of Waldemar the Great who brings the provinces under central control.

1167

The Lombard League is founded by cities in northern Italy to assert their independence as communes (city republics) and to resist the Holy Roman Emperor Frederick I, Barbarossa.

Anglo-Norman adventurers invade Ireland and conquer much of the island. They originate the 'Anglo-Irish' minority, known as the 'Ascendancy', who dominate Irish affairs until 1922.

1168

In central Mexico the last Toltec king is driven from the capital, Tula, by northern tribes including the Aztecs.

1170

In England, Thomas Becket (b.1118), Archbishop of Canterbury, is murdered in his cathedral by knights claiming to act on behalf of King Henry II.

1171

The Sunni Kurdish warrior Saladin (1138–93) overthrows the Shia Fatimid Dynasty and founds the Ayyubid Dynasty, which rules Egypt, Syria and Mesopotamia (modern-day Iraq) until 1250.

Henry II of England, concerned at the increasing power in Ireland of the Earl of Pembroke (Strongbow), is declared lord of Ireland, and grants Irish estates to some of his courtiers.

1173

Henry II's son, Henry, having been crowned his father's associate and successor, flees from England to ally with Louis VII of France. Henry II's sons John and Richard rebel unsuccessfully against their father's rule.

1175

Saladin is recognized as the Sultan of Egypt and Syria by the Caliph of Baghdad. He expands his empire by taking Edessa (1182), Aleppo (1183) and Jerusalem (1187).

1177

The Treaty of Venice restores a single papacy.

1180–5

The Gempei War in Japan leads to the triumph of the Minamoto (or Genji) and the downfall of the Taira (or Heike) as the most powerful noble family and as guardians of the powerless but sacred emperors.

1186

The Bulgarians rebel against Byzantine rule, creating the second Bulgarian Empire, which becomes the most powerful state in the Balkans.

1189

Richard I, the Lion Heart (1157–99), becomes king of England in succession to his father, Henry II.

1189–92

The Third Crusade takes place, led by Emperor Frederick I, Barbarossa, Philip II of France and Richard I of England. It ends having failed to recapture Jerusalem, but with a successful siege of the city of Acre and the capture of Cyprus.

c.1190

Having abandoned most of their major cities (for reasons that are still not clear), the Maya of Central America establish their last capital at Mayapan.

1191

Zen Buddhism is introduced into Japan from China by the monk Eisai (1141–1215), who is now regarded as the founder of the Rinzai sect.

1192

In Japan, Minamoto Yoritomo (1147–99) takes the title *shogun* ('generalissimo') and institutes the first shogunate, a military government based in Kamakura, far to the east of the imperial capital Kyoto.

Muhammad Ghuri (d.1206) gains control of the whole of northern India, with victory over the Ghaznavids of Lahore in 1186 and other rivals in the second Battle of Tarain. He establishes the first of the Delhi Sultanates.

1194

The Hohenstaufen Dynasty in Germany expands under Emperor Henry VI. He takes control of the kingdom of Sicily.

1197

After Henry VI's death, problems that have been brewing for some time emerge between the Guelf party under Henry the Lion and the Hohenstaufens led by Philip of Swabia.

1198

German and Scandinavian knights launch the 'Livonian Crusade', conquering and Christianizing large parts of what are now Finland, Estonia, Latvia and Lithuania and creating aristocracies that retain power until 1918.

1200–1299

c.1200

Emperor Lalibela of Ethiopia has eleven great churches hewn out of solid rock at Roha, which has since been renamed Lalibela.

Roof of a church hewn from rock at Lalibela

1202–4

Philip II Augustus of France annexes King John's lands in France.

The Fourth Crusade, proclaimed by Pope Innocent III in 1198 to liberate Jerusalem, takes place. Financed by the Venetians, it takes Zara, then Constantinople, expelling the Byzantine emperor and establishing the 'Latin Empire', which lasts until 1261.

1206

Temujin (c.1162–1227) establishes the Mongol Empire, taking the title Genghis Khan ('Universal Ruler').

1209–10

The Papacy grants approval to the Franciscan religious order founded by Francis of Assisi (1181–1226). Its Grey Friars ('brothers' dressed in grey) largely abandon monastic life to care for the sick and the poor.

1209–28

A crusade in the south of France destroys the heretical movement known as the Albigensians (or Cathars).

1211

Mongol armies first enter China, beginning their conquests.

1212

The Children's Crusade, involving thousands of children and youths from France, Germany and other lands in western Europe, sets out for Palestine, but most die or are enslaved as they travel.

1215

At Runnymede, on the River Thames, King John of England (1167–1216) seals the Magna Carta (the 'Great Charter') imposed on him by the leading barons. Its listing of the barons' rights is used in later centuries as a basis for the concepts of civil rights and the rule of law in English-speaking countries.

Facsimile of the Magna Carta

1216

The Papacy grants approval to the Dominican order founded by Dominic de Guzman (1170–1221). Called the 'Black Friars' because of their black robes, they work mainly as preachers and teachers.

1217–21

The Fifth Crusade captures the port of Damietta in Egypt, but fails in the Nile Delta.

1217–1389

The Serbs create an empire that, at its height, rules most of the Balkans.

1219

Mongols invade Persia, Iraq and Anatolia (now in Turkey). The city of Samarkand falls to Genghis Khan in 1220.

1220

Frederick II (1194–1250), son of Henry VI, is crowned Holy Roman Emperor. However, the Hohenstaufen Empire begins to falter with his excommunication and the rebellion of his son, Henry VII.

1228–9

The Sixth Crusade takes Jerusalem, but loses it to a Muslim army in 1244.

1229

The Berber Hafsid Dynasty replaces the Almohads in Tunisia and eastern Algeria.

1230–95

The Order of the Teutonic Knights carves out a state for itself in the disputed borderlands of Germany and Poland, converting the remaining pagans to Christianity.

1231

Mongols invade Korea.

c.1235

Sundiata (d.1255) founds the Mali Empire in western Sudan.

1237–8

A Mongol army, led by Genghis Khan's grandson Batu (d.c.1255), captures the cities of Moscow and Vladimir, initiating the rule of Russia by the Kipchaks, known as the Golden Horde, which lasts until 1480.

1240

Alexander Nevsky, Grand Prince of Vladimir (c.1220–63), defeats German and Swedish forces in a battle on the River Neva, saving Russia from European invaders but leaving it open to domination by the Golden Horde, with which Alexander collaborates.

1248–54

King Louis IX of France (1214–70) leads the largely ineffectual Seventh Crusade, which ends with his brief imprisonment in Egypt.

1250

Saladin's Ayyubid Sultanate in Egypt is overthrown by the Mamelukes, originally slaves employed in the Ayyubid armies.

1254

The Hohenstaufen Dynasty declines rapidly after the death of Emperor Conrad IV (1228–54). St Louis IX of France (r.1226–70) becomes the most powerful western ruler.

1258

The English barons, led by Simon de Montfort (1208–65), revolt against the autocratic rule of Henry III (c.1207–72). The king is forced to capitulate in 1259 and allows the barons to increase their power.

1258–1339

The Ilkhanids, a Mongol dynasty founded by Hulagu (c.1217–65), replace the 'Abbasid caliphs, and rule Persia and the central Islamic lands from Baghdad.

1260

Mamelukes from Egypt defeat a Mongol army led by Hulagu at the Battle of Ayn Julut in Palestine, effectively stopping the Mongols' westward advance.

1261

Michael VIII of Nicaea (c.1225–82) captures Constantinople, overthrows the Latin Empire and founds the Palaeologus Dynasty, the last ruling family of Christian Byzantium.

1265

The first English parliament takes place, formed by Simon de Montfort's expansion of the Council of the Barons. Later in the year de Montfort is killed at the Battle of Evesham.

1269

The Berber Marinid Dynasty replaces Almohad rule in Morocco.

1271

The Italian merchant Marco Polo (1254–1324) may have begun a journey through Central Asia and the Gobi Desert to China. His reports, which have been questioned ever since, became the main source of European knowledge (and legends) about east Asia until the 16th century.

1273

Rudolf I (1218–91) becomes king of Germany, founding the Habsburg Dynasty, which gradually becomes the most powerful family in central Europe and monopolizes the imperial throne from 1439 to 1806 and then, in a different form, to 1918.

1277–84

Wales, which has been divided and ruled by native princes since the departure of the Romans, is conquered by the English under Edward I (1239–1307) and becomes a principality of the English crown.

1278

Bohemia and Moravia are united under the rule of King Wenceslas II.

1279

In China the Sung (Song) Dynasty is destroyed by the Mongols. Kublai Khan (1214–94), a grandson of Genghis Khan, becomes Emperor of China and founder of the Yuan Dynasty, which rules the empire until 1368.

1282

Sicilians rebel against Charles I of Anjou, the French ruler of the island. Their massacre of French residents is called the 'Sicilian Vespers' because it began during vespers (the evening service in churches).

1290

Jews are expelled from England by the Edict of Expulsion, in a dispute over moneylending.

1298

King Edward I of England, claiming to be overlord of Scotland, defeats a Scottish army led by William Wallace (c.1274–1305) at Falkirk, but the wars of Scottish independence continue even after Wallace is captured and executed.

1300–1399

c.1300

Sultan Osman I (c.1259–c.1326) founds the Ottoman Empire in Turkey and begins the Ottoman attack on the Byzantine Empire.

The kingdom of Benin, famous for its bronze artifacts, is founded in West Africa.

1306

Jews are expelled from France.

1307

Mansa Musa becomes ruler of the empire of Mali. Control of trade across the Sahara makes this the richest Muslim state.

The military order of the Knights Templar is disbanded on the order of Pope Clement V, influenced by Philip IV of France.

1309

Pope Clement V (c.1260–1314) moves the seat of the papacy from Rome to Avignon, France. As a result, the Church loses much of its authority.

1310

Öljeitü (1280–1316; also known as Khudabanda), the Mongol ruler of Persia, Iraq and other territories, declares Shia Islam the official religion of his empire.

1314

Under Robert Bruce (1274–1329) the Scots gain a decisive victory over the English forces of Edward II (1284–1327) at the Battle of Bannockburn.

1325–41

Ivan I Kalita ('Moneybags') rules as Grand Prince of Moscow. He is regarded as the first ruler to unify Russia.

c.1325

Aztecs found the city of Tenochtitlán on Lake Texcoco in Mexico, the site of modern-day Mexico City.

1328

The last Capetian king of France, Charles IV, the Fair (b.1294), dies leaving no sons. The nobles of France favour Charles's cousin Philip VI (1293–1350), who founds the Valois Dynasty.

c.1333

The 'Black Death', a bubonic plague, appears in China.

1337

Edward III of England declares war on Philip VI of France, beginning a series of wars (1337–1453) over the French throne and English lands in France known since the 19th century as the Hundred Years War.

1338

In Japan the Ashikaga Shogunate is founded, with its headquarters at Muromachi in Heian-kyo (now Kyoto).

1340

An English army under Edward III defeats the French at the Battle of Crécy.

c.1340

The Hindu Empire based in Vijayanagar ('City of Victory') in southern India becomes the centre of resistance to Islam.

1341

Öz Beg or Uzbek (r.1313– 41), Khan (ruler) of the Golden Horde, dies, having converted to Islam.

Statue of Öz Beg in Samarkand, Uzbekistan

1347–51

The Black Death ravages Europe. It may have killed about 25 million people, one third of the population, as well as millions in western Asia. A second major outbreak occurs in 1361–3.

1349

Casimir the Great, king of Poland, welcomes Jews fleeing from persecution in Germany. Poland soon becomes home to the largest Jewish community in the world, lasting until the Holocaust of World War II (1939–45).

1356

The English Army under Edward the Black Prince (son of King Edward III) defeats the French at the Battle of Poitiers and captures King John II of France. The French king agrees to return French possessions which had previously been held by Henry II of England.

1358

A group of mainly German cities involved in trade around the Baltic Sea and along the River Rhine creates the Hanseatic League. The League goes on to dominate trade throughout north-western Europe, having, at its height, 160 member cities as well as trading posts in Flanders, Norway, Russia and England.

1360

In the Peace of Bretigny, the English king Edward III takes sovereignty over south-western France and ends his claims to the French Crown, but t he Hundred Years War begins once more in 1369.

1368

Zhu Yuanzhang (1328–98) drives the Mongols out of China and, as Emperor Hong Wu, founds the Ming Dynasty, with its capital at Nanking ('southern capital') until 1421.

1369

Timur (1336–1405), also known as Tamerlane ('Timur the Lame'), seizes the throne of Samarkand, claiming to be a descendant of Genghis Khan.

1370

Under the Treaty of Stralsund, Denmark accepts the Hanseatic League's control of trade in the Baltic region.

c.1370

In Peru, Nançen Pinco becomes ruler of the Chimú, and the Chimú state begins to expand.

1371

Robert II of Scotland (1316–90) establishes the Stuart Dynasty, which rules Scotland until 1714.

1378

The return of the Papacy to Rome causes the Great Schism, a period of deep crisis for the Western Church when there were two, and later three, rival popes.

1381

Wat Tyler (d.1381) and John Ball (d.1381) lead the Peasants' Revolt in south-eastern England after three oppressive poll taxes are imposed in 1377–81. They are both executed.

1383–1580

The Aviz Dynasty, founded by John I (1357–1433), secures the frontiers of Portugal against the neighbouring kingdom of Castile, and launches the 'golden age' of Portuguese trade and discovery.

1386

The marriage of Queen Jadwiga of Poland and Grand Duke Jagiello of Lithuania, following his conversion from paganism to Christianity, creates the Union of Poland–Lithuania.

1386–95

Timur subdues nearly the whole of Persia, as well as Mesopotamia, Georgia and the Russian territories of the Golden Horde.

c.1387

Geoffrey Chaucer (c.1345–1400), the first great English author, begins to write *The Canterbury Tales*, which takes the form of stories told by a group of pilgrims on its journey to Canterbury.

1389

Serbia falls to the Ottoman Turks in the Battle of Kosovo.

1391

Jews in Spain are killed or forced to accept Christianity.

1397

The Hanseatic League begins to decline following the Union of Kalmar between crown councils of Sweden, Denmark and Norway (including Iceland). Plans for a Great Northern Empire, however, do not succeed because the other countries refuse to accept an overall Danish ruler. The Union ends in 1523.

1398–9

Timur invades India, destroying Delhi and annexing the Punjab.

1400–1499

1400

The Welsh, led by nationalist hero Owen Glendower (c.1350–c.1416), rebel unsuccessfully against Henry IV of England (c.1366–1413).

1402–05

Ottoman Turks are defeated by Timur, the Mongol emperor, at the Battle of Ankara, leading to the collapse of the Empire of Asia Minor. In 1405 Timur dies, with fighting among his descendants leading to the eventual crumbling of his empire.

1405–33

Chinese admiral Zheng He (1371–1433) directs the voyages of seven fleets to India, Arabia and East Africa, creating trade links and leading to Chinese emigration to south-east Asia.

1410

Polish–Lithuanian forces defeat the Teutonic Knights, a German religious-military order, at the Battle of Tannenberg.

1413

Thai armies sack Angkor Thom, the ancient capital of the Khmer Empire. The city is abandoned and not rediscovered until 1861.

1414–18

The Council of Constance, an ecumenical council of Christian churches, is held. In 1417 the election of Martin V (1368–1431) as pope ends the Great Schism, a period when there have been rival popes.

1415

An English army commanded by Henry V (1387–1422) defeats the French at the Battle of Agincourt.

1415–36

The burning at the stake of the Czech religious reformer John Huss (Jan Hus, c.1369–1415) sparks a civil war in his native Bohemia. The subsequent Hussite Wars eventually lead to Bohemia becoming the first Christian country to tolerate two separate churches (Catholic and Hussite).

1421

With the completion of 'The Forbidden City', the new Chinese imperial palace, the Ming Dynasty moves the Chinese capital to Beijing to improve northern defences and extends the Great Wall to 2,450km.

c.1430

Itzcoatl, the Aztec ruler of the Mexican city of Tenochtitlán, establishes control over the cities of Texcoco and Tlacopan.

1431

After helping to halt the English advance into France during the Hundred Years War, the semi-legendary female soldier Joan of Arc (b.c.1412) is burned at the stake.

c.1437

Montezuma I (c.1390–1464) becomes Aztec emperor of Mexico.

1439

The Russian Orthodox Church separates from the Greek Church.

1448

The Russian Orthodox Church becomes independent of the Byzantine Orthodox Church of Constantinople, but quickly submits to the Russian princes.

At Arguin in Mauritania, Portuguese traders build a fort, the first known European colonial building in Africa.

c.1450

German goldsmith Johannes Gutenberg (1400–68) invents a mould for casting movable metal type and the first printing press. In 1455 he produces the Gutenberg Bible, believed to be the first European book printed with movable type.

1452

Italian painter, sculptor, architect and engineer Leonardo da Vinci is born (d.1519). His works include *The Last Supper* (1498) and the *Mona Lisa* (1504).

1453

The Hundred Years War (which started in 1337) ends with a French victory over the English at the Battle of Castillon. Of all the former English lands in France, only Calais (eventually lost in 1558) and the Channel Islands remain in English hands.

The Ottoman Sultan Mehmet II (1432–81) directs the capture of Constantinople, capital of the Byzantine Empire, and makes it his base. With the death of the emperor Constantine XI (b.1404) while fighting on the city wall, the Byzantine Empire comes to an end.

1454

Under the Treaty of Lodi the leading states of the Italian peninsula (Milan, Venice, Naples, Florence and the Papal States) create the Italian League.

1455–85

The Wars of the Roses divide England as two rival branches of the Plantagenet Dynasty, the House of York (white rose) and the House of Lancaster (red rose), fight repeatedly over the throne.

1460

The world's first stock exchange is opened at Antwerp in Flanders.

c.1460

The Songhai Empire rises to power in West Africa.

1466

Poland, involved in power struggles with Lithuania and Prussia for several decades, gains control of Prussia.

1467–77

The Onin War in Japan is the first in a series of civil wars among rival *daimyo* (feudal lords) that continues until 1600.

1469

The marriage of Ferdinand V of Aragon (1452–1516) and Isabella I of Castile (1451–1504) unites the whole of modern Spain except the region around Granada in the south, which remains in Muslim hands.

Guru Nanak is born (d.1539). He is the founder of Sikhism, the principles of which are set out in the *Guru Granth Sahib* in 1604.

1470

The Incas overthrow the Chimú state (in what is now Peru) in the course of creating an empire covering modern Peru, Bolivia and Ecuador, and parts of Chile and Argentina.

1472

Ivan III 'the Great', Grand Prince of Muscovy (1440–1505), marries Zoe Palaiologa, heiress of the last Byzantine ruling family. He declares Moscow the 'Third Rome' (after Rome and Constantinople), reinforcing his links with the Russian Orthodox Church. He styles himself 'tsar of all Russia'.

1475

The Italian sculptor, painter and poet Michelangelo is born (d.1564). His works include the statue of David in Florence and the ceiling of the Sistine Chapel in Rome.

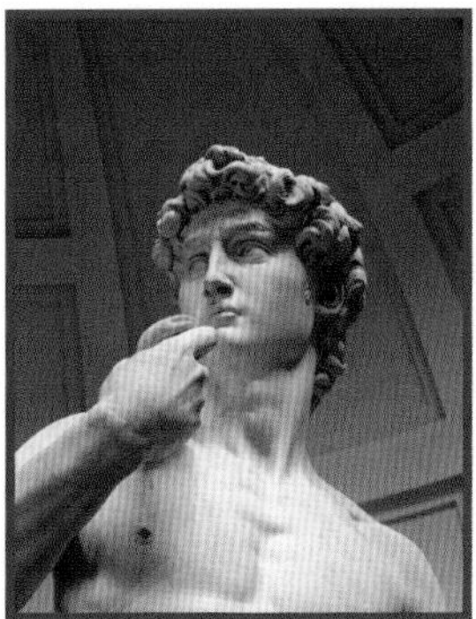

Part of the statue of David by Michelangelo

William Caxton (c.1422–1491) produces the first printed book in English, *The Recuyell of the Historyes of Troye*, at Bruges, Belgium.

1478

The Spanish Inquisition, an organization for judging cases of heresy, is founded by the Papacy. A writer of the time estimated that in its first ten years it burnt 2,000 people at the stake and punished 15,000 others.

1480

Ivan III, Grand Prince of Muscovy, decisively defeats the Mongols of the Golden Horde, and ends his payment of a tribute (a payment made to acknowledge submission) to them. The Golden Horde then splinters into several small khanates.

1483–98

Charles VIII of France (1470–98) attempts to re-create the Byzantine Empire, claiming control over the Kingdom of Naples and making alliances with England, Barcelona and the Habsburgs of Germany.

1485

In England, the Wars of the Roses end when Henry Tudor (1457–1509) defeats Richard III (1452–85) at the Battle of Bosworth Field and becomes Henry VII, founding the Tudor Dynasty.

1488

The Portuguese explorer Bartolomeu Diaz rounds the Cape of Good Hope. The Portuguese go on to open up a sea route to Asia from the Atlantic.

1492

The Christian kingdoms of Aragon and Castile conquer Granada, the last Muslim realm in Spain, and expel hundreds of thousands of Muslims and Jews.

Ferdinand and Isabella of Spain commission the expeditions of the Italian navigator Christopher Columbus, who reaches the Bahamas and explores Cuba and Hispaniola.

The Spaniard Rodrigo Borgia (1431–1503) becomes Pope Alexander VI, now considered to be one of the most corrupt popes of the Renaissance period. His daughter, Lucrezia Borgia (1480–1519), is notorious in legend, perhaps unfairly, for vice and crime.

1494

The Italian Wars, a long series of conflicts lasting until 1559, follow the collapse of the Italian League.

Spain and Portugal sign the Treaty of Tordesillas, as recommended by the Pope. It divides possessions in the 'New World' of the Americas between them. Lands to the east of an arbitrary line become Portuguese, those to the west, Spanish.

1494–1530

Babur (1483–1530), a descendant of the Mongol emperors Genghis Khan and Timur, heads the final Muslim advances into India.

1495–1521

Manuel I, the Great, of Portugal establishes Portuguese commercial power in India, east Asia, Africa and Brazil.

1497

John Cabot (c.1450–c.1499), an Italian navigator employed by Henry VII of England, lands in Newfoundland, North America.

1497–9

The Portuguese navigator Vasco da Gama (c.1469–1525) completes the first recorded sea voyage from Europe to India and back, generating European interest in India.

1499

Switzerland gains its independence from the German Empire in the Peace of Basle.

1499–1502

Amerigo Vespucci (1451–1512) makes reports of his coastal travel in the Americas, making the region known.

1500–1599

1500

Portuguese navigator Pedro Cabral (c.1467–c.1520) lands on the coast of Brazil and claims it for the Portuguese Crown.

1501

Isma'il I (1487–1524) founds the Safavid Dynasty in Persia.

1502

Montezuma II (1466–1520) becomes the last Aztec emperor of Mexico.

1503

The Portuguese start to send African slaves to their new colony in Brazil, the first of about 12 million carried to the Americas over the next three centuries.

1505–15

The viceroys Almeida and Albuquerque establish the Portuguese commercial empire in Goa, on the western coast of India, Ceylon, Malacca and the East Indies. They enjoy huge profits until the English and Dutch seize trading power in the 16th century.

1512–20

Ottoman Emperor Selim I acquires Arabia, Egypt and Syria.

1515

Switzerland is defeated by France at the Battle of Marignano, forfeiting its claim to be a major power and adopting the policy of neutrality that it still has today.

1517

The German theologian Martin Luther (1483–1546) draws up his list of 95 theses that question the authority of the Pope, and nails them to the door of Wittenberg Church. This act launches the Protestant Reformation.

Portrait of Martin Luther, 1533

1519

Ferdinand Magellan (c.1480–1521) discovers a

passage running from the Atlantic into another ocean, which he names the Pacific. Although he is murdered in the Philippines, his ships complete the first circumnavigation of the Earth.

1519–21

Hernán Cortés (1485–1547), a Spanish adventurer, forms alliances with native rebels against Montezuma II (1466–1520), Aztec emperor since 1502. Montezuma is killed in battle, and Cortés captures the Aztec capital Tenochtitlán.

1520

Martin Luther composes three essays against the doctrine of the Roman Church, resulting in a papal bull (an order from the Pope) issued against him and eventually his excommunication from the Church.

Süleyman I, the Magnificent, or the Lawgiver (1494–1566), becomes Ottoman Sultan. He enlarges the empire to its greatest extent and rebuilds much of Constantinople (modern-day Istanbul).

1523

Gustav I Vasa (1496–1560) breaks the Union of Kalmar, signed in 1397 between the Crown Councils of Sweden, Denmark and Norway, by establishing the kingdom of Sweden (including Finland). He imposes Lutheranism, the teaching of the Protestant reformer Martin Luther, on the country in 1527.

1526

The Delhi Sultanate is destroyed by Babur, who makes himself the first Mogul emperor of India.

The Ottomans conquer most of Hungary, while the Habsburgs take control of the remainder of Hungary and the whole of Bohemia until 1918.

1531

Protestant German princes form the Schmalkaldic League to defend Protestantism against the Holy Roman Emperor, Charles V. The League is destroyed in 1547 at the Battle of Mühlberg.

1533

Francisco Pizarro (c.1478–1541), a Spanish adventurer, takes the Inca capital, Cuzco, in Peru and has the last Inca ruler, Atahualpa (b.c.1500), murdered.

1534

The Act of Supremacy ends the pope's authority in England, three years after Henry VIII (1491–1547) is made Supreme Head of the English Church (1531). With the Dissolution of the Monasteries, the property of Catholic monasteries is confiscated.

Ignatius of Loyola (1491–1556) founds the missionary religious order of the Society of Jesus (Jesuits), which preaches complete obedience to Church doctrine.

1536

Denmark, Norway and Iceland are converted to Lutheranism, the teachings of Martin Luther.

William Tyndale (b.c.1494), Protestant translator of the Bible into English, is executed in Spain. His translation later forms the basis of the Authorized Version of the Bible published in 1611.

1543

The Polish astronomer Nicolaus Copernicus (1473–1543) publishes his theory that the Earth revolves around the Sun.

1545–63

In Italy the Council of Trent, a series of councils of the Catholic Church, revises many of its doctrines, contributing to the Counter-Reformation (or Catholic Reformation) in response to the rise of Protestantism.

1547

Ivan IV, the Terrible (1530–84), takes the title 'Tsar of Russia' and begins a series of conquests of the remaining Mongol khanates.

1555

Under the Peace of Augsburg, each state of the Holy Roman Empire is allowed to choose whether its subjects are to be Catholics or Lutherans.

1556

Akbar the Great (1542–1605) becomes Mogul emperor of India, defeating Afghan invaders and extending the empire's territories.

1556–9

Spain, under the rule of Philip II (1527–98), takes Burgundy and Naples from France.

1557

China allows Portuguese settlement in Macao.

1558

Elizabeth I (1533–1603) becomes queen of England. Her reign is often seen as a 'golden age' of exploration and flourishing culture in England, although it was also characterized by violent repression of English Catholics.

1560

The Church of Scotland is founded by Protestant reformer John Knox (c.1513–72).

1562–98

France is divided by the Wars of Religion, a series of conflicts over Protestantism and the succession to the throne. In the 'St Bartholomew's Day Massacre' (1572), French Huguenots (Protestants) are slaughtered at the order of Charles IX (1550–74). The Wars end when the Huguenot Henry IV (1553–1610), founder of the Bourbon Dynasty, succeeds to the throne, converts to Catholicism and issues the Edict of Nantes (1598), which grants freedom of worship throughout France until 1685.

1565–72

Tsar Ivan IV divides the Russian Empire into separate territories of the tsar and of the boyars (aristocracy), initiating a period of terror.

1568

William I, the Silent, Prince of Orange (1533–84), leads a revolt of 17 of the Spanish-ruled provinces in the Low Countries, starting the Eighty Years War with Spain, which lasts until 1648.

1571

The 'Holy League' of Elizabeth I of England and Philip II of Spain defeats the Ottoman navy at the Battle of Lepanto, accelerating the decline of its empire.

1577

Guru Ram Das (1534–81) founds the city of Amritsar, later the centre of Sikhism.

1577–80

English explorer Sir Francis Drake (c.1540–96) becomes the first man to circumnavigate the globe in a single journey.

1580

Portugal is united with Spain for 60 years after Sebastian, the last Portuguese king of the Aviz Dynasty, dies (1578) leaving no heir.

1581

Tsar Ivan IV of Russia conquers the Tartar territory of Sibir, and begins the gradual exploration and conquest of Siberia.

The Netherlands defect from Spanish control as Philip II of Spain attempts to crush Protestantism there.

1582

The Japanese warrior Hideyoshi Toyotomi (1536–98) becomes chancellor and establishes a administration, reducing the power of the *daimyo* (feudal nobles).

Pope Gregory XIII introduces the 'Gregorian' calendar. It is adopted almost at once throughout Catholic Europe, but the Julian calendar long remains in force in Protestant and Orthodox countries.

1584

The first English colony in Virginia in North America is established by Sir Walter Raleigh (1552–1618).

1587

Queen Elizabeth I of England has her cousin Mary, Queen of Scots (1542–87), the leading Catholic claimant to her throne, executed.

1588

The Spanish Armada, a fleet of 130 ships sent by Philip II of Spain to invade England, is defeated.

1590

The Italian astronomer, mathematician and natural philosopher Galileo Galilei (1564–1642) proves that all bodies fall at the same rate, contrary to Aristotle's belief that the rate at which a body falls is proportional to its weight.

Telescopes belonging to Galileo Galilei

1594

The English playwright, poet and actor William Shakespeare (1564–1616) begins his career with the Lord Chamberlain's Company of players, later the King's Men, the company for which he wrote many of his 37 plays.

1600–1699

1600

The British East India Company is founded, the most powerful of the merchant adventurer companies that helped to establish England as the leading trading power.

In Japan, Tokugawa Ieyasu (1543–1616) becomes overlord of the *daimyo* (feudal nobles) and establishes the Tokugawa Shogunate, which runs until 1867.

1603

On the death of Queen Elizabeth I, the last Tudor monarch, the throne passes to James VI of Scotland (and I of England), beginning the rule of the Stuart Dynasty in England as well as Scotland.

French control in Canada begins with the first governor, Samuel de Champlain (c.1567–1635), who holds Newfoundland, Nova Scotia and New France.

1604

The foremost Sikh scripture, the *Guru Granth Sahib*, is compiled by the fifth guru, Guru Arjan (1536–1606), and installed in the newly completed Golden Temple in Amritsar.

1605

The Gunpowder Plot, a Catholic conspiracy to blow up the English Parliament, is uncovered. The capture of Guy Fawkes, a leading conspirator, is still celebrated every 5 November (Bonfire Night).

1609

The Catholic League is established between Spain and Bavaria, marking several decades of Counter-Reformation, a reform of activity in the Catholic Church stimulated by the Reformation.

1609–19

German astronomer Johannes Kepler (1571–1630) formulates the laws of planetary motion, describing elliptical orbits and forming the starting point of modern astronomy.

1610

Galileo perfects the refraction telescope and uses it to discover the mountains of the Moon and four of Jupiter's moons.

1613

Following the 'Time of Troubles', a period of civil war and foreign intervention, an assembly of the Russian Empire chooses Mikhail Romanov (1596–1645) as tsar. Founder of the Romanov Dynasty, he makes peace with Sweden and Poland.

1618–48

The Thirty Years War, initially a dispute over the rights of Calvinists (followers of beliefs of the French theologian John Calvin) in the Holy Roman Empire, becomes an intermittent power struggle among the leading European powers: France, the various German states, the Habsburg emperors and their cousins the kings of Spain, and Sweden.

1619

The Dutch empire of the East Indies (modern Indonesia) begins with the establishment of a settlement at Batavia (now Jakarta).

1620

The Puritan 'Pilgrim Fathers', early English religious settlers, establish the Plymouth colony in North America.

1624

Dutch colonists establish New Amsterdam (now New York City).

Cardinal Armand Richelieu (1585–1642), Minister of State to the French Crown, begins a period of absolutist rule in France. The era comes to be symbolized by buildings such as the Palace of Versailles, and classically styled artistic works.

1629

The English parliament is dissolved after it has disagreements with King Charles I (1600–49) over religious policy and taxation revenue. Charles rules without Parliament for eleven years.

c.1632–43

The Mogul emperor Shah Jahan oversees the building of the Taj Mahal, the mausoleum of his wife, Mumtaz Mahal, outside Agra.

1637–9

The Japanese Shogunate, fearful of the united Spanish–Portuguese Empire, bans Christianity and reduces contact with foreigners to closely controlled trade within east Asia. Ports remain closed until 1853.

1640

Portugal rebels against Spanish rule, regains its independence, and gains control of Brazil and other colonies, under the Braganza Dynasty.

1642

The Dutch navigator Abel Tasman begins voyages during which he discovers Tasmania and New Zealand, and explores the coast of Australia.

1642–8

Parliamentarians (Roundheads) and supporters of Charles I (Royalists or Cavaliers) engage in the English Civil Wars, a series of conflicts over the extent of royal power and the character of the national Church. The Parliamentarians defeat the Royalists at the Battle of Marston Moor (1644).

1644

The Manchus conquer China, overthrowing the Ming Dynasty and establishing the Ch'ing (Qing) Dynasty.

1646

The English mystic George Fox (1624–91) founds the Society of Friends (Quakers), which is formally organized in 1667.

1648

The Peace of Westphalia ends the Thirty Years War and the Eighty Years War, recognizes Dutch independence and introduces the principle of non-interference in the internal affairs of sovereign states. It leaves the Holy Roman Emperor with only nominal authority in Germany.

1649

Charles I of England is executed, the monarchy is abolished, and the English Parliament turns the entire British Isles into a republic known as the Commonwealth.

1652

The Dutch East India Company founds Cape Town.

1652–74

A series of three naval wars between England and the Dutch Republic, known as the Anglo-Dutch Wars, result from rivalry over commercial interests and colonies.

1653–8

Oliver Cromwell (1599–1658), the Puritan general who led the Parliamentary armies in the English Civil Wars and who suppressed a Catholic uprising in Ireland, rules as Lord Protector of Great Britain.

Portrait of Oliver Cromwell, c.1649

1654–67

The Thirteen Years War between Poland–Lithuania and Russia ends in the transfer of what are now Belarus and eastern Ukraine to Russian rule.

1656–7

Frederick William I, Elector of Brandenburg, is recognized as ruler of the Brandenburg–Prussian nation state that he has created, just one of the German principalities emerging from the fragmentation of the German Empire.

1658

Aurangzeb (1618–1707) becomes the last and most magnificent of the Mogul emperors of India.

Oliver Cromwell dies, and is succeeded as Lord Protector by his son Richard Cromwell (1626–1712). Richard proves incapable of ruling and is forced to resign in 1659.

1660

The monarchy is restored in England, Scotland and Ireland when Charles II (1630–85), son of Charles I, returns to England from exile in France. However, his absolutist rule resurrects the tensions between the Crown and Parliament that were typical of the reign of his father.

Samuel Pepys (1633–73), an official of the English Admiralty, begins his diary, which becomes famous when it is deciphered and published in the 19th century.

1661

After the death of his premier minister Cardinal Mazarin, Louis XIV (1638–1715), 'The Sun King', assumes total control of the government. His absolutist rule is the longest reign in French history.

1664–5

The Great Plague of London kills more people than any other single epidemic in the city, with an estimated 70,000 casualties.

1664

In North America, the English take control of the Dutch colony of New Amsterdam, renaming it New York.

1666

The Great Fire of London destroys the city. The rebuilding programme is directed by Christopher Wren (1632–1723) and includes a rebuilt St Paul's Cathedral and many new churches. His plans to re-model the old street patterns are discarded.

1669

The Hanseatic League, a powerful federation of trading guilds, is weakened by the rise of Dutch and English traders and holds the last meeting of its assembly.

1678

The 'Popish plot', an alleged Roman Catholic conspiracy to assassinate Charles II of England and place James, Duke of York (later James VII and II), on the throne, is discovered. It leads to the execution of 35 plotters and the weakening of the government.

1679

Political parties start to emerge in the English Parliament for the first time: the Whigs, opponents of the Catholic Stuart Dynasty, and the Tories, who are Anglican but loyal supporters of the Stuart King James II.

1680

The English astronomer Edmond Halley (1656–1742) makes his prediction for the return (in 1758) of a comet that had previously been observed in 1066 and 1583. It is now called Halley's comet in his honour.

1682

The French explorer René-Robert Cavelier de la Salle (1643–87) explores the Mississippi River to its mouth and claims the whole of the Mississippi Basin for France, naming the region 'Louisiana' after the French king Louis XIV (1638–1715).

1685

After Louis XIV revokes the Edict of Nantes, which guaranteed freedom of worship in France, many Huguenots (Protestants) leave the country to settle in England and the Dutch Republic.

1686–97

The Holy Roman Empire, Spain and Bavaria form the League of Augsburg, an alliance against French territorial expansionism under Louis XIV. Later, the Dutch Republic, England, Sweden and Savoy (a kingdom in northern Italy) join during the War of the League of Augsburg, creating the Grand Alliance against France. Simultaneously, King William's War becomes the first of the great wars between France and England for control of North America.

1687

Isaac Newton publishes his greatest work, *Philosophiae Naturalis Principia Mathematica* ('The Mathematical Principles of Natural

Philosophy'), which includes his three laws of motion.

1688–9

The Catholic King James VII and II flees England for France. Parliament carries out the 'Glorious Revolution', inviting the Protestant Dutch prince William of Orange (1650–1702) and his wife Mary (1662–94), James's daughter, to become joint Protestant monarchs. William III and Mary II are crowned in April 1689. However, the Jacobites (from *Jacobus*, the Latin for 'James') continue actively to support James and his descendants for the next half-century, especially in Scotland.

1689

In West Africa Osei Tutu (d.1712) founds the Ashanti confederacy, a powerful confederacy of chiefdoms.

1690

At the Battle of the Boyne in Ireland the forces of Protestant King William III defeat those of former king James VII and II who was attempting to regain the throne.

1692

The small Puritan community of Salem in Massachusetts holds the infamous Witchcraft Trials. The convictions lead to 20 deaths.

1696

Peter I, the Great (1672–1725), becomes sole tsar of Russia on the death of his half-brother Ivan, and he takes the title Emperor in 1721. His organization and reforms revolutionize Russia from above and initiate the rise of Russia as a great world power.

1699

Austria drives the Ottomans out of Hungary (then including Slovakia, Transylvania and Croatia), which becomes another Habsburg family territory until 1918.

Gobind Singh (1666–1708), the last of the ten Sikh Gurus, institutes the Khalsa, an order marked by the wearing of the 'Five Ks', symbols of allegiance to Sikhism.

1700–1799

1700–21

The Great Northern War between Sweden and an alliance of Russia, Denmark and Poland–Lithuania leads to Russian domination of the Baltic region.

1700–40

The multinational state of Austria–Hungary thrives under Habsburg rule and unites against the Ottoman threat.

1701

Elector Frederick III of Brandenburg (1657–1713), ruler of the largest single state within the Holy Roman Empire as well as parts of Poland outside the Empire, is crowned King Frederick I of Prussia.

1701–13

The death of Charles II (1661–1700), the last Habsburg king of Spain, leads to the War of the Spanish Succession over his titles. Great Britain, Habsburg Austria and the Dutch Republic support Archduke Charles of Austria (1685–1740), while France and Spain support Philip, Duke of Anjou (1683–1746), a grandson of Louis XIV. The war is resolved by the Peace of Utrecht, which makes Philip the king of Spain, founder of the Bourbon Dynasty, but surrenders the lands of the Spanish Netherlands (now Belgium), Milan, Naples and Sardinia to Austria, and Gibraltar to Great Britain.

1702–13

Queen Anne's War is waged by Britain and France for control of North America.

1703

Peter I, the Great, founds St Petersburg, which replaces Moscow as the capital of Russia in 1712. (Moscow becomes the capital once more in 1918.)

1707

The Act of Union unites the kingdoms and parliaments of England and Scotland.

The last great Grand Mogul, Aurangzeb, dies. His rule saw the greatest extent of the Mogul Empire in 1691, but also saw persecutions of Hindus and Sikhs that were to provoke uprisings.

1709

The English ironmaster Abraham Darby (c.1678–1717) is the first to use coke successfully in the smelting of iron.

1714–1837

On the death of Queen Anne, the last of the Stuart Dynasty, the throne passes to George I (1660–1727), the Elector of Hanover. The Hanoverian Dynasty rules both the British Isles and the German kingdom of Hanover.

1715

Jacobites, supporters of the claim to the British throne of the Catholic James VII and II and his descendants, launch a short-lived unsuccessful rebellion in support of the former king's son James (1688–1766), known as the 'Old Pretender'.

1715–74

The reign of French king Louis XV sees massive excesses that herald the loss of authority of the *ancien régime* ('old order'), leading eventually to the French Revolution in 1789.

1720

The 'South Sea Bubble', a financial crisis

following the collapse of the South Sea Company, ruins many investors in Great Britain.

1722

Afghans overthrow the Safavid Dynasty, rulers of the Persian Empire since 1501.

1725

The Japanese playwright Chikamatsu Monzaemon (b.1653) dies, having written more than 100 plays, many of which are still performed in Kabuki (a stylized form of drama, with singing and dancing, performed by men) or Bunraku (a form of puppet theatre in which each puppet is manipulated by three men who remain visible).

1728

Vitus Bering (1681–1741), a Danish navigator employed by the Russian court, discovers the Bering Strait between Russia and Alaska.

1733

The English inventor John Kay (1704–c.1780) devises the flying-shuttle loom, advancing the mechanization of the textile industry.

1735

The Swedish naturalist Carolus Linnaeus (1707–78) publishes his *Systema Naturae* ('System of Nature'), beginning the classification of plants and animals by a system of Latin names, which is still used today.

1736

Nadir Shah (1688–1747), a former bandit, becomes Shah of Persia. He goes on to invade Bahrain, Oman, northern India and Central Asia, but is murdered by his own troops.

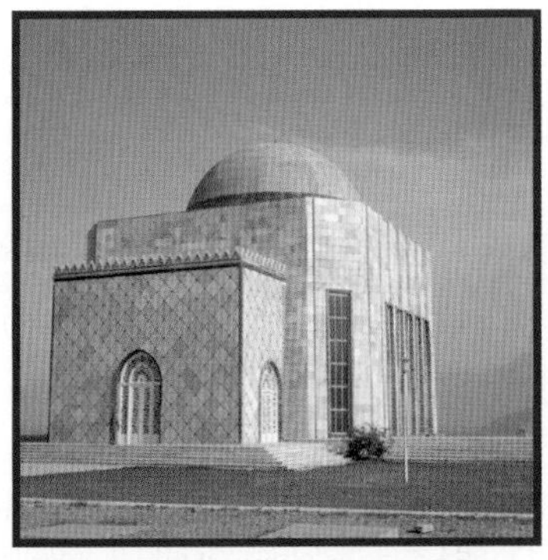

Mausoleum of Nadir Shah, Kabul, Iraq

1736–96

The Chinese Empire under Qianlong (1711–99) expands to include Tibet, Mongolia, Turkestan, Annam, Burma and Nepal.

1738

John Wesley (1703–91) and his brother Charles (1707–88) begin the preaching of Methodism, initially an evangelical movement within the Church of England, but the basis of a separate church from 1795.

1740–8

The complex War of the Austrian Succession sees Maria Theresa (1717–80) attempt to succeed her father and become the first woman to rule Habsburg Austria. The conflict, which comes to involve most of Europe, begins when the Prussian king Frederick II, the Great (1712–86) seizes the Austrian-held province of Silesia, while Great Britain comes to Austria's aid. France and Britain fight in other theatres of war in North America (King George's War) and India. The War ends with the Treaty of Aix-La-Chapelle (1748), which largely restores the status quo.

1744

Guided by the puritanical Muslim teacher Muhammad ibn 'Abd al-Wahhab (1703–92), the Saud family begins the creation of its kingdom in Arabia, which still officially practises Wahabism, a strict Islamic doctrine.

1745–6

Jacobites launch a rebellion in Great Britain in support of James VII and II's grandson Charles Edward Stuart (1720–88, the 'Young Pretender' or 'Bonnie Prince Charlie'). The insurgency, which becomes known as the Forty-Five Rebellion, aims to place James on the throne. The Jacobites are defeated at the Battle of Culloden (1746) and the British government suppresses the Scottish Highland clans that took part in the Rebellion (1747).

c.1750

The Polish Jewish teacher and healer Baal-Shem-Tov (1699–1760) founds modern Hasidism, a devout strain of Judaism, which spreads throughout eastern Europe.

1751

The French philosophers Denis Diderot (1713–84) and Jean Le Rond d'Alembert (1717–83) publish the first volume of the *Encyclopédie*, the major reference work of the Enlightenment – the name given to the spirit of the French philosophers of the 18th century who believed in reason and human progress, questioning tradition and authority.

1752

The Gregorian calendar, introduced in most European countries after 1582, is adopted in Great Britain and Ireland.

1756–63

In the Seven Years War, a conflict fought in Europe, North America and India, a bloc of countries comprising Austria, France, Russia, Sweden and Saxony opposes Prussia, Great Britain, Hanover and Portugal. It ends with the Treaty of Paris, whereby Spain and France concede colonial territory to Britain, most significantly in North America.

1757

Forces of the British East India Company, under Robert Clive (1725–74), defeat Siraj ud-Daula (c.1732–57), Nawab of Bengal, initiating the creation of the British 'Raj' (empire).

1759

British and Hanoverian forces defeat the French at the Battle of Minden during the Seven Years War. Also, at the Battle of Quebec, the British general James Wolfe (1727–59) defeats the French on the Plains of Abraham, winning New France (now the southern parts of Quebec Province and Ontario) for Britain, but dying in battle.

1761

The Afghans defeat the Marathas, the dominant people of south-west India, at Panipat, ending Maratha conquests of parts of northern India and weakening the Mogul empire.

1765

The Scottish engineer James Watt (1736–1819) improves the steam engine by adding a separate condenser, probably the greatest single improvement ever made to the steam engine.

1768

Ali Bey (1728–73) becomes Sultan of Egypt and establishes independence from the Ottoman Empire.

1768–79

The English navigator Captain James Cook (1728–79) makes scientific expeditions (1768–71 and 1772–5) along the east coast of Australia (landing at Botany Bay in 1770), New Caledonia, Tonga and the Sandwich Islands.

1771

Swedish chemist Carl Scheele (1742–86) discovers oxygen. However, an independent discovery by English chemist Joseph Priestley (1733–1804) in 1774 is more widely known.

1772

Russia, Austria and Prussia agree on the first partition of Poland–Lithuania, leaving that state greatly reduced in size. Following two more partitions (1793 and 1795), Poland and Lithuania disappear from the map of Europe.

1773

Conflict in North America between the colonies and the British government begins after the imposition of a tax on tea imported there. Cargoes from tea ships are thrown into Boston Harbour by the colonists in protest, an incident dubbed the Boston Tea Party.

1775–83

Growing tension between the 13 North American colonies and Britain, based on the colonists' resentment of taxation without political representation, leads to the American Revolution. Hostilities break out at Lexington and Concord, and then Bunker Hill (all 1775). In 1776 a Continental Congress led by George Washington (1732–99) drafts the Declaration of Independence (4 July), the work of Thomas Jefferson (1743–1826). The independence of the United States of America is recognized under the Treaty of Paris (1783).

1776–86

The Fulani Emirates are founded in what is now northern Nigeria.

1780

Joseph II (1741–90) becomes sole ruler of Austria on the death of his mother, Maria Theresa, and introduces reforms, abolishing serfdom and granting religious tolerance.

French chemist Antoine Lavoisier (1743–94) discovers the true nature of oxygen and its role in combustion and gives it its name.

1781

The British Army surrenders at Yorktown in Virginia during the American Revolution. The defeat destroys the political will of the British to continue the war.

The German-born English astronomer Sir William Herschel (1738–1822) discovers Uranus, the first planet to be found that is not visible to the naked eye.

1783

In France, Joseph Montgolfier (1740–1810) and his brother Jacques (1745–99) conduct the world's first manned balloon flight.

1785

The power loom for spinning cotton is invented by Edmund Cartwright (1743–1823).

1787

The USA adopts its Constitution (now the oldest written constitution still in force in any nation state) and George Washington becomes the country's first president.

1788

Britain founds the penal colony of New South Wales, Australia's first permanent European settlement.

1789

The French Revolution begins with the storming of the main prison in Paris, the Bastille. The Declaration of the Rights of Man, famously proclaiming *liberté, égalité, fraternité* ('freedom, equality, brotherhood'), is produced, influenced by the American Bill of Rights of 1776.

1791

Toussaint Louverture (c.1743–1803) leads a slave revolt against the French in Haiti, the first successful uprising by a non-white people against a white colonial empire.

1792

The French Revolutionary Wars (1792–1802) begin when the French declare war on Austria and Prussia in fear that the Habsburgs might intervene in France. The success of France at the Battle of Valmy secures the success of the French Revolution.

1793

Louis XVI (b.1754), King of France, is executed by the Revolutionary authorities. Later that year his wife, Marie Antoinette (b.1755), is also guillotined.

Portrait of Marie Antoinette, 1793

1794

Agha Muhammad seizes the throne of Persia and establishes the Qajar Dynasty, which rules until 1925.

1796

The English physician Edward Jenner (1749–1823) successfully inoculates a child against smallpox, inaugurating vaccination.

1798

English poets William Wordsworth (1770–1850) and Samuel Taylor Coleridge (1772–1834) jointly publish *Lyrical Ballads*, often regarded as pioneering the Romantic movement in verse.

At the Battle of the Nile a French naval force led by Napoleon Bonaparte (later Napoleon I, 1769–1821) attempts to conquer Egypt. It is stopped by British naval forces under Horatio Nelson (1758–1805).

1799

Napoleon Bonaparte becomes First Consul of France (1799–1804).

Tipu Sultan (c.1753–99), ruler of Mysore (in India), is killed by British forces.

1800–1899

1800

The Italian physicist Alessandro Volta (1745–1827) invents the electrochemical battery, the first source of continuous electricity.

1801

Following the abolition of the Irish Parliament under the Act of Union, Great Britain and Ireland form the United Kingdom.

1803

The USA doubles in size with the Louisiana Purchase from France, the new nation acquiring full control of lands to the west of the Mississippi River.

1804

Napoleon Bonaparte, the French general who has already made France the dominant power in western Europe, makes himself Napoleon I, Emperor of the French and King of Italy. He issues the Code Napoleon, which has had a major influence on other law codes.

The Islamic religious leader Usman dan Fodio (1754–1817) launches the war that establishes the Fulani Empire in central Africa.

1804–6

The Lewis and Clark expedition, named after its leaders Meriwether Lewis and William Clark, opens up a route across the USA to the Pacific Ocean.

Pocket compass used in the Lewis and Clark expedition

1805

At the Battle of Trafalgar, south of Spain, Horatio Nelson, commanding the British fleet, defeats the combined fleets of France and Spain, but is mortally wounded.

Following France's defeat of Austria at the Battle of Austerlitz, the Treaty of Pressburg (Bratislava) sees Austria renounce all interests in Italy and lose most of its western Alpine lands.

1806

The Holy Roman Empire comes to an end when Emperor Francis II (1768–1835) is forced to abdicate by Napoleon. Francis becomes Francis I of the new Austrian Empire, which includes the extensive Habsburg family domains in central and eastern Europe.

1807

Russian armies are sent to support Prussia fight an inconclusive campaign against the French. France and Russia effectively partition Europe between them.

Following a similar decision by Denmark in 1804, Britain makes the slave trade illegal. British naval vessels start to patrol the coasts of Africa to suppress the trade.

1808

The USA bans the importation of slaves into the country, but trading slaves within the USA remains legal.

The English chemist John Dalton (1766–1844) propounds atomic theory.

1808–14

A French invasion of Spain and Portugal begins a series of Peninsular Wars.

1809

Finland is ceded from Sweden to Russia.

1810–26

In the South American Wars of Independence the creole (mixed-race) élites in the Spanish colonies in Central and South America rebel against Spanish rule, creating a series of republics, and reducing Spain's empire to Cuba, Puerto Rico and the Philippines. Simon Bolivar, the revolutionary politician and military leader known as 'the Liberator', is largely credited with the independence of Bolivia, Colombia, Ecuador, Peru and Venezuela.

c.1810–20

Thousands of crofting families in the Scottish highlands are evicted by their landlords, who want the land for sheep farming. This becomes known as the 'Highland Clearances'.

1812

Napoleon I invades Russia, but his army suffers disastrous losses with the approach of winter and makes a forced retreat.

1812–14

During the War of 1812, between the USA and Britain, US forces burn parts of York (now Toronto) and British forces burn parts of Washington, DC.

1813–14

Napoleon I is defeated at the 'Battle of the Nations' in Leipzig by the combined forces of Austria, Prussia, Russia and Sweden. He is forced to abdicate and is exiled to the Italian island of Elba.

1815

Napoleon I, having regained power, is finally defeated at the Battle of Waterloo by British forces under the Duke of Wellington (1769–1852) and Prussian forces under Gebhard Leberecht von Blücher (1742–1819), and is exiled to St Helena, where he dies in 1821.

At the Congress of Vienna the great European powers confirm the transfer of Finland from Sweden to Russia (1809), and of Norway from Denmark to Sweden (1814); award the Austrian Netherlands (Belgium) to the new Kingdom of the Netherlands, and most of Poland to Russia; and create the German Confederation.

1816

A French scientist, Nicéphore Niepce (1765–1833), produces the world's first photographic image on metal.

1818

Shaka (1787–1828) founds the Zulu Kingdom in southern Africa.

1819

Stamford Raffles (1781–1826) acquires Singapore for the British East India Company.

1821–7

The Greek War of Independence against the Ottoman Empire ends with the decisive defeat of the Turkish and Egyptian fleet at the Battle of Navarino by the British and French fleets.

1822

Brazil achieves independence from Portugal.

A group of freed US slaves founds a colony in Liberia, on the coast of West Africa.

1823

US President James Monroe (1758–1831) announces the Monroe Doctrine, declaring US hostility to further European colonization or political interference in the Western Hemisphere.

1824–26

The First Anglo-Burmese War begins the colonization of Burma by Britain, which is continued and expanded in two further wars (1852–3 and 1885).

1825–8

Argentina and Brazil fight a war over a border region known as the Banda Oriental, which becomes the independent republic of Uruguay.

1829

Following agitation by Irish political leader Daniel O'Connell (1775–1847; known as 'the Liberator'), the Catholic Emancipation Act in Britain allows Catholics to hold public office.

1830

Belgium achieves independence from the Netherlands.

1830–1

Poland attempts revolution but becomes a Russian province.

1833

The Slavery Abolition Act abolishes slavery in the British Empire.

English mathematician Charles Babbage (1792–1871) initiates a major step towards modern computers with his unrealized design for an 'analytical engine'.

1836

The Boers, Europeans who had been born in the Dutch colony at the Cape in South Africa, begin their Great Trek northwards from the Cape to escape British rule. They create republics in the Transvaal and the Orange Free State.

Texas declares its independence from Mexico, and defends it at the siege of the Alamo in San Antonio, but later (1846) joins the USA as the 28th state.

Charles Dickens (1812–70) begins his first novel, *The Pickwick Papers*, believed to be the first work of fiction ever published in serial form.

1836–42

The first of three Anglo-Afghan Wars is fought (the others following in 1878–80 and 1919) to determine the border between British India and Afghanistan.

1837

Victoria (1819–1901) becomes queen of Great Britain and Ireland, but, being a woman, is prevented from ruling Hanover like her immediate predecessors.

1838

The first in a series of Zulu Wars breaks out between Boers and Zulus after Boer settlers are massacred in Zululand; the Boer forces emerge victorious. In an Anglo–Zulu War, British forces destroy the Zulu Kingdom in southern Africa by 1879.

1839

The Chinese government's attempt to block the British trade in opium leads to the First Opium War. Under the Treaty of Nanking (1842), Hong Kong is ceded to Britain and China is forced to open five 'treaty' ports to European trade. China's arrest of a British ship, the *Arrow*, leads to the Second Opium War, which is won by a combined British and French force. Under the Treaty of Tianjin (1860), Kowloon is ceded to Britain.

1840

Britain annexes New Zealand under the Treaty of Waitangi, which formally recognizes the rights of the native Maori people.

1845–c.1850

The Great Irish Famine, caused by the failure of the potato crop, leads to massive population loss through starvation and emigration.

1846

The German astronomer Johann Galle (1812–1910) becomes the first person to observe the planet Neptune.

1846–8

The Mexican War results in Mexico's loss to the USA of a swathe of territory from California to Texas.

1848

In a chain reaction known as the 'Springtime of Nations', nationalist revolutions erupt in France, Germany, Austria, Hungary and Italy. The Second Republic is established in France, but elsewhere the old order is restored.

Two German revolutionaries living in exile in England, Karl Marx (1818–83) and Friedrich Engels (1820–95), publish *The Communist Manifesto*, the founding text of Marxism.

1850–64

The Taiping Rebellion against the Ch'ing (Qing) Dynasty in China costs millions of lives before it is crushed.

1851

The Great Exhibition in London sets out to celebrate the 'works of industry of all nations', but in reality symbolizes Britain's industrial supremacy.

1852

President Louis-Napoleon Bonaparte of France (1808–73), a nephew of Napoleon I, suspends the Constitution of the Second Republic and assumes the title of Emperor Napoleon III.

1853

A US fleet under Commodore Matthew Perry (1794–1858) enters Tokyo Bay and the Japanese Shogunate opens relations with a country outside north-east Asia for the first time since 1637–9.

1854

Britain and France join in the Crimean War on the side of the Ottoman Empire against Russian expansionism. Major battles are fought at the River Alma, Balaclava, and Inkerman. The war ends with the Treaty of Paris in 1856, and Russia returning much of the territory it took.

1855

The English metallurgist Henry Bessemer (1813–98) patents his process for converting pig iron into steel.

1856

In the Neanderthal (the valley of the River Neander) in Germany, the first known remains are found of a species of human beings other than *Homo sapiens*.

1857

The Sepoy Mutiny or Indian Mutiny, an uprising against British rule in India, begins when Indian troops in British service (sepoys) revolt. It leads to the transfer of government from the East India Company to the British Crown.

1859

Following an uprising against Austrian rule in northern Italy, the Kingdom of Italy is proclaimed, with Florence as its capital. The movement gradually expands, under the leadership of Giuseppe Garibaldi (1807–82), to take in the whole peninsula including, by 1870, Rome.

The English naturalist Charles Darwin (1809–82) publishes *On the Origin of Species*, setting out his idea of 'natural selection' (evolution), partly developed from discoveries that he made during the voyage of the *Beagle* to South America (1831–35).

1861

Emperor Alexander II of Russia (1818–81) declares the emancipation of the serfs, but requires them to pay compensation to their former owners.

Moldavia and Wallachia, liberated from the Ottoman Empire, unite to form Romania.

1861–5

The American Civil War between the anti-slavery North (the Union) and the slave-holding states of the South (the Confederacy) results in the abolition of slavery and the emancipation of the slaves, but is also followed by the assassination of President Abraham Lincoln (1809–65).

1863

Mirza Huseyn Ali (1817–92) founds the Bahai faith in Persia. It follows the teachings of Babism and emphasizes world unity and peace.

1864

Karl Marx (1818–1883) founds the International Working Men's Association, usually known as 'The First International', the first international socialist organization.

1866

The Seven Weeks War (the Austro-Prussian War) results in the exclusion of Austria from the German Confederation and the dominance of Prussia over the 37 other German states.

1867

The Austrian Empire is refounded as Austria–Hungary, a 'dual monarchy' in which the Austrians dominate Czechs and Poles, and the Hungarians rule the other Slav peoples of the empire.

Four British colonies in eastern North America form the self-governing federal Dominion of Canada, which then purchases the lands of the Hudson's Bay Company and (1871) takes in British Columbia.

Russia sells Alaska to the USA.

The Meiji Restoration in Japan sees the overthrow of the last Shogun by a modernizing movement that formally 'restores' rule by the figurehead emperors.

1868

Britain ends the transportation of convicts to Australia.

1869–70

The First Vatican Council adopts the belief of papal infallibility.

1870–1

A crushing defeat for France in the Franco-Prussian War leads to the fall of Napoleon III.

1871

On the initiative of the Prussian prime minister, Otto von Bismarck (1815–98), the separate German states form a federal German Empire; the King of Prussia becomes the German Emperor Wilhelm I (1797–1888); and Bismarck becomes Chancellor of the unified Germany.

1874

Impression, soleil levant ('Impression, Rising Sun'), a painting by the French artist Claude Monet (1840–1926), gives the name to the Impressionist school of painters.

Impression, soleil levant by Claude Monet

1876

Queen Victoria is declared Empress of India.

A Scots-born US inventor, Alexander Graham Bell (1847–1922), patents the telephone.

1877

The US inventor Thomas Alva Edison (1847–1931) devises the phonograph, the first practical machine for recording sound.

1878

Following intervention by the Western powers, Serbia and Bulgaria are granted independence from the Ottoman Empire.

1880–1

The First Boer War, fought between the Boers (Afrikaners or Dutch settlers) and the British in southern Africa, ends with the defeat of British forces at Majuba Hill.

1881

Emperor Alexander II of Russia is assassinated by revolutionary terrorists.

1882–98

In the Sudan, Muhammad Ahmed (1844–85) claims to be the Islamic saviour the Mahdi ('the Divinely Guided One') and goes on to launch a war against British–Egyptian rule. In 1885 Mahdist followers capture the capital, Khartoum, but are eventually defeated at the Battle of Omdurman in 1898.

1884

The German engineers Gottlieb Daimler (1834–1900) and Karl Benz (1844–1929) each develop a petrol-burning internal-combustion engine.

1885

A group of Indian nationalists and British sympathizers found the Indian National Congress, aimed at securing independence from Britain.

At the Berlin Conference the great powers of Europe recognize Belgian control of the Congo. They also formalize the European 'Scramble for Africa' (the term given to the division of land on the continent between them) that leaves Ethiopia and Liberia as the only independent states in Africa by 1900.

1886

The first women's suffrage bill to allow votes for women is introduced into the UK Parliament, but it is unsuccessful. Several more bills are introduced between 1886 and 1911, but all are defeated.

1887

France, which has engaged in colonial ventures in south-east Asia since 1858, merges Vietnam, Cambodia and Laos into a federation called the Indochinese Union or French Indo-China.

1888

Brazil becomes the last state in the Americas formally to abolish slavery.

1892

James Keir Hardie (1856–1915) becomes the first member of the British House of Commons from a working-class background.

1893

New Zealand becomes the first country in the world to give women the vote.

1894

Alfred Dreyfus (1859–1935), a French army captain of Jewish descent, is wrongly convicted of passing military secrets to Germany. His case becomes an international *cause célèbre* until he is cleared of all charges and returns to the army (1906).

1894–5

Conflict between Chinese and Japanese interests in Korea leads to a war in which China is defeated and obliged to recognize Korea's independence.

1895

A German physicist, Wilhelm Röntgen (1845–1923), discovers X-rays.

In Paris, Auguste Lumière (1862–1954) and his brother Louis (1864–1948) conduct the first public showing of moving pictures recorded on celluloid: the cinema is born.

1898

Following the Spanish–American War, the USA gains the Philippines (until its independence in 1946), Puerto Rico and naval bases in Cuba, although Cuba itself becomes formally independent in 1902.

Two French physicists, Polish-born Marie Curie (1867–1934) and her husband Pierre (1859–1906), isolate the elements polonium and radium in their work on magnetism and radioactivity.

1898–1900

An anti-foreign uprising in China by rebels belonging to a secret society is suppressed when foreign powers send a combined force to occupy Beijing. The Boxer Rising is the name given to the uprising by Westerners after the martial arts rituals of the rebels.

1899–1902

The Second Boer War between the Boer republics of Orange Free State and the Transvaal and the British Empire in South Africa ends in military defeat for the Boers. The peace is concluded by the Treaty of Vereeniging.

1900–1999

1900

The Labour Representation Committee is established to represent trade unions and socialist groups in the UK parliament. The committee is renamed the Labour Party in 1906.

The German physicist Max Planck (1858–1947) proposes quantum theory, which assumes that energy changes take place in small discrete instalments (or quanta).

1901

Queen Victoria of Great Britain and Ireland dies after a reign of 64 years.

Six British colonies combine to form the Commonwealth of Australia.

Guglielmo Marconi (1874–1937), an Italian inventor, sends the first wireless (radio) message across the Atlantic Ocean.

1903

Orville Wright (1871–1948) and his brother

Wilbur (1867–1912) carry out the first powered flight of a heavier-than-air craft at Kitty Hawk, North Carolina.

1904–5

Russia suffers naval and military disasters before eventual defeat in the Russo-Japanese War, a conflict based on rival imperial expansionism.

1905

Norway achieves independence from Sweden.

The German physicist (later a US citizen) Albert Einstein (1879–1955) publishes a paper on his special theory of relativity.

1905–6

The first revolution in Russia is defeated, but Tsar Nicholas II (1868–1918) allows a constitution and the empire's first legislature, the Duma.

1907

Women in Finland are the first in Europe to be elected as MPs.

1908

In the Ottoman Empire the reformist Young Turks organization stages a revolution, replacing Sultan Abd-ul-Hamid II (1842–1918) with Mehmet V (1844–1918), and giving the legislature (founded in 1876) real powers for the first time.

The US engineer and entrepreneur Henry Ford (1863–1947) begins production of the Model T car.

A Model T Ford motor car

1909

A US explorer, Robert E Peary (1856–1920), becomes the first to reach the North Pole.

The French aviator Louis Blériot (1872–1936) makes the first aeroplane flight across the English Channel.

1910

In Portugal the monarchy is replaced by a republic; the country is governed by a series of dictators until 1974.

Britain creates the Union of South Africa, granting self-government to its white inhabitants, abolishing the voting rights of the Cape Coloureds (those of mixed descent) and maintaining the exclusion of its black majority from politics.

Japan announces the formal annexation of Korea.

1911

A revolution in Mexico overthrows Porfirio Diaz (1830–1915), dictator since 1877.

The New Zealand-born British physicist Ernest Rutherford (1871–1937) discovers the nucleus of the atom. In 1919 he splits the atom and in 1934 he produces the first nuclear fusion reaction.

A team led by Norwegian explorer Roald Amundsen (1872–1928) reaches the South Pole.

1911–12

Revolution in China leads to the overthrow of the Ch'ing (Qing) Dynasty, and the establishment of an unstable and fragmented republic.

1912

A British exploration team led by Captain Robert Falcon Scott (b.1868) reaches the South Pole, only to find that Roald Amundsen had reached it first in December 1911. Scott and his companions die on their return journey.

The *Titanic*, a British luxury liner, hits an iceberg off Newfoundland and sinks, with the loss of more than 1,500 lives.

1912–13

In two Balkan Wars the Ottoman Empire loses almost all of its remaining territory in Europe. Albania becomes independent, but the majority-Albanian province of Kosova (Kosovo) is conquered by Serbia.

1913

Suffragette Emily Davison (b.1872) is killed when she throws herself under the King's horse at the Derby horse race in England.

1914

The US Corps of Engineers completes the building of the Panama Canal, linking the Caribbean Sea with the Pacific Ocean.

1914–18

The initial cause of World War I is the assassination in 1914 of Archduke Franz Ferdinand, heir presumptive of the Austro-Hungarian throne, by the Serbian nationalist Gavrilo Princip (June 28). The 'Central Powers' (Germany, AustriaHungary, the Ottoman Empire and Bulgaria) fight the 'Allied Powers' (Britain, France, Russia, Serbia and Japan) in a global war fuelled by nationalism, empire and expansionism.

1915

Allied forces, including ANZAC units from Australia and New Zealand, fail to take the Gallipoli peninsula from the Ottoman Empire.

The passenger liner *Lusitania* is torpedoed by a German submarine, with the loss of more than 1,000 lives.

1915–16

An estimated 600,000 Armenians are killed or left to die of starvation while being deported from the Ottoman Empire.

1916

On the Western Front, the Battle of the Somme sees hundreds of thousands of soldiers die in trench warfare over a strip of French land. July 1, the first day of the 'Big Push', results in the British army suffering 57,470 casualties, the costliest day in the army's history. In September during the same battle the British Army makes the first use of the military tank.

In Dublin, Irish nationalists stage a rebellion, the unsuccessful Easter Rising. It is suppressed after a week and 16 of its leaders are executed.

Encouraged by Great Britain, the sharif of Mecca, Husayn ibn Ali, begins the Arab Revolt against Turkish rule. At the end of World War I, he is left bitter by the failure of the Allies to honour promises made to him over Arab territories.

1917

The USA enters World War I on the side of the Allied Powers.

In Russia the February (or March) Revolution overthrows the imperial regime and the October (or November) Revolution brings the first communist government to power under Vladimir Ilyich Lenin (1870–1924) and his Bolshevik Party. Russia withdraws from World War I.

The Balfour Declaration, issued by the British Foreign Secretary Arthur Balfour (1848–1930), promises Zionists, supporters of a Jewish state, a national home for Jews in Palestine.

1918

World War I ends with the collapse of four empires. Germany loses land to France and Poland, and becomes a republic. Austria–Hungary is replaced by the independent states of Austria, Czechoslovakia, Hungary and Yugoslavia (dominated by Serbia). Russia recognizes the independence of Poland, Finland, Estonia, Latvia and Lithuania. In place of the Ottoman Empire, Britain and France divide the Arab world between them, while Turkey and Greece battle over their respective Greek and Turkish minorities.

The Bolshevik government in Russia moves the capital back to Moscow from St Petersburg, adopts the Julian calendar, nationalizes industry and attempts other reforms, while fighting a brutal civil war with the 'Whites' (anti-communists) and intervention by foreign armies.

In Britain women over the age of 30 receive the vote.

1919

At the Versailles Peace Conference the great powers impose reparation payments on Germany and found the League of Nations (1920–46), which is proposed by US President Woodrow Wilson (1856–1924), but which the USA decides not to join.

1919–21

During the Irish Revolution, the Irish Republican Army carries out guerrilla attacks on British forces. The British authorities react by deploying militarized police officers, the 'Black-and-Tans' (so called because of the colour of their uniforms) and the 'Auxiliaries'.

1920

The Government of Ireland Act is passed by the UK parliament, and creates two devolved parliaments: one in Belfast, representing six (predominantly Protestant) of the nine counties of Ulster, and the second in Dublin.

1921

The Chinese Communist Party is formed.

1922

The Union of Soviet Socialist Republics (USSR) is formed, with Russia as the dominant force.

The Fascist leader Benito Mussolini (1883–1945) seizes power in Italy.

Propaganda poster of Benito Mussolini

The Irish Free State is proclaimed and an independent Irish parliament and government takes office after elections. However, the year-long Irish Civil War breaks out between opponents and supporters of the treaty, which is eventually won by the pro-treaty side.

1923

Mustapha Kemal Atatürk (1881–1938) abolishes both the Ottoman Sultanate and the Islamic caliphate linked to it, and becomes president of Turkey.

1924

Adolf Hitler (1889–1945) writes *Mein Kampf* ('My Struggle') while in prison. It contains many of the political ideas that he would later seek to realize.

1925

Reza Khan (1878–1944) of Persia becomes its ruler, or shah, and renames the country Iran.

A Scottish electrical engineer, John Logie Baird (1888–1946), gives the first public demonstration of a television image, having made the apparatus almost entirely from scrap materials.

1926

The Trades Union Congress (TUC) in the UK organizes the General Strike in support of an existing miners' strike to resist wage cuts. It lasts for eight days, before ending in the face of government resistance.

1926–8

In China, Nationalists under Chiang Kai-shek (1887–1975) subdue the warlords, the provincial military rulers, and reunify the country.

1927

Joseph Stalin (1879–1953) wins the struggle for power in the USSR after the death of Lenin in 1924, and sends his main rival, Leon Trotsky (1879–1940), into exile.

The US aviator Charles Lindbergh (1902–74) makes the first non-stop solo transatlantic flight.

The British Broadcasting Corporation (BBC) begins its radio service.

1928

In the USSR, Stalin begins the forced merger of land into collective farms, a process known as collectivization, as well as the first 'five-year plan' for industrialization. By 1934, millions of people have died from the resulting famines.

A Scottish bacteriologist, Alexander Fleming (1881–1955), accidentally discovers penicillin, the first widely used antibiotic.

1929

The New York Stock Exchange, located on Wall Street in the city, crashes, causing the worldwide Great Depression. The event comes to be known as 'the Wall Street Crash'.

The US astronomer Edwin Hubble (1889–1953) announces his experimental evidence of galaxies moving away from each other in an expanding universe, supporting the 'Big Bang' theory already proposed by Belgian astrophysicist Georges Lemaître (1894–1966).

1930

The US astronomer Clyde Tombaugh (1906–97) discovers Pluto.

1931

Japan invades Manchuria in north-eastern China and uses it as a base to conquer most of the rest of China.

King Alfonso of Spain (1886–1941) is sent into exile, and a republic is declared.

The UK enacts the Statute of Westminster, which recognizes the sovereignty of the 'Dominions' – Canada, Australia, New Zealand, South Africa, Newfoundland (which joins Canada in 1949) and the Irish Free State – as part of the Commonwealth of Nations.

1932

The kingdoms of Saudi Arabia and Iraq become the first fully independent Arab states (followed by Egypt in 1936).

1933

Adolf Hitler becomes chancellor of Germany.

US President Franklin D Roosevelt (1882–1945) begins to implement his 'New Deal' programme for national recovery from the Great Depression.

1934–5

Approximately 100,000 Chinese Communists under Mao Zedong (1893–1976) begin their 'Long March': withdrawing from south-eastern to north-western China after their base has been encircled by Nationalist government troops.

1934–8

Soviet leader Stalin inaugurates a massive purge of the Communist Party, government, armed forces and intelligentsia in which millions are killed, imprisoned, sent to labour camps or exiled.

1935

Nazi Germany introduces the Nuremberg Laws, depriving German Jews of citizenship and expelling them from most professions.

1936

German forces reoccupy the Rhineland, held by France since 1919.

In the UK, King Edward VIII, who has been king for under a year, is forced to abdicate over disapproval of his proposed marriage to divorcée Wallis Simpson.

1936–9

The Spanish Civil War ends in 1939 with the overthrow of the Republican government by General Francisco Franco (1892–1975), who remains dictator of Spain until his death.

1937

The Peel Commission, appointed by the British Prime Minister Stanley Baldwin (1867–1947) to investigate the working of the British administration of Palestine, recommends the partition of Palestine into separate Arab and Jewish states; the proposal is rejected by the Arabs.

1937–41

In China, both the Nationalists and Communists fight the invading Japanese army, but their forces continue to clash and the alliance disintegrates by 1941.

1938

Nazi Germany occupies Austria and proclaims the Anschluss, the union of the two countries. It also seizes the German-speaking Sudeten districts of Czechoslovakia, with the acceptance of Britain and France.

1939

World War II breaks out when Germany invades Poland, prompting Britain and France to declare war. The 'Axis Powers' (Germany, Italy, Japan and Hungary) are ranged against the 'Allied Powers' (initially, Britain, France and their empires). Poland is subsequently divided between Germany and the USSR, which also occupies the Baltic states of Estonia, Latvia and Lithuania. Italy occupies Albania.

1940

Germany invades and occupies France, Belgium, the Netherlands, Denmark and Norway, but the victory of the Royal Air Force over the German air force, the *Luftwaffe,* in the Battle of Britain leads Hitler to postpone his plans to invade Britain.

1940–1

The Blitz (from German *Blitzkrieg*, 'lightning war'), a series of German air raids on British cities, causes devastation, particularly in London and Coventry.

London on fire during the Blitz

1941

Germany and its allies launch Operation Barbarossa, the invasion of the USSR. They lay siege to Leningrad (now St Petersburg) for 900 days before retreating. The siege costs an estimated 1.25 million Russian lives.

An unprovoked Japanese air attack on the US base at Pearl Harbor, Hawaii, brings the USA into World War II.

1942

The British victory over the German Afrika Corps at El Alamein in Egypt is a turning point in the North Africa campaign.

Japanese forces capture the British military base at Singapore and begin creating the 'Greater East Asia Co-Prosperity Sphere', covering most of south-east Asia.

In the UK, economist William Beveridge produces the Beveridge Report, a blueprint for the creation of a welfare state.

1942–3

The battles of Stalingrad and Kursk see decisive defeats of Germany by the USSR, and mark turning points in the war.

1943

The Italian dictator Benito Mussolini (b.1883) falls from power; he is executed in 1945. Italy subsequently surrenders to the Allies.

1943–4

The first computer, 'Colossus', is built by British engineers to break the German 'Enigma' codes that are being used to encrypt military and governmental communications.

1944

Operation Overlord begins the Allied liberation of Europe with naval landings in Normandy in northern France starting on D-Day (6 June).

1945

World War II ends. Adolf Hitler commits suicide in his Berlin bunker (April). Germany surrenders (May); Japan also capitulates (August) after the USA drops atomic bombs on the Japanese cities of Hiroshima and Nagasaki, killing an estimated 250,000 people.

By the end of the war in Europe about six million Jews, 500,000 Gypsies and thousands of other prisoners have been murdered by the Nazis in the Holocaust.

The United Nations is formed to replace the League of Nations.

1945–6

The Nuremberg Trials are held by the Allies to try Nazi war criminals. Some defendants, including Hermann Goering (1893–1946), are sentenced to death.

1946

Communist Ho Chi Minh (1890–1969) establishes the Democratic Republic of Vietnam.

In the USA John Mauchley (1907–80), John Eckert (1919–95) and others complete work on ENIAC, the first functioning computer with a memory.

1946–54

A nationalist revolt in French Indo-China leads to the withdrawal of France in 1954.

1947

US President Harry S Truman (1884–1972) announces the Truman Doctrine, promising aid to countries threatened by communist interference. He also promotes the Marshall Plan prepared by his Secretary of State, George C Marshall (1880–1959), for economic aid to rebuild war-torn Europe.

India is given independence from Britain, and the Indian Independence Act partitions the Indian subcontinent into two independent countries, a predominantly Hindu India and a predominantly Muslim Pakistan. The region of Kashmir has been disputed between them ever since.

The United Nations supports the formation of two states in Palestine, one Arab and one Jewish.

1948

Israel, Burma and Ceylon (Sri Lanka) become independent from Britain.

Mohandas Karamchand Gandhi (b.1869), known as the Mahatma ('great soul') and the leader of the Indian independence movement, is assassinated by a Hindu extremist.

Britain withdraws from Palestine and the independent State of Israel is proclaimed. Israel is invaded by its Arab neighbours but the Israelis win the first Arab-Israeli war, gaining more land. Over 700,000 Arabs leave the Israeli-occupied areas, many for refugee camps in the Gaza Strip and West Bank.

In South Africa the National Party comes to power and begins to expand discrimination against non-whites, creating a system of *apartheid* ('separateness' of blacks and whites).

Joseph Stalin begins a blockade of traffic between the Soviet-occupied east of Berlin and the US, British and French zones in the west, in the hope that the Allies will withdraw and allow him to secure his control over eastern Europe. The city is relieved by airlifts of supplies, the Berlin Airlift, for eleven months until the blockade is lifted in May 1949.

Three US physicists, John Bardeen (1908–91), Walter Brattain (1902–87) and William Shockley (1910–89), invent the transistor, which contributes greatly to the development of computers and other electronic devices.

1949

The USA, Canada and their European allies form a defence alliance, the North Atlantic Treaty Organization (NATO).

The US, British and French occupation zones of Germany merge into the Federal Republic (West Germany) and the Soviet zone becomes the Democratic Republic (East Germany).

Communists take power in China after a civil war that has raged since 1945. President Chiang Kai-shek withdraws to the island of Taiwan, and Mao Zedong formally proclaims the People's Republic of China.

Indonesia achieves independence from the Netherlands.

1950

India becomes a republic within the Commonwealth.

Senator Joseph McCarthy (1909–57) launches an attack on what he claims are communist elements in the US Government. His anti-communist witch-hunt becomes known as 'McCarthyism'.

1950–3

The Korean War sees United Nations forces defend South Korea against an invasion by communist North Korea and China.

1952

The charismatic leader Eva Peron (b.1919) dies in Argentina. As the president's wife from 1945 until her death, her charitable work made her beloved by the people of Argentina.

The Mau Mau rebellion, an independence movement in Kenya, begins, and lasts until 1960. Kenya finally gains independence from Britain in 1963.

The USA tests the world's first hydrogen bomb.

1953

New Zealand mountaineer Edmund Hillary (1919–) and the Nepalese Sherpa Tenzing Norgay (1914–86) are the first men to conquer Mount Everest.

Four biologists, Francis Crick (1916–2004), Rosalind Franklin (1920–58), James Watson (1928–) and Maurice Wilkins (1916–2004) discover the helical structure of the genetic material DNA and the existence of a genetic code, revolutionizing the science of genetics.

1954

The French withdraw from Indo-China (Vietnam, Cambodia and Laos). Vietnam is divided into the Communist 'Democratic Republic' in the north and the 'State' of Vietnam in the south.

Algeria begins its war of independence against colonial power France, and fighting continues until the North African country becomes independent in 1962.

1955

The USSR and its Communist allies in Central and Eastern Europe sign the Warsaw Pact, forming a military alliance under Soviet command to rival NATO.

US civil-rights activist Rosa Parks (1913–2005) refuses to give up her seat to a white man on a bus in Alabama, USA, sparking a boycott of segregated buses in that state. In 1956 the American Supreme Court declares such segregation illegal.

1956

Egypt nationalizes the Suez Canal, prompting an invasion by Britain, France and Israel, who are forced to withdraw after US and Soviet pressure.

Israel invades the Gaza Strip and the Sinai Peninsula. The United Nations votes to create a peace force for the Middle East.

The Hungarian Uprising, a revolution against Communist rule in the country, is suppressed by the USSR.

1957

The Treaty of Rome establishes a European Economic Community comprising France, West Germany, Italy, Belgium, the Netherlands and Luxembourg.

The Gold Coast becomes the first British colony in Africa (other than South Africa) to be granted independence, and it is renamed Ghana.

The USSR launches the world's first artificial satellite, Sputnik 1.

1958

In the USA Jack Saint Clair Kilby (1923–2005) invents the integrated circuit (or 'microchip').

1959

In Cuba, Fidel Castro (1927–) and the Argentine revolutionary Ernesto 'Che' Guevara (1928–67) lead a revolution by Communists and other radical groups that overthrows the dictator Fulgencio Batista (1901–73).

China suppresses nationalists in Tibet. The Dalai Lama, the Buddhist leader, flees to India.

1960

Having already granted independence to Morocco and Tunisia (1956), France grants independence to 16 other former colonies in Africa, while Britain grants independence to Nigeria, soon to be followed by other colonies throughout the continent.

1961

1,500 anti-Castro Cuban exiles sponsored by the USA invade Cuba, landing at Bahía de Cochinos ('Bay of Pigs') on the southern coast, but they fail to win local support and are rapidly defeated by Cuban troops.

East Germany builds the Berlin Wall, a wall between West Berlin and East Berlin, to end the mass illegal emigration to the West.

A Soviet cosmonaut, Yuri Gagarin (1934–68), becomes the first human being to travel into space.

1961–4

Civil war breaks out between North and South Vietnam after plans to reunify the country fail. The USA provides aid and military advisers to South Vietnam in an attempt to stop the spread of Communism in south-east Asia.

1962

The Cuban Missile Crisis is resolved when US President John F Kennedy (1917–63) persuades the Soviet leader Nikita Khrushchev (1894–1971) not to station nuclear missiles in Cuba.

Telstar I communications satellite

The USA launches Telstar I, a communications satellite that relays the first transatlantic television signals.

1963

US President John F Kennedy (b.1917) is assassinated.

Indonesia, under President Ahmed Sukarno (1902–70), invades territory in the newly created and British-backed Federation of Malaysia. However, his power declines after a coup in 1965.

Britain, USA and the USSR are among 100 governments to sign the Nuclear Test Ban Treaty, prohibiting the testing of nuclear weapons on or above the surface of the Earth.

1964

In the USA a new Civil Rights Act prohibits discrimination in all public places, government, employment, and union membership.

The Palestine Liberation Organization (PLO) is created in Jerusalem. Its charter denies the right of Israel to exist and calls for Palestine to be liberated by armed conflict.

In South Africa, Nelson Mandela (1918–), a leader of the African National Congress (ANC), is sentenced to life imprisonment for treason.

1964–75

In the Vietnam War, the Communist government founded in the North fights and defeats the pro-Western government in the South, which (until 1973) is supported by US and other Western forces.

1966

Rhodesia leaves the Commonwealth.

1966–76

During the 'Cultural Revolution' in China, Mao Zedong encourages the Red Guards, a youth movement, to persecute intellectuals.

1967

In the Six-Day War, or June War, Israel quickly defeats an alliance of Egypt, Syria and Jordan, and occupies East Jerusalem, the West Bank and the Gaza Strip. Violence and peace talks have alternated ever since.

The Igbo people of eastern Nigeria form the Republic of Biafra, resulting in a war that ends with the surrender of Biafra in 1970.

1968

Student protests lead to a general strike in France, and political upheaval in Mexico, Italy, Germany, Japan and elsewhere.

The US civil-rights leader Martin Luther King, Jr (b.1929) is assassinated.

Warsaw Pact troops invade Czechoslovakia to crush the regime of Alexander Dubček (1921–92), who had introduced the liberalizing reforms known as the 'Prague Spring'.

1969

After serious civil disturbances in Northern Ireland because of Protestant political dominance and discrimination against the Catholic minority, British troops are sent to restore order. However, the situation worsens and the province enters a long period of unrest and violence known as the 'Troubles'.

The US astronaut Neil Armstrong (1930–) becomes the first man to set foot on the Moon, during the Apollo 11 mission.

1970

Head of state Norodom Sihanouk (1922–) of Cambodia is deposed in a coup. A right-wing government is formed and the country is renamed the Khmer Republic. Subsequent fighting throughout the country draws in troops from North and South Vietnam and the USA.

1971

Civil war in Pakistan ends with independence for Bangladesh (formerly named East Pakistan).

In Uganda, Commander-in-Chief Idi Amin (1925–2003) seizes power following a coup, expelling Ugandan Asians with British passports.

1972

US President Richard Nixon (1913–94) opens diplomatic relations with Communist China, which the USA has boycotted since 1949.

1973

The Vietnam War is officially ended by the Paris Peace Treaty.

The UK, the Irish Republic and Denmark join the European Community.

The Yom Kippur War, or October War, follows a surprise attack by Egypt and Syria on Israel.

Salvador Allende (b.1908), socialist president of Chile since 1970, is killed when his government is overthrown by armed forces under General Augusto Pinochet (1915–2006), who becomes dictator until 1990.

1974

A revolution in Portugal overthrows the authoritarian government of Marcelo Caetano (1906–80) and grants independence to the African nations of Angola, Guinea-Bissau and Mozambique.

Cyprus is divided into two parts after a Turkish invasion leads to occupation of over one-third of the island.

Republican Richard Nixon resigns the US presidency when he is threatened with impeachment over his involvement in the burglary in 1972 of the Democratic Party's campaign headquarters in the Watergate complex in Washington, DC.

1975

The death of Francisco Franco in Spain is followed by the restoration of parliamentary democracy and of the monarchy, with Juan Carlos (1938–) named king.

Vietnam is reunified under the Communist government in the north, while neighbouring Cambodia and Laos also become Communist states.

The Khmer Rouge, a genocidal revolutionary movement led by Pol Pot (1928–98), takes power in Cambodia. The regime murders about 1.5 million people before being overthrown by the Vietnamese in 1979.

1976

Chinese Communist Party chairman Mao Zedong dies; Hua Guofeng (1920–) becomes leader and arrests the 'Gang of Four' that promoted the Cultural Revolution.

1977

Millions mourn the death of 'The King of Rock and Roll', Elvis Presley (b.1935).

1978

A Soviet-backed regime takes power in Afghanistan; the USSR invades eight months later to support the fragile regime, but meets resistance from Muslim guerillas (the Mujaheddin), who proclaim a *jihad* ('holy war'). Withdrawal of the forces begins in 1988, although the Communist government stays in power until 1992.

A Polish cardinal, Karol Wojtyla (1920–2005), becomes Pope John Paul II, the first non-Italian pope since the 16th century.

1979

In Nicaragua the left-wing Sandinista movement led by Daniel Ortega (1945–) overthrows Anastasio Somoza Debayle (1925–80), whose family has ruled there since 1937. Civil war ensues and continues until 1990.

The Shah of Iran (1919–80) is deposed and an Islamic republic is set up under Ayatollah Khomeini (1900–89).

1980

Black majority rule comes into force in Zimbabwe (formerly Rhodesia).

Shipyard workers in Gdansk, Poland, form Solidarity, the first independent labour union to function openly in a Communist country.

1980–8

Millions of lives are lost in the Iran–Iraq War.

1981

Greece joins the European Community.

The US Space Shuttle, a reusable crewed launch vehicle, comes into use.

1982

The USA and the USSR begin Strategic Arms Reduction Talks (START).

In the short Falklands War, Britain retakes the Falkland Islands after an invasion by Argentina.

The military regime established in Argentina in 1976 falls soon afterwards.

1982–5

Israeli forces invade Lebanon to drive out PLO (Palestine Liberation Organization) and Syrian guerrillas, reaching Beirut, and remaining for three years.

1984

The Indian prime minister Indira Gandhi (b.1917) is assassinated by Sikh extremists.

A gas leak at a pesticide plant owned by the Union Carbide Corporation in Bhopal, India, kills an estimated 3,000 people immediately, and many thousands more die in subsequent years as a result of poisoning.

1985

Mikhail Gorbachev (1931–) becomes leader of the USSR, and initiates a programme of reconstruction (*perestroika*) and greater openness (*glasnost*).

In London and Philadelphia two large pop concerts are held under the name 'Live Aid' to raise money for victims of famine in Ethiopia, and 1.5 billion people around the world watch the events live on television.

1986

In Ukraine the Chernobyl nuclear reactor explodes, causing an environmental and medical disaster. A World Health Organization Report (2005) claimed 56 people died as a direct result of the accident, but that up to 9,000 people could die from related diseases in future.

The USSR launches Mir, the first permanently manned space station.

1987–93

An intermittent uprising (*intifada*) by Palestinians in the Gaza Strip and West Bank is put down by Israeli forces.

1989

The Chinese army crushes mass anti-government protests in and around Tiananmen Square in the capital, Beijing.

Communist governments fall from power across Central and Eastern Europe, culminating in the dismantling of the Berlin Wall and the 'Velvet Revolution' in Czechoslovakia, and the largely televised overthrow and execution of Nicolae Ceauşescu (b.1918) and his wife Elena Ceauşescu (b.1919), who have ruled Romania since 1965.

The English computer scientist Sir Tim Berners-Lee (1955–) devises a system of linking information stored on diverse computers, thereby extending the use of the Internet that was set up for US universities in 1984, to create a global repository of interlinked information (the 'World Wide Web').

1990

The former East Germany is reunited with the Federal Republic of Germany.

The dismantling of the Berlin Wall

In Burma, following the election victory of the National League for Democracy led by Aung San Suu Kyi (1945–), the army nullifies the results and imposes martial law. Aung San Suu Kyi is placed under almost continual house arrest.

The Human Genome Organization publishes the first draft of the human genome and completes its sequencing in 2003.

1991

In the Gulf War a US-led United Nations coalition expels invading Iraqi forces from Kuwait.

The USSR collapses and is replaced by 15 independent republics.

1992

Yugoslavia breaks up into five separate republics, one of which, Bosnia-Herzegovina, is plunged into war among Serbs (supported by Serbia), Croats (supported by Croatia) and Bosnians (Muslims) until 1995.

1993

Czechoslovakia peacefully splits into the Czech Republic and Slovakia.

The European Community is relaunched as the European Union.

1994

In South Africa, following the abolition of apartheid, Nelson Mandela (1918–), released from prison in 1990 after 26 years' imprisonment, is elected as the country's first black president.

In Rwanda, following the assassination of President Juvénal Habyarimana (b.c.1937), members of the majority Hutu people massacre about 800,000 people, mostly from the Tutsi minority, but also moderate Hutus. In 2006 the International Criminal Tribunal for Rwanda (ICTR) legally recognizes the massacre as genocide.

In Afghanistan the Islamic fundamentalist group the Taliban emerges, seeking to impose strict Islamic law on the country. Within two years the Taliban has taken the capital Kabul, and by 1998 almost 90 per cent of the country is under Taliban control.

1995

Austria, Finland and Sweden join the European Union.

1996

A peace process begun in 1991 between Israel and Palestine falters after an Israeli general election brings to power a coalition led by right-wingers opposed to a Palestinian state.

1997

Tutsi rebels led by Laurent Kabila (1939–2001) invade Zaire and stage a coup, renaming the country the Democratic Republic of Congo. Civil war with extensive foreign intervention follows.

Britain returns Hong Kong (including Kowloon) to China.

The Kyoto Treaty is drawn up in Kyoto, Japan, as part of a UN effort to reduce emissions of environmentally harmful gases and curtail global warming.

The first successful cloning of an animal, at the Roslin Institute in Scotland, results in Dolly the sheep.

1998

A tentative peace agreement is reached in Northern Ireland (the Good Friday Agreement).

1999

Serbia's persecution of the Albanian majority in Kosova (Kosovo) is ended by a campaign of NATO air-strikes.

2000–

2001

The World Trade Center in New York is destroyed in a terrorist attack when suicide bombers hijack commercial airliners and fly them into the building's twin towers, killing thousands. The Pentagon (Defense Department) in Washington, DC, is attacked in the same manner on the same day.

The USA and its allies overthrow the Taliban regime in Afghanistan, which it claims was sheltering the leaders of Al Qaeda, the Muslim fundamentalist network which claimed responsibility for the attacks.

2002

The euro is adopted as the currency of twelve states in the European Union.

East Timor gains its independence from Indonesia.

2003

In the Iraq War the USA, the UK and their allies invade Iraq, overthrow the dictatorship of Saddam Hussein (1937–2006), and establish an interim government.

The 'road map' peace plan, set out by the European Union, Russia, the USA and the United Nations, is endorsed by the Israeli and Palestinian prime ministers. However, despite a three-month truce by militant groups, the peace process makes little progress as the *intifada* and severe Israeli reprisals continue.

An uprising in Darfur, Sudan, by black African rebels is opposed by the government's Arab militia. By 2006 an estimated 400,000 civilians had been killed and two and a half million had fled their homes.

2004

In Iraq the coalition of the USA, the UK and their allies formally hand over power to a new government under Prime Minister Ayad Allawi (1945–).

A massive earthquake off the coast of Indonesia causes a series of huge waves to hit coastal areas around the Indian Ocean. Over 200,000 people are killed.

2005

Elections in Iraq lead to a new government under Prime Minister Nouri (or Jawad) al-Maliki (1950–), which sits for the first time in 2006.

2006

Montenegro declares its independence from Serbia, formally marking the end of Yugoslavia.

The Israeli military bombards Lebanese cities including the capital Beirut and then launches a land invasion in retaliation for the abduction of two Israeli soldiers by Iranian-backed Shiite Hezbollah (Party of God) fighters. A UN peacekeeping force is sent to the region.

The Iraqi insurgence continues to escalate. Diverse armed groups opposed to the new government attack Iraqi security forces and civilians as well as coalition troops.